# 1897
# SEARS, ROEBUCK
## CATALOGUE

# 1897

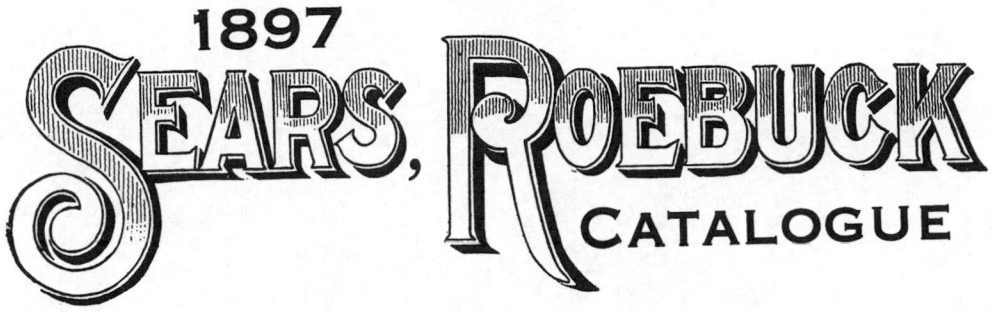

# Sears, Roebuck Catalogue

INTRODUCTION BY
**S. J. PERELMAN**

**FRED L. ISRAEL**
GENERAL EDITOR

CHELSEA HOUSE
PUBLISHERS
An imprint of Infobase Publishing

Printed and bound in the United States of America

10 9 8

ISBN 0-87754-045-4
0-7910-4626-5 (pbk.)

# PREFACE

If all the records for the 1890's should be lost, a scholar in the remote future who stumbled upon this book could obtain a fairly accurate description of American life during the last decade of the nineteenth century. The items displayed represent artifacts people really wanted and bought. Sears Roebuck did not as a rule experiment with fads. Nevertheless, the catalogue does record technological advances, changes from earlier ways of living, but changes that were rapidly becoming engrained in the American life style. Hence, the panoramic view drawn from the Sears catalogue is revealing and valid. For this reason alone, this catalogue occupies a unique place as authentic Americana, a companion to the faded family album. Today we chuckle at the wordy descriptions and repetitious phrases, but in its day the catalogue earnestly—and I think sincerely—satisfied the ravenous appetite for detail that characterized the rural mail order customer. Although Sears' catalogues from the 1890's are now collector's items, millions of Americans once considered these crowded pages as required reading.

The catalogue was designed and maintained as a business instrument. Its friendly descriptions convinced the reader how easy it was to order by mail—"in any language." "Don't be afraid you will make a mistake. We receive hundreds of orders every day from young and old who never before sent away for goods. We are accustomed to handling all kinds of orders. Tell us what you want in your own way, written in any language, no matter whether good or poor writing, and the goods will promptly be sent to you." The company offered fantastic guarantees —the sewing machine could not only sew and sew satisfactorily, but it could also sew better than any other sewing machine in the world. Sears guaranteed the bobbin, the shuttle, the treadle, the leather belt for the treadle, the solid golden oak cabinet, the varnish, and the linseed oil used to bring out the grain. Sears guaranteed safe arrival and pioneered in early status-striving motivation: "the neighbors would admire it once they were permitted to inspect it."

The Sears Roebuck Company, capitalized at $150,000 in 1895, listed its assets in excess of one hundred million dollars twenty years later. Half of the 1895 capitalization was provided by Aaron Nussbaum who had amassed a considerable sum of money selling ice cream at the Chicago World's Fair (Columbian Exposition). It was Aaron Nussbaum who subsequently brought into the business his brother-in-law, Julius Rosenwald, who became its dominant force.

Recently I decided to assign an 1890's Sears Roebuck catalogue to my students in American History survey courses so they might better understand the sense of the period. To my surprise neither my college library nor the Library of Congress, not even the Smithsonian, possessed these early volumes of authentic Americana. Used book stores referred me to antique dealers—but to no avail. Out of interest and determination, I placed classified advertisements in leading mid-Western newspapers which brought many nostalgic letters—and just one 1897 catalogue. The Sears 1897 catalogue is reprinted now (with its original, and sometimes inconsistent, pagination) because it is an authentic part of American culture, sociology, and history, an invaluable record from which we can gain insight into a by-gone era.

Fred L. Israel

City College of New York

# CONTENTS

*Preface*                                                    v

*Browsers' Delight* by S. J. Perelman                        ix

*What America Was Like: 1895–1905*                           xv


Ordering Instructions                                        1

Groceries                                                    8

Drugs                                                        26

General Hardware                                             38

Tools                                                        64

Refrigerators                                                104

Bells                                                        106

Cutlery                                                      107

Stoves and Household Utensils                                115

Agricultural Implements                                      148

Men's and Boys' Clothing                                     166

Boots, Shoes, and Rubbers                                    190

Men's and Boys' Furnishings                                  210

General Accessories                                          225

Trunks                                                       250

Dry Goods                                                    254

Women's and Girls' Clothing                                  268

Carpets, Curtains, and Linens                                284

Women's Accessories                                          301

Books and Stationery                                         336

Watches and Jewelry                                          362

Silverware                                                   438

Clocks                                                       457

Optical Goods                                                462

Surveyors' Instruments                               467

Thermometers                                         469

Electrical Goods                                     470

Cameras and Equipment                                473

Talking Machines and Records                         485

Organs and Pianos                                    510

Musical Goods                                        515

Sporting Goods                                       562

Bicycles                                             611

Furniture                                            642

Crockery and Glassware                               678

Baby Carriages                                       692

Sewing Machines                                      697

Harness and Saddlery                                 708


*Index*                                              775

# BROWSERS' DELIGHT

## S. J. Perelman

The years 1896–1897 produced a number of best-sellers the names of which still create a ripple of recognition, if no particular nostalgia, after three quarters of a century. Frances Hodgson Burnett, Paul Leicester Ford, J. M. Barrie, and several other merchants of glucose rang the bell with such works as *A Lady of Quality, Sentimental Tommy,* and *Margaret Ogilvy.* The portentous semi-religious books of Hall Caine and Harold Frederic—*The Christian* and *The Damnation of Theron Ware*—exalted churchgoers who in the normal course of events regarded novel reading as sinful, a pastime as dubious as Kelly pool or draw poker. The top favorite of 1897, of course, was *Quo Vadis,* by Henryk Sienkewicz, which was destined for a long, vigorous success not only in print but on celluloid. It is noteworthy that of the twenty titles listed in those two years, only one achieved a semblance of immortality, Stephen Crane's *The Red Badge of Courage*—a statistic hardly calculated to inspire youth to undertake the literary life.

Of all these widely-circulated works, however, not one was read with the rapt attention, the consuming interest, paid to a bulky volume issued in Chicago and sent post-free to millions of American homes—the Sears Roebuck catalogue, or, as it was then called, Consumers Guide. The 1897 issue sports an artistic cover depicting a rather overweight divinity—Ceres, the corn and earth goddess, I judged—posed beside a cornucopia from which gush forth a variety of goodies—upright pianos, wardrobes, stoves, *et cetera.* Off in the distance is a rich farmstead, overhead a globe of the world proclaiming "Sears, Roebuck and Co. Cheapest Supply House on Earth. Our Trade Reaches Around the World." Its 770-odd pages list a dizzying variety of merchandise intermingled with sales appeals, testimonial letters, and colorful engravings illustrating the wealth of articles available to the customer. The profusion of goods shown in the index, in which there are over six thousand items, ranges through every conceivable form of artifact, from autoharps to kraut cutters, from dulcimers to teething rings, from foot scrapers to feather boas. One can well imagine some archaeologist of the twenty-fifth century scratching his head (if our posterity will indeed have heads to scratch) over this gigantic kitchen midden, vainly attempting to adumbrate a vanished civilization from its household machinery.

Though never less than awe-inspiring, the Sears catalogue exercised an effect on me not unlike Marcel Proust's madeleine and limeflower tea; whole areas of my remote youth leaped back into focus as I thumbed through its pages. There was, for example, the instrument numbered No. 14954 and known as Brown and Sharp's Latest Pattern Hair Clipper. Now, Brown and Sharp (which, incidentally, should be Sharpe) is a renowned machine tool concern in Providence, Rhode Island. I worked there throughout the summer of 1919 for what is known as a pittance, filing myriads of tiny flanges or grommets or something of the sort that later became part of a mechanism I never saw. The atmosphere and my fellow-employees were Dickensian, of an unparalleled grimness and straight out of the shoe-blacking factory where David Copperfield toiled, and I conceived such a revulsion for that apprenticeship that it haunted my dreams for years. Similarly, No. 15463 in the catalogue, Shepard's Lightning Ice Cream Freezer. No doubt it will excite skepticism if not forthright derision from young folk nowadays, but fifty years ago it was the custom to brew ice cream at home. The ingredients were mingled in a cylinder in the center of a wooden bucket, the rest of which was packed with shaved ice and coarse salt. The youngest member of the family, which happened to be yours truly by a coincidence, was then keelhauled into turning a handle attached to the cylinder until the mixture froze. Apart from the endless dreary labor of grinding, I detested the finished product; I much preferred cheap, store-bought ice cream gaudily colored like the rainbow, even though my parents asserted it was sheer poison. The warning didn't faze me in the least. One lived dangerously in those days.

Leafing through the catalogue at random, the reader gleans not only a fascinating spectrum of life in the closing years of the nineteenth century, but an astonished sense of how inexpensive it was. Take ladies' corsets, for instance (an invitation I'm sure no red-blooded male will decline). No. 24810, a model known as "Exposition", is thus described: "Perfectly shaped and a fine fitting corset, equal to any retailed at 80 cents. Price, $0.40." Could any late Victorian wolf, encircling his inamorata's hourglass waist, ever have dreamed that the treasures in his grasp were packaged in forty cents' worth of whalebone and cambric? If Milady wanted something really *de luxe,* there was No. 24813: "This corset is modeled after the finest French shapes [which, incidentally, Toulouse-Lautrec was busy immortalizing at that very point in history, brother, and hot ziggety] and will fit any lady of average proportions. It is made with soft busts and stayed with unbreakable French wire. $0.75." Unbreakable, obviously, in order to repel the forays of the above-mentioned Victorian wolf. The reader, refreshed by this stroll down Mammary Lane, can now turn to Men's Wear and find a wide selection of toggery designed for individuals of every conceivable category. No. 453, to illustrate, was "our $23.95 Broadcloth Professional Suit. Just the suit for ministers, physicians, and professional men." For flashier types—pinochle players, pool sharks, and hustlers like Get-Rich-Quick Wallingford and Blackie Daw—No. 4442 was certain to set the pulses drumming: "Fur Overcoats. $8.90 buys a regular $15.00 Spotted Dog Overcoat. Made from carefully selected black spotted pelts." Presumably these skins

were tailored from Dalmatians who had outlived their usefulness as coach-dogs and mascots on fire-engines. The text also noted that Yellow Dog Overcoats and Gray Dog Overcoats were purchasable at the same reasonable figure. Today the average person might justifiably blanch at the thought of wearing his Airedale or schnauzer to repel the wintry blast, but people took a much less sentimental view of Fido in the Nineties. He was expected to pull his weight in the boat, as No. 16922 in the catalogue evidences. This was a machine known as Lamb's Adjustable Animal Power, a treadmill operated by the household's dog, goat, or sheep that worked a cream separator, corn sheller, or dairy churn. "If you keep a dog, make him work his passage," the accompanying text growls. And somewhere in the adjoining pages, no doubt, there was a spiked club available to beat the daylights out of man's best friend if he shirked his task.

However remote Sears Roebuck's customers may have been from the main depot in Chicago, their health was safeguarded by a vast array of patent medicines and proprietary articles. Twenty close-knit pages of elixirs, specifics, boluses, capsules, chemicals, tinctures, pills, and granules undertook to combat practically any malaise on earth. A typical sample is No. G-3059—Dr. Chaise's Complexion Wafers. "Highly recommended by the celebrated Madame La Ferris of Paris and many others," the letterpress asserts. "They are unequalled for producing a clear complexion and a plump figure." That Madame La Ferris must have possessed a strikingly voluptuous figure seems implicit, but the nature of the wafers eluded me until I stumbled on No. G-3030½, which specified, "Arsenic Complexion Wafers. Can be taken with impunity, according to directions. For a clear complexion and plump figure have no equals." It is interesting to speculate how many arsenic wafers were slipped into hubby's coffee on those lonely farms, with nobody around but the dog endlessly operating the treadmill, and the hired man, who might be expected to appreciate the virtues of a plump figure. Another entry in the pharmacopeia exceptional for its downright honesty is No. G-4200, a remedy for excess poundage: "Obesity Powders. These powders are recommended for and are very successful in reducing the flesh of corpulent people. Follow the directions and do not look for immediate results." Far and away the prize nostrum of all, however, and the answer to a universal problem is No. G-4261, Sear's Sure Cure to Stop Drinking, characterized in these eloquent words: "Guaranteed to cure the habit of drinking ardent spirits, or money refunded. It is the greatest temperance worker the world has ever known. It creates a desire for food instead of drink; it supplies and satisfies the desire instantly for liquor; without so doing no man could be cured. It is not intoxicating, but stimulates the entire system to healthy action without after-prostration. It quiets the nervous excitement, vertigo, muscular trembling, etc., improves the appetite and digestion, regulates the bowels, repairs waste and makes him feel like a man again; it acts promptly, and the man who takes it when the desire comes on will find he has conquered the terrible craving. Special prices to temperance societies." Perplexed that medical science has still to adopt this panacea, I forthwith rang up my doctor and read him the entire panegyric. His only answer was a savage bark of laughter, which confused me more than ever.

The next day, however, his nurse confided to me that old Doc Savage had been on a three-day drunk. There may be something to G-4261 after all.

While the purpose of most of Sears and Roebuck's merchandise in this particular epoch is abundantly clear, there are nevertheless a few items that plunge one into a brown study. What, for example, are we to make of No. 63632: "Universal Wolf Tooth Forceps for extracting wolf teeth. Length 9 inches, weight ¾ pound; nickel plated. Price $3."? Granted our forebears were hardy folk and made of sterner stuff than today's milksops, it seems curious that they should have practiced orthodontia on wolves. And even assuming they did, what added value should there be in a toothless wolf? Perhaps the extraction was an initial step in converting him into a fur coat like No. 4442, the Spotted Dog. On the other hand, the legend of Count Dracula was fresh in people's minds in that era, and eradicating wolf molars may have been visualized as helping to stamp out vampirism. Equally mystifying in the catalogue was No. 3908, an article classified as "Ladies' Fine Felt Nullifier, Fur Trimmer". I supposed at first that this must be some sort of weapon like a persuader or blackjack, an instrument for ridding oneself of unwelcome suitors—a fur-trimmed billy, that is, or a spray-gun equipped with sneeze powder—, but then it developed that there was a Men's Nullifier as well. Eventually, a description did emerge reluctantly, *viz.*: "The Nullifier is fast becoming the most popular slipper on the market, and it deserves to be. Made from a very fine selection of tan or russet goat, etc., etc." Palpably my original suspicion had been correct; it was a boot designed to administer a kick in the *Sitzfleisch* to anyone whose society had become repellent.

Almost as perplexing an item of merchandise was the false beard, two types of which were offered—No. 24791 on wire at $1.00 and No. 24792 at $2.00, the latter described as "ventilated". It does not require the mentality of a Sherlock Holmes to reason that an individual affecting a false beard is up to no good, and whether the beard is ventilated or not couldn't matter a tinker's dam. The section on wigs attached to the foregoing, by the by, is worth passing mention. "To measure for a toupee," it states, "cut a piece of paper the exact size and shape of the bald spot." Anybody agile enough to measure his own bald spot, even with a series of reflecting mirrors, would qualify as a circus acrobat, and as for asking wife, concubine, or secretary to assist him in the task, the thought is too humiliating to entertain. To further bewilder students of the catalogue, finally, there is a version of that popular Victorian pastime, the stereopticon, that furnished 100 rather unsettling colored slides. The following were fairly representative: "Dentist drawing teeth; bull tossing dog; woman beating boy; parson carrying pig; Vesuvius in eruption; man swallowing rats; treading in father's shoes." A tasty collation indeed for the family to feast their eyes on as they sat around the parlor of a winter evening. Television with its noisy mayhem was still half a century away, but I doubt whether it has yet produced anything quite as toothsome.

The majority of the books advertised by Sears, speaking of matters cultural, were

in contrast highly moral and inspirational in that vanished period—the novels of Augusta J. Evans, Marie Corelli, Mrs. Humphrey Ward, *et al.* As might be expected, Horatio Alger, the foremost apostle of the American success myth, was represented with a good-sized sprinkling of titles, including these favorites: *"Dan the Newsboy, Frank Fowler the Cash Boy, Tom the Bootblack, Tony the Hero, Joe's Luck, The Train Boy,* and *Tom Temple's Career."* All of these homilies, which, parenthetically, I read from cover to cover in my own youth, stressed virtues like honesty, manliness, and frugality; so it is refreshing to turn from so much sugary sentiment to the boys' clothing section of the catalogue and discover that youthful egotism was kept firmly under control. "Special prices on knee pants for boys from 4 to 14 years of age," declared a streamer. "A glance at our price and you will wonder how it is possible to furnish a pair of boy's knee pants at the price we offer them (15¢, 25¢, 38¢); but in our tailoring department we have many remnants which can be used only to advantage in boy's pants." It must have been a salutary experience for some bumptious little weasel, brimful of Alger's cant, suddenly to comprehend from the foregoing that his breeches were no more than scraps.

Again and again throughout these 700 diverse pages, the reader is exhorted, besought, entreated, and begged to take advantage of the multitudinous bargains clogging the warehouses in Chicago, and the prose these appeals are couched in provides an interesting contrast with today's merchandising methods. There is, for example, the sexy approach, typified by this appeal lurking in the ladies' millinery section: "We are naming such prices as will bring out many a dollar that has been hidden away in a stocking." Then there is the fiscal ploy, inspired, no doubt, by the then current activities of William Jennings Bryan: "You can talk about free silver and free gold. Wherever high prices prevail there is little freedom of any kind of money. It's such prices as are named in this book that loosens the money market." Emotion, obviously, had got the better of the copywriter's syntax in his closing sentence, but I question whether the catalogue was beamed primarily at grammarians. Still another type of bait is the philanthropic, in which Sears and Roebuck portrayed themselves as public benefactors clothed in white samite: "It is safe to say that we are doing more for the farmer and the laborer than all the political demagogues in the country. The economy of any man's life resolves itself into a judicious expenditure of what money he has, whether the amount is large or small. Our factory-to-consumer system brings about a revolution in profits, and is in reality a profit-sharing enterprise, as the consumer benefits by the middleman's profits which are cut off by our methods of merchandising." This sanctimonious pose gives way later to one in which the firm adopts the role of a publishing titan like Pulitzer or Hearst: "Once in a while you will get circulars from us. These circulars are worth as much to you as most of the newspapers you get. They contain News that touches your pocketbook. They tell of War on prices. They tell of Killing Competition. They tell of the Science of systematic merchandising. They tell of High Art in wearing apparel. If you want news of War, Sensation, Science, and Art, read our circulars." Perhaps the most succinct policy statement of all is that contained in the

footwear division, which states flatly, "Our boot and shoe department is admirable. If we can't suit you in quality and price, there is no use looking further." In other words, go barefoot and be damned, runs the assumption, because nobody could satisfy a *nudnick* like you. It is a breath of sheer ozone, the storekeeper's basic malevolence toward the customer boiling up to the surface, and one too rarely met with in today's marketplace.

"Backward o backward, turn time in thy flight," the poet implores, and it is a privilege of sorts to reverse the clock threescore years and ten and see how Grandpa's generation lived. The automobile, the supermart, and the TV commercial, all of which were to revolutionize our existence for better or worse, lay far in the future; here, in the Sears catalogue, was a fairyland for kiddies from nine to ninety, a garden of wonders appealing to every taste. How universal it was may be summed up in a final testimonial letter embalmed in the text from a Mr. M. C. Kessler of Frametown, West Virginia, who wrote this touching tribute: "Sirs: Your shipment of the revolvers was received some time ago, but I have been very busy and did not write. They have proven very satisfactory, and if I ever want anything of the kind again, you will get my orders." Exactly on whom the writer used his purchase, what dramatic occurrence underlies his words, we shall never know, but it hardly matters. At the moment he wrote, he was a satisfied customer and a happy man, and whether in 1897 or 1968, that's rare enough.

# WHAT AMERICA WAS LIKE:

## 1895–1905

If turn-of-the-century Americans had a favorite word it was *progress*. The country's future seemed limitless; each generation would be taller, more widely educated, healthier, richer—in short, *better*—than the one it succeeded. Science and medicine knew no boundaries; Americans would one day free themselves from disease, poverty, even from their ties to the earth. Such a faith went hand in hand with both generosity and acquisitiveness. America opened its doors to millions of people "yearning to breathe free"; after all, thought the sprawling nation, its resources were inexhaustible. Americans also wanted their own share.

Into this burgeoning and optimistic society dropped an object of nearly magical power: a book that offered almost every item anyone could need to make life complete. Readers of the *Consumers' Guide*, a new catalogue published by a young company called Sears, Roebuck, could discover—and, if they chose, *own*—anything from a new baby carriage to a new house to a new corset. In the book's hundreds of densely illustrated pages lay a profusion of dreams. Along with objects familiar but "improved," there were strange and wonderful things people never knew they needed until they saw them in the "Wish Book" (as Americans soon fondly tagged the bulky catalogue).

People's desires are shaped in part by the world around them. At the turn of the century, Americans read newspapers, books, and magazines; talked with friends, neighbors, and fellow workers; sang together at church, in the saloon, or at Fourth of July picnics; examined photograph albums and peered through stereopticons together in the parlor. Some of their images and books and songs are fresh today; others shimmer only dimly in the half-light of cultural history.

Readers of the early Wish Book might have inhabited any state of the Union. They might be well-to-do or working class, old or young. They might be black or white or yellow, native born or recently immigrated. Whoever they were, their needs and dreams reflected a busy, ambitious, patriotic, confident—even cocky—national ethos. But what made them tick? What caught their interest, what worried them, what made them so sure of their bright, expanding future? And when they reached it, what did they expect to find on their plates? The answers lie in their daily menu of news; then as now, events, trends, and personalities that occupied the national press both shaped and mirrored the national mind. Here, offering a glimpse of that mind, are some of the news items reported between 1895 and 1905.

**1895**

Sears, Roebuck establishes a mail-order business, selling its wares through a large, inviting catalogue. At first appealing mostly to remote farm families, the "Wish Book" soon finds customers in towns and cities as well.

The decade's best-selling books—all of them romances—include *The Prisoner of Zenda*, by Anthony Hope; *Graustark*, by George Barr McCutcheon; *Quo Vadis?*, by Henryk Sienkiewicz; and *When Knighthood Was in Flower*, by Charles Major. Also popular is Stephen Crane's 1895 Civil War masterpiece, *The Red Badge of Courage*.

Future author, editor, and educator W. E. B. Du Bois becomes the first black to receive a degree from Harvard University.

The number of automobiles registered in the United States rises to 300.

At Wisconsin's Yerkes Observatory, University of Chicago scientists install the world's most powerful telescopes, giving American astronomers a substantial edge over global competition.

Fashion decrees that women's skirts may be raised as much as two inches from the ankle, but only in bicycling outfits and only when the hem contains lead weights to keep it down.

Illustrator Charles Henry Gibson creates an idealized female with upswept hair, a generous bosom, wasp waist, and "ladylike" expression. The Gibson Girl will become America's ideal of feminine beauty for the rest of the decade.

**1896**

Utah joins the Union, becoming the nation's 45th state and the first to give women the vote.

In June, inventor Charles E. Duryea becomes the first American to receive a patent for a gasoline-driven automobile. Five months later, Chicago hosts the nation's first race for self-propelled vehicles; the winner is an imported Benz, the only car to make it to the finish line.

Latrobe, Pennsylvania, is the site of the nation's first professional football game, a match between the home team and one from nearby Jeannette, Pennsylvania.

Bowling enthusiasts establish the American Bowling Congress, a body that helps repopularize the old sport.

A U.S. Supreme Court case, *Plessy v. Ferguson*, legalizes racial segregation in the United States.

"The Yellow Kid," America's first comic strip, appears in the New York *World*. "Mr. Dooley," Finley Peter Dunne's phenomenally popular, Irish-accented humor column, debuts in a Chicago newspaper. "Dorothy Dix," America's favorite giver of advice to the lovelorn, meets her public via the *New Orleans Picayune*.

Former professional baseball player Billy Sunday, America's best-known and most flamboyant preacher, is ordained in April.

Revolution breaks out in Nicaragua; the United States sends the Marines.

Olympic Games are staged in Athens, Greece. Dominated by American athletes, they are the first such events to be held in 15 centuries.

In one of America's most electrifying political speeches, William Jennings Bryan—Nebraska Democrat, presidential hopeful, and silver-standard enthusiast—thunders, "You shall not crucify mankind upon a cross of gold!"

*Evangelist Billy Sunday*

The country's most popular song is "There'll Be a Hot Time in the Old Town Tonight."

Working in a Detroit shed, Henry Ford and his aides put the last touches on the first Ford automobile.

Miners discover gold in northwest Canada's Klondike Creek; within months, some 30,000 American prospectors have raced across the border.

A Manhattan music hall shows the first publicly screened movie, a collection of brief scenes involving dancing, comic boxing, and ocean waves. "Wonderfully real and singularly exhilarating," comments the *New York Times*.

*1897*

Republican William McKinley becomes the nation's 25th president.

*In His Steps*, a collection of sermons by Charles M. Sheldon, a hitherto unknown minister from Topeka, Kansas, becomes the year's runaway best-seller. The year's most popular song is "On the Banks of the Wabash."

America's first subway system opens in Boston.

Prizefighter Bob Fitzsimmons defeats popular world champion "Gentleman Jim" Corbett with a brand-new move—the "solar plexus punch"—after 14 bruising rounds.

*1898*

The United States annexes Hawaii.

The U.S. battleship *Maine* blows up in the harbor of Havana, Cuba, killing 260 American sailors; allegedly engineered by Spanish agents ("Remember the *Maine*! To hell with Spain!" chant furious Americans), the explosion leads to the brief but violent Spanish-American War, won by the United States with the aid of future president Theodore (Teddy) Roosevelt and his "Rough Riders." Also instrumental in gaining the victory are 20 black regiments and Commodore George Dewey, who destroys the Spanish fleet at Manila Bay, the Philippines.

The United States takes Puerto Rico from Spain. Along with Hawaii, Puerto Rico will become a U.S. territory in 1900.

*Theodore Roosevelt*

*1899*

With the publication of Scott Joplin's "Maple Leaf Rag," ragtime becomes one of the nation's hottest musical styles. Another big song of the year is the gaudily sentimental "She Was Only a Bird in a Gilded Cage."

For the first time, an American president, William McKinley, rides in an automobile (a Stanley Steamer). Nevertheless, sniffs the conservative *Literary Digest*, "the horseless carriage . . . will never come into as common use as the bicycle." (At this time, the country boasts 4,000 automobiles and 10 million bikes.)

Congress approves the first use of voting machines for federal elections.

The Gideons, a group of Christian traveling salesmen, place a Bible in the Superior Hotel of Iron Mountain, Montana. The move introduces the Gideons' ambitious—and eventually successful—plan to put a Bible in every hotel room in America.

*1900*

The number of immigrants since 1880 reaches almost 4 million; the entire U.S. population hits 75,994,575. Collectively, these people use 1.3 million telephones, drive 8,000 cars, and smoke 4 billion cigarettes a year. (Cigars, chewing tobacco, and pipes, however, remain far more popular than cigarettes.)

*Prohibitionist Carry Nation*

Life expectancy at birth is 51 years for women, 48 years for men. American adult illiteracy stands at 10.7 percent, down from 20 percent in 1870.

A Galveston, Texas, hurricane kills 6,000 people and causes more than $20 million in property damage. In Hoboken, New Jersey, a steamship fire kills 326 people.

The year's biggest hit songs are "Good-Bye, Dolly Gray" and "In the Good Old Summertime."

Hoping to obtain more than the prevailing 30 cents a day for seamstresses, union organizers establish the International Ladies' Garment Workers' Union.

Antiliquor activist Carry Nation kicks off her crusade for Prohibition (which will finally arrive in 1919) by leading an ax-wielding group of women through the saloons of Kansas.

Trying to save his passengers, veteran railroad engineer Casey Jones refuses to leave his hurtling, out-of-control "Cannonball Express"; he dies at the throttle and becomes an instant folk hero.

## 1901

McKinley is assassinated in September, catapulting Vice-president Theodore Roosevelt into the White House. The new chief executive delights voters with his motto: "Speak softly and carry a big stick."

Financier J. P. Morgan incorporates the United States Steel corporation, a gigantic trust capitalized at $400 million. At this point, one percent of the population owns seven-eighths of the nation's wealth.

Although he is a renowned marksman, President Theodore Roosevelt refuses to shoot a baby bear during a hunt, charming the nation and resulting in a much-loved new toy: the Teddy Bear.

The great Texas oil boom begins with the discovery of Spindletop, a spectacular gusher near Beaumont.

President Theodore Roosevelt surprises the nation and horrifies the white South by inviting black educator Booker T. Washington to a White House lunch.

## 1902

*In Dahomey,* a wildly popular musical by poet Paul Laurence Dunbar and composer Will Marion Cook, opens in Boston; the most successful black musical to date, the show will run for three years.

Inventor-businessman King C. Gillette begins to manufacture safety razors with disposable blades.

Ida Tarbell publishes a stunning exposé of the oil business: *History of the Standard Oil Company.* The report is one of several sensational "muckraking" works including Frank Norris's *The Octopus* and *The Pit,* Lincoln Steffans's *The Shame of the Cities,* Upton Sinclair's *The Jungle,* and Jack London's *The Iron Heel.*

Congress passes the Reclamation Act, which starts the federal national park system and opens an era of natural-resource conservation. Legislators also pass the Isthmian Canal Act, which will lead to U.S. construction of the strategically and commercially crucial Panama Canal (to be completed in 1920).

Two books dominate the literary year. The first is Owen Wister's best-selling western novel *The Virginian.* The second is Helen Keller's *The Story of My Life,* the autobiography of a 23-year-old woman who has been blind and deaf since infancy.

In posh Saratoga, New York, a society matron creates a national furor by wearing a split skirt and riding astride her horse. The daring equestrian claims her system beats riding sidesaddle and is just as modest.

W. E. B. Du Bois publishes *The Souls of Black Folk*, a precedent-shattering approach to social reform for black Americans that advocates patriotic, nonviolent activism. Jack London's *The Call of the Wild*, his most popular novel, appears.

1903

Florida's Pelican Island becomes the first U.S. federal wildlife refuge.

A fire in Chicago's Iroquois Theatre kills 588 people and leads to passage of public-safety laws.

In the first transcontinental trip for a gasoline-powered vehicle, a Packard car travels from San Francisco to New York in 52 days.

In baseball's first World Series, the American League's Boston Red Sox trounce the National League's Pittsburgh Pirates five games to three.

Director Edwin S. Porter releases a 14-minute western, *The Great Train Robbery*, the first American film with a plot.

President Theodore Roosevelt sends the first around-the-world cable message; transmitted in part by the new Pacific Cable, the message returns to the president in exactly 12 minutes.

1904

At Kitty Hawk, North Carolina, Orville and Wilbur Wright achieve the first successful flight of a large, heavier-than-air machine—the 12-HP *Flyer*, which travels 120 feet in 12 seconds.

New York State passes the first U.S. speed law: the limits are 10 MPH in cities, 15 in villages, and 20 on country roads.

Theodore Roosevelt wins election to his first full term as president.

Opening in the Broadway play *Sunday*, Ethel Barrymore ad libs her best-known line: "That's all there is, there isn't any more."

Competing transatlantic steamship companies reduce rates for steerage passengers to $10. At this point, one million immigrants are entering the United States each year.

A New York City woman lights a cigarette, then finds herself under arrest. "You can't do that on Fifth Avenue," says the arresting policeman.

*Actress Ethel Barrymore*

UPI/Bettmann Newsphotos

1905

The Rules Committee of Football makes sweeping revisions: forward passes are legalized, for example, but many violent scrimmage plays are made illegal. A black athlete, Bob Marshall of the University of Minnesota, is selected for the All-American Football team.

Radical labor leaders meet in Chicago to establish a new union, the Industrial Workers of the World, which will also become known as the IWW or the Wobblies. "The working class and the employing class have nothing in common," declare IWW founders.

On its Chicago-to-California run, the Chicago and North Western Railway introduces the first electrically lighted train.

Automobile registrations rise to 77,988.

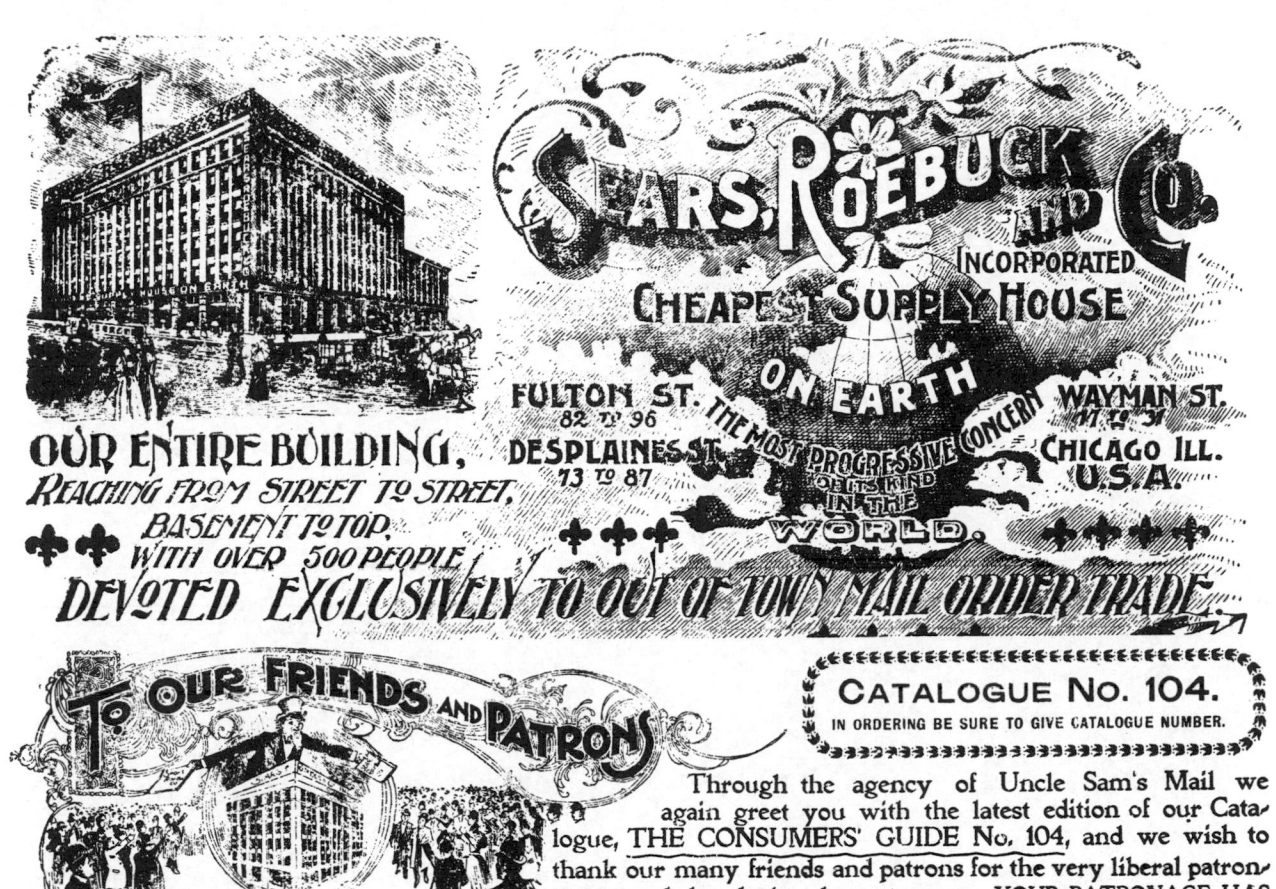

**SEARS, ROEBUCK AND CO.**
INCORPORATED
CHEAPEST SUPPLY HOUSE ON EARTH
THE MOST PROGRESSIVE CONCERN OF ITS KIND IN THE WORLD.

FULTON ST. 82 TO 96
DESPLAINES ST. 73 TO 87
WAYMAN ST.
CHICAGO ILL. U.S.A.

OUR ENTIRE BUILDING, REACHING FROM STREET TO STREET, BASEMENT TO TOP, WITH OVER 500 PEOPLE DEVOTED EXCLUSIVELY TO OUT OF TOWN MAIL ORDER TRADE.

TO OUR FRIENDS AND PATRONS

**CATALOGUE No. 104.**
IN ORDERING BE SURE TO GIVE CATALOGUE NUMBER.

Through the agency of Uncle Sam's Mail we again greet you with the latest edition of our Catalogue, THE CONSUMERS' GUIDE No. 104, and we wish to thank our many friends and patrons for the very liberal patronage accorded us during the past season. YOUR PATRONAGE HAS BEEN SO VERY LIBERAL that our business has grown beyond our most sanguine expectations; in fact, we honestly believe the remarkable growth of our business is without a parallel in the history of mercantile concerns.

WE CAN ASSURE YOU THAT YOUR TRADE HAS BEEN GREATLY APPRECIATED, and at no time have we been blind to the great responsibility taken in the endeavor to fill promptly the thousands of orders and answer the thousands of inquiries that reach us daily.

WE HAVE SPARED NEITHER TIME NOR MONEY to care for our customers' every want. It has been our constant aim to so please every customer that he would become our friend, and as a friend would use his kind influence among his friends and neighbors in our behalf.

THE VERY REMARKABLE GROWTH OF OUR BUSINESS IS THE MOST SATISFACTORY PROOF to us that we have succeeded; and yet at times the volume of business offered us by our country friends has been almost beyond our maximum capacity. But experience has taught us that it is safe to anticipate the wants of our customers. Experience has taught us that the people throughout the length and breadth of the land are anxious to give their material support to a house WHERE THEY CAN BUY THEIR GOODS AT WHOLESALE PRICES, where they can send their orders and their money with the positive assurance that they will be treated in exactly the same way as we would like to be treated were we in their place.

THE THOUSANDS OF UNSOLICITED TESTIMONIALS which reach us from prominent people in every state and territory, THE FLATTERING NOTICES WHICH APPEAR IN THE PRESS, the very apparent increase in the number of orders we receive each succeeding month, demonstrate to us beyond any question of doubt that WE HAVE THE CONFIDENCE OF OUR CUSTOMERS, that they are in favor of this method of merchandising, that they are using their influence everywhere in our behalf, and in consequence of this assurance we are making very extensive preparations for the future, and, though pointing to the past with no little pride, for the future we can safely assure you even better values, prompter shipments, and we believe such treatment in general as can be secured from no other concern.

OUR FACILITIES FOR HANDLING MERCHANDISE on a very large scale, and yet on a most economical basis, are unexcelled.

WE OCCUPY ONE OF THE LARGEST BUSINESS BLOCKS FOR BLOCKS AROUND. The above illustration engraved from a photograph will give you a very good idea of the appearance of the building. It was built expressly for us, and to facilitate the accurate, rapid and economical handling of merchandise. The building extends one whole block long on Desplaines St., reaching from Fulton to Wayman, and about half a block on Fulton St. It has six full stories and basement, and we occupy it entire. We also utilize other space in other buildings for storage.

IN THIS BUILDING WE EMPLOY BETWEEN 600 AND 700 PEOPLE, whose entire time is devoted to the wants and needs of our country customers who send their orders to us by mail, and receive in return the merchandise by freight, express or mail; in other words, OUR BUSINESS IS DEVOTED EXCLUSIVELY TO THE OUT-OF-TOWN MAIL ORDER TRADE.

# SEARS, ROEBUCK AND CO.
## CONSUMERS GUIDE
### INCORPORATED — CHEAPEST SUPPLY HOUSE ON EARTH — OUR TRADE REACHES AROUND THE WORLD
### NUMBER 104

## THE POLICY OF OUR HOUSE

**It is the Policy of Our House to Supply the Consumer Everything on which we can save him money,** goods that can be delivered at your door anywhere in the United States for less than they can be procured from your local dealer; and although our line covers about everything the consumer uses, there is scarcely an article but what will admit of a saving of at least 15%, and from that to 75%, to say nothing of the fact that our goods are as a rule of a higher grade than those carried by the average retailer or catalogue house, and we earnestly believe a careful comparison will convince you that we can furnish you more and better goods for your dollar than you can obtain from any other establishment in the United States.

### We Aim to Illustrate Honestly and Correctly Every

**Article.** So far as possible, illustrations are engraved from photographs taken directly from the article. Our illustrations and descriptions are such as will enable you to order intelligently; in fact, so that you can tell what you are getting as well as if you were in our store selecting the goods from stock.

### We Employ No Agents.
By the aid of our numerous catalogues our customers can deal with us direct. Thus the **Farmer, Miner, Mechanic, Business Man,** in fact anyone, can send in his or her own order and save money.

### Our Terms are Alike to All.

### Our Employees are Instructed to Treat Every Customer

### at a Distance Exactly as They Would Like to be Treated

were they in the customer's place; in fact, if you favor us with your patronage we will feel under obligations to do everything in our power to merit your trade, and no matter how small your order may be it will receive the same prompt and careful attention as if it were ever so large.

### We Aim to Treat Our Customers
in a manner calculated to secure their permanent patronage. **The unprecedented growth of our business proves that we have succeeded in supplying the wants of the people in a satisfactory manner and at lower prices than** they could possibly secure elsewhere.

### We Deem that the Best Advertisement Any Firm Can

**Have** is a well satisfied customer. **We aim to bring the manufacturer and consumer closer together.** The closer the relation between the manufacturer and consumer, the more economy to all concerned, and in a great measure it does away with the long chain of profits in the handling of merchandise.

### We are Able by Reason of Our Enormous Output of

**Goods** to make contracts with representative manufacturers and importers for such large quantities of merchandise that we can secure the lowest possible prices. To this we add the smallest percentage of profit possible, and through the medium of catalogues offer the goods to our customers, and on our economic one-small-profit plan, direct from manufacturer to consumer, a large percentage of the merchandise we handle is owned by the purchaser at less than local dealers can buy in quantities.

### A Trial Order Will Convince You of the Saving
worked by our economic one-small-profit plan. If you contemplate purchasing any article of merchandise, we would consider it a privilege to quote you our lowest price, irrespective of whether you buy from us or not. **It will be a safeguard against your paying someone else too much money.** It will also open up a correspondence between us, and may eventually lead to our selling you some article of merchandise by which we may be able to demonstrate the saving of our method.

## WHERE WE SELL GOODS

**Our Catalogues and Other Printed Matter may Fall into the Hands of those Living at Remote Distances** who will not think of buying owing to the great distance. Don't think you live too far away. **THERE IS NOT A TOWN IN THE UNITED STATES WHERE WE HAVE NOT SOLD GOODS.** Our goods go into every city, town and hamlet in every state, as well as to almost every country on the globe. **DISTANCE CUTS NO FIGURE.** We can serve you at any time and in any place. Our largest trade is in Pennsylvania, next in New York, third Illinois, fourth Ohio, and so on according to the population of the different states.

### Freight and Express Rates are Usually Low
and we have special facilities for shipping, carefully consulting the various classifications so as to pack your goods in such a manner as will entitle them to the lowest possible transportation charges.

### Get Other Information Concerning Express and Freight

**Rates** on the following pages, and you will see that the transportation amounts to next to nothing as compared with what you save in price.

### Consider You Pay Freight or Express no matter Where

### You Live or Where You Buy.
You may as well pay it to the railroad company and be dealing direct with first hands, as to pay it in the way of an exorbitant price to local dealers.

## ABOUT UNPROFITABLE SHIPMENTS.

### We Not Infrequently Receive Orders which we Term

**"Unprofitable" Shipments.** For example: A party living far distant may order a dollar's worth of sugar to go by express. The express charges would equal the cost of the sugar. We occasionally get an order for heavy hardware, the order amounting to perhaps less than $5.00. The goods weigh 100 pounds. We are asked to ship them by express. This is usually an unprofitable shipment. A single pair of heavy cheap boots to go a great distance by express, or of very bulky woodenware, or furniture, or other merchandise, might be what we term an unprofitable shipment.

### We Would Advise Our Customers to Study the Freight

### and Express Rates
as given on the following pages, for we do not wish you to send us a dollar for anything unless we can save you money on the purchase.

### Orders that Would Be Unprofitable to Ship by Mail

### or Express May Be Very Profitable When Sent by

**Freight,** but as 100 pounds is usually carried by freight for the same charge as 10 pounds, by adding other merchandise to your order, either for yourself or by getting your neighbors to join you in making up a large order, it will make the shipment very profitable.

# About our Prices

**It will ever be our aim to maintain the reputation we have earned as THE CHEAPEST SUPPLY HOUSE ON EARTH.**

**WE EMPLOY THE MOST COMPETENT BUYERS** that money can obtain, and their long experience with us places them in a position to understand our customers' wants.

**WE PAY CASH** for all goods, no matter how large the quantity, and our established reputation gives our buyers the inside track with every manufacturer in the country, thereby giving us the benefit of first choice on the market.

**IF YOU BUY FROM US** you will get your goods for as little or less money than your local dealer does. As our immense trade requires us to purchase in such large quantities from American and European manufacturers, and always for cash, we are assured of the lowest possible prices.

**THEN WE SELL FOR CASH,** having no bad debts, no traveling men's expenses, no expenses for collections, hence we can sell at a far lower margin of profit than any other dealer, and when you buy from us you are not helping to pay for all such useless expenses,

**OUR BUYERS ARE ALWAYS ON THE ALERT FOR SPECIAL SALES.** If there is a manufacturer or importer who is temporarily embarrassed and must have money, we are ready to buy, and our customers always get the benefit of our bargains.

**FROM TIME TO TIME YOU WILL BE OFFERED MERCHANDISE,** even many of the articles quoted in this catalogue, at less money than the actual cost to produce. Our bargains are our customers' bargains. No matter how cheap we buy, we add the smallest percentage of profit possible consistent with honest goods and honest representations, and that is our net price to one and all, the price against which no other concern can compete; prices that establish us as the **CHEAPEST SUPPLY HOUSE ON EARTH.**

# About our RELIABILITY

**As this Catalogue may fall into the Hands of some who are not Acquainted WITH OUR REPUTATION FOR FAIR AND HONORABLE DEALING** and do not know of our financial standing, would say we are authorized and incorporated under the laws of the State of Illinois with a cash capital and surplus of $250,000.00, paid in full.

**WE REFER BY SPECIAL PERMISSION** to the **NATIONAL BANK OF THE REPUBLIC,** to any Express Company in Chicago, any old reliable business house or financial institution in this city, or, if you have any friends residing in this city, write **them** and ask them concerning our house.

**ON ANOTHER PAGE** we show a fac simile copy of the letter given us by the **National Bank of the Republic.** Such a letter would not be given to any concern unless **their** reputation was beyond any question of doubt. Should you write for information to any of the references given, be sure to enclose a two cent stamp for **reply.**

**WE GIVE YOU THIS PRIVILEGE: IF YOU HAVE ANY DOUBT** as to our reliability you can send **your** order and money to the National Bank of the Republic, or any express **company** in Chicago, with instructions not to turn it over to us unless they know **us to be** thoroughly reliable and a concern that will do exactly as we agree.

## RULES, CONDITIONS OF SHIPMENT, TERMS, ETC.

**PLEASE READ THE FOLLOWING RULES AND CONDITIONS VERY CAREFULLY: To conduct our business** in a gratifying, prosperous and beneficial manner, it is necessary that **we** establish certain rules to govern our movements so as to enable us to handle **all** orders and correspondence in a successful and satisfactory way. To prevent **any** misunderstanding we therefore ask your careful attention to the following rules and **conditions from** which we cannot deviate under any circumstances.

**The Prices we Quote for Goods in Our Store.** All expense of transportation **of goods and Money MUST BE BORNE BY THE PURCHASER.** All quotations are **subject to** fluctuation of the market without notice to the purchaser. **IF THERE IS A DECLINE WE WILL GIVE YOU THE BENEFIT OF THE DECLINE** and refund the difference. **IF THERE IS AN ADVANCE,** we will charge you for such advance. The prices quoted in this book are correct at the time of printing, and as a rule there is very little variation until the next time following.

# TERMS

**We Desire to Make Our Terms of Shipment as Liberal as Possible,** consistent with absolute safety and without loss, which would otherwise add to our selling price.

**ALL GOODS EXCEPT CUT PIECE OR DRESS GOODS** will be shipped by **FREIGHT** or **EXPRESS C. O. D.** subject to examination where a sufficient amount accompanies the order to cover transportation charges both ways, in case goods are not accepted, and unless otherwise specified one-fourth the amount of bill should accompany the order, the balance to be paid after goods have been received.

**WE POSITIVELY REQUIRE CASH IN ADVANCE** for goods and postage when goods are to be sent by mail. Send enough and we will refund the amount overpaid, if any, but do not fail to include enough for postage if to go by mail.

**MANY ARTICLES OF MERCHANDISE** will be shipped by freight or express C. O. D. subject to examination upon receipt of a very small deposit. In such cases special terms are plainly stated under the descriptions of the article.

**FOR EXAMPLE,** watches are sent C. O. D., subject to examination upon receipt of a 50 cent deposit; Clothing on receipt of $1.00; Vehicles on receipt of $5.00 to $10.00, but unless otherwise specified one-fourth the amount of bill should accompany the order.

☞ No Cash Discount will be allowed on C. O. D. Shipments.

☞ See our Special Offer of Discount on Cash Orders, page 3.

# Express Shipments

**Goods will be Sent by Express C.O.D.**

(collect on delivery) and subject to examination, in compliance with our terms as above explained, and may be examined at the express office in the presence of the Express Company's Agent.

**PLEASE DO NOT ABUSE THIS PRIVILEGE** by occupying the agent's time, but endeavor to cause him as little trouble as possible.

**WE ARE WILLING** to have our customers examine the goods and be satisfied they are the same as ordered before paying for them, but that privilege is gratuitous on the part of the express company and should be appreciated.

**WE USE BOXES** or cases for express shipments only when necessary to insure safe transportation, but make no charge for such.

**WE PACK ALL EXPRESS SHIPMENTS** so as to make the lightest package possible, thus reducing the express charges to the minimum.

**THERE IS NO NECESSITY OF PREPAYING CHARGES** unless you are sending goods to a friend inasmuch as the charges are the same at either end of the line.

**ON ANOTHER PAGE WE SHOW EXPRESS RATES** on packages of different weights to different points of the United States, from which you can approximate the express rates to your place.

# Freight Shipments

**We will Forward Goods by Freight to Anyone** who sends the money with the order.

**WE WILL ALSO SHIP THE GOODS** by freight in our name and collect through your express agent or nearest bank, if sufficient money is sent with your order to cover freight charges, as before explained. Freight charges must be prepaid to points where there is no Railroad Station; otherwise it is not necessary as the rates are the same whether prepaid or collected at destination.

**REMEMBER OUR LIABILITY** ceases as soon as we receive a clear receipt from the transportation company. We will make claim on the transportation company for loss or damage to goods in transit for your account if so desired, and we will cheerfully render you all assistance in our power to make prompt collection.

**TO ASCERTAIN THE FREIGHT RATE** on any goods wanted consult your local freight agent or compute the freight rates by the cwt. on the different classes of merchandise to the town nearest you as shown on the following pages, from which you can approximate the rate to your town; or, when so desired, we will quote you the freight rate.

**WE MAKE NO CHARGES** for Boxes or Cases, but pack and deliver all goods on board the cars in Chicago, except Vehicles, which are quoted F. O. B. factory.

# Mail Shipments

**Postage on Goods by Mail is One Cent per Ounce** or fraction thereof, being 16c per pound.

**NO ONE PACKAGE** must exceed 4 pounds, but any number of packages may be sent to the same address weighing 4 pounds or less each.

**PACKAGES CAN BE SENT** by registered mail for 8c per package extra.

**WE WOULD ADVISE** insuring all mail shipments. (See insurance information under next heading.) **The insurance** fee is usually less than the cost of registering and in case of loss we will duplicate the shipment. The invoice or bill generally follows the goods within two days.

**EXPLOSIVES, POISONOUS OR INFLAMMABLE ARTICLES** are unmailable. Sharp pointed instruments, and glass, such as needles, knives, pens, lantern slides, etc., can go in mailable cases at an extra cost of 5c. Liquids not more than 4 oz. may be enclosed in vials and packed in wooden boxes as provided for by the United States Postal Laws. Allow 5c for liquid cases.

**WE ARE CONSTANTLY SENDING OUT** large quantities of goods by mail to all parts of the Union, and with very few exceptions goods reach their destination.

**ALL GOODS SENT BY MAIL** are at purchaser's risk unless insured,

**WE CAN ASSUME NO RESPONSIBILITY** after goods are deposited in the postoffice. We would advise insuring everything of value,

# Insure Mail Shipments

We have Perfected a Plan of Postal **Insurance** and will, until further notice, insure small packages when so **instructed** for 5¢ for each package, $5.00 or under in value; 10¢ for packages valued at from $5.00 to $10.00, and 5¢ for each additional $5.00 in value.

**IF YOU WANT YOUR PACKAGES INSURED** be sure to write "insure" in your order and inclose the insurance fee. ☞ **Prompt notification of the failure to receive packages is necessary to secure adjustments.**

**ALWAYS MENTION YOUR INVOICE NUMBER** When it is necessary to write us Regarding any Shipment or any portion of an Order.

**AS SOON AS WE RECEIVE YOUR ORDER** we notify you by postal card, giving the invoice number of the order. **FAILURE TO RCEIVE SUCH NOTICE** indicates that your order has not reached us. **ALL CLAIMS** for shortage, damage, etc., must be made within 5 days from receipt of invoice.

## HOW TO ORDER

### Fill out Closely all the Blank Spaces in Our Order Sheet

as shown in filled out sample order blank on page 9. and if you do not have an order sheet CLOSELY FOLLOW THESE INSTRUCTIONS:

WRITE YOUR NAME CLEARLY AND DISTINCTLY. Many people forget to sign their name. In such case order has to be held till customer complains.

Give your POSTOFFICE, NAME, also street address, shipping point, and then say what county and state.

SAY FROM WHAT CATALOGUE ORDERED, and always give the catalogue number and price of each article wanted, being particular to mention the size, color and other necessary references. Give other necessary descriptions.

STATE PLAINLY HOW MUCH MONEY INCLOSED and, after noting our rules for shipments, say how you wish your goods forwarded, whether by mail, express or freight.

IF YOU DESIRE ANY INFORMATION, or wish to refer to any other matters, DO NOT WRITE ABOUT THEM ON YOUR ORDER, but communicate with us in a separate letter, as our correspondence and orders are handled in separate and distinct departments.

PLEASE DO NOT FAIL TO ADHERE TO THIS RULE: WRITE YOUR ORDER ONLY ON ONE SHEET and any letter or remarks on a separate sheet.

IT IS BEST to make express orders exceed $5.00 in value and freight orders exceed 100 pounds in weight.

WE DESIRE THAT OUR GOODS shall cost you less under all circumstances than you can possibly obtain them elsewhere.

WE ADVISE SENDING CLUB ORDERS so as to make a freight order of 100 pounds or more to get lowest transporation rate and best cash discount.

See Cash Discounts on this page. All about Club Orders Page 4.

## HOW TO SEND MONEY

### Remit by Postoffice Money Order, Express Money Order, Bank Draft or in Cash.

IF YOU SEND YOUR INDIVIDUAL CHECK on a local bank your order will be delayed until we make collection, and the expense of collection will be deducted.

POSTAGE STAMPS will be accepted in any amount as an accommodation to our customers.

WE RECOMMEND THE EXPRESS MONEY ORDER system because it is inexpensive, of less trouble and is safe; besides this, if it should get lost or miscarried your loss will be made good. Do not, under any circumstances, send money or stamps in a letter by open mail, as many such letters never reach us, and in such a case a great amount of trouble and inconvenience is caused, as well as the loss you sustain. If you prefer to remit by registered mail we advise the use of two envelopes, one inside of the other, and the outer one carefully and securely sealed. Do not send Gold or Silver coin that is defaced, as light weight coins are worth no more than bullion, and that is less than the face value of the coin.

WHEN WRITING TO US FOR PRICES, or when ordering goods not in catalogue, be careful to give full and complete description of the article wanted.

STATE IN WHAT QUANTITIES you wish to purchase and where there is a large range in prices, about what price you wish to pay.

IF POSSIBLE, SEND A PICTURE of the article desired, or make a drawing if it is difficult to describe.

IF YOU STATE FOR WHAT USE THE GOODS ARE INTENDED, we have practical experts in each department who can often suggest something better for less money.

THE FOLLOWING NECESSARY POINTS are often not given, viz.: Size, quality, finish, weight, color, maker's name, maker's number, material, width, height, length, depth, etc. We are at all times ready to serve you; but, please remember our clerks are not mind readers.

## ABOUT FREE SAMPLES

### For the Convenience of Our Customers

who wish to see samples of cloth before ordering we have prepared special separate sample cards on the following lines: Men's and boys' clothing, ladies' cloaks and capes, ladies' and men's mackintoshes, ladies' tailor made dresses, wrappers, waists and skirts.

THE ABOVE NAMED SPECIAL SAMPLE CARDS show the choicest selections from our entire stock; and to insure prompt attention we would recommend that you send for one of these sample cards in preference to selecting any special numbers from the catalogue. These sample cards are arranged to show the lines to better advantage, and besides will prevent unpleasant delays in cases where we might be out of the exact samples you might select from the numbers. However, should you desire to see a cloth sample of any special number in this catalogue, be sure to state the exact number and ask for no other samples except the numbers in which you are interested.

WHEN REQUESTED, we will furnish cloth samples of dry goods, carpets, etc.; but we would consider it a special favor if you would confine your request to the exact numbers and styles interested in. We are anxious that you should have the samples needed to make up your order, but as matter of economy of TIME we are compelled to urge our customers to confine themselves strictly to the exact number or kinds and prices of the goods interested in, and not ask for samples which will be of no use to them and considerable expense to us. The TIME used in supplying one applicant with samples amounts to very little, but in supplying several thousand daily it is very great; and in order to prevent any delay we trust you will adhere as closely as possible to our rules above in requesting our special sample cards. Furthermore, the cost of material used in supplying several thousand requests for samples daily is considerable, and you will be benefited by preventing the necessity of advancing prices of the goods as the cost of the samples very naturally increases the cost of the goods; at the same time we assure you we will deem it a privilege to supply you with the needed samples, and we thank you in advance for this privilege as well as for your consideration in making the request for samples as inexpensive for us as possible.

## HOW TO RETURN GOODS

### The United States Postal Laws and Regulations

require that all packages of merchandise sent in the mails must be wrapped or enveloped in such a manner that their contents may be readily examined by the postmaster without destroying the wrapper.

NEVER SEAL PACKAGES RETURNED BY MAIL, but tie them securely with twine.

DO NOT INCLOSE WRITTEN MATTER of any kind in mail packages, as by so doing you are liable to double letter postage or a fine of $10.00, and we in such cases deduct the extra postage from the value of the goods.

WHEN RETURNING A PACKAGE BY MAIL, address it plainly, and in the upper left hand corner write whom it is from, providing you do not have one of the labels we furnish for the purpose. Send us by separate mail the particulars or instructions.

NEVER RETURN GOODS BY EXPRESS if the weight is more than 25 pounds, as it is cheaper to send heavy packages by freight.

WHEN YOU RETURN GOODS BY EXPRESS OR FREIGHT be sure to inclose in the package your letter of instructions or particulars.

BEFORE RETURNING THE GOODS to us in any manner, we would ask that you communicate with us in regard to them.

IN ALL CASES, WHEN NECESSARY TO WRITE to us regarding an order, be sure to advise us the INVOICE NUMBER of the order you refer to.

DON'T FORGET the letter of full instructions should be in all express and freight shipments returned.

DON'T FORGET we must always have your INVOICE ORDER NUMBE Never write us about a shipment and omit the number.

## DISCOUNTS FOR CASH.

On C. O. D. Orders no Cash Discount will be allowed. THREE PER CENT. DISCOUNT will be allowed on all orders no matter how small IF ACCOMPANIED BY CASH IN FULL.

ON ORDERS AMOUNTING TO $50.00 and up to $100.000. 4% discount provided cash in full accompanies your order.

ON ORDERS AMOUNTING TO OVER $100.00 5% discount provided cash in full accompanies your order.

The above cash discounts DO NOT APPLY TO GROCERIES, BARB WIRE OR NAILS. On orders for Groceries amounting to $20.00 or over, accompanied by cash in full we allow 2% cash discount, except on sugar. Sugar, Nails and Barbed Wire are NET in all cases (no discount).

NEARLY ALL OUR CUSTOMERS SEND CASH IN FULL. It's the best way. You save the cash discount, save the return charges on money to us, besides we can, as a rule, make prompter shipment of cash in advance order than of C. O. D. order.

YOU TAKE NO RISK in sending cash in full with your order, for we will immediately refund your money if goods are not found exactly as represented.

IF YOU SEND TOO MUCH MONEY we will always refund the balance with the bill. Please don't forget this and always be sure to include enough extra to cover postage when gooods are to be sent by mail.

## WE ISSUE THE FOLLOWING CATALOGUES

### OUR BIG CATALOGUE— "THE CONSUMERS' GUIDE"

—is issued in MARCH and SEPTEMBER of EACH year,

and will be MAILED or sent by EXPRESS to any address on receipt of 15 cents to PARTLY PAY postage or express. THE BOOK IS FREE—the 15 cents you send merely helps to pay transportation.

WE SEND THE FOLLOWING SPECIAL CATALOGUES FREE on application: We name the amount of postage required to mail each book, and while we will gladly send them free on application, WE WOULD DEEM IT A COURTESY if you would enclose enough to pay postage. The small amount necessary to cover postage is all you pay.

postage amounts to but little to the applicant, but when we send out **THOUSANDS DAILY IT MEANS A GREAT DEAL TO US.**

| | | | | |
|---|---|---|---|---|
| Agricultural Implements...Postage 2c | | Furniture.....................Postage 7c | |
| Accordeons (only),........... " 2c | | Groceries..................... " 1c | |
| Baby Carriages............. " 3c | | Guitars (only)................ " 1c | |
| Bicycles................... " 2c | | Musical Instruments........ " 3c | |
| Blacksmith Tools......... " 3c | | Mandolins (only)........... " 1c | |
| Books..................... " 5c | | Pianos and Organs........ " 3c | |
| Bibles (only)............... " 1c | | Saddles (only)............. " 2c | |
| Boots and Shoes........... " 2c | | Sewing Machines... ...... " 2c | |
| Carpenters' Tools.......... " 2c | | Violins (only)............. " 1c | |
| Cloaks and Capes........... " 2c | | Vehicles and Harness...... " 5c | |
| Clothing................... " 4c | | Watches and Jewelry... ... " 4c | |
| Dresses. Waists and Skirts. " 3c | | Wagon Makers' Stock Tools. " 3c | |

**THE ABOVE CATALOGUES** are special separate books. **IN THESE SPECIAL CATALOGUES** much more space is devoted to large beautiful illustrations and complete description of the articles. **A MORE COMPLETE LINE** is also shown.

**WE WOULD RECOMMEND** that you send for such special catalogues as will furnish you full information concerning any article covered in the above lines which you contemplate purchasing.

## CLUB ORDERS

### OUR CLUB ORDER PLAN.

**It pays for neighbors to club**

**TOGETHER** and send their orders. **iT PAYS YOU** to get your neighbors to make up their orders and send with yours.

☞ See How It Pays You Both.

| Your order...... $10 00 | His share of discount........ $1 05 |
|---|---|
| Neighbor A.............. 35 00 | His share of discount......... 45 |
| Neighbor C.............. 15 00 | His share of discount......... 45 |
| Neighbor D.............. 25 00 | His share of discount........ 75 |
| Neighbor E.............. 30 00 | His share of discount........ 90 |
| Neighbor F.............. 20 00 | His share of discount........ 60 |
| Neighbor G... .......... 20 00 | His share of discount........ 60 |
| $155 00 | $ 4 35 |

**YOU GET FIVE PER CENT. DISCOUNT ON $155.00,** which is $7.75, and pay $4.35 to your neighbors, leaving you a profit of $3.40 or 34% on your own purchase, or in other words you get for yourself $10.00 worth of goods for $6.60, besides your neighbors save money. They get our **LOWEST PRICES** and the regular discount and **SAVE IN FREIGHT.**

**CLUB ORDERS MAKE FREIGHT VERY LOW** for we ship all goods together in one or more boxes to the one person. You divide the freight charges among yourselves according to the amount of each one's purchase, and for each one **YOU WILL FIND IT VERY LITTLE.**

**IN MAKING A CLUB ORDER** have each one ordering make out a separate order, put all the orders together, tell us whom to ship the goods to; we will carefully **PACK EACH ORDER SEPARATELY,** plainly mark each box or package for the party for whom it is intended, box all packages in one or more big boxes, and make a freight shipment, thus securing for you the lowest possible freight rate.

**LET EACH NEIGHBORHOOD,** three, four or five families join together twice a year, make up a club order and send to us. **The saving will surprise you.**

## ABOUT MISTAKES.

We make mistakes—so do all houses; but when we do make them **we are** always glad and anxious for an opportunity to rectify the mistake. Notwithstanding we employ every known modern convenience in conducting our business. errors will occasionally creep in, and unless our customers report such errors we have no opportunity of righting the wrong.

**WE HAVE LEARNED** in several cases where a small error has cost us the loss of a valuable customer, although the error was unavoidable, and we would have gladly corrected it if given opportunity. In this way we are sometimes blamed for things of which we are entirely innocent.

**DON'T FAIL TO REPORT** any oversight, shortage, inattention or error on our part. Do it pleasantly, if possible, if not pleasantly report it anyway, and you will find us quick to right any wrong.

### To Avoid Unpleasant Delays, Useless Correspondence, Etc., Please Observe the Following Fixed Rules. Regulations and General Instructions:

**TWO TO FIVE FIVE DAYS ARE REQUIRED** to fill all orders. Consider the time for your order to reach us, the time for freight or express to reach you, then add two to five days and you will seldom, if ever be disappointed in getting your goods on time; besides freight and express matter is sometimes delayed a few days in transit. **DO NOT GET IMPATIENT**—allow a little extra time—and you will seldom, if ever need to write to us concerning a delayed shipment. **If necssary to write concerning** a delayed shipment be sure to give your order number as plainly written on postal acknowledgment of your order.

**QUESTIONS ARE OFTEN ASKED US** which are fully explained in this catalogue. Kindly look to this catalogue for desired information, and you may often save yourself and us delay and trouble.

**DO NOT ASK FOR QUANTITY PRICE** or concessions of any kind. Our prices are fixed, and no matter how little or how much you buy the price is the same, the only allowance being our extra cash discount.

**AFTER WRITING AN ORDER,** check it over closely to see you have figured the right prices and discounts; be sure your extensions, additions and subtractions are correct; be sure size, colors, weights or measurements are absolutely correct; be sure you have followed our rules carefully, that the proper amount is inclosed, including enough to pay postage if to be sent by mail; be sure your name and address is plainly written in full, that your shipping directions are plainly stated, the exact amount and kind of money inclosed is plainly stated, and you will seldom, if ever, have any delay or inconvenience.

**DON'T ASK US TO SHIP ANY GOODS** in any way that does not conform fully with our rules, terms and conditions.

**SHOULD YOU WRITE FOR ANY SPECIAL CATALOGUE OR SAMPLES** and do not receive them in four or five days, it is needless to inquire concerning them. In the rush of business we may for a few days run out of certain catalogues or samples, but they will always be forwarded to you promptly as soon as possible.

**CONSIDER.** We have several thousand orders and several thousand letters to handle every day, and while we have over 600 people to do this work and will gladly answer communications, the necessity of writing, unnecessary delays, time and labor may be avoided by carefully reading our catalogue and studying our terms and methods of doing business.

**OUR AIM IS TO HANDLE YOUR ORDER** with the greatest possible dispatch and accuracy, to treat every customer alike and that the very best we know how, and to enable us to accomplish the very best results we desire to obviate unnecessary correspondence and the unnecessary delay arising from same.

---

# YOU ARE INVITED TO COME AND SEE US . . . .

## x x x x IF YOU EVER COME TO CHICAGO.

### TELL YOUR FRIENDS
#### COMING TO CHICAGO TO CALL AND SEE US.

# MAKE OUR STORE YOUR HEADQUARTERS WHILE IN THE CITY....

We will try and make it pleasant for you. YOU WILL NOT BE ASKED TO BUY, but gentlemanly ushers will show you through our house and we feel sure you will be interested in seeing how a GREAT MAIL ORDER BUSINESS is conducted, how 10,000 to 20,000 letters are disposed of daily, and many thousands of packages dispatched each day.

ANYONE CAN DIRECT YOU TO OUR STORE. Three car lines pass our doors; we are located at the corner of Fulton, Desplaines, and Wayman Streets. OUR BUILDING IS THE LARGEST FOR BLOCKS AROUND. You can't miss it.

## .......YOU WILL ALWAYS BE MADE WELCOME HERE.......

---

## Greatest Mail Order House on Earth

# ABOUT FREIGHT AND EXPRESS.

**YOU MUST PAY THE FREIGHT OR EXPRESS,** but it will **AMOUNT TO NEXT TO NOTHING** compared with what you will save in price.

**THE FOLLOWING TABLES** show just what the freight or express rate is per 100 pounds to different points in the different states and territories.

**TAKE THE NEAREST TOWN IN YOUR STATE** as given in our table and the freight or express rate to your town will be almost, if not exactly, the same rate, and in this way you can calculate very closely the freight or express charges you will have to pay.

**FREIGHT IS THE CHEAPEST WAY TO SHIP,** and by freight we recommend shipments of 100 pounds or more to a shipment.

**IT ISN'T NECESSARY** to write us for freight rates. From the table you can tell almost exactly the cost of freight or express to any point. Almost all heavy articles, such as groceries, nails, etc., go at fourth class freight rate. Light and bulky goods, such as vehicles, clothing, furniture, dry goods, etc., go at first and second-class freight rate.

## APPROXIMATE FREIGHT AND EXPRESS RATES TO CENTRAL POINTS IN EVERY STATE AND TERRITORY.

| | 1st class freight per 100 lbs. | 2d class freight per 100 lbs. | 3d class freight per 100 lbs. | 4th class freight per 100 lbs. | Express per 100 lbs. |
|---|---|---|---|---|---|
| **ALABAMA—** | | | | | |
| Ashby | 1 43 | 1 23 | 1 01 | 80 | 4 00 |
| Decatur | 1 15 | 96 | 80 | 63 | 3 25 |
| Birmingham | 1 19 | 1 03 | 83 | 64 | 3 75 |
| Mobile | 1 10 | 90 | 75 | 58 | 4 00 |
| Montgomery | 1 38 | 1 26 | 1 03 | 80 | 3 75 |
| **ARIZONA TERRITORY—** | | | | | |
| Benson | 3 42 | 3 01 | 2 66 | 2 10 | 11 25 |
| Flagstaff | 3 90 | 3 40 | 2 70 | 2 10 | 10 75 |
| Prescott | 3 72 | 3 25 | 2 90 | 2 30 | 12 25 |
| Phoenix | 3 72 | 3 25 | 2 90 | 2 30 | 13 00 |
| Tucson | 3 52 | 3 05 | 2 70 | 2 10 | 12 00 |
| Yuma | 3 52 | 3 05 | 2 70 | 2 10 | 12 00 |
| **ARKANSAS—** | | | | | |
| Fort Smith | 1 35 | 1 18 | 92 | 72 | 4 00 |
| Knobel | 1 18 | 96 | 75 | 57 | 3 25 |
| Little Rock | 1 35 | 1 13 | 90 | 62 | 3 50 |
| Newport | 1 22 | 1 01 | 80 | 62 | 3 25 |
| Pine Bluff | 1 35 | 1 16 | 90 | 62 | 3 50 |
| Texarkana | 1 44 | 1 26 | 1 05 | 86 | 4 00 |
| Van Buren | 1 35 | 1 18 | 92 | 72 | 4 00 |
| **BRITISH COLUMBIA—** | | | | | |
| Vancouver | 2 45 | 2 20 | 2 05 | 1 75 | 13 25 |
| **CALIFORNIA—** | | | | | |
| Fresno | 3 02 | 2 75 | 2 56 | 2 22 | 12 00 |
| Los Angeles | 2 40 | 2 15 | 2 00 | 1 70 | 12 00 |
| Needles | 3 90 | 3 40 | 2 70 | 2 10 | 11 75 |
| Redding | 3 01 | 2 71 | 2 50 | 2 12 | 12 00 |
| Sacramento | 2 40 | 2 15 | 2 00 | 1 70 | 12 00 |
| San Diego | 2 40 | 2 15 | 2 00 | 1 70 | 12 00 |
| San Francisco | 2 40 | 2 15 | 2 00 | 1 70 | 12 00 |
| Ukiah | 2 90 | 2 57 | 2 38 | 2 05 | 13 50 |
| **COLORADO—** | | | | | |
| Denver | 2 05 | 1 65 | 1 25 | 97 | 6 00 |
| Grand Junction | 3 80 | 3 20 | 2 50 | 1 92 | 6 00 |
| Greeley | 2 05 | 1 65 | 1 25 | 97 | 6 00 |
| Gunnison | 3 20 | 2 65 | 2 10 | 1 72 | 6 00 |
| Pueblo | 2 85 | 1 65 | 1 25 | 97 | 6 00 |
| Trinidad | 2 05 | 1 65 | 1 25 | 97 | 6 00 |
| **CONNECTICUT—** | | | | | |
| Bridgeport | 82 | 71 | 55 | 39 | 3 00 |
| Hartford | 82 | 71 | 55 | 39 | 3 00 |
| New Haven | 82 | 71 | 55 | 39 | 3 00 |
| New London | 82 | 71 | 55 | 39 | 3 00 |
| Willmantic | 82 | 71 | 55 | 39 | 3 00 |
| **DELAWARE—** | | | | | |
| Dover | 75 | 65 | 50 | 35 | 2 00 |
| Newark | 73 | 63 | 48 | 33 | 2 25 |
| Wilmington | 73 | 63 | 48 | 33 | 2 25 |
| **DISTRICT OF COLUMBIA—** | | | | | |
| Washington | 72 | 62 | 47 | 32 | 2 25 |
| **FLORIDA—** | | | | | |
| Gainesville | 1 91 | 1 64 | 1 44 | 1 23 | 5 50 |
| Jacksonville | 1 35 | 1 14 | 1 00 | 87 | 5 00 |
| Pensacola | 1 30 | 1 09 | 90 | 67 | 4 25 |
| Tallahassee | 2 19 | 1 88 | 1 63 | 1 41 | 5 25 |
| Tampa | 2 27 | 1 96 | 1 68 | 1 49 | 6 00 |
| **GEORGIA—** | | | | | |
| Atlanta | 1 47 | 1 26 | 1 06 | 85 | 3 75 |
| Brunswick | 1 35 | 1 14 | 1 00 | 87 | 4 25 |
| Macon | 1 47 | 1 26 | 1 06 | 85 | 4 25 |
| Rome | 1 47 | 1 26 | 1 06 | 85 | 4 25 |
| Savannah | 1 35 | 1 14 | 1 00 | 87 | 5 00 |
| **IDAHO—** | | | | | |
| American Falls | 3 30 | 2 80 | 2 20 | 1 82 | 8 75 |
| Boise City | 3 30 | 2 80 | 2 45 | 2 02 | 10 00 |
| Idaho Falls | 3 30 | 2 80 | 2 20 | 1 82 | 8 00 |
| Moscow | 3 60 | 3 10 | 2 60 | 2 10 | 10 00 |
| Mountain Home | 3 30 | 2 80 | 2 45 | 2 02 | 10 00 |
| Pocatello | 3 30 | 2 80 | 2 20 | 1 82 | 8 00 |
| **ILLINOIS—** | | | | | |
| Cairo | 56 | 48 | 39 | 25 | 2 00 |
| Danville | 30 | 25 | 20 | 14 | 1 00 |
| Freeport | 40 | 32 | 24 | 18 | 1 00 |
| Joliet | 22 | 19 | 15 | 10 | 50 |
| Peoria | 40 | 32 | 24 | 18 | 1 00 |
| Quincy | 47 | 38 | 29 | 22 | 1 25 |
| Springfield | 47 | 38 | 29 | 22 | 1 00 |
| **INDIANA—** | | | | | |
| Elkhart | 25 | 22 | 20 | 13 | 75 |
| Evansville | 40 | 34 | 25 | 17 | 1 75 |
| Fort Wayne | 29 | 25 | 20 | 14 | 75 |
| Goshen | 25 | 22 | 20 | 13 | 75 |
| Indianapolis | 32 | 27 | 22 | 14 | 1 25 |
| LaFayette | 30 | 25 | 20 | 13 | 75 |
| New Albany | 40 | 34 | 25 | 17 | 1 50 |
| Terre Haute | 32 | 27 | 22 | 14 | 1 25 |
| **INDIAN TERRITORY—** | | | | | |
| Atoka | 1 50 | 1 29 | 1 07 | 96 | 3 75 |
| Eufaula | 1 35 | 1 18 | 92 | 73 | 3 75 |
| Kiowa | 1 42 | 1 10 | 1 00 | 82 | 3 75 |
| Wagoner | 1 30 | 1 10 | 85 | 60 | 3 50 |
| **IOWA—** | | | | | |
| Burlington | 47 | 38 | 29 | 22 | 1 25 |
| Council Bluffs | 80 | 65 | 45 | 32 | 2 00 |
| Centerville | 68 | 56 | 40 | 22 | 1 75 |
| Davenport | 46 | 36 | 28 | 22 | 1 25 |
| Des Moines | 68 | 57 | 40 | 29 | 1 75 |
| Keokuk | 47 | 38 | 29 | 22 | 1 25 |
| Mason City | 63 | 52 | 42 | 26 | 2 00 |
| Muscatine | 47 | 38 | 29 | 22 | 1 25 |
| Ottumwa | 61 | 50 | 36 | 26 | 1 75 |
| Sioux City | 80 | 65 | 45 | 32 | 2 00 |
| Webster City | 72 | 61 | 42 | 29 | 2 00 |

| | 1st class freight per 100 lbs. | 2d class freight per 100 lbs. | 3d class freight per 100 lbs. | 4th class freight per 100 lbs. | Express per 100 lbs. |
|---|---|---|---|---|---|
| **KANSAS—** | | | | | |
| Atchison | 80 | 65 | 45 | 32 | 2 00 |
| Dodge City | 1 67 | 1 43 | 1 16 | 92 | 4 50 |
| Leavenworth | 80 | 65 | 45 | 32 | 2 00 |
| Norton | 1 52 | 1 29 | 1 04 | 84 | 4 00 |
| Topeka | 1 09 | 89 | 64 | 47 | 2 75 |
| Fort Scott | 97 | 81 | 60 | 43 | 2 75 |
| Wichita | 1 10 | 1 18 | 91 | 70 | 3 75 |
| Winfield | 1 43 | 1 21 | 94 | 73 | 3 75 |
| **KENTUCKY—** | | | | | |
| Ashland | 45 | 39 | 30 | 21 | 2 00 |
| Frankfort | 60 | 51 | 40 | 30 | 2 00 |
| Louisville | 42 | 36 | 27 | 19 | 1 50 |
| Hopkinsville | 47 | 41 | 36 | 31 | 2 75 |
| Paducah | 60 | 50 | 40 | 25 | 2 50 |
| Paris | 68 | 59 | 46 | 32 | 2 00 |
| **LOUISIANA—** | | | | | |
| Baton Rouge | 1 10 | 90 | 75 | 58 | 4 50 |
| New Orleans | 1 10 | 90 | 75 | 58 | 4 20 |
| Shreveport | 1 30 | 1 10 | 92 | 78 | 4 50 |
| **MAINE—** | | | | | |
| Augusta | 94 | 81 | 64 | 45 | 3 00 |
| Bangor | 98 | 85 | 65 | 47 | 3 25 |
| Lewiston | 82 | 71 | 55 | 39 | 3 00 |
| Portland | 82 | 71 | 55 | 39 | 3 00 |
| **MANITOBA—** | | | | | |
| Winnipeg | 1 53 | 1 29 | 1 05 | 81 | 5 25 |
| **MARYLAND—** | | | | | |
| Annapolis | 72 | 62 | 47 | 32 | 2 50 |
| Baltimore | 72 | 62 | 47 | 32 | 2 55 |
| Hagerstown | 72 | 62 | 47 | 32 | 2 55 |
| **MASSACHUSETTS—** | | | | | |
| Boston | 82 | 71 | 55 | 39 | 2 50 |
| New Bedford | 82 | 71 | 55 | 39 | 3 25 |
| Springfield | 82 | 71 | 55 | 39 | 2 50 |
| Worcester | 82 | 71 | 55 | 39 | 2 50 |
| **MICHIGAN—** | | | | | |
| Adrian | 26 | 23 | 20 | 13 | 1 25 |
| Alpena | 55 | 45 | 35 | 26 | 2 50 |
| Bay City | 37 | 32 | 24 | 16 | 1 75 |
| Detroit | 37 | 32 | 24 | 16 | 1 25 |
| Grand Rapids | 36 | 31 | 23 | 16 | 1 25 |
| Kalamazoo | 30 | 26 | 23 | 16 | 75 |
| Lansing | 36 | 31 | 23 | 16 | 1 25 |
| Manistee | 47 | 41 | 31 | 23 | 2 00 |
| Marquette | 60 | 50 | 40 | 28 | 2 50 |
| Petoskey | 51 | 44 | 33 | 25 | 2 00 |
| **MISSISSIPPI—** | | | | | |
| Holly Springs | 1 09 | 93 | 77 | 64 | 3 10 |
| Jackson | 1 18 | 99 | 80 | 67 | 4 00 |
| Meridian | 1 18 | 99 | 80 | 67 | 4 00 |
| Mississippi City | 1 53 | 29 | 1 04 | 82 | 4 25 |
| Natchez | 1 10 | 90 | 75 | 58 | 4 50 |
| Vicksburg | 1 10 | 90 | 75 | 58 | 4 00 |
| West Point | 1 54 | 1 28 | 99 | 80 | 3 50 |
| **MINNESOTA—** | | | | | |
| Albert Lea | 60 | 50 | 40 | 25 | 2 00 |
| Crookston | 1 46 | 1 23 | 96 | 68 | 4 25 |
| Duluth | 65 | 55 | 42 | 28 | 2 50 |
| Edgerton | 86 | 70 | 49 | 38 | 2 25 |
| Marshall | 85 | 72 | 55 | 40 | 3 00 |
| Minneapolis | 60 | 50 | 40 | 25 | 2 00 |
| Redwood Falls | 70 | 56 | 45 | 34 | 3 00 |
| Winona | 50 | 42 | 33 | 23 | 1 75 |
| **MISSOURI—** | | | | | |
| Chillicothe | 80 | 65 | 45 | 32 | 2 00 |
| Hannibal | 47 | 38 | 29 | 22 | 1 25 |
| Jefferson City | 75 | 61 | 42 | 29 | 3 25 |
| Kansas City | 80 | 65 | 45 | 32 | 2 00 |
| Poplar Bluff | 1 22 | 96 | 79 | 63 | 2 75 |
| St. Louis | 47 | 38 | 29 | 23 | 1 50 |
| St. Joseph | 80 | 65 | 45 | 32 | 2 00 |
| Springfield | 1 03 | 84 | 64 | 45 | 2 00 |
| **MONTANA—** | | | | | |
| Big Timber | 2 90 | 2 50 | 2 02 | 1 67 | 7 75 |
| Billings | 2 85 | 2 45 | 1 08 | 1 05 | 7 00 |
| Butte | 3 10 | 2 65 | 2 15 | 1 75 | 8 00 |
| Glendive | 2 15 | 1 76 | 1 46 | 1 19 | 5 50 |
| Helena | 3 10 | 2 76 | 2 15 | 1 75 | 8 00 |
| Livingston | 2 95 | 2 55 | 2 05 | 1 70 | 8 00 |
| Missoula | 3 20 | 2 75 | 2 25 | 1 85 | 9 00 |
| **NEBRASKA—** | | | | | |
| Ainsworth | 1 57 | 1 33 | 1 06 | 82 | 3 75 |
| Crawford | 2 02 | 1 76 | 1 43 | 1 17 | 4 75 |
| Hastings | 1 31 | 1 11 | 83 | 62 | 3 50 |
| Hemingford | 1 85 | 1 62 | 1 31 | 1 03 | 5 00 |
| Omaha | 80 | 65 | 45 | 32 | 2 00 |
| Lincoln | 85 | 70 | 49 | 36 | 2 75 |
| O'Neill | 1 43 | 1 18 | 89 | 68 | 3 25 |
| Ogallala | 1 63 | 1 41 | 1 16 | 91 | 4 50 |
| Valentine | 1 64 | 1 41 | 1 11 | 87 | 4 00 |
| **NEVADA—** | | | | | |
| Carson City | 3 90 | 3 40 | 2 70 | 2 10 | 12 75 |
| Elko | 3 90 | 3 40 | 2 70 | 2 10 | 12 00 |
| Reno | 3 69 | 3 28 | 2 70 | 2 10 | 12 00 |
| **NEW JERSEY—** | | | | | |
| Newark | 75 | 65 | 50 | 35 | 2 50 |
| Trenton | 75 | 65 | 50 | 35 | 2 50 |
| **NEW MEXICO—** | | | | | |
| Deming | 2 32 | 2 06 | 1 88 | 1 67 | 7 50 |
| Las Vegas | 2 32 | 2 06 | 1 88 | 1 67 | 7 25 |
| Lordsburg | 2 58 | 2 31 | 2 07 | 1 88 | 9 25 |
| Albuquerque | 2 32 | 2 06 | 1 88 | 1 67 | 7 25 |
| Raton | 2 24 | 1 79 | 1 37 | 1 07 | 6 50 |
| Santa Fe | 2 32 | 2 06 | 1 88 | 1 67 | 7 25 |
| Socorro | 2 32 | 2 06 | 1 88 | 1 67 | 7 50 |

## FREIGHT AND EXPRESS RATES—Concluded.

| | 1st class freight per 100 lbs. | 2d class freight per 100 lbs. | 3d class freight per 100 lbs. | 4th class freight per 100 lbs. | Express per 100 lbs. |
|---|---|---|---|---|---|
| **NEW HAMPSHIRE—** | | | | | |
| Concord | $ 82 | $ 71 | $ 55 | $ 39 | $ 2 75 |
| Keene | 82 | 71 | 55 | 39 | 3 00 |
| Portsmouth | 82 | 71 | 55 | 39 | 2 50 |
| **NEW YORK—** | | | | | |
| Albany | 72 | 63 | 48 | 34 | 2 25 |
| Buffalo | 45 | 39 | 30 | 21 | 1 75 |
| Elmira | 65 | 56 | 43 | 30 | 2 25 |
| New York City | 75 | 65 | 50 | 35 | 2 50 |
| **NORTH CAROLINA—** | | | | | |
| Charlotte | 1 40 | 1 20 | 95 | 70 | 4 00 |
| Salisbury | 1 40 | 1 20 | 95 | 70 | 3 75 |
| Raleigh | 1 33 | 1 13 | 89 | 64 | 4 00 |
| Wilkesboro | 1 43 | 1 22 | 97 | 71 | 4 00 |
| Wilmington | 1 27 | 1 07 | 87 | 62 | 4 25 |
| **NORTH DAKOTA—** | | | | | |
| Bathgate | 1 68 | 1 42 | 1 16 | 89 | 4 75 |
| Bismarck | 1 80 | 1 52 | 1 24 | 97 | 4 75 |
| Fargo | 1 90 | 1 60 | 1 25 | 85 | 4 00 |
| Grand Forks | 1 50 | 1 27 | 99 | 70 | 4 25 |
| Minot | 1 75 | 1 49 | 1 21 | 95 | 5 50 |
| Wahpeton | 1 20 | 1 00 | 80 | 55 | 4 00 |
| Jamestown | 1 55 | 1 31 | 1 02 | 73 | 4 25 |
| **OHIO—** | | | | | |
| Canton | 41 | 35 | 26 | 18 | 1 50 |
| Cincinnati | 40 | 34 | 25 | 17 | 1 50 |
| Cleveland | 41 | 35 | 26 | 18 | 1 50 |
| Columbus | 41 | 35 | 26 | 18 | 1 50 |
| Lima | 37 | 32 | 24 | 16 | 1 25 |
| Steubenville | 45 | 39 | 30 | 21 | 1 75 |
| Toledo | 37 | 32 | 24 | 16 | 1 25 |
| Youngstown | 44 | 38 | 29 | 19 | 1 50 |
| **OKLAHOMA TERRITORY—** | | | | | |
| El Reno | 1 50 | 1 29 | 1 07 | 89 | 4 75 |
| Guthrie | 1 50 | 1 29 | 1 07 | 87 | 4 00 |
| Kingfisher | 1 50 | 1 29 | 1 07 | 87 | 4 25 |
| Oklahoma | 1 50 | 1 29 | 1 07 | 89 | 4 00 |
| **OREGON—** | | | | | |
| Arlington | 3 05 | 2 75 | 2 54 | 2 16 | 11 00 |
| Baker City | 3 60 | 3 10 | 2 60 | 2 10 | 10 00 |
| La Grande | 3 60 | 3 10 | 2 60 | 2 10 | 10 00 |
| Portland | 2 40 | 2 15 | 2 00 | 1 70 | 12 00 |
| Roseburg | 3 16 | 2 79 | 2 60 | 2 10 | 13 50 |
| Salem | 2 73 | 2 43 | 2 23 | 2 89 | 12 50 |
| **PENNSYLVANIA—** | | | | | |
| Erie | 45 | 39 | 30 | 21 | 2 00 |
| Harrisburg | 72 | 62 | 47 | 32 | 2 25 |
| Philadelphia | 73 | 63 | 48 | 33 | 2 25 |
| Pittsburg | 45 | 39 | 30 | 21 | 1 75 |
| Sharpsville | 44 | 38 | 29 | 19 | 1 75 |
| Scranton | 73 | 63 | 48 | 33 | 2 50 |
| **RHODE ISLAND—** | | | | | |
| Newport | 82 | 71 | 55 | 39 | 3 00 |
| Providence | 82 | 71 | 55 | 39 | 2 50 |
| **SOUTH CAROLINA—** | | | | | |
| Columbia | 1 48 | 1 26 | 1 06 | 82 | 4 50 |
| Charleston | 1 35 | 1 14 | 1 00 | 87 | 4 75 |
| Florence | 1 57 | 1 37 | 1 09 | 82 | 4 50 |
| Greenville | 1 56 | 1 41 | 1 11 | 84 | 4 50 |
| Ridgeway | 1 56 | 1 34 | 1 11 | 83 | 4 50 |
| **SOUTH DAKOTA—** | | | | | |
| Aberdeen | 1 25 | 1 05 | 75 | 56 | 3 25 |
| Deadwood | 2 25 | 1 95 | 1 60 | 1 32 | 6 50 |
| Canton | 83 | 68 | 47 | 34 | 2 50 |
| Eureka | 1 40 | 1 15 | 90 | 67 | 3 50 |
| Huron | 1 24 | 1 05 | 75 | 51 | 3 25 |
| Redfield | 1 25 | 1 05 | 75 | 56 | 3 50 |
| Pierre | 1 30 | 1 10 | 80 | 60 | 4 00 |
| Watertown | 1 15 | 90 | 65 | 47 | 3 50 |
| Vermillion | 89 | 73 | 51 | 37 | 2 50 |
| Yankton | 91 | 73 | 51 | 37 | 2 50 |

| | 1st class freight per 100 lbs. | 2d class freight per 100 lbs. | 3d class freight per 100 lbs. | 4th class freight per 100 lbs. | Express per 100 lbs. |
|---|---|---|---|---|---|
| **TENNESSEE—** | | | | | |
| Bristol | $ 1 14 | $ 98 | $ 74 | $ 52 | $ 3 75 |
| Chattanooga | 1 16 | 99 | 82 | 64 | 3 00 |
| Knoxville | 1 16 | 99 | 82 | 64 | 3 50 |
| Greenfield | 91 | 75 | 60 | 49 | 2 75 |
| Memphis | 85 | 65 | 55 | 43 | 3 00 |
| Jackson | 1 03 | 85 | 70 | 57 | 2 90 |
| Jonesboro | 1 60 | 1 38 | 1 17 | 90 | 4 25 |
| Nashville | 78 | 67 | 53 | 40 | 2 75 |
| **TEXAS—** | | | | | |
| Corpus Christi | 1 50 | 1 29 | 1 09 | 1 00 | 7 00 |
| Austin | 1 50 | 1 29 | 1 09 | 1 00 | 5 50 |
| Beaumont | 1 50 | 1 29 | 1 09 | 1 00 | 6 25 |
| Dallas | 1 50 | 1 29 | 1 09 | 1 00 | 4 25 |
| Abilene | 1 50 | 1 29 | 1 09 | 1 00 | 5 50 |
| Houston | 1 50 | 1 29 | 1 09 | 1 00 | 5 25 |
| Laredo | 1 62 | 1 42 | 1 27 | 1 20 | 6 75 |
| El Paso | 1 62 | 1 42 | 1 27 | 1 20 | 7 25 |
| Tascosa | 1 69 | 1 47 | 1 26 | 1 16 | 6 50 |
| San Antonio | 1 50 | 1 29 | 1 09 | 1 00 | 5 75 |
| **UTAH—** | | | | | |
| Frisco | 3 65 | 3 18 | 2 66 | 2 24 | 10 50 |
| Milford | 3 60 | 3 13 | 2 61 | 2 19 | 10 25 |
| Ogden | 3 10 | 2 65 | 2 15 | 1 75 | 8 00 |
| Thompson's | 3 10 | 2 65 | 2 15 | 1 75 | 10 00 |
| Nephi | 3 30 | 2 83 | 2 31 | 1 89 | 8 75 |
| Salt Lake City | 3 10 | 2 65 | 2 15 | 1 75 | 8 00 |
| **VERMONT—** | | | | | |
| Bradford | 82 | 71 | 55 | 39 | 3 25 |
| Hartford | 82 | 71 | 55 | 39 | 3 10 |
| **VIRGINIA—** | | | | | |
| Lexington | 72 | 62 | 47 | 32 | 2 75 |
| Richmond | 72 | 62 | 47 | 32 | 3 00 |
| Suffolk | 72 | 62 | 47 | 32 | 3 00 |
| Salem | 72 | 62 | 47 | 32 | 3 25 |
| **WASHINGTON—** | | | | | |
| Colfax | 3 60 | 3 10 | 2 60 | 2 10 | 10 00 |
| Tacoma | 2 40 | 2 15 | 2 00 | 1 70 | 12 00 |
| Kalama | 2 40 | 2 15 | 2 00 | 1 70 | 12 00 |
| Pomeroy | 3 60 | 3 10 | 2 60 | 2 10 | 10 00 |
| Spokane | 3 60 | 3 10 | 2 60 | 2 10 | 10 00 |
| Olympia | 2 40 | 2 15 | 2 00 | 1 70 | 12 00 |
| New Whatcom | 2 40 | 2 15 | 2 00 | 1 70 | 12 00 |
| **WEST VIRGINIA—** | | | | | |
| Confluence | 78 | 69 | 55 | 39 | 2 70 |
| Charleston | 52 | 44 | 35 | 26 | 2 50 |
| Grafton | 72 | 62 | 47 | 32 | 2 00 |
| Wheeling | 45 | 39 | 30 | 21 | 1 75 |
| Harpers Ferry | 72 | 62 | 47 | 32 | 2 25 |
| **WISCONSIN—** | | | | | |
| Beloit | 37 | 31 | 24 | 18 | 75 |
| Ashland | 65 | 55 | 44 | 28 | 2 25 |
| Madison | 40 | 35 | 26 | 18 | 1 25 |
| Milwaukee | 25 | 20 | 15 | 12 | 60 |
| Prairie du Chien | 50 | 42 | 33 | 23 | 1 50 |
| Grand Rapids | 50 | 42 | 33 | 23 | 1 50 |
| Superior | 65 | 55 | 44 | 28 | 2 50 |
| Chippewa Falls | 60 | 50 | 40 | 25 | 1 75 |
| Wausau | 58 | 43 | 37 | 23 | 1 75 |
| Green Bay | 43 | 36 | 29 | 20 | 1 25 |
| **WYOMING—** | | | | | |
| Cheyenne | 2 05 | 1 65 | 1 25 | 97 | 6 00 |
| Casper | 2 70 | 2 35 | 1 90 | 1 55 | 6 50 |
| Evanston | 3 10 | 2 65 | 2 15 | 1 75 | 8 00 |
| Green River | 3 10 | 3 65 | 2 15 | 1 75 | 8 00 |
| Laramie | 2 50 | 3 10 | 1 64 | 1 29 | 6 75 |
| Rawlins | 3 09 | 2 54 | 1 94 | 1 56 | 8 00 |

# SOME POINTS ABOUT EXPRESS.

**All bulky and heavy goods should be shipped by freight.** Whenever a shipment weighs less than 30 or 40 pounds it should be shipped by express. In most cases freight shipments weighing less than 100 pounds, **no difference how small or how light,** are charged by the railroad companies at the full 100-pound rate. In some few instances we can secure a minimum charge of less than the 100-pound rate when shipment weighs less than that amount.

☞ **N. B.**—Where shipments are to be sent to points at which there are no agents, freight or express **must be prepaid.** In such orders we request full cash with order, together with sufficient additional to prepay express or freight.

The foregoing table also gives the official rates of express for each 100 pounds. **In most cases the express on 50 pounds is just half of the 100-pound rate,** and weights between 50 and 100 pounds are in the same proportion. Where the shipment is less than 50 pounds the rate is slightly higher in proportion to the weight. We give below, as an example, the graduated scale for various weights, where the rate is $3.00 per 100 pounds:

| | |
|---|---|
| 1 pound | $0 25 |
| 2 pounds | 30 |
| 3 pounds | 45 |
| 4 pounds | 55 |
| 5 pounds | 65 |
| 7 pounds | 70 |
| 10 pounds | 75 |
| 15 pounds | 85 |
| 20 pounds | 1 00 |
| 25 pounds | 1 10 |
| 30 pounds | 1 25 |
| 35 pounds | 1 35 |
| 40 pounds | 1 45 |
| 50 pounds | 1 50 |
| 60 pounds | 1 80 |
| 70 pounds | 2 10 |
| 80 pounds | 2 40 |
| 90 pounds | 2 70 |
| 100 pounds | 3 00 |

Up to 50 pounds the scale is graduated, and where e weight is more than 50 pounds, pound rate is charged. This rule applies where the rates are $2.00 per 100 pounds or more.

We trust that we have fully explained these matters. We are always willing and ready to answer questions relating to freight and express, but by going into detail we hope we may not only save you the bother of writing us, but may also at the same time enable you to determine just what your goods will cost you delivered in your home. We want you to feel that we will do what we say we will. **When we advertise** a thing, it's so. By our full explanation regarding freight and express, you can figure out for yourself just what you can save by taking advantage of the marvelous offers made in the pages of this catalogue.

We realize that our prices are so small that many doubts might arise in the minds of some, as to whether or not the goods we advertise are first-class, new and up-to-date. To answer all questions with a word, to set all doubts forever at rest, and to satisfy new customers of our good faith, we have arranged with all express and freight companies that many lines of goods may be examined at the depot. We have gone to the extreme of liability in terms, and in a large number of lines allow you the privilege of examining your purchase at your own depot. At the head of each department in this catalogue you will find a clear and liberal statement of the terms on which we ship each particular line of goods.

However, our trade is so established and our name so well known that nine-tenths of our orders contain full cash in advance. In sending full cash with order you not only obviate the inconvenience of C. O. D. shipments, but you have the advantage **on most goods,** saving express charges on return of money to us.

**EXPRESS OR FREIGHT CHARGES** add next to nothing to the cost of goods you order from us as compared with what you will save in price.

**ONE ORDER** will convince you that it pays to buy everything in merchandise from headquarters.

☞ **Be sure to read about Our Prices and the Policy of our House on page 1 of this Catalogue.** ☜

# WHAT OUR BANKERS SAY.

No 3179.

*E. G. Keith, President*
*Wm. J. Watson, Vice President*

*Capital $2,000,000.*
*Surplus $1,000,000.*

*H. H. Hitchcock, Cashier.*
*Edward Dickinson, Asst. Cashier.*

## The Metropolitan National Bank
### OF CHICAGO

CHICAGO, ILL., January 27th, 1897.

TO WHOM IT MAY CONCERN:

We take pleasure in testifying to the responsibility of Messrs. Sears, Roebuck & Company, Incorporated under the laws of the State of Illinois, with a capital of $150,000 fully paid up. They are one of the representative business houses of Chicago, occupying commodious quarters, and employing in the neighborhood of five hundred people. The officers and stockholders of the Company are well and favorably known to us, and we have full confidence in any representations they may make.
Very truly yours,

*H. H. Hitchcock*

(17) 5M. 9-25-96.

(1867)

CAPITAL, $1,000,000.
SURPLUS, $1,000,000.

# THE NATIONAL BANK OF ILLINOIS,

GEO. SCHNEIDER, PREST.
WALTER L. PECK, VICE PREST.
WM. A. HAMMOND, 2D VICE PREST.
CARL MOLL, CASHIER.
HENRY D. FIELD, ASST. CASHIER.
HENRY R. KENT, 2D ASST. CASHIER.

ILLINOIS BANK BUILDING, 115 DEARBORN ST.

CHICAGO, January 29th, 1896.

TO WHOM IT MAY CONCERN:-

The stockholders of the firm of Sears, Roebuck & Co. are personally known to us, and we take pleasure in stating that from our experience the concern is a reputable one and thoroughly responsible. They keep a very desirable account with us.

They are incorporated under the laws of the State of Illinois, with a cash capital of $150,000, paid in full. They occupy a large five story building, employ between four and five hundred people, and are doing one of the largest businesses in the country in their line.

We have full confidence in any representations they may make.
Yours truly,

*Carl Moll*

Cashier.

# SEARS ROEBUCK & Co
## GROCERY DEPT

BUY YOUR GROCERIES AT WHOLESALE. In no other Line of Merchandise can you save so much money in a year. GROCERIES ARE USED THREE TIMES EVERY DAY in every family. We can not save you very much on one meal, BUT ON 1,095 MEALS, the number you and your family eat every year, WE CAN SURPRISE YOU on the amount of money we can save you. YOUR LOCAL DEALER buys at wholesale and makes money on the groceries he sells you. YOU CAN BUY AT WHOLESALE PRICES and save this profit; and isn't it your duty to buy as cheap as possible? to make your dollar go as far as possible? OUR GROCERY DEPARTMENT IS VERY COMPLETE. We carry a very large and complete stock of all the goods quoted in this Catalogue. OUR GROCERIES ARE IMPORTED DIRECT or bought from the GROWERS or MANUFACTURERS, hence we are able to offer you the same or lower prices than the largest jobbers can give to the largest wholesale dealers. HIGHEST STANDARD OF QUALITY is maintained in this department. Our Grocery Department is in charge of a competent manager who has made this business a life study. IN THE INSPECTION OF GOODS he is assisted by a VERY ABLE CHEMIST, and nothing is allowed to remain in stock or go to our customers which is not up to the highest standard of quality. FROM US YOU CAN BE SURE of getting all strictly fresh, carefully inspected, high standard goods, and BETTER IN QUALITY than the goods carried by the average retail dealer.

**FREGHT RATES ARE LOW ON GROCERIES.** Most goods in this line take the lowest freight rate (4th class). (See 4th class freight rate per 100 pounds to different points on preceding page.) All groceries should be shipped by freight and in not less than 100 pound lots to secure lowest transportation charges. Express shipments are seldom profitable on anything in this line. If your grocery order doesn't amount to 100 pounds add the necessary 20, 30 or 40 pounds by making the weight up in sugar, soap, coffee, syrup, fish or other heavy goods, it will pay you.

**OUR CLUB ORDER PLAN** works nicely in ordering groceries, some of your neighbors would surely like to join with you in ordering, save the retailer's profit, make up the 100 pounds or more and secure the lowest transportation charges. Read all about club offer on page 3.

Old customers find the grocery department a great advantage not only for the money they save on the groceries bought, but in ordering other merchandise they add just enough needed groceries, often only sugar, 20, 30, 40 and often 80 or 90 pounds and let the goods come in one 100 pound freight shipment. IT PAYS. Freight shipments of 100 pounds or over are the cheapest way to receive goods.

**OUR TERMS.** We will ship groceries by freight C. O. D., subject to examination, on receipt of a sufficient amount of cash to cover freight charges both ways. You can examine the goods at your railroad station and if found perfectly satisfactory and exactly as represented, pay the freight agent our price and charges less the amount sent us with order. WE ALLOW A CASH DISCOUNT of two per cent.. (2%) on all groceries, (except sugar, which is always net). If you send cash in full with your order you can deduct 2% from our prices on all groceries but sugar. WE RECOMMEND CASH ORDERS, you save the cash discount, avoid the expense of collection through Bank, Express or Railroad Co., return of money to us, etc., besides cash orders are not so liable to delays.

## TEA DEPARTMENT

### ON TEA xxxxxxxxxxxxxx

You can save so much money by buying direct that you can't possibly afford to pay retail prices. **Order 10 or 20 pounds**—order enough to last six months. It will pay you, and it will pay your neighbors to join in with you. Try to make the entire order 100 pounds and let us ship by freight. **You need not send all the money at once**—send part and pay the freight agent the balance when received.

### Our Own Importations.

We are direct importers of teas and can at all times meet every requirement as to quality, style of leaf or variety of growth. For convenience of those ordering by mail we simply grade by number, and guarantee exceptional quality and values at prices quoted.

### Fancy Garden Teas.

About 35 pounds to the half chest.

| | ½ chests. | 5-lb pkgs. | Per lb. |
|---|---|---|---|
| G 500 Golden Tips......... | $0 52 | $0 55 | $0 60 |
| G 501 Ungalora Black Oolong | 52 | 55 | 60 |
| G 502 Moning Congou...... | 68 | 70 | 75 |
| G 503 Ceylon Pekoe......... | 52 | 55 | 60 |

### Japan—Sun Dried, Green.

For purity and richness of flavor they are unexcelled. Send us a trial order on our guarantee that they will give entire satisfaction or no sale.

| | ½ chests | 5-lb pkgs | Per lb |
|---|---|---|---|
| G 509 Extra choicest......... | $0 43 | $0 45 | $0 50 |

Extra choicest garden cultivated leaf. Finest tea of this description in the market..

| G 510 Extra choice............. | 28 | 30 | 35 |
|---|---|---|---|

Choice selected leaf. A perfect tea in the cup.

| | ½ chests. | 5-lb pkgs. | Per lb. |
|---|---|---|---|
| G 511 Choice.................. | 22 | 23 | 25 |

Full body, toasty flavor. We offer this as a special bargain

| G 512 Bargain.............. | 20 | 21 | 22 |
|---|---|---|---|

This tea is our leader in regular Japans.

### Japan—Basket-Fired, Black.

| G 514 Extra choicest............ | 43 | 45 | 50 |
|---|---|---|---|

As good a basket-fired Japan, in every way, as was ever brought to Chicago.

| G 515 Extra choice............. | 28 | 30 | 35 |
|---|---|---|---|

A wire leaf tea resembling No. G516, but better in the cup.

| G 516 Choice.................. | 22 | 23 | 25 |
|---|---|---|---|

Straight wire leaf.

| G 517 Bargain................ | 19 | 21 | 23 |
|---|---|---|---|

An excellent tea, both in style and draw.

### Japan—Siftings.

| G 520 Best grade............... | 10 | 11 | 12 |
|---|---|---|---|
| G 521 Best grade Japan Dust.. | 09 | 10 | 12 |

### New Tea Siftings.

| G 524 Extra choicest siftings. | 12 | 13 | 14 |
|---|---|---|---|

| | ½ chests. | 5-lb. pkgs. | Per lb. |
|---|---|---|---|
| G 525 Extra choice......... ... | 43 | 45 | 50 |
| G 526 Choice.................. | 28 | 30 | 35 |

### Gunpowder—Moyune.

| G 528 Extra choicest............ | 53 | 55 | 60 |
|---|---|---|---|

Fancy flower leaf, true Nankin Moyune. The perfection of gunpowder tea.

| G 529 Extra choice............. | 43 | 45 | 50 |
|---|---|---|---|

A very fine drawing fancy Nankin Moyune.

| G 533 Choice.................. | 28 | 30 | 35 |
|---|---|---|---|

Strictly choice, toasty, drawing Moyune.

| G 534 Good................... | 22 | 23 | 25 |
|---|---|---|---|

Choice, true Moyune. A tea that will cause the request: "Same tea as we had last time."

### Imperial Green.

| G 536 Extra choicest.. ........ | 30 | 33 | 37 |
|---|---|---|---|

### Young Hyson—Moyune.

| G 538 Extra choicest.......... | 50 | 55 | 60 |
|---|---|---|---|

Very clean, select leaf, perfect in style and draw. We can obtain nothing better at retail.

| G 539 Extra choice............. | 33 | 35 | 40 |
|---|---|---|---|

Handsome leaf. Desirable in all respects.

| G 541 Choice.................. | 28 | 30 | 35 |
|---|---|---|---|

Fine, small-rolled leaf. A superb tea in the cup.

| G 543 Good.................... | 20 | 22 | 25 |
|---|---|---|---|

An extra sifted tea; bold style and of rich, full-bodied flavor.

### Green Japan.

| G 544.......................... | 30 | 32 | 35 |
|---|---|---|---|
| G 546.......................... | 20 | 22 | 25 |

### Oolong—Formosa.

This tea is the very choicest of first growth pickings. There is no such tea to be found in ordinary retail stores. Our No. 547 was on exhibition at the World's Fair for $1.50, and the No. 548 sold as a specialty at $1 per pound.

| G 547 Extra choicest.......... | 53 | 55 | 60 |
|---|---|---|---|

A fine, rich, toasty tea; excellent in style. (In quarter chest.)

| G 548 Extra choice............ | 43 | 45 | 50 |
|---|---|---|---|

Good style and excellent cup qualities.

| G 549 Choice.................. | 28 | 30 | 35 |
|---|---|---|---|

Good steeper; will give satisfaction anywhere; retailed at 50 cents.

| G 550 Good.................. | 22 | 23 | 25 |
|---|---|---|---|

Of good leaf, flavor and strength.

| G 551 Very fair quality; makes a nice liquor...... | 20 | 22 | 23 |
|---|---|---|---|

## TEAS.—Continued.

### English Breakfast.—Moning Congou.

| | | ½ chests | 5-lb. pkgs. | Per lb. |
|---|---|---|---|---|
| G 553 | Extra choicest | $ 53 | $ 55 | $ 60 |

Fancy Moning Congou will please any lover of black tea.

| | | | | |
|---|---|---|---|---|
| G 554 | Choicest | 43 | 45 | 50 |

A sightly, desirable tea, in appearance—draws as well as it looks. You will find difficulty in matching it at this figure.

| | | | | |
|---|---|---|---|---|
| G 555 | Choice | 28 | 30 | 35 |

A sweet, good drawing tea.

| | | | | |
|---|---|---|---|---|
| G 557 | Good | 20 | 22 | 25 |

Plain drawing—the best we can find to sell at this price.

### India—In 1-lb. Packages.

The World's Fair created a widespread demand for these very choicest grades of teas. We offer the best known and by all odds, the most select and delightful of the scores of attractively named teas on the market.

The lover of a drink—the finest that can be brewed—will be charmed by its delightful flavor.

| | | Case 60 lbs. | 5 lbs | 1 lb. |
|---|---|---|---|---|
| G 561 | Light of Asia | $ 90 | $ 95 | $1 00 |
| G 562 | Star of India | 62 | 65 | 70 |
| G 563 | Lalla Rookh | 40 | 45 | 50 |
| G 564 | Monsoon White Label. 40 lbs in case | 55 | 58 | 60 |
| G 565 | Monsoon Yellow Label 40 lbs in case | 35 | 38 | 40 |
| G 566 | Nabob or Naban | 55 | 58 | 60 |

**BUY YOUR COFFEE DIRECT**; you can just as well save the profit of the retailer; it will amount to **a great deal in a year. Order 50 pounds of coffee**, get your neighbor to join with you on a 100 pound order of groceries and other goods; you will be surprised how much you will save in cost. **The freight will amount to very little**, especially if several neighbors order together and divide it up; 100 pounds for 500 miles will be about 60 cents, and if the order contains goods for four families, it is 15 cents for each family. Consider this, then compare our prices with your local dealer's prices. **So much can be saved** by buying coffee and other groceries at wholesale that we know one order will insure our receiving all future orders.

**MAKE UP A FREIGHT ORDER** of groceries and add the other needed merchandise. **Read our Club Order Inducements**; it reduces freight, **makes it cheaper for all** and you make money for your efforts. Surely some of your neighbors will order with you; **ask them. We encourage freight shipment.** It's cheap. Include all the goods you need **and don't forget the groceries.**

A delicious cup of coffee makes a good breakfast. Our coffees we import direct. Everybody praises their delicious aroma and flavor. It is very important to get fresh roasted coffee. Once the bean becomes stale and absorbs moisture, the flavor and good drinking qualities leave the bean, and render it unfit for use. Often the merchant has coffee on hand for months; in such cases it loses both strength and flavor. If you want strictly fresh roasted coffee, place your orders with us. We guarantee every pound to be fresh and crisp. Coffee must be kept in an air-tight can or jar if you wish it to retain its strength and flavor.

### Coffees—Green.

| No. | | By the Sack per lb. | Less than Sack per lb. |
|---|---|---|---|
| G 570 | Rio, ordinary (not selected) sacks 125 lbs | $ 16 | $ 17 |
| G 571 | Rio, prime, medium dark bean, sacks 125 lbs | 17 | 18 |
| G 572 | Rio, good, dark bean, heavy drinker, sacks 125 lbs | 18 | 19 |
| G 573 | Selected Rio, medium dark bean, sacks 125 lbs | 19 | 20 |
| G 574 | Extra choice, golden, sacks 125 lbs. | 19½ | 20½ |
| G 575 | Costa Rica, prime, sacks 125 lbs | 21 | 22 |
| G 576 | Santos, extra fine, sacks 125 lbs. | 22 | 23 |
| G 577 | Maricaibo extra choice, sacks 125 lbs | 22 | 23 |
| G 578 | Peaberry Santos, sacks 125 lbs | 20 | 21 |
| G 579 | O. G. Java, prime | 23½ | 24½ |
| G 580 | O. G. Java, choice old | 27 | 28 |
| G 581 | Private Garden Growth O. G. Java, very finest obtainable | 31 | 32 |
| G 582 | Arabian Mocha (genuine) best | 25 | 26 |
| G 583 | Pamanockan Liberia Java coffee, 140-lb sacks | 23 | 24 |

### Coffees—Roasted.

All our roasted coffees are **choice**. We avoid complaints by giving in all cases and at all prices, coffee that looks good, tastes good, saves your money and preserves your temper. A trial order will tempt you to order again. Give this department an early trial.

| No. | | 10 lbs and up | Pounds for $1. | Per lb |
|---|---|---|---|---|
| G 590 | Arabian Mocha | $ 32 | 3 | $ 35 |
| G 591 | Peaberry (male berry) Mocha | 28 | 3½ | 30 |
| G 592 | Mandahling Java | 32 | 3 | 35 |
| G 593 | Old Gov't Java | 28 | 3½ | 30 |
| G 594 | Ceylon Java | 27 | 3¾ | 28 |
| G 595 | African Java | 27 | 3½ | 30 |
| G 596 | Mocha and Java Blend | 22 | 4½ | 23 |
| G 597 | Golden Santos Peaberry | 23 | 4 | 25 |
| G 598 | Choice Santos | 21 | 4½ | 23 |
| G 599 | Golden Rio | 23 | 4 | 26 |
| G 600 | Select Rio | 19 | 5 | 20 |
| G 601 | Good Roast Santos and Rio, mixed | 16 | 6 | 17 |

### Coffee—Special Blends—Ground.

| | | 10 lbs and up | For $1.00 | Per lb |
|---|---|---|---|---|
| G 605 | Royal Blend | $ 27 | 3½ lbs | 30 |

A combination of the finest Java and Mocha coffees, with the addition of a portion of the best English chicory.

| | | 10 lbs and up | For $1.00 | Per lb |
|---|---|---|---|---|
| G 606 | Holland Blend | $ 22 | 4½ lbs | 25 |

This celebrated combination is a mixture of fine Old Gov't Java and other high grade coffees skillfully blended to produce a rich, strong, full-bodied and high flavored beverage. The old soldier or sailor who sighs for a coffee "like we used to get in the army," will find in this the realization of a long cherished desire.

| | | 10 lbs and up | For $1.00 | Per lb |
|---|---|---|---|---|
| G 607 | After Dinner Java | $ 18 | 5 lbs | 22 |

We have sold this well known and highly appreciated brand for many years. It has given invariable satisfaction and won for itself great popularity. We have put forth every effort in making this coffee a favorite with the large number of people who want a first-class article at this popular price.

| | | 10 lbs and up | For $1.00 | Per lb |
|---|---|---|---|---|
| G 608 | French Breakfast | $ 15 | 6 lbs | 18 |

A rich, strong combination, blended from coffees possessing the prime requisites of great strength, with full, rich flavor. Will give unqualified satisfaction to customers desiring good coffees at an extremely low price.

| | | 10 lbs and up | For $1.00 | Per lb |
|---|---|---|---|---|
| G 609 | Chicago Blend | $ 13 | 7 lbs | 15 |

### Crushed Java Coffee.

| | | 10 lbs and up | For $1.00 | Per lb |
|---|---|---|---|---|
| G 610 | Java Coffee crushed, excellent flavored drink | $ 15 | 6½ lbs | 16 |

#### Roasted Coffee—Packages.

G 611 McLaughlin's XXXX, per lb, in 100-lb cases, 19¼c. Per lb, 20c.
G 612 Arbuckle's Ariosa, per lb. in 100-lb cases, 19¼c. Per lb, 20c.

### Chicory and Coffee Essence.

It is admitted by patrons of our grocery department that these goods are the cleanest and best on the market.

| | | Per lb. |
|---|---|---|
| G 620 | Chicory, 5 papers to lb. | $0 05 |
| | Yellow Papers, 65 lb cases | 04¼ |
| G 621 | English Chicory, bulk | 06 |
| | 50-lb sacks | 05½ |
| G 622 | Coffee Essence, Hummel's, in tin cans. 6 doz. in a box, per box, $1.40; doz 25c; ea, | 02½ |

### Cocoa.

Lovers of this delightful drink will find our assortment is the best. The manager of this department takes pride in the general superiority of his stock.

| | | Box. | Lb. | Can. |
|---|---|---|---|---|
| G 624 | Wilbur's Breakfast, 12 ½-lbs | $2 20 | $ 38 | $ 20 |
| G 625 | Wilbur's Breakfast 5-lb cans | .... | .... | 1 80 |
| G 626 | Brooks' 1-lb tins, 12 in case | 6 25 | .... | 55 |
| G 627 | Brooks' 5-lb cans | .... | .... | 2 50 |
| G 628 | Huyler's, ½-lbs, 24 in case | 5 25 | .... | 23 |

#### Baker's.

| | | Box. | lb. | Pkg. |
|---|---|---|---|---|
| G 629 | Cracked, 24 ½-lb pkgs. in box | $3 84 | 35 | 20 |
| G 630 | Pure, 24 ½-lb pkgs. in box | 4 80 | 45 | 25 |
| G 631 | Breakfast, 12 ½-lb pkgs. in box | 2 55 | 45 | 23 |
| G 632 | Broma, ½-lb pkgs. 12 lbs in box | 4 50 | 40 | 20 |

#### Epps'.

| | | Box. | Lb. | Can. |
|---|---|---|---|---|
| G 633 | Homeopathic, 28 ½-lb cans in box | $5 32 | 40 | 20 |

#### Van Houten's.

| | | Box. | Lb. | Can. |
|---|---|---|---|---|
| G 634 | ⅛-lb cans, 48 cans in case | $5 75 | $1 15 | 15 |
| G 635 | ¼-lb cans, 24 cans in case | 4 80 | 90 | 23 |
| G 636 | ½-lb cans, 24 cans in case | 9 60 | 90 | 45 |
| G 637 | 1-lb cans, 12 cans in case | 8 64 | 80 | 80 |

#### Frey's Homeopathic.

| | | Box. | Lb. | Can. |
|---|---|---|---|---|
| G 640 | ½-lb tins, 2 doz. in case | $3 96 | 35 | 18 |

#### Bulk.

| | | 5-lbs. and up. | Lb. |
|---|---|---|---|
| G 641 | Cocoa in bulk | 23 | 25 |

### Cocoa Shells.

| | | Box. | Per lb. |
|---|---|---|---|
| G 642 | Baker's 1-lb. pkgs., boxes 10 lbs. | 80 | 10 |
| G 643 | Maillard's 1-lb pkgs., boxes 10 lbs. | 90 | 10 |
| G 644 | Bulk, bags about 45 lbs | 2½ | 3 |

### Chocolates.

A delicious cup of chocolate cannot be made by the best cook in the world if the chocolate itself is poor. We greatly simplify the art of preparing this superb drink by quoting the best at prices charged by retail dealers for inferior and unknown brands.

#### Wilbur's.

| | | Box. | lb. |
|---|---|---|---|
| G 645 | Wilbur's Premium, 1-lb, 12 in case | $3 60 | 32 |
| G 646 | Wilbur's Vanilla, ½-lb, 24 in case | 5 60 | 50 |
| G 647 | Wilbur's German, sweet, ½-lb, 24 in case | 2 16 | 20 |
| G 653 | Whitman's Instantaneous, 12-lb pkgs. | 7 92 | 72 |
| G 656 | Imperial, sweet, 12-lb boxes | 2 40 | 22 |

#### Baker's.

| | | Box. | lb. |
|---|---|---|---|
| G 658 | German Sweet, ¼-lb pkgs., 12-lb boxes | $2 64 | 25 |
| G 648 | Baker's Premium, 12-lb boxes | 4 08 | 35 |
| G 649 | Baker's Triple Vanilla, 12-lb boxes | 4 40 | 37 |
| G 654 | Baker's, 10-lb cakes, for bakers' use | | 22½ |

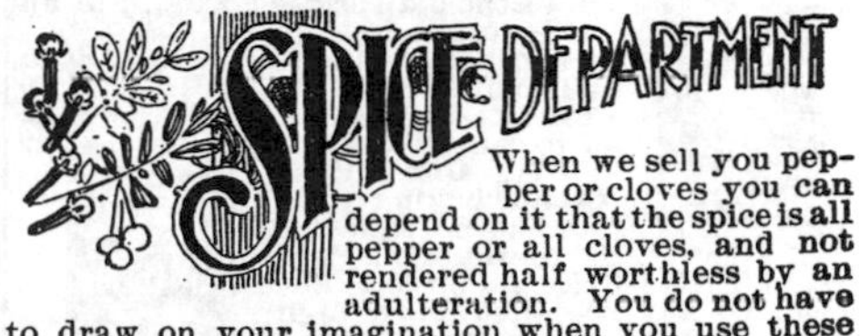


When we sell you pepper or cloves you can depend on it that the spice is all pepper or all cloves, and not rendered half worthless by an adulteration. You do not have to draw on your imagination when you use these goods. So constant has been the trade in these lines that we ascribe it to their general excellence.

### Plymouth—Pure Ground Spices.

| | | 5 lbs | Per lb |
|---|---|---|---|
| G 660 | Black Pepper | $ 15 | $ 20 |
| G 661 | Cayenne Pepper | 35 | 40 |
| G 662 | White Pepper | 20 | 25 |
| G 663 | Cinnamon—Saigon | 29 | 38 |
| G 664 | Cinnamon-Cassia | 17 | 24 |
| G 665 | Mustard | 20 | 25 |
| G 666 | Ginger—Jamaica | 20 | 25 |
| G 667 | Allspice | 18 | 23 |
| G 668 | Cloves | 25 | 30 |
| G 669 | Mace | 65 | 75 |
| G 671 | Nutmegs | 65 | 75 |

| | | Doz | Each |
|---|---|---|---|
| G 672 | Paprika—Hungarian (¼ lb boxes), sweet pepper | 2 50 | 25 |

When desired, above goods in 1, 2 and 5-lb decorated, screw-top tin canisters, without extra charge.

#### Standard Ground.

| | | 5 lbs and up | Per lb |
|---|---|---|---|
| G 673 | Black Pepper | $ 12 | $ 15 |
| G 674 | Cayenne Pepper | 25 | 30 |
| G 675 | White Pepper | 20 | 25 |
| G 676 | Cinnamon | 25 | 30 |
| G 677 | Mustard | 15 | 20 |
| G 678 | Ginger | 20 | 25 |
| G 679 | Allspice | 12 | 15 |
| G 681 | Cloves | 15 | 20 |

When desired, above goods in 1, 2 and 5-lb decorated, screw-top tin canisters, without extra charge.

#### Whole Spices.

| | | 5 lbs and up | Per lb |
|---|---|---|---|
| G 683 | Pepper, black | $ 9 | $ 10 |
| G 684 | Pepper, double sifted | 11 | 12 |
| G 685 | Allspice | 10 | 12 |
| G 686 | Cassia Cinnamon | 16 | 18 |
| G 687 | Cloves | 8 | 10 |
| G 688 | Ginger, Jamaica | 20 | 25 |
| G 689 | African Ginger | 15 | 20 |
| G 690 | Mace | 50 | 55 |
| G 691 | Nutmegs, Penang | 45 | 50 |
| G 692 | Nutmegs, Macassar | 50 | 55 |
| G 693 | Mixed, for pickling | 18 | 20 |
| G 694 | Cassia Buds | 25 | 30 |

**SPEND SOME TIME LOOKING THROUGH THIS CATALOGUE. IT WILL SURPRISE YOU TO FIND HOW MUCH MORE THAN NECESSARY YOU HAVE BEEN PAYING FOR WHAT YOU BUY.**

## Mustard.

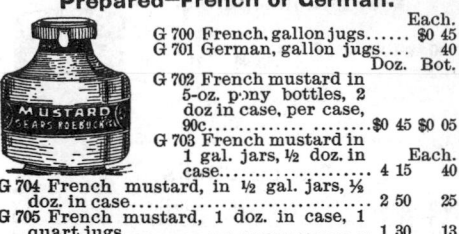

| | Per case | Each |
|---|---|---|
| G 695 Colman's D. S. F. in ¼-lb tins, 4 doz. | $5 80 | 15 |
| G 696 Colman's D. S. F. in ½-lb tins, 2 doz. | 5 10 | 25 |
| G 697 Colman's D. S. F. in 1-lb tins, 1 doz. | 5 10 | 45 |
| G 698 Colman's D. S. F. in 10 lb cans. | 3 00 | |
| G 699 Keene's English, 1-lb cans. | 5 10 | 45 |

### Prepared—French or German.

| | | Each. |
|---|---|---|
| G 700 French, gallon jugs | | $0 45 |
| G 701 German, gallon jugs | | 40 |
| | | Doz. Bot. |
| G 702 French mustard in 5-oz. pony bottles, 2 doz in case, per case, 90c. | $0 45 | $0 05 |
| | | Each. |
| G 703 French mustard in 1 gal. jars, ½ doz. in case. | 4 15 | 40 |
| G 704 French mustard, in ½ gal. jars, ½ doz. in case. | 2 50 | 25 |
| G 705 French mustard, 1 doz. in case, 1 quart jugs. | 1 30 | 13 |

# BAKING POWDER

It costs manufacturers of certain well-known brands of baking powders thousands and tens of thousands of dollars a year for advertising. The tremendous cost of this advertising comes out of the pockets of the people who buy.

The ingredients necessary to make a good baking powder are not so expensive. The cost comes in, in creating a demand, and in selling the goods. Our special brands quoted below have stood the most rigid tests, and in buying them you pay for what the ingredients cost, without a high-sounding name and expensive advertising.

### Home Baking Powder.

G 710  A pure baking powder, guaranteed to make as good a baking as the high priced goods. Put up in 10, 5 and 1 lb cans.

| | |
|---|---|
| 10 lb can, per can | $1 65 |
| 5 lb can, per can | 90 |
| 1 lb can, per can | 22 |
| 1 lb cans, per doz | 2 40 |

G 711  Our Silver Cream baking powder has no equal; it is absolutely Pure Cream Tartar Baking Powder. Superior to any so-called pure high priced monopoly baking powder. More than twenty years ago cream tartar was worth 49 cents per pound, and bi-carbonate of soda 6 cents; now cream tartar and soda about half former prices and yet the monopoly goods remain the same. Will you be imposed upon longer? Any lady can put up a pure baking powder. It is no secret. Will you patronize monopolies that are robbing the public when you can get perfectly pure goods at a reasonable price? We guarantee ours to please or money refunded.

| | 1 lb | 5 lbs | 10 lbs |
|---|---|---|---|
| Silver Cream baking powder, put up in 10, 5 and 1 lb round cans, ½ lb cans 18 cents. | $0 33 | $1 50 | $2 80 |

### Price's.

G 713

| | Doz. | Each. |
|---|---|---|
| Dime cans | $0 90 | $0 09 |
| 4-oz. cans | 1 35 | 12 |
| 8-oz. cans | 2 50 | 23 |
| 16-oz. cans | 4 70 | 43 |
| 2½-lb cans | 11 25 | 1 00 |
| 5-lb cans | 21 50 | 1 95 |
| 10-lb cans | 42 00 | 3 80 |

### Crown.

| | Doz. | Each. |
|---|---|---|
| G 715  5-lb cans, 1 doz. in case | $9 00 | $0 90 |

### Royal.

G 717

| | Doz. | Each. |
|---|---|---|
| 10-cent size | $0 95 | $0 09 |
| ¼-lb cans | 1 40 | 15 |
| ½-lb cans | 2 55 | 25 |
| 1-lb cans | 4 95 | 45 |
| 2½-lb cans | 11 25 | 1 00 |
| 5-lb cans | 22 00 | 2 00 |

# Color Card of Paints FREE.

## Saleratus, or Bi-Carb. of Soda

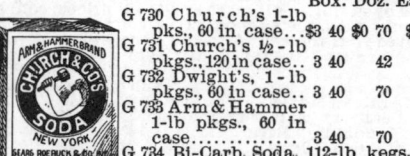

| | Box. | Doz. | Each. |
|---|---|---|---|
| G 730  Church's 1-lb pks., 60 in case | $3 40 | $0 70 | $0 06 |
| G 731  Church's ½-lb pkgs., 120 in case | 3 40 | 42 | 04 |
| G 732  Dwight's, 1-lb pkgs., 60 in case | 3 40 | 70 | 06 |
| G 733  Arm & Hammer 1-lb pkgs., 60 in case | 3 40 | 70 | 06 |
| G 734  Bi-Carb. Soda, 112-lb kegs, per keg, $2.70; per lb, 4c. | | | |
| G 735  Sal Soda, kegs, 175 lbs, per keg, $2.00; over 25 lbs and less than keg, per lb, 2c; per lb, 3c. | | | |

## Cream of Tartar.

Guaranteed hetbest on the market. If any item is not as we say, it is your privilege to send it back.

| | Box. | Lb. |
|---|---|---|
| G 718  Bulk, strictly pure | $0 25 | $0 30 |
| G 719  Standard | 15 | 20 |

## Magic Yeast—Quickest and Best.

We get our yeast fresh each day. It will pay you to save the pennies as well as the dollars.

| | Box. | Pkg. |
|---|---|---|
| G 721  10-cent size, 3 doz. in box | $1 70 | $0 06 |
| G 722  5-cent size, 3 doz. in box | 95 | 04 |
| G 723  Yeast Foam, purity and excellence, 5-cent size, 3 doz. in box | 95 | 04 |

## Twin Bros'. Yeast.

| | Box. | Pkg. |
|---|---|---|
| G 725  10-cent size, 3 doz. in box | $1 50 | $0 06 |
| G 726  5-cent size, 3 doz. in box | 1 00 | 04 |

# EXTRACTS

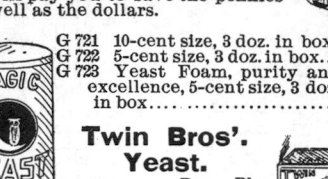

In order that we may fully assure our customers of the best extracts and essences, we put up special brands in our own establishment. One of the gentlemen connected with this department is a practical chemist of many years experience, and he has full instructions from the house to give such values as were never known of before. Retail dealers take advantage of comparative ignorance of customers on the relative value of extracts and secure very large profits on the inferior and usually adulterated line they carry. Try our brands and you will be more than pleased.

### Lemon.

| | | Each. | Doz. |
|---|---|---|---|
| G 740  2 oz | | $0 09 | $1 00 |
| G 741  4 oz | | 18 | 2 00 |
| G 742  8 oz | | 33 | 3 75 |
| G 743  Pts. (16 oz) | | 65 | 7 55 |
| G 744  Per gallon | | 4 50 | |

### Vanilla.

| | | Each. | Doz. |
|---|---|---|---|
| G 746  1 oz | | $0 10 | $1 10 |
| G 747  2 oz | | 16 | 1 70 |
| G 718  4 oz | | 30 | 3 20 |
| G 749  8 oz (½-pints) | | 60 | 6 25 |
| G 751  16 oz (pints) | | 1 00 | 11 50 |

### Standard Grade— Lemon.

| | | Each. | Doz. |
|---|---|---|---|
| G 753  2-oz panel | | $0 05 | $0 40 |
| G 754  4-oz panel | | 07 | 70 |
| G 755  ½ pint, round | | 14 | 1 50 |
| G 756  Pints, round | | 27 | 3 00 |
| G 757  Per gallon, bulk | | 2 25 | |

### Vanilla.

| | | Each. | Doz. |
|---|---|---|---|
| G 760  2-oz panel | | 06 | 50 |
| G 761  4-oz panel | | 10 | 90 |
| G 762  ½ pint, round | | 17 | 1 75 |
| G 763  Pints, round | | 30 | 3 00 |
| G 764  Per gallon | | 2 50 | |

### Dr. Price's Flavoring Extracts. Lemon.

| | | Each. | Doz. |
|---|---|---|---|
| G 766  1 oz | | $0 09 | $1 05 |
| G 767  2 oz | | 17 | 1 80 |
| G 768  4 oz | | 30 | 3 50 |
| G 769  8 oz | | 60 | 6 75 |

### Vanilla.

| | | | |
|---|---|---|---|
| G 770  1 oz | | 14 | 1 55 |
| G 771  2 oz | | 25 | 2 80 |
| G 772  4 oz | | 50 | 5 50 |
| G 773  8 oz | | 95 | 10 75 |

## Gillett's.

Other flavors—double strength.

2-oz bottles.

| | | Each. | Doz. |
|---|---|---|---|
| G 775  Raspberry | | $0 17 | $1 75 |
| G 776  Strawberry | | 17 | 1 75 |
| G 777  Pineapple | | 17 | 1 75 |
| G 778  Rose | | 23 | 2 50 |
| G 779  Celery | | 17 | 1 75 |
| G 780  Almond | | 17 | 1 75 |
| G 781  Cloves | | 17 | 1 75 |
| G 782  Orange | | 17 | 1 75 |
| G 783  Peach | | 17 | 1 75 |
| G 784  Banana | | 17 | 1 75 |
| G 785  Raspberry | | 14 | 1 50 |
| G 786  Strawberry | | 13 | 1 40 |
| G 787  Pineapple | | 14 | 1 50 |
| G 788  Rose | | 18 | 2 00 |
| G 789  Celery | | 14 | 1 50 |
| G 790  Almond | | 14 | 1 50 |
| G 791  Cloves | | 14 | 1 50 |
| G 792  Orange | | 14 | 1 50 |
| G 793  Peach | | 11 | 1 50 |
| G 794  Banana | | 14 | 1 50 |

### Our Celebrated Pink Label Brand.

Quadruple Strength Essences.

| | | | |
|---|---|---|---|
| G 800  Peppermint, 2 oz | | $0 05 | $0 50 |
| G 801  Peppermint, 4 oz | | 08 | 80 |
| G 802  Wintergreen, 2 oz | | 05 | 50 |
| G 803  Wintergreen, 4 oz | | 08 | 80 |
| G 804  Cinnamon, 2 oz | | 05 | 50 |
| G 805  Cinnaman, 4 oz | | 08 | 80 |

### Extracts,—Other Flavors.

(2 ounce size.)

These Extracts and Essences are prepared by our own registered pharmacist, a gentleman of broad experience in everything pertaining to the trade. We offer this complete line with the double assurance, they are pure as the best and better value than you can get elsewhere for double the money. Every housewife knows the desirability of these choice flavors in the art of cooking. Include what you need with your freight order and they will add scarcely any weight to the shipment.

| | | Each. | Doz. |
|---|---|---|---|
| G 815  Pear | | $0 23 | $2 50 |
| G 816  Apple | | 23 | 2 50 |
| G 817  Rock and Rye | | 23 | 2 50 |
| G 818  Cherry (red, black or wild) | | 23 | 2 50 |
| G 819  Gooseberry | | 23 | 2 50 |
| G 820  Plum | | 23 | 2 50 |
| G 821  Blackberry | | 23 | 2 50 |
| G 822  Coffee | | 23 | 2 50 |
| G 823  Chocolate | | 23 | 2 50 |
| G 824  Sherbet | | 23 | 2 50 |
| G 825  Quince | | 23 | 2 50 |
| G 826  Pistachio | | 23 | 2 50 |
| G 827  Nutmeg | | 23 | 2 50 |
| G 828  Sarsaparilla | | 23 | 2 50 |
| G 829  Mead | | 23 | 2 50 |
| G 830  Currant | | 23 | 2 50 |
| G 831  Tropical Melon | | 23 | 2 50 |
| G 832  Ginger | | 23 | 2 50 |
| G 833  Wild Strawberry | | 23 | 2 50 |
| G 834  Wild Raspberry | | 23 | 2 50 |
| G 835  Walnut | | 23 | 2 50 |
| G 836  Mandrin | | 23 | 2 50 |
| G 837  Tutti Frutti | | 23 | 2 50 |
| G 838  Orgeat | | 23 | 2 50 |
| G 839  Allspice | | 23 | 2 50 |
| G 840  Cinnamon | | 23 | 2 50 |
| G 841  Coriander | | $0 23 | $2 50 |
| G 842  Curry | | 23 | 2 50 |
| G 843  Lavender | | 23 | 2 50 |
| G 844  Lime Fruit | | 23 | 2 50 |
| G 846  Raspberry (black) | | 23 | 2 50 |
| G 847  Red Raspberry | | 23 | 2 50 |

### Flag Brand Essences.—Quadruple Strength.

| | | Each. | Doz. |
|---|---|---|---|
| G 850  Hops | | $0 23 | $2 50 |
| G 851  Ginger Ale | | 23 | 2 50 |

### Brandy Flavoring Extracts.

(2 ounce sizes.)

| | | Each. | Doz. |
|---|---|---|---|
| G 853  Cognac | | $0 33 | $3 75 |
| G 854  Apple | | 23 | 2 50 |
| G 855  Cherry | | 23 | 2 50 |
| G 856  Peach | | 23 | 2 50 |
| G 857  Armagnac | | 23 | 2 50 |

### Gin Flavoring Extracts.

(2 ounce size.)

| | | Each. | Doz. |
|---|---|---|---|
| G 860  Holland | | $0 35 | $3 50 |
| G 861  Old Tom | | 35 | 3 50 |
| G 862  London Dock | | 35 | 3 50 |
| G 863  Rye | | 35 | 3 50 |
| G 864  St. Croix | | 35 | 3 50 |

### Whisky Flavoring Extracts.

| | | Each. | Doz. |
|---|---|---|---|
| G 865  Irish | | $0 35 | $3 50 |
| G 866  Scotch | | 35 | 3 50 |
| G 867  Monongahela | | 35 | 3 50 |

### Cordial Flavoring Extracts.

| | | Each. | Doz. |
|---|---|---|---|
| G 868  Annis Seed | | $0 23 | $2 50 |
| G 869  Benedictine | | 23 | 2 50 |
| G 871  Kirschenwasser | | 23 | 2 50 |

**DON'T SEND AN ORDER IF YOU CAN HELP IT WITHOUT INCLUDING WHAT GROCERIES YOU NEED TO MAKE UP A FREIGHT SHIPMENT, AND THUS SAVE CHARGES.**

### Jamaica Ginger.

A strictly pure essence, worth double what retailers sell.

| | Each. | Doz. |
|---|---|---|
| G 880 2 oz bottle | $0 15 | $1 50 |
| G 881 4 oz bottle | 25 | 2 50 |

### Blackberry Brandy.

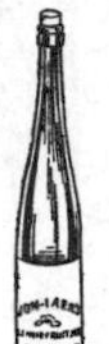

We have a very large demand for this pure medicinal beverage prepared from the juice of the blackberry. Prescribed by the best physicians.

| | Case. | Each |
|---|---|---|
| G 884 G. M. Jarvis Co., qts. 1 doz in case | $5 50 | $0 55 |
| G 885 G. M. Jarvis Co., pts. 2 doz in case | 5 75 | 30 |

### Beverages.

At all seasons of the year a refreshing drink is very acceptable. We quote an assortment including the most desirable beverages. At a very little outlay one can manufacture strictly pure temperance drinks for family use, or for sale, at a large profit.

| | Doz | Each |
|---|---|---|
| G 887 Lemon Sugar, for making lemonade, no lemon required, 1-lb cans, 2 doz. in case | $2 40 | $0 24 |
| G 888 Lemon sugar, ½-lb cans, 2 doz. in case | 1 50 | 14 |

| | Doz. | Each |
|---|---|---|
| G 889 Lime Juice, finest quality, quart bottles, 1 doz. in case | $3 10 | $0 27 |
| G 891 Lemon Juice, clarified, quart bottles, 1 doz. in case, | 4 00 | 38 |
| G 892 Raspberry Vinegar | 4 10 | 38 |
| G 893 Grape Juice, Stevens', healthy, palatable and refreshing; pint bottles, 2 doz. in case | 4 00 | 36 |
| G 894 Same, quart bottles | 6 50 | 60 |

**Thompson's Hygeia Wild Cherry Phosphate**, a delicious beverage in extract form.

| | Doz. | Each |
|---|---|---|
| G 896 25-cent size makes 6 quarts | $1 75 | $0 18 |
| G 897 40-oz size makes 80 quarts | 7 00 | 65 |
| G 898 C & C Ginger Ale, imported | 1 35 | 14 |

### Root Beer.

This is a strict temperance drink, one that has a very large sale. It is so well known that nothing more can be said than that the brands sold by us have no superior.

| | Bot. | Doz. |
|---|---|---|
| G 899 Atlantic Brand Root Beer Preparation. Each bottle will make 5 gallons of beer | $0 10 | $1 10 |
| G 900 Hires' Extract | 15 | 1 75 |

### Wild Cherry Phosphate.

One ounce of this Phosphate will make 2 quarts of the finest drink imaginable; 15 cents for two gallons of a delicious beverage makes it pretty cheap.

| | Doz. | Each |
|---|---|---|
| G 902 Walhalla, 4 oz. bottles | $1 45 | $0 15 |
| G 903 Walhalla, 1-gal. jugs | .... | 2 50 |
| G 904 Thompson's, 8-oz | 2 00 | 25 |
| G 905 Thompson's, 24-oz | 4 00 | 50 |

### Desiccated Cocoanut.

We buy Schepp's in bulk and in large quantities, and put up in our own packages.

| | Pkg |
|---|---|
| G 906 In 1-lb paper cartons | $0 21 |
| G 907 In ½-lb paper cartons | 12 |
| | lb. |
| G 908 Bulk, shredded 20-lb pails | 13 |
| Less quantity | 14 |

**Dunham's.**

| | Lb. | Pkg |
|---|---|---|
| G 910 Shredded, 15-lb cases, ¼-lb | 30 | 09 |
| G 911 Shredded, 15-lb cases, ½-lb | 30 | 16 |

### Herbs.

These are genuine herbs, and nothing is mixed with them in order to increase profits. We are not on hand to talk for our goods and so let our goods talk for themselves. We don't want only a part of your trade, but want to treat you so well that we will deserve all of it.

| | Doz. | Each. |
|---|---|---|
| G 915 Leaf—Sage, Thyme, Savory, Marjoram, Bay Leaves, 2-oz. pkgs | $0 40 | $0 05 |
| G 916 Leaf—Sweet Basil and Mint | 75 | 10 |
| G 917 Ground Sage, ¼-lb. pkgs | 1 00 | 10 |
| G 918 Ground Thyme, ¼-lb. pkgs | 1 00 | 10 |
| G 919 Ground Summer Savory, ¼-lb pkgs | 1 00 | 10 |
| G 920 Ground Sweet Marjoram, ¼-lb. pkgs | 1 00 | 10 |
| G 921 Ground Sweet Basil, ¼-lb. pkgs | 1 00 | 10 |
| G 922 Imported Mint, 2-oz. bots | 2 50 | 25 |
| G 923 Imported Parsley, 2-oz. bots | 2 50 | 25 |
| G 924 Pressed Hops; best standard hops. ½ lb packages | 60 | 07 |
| G 925 Pressed Sage; standard. ½ lb packages | 60 | 07 |
| G 929 Bay Leaves, per pound, 25c. | | |

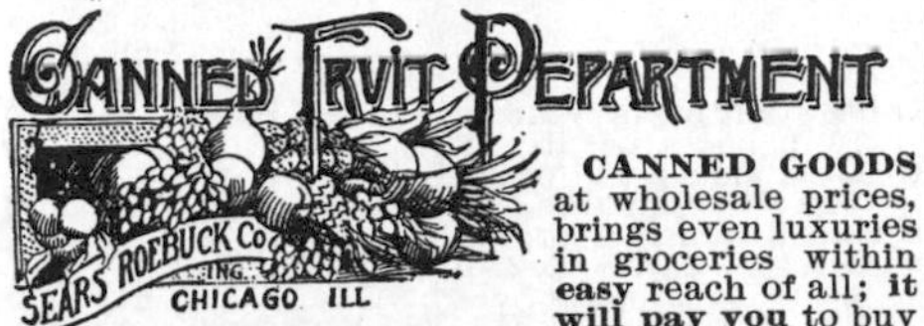


**CANNED GOODS** at wholesale prices, brings even luxuries in groceries within **easy** reach of all; **it will pay you** to buy these goods **in dozen lots; two or three families** should join in making up the order so as to get the **dozen price** and the lowest freight rate and that divided up.

**We are so anxious for your order**, so anxious to show the value we can give, the amount you can save, that **you need not send us all the money** at once if you don't wish; send **one-fourth** the amount with your order, **pay the balance** to your freight agent when the goods are received.

**Go over this Grocery List carefully**, order just what you want, **no more, no less**, but don't forget the other departments, remembering a few things in other merchandise will add nothing to the freight.

Our stock includes only the **newest goods of the latest pack**. We ask you to remember that while price is a great object in buying anything, quality deserves great consideration in this department. **We claim for our goods** that they are superior, pure and new. We take particular pains that our canned goods shall be of such desirability that we may gain a customer in each sale. We have **made the prices just as low** as such excellent goods can be put on the market at, and we agree to refund every cent where goods are returned immediately, if they are not found as represented. Canned goods come two dozen in a case, unless otherwise specified. **We will assort cases** at dozen rates when not more than six kinds are ordered, thus giving you an opportunity to obtain these goods at as near cost price as possible.

| | Doz. | Can. |
|---|---|---|
| G 930 Apricots, heavy syrup | $1 50 | $0 14 |
| G 931 Apricots, extra gal. cans | 5 50 | 50 |
| G 932 Apricots, standard goods | 4 50 | 40 |
| G 933 Apricots, for pies, gal. goods | 3 60 | 32 |
| G 934 Crawford peaches | 1 70 | 16 |
| G 935 Crawford peaches for table, gal. cans, extra | 6 05 | 52 |
| G 936 Crawford Peaches, gal. cans, standard | 4 00 | 38 |
| G 937 Lemon Cling Peaches | 1 50 | 13 |
| G 938 White Health Peaches | 1 50 | 13 |
| G 939 White Cherries | 2 10 | 20 |
| G 940 Egg Plum | 1 35 | 12 |
| G 942 Green Gage Plums | 1 35 | 12 |
| G 943 Muscat Grapes | 1 35 | 12 |
| G 944 Bartlett Pears | 1 50 | 14 |
| G 945 Bartlett Pears | 1 85 | 18 |

The extra following prices are for **California Extras** the very highest grade. California Preserved Fruits, better than Golden Gate Extras.

| | Doz. | Can. |
|---|---|---|
| G 946 Apricots | $1 25 | $0 12 |
| G 947 Lemon Cling Peaches | 2 00 | 20 |
| G 948 Crawford Peaches | 1 75 | 16 |
| G 949 Bartlett Pears | 2 00 | 19 |
| G 950 Muscat Grapes | 1 55 | 14 |
| G 951 Green Gage Plums | 1 40 | 13 |
| G 952 Egg Plums | 1 40 | 13 |
| G 953 White Cherries | 2 25 | 20 |
| G 954 Black Cherries | 2 10 | 19 |
| G 955 Peaches, sliced, very choice | 2 35 | 23 |

**Eastern Fruits**, all 2-lb. cans, except those otherwise quoted, and selected with great care as to quality and weight; 2 dozen in case.

| | Doz. | Can. |
|---|---|---|
| G 960 Blackberries, extra standard | $1 15 | $0 10 |
| G 961 Blackberries, preserved | 1 25 | 12 |
| G 962 Blueberries, standard | 95 | 9 |
| G 963 Strawberries, standard | 95 | 9 |
| G 964 White Cherries | 1 50 | 14 |
| G 965 Red Cherries, standard | 1 25 | 12 |
| G 966 Egg Plums, standard | 90 | 8 |
| G 967 Green Gage Plums, standard | 90 | 8 |
| G 968 Gooseberries, standard | 80 | 8 |
| G 969 Pineapple, extra standard | 1 25 | 11 |
| G 970 Pineapple, Genesee brand, sliced extra | 2 00 | 20 |
| G 971 Pineapple, Genesee brand, grated extras | 2 40 | 22 |
| G 972 Shredded Pineapple, 2-lb. cans, Curtice Bros.' finest thing put up in tin | 2 60 | 25 |
| G 973 White Ox-Heart Cherries, 2-lb. can, preserved and pitted, very finest quality | 3 00 | 27 |
| G 974 Preserved Cranberries | 2 30 | 22 |
| G 975 Rhubarb, 3-lb. cans, in syrup; extra | 1 50 | 15 |
| G 976 Figs, preserved in heavy syrup; finest | 2 00 | 23 |
| G 977 Black Raspberries, extra quality, standards; preserved in heavy sugar syrup | 1 45 | 14 |
| G 978 Black Raspberries, stand'rd quality | 95 | 9 |
| G 980 Apples, gallon can, best goods | $2 25 | $0 20 |
| G 981 Apples, 3-lb cans, best goods | 75 | 09 |
| G 982 Strawberries, 2-lb cans, preserved in refined sugar. Very finest; better than if put up at home | 3 00 | 28 |
| G 983 Pears, 3-lb cans, eastern fruit | 1 25 | 12 |
| G 984 Peaches, 3-lb tins, pie goods | 85 | 09 |
| G 985 Peaches, 3-lb tins, all yellow seconds, good goods | 1 25 | 11 |
| G 986 Peaches, extra standard, all yellow | 1 85 | 18 |
| G 987 Peaches for Pies, gallon cans | 2 35 | 23 |

**The Canned Vegetables** on our shelves are always up to a general high standard of excellence. When you buy of us we sell you what you pay for, and that isn't an attractive can, only two-thirds full of inferior goods. Full measure and big value is the rule in this department. Buy and you will buy again. It pays to make up a hundred pound order by adding such canned goods as you need. Freight is very little when compared with what we save you.

| (2 dozen in case.) | Doz. | Can. |
|---|---|---|
| G 990 Marrowfat Peas, standards | $1 05 | $0 09 |
| G 991 Early June Peas, standards | 1 20 | 11 |
| G 992 Pumpkin, 3-lb cans, best quality | 95 | 09 |
| G 993 Succotash, very best | 95 | 09 |
| G 994 White Wax Beans, extras | 1 00 | 09 |
| G 995 White Wax Beans, very finest quality | 1 50 | 14 |
| G 996 Marrowfat Peas, best quality | 1 35 | 12 |
| G 997 Extra Sifted Peas | 1 40 | 13 |
| G 998 String Beans, standards | 70 | 07 |
| G 999 Sweet Potatoes, best goods | 1 40 | 13 |
| G 1000 Squash, extra quality | 1 00 | 09 |
| G 1001 Lima Beans, extra quality | 1 10 | 11 |
| G 1002 Lima Beans, standard | 75 | 08 |
| G 1003 Gallon Pumpkin | 2 25 | 23 |

| | Doz. | Can. |
|---|---|---|
| G 1004 Elgin Corn | $0 95 | $0 09 |
| G 1005 Corn, Paris, 2-lb cans, B. & M. | 1 00 | 10 |
| G 1006 Corn, standard | 70 | 06 |
| G 1007 Corn, Illinois, standard, good | 50 | 05 |
| G 1008 Corn, Loomis, Portland, Maine, very fancy and sweet | 1 00 | 09 |
| G 1009 Beans, Boston Baked, 3-lb cans | 1 00 | 09 |

| | Doz. | Can. |
|---|---|---|
| G 1010 Tomatoes, gal. cans, best grades | $2 60 | $0 23 |
| G 1011 Tomatoes, standard, gal. | 2 40 | 22 |
| G 1012 Tomatoes, whole packed solid, 3-lb tins, very fine | 85 | 08 |
| G 1013 Tomatoes, 3-lb tins, extra standards | 75 | 07 |
| G 1014 Imported French Peas, best quality | 1 85 | 17 |
| | Doz. | Each. |
| G 1015 Mushrooms, imported, in tins | 2 40 | 22 |

### Plum Pudding.

Richardson & Robbins', a marvel of cooking. Better than home-made, and at no greater cost.

| | Doz. | Can. |
|---|---|---|
| G 1120 1-lb tins | $2 50 | $0 24 |
| G 1121 Same, 2-lb tins | 4 50 | 40 |
| G 1122 R. & R. Plum Pudding Sauce, 1-lb tins | 1 75 | 20 |
| G 1123 Same, 2-lb tins | 3 00 | 30 |
| G 1124 Fruit Pudding, assorted | 1 00 | 09 |

### Jams and Jellies.

#### Jellies in Pails.

Prepared from ripe fruit, Currant, Strawberry, Raspberry, Quince or Grape. Extra quality; finest to be had.

| | Doz. | Each |
|---|---|---|
| G 1130 5-lb tin pails | $6 00 | $0 65 |
| 10-lb tin pails | 10 60 | 1 25 |
| 20-lb wood pails | | 2 00 |

#### Jelly in 20 and 30 lb Kits.

New style packages. Railroads take them as fourth class freight.

| | Each. |
|---|---|
| G 1131 30-lb wood pails | $0 55 |
| 20-lb wood pails | 40 |

**WE ASK YOU TO WRITE US, IF AT ANY TIME YOU ARE NOT COMPLETELY SATISFIED WITH WHAT WE DO FOR YOU. WE DO NOT CLAIM TO BE ABSOLUTELY FREE FROM MISTAKES, AND ARE ANXIOUS TO SATISFY YOU.**

### Jellies in Tumblers.

Challenge Brand, very nice Currant, Strawberry, Raspberry, Quince, Apple, Peach, Plum or Grape. Doz. Each.
G 1132 Nice table tumblers, ½ lb each, 2 doz in case..........$0 75 $0 07
G 1134 Same in 1-lb tumblers, 2 doz. in case... 1 10 20

### Preserves in Pails.

Strawberry, Blackberry, Raspberry, Plum, Peach, Cherries and Quince. Extra quality, pure sugar and fruit goods, best in the market and very popular:

| | Doz. | Each |
|---|---|---|
| G 1136 5-lb tin pails | $7 35 | $0 75 |
| 10-lb tin pails | 14 00 | 1 35 |
| 20-lb wood pails | .... | 2 15 |

### S., R. & Co. Fine Preserves.

G 1138 1-lb tin cans, choice, clean goods, and are prepared from the ripe fruit: we fully guarantee them. Strawberry, Red and Black Raspberry, Blackberry, Apricot, Peach, Pineapple, Green Gage, Quince. They come packed 4 dozen in case. We will give you assorted cases
Price, per case of 4 dozen..........$5 00
Price, per dozen..........1 25
Price, per can..........12
Try a small order; you will want more.

### Various Brands.

These preserves are put up by one of the largest establishments in the country, a concern whose reputation for fine goods is unequalled. We hence offer them with an assurance based on experience that you will be more than pleased.

| | Doz. | Each |
|---|---|---|
| G 1143 Apricot preserves, 20-lb kanakins | .... | 1 40 |
| G 1144 Raspberry, Strawberry and Peach, 20-lb kanakins | .... | 1 60 |
| G 1145 **Orange Marmalade** imported, 1-lb jars, 2 doz. in case | $2 00 | $0 20 |

### Fruit Butter.

Put up in hermetically sealed cans containing 5 lbs each. Will keep for years in any climate. Clean and wholesome.

| | Doz. | Can. |
|---|---|---|
| G 1147 Apple, 1 doz. in case | $4 25 | $0 40 |
| G 1148 Peach, 1 doz. in case | 4 85 | 45 |
| G 1149 Plum, 1 doz. in case | 4 85 | 45 |
| G 1150 Quince, 1 doz. in case | 4 85 | 45 |
| G 1151 Pear, 1 doz. in case | 4 85 | 45 |

### Gelatine.

(Packed in 2-oz. boxes.)

A preparation that is indispensable to the housewife who is fond of making jellies. These are the purest on the market.

| | Doz. | Each |
|---|---|---|
| G 1154 Crystal Brilliant Gelatine, white | $1 00 | $0 10 |
| G 1155 Cox's Brilliant Gelatine, white | 1 60 | 15 |
| G 1156 Sheet, French, per lb. | .... | 50 |
| G 1157 Nelson's | 1 65 | 14 |

SHOULD NOT BE OMITTED in making up your order. **JUST LOOK AT OUR PRICES.** What have you been paying? What do we ask? What's the difference? Don't it pay to order here? **REMEMBER, TO MOST POINTS THE FREIGHT ON 100 POUNDS** is no more than on 50 pounds. **So keep adding** to your order until you have **100 pounds. If necessary** ask your neighbor to help make up the 100 pounds. **It will pay you so well. Remember cash in full less 2% or C. O. D.** on receipt of **one-fourth the amount.** Take your choice.

We carry in our store only the latest season's products. In fact our stock is always changing and we are receiving constant fresh consignments from home and foreign markets. This enables us to offer at all times and seasons clean and fresh fruits, the very nicest that can be bought. We save you from 25 to 40% and give you better goods.

Eighteen pounds of dried fruit are equal to three bushels of green, or one pound of dried fruit is equal to six pounds of green. This applies to all fruits and is the same whether fruits are evaporated or sun-dried.

| | Full Pkg | Br'k'n Pkg Lb |
|---|---|---|
| G 1160 Raisins, California, London layers, 20-lb box, 1896, extras; 3 crown, large fruit | $1 50 | $0 10 |
| G 1161 Raisins, California London layers, 5-lb boxes. Each | 43 | |
| G 1162 Raisins, California, London layer; very fine, 4 crown, 20-lb boxes | $1 75 | $0 11 |
| G 1163 California Valencia raisins, 1896, 50-lb. boxes, per lb | 08½ | 10 |
| G 1164 Raisins, California, Sultana, seedless; boxes of 50-lb., 1896 | 08 | 09 |
| G 1165 Raisins, Imported Sultanas, seedless; boxes about 25-lbs.; all fancy bleached, crop 1896 | 11 | 13 |
| G 1166 Raisins, new 1896, 3 crown loose Muscatels, in 50-lb. boxes. Very nice | 05½ | 06½ |
| G 1167 Raisins, new, 1896; 4 crown loose Muscatels in 50-lb. boxes; very choice; sell any quantity | 07 | 08 |
| G 1168 Currants, English, crop 1896, about 375 lbs, in a bbl. Our own importation, clean | 06 | 07 |
| G 1169 Currants, Vostizza (Royal Crown Brand), the very fanciest currant that grows; 25 and 50 lb. boxes | 07 | 08 |
| G 1171 California French Prunes; very large and extra choice, 1896. Bags of 85 lbs., 50 and 25 lb. boxes | 08 | 09 |
| G 1172 California French Prunes medium size, very nice. Bags of 85 lbs. | 07 | 08 |
| 50 and 75 lb. boxes | 07 | |
| G 1173 French California Prunes, small and very good. Barrels of 325 lbs. | 06 | 07 |
| Bags of 85 lbs | 06¼ | 07 |
| 50 and 25 lb. boxes | 06½ | 07 |
| G 1174 California Cherry or Ruby Prunes, very bright and fancy. Bags of 85 lbs. | 07 | 08 |
| 50 and 25 lb. boxes | 07 | |
| G 1175 Apples, Dried apples, Michigan, in 60-lb. sacks, or bbls. of about 200 lbs. each; choice, quarters | 04 | 05 |
| G 1176 Evaporated Apples, XXXX in 50-lb. boxes; fancy ring cut, best grade | 06 | 08 |
| G 1177 Evaporated Apples, second grade, 50-lb. boxes | 05 | 06 |
| G 1178 Nectarines, California, in 25 and 50 lb. boxes | 08 | 10 |
| G 1179 Peaches, California, halves, choice, new; bags 75-lbs., snap trade | 08 | 09 |
| G 1180 Peaches, California, 50-lb. boxes, snap trade | 09 | |
| G 1181 Peaches, California, 50-lb. boxes, snap trade | 08½ | |
| G 1182 Pears, California, halves, nice goods, in sacks of 80-lbs | 08 | 09 |
| G 1183 Peaches, sun-dried, light color, sound fruit; bags about 85 lbs., choice. | 07 | 08 |
| G 1184 Sun-dried Peaches, dark, 75-lb. bag | 05 | 06 |
| G 1185 Peaches, Jumbo California, halves, large, nice fruit, 25 and 50 lb. boxes | 11 | 12 |
| Sacks of 70 lbs | 10 | |
| G 1186 Apricots, California, 25-lb. boxes; very bright and fancy | 14 | 15 |
| G 1187 Apricots, in bags, 85 lbs | 11½ | 13 |
| G 1188 Blackberries, evaporated, new. 25 and 50 lb. boxes | 08½ | 09½ |
| G 1189 Raspberries, evaporated, new, 25 and 50 lb. boxes | 18 | 20 |
| G 1190 Plums, pitted, California, 80-lb. sacks, golden, clean fruit | 09 | 10 |
| G 1191 Figs, 10-lb. boxes 1896, very choice fruit | 12 | |
| G 1192 Imported Smyrna Figs, very choice; boxes 6 and 12 lbs. Full pkg. per lb | 12 | |

We do not break packages of figs.

### Citron, Lemon Peel, Etc.

These are selected, fresh, nice goods and the prices are right. If you ever use these goods be sure to include what you want with your next order.

| | By the drum per lb. | Less than drum per lb. |
|---|---|---|
| G 1200 Citron, best, 25-lbs. in drum | $0 12 | $0 14 |
| G 1201 Lemon peel, 25-lbs. in drum | 13 | 15 |
| G 1202 Orange Peel, 25-lbs. in drum | 13 | 15 |
| G 1203 Dates, Fard, dark, in about 12-lb. carton | 07 | 08 |
| G 1204 Dates, Select Persian, 12-lb. boxes | 08 | 10 |
| G 1205 Dates, Fard, 60-lb. boxes | 06 | 08 |

### Sauerkraut.

#### Johnson's Silver Thread.

The maker of this Sauerkraut knows his business, and he makes it his business to furnish us the choicest you can find anywhere. Your money back if the kraut isn't just right.

| | Bbl |
|---|---|
| G 1210 15 gal. kegs | $2 25 |
| G 1211 Barrels, 30-gal | 3 50 |
| G 1212 Barrels, 42-gal | 4 75 |

**FREIGHT** IS CHEAPER THAN EXPRESS.
**BIG ORDERS Save More Money than Small.**

**WE SELL ALL KINDS** of Sauces and Condiments at **Wholesale.** In this department you **can have the best** at what the cheapest are sold in retail stores. We take particular pains to have on hand such an assortment of goods as are found on the shelves of the **finest grocery stores** of large cities. **A saving of from 20 to 50 per cent.** is effected for you by **buying in large quantities** from the maker and adding the narrowest possible margin of profit. **DO NOT FORGET** to include some of these **fine table sauces in your next order.**

### Horse Radish.

We sell prepared Horse Radish at 30% less than usual retail prices.

| | Doz. | Each. |
|---|---|---|
| G 1220 Valhalla Cream, 8-oz. bottles | $2 00 | $0 18 |
| G 1221 Valhalla Plain, 8-oz. bottles | 95 | 10 |
| G 1222 Best quality, 1-gallon jugs | .... | 75 |
| G 1223 Best Quality, per qt. | ... | 25 |
| G 1224 Best Quality, half-pint bottles | 95 | 10 |

### Catsup.—In Glass.

There are hundreds of brands of Catsup on the market, a few of them good. We sell the best of those few, at less than retail prices for the many bad makes.

| | Case. | Doz. | Each. |
|---|---|---|---|
| G 1226 Snider's, quarts | $3 30 | $3 30 | $0 25 |
| G 1227 Snider's, pints | 4 60 | 2 30 | 25 |
| G 1228 Snider's, ½ pint | 2 70 | 1 35 | 15 |
| G 1229 Curtice Bros.' Blue Label, ½ pts., 25 bottles | 2 60 | 1 35 | 20 |
| G 1231 Curtice Bros.' 1 pts., 25 bot. | $4 25 | $2 20 | $0 20 |
| G 1232 Curtice Bros.' Blue Label, qts. 12 bottles | 3 25 | 3 25 | 30 |

| | Doz. | Each. |
|---|---|---|
| G 1233 Wicherts', ½ pt. bot. | $1 15 | $0 10 |
| G 1234 Wicherts', pt. bot. | 2 10 | 18 |
| G 1235 Wicherts', qt. bot. | 3 00 | 27 |

### Catsup in Jugs.

| | Each |
|---|---|
| G 1236 Extra choice, gallon jug | $0 75 |
| G 1237 Premium, gallon jugs | 50 |
| G 1238 People's choice, gallon jugs | 35 |

### Worcestershire Sauce.

Lea & Perrin were the originators of this particular sauce, and it is acnowledged that their make is the choicest that can be bought.

| | Doz. | Each. |
|---|---|---|
| G 1241 Lea & Perrin's, half pints | $2 75 | $0 24 |
| G 1242 Lea & Perrin's, pints | 5 00 | 45 |
| G 1243 Lea & Perrin's, quarts | 8 25 | 75 |

Equal to any manufactured. Give it a trial; you will be pleased with it.

| | Doz. | Each. |
|---|---|---|
| G 1245 ½ pint bottles, 2 doz. in case | $0 90 | $0 08 |
| Pint bottles, 2 doz. in case | 1 50 | 13 |
| Quart bottles, 1 doz. in case | 2 80 | 25 |

### Salad Dressing.

This dressing is prepared from the recipe of a famous French chef, and is very fine.

| | Doz. | Each |
|---|---|---|
| G 1247 Durkee's, large | $4 75 | $0 42 |
| G 1248 Durkee's, small | 2 75 | 25 |

### India Soy.

A very fine Condiment that when once bought will always be in favor and kept constantly on hand.

| | Dox. | Ea |
|---|---|---|
| G 1250 Crosse & Blackwell's pint bottles 1 doz. in case | $3 50 | $0 35 |

### Capers.

Make a fine sauce for meats. Very popular and meet a large sale.

| | Doz. | Each. |
|---|---|---|
| G 1254 Spanish, Capers capotes, 6-oz. bottles | $1 50 | $0 14 |
| G 1255 French, Capers Nonpareilles, 6-oz. bottles | 2 70 | 25 |

### Tobasco Pepper Sauce.

| | Doz. | Each. |
|---|---|---|
| G 1257 2-oz. bottles, 1 doz. in box | $4 00 | $0 40 |

### Curry Powder.

always in favor with the best cooks. Order a bottle and you will be more than pleased.

| | Doz. | Each. |
|---|---|---|
| G 1259 Crosse & Blackwell's, 1-oz. bottles | $1 35 | $0 12 |
| G 1260 Crosse & Blackwell's, 2-oz. bottles | 1 75 | 18 |

### Miller's Chili Sauce.

Always keep it on hand. We sell it so cheap, and it will cost you next to nothing when sent with other goods.

| | Doz. | Each. |
|---|---|---|
| G 1262 Half pints | $2 25 | $0 18 |
| G 1263 Pints | 3 30 | 28 |
| G 1266 Wichert's, pints | 2 00 | 20 |

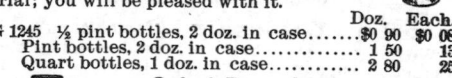

ALWAYS SAY WHAT CATALOGUE YOU ORDER FROM. ALWAYS GIVE THE ARTICLE NUMBER AND PRICE. AVOID MISTAKES BY USING THE UTMOST CARE AND GIVING FULL INSTRUCTIONS.

### Bengal Club Chutney.

| | Doz. | Each. |
|---|---|---|
| G 1252 Crosse & Blackwell's, pints | $6 00 | $0 55 |

### Pepper Sauce.

A sauce that has a very large sale, and many people prefer it to any other. As usual, our stock contains only the best.

| | Doz. | Each |
|---|---|---|
| G 1270 Red or Green, small bottles, ring | $0 70 | $0 07 |
| G 1271 Red Ring, large bottles | 1 10 | 10 |

### Olives.

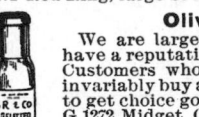

We are large importers of olives, and have a reputation for a most select stock. Customers who have bought of us once invariably buy again, for they know where to get choice goods.

| | Doz. | Each |
|---|---|---|
| G 1272 Midget Olives, 8-oz bottles, 2 doz. in case | $0 85 | $0 08 |
| G 1273 S., R. & Co.'s Queen Olives, 2 doz. in case; very finest; 10-oz. bottles | 2 30 | 22 |
| G 1274 Same, pint bottles; 16-oz. | 4 50 | 40 |
| G 1275 Same, quart bottles; 32-oz. | 7 00 | 65 |

| | 5 and 10 gal. kegs. | 1 gal. jugs. |
|---|---|---|
| G 1276 Olives in bulk: | | |
| X, small, per gallon | $0 75 | $0 80 |
| XX, medium, per gallon | 90 | 95 |
| XXX, large, per gallon | 1 00 | 1 05 |

### Olive Oil.

Always include such articles with your freight shipment. It always pays to ship by freight, as you can save very much more than on express shipments.

| | Case. | Bot. |
|---|---|---|
| G 1277 Domestic, half pints, 2 doz. in case | $1 15 | $0 07 |
| G 1278 Domestic, pints, 2 doz. in case | 2 00 | 10 |
| G 1279 Domestic, quarts, 1 doz. in case | 2 00 | 20 |

### Rae's Pure Olive Oil.

This oil, imported steadily for over thirty-five years, has been repeatedly tested by prominent chemists, and pronounced Pure Olive Oil.

| | Case. | Bot. |
|---|---|---|
| G 1280 ½-pints, 2 doz. in case | $5 50 | $0 28 |
| Pints, 2 doz. in case | 9 00 | 45 |
| Quarts, 1 doz. in case | 8 00 | 75 |

### Rae's Sublime Olive Oil.

This oil is absolutely pure and of the very finest quality. Put up in tins, ½ gal. and 1 gal. each. Being tin it insures full measure, and loss against breakage in handling; 10 gals. in case.

| | Case. | Each |
|---|---|---|
| G 1282 ½-gal. cans | $25 00 | $1 75 |
| G 1283 1-gal. cans | 25 00 | 2 50 |

In order to get good Pickles we compel the manufacturer to guarantee them put up in absolutely pure vinegar, and positively free from sulphuric acid. We also assure that you get full measure and full count. Our pickles are all first quality. We let the seconds go to your retail dealer, to whom you would pay fancy prices.

### Pickles.—In Glass.

These are specially fine goods. Money doesn't buy better. You can make up a freight order and include a few bottles of these pickles without adding anything to speak of to the freight.

### Crosse & Blackwell's English

| | Doz. | Each |
|---|---|---|
| G 1340 Crosse & Blackwell's Midgets, put up in full pint bottles. It is a very small, crisp pickle; just the thing for lunch and party | $3 25 | $0 28 |
| G 1341 Gherkins, C. & B.'s, pints | 3 60 | 30 |
| G 1342 Chow Chow, C. & B.'s, pints | 3 60 | 30 |
| G 1343 Mixed Pickles, C. & B.'s, pints | 3 60 | 30 |
| G 1344 Chow Chow, C. & B.'s, quarts | 5 50 | 48 |
| G 1345 Gherkins, C. & B.'s, quarts | 5 50 | 48 |
| G 1346 Mixed Pickles, C. & B.'s, quarts | 5 50 | 48 |

### Extra Choice Pickles.

| | Doz. | Ea. |
|---|---|---|
| G 1350 Fancy mixed in glass jars, 1 doz. in a case, quarts | $3 00 | $0 30 |
| G 1351 Fancy mixed, in glass jars, 1 doz. in a case, pints | 2 00 | 20 |
| G 1352 Chow Chow, 1 doz. in a case, quarts | 3 00 | 30 |
| G 1353 Chow Chow, 1 doz. in a case, pints | 2 00 | 20 |
| G 1354 White Holland Onions, extra small, pts. | 2 25 | 23 |
| G 1355 White Holland Onions, extra small, quarts | $3 25 | $0 30 |

### American Style.

| | Doz. | Bot. |
|---|---|---|
| G 1356 Gherkins, pints, 1 doz. in a case | $0 95 | $0 10 |
| G 1357 Gherkins, quarts, 1 doz. in a case | 1 40 | 12 |
| G 1358 Fancy mixed, pints, 1 doz. in a case | 95 | 10 |
| G 1359 Fancy mixed, quarts, 1 doz. in a case | 1 40 | 12 |

### Pickles—in Wood.

| | Pkg. |
|---|---|
| G 1310 Medium, barrels, 30 gals | $3 85 |
| G 1311 Medium, ½ barrels, 15 gals, count 600 | 2 50 |
| G 1312 Medium, 10 gal kegs | 2 25 |
| G 1313 Medium, 5 gal kegs | 1 35 |
| G 1314 Small, barrel, 30 gals | 5 00 |
| G 1315 Small, ½ barrels, count 1,200 | 3 00 |
| G 1316 Small, 10 gal kegs | 2 60 |
| G 1317 Gherkins, barrels, 30 gals | 6 05 |
| G 1318 Gherkins, ½ barrels, count 1,750 | 3 60 |
| G 1319 Gherkins, 10 gallon kegs | 3 00 |
| G 1320 Gherkins, 5 gal kegs | 1 90 |
| G 1321 Gherkins, 3 gal kegs | 1 40 |
| G 1322 Gherkins, 2 gal kegs | 1 20 |
| G 1323 Gherkins, 1 gal kegs | 75 |
| G 1324 Fancy Mixed, No. 3, ½ barrels | 6 00 |
| G 1325 Fancy Mixed, 10 gal kegs | 5 00 |
| G 1326 Fancy Mixed, 5 gal kegs | 2 20 |
| G 1327 Fancy Mixed, 2 gal kegs | 1 20 |
| G 1328 Fancy Mixed, 1 gal kegs | 85 |
| G 1329 White Holland Onions, in vinegar, small, 5 gal kegs | 4 50 |
| G 1330 White Onions, in vinegar, 1 gal kegs | 1 25 |
| G 1331 Chow Chow, No. 2, 5 gal kegs | 2 85 |
| G 1332 Chow Chow, 1 gal pails | 90 |
| G 1333 Sweet Spiced Gherkins, finest article in the market, 1 gal buckets | 90 |

### Vinegar.

Give our vinegar a trial—you cannot equal it for the money. No charge for barrels, which is equal to 2½ cents per gallon from quotations. Barrels contain from 45 to 50 gallons. We do not sell less than original packages.

G 1359½ Cider Vinegar, bbls. only, 50 gal.; per bbl., $6.00.

S. R. & Co.'s Apple Juice Cider Vinegar, guaranteed absolutely pure; made only from pure apple juice.

| | Gal. | Keg. |
|---|---|---|
| G 1360 Barrels, 47 gals, 40 grain | $0 13 | |
| G 1361 Barrels, 45 gals., 45 grain | 15 | |
| G 1362 ½ barrels, 30 gals., 45 grain | 16 | |
| G 1363 ½ barrels, 30 gals., 40 grain | 14 | |
| G 1364 15-gal. kegs, 40 grain | | $2 05 |
| G 1365 15-gal. kegs, 45 grain | | 2 20 |
| G 1366 10-gal. kegs, 40 grain | | 1 55 |
| G 1367 10-gal. kegs, 45 grain | | 1 70 |
| G 1368 White Wine, 40 grain, 29 gal | 11 | |
| G 1369 White Wine, 50 grain, bbl., 29 gal | 15 | |
| G 1370 White Wine, triple strength, 60 grain; very fine, in ½ barrels containing about 29 gal. No charge for bbl. | 18 | |

| | Bot. | Doz. |
|---|---|---|
| G 1372 Imported Malt Vinegar, C. & B., quart bottles | $0 20 | $2 10 |

### SALT.

| | Per bbl. | Per sack. |
|---|---|---|
| G 1380 Salt No. 1, Michigan, fine, 280-lb. bbl. | $1 00 | .... |
| G 1381 Michigan, fine dairy salt, 280-lbs. | 1 50 | .... |
| G 1382 Coarse Rock Salt | 1 50 | .... |
| G 1383 Higgins' or Ashton's fine dairy salt, 224-lb. sack | .. | $2 55 |
| G 1384 Michigan fine table salt, in 10-lb. sacks, 28 sacks in bbl | 1 40 | 06 |

| | Case. | Each. |
|---|---|---|
| G 1385 Crystal Diamond Table Salt, very dry and pure, in cartoons weighing 3 lbs. each, 24 packages in case | $1 60 | $0 08 |

| | Barrel. |
|---|---|
| G 1386 Rock Lump Salt for stock, first quality, 280-lb. bbls | $1 95 |

### Celery Salt.

| | Doz. | Each. |
|---|---|---|
| G 1387 4-oz. sifting top bottles | $0 90 | $0 08 |
| G 1388 Durkee's 4-oz. bottles | 1 50 | 15 |
| G 1389 Crown, 1-lb. tins | 4 80 | 40 |



## MEATS.

Prices of meats are fluctuating. We will charge you market rates on the day your order is received.

We handle only the best grades, and meats once cut cannot be returned. Sold only according to weight quoted. Our dealings are confined to two of the leading packers in Chicago, and we hence can guarantee that the meat when it leaves our store is pure and sweet.

We make it pay you to deal with us, for we save you the extra profits. Freight on this class of goods is very small and it will cost you very little for shipping a hundred pounds. You can almost always make up a freight order. Order such meat and flour and sugar as you will need, when you order your clothing or dry goods.

### In Lots of 100 Lbs. or More, 1 Cent per Pound Less.

| | Lb. |
|---|---|
| G 1400 Boneless Hams, about 3 to 4 lbs. each; best goods | $0 10 |
| G 1401 Summer Sausage, best quality, 50-lbs. in box | 13 |
| G 1402 Ham, very best sugar cured, 12 to 14 lbs. average | 11¼ |
| G 1403 Ham, same as G1402, 16-lbs. average | 11 |
| G 1404 Shoulders, 10 to 15 lbs. each, smoked | 07 |
| G 1405 Picnic Hams | 07 |
| G 1406 Dried salt sides, 40 to 60 lbs. each | 06 |
| G 1407 Bacon, smoked, clear sides, 40 to 50 lbs. each | 06¾ |
| G 1408 Bacon, bellies, smoked, 34-lbs. each | 06¾ |
| G 1409 Bacon, breakfast, smoked, 5 to 6 lbs. each | 10 |
| G 1410 Dried Beef Hams, 10 to 14 lbs. each, inside tenders | 13 |
| G 1411 Dried Beef, knuckle pieces, 5 to 7 lbs. each | 15 |

### Pig's Feet.

**The best the market affords.**

| | |
|---|---|
| G 1414 15-lb. kit | $0 75 |
| 40-lb., ¼ bbls | 1 55 |
| 80-lb., ½ bbls | 2 90 |

### Tripe.

We get these goods direct from the largest packing houses, and hence can assure you the finest.

| | Bbl. or kit. |
|---|---|
| G 1416 Kits, containing 10-lbs | $0 60 |
| G 1417 Kits, containing 15-lbs | 70 |
| G 1418 Quarter barrels, 40-lbs | 1 40 |
| G1419 Half barrels, 80-lbs | 2 50 |

### Pork.

The freight on 100 lbs. of pork will be very small, when you consider the saving. You can order other articles sent with the freight shipment and there will be very little if any additional charges.

Prices subject to market changes.

| | Bbl. |
|---|---|
| G 1421 Heavy Butts | $9 75 |
| G 1422 Short Cut Pork | 10 00 |
| G 1423 Mess Pork, new | 9 50 |
| G 1424 Clear Back Pork, new | 9 50 |
| G 1425 Lean Family Pork | 11 00 |
| G 1426 Boneless Bean Pork | 8 50 |

### Beef.

Prices subject to market changes.

| | Each |
|---|---|
| G 1427 Extra Mess Corned Beef, 200 lb. bbls. | $9 00 |
| G 1428 Extra Mess Corned Beef, 100 lb. ½ bbls. | 5 00 |
| G 1429 Plate Corned Beef, 200 lb. bbls. | 9 75 |
| G 1430 Plate Corned Beef, 100 lb. ½ bbls | 5 50 |
| G 1431 Extra Plate Corned Beef, 200 lb. bbls. | 11 00 |
| G 1432 Extra Plate Corned Beef, 100 lb. ½ bbls. | 6 00 |
| G 1433 Boneless Rolls, corned, 200 lb. bbls | 11 50 |
| G 1434 Boneless Rolls, corned, 100 lb. ½ bbls. | 6 25 |
| G 1435 Boneless Rump Butts, corned 200 lb. bbl | 12 00 |
| G 1436 Boneless Rump Butts, corned, 100 lb. ½ bbls | 6 50 |

### Mince Meat.

#### Challenge Brand—(Wet).

| | lb |
|---|---|
| G 1294 Quarter Barrels, about 100 lbs. | .06 |
| G 1295 Pails, 25 lbs ea. | .06½ |
| G 1296 Kannakins, 9 lbs each, 6 in crate | .07½ |
| G 1297 Kannakins, 4½ lbs each, 6 in crate | .08½ |
| G 1298 Glass Pails, 5 lbs each, ½ doz. in case per doz. | $5 75 |

#### Richelieu Condensed—(Dry).

☞ Best in the market.

G 1300 Kegs, 25, 50 and 100 lbs. per lb. .10¾

G 1301 3-lb Glass Jars, 1 doz. in case, doz. $6 05 Ea 55

G 1302 5-lb Glass Jars, 1 doz. in case, doz. 8 70 Ea 80

G 1303 New England Meat, 3 doz. in a case, per case $3 10; each 10

## Mince Meat.—Continued.
### Batavia Brand Condensed—(Dry).

| | Doz. | Each |
|---|---|---|
| G 1290 In cases containing 3 doz. pkgs.. | $0 80 | $0 07 |
| G 1291 In tins, (handsomely decorated), 10 lbs each, 1 doz. in case, per lb... | | 11 |

### Cow Boy Brand, Condensed.

| | Doz. | Each |
|---|---|---|
| G 1292 In cases containing 3 doz. packages | $0 75 | $0 07 |
| G 1293 In kegs or half bbls., per lb... | | 09 |

## LARD.
### Strictly Pure Leaf Lard.

Prices subject to market changes. While we are compelled to follow the changes of the market, we are as quick to grant reductions where prices fall as we are to ask an advance when the market rises. Kettle rendered absolutely pure.

| | Full Pkg. per lb. | Per pail |
|---|---|---|
| G 1440 Half-barrels, 120-lbs | $0 06½ | |
| G 1441 50-lb. can in case | 06¾ | |
| G 1442 Buckets, 20-lbs. | 07 | |
| G 1443 Pails, 10-lb each. 60-lbs. in case... | 07¼ | 70 |
| G 1444 Pails, 5-lbs. each. 60-lbs. in case... | 07½ | 40 |
| G 1445 Cottolene, substitute for lard, 5-lb. pail, each | | 45 |
| 50-lb. pails, each.. | | 3 25 |

### Cottosuet.

Most people prefer Cottosuet to Lard. It is prepared by the largest manufacturer of such compounds and once used will always be used.

| | | Doz. | Each |
|---|---|---|---|
| G 1446 3-lb. pail, 20 pails in case | $3 95 | $0 25 |
| G 1447 5-lb. pail, 12 pails in case | 3 85 | 40 |
| G 1448 10-lb. pail, 6 pails in case | 3 75 | 40 |
| G 1449 50-lb. tins | | 2 80 |

### Butter Color, Rennet, Cheese Color, Etc.

| | Doz. | Each |
|---|---|---|
| G 1452 Rennet Extract, 1 gal bottles... | $2 00 | |
| G 1453 Tablets, per box of 100 No. 1 Tablets | 3 75 | |
| G 1454 Tablets, per box of 200 No. 2 Tablets | 2 00 | |
| G 1455 Sample Boxes, containing 50 No. 2 Tablets | | 70 |
| G 1456 Hansen's Household Rennet Tablets, for making junket or curd and whey, 12 tablets in glass | 1 20 | 15 |
| G 1457 Bavarian Rennets, dry | 1 20 | 12 |
| G 1458 Hansen's Cheese Color, 1 gal. bot's.. | | 190 |
| G 1459 Hansen's Cheese Color, 4-oz. sample bottle.. | 1 90 | 16 |

### Sears, Roebuck & Co.'s Butter Color.

| | | Each |
|---|---|---|
| G 1461 Large $1.00 size | | $0 75 |
| G 1463 Medium, 50c size | | 37 |
| G 1464 Small, 25c size | | 18 |

## PRESERVED MEATS.

No family should be without a nice supply of these preserved meats. Handy for quick lunches, outings, traveling and very palatable. As usual, we keep, only the best, and you must be sure to include some in your freight order.

### Tongue.

| | Doz. | Each |
|---|---|---|
| G 1472 1-lb. Lunch Tongue | $2 75 | $0 25 |

### Ham.

| | Doz. | Each |
|---|---|---|
| G 1473 Potted, ½-lb. tins | $1 00 | $0 10 |

### Corned Beef.

| | Doz. | Each |
|---|---|---|
| G 1475 1-lb. cans | $1 25 | $0 12 |
| G 1476 2-lb. cans | 2 25 | 20 |
| G 1477 5-lb. cans | 4 50 | 40 |
| G 1478 6-lb. cans | 7 00 | 60 |
| G 1479 14-lb. cans | 15 00 | 1 35 |

### Lamb's Tongue.

| | |
|---|---|
| G 1481 Pond's 10-lb. kits | $2 00 |
| 15-lb. kits | 2 75 |
| ¼ barrel | 7 00 |

### Chipped Dried Beef.

| | Doz. | Each |
|---|---|---|
| G 1483 1-lb. cans | $2 10 | $0 20 |

### Extract of Beef.

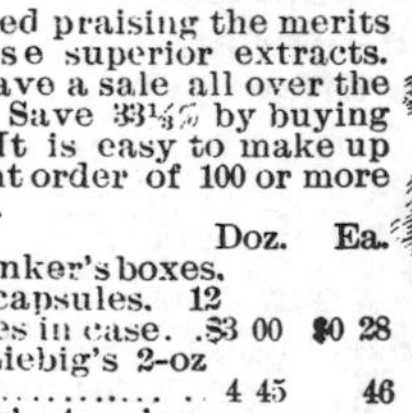

No need praising the merits of these superior extracts. They have a sale all over the world. Save 33⅓% by buying of us. It is easy to make up a freight order of 100 or more pounds.

| | Doz. | Ea. |
|---|---|---|
| G 1500 Anker's boxes, 10 capsules, 12 boxes in case | $3 00 | $0 28 |
| G 1501 Liebig's 2-oz jars | 4 45 | 46 |

| | Doz. | Each |
|---|---|---|
| Liebig's 4-oz jars | $ 8 20 | $0 80 |
| Liebig's 8-oz jars | 15 25 | 1 45 |
| Liebig's 16-oz jars | 28 25 | 2 60 |
| G 1502 Armour's solid extract, 2-oz | 4 20 | 40 |
| Armour's solid extract, 4-oz | 7 75 | 70 |
| Armour's solid extract, 8-oz | 14 50 | 1 25 |
| Armour's solid extract, 16-oz | 27 00 | 2 25 |
| G 1903 Armour's fluid extract, 2-oz | 3 70 | 30 |
| Armour's fluid extract, 4-oz | 7 00 | 60 |
| Armour's fluid extract, 8-oz | 12 00 | 1 10 |
| Armour's fluid extract, 16-oz | 22 00 | 2 05 |

---

## FISH DEPARTMENT
### FOR FISH

**WE ARE HEADQUARTERS;** our prices should interest you; **no dealer can buy cheaper;** you can save 25% to 50% in price, **20 or 50 pounds** of fish may just make up the **100 pounds** shipment, if so be sure to **add it,** even if you get a neithbor to join with you, take part of the goods and pay part of the freight.

**WE PREFER MAKING FREIGHT SHIPMENT**—because its cheaper for you. We urge club orders—because its cheaper for you. We urge Grocery orders—because it helps to make up the 100 pounds weight, reduces the freight charge on each article to next to nothing and will surely result in your buying everything from us.

**Send all the money in advance and get 2% cash discount,** or send 25% in advance and pay the freight agent the balance when goods are received.

### Herring, Imported, Spiced.

| | Pail. |
|---|---|
| G 1535 Hamburg, nicely spiced and vinegared (our specialty), in pails, 12-lbs. fish | $0 85 |

### Holland Herrings, Imported Kegs.

| | Keg. |
|---|---|
| G 1536 Dark Hoops | $0 70 |
| G 1537 Dark Hoops, extra, new | 75 |
| G 1538 Milchner | 85 |

---

### Smoked Fish,

| | Box. | Doz. |
|---|---|---|
| G 1539 Herring, scaled, about 45 fish in box | $0 15 | $1 65 |

### Whole Fish.

| | Full bundle per lb. | Less qty. per lb. |
|---|---|---|
| G 1520 Pollock, about 5-lbs. each, 50-lbs. in bundle | $0 03½ | $0 05 |
| G 1521 Codfish. Grand Bank. about 5-lbs. each, 50-lbs. in bundle | 05 | 07 |
| G 1522 Genuine George's Whole Cod, 7-lbs. each, 50-lbs. in bundle | 06 | 08 |
| G 1523 Stockfish Norwegian, large genuine, 110-lbs. in bundle | 08½ | 09½ |
| G 1524 Stockfish, medium | 08¼ | 09¼ |
| G 1525 Stockfish, small | 06 | 08 |

### Boneless Codfish.

| | Box. | Lb. |
|---|---|---|
| G 1528 Grand Bank. 2-lb. blocks, 40-lb. boxes | $2 25 | $0 07 |
| G 15.. George's very best, 2-lb. blocks, 40-lb. boxes | 2 60 | 08 |
| G 1530 Snow White, 1-lb. blocks, 5-lb. boxes | 40 | |
| G 1531 Grand Bank Strips, fancy 40-lb. boxes | 2 85 | 09 |
| G1532 George's Strips, fancy 40-lb. boxes | 3 40 | 10 |

| | |
|---|---|
| G 1533 Beardsley's Shredded Genuine Codfish. The best thing in the market, 2 doz. packages in case. Price per case | 1 90 |
| Per doz. | 95 |
| Per package | 10 |

---

## FISH IN BRINE.

Should they become dry rebrine them, and you will have no trouble with rusty fish. Always keep fish out of the sun.

| | Bbls. 200 lbs. | ½ Bbls. 100 lbs. | ¼ Bbls. 50 lbs. | Tubs. 40 lbs. | Pails. 20 lbs. | Pails. 15 lbs. | Pails. 10 lbs. |
|---|---|---|---|---|---|---|---|
| **LAKE FISH.** | | | | | | | |
| G 1550 No. 1 White Fish, large | | $ 7 15 | $ 3 85 | $ 3 15 | $ 1 60 | $ 1 25 | $ 0 90 |
| G 1551 No. 1 White Fish, medium | | 6 05 | 3 30 | 2 50 | 1 40 | 1 10 | 80 |
| G 1552 Family White Fish, very small | | 1 95 | 1 25 | 1 05 | 55 | 50 | 40 |
| G 1553 No. 1 Trout | | 3 85 | 2 20 | 1 80 | 95 | 75 | 55 |
| G 1554 No. 1 Bay Fish | | 1 95 | 1 25 | 1 05 | 55 | 50 | 40 |
| G 1555 Flat Lake Herring | | 1 95 | 1 25 | 1 05 | 55 | 50 | 40 |
| **MACKEREL.** | | | | | | | |
| G 1556 Norway Bloater, Mess, heads and tails off.. | $36 35 | 18 70 | 9 35 | 7 50 | 3 80 | 3 00 | 1 95 |
| G 1557 Norway Bloaters | 33 00 | 17 05 | 8 52 | 6 90 | 3 50 | 2 65 | 1 80 |
| G 1558 Block Island Bloater | 27 50 | 14 30 | 7 15 | 5 80 | 2 90 | 2 25 | 1 55 |
| G 1559 Extra No. 1 Shore, large | 24 20 | 12 65 | 6 35 | 5 10 | 2 60 | 2 00 | 1 40 |
| G 1560 No. 1 Shore, medium size | 19 80 | 10 45 | 5 25 | 4 25 | 2 15 | 1 65 | 1 15 |
| G 1561 Large Family | 15 40 | 8 25 | 4 15 | 3 35 | 1 70 | 1 35 | 95 |
| **HERRING.** | | | | | | | |
| G 1562 Round Shore, new | 4 50 | 2 75 | 1 40 | 1 20 | 65 | 55 | 50 |
| G 1563 Gibbed | | | | | | | |
| G 1564 Labrador, split | 7 15 | 4 15 | 2 05 | 1 70 | 90 | 70 | 55 |
| G 1565 Halifax, split, large | 6 60 | 3 85 | 1 95 | 1 60 | 85 | 65 | 50 |
| G 1566 Norway, K.K.K., fat | 9 90 | 5 50 | 2 75 | 2 25 | 1 10 | 90 | 65 |
| G 1567 Holland, imported | 8 80 | 4 40 | 2 20 | 1 80 | 95 | 75 | 55 |
| G 1568 Scotch, imported, very nice | 9 90 | 5 50 | 2 75 | 2 25 | 1 10 | 90 | 65 |
| **OTHER KINDS.** | | | | | | | |
| G 1669 California Salmon | 12 10 | 6 60 | 3 20 | 2 75 | 1 40 | 1 10 | 80 |
| G 1570 Bristlings or Sprats | 7 75 | 4 50 | 2 25 | 1 80 | 95 | 75 | 60 |
| G 1571 Tongues and Sounds | 13 20 | 7 15 | 3 60 | 2 90 | 1 50 | 1 15 | 85 |
| G 1572 Anchovies, genuine spiced | | 6 05 | 3 30 | 2 70 | 1 40 | 1 10 | 80 |

---

### Canned Fish.

| | Doz. can. | Can. |
|---|---|---|
| G 1580 Cove Oysters, No. 1, 5-oz. full weight cans | $0 90 | $0 09 |
| G 1581 Cove Oysters, No. 2, 10-oz., full weight cans | 1 55 | 14 |
| G 1582 Cove Oysters, best brand, extra select, 2 lb | 2 40 | 22 |
| G 1583 Lobsters, extra quality, No. 1 can | 2 65 | 25 |
| G 1584 Lobsters, extra quality, No. 2 cans | 3 65 | 33 |
| G 1585 Salmon, finest Columbia river, 1-lb. cans | 1 40 | 13 |
| G 1586 Salmon, extra quality, Alaska, No. 1 cans | 1 25 | 12 |
| G 1587 Salmon, fine quality Alaska, 1-lb. cans | 1 10 | 10 |
| G 1588 Salmon, extra quality Columbia river, No. 1 can | 1 80 | 16 |
| G 1590 Clams, Little Neck, B & M brand, extra quality No. 1, large cans, full weight | 1 15 | 10 |
| G 1591 Clams, 2-lb., B & M, full weight | 1 85 | 17 |
| G 1592 Clams, Little Neck, Doxie's No. 2 cans | 2 60 | 22 |
| G 1593 Shrimps, Barataria, Dunbars, 2 doz, in case | 2 35 | 22 |
| G 1594 Sardines, domestic, best domestic packing, ¼ boxes | 45 | 04 |

(Sardines packed in best olive oil.)

| | | |
|---|---|---|
| G 1595 Sardines, domestic, best domestic packing, ½ boxes | 85 | 08 |

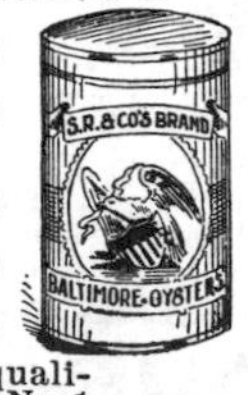

### Something for Nothing

We can't give you. But we can give you

### A Great Deal for Little.

---

| | Doz. Can | |
|---|---|---|
| G 1596 Sardines, imported, good grade, 12 to 14 fish, ¼ box | 1 45 | 13 |
| G 1597 Sardines, imported, ¼s, stuffed with truffles, key | 2 50 | 25 |
| G 1598 Sardines, imported, fine grade, 18 to 20 fish, ½ box.. | 2 40 | 23 |
| G 1599 Sardines in mustard, ¾ boxes | 98 | 09 |
| G 1600 Sardines in mustard, ½ boxes | 50 | 05 |
| G 1601 Boneless Sardines, finest imported, ½ boxes, with key | 3 50 | 33 |
| G 1602 Boneless Sardines, finest imported, ¼ boxes, with key | 2 75 | 25 |

### Mackerel—Canned.

| | Doz. | Can. |
|---|---|---|
| G 1603 Blue Back, fresh, 1-lb. cans | $1 00 | $0 10 |
| G 1604 Fresh Broiled Mackerel in tomato sauce, 3-lb. cans | 2 25 | 20 |
| G 1605 Fresh Broiled Mackerel in mustard sauce, most delicious, 3-lb. can | 2 25 | 20 |
| G 1606 Fresh Mackerel, genuine, 1-lb. can, 4 doz. in case | 1 50 | 14 |

### Deviled Crabs.

| | Doz. | Each. |
|---|---|---|
| G 1607 McMenamin's, 1-lb. cans, with shells | $2 35 | $0 22 |
| G 1608 McMenamin's, 2-lb. cans, with shells | 3 50 | 32 |

### Russian Caviar.

| | | |
|---|---|---|
| G 1610 Dittman's extra. 2-lb.. 2 doz. in case | 7 20 | 65 |
| G 1611 Dittman's extra. 1-lb., 2 doz. in case | 4 90 | 45 |
| G 1612 Dittman's extra, ½-lb., 4 doz. in case | 3 00 | 28 |
| G 1613 Dittman's extra, ¼-lb., 5 doz. case | 2 00 | 18 |

---

**WE HAVE A SPECIAL CATALOGUE OF VEHICLES THAT WILL TELL YOU MORE ABOUT LOW PRICES IN FIVE MINUTES THAN YOU COULD GET OUT OF YOUR RETAIL DEALER IN FIVE YEARS. CATALOGUE IS MAILED FREE.**

# SOUPS

These Soups sell well because they are made well. They help the housewife wonderfully when she runs a little short of provisions. We sell them at prices very little above the cost to make. You can have a few cans packed with your large freight order, and you'll be surprised how little the charges will be. We will make any assortment of one dozen or more and sell at the regular dozen prices.

## White Label—Armour Packing Co.

G 1485—

Puree of White Beans............
Puree of Lentils with Small Sausage..................
Clear Turtle..................
Chicken.................
Chicken Gumbo (okra)......
Mulligatawny..............
Consomme.................
French Bouillon...........
Julienne................
Printanier...............
Vegetable...............
Beef..................
Mutton..............

| | |
|---|---|
| Tomato.......... | Puree of Green Peas.... |
| Oxtail.......... | Mock Turtle.... |
| Kidney.......... | Puree of Game.... |

Solo Puree..................
Per case, 2 doz. 3-lb. cans..........$5 00
Per doz..........$2 50    Per can..........25

## Various Soups.

| | Case | Doz. | Each |
|---|---|---|---|
| G 1487 Snider's Tomato, gallon.....$.... | $6 25 | $0 55 |
| G 1488 Snider's Tomato 3 lbs....... 5 30 | 2 75 | 25 |
| G 1489 Snider's Tomato, 1 lb......... .... | 1 35 | 12 |
| G 1490 Dunbar's Okra and Gumbo, 3 lbs......... 6 50 | 3 25 | 28 |
| G 1491 Huckin's Tomato, Mock Turtle, Julienne, Pea, | | |

Macaroni, Vermicelli, Consomme, Beef, Vegetable and Mutton

| | | | |
|---|---|---|---|
| Broth.......... | 6 50 | 3 40 | 30 |
| G 1493 Chicken.......... | 7 40 | 3 75 | 35 |
| G 1494 Green Turtle.......... | 15 00 | 8 00 | 75 |
| G 1495 Terrapin.......... | 16 00 | 8 50 | 80 |

## Condensed Milk.

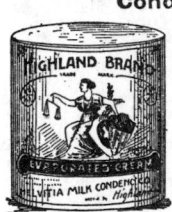

You will find it to your advantage to include a half a dozen or a dozen cans of condensed milk with your freight order. We make the prices right, and will save you money; in fact, a large percentage of what you pay your retail dealer.

| | Case. | Doz. | Ea. |
|---|---|---|---|
| G 1505 St. Charles unsweetened evaporated cream, 4 doz. in case......... $4 25 | $1 10 | $0 10 |
| G 1507 Evaporated cream, Highland brand, 4 doz in case......... 6 00 | 1 75 | 15 |
| G 1508 Eagle brand 1 lb cans, 4 doz in case......... 7 50 | 1 90 | 17 |

| | Case | Doz. | Ea. |
|---|---|---|---|
| G 1509 Crown brand, 1 lb cans. 4 doz. in case......... $6 00 | $1 50 | $0 15 |
| G 1510 Genuine Anglo-Swiss milk cham, 4 doz. 1-lb cans in case... 8 00 | 2 10 | 20 |

## Imported Malt Extract.

A most strengthening and valuable medicine, prescribed by the best physicians. If you feel run-down or nervous you will find no tonic better than malt extract. This brand is the best made.

| | Doz. | Each |
|---|---|---|
| G 1619 Leopold Hoff's size bottle..........$3 25 | $0 29 |

The only genuine, imported by Torrant & Co,

# FREIGHT YOUR ORDERS.....

Save all you can, and that can best be done by making your orders of sufficient size so that it will pay to make a freight shipment

---

# FLOUR DEPARTMENT

**We want your orders for Flour.** We want the orders because we are in a position to save you money on the best flour there is made. By saving money for you and pleasing you, we can count on you as a steady customer and friend. There isn't a cent in the flour business for us, and it may seem strange that we should urge you to buy goods from us on which we make no money. But the fact is, we want to encourage you to make up freight orders. You can save more money when you ship by freight than by express.

Order your flour at the same time with your suit, or some hardware, dry goods or other smaller articles, and all will come by freight at small expense.

| | Bbl. |
|---|---|
| G 1620 White Winter Wheat, best St.Louis grade, used principally for pastry.... | $4 75 |
| G 1621 Minnesota Patent (Pillsbury's best) barrels only......... | 4 85 |
| G 1622 Minnesota Patent, barrels only, Washburn's Superlative......... | 4 85 |

| | Bbl. | Sack 49 lbs. |
|---|---|---|
| G 1623 Pink Label, Minnesota Patent Fancy, best quality, 196-lbs............$4 60 | $1 20 |
| G 1624 Pink Label Winter Wheat....... 4 60 | 1 20 |
| G 1625 Pink Label Wisconsin Rye Flour.. 3 25 | 90 |
| G 1626 Bohemian Rye Flour, genuine Bohemian......... 3 35 | 90 |
| G 1627 Graham, extra winter wheat ... 3 40 | 90 |
| G 1628 Buckwheat Flour, genuine New York..........per lb. 2¼c. 4 25 | 1 10 |
| G 1629 Gluten, entire wheat flour, manufactured at Lockport. New York ... 5 50 | |

Per pound in any quantity, 3 cents

| | | |
|---|---|---|
| G 1630 ½ bbl. sacks......... | 1 75 |
| G 1631 ¼ bbls., 48 lb. sacks......... | 1 45 |

## FARINACEOUS GOODS.

**Our stock is most complete.** We keep the best because it sells best, and people keep on buying, because they are pleased. Everything new and fresh. We receive new consignments almost daily.

When you make your next order, include a supply of these goods to the amount of 100 pounds or so, and let the goods go by freight. Money saving is money getting and we make both easy. More than that, we keep you supplied with nice goods, which ought to be a big object to you.

## Self-Raising Buckwheat Flour.

| | Case | Pkg. |
|---|---|---|
| G 1635 Packed 50(2 lb) pkgs, in case......... $3 50 | $0 10 |
| G 1636 Packed 20(5 lb) pkgs. in case......... 3 50 | 23 |

## Pancake Flours.

| | Case. | pkg. |
|---|---|---|
| G 1637 Uncle Jerry's, cases 36 (2-lb) packages......... $3 25 | $0 10 |
| G 1638 Aunt Jemima's, cases 35 (2-lb). packages... 3 25 | 10 |

## Self-Raising Pancake Flour.

| | | |
|---|---|---|
| G 1640 Packed 36 (2 lb) packages in case......... $2 80 | $0 10 |
| G 1641 Packed 12 (5-lb) packages in case.. 2 25 | 23 |

## Oatmeal—Very Best Quality.

| | Each | Lb. |
|---|---|---|
| G 1643 Oatmeal, A, fine ground, bbls, 200 lbs..$4 90 | $0 03 |
| G 1644 Oatmeal, A, fine ground, half bbls, 100 lbs................. 2 65 | |
| G 1645 Oatmeal, B, medium steel cut. bbls, 200 lbs................. 4 90 | 03 |
| G 1646 Oatmeal, B, medium steel cut, half bbls., 100 lbs................. 2 65 | |
| G 1647 Oatmeal, C, coarse steel cut, bbls, 200 lbs................. 4 90 | 03 |
| G 1648 Oatmeal, C, coarse steel cut. half bbls, 100 lbs................. 2 65 | |

| | Case | Pkg |
|---|---|---|
| G 1649 Steel Cut Oatmeal, 36 (2 lb) pkgs in case......... 2 75 | 08 |
| G 1650 Steel Cut Oatmeal, 12 (5 lb) pkgs in case......... 2 50 | 20 |
| G 1651 Scotch Ground Oatmeal, 36(2lb) pkgs in case......... 3 25 | 12 |
| G 1652 Scotch Ground Oatmeal, 12(5lb)pkgs in case......... 2 85 | 23 |

## Rolled Oats.

| | Bbl. | Lb. |
|---|---|---|
| G 1653 Rolled Oats, bbls, 180 lbs........$4 25 | $0 03 |
| G 1654 Rolled Oats, half bbls, 90 lbs........ 2 35 | |
| G 1655 Rolled Oats, bulk, all new oats........ | |
| G 1657 Rolled Oats (Avena) partly cooked. a superior article, easily prepared, none finer, 36 (2-lb) pkgs in case......... 2 75 | Case Pkg. 08 |

---

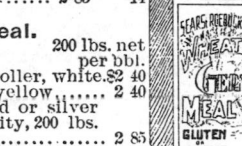

**Don't Omit Rice** from your grocery order. Our Lousiana Rice we buy in car load lots direct from one of the largest growers of finest **Lousiana Rice. We import** direct our **Japan Goods** and can therefore name you the prices, quality considered, which can not be duplicated by any other firm.

**Rice takes lowest freight rate;** always fourth-class so freight adds very little to cost and in **many cases nothing.** Your order may weigh 75 pounds when you can add 25 pounds of our finest Lousiana Rice costing you $1.12, without adding **one cent** to freight charges. For the same goods your dealer would ask you $2.00. **A discount of 2%** allowed if cash in full accompanies your order, **we ship C. O. D.** if a deposit accompanies your order.

☞ **DON'T FORGET OUR BARGAINS IN RICE** when ordering groceries.

Barrels contain about 330 pounds.

| | Price pr lb. by bbl. | Sack of 50 lbs. | Sack of 25 lbs. | Per lb. |
|---|---|---|---|---|
| G 1720 Lou. fair white | $0 03½ | $2 00 | $1 06 | $0 04½ |
| G 1721 Lou. best quality | 04 | 2 13 | 1 12 | 05 |
| G 1722 Car. choice head | 04½ | 2 40 | 1 25 | 05½ |
| G 1723 Car. fancy head | 05½ | 2 90 | 1 50 | 06 |
| G 1724 Japan, best | 05 | 2 65 | 1 40 | 06 |
| G 1725 Best Carolina, broken cleaned | 02½ | 1 40 | 75 | 03 |

| | Pkg. | Case |
|---|---|---|
| G 1726 Rice Flour, imported stock, finest quality, S. R. & Co. pack. 1 lb. pkg. 40 lbs. in case | $0 08½ | $0 10 |

## Imported Macaroni.

If you like macaroni you will find nothing better. A large package weighs so little that you can have it sent along with a freight order at **no additional expense.**

| | Full Box lb. | Less qnty. lb. |
|---|---|---|
| G 1730 Barton's Fils Macaroni, made from pure African Farina. Guaranteed equal to any in the market; 24 1-lb pkgs, in case | $0 10½ | $0 13 |
| G 1731 Domestic, bulk, best, about 12 lbs in box, finest made, per box | 60 | |
| G 1732 Domestic, good quality, in 1-lb pkgs about 25 lbs in box | 07 | 08 |

## Spaghetti.

Finest in the world and half price at that.

| | Box. | lb. |
|---|---|---|
| G 1733 Marge Fils, new importation, 25-lb boxes | $3 25 | $0 14 |
| G 1734 Domestic, 25-lb boxes | 1 50 | 07 |

## Vermicelli.

Costs but little, and elegant in quality.

| | Box. | Pkg. |
|---|---|---|
| G 1735 Domestic, bulk, 12-lb boxes, finest make | $0 60 | |
| G 1736 Domestic, 1-lb pkgs, 25 lbs in box | 1 80 | 08 |
| G 1737 Imported, finest quality, 25 1-lb packages in case | 2 75 | 13 |

## Tapioca.

A great favorite for puddings. Have a few packages packed in with your freight order.

| | | Case of 2 Doz. |
|---|---|---|
| G 1738 Rio Tapioca, the most delicate and pure known. Makes excellent puddings, etc. Per pkg | 16c | $3 12 |

| | Full sks | lb |
|---|---|---|
| G 1739 Flake Tapioca, sacks contain about 115 lbs | $3 45 | $0 04 |
| G 1742 Pearled, sacks contain about 135 lbs | 3 50 | 04 |

| | Case. | Pkg. |
|---|---|---|
| G 1743 Flake Tapioca, selected; none finer, 36 2-lb pkgs in case | $3 50 | $0 12 |
| G 1744 Pearled Tapioca, selected, none finer, 36 2-lb pkgs in case | 3 75 | 12 |

## Manioca.

A trial order will induce you to keep a constant supply.

| | Case. | Pkg. |
|---|---|---|
| G 1745 Hill's East India Manioca, 24 1-lb pkgs in case | $ 4.25 | $0 20 |

## Sago.

**All we ask is one trial** to convince you that there is none better, and that **our prices are the lowest.**

| | Full sack per lb. | Less qty. |
|---|---|---|
| G 1750 Fine German Sago, sacks about 120 lbs | $0 03 | $0 04 |
| G 1751 Sago, pearled, fine German, extra-quality, packed 36 2 lb. pkgs. in case, guaranteed, per case | 3 50 | 12 |

## Gloss Starch.

**Inferiority is a quality entirely unknown in our stock. The sale of good goods holds our trade.** This applies to starch and you ought to get a supply with your next freight order.

| | Box. | Lb. |
|---|---|---|
| G 1754 Laundry bulk starch in 50 lb. boxes | $1 75 | $0 04 |
| G 1755 Extra quality Gloss, in 6 lb. wood boxes, fully equal to any; price per 6 lb. box | | 25 |

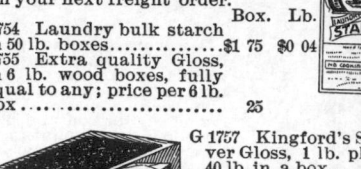

| | Per lb |
|---|---|
| G 1757 Kingford's Silver Gloss, 1 lb. pkgs. 40 lb. in a box | $0 08 |
| G 1758 Kingford's Silver Gloss, in 6 lb. wood boxes, per box | 45 |

## Celluloid Starch.

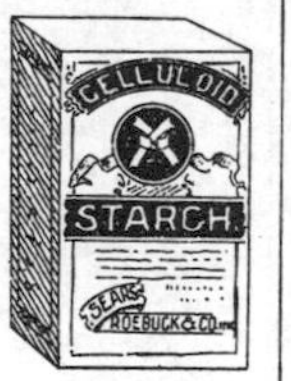

| | Case. | Pkg. |
|---|---|---|
| G 1760 Buy the best and only original Celluloid Starch. No rubbing, no boiling is required. Great invention; 64 pkgs. in a case | $5 00 | $0 08 |

## Corn Starch.

| | Box. | Doz. | Pkg. |
|---|---|---|---|
| G 1761 Superior, 50 1 lb. pkgs. in a box | $2 00 | $0 50 | $0 05 |
| G 1762 Kingsford's 40 1 lb. pkgs. in box | 2 65 | 85 | 08 |

**We save you from 4 to 6 cents a pound on Cheese.** The freight is very small on a hundred pounds and when you buy of us you don't pay a profit on the freight. Furthermore when you buy of us, you get fresh new goods, and not such as you have been buying from the shelves of the retail dealer. We guarantee to ship goods that are all right. Each shipment is carefully examined before shipping.

### Domestic.

We do not cut cheese unless so stated.

| | Lb. |
|---|---|
| G 1772 Plymouth Brand, Cheddar, 60-lb. boxes | $0 11 |
| G 1774 Twin Cheese, 2 in box, about 34 lbs. each; Plymouth Brand, finest made | 11 |
| G 1775 Full Cream, Herkimer Co., N. Y., about 60 lbs. each | 11 |
| G 1776 Young America, full cream, October, about 9 lbs. per lb | 12 |
| 4 cheese in box, price per lb. per box | 11 |

| | Case. | Each. |
|---|---|---|
| G 1777 Pineapple, Norton, medium size, 4 in case, about 4 lbs. each | $3 65 | $1 00 |
| G 1778 Pineapple, Norton, picnic size, 7 in case, about 2 lbs. each | 3 40 | 60 |

| | Case. | Lb. |
|---|---|---|
| G 1779 Domestic Swiss, about 25 lbs, 6 cheese in a box, 14c. per lb; less than a box, 16c. | | |
| G 1780 Limburger, very best, about 2-lb bricks; we do not cut; cases about 120-lb boxes | $0 10 | $0 11 |
| G 1781 Brick, finest Wisconsin make, about 5-lb bricks. 120-lb boxes | 10 | 12 |

### Imported.

| | Per lb. | Less Qnt'y Per lb. |
|---|---|---|
| G 1783 Swiss, 100 to 160 lbs each; we cut any quantity; price for full cheese | $0 30 | $0 35 |
| G 1784 Sap Sago, or green cheese, 3 or 4 to the pound; per loaf, each 10c | 25 | |
| G 1785 Edam, Van Rossem's, wrapped in tin foil, each | | 85 |
| G 1786 Roquefort, about 5 lbs; per lb | | 50 |

## Seeds.

| | Per lb |
|---|---|
| G 1790 Canary | $0 04 |
| G 1791 Hemp, 100-lb lots 3½c | 04 |
| G 1792 Rape, imported, best | 04 |
| G 1793 Millet, native | 04 |
| G 1794 Caraway | 12 |
| G 1795 Celery | 18 |
| G 1796 Anise, Italian | 20 |
| G 1797 Flaxseed | 05 |
| G 1798 Poppy, red—blue (Maw) | 18 |
| G 1799 Mustard, yellow | 10 |
| G 1800 Fennel | 17 |
| G 1801 Coriander | 10 |
| G 1802 Cardamon, No. 1 | 1 00 |

## Mixed Bird Seed.

**Our Bird Seed is thoroughly sifted and cleansed, and is packed under our own supervision.**

| | Case. | Pkg. |
|---|---|---|
| G 1804 Hemp, Rape, Canary and Millet, mixed 1-lb packages, 60 lbs in case | $2 40 | $0 05 |
| G 1805 Same, 5-lb packages, with 1 full-sized cuttlebone in each pkg 60 lbs in case | 2 40 | 23 |
| G 1806 Cuttlebone, per lb, 22c. | | |
| G 1807. Bird Gravel, 3 doz pkgs in cases, with whole cuttlebone in each package | 1 60 | 06 |

**TONS OF FLOUR** are necessary to manufacture Crackers and Biscuit sufficient to meet the demands of our trade. Our friends have learned by personal experience the **really fine and fresh goods** we handle in this line. Not only are old customers sending in their constant renewals of previous orders, but new trade is attracted by the **high class article** and the **extremely low prices.** We shall continue to maintain this high standard of excellence. We have every reason to hope for your trade and that of your neighbor. When you need any article, no difference how small, it is well to look into your pantry and find out if **you need some groceries.** Perhaps some flour, meat, extracts, pickles, baking powder and of course, a small or large box of crackers are wanted. **You can easily make up a freight order,** and you know the **freight is little or nothing** compared with what we save you.

Butter, oyster and soda crackers come in about 25-lb boxes and 50-lb barrels. All others in about 35-lb boxes and 70-lb barrels. No charge for barrels or boxes.

| | Bbls. or bxs. lb. | 2-lb cart. lb. | 3-lb cart. |
|---|---|---|---|
| G 1820 Soda crackers, very fine; the regular grade | $0 05½ | $ | $0 06½ |
| G 1821 Soda cracers, city, superfine, light and flaky | 07 | 08 | .... |
| G 1822 Soda crackers, Princess, best grade | 09 | 10 | .... |
| G 1823 Oyster crackers, cream, best quality, picnic | 05½ | .... | 06½ |
| G 1824 Oyster, fancy | 06½ | .... | 07½ |
| G 1825 Butter crackers, wafers, very fine | 05½ | .... | 06½ |
| G 1826 Boston Butters | 07½ | .... | 08½ |
| G 1827 Kenosha crackers | 07½ | .... | .... |
| G 1828 Milk crackers, delicious | 08 | 09 | .... |
| G 1829 Graham crackers | 08 | 09 | .... |
| G 1830 Oatmeal crackers | 08 | 09 | .... |
| G 1831 Pilot Bread, best made | 06½ | .... | 07½ |
| G 1832 Cracknells, egg biscuit | 15 | 16 | .... |
| G 1833 Pretzels, hand made | 08 | 09 | .... |
| G 1834 Lemon Wafers | 14 | 15 | .... |
| G 1835 Grandma's Cookies, assorted | 10½ | .... | 11½ |
| G 1836 Frosted Cream Crackers | 08 | 09 | .... |
| G 1837 Vanilla Wafers | 14 | 15 | .... |
| G 1838 Ginger Snaps, best | 08 | 09 | .... |
| G 1839 Lemon Snaps, best | 11½ | 12½ | .... |
| G 1840 Animals | 11½ | 12½ | .... |
| G 1841 Assorted Jumbles | 11 | 12 | .... |
| G 1842 Jelly Fingers | 14 | 15 | .... |
| G 1843 Sultana Fruit Biscuit, finest in the world. These are very popular, and are one of our specialties | 11 | 12 | .... |
| G 1844 Honey Jumbles, iced | 12½ | 13½ | .... |

G 1845 **A LEADER**—Superior Soda, Butter or Oyster Crackers, a 25-lb box for $1.00.

### Fancy Crackers, Discuits, Etc.

| | Doz | Each |
|---|---|---|
| G 1846 Long Branch Flakes, 1-lb tins | $2 40 | $0 22 |
| G 1847 Albert Biscuit, 1-lb tins | 2 50 | 23 |
| G 1848 Thin Water Biscuits, 1-lb tins | 2 50 | 23 |
| G 1849 Graham Wafers, 1-lb tins | 2 50 | 23 |
| G 1850 Ginger Wafers, 1-lb cans | 2 50 | 23 |
| G 1851 Oatmeal Wafers, 1-lb papers | 1 40 | 13 |
| G 1852 Zephyr, Extra Fancy Sodas, 1-lb packages | 1 40 | 13 |
| G 1853 Graham Wafers, 1-lb papers | 1 40 | 13 |
| G 1854 Vanilla Wafers, 1-lb tin boxes | 2 50 | 23 |
| G 1855 Brownies, in 1-lb papers | 1 50 | 14 |
| G 1856 Sugar Wafers, in 1-lb tins | 2 50 | 23 |
| G 1857 Cocoanut Macaroons | 2 50 | 23 |

**FOR LATEST STYLES........**

**......CONSULT OUR......**

**Dry Goods and Clothing Departments.**

**READ WHAT WE SAY IN FRONT PAGES OF THIS BOOK ABOUT CLUB ORDERS. IT WILL PAY YOU TO TAKE THIS MATTER UP WITH YOUR NEIGHBORS AND YOU CAN ALL SAVE MONEY.**

# CANDY DEPARTMENT

**A SWEET TOOTH** is sure to be found amongst everyone's "grinders." To satisfy your taste for sweets we carry an extensive line of strictly choice candies. These are made especially for us by one of the leading manufacturers. **NOTE ONE FACT. We never ship** candy that has been made over a week. Fresh consignments are received daily. **The finer grades are made after the order is received.** This insures nice, fresh, clean goods, and it is worth your while when buying candies to consider **this** special advantage. Most goods you can buy at retail are all the way from two months to a year old.

**PRICES AND PROFITS** are cut indiscriminately. We sell at the narrowest margin over the actual cost to make.

You can include a nice 5-lb. box or a pail with your freight order and you'll scarcely know the difference n the amount of your bill. **Give us one trial and we will please you.**

## Five Pounds Fancy Mixed Candy for 35 Cents

G 1865.

G 1865 A Pail of Fancy Mixed Candy, 30 lbs. in good wooden pail, for **$1.95.**

Buy a pail of fine candy and divide it among your neighbors. They will all want candy. Three or four order together and get a pail (30 lbs) of candy for $1.95. and you get the candy at 6½c per pound and the pail for nothing.

An Extra Quality Fancy Mixed Candy, usually sold by retail dealers at 20c per pound. Our offer of 5 lbs (in box) for **35c**, or 30 lbs in wooden pail for **$1.95**, is special, and shows how low it is possible to sell staple goods direct to consumers on our one-small-profit plan.

## Special Bargain in Gum Drops.

G 1866 Five pounds Fancy Gum Drops for **25c** or 35 pounds Fancy Gum Drops in good wooden pail for **$1.65. Your retail dealer** would pay about $3.00 for such a 35-lb pail of gum drops and would sell it for $7.00. Buy 5 pounds at retail and you would pay $1.00 —35 pounds and you would pay $7.00. You see it will pay you to get several to order with you and get your candy by the pail.

## Your Choice for 55 Cents.

G 1867 Five Pounds Fancy Candy in box for **55c. $1.50 a box—30c a pound, is the retail price.**

Get your friends to join you and make up an order for all and save the **enormous profit of the retailer.**

| | Per box. |
|---|---|
| Iceland Moss Squares, 5 lbs in a box...... | $0 55 |
| Hoarhound Squares, finest quality made, 5 lbs in a box... | 55 |
| Fancy Lemon Drops, 5 lbs in a box.......... | 55 |
| Fancy Strawberry Drops, 5 lbs in a box......... | 55 |
| Fancy Pineapple Drops, 5 lbs in a box......... | 55 |
| Fancy Cream Balls, 5 lbs in a box.... | 55 |
| Fancy Lady Kisses, 5 lbs in a box......... | 55 |

## Fancy Chocolate Creams at 14 Cents Per Pound.

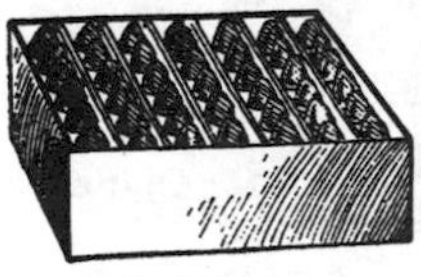
G 1868.

G 1868. In 5-pound boxes, **70c for the box.** Retail everywhere at 25c to 40c per pound. These are very fancy goods and at our price you can't afford to miss this offer. **Not less than a 5-pound box sold to any-one.** Make up a $10.00 order by getting your friends and neighbors to order with you and we will ship the goods by freight, which will add very little to the cost.

## Special Drive in Fancy Caramels.

G 1869 Fancy Wrapped Caramels, for box of 5 lbs, **55c.**

Snow Drop Caramels, iced, new, for box of 5 lls, **59c.**

G 1870 200 Licorice Jaw Breakers in 5-lb box for **59c.**

Retail everywhere at 2 for one cent—$1.00 for the box.

G 1870.

## Great Drive in Fancy Stick Candy.

G 1872.

G1872 This fancy grade stick candy retails at 20 cents per pound in every retail store. Our special offer price is **7c.** per pound, **35c.** for 5 lb. box. Not less than one box sold.

Your choice Fancy Colored Stick Candy.

Fancy Excelsior Twist Stick Candy.

Fancy Grade Hoarhound Stick Candy.

A full wooden pail, 30-lbs. for **$2.10.** It will pay you to order by the pail,

## Special Bargains in Fancy Candy.

G 1873 Candy that retails at three times our prices.

This candy comes in 5-lb. boxes; not sold in less quantity.

G 1873.

Fancy Cocoa Tablets, cocoanut center, transparent covering, Price per box of 5 lbs., **75c.** Your retail dealer would ask $1.50 or more,

G 1874 100 Cocoa Tea Biscuits, retail price, $1.00. Our price, **59c.**

G 1874.

100 Lady Fingers, retail price, $1.00. Our price, **59c.**

100 Penny Fig Paste Squares, assorted lemon, vanilla, etc., retail price, $1.00. Our price, **49c.**

## Great Bargains in Candy.

G 1875 100 Daisy Squares, assorted colors. Regular retail price, $1.00. Our special price, **59c.** per box.

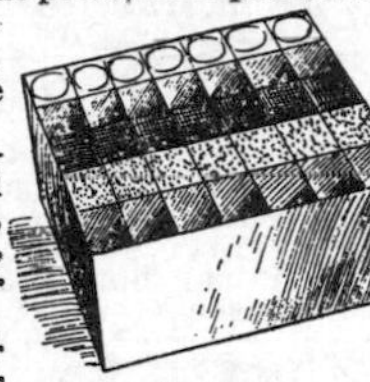
G 1875.

100 Mince Pie Cuts, assorted colors. Regular retail price, $1.00. Our special price **59c.** per box.

100 Princess Squares, assorted colored tops, decorated with cocoanut, nonpareils, etc. Regular retail price, $1.00. Our special price, **59c.** per box.

100 Yum Yum Squares, fancy tops, assorted colors, Regular retail price, $1.00. Our special price, **59c.** per box.

100 Liberty Bells, Italian cream topped with bell. Regular retail price, $1.00. Our special price, **59c.** per box.

100 Assorted Chocolate Bars, three inches long. Regular retail price, $1.00. Our special price, **59c.** a box.

G 1877.

100 Vanilla Assorted Bars, three inches long. Regular retail price, $1.00. Our special price, **59c.** per box.

G 1876 100 M. M. Bananas, 6½ inches long, very fancy goods, Regular retail price $1.00. Our special price, **59c.** per box.

200 M. M. Elephants. Regular retail price, $1.00. Our special price, **59c.** per box.

200 M. M. Fish Cakes. Regular retail price, $1.00. Our special price, **59c.** per box.

100 M. M. Royal Cakes, Regular retail price, $1.00. Our special price, **59c.** per box.

## Very Fancy French Creams.

No. G 1877.

G 1877 Packed in fancy 5-lb wooden boxes, dove tailed corners. **Our special offer price** is less than one-half the regular retail price.

| | Box 5 lbs |
|---|---|
| Assorted Fine Creams, | $1 20 |
| Maple Walnut Creams, | 1 20 |
| Pineapple Bon Bons... | 1 20 |
| Jelly Diamonds........ | 1 20 |
| Apricot Jelly Walnuts, | 1 20 |
| Peraline Creams..... | 1 20 |
| Pistachio Creams.......... | 1 20 |
| Pistachio Bon Bons........ | 1 20 |
| Walnut Bon Bons..... | 1 20 |
| Pecan Bon Bons.... | 1 20 |
| Walnut Jenilles... | 1 20 |
| English Walnut Creams.... | 1 20 |
| Walnut Paste Bon Bons..... | 1 20 |
| Assorted Jelly Ices..... | 1 10 |
| Almond Nougatines..... | 1 20 |
| Apricot Lemon Slices..... | 1 20 |

## Almonds.

| | | 5-lb. boxes. Per box. |
|---|---|---|
| G 1880 | Cream.... | $0 75 |
| G 1881 | French Burnt...... | 95 |
| G 1882 | Burnt Peanut...... | 60 |
| G 1883 | Cream Peanut...... | 60 |

## Bon Bons.

| | | |
|---|---|---|
| G 1884 | Imperials.... | 55 |
| G 1885 | Peerless.... | 60 |
| G 1886 | Flat Raspberries.... | 60 |
| G 1887 | Lady Creams.... | 60 |
| G 1888 | Cream Mice.... | 75 |
| G 1889 | Small Cream Varieties.... | 55 |
| G 1890 | Cream Roses.... | 55 |
| G 1891 | Maple Bon Bons.... | 55 |
| G 1892 | Double Color.... | 60 |
| G 1893 | Lemon XXX.... | 60 |
| G 1894 | Orange XXX.... | 60 |
| G 1895 | Cream Strawberries.... | 60 |
| G 1896 | Royal Creams.... | 60 |

## Nuts.

| | Bag pr lb. | Less pr lb. |
|---|---|---|
| G 1900 Almonds, Jordan, shelled, 28-lb. boxes.... | $0 35 | $0 40 |
| G 1901 Almonds, Taragona, soft shell, 150-lb. bags.... | 12 | 15 |
| G 1902 Almonds, Cal. Princess, paper shells, 100-lb. bags.... | 12 | 15 |
| G 1903 Brazils, new crop, 150-lb. bags...... | 6½ | 8 |
| G 1904 Filbert's, new crop, 150-lb bags.... | 09 | 11 |
| G 1905 English Walnuts, Grenobles, new crop, 150-lb. bags; fancy stock.... | 11 | 12 |
| G 1906 California Walnuts, new crop, 130-lb. bags fine goods....... | 11 | 12 |
| G 1907 Pecans, new crop, 130-lb. bags.... | 07 | 10 |
| G 1908 Virginia Peanuts, green, 100-lb. bags; fancy.... | 05½ | 06½ |
| G 1909 Virginia Peanuts, roasted, 100-lb. bags; fancy.... | 06 | 07 |
| G 1910 Mixed Nuts, finest brand; fine selections....... | | 11 |

## Chewing Gum.

We do not sell less than a box.

| | Box. |
|---|---|
| G 1911 Adams' New York Rubber Gum, 100-pieces in box.... 6 cents extra, by mail. | $0 25 |
| G 1912 Adams' Pepsin Tutti Frutti Gum, 20 foil covered bars, 5 pieces in each bar.... 19 cents extra, by mail. | 60 |
| G 1913 Adams' Sweet Fern Gum, 200 pieces in a box, retails 2 for 1 cent.... 19 cents extra, by mail. | 55 |
| G 1914 Betham's Pepsin Celery Gum, 20 packages in a box, 5 pieces in a package...... 18 cents extra by mail. | 55 |
| G 1915 Old Fashioned Pure Spruce Gum, 20 pieces in a box, 5 pieces in a package.... 17 cents extra by mail. | 60 |
| G 1916 Taffy Tolu Gum, 72 pieces in a box..... 8 cents extra, by mail. | 20 |
| G 1917 White's Yucatan Gum, 20 packages in a box, 5 sticks in a package.... 20 cents extra, by mail. | 51 |

**ORDER YOUR SUGAR FROM US.** We guarantee for you the lowest importation price on day your order is received. **WE ASK NO PROFIT ON SUGAR**—we are willing to supply all our customers with their sugar at actual cost to import. **We don't want one cent of profit on sugar. SUGAR IS OUR ACCOMMODATION LINE**—our old customers appreciate it—**all new customers** will also appreciate it when they learn what a saving it is for them. **PRICES CHANGE SO OFTEN** we cannot quote prices in this book, but we will cheerfully quote prices on application, or you will find them in our **Free Grocery Catalogue.**

**IT ISN'T NECESSARY** to get quotations—in making up your order just say how much is for sugar and what kind is wanted, and you will get the **very lowest prices** of the market on the day your order is received **Sugar, like grain, cotton, pork or beef, is** changing more or less every day.

**NO DISCOUNT (NO 2 PER CENT.)** will be allowed on **SUGAR.** You will get it at **COST, no profit, no loss,** and we will save you a great deal of money in a year.

**FREIGHT ON SUGAR** is very low—**4th class, the lowest freight rate.** (See 4th class freight rate to the different states on page 7. **You will see freight on this class of goods amounts to next to nothing.)**

**SUGAR IS THE BEST** commodity with which to make up your 100-pound freight order; **a great many** of our customers make up their order of all the goods wanted from the different departments and then add **sugar** to make up the 100 pounds. **That brings the other goods practically free of all freight charges, free of all transportation cost.**

**YOUR NEIGHBORS** will surely take from you any **sugar** you do not want.

| | |
|---|---|
| G 1920 | Dominoes.... |
| G 1921 | H. & E. Cut Loaf.... |
| G 1922 | Cubes.... |
| G 1923 | XXXX Powdered.... |
| G 1924 | H. & E. Powdered.... |
| G 1925 | Standard Powdered.... |
| G 1926 | Revere Fine Granulated.... |
| G 1927 | Fine or Standard Granulated.... |
| G 1928 | Mould A.... |
| G 1929 | Confectioners' A.... |
| G 1930 | Off A.... |
| G 1931 | White Phœnix Extra C.... |
| G 1932 | Phœnix Extra C No, 1.... |
| G 1933 | Phœnix C No. 2.... |
| G 1934 | Yellow No. 3.... |
| G 1935 | Yellow No. 4.... |
| G 1936 | Yellow No. 5.... |
| G 1937 | Golden Brown No. 6.... |
| G 1938 | Cuban Dark No. 7.... |

**WE CAN GRATIFY YOUR TASTES JUST AS WELL AS THOUGH YOU SELECTED FROM A RETAIL STORE. IT IS OUR BUSINESS TO PLEASE YOU, FOR OUR FUTURE TRADE DEPENDS ON IT.**

# SYRUP AND MOLASSES

**SYRUP AT FIRST COST** means to own it at about one-half the price charged by retail dealers. **WE SELL SYRUP AND MOLASSES** at lowest wholesale prices. No retail dealer can buy it any cheaper than you can buy from us. **A 5-GALLON KEG OF SYRUP** is a nice family order, costs but little when bought at our prices, **weighs about 40 pounds**, and takes lowest freight rate, **4th class**, which amounts to next to nothing. **JUST THINK! You can buy 5 gallons of syrup, keg and all, for about $1.00.** It goes a long way towards making up a 100-pound order, and helps you to own your groceries and other goods as cheap as any dealer can buy.

**Send the full amount with your order** and deduct 2% cash discount, or send 25% and pay your freight agent the balance when goods are received.

A barrel of syrup or mollasses contains 50 gallons; half-barrels, 25 gallons.

Always give name when ordering syrup or molasses. Two and half gallon kits now take lowest rate of freight, same as barrels.

No extra charge for barrels, kegs or kits.

| | Per gal. bbl. | Per gal. ½-bbl. | By 5 & 10 gal. keg. | 2½ g'l & 10 Kits. kit. |
|---|---|---|---|---|
| G 1945 Sugar-loaf Drips, amber, **Strictly Choice**... | $0 19 | $0 21 | $0 22 | $0 65 |
| G 1946 Sunshine, light amber | 21 | 23 | 24 | 70 |
| G 1947 Dew Drop Drips, dark rich body | 16 | 18 | 20 | 60 |
| G 1948 Morning Glory, pure syrup | 22 | 24 | 26 | 80 |
| G 1949 Honey Drips | 23 | 25 | 27 | 85 |
| G 1950 Revere, pure sugar syrup | 30 | 32 | 37 | 1 00 |

The Revere has a strong taste like molasses.

## Molasses.

| | Per gal. bbl. | Per gal. ½-bbl. | By 5 & 10 gal. kit. | 2½ g'l kit. |
|---|---|---|---|---|
| G 1952 Molasses, black strap, cheap grade of molasses mostly used for baking | $0 13 | $0 15 | $0 17 | $0 50 |
| G 1953 Molasses, Porto Rico. | 30 | 32 | 34 | 1 00 |
| G 1954. New Orleans P | 19 | 21 | 23 | 65 |
| G 1955 New Orleans R, prime new open kettle | 23 | 24 | 26 | 85 |
| G 1956 New Orleans, finest golden, very best in market | 38 | 39 | 41 | 1 20 |

## MAPLE SYRUP.
### Pure Vermont.

| | Per gal. | Ea. |
|---|---|---|
| G 1957 Very fine, by the barrel | $0 82 | |
| G 1958 Half barrels | 87 | |
| G 1959 5 gallon cans | 97 | |
| G 1960 Gallon tins | $1 15 | |
| G 1961 Half-gallon tins | | 65 |
| G 1962 Quarts | | 40 |
| G 1963 Gallon tins, choice grade | | 75 |
| G 1964 Half-gallon tins | | 45 |
| G 1965 Quarts | | 25 |

### In Bulk.

| | Gal. |
|---|---|
| G 1966 Vermont. No. 1.5 or gal. kegs | $0 70 |
| G 1967 Canada. No. 2.5 or 10 gal. kegs | 45 |
| G 1968 Canada. No. 2, per gal | 50 |

| | Doz. |
|---|---|
| G 1970 Richelieu 1 lb. hermetically sealed glass jars, piece of comb in each. This is Century Rose California honey, probably the finest produced (2 doz. jars in case) | $2 50 |

### White Clover Strained.

| | Doz. | Ea. |
|---|---|---|
| Glass Tumblers. 1 lb. each. 2 doz. in case | $2 00 | $0 20 |
| Glass jars. 1 lb. each. 2 doz. in case | 2 25 | 22 |
| Glass jars. 2 lb. each. 1 doz. in case | 3 50 | 34 |
| Glass jars. 3 lb. each. 1 doz. in case | 4 90 | 47 |

# WE MAKE PRICES

## On Musical Instruments against which none can compete.....

$1 75    $2 95    $2 95

## Special Music Catalogue

Free on Application.

**All Instruments Fully Warranted and Satisfaction Absolutely Guaranteed.**

---

# SOAP DEPARTMENT.

**HEADQUARTERS FOR LAUNDRY SOAP. Our Sales of Laundry Soap** are enormous, and it's on account of the quality and price. **DON'T PAY RETAIL PRICES FOR LAUNDRY SOAP.** You can't afford it, for it's a willful waste of money. You can buy it as cheap as your dealer can. Why not save his profit?

**Make Your Order 100 Pounds** by buying a full case of Laundry Soap, weighing 60 to 75 pounds, your neighbor will want part of it if you don't want all, by buying case lots you get the lowest price and lowest freight rate.

**LAUNDRY SOAP** goes at fourth-class freight rate the **very lowest,** about 20 cents per 100 pounds for 500 miles, buy a case of 60 pounds of Laundry Soap, make up the 40 pounds or more in other goods and just see how much money we can save you.

| | | Bar. | Box. |
|---|---|---|---|
| G 1980 Old Glory Mottled German Laundry Soap, very superior quality; 60 bars in box | | $0 04 | $2 25 |

G 1981 Try our celebrated Badger family soap; a thick, fancy shaped hard pressed and wrapped, made of the best material that enters into the making of a strictly first class soap. We guarantee this brand, and will refund the price paid if dissatisfied with your bargain

| | | Bar. | Box. |
|---|---|---|---|
| Put up in family size boxes, 30 bars... | | | 1 10 |
| G 1982 100 bars in box 75 pounds net | | 03½ | 3 00 |

G 1983 Our Royal Mottled German unequaled by any Mottled German soap, on the market. Guaranteed to give satisfaction: 60 lb. bars... 04  2 10

G 1984 Royal Long Bar, same as Fairbanks, 80 bars to box ... 04½  3 05

G 1985 Globe Brag Soap, biggest cake and best value for the money ever offered. Each weighs 1¼ lbs., 48 cakes to a box ... 05  2 20

G 1986 China Soap Far exceeds any soap on the market. Best in the world for the laundry. Is bought by thousands and prefered to any other for the toilet. Better than Ivory; 100 eight oz. cakes to a box ... 04  3 50

G 1987 White Floating Soap, for the toilet, 100 bar box 6 oz. cakes ... 04  3 00
50 bar box, 6 oz. cakes ... 04  1 50

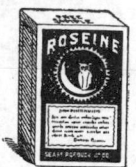

## WOOL SOAP?
### For Washing Woolens and for the Bath~

### Sears, Roebuck & Co.,
### Selling Agents.

G 1988   This soap has such a wide reputation gained through its great merits, that little we can say will increase the very great demand. It is the only soap that does not shrink woolens when washed. Egen if this were its only merit it would deserve the greatest sale of any soap made. Yet it is in every other way the peer of any laundry soap in the market. Guaranteed **absolutely pure,** and unexcelled for Laundry, Toilet or Bath. Put up in neat, attractive form, in boxes of 100 cakes.
Per box of 100 10-oz. cakes, per case ... $7 25
Per doz cakes ... 95

G 1989   We have Wool Soap also in convenient 6-oz size for Toilet or Bath, and there is none better.
Per box of 100 6-oz cakes ... 4 50
Per doz cakes ... 60

G 1990   **Cream Laundry Soap.** A wonderful laundry soap that is fast taking the place of old lines, sold at high retail prices, where you paid 50% for the name. The strict purity of this soap makes the price seem ridiculously low.
60-lb boxes, 1-lb bars, per box ... 2 65

G 1992 Proctor & Gamble's Mottled German. 60 bars. 60 lb ... 05  2 45
G 1993 Proctor & Gamble's Denox, 100

---

twelve ounce cakes ... 04  2 85
G 1994 Proctor & Gamble's Ivory Soap, 50 bars ... 07  4 35
G 1995 Proctor & Gamble's Ivory Soap, 100 10 oz. cakes in box ... 07  6 75
G 1996 Babbitt's Best, 100 pressed cakes, 75 lbs ... 05  4 10
G 1997 Dobbin's Electric, 60 bars in box ... 08  4 50

## Chinese Laundry Wax.

| | | |
|---|---|---|
| G 1998 Per doz | | $0 40 |
| Each | | 05 |
| G 1999 Beeswax, 3 doz. cakes in box, per box | | 1 25 |
| Per doz | | 50 |
| Each | | 05 |

## Roseine.

The greatest Washing Powder known, superior to anything else on the market.

| | Case. | Pkg. |
|---|---|---|
| G 2000 50 half pound packages in case | $1 75 | $0 04 |
| G 2001 100 half pound packages in case | 3 25 | 04 |

## Castile Soap.

Not less than single bar sold.

| | Lb. | Case pr lb. |
|---|---|---|
| G 2004 Pale Green Castile Soap, imported' 4 lb. bars, case of 9 bars | $0 15 | $0 13 |
| G 2005 Mottled Imported, 3½ to 3¾ lb bars, case of 9 bars | 09 | 08 |
| G 2006 White, Domestic, 3½ to 3¾ pound bars. case of 9 bars | 09 | 08 |
| G 2007 White Imported, fine quality, warranted made from pure olive oil. 3½ to 3¾ lb bars; note the price; 9 bars in box | 15 | 13 |

**We import our castile soaps direct, therefore we can vouch for their purity.**

| | Cake | Box |
|---|---|---|
| G 2008 Mottled Domestic Castile, ¼-lb cakes, 12 in box | 04 | 32 |
| G 2009 White Domestic Castile, ¼-lb cakes 12 in box | 03 | 29 |
| G 2010 Scouring Soap, the best polishing soap, equal to Sapolio, yet much lower in price; 72 cakes in box | 05 | 2 85 |
| G 2011 Sapolio, Enoch Morgan's Sons House, 10-cent size 6 doz in box | 08 | 4 75 |

## Coal Oil Johnny's Petroleum Soap.

G 2012   The modern soap. For the laundry, bath, toilet or shaving. For laces, flannels. china or glassware, its equal is unknown. The only pure soap. The only soap that will do good work in hard water or sea water. One cake is worth as much as two of any other.
Our price, per cake ... $0 05
Per box of 100 cakes ... 4 50

## Dr. Raub's Celebrated Cutaneous Soap,

G 2013   **The greatest skin beautifier and preserver known.** Thirty years of study have given the world the greatest of all soaps; a truly antiseptic toilet preparation. A marvel for the complexion and prevents all skin diseases. Regular 25-cent value. Our price per cake ... $0 10
Per box of 3 cakes ... 25

## Buttermilk Glycerine Soap.

G 2014   The materials used in this soap are the finest and its continuous use will greatly benefit the skin. It is entirely free from alkali or any injurious substances, and guaranteed **absolutely pure.**
Per cake ... $0 05
Per box of 3 cakes ... 12

## Kirk's "Topaz" Transparent Glycerine Toilet Soap.

G 2016   This is a marvelous value and we shall look for many repeated orders for it; 12 good size cakes in neat paper box; per box, only ... $0 45

## Castile Toilet Soap.

G 2017   For purity and excellence this is not surpassed by any similar soap made. It is really an **immense bargain;** 12 good size cakes, assorted variegated and white, in neat paper box. Per box, $0 45

---

**A STRAIGHT LINE IS THE SHORTEST DISTANCE BETWEEN TWO POINTS. WE SELL DIRECT FROM FACTORY TO CONSUMER. THERE IS NO MORE DIRECT WAY.**

## Genuine "Turkish Bath" Toilet Soap.

G 2018 This is a bargain you should not overlook. Retails in almost every store at twice our price; 12 good size cakes in neat paper box. Per box, only.................... $0 45

## "Congo Cocoa" Toilet Soap.

G 2019 Made from pure cocoa oil. These are about the size cakes usually retailed at 5 cents each, and four low price is exceptionally favorable to our customers; 12 cakes in neat paper box, per box, only............ $0 25

## Cocoanut Oil Toilet Soap.

G 2020 **Pure Cocoanut Oil Soap.** This soap gives the same results when used in very hard water that an ordinary soap would have in soft water. Made expressly for Dakota, Utah, Arizona trade, or wherever there is a trace of alkali in the water. Cocoanut Oil Soap can, of course, be used in soft as well as hard water. It makes wonderful suds, possesses a decided cocoanut odor, and many persons will use no other. Cakes ⅝x1⅞x3 inches; 1 dozen cakes in a box. Per doz........$0 20
Per gross.................................................. 2 00

## "Oat Meal" Toilet Soap.

G 2021 This is a superior quality, and has become recognized for its excellence. You will do well to place this on your next order. Six good size cakes in neat paper box. Per box, only..............$0 23

| | Box | Cake |
|---|---|---|
| G 2022 Honey, No. 197, 3 cakes in box | $0 20 | $0 7½ |
| G 2023 Glycerine, No. 198, 3 cakes in box | 20 | 7½ |
| G 2024 Pears' Unscented, universally known the world over as the best; 3 cakes in box | 30 | 10 |
| G 2025 Pears' scented, highest quality made in toilet soaps; 3 cakes in box | 42 | 14 |
| G 2026 Cashmere Bouquet, Colgate's, the par excellence of all; 3 cakes in box | 65 | 23 |
| G 2027 Old Black Joe, unrivaled as complexion soap; 3 doz in box | 1 65 | 05 |
| G 2028 **Cuticura Toilet Soap.** Everybody knows this soap. **Finest in the world.** 3 cakes in box | 42 | 14 |

## Shaving Soap.

G 2029 Yankee Shaving, very choice, 1 doz in box; per box, $1.00; per cake, 9c.
G 2030 Williams' Shaving, finest made, 6 cakes to pound. Per lb, 30c; per cake, 6c.

## Sal Soda.

Whenever you need Sal Soda let us send what you want, and **we'll guarantee the goods.**

| | Kegs. | Lb. |
|---|---|---|
| G 2033 Sal Soda, kegs, 160 lbs | $1 60 | $.... |
| G 2034 Sal Soda, bulk, per lb | | 01½ |

## Lye.

**No better Lye made** than what we sell. A dozen or two cans will cost you little additional freight.

| | Doz. | Each. |
|---|---|---|
| G 2035 Lewis, 4 doz. in case | $1 05 | $0 09 |
| G 2036 Babbitt's, 4 doz. in case | 1 00 | 09 |
| G 2037 Vulcan, 4 doz. in case | 85 | 08 |
| G 2038 Star Scrubbing Lye, 4 doz. in case | 45 | 04 |

## Blueing.

**Very fine, the best made, sold strictly on its merits.**

| | Doz. | Each. |
|---|---|---|
| G 2040 Quart bottles | $0 85 | $0 08 |
| Pint bottles | 50 | 05 |
| Half-pint bottles | 25 | 03 |

## Dry Blueing—Purest Quality.

| | | |
|---|---|---|
| G 2041 No. 1, small sifting top boxes, 3 doz. in carton | 25 | 03 |
| G 2042 No. 2 large sifting top boxes, 3 doz. in carton | 45 | 05 |

## Ammonia.

| | Doz. | Each. |
|---|---|---|
| G 2043 Quart bottles | $1 00 | $0 12 |
| G 2044 Pints | 75 | 07 |

## Borax.

| | Doz. | Each. |
|---|---|---|
| G 2045 1-lb. pkgs | $1 00 | $0 10 |
| G 2046 ½-lb. pkgs | 70 | 07 |
| G 2047 Bulk, per lb | | 10 |

## Queen Victoria Perfumes

Give universal satisfaction and are the handsomest preparation ever offered to the public, at less than half the regular price. We make these extracts in our own laboratory and can vouch for their lasting qualities and delicate odor. These perfumes are put up in lapidary cut stopper bottles of diamond brilliancy.

| | 2-oz. size. | 4-oz. size. |
|---|---|---|
| G 2048 Carnation Pink | $0 48 | $0 89 |
| Columbia Bouquet | 48 | 89 |
| Jockey Club | 48 | 89 |
| Lilac Blossoms | 48 | 89 |
| Lily of the Valley | 48 | 89 |
| Moss Rose | 48 | 89 |
| Musk | 48 | 89 |
| New Mown Hay | 48 | 89 |
| Violet | 48 | 89 |
| Indian Violet | 48 | 89 |
| White Heliotrope | 48 | 89 |
| White Rose | 48 | 89 |
| Ylang Ylang | 48 | 89 |
| English Violet | 48 | 89 |
| Meadow Blossom | 48 | 89 |
| Sweet Clover | 48 | 89 |
| Jasamine | 48 | 89 |
| Crab Apple | 48 | 89 |
| Mignonette | 48 | 89 |
| Sweet Pea | 48 | 89 |
| Tea Rose | 48 | 89 |
| Tuberose | 48 | 89 |
| Wood Violet | 48 | 89 |
| Shandon Bells | 48 | 89 |
| Rose Geranium | 48 | 89 |

### Colognes.

| | | |
|---|---|---|
| G 2049 Eau de Cologne | 35 | 60 |
| Hawthorne | 35 | 60 |
| Nadjy | 35 | 60 |
| Violet | 35 | 60 |
| Zenithia | 35 | 60 |

### Toilet Waters.

| | | |
|---|---|---|
| G 2050 Lavender | 35 | 60 |
| Ylang Ylang | 35 | 60 |
| Violet | 35 | 60 |
| White Rose | 35 | 60 |
| Jasamine | 35 | 60 |
| Jockey Club | 35 | 60 |
| White Heliotrope | 35 | 60 |
| G 2051 Hoyts German Cologne, trial size, each | | $0 20 |
| Medium size | | 40 |
| Large size | | 75 |
| G 2052 Sears, Roebuck & Co.'s German Cologne, 4 ounce | | 50 |
| 8 ounce | | 90 |

**For Home, School or Office use, our Diamond Inks are far ahead of anything sold.** We are supplying schools and colleges with full supplies in **this line,** and invariably to their highest satisfaction. If you have never tried this ink, buy a trial bottle. Have a supply sent with your next freight order at no additional expense for shipping.

### Diamond Black Ink.

| | Gro. | Doz. | Bot. |
|---|---|---|---|
| G 2055 2 oz. paper bottles, 3 doz. in box | $2 50 | $0 28 | $0 03 |

### Diamond Magic Black Ink.

| | | |
|---|---|---|
| G 2056 One-half pint bottles, with spouts, 1 doz. in box | 1 50 | 14 |
| G 2057 One pint bottles, with spouts, 1 doz in box | 2 40 | 22 |
| G 2058 One quart bottles with spouts, 1 doz. in box | 4 20 | 42 |

### Diamond Chemical Writing Fluid.

Writes a beautiful blue color which changes to a coal black. This is the ink for bookkeeping and fine writing.

| | Doz. | Bot. |
|---|---|---|
| G 2059 4 oz. desk stands, enameled top, 3 doz. in box | $0 65 | $0 06 |
| G 2060 One-half pint bottles with spouts, 1 doz. in box | 1 65 | 15 |
| G 2061 One pint bottles with spouts, 1 doz. in box | 2 55 | 24 |
| G 2062 One quart bottles with spouts, 1 doz. in box | 4 50 | 42 |

### Diamond Cardinal Red Ink.

| | | |
|---|---|---|
| G 2063 2 oz. square stands, enameled tops; 1 doz. in box | 1 20 | 11 |

### Diamond Violet Ink.

| | Gro. | Doz. | Bot. |
|---|---|---|---|
| G 2064 1½ oz. round stands, wood tops, 3 doz. in box | $3 65 | $0 35 | $0 04 |

### Diamond Violet Writing and Copying Ink.

| | Doz. | Bot. |
|---|---|---|
| G 2065 ½ pint bottles, with spouts, 1 doz. in box | $2 10 | $0 19 |
| G 2066 Piut bottles, with spout, 1 doz. in box | 3 60 | 33 |
| G 2067 Quart bottles, with spouts, 1 doz. in box | 6 00 | 55 |

### Diamond Green Ink.

| | Gro. | Doz. | Bot. |
|---|---|---|---|
| G 2068 2 oz. square stands, enameled tops, 3 doz. in box | $5 65 | $0 50 | $0 05 |

### Diamond Chemical Combined Writing and Copying Fluids

| | | |
|---|---|---|
| G 2069 ½ pint bottles, with spouts, 1 doz. in box | $2 40 | $0 22 |

### Sanford's Ink.

| | Box. | Doz. | Bot. |
|---|---|---|---|
| G 2071 Sanford's Black, 2-oz, 3 doz in box | $0 57 | $0 30 | $0 03 |
| G 2072 Thomas' Black, 2-oz, 3 doz in box | 75 | 30 | 03 |
| G 2073 Thomas' Black, 4 oz, 3 doz in box | 1 75 | 60 | 06 |

## Stove Polish.

We sell only such grades as as give a **full and lasting lustre.** A poor polish is worse than useless, for your work will count for nothing. **Don't forget these small items** when you are making up your freight order.

G 2076 Enameline Stove Polish, applied with a cloth, no smell, no dust, quick and clean;

| | Box. | Doz. | Each. |
|---|---|---|---|
| 5c size, 3 doz in box | $1.20 | $0 45 | $0 04 |
| 10c size, 3 doz in box | 1 85 | 70 | 07 |

| | | | |
|---|---|---|---|
| G 2077 Rising Sun, 10-cent size. Gross box | 5 90 | 0 55 | 0 05 |
| G 2078 Parlor Pride Stove Polish | | 80 | 08 |

G 2080 Sun Paste Stove Polish, 5-cent size, ¼ gross in box. Box $4.75; doz. 45c; each 4c.
G 2081 Sun Paste Stove Polish, 10c size, ¼ gross in box. Box $7.85; doz. 70c; each 7c.

## Burnishine.

**The most marvelous Metal Polish now in use;** will produce a most brilliant lustre to brass, copper, zinc, steel, bronze, tin, gold, silver and all metals; really a household necessity. Contains no acid, grease, or anything injurious. Put up in screw-top tin cans, ½ pints, pints, quarts and gallons.

| | Doz. | Ea. |
|---|---|---|
| G 2082 ½-pint tins | $1 75 | $0 18 |
| G 2083 Pint tins | 3 15 | 28 |
| G 2084 Quart tins | 5 75 | 50 |
| G 2085 Gallon tins | 19 00 | 1 80 |

## Bath Brick.

| | Case. | Ea. |
|---|---|---|
| G 2087 Bath Brick, 2 doz. in case, imported | $0 85 | $0 04 |
| G 2088 Bath Brick, domestic, 2 doz in case | 75 | 03 |

G 2089 Bath Brick, pulverized, 1-lb packages, Per doz. 65c; each, 6c.

## Blacking and Shoe Dressing.

Everyone recognizes these brands of Polishes and Blackings. We sell them because **our customers want the best;** and they get the **best at the price of the cheapest.** Keep these goods in mind when you are making up your big order.

| | Doz. | Box. |
|---|---|---|
| G 2090 Shoe Blacking, Bixby's best, 5-cent size, No. 2 | $0 25 | $0 03 |
| G 2091 Shoe Blacking, Bixby's best, 10-cent size, No. 4 | 50 | 05 |
| G 2092 Bixby's B B B Blacking, with patent handle | 70 | 08 |

## The E. W. Brand of Imported Holland Russet Polish.

G 2093 Absolutely free from injurious substances. Is of the very best quality, gives a beautiful polish. The largest box of Russet Polish ever put up.
Price, per doz................$1 10
Per box.................... 10

## The E. W. Brand of Improved Holland Patent Leather Polish.

G 2094 The E. W. Brand of Improved Holland Patent Leather Polish, producing a patent leather finish without exertion. The best article in the market, at the same time the largest box ever put up. Price, per doz.. $1 10
Per box.................. 10

G 2095 The E. W. Brand of Imported Holland Shoe Blacking beats any blacking that was ever introduced. Produces the most brilliant lustre and lasting shine. Will never get hard. Price, per doz, 45c; Per box .... $0 04

| | Case | Ea. |
|---|---|---|
| G 2100 Bixby's Royal Shoe Dressing, for ladies' and children's shoes, 1 doz in case | $0 80 | $0 07 |
| G 2101 Phoenix Shoe Dressing, put up in 4-oz full weight glass bottles, brush attached to cork. Just the thing for ladies' and children's shoes. **Note the price.** 1 dozen in case | 80 | 06 |

**WE NEED NO INTRODUCTION TO OUR OLD CUSTOMERS. IF YOU HAVE NEVER DEALT WITH US, PERHAPS YOUR NEIGHBOR HAS, AND CAN TELL YOU ABOUT OUR METHODS IF YOU WILL ASK HIM.**

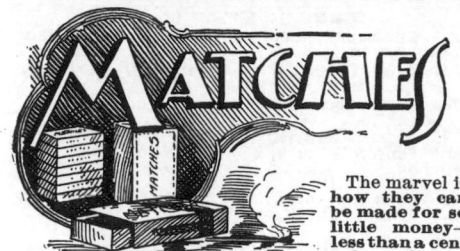

The marvel is **how they can be made for so little money—less than a cent a box.** Only 8 cents a thousand. A case will last a long time and the price is small. **Be sure to include a case or caddy with your next order.** Something you can't be without. We do not sell less than a case or caddy.

G 2105 Parlor Matches, put up in boxes containing 100 matches; 144 boxes in a case, making 14,400 matches. Every match is perfect and full count warranted. Price per case.......... $1 15
In lots of 5 cases, crated 5 50
G 2106 Telegraph Matches, sulphur, 200 matches in each box, 24 boxes in a wood caddy, making 4,800 matches. Price per caddy .......... $0 35
5 caddies in a rack, price per rack.......... 1 45
G 2107 Bridal Match, 200 matches in slide box 100 boxes in case, making 20,000 matches.
Price per case.......... 1 25
Price in lots of 5 cases.......... 6 00
G 2108 Italian Wax Matches, 50 matches in patent box; vest pocket size; 2 boxes for 3 cents; per doz boxes 15 cents; 144 boxes.......... 1 60

G 2109 Red Top Safety Match, 60 matches in box, 1 doz boxes in package. Price per package, 10c; 1 doz packages, 144 boxes, 70c; 60 packages, 720 boxes, in a 5-gross case; price per case .... 3 50
G 2110 Swedish Sulphur Midget, 80 matches in box; 1 doz boxes in package. Price per package, 8c; 1 doz packages, 65c; 60 packages in a case. Price per case 3 00
G 2111 Blazers Anti-Wind Matches, 20 in box. 12 boxes in package. Per package.......... 10
Per doz packages.......... 85

## Candles.

We are in constant receipt of **commendation from our old customers** who have bought these goods from us. We hence have every confidence in **their high quality** and offer them as the **best that can be bought.**

| | By box per lb. | Per lb. |
|---|---|---|
| G 2200 Star Candles, 40-lb boxes, 8 to the lb, full weight | $0 10 | $0 11 |
| G 2201 Granite Wax Mining Candles, 6's 14 oz, 40 lbs in box | 8½ | 10 |
| G 2202 Adamantine mining Candles, 6's 14 oz, 40 lbs in box | 9 | 11 |
| G 2203 Paraffine Wax Candles, 4's and 6's to lb, 36 lbs in case | 8½ | 11 |
| G 2204 Paraffine Wax Candles, 12 to lb, 36 lbs in case | 8½ | 11 |
| G 2205 'Xmas Candles, 24's, 36's or 48's, per box | | 15 |
| G 2206 Paraffine Wax, hard cakes, for waxing dancing floors | | 15 |
| G 2207 Carriage Candles, 1 doz in a box, per box | | 75 |
| G 2208 Ball Candle Holders, to use on 'Xmas trees. Per doz | | 10 |
| Per gross | | 90 |

Prices on Cordage change considerably from time to time, and we **always give you the benefit** where there is a fall. **We guarantee our Cordage** to be perfect in quality and make. Send to us for anything you want in this line.

We sell rope in any quantity, but rope once cut from the coil cannot be returned.

| | | Per lb. |
|---|---|---|
| G 2115 | Manila Rope, diameter ¼ and ⅜ inch | $0 09 |
| G 2116 | Manila Rope, diameter ½, ⅝, ¾, ⅞ or 1 inch | 08 |
| G 2117 | 1¼, 1½, 1¾ and 2 inch | 08 |
| G 2118 | Jute Rope, ¼ to ¾ inch in diameter | 07 |
| G 2119 | Cotton Rope, about 130 lb. coils, ¼ to ⅜ inch in diameter | 18 |
| G 2120 | By coil | 16 |
| G 2121 | ⅝, ¾, ⅞ and 1 inch | 20 |
| G 2122 | By coil | 18 |
| G 2123 | Fodder Twine, coils about 100 lbs. Bale. each. We sell any quantity | 04¾ 05 |
| G 2124 | Wool Twine, 1 lb. balls, 125 lb. bales | 05¼ 07 |
| G 2125 | Bag Strings, best quality | 25 |
| G 2126 | Cotton Twine, 5 balls to pound | 20 |

In ordering cordage, always give the diameter wanted. Estimated weight per foot of the different sizes given upon application.

**Ropes once cut from the coil cannot be returned.**

You cannot help but find just the kind of clothes line you want in our very large stock. Give us your order.

| | | Doz. | Each. |
|---|---|---|---|
| G 2130 | India hemp cable laid sash cord and clothes line combined; very durable; eighty feet long, best clothes line on the market | $2 00 | $0 20 |
| G 2131 | Manila, 60 feet, very best | 1 25 | 12 |
| G 2132 | Manila, 80 feet, very best | 1 75 | 16 |
| G 2133 | Manila, 100 feet, very best | 1 95 | 22 |
| G 2134 | Jute, 60 feet, extra quality | 60 | 06 |
| G 2135 | Jute, 90 feet, extra quality | 1 00 | 10 |
| G 2136 | Cotton, 60 feet | 1 15 | 11 |
| G 2137 | Cotton, 80 feet | 1 45 | 15 |
| G 2138 | Cotton, 100 feet | 1 75 | 18 |
| G 2139 | Wire Galvanized, No. 20, 100 feet | 1 85 | 17 |
| G 2140 | Wire Galvanized, No. 18, 100 feet | 2 25 | 20 |
| G 2141 | Cotton Mop Heads, 9 lbs. to dozen | 1 10 | 10 |
| G 2142 | 12 pounds to dozen | 1 45 | 15 |
| G 2143 | Fancy Braided Cotton Clothes lines will not kink, are waterproof and make a good sash cord; 50 feet | 2 25 | 20 |
| | 75 feet | 3 30 | 30 |
| | 100 feet | 4 25 | 40 |

## Sash Cord.

Braided Sash Cord is put up in bundles of 100 feet. We do not sell less than a bundle.

| | | Size. | Length Pr lb. | Pr lb. |
|---|---|---|---|---|
| G 2145 | American Hemp Unbleached | 8-32 | 38 ft. | $0 18 |
| G 2146 | Indian Hemp Bleached | 7-32 | 46 ft. | 20 |
| G 2147 | Silver Lake Braided | 7-32 | 55 ft. | 26 |
| G 2148 | Silver Lake Braided | 8-32 | 46 ft. | 26 |
| G 2149 | Silver Lake Braided | 9-32 | 40 ft. | 26 |
| G 2150 | Silver Lake Braided | 10-32 | 36 ft. | 26 |

7-32 weighs about 2¼ lbs. to the bundle.
8-32 weighs about 2¼ lbs. to the bundle.
9-32 weighs about 2½ lbs. to the bundle.
10-32 weighs about 2¾ lbs. to the bundle.

All our broom handles are **thoroughly seasoned.** The brooms are **warranted not to come off the handles.**

| | | Doz. | Each. |
|---|---|---|---|
| G 2155 | No. 52, Whisk Brooms, corn small | $0 90 | $0 08 |
| G 2156 | No. 51, Whisk Brooms, fine corn medium size | 1 10 | 10 |
| G 2157 | No. 95, Whisk Brooms, fine corn | 1 45 | 13 |
| G 2158 | No. 100, Whisk Brooms, fine corn, extra size | 2 00 | 20 |
| G 2159 | No. 106, Whisk Broom for barber's use, extra long | 1 10 | 10 |

We do not sell less than quarter dozen where dozen prices only are given.

| | | Doz. | Each. |
|---|---|---|---|
| G 2160 | No. 2, House Broom | $2 00 | $0 20 |
| G 2161 | No. 1, House Broom | 2 25 | 22 |
| G 2162 | No. 1, Parlor Broom | 2 60 | 25 |
| G 2163 | Fancy Carpet Parlor Broom | 3 00 | 28 |
| G 2164 | Extra Fancy Carpet Parlor Broom best | 3 25 | 30 |
| G 2165 | Stable or Warehouse | 3 00 | 28 |
| G 2166 | Extra weight Warehouse, rattan reed center | 3 72 | 35 |
| G 2167 | Toy Brooms, common | 1 00 | 09 |
| G 2168 | Toy Brooms, extra | 1 25 | 11 |
| G 2169 | Stable Brooms, rattan, 14 inch long | 4 00 | 40 |
| G 2170 | Stable Brooms, rattan, 16 inch. long, 6 rows | 5 00 | 50 |

## Brushes.

All sorts of brushes are needed about the house. **WE carry the best there are,** and if you are in need of one have it added to your next order and the charges will be nothing. **See our Hardware Department for Paint, Varnish, Calsomine or other brushes not quoted here.**

| | | Per Doz. | Each |
|---|---|---|---|
| G 2180 | Stove Brushes | $1 75 | $0 18 |
| G 2181 | Stove Brushes, No. 2. | 1 50 | 14 |
| G 2182 | Scrub Brushes, Mexican rice root, 9 inches long | 55 | 05 |
| G 2183 | Scrub Brushes, gray stock, 11 inches long | 1 75 | 18 |
| G 2184 | Scrub Brushes, palmetto, 11 inches; will outwear 3 ordinary brushes | 2 40 | 22 |
| G 2185 | Deck Scrub Brushes, with rubber edge, used for scrubbing floors | 2 20 | 20 |
| G 2186 | Scrub Brushes, white stock, with pointed ends, 11 inches long | 1 05 | 10 |
| G 2187 | Scrub Brushes, Tampico No. 53 | 75 | 07 |
| G 2188 | Scrub Brushes, handy house, for sinks, etc | 45 | 04 |

| | | | |
|---|---|---|---|
| G 2189 | Scrub Brush, Mexican rice root, 11 inches long | 1 50 | 15 |
| G 2190 | Scrub Brush, No. 232, same a No. G 2189, but made of bristles. This is a fine brush | 2 50 | 23 |
| G 2191 | Bristle Brush, with handle No. 1 | 2 75 | 25 |
| G 2192 | Scrub Brushes, American crown, new style, white stock, 10 inches long | 1 05 | 10 |
| G 2193 | Scrub Brushes, American Elk, new style gray stock, 10 inches long | 1 05 | 10 |
| G 2194 | Scrub Brushes, American Empire, new style, rice root stock | 1 05 | 10 |
| G 2195 | Scrub Brush, No. 760, solid back, white Tampico centre, palmetto pointed ends, 8 inches long | 1 35 | 13 |

**THE DIFFERENCE BETWEEN GOOD OIL AND BAD OIL** cannot be measured by the difference in price. Poor oil is for most purposes worse than useless. **We avoid all complaint** by quoting and handling only the best of all grades. **The freight** on oils is at the lowest rate, and hence you can feel assured of a handsome saving in price after all charges are paid. No use paying 18 cents a gallon for what we furnish at 11 cents. No use paying 60 cents a gallon for what we furnish at 43 cents. **And we charge no profit on the freight.**

If you need a barrel of oil, have such Groceries, or Clothing, or Harness, or Furniture, or Dry Good as you need, sent along at the same time, and the **freight will be very little.**

## Kerosene Oils.

We do not sell less than a barrel of kerosene oil, except our Climax oil, G 2230. No charge for barrels. Barrels contain about 52 gallons. We do not solicit kerosene oil trade in the state of Iowa, owing to the annoying inspection laws. The only oil we can ship into Iowa is our 175 degree fire test, and all kerosene oil shipped into Iowa is entirely at the purchaser's risk. Prices are subject to market changes.

| | | Per Gal. |
|---|---|---|
| G 2220 | Electric brand, 150 degrees; a fine white oil | $0 09¼ |
| G 2221 | Illinois legal test, prime white, 150 degrees test | 07¾ |
| G 2222 | Illinois Water White, 150 | 08¾ |
| G 2223 | Indiana legal test, prime white | 08¾ |
| G 2224 | Indiana legal test, water white | 10¼ |
| G 2225 | Michigan legal test, prime white | 08¾ |
| G 2226 | Michigan legal test, water white | 10¼ |
| G 2227 | Wisconsin legal test, prime white | 07¾ |
| G 2228 | Wisconsin legal test, water white | 08¾ |
| G 2229 | Headlight Carbon Oil, 175 legal test | 09¾ |
| G 2230 | Climax kerosene, 150 degrees, absolutely the best carbon oil at any price. No need of paying fancy prices for fancy names. Fully guaranteed. If not perfectly satisfied after trying, return at our expense | 15 |
| G 2231 | Perfect oil, in cases containing two 5-gallon cans, per case | 2 10 |
| G 2232 | Gasoline, 88 degrees, best on earth for gas machines, barrels only | 15½ |
| G 2233 | Stove gasoline, 74 degrees, deodorized. barrels only | 10 |
| G 2234 | Naphtha, or benzine, 63 degrees, barrels only | 11 |

## Family Oil Tank.

G 2240 Capacity 60 gallons; diameter 25½ inches, heighth 40½ inches. Force pump diameter 1½ inches. Will hold full barrel of oil and 10 gallons to spare.

Made of best galvanized iron in body and bottom, wood bottom under metal, tin hood, portable, steady stream pump, which can be taken out and used for pumping oil from barrel into tank. Painted, weight, crated for shipment, 50 pounds,
Price, with pump complete.......... $3 57
G 2241 Extra pumps, each.......... 90
G 2242 Gasoline Tanks, holding 60 gallons, 4-inch. screw top, ½ inch. brass faucet, each.... 3 40

We cannot ship oil tanks filled, as railroad will not receive them.

G 2243 **Home Oil Tank** is made from the highest grade of galvanized iron, with wood bottom underneath the metal one to protect it from rust and damage, and is provided with straight lift; steady-stream force pump, made of tin, with improved brass valve. The pump is removable, for transferring oil from the barrel to tank.
60 Gallon tank with Pump.. $4.37

G 2244 **S., R. & Co.'s Family Oil Can.** This fills the bill for **a clean and handy family can.** It is a surprise in its operation as well as in name. The can is made of the best galvanized iron, with removable steady stream force pump, made of all metal and no packing of any kind to give out. Cover when closed prevents dust from getting in and odors from getting out. This means no evaporation and no loss of oil, as well as being clean and agreeable. Made in five gallon sizes only. Price, each.......... 83c.

**A CAREFUL COMPARISON OF OUR PRICES WITH THOSE FOUND IN CATALOGUES OF WOULD-BE COMPETITORS WILL CONVINCE YOU THAT IT PAYS BEST TO DO BUSINESS WITH THE OLD RELIABLE.**

## Lard, Neatsfoot. Cylinder, Engine, Machine, Linseed, Java and Baltic Oils, Turpentine, Etc.

**Special Notice.**

We sell any quantity over one gallon, but nothing less than one gallon. Barrels contain 52 gallons, half barrels contain 28 gallons. Less quantities than half barrel 5c a gallon higher than the quoted prices. No charge for barrel in original packages. One-half barrels 75c. each, 10 gallon can 50c., 5 gallon can 35c., 2 and 3 gallon cans 30c., 1 gallon cans 20c. each. In ordering less quantities than half barrels be sure and allow the extra 5c. per gallon and also allow money for the cans. Samples will be sent free on application when stating kinds desired, provided you will remit 10c. to cover expenses of mailing tubes for each sample.

### Lard Oils.—Cans Extra.

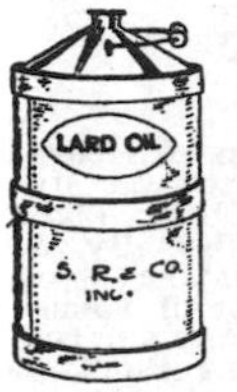


Prices on these oils subject to market changes. Gal.

G 2250 Extra Winter Strained Lard Oil, used extensively by plumbers, brass spinners, etc. For all kinds of lubricating and for miners' lamps, railroad lanterns, etc., etc. $0 45

G 2251 No. 1 Lard Oil, used for lubricating and mixing, a very good oil, but not so white and clear as the winter strained.... 38

### Neatsfoot Oil.—Cans Extra.

Prices on these oils subject to market changes.

G 2253 Pure Neatsfoot Oil, used in dressing leather, oiling guns, etc. We are headquarters and sell at right prices. 63

G 2254 Extra Neatsfoot Oil, commonly sold for purest. 53

G 2255 No. 1 Neatsfoot Oil, commonly sold for extra. 43

### Cylinder Oils.—Cans Extra.

G 2257 Extra Valve Cylinder, the very best cylinder oil; the jobbing price on this kind of oil in single bbl. is 75c per gal. and oftentimes more money. 40

G 2258 Midnight Black Cylinder Oil, 650 degrees fire test, gravity 22. 36

G 2259 Victor Cylinder, used for cylinders and heavy machinery, our price. 33

G 2260 Pure Natural W. Va. Lubricating Oil; the best below zero, will flow in cold weather. 21

### Engine Oils.—Cans Extra.

| | | |
|---|---|---|
| G 2262 | Dynamo Engine Oil | 35 |
| G 2263 | Rose Engine Oil | 22 |
| G 2264 | Golden Engine | 19 |

### Harness Oil.—Cans Extra.

G 2266 Perfect Harness Oil No. 1, contains no acid. It preserves the leather and keeps it pliable. 42

### S. R. & Co. Harness Oil.

Is guaranteed equal to anything in the market for softening and preserving the leather, harness, etc., though it is sold at a lower price than any other make.

| | | Can. | Doz. |
|---|---|---|---|
| G 2310 | Pt cans | $0 12 | $1 25 |
| G 2311 | Qt. cans | 20 | 2 25 |
| G 2312 | Gal. cans | 50 | 5 00 |
| G 2313 | 5 gal. cans, price per 5 gals | | 2 40 |
| G 2314 | 10 gal. cans, price per 10 gals | | 4 60 |

### Machine Oil.—Cans Extra.

| | | |
|---|---|---|
| G 2268 | Excelsior Machine Oil | 22 |
| G 2269 | Summer Black Oil | 12 |
| G 2270 | 15 degrees | 15 |
| G 2271 | Zero | 18 |
| G 2272 | Castor No. 1, white, very best grade used for medicinal use, etc. | 1 25 |
| G 2273 | Castor No. 3, for lubricating, etc. | 1 00 |
| G 2274 | Castor, lubricating | 54 |
| G 2275 | Castor, machine | 30 |
| G 2276 | Castor, machine No. 1 | 28 |
| G 2277 | Spirits Turpentine | 38 |
| G 2278 | Cup Grease, 10 lb. pails, each | 1 15 |
| G 2279 | Cup Grease, hard or soft, 25 lb. pails each | 2 50 |
| G 2280 | Cup Grease, 50 lb. pails each | 4 75 |

| | | 2 oz. panel bottles. Each. | 2 oz. panel bottles. Doz. | 4 oz. panel bottles. Each. | 4 oz. panel bottles. Doz. |
|---|---|---|---|---|---|
| G 2281 | Castor Oil, cold pressed | $0 10 | $1 00 | $0 15 | $1 50 |
| G 2282 | Castor Oil, cold pressed, pint bottles | 28 | 2 75 | | |
| G 2283 | Glycerine, pure | 10 | 1 00 | 15 | 1 50 |
| G 2284 | Sewing Machine Oil | 05 | 50 | 09 | 85 |
| G 2285 | Sweet Oil | 07 | 65 | 10 | 1 10 |
| G 2286 | Benzine | 07 | 65 | 10 | 1 10 |
| G 2287 | Turpentine | 07 | 65 | 10 | 1 10 |
| G 2288 | Cod Liver Oil, strictly pure, pints | 40 | 4 25 | | |

G 2289 Walrus Sewing Machine Oil, 4-oz. tin cans, with oiler spout; best quality oil. Packed 6 doz. cans in case. Price per case $4.75. Can. $0 10 Doz. $0 90

### Harvester Oil.

| | | Ea. | Doz. |
|---|---|---|---|
| G 2291 | For threshing machines, wind mills, harvesters, mowers, and heavy farm machinery of all kinds. Is highly recommended by those who have used it. Quart cans, 1 doz. in case | 20 | 2 15 |
| G 2292 | Gal. cans, 6 in case | 45 | 4 75 |
| G 2293 | 5 gal. cans, 2 in crate; price per case of 10 gal. | | 3 85 |
| G 2294 | 5 gal can, 1 in case, price for 5 gal. | | 2 00 |
| G 2295 | ½ bbl., 28 gal., no charge for pkgs, 30 cents per gal. | | |
| G 2296 | Bbls. 52 gals, price per gal. 26 cents | | |

### Electric Cycle Oil.

| | | | |
|---|---|---|---|
| G 2297 | For bicycles, lawn mowers and light machinery of all kinds, 4 oz. screw top can | 12 | 1 35 |
| G 2298 | Same oil in 8 oz. cans with oiler spout | 20 | 2 25 |

### Coach Oil.

| | | | |
|---|---|---|---|
| G 2300 | Quart cans | 26 | 2 80 |
| G 2301 | Gallon cans | 65 | 7 50 |
| | | | Per crate. |
| G 2302 | One 5 gal. in crate, price per 5 gals | | $2 80 |
| G 2303 | Two 5 gal can in crate, price per crate | | 5 35 |
| | | | Per Gal. |
| G 2304 | ½ bbl. 28 gal., price per gal | | $0 43 |
| G 2305 | Bbls. 52 gal., price per gal | | 39 |

### Linseed Oil.

These prices subject to market changes. Cans extra. Write us for prices.

| | | Gal. |
|---|---|---|
| G 2316 | Strictly pure raw | $0 33 |
| G 2317 | Strictly pure boiled | 35 |

Barrels containing 52 gals; ½ bbls, 30 gals, and cans as wanted. Less quantities than ½ bbl., 5 cents per gallon higher. No charge for bbls., ½ bbls. 75 cents each. 5 gal 50c.; 10 gal. cans 75c.

### Java and Baltic Oils.

These oils will not mix with white lead or zinc, only mineral paints for rough work, such as barns, fences, etc. Cans extra. We do not sell less than 5 gallons of these oils. Less quantities than ½ bbl., 5c. per gallon higher than the following prices.

### Boiled Java Oil.

| | | Per gal. |
|---|---|---|
| G 2320 | Use exactly the same as boiled linseed oil. Needs no dryer. Dries in 24 hours | $0 27 |
| G 2321 | Raw Java Oil. Use same as raw linseed. Requires 25 per cent good drier | 24 |
| G 2322 | Baltic Oil. Use same as boiled Java. Adapted for all colors except white; gives white a creamy tint. Used by car and bridge painters | 20 |

The S. P. Shotter Co., manufacturers, guarantee these oils to be absolutely pure vegetable oils, free from any adulteration whatever Less quantity than barrel, cans extra, 5 gal. 50c.; 10 gal. 75c.

### Hoof Dressing.

G 2324 A Hoof Dressing that should be kept on hand for constant use. Recommended by all horse owners. Quart cans. per can, 56 cts.

## Diamond Liquid Glue.

**Mends Anything Strong as a Rock.**

| | | Doz. | Ea. |
|---|---|---|---|
| G 2484 | 1½-oz bottles Glue, 1 doz in box | $0 70 | $0 07 |
| G 2485 | 2-oz patent tin cans, 1 doz in box | 1 28 | 12 |
| G 2486 | 4-oz patent tin cans, 1 doz in box. | 2 00 | 18 |
| G 2487 | ½-pt tin cans, 1 doz in box | 2 40 | 22 |
| G 2488 | Pint tin cans 1 doz in box | 3 95 | 35 |
| G 2489 | Quart tin cans 1 doz in box | 6 75 | 54 |
| G 2490 | ½-gal tin cans ½ doz in box | 10 70 | 66 |
| G 2891 | 1-gal tin cans ½ doz in box | 19 15 | 1 70 |

## Mucilage and Liquid Cement.

| | | Doz. | Ea. |
|---|---|---|---|
| G 2493 | Diamond Gum Mucilage, 3-oz flat stand bottles, 1 doz in box | $0 75 | $0 07 |
| G 2494 | Diamond Gum Mucilage, 2-oz cone shape bottles, 3 doz in box | 40 | 04 |
| G 2495 | Diamond Gum Mucilage, pint bottles, 1 doz in box | 2 70 | 25 |
| G 2496 | Diamond Gum Mucilage, quart bottles, 1 doz in box | 4 80 | 44 |
| G 2497 | Diamond Cream Mucilage, the quickest sticker there is, 3-oz bottles, 1 doz in box | 75 | 07 |
| G 2498 | Diamond Magic Invisible Cement, for mending china, glassware, crockery, ornaments, etc.; small bottles, 1 doz. in box | 80 | 08 |



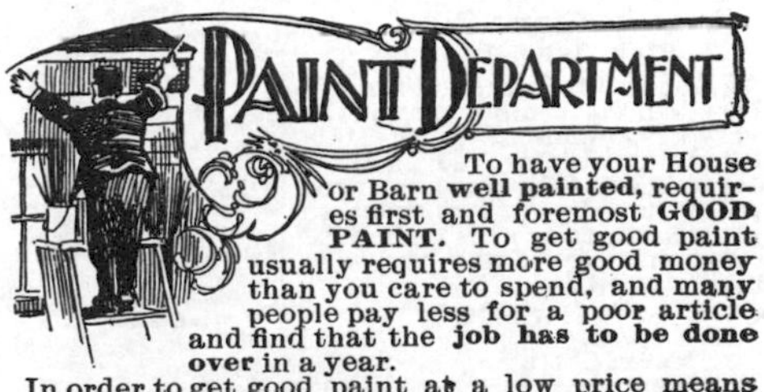


To have your House or Barn **well painted**, requires first and foremost **GOOD PAINT.** To get good paint usually requires more good money than you care to spend, and many people pay less for a poor article and find that the **job has to be done over** in a year.

In order to get good paint at a low price means that some **profit and expense must be cut off** entirely. By our economic system, we ship to you from the door of the factory. **No middleman's profit. No adulteration** to increase retailer's profits. We give you a square deal and furnish **the best paints you ever saw** and for 50 per cent less money.

The freight rate on Paints is very low. You can get your supply from us, get the best there is made, and the freight will be very little compared with what we save you. We want to get you started to buying your paints from us, we are quoting exceedingly low prices in order to keep your trade. We are selling nothing but the best. Every house, barn or buggy coated with our paint will be a lasting advertisement for us.

**SPECIAL OFFER.**—We will allow a **SPECIAL CASH DISCOUNT OF 5%** to each customer who buys 20 gallons or more of **House or Barn Paint**, and who will agree to put up in a suitable and conspicuous place, a small metal sign, stating that the paint for the job was furnished by us.

**We issue fine color cards** of our various paints; send at once, **costs you nothing** and it will **help you** in making your selection.

**BE SURE TO STATE** what kind of paint you want to buy when you send for the card.

## Paste Paints for 1897.

### Pink Label Brand.

Quality guaranteed equal to any in the world. A new departure in our paint and oil department for 1897. Paste paints are made in all colors, same as our Pink Label Brand Ready Mixed Paints, except the following four: Emerald Green, Vermillion, Dark Blue and Tuscan Red. Parties who wish to do their own mixing will find our paste paints to be the very best pigments ground in pure linseed oil, and are ready for immediate use with the addition of oils for thinning. Packed in 12½ and 25 lb. pails. Directions: With every 25 lb. pail of paste paint add 2½ gallons of boiled linseed oil for the first coat (primal coat). For every additional coat add only 2 gallons of boiled linseed oil. Price for all colors, 12½ pound pails, 95 cents; 25 lb. pails, $1.75. Color card sent free on application.

### Prepared Paints.

Send for illustrated color card and hints on selecting colors of our Pink Label Brand, absolutely pure. We fully guarantee our prepared paint to give better satisfaction as to durability and appearance, than any paint mixed by hand. Write us for our 1897 color card and hints on selecting colors, showing 16 combinations, selected with careful regard to harmony which can be relied upon as being in good taste. Remember the Pink Label Brand Barn, Floor and Carriage Paints are equally as good as the house paint. We guarantee every gallon to be full weight and measure and to give perfect satisfaction if properly used, and any failure to do so will be made good. If it pleases you, as we are sure it will, kindly tell your neighbors about it, what it costs, and how they can get it.

Don't be afraid of these paints because the price is low. They are the best we could buy at any price and our label is on every package to prove our faith in the goods.

One gallon of this paint will cover (two coats) over 300 square feet of surface.

**Always order by color number as well as catalogue number.**

G 2330—
201 French Gray.
202 Lavender.
203 Straw.

| | |
|---|---|
| 204 Pea Green. | 221 Leather Brown. |
| 205 Light Drab. | 222 Pure Gray. |
| 206 Canary. | 223 Light Blue. |
| 207 Lemont Stone. | 224 Maroon. |
| 208 Pearl. | 225 Bronze. |
| 209 Beaver | 226 Willow Green. |
| 210 Pink. | 227 Drab. |
| 211 Milwaukee Brick. | 228 Olive. |
| 212 Quaker Drab. | 229 Red. |
| 214 Olive Drab. | 230 Brown. |
| 215 Cream. | 232 Myrtle Green, |
| 216 Fawn. | 234 Vermillion. |
| 217 Pure Blue. | 236 Emerald Green. |
| 218 Buff. | IW Inside White. |
| 219 Terra Cotta. | OW Outside White. |
| 220 Apple Green. | Blk Black. |

| Prices for all colors except 232, 234, 236. | Each. | Gal. |
|---|---|---|
| 1 quart can | $0 30 | |
| 2 quart cans | 55 | |
| 1 gallon cans | 1 00 | |
| 5 gallon buckets | | $0 95 |
| 10 gallon kegs | | 95 |
| 25 gallon half barrels | | 90 |
| 50 gallon barrels | | 90 |

| | | 1 pt. | 2 qts. | 1 gal. |
|---|---|---|---|---|
| No. 232 | Myrtle Green | $0 50 | $0 95 | $1 80 |
| No. 236 | Emerald Green | 50 | 95 | 1 80 |
| No. 234 | Vermillion | 65 | 1 20 | 2 20 |

**Write for color cards.**

**WE MAKE IT A CONSTANT STUDY TO SERVE OUR PATRONS IN A MANNER THAT WILL PAY THEM BEST. OUR REWARD LIES IN THE CONSTANT TRADE OF SATISFIED CUSTOMERSS.**

## Liquid Floor Paints.

**Pink Label Brand.**

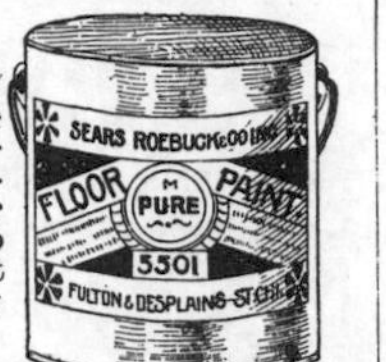


Floor paints improved for 1897. New colors. Made from the very best pigments, by the latest and most improved machinery. Absolutely the best floor paint made; guaranteed to please, or can be returned at our expense. Paint will dry in one night.

G 2332— 500 Dark Drab.

| | |
|---|---|
| 510 Yellow. | 540 Lead |
| 520 Terra Cotta. | 550 Maroon. |
| 530 Leather, | 560 Oxide Red. |

1 gallon, $1.00; Half gallon, 55c.; 1 quart, 30c.

Prices for larger quantities same as Liquid House Paints.

## Iron Paints.

| | | Bbl. pr lb. | Per lb. |
|---|---|---|---|
| G 2342 | Dark Red Iron Paint, 350 lbs.... | $0 01¼ | $0 01¾ |
| G 2343 | Rossie Red (genuine) 350 lbs..... | 01¼ | 01¾ |

## Zinc and Putty.

**Pink Label Brand.**

G 2345 Strictly Pure French Zinc, in oil 12½ Lb. and 25-lb cans........ $0 11½

G 2346 Pure Red Seal French Zinc, in oil, 1 to 5 lb cans........ 15

G 2347 Zinc in oil; American Snow White, 12½ and 25-lb pails........ 06

G 2348 Putty, in bladders, 10 to 25 lbs........ 02½

## Roof, Fence and Barn Paint.

**Pink Label Brand**

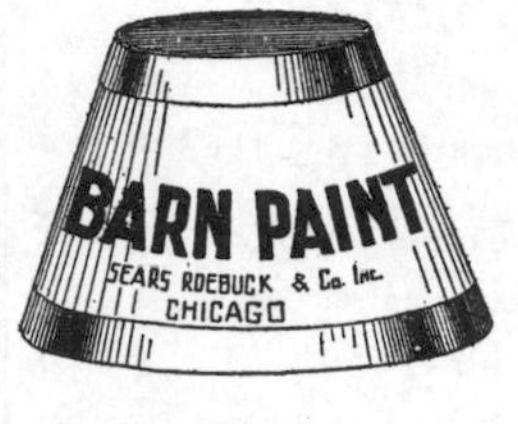


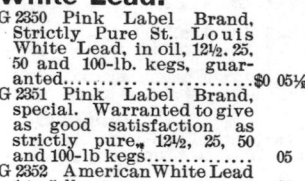

These are composed of the most durable mineral paints, finely ground and thinned with linseed oil. They are recommended for their durability. Color card upon application. The colors are: 730 Yellow, 720 Drab, 740 Pure Brown, 730 Oxide Red, 710 Lead Color, 750 Tuscan Maroon.

| | | Gal. |
|---|---|---|
| G 2336 | 1 gallon cans........ | $0 65 |
| G 2337 | 5 gallon kits........ | 60 |
| G 2338 | 10 gallon kits........ | 60 |
| G 2339 | 25 gallon barrels........ | 55 |
| G 2340 | 50 gallon barrels........ | 50 |

## White Lead.

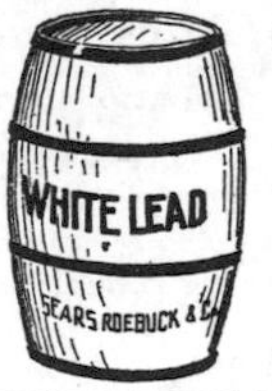


G 2350 Pink Label Brand, Strictly Pure St. Louis White Lead, in oil, 12½, 25, 50 and 100-lb. kegs, guaranteed........ $0 05⅛

G 2351 Pink Label Brand, special. Warranted to give as good satisfaction as strictly pure, 12½, 25, 50 and 100-lb kegs........ 05

G 2352 American White Lead 1 to 5-lb. cans........ 06

## Dry Colors.

We handle only best qualities.

| | | Bbl. pr lb. | Per lb. |
|---|---|---|---|
| G 2354 | Rochelle Ochre, 400 lbs........ | $0 01¼ | $0 02 |
| G 2355 | Golden Washed Ochre, 400 lbs.... | 01 | 02 |
| G 2356 | Italian Buff (light), 500 lbs...... | 01 | 02 |
| G 2357 | Cookson English Venetian Red, 336 lbs...... | 01⅜ | 02 |
| G 2358 | Imperial English Venetian Red, 336 lbs........ | 01⅜ | 02 |
| G 2359 | Snow White Wood Filler, 550 lbs.. | 01½ | 02¼ |
| G 2360 | Silver White Wood Filler, 550 lbs........ | 01½ | 01¾ |
| G 2361 | White Mineral Primer, 550 lbs.... | 01½ | 02 |
| G 2362 | Lampblack, Germantown, 35 lbs | 10 | 11 |
| G 2363 | Burnt Umber, 350 lbs........ | 05 | 06 |
| G 2364 | Raw Umber, 350 lbs........ | 05 | 06 |
| G 2365 | Burnt Sienna, 350 lbs........ | 08 | 09 |
| G 2366 | Red Lead........ | | 10 |
| G 2367 | Raw Sienna........ | 08 | 09 |
| G 2368 | Chrome Green, best........ | | 10 |
| G 2369 | Chrome Yellow........ | | 15 |

## Wood Stains.

**Pink Label Brand.**

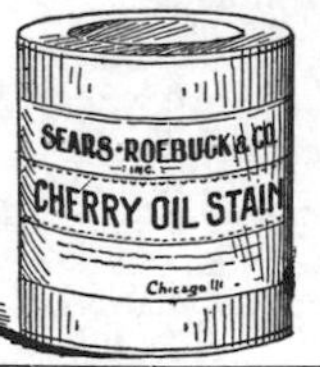


Perfect imitations of natural woods, Cherry, Rosewood, Mahogany, Walnut, Ebony, Light Oak, Dark Oak, Specially intended for refinishing wood work in the interior of homes. Can be applied on any surface.

| | |
|---|---|
| G 2370 Gallons, per gallon | $1 45 |
| Half gallons, per can..... | 80 |
| Quarts, per can........ | 45 |
| Pints, per can........ | 25 |
| Half pints, per can........ | 18 |

# PINK LABEL VARNISHES, ETC.

These goods are guaranteed equal in quality to any like goods made. We have placed them on the market at prices that will at once command your attention. Put up in all sizes, from pints to 50 gallon barrels. No charge for packages.

| | | Pints Each. | Pints Dozen. | Quarts Each. | Quarts Dozen. | ½ Gal. Each. | ½ Gal. Dozen. | 1 Gal. Each. | 5 Gal. Each. | 1 Gal. Each. | ½ Bbl. 25 gals. Per gal. | Barrel 50 gals. Per gal. |
|---|---|---|---|---|---|---|---|---|---|---|---|---|
| G 2372 | No. 1 Furniture Varnish........ | $0 22 | $2 25 | $0 40 | $4 00 | $0 60 | $6 00 | $1 00 | $4 50 | $9 00 | $0 80 | $0 75 |
| G 2373 | No. 1 Coach Varnish........ | 25 | 2 50 | 45 | 4 50 | 85 | 8 50 | 1 60 | 7 00 | 14 00 | 1 10 | 1 05 |
| G 2374 | Extra Light Coach Varnish........ | 30 | 3 00 | 55 | 5 50 | 95 | 9 50 | 1 70 | 7 50 | 15 00 | 1 35 | 1 30 |
| G 2375 | Light Hard Oil Finish........ | 25 | 2 50 | 45 | 4 50 | 85 | 8 50 | 1 60 | 7 00 | 14 00 | 1 10 | 1 05 |
| G 2376 | Extra Light Hard Oil Finish........ | 30 | 3 00 | 55 | 5 50 | 95 | 9 50 | 1 70 | 7 50 | 15 00 | 1 35 | 1 30 |
| G 2377 | Pure Imported Damar Varnish........ | 35 | 3 50 | 60 | 6 00 | 1 00 | 10 00 | 1 80 | 8 50 | 17 00 | 1 60 | 1 50 |
| G 2378 | Durable Floor Varnish........ | 35 | 3 50 | 60 | 6 00 | 1 00 | 10 00 | 1 80 | 8 50 | 17 00 | 1 60 | 1 50 |
| G 2379 | B. & T. Dryer........ | 18 | 2 00 | 30 | 3 00 | 40 | 4 00 | 60 | 2 25 | 4 50 | 40 | 35 |
| G 2380 | Enamel Leather Top Dressing........ | 40 | 4 00 | 75 | 7 50 | 1 35 | 13 50 | 2 50 | 11 00 | 22 00 | 2 20 | 2 10 |
| G 2381 | Extra Turpentine Japan Dryer........ | 25 | 2 50 | 45 | 4 50 | 85 | 8 50 | 1 60 | 7 00 | 14 00 | 1 10 | 1 05 |
| G 2382 | House Painters Japan........ | 22 | 2 25 | 40 | 4 00 | 60 | 6 00 | 1 00 | 4 50 | 9 00 | 80 | 75 |
| G 2383 | No. 1 Black Asphaltum........ | 20 | 2 00 | 35 | 3 50 | 50 | 5 00 | 80 | 3 50 | 7 00 | 65 | 60 |
| G 2384 | Oil Shellac........ | 25 | 2 50 | 45 | 4 50 | 85 | 8 50 | 1 60 | 7 00 | 14 00 | 1 10 | 1 05 |
| G 2385 | Liquid Wood Filler, for soft woods........ | 30 | 3 00 | 55 | 5 50 | 95 | 9 50 | 1 70 | 7 50 | 15 00 | 1 35 | 1 30 |
| G 2886 | Inside Coach Rubbing Varnish........ | 35 | 3 50 | 60 | 6 00 | 1 00 | 10 00 | 1 80 | 8 50 | 17 00 | 1 60 | 1 50 |
| G 2387 | Outside Body Varnish........ | 55 | 5 50 | 1 00 | 10 00 | 1 60 | 16 00 | 3 00 | 12 50 | 25 00 | 2 40 | 2 35 |
| G 2388 | Coach Body Varnish........ | 55 | 5 50 | 1 00 | 10 00 | 1 60 | 16 00 | 3 00 | 12 50 | 25 00 | 2 40 | 2 35 |
| G 2389 | Rubbing Body Varnish........ | 40 | 4 00 | 75 | 7 50 | 1 35 | 13 50 | 2 50 | 11 00 | 22 00 | 2 20 | 2 10 |
| G 2390 | Shellac Varnish, orange grain alcohol........ | 50 | ---- | 85 | ---- | 3 15 | ---- | ---- | ---- | ---- | ---- | ---- |
| G 2391 | Shellac Varnish, white grain alcohol........ | 60 | ---- | 1 00 | ---- | 3 75 | ---- | ---- | ---- | ---- | ---- | ---- |
| G 2392 | Shellac Varnish, white wood grain alcohol........ | 50 | ---- | 85 | ---- | 3 15 | ---- | ---- | ---- | ---- | ---- | ---- |
| G 2393 | Shellac Varnish, orange wood grain alcohol........ | 40 | ---- | 75 | ---- | 2 50 | ---- | ---- | ---- | ---- | ---- | ---- |

## Pure Colors in Oil.

**Pink Label Brand.**

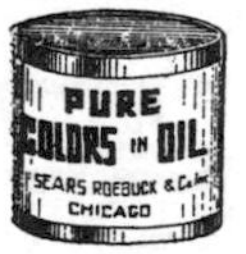


| | | 1-lb. cans. | 5-lb. cans. |
|---|---|---|---|
| G 2395 | Drop Black........ | $0 16 | $0 75 |
| G 2396 | Ivory Black........ | 16 | 75 |
| G 2397 | Coach Black........ | 16 | 75 |
| G 2398 | Prussian Blue... | 36 | 1 65 |
| G 2399 | Ultramarine Blue........ | 20 | 95 |
| G 2400 | Italian Sienna, raw or burnt........ | 14 | 65 |
| G 2401 | Turkey Umber, raw or burnt........ | 12 | 55 |
| G 2402 | Van Dyke Brown........ | 14 | 65 |
| G 2403 | Chrome Green........ | 16 | 75 |
| G 2404 | Scarlet Vermilion........ | 26 | 1 20 |
| G 2405 | Tuscan Red........ | 20 | 95 |
| G 2406 | Venetian Red........ | 08 | 35 |
| G 2407 | Indian Red........ | 15 | 70 |
| G 2408 | Chrome Yellow........ | 20 | 90 |
| G 2409 | Yellow Ochre........ | 10 | 45 |
| G 2410 | Graining Colors (Antique, Mahogany, Cherry, Walnut)........ | 15 | 70 |
| G 2411 | Red Lead........ | 13 | 60 |

## Buggy Paints.

**Pink Label Brand.**

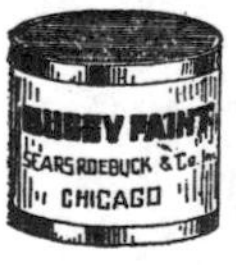


Ground in best coach varnish. Ready for use. Prepared expressly for painting buggies, coaches, carriages, garden chairs, settees, benches, etc. One coat will make a beautiful and durable finish. No varnishing required. An assortment at a dozen prices. Be sure and give number of color.

| | |
|---|---|
| 600 Yellow | 640 Brewster Green |
| 610 Vermilion | 650 Blue |
| 620 Light Wine | 605 Wine Color |
| 630 Coach Green | 670 Coach Black |

| | | Each. | Doz. |
|---|---|---|---|
| G 2413 | Quart cans........ | $0 60 | $6 00 |
| | Pint cans........ | 35 | 3 26 |
| | Half-pint cans........ | 20 | 2 25 |
| | Also best vermilion and white. | | |
| G 2414 | Quart cans........ | 75 | 8 50 |
| | Pint cans........ | 40 | 4 50 |
| | Half-pint cans........ | 25 | 2 85 |

## Enamel Paint.

In twelve beautiful and delicate shades adapted for general decorative purposes. Especially desirable for picture frames, chairs, tables, flower pots, wicker work and bric-a-brac. Dries hard in forty-eight hours with a very high luster. These goods are specially adapted for bicycles and are in the following shades: White, Ultra Blue, Vermillion, Rose, Ivory, Terra Cotta, Dark Green, Maroon, Azure Blue, Deep Blue, Yellow, Black.

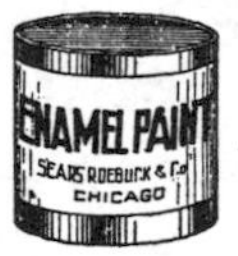


| | | Each. | Doz. |
|---|---|---|---|
| G 2416 | Half pound cans.... | $0 20 | $2 00 |
| | One pound cans........ | 40 | |
| | One quart cans........ | 75 | |
| | One gallon cans........ | 2 50 | |

## Monarch Iron Paint.

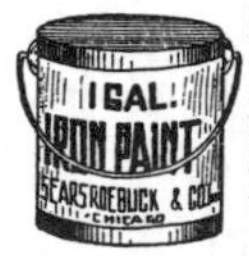


Can not be excelled for general durability and preservative qualities. It is made especially for covering all kinds of metal work, dries rapidly with a hard, glossy black finish, and is absolutely water and acid proof. One gallon will cover about 300 square feet.

| | | Pr gal. |
|---|---|---|
| G 2450 | 2 gal cans........ | $0 80 |
| | 5 gal cans........ | 68 |
| | 10 gal cans........ | 60 |
| | 25 gal barrels........ | 47 |
| | 50 gal barrels........ | 35 |

We furnish iron paint only in black.

## Liquid Wood Filler.

Dries quickly, fills pores absolutely, makes a hard, smooth finish. Superior to any in the market in color, working qualities, and durability.

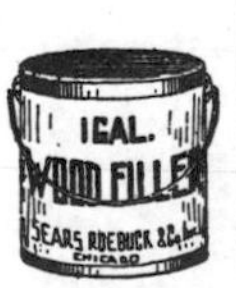


| | |
|---|---|
| G 2417 By the barrel, per gallon | $1 15 |
| By the half barrel, per gallon... | 1 20 |
| By the 10 gallon can, per gallon.. | 1 25 |
| By the 5 gallon can, per gallon.. | 1 30 |
| By the 1 gallon can, per gallon.. | 1 40 |
| By the quart can, each........ | 40 |

No charge for packages.

## Liquid Cement.

G 2418 Pink Label Brand Cement will mend china, glass, stoneware, wood, etc. Put up in 2, 4, 8, and 16 oz. bottles; 2 oz. 12c.; 4 oz. 18c.; 8 oz. 22c.; 16 oz. 40c.

## Mucilage and Liquid Glue.

G 2419 Pink Label Brand, put up in flat bottom bottles; 2 oz.. 4c.; 3 oz., 7c.; 8 oz,. 15c.; pint, 25c., 1 quart 44c.

## Rubber Cement.

G 2420 Pink Label Brand Rubber Cement, for mending all kinds of rubber and leather goods, glass, china, and stoneware, bicycle tires, tubes, etc., also boots, shoes, rubbers, etc. Put up in tubes and cans; 2 oz. tubes, 10c.; 4 oz., 17c.; 8 oz., 25.

## Kerosene Emulsion.

G 2422 For spraying and washing trees, vines, plants field crops and domestic animals. Guaranteed to kill plant lice, red spider, scales, mealy bugs, lice on cattle and hogs, tick on sheep. One can is sufficient for 25 to 50 gallons of water. Price, 23c.; per case of 1 dozen, $2.65.

## Bordeaux Mixture.

G 2423 Is the greatest destroyer of fungus growth on vegetation, viz: mildew, rust, blight. One can is sufficient to dilute with 35 to 50 gallons of water. Price per can, 33c.; per dozen, $2.25.

## S., R. & Co.'s Kalsomine.

One coat will cover as well and give a finer finish than two coats of ordinary kalsomine. Is prepared dry and made ready for use by simply adding hot water. Full directions on each package. Can be used on iron, wood, brick, stone or plaster walls, wooden partitions, etc., one package covering about 400 square feet. Sixteen tints and pure white.

| | | |
|---|---|---|
| G 2424 | White, per package........ | $0 30 |
| G 2425 | Tints, per package........ | 35 |
| G 2426 | 25 packages in case, per case white........ | 7 00 |
| G 2427 | 25 packages in case, per case, tints........ | 7 50 |
| G 2428 | 100 lb. drums, white........ | 6 00 |
| G 2429 | 100 lb. drums, tints........ | 6 50 |

Four fresco colors for bordering, striping, etc. Color card mailed free. Send for one.

## Wall Paper Cleaner.

G 2432 Index Wall Cleaner. It makes old wall paper look like new; removes smoke, dust, etc. Is a dry compound put up in neat packages with directions for use. Per doz. $1.50; each, 15c.

## Pumice Stone.

| | | Doz. | Each. |
|---|---|---|---|
| G 2433 | Compressed, bricks........ | $2 25 | $0 22 |
| G 2434 | Powdered, per lb........ | | 08 |

REMEMBER OUR 3% CASH DISCOUNT WHEN FULL AMOUNT ACCOMPANIES ORDER. MOST OF OUR CUSTOMERS SEND CASH WITH ORDER. WE DON'T ASK YOU TO KEEP THE GOODS IF THEY ARE NOT ALL RIGHT.

## Lime, Cement, Tar, Hair, Etc.

| | | Bbl. |
|---|---|---|
| G 2451 | Lime | $1 10 |
| G 2452 | Cement, natural | 1 25 |
| G 2453 | Portland Cement, imported | 3 40 |
| G 2454 | Plaster Paris | 2 00 |
| | | Per bu. |
| G 2455 | Hair, washed | 30 |
| G 2456 | Pine Tar, Carolina, bbls only, per bbl, about 30 gals | 3 50 |

| | | Gro. | Doz. | Each. |
|---|---|---|---|---|
| G 2436 | Quarts | $9 50 | $ 90 | $0 10 |
| G 2437 | Half gallons | 19 00 | 1 75 | 18 |
| G 2438 | Gallons | 30 00 | 3 10 | 28 |
| G 2457 | Coal Tar, per bbl | | | 6 25 |
| G 2458 | 3 gal cans, per can | | | 1 50 |

## Roofing Felt.

**S., R. & Co.'s Prepared Roofing.**

With each roll we furnish 2 gallons Roof Coating, 1½ pounds tin caps, and 1 pound barbed wire roofing nails. Each roll contains 108 square feet. Pr roll.

G 2440 2-ply Roofing Felt. Weight about 75 lbs per roll. Price, with cement, caps and nails.. $1 60
In lots of 5 rolls or more ... 1 40

G 2442 3-ply Roofing Felt. Weight about 100 lbs per roll. Price, complete with cement, caps and nails ... 1 90
In lots of 5 rolls or more ... 1 65

G 2443 Roofing Brushes, made expressly for applying the cement; 2-knot brush, each ... 70
3-knot brush ... 90

| | | Per lb. |
|---|---|---|
| G 2444 | Tin Roofing Caps | $0 07 |
| G 2445 | Barbed Roofing Nails | 04 |

## Roofing Cement.

G 2446 The price on this varies according to the quantity desired, the cost of the cask being included in the price of the cement. Per gal.

| | Per gal. |
|---|---|
| 50 gallon lots or more | $0 14 |
| 21 to 40 gallon lots | 16 |
| 11 to 20 gallon lots | 18 |
| 6 to 10 gallon lots | 20 |
| 5 gallons | 25 |
| 2 gallons and less | 30 |

## Sheathing Paper. Pr roll.

G 2447 Union Brand Red Rosin sized sheathing, strong, durable, no shrinkage, put up in rolls 36 inches wide, 500 square feet in each roll weighing about 35 lbs ... $1 05

G 2448 Peerless Brand Gray Rosin sized sheathing, the cheapest paper in the market; is waterproof, clean to handle and durable, 500 square feet in roll, 36 inches wide, weighs about 25 lbs ... 75

See our Hardware Department for other brands of building paper.

## Elastic Cement.

For repairing leaks on all kinds of roofs, gutters, eave troughs, etc. You can apply it yourself with a putty knife or paddle; no tinner or roofer required. Where once applied it will stay. The weather does not affect it, and it will last for years.

G 2460 2 lb. cans, each ... $0 30
5 lb. cans, each ... 60

## Paper, Wrapping.

We sell any quantity at prices given, except waxed butter and tissue. Per Ream.

G 2462 Waxed butter paper, grease proof, 9 x 12 inches, 480 sheets ... $0 15
12 x 18 inches, 480 sheets ... 30

G 2463 Tissue paper, 320 sheets to ream, 10 x 15.. 15

G 2464 Fine manila paper, for general wrapping, sizes, 12 x 18, 15 x 20, 18 x 24, or 24 x 36 ... Lb. 04

G 2465 Rag Paper, same sizes as manila ... 2½

## Paper Bags.

500 in bundle.

| | | 100. | Bun. |
|---|---|---|---|
| G 2466 | No. 1 | $0 12 | $0 42 |
| | No. 2 | 13 | 53 |
| | No. 3 | 15 | 64 |
| | No. 5 | 20 | 90 |
| | No. 10 | 30 | 1 35 |
| | No. 12 | 40 | 1 65 |
| | No. 16 | 50 | 2 37 |
| | No. 20 | 60 | 2 63 |
| | | Doz. | 100. |
| G 2467 | 1-16 barrel paper flour sacks | $0 12 | $0 70 |
| G 2468 | ⅛ barrel paper flour sacks | 15 | 1 00 |
| G 2469 | ¼ barrel paper flour sacks | 27 | 1 90 |

## Toilet Paper.

**We sell only in original cases** and will not break cases under any circumstances. A year's supply of Toilet Paper costs you but little by our economic, one small profit system, as we ship direct from the factory. **We would suggest** that you club your order with neighbors and make up a freight shipment of several hundred pounds. Include what toilet paper you need and the freight will be little.

### Toilet Paper in Rolls.

G 2470 **Little Jewel.** A special medium sized perforated roll, fair grade paper and a big bargain. Per case of 100 rolls ... $2 25

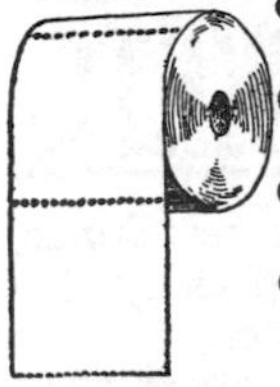

G 2471 **Era.** A good sized, perforated roll, excellent paper. Per case of 100 rolls ... 2 85

G 2472 **Climax.** A fine large perforated roll, very excellent paper. Per case of 100 rolls... 3 95

G 2473 **Lyndon.** A pure tissue manila paper, large perforated rolls. Per case of 100 rolls 4 75

G 2474 **Envoy.** A very superior and extra large roll of pure tissue manila. Retails at 3 rolls for a quarter. Per case of 100 rolls ... 5 00

G 2475 **Winner.** The biggest roll of the best tissue toilet paper made. Guaranteed, 1000 sheets perforated. A special grade at half price. Per case of 100 rolls ... 6 15

### Toilet Paper in Packages.

G 2476 **Clover Leaf.** A fine tissue manila paper in sheets. Each package has a riveted hanger. Per case of 100 packages... 2 45

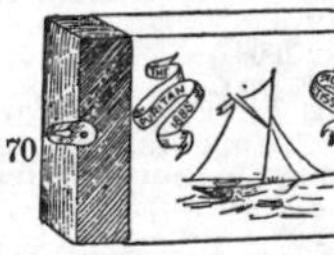

G 2477 **Crescent.** A very nice genuine tissue manila toilet paper. Large package, riveted hanger. Per case of 100 packages ... 3 70

G 2478 **Diana.** A choice grade of tissue manila. Large package with riveted hanger. Per case of 100 packages ... 5 15

G 2479 **The Puritan.** The finest grade of special tissue manila, guaranteed free from injurious chemicals. Very large packages. Per case of 100 packages ... 6 15

## Axle Grease.

### S., R. & Co.'s Perfection Axle Grease.

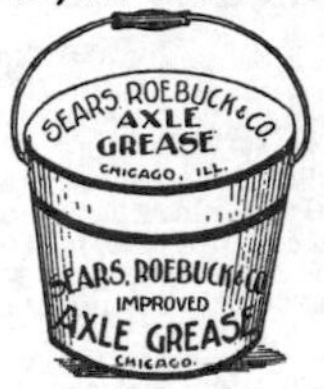


We have secured control of the total product of the best equipped axle grease factory in the United States and can now offer you a grease that will outwear by 5 to 15 days any grease on the market. No matter how low this price may seem to you, we have faith enough in the goods to place our name on every package, and if not satisfactory you may return the goods at our expense.

| | | Case. | Ea. |
|---|---|---|---|
| G 2481 | Trial box, 1 doz. 1 lb. boxes | $0 55 | $0 05 |
| G 2482 | 2 doz. in case, 1 lb. boxes | 95 | 05 |
| G 2483 | 3 doz. in case, 1 lb. boxes | 1 40 | 05 |
| G 2484 | ½ doz. in crate, 10 lb bkts | 2 00 | 38 |
| G 2485 | 1 doz. in crate, 10 lb. buckets | 3 95 | 38 |
| G 2486 | ½ doz. in crate, 25 lb. buckets | 4 75 | 85 |
| G 2487 | 1 doz. in crate, 25 lb. buckets | 8 50 | 85 |
| G 2488 | Kegs about 60 lbs. | | 1 95 |
| G 2489 | 100 lb. kegs | | 3 00 |
| G 2490 | 200 lb. kegs | | 5 75 |

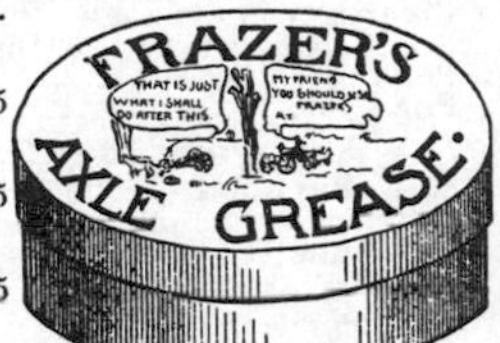


| | | Case. | Doz. | Box. |
|---|---|---|---|---|
| G 2492 | Frazer's small 1 lb. wood boxes 4 doz. in case | 3 20 | 82 | 07 |

## Can Openers.

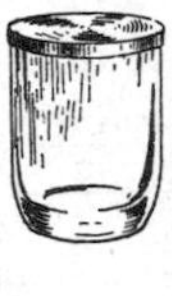

| | | Doz. | Ea. |
|---|---|---|---|
| G 2499 | Can Opener, 1 doz. in box, iron handles | $0 50 | $0 05 |

## Jelly Tumblers.

Prices subject to change. Case

G 2500 Jelly Tumblers, tin top, hold ⅓ pint each, 6 dozen in case ... $1 70

G 2501 Jelly Tumblers, tin top, hold ½ pint, 6 doz. in case ... 1 95

## Mason's Fruit Jars.

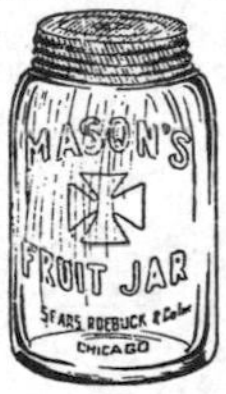


| | | Case. |
|---|---|---|
| G 2503 | Pints, per case of 6 doz. | $3 75 |
| G 2504 | Quarts, per case of 8 doz. | 6 00 |
| G 2505 | ½ gallon, per case of 6 doz. | 5 50 |
| G 2506 | Extra rubber bands, per doz. | 05 |

Extra Caps and Rubbers for the three sizes, 45 cents per dozen.

These prices are subject to changes.

## Stock Food.

### This Price is Net Cash—No Discount.

| | For Feeding to Stock. | Sack. |
|---|---|---|
| G 2509 | Ground Oil Cake, 100-lb sack | $1 10 |
| G 2510 | Ground Oil Cake, per ton only | $20 00 |

## Middlings and Bran.

Prices are net and subject to market changes. The prices we make show what the market was when list was printed. Send us your orders and we will supply you at the lowest market price on the day your order is received.

| | | |
|---|---|---|
| G 2512 | Middlings, per ton, 100-lb sacks | $10 75 |
| | 100-lb sacks | 65 |
| G 2513 | Bran, per ton, in 100-lb sacks | 9 75 |
| | 100-lb sacks each | 60 |

## Horse and Cattle Powders.

| | | |
|---|---|---|
| G 2515 | 5-lb packages | $0 50 |
| | 10-lb packages | 1 00 |

## Cracked Bone for Poultry.

| | | |
|---|---|---|
| G 2517 | 25-lb sacks | $0 50 |
| | 50-lb sacks | 95 |
| | 100-lb sacks | 1 85 |

## Ground Oyster Shells for Poultry.

| | | |
|---|---|---|
| G 2519 | 25-lb sacks | $0 45 |
| | 50-lb sacks | 75 |
| | 100-lb sacks | 1 20 |

## Blatchford's Calf Meal.

| | | |
|---|---|---|
| G 2520 | 25-lb sacks | $1 25 |
| | 50-lb sacks | 2 00 |
| | 100-lb sacks | 3 50 |

## Pure Ground Beef Scraps for Poultry.

| | | |
|---|---|---|
| G 2522 | 25-lb sacks | $0 60 |
| | 50-lb sacks | 1 10 |
| | 100-lb sacks | 2 00 |

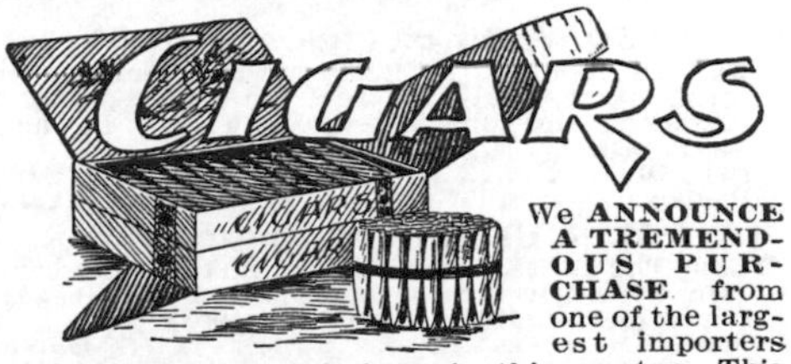


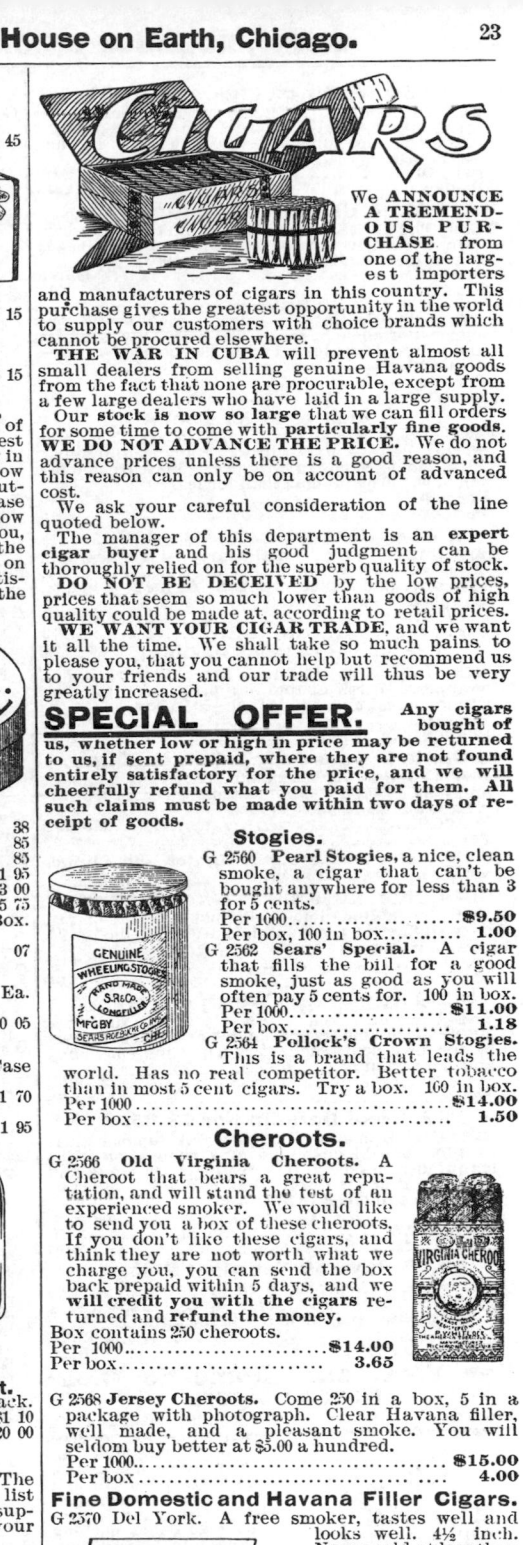

We **ANNOUNCE A TREMENDOUS PURCHASE** from one of the largest importers and manufacturers of cigars in this country. This purchase gives the greatest opportunity in the world to supply our customers with choice brands which cannot be procured elsewhere.

**THE WAR IN CUBA** will prevent almost all small dealers from selling genuine Havana goods from the fact that none are procurable, except from a few large dealers who have laid in a large supply.

Our **stock is now so large** that we can fill orders for some time to come with **particularly fine goods. WE DO NOT ADVANCE THE PRICE.** We do not advance prices unless there is a good reason, and this reason can only be on account of advanced cost.

We ask your careful consideration of the line quoted below.

The manager of this department is an **expert cigar buyer** and his good judgment can be thoroughly relied on for the superb quality of stock.

**DO NOT BE DECEIVED** by the low prices, prices that seem so much lower than goods of high quality could be made at, according to retail prices.

**WE WANT YOUR CIGAR TRADE**, and we want it all the time. We shall take so much pains to please you, that you cannot help but recommend us to your friends and our trade will thus be very greatly increased.

## SPECIAL OFFER.

**Any cigars bought of us, whether low or high in price may be returned to us, if sent prepaid, where they are not found entirely satisfactory for the price, and we will cheerfully refund what you paid for them. All such claims must be made within two days of receipt of goods.**

## Stogies.

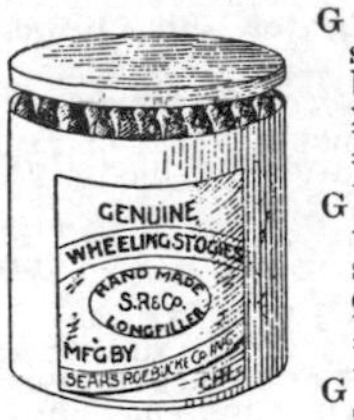


G 2560 **Pearl Stogies**, a nice, clean smoke, a cigar that can't be bought anywhere for less than 3 for 5 cents.
Per 1000 ... **$9.50**
Per box, 100 in box ... **1.00**

G 2562 **Sears' Special.** A cigar that fills the bill for a good smoke, just as good as you will often pay 5 cents for. 100 in box.
Per 1000 ... **$11.00**
Per box ... **1.18**

G 2564 **Pollock's Crown Stogies.** This is a brand that leads the world. Has no real competitor. Better tobacco than in most 5 cent cigars. Try a box. 100 in box.
Per 1000 ... **$14.00**
Per box ... **1.50**

## Cheroots.

G 2566 **Old Virginia Cheroots.** A Cheroot that bears a great reputation, and will stand the test of an experienced smoker. We would like to send you a box of these cheroots. If you don't like these cigars, and think they are not worth what we charge you, you can send the box back prepaid within 5 days, and we **will credit you with the cigars** returned and **refund the money.**
Box contains 250 cheroots.
Per 1000 ... **$14.00**
Per box ... **3.65**

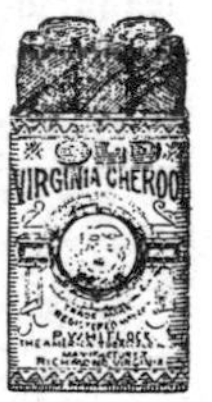


G 2568 **Jersey Cheroots.** Come 250 in a box, 5 in a package with photograph. Clear Havana filler, well made, and a pleasant smoke. You will seldom buy better at $5.00 a hundred.
Per 1000 ... **$15.00**
Per box ... **4.00**

## Fine Domestic and Havana Filler Cigars.

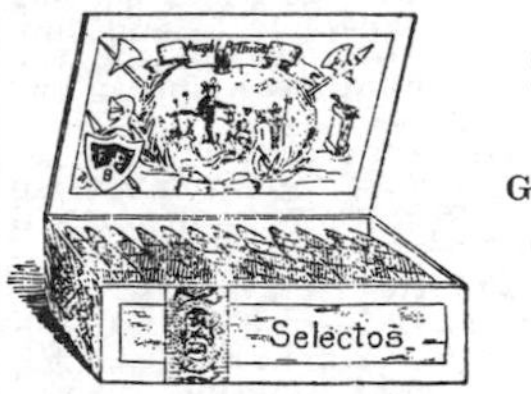


G 2570 Del York. A free smoker, tastes well and looks well. 4½ inch. Never sold at less than two for 5 cents. 50 in box.
Per 1000 ... **$10.50**
Per box ... **60**

G 2572 Muy Gracias. A special brand put up especially for us, and warranted to please. 4½ inch, 50 in box.
Per 1000 ... **$10.50**
Per box ... **65**

## A Fine 5 Cent Cigar—Only 70 Cents for 50.

G 2574 The Princess 5 cent Cigar. Best smoke ever had for the money. The tobacco is fine Domestic, with a smooth wrapper. Looks like most ten cent cigars. 50 in a box.
Per 1000 ... **$13.50**
Per box ... **70**

## Try a Box at 80 Cents.

G 2576 The Clandin's Imperator. Scarcely more than 1½ cents apiece and worth 5. Nice flavor, good taste and handsome color. One of our choicest cheap brands. 4½ inch—50 in box.
Per 1000 ... **$15.00**
Per box ... **80**

**YOU WILL SAVE US A GREAT DEAL OF TIME AND TROUBLE BY ALWAYS GIVING THE PAGE AND ARTICLE NUMBER OF GOODS YOU ORDER. IT IS BETTER TO PREVENT MISTAKES THAN TO CORRECT THEM.**

### $2.50 Worth of Cigars for $1.00.

G 2578 Our Colors. A Cigar you will seldom see in retail stores: Only the best dealers keep them. Buy a box, and you will keep on buying. 4½ inch —50 in box.
Per 1000.................... $19.00
Per box.................... 1.00

### A Rare Bargain at 48c for 50.

G 2580 The Best. If you do not think this is a bargain, we will never ask you to patronize our Cigar Department again. 4½ inch—50 in box.
Per 1000.................... $9.25
Per box.................... 48

### $2.50 for 145.

G 2582 Peria de Cuba. A trade maker and the choicest of cheap cigars. The price only is cheap, and you will be pleased with the goods. 4¼ inch—50 in a box.
Per 1000.................... $27.00
Per box.................... 1.45

### A Leader at 3½ Cents.

G 2584 City of Havana, 4½ inch, 50 in box. The filler of this cigar is fine selected Havana Clippings, with choice Sumatra wrapper. More frequently sold as a 10 cent cigar than for less.
Per 1000.................... $35.00
Per box.................... 1.88

### A Rare Bargain at $2.00 per Box.

G 2586 Little Joker. Particularly well made, and often sold at two and a half times our price. Fine filler and choice wrapper. 4¼ inch—50 in box. Wrapped in two bundles.
Per 1000.................... $37.00
Per box.................... 2.00

### The Famous K. of P. Cigar.

G 2588 Knights of Pythias. Long filler with fine wrapper. Worth double our price. A cigar you will keep on buying. 4½ inch—50 in box.
Per 1000.................... $28.00
Per box.................... 1.53

### 4 Cents Buys a 3 for a Quarter Cigar.

G 2590 Cookies. A good smoke, just as free a smoker and just as good a flavor as most three for a quarter goods. 4⅜ inch. 50 in box.
Per 1000.................... $38.00
Per box.................... 2.00

☞ **We give a nice Cigar Lighter and Clipper Free with 750 Cookie Cigars.**

### 90 Cents Buys Cigars Worth $2.00.

G 2592 Queen Bouquet. A distinct leader in cigars, very well flavord and a special bargain. 4 inch. with bands, 25 in box.
Per 1000.................... $33.00
Per box.................... 90

### $1.53 Buys $2.50 Worth of Cigars.

G 2594 Upmann's Red Cross. 4⅛ inch, Exquisitos. These special cigars are banded and you can't buy better for 10 cents each. Try a box and you'll buy another. 25 in box.
Per 1000.................... $53.50
Per box.................... 1.53

### A Great Bargain For $3.35.

G 2596 Carl Upmann's Bouquet. A famous cigar that has the biggest kind of a reputation. The manufacturers make it a leader at 10 cents and many retailer's will sell it at two for a quarter. They come in boxes of 25 and 50.
Per 1000.................... $65.00
Per box of 50.................... 3.35
Per box of 25.................... 1.80

### $3.25 Buys 50 Ten Cent Cigars.

G 2598 Sports. A strictly high grade cigar, a product of one of the best factories, well made and a free, well flavored smoker. 4 inch., 50 in box,
Per 1000.................... $63.00
Per box.................... 3.25

## Key West and Domestic Clear Havana Cigars.

**We are the agents for the celebrated Juan F. Portuondo's Cigars,** and are in a position to give the best bargains in strictly high grade goods.

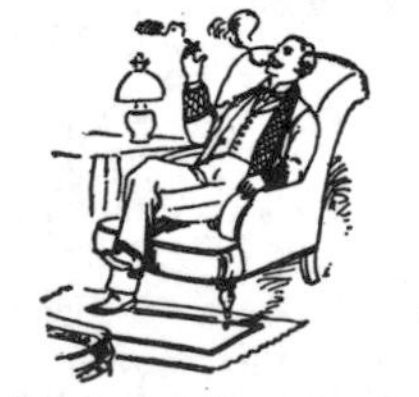

Lovers of the weed will find their tastes fully satisfied with our line, and a connoisseur will find nothing to complain of, and only **words of praise for the general excellence** of the goods.

We want your trial order, and if we get you started with us, we know you will buy your cigars nowhere else.

### Choice of the Market at 4 cents.

G 2600 La Flor de Portuondo, Chicos. A fine 4¼ inch cigar, that comes 50 in box. A delightful smoke, warranted to please the most exacting. If you don't think these cigars are worth what we ask for them, after you have smoked a few, we will allow you to return the balance to us prepaid, and we will refund what you paid for them.
Per 1000.................... $38.00
Per box.................... 2.00

### Save 30 to 40 per cent. on these Elegant Cigars.

G 2602 La Flor de Portuondo Londres Grande. A choice 5 inch cigar, made of select tobacco, and worth double our price. Our reputation is at stake on these goods and we are willing to risk it. 50 in box.
Per 1000.................... $65.00
Per box.................... 3.40

### A Genuine 2 for a quarter Cigar.

G 2604 La Flor de Portuondo, Perfectos. A 5 inch cigar that has met with a tremendous sale since we secured the agency. A splendidly flavored smoke. Well made and of the best tobacco. 25 in box.
Per 1000.................... $75.00
Per box.................... 2.00

G 2606 La Flor de Portuondo, Preferido Perfectos. The same elegant cigar as G2604 above, but larger, being 5½ inches in length. 25 in box.
Per 1000.................... $90.00
Per box.................... 2.35

G 2608 **Bride of Key West.** This is one of the best additions to our stock, and we offer it in competition with the choicest 10 cent goods on the market. 50 in box.
Per 1000.................... $60.00
Per box.................... 3.25

G 2610 **La Matilde Especiales.** A cigar that can scarcely be kept constantly in stock, so great is the demand. You will find it even more than we can say in its praise. 50 in box.
Per 1000.................... $65.00
Per box.................... 3.50

## Imported Havanas.

**It is well known** that the stock of **Genuine Havana Tobacco** is very small. Only by large recent purchases from an importer whose supply is fortunately larger than that of other houses, are we able to **offer these choice goods** at the prices named.

### You Never Buy Better at 2 for a Quarter.

G 2612 **El Pervenir, Conchas.** As nice a 4¼ inch Cigar as you ever saw. The flavor is delicious, and it is a trade winner. 50 in box.
Per 1000.................... $95.00
Per box.................... 4.35

### Always Sold at 25 Cents Each.

G 2614 **Bachelors.** The kind of a Cigar that just suits. Not too mild and not too strong. Pleases the connoiseur, and saves the purse. 25 in box.
Per 1000.................... $112.00
Per box.................... 2.90

### $6.25 worth of Cigars for $4.15.

G 2616 **Rosa Bouquets.** A dainty little Cigar worth its weight in gold. Made of the choicest tobacco by the most expert cigar makers, workmen who make only the finest goods. 3⅞ inch—50 in box.
Per 1000.................... $80.00
Per box.................... 4.15

## Cigarettes.

We do not sell less than a box of 500. Box.

G 2640 Old Judge, 10 or 20 in package, 500 in box. $2 00
G 2642 Richmond Straight Cut No. 1, 10 or 20 in package, 500 in box.................... 3 15
G 2644 Preferred Stock "Dukes," 10 or 20 in package, 500 in box.................... 3 25
G 2646 Sporting Extras, "Kinney Bros.," 20 in package, 500 in box.................... 3 25
G 2648 Cameo. "Dukes" 10 in package, 500 in a box.................... 2 15
G 2650 Mexican Yellow Cigarette Paper, 200 leaves in bundle, 50 bundles in box. Per box. 50
Per dozen bundles.................... 15
G 2652 Cigarette Paper, Riz-La, per book, 3 cts; per dozen books, 25 cts.

## Plug Tobacco.

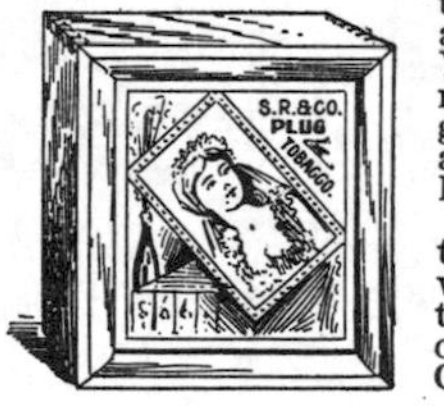


**We are Headquarters** for the best brands of tobaccos and our **prices are right.** You can include what you need with your order for groceries and other goods and your freight will be little if any more.

We are anxious to get you to dealing with us and we will make it so satisfactory that you will always be our customer.

G 2670 **Battle Ax Plug.** Biggest in the world for 10 cents. 3 ten cent pieces to the pound. Butts of 12 or 24 lbs. Per lb...... 22c

Per lb.

G 2672 **Sure Pop.** A good chew and costs little. 14 oz. plugs, size 2x12. 24 lb butts.......... 22c
G 2674 **Kylo Plug.** 3x12, 20 oz. plugs. **A big piece for a little money**.......... 25c
G 2676 Out of Sight. A good favorite with many customers. Very cheap in price. 3x12 plugs. Come in butts of 15 or 30 lbs.......... 21c
G 2678 Even Change. The Best Big Piece in the world for the money. Just as good as many kinds you pay double for. 16 oz. plugs. Butts of 16 lbs.......... 20c
G 2680 J. T. or Big Chunk. An old favorite and the manufacturers are keeping it up to the highest standard of excellence. 80 oz. plugs. Butts weigh 8, 12 or 24 lbs.......... 33c

| | In butts. | Single Lb. |
|---|---|---|
| G 2682 Boot Jack, plug, bright, White Burley, fancy tobacco, 3 plugs to the lb. in 12 lb. butts | $0 73 | $0 75 |
| G 2684 Spear Head, known the world over 30-lb. butts, 16-oz. plugs | 36 | 38 |
| G 2686 Newsboy Plug, 8 and 16 lb. butts | 30 | 32 |
| G 2688 Piper Heidsieck, 3 plugs to the lb., 7 and 14 lb. butts | 53½ | 55 |
| G 2690 Five Bros. High Grade; John Finzer & Co.; 3x3, 8-lb. tins | 56 | 58 |
| G 2692 Jolly Tar, bright navy, 4 plugs to the pound, 28-lb. butts, full weight | 33 | 35 |
| G 2693 Black Thirds, dark navy, 10-lb. butts, 3 plugs to lb | 29 | 31 |

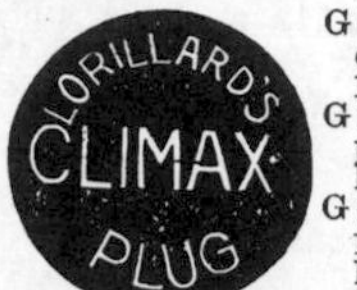


| | | |
|---|---|---|
| G 2694 Climax, 16-oz. clubs, 2x12-30 lb. and 12 lb. butts | 33 | 34 |
| G 2695 Climax, 6 to lb. plugs, twin, 4s, 12 to 28 lb. butts | 35 | 36 |
| G 2696 Battery Plug, 3x12, 3 space, Burley filler, good sweet chew. 24-lb. butts | 18 | 20 |
| G 2697 Mechanics Delight, Dark Navy, double thick 3 to lb., 10½ lb. caddies | 34 | 36 |
| G 2698 Horseshoe, 16-oz. plugs, 2x12, 24 lb. butts | 37 | 38 |
| G 2699 Horseshoe, 12 butts, 16 oz. plugs | 37 | 38 |

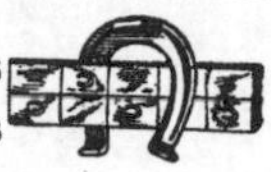

## Fine Cut Tobaccos.

Pail

G 2700 Cyclone. Light or dark, 10 lb pails.......... $3 00
G 2701 Our Pet, 10 lb pails.......... 2 00
G 2702 Square Deal. Light or dark, fine durable chew, 10 lb pails.......... 2 51
G 2703 Jack. Light or dark, fine chew, 10 lb pail 2 62
G 2704 Seashore. Light or dark, 10 lb pails, standard quality.......... 2 35
G 2705 Old Settler. Light or dark, extra fine quality, 10 lb pails.......... 3 25
G 2706 Full Dress. Light or dark, 10 lb pails, none better at any price.......... 5 25

## Smoking Tobacco.

Only such as are **time tried and found perfect** are contained in this list. If you enjoy the weed make your selection from our complete stock and we are bound to please you. Lb.

G 2720 "Powhattan," granulated, 2 oz cloth, 10 and 25 lb boxes. We give a fine Powhattan pipe with each 2 oz package.......... $0 30
G 2721 Must Go. 16 oz cloth, 25 lb, a corncob pipe with each package.......... 20
G 2723 Havana Cigar Clippings. 1s, paper, 25 lb cases.......... 24
G 2725 "Sweet Clippings," fine old stock, ¼'s and ½'s, paper, 25-lb cases.......... 15
G 2726 Kentucky Standard, ¼'s, 25 lb. cases.. 14
G 2727 "Sweet Kentucky," sweet smoke, ¼'s and ½'s, paper, 25 lb. cases.......... 15
G 2728 Canada Chop, 3 oz., foil, 6 lb., cartons, 24 lb. cases. We give 6 pounds but only charge for 5 pounds, making 1 pound free with every 5 pounds.......... 41
G 2729 Plow Boy, ¼'s, foil, 5 lb., cartons, 24 lb. cases.......... 31
G 2730 ⅛'s foil, 6 lb., cartons, 24 lb. cases.......... 32
G 2731 16 oz., tin pails, 24 lb. cases.......... 33
G 2732 Brair Pipe, ¼'s and ⅛'s, 24 lb. cases.......... 30
G 2734 Corn Cake, 1 lb. bags, 25 lb. cases, cob pipe with each pound.......... 16
G 2735 Yum Yum, ¼'s and ⅛'s, foil, cartons, 30 and 60 lb. cases.......... 33
G 2736 1 lb. tin cans, 36 and 54 lb. cases.......... 33
G 2737 1 lb. pails, 30 and 60 lb. cases.......... 33

Genuine Bull Durham. With each 25 lb. lot we will include, free, a box of Fairbank's White Star Soap, or, less than 25 lb., 1 novel free with each lb.

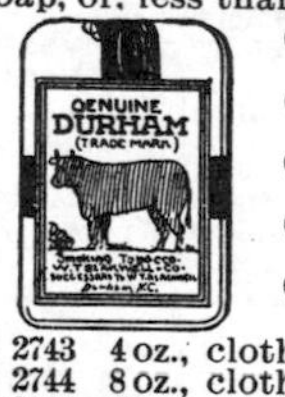


G 2738 1 lb., cloth bags, 25 lb. bales.......... 45
G 2739 ½ lb., cloth bags, 25 lb. bales.......... 47
G 2740 ¼ lb., cloth bags, 25 lb. bales.......... 50
G 2741 ⅛ lb., cloth bags, 25 lb. bales.......... 52
G 2742 Seal of North Carolina, granulated, 2 oz. cl.......... 51
G 2743 4 oz., cloth.......... 49
G 2744 8 oz., cloth.......... 44
G 2745 16 oz., cloth.......... 42
G 2746 16 oz., wood.......... 44
G 2747 Mail Pouch, W. Va., ¼'s papers, 30 lb. cases, loose 29.......... 31
G 2748 ⅛'s, papers, 30 lb. cases, loose.......... 32
G 2749 Sweet Tip Top, ¼'s and ⅛'s, foil.......... 33
G 2750 Old Tip Top, ¼'s and ⅛'s, plain.......... 28
G 2751 Fashion, cut plug, 2 and 4 oz., foil, 5 lb. cartons.......... 33

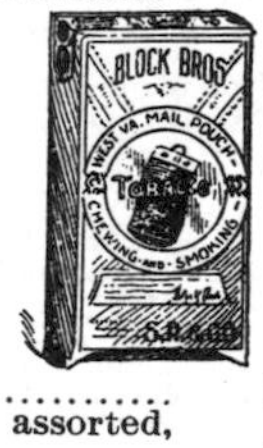


G 2752 Navy Clippings, ¼'s, 25 lb. cases.......... 22
G 2753 Badger, ¼'s, ½'s and 1's, or assorted, 30 and 50 lb. cases.......... 13
G 2754 Peerless, ¼'s, ½'s and 1's, or assorted, 30 and 50 lb. cases.......... 27
G 2755 ⅛'s, in foil, 30 lb. cases.......... 29

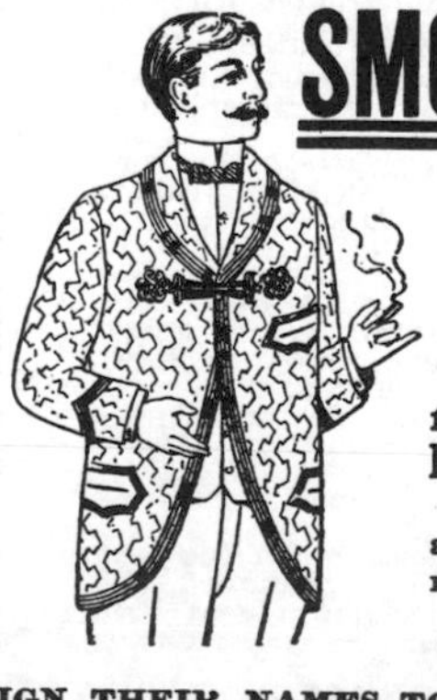

# SMOKING JACKETS.

The Newest Styles, made especially for Fine Trade.

**We make prices right, and you save half or more.**

**See Our Clothing Dept.**

**IT MAY SEEM STRANGE, BUT IT IS STILL A FACT THAT SOME PEOPLE DO NOT EVEN SIGN THEIR NAMES TO THEIR LETTER OR ORDER. MANY MORE FAIL TO GIVE POSTOFFICE ADDRESS. BE CAREFUL THAT YOU MAKE NO SUCH MISTAKES.**

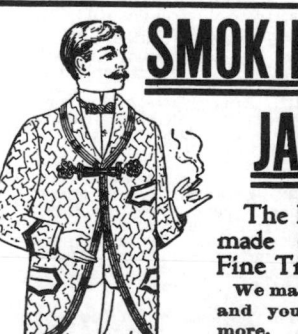

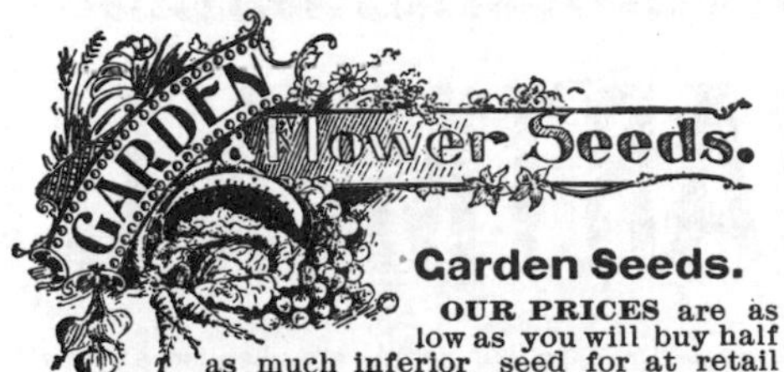


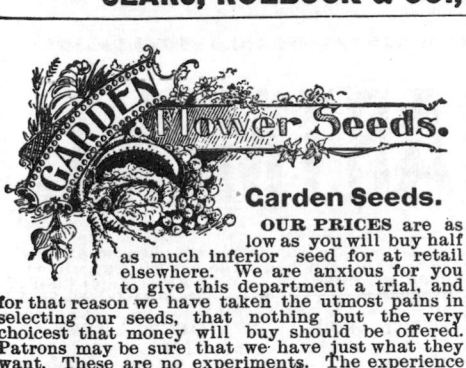

## Garden Seeds.

**OUR PRICES** are as low as you will buy half as much inferior seed for at retail elsewhere. We are anxious for you to give this department a trial, and for that reason we have taken the utmost pains in selecting our seeds, that nothing but the very choicest that money will buy should be offered. Patrons may be sure that we have just what they want. These are no experiments. The experience of hundreds of Gardeners is sufficient to prove that there is no better garden truck grown than the products grown from these specialties. Nothing fancy about them. Good, honest, desirable varieties, that are just right.

Let us put up what you need with your freight or express order and you'll not know the difference when you pay the charges, for they will add little or nothing to the weight.

| | | |
|---|---|---|
| **Artichoke.** | lb. | pr oz |
| G 2800 Large Green Globe | $3 50 | $ 30 |
| **Asparagus.** | | |
| G 2802 Conover's Colossal | 21 | |
| **Beans—Dwarf or Bush.** Green Podded Varieties. | bu. | pr. lb |
| G 2803 Burpee's Bush Lima | $8 00 | $ 20 |
| G 2804 Henderson's Bush Lima | 4 80 | 15 |
| G 2805 Early Mohawk | 3 25 | 10 |
| G 2806 Early Improved Red Valentine—Round Pod. | 3 25 | 10 |
| G 2807 Extra Early Refugee | 3 25 | 10 |
| **Wax Podded Varieties.** | | |
| G 2810 Improved Golden Wax Rust Proof | 3 50 | 10 |
| O 2812 Challenge Black Wax | 4 25 | 12 |
| G 2813 Wardwell's Kidney Wax | 3 75 | 10 |
| **Beans--Pole or Running.** | | |
| G 2814 New Jersey Extra Early Lima | 6 00 | 18 |
| G 2815 King of the Garden Lima | 6 00 | 18 |
| G 2816 Red Speckeled Cut Short or Corn Hill | 6 00 | 18 |
| G 2817 Early Golden Cluster Wax | 6 00 | 18 |
| **Beets—Table.** | lb. | oz |
| G 2818 S., R. & Co.'s Extra Early Egyptian | $0 45 | 04 |
| G 2819 Eclipse Blood Turnip | 25 | 03 |
| G 2820 Edmand's Early Blood Turnip | 22 | 03 |
| G 2821 Long Smooth Blood Red | 22 | 03 |
| **Beets--For Stock.** | | |
| G 2822 S., R. & Co.'s Improved Mammoth Long Red | 18 | |
| G 2824 Vilmorin's Improved Imperial Sugar | 18 | |
| **Brussel's Sprouts.** | | |
| G 2825 Dwarf Improved | 85 | |
| **Carrot.** | | |
| G 2830 Guerande or Ox Heart | 35 | |
| G 2831 Chanteney (Best for Bunching) | 35 | |
| G 2832 Danvers | 35 | |
| G 2833 Improved Long Orange | 32 | |
| **Cabbage.** | lb. | 4 oz. |
| G 2840 Extra Eearly Express | $ 0 75 | $0 25 |
| G 2841 Early Jersey Wakefield Select | 1 45 | 50 |
| G 2842 Henderson's Early Summer Select | 1 10 | 35 |
| G 2843 S., R. & Co.'s Faultless | 2 10 | 65 |
| G 2844 S., R. & Co.'s Bridgeport Drumhead | 2 95 | 90 |
| G 2845 Premium Flat Dutch | 1 05 | 32 |
| G 2846 Large Late Drumhead | 85 | 25 |
| G 2850 Mammoth Rock | 1 25 | 40 |
| G 2851 Early Dwarf Flat Dutch | 1 05 | 32 |
| Our strains of Cabbage Seeds are very popular with market gardeners in all sections. | | |
| **Collards.** | | |
| G 2853 Georgia | 55 | 18 |
| **Cress.** | | |
| G 2854 Extra Curled | 25 | |
| G 2855 True Water | 2 45 | 80 |
| **Chicory.** | | |
| G 2856 Large Rooted | 50 | |
| **Cauliflower.** | | oz |
| G 2857 Henderson's Snowball | | 3 50 |
| G 2858 Leonard's Earliest Erfurt | | 2 95 |
| G 2859 Early Snowball | | 1 45 |
| G 2860 Autumn | | 50 |
| **Delery.** | | 4 oz |
| G 2864 New Golden Self-Blanching | 2 65 | 80 |
| G 2865 Giant Golden Heart | 1 35 | 40 |
| G 2866 Dwarf White Kalamazoo | 1 05 | 30 |
| G 2867 White Plume | 1 45 | 45 |
| G 2868 New Giant Pascal | 1 20 | 35 |
| **Corn—Sweet.** | bu. | |
| G 2870 Cory | 1 75 | |
| G 2871 Crosby's Early | 2 10 | |
| G 2872 Shoe Peg | 2 10 | |
| G 2875 Stowell's Evergreen—True Stock. | 1 90 | |
| **Corn—Pop.** | lb. | |
| G 2880 Monarch White Rice | $ 0 05 | |
| G 2881 Pearl | 05 | |
| G 2882 Red Rice | 05 | |
| **Cucumber.** | | 4 oz |
| G 2886 Evergreen White Spine | 30 | $ 09 |
| G 2887 Westerfield's Imp. Chicago Pickle | 30 | 09 |
| G 2888 Parisian Pickle | 1 20 | 40 |
| G 2889 Improved Long Green | 30 | 09 |
| **Egg Plant.** | | oz |
| G 2890 S., R. & Co.'s Improved New York Purple Spineless | 2 95 | 35 |
| G 2891 Early Long Purple | 1 70 | 18 |
| **Herbs.** | | oz |
| G 2900 Anise | 65 | 06 |
| G 2901 Balm | 2 10 | 18 |
| G 2902 Basil | 95 | 08 |
| **Herbss—Continued.** | lb. | oz. |
| G 2903 Borage | 1 40 | 10 |
| G 2904 Caraway | 50 | 04 |
| G 2905 Coriander | 60 | 06 |
| G 2906 Dill—Mammoth | 95 | 08 |
| G 2908 Fennel | 65 | 06 |
| G 2909 Horehound | 1 75 | 14 |
| G 2910 Hyssop | 2 10 | 18 |
| G 2911 Lavender | 95 | 08 |
| G 2912 Sweet Marjoram | 95 | 08 |
| G 2913 Rosemary | 2 30 | 20 |
| G 2914 Rue | 95 | 08 |
| G 2915 Sage—Broad Leaved | 2 20 | 20 |
| G 2916 Saffron | 95 | 08 |
| G 2917 Summer Savory | 60 | 05 |
| G 2918 Thyme | 1 45 | 10 |
| **Leek.** | Lb. | 4 oz. |
| G 2935 London Flag | 85 | 25 |
| G 2936 Large Musselburg | 1 05 | 30 |
| **Lettuce.** | | |
| G 2940 Tilton's White Star | 65 | 20 |
| G 2941 Grand Rapids (forcing) | 65 | 20 |
| G 2942 Early Curled Simpson, black seed | 65 | 20 |
| G 2944 Salamander | 60 | 20 |
| G 2945 St. Louis Head | 60 | 20 |
| G 2946 Denver Market | 60 | 20 |
| G 2947 Early Prize Head | 60 | 20 |
| **Mustard.** | | |
| G 2950 White | 18 | |
| G 2951 Southern Giant Curled | 40 | 15 |
| **Melon—Musk.** | | |
| G 2960 Banquet | 50 | 20 |
| G 2961 New Orleans or Creole | 32 | 10 |
| G 2963 New Early Hackensack | 32 | 10 |
| G 2964 Chicago Market Nutmeg | 32 | 10 |
| G 2967 Shumway's Giant | 45 | 15 |
| **Melon—Water.** | Lb. | 4 oz. |
| G 2970 Dixie, new and very good | $0 25 | $0 08 |
| G 2971 Light Icing | 25 | 08 |
| G 2972 Jumbo | 25 | 08 |
| G 2973 Phinney's Early | 25 | 08 |
| G 2974 The Boss | 25 | 08 |
| **Okra.** | | |
| G 2983 Dwarf Green, Improved | 30 | |
| G 2984 Long Green | 30 | |
| **Parsley.** | | |
| G 2986 Double Curled | 32 | 10 |
| G 2987 Champion Moss Curled | 32 | 10 |
| **Pepper.** | | |
| G 2988 Large Bell or Bull Nose | 1 30 | 40 |
| G 2989 Sweet Mountain | 1 30 | 40 |
| G 2990 Ruby King | 1 45 | 45 |
| **Parsnip.** | | |
| G 2991 Guernsey Improved | 18 | |
| G 2992 Hollow Crown | 18 | |
| G 2993 Market Gardner's—Very Select | 35 | |
| **Pumpkin.** | | |
| G 2995 S., R. & Co. Mammoth Prize | 48 | |
| G 2996 Tennessee Sweet Potatoe | 50 | |
| G 2997 Large Cheese | 35 | |
| G 2998 Connecticut Field—Large Yellow | 16 | |

## Onion Seed.

Upon no other crop does the quality of the seed have a greater influence than upon onions. Special care should be exercised by all dealers to obtain pure stock.

**Sears, Roebuck & Co. Onion Seed** is indorsed by market gardeners everywhere. Each succeeding year adds to its popularity with them. This is the surest indication of merit.

| | Lb. | 4 oz. |
|---|---|---|
| G 3000 Extra Early Flat Red | $1 25 | $0 40 |
| G 3001 Yellow Danvers Flat | 75 | 25 |
| G 3002 S., R. & Co. Yellow Globe | 1 55 | 45 |
| G 3003 Yellow Dutch, or Strasburg | 90 | 30 |
| G 3004 White Portugal (American Silver Skin) | 1 95 | 60 |
| G 3005 Early White Queen | 1 05 | 30 |
| G 3006 Mammoth Silver King | 1 00 | 30 |
| G 3007 Red Bermuda | 1 55 | 45 |
| **Radish.** | lb. | 4 oz. |
| G 3010 Leonard's Three Leaf | 40 | 13 |
| G 3011 Early Deep Scarlet Turnip Forcing | 40 | 13 |
| G 3012 Scarlet Turnip, White Tip Forcing | 40 | 13 |
| G 3015 French Breakfast | 30 | 10 |
| G 3016 California Mammoth White Improved | 42 | 14 |
| **Rhubarb.** | | |
| G 3021 Victoria | 95 | 30 |
| G 3022 Linnæus | 1 00 | 30 |
| **Spinach.** | | |
| G 3025 Extra Large Round Leaf | 15 | |
| G 3026 Savoy Leaved | 18 | |
| G 3027 Long Standing | 18 | |
| **Squash.** | | |
| G 3030 S. R. & Co. Improved Giant Summer Crookneck | 50 | 15 |
| G 3032 Summer Crookneck | 40 | 13 |
| G 3033 Colvin's Orange Marrow | 40 | 13 |
| G 3034 Hubbard | 40 | 13 |
| **Tobacco.** | | |
| G 3040 Connetticut Seed Leaf | 1 35 | 40 |
| G 3041 Havana | 2 95 | 90 |
| G 3042 White Burley | 1 75 | 50 |
| **Tomato.** | | |
| G 3050 Ponderosa | 2 35 | 70 |
| G 3051 Atlantic Prize | 1 50 | 45 |
| G 3052 Royal Red | 1 50 | 45 |
| G 3053 Early Optimus | 1 40 | 40 |
| G 3054 Dwarf Champion | 1 40 | 40 |
| G 3055 Livingston's Beauty | 1 40 | 40 |
| G 3057 Early Ruby | 1 40 | 40 |
| **Turnip.** | | |
| G 3060 Extra Early Milan Strap Leaf | 85 | 25 |
| G 3061 Purple Top Strap Leaf | 35 | 12 |
| G 3062 Early Snowball | 30 | 10 |
| G 3066 Sweet German | 30 | 10 |
| G 3067 Large White Norfolk | 25 | 08 |

## Lawn Grass Seed.

| | Lb. pkg. | Bu. |
|---|---|---|
| G 3075 Our Celebrated Lawn Grass Seed has won a wide reputation. Our old customers will buy no others. Try a pound or more. Include it with your freight order. Get your neighbors to club with you for a bushel. We send full directions for beautifying yards and lawns. 14 lbs. to the bushel | $0 20 | $2 30 |

## Timothy Seed.

The prices are subject to market changes. We quote only clean seeds of the very choicest grades in the market.

| | Bushel. |
|---|---|
| G 3080 Fancy Timothy Seed | $4 50 |
| G 3081 Choice Timothy Seed | 4 00 |
| G 3082 Fair Timothy Seed | 3 50 |

## Clover Seeds.

Prices subject to market fluctuations.

| | |
|---|---|
| G 3086 Choice Red Clover Seed | 8 00 |
| G 3087 Prime Red Clover Seed | 7 50 |
| G 3088 Flax Seed, 56-lb. to bushel | 1 75 |
| G 3089 Hungarian Grass Seed....... per 100-lbs., | 1 75 |
| G 3090 Millet ....... per 100-lbs., | 1 50 |
| G 3091 Buckwheat ....... per bushel, | 1 50 |

## Great Sale of Garden Seeds.

**Take your choice, 13 regular 5 cent packages for 25 cents.** Sell 5 packages to your neighbors, and the balance will **cost you nothing.** Not fewer than 13 packages sold; make your selection.

G 3095 **Flat Five Cent Papers Vegetable Seeds.** Beet—Eclipse, Early Blood Turnip; Cabbage—Early Dwarf Flat Dutch, Large Late Drumhead; Carrot—Early Red Half Long Stump Root, Early Scarlet Short Horn; Cauliflower—Snowball; Celeriac—Turnip Rooted Celery; Celery—White, Solid; Cucumber—Early Frame, Improved Long Green, Early Short Green; Herbs—Sweet Majoram, Sage, Summer Savory, Summer Thyme; Kohl Rabi—Early White; Leek—American Flag; Lettuce—Early Curled Simpson, Prize Head; Musk Melon—Round Yellow Canteloupe, Green Nutmeg; Water Melon—Phinney's Early, Kolb's Gem; Onion—Large Red Wethersfield, Yellow Globe Danvers; Parsley—Double Curled; Parsnip—Long white Sugar; Pepper—Long Red Cayenne; Pumpkin—Sugar; Radish—Early Scarlet Turnip, French Breakfast, Chinese Rose, Winter; Salsify—Long White; Spinach—Bloomsdale; Squash—Hubbard; Turnip—Early White Dutch, Purple Top White Globe; Rutabaga—Skirving's Purple Top; Tomato—Acme, Livingston's Favorite, Red Trophy (selected), Paragon.

## Great Sale of Choice Flower Seeds

**You can make money** by buying an ounce of these flower seeds and supplying your neighbors. You not only save 50 per cent. but you will get such quality and desirable varieties as you never saw in a retail store.

Always include such seeds as you need in your freight order. Make your selections, and always give **name and quantities wanted.**

**No. G 3100.—**

| | Per ½ oz. |
|---|---|
| Adonis—Autumnalis | $ 0 06 |
| Ageratum—Mexicanum | 09 |
| Alyssum—Sweet | 09 |
| Antirrhinum—Mixed | 12 |
| Asters—Victoria Red | 60 |
| Asters—Victoria White | 60 |
| Asters—Victoria Pink | 60 |
| Asters—Victoria Blue | 60 |
| Bachelors' Button—Mixed Corn Flower. | 06 |
| Balsam—Double Mixed | 17 |
| Calliopsis—Mixed | 06 |
| Candytuft—Mixed | 06 |
| Canna—Mixed | 06 |
| Carnation—Double Dwarf Vienna | 60 |
| Margaret | 80 |
| Castor Beans—Mixed | 06 |
| Chrysanthemum—Coronarium Mixed | 06 |
| Cypress Vine—Mixed | 09 |
| Dahlia—Double Mixed | 60 |
| Daisy—Double Mixed, Very Fine | 1 35 |
| Forget Me Not | 28 |
| Four O'Clocks—Mixed | 06 |
| Gourds—Pear-Shaped | 09 |
| Gourds—White Egg | 06 |
| Gourds—Dipper | 06 |
| Hollyhock—Very Double Fine Mixed | 35 |
| Love In A Mist—Double Mixed | 06 |
| Marigold—African double | 09 |
| Mignonette—Sweet | 06 |
| Morning Glory—Mixed | 06 |
| Mourning Bride—Double Dwarf Mixed | 06 |
| Nasturtium—Tall Mixed | 06 |
| Nasturtium—Dwarf Mixed | 06 |
| Pansy—Fine Mixed | 30 |
| Petunia—Extra Fine Mixed | 17 |
| Phlox Drummondii—Mixed, | 14 |
| Pink—China Double Mixed | 12 |
| Poppy—Carnation Double Mixed | 06 |
| Portulacca—Single Large Flowered Mixed | 12 |
| Sweet Peas—Emily Henderson | 06 |
| Sweet Peas—American Belle | 06 |
| Sweet Peas—Cardinal | 06 |
| Sweet Peas—Light Blue and Purple | 06 |
| Sweet Peas—Choice Mixed | 06 |
| Sweet William—Mixed | 06 |
| Verbena—Mixed | 23 |
| Zinna—Double Mixed | 09 |

**JUSTICE COMPELS US TO ADMIT THAT IF OUR COMPETITORS COULD MEET US ON PRICES, THEY WOULD BE GLAD TO DO SO. BUT THEY CAN'T, AND THERE'S AN END O' IT.**

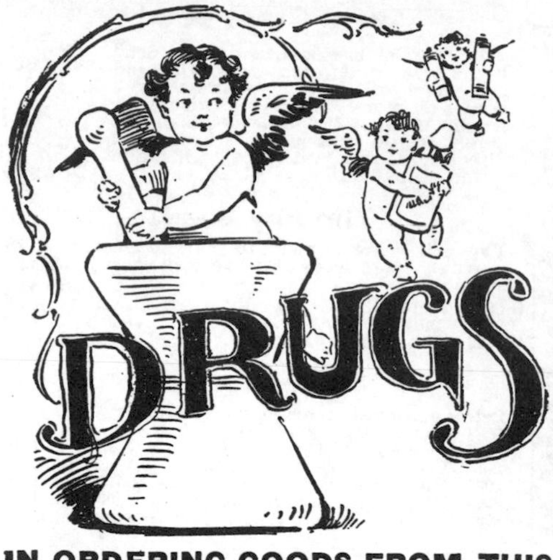


# DRUG DEPARTMENT.

**THIS SPECIAL BRANCH** of our business is in charge of competent chemists and registered pharmacists who have had large experience both in this country and Europe in handling and compounding **DRUGS AND CHEMICALS. THEY HAVE STRICT INSTRUCTIONS TO EXAMINE THOROUGHLY** every article received in this department, to note its **QUALITY AND FRESHNESS**, to apply tests to ascertain its **STRENGTH AND PURITY**, and to reject everything which does not come up to **THE FULL STANDARD REQUIRED BY THE DRUG INSPECTORS OF THE UNITED STATES GOVERNMENT.**

**WE ARE IN A POSITION** and will be pleased to **ANSWER ANY INQUIRIES** concerning Drugs, Patent Medicines, etc., etc., either as regards their appearance, medicinal properties, or special purposes they are used for. **THIS INFORMATION** we will give to our customers **FREE** and it is valuable on account of the long and varied experience of our staff of Chemists and Pharmacists.

**THE PRICES** will be on the same footing as in our other branches—**THE LOWEST THAT IT IS POSSIBLE** to sell these goods and make only our usual small profit. We think this is a much better plan than putting the prices up to the highest figure that we might think the public would stand, as is done by many who engage in this line of business. **WE ARE SURE OUR PLAN** will be appreciated by the intelligent class of consumers. It is no crime to **SAVE MONEY**, but it is criminal to foolishly throw it away.

**IN ORDERING GOODS FROM THIS DEPARTMENT WE MUST REQUEST YOU TO SEND CASH TO THE FULL AMOUNT. WE WILL NOT SEND C, O. D.** All prices in this list are **NET—NO DISCOUNT.** Four ounce bottles of liquids and smaller sizes can be sent by mail if packed in a special box approved by the postal authorities. You must remember to allow us 10 or 18 cents, according to size, for these mailing boxes. Poisons, inflammable or explosive materials cannot be mailed.

## Special Medicines.

The following special medicines, patented by Sears, Roebuck & Co., are compounded by our chemists from the prescriptions of celebrated physicians, who have made specialties of the diseases to which each medicine refers to. They have been before the public for a number of years, and have given great satisfaction to everyone who has tried them. Each one is a reliable medicine skillfully compounded from the freshest and purest materials; for merit and curative properties they cannot be excelled. We guarantee each to accomplish all that we claim for them.

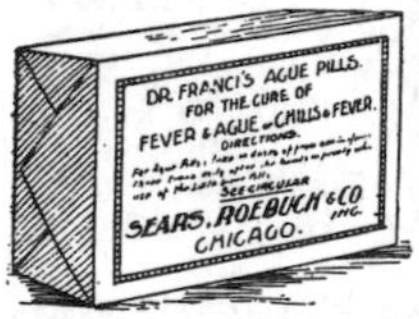


**D 100 Ague Pills.** For the cure of chills and fever. We were very fortunate to obtain the recipe for these pills from a physician who had used it constantly and successfully in his practice for thirty years in the West and South. They are an infallible remedy for this disease so very common in certain parts of our States, and never fail to stop its progress, and always effect a cure when the use of them is continued.
Price, per box, **50c**; per dozen.......... **$5.00**

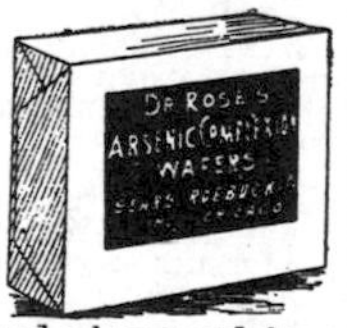


**D 102 Arsenic Complexion Wafers.** These wafers are from the prescription of a famous French physician, and are perfectly harmless when used according to the directions on each box. They are an excellent remedy for rough and discolored skin. They clear the complexion and make the skin soft and smooth. They tone up the whole system and when used for a length of time will make thin persons plump and keep them so.
Small box, **40c**; per dozen.......... **$4.25**
Large " **79c**; " .......... **8.00**

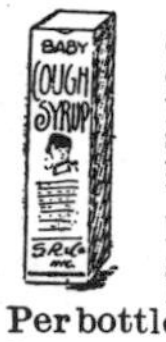


**D 104 Baby Cough Syrup.** This is an old-fashioned Mothers' remedy carefully compounded specially for the baby. It is pleasant to take and will give the little sufferers quick relief and cure whenever they have Coughs, Colds, Hoarseness, Whooping Cough, etc. It is perfectly harmless. No mother need be afraid to give it to her children. Full directions how to give it on every bottle.
Per bottle, **20c**; per dozen.......... **$2.25**

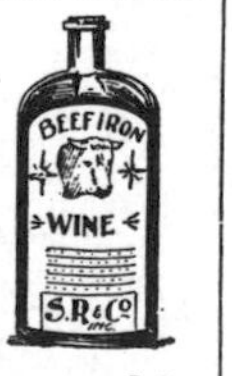


**D 106 Beef, Wine and Iron.** This is an old time tonic. Universally known for its great strength giving and flesh producing qualities. The great trouble with most of the Beef, Wine and Iron found in the market is the poor quality of materials used in making it. It is often found in a state quite unfit for use on that account. We take special pains with this preparation using only the finest imported sherry wine, fresh made extract of beef and pure salts of iron in a form specially prepared for the blood. This is one of the finest preparations to build up the system, and make blood; it will bring color to the cheeks and strength to the muscles.
Pint bottle, **35c**; per dozen.......... **$4.00**

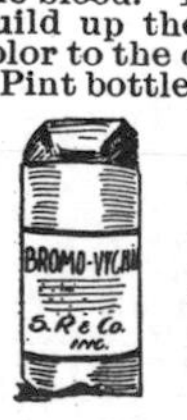


**D 108 Bromo Vichy.** This is a speedy and excellent remedy for Nervous Headaches, Neuralgia, Sleeplessness, Over Brain Work, Depression following alcoholic excesses and all nervous troubles. A fine bracer in the morning. Full directions on the bottle. Makes a pleasant drink when thirsty.
Small size, **8c**; large.......... **20c.**

**D 110 Blackberry Brandy.** A delicious cordial expressly bottled for medical use. It has been found so beneficial and efficacious to stomach and bowel complaints that the U. S. Gov't allows it to be sold without a license.
Pints, per bottle, **35c**; case of 2 dozen...... **$5.75**
Quarts, " **50c**; " 1 " ...... **5.25**

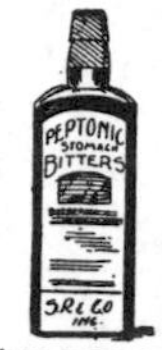


**D 112 Bitters. Peptonic Stomach Bitters.** Put up in large bottles holding 1½ pints. This is a very agreeable, pleasant Bitters to take. It is compounded from seventeen different roots and herbs in such a manner that the greatest beneficial effects are obtained from them. It is an excellent appetizer and sure cure for dyspepsia when its use is continued. A general bracer up of the whole system. A wineglassful taken before meals will give you an appetite and a satisfied feeling and enable you to enjoy what you eat and digest it well.
Large bottle, **78c**; per doz.......... **$8.50**

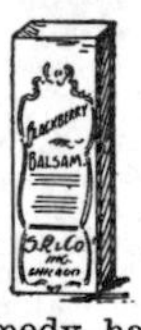


**D 114 Blackberry Balsam.** This is a remedy which should be kept in every family in readiness for sudden attacks of bowel troubles and especially so in times of prevailing cholera. It cannot be excelled in curing all relax conditions of the bowels. It is cleansing, regulating, quieting and healing.
Bottle **20c.**, per doz.......... **$2.00**

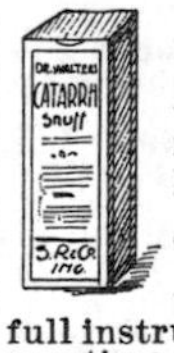


**D 116 Catarrh Snuff.** This remedy has been used for the past 20 years by a physician who is a specialist on diseases of the throat and nose, we guarantee it to give immediate relief in all ordinary cases of nasal catarrh, hay fever, cold in the head. Everyone who is subject to this distressing complaint ought always to carry with them a bottle of this remedy. We enclose a Perfect Powder Blower in each package with full instructions how to use it and can be used at any time without inconvenience.
Complete with blower, **20c**; per dozen...... **$2.25**

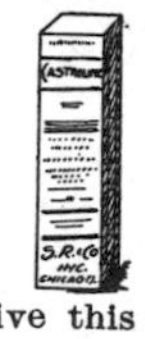

**D 118 Castroline.** This is a perfect substitute for castor oil, especially adapted for infants and children who take it readily. It is perfectly harmless, being a vegetable compound. It will cure constipation in children, regulate the bowels and expel worms, and correct all stomach trouble with which they are generally much troubled, and which causes sleeplessness, loss of appetite, fevers etc. We would ask mothers to give this a trial, they will find it a blessing.
Bottle **20c**; per doz.......... **$2.25**

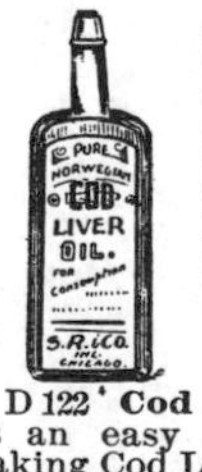


**D 120 Cod Liver Oil.** This oil we import from Norway at certain seasons of the year and can therefore guarantee its freshness and purity. It is carefully selected for us from the first pressings of the livers of the Norwegian cod. It has a pleasant bland taste, and is an invaluable medicine to those who have weak lungs, and are subject to coughs, colds etc.
Pint bottle **50c**; per doz.......... **$5.50**

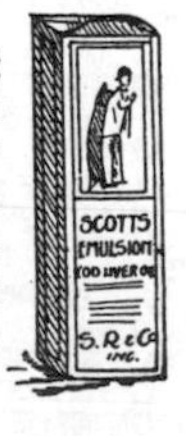


**D 122 Cod Liver Oil Emulsion.** This is an easy and pleasant method of taking Cod Liver Oil for those who cannot digest the raw oil. It tastes like flavored cream. It will strengthen the lungs, make flesh and blood. A thin weak person will get stout and strong by continued use, and need never fear of catching cold or having lung trouble, if a little is used every day. Full directions on the bottle.
Bottle, **60c**; dozen.......... **$5.50**

**D 124 Cure to Stop the Drinking Habit.** We guarantee this to cure anyone of the habit of drinking alcoholic stimuulants. It is the greatest temperance worker the world has ever known. It creates a desire for food instead of drink. It stops the craving for liquor instantly and stimulates the entire system to healthy action. It quiets nervous excitement, improves the appetite and regulates digestion, regulates the bowels, repairs the waste caused by over indulgence in liquor and makes one feel like a new man again. We will give special prices to any temperance society who would wish to give it a trial and test its merits. Treat yourself at home and become a new man.
Box containing 24 doses, **50c**; doz.......... **$5.00**
Box containing 48 doses, **$1.00**; doz.......... **$9.00**

**D 126 Cough Syrup.** This is a preparation we can honestly recommend to anyone suffering from a cold, cough, sore throat, or any trouble of the lungs, throat or bronchial tubes. It will give relief from a distressing cough from the first dose taken, and will cure one of long standing when persevered in. Full directions with each bottle.
Price per large bottle, **30c**; doz.......... **$3.00**

**D 128 Corn, Bunion and Wart Remover.** This is a very effective remedy for these troublesome and very painful afflictions. It will give instant relief and effect a permanent cure. We have tried it ourselves, therefore we can testify knowingly to its great merits.
Each, **9c**: doz.......... **$0.90**

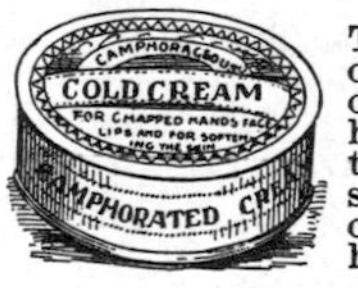


**D 130 Camphor Cold Cream.** This is a very healing salve and of great value when the skin is chapped from cold, especially the hands and lips. It will heal up the crack and render the skin smooth again. Also a fine application to burns, soothing and healing.
Per pot, **15c**; doz.......... **$1.50**

**D 131 Carbo Wafers.** These wafers are a true specific for sour stomach, heartburn, distress after eating. One or two taken immediately after eating never fail to give relief.
Box, **25c**; doz.......... **$2.50**

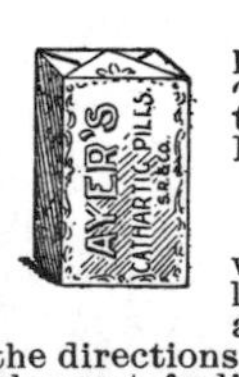


**D 132 Cathartic Pills.** This is a pleasant purgative pill having thorough action on the liver and moving the bowels gently without griping. Full directions on each box.
Box **10c.**; doz.......... **75c.**

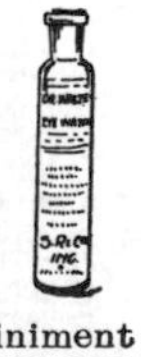

**D 134 Eye Water.** This water is prepared by an oculist especially for inflamed and sore eyes; by following the directions on the bottle, a soothing and pleasant feeling will result and the eyes will be restored to health. Will not harm the youngest child.
Bottle **15c.**; doz.......... **$1.40**

**D 136 Electricating Liniment.** This liniment ought to be in every household for emergency cases. It is a valuable remedy for sprains, bruises, stiff joints, swellings. It has a wonderful soothing effect and is very penetrating.
Large bottle, **29c**; doz.......... **$3.00**

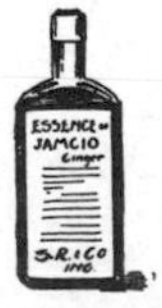

**D 138 Essence of Jamaica Ginger.** This is a strong essence prepared from selected Jamaica Ginger Root, it contains all the stimulating warming and healing properties of good ginger and will be found very valuable in stomach and bowel troubles.
This size usually sold poor in quality at **25c.** Our price full strength **18c.**
Regular **50c** size; our price, **36c.**

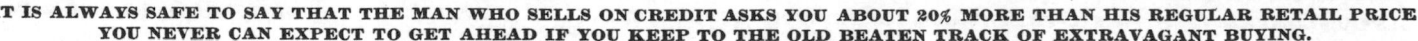

**IT IS ALWAYS SAFE TO SAY THAT THE MAN WHO SELLS ON CREDIT ASKS YOU ABOUT 20% MORE THAN HIS REGULAR RETAIL PRICE**
**YOU NEVER CAN EXPECT TO GET AHEAD IF YOU KEEP TO THE OLD BEATEN TRACK OF EXTRAVAGANT BUYING.**

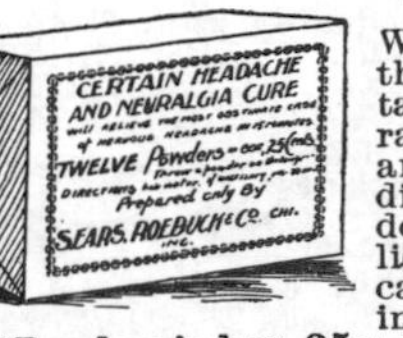


D 140 **Headache Cure.** We can highly recommend this preparation as a Certain Headache and Neuralgia Cure. Headaches are very common and very distressing. One or two doses of this cure will relieve the most obstinate case of Nervous Headache in ten minutes.
12 Powders in box, **25c**; Per doz. boxes....... **$2.25**

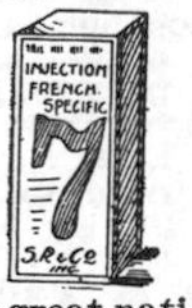


D 142 **Injection No. 7.** This is a French Specific for trouble of the Urinary Organs in either male or female, has a very quick effect and leaves no bad results from its use. Will cure Gonorrhea or Gleet in from 1 to 5 days. Full instructions and useful information with each bottle.
Price **79c**; Doz.................. **$8.00**

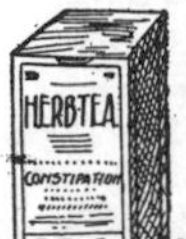


D 144 **Herb Tea.** This is the great national German regulator for all disorders of the system. A positive cure for constipation and also for dyspepsia. Easy to prepare and pleasant to take.
Small box, **20c**; Doz............ **$2.25**
Large box, **40c**; Doz.............. **$4.50**

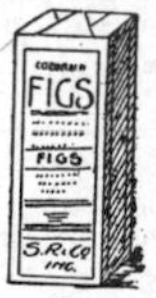


D 146 **Fig Laxative.** This very agreeable preparation is prepared from California fruits. It cannot be equaled as a system renovator and a most effective remedy in constipation. It is especially valuable to ladies and children and they enjoy taking it, it is so pleasant.
Bottle, **29c**,; Doz.................. **$3.00**

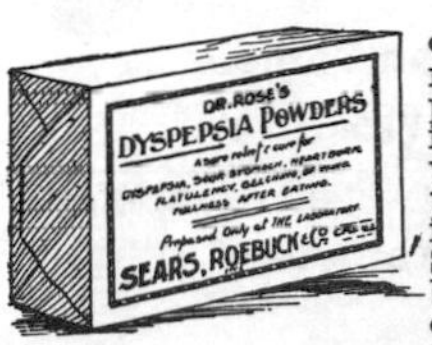


D 148 **Dyspepsia Powders.** This is a remedy of remarkable efficacy in Dyspepsia. One powder taken immediately after a meal will prevent many of the troubles brought on by an irritable and weak stomach. Such as sour stomach, heartburn, indigestion, belching of wind. If used for a few weeks all stomach distress will disappear as if by magic and eating will be a pleasure. Full directions on each box.
12 powders in a box, **40c**. Doz. boxes......... **$4.00**

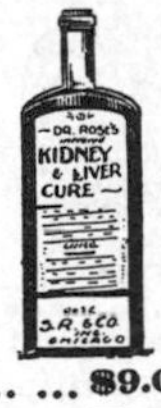


D 150 **Kidney and Liver Cure.** This is a scientific preparation of vegetable ingredients, highly esteemed for its soothing and healing qualities in all diseases of the Kidneys, Liver and Bladder. It is one of the recognized remedies for Brights Disease and has performed some remarkable cures. It is very valuable in female complaints of the urinary organs, change of life, irregularities, prolapsus, etc. Full directions accompany each bottle.
Pint bottle, **85c.**; per doz............... **$9.00**

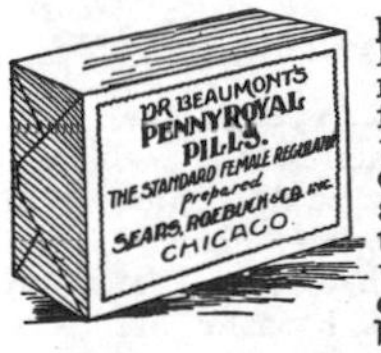


D 152 **Female Pills.** These pills are a combination of Pennyroyal, Tansy, Cottonroot Bark in a concentrated form, with other ingredients which increase the peculiar effect of these medicines. They are very powerful and require to be used cautiously, but if the very complete directions which can be found separately in each box, will be followed closely, all will be well.
Full treatment in each box. Per box, **85c.**; per doz. boxes.................. **$8.50**
With useful information and instructions to ladies concerning their troubles.

D 154 **Little Liver Pills.** This is a very small pill, easily swallowed even by children. It acts specially on the Liver, regulating the flow of the bile and causing the bowels to act in a regular manner. It is especially a good pill for any one inclined to biliousness, and a sure cure for headaches and stomach troubles arising from too much bile in the stomach.

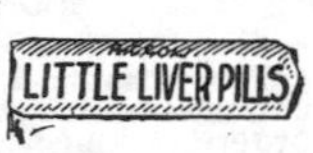


Per bottle, **12c**. Per doz. bottles... **$1.00**

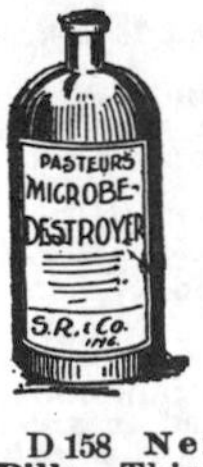


D 156 **Microbe Killer.** This is Dr. Pasteur's Microbe Killer, which, if taken once or twice a day, will prevent La Grippe, Catarrh, Consumption, Malaria, Blood Poison, Rheumatism and all disorders of the blood. It acts as an antiseptic, killing the germs which are the cause of these diseases. This preparation of Dr. Pasteur's will eradicate any form of disease and purify the whole system.
½ gallon bottles, each, **97c.**; per doz...... **$11.50**

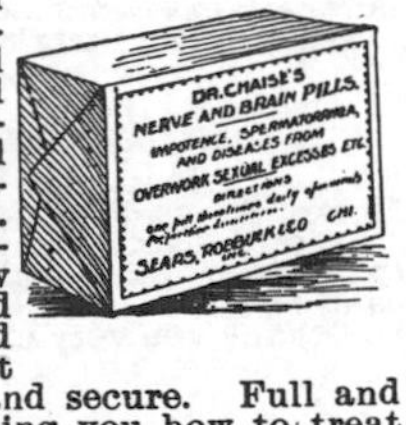


D 158 **Nerve and Brain Pills.** This pill has a remarkable effect on both old and young. It cannot be equaled by any others as a cure for Impotence, Spermatorrhœa and all diseases arising from excesses and abuses of any kind. It will tone up the whole nervous system, no matter how much worn out, overworked and depressed you may be, and give you a new lease of life. It can be sent by mail, private and secure. Full and very explicit directions telling you how to treat yourself to get thoroughly well and strong again.
Per box, **88c**. Doz. boxes..... **$9.00**

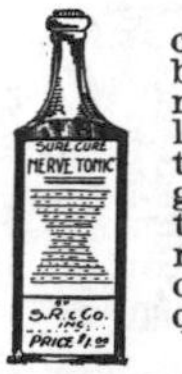


D 160 **Nerve Tonic.** This is a sure cure Nerve Tonic and Stimulant with blood purifying properties. There are many on the market most of them worthless. This has our guarantee to be all that we claim for it. It is valuable in general nervous debility, strengthening the nerves, invigorating the brain and restoring the health. A few doses will convince anyone using it of its sterling qualities.
Large bottles, **60c**; Doz.......... **$7.00**

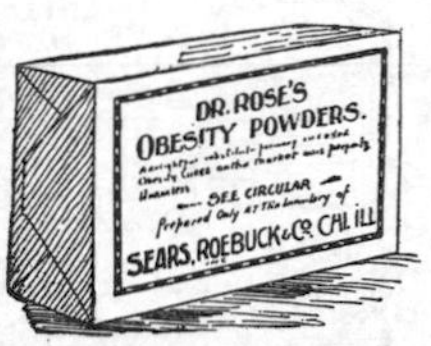


D 162. **S., R. & Co.'s Obesity Powders.** If any one wishes to get rid of superfluous fat without injury to their general health this is the remedy to take. Full directions how to take the powders, what to eat and drink and exercise accompany each box.
Price, **88c**; Doz ..... **$9.00**

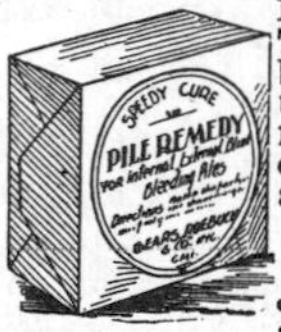


D 164 **Pile Remedy.** This is a guaranteed cure for blind, bleeding or itching Piles. If you have tried other remedies without getting relief, we advise you to send for a box of this. It never fails to give relief and a cure.
Box, **25c**. Doz. boxes......... **$2.00**

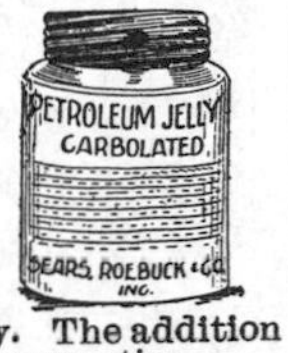


D 166 **Petroleum Jelly.** This is another name for the preparations called Vaseline, Cosmoline, etc., all made from Petroleum. It is excellent for healing cuts, bruises, burns, etc.
Plain, 2 oz. bottles, **6c**; Doz... **50c**
One lb cans........ **20c**; Doz **$2.00**

D 168 **Carbolized Petroleum Jelly.** The addition of carbolic acid increases its healing properties.
2 oz. bottles, **15c**; Doz.......................... **$1.50**

D 170 **Perfumed Petroleum Jelly.** This can be used as a dressing for the hair.
2 oz. bottles, **15c**; Doz.......................... **$1.50**

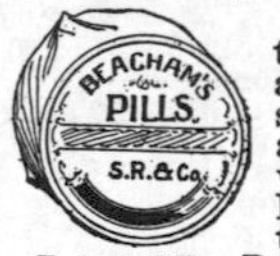


D 172 **Pink Pills for Pale People,** the great blood builder. Cures pale and sallow complexions. Suppression of the Periods. Rheumatism and all diseases arising from mental worry, overwork, early decay, etc. Full directions on circular around the box.
Price, **25c** Doz. boxes.......................... **$2.00**

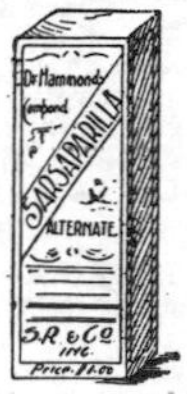


D 174 **Sarsaparilla.** This combines in an agreeable form the medicinal properties of the most approved blood purifying remedies of the vegetable kingdom. It is undoubtedly the best Blood Purifier in the market, and the best value for the money. Try a bottle when you feel out of sorts. We are sure you will recommend it to your friends.
Large bottle, **59c**; Doz......... **$6.00**

D 176 **Toothache Wax.** Will cure the worst case of toothache in one minute. All ready to use. No cotton to look for, only to pick a piece out of the bottle and apply it to the tooth.
Single bottle, **10c**. Doz. bottles.............. **90c**

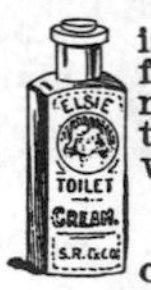


D 178 **Witch Hazel Toilet Cream.** This is an elegant preparation for chapped hands, face, lips and all roughness of the skin. It makes the skin soft and velvety and protects it from chapping or getting rough when exposed to cold weather.
4 oz. bottles, **20c**; Doz.... **$2.00**

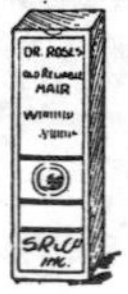


D 180 **Rheumatic Cure.** One of the blessings of the age. A positive cure for Rheumatism, Sciatica, Lumbago. Try a bottle and get relief.
Each, **70c**; Doz.................. **$7.50**

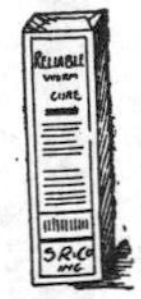


D 182 **Worm Syrup.** This is a reliable preparation for expelling worms from children. It is pleasant to take and does not require any medicine to be given afterwards to move the bowels.
Bottle, **20c**; Doz.................. **$2.25**

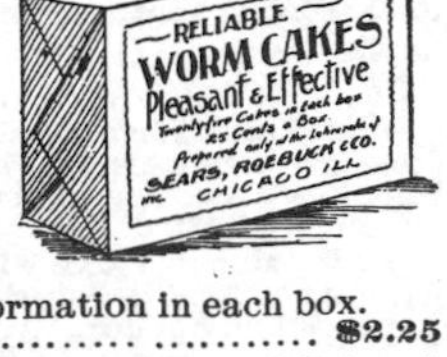


D 184 **Worm Cakes.** This is a very satisfactory remedy for destroying worms and removing them from the system. It is in convenient form for children to take, which they readily do, thinking it is a candy. Full instructions how to give them, and other useful information in each box.
Price **20c**; Doz.......................... **$2.25**

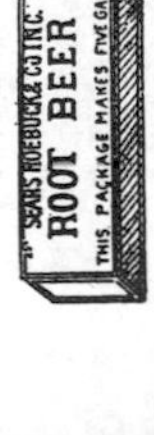


D 186 **Root Beer.** A healthy and delicious beverage. One bottle makes 5 gallons of not only a **healthy temperance beverage** but one of the most pleasant and invigorating that can be found for the warm weather, producing a gentle stimulation throughout the entire body without any deleterious effects. It is also a blood purifier, easily prepared and costs very little.
Per bottle, **12c**; Doz......... **$1.25**

## SPECIAL FAMILY REMEDIES.

The following few well known household remedies and other useful articles are carefully put up in our own laboratory, in a convenient form expressly for family use. We guarantee their strength, freshness and purity. Each and every one of them is a necessary article in every house, for when they are wanted they are wanted **quick.** When they are in reach they often save severe pain, avert sickness and sometimes save life, and the expense of having them is very small when purchased from us. Study the list well.

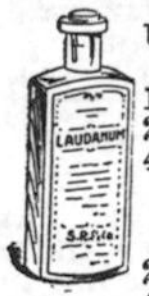
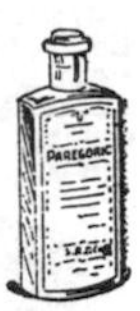

D 188 **Laudanum (Tinct. Opium) U. S. P. Strength.**

| | Each. | Doz. |
|---|---|---|
| 1 oz. bottle | $0 10 | $1 00 |
| 2 oz. bottle | 18 | 2 00 |
| 4 oz. bottle | 29 | 3 00 |

D 190 **Paregoric.**

| | Each. | Doz. |
|---|---|---|
| 2 oz. bottle | $0 12 | $1 25 |
| 4 oz. bottle | 18 | 1 75 |

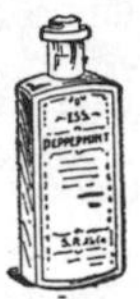
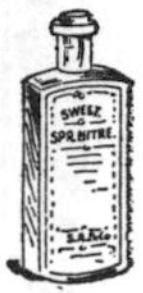

D 192 **Ess. Peppermint.**

| | Each. | Doz. |
|---|---|---|
| 2 oz. bottle | $0 13 | $1 30 |
| 4 oz. bottle | 20 | 2 00 |

D 194 **Sweet Spirits of Nitre.**

| | Each. | Doz. |
|---|---|---|
| 2 oz. bottle | $0 13 | $1 30 |
| 4 oz. bottle | 20 | 2 00 |

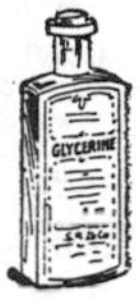

D 196 **Glycerine.** Absolutely pure.

| | Each. | Doz. |
|---|---|---|
| 2 oz. bottles | $0 10 | $1 00 |
| 4 oz. bottles | 15 | 1 50 |
| ½ lb. bottles | 20 | 2 00 |
| 1 lb. bottles | 35 | 3 25 |

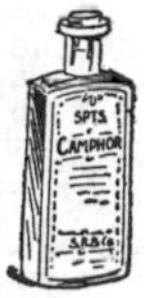

D 198 **Spirits of Camphor.** In 4 oz. bottles, guaranteed to be strong and pure ...... 18 1 75

D 200 **Tincture of Arnica.** Made according to U. S. P. strength.

| | Each. | Doz. |
|---|---|---|
| ¼ pint | $0 16 | $1 90 |
| ½ pint | 25 | 2 75 |
| 1 gallon | 3 00 | |

D 202 **Essence Jamaica Ginger.** Extra strength and quality

| | | |
|---|---|---|
| 2 oz. bottle | 15 | 1 50 |
| 4 oz. bottle | 25 | 2 50 |

D 204 **Extract Lemon Peel.** Fine flavor.

| | | |
|---|---|---|
| 2 oz bottles | 15 | 1 50 |
| 4 oz bottles | 25 | 2 50 |

D 206 **Extract of Vanilla.** Extra strength and purity

| | | |
|---|---|---|
| 2 oz. bottles | 18 | 2 15 |
| 4 oz. bottles | 32 | 4 00 |

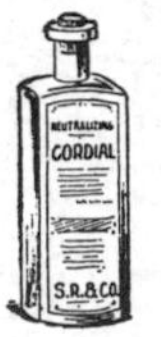


D 208 **Neutralizing Cordial.** Composed of Rhubarb, Peppermint, Golden Seal, Cassia, Brandy, etc. A general corrector of the stomach and bowels, also useful in diarrhaea, dysentery, cholera morbus, dyspepsia, etc.

| | Each | Doz. |
|---|---|---|
| 4 oz. bottles | $0 28 | $2 75 |

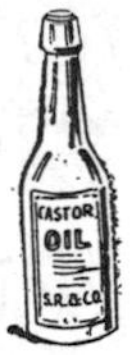


D 210 **Castor Oil.** Pure cold drawn East India almost tasteless.

| | Each | Doz. |
|---|---|---|
| 4 oz. bottles | $0 15 | $1 50 |
| ½ pints | 0 25 | 2 50 |
| **Sweet Oil,** (the finest Olive.) | | |
| 4 oz. bottles | 0 19 | 2 00 |
| ½ pint | 0 25 | 2 75 |

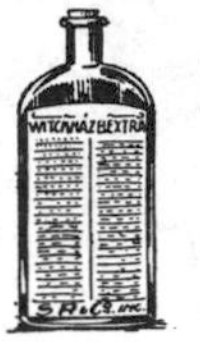


D 212 **Extract Witch Hazel.** (Hamamelis). This is the same as Pond's Extract. It is a valuable medicine to have in every house, ready for sore throats, sore eyes, hemorrhage, sprains, bruises, etc., in fact useful in nearly every accident; we guarantee this to be pure and full strength such as is not often found in small stores.

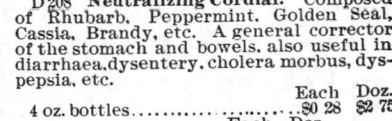

| | Each | Doz. |
|---|---|---|
| ½ pint bot. usually sold at 50c. our price | $0 15 | $1 50 |
| 1 " " " " 1 00 " | 0 25 | 2 50 |
| 2 " " " " 1 50 " | 0 40 | 4 00 |

In gallon lots, 75c. per gallon, jug 10c. extra.

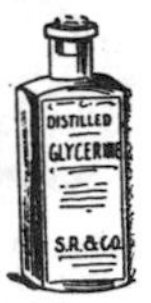


D 214 **Glycerine and Rose Water.** A very agreeable and useful combination for roughness of the skin and chapped lips.

| | Each | Doz. |
|---|---|---|
| 2 oz. bottles | 0 10 | 1 00 |
| 4 oz. bottles | 0 18 | 1 75 |

D 216 **Compound Licorice Powder.** A well known pleasant and gentle laxtive and carefully prepared according to the instructions in the German Pharmacopeia dose in each package.

| | |
|---|---|
| 2 oz. boxes | 10c. |
| 4 oz. boxes | 15c. |
| 8 oz. boxes | 25c. |
| 1 lb. boxes | 40c. |

Dose on each package.

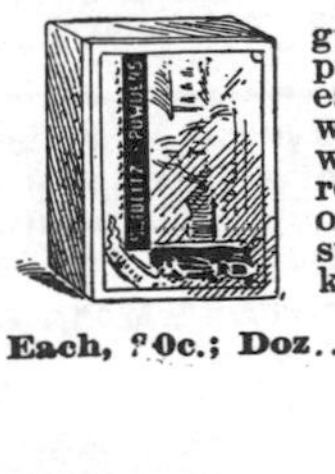

D 218 **Seidlitz Powders.** We guarantee these to be genuine pure, full strength; in order that each customer may get them fresh with their strength unimpaired, we prepare them just when we receive the order for them; most of these powders bought from small stores are worthless from being kept too long.
In boxes containing 10 powders.
**Each, 20c.; Doz**.......................... **$2.00**

**D 220 Opedeldoc.** This is a superior old fashioned remedy for applying to sprains, bruises, stiff joints, rheumatism, lumbago, bunions or any inflamed surface.     Each.   Doz.
2 oz. bottles............................ 20   2 25
4 oz. bottles............................ 35   4 00

**D 222 Camphorated Oil.** An excellent article for rubbing on children's chests and throats in cases of croup, difficulty of breathing, sore throat, coughs, colds. A small quantity of Spirits of Turpentine added to it will increase its effectiveness in many cases. 4 oz. bottles, 18c.; 8 oz. bottles ............35c

**D 224 Balsamic Court Plaster.** Often a very useful article to have near at hand. Envelopes containing 3 sheets, black, white and flesh colors.
Each, 03c.; per doz...........25c

**D 226 Nursery Powder.** A finely perfumed powder especially adapted for use in the chafing of infants, very soothing when applied to any raw and inflamed surface.
4 oz. package, each, 17c.; per doz...........................$1.60

**D 228 Turpentine.** Pure spirits of turpentine, for internal or external use.
4 oz bottles, each 10c; per doz $1.10

**D 230 Ammonia.** Extra quality. Pint bottles expressly for household use.
Each, 7c.; per doz.................... 75c

**D 232 Epsom Salts.** These salts lose their strength when kept long lying loose in drawers, as is done in some stores. We only use fresh and selected stock.
1 lb package freshly packed to order, 5c; doz..50c

**D 234 Rochelle Salts.** Only the best quality, not at all disagreeable to take.
¼ lb. packages, each, 15c; dozen........$1.50
½ lb. " " 30c; " ...........2.85
1 lb. " " 40c; " ...........4.50

**D 236 Sulphur,** powdered and refined for medicinal use. 1 lb. packages, each, 10c; dozen.......50c

**D 238 Insect Powder.** Warranted a strictly pure Dalamation powder, sure death to all insects. Put up in air-tight containers.
Each, 15c.; dozen...................$1.50
Powder guns for using the above, each, 6c; dozen...........50

**D 240 Borax,** refined and powdered, put up by ourselves expressly for family use and guaranteed perfect.
1 lb. packages, each, 10c; dozen........$1.00

**D 242 Rat Killer.** A sure thing, never fails to rid the premises of rats, mice, cockroaches, etc. They go away from the house and die.
Box, each, 11c; dozen..$1.10

**D 244 Blue Seal Vaseline.** Cheeseborough Mfg. Co. Useful when a salve is needed for the skin.
Each, 4c; dozen....................45c

**D 246 Quinine Pills.** Sugar or gelatine coated. 100 in each bottle. A medicine no family should be without.
Per bottle......................24c

**D 248 Electric Ring for Rheumatism.**
These are the first rings introduced into the United States, all others being imitations. Their popularity has caused many rings to be placed on sale that are without any curative properties. Gray metal polished, price, each.....85c
Gray metal, gold plated on outside, price each...........................$1.25

**D 250 The Remedial Heater or Pocket Stove.** Designed for the treatment of ear or toothache, colic, diseases of women and children where the application of external heat is necessary. It can be carried in the overcoat pocket and used as a finger warmer. It is made of metal, nickel plated, and measures 3½x1 inch. There is nothing about it to get out of order and no possible danger of fire escaping from the heat chamber. Heat is produced by the burning of a small tablet of a slowly combustible substance, principally made up of a carbon. One of these will burn with an even heat for about two hours, and continuous heat may be obtained by replacing the consumed carbon by another.
Price, complete, packed in neat wood box, with one dozen carbons, 35c; postage, 15c; extra carbons per dozen, 10c.

**POSTAGE** must always be included with mail orders. When Liquids are ordered by mail, send 5 cents extra for mailing tube.

---

## NURSERY DEPARTMENT.

### Baby Foods, Medicine etc.

| | Usual price each. | Our price each. | Our price per doz. |
|---|---|---|---|
| **D 252** Battle Creek Sanitarium Infant Food.... | .75 | .65 | 6.00 |
| **D 254** Horlick's Food for Infants, large... | .75 | .60 | 7.00 |
| **D 256** Horlick's Food for Infants, small... | .40 | .35 | 3.80 |
| **D 258** Horlick's Malted Milk, small... | .50 | .45 | 4.50 |
| **D 260** Horlick's Malted Milk, large... | 1.00 | .85 | 9.00 |
| **D 262** Horlick's Malted Milk, hospital size... | 3.75 | 3.00 | |
| **D 264** Imperial Granum small... | .75 | .65 | 7.20 |
| **D 266** Imperial Granum, large... | 1.25 | 1.00 | 11.25 |
| **D 268** Lactated Food, Wells, Richardson & Co., small... | .25 | .20 | 2.20 |
| **D 270** Lactated Food, Wells, Richardson & Co., large... | 1.00 | .80 | 8.80 |
| **D 272** Lactated Food, Wells, Richardson & Co., hospital size... | 2.50 | 2.25 | 25.00 |
| **D 274** Mellin's Infant Food, large... | .75 | .60 | 6.50 |
| **D 276** Mellin's Infant Food, small... | .35 | .40 | 4.00 |
| **D 278** Nestle's Milk Food... | .50 | .40 | 4.50 |
| **D 280** Lactopreparata R. & C., large... | 1.00 | .70 | 8.00 |
| **D 282** Lactopreparata R. & C., small... | .50 | .35 | 4.00 |
| **D 284** Ridges' Food for Infants, small... | .35 | .30 | 3.10 |
| **D 286** Ridges' Food for Infants, 2d size... | .50 | .45 | 5.25 |
| **D 288** Ridges' Food for Infants, 3d size... | 1.25 | .85 | 10.10 |
| **D 290** " " 4th " | 1.75 | 1.25 | 14.20 |
| **D 292** Wagner's Infant Food... | .50 | .30 | 3.25 |
| **D 294** Baby Cough Syrup, a reliable remedy expressly prepared for young children, harmless... | .25 | .20 | 2.25 |
| **D 296** Bull's Baby Syrup, soothing and quieting... | .25 | .20 | 2.00 |
| **D 298** Winslow's Soothing Syrup... | .25 | .18 | 1.90 |
| **D 300** Nursery Powder for chafing, etc... | .25 | .10 | 1.00 |
| **D 302** Bonated Talcum Powder, in decorated metal box with perforated top for the nursery and for the toilet... | .25 | .12 | 1.00 |
| **D 304** Castroline. An excellent substitute for castor oil, pleasant to take, safe, mild and sure, just the thing for the baby when it is cross. It will sweeten the stomach and regulate the bowels... | .25 | .20 | 2.25 |

### Rubber Teething Rings.

**D 306 Rubber Teething Ring,** seamless, full size, best white rubber.
Each .......................$0.03

**D 308 Rubber Teething Ring,** full size, seamless, best black rubber.
Each........................$0.04

**D 310 Bone Teething Ring,** 1¾ inches, nicely finished. Each...............$0.04

**D 312 Vegetable Ivory Teething Ring.** Teething ring of real vegetable ivory and large seamless black rubber nipple.
Each.......................$0.10

**D 314 Bailey's Teething Pad.**
Each........................$0.10

### Rubber Nipples.

**D 316 Rubber Nipples** for tube fittings. White, black and maroon.
Each, 2c; doz...............$0.20

**D 318 Rubber Nipples** to fit over bottle. White, black and maroon.
Each 3c; doz................$0.25

**D 320 Rubber Nipples,** Davidson's Patent. Black, white or maroon, to fit over bottle.
Each 3c; doz................$0.30

**D 322 Davidson's Health Nipple,** made from the finest Para rubber; is constructed so that the infant can obtain a strong hold and renders nursing easy.
Each, 4c.; per doz..........$0.45c

**D 324 Mispah Valve Nipple.** Makes nursing easy. Allows the food to flow slowly and easily. Prevents colic. Each, 5c; doz...........$0.50

**D 326 Nursing Bottles,** Burr Patent, white rubber fittings.
Each, 10c; doz........$0.95

**D 328 S. R & Co. Nurser No. 1.** Fitted with white, black or maroon fittings. Complete with 2 brushes in each box. Each, 20c; doz.......$2.25

---

**D 330 Nursing Flask,** graduated, white flint.
To hold 6 oz., each, 5c; doz................$0.50
To hold 8 oz., each, 7c; doz................$0.65
To hold 12 oz., each, 10c; doz..............$1.00

**D 332 Nursing Bottle Fittings,** complete in white, black or maroon.
Each, 6c; doz......$0.60

**D 334 Borated Talcum Powder.** Perfumed.
Per box....................$0.10

**D 346 Toilet Powder Puffs** for infants' use. Satin top, lion handle.
Each.......................$0.20

**D 358 Puff Boxes.** Papier Mache, handsomely decorated.
Each.......................$0.20

**D 350 Best Nursery Powder.**
Per package................$0.10

### A Few Handy Pocket Goods
In screw top air tight glass vials.

#### Aromatic Cachou.
    Each.   Doz.
**D 352 Aromatic Cachou** Lozenges, for perfuming the breath. Makes a delicious confection.............$0 08   $0 85

#### Silver Cachous.
    Each.   Doz.
**D 354 Silver Cachous,** for perfuming the breath. Vest pocket size...............$0 08   $0 85

#### Chlorate Potash Tablets
    Each.   Doz.
**D 356 Chlorate Potash Tablets.** 5 grains each. For sore throat, hoarseness, etc.........$0 08   $0 85

#### Soda Mint Tablets.
    Each.   Doz.
**D 358 Soda Mint Tablets.** For sour stomach, flatulency, nausea, etc................$0 08   $0 85

#### Bronchial Troches.
    Each.   Doz.
**D 360 Bronchial Troches.** For coughs, colds, sore throat, hoarseness, etc..............$0 08   $0 85

#### Licorice Lozenges.
    Each.   Doz.
**D 326 Licorice Lozenges.** Pure, very soothing to the throat and bronchial tubes....$0 08   $0 85

#### Slippery Elm Lozenges.
**D 364 Slippery Elm Lozenges.** Demulcent for roughness in the throat and irritating cough..$0 08   $0 85

**D 366 English Smelling Salts.** Each. Doz. For faintness, headaches, etc.
Pretty glass stoppered vials....$0 20   $1 83

**D 368 Pepsin Tablets.** For dyspepsia, indigestion, etc...... 15   1 50

**D 370 Trix.** For the breath.. 03   30

**D 372 Sen Sen**................ 03   30

---

**IF YOU ARE OF THE OPINION THAT MAIL ORDER BUYING DOES NOT PAY, GIVE US ONE TRIAL AND WE WILL GUARANTEE THAT YOU WILL CHANGE YOUR MIND,**

# Patent and Proprietary Medicine.

The following list contains only a few of the more prominent Patent Medicines, such as those which are kept before the public by constant advertising. This will give you an idea of our low prices. The number of Patent and Proprietary medicines on the market at the present time is so enormous that it is not possible for us to put them all on our list, and keep the size of this catalogue within ordinary bounds, but our facilities in buying are so great that we can supply you with any Patent Medicine or Proprietary Article that is manufactured. If you do not find it mentioned here, write to us about it, or send what money you think it is worth; if you send more than our price we will return to you the surplus with the goods. Our great aim in conducting our business is, that when we get your first order, to try our very best to keep you a customer for life. We can only accomplish this by acting honestly with you; by faithfully fulfilling our promises to you; by sending to you exactly what you ordered of the best quality and at the lowest price. Old, experienced, fully registered pharmacists employed in our drug department.

| | | Retail price each | Our price each | Our price doz. |
|---|---|---|---|---|
| D 380 | Atlophoros | $1 00 | $0 75 | $8 50 |
| D 382 | Ayer's Ague Cure | 1 00 | 75 | 7 75 |
| D 384 | Ayer's Cherry Pectoral | 1 00 | 68 | 7 75 |
| D 386 | Ayer's Hair Vigor | 1 00 | 58 | 6 75 |
| D 388 | Ayer's Sarsaparilla | 1 00 | 68 | 7 78 |
| D 390 | Ayer's Pills | 25 | 14 | 1 50 |

| | | Retail price each | Our price each | Our price doz. |
|---|---|---|---|---|
| D 392 | Beecham's Pills | $0 25 | $0 18 | $1 85 |
| D 394 | Benson's Capcine Plaster | 25 | 18 | 1 75 |
| D 396 | Boschee's German Syrup | 75 | 50 | 5 25 |

| | | Retail price each | Our price each | Our price doz. |
|---|---|---|---|---|
| D 398 | Brandreth's Pills | 25 | 14 | 1 50 |
| D 400 | Bromo-Caffeine, large | 1 25 | 85 | 9 50 |
| D 402 | Bromo-Caffeine, medium | 75 | 55 | 6 00 |
| D 404 | Bromo-Caffeine, small | 40 | 30 | 3 00 |
| D 406 | Bromo-Caffeine, trial size | 10 | 08 | 75 |
| D 408 | Bromo Seltzer, trial size | 10 | 08 | 96 |
| D 410 | Bromo Seltzer, sm. | 25 | 20 | 2 00 |
| D 412 | Bromo Seltzer, med | 50 | 40 | 4 00 |
| D 414 | Bromo Seltzer, lge | 1 00 | 80 | 8 00 |
| D 416 | Bull's Cough Syrup, med. | 50 | 35 | 4 00 |
| D 418 | Bull's Cough Syrup, small | 25 | 18 | 2 00 |
| D 420 | Brown's Troches | 25 | 17 | 1 75 |
| D 422 | Carter's Little Liver Pills | 25 | 13 | 1 50 |
| D 424 | Carter's Iron Pills | 50 | 32 | 2 75 |
| D 426 | Carbolic Salve | 25 | 20 | 2 25 |
| D 328 | Carbolic Salve, (vetinary) | 50 | 35 | 4 00 |
| D 430 | Castoria | 35 | 24 | 2 80 |
| D 432 | Cuticura Ointment large | 1 00 | 75 | 8 80 |
| D 434 | Cuticura Ointment, small | 50 | 40 | 4 40 |
| D 436 | Cuticura Resolvent | 1 00 | 75 | 8 80 |
| D 438 | Cuticura Plaster | 25 | 18 | 2 00 |
| D 440 | Damina Wafers, pink for men | 1 00 | 75 | 8 00 |
| D 442 | Damina Wafers, white for women | 1 00 | 75 | 8 00 |
| D 444 | Diamond Dyes, all colors | 10 | 08 | 85 |
| D 446 | Dyes, S. R. & Co. family dye superior for cotton, wool, silk, ribbons, feathers, all colors | 10 | 5 | 50 |
| D 448 | Fellow's Hypophosites | 1 50 | 1 15 | 12 00 |
| D 450 | Garfield Tea, small | 50 | 18 | 2 00 |
| D 452 | Garfield Tea, medium | 50 | 35 | 4 00 |
| D 454 | Garfield Tea, large | 1 00 | 75 | 8 00 |
| D 456 | Gleet and Gonorrhœa cure | 1 00 | 80 | 8 00 |
| D 458 | Greene's August Flower | 75 | 50 | 5 25 |
| D 460 | Greene's Nervura | 1 00 | 75 | 8 75 |
| D 462 | Gunning's Bird Tonic | 25 | 18 | 2 00 |
| D 464 | Gumbault's Caustic Balsam | 1 50 | 1 25 | 12 00 |
| D 466 | Harlem Oil, genuine | 15 | 07 | 40 |

| | | Retail price each | Our price each | Our price doz. |
|---|---|---|---|---|
| D 468 | Hamlins' Wizard Oil | 50 | 35 | 4 00 |
| D 470 | Hall's Catarrh Cure | 75 | 50 | 5 50 |
| D 472 | Hall's Hair Renewer | 1 00 | 60 | 6 75 |
| D 474 | Hamburg Drops | 50 | 35 | 3 75 |
| D 476 | Hamburg Breast Tea | 25 | 20 | 2 00 |
| D 478 | Harter's Lung Balm | 25 | 15 | 1 50 |

| | | Retail price each | Our price each | Our price doz. |
|---|---|---|---|---|
| D 480 | Himrods' Asthma Cure | 1 00 | 80 | 8 00 |
| D 482 | Kennedy's Medical Discovery | 1 50 | 1 12 | 13 00 |
| D 484 | Kennedy's Favorite Remedy | 1 00 | 85 | 8 80 |
| D 486 | Kennedy's Salt Rheum Ointment | 50 | 40 | 4 00 |

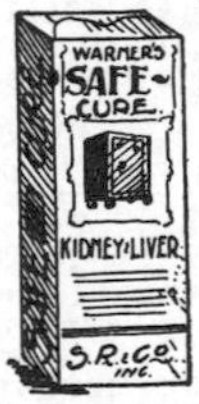

| | | Retail price each | Our price each | Our price doz. |
|---|---|---|---|---|
| D 488 | Hire's Root Beer | 25 | 15 | 1 75 |
| D 490 | Hoble's Sprague Kidney Pills | 50 | 40 | 4 00 |
| D 492 | Hood's Sarsaparilla | 1 00 | 67 | 8 00 |
| D 494 | Hood's Vegetable Pills | 25 | 18 | 2 00 |
| D 496 | Hanford's Acid Phosphates | 50 | 35 | 4 00 |
| D 498 | Hostetter's Stomach Bitters | 1 00 | 75 | 8 40 |
| D 500 | Hunyadi Waters (German Bitter Waters) | 50 | 23 | 2 75 |
| D 501 | Hunyadi Janas | 50 | 25 | 2 90 |
| D 502 | Injection Brou | 1 00 | 80 | 8 50 |
| D 503 | Jaynes Expectorant | 1 00 | 65 | 7 00 |
| D 504 | Jaynes Tonic Vermifuge | 35 | 30 | 3 20 |
| D 505 | Jaynes Pills | 25 | 18 | 1 80 |
| D 506 | Kæmpfers' Mocking Bird Food | 40 | 30 | 3 20 |
| D 514 | Kidney Wort, dry or liquid | 1 00 | 75 | 8 50 |
| D 516 | Koenig's (Father) Nerve Tonic | 1 00 | 85 | 9 50 |
| D 518 | Lane's Family Medicine, small | 25 | 20 | 2 00 |
| D 520 | Lane's Family Medicine, large | 50 | 40 | 4 00 |
| D 522 | Listerine | 1 00 | 70 | 8 00 |
| D 524 | Mustang Liniment, small | 25 | 18 | 2 10 |
| D 526 | Pettit's Eye Salve | 25 | 18 | 1 65 |
| D 528 | Paine's Celery Compound | 1 00 | 75 | 8 75 |
| D 530 | Pierce's Favorite Prescription | 1 00 | 68 | 7 75 |
| D 532 | Pierce's Golden Medical Discovery | 1 00 | 68 | 7 75 |
| D 534 | Pierce's Pellets | 25 | 14 | 1 60 |
| D 536 | Pinkham's (Lydia) Compound | 1 00 | 67 | 8 00 |
| D 538 | Pinkham's Vegetable Pills | 25 | 18 | 1 85 |
| D 540 | Pinkham's Sanative Wash | 25 | 20 | 2 00 |
| D 542 | Pennyroyal Pills | 2 00 | 88 | 8 50 |
| D 544 | Pink Pills | 50 | 25 | 2 50 |
| D 546 | Piso's Consumption Cure | 25 | 18 | 2 00 |
| D 548 | Pond's Extract, large | 1 75 | 1 40 | 16 00 |
| D 550 | Pond's Extract, medium | 1 00 | 75 | 8 75 |
| D 552 | Pond's Extract, small | 50 | 40 | 4 25 |
| D 554 | Radway's Ready Relief | 50 | 40 | 4 00 |
| D 556 | Radway's Pills | 25 | 14 | 1 60 |
| D 558 | Rat Poison | 15 | 10 | 1 00 |
| D 560 | Schenck's Mandrake Pills | 25 | 14 | 1 65 |
| D 562 | Schenck's Pulmonic Syrup | 1 00 | 80 | 8 00 |
| D 564 | Scott's Emulsion | 1 00 | 70 | 8 00 |
| D 566 | Shaker Extract of Roots | 60 | 50 | 5 50 |
| D 568 | Sage's Catarrh Cure | 50 | 35 | 3 75 |
| D 570 | Spratt's Dog Soap | 25 | 15 | 1 65 |
| D 572 | St. Jacob's Oil | 50 | 35 | 4 00 |
| D 574 | Syrup of Figs | 50 | 40 | 4 00 |
| D 576 | Sears's Fig Laxative (A pleasant syrup of figs for constipation.) | 50 | 40 | 4 50 |
| D 578 | Sears's Sarsaparilla (The great blood purifier.) | 1 00 | 59 | 6 00 |
| D 580 | Tansy Pills | 1 00 | 83 | 8 50 |
| D 582 | Toothache Wax | 10 | 08 | 90 |
| D 584 | Tarrant's Seltzer Aperient, large | 1 00 | 80 | 8 80 |
| D 585 | Tarrant's Seltzer Aperient, small | 50 | 40 | 4 00 |
| D 586 | Warner's Safe Kidand Liver Cure | 1 25 | 85 | 10 00 |
| D 588 | Winslow's Soothing Syrup | 25 | 18 | 1 90 |

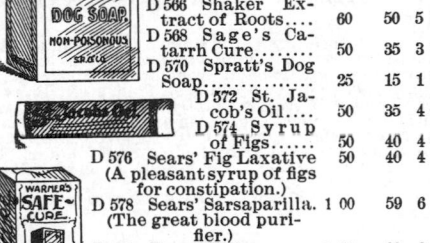

If you cannot find what you want mentioned in the above list, write to us about it. We can supply you with any patent medicine and proprietary article that is on the market cheaper than you can get them elsewhere. The most economical method of ordering goods from us is for you to look through all the different departments in this catalogue at least once a month, select every article you know you will need to have pretty soon, add to your selection what goods you must have right away, send us the order, complying with our terms printed on the first and second pages. We will select the articles ordered carefully and ship them to you without delay. At the end of the month you will be filled with astonishment at the large surplus of money you have laying around loose and with admiration for our system of conducting business and besides having all the necessaries of life of the best quality.

## Prescription Department.

We have unequaled facilities for preparing prescriptions and family recipes. In this branch of our Drug Department we employ only registered druggists having long experience. Our medicines are always fresh and of the best quality. Send your prescriptions and recipes to us—you can always feel well assured of having them prepared with the greatest care by competent and skilful druggists and chemists, using only the purest and freshest drugs, and at a price very much cheaper than you could have them prepared elsewhere. Our prices for prescriptions in general average: For liquid prearations, 7 cents per ounce; for powders and pills, 17 cents per doz. These prices can be applied to the majority of prescriptions and recipes but there are exceptional cases where we charge more, but our prices are always far below the retail druggists' prices.

**SAVE THE ENORMOUS PROFITS.....**
**OF RETAIL DRUGGISTS.**

## Drugs, Chemicals, Pills, Extracts, etc.

We have always in stock a full assortment of Drugs, Acids, Chemicals, Fluid Extracts, Pills and Granules, Compressed Tablets, Hypodermic Tablets, Elixirs, Wines, Liniments, Ointments, Tinctures, Druggists' Sundries, in fact every article that

 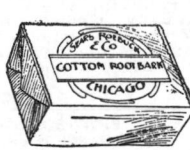 

is generally kept in large, first-class drug stores. You can safely send us your order for any drug or chemical, either in the crude state, or prepared in the form of Extract, Tincture, Elixir, etc., and rest assured of receiving exactly what you ordered in a fresh condition and pure quality, and at a price far below what is usually charged for such articles in retail stores, which is a very important item for you to consider. A special catalogue containing a full list of Drugs, Patent Medicines and Drug Sundries mailed to anyone on application.

Poisons cannot be sent by mail, and a four ounce bottle of liquid is the largest that can be mailed. As articles in our drug department do not as a rule weigh much, they can be sent by express at very little cost, but the most economical method is for you to include an order for drugs when you are ordering goods from our other departments.

## Homeopathic Remedies.

Our Homeopathic Specifics are prepared under the supervision of an old experienced Homeopathic Physician. Great care is taken in preparing them according to the rules laid down by the highest authorities on homeopathy, and only the purest drugs used. Every one of the following specifics is a special cure for the disease named on it; the dose is on each bottle, and from two to four doses are to be taken every day according to the severity of the case.

| | | Usual Price | Our Price |
|---|---|---|---|
| D 600 | Cures rheumatism or rheumatic pains | $0 25 | $0 18 |
| D 602 | Cures fever and ague, intermittent fever, malaria | 25 | 18 |
| D 604 | Cures piles, blind or bleeding, external or internal | 25 | 18 |
| D 606 | Cures opthalmia, weak or inflamed eyes | 25 | 18 |
| D 608 | Cures catarrh, influenza, cold in head | 25 | 18 |
| D 610 | Cures whooping cough, spasmodic cough | 25 | 18 |
| D 612 | Cures asthma, oppressed difficult breathing | 25 | 18 |
| C 614 | Cures fevers, congestions, inflamations | 25 | 18 |
| C 616 | Cures worm fever or worm disease | 25 | 18 |
| D 618 | Cures cholic, crying and wakefulness of infants; teething | 25 | 18 |
| D 620 | Cures diarrhœa of children and adults | 25 | 18 |
| D 622 | Cures dysentery, gripings, bilious colic | 25 | 18 |
| D 624 | Cures cholera, cholera morbus, vomiting | 25 | 18 |
| D 626 | Cures coughs, colds, bronchitis | 25 | 18 |
| D 628 | Cures toothache, faceache, neuralgia | 25 | 18 |
| D 630 | Cures headache, sick headache, vertigo | 25 | 08 |
| D 632 | Cures dyspepsia, indigestion, weak stomach | 25 | 18 |
| D 634 | Cures supressed menses, or scanty | 25 | 18 |
| D 636 | Cures leucorrhœa, or profuse menses | 25 | 18 |
| D 638 | Cures croup, hoarse cough, difficult breathing, laryngitis | 25 | 18 |
| D 640 | Cures salt rheum, eruptions, erysipelas | 25 | 18 |
| D 642 | Cures ear discharge, earache | 25 | 18 |
| D 644 | Cures scrofula, swellings, ulcers | 25 | 18 |
| D 646 | Cures general debility, physical weakness, brain fag | 25 | 18 |
| D 648 | Cures dropsy, fluid accumulations | 25 | 18 |
| D 650 | Cures seasickness, nausea, vomiting | 25 | 18 |
| D 652 | Cures kidney disease, gravel, calculi | 25 | 18 |
| D 654 | Cures nervous debility, vital weakness | 1 00 | 77 |
| D 656 | Cures sore mouth and canker | 25 | 18 |
| D 658 | Cures urinary incontinence, wetting bed | 25 | 18 |
| D 660 | Cures painful menses, pruritis | 25 | 18 |
| D 662 | Cures disease of the heart, palpitations | 1 00 | 77 |
| D 664 | Cures epilepsy, St. Vitus dance | 1 00 | 77 |
| D 666 | Cures sore throat, quinsy or ulcerated sore throat | 25 | 18 |
| D 668 | Cures chronic congestions, headaches | 25 | 18 |
| D 669 | Cures grip and summer colds | 25 | 18 |
| D 670 | A strong cardboard case covered with black muslin, containing 12 specifics | | 1 50 |
| D 671 | A polished hardwood case with lock and key, containing 24 remedies | | 4 50 |
| D 672 | A full line of Humphrey's, Munyon's and Ballantine's Cures in stock. The size usually sold for 25c our price | | 20 |
| | The size usually sold for $1, our price | | 80 |

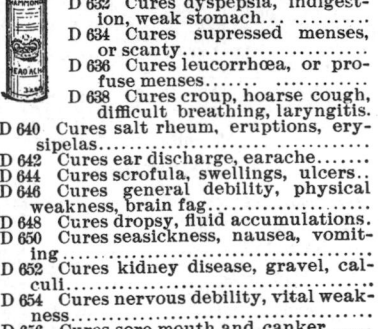

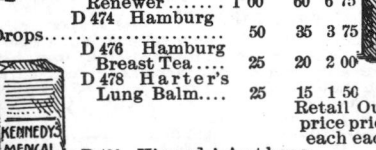

**IF WE COULD ONCE GET YOU STARTED ON THE CLUB ORDER PLAN, YOU WOULD FIND SUCH AN INCREASE OF AN ALREADY LARGE SAVING THAT YOU WOULD SOON HAVE ALL YOUR NEIGHBORS BUYING WITH YOU**

## Homeopathic Cases.

**We make Special Medicine Cases to order** to contain 12, 24, 36 or 48 remedies. We will fill these cases with **any assortment of remedies** you wish and any size bottles. With each case we send a **Homeopathic Manual,** giving full directions how to use the remedies, also a **general description of diseases,** and how to treat sick people to get them well again. **Our prices are very low** for these cases **and they are worth from four to five times the amount we ask for them.** Send us a description of the remedies wanted and we will send you the cost. There ought to be one in every household, especially where there are children.

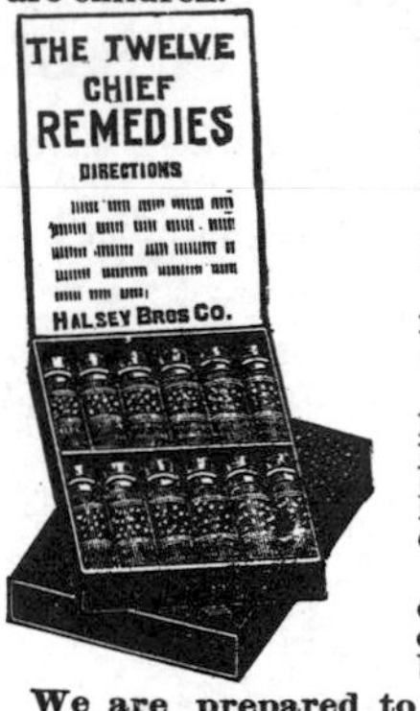


### Our 85c Homeopahtic Cases.

D 679 Contains 12, 1 dr. remedies with directions. ....................$0.85

### Our $1.50 Homeopahtic Cases.

D 680 Contains 12, 2 dr. remedies with directions. ....................$1.50

D 681 This is a durable polished hardwood case, containing 24, 2 dr. and 4, 1 oz. bottles, fitted with lock and key, complete with Ruddock's Stepping Stone. $5.00

D 682 Similar to above containing 36, 2 dr. and 4 1 oz. bottles, complete with book....................$6.75

**We are prepared to furnish anything in the line of Homeopathic supplies, and guarantee them to be full strength and fresh condition.** We mention a few of the more prominent. A more complete list will be found in our **special Drug Catalogue.** We will be pleased to furnish information on Homeopathic medicines if you are in doubt as to what to order. We will also send a copy of **Halsey's Manual,** (152 pages), **a complete homoepathic treatise, free on request.** When ordering the following remedies please specify what form you wish them in; pills, powder, discs or liquid.

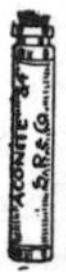
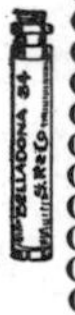
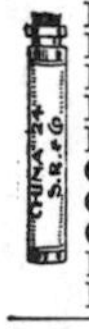
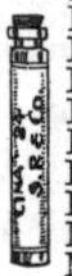
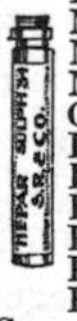

| Name. | Strength. | Name. | Strength. |
|---|---|---|---|
| Aconite.......... | 3x | Hydrastis........ | 1x |
| Antimon crud.... | 3x | Hyoscyamus..... | 3x |
| Apismel .......... | 3x | Ignati............ | 3x |
| Arnica............ | 3x | Iodium ........... | 3x |
| Arsenic alb....... | 3x | Ipecac............ | 3x |
| Baptisa........... | 1x | Kali bichr........ | 3x |
| Belladonna....... | 3x | Lachesis......... | 6x |
| Bryonia alba..... | 3x | Lycopodium...... | 3x |
| Calcarea carb.... | 3x | Mercurius biniod | 3x |
| Cantharis ........ | 3x | Mercurius corros | 3x |
| Carby veg........ | 3x | Mercurius sol.... | 3x |
| Caulophyllum ... | 0 | Mercurius viv.... | 3x |
| Causticum........ | 3x | Natrum mur..... | 6x |
| Chamomilla....... | 3x | Nitric Acid. ..... | 6x |
| China............. | 2x | Nux vomica...... | 3x |
| Chinin, arsen.... | 2x | Opium........... | 3x |
| Chimicifuga...... | 1x | Phosphorus....... | 3x |
| Cina.............. | 2x | Phosphoric acid. | 3x |
| Cocculus......... | 3x | Phytolacca....... | 0 |
| Coffea crud....... | 3x | Podophyllin...... | 3x |
| Colchicum........ | 3x | Pulsatilla ........ | 3x |
| Colocynthis ...... | 3x | Rhus tox ......... | 3x |
| Cuprum met..... | 3x | Sanguinaria .......... | 2x |
| Digitalis.......... | 2x | Secale cor............. | 1x |
| Drosera.......... | 2x | Sepia ................. | 3x |
| Dulcamara....... | 3x | Silicea................ | 6x |
| Eupatorium perf | 1x | Spigelia .............. | 3x |
| Ferrum phos..... | 3x | Spongia .............. | 3x |
| Gelsemium....... | 1x | Staphysagria......... | 6x |
| Glonoine ......... | 3x | Sulphur.............. | 3x |
| Graphites ....... | 6x | Tartar emetic........ | 3x |
| Hamamelis....... | 1x | Veratrum alb......... | 3x |
| Hepar sulphtr... | 3x | | |

D 683 ¼ oz. phials each **10** cents. By mail **15** cents
D 684 ½ oz. phials each **15** cents. By mail **20** cents
D 685 1 oz. phials each **20** cents. By mail **25** cents
D 686 2 oz. phials each **40** cents. By mail **45** cents

## Halsey's Specialties.

| | | Bottle |
|---|---|---|
| D 692 | Carbo Peptine Wafers.............................. | $0 40 |
| D 694 | Burn and Frost Liniment........................... | 0 40 |
| D 696 | Camphor Pills........................................ | 0 20 |
| D 708 | Catarrh Tablets...................................... | 0 40 |
| D 700 | Catarrh Treatment Complete...................... | 2 75 |
| D 702 | Chestnut Pile Crate................................. | 0 40 |
| D 704 | Elixir Hydrastis and Coca.......................... | 8 00 |
| D 706 | General Debility Specific........................... | 0 80 |
| D 718 | Goitre Tablets........................................ | 0 50 |
| D 710 | Hensel's Tonic........................................ | 0 90 |
| D 712 | Infant Tablets......................................... | 0 40 |
| D 714 | LaGrippe Specific.................................... | 0 60 |
| D 716 | Liver Tablets.......................................... | 0 40 |
| D 728 | Nerve Salt............................................. | 1 60 |
| D 720 | Neuralgia Cure........................................ | 0 40 |
| D 722 | Rhus and Bryonia Plaster. Small.............. | 0 20 |
| D 724 | " " " " Yard rolls ... | 0 75 |
| D 726 | Sore Throat Tablets.................................. | 0 20 |
| D 728 | Tape Worm Remedy................................. | 0 75 |
| D 730 | Uterine Wafers....................................... | 0 75 |
| D 732 | Whooping Cough Syrup............................ | 0 40 |
| D 734 | Witch Hazel Cream.................................. | 0 20 |

## Homeopathic Books.

D 736 Ruddock's Stepping Stone to Homeopathy and Health. 258 pages....................$0.80

D 738 Ruddock's Homeopathic Guide, containing the Stepping Stone and The Ladies Manual in one volume, 592 pages....................$1.60

## Homeopatnic Remedies for Farm and Stable.

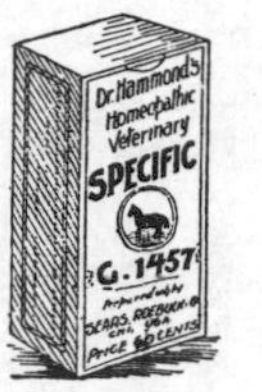


**These remedies cure all diseases of horses, cows, dogs, sheep, Poultry and other animals.** Many a valuable animal has been saved by the timely use of these specifics. They are easy to give, quick to act, and harmless, always leave the animal in good condition. Full instructions to give the medicine and how to treat the case are inclosed with every bottle.

Single bottles containing over 50 doses, usual price............ $0.60
Our price ....................... .40

The complete set packed in a neat box forming a valuable medicine chest, only .......... ...$3.00

D 760 For fevers, chills, congestion, etc.
D 762 For strangles, glanders, distemper, influenza, quinsy, nasal catarrh, sore throat, etc.
D 764 For bronchitis, coughs, pleuro-pneumonia, inflammation of lungs, etc.
D 766 For indigestion, constipation, ill condition, overfed, staggers.
D 768 For rheumatism, strains, spavin, lameness, etc.
D 770 For urinary and kidney difficulties, diseases of the bladder, difficult and painful urination, etc.
D 772 For worms, botts, grubbs, debility.
D 774 For colic, diarrhœa, dysentry. stomach ache.
D 776 For manage, grease and skin diseases.

## Special Veterinary Remedies.

**We have a most valuable and complete line of veterinary medicines,** specially prepared for us by **a veterinary surgeon of long experience.** To the farmer, stockraiser, and to everyone who keeps animals, either for profit or pleasure, they are **worth a hundred times their cost.** When your animals are sick and out of condition, give these remedies a trial. You will find complete instructions how to use them and how to treat the sick animals with each package. When you have given them a fair trial, you will be surprised how soon your cattle will return to a healthy condition again. The following we guarantee all that is claimed for them.

D 780 **Veterinary Colic Cure.** Unexcelled for all stomache and bowel troubles accompanied with colic pains, such as Wind Colic, Spasmodic Colic, Engorgement of Stomach, Botts, Stoppage of Water, Indigestion, etc. It relieves pain and relaxes the muscular coat of the stomache, bowels and bladder, causing a normal action and free evacuation of the organs.
Each....................$0.85

D 782 **Veterinary Fever Remedy.** Give in all diseases that are accompanied by fever. Give early in Lung Fever, Pneumonia, Bronchitis, Pleurisy, Laryngitis, Sore Throat, Distemper, Cold, etc. It is a positive cure if given promptly in an attack of Laminitis, or Founder, and accompanied by hot poultices to the horse's feet. It will remove the congestion and effect a permanent cure in a few hours. In case of Inflammation of the Bowels, given with Star-Crescent Colic Cure, and hot applications to the belly, gives relief to the patient and cures the disease in a few hours.
Each....................$0.40

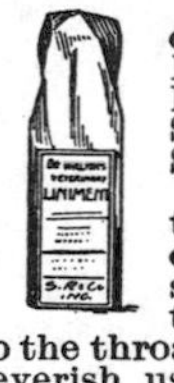


D 784 **Veterinary Liniment.** Recommended in Sore Throat, Laryngitis, Distemper, Pneumonia, Bronchitis, Lung Fever, Sprains of Muscles or Tendons, Sweeny or Atrophy of the Muscles of the Shoulders or Hips.

**Directions:**—Apply freely and rub thoroughly. Its effect depends somewhat on the amount applied, and the time spent in rubbing. In throat and lung troubles it should be thoroughly applied to the throat or sides of the chest. If the animal is feverish, use Star-Crescent Fever Cure as directed. If a cough should accompany the case, use Star-Crescent Cough Powder.
Each ....................$0.25

D 786 **Veterinary Wire Cut Remedy.** Heals cuts and wounds in all parts of the body without leaving a scar. The best remedy for cuts from barbed wire. It heals them the quickest. It is an antiseptic, destroying all germs and foul odors. A preventive from flies and insects. When used in cold weather it prevents the animal from taking cold in the cuts.
Each ....................$0.40

D 788 **Veterinary Cough Powder.** Star Cough Powder is a sure cure for all Coughs, Colds, Distemper, Bronchitis, Laryngitis, Pneumonia, Pleurisy, etc. **Symptoms of Distemper:** Standing coat, loss of condition, dullness, cough with redness of membrane of nose, watery discharges from eyes and nose, scanty high colored urine. increased thirst, soreness of throat; soon a swelling arises between the bones of lower jaw, hot, tender and hard at first but gradually becoming soft and pus is formed. Breathing loud and difficult. After opening the abscess and letting the pus escape, relief is obtained.
Per box....................25c.

D 790 **Veterinary Black Leg Remedy.** Is a sure and positive cure for Black Leg in young Calves and Stock and a positive preventive against the disease. Black Leg, Black Quarter, Bloody Urine, extensive engorgement of a Shoulder, Quarter, Neck, Side or Breast. It is most frequent in young or rapidly growing and thriving stock, attacking first the best of the herd and rapidly running its way through.
Each....................25c.

D 792 **Veterinary Blister.** Unexcelled for Bone Spavin, Ring Bone, Splint, Curb, Bog Spavin, Blood Spavin, Thoroughpin, etc. Removes Wind Puffs, Calouses, etc., from kicks or bruises, Thickening of Tendons, etc.
Package....................40c.

D 794. **Star-Crescent Lice and Insect Destroyer.** Positively kills Lice, Ticks, Fleas, Flies and all Insects. **Directions.**—Sprinkle thoroughly.

All animals—the younger ones particularly—are commonly troubled by the long hair in the winter months becoming filled with Lice. These little pests will so annoy and eat at the young animals that they will lose flesh, refuse to eat, and in many cases unless relieved, die from the tormenting of these insects. One thorough application of this Powder kills all vermin.
Package....................15c.

D 796 **Veterinary Tonic Condition Powders.** This Powder may be given with great advantage in all cases of loss of appetite, roughness of the hair or coart, stopping of water and bowels, Cough, Colds, Inflammation of the lungs and bowels, recent Founders, Swelling of the Glands of the Throat, Horse Distemper, Hidebound; will also backen the Heaves and in recent cases effect a cure. There is no disease among Horses and Cattle where this valuable Powder is not called for; and by its timely use will save the lives of many valuable animals. The superiority of this Powder over every other preparation of its kind is only known to those who have seen its astonishing result on horses and cattle. This powder acts upon tne secretions, consequently will arrest disease promptly.
Each package....................20c.
In bulk....................per lb., 15c.

D 798 **Star-Crescent Worm Powder. Veterinary.** Expels Worms from Horses, etc. Worms cause Indigestion, Colic, Constipation, Loss of Flesh and General Debility. Study the symptoms. To expel worms give one powder a day, then give one pint raw linseed oil for a physic.
Box....................25c.

D 800 **Veterinary Eye Water. Directions.**—Apply to the eye three times a day by dropping three or four or several drops in the ball of the eye. If the eye is red and swollen on the inside of the lids, foment it several times a day with hot water and keep the animal in a darkened and well ventilated stable. Feed on light and easy digested food, such as bran, mash, carrots, etc.
Each....................25c.

D 802 **Liniment. The Best Liniment for Man or Beast,** for Cuts, Wounds, Bruises, Strains, Swellings, Burns, Scalds, Sprains, Pains, Aches, Sores, Cracked Hands, Frost bites, Chilblains, Spavin, Ring Bone, Wind Gall, Sweeny, Scratches and all flesh bone and muscular ailments.
Each....................25c.

D 804 **Veterinary Fattening Condition Powder.** Use this Remedy in time. Do not wait until your stock is silk, but give it to ward off sickness. It pays for itself, keeping the animal in a strong, healthy condition, easy to fatten. Give for loss of Appetite, Roughness of the Hair or Coat, Stoppage of Water and Bowels, Coughs, etc. Will also backen the Heaves and in recent cases effect a cure.
Per lb....................8c.

D 806 **Feverine, A Safe and Sure Cure for Milk Fever.** Dairyman should ever have a bottle of this remedy on hand, and upon the first appearance of the malady follow the directions closely. There is not a dairyman in the country who has not lost valuable cows with milk fever. At last science has come to our aid and given us Feverine, a positive cure and an infallible preventive.
Price, per bottle....................90c.

## Cracked Bone for Poultry.

| | | |
|---|---|---|
| G 2577 | 25 lb sacks.................... | $0 50 |
| | 50 lb sacks.................... | 95 |
| | 100 lb sacks.................... | 1 85 |

## Ground Oyster Shells for Poultry.

| | | |
|---|---|---|
| G 2519 | 25 lb sacks.................... | 45 |
| | 50 lb sacks.................... | 75 |
| | 100 lb sacks.................... | 1 20 |

## Blatchford's Half Meal.

**For Prparing Milk to Feed Calves.**

| | | |
|---|---|---|
| G 2520 | 25 lb sacks.................... | 1 25 |
| | 50 lb sacks.................... | 2 00 |
| | 100 lb sacks.................... | 3 50 |

## Pure Ground Beef Scraps for Poultry.

| | | |
|---|---|---|
| G 2522 | 25 lb sacks.................... | 60 |
| | 50 lb sacks.................... | 1 10 |
| | 100 lb sacks.................... | 2 00 |

D 808 **Kennel Club Soap.** For washing all domestic animals. It will destroy insects, cleanse the skin and keep it healthy; leaves the hair soft and glossy; will not injure the hands; not poisonous.
Per cake; **8 cents**; per doz....................**$0.75**

D 810 **Black Harness Soap.** This is the finest harness soap made. Will clean, polish and preserve your harness, making it look better and wear longer.
Per cake, **15 cents**; per doz....................**$1.50**

## "Milk Oil" Sheep Dip.

"Milk Oil" Sheep Dip never fails to cure **Scab** or **Mange,** and is sure death to **Lice, Ticks and Fleas.** It is the best sheep dip for farmers to use, as it is not poisonous, and no expert is required to apply it. Directions for using on every can. One gallon makes 50 gallons of wash.

D 811 One gallon can, each....................**$ 1.20**
D 812 Five gallon cans, each....................**5.00**
D 813 Ten gallon cans, each....................**10.00**

## Cooper's Dip.

Every sheep grower knows this dip. We sell the **Genuine** which is made in Berkhamsted, England.

D 814 Packet to make 100 gallons....................**$ 2.00**
D 815 Case to make 1,000 gallons....................**16.00**

**WE ALLOW SPECIAL DISCOUNTS FOR CLUB ORDERS. IT WILL PAY YOU AND YOUR NEIGHBORS TO ORDER AT THE SAME TIME, HAVE YOUR GOODS SHIPPED BY FREIGHT, SAVE CHARGES AND GET THE BIGGEST DISCOUNT.**

# THE PRINCESS BUST DEVELOPER AND BUST CREAM OR FOOD

**Regular retail price, each.............$5.00**
**OUR PRICE, EACH ............... 1.46**
**With one bottle Bust Expander, and
one jar Bust Food FREE.**
**OUR PRICE, PER DOZEN........ $15.60**

**WILL ENLARGE ANY LADY'S BUST FROM 2 TO 3 INCHES. PRICE FOR DEVELOPER, BUST
EXPANDER AND BUST FOOD, COMPLETE - - - - - - - $1.46**

With every order for Princess Bust Developer and Bust Food, we furnish FREE one
bottle of the GENUINE FLEUR DE LIS BUST EXPANDER and TISSUE BUILDER (retail
price, 75 cents) without extra charge.

## THE PRINCESS BUST DEVELOPER
### IS A NEW SCIENTIFIC HELP TO NATURE.

**COMBINED WITH THE USE OF THE BUST CREAM OR FOOD, FORMS
A FULL, FIRM, WELL DEVELOPED BUST.**

It is designed to build up and fill out shrunken and
undeveloped tissues, form a rounded, plump, perfectly
developed bust, producing a beautiful figure.

THE PRINCESS BUST DEVELOPER AND CREAM
FOOD is absolutely harmless, easy to use, perfectly safe
and considered the most successful bust developer on
the market.

**IF NATURE HAS NOT FAVORED YOU** with that greatest charm,
a symmetrically rounded
bosom, full and perfect, send for the Princess Bust
Developer and you will be pleased over the result of a
few weeks' use. The Princess Developer will produce the
desired result in nearly every case. If you
are not entirely satisfied with the result after
giving it a fair trial, please return it to us
and we will gladly refund your money.

**Unmailable
on account of
weight.**

**PRINCESS BUST DEVELOPER.**

Comes in two sizes, 4 and 5 inches in diameter. State
size desired. The 4-inch Developer is the most
popular as well as the most desirable size.

**THE DEVELOPER** is carefully made of nickel and aluminum, very finest
finish throughout. Comes in two sizes, 4 and 5 inches
diameter. In ordering please state size desired. The developer gives the
right exercise to the muscles of the bust, compels a free and normal circulation of the blood through the capillaries, glands and tissues of the flabby, undeveloped parts, these parts are soon restored to a healthy condition, they
expand and fill out, become round, firm and beautiful.

## THE BUST CREAM OR FOOD
### IS APPLIED AS A MASSAGE.

It is a delightful cream preparation, put up by an eminent
French chemist, and forms just
the right food required for the
starved skin and wasted tissues.
The ingredients of the Bust Food
are mainly pure vegetable oils,
perfectly harmless, combined
in a way to form the finest nourishment for the bust glands. It is
delicately perfumed and is

**UNRIVALED FOR DEVELOPING
THE BUST, ARMS AND NECK,**

making a plump, full, rounded
bosom, perfect neck and arms, a
smooth skin, which before was
scrawny, flat and flabby.

**FULL DIRECTIONS ARE FURNISHED.
SUCCESS IS ASSURED.**

You need no longer regret that
your form is not what you would
like it to be. Ladies everywhere
welcome the Princess Bust Developer and Cream Food as the
greatest toilet requisite ever offered.

**THE PRINCESS BUST DEVELOPER AND FOOD** is a treatment that will
when properly used for
a reasonable length of time develop and enlarge the bust, cause it to fill out
to full and natural proportions, give that rounded, firm bosom which belongs to a perfect symmetrical figure.

**$1.46 is our Combination Price for the PRINCESS DEVELOPER, BUST FOOD and BUST EXPANDER, Complete, the Lowest Price Ever Made on this Article.**

**DON'T PAY** an extravagant price for a so called bust developer.
Send for the Princess Developer, complete with the Bust Food and Bust Expander, at our special reduced price of $1.46, state whether
you wish the 4 or 5-inch developer, and if you are not entirely satisfied with the results, if it does not meet your expectations, without the slightest harm
or inconvenience, return it, after giving it a trial, and we will refund your money. Don't put off ordering. Nowhere else can you buy a Princess Bust
Developer for only $1.46.
**No. 8E1098 Our Princess Bust Developer, with one bottle Bust Expander and one jar Bust Food, FREE. Price, complete........................$1.46**

# OUR 57-CENT PRINCESS TONIC HAIR RESTORER
## A RELIABLE NEW HAIR TONIC AND PRODUCER

**No,
8E1101**

**Per Bottle
57c.**

**RESTORES THE NATURAL COLOR, PRESERVES AND STRENGTHENS THE
HAIR, PROMOTES THE GROWTH, ARRESTS FALLING HAIR, FEEDS AND
NOURISHES THE ROOTS, REMOVES DANDRUFF AND SCURF AND ALLAYS
ALL SCALP IRRITATIONS. THE ONLY INVARIABLY EFFECTIVE, UNIFORMLY
SUCCESSFUL, PERFECTLY HARMLESS, POSITIVELY NO-DYE PREPARATION
ON THE MARKET** that restores gray hair to its natural and youthful color, removes
scales and dandruff, soothes irritating, itching surfaces, stimulates the hair follicles,
supplies the roots with energy and renders the hair soft and makes the hair grow.
**EVERY SINGLE BOTTLE** of PRINCESS TONIC HAIR RESTORER is compounded especially in
our own laboratory by our own skilled chemists and according to the
prescription of one who has made the hair and scalp, its diseases and cure, a life study.
**PRINCESS TONIC HAIR RESTORER IS NOT AN EXPERIMENT,** not an untried, unknown
remedy, depending upon
advertisements for sale, but it is a preparation made of ingredients that will effectively prevent
the falling of hair, stimulate the growth of new hair, remove dandruff and other scalp diseases.

| | |
|---|---|
| Regular retail price, per bottle........................ | $1.00 |
| Our price, per bottle................................ | .57 |
| Our price, per dozen bottles...................... | 5.75 |

**Unmailable on account of weight.**

**ARE YOU INCLINED TO BALDNESS?** Is your hair thin or falling out? Does your hair
come out easily and gather on the comb and
brush when you brush it? Does your head itch? Do you have dandruff or scurf, and do white
dust like particles settle on your coat collar? Is your hair stiff and coarse and hard to
brush? Is your hair fading or has it turned prematurely gray? If your hair suffers in any
one or more of these particulars, you can order a bottle of PRINCESS TONIC HAIR
RESTORER as a trial, for speedy relief. Use it according to directions and you will be surprised and delighted at the good results. It acts direct on the tiny roots of the hair, giving
them required fresh nourishment, starts quick, energetic circulation in every hair cell, tones
up the scalp, freshens the pores, stops falling and sickly hair, changes thin hair to a fine heavy
growth, puts new life in dormant, sluggish hair cells, producing in a comparatively short time
a new growth of hair. If your hair is fading or turning gray, one bottle of Princess Tonic
Hair Restorer will give it healthy life and renew its original color. PRINCESS TONIC HAIR
RESTORER is good for both men and women. Is equally effective on men's and women's hair.

**PRINCESS TONIC HAIR RESTORER IS ABSOLUTELY HARMLESS.** IT IS NOT A DYE. It can
be applied to the most delicate
hair, it will not stain the daintiest head dress. Princess Tonic Hair Restorer is made under a special process,
perfectly pure and clear, without any sediment, and containing the following named ingredients, recognized as
the best constituents of highest efficiency for hair and scalp treatment for restoring them to a natural, healthy
condition. Princess Tonic Hair Restorer contains in correct proportions: LEAD ACETATE, SOLUBLE SUL-
PHUR, NATRIUM MURIATE, RESORCIN, CANTHARIDES, CAYENNE, GLYCERINE.
**ORDER A BOTTLE AT 57 CENTS** and if you do not find it just the hair tonic you want, stimulating
the growth, cleansing the scalp, stopping hair from falling out, restor-
ing natural color, curing dandruff or promoting a new growth of hair, return it to us at once and we will cheerfully refund your money.
**EVERY BOTTLE OF THE GENUINE PRINCESS TONIC HAIR RESTORER IS STAMPED WITH
THIS LABEL AS SHOWN IN THE ILLUSTRATION—OUR GUARANTEE OF HIGHEST QUALITY.**
**YOU WILL FIND VARIOUS SO CALLED HAIR TONICS** and hair restorers widely advertised in the
newspapers and magazines. Some of them
possess merit and others do not. Those that possess merit are sold for two and three times the price we ask
for genuine Princess Tonic Hair Restorer, and are not equal to the preparation that we put out under our binding guarantee for quality. If you have any doubt as to the merit of the Princess Tonic Hair Restorer as
against the preparations advertised and offered by others, we would be willing for you to order our preparation, and then send for any other preparation on the market, give both preparations a fair and honest trial, and
if you do not find the Princess Tonic Hair Restorer better by far than any other hair tonic, you need only write
us to this effect and we will return your money. By using the remedy properly it will overcome almost any
hair trouble, and a single month's treatment is often sufficient to accomplish result, sometimes a few weeks will
do the work, it depending somewhat on the length of time the trouble has existed.
**No. 8E1101** Price, per dozen bottles, $5.75; per bottle........................ **57c**

**This Label is your
Protection.**
It shows that only the
purest and finest in-
gredients are used.

## ATTENTION LADIES!

The world renowned Doctor Eramus Wilson gives the following advice: "In offering the following advice on the cultivation of natural beauty, I am fully aware of the vast responsibility attending my efforts in this direction, therefore I have carefully avoided making use of any doubtful conclusions, but instead have employed wholesome practical truths only. Now if you expect to succeed in your undertaking, then the very first thing for you to observe is your personal appearance, it matters not whether you belong to the gentle or the opposite sex, this advice is applicable to either.

"My lifelong experience has perfected me to diagnose every blemish of the skin and confidently say there is nothing to equal Maison Riviere's preparations to attain the desired result.

"As the eye conveys the impression—good or bad, pleasing or offensive—therefore it is of the utmost importance that we should make friends with the eye and hold ourselves in readiness for its critical inspection. A bad complexion will immediately place its possessor in an unfavorable light and blind the eye to every other good quality, either of features or intellect. Not only this, but in many cases will stamp its victims as being vulgar and common, and make it impossible for them to rise above these impressions. We judge people immediately by their appearance.

"Now a bad complexion is always an eye-sore to any one, and it matters not how often seen, we can never help picturing to ourselves how different the person would look if she had a good complexion. Any body with the proper kind of pride should shrink from placing herself in such a position as to require her friends and those whom she is thrown in contact with the necessity of apologizing, even to themselves for her bad complexion. That is not what women appreciate; love and admiration are the two great wants in every woman's nature, and beauty alone can aid them in being loved and admired. It is against the laws of nature to admire and love those who do not please us by an attractive appearance and a pleasing manner. A perfect complexion is all that is lacking in most cases to complete a very winning personality, therefore to attain the above results, use the following, as I have much pleasure in stating Maison Rivieres' preparations are absolutely harmless and of great benefit to the skin."

### FRECKLES.

G 6174 These blemishes are excessively disfiguring and annoying—more so because they invariably take possession of the otherwise prettiest complexions. They are caused by a congested condition of the coloring matter, which becomes mottled and dotted on the mucous network, and drawn to the surface by the hot rays of the sun and wind, and in many other cases cold weather will increase them. Maison Revieres celebrated and world-famed Ninon del Enclos will speedily remove all traces of freckles. Full directions on the bottle. $1.00. Our price, 75c.; per doz., $8.50.

### CREME RIVIERE.

G 6175 This is a healing, cooling and penetrating ameliorative cleanser of the skin. In a single night it makes the roughest chapped skin soft and fine grained; also is an excellent wrinkle remover. This elegant preparation is unrivaled for its purity. Full directions on jars. $1.00. Our price, 75c.; per doz., $8.50.

### SUPERFLUOUS HAIR.

G 6176 No worse affliction can befall a woman's face than to see a horrible growth of coarse hairs springing out like bristles, making it harsh and repulsive to the touch and disfiguring to behold. It is unwomanly and should be removed, by the use of Maison Riviere's celebrated preparation. See full particulars on bottle. $1.00. Our price, 75c.; per doz., $8.50.

### CREME INCOMPARABLE.

G 6177 Think of a remedy having the power of summoning instantly to the face and neck the color and beauty of youth! It gives the face a soft, beautiful flush and brilliancy. It is fragrant and refreshing. Maison Riviere's Creme Incomparable is the most elegant beautifier known. Directions on the bottle. $1.00. Our price, 75c.; per doz., $8.50.

### ROUGE ORIENTAL.

G 6178 For ladies who are troubled with pallor or have no color in their cheek, Rouge Oriental is a treasure. It is a beautiful and effective compound for tinting the cheeks. It gives a perfectly natural color, which is only removed by warm water and soap. Rouge Oriental is not affected by the bath, but remains fresh and rosy until removed by soap and warm water. $1.00. Our price 75c.; per doz., $8.50.

### HAIR TONIC AND RESTORER.

G 6179 What is more beautiful than a luxuriant growth of hair in man or woman? The discovery of and successful combination of chemical forces that unite with and aid nature's subtle workings in the scalp, and which produce nourishment for and growth of the human hair is one of the marvelous discoveries of Maison Riviere. It also prevents dandruff and incipient baldness. Full directions on each bottle. $1.00. Our price, 75c.; per doz., $8.50.

### DENTIFRICE.

G 6180 The most perfect preparation for the teeth. Will keep them entirely free from stains or discolorations. It will effectually remove the tartar, hardens the gums and keeps the teeth as lovely as pearls, leaving a delicious aftertaste in the mouth for hours. 50c. Our price, 35c.; per doz., $4.00.

### EAU DE LA JENNESSE.

G 6181 This Complexion Bleach purifies the flesh and makes the skin fresh, healthy and beautiful, it does not bleach out the rosy color of the cheeks as its name might seem to imply, on the contrary, it increases the brilliancy and frees the skin from all foreign matter that gives one that leaden, sallow complexion so often seen, prepared by Maison Riviere. Full directions on every bottle. $1.00. Our price, 75c.; per doz., $8.50.

### TRIANON.

G 6182 This elegant preparation will allay and soothe all irritation of the skin and is highly agreeable to gentlemen after shaving. $1.00. Our price, 75c.; per doz., $8.50.

### POUDRE MERVEILLEUX.

G 6183 This preparation gives the nails a splendid, lustrous and rosy appearance, which enhances so greatly the charms of a lovely and beautiful hand. Full directions on the box. 50c. Our price, 35c.; per doz., $4.00.

### QUEEN VICTORIA PERFUMES

gives universal satisfaction and are the handsomest preparations ever offered to the public, at less than half the regular price. We make these extracts in our own laboratory and can vouch for their lasting qualities and delicate odor. These perfumes are put up in lapidary cut stopper bottles of diamond brilliancy.

| | | 2-oz. size. | 4-oz. size. |
|---|---|---|---|
| G 6184 | Carnation Pink | $0 48 | $0 89 |
| | Columbia Bouquet | 48 | 89 |
| | Jockey Club | 48 | 89 |

| | | 2-oz. size. | 4-oz. size. |
|---|---|---|---|
| | Queen Victoria Perfumes.—Continued. | | |
| | Lilac Blossoms | 48 | 89 |
| | Lily of the Valley | 48 | 89 |
| | Moss Rose | 48 | 89 |
| | Musk | 48 | 89 |
| | New Mown Hay | 48 | 89 |
| | Violet | 48 | 89 |
| | Indian Violet | 48 | 89 |
| | White Heliotrope | 48 | 89 |
| | White Rose | 48 | 89 |
| | Ylang Ylang | 48 | 89 |
| | English Violet | 48 | 89 |
| G 6185 | Meadow Blossom | 48 | 89 |
| | Sweet Clover | 48 | 89 |
| | Jasmine | 48 | 89 |
| | Crab Apple | 48 | 89 |
| | Mignonette | 48 | 89 |
| | Sweet Pea | 48 | 89 |
| | Tea Rose | 48 | 89 |
| | Tuberose | 48 | 89 |
| | Wood Violet | 48 | 89 |
| | Shandon Bells | 48 | 89 |
| | Rose Geranium | 48 | 89 |

### COLOGNES.

| | | 2-oz. size. | 4-oz. size. |
|---|---|---|---|
| G 6186 | Eau de Cologne | 48 | 89 |
| | Hawthorne | 48 | 89 |
| | Nadjy | 48 | 89 |
| | Violet | 48 | 89 |
| | Zenithia | 48 | 89 |

### TOILET WATERS.

| | | 2-oz. size. | 4-oz. size. |
|---|---|---|---|
| G 6187 | Lavender | 48 | 89 |
| | Ylang Ylang | 48 | 89 |
| | Violet | 48 | 89 |
| | White Rose | 48 | 89 |
| | Jasmine | 48 | 89 |
| | Jockey Club | 48 | 89 |
| | White Heliotrope | 48 | 89 |

### RUBBER GOODS.

| | | Each. |
|---|---|---|
| G 6188 | Bulb Syringes in Box with hard Rubber Pipes— | |
| | No. 1 | $1 50 |
| | No. 2 | 90 |
| | No. 4 | 56 |
| G 6189 | Goodyear Syringe No. 13 | 1 01 |
| | Fountain Syringes, with three hard Rubber Pipes, in paper box— | |
| | 1 quart | 68 |
| | 2 quart | 80 |
| | 3 quart | 82 |
| | In wood box— | |
| | 1 quart | 1 13 |
| | 2 quart | 1 25 |
| | 3 quart | 1 37 |
| G 6190 | The Pioneer Fountain Syringe— | |
| | 2 quart | 1 06 |
| | 3 quart | 1 04 |
| G 6191 | Columbian Syringe— | |
| | No. 1, 3 quart | 1 08 |
| | No. 4, 4 quart | 1 25 |
| G 6192 | Goodyear Rubber Syringe, 2-ounce vaginal ring handle | 69 |
| G 6193 | " " " 1 " " " " " | 56 |
| G 6194 | " " " ½ " " " " " | 51 |
| G 6195 | " " " ¼ " " " " " | 45 |
| G 6196 | Ladies' Syringe | 2 68 |
| G 6197 | Rubber Water Bottles— | |
| | 1 quart | 75 |
| | 2 quart | 87 |
| | 3 quart | 99 |
| | 4 quart | 1 11 |
| G 6198 | Plain Atomizer, No. 10, Goodyear | 68 |
| G 6199 | Vaseline Atomizer, No. 15, Goodyear | 1 05 |
| G 6200 | Automatic Plant Spray Atomizer | 93 |
| G 6201 | Our Darling Nursing Bottle | 26 |
| G 6202 | Ladies' Gauntlet Rubber Gloves, all sizes | 1 40 |
| G 6203 | Gents' Gauntlet Rubber Gloves | 1 51 |
| G 6204 | Oval Bed Pan | 3 56 |
| G 6205 | No. 2a Round Bed Pan | 3 51 |
| G 6206 | No. 1 Round Bed Pan, without outlet | 2 36 |
| G 6207 | Invalid Air Cushions— | |
| | No. 5 | 1 89 |
| | No. 6 | 2 01 |
| | No. 7 | 2 13 |
| | No. 8 | 2 25 |
| G 6208 | Air Pillows— | |
| | Size 9x13 | 1 59 |

### RUBBER BATH BRUSH.

G 6209 Three styles of this brush are made, first the electric bath for the body, an excellent thing for rheumatic trouble. Use morning and night and in the bath. Price, each..................$ 60

### RUBBER HAND BRUSH.

G 6210 Used especially for the hands in removing stains, dirt, etc. Does not scratch or deface the skin. Is very effective. Price, each..................$ 25

### RUBBER TOILET BRUSH.

G 6211 For the nails and hands. A ladies' hand brush, is soft and pliable and universally used as a toilet brush. Price, each..................$ 15

### RUBBER BATH MITTEN.

G 6212 The Bath Mitten is made to button over the hand. This mitten is one of the most useful toilet articles for the bath introdued. No family should be without one. In its use it creates a healthful action of the blood and keeping the skin soft and giving a beautiful tint as to nature. Price, each..........$ 75

### BABY BATH MITTEN.

G 6213 Quite similar in construction to the bath mitten, but of softer texture; so delicate, indeed, the young child will welcome the touch. Used in the bath or after drying. Price, each..................$ 45

**Use care in making out your orders. Always use our order blank, if you have one handy. We mail blanks and envelopes free on application.**

# .....DRUG DEPARTMENT.....

**THIS SPECIAL BRANCH** of our business is in charge of competent chemists and registered pharmacists who have had large experience both in this country and Europe in handling and compounding drugs and chemicals. They have strict instructions to examine thoroughly every article received in this department, to note its quality and freshness, to apply tests to ascertain its strength and purity, and to reject everything which does not come up to **full standard** required by the drug inspectors of the United States Government. **WE ARE IN A POSITION** and will be pleased to answer any inquiries concerning drugs, patent medicines, etc., either as regards their appearance, medicinal properties, or special purposes they are used for. **IN ORDERING GOODS FROM THIS DEPARTMENT** we must request you to send cash to the full amount. We will not send C. O. D. All prices in this list are net—no discount. Four-ounce bottles of liquids and smaller sizes can be sent by mail if packed in a special box approved by the postal authorities. You must remember to allow us 10 or 18 cents, according to size, for these mailing boxes. Poisonous, inflammable or explosive materials cannot be mailed.

## OUR 60c
## Nerve and Brain
## PILLS.

**GUARANTEED THE HIGHEST GRADE ON THE MARKET.**

**Six Boxes Positively Guaranteed to Cure any Disease for which they are intended.**

**THIS WILL CURE YOU** if you feel generally miserable or suffer with a thousand and one indescribable bad feelings, both mental and physical, among them low spirits, nervousness, weariness, lifelessness, weakness, dizziness, feeling of fullness, like bloating after eating, or sense of goneness, or emptiness of stomach in morning, flesh soft and lacking firmness, headache, blurring of eyesight, specks floating before the eyes, nervous irritability, poor memory, chilliness, alternating with hot flushes, lassitude, throbbing, gurgling or rumbling sensations in bowels, with heat and nipping pains occasionally, palpitation of heart, short breath on exertion, slow circulation of blood, cold feet, pain and oppression in chest and back, pain around the loins, aching and weariness of the lower limbs, drowsiness after meals, but nervous wakefulness at night, languor in the morning, and a constant feeling of dread, as if something awful was going to happen.

If you have any of these symptoms our **NERVE AND BRAIN PILLS** will cure you. No matter what the cause may be or how severe your trouble is, **DR. CHAISE'S NERVE AND BRAIN PILLS** will cure you. These pills have a remarkable effect on both old and young. They can not be equalled by any other medicine as a cure for impotence, spermatorrhœa, night sweats, emissions, varicocele (or swollen veins), weakness of both brain and body, arising from excesses and abuses of any kind. It will **tone up the whole nervous system**, no matter how much worn out, overworked or depressed you may be; the weak and timid young man made strong and bold again; they will give youthful vigor and a new lease of life to the old.

**BEWARE OF QUACK DOCTORS** who advertise to scare men into paying money for remedies which have no merit. Our Nerve and Brain Pills are compounded from a prescription of one of the most noted German scientists, and are the same as has been used in German hospitals for years with marvelous success. **HOW TO CURE YOURSELF,** and full and explicit directions, are enclosed with every box. All orders and inquiries concerning these pills will be treated **confidentially**, and all shipments made in plain sealed package.

**ONLY $3.00 FOR 6 BOXES.** Enough to cure any case, no matter how severe, no matter how long standing, whether old or young, no matter from what cause. Send us **$3.00** and we will send you 6 boxes by return mail, postpaid, in plain sealed package, with full instructions, full directions.

No. D1500 Price, per box, 60c; 6 boxes (an amount to cure anyone)....$3.00

If you need these pills don't delay, this is the first time the American people have had an opportunity of getting the genuine Dr. Chaise's Pills, and the first time they have been sold any where at anything like our price.

## 75c B B B 75c
### BLOOD BLOOD BLOOD

**READ CAREFULLY AND FIND OUT WHAT OUR B B B MEDICINE IS**

**THESE THREE LETTERS STAND FOR**

## DR. BARKER'S BLOOD BUILDER

Nature's most wonderful remedy for destroying poisons in the blood and building up a pure healthy blood, no matter how diseased the system is.

It is universally conceded that seventy-five per cent of the diseases with which the human family suffer to-day are produced by some poisonous germs in the blood or some derangement of that life giving and sustaining fluid. Physicians tell us that one in every twenty persons is infected with poisonous microbes. It is easy then to understand how blood diseases are so prevalent and needs but little argument to show why a simple vegetable remedy, which destroys and expels these poisonous germs, is the only true blood purifier. It will cure scrofula, cancer, rheumatism, especially that arising from mercurial poisoning; eczema and other skin diseases that arise from impurity of the blood, nasal catarrh, acne or pimples, chronic ulcers, carbuncles, boils. It is a true specific for syphilis in its primary, secondary or tertiary form, eradicating all unclean matter from the blood, removing all taint of this disease. A few bottles taken in the spring will prepare the system to stand the heat and corrupting influence of the hot summer days and ward off sickness. Taken in the fall it braces the system to stand the blasts of winter. As a general tonic and builder up of pure blood **DR. BARKER'S BLOOD BUILDER** is the most valuable of all medicines, cleansing the system, freeing it from all poisonous germs. It is a powerful remedy, yet no one need be afraid to take it, as it is purely vegetable. It will cure you and make your skin smooth and give to it a healthy appearance.

No. D1502 Large bottles.............................75c

## Our 50c
## LIQUOR
## HABIT
## CURE.

**STOP DRINKING GERMAN LIQUOR CURE GUARANTEED TO DESTROY ALL DESIRE FOR LIQUOR SOLD ONLY BY SEARS ROEBUCK & CO.INC. CHICAGO ILL**

**Every man can be permanently cured of the habit or desire for intoxicating drink of any kind.**

**WE GUARANTEE A COMPLETE CURE.** Our remedy is perfectly harmless, none of the bad effects produced by many so called liquor cures so widely advertised. That drunkenness is a disease that can be cured by medicine, just the same as other diseases can, is a fact becoming well known. Thousands of cases have been cured by this medicine; in fact, its wonderful curative properties are now well known throughout the entire world. We bring this cure within the reach of everyone. It is now not necessary to go to an institute for treatment; home treatment is just as successful. The impression has been cultivated by interested parties that cures could not be effected except by hypodermic injections, but nothing is more absurd. Any medicine taken into the stomach will be as effective as if used hypodermically. No medicine has had such a wonderful success in this age of progress as **OUR LIQUOR HABIT CURE**. It creates an appetite for food instead of liquor, it stimulates the whole system to healthy action, it quiets nervous excitement, vertigo, muscular trembling and all the dangerous effects of excessive use of liquor. It improves the appetite and digestion and regulates the bowels. It is, in fact, a perfect cure for the drink habit.

**WE URGE EVERYONE** who have accustomed themselves to the excessive use of liquor, and who wish to stop the practice, to send for even a small box as a trial. We know our remedy will cure you. We are sure that after using a few doses you will feel the craving for liquor disappearing and a warm healthy glow spreading from the stomach over the whole system; you will have a desire for food instead of rot gut. This will be the commencement of the cure, and if you will follow it up faithfully for a few weeks it will effect a permanent cure. When you have used a small box, we know you will send for 12 more boxes for $5.00, to thoroughly complete the cure.

No. D1504 Price for small box containing 24 doses................$ .50
Per dozen..........................5.00
Price for large box containing 48 doses................1.00
Per dozen..........................9.10

12 small boxes, our $5.00 lot, will cure almost any case. 12 large boxes, our $9.10 lot, will cure any case, no matter how severe.

## OUR 70c. POSITIVE
## Rheumatic Cure.

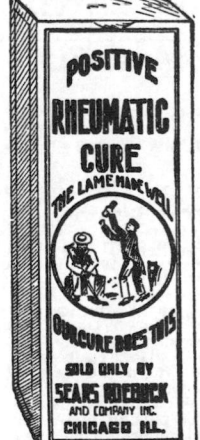

**POSITIVE RHEUMATIC CURE THE LAME MADE WELL OUR CURE DOES THIS SOLD ONLY BY SEARS ROEBUCK AND COMPANY INC. CHICAGO ILL.**

**WHAT IS RHEUMATISM?** This Dreadful disease, this scourge of humanity, is a blood disease, always due to one cause, namely the presence in the system of urea, and uric acid, which poisonous elements could not be retained unless there was a defective kidney action underlying the Rheumatic disease. Rheumatism may be divided into two classes, Acute and Chronic Rheumatism. Acute or commonly called inflamatory rheumatism announces itself through piercing pains in the joints and muscles in the back, the knees, the hips, etc., and generally spreads through the whole body. Chronic Rheumatism on the other hand is accompanied by no fever, the joints are very painful, swollen, sensitive and often stiff. If this disease is of long duration the joints will swell or expand, and dislocation take place. The resulting deformity and crippling of the joints can be cured if correctly treated. We can say inflammatory Rheumatism is the most dangerous of the two, owing to its rapid spreading over the body, implicating certain internal organs and structures, especially the heart, often producing pleurisy, pneumonia, bronchitis, cerebral and spinal meningitis. If the disease has thus far advanced without receiving proper treatment relapses are frequent and death often results, which is generally due to complications. There is but one satisfactory way to treat rheumatism and that is in a constitutional manner, by giving internal medicines which act on the blood.

Our Positive Rheumatic Cure will positively cure Rheumatism in all forms and in all its different stages, by reason that it removes from the system the urea and uric acid upon which the disease feeds. This remedy has a specific action on the blood, it increases the number of the red blood corpuscles, which are morbidly deficient in cases of rheumatism.

Our Positive Rheumatic Cure is compounded from a prescription of a celebrated French Scientist who spent the greater part of his life in prescribing for rheumatism in all its forms. Our Remedy Will Cure when all others fail. If you have rheumatism in any form you should get this remedy at once. If you have been suffering for years you will find quick relief and final cure in this remedy. If your case is chronic order six bottles for, in severe cases and cases of long standing there is a necessity to use this remedy for a longer period; several months may be needed to fully secure exemption from the disease. We recommend ordering six bottles, it will cause a complete reconstruction of the system.

No. D1506 Price, per bottle, 70c; per six bottles................$3.75

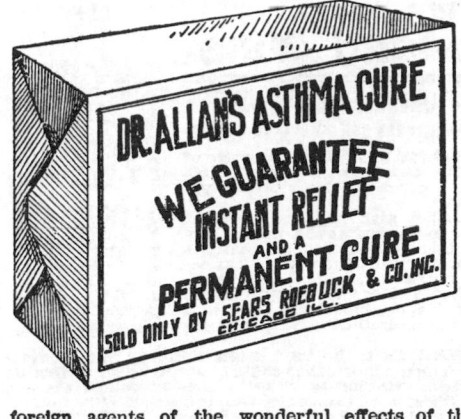

## NUTRITIVE TONIC.
# Beef, Iron and Wine.

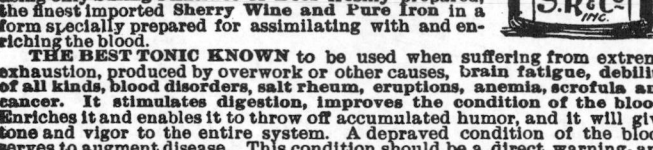

### GUARANTEED HIGHEST GRADE EVER PRODUCED.
**OUR PRICE 35c.** Inferior grades sell at 50c to $1.00.

**NO FAMILY SHOULD BE WITHOUT** a bottle of **BEEF IRON AND WINE.** This is an old time TONIC, universally known for its great strength giving and flesh producing qualities.

**THE GREAT TROUBLE** with most of the Beef Wine and Iron found in the market at the present day is the poor quality of materials used in making it. It is often found in a state quite unfit for use on that account. We take great pains with this preparation, using only Suling's Extract of Beef freshly prepared, the finest imported Sherry Wine and Pure Iron in a form specially prepared for assimilating with and enriching the blood.

**THE BEST TONIC KNOWN** to be used when suffering from extreme exhaustion, produced by overwork or other causes, brain fatigue, debility of all kinds, blood disorders, salt rheum, eruptions, anemia, scrofula and cancer. It stimulates digestion, improves the condition of the blood. Enriches it and enables it to throw off accumulated humor, and it will give tone and vigor to the entire system. A depraved condition of the blood serves to augment disease. This condition should be a direct warning, and by taking it as such and using a corrective, much ill health can be avoided.

**WE HAVE THOUSANDS OF TESTIMONIALS** as to the wonderful good this medicine has done for those that are weak, nervous and debilitated. **OUR PRICES ARE VERY LOW.** Inferior goods are sold everywhere at nearly double our prices.

| | | |
|---|---|---|
| **No. D1515.** | Price for full pint bottles | $0.35 |
| | Price for ¼ dozen pint bottles | 2.00 |
| | Price for 1 dozen pint bottles | 3 75 |
| | Price for ½ gallon bottle | 1.50 |
| | Price for 1 gallon bottle | 2.50 |

**ORDER A GALLON BOTTLE** of our Beef Wine and Iron and you will find it the best investment you ever made.

## Our Celery Malt Compound

### FOR 55 CENTS.

**We sell the highest grade Celery Malt Compound for 55 cents in large bottles.**

It retails everywhere, even in inferior qualities, at $1.00 and upwards.

We guarantee our Celery Malt Compound to be absolutely pure, unadulterated and superior to any other celery compound on the market regardless of name or price.

Our Celery Malt Compound is a true nerve tonic, a genuine appetizer, a stimulant both for the young and old. We do not pretend that it is an absolute specific for any chronic disease, but it has a much wider range of usefulness as it is especially beneficial in hundreds of the ills that flesh is heir to.

A glance at its composition, which we give below, will show any person of ordinary intelligence why it is such a useful preparation and should be kept in every household.

Our Celery Malt Compound contains in a concentrated form the active medicinal properties of the Italian celery seed, well known to physicians as one of the best and most active controlling and strengthening agents for the nerves, also the phosphates in the same state as found in the strong, healthy, vigorous, natural body, and in quantities approved of by the medical profession, the value of which has been so thoroughly demonstrated in all brain and nervous affections and in emaciated conditions. In addition it contains a large percentage of malt, which is very strengthening and fattening.

You will see it is an ideal combination which is not only a most useful tonic and stimulant but a delicious beverage as well.

As a brain and nerve tonic, appetizer and stimulant, it is certainly unqualed in the realm of medicine.

For insomnia, nervousness, mental or physical exhaustion, loss of appetite, impoverished blood and for that tired feeling that comes from close confinement or sedentary habits, it is really magical in its effects, infinitely better than all stimulants of an alcoholic nature.

If you are nervous, exhausted, can't sleep, or if the body is poor and your digestion imperfect and you are out of sorts generally and in a low physical condition, do not fail to try Celery Malt Compound. It will give you new life and vigor and build up your entire system.

Ask your neighbors about our Celery Malt Compound. Some of them doubtless have used it, and if they have they can tell you of its merits. No family can afford to be without it.

If you have bought compound of any other make from your local druggist, order a bottle of Celery Malt Compound at 55 cents. Try it. Compare it, and if you do not find our Celery Malt Compound better than any other like preparation on the market, return it at our expense and we will refund your money.

Our Celery Malt Compound is prepared under our special direction by a very able chemist. Every ingredient is carefully tested to know that it is of the very highest quality, and it is sent out under our guarantee that there is no other preparation of the kind that compares with it.

| | | |
|---|---|---|
| **No. D1517** | Our special price for large bottles | $0.55 |
| | For half dozen bottles | 3.00 |
| | For one dozen bottles | 5.50 |

**Order a dozen bottles at $5.50.** You can sell half of them at $1.00 each and the half dozen will cost you nothing.

# Our Drug Department is under the management of a
## MOST COMPETENT CHEMIST OF MANY YEARS EXPERIENCE.

**YOUR ORDERS** when placed with us are in MORE CAREFUL HANDS than when placed with two-thirds of the local druggists.

---

## MOTHERS
### Read What we Say About Our
# RELIABLE WORM SYRUP AND
## WORM CAKES.

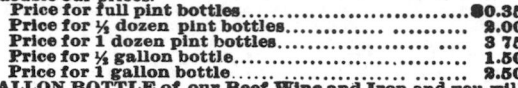

You can save your children from much suffering and in many cases save their lives. No other disease is so fatal to children as worms. Unfortunately they are seldom free from them, and as the symptoms resemble those of almost every other complaint, they often produce alarming effects without being suspected. Worms are not only a cause of disease in themselves, but by their irritation aggravate all other diseases, wandering from one part of the body to another, winding themselves up into large balls, obstructing the bowels and frequently the throat, causing convulsions and too often death. **OUR RELIABLE WORM SYRUP** effectually destroys the worms and removes the nest in which their young are deposited. It moves the bowels very gently, the worms being to a greater or less extent dissolved by the action of the medicine, can scarcely be recognized in the stools, but the improvement in the health of the child will be sufficient evidence of the beneficial effects of the medicine. Every mother ought to have a bottle of the syrup or a box of the cakes always in the house. The syrup and the cakes are the same medicines in different forms. The syrup is more pleasant to the taste and more suitable for very young children. The cakes can be given to older people, even adults can be benefitted by using them, as grown up folks, as well as children, often suffer from worms. These reliable worm medicines are not only worm destroyers, but act as a general tonic, destroying sourness of the stomach and producing a healthy appetite. Mothers, keep your children healthy.

| | | |
|---|---|---|
| **No. D1519** | Each bottle of syrup, 20c; per doz | $2.25 |
| | Each box of cakes, 20c; per doz | 2.25 |

# PERUVIAN WINE OF COCA.

A Genuine Rich Wine Imported by Ourselves and well known throughout Europe for its Strengthening and Nourishing Qualities.

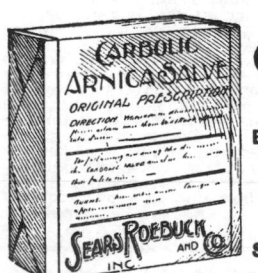

It sustains and refreshes both the body and the brain, and has deservedly gained its excellent reputation and great superiority over all other tonics. It is more effective and rapid in its action. It may be taken for any length of time with perfect safety without causing injury to the system, the stomach and gastric juices. On the contrary, Peruvian Wine of Coca aids digestion, removes fatigue and improves the appetite, never causing constipation. For many years past it has been thoroughly tested and has received the endorsements of hundreds of the most eminent physicians of the world, who assure us of their utmost satisfaction with the results obtained by using it in their practice. They urgently recommend its use in the treatment of Anemia, Impurity and Impoverishment of the Blood, Consumption, Weakness of the Lungs, Asthma, Nervous Debility, Loss of Appetite, Malarial Complaints, Biliousness, Stomach Disorders, Dyspepsia, Languor and Fatigue, Obesity, Loss of Forces and Weakness caused by excesses, and similar Diseases of the Same nature. It is specially adapted for persons in delicate health and for convalescents. It is very palatable and agreeable to take and can be born by the most enfeebled stomach where everything else would fail.

If you wish to accomplish double the amount of work or have to undergo an unusual amount of hardship always keep a bottle of our Peruvian Wine of Coca near you. Its sustaining powers are wonderful.

It is used in most of the Hospitals in Europe, and many of our American public institutions are adopting it. After many severe tests it has been effectually proven that in the same space of time more than double the amount of hardship and work could be undergone when Peruvian Wine of Coca was used and positively no fatigue experienced.

Expecting a large demand for this wine we have made arrangements for an extra large shipment, which enables us to let our customers in at the very lowest price.

**No. D1521** Per bottle, 95c; per dozen ................ $10.00

## ARNICATED
# CARBOLIC SALVE
### The Best in the World for

**BURNS, FLESH WOUNDS, CHILBLAINS, BOILS, FELONS, SORES, PILES, ULCERS AND FEVER SORES.**

EXCELLENT FOR
**Salt Rheum, Eczema, and Ringworm.**

| | | |
|---|---|---|
| **No. D1522** | Per Box | $0.25 |
| | Per Doz | 2.00 |

# ...WONDERFUL...
# LITTLE . LIVER . PILLS.

### ENTIRELY VEGETABLE IN THEIR COMPOSITION.

These wonderful little pills operate without disturbance to the system, diet or occupation.

CONSTIPATION, that most hideous and deathly demon of sickness, is an easy enough thing to cure if you will only persist in taking proper treatment. It is one of the commonest troubles and often thought to be a very little thing. Yet, we say that nine-tenths of all human sickness is due to this one thing. When the bowels do not move regularly the natural drainage tract in the human system is damned up, decomposition ensues and poisonous gases and liquids are carried all through the system. The result is jaundice, torpid liver, biliousness, sallow skin, indigestion, foul breath, coated tongue, loss of appetite, pimples, belching foul gases, blotches, boils, dizziness, headache, cramps, colic, etc. You can easily avoid all these troubles and keep your system pure and healthy by taking from time to time one or two of our WONDERFUL LITTLE LIVER PILLS. Some of our customers call them "LITTLE GIANTS," they are so small in size and easy to swallow, yet so effective and mild in their operation. Whenever your stomach, liver and bowels get out of order take one or two of our LITTLE WONDERS and notice the quick effect and great relief you will experience. Keep a bottle always beside you. Use them occasionally and you will always feel well and look the picture of health.

No. D1525  Per bottle, only 12c; per doz............................$1.00

## Ague Cure.

### FOR CHILLS AND FEVER THIS IS A TRUE SPECIFIC.

We are selling thousands of boxes to those living in the Southern and Western states and not a case of failure to cure has as yet been reported to us; we were fortunate to obtain the recipe for this cure from a physician who had used it constantly in his practice for thirty years with great success. It is an infallable remedy for this disease and those living in low and swampy localities, ought to have it always at hand. It is much superior and less harmful to the systum than quinine. It acts more promptly and the cure is more complete. With every package is enclosed a small vial of vegetable liver pills, with explicit directions how to keep the system in condition to guard against malaria.

No. D1527.  Per box, 50c; per doz.................................$5.00

## Orange Wine
## Stomach Bitters.

Guaranteed Absolutely Pure and the Highest Grade on the Market.

Put up in extra large bottles holding 1 1-2 pints.

DO NOT COMPARE OUR ORANGE WINE STOMACH BITTERS with the bitters that are being sold by retail druggists generally at $1.00 to $1.50 a bottle, bitters that are made from the very cheapest ingredients. Our Orange Wine Stomach Bitters are made from wine distilled from the fruit of the Seville Orange tree in combination with herbs well known for their tonic and healing effect on the stomach. Order 1 dozen bottles. You can sell them at $1.00 each with profit enough so that several bottles will cost you nothing.

This is a pleasant bitters. As before explained, it is made from a wine distilled from the fruit of the Seville orange tree in combination with herbs well known for their tonic and healing effects on the stomach. As an appetizer there is no bitters made that will equal it, and it is a guaranteed cure for dyspepsia when its use is continued for some time. As a general bracer up of the whole system it has no equal, and the taste is so delicious that the most fastidious enjoy taking it. Owing to the intrinsic and widely established therapeutic value of its chief constituents, which are necessary to good digestion, this preparation stands unequaled. While furnishing admirable means for treating gastric ailments, indigestion, want of appetite, malarial diseases, low spirits, and nervousness, it removes that tired feeling and heals the derangements generally, will purify the blood, the bones, muscles, and the nerves receive new force, brain power is supplied and health and vigor restored. It exerts a most wonderful power in sustaining the system during arduous labors and journeys. It stimulates respiration and the brain by increasing the blood supply, increases the heart's action, and under its daily use an extra amount of labor can be borne without suffering. It is an agreeable and wholesome stimulant, and imparts a pleasant taste with an agreeable sense of warmth which permeates the entire system. Don't buy bitters from your local druggist unless you are acquainted with the reputation of the manufacturers and thus know that the ingredients contained are of the highest grade. Understand, every bottle of the Orange Wine Stomach Bitters is sold with our positive guarantee that they are made from the fruits of the Seville orange tree in combination with 17 different roots and herbs in such a manner that the greatest beneficial effects are obtained.

OUR OFFER.  Send us 85c for a bottle of our Orange Wine Stomach Bitters, and if you are not greatly benefitted, if you do not find it superior to any bitters on the market, return it at our expense and we will cheerfully refund your money.

No. D1529  Our special price for bottles holding 1½ pints..........$0.85
½ dozen bottles ...........................................  4.50
1 dozen bottles............................................  8.50

# Our Famous
# BLOOD PILLS.

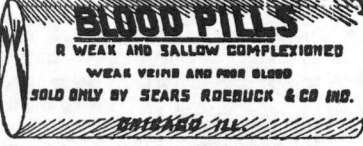

### FOR MEN AND WOMEN THAT REQUIRE A NERVE TONIC, BLOOD PURIFIER OR BUILDER.

Over one hundred thousand sold last year, which shows what is thought of these pills when known. Others sell them at 50 cents per box.

### Our Price is 25c per box; $2.00 per dozen.

FOR FEMALE TROUBLE they are an unfailing remedy, and guaranteed far superior to any other pills on the market at any price. They give tone to the whole system, making the eyes bright, the cheeks rosy, and, through strength and buoyancy, the step is firm and elastic. Our BLOOD PILLS can be taken according to directions without any danger, by either sex, and if carefully followed will result in quick results and permanent relief. Weakness, poor thin blood, giving a sallow or pale complexion, loss of appetite, Chlorosis or Green Sickness, Pain in the Back, Palpitation of the Heart, Nervous Headaches, Suppression of Menses, Leucorrhœa, Tardy or Irregular Periods, Hysteria, Paralysis, and all diseases resulting from humors in the blood, which cause Erysipelas, Sores, Swellings, and even Consumption, also in cases where the system is broken down by overwork of mind or body, or from excesses and indiscretions of living. THE EFFECT IS WONDERFUL. These pills are not of a cathartic nature, they do not nor are they intended to purge. They are intended to act on the blood, and supply what is needed in restoring the tone and lacking constituents, stimulating to activity the sluggish system.

FOR WOMEN, in case of Suppression of Menses, Leucorrhœa or Whites, Chlorosis, Anemia, Locomotor Ataxia, a quick and permanent cure can be effected; in fact, it is the greatest remedy known.

FOR MEN, these pills stand without a rival. They build up the system and cure Spermatorrhœa, Impotence, Nervous Despondency, Loss of Memory, Confusion of Ideas, Irritability of Temper, Pain in Back and Perinæum, draining of Prostatic Fluid. These pills retail everywhere at 50c to $1.00.

No. D1531, Price, per box, 25c; per doz............................$2.00

# ....OUR....
# EARLING FIG LAXATIVE.

### ....FOR THE....

### Bowels, Liver, Kidney and Stomach

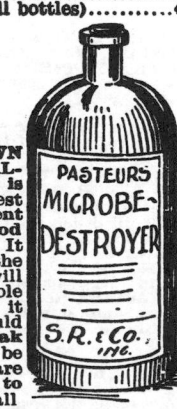

The great remedy of the age for above troubles.

### Our Price for Small Bottle............20c
### Our Price for Large Bottle............40c
### (EQUAL TO THREE SMALL BOTTLES).

EARLING FIG LAXATIVE was never retailed for less than 50 cents. OUR SPECIAL PRICE IS 20 CENTS. If you have bowel, kidney, liver or stomach trouble in any form order a large bottle of Earling Fig Laxative and you will find immediate relief and a speedy and permanent cure. EARLING FIG LAXATIVE will cure you speedily and permanently, even if physicians have been unable to help you. Earling Fig Laxative is nature's own remedy for restoring the bowels to a healthy and normal condition. Unlike pills and purgatives it strengthens instead of weakening and enfeebling their action. For Chronic Constipation, to effect a permanent cure a remedy is required that will not only act quickly on the bowels, but will produce a tone and stimulating effect upon the inner coating of the intestines, strengthen the muscular action and restore the paralyzed functions. Earling Fig Laxative, if taken regularly, will cure constipation with its attending ills. Earling Fig Laxative is perfectly harmless. It is a liquid made from fruits, plants and herbs, is mild in form, easy to take, and in all cases of bowel, stomach, kidney and liver complaints its effect upon the entire system is magic.

No. D1533  Price per small bottle.................................20c
Price per large bottle (equal to 3 small bottles)...........40c

## PASTEUR'S
## Microbe Killer.

NONE GENUINE UNLESS BEARING OUR OWN LABEL. OUR SPECIAL PRICE. ONE-HALF GALLON BOTTLE 97c. Others sell it at $2.00. This is Dr. Pasteur's Microbe Killer, one of the grandest remedies known to the present age. It will prevent LaGrippe, Catarrh, Consumption, Malaria, Blood Poison, Rheumatism and all diseases of the blood. It acts as an antiseptic, killing the germs which are the cause of the disease. Dr. Pasteur's Microbe Killer will eradicate any form of disease, and purify the whole system. By taking it regularly once or twice a day it will ward off many attacks of disease which would otherwise cause much suffering. If you have weak lungs don't fail to keep this remedy on hand to be taken fall and spring and at other times when there are sudden climatic changes. If you are subject to Catarrh take this remedy once or twice a week and all trouble will be ended. If you are subject to Rheumatism it will save you all pain. You will never again be bothered with rheumatism if you use Pasteur's Microbe Killer. If you are subject to fever and LaGrippe, use Dr. Pasteur's Microbe Killer as a preventative and you will never have trouble. No family should be without this wonderful remedy. It will save its cost a hundred times every year. See it make the difference.

No. D1535  Price per half gal. 97¢; per gallon............$1.75

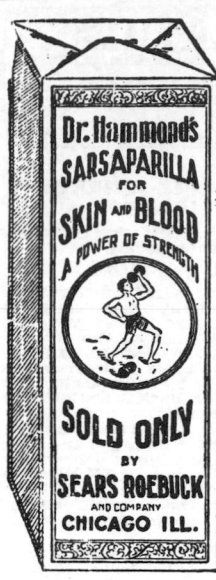

# HAMMOND'S SARSAPARILLA.

### Guaranteed the Best on the Market.

**There is no other Sarsaparilla made that will compare with it.**

Our price, per large bottle, 59c; per doz., $6.00. Never retails at less than $1.00.

Dr. Hammond's Sarsaparilla combines in an agreeable form the medicinal properties of the most approved alterative and blood purifying remedies of the vegetable kingdom. Dr. Hammond's Sarsaparilla will not cure everything, but the fact that on the purity and vitality of the blood depends the vigor and health of the whole system, and that disease of various kinds is often only the sign that nature is trying to remove the disturbing cause, lead to the conclusion that a remedy which gives life and vigor to the blood and eradicates scrofula and other impurities, as this preparation undoubtedly does, must cure and prevent many diseases. Hence the field of its usefulness is an endless one, and we are warranted in recommending it for all derangements caused by an unnatural state of the blood.

FOR SCROFULA. Dr. Hammond's Sarsaparilla is the greatest known remedy for scrofula, and there is no other disease that is so general among our population. ALMOST EVERY INDIVIDUAL HAS THIS LATENT POISON COURSING THE VEINS. Its alarming fatality is not realized because consumption and other diseases are reported as the causes of deaths, many of which are the result of scrofula. This scrofulous taint weakens the energies of life, and constitutions contaminated by it are more susceptible to disease and have less physical force to withstand it. Persons afflicted with scrofulous sores endure intense suffering which, like the gratitude they feel to a remedy which cures them, cannot be fully appreciated by others. Scrofulous affection is hereditary, and may be transmitted, without appearing, through several generations, and then assume its worst forms. The indications of scrofula are many and varied. The following are among its prominent characteristics: Pallid countenance, a bluish white transparent complexion, inflamed eyelids, eruptions on the scalp and various parts of the body, irregular appetite, sometimes keen, at others, dainty; bowels irregular, a general lassitude and debility which takes away all energy or desire for action, business or labor. Scrofula is most dangerous when it seats itself upon the lungs, producing tubercular consumption. It is not, however, confined to any part of the body, as it attacks the lungs, liver and kidneys, also the digestive and uterine apparatus, inducing and often resulting in a long train of diseases such as consumption, ulceration of the liver, stomach or kidneys, eruptions and eruptive diseases of the skin, ulcers, tumors, erysipelas, salt rheum, blotches, postules, tetter, pain in the bones, side or head, ring worm, scald head, catarrh, dyspepsia, female weaknesses, leucorrhœa arrising from internal ulceration and uterine diseases aggravated by low condition of the system or impure state of blood, dropsy, emaciation, general debility, that tired feeling.

OUR SARSAPARILLA is a purely scientific preparation. It is carefully prepared from the most powerful, yet perfectly safe and harmless alteratives and blood purifying agents, selected from the vegetable kingdom. This preparation does not contain mercury or arsenic in any form or combination whatever. OUR SARSAPARILLA CURES where all others fail. It combines the merits of all other sarsaparilla compounds with defects of none. For blood making, blood cleansing, flesh and appetite producing OUR SARSAPARILLA is unequaled. No family can afford to be without it. For infants, children, grown people, it should be taken regularly. OUR PRICES ARE VERY LOW.

No. D1540 Price, per large bottle, 59c; per doz............ ......$6.00
NEVER RETAILED AT LESS THAN $1.00.

# Dr. Rose's KIDNEY and LIVER CURE.

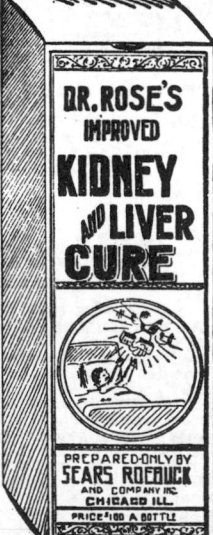

THIS IS THE FIRST TIME DR. ROSE'S REMEDY HAS BEEN OFFERED DIRECT TO THE PATIENT. Heretofore it has been prescribed by doctors and then sold at $1.50 to $2.00 per bottle.

## OUR PRICE IS 85c; PER DOZ. $9.00.

GUARANTEED THE GREATEST KIDNEY AND LIVER REMEDY EVER KNOWN. This is a great remedy which will effect a speedy cure where all other remedies fail. For all diseases arising from disordered Kidneys, Liver or Bladder there is nothing known that will equal Dr. Rose's Kidney and Liver Cure. It cures Bright's Disease, Diabetis, Catarrh of the Bladder, Incontinence of the Urine, Irregular Menses, Leucorrhœa, Dysmenorrhœa, Female Weakness and General Debility. The medicine acts directly on the organs, its cleansing properties add vigor and tone to the whole system. If you have Kidney, Liver or Urinary trouble of any nature don't delay, order a bottle at once and you will be surprised at the results.

D1542 Price, per bottle 85c; per doz....................... $9.00

# Dr. Rose's French Arsenic Complexion Wafers......

OUR SPECIAL PRICE
Per box, 40c; per dozen, $4.25.
OUR SPECIAL PRICE
For larger box, 79c; per dozen, $8.00.

### RETAILS GENERALLY FOR MORE THAN DOUBLE THE PRICE.

PERFECTLY HARMLESS when used in accordance with our directions, it possesses the "wizard's touch" in producing, preserving and enhancing beauty of form and person in male and female by surely developing a transparency and pellucid clearness of complexion, shapely contour of form, brilliant eyes, soft and smooth skin, where by nature the reverse exists. The great trouble hitherto has been how to make this beautifying principle safely available and at the same time avoid what is detrimental and injurious. Arsenical solutions have utterly failed, and until a recent discovery by a French physician and chemist, the internal administration of arsenic has been attended with more or less danger as well as disappointing results. In the direction for which they are intended their effect is simply magical, the most astounding transformation in personal appearance being brought about by their steady use. Even the coarsest and most repulsive skin and complexion, marred by freckles and other disfigurements, slowly change into an unrivaled purity of texture, free from any spot or blemish whatever, the pinched features become agreeable, the form angular gradually transforms itself into the perfection of womanly grace and beauty. These pills are used by men, the favorable results are the same.

All Danger is Averted in these Complexion Wafers, prepared by our experienced chemist, and the remedy taken in the manner directed on each box is absolutely innocuous while the peculiar virtues of the remedy remain unimpaired and intact. Taken as directed the wafers will be found a positive, safe and magical specific for all sorts of skin troubles, unsightliness and imperfections, being in reality the only beautifier of the complexion, skin and form known. Guaranteed a sure cure for freckles, moth, blackheads, pimples, vulgar redness; rough, yellow or muddy skin, and other facial disfigurements are permanently removed and a deliciously clear complexion and rounding up of angular forms assured.

Ladies, you can be beautiful. No matter who you are, what your disfigurements may be, you can make yourself as handsome as any lady in the land by the use of our French Arsenic Wafers. We recommend ordering one dozen large boxes and then carefully follow our directions.

No. D1544. Price, per small box, 40c; per doz...................... $4.25
Price, per large box, 75c; per doz...................... $8.00

# Dr. Hammond's Tar Expectorant.

## THE GREAT CONSUMPTION CURE.

More cases of Consumption have been cured by the timely use of Dr. Hammond's Tar Expectorant than by all other remedies combined.

For the cure of Colds, Coughs, Croup, Influenza, Bronchitis Quinsy, Laryngitis, Hoarseness, Sore Throat, Night Sweats, Catarrh and for the immediate relief of Consumptive patients.

DR. HAMMOND'S TAR EXPECTORANT is the most wonderful remedy ever offered to the public. It wonderfully increases the power and flexibility of the voice, strengthens weak lungs, allays pulmonary irritation and affords the most effectual relief for Whooping Cough and even for Consumption in its advanced stages. It is especially beneficial in those diseases which are too often regarded as simply annoying, such as common colds and coughs, but which are really dangerous in their tendency and demand prompt and active treatment. For the more serious forms of Throat and Lung Troubles its value can not be overestimated to anyone worn out with constant coughing and loss of sleep.

DR. HAMMOND'S TAR EXPECTORANT is a blessing, as it gives immediate relief, and sweet rest follows.

WE GUARANTEE that every case of pulmonary disease, not already beyond the reach of human aid, can be relieved and cured by being promptly treated with Dr. Hammond's Tar Expectorant. DELAYS ARE DANGEROUS.

Keep a bottle always in the house and use it promptly whenever the first symptom of a cough shows itself. Both suffering and money will be saved. PRICE WAS NEVER SO LOW BEFORE. It is retailed at 75 cents per bottle when sold by dealers.

No. D1546 Price per bottle.............30c; per dozen...... .....$3.00

# CATHARTIC PILLS.

This is the old fashioned sugar coated Cathartic Pill of the U. S. Pharmacopœia, the same as Ayer's, Brandreth's, Jaynes' and other much advertised pills. They act principally on the liver, and move the bowels gently without griping. These pills are carefully prepared from fresh vegetable extracts, and can be thoroughly relied upon. For this reason they are much superior to many others sold at double their price.

No. D1548 Box containing 25 pills, 10c; doz........ ......... ......75c

## SAVE EXORBITANT DOCTOR'S BILLS.

# ELECTRICATING LINIMENT.

## A NEW AND GREAT DISCOVERY.

NOTHING BEFORE HAS BEEN KNOWN LIKE IT. By a newly discovered process this liniment is electrically charged by a powerful current of electricity, whereby the ingredients undergo a powerful change which, when applied to the most severe cases of Rheumatism, Sprains and Bruises, effects immediate relief. It never fails in its Magical Effect.

Certain cure for Rheumatism, Cuts, Sprains, Wounds, Old Sores, Corns, Galls, Bruises, Growing Pains, Contracted Muscles, Lame Back, Stiff Joints, Frosted Feet, Chilblains, Etc. Persons suffering from partial paralysis of arms and legs will be rendered great benefit by its use, frequently regaining complete use of these members, also an application to the Throat and Chest and externally for Lung Troubles; great relief will be experienced by rubbing the chest with this, the most penetrating liniment in the world. TRY IT.

No. D1550. Price, bottles, 29c; per doz. $3.00

# CORNS, BUNIONS AND WARTS.

THE GREAT CHINESE CORN, BUNION AND WART REMOVER never fails to give immediate relief and a complete cure is certain when directions are faithfully followed. No one suffering from Corns, Bunions or Warts should fail to give our great Chinese Corn, Bunion and Wart remover a trial. We have tried it ourselves and found relief, therefore can testify knowingly as to its great merits.

No. D1552 Price, each, only 10c; per doz. $1.00

# Injection No. 7.

## CURES IN ONE TO FIVE DAYS

**No Other Medicine Required**
**No Fear of Stricture**
**No Bad Results**

### An Absolute Cure.

A French Specific having a great reputation abroad as a reliable cure for all troubles of the urinary organs in either male or female, has a very quick effect and leaves no bad result, no matter how severe the case. Either gonorrhœa or gleet quickly and easily cured. Full instructions and valuable information with each package.

No. D1554 Price per bottle............79c
Per doz....................$8.00

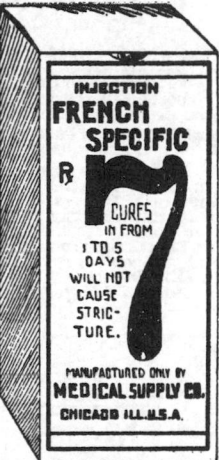

# BROMO VICHY.

**A Morning Bracer. A Headache Reliever.**
**A Brain Cleaner.     A Nerve Steadier.**

This is by far the best "Bromo" preparation at present offered to the public. One or two teaspoonfuls taken in half a tumbler of cold water will instantly dispel any sickness of the stomach, relieve a severe headache, clear up the brain and steady the nerves. It is a thirst quencher, and causes a pleasant feeling to prevail all through the body. It is a quick remedy for nervous Headaches, Neuralgia, Sleeplessness, Over Brain Work, depression following alcholic excesses, and all nervous troubles. A little should always be on one's bureau table for use in the morning or at night.

No. D1556 Small trial size, only 8c; large size.........20c

# DO YOU SNEEZE?

# CAMPHOR PILLS

Have been long used by the homeopathic physicians as a remedy for cold in the head, cramps, colic, diarrhœa and cholera morbus and other annoying troubles resulting from catching cold. Also for menstrual colic. A bottle of these pills ought to be carried in the pocket continually by those who are traveling, or outside most of the day exposed to all weathers. Though very effective in performing cures, they are small and can be conveniently kept in the vest pocket. They attained their first reputation many years ago by the remarkable success following their use in preventing and curing Asiatic cholera. Since then the have become a household necessity with thousands of people.

No. D1558 Small vial, 20c; doz....................$2.00
Large home vial, containing as much as 4 small vials...59c

# CAMPHOR COLD CREAM.

A SALVE OF REMARKABLE HEALING QUALITIES. Of great value when the skin is chapped from cold; it will heal up the cracks and make the skin soft and smooth again, also it cannot be excelled as a soothing and healing application to burns, and dressing for abraisons of the skin, pimples, boils, etc.

No. 1559. Price, per pot......... ........15c
Per doz ....................$1.50

# Rr. Rose's Dyspepsia Powders.

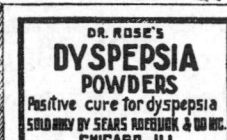

DYSPEPSIA RELIEF SURE FOR 40c. A remedy of remarkable efficacy in Dyspepsia and all troubles of like nature. It acts upon the food as digester and transforms starchy food into soluble and easily digested principles, thus relieving the stomach and allowing rest and also giving tone to that organ. By taking a powder just before a meal you prevent many of the ills brought on by an irreliable stomach such as dyspepsia, sour stomach, heartburn, indigestion, constipation, distress after eating, belching of wind, and in truth, it can be said that it is a true assistant to digestion. It never fails to relieve, no matter how severe the case may be. A trial is all that is asked for. A single box even will convince any sufferer of the remarkable results obtained from the use of these powders.

No. D1561 Price per box 40c; per doz.... .........................$4.00

# Baby Cough Syrup.

## MOTHER'S FAVORITE REMEDY.

NO MOTHER OUGHT TO GIVE HER CHILD MEDICINE WITHOUT KNOWING WHAT IT CONTAINS. Babies take cold easy, their lungs are weak, and at the first symptom of cold, such as watering at the lips or nose, hoarseness, slight cough, feverish skin, a simple remedy which is known to have healing properties ought to be given, as delay is more dangerous than in adults. Our "MOTHER'S FAVORITE REMEDY," carefully made from the purest materials, thoroughly tested by our chemist, composed of Tulu, Squills, Arabian Healing Gum, Rock Candy, compounded by our chemists from the prescription of a famous English physician, who years ago attended the Royal Family of England, is a good remedy and perfectly harmless.

No. D1562 Price, per bottle, 20c; per doz ...$2.25

# Castroline.

## SAME AS CASTORIA.

### 1100 Drops for Only 20c.

Keep Your Children Healthy and Cheerful by Using Castroline Only.

YOU NEED NOT HAVE ANY OTHER MEDICINE IN THE HOUSE FOR YOUR CHILDREN. It is unquestionably the best thing for infants and children the world has ever known. It is harmless, and children like it. It gives them health and may save their lives. Mothers, keep it beside you, and you will always have something absolutely safe, pleasant to take, and the acme of perfection as a child's medicine for every ailment they are subject to.

CASTROLINE WILL DESTROY WORMS, allay fever, prevent vomiting, cures diarrhœa and wind colic, relieves teething troubles. Cures constipation and flatulency. It assimilates the food, regulates the stomach and bowels, and gives to the child a healthy and natural sleep. When your baby cries give it a dose of CASTROLINE, its effect will be soothing to the baby and pleasant to you. It contains neither morphine or opium or any other narcotic property. It is much superior to the so-called soothing syrups which are being advertised daily. It will cause the baby to sleep when fretful, giving the mother her much needed rest. One size bottle only.

No. D1563 Price, per bottle 20c; per doz.........................$2.25

# FOR THOSE WHO SUFFER.

# Carbo Wafers.

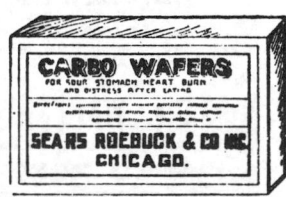

AN AID TO DIGESTION. From personal experience we believe these wafers to be unexcelled as a cure for the most stubborn cases of dyspepsia. They contain in a concentrated form the natural peptic principles of the stomach combined with French willow charcoal. We can truly recommend them as a curative in all disordered conditions of the digestive functions such as heartburn, sour bitter fluid rising in the throat, belching of gas, water brash, weight pain and fullness in the stomach after eating, with palpitation of the heart, nausea, and bad effects from abuse of stimulants. Morning sickness is greatly relieved by their use.

No. D1564 Price, per box containing 25 doses, 25c; per doz........$2.50

# Blackberry Balsam.

**A REMEDY WHICH SHOULD BE KEPT CONSTANTLY AT HAND.**

The poorest in the land can afford it at only 20 cents a bottle. It will prevent serious illness used promptly, and often be the means of saving life. It is a pleasant, safe, speedy, and effectual remedy for Dysentery, Diarrhœa, Looseners, Asiatic Cholera, Cholera Morbus, Cholera Infantum, Summer Complaint, Colic, Cramps, Griping Pains, Sour Stomach, Sick and Nervous Headache, Pain or Sickness of the Stomach, Vomiting, Restlessness and Inability to Sleep, Wind in the Stomach and Bowels, Hysterics, and for all bowel affections. We have received thousands of certificates from physicians, clergymen, and families of the first respectability bearing the strongest testimony in its favor.

No. D1565   Price, single bottle.................$ .20
Per doz............................2.25

## PILES! PILES!! PILES!!!

## Speedy-Cure Pile Remedy.

**WHY SUFFER** when one quarter of a dollar spent for our SPEEDY-CURE PILE REMEDY will give relief and perform a cure. This preparation affords immediate relief and a prompt cure in all cases. It allays at once the extreme soreness and tenderness of all parts, reduces the inflammation and heals all ulcerative conditions. It is equally serviceable for itching piles. We have sold thousands of boxes and do not know of a single case where a permanent cure has not been effected. If you have tried other remedies without getting relief, try our SPEEDY-CURE, IT NEVER FAILS.

No. D1566   Price, per box, 25c; per doz. boxes.......................$2.00

## THE GENUINE
# German Herb Tea.

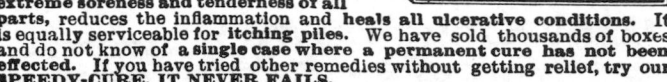

A HARMLESS VEGETABLE REMEDY AND A POSITIVE CURE FOR CONSTIPATION, with no bad after affects. It is composed of herbs and roots familiar to the peasant of Germany, especially those who nurse the sick. Through irregular living, poorly cooked food, improper habits of eating, nearly all persons are suffering more or less from constipation and the resultant sick-headaches; although there may be a daily movement of the bowels, there is still much fecal matter adhering to the intestines and poisoning the blood. Our Herb Tea, made of simple, harmless herbs, will, when taken regularly for a short time, thoroughly cleanse the stomach and bowels of all unclean matter. The blood becomes purified and the person greatly improved in health.

No. D1567   Price, per small box, 20c; per doz.......................$2.25
Price, per large box, 40c; per doz. .....................4.25

## —DR.— HAMMOND'S INTERNAL CATARRH CURE.

**A RADICAL CURE FOR CATARRH.**

Reduced to 50 cents.          Formerly sold at $1.00.

IF YOU HAVE CHRONIC CATARRH order Dr. Hammond's Internal Catarrh Cure and you will get instant relief and a speedy and permanent cure. A great many people cannot understand how our internal remedy can affect catarrh when located in the head, where most people feel the catarrh first, but whether in the head, stomach, bowels, bladder or throat it is all the same. Dr. Hammond's Internal Catarrh Cure will destroy the disease and make you well again. Catarrh is a chronic inflammation of the mucous surface and it is the same wherever you find it, you cannot completely cure it until the whole system has been put in perfect health. Local treatment will give you relief but can not cure. When the hearing has become affected we have never failed to give relief and often completely restore it by the use of this great remedy. Full directions accompany each bottle, also fuller particulars concerning it. Cure your catarrh with Dr. Hammond's Internal Catarrh Cure. Try a bottle, and you will surely use it until well again.

No. D1568   Price, per bottle, 50c; per doz... ...........$5.00

# DR. WALTER'S CELEBRATED EYE WATER.

## ☞NO MORE WEAK OR SORE EYES.☜

WHEREVER THIS REMARKABLE EYE-WATER HAS BEEN INTRODUCED A MARKED IMPROVEMENT IN THE HEALTH OF THE EYES HAS BEEN THE RESULT. Dr. Walter, a celebrated Specialist on Eye Diseases, used this water 25 years in his practice, performing wonderful cures. For weakness or inflammation of the eyes it has no equal, absolutely harmless to the youngest child.

No. D1569   Bottle, 15c; per doz......................$1.40

---

# MEXICAN HEADACHE CURE.

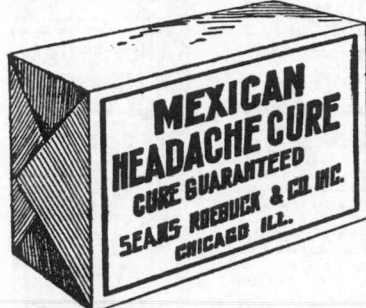

A Splitting Headache Cured Immediately by our Positive Headache and Neuralgia Cure.

Almost every one is more or less troubled with a headache at some time or other. Some persons are hardly ever free from them, and suffer martyrdom. We confidently say to our customers that it is not necessary to suffer longer than the time it takes to get a package of our Positive Headache Cure. We positively guarantee relief within fifteen minutes after the first dose has been taken. Rarely is a second dose required except in very obstinate cases. No matter from what cause, whether a nervous headache, or from the stomach, or a severe case of neuralgia, we guarantee complete relief. It is perfectly harmless, no bad results follow its use. Give it a trial when you suffer and you will be sure to speak of us as your friends.

No. D1570   Box, 25c; dozen...............................$2.25

## INDIAN COUGH SYRUP.

An old Indian remedy for coughs, colds, sore throat, bronchitis, croup, and all diseases of the throat and lungs, prepared by White Cloud of the Indian Medicine Company. Each bottle usually sold for 50c.

No. D1571   Price, per bottle........ 20c
Per doz.........$2.25

# COD LIVER OIL.

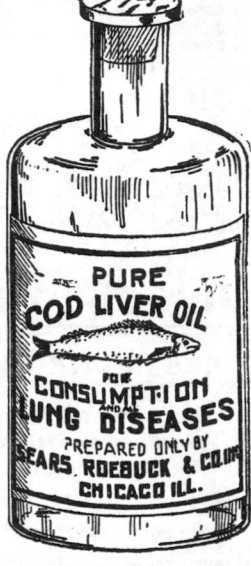

**Guaranteed Absolutely Pure. Highest Grade Made.**

Look at Our Prices : { Full Pint Bottles....$ .50
{ Per Dozen........... 5.50

You will save one-half in price and get the best goods possible to put up if you place your order with us.

☞You can't afford to buy Cod Liver Oil unless you know it is absolutely pure.

If you buy from us you will have our guarantee and know it is absolutely pure and fresh, imported direct from Norway, in original packages, where it is prepared from strictly fresh livers, pure and sweet.

For Consumption, Severe Colds, Lung and Throat Troubles, NORWAY COD LIVER OIL should be taken regularly.

No. D1572   Per pint bottle............50c
Per dozen...............$5.50

# OUR COD LIVER OIL EMULSION.

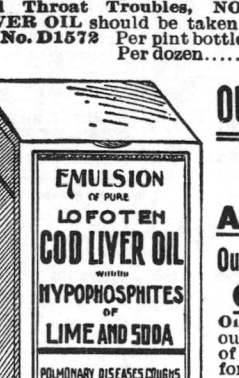

**Pure Cod Liver Oil with Hypophosphites of Lime and Soda.**

## A CONSUMPTION CURE.

Our price for large bottle, 60c; per doz., $5.50

**60 cents** is the lowest price at which the highest quality Cod Liver Oil Emulsion was ever sold and we feel sure our customers will appreciate this opportunity of getting for 60 cents what they have heretofore been compelled to pay $1.00 or more for.

IT IS THE GREATEST REMEDY EVER DISCOVERED for Phthisis or Consumption, Colds and Chronic Coughs, Scrofula in its various forms, Rheumatism, Skin Diseases, Diseases of Children, Anaemia, or poor condition of the blood, and General Debility. In all the above diseases a remedial agent most essential and productive of the best results is a nutrient, an alterative for the body and a tonic for the brain and nervous system. FOR CONSUMPTION there is nothing known to equal our Cod Liver Oil Emulsion and in the first and second stages will effect a quick and permanent cure. FOR COUGHS AND CHRONIC COLDS there is nothing known to equal our Cod Liver Oil Emulsion, and no family can afford to be without it. Doctor bills can be avoided, often lung fever and other diseases averted by the time use of Cod Liver Oil Emulsion. We would advise mothers to always have a bottle on hand to give to their children or any member of the family when they have a cold or stubborn cough. AS A CURE FOR SCROFULA in its various forms Cod Liver Oil Emulsion is of the greatest benefit. FOR RHEUMATISM, Cod Liver Oil Emulsion is a valuable remedy and it has often cured the most stubborn cases, when all other remedies have failed. FOR SKIN DISEASES Cod Liver Oil Emulsion should always be used, there is perhaps no other remedy that exerts so powerful an influence over skin diseases. For GENERAL DEBILITY AND EMACIATION. Our Cod Liver Oil Emulsion taken regularly after meals will quickly recuperate and build you up to renewed strength, health and vigor. FOR PURE BLOOD nothing will do so much good as our Cod Liver Oil Emulsion, it will enrich and purify the blood, give it heat and life and tone and strengthen the entire nervous system. FOR DISEASES OF CHILDREN our Emulsion of Cod Liver Oil should always be used.

No. D1573   Price for large bottle, 60c; 1 dozen bottles............$5.50

# SPECIAL FAMILY DEPARTMENT.
## FAMILY REMEDIES.

### Simple, Useful, Necessary, and Known to Everyone.

We list here a few useful articles which will be recognized by everyone as valuable to have in every household. We guarantee the freshness, strength and purity of each, as they are carefully put up by our experienced chemists in our own laboratory. It is scarcely necessary for us to endeavor to impress on every head of a family the great importance in a time of sickness of having a few simple remedies not only near at hand, but also of full strength and purity. Useless medicines not only waste your money but also cause much bodily harm and lead to more serious sickness. We will stake our reputation on the strength and purity of our Family Remedies and Useful Articles. Let this be your motto always, buy from a responsible house whose reputation is established for honorable dealing. We wish our customers to know that we look on them as friends and endeavor to treat them as such. We sympathize with them in their troubles, and are only too happy when we are able to help them either in giving advice or saving them money. Study the following list well. Our prices are so low that the expense of having a few of them in the house is very small, and besides having the satisfaction of knowing of their good quality.

## ...BORAX...

### THE HOUSEKEEPER'S FRIEND.
HAS MORE USE ABOUT THE HOME THAN EVEN THAT OF COMMON SALT.

For the laundry, the kitchen, the bath and for various medical uses it is indispensible.

Chemically pure and finely powdered. We put it up in one-pound boxes with complete directions for using in washing, starching, keeping away moths, killing cockroaches, dressing wounds and bruises, arresting fermentation, cleaning clothes, etc.

You can rely on getting from us the pure powdered borax, which will be much satisfaction to you, as it is a much adulterated article.
No. D1580. 1 pound boxes, 10c; doz....$1.00

## LAUDANUM.

#### (Tinct. Opium.)

U. S. P. Strength. Directions on each bottle for old and young.
No. D1581
1 oz. bottle, 10c; per doz..............$1.10
2 oz. bottle, 18c; per doz.............. 2.00
4 oz. bottle, 28c; per doz.............. 3.00

## PAREGORIC.

### ALWAYS USEFUL.
### BOTH FOR CHILDREN AND ADULTS.
#### Full directions.
No. D1582 2 oz. bottle, 12c; per doz............$1.25
4 oz. bottle, 18c; per doz. ................ 1.75

## Sweet Spirits of Nitre.

This article is more liable to adulteration than any other medicine. You seldom can get it pure and full strength from a drug store. It is a valuable medicine when fresh and unadulterated. We guarantee what we sell to be absolutely pure.
No. D1583 2 oz. bottles, 15c; per doz................$1.60
4 oz. bottles, 25c; per doz................ 2.50
Per pint.................................. 75

## Essence Peppermint.

#### Pure and Strong, Best Quality for Medical Use.
No. D1584 2 oz. bottles each, 15c; per doz..........$1.50
4 oz. bottles each, 25c; per doz.......... 2.50

## Essence Jamaica Ginger.

PREPARED OF GREAT STRENGTH FROM THE FINEST QUALITY OF JAMAICA JINGER, imported by ourselves. Ginger has healing properties peculiar to itself; many preparations are offered for sale which are represented as containing ginger, when generally they owe their hot taste to pepper alone. Buy our genuine essence and get the full benefit of its valuable properties.
No. D1585 2 oz. bottles, each, 15c; per doz... ...........$1.50
4 oz. bottles, each, 25c; per doz............... ...........2.50

**SAVE 40 TO 75 PER CENT ON ALL MEDICINES, DRUGS, ETC. GET THE PUREST OF INGREDIENTS IN EVERYTHING YOU BUY.**

## Castor Oil.

#### Cold Pressed and Almost Tasteless.
No. D1586 4 oz. bottles, each, 15; per doz.........$1.50
Half pint bottles, each, 25; per doz......... 2.50

## Olive Oil. (Sweet Oil.)

THIS IS A FINE OIL IMPORTED BY US FROM OLIVE VINEYARDS OF ITALY, for either internal or external use. Any one wishing to use an absolutely pure Olive Oil should send for this.
No. D1587 4 oz. bottles, each, 19c; per doz..........$2.00
Half pint bottles, each, 25c; per doz..... 2.75

## ..SPIRITS OF CAMPHOR..

#### MADE FROM PURE GUM CAMPHOR, IMPORTED BY OURSELVES FROM FORMOSA, CHINA.

No. D1588 2 oz. bottles, each, 10c; per doz..........$1.00
4 oz. bottles, each, 18c; per doz.......... 1.15
Per pint, 60 cents.

## Tincture of Arnica

We are careful to make this of great strength from recently picked Arnica Flowers, thereby getting the full virtues of the herb . . . . . .

The value of Arnica is well known as an application to Bruises, Sprains, Cuts, Swelling, &c., but to secure any benefit it is necessary to have a strong well prepared tincture, such as ours.
No. D1590 4 oz. bottles each, 16c; per doz..........$1.95
Half pint bottles each, 24c; per doz..... 2.75
1 pint bottles each, 45c; per doz......... 4.50
($3.00 per gallon.)

## CAMPHORATED OIL.

An excellent article for rubbing on children and grown up person's chests and throats in cases of croup, difficulty in breathing, sore throat, coughs. A small quantity of pure spirits of turpentine added to it will increase its effectiveness in many cases.
No. D1591 4 oz. bottles 18c; 8 oz. bottles............................35c

## SPIRITS OF TURPENTINE.

### Pure, for Internal or external use.

When you wish to use turpentine as a medicine whether internally or externally, always get a pure article, never use the common oil of turpentine that is generally sold for mixing with paints.

### WE SELL THE PURE.

No. D1592 Price, 4 oz. bottles for only 10; per doz........ $1.00
8 oz. bottles for only 15c; per doz. ............. 1.50
16 oz. bottles for only 25c; per doz............ .. 2.00

## Glycerine.

WARRANTED ABSOLUTELY PURE. Can be used either externally or internally.
No. D1594 2-oz. bottles, 10c; per doz ........ .. ....................$1.00
4-oz. bottles, 15c; per doz........................ 1.50
½-lb. bottles, 20c; per doz........................ 2.00
1-lb. bottles, 35c; per doz........................ 3.25

## Petroleum Jelly.

This is another name for Pure Vaseline or Cosmoline, and other titles given to it. It is one of the most valuable and also the most harmless and simple articles to have at hand in cases of bruises, cuts, burns, chaps, roughness of the skin, etc. For convenience, we put it in 2-oz. screw top glass jars.
No. D1596 Price, each, 6c; per doz............$ .50
1-lb. cans, 20c; per doz............ 2.00

## Carbolized Petroleum Jelly.

This is the same as the above, with the addition of Pure Carbolic Acid, which increases to a great extent its powers of healing.
No. D1598 2-oz. bottles, 15c; per doz..................................$1.50
1-lb. cans, 45c; per doz.............................. 5.00

# Neutralizing Cordial.

### A WELL-KNOWN HOUSEHOLD REMEDY.

Useful in treatment of Diarrhœa, Dysentery and Cholera Morbus. Also a great remedy for Dyspepsia, a general corrector of the Stomach and Bowels.
No. D1600 4-oz. bottles, 28c; per doz..............$2.75

## FLAKE TAR CAMPHOR.

A Chemically Pure Product of Coal Tar for the Preservation of Furs, Clothing, etc., from Moths.

It will not injure the most delicate fabrics and is a certain preventative of moth attacks which are so distructive to winter clothing, woolen goods especially.
No. D1602 Put up in 1-lb. pkgs....... ..........25c
Per doz... .................$2.00

## Sulphur Candles.

For fumigating infected rooms and clothing in times of cholera, diphtheria, typhoid and scarlet fevers and all contagious diseases.

The most powerful disinfectant known. Kills all insects. Destroys noxious vapors. When you wish to fumigate with sulphur use these, no danger of fire, easily lighted, burns steady, a most convenient article to have.
No. D1604 Price, per candle only, 8c; per dozen..................65c

## Perfumed Petroleum Jelly.

THIS MAKES AN EXCELLENT DRESSING FOR THE HAIR, much superior to all pomades containing animal fats, which become rancid and spoil and injure the hair.
No. D1606 Price per 2-oz. bottle, 15c; per doz.....................$1.50

## Compound Licorice Powder.

THIS IS A WELL-KNOWN GENTLE LAXATIVE, pleasant to take. Children take it readily. It has an effective and healing action on the bowels. We prepare it carefully, according to the instruction of the German Pharmacopeia.
No. D1608 4-oz. package, 20c; 8-oz. package, 35c; 1-lb. package....65c

## Seidlitz Powders.

WE ALWAYS MAKE OUR SEIDLITZ POWDERS FRESH WHEN WE RECEIVE THE ORDER FOR THEM.

Most of these powders bought in stores are worthless from being kept too long; they lose their strength. We guarantee all Seidlitz Powders we send out to be made from pure materials and full strength. Put up in tin boxes, containing in each 10 blue and 10 white papers.
No. D1610 Price, each box, 20c; per doz..................$2.00

# CARBOLIC ACID.

A Saturated Solution of Carbolic Acid for Disinfecting Purposes, Destroying Contagion, Cleansing Purposes, etc.

Excellent for keeping away disease, destroying bad smells. Put up expressly for household use.
No. D1612
1-lb. bottles, each....... $ .25
Per doz.................... 2.50

## AMMONIA.

STANDARD QUALITY.
Extra Purity and Strength.
Put up expressly for home use.
It lightens work and brightens the home. Makes the washing cleaner and polishing easier.
In pint bottles, with full directions for using in the laundry, for the toilet, and for cleaning glass, crockery, paint, taking out stains, etc.
No. D1614 Each, 7c; per doz.....................75c

## Quinine Pills.

2 grs. each, sugar or gelatine coated. We have made a special contract with one of the best known and largest manufacturers of quinine pills in the world to supply us with these pills made full strength and with absolutely pure quinine. For the convenience of our customers we have them put up in wooden boxes containing 25 pills, 2 grains of pure quinine each, sugar coated.
No. D1616 Price, per box, 12c; per doz......................$1.25
Also, we have them in bottles. Each bottle contains 100 2-grains pure quinine pills, either gelatine or sugar coated.
No. D1618 Per bottle, 25c; per doz................................$2.50

# EPSOM SALTS.

These salts lose their strength when kept long in open drawers and boxes, as is the custom in most retail stores. We furnish this salt always fresh and its valuable qualities unimpaired by exposure to the atmosphere.
No. D1620 Price, per pkg. freshly put up to order, 5c; per doz..................50c

## ROCHELLE SALTS.

When Pure this Salt is almost tasteless

We are particular to get it straight from the manufacturer and know that it is of pure quality.
No. D1622
¼ lb. packages.....15c
½ lb. packages.....25c
1 lb. packages.....40c

## SUBLIMED SULPHUR.

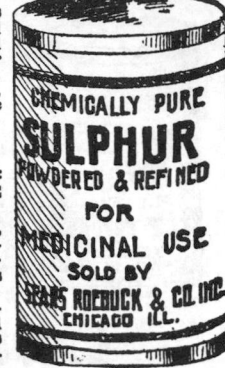

The finest Flowers of Sulphur prepared especially for medical use and packed by our chemist.
No. D1624 1 lb. pkgs., each 5c; per doz.....50c

## GENUINE HAMAMELIS WITCH HAZEL EXTRACT.

BUY DIRECT AND SAVE ALL RETAIL PROFITS.

We can save you money, save you one-half on anything in this line, and Guarantee Highest Grade Goods on the market.

Our Extract of Hamamelis Witch Hazel, you will find even better than Pond's Extract, a universal all-healing remedy.

Should be in every household, useful for sore throat, hemorrhage, wounds, sprains, bruises, sore eyes, stiff joints, burns, and in nearly every accident that one can have.

We guarantee this to be pure full strength and such as is not often found in retail stores.

Our Price is so low that every family can afford to keep a supply in their homes.
Look at Our Prices.
No. D1626.
½ pint bottle, retail price, $ .50; our price.......15c
1 pint bottle, retail price, 1.00; our price.......25c
1 quart bottle, retail price, 1.50; our price.......40c
½ gallon, retail price........2.75; our price.......70c
1 gallon, retail price........3.50; our price ...$1.00

## RAT KILLER.

### THE GREAT VERMIN DESTROYER.

The most efficient poison for Rats, Mice, Cockroaches, Ants, Flies, Squirrels, Crows, Bed Bugs, and all kinds of troublesome vermin. This is a sure destroyer. Rats and mice do not die in the house after eating it, but go outside for air and water.
No. D1628 Price, per box, each, 11c; per doz..$1.00

# INSECT POWDER.

A true Dalmatian Insect Powder, warranted free from all adulterations. Fresh and Strong. Sure death to Bed Bugs, Croton Bugs, Potato Bugs, Cockroaches, Fleas, Lice, Moths, Flies, Ants and all insects. This article is very much subject to adulteration. Buy from us and get it PURE.
No. D1630 Put up in ¼ lb. tin boxes, each, 15c; per dozen....$1.50
Put up in 1 lb. boxes, each, 40c; per dozen.. .........$4.50

## Insect Powder Gun.

For using the above.
No. D1632 Price, each, 6c; per doz....60c

### Large or Jumbo Powder Gun.

Holds ¼ lb. of powder, button and spout screw off. Large opening for filling.
No. D1634 Price, each, 20c; per dozen...........................$2.00

# STRANGLE FOOD.

### THE SUREST AND QUICKEST DEATH TO BUGS.

It instantly strangles. Kills cockroaches, bedbugs, croton bugs, ants, moths, fleas, lice and all other vermin. Harmless to man, beast or bird.
No. D1636 Price, per can, 25c; per doz. $1.50

## A FEW HANDY POCKET GOODS

### In Screw Top Air Tight Glass Vials.

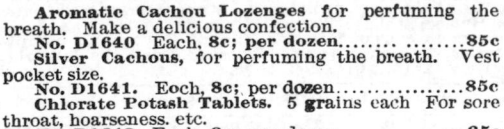

**Aromatic Cachou Lozenges** for perfuming the breath. Make a delicious confection.
No. D1640  Each, 8c; per dozen..............85c
**Silver Cachous**, for perfuming the breath. Vest pocket size.
No. D1641.  Each, 8c; per dozen...............85c
**Chlorate Potash Tablets.** 5 grains each  For sore throat, hoarseness. etc.
No. D1642  Each, 8c; per dozen...............85c
**Soda Mint Tablets**, for sour stomach, flatulency, nausea, etc.
No. D1643  Each, 8c; per dozen...............85c
**Bronchial Troches**, for coughs, colds, sore throat. hoarseness.
No. D1644  Each, 8c; per dozen...............85c
**Licorice Lozenges.**  Pure, very soothing to the throat and bronchial tubes.
No. D1645  Each, 8c; per dozen...............85c
**Slippery Elm Lozenges.** Demulcent for roughness in the throat and irritating cough.
No. D1646  Each, 8c; per dozen...............85c
**Paregoric Tablets.**  Each tablet equals 15 drops of paregoric; dose 1 to 4 according to age.
No. D1647  Price, each, 8c; per dozen...........85c
All of the above tablets furnished at 65c per pound in bulk.
**Pepsin tablets.** Made from pure pepsin, for dyspepsia, indigestion, etc.
No. D1648  Price, per bottle, 15c; per doz....$1.50
**Trix for the breath.**
No. D1649  Price, per package, 3c; per doz.....35c
**Sen Sen.**
No. D1650  Price, per package, 3c; per doz.....35c

# NURSERY DEPARTMENT.

### For Baby Foods See Special Drug Catalogue.

| | Usual price, each. | Our price, each. | Our price, per doz. |
|---|---|---|---|
| No. D1666  Baby Cough Syrup, a reliable remedy expressly prepared for young children, harmless...... | $0.25 | $0.20 | $2.25 |
| No. D1667  Bull's Baby Syrup, soothing and quieting | .25 | .20 | 2.00 |
| No. D1668  Winslow's Soothing Syrup...... | .25 | .18 | 1.90 |
| No. D1669  Nursery Powder, for chafing. etc. | .25 | .10 | 1.00 |
| No. D1670  Borated Talcum Powder, in decorated metal box with perforated top, for the nursery and for the toilet......... | .25 | .10 | 1.00 |
| No. D1671  Castroline.  An excellent substitute for castor oil, pleasant to take, safe, mild and sure, just the thing for the baby when it is cross.  It will sweeten the stomach and regulate the bowels.......... | .25 | .20 | 2.25 |

## Rubber • Teething • Rings.

**Rubber Teething Rings**, seamless, full size, best white rubber.
No. D1672  Price each..............3c
**Rubber Teething Rings**, full size, seamless, best black rubber.
No. D1673  Price each............4c
**Bone Teething Ring**, 1¾ inches, nicely finished.
No. D1674  Price each.................4c
**Vegetable Ivory Teething Ring.**  Teething ring of real vegetable ivory and large seamless black rubber nipple.
No. D1675  Price each........................10c
**Bailey's Teething Pad.**
No. D1676  Price each.....•................70c

# NURSERY BOTTLE FITTINGS.

**Best quality**, all complete, in white, black or maroon.
No. D1677  Each, 6c; per doz.....60c

## Nursing Flasks.

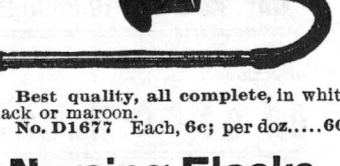

**Graduated to hold 8 ounces**, oval shape with sloping sides.  No corners, therefore easy to clean.
No. D1678  Each, 7c; per doz.....70c

### Borated Talcum Baby Powder.

**For the toilet and nursery.** Preserves, softens and whitens the skin.  For chafing it is an excellent powder.  Absorbs moisture and keeps the skin cool and soft.  Nicely perfumed and put up in handsomely decorated metal boxes with sprinkler top.
No. D1679  Price per box, 10c; per doz...........................$1.00

## Rubber Nipples.

**Rubber Nipples** for tube fittings.  White, black and maroon.
No. D1680  Price, each, 2c; per doz..............20c
**Rubber Nipples** to fit over bottle.  White, black or maroon.
No. D1681  Price, each, 3c; per doz.................25c
**Rubber Nipples**, Davidson's patent.  Black, white or maroon.  To fit over bottle.
No. D1682  Price, each, 3c; per doz.................30c
**Davidson's Health Nipples.**  Made from the finest Para rubber; is constructed so that the infant can obtain a strong hold and renders nursing easy.
No. D1683  Price, each, 4c; per doz.................45c
**Mispah Valve Nipple.**  Making nursing easy.  Allows the food to flow easily.  Prevents colic.
No. D1684  Price, each, 5c; per doz.................50c
**Nursing Bottles**, Burr patent, white rubber fittings.
No. D1685  Price, each, 10c; per doz........95c
**S. R. & Co. Nurser No. 1.**  Fitted with white, black or maroon fittings.  Complete with two brushes in each box.
No. D1687  Price, each, 20c; per doz......$2.25

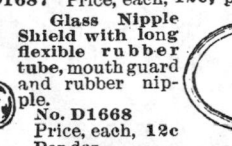

**Glass Nipple Shield with white rubber nipple and bone guard.**
No. D1687  Price, each, 12c; per doz.........$1.00

**Glass Nipple Shield** with long flexible rubber tube, mouth guard and rubber nipple.
No. D1668  Price, each, 12c  Per doz.....................$1.10
**English Breast Pump**, with white rubber bulb.  One in box.
No. D1689  Price, each, 20c; per doz.................$2.00

# TOILET POWDER PUFFS.

**For ladies' and infants' use.**  Satin tops, ivory handle.
No. D1690  Price, each, 20c; per doz..........$2.25

# PUFF BOXES.

**Celluloid**, in ivory, pink or blue.  Very light and handsome.
No. D1691  Each, 45c; per doz..$5.00
**White metal**, handsome gilt covers, ornamental tops.
No. D1692  Each, 25c; per doz..$2.50

## SUPERFINE NURSERY POWDER.

**One-quarter pound Packages.**
No. D1693  Price, each, only 10c; per doz........$1.00

# BABY • SOOTHING • SYRUP.

**A blessing to parents**, harmless and effectual in soothing and quieting children of any age.  We guarantee it to contain no opium or morphine; prepared from simple herbs and has a wonderful effect in soothing and quieting a child who may be cross, no matter from what reason.  A remedy for colic, excellent during teething time.
No. D1720  Price, per bottle, 18c; per doz...........$2.00

# RUBBER TUBING.

**Smooth or corrugated white**, for bulb and fountain syringes.
No. D1700  Price, per foot.............................5c
**White, black or maroon rubber** tubing for feeding bottles.
No. D1702  Price, per foot.......................4c
**Glass tubes for nursing-bottle fittings.**
No. D1704  Price, per doz..............................10c

# NURSERY RUBBER SHEETING.

| White. | Width, | 27 inch. | 36 inch. | 45 inch. | 54 inch. |
|---|---|---|---|---|---|
| No. D1710  Price, per yard.............. | | 37c | 48c | 64c | 80c |

**Tan Rubber Sheeting**, soft as silk, very light in weight, strong and absolutely waterproof.  For hospital and nursery use, also for making bathing caps, diapers, etc.
No. D1712  27 inches wide, per yard.................45c
No. D1714  26 inches wide, per yard.................60c

# OUR HOMEOPATHIC REMEDIES.

Our Homoepathic Specifics are prepared under the supervision of an old experienced Homeopathic physician. Great care is taken in preparing them according to the rules laid down by the highest authorities on homeopathy, and only the purest drugs used. Every one of the following specifics is a special cure for the disease named on it. Adults take 6 pellets, children from 1 to 3 according to age, and from two to four doses are to be taken every day according to the severity of the case. We ask the special attention of all our customers to these high grade remedies. If you have them near at hand, we guarantee they will save you many a doctor's bill, and what of more consequence, quickly relieve any suffering member of the family and ward off more serious sickness. We make the price as low as we possibly can in order that they may be within reach of every one of our customers, only 18c each bottle, with the exception of three rare ones which of necessity we require to make a higher price.

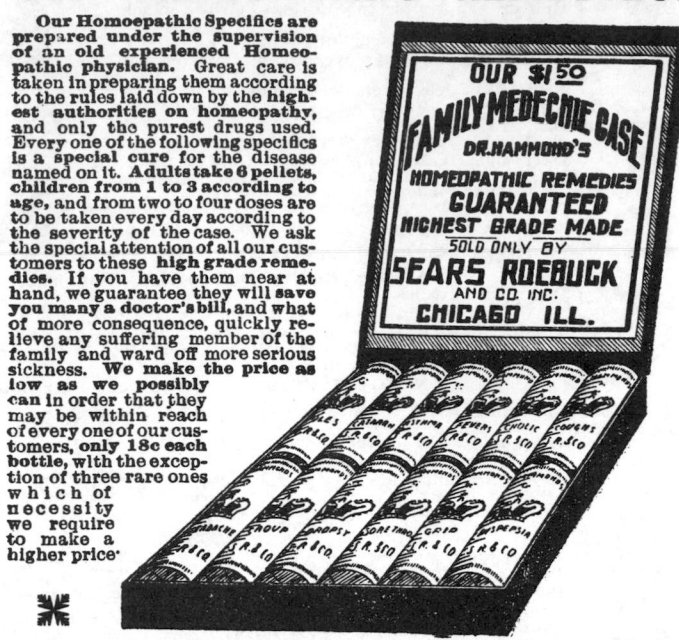

OUR $1.50 FAMILY MEDICINE CASE DR. HAMMOND'S HOMEOPATHIC REMEDIES GUARANTEED HIGHEST GRADE MADE SOLD ONLY BY SEARS ROEBUCK AND CO. INC. CHICAGO ILL.

## A SPECIAL OFFER.

As an inducement to give these Remedies a thorough trial, we will allow you to select 12 cures, including the 60c ones. Make your own selection, one or more of any kind, and we will put them in a neat case such as we represent here and only charge you $1.50. No family can afford to neglect this great offer.

A 12 BOX CASE will save you many dollars doctor's bills in a year and may save your life. No family should be without a case of our Homeopathic Remedies.

| | | Usual Price. | Our Price. |
|---|---|---|---|
| No. D1751 | Cures rheumatism or rheumatic pains | $0.25 | $0.18 |
| No. D1752 | Cures fever and ague, intermittent fever, malaria etc. | .25 | .18 |
| No. D1753 | Cures piles, blind or bleeding, external or internal. | .25 | .18 |
| No. D1754 | Cures opthalmia, weak or inflamed eyes | .25 | .18 |
| No. D1755 | Cures catarrh, influenza, cold in the head | .25 | .18 |
| No. D1756 | Cures whooping cough, spasmodic cough | .25 | .18 |
| No. D1757 | Cures asthma, oppressed or difficult breathing | .25 | .18 |
| No. D1758 | Cures fevers, congestions. inflammation | .25 | .18 |
| No. D1759 | Cures worm fever or worm diseases | .25 | .18 |
| No. D1760 | Cures cholic, crying and wakefulness of infants teething | .25 | .18 |
| No. D1761 | Cures diarrhœa of children and adults | .25 | .18 |
| No. D1762 | Cures dysentery, griping, bilious colic | .25 | .18 |
| No. D1763 | Cures cholera, cholera morbus, vomiting | .25 | .18 |
| No. D1764 | Cures coughs, colds, bronchitis | .25 | .18 |
| No. D1765 | Cures toothache, faceache, neuralgia | .25 | .18 |
| No. D1766 | Cures headache, sick headache, vertigo | .25 | .18 |
| No. D1767 | Cures dyspepsia, indigestion, weak stomach | .25 | .18 |
| No. D1768 | Cures suppressed menses, or scanty | .25 | .18 |
| No. D1769 | Cures leucorrhœa, or profuse menses | .25 | .18 |
| No. D1770 | Cures croup, hoarse cough, difficult breathing, laryngitis | .25 | .18 |
| No. D1771 | Cures salt rheum, eruptions, erysipelas | .25 | .18 |
| No. D1772 | Cures ear discharge, earache | .25 | .18 |
| No. D1773 | Cures scrofula, swellings, ulcers. | .25 | .18 |
| No. D1774 | Cures general debility, physical weakness, brain fag. | .25 | .18 |
| No. D1775 | Cures dropsy, fluid accumulations | .25 | .18 |
| No. D1776 | Cures seasickness, nausea, vomiting. | .25 | .18 |
| No. D1777 | Cures kidney disease, gravel, calculi | .25 | .18 |
| No. D1778 | Cures nervous debility, vital weakness | 1.00 | .60 |
| No. D1779 | Cures sore mouth and canker. | .25 | .18 |
| No. D1780 | Cures urinary incontinence, wetting bed. | .25 | .18 |
| No. D1781 | Cures painful menses, pruritis. | .25 | .18 |
| No. D1782 | Cures disease of the heart, palpitations. | 1.00 | .60 |
| No. D1783 | Cures epilepsy, St. Vitus dance. | 1.00 | .60 |
| No. D1784 | Cures sore throat, quinsy or ulcerated sore throat. | .25 | .18 |
| No. D1785 | Cures chronic congestions, headache. | .25 | .18 |
| No. D1786 | Cures grip and chronic colds. | .25 | .18 |
| No. D1787 | A strong cardboard case covered with black muslin, containing 12 specifics, your own selection from above list. | | 1.50 |
| No. D1788 | A polished hardwood case, with lock and key, containing 24 remedies. | | 4.50 |
| No. D1789 | A full line of Humphrey's, Munyon's and Ballentine's cures in stock. The size usually sold for. | .25 | .20 |
| | The size usually sold for. | 1.00 | .80 |

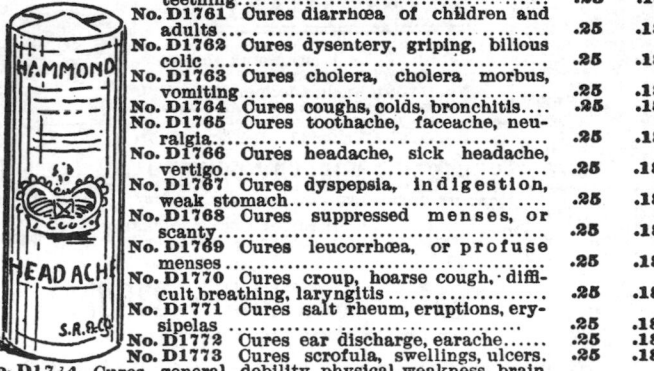

HAMMOND HEAD ACHE S.R.&CO.

**YOU MAY LIVE MILES FROM A REGULAR PHYSICIAN.** If so, you are in danger without these remedies in your home. They are always handy, always convenient, easy to take, act quick, will relieve your suffering and may save your life while waiting a doctor's arrival.

ONLY $1.50 FOR A CASE OF 12 BOTTLES, your own selection. Take our warning notice, don't be without them.

# Homeopathic Medicines.

We are prepared to furnish anything in the line of Homeopathic supplies, and guarantee them to be full strength and fresh condition. We mention a few of the more prominent. We will be pleased to furnish information on Homeopathic medicines if you are in doubt as to what to order. We will also send a copy of Halsey's Manual (152 pages), a complete homeopathic treatise, free on request. When ordering the following remedies please specify what form you wish them in—pills, powder, discs or liquid.

| Name. | Strength. | Name. | Strength. | Name. | Strength. |
|---|---|---|---|---|---|
| Aconite | 3x | Cuprum met. | 3x | Mercurius viv | 3x |
| Antimon crud. | 3x | Digitalis | 2x | Natrum mur. | 6x |
| Apismel | 3x | Drosera | 2x | Nitric Acid. | 6x |
| Arnica | 3x | Dulcamara | 3x | Nux vomica. | 3x |
| Arsenic alb. | 3x | Eupatorium p'r | 1x | Opium | 3x |
| Baptisa | 1x | Ferrum phos. | 3x | Phosphorus | 3x |
| Belladonna. | 3x | Gelsemium | 1x | Phosphorus aci | 3x |
| Bryonia alba. | 3x | Glonoine | 3x | Phytolacca | 0 |
| Calcarea carb. | 3x | Graphites | 6x | Podophyllin | 3x |
| Cantha-is. | 3x | Hamamelis | 3x | Pulsatilla | 3x |
| Carby veg. | 3x | Hepar sulphtr. | 3x | Rhus tox. | 3x |
| Caulophyllum. | 1x | Hydrastis | 1x | Sanguinaria | 2x |
| Causticum. | 3x | Hyoscyamus | 3x | Secale cor. | 1x |
| Chamomilla | 3x | Ignati | 3x | Sepia | 3x |
| China. | 2x | Iodium | 3x | Silicea | 6x |
| Chinin, arsen. | 2x | Ipecac | 3x | Spigelia | 3x |
| Chimicifuga | 1x | Kali bichr. | 3x | Spongia | 3x |
| Cina | 2x | Lachesis | 6x | Staphysagria. | 3x |
| Cocculus | 3x | Lycopodium | 3x | Sulphur. | 3x |
| Coffea crud | 3x | Mercurius bnod | 3x | Tartar emetic. | 3x |
| Colchicum | 3x | Mercurius corr | 3x | Veratrum alb. | 3x |
| Colocynthis. | 3x | Mercurius sol. | 3x | | |

| | | |
|---|---|---|
| No. D1790 | ¼ oz. phials each, 10c; by mail | 15c |
| No. D1791 | ½ oz. phials each, 15c; by mail | 20c |
| No. D1792 | 1 oz. phials each, 20c; by mail | 25c |
| No. D1793 | 2 oz. phials each, 40c; by mail | 45c |

## HALSEY'S SPECIALTIES.

| | | Bottle. |
|---|---|---|
| No. D1794 | Carbo Peptine Wafers | $ .40 |
| No. D1795 | Burn and Frost Liniment | .40 |
| No. D1796 | Camphor Pills | .20 |
| No. D1797 | Catarrh Tablets | .40 |
| No. D1798 | Catarrh Treatment Complete | 2.75 |
| No. D1799 | Chestnut Pile Crate | .40 |
| No. D1800 | Elixir Hydrastis and Cocoa | 8.00 |
| No. D1801 | General Debility Specific | .80 |
| No. D1802 | Goitre Tablets | .50 |
| No. D1803 | Hensel's Tonic | .90 |
| No. D1804 | Infant Tablets | .40 |
| No. D1805 | LaGrippe Specific | .60 |
| No. D1806 | Liver Tablets | .40 |
| No. D1807 | Nerve Salt | 1.60 |
| No. D1808 | Neuralgia Cure | .40 |
| No. D1809 | Rhus and Bryonia Plaster. Small | .20 |
| No. D1810 | Rhus and Bryonia Plaster. Yard rolls. | .75 |
| No. D1811 | Sore Throat Tablets | .20 |
| No. D1812 | Tape Worm Remedy | .75 |
| No. D1813 | Uterine Wafers | .75 |
| No. D1814 | Whooping Cough Syrup | .40 |
| No. D1815 | Witch Hazel Cream | .20 |

## HOMOEPATHIC BOOKS.

Rnddock's Stepping Stone to Homœopathy and Health. 258 pages.
No. D1816 Price ... $0.80
Ruddock's Homœopathic Guide, containing the Stepping Stone and The Ladies' Manual in one volume. 592 pages.
No. D1817 Price ... $1.60

We make Special Medicine Cases to order to contain, 12, 24, 36 or 48 remedies. We will fill these cases with any assortment of remedies you wish, and any size bottles. With each case we send a Homeopathic Manual, giving full directions how to use the remedies, also a general description of diseases, and how to treat sick people to get them well again. Our prices are very low for these cases, and they are worth from five to six times the amount we ask for them. Send us a description of the remedies wanted and we will send you the cost. There ought to be one in every household, especially where there are children.

THE TWELVE CHIEF REMEDIES DIRECTIONS HALSEY BROS CO.

## Our 85c Homeopathic Cases.

No. D1818 Contains 12 1-dr. remedies with directions ... 85c

## Our $1.50 Homeopathic Cases.

No. D1819 Contains 12 2-dr. remedies with directions ... $1.50

No. D1820 This is a durable polished hardwood case, containing 24 2-dr. and 4 1-oz. bottles, fitted with lock and key, complete with Ruddock's Stepping Stone ... $5.00

No. D1821 Similar to above. containing 36 2-dr. and 4 1-oz. bottles, complete with book ... $6.75

## ROBB'S FAMILY PHYSICIAN.

No. 29140 A concise and comprehensive treatise on diseases as they occur in everyday life. The causes, the symptoms and treatment, demonstrating the cure of the various ills humanity is subject to. By J. V. Bean, M. D., R. L. Robb, M. D., and Sarah L. Robb, M. D. Illustrated with numerous engravings. Cloth. Size, 5½x8 inches.
Retail price, $3.50; our price ... $1.10
Postage, extra, 23 cents.

# Saves Money

## $1.50

## Saves Life

### Sears, Roebuck & Co.'s Family Medicine Case.

:: CONVENIENT AND RELIABLE ::

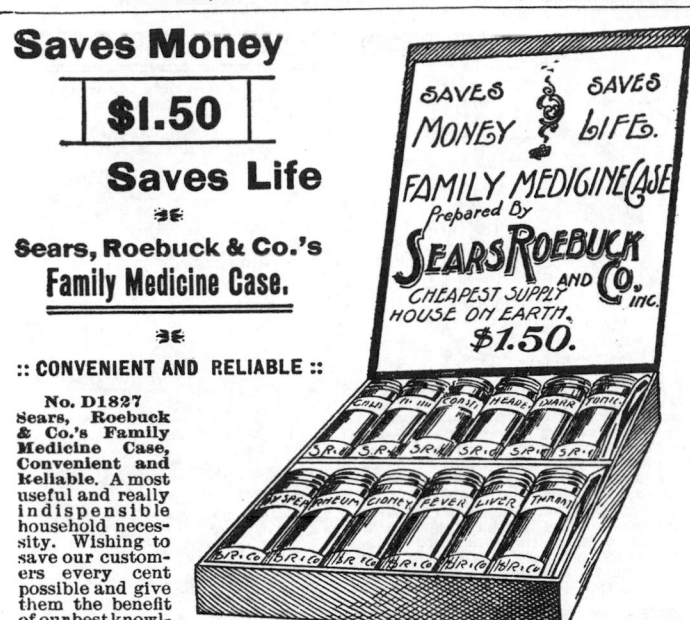

No. D1827 Sears, Roebuck & Co.'s Family Medicine Case, Convenient and Reliable. A most useful and really indispensible household necessity. Wishing to save our customers every cent possible and give them the benefit of our best knowledge and experience we have had our physician and chemist prepare in convenient form a number of reliable remedies such as are daily used by the leading physicians in the country when called in to prescribe in cases of sickness. We do not wish altogether to supplant the doctor, as we consider him a necessary factor in society. But we recognize the fact that many useful lives are lost because help is not obtained in time, and therefore desire to place within the reach of all our customers at a nominal price the means to avert serious sickness, or at least hold such cases in check till a doctor can be obtained. We also know that a doctor's bill and a druggist's account is frequently a great drain on many a pocketbook, already sadly depleted by the ordinary calls of existence. We thus offer you the means to combat the simple ailments of life without such expense. The following are the remedies we have selected as being the most useful.

No. 1. **COLD IN THE HEAD**—Will cure quinsy, tonsilitis, cold in the head, influenza, and many of the milder troubles arising from cold.
No. 2. **COLIC**—Very useful for all childish pains, such as in cramps, colic, or for the restlessness of teething, diarrhœa, etc.
No. 3. **COUGH**—Valuable in coughs, bronchitis, hoarseness and any trouble in throat and chest arising from cold.
No. 4. **CONSTIPATION**—Will relieve obstinate cases of constipation, which is often the cause of headache, biliousness, offensive breath, etc.
No. 5. **DIARRHŒA**—Useful and a sure cure for any form of diarrhœa, cholera morbus, cholera infantum, sour stomach, etc.
No. 6. **HEADACHE**—Good for headache of any sort, fever, cold, nervousness, la-grippe, etc.
No. 7. **TONIC**—For any weakened condition of the system.
No. 8. **ALTERATIVE**—For impure blood, boils, scrofula, ulcers, eczema, etc.
No. 9. **DYSPEPSIA**—From any of the ordinary causes.
No. 10. **KIDNEY AND LIVER**—To remove or cure all diseases of the organs.
No. 11. **MALARIAL**—To be used when quinine fails, or when the patient cannot take it.
No. 12. **RHEUMATIC**—A true remedy.
No. 13. **NERVOUS TROUBLES**—Calms and sooths; will relieve nervousness in any form.
No. 14. **HEART REGULATOR**—A splendid tonic for the heart.
No. 15. **LIVER CORRECTOR**—For biliousness, jaundice, sallow complexion, sour stomach, &c.
No. 16. **KIDNEY DISORDERS**—Gently stimulates the kidneys and relieves urinary troubles in both old and young.
No. 17. **BRONCHIAL**—For difficult breathing, pain in the chest, cold in the bronchial tubes.
No. 18. **THROAT**—For hoarseness, tickling in throat; useful for speakers and singers.
No. 19. **NEURALGIA**—For the relief of neuralgia, sciatica, &c.
No. 20. **FEVER**—For all kinds of fever, especially that arising from cold.
No. 21. **CROUP**—For children; to be given when the first symptom appears.
No. 22. **MUMPS**—Give regularly and follow instructions in our Medical Guide.
No. 23. **PLEURISY**—For pain in the chest on breathing and coughing.
No. 24. **PIMPLES**—For skin blemishes.

## OUR GREAT OFFER
We will allow you to select any 12 of the above remedies, which selection we will put up in a **handsome black cloth covered case for $1.50.** We will send with each case a **book giving full instructions** how to use these remedies and containing other valuable information for the care of the sick.

**FOR $2.50** we will send you the 24 remedies complete with our valuable book of instructions.

Remember that we are the only firm in the country putting up a **reliable Medicine Case** for family use.

### In Offering Our
### : CASE OF MEDICINE :
#### and
#### BOOK OF INSTRUCTIONS

It is needless to say we give much more for the money than can be obtained in any other way. These medicines, if obtained in the ordinary way, would cost you from
## $10.00 to $20.00

---

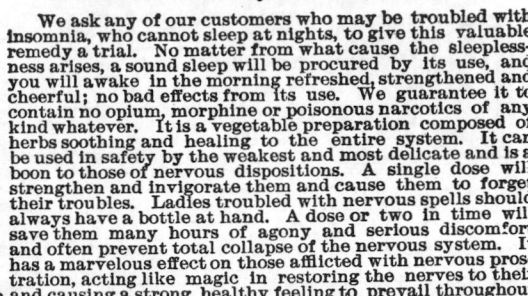

# ‡SOMONE Sweet refreshing sleep

## A Reliable Remedy for Sleeplessness.

We ask any of our customers who may be troubled with insomnia, who cannot sleep at nights, to give this valuable remedy a trial. No matter from what cause the sleeplessness arises, a sound sleep will be procured by its use, and you will awake in the morning refreshed, strengthened and cheerful; no bad effects from its use. We guarantee it to contain no opium, morphine or poisonous narcotics of any kind whatever. It is a vegetable preparation composed of herbs soothing and healing to the entire system. It can be used in safety by the weakest and most delicate and is a boon to those of nervous dispositions. A single dose will strengthen and invigorate them and cause them to forget their troubles. Ladies troubled with nervous spells should always have a bottle at hand. A dose or two in time will save them many hours of agony and serious discomfort and often prevent total collapse of the nervous system. It has a marvelous effect on those afflicted with nervous prostration, acting like magic in restoring the nerves to their normal condition and causing a strong healthy feeling to prevail throughout the whole body. It quiets the nervous excitement and muscular trembling caused by the excessive use of liquor, and acts as an antidote to the liquor habit. Full directions accompany each bottle how to use it both for sleeplessness and nervous troubles,

D1830 Price, per bottle .... .................................. $0.75
　　　　 Per dozen................................................. 8.00

---

## ◄—: CURE :—►
### FOR THE
### .. OPIUM ✱ AND ✱ MORPHIA ✱ HABIT ..

We here offer a perfectly safe and reliable cure to those addicted to the habit of using opium or morphia in any form or manner whatever. We guarantee this preparation to be absolutely harmless, to contain no poisonous narcotics. Can be taken freely without producing any of the deleterious effects on the system, such as are caused by the use of opium and morphia. Immediately on taking a dose of this remedy a calming and soothing effect is produced. It acts as a tonic to the nerves; its use will completely destroy that terrible craving for morphine in those who are victims to the deadly habit of taking these poisonous drugs and free them from their bondage, restoring their health and make them feel like living again. A dose can be taken whenever a craving for morphia or opium exists; it will act at first as a perfect substitute, rendering the patient independent of these poisonous drugs, and after continued use for a short period the nerves will become strong and the general health improved, so that the remedy can be taken at longer intervals and soon altogether discontinued, then the cure is complete.

D1835 Price per bottle........................ ................. $0.75
　　　　 Per dozen.............................................. 8.00

---

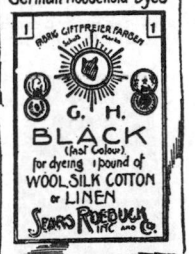

## .. GERMAN ✱ HOUSEHOLD ✱ DYES ..

These Dyes are imported by ourselves from Germany, and we warrant them to be the best in the market. Many dollars can be saved by using them; old, worn and faded dresses and ribbons, feathers, etc., made to look new and fresh again. We can send you color and shade you desire, if you send us a sample we will match it. The directions on every package are very plain and simple.

**Will dye Wool, Silk, Cotton,
Linen or Feathers - - - -**

D1838 Each package.......................... 5c
　　　　 Per dozen............................... 55c

---

# SANITARY DISINFECTANT.

| A GOOD RELIABLE DISINFECTANT ... | .....IS WORTH..... | Its Weight .. In Gold .. |
|---|---|---|

We here offer to our customers the most powerful Disinfectant, Deodorizer and Antiseptic known to science. It is non-poisonous, and when diluted with water, as described on the label of each can, it is the cheapest disinfectant ever offered to the public. Can be used to disinfect drains, sinks, gullies, urinals, water closets, farm yards and buildings, chicken pens, rabbit-hutches, bird cages, cattle trucks, slaughter houses, stables, kennels, ash barrels, garbage cans. It kills all disease germs and should be used for general disinfecting purposes. It is also one of the best insecticides; will destroy fleas on dogs and other animals, lice on chickens, cures mange on animals, makes an excellent and cheap sheep dipping; will also protect animals from the torment of flies, mosquitoes, midges, gnats, etc. It will also destroy insects on plants and trees without any injury to the plants or trees themselves, and destroy weeds on garden paths.
It will purify the air wherever it is used, remove all foul smells, destroying all germs and pests of every kind.
In order to save all the money possible to our customers we prepare this Sanitary Disinfectant in a very concentrated form. One pint will make from one to five gallons according to the purpose required. It mixes readily with water, forming a white, milky fluid. Agreeable and pleasant to use by the most delicate.

D1841 Pint cans, only........................................... $0.35
D1842 Quart cans, only.......................................... 0.50
D1843 Gallon cans, only......................................... 1.50

# HYPODERMIC SYRINGES.

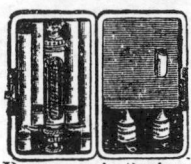

Hypodermic Syringe, nickel plated, with two needles, two vials and extra wire, in neat morocco case.

No. D2200 Price, each..................$1.50
Postage, 8 cents.

Hypodermic Syringe, nickel plated, more complete instrument than above, with two needles, four vials, extra wire, etc., in morocco case.

No. D2202 Price, each..................$2.00
Postage, 8 cents.

Hypodermic Syringe, best grade, four vials, two needles, extra wire and washers, in closed end, aluminum pocket case.

No. D2204 Price, each..................$2.50
Postage, 8 cents.

Needles for Hypodermic Syringes. Assorted sizes.

No. D2206 Price, each, 25c; per doz........$2.70

## Hypodermic Syringe.

### WITH GLASS BARREL.

Protected by a metal cylinder, open both sides, with graduations on piston rod, finger rests same as cut, and cap on end to prevent wearing out of plunger, in fine nickel case with spring cover. Needles screw into case.

No. D2209 Price, each..................$2.75

## CRUTCHES.

Plain style, made of one piece, half round finish, second growth hickory or elm. Upper half is split and bent into shape, arm piece is firmly connected with the ends by bolts; made in all sizes from 42 inches up.

No. D2212 Price, per pair..................75c

Polished natural wood finish, constructed of two pieces tough hickory bent into shape, firmly glued and riveted together at lower end, bolted to a bent arm piece at upper end, also furnished with an iron ferrule. All sizes.

No. D2214 Price, per pair..................$1.25

Second growth hickory, lower ends well glued and riveted and supplied with neatly shaped nickel plated socket and rubber cushion. Upper ends are fitted with wood arm piece, finished in natural color of the wood. Any size made to order.

No. D2216 Price, per pair..................$2.25

Crutches of selected second growth hickory, natural wood finish, firmly connected. supplied with patent jaw socket with rubber cushions and elastic arm piece of leather, stuffed with curled hair, nickel plated sockets and bands. Made any size.

No. D2218 Price, per pair..................$4.00

Same style in rosewood, with patent jaw sockets.

No. D2220 Price, per pair..................$8.00

Note—In ordering crutches please give precise measure from under the arm to floor when standing erect, or if patient is in a horizontal position, length from under arm to sole of foot.

## RUBBER CRUTCH BOTTOMS.

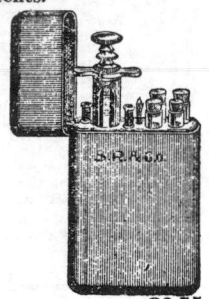

Rubber rasp style. Crutch tips or bottoms. Made in ¾, ⅞ and 1 inch diameter.

No. D2223 Price, per pair..................20c

## Electric Ring for Rheumatism.

These are the first rings introduced into the United States, all others being imitations. Their popularity has caused many rings to be placed on sale that are without any curative properties.

No. D2226 Gray metal polished, price, each..................85c

No. D2228 Gray metal gold plated, on outside, price, each..................$1.25

## EAR TRUMPETS AND CONVERSATION TUBES.

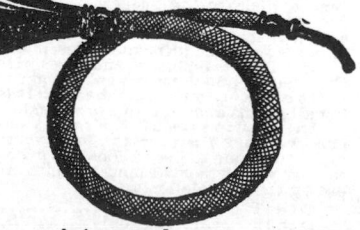

We wish to call your attention to the superior quality of our Conversation Tubes. Made of elastic spiral twine tubing, covered with rubber and overspun with silk or mohair, with mouth and ear pieces of highly polished hard rubber. Made conical cylindrical in shape and in various lengths.

No. D2234

Conversation Tubes, conical, 5 feet long, silk covered....$6.00
Conversation Tubes, conical, 3 feet long, silk covered.... 4.50
Conversation Tubes, conical, 5 feet long, mohair covered..................$5.00
Conversation Tubes, conical, 3 feet long, mohair covered.................. 3.50
Conversation Tubes, cylindrical, 3 feet long, silk covered.................. 2.50
Conversation Tubes, cylindrical, 3 feet long, mohair covered............. 2.00

## LONDON HEARING TUBES.

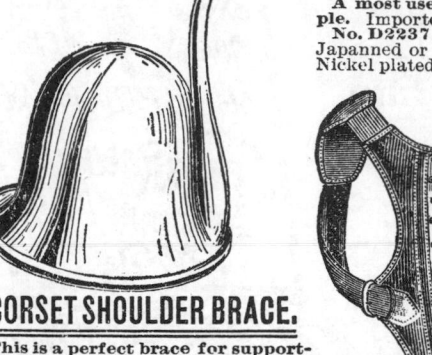

A most useful article for deaf people. Imported by ourselves

No. D2237

|  | Small. | Medium. | Large. |
|---|---|---|---|
| Japanned or Nickel plated.. | $3.00 | $3.50 | $4.00 |

## CORSET SHOULDER BRACE.

This is a perfect brace for supporting the back, and at the same time drawing the shoulders back so as to expand the chest and throw the body into an erect, graceful position. All tendency to round shoulders is thus avoided, and this to young people at the period when the bones and muscles are growing and hardening is of the utmost importance.

No. D2240 Price..................$1.25

## S. R. & Co.'s

### Improved Washington

### Shoulder Brace.

This Brace is well arranged to draw the shoulders gently back without cutting or chafing under the arms, thus inclining the body to a graceful, correct position, expanding the chest and correcting all tendency to stooping or round shoulders. Made of strong silk webbing calf back, webbing rolled under arm so as not to cut. Suspender attachment is of the strongest and finest material.

No. D2243 Price......$1.50

## IMPROVED ABDOMINAL and UTERINE SUPPORTER.

Extra fine pebbled morocco or russet leather with elastic side straps. New form passary of highly polished hard rubber held in position by strong smooth rubber tubing; made in all sizes.

No. D2246 Price..................$2.75

When ordering give circumference of abdomen at largest part.

## THE LONDON ABDOMINAL SUPPORTER,

Well known as the best and strongest supporter in the market. We guarantee it to be made from the finest and stoutest material that can be procured, any part perfect.

No. D2247 Price, all sizes up to 40 in., $1.50

No. D2248 Price, all sizes above 40 inches..................1.75

When ordering give circumference of abdomen at largest part.

## Veterinary Instruments.

In veterinary goods we illustrate only a few instruments that are commonly used by every one owning a horse, but we are in a position to supply anything made in this line, and will quote prices upon application.

**D 820** Universal Wolf Tooth Forceps for extracting wolf teeth. Length 9 inches; weight ¾ pound; nickel plated. Price, **$3.00**

**D 822** Wolf Tooth Forceps, bayonet pattern; length 13 inches; nickel plated. Price.... **$3.00**

**D 824** Wolf Tooth Forceps curved nickel plated; length 9 inches. Price, each..... **$2.50**

**D 826** Small Molar Splinter Forceps, nickel plated, 13 inches, Each..... **$3.00**

**D 828** Straight Incisor Cutters. Each... **$3.00**

**D 830** Molar Extracting Forceps. Handle extra. Each.... **$7.50**

**D 832** Closed Molar Cutters. Handles extra. Each.. **$7.50**

**D 834** Open Molar Cutters. Handles extra. Each.... **$7.50**

**D 836** Handles for Cutters and Extractors Per pair..**$3.**

**D 838** Reversible Float, nickel plated, plain; length 19 inches. Price... **$1.00**

**D 840** Reversible Float, nickel plated, jointed. Price... **$1.50**

**D 842** House's Reversible Float, nickel plated, jointed. Each..... **$2.00**

**D 844** House's Reversible Float, nickel plated, plain. Each... **$1.50**
Extra blades for House's Float... **25c**

**D 846** Palmer's Dental File. Each.... **$1.00**

**D 848** Plain Double File, 10 inch. Each.... **50c**
**D 850** Separating Saw. Each... **$1.00**
**D 852** Simmon's Pus Scoop Each... **$1.75**

**D 854** Balling Iron; weight 1¼ lbs. plain, Each... **75c**
Nickel plated.. **$1.50**
**D 856** Green's Extension Bit Mouth Specula. Each... **$4.50**

**D 858** Castrating Knife, spring back, Each..**$1.25**
**D 860** Zieglers' Castrating Knife. Each....**$2.00**
Postage, 4c.

### Horse Flems.

**D 862** Horse Flems, brass handle.
Each two-blade... **65c**
Three-blade... **75c**
Postage, 50c.

---

## Spring Lancet.

**D 864** Spring Lancet, guarded. Each.. **$2.25**

**D 866** Seton Needles, plain. Each. 6 inch,.....**50c**
12 inch......**90c**
18 inch......**$1.00**
Postage, 10c.

**D 868** Seton Needles, jointed. Price, 12 inch, 1 joint......**$1.75**
18 inch, 2 joints......**$2.25**
Postage, 15c.

**D 870** Fetlock Shears. Price......**$1.00**
**D 872** Roweling Shears, best quality. Price...**$2.25**

**D 874** Braided Silk, 4 sizes, on card, white. Price per card....**50c**

**D 876** Twisted Silk, one size, on card, white. Per card....**10c**
**D 877** Half Curve Needles in sizes from 2 to 4 inches, Price each, 15c.; per doz......**$1.00**
**D 878** Full Curve Needles, in sizes 2 to 4 inches. Price, each, 15c, per doz......**$1.00**
**D 880** Straight Needles, sizes 2 to 4 inches. Price, each, 15c, per dozen......**$1.00**

**D 882** Hoof Knife, double edge. Price, each..**$1.25**
Postage, 5c.
**D 884** Hook Knife, single edge, right or left. Price, each ......**$1.00**
Postage, 5c.

**D 886** Sand Crack Forceps and Cautery Iron. Price......**$6.00**

**D 888** Farmer Miles' Castrating Ecraseur; weight 1 lb. Price..**$10**

**D 890** The S. and S. patent improved Ecraseur. Price, each ......**$15**

**D 892** Halstead's patent Ecraseur. Price each......**$9.75**

**D 894** Miles' Spaying Shears. Price, each...**$6.00**

**D 896** Horse Trocar, reversible.
Price, each......**$1.50**

**D 898** Cattle Trocar and Camula, for opening and draining abscesses, etc. Price, each......**$1.50**
Postage, 4c.

**D 899** Veterinary Thermometer 6 inch sensitive, self-regestering; in pocket case. Price..... **$1.50**

**D 900** The Boss Pig Extractor and Tooth Forceps, with treatise on the raising of the pig. This instrument was given first premium at Iowa State Fair, 1895, and is the newest invention of the kind. The outfit is put up neatly in box and complete weighs only 18 ounces. Once tried always used, is the general prediction. Price of outfit, complete......**$1.50**

---

## Improved Pig Forceps.

**D 902** The improved Pig Forceps has points of excellence which make it a most practical instrument, and may be used upon either small or large sows with equal satisfaction. The instrument is made of malleable iron, tinned to prevent rusting; will not tear the sow or otherwise injure the animal in operation. Price, each......**75c**

**D 904** Drenching horn for administering medicine to horses; japanned; weight 1½ lbs. Each......**85c**

### Drenching Bit.

**D 906** Burton's Drenching Bit. No longer any trouble to give your horse medicine. One man can do it; used by horsemen throughout the country; weight, 1¼ lbs. Price......**$2.75**

### Mouth Speculum.

**D 908** Mouth Speculum. S. & S. patent, easy of operation; it holds the mouth open so that an examination of the teeth can be made with the greatest ease. Nickel plated; weight 4 lbs. Price......**$9.50**

### Horse Catheter.

**D 912** Horse Catheter, best quality. Price. **$2.00**
**D 913** Horse Catheter, same as above, second quality. Price......**$1.75**
**D 914** Metal Mare Catheter. Price......**$1.50**
**D 916** Metal Mare Catheter, jointed. Price......**$2.00**

**D 918** Injection Syringes; metal; 16 ounces, weight 1½ lbs., price, $1; 24 ounces, weight, 2½ lbs. $2; 36 ounces, weight 3¼ lbs......**$2.50**
**D 920** Veterinary Balling Gun, nickel plated, 15 inch length. Price......**$2.25**
**D 922** Veterinary Scalpel, ebony handle, right or left; specify which is wanted. Price......**1.25**
**D 924** Veterinary Scalpel, ebony handle, double edge, Price......**1.50**
**D 926** Veterinary Hypodermic Syringe, complete with three needles, needle trocar, etc. Price......**3.50**
**D 928** Veterinary Surgeons' Gum Lancet, folding, black handle. Price......**1.50**
**D 930** Veterinary Surgeons' Pocket Case, made of best morocco, and containing an assortment of twelve instruments. Price......**20.00**

**D 932** Syringes, for administering medicine to horses and other animals. Quittor hard rubber, two pipes. Price..**$1.50**
**D 934** Syringes, same as preceeding, but of metal, nickel plated, Quittor two pipes. Price each......**$2.50**
**D 936** Veterinary Hard Rubber Horse Syringes, capacity, 24 ounces. Each......**$3.75**

**D 938** Dehorning Saw, best quality, nickel plated. Each......**$1.50**

**D 940** Gouging Forceps, nickel plated. Each......**$3.50**

### Dehorning Shears.

**D 942** The Adsit Dehorning Shears, sure, simple and strong, makes a drawing cut completely encircling the horn, which it removes almost instantly; by the use of these shears you save time, expense and unnecessary excitement to the animal. Price in regular finish, $9; in nickel plated and polished handles......**$13.50**

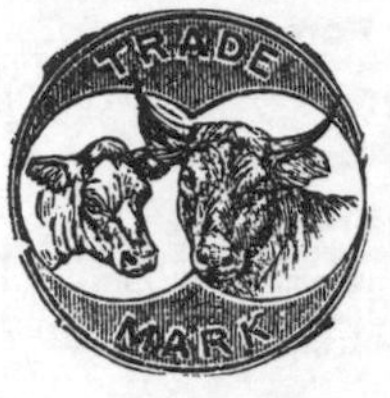


D 943 **For Dehorning Cattle.** Dehorn your calves easily, safely and perfectly at one cent a horn by our Chemical Dehorner. The application is so simple that anyone can use it. When it is used for about two generations of cattle, a breed will be raised without horns, perfectly harmless. Full directions with each package. Each........................ 80c

### Coin Silver Milking Tubes, Etc.

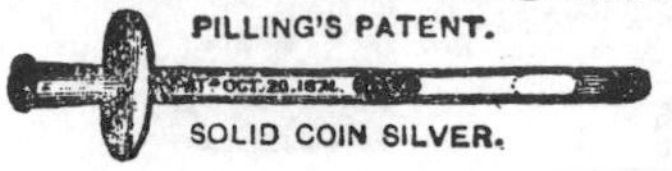


D 944 **Coin Silver Milking Tubes,** for sore and obstructed teats and hard milking cows; made of pure coin silver and can be used with absolute safety. set of four tubes, 1¾ inches long, in a neat box, with full directions for use. Each, **$1.60;** single tubes, each..............43c

| Special lengths, inches, | 2¼ | 2¾ | 3¼ | 3¾ |
|---|---|---|---|---|
| Each, | $0.55 | .70 | .80 | .95 |

**Postage 2 cents.**

D 946 **Grooved Director,** or instrument for opening cows' teats, with full directions for using. Each **60c;** per doz........................**$6.00**

**Postage 2 cents.**

D 948 **Lead Probes,** for treatment of stricture and obstructed teats, also for enlarging the opening in cows' teats; made in three sizes, small, medium and large; full directions for using with each probe. Each **20c**

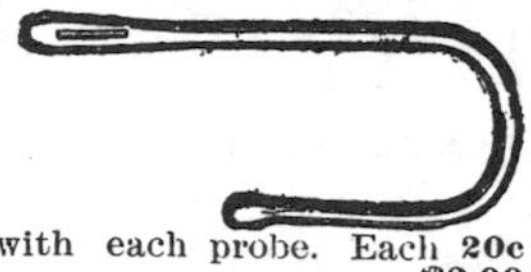

Per doz........................**$2.00**

D 950 **Cow Teat Slitter,** best implement, steel, nickeled sheath, 5 inch length. Each....... **$1.25**

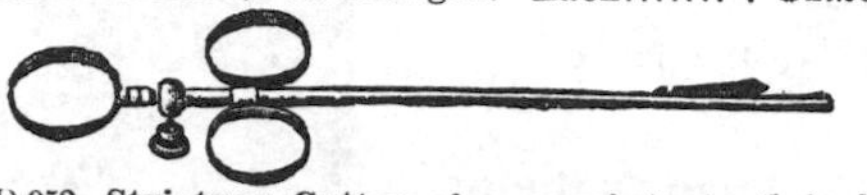

D 952 **Stricture Cutter,** for cows' teats, 7 inch length, made of best implement steel. Each. **$2.60**

### Poultry Instruments.

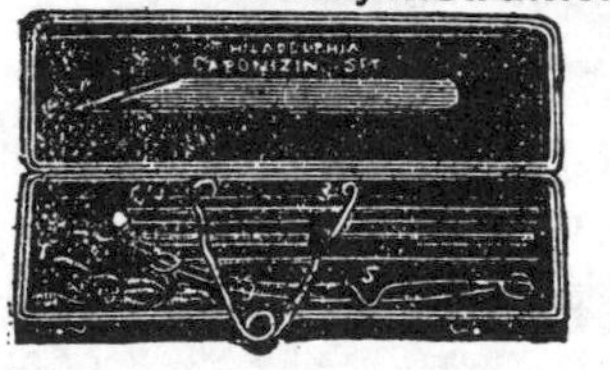

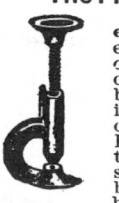

D 954 **It is well understood** that poultrymen can double their profits by caponizing their chicks. The operation is very simple, the instructions being so explicit that anyone after a careful reading, will be able to perform the operation with proper instruments. The demand for capons far exceeds the supply, even at an advanced price. The Philadelphia Caponizing Set contains the best instruments on the market, and at the price at which they are offered no one who keeps chickens can afford to neglect the opportunity of increasing their profits. Price, per set. in velvet lined case(see cut) with book, "Complete Guide for Caponizing.........................**$2.50**

**Postage 10 cents.**

### French Poultry Killing Knife.

D 956 **Every Poultry Raiser** should have one. They are made of finely tempered instrument steel, with nickeled handle; will last a lifetime. Each.............. **40c**

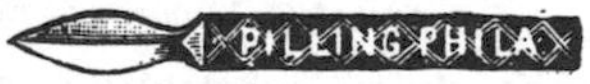


**Postage 5 cents.**

### The Philadelphia Poultry Marker.

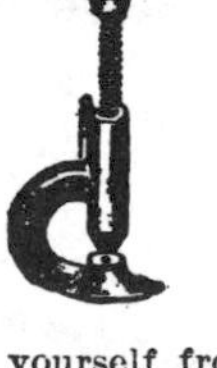

D 958 **Do you keep a record of chickens?** The different breeds, hatches, etc., should be kept. There is no better or quicker way than by this marker, as over two hundred different marks can be made by punching between toes; for instance, between first and second toes of right foot can mean Wyandotte or Plymouth Rock; between second and third toes, White Leghorn or Langshan, so that hundreds of private marks can be made, not only to keep records, but by your private marks you can secure yourself from the chicken thief. They are well made, with steel spring and cutter, nicely nickel plated. Price. **(Postage 5c.)**................ **18c**

### Gape Worm Extractor.

D 960 **The Disease commonly known as gape** is caused by a small worm in the windpipe of fowls. When the chick seems to gasp frequently it is a sure indication of gapes, and it should receive attention at once. The only sure cure is to remove the worms by mechanical means. You will save time and money by having on hand a Gape Worm Extractor. The Extractor quickly removes, without injury to the chick, the worms and the matter from the windpipe, and effects an instant cure. The cut shows the manner of using the instrument. One chick saved pays price of instrument. Price. **(Postage 2c.)**..**20c**

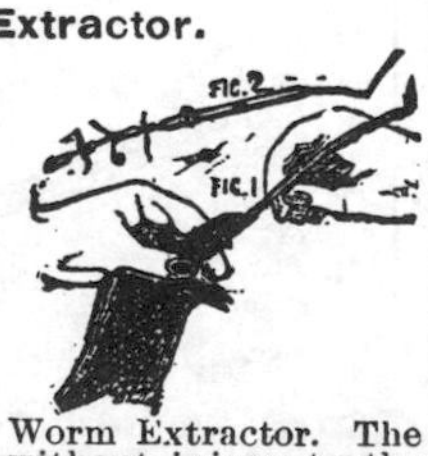


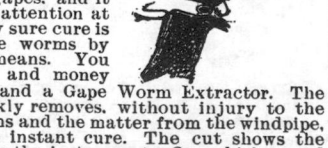

### Suspensory Bandages.

D 963 **Red Cross Suspensory, Army and Navy Style.** Large, medium and Small.

| | Each. | Doz. |
|---|---|---|
| Cotton, non-elastic | **$0.20** | **$2.00** |
| Lisle thread, elastic band | .35 | 4.00 |
| Silk, elastic band | .50 | 5.00 |

D 964 **J. P. Suspensory, Single Band.** Large, medium and small.

| | Each | Doz. |
|---|---|---|
| Cotton Sack | **$0.20** | **$2.00** |
| English Web Sack | .25 | 2.50 |
| Silk Sack | .35 | 3.75 |

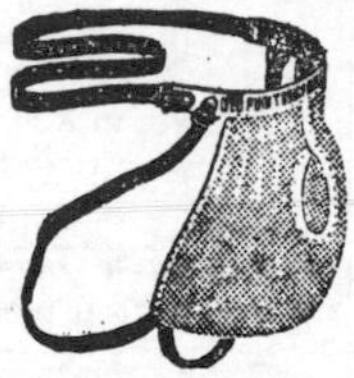

D 965 **O. P. C. Suspensory.** Automatically adjustable and never fails to fit and give satisfaction; for comfort, security, durability and elegance the best in the world. Order by number. Give size, large medium or small.

| | Each |
|---|---|
| No. 2, lisle | **$0.75** |
| No. 3, silk | 1.25 |
| No. 4, all silk | 1.75 |
| No. 5, all silk, fancy colors | 2.25 |

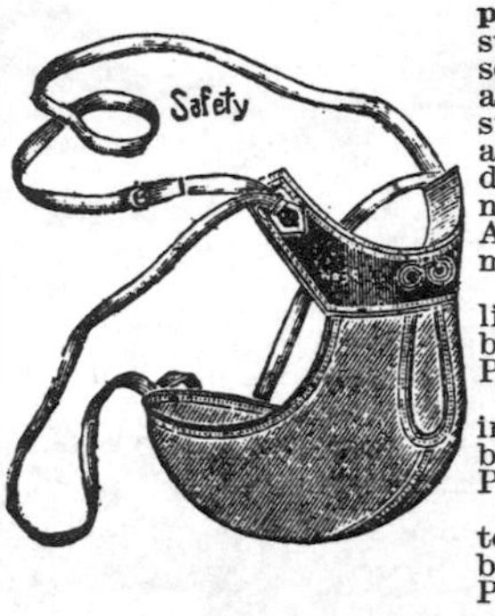


D 966 **Safety Suspensory.** The construction of the Safety secures a perfect self-adjusting, sliding-loop suspensory, which enables the sack to be detached for washing; no buckles on sack. Assorted sizes: large medium and small.

No. 52. Safety, English web sack, elastic band. Each.....**$0.50**
Per dozen........ 4.50

No. 53. Safety, bolting silk sack, elastic band. Each.....**$0.60**
Per dozen........ 5.00

No. 54. Safety, knitted silk sack, elastic band. Each.....**$0.70**
Per dozen........ 6.00

### Covered Elastic Bandages.

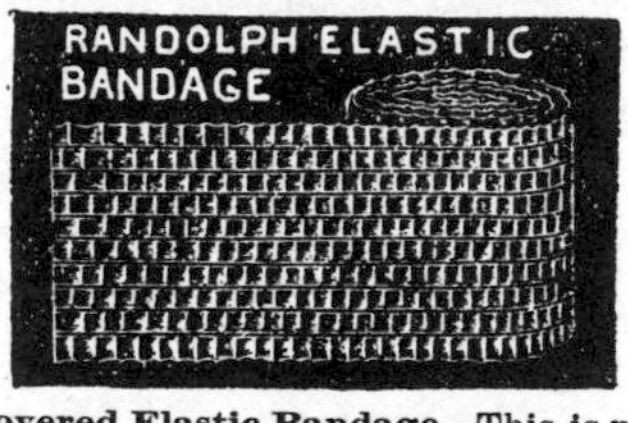


D 967 **Covered Elastic Bandage.** This is made of a rubber thread and soft lisle thread; best quality, making a soft bandage that is light and porous.

| | |
|---|---|
| 2 inches wide by 9 feet long (stretched), each | $0 50 |
| 2 inches wide by 15 feet long (stretched), each | 0 80 |
| 2 inches wide by 24 feet long (stretched), each | 1 10 |
| 2½ inches by wide 9 feet long (stretched), each | 0 60 |
| 2½ inches wide by 15 feet long (stretched), each | 0 95 |
| 3 inches wide by 9 feet long (stretched), each | 0 75 |
| 3 inches wide by 15 feet long (stretched), each | 1 15 |

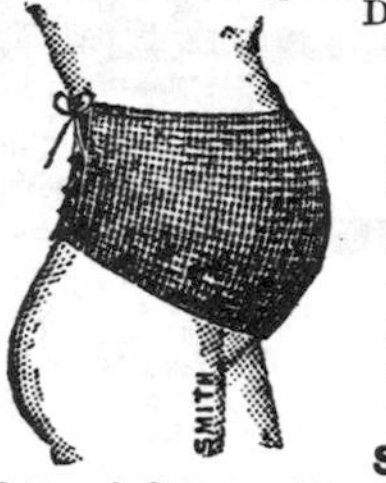


D 968 **Covered Elastic Abdominal Supporter,** made of soft lisle thread, interwoven with protected rubber thread making it superior to any other supporter of its kind; may be washed in lukewarm water and thereby kept clean; is very light and comfortable, weighs about two ounces; made in all sizes to order.

Price each, 8 inches wide. $2.00
Price 10 inches wide...... 2 25
Price 12 inches wide...... 2 50

### Soft Rubber Catheters.

D 969 **A fine quality soft Rubber Catheter** in all sizes. "American scale," from the small No. 5 to the large No. 20. Each........................**$0.25**

We are prepared to furnish prices of abdominal female, elastic stockings, deformity apparatus, trus-supporters made of different materials for male or ses, surgical appliance, instruments, etc.

D 970 **Ladies' Elastic Doily Belt,** Silk Trimmings and Silk Elastic. This belt, made in both silk and thread elastic, is worn by ladies during their menstrual period, for the convenience of attaching the napkin and is indespensable for comfort. In walking or sitting, it conforms to the varying positions of the body, thereby preventing all tendency to chafe. It is easily adjusted, and will not interfere with the other garments.

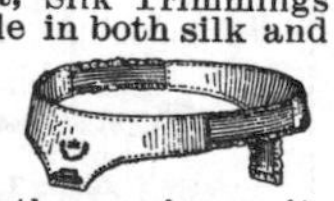

Each...........................................**$0.65**

D 971 **Antiseptic and Absorbent Pad.** These pads, made from cotton, gauze and bandage, have been rendered "Antiseptic," thus making a very convenient and entirely safe substitute for the old style napkin and are highly recommended by all our prominent medicial authorities. For traveling and especially for long voyages, they are a necessity, as their antiseptic nature prevents them from carrying germs of disease and enables their being kept until convenient to burn, or otherwise disposed of. Their cheapness combined with their downy softness, absorbent and antiseptic properties, recommend them for regular use, as a good substitue for the old style cumbrous, hot and chafing napkins. Box of one doz............................**$0.40**

### Syringes and Rubber Goods.

Only the best qualities quoted; made by the Goodyear company, which is a well-known, reliable manufacturer; they will not put their name on anything that is not first class in every particular. Notice our prices; they are less than half drug store prices, and goods received from us are all fresh, nice goods, everything guaranteed to be satisfactory, or you can return the same at our expense. Allow about 15 cents postage on syringes.

### Hard Rubber Syringes.

| | | |
|---|---|---|
| D 972 | Safety point ⅛ oz., each | **$0.15** |
| | Safety point ¼ oz., each | .20 |
| D 973 | Long point ⅛ oz., each | .15 |
| | Long point ¼ oz., each | .20 |
| | Long point ½ oz., each (Infant's rectal.) | .35 |
| | Long point 1 oz., each | .45 |
| D 974 | Vaginal 1 oz., each | .35 |
| | Vaginal 2 oz., each | .45 |

### Goodyear Bulb Syringes.

D 975 The Goodyear Improved Enema with two metal pipes, the best cheap syringe made. Each.........................**$0.30**

D 976 Goodyear's Union Syringe with three hard rubber pipes in neat box, an extraordinary syringe for the money; weight, 10 oz. Each...........**$0.50**

D 977 Extra Quality Goodyear Union Syringe, constructed of the best quality soft rubber, with three hard rubber fittings. Each in wooden box; weight 12 oz. Each.........................**$1.00**

D 978 Goodyear's Original Syringe, in handsome wood box; very well known as a high-priced syringe and always gives satisfaction, with three hard rubber fittings; weighs, packed, 12 oz. Each.....**$0.75**

D 979 **Columbia Fountain Syringe.** Made from white rubber with hard rubber fitting; 3 hard rubber pipes; in neat box; long rubber pipe, with patent shut-off.

| | |
|---|---|
| Each, 2 quart | **$0.50** |
| Each, 3 quart | .60 |
| Each, 4 quart | .70 |

D 979½ **Pioneer Fountain Syringe;** in fine wood box· made of extra quality rubber; extra long rubber pipe; patent shut-off; fine hard rubber pipes; an excellent thing to have in the family.

| | |
|---|---|
| Each, 2 quart | **$0.78** |
| Each, 3 quart | .88 |
| Each, 4 quart | .95 |

### The Ladies' Syringe.

D 980 **"Tyrian" Female Syringe;** for cleansing the vaginal passages of all discharges; especially adapted **for injection of hot water,** the liquid being driven from the syringe when bulb is compressed and drawn back into it on relaxing the pressure, thus giving an opportunity to thoroughly wash the diseased parts. Capacity 8 ounces. Made of one piece of **soft rubber,** with removable hard rubber shield. Having no valves or connections, cannot get out of order; weight, packed, 13 oz. Each..**$1.25**

D 981 English Breast Pump, one in a box,
Each.........................**$0.18**
Dozen........................ **2.00**

D 982 Nipple Shield Glass with rubber nipple.
Each.........................**$0.12**

D 983 Nipple shield with long tube. Each...**$0.15**

D 984 **Goodyear's Best Rubber Water Bottle.** Extra quality; **every one** warranted; everyone should have one. **Notice our price:**

| | |
|---|---|
| Each, 2 quart | **$0.75** |
| Each, 3 quart | .80 |
| Each, 4 quart | .85 |

### Hypodermic Syringes.

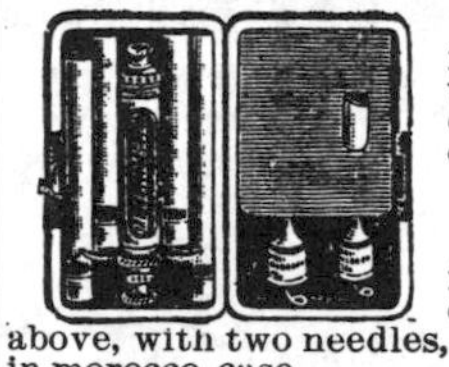

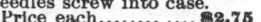

D 985 Hypodermic Syringe, nickel plated, with two needles, two vials and extra wire, in neat morocco case.
Price, each..........**$1.50**

**Postage 8c.**

D 986 Hypodermic Syringe, nickle plated, more complete instrument than above, with two needles, four vials, extra wire etc., in morocco case.
Price.........................**$2.00**

**Postage 8c.**

D 987 Hypodermic Syringe, best grade, four vials, two needles, extra wire and washers, in closed end, aluminum pocket case.
Price.........................**$2.50**

**Postage 8c.**

D 988 Needles for Hypodermic Syringes.
Price, each **25c.,** per dozen assorted sizes..**$2.70**

### Hypodermic Syringe with Glass Barrel.

D 989 Protected by a metal cylinder, open both sides, with graduations on piston rod, finger rests same as cut, and cap on end to prevent during out of plunger, in fine nickel case with spring cover. Needles screw into case.
Price each......... **$2.75**

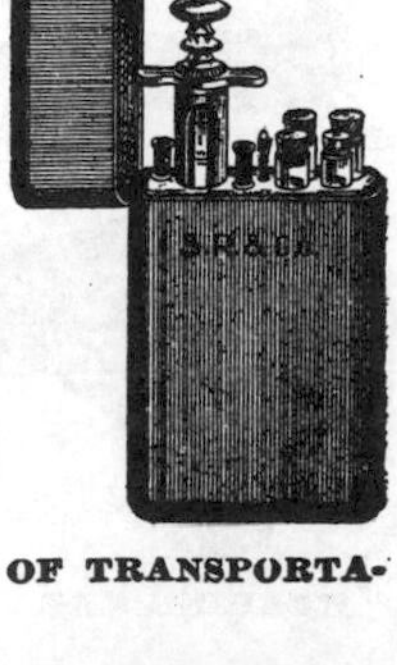


**YOU CAN INCLUDE WHAT MEDICINES OR INSTRUMENTS YOU NEED WITH YOUR FREIGHT ORDER AND THE COST OF TRANSPORTATION WILL NOT BE INCREASED.**

## Chemical and Clinical Thermometers.

D 981 Solid glass Chemical Thermometers, graduations etched on tube or porcelain scale up to 300 degrees and 600 degrees.
Price, each........................................**$2.00**

D 982 Clinical Thermometers, self-registering, 4 inches, in neat hard rubber case, straight pattern, with bulb. Very accurate.
Price, each........................................**$1.00**

D 983 Clinical Thermometers, self-registering, 4 inches in black enameled case with gilt band, safety chain and clasp. Cannot be lost out of pocket. A clinical certificate for accuracy accompanies each thermometer.
Price, each........................................**$2.00**

## The Health Inhaler.

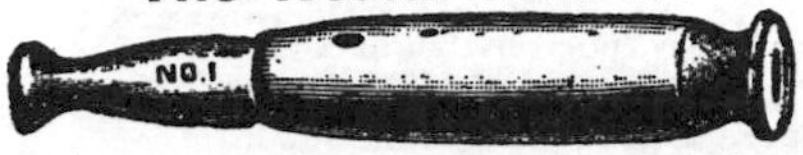


D 984 An improved breathing tube with valve for systematic chest expansion (by use of common air) and the cure of diseases of the lungs, throat and other air passages, and disorders of circulation, digestion and assimilation; full information and explanation regarding its use with each inhaler.
Price, each (post paid)........................................**$1.00**

## Improved Corn Knife.

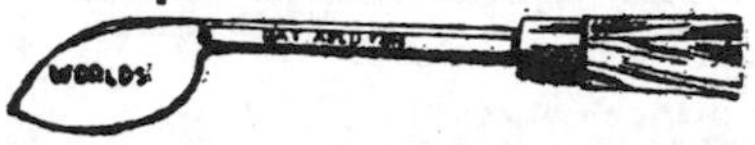

D 985 This instrument is especially designed to be used in cutting or piercing corns, made of best steel, and so shaped that it is firmly held and does the work rapidly, and superior to any other instrument heretofore in the market.
Price, with protecting sheath each..............**25c.**

## Strongest, Cheap Crutch in the Market.

D 986 New Style A. A plain crutch, made of one piece of wood; half round, hickory elm. The upper half is split and bent into shape; the arm piece is also made of bent wood, and is firmly connected with the ends by two strong bolts, which makes it the strongest cheap crutch in the market. We keep in stock all sizes from 42 inches up.

| | | Per pair net. |
|---|---|---|
| No. 1. | No ferrule | $1 10 |
| No. 2. | With iron ferrule | 1 35 |
| No. 3. | With nickel plated socket and rubber cushions | 1 80 |
| No. 4. | With nickel plated jaw sockets and rubber cushions | 2 40 |

Above crutches stuffed and padded with oil cloth, 50 cents net per pair

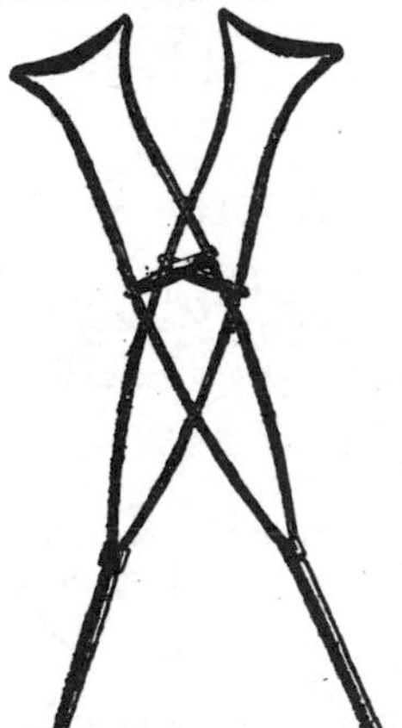

D 987 Plain style, made of one piece, half round finish, second growth hickory elm. Upper half is split and bent into shape, arm piece is firmly connected with the ends by bolts, made in all sizes from 42 inches up. Price per pair..**75c.**

D 989 Polished natural wood finish, constructed of two pieces tough hickory bent into shape, firmly glued and riveted together at lower end, bolted to a bent arm piece at upper end, also furnished with an iron ferrule. **All sizes.**
Price, per pair...**$1.25**

D 990 Second growth hickory, lower ends well glued and riveted, and supplied with neatly shaped nickel plated socket and rubber cushion. Upper ends are fitted with wood arm piece, finished in natural color of the wood. Any size made to order.
Price, per pair........................................**$2.25**

D 991 Crutches of selected second growth hickory, natural wood finish, firmly connected, supplied with patent jaw socket with rubber cushions, and elastic arm piece of leather, stuffed with curled hair, nickel plated sockets and bands. Made any size.
Price, per pair........................................**$4.00**
Sagme style in rosewood, with patent jaw sockets.
Price, per pair........................................**$8.00**

**Note**—In ordering crutches please give precise measure from under the arm to floor when standing erect; or if patient is in a horizontal position, length from under arm to sole of foot.

## Rubber Crutch Bottoms.

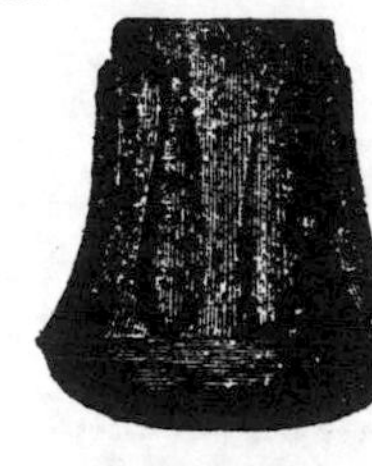

D 992 Rubber rasp style, Crutch Tips or Bottoms, made in ¾, ⅞ and 1 inch diameter.
Price, per pair........**20c.**

## Toilet and Complexion Brushes.

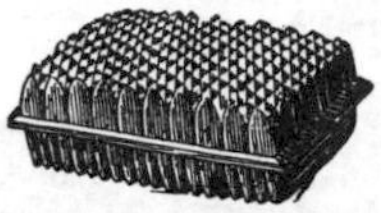

D 1002. **The "Salamander" Rubber Toilet Brush.** Patented July 8, 1890. This improved rubber toilet brush having two different surfaces, makes it the best toilet brush ever made. The side with the diamond points will cleanse the hands of all mechanics, and will keep their hands soft and in good condition. Machinists, Printers, Blacksmiths, Penmen, Shoemakers, and in fact all whose hands become stained by their labor. The surface that has the heavy corrugations will clean the hands of the most delicate lady or any whose flesh is tender, without hurting the skin or making it rough. This brush will remove paint, tar or grease from clothing by simply using soap and water. All who use pumice to clean their hands will find that this brush removes the stains cleaner, and will not leave the hands sore, but soft and clean. For bath use this brush has no equal, and is the only brush that will float in water.
Price, **20c.**, per doz........................................**$2.00**

D 1003 **Complexion Brush.** It is especially constructed for massaging the skin. It removes all roughness and dead cuticle, smoothing out the wrinkles, rendering the skin soft and pliant, and tinted with a healthy glow.
For the bath it will be found a perfect luxury by both old and young. The brush is all one piece and as soft as silk.
Price, **50c.**, per doz........................................**$5.00**

D 1004. **Rubber Toilet Brush.** For the nails and hands. A ladies' hand brush, is soft and pliable and universally used as a toilet brush.
Price, small, **15c.**; per doz........................................**$1.75**
Price, large, **25c.**; per doz........................................**$2.75**

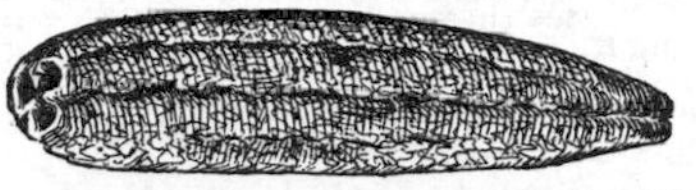

D 1005. **Japanese Loofah.** (Flesh Brush) The Loofah is a fibrous part of a gourd that grows in the south of Japan. Its health-giving properties, when used as a flesh brush or sponge, have been known to the Japanese for ages. In England, where they have been used for some years, they are rapidly taking the place of the ordinary sponge for bath purposes. Their use gives a healthy glow to the body, removes all accumulations from the pores of the skin, increases the circulation of the blood, and leaves a pleasant sensation.
**Directions.** The Loofah may be used as a sponge, just as it is, or to make it a trifle more handy, soak in water until it expands full size; cut lengtwise and remove the inner substance so that the Loofah opens out like a cloth. Price, **9c.**; per doz....**$1.00**

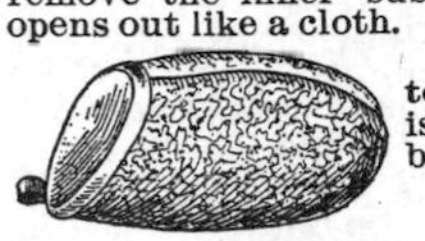

D 1006. **Loofah Bath Mitten.** Loofah front with Turkish toweling back. The best bath mitten in the market.
Price, **20c.**; per doz...**$2.00**

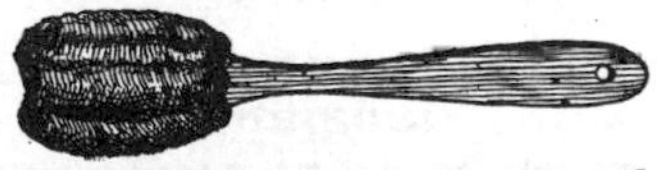

D 1007 **Loofah Bath Brush.** Try one and satisfy yourself that
1st. It is the best bath brush made.
2d. It is light, cheap and durable.
3d. It is very porous and easily dried.
4th. It is a pleasant and perfect friction brush.
5th. It is nature's own medicine.
6th. It is recommended by all as the best Sanitary and Hygienic brush known for the bath.
Price, **18c.**; per doz........................................**$2.00**

## Toilet and Medicated Soaps.

We are large buyers of fine Toilet and Medicinal Soaps, therefore we can give you good bargains in this line. We buy only soaps that we know to be of good quality and made of pure ingredients; soaps that we use in our own families.

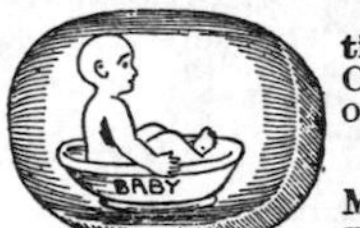


G 2017 **Imported White Castile Soap.** This is a genuine Castile soap, made from pure olive oil, not perfumed.
Large cakes, per doz........**45c**

D 1009 **Tuscan Castile Soap.** Made from the green olive oil, guaranteed to be absolutely pure and free from animal fats and cottonseed oil and to contain no free alkali.
Per cake, **5c**; per dozen........................................**50c**

G 2018 **Turkish Bath Soap.** A fine soap made by Colgate & Co., the celebrated soap and perfume manufacturers of New York.
Each cake, **5c**; dozen........................................**45c**

D 1011 **Rico Toilet Soap.** A nicely perfumed complexion soap made especially for ourselves from pure materials by Colgate & Co., New York. Each cake stamped with their name as a guarantee of purity. This is a high class soap usually sold for 25c.
Per cake, **7c**; dozen........................................**75c**

D 1012 **Colgate'e 7th Regiment Banquet Soap.** This is a high grade toilet soap, sold in drug stores for 25 cents; highly perfumed; 3 cakes in handsome paper box.
Per cake, **14c**; per box........................................**40c**

D 1013 **Geranial Toilet Soap.** Complexion toilet soap, delicately perfumed with roses, oval cakes, each wrapped and packed, 3 in a neat bon-bon box.
Each cake, **9c**; per box........................................**24c**

G 2022 **Colgate's Glycerine Soap.** This well-known soap usually sold for 15 cents.
Per box of 3 cakes........................................**20c**

G 2023 **Colgate's Honey Soap.** Comes 3 cakes in neat paper box, usual price 15 cents a cake
Per box of 3 cakes........................................**20c**

G 2019 **Dr. Raub's Cutaneous Soap.** Try this soap once and you will always use it, it is the most perfect skin and complexion soap made. It is recommended by physicians for its great healing qualities in skin troubles. Highly medicated, delicately perfumed; the price usually asked for it is 25c.
Our price, **10c**; Box of 3 cakes........................................**25c**

D 1018 **Juvenile Toilet Soap.** This exquisitely perfumed soap has become a great favorite all through the country.
We sell it at **18c.** each and........................................**50c box**

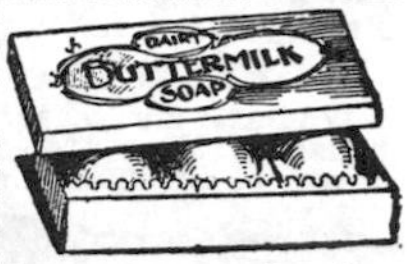


D 1019 **Dairy Buttermilk Soap.** This is the little giant bargain, 3 sweet little cakes in a box.
Each box of three cakes only **5c**; per doz. cakes **20c**

D 1020 **Sulphur Soap.** This is a soap very beneficial in skin diseases. It is pleasant to use, makes the skin healthy and of good color, and when used constantly will keep it so.
Price per cake, **8c**; dozen........................................**80c**

D 1021 **Tar Soap.** Has all the healing properties of tar; an excellent soap for cleansing the scalp and keeping the scalp in a healthy condition, soft and glossy; valuable also as a nursery and toilet soap.
Price per cake, **8c**: dozen........................................**80c**

D 1022 **Carbolic Soap.** A pure sanitary soap containing the healing properties of carbolic acid and vegetable oils, for washing old sores, bruises, cuts, burns, etc.
Price per cake, **8c**; dozen........................................**80c**

## Shaving Soaps.

D 1023 **Barbers' Bar Soap.** The finest shaving soap made. In constant use by first-class barbers all through the country. Round bars cut in six cakes.
Price, per cake, **4c**; per bar of 6 cakes ..........**22c**

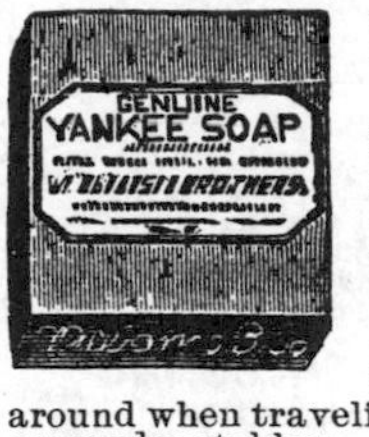


G 2029 **Yankee Shaving Soap.** A favorite shaving soap. In square cakes.
Per cake, **9c**; per doz....**$1.00**

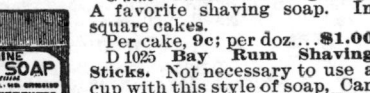

D 1025 **Bay Rum Shaving Sticks.** Not necessary to use a cup with this style of soap, Can use cold or warm water. Each stick in box with directions for using.
Per stick, **15c**; per doz..**$1.50**

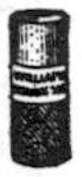

D 1026 **Williams' Travelers' Favorite Shaving Stick.** Convenient to carry around when traveling. Each in leatherette covered metal box. Perfumed with roses.
Each, **19c**; per doz........................................**$1.90**

## Perfumes.

D 1027 **Sears, Roebuck & Co.'s Perfume Extracts** have given great satisfaction to everyone who has used them. They are **sweet and lasting perfumes**, put up in handsome packages. We import these perfume extracts in bulk from the flower gardens of France, and put them up ourselves in different sized bottles. By this method we can afford to give the choicest full strength perfume in a pretty bottle for a low price.

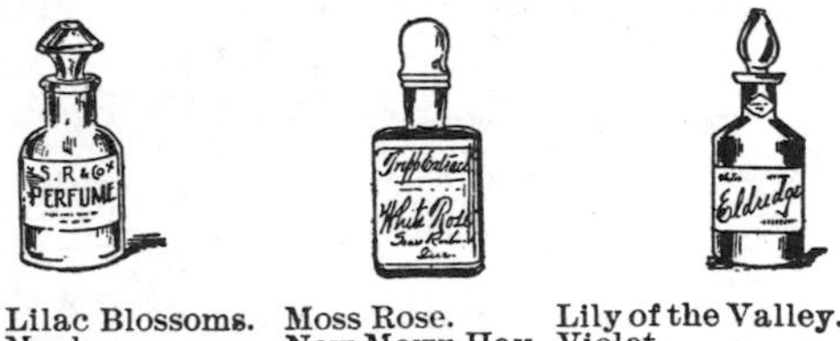

| | | |
|---|---|---|
| Lilac Blossoms. | Moss Rose. | Lily of the Valley. |
| Musk. | New Mown Hay. | Violet. |
| Indian Violet. | White Rose. | Wh'te Heliotrope. |
| Ylang Ylang. | English Violet. | Sweet Clover. |
| Jasamine. | Crab Apple. | Mignonette. |
| Sweet Pea. | Tea Rose. | Tuberose. |
| Wood Violet. | Shandon Bells. | Rose Geranium. |
| Carnation Pink. | Jockey Club. | Meadow Blossom. |
| Columbia Bouquet. | | |

Put up in glass stoppered bottles, 1 oz., each...**25c**
Put up in glass stoppered bottles, 2 oz., each...**48c**
Put up in glass stoppered bottles, 4 oz., each...**89c**
Put up in glass stoppered bottles, 8 oz., each.**$1.60**

D 1028 **Colgate's Cashmere Boquet Extract.**
1 oz. glass stoppered bottles........................................**46c**
2 oz. glass stoppered bottles........................................**68c**
4 oz. glass stoppered bottles........................................**$1.00**

D 1029 **Sears, Roebuck & Co.'s Toilet Waters.** Lavender, Ylang Ylang, Violet White Rose, Jasamine, Jockey Club, White Heliotrope.
Put up in 4 oz. bottles, each ........**$0.25**
Put up in ½ pint bottles, each ...... **.50**

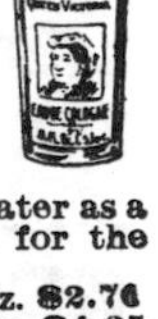

D 1030 **Colgate's Cashmere Bouquet Toilet Waters.**
Put up in 3 oz. bottles..**$0.38**
Put up in ½ pint bottles **.74**

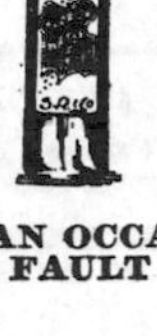

D 1031 **Sears, Robuck & Co.'s Genuine Florida Water.** Used as a perfume for the handkerchief, or mixed with water as a cooling and refreshing lotion for the skin.
Put up in 4 oz. bottles...**25c**; doz. **$2.76**
Put up in ½ pint bottles, **45c**; doz. **$4.85**

WHILE WE HAVE A MOST PERFECT SYSTEM OF HANDLING OUR ENORMOUS BUSINESS, AN OCCASIONAL MISTAKE CANNOT BE ABSOLUTELY PREVENTED. WE PAY ALL EXPENSES WHERE THE FAULT IS OURS.

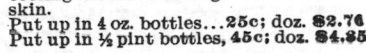

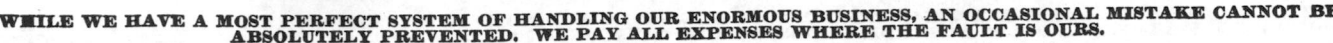

**D 1032 Sears, Roebuck & Co.'s Colognes.** These are specially prepared by us for the toilet and handkerchief and will compare favorable with the finest made; of great value in sick rooms. When used freely they act as a pleasant disinfectant destroying bad odors and rendering the air in the room fresh and pleasant. Eau de Cologne, Hawthorne, Nadjy, Violet, and Zenithia.

Put up in 4 oz. bottles............$0.35
Put up in 8 oz. bottles............ .60

**D 1033 Genuine Imported Farina Cologne.** This is the well-known branch of Farina Cologne imported by ourselves from Germany.

Put up in 1 oz. bottles............$0.15
Put up in 2 oz. bottles............ .25
Put up in 4 oz. bottles............ .45

## Japanese Tooth Brushes.

We have just received a large importation of these brushes. They are the finest tooth brush and most handsome designs of any ever imported to this coun-

try. We are going to sell them at a very low price considering the quality of the brush. They are attractively boxed and finished. We quote and describe but a few. Order by number.

|  | Each | Doz. |
|---|---|---|
| D 1034 "Sergo" a 3 row child's brush waxed back, handles decorated in colors, in fancy paper box | $0 08 | $0 95 |
| D 1037 A four row ladies' brush, assorted colored decorations on handles, ½ dozen in fancy bamboo box | 15 | 1 70 |
| D 1038 A four row gent's good quality decorated, assorted cut of bristles and and handles, ½ doz. in fancy bamboo box | 19 | 2 25 |
| D 1040 Extra quality carved handles, assorted, wood box | 20 | 2 25 |
| D 1041 A four row assorted wood handle, medium quality | 05 | 55 |
| D 1042 A 4 row cone handle assorted, good quality | 06 | 65 |
| D 1043 An extra fine quality, 4 row, elaborately decorated handles, ½ doz in box | 25 | 2 75 |

## For the Teeth.

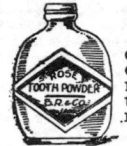

**D 1043½ Rose Tooth Powder.** An excellent powder for cleansing, whitening and preserving the teeth. Will remove tartar and prevent decay. Contains nothing injurious. Put up in metal screen top boxes.
Price each......15c; Doz......$1.75

## Liquid Dentifrice Imperial.

**D 1044** The most perfect preparation for the teeth. Will keep them entirely free from stains or discolorations. It will effectually remove the tartar, hardens the gums and keeps the teeth as lovely as pearls, leaving a delicious aftertaste in the mouth for hours.
Each......25c; Doz..........$2.50

## Tooth Soap.

**D 1045** "Sanitary," the Perfect Tooth Soap, for cleaning, beautifying and preserving the teeth, hardening the gums and keeping the breath sweet; warranted not injurious; in metallic box. Retail price. 25c.
Our price, per box....12c; Per doz. boxes..$1.25

## Tooth Preparations.

**Miscellaneous. Each**
D 1046 Bazin's Charcoal Paste..................$0 30
D 1047 Brown's Camphorated Dentifrice............ 19
D 1048 Buchan's Carbolic Tooth Soap............ 16
D 1049 Calder's Saponaceous Dentine............ 20
D 1050 Colgate's Antiseptic Dental Powder........ 19
D 1051 Colgate's Rince Bouche................ 40
D 1052 Fougera's Eau Angelique............ 70
D 1053 Gosnell's Cherry Tooth Paste........ 40
D 1054 Hood's Tooth Powder, small............ 46
D 1055 Jewsbury & Brown's Oriental Paste, small........ 45
D 1056 Lyon's Tooth Powder... 20
D 1057 Lyon's Tooth Tablets... 40
D 1058 Rubifoam............ 20
D 1059 Sheffield's Creme Dentifrice, tubes............ 19
D 1060 Strong's Arnica Tooth Soap............ 19
D 1061 Sozodont............ 60
D 1062 Sozodont Tooth Powder.. 19
D 1063 Teaberry Tooth Powder.. 19
D 1064 Thurston's Tooth Powder.. 20
D 1065 Zonweiss............ 20

**D 1066 Ear Cleaner.** Improved Ear Cleaner, spoon and ear sponge combined. A very useful and pretty little ivory toilet article.
Each..................10c; Per doz..........$1.00

## For the Hair.

**D 1067 S. R. & Co. Hair Tonic Restorer.** A luxuriant growth of hair is a thing of beauty and a joy forever. This preparation will prevent the hair from falling out, increase its growth and if it is fading, turning grey and loosing its lustre, it will restore it to its natural color and strength.
Each 75c; doz..........$8.00

**D 1068 Hair Elixir.** A beautiful dressing for the hair, making it soft and glossy, prevents it from splitting and falling out. Cures dandruff and makes the hair grow. Each 50c; doz..........$5.00

**D 1069 Old Reliable Hair and Whisker Dye.** In use since 1860; will change the color of the hair to a light or dark brown or black in a few hours without doing any injury to it; used according to directions any shade of brown or black can be obtained. Each 40c; doz..........$4.50

**D 1070 Hair Curling Fluid.** This preparation will keep the hair in curl during the dampest or warmest weather; quite harmless to the hair; directions on each bottle. Each 25c; doz..........$2.50

**D 1071 Blonde Hair.** This is a perfectly harmless preparation that will gradually turn the hair from any color to a beautiful blonde color. Any shade of color can be obtained. from light brown to golden by following the simple instructions which go with each bottle. We guarantee that no harm to the hair will result in using it, but rather it is cleansing and strengthening.
Small trial size, each 50c; doz..........$5.00
Large................ 90c; doz.......... 8.00

### Hair Oils. Imported.

D 1072 Coudray's Brilliantine... $0.40
D 1073 Pinaud's Brilliantine... .38
D 1074 Societe Hygienique Oil... .60
D 1075 S. R. & Co's. Brilliantine for making the hair soft and glossy................ .20

### Shampoo Paste.

**D 1076 Shampoo Paste.** Removes dandruff, leaves the hair soft and keeps the scalp in healthy condition; produces the finest foam, is the most economical shampoo and is unexcelled as a cleanser Per box...25c; doz..........$2.50

### Pomatum and Cosmetiques.

**D 1077 Olive Wax Pomatum,** for fixing and laying the hair, whiskers and mustaches. Highly perfumed; each stick wrapped in tinfoil.
Each 10c; doz..................75c

**D 1078 French Cosmetique,** round stick, wrapped in foil; black, pink or white. Retail price, 10c; our special price. Per stick 5c; doz..................45c

## Highly Recommended Toilet Preparations.

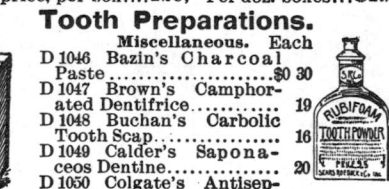

**Our special line of articles for the toilet cannot be equaled by any other house** either in this country or in Europe, on account of their good and harmless quality and the magical effects produced. They are prepared by a specialist who has made a life study of the science of improving and beautifying the skin, hair and teeth. It is in the nature of the human family from the savage to the most civilized to use the best means obtainable, by which they can render themselves more pleasing and attractive to others. It is a duty and a pleasure we owe to one another. It is almost criminal to go about with a repulsive complexion, etc., when the means to render yourself attractive are so easily obtainable.

**D 1079 Lavender Lotion.** This lotion is composed of the purest ingredients selected without regard to expense. Nothing on the market can compare to it as a beautifier of the complexion. Full directions with each bottle. Each Doz. ..........$.75 7.50

**D 1080 Almond Nut Cream.** A cleansing, cooling, excellent face cream, clears the skin from wrinkles, tan, freckles, etc., rendering it soft and white .50 5.00

**D 1081 Secret de Ninon.** For freckles. These blemishes are very annoying especially to those with pretty complexions. This preparation will remove freckles if the directions on the bottle are followed, and will leave the skin in a natural healthy condition. .75 8.50

**D 1082 Depilatory.** For removing superfluous hair. Nothing disfigures a woman's face so much as an unnatural growth of hair. This preparation removes all hair from the skin in one or two applications, when the directions on the bottle are carefully followed.. .75 8.50

**D 1083 Witch Hazel Toilet Cream.** Each Doz. This is an elegant preparation for the skin when it is chapped and rough. A few applications well rubbed in render the skin soft and velvety. It is also good for removing sunburn and freckles. It will prevent the skin from chapping or discoloring when exposed to the cold, if used before going out. It does not leave the skin greasy or sticky. Gloves can be worn immediately after using it without soiling them............$.25 $2.50

**D 1184 Camphorated Cold Cream.** Very fine for chapped Lips, Face or Hands. Keeps the skin smooth..................0.15 1.50

**D 1185 Arsenic Complexion Wafers.** These Wafers can be taken without any fear of any harm resulting from their use. They are an excellent medicine for giving to the complexion a clearness and brilliancy not obtainable by external applications, at the same time they improve the general health, causing the figure to grow plump and round.
Small size..................0.40 4.25
Large size..................0.75 8.00

**D 1186 Water of Youth.** Each Doz. This is a simple preparation much used by a famous French beauty of the last century. After using it for a few days, it gives the skin a youthful fresh softness with a perfect tint..$0.75 $8.50

**D 1187 Rouge.** A harmless preparation for giving color to the cheeks and lips; it gives a perfectly natural pretty color..................0.50 5.00

**D 1188 Face Powder.** There are a good number of powders for the face on the market. ours we claim to be the superior of any; it is harmless, almost invisible when used rightly with a very enchanting effect. It is put up in three shades to suit the different complexions. white, pink and brunette.
Each..................$0.15
Dozen..................1.50

## Powders and Cosmetics.
**MISCELLANEOUS.**

D 1188½ Ayer's Recamier Cream. with or without glycerine......$1 15
D 1189 Ayer's Moth and Freckle Lotion.. .. 1 15
D 1190 Ayer's Recamier Balm.. .. 1 15
D 1191 Ayer's Recamier Powder.. .. 0 42
D 1192 La Blanche Powder.. .. 0 35
D 1193 Pear's Fuller's Earth.. .. 0 19
D 1194 Pozzoni's Complexion Powder..................$0 40
D 1195 Pozzoni's Dove Face Powder.. .. 0 20
D 1196 Tetlow's Swan's Down. 0 13
D 1197 Vaseline Camphor Ice. 0 10
D 1198 Cold Cream Vaseline.. 0 17
D 1199 Elsie Toilet Cream, the best known remedy for sunburn, freckles and chapped hands and for keeping the skin soft and white..$0 25
D 1200 Blush of Roses.. .. 0 65
D 1201 Couelray's Blanc De Pearl.. .. 0 55
D 1202 Champluis Liquid Pearl.. .. 0 40
D 1203 Elgin Phantom Powder.. .. 0 18
D 1204 Gourad's Oriental Cream.. .. 1 05
D 1205 Hagaus Magnolia Balm..................$0 50
D 1206 Dorins Rouge de Theatre.. .. 0 18
D 1207 Blanc de Pearl Powder.. .. 0 18
D 1208 Eye Brow Pencils, Black or Brown, in nickel plated cases.. .. 0 10
D 1209 Strong's Arnica Jelly.. .. 0 15
D 1210 Blue Seal Vaseline.. .. 0 04
D 1211 Cold Cream of Roses.................. 0 20

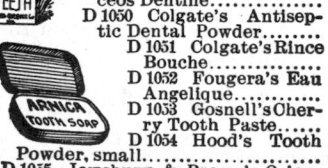

## Funnels.

| | | Each. |
|---|---|---|
| D 1212 | ½ pint, glass | $0.15 |
| | 1 pint, glass | 20 |
| | 1 quart, glass | 25 |
| | 2 quart, glass | 35 |
| | ¼ pint, hard rubber | 40 |
| | ½ pint, hard rubber | 45 |
| | 1 pint, hard rubber | 50 |
| | 1 quart, hard rubber | 60 |

## Mortars.

| | | Each. | | Each. |
|---|---|---|---|---|
| D 1213 | Glass, 1 oz | $0.15 | 2 oz | 20 |
| | 4 oz | 25 | 8 oz | 35 |
| D 1214 | Iron, Pint | 50 | Quart | 60 |
| | ½ gallon | 85 | Gallon | 1.40 |
| | 2 gallons | 2.00 | | |

| | | |
|---|---|---|
| D 1215 | Wedgewood, 5 oz | 50 |
| | 8 oz | 55 |
| | 16 oz (pint) | 70 |
| | 32 oz (quart) | 1.30 |
| | ½ gallon | 1.60 |
| | 1¼ gallon | 2.90 |

## Graduates or Measuring Glasses.

| | Each. | | | Each. |
|---|---|---|---|---|
| D 1216 | 1 oz | $0.20 | 2 oz | $0.25 |
| | 4 oz | 30 | 8 oz | 45 |
| | 16 oz | 75 | | |

## Glass Spirit Lamps.

With ground glass cap.

| | | Each. |
|---|---|---|
| D 1217 | 2 oz | $0.25 |
| | 4 oz | 35 |
| | 8 oz | 50 |

## Scales and Weights.

D 1218 Hand scales, with weight, 5 in. beam, 2¼ in. pans, neatly put up in lined folding box. Price, **50c**; postage, 10c.

D 1222 Prescription Scales, with pillar and beam on polished walnut or cherry box, with drawer. 6 inch beam, 2½ inch pans, and includes full set weights, Price, **$3.50.** Weight, 1½ lbs.

D 1222 The Lakeside Prescription Scales, with pillar and 8 inch beam on finished ashwood box, with drawer. Finished in lacquered brass, and has nickle-plated pans, 2¾ inch diameter. Full set weights. Price, **$4.25.** Weight, 1¾ lbs.

## Hydrometers.

D 1223 Can furnish Hydrometers for any of the following purposes (give name and number when ordering):

1. Acid.
2. Alkali.
3. Sugar and Syrup.
4. Vinegar.
5. Salt, 0 to 50.
6. Salinometer, 0 to 100.
7. Cider.
8. Shellac.
9. Spirit plain.
10. Bark (for tanners).
11. Liquids heavier than water.
12. Liquids lighter than water.
13. Sacchrometers.
14. Ammonia.
15. Coal Oil.

Price of any of the above, **50c.**

## Urinometers.

D 1224 Urinometers for determining the specific gravity of the urine; is an indicator of the condition of the same as related to the general health. A circular accompanies each instrument, giving full instructions as to how it should be used. Urinometer, complete with jar, iuclosed in round wood box. Each .......... **$0.35**

## Empty Gelatine Capsules.

Readily Soluble.

No. 5 holds ½ grain of dry quinine.
No. 2 holds 3 grains of dry quinine.
No. 4 holds 1 grain of dry quinine.
No. 1 holds 4 to 5 grains of dry quinine.
No. 3 holds 2 grains of dry quinine.
No. 0 holds 6 grains of dry quinine.
No. 00 holds 8 grains of dry quinine.

They come in boxes of 100 and 1000 capsules—one size only in a box. Retail at double our prices.

We do not assort or sell less than one box.

D 1225 In boxes of 100, any one size .......... $0.12
D 1226 In boxes of 1000, any one size .......... .85

## Empty Capsules.

For Veterinary Use.

| | | Per Box. |
|---|---|---|
| D 1227 | No. 10 holds 1 oz., 10 capsules in a box | $0.25 |
| D 1228 | No. 11 holds ½ oz., 10 capsules in a box | .23 |
| D 1229 | No. 12 holds ¼ oz., 10 capsules in a box | .20 |

See Nos. 1640 to 1650 for filled capsules.

## Filtering Paper.

D 1230 12 inch diameter, 100 in package, per package .......... $0.40
We do not sell less than package.

**THE INDEX** To this Catalogue is contained in the last pages. Search the Index TO FIND WHAT YOU WANT.

## Druggist Twine.

D 1231 All colors (8 balls to the lb.) per pound...$0.45
We do not sell less than a pound.

## Cold Cream Jars.

Empty.

| | | Each. | Per Dozen Lots Only. |
|---|---|---|---|
| D 1232 | ½ oz | $0.12 | $1.10 |
| | 1 oz | .15 | 1.20 |
| | 2 oz | .18 | 1.20 |

## Ointment Pots.

Flint Glass. Nickle Screw Cap.

| | | Per Doz. | | Per Dozen. |
|---|---|---|---|---|
| D 1233 | ¼ oz | $0.50 | ½ oz | .55 |
| | 1 oz | .65 | 2 oz | .75 |
| | 4 oz | 1.05 | 8 oz | 1.75 |
| | 16 oz | 2.70 | | |

## Turned Wood Boxes.

| | | Per Gross. | | Per Gross. |
|---|---|---|---|---|
| D 1234 | ¼ oz | $0.50 | ½ oz | .60 |
| | 1 oz | .70 | 2 oz | .90 |
| | 3 oz | 1.20 | 4 oz | 1.40 |

Jaynes' Wooden Pill Boxes .......... .60

## Tin Ointment Boxes.

Seamless, Plain.

| | | Per 100. | | Per 100. |
|---|---|---|---|---|
| D 1235 | ¼ oz | $0.25 | ½ oz | .35 |
| | 1 oz | .60 | 2 oz | 1.00 |
| | 3 oz | 1.25 | 4 oz | 2.25 |

## Baking Powder Cans, Round.

| | | Per 100 plain. | | Per 100 plain. |
|---|---|---|---|---|
| D 1236 | 4 oz | $ 1.16 | 8 oz | 2.00 |
| | 1 pound | 3.40 | 2 pound | 7.20 |
| | 2½ pound | 8.00 | 5 pound | 1.50 |

## Corks.

Always mention our stock numbers when ordering goods.

| | Numbers. | Fine (X) Per gross. | Fine (X) Per 5 gross bag. | Superf' (XX) Per gross | Superf' (XX) Per 5 gross bag. |
|---|---|---|---|---|---|
| G 1238 | 1 to 6 assorted | $0 17 | $0 50 | $0 33 | $0 97 |
| | 3 to 6 assorted | 20 | 60 | 37 | 1 10 |
| | 0, 1 and 2 | 11 | 33 | 25 | 73 |
| | 3 | 13 | 38 | 28 | 84 |
| | 4 | 15 | 45 | 33 | 99 |
| | 5 | 25 | 75 | 38 | 1 14 |
| | 6 | 30 | 90 | 48 | 1 44 |
| | 7 | 45 | 1 20 | 68 | 2 04 |
| | 8 | 52 | 1 57 | 85 | 2 55 |
| | 9 | 59 | 1 77 | 1 00 | 3 00 |
| | 10 | 74 | 2 20 | 1 23 | 3 69 |
| | 6 to 10 assorted | 85 | 2 55 | 52 | 1 54 |
| | 7 to 20, assorted, jug | 1 18 | 3 54 | .... | .... |
| | 11 to 20, assorted, jug | 1 43 | 4 26 | .... | .... |

## Wine Corks.

| | | Fine (X) Per gross. | Fine (X) Per 5 gross bag. | Superf' (XX) Per gross | Superf' (XX) Per 5 gross bag. |
|---|---|---|---|---|---|
| G 1239 | No. 7, 1½ in. long | $0 77 | $3 36 | $1 00 | $4 41 |
| | No. 8, 1½ in. long | 95 | 4 13 | 1 20 | 5 25 |
| | No. 9, 1½ in. long | 1 05 | 4 62 | 1 34 | 5 88 |
| | No. 10, 1½ in. long | 1 13 | 4 97 | 1 50 | 6 58 |

## Rubber Corks.

G 1240 The number and size of our rubber corks correspond to the regular cork. 100 in a box. We do not sell less.

| Nos. | Per 100 | Nos. | Per 100 |
|---|---|---|---|
| 0 | $0 50 | 6 | $0 85 |
| 1 | 50 | 7 | 1 35 |
| 2 | 50 | 8 | 1 65 |
| 3 | 60 | 9 | 1 95 |
| 4 | 60 | 10 | 2 95 |
| 5 | $0.85 | | |

## Specie, or Jar Corks.

| | Measure large end. | Per gross. | | Per gross, |
|---|---|---|---|---|
| G 1241 | 1 inch | $0 44 | 1⅛ inch | 65 |
| | 1¼ inch | 68 | 1⅜ inch | 80 |
| | 1½ inch | 96 | 1⅝ inch | 1 16 |
| | 1¾ inch | 1 40 | 1⅞ inch | 1 60 |
| | 2 inch | 1 80 | 2¼ inch | 2 28 |
| | 2½ inch | 3 36 | 2¾ inch | 4 24 |
| | 3 inch | 5 12 | | |

## Bottles.

G 1242 Always mention number at top of quotation when ordering goods. Flint precription bottles, French square, oval or round.

| Capacity. | Per gross in full cases. | Per gross in less than full cases. | Per doz. in less than gross lots. |
|---|---|---|---|
| ½-oz., 5 gross in case | $1 20 | $1 50 | $0 15 |
| 1-oz., 5 gross in case | 1 40 | 1 70 | 18 |
| 2-oz., 3 gross in case | 1 80 | 2 25 | 20 |
| 3-oz., 2 gross in case | 2 00 | 2 20 | 25 |
| 4-oz., 2 gross in case | 2 40 | 3 00 | 30 |
| 6-oz., 1 gross in case | 2 80 | 3 50 | 35 |
| 8-oz., 1 gross in case | 3 20 | 4 00 | 38 |
| 16-oz., ½ gross in case | 5 20 | 5 72 | 42 |
| 32-oz., ½ gross in case | 8 00 | 8 80 | 80 |

Assorted, 1 gross in case, ½ to 8 ounces, per case, $2.00.

Oval and round bottles furnished at same price as French square. Wide mouth bottles, all shapes, $1.00 a gross higher.

These bottles are best white flint. The common green glass bottles we do not handle, except in full cases on special orders. Unless otherwise instructed, we will ship the round bottles.

## Glass Stoppered Bottles.

| | | Per doz. wide mouth. | Per doz. narrow mouth. |
|---|---|---|---|
| G 1243 | 1-oz | $0 60 | $0 54 |
| | 2-oz | 64 | 62 |
| | 4-oz | 87 | 81 |
| | 8-oz | 1 12 | 1 04 |
| | 16-oz. or pints | 1 65 | 1 60 |
| | 32-oz. or quarts | 2 21 | 2 20 |
| | ½-gal | 4 10 | 3 90 |

## Shoo-Fly Flasks.

| | | Case lots, Per gross. | Per dozen |
|---|---|---|---|
| G 1244 | ½ pints, ½ gross in case | $ 4 40 | $0 45 |
| | Pints, ½ gross in case | 6 80 | 60 |
| | Quarts, ½ gross in case | 10 40 | 95 |

## Ball Neck Panels or Essence Bottles.

| | | Case lots, Per gross. | Per gross, less than a case. |
|---|---|---|---|
| G 1245 | ¾-ounce, 5 gross in case | $1 60 | $1 76 |
| | 1¼-ounce, 3 gross in case | 1 80 | 1 98 |
| | 1¾-ounce, 3 gross in case | 2 00 | 2 20 |
| | 2-ounce, 2 gross in case | 2 20 | 2 42 |
| | 3-ounce, 2 gross in case | 2 60 | 2 82 |
| | 4-ounce, 1 gross in case | 3 20 | 3 52 |

These are full measure and of flint glass.

## Pomades--Wide Mouth, Round.

| | | | |
|---|---|---|---|
| G 1246 | 1-oz., 5 gross in case | $1 80 | $2 25 |
| | 2-oz., 3 gross in case | 2 20 | 2 75 |
| | 4-oz., 2 gross in case | 2 80 | 3 50 |

## Homeopathic Vials.

One gross in a box. We do not sell less.

| | | Per gross. | | Per gross. |
|---|---|---|---|---|
| G 1147 | ¼ drachm | $0 60 | ½ drachm | 60 |
| | 1 drachm | 65 | 2 drachm | 75 |
| | 3 drachm | 1 00 | 4 drachm | 1 50 |

## Corn and Bunion Plasters.

| | | Each. | Doz. |
|---|---|---|---|
| D 1248 | Allcock's Corn Plasters, 3 in envelope | $0.08 | $0.75 |
| D 1249 | Allcock's Corn Plasters, 12 in box | .15 | 1.50 |
| D 1250 | Allcock's Bunion Plasters, 6 in box | .15 | 1.50 |
| D 1251 | Round or oval Corn Plasters, thick or thin 1 doz in box per bx | .10 | 1.00 |

| | | Each. | Doz. |
|---|---|---|---|
| D 1252 | Square, round or oval Plaster ½ doz. in box, per box | $0.12 | $1.25 |
| D 1253 | London Medicated Corn Plaster per box | .17 | 2.00 |
| D 1254 | London Medicated Bunion Plasters per box | .17 | 2.00 |
| | Lonas Corn Leaf | .08 | .85 |
| D 1255 | Sears, Roebuck & Co.'s Russian Corn, Bunion and Wart Cure. We Guarantee this remedy to cure Corns and Bunions, to destroy warts; if persevered with, it will give relief on the first application, no trouble to use | .10 | .90 |

## Medicated Plasters.

**We guarantee all our Plasters to be fresh and good quality.** They are excellent for pains in the back, chest, kidneys or other parts of the body, arising from colds, rheumatism, sprains, etc. We quote only a few of the more frequently used ones, but we can furnish plasters of any description, either spread on linen or cotton, or in the original mass.

### Porous Plasters.

| | | each. | doz. |
|---|---|---|---|
| D 1256 | Belladonna Plaster | **$0.10** | **$1.00** |
| D 1257 | Poor Man's Plaster | **.15** | **1.25** |
| D 1258 | Strengthening Plaster | **.10** | **1.00** |
| D 1259 | Capsicum Plaster | **.15** | **1.25** |
| D 1260 | Belladonna and Capsicum Plaster | **.15** | **1.25** |
| D 1261 | Kidney Plaster, large size to cover both kidneys | **.25** | **2.25** |

### Mustard Plasters.

Always ready for use. Very handy to have at hand when needed.

D 1262 3 plasters in tin box, per box .......... **10c**
D 1263 6 plasters in tin box, per box .......... **15c**
D 1264 10 plasters in tin box, per box .......... **20c**
D 1265 One yard roll, each .......... **30c**
D 1266 **Rubber Adhesive Plaster.** 1 yd. rolls, each .......... **25c**
D 1267 **Isinglass Adhesive Plaster.** White, flesh or black color. 1 yd. rolls in tin box, each .......... **50c**



**IF WE COULD GET ALL OUR CUSTOMERS TO USE OUR SIMPLE RULES IN ORDERING GOODS, WE COULD PREVENT NINE OUT OF TEN OF MISTAKES THAT OCCUR. READ THE FIRST PAGES OF THIS BOOK AND YOU WILL HAVE NO TROUBLE.**

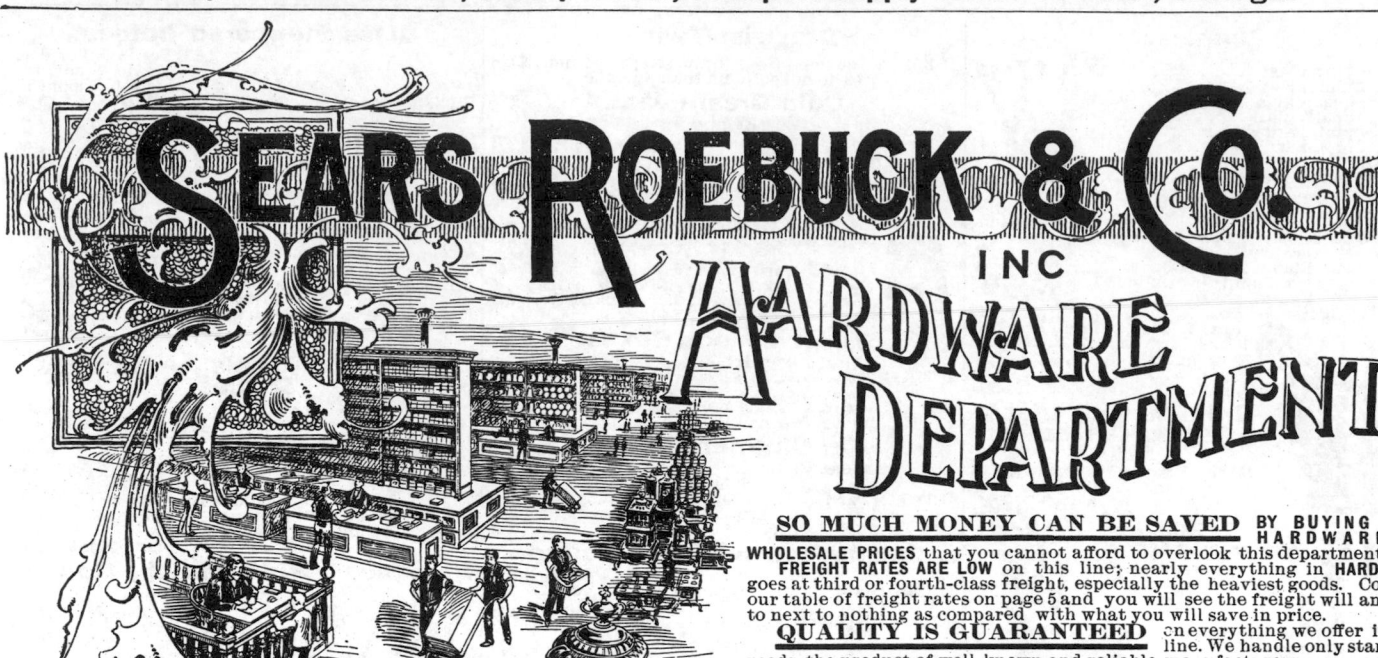

# SEARS ROEBUCK & CO. INC — HARDWARE DEPARTMENT

**SO MUCH MONEY CAN BE SAVED** BY BUYING YOUR HARDWARE AT **WHOLESALE PRICES** that you cannot afford to overlook this department. **FREIGHT RATES ARE LOW** on this line; nearly everything in **HARDWARE** goes at third or fourth-class freight, especially the heaviest goods. Consult our table of freight rates on page 5 and you will see the freight will amount to next to nothing as compared with what you will save in price.

**QUALITY IS GUARANTEED** on everything we offer in this line. We handle only standard goods, the product of well-known and reliable manufacturers. **WE DO NOT HANDLE TRASHY GOODS;** we believe the best is always the cheapest, and we can save you 25% to 50% on everything in the hardware line. If you place your order with us it will mean we will get your future orders, as well as the orders of your friends and neighbors.

**IF YOU CONTEMPLATE BUILDING** A HOUSE, BARN, GRANARY or other building. consult this catalogue for prices on your Hardware, Doors, Sash, Paper, Paints etc., or get your carpenter to make out a bill of just what material you will require in this line and let us quote you prices. We will save you money; if we don't sell you, we will compel some dealer to sell you the cheapest bill he ever sold in his life. **WHEN BUILDING, DON'T BUY THIS CLASS OF GOODS** from your dealer until you have got our figures. We will open your eyes in the saving.

**CARPENTERS AND BUILDERS** are especially requested to consult this Catalogue for prices on Tools of all descriptions, and for further information **Send for our Free Tool Catalogue. BLACKSMITHS AND WAGONMAKERS** are invited to carefully note our prices on everything in their line and for further particulars **SEND FOR OUR FREE CATALOGUE** of Blacksmiths' and Wagonmakers' Tools and Supplies.

**SPECIAL SEPARATE BOOKLETS** are issued showing large illustrations and very complete descriptions of the following special lies: AGRICULTURAL IMPLEMENTS; POULTRY NETTING and WIRE FENCING; SCALES; FARM, CHURCH and SCHOOL HOUSE BELLS; LAWN MOWERS; PORTABLE FORGES; STEEL SAFES; ICE CREAM FREEZERS; REFRIGERATORS; WRINGERS; WASHING MACHINES; OIL and GASOLINE STOVES and WOOD and COAL STOVES. **THESE BOOKLETS ARE FREE** and will be sent to any address by mail, postpaid, on application.

**OUR LIBERAL TERMS:** All hardware (except such as must be paid for in advance) will be sent to any address by **Freight or Express, C. O. D.,** subject to examination, on receipt of **one-fourth** the amount of purchase, balance and transportation charges payable after goods are received. **THREE PER CENT. CASH DISCOUNT** allowed if cash in full accompanies your order, **EXCEPT on NAILS and BARBED WIRE, which are NET CASH** in all cases.

**OUR CLUB ORDER PLAN** as fully explained on page 4, is especially recommended to your consideration when ordering hardware. **Your neighbors** will surely want something in this line and gladly join with you in making up an order.

---

## NAILS

**WE ARE HEADQURTERS ON NAILS** and will not be undersold by anyone. **It is a common practice** with hardware dealers to offer nails at cost or below cost with the condition that the other goods be bought from them. **This gives them a chance to get** their profit on nails by adding to the other goods.

**BEWARE OF THIS SCHEME.** Our prices on nails are without any such conditions. **If you want other goods** we will be glad to receive your order for them at our regular prices. **But we want to sell the nails anyway.**

**AS PRICES ON NAILS ARE CONSTANTLY FLUCTUATING** we cannot print prices which will hold for the season, but you can always find them quoted in our Grocery Price List, which is revised and issued weekly and is sent free to anyone on request. If you should send us an order for nails, they will be charged at the **lowest price on the day** your order is received.

**NAILS TAKE THE LOWEST FREIGHT RATE, FOURTH-CLASS.**

☞ See rates on pages 5 and 6.

The length of various nails is as follows:

| Size, | 2d | 3d | 4d | 5d | 6d | 7d | 8d | 9d |
|---|---|---|---|---|---|---|---|---|
| Inches, | 1 | 1¼ | 1½ | 1¾ | 2 | 2¼ | 2½ | 2¾ |
| Size, | 10d | 12d | 16d | 20d | 30d | 40d | 50d | 60d |
| Inches, | 3 | 3¼ | 3½ | 4 | 4½ | 5 | 5½ | 6 |

### Price List of Nails in Kegs of 100 lbs Each.

**Cash in Full must be sent with orders for nails.**

THE **BASE PRICE** of nails is constantly changing, so we cannot print a **Base Price** which will hold good for more than ten days from date of issue of this catalogue. The list of advances (which remains the same at all times) is the amount to be added to the base price to find the cost of any certain size nail. The **Base Price** is for nails 20d to 60d. Our Base Price today is **$1.65 per keg** for Wire Nails and **$1.60 per keg** for Cut Nails.

### List of Common, Fence, Shingle and Flooring Nails.

| | |
|---|---|
| 20d, 30d, 40d, 50d, 60d | Same as Base Price |
| For 10d, 12d and 16d | add $0 05 to Base Price |
| For 8d and 9d | add 0 10 to Base Price |
| For 6d and 7d | add 0 20 to Base Price |
| For 4d and 5d | add 0 30 to Base Price |
| For 3d | add 0 45 to Base Price |
| For 3d fine | add 0 50 to Base Price |
| For 2d | add 0 70 to Base Price |
| For 2d fine | add 1 00 to Base Price |

These prices are for full kegs of 100 lbs. We will furnish any quantity at an advance of ½c per lb. above the keg price.

**No. 109. Clinch or Wrought Nails** sold in any quantity.

| Length. | Per lb. |
|---|---|
| 6d......2 inch.. | 4 c |
| 8d......2½ inch.. | 3¾c |
| 10d......3 inch.. | 3½c |

If full kegs are wanted price will be quoted on application.

### Nails in Small Packages.

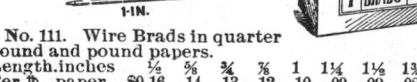

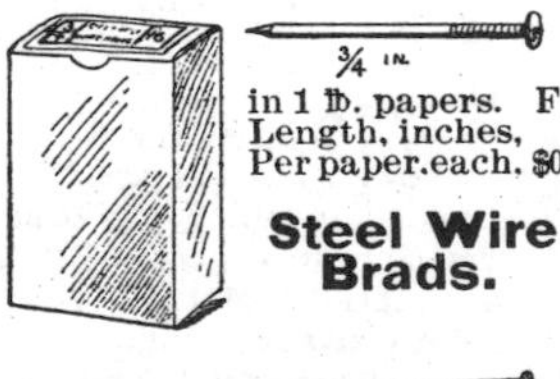

**No. 110. Wire Nails** in 1 lb. papers. Flat heads.

| Length, inches, | ¾ | ⅞ | 1 | 1¼ | 1½ |
|---|---|---|---|---|---|
| Per paper.each. | $0.12 | .10 | .09 | .08 | .08 |

### Steel Wire Brads.

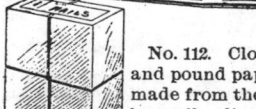

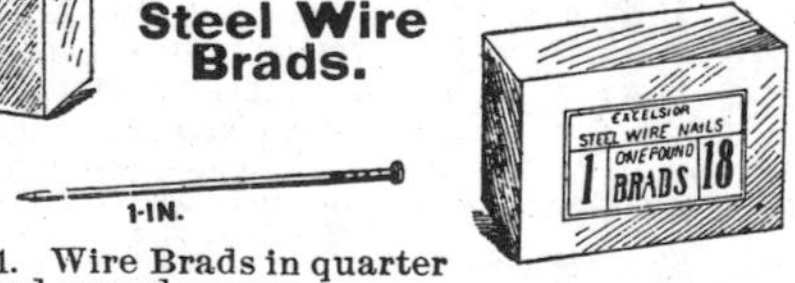

**No. 111. Wire Brads** in quarter pound and pound papers.

| Length.inches | ½ | ⅝ | ¾ | ⅞ | 1 | 1¼ | 1½ | 1¾ | 2 |
|---|---|---|---|---|---|---|---|---|---|
| Per lb., paper. | $0.16 | .14 | .13 | .12 | .10 | .09 | .09 | .08 | .08 |
| Per ¼ lb., paper. | .06 | .05 | .05 | .04 | .04 | .03 | .03 | .03 | .03 |

### Clout Nails.

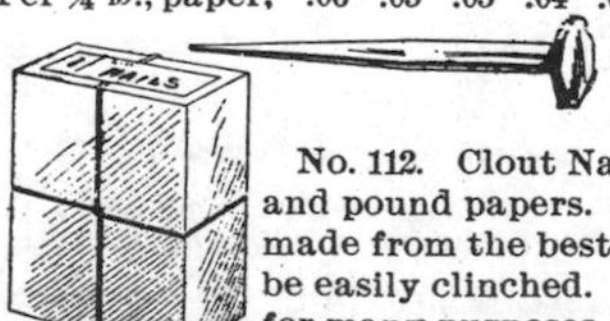

**No. 112. Clout Nails** in half pound and pound papers. Clout Nails are made from the best soft iron and can be easily clinched. Very convenient for many purposes.

| Length,inches. | ½ | ⅝ | ¾ | ⅞ | 1 | 1¼ | 1½ | 1¾ | 2 |
|---|---|---|---|---|---|---|---|---|---|
| Per lb., | $0.14 | .12 | .10 | .08 | .07 | .07 | .07 | .07 | .07 |
| Per ½ lb., | .08 | .07 | .06 | .06 | .05 | .05 | .05 | .05 | .05 |

### Brass Head Furniture Nails.

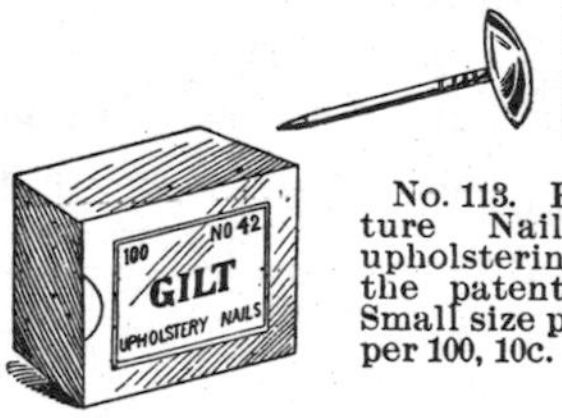

**No. 113. Brass Head Furniture Nails** are used for upholstering or for nailing on the patent wood chair seats. Small size per 100, 7c; large size, per 100, 10c.

### Cut Tacks.

Tacks are sold in packages of various sizes, known as fullweights, half weights, quarter weights and skins. The latter mostly paper and twine. The size known as half weights is most convenient for ordinary use and is what is sold by the best and most reliable dealers. All tacks quoted by us are guaranteed to be strictly genuine half weight papers. For ingrain carpet use 8 oz. tacks; for Brussels carpet use 10 oz. tacks; for extra thick Brussels carpet use 12 oz. tacks. To tack curtains on spring shade rollers use 1 oz. tacks. There are 370 tacks in a **half weight** paper of 8 oz. cut tacks or nearly four times as many as in **count** tacks of 100 in a paper.

**No. 114. American Iron Cut Tacks.**

| Ounces. | 1 | 2 | 3 | 4 | 6 | 8 | 10 | 12 | 16 |
|---|---|---|---|---|---|---|---|---|---|
| Per paper. | $0.02 | .02 | .02 | .02 | .03 | .03 | .03 | .03 | .04 |
| Per doz. papers. | .14 | .15 | .18 | .21 | .23 | .25 | .27 | .29 | .31 |

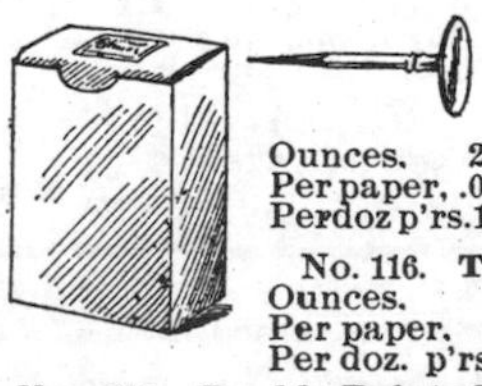

**No. 115.**

**Wire Cut Tacks.**

| Ounces. | 2 | 3 | 4 | 6 | 8 | 10 | 12 | 16 |
|---|---|---|---|---|---|---|---|---|
| Per paper, | .02 | .02 | .02 | .02 | .02 | .02 | .02 | .03 |
| Per doz p'rs. | .11 | .15 | .16 | .17 | .18 | .19 | .21 | .27 |

**No. 116. Tinned Carpet Tacks.**

| Ounces. | 6 | 8 | 10 | 12 |
|---|---|---|---|---|
| Per paper. | $0.03 | .03 | .03 | .04 |
| Per doz. p'rs | .25 | .27 | 30. | .35 |

**No. 117. Double Pointed Tacks, Blued.**

| Ounces. | 10 | 11 | 12 |
|---|---|---|---|
| Per paper. | $0.02 | .02 | .03 |
| Per dozen papers, | .15 | .15 | .18 |

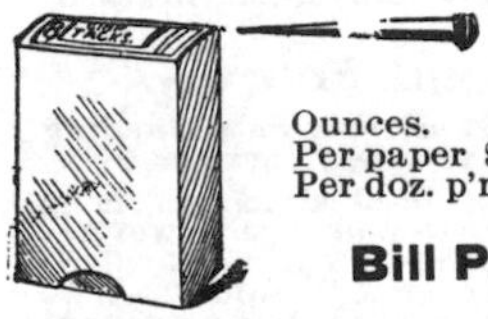

## Gimp Tacks.

No. 118.

| | | | | | | | |
|---|---|---|---|---|---|---|---|
| Ounces. | 1 | 2 | 3 | 4 | 6 | 8 | 10 |
| Per paper | $0.02 | .02 | .03 | .03 | .03 | .04 | .04 |
| Per doz. p'rs | .18 | .21 | .24 | .26 | .28 | .30 | .34 |

## Bill Posters' Tacks.

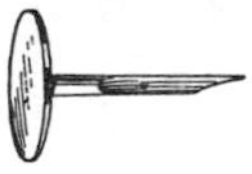

No. 119. Put up in 1 lb. papers.

| | | | |
|---|---|---|---|
| Ounces, | 4 | 6 | 8 |
| Per pound, | $0.11 | .10 | .07 |

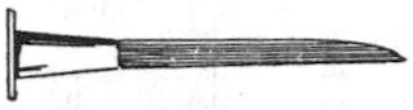

## Swede's Iron Upholsterer's Tacks.

No. 120.

| | | | | | | |
|---|---|---|---|---|---|---|
| Ounces, | 4 | 6 | 8 | 10 | 12 | 16 |
| Per paper, | $0.02 | .02 | .02 | .03 | .03 | .04 |
| Per doz. papers, | .13 | .16 | .19 | .20 | .24 | .32 |

## Swede's Iron Upholsterer's Tacks.

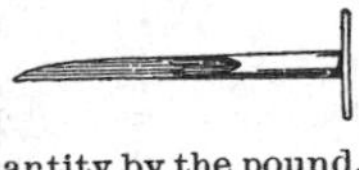

No. 121. In bulk, sold in any quantity by the pound.

| | | | | |
|---|---|---|---|---|
| Ounces, | 4 | 6 | 8 | 10 |
| Per pound, | $0.11 | .10 | .09 | .08 |

## Copper Tacks.

No. 122. Put up in 1 lb. papers.

| | | | | | | | |
|---|---|---|---|---|---|---|---|
| Length, inches. | ½ | ¾ | ⅞ | 1 | 1⅛ | 1¼ | 1½ |
| Per pound. | $0.30 | .29 | .28 | .27 | .27 | .27 | .27 |

## Trunk Nails.

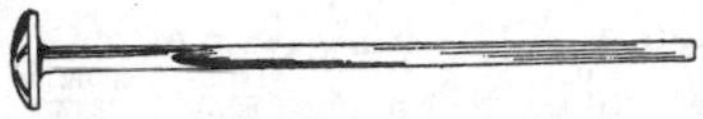

No. 123. Tinned Heads.

| | | | | | | | | | | |
|---|---|---|---|---|---|---|---|---|---|---|
| Length, inches, | ⅜ | ½ | ⅝ | ¾ | ⅞ | 1 | 1¼ | 1½ | 1¾ | 2 |
| Per pound, | $0.18 | .13 | .12 | .10 | .10 | .10 | .09 | .09 | .09 | .09 |

## Glaziers' Points.

No. 124. Zinc Glaziers' Points for fastening glass in sash, put up in ¼ lb. papers; price per paper, 6c.; per doz., 65c.

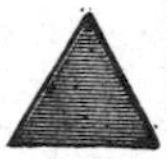

## Carriage Bolts.

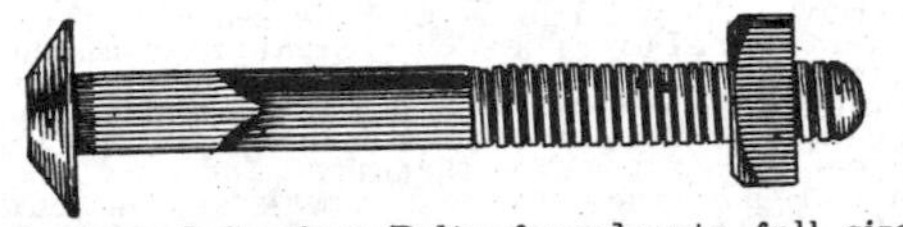

Oval head Carriage Bolts, forged nuts, full size square shoulder, well cut thread in nut and on bolt, made from soft iron which will not break easily.

No. 125. Carriage Bolts, ¼ inch in diameter.

| | | | | | | | | |
|---|---|---|---|---|---|---|---|---|
| Length, | 1½ | 2 | 2½ | 3 | 3½ | 4 | 5 | 6 |
| Per doz., | $0.05 | .05 | .06 | .06 | .07 | .07 | .08 | .09 |
| Per 100, | .36 | .39 | .42 | .45 | .49 | .51 | .55 | .63 |

No. 125½. Carriage Bolts, 5-16 inch in diameter.

| | | | | | | | | | |
|---|---|---|---|---|---|---|---|---|---|
| Length, | 2 | 2½ | 3 | 3½ | 4 | 4½ | 5 | 5½ | 6 |
| Per doz., | $0.07 | .07 | .08 | .08 | .08 | .09 | .10 | .10 | .10 |
| Per 50, | .24 | .26 | .27 | .29 | .31 | .33 | .35 | .36 | .38 |
| Per 100, | .47 | .51 | .54 | .58 | .62 | .65 | .69 | .72 | .76 |

No. 126. Carriage Bolts. ⅜ inch in diameter.

| | | | | | | | | | | |
|---|---|---|---|---|---|---|---|---|---|---|
| Length, | 2½ | 3 | 3½ | 4 | 4½ | 5 | 5½ | 6 | 7 | 8 |
| Per doz., | $0.08 | .09 | .10 | .10 | .11 | .12 | .12 | .13 | .14 | .15 |
| Per 50, | .30 | .32 | .35 | .37 | .40 | .42 | .45 | .47 | .55 | .60 |
| Per 100, | .60 | .64 | .70 | .74 | .80 | .84 | .90 | .94 | 1.05 | 1.15 |

No. 126½. Carriage Bolts ½ inch in diameter.

| | | | | | | | |
|---|---|---|---|---|---|---|---|
| Length, | 3 | 3½ | 4 | 4½ | 5 | 5½ | 6 |
| Per doz., | $0.15 | .16 | .17 | .18 | .20 | .21 | .22 |
| Per 50, | .54 | .58 | .62 | .65 | .68 | .72 | .76 |
| Per 100, | 1.08 | 1.16 | 1.23 | 1.30 | 1.37 | 1.44 | 1.52 |
| Length, | 6½ | 7 | 8 | 9 | 10 | 11 | 12 |
| Per doz., | $0.23 | .24 | .25 | .26 | .29 | .31 | .33 |
| Per 50, | .80 | .83 | .90 | .98 | .1.05 | 1.12 | 1.19 |
| Per 100, | 1.59 | 1.66 | 1.80 | 1.95 | 2.09 | 2.24 | 2.38 |

**Weight of carriage bolts per 100.** ¼ inch carriage bolts weigh about 2½ lbs. per 100 for each inch in length, 5-16 inch carriage bolts about 4¼ lbs. per 100 for each inch in length. ⅜ inch carriage bolts weigh about 6 lbs. per 100 for each inch in length, ½ inch carriage bolts weigh about 13 lbs. per 100 for each inch in length.

## Iron Washers

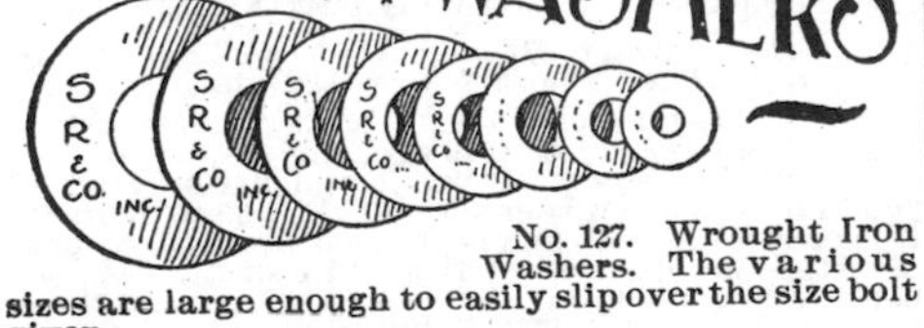

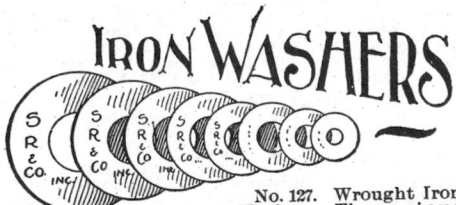

No. 127. Wrought Iron Washers. The various sizes are large enough to easily slip over the size bolt given.

| | | | | |
|---|---|---|---|---|
| For bolt, inches, | ¼ | 5-16 | ⅜ | ½ |
| Per doz., | $0.02 | .02 | .03 | .05 |
| Per lb. | .08 | .07 | .06 | .05 |
| No. in lb. | 139 | 119 | 119 | 20 |

## Machine Bolts

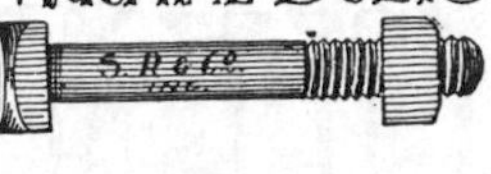

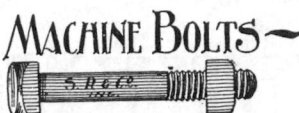

Machine Bolts have square heads and nuts, and are round all the way up to the head. Weights about the same as carriage bolts. (See numbers 129 to 132.)

No. 128. Diameter, ¼ inch.

| | | | | | | | | | | |
|---|---|---|---|---|---|---|---|---|---|---|
| Length, | 1½ | 2 | 2½ | 3 | 3½ | 4 | 4½ | 5 | 5½ | 6 |
| Per doz., | $0.08 | .08 | .08 | .08 | .08 | .09 | .10 | .10 | .10 | .11 |
| Per 100, | .59 | .60 | .62 | .65 | .67 | .70 | .73 | .76 | .78 | .81 |

No. 129. Diameter, 5-16 inch.

| | | | | | | | | | | | | |
|---|---|---|---|---|---|---|---|---|---|---|---|---|
| Length, | 1½ | 2 | 2½ | 3 | 3½ | 4 | 4½ | 5 | 5½ | 6 | 6½ | 7 |
| Per doz. | $0.08 | .08 | .10 | .11 | .12 | .12 | .12 | .12 | .12 | .15 | .15 | .16 |
| Per 100. | .67 | .70 | .73 | .77 | .80 | .83 | .87 | .90 | .93 | .97 | 1.00 | 1.03 |

No. 130. Diameter, ⅜ inch.

| | | | | | | | |
|---|---|---|---|---|---|---|---|
| Length, | 1½ | 2 | 2½ | 3 | 3½ | 4 | 4½ |
| Per doz. | $0.10 | .11 | .12 | .15 | .15 | .16 | .16 |
| Per 100, | .80 | .84 | .88 | .92 | .96 | 1.00 | 1.04 |
| Length, | 5 | 5½ | 6 | 6½ | 7 | 7½ | 8 |
| Per doz., | $018 | .18 | .18 | .18 | .19 | .19 | .19 |
| Per 100, | 1.10 | 1.15 | 1.20 | 1.25 | 1.30 | 1.35 | 1.40 |

No. 131. Diameter, ½ inch.

| | | | | | | | | | | | |
|---|---|---|---|---|---|---|---|---|---|---|---|
| Length, | | 1½ | 2 | 2½ | 3 | 3½ | 4 | 4½ | 5 | 5½ | 6 |
| Per doz., | | $0.18 | .19 | .20 | .20 | .20 | .22 | .22 | .23 | .24 | .25 |
| Per 100, | | 1.20 | 1.27 | 1.35 | 1.40 | 1.45 | 1.54 | 1.60 | 1.70 | 1.74 | 1.80 |
| Length, | 6½ | 7 | 8 | 9 | 10 | 11 | 12 | 14 | 16 | 18 | 20 |
| Per doz., | $0.25 | .27 | .29 | .30 | .34 | .36 | .38 | .40 | .42 | .45 | .50 |
| Per 100., | 1.87 | 1.94 | 2.07 | 2.20 | 2.34 | 2.47 | 2.60 | 2.87 | 3.14 | 3.40 | 3.70 |

## Stove Bolts

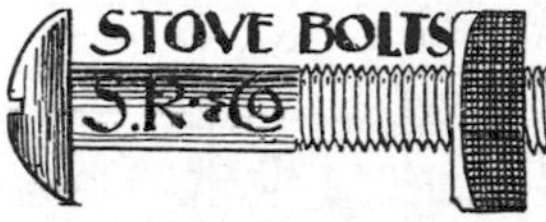

Stove bolts are useful for many purposes. For fastening hinges they are cheap and good. For many uses they take the place of carriage bolts at much less cost.

No. 132. 3-16 inch round head.

| | | | | | | | | | | | |
|---|---|---|---|---|---|---|---|---|---|---|---|
| Length, | ½ | ⅝ | ¾ | ⅞ | 1 | 1¼ | 1½ | 1¾ | 2 | 2½ | 3 |
| Per doz. | $0.05 | .06 | .06 | .06 | .06 | .06 | .07 | .07 | .07 | .08 | .08 |
| Per 100. | .29 | .30 | .30 | .31 | .31 | .32 | .34 | .35 | .37 | .40 | .44 |

No. 133. ¼ inch round head.

| | | | | | | | | | | | |
|---|---|---|---|---|---|---|---|---|---|---|---|
| Length. | ½ | ⅝ | ¾ | ⅞ | 1 | 1¼ | 1½ | 1¾ | 2 | 2½ | 3 |
| Per doz. | $0.06 | .06 | .06 | .06 | .06 | .07 | .07 | .07 | .08 | .08 | .08 |
| Per 100. | .32 | .32 | .32. | .23 | .33 | .35 | .36 | .38 | .40 | .43 | .47 |

No. 134. 5-16 inch round head.

| | | | | | | | | |
|---|---|---|---|---|---|---|---|---|
| Length, | ¾ | ⅞ | 1 | 1¼ | 1½ | 2 | 2½ | 3 |
| Per doz. | $0.08 | .09 | .09 | .09 | .10 | .10 | .11 | .12 |
| Per 100. | .45 | .46 | .48 | .51 | .54 | .58 | .61 | .64 |

## Flat Head Stove Bolts.

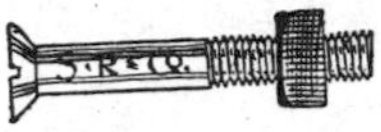

No. 135. 3-16 inch flat head.

| | | | | | | | | | | |
|---|---|---|---|---|---|---|---|---|---|---|
| Lingth, | ½ | ⅝ | ¾ | ⅞ | 1 | 1¼ | 1½ | 2 | 2½ | 3 |
| Per doz. | $0.04 | .04 | .04 | .04 | .05 | .05 | .05 | .06 | .06 | .07 |
| Per 100. | .20 | .20 | .20 | .22 | .22 | .24 | .24 | .28 | .32 | .35 |

No. 136. ¼ inch flat head.

| | | | | | | | | | |
|---|---|---|---|---|---|---|---|---|---|
| Length, | ⅝ | ¾ | ⅞ | 1 | 1¼ | 1½ | 2 | 2½ | 3 |
| Per doz., | $0.05 | .05 | .05 | .05 | .05 | .05 | .06 | .06 | .07 |
| Per 100. | .22 | .22 | .23 | .23 | .25 | .27 | .30 | .34 | .36 |

No. 137. 5-16 inch flat head.

| | | | | | | | | |
|---|---|---|---|---|---|---|---|---|
| Length, | ¾ | ⅞ | 1 | 1¼ | 1½ | 2 | 2½ | 3 |
| Per doz., | $0.06 | .07 | .07 | .07 | .07 | .07 | .08 | .08 |
| Per 100, | .35 | .36 | .37 | .39 | .40 | .44 | .47 | .50 |

## Lag Screws

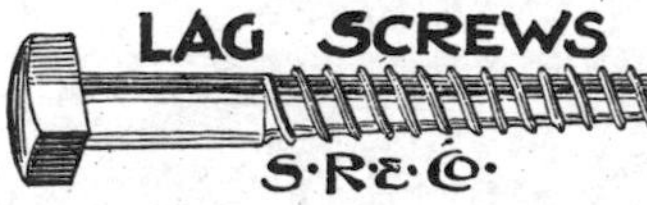


No. 138. Lag or coach screws with square heads. Weights about the same as carriage bolts. (See numbers 129 to 132.)

Diameter 5-16th inch.

| | | | | | | | | | | |
|---|---|---|---|---|---|---|---|---|---|---|
| Length, | 1½ | 2 | 2½ | 3 | 3½ | 4 | 4½ | 5 | 5½ | 6 |
| Per doz., | $0.10 | .10 | .11 | .11 | .12 | .12 | .13 | .13 | .14 | .15 |
| Per 100. | .56 | .60 | .64 | .68 | .71 | .75 | .80 | .83 | .86 | .90 |

No. 139. Diameter. ⅜ inch.

| | | | | | | | | | | |
|---|---|---|---|---|---|---|---|---|---|---|
| Length, | 1½ | 2 | 2½ | 3 | 3½ | 4 | 4½ | 5 | 5½ | 6 |
| Per doz., | $0.11 | .11 | .12 | .12 | .13 | .13 | .14 | .15 | .16 | .17 |
| Per 100, | .68 | .72 | .77 | .81 | .86 | .90 | .95 | .99 | 1.04 | 1.08 |

No. 140. Diameter ½ inch.

| | | | | | | | | |
|---|---|---|---|---|---|---|---|---|
| Length, | 1½ | 2 | 2½ | 3 | 3½ | 4 | 4½ | 5 |
| Per doz., | $0.14 | .16 | .18 | .19 | .19 | .20 | .22 | .23 |
| Per 100. | .95 | 1.02 | 1.09 | 1.16 | 1.28 | 1.31 | 1.40 | 1.46 |

No, 141. Diameter. ½ inch.

| | | | | | | | | |
|---|---|---|---|---|---|---|---|---|
| Length, | 5½ | 6 | 7 | 8 | 9 | 10 | 11 | 12 |
| Per doz., | $0.24 | .25 | .28 | .30 | .32 | .34 | .36 | .38 |
| Per 100, | 1.54 | 1.61 | 1.76 | 1.92 | 2.06 | 2.21 | 2.36 | 2.51 |

## Bolt Ends.

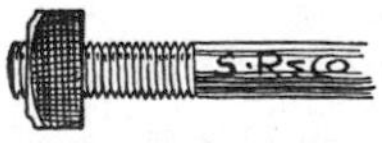

No. 142. Bolt ends with square nuts, made of a superior grade of soft iron which is very tough. By welding bolt end to round iron of same size bolts of any required length may be made.

| | | | | | |
|---|---|---|---|---|---|
| Diameter of iron, | ½ | ⅝ | ¾ | ⅞ | 1 in. |
| Length of ends, | 8 | 9 | 10 | 11 | 12 |
| Price, per doz., | $0.25 | .28 | .45 | .84 | 1.20 |
| Av. weight, per doz., | 6 | 8 | 13 | 25 | 48 lbs. |

## What the People Say.

### All His Dealings with us Have Been Satisfactory.

WAYCROSS, GA., Jan. 13th, 1897.

MESSRS, SEARS, ROEBUCK & CO.

GENTS:—Would say invoice No. 326670 was duly received, and so far proves very satisfactory, in fact all the dealings I have had with your house have been satisfactory, and I will try and do you all the good I can.

Respectfully yours,
JAS. G. REDMOND.

### Neighbors Think his Stove very Cheap.

SHARRARD. MERCER CO., ILL.. Jan. 13, 1897.

TO SEARS, ROEBUCK & CO., Chicago, Ill.

DEAR SIRS:—I wish to acknowledge the receipt of stove in good condition, and must say we are well pleased with the stove, think we have a good bargain. All our neighbors think it real cheap when we tell them the price, invoice No. 325086. Thanking you for your prompt attention to my order, and can assure you we will try to have other orders for your house in the near future, we remain.

Yours respectfully,
JACOB DOUGLAS.

### Will do all He Can for Us.

TECUMSEH, MICH., Jan. 20, 1897.

MESSRS. SEARS, ROEBUCK & CO., Chicago. Ill.

DEARS SIRS: I received the clothes and samples all in good order. The clothes were good value and fit all right. I am well pleased with them for the money. Will try and send you some orders, if I do not, I will certainly advertise your business for you all I can.

Very truly yours,
J. F. SOUTHWICK.
Tecumseh, Lenawee Co., Mich.

### Would not take Double what he Paid for the Suit.

PRINCETON, ILL., Jan. 10th, 1897.

SEARS. ROEBUCK & CO.,

GENTLEMEN: Inclosed please find fifteen cents in stamps for one of your large catalogues the Consumers' Guide, as I wish to make up an order in a week or two, and send for some more goods. The suit I received from you proved perfectly satisfactory in every way, am very much pleased with it, would not take double what I paid for it if I could not replace it. So far you have dealt white with me. Hoping to be able to favor you with another order soon, I am

Yours truly.
PETER J. MAAS.

### Takes Great Pleasure in Showing New Suit to His Friends.

NEW ORLEANS, LA., Jan. 9, 1897.

MESSRS. SEARS ROEBUCK & CO.

DEAR SIRS:—I received, by express, my suit and found it just as represented by you, and the fit is perfect. I take great pleasure in showing it to my friends. Trusting to have more orders for you in the future, I remain.

Yours truly.
1831 Chippewa St. THOS. J. FOLEY.

### Goods Beyond His Expectations.

DELEMAR. Jan. 9. 1897.

DEAR SIRS:—I have received the goods sent me by you a few days ago. I must say, in regard, I am very highly pleased with them. They are beyond my expectations. Shall recommend your firm to all friends.

Yours truly.
THOMAS CRETNEY.

### He is Busy Telling his Friends and Neighbors how to Save their Dollars.

CHARLES CITY, IA., Jan. 29, 1897.

DEAR SIRS: I take pleasure in writing and acknowledging the safe arrival of the goods, and they are the best fit I ever had, and good quality combined. Now I must thank you for the prompt response, and I shall do all in my power for your future orders from this locality, and I am willing to admit that you have succeeded in capturing my future trade for one, and I hope to send in a big order soon. I appreciate what you have done for me and shall always feel indebted to you, and shall always say a good word in your favor, and I must say that if times were not so hard I would have been able to order sooner; but my neighbors say that as soon as they can they want me to order for them, as some of them cannot write but German, and others cannot write any. So I am waiting and hoping, for I am busy telling them how to save a dollar on two dollars,

Your servant,
JOHN M. BILGO.

### Cape Proves Satisfactory.

PARKERVILLE, KAN.. Jan, 17, 1897.

SEARS, ROEBUCK & CO.

DEAR SIRS: I have received the cape in good order, have tried it and it proves more than satisfactory. It is as good as a $6.00 cape here. It is a perfect one and I am well pleased with it. With many thanks to you, I am, till I send for another order soon,

Yours truly, E. SAWYER.

### Will Recommend us to His Friends.

NO. BANNFORD. CT., Jan. 19, 1897.

SEARS, ROEBUCK & CO.

DEAR SIRS: I received things all right and must say I was more than pleased with them. Everything is more than represented to be. I shall recommend you to all of my friends. Those who have seen the fascinator say they don't see how you can sell them for such a price. You cannot get them here for that price like this.

I am respectfully yours,
MISS F. BARKER.

**CUSTOMERS WILL BEAR IN MIND THAT POSTAGE RATE IS 1 CENT PER OUNCE FOR MERCHANDISE. ALWAYS SEND EXTRA FOR POSTAGE.**

The cut below shows exact sizes of all screws up to 3 inches in length and No. 20 in diameter. Hence in ordering wood, blued, brass or nickel plated screws, you can tell from the cut what size you will need.

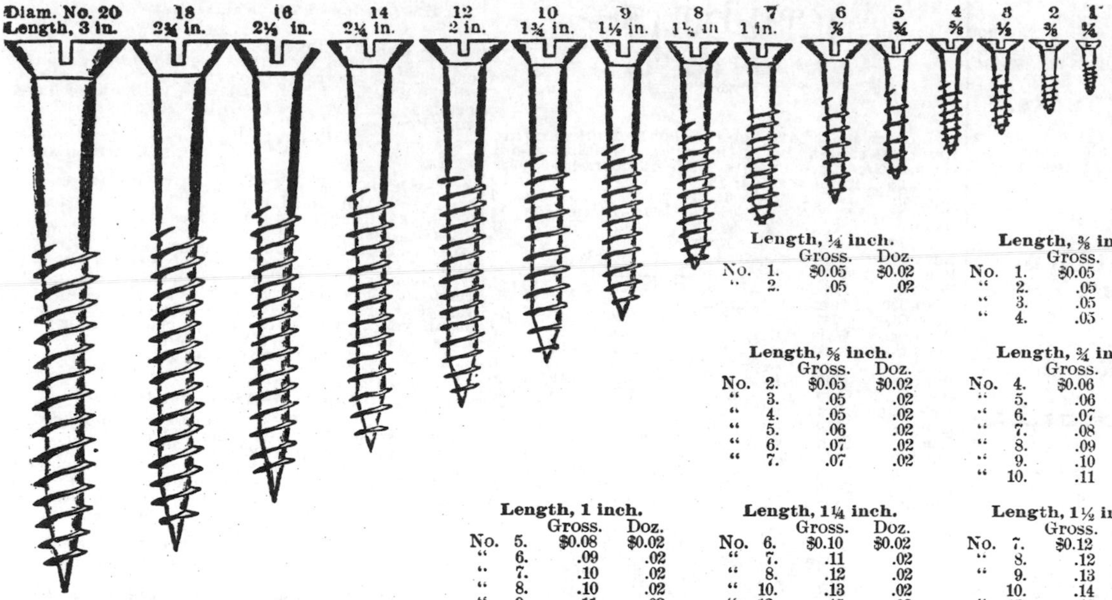

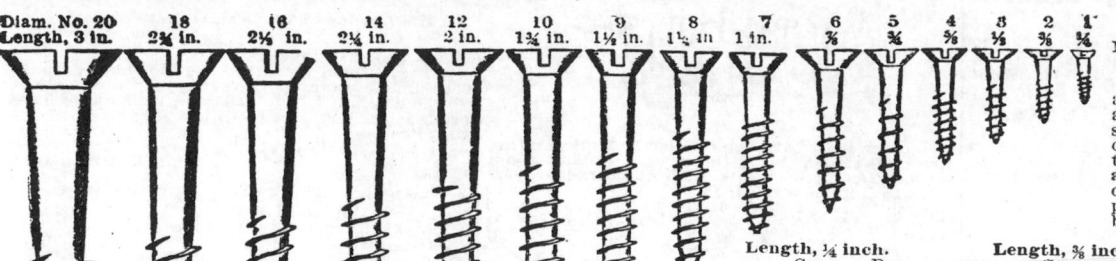

Diam. No. 20 18 16 14 12 10 9 8 7 6 5 4 3 2 1
Length, 3 in. 2¾ in. 2½ in. 2¼ in. 2 in. 1¾ in. 1½ in. 1¼ in. 1 in. ⅞ ¾ ⅝ ½ ⅜ ¼

## Wood Screws.

**No. 143. Full size cuts showing actual size of screws.**

Screws are now almost as cheap as nails. Better goods than we offer are not made. We list below the sizes most commonly sold which we carry in stock and sell in any quantity. We can furnish **full packages of 1 gross** of any size or kind of screw wanted, but do not break packages on sizes other than listed below.

**Length, ¼ inch.**

| No. | Gross. | Doz. |
|---|---|---|
| 1. | $0.05 | $0.02 |
| 2. | .05 | .02 |

**Length, ⅜ inch.**

| No. | Gross. | Doz. |
|---|---|---|
| 1. | $0.05 | $0.02 |
| 2. | .05 | .02 |
| 3. | .05 | .02 |
| 4. | .05 | .02 |

**Length, ½ inch.**

| No. | Gross. | Doz. |
|---|---|---|
| 2. | $0.05 | $0.02 |
| 3. | .05 | .02 |
| 4. | .05 | .02 |
| 5. | .05 | .02 |
| 6. | .06 | .02 |

**Length, ⅝ inch.**

| No. | Gross. | Doz. |
|---|---|---|
| 2. | $0.05 | $0.02 |
| 3. | .05 | .02 |
| 4. | .05 | .02 |
| 5. | .06 | .02 |
| 6. | .07 | .02 |
| 7. | .07 | .02 |

**Length, ¾ inch.**

| No. | Gross. | Doz. |
|---|---|---|
| 4. | $0.06 | $0.02 |
| 5. | .06 | .02 |
| 6. | .07 | .02 |
| 7. | .08 | .02 |
| 8. | .09 | .02 |
| 9. | .10 | .02 |
| 10. | .11 | |

**Length, ⅞ inch.**

| No. | Gross. | Doz. |
|---|---|---|
| 5. | $0.07 | $0.02 |
| 6. | .08 | .02 |
| 7. | .09 | .02 |
| 8. | .10 | .02 |
| 9. | .10 | .02 |
| 10. | .11 | .02 |
| 11. | .12 | .02 |
| 12. | .14 | .02 |

**Length, 1 inch.**

| No. | Gross. | Doz. |
|---|---|---|
| 5. | $0.08 | $0.02 |
| 6. | .09 | .02 |
| 7. | .10 | .02 |
| 8. | .10 | .02 |
| 9. | .11 | .02 |
| 10. | .12 | .02 |
| 12. | .14 | .02 |
| 14. | .17 | .02 |

**Length, 1¼ inch.**

| No. | Gross. | Doz. |
|---|---|---|
| 6. | $0.10 | $0.02 |
| 7. | .11 | .02 |
| 8. | .12 | .02 |
| 10. | .13 | .02 |
| 12. | .15 | .02 |
| 14. | .20 | .02 |
| 16. | .25 | .03 |

**Length, 1½ inch.**

| No. | Gross. | Doz. |
|---|---|---|
| 7. | $0.12 | $0.02 |
| 8. | .12 | .02 |
| 9. | .13 | .02 |
| 10. | .14 | .02 |
| 12. | .17 | .02 |
| 14. | .21 | .02 |
| 16. | .26 | .03 |

**Length, 1¾ inch.**

| No. | Gross. | Doz. |
|---|---|---|
| 8. | $0.13 | $0.02 |
| 9. | .14 | .02 |
| 10. | .15 | .02 |
| 12. | .19 | .03 |
| 14. | .24 | .03 |
| 16. | .29 | .03 |
| 18. | .33 | .03 |

**Length, 2 inch.**

| No. | Gross. | Doz. |
|---|---|---|
| 10. | $0.17 | $0.02 |
| 12. | .20 | .02 |
| 14. | .25 | .03 |
| 16. | .30 | .03 |
| 18. | .37 | .04 |

**Length, 2¼ inch.**

| No. | Gross. | Doz. |
|---|---|---|
| 12. | $0.22 | $0.03 |
| 14. | .27 | .03 |
| 16. | .32 | .04 |
| 18. | .38 | .04 |

**Length, 2½ inch.**

| No. | Gross. | Doz. |
|---|---|---|
| 14. | $0.29 | $0.03 |
| 16. | .35 | .04 |
| 18. | .42 | .05 |
| 20. | .50 | .05 |

**Length, 3 inch.**

| No. | Gross. | Doz. |
|---|---|---|
| 14. | $0.34 | $0.04 |
| 16. | .42 | .05 |
| 18. | .52 | .06 |
| 20. | .60 | .06 |

**Length, 3½ inch.**

| No. | Gross. | Doz. |
|---|---|---|
| 16. | $0.49 | $0.05 |
| 18. | .60 | .06 |
| 20. | .70 | .07 |
| 22. | .78 | .07 |

**Length, 4 inch.**

| No. | Gross. | Doz. |
|---|---|---|
| 18. | $0.70 | $0.07 |
| 20. | .80 | .08 |
| 24. | 1.00 | .10 |

## Round Head Blued Screws.

**No. 144.**

**Length, ½ inch.**

| No. | Gross. | Doz. |
|---|---|---|
| 3. | $0.10 | $0.02 |
| 4. | .10 | .02 |
| 5. | .11 | .02 |

**Length, ¾ inch.**

| No. | Gross. | Doz. |
|---|---|---|
| 4. | $0.10 | $0.02 |
| 5. | .12 | .02 |
| 6. | .13 | .02 |

**Length, ⅞ inch.**

| No. | Gross. | Doz. |
|---|---|---|
| 5. | $0.13 | $0.02 |
| 6. | .15 | .02 |
| 7. | .18 | .02 |
| 8 | .19 | .02 |

**Length, 1 inch.**

| No. | Gross. | Doz. |
|---|---|---|
| 6. | $0.16 | $0.02 |
| 7. | .18 | .03 |
| 8. | .19 | .03 |
| 10. | .23 | .04 |

**Length, 1¼ inch.**

| No. | Gross. | Doz. |
|---|---|---|
| 6. | $0.19 | $0.03 |
| 7. | .20 | .03 |
| 8. | .22 | .03 |
| 9. | .24 | .04 |
| 10. | .25 | .04 |

**Length, 1½ inch.**

| No. | Gross. | Doz. |
|---|---|---|
| 10. | $0.27 | $0.04 |
| 12. | .32 | .05 |
| 14. | .42 | .05 |

**Length, 1¾ inch.**

| No. | Gross. | Doz. |
|---|---|---|
| 12. | $0.38 | $0.04 |
| 14. | .48 | .05 |
| 16. | .57 | .06 |

## Flat Head Brass Screws.

**No. 145.**

**Length, ⅜ inch.**

| No. | Gross. | Doz. |
|---|---|---|
| 2. | $0.14 | $0.03 |
| 3. | .15 | .03 |
| 4. | .16 | .03 |

**Length, ½ inch.**

| No. | Gross. | Doz. |
|---|---|---|
| 2. | $0.15 | $0.03 |
| 3. | .16 | .03 |
| 4. | .17 | .03 |
| 5. | .18 | .03 |

**Length, ⅝ inch.**

| No. | Gross. | Doz. |
|---|---|---|
| 3. | $0.16 | $0.03 |
| 4. | .18 | .03 |
| 5. | .20 | .03 |
| 6. | .22 | .03 |

**Length, ¾ inch.**

| No. | Gross. | Doz. |
|---|---|---|
| 5. | $0.22 | $0.03 |
| 6. | .24 | .04 |
| 8. | .32 | .04 |
| 10. | .36 | .04 |

**Length, ⅞ inch.**

| No. | Gross. | Doz. |
|---|---|---|
| 6. | $0.24 | $0.04 |
| 7. | .27 | .04 |
| 8. | .30 | .04 |
| 9. | .36 | .04 |

**Length, 1 inch.**

| No. | Gross. | Doz. |
|---|---|---|
| 7. | $0.32 | $0.04 |
| 8. | .38 | .04 |
| 9. | .39 | .04 |
| 10. | .45 | .05 |

**Length, 1¼ inch.**

| No. | Gross. | Doz. |
|---|---|---|
| 8. | $0.40 | $0.04 |
| 9. | .45 | .05 |
| 10. | .50 | .05 |
| 12. | .66 | .06 |

**Length, 1½ inch.**

| No. | Gross. | Doz. |
|---|---|---|
| 9. | $0.53 | $0.05 |
| 10. | .60 | .06 |
| 12. | .75 | .08 |
| 14. | .95 | .10 |

## Round Head Nickel Plated Screws.

**No. 146.**

**Length, ½ inch.**

| No. | Gross. | Doz. |
|---|---|---|
| 4. | $0.55 | $0.06 |
| 5. | .56 | .06 |
| 6. | .58 | .07 |

**Length, ⅝ inch.**

| No. | Gross. | Doz. |
|---|---|---|
| 4. | $0.56 | $0.06 |
| 5. | .57 | .06 |
| 6. | .58 | .07 |
| 7. | .59 | .07 |

**Length, ¾ inch.**

| No. | Gross. | Doz. |
|---|---|---|
| 5. | $0.57 | $0.06 |
| 6. | .58 | .06 |
| 8. | .60 | .07 |
| 10. | .68 | .07 |

**Length, ⅞ inch.**

| No. | Gross. | Doz. |
|---|---|---|
| 6. | $0.58 | $0.06 |
| 7. | .60 | .06 |
| 8. | .62 | .07 |
| 9. | .65 | .08 |

**Length, 1 inch.**

| No. | Gross. | Doz. |
|---|---|---|
| 7. | $0.63 | $0.07 |
| 8. | .65 | .07 |
| 9. | .68 | .08 |
| 10. | .70 | .08 |

**Length, 1¼ inch.**

| No. | Gross. | Doz. |
|---|---|---|
| 8. | $0.66 | $0.07 |
| 9. | .72 | .08 |
| 10. | .78 | .08 |
| 12. | .92 | .09 |

**Length, 1½ inch.**

| No. | Gross. | Doz. |
|---|---|---|
| 9. | $0.82 | $0.09 |
| 10. | .86 | .09 |
| 12. | 1.00 | .11 |
| 14. | 1.26 | .12 |

**Length, 2 inch.**

| No. | Gross. | Doz. |
|---|---|---|
| 10. | $1.00 | $0.11 |
| 12. | 1.20 | .13 |
| 14. | 1.50 | .17 |

## Drive Screws.

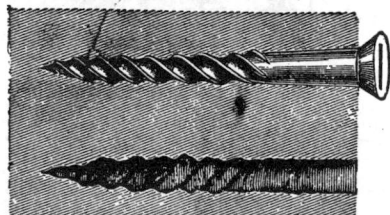

**No. 147.** The drive screws are preferred by some mechanics, as they can be driven with a hammer without breaking the hold in the wood. We will not break packages, and prices are for a box containing 144 drive screws. We carry in stock the following sizes, but can furnish any size made.

| Length... | ⅝ | ⅞ | 1 | 1 | 1¼ | 1¼ | 1¼ | 1½ | 1½ | 1½ | 2 |
|---|---|---|---|---|---|---|---|---|---|---|---|
| Diameter. | 7 | 8 | 8 | 10 | 9 | 10 | 12 | 9 | 10 | 12 | 12 |
| Per gross. | $0.10 | .12 | .12 | .13 | .13 | .14 | .17 | .14 | .16 | .18 | .22 |

**For a First-Class Chance To Buy Nice Pants, We Need Say No More,,**

☞ PAGE 164.

**ALWAYS MAKE UP FREIGHT ORDERS WHEN YOU WANT HARDWARE, SO AS TO SAVE ALL YOU CAN. REMEMBER OUR DISCOUNTS FOR CLUB ORDERS. IT WILL PAY YOU TO GET YOUR NEIGHBORS TO JOIN YOU.**

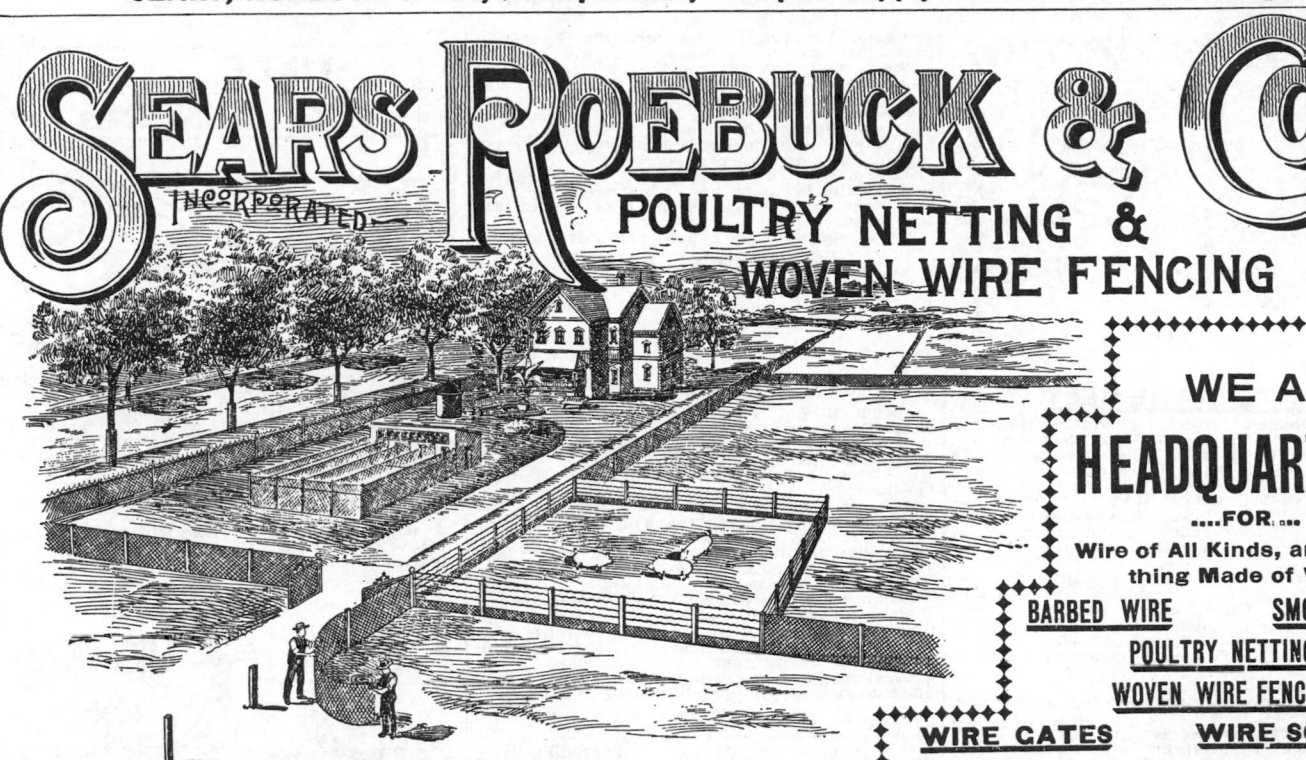

# SEARS ROEBUCK & CO.
### Incorporated
## POULTRY NETTING & WOVEN WIRE FENCING

## WE ARE
# HEADQUARTERS
#### ....FOR....
### Wire of All Kinds, and Everything Made of Wire.

| BARBED WIRE | SMOOTH WIRE |
|---|---|

### POULTRY NETTING
### WOVEN WIRE FENCING

| WIRE GATES | WIRE SCREENS |
|---|---|

Everything in Wire at Manufacturers' Lowest Prices.

**WE CAN SAVE YOU MONEY** ON YOUR BARBED WIRE FENCE, YOUR SMOOTH WIRE FENCE, YOUR POULTRY NETTING, YOUR SHEEP AND HOG FENCING your wire screen cloth and screen doors. DON'T BUY ELSEWHERE until you have consulted our prices.

**ABOUT BARBED FENCE WIRE.** For this season's supply of barbed wire we have arranged with three of the largest manufacturers in America at JOLIET, ILL., PITTSBURG, PA., ST. LOUIS, MO., and will make shipment from the point nearest our customers. The barbed wire we offer will be the highest grade made, and our prices will be below any competition, but as the price is constantly changing we can ONLY QUOTE PRICE ON APPLICATION. BARBED FENCE WIRE will always be NET CASH WITH ORDER—NO DISCOUNT

**WOVEN WIRE NETTING** FOR POULTRY, FENCE, SCREEN, ETC. **WE OFFER ONLY THE BEST GRADE OF GOODS MANUFACTURED** and for less money than inferior goods are sold by others.

**YOU SHOULD HAVE THE BEST** and that you may have the best and that at a lower price than you can possibly buy elsewhere, we have critically examined the products of each of the leading manufacturers and have selected in each line the VERY BEST GOODS MADE. WE HAVE REJECTED ALL SECOND GRADE GOODS and made our contracts for such large quantities for cash that we can name you prices heretofore unknown.

**OUR WIRE GOODS WILL BE FOUND SUPERIOR** to that carried by the average retail dealer or offered by other mail order houses. OUR WIRE GOODS are only the highest grade products of the very largest and most reliable manufacturers in America. WE OFFER YOU THESE GOODS IN ALL THE VARIOUS SIZE MESHES AND SIZE WIRE suitable for the different uses for the RANCH, FARM, LAWN AND GARDEN.

**OUR BINDING GUARANTEE.** We guarantee all our Fencing and Netting to be made of size wire as stated in our description. WHEN COMPARING OUR PRICES WITH OTHERS please remember this and be sure competing price is of the same size wire. WE GUARANTEE EACH BALE to contain quantity specified

**ABOUT THE FREIGHT.** Freight amounts to next to nothing compared with what you will save in price. For 500 miles it will, as a rule, add not more than FIVE PER CENT to our cost, and THIS THE CASH DISCOUNT NEARLY COVERS.

**TERMS.** We will ship all wire goods, except barbed and smooth wire, by freight, C. O. D., subject to examination, on receipt of ONE-FOURTH the amount of purchase, balance and freight charges payable at your freight depot. DISCOUNT OF THREE PER CENT. allowed if cash in full accompanies your order, except on barbed or smooth wire, which are net cash with order. NEARLY ALL OUR CUSTOMERS SEND CASH IN FULL.

---

## Barbed Fence Wire.

There is hardly anyone who now uses 4-point wire, as they have found by experience that 2-point Glidden patent wire turns all stock, looks better and is not so liable to breakage. There is also a little more in length to the pound. We can furnish 4-point wire if our customers insist on having it. The hog wire has barbs about three inches apart, cattle wire about six inches apart. Price is liable to advance or decline any day so we cannot quote a price for the season. For price see our grocery list which is issued weekly and sent free on request. If you haven't our grocery list write us for price.

Barbed wire takes very lowest freight rate. 4th class; see pages 5 and 6 for freight rates.

Don't build a rod of fence until you get our latest quotations on wire, staples, etc.

It's always in our latest grocery list, revised and issued weekly.

We will save you money when you get ready to fence.

## GREAT ....
### .....GUNS
#### ON THE......
#### MOST........
#### LIBERAL......
#### TERMS......

See Page 562 and note the LOWEST PRICES at which Fine Firearms were ever offered.

---

# SMOOTH WIRE

9  10  11  12  13  14 15 16 17 18 19 20

The above illustration shows the different sizes exact. The illustrations are full size of wire and the number indicates the exact size. When we quote wire size by number refer to above and you can tell the exact size of wire.

No. 135  Smooth wire, plain.
No. 136  Galvanized.

**In 100 lb. bundles. We do not break bundles.**

| Number, | 8 | 9 | 10 | 11 | 12 | 13 |
|---|---|---|---|---|---|---|
| Plain, | $1.45 | 1.45 | 1.50 | 1.55 | 1.65 | 1.75 |
| Galvanized, | 1.75 | 1.75 | 1.80 | 1.85 | 1.95 | 2.05 |

**NOTICE: We are selling Smooth wire to-day** at above price, but this price is liable to change at any time. No matter if it declines or advances, it will be sold at price quoted in the latest issue of our grocery list which is issued weekly and sent free on request.

This wire goes at 4th class freight rate; see pages for rates. Freight will add next to nothing in cost compared with the saving our prices afford you.

IF YOU DON'T SEE WHAT YOU WANT LOOK IN INDEX AT END OF BOOK.

---

## Wire Gauge.

No. 160 English standard wire gauge, polished cast steel. Gauge numbers 6 to 36. Price each, 90c.

### Wire on 1-2 lb Spools.

No. 161. Wire put up in this shape does not get snarled or kinked. The wire is shellac coated, which prevents rusting. Keep a spool of this wire in your tool chest and it's sure to come handy some day.

| Number, | 16 | 18 | 20 | 22 | 24 | 26 | 28 |
|---|---|---|---|---|---|---|---|
| Annealed Steel, | $0.07 | .07 | .08 | .08 | .09 | .09 | .10 |
| Spring brass, | .18 | .18 | .19 | .20 | .22 | .22 | .29 |
| Soft copper, | .20 | .20 | .20 | .22 | .24 | .25 | .31 |

### Hair Wire on Spools.

No. 162. Black hair wire on spools. Per spool 3c. Per dozen spools, 30c.
No. 163 Plated hair wire, on spools. Per spool, 4c. Per dozen spools, 33c.

No. 4

No. 2

No. 0

### Picture Wire.
Braided wire picture cord silver finish. Moths can't eat it off; comes in coils of 25 yards. We do not cut coils.

No. 165 Braided wire picture cord as above No. 0, suitable for small light pictures. Pr coil of 25 yds., 4c.

No. 166 Braided wire picture cord, as above, No. 2. suitable for medium weight pictures. Per coil of 25 yards, 8c.

No. 167 Braided wire picture cord as above No. 4. suitable for heavy pictures. Per coil of 25 yards, 14c.

---

**WHENEVER YOU FIND IT NECESSARY TO WRITE US ABOUT AN ORDER ALWAYS MENTION THE INVOICE NUMBER SO THAT THE MATTER MAY BE REFERRED TO WITH THE LEAST POSSIBLE DELAY.**

# POULTRY NETTING

## GUARANTEED THE BEST

Genuine **ACME** Galvanized Bessemer Steel Wire Netting Made for Poultry Fences, Vine Supports, Trellises, etc.

**SUPERIOR IN QUALITY** to what we were able to offer last season, **and better wire than you will be likely to get elsewhere** this season.

**THIS MANUFACTURER HAS THE REPUTATION** of making the best Netting on the market, and by reason of our very favorable contract we can quote it at even less than light and inferior goods are offered.

**THE ACME NETTING** will give twice the service of cheaper grades, and makes the **best and cheapest** poultry fences; cannot blow down; very easily put up; also excellent for pea vine supports and training ornamental vines.

A 150 foot bale, No. 19 wire, 48 inches wide, weighs about 47 pounds, others in proportion. You see freight adds but little to cost.

**No. 170. Galvanized Poultry Netting** with 2 inch mesh, made from **No. 19 wire** (see illustration on page 41 for exact size of No. 19 wire) with double and twisted selvage. Full rolls are 150 feet long. This is the standard size mesh most generally used for poultry yards and light farm purposes.

| Width. | Per Bale of 150 ft. | Per Foot cut piece | Width. | Per Bale of 150 ft. | Per Foot cut piece |
|---|---|---|---|---|---|
| 12 inch | $0 67 | ¾c | 48 inch | $2 67 | 2½c |
| 18 inch | 1 00 | 1 c | 54 inch | 3 00 | 2¾c |
| 24 inch | 1 34 | 1½c | 60 inch | 3 34 | 3 c |
| 30 inch | 1 67 | 1¾c | 72 inch | 4 00 | 3¾c |
| 36 inch | 2 00 | 2 c | 84 inch | 4 69 | 4½c |
| 42 inch | 2 34 | 2¼c | 96 inch | 5 34 | 5 c |

**No. 171. Galvanized Poultry Netting** with 1½ inch mesh, made from **No. 19 wire** (see illustration on page 41 for exact size of No. 19 wire) with double and twisted selvage. Full rolls are 150 feet long. Used for poultry yards, pigeon cotes, etc.

| Width. | Per Bale of 150 ft. | Per Foot cut piece | Width. | Per Bale of 150 ft. | Per Foot cut piece |
|---|---|---|---|---|---|
| 12 inch | $0 95 | 1 c | 48 inch | $3 80 | 4 c |
| 18 inch | 1 42 | 1½c | 54 inch | 4 28 | 4½c |
| 24 inch | 1 90 | 2 c | 60 inch | 4 75 | 5 c |
| 30 inch | 2 38 | 2½c | 72 inch | 5 70 | 6 c |
| 36 inch | 2 85 | 3 c | 84 inch | 6 65 | 7 c |
| 42 inch | 3 33 | 3½c | 96 inch | 7 60 | 8 c |

**No. 172. Galvanized Poultry Netting** with 1 inch mesh, made from **No. 20 wire** (see illustration on page 41 for exact size of No. 20 wire) with double and twisted selvage. Full rolls are 150 feet long. This netting is used at the bottom of fences to keep the small chickens inside and prevent vermin intruding.

| Width. | Per Bale of 150 ft. | Per Foot cut piece | Width. | Per Bale of 150 ft. | Per Foot cut piece |
|---|---|---|---|---|---|
| 12 inch | $1 48 | 1½c | 36 inch | $4 44 | 4½c |
| 18 inch | 2 22 | 2¼c | 42 inch | 5 18 | 5¼c |
| 24 inch | 2 96 | 3 c | 48 inch | 5 92 | 6 c |
| 30 inch | 3 70 | 3¾c | | | |

# WOVEN LAWN, GARDN & FARM FENCING

**No. 173. Galvanized Acme Woven Steel Wire Fencing** Mesh made from No. 15 (see illustration on page 41 for exact size of wire) wire, with twisted wire rope selvage made from three strands of No. 14 wire, size of mesh 2x4 inches. This is a cheap, strong fence suitable for lawn, gardens, etc.

☞**REMEMBER.** This is the **genuine ACME NETTING. The very best** made.

**CONSIDER** the Quality and our 3% cash discount from above prices when ordering.

**YOUR MONEY REFUNDED** if goods are not found exactly as represented.

Take nothing but the Acme Netting if you buy elsewhere.

**The Highest Grade Wire Fencing on the Market.**

In the different sizes it is made suitable for all purposes. For lawn, gardens, orchards, cemeteries, parks, farm, pasture, railroads, or elsewhere.

**The Acme is the only fencing made of the Best Bessemer Steel** wire and having the heaviest possible galvanized plate, insuring it against rust.

**This our No. 173 Fence**, for lawn, garden, etc., can be made very ornamental and beautiful by adding our No. 178 fence ornaments or pickets which we furnish as low as 6½ cents per foot.

**Our No. 173 Wire Fencing** is especially adapted for beautiful lawn fencing, it is strong enough to stop large animals and small ones cannot get through it.

**It is compactly rolled** in bales of 20 rods or 330 feet.

| Width. | Per rod of 16½ feet. | Per bale 330 ft. or 20 rods | Width. | Per rod of 16½ feet. | Per bale 330 ft. or 20 rods |
|---|---|---|---|---|---|
| 19 in. | $0.41 | $7.31 | 49 in. | $0.88 | $15.75 |
| 25 in. | .47 | 8.44 | 55 in. | .97 | 17.43 |
| 31 in. | .56 | 10.12 | 61 in. | 1.06 | 19.12 |
| 37 in. | .67 | 12.15 | 67 in. | 1.16 | 20.80 |
| 13 in. | .78 | 14.06 | 73 in. | 1.25 | 22.50 |

**DON'T BUY A POOR WIRE FENCE.** The Acme Bessemer steel wire fencing is so far superior to all other grades, that it would be cheap at double the price of many.

**The Acme will never break, never rust**, and the tensile strain it will stand is simply wonderful.

**When all other fences give away** buy the **Acme** for your Pasture, your Cowyard or will endure any general purpose.

**Consider our liberal C. O. D. terms** and don't forget our 3 per cent discount for cash when ordering and comparing our prices with others.

**Genuine Acme Galvanized Woven Bessemer Steel Wire Fencing**, mesh made from No. 14 wire (see illustration on page 51 for exact size of wire) with twisted wire rope selvage made from three strands of No. 14 wire. Size of mesh 3x6 inches. This the best general purpose fence, strong enough to stop a bull, fine enough to stop dogs and other small animals.

### No. 174.

| Width. | Per rod of 16½ feet. | Per bale 20 rods or 330 ft. | Width. | Per rod of 16½ feet. | Per bale 20 rods or 330 ft. |
|---|---|---|---|---|---|
| 20 inch | $0 38 | $6 75 | 47 inch | $0 63 | $11 47 |
| 23 " | 41 | 7 32 | 53 " | 68 | 12 62 |
| 26 " | 44 | 7 88 | 59 " | 74 | 13 27 |
| 29 " | 47 | 8 55 | 65 " | 79 | 14 17 |
| 35 " | 54 | 9 67 | 71 " | 85 | 15 19 |
| 41 " | 59 | 10 57 | 77 " | 91 | 16 31 |

**Genuine ACME Galvanized Woven Bessemer Steel Wire Fencing**, mesh made from No. 13 wire (see illustration on page 51 for exact size of wire) with twisted wire rope selvage made from three strands of No. 13 wire. Size of mesh, 4x8. This makes a strong, durable fence.

**This is one of the heaviest, strongest, woven wire fences made** and is suitable for all purposes, Farm, Pasture, Railroads or elsewhere.

**Remember the Acme** is far superior to all other fencing and yet our prices are as low or lower than others can sell the poorer grades.

### No. 175.

| Width. | Per rod of 16½ feet. | Per bale 20 rods or 330 ft. | Width. | Per rod of 16½ ft. | Per bale 20 rods or 330 ft. |
|---|---|---|---|---|---|
| 18 in. | $0 35 | $ 6 19 | 50 in. | $ 62 | $11 25 |
| 22 in. | 38 | 6 75 | 54 in. | 66 | 11 81 |
| 26 in. | 41 | 7 32 | 58 in. | 69 | 12 38 |
| 30 in. | 45 | 8 10 | 62 in. | 72 | 12 94 |
| 34 in. | 50 | 9 00 | 66 in. | 75 | 13 50 |
| 38 in. | 53 | 9 56 | 70 in. | 79 | 14 06 |
| 42 in. | 56 | 10 12 | 74 in. | 81 | 14 63 |
| 46 in. | 60 | 10 69 | 78 in. | 85 | 15 18 |

**Genuine Acme Galvaized Woven Bessemer steel Wire Fencing**, mesh made from No. 13 wire. See illustration on page 51, for extra size of wire, with twisted wire rope selvage made from three strands of No. 13 wire. Size of mesh 5½x10½ inches.

**NOTICE SIZE OF WIRE FROM WHICH THIS FENCING IS MADE.**

**Don't compare this** with inferior fencing made from No. 14 wire.

**FOR AN EXTRA HEAVY, STRONG, NEVER-GIVE-OUT, ALL PURPOSE** fence, there is nothing better made.

**Our Acme Wire Fencing is guaranteed the best** on the market at any price.

### No. 176.

| Width. | Per rod of 16½ feet. | Per Bale 20 rods or 330 ft. | Width. | Per rod of 16½ feet. | Per Bale 20 rods or 330 ft. |
|---|---|---|---|---|---|
| 20 in. | 32c | $5 62 | 42 in. | 47c | $8 44 |
| 25½ in. | 36c | 6 40 | 47½ in. | 50c | 9 00 |
| 31 in. | 40c | 7 10 | 53 in. | 53c | 9 56 |
| 36½ in. | 44c | 7 88 | | | |

# SHEEP AND HOG FENCING

**No. 177. Genuine Acme Galvanized Hog Fencing.** Mesh 4x8, made from No. 14 steel wire with twisted rope selvage made from three strands No. 13 wire.

Put up in bales of 20 rods, or 330 ft. long and sold only in full bales. The above illustration shows how this fencing can be used in connection with common or barbed wire.

There are many inferior grades on the market and even such grades are sold at more than our price.

It will pay you when buying wire fencing or wire netting to get **THE ACME**, the highest grade Bessemer steel galvanized wire made.

22 in. wide, per bale of 330 ft. ..................**$5.95**

# FENCE ORNAMENTS

**No. 178. Malleable Iron Fence Picket, japanned.** Length, 12 inches; height, 5 inches. They are especially adapted for the top rail of any fence, board partitions, veranda roofs, etc. They may be used inverted for ornament under veranda roofs.

| | |
|---|---|
| Price each | 8c. |
| Price for 50 or more, each | 7c. |
| Price for 500 or more, each | 6½c. |

# EVERYTHING IN GATES

## OUR WOVEN WIRE GATES

are the best made. We use only the **Acme Bessemer Steel Galvanized Wire**, and the workmanship, ornamentation and general finish is of the best.

**Compare our prices** with others. Consider quality, our 3 per cent cash discount, our liberal terms of shipment, our binding guarantee.

**No. 179. Small Single Gates**, with T steel frames and ornamental top, complete with hinges and latch. Posts should be placed 40 inches apart. Mesh suitable to match fencing ordered with gate. Heights, 36, 42, 48, 54 inches. Be sure to state what height is wanted when ordering.

Price, each ................................**$2.65**

Posts not furnished.

**No. 180. Small Single Gate** with wooden frames. Plain top, complete with hinges and latch. Same sizes as above. Give height wanted when ordering.

Price each ................................**$2.00**

# SINGLE GATE

**No. 181. Large single gate** for driveway with T steel frame and ornamental top complete with hinges and latch. Mesh suitable to match fencing ordered. Height 36, 42, 48, 54 inches. Be sure to state what height gate is wanted when ordering. Posts should be set 10 feet 5 inches apart. Posts not furnished.

Price, each ................................**$6.25**

**No. 182. Large single gate** for driveway with wooden frame. Plain top complete with hinges and latch. Sizes same as above. Be sure to state height wanted when ordering.

Price, each ................................**$3.65**

**IF YOU DO NOT NEED A WHOLE BALE OF WIRE PERHAPS YOUR NEIGHBOR NEEDS SOME. YOU CAN DIVIDE IT UP BETWEEN YOU AND BOTH SAVE MONEY.**

## Large Double Gates.

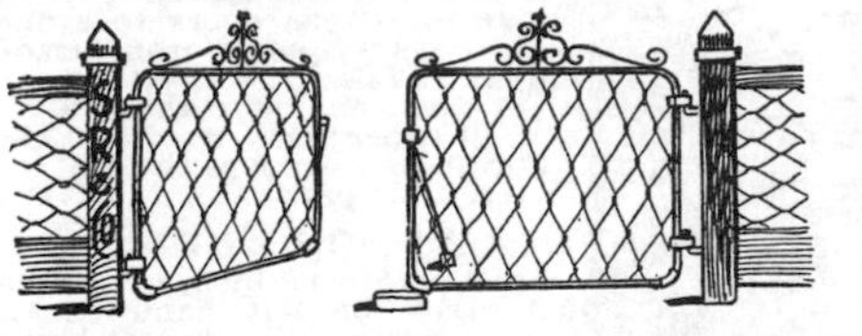

No. 183. Large double gate for driveway with T steel frame and ornamental top for opening 10 feet 5 inches between posts, complete with hinges and latch. Mesh suitable to match fencing ordered. Height 36, 42, 48 and 54 inches. **Be sure to state height wanted when ordering.**
Price, per pair.......................................**$6.88**

No. 184. Large double gate for driveway with wooden frame and plain top complete with hinges and latch, same sizes as above. **Be sure to state height wanted when ordering.**
Price, per pair.......................................**$4.25**

## Steel Fence Post.

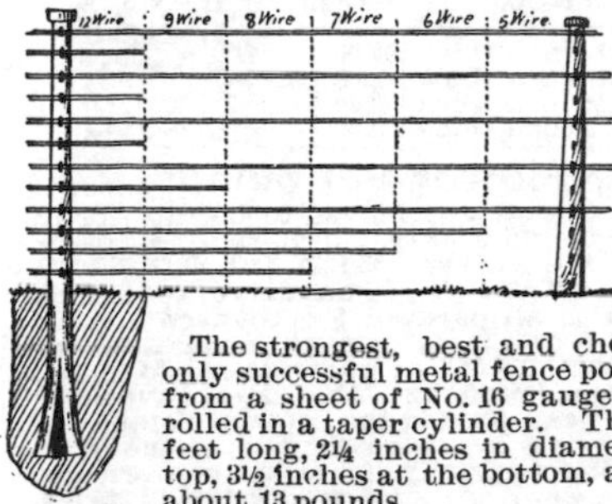


The strongest, best and cheapest—the only successful metal fence post—is made from a sheet of No. 16 gauge steel, cold rolled in a taper cylinder. This post is 7 feet long, 2¼ inches in diameter at the top, 3½ inches at the bottom, and weighs about 13 pounds.

**ADVANTAGES.**—No post holes are required; it is driven into the ground. As it is driven it spreads at the bottom and automatically anchors itself. Frost cannot heave it nor fire burn it. It is covered with a solvent guaranteed to resist rust in the ground for 15 years. It will last a lifetime. Five of these posts can be set in the same time required to dig a hole for a wood post. For full description send for our special fence post catalogue, mailed free.

No. 185. The only special tools required for driving our Steel Posts are a Driving Cap, which is placed on the post while setting it, a pair of Tongs for compressing the top of post for the permanent cap, a Wooden Maul. The driving cap must be used.
Price per 100.......................................**$40.00**
Price each.......................................**45c.**
Plain caps furnished free.

## Steel Post for Woven Wire.

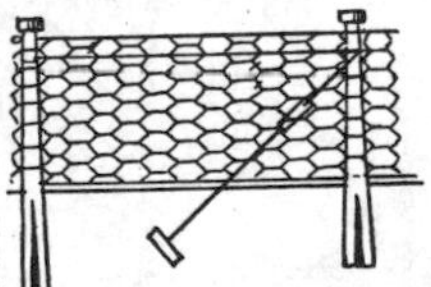

No. 185½. For woven wire the post is punched near the top and below for the cable—just the width of the netting. Fasten one end of the web to the end post, notice that it is square, that is, that the twists are above each other true. At the other end pass the top cable through the post and with a ratchet stretcher draw tight, then draw the lower cable until the intermediate wires are straight and even with the cables. Before stretching tight, the top cable should be stapled at intervals to hold it upright. Do not try to stretch the web unnaturally wide. In going over a hill, at the highest post fold the bottom cable back until the web will pass down straight on the other side. In starting up a hill fold the cable back. We can make posts for any other fence and have them ready for shipment in four days after receiving the order. State the kind of fence material you intend to use, and give spacing of the wires.
Price per 100.......................................**$40.00**
Price each.......................................**45c.**
No. 186. Ornamental Caps, each.......................................**10c.**
No. 186½. Driving Caps, each.......................................**$1.75**
No. 187. Tongs, each.......................................**1.50**

## STEEL FENCE STAPLES

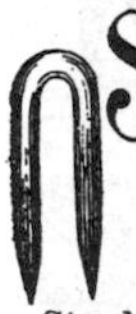

Staples are **sharp pointed**, will **drive well** and are perfectly bent and cut. The ¾ inch are for poultry netting. The 1 inch for woven fencing and the 1¼ or 1½ inch for barbed or smooth wire fencing.
No. 188. ¾ inch staples, 550 to the lb., per lb....5½c.
No. 189. 1 inch staples, 230 to the lb., per lb......5c.
No. 190. 1¼ inch staples, 100 to the lb., per lb....3¼.
No. 191. 1½ inch staples, 80 to the lb., per lb....3¼.
Lowest (4th class) freight rate goods. See pages 5 and 6 for freight rates.

**WE CAN SAVE YOU ENOUGH.....**
**On Your Wire Fencing to Pay for the Expense of Putting It Up.**

## WIRE STRETCHER

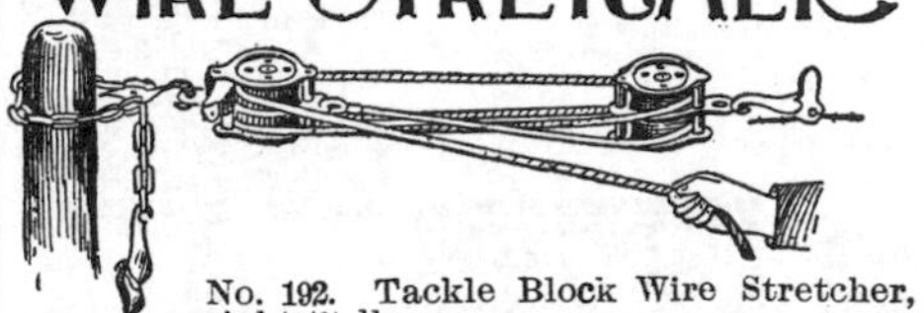

No. 192. Tackle Block Wire Stretcher, weight 4½ lbs.
Price complete with 16 foot rope, 90c.
This stretcher is provided with all grapples for stretching barbed wire, strand and woven wire fencing. It also is a complete set of tackle blocks for ordinary use.

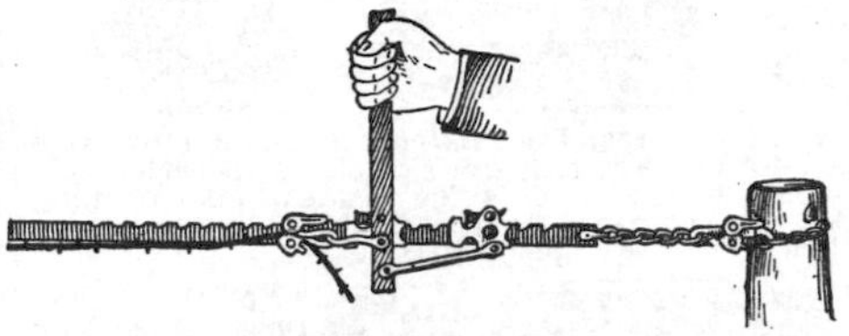

No. 193. The above cut shows this stretcher in such a manner and the article is so well known that further description is not necesssry. Weight, 2 lbs. We sell them for, each 35c.

## Wire Fence Ratchets.

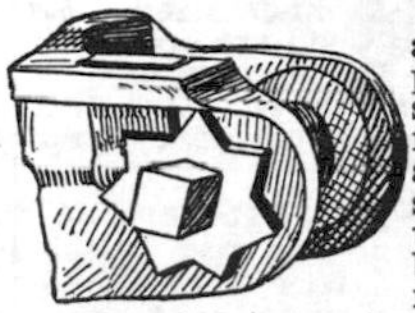

No. 194. Wire Fence Ratchets are intended to be placed permanently on the post in sections of abont 50 rods of fence. When cold weather approaches fence can be slackened in a few minutes, thus avoiding liability of breakage during the winter months. In the spring or at any time, fence may be easily and quickly tightened. Saves time and breakage of fence.
Price, each **6c**; per dozen, **55c**; per 100.......**$4.00**

## Hens' Nests.

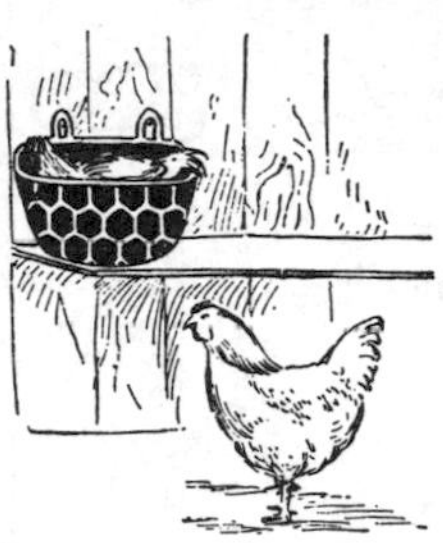

These nests are made from steel wire japanned. They are clean, afford no place for vermin and are recommended by poultry raisers everywhere. Intended to be fastened to the wall with two screws.
No. 197. Price each, **7c.**; Per doz., **75c.**

## Wire Cloth.

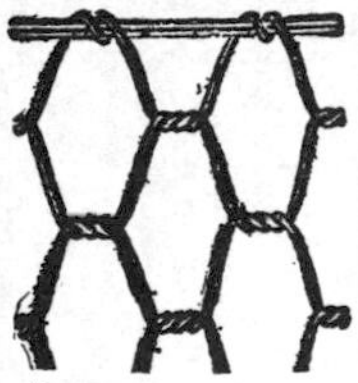

This cut shows meshes just one-half the actual size. This wire is used largely for cages and window guards for churches, school houses etc. Meshes are 1x½ inches; made from No. 19 wire with double and twisted selvage.
No. 198. Galvanized twist wire cloth as above.
Price per running foot.

| In. wide. | Price. | In. wide. | Price. | In. wide. | Price. |
|---|---|---|---|---|---|
| 12 | .05 | 28 | .11¾ | 44 | .18¼ |
| 14 | .06 | 30 | .12½ | 46 | .19¼ |
| 16 | .06¾ | 32 | ,13¼ | 48 | .20 |
| 18 | .07½ | 34 | .14 | 50 | .22½ |
| 20 | .08¼ | 36 | .15 | 54 | ,25 |
| 22 | .09¼ | 38 | .15¾ | 60 | .27 |
| 24 | .10 | 40 | .16¾ | 72 | .30 |
| 26 | .11 | 42 | .17½ | | |

Prices of bales of 150 ft. quoted upon application.

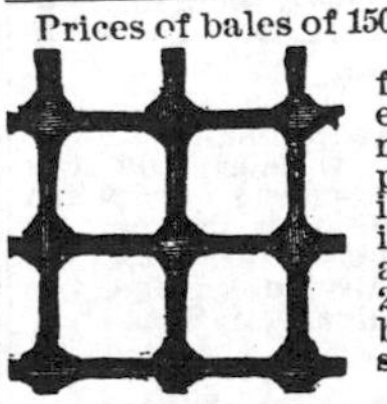

No. 199. This wire cloth is used for cages, window guards, fruit evaporators, grain cleaning machinery and many other purposes. We carry it in stock in the following meshes: ½ inch, ⅜ inch, ¼ inch, 1-6 inch, and in widths as follows: 18, 24, 30, 36, 48 inches. In ordering be sure and give width and **size mesh** desired.
Price per running foot:

| In. wide. | Price. | In. wide. | Price. | In. wide. | Price. |
|---|---|---|---|---|---|
| 14 | $0 06 | 24 | $0 10 | 36 | $0 15 |
| 16 | 06¾ | 28 | 11¾ | 42 | 17½ |
| 18 | 07½ | 30 | 12½ | 48 | 20 |
| 20 | 08¼ | 32 | 13¼ | | |

Prices for full bales quoted on application.

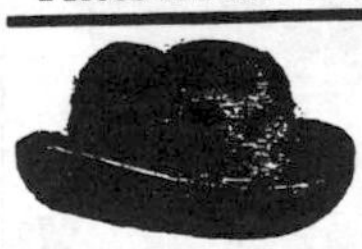

**WE SELL GOOD HATS...**

**Cheaper than any other Concern in the world.** See our quotations in hat department. Include a **Nutria Fur Hat** in your next order. We can furnish any style you wish, and will give you such value as you have never had before.

## WIRE SCREEN CLOTH
### FOR WINDOWS DOORS ETC.

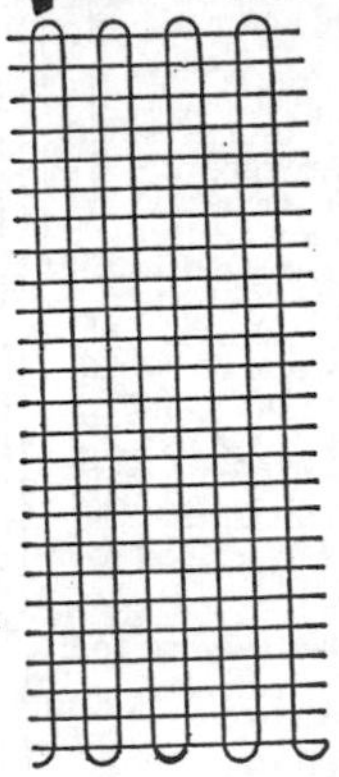

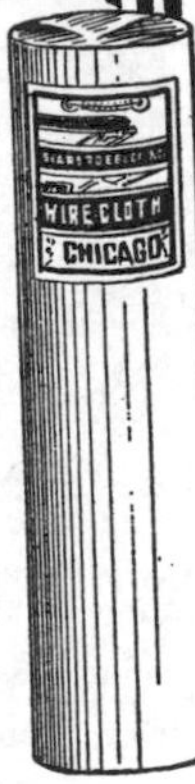


The two illustrations are made, one to show you the exact size of mesh, the other a roll to show you in what shape it comes for shipment. **You can make your own Screen Doors and Windows.** Order just what wire cloth you require, but note the reduction in price when ordering in full rolls.

**Best Acme Bessemer Steel Wire** painted **Black** or **Green** (double selvage) standard mesh.

**Consider our 3 per cent cash discount,** also our liberal terms of shipment when comparing our prices with others.

No. 1100. Green painted wire cloth,
No. 1101. Black painted wire cloth.

| Width. | Per Lineal foot. | Per roll of 100 running ft. |
|---|---|---|
| 24 in. | 3¾c. | $2 60 |
| 26 in. | 4 c. | 2 82 |
| 28 in. | 4¼c. | 3 03 |
| 30 in. | 4½c. | 3 25 |
| 32 in. | 4¾c. | 3 47 |
| 34 in. | 5 c. | 3 68 |
| 36 in. | 5¼c. | 3 90 |
| 38 in. | 5½c. | 4 12 |
| 40 in. | 5¾c, | 4 33 |
| 42 in. | 6 c. | 4 55 |
| 44 in. | 6½c. | 4 77 |
| 46 in. | 7 c. | 4 98 |
| 48 in. | 7½c. | 5 20 |

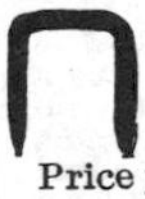

No. 1105. Wire cloth staples are much superior to common tacks. Two points enter the wood. They lap over three wires, hence hold the wire better, and not so many tacks required.
Price per pound. **17c**; per paper of 120 staples, **4c.**

## WIRE LATH

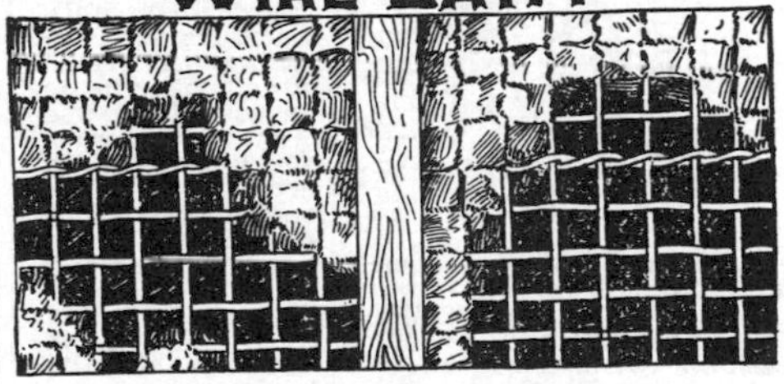

No. 1106. **This Wire Lath** is a wire cloth made from No. 20 wire with 2½ meshes to the inch and is fastened to the wall or ceiling as a foundation on which to plaster, It has double and twisted wires running through the warp, or length, every six inches, adding greatly to the strength of the fabric. Experiments have demonstrated that wire lath will hold mortar under any degree of heat without crack or fracture. Therefore plaster on wire lath is the best known system of fire-proof construction. It is 36 inches wide, put up in rolls 200 ft. long.
Price per roll 200 ft. long,.......................................**$9.75**
Price per yard, cut pieces.......................................**0.16**

## Window Screens.

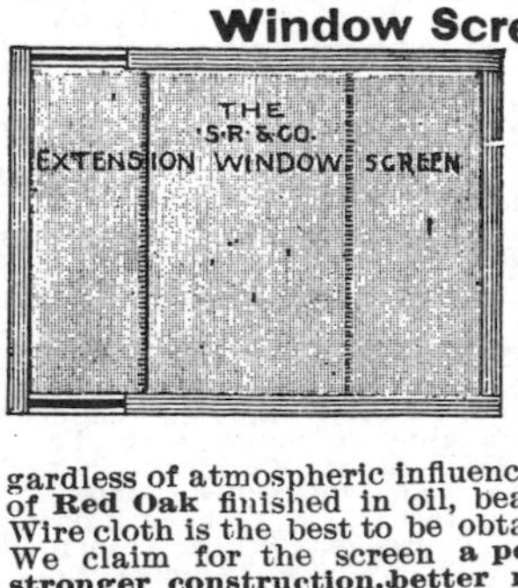


No. 1107. "Our Own" extension window screen **has** a perfect adjustment by means of double dove-tail tongues made of spring steel **that** will expand or contract and **at all** times adapt themselves to the dove-tail grooves **in** which they slide regardless of atmospheric influence; frames are made of **Red Oak** finished in oil, beaded on both sides. Wire cloth is the best to be obtained in the market. We claim for the screen **a perfect adjustment, stronger construction, better material and smother finish** than can be found in any other. Made in the following sizes and no other size furnished.

| High. | Width Adjustable. | Price Each | Price Per Doz. |
|---|---|---|---|
| 18 inches. | From 20 to 33 inches. | 23c. | $2.47 |
| 24 " | " 24 " 37 " | 29c. | 3.07 |
| 30 " | " 24 " 37 " | 35c. | 3.73 |

**REMEMBER OUR THREE PER CENT. CASH DISCOUNT FOR CASH IN FULL ON ALL ORDERS EXCEPT SUGAR, NAILS AND BARBED WIRE**
**LOOK INTO OUR CLUB ORDER PLAN AND SPECIAL DISCOUNT.**

## Window Screen Frames.

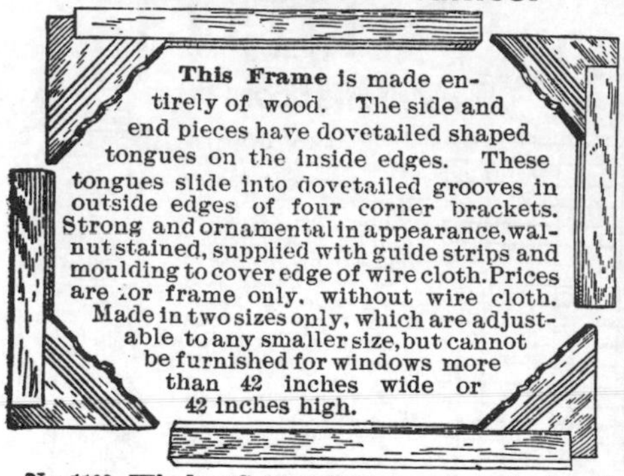

**This Frame** is made entirely of wood. The side and end pieces have dovetailed shaped tongues on the inside edges. These tongues slide into dovetailed grooves in outside edges of four corner brackets. Strong and ornamental in appearance, walnut stained, supplied with guide strips and moulding to cover edge of wire cloth. Prices are for frame only, without wire cloth. Made in two sizes only, which are adjustable to any smaller size, but cannot be furnished for windows more than 42 inches wide or 42 inches high.

No. 1108 **Window Screen Frame** as described to fit window 36x36 inches or any smaller size.
Price, each, **18c**; per doz. ............ **$1.94**
Window Screen Frame as described above to fit window 42x42 inches or any smaller size,
Price, each, **20c**; per doz. ..................... **$2.32**

## Screen Corner Irons.

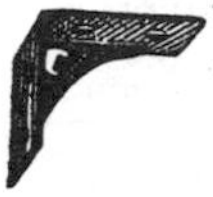

No. 1109 **Cast Window Screen Corner Irons** for those who wish to make their own frames add to the strength and appearance of the frame at a trifling cost. No need of tennon and mortise. Simply saw ends of sticks off square, drive in a long wire nail, or use a hardwood dowelpin. See that frames are square, screw on bracket and you have a strong frame that looks nice for little money. Made of cast iron, japanned.
Price per set of 4 corners, **6c**; per doz. sets... **$0.65**

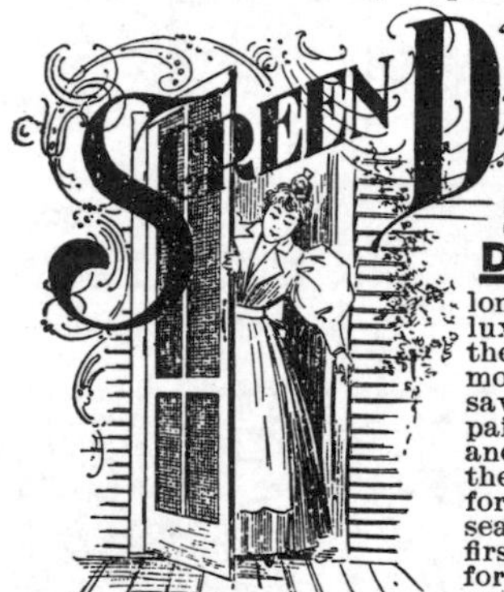

**SCREEN DOORS** are no longer considered a luxury but one of the necessities of modern life. The saving of damage to paint, paper, ceiling and furniture, and the saving of labor for cleaning in one season will pay the first cost of screens for a house. The screens which we sell (if given a coat of paint when needed) are practically indestructible and (barring accidents) should last as long as any other door. We have a superior line of these goods, but by buying them direct from the factory in large quantities for cash and selling them direct to the consumer with one small profit added we are able to offer them at prices as low as is usually got for the cheapest screen that can be procured.

No. 1110. Four Panel Screen Doors (same style as shown in picture above) made from kiln dried pine with stiles 3 inches wide. Bottom rail 7 inches wide. Flush mouldings. Put together with hardwood dowels and glued joints. They are finished and painted green with light mouldings, black or green wire cloth—the best in the market—is fastened to the frame by pressing into a groove and made secure with a wedge, avoiding the use of tacks. Cannot sag or stretch out. **Made only in the following sizes and no other sizes furnished.**

| Thickness. | Width. | Height. | Price each. |
|---|---|---|---|
| ⅞ inch. | 30 inches. | 78 inches. | 64c |
| ⅞ inch. | 32 inches. | 80 inches. | 65c |
| 1⅛ inch. | 30 inches. | 78 inches. | 67c |
| 1⅛ inch. | 32 inches. | 80 inches. | 68c |
| 1⅛ inch. | 32 inches. | 84 inches. | 69c |
| 1⅛ inch. | 34 inches. | 82 inches. | 70c |
| 1⅛ inch. | 34 inches. | 84 inches. | 72c |
| 1⅛ inch. | 36 inches. | 84 inches. | 75c |

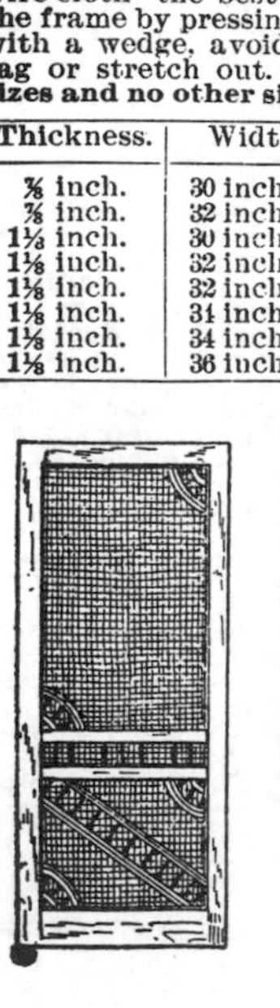

No. 1111. Fancy screen doors made with flush mouldings, from hard pine lumber thoroughly kiln dried, put together with heavy maple dowels set in glue. Covered with best black hard steel wire cloth stretched and securely fastened to the frame with a groove and wedge. Stiles 3 inches wide, bottom rail 7 inches wide. Finished natural color of the wood with two coats of varnish. Securely packed for shipment. Made in the following sizes and no other sizes furnished.

| Thickness | Wfdth | Height | Price Each |
|---|---|---|---|
| 1⅛ in | 30 in | 78 in | $1.20 |
| 1⅛ in | 32 in | 80 in | 1.22 |
| 1⅛ in | 34 in | 82 in | 1.25 |
| 1⅛ in | 36 in | 84 in | 1.27 |

## Screen Door Catches.

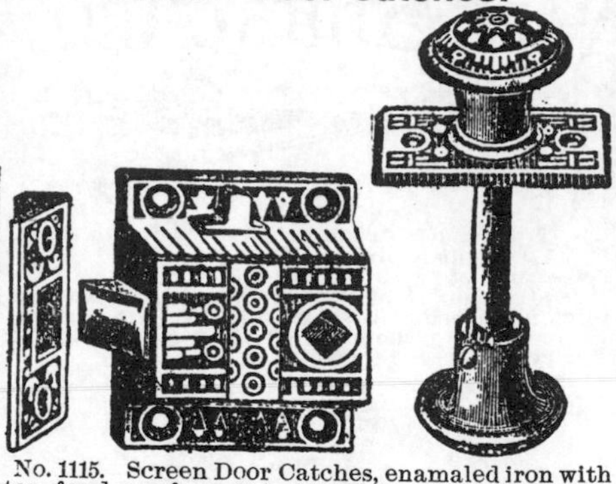

No. 1115. Screen Door Catches, enameled iron with stop, for doors from ⅞ to 1⅜ thick. This is the style commonly used and is for inside of door opening out. Packed complete with knobs and screws.
Price, each **14c.**; per doz. **$1.52.**

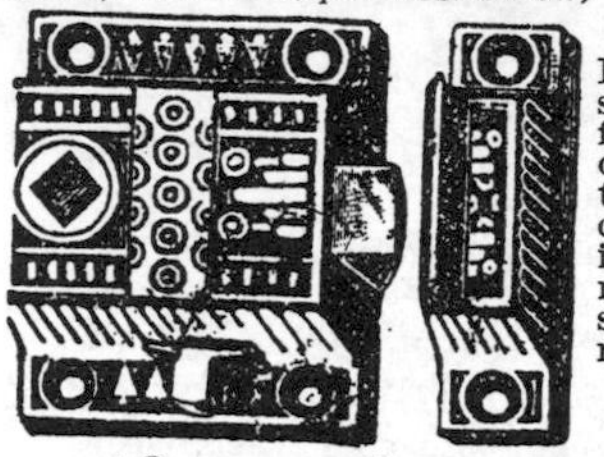

No. 1116. Screen Door Catches same pattern and finish as above for doors ⅞ to 1⅜ in. thick, for inside of doors opening in. This is not much used. Be sure to order the right catch.
Price each, **15c.** per doz., **$1.62.**

## Screen Door Springs.

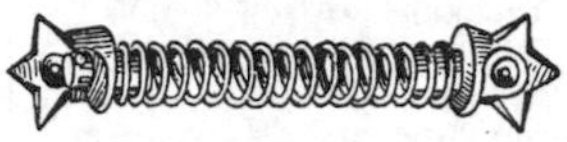

No. 1117. Coiled Wire Door Spring, made of heavy steel spring wire, japanned, adjustable tension, weight 11 oz.
Price, each, **8c.**, per doz., **87c.**

No. 1118. Torrey Door Spring is without doubt the best cheap door spring made. So well known description is not necessary. Weight 12 oz.
Price, each ..................... **12c**
Per doz. ......................... **$1.32**

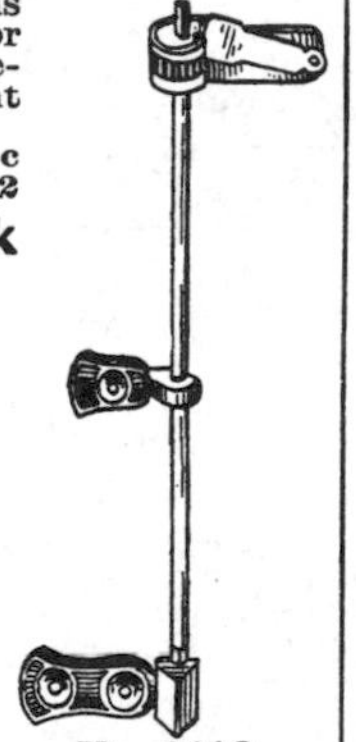

No. 1118.

## Door Spring and Check

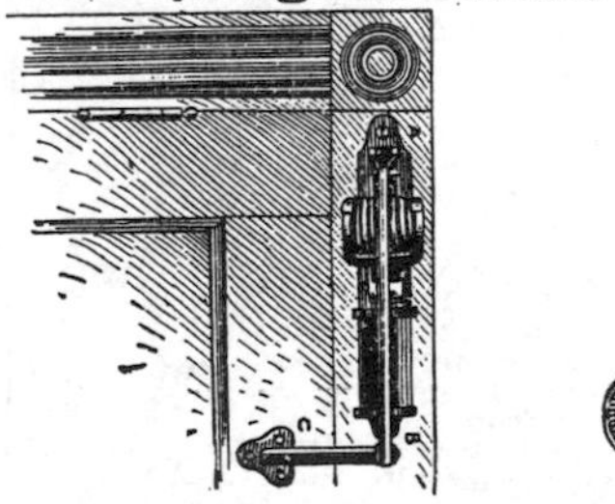

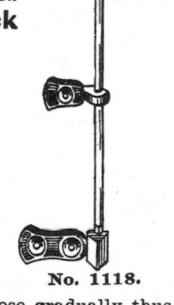

A check causes the door to close gradually thus avoiding the noise of slamming doors. Prevents breaking glass in doors and saves the lock the hardest wear it gets. For durability, easy adjustment, facility for putting in position, reasonable cost, efficiency in use and good appearance, we claim the Spring and Check cannot be excelled. It may be used on either right or left hand doors.

No. 1119. Suitable for screen doors ............ $2 47
No. 1120. Suitable for light inside doors ......... 2 47
No. 1121. Suitable for light outside doors ........ 2 69
No. 1122. Suitable for ordinary outside doors .... 3 08
No. 1123. Suitable for heavy outside doors ...... 4 20

## Spring Hinges.

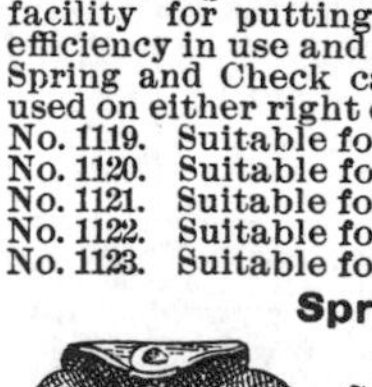

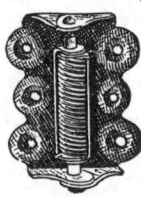

No. 1125 The Pullman Wrought Steel Spring Hinges hold the door tightly closed, or when opened past the center, as securely open. Size 2½x3¼; weight per pair, 9 oz. Price, per pair, **8c**; per doz. pair, **87c.**

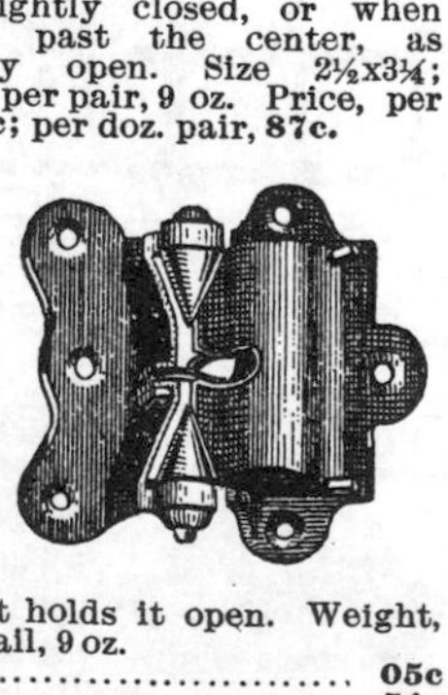

No. 1126 The "**Beat them all**" spring hinge holds door tightly closed as the greatest tension is when door is nearly closed. The working strain upon its coil spring is less than one-half of that of any other, making it efficient and durable. When door is opened past the center it holds it open. Weight, per pair, packed for the mail, 9 oz.
Price per pair ..................................... **05c**
Price per doz. pair ................................ **54c**

**BY REFERRING TO INDEX** you will find many articles you might not know are in the Catalogue. See back of book.

## Double Action Spring Hinges.

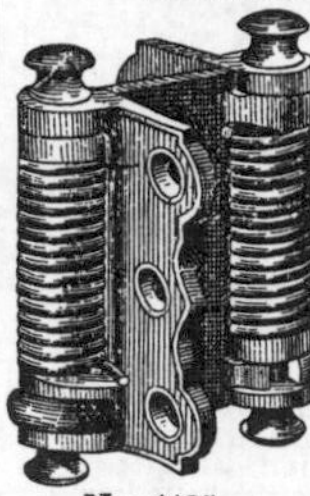

No. 1127.

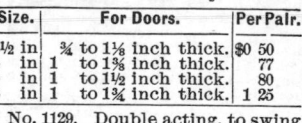

No. 1127 Double Acting Spring Hinge for screen doors to swing both ways—japaned iron—made only in two sizes.
For doors not more than 1⅛ in. thick, per pair ............... **15c**
For doors not more than 1⅜ in. thick, per pair ............... **19c**

## Spring Butts.

The Gem Spring Butt, reversible for right or left hand doors; japanned iron. The largest hinge that the thickness of the door will permit will work the best.

No. 1128. Single acting, to swing one way.

| Size. | For Doors. | Per Pair. |
|---|---|---|
| 3½ in | ¾ to 1⅛ inch thick. | $0 50 |
| 4 in | 1 to 1⅜ inch thick. | 77 |
| 5 in | 1 to 1½ inch thick. | 80 |
| 6 in | 1 to 1¾ inch thick. | 1 25 |

No. 1129. Double acting, to swing both ways.

| Size. | For Doors. | Per Pair. |
|---|---|---|
| 3½ in | ¾ to 1⅛ inch thick. | $1 00 |
| 4 in | 1 to 1⅜ inch thick. | 1 33 |
| 4 in | 1 to 1½ inch thick. | 1 60 |
| 6 in | 1 to 1¾ inch thick. | 2 40 |

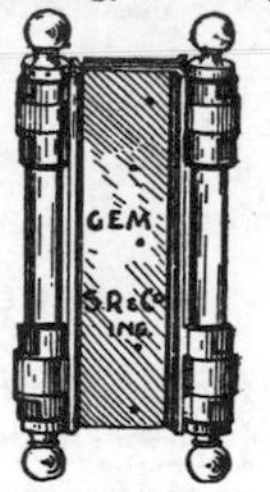


Nos. 1128-1129.

## Wire Flower Pot Stands.

Our stands are all guaranteed to be superior in design, strength, durability and finish to any other make now in the market. **THEY DO NOT NEED BOXING OR CRATING.** Thousands of them have been shipped to all parts of the country without complaint of breakage or damage. They are very light and if not crated or boxed go at **ACTUAL WEIGHT** instead of 100 lbs. The casters have heretofore been a weak point in the flower pot stand but by using an extra heavy caster and attaching it without cutting away any of the leg we overcome this difficulty, we have seen a man weighing 225 lbs. stand with his whole weight on one leg of our stand without injuring it in any way. All our stands are handsomely finished in green and gold. **We guarantee safe delivery anywhere.** We guarantee against breakage in usage for two years.

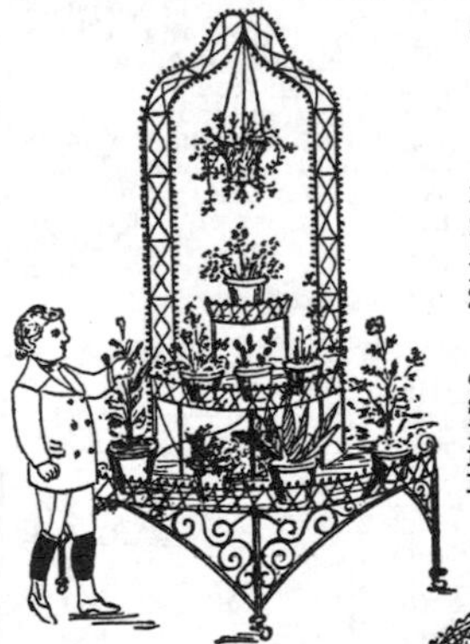

### Small Semi-Circular Flower Stand.

**With Trellis.**

No. 1130. 3 feet 6 inches wide, 28 inches deep, 5 ft. 8 inches high, will hold from 18 to 24 pots, weight 21 lbs.
Price each .. **$4.67**

No. 1131. Small semi-circular flower stand same as above except it has no trellis, 36 inches high, weight 15 lbs.
Price each... **$3.67**

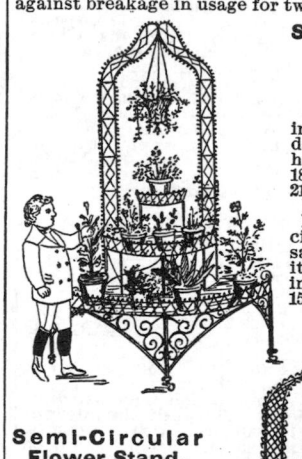

### Semi-Circular Flower Stand.

**With Trellis.**

No. 1132. 6 feet 8 inches high, 4 ft. long, 32 inches deep, weight 30 lbs.
Price each... **$6.67**

No. 1133. Stand same as above without the trellis, 3 ft. 8 inches high, weight 24 lbs.
Price each... **$4.33**

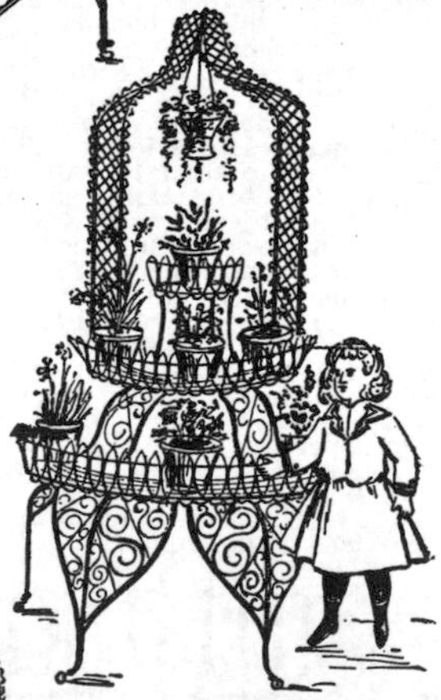

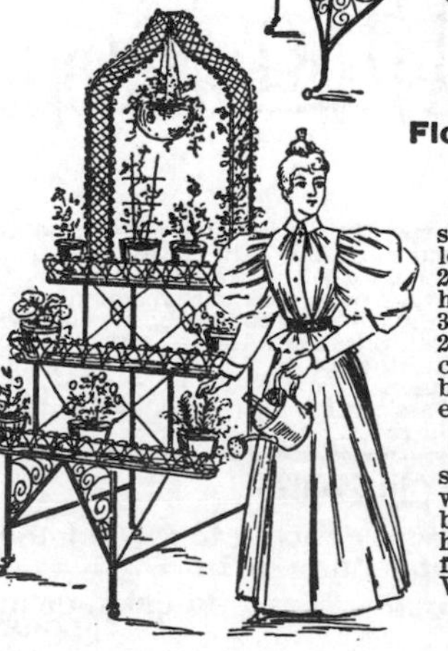

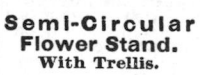

### Flower Stand.

**With Arch.**

No. 1134. Three shelves 3 ft. 3 in. long, 6 in. high, 20 in. deep. Will hold from 24 to 30 pots. Weighs 25 lbs. Price includes arch and basket. Price, each...... **$5.33**

No. 1135. Stand same as above, without arch or basket. 12 in. high, shelves 3 ft. 2 in. long. Weighs 20 lbs.
Price each..
........ **$4.33**

## Our Finest Flower Stand.

No. 1136. Pyramid flower stand with gothic arch and basket, 6 feet 6 in. high, 4 feet wide and 22 inches deep. Will hold from ?5 to 40 pots. Weighs 35 lbs. Price, each.. **$6.67**

No. 1137. Stand same as above, without arch. 42 in. high. Weighs 29 lbs. Price, each.. **$5.65**

*Retails at $10.00.*

## Special Acquarium Flower Stand.

No. 1138. **Aquarium Flower Stand.** This combination of an ornamental wire stand and aquarium makes a very attractive appearance. The plants being near water become very thrifty in growth. This aquarium is 24 inches long, 15 inches wide and 13 inches deep. The stand is 3 feet long and 2 feet wide.

Price of aquarium and stand (weight 117 lbs.) ............ **$13.35**

Price of aquarium only (weight 106 lbs.).... **$8.00**

No. 1139. Aquarium Flower Stand. Size of aquarium, 18 inches long, 13 inches wide and 13 inches deep. Size of stand, 2 feet 6 inches long and 2 feet wide. Price of aquarium and stand, (w'g't 71½ lbs.), **$10.00** Price of aquarium only, (weight 54 lbs.)...... **6.00**

## Window Flower Pot Shelves.

No.1140. **Window Flower Pot Shelves** are intended to be put on the outside of window frame sill or they may be used inside to set flower pots on. They are 7 inches wide with border 4½ inches high, finished in green and gold.

33 inches long, each, 75c; doz................ **$8.00**
36 inches long, each, 76c; doz................ **8.10**
39 inches long, each, 80c; doz................ **8.50**

## Wire Spark Guards.

No. 1141. These guards are made of plated steel wire, the wire being plated after they are made, which gives them a brilliant and durable covering and holds the mesh and guards in shape. The mesh is ¾ inch and each guard is lined with a fine wire cloth which prevents sparks flying out.
24 inches wide by 30 inches high, each.......... **$1.95**
30 inches wide by 30 inches high, each.......... **2.10**

## Grave Guards and Arches.

No. 1142. This is a neat and substantial pattern of moderate cost. It is made of round iron frame work with coiled wire tassels on each post. Made only in following sizes. Painted a handsome green.

| Length. | Width. | Height. | Price each. |
|---|---|---|---|
| 4 ft. | 21 inches. | 24 inches. | $4 80 |
| 5 ft. | 24 inches. | 24 inches. | $6 00 |
| 6 ft. | 30 inches. | 27 inches. | $7 20 |
| 7 ft. | 30 inches. | 27 inches. | $8 40 |

## Wire Chairs and Settees.

No. 1143. Steel Wire Chairs for Cemeteries, Lawns, Porches, are strong, durable and ornamental. If kept properly painted they are practically indestructible. This is an **extra large steel wire arm chair** and is painted green and gold. Cool and very comfortable. Every veranda and lawn should be furnished with them. Made in two styles.

Painted with border as shown in cut, each **$5.25**
Painted without border, each........... **$4.80**

## Our Elegant $7.20 Settee.

No. 1144. Steel Wire Settees. Large and roomy for two people. Notice the large foot shown in picture which prevents injury to floor or lawns. Correctly proportioned; handsome design; neatly finished in green and gold. Made in two styles.
Painted with border as shown in cut, each.. **$7.20**
Painted without border, each........... **$5.75**

## Galvanized Rigid Frame Door Mats

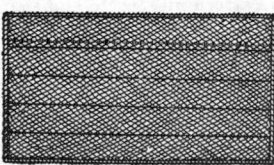

No. 1145. These are the strongest, most durable and attractive ever manufactured. **Guaranteed to keep in perfect shape** under any usage. They are made of hard steel wire, galvanized.

| | | | |
|---|---|---|---|
| 16 x 24 in. | Each 75c. | 30 x 48 in. | Each $2.62 |
| 18 x 30 in. | Each $1.00 | 36 x 48 in. | Each 3.25 |
| 22 x 36 in. | Each 1.50 | 36 x 60 in. | Each 4.00 |
| 26 x 48 in. | Each 2.25 | 36 x 72 in. | Each 5.00 |

## Sand Screens.

No. 1146. Sand Screens. This Sand Screen is so made that **the wires cannot be displaced** or become separated from the heavy cross rods. The frames are strong and the wires are heavy steel. Will outwear any other and sand can be screened rapidly. Made in two sizes; small size weighs about 35 lbs; large size about 42 lbs.
22x61, price each.... **$3.75**
28x67, price each.... **4.69**

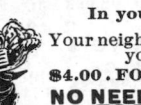

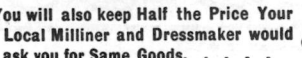
## STOCK RAISERS' GOODS.

Our trade among the stock growers of the south and west indicates that we are headquarters in this line of goods.

No one competes with us in price, and our line embraces the best made goods in the market. We can save you 25 to 50 per cent., besides insuring you at all times strictly high grade standard goods. One order in this line will convince you we have no competitors.

### Hog Ringers.

No. 1200. Hill's Pattern Hog Ringer. Price,.. **9c**
No. 1203. Hill's Pattern Hog Rings for above ringer; 100 rings in a box.
Price, per box 7c., per dozen boxes .......... **$0.78**
No. 1204. Hill's Pattern Shoat Rings for above ringer; 100 rings in a box.
Price, per box 7c., per dozen boxes.......... **$0.78**
No. 1205. Hill's Pattern Pig Rings for above ringer; 100 rings in a box.
Price, per box 7c., per dozen boxes.......... **$0.78**
No. 1207. Perfection Hog Ringer. Price, each.. **$0.11**

No. 1209. Perfection Hog Rings to be used with above ringer; 100 rings in a box.
Price, per box 10c., per dozen boxes.......... **$1.08**

### Stock Marks.

Stock Mark to use with Perfection ringer and rings. Made of brass about the size and thickness of a silver quarter dollar. The initial is stamped on mark with a steel stamp. **State letter wanted** when ordering. Ringer or rings are not included in prices quoted.
No. 1212. Stock Mark with any one letter or figure on one side. Price per doz. 10c., per 100, 75c.
No. 1213 Stock Marks with any two letters or figures on one side Price per dozen, 18c., per 100, **$1.25**.
No. 1214. Stock Marks with any three letters or figures on one side.
Price, per dozen, 25c., per 100. ............. **$1.75**
No. 1215. Stock Marks with consecutive numbers, on one side only—1-2-3-4-5—or any set of consecutive numbers not having more than three figures in the number. Price, per doz., 25c., per 100......... **$1.75**
No. 1216. Stock Marks with consecutive numbers on one side, any one letter or figure on the other.
Price, per dozen, 30c., per 100.................. **$2.25**
No. 1217. Stock Marks with consecutive numbers on one side, any two letters or figures on the other.
Price, per dozen, 35c., per 100.................. **$2.75**
No. 1218. Stock Marks with consecutive numbers on one side, any three letters or figures on the other.
Price, per dozen, 50c., per 100....... ....... **$3.50**

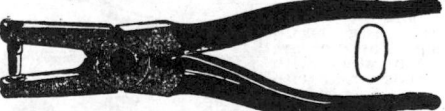

No. 1219. Oval Ear Punch for punching the ear and closing the metal ear labels. Price, each...... **$1.25**

### Stock Markers.

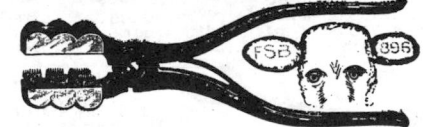

**The Burch Tattoo Ear Marker** for horses, cattle, sheep, swine and dogs.

It is well known that a mark tattooed into the skin of a man or animal will remain visible as long as the wearer lives. It cannot be changed or removed as ear labels or buttons frequently are, and will, therefore, prevent fraud and stop all controversies as to the identification of registered animals. It is the only brand or mark which may be applied to a horse without disfiguring.

The markers are fitted with three letters or figures, whichever the purchaser desires, at **$1.80 each**. The letters are interchangeable, and can be quickly removed and others attached in their place. The letters are ½ inch square, and cut out of solid metal. If the letters are kept oiled they should last a life time.

**Directions for Using.**—First smear the letters with the tattoo oil, punch the ear, and then rub the oil well into the punctures with the thumb or fingers.

It takes three to five days for the ear to heal and the brand to show out clear and distinct.

On a white, pink or yellow skin the brand is a jet black, but on a brown or black skin it makes a clear blue brand.
No. 1220. Marker fitted with three letters or figures..................................... **$1.80**
No. 1221. Extra letters or figures, each ...... **$0.35**
No. 1222. Tattoo Oil, per bottle (marks 500 ears)..................................... **$0.50**
We can send the Markers by mail when desired. The postage on each is 25 cents.

## The Burch "Bar Brand" Punch.

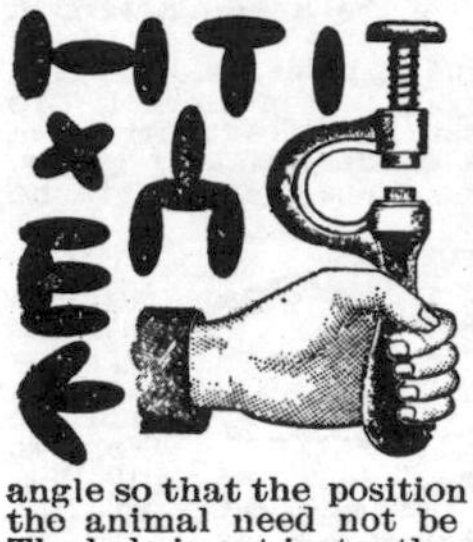

No. 1223. This instrument is for cutting holes in the ears of animals. The die in this punch cuts out a half-inch oval slit in the ear. **An endless variety of designs and combinations** may be punched in the animal's ear. also the following letters of the alphabet may be made with it; **A, E, F, H, I, K, L, M, N, T, V, W, X** and **Z**. The die in the punch can be turned around to any angle so that the position of the punch and ear of the animal need not be changed while branding. The hole is cut instantly; the die being very sharp, tht animal suffers little or no pain. Owners of stock can register their brand at any county seat and it then becomes their private property. This instrument is one of the cheapest and most durable ever brought out for marking stock. The mark cannot be altered or removed and the holes are not large enough to disfigure the ears. In the accompanying illustration we show a few of the 200 designs that can be produced with this punch. The illustrations are full size. The smallest lamb or pig can be marked with success. The die is made of the finest tool steel and will last for years, in case it should become broken by accident, we can furnish duplicates which can be inserted instantly.

Price, each..............................**$2.00**

**Postage 30 cents extra if sent by mail.**

## Ear Labels.

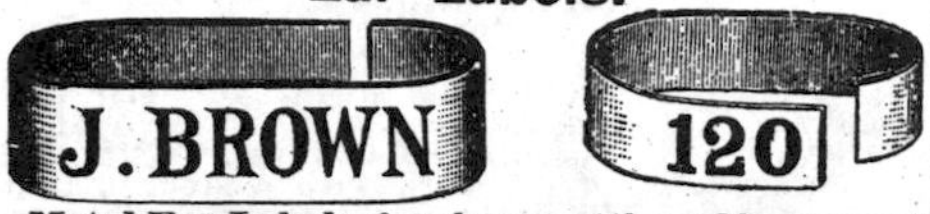


**Metal Ear Labels,** for sheep, cattle and hogs; used by all live stock record associations, your name on one side and numbered from 1 upward, or any numbers desired on the reverse side; they are very light and will not tear out. If there are more than seven letters in your name the initials only can be put on labels. If you desire labels sent by mail add 20 cts per hundred for postage.

No. 1225. Sheep and hog size. Price, per 50..**$1.00**
Per 100................................ 2.00
No. 1226. Cattle size. Price, per 50.......... 1.00
Per 100................................ 2.00

**We cannot furnish in quantities less than 50.**

## Mark Your Poultry.

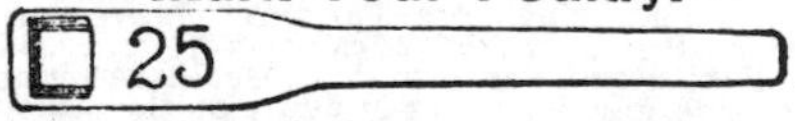


No. 1232. **Champion Leg Bands.** Light as a feather; cannot come off; made of Aluminum. For turkeys, geese, ducks and chickens. Prices 1 doz. **30c**; 25 for **50c**; 50 for **75c**; 100 for....................**$1.25**

All leg bands are numbered from 1 up, or can furnish any numbers desired.

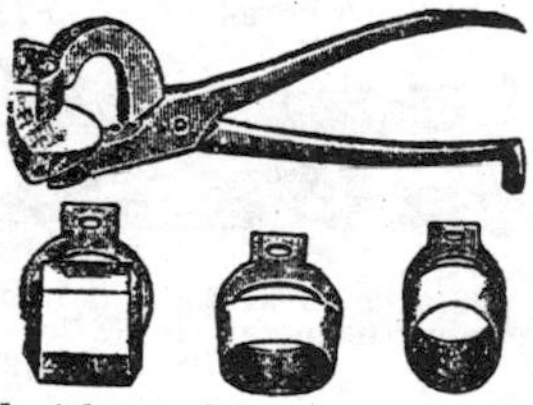

**Stock Marking Tongs.** For marking the ears of horses, cattle, hogs and sheep. The dies are made of steel, with razor edge, and with proper care will last for years. The dies are interchangeable, and can be attached to or removed from tongs in one minute.

No. 1233 Tongs fitted with round die.........**$2.50**
No. 1235 Tongs fitted with square or oval die.
Price, each..............................**$3.00**

## Hog Tamers.

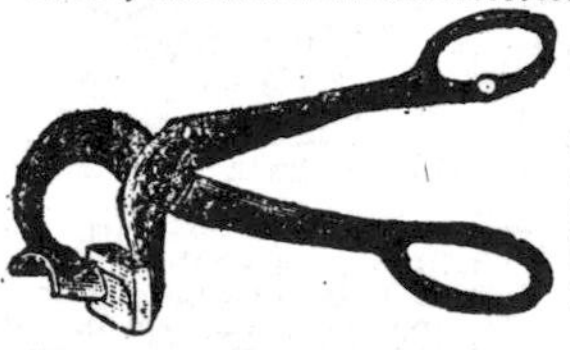

No. 1236 **Hurd's Hog Tamer.** Three different sizes of steel knives furnished with each Tamer.
Price, each...**$0.50**

## Newton & McGee's Draw Cut Patent Dehorner with latest Improvements.

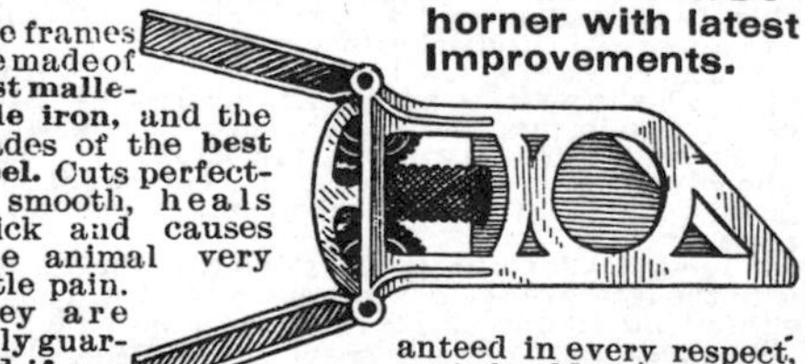

The frames are made of **best malleable iron**, and the blades of the **best steel.** Cuts perfectly smooth, heals quick and causes the animal very little pain. They are fully guaranteed in every respect, and if any part should break from a flaw or defect **we will replace same without expense to the purchaser.** They are made in three sizes.

No. 1250. No. 1 Draw Cut Dehorner, is for calves only. Has a 2-inch opening. Length, 2 feet 3 inches; weight, 4½ lbs. Price each.............**$3.00**

No. 1251 No. 2 Draw Cut Dehorner, as described above, for young and medium aged cattle. Has a 3¼ inch opening. Length, 3 feet 4 inches; weight, 12 lbs. Price each..............................**$5.25**

No. 1252 No. 3 Draw Cut Dehorner, as described above, is for either young or old cattle. Has 4½ inch opening. Length, 3 feet 8 inches. Weighs, 17 lbs Price each..............................**$6.75**

**For prices Sheep Dip, &c., see Drug department.**

## Dehorning Tools.

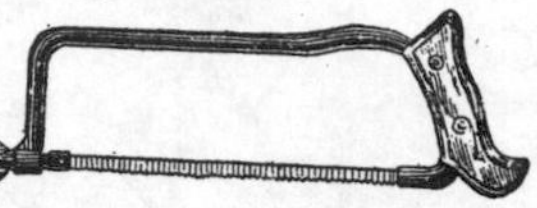

No. 1253 **Dehorning Saw** with japanned malleable iron frame, beech handle, complete, with blade 9½ inches long, ¼ inch wide.
Price, each..............................**$0.65**
Extra blades for this saw, each .............. 0.10
Per doz.................................. 1.08

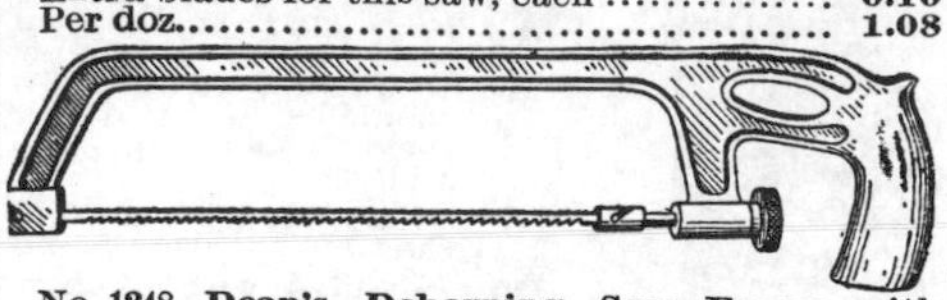

No. 1248 **Dean's Dehorning Saw Frame** with Disston 12-inch blade; malleable iron frame, nicely enameled. Price, each.... ........ .........**$1.00**
No. 1249 Extra blades for this saw. Each... 0.25

## Cow Ties.

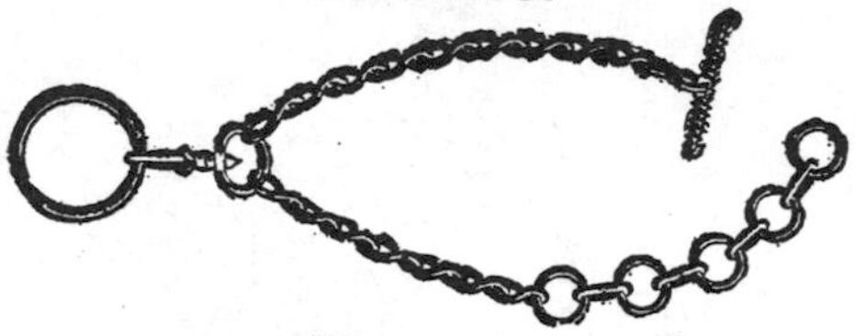

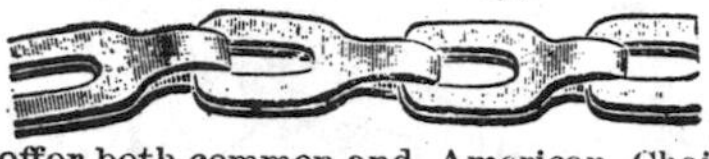

We offer both common and American Chain Cow Ties. The American Chain Link is stamped from a piece of soft steel; has no welds, which is the weak part of common style chains.

No. 1260 **The Common Pattern** closed ring Cow ties with toggle. Price each, **16c**; per doz .. **$1.80**
No. 1261 **The same Tie,** American pattern chain. Price each, **18c**; per doz........................**$1.95**

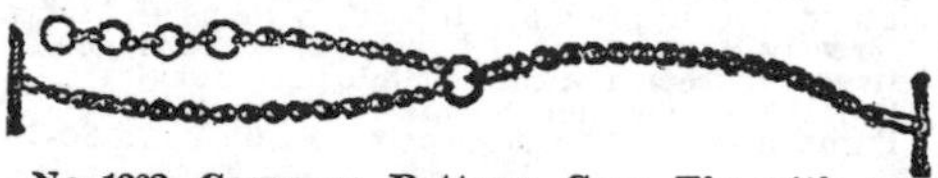

No. 1262 **Common Pattern Cow Tie** with two toggles. Price each **16c**; per doz.... .........**$1.80**
No. 1263 **American Pattern** with toggle and snap Price each, **20c**; per doz........................**$2.16**

## Hay Racks and Feed Boxes.

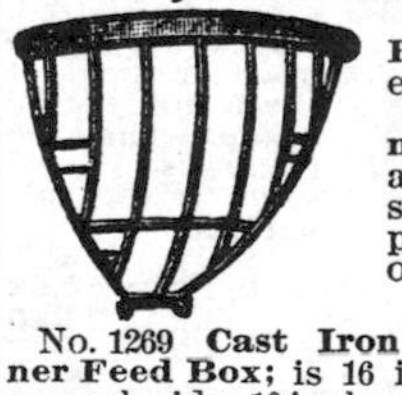

No. 1267 **Cast Iron Corner Hay Rack.** Weigh 29 lbs. Price each................................**$1.10**

No. 1268 **Wrought Steel Corner Hay Rack;** same shape as above but made of bent ½-inch steel rods. State if to be placed on "off" or "near" side of the horse. Price each **$1.50**

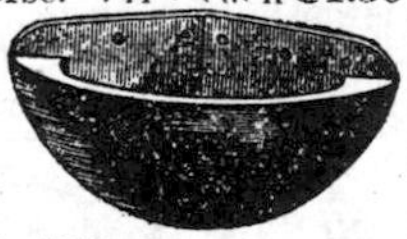

No. 1269 **Cast Iron Corner Feed Box;** is 16 inches on each side; 10 inches deep; weight 28 pounds.
Price each............. **80c**

## Cattle Tie Irons.

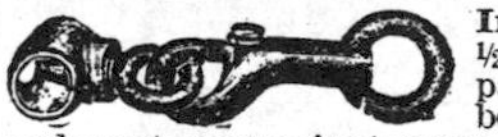

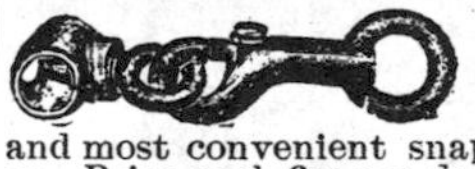

No. 1275 **Cattle Tie Irons.** Tinned; for rope ½ inch in diameter, with patent covered spring bolt snap. The safest and most convenient snap made. Weight, each, 6 oz. Price each **6c**; per doz..........................**60c**

## Picket Pins.

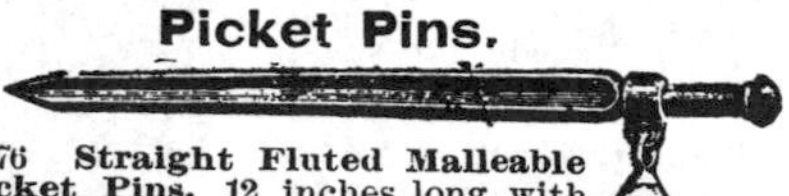

No. 1276 **Straight Fluted Malleable Iron Picket Pins.** 12 inches long with swivel. Weight 1½ lbs. Price each....**6c**

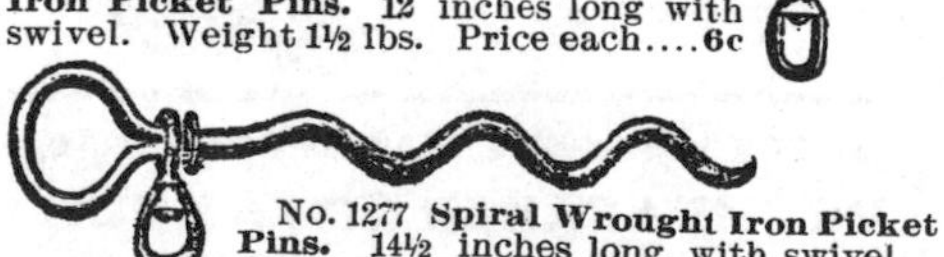

No. 1277 **Spiral Wrought Iron Picket Pins.** 14½ inches long, with swivel.
Each.. .................................. **13c**

## Swivels.

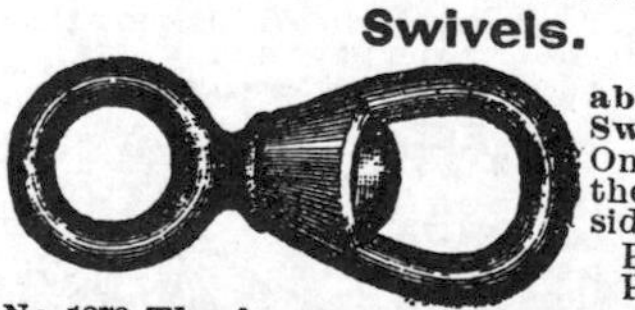

No. 1278 **Malleable Iron Lariat Swivels,** 3 in. long. One eye ⅝ in. inside. the other ¾ in. inside.
Price each.....**3c**
Per doz.........**30c**

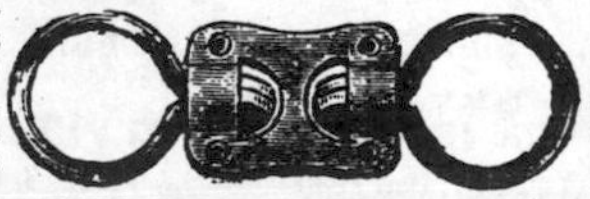

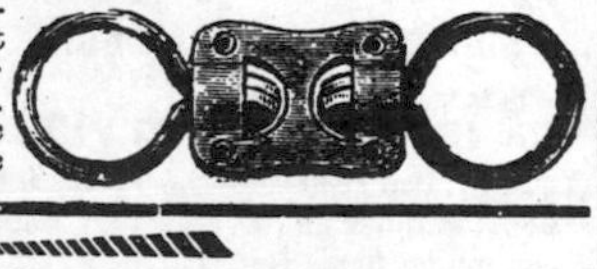

No. 1279 **The American Wrought Steel Lariat Swivel,** eyes ⅝ in, inside.
Price each.....**4c**
Per doz........**33c**

**IF YOU**
**Ever have had or will have the slightest cause for complaint**
**WRITE US**
**Stating the facts, and we will take pains to straighten the matter out to your satisfaction**

## Picket Chains.

No. 1280 **The Triumph Tie-out or Picket Chains,** 20 feet long; stronger, better and more durable than a rope. Price each. **65c**; per doz...................**$6.90**

## Cattle Leaders.

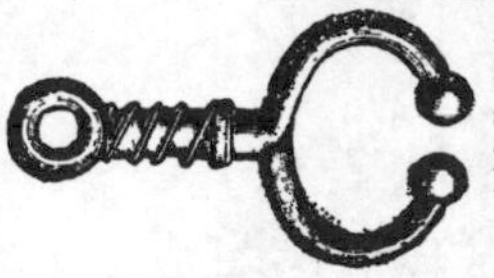

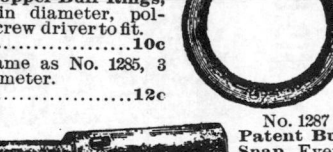

No. 1283 **Malleable Iron Cattle Leaders,** with brass spring; full size, regular goods, same as you pay double the price for or more.
Price each..........**4c**
Per doz............**45c**

## Bull Rings.

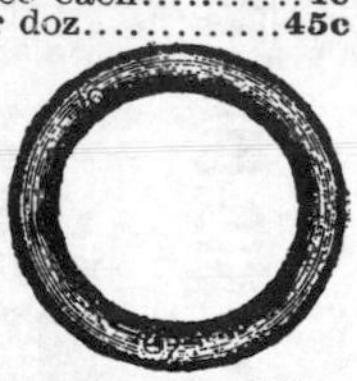

No. 1285 **Copper Bull Rings,** 2½ inches in diameter, polished, with screw driver to fit.
Price each....................**10c**
No. 1286 Same as No. 1285, 3 inches in diameter.
Price each....................**12c**

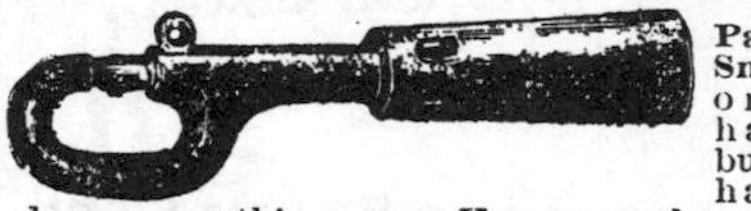

No. 1287 **Patent Bull Snap.** Every one who handles a bull should have and always use this snap. You never know at what minute they will become vicious. We furnish with snap three feet of chain with ring on end and three screw eyes. No wood handle furnished.
Price each................................**25c**

## Ox Balls.

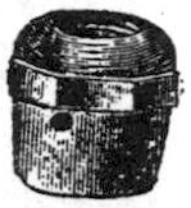

No. 1289 **Brass Ox Balls,** to put on the tips of the horns of vicious cattle. Octagon pattern.
Medium size, ¾ in. Each, **3c**; per doz. **32c**
Large size, ⅞ in. Each, **4c**; per doz. **40c**

## Crooks.

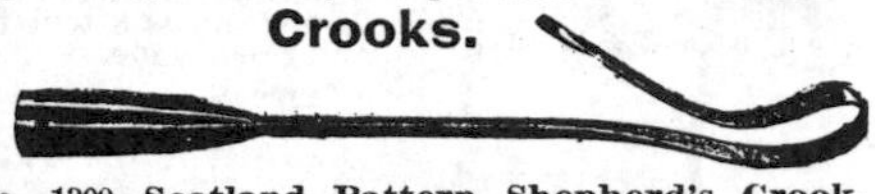

No. 1309 **Scotland Pattern Shepherd's Crook,** light polished cast steel, no handle. Price each, **75c**
No. 1310 **American Pattern Shepherd's Crook,** heavy polished cast steel, no handle. Price each. **85c**

## Sheep Shears.

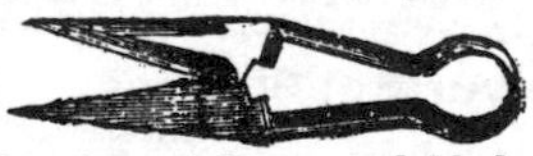

No. 1315 **The Celebrated Burgon & Ball's Sheep Shears,** double bow, (cut shows single bow,) straight swaged blades, polished; the kind that is used by professional sheep shearers.

| Size, inches...... | 6½ | 7 |
|---|---|---|
| Each............ | **$1.20** | **$1.25** |

**No. 1316. A Good Sheep Shears with Single Bow,** bent handles, half polished. Good enough for anyone who is not a professional sheep shearer.

| Size, inches...... | 5 | 5½ | 6 |
|---|---|---|---|
| Each........... | **60c** | **62c** | **65c** |

## Ox Yokes.

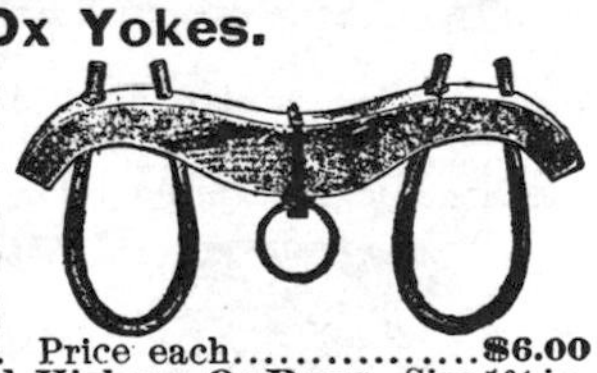

No. 1320 **Medium Sized Ox Yokes,** ironed, complete with bows and pins.
Price each, **$5.00**
No. 1321 **Large Sized Ox Yokes,** ironed, complete with bows and pins. Price each...............**$6.00**
No. 1322 **Selected Hickory Ox Bows.** Size 1¾ in. per pair, **56c**; size 2 inch, per pair..........**60c**

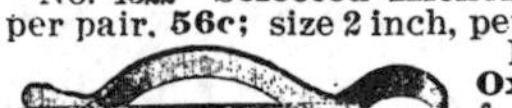

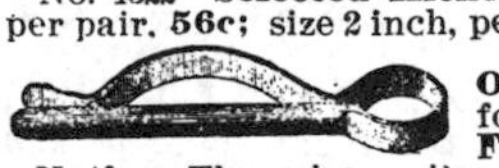

No. 1323 **Cast Steel Ox Bow Pins.** Price each for 1¾ inch bows........**5c**
For 2 inch bows..........**6c**

**Notice**—The price on Bow Pins is for one only.

## Calf Weaners.

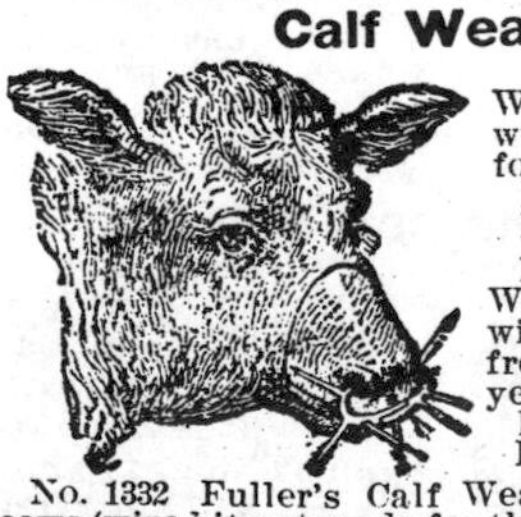

No. 1330 Fuller's Calf Weaners. Small size with wire bit for calves from four to eight months old.
Price, each... ......**17c**
Per doz..........**$1.80**

No. 1331 Fuller's Calf Weaners. Medium size with wire bit for calves from eight months to two years old.
Price, each. ......**20c**
Per doz. .........**$2.10**

No. 1332 Fuller's Calf Weaners. Large size for cows (wire bit not made for this size).
Price, each, **25c.**; per doz..........................**$2.75**

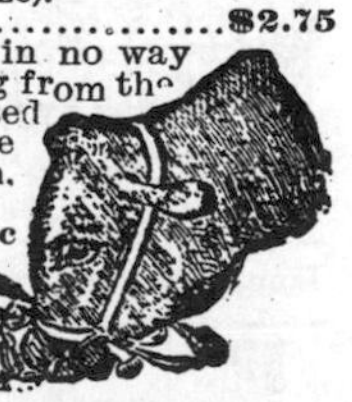

No. 1333 The Hoosier Weaner in no way prevents the animal from feeding from the ground. but when the head is raised in an attempt to suck, the muzzle automatically covers the mouth, complete with strap.
Price, each............**40c**
Per doz........**$4.55**
Weaners cannot be sent by mail.

## ANIMAL POKES.

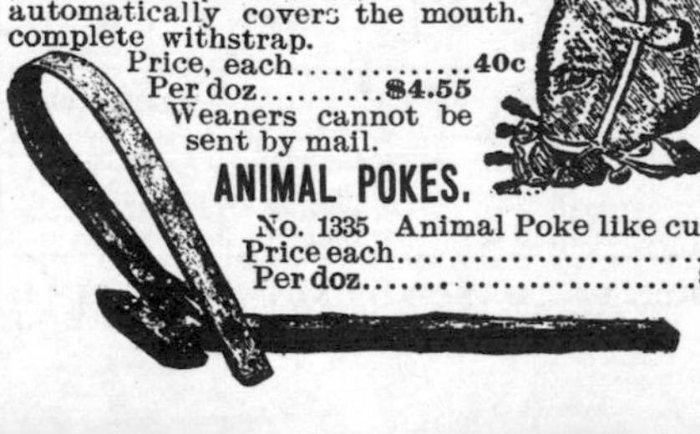

No. 1335 Animal Poke like cut.
Price each................................**30c**
Per doz.................................**$3.30**

# EVERYTHING IN SCALES

**YOU CANNOT AFFORD** to be without Scales to weigh **EVERYTHING YOU BUY** and **EVERYTHING YOU SELL.**

**EVERY FARMER** should own either a set of **WAGON SCALES** or **PLATFORM SCALES.**

**A FARMER SHOULD NOT** sell a load of Grain, a Bale of Cotton, a Hog or a Steer that has not been weighed on his own Scales.

**YOUR SCALES** will check mistakes and detect dishonesty and will pay the cost ten fold in a few years.

**WE ARE HEADQUARTERS** for everything in the line of Scales. We offer only the **best goods** and at prices that cannot be undersold.

**OUR TERMS ARE LIBERAL.** We will ship Scales to any address, by freight or express, C. O. D., subject to examination, on receipt of sufficient deposit to pay transportation charges both ways, balance and freight or express charges payable after the goods are received.

**DISCOUNT OF THREE PER CENT.** allowed if cash in full accompanies your order.

**FREIGHT RATES ARE LOW** on Scales, they take second and third class rate, and the freight will amount to next to nothing compared with what you will save in cost.

**OUR GUARANTEE.** We guarantee all Scales to be absolutely perfect as to weight, made of the best material and the **HIGHEST STANDARD ON THE MARKET. There are many cheaper grades on the market. WE HANDLE ONLY THE VERY BEST.**

## Best Farm Wagon Scale Made.

We have contracted for a large number of these Scales and at prices that enable us to give values never before given.

**WE GUARANTEE THIS THE BEST WAGON SCALE EVER MADE.** The construction is very simple and great care has been taken to arrange it so anyone with even ordinary mechanical ideas can erect it successfully. All the materials are the very best possible. Brass beams, sliding poise and steel pivots.
**BUILDING PLAN AND FULL DIRECTIONS SENT WITH EACH SCALE.**

No. 1400 Capacity, 2 tons; shipping wgt, 600lbs; size of platform, 7x13 ft; single beam. Price, each **$50.00**
No. 1402 Capacity, 3 tons; shipping wgt, 600lbs; size of platform, 8x14 ft; double beam. Price, each **46.00**
No. 1404 Capacity, 4 tons; shipping wgt, 675lbs; size of platform, 8x14 ft; double beam. Price, each **49.50**
No. 1406 Capacity, 5 tons; shipping wgt, 675lbs; size of platform, 8x14 ft; double beam. Price, each **53.50**
Write us for price delivered at your railroad depot, or approximate freight from our information on freight. These Scales take **third class freight rate.**
**DON'T COMPARE THE SCALES WE OFFER** with the many cheap, worthless Wagon Scales on the market. **OUR SCALES ARE GUARANTEED THE VERY BEST,** and, quality considered, our prices are at least 33⅓ PER CENT. BELOW THE MARKET.

## Our $11.50 Platform Farm Scale.

Guaranteed the Best Platform Scale on the market.

**No Farmer can afford** to be without a set of these scales. Capacity from 400 to 1500 pounds (according to price). **You can weigh every load of grain you sell before going to market.**

Everything grown on the farm should be weighed, it isn't safe to do otherwise.

These Scales will serve you better than any other Platform Scales made.

**REMEMBER, OUR 3 PER CENT. CASH DISCOUNT** when cash in full accompanies your order, when comparing our prices with those of other houses.

**DON'T FORGET OUR LIBERAL C. O. D.,** subject to examination, **TERMS.**

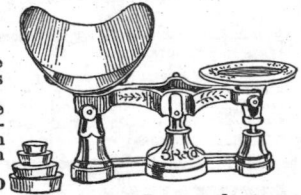

| | Capacity, Lbs. | Ship.Wt. Lbs. | Price. |
|---|---|---|---|
| No. 1410 | 400 | 155 | $11.50 |
| No. 1411 | 600 | 170 | 12.67 |
| No. 1412 | 800 | 180 | 14.00 |
| No. 1413 | 1,200 | 265 | 16.00 |
| No, 1414 | 1,500 | 270 | 20,00 |

These scales are unquestionably the best scale made for the money. They are provided with the best of **steel pivots** carefully hardened—have **no check rods** to bind and get out of place. The platform rests on adjustable chill bearings which takes the wear directly off from the steel pivots, and the pivots remaining sharp, **the scale acts quick and sensitive.** Has wheels, wood center platform, sliding poise beam, sealed and tested. The greatest care is exercised in packing these scales for shipment.
**DON'T BUY A CHEAP MADE PLATFORM SCALE,** They are dear at any price.

## Our $1.00 Family Scales.

No. 1416 **Our $1.00** price should induce every family in the land to own a pair of these 4 pound scales.

**You may save the cost in one day's use.**

Even balance scales. Plain Japanned. To weigh 4 pounds. With good tin scoop.
Our Price....**$1.00**

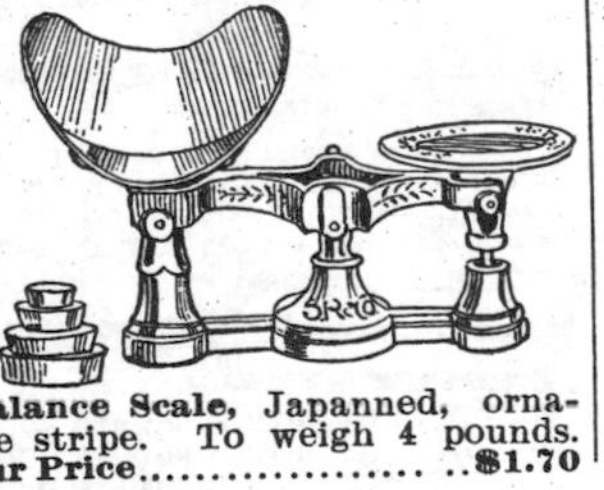

No. 1430 **Even Balance Scale,** Japanned, ornamented with bronze stripe. To weigh 4 pounds. With tin scoop. Our Price.......................**$1.70**

## Our $2.15 Leader.

**JUST THINK** a 240 Pound Platform Counter Scale for $2.15. This scale would retail at more than double the price.
**$2.15 SHOULD INTEREST YOU.** This is an all purpose scale, weighing from ½ ounce to 240 pounds. This will take the place in many ways of a regular platform scale. It has fine steel bearings, tin scoop, brass beam. Weighs, boxed for shipment, 43 pounds.

There are several similar scales on the market offered in a wholesale way at, or near our price, but not to compare in quality within 50 per cent. of our **SPECIAL PRICE OF $2.15.**

## Our 25 Pound $1.65 Family Scales.

No. 1425 This is a regular **$3.50 scale,** never sold at retail for less than $3.50.

**We make the price $1.65 complete.** We bought a large number at a low price, to which we add our one small percentage of profit. The result is $1.65.

**It will pay you to buy these scales** and weigh your grocery and meat purchases. Weigh the butter. Scale weighs ¼ oz. or 25 pounds. The accompanying cut is a perfect illustration of **Our Special $1.65 Family Scales.** No better family scale made. Guaranteed absolutely accurate and well made. Can be used with or without scoop. Weighs from ¼ ounce to 25 pounds. Retails at **$3.50.** We sell it for **$1.65**

## Our $3.50 Beauty.

Retails at $5 to $7.
We can sell them at $3.50.
Very handsome counter scale, suitable for family or grocery store use, guaranteed perfectly accurate. Made throughout of steel, beautifully japanned, striped, ornamented. Large 7½ inch glass sash. Weighs from ½ ounce to 25 pounds. 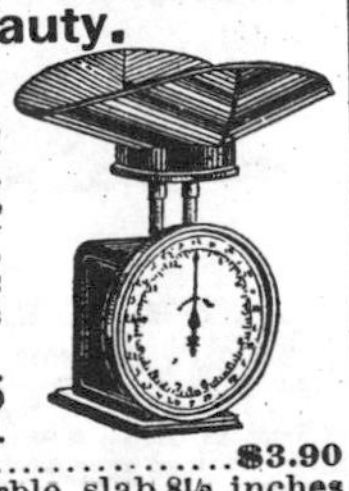
No. 1446 Scale, with tin scoop.
Each........................**$3.50**
No. 1447 Scale, with brass scoop.
Each........................**$3.90**
No. 1448 Same scale with marble slab 8½ inches square, instead of scoop........**$4.20**

## Our $2.50 Family Scale.

Your dealer would ask $5 for same scale.
No. 1452 These family scales weigh from 1 oz. to 25 lbs, made of finest steel throughout, beautifully japanned and ornamented throughout. Large brass dial, black figures, Aluminum hand, very sensitive, tin scoop.
Our special price, **$2.50**

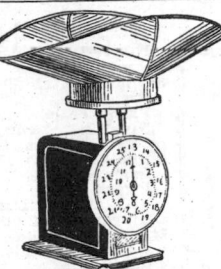

## Our $2.75 Scales.

Worth double our price.

No. 1456 This is the handsomest, and most attractive 4 pound candy, lard, tea, spice or kitchen scale on the market. Beautifully finished in brass, nickel plated. Weighs 4 pounds by ounces. Every scale warranted accurate. Celluloid dial, large black figures.
Our price...........**$2.75**

**ORDER BY NUMBER.**

## Our $1.90 Family Scale.

Sold by many at $4.

This is a very attractive scale for family, grocer or general use, extremely sensitive and entirely free from friction. All steel, japanned, upright brass dial, large black figures, easily read, absolutely unbreakable, tin scoop.
No. 1460 Weighs 12 pounds by ounces...............**$1.90**
No. 1461 Weighs 24 pounds by 2 ounces............**$2.10**

## Our $2.95 Scale.

Nothing Finer in a 6 or 12 pound Scale.

The latest, most attractive Kitchen, Tea, Candy, Spice or Tobacco Scale made. Beautifully finished in nickel plate, **Brass Dial.** Large black figures.
No. 1466 Weighs 6 pounds by ½ ounces..................**$2.95**
No. 1468 Weighs 12 pounds by ounces..................**$3.30**

## Our $3.00 National Postal Scale.

No. 1470 **The National Postal Scale** indicates instantly the exact amount of postage in cents required for letters, books, newspapers and merchandise to any part of the United States or Canada.
Weighs up to 4 pounds by ½ ounces. Made of finest steel, japanned and nickel trimmed.
Price........................**$3.00**

## Our $2.20 Hanging Scale.

No. 1472 Brass Dial, Large Black Figures. Very sensitive and accurate. Weighs 25 pounds by ounces. Bow and steel pan galvanized. Can be instantly adjusted. Price....**$2.20**

## Butcher's Peerless Scale.

One of the finest Scales made.

No. 1474 Double Dial with Nickel Trimming. Weighs 20 pounds by ozs. Very sensitive and accurate. Steel porcelain pan.
Our Special price...............**$5.10**

No. 1480 Butcher's Scales, with marble slab; to weigh 32 pounds by ounces; weight carefully packed in box for shipment, 40 lbs. Price..............**$8.70**
No. 1481 Same as No. 1480; to weigh 64 lbs. by 2 ounces; weight carefully packed in box for shipment, 40 lbs. Price..............**$9.95**

**POSTAGE IS ONE CENT PER OUNCE, 16 CENTS PER POUND AND MUST BE PREPAID. WHEN YOU WANT GOODS SENT BY MAIL, YOU MUST NOT FAIL TO SEND POSTAGE IN FULL.**

## Spring Balances.

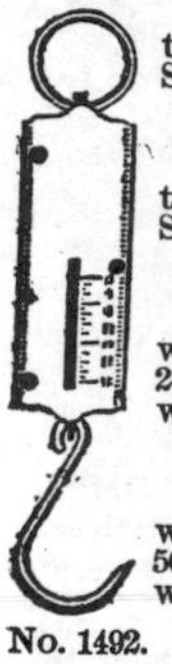

No. 1492.

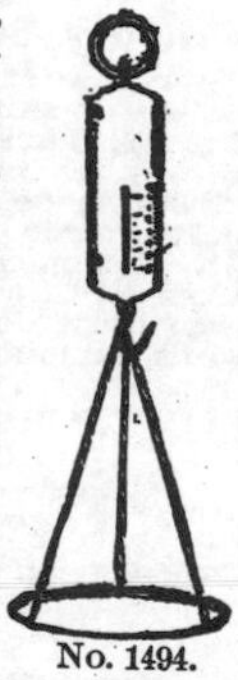

No. 1494.

No. 1492 **Spring Balance,** to weigh 24 lbs. by ½ lbs. Shipping weight, 9 oz.
Price each ........... **$0.08**
Price per doz ......... **.87**

No. 1493 **Spring Balance,** to weigh 48 lbs. by pounds. Shipping weight, 12 oz.
Price each ........... **$0.16**
Price per doz ......... **1.73**

No. 1494 **Spring Balance,** with round tin dish; weighs 24 lbs. by ½ ponnds. Shipping weight, 1¾ pounds.
Price each ........... **$0.20**
Price per doz ......... **2.00**

No. 1495 **Spring Balance,** with round tin dish; weighs 50 lbs. by pounds. Shipping weight, 2½ lbs.
Price each ........... **$0.35**
Price per doz ......... **3.88**

## Finest Straight Spring Scale Made.

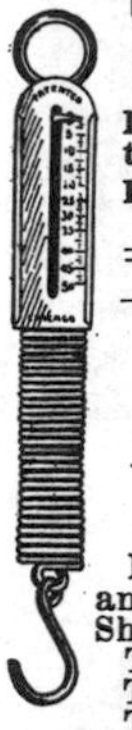

**These scales are more compact, and have longer dials than other makes. While better in many ways than the old style, comparison will show that our prices are lower.**

**PRICES:**

| No. | Weight. | Price. |
|---|---|---|
| 1496 | 50 pounds x ½ pound. | $0.38 |
| 1497 | 75 pounds x ½ pound. | 0.88 |
| 1498 | 100 pounds x 1 pound. | 1.05 |
| 1499 | 150 pounds x 1 pound. | 1.33 |
| 1500 | 210 pounds x 2 pounds. | 1.58 |

## Ice Balances.

No. 1502 **Ice Balances,** strong and durable; weighs by 5 pounds. Shipping weight 4¼ lbs.
To weigh 200 lbs ........... **$2.15**
To weigh 300 lbs ........... **2.56**
To weigh 400 lbs ........... **3.00**

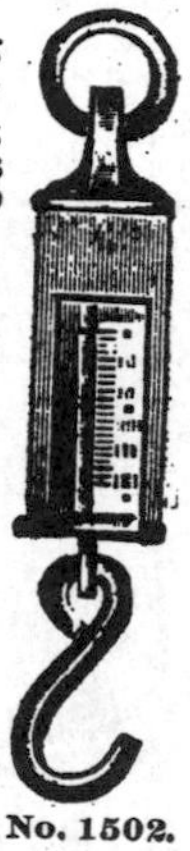

No. 1502.

## 30-Cent Professional Scale.

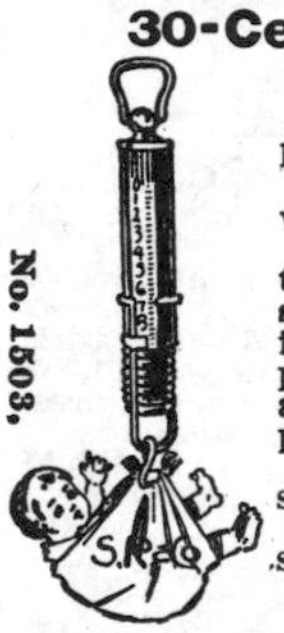

No. 1503.

**Every doctor should have one.**

**No family should be without one.**

**This is a very beautiful and accurate scale,** beautifully finished in brass, nickel plated, and offered at about one-half retail price.

No. 1503 10 pound scale ........... **$0.30**
No. 1504 20 pound scale ........... **0.40**

## Steelyards.

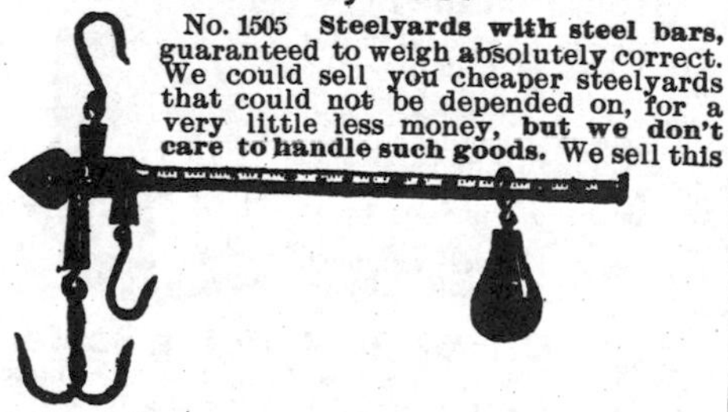

No. 1505 **Steelyards with steel bars,** guaranteed to weigh absolutely correct. We could sell you cheaper steelyards that could not be depended on, for a very little less money, **but we don't care to handle such goods.** We sell this grade as low as you get the common grade elsewhere. The 50 lb. size weighs by ¼ lbs., larger sizes by ½ lbs.

| Capacity, lbs. | 50 | 100 | 150 | 200 | 250 | 300 |
|---|---|---|---|---|---|---|
| Price, each. | $0.45 | .50 | .63 | .80 | .95 | 1.05 |

## Scale Beams.

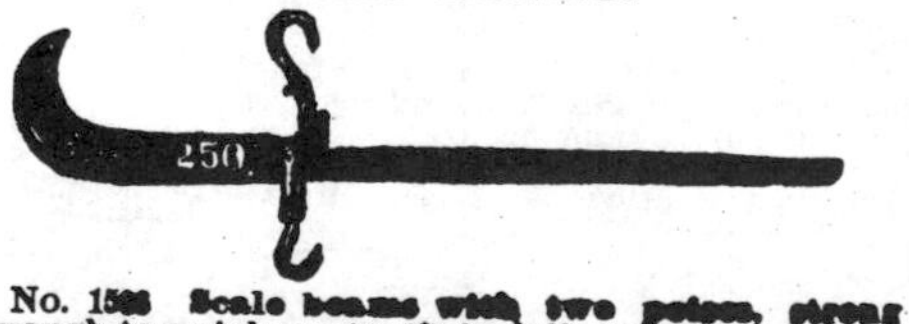

No. 1506 **Scale beams with two poises, strong enough to weigh up to their full capacity without injury. With each scale beam we furnish poises as** follows: 250-lb. beam, one 2-lb. and one 8-lb. poise; 400-lb beam, one 3-lb. and one 12-lb. poise; 600-lb. beam, one 8-lb. and one 16-lb poise; 1,000-lb beam, one 8-lb. and one 32-lb. poise; 1,200-lb. beam, one 16-lb. and one 32-lb. poise.

| Capacity, lbs. | 250 | 400 | 600 | 1,000 | 1,200 |
|---|---|---|---|---|---|
| Price, complete | $0.95 | 1.50 | 2.00 | 3.30 | 4.00 |

**YOU CAN SAVE THE PRICE OF YOUR SCALES......**
in a week by
**"KEEPING TAB" ON ......WHAT YOU BUY AND SELL**

## DEPARTMENT OF GARDEN TOOLS.

**In this line we offer only strictly high grade goods, made by concerns of well known and established reputation, and on this class of goods we are prepared to save you money. We can supply you at as little or less money than your dealer can buy in quantities.**

**It will pay you** to include all these goods in your order. Let us ship by freight and get you the correct freight rate. **One trial order** will demonstrate. Our economic one small profit plan works a great saving to the buyer.

## D Handle Spades.

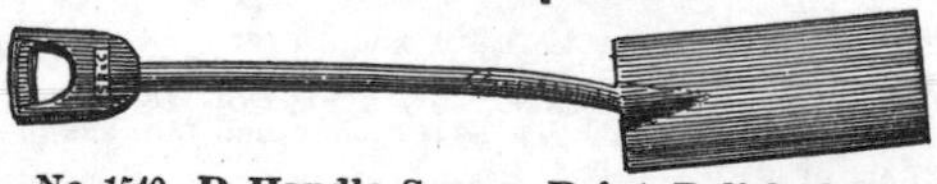

No. 1540 **D Handle Square Point, Polished Steel Spades.** Back and front strap, riveted. Size 7½x12 inches, which is full regular size. Every spade warranted. Each, **$0.50;** per dozen ........... **$5.50**

No. 1541 **D Handle Square Point Polished Spade.** made of solid crucible cast steel. Plain back socket straps. This is the highest grade spade on the market, every blade being made of selected crucible cast steel, fully warranted. Nothing better made. Size 7¼x12 inches. Each, **80c;** per dozen ....... **$8.75**

## Long Handle Spades.

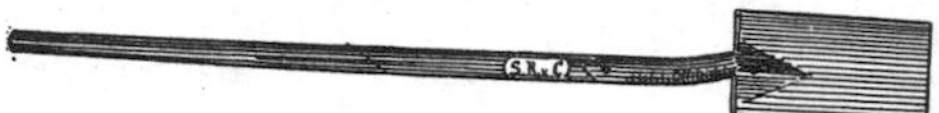

No. 1542 **Long Handle Square Point Polished Steel Spades.** Back and front strap riveted. Size 7¼x12 inches, full regular size. Warranted selected hickory handles. Each, **50c;** per dozen ....... **$5.50**

No. 1543 **Long Handle Square Point Polished Spade.** Made of solid crucible cast steel. Plain back socket straps, Same grade as our No. 1541. Fully warranted. Each, **80c;** per dozen ....... **$8.75**

## Square Point, Plain Back Shovels.

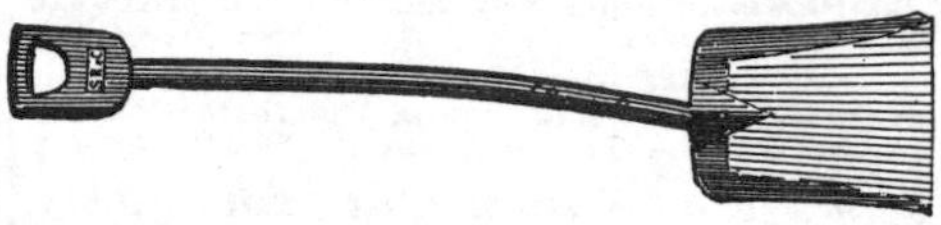

No. 1544 **D Handle Square Point Polished Shovels.** Back and front strap riveted. Size 9¾x12 inches, full regular size. Made of the best selected steel. Warranted. Each, **50c;** per dozen ..... **$5.50**

No. 1545 **D Handle Square Point Polished Shovels.** Made of solid crucible cast steel. Plain back socket straps. Made of selected stock. Nothing better made. Size 9¾x12 inches. Every spade fully warranted. Each, **80c;** per dozen ........... **$8.75**

## Long Handle Square Point Shovels

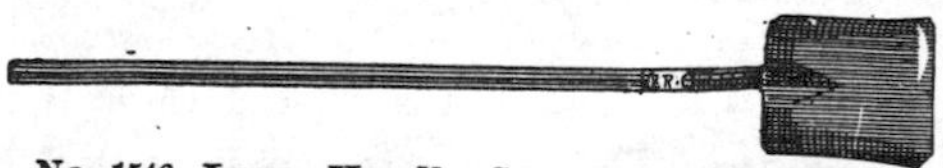

No. 1546 **Long Handle Square Point Polished Steel Shovels.** Back and front strap riveted. Size 9¾x12 inches. Made of selected steel. Each, **50c;** per dozen ........... **$5.50**

No. 1547 **Long Handle Square Point Shovels.** Made of solid crucible cast steel. Plain smooth back and socket straps, same grade as our No. 1545. Every shovel warranted. Best selected hickory handles. Each, **80c;** per dozen ........... **$8.75**

## Round Point, Solid Steel Shovels.

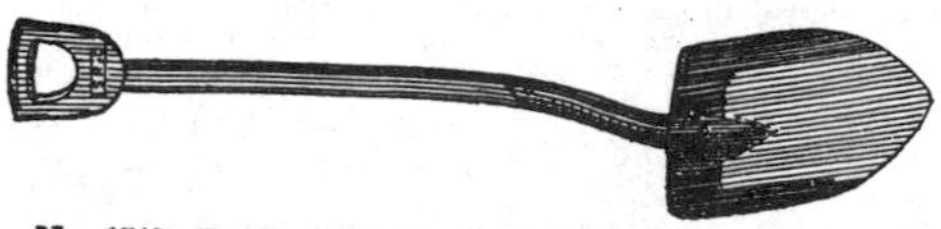

No. 1548 **D Handle, Round Point, Polished Steel Shovels.** Back and front straps riveted. Made of **steel, not iron.** Size, 9¾x12 in.
Each, **50c;** per doz ........... **$5.50**

No. 1549 **D Handle, Round Point, Polished Solid Crucible Cast Steel Shovels.** Made of the highest grade cast steel. Nothing better made. Plain back socket straps. Every shovel warranted.
Each, **80c;** per doz ........... **$8.75**

## Long Handle Shovels.

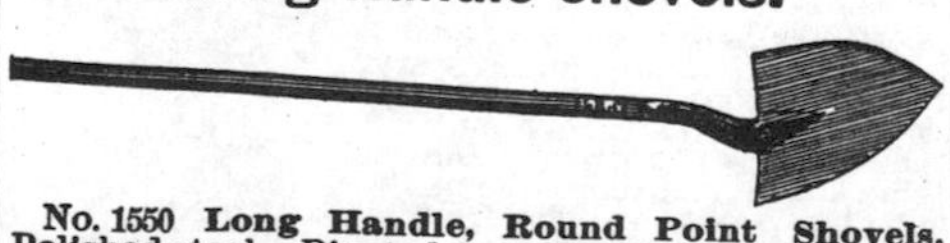

No. 1550 **Long Handle, Round Point Shovels.** Polished steel. Riveted front and back straps. Size 9¾x12 in., full regular size. Each, **50c;** per doz **$5.50**

No. 1551 **Long Handle, Round Point, Polished Solid Crucible Cast Steel Shovels.** Plain smooth back socket straps. Made of the finest cast steel. Nothing better made. Fully warranted.
Each, **80c;** per doz ........... **$8.75**

## Coal Shovels.

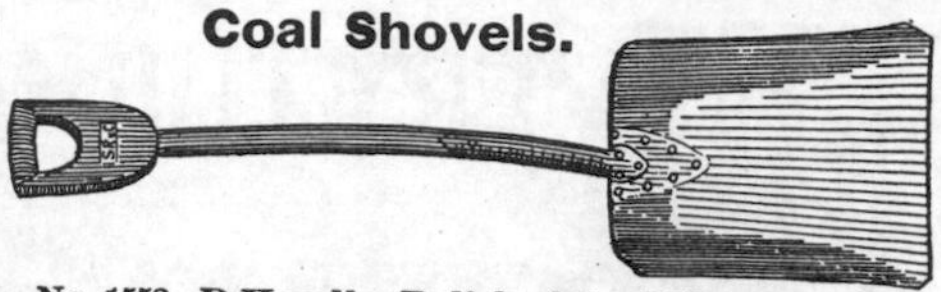

No. 1552 **D Handle, Polished Coal Shovels.** Made of extra fine cast steel. Plain back socket straps. Made of selected stock. Makes an excellent shovel for snow, grain or sawdust. Made in three sizes, as follows:

| | Size of Blades. | Each. | Per Doz. |
|---|---|---|---|
| No. 1. | 13 in. wide, 14½ in. long. | **$0.75** | **$ 8.10** |
| No. 2. | 14½ in. wide, 15 in. long. | **.85** | **9.20** |
| No. 3. | 15⅝ in. wide, 15⅝ in. long. | **.95** | **10.25** |

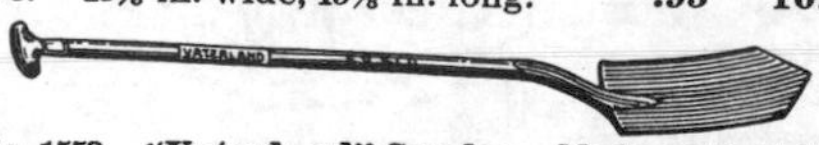

No. 1553. **"Vaterland" Spades.** Made of the highest grade steel, full polished. The cutting edges being angular, no steps are required, which allows the blade to scour from end to end. You can do more work with this spade than any tool made. We use extra all white hickory handles. Every spade fully warranted. **Try one.** Each, **85c;** per doz.. **$9.00**

## Scoop Shovels.

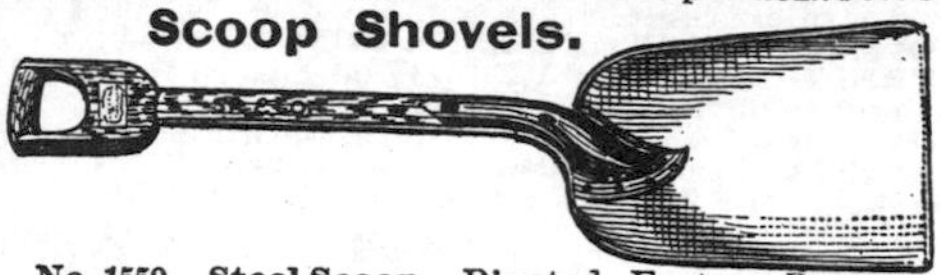

No. 1559. **Steel Scoop.** Riveted. Eastern Pattern, polished. **A good farmer's scoop.**

| | No. 3 | No. 5 | No. 7 | No. 9 |
|---|---|---|---|---|
| Width | 12½ in. | 12 in. | 13⅜ in. | 14¼ in. |
| Length | 15½ in. | 16½ in. | 17½ in. | 18¼ in. |
| Each | **$0.67** | **$0.72** | **$0.78** | **$0.83** |

No. 1560. **Steel Scoop.** Riveted, Eastern Pattern, socket strap, polished. This is a strong, well made, durable scoop, and is warranted.

| | No. 3 | No. 5 | No. 7 | No. 9 |
|---|---|---|---|---|
| Width | 12½ in. | 12 in. | 13⅜ in. | 14¼ in. |
| Length | 15½ in. | 16½ in. | 17½ in. | 18¼ in. |
| Each | **$0.82** | **$0.88** | **$0.95** | **$1.00** |

## Wire Potato Scoop.

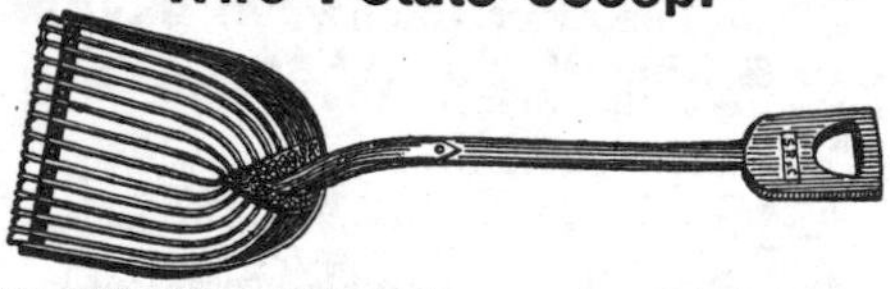

No. 1562. **Wire Potato Scoop.** Size 13½x16 inches.
Price, each ........... **$ 1.00**
Price, per doz ........... **11.88**

## The Potato Scoop Fork.

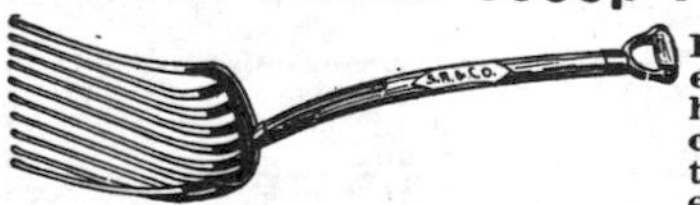

No. 1564. **This Fork is unequalled for handling corn,** potatoes, onions, etc. Made of one solid piece of cast steel. Will screen dirt from vegetables; handle corn without sticking in the cobs; pitch fine manure better than any fork or shovel made. Made in two sizes, as follows:
10 tines 14 in. wide and 16 in. long. Each... **$1.15**
Per doz ........... **12.25**
12 tines, 18 in. wide and 17 in. long. Each .. **1.45**
Per doz ........... **15.90**

## Drain Spades.

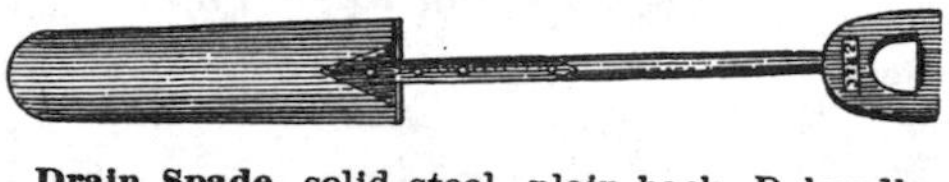

**Drain Spade,** solid steel, plain back, D handle, round point, blade tapers from 5½ inches at the step to 4½ inches at the point.
No. 1566 Length, 18 inches. Price, each...... **95c**
No. 1568 Length, 20 inches. Price, each...... **$1.c0**

## Post Spade.

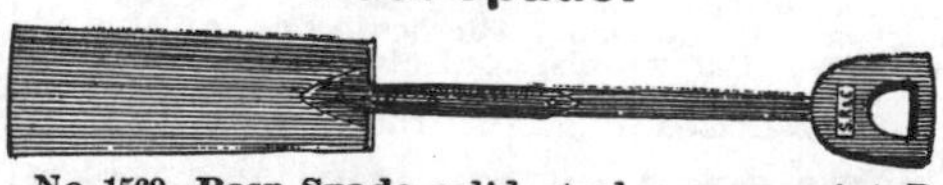

No. 1569 **Posr Spade,** solid steel square point, D handle, plain back; size 6¼x18 inchces. Each..... **95c**
No. 1570 **Same as No. 1569,** 6½x20 inches.
Price, each ........... **$1.00**

## Tiling Soades.

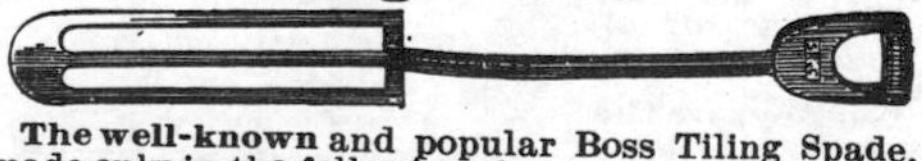

**The well-known** and popular Boss Tiling Spade, made only in the following sizes:
No. 1572 Size, 4¼x18, round point. Each..... **$1.55**
No. 1573 Size, 4½x20, round point. Each..... **$1.60**

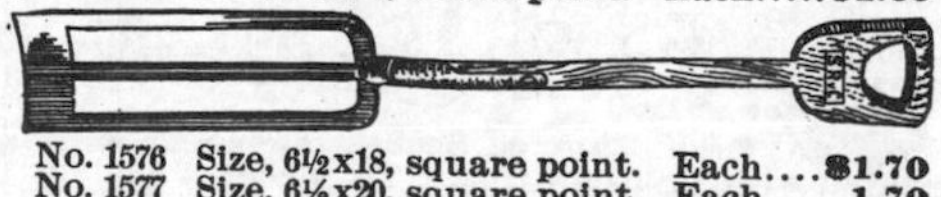

No. 1576 Size, 6½x18, square point. Each.... **$1.70**
No. 1577 Size, 6½x20, square point. Each.... **1.70**
No. 1578 Size, 6½x22, square point. Each.... **1.75**

**WE WANT TO [illegible] BEST. YOU MUST COOPERATE WITH US BY USING THE UTMOST CARE IN MAKING OUT YOUR**

## Drain Cleaners.

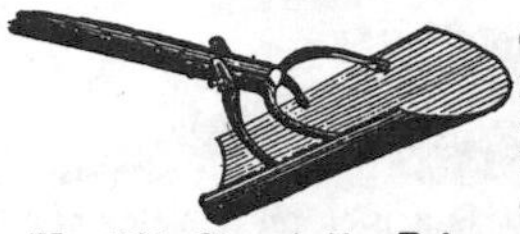

Adjustable Drain Cleaner, to push or pull, cast steel, polished. The strongest and best Drain Cleaner on the market.

No. 1580 Size, 4x16. Price, each....................85c
No. 1581 Size, 5x16. Price, each....................90c
No. 1582 Size, 6x16. Price, each....................95c

## Spading Forks.

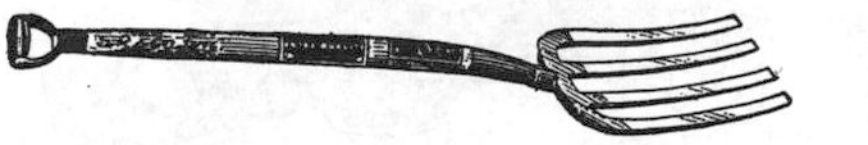

No. 1585 D handle, capped ferrule, Spading Fork, 4 flat steel tines. Price, each, 50c; Per dozen..$7.50
No. 1586 D handle, capped and strapped ferrule, Spading Fork, 4 heavy angular steel tines. The strongest and best spading fork made.
Price, each.........60c; Per dozen.........$6.50

## Coke Forks.

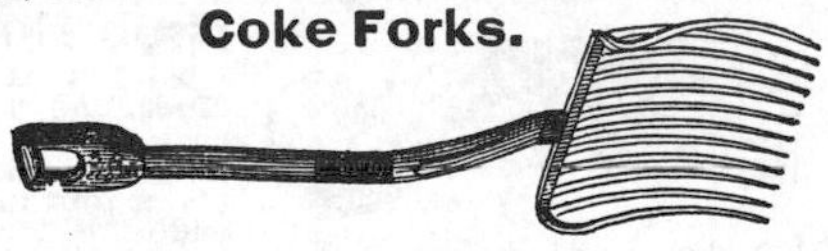

Coke Forks. Made of the best cast steel, strapped ferrule, D handle.
No. 1587 Price, each, 10 tooth....................$1.35
No. 1588 Price, each, 12 tooth....................1.75
No. 1589 Price, each, 14 tooth....................1.90

## Manure and Potato Hooks.

No. 1591 Manure Hooks, 4 tines, plain ferrule, made from one piece of best crucible steel. Each....................32c

## Potato Hooks.

No. 1593 Potato Digger, 4 round tines.
Price, each.........25c; Per dozen..........$2.90
No. 1594 Potato Digger, 4 flat tines.
Price, each.........25c; Per dozen..........$2.90

## Shovel Handles.

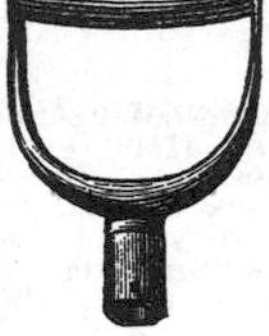

No. 1596. Malleable "Ds" for fork or shovel handles.
Price, each....................$0.07
Per doz .................... 0.70

**Get your neighbors interested, and club together for a mixed freight order.**

## Hay Forks.

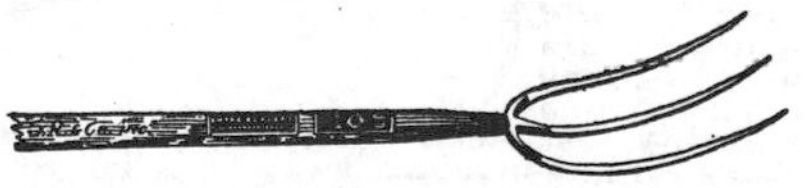

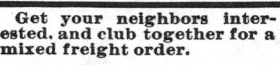

This cut shows the Plain Ferrule.

Straight handle, Plain Capped Ferrule Hay Forks, 3 oval tines, standard size and length; selected handles.

| | No. 1597 | No. 1597 | No. 1598 | No. 1599 | No. 1600 |
|---|---|---|---|---|---|
| Length of handle, ft.. | 4 | 4½ | 5 | 5½ | 6 |
| Price, each........... | $0.29 | $0.29 | $0.29 | $0.30 | $0.31 |
| Price, dozen.......... | 3.25 | 3.25 | 3.25 | 3.33 | 3.45 |

Straight handle, capped and strapped ferrule Hay Forks, 3 oval tines, standard size and length; selected handles.

| | No. 1605 | No. 1806 | No. 1606 | No. 1607 | No. 1608 |
|---|---|---|---|---|---|
| Length of handle, ft.. | 4 | 4½ | 5 | 5½ | 6 |
| Price, each........ | $0.34 | $0.34 | $0.34 | $0.35 | $0.36 |
| Price, dozen | 3.75 | 3.75 | 3.75 | 3.87 | 4.00 |

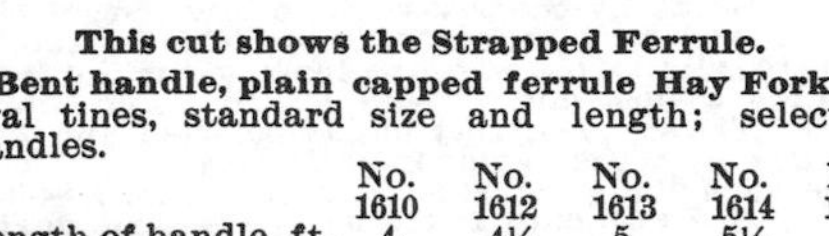

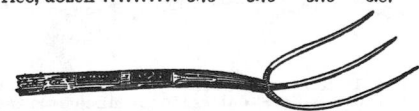

This cut shows the Strapped Ferrule.

Bent handle, plain capped ferrule Hay Forks, 3 oval tines, standard size and length; selected handles.

| | No. 1610 | No. 1612 | No. 1613 | No. 1614 | No. 1616 |
|---|---|---|---|---|---|
| Length of handle, ft.. | 4 | 4½ | 5 | 5½ | 6 |
| Price, each........... | $0.30 | $0.30 | $0.30 | $0.32 | $0.33 |
| Price, dozen.......... | 3.39 | 3.36 | 3.39 | 3.50 | 3.62 |

Bent handle, capped and strapped ferrule Hay Forks, 3 oval tines, standard size and length; selected handles.

| | No. 1618 | No. 1620 | No. 1621 | No. 1622 | No. 1624 |
|---|---|---|---|---|---|
| Length of handle ft.. | 4 | 4½ | 5 | 5½ | 6 |
| Price, each........... | $0.35 | $0.35 | $0.35 | $0.36 | $0.37 |
| Price, dozen........... | 3.92 | 3.92 | 3.92 | 4.04 | 4.17 |

**REMEMBER OUR LIBERAL DISCOUNT OF 3 PER CENT....... When cash in full accompanies order.**

## Four Tine, Bent Handle Hay Fork.

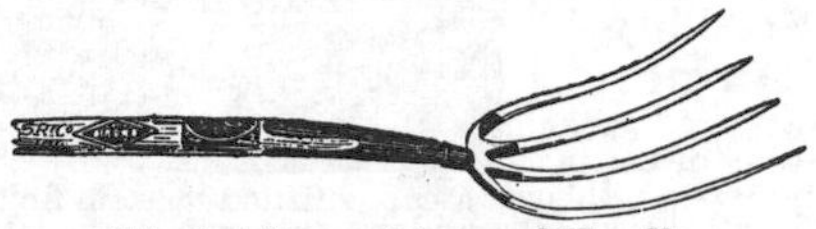

This Cut Shows Strapped Handle.

No. 1630 Bent Handle Capped and Plain Ferruled. 4 oval tines. Selected handles.

| Length of Handles, feet......... | 4½ | 5 | 5½ |
|---|---|---|---|
| Price each........ | $0.41 | $0.41 | $0.45 |
| Price, doz.................... | 4.30 | 4.30 | 4.85 |

No. 1631 Bent Handle Capped and Strapped Ferrule. 4 oval tines. Selected handles.

| Length of Handles, feet......... | 4½ | 5 | 5½ |
|---|---|---|---|
| Price, each.................... | $0.46 | $0.46 | $0.50 |
| Price, doz .................... | 5.10 | 5.10 | 5.50 |

## Manure Forks.

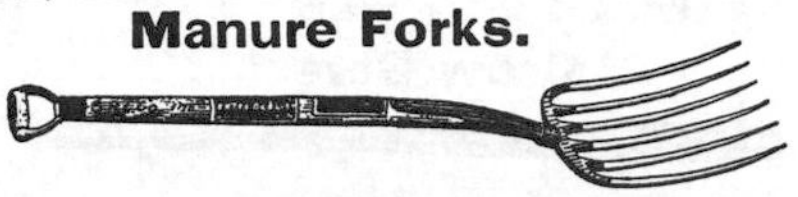

Made of best crucible steel, gold bronze finish, D handle, plain ferrule Manure Forks, oval tines 12 inches long. No better goods made anywhere.
No. 1635 4 tines; price, each 40c; doz........ $4.75
No. 1636 5 tines; price, each 57c; doz........ 6.75
No. 1637 6 tines; price, each 70c; doz........ 8.00
D Handle Capped and Straped Ferrule Manure Forks. Oval tines 12 in. long.
No. 1640 4 tines; price each 43c; doz........ $4.75
No. 1641 5 tines; price each 60c; doz........ 8.00
No. 1642 6 tines; price each 72c; doz........ 8.50

## Long Handle Manure Forks.

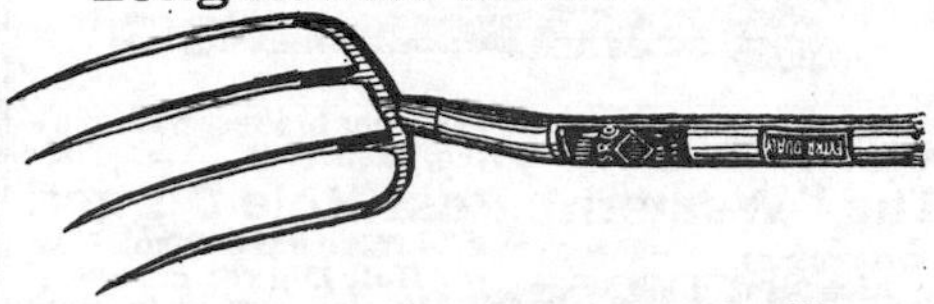

Long Handle Capped Plain Ferrule Manure Forks. Oval tines, 12 in. long.
No. 1644 4 Tines. Each, 37c; per doz.......... $4.25
5 Tines. Each, 57c; per doz.......... 6.56
6 Tines. Each, 66c; per doz.......... 7.65
Long Handle Capped and Strapped Ferrule Manure Forks. Oval tines 12 in. long.
No. 1645 4 Tines. Each, 40c; per doz.......... $4.62
5 Tines. Each, 62c; per doz.......... 7.05
6 Tines. Each, 70c; per doz.......... 8.10

## Barley Fork.

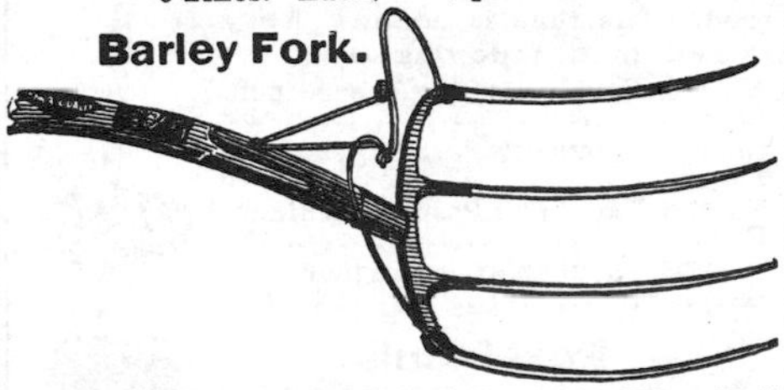

Steel Barley Fork with Adjustable Wire Bail and Brace. 4 tines 18 in. long. Long Handles.
No. 1648 Plain ferrule, each 65c; doz........$7.60
No. 1649 Strapped ferrule, each 69c; doz ...$8.51

## Hoes.

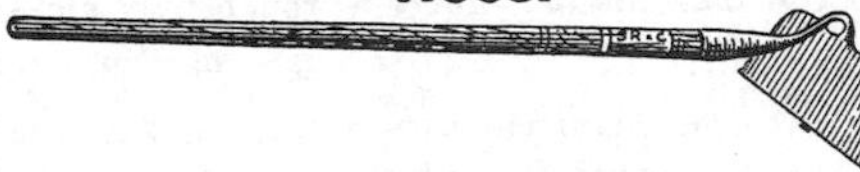

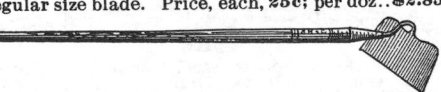

No. 1651 Common Shaped Hoes, with Cast Steel Blade wielded to Shank. Selected handles, full regular size blade. Price, each, 25c; per doz..$2.85

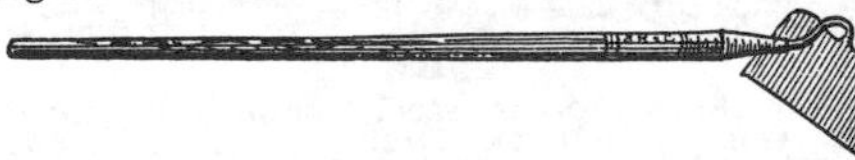

No. 1652 Common Shaped Hoes, with Cast Steel Blade welded to Socket. Selected handles, full regular size blade. Price, each, 28c; per doz..$3.00

## Boys' Hoes.

Common Shaped Boys' Hoes. Cast steel blade, solid shank. Selected handles, small size blade.
No. 1653 Each, 21c; per doz....................$2.40

## Solid Shank Mortar Hoes.

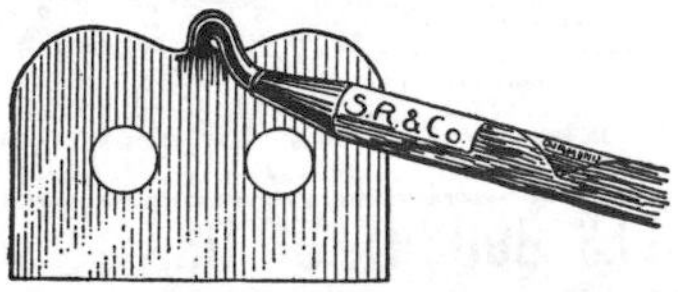


Solid Shank Mortar Mixer. Finest hoe made for mixing mortar. Also an excellent hoe for cleaning irrigating ditches, as it allows the water to pass through the holes while the mud and refuse is drawn out. Blade 10 in. wide. Each, 50c; per doz....$.580
No. 1655 Same as above, without Holes in Blade. Each, 45c; per doz....................$5.20

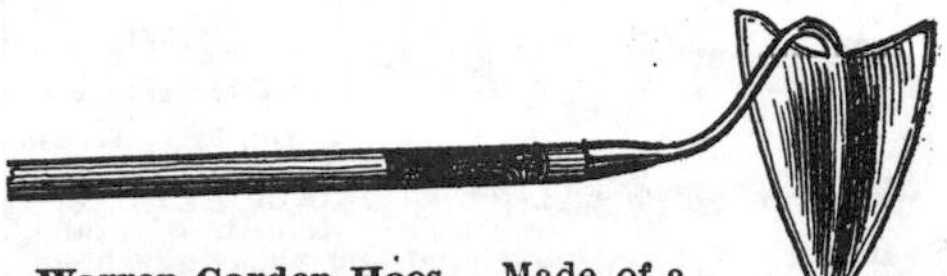

Warren Garden Hoes. Made of a piece of cast steel. Polished Blades.
No. 1657 Garden Size. Each, 45c; per doz...$4.80
No. 1658 Field Size. Each, 55c; per doz... .$5.47

## Weeding Hoe and Rake.

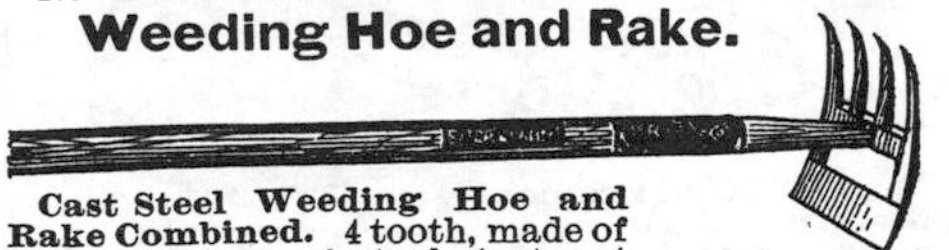

Cast Steel Weeding Hoe and Rake Combined. 4 tooth, made of one solid piece of steel, (not cast iron.) No. 1660 Each, 27c; per doz............$3.25

## Scuffle Hoes.

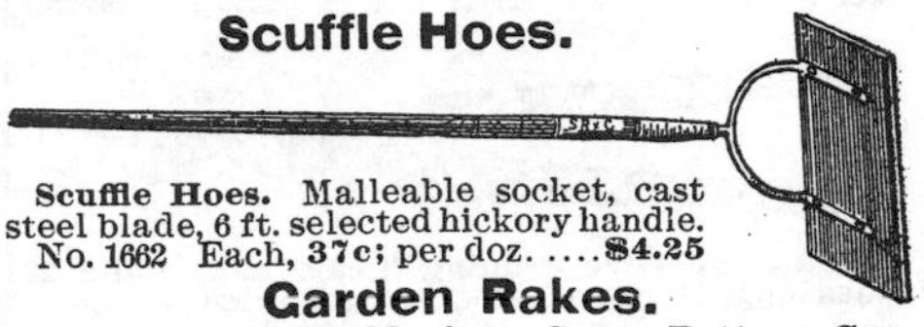

Scuffle Hoes. Malleable socket, cast steel blade, 6 ft. selected hickory handle.
No. 1662 Each, 37c; per doz. ....$4.25

## Garden Rakes.

Malleable iron Curve Pattern Garden Rake.

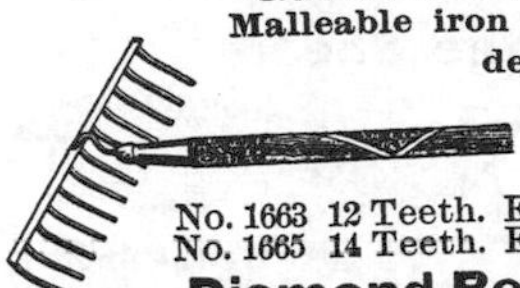

**ORDER BY NUMBER.**

No. 1663 12 Teeth. Each, 20c.; doz...$2.00
No. 1665 14 Teeth. Each, 23c.; doz... 2.25

## Diamond Bow Steel Rakes.

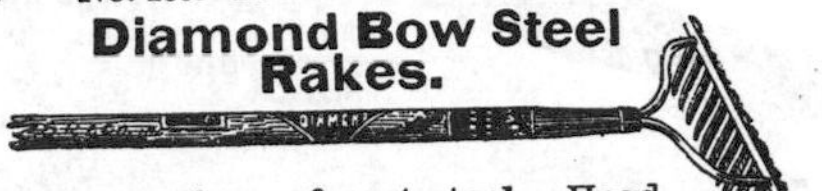

Made of one piece of cast steel. Head, teeth, braces full polish—selected handles.
No. 1667 12 Teeth. Each, 40c.; doz...$4.60
No. 1668 14 Teeth. Each, 45c.; doz... 5.25

**The Hustler Lawn Rake**

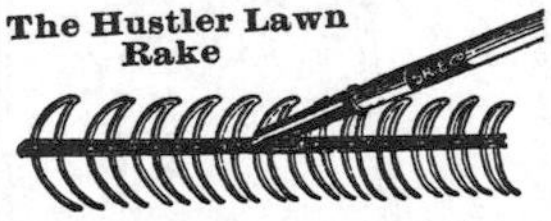

Braced steel head with 24 steel teeth wire teeth—light and durable. The best rake ever made for the money.
No. 1669 Price, each, 35c.; per doz..........$4.00

**The Gibbs Lawn Rake.** Solid malleable iron frame—30 wire teeth.
No. 1671 Each...50c
Per doz.......$5.95

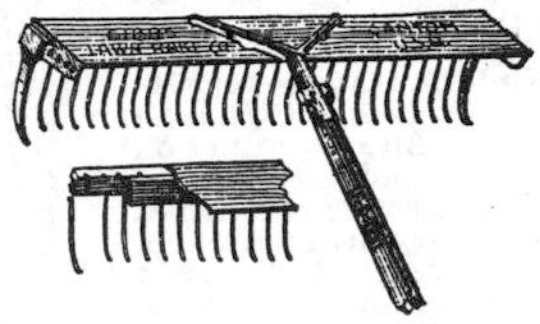

## Garden Trowels.

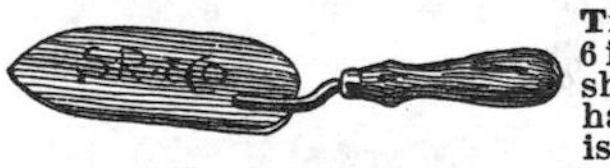

No. 1672 Garden Trowel. Steel blade 6 inches long, steel shank. Hardwood handle, cherry finish.
Each ........ ......$0.05 Per doz..........$0.54

## Strawberry Fork.

No. 1674 Garden Fork. Malleable hardwood handle.
Price, each..$0.05
Per doz..... 0.54

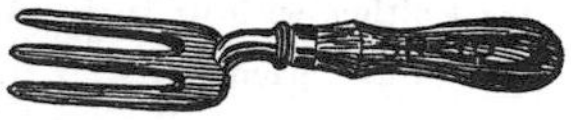

## Excelsior Weeder.

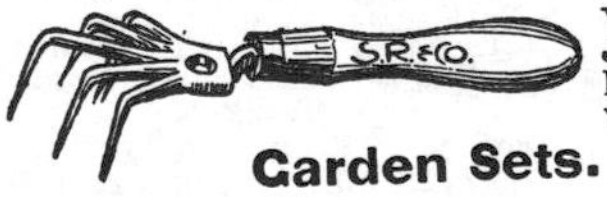


No. 1675 Excelsior Weeder, 5 Prongs, Japanned. Malleable iron hardwood handle.
Price, each..$0.05
Per doz..... 0.54

## Garden Sets.

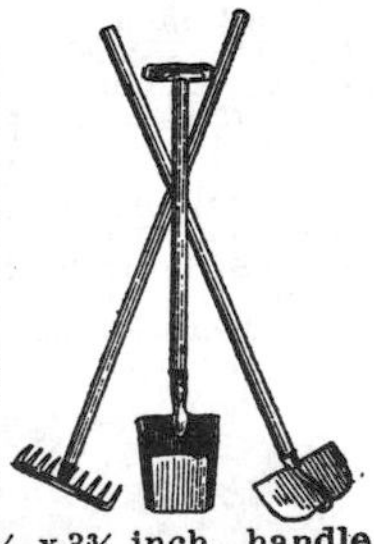

No. 1678 The Wonder Garden Set. Consisting of three pieces; spade—polished steel blade 4½ x 3½ inches with handle 16 inches long; hoe, polished steel blade 3¾ x 2¼ inches with handle 24 inches long; rake, malleable iron japanned 3 inches in breadth with handle 22 inches long. all handles of hardwood varnished.
Price per set of 3 pieces as described above........$0.15
No. 1680 The Marvel Garden Set. Same style as 1678 set but larger and better finished. Consists of three pieces as follows, spade, polished steel blade 5½ x 3¾ inch, handle 18 inches long, hoe polished steel blade 5¼ x 3½ inch, handle 30 inches long. rake malleable iron turned, 5¾ inch, broad handle 30 inches long. All handles of hardwood varnished.
Price per set of three pieces as described above ..............................................$0.20

**IF YOU WILL MAKE UP AN ORDER OF GROCERIES AT THE SAME TIME YOU WANT OTHER GOODS, YOU CAN HAVE THE WHOLE SHIPMENT SENT BY FREIGHT AT A MINIMUM COST OF TRANSPORTATION.**

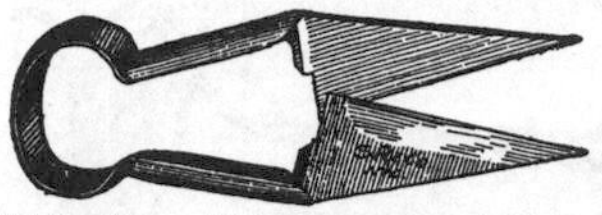

## Grass Shears.

No. 1682 **Grass Shears,** like cut; bent handles; length of blade, 5½ inches. Not recommended for shearing sheep. Price, each, **20c**; per dozen....................**$2.25**

## Pruning Shears.

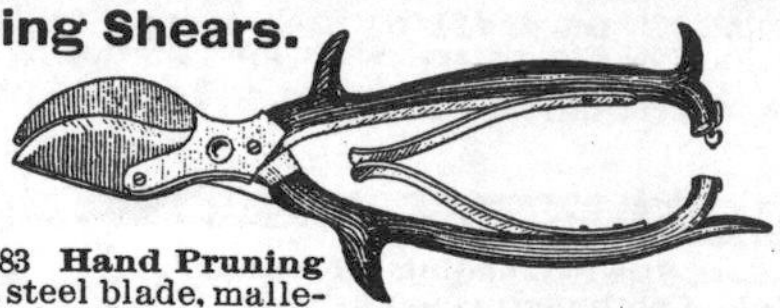

No. 1683 **Hand Pruning Shears,** steel blade, malleable iron handles, brass springs. The most popular hand pruning shear made. Price, each, **20c**; per dozen....................**$2.35**

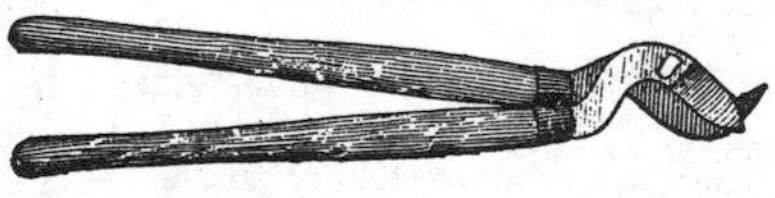

No. 1684 **Buckeye Pruning Shears,** ash handle, 22 inches long, 2 inch cast steel cutter. Price, each.**55c**

## Hedge Shears.

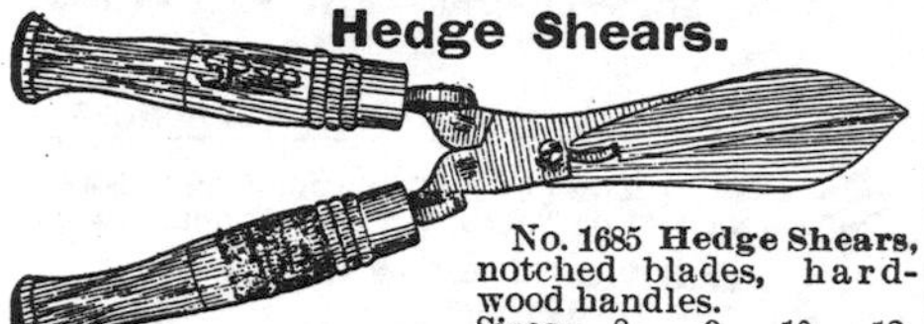

No. 1685 **Hedge Shears,** notched blades, hard-wood handles.

| Sizes, | 8 | 9 | 10 | 12 |
|---|---|---|---|---|
| Each, | $0.85 | $1.00 | $1.10 | $1.65 |

## Tree Pruner.

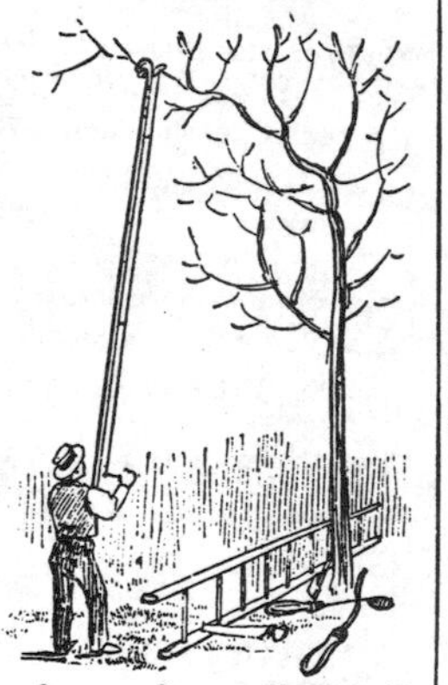

No. 1686 **The Standard Tree Pruner,** with latest improvements, is considered by fruit growers and gardeners **the best in the market.** Although the cutting blade is very thin, it being supported on **both sides** by the hook, makes **it strong and durable.** It will cut off the largest bough the hook will admit, and also clip the smallest twig. **No ladders are required,** as pruning can be done while standing on the ground.

No. 1687 Extra knives for above pruners, each, ....................**20c**

| Length, feet, | 4 | 6 | 8 | 10 | 12 |
|---|---|---|---|---|---|
| Weight, lbs., | 2¼ | 3 | 3½ | 4 | 4½ |
| Price, each, | $0.40 | $0.45 | $0.50 | $0.55 | $0.60 |

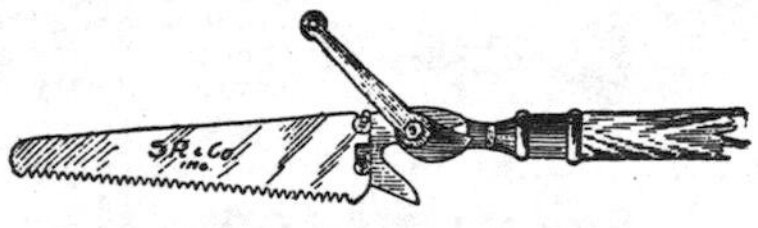

No. 1688 **Disston's Pruning Hook and Saw,** can be used either with or without saw, as the saw is easily and quickly taken off. The pole is not furnished. Price, each....................**$1.20**

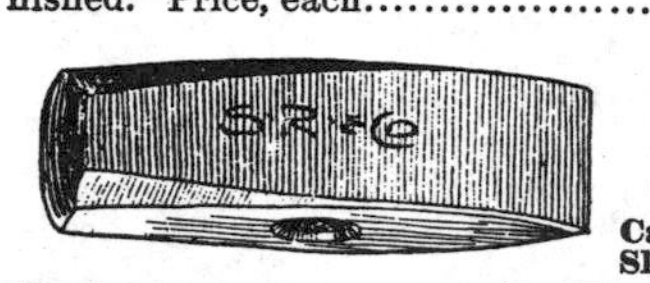

## Stone Sledges.

No. 1690 **Solid Cast Steel Stone Sledges.**

| Weight, lbs., | 8 | 9 | 10 | 11 | 12 | 13 | 14 | 15 | 16 |
|---|---|---|---|---|---|---|---|---|---|
| Price, each, | $0.64 | .72 | .80 | .88 | .96 | 1.04 | 1.12 | 1.20 | 1.28 |

No. 1691. **Sledge Handles,** second growth hickory, XXX grade. Each **10c**; per doz.......... **$1.00**

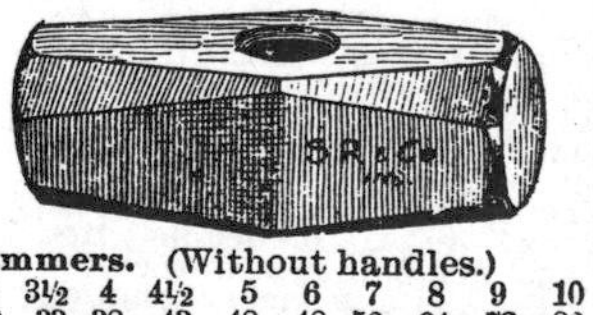

No. 1692 **Solid Cast Steel Drilling or Striking Hammers.** (Without handles.)

| Weight, lbs., | 2½ | 3 | 3½ | 4 | 4½ | 5 | 6 | 7 | 8 | 9 | 10 |
|---|---|---|---|---|---|---|---|---|---|---|---|
| Price, each, | $0.30 | .29 | .33 | .38 | .43 | .48 | .48 | .56 | .64 | .72 | .80 |

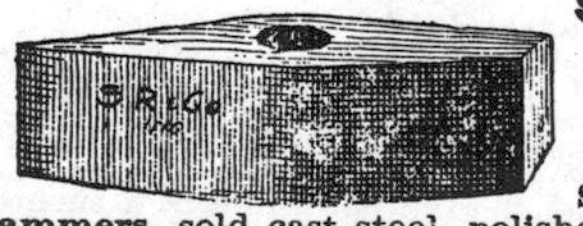

## Single Face Spalling Hammers.

**Single Face Spalling or Stone Hammers,** sold cast steel, polished face, oil finish. Nothing better made.

No. 1694 Price, 3 lbs. and under, per lb..........**10c**
No. 1695 " 3 to 5 lbs., " ..........**9½c**
No. 1696 " 5 lbs. and over, " ..........**9c**

## Double Fac Spalling Hammers.

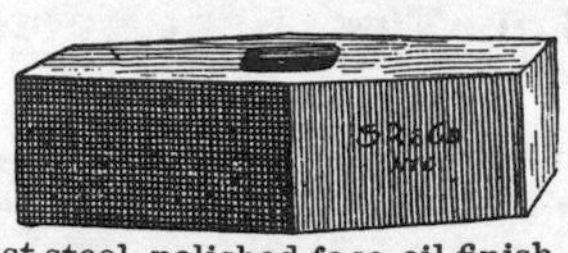

**Double Face Spalling or Stone Hammers.** Solid cast steel, polished face, oil finish.
No. 1700 Price, 3 lbs. and under, per lb..........**10c**
No. 1701 " 3 to 5 lbs., " ..........**9½c**
No. 1702 " 5 lbs. and over, " ..........**9c**

## Stone Axe.

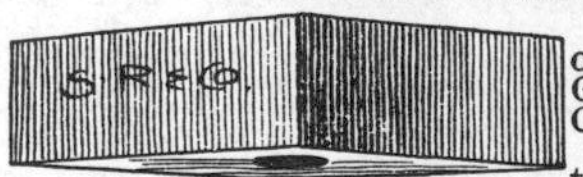

**Stone Axe.** Made of the Highest Grade Tool Steel. Oil finish.
No. 1703 Price, 3lb to 5 lb, per lb.**16½c**
No. 1704 Price, 5lb to 12lb, per lb.......... **16c**

## Crow Bars.

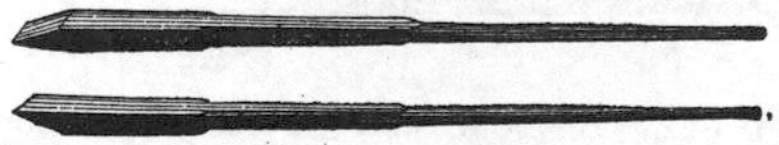

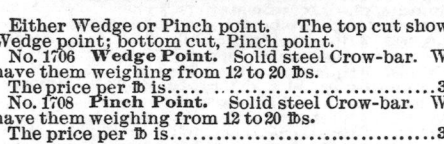

Either Wedge or Pinch point. The top cut shows Wedge point; bottom cut, Pinch point.

No. 1706 **Wedge Point.** Solid steel Crow-bar. We have them weighing from 12 to 20 lbs.
The price per lb is....................**3c**

No. 1708 **Pinch Point.** Solid steel Crow-bar. We have them weighing from 12 to 20 lbs.
The price per lb is....................**3c**

## Eureka Post Hole Digger.

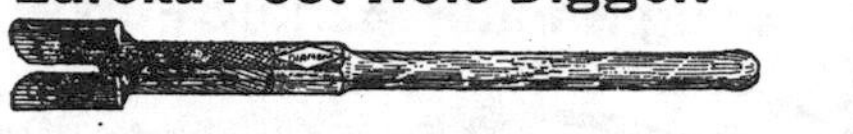

No. 1709 **The Eureka,** cast steel blades with malleable iron mounting. Price, each....................**85c**

## The "Western" Post Hole Digger.

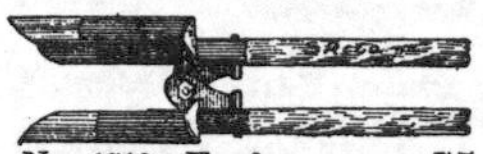

**The "Western" Post Hole Digger,** cast steel blades, heavy malleable mounting, selected handles.
No. 1710 Each..........**75c**; Per dozen......**$8.75**

## Post Hole Augers.

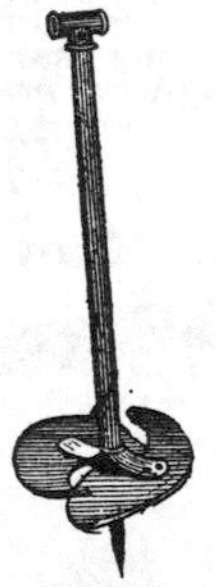

**These are the well known goods made by Vaughan & Bushnell; blades are of solid cast steel, spring tempered. The tube is hollow. They are made in the following sizes:**

No. 1712 Vaughan's Post Auger 6 inch. Each....................**45c**
No. 1713 Vaughan's Post Auger 7 inch. Each....................**45c**
No. 1714 Vaughan's Post Auger 8 inch. Each....................**45c**
No. 1715 Vaughan's Post Auger 9 inch. Each....................**45c**

## Post Mauls.

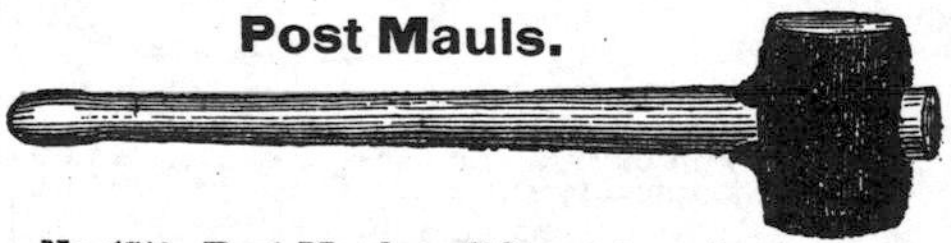

No. 1716 **Post Mauls,** solid cast iron, heavy, hickory handles.

| Weight, lbs.......... | 10 | 13 | 16 | 18 | 20 |
|---|---|---|---|---|---|
| Price, each.......... | $0.22 | .25 | .30 | .40 | .45 |

No. 1717 **Post Maul Handles,** each..........**8c**

## Railroad Picks.

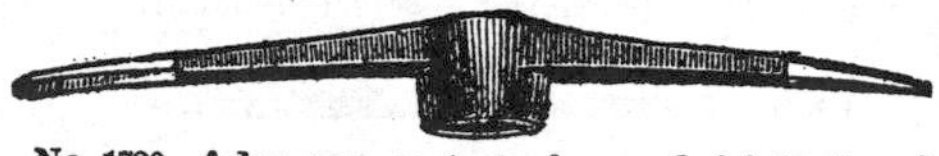

No. 1720 **Adze eye,** cast steel, axe finish Railroad Picks. Weights, 5 to 6 lbs. Each....................**30c**
No. 1721 **Hickory handle,** 36 inches long, for above picks. Each....................**9c**

## Drifting Picks.

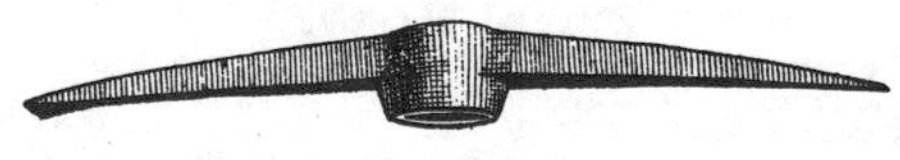

No. 1724 **Drifling Picks,** adze eye, oil finish.

| No.......... | 1 | 2 | 3 | 4 |
|---|---|---|---|---|
| Weight.......... | 3 lbs. | 4 lbs. | 4½ lbs. | 5 lbs. |
| Each.......... | 30c. | 34c. | 36c. | 39c. |
| Dozen.......... | $3.50 | $3.80 | $4.10 | $4.25 |

No. 1725 **Hickory handles for above picks,** 36 inches long. Each....................**9c**



## Pick Mattocks.

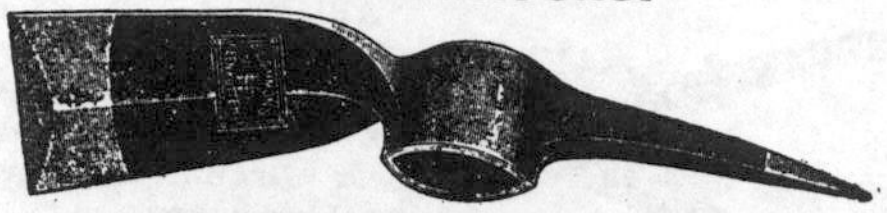

No. 1727 **Pick Mattock** is a pick on one side and a mattock on the other, as shown in above cut. Adze eye, extra tool steel, axe finish. Price. each.....**45c**
No. 1728 **Handle for above.** Each....................**9c**

## Mattocks.

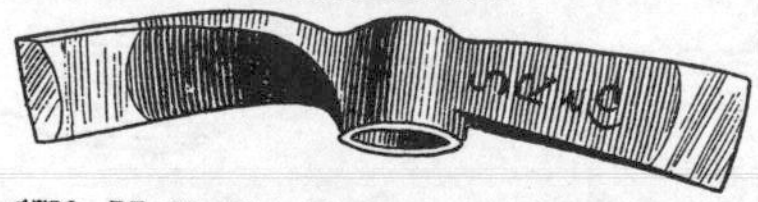

No. 1730 **Mattock.** Long cutter, cast steel, adze eye, axe finish; weight 5 to 6 lbs. Each....... **$0.37**
No. 1731 **Mattock.** Short cutter, same as above; weight 4½ lbs. Each....... **$0.35**
No. 1732 **Handles for above.** Hickory, 36 inches long. Each....................**$0.09**

## Grub Hoes.

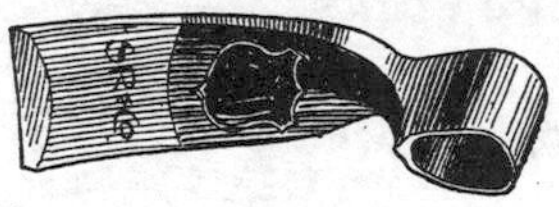

No. 1734 **Grub Hoes,** adze eye, cast steel, axe finish, blade is about four inches wide.
Price, each....................**$0.35**
No. 1735 **Handles for above.** Each.......... **.10**

## Hazel Hoes.

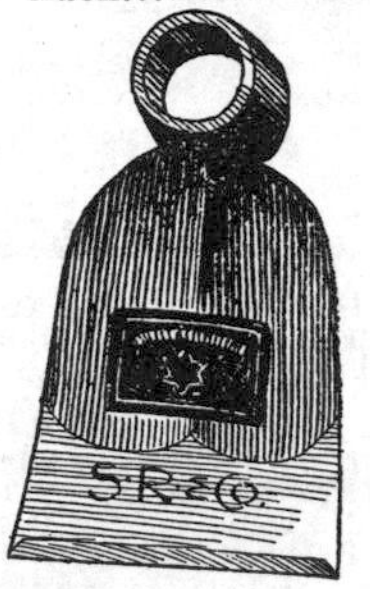

No. 1737 **Hazel Hoes.** Size is about 6 inch cut, 10 inch long, and weighs about 3 lbs. Adze eye, cast steel, axe finish.
Price, each.......... **$0.40**
No. 1738 **Handles for above.**
Price each.......... **$0.15**

**ORDER BY NUMBER.**

## Bush Hooks.

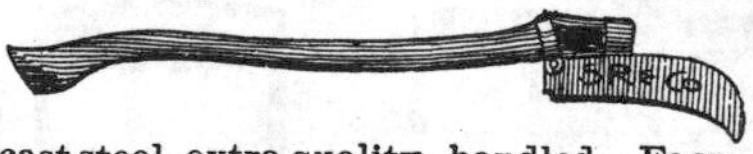

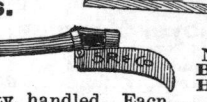

No. 1749 **Bush Hooks,** cast steel, extra quality, handled. Eacn..... **$0.60**

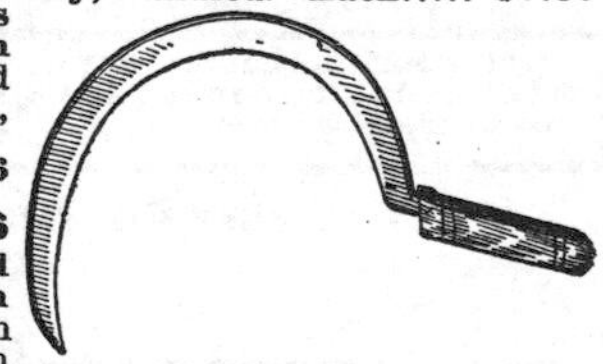

No. 1741 **Grass Hook or Smooth Edge Sickle,** good quality cast steel, medium size.
Price, each. **$0.16**

## Grain Sickles

No. 1742 **The Old Fashioned Grain Sickle** with rough edge, made from extra quality cast steel. Price, each, small **20c**; medium, **25c**; large....................**$0.30**

## Grain Cradles.

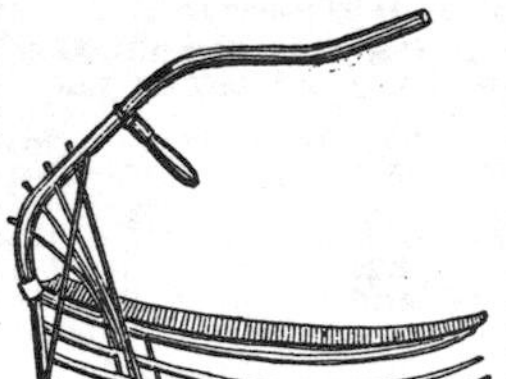

No. 1744 **Morgan Grain Cradle,** 4 fingers, grape vine pattern, wood brace, ring fastening, silver steel scythe.
Price, each...... **$2.25**
No. 1745 **Grain Cradle,** same as above, with iron brace.
Price, each...... **$2.25**

## Scythes.

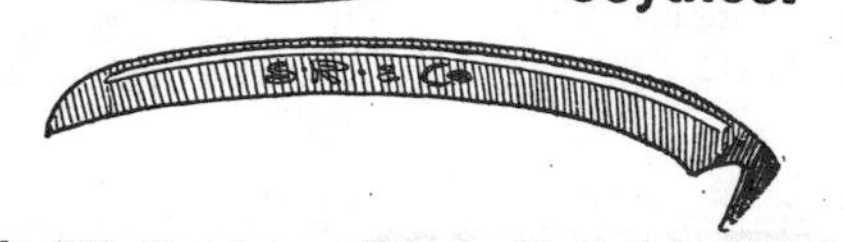

No. 1746 **Dutchman Patern, Steel Back Scythe,** made of the very finest cutlas steel. Made from the best material, by the best workmen, by one of the largest and best manufacturers. This scythe is made to sell to those who are looking for the **best possible goods,** and is sold at our usual small profit. The scythe is very highly polished and has no paint or bronze to hide imperfection.
Priee, each **45c**; per doz....................**$5.25**
No. 1748 **Dutchman Pattern Scythe,** same shape as above, painted aud bronzed.
Price, each, **40c**; per doz....................**$4.45**

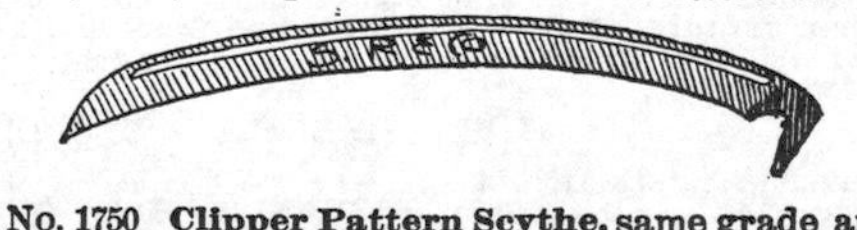

No. 1750 **Clipper Pattern Scythe,** same grade and finish as 1746, only a different shape.
Price, each, **50c**; per doz....................**$5.75**
No. 1751 **Clipper Pattern Scythe,** bronzed, polished web, ground sharp, good or better than is usually sold. Price, each, **45c**; per doz....................**$4.85**

**WE MAIL AN ELABORATE BABY CARRIAGE CATALOGUE FREE ON APPLICATION. OUR SPECIAL BICYCLE CATALOGUE ALSO ILLUSTRATES BABY SEATS TO CARRY THE BABY ON YOUR BICYCLE WITH YOU.**

## Weed Scythe.

No. 1753. Weed Scythes. Extra cast steel.
nch...... $0.40 Per dozen.........$4.50

## Bush Snath.

No. 1754. Cast Steel
Bush Snath.
Price, each, $0.40

## Grass Snath.

No. 1756. Patent loop Scythe Snath for grass scythes (not heavy enough for brush scythes), complete with wrench. Price, each..................$0.55

## Bush Snath.

No. 1757. Bush Snath for Bush Scythes.
Price................................$0.60

## Scythe Stones.

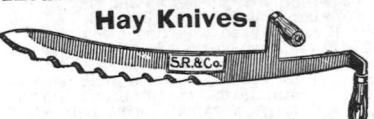

No. 1759. The celebrated Indian Pond Scythe Stones.
Price, each....$0.05
Per dozen...... 0.50
No. 1760. The Ragg Scythe Stone, flat.
Price, each....... $0.06 Per dozen .........$0.67
No. 1761. The Black Diamond Stone, (see cut) finest stone on the market. Nothing better.
Price, each........$0.07 Per dozen ..........$0.75
The above are full size, Regular Goods.

## Hay Knives.

No. 1764. The old well known Lightning Pattern Hay Knife, so well known an illustration is all that is necessary to describe it. Price, each.......$0.50

No. 1766. The Heath Upright Hay Knife. Made of the best material. Cast steel sections same as used on a mowing machine. Each............$ 1.00
Per dozen........................ 11.00

## Corn Knives.

No. 1767. The Acorn Corn Knife. Cast Steel blade. 3 rivets. Price, each .....................$0.22
Per dozen........................... 2.40

No. 1796. The Clipper Corn Knife. Cast steel blade; handle riveted on. Price, each.........$0.20
Per dozen ......................$2.30

## Corn Hooks.

No. 1771. Corn Hook. Common pattern, cast steel blade, two rivets. Price, each, $0.15
Per dozen .. 1.75

## Lightning Corn Knife.

No. 1772. Made of the finest oil tempered steel, full polished. Each, $0.15
Per dozen.......... 3.33

## OUR ACME HIGH GRADE LAWN MOWERS.

For the coming season we offer the **Highest Grade Lawn Mowers** at prices that will defy competition. The enormous grade we were favored with last year has induced us to make very extensive preparations for the coming season. We have contracted with one of the largest and most reliable makers in the country for such a large quantity on the basis of cost to produce, that we can now offer our customers a strictly high grade guaranteed Lawn Mower for about one-half the price they would be compelled to pay local dealers. **OUR ACME LAWN MOWERS** are guaranteed the best made. While we invite a close comparison of our prices with those of any other house on strictly high grade machines, we do not wish them compared with inferior machines, which were made to sell and not for service. Every Acme Machine is guaranteed to give perfect satisfaction. The Acme has many reliable improvements not found in other makes.

**THE ACME MOWERS** **Have the Latest Patent Micrometer Adjustment.** The adjusting box is held in position on the frame by a bolt and nut at the end opposite the set screw. By moving the set screw the adjusting box is carried upward or downward, enabling the reel knives, which are carried on the axle. to be adjusted to the cutter bar as may be desired or is necessary. Tightening one screw and loosening the other, brings the reel bars closer to the cutter bar, and vice versa. **We claim this to be the greatest improvement ever made in Lawn Mowers.** The adjustment is not only easy, simple and accurate, but it allows the reel knives or more delicate parts of the apparatus to be adjusted to the cutter bar or heavier part, instead of the reverse, as on other makes. The application of this principle makes another advantage possible, that of a solid and permanent attachment for the cutter bar, thus greatly increasing the strength and wearing qualities of the Mower.

### Our $2.35 Razor Blade Acme Lawn Mower.

At $2.35 we offer a lawn mower which will compare favorably with any machine you can buy in your local market at double the price. After thorough and exacting tests we offer this lawn mower, confident that it will justify every claim we make for it. It is especially adapted to small lawns. It is extremely light, making it easy to carry from place to place. **Special care** has been taken in the selection of all the material entering into its construction. Simplicity of construction, easy and accurate operation, durability and finish make this undoubtedly the best light mower on the market. The mower has an improved cutter-bar of solid tool steel, tempered and oiled. **The knives** have a positive shear cut and are regulated by the improved micrometer adjustment. The shafts run in phosphor bronze bearings, adding greatly to the ease and smoothness of running. New malleable iron handle brace made in one piece. Diameter of traction wheel, 7 inches; reel, 5 inches. All parts are interchangeable and can be replaced at once with little expense in case of breakage or wear.
No. 1774. Your choice of 10-inch, 12-inch, 14-inch or 16-inch..........................................$2.35
**Remember there is a 3 per cent. cash discount if cash in full accompanies your order.**

### Our Acme Lawn Mowers At $3.50 to $4.20.

12, 14 and 16 inch Mower at $3.50; 18 inch at $3.85 and the 20 inch at $4.20. Three per cent. discount allowed if cash in full accompanies your order.
**This is our standard high grade Acme machine** and is greatly improved for this season. The drive wheels are open for one-inch below the tread, though the working parts are completely enclosed. **It is the easiest running lawn mower made** because the handle brace is so attached to the drive wheel that the power is applied to the center of motion. **This machine** is especially designed for cutting thick and heavy grass with ease, the handle having a malleable iron hook which is adjusted to the shrubbery guard, thus holding the machine rigidly to the ground no matter how heavy the grass. In light grass this hook is thrown back on the handle. This mower has our patent micrometer adjustment, solid steel cutter bar, noiseless ratchet, new malleable iron brace, bearings of phosphor bronze. The body of this machine is hand painted in cream white and decorated in maroon and gold. **Diameter of traction wheel**, 8½ inches; diameter of reel, 5½ inches. **All parts are interchangeable** and can be duplicated at once in case of breakage or wear.

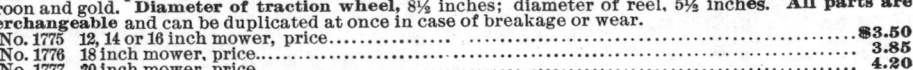

No. 1775  12, 14 or 16 inch mower, price.........................................................$3.50
No. 1776  18 inch mower, price............................................................... 3.85
No. 1777  20 inch mower, price................................................................ 4.20

### Our High Grass Acme Lawn Movers at $5.60 to $6.50.

$5.60 for 14 and 16 inch; $5.90 for 18 inch; $6.25 for 20 inch; $6.50 for 22 inch.
**Three per cent. discount** allowed if cash in full accompanies your order. When comparing our prices with others please consider this 3 per cent cash discount.
**This mower** has been greatly improved for this season. The drive wheel has been made open for 2 inches down from the tread, thus making it lighter and of a more elegant appearance. Its working parts are entirely enclosed. It is the lightest running high grass machine made. Has our patent micrometer adjustment, has solid steel cutter bar, has reel knives of highest grade crucible steel, so formed as to give a spiral and shear cut, has our patent noiseless ratchet, the most perfect mechanism of the kind. Reel shafts in phosphor bronze bearings with a perfect arrangement for taking up any wear. Has our improved handle brace of malleable iron in one piece, which is attached to machine before leaving the factory, thus reducing the work of setting up to the minimum, it being only necessary to insert the handle and fasten the bolts. The body of the machine is hand painted in cream white and decorated in maroon and gold. Ratchet wheel 10 inches in diameter, reels 7 inches in diameter. Has 4 knives. All parts are interchangeable and can be duplicated at once.

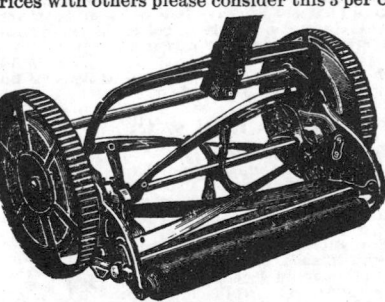

No. 1778  Price, 14 or 16 inch.......................................................$5.60
No. 1779  Price, 18 inch............................................................... 5.90
No. 1780  Price, 20 inch.............................................................. 6.25
No. 1781  Price, 22 inch.............................................................. 6.50

### Our Acme Universal Catcher for $1.00.

**This is a grass catcher** that will fit any lawn mower made. Heavy canvas body, blacked sheet steel bottom. **The catcher is** attached to the handle only and is entirely independent of the mower proper. Can be attached or taken off in an instant. Can be used on any lawn mower made. Is guaranteed to give satisfaction in every case.
No. 1782  To fit 10, 12, 14 or 16-inch mower...................$1.00
No. 1783  To fit 18 or 20-inch mower ...................... 1.05
**OUR LIBERAL DISCOUNT** OF 3 PER CENT. MUST NOT BE OVERLOOKED. MOST OF OUR CUSTOMERS SEND CASH IN FULL.

WE QUOTE ALL SORTS OF GRASS SEEDS AND GARDEN SEEDS IN FULL. SEEDS ON PAGE 25. WE SAVE YOU HALF THE RETAIL PRICE.

# PUMP DEPARTMENT.

**PROBABLY THERE IS NO OTHER LINE OF GOODS THAT WE SELL ON WHICH WE CAN SAVE OUR CUSTOMERS MORE MONEY THAN WE CAN ON PUMPS.** We fit all our pumps, so any one can set them in the well without any trouble. The only special tool required is a pipe tong. We sell a pipe tong for $1.00, and everyone who has a pump should have one. We have tried to make explanations of pumps so plain that anyone will be able to select the pump best adapted to his needs. **If in doubt, write us, giving us this information: How deep is well? Is force pump or lift pump wanted? How much water is wanted per day? When water is to be drawn from a distance or forced to a distance, send a rough drawing showing position of pump, position of well, and giving all angles and measurements. Also state quantity of water wanted.** We will select the outfit, which our pump man, with an experience of twenty years, thinks will give you the best satisfaction, and name you our best price for the outfit. **Don't forget our liberal 3% cash discount, when cash in full accompanies your order.**

## Pitcher Spout Pump.

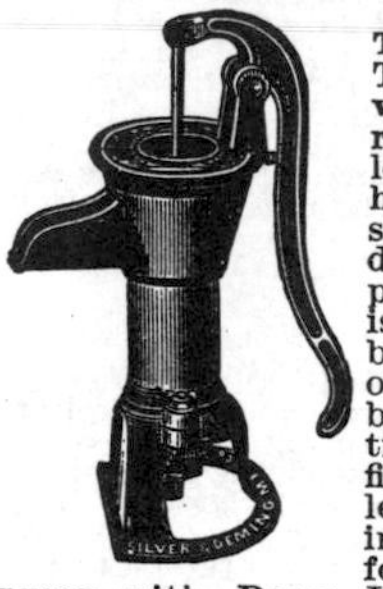


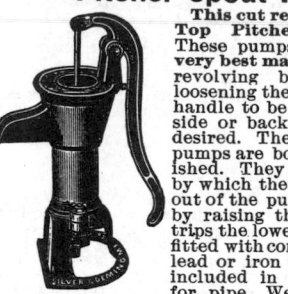

**This cut represents our Close Top Pitcher Spout Pump.** These pumps are made in the **very best manner** and have the revolving bearer which by loosening the set screw allows handle to be placed on either side or back, in any position desired. The cylinders of these pumps are bored true and polished. They have Trip Valves, by which the water may be let out of the pump in the winter by raising the handle until it trips the lower valve. They are fitted with connection for either lead or iron pipe. Pipe is not included in price. See index for pipe. We also make this pump with Brass Lined Cylinder. It is a well known fact that leather plungers operating in brass cylinders are almost indestructible. **We can fully recommend them where the best is wanted.**

**Sizes and Prices. No. 1807.**

| | | Iron. | Brass-Lined |
|---|---|---|---|
| No. 1 | 2½ inch calibre, for 1 inch pipe. | $0.90 | $1.39 |
| No. 2 | 3 inch calibre, for 1¼ inch pipe. | 1.00 | 1.55 |
| No. 3 | 3½ inch calibre, for 1¼ inch pipe. | 1.12 | 1.80 |
| No. 4 | 4 inch calibre, for 1½ inch pipe. | 1,23 | 1.92 |

## Iron and Brass Lined Force Pump.

**With Air Chamber, Revolving Bearer and Brass Piston Rod.**

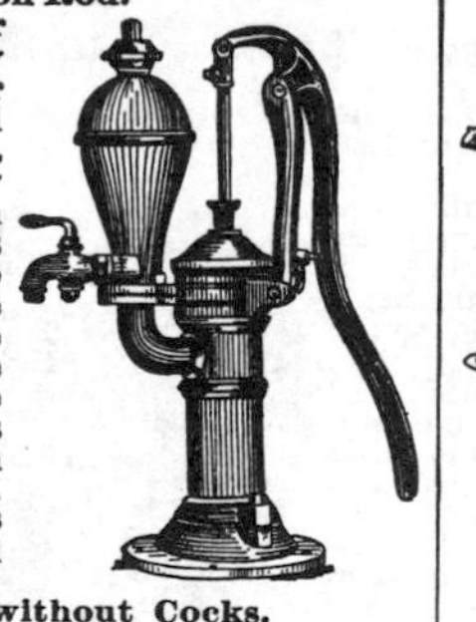

**This is a Staple Pump for House Use.** It is usually placed on a kitchen sink or elevated platform, and used to force water up into a tank or reservoir to supply bath rooms and wash basins. The air chamber is fitted with an outlet into which a draw cock may be screwed if desired. Hose may also be attached to the cock for sprinkling or fire purposes, in which case it is best to put a stop-cock on the upward discharge. These pumps have **brass valve seats,** and are fitted for iron or lead pipe.

**Sizes and Prices without Cocks.**

| | Iron | Brass lined. |
|---|---|---|
| No. 1808 No. 1, 2½ in. Cylinder for 1 in. pipe | $4.53 | $5.63 |
| No. 1809 No. 2, 2½ in. Cylinder for 1 in. pipe | 4.90 | 6.12 |
| No. 1810 No. 4, 3 in. Cylinder for 1¼ in. pipe | 5.88 | 7.35 |
| **Prices with Cock, as in cut.** | | |
| No. 1812 No. 1, To fit ¾ in. hose coupling. | 5.50 | 6.60 |
| No. 1813 No. 2, To fit ¾ in. hose coupling. | 6.10 | 7.32 |
| No. 1815 No. 4, To fit 1 in. hose coupling. | 7.10 | 8.57 |

**We can fully recommend our Brass-Lined Pumps to be equal to an all brass one and much cheaper.** The cylinder is lined with a seamless drawn brass tube. The plunger, piston rod, stuffing nut, and all working parts are brass, and as leather plungers operating in brass cylinders are known to be almost indestructible. **parties wishing a first-class Pump will give them the unhesitating preference.**

## Anti-Freezing Wrought Iron Lift Pump.

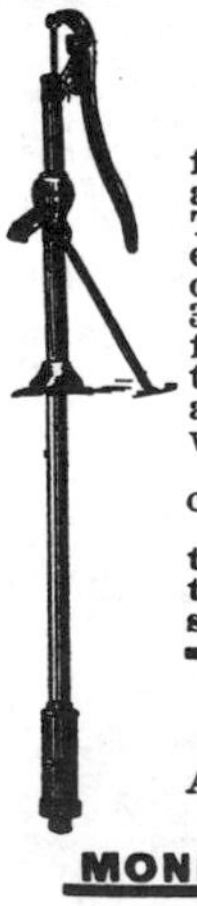

Suitable for wells not more than 30 feet deep. It measures 4 feet from flange at platform to bottom of cylinder. The flange is adjustable, which makes it especially suitable for drive wells. Shape of spout prevents flooding at the top. Has 3x10 iron cylinder of good quality, fitted for 1¼ inch iron pipe. If well is more than 20 feet deep we recommend placing a foot valve on end of pipe at bottom of well.

No. 1817 Price for pump as shown in cut........................................$2.47

**NOTICE.—This price does not include the pipe to reach from the bottom of the cylinder to bottom of well. For pipe see 1955.**

## OUR PUMPS

**ARE MADE BY THE LEADING MANUFACTURER IN HIS LINE.**

**MONEY DOESN'T BUY BETTER.**

## Anti-Freezing Closed Top Lift Pump.

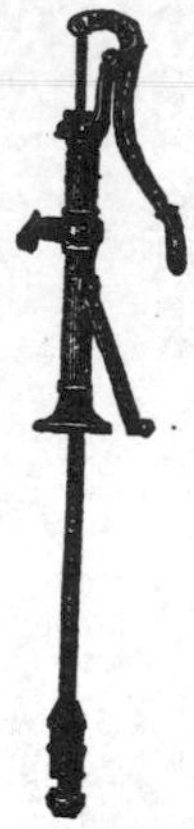

Adapted for wells not more than 30 feet deep. Has revolving top so handle may be placed on either side or at back of spout in any position desired. It measures four feet from platform to bottom of cylinder. The pipe connecting cylinder and pump, screws into the pump at the spout, thus leaving an air space around the pipe above the platform which is a preventative against freezing. The cylinder is of the best quality and is fitted for 1¼ inch pipe unless otherwise ordered. If well is more than 20 feet deep we recommend placing a foot valve on end of pipe at bottom of the well. Pipe to reach from bottom of cylinder to bottom of well is not furnished at prices named below.

**Sizes and Prices.**

No. 1820 No. 2, 2½ inch cylinder... $2 60
No. 1822 No. 3, 2¾ inch cylinder... 2 70
No. 1824 No. 4, 3 inch cylinder... 2 80
No. 1826 No. 5, 3¼ inch cylinder... 3 35
No. 1828 No. 6, 3½ inch cylinder... 3 65

## Heavy New Pattern Close Top Lift Pump.

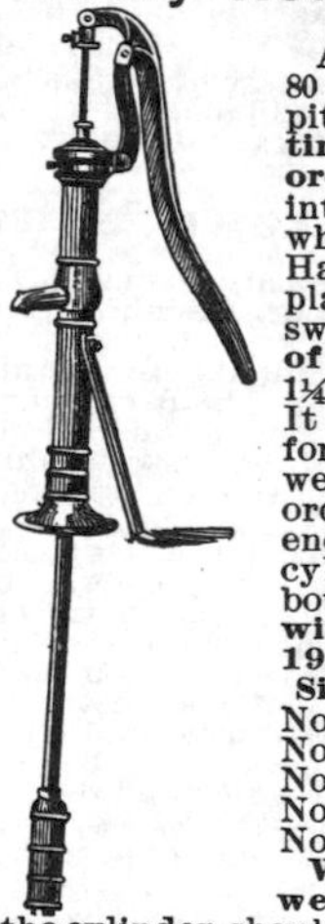

Adapted for wells not more than 80 feet deep. The bolts on cap and pitman are large, and will **many times outwear the small ones in ordinary use.** The pipe is screwed into pump just below the spout, which prevents freezing in winter. Has revolving top so handle may be placed in any desired position. Has swinging fulcrum. **The cylinder is of the best quality,** and fitted for 1¼ in. pipe unless otherwise ordered. It measures 4 ft. from flange at platform to bottom of cylinder. For wells not more than 25 or 30 ft. deep order the pump as shown in cut, and enough pipe to reach from bottom of cylinder (4 ft. from platform) to the bottom of well. **Pipe is not included with pump. For price of pipe see 1955.**

**Sizes and Prices as Shown in Cut.**

No. 1830. No. 2. 2½ in. cylinder. $3.28
No. 1831. No. 3. 2¾ " 3.39
No. 1832. No. 4. 3 " 3.57
No. 1833. No. 5. 3¼ " 3.78
No. 1834. No. 6. 3½ " 3.96

**When this pump is ordered for well more than 25 or 30 feet deep,** the cylinder should be placed within 10 feet of the bottom of well. When so ordered it takes more pump rod and pump rod couplings, and requires extra labor, for which we make an extra charge of 5 cents per foot for each foot the cylinder is put down. This charge is to be added to cost of pump and pipe complete.

**NOTICE.—The cost of pipe is not included in above extra charge. We give below a sample order for pump and pipe complete to reach 74 feet from platform with cylinder put down 65 feet.**

No. 1832 1 pump, No. 4........................$ 3.57
No. 1955 70 feet black iron pipe, 1¼ inch. at 5½c 3.85
To putting cylinder down 65 feet, at 5c..... 3.25
$10.67

## Heavy Lift Pump with Windmill Head.

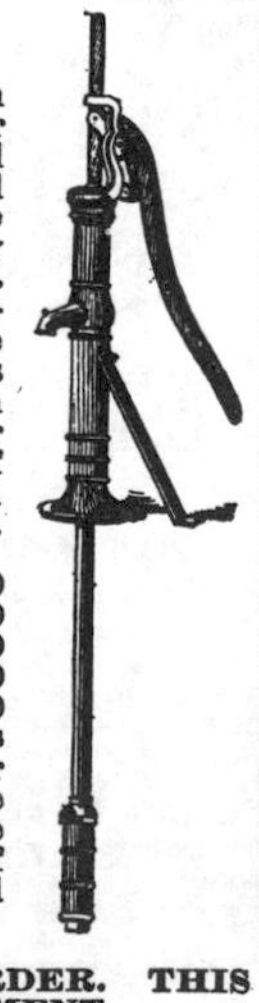

Adapted for wells not more than 80 feet deep. May also be used for hand use. Pipe screws into standard at the spout. Has revolving top and swinging fulcrum. **All parts are strong and durable. We can fully recommend it as a first-class pump.** Measures 4 feet from platform to bottom of cylinder. For wells not more than 25 or 30 feet deep order pump as shown in cut and enough 1¼ inch iron pipe to reach from bottom of cylinder (4 feet below platform) to bottom of well. Price of pipe is not included in price of pump. For price of pipe see 1955.

**Sizes and Prices as Shown in Cut.**

No. 1840. No. 2. 2½ inch cylinder. $3.40
No. 1841. No. 3. 2¾ inch cylinder. 3.50
No. 1842. No. 4, 3 inch cylinder. 3.60
No. 1843. No. 5. 3¼ inch cylinder. 3,70
No. 1844. No. 6. 3½ inch cylinder. 3.90

**When this pump is ordered for wells more than 25 or 30 feet deep** cylinder should be placed within 10 feet of the bottom of the well for which we make an extra charge in addition to cost of pump and pipe same as explained under pump No. 1834.

## Extra Heavy Lift Pump.

**For Stockyard and Heavy Work.**

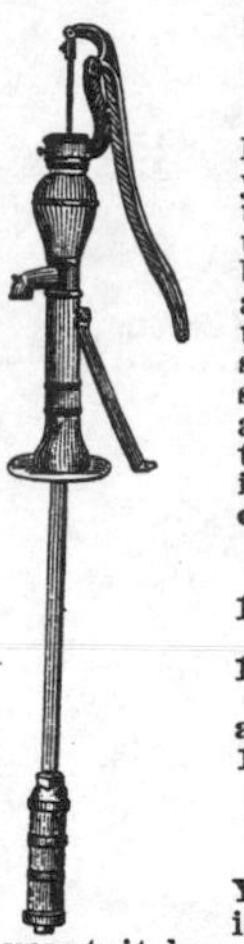

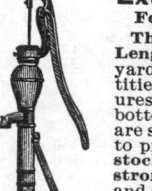

**This cut represents our Heavy Set-Length Lift Pump,** adapted for stockyards and wells, where large quantities of water are required. It measures 4 feet from flange at platform to bottom of cylinder. **The Set-Lengths** are screwed in the pumps at the spout to prevent freezing in winter. **The stocks are made very heavy and strong,** and the cylinders are large and capable of throwing large quantities of water. **We fully recommend it where a large amount of water is desired.**

**Sizes and Prices.**

No. 1850 3½ inch cylinder, fitted for 1½ inch pipe........................$4.52
No. 1851 4 inch cylinder, fitted for 1½ inch pipe........................$4.91

**Price of pipe is not included in above prices. For Pipe see No. 1955.**

## Extra Heavy Lift Pump.

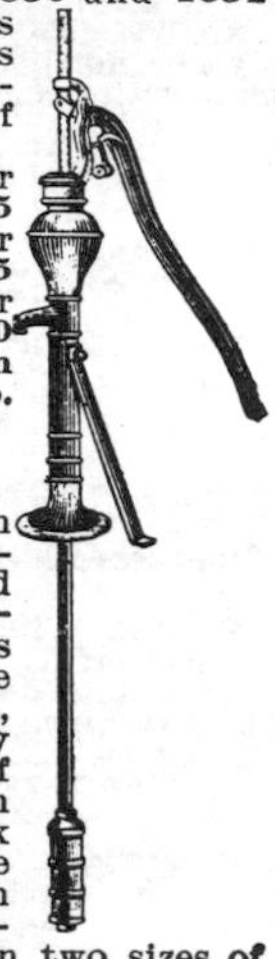

**Extra Heavy Lift Pump for Stock Yard and Heavy Work.** This pump is exactly like **No. 1850** and **1851** except it has windmill head and is made in three sizes. When well is more than 20 feet deep, we recommend putting a foot valve at end of pipe in bottom of well.

No. 1854 3½ inch cylinder, fitted for 1½ inch pipe.................. $5.35
No. 1855 4 inch cylinder, fitted for 1½ inch pipe.......... ........ $5.65
No. 1856 4 inch cylinder, fitted for 2 inch pipe.................. $6.00

**Price of Pipe is Not Included in Above Prices. For Pipe See No. 1955.**

## Heavy Force Pump.

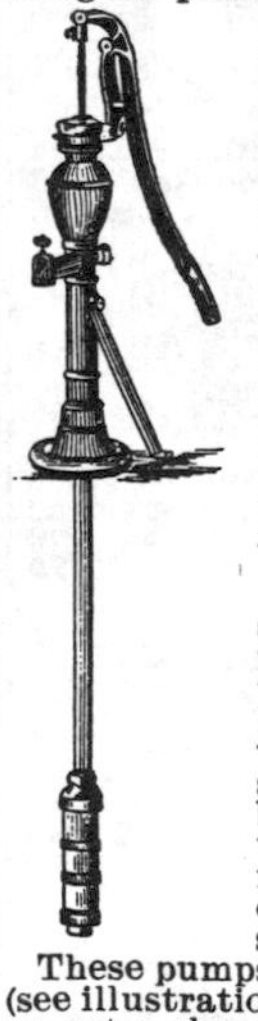

Adapted for wells not more than sixty feet deep. The pipe which connects cylinder to pump is screwed into pump at the spout, **thus preventing freezing in winter.** It has an outlet in rear of spout where a one inch pipe may be attached if desired, as shown in cut of No. 1870. Hose may be attached to the spout by means of the clevis which we furnish as shown in cut. We can also furnish with cock at spout if so ordered at extra price named below. It measures 4 feet from flange at platform to bottom of cylinder. They are made in two sizes of standards, medium and large. The large pump will give best results in deep wells; fitted for 1¼ inch pipe unless otherwise ordered. When used for force pump, set the thumb screw down tightly; when used as a lift pump, loosen the screw.

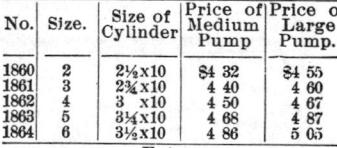

| No. | Size. | Size of Cylinder | Price of Medium Pump | Price of Large Pump. |
|---|---|---|---|---|
| 1860 | 2 | 2½x10 | $4 32 | $4 55 |
| 1861 | 3 | 2¾x10 | 4 40 | 4 60 |
| 1862 | 4 | 3 x10 | 4 50 | 4 67 |
| 1863 | 5 | 3¼x10 | 4 68 | 4 87 |
| 1864 | 6 | 3½x10 | 4 86 | 5 05 |

**Extras.**

**The above prices are for pump as shown in cut.** Price of pipe to reach from bottom of cylinder to bottom of well is not included. For pipe see 1955. If this pump is ordered for well more than 25 or 30 feet deep, the cylinder should be placed within 10 feet of the bottom of the well. When so ordered we make an extra charge of 5 cents per foot for each foot the cylinder is put down. For full information read description of pump No. 1834.

These pumps can also be fitted with cock at spout, (see illustration of pump No. 1870) for which we make an extra charge of 50 cents.

These pumps can also be fitted with back attachment, (see illustration of pump No. 1870) for which we make an extra charge of 90 cents.

## Wind Mill Force Pump.

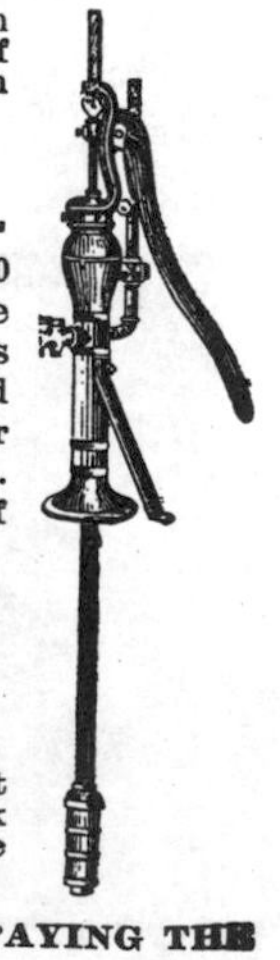

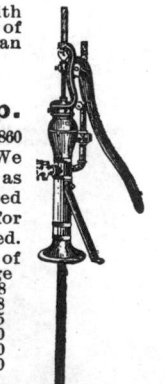

This pump is exactly like No. 1860 except it has a windmill head. We can fully recommend both of them as powerful force pumps. Size 8 is fitted for 1½ inch pipe, other sizes fitted for 1¼ inch pipe, unless otherwise ordered.

| | Size | Size of Cylinder | Price of Medium | Price of Large |
|---|---|---|---|---|
| No. 1870 | 2 | 2½x10 | $4 68 | $4 88 |
| No. 1871 | 3 | 2¾x10 | 4 78 | 5 08 |
| No. 1872 | 4 | 3x10 | 4 87 | 5 25 |
| No. 1873 | 5 | 3¼x10 | 5 05 | 5 40 |
| No. 1874 | 6 | 3½x10 | 5 22 | 5 60 |
| No. 1875 | 8 | 4x10 | 5 76 | 6 00 |

**Extras same as pump No. 1834.**

**Above prices are for pump without cock at spout and without back attachment. For prices of these extras see pump No. 1864.**

**REMEMBER OUR SPECIAL DISCOUNT OF 3 PER CENT. FOR FULL CASH WITH ORDER. THIS DISCOUNT WILL GO TOWARD PAYING THE FREIGHT ON YOUR SHIPMENT.**

## Hand Force Pump.

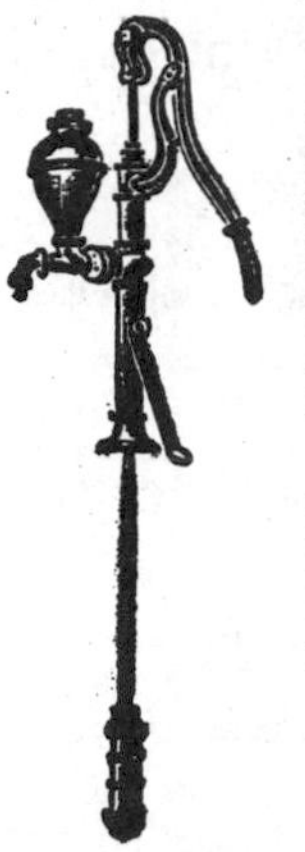

**This is a popular and powerful Force Pump,** and when cylinder is put down is adapted for wells not more than 80 feet deep. We furnish hose attachments, free. Back attachment as shown in illustration of pump No. 1870, and cock at spout can be furnished at extra charge named below. It is a most excellent force pump and cannot fail to give satisfaction.

**Prices.**

No. 1881 2¾ inch cylinder.... **$5.04**
No. 1882 3 inch cylinder.... **5.06**
No. 1883 3¼ inch cylinder.... **5.25**
No. 1884 3½ inch cylinder,... **5.40**

**Extras same as pump No. 1870.**

## Extra Heavy Force Pump Standard only with Windmill Head.

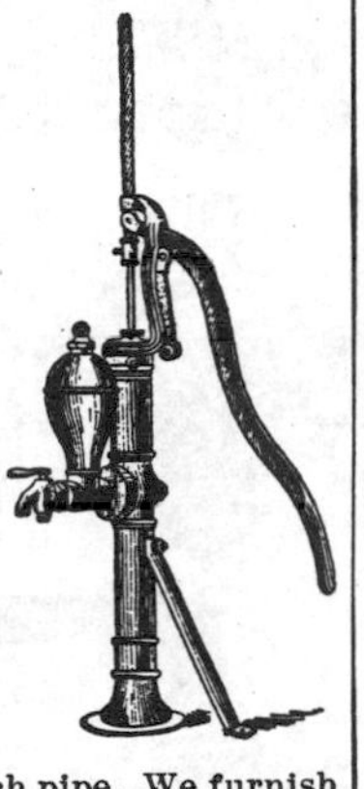

For very deep wells we offer this standard only with windmill head and cock spout. Back attachment as shown in illustration of pump No. 1870 can be furnished at extra charge of 50c. if ordered. To make complete outfit besides the standard select the cylinder desired. (See No. 1926 to 1943) Order the required pipe. (See No. 1955) Say how many feet you want cylinder put down, and to cost of standard cylinder and pipe add 5c. per foot for each foot the cylinder is put down, which covers cost of pipe rod, rod couplings, labor, etc. As a guide to making order see No. 1834, adding cost of cylinder selected. We have this standard in two sizes and can have fitted for pipe as large as 3 inches if so ordered, and top outlet auy size requested. When no size is mentioned we fit it for 1¼ pipe and tap back outlet for 1 inch pipe. We furnish regular for 6 inch stroke, but can furnish 10 inch stroke if ordered at extra charge named below. When ordered 10 inch stroke state if for tube well purposes or if forked rod is desired.

| | **Sizes and Prices.** | List. |
|---|---|---|
| 1886 | No. 1. With Brace, 6 inch stroke .......... | $5.95 |
| 1888 | No. 2. With Brace, 6 inch stroke,........... | 6.60 |
| | Extra for 10 inch stroke........................ | .50 |
| | Extra for back attachment .................... | 90 |

## Underground Valve Force Pump.

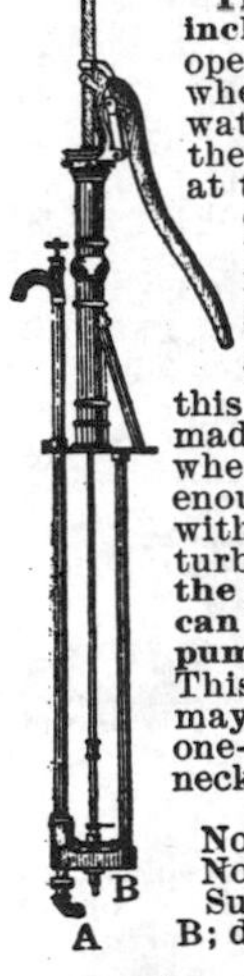


**This Pump is especially adapted for 2 inch tubular wells,** also 1¼ inch pipe for open or drilled wells. By operating the wheel in the top of the goose neck, the water may be discharged either through the spout or through the underground pipe at the bridge piece below. It differs from other three-way valve pumps in that the operating screw, which is of brass, is below, near the valve, and not at the goose-neck, consequently there is no liability to chill and freeze. The pipe on the right forms the air chamber. When this pump is used for tubular wells, it is made with a cap at the stuffing box which, when unscrewed, leaves an opening large enough to pull the plunger up through without disconnecting the pipe, or disturbing the pump in any way. **All parts of the pump are strong and well made. We can most unhesitatingly recommend this pump as the best of its kind in the market.** This pump is always sent for 2 inch pipe, but may be bushed for smaller sizes. One and one-fourth inch discharge pipe. Goose neck to fit 1 inch hose coupling.

**Prices.**

No. 1890 6 inch stroke........... ...**$7.00**
No. 1892 10 inch stroke............... **8.00**

Suction pipe and rod coupling connect at B; discharge pipe connects at A.

**Extras.**

**To make complete outfit** select cylinder desired, and quantity of pipe wanted for suction, also number of feet of pipe wanted for discharge. State number of feet cylinder shall be put down and in addition to cost of standard cylinder and pipe add 5 cents per foot for each foot the cylinder is put down. For sample order see No. 1886-87.

## A $25.00 GUN

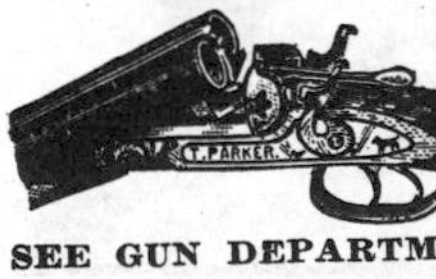


**FOR**

**$16.35.**

**SEE GUN DEPARTMENT, PAGE 569. OUR LINE OF SPORTING GOODS IS MOST COMPLETE.**

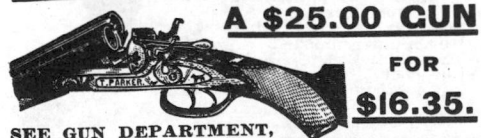

## Tank Pump.

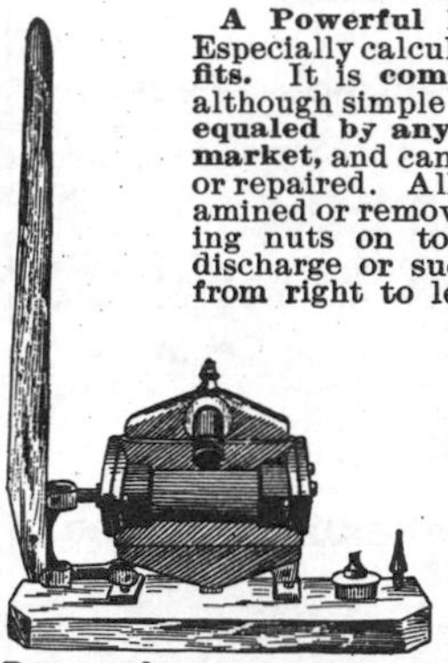

**A Powerful Double-Acting Pump.** Especially calculated for **thresher's outfits.** It is **compact and strong,** and although simple in construction, **is unequaled by any other pump in the market,** and can be easily taken apart or repaired. All the valves can be examined or removed by simply unscrewing nuts on top and bottom. The discharge or suction can be changed from right to left by reversing caps. Handles can be changed to either end, making it either right or left. This Tank Pump is so well known it needs no special description. The large number sold in past years is sufficient evidence of its value.

**Prices.**

No. 1894 Diameter cylinder, 5 in.; suction, 2 in.; discharge, 2 in., Pump only....................................**$6.00**
No. 1896 **2 in. Wire Lined Smooth Bore Suction Hose,** per foot...................................**$0.35**

## Double-Acting Tank Pumps with Air Chamber.

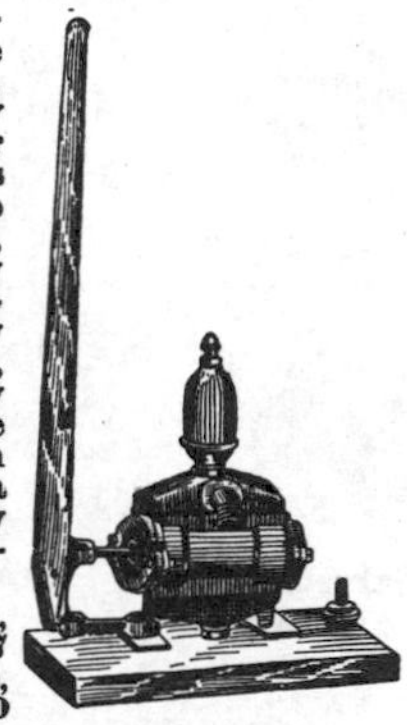

**These Pumps are duplicates of No. 1894** with the exception of air chambers. These pumps are **especially valuable on board ship for washing deck, wetting sails or extinguishing fires,** also around wharves, factories, mills, warehouses, livery stables, lumber yards, irrigating from ditches or shallow wells, spraying fruit trees, shrubs, drives, etc., and any other purpose where a force pump is needed, and when used with our double brake is a powerful fire pump, quickly placed in position in any location.

No. 1898 With single brake, mounted on plank... **$7.67**
No. 1899 With double brake, mounted on plank..... **$ 9.00**

## Wood Pumps.

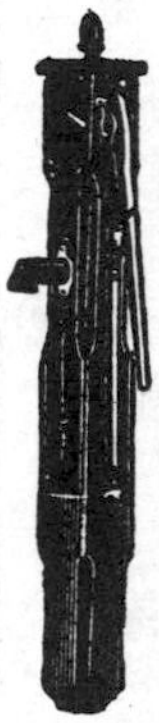

**Our Wood Pumps are made from selected stock, thoroughly painted, striped and varnished.** They are carefully wrapped in strong paper for shipment. They are furnished with iron handle brackets and iron spouts. The plunger which is the vital part of a suction pump is of the latest improved pattern. Adapted for wells not more that 30 feet deep.

**To Seleet a Pump.**

For wells 20 ft. or less deep use 6 ft, pump.
" 20 to 25 ft, " " 7 ft. "
" 25 to 30 ft. " " 8 ft. "

Bottom of 6 ft. pump comes 2 ft. below platform. Bottom of 7 ft. pump comes 3 ft, below platform. Bottom of 8 ft. pump comes 4 ft. below platform.

Besides the pump order enough tubing of size to match pump to reach from bottom of pump to bottom of well. Tubing comes in lengths of 12 ft. and less. When more than 12 ft. of tubing will be required order a coupling to connect the tubing. Prices of tubing and couplings will be found with each pump.

## Stock Pump.

**Stock Pump** is 7 inches square, 4 inch bore, 10 inch stroke. Capacity 80 gals. per minute. These pumps are particularly adapted to the wants of farmers and stockmen using large quantities of water. They should not be used in wells where the water is more than 15 or 20 ft. from the platform, as the quantity of water which the pump lifts at each stroke would cause it to work hard in deep wells.

| No. | Length, | Price Plain Pump. | Price Porcelain Lined Cylinder. |
|---|---|---|---|
| 1901 | 6 feet. | $2.80 | $3.50 |
| 1902 | 7 feet. | 3.10 | 3.85 |
| 1903 | 8 feet. | 3.40 | 4.10 |

No. 1904 Tubing for above pump 4½ inches square, 2 inch bore, per feet...................................**$0.09**
No. 1905 Couplings for tubing, each.......... **.25**

## Farm Pump.

**General Purpose Pump** is 6 inches square 3½ inch bore, 9 inch stroke. **Capacity, 60 gallons per minute.** While this pump throws an ample supply of water, ladies and children can work the pump with ease.

| No. | Length. | Price Plain Pump. | Price with Porcelain lined cylinder. |
|---|---|---|---|
| 1906 | 6 feet. | $2.25 | $3.00 |
| 1907 | 7 feet. | 2.50 | 3.25 |
| 1908 | 8 feet. | 2.80 | 3.60 |

No. 1909 **Tubing to fit above pump 4 inches square with 1¾ inch bore. Per foot.........$0.08**
No. 1910 Coupling for above tubing, each.... **.25**

## Cistern Pump.

**Cistern Pump** is 5 inches square, 3 inch bore, 8 inch stroke. **Capacity 40 gallons per minute.** This pump is adapted to cisterns and shallow wells where a moderate quantity of water is required.

| No. | Length. | Price Plain Pump. | Price with Procelain lined cylinder. |
|---|---|---|---|
| 1911 | 6 feet. | $1.95 | $2.60 |
| 1912 | 7 feet. | 2.05 | 2.75 |

**Tubing to fit above pump 3½ inches square, 1¼ inch bore.** Per foot, 6c; Couplings for above tubing. Each.......................................**$0.18**

## Rubber Bucket Chain Pumps.

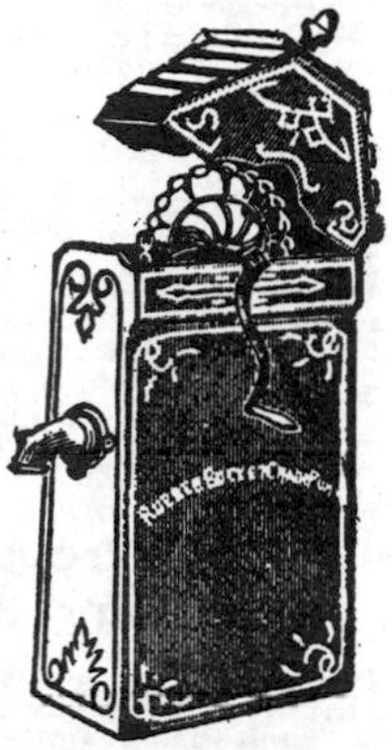

No. 1913 **Rubber Bucket Chain Pump,** complete for well ten feet deep.... **$3.25**
No. 1914 **Rubber Bucket Chain Pump,** complete for well 12 feet deep...... **$3.50**
No. 1915 **Rubber Bucket Chain Pump,** complete for well 15 feet deep..... **$4.00**
No. 1916 **Rubber Bucket Chain Pump,** complete for well 18 feet deep...... **$4.25**
No. 1917 **Rubber Bucket Chain Pump,** complete for well 20 feet deep...... **$4.50**

**We do not advise the use of chain pumps for wells deeper than 20 feet.**

No. 1918 **Bubber Buckets for Chain Pump.** Each 6c; per doz..... **$0.60**

## Spraying Pump.

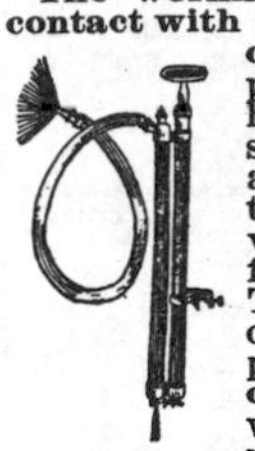

**The working parts and all parts coming in contact with the liquids are constructed entirely of brass.** The construction of the pump requires the pressure on the handle to be all done on the down stroke, the pressure on the cylinder acting as a cushion, and partly forcing the handle up again, thus making it very easy of operation, requiring no foot rest or other device to steady it. The hose can be detached at the top of pump and a nozzle attached in its place, either for **spraying, sprinkling, or throwing a solid stream.** No wrench or other tool is required to make this change. **This feature is peculiar to this pump only.** It is also arranged so that a small stream is discharged with great force from the bottom of the pump into the bucket or barrel, serving to thoroughly agitate the mixture at all times when the pump is in use. The agitator does not lessen the force of the spry at the nozzle. It will be readily seen that the arrangement for attaching the hose 'at the top of the pump has this advantage over attaching it at the bottom: it does not bring the outside surface of the hose into contact with the acids contained in the solutions, thus adding to the life of the hose. It will throw a solid stream seventy-five feet, and for washing buggies, windows, etc., it is very useful. **It can also be usee for whitewashing trees, barns, outhouses, etc., and for extinguishing fires.**

No. 1921 Price, each..................................**$2.35**

## Pump Cylinders.

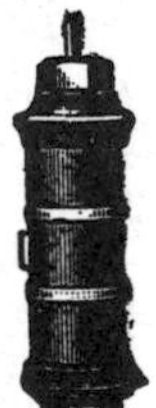

**By means of the cylinder water is raised, and unless the cylinder is well made no good results can be obtained.** A good cylinder must be bored true and plunger must fit accurately. Valves must be simple and durable. The cost of repairing a cylinder is usually more than its first cost, so it pays to get the best. Our cylinders are the best that skilled workmen can produce, and our price as low as equally well made goods can be sold for. Cylinders 10 long have 6 inch stroke and can be used in wells up to 35 feet deep. Cylinders 12 inches long have 6 inch stroke and can be used in wells up to 75 feet deep. Cylinders 16 inches long have 10 inch stroke and can be used in wells up to 200 feet deep. Cylinders 2 inches inches in diameter are fitted for 1 inch pipe. Cylinders 3½ inches in diameter are fitted for 1½ inch pipe. Cylinders 4 inches in diameter are fitted for 2 inch pipe. All others fitted for 1¼ inch pipe.

| | Diameter. | 10 in. long. | 12 in. long. | 16 in. long. |
|---|---|---|---|---|
| No. 1926 | 2 inch | $0 75 | $1 10 | $1 22 |
| No. 1927 | 2¼ inch | 80 | 1 15 | 1 28 |
| No. 1928 | 2½ inch | 87 | 1 20 | 1 38 |
| No. 1929 | 2¾ inch | 94 | 1 30 | 1 48 |
| No. 1930 | 3 inch | 1 00 | 1 40 | 1 58 |
| No. 1931 | 3¼ inch | 1 06 | 1 50 | 1 70 |
| No. 1932 | 3½ inch | 1 12 | 1 60 | 1 80 |
| No. 1933 | 4 inch | 1 29 | 1 85 | 2 10 |

**Brass Body Cylinders are practically as good as the solid brass, and much cheaper.** The barrel is made of a seamless brass tube and wookmanship, stroke, and capacity are all same as iron cylinders.

| | Diameter. | 10 in. long. | 12 in. long. | 16 in. long. |
|---|---|---|---|---|
| No. 1936 | 2 in. | $1 88 | $2 00 | $2 27 |
| No. 1937 | 2¼ in. | 1 94 | 2 06 | 2 42 |
| No. 1938 | 2½ in. | 2 05 | 2 12 | 2 55 |
| No. 1939 | 2¾ in. | 2 13 | 2 25 | 2 69 |
| No. 1940 | 3 in. | 2 26 | 2 37 | 2 81 |
| No. 1941 | 3¼ in. | 2 43 | 2 56 | 3 00 |
| No. 1942 | 3½ in. | 2 62 | 2 82 | 3 70 |
| No. 1943 | 4 in. | 3 50 | 3 75 | 4 38 |

**WE CAN DO ALL THE FITTING FOR YOUR PUMP CHEAPER AND BETTER THAN YOU CAN DO IT AT HOME. ALWAYS GIVE FULL SPECIFICATIONS WHEN ORDERING FROM THIS DEPARTMENT.**

## Foot Valves.

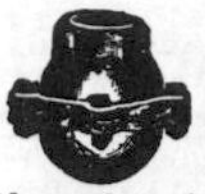

**We recommend that Foot Valve and Strainer** should be placed on lower end of pipe in wells more than 15 or 18 ft. deep. It makes pump work much easier and the strainer prevents anything from entering the pipe which might clog the valves in cylinder. Made in two sizes.

No. 1946 For 1¼ inch pipe, price each.... .. $0 40
No. 1947 For 1½ inch pipe, price each. .... 50

## Drive Well Points.

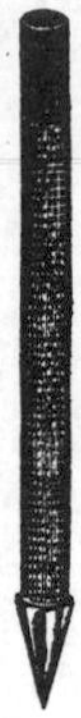

No. **1950 Drive Well Points** are made of wrought iron pipe, galvanized inside and out after the holes are punched. It is covered with a brass gauze and gauze is covered and protected by a perforated brass jacket. No. 60 guaze is most commonly used. No. 100 gauze is for quick sand.

| Diameter. | Length. | No. 60 gauze. Each. | No. 100 gauze. Each. |
|---|---|---|---|
| 1¼ in. | 24 in. | $0.65 | $1.42 |
| 1¼ in, | 30 in. | 1.00 | 2.13 |
| 1¼ in. | 36 in. | 1.17 | 2.50 |
| 1¼ in. | 42 in. | 1.34 | 2.84 |
| 1½ in. | 30 in. | 1.06 | 2.10 |
| 1½ in. | 36 in. | 1.49 | 2.94 |
| 2 in. | 36 in. | 1.86 | 3.37 |
| 2 in. | 48 in. | 2.42 | 4.43 |

## Standard Wrought Iron Pipe. Black and Galvanized.

**For Steam, Gas and Water. When pipe is ordered in full lengths one coupling is furnished free with each Piece.** Full lengths are from 16 to 20 feet long. **When pipe is cut to exact lengths we charge for threads on both ends as per list below.** No coupling with pipe cut to exact length.

Prices of pipe subject to fluctuations of the market. Orders will always be filled at the lowest possible prices.

**No. 1955 Black Iron Pipe.**
**No. 1956 Galvanized Iron Pipe.**

| Inside Diameter. | Black Per foot. | Galvanized Per foot. | Extra threads Per cut. | Pounds Per foot. |
|---|---|---|---|---|
| ⅛ in. | $0.02½ | ...... | $0.03 | ¼ |
| ¼ in. | .02½ | .03½ | .03 | ⅔ |
| ⅜ in. | .02½ | .03½ | .03 | ½ |
| ½ in. | .03 | .04 | .03 | 4-5 |
| ¾ in. | .03¼ | .04¾ | ,03 | 1 1-10 |
| 1 in. | .04½ | .06¼ | .04 | 1⅔ |
| 1¼ in. | .05½ | .08½ | .04 | 2⅔ |
| 1½ in | .07½ | .11½ | .05 | 3⅓ |
| 2 in. | .10 | .15½ | .06 | 3⅔ |
| 2½ in. | .14 | .22 | .08 | 5¾ |
| 3 in. | .18 | ,29 | .10 | 7½ |
| 3½ in. | .22½ | .35 | .15 | 9 |
| 4 in. | .26 | .42 | .20 | 10⅔ |
| 4½ in. | .32 | .55 | 30 | 12½ |
| 5 in. | .38 | .62 | .35 | 14½ |
| 6 in. | .49 | .78 | .40 | 18¾ |

**BE SURE TO ALLOW FOR COST OF CUTTING THREADS WHEN PIPE IS ORDERED CUT TO EXACT LENGTHS.**

## Iron Pipe Fittings.

**We illustrate the fittings that are commonly used,** but can furnish any fitting that is made. If you want any fitting not quoted here, you can safely order it from us, allowing sufficient money to pay for it and we will fill your order promptly; or, if you prefer, write us and we will promptly and cheerfully quote price.

**ABOUT SIZES.**

**Remember that the size of iron pipe is inside measure and that fittings are for pipe of corresponding size.** We show below the comparative sizes of iron pipe.

| Pipe Size | ⅛ in. | ¼ in. | ⅜ in. | ½ in. | ¾ in. |
|---|---|---|---|---|---|
| Outside Measure | 40/100 in. | 54/100 in. | 67/100 in. | 84/100 in. | 1 5/100 in. |

| P'pe Size.. | 1 in, | 1¼ in. | 1½ in. | 2 in. |
|---|---|---|---|---|
| Outside Measure... | 1 31/100 in. | 1 66/100 in. | 1 9/10 in. | 2 37/100 in. |

## Wrought Iron Couplings.

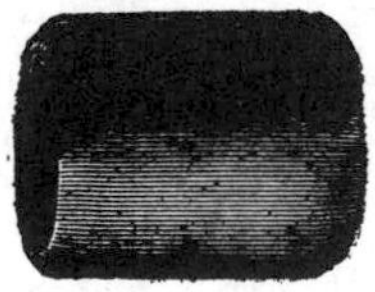

No. 1957.

| Por Pipe, inch, | ¼ | ⅜ | ½ | ¾ | 1 | 1¼ | 1½ | 2 |
|---|---|---|---|---|---|---|---|---|
| Black, each, | $0.03 | .03 | .03 | .04 | .05 | .06 | .08 | .10 |
| No. 1958. Galvanized, each, | $0.04 | .04 | .04 | .06 | .08 | .09 | .10 | .12 |

## Malleable Elbows.

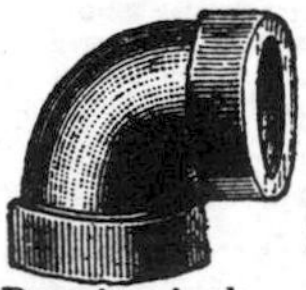

No. 1961.

| Por pipe, inch, | ¼ | ⅜ | ½ | ¾ | 1 | 1¼ | 1½ | 2 |
|---|---|---|---|---|---|---|---|---|
| Black, each, | $0.02 | .03 | .04 | .05 | .07 | .08 | .12 | .15 |
| No. 1962. Galvanized, each, | $0.03 | .04 | .05 | .06 | .08 | .10 | .16 | .22 |

## Malleable Tees.

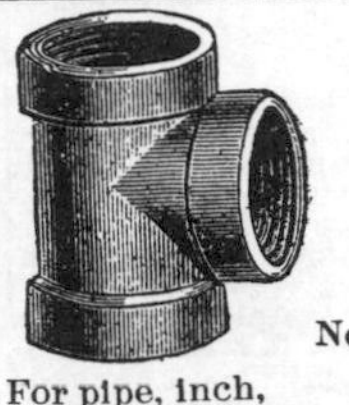

No. 1963.

| For pipe, inch, | ¼ | ⅜ | ½ | ¾ | 1 | 1¼ | 1½ | 2 |
|---|---|---|---|---|---|---|---|---|
| Black, each, | $0.03 | .04 | .05 | .06 | .08 | .09 | .12 | .16 |
| No. 1964. Galvanized, each, | $0.04 | .05 | .06 | .07 | .09 | .12 | .18 | .25 |

## Malleable Crosses.

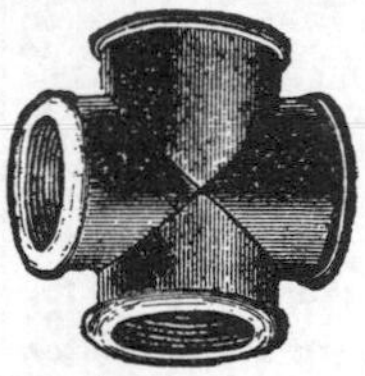

No. 1965.

| For pipe, inch, | ¼ | ⅜ | ½ | ¾ | 1 | 1¼ | 1½ | 2 |
|---|---|---|---|---|---|---|---|---|
| Black, each, | $0.04 | .04 | .05 | .06 | .08 | .12 | .18 | .28 |
| No. 1966. Galvanized, each, | $0.05 | .05 | .06 | .08 | .12 | .18 | .25 | .40 |

## Malleable Unions.

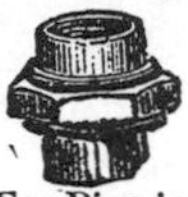

No. 1967.

| For Pipe in., | ¼ | ⅜ | ½ | ¾ | 1 | 1¼ | 1½ | 2 |
|---|---|---|---|---|---|---|---|---|
| Black, each, | $0.07 | .08 | .08 | .10 | .12 | .16 | .20 | .25 |
| No. 1968. Galvonized, each.... | 0.09 | .10 | .12 | .14 | .18 | .25 | .32 | .40 |

## Malleable Reducers.

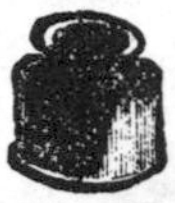

No. 1971—
To reduce one size—size given is big end.

| For pipe, in. | ¼ | ⅜ | ½ | ¾ | 1 | 1¼ | 1½ | 2 |
|---|---|---|---|---|---|---|---|---|
| Black, each. | $0.02 | .03 | .03 | .04 | .07 | .08 | .10 | .14 |
| No. 1972— Galvanized, each.... | $0.03 | .03 | .04 | .05 | .10 | .12 | .15 | .22 |

## Cast Iron Plugs.

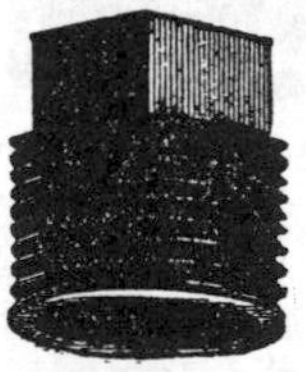

No. 1975.

| For pipe, in.. | ¼ | ⅜ | ½ | ¾ |
|---|---|---|---|---|
| Black, each, | $0.02 | .02 | .02 | .03 |
| For pipe, in.. | 1 | 1¼ | 1½ | 2 |
| Black. each, | .03 | .04 | .05 | .06 |

No. 1976. Galvanized, each—

| ¼ | ⅜ | ½ | ¾ | 1 | 1¼ | 1½ | 2 |
|---|---|---|---|---|---|---|---|
| $0.03 | .03 | .03 | .04 | .04 | .05 | .06 | .08 |

## Bushing.

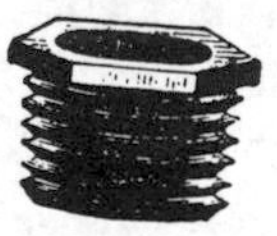

Reducing one size, outside size is given.

No. 1979.

| For pipe, in., | ⅜ | ½ | ¾ | 1 |
|---|---|---|---|---|
| Black, each, | $0.03 | .04 | .04 | .04 |
| For pipe, in., | 1¼ | 1½ | 2 | |
| Black, each, | .05 | .06 | .06 | |

No. 1980. Galvanized, each—
$0.04 .05 .05 05 .06 .08 .10

## Lock Nuts.

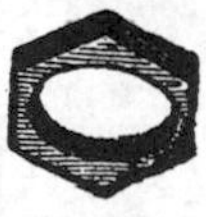

No. 1981.

| For pipe, in. | ¼ | ⅜ | ½ | ¾ | 1 | 1¼ | 1½ | 2 |
|---|---|---|---|---|---|---|---|---|
| Each, | $0.02 | .02 | .02 | .03 | .03 | .03 | .04 | .05 |

## Pipe Caps.

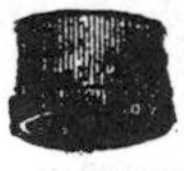

No. 1983.

| For pipe in. | ¼ | ⅜ | ½ | ¾ | 1 | 1¼ | 1½ | 2 |
|---|---|---|---|---|---|---|---|---|
| Black, each, | $0.02 | .03 | .03 | .04 | .04 | .05 | .06 | .08 |
| No, 1984. Galv'd each, | $0.03 | .04 | .04 | .05 | .05 | .06 | .07 | .09 |

## Nipples.

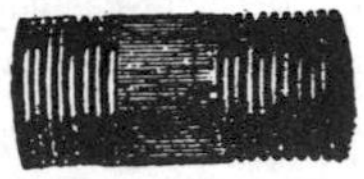

State length wanted.

| No. 1987. Size, in., | ¼ | ⅜ | ½ | ¾ | 1 | 1¼ | 1½ | 2 |
|---|---|---|---|---|---|---|---|---|
| Black, short, price ea., | $0.02 | .02 | .03 | .04 | .04 | .05 | .06 | .07 |
| No. 1988. Galv'd short, price ea., | .03 | .03 | .04 | .05 | .05 | .06 | .07 | .10 |
| No. 1989. Black, long, price ea., | .03 | .03 | .04 | .05 | .05 | .06 | .08 | .09 |
| No. 1990. Galv'd long, price ea., | .04 | .04 | .05 | .06 | .06 | .08 | .10 | .12 |

## Malleable Return Bends, Open Pattern

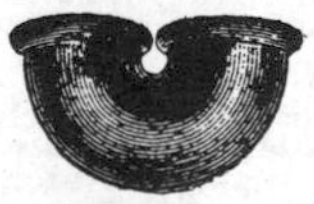

No. 1991.

| For Pipe, in., | ¾ | 1 | 1¼ | 1½ | 2 |
|---|---|---|---|---|---|
| Black each, | $0.09 | .12 | .15 | .23 | .38 |

## Brass Globe Valves.

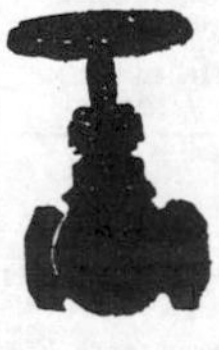

No. 1993.

| For pipe, in., | ¼ | ⅜ | ½ | ¾ |
|---|---|---|---|---|
| Price, each, | $0,20 | .25 | .30 | .35 |
| For pipe, in., | 1 | 1¼ | | |
| Price, each, | .50 | .70 | | |
| For pipe. in., | 1½ | 2 | 2½ | 3 |
| Price, each, | .95 | 1.40 | 2,85 | 3.90 |

## Brass Angle Valves.

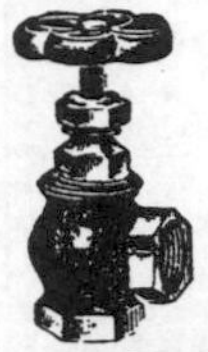

No. 1994.

| For pipe, in., | ¼ | ⅜ | ½ | |
|---|---|---|---|---|
| Price, each, | $0.20 | .26 | ,32 | |
| For pipe, in., | ¾ | 1 | 1¼ | |
| Price, each, | .36 | .55 | .72 | |
| For pipe, in., | 1½ | 2 | 2½ | 3 |
| Price, each, | .98 | 1.45 | 2.90 | 3.95 |

## Brass Cross Valves.

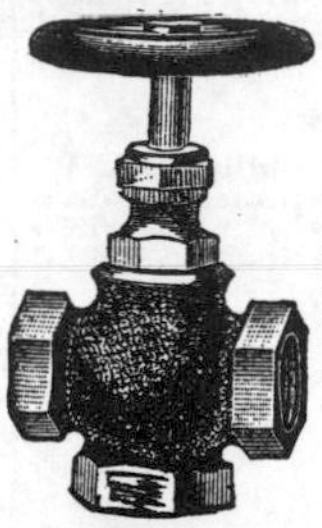

No. 1995.

| For pipe, in.. | ¼ | ⅜ | ½ | ¾ |
|---|---|---|---|---|
| Price, each, | $0.34 | .35 | .40 | .55 |
| For pipe, in., | 1 | 1¼ | 1½ | |
| Price, each, | .68 | 1.00 | 1.30 | |
| For pipe, in., | 2 | 2½ | 3 | |
| Price, each, | 2.15 | 4.25 | 6.50 | |

## Horizontal Check Valves.

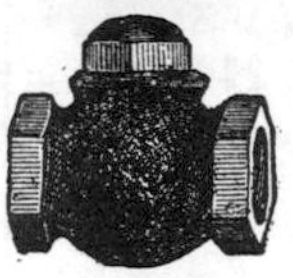

No. 1996.

| For pipe, in., | ¼ | ⅜ | ½ | ¾ | 1 | 1¼ |
|---|---|---|---|---|---|---|
| Price, each, | $0.20 | .22 | .25 | .32 | .45 | .60 |
| For pipe, in., | 1½ | 2 | 2½ | 3 | | |
| Price, each, | .85 | 1.10 | 2.40 | 3.50 | | |

## Brass Three-Way Cocks.

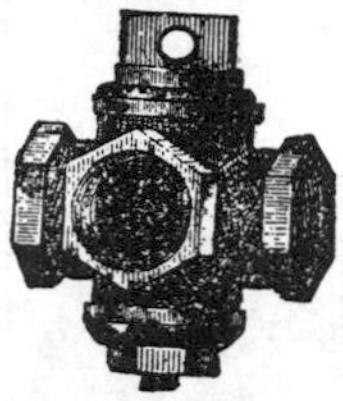

No. 1997—

| For pipe, in..... | ½ | ¾ | 1 | 1¼ |
|---|---|---|---|---|
| Price, each.... | $0.68 | .80 | $1.00 | $1.55 |
| For pipe, in... | 1½ | 2 | 2½ | 3 |
| Price, each.... | $1.95 | $2.95 | $5.00 | $6.50 |

## Water Pipe Stops.

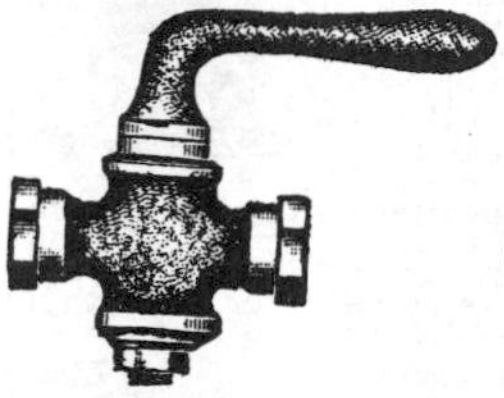

No. 1998. **Brass Rough Stop,** lever handle, screwed for iron pipe.

| Size, inches, | ½ | ¾ | 1 | 1¼ | 1½ | 2 |
|---|---|---|---|---|---|---|
| Price, plain, each, | $0.32 | .52 | .75 | 1.20 | 1.65 | 2.75 |

No, 1999. **Rough Brass Stop T handle, screwed for iron pipe.**

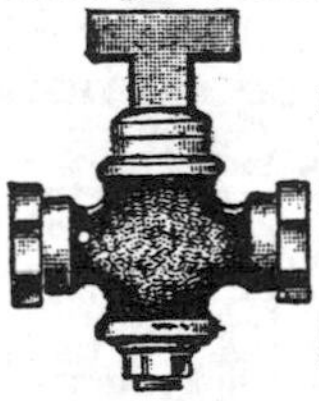

| Size. | ½ | ¾ | 1 |
|---|---|---|---|
| Each, | $0.30 | .50 | .70 |
| Size, | 1¼ | 1½ | 2 |
| Each, | $1.15 | 1.60 | 2.60 |

## Bibbs.

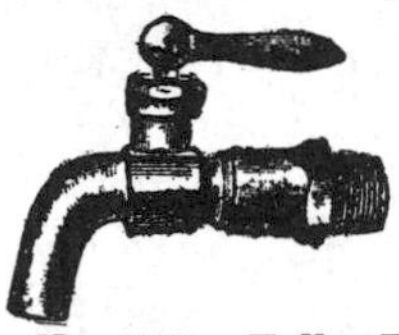

No. 11001. **Fuller Pattern. Plain Bibb** for iron pipe, finished brass.

| Size, in., | ½ | ⅝ | ¾ | 1 |
|---|---|---|---|---|
| Price, each, | $0.55 | .62 | .82 | 1.05 |

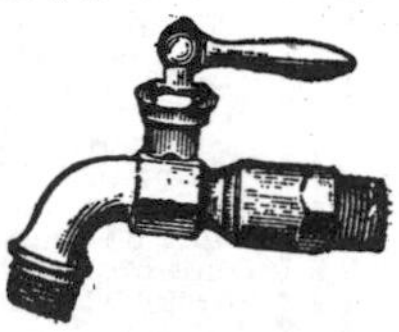

No. 11003. **Fuller Pattern. Hose Bibb** for iron pipe, finished brass.

| Size, in., | ½ | ⅝ | ¾ | 1 |
|---|---|---|---|---|
| Price, each | $0.62 | .70 | .85 | 1.20 |

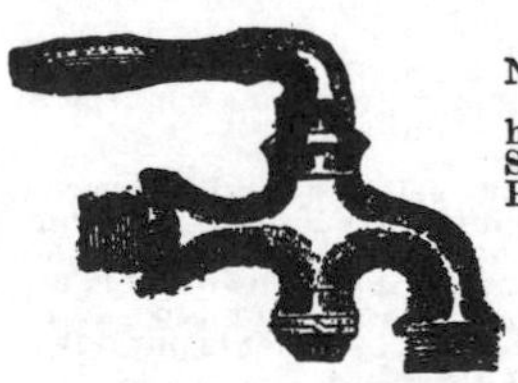

No. 11004. **Hose Bibbs.** For iron pipe. Lever handle finished.

| Size, inches, | ½ | ⅝ | ¾ | 1 |
|---|---|---|---|---|
| Price, each, | $0.48 | .62 | .80 | 1.20 |

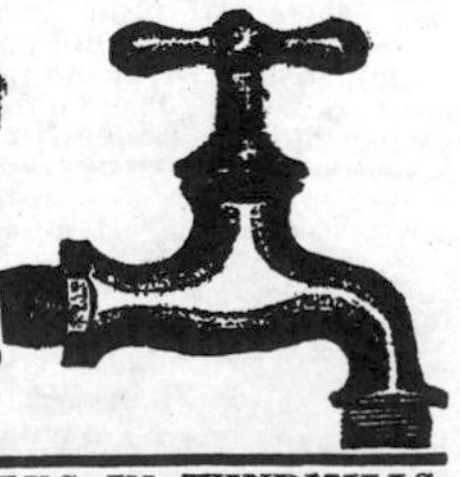

No. 11006. **Compression Hose Bibbs.** Screwed for iron pipe with shoulder, finished.

| Size, inches, | ⅜ | ½ | ⅝ | ¾ | 1 |
|---|---|---|---|---|---|
| Price, each, | $0.42 | .45 | .50 | .75 | 1.20 |

**WONDERFUL** VALUES IN WINDMILLS.
SEE INDEX.....

**DON'T ORDER ONE OF THE SMALL ITEMS ON THIS PAGE SENT ALONE BY MAIL OR EXPRESS, UNLESS YOU CANNOT GET IT AT HOME. WHEN YOU ARE IN NEED OF SMALL ITEMS, MAKE UP A FREIGHT ORDER OF GROCERIES AND SHIP ALL TOGETHER.**

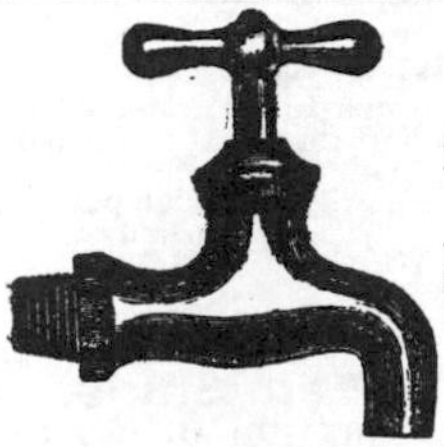

No. 11007. **Compression Plain Bibbs.** Screwed for iron pipe, with shoulder, finished.

| Size, inches, | ⅜ | ½ | ⅝ | ¾ | 1 |
|---|---|---|---|---|---|
| Price, each, | $0.37 | .40 | .45 | .62 | 1.15 |

## Brass Air Cocks.

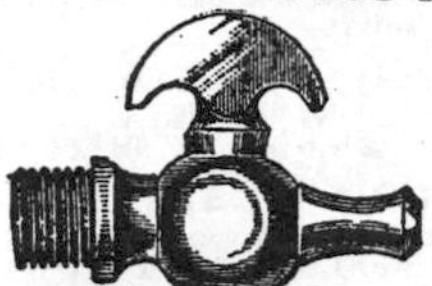

No. 11009.

| Pipe size, in., | ⅛ | ¼ | ⅜ | ½ |
|---|---|---|---|---|
| Price, ea., | $0.12 | .13 | .15 | .18 |

## Brass Oil Cups.

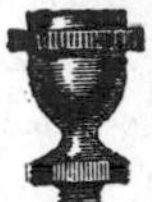

No. 11010. **All brass with screw tops,**

| | | | | | |
|---|---|---|---|---|---|
| Pipe, size of shank, in., | ⅛ | ¼ | ¼ | ⅜ | ⅜ |
| Diameter of body, in.. | ¾ | 1 | 1¼ | 1½ | 2 |
| Price. each, | $0.10 | .12 | .18 | .25 | .50 |

## PIPE FITTERS' TOOLS.

### Open Hinge Malleable Iron Pipe Vise

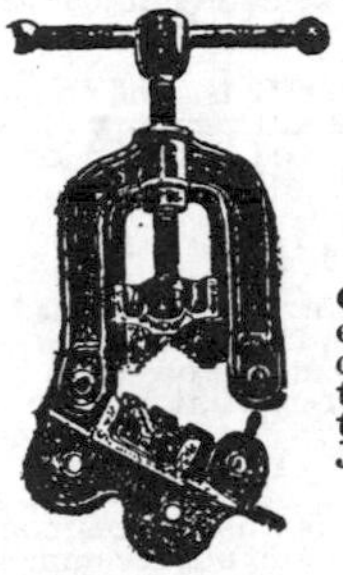

No. 11011. **Has interchangeable Cut Steel Jaws,** and is constructed to do the heaviest work. Great care has been taken in manufacturing the various parts, putting the strength where most desired. Jaws are warranted.

| | No. 1 | No. 2 |
|---|---|---|
| Holds pipe from | ¼ to 2 in. | ¼ to 3 in. |
| Weight, pounds | 20 | 26 |
| Price, each | $2.30 | $3.30 |
| No. 11012. **Extra Jaws** | 1.25 | 1.88 |

### One-Wheel Pipe Cutter.

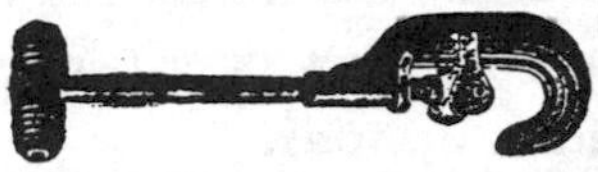

No. 11013. **Made of Malleable Iron** with steel rod and tool steel cutter; lighter and stronger than any other one-wheel cutter made.

| | No. 1 | No. 2 | No. 3 |
|---|---|---|---|
| Cuts pipe from | ⅛ to 1 in. | 1 to 2 in. | 2 to 3 in. |
| Price, each, | $0.80 | $1.65 | $3.30 |
| Extra wheels, | 0.12 | 0.18 | 0.25 |

### Three-Wheel Pipe Cutter.

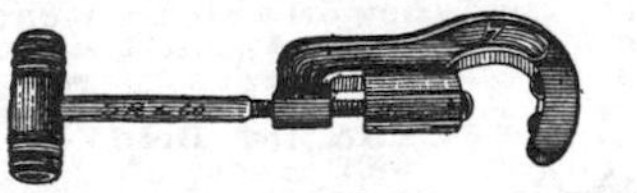

No. 11015. **Made of malleable and wrought iron,** with steel pins and wheels of Jessop's best tool steel. Simple and strong in construction and cuts rapidly and easily.

| | No. 1 | No. 2 | No. 3 |
|---|---|---|---|
| Cuts from | ⅛ to 1 | 1 to 5 | 2 to 3 |
| Price, each, | $1.35 | 1.80 | 3.20 |
| Extra wheels, each, | .12 | .18 | 25 |

### Stanwood Pipe Cutters, Case Hardened.

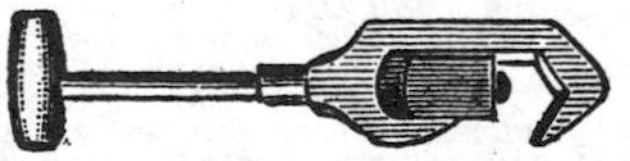

Order No. 11016. Weight, 3¾ lbs., 8½ lbs., 24 lbs.

| | No. 1 | No. 2 | No. 3 |
|---|---|---|---|
| Cuts pipe from | ⅛ to ¾ | 1 to 2 | 2 to 3 |
| Price, each, | $1.20 | $1.55 | $4.67 |
| No. 11017. Cutter wheels. Price, each, | $0.10 | .15 | 20 |
| No. 11018. Cutter Bl'ks and wheels, Price | .35 | .45 | .90 |

### Saunder's Pipe Cutter.

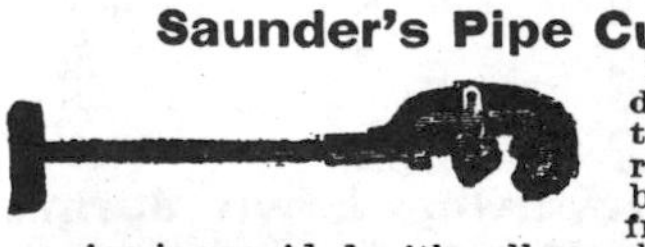

No. 11019. **Saunder's Pipe Cutters.** By referring to cut it will be seen that the front that rubs on pipe is provided with rollers which reduce the friction, making it a very easy cutting tool; weight, 3¾ to 6¾ pounds.

| | No. 1 | No. 2 | No. 3 |
|---|---|---|---|
| Cuts pipe, | ⅛ to 1 | 1 to 2 | 2 to 3 |
| Complete, | $1.65 | $2.50 | $7.87 |
| Wheels, | .24 | .32 | .50 |

### Lightning Screw Plate.

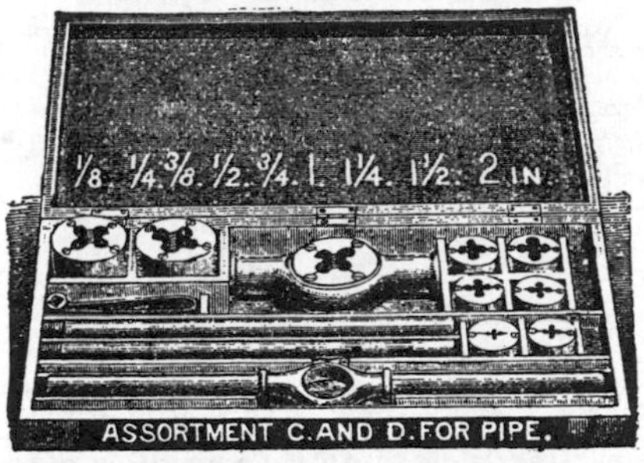


No. 11021. **The Lighting Screw Plate** for pipe; cuts 9 sizes (from ⅛ to 2 inches); weight, 62 pounds. Price, complete in wood case.................. **$21.60**

### Pipe Stock Dies.

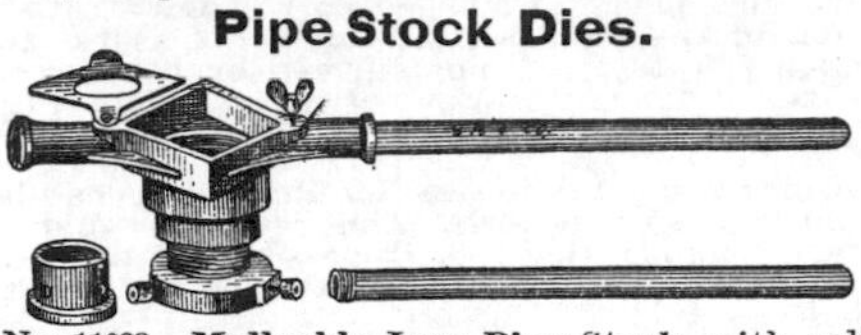

No. 11023. **Malleable Iron Pipe Stock,** with solid steel die. No taps. See No. 11025 for taps. Weights range from 15 to 35 pounds.

| | No. 0 | No. 1 | No. 1½ |
|---|---|---|---|
| Pipe size of dies, | ⅛,¼,⅜,½ | ¼,⅜,½,¾,1 | ¾,1,1¼ |
| Dimension of dies, | 2x1½ | 2½x¾ | 3x¾ |
| Complete with dies, | $2.85 | 3.60 | 3.25 |
| Extra dies, | .52 | .75 | .90 |
| Extra guides, | .12 | .15 | .22 |
| | No. 1¾ | No. 2 | No. 3 |
| Pipe size of dies, | 1, 1¼, 1½ | 1¼,1½, 2 | 2½, 3 |
| Dimension of dies, | 3x¾ | 4x⅞ | 5x1¼ |
| Complete with dies, | $3.25 | 4.75 | 10.00 |
| Extra dies, | .95 | 1.40 | 3 35 |
| Extra guides, | .30 | .30 | .45 |

### Pipe Taps.

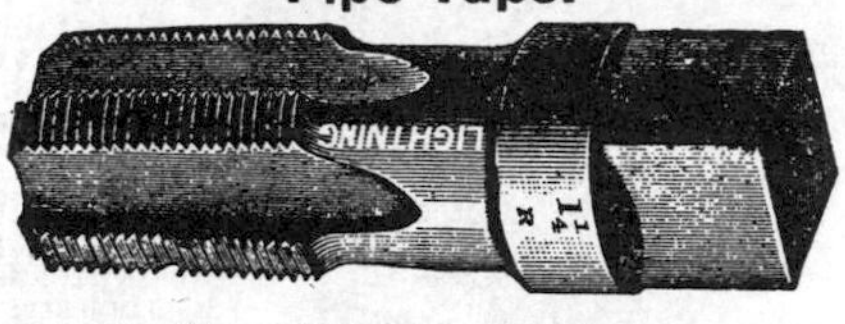

No. 11025 **Pipe Taps.**

| | | | | | | |
|---|---|---|---|---|---|---|
| Size, in., | ⅛ | ¼ | ⅜ | ½ | ¾ | |
| Each, | $0.25 | $0.28 | $0.33 | $0.42 | $0.55 | |
| Size, in., | 1 | 1¼ | 1½ | 2 | 2½ | 3 |
| Each, | $0.70 | $0.74 | $0.92 | $1.25 | $2.10 | $3.00 |

### Brown's Adjustable Pipe Tongs.

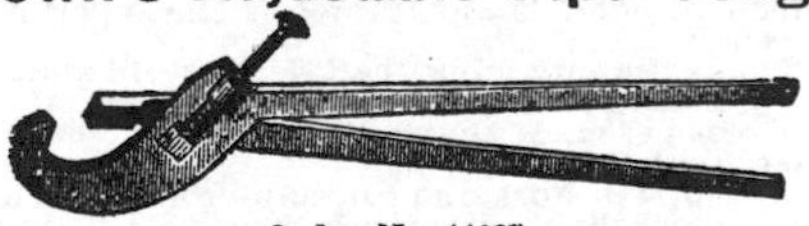

Order No. 11027.

| | No. 1 | No. 1½ | No. 2 | No. 3 | No. 4 |
|---|---|---|---|---|---|
| Takes pipe from | ⅛ to ¾ | ⅜ to 1 | ½ to 1¼ | 1 to 2 | 1¼ to 3 |
| Price. each, | $0.44 | .50 | .65 | .95 | 2.10 |

### Alligator Pipe Wrench.

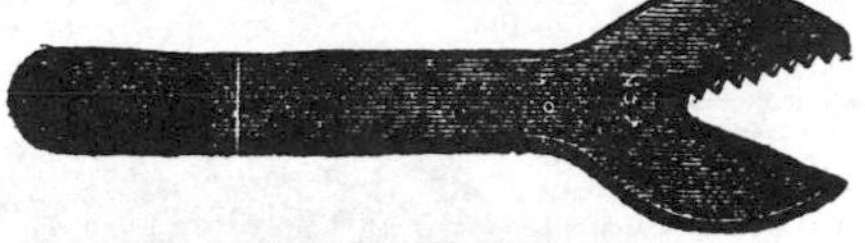

Order No. 11028.

| | | | | | |
|---|---|---|---|---|---|
| Length, inches | 5¾ | 9 | 16 | 22 | 27 |
| Takes pipe, | ⅛ to ⅜ | ⅜ to ¾ | ½ to 1¼ | 1¼ to 2 | 2 to 3 |
| Price, each, | $0.15 | .40 | .75 | 1.15 | 1.80 |
| Weight, lbs., | ¼ | ¾ | 2¾ | 6¼ | 13 |

### Trimo Pipe Wrench.

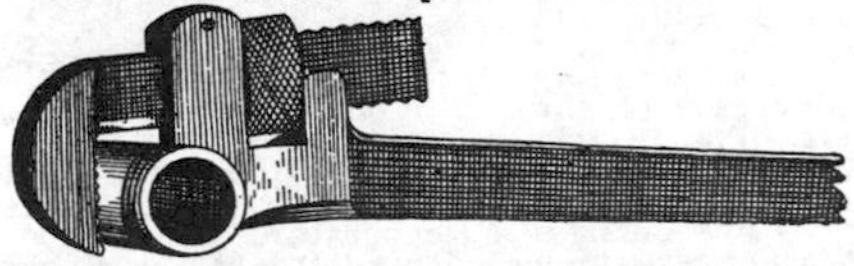

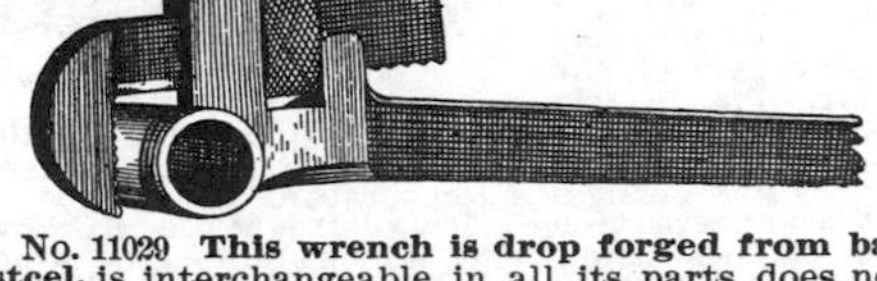

No. 11029 **This wrench is drop forged from bar steel,** is interchangeable in all its parts, does not lock upon the pipe, but releases its hold readily; grips the pipe firmly without lost motion; does not crush the pipe or slip. The movable jaw and the nut are made with a round top and bottom thread, guaranteed not to strip or burr. **An inserted jaw is placed in the handle, which can be renewed for little expense when dull or worn.**

| | | | | |
|---|---|---|---|---|
| Length, open, inches | 10 | 14 | 18 | 24 |
| Takes pipe from..... | ⅛ to ½ | ¼ to ½ | ¼ to 2 | ¼ to 2½ |
| Price, each........... | $1.00 | $1.50 | $1.75 | $2.60 |

**SPECIAL TERMS** ON CLUB ORDERS. SEE PAGE 4.

### The Wright '96 Wrench.

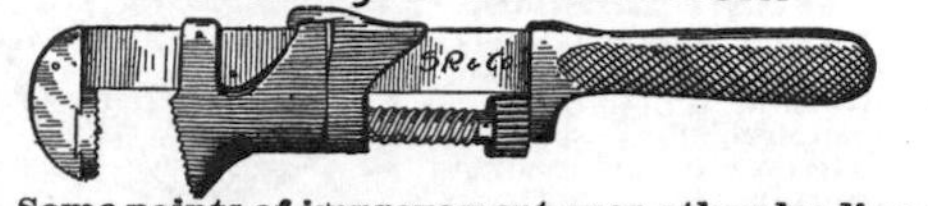

**Some points of improvement over other leading pipe wrenches.**

Will not crush the pipe; is narrower back of the jaw—can get into closer quarters; can be easier operated with one hand; it will always release its grip when its work is done; more surface of thread on screw and nut, which makes it more durable; its checked handle; it being made of iron, will not split or break; it is better balanced, which makes it easier for the operator; in putting on pipe for extention, the handle does not become marred as the wood handle; it has less parts, which makes it less trouble to keep in repair; the jaws can replaced for less money; the spring is so covered there is no danger of its breaking.

No. 11031. 6 inch, opens 1⅛ inch, price each.....$0.95
No. 11032. 8 inch, opens 1½ inch, price each..... 1.00
No. 11033. 10 inch, opens 1¾ inch, price each..... 1.25
No. 11034. 14 inch, opens 2½ inch, price each..... 1.50
No. 11034. 18 inch, opens 3½ inch, price each... . 2.00

### Bemis & Call's Pipe Wrench.

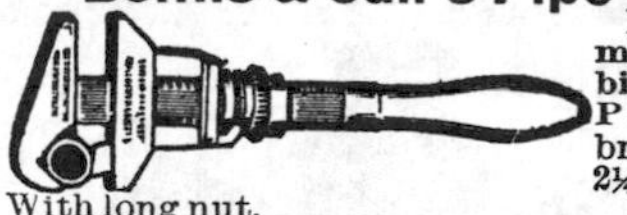

No. 11037 **Bemis & Call's Combination Nut and Pipe Wrench,** bright finish, weight 2¼ to 3¼ pounds. With long nut.

10 inch takes pipe ⅛ to 1 inch. Each..........**$1.42**
12 inch takes pipe ½ to 1¾ inch. Each........ **1.60**
15 inch takes pipe ½ to 2 inch..... ............ **2.25**

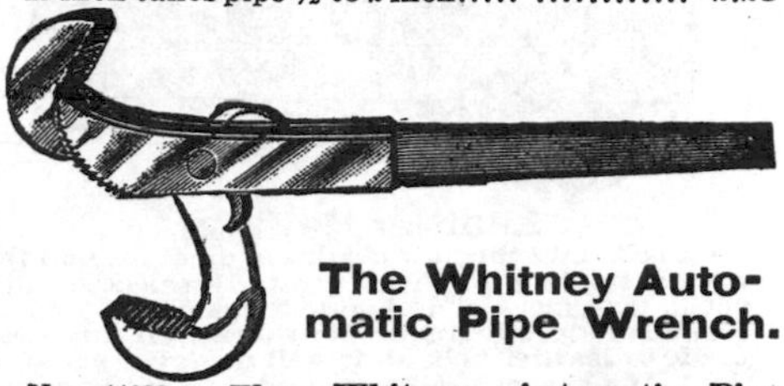

### The Whitney Automatic Pipe Wrench.

No. 11038. **The Whitney Automatic Pipe Wrench,** as illustrated above, shows the jaw open and closed. This is the strongest, lightest, simplest, and most perfect working Pipe Wrench we have ever seen. Carefully made from **selected tool steel** of superior quality. Material and workmanship is fully guaranteed. The harder you pull on this wrench the tighter the grip. **But the grip relaxes instantly when pressure is removed.** The grip being distributed over a larger surface, it is **not so liable to crush** the pipe by a severe strain.

| | | | |
|---|---|---|---|
| Length, inches. | 8 | 14 | 18 |
| Takes pipe, | ⅛ to 1 | ⅛ to 1½ | ¼ to 2½ |
| Price, each, | $0.90 | $1.35 | $1.80 |

### Gas Pliers.

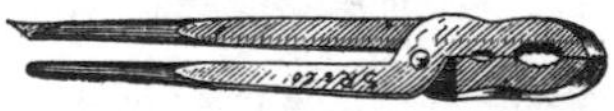

| Length in. | No. 11040. | 6 | 8 | 10 |
|---|---|---|---|---|
| Each, | | $0.25 | .35 | .40 |

### Pipe Lifter.

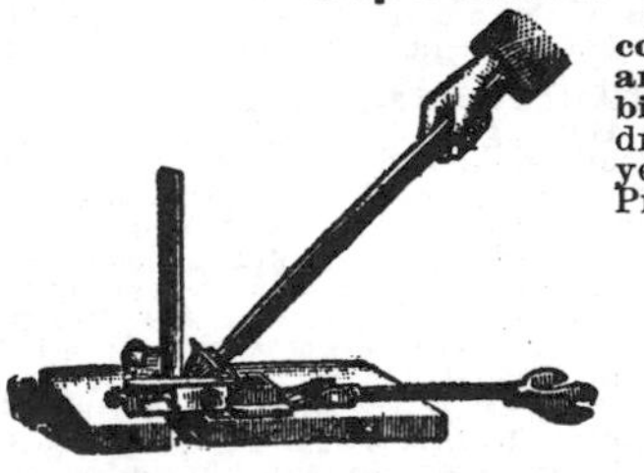

No. 11044 **Babcock Pipe Lifter and Holder combined.** For well drillers; a simple yet complete tool. Price, each, **$4.95**

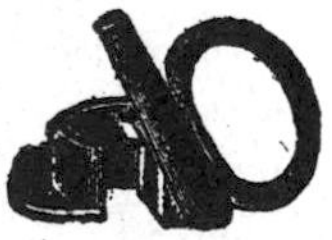

No. 10045 **Pipe Lifting Clevis.** A handy device to prevent pipe from slipping when being taken from well.
Price, each..............**$0.95**

### Sinks.

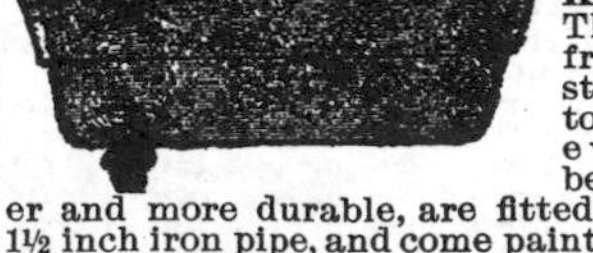

**Wrought Steel Kitchen Sinks.** These sinks are made from one plate of steel and are superior to cast iron sinks in every particular, being lighter, stronger and more durable, are fitted for 1¼ inch lead or 1½ inch iron pipe, and come painted or galvanized in the following sizes:

Order No. 11047. **Painted.**

| Size, | Weight, lbs. | Each. | Size. | Weight, lbs. | Each. |
|---|---|---|---|---|---|
| 16x24x6 | 13 | $1.35 | 20x30x6 | 21¾ | $2.30 |
| 18x30x6 | 15½ | 1.87 | 20x36x6 | 23 | 2.77 |
| 18x36x6 | 18½ | 2.25 | 20x40x6 | 25½ | 3.00 |

Order No. 11048. **Galvanized.**

| Size. | Weight, lbs. | Each. | Size. | Weight, lbs. | Each. |
|---|---|---|---|---|---|
| 16x24x6 | 13 | $2.00 | 20x36x6 | 21¾ | $3.12 |
| 18x30x6 | 15½ | 2.55 | 20x36x6 | 23 | 3.75 |
| 18x36x6 | 18½ | 3.25 | 20x40x6 | 25½ | 4.25 |

**YOU MAY BE SURE OF NOT GETTING AN ANSWER TO YOUR LETTER, IF YOU FAIL TO SIGN YOUR NAME OR GIVE YOUR POST OFFICE ADDRESS. SOME PEOPLE TAKE PAINS TO OMIT THESE IMPORTANT MATTERS.**

## Wash Basins.

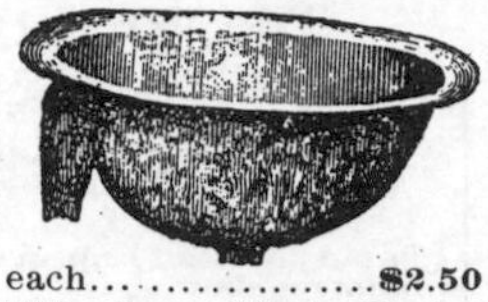

No. 11050 **Iron Wash Basins**, enameled; common overflow; diameter, 14 in. complete with stopper, fitted for either lead or iron pipe.
Price, each.................$2.50

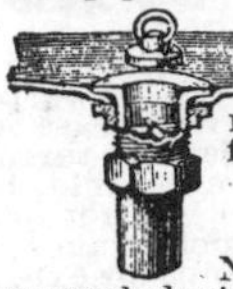

No. 11051 **Iron Wash Basins** enameled; patent overflow; diameter, 14 in., complete with stopper, fitted for either iron or lead pipe.
Price each,...........$2.80

## Urinals.

No. 11051½ **Iron Corner Urinal**, enameled; size, 9 in., fitted for lead pipe.
Price, each..........................$1.70
No. 11053 **Iron Half Circle Urinal**, enameled; size, 12 in., fitted for lead pipe. Price, each........$1.90

## Lead Pipe.

No. 11055

**Lead Pipe**, 1 in. in diam.. 2½ lbs. to ft. Per foot 16c
Lead Pipe, 1¼ " " 3 lbs. " " " 19c
Lead Pipe. 1½ " " 4 lbs. " " " 25c

## Sheet Lead.

No. 11057 **Sheet Lead.** In ordering give thickness wanted. Price per lb.................... $0.07

## BELTING.

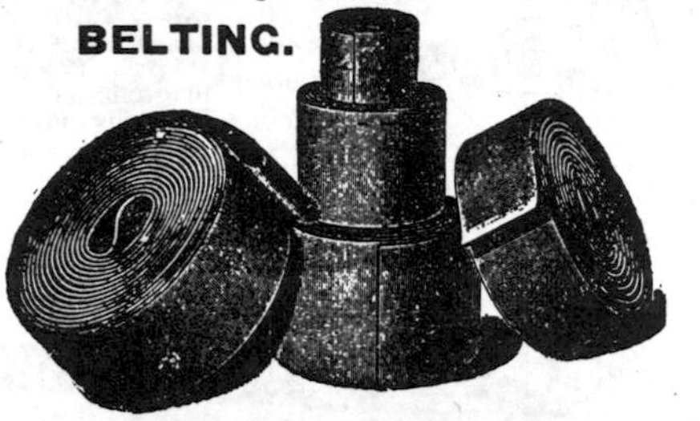

## Leather Belting.

**We sell only the best grades in medium and full weight stock,** made from carefully selected hides of oak tannage, and designate the same as Standard A and Standard B grades. **We do not sell the cheap grade of leather belt, as it will not give satisfaction.** If a cheaper belt is wanted we advise the use of a rubber belt.

No. 11068 **Standard A,** white oak tanned.
No. 11069 **Standard B,** white oak tanned.

| Width. | Price per foot. Standard A. | Standard B. | Width. | Price per foot. Standard A. | Standard B. |
|---|---|---|---|---|---|
| 1 | 6 | 4¾ | 4 | 30 | 24 |
| 1¼ | 8 | 6½ | 4½ | 34 | 27 |
| 1½ | 10 | 8 | 5 | 38 | 30½ |
| 1¾ | 12 | 9½ | 5½ | 42 | 33½ |
| 2 | 14 | 11 | 6 | 46 | 37 |
| 2¼ | 16 | 13 | 7 | 54 | 43 |
| 2½ | 18 | 14½ | 8 | 62 | 49½ |
| 2¾ | 20 | 16 | 9 | 70 | 56 |
| 3 | 22 | 17½ | 10 | 78 | 62½ |
| 3¼ | 24 | 19 | 11 | 86 | 69 |
| 3½ | 26 | 21 | 12 | 94 | 75 |
| 3¾ | 28 | 22½ | | | |

**Double Belts twice the price of single.**
**Extra heavy belts extra prices.**

☞ **In ordering state where belts are to run.** We do not guarantee belts run on the quarter turn, unless they are especially made for that purpose.

**Endless belts made to order at short notice.** The cost of making endless equals the price of 3 feet of belt.

## Rubber Belting.

**Our Rubber Belting is composed of the best quality of Cotton Duck and India Rubber, made in the best manner possible.** These belts will stretch less than any other belts made. On this account the friction always remains firm. Not only is stretch an exceedingly troublesome defect, but it also loosens the friction, and destroys the strength of the belt. **These belts are especially adapted to moist places and agricultural purposes. They are not suitable for thresher or saw-mill belts.** We have this belt in two grades, which we designate as Standard and Extra. We do not guarantee the Standard belt, but it is **all right** for nearly any place where a light, narrow belt is used. For large widths, quick running machinery or extra heavy work, our Extra belt should be used. **We make endless belts only in Extra quality,** For making endless, we charge as much as three feet of belt would cost. **Be careful in making orders for belt, for it is sent as ordered, it will not be taken back or exchanged.**

## 2-Ply Rubber Belting.

No. 11072 **Standard Quality, not Guaranteed. Extra Quality, Guaranteed.**

| Size. | Standard. per ft. | Extra. per ft. | Size. | Standard. per ft. | Extra. per ft. |
|---|---|---|---|---|---|
| 1 in. | $0 02 | $0 03 | 2½ in. | $0 05½ | $0 07½ |
| 1¼ in. | 02¾ | 03¼ | 3 in. | 06½ | 09 |
| 1½ in. | 03¾ | 04½ | 3½ in. | 07½ | 10½ |
| 2 in. | 04½ | 06 | 4 in. | 09 | 12 |

## 3-Ply Rubber Belting.

No. 11073 **Standard Quality, not guaranteed. Extra quality, guaranteed.**

| Size. | Standard, per ft. | Extra, per ft. | Size. | Standard, per ft. | Extra, per ft. |
|---|---|---|---|---|---|
| 2 in. | $0.05 | $0.07 | 8 in. | $0.21½ | $0.28 |
| 2½ in. | .06½ | .10 | 9 in. | .23½ | .32 |
| 3 in. | .07½ | .10½ | 10 in. | .26½ | .36 |
| 3½ in. | .09 | .12 | 11 in. | .29 | .40 |
| 4 in. | .10 | .13½ | 12 in. | .31 | .43 |
| 5 in. | .12½ | .17 | 13 in. | .35 | .47 |
| 6 in. | .15 | .21 | 14 in. | .38 | .51 |
| 7 in. | .18 | .24 | | | |

## 4-Ply Rubber Belting.

No. 11074. **Standard quality, not guaranteed. Extra quality, guaranteed.**

| Size. | Standard, per ft. | Extra. per ft. | Size. | Standard, per ft. | Extra, per ft. |
|---|---|---|---|---|---|
| 3 in. | $0.09 | $0.12½ | 10 in. | $0.34 | $0.43 |
| 3½ in. | .11 | .15 | 11 in. | .38 | .47 |
| 4 in. | .12 | .17 | 12 in. | .42 | .52 |
| 4½ in. | .14 | .19 | 13 in. | .44 | .57 |
| 5 in. | .15 | .21 | 14 in. | .49 | .62 |
| 6 in. | .18 | .25 | 15 in. | .53 | .66½ |
| 7 in. | .20 | .29 | 16 in. | .57 | .71 |
| 8 in. | .23 | .34 | 18 in. | .64 | .81 |
| 9 in. | .26 | .38 | | | |

## Stitched Cotton Belt.

**We have the strongest Stitched Cotton Belting that is manufactured.** The rows of stitches are sewed so close together that the plies **cannot separate. It is Painted with a Composition of a Red Color which Gives it a Good Friction, and Makes it Thoroughly Waterproof.** Oil (no matter in what quantity,) will not injure the belting in the least. We feel confident that the belt will **Give Satisfaction on Any and All Kinds of Works,** as it is thoroughly waterproof, not affected by heat or cold, steam or dampness, or any of the injurious gasses, and will always be found soft and pliable. **Stitched Cotton Belting is Cheaper, More Durable and Much Stronger than Leather Belting,** as has been shown by various tests. This belting is folded in such a manner that it is **Impossible for the Edges to Fray out.** All belting is thoroughly stretched before leaving the factory.

No. 11078 **Four ply Stitched Cotton Belt.**

| Width, in., | 1½ | 2 | 2½ | 3 | 3½ | 4 | 4½ | 5 | 6 | 7 | 8 | 9 | 10 | 12 |
|---|---|---|---|---|---|---|---|---|---|---|---|---|---|---|
| Price, per ft., | $0.07 | .09 | 11 | .13 | .16 | .18 | .20 | .22 | .27 | .31 | .36 | .40 | .45 | .54 |

No. 11079 **Six ply Stitched Cotton Belt.**

| Width, in., | 5 | 6 | 7 | 8 | 9 | 10 | 12 |
|---|---|---|---|---|---|---|---|
| Price per ft., | $0.30 | .36 | .42 | .48 | .54 | .60 | .72 |

## Thresher Belt.

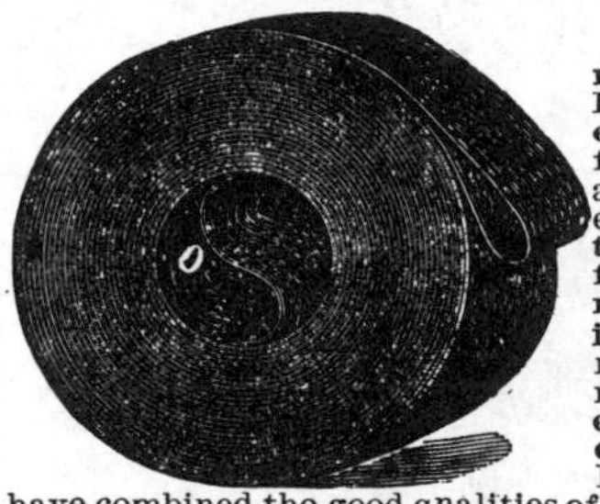

No. 11086 **Strongest and most durable Rubber Thresher Belt manufactured.** It is a well established fact that **cotton belting is far superior to rubber belting** in a great many respects, but rubber belting excels because it does not stretch. In this belt we have combined the good qualities of the cotton belting with the superior qualities of the rubber, and produced the **only belt that will meet all the requirements of a good thresher belt.** This belt is adhered together with rubber friction, and is also sewed closely by the celebrated **"Cross-Stitch,"** which, of itself, is a guarantee of the superiority of this belt.

**This is the only rubber belt that we will guarantee for thresher purposes, and in fact is the only rubber belt yet made that will stand the abuse that thresher belts get.**

We carry in stock and can ship promptly the following lengths of this endless Thresher belt, all 4-ply. **Actual length is three feet less than stated.**

| Length, ft. | 6 in. 4-ply. | 7 in. 4-ply. | 8 in. 4-ply. |
|---|---|---|---|
| 120 | $33 60 | $39 60 | $43 20 |
| 130 | 36 40 | 42 90 | 46 80 |
| 140 | 39 20 | 46 20 | 50 40 |
| 150 | 42 00 | 49 50 | 54 00 |
| 160 | 44 80 | 52 80 | 57 60 |

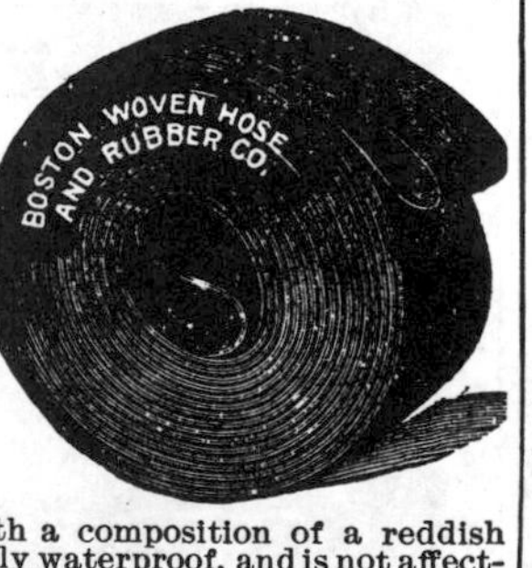


No. 11088. **Grain King Endless Stitched Canvas Thresher Belt** is far superior to all other canvas thresher belting on account of the process of its manufacture. The splice is made in such a manner that the belt is no thicker at this point, and **is just as strong and flexible as any other part of the belt.** The **"Grain King"** is painted with a composition of a reddish color and is thoroughly waterproof, and is not affected by any change of temperature, neither by oil. **It is a cheap, strong belting.** It is sewed with rows of stitches throughout its entire length, which makes it practically **impossible for the plies to separate.** We carry the following length of this 4-ply belt in stock and can ship promptly. The actual length of these Belts is three feet less than stated.

| Length. | 6 in. 4 ply. | 7 in. 4 ply. | 8 in. 4 ply. |
|---|---|---|---|
| 120 | $25.60 | $30.40 | $35.20 |
| 130 | 27.74 | 32.94 | 38.14 |
| 140 | 29.88 | 35.48 | 41.08 |
| 150 | 32.02 | 37.02 | 44.02 |
| 160 | 34.16 | 39.56 | 46.96 |

## Rawhide Lace Leather.

No. 11090. **We sell the best grade of Rawhide Lace Leather** in sides of from 5 to 15 square feet (we do not cut) for **20c** per square foot.

No. 11092. **Lace Leather Cutters,** adjustable to cut varions widths. Price, each...............$0.40

## Cut Rawhide Lace.

No. 11094. **Cut Lacing comes in bunches of 100 feet.** Will sell a half bunch at one-half the price of full bunch.

| Width. | Price per bunch of 100 feet. | Width. | Price per bunch of 100 feet. |
|---|---|---|---|
| ¼ | $0.50 | ½ | $1.00 |
| 5-16 | .60 | ⅝ | 1.35 |
| ⅜ | .70 | ¾ | 1.60 |

## Belt Studs.

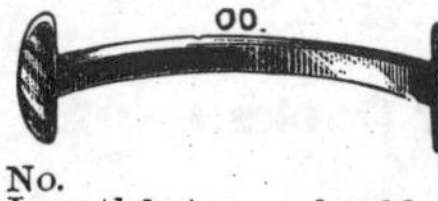


No. 11096. **Blake's Belt Studs.** Recognized as the best belt fastener made.

| No. | 00 | 0 | 1 | 2 | 3 | 4 | 5 |
|---|---|---|---|---|---|---|---|
| Length between shoulders, | 15-16 | 11-16 | ¾ | 9-16 | ½ | 7-16 | ⅜ |
| Per 100, | $0.90 | .71 | .60 | .45 | .30 | .30 | .23 |
| Per dozen, | .12 | .10 | .08 | .06 | .04 | .04 | .03 |

## Rubber Garden Hose.

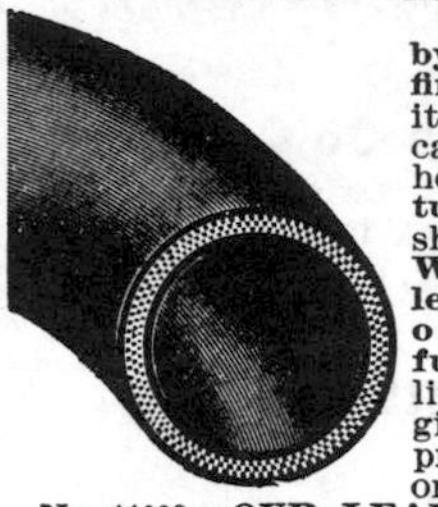

**Our Hose is made entirely by machinery from start to finish,** so there is no possibility of poor goods caused by careless operatives. All our hose is made with **seamless tube.** When not in use hose should be kept in a cool place. **We sell Garden Hose in lengths of 25 and 50 feet only. Couplings are not furnished.** If you want couplings, order them separately, giving catalogue number and price, and we will put them on for you.

No. 11098. **OUR LEADER HOSE** is good enough for ordinary use. In fact, there are very few places where this would not give as good satisfaction as higher priced hose. Without couplings.

| | 3-ply. | | 4-ply. | |
|---|---|---|---|---|
| Diameter, inches, | ¾ | 1 | ¾ | 1 |
| Per foot, | $0.07 | .11 | .10 | .14 |

No. 11100. **Our Best Grade Hose** is constructed of best possible material. Will stand more pressure and wear longer than the Leader grade. **Yon can't buy better hose than this, no matter what you pay.**

| | 3-ply. | | 4-ply. | |
|---|---|---|---|---|
| Diameter, inches | ¾ | 1 | ¾ | 1 |
| Per foot, | $0.08½ | .12 | .11 | 15 |

No. 11102. **Competition Hose** is what is commonly sold. It is not guaranteed and we do not recommend it. We have this season secured the best hose of this grade that we have ever seen. We sell it in 50 ft. lengths only, without couplings, ¾ inch, 3-ply. Price per length of 50 ft............................ $2.35

## Hose Couplings.

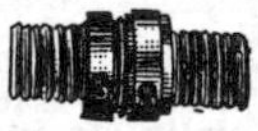

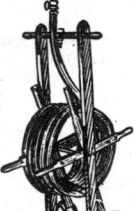

No. 11102 **Brass Hose Couplings.** Will fit any kind of hose of inside measure as given.

| Inch, | Per pair, | Inch, | Per pair, |
|---|---|---|---|
| ¾ | $0 06 | 1¼ | $0 40 |
| 1 | 20 | 1½ | 55 |

## Hose Splicer.

No. 11104 **Hose Splicer for mending Hose,** or joining short pieces together.
Size, ¾ inch, price, **5e** each; size, 1 inch, price, **5c** each.

## Hose Clamps.

No. 11105 **Hose Clamps,** made of brass, for fastening hose to couplings or splicer. Cheap as a wire band and very much better, as no tools are required except a small screw driver to put it on or remove it.
Size, ¾ in., price each, **4c**; size, 1 in., price each, **8c.**

## Hose Reels.

No. 11107 **Hose Reel,** strong and well made of hardwood, iron wheels. No hose included.
Price each...................$0.65

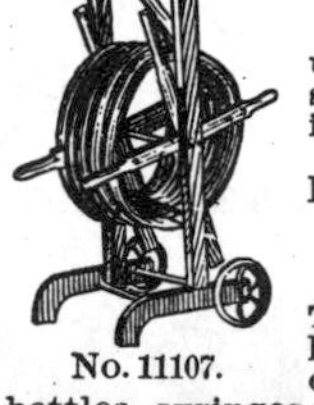

No. 11107.

## Hose Nozzles.

No. 11108 **This Nozzle can be regulated to throw either a solid stream or a spray by simply turning the cock.**

¾ in. 1 in.
Price, each...**$0.45 $0.58**

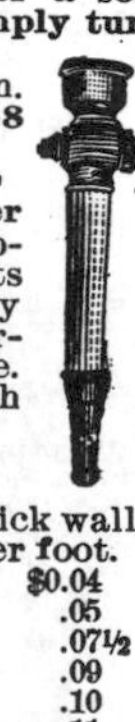

No. 11108

## Rubber Tubing.

No. 11109 **Pure Rubber Tubing,** is used for siphoning liquors out of vats or barrels; for nursery bottles, syringes, and numerous other purposes. It will not stand much pressure. Made in twogrades. Thin wall is 1-16 inch thick. Thcik wall is 3-32 inch thick.

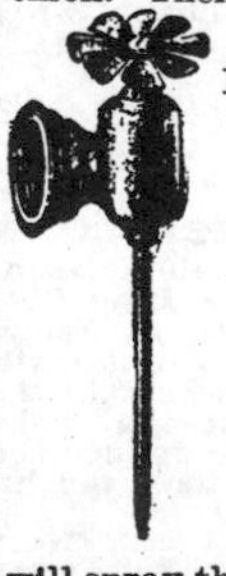

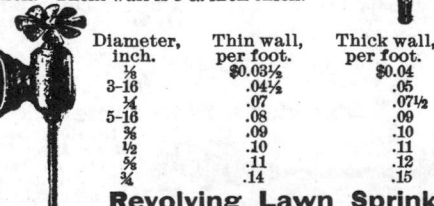

| Diameter, inch. | Thin wall, per foot. | Thick wall, per foot. |
|---|---|---|
| ⅛ | $0.03½ | $0.04 |
| 3-16 | .04½ | .05 |
| ¼ | .07 | .07½ |
| 5-16 | .08 | .09 |
| ⅜ | .09 | .10 |
| ½ | .10 | .11 |
| ⅝ | .11 | .12 |
| ¾ | .14 | .15 |

## Revolving Lawn Sprinklers to Stick in the Ground.

No. 11111. **The Crown Sprinkler** will spray the water perfectly for 10 to 20 feet each way. Made of brass, nickel plated, fits ¾ inch hose only. Price, Each..............................**25c**

No. 11112 **The Little Wonder Lawn Sprinkler** is one of the best sellers we have. It is strong, durable, and does the work. Price, each..................**18c**

## CARRIAGE HARDWARE AND SUPPLIES,

**In calling your attention** to this complete department, we are confident that we can supply the great need of thousands of our customers who find it constantly necessary to replace various parts of their vehicles, but who have been paying exorbitant retail prices. **We offer a line** that has no equal in general excellence of material and finish. At the same time our contracts with manufacturers are so advantageous that we are in a position to make unusually low prices.

### Buggy Tops.

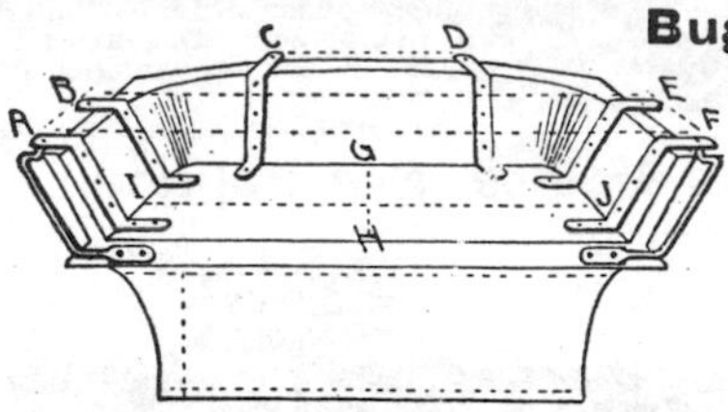


**In ordering buggy tops** give measurements from center to center of holes in irons, as shown in above cut; width from A to F, from B to E, from A to B, from C to D. State whether you want 3 or 4 bows, and give choice of color of lining.

**In ordering cushions** give measurements from I to J on bottom of seat, from G to H width of seat at bottom, and state if square or round corners are wanted.

**In ordering cushions with fall** give measurements of cushion as above, and also width of fall at the bottom and distance from bottom of seat to floor of buggy. Our buggy tops are shipped in light but strong crates, and are not liable to injury in transportation.

### Our Terms of Shipment Are Liberal.

Any of these goods will be sent by freight C. O. D., subject to examination on receipt of $5, balance and freight charges to be paid after goods are received. **A Discount of 3 per cent.** allowed if cash in full accompanies your order.

**You will save money** by buying your own needed repairs direct from us at manufacturers' lowest prices. **Freight** amounts to nothing compared with what you save in price. Nearly all these goods are taken at second-class rate or lower.

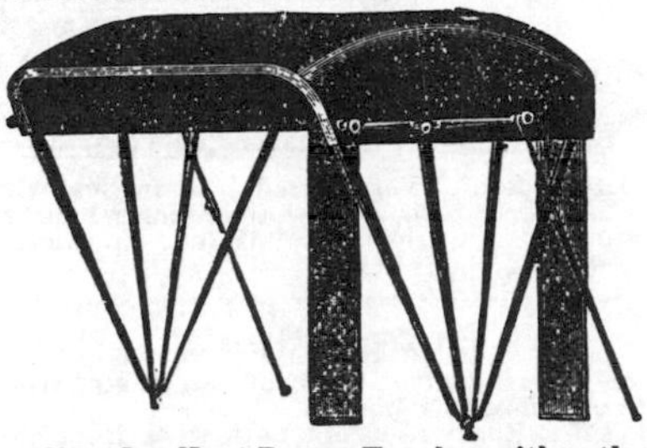

No. 11200. Our No. 1 Buggy Top has either three or four bows as desired. This is a full rubber top with steel bow sockets, second growth top bows, wrought iron joints, japanned nuts, iron rivets, Thomas top props, concealed joints between two back bows. Top lined with wool cloth, back stays lined, back curtain lined, rubber side curtains, Indigo dyed back, glass in back curtains. Our special price for No. 1 top, as above described .......... **$8.35**

No. 11201. Our No. 2 Buggy Top is in appearance just like No. 1 shown above. However, our No. 2 has leather quarters and stay top, steel bow sockets, second growth top bows, wrought iron joints, japanned nuts, iron rivets, Thomas top props, top lined with all-wool cloth, back stays lined, back curtains lined, rubber side curtains, front valance sewed on, Indigo dyed No. 12 back, glass in back curtain. Three or four bows, as desired. Our special price, as described .......... **$10.00**

No. 11202. Our No. 3 Buggy Top is full leather, guaranteed to be genuine leather. This top is lined with all-wool cloth, back stays lined, rubber side curtains, Indigo dyed No. 12 back, glass in back curtain. Three or four bows as desired. Steel bow sockets, second growth top bows, wrought iron joints, japanned nuts, iron rivets, Thomas top props, concealed joints between two back bows. Our special price on our No. 3 full leather top .......... **$13.65**

### Extras.

No. 11205. For quarter rail attached to above top add .......... **$1.35**

No. 11206. For our No. 2 rail welded to fit seat, with lazy back, wood and attached to above top, add .. **$1.35**

No. 11207. Extra rubber side curtains. Per pair, **$2.00**

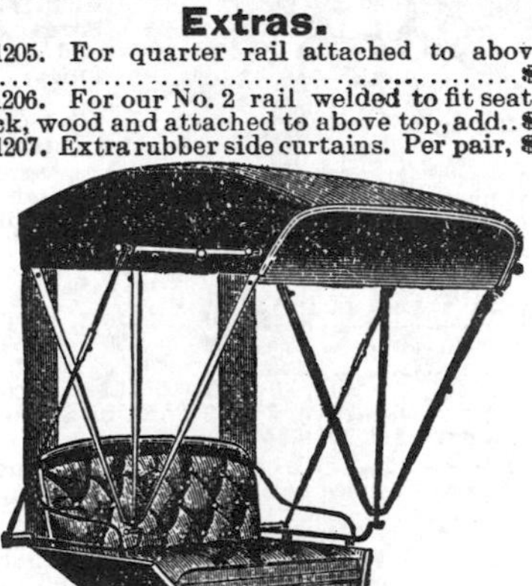

No. 11210. The accompanying illustration shows our No. 4 Buggy Top complete, with seat, full back and cushion with fall. This top is made of 22 ounce rubber, with seat, wrought rail and joints. Three or four steel socket bows. Top, back stays and back curtain lined with all wool fast color cloth, either blue or green, side curtains indigo dyed rubber, 12 ounce blue or green cloth on full back and cushion. These are either biscuit or diamond tufted, and filled with selected moss. Front and back valance nailed on. Black nuts and iron rivets. Our special price on No. 4 Top, complete, as described .......... **$14.65**

No. 11211. Our No. 5 Buggy Top, complete, with full back and cushion, is made like shown in the picture of our No. 4, but has leather quarter and stay, and is complete with seat, wrought rail and joints, three or four steel bows, top, back stays and back curtain lined with all wool fast color cloth. Rubber side curtains, 14 ounce blue or green cloth in full back and cushions. Front valance sewed on. Black nuts and iron rivets. Our special price .......... **$18.00**

No. 11212. Our No. 6 Top is the finest Buggy Top made. It has machine buffed leather top and is complete with seat, cushion and full back. Wrought rail and joints. Three or four steel bows as desired. Lined throughout, except side curtains, with 10 ounce all wool fast color cloth. Rubber side curtains, 14 ounce blue or green cloth on full back and cushion. The latter is tufted in biscuit and diamond style, and stuffed with moss. Black nuts and iron rivets. Valance sewed on. Style same as shown in picture of No. 4 Buggy Top. Our special price .......... **$25.00**

### Extras.

No. 11215. Extra rubber back curtains. Each .. **$1.50**

No. 11216. Extra rubber back stays. Each ..... **$1.50**

### Extension Tops.

In measuring for Extension Tops, give length of seat from outside to outside in top of rim, in widest place, and state if wood or iron seat. Also give the distance from front of front seat to front of back seat on bottom of seats, and state if back seat is higher or lower than front seat.

No. 11219. Our No. 7 Extension Top is a 4-bow, 26 ounce rubber top, lined throughout with all wool cloth, except side curtains, which are indigo dyed rubber.

Wrought iron joints, japanned nuts and iron rivets. Front valance sewed on. No rail. Our special price .......... **$12.65**

No. 11220. Our No. 8 Extension Top, just the same as our No. 7 above described, but has leather quarter and stay. Our special price .......... **$16.65**

No. 11222. Our No. 9 is a full leather Extension Top, otherwise just the same as No. 7, described above. Our special price .......... **$22.65**

All tops over 42 inches wide cost from **65c** to **$2.00** extra, in accordance with the extra width.

### Canopy Tops.

In measuring for Canopy Top give exact distance from back of back seat to front end of body. Give exact width of seats from outside to outside on top. These canopy tops are the best the market affords.

No. 11224. Our No. G 100 Canopy Top is covered with black drill, lined with all wool cloth, and ornamented with all wool fringe. Price, for 5 foot length or less, without standards or curtains .......... **$7.30**

For larger sizes add extra for each additional foot .......... **$1.35**

No. 11226. Complete set side and back curtains, indigo dyed rubber .......... **$5.65**

### Canopy Top Standards.

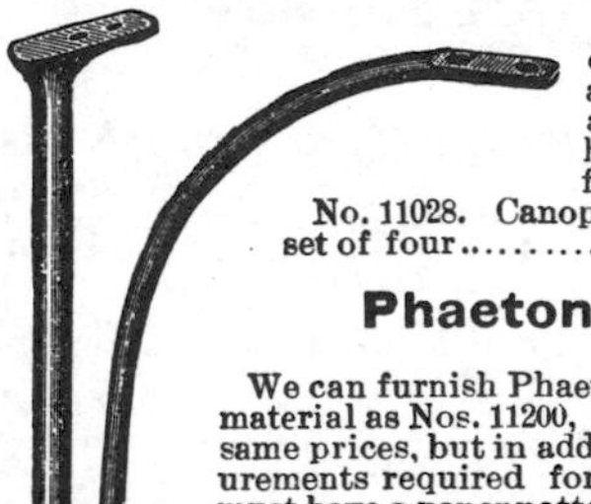

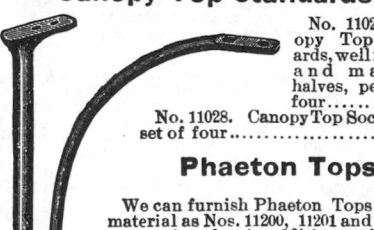

No. 11027. Canopy Top Standards, well finished, and made in halves, per set of four ....... **$2.65**

No. 11028. Canopy Top Sockets per set of four .......... **66c**

### Phaeton Tops.

We can furnish Phaeton Tops of same material as Nos. 11200, 11201 and 11202 at same prices, but in addition to the measurements required for buggy tops we must have a paper pattern showing exact shape and size of back of seat. State how much higher the back gooseneck is than the front one. The measurements must be made very carefully and phaeton top cannot be returned if sent as ordered. Cash in full must accompany orders for phaeton tops.

### Wagon Sunshade Top.

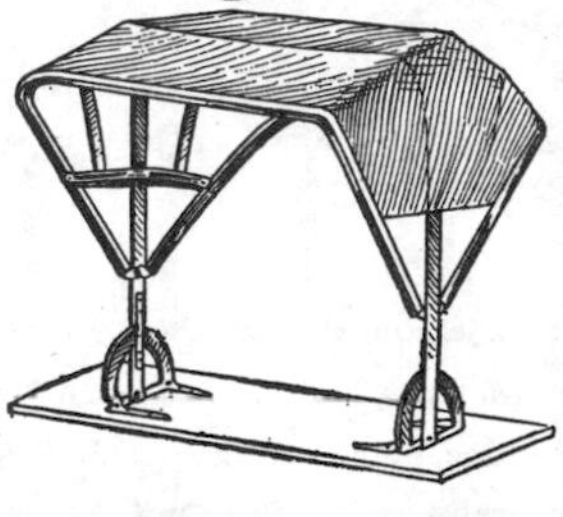

Especially adapted for express and farm wagons.

This top is furnished complete with irons and bolts, ready to attach to seat. The irons will fit any kind of a seat. The sizes we keep in stock are for seats measuring from 32 to 44 inches. For extra wide tops the additional cost of making will be added. When ordering give width of seat outside to outside on top of seat at back corner.

No. 11230. Covered with brown duck and fringed. Price .......... **$3.75**

No. 11231. Covered with awning stripe and fringed. Price .......... **$4.25**

No. 11232. Covered with enameled drill and fringed. Price .......... **$3.85**

No. 11233. Covered with rubber and fringed. Price .......... **$4.50**

### Storm Wagon Top.

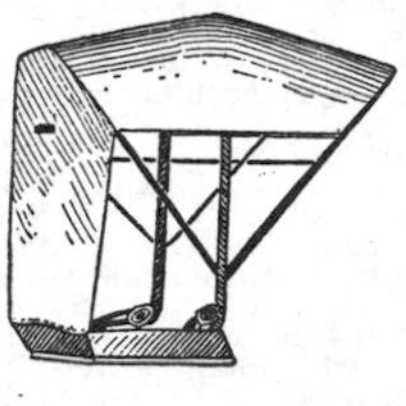

It is adapted for any style wagon. Not suitable for a buggy; seat not furnished. This top, with all irons complete, ready to attach to a seat, is made with side and back curtains, side curtains can be detached; back curtains to roll up; made to fit seats from 32 to 44 inches across top of flare. Be sure to send measure of seat from out to out on top of seat, at back corner.

| | | Price. |
|---|---|---|
| No. 11236. | Covered with brown duck .......... | **$6.12** |
| No. 11237. | Covered with awning stripe .......... | **6.65** |
| No. 11238. | Covered with enameled drill .......... | **6.30** |
| No. 11239. | Covered with rubber drill .......... | **7.70** |
| No. 11240. | Covered with sail duck .......... | **5.75** |

### $1.95 For the Best Wagon Umbrella Made.

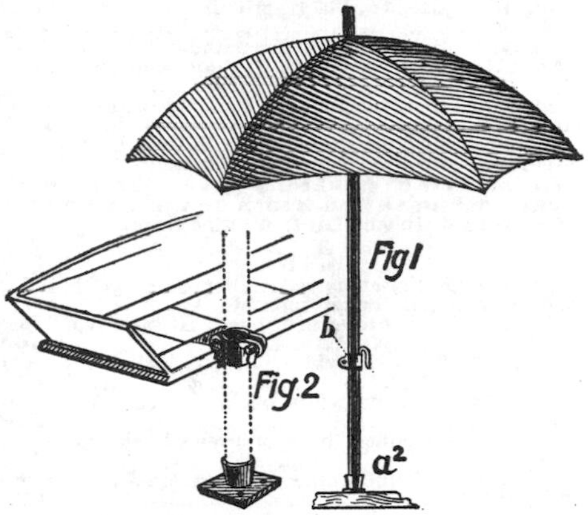


This is the most popular Umbrella on the market, **very latest and best.** This Umbrella has **heavy duck covering,** in blue, brown or white, or in following stripes: Tan and white, red and white, or blue and white. **Guaranteed the strongest** Umbrella made. Six steel ribs, 1½ inch white ash handle, 5 feet 8 inch spread, cover removable. Price includes all fixtures complete.

**This is the Umbrella to buy,** and our special price below all others is $1.95.

No. 11240½. Price .......... **$1.95**

### Wagon Umbrellas with Fixture Sockets,

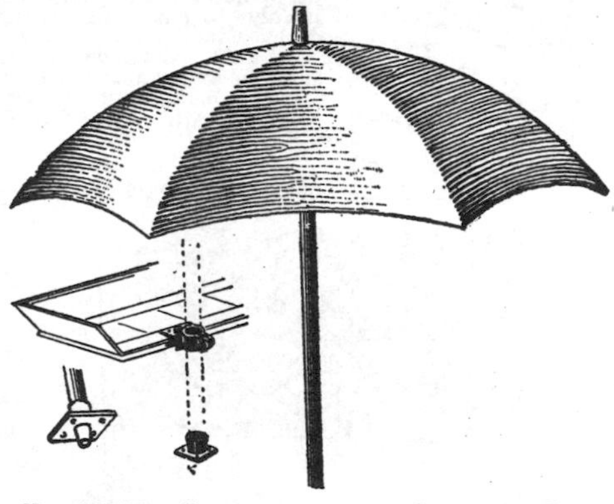

No. 11241½. **Compare our prices on these** goods with those of other houses and see if we cannot save you 25 to 50 per cent. on price.

**Our price .......... $1.50 to $2.20**

These Umbrellas come with best quality heavy steel ribs and fixtures. Handles, 1¼ inch seasoned white ash, oiled and varnished.

**Colors** blue, drab, buff or black. Heavy muslin.

☞ **Be sure to state color wanted.**

The most complete fixtures yet produced. Made of the best malleable iron, light and strong, quickly applied, and holds the Umbrella secure. We furnish all extras complete without extra charge.

| | | |
|---|---|---|
| 36-inch, 8 ribs, with fixtures .......... | each, | **$1.50** |
| 36-inch, 10 ribs, with fixtures .......... | " | **1.60** |
| 38-inch, 8 ribs, with fixtures .......... | " | **1.65** |
| 38-inch, 10 ribs, with fixtures .......... | " | **1.75** |
| 40-inch, 10 ribs, with fixtures .......... | " | **1.90** |
| 40-inch, 10 ribs, double face duck, green inside, duck outside, with fixtures .......... | each, | **2.20** |

## Buggy Cushions and Falls and Full Backs.

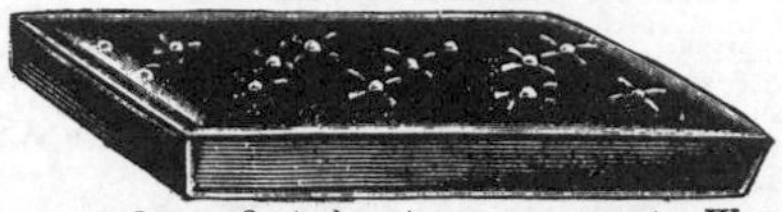

These goods are first-class in every respect. We make strictly inside prices on these goods and can save you a large percentage on each purchase. The price of full back is just the same as that of the cushion with fall. If you want both the full back and cushion with fall, the price will be just twice that of the cushion and fall alone.

No. 11244. Black drill Cushion and Fall ........**78c**
No. 11245. Black drill Cushion without Fall......**65c**
No. 11246. Rubber Cushion with Fall..............**94c**
No. 11247. Rubber Cushion without Fall..........**80c**
No. 11248. Blue or green cloth Cushion, plain top, with Fall........................................**$1.67**
No. 11249. Blue or green cloth Cushions, with Fall, biscuit or diamond tufted, filled with moss......**$2.00**
No. 11250. Fancy leather Cushions and Fall, plain top..................................................**$3.00**
No. 11251. Fancy leather Cushions, without Fall, plain top..........................................**$2.50**
No. 11252. Black leather Cushion, with Fall, plain top..................................................**$2.95**
No. 11253. Black leather Cushions, without Fall, plain top..........................................**$2.50**
No. 11254. Black split leather Cushions, with Fall, plain top..........................................**$2.55**
No. 11255. Black split leather Cushions, without Fall, plain top..........................................**$2.00**
No. 11256. Green or black artificial leather Cushions and Falls..........................................**$1.66**
No. 11257. Same as No. 11256 without Fall..... **1.35**
No. 11258. Brown corduroy Cushions and Falls, plain top..................................................**$2.00**
No. 11259. Brown corduroy Cushions, without Falls, plain top..........................................**$1.75**

All above Cushions are based on 34-inch length. All larger sizes we charge 7c per inch extra.

**In ordering Cushions give size of seat. Measure length and width on inside bottom of seat and do not include the flare.**

## Drill.

Standard quality embossed rubber Carriage Drill for mending cushions, buggy tops, etc.

No. 11261. 18 ounce, white back, 50 inch wide, per yard..................................................**40c**
No. 11262. 22 ounce, white back, 50 inches wide, per yard..................................................**47c**
No. 11263. 28 ounce, white back, 50 inches wide, per yard..................................................**54c**
No. 11264. 22 ounce, blue or green back, 50 inches wide, per yard..........................................**60c**
No. 11265. 22 ounce, blue or green back, 36 inches wide, per yard..........................................**47c**

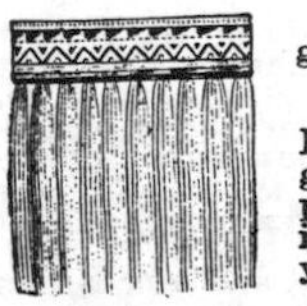

No. 11267. Carriage fringe, blue or green, 5 inches deep, per yard....**42c**

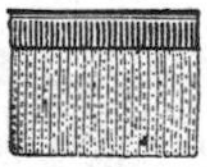

No. 11269. Worsted Boullion, blue or green, 4 inches deep, per yard, **22c**; 5 inches deep, per yard............**25c**

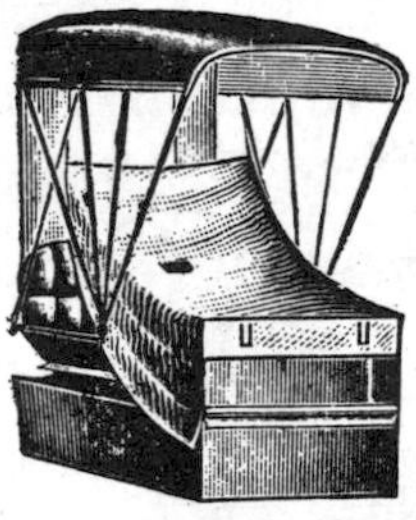

## Buggy Aprons.

No. 11271. Holden's patent Buggy Apron, made of waterproof cloth, extra heavy, adjustable to any width buggy dash. Each...........**$1.10**

No. 11272. Carriage Apron, same as buggy apron, except in size, being much larger. Each..................**$1.55**

## Buggy Dashes.

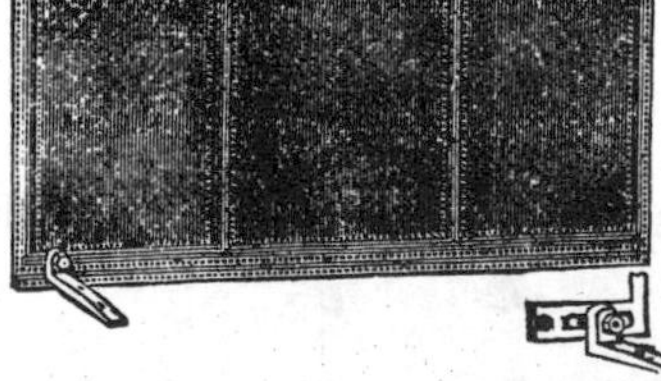

Made of best leather molding, completely ironed and ready to put on your buggy. All have patent extensions to fit bodies not exact measurement of the dash.

No. 11274. Buggy Dashes, 11 inches high by 21 inches long. Price, each..........................................**$1.20**
For each additional inch in length with same height add **3** cents to above price.
No. 11275. Buggy Dashes, 13 inches high by 24 inches long. Price, each..........................................**$1.40**
For each additional inch in length, same height, add **5** cents to price of 13x24 Dash.
No. 11276. Buggy Dashes, 15 inches high by 24 inches long. Price, each..........................................**$1.60**
For each additional inch in length for 15 inch height add **5** cents to the price of the 15x24 Dash.

Irons for square end bodies sent unless ordered for flaring end bodies.

## Carriage Lamps.

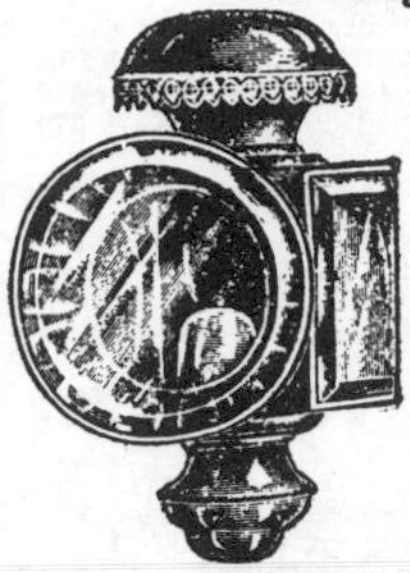

Latest style, very handsome black japanned, with nickel trimmings.

No. 11278. Small size, plain glass, suitable for buggies, phaetons, etc. Price, per pair..........................**$3.25**
No. 11279. Large size, having beveled glass, suitable for surreys, carriages, etc. Price, per pair..................**$4.00**

For Dash Lamps and Driving Lanterns, see index.

## Curtain Lights.

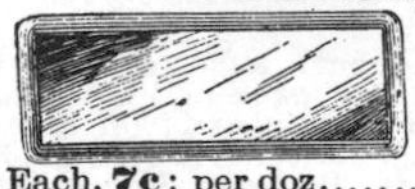

No. 11281. Buggy Curtain Lights, square corners, japanned frame, 1¼x5 inch opening, complete with glass and frame. Each, **7c**; per doz.........................................**75c**
No. 11282. 1¾x5½. Each, **9c**; per doz...........**96c**

## Button Holes.

No. 11284. Talcott's Elastic Button Holes for carriage or wagon curtains, round hole, japanned frame, rubber center.
Per doz., **30c**; per gross....... **$3.00**

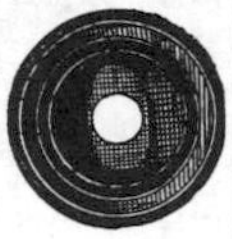

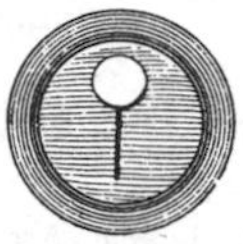

## Knob Eyelets.

No. 11286. Knob Eyelets, japanned frame, goat leather center.
Per doz., **10c**; per gross...... **65c**

## Metallic Loops and Buckles.

Metallic Loops are stamped from metal to imitate patent leather.

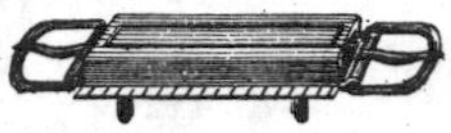

No. 11288. Double buckle Loop, 2½ inches long. Each, **4c**; per doz..**30c**

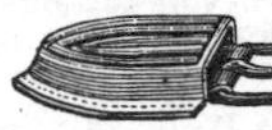

No. 11289. Single Buckle and Loop.
Each, **3c**; per doz ......... **25c**

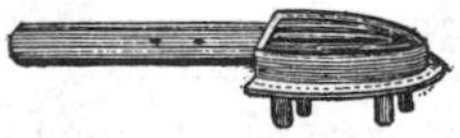

## Metallic Strap Loops.

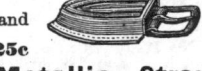

11291 Each..........**$0.04**
Per doz.......... **.26**

## Curtain Straps and Fasteners.

11292 Price, each.......**$0.03**
Per doz................. **.25**

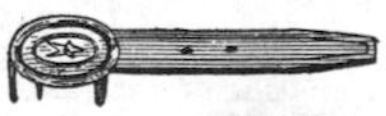

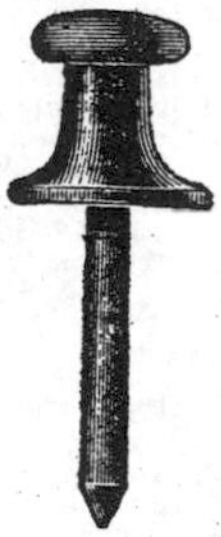

## Japanned Carriage Knobs.

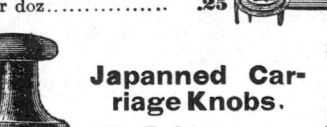

11293 To drive.
Per doz..... ....**$0.05**
Per gross......... **.35**
11294 To screw. For single or double curtains.
Per doz..........**$0.08**
Per gross........ **.65**

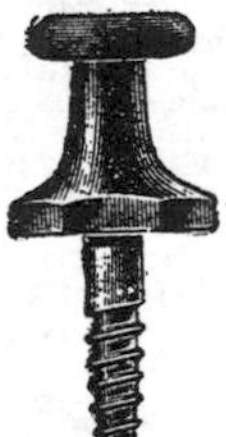

## Carriage Top Prop Nuts.

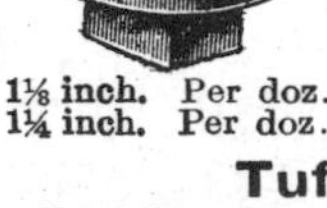

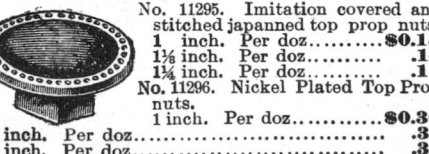

No. 11295. Imitation covered and stitched japanned top prop nuts.
1 inch. Per doz..........**$0.13**
1⅛ inch. Per doz.......... **.14**
1¼ inch. Per doz.......... **.15**
No. 11296. Nickel Plated Top Prop nuts.
1 inch. Per doz...........**$0.30**
1⅛ inch. Per doz.......................................... **.31**
1¼ inch. Per doz.......................................... **.32**

## Tufting Buttons.

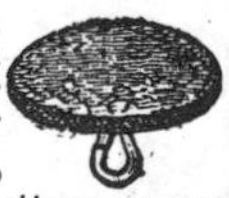

No. 11298. Japanned Tufting Buttons.
Per paper of 1 gross, **20c**; per dozen papers......................................**$2.16**
No. 11299. Cloth Covered Tufting Buttons, green or blue.
Per dozen, **4c**; per gross.........**$0.40**
No. 11300. Leather Covered Tufting Buttons, green.
Per dozen, **5c**; per gross.................................**$0.50**

## Lining Nails.

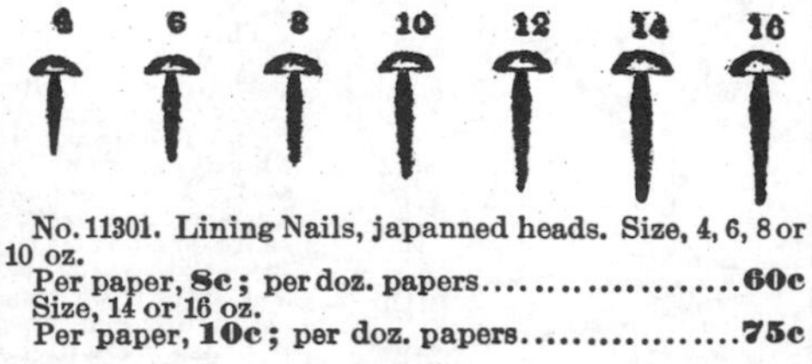


No. 11301. Lining Nails, japanned heads. Size, 4, 6, 8 or 10 oz.
Per paper, **8c**; per doz. papers....................**60c**
Size, 14 or 16 oz.
Per paper, **10c**; per doz. papers....................**75c**

## Toe Pads.

11303. Patent Leather Toe Pads or Panel Protectors, placed on the side of the buggy, prevent the varnish from being scratched by the shoe while getting in or out of the buggy. The ornamental designs are embossed. They are an addition to the appearance of any buggy.
Per pair..........................**$0.30**

## Bodies, Not Painted.

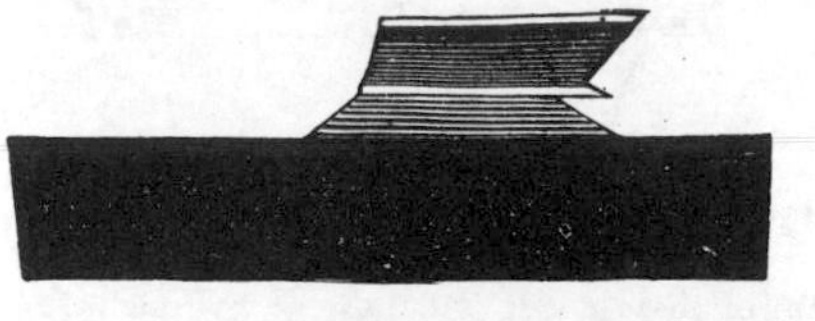

No. 11305. Piano Buggy Body, 24 inches wide and 48 inches long, or 25 inches wide and 50 inches long, panels 8 inches deep; weight, about 50 lbs.
Finished and crated for shipping..............**$3.95**

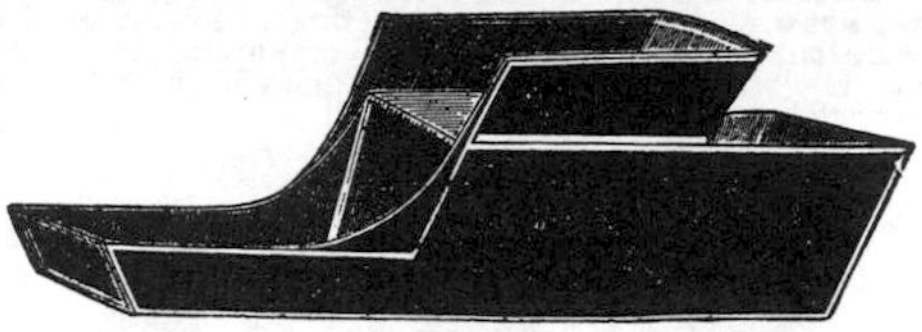

No. 11306. Road Wagon Body, 24 inches wide, 48 inches long, or 25 inches wide and 50 inches long; crated for shipment; not ironed or painted, but finished in white; weight, about 58 lbs.
Each.................................................**$4.05**

## Buggy Seats.

When ordering, give length of buggy seat from outside to outside on the bottom.

No. 11307. Buggy seat, not painted or ironed, but in the white, all ready for finishing, square corners, 26 to 38 inches wide on the bottom, 15 inches deep; weight, 11 lbs.
Each.................................................**$1.00**
No. 11309. Buggy seat, same as above, ironed, ready for buggy top or lazy back, sizes same as above.
Price each.........................................**$1.85**

## Sarven Patent Wheels.

**(Not Tired.)**

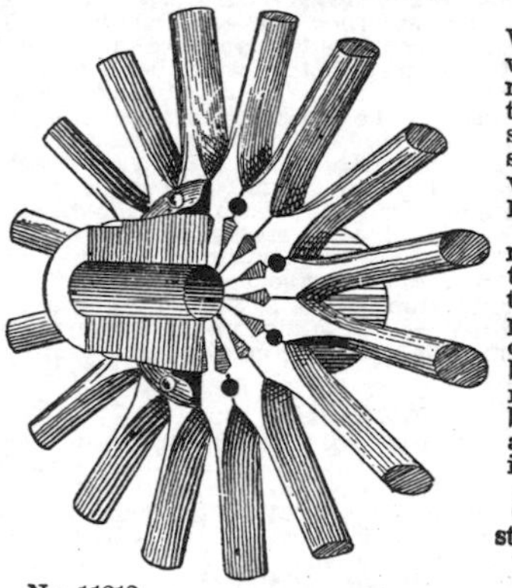

Sarven Patent Wheels are too well known to need description. The sizes shown below are standard and we can ship promptly.

The prices named are for the wheels in the white (not painted) without tires or boxes. We cannot furnish boxes. For tires and axles see index.

(Cut shows construction of hub.)

No. 11312.

| | | | | |
|---|---|---|---|---|
| Size of spoke, inches...... | 1 | 1⅛ | 1¼ | 1⅜ |
| Length of hub, inches.... | 6½ | 6½ | 7 | 7 |
| Tread | ⅞ | 1 | 1⅛ | 1¼ |
| Depth of rim.............. | 1⅛ | 1¼ | 1⅜ | 1½ |
| A grade.................... | $10.00 | 10.10 | 11.30 | 12.50 |
| B grade.................... | 8.20 | 8.30 | 9.50 | 10.75 |
| C grade.................... | 6.45 | 6.55 | 7.15 | 8.30 |
| D grade.................... | 5.25 | 5.35 | 6.00 | 6.25 |

Diameter of the above: 3 ft., 3 ft. 2 in., 3 ft. 4 in., 3 ft. 6 in., 3 ft. 8 in., 3 ft. 10 in., 4 ft.

**Give height of Wheels wanted.** If no height is mentioned we use our judgment in filling orders. These prices are for a set of 4 wheels any height listed above. Half sets furnished at one-half the price of a set. **The Hub length** is length of box which goes in the hub; rim band and hub or sand band not being measured. Write us for prices on heavier Sarven Wheels, being careful to give size of spoke, length of hub, tread, depth of rim and height of wheels wanted. Thimble skeins cannot be used in Sarven Wheels. Steel axles must be used.

## Iron Tires.

No. 11314. In sets of 54 feet, which is the correct amount for ordinary sets of wheels. Prices subject to change of market.

| Size. | Weight. lbs. | Price per set. | Size. | Weight lbs. | Price per set. |
|---|---|---|---|---|---|
| 1¼x⅜ | 85 | $1.48 | 2½x½ | 227 | $3.40 |
| 1⅜x⅜ | 94 | 1.53 | 3 x½ | 273 | 4.09 |
| 1½x½ | 137 | 2.40 | 3½x½ | 319 | 4.78 |
| 1⅝x½ | 148 | 2.60 | 4 x½ | 364 | 5.46 |
| 1¾x½ | 160 | 2.80 | 4 x⅝ | 455 | 6.82 |
| 2 x½ | 180 | 3.15 | | | |

**No difference how far away you are, we can save you money. The freight is but a small item when you consider the saving.**

## Steel Tire.

No. 11316.

| | | | | |
|---|---|---|---|---|
| Size | ¾x$\frac{3}{16}$ | ⅞x$\frac{3}{16}$ | 1x¼ | 1¼x¼ |
| Weight, per set | 27 lbs. | 30 lbs. | 48 lbs. | 60 lbs. |
| Price, per set | $0.75 | .85 | 1.10 | 1.35 |

## Tire and Iron Work Bolts.

No. 11318.

Diameter, 3-16 inch.

| | | | | | | | |
|---|---|---|---|---|---|---|---|
| Length, | 1½ | 1¾ | 2 | 2¼ | 2½ | 2¾ | 3 |
| Per doz., | $0.03 | .03 | .03 | .04 | .04 | .04 | .04 |
| Per 100, | .17 | .18 | .19 | .21 | .22 | .23 | .25 |

Diameter, ¼ inch.

| | | | | | | |
|---|---|---|---|---|---|---|
| Length, | 1¾ | 2 | 2¼ | 2½ | 2¾ | 3 |
| Per doz., | $0.04 | .04 | .04 | .04 | .05 | .05 |
| Per 100, | .23 | .25 | .26 | .27 | .29 | .31 |

Diameter, 5-16 inch.

| | | | | | | | |
|---|---|---|---|---|---|---|---|
| Length, | 1¼ | 1¾ | 2 | 2¼ | 2½ | 2¾ | 3 |
| Per doz., | $0.05 | .05 | .05 | .05 | .05 | .05 | .06 |
| Per 100, | .30 | .30 | .32 | .34 | .36 | .38 | .46 |

For other bolts see index.

## Tired and Banded Wheels.

**(Sarven Patent.)**

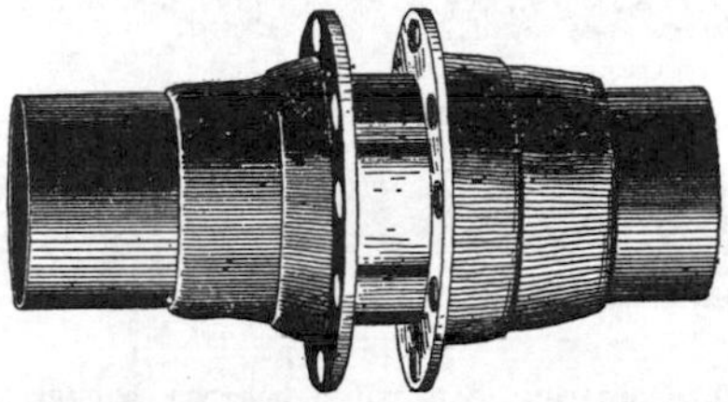

Cut shows style of flange used on our tired wheels.

The wheels and axles on a buggy are usually completely worn out while the other parts, with slight repairs, would be good for several more years' service. If you have a buggy in this condition, a set of our tired wheels, a set of short bed axles and a coat of paint give you a buggy which will probably last just as long as a new one. Our wheels are made by a reliable factory and closely inspected when we receive them, and any wheels not right are refused. They are tired with a round edge tire, bolted between every spoke. The flange and hub band are shown in above cut. The length of hub is the length where the box goes. We do not set boxes, or weld axles, and cannot furnish boxes only, as they would probably not fit your axles. We do not furnish painted wheels. Buggy paint, varnish, etc., is sold by our grocery department. See index.

| No. | Thickness of tire. | Size of spoke. | Length of hub. | Width of rim. | Depth of rim. |
|---|---|---|---|---|---|
| 11320 | 7-32 | 1 1-16 | 6½ | ⅞ | 1⅛ |
| 11321 | ¼ | 1⅛ | 6½ | 1 | 1¼ |
| 11322 | 5-16 | 1¼ | 7 | 1⅛ | 1⅜ |
| 11323 | ⅜ | 1⅜ | 7½ | 1¼ | 1½ |

| No. | Height of front wheel. | Height of rear wheel. | Price per set. | Weight per set. |
|---|---|---|---|---|
| 11320 | 3 ft. 8 | 4 ft. | $7.75 | 90 |
| 11321 | 3 ft. 8 | 4 ft. | 8.00 | 100 |
| 11322 | 3 ft. 8 | 4 ft. | 9.50 | 125 |
| 11323 | 3 ft. 8 | 4 ft. | 11.25 | 160 |

The above sizes of wheels are those most used, and we aim to carry them in stock at all times ready to fill orders as soon as received, Can also usually furnish wheels in heights of 3 feet 6 inches and 3 feet 10 inches and 3 feet 4 inches and 3 feet 8 inches at same prices without delay, if all other sizes are regular. If no height is mentioned we send 3 feet 8 inches and 4 feet wheels. **In ordering wheels for repair work give length of box in your old wheel, which will be the length of hub required.** All wheels warranted against defects in material or workmanship. Two wheels sold at half the price of a set, one wheel at one-quarter the price of a set. In ordering parts of sets be sure to give height.

## Steel Axles.

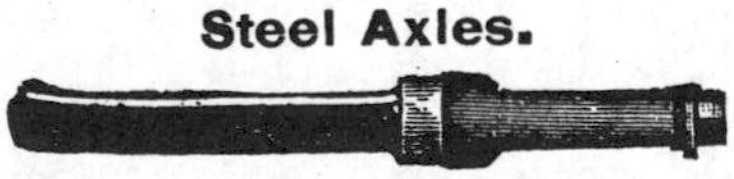

We sell half patent solid collar swelled shoulder steel axles complete with boxing. We cannot furnish boxes only, nor axles without boxes. **A set of short bed axles** (commonly called axle stubs) consists of 4 axles with short bed, which are intended to be welded to old axles. **A set of long bed axles** consists of 4 axles with bed long enough to make axle complete by welding in the center. We sell one half set at one half the price of a full set, and one quarter set at one quarter the price of full set. We cannot weld axles or set boxes.

No. 11330. Short bed.
No. 11331. Long bed.

| Size. | Price short bed. | Price long bed. | Size. | Price short bed. | Price long bed. |
|---|---|---|---|---|---|
| ⅞x6½ | $2.05 | $2.65 | 1¼x7½ | $3.10 | $4.10 |
| 1 x6½ | 2.15 | 2.80 | 1⅜x7 | 4.75 | 6.00 |
| 1⅛x6½ | 2.45 | 3.25 | 1⅜x7½ | 4.85 | 6.05 |
| 1⅛x7 | 2.50 | 3.30 | 1½x8 | 6.30 | 7.55 |
| 1⅛x7½ | 2.55 | 3.35 | 1⅝x8½ | 7.90 | 9.30 |
| 1¼x6½ | 3.00 | 4.00 | 1¾x9 | 10.00 | 11.50 |
| 1¼x7 | 3.05 | 4.05 | | | |

**In ordering parts of sets be sure and state whether right or left hand is wanted.**

## Thimble Skeins.

With boxes to fit.

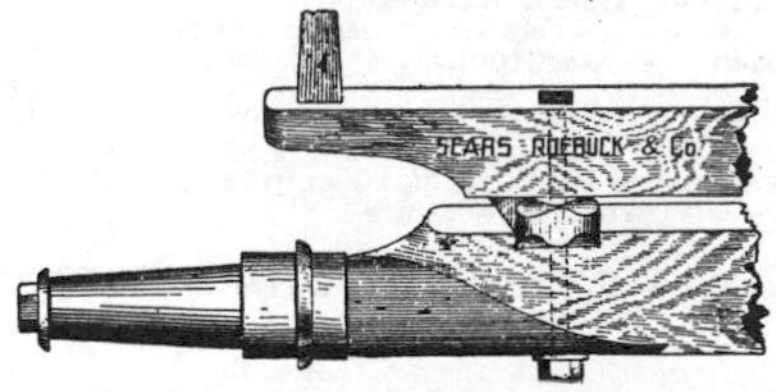


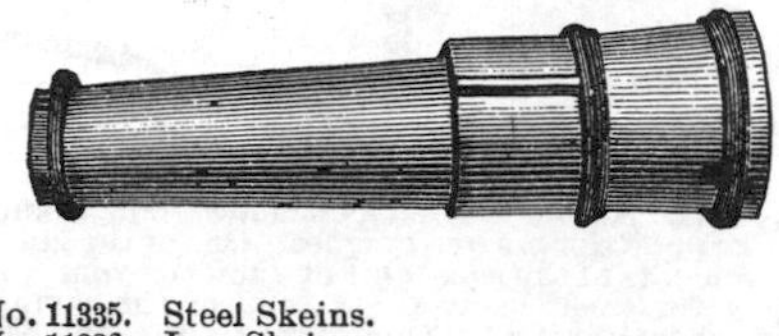

No. 11335. Steel Skeins.
No. 11336. Iron Skeins.

These Thimble Skeins are seamless and have cut threads. Set consists of 4 skeins, but we will sell one only at ¼ the price of full set, or 2 only at ½ the price of full set.

**When ordering one skein only, state whether right or left is wanted.**

| Size, Inches. | Weight, lbs. Iron. | Price Per Set Iron. | Price Per Set Steel. | Weight, lb. Steel. |
|---|---|---|---|---|
| 2 x 6 | 24 | $0.82 | | |
| 2 x 6½ | 26 | .82 | | |
| 2⅛x 6½ | 26 | .88 | | |
| 2¼x 7 | 28 | .94 | $3.74 | 44 |
| 2¼x 7½ | 30 | 1.00 | 3.80 | 46 |
| 2⅜x 7 | 30 | 1.00 | | |
| 2⅜x 7½ | 32 | 1.00 | | |
| 2½x 7 | 32 | 1.13 | | |
| 2½x 7½ | 34 | 1.13 | 3.80 | 48 |
| 2½x 8 | 36 | 1.19 | 3.87 | 50 |
| 2¾x 8 | 40 | 1.32 | 4.07 | 51 |
| 2¾x 8½ | 48 | 1.35 | 4.14 | 53 |
| 2¾x 9 | 52 | 1.50 | 4.20 | 60 |
| 3 x 9 | 56 | 1.50 | 4.34 | 66 |
| 3 x10 | 60 | 1.60 | 4.47 | 70 |
| 3¼x 9 | 65 | 1.75 | 4.96 | 70 |
| 3¼x10 | 70 | 1.88 | 5.00 | 76 |
| 3¼x11 | 74 | 1.94 | 5.06 | 80 |
| 3½x10 | 74 | 2.00 | 5.54 | 80 |
| 3½x10½ | 80 | 2.00 | 5.60 | 88 |
| 3½x11 | 84 | 2.08 | 5.67 | 94 |
| 3½x12 | 92 | 2.20 | 6.00 | 100 |
| 3¾x11 | 92 | 2.25 | 6.66 | 100 |
| 3¾x12 | 96 | 2.85 | 6.66 | 108 |
| 4 x12 | 116 | 2.65 | 8.00 | 112 |
| 4¼x12 | 122 | 3.75 | 8.67 | 135 |
| 4½x12 | 130 | 4.50 | | |
| 4½x13 | 138 | 5.00 | 12.00 | 150 |

## Wide Tire Metal Wheels.

**If you and your neighbors would use wide tired wheels, you would have good roads. Made and shipped from Davenport, Iowa, or Springfield, Ohio, according to which is nearest. In ordering give dimensions as indicated below.**

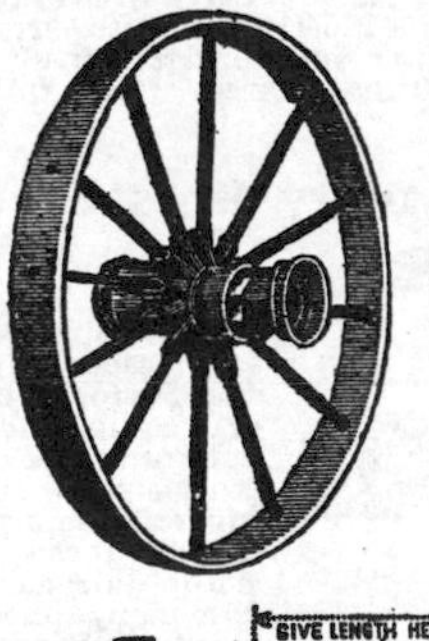

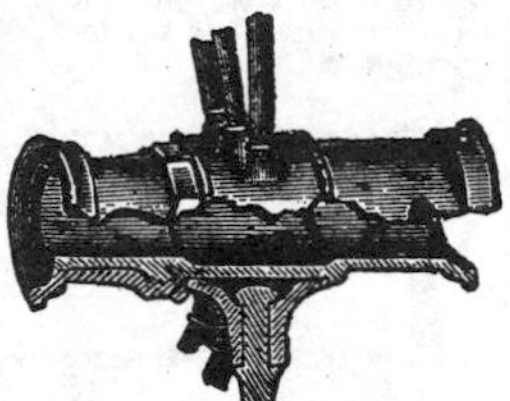

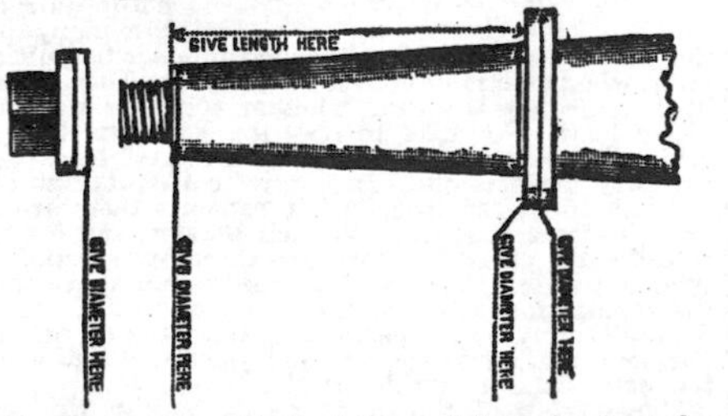


The demand for wide tired low metal truck wheels has led us to study the demands of our customers, and caused us to catalogue standard wheels which are made by the best manufacturers, and which can be furnished at the lowest possible cost. The low wheel with wide tire has come to stay. Economy and strength are served when you have a set for use in the hundred and one emergencies arising where they may be used to great advantage. If you now have a new wagon, the gear will outlast two sets of common wood wheels. Buy a set of these up to date wide tired metal wheels, and avoid further expense that is bound to come in the constant use of wood wheels. At the same time, a day's use of these low

## Wide Tire Metal Wheels—Continued

metal wheels will convince you that you will save the cost of them in a year. You can do alone with them what would require an extra hand with the old style wheels. You can load your wagon twice as easily, and you can haul twice as much more with the same team.

We warrant all these wheels against defective workmanship or material, and if found defective under our guarantee, we will repair or replace them free of charge if delivered to our factory.

We urge you to give these wheels a trial. The increased demand proves their absolute success and makes other orders certain where they are once introduced. In making out your order, be sure to state size of skein wheel is intended for. These wheels have 4 inch tire. The hub is malleable iron, with a removable box, so that when worn, it can be replaced with a new one. The spokes are of straight steel, oval in form and 1 inch in diameter.

We make these wheels in 30 inch, 34 inch, or 38 inches in diameter; with 10, 12, and 14 oval steel spokes respectively.

No. 11341. Price of 30 in. wheel. Each......... **$3.15**
No. 11342. Price of 34 in. wheel. Each......... **3.60**
No. 11343. Price of 38 in. wheel. Each......... **4.00**

## Wagon Jacks.

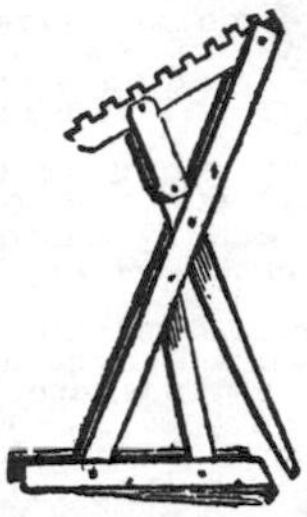

No. 11344. Eclipse Wagon Jack, strong and durable.
Price each......................... **70c**

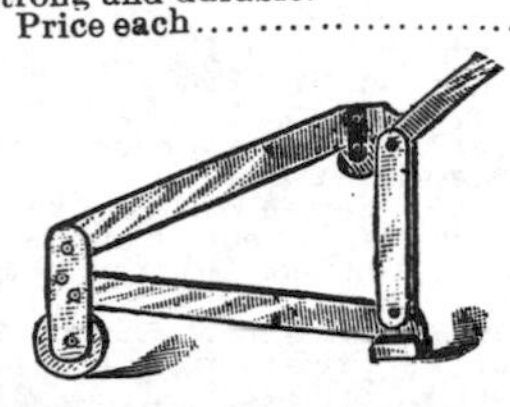

No. 11346. Miller's patent Wagon Jack. For buggy, each, **$1.00**; for wagon, each, **$1.25**; for truck, each..... **$1.65**

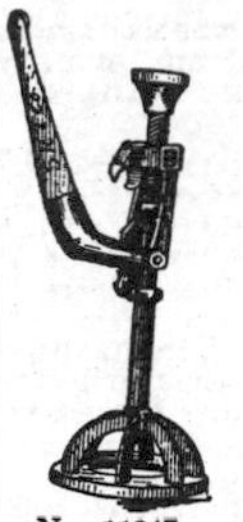

No. 11347.

No. 11347. The Meeker Wagon Jack is the strongest and lightest, most compact and neatest of all the wagon jacks in the market. Will lift more and easier than any other jack in the market. It is all metal but the handle. We carry in stock three sizes.

No. 2. Weight, 24 lbs.; will lift 3,000 lbs. Price......................... **$2.90**
No. 3. Weight, 13 lbs.; will lift 2,000 lbs. Price......................... **$1.20**
No. 4. Weight, 7 lbs.; will lift 1,000 lbs. Price......................... **$1.00**

## Wagon Hubs.

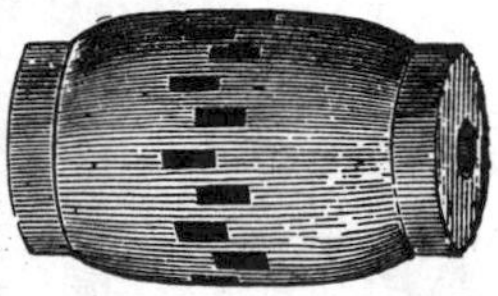

No. 11349. Made of selected oak and birch, cupped patterns, measurements are made inside of hub, the cupping not being included in the lengths given. Always give sizes. We cannot furnish less than full sets.

| Size. Diam., in. | Length, in. | Style mortise. | Price per set, Oak. | Price per set, Birch. | Weight per set, lbs. |
|---|---|---|---|---|---|
| 6 | 7 | Part Dodged | $0.85 | $0.85 | 20 |
| 6 | 7½ | " | | | 20 |
| 6 | 8 | " | | | 20 |
| 6½ | 7½ | " | | | 25 |
| 6½ | 8 | " | | | 25 |
| 6½ | 8½ | " | | | 25 |
| 7 | 8 | Straight & " | .97 | .91 | 30 |
| 7 | 8½ | " | | | 30 |
| 7 | 9 | " | | | 30 |
| 7½ | 8½ | " | 1.12 | 1.00 | 35 |
| 7½ | 9 | " | | | 35 |
| 8 | 9 | " | 1.18 | 1.12 | 40 |
| 8 | 10 | " | 1.25 | 1.18 | 40 |
| 8¼ | 10 | " | 1.31 | 1.25 | 45 |
| 8½ | 10 | " | 1.37 | 1.31 | 50 |
| 8½ | 11 | Straight. | 1.44 | 1.37 | 50 |
| 9 | 11 | " | 1.50 | 1.44 | 60 |
| 9 | 12 | " | 1.56 | 1.44 | 60 |
| 9½ | 11 | " | 1.56 | 1.44 | 75 |
| 9½ | 12 | " | 1.56 | 1.50 | 75 |
| 10 | 12 | " | 1.87 | 1.68 | 85 |
| 10½ | 12 | " | 2.18 | 1.81 | 95 |
| 11 | 13 | " | 3.25 | 2.25 | 110 |
| 12 | 14 | " | 3.68 | 2.87 | 125 |

These hubs are bored for thimble skeins and will be sent that way unless it is specified that they are wanted for iron axles. Be sure and give dimensions in ordering.

## Buggy Hubs.

No. 11351. Select elm Buggy Hubs, painted ends. Always give size. Nothing but full sets furnished.

| Diameter. | Length. | Size mortise. | No. of mortises. | Price per set. |
|---|---|---|---|---|
| 3½ | 6½ | 1$\frac{3}{16}$x$\frac{5}{16}$ | 14 and 16 | $0.60 |
| 4 | 7 | 1$\frac{5}{16}$x⅜ | 14 and 16 | .75 |
| 4¾ | 7 | 1$\frac{1}{16}$x$\frac{7}{16}$ | 14 and 16 | .90 |
| 5 | 6½ | 1$\frac{3}{16}$x½ | 14 and 16 | 1.10 |
| 5 | 7 | 1$\frac{3}{16}$x½ | 14 and 16 | 1.20 |
| 5¾ | 7½ | 1$\frac{5}{16}$x½ | 14 and 16 | 1.25 |
| 6 | 7 | 1⅜x$\frac{9}{16}$ | 12 and 14 | 1.30 |
| 6½ | 8 | 1½x⅜ | 12 and 14 | 1.55 |
| 6½ | 9 | 1½x⅜ | 12 and 14 | 1.80 |
| 7 | 8½ | 1⅝x⅝ | 12 and 14 | 1.95 |
| 7 | 9 | 1⅝x⅝ | 12 and 14 | 2.10 |

**Remember that we stand back of our goods with a binding guarantee that they shall be just as represented, or they may be returned and money refunded.**

## Wagon Spokes.

No. 11353. Wagon Spokes, forest oak, 52 to a set. Always state what size and grade is wanted.

Price per set.

| Size, inches. | C | B | B select. | A | A select. | Weight, lbs. |
|---|---|---|---|---|---|---|
| 2 | | $1.80 | $2.19 | $2.69 | $2.72 | 55 |
| 2⅛ to 2½ | $1.44 | 1.80 | 2.19 | 2.69 | 2.72 | 60–80 |
| 2⅝ | 1.75 | 2.12 | 2.50 | 3.00 | 3.13 | 90 |
| 2¾ | 1.80 | 2.15 | 2.55 | 3.00 | 3.16 | 95 |
| 3 | 1.85 | 2.20 | 2.60 | 3.00 | 3.20 | 110 |

A set consists of two bundles, one front and one hind, the two bundles containing enough spokes for one set of wheels.

Front bundles are half the price of a full set.

Hind bundles are half the price of a full set, plus 25c.

## Buggy Spokes.

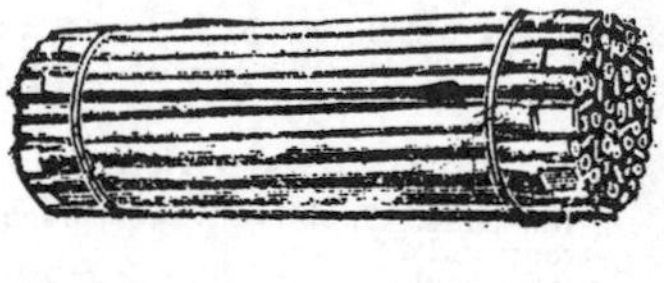

No. 11357. Buggy Spokes, hickory, 1 to 1⅜, 60 to a set, 1½ to 2 inch, 52 to set. We do not break sets. Can be used only in wood hub wheels.

| Size, inches, | 1 | 1⅛ | 1¼ | 1⅜ | 1½ | 1⅝ | 1¾ | 1⅞ | 2 |
|---|---|---|---|---|---|---|---|---|---|
| Weight, per set, lbs. | 25 | 28 | 32 | 35 | 40 | 46 | 48 | 54 | 60 |

Prices, C grade, $1.25 per set; B select, $2.00; A extra select, $2.50. All sizes are the same price. **Be sure to state size wanted.**

No. 11359. Sarven Wheel Spokes; can be used only in Sarven wheels; not put up in sets; will sell any quantity at prices quoted. **Be sure to give size wanted.**

| Size. | | A | B | C |
|---|---|---|---|---|
| ¾ to 1¼. | Price each | 9c | 6c | 5c |
| 1 5-16 to 1⅜. | Price each | 10c | 7c | 5c |
| 1 7-16 to 1½. | Price each | 11c | 8c | 6c |
| 1 9-16 to 1⅝. | Price each | 12c | 9c | 7c |

No. 11361. **Club Spokes,** for iron hub wheels. Grade, B select. Size 1 inch to 2 inch. We sell any quantity at prices quoted. **Be sure to give size wanted.**

| Size. | | |
|---|---|---|
| 1 to 1¼ inch. | Price each | 5c |
| 1 5-16 to 1⅜ inch. | Price each | 6c |
| 1 7-16 to 1½ inch. | Price each | 7c |
| 1 9-16 to 1⅝ inch. | Price each | 8c |
| 1 11-16 to 1¾ inch. | Price each | 9c |
| 1⅞ to 2 inch. | Price each | 10c |

No. 11362. Shell Band Wheel Spokes. Can be used only in shell band wheels. We carry in stock B grade only. Sell any quantity at prices quoted. **Be sure to give size wanted.**

| Size. | | |
|---|---|---|
| 1 to 1¼ inch. | Price each | 6c |
| 1 5-16 to 1⅜ inch. | Price each | 7c |

## Sawed Felloes.

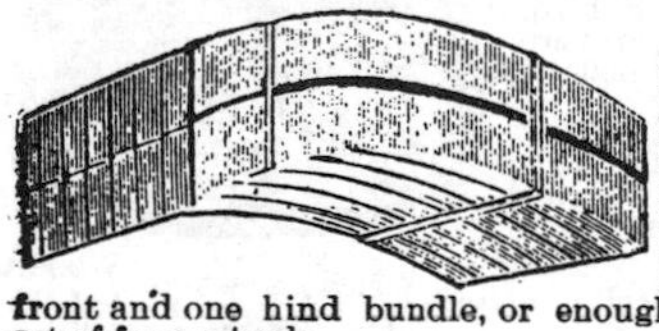

No. 11363. Sawed Felloes, select white oak, rough; 26 to set. Nothing less than one front or one hind bundle furnished. A set consists of one front and one hind bundle, or enough felloes for one set of four wheels.

Diameter, 3 ft. 8 in. and 4 ft. 6 in.

| | Weight. | Per Set. |
|---|---|---|
| 1¾ tread x 2¼ depth | 75 lbs. | $1.25 |
| 1¾ tread x 2½ depth | 80 lbs. | 1.30 |
| 2 tread x 2½ depth | 85 lbs. | 1.35 |
| 2 tread x 2⅝ depth | 90 lbs. | 1.37 |
| 2 tread x 2¾ depth | 95 lbs. | 1.40 |
| 2¼ tread x 3 depth | 130 lbs. | 2.00 |
| 2½ tread x 3 depth | 160 lbs. | 2.30 |
| Diameter, 3 ft. 2 in., 4 ft. 2 in. | | |
| 2¼ tread x 3 depth | 130 lbs. | $2.05 |
| 2½ tread x 3 depth | 160 lbs. | 2.35 |

Special diameters sawed to order. Prices on application.

## Bent Felloes or Rims.

Nothing less than rims for two wheels furnished in each diameter.

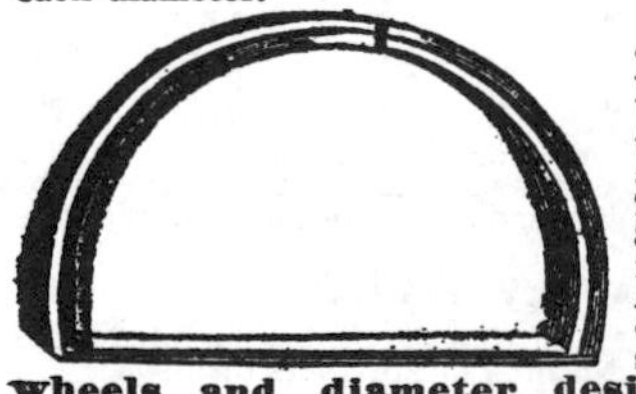

No. 11365. Bent of the choicest woods obtainable. We can furnish the following diameters: 3 ft., 3 ft. 2 in., 3 ft. 6 in., 3 ft. 8 in., 3 ft. 10 in., 4 ft., and 4 ft. 2 in. **Always state diameter desired for front wheels and diameter desired for hind wheels.**

Price per set (4 wheels).

| Tread. | Depth. | Weight. | Select Hickory. | Black Hickory. |
|---|---|---|---|---|
| ⅞ | 1 | 25 lbs | $0.70 | $0.90 |
| 1 | 1⅛ | 30 lbs | .75 | .92 |
| 1⅛ | 1¼ | 35 lbs | .78 | 1.00 |
| 1¼ | 1⅜ | 45 lbs | .85 | 1.25 |
| 1⅜ | 1½ | 50 lbs | .95 | 1.30 |
| 1½ | 1⅝ | 55 lbs | 1.10 | 1.52 |
| 1⅝ | 1¾ | 65 lbs | 1.30 | 1.75 |
| 1¾ | 2 | 75 lbs | 1.70 | 2.12 |
| 2 | 2 | 80 lbs | 1.75 | 2.31 |

## Bent Truck and Wagon Rims.

No. 11370. Select White Oak.

| Tread size. | Depth. | Price, per set. | Weight. |
|---|---|---|---|
| 3 inch. | 1¾ inch. | $2.00 | 120 lbs. |
| 3 inch. | 2 | 2.25 | 125 lbs. |
| 4 inch. | 1¾ | 2.65 | 155 lbs. |
| 4 inch. | 2 | 2.88 | 160 lbs. |

In circles of 30, 36, 42, 44, 50 and 54 inches, all same price. State diameter wanted.

## Our Common Sense Tongue Support.

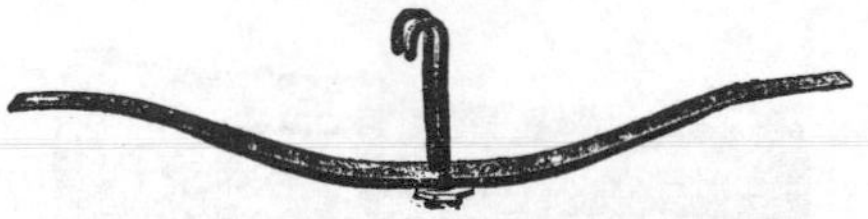

No. 11371. Accompanying cut shows our Common Sense Support for wagon tongues. One of the greatest improvements of the age. One of these on your wagon will pay for itself many times over in the saving of horse flesh. Give it a trial and you will be convinced of its advantages and utility. You can put it on any common wagon, and it can be adjusted to any desired height. We consider it the most efficient tongue support made; can be put on or taken off in less than a minute. Our special price ........ **$1.00**

# BOLSTER SPRINGS.

## Our Celebrated Low Down Easy Bolster Spring.

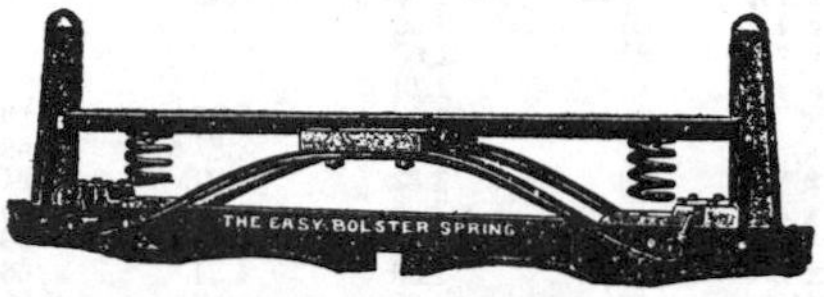


No. 11373. The accompanying cut shows our Easy Bolster Spring, positively the best wagon spring made. The illustration shows just how the spring sets on the Bolster. It raises the wagon bed less than any first-class spring in the market. There are many imitations of this spring, which fact is the best proof of its value. The medium weight leaf springs serve to convert the common farm wagon into a spring vehicle that rides as easy as a buggy empty, or with a light load. When you have a heavy load, the relief coil springs render the wagon just as easy riding, and take from the leaf springs a part of the weight. This spring is the outcome of several years' experiments. We feel that we are offering as a result a bolster spring that is the height of perfection. Where one of these sets goes into a neighborhood, a dozen more will follow.

We make these Bolster Springs for 36 inch, 38 inch, 42 inch, and 44 inch bolsters. In ordering, give careful measurements of exact width between bolster stakes. Our special prices are as follows:

Capacity to carry up to 1,200 lbs., per set of two full springs, **$5.25**; capacity to carry up to 2,000 lbs., per set of two full springs, **$6.00**; capacity to carry up to 3,000 lbs., per set of two full springs, **$7.50**; capacity to carry up to 4,000 lbs., per set of two full springs, **$9.00**; capacity to carry up to 6,000 lbs., per set of two full springs, **$12.00.**

## Our Fruit and Dairy Bolster Springs.

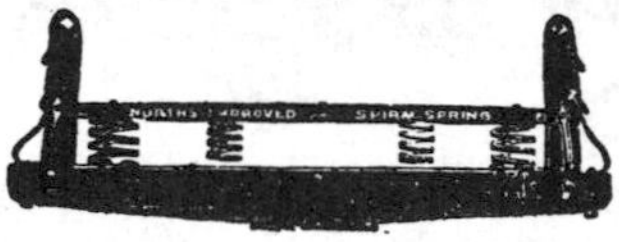

No. 11374. Order by number.

Our No. 11374 Bolster Springs are especially adapted for fruit or dairy hauling, but are used extensively on all kinds of wagons. Truck farmers and dairymen lose many times the price of these springs through damage to fruit and milk, when being jolted over rough roads. These Bolster Springs are equally easy, whether you have a light or heavy load. For 1,000 to 1,500 lbs. capacity there are two coil springs to each Bolster. For 2,000 to 3,000 lbs. capacity there is one extra relief coil spring to each Bolster. For 4,000 to 5,000 lbs. capacity there are two extra relief coil springs to each Bolster, and for 5,000 to 6,000 lbs. capacity there are three extra relief coil springs to each Bolster. The illustration above shows the springs for 4,000 to 5,000 lbs. capacity. This Bolster Spring is simple in construction, reliable and durable. Farmers, fruit growers, and dairymen will find a long felt want satisfied in this article.

They obviate all the annoyances as well as the losses occasioned by traveling over rough roads. We put them up to fit 36, 38, 42 or 44 inch bolsters, and they have extension end shoes to fit odd sized Bolsters. Any one can instantly adjust them to fit any ordinary wagon.

We warrant every set to give entire satisfaction. In ordering, always give exact size between Bolster stakes.

Our special prices for set of two Springs:

To carry 1,000 lbs., per set, **$3.00**; to carry 1,500 lbs., per set, **$3.35**; to carry 2,000 lbs., per set, **$3.75**; to carry 2,500 lbs., per set, **$4.15**; to carry 3,000 lbs., per set, **$4.50**; to carry 4,000 lbs., per set, **$5.25**; to carry 5,000 lbs., per set, **$6.00**; to carry 6,000 lbs., per set, **$6.75**; to carry 8,000 lbs., per set, **$7.50.**

## Our Common Sense Bolster Spring.

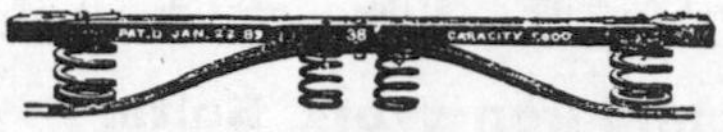

No. 11376. Order by number.

We illustrate here our Common Sense Bolster Spring. This spring is made to meet the demand for an easy article at a small price. A set will transform your common wagon into an easy riding vehicle. This one in particular is as perfectly graduated as any spring on the market. Adapted alike for light or heavy use; we guarantee every set to give entire satisfaction. One set in your neighborhood is bound to sell others. At our low prices you can sell enough sets to your neighbors, who see yours, to pay you for your own.

The prices below are for two springs, for rear and front bolsters. Always give exact width between bolster stakes when ordering. Our special prices:

To carry 1,000 lbs., per set of 2 springs, **$2.95**; to carry 1,500 lbs., per set of 2 springs, **$3.25**; to carry 2,000 lbs., per set of 2 springs, **$3.75**; to carry 2,500 lbs., per set of 2 springs, **$4.15**; to carry 3,000 lbs., per set of 2 springs, **$5.25**; to carry 4,000 lbs., per set of 2 springs, **$6.00**; to carry 5,000 lbs., per set of 2 springs, **$6.75**; to carry 6,000 lbs., per set of 2 springs, **$7.50**; to carry 8,000 lbs., per set of 2 springs, **$8.25**; to carry 10,000 lbs., per set of 2 springs, **$9.00.**

## Racine Bolster Springs.

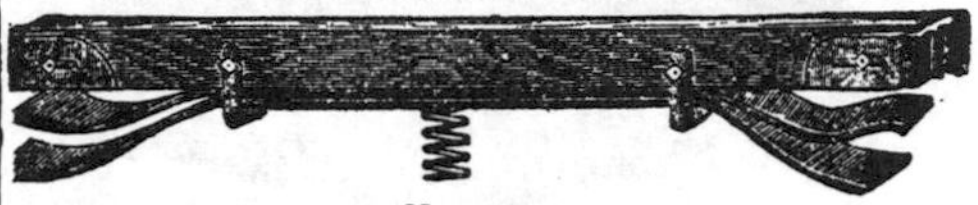

No. 11377.

When ordering state width between bolster stakes and weight you wish wagon to carry.

These heavy spring steel leaves are more durable and far superior to coil springs, and are taking their place wherever tested. Fits any farm wagon.

No. 11377. 1,000 lbs. capacity; weight, 30 lbs. Per pair ........ **$3.00**

No. 11379. 2,000 lbs. capacity; weight, 40 lbs. Per pair ........ **$3.50**

No. 11380. 4,000 lbs. capacity; weight, 50 lbs. Per pair ........ **$4.50**

No. 11382. 6,000 lbs. capacity; weight, 75 lbs. Per pair ........ **$5.50**

Price is for two springs.

## Carriage Springs.

Oil tempered, half bright.

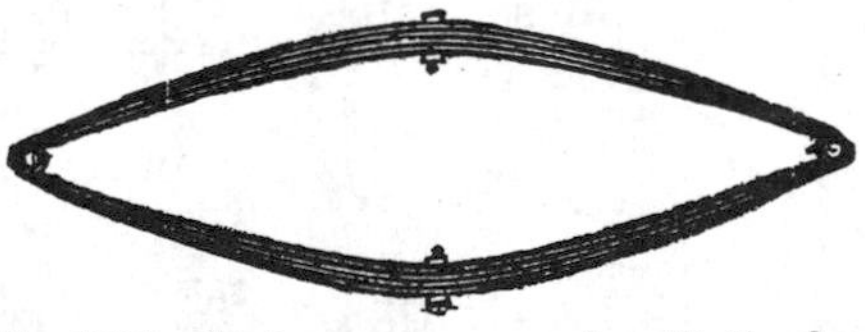

No. 11384. Carriage springs, regular elliptic shape. Will furnish only one spring at half the price of pair; double sweep same price as single.

| Width, Inches. | No. of Leaves. | Length. Inches. | Av. Weight, Per Pair, lbs. | Price, Per Pair. |
|---|---|---|---|---|
| *1¼ | 3 | 34 | 33 | $1.82 |
| *1¼ | 3 | 36 | 35 | 1.95 |
| *1¼ | 4 | 34 | 37 | 2.08 |
| *1¼ | 4 | 36 | 40 | 2.27 |
| *1¼ | 5 | 36 | 43 | 2.47 |
| 1⅜ | 3 | 34 | 36 | 2.01 |
| *1⅜ | 3 | 36 | 38 | 2.14 |
| *1⅜ | 4 | 34 | 40 | 2.40 |
| *1⅜ | 4 | 36 | 45 | 2.53 |
| *1⅜ | 5 | 36 | 47 | 2.73 |
| *1½ | 3 | 36 | 41 | 2.24 |
| *1½ | 4 | 36 | 47 | 2.73 |
| 1½ | 4 | 38 | 51 | 2.99 |
| *1½ | 5 | 36 | 55 | 3.25 |
| 1½ | 5 | 38 | 56 | 3.31 |
| *1½ | 6 | 36 | 63 | 3.83 |
| 1½ | 6 | 38 | 69 | 4.16 |
| *1¾ | 4 | 36 | 55 | 3.25 |
| 1¾ | 4 | 38 | 58 | 3.44 |
| *1¾ | 5 | 36 | 65 | 3.90 |
| 1¾ | 5 | 38 | 71 | 4.29 |
| 1¾ | 6 | 36 | 74 | 4.48 |
| 1¾ | 6 | 39 | 80 | 4.87 |
| *1¾ | 7 | 36 | 82 | 5.00 |
| 1¾ | 7 | 38 | 85 | 5.20 |
| 2 | 4 | 36 | 59 | 3.51 |
| 2 | 4 | 38 | 65 | 3.90 |
| *2 | 5 | 36 | 74 | 4.48 |

Springs marked * are stock sizes. All other sizes must be made to order, for which allow five days.

## Sweet's Seat Springs.

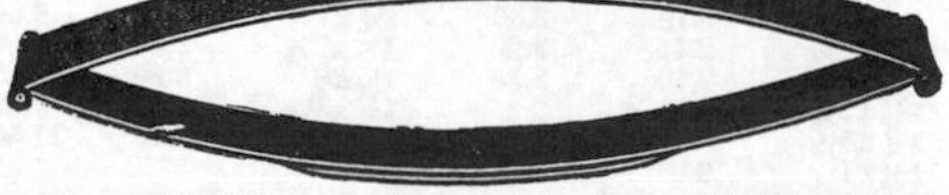

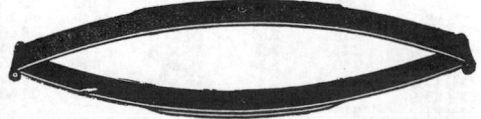

No. 11388. Seat Springs, two leaf, 1½x26 inches. Weight, per pair, 12 lbs. Per pair ........ **50c**

## Carriage Steps.

Malleable Body Step.

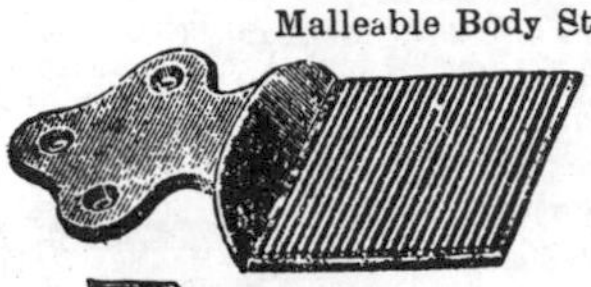

No. 11389. ¾ inch drop, 3½x3⅜ inch pad, 1⅞ inch center to center of holes, 5-16 inch holes. Weight, 1 lb. Price per pair........**16c**

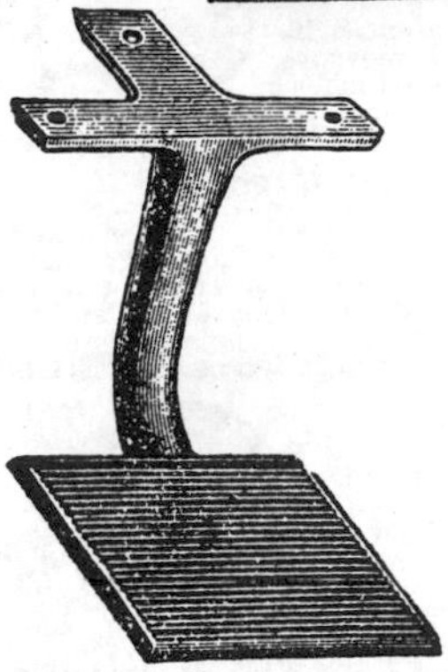

No. 11390. Malleable Body Step, without brace, 4 inch drop, 4¾ inch projection. 3½x4 pad, 3⅝ inches center to center holes. Price, per pair....**32c**

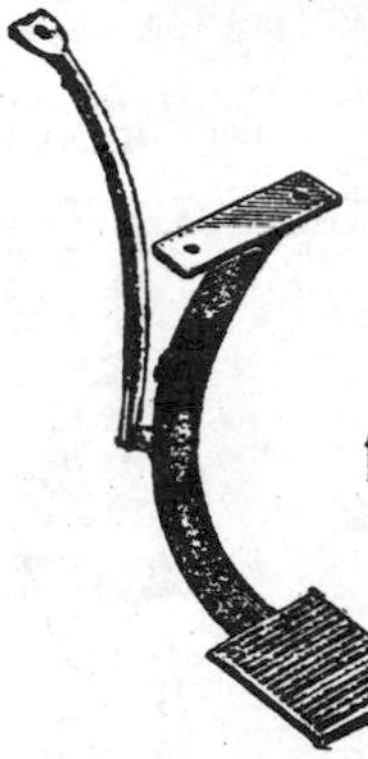

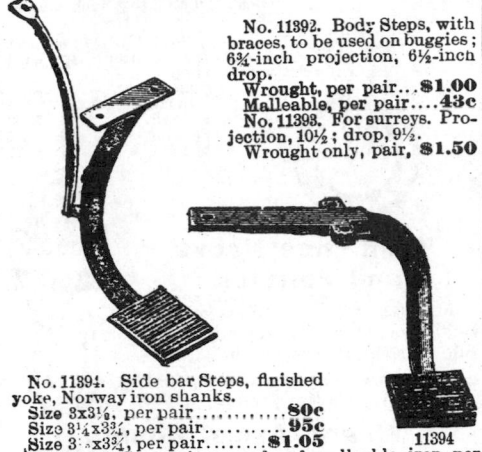

No. 11392. Body Steps, with braces, to be used on buggies; 6¾-inch projection, 6½-inch drop.
Wrought, per pair...**$1.00**
Malleable, per pair....**43c**
No. 11393. For surreys. Projection, 10½; drop, 9½.
Wrought only, pair, **$1.50**

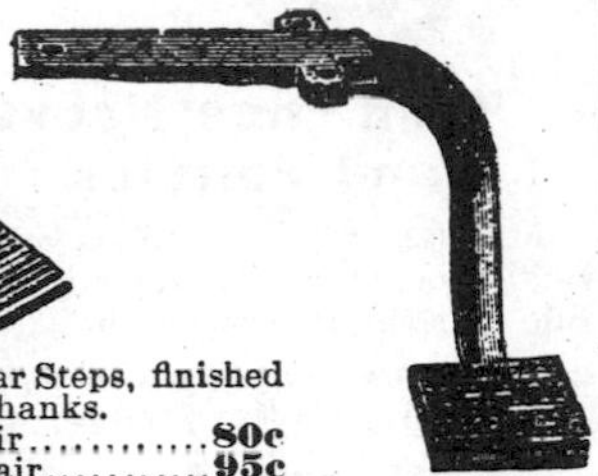

11394

No. 11394. Side bar Steps, finished yoke, Norway iron shanks.
Size 3x3¼, per pair............**80c**
Size 3¼x3¾, per pair...........**95c**
Size 3½x3¾, per pair.........**$1.05**
No. 11395. Same sizes, made of malleable iron, per pair, **40c**, **45c** and **60c**, respectively.

## Anti-Rattlers.

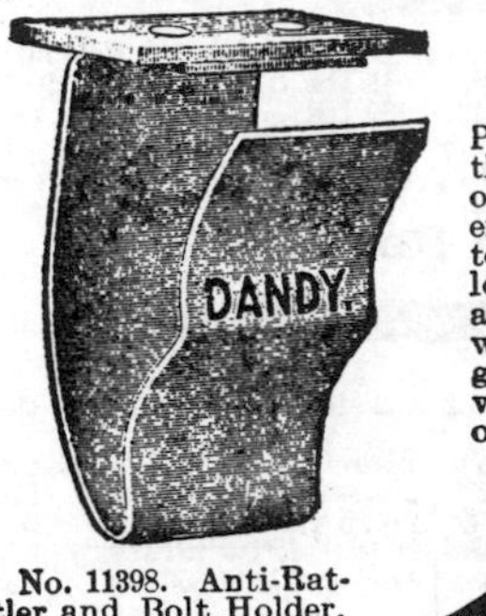


No. 11397. Shaft and Pole Coupling, Anti-Rattlers, "The Dandy," made of steel, the head strengthened by a plate riveted on; to place in position set the lower part in the coupling and drive them in; they will not break; the corrugation on the side prevents them from working out.
Per pair...........**10c**
Per doz. pairs....**$1.00**

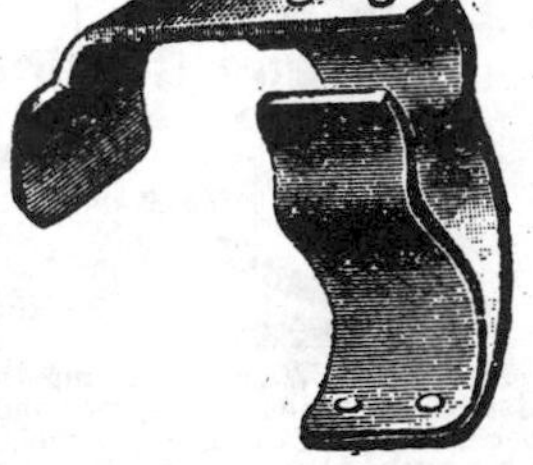

No. 11398. Anti-Rattler and Bolt Holder, made of Crescent patent cold rolled steel. It insures against the rattling of the shafts of any spring vehicle, is perfectly noiseless, will last as long as the buggy, and shafts can be taken off without trouble and replaced by a pole in a minute.
Per pair.............**12c**
Per dozen....**$1.10**

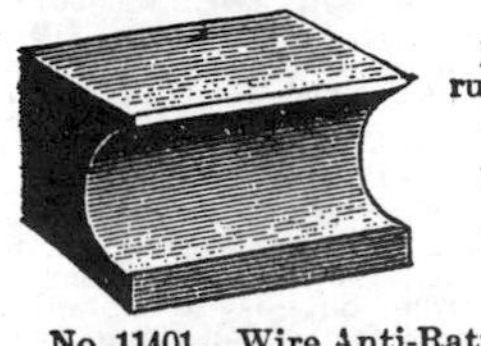

No. 11399. Common pattern, rubber Anti-Rattlers.
⅞ in., per pair, **4c**; per doz. pairs................**40c**
1 in., per pair, **4c**; per doz. pairs................**45c**
1⅛ in., per pair, **5c**; per doz. pairs..............**50c**

No. 11401. Wire Anti-Rattler, made of steel wire; prevents rattling of the shafts.
Price, per pair, **5c**; per doz. pairs..................**50c**

**It will not pay you to order small items alone by express. Make up a freight order of groceries and hardware, such as you will need, and the saving will be large.**

## Shaft Couplings, Etc.

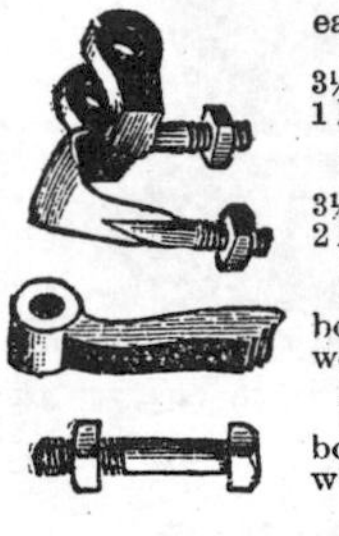

Shaft Couplings, finished beveled ears.
No. 11403. ⅞ inch eye, 5-16 inch bolt, 3⅛ inch clip, 5-16 inch shank; weight, 1 lb.
Per pair, **25c**; doz. pairs...**$2.75**
No. 11404. 1 inch eye, ⅜ inch bolt, 3⅛ inch clip, 5-16 inch shank; weight, 2 lbs. 9 oz.
Per pair, **25c**; doz. pairs...**$2.75**
No. 11405. 1⅛ inch eye, 7-16 inch bolt, 4 inch clip, 5-16 inch shank; weight, 3½ lbs.
Per pair, **30c**; doz. pairs...**$3.25**
No. 11406. 1¼ inch eye, 7-16 inch bolt, 4 inch clip, ⅜ inch shank; weight, 3½ lbs.
Per pair, **45c**; doz. pairs...**$5.00**

## Fifth Wheels.

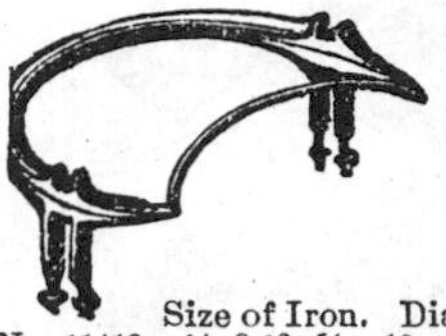

Fifth Wheels, Derby pattern, plain front. When ordering, give size of axle, size of iron and diameter.

| | Size of Iron. | Diameter. | Each. |
|---|---|---|---|
| No. 11410. | ½, 9-16, ⅝ | 10 and 16 in | $0.60 |
| No. 11411. | ¾ | 12 and 16 in | .70 |
| No. 11412. | ⅞ | 14 and 16 in | 1.15 |
| No. 11413. | 1 | 14 and 16 in | 1.65 |
| No. 11414. | 1⅛ | 14 and 16 in | 1.90 |
| No. 11415. | 1¼ | 14 and 16 in | 2.50 |

## Clip King Bolts, Flanged with Finished Ends.

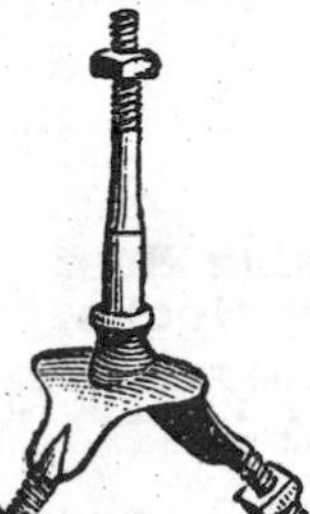

No. 11417. No. 1, ½ inch at collar, light, weight 11 oz.
Each, **15c**; per doz.....**$1.50**
No. 11418. No. 2, 9-16 inch at collar, medium, weight 12 oz.
Each, **15c**; per doz.....**$1.50**
No. 11419. No. 3, ⅝ inch at collar, heavy, weight 15 oz.
Each, **20c**; per doz.....**$2.25**
No. 11420. No. 4, ¾ inch at collar, extra heavy, weight 1 lb. 4 oz.
Each, **27c**; per doz.....**$3.00**

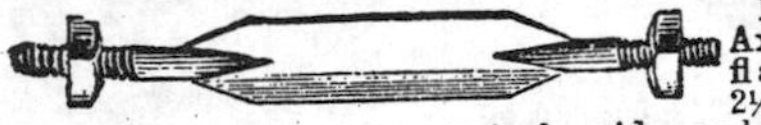

No. 11422. Axle Clips, flat part 2½, 2¾, 3¼, 3¾, 4¼, 4¾ inches long, ⅞ inch wide and 5-16 inch shank. Clips, 2½ and 2¾, weight 3 oz. each; 3¼ to 4¾, 5 oz. each.
Each, up to 3¾ inch, **3c**; per doz.........**30c**
Each, 4¼ and 4¾, **5c**; per doz.............**50c**
No. 11423. Same, ⅜ shank.

| | Each. | Per Doz. |
|---|---|---|
| Flat part, 1⅛x4 | .4c | 45c |
| Flat part, 1⅛x4½ | .4c | 45c |
| Flat part, 1⅛x5 | .5c | 55c |
| Flat part, 1⅛x5½ | .5c | 55c |
| Flat part, 1⅛x6 | .6c | 65c |
| Flat part, 1⅛x6½ | .6c | 65c |
| Flat part, 1⅛x7 | .7c | 75c |
| Flat part, 1⅛x7½ | .7c | 75c |

## Axle Clip Yokes.

Wrought iron. Punched holes.

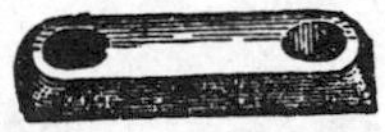

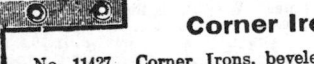

No. 11424. Axle Clip Yokes with 5-16 inch holes; distance between holes ⅞ to 1½ inches. State size wanted in ordering.
Price, each, **3c**; per doz. **25c**
No. 11425. Axle Clip Yokes with ⅜ inch holes; distance between holes from 1 to 2 inches. State size wanted.
Price, each, **5c**; per doz..........**50c**
No. 11426. Axle Clip Yokes with 7-16 inch holes; distance between holes from 1⅜ to 2¼ inches. State size wanted.
Price, each, **7c**; per doz..........**75c**

## Corner Irons.

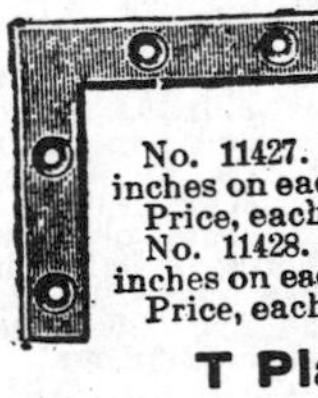

No. 11427. Corner Irons, beveled edge, 3½ inches on each side, ⅝ inch wide.
Price, each, **3c**; per doz..........**22c**
No. 11428. Corner Irons, beveled edge, 3½ inches on each side, ¾ inch wide.
Price, each, **3c**; per doz..........**22c**

## T Plates.

| | Long | High | Wide | Each | Doz. |
|---|---|---|---|---|---|
| No. 11429. | 2¾ | 2⅛ | ⅝ | 3c | 22c |
| No. 11430. | 3⅜ | 2½ | ¾ | 3c | 22c |
| No. 11431. | 3¾ | 2¾ | ¾ | 3c | 22c |

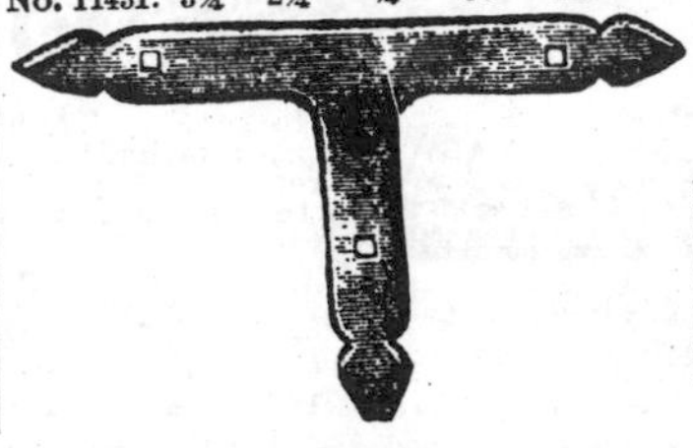

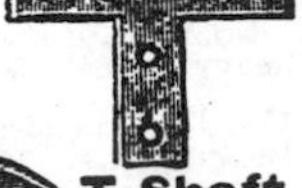

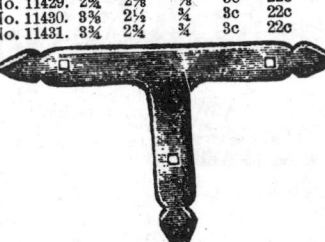

## T Shaft Irons.

No. 11432. Shaft Irons, 8 inches long, 5 inches high, ⅞ inches wide, ¼ inch holes; in pairs, rights and lefts.
Per pair, **8c**

## Rivets.

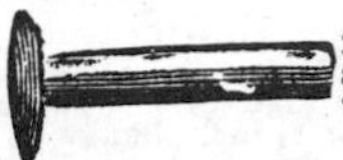

No. 11434. Rivets, flat head. The number of rivets to the pound is approximated. ¼ inch in diameter, any length.
Per lb.................................**7c**

| | | | | | | |
|---|---|---|---|---|---|---|
| Length | 1 | 1⅛ | 1¼ | 1⅜ | 1½ | 1⅝ |
| No. rivets to lb. | 58 | 56 | 54 | 53 | 50 | 48 |
| Length | 1¾ | 1⅞ | 2 | 2⅛ | 2¼ | 2⅜ |
| No. rivets to lb. | 46 | 44 | 42 | 40 | 38 | 36 |
| Length | | 2½ | 2⅝ | 2¾ | 2⅞ | 3 |
| No. rivets to lb. | | 34 | 32 | 30 | 28 | 26 |

Give size when ordering.

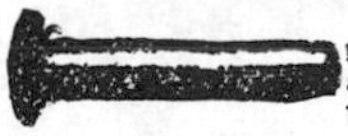

No. 11436. Rivets, oval head. The number of rivets to the pound is approximated. ¼ inch in diameter, any length.
Per lb.................................**7c**

| | | | | | | |
|---|---|---|---|---|---|---|
| Length | 1 | 1⅛ | 1¼ | 1⅜ | 1½ | 1⅝ |
| No. rivets to lb. | 56 | 54 | 52 | 50 | 48 | 46 |
| Length | 1¾ | 1⅞ | 2 | 2⅛ | 2¼ | 2⅜ |
| No. rivets to lb. | 44 | 40 | 37 | 35 | 33 | 30 |
| Length | | 2½ | 2⅝ | 2¾ | 2⅞ | 3 |
| No. rivets to lb. | | 28 | 25 | 23 | 22 | 20 |

Give size when ordering.

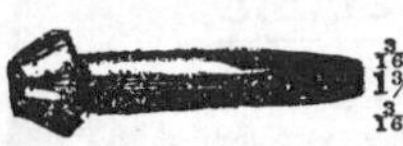

No. 11438. Wagon Box Nails, 3/16 inch in diameter, lengths 1¼, 1⅜, 1½, 1⅝, 1¾, 1⅞ and 2 inch; 3/16, any length.
Per lb.....................**12c**
Give size when ordering.

## Riveting Burrs.

No. 11439. Riveting Burrs, for ¼ inch rivets. Outside diameter ⅝ inch, hole 1/4.
Per lb....................................**12c**
For 3/16 inch rivets. Outside diameter ½ inch, hole 3/16.
Per lb....................................**15c**

## Whiffletree Plates.

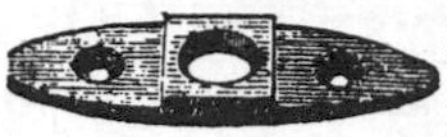

No. 11440. Whiffletree Plates 3¼ inches long; 5/16 inch round hole; weight per set, 4 oz. Per set, **4c**; per doz. sets......**25c**

## Felloe Plates.

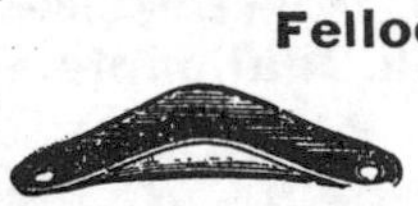

No. 11442. Wrought Iron Felloe Plates. Philadelphia pattern.

| | | | | | | | | | |
|---|---|---|---|---|---|---|---|---|---|
| Sizes | ¾ | ⅞ | 1 | 1¼ | 1⅜ | 1½ | 1⅝ | 1¾ | 2 in. |
| Weight per doz. | 6 | 7 | 11 | 15 | 21 | 21 | 22 | 35 | 36 oz. |
| Per doz | 5c | 6c | 8c | 12c | 16c | 18c | 20c | 24c | 27c |

## Pole Tips.

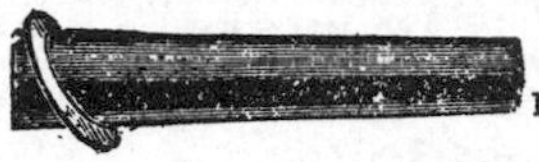

No. 11443. Silver plated Pole Tips.

| | | | | | |
|---|---|---|---|---|---|
| Length | 6¼ | 6½ | 6¾ | 7 | 7¼ in. |
| Size of hole | 1 | 1⅛ | 1¼ | 1⅜ | 1½ in. |
| Weight | 14 | 14 | 17 | 18 | 23 oz. |
| Silver plated. Each | 60c | 65c | 70c | 75c | 95c |
| No. 11444. Plain malleable. Each | 12c | 16c | 22c | 28c | 33c |

## Shaft Tips.

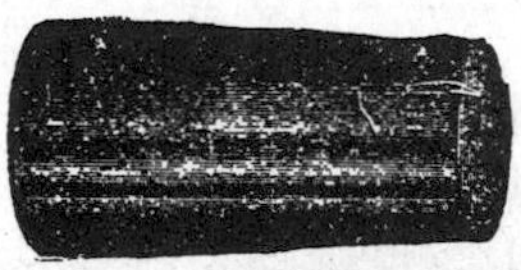

No. 11445. Size of hole, ⅞ inch. Silver plated.
Per pair **10c**; per doz. pairs......**80c**
Size of hole, 1 inch. Silver plated.
Per pair, **12c**; per doz. pairs....**$1.10**

| | | |
|---|---|---|
| No. 11446. Size of hole | ⅞ inch. | 1 inch. |
| Wrought brass. Per pair | $0.15 | $0.20 |
| Wrought brass. Per doz. pairs | 1.25 | 1.40 |
| No. 11454. Malleable Shaft Tips. Per pair | | .06 |
| Malleable. Per doz. pairs | | .57 |

## Whiffletree Tips.

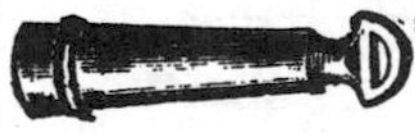

No. 11447. Length, 3¼ inches; size of hole, ¾ inch; weight per pair, 8 oz. Silver plated.
Per pair.....................**$0.45**
Per doz. pairs..............**4.85**

| | | | | |
|---|---|---|---|---|
| Length | 3¼ | 4 | 4 | 4 |
| Size of hole | ⅞ | 1 | 1⅛ | 1¼ |
| Weight per pair, oz | 8 | 13 | 14 | 21 |
| Silver plated. Per pair | $0.46 | $0.53 | $0.80 | $1.13 |
| Silver plated. Per doz. pairs | 4.90 | 5.73 | 8.65 | 12.15 |

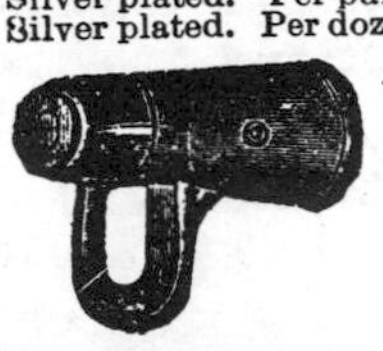

No. 11448. Hawley's Patent Whiffletree Hooks.

| | | | |
|---|---|---|---|
| Diameter, in | ⅞ | 1 | 1⅛ |
| Weight per pair | 11 | 12 | 13 oz. |
| Per pair | $0.21 | $0.23 | $0.30 |
| Per doz. pairs | $2.20 | $2.25 | $2.65 |
| Diameter, in | | 1¼ | 1⅜ |
| Weight per pair, lbs. | | 1 | 1⅛ |
| Per pair | | $0.33 | $0.33 |
| Per doz. pairs | | 2.90 | 3.55 |

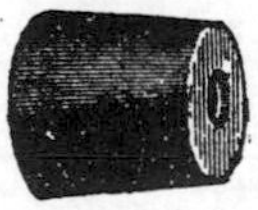

No. 11450. Closed end—core malleable

| | | | | | |
|---|---|---|---|---|---|
| Size inside large end, | ¾ | ⅞ | 1 | 1⅛ | 1¼ in. |
| Depth | 1 | 1 | 1⅛ | 1⅛ | 1½ in. |
| Each | 2c | 2c | 3c | 3c | 4c |
| Per doz | 15c | 17c | 22c | 25c | 30c |

**Undoubtedly some of your neighbors have never bought by mail, and think it don't pay. If you can persuade them differently, we make it worth your while.** **See special club order terms on page 4.**

## Malleable Whiffletree Tongues.

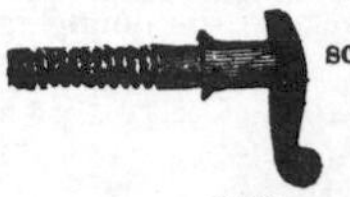

No. 11451. With shoulder. To screw. 3 inches long, 7/8 inch shank. Each, **3c**; per doz............ **24c**
2⅜ inches long, ⅜ inch shank. Each, **2c**; per doz........... **15c**

## Wagon Box Rods.

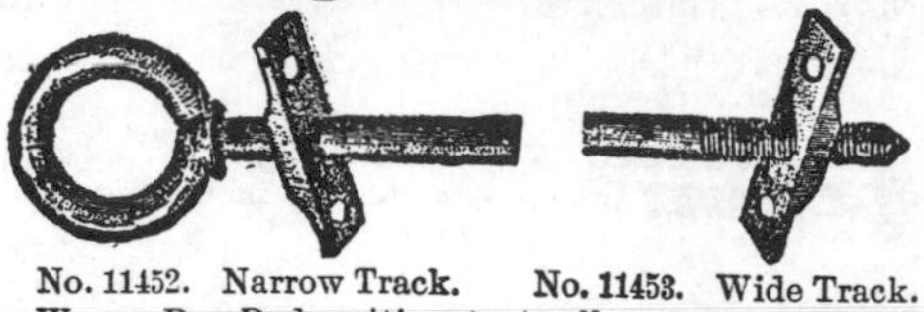

No. 11452. Narrow Track. No. 11453. Wide Track.
Wagon Box Rods, with patent collar; both wide and narrow track; state which you want; wide track are 3 feet 7 inches between collars, and narrow track 3 feet 3 inches; weight about 1¾ lbs.
Each, **9c**; per doz ........................................ **98c**

## Wagon Bow Staples.

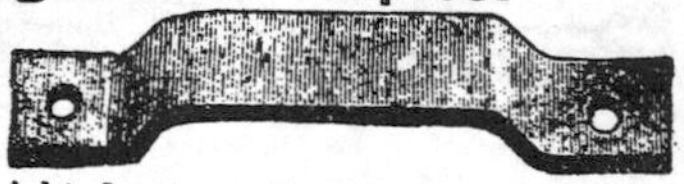

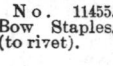

No. 11455. Bow Staples, (to rivet).

| Size. | Weight, doz. | Per doz. | Per gross. |
|---|---|---|---|
| 1½ | 17 oz. | 7c | $0.80 |
| 1¾ | 20 oz. | 8c | .90 |
| 2 | 24 oz. | 9c | 1.00 |

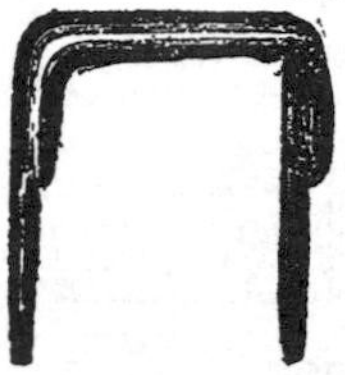

## Wagon Bow Staples.

(To drive.)

**State size wanted.**

No. 11457. Wagon Bow Staples, 1¼, 1¾ and 2 inch. Weight per doz., 15 oz.
Per doz., **7c**; per gross.... **80c**

## Wear or Rub Irons, Malleable.

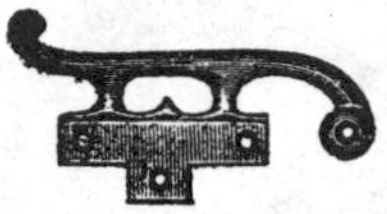

No. 11458. Length, 6½ in.; width, 2 inches.
Per pair .................. **10c**
Per doz. pairs ....... **$1.10**

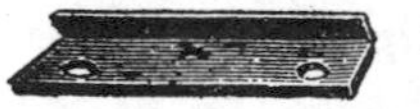

No. 11459. 1¼ inch bearing. Length, 5 inches.
Per pair.................... **8c**
Per doz. pairs.......... **85c**

No. 11461. Length, 6¼ inches; bearing, 1⅜ inch.
Per pair, **10c**; per doz. pairs.................. **$1.00**

## King Bolts.

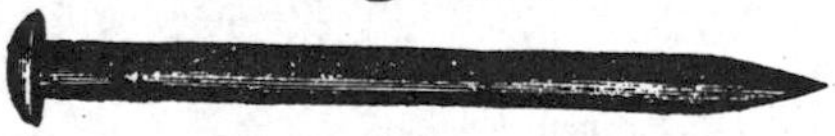

No. 11462. Button head steel wagon King Bolt.

| Size. | Each. | Per doz. |
|---|---|---|
| ⅞ inch | 15c | $1.50 |
| 1 inch | 20c | 2.00 |
| 1⅛ inch | 25c | 2.50 |
| 1¼ inch | 30c | 3.00 |

## Hammer Straps.

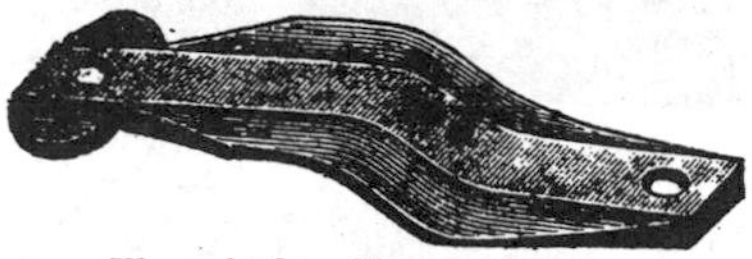

Wrought Iron Hammer Strap.
No. 11463. Heavy, each, **5c**; doz .................. **55c**
No. 11464. Light, each, **4c**; doz.................. **45c**

## Pole Caps.

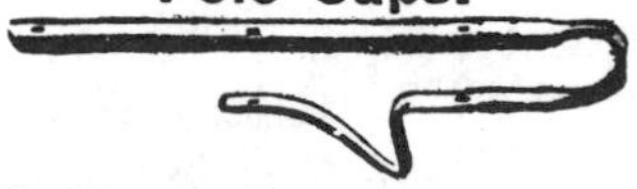

No. 11465. Wrought Iron Pole Cap, with holdback. Weight, 2 lbs. 10 oz.
Each, **16c**; per doz. ................................ **$1.75**

## Wagon Box Straps.

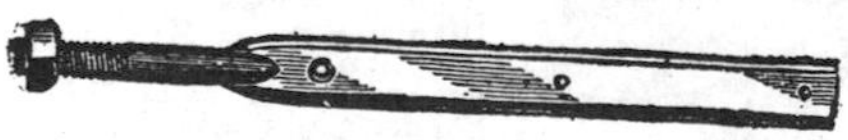

No. 11467. Wagon Box Strap Bolts. A set consists of 8.

| | | | | | |
|---|---|---|---|---|---|
| Length, inches | 10 | 12 | 14 | 16 | 18 |
| Weight per set, lbs. | 4¼ | 6 | 7¼ | 9½ | 10 |
| Diameter at screw | ½ | ½ | 9/16 | 9/16 | ⅝ |
| Per set | 28c | 30c | 33c | 42c | 58c |

**Special attention is directed to page 4 of this Catalogue, where our liberal terms on club orders are explained. It will pay you to interest your neighbors in this Catalogue.**

## Bolster Plates.

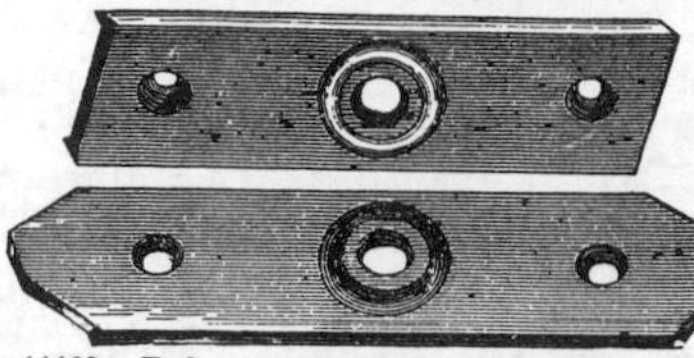

No. 11468. Bolster Plates, wrought iron, common pattern.

| | | | | |
|---|---|---|---|---|
| Width | 2¾ | 3 | 3¼ | 3½ |
| Weight | 5½ lb. | 5½ lb. | 5½ lb. | 6 lb. |
| Per set | 20c | 25c | 30c | 32c |

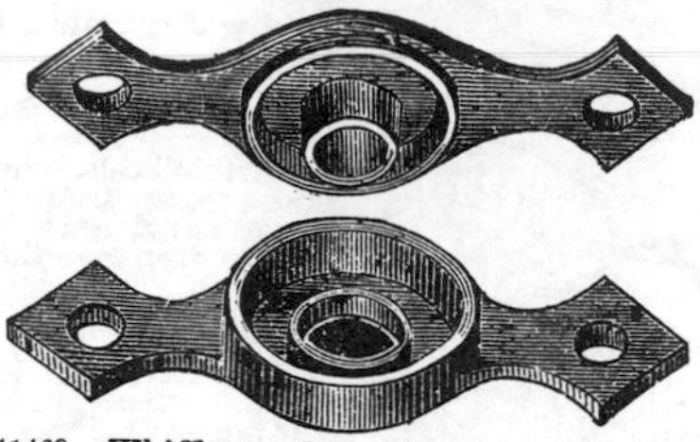

No. 11469. Whiffletree Couplings, low pattern.

| Width. | Length. | Size of hole. | Weight, oz. | Per pair. | Per doz. pairs. |
|---|---|---|---|---|---|
| 1½ | 4 | ⅜ | 4 | 4c | 25c |
| 1¾ | 4¾ | ⅜ | 8 | 5c | 30c |
| 2 | 4¾ | ⅜ | 9 | 5c | 30c |
| 2½ | 5¼ | 7/16 | 10 | 6c | 40c |
| 3 | 6½ | 7/16 | 15 | 6c | 60c |

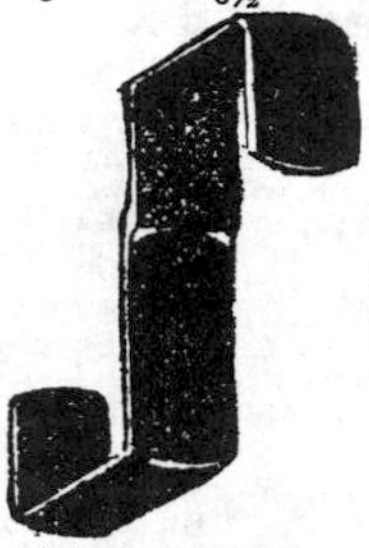

## Malleable Seat Spring Hooks.

No. 11472. Seat Spring Hooks, 3½ inches long; 1⅛ and 1½ inch hooks. Weight per set, 2 lbs. 13 oz.
Per set of 4 hooks........... **8c**

## Neck Yoke Attachment.

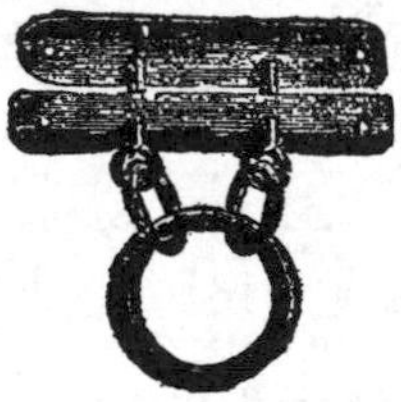

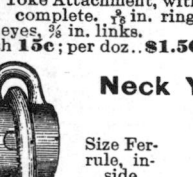

No. 11474. Wrought Iron Neck Yoke Attachment, with plate, complete. 9/16 in. ring, 7/16 in. eyes, ⅜ in. links.
Each **15c**; per doz.. **$1.50**

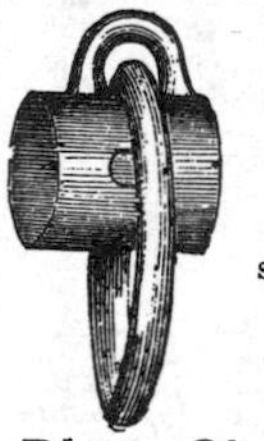

## Neck Yoke Ferrules.

No. 11475.

| Size Ferrule, inside small end. | Size Ring. | Price, each. | Price, doz. |
|---|---|---|---|
| 1¼ in. | 3½x⅜ in. | $0.04 | $0.40 |
| 1⅜ in. | 3½x⅜ in. | .05 | .54 |
| 1½ in. | 3½x 7-16 in. | .06 | .64 |

## Plow Clevises.

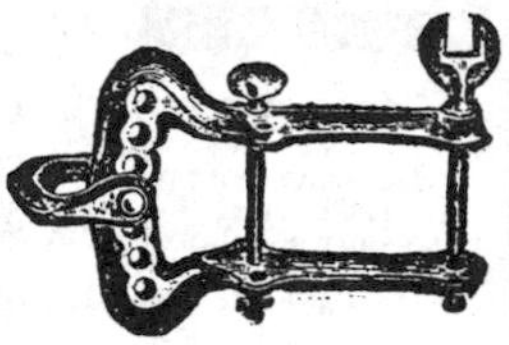

No. 11476. Malleable Plow Clevis, for 2½ inch beam. Extreme length, 8 inches; 5 holes. Weight, 3¼ lbs.
Each **26c**; per doz. **$2.80**

No. 11477. Malleable Plow Clevis, for 2¾ inch beam. Extreme length, 8¼ inches; 7 holes. Weight, 3¼ lbs.
Each, **28c**; per doz.......................................... **$3.00**

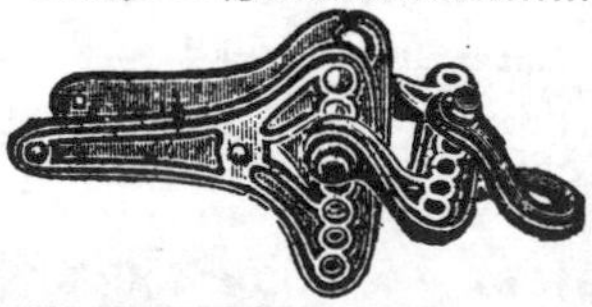

No. 11479. Malleable Iron Plow Clevis, for 3 inch wood beam, 4¾ inch to center of beam holes; 9 holes in cross clevis. Weight 5¼ lbs. Complete, as shown in cut.
Each.......... **38c**

No. 11480. Cross Link for iron heavy plow clevis.

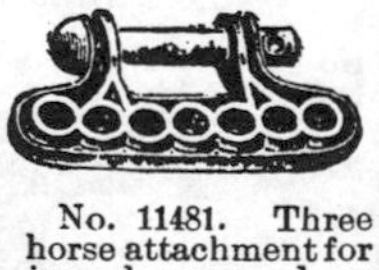

| | A. | B. | C. |
|---|---|---|---|
| Width, in., inside lugs. | 2¼ | 2 | 3¼ |
| Length, in | 5 | 6 | 6½ |
| Holes | 6 | 7 | 8 |
| Each | 8c | 10c | 12c |

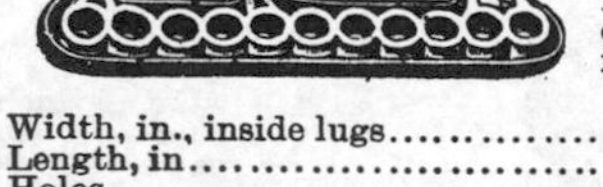

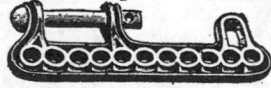

No. 11481. Three horse attachment for iron beam plow clevis. Malleable iron.

| | A. | B. | C. |
|---|---|---|---|
| Width, in., inside lugs | 2 | 2⅜ | 3⅜ |
| Length, in | 7¾ | 9½ | 9½ |
| Holes | 9 | 11 | 11 |
| Each | 11c | 14c | 16c |

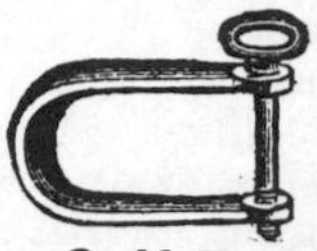

## Screw Pin Clevis.

No. 11482. Malleable Clevis, with screw pin, 2½ inches inside measure, 4½ inches in length. Weight, 1 lb. 10 oz.
Each, **10c**; per doz........... **90c**

## Self-Fastening Pin Clevis.

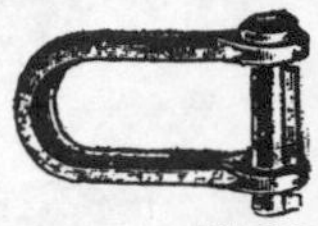

No. 11484. Malleable Patent Self-fastening Pin Clevis; inside measure 2½ inches; whole length, 4½ inches. Weight, 1 lb. 12 oz.
Each, **10c**; per doz................................. **$1.00**

## Swivel Hook Clevis.

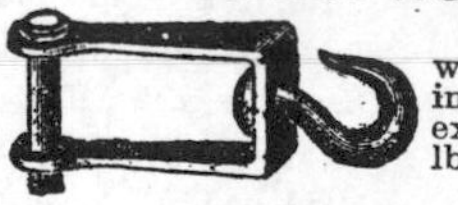

No. 11486. Evener Clevis with swivel hook, 2½ inches inside measurement, 9 inches extreme length. Weight, 3 lbs. 9 oz.
Each, **15c**; per doz.. **$1.62**

## End Clevis.

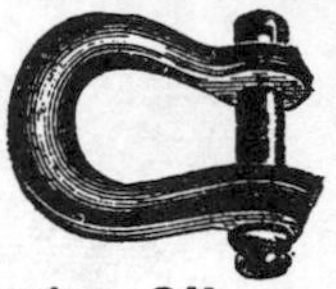

No. 11487. Malleable End Clevis, inside measure ¾ inch, whole length 3 inches. Weight, 12 oz.
Each, **4c**; per doz.......... **44c**

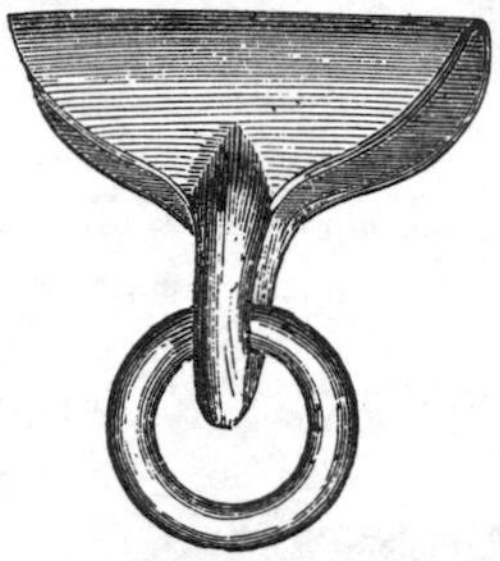

## Center Clips.

For 2 to 3 inch single trees.

No. 11491. Wrought Iron Center Clip, with rings.

| Size of iron in ring. | Each. | Doz. |
|---|---|---|
| ½ inch, | $0.05 | $0.50 |
| 9/16 inch, | .06 | .64 |
| ⅝ inch, | .07 | .75 |

## Whiffletree Hooks and Ferrules.

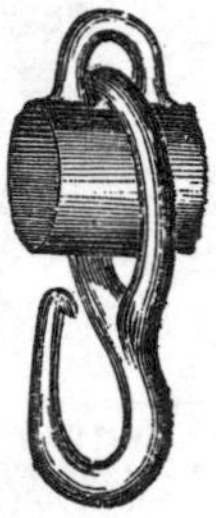

No. 11492. Singletree Hook and Ferrule; wrought iron hook, malleable ferrule. Weight, 11 ounces each.
1¼ inches, each, **4c**; per doz...... **44c**
1½ inches, each, **5c**; per doz....... **52c**

## Wagon Axles, Rough.

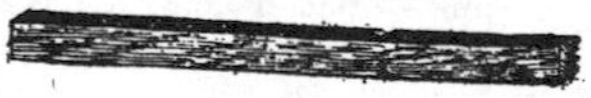

No. 11494. Wagon Axles, shell bark hickory.

| Size. | Weight per pair. | Per pair. |
|---|---|---|
| 3x4 inches by 6 feet long, | 48 lbs. | $0.70 |
| 4x5 inches by 6 feet long, | 80 lbs. | 1.40 |
| 4x6 inches by 6 feet long, | 96 lbs. | 1.65 |
| 5x6 inches by 6 feet long, | 120 lbs. | 2.25 |
| 5x7 inches by 6 feet long, | 142 lbs. | 2.65 |

## Wagon Reaches.

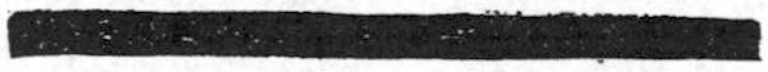

No. 11496. Wagon Reaches, select white oak in the rough.

| Size. | Length. | W't. | Each. | Size. | Length. | W't. | Each. |
|---|---|---|---|---|---|---|---|
| 2x4 in. | 8 ft. | 11 lbs. | 25c | 2½x4½ | 12 ft. | 47 lbs. | 57c |
| 2x4 | 10 ft. | 13½ lbs. | 33c | 2½x5 | 10 ft. | 45 lbs. | 50c |
| 2x4 | 12 ft. | 16 lbs. | 38c | 2½x5 | 12 ft. | 57 lbs. | 60c |
| 2½x4½ | 8 ft. | 31 lbs. | 38c | 3x5 | 12 ft. | 60 lbs. | 71c |
| 3¼x4½ | 10 ft. | 40 lbs. | 43c | | | | |

## Wagon Gearing, Rough.

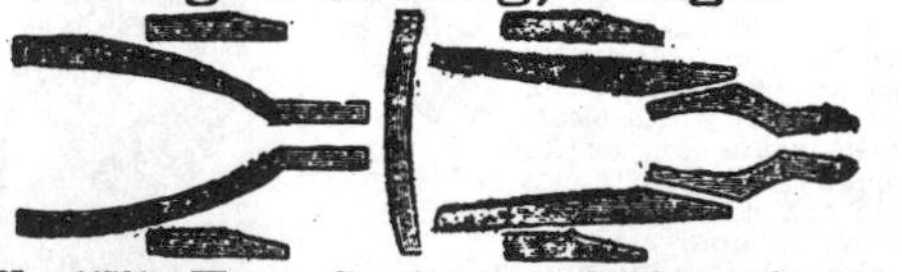

No. 11501. Wagon Gearing, sawed select oak, consisting of 2 front hawns, per pair, **25c**; 2 hind hawns, per pair, **27c**; 2 tongue hawns, per pair, **25c**; 1 sway bar, each **12c**; 4 stakes, per set, **10c**; set complete ........................................................ **99c**
(Weight, per set, 55 pounds.)
No. 11502. Bent Hawns, wide or narrow track, 2x3 in. Weight, 20 lbs. Each.................................. **51c**

## Wagon Bows.

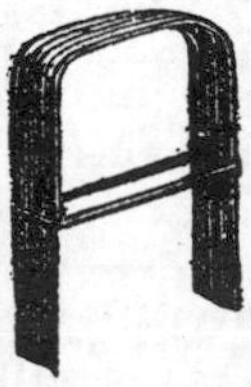

No. 11504. Express Wagon Bows, white ash, oval top or square top, 5 pieces to a set. When ordering bows, give width from outside to outside, 1⅛x⅜, 3 feet to 4 feet wide; weight, per set, 25 lbs. Square top, **$1.30**; oval top.................................. **$1.13**
No. 11505. Wagon Bows, round or square top, 5 pieces to a set (be sure to say whether for narrow or wide track). Weight, per set, 30 lbs. Size, 1⅜x¼ inches. Per set, round top, **60c**; square top.................................. **65c**

**We have a most complete line of Agricultural Implements on pages 136 to 154. Our prices and terms are beyond competition.**

## Wagon Bolster.

No. 11507. Wagon Bolster, select white oak in the rough.

| Size. | Length. | W't. | Each. | Size. | Length. | W't. | Each. |
|---|---|---|---|---|---|---|---|
| 2½x3 in. | 4 ft. | 14 lbs. | 18c | 4x5 | 4½ ft. | 33 lbs. | 43c |
| 3x4 | 4 ft. | 16 lbs. | 21c | 4x6 | 4 ft. | 33 lbs. | 45c |
| 3x4 | 4½ ft. | 18 lbs. | 25c | 3½x4½ | 4 ft. | 21 lbs. | 31c |
| 3½x4½ | 4 ft. | 21 lbs. | 29c | 4x5 | 4 ft. | 28 lbs. | 41c |
| 3½x5 | 4 ft. | 23 lbs. | 32c | 4x6 | 4½ ft. | 36 lbs. | 51c |

## Wagon Tongues.

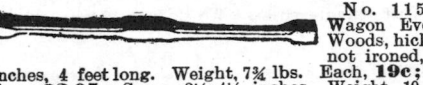

No. 11507. Wagon Tongues, select white ash, rough size at butt, 3x3, tip 2x3, 12 feet long. Weight, 30 lbs. Each ........ **75c**

No. 11508. 4x4, 12 feet long; tip, 2x4. Weight, 50 lbs. Each ........ **95c**

## Singletree and Evener Woods, Etc.

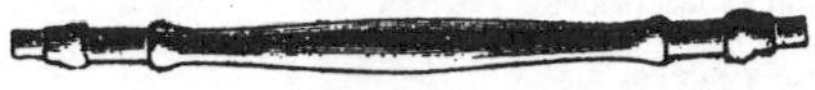

No. 11509. Wagon Neck Yoke Wood, round hickory, 2 inch center, 38 inches long, not ironed. Weight, 3 lbs. 3 oz. Each, **10c**; per doz ........ **$1.10**

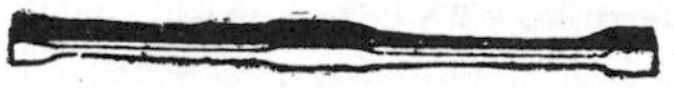

No. 11510. Wagon Evener Woods, hickory not ironed, 2x4 inches, 4 feet long. Weight, 7¾ lbs. Each, **19c**; per doz., **$2.05.** Same, 2½x4½ inches. Weight, 10 lbs. Each, **27c**; per doz ........ **$3.00**

No. 11511. Singletree Woods, round hickory, not ironed; 2½ inch center. Weight, 3½ lbs. Each, **9c**; per doz ........ **$1.00**

No. 11512. Singletree Woods, oval hickory, not ironed, 2½ inch center. Weight, 3¾ lbs. Each, **9c**; per doz ........ **$1.00**

## Ironed Neck Yoke.

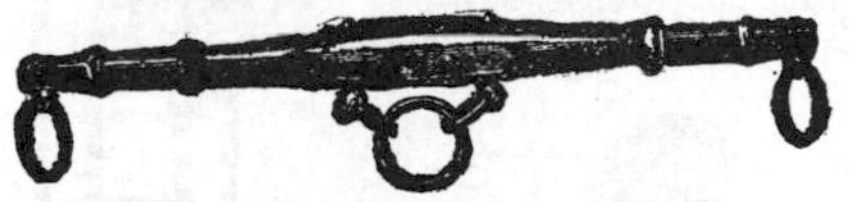

No. 11513. Neck Yokes, 38 inch; hickory, ironed complete. Weight, 7¼ lbs. Each, **40c**; per doz ..... **$4.50**

## Ironed Evener.

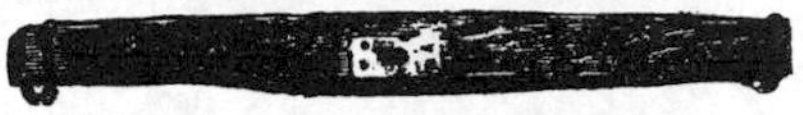

No. 11514. 2x4x48 wrought iron plates and malleable clevis, complete, as shown in cut, oiled. Each ..... **42c**

## Plow Evener.

No. 11516. Select hickory, 36 inches long, 3 inches thick, with hook in center, about 8 lbs. Each ...... **40c**

## Ironed Wagon Singletrees.

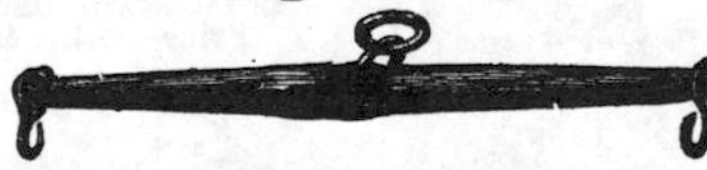

These are very fine Singletrees, made of selected woods, equipped with center clip hook and ferrule.

No. 11518. These Singletrees are not painted, but finished smooth and carefully oiled. Singletrees, 26 inch (plow), hickory, ironed. Weight, 3¼ lbs. Each, **17c**; per doz ........ **$1.84**

No. 11519. Singletrees, 30 inch, plow, hickory, ironed. Weight, 3¾ lbs. Each, **19c**; per doz ........ **$2.00**

No. 11520. Singletrees, 36 inch, wagon, hickory, ironed, with ferrules and hooks. Weight, 6 lbs. Each, **32c**; per doz ........ **$3.25**

## Shafts.

IRONED (NOT PAINTED).

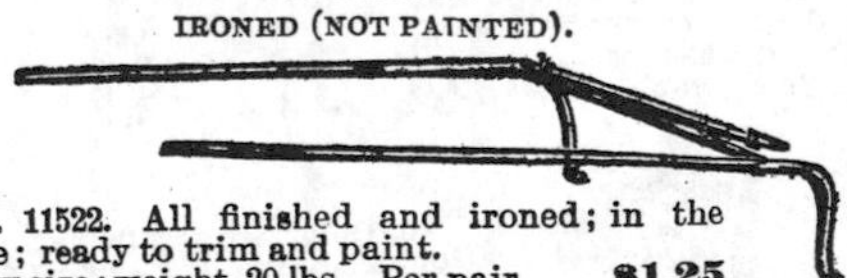

No. 11522. All finished and ironed; in the white; ready to trim and paint.
Buggy size; weight, 20 lbs. Per pair...... **$1.25**
Spring wagon size: weight, 30 lbs. Per pair..... **$1.45**

## Bent Heel Buggy or Cutter Shafts

Finished, bars included. **Give size when ordering.**

| | Size. | NOT IRONED. Weight. | | | Black. XXX Hick'y, |
|---|---|---|---|---|---|
| No. 11523. | 1⅜x1⅞ | 11¼ lbs. | Per pair, | 65c | 95c |
| No. 11524. | 1⅜x2 | 12¼ lbs. | | | |
| No. 11525. | 1½x2 | 12½ lbs. | | | |
| No, 11526. | 1½x2¼ | 14½ lbs. | | | |
| No. 11527. | 1⅝x2¼ | 15 lbs. | | | |

## Buggy Singletree Woods.

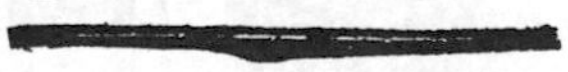

No. 11530. Buggy Singletree Woods, forest hickory, 1½, 1⅝, 1¾, 1⅞ inch center. **Give size when ordering.** Each, **12c**; per dozen ........ **$1.30**

No. 11531. Second growth hickory. Each, **18c**; per dozen ........ **$2.00**

## Buggy Poles.

No. 11533. Single bend Poles.
No. 11535. Double bend Poles.
Give size when ordering.

Buggy Poles, finished, including finished circles. The prices below are for one single bend pole and circle, which are called a set.

| Size. | XXX. | Black Hickory. | Weight. |
|---|---|---|---|
| 1¾x2¼ | 75c | $0.95 | 14 lbs. |
| 2 x2¼ | 80c | 1.05 | 15 lbs. |
| 2 x2¾ | 92c | 1.25 | 17 lbs. |
| 2 x3 | 95c | 1.28 | 19 lbs. |

Above prices are for single bend poles.
Double bend Poles, add 5 cents to price of single bend.

## Trimmed Neck Yokes.

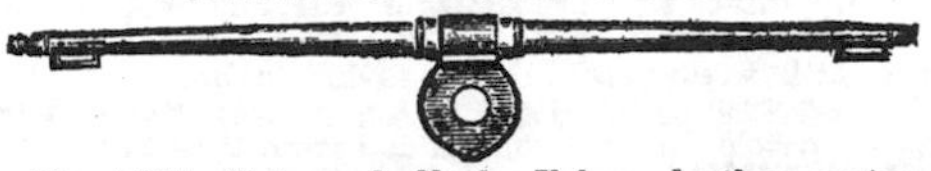

No. 11537. Trimmed Neck Yokes, leather center, acorn tips, 42 inches long; weight, 2 lbs. 10 oz. Each (not painted) ........ **50c**

## Buggy Neck Yoke Woods.

No. 11540. Buggy Neck Yoke Woods, 42 inches long, second growth hickory, acorn tips, 1⅝ to 2 inch center; weight, 2¼ lbs. Each, **25c**; per doz .... **$2.50**

## Bob Woods.

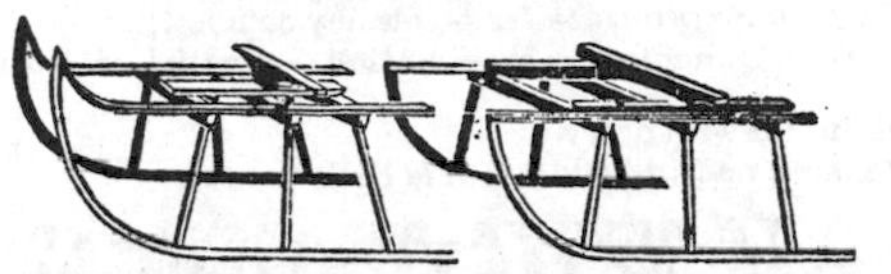

No. 11542. Finished grocery Bob Woods, all made with 3 knees front and 2 hind, extra well finished, not ironed or painted, but ready for finishing.
1⅛x1⅛ tread. Per set ........ **$5.95**
1¼x1¾ tread. Per set ........ **6.85**

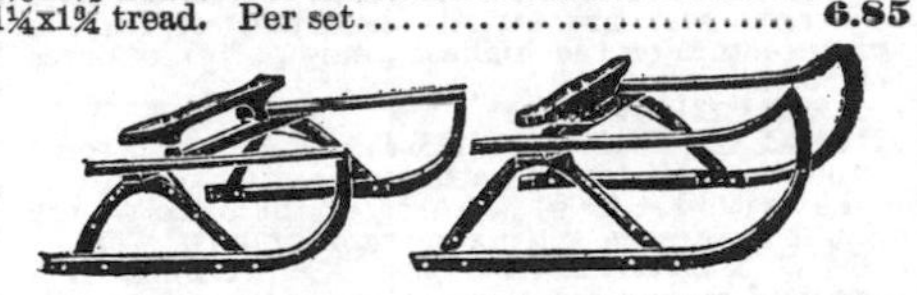

No. 11544. This is a new style and is giving good results; completely ironed, except draw irons and shoes; in the white, ready to paint; just the thing for a pleasure, grocery, express or light delivery sleigh. We want your order for a set.
1⅛ tread. Per set ........ **$8.45**
1¼ tread. Per set ........ **9.10**

## Special Bargains in Bob Sleds.

**Our Bob Sleds** are made and shipped from Abingdon, Ill., by a concern who have a reputation in this line second to none. The manufacturers of these goods are recognized by all dealers as the makers of the best bobs in the country, and only the best are good enough for us to offer to our trade. We contracted for this line of goods, for the reason that we learned by investigation that nothing but the best of material entered into the construction of this work, that this line of bobs was the best on the market regardless of price.

**These Sleighs** are all covered by the most binding two years' guarantee, during which time, if any piece or part gives out by reason of defect in material or workmanship, we will replace it free of charge. With care they will last a natural lifetime.

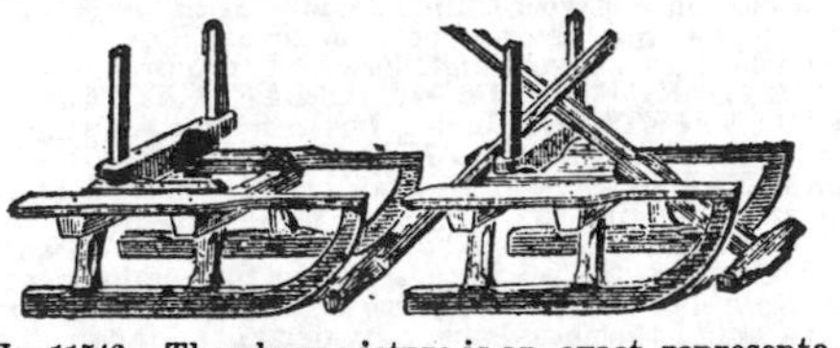

No. 11546. The above picture is an exact representation of our 2x3—two knee Bob Sled, engraved from a photograph.

**Our Bobs** are made of the very best selected material throughout; best workmanship, painted in four coats vermilion paint, striped, ornamented and varnished.

**Our special offer price** on the above Bob Sled complete is **$11.90.** Well ironed throughout; complete in every respect.

No. 11547. Size of runners, 2x3 inches; capacity, 4,000 lbs.; size of runners, 2x3½ inches; capacity, 6,000 lbs. Price ........ **$12.75**

No. 11548. **We make the same Bobs** with our special patent steel knees as follows:
Size 2x2½ inch runners, for grocery express; capacity, 3,000 lbs ........ **$11.85**
Size 2x3 inch runners, for farm use; capacity, 6,000 lbs ........ **$11.95**
Size 2x3½ inch runners, for heavy teaming; capacity, 8,000 lbs ........ **$12.75**

**The Biggest Buggy**
CATALOGUE EVER PUBLISHED
WILL BE MAILED TO YOU. . .
**Free on Application.**

No. 11549. **We also furnish** the celebrated Spies Oscillator Bobs, which we claim to be superior to any on the market. It has its steel knee on the same plan as our steel knee bob. Its construction is as simple and durable as any oscillator bob on the market. It has long runners, grooved shoes, and has two draft rods from the beam to the tongue, to prevent the great strain from the tongue to the runner. These sleds are made in three different sizes:
2x3 inch runners, for grocery express use; capacity, 3,000 lbs. Price ........ **$13.50**
2x3½ inch runners, for farm use; capacity, 6,000 lbs. Price ........ **$13.80**
2x4 inch runners, for heavy teaming use; capacity, 8,000 lbs. Price ........ **$14.95**

## Bob Runners.

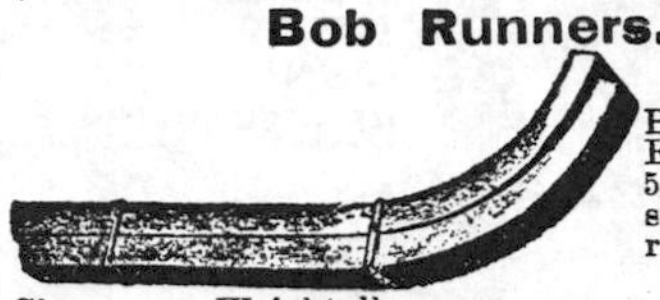

No. 11551. Bent Bob Runners. Entire length, 5½ feet. Set consists of 4 single runners.

| Size. | Weight, lbs. | Per set. |
|---|---|---|
| 2x3 | 45 | $1.44 |
| 2x3½ | 60 | 1.68 |
| 2x4 | 65 | 2.08 |

## Long Sleigh Runners.

No. 11554. White Oak Bent solid, 10½ feet long.

| | Per pair. | | Per pair. |
|---|---|---|---|
| 1⅝x2 | $1.00 | 2 x3 | $2.00 |
| 1⅝x2¼ | 1.10 | 2 x3½ | 2.10 |
| 1¾x2½ | 1.49 | 2⅛x4 | 2.40 |
| 2 x2¾ | 1.60 | 2⅜x4½ | 2.80 |

## Bob Sleigh Gearing.

No. 11556. Bob Beams, 5 to a set, 3x3½; weight, 60 lbs. Per set ........ **72c**
No. 11557. Bob Knees, 10 to a set, 3x3½; weight, 40 lbs. Per set ........ **40c**
No. 11558. Bob Raves, 4 to a set, 1¾x6¾x54; weight, 40 lbs. Per set ........ **68c**
No. 11559. Bob Rollers, 2 to a set, 3x3½x36; weight, 5 lbs. Per set ........ **23c**
No. 11561. Bob Saddles, 1 to a set, 2x12x24; weight, 10 lbs. Per set ........ **17c**
No. 11562. Bob Reaches, 1 to a set, 2x4x48; weight, 7½ lbs. Per set ........ **10c**
No. 11563. Sawed Bob Benches, white Oak; wide track 3 feet 6; narrow track 3 feet 2; size 3x9, each, **45c**; 3½x9, each, **54c**; 4x9, each ........ **63c**
Bob Benches weigh 120 pounds to a set.

## Cast Bob Shoes.

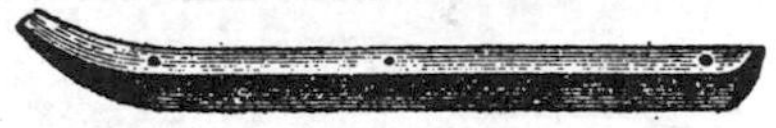

Cast iron Bob Sleigh Shoes, interchangeable for right or left hand; 1½ tread, 2 on top and 1¾ thick.

No. 11565.

| Length. | Weight, per set of four. | Per set. |
|---|---|---|
| 36 inches. | 64 pounds | $1.28 |
| 38 inches. | 66 pounds | 1.32 |
| 40 inches. | 68 pounds | 1.36 |
| 42 inches. | 70 pounds | 1.40 |
| 44 inches. | 72 pounds | 1.44 |
| 48 inches. | 76 pounds | 1.52 |

## Sleigh Shoe Bolts.

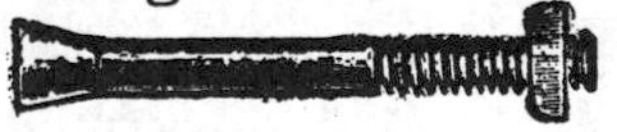

No. 11567.

| Length. | Diameter. | Price per set of 16. |
|---|---|---|
| 4½ inches. | 7/16 | 20c |
| 5 inches. | 7/16 | 22c |
| 5½ inches. | 7/16 | 25c |
| 6 inches. | 7/16 | 28c |

## Cutter Stuff.

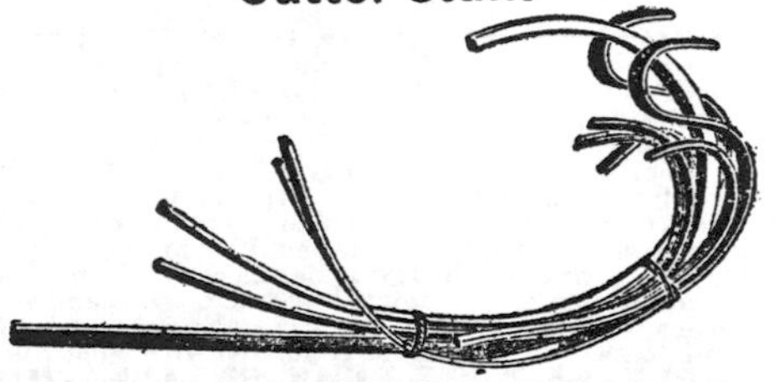

No. 11569. Bent Cutter Stuff for Portland cutters, consisting of runners, raves and fenders, put up in the rough, 1 set in a bundle. 1½ inch, one seat, weight 35 lbs., per set, **$1**; 1½ inch, two seats, weight, 40 lbs., per set ........ **$1.10**

No. 11571. Same for swell body cutters; 1¼ inch, one seat, weight, 35 lbs., per set, **$1.50**; 1½ inch, two seats, weight, 40 lbs., per set ........ **$2.20**

No. 11572. Same for square box cutter; 1¼ inch, one seat, weight, 30 lbs., per set, **85c**; 1½ inch, two seats, weight, 35 lbs., per set ........ **95c**

## Cutter Shoes.

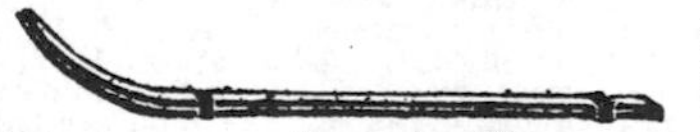

No. 11574. Steel Cutter Shoes, tapered and bent.

| Size. | Per pair. | Size. | Per pair. |
|---|---|---|---|
| ⅜x¾ | $0.75 | ⅜x1 | $0.85 |
| ½x1 | 1.10 | ½x¾ | .95 |
| ⅝x1¼ | 1.15 | ½x1¼ | 1.20 |

Weight, about 28 lbs. per set.

**Our special Bicycle Catalogue shows such a line of wheels at such prices that you should not send for it if you have not the will power to resist temptation.**

# SEARS ROEBUCK & CO'S BLACKSMITH TOOLS

**EVERY FARMER HIS OWN BLACKSMITH**

## DO YOUR OWN WORK
### ...ON THE FARM...
**Sharpen the Plows, Shoe the Horses,**
**Set the Loose Tires, Mend the Machinery.**

**WITH AN OUTFIT** selected from this list, every farmer, ranchman and mechanic can be his own blacksmith.

**NO DELAY FOR REPAIRS IN A BUSY SEASON** while the team and a man has gone to the blacksmith shop. Again, if you have an outfit you will improve rainy days to fix up things that are showing wear, and avoid costly vexations and dangerous breakage in a busy time.

**THE COST OF A COMPLETE OUTFIT** is but little. You will save it all in one year's blacksmith bills, to say nothing of the saving in time.

**DON'T SAY YOU CAN'T DO THE WORK.** Thousands of farmers have bought outfits from us, few articles at first, then added from time to time, and now have a complete outfit, **DO ALL THEIR OWN WORK,** and many take in work from neighbors, who are willing to pay well for the work and thus save the time of going to the town blacksmith.

**A PORTABLE FORGE, ANVIL, DRILL, VISE, STOCK AND DIES, TAPER TAPS, TONGS AND SHOEING OUTFIT,** and you are prepared for any kind of blacksmith work.

**$25.00 WILL BUY SUCH AN OUTFIT.** On the start you may not want a complete outfit, but later you will surely add until you have a complete outfit, and you will call it the best investment you ever made.

**SPACE WILL NOT PERMIT** our showing everything in the line. We show here the tools most commonly used.

**WE ISSUE A SPECIAL CATALOGUE** of blacksmith tools, showing everything in the line, and will gladly mail it free on application.

**EVERY TOOL WE SELL IS GUARANTEED STANDARD QUALITY,** the product of the best manufacturers. We do not handle cheap, trashy or second grade goods.

**OUR PRICES,** quality considered, you will find by comparison, are far below any competition.

**OUR TERMS:** Any goods will be sent by freight, C. O. D., subject to examination, on receipt of **ONE-FOURTH** the amount of order, balance to be paid at freight depot.

**THREE PER CENT. DISCOUNT,** for cash in full with order.

**FREIGHT IS VERY LOW** on this class of goods, and will add but very little to cost.

## BARGAINS IN PORTABLE FORGES
### OUR LEADER for $7.95

No. 11600.

**WE BELIEVE WE ARE HEADQUARTERS FOR EVERYTHING DESIRABLE IN PORTABLE FORGES.**

**WE HAVE MADE OUR CONTRACTS WITH SEVERAL OF THE** very largest and most reliable manufacturers in the country, concerns who are strictly headquarters for the manufacture of the highest grade portable forges on the market.

**THERE ARE MANY CHEAP, INFERIOR FORGES OFFERED,** and even some of our competitors may attempt to meet or cut our prices, but when a forge is offered at within 10 or 20 per cent. of the price we are able to name, you can depend upon it you are not getting the same grade of work.

**WE GUARANTEE OUR FORGES TO BE EXACTLY AS REPRESENTED,** and if not found so, you can return them to us and we will cheerfully refund your money.

**ALL OUR FORGES ARE MADE OF THE VERY BEST MATERIAL,** are thoroughly well put together, and guaranteed to give the best of service. The prices we quote are for the Forges carefully packed and delivered on board the cars in Chicago. You pay the freight, but you will find the freight will amount to next to nothing, as compared with what you will save in price. There is perhaps no more necessary or economic machine on a farm than one of our strictly high grade portable Forges. In one year it will save its cost ten times over in time, to say nothing of the saving in blacksmiths' bills.

**WE BELIEVE THAT WE OFFER THE MOST POPULAR LINE OF FORGES,** from the fact that our Forge trade has grown until we believe we are without an exception the largest dealers in the land direct with the consumer.

**WE WOULD ASK YOU TO COMPARE OUR PRICES CLOSELY WITH THOSE** of other houses, compare the illustrations and descriptions, and then if you are not thoroughly satisfied that we are offering you a better Forge for less money than you could possibly buy elsewhere, send to us for a Forge and compare it with the Forge you can buy elsewhere, and if you do not say ours is better and cheaper, the best Forge ever seen for the money, return it at our expense and we will cheerfully refund your money.

**No. 11600. OUR SPECIAL LEADER AT $7.95.**

**AT $7.95 WE OFFER YOU A STRICTLY HIGH GRADE,** fully guaranteed Forge, which you could not duplicate elsewhere in a wholesale way at less than $10.00, and a Forge that would retail at $12.00 or more.

**THIS FORGE IS ESPECIALLY DESIGNED FOR** bridge, boiler and tank builders, miners, prospectors, elevated railroad builders, farmers, etc.

**WE ARE ABLE TO GET THE PRICE SO LOW, $7.95,** that every farmer in selecting a Forge should order this in preference to a cheaper one. The motion is a very simple device. It has a self-acting ratchet, no springs or anything to get out of order. It is made from the very best material. The lever is connected with a segment of gears which speeds the driving wheel up to a very high speed. It requires a very slight movement of the lever to get the strongest blast. **THIS FORGE IS SUPPLIED WITH A 9-INCH FAN, HEARTH IS 22 INCHES IN DIAMETER.** Having but three legs, it stands very firmly on an uneven foundation, and is purposely made for the work we claim. **HEIGHT OF FORGE, 30 INCHES; HEARTH, 22 INCHES IN DIAMETER; FAN, 9 INCHES; WEIGHT, 80 LBS.** This is the largest Forge we ever saw offered at anything like the price, and we would ask you to compare the size of hearth and fan with other Forges at about the same price, and draw your own conclusions.

**WE WANT TO SELL 5,000 OF THESE SPECIAL $7.95** Forges during the coming year, and with the expectation that we will sell this number, we are able to make our price $7.95. By making our contract on this basis, we were able to get the price down to about the actual cost of material and labor. To this we have added only our one small percentage of profit, and as a result, in buying a single Forge from us at $7.95, you are practically buying on the basis of a contract for 5,000 Forges. These Forges are accepted by the railroad companies at second class freight rate, and its weight is 80 lbs. By referring to the freight rates in the front part of the book, you can calculate very closely what the freight will be, which you will find will amount to next to nothing, as compared with what you will save in price.

**PLEASE NOTE THAT ON ALL THIS CLASS OF GOODS WE WILL SHIP C. O. D.,** subject to examination, by freight, where a sufficient amount accompanies order to cover freight charges both ways. You can examine the goods at your freight depot, and if found perfectly satisfactory and exactly as represented, pay the freight agent our special price, $7.95, and freight charges, less the amount sent with order.

**A DISCOUNT OF 3 PER CENT. IS ALLOWED** on all blacksmith tools, where cash in full accompanies your order. Do not overlook our 3 per cent. cash discount when comparing our prices with those of other houses. Bear in mind that the 3 per cent. cash discount on this Forge would mean to you a saving of 24c., and when comparing our prices with the prices of other houses, always deduct the 3 per cent. cash discount, which brings this Forge down to $7.71. There are Forges on the market, some offered by catalogue houses, you may have seen them illustrated and quoted. Compare this Forge with anything you can find in any catalogue at $10.00, and if you do not from the illustration and description consider ours equal or better, we will not expect you to give us your order.

**EVERY ONE IN WANT OF A FORGE SHOULD PLACE THEIR ORDER WITH US,** or, if in want of anything in the line of blacksmiths' tools, we should have their order. We feel we are entitled to it by reason of the prices and terms of shipment we offer. First, we have arranged with the different manufacturers to supply only the highest grade of goods that can be obtained. We have fixed the prices at the manufacturers' lowest prices. By a careful comparison of our prices with those of other reliable houses, we have found without a single exception, when quality is considered, we are much lower in price. Different from other houses, we offer to send these goods by freight C. O. D., subject to examination on receipt of a deposit only to cover freight charges. We fully guarantee everything in this line that we offer you. If not found as represented, your money is always ready, and on the basis of excellency in material and make, liberalness in terms of shipment, prices lower than any of our competitors, a 3 per cent. discount for cash, we shall hope to receive your order.

**DO NOT OVERLOOK THIS FORGE AT $7.95 ON OUR REGULAR TERMS, OR $7.71 IF CASH IN FULL ACCOMPANIES YOUR ORDER. THERE IS NOTHING LIKE IT ON THE MARKET, AND YOU WILL FIND NO SUCH A BARGAIN IN ANY OTHER BOOK.**

No. 11602. Sears, Roebuck & Co. Portable Forge. It is especially built for farmers' use or for light repairing. Blacksmiths should buy a larger forge. This lever forge has pipe legs; stands 30 inches high. Hearth is 18 inches in diameter. Weight, 65 lbs.
Price, each .............. **$6.30**

No. 11604. Sears, Roebuck & Co. Double Ratchet Forge, with shield. This forge is intended for bridge, boiler and tank builders, miners, prospectors, farmers and mechanics. Hearth is 18 inches in diameter.
Price, each ... **$9.00**

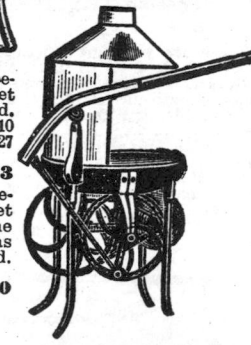

No. 11606. Sears, Roebuck & Co. Double Ratchet Forge, with half hood. Height, 29 inches; fan, 10 inches; hearth, 21x27 inches. Weight, 140 lbs.
Price, each ..... **$14.33**

No. 11608. Sears, Roebuck & Co. Double Ratchet Forge, with shield. Same as No. 11606, except has shield instead of half hood. Weight, 130 lbs.
Price, each ..... **$13.50**

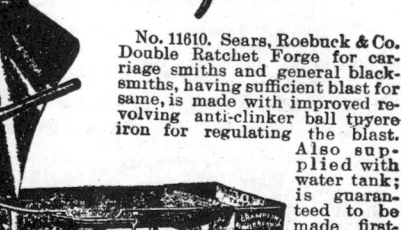

No. 11610. Sears, Roebuck & Co. Double Ratchet Forge for carriage smiths and general blacksmiths, having sufficient blast for same, is made with improved revolving anti-clinker ball tuyere iron for regulating the blast. Also supplied with water tank; is guaranteed to be made first-class in every respect. Hearth, 28x40 in.; height, 30 inches; weight, with water tank, 300 pounds; weight, without water tank, 250 lbs.
Price, with water tank, ..................... **$17.75**
Price, without water tank ..................... **16.00**

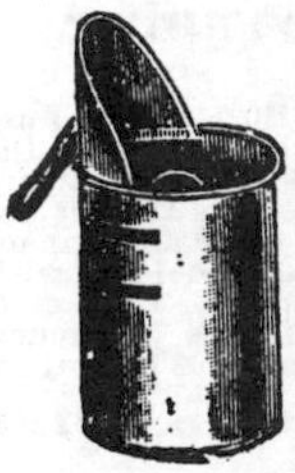

No. 11612. Sears, Roebuck & Co.'s Railroad and Bridge Builders' Forge, with galvanized iron drum and shield. This forge is specially designed for bridge and tank builders, all the working parts being enclosed in a galvanized drum made of wrought iron. The shield is also made of galvanized iron. The working parts are easy of access, simply by drawing a small slide to one side. This forge is made of the best material, and capable of the roughest kind of handling. This forge is made with the ball tuyere iron.

Forge No. 9. Size of hearth, 18 in.; fan, 9 in.; height, 30 in.; weight, 115 lbs. Price....................$14.75

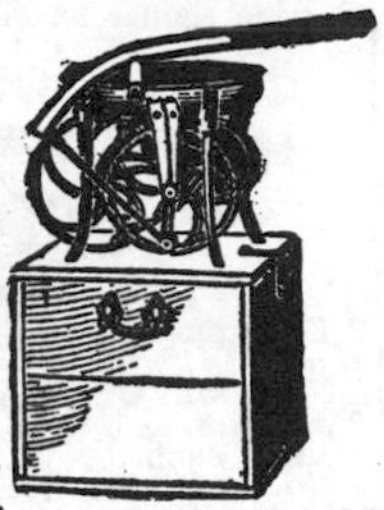

No. 11614. Sears, Roebuck & Co.'s Miners' Forge. Size of hearth is 18 inches; diameter of fan, 9 inches. The capacity of the forge is such as to give the miner and prospector entire satisfaction. It is made with short legs, and we place it in a case, making it very handy for transportation. The case has also ample room for a full line of blacksmiths' tools. Complete with case. Price....................$10.00

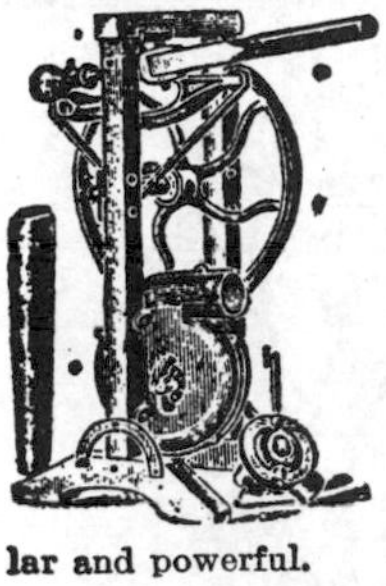

No. 11616. Sears, Roebuck & Co.'s Lever Blacksmith Blower. Fan is 16 inches in diameter and fly wheel 28 inches in diameter. Has the capacity of a 50-inch bellows. With patent tuyere iron and piping complete. Price............$8.00

Neither skill, money nor labor has been spared in designing and constructing this strictly first-class blower. The automatic lever motion is absolutely perfect in its construction; cannot get out of order; durable and light running; giving a continuous blast, regular and powerful.

## Blacksmiths' Bellows.

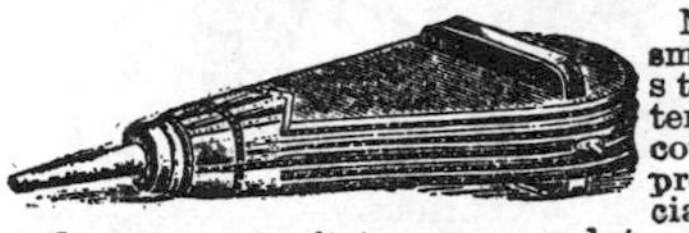

No. 11618. Blacksmith's Bellows, standard patterns. We use cowhide leather, prepared especially for our use, and we guarantee it to wear equal to any made. We use whitewood, basswood and pine in the woodwork, which is kiln-dried, making it perfectly dry, that it may not be affected by the change of climate. We aim to use nothing but the best and most suitable materials in their construction. The weight of our bellows is about as follows. They may vary a little, but not much:

| | | | | |
|---|---|---|---|---|
| Width, in............. | 26 | 28 | 30 | 32 |
| Weight, lbs........... | 32 | 40 | 50 | 60 |
| Price, each........... | $3.30 | $3.60 | $3.90 | $4.20 |
| Width, in............. | 34 | 36 | 38 | 40 |
| Weight, lbs........... | 70 | 80 | 90 | 100 |
| Price, each........... | $4.80 | $5.40 | $6.00 | $6.90 |

## Moulders' Bellows.

No. 11620. Moulders' Bellows. Weight, 3¾ lbs. Width, 12 inches. Each..............................$1.10

## Tuyere Iron.

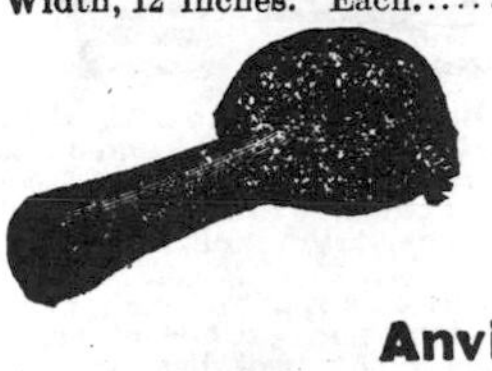

No. 11622. Single ducks' nest Tuyere Iron. Weight, 14 lbs. Price, each..........40c

## Anvils.

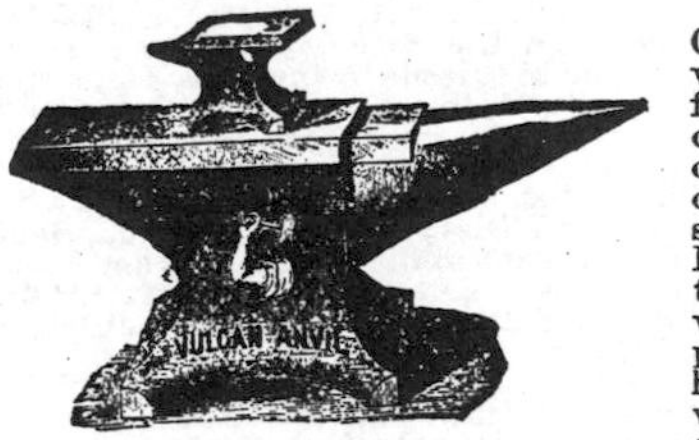

No. 11624. Cast Iron Anvils, with steel face. The face of this anvil is one solid piece of English tool steel thoroughly welded to the body of anvil by a patent process. The horn is covered with and its extremity made entirely of cast steel. The face and horn are then accurately ground and tempered. We do not guarantee this anvil, but it will give excellent satisfaction for light work.

| | | | | |
|---|---|---|---|---|
| No. | 2 | 3 | 4 | 5 |
| Weight, lbs., | 20 | 30 | 40 | 50 |
| Price, | $2.40 | $2.75 | $3.20 | $3.65 |
| No. | 6 | 7 | 8 | 9 |
| Weight, lbs., | 60 | 70 | 80 | 90 |
| Price, | $4.00 | $4.50 | $4.90 | $5.55 |

**Refer to the index in end of book for what you can't find. You are liable to overlook many needed articles when you glance through the Catalogue.**

## Peter Wright Anvils.

Wrought Iron with Steel Face.

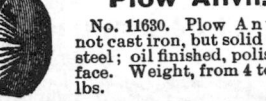

No. 11626. This well known anvil has stood the test for years and is to-day the most popular anvil in the world. It is cheap enough for any body and good enough for any one. Don't buy an anvil too light for your work. A light anvil when struck a hard blow with a heavy hammer is sure to jump. We carry a large stock but occasionally are not able to send exact weight ordered, but can always cover within 5 lbs. of the weight ordered. This anvil is sold by the pound and price per pound varies with the size.

85 lbs. to 500 lbs. Per lb..............................10½c
61 lbs. to 84 lbs. Per lb..............................13c
50 lbs. to 60 lbs. Per lb..............................13½c

## Plow Anvil.

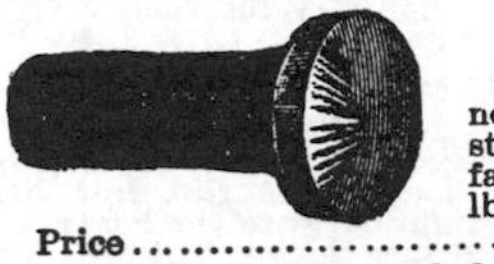

No. 11630. Plow Anvil, not cast iron, but solid cast steel; oil finished, polished face. Weight, from 4 to 4½ lbs.

Price..............................................60c

## Blacksmiths' Drills.

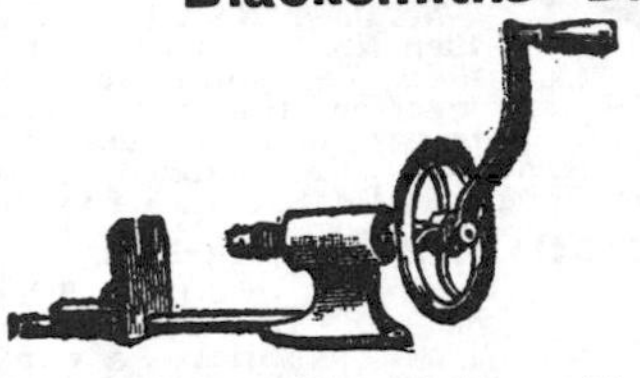

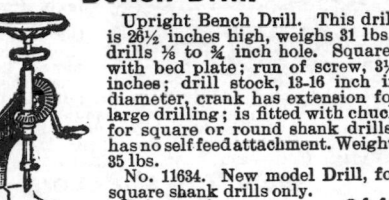

No. 11632. The old standard Blacksmiths' Drill. Length, 29 inches; screw feed. The hole in mandrel is square to hold drill points, which the blacksmith must make for himself. We cannot furnish drills to fit this machine. Weight, 29 lbs. Price, each..............................$1.50

## Bench Drill.

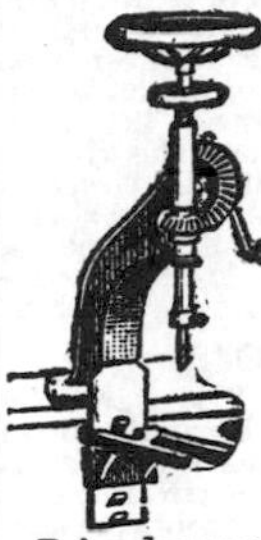

Upright Bench Drill. This drill is 26½ inches high, weighs 31 lbs., drills ⅛ to ¾ inch hole. Squares with bed plate; run of screw, 3½ inches; drill stock, 13-16 inch in diameter, crank has extension for large drilling; is fitted with chuck for square or round shank drills; has no self feed attachment. Weight, 35 lbs.

No. 11634. New model Drill, for square shank drills only. Price, each................$4.40

No. 11635. New model Drill, for ½-inch round shank drills only. Price, each................$4.40

Price does not include drill bits. See index for drill bits.

## Post Drills.

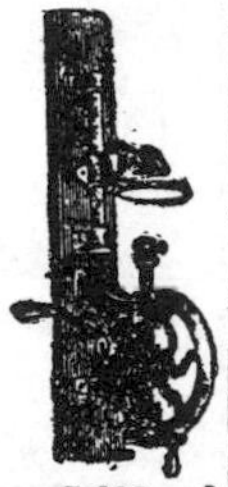

No. 11637. Blacksmith Self Feed Drill, weighs 100 pounds; drills to center of a 14 inch circle; has back gear; will drill from 0 to 1 inch hole; made of the best material; well finished; spindle bored to take in ½ inch straight shank drills.

In material and finish this drill is equal to any that's made.

Price, each..........................$6.00

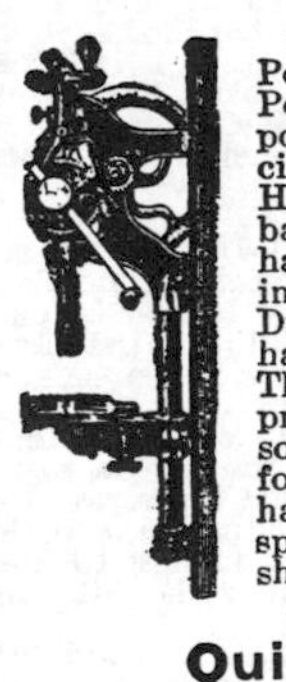

11639. World's Champion Self-Feed Post Drill, 1893 pattern. The World's Popular Drill for $10.00. Weight, 125 pounds. Drills to the center of a 15-inch circle, and from 1-64 to 1¼ inch hole. Has double journal bearings with full back gear; also, two speeds on right hand side of drill, which can be changed in an instant to suit all kinds of work. Diameter of spindle, 1¼ inches. The screw has an up and down run of 4¼ inches. The automatic self-feed is the latest improved. The table is large and slotted, so operator can securely bolt work on for drilling. This drill is mounted on a hard wood plank, 2 inches thick. The spindle is bored to take in ½ inch straight shank drills.

Our price..........................$7.50

## Quick Return Drill.

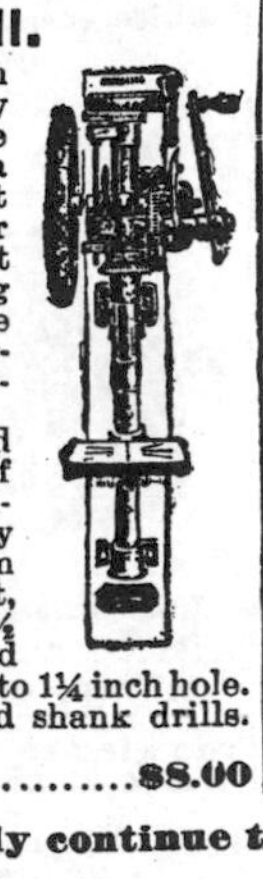

No. 11641. This drill is supplied with our patent quick-return attachment, by which the drill bit is removed from the work in an instant, by simply pushing a lever with the left hand, while the right hand continues turning the handle or crank which raises the bit to any height desired, and at the same time cleaning the hole bored as the bit revolves while being raised. It has two journal bearings, which are double, as in our 1893 pattern.

The drill is supplied with two true and honest speeds on the right hand side of the drill. First speed for light and medium work, and second speed for heavy work. You simply change the hub from first speed to second speed. Actual weight, 130 pounds. Will drill to a center of 15½ inches. The spindle has a run up and down of 3½ inches, and will bore from 0 to 1¼ inch hole. Spindle is bored to take in ½ inch round shank drills. No drills furnished at this price.

Price, each..............................................$8.00

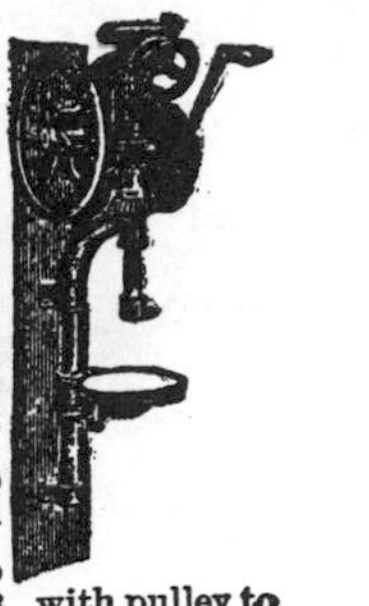

No. 11642. The (No. 4) Upright Self-feed Drill. This machine has nearly a continuous feed, which may be quickly adjusted by a thumb-screw, for two rates of speed. Has swing table which is very convenient, is out of the way when not in use, and may be quickly swung into position when wanted; will drill to the center of an 18-inch circle. Spindle bored to take drills with ½ inch round shank; will drill from ⅛ to 1½ inch hole. Length, 45 inches; weight, 185 lbs. No drill bits furnished with this machine at prices quoted. See index for bits.

Price, each..............................$12.50

No. 11643. **With quick-return attachment** (4½).

Price, each..............................$13.50

No. 11644. Post Drill, like No. 11643, with pulley to be run with power. Each..............................$15.00

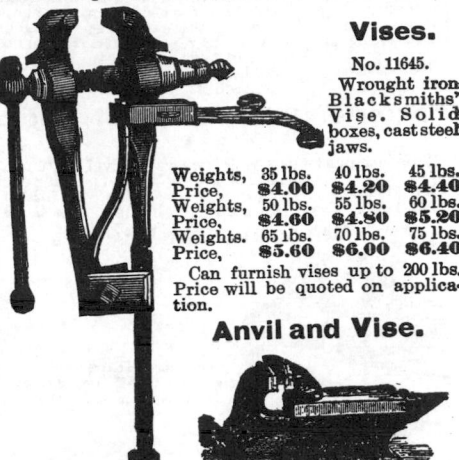

## Vises.

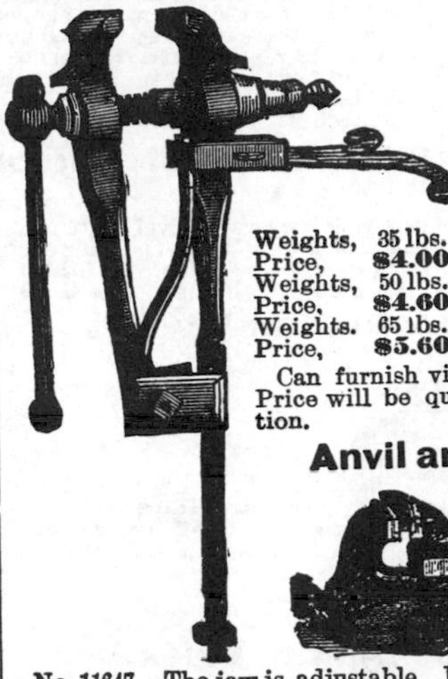

No. 11645.

Wrought iron Blacksmiths' Vise. Solid boxes, cast steel jaws.

| | | | |
|---|---|---|---|
| Weights, | 35 lbs. | 40 lbs. | 45 lbs. |
| Price, | $4.00 | $4.20 | $4.40 |
| Weights, | 50 lbs. | 55 lbs. | 60 lbs. |
| Price, | $4.60 | $4.80 | $5.20 |
| Weights. | 65 lbs. | 70 lbs. | 75 lbs. |
| Price, | $5.60 | $6.00 | $6.40 |

Can furnish vises up to 200 lbs. Price will be quoted on application.

## Anvil and Vise.

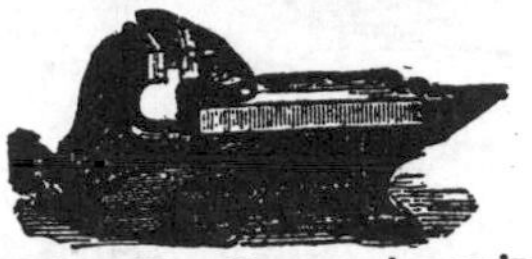

No. 11647. The jaw is adjustable. By removing a pin, the inner jaw can be swung round so as to hold wedge or irregular shape. The anvil has a chilled, hardened and polished surface. This is the best anvil and vise of its kind.

| | | | |
|---|---|---|---|
| No. 11646. | 3½ in. jaw, 25 lbs. | Price, each...... | $3.40 |
| No. 11647. | 4 in. jaw, 35 lbs. | Price, each...... | 4.10 |
| No. 11648. | 4½ in. jaw, 40 lbs. | Price, each...... | 4.70 |

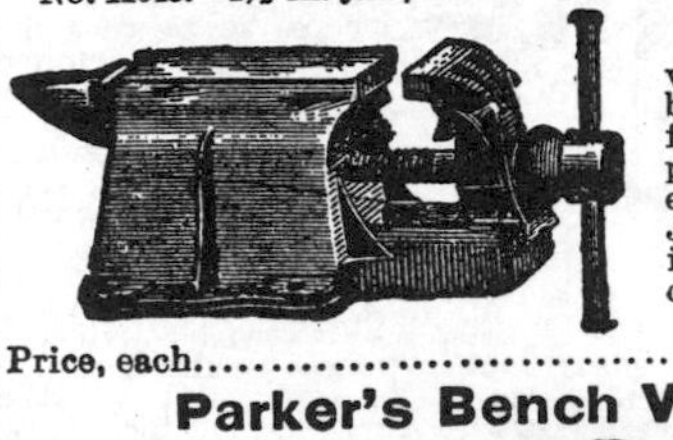

No. 11649. Anvil and vise combined, with jaws for holding pipes. Has chilled face and jaws. Jaws are three inches wide; open 5 inches. Weighs 28 lbs.

Price, each..............................................$1.12

## Parker's Bench Vise.

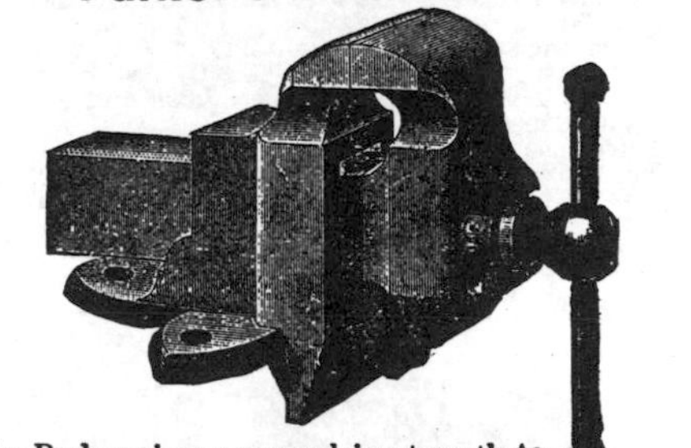

The Parker vises are equal in strength to any bench vise on the market, and the steel faces are milled and fitted to the jaws, and can be renewed at a trifling cost.

| | Length of jaws. | Weight. | Price each. |
|---|---|---|---|
| No. 11651. | 3¼ inches. | 23 lbs. | $4.00 |
| No. 11652. | 4⅛ inches. | 41½ lbs. | 6.15 |

## Parker's Swivel Vise.

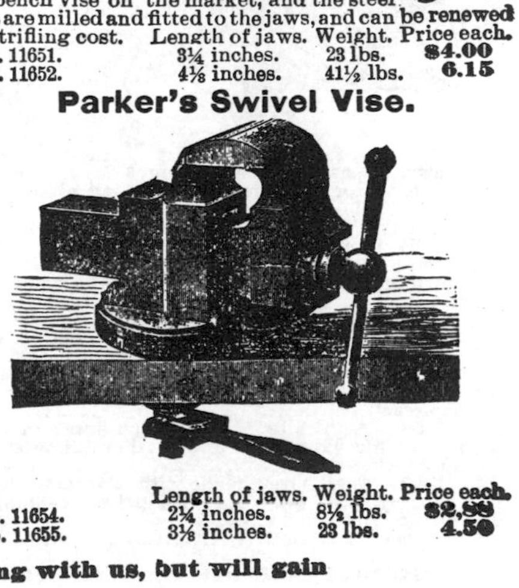

| | Length of jaws. | Weight. | Price each. |
|---|---|---|---|
| No. 11654. | 2¼ inches. | 8½ lbs. | $2.88 |
| No. 11655. | 3⅛ inches. | 23 lbs. | 4.50 |

**Our aim is to so satisfy our customers, that they will not only continue trading with us, but will gain new patrons for us.**

## Parker's Patent Victor Vises.

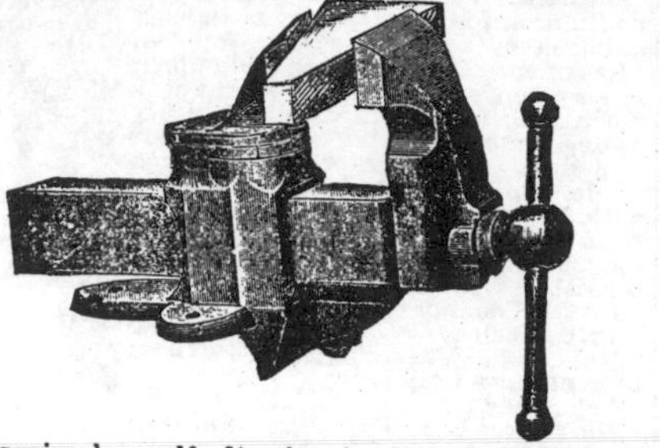

This vise has self-adjusting back jaws, which automatically adapt themselves for holding wedge-shaped pieces. The steel faces of these vises are milled and fitted to the jaws, and can be renewed at a trifling cost.

| | Length of jaws. | Weight. | Price each. |
|---|---|---|---|
| No. 11660. | 3¼ inches | 25 lbs. | $5.15 |
| No. 11661. | 3⅞ inches | 39 lbs. | 5.50 |

## Parker's Patent Swivel Victor Vises.

This vise has swivel back jaws and swivel bottom.

| | Length of jaws. | Weight. | Price each. |
|---|---|---|---|
| No. 11663. | 3¼ inches | 30 lbs. | $5.50 |
| No. 11665. | 3⅞ inches | 42 lbs. | 6.70 |

## Combination Vise.

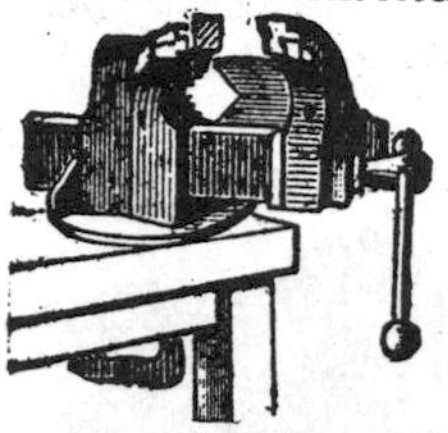

No. 11667.

| No. | 1 | 2 |
|---|---|---|
| Weight, | 41 lbs. | 50 lbs. |
| Each, | $7.50 | $9.50 |
| Take pipe, | ⅛ to 2, | ¼ to 3. |

## Light Clamp Vises.

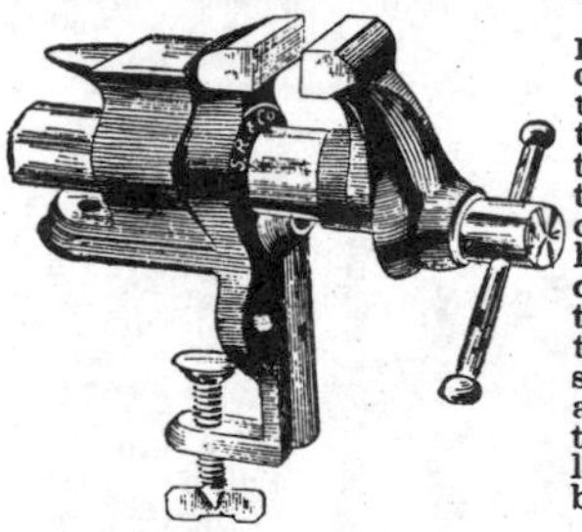

A very important improvement in this vise consists in widening the clamp at its junction with the body of the vise and providing the same with two countersunk screw holes so in case the clamp is ever broken the vise can be attached to the bench by screws. In the ordinary style of clamp vises they are utterly worthless if the clamp ever breaks.

No. 11669. Clamp Vise with Anvil has 1½ inch jaws, opens 1¾ inches, weighs 1¼ lbs.
Price, each........................25c

No. 11670. Clamp Vise with Anvil, has 1¾ inch jaws, opens 2 inches, weighs 2¾ lbs.
Price each........................45c

No. 11671. Clamp Vise with Anvil, has 2-inch jaws, opens 2¼ inches, weighs 4½ lbs. Jaws and anvil face chill hardened.
Price, each........................65c

No. 11672. Clamp Vise and Anvil, has 2½ inch jaws, opens 2⅜ inches, weighs 9½ lbs. Jaws and anvil face chill hardened.
Price, each........................$1.00

## Light Anvil Vises.

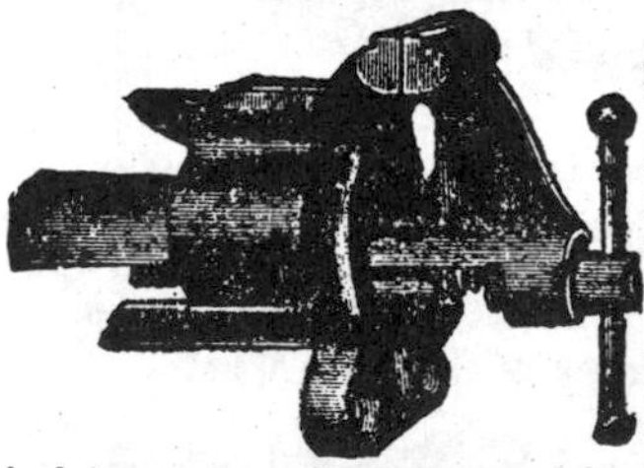

No. 11676. This little vise is made in the finest manner. The body is japanned; the jaws and bar are accurately ground and polished; the screw and lever made from best polished steel. It does not have anvil as shown in cut. Has 1 inch jaws, opens 1¼ inches, weighs 5 oz. and is intended only for jewelers, dentists and similar light work.
Price, each........................15c

No. 11677. Anvil Vise. This vise is made with 1¼ inch jaws; opens 1¾ inches; weighs 1¼ lbs. Has anvil as shown in cut. It's one of the cheapest tools we have.
Price, each........................18c

No. 11678. Anvil Vise. Made with 1¾ inch jaws: opens 2 inches; weighs 2½ lbs. Has anvil as shown in cut.
Price, each........................38c

No. 11679. Anvil Vise. Two-inch jaws; opens 2¼ inches; weighs 4 lbs. The jaws and anvil chill hardened.
Price, each........................48c

No. 11680. Anvil Vise. Has 2½ inch jaws; opens 2¾ inches; weighs 9 lbs.; jaws and anvil chill hardened.
Price, each........................$1.00

No. 11681. Anvil Vise. Made with 2½ inch checked and tempered steel jaws; opens 2¾ inches: weighs 9 lbs.; chilled and hardened anvil.
Price, each........................$1.20

## Bench Vise.

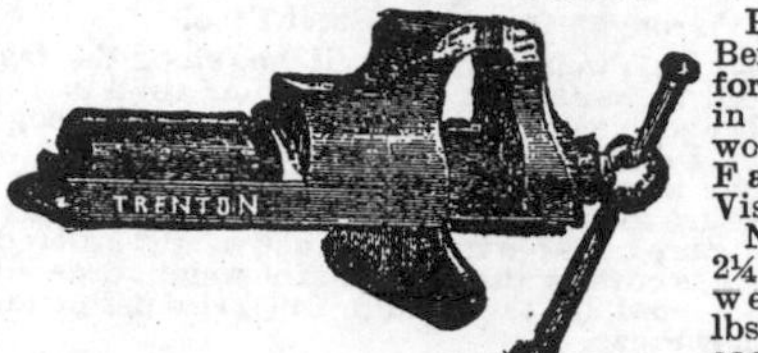

Parallel Bench Vises for light work in metal or wood, "The Farmer's Vise."

No. 11683. 2¼ inch jaws; weight, 7½ lbs. Price, each..$1.00

No. 11684. 3 inch jaws: weight, 17½ lbs.
Price, each........................$1.70

No. 11685. 4 inch jaws; weight, 38¼ lbs.
Price, each........................$2.85

## Little Giant Tire-Upsetter.

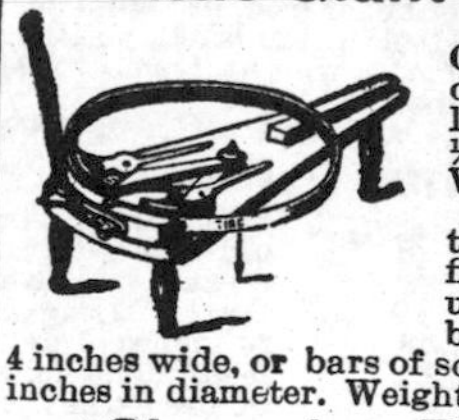

No. 11686. No. 1 Little Giant will upset any size or diameter of tire, from the light buggy to the heavy tire ½ inch thick to 2 inches wide. Weight, 100 lbs. Price $8.00

No. 11687. No. 2 is heavier than No. 1, and lies on the floor. Both jaws move. Will upset any tire, from a light buggy tire to a truck tire 4 inches wide, or bars of square or round iron up to 1¼ inches in diameter. Weight, 160 lbs. Price each.$11.00

## Champion Tire Shrinkers.

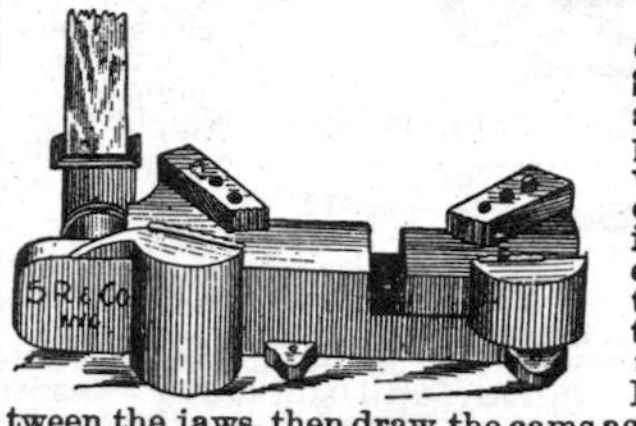

No. 11690. The Champion Tire Shrinker, a very simple and inexpensive machine, which saves all cutting and welding of tires. Works equally as well on the lightest steel tire, and on wagon tires 4x1 inch. Place the tire between the jaws, then draw the cams against the tire, then with but little pressure on the handle you can shrink the tire to suit. Weight, 140 lbs.; floor space required for it 18x10 inches; will shrink tire 1x4, and axles 1¼x1¼. Price, each........................$7.50

## Mole Tire Shrinkers.

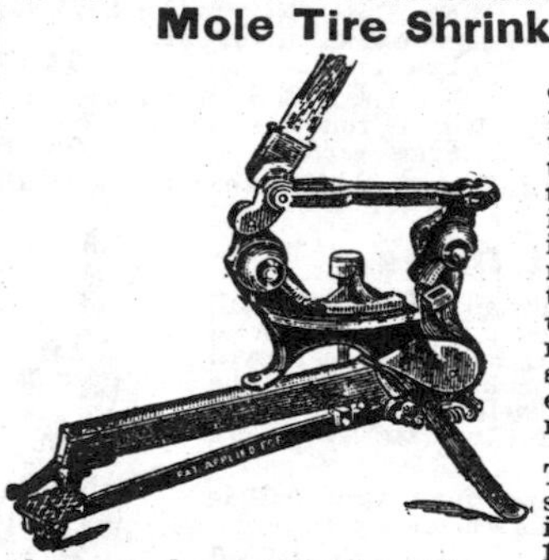

The operation of bringing down the lever grasps the tire and does the work; raising the lever opens it. By this means it is not necessary to remove the tire until it is upset as much as required. Can be successfully operated by one man.

No. 11691. Mole Tire Shrinker, size 1. Bed is 2¼ inches; weight, 150 lbs. Is adapted to general custom work. Price, each........$6.67

No. 11692. Mole Tire Shrinker, size 2. Bed is 3 inches; weight, 225 lbs. Will do all but the heaviest work. Price, each........................$9.35

No. 11693. Mole Tire Shrinker, size 3. Bed is 4 inches; weight, 300 lbs. Will shrink all sizes, including heavy wagon and truck tires. Price, each.....$12.00

## Tire Benders.

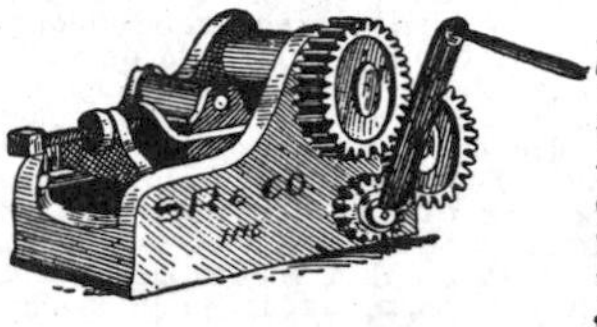

11695. The Champion Tire Bender. The frame is one solid piece; is double back geared, and worked with two cranks. The height of the tire is regulated by a screw; its bending capacity is 3x⅝ inches to the lightest tire; it will take in 5 inches in width; it will bend fifth wheels as well as tires.
Price, each........................$6.50

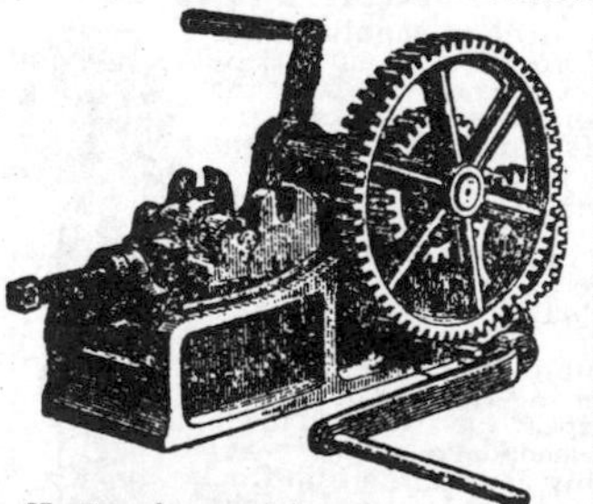

No. 11696. The Eureka Tire Bender is strong and powerful; the two end rolls are provided with wrought iron collars in order to keep the tire from twisting; the height of the tire is regulated by a screw. The No. 1 size will bend 4x1 tire; the No. 2, 6x1¼ inches to the lightest tire.

No. 1, price, each........................$10.00
No. 2........................15.50

**We try our best to please you. We occasionally make a mistake, which we are only too glad to correct. If an error should occur, write us and always give invoice number.**

## Graduated Tire Measuring Wheel.

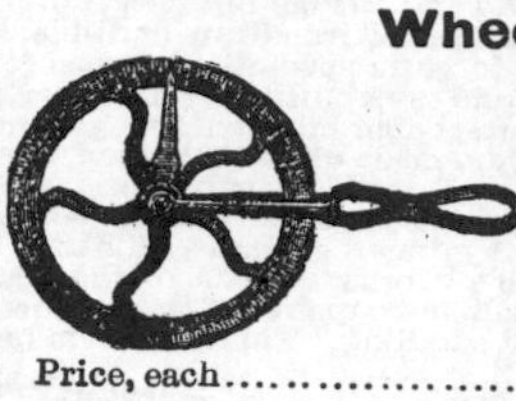

No. 11697. A drop forging is made, so that the figures and lines are raised above the surface of the wheel and cannot be filled or defaced with rust or dirt. It is exactly 24 inches in circumference, with index hand.
Price, each........................$1.25

## Oil Trough.

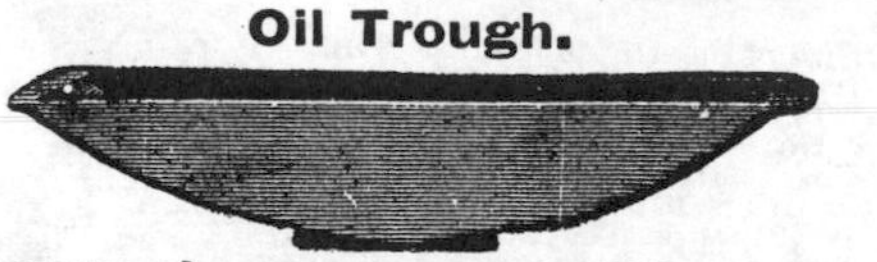

Every one who owns a wagon should have one of these.

No. 11700. Oil Trough, for oiling wagon wheels, for 2 inch tire, made of cast iron; weight, 10 lbs.
Price, each........................33c

No. 11701. Oil Trough, larger size than No. 11700 for wheels with tire as wide as 4 inches. Weight, 15 lbs.
Price, each........................48c

## Self Heating Oil Troughs.

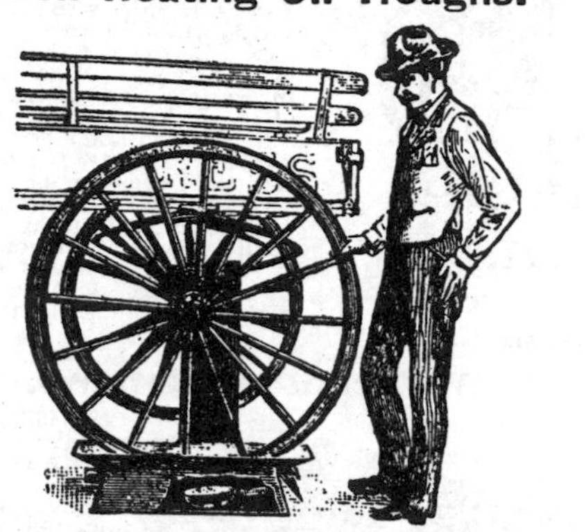

DIRECTIONS.

Place the oil trough as shown in the illustration, after having poured into the chamber two quarts of linseed oil. Saturate the mineral wool torch with coal oil or gasoline, and apply match, and place the same under trough, and heat the oil to boiling point. Revolve the wheel slowly in the trough, as shown in cut, until the wood is thoroughly saturated with the oil, taking care that the boiling oil covers the felloe.

Made in two sizes.

No. 11703. For 3½ tire or narrower; weight, 10 lbs.
Each........................$1.75

No. 11704. For tire up to 4 inches; weight, 14 lbs.
Each........................$2.00

## Blacksmiths' Stocks and Dies.

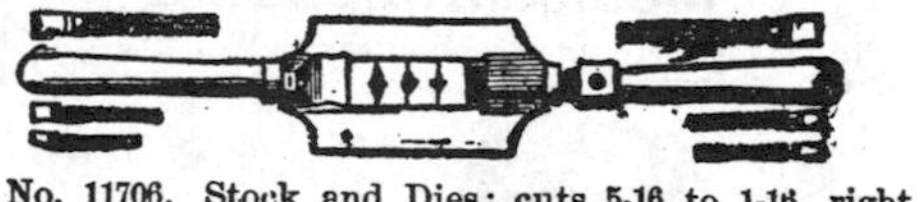

No. 11706. Stock and Dies; cuts 5-16 to 1-16, right hand, 18, 24, and 32 threads to the inch, 4 taps and 3 sets of dies, complete; weight. 1 lb........................$1.50

No. 11707. Stock and Dies; cuts 5-16 to 1-16 inch, right hand, 16, 20, 24, and 32 threads to the inch, 4 taps and 1 set of 4 dies; weight, 1 lb........................$1.65

No. 11708. Stock and Dies; cuts ½ to 3-16 inch, right hand, 14 to 20 threads to the inch, and ½ to 5-16 left hand, 14 threads to the inch, 6 taps and 3 sets of dies; weight, 2¼ lbs........................$2.10

No. 11709. Stock and Dies; cuts ½ inch to ⅛ inch, right hand, 16, 20, and 26 threads to the inch, 6 taps and 1 set of 3 dies; weight, 2¼ lbs........................$1.95

No. 11710. Stock and Dies; cuts ⅝ to 3-16 right hand, 14, 18, and 22 threads to the inch; 6 taps and 1 set of 3 dies; weight, 3 lbs. 5 oz........................$2.50

No. 11711. Stock and Dies; cuts ¾ to 5-16 inch, right hand, 12, 14, and 16 threads to the inch, 3 taps and 3 sets of dies; weight, 2¼ lbs........................$2.68

No. 11712. Stock and Dies; cuts ¾ to 5-16 inch, right hand, 10, 12, and 14 threads to the inch, 3 taps and 3 sets of dies; weight, 2¼ lbs........................$2.70

No. 11713. Stock and Dies; cuts ¾ to 5-16 inch, right hand, 10, 12, and 16 threads to the inch, 3 taps and 3 sets of dies; weight, 2¼ lbs........................$2.72

No. 11714. Stock and Dies; cuts 1 inch to ⅜ inch, right hand, 9, 10, and 14 threads to the inch, 3 taps and 3 sets of dies, complete; weight, 4 lbs. 2 oz........................$3.00

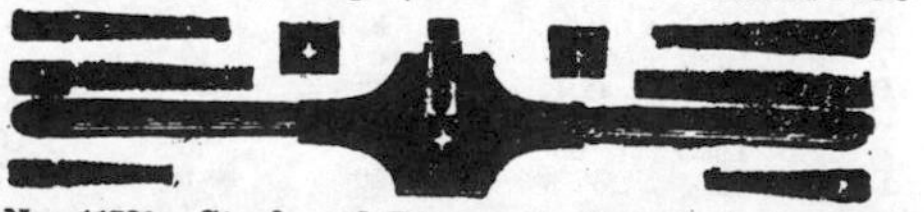

No. 11720. Stock and Dies; cuts ¾ to ⅛ inch, right hand, 10, 12, 14, and 18 threads to the inch, 4 taps and 4 pairs of dies. Price, per set........................$3.90

No. 11721. Stock and Dies; cuts ¾ to ⅜ inch, right hand, 10, 12, and 16 threads to the inch, 6 taps and 3 pairs of dies; weight, 5 lbs........................$3.95

**Our discount of 3 per cent. for cash is very liberal, and it will, in many cases, be sufficient to pay the freight. Most of our customers send cash in full.**

## Blacksmiths' Dies.

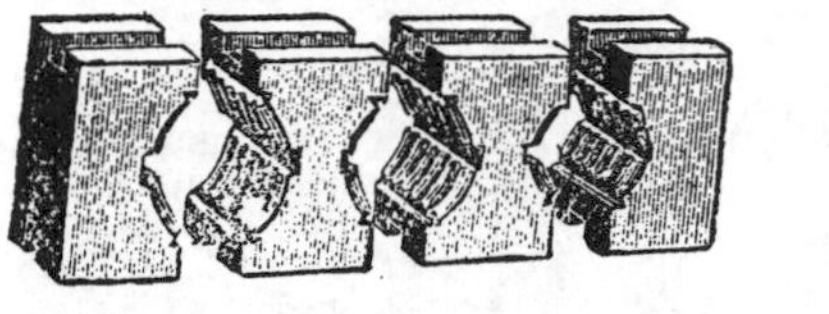

Blacksmiths' Dies, in sets only, to fit stocks as given above.

We cannot furnish extra dies to fit every number of stock, as they are not all interchangeable.

| | | Per set. |
|---|---|---|
| No. 11726. | For No. 11706 stock and die | $1.30 |
| No. 11727. | For No. 11707 stock and die | 1.30 |
| No. 11728. | For No. 11708 stock and die | 1.30 |
| No. 11729. | For No. 11709 stock and die | 1.30 |
| No. 11730. | For No. 11710 stock and die | 1.30 |
| No. 11731. | For No. 11711 stock and die | 1.70 |
| No. 11732. | For No. 11712 stock and die | 1.70 |
| No. 11733. | For No. 11713 stock and die | 1.70 |
| No. 11734. | For No. 11714 stock and die | 1.70 |
| No. 11735. | For No. 11720 stock and die | 1.92 |
| No. 11736. | For No. 11721 stock and die | 1.92 |

## Blacksmiths' Taper Taps.

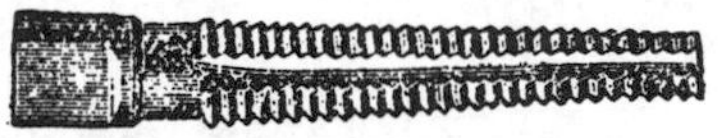

**Give size and threads when ordering.**

No. 11740. Right Hand Taps.
No. 11741. Left Hand Taps.

| Size, inches. | Hand. | Threads to the inch. | Price, each. |
|---|---|---|---|
| 1½ | R | 6 7 & 8 | $1.20 |
| 1½ | L | 6 7 & 8 | 1.20 |
| 1¼ | R | 6 7 8 & 9 | .70 |
| 1¼ | L | 8 & 9 | .70 |
| 1 | R | 7 8 9 & 10 | .50 |
| 1 | L | 8 & 9 | .50 |
| ⅞ | R | 8 9 & 10 | .36 |
| ⅞ | L | 9 | .36 |
| ¾ | R | 7 8 9 10 12 & 14 | .26 |
| ¾ | L | 10 & 12 | .26 |
| ⅝ | R | 10 11 12 14 & 16 | .20 |
| ⅝ | L | 10 & 12 | .20 |
| 9/16 | R | 10 12 14 & 16 | .20 |
| 9/16 | L | 12 | .20 |
| ½ | R | 10 12 14 16 & 18 | .16 |
| ½ | L | 12 & 14 | .16 |
| 7/16 | R | 10 12 14 16 & 18 | .16 |
| 7/16 | L | 14 | .16 |
| ⅜ | R | 10 12 14 16 18 & 20 | .15 |
| 5/16 | R | 14 16 18 20 & 22 | .12 |
| ¼ | R | 16 18 20 22 24 & 26 | .12 |
| 3/16 | R | 24 26 & 28 | .12 |
| ⅛ | R | 80 & 32 | .12 |

## Bicycle Screw Plate.

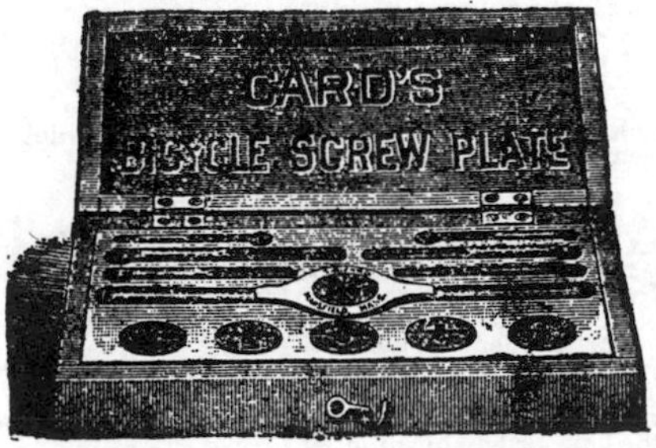


These plates will be found very convenient as they are especially adapted to bicycle work. The dies are adjustable for making tight or loose fits. Plug taps are furnished with these plates.

No. 11744. Set No. 1. Stock 5 inches long, dies ⅝ of an inch in diameter, 6 dies and 6 taps.

Cutting 3-32, 54; ⅛, 40; ⅛, 42; 3, 48; 3, 56; 6, 38, or an equal number of regular sizes.

Price, complete, in hardwood case............**$4.00**

No. 11745. Set No. 2. Stock 5 inches long, dies ⅝ of an inch in diameter, 6 dies and 6 taps.

Cutting 3-32, 56; 7-64, 56; 9-64, 40; 1, 64; 1½, 56; 2, 48, or an equal number of regular sizes.

Price, complete, in hardwood case............**$4.10**

No. 11746. Set No. 3. Stock 5 inches long, dies ⅝ of an inch in diameter, 14 dies and 14 taps.

Cutting 3-32, 52; 3-32, 54; 3-32, 56; 7-64, 56; ⅛, 40; ⅛, 42; 9-64, 40; 1, 64; 1½, 56; 2, 48; 3, 48; 3, 56; 4, 42; 6, 38, or an equal number of regular sizes.

Price, complete, in hardwood case............**$8.00**

## Screw Plates.

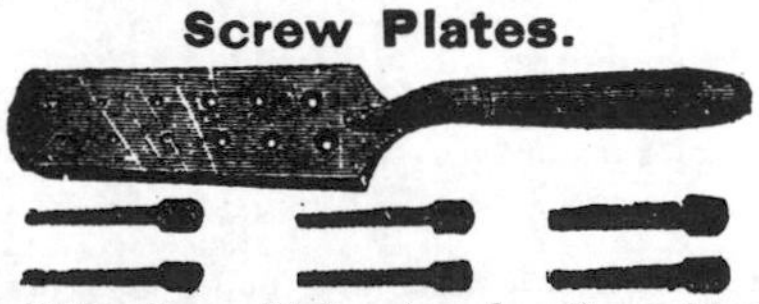

No. 11748. Screw Plates, iron handles, will cut 1- different sizes from ⅜ to 1/8, intended for gunsmiths', jewelers' or model makers' use; weight, 10 oz.

Each, 90c; by mail, 10c extra.

## Electric Screw Plates.

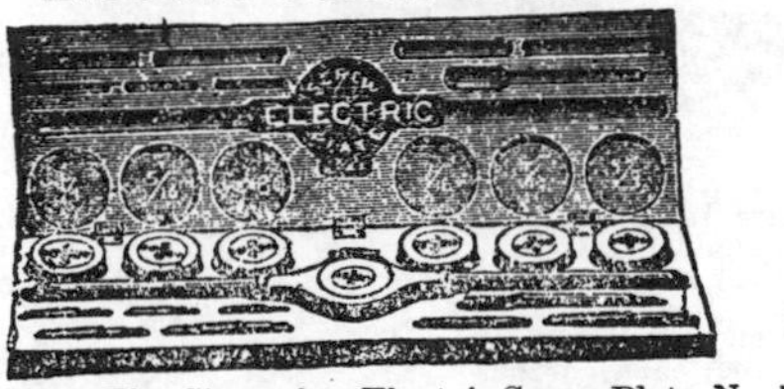


No. 11751. The Champion Electric Screw Plate, No. 5. Length of stock, 23 inches, cuts ¼x20, 5/16x18, ⅜x16, 7/16x14, ½x12, ⅝x11, ¾x10.

Price, with tap wrench............**$10.40**

No. 11752. The "Champion" Electric Screw Plate, No. 2. Length of stock, 23 inches, cutting ¼-20, ⅜-16, ½-12, ⅝-11, ¾-10. Complete in box with tap wrench.

Price, each............**$8.75**

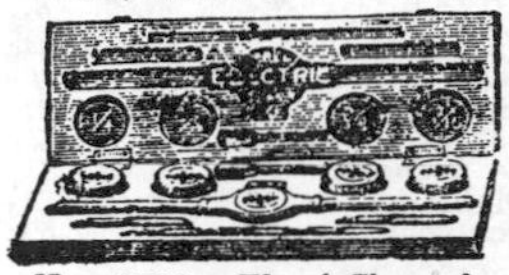


No. 11753. The Champion Electric Screw Plate, No. 4. Length of stock, 26 inches, cuts ½x12, ⅝x11, ¾x10, ⅞x9, 1x8 threads.

Price, with tap wrench............**$11.25**

No. 11754. The "Champion" Electric Screw Plate, No. 7. Length of stock 26 inches. Cutting ¼-20, 5/16-18, ⅜-16, 7/16-14, ½-12, ⅝-11, ¾-10, ⅞-9, 1-8. Complete in box.

Price, each............**$16.50**

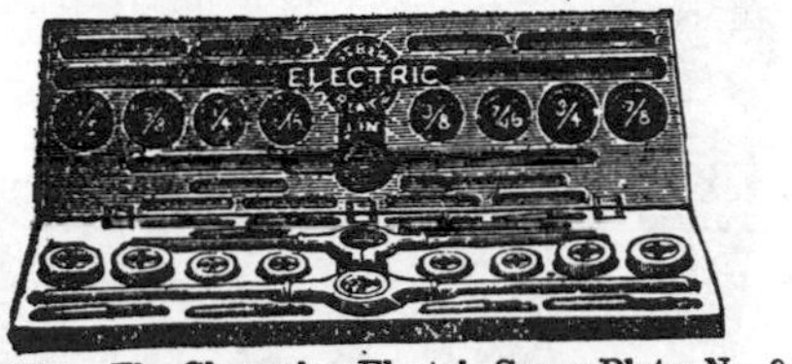


No. 11756. The Champion Electric Screw Plate, No. 9; has two stocks, one 14½ inches long for the first four sizes, and the other 26 inches long for the larger sizes, cuts ¼x20, 5/16x18, ⅜x16, 7/16x14, ½x12, ⅝x11, ¾x10, ⅞x10, 1x8.

Complete in case, with tap wrench............**$17.85**

## Electric Full Mounted Screw Plates.

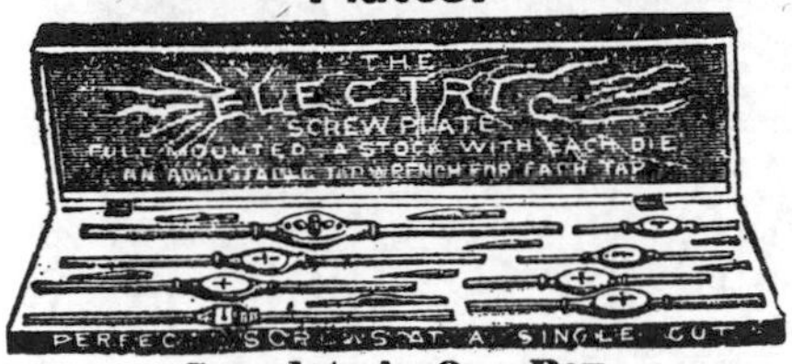


**Complete in One Box.**

Every set supplied with our patent adjustable electric tap wrench. The best screw plate in the market.

No. 11760. Electric Screw Plate, No. 102, cutting ¼-20, ⅜-16, ½-12, ⅝-11, ¾-10 threads.

Price, each............**$10.10**

No. 11761. Electric Screw Plate, No. 104, cutting ½-12, ⅝-11, ¾-10, ⅞-9, 1-8 thread.

Price, each............**$12.68**

No. 11762. Electric Screw Plate, No. 105, cutting ¼-20, 5/16-18, ⅜-16, 7/16-14, ½-12, ⅝-11, ¾-10 thread.

Price, each............**$11.70**

No. 11763. Electric Screw Plate, No. 107, cutting ¼-20, 5/16-18, ⅜-16, 7/16-14, ½-12, ⅝-11, ¾-10, ⅞-9, 1-8 thread.

Price, each............**$19.15**

## Green River Screw Plates.

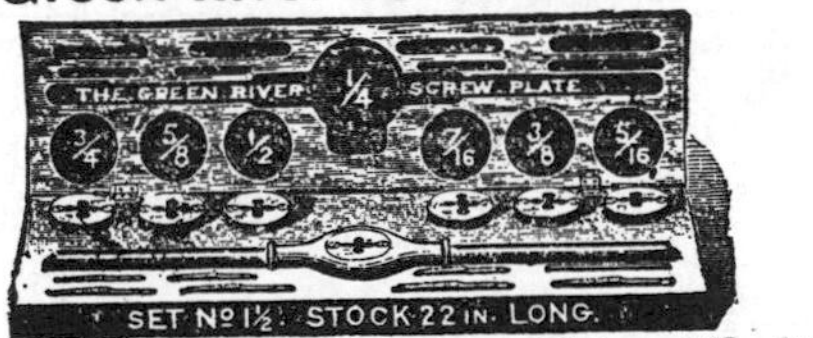


No. 11765. The Green River Screw Plate, set No. 1½, cuts from ¼ to ¾ inch; stock 22 inches long, 7 sizes; ¼, 5/16, ⅜, 7/16, ½, ⅝, ¾ inch taps; dies and guides complete in case.

Per set............**$10.50**

No. 11766. The Green River Screw Plate, set No. 3, from ¼ to 1 inch; stock, 29 inches in length, 5 sizes; ½, ⅜, ¾, ⅞, 1 inch taps, dies and guides complete in case. Weight, 18 lbs.

Per set............**$14.25**

Other numbers of Green River Screw Plates quoted on request.

**$4.98 FOR A LADIES' $7.00 SILK SKIRT.**

*"WHATEVER YOU DO, DO IT WELL."*

That's the motto we follow in our skirt department, and that's the reason why we can offer you a ladies' fine black figured taffeta silk skirt, made up in the very latest style and finished in first-class manner throughout for **$4.98.** **You would pay $7.00 for this skirt elsewhere.** For full description see our skirt department.

## Hammers.

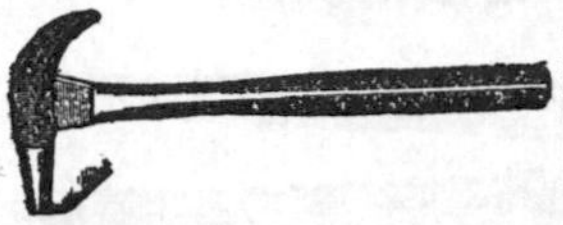

No. 11768. Farriers' Hammer; weight (not including handle), 10 oz.; adze eye, cast steel, round pole, polished.

Price, each......**40c**

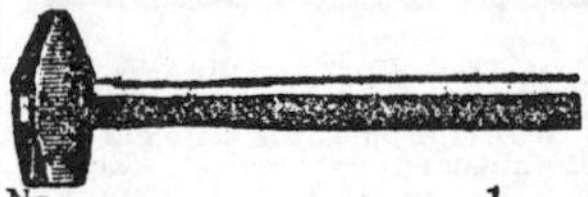

No. 11769. Blacksmiths' Hand Hammer, extra fine steel. Fully warranted; handles not included in weights.

| No. | 1 | 2 | 3 |
|---|---|---|---|
| Weight | 2 lbs. | 2 lbs. 10 oz. | 3 lbs. |
| Price, each | 50c | 55c | 60c |

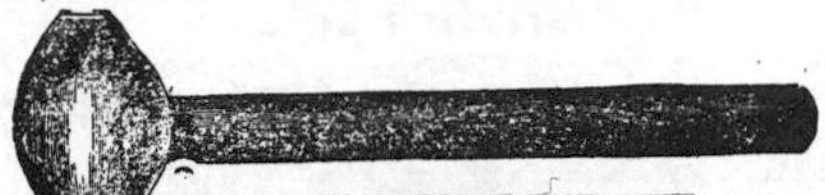

FARRIERS' TURNING HAMMERS.

No. 11771. Farriers' Turning Hammers, Chicago pattern, solid cast steel, with handles. Weights, without handles, 2, 2½ and 3 lbs.

Price each, any weight............**95c**

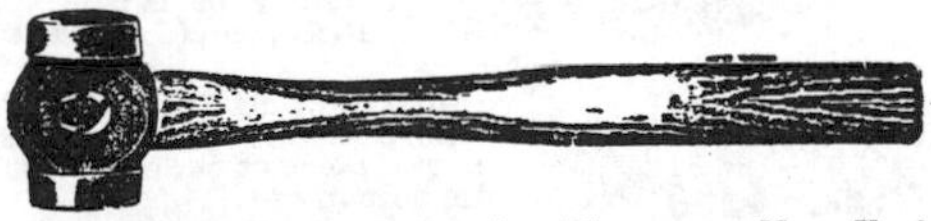

No. 11772. Farriers' Turning Hammers, New York pattern. Weights, 2, 2½ and 3 lbs.; weights do not include handle.

Price, each............**$1.20**

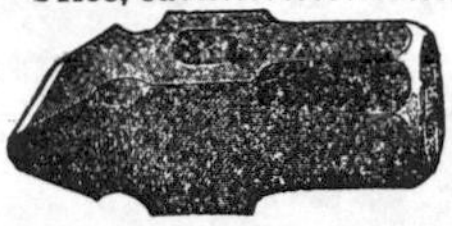

No. 11774. Solid cast steel Blacksmiths' Sledges, without handles.

| Size, pounds | 8 | 9 | 10 | 11 | 12 | 13 | 14 | 15 | 16 | 17 |
|---|---|---|---|---|---|---|---|---|---|---|
| Price, each | 56c | 63c | 70c | 77c | 84c | 91c | 98c | $1.05 | $1.12 | $1.19 |

No. 11775. Handles for above, 36 inches long, shaved hickory.

Price, each, **20c**; doz............**$2.16**

## Farriers' Knives.

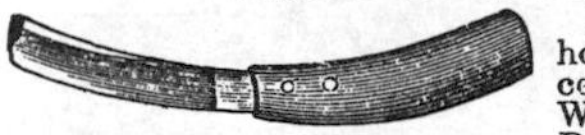

No. 11778. Wostenholm Farriers' Knife, celebrated IXL brand. Weight, 7 oz.

Price, each.......**28c**

## Buttress.

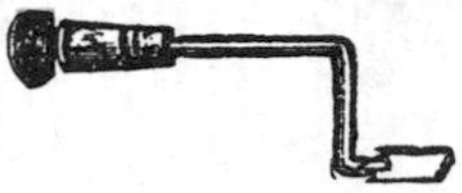

No. 11779. Cast steel Farriers' Buttress, half polished. Weight, 1 lb, 7 oz.

Price, each........**50c**

## Bolt Clippers.

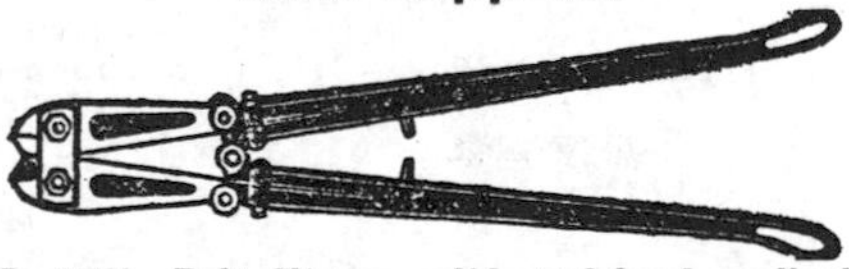

No. 11780. Bolt Clipper, solid steel head, malleable iron handles, very strong, simple adjustment. Don't buy too small size.

No. 0 cuts ¼ inch bolts in the thread only. Price, each, **$2.50.** No. 1 cuts ⅜ inch bolts in the thread only. Price, each, **$3.00.** No. 2 cuts ½ inch bolts in the thread only. Price, each, **$4.00.** No. 3 cuts ⅝ inch bolts in the thread only. Price, each, **$7.50.**

## Tongs.

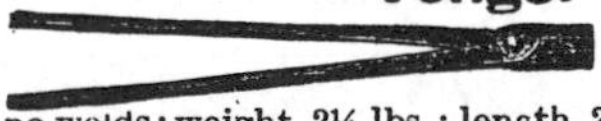

No. 11782. Blacksmiths' Straight Lip Tongs, drop forged, no welds; weight, 2¼ lbs.; length, 20 inches.

Price, each............**26c**

No. 11783. Length, 22 inches; weight, 2¾ lbs.

Price, each............**30c**

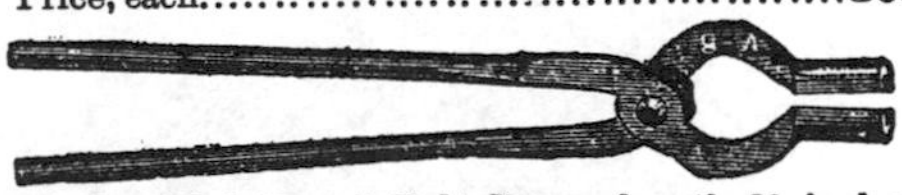

Blacksmiths' Round Bolt Tongs, length 20 inches. State what size bolts tongs are wanted for.

No. 11785. For bolts 5/16 to ½ inch, weight from 1¾ to 2½ lbs.

Price, each, any one size............**40c**

No. 11786. For bolts ⅝ to ¾ inch, weight 2¾ lbs.

Price, each............**50c**

No. 11787. For bolts ⅞ to 1 inch, weight 3½ lbs.

Price, each............**55c**

## Pincers.

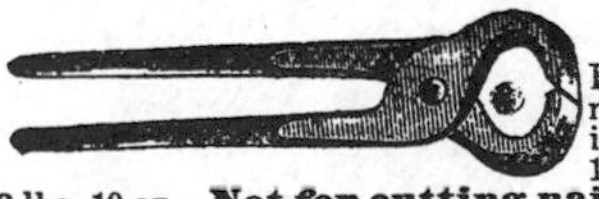

No. 11767. Farriers' Pincers, solid hammered cast steel polished jaws, length 14 inches; weight, 2 lbs. 10 oz. **Not for cutting nails.**

Price, each............**70c**

**We will consider it a great favor if you will interest a neighbor in our house, show him our Catalogue and induce him to send for one.**

## Cutting Nippers.

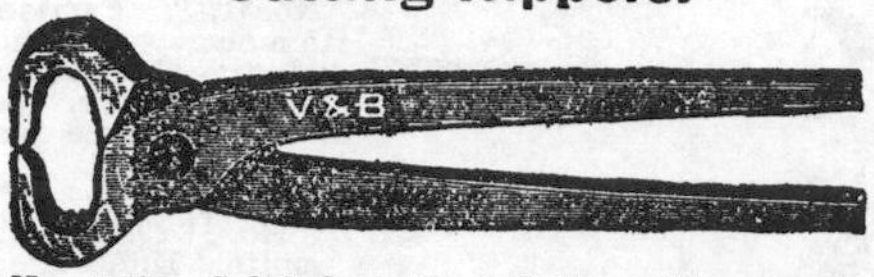

No. 11790. Solid Cast Steel Cutting Nippers. For cutting wire nails, etc. Also used for cutting horses' hoofs. Do not pry with this nipper, for it is hardened to cut and prying will almost surely break it. Length, 14 inches.

Price, each ........................................ **70c**

## Anvil Tools.

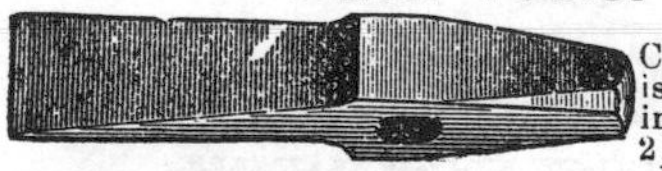

No. 11791. Hot Cutter (no handle is furnished), 1⅜ inch cut; weight, 2 lbs. 2 oz.

Price, each. **35c**

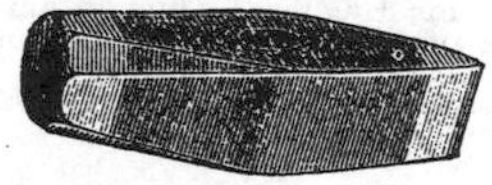

No. 11793. Cold Cutter (handle is not furnished), 1⅜ inch cut; weight, 2 lbs. 14 oz.

Price, each ....... **36c**

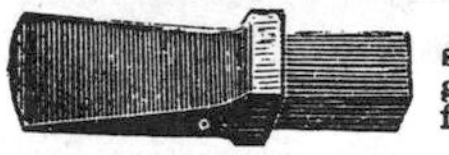

No. 11795. Blacksmiths' solid cast steel Hardie; size given is size of shank, which fits hole in anvil.

| | | | | | |
|---|---|---|---|---|---|
| Size, inches | ½ | ⅝ | ¾ | ⅞ | 1 |
| Weight, lbs | ½ | ¾ | 14 oz. | 1¾ | 2 |
| Price, each | 15c | 16c | 28c | 32c | 38c |

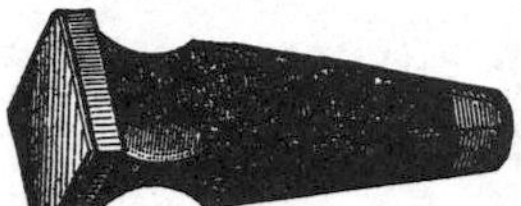

No. 11797. Blacksmiths' solid steel square Flatters.

| | | | | | |
|---|---|---|---|---|---|
| Size of face, inches | 2 | 2¼ | 2½ | 2¾ | 3 |
| Weight, lbs. | 2⅜ | 2¾ | 3¾ | 4 | 5 |
| Price, each | 31c | 40c | 51c | 58c | 68c |

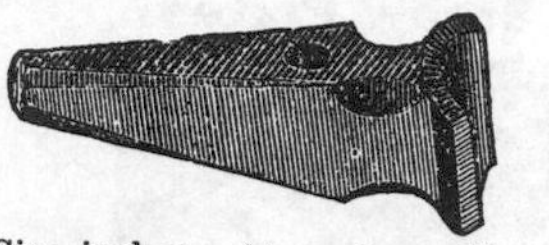

No. 11798. Solid crucible steel Top Swages; weight from 2½ to 3 lbs.

| | | | | | | | |
|---|---|---|---|---|---|---|---|
| Size, inches, | ¼ | 5/16 | ⅜ | 7/16 | ½ | ⅝ | ¾ |
| Weight, lbs., | 1½ | 1½ | 2 | 2 | 2 | 2 | 2¾ |
| Price, each, | 25c | 25c | 30c | 30c | 30c | 30c | 42c |
| Size, inches, | ⅞ | 1 | 1⅛ | 1¼ | 1½ | 2 | |
| Weight, lbs., | 2¾ | 2¾ | 3 | 3 | 4 | 4 | |
| Price, each, | 42c | 42c | 45c | 45c | 60c | 60c | |

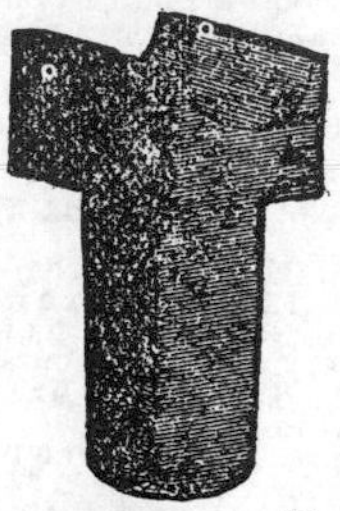

No. 11799. Solid crucible steel Bottom Swage; shanks are from ⅞ to 1¼ inches.

| | | | |
|---|---|---|---|
| Size, inches | ¼ | 5/16 | ⅜ |
| Weight, lbs. | 2¼ | 2¼ | 2¼ |
| Price, each | 34c | 34c | 34c |
| Size, inches | 7/16 | ½ | ⅝ |
| Weight, lbs | 2¼ | 2¼ | 2¼ |
| Price, each | 34c | 34c | 34c |
| Size, inches | ¾ | ⅞ | 1 |
| Weight, lbs | 2½ | 2¾ | 3 |
| Price, each | 38c | 42c | 45c |
| Size, inches | | 1⅛ | 1¼ |
| Weight, lbs | | 3 | 3¼ |
| Price, each | | 45c | 50c |

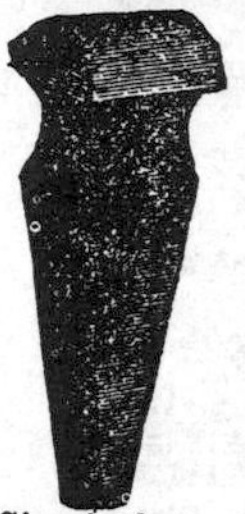

No. 11800. Solid crucible steel Top Fuller.

| | | | | | |
|---|---|---|---|---|---|
| Size, inches | ¼ | ⅜ | | ½ | ⅝ |
| Weight, lbs | 2 | 2 | | 2¼ | 2¼ |
| Price, each | 30c | 30c | | 40c | 40c |
| Size, inches | ¾ | ⅞ | 1 | 1⅛ | 1¼ |
| Weight, lbs | 3 | 3 | 3¼ | 3¼ | 4¼ |
| Price, each | 45c | 45c | 50c | 50c | 65c |

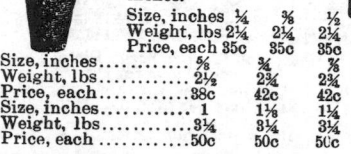

No. 11802. Solid crucible steel Bottom Fuller; shanks are from ⅞ to 1¼ inches.

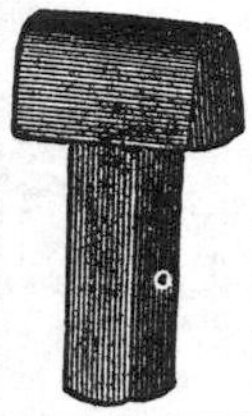

| | | | |
|---|---|---|---|
| Size, inches | ¼ | ⅜ | ½ |
| Weight, lbs | 2¼ | 2¼ | 2¼ |
| Price, each | 35c | 35c | 35c |
| Size, inches | ⅝ | ¾ | ⅞ |
| Weight, lbs | 2½ | 2¾ | 2¾ |
| Price, each | 38c | 42c | 42c |
| Size, inches | 1 | 1⅛ | 1¼ |
| Weight, lbs | 3¼ | 3¼ | 3¼ |
| Price, each | 50c | 50c | 50c |

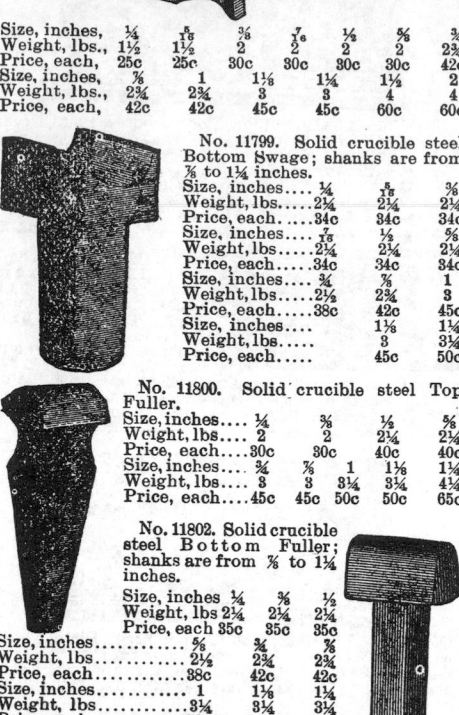

## Horse Nails.

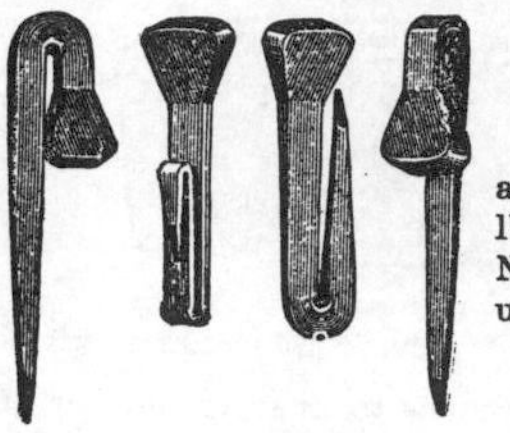

No. 11804. Horse Nails are put up in boxes of 25 lbs. We sell any quantity. Nos. 6 and 7 are most used.

| | | | | | | |
|---|---|---|---|---|---|---|
| No. | 5 | 6 | 7 | 8 | 9 | 10 |
| Length, inches, | 1⅞ | 2 | 2¼ | 2⅜ | 2½ | 2⅝ |
| Per lb | $0.18 | $0.17 | $0.16 | $0.15 | $0.14 | $0.11 |
| Per box | 4.25 | 4.05 | 3.75 | 3.50 | 3.25 | 2.60 |

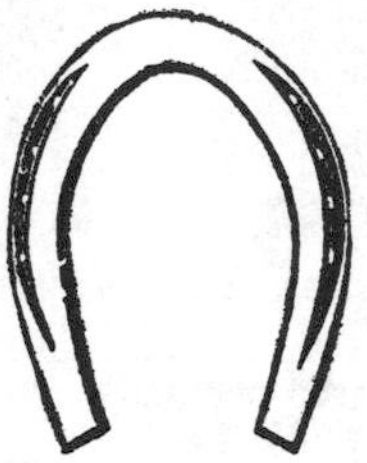

## Horse Shoes.

No. 11806. Horse Shoes, not ready to put on, as they must be fitted. A set consists of 2 front and 2 hind shoes.

| | | | | | | |
|---|---|---|---|---|---|---|
| No | 1 | 2 | 3 | 4 | 5 | 6 |
| Length from outside of front shoe, inches | 5½ | 6 | 6½ | 6⅞ | 7¼ | 7⅝ |
| Width from outside to outside of front shoe, inches | 4½ | 4¾ | 5⅛ | 5⅜ | 6 | 6¾ |
| Price per set, front and hind | $0.18 | $0.20 | $0.30 | $0.35 | $0.40 | $0.50 |
| Price per keg of 100 lbs., front and hind | 3.75 | 3.75 | 3.75 | 3.75 | 3.75 | 3.75 |

## Toe Calks.

No. 11807. Toe Calks, admitted to be the best in the market, made of Bessemer steel.

| | | | | | | |
|---|---|---|---|---|---|---|
| No | 1 | 2 | 3 | 4 | 5 | 6 |
| Number calks to lb | 20 | 12 | 8 | 6 | 5 | 4 |

Price per pound, any size ........................ **6c**

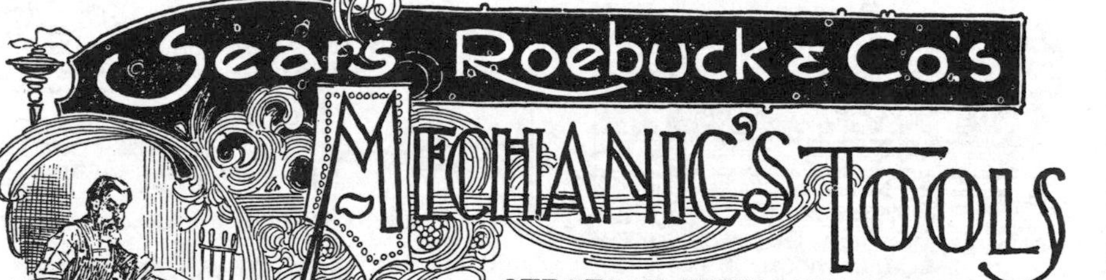


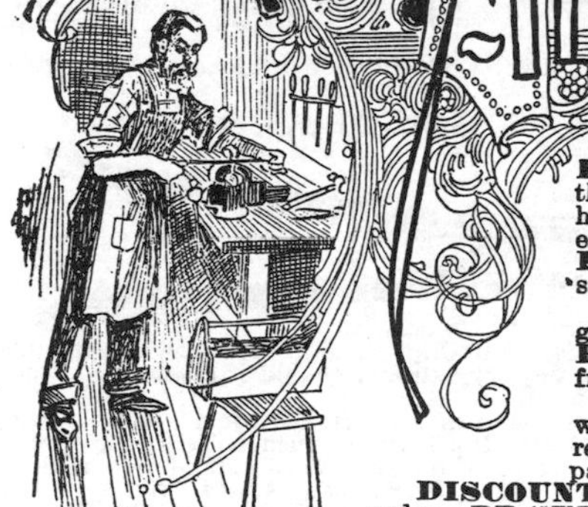

**OUR STOCK EMBRACES ALMOST EVERYTHING MADE IN MECHANICS' TOOLS,** and the goods we offer are all of the highest standard of quality. We handle nothing in this line that is not made by manufacturers of established and well-known reputation. **EVERY ARTICLE IS FULLY GUARANTEED,** and if not found perfectly satisfactory, can be returned and your money will be refunded. **WE CAN SAVE YOU SO MUCH MONEY** on these goods that you cannot afford to pay retail prices. Every **CARPENTER, BLACKSMITH** or other mechanic once buying from us ever after is a regular customer. **OUR TERMS ARE LIBERAL.** Any goods in this line will be sent to any address by **FREIGHT OR EXPRESS** on receipt of a sufficient deposit to cover charges both ways, balance payable when received. **DISCOUNT OF 3 PER CENT.** allowed if cash in full accompanies your order. **BE SURE TO CONSIDER THE CASH DISCOUNT** when comparing our prices with others.

## Saws.

**Patent Gullet-Tooth Circular Saws.**

Henry Disston & Sons'.

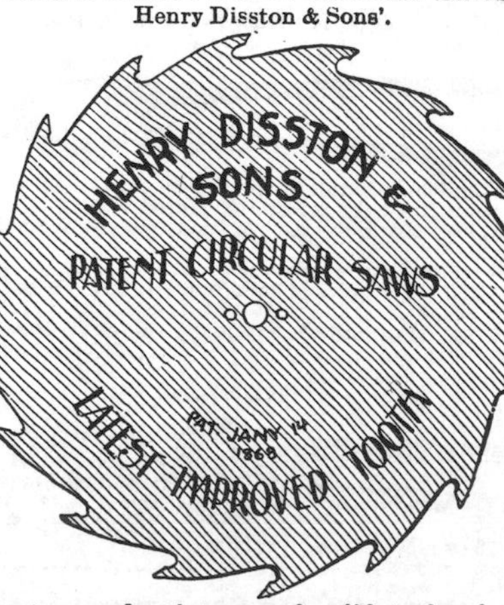


Patent ground and tempered solid teeth, of extra quality, superior workmanship.

**Order style wanted by number below.**

| Diameter, inch. | Thickness, gauge. | Size of hole, inch. | Price, each. |
|---|---|---|---|
| 4 | 19 | ¾ | $0.53 |
| 5 | 19 | ¾ | .62 |
| 6 | 18 | ¾ | .75 |
| 7 | 18 | ¾ | .93 |
| 8 | 18 | ⅞ | 1.05 |
| 9 | 17 | ⅞ | 1.35 |
| 10 | 16 | 1 | 1.60 |
| 12 | 15 | 1 | 2.00 |
| 14 | 15 | 1⅛ | 2.35 |
| 16 | 15 | 1⅛ | 2.85 |
| 18 | 13 | 1¼ | 3.60 |
| 20 | 13 | 1 5/16 | 4.35 |
| 22 | 12 | 1 5/16 | 5.15 |
| 24 | 11 | 1⅜ | 6.15 |
| 26 | 11 | 1⅜ | 7.20 |
| 28 | 10 | 1½ | 8.25 |
| 30 | 10 | 1½ | 9.25 |
| 32 | 10 | 1⅝ | 11.00 |
| 34 | 9 | 1⅝ | 12.00 |
| 36 | 9 | 1⅝ | 13.25 |
| 38 | 9 | 1⅝ | 15.75 |
| 40 | 9 | 2 | 18.25 |
| 42 | 8 | 2 | 21.00 |
| 44 | 8 | 2 | 25.00 |
| 46 | 8 | 2 | 30.00 |
| 48 | 8 | 2 | 35.00 |
| 50 | 7 | 2 | 40.00 |
| 52 | 7 | 2 | 45.00 |
| 54 | 7 | 2 | 50.00 |
| 56 | 7 | 2 | 57.50 |
| 58 | 7 | 2 | 65.00 |
| 60 | 6 | 2 | 72.50 |
| 62 | 6 | 2 | 80.00 |
| 64 | 6 | 2 | 90.00 |
| 66 | 6 | 2 | 100.00 |

## EVERY SEARS, ROEBUCK & CO. SAW

### Is warranted as follows:

**If this Saw** does not prove as good or better than any Saw you ever had return it and money will be refunded. **Why pay more than our prices?**

**Be sure to read our special notice before making out your order for Circular Saws.** The above saws are standard gauge and size hole for each diameter. We can furnish saws with any size hole at same price. We can furnish saws of different gauge, for which an extra charge will be made. The standard saws can be shipped promptly; special saws are shipped soon as possible; but if other orders are ahead of yours it must take its turn. In writing us for price of special saws be very particular to give full description, and you will receive a prompt reply. We furnish blanks which will aid you in making specifications, which will be sent free on request.

### SPECIAL NOTICE.

No. 12000. Rip Saw, standard gauge and hole. If you want the standard Rip Saw, exactly as above list, order this number.

No. 12001. Cross Cut Saw, standard gauge and hole. If you want the standard Cross Cut Saw, exactly as above list, order this number.

No. 12002. Rip or Cross Cut Saws. If you want either Rip or Cross Cut Saws, different in any way from the standard list above, or with special number of teeth to the saw, order this number.

## Saw Mandrels.

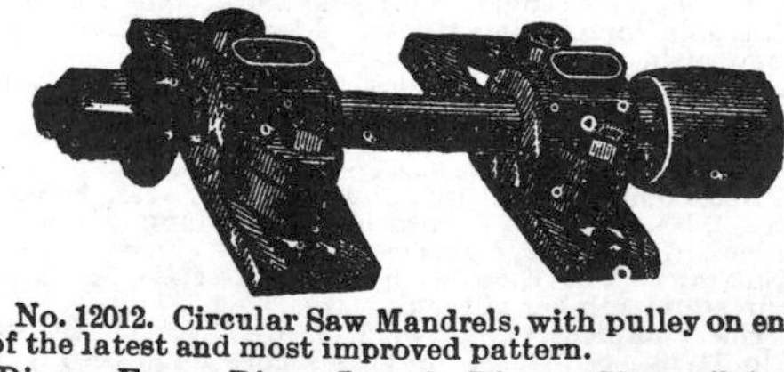

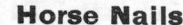

No. 12012. Circular Saw Mandrels, with pulley on end, of the latest and most improved pattern.

| Diam. of Pulley, inches. | Face of Pulley, inches. | Diam. of Flange, inches. | Length of Shaft, inches. | Diam. of Shaft, inches. | Size of hole in Saw, inches. | Price of Mandrel C'mp'e. |
|---|---|---|---|---|---|---|
| 2½ | 3½ | 2½ | 16 | 1 1/16 | 1 | $ 5.26 |
| 3 | 4½ | 3 | 19 | 1 3/16 | 1⅛ | 5.81 |
| 3¼ | 4½ | 3½ | 20 | 1 5/16 | 1¼ | 6.15 |
| 4 | 5 | 4 | 24 | 1 7/16 | 1 5/16 | 7.36 |
| 4½ | 5½ | 4½ | 26 | 1 7/16 | 1 5/16 | 8.20 |
| 5 | 6 | 5 | 28 | 1 7/16 | 1⅜ | 9.41 |
| 5½ | 6½ | 5½ | 30½ | 1 7/16 | 1⅜ | 10.26 |
| 6 | 7 | 6 | 32½ | 1 9/16 | 1½ | 13.35 |
| 7 | 8 | 6 | 37 | 1 11/16 | 1⅝ | 16.10 |
| 8 | 8 | 6 | 41 | 1 13/16 | 1⅝ | 19.15 |

Our Mandrels are made with pulley on right hand side (when saw is running toward you), with left hand thread, unless otherwise ordered.

**Do not expect us to fill your orders correctly unless you are careful to comply with the simple rules for ordering, as explained in the front part of book.**

## Cross Cut Saws.

Sears, Roebuck & Co. Saws are sold without dictation from any combination or trust at our usual small profit. Our guarantee is fair and complete, and without conditions that would make it practically worthless. Each and every Sears, Roebuck & Co. Saw is etched with our trade mark and this guarantee: **If this Saw does not prove as good or better than any Saw you ever had, return it and money will be refunded.** We have these Saws made for our trade by a manufacturer whose reputation for making first-class Saws is not excelled by any one anywhere. We have contracted for an immense quantity and are able to sell them to consumer for less than the average dealer can buy at wholesale. These Saws are all ground thin back with a true taper from edge of teeth to the back. You can't possibly buy better Saws. Why pay more?

No. 12015. Sears, Roebuck & Co., two-man, narrow Cross Cut Saws. **Warranted.** Champion tooth, complete with handles.

5½ foot. Weight, 5¼ lbs..........Price, each, **$0.92**
6 foot. Weight, 5¾ lbs..........Price, each, **1.00**

No. 12016. Sears, Roebuck & Co. regular width, Champion tooth, two-man Cross Cut Saws. **Warranted.** Complete with handles.

| Length, feet. | Weight, lbs. | Price, each. | Length, feet. | Weight, lbs. | Price, each. |
|---|---|---|---|---|---|
| 5 | 6 | $1.65 | 6 | 8 | $1.95 |
| 5½ | 7 | 1.83 | 6½ | 8¾ | 2.25 |

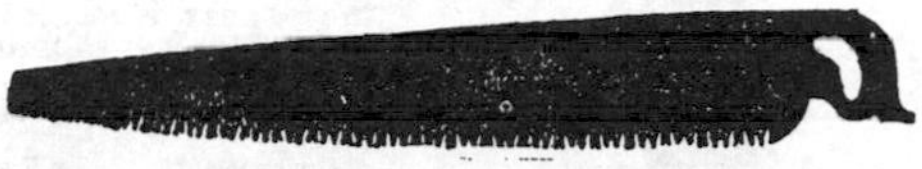

No. 12018. Sears, Roebuck & Co. one-man Cross Cut Saws. Champion tooth, supplementary handle. **Warranted.**

| Length, feet. | Weight, lbs. | Price, each. | Length, feet. | Weight, lbs. | Price, each. |
|---|---|---|---|---|---|
| 3 | 3½ | $1.05 | 4 | 4¾ | $1.40 |
| 3½ | 4 | 1.18 | 4½ | 5¾ | 1.53 |

## Cross Cut Saw Handles.

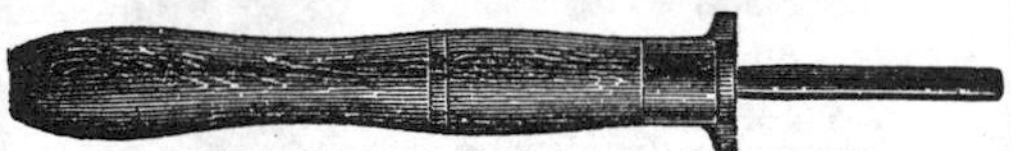

No. 12026. Patent Loop Cross Cut Saw Handles. Per pair..............................**12c**

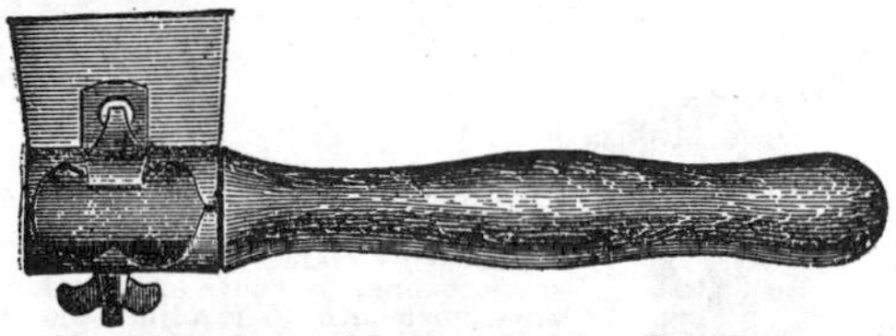

No. 12027. Reversible Cross Cut Saw Handles. Per pair..............................**18c**

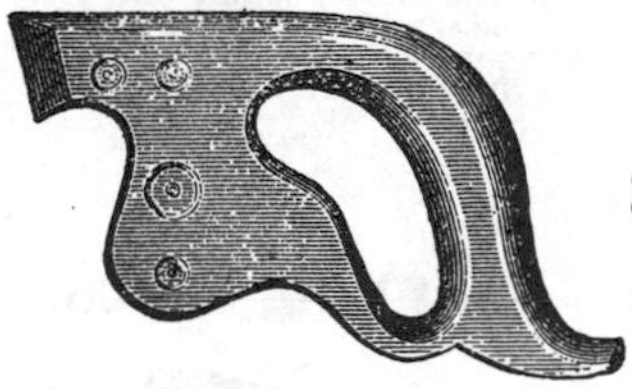

No. 12030. Handle for one-man Cross Cut Saw. Each........**18c**

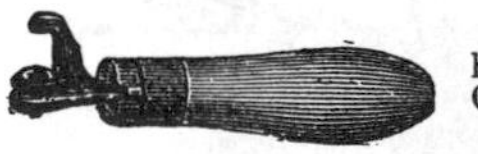

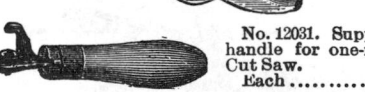

No. 12031. Supplementary handle for one-man Cross Cut Saw. Each...................**8c**

## Kitchen Saws.

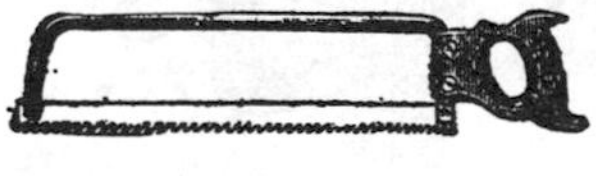

No. 12036. Kitchen Saws, wood handle, oval frame, 12-inch blade. Every one who cuts meat should have one. Price, each..............................**22c**

## Butchers' Saws.

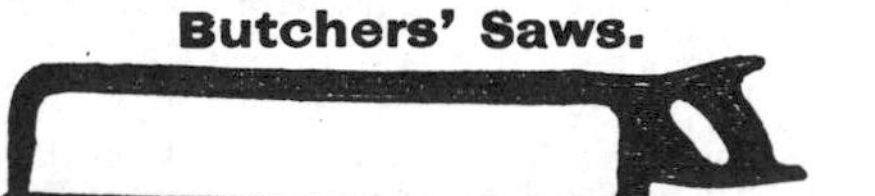

No. 12037. Flat Frame Butcher Saw, wood handle, polished blade.

| Size, inches | 20 | 22 | 24 |
|---|---|---|---|
| Each | 75c | 80c | 85c |

## Butchers' Saw Blades.

| No. 12039. Length, inches.. | 20 | 22 | 24 | 26 |
|---|---|---|---|---|
| Each | $0.30 | $0.34 | $0.36 | $0.42 |
| Per dozen | 3.55 | 4.00 | 4.20 | 4.50 |

## Buck Saws.

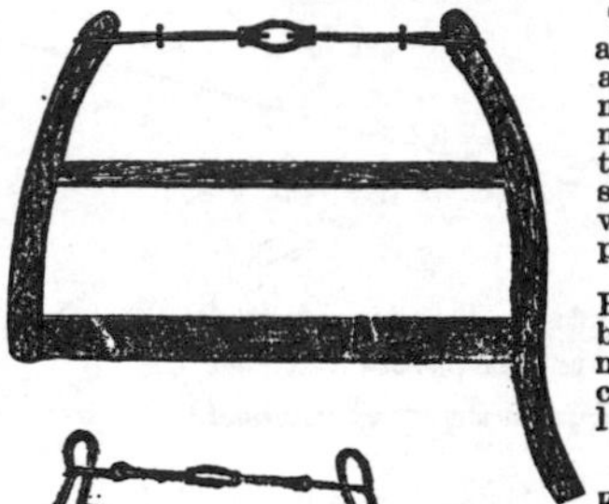

The frames of all our Buck Saws are made of hard maple, and are much better than those usually sold. Buck Saws weigh from 3 to 4 pounds each.

No. 12054. Plain Frame Wood Saw, blade 30 inches, not warranted, complete with loop saw rod. Price, each.**40c**

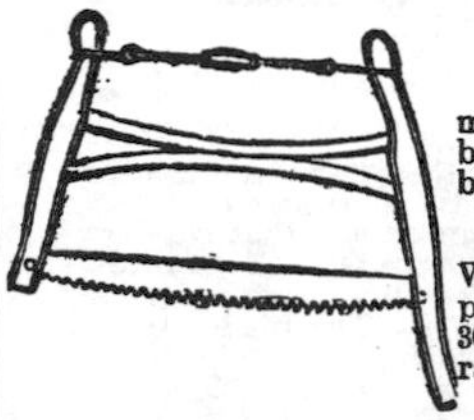

No. 12055. Braced Frame Wood Saw, maple frame, painted red, best tinned rod, 30 inch blade. **Warranted.** Price, each............**55c**

No. 12056. Braced Frame Wood Saw, maple frame, painted red, best tinned rod, 30-inch blued blade. Warranted. Price, each............**60c**

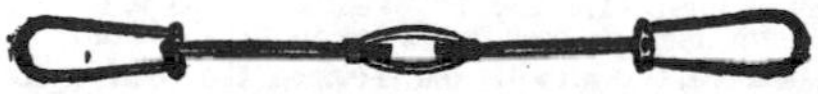

No. 12062. Loop Buck Saw Rods, will span from 19 to 22 inches; weight, 10 oz. Price, each..............**5c**

No. 12063. Best tinned Loop Saw Rods, span from 19 to 22 inches. Price, each..............**8c**

No. 12066. Buck saw Blades, same as used in No. 12055 bucksaw, each..............**38c**

No. 12067. Buck Saw Frames, same as used in No. 12055 bucksaw, each..............**25c**

## Foot Power Bracket Saw.

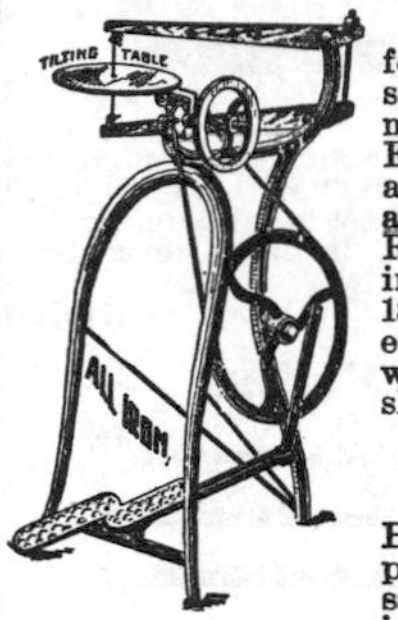


No. 12068. To meet the demand for a cheap and good foot power saw, we have had made an all iron machine which we offer for $2.25. For scroll sawing alone it is about as good as the higher price saws, and the finish is the same as our Rogers Saws. It has an iron tilting table, second growth ash arms, 18 inches long, improved clamps, etc. Weight of saw, 17 lbs.; weight when boxed, 35 lbs. Boxed for shipping without extra charge. Price....................**$2.25**

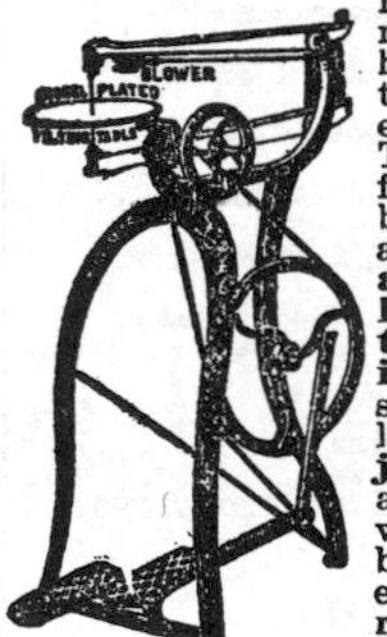


No. 12069. **Bracket Saw.** Has a rubber dust blower, improved clamps for holding the saw blade and a roller inserted in the table back of the saw, which makes it run perfectly true. We have no hesitancy in declaring this to be the best cheap saw ever offered to the public. The entire frame work is made from iron, painted and japanned black, and ornamented with red and gilt stripes. **The arbors are made of steel, carefully gauged and fitted to their bearings. The bearings** to the arms are carefully sized to bring them in perfect line. **The stretcher rod is jointed,** which allows the upper arm to be thrown out of the way when adjusting work or saw. The balance wheel is 4½ inches in diameter, with iron spoke center and rim of solid emery. The attachment for drilling is on the **right hand** side of machine, which is an advantage. With each machine we give 12 saw blades, wrench, sheet of designs and 3 drill points. The saw alone weighs 25 lbs.; when boxed for shipment, about 42 lbs. Price..............................**$3.30**

## Lathe and Saw.

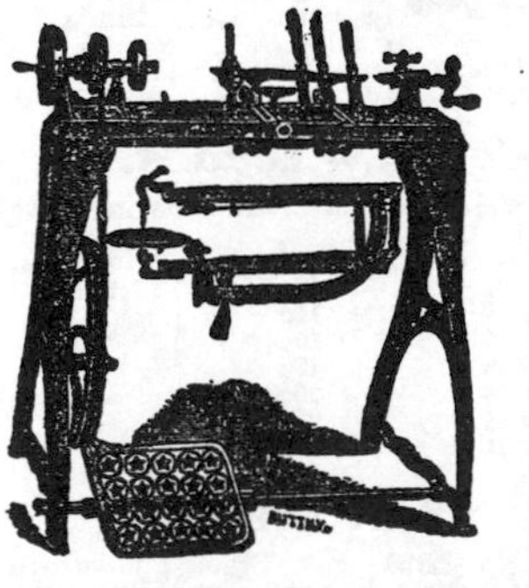

No. 12070. This lathe is provided with a long and short tool rest, five turning tools, wrench and drill points. Swing of lathe, five inches; length of bed, 24 inches; distance between center, 15½ inches. The large drive wheel has two grooves of varying depths on its face to give it a change of speed; the higher speed is 11 to 1; the lower, 7 to 1; the lathe head has a two inch face plate, a spur center, a screw center for turning cups and also a drill chuck to hold from 1-32 to ¼ inch round twist drills for drilling wood or iron. The lathe is thoroughly built and highly finished, the plain and polished parts being nickel plated. Price..........**$8.25**

No. 12071. Same lathe, with scroll saw attachments. Price..............................**$10.00**

## Mitre Boxes.

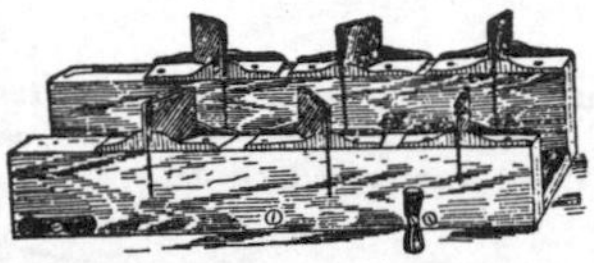

No. 12072. **Olmstead Improved Mitre Boxes.** In this mitre box the irons which guide saw are adjustable to any thickness of saw. When putting the saw into the slots have the teeth of saw below the irons.

Size A will saw molding 1½ in. x 3 in..............**$1.00**
Size B " " 2½ in. x 4 in..............**1.50**

**The New Langdon Mitre Box, Improved.**

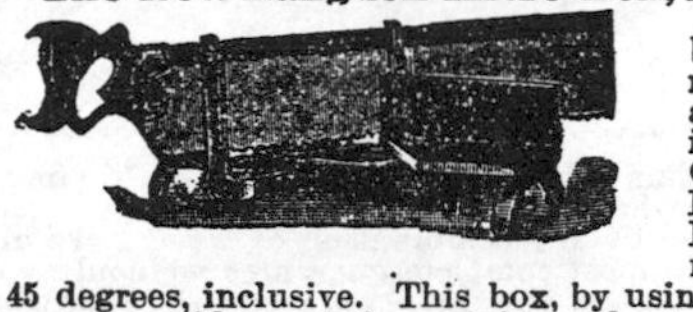

This is the best mitre box made, and has all the latest improvements. Ordinary New Langdon Mitre Box cuts from right angles to 45 degrees, inclusive. This box, by using the circular arms or guides, cuts from right angles to 75 degrees on 2¾ inch stuff, varying more or less with width of stuff. It is the only box adjustable for mitreing circular worl in patterns and segments of various kinds.

No. 12073. The Langdon New Improved Mitre Box, with saw, 22x4, gives 6 inches width at right angles and 4 inches at mitre. Weight, 10½ lbs. Price, each..............................**$8.20**

No. 12074. The Langdon New Improved Mitre Box, with saw 24x4, gives 9½ inches at right angles and 6¾ at mitre; weight, 11½ lbs. Price, each, with saw..............................**$10.35**

No. 12075. The Langdon New Improved Mitre Box, with saw, 28x5, gives 9½ inches width at right angles and 6¼ inches at mitre; weight, 12½ lbs. Price, each, with saw..............................**$11.75**

Should any part get broken at any time we can furnish repairs cheaply. Parts are all interchangeable, so any one can repair them. When ordering part, state size and number of the box it is for, and, if possible, send a drawing.

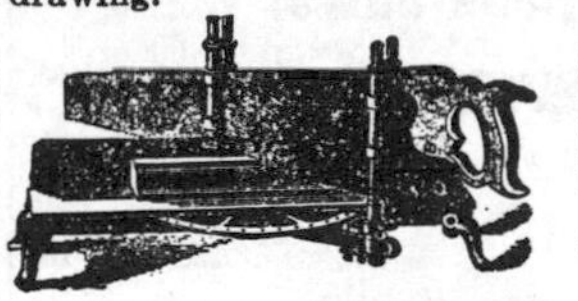

No. 12076. The Stanley Improved Mitre Box, for use with either back or panel saw. Adjustable. Length, 20 inches. Price, without saw..............**$5.75**

## Hand Saws.

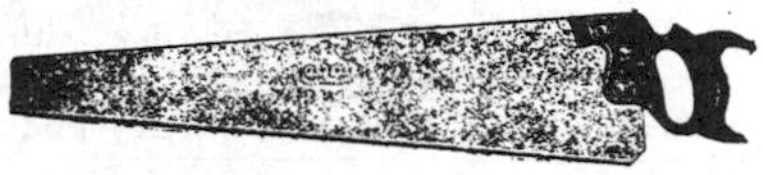

No. 12078. This Saw is not intended for mechanics use, but for a household saw or for any one who has but little use for a saw. It is not warranted. Length given is length of blade. Handle is not included in measurements. Beech handle, three brass screws, filed and set.

| Length, inches...... | 12 | 14 | 16 | 18 | 22 | 26 |
|---|---|---|---|---|---|---|
| Each | **20c** | **22c** | **25c** | **27c** | **30c** | **35c** |

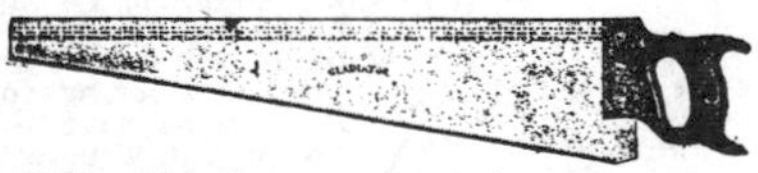

No. 12079. This Saw, as shown in cut, is a combination of hand saw, square, rule and straight edge. It is not warranted, but is as good or better than any combination saw made. Beech handle, three brass screws, ruled back, filed and set. Made one size only. Length, 26 inches. Price, each..............................**50c**

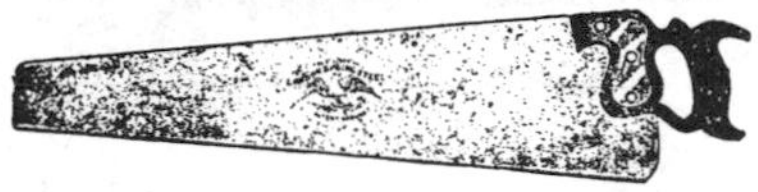

No. 12080. While this Saw is not warranted, it is a fair grade Saw, and has given excellent satisfaction. Blade is cast steel, patent ground and tempered, walnut handle with steel plate on handle, three brass screws, filed and set.

| Length, inches......... | 18 | 22 | 26 | Rip. 28 |
|---|---|---|---|---|
| Price, each .......... | 45c | 50c | 55c | 65c |

## Saw Handles.

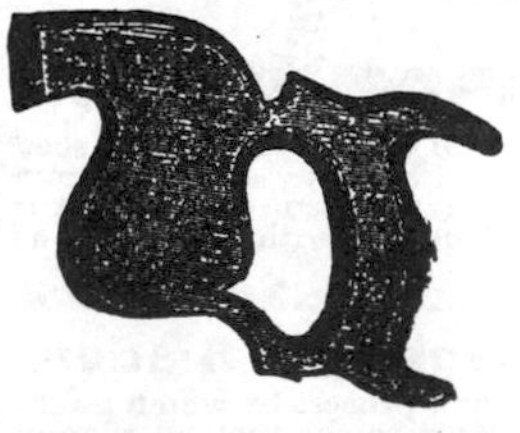

No. 12081. Hand Saw Handle, common beechwood, with varnished edges. Weight, 10 oz. Each.......**7c**

## Saw Handle Screws.

No. 12082. Brass.

| No. | Each. | Per doz. |
|---|---|---|
| 2 | 2c | 17c |
| 3 | 3c | 22c |
| 4 | 5c | 25c |
| 5 | 2c | 20c |

No. 3.

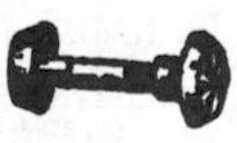

No. 5.

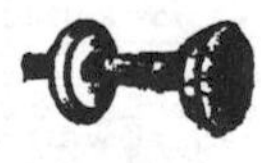

No. 2.

**This book is so crowded with bargains in every line you need to purchase, that you should refer constantly to the index to prevent overlooking some of them.**

## A STRICTLY GUARANTEED SAW. NO BETTER MADE.

During the year 1896 we did not have a Sears, Roebuck & Co. Saw returned to us.

If this saw does not prove as good or better than any saw you ever had return it and money will be refunded

Now made with Carved Handle.

**No. 12085.** This is **the best Saw made.** We have it made especially for our trade by a manufacturer whose reputation for making first-class goods is not excelled by any one anywhere. We contract for immense quantities, and are able to sell to consumer at less than retail dealers can buy at wholesale. Our selling price is not controlled by any combination or trust. We give our customers the same guarantee that we demanded and secured from the manufacturers, and that is the best, fairest, and most complete guarantee we could write. No other saw is sold with any such guarantee, free from all restrictions and conditions. On the blade of each Saw is etched our trade-mark and the following guarantee: If this Saw does not prove as good or better than any Saw you ever had, return it and money will be refunded. **You can't possibly buy a better Saw. Why pay more?** The blade is made from selected spring steel, patent ground and tempered, handle carved and polished, five improved screws, hand filed and set. Order No. 12085.

| | | | Rip. | |
|---|---|---|---|---|
| Length, inches | 18 | 20 | 22 | 26 | 28 |
| Each | 90c | $1.00 | 1.10 | 1.25 | 1.40 |

The 18, 20 and 22-inch Saws come 9, 10 and 12 points to the inch. The 26-inch Saws come 7, 8, 9, 10 and 12 points to the inch; 28-inch Rip Saws come 4, 4½, 5, 5½ and 6 points to the inch. If you don't state what is wanted we use our best judgment in filling order.

**Read the Guarantee given on Sears, Roebuck & Co. Saws.**

### Back Saws

No. 12099. Sears, Roebuck & Co.'s Back Saw, apple handle, polished edges, blued back.

| Size, inches | 10 | 12 | 14 | 16 |
|---|---|---|---|---|
| Each | 80c | 90c | $1.00 | 1.10 |

### Compass Saws.

No. 12100. Compass Saw, cast steel.

| Size, inches | 10 | 12 | 14 |
|---|---|---|---|
| Each | 12c | 15c | 16c |

### Keyhole Saws.

No. 12101. Keyhole Saw, with iron pad. This is a cheap and convenient combination of a Keyhole Saw, Saw Pad and Screwdriver.

Each ..........12c

No. 12102. Keyhole Saw Blades can be used in above Pad or in an ordinary file handle or chisel handle.

Price each..........8c

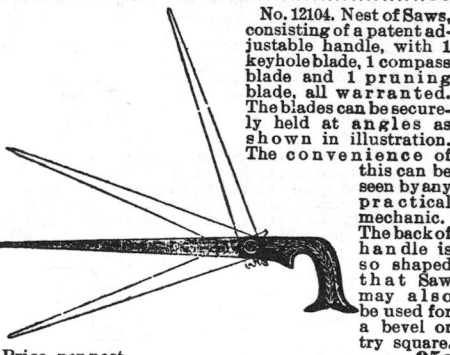

No. 12104. Nest of Saws, consisting of a patent adjustable handle, with 1 keyhole blade, 1 compass blade and 1 pruning blade, all warranted. The blades can be securely held at angles as shown in illustration. The convenience of this can be seen by any practical mechanic. The back of handle is so shaped that Saw may also be used for a bevel or try square.

Price, per nest..........95c

No. 12105. **Nest of Saws, not adjustable,** consisting of 1 handle, 1 keyhole blade, 1 compass blade, 1 table or pruning blade; all interchangeable in the handle.

Price complete..........65c

### Extension Hack Saw Frame.

No. 12110. This tool is made of steel, highly finished and so constructed that it can be easily extended from 8 to 12 inches, and when saw is inserted in position it is as firm as a solid frame. Complete with one blade, as shown in cut.

Price each..........78c

### Griffin's New Hack Saw Blades.

These are tempered by a new process by which a very high degree of temper is given to the toothed edge of the blade, diminishing in hardness to the back, which is of a low spring temper.

This process enables us to produce a blade which combines the best cutting and wearing quality with the least liability to breakage, and is stiffer, holds its shape better, and will not stretch when used in a machine.

| No. 12112. Length, inches.. | 6 | 7 | 8 | 9 | 10 | 12 |
|---|---|---|---|---|---|---|
| Per doz | 42c | 45c | 48c | 55c | 57c | 65c |

### Hand Bracket Saw.

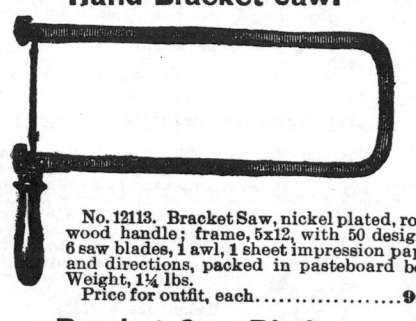

No. 12113. Bracket Saw, nickel plated, rosewood handle; frame, 5x12, with 50 designs, 6 saw blades, 1 awl, 1 sheet impression paper and directions, packed in pasteboard box. Weight, 1¼ lbs.

Price for outfit, each..........90c

### Bracket Saw Blades.

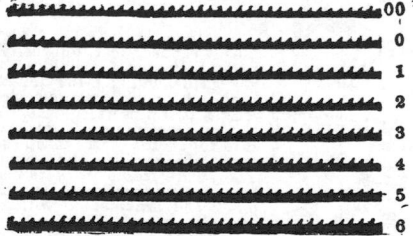

| | |
|---|---|
| | 00 |
| | 0 |
| | 1 |
| | 2 |
| | 3 |
| | 4 |
| | 5 |
| | 6 |

No. 12114. Bracket Saw Blades, 5 inches long. Any number. We do not sell less than a dozen of any one size.

Nos. 0 to 6, per doz., 6c; per gross..........60c
Nos. 7 and 8, per doz., 7c; per gross..........70c
Nos. 9 and 10, per doz., 8c; per gross..........80c

The above Blades also fit our No. 12068, 12069, 12070 and 12071 saws.

### Turning Saw.

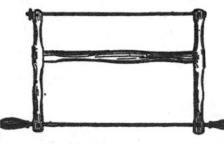

No. 12115. The frame is made of birch wood, with ebonized handles. There is an index on each handle to show the operator just how far to turn each. The friction is regulated by screws. It is quite superior to most other kinds in market.

Frame, with one blade, each..........$0.87
18-inch blades, each 15c; per doz..........1.75

### Felloe Web Saw Blades.

No. 12116. Felloe Web Saw Blades. In ordering state width wanted.

| Length | Width | Each | Per doz. |
|---|---|---|---|
| 12 | ¼ to ⅜ | 12c | $1.25 |
| 14 | ¼ to ½ | 14c | 1.42 |
| 16 | ¼ to ½ | 15c | 1.55 |
| 18 | ¼ to ⅝ | 17c | 1.85 |
| 20 | ¼ to ⅝ | 20c | 2.05 |
| 22 | ¼ to ⅝ | 22c | 2.25 |
| 24 | ¼ to ¾ | 25c | 2.50 |

### Saw Clamps.

No. 12120. Saw Clamp; jaws are 9½ inches. To open clamp, throw the lever down; place saw between the jaws and bring the lever back, and saw is securely held for filing; nicely japanned; weight, about 3½ lbs.

Price each..........32c

No. 12124. Ball and socket adjustable Saw Clamp; is adjustable in every direction; length of jaw, 9½ inches; saw is secured by tightening thumb screw; nicely japanned. Weight about 10½ lbs.

Price each..........65c

No. 12125. Silent Saw Vise with **third jaw faced with rubber,** which is pressed against the blade of saw, preventing all noise of vibration; weight about 3¾ lbs.

Price each..........88c

No. 12126. Adjustable Saw Clamp, with malleable screw clamp to secure it to bench or table. This clamp holds saw in same manner as above and jaws are same length. The adjustable feature, which can be readily understood by looking at cut, makes this the most popular and best selling saw clamp in the market. Weight about 5 lbs.

Price each..........48c

### Saw Clamp with Filing Guide.

No. 12127. Henry Disston & Sons' Saw Clamp and Guide. This enables any one to file a saw correctly, even if they are not skilled in the art of saw filing. Full directions for use accompany each outfit. The clamp is not shown in full in the illustration. It is very similar to No. 12120 clamp, with the addition of the guide. Ordinary files can be used.

Price for Clamp-Filing Guide, file and handle, all complete in wooden box..........$1.75

### Saw Sets.

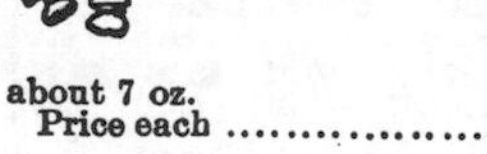

No. 12132. Lever Saw Sets with wood handle. The depth of set on tooth and amount of set can be regulated by means of gauges on the set. Weight about 7 oz.

Price each..........9c

**When you need some Hardware, order enough Groceries to make up a freight order and you will cut down the cost of transportation to a minimum.**

## The Old Reliable Morrell's Saw Set.

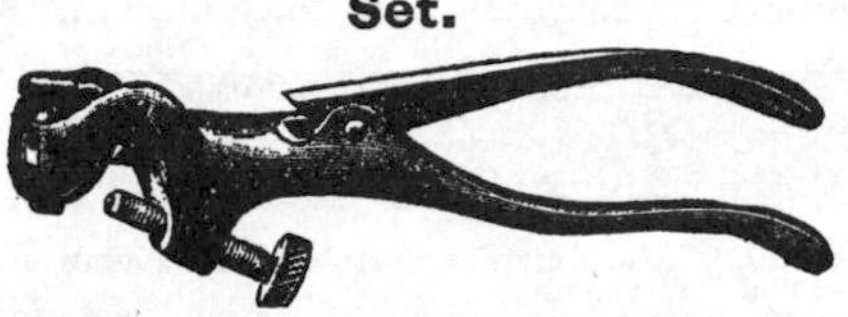

If this Saw Set is used intelligently it will be impossible to break a tooth out of a saw while setting it. No prying required. Simply shutting the handles sets the tooth. The point of tooth when in position on anvil can be seen by the operator. We have the following sizes:

No. 12133. Morrell's Perfect Saw Set No. 1, for setting hand, band, panel, buck and meat saws. Each.................................. **60c**

No. 12134. No. 3, for common tooth circular and cross cut saws from 20 to 14 gauge. Weight, 1 lb. 6 oz. Price, each.................................. **$1.00**

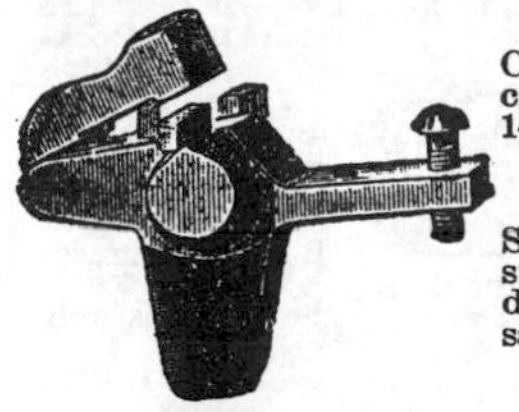

No. 12135. No. 4, for Champion or M tooth cross cut saws from 22 to 14 gauge. Weight, 1½ lbs. Price, each...... **$1.12**

No. 12136. Hammer Saw Set, Aiken's genuine cast steel. So well known, a description is not necessary. Price, each......... **50c**

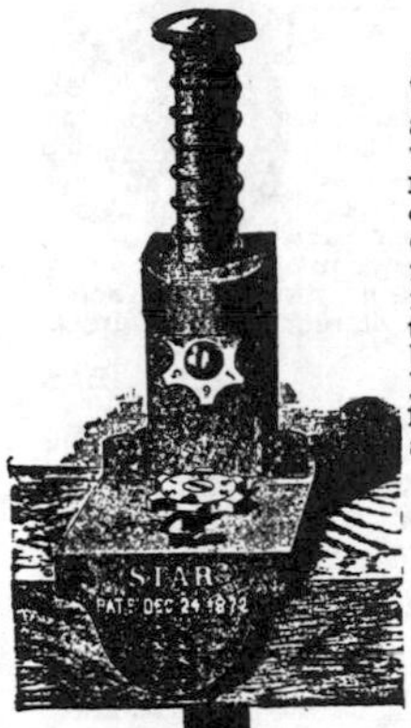


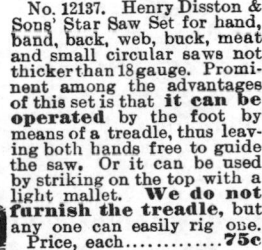

No. 12137. Henry Disston & Sons' Star Saw Set for hand, band, back, web, buck, meat and small circular saws not thicker than 18 gauge. Prominent among the advantages of this set is that **it can be operated** by the foot by means of a treadle, thus leaving both hands free to guide the saw. Or it can be used by striking on the top with a light mallet. **We do not furnish the treadle**, but any one can easily rig one. Price, each............ **75c**

## The Practical Saw Jointer.

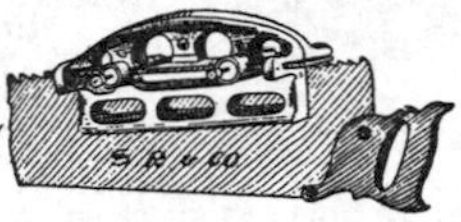

No. 12142. It is simple and effective. A very useful tool for carpenters, cabinetmakers, patternmakers, carriagemakers, and in fact for all using, making and repairing saws, as it makes a great saving in time and insures accuracy in jointing the teeth to an equal length. It is used on the saw as shown in the cut, and the file in the slot is adjustable, so that the full width of the file may be utilized on one side, then the file reversed and used in the same way until it is all worn out. Its good qualities will be appreciated by those having gone on so long in the old way, by the saving of the wear and tear on the fingers, and the ease and facility with which it can be used. No mechanic's kit is complete without one. Price.................................. **30c**

## FILES.

We will carry in stock this season a brand of files which our buyer considers as good as it's possible to make. Having had an experience of twenty years, his opinion is certainly worthy of consideration. **We do not handle seconds.** The manufacturer requests us not to print the maker's name this year, as we are selling to any one at his regular wholesale price to dealers. The maker's name is on each package, and each file has the manufacturer's brand on it. They are goods of acknowledged excellence and the favorite with many of the largest file users in the country. The **"Tang,"** or part which goes in the handle, is not included in size of files.

## Taper Files.

No. 12165. Taper Files.

| Size, inches. | Weight, oz. | Each. | Per doz. |
|---|---|---|---|
| 3 | 2 | 4c | $0.33 |
| 3½ | 2 | 4c | .34 |
| 4 | 3 | 5c | .36 |
| 4½ | 3 | 5c | .42 |
| 5 | 4 | 6c | .51 |
| 5½ | 4 | 7c | .60 |
| 6 | 4 | 8c | .72 |
| 7 | 4 | 10c | .90 |
| 8 | 6 | 12c | 1.14 |

## Slim Taper Files.

No. 12166. Slim Taper Files.

| Size, inches. | Weight, oz. | Each. | Per doz. |
|---|---|---|---|
| 3 | 2 | 4c | 35c |
| 3½ | 2 | 4c | 36c |
| 4 | 3 | 5c | 39c |
| 4½ | 3 | 5c | 44c |
| 5 | 4 | 6c | 51c |
| 5½ | 4 | 6c | 57c |
| 6 | 4 | 7c | 63c |
| 7 | 4 | 8c | 75c |
| 8 | 6 | 10c | 90c |

## Double Enders.

No. 12167. Double End Files. Very popular with all mechanics. Price includes handle. Length given is whole length of file.

| Size, inches | 7 | 8 | 9 | 10 |
|---|---|---|---|---|
| Weight, each, oz | 2 | 2 | 3 | 4 |
| Each | 8c | 9c | 10c | 12c |
| Per dozen | 72c | 80c | 91c | $1.10 |

## Mill Files.

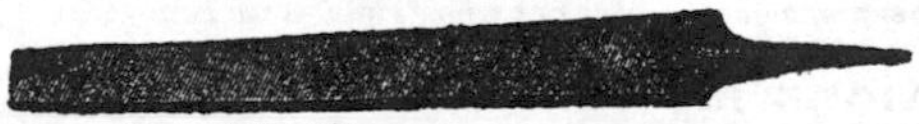

No. 12168. Mill Files.

| Size, inches. | Weight, oz. | Each. | Per doz. |
|---|---|---|---|
| 6 | 6 | 7c | $0.68 |
| 8 | 7 | 10c | .87 |
| 10 | 10 | 12c | 1.20 |
| 12 | 16 | 17c | 1.62 |
| 14 | 31 | 22c | 2.34 |

## Flat Bastard Files.

No. 12169. Flat Bastard Files. Same shape as mill files, but with coarse cut. Will cut away faster than mill files, but are not suitable for saws. Sometimes called a plow file. Also, sometimes used to file wood, as they give a smoother finish than the regular wood rasp.

| Size, inches. | Weight, oz. | Each. | Per doz. |
|---|---|---|---|
| 4 | 2 | 7c | $0.60 |
| 5 | 4 | 7c | .66 |
| 6 | 4 | 8c | .75 |
| 8 | 7 | 11c | 1.02 |
| 10 | 12 | 15c | 1.41 |
| 12 | 20 | 21c | 2.00 |
| 14 | 29 | 30c | 2.85 |

## Half Round Files.

No. 12170. Half Round Bastard File. One side is same as Flat Bastard. The other side is half round. Used for same purposes as Flat Bastard Files.

| Size, inches. | Weight, oz. | Each. | Per doz. |
|---|---|---|---|
| 6 | 4 | 10c | $0.96 |
| 8 | 8 | 14c | 1.29 |
| 10 | 11 | 19c | 1.74 |
| 12 | 18 | 25c | 2.34 |

## Round Files.

No. 12172. Round Bastard Files. Sometimes called Rat Tail Files.

| Size, inches. | Weight, oz. | Each. | Per doz. |
|---|---|---|---|
| 4 | 2 | 6c | $0.54 |
| 5 | 4 | 7c | .60 |
| 6 | 5 | 7c | .68 |
| 8 | 6 | 10c | .87 |
| 10 | 8 | 12c | 1.20 |
| 12 | 12 | 17c | 1.62 |

## Wood Rasps.

No. 12174. Wood Rasps. Flat on one side, half round on the other. With tang.

| Size, inches | 10 | 12 | 14 |
|---|---|---|---|
| Weight, oz | 11 | 18 | 28 |
| Each | $0.25 | $0.32 | $0.45 |
| Per dozen | 2.50 | 3.50 | 4.82 |

## Cabinet Rasps.

No. 12175. Cabinet Rasp. Same as above, only not as coarse cut. Leaves the work much smoother than the regular wood rasp. With tang.

| Size, inches | 10 | 12 |
|---|---|---|
| Each | $0.30 | $0.40 |
| Per dozen | 3.36 | 4.50 |

## Horse Rasps.

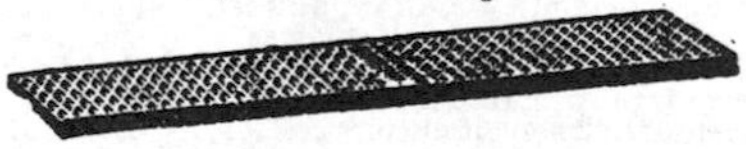

No. 12176. Horse Rasps. We have sold a great many Horse Rasps of this brand. Our trade is increasing and we are getting orders again and again from same parties. Order a sample, give it a trial, and see if it's not just as good or better than those for which you must pay more.

| Size, inches | 12 | 14 | 16 |
|---|---|---|---|
| Each | $0.24 | $0.32 | $0.44 |
| Per dozen | 2.57 | 3.64 | 5.00 |

No. 12177. Heller's Horse Rasps. Flat; **not tanged.**

| Size, inches | 12 | 14 | 16 |
|---|---|---|---|
| Each | $0.28 | $0.40 | $0.56 |
| Per dozen | 3.29 | 4.64 | 6.47 |

## File Handles.

No. 12179. File Handles, with brass ferrule, assorted sizes, suitable for files quoted above. When ordering state if wanted large, medium or small. Weight, 2 oz. Each, **2c**; per dozen.................................. **20c**

## File Cleaners.

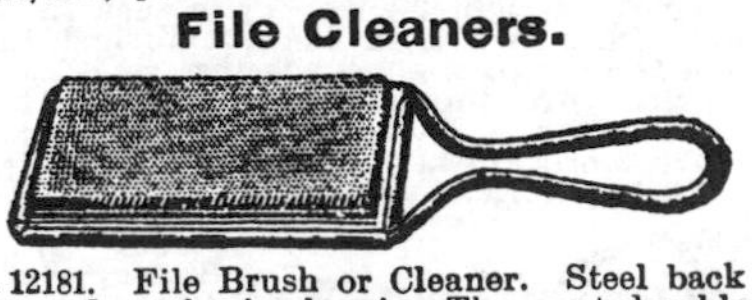

No. 12181. File Brush or Cleaner. Steel back and frame, and steel wire brush. The most durable and nicest finish file brush in the market. Each........ **14c**



## EMERY GOODS.

We are headquarters for everything in this line. We handle only the highest grade goods made, and on this class of goods we have no competition. **We can save you 25 per cent.** or more on emery goods, and only one order will convince you.

## Emery Oil Stones.

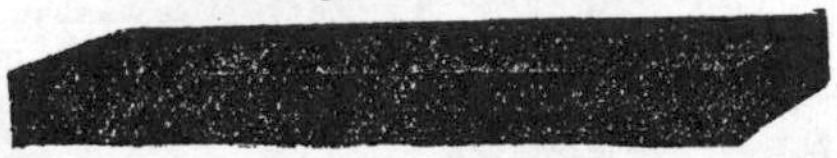

These stones are destined to supersede all other stones used with oil. The lightning rapidity with which they sharpen a tool, without taking the temper from the steel, is marvelous. A keen edge may be obtained in half the time required by the use of the quarried stone. They are made with a coarse and fine side, thus combining two stones in one, the coarse side to be used for taking out nicks and for rapid cutting; the fine side for putting on a fine, keen edge. Their phenomenal sale attests their merits and growing popularity.

No. 12183.

| Size. | Price each. | Size. | Price each. |
|---|---|---|---|
| 8x2x1 | **42c** | 7x2½x¾ | **40c** |
| 7x2x1 | **38c** | 6x2x¾ | **30c** |
| 4x1½x½ | **20c** | | |

## Emery Gouge Slips.

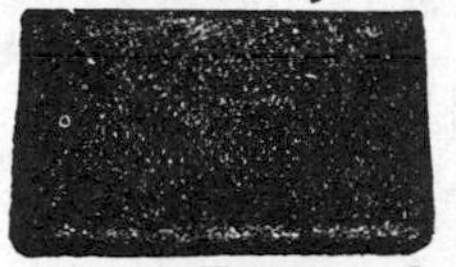

No. 12184. Emery Gouge Slips are 4 inches long, 2¼ inches wide, ½ inch thick on one edge and ⅛ inch thick on the other. Price each.......... **20c**

## Emery Ax Stones.

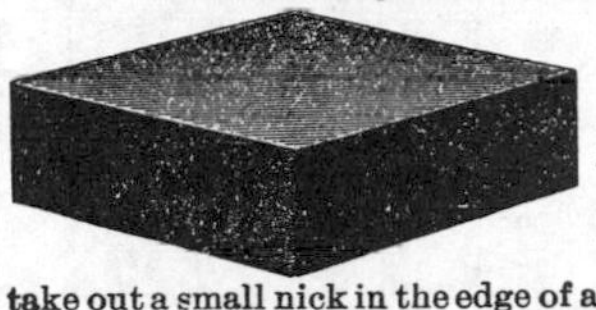

No. 12185. Emery Ax Stone is of a convenient size to carry in the pocket. Don't chop wood with a dull ax. It is surprising to see how quickly one of these stones will take out a small nick in the edge of an ax. Made in 2 sizes.

2½x2½x¾, Price each.................................. **20c**

2x2x⅝, Price each.................................. **15c**

## Emery Scythe Stones.

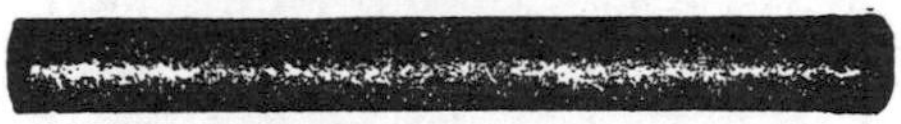

No. 12186. Emery Scythe Stones are having a phenomenal sale and some of our customers are ordering them by the dozens to sell to their neighbors. They will put the right kind of an edge on a scythe and do it quickly. Made in two sizes, oval shape.

12x1¼x½ inches. Price each, **25c**; per doz..... **$2.50**

9x1¼x½ inches. Price each, **20c**; per doz..... **2.10**

## Emery Razor Hone.

No. 12188. **Emery Razor Hone** is far superior to natural stone and at the same time much lower in price; size, 6x2x½ inches. Price, each .................... **75c**

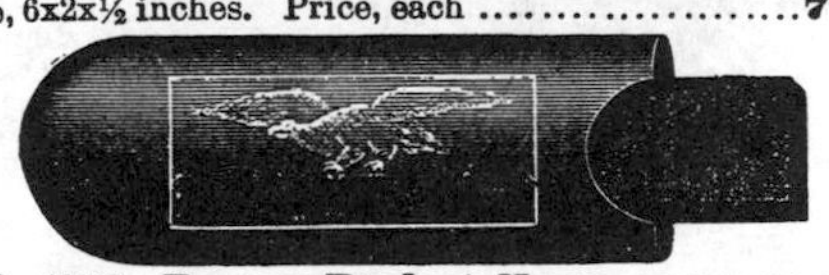

No. 12189. **Emery Pocket Hone,** coarse on one side, for sharpening lead pencils, taking nicks out of knife blades, and quick sharpening; the other side fine to put a razor edge on pocket knives, etc.; is furnished with a handsome leather case, convenient size to carry in vest pocket; weight, packed for the mail, 3 oz. Price, each .................................. **25c**

## Emery Knife Sharpener, or Steel.

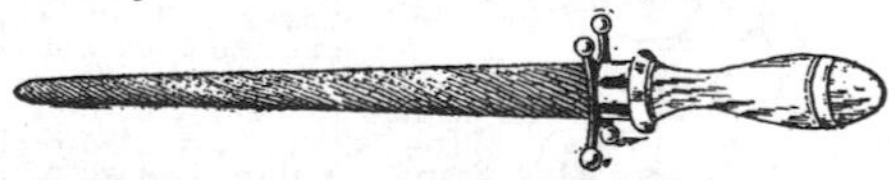

A new and useful device for imparting a keen edge to the dullest knife or scissors in half the time required by other means.

This knife sharpener is composed of a solid shaft of emery, firmly secured to a handsomely finished handle by means of a steel rod extending its entire length, making it strong and durable.

It is one of the most popular household articles we have and every kitchen should have one in it. Although our price is low, we guarantee it to be exactly as represented and of the best quality it's possible to make. It's not a wood stick covered with sand and glue, although that kind is usually sold at this price. Made in two sizes with nickel plated shield and hardwood handle with nickelplated ferrule.

No. 12190. **Emery Knife Sharpener,** emery 8 inches long, whole length (including handle), 12 inches; weight, 6 oz. Price, each.................................. **10c**

Per dozen.................................. **$1.08**

No. 12191. **Emery Knife Sharpener,** emery 10 inches long, whole length (including handle), 14 inches; weight, 8 oz. Price, each.................................. **15c**

Per dozen.................................. **$1.50**

## EMERY WHEELS.

The Acme Emery Wheel is made especially for our trade by manufacturers who have established a most enviable reputation for making high grade satisfactory wheels. The wheels made for us are exactly the same grade in every respect as those which they have made for years and on which they have built up their business and reputation. The only way they differ is in the label. Our label instead of theirs don't detract a particle from the value of the wheels, but it makes the price lower. The manufacturers sell this wheel to the consumer at nearly twice the price we charge and would not furnish us with goods with their labels to sell at our prices. But they will take off their labels and put on our label and they think we couldn't give them away to their customers. Perhaps they are right. But if any user of emery wheels will give our wheels a trial we believe he will recognize their merit and give us all his future trade.

### Directions for Ordering.

Always state Diameter, Thickness, **Size of Arbor Hole** and shape of face, the kind of material to be ground, whether surface or edge grinding and fine or coarse work is required; whether the work is light or heavy; speed at which wheel is to run.

### Directions for Using.

Acme Emery Wheels will do the best work when run at a surface speed of one mile a minute, but for hardened tool grinding a slower speed is advisable. Before putting a wheel on the mandrel tap it lightly with a hammer to ascertain that it is sound. If it rings it has not suffered from ill usage, and may be safely put to use.

All our wheels are thoroughly tested at a very much higher strain than that to which they are subjected in use and all are packed carefully. In transportation they may be broken, hence the necessity of testing immediately before running them.

Always use iron flanges on both sides of the wheel. The flanges ought to be about one-third of the diameter of the wheel or larger. Rubber or leather washers should be used, especially with thin wheels.

All emery machines should be provided with rests on which the article to be ground is held.

Wheels should run toward the operator, with the rests close to the face of the wheel. Very often wheels are broken by castings being caught between the wheels and rests by getting out of the workman's hands.

### Price List of Emery Wheels.

No. 12196. Flat Face Emery Wheels.      No. 12198. Round Face Emery Wheels.
No. 12197. Bevel Face Emery Wheels.

**Give diameter, thickness and size of hole.**

| Diameter of Wheel | ¼ | ⅜ | ½ | ⅝ | ¾ | 1 | 1¼ | 1½ | 1¾ | 2 | 2¼ | 2½ |
|---|---|---|---|---|---|---|---|---|---|---|---|---|
| | | | | | | | THICKNESS. | | | | | |
| 2 | $0.11 | $0.14 | $0.15 | $0.16 | $0.17 | $0.18 | $ 0.19 | $ 0.20 | $ 0.21 | $ 0.22 | $ 0.23 | $ 0.24 |
| 2½ | .12 | .17 | .20 | .21 | .22 | .23 | .24 | .27 | .30 | .32 | .35 | .37 |
| 3 | .15 | .20 | .24 | .25 | .26 | .27 | .28 | .29 | .40 | .43 | .47 | .50 |
| 3½ | .18 | .24 | .29 | .30 | .31 | .32 | .33 | .35 | .50 | .55 | .60 | .65 |
| 4 | .23 | .25 | .30 | .32 | .35 | .40 | .47 | .53 | .60 | .65 | .72 | .78 |
| 4½ | .27 | .28 | .32 | .35 | .40 | .47 | .55 | .62 | .70 | .77 | .85 | .92 |
| 5 | .30 | .31 | .35 | .40 | .45 | .55 | .65 | .75 | .85 | .95 | 1.05 | 1.15 |
| 6 | .42 | .43 | .45 | .58 | .60 | .77 | .93 | 1.10 | 1.25 | 1.42 | 1.58 | 1.75 |
| 7 | .47 | .50 | .55 | .65 | .75 | .97 | 1.18 | 1.40 | 1.60 | 1.82 | 2.03 | 2.25 |
| 8 | .53 | .60 | .65 | .78 | .90 | 1.15 | 1.40 | 1.65 | 1.90 | 2.15 | 2.40 | 2.65 |
| 9 | .63 | .70 | .78 | .93 | 1.07 | 1.35 | 1.65 | 1.93 | 2.22 | 2.50 | 2.79 | 3.08 |
| 10 | .75 | .85 | .92 | 1.10 | 1.25 | 1.60 | 1.93 | 2.27 | 2.60 | 2.94 | 3.28 | 3.62 |
| 12 | .90 | .95 | 1.00 | 1.25 | 1.50 | 1.85 | 2.25 | 2.68 | 3.19 | 3.50 | 3.93 | 4.35 |
| 14 | 1.02 | 1.29 | 1.57 | 1.83 | 2.12 | 2.65 | 3.22 | 3.77 | 4.32 | 4.87 | 5.42 | 5.97 |
| 16 | | | | | 2.72 | 3.43 | 4.14 | 4.85 | 5.57 | 6.25 | 6.98 | 7.70 |
| 18 | | | | | 3.32 | 4.25 | 5.19 | 6.13 | 7.07 | 8.00 | 8.94 | 9.88 |
| 20 | | | | | | 5.07 | 6.19 | 7.32 | 8.44 | 9.57 | 10.69 | 11.82 |
| 22 | | | | | | 6.25 | 7.75 | 9.25 | 10.75 | 12.25 | 13.75 | 15.25 |
| 24 | | | | | | 7.25 | 9.00 | 10.75 | 12.50 | 14.25 | 16.00 | 17.75 |
| 26 | | | | | | | 10.75 | 12.75 | 14.75 | 16.75 | 18.75 | 20.75 |
| 30 | | | | | | | | 15.25 | 18.00 | 20.75 | 23.50 | 26.25 |
| 36 | | | | | | | | 23.75 | 27.63 | 31.50 | 35.38 | 39.25 |

**Don't forget to give size of hole, diameter and thickness.**

### Emery Wheel Stands.

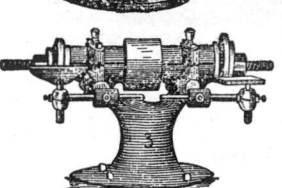

No. 12199. Emery Wheel Stand, for power. Will run two 6-inch emery wheels, 1 inch thick, has ¾ inch steel spindle, ⅝ inch between flanges, pulley 2 inches in diameter, 1⅜ inch face, Weight, 9 lbs. Price, each......**$3.95** Price does not include wheels.

No. 12200. Emery Wheel Stand, for power, will run two wheels 10 inches in diameter and 1½ inches thick, has steel spindle 1 inch in diameter in bearings, ¾ inch between flanges. The bearings are 2 inches long and adjustable, mounted with brass oil cups. Pulleys 2½ inches diameter, 1¾ inch face. Two adjustable knuckle joint rests, as shown in cut. Weight, 25 lbs. Price......**$8.00**

No. 12201. Emery Wheel Stand. Will run two wheels 12 inches in diameter and 2 inches thick, has steel spindles 18 inches long and 1 inch diameter in bearings, ¾ inch between flanges. The bearings are 3 inches long and same style as engine lathe bearings, mounted with brass oil cups. Pulleys 3½ inches diameter, 2¼ inch face. Exactly like cut of No. 12200 only larger. Weight, 40 lbs. Price......**$12.00**

No. 12202. Emery Wheel Stand. Will run two wheels 16 inches in diameter and 2½ inches thick; has steel spindles 1 3-16 inch diameter in bearings, 1 inch between flanges. The bearings are 4 inches long and same style as engine lathe bearings, mounted with brass oil cups. Pulley 3¾ inches diameter, 2½ inch face.

These stands are provided with two rests which are knuckle jointed, and can be set at any desired angle, as shown in cut of 12200; weight, 65 lbs. Price....**$16.00**

**Notice.**—An important feature of all these stands, establishing their superiority over all others, is the bearing protectors, which not only keeps the emery dust from off the journals, but also the oil from penetrating the emery wheels, which when saturated with oil, become worthless, a notable defect in other emery wheel stands which has hitherto not been overcome.

### Emery Wheel Dresser.

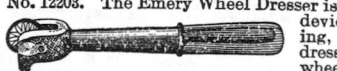

No. 12203. The Emery Wheel Dresser is a very simple device for sharpening, trueing, or dressing an emery wheel on its arbor at full speed. It leaves the wheel clean and sharp and in the best possible condition for cutting. An emery wheel is a cutting tool composed of innumerable sharp grains of emery, which become dull by use. To sharpen the wheel these grains must be brought to the surface, and this dresser is the best tool in the market for the purpose. Price, each with 2 sets of cutters ..................**95c** Extra cutters, each..................**20c**

### Levels.

No. 12220. Cherry stained Level **without plumb. Not adjustable.** Length, 12 inches. Price, each...........**20c**

No. 12221. Plumb and Level. Arch top plate. Two side views. Polished. Not adjustable. Lengths, 24, 26, 28 or 30 inch. Weight, 3½ lbs. Price, each........**38c**

No. 12224. Improved adjustable Plumb and Level. Polished mahogany arch top plate. Two side views. Lengths, 26, 28 or 30 inch. Weight, 3½ lbs. Price, each......**50c**

No. 12225. Improved adjustable Plumb and Level made from three pieces, glued together so it cannot warp or spring. Arch top plate. Two ornamental brass tipped side views. Finely polished and tipped. Lengths, 26, 28 or 30 inch. Weight, 3½ lbs. Price, each..................**80c**

No. 12227. Stanley Hand-y Plumb and Level. Arch top plate. Two side views. Polished and tipped. Lengths, 26, 28 or 30 inch. Cheapest Level. Price, each..................**71c** The shallow grooves on each side of the level afford an excellent grip on the tool. This will be especially appreciated for house framing, bridge building and general outside work.

---

No. 12230. Glasses for Plumbs and Levels. Lengths, 1½ to 4 inches. In ordering state length wanted. Price, each..................**5c**

No. 12234. Machinists' adjustable iron Plumb and Level and Inclinometer.

| Length, inches | 6 | 12 | 18 |
|---|---|---|---|
| Price, each | $1.90 | 2.15 | 2.55 |

No. 12236. Adjustable Double Plumb and Level for carpenters' and machinists' use. Made of gray iron with steel bars extending through each column.

| Size, inches | 6 | 12 | 18 | 24 |
|---|---|---|---|---|
| Price, each | $1.15 | 1.35 | 1.45 | 1.88 |

No. 12250. Pocket Level, which can also be quickly attached to the edge of a steel square or a straight edge. Body is japanned. iron, brass top plate. Weight, 6 oz. Price, each..................**7c**

No. 12251. Brass Pocket Level. Same as above only all brass. Price, each..................**20c**

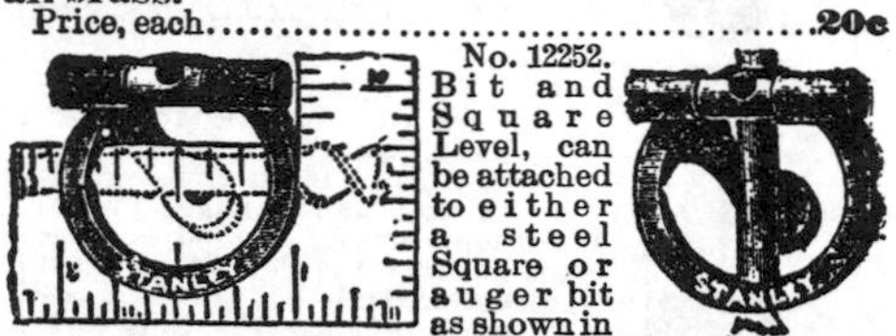

No. 12252. Bit and Square Level, can be attached to either a steel Square or auger bit as shown in illustration. On a bit it serves as a guide to bore accurately at either plumb level or at an angle of 45 degrees. Has brass frame. Weight, 4 oz. Price, each..................**21c**

### Stanley's Improved Level Sights.

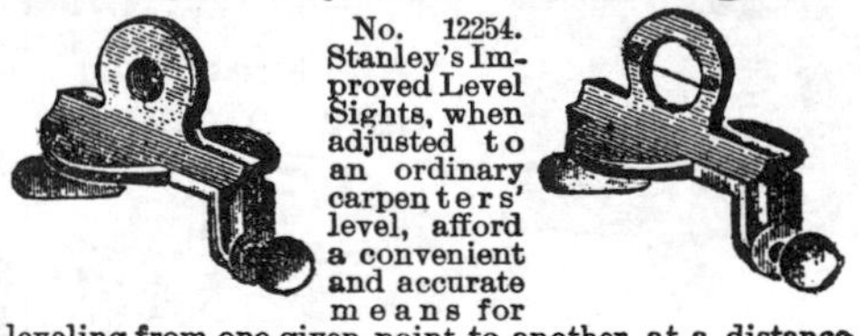

No. 12254. Stanley's Improved Level Sights, when adjusted to an ordinary carpenters' level, afford a convenient and accurate means for leveling from one given point to another at a distance away. The price given below is for sights only. Level is not included. Price, per pair..................**43c**

### Plumb Bobs.

No. 12256. Japanned Iron Plumb Bob. Weight, 9 oz. Price, each...**5c**
No. 12258. Brass Plumb Bob with hardened steel point. Weight 6 oz. Price, each ..................**20c**

### Adjustable Plumb Bobs.

No. 12258. By dropping the Bob with a slight jerk while the ring is held in the hand any desired length of line may be reeled off, a spring which has its bearing on the reel will check and hold the Bob firmly at any point on the line. A suitable length of line comes reeled on each Bob.

No. 12262. Adjustable Plumb Bob, as described above, made of bronze metal with hardened cast steel point, No. 1 or small size. Price, each..................**$1.00**

No. 12263. Same as above, No. 2 or large size. Price, each..................**$1.20**

No. 12264. Adjustable Plumb Bob, described as above, made of iron with steel point, large size. Price, each..................**75c**

...When you want...

## GUNS, REVOLVERS, AMMUNITION, or SPORTING GOODS

### of any kind,

Refer to our Catalogue, and you will find just what you want, at prices you can afford.

---

**Every man who buys goods of us is at least 25 per cent. of his purchase better off. We'll make it pay you.**

## Carpenters' Squares.

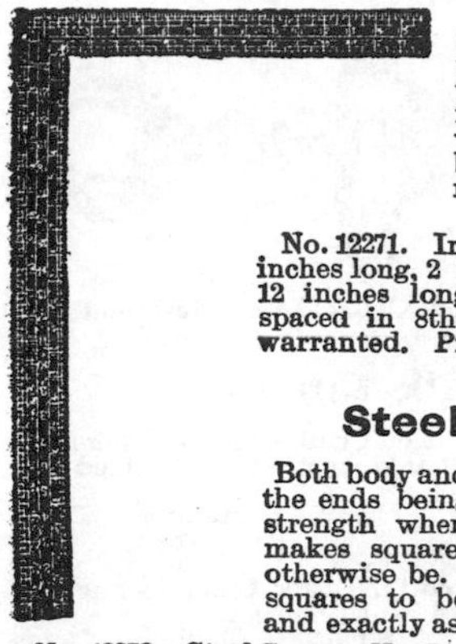

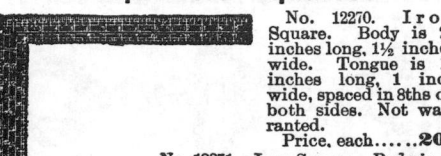

No. 12270. Iron Square. Body is 24 inches long, 1½ inches wide. Tongue is 12 inches long, 1 inch wide, spaced in 8ths on both sides. Not warranted.
Price, each......20c

No. 12271. Iron Square. Body is 24 inches long, 2 inches wide. Tongue, 12 inches long, 1½ inches wide, spaced in 8ths on both sides. Not warranted. Price, each .........25c

## Steel Squares.

Both body and tongue are **tapered**, the ends being thinner. This gives strength where it is needed, and makes square lighter than it would otherwise be. We guarantee these squares to be equal to any made, and exactly as represented.

No. 12272. Steel Square, No. 7, extra quality, 2 inches wide, marked on both sides, spaced ⅛, ¼ and 1 inch. Essex new board measure, giving feet and inches in full.
Size of body, 24x2 inches; size of tongue, 16x1½ inches. The face is marked ⅛-¼; back is marked ¼-1-¼-¼. Price, each ......................................40c

No. 12273. Steel Square, No. 3, extra quality; size of body, 24x2 inches; size of tongue, 16x1½. Marked on face, 1/16-1/4-1/16; marked on back, 1/12-1/4-1/12-1/4; with brace measure and Essex new board measure, giving feet and inches in full. Price, each ...............................45c

No. 12274. Steel Square, No. 03, same description as 12273, nickel plated. Price, each ....................60c

No. 12275. Steel Square, No. 112, nickel plated; size of body, 12x1½ inches; size of tongue, 8x1 inch; marked on face, 1/16-1/8-1/16-1/8; marked on back, 1/12-1/8-1/12-1/8. This square will be found very convenient, as it may be put in an ordinary tool chest. Price, each ............................50c

No. 12276. Steel Square, No. 14; size of body, 24x2 inches; size of tongue, 16x1½; with brace measure and Essex board measure; marked on face, 1/8-1/4-1/8-1/4; marked on back, 1/4-1-1/4-1/4, giving feet and inches in full. Price, each ..................................................40c

No. 12277. Steel Square, No. 100, extra quality. Body 24x2 inches; tongue, 16x1½; brace measure, 8 square and Essex's board; measure giving feet and inches in full marked on face, 1/16-1/8-1/16-1/8; marked on back, 1/12 and 1/32-1/12-1/10. Price, each ..............................75c

No. 12278. Same Square as No. 12277, only nickel plated. Price, each ...................................90c

No. 12279. Steel Square, calculated for making a tenon or mortise. The tongue of the square has notches in the edge which hold an awl or pencil from slipping; a very convenient tool for mechanics' use, spaced the same as No. 12273; not plated. Each ....................$1.00

No. 12280. Same as No. 12279, nickel plated. Price, each .................................................$1.15

## Try Squares.

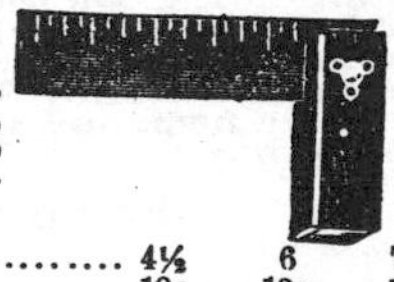

No. 12294. Try Square. Brass lined, rosewood handle, graduated steel blade, square inside or out. Blade is measured from inside of handle.

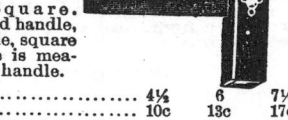

| Size blade, inches | 4½ | 6 | 7½ |
|---|---|---|---|
| Price each | 10c | 13c | 17c |

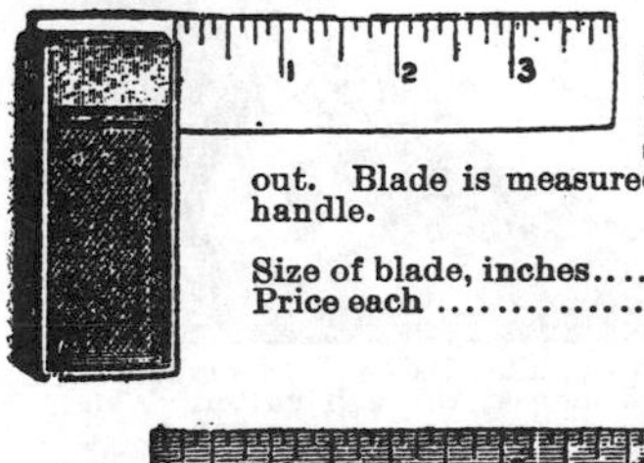

No. 12295. Try Square. Iron handle, graduated steel blade, square inside and out. Blade is measured from inside of handle.

| Size of blade, inches | 4 | 6 | 8 |
|---|---|---|---|
| Price each | 15c | 17c | 20c |

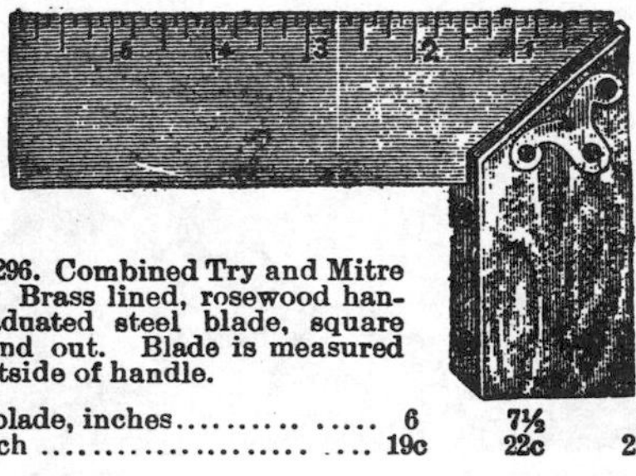

No. 12296. Combined Try and Mitre Square. Brass lined, rosewood handle, graduated steel blade, square inside and out. Blade is measured from outside of handle.

| Size of blade, inches | 6 | 7½ | 9 |
|---|---|---|---|
| Price each | 19c | 22c | 25c |

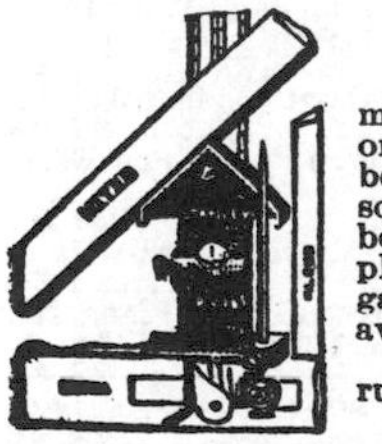

No. 12302. Combination Attachment. When this is attached to an ordinary carpenters' rule, it may be used for a try square, mitre square, T square, inside square, beam compass, spirit level and plumb mortise gauge, marking gauge, depth gauge or scratch awl. Weight, 10 oz.
Price, with 12-inch graduated ruler..........................50c

## Bevels.

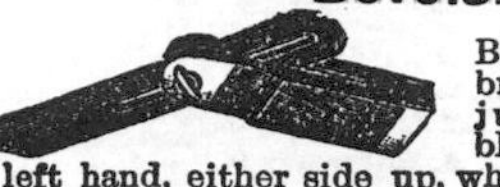

No. 12310. Sliding T Bevel, rosewood handle, brass tipped, flush adjusting screw steel blade, can be used right or left hand, either side up, which is a great convenience. Weight, 7 to 10 oz.

| Length, inches | 6 | 8 | 10 |
|---|---|---|---|
| Price | 15c | 16c | 18c |

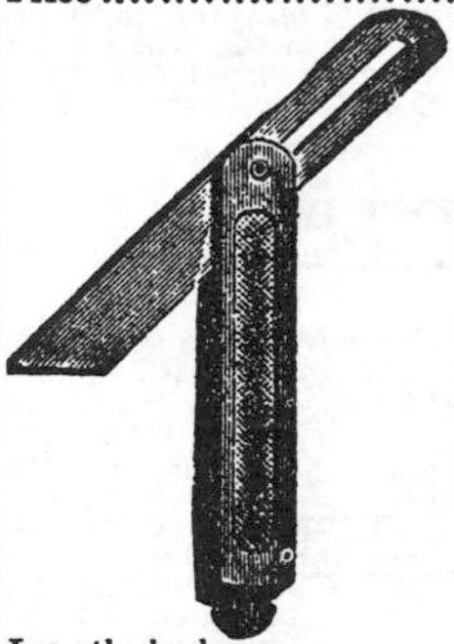

No. 12311. Eureka Sliding T Bevel, iron handle, steel blade. Blade can be secured at any angle by turning thumb screw at the end of handle. This bevel is the same on both sides. No screws or depressions to bother in use.

| Length, inches | 6 | 8 | 10 |
|---|---|---|---|
| Price each | 27c | 29c | 35c |

## Carpenters' Boxwood Rules.

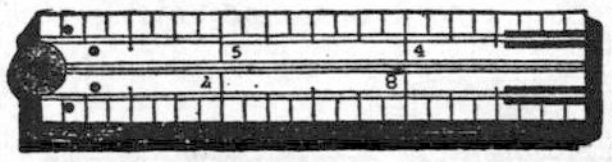

No. 12315. **One Foot Rule.** Round joint, middle plates, spaced 8ths and 16ths, four fold, ⅝ inch wide; weight, 3 oz. Price, each, **4c**; per doz...............40c

No. 12316. **Two Foot Rule.** Round joint, middle plates, spaced 8ths and 16ths, four fold, 1 inch wide, weight, 5 oz. Price, each, **5c**; per doz...............55c

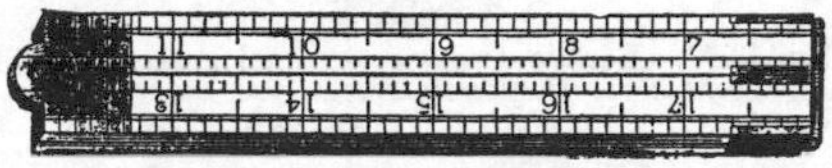

No. 12317. **One Foot Rule.** Square joints, middle plates, spaced 8ths and 16ths, four fold, ⅝ inch wide, weight, 4 oz. Price, each, **5c**; per doz...............54c

No. 12318. Two Foot Rule. Square joints, edge plates, spaced 8ths, 10ths, 12ths and 16ths, with drafting scale, four fold, 1 inch wide; weight, 6 oz. Price, each, **10c**; per doz...............$1.08

No. 12319. Two Foot Rule. Square joints, edge plates, spaced 8ths, 10ths and 16ths, and drafting scale, four fold, 1⅜ inches wide; weight, 6 oz. Price, each, **12c**; per doz...............$1.32

No. 12320. Two Foot Rule. Square joints, **full brass bound**, spaced 8ths, 10ths, 12th and 16ths, and drafting scale, four fold, 1 inch wide. Price, each, **24c**; per doz...............$2.64

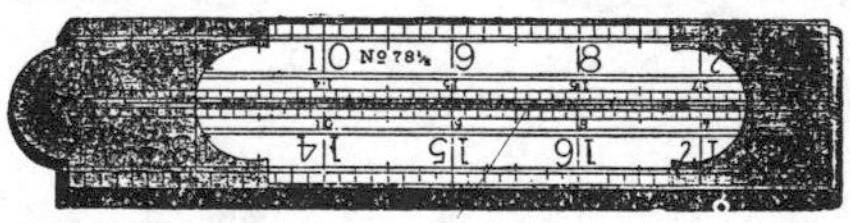

No. 12324. One Foot Rule. Arch joints, edge plates, spaced 8ths and 16ths, four fold, ⅝ inch wide. Price, each...............8c

No. 12325. One Foot Rule. Arch joints, full brass bound, spaced 8ths and 16ths, four fold, ⅝ inch wide. Price, each...............16c

No. 12326. Two Foot Rule. Arch joints, outside edges brass bound, spaced 8ths, 10ths, 12ths and 16ths, and drafting scale, four fold, 1 inch wide. Price, each...............18c

No. 12327. Two Foot Rule. Arch joint, full brass bound, spaced 8ths, 10ths, 12ths, 16ths, and drafting scale, four fold, 1 inch wide. Price, each...............22c

No. 12328. Two Foot Rule. Arch joint, full brass bound, spaced 8ths, 10ths, 16ths, and drafting scale, four fold, 1⅜ inches wide. Price, each...............27c

No. 12329. Two Foot Rule. Double arch joints, full brass bound, spaced 8ths, 10ths, 12ths and 16ths, drafting scale four fold, 1⅜ inches wide. **The best boxwood rule made.** Price each ...............32c

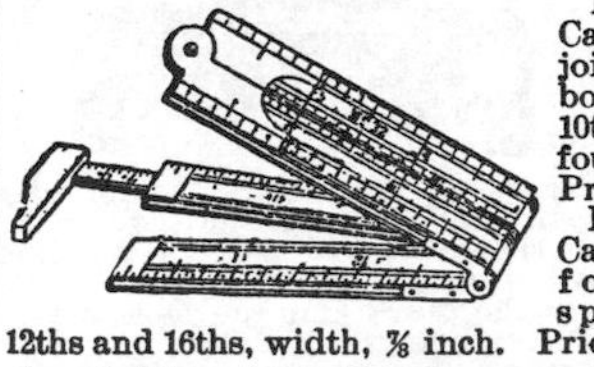

No. 12336. One Foot Caliper Rule. Arch joints, full brass bound, spaced 8ths, 10ths, 12ths and 16ths, four fold, width, 1 inch. Price, each...............27c

No. 12337. Six Inch Caliper Rule. Two fold square joints, spaced 8ths, 10ths, 12ths and 16ths, width, ⅜ inch. Price, each...............10c

## Architects' Rules with Beveled Edges.

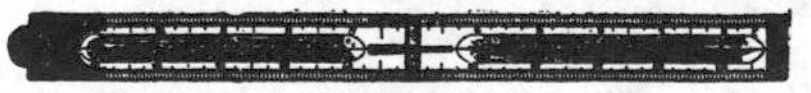

No. 12342. Two Foot Architects' Rule. Arch joint, edge plates, spaced 8ths, 10ths, 12ths and 16ths with inside beveled edges and architects' drafting scale, four fold, 1 inch wide. Price, each...............20c

## Slide Rule.

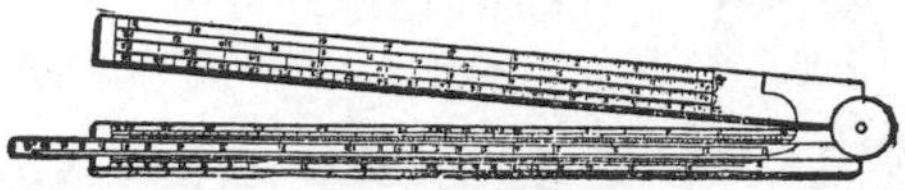

No. 12344. The old standard Slide Rule, two foot, two fold, arch joints bitted. Gunter's slide spaced 8ths, 10ths and 16ths inch, 100th of a foot drafting and octagonal scale, 1⅜ inches wide. Price, each...............25c

## Ivory Rules.

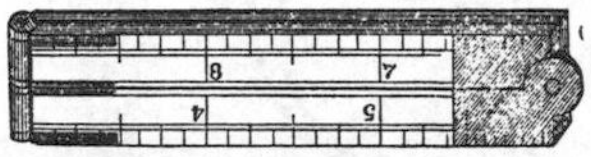

No. 12345. Ivory Rule, 1 foot, four fold, square joints, German silver edge plates as shown in cut, spaced 8ths and 16ths of an inch, ⅝ inch wide. Price each...............75c.

No. 12346. Ivory Rule, 1 foot, four fold, round joints, middle plates, spaced 8ths and 16ths of an inch, ⅝ inch wide. Price each...............50c.

No. 12347. Ivory Rule, 1 foot, four fold, square joints, German silver edge plates, spaced 8ths, 10ths, 12ths and 16ths of an inch, ¾ inch wide. Price each.......$1.00

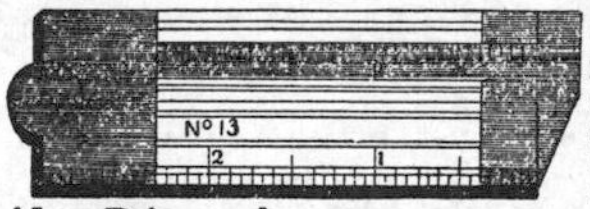

No. 12348. Ivory Caliper Rule, 6 inch, two fold, square joints, spaced 8ths, 10ths, 12ths and 16ths of an inch, ⅞ inch wide. Price each...............67c

No. 12349. Ivory Caliper Rule, 6 inch, two fold, square joints, German silver bound, spaced 8ths and 16ths of an inch, ⅞ inch wide. Price each...............$1.10

No. 12349½. Ivory Caliper Rule, 1 foot, four fold, square joints, German silver bound, spaced 8ths and 16ths of an inch, ⅝ inch wide. Price each.......$1.95

## Log Rules.

These Rules are made of the finest second growth hickory, the butt or first cut only being used. They are rived out and shaved down by hand, and no cross-grained stocks are used. The figures are burned on the wood. No amount of use in rain or snow will efface them.

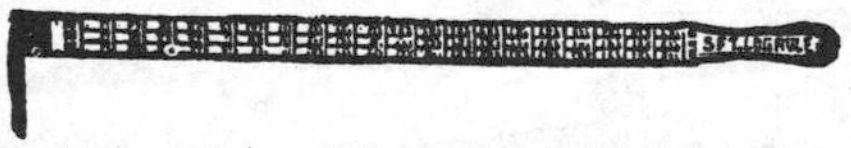

No. 12350. Scribner's Log Rule Solid Hook, figured to 48 inches, handle 8 inches. Price each...............$1.15

No. 12351. Doyle's Log Rule, same as above. Price each...............$1.15

## Board Rules.

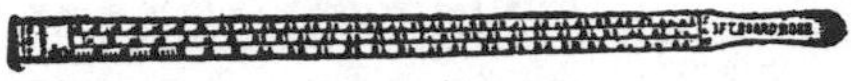

No. 12354. Inspectors' Board Rule, three tier, 3½ feet, extra heavy brazed heads (steel caps and brass shoulder). Price each...............$1.15

No. 12355. Inspectors' Board Rule, three tier, 3 feet, extra heavy brazed head. Price each...............$1.00

No. 12356. Octagon Walking Cane Board Rule, 3 feet, eight lines, Doyle scale only, brass head and end. Price each...............79c

## Measuring Tapes.

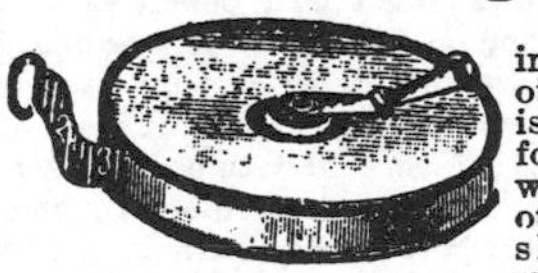

Brass bound case, folding handle with ½ inch oiled cotton tape. This is a good low priced tape for family use. Millwrights, surveyors and others who use line much should buy a higher priced one.

No. 12363. To measure 25 feet. Price, each ......20c
No. 12364. To measure 50 feet. Price, each ......25c
No. 12365. To measure 100 feet. Price, each ......45c

## Chesterman's Tape Line.

This Tape Line is well known as a durable, reliable, accurate and strong tape line. Wire is woven in with the linen, which prevents stretching. Has a heavy red leather case, folding handle, spaced in 12ths.

No. 12369. To measure 50 feet. Price, each....$1.95
No. 12370. To measure 66 feet. Price, each....2.25
No. 12371. To measure 100 feet. Price, each....3.15

## Steel Tape Lines.

No. 12374. Steel Tape Line, nickel plated, brass case, flush handle, flexible steel tape ⅜ inch wide.
To measure 50 feet. Price, each...............$3.00
To measure 75 feet. Price, each...............5.00
To measure 100 feet. Price, each...............6.40

## Pocket Tape Measures.

No. 12375. Pocket Tape nickel plated case; patent spring with stop, ¼ inch linen tape.
To measure 3 feet. Price, each...............35c
To measure 5 feet. Price, each ...............40c

When you build your House, we can save you enough on the
**Hardware, Sash, Doors, Blinds, Building Paper, Paint, Etc., . .**
to pay part of the carpenter's bill.

**We would rather lose a dollar than be the cause of a customer losing ten cents. We propose that you shall save money by dealing with us, and we are in a position to help you.**

## Calipers.

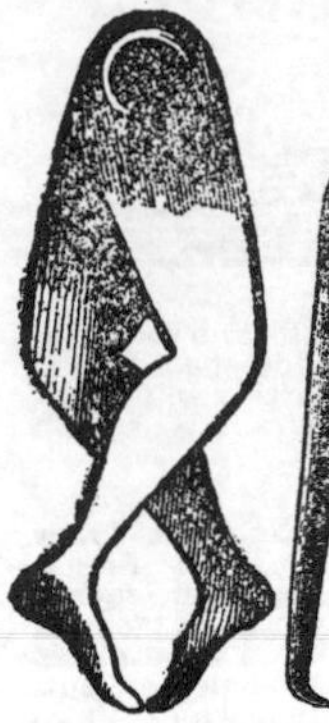
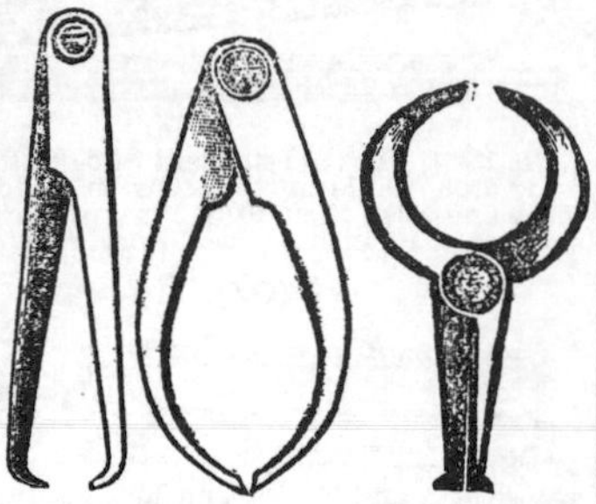

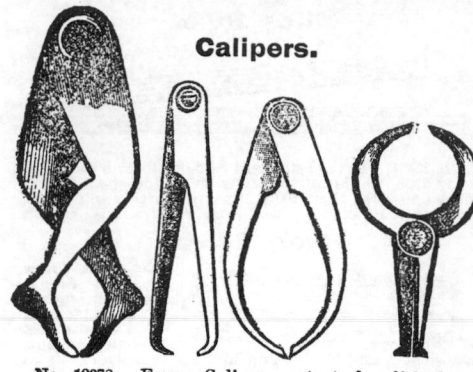

No. 12378. Fancy Caliper, cast steel polished, 2½ inches. Calipers inside or outside; weight, 3 oz. Price ........ **8c**

No. 12379. Inside Caliper, cast steel polished; length, 4 inches; weight, 4 oz. Calipers inside only. Price, **8c**

No. 12380. Inside Caliper, same as above; length, 6 inches; weight 5 oz. Price ........ **12c**

No. 12383. Outside Caliper, cast steel polished; length, 4 inches; weight, 4 oz. Price ........ **8c**

No. 12384. Outside Caliper, same as above; length, 6 inches; weight, 5 oz. Price ........ **12c**

No. 12385. Outside Caliper, same as above; length 8 inches; weight, 6 oz. Price ........ **15c**

No. 12388. Double Caliper, cast steel polished calipers inside and out; length, 4 inches; weight, 4 oz. Price ........ **11c**

No. 12389. Double Caliper, same as above. Length, 6 inches; weight, 5 oz. Price ........ **15c**

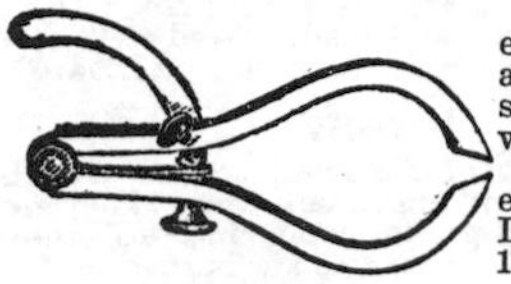

No. 12392. Wing Calipers, with adjusting spring and screw, polished cast steel. Length, 6 inches; weight, 6 oz. Price.. **15c**

No. 12393. Wing Calipers, same as above. Length, 8 inches; weight, 12 oz. Price........ **20c**

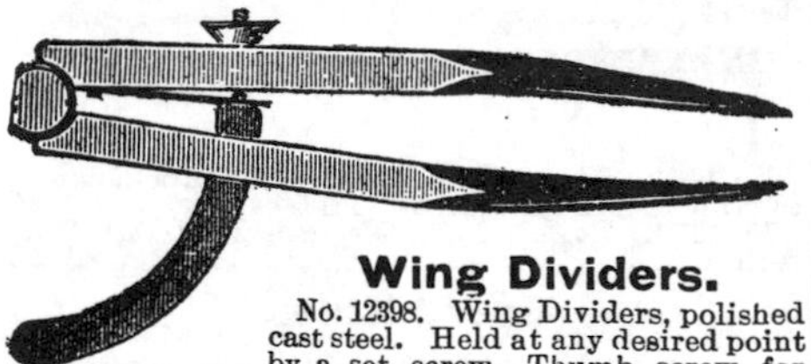

## Wing Dividers.

No. 12398. Wing Dividers, polished cast steel. Held at any desired point by a set screw. Thumb screw for slight and accurate adjustment not shown in cut.

| | | | |
|---|---|---|---|
| Size, inches, | 6 | 8 | 10 |
| Price, each, | $0.12 | .16 | .22 |
| Weight, ounces, | 6 | 8 | 12 |

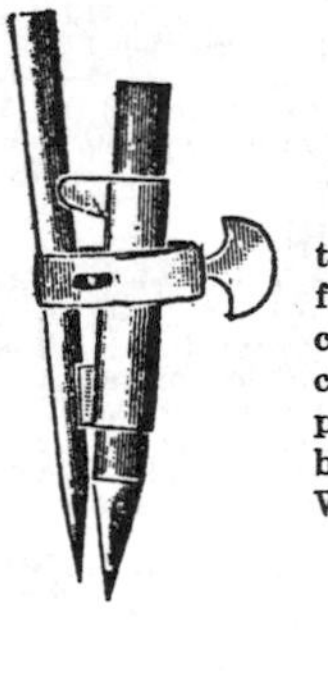

## Pencil Holders.

No. 12400. By means of this invention a common lead pencil can be fastened on one leg of any ordinary compass or divider; one screw clamps it in place. A short piece of pencil is furnished with each holder, but no compass or divider is given. Weight, 3 oz. Price each........ **18c**

## Trammel Points.

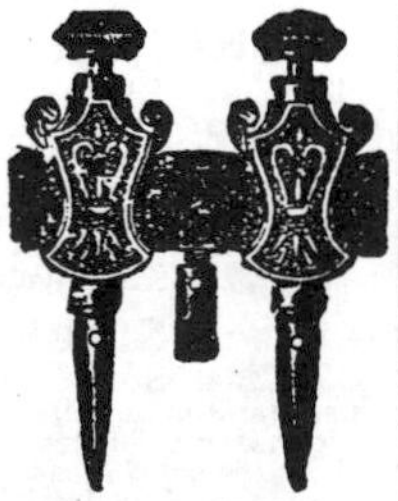

No. 12402. Stanley's Improved Trammel Points, bronze metal, steel points. The steel points are removable, and the pencil socket, which is given with each pair, can be substituted when desired. No. 2. Medium. Price, each........ **75c**

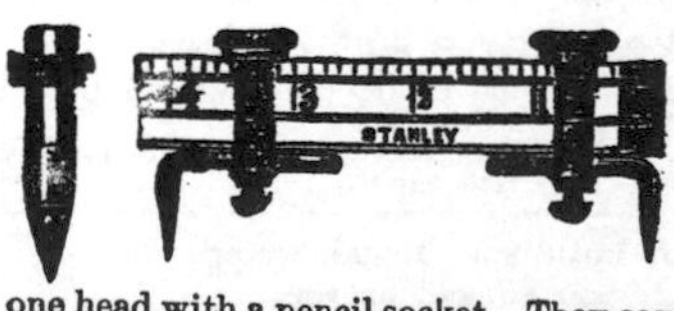

No. 12403. Rule Trammel Points. A set consists of 2 brass trammel heads, with movable steel points, and one head with a pencil socket. They can be attached to carpenters' rules of ordinary width, and on many kinds of work will take the place of regular trammel points, calipers or dividers, panel or marking gauges. Weight, 8 oz. Price, per set........ **36c**

## Marking Gauges.

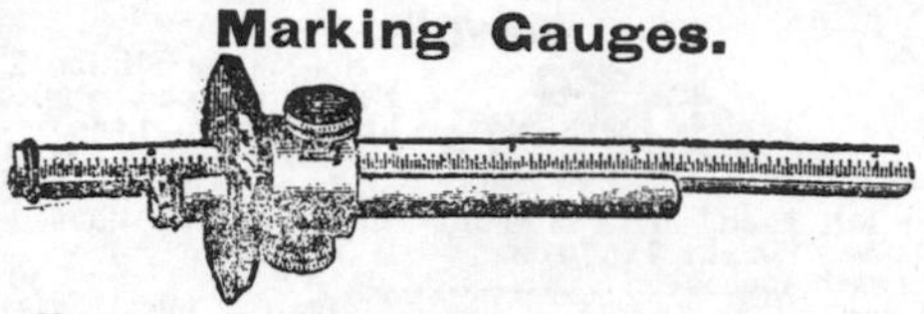

No. 12412. Barrett's combination marking and mortise Roller Gauge. Made entirely of metal. The marker is a revolving steel wheel, which will not follow the grain of the wood. Weight, 15 oz. Price, each.... **62c**

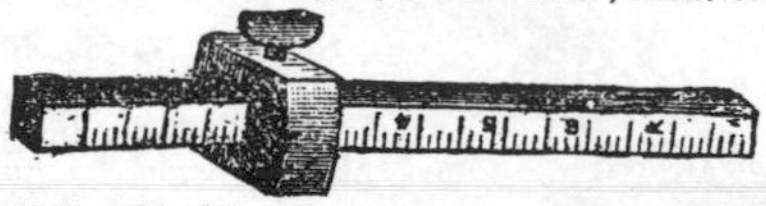

No. 12413. Marking Gauge, beechwood bar and head, boxwood thumb screw, marked bar, steel point. Weight, 7 oz. Price, each, **4c**; per doz........ **40c**

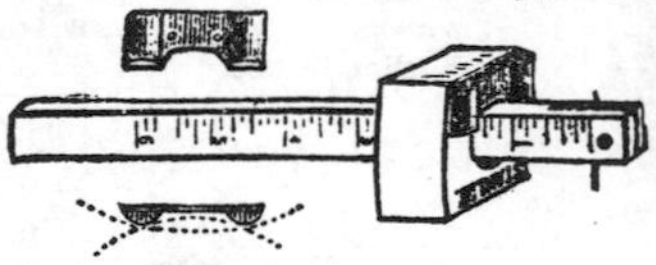

No. 12415. Improved marking gauge; will run a gauge line with accuracy, either straight or around curves of any degree, either concave or convex; beechwood, boxwood thumb screw, oval bar, marked in inches. Price, each........ **6c**

No. 12416. Improved marking Gauge, boxwood, brass thumb strew and shoe, plated head, adjustable steel point. Price, each........ **15c**

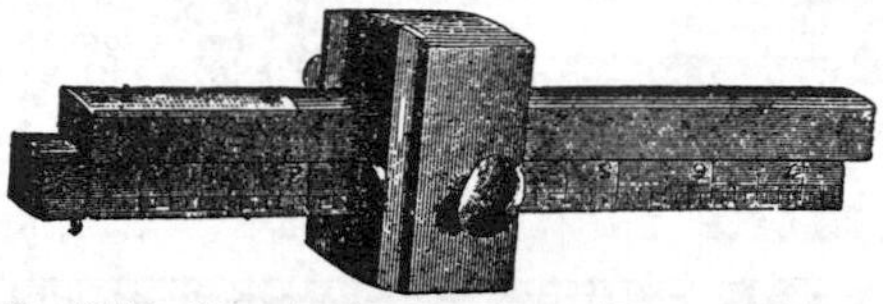

No. 12418. Double Gauge. A marking and mortise gauge combined, beechwood, polished boxwood thumb screw, marked in inches. Price, each........ **15c**

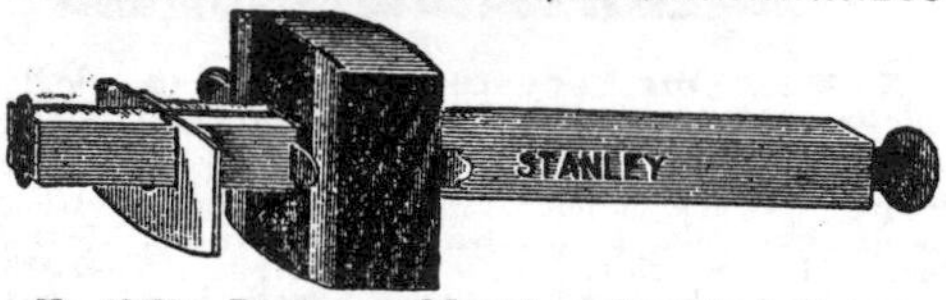

No. 12420. **Improved butt and rabbet Gauge.** The most convenient gauges for hanging doors, mortising, marking, etc. Weight, 15 oz. Price, each.... **80c**

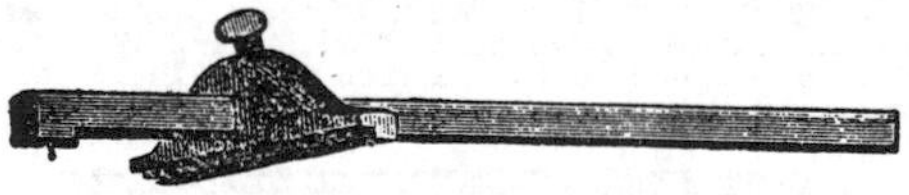

No. 12422. **Panel Gauge.** Beechwood, boxwood thumb screw, oval bar, 17 inches long. Price, each.. **10c**

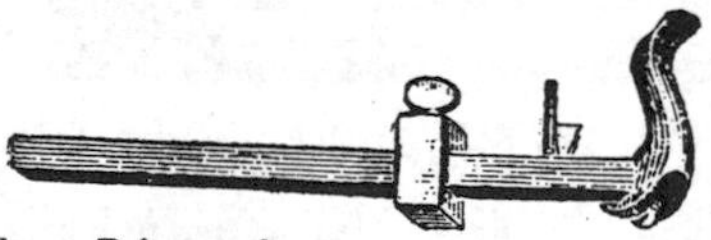

No. 12423. **Slitting Gauge.** Beechwood; handled with roller; cast steel slitter, 17 in. bar. Price, each........ **31c**

## Clapboard Gauge.

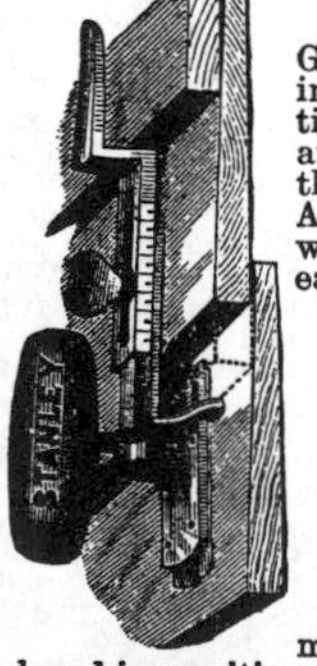

No. 12425. Clapboard or siding Gauge or holder is used as is shown in illustration. When in this position, press the handle over sidewise and it will be held securely. Two of them are as good as an extra man. Adjustable to lay clapboards to the weather any width desired. Price, each........ **32c**

## Clapboard Marker.

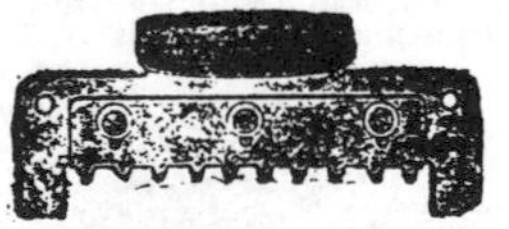

No. 12428. Clapboard Marker. By moving this tool half an inch (when placed in position as shown) it will make a full line across the clapboard exactly over the edge of the corner board. Saw to the mark and you have a perfectly close joint. Price, each........ **35c**

## Shingling Brackets.

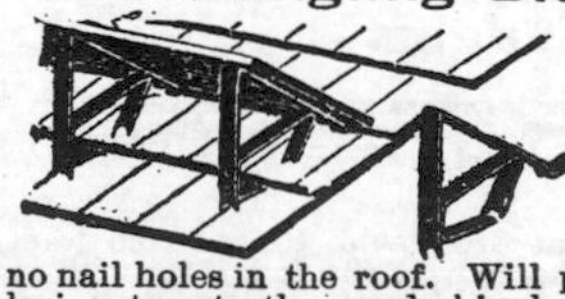

No. 12429. Shingling Brackets. The parts are of spring steel, firmly riveted together. **Light, Strong, Safe.** Quickly put up and taken down, leaving no nail holes in the roof. Will pay for themselves in laying twenty thousand shingles and last a lifetime. Price, each, **20c**; per doz........ **$2.25**

## Chalk Line, Reels and Awls.

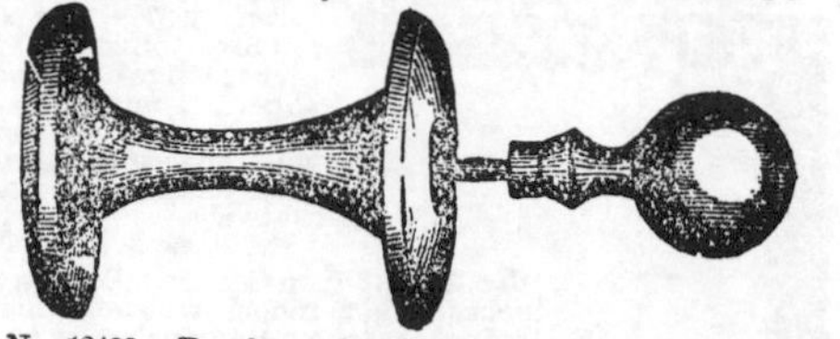

No. 12433. Beechwood Chalk Line, Reel and Awl. Weight, 6 oz. Each........ **5c**

## Chalk Lines.

No. 12435. Braided cotton Chalk Lines, in hanks of 18 feet each. One dozen hanks connected. Braided lines do not kink or snarl.

| | Small. | Medium. | Large. |
|---|---|---|---|
| Per hank........ | 2c | 3c | 4c |
| Per doz........ | 18c | 22c | 33c |

No. 12436. Common cotton Chalk Lines, in hanks of 18 feet each. One dozen hanks connected.

| | Small. | Medium. | Large. |
|---|---|---|---|
| Per hank........ | 2c | 3c | 4c |
| Per doz. hanks........ | 10c | 20c | 30c |

## Carpenters' Chalk.

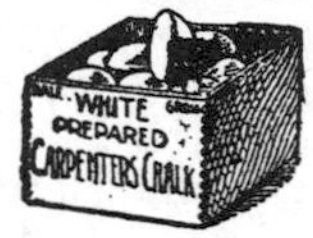


| | | Per doz. | Per box. |
|---|---|---|---|
| No. 12437. | White.. | **5c** | **27c** |
| No. 12438. | Red.... | **6c** | **30c** |
| No. 12439. | Blue... | **7c** | **35c** |

Six dozen in a box.

## Carpenters' Pencils.

No. 12440. Oval white wood Carpenters' Pencil, 12 inches long, with rule marked on it. Price, each, **3c**; per doz, **25c.**

No. 12441. Oval red cedar Carpenters' Pencil, 12 inches long. Extra quality lead. Price, each, **4c**; per doz, **40c.**

## PLANES.

The Genuine Bailey Planes, made by the Stanley Rule & Level Company, are so well and favorably known to mechanics **the world over,** that they need no recommendation from us. The cutter is stamped from a solid piece of the best quality of **English cast steel,** of equal thickness throughout, finely tempered and ground sharp ready for use. By means of a lever, located under the plane iron, and working sidewise, the cutting edge can easily be brought into a position exactly square with the bottom of the plane. The patents having expired, planes of same style and description are now made by various manufacturers and are sometimes offered as Bailey Pattern, or even for the genuine goods. We have designated such planes as **Imitation Bailey Planes,** as we want customers to perfectly understand what they are ordering. **Our Imitation Bailey Planes are made by a reliable firm, and will give satisfaction in every way.**

## Bench Planes.

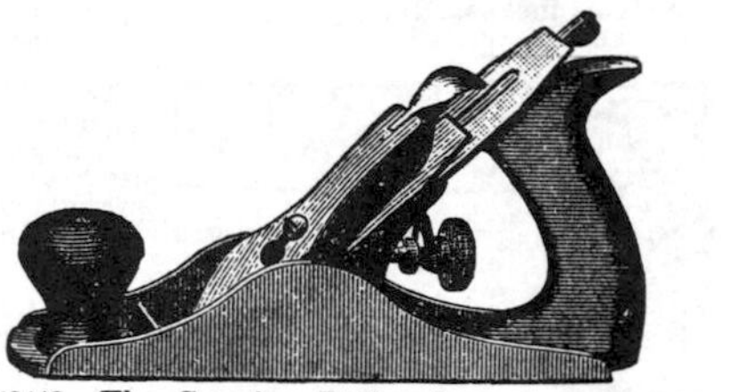

No. 12448. The Genuine Bailey Iron Smooth Plane No. 3. Length, 8 inches; 1¾ inch cutter. Weight, 3 lbs. Price, each........ **$1.14**

No. 12449. An imitation of the above plane. Weight, 3 lbs. Price, each........ **$1.08**

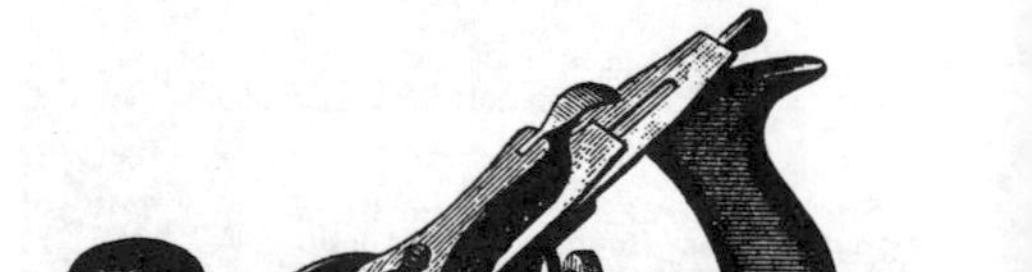

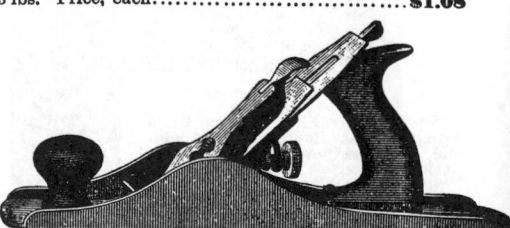

No. 12450. The Genuine Bailey Iron Jack Plane No. 5, Length, 14 inches; 2 inch cutter. Weight, 4¾ lbs. Price, each........ **$1.45**

No. 12451. An imitation of the above plane. Weight, 4¾ lbs. Price, each........ **$1.28**

No. 12452. The Genuine Bailey Iron Fore Plane No. 6. Length, 18 inches; 2⅜-inch cutter; weight, 7 lbs. Price, each........ **$1.81**

No. 12453. An imitation of the above plane; weight, 7 lbs. Price, each........ **$1.62**

No. 12454. The Genuine Bailey Iron Jointer Plane, No. 8; length, 24 inches; 2⅝-inch cutter; weight, 9¾ lbs. Price, each........ **$2.47**

No. 12455. An imitation of the above plane; weight, 9¾ lbs. Price, each........ **$2.25**

**We sell only such goods as are perfectly made and durable. We want the constant use of an article to give you as much satisfaction as its first appearance upon receipt.**

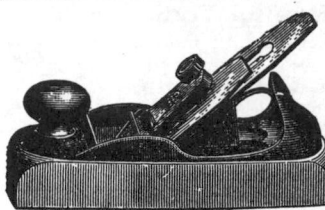

No. 12466. The Genuine Bailey Wood Smooth Plane, No. 22; length, 8 inches; 1¾-inch cutter; weight, 2¾ lbs. Price, each......**76c**

No. 12467. An imitation of the above plane; weight, 2¾ lbs. Price, each,**70c**

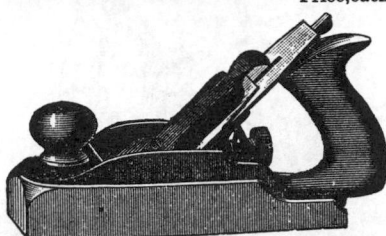

No. 12468. The Genuine Bailey Wood Smooth Plane, with handle, No. 35; length, 9 inches; 2-inch cutter; weight, 3½ lbs. Price, each......**95c**

No. 12469. An imitation of the above plane; weight, 3½ lbs. Price, each......**90c**

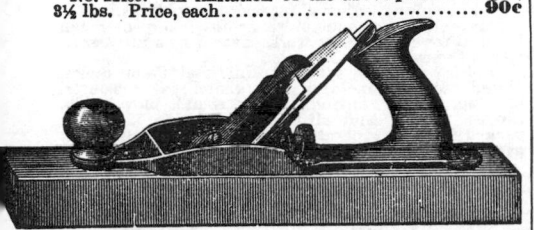

No. 12470. The Genuine Bailey Wood Jack Plane No. 27; length, 15 inches; 2⅜-inch cutter; weight, 4 lbs. Price, each......**96c**

No. 12471. An imitation of the above plane; weight, 4 lbs. Price, each......**90c**

No. 12472. The Genuine Bailey Wood Fore Plane, No. 29; length, 20 inches; 2⅜-inch cutter; weight, 5¾ lbs. Price, each......**$1.05**

No. 12473. An imitation of the above; weight, 5¾ lbs. Price, each......**$1.00**

No. 12474. The Genuine Bailey Wood Jointer Plane, No. 32; length, 26 inches; 2⅜-inch cutter; weight, 7¼ lbs. Price, each......**$1.23**

No. 12475. An imitation of the above plane; weight, 7¼ lbs. Price, each......**$1.15**

## Stanley Wood Planes.

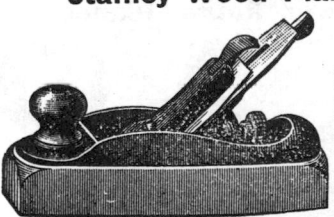

No. 12480. The Stanley Wood Smooth Plane No. 122; length, 8 inches, 1¾ inch cutter; weight, 2 lbs. Price—Each......**57c**

No. 12481. The Stanley Wood Smooth Plane, with handle, No. 135; length, 10 inches, 2⅛ inch cutter; weight, 3¼ lbs. Price, each......**76c**

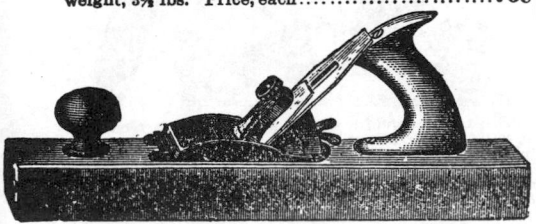

No. 12482. The Stanley Wood Jack Plane No. 127; length, 15 inches, 2¼ inch cutter, weight, 3½ lbs. Price, each......**78c**

No. 12483. The Stanley Wood Fore Plane No. 129; length, 20 inches, 2⅜ inch cutter; weight, 5 lbs. Price, each......**84c**

No. 12484. The Stanley Wood Jointer Plane No. 132; length, 26 inches, 2⅜ inch cutter; weight, 6 lbs. Price, each......**95c**

**Your money is as safe with us as in a bank.**

## Wood Bench Planes.

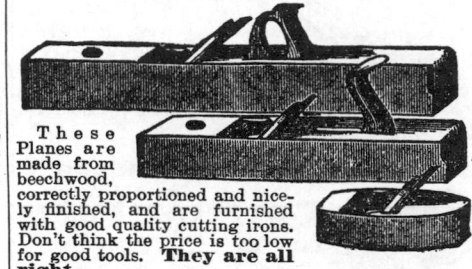

These Planes are made from beechwood, correctly proportioned and nicely finished, and are furnished with good quality cutting irons. Don't think the price is too low for good tools. **They are all right.**

No. 12494. Beechwood Smooth Plane; length, 8¼ inches; 2 inch double iron; weight, 2½ lbs. Price, each......**36c**

No. 12495. Beechwood Jack Plane; length 16 inches, 2¼ inch double iron; weight, 4½ lbs. Price, each, **40c**

No. 12496. Beechwood Fore Plane; length, 22 inches, 2½ inch double iron; weight, 6½ lbs. Price, each..**58c**

No. 12497. Beechwood Jointer Plane; length, 26 inches, 2½ inch double iron; weight, 9 lbs. Price, each ...**63c**

No. 12498. Set of 4 Planes, one each of the above wood bench planes. Per set......**$1.90**

## Block Plane.

No. 12500. Iron Block Plane; length, 3½ inches, 1 inch cutter. Not a toy, but a practical tool for light work; weight, 9 oz. Price, each......**8c**

No. 12501. Iron Block Plane; length, 5½ inches, 1¼ inch cutter; weight, 14 oz. Price, each ..**15c**

No. 12502. Iron Block Plane; length, 7½ inches. 1¾ inch cutter; weight, 1 lb. 14 oz. Price, each.....**22c**

No. 12503. Iron Block Plane (double ender); length, 8 inches, 1¾ inch cutter. By reversing the cutter and clamping wedge, as shown by dotted lines in cut, this plane can be made to plane close up into corners; weight, 1 lb. 14 oz. Price, each......**30c**

## Bailey's Block Planes, with Adjustable Mouth.

These planes are made by the Stanley Rule & Level Co. All have the lateral adjustment to set the cutting iron square with the face of the plane. The advantage of the adjustable mouth is that the mouth of plane may be made larger or smaller for different kinds of work.

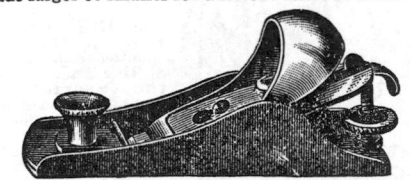

No. 12525. Bailey's patent iron Block Plane. Length, 8 inches, 1¾ inch cutter. Adjustable cutter, adjustable mouth. Weight, 1 lb. 10 oz. Price, each......**60c**

No. 12526. Same shape and adjustments as above, 7 inches long, 1¾ inch cutter. Weight, 1 lb. 14 oz. Price, each......**65c**

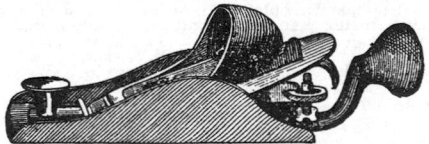

No. 12527. Bailey's Block Plane. Adjustable cutter, adjustable mouth, rosewood handle. Length, 6 inches, with 1¾ inch cutter. Price, each......**70c**

No. 12528. Bailey's Block Plane. Same as above. Length, 7 inches, with 1¾ inch cutter. Price, each..**75c**

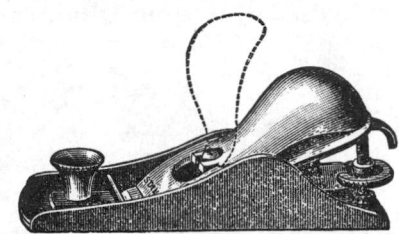

This plane has a knuckle joint in the cap, and placing the cap in position clamps the cutter securely in its seat. Has nickel-plated trimmings and all adjustments same as above planes.

No. 12532. Knuckle Joint Plane, as above. Length, 6 inches, 1¾ inch cutter. Weight, 1 lb. 10 oz. Price, each......**70c**

No. 12533. Knuckle Joint Plane, as above. Length, 7 inches, 1¾ inch cutter. Weight, 1 lb. 14 oz. Price, each......**75c**

## Plane Irons.

No. 12540. **Plane Irons for Bailey or Stanley Planes.**

In ordering these plane irons BE SURE to state the **manufacturers' number of the plane for which they are wanted.**

| Size, inches, | 1¾ | 2 | 2¼ | 2⅜ | 2⅝ |
|---|---|---|---|---|---|
| Cut Irons, each, | 15c | 16c | 19c | 23c | 42c |
| Double Irons, each, | | 33c | 35c | 40c | 42c |

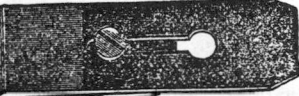

No. 12541. Extra quality Plane Irons for wood bench planes. Best of material and workmanship, and finely tempered.

| Size, inches, | 1¾ | 2 | 2¼ | 2½ |
|---|---|---|---|---|
| Cut Irons, each, | 10c | 13c | 15c | 18c |
| Double Irons, | 24c | 25c | 27c | 32c |

## Cutters for Block Planes.

No. 12543. Steel Cutter for iron block plane No. 12443 or No. 12444. Price, each......**8c**

No. 12544. Steel Cutter for iron block plane No. 12445 or No. 12447. Price, each......**10c**

No. 12545. Steel Cutter for iron block plane Nos. 12525, 12526, 12532 and 12533. Price, each......**12c**

Be sure to state for which plane cutter is wanted.

## Stanley's Rabbet and Block Plane.

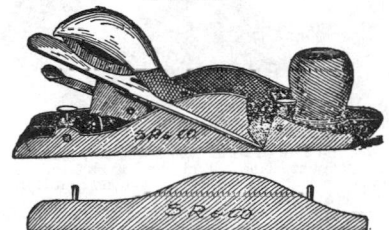

A detachable side will easily change this tool from a Block Plane to a Rabbet Plane, or vice versa. The cutter is set on a skew.

No. 12549. Rabbet and Block Plane, with detachable side, 7 inches in length, 1¾ inch cutter. Price......**85c**

## Bench Plane Handles.

No. 12550. Jack Plane Handles, beechwood. Each, **3c**

No. 12551. Fore or Jointer Plane Handles, beechwood. Each......**5c**

## Stanley's Adjustable Planes.
### Stanley's Circular Plane.

No. 12570. Stanley's Adjustable Circular Plane, with flexible steel face, which, by turning the knob on the front of the plane, can be easily shaped to any required arc, either concave or convex. Weight, 3¾ lbs. Price, each......**$1.52**

## Stanley's Adjustable Chamfer Plane.

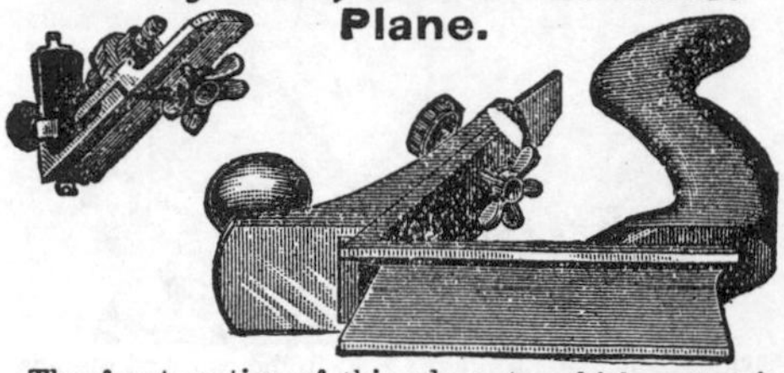

The front section of this plane, to which cutter is attached, can be moved up and down. It can be firmly secured to the rear section, at any desired point, by means of a thumb screw. Without the use of any other tool this plane will do perfect chamfer, or stop chamfer work of all ordinary widths. When the faces of both sections are even it can be used as an ordinary bench plane.

No. 12571. Adjustable Chamfer Plane, as above. Length, 8 inches; 1⅝ inch cutter. Weight, 3 lbs. Price, each ....... **$1.18**

No. 12572. Beading Attachment for above chamfer plane. For beading or molding a chamfer an additional attachment can be furnished, with six cutters, sharpened at both ends, including a large variety of ornamental forms. This attachment is not included with above plane. Price, for attachment ....... **60c**

## Stanley's Improved Rabbet Plane.

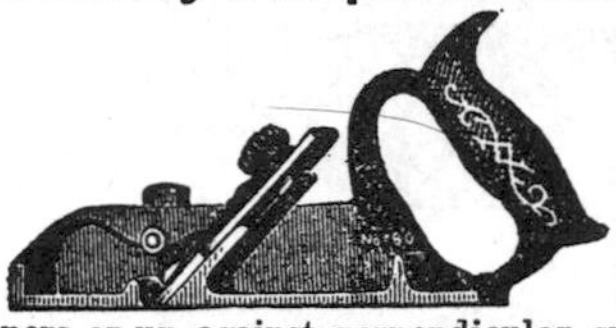

No. 12573. Stanley's Improved Rabbet Plane. This plane will lie perfectly flat on either side, and can be used with right or left hand equally well while planing into corners or up against perpendicular surfaces; has spur, which can be removed when not wanted. Length, 8 inches; 1½ inch cutter; weight, 3½ lbs. Price, each ....... **60c**

## Stanley's Duplex Rabbet Plane and Fillister.

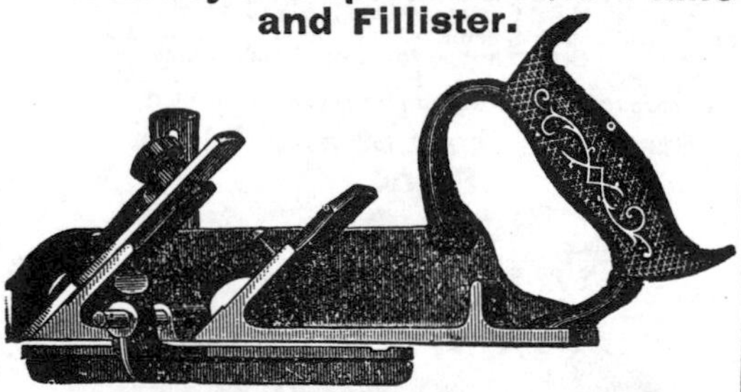

Remove the arm to which the fence is secured and a Handled Rabbet Plane is had, and with two seats for the cutter, so that the tool can be used as a Bull-Nose Rabbet if required.

The arm to which the fence is secured can be screwed into either side of the stock, thus making a superior right or left hand fillister with adjustable spur and depth gauge.

No. 12574. Duplex Rabbet Plane and Fillister as above. Length, 8½ inches; 1½ inch cutter; weight, 3¼ lbs. Price, each ....... **89c**

## Stanley's Adjustable Tonguing and Grooving Plane.

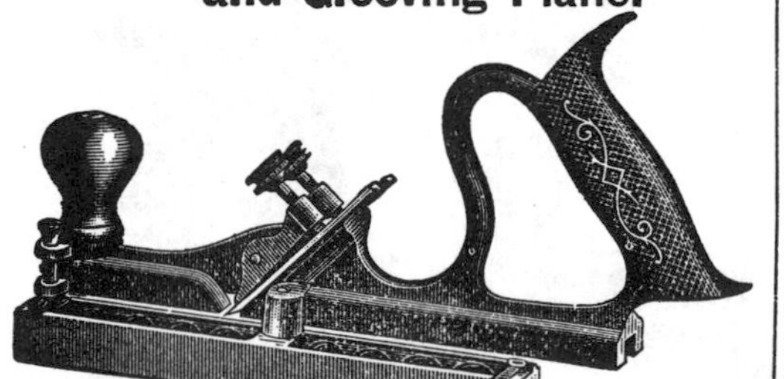

These planes have two separate cutters a suitable distance apart. When the guide or fence is set as shown above, both cutters work and a tongue can be made.

The fence is hung on a pivot, and can be swung around end for end. This movement covers one of the cutters, and also furnishes a guide for grooving an exact match for the tongue.

In working thicker than 1 inch stuff, with No. 48 Plane, or ½ inch stuff with No. 49, place the extra wide cutter in right hand side of the plane. The tongue and the groove will be equally removed from the center of the edges, on extra thick or thin boards, but a perfect match will be made.

No. 12575. Tonguing and Grooving Plane (commonly called Match Plane), as above, which will match board of any thickness from ¾ to 1¼ inches thick. (No. 48.) Weight, 2¾ lbs. Price, each ....... **$1.48**

No. 12576. Tonguing and Grooving Plane, as above, which will match board any thickness from ⅜ to ¾ inch. (No. 49.) Weight, 2¾ lbs. Price, each ....... **$1.50**

## Stanley Bull-Nose Rabbet Plane.

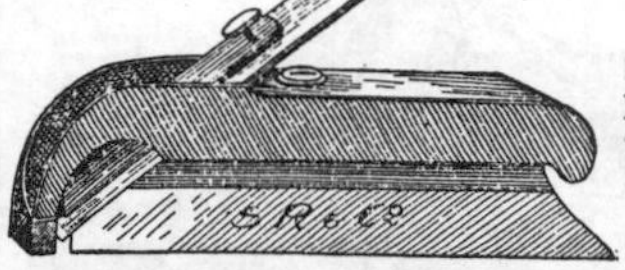

No. 12577. Iron Stock, 4 inches in length, 1 inch cutter. Price, each ... **20c**

## Stanley's Side Rabbet Plane.

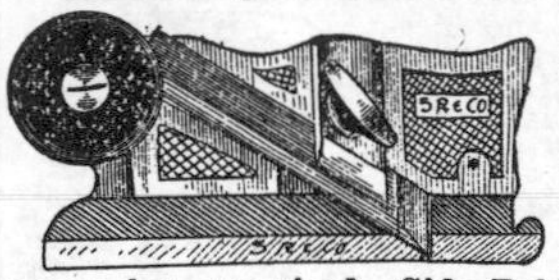

No. 12578. A convenient tool for side-rabbeting and trimming dados, mouldings and grooves of all sorts. A reversible nose-piece will give the tool a form by which it will work close up into corners when required. Side Rabbet Plane, 4 inches in length, price, each ....... **75c**

## Stanley's Adjustable Beading Plane.

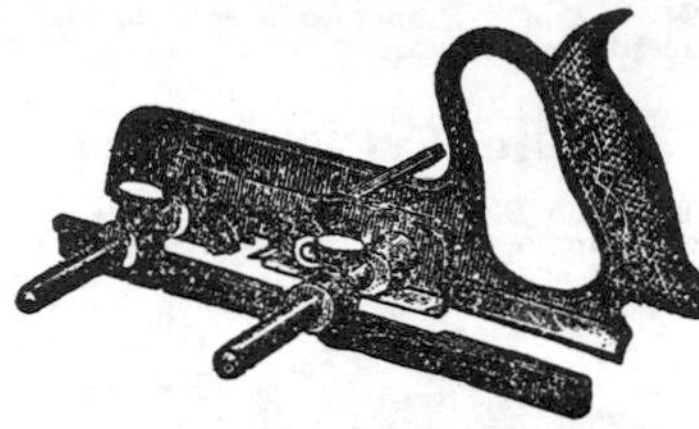

No. 12579. Patent Adjustable Beading Plane. This plane will do all the work for which 14 common wood bead planes would be required. Has spur cutter for use when beading across the grain. By adjustment of the fence center beading can be done any distance up to 5 inches from the edge of a board. Price, complete, including 7 bits, sizes ⅛, 3/16, ¼, 5/16, ⅜, 7/16, ½ inch. Price, each ....... **$2.30**

## Stanley's Patent Adjustable Beading, Rabbet and Slitting Plane.

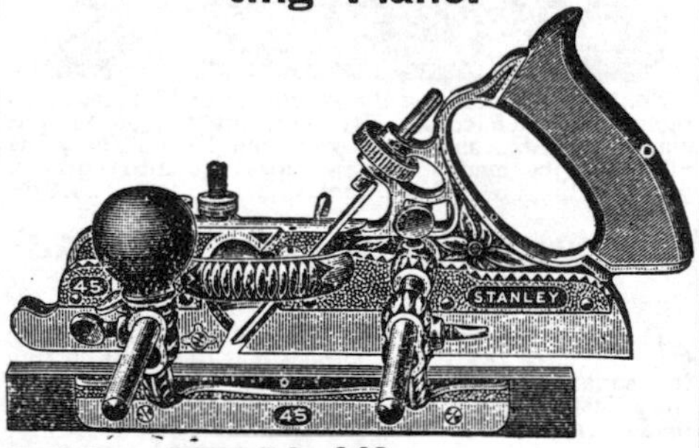

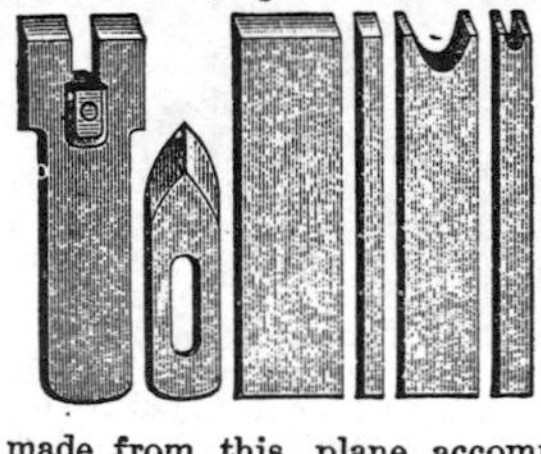

No. 12583. Stanley's Patent Adjustable Beading Rabbet and Slitting Plane. This is **the favorite** with first class carpenters, and in each of its several forms will do first class work, even in the hands of an ordinary mechanic. Directions for forming the different tools which can be made from this plane accompany each plane, and are easily understood by any one of ordinary intelligence. This plane embraces (1) beading and center beading plane; (2) rabbet and fillister; (3) dado; (4) plow; (5) matching plane; (6) sash plane, and (7) a superior slitting plane. Each plane has seven beading tools (⅛, 3/16, ¼, 5/16, ⅜, 7/16, and ½ inch), ten plow and dado bits (⅛, 3/16, ¼, 5/16, ⅜, 7/16, ½, ⅝, ¾, and ⅞ inch), a slitting blade, a tonguing tool, and a sash tool. Weight, 6¼ lbs. Price, complete with tools as above. Each ....... **$4.60**

## Extras.

The following tools can be used with above plane, but are not included in above combination:

## Hollows and Rounds.

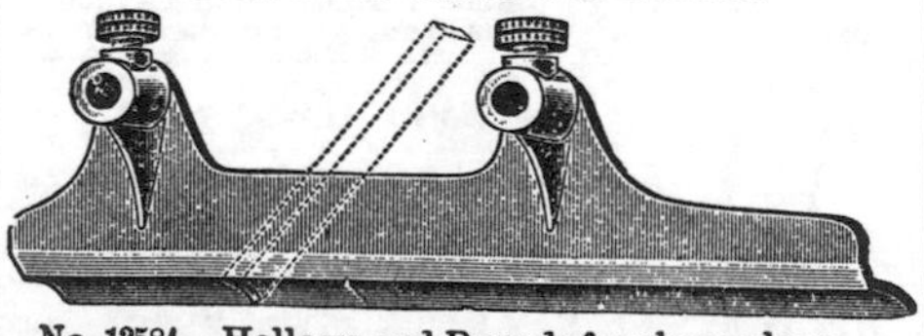

No. 12584. Hollows and Rounds for above plane.

| No. | 6 | 8 | 10 | 12 |
|---|---|---|---|---|
| Cutter, width, inches | ½ | ⅝ | ¾ | 1 |
| Works, circle, inches | ¾ | 1 | 1¼ | 1½ |
| Price, per pair | $0.88 | .88 | .88 | .88 |

## Nosing Tool.

No. 12585. Nosing Tool, 1¼ inch (attach same as above). Each ....... **60c**

## Reeding Tools.

No. 12586. Size of beads, either ⅛, 3-16 or ¼ inch, are same price. State size wanted when ordering.

| No. beads | 2 | 3 | 4 | 5 |
|---|---|---|---|---|
| Price, each | $0.20 | .30 | .40 | .50 |

## Stanley's Patent Universal Plane.

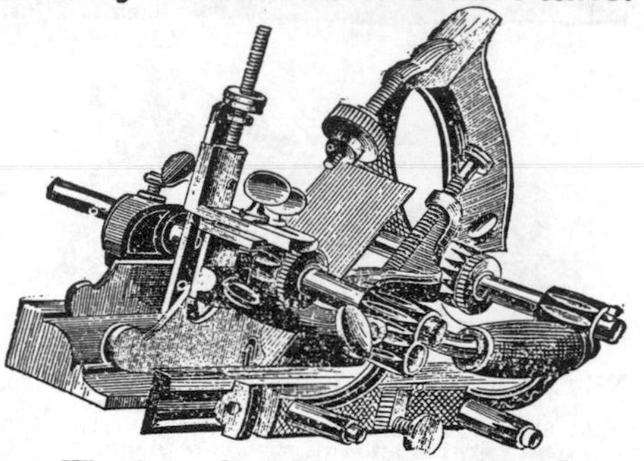

[The plane, adjusted for making moldings.]

This tool, in the hands of an ordinary carpenter, can be used for all lines of work covered by a full assortment of so-called fancy planes.

No. 12587. Stanley's Patent Universal Plane, nickel plated, including molding plane, match, sash, chamfer, beading, reeding, fluting, hollow, round, plow, dado, rabbet, fillister and slitting plane, with 52 cutters packed in four separate cases and the whole outfit packed in a neat wooden box. Price, complete.. **$9.30**

## Hand Beader.

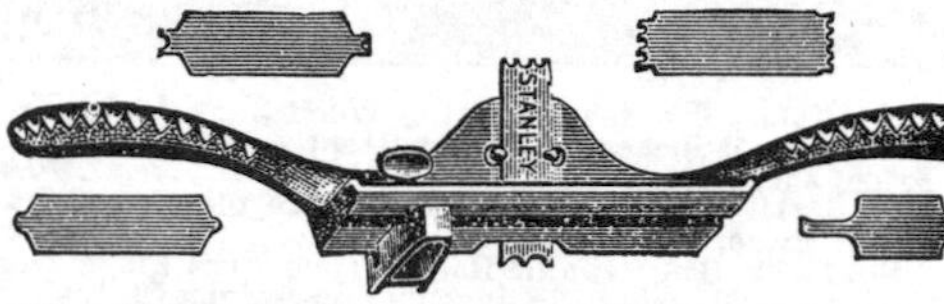


No. 12590. Stanley's Universal Hand Beader, for beading, reeding or fluting straight or irregular surfaces and for all kinds of light routering, with a square gauge for straight work and an oval gauge for curved work. Both ends of the cutters are sharpened, thus embracing in a compact form six ordinary sizes of beads, four sets of reeds, two fluters and a double router iron (size ⅛ and ¼ inch). Weight, 1 lb. 10 oz. Price, complete as above, nickel plated ....... **65c**

## Stanley's Router Planes.

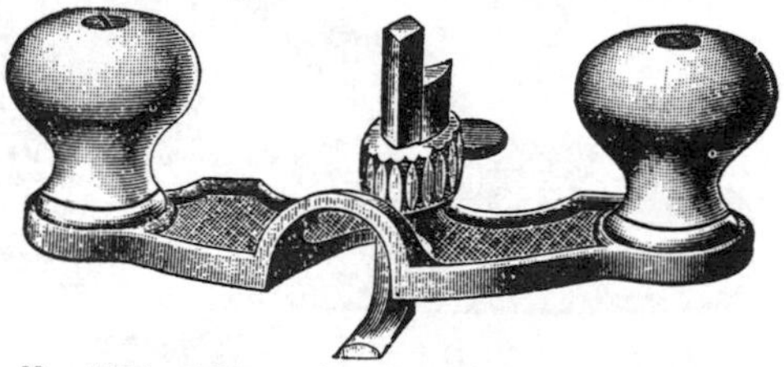

No. 12594. This tool will smooth the bottom of grooves, panels or all depressions below the general surface of any wood work, and will rapidly router out mortises for sash, frame, pulleys, etc. The bits can also be clamped to the backside of the upright post and outside of the stock; in this position they will plane into corners which can not be easily reached with any other tool; has iron stock and steel bits (¼ and ½ inch). Price, complete ....... **88c**

## Scraper Plane.

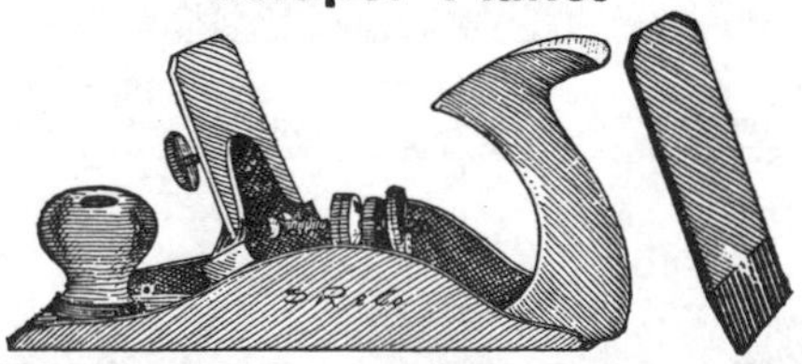

This tool is used for scraping and finishing veneers or cabinet-work. It can be used equally well as a tooth plane; and will do excellent work in scraping off old paint and glue.

No. 12595. Adjustable Scraper, 9 inches, 3 in. cutter ....... **$1.15**

Cutters, for veneer scraping ....... **.15**

Cutters, for toothing, Nos. 22, 28, 32 (22, 28 or 32 teeth per in.) ....... **.18**

## Stanley's Improved Wood Scraper.

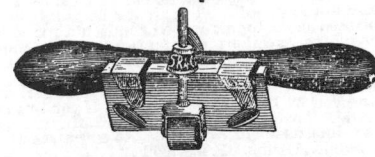

This Scraper can be adjusted to any desired pitch; and may be worked toward or from the person using it. The roller acts as a support to relieve the strain on the wrist and hands of the workman. The handle can be detached for working into corners.

No. 12596. Scraper, with handle and roller, 4 in. blade..................................................**88c**
Cast steel blades, for above Scraper..........**20c**

## Miscellaneous Planes.
### Hollows and Rounds.

No. 12620.
No.   1 2 3 4 5 6
Works. ¼ ⅜ ½ ⅝ ¾ ⅞ in. Per pair....**54c**

No. 12621.
No.    7    9
Works,   1   1¼ in.
Per pair.........**60c**

No. 12622.
No. 11, works 1½ in.
Per pair.........**70c**

**We do not break pairs.**

No. 12622½. Set of 9 pairs of Hollow and Rounds, one pair each of the above size. Per set.............**$5.10**

### Nosing Planes.

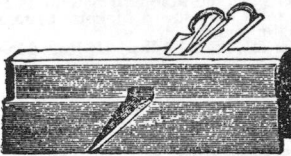

No. 12623. Nosing Plane for steps to work ⅞, 1, 1⅛ or 1¼ inch; any one size.
Each.........**64c**
No. 12624. To work 1⅜ or 1½ inch; any one size.
Each.........**70c**

### Molding Planes.

No. 12625. Quarter round Plane. The lower part of cut shows shape of molding made with this plane.

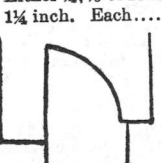

Either ½ or ⅝ inch. Each..**28c**
Either ¾, ⅞ or 1 inch. Each.**35c**
1¼ inch. Each..............**40c**

No. 12626. Quarter round with fence; lower part of cut shows shape of molding made with this plane.
Either ½ or ¾ inch. Each..**43c**
Either ⅞ or 1 inch. Each..**49c**

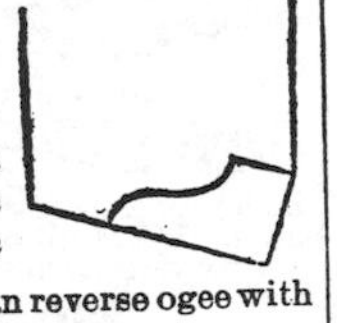

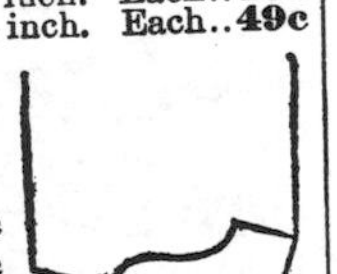

No. 12627. Roman reverse ogee.
Either ⅜, ½ or ⅝ inch. Each..**40c**
Either ¾, ⅞ or 1 inch. Each....**45c**
1¼ inch. Each.................**54c**

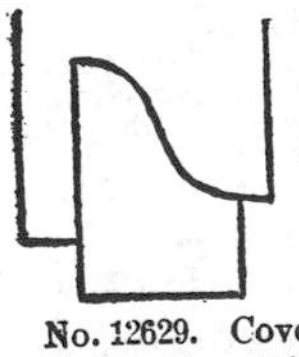

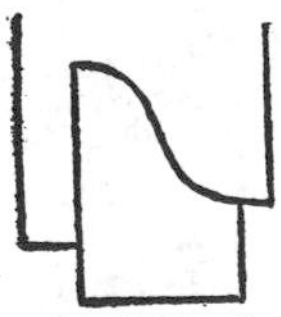

No. 12628. Roman reverse ogee with fence.
Either ½ or ⅝ inch. Each.....**43c**
Either ¾, ⅞ or 1 inch. Each..**48c**

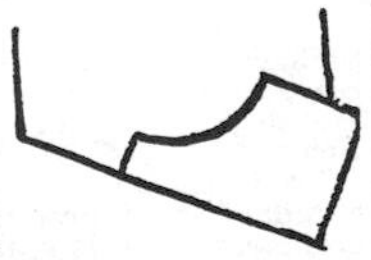

No. 12629. Cove Plane.
Either ½ or ¾ inch. Each..**27c**
Either ⅞ or 1 inch. Each..**35c**

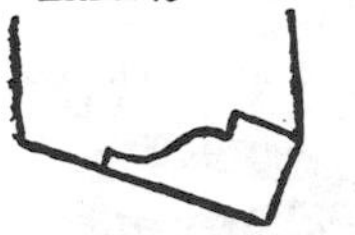

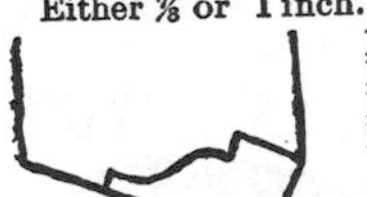

No. 12630. Ogee Plane.
Either ⅜, ½, ⅝, ¾, ⅞ or 1 inch.
Each........................**35c**
Either 1¼ or 1½ inch. Each..**46c**

No. 12636. Side bead Plane, single boxed.
Either ⅛, 3-16, ¼, 5-16, ⅜ or ½ inch.
Each........................**28c** 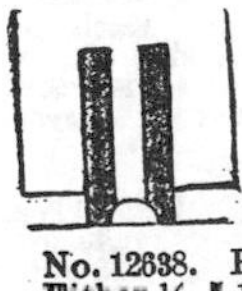
No. 12637. Center bead Plane, double boxed.
Either ⅛, 3-16, ¼, 5-16, ⅜ or ½ inch.
Each........................**33c**

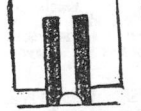 

No. 12638. Reeding Planes.
Either ¼, 5-16 or ⅜ inch; cuts 2 beads.
Price, each, any one size..**$1.03**

## Panel Plows.

No. 12644. Beechwood Panel Plow, Handled. Screw stop and arms, complete with set of eight cast steel bits.
Price, each..................................**$3.25**
No. 12646. Boxwood or Rosewood Panel Plow, Handled, boxwood arms and fence, complete with set of eight cast steel bits.
Price, each..................................**$5.50**

## Sash Planes.

No. 12648. Adjustable Sash Plane Screw Arms, boxed, to cut bevel or ovalo molding. State which is wanted in your order.
Each...**$1.20**

## Rabbet Planes.

No. 12650. Skew Rabbet Plane, either ½, ⅝, ¾, ⅞ or 1 inch.
Each.............**33c**

Size, inches,   1¼    1½    1¾     2
Each,     $0.37   .40   .45   .59
No. 12651. Jack Rabbet Plane, with handle and spur cutter, either 1½ or 2 inch.
Price, each........................**$1.00**

## Special Notice.

If you don't see what you want, ask for it. We advertise here the Planes we sell most, but can furnish anything in the plane line at correspondingly low prices if it's to be had in this market.

## Jointer Gauges.

No. 12654. Jointer Gauges; an invention to attach to an ordinary jointer plane. It holds the face of the plane at any desired angle, so to joint edge of board either square or at any bevel desired. No trouble to get edge of lumber "out of wind" when you use this gauge. Weight, 2¼ lbs.
Price, each........................**$1.20**

## Cabinet Scraper.

No. 12660. Cabinet Scraper, a sheet of finely tempered saw steel about 3x5 inches.
Price, each........................**6c**

## Sand Paper.

No. 12664. We carry the following numbers in stock: Nos. 00, 0, ½, 1, 1½, 2 and 3; Nos. 1 and 1½ are commonly used. No. 00 is the finest and No. 3 coarsest. State numbers wanted when ordering.
Price, per sheet, **1c**; per bundle of 24 sheets.....**15c**

## Emery Cloth.

No. 12665. We carry same numbers as sand paper, except the No. 3, which is not made.
Price, per sheet......................................**3c**
Per bundle of 24 sheets...........................**48c**

## Men's Overshirts...

and *FURNISHING GOODS* of every description in the complete department devoted to that line of goods. Refer to pages 206 to 249.

## Axes.

We offer you a line of Axes which are acknowledged by all to be the standard of the world. We know there is no better made.

No. 12685. The Kelly Axe. It's the shape and good cutting qualities which have made this one of the most popular axes in the market. It is made of the finest steel, hand-hammered, tempered, and tested before leaving the factory. The blade is so shaped it will cut deepest but will not bind in the timber. It will burst the chip, and will not become stubbed after grinding. It has a taper eye which binds the handle. We have them in all weights, from 3 to 5 lbs.
Price, each.................**48c**
Doz....................**$5.62**

## Hunt's Axe.

No. 12686. The genuine old reliable Hunt's Axe. Northwestern pattern like cut. Weights are from 3 to 5 lbs.
Price, each..................**60c**
Doz.....................**$6.00**

No. 12689. Handled Axe. A good axe all complete, with handle put in. It weighs from 3¼ to 4¼ lbs. Handle not included in weight.
Each....**60c**
Doz....**$6.84**

No. 12692. Boy's Axe. Give the boys a chance. Boy's Axe complete with handle; cast steel; gold bronzed. Weight, 2½ lbs. Length of handle, 26 inches.
Price, each........................**45c**
Doz..................................**$4.80**

## Double Bitted Axe.

No. 12693. Kelly's well-known Double Bitted Axe. Same workmanship and material as No. 12685. Weights are from 3½ to 5½ lbs.
Price, each........................**75c**
Doz..................................**$8.75**

## Hunter's Axe.

No. 12694. An axe-shaped Hatchet, all complete, with handle. Weight, 1¼ lbs. Handle not included in weight. Length of handle, 16 inches.
Price, each..................**40c**

## Axe Handles.

No. 12698. Octagon hand shaved, all white, second growth hickory. Selected and oiled, 36 inches long. The best axe handle made. Price, each, **25c**; per doz........................**$2.70**
No. 12699. Oval shaved, second growth hickory, 36 inches long. A first rate handle. Each, 20c; per doz........................**$2.16**
No. 12700. Extra turned hickory, second growth, 36 inches long. Each, 18c; per dozen.............**$2.00**
No. 12701. No. 2 turned hickory, 36 inches long. Each, 10c; per doz........................**$1.10**
No. 12702. Double Bitted Axe Handle. Shaved hickory. Second growth, 36 inches long. Each, 20c; per doz........................**$2.16**

## Boys' Axe Handles.

No. 12703. Handles for boys' axe. Turned hickory, 28 inches long. Each, 20c; per doz..............**$2.16**

## Axe Handle Wedge.

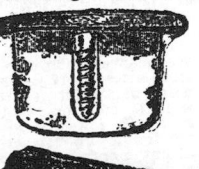

No. 12709. So well known description is not necessary. Weighs 5 oz. Each, **3c**; per doz.........................**38c**

## Wood Wedges.

No. 12710. Solid cast steel wood wedges. Weight, 4 lbs., each, **16c**. Weight, 5 lbs., each.........**20c**

## Beetle Rings.

No. 12712. Wrought Iron Beetle Rings, made of flat iron 1 inch wide. 3-16 inch thick.

| Diameter, inches, | 4½ | 5 | 6 |
|---|---|---|---|
| Weight, lbs., | 1 | 1½ | 2¼ |
| Price, each, | 10c | 15c | 20c |

## Hatchets.

All hatchets sold by us have handles, but weight of handle is not included when we state weight of hatchet. The cheapest hatchet we sell is a good reliable tool, and the higher priced ones are only superior in finish.

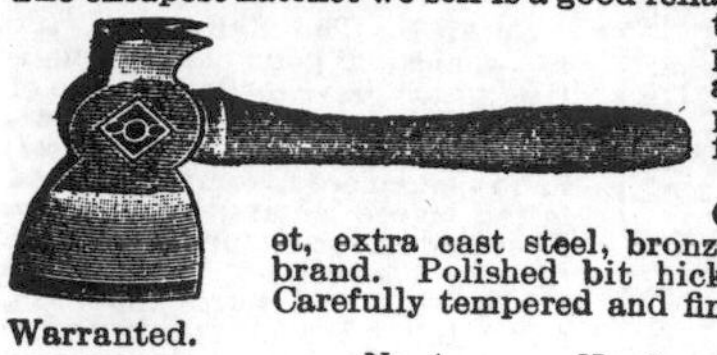

No. 12716. Claw Hatchet, extra cast steel, bronzed. Y and P brand. Polished bit hickory handle. Carefully tempered and finely finished. Warranted.

| | No. 1. | No. 2. | No. 3. |
|---|---|---|---|
| Width, inches, | 3½ | 4 | 4½ |
| Weight, | 1 lb. 3 oz. | 1 lb. 9 oz. | 1 lb. 15 oz |
| Price, each, | $0.42 | .45 | .48 |

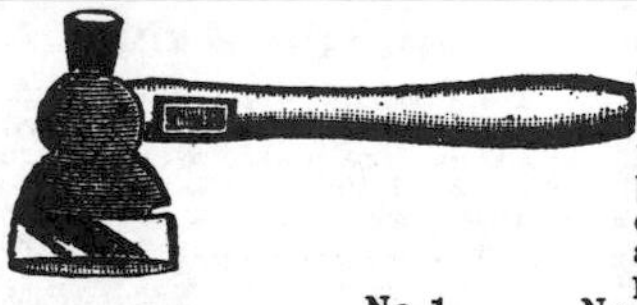

No. 12718. Shingling Hatchets, Y and P brand, common pattern, extra cast steel, bronzed, polished bit, hickory handle, finely finished and carefully tempered.

| | No. 1. | No. 2. | No. 3. |
|---|---|---|---|
| Width, inches, | 3½ | 4 | 4½ |
| Weight, | 1 lb. 1 oz. | 1 lb. 7 oz. | 1 lb. 13 oz. |
| Price, each, | $0.40 | .43 | .45 |

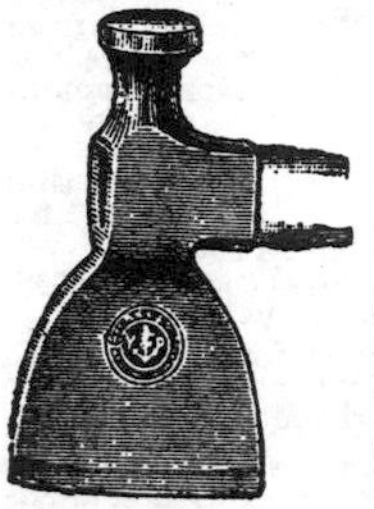

12720

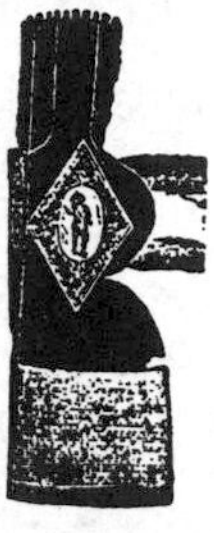

12724

No. 12720. **The best Shingling Hatchet made.** Y and P brand. Adze eye, bell poll, solid cast steel, full polished hickory handles, thin blade, width of bit 3½ inches, weight, 1 lb. 4 oz., warranted. Price, each.......... **65c**

No. 12724. Lathing Hatchet. Y and P brand. Extra cast steel, bronzed, polished bit, common pattern, hickory handle.

| | No. 0. | No. 1 | No. 2 |
|---|---|---|---|
| Width, inches | 2 | 2¼ | 2½ |
| Weight, | 10 oz. | 14 oz. | 1 lb. 1 oz. |
| Price, each, | $0.38 | .40 | .43 |

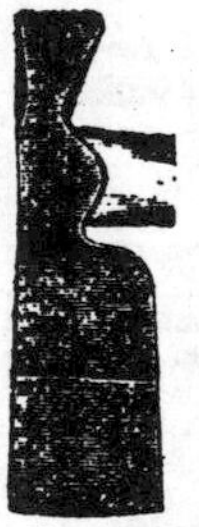

No. 12726.

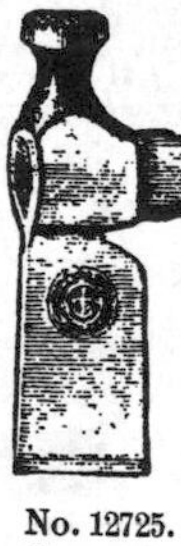

No. 12725.

No 12725. Full polished Lathing Hatchet, Y and P brand, solid cast steel, thin blade, adze eye, hickory handle; width of bit, 2¼ inches; weight, 1 lb.; warranted. Price, each.......... **65c**

No. 12726. The Underhill Star Pattern Lathing Hatchet, Y and P Brand, full polished, solid cast steel, extra thin blade, 2 inches wide; weight, 1 lb. Price, each........ **73c**

No. 12727. Handles for Hatchets; give Catalogue Number and size of hatchet for which handle is wanted. Price, each, **5c**; doz., **54c.**

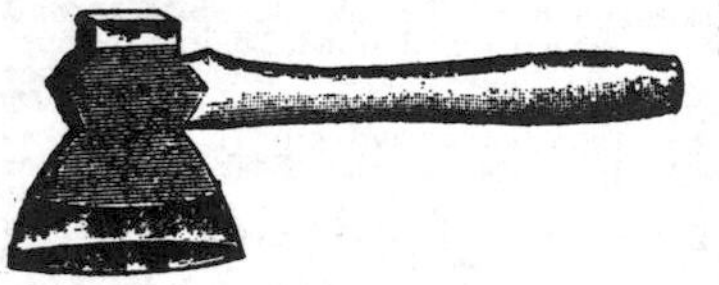

No. 12732. Broad hatchets or carpenter bench axes, Y and P brand; extra cast steel, bronzed polished bit, hickory handle.

| Width, | 4¼ | 5 | 5½ | 6 inch. |
|---|---|---|---|---|
| Weight, | 1 lb. 12 oz. | 2 lb. 2 oz. | 2 lb. 8 oz. | 2 lb. 14 oz. |
| Price, each, | $0.60 | .65 | .75 | .85 |

No. 12733. Handles for No. 12732 hatchets. (State size wanted.) Price, each.......... **6c**

## Broad Axes.

No. 12736. Carpenter's Broad Axe; western pattern, extra cast steel, bronzed polished bit; weight, 6 to 9 lbs., cut 10 to 13 inches. We can not always fill orders with weight and cut as ordered. We do so as nearly as possible always. If you are most particular about weight, mention weight first. If you are most particular about width of cut, mention cut first, and we will do the best we can for you. Price, each....... **$1.45**

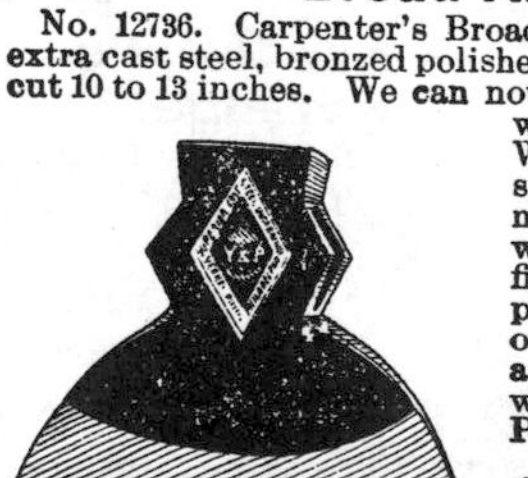

No. 12737. Handles for the above broad axe, right or left hand, 26 inches long. Price, each...**18c**

## Carpenters' Adze.

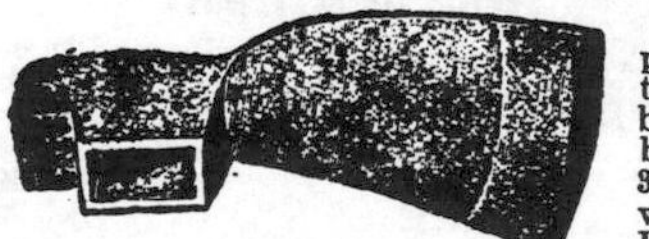

No. 12740. Carpenters' Adze; extra cast steel, bronzed polished bit; width of cut, 3½ to 4 inches; weight, 3¾ lbs. Price, each...**90c**

No. 12741. Handles for the above adze, second growth hickory, 34 inches long. Price, each.............. **40c**

## Tack Hammers.

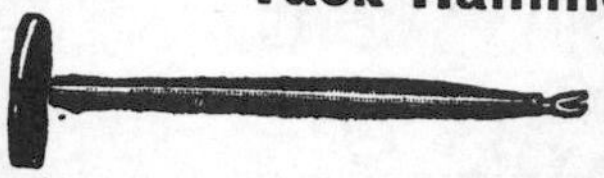

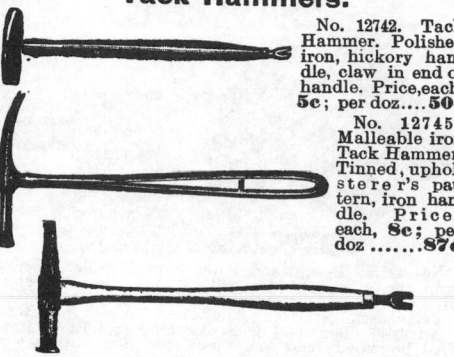

No. 12742. Tack Hammer. Polished iron, hickory handle, claw in end of handle. Price, each, **5c**; per doz.... **50c**

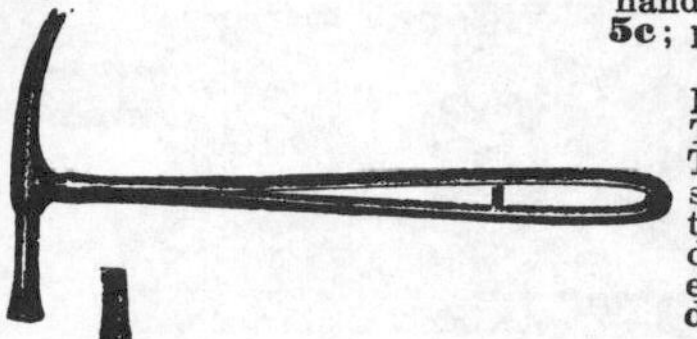

No. 12745. Malleable iron Tack Hammer. Tinned, upholsterer's pattern, iron handle. Price, each, **8c**; per doz....... **87c**

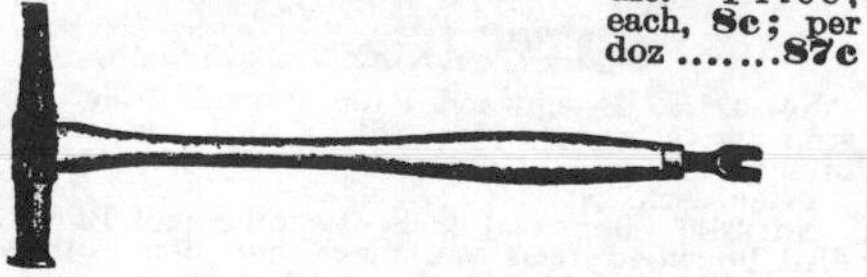

No. 12746. The head of this hammer is magnetic, and it will pick up and hold tack for driving; hickory handle with steel claw. Price, each, **10c**; per doz. **$1.08**

## Tack Pullers.

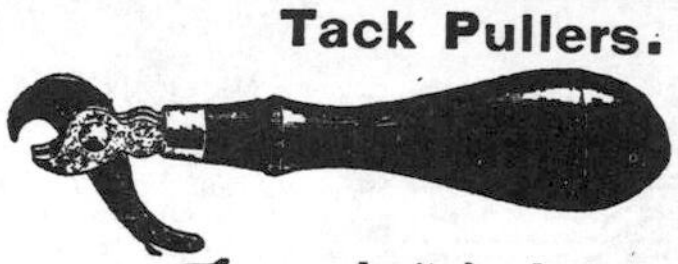

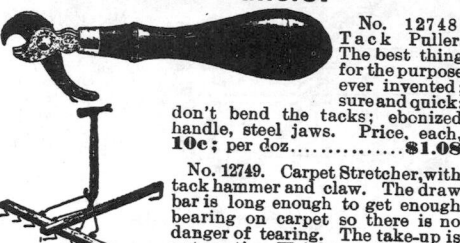

No. 12748. Tack Puller. The best thing for the purpose ever invented; sure and quick; don't bend the tacks; ebonized handle, steel jaws. Price, each, **10c**; per doz.............. **$1.08**

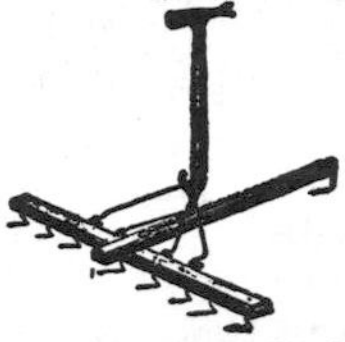

No. 12749. Carpet Stretcher, with tack hammer and claw. The draw bar is long enough to get enough bearing on carpet so there is no danger of tearing. The take-up is automatic. Weight, 1 lb. 11 oz. Price, each .................. **40c**

## Nail Hammers.

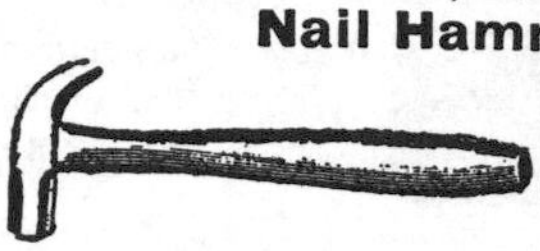

No. 12754. Cast Iron Hammers are **strictly no good.** We have a few of these hammers in stock, which we would rather keep than sell to our customers. If you **must have them,** we sell you a light one for 10 cents, or a full size for 15 cents. You will be sorry if you buy one. Can't you afford to buy a first-class hammer at our prices for them? See how cheap they are.

## Nail Holding Hammers.

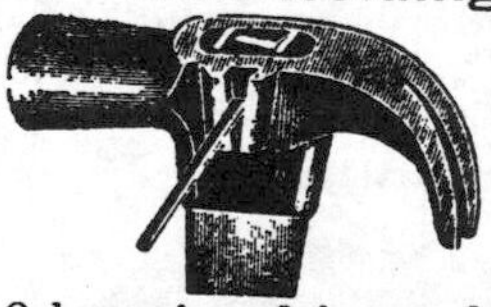

By the improved form of the groove this Hammer will hold any size or shape of cut or wire nails. With it one can drive nails beyond ordinary reach.

No. 12755. Nail Holding Hammer, made from the best quality crucible steel. Only one size and shape made. Weight, 1 lb. 3 oz., without handle. Price, each, with handle.............. **75c**

## David Maydole's Nail Hammers.

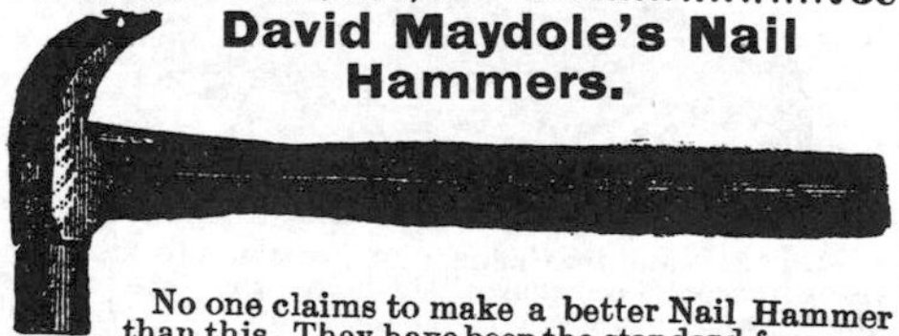

No one claims to make a better Nail Hammer than this. They have been the standard for more than 50 years and still maintain their high reputation. They are proportioned right; they hang right; claws are right shape to draw a nail without breaking the claw; temper is right. **Every Hammer is fully warranted.**

No. 12756. **The genuine David Maydole Nail Hammers.** Adze eye, polished hickory handles. Weights do not include handles.

| No. | 1 | 1½ | 2 | 3 |
|---|---|---|---|---|
| Weights, | 1¼ lbs. | 1 lb. | 13 oz. | 7½ oz. |
| Price, each, | $0.54 | .48 | .45 | .40 |

## Adze-Eye Bell-Face Nail Hammer.

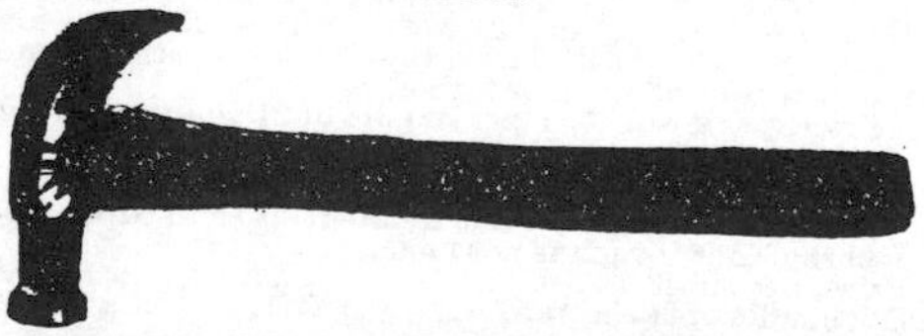

No. 12757. **The genuine David Maydole Nail Hammers.** Adze-eye bell-face, polished; hickory handle. Weights do not include handles.

| No. | 11 | 11½ | 12 | 13 |
|---|---|---|---|---|
| Weight, | 1 lb. 3 oz. | 1 lb. | 12 oz. | 7 oz. |
| Price, each, | $0.55 | .49 | .46 | .42 |

Bell-face Hammers are rounded on the face. They do not slip from the head of the nail, and there are no sharp corners to mar the surface of the wood when nail is driven home.

## Steel Nail Hammers.

The following Hammers, No. 12758 and No. 12759, are made from the best cast steel and are warranted against flaws and not to be soft. They are not so highly finished and polished as the higher priced goods, but for common use they give excellent satisfaction. Don't compare these hammers with cast iron goods like No. 12754. We tell you that No. 12754 hammers are no good and you will find them so. We tell you that these hammers are all right and you will not be disappointed if you buy one.

No. 12758. Adze Eye Plain Face Nail Hammer, same shape as illustration of No. 12756. **Warranted.**

Size 1, weight, 1¼ lbs. Price, each.................. **30c**
Size 2, " 1 lb. " .................. **28c**
Size 3, " 13 oz. " .................. **25c**

Weight of handle not included in stating weight.

No. 12759. Adze Eye Bell Face Nail Hammers, same shape as illustration of No. 12757. **Warranted.**

Size 11, weight, 1¼ lbs. Price, each.................. **32c**
Size 11½, " 1 lb. " .................. **30c**
Size 12, " 13 oz " .................. **27c**

## Riveting Hammers.

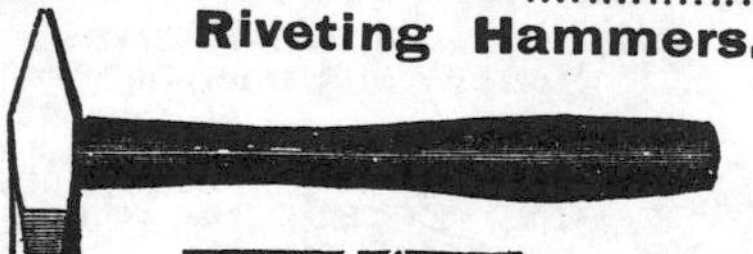

RIVETING HAMMERS.

No. 12768. The Y. & P. Brand Riveting Hammers polished extra cast steel. Handles not included in weights.

| Weight, | 7 oz. | 9 oz. | 12 oz. | 18 oz. | 26 oz. |
|---|---|---|---|---|---|
| Price, each, | $0.21 | .22 | .23 | .25 | .30 |

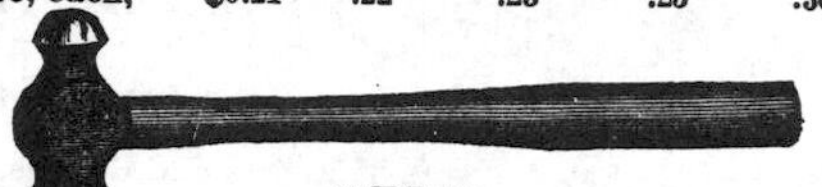

Ball Pene.

No. 12769. The Y. & P. Brand Machinists' Ball Pene Hammers, polished solid cast steel; hickory handle. Handles not included in weights.

| Weight, | 12 oz. | 1 lb. | 1¼ lbs. | 1½ lbs. | 1¾ lbs. | 2 lbs. |
|---|---|---|---|---|---|---|
| Price, each, | $0.43 | .48 | .50 | .53 | 58 | 62 |

## Mallets.

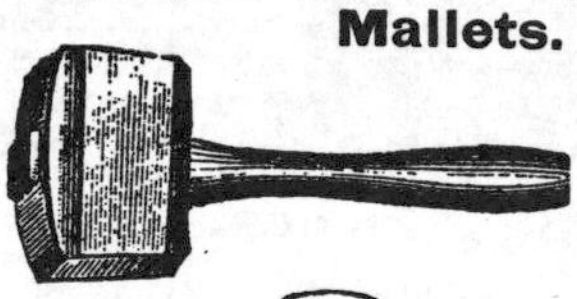

No. 12772. Square hickory Mallets. Head is 6½x2¾x3¾. Mortised handle. Weight about 1¾ lbs. Price, each .... **11c**

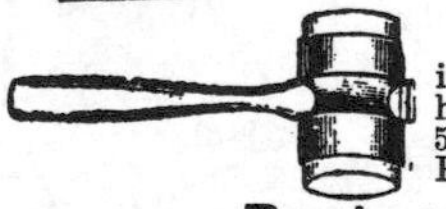

No. 12775. Round malleable iron Mallet, with inserted hickory faces. Head is 5¾x3 inches. Weight, 3⅛ lbs. Price, each.............. **38c**

## Pocket Wrench.

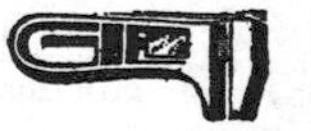

No. 12778. Pocket Screw Wrench, all iron, tinned; whole length when closed, 3¾ inches. Takes nut ⅝ in. Weight, 7 oz. Price, each.......... **6c**

## Alligator Wrench.

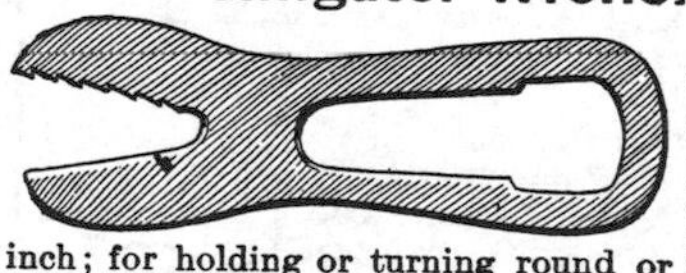

No. 12779. Solid cast steel Alligator Wrench. Length, 5¾ inches. Capacity, ¼ to ⅝ inch; for holding or turning round or square bolts or nuts. Weight, 7 oz. Price, each.................. **15c**

**For other wrenches see index.**

## Monkey Wrenches.

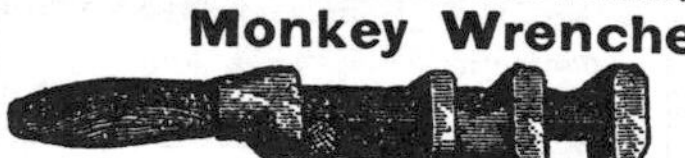

No. 12781. Screw Wrench, wrought iron bar, head and screw. The 10 inch size is best for general purposes.

| Size, inches, | 6 | 8 | 10 | 12 | 15 |
|---|---|---|---|---|---|
| Weight, | 1 lb. | 1 lb. 6 oz. | 2 lbs. | 2½ lbs. | 3½ lbs. |
| Price, each, | $0.17 | .18 | .20 | .25 | .42 |

No. 12782. "Coe's" knife handle Screw Wrench. The standard high-grade wrench. The favorite with engineers, machinists and all first-class workmen. Best wrought iron bar head and screw.

| Size, inches, | 8 | 10 | 12 | 15 |
|---|---|---|---|---|
| Weight, | 1 lb. 6 oz. | 2 lb. 3 oz. | 3 lbs. | 4 lb. 5 oz. |
| Price, each, | $0.47 | .56 | .65 | 1.10 |

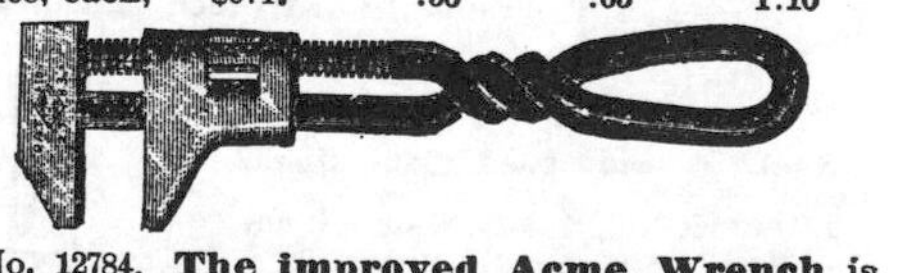

No. 12784. **The improved Acme Wrench** is made entirely of best quality wrought iron. Each size will take larger nut than corresponding size of any other wrench made. **The 5-inch size is nickel plated,** and makes an excellent pocket or bicycle wrench.

| Size, inches, | 5 | 6 | 8 | 10 |
|---|---|---|---|---|
| Weight, | 9 oz. | 14 oz. | 1 lb. | 2 lbs. 10 oz. |
| Price, each, | $0.50 | .33 | .38 | .48 |
| Size, inches, | 12 | 15 | 18 | |
| Weight, | 4 lbs. 6 oz. | 6 lbs. | 8 lbs. | |
| Price, each | $0.50 | .95 | $1.18 | |

**Never cut a picture from your Catalogue to send with your order. It is never necessary, if you will follow instructions in front of book.**

## Froes.

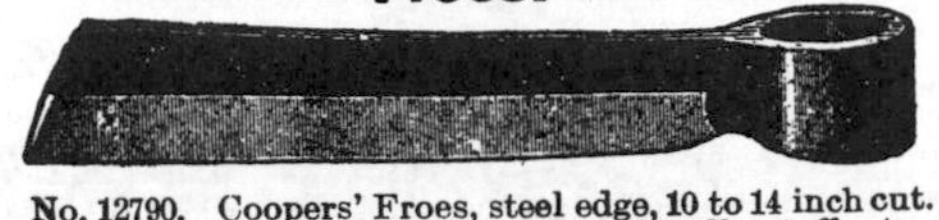

No. 12790. Coopers' Froes, steel edge, 10 to 14 inch cut. Used for splitting shingles, staves, handle stuff, etc., from the log. Weight, 2½ lbs. Price, each........**60c**

## Coopers' Adze.

No. 12791. Barton's Coopers' Adze, flour barrel size, handled and bolted. Price, each................**$2.10**

## Hoop Knives.

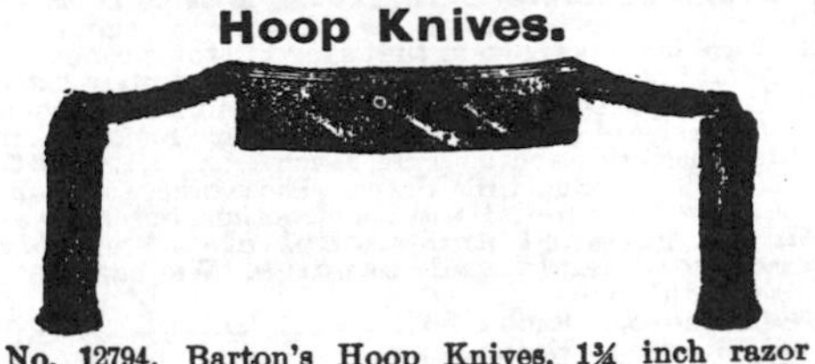

No. 12794. Barton's Hoop Knives, 1¾ inch razor blade, walnut handles, 8 inch cut. Price, each.....**95c**

## Shingle Knives.

No. 12795. Shingle Knives, 1¾ inch, cast steel blade, beechwood handles, cut 14 inches. Price, each.....**85c**

## Drawing Knives.

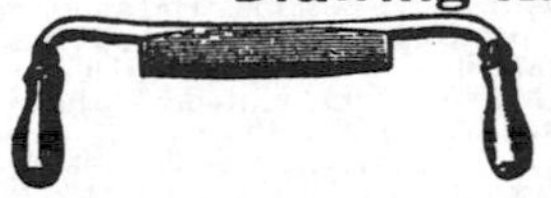

No. 12798. Carpenters' Draw Knives, oval cast steel blade, extra capped handle. Good tools, finely finished.

| | | | |
|---|---|---|---|
| Size, cut, inch, | 8 | 10 | 12 |
| Weight, lbs., | 1¼ | 1½ | 1¾ |
| Price, | $0.40 | .45 | .50 |

## Adjustable Folding Handle Drawing Knife.

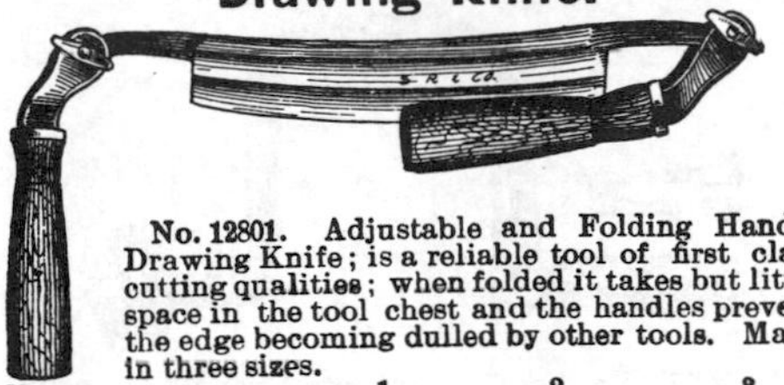

No. 12801. Adjustable and Folding Handle Drawing Knife; is a reliable tool of first class cutting qualities; when folded it takes but little space in the tool chest and the handles prevent the edge becoming dulled by other tools. Made in three sizes.

| | | | |
|---|---|---|---|
| No. | 1 | 2 | 3 |
| Length of blade, | 6 in. | 7 in. | 8 in. |
| Size when folded, | 11½x2 | 12¾x2 | 14x2 |
| Price each, | 1.10 | 1.15 | 1.25 |

## Chamfer Gauge for Drawing Knives.

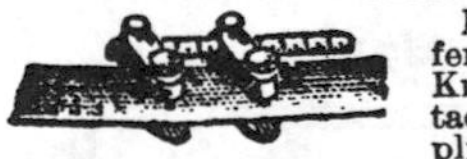

No. 12802. Improved Chamfer Gauge for Drawing Knives. The use of this attachment and method of applying it to blade can easily be seen by referring to the illustration. It is made of iron, nickel plated.

| | | | |
|---|---|---|---|
| Size, inches, | 1¼ | 1½ | 1¾ |
| Fits blade, in. wide, | 1⅛ to 1¼ | 1⅜ to 1¾ | 1⅝ to 1¾ |
| Price, each, | $0.50 | .50 | .50 |

## Spoke Shaves.

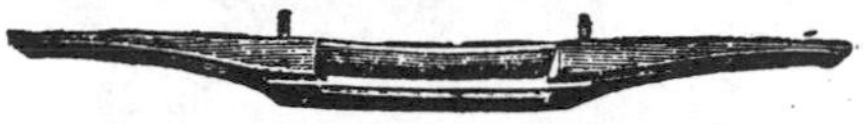

No. 12803. Beechwood Spoke Shaves, with 2½ inch cast steel cutter; weight, 8 oz. Price, each.........**18c**

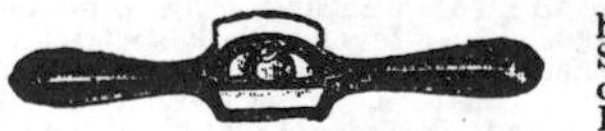

No. 12804. Iron handle Spoke Shave, with 1¾ in. cast steel cutter. Price, each ...**12c**

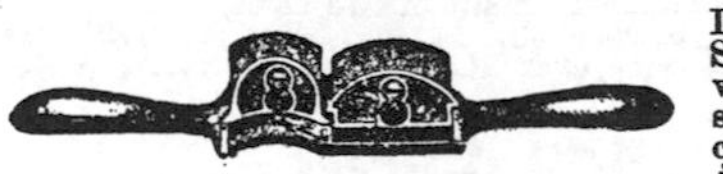

No. 12805. Iron handle Spoke Shave, with two cast steel cutters, concave 1½ inch and straight 1⅝ inch wide. Price, each..........................**15c**

No. 12806. Iron handle Spoke Shave, with adjustable cap, 2⅛ inch cast steel cutter. Price, each..........**22c**

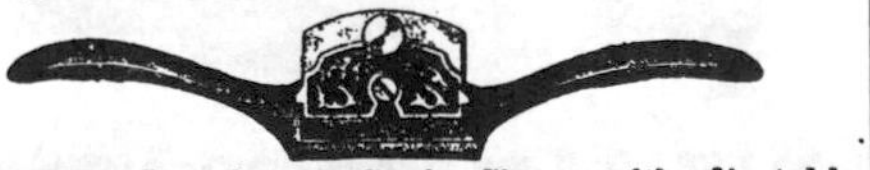

No. 12807. Iron handle Spoke Shave, with adjustable cap, raised handles, 2⅛ inch cast steel cutter. Price, each..........................................**23c**

No. 12809. Chamfer Spoke Shave, iron handles, 1½ inch cast steel cutter; chamfer gauge is adjusted by two thumb screws in handles and will accurately chamfer any width up to 1½ inches; weight, 14 oz. Price, each..........................................**25c**

No. 12812. Goodell's Spoke Shave, rosewood handles, 2 inch cast steel cutter; the angle of the knife is such that it cuts instead of scraping the grain of the wood; either handle may be removed to work in close places; will work in smaller circles than any other shave made. Price, each..........................................**65c**

## Chisels and Gouges.

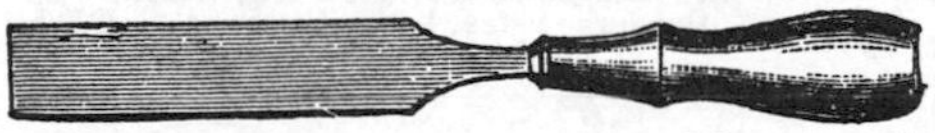

No. 12822. Tanged Firmer Chisels, solid cast steel, polished, **with handle** included.

| | | | | | | | | | | | |
|---|---|---|---|---|---|---|---|---|---|---|---|
| Size, | ¼ | ⅜ | ½ | ⅝ | ¾ | ⅞ | 1 | 1¼ | 1½ | 1¾ | 2 |
| Price, each, | $0.15 | .16 | .17 | .18 | .19 | .20 | .23 | .30 | .35 | .42 | .50 |

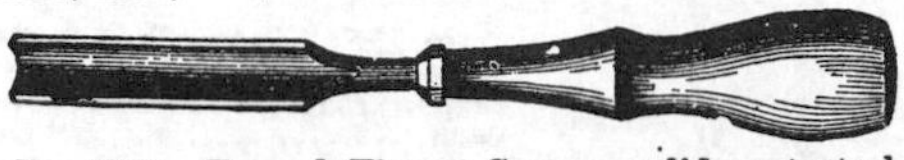

No. 12823. Tanged Firmer Gouges, solid cast steel, polished. Outside bevel, **with handles included.**

| | | | | | | | | | | | |
|---|---|---|---|---|---|---|---|---|---|---|---|
| Size, | ¼ | ⅜ | ½ | ⅝ | ¾ | ⅞ | 1 | 1¼ | 1½ | 1¾ | 2 |
| Each, | $0.18 | .19 | .20 | .21 | .22 | .23 | .28 | .35 | .43 | .55 | .65 |

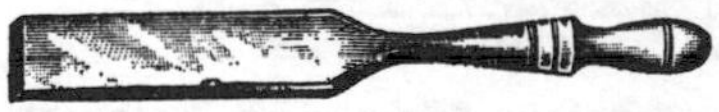

No. 12824. Socket Firmer Chisels; blades are 6 inches long. For quality of material, finish and cutting qualities these chisels can not be equaled at the price. They are high grade, first-class tools; handles included.

| | | | | | | | | | | | |
|---|---|---|---|---|---|---|---|---|---|---|---|
| Size, | ¼ | ⅜ | ½ | ⅝ | ¾ | ⅞ | 1 | 1¼ | 1½ | 1¾ | 2 |
| Price, | $0.15 | .16 | .17 | .19 | .21 | .22 | .23 | .25 | .27 | .29 | .32 |

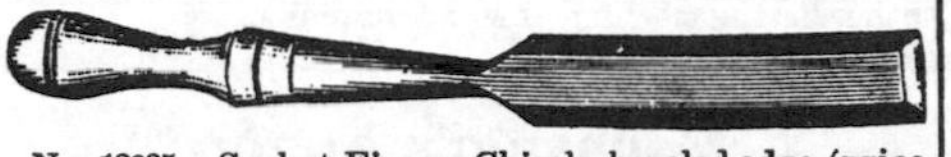

No. 12825. Socket Firmer Chisels, beveled edge (price includes handles). These are high grade tools, made in the best manner of the best materials. Bevel blade, 6 inches long, applewood handles.

| | | | | | | | |
|---|---|---|---|---|---|---|---|
| Size, | ⅛ | ¼ | ⅜ | ½ | ⅝ | ¾ | ⅞ |
| Price, each, | $0.20 | .21 | .22 | .23 | .25 | .26 | .27 |
| Size, | 1 | 1¼ | 1½ | 1¾ | 2 | | |
| Price, each, | $0.30 | .31 | .33 | .35 | .40 | | |

## Socket Framing Chisels.

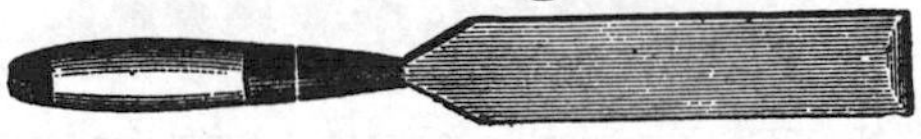

No. 12830. Socket Framing Chisel; blade 8 inches long; high grade; fine finish, with handles. Handles have iron ring on end to prevent splitting.

| | | | | | | |
|---|---|---|---|---|---|---|
| Size, inches, | ½ | ¾ | 1 | 1¼ | 1½ | 2 |
| Price, each, | $0.24 | .27 | .30 | .34 | .38 | .45 |

## Socket Corner Chisels.

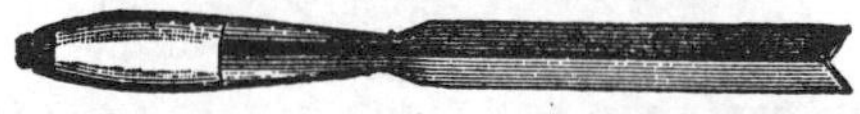

No. 12831. Socket Corner Chisel; extra cast steel, polished outside, with handle. Handle has iron ring on end to prevent splitting. Each face of chisel measures 1 inch. Price, each..........................................**60c**

## Carpenters' Slick.

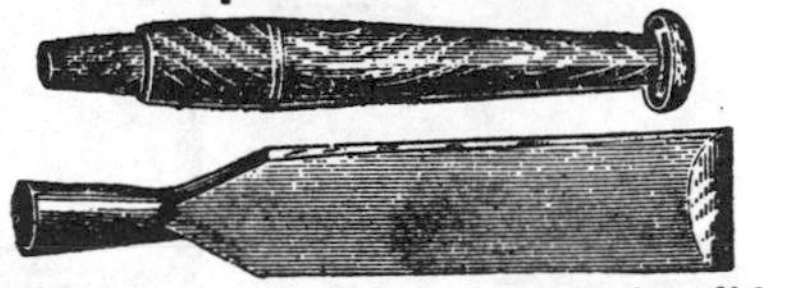

No. 12832. Socket Slick; extra cast steel, polished; with handle, as shown in illustration.

| | | | | |
|---|---|---|---|---|
| Size, inches, | 2½ | 3 | 3½ | 4 |
| Price, each, | $0.75 | .83 | 1.00 | 1.15 |

## Buck's Chisels.

Buck's Chisels and Gouges have attained a reputation for excellence of their fine cutting qualities known everywhere. When you get a tool stamped Buck you are getting the finest tempered and keenest cutting tool that can be bought. Three generations have made the work of forging, hardening and tempering edge tools a practical life study, and now have attained a standard that cannot be excelled. All goods warranted against flaws and not to be too soft. Do not condemn the cutting quality of any new tool until you have ground it more than once, as you will often find a perfect edge on the second if not on the first grinding.

## Buck's Tanged Firmer Chisels.

**With Polished Appletree Handle.**

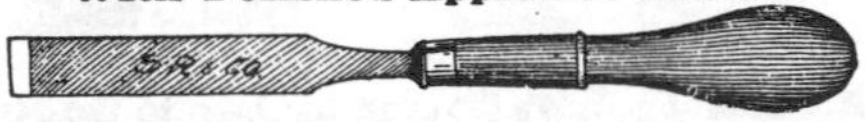

No. 12835. Buck's Tanged Firmer Chisels, ground sharp and honed, with polished appletree handles. The 1 inch chisel blade is 5½ inches long from the bolster. Other sizes in proportion.

| | | | | | | | |
|---|---|---|---|---|---|---|---|
| Size, inches, | ⅛ | 3/16 | ¼ | 5/16 | ⅜ | ½ | ⅝ |
| Price, each, | $0.18 | .19 | .20 | .21 | .22 | .24 | .25 |
| Size, inches, | ¾ | ⅞ | 1 | 1¼ | 1½ | 1¾ | 2 |
| Price, each, | $0.27 | .30 | .32 | .41 | .50 | .60 | .70 |

No. 12836. Set of 9 of the above chisels, one each, size, ⅛, ¼, ⅜, ½, ¾, 1, 1¼, 1½ and 2 inch. Per set....**$2.90**

No. 12837. Set of 14 of the above chisels, one each, size from ⅛ to 2 inch. Per set..........................**$4.35**

## Buck's Tanged Firmer Gouges.

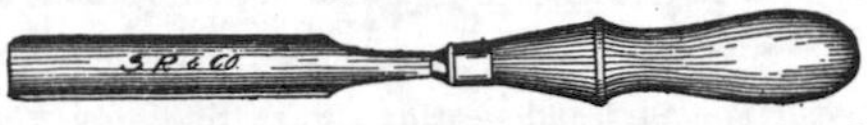

No. 12838. Buck's Tanged Firmer Gouges, beveled outside, ground sharp, with best quality applewood handles. The 1 inch blade is 5½ inches long from the bolster. Other sizes in proportion.

| | | | | | | | |
|---|---|---|---|---|---|---|---|
| Size, inches, | ⅛ | 3/16 | ¼ | 5/16 | ⅜ | ½ | ⅝ |
| Price, each, | $0.23 | .24 | .25 | .26 | .27 | .29 | .30 |
| Size, inches, | ¾ | ⅞ | 1 | 1¼ | 1½ | 1¾ | 2 |
| Price, each, | $0.33 | .36 | .38 | .50 | .60 | .70 | .83 |

No. 12839. Set of 9 of the above gouges, one each., size ⅛, ¼, ⅜. ½, ¾, 1, 1¼, 1½ and 2 inch..............**$3.00**

No. 12840. Set of 14 of the above gouges, one each, size from ⅛ to 2 inches. Price, per set..............**$5.25**

## Buck's Socket Firmer Chisels.

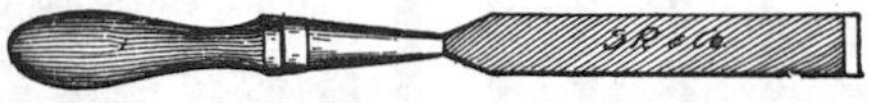

No. 12841. Buck's Socket Firmer Chisels, furnished with the best applewood handles. The 1 inch blade is 6 inches long from the shoulder.

| | | | | | | | |
|---|---|---|---|---|---|---|---|
| Size, inches, | ⅛ | 3/16 | ¼ | 5/16 | ⅜ | ½ | ⅝ |
| Price, each, | $0.28 | .29 | .30 | .31 | .32 | .33 | .36 |
| Size, inches, | ¾ | ⅞ | 1 | 1¼ | 1½ | 1¾ | 2 |
| Price, each, | $0.39 | .42 | .46 | .50 | .54 | .62 | .70 |

No. 12841½. Set of 9 of the above chisels, one each, size ⅛, ¼, ⅜, ½, ¾, 1, 1¼, 1½ and 2 inch.
Price, per set..........................................**$4.25**

No. 12842. Set of 14 of the above chisels, one each, size from ⅛ to 2 inches. Per set..................**$5.45**

## Buck's Socket Firmer Chisels.

**With Beveled Edges and Fancy Applewood Handles.**

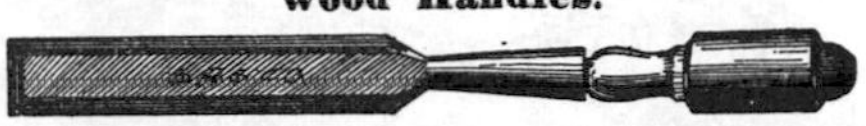

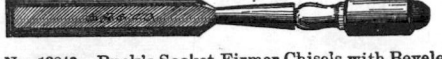

No. 12843. Buck's Socket Firmer Chisels with Beveled edges and fancy applewood handles. The one inch blade is 6 ½ inches long, other sizes in proportion.

| | | | | | | | |
|---|---|---|---|---|---|---|---|
| Size, inches, | ⅛ | 3/16 | ¼ | 7/16 | ⅜ | ½ | ⅝ |
| Price, each, | $0.46 | .47 | .48 | .49 | .50 | .54 | .57 |
| Size, inches, | ¾ | ⅞ | 1 | 1¼ | 1½ | 1¾ | 2 |
| Price, each, | $0.60 | .64 | .68 | .75 | .79 | .99 | 1.08 |

No. 12843½. Set of 9 of the above chisels, one each, size, ⅛, ¼, ⅜, ½, ¾, 1, 1¼, 1½ and 2 inch.
Price, per set..........................................**$5.60**

No. 12844. Set of 14 of the above chisels, one each, size from ⅛ to 2 inches. Price, per set...........**$8.60**

## Buck's Turning Chisels.

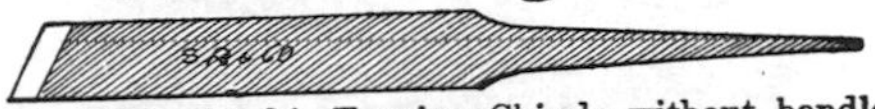

No. 12845. Buck's Turning Chisels, without handles. The 1 inch size is 10¼ inches over all.

| | | | | | | | |
|---|---|---|---|---|---|---|---|
| Size, inches, | ⅛ | 3/16 | ¼ | 5/16 | ⅜ | ½ | ⅝ |
| Price, each, | $0.17 | .18 | .18 | .18 | .19 | .20 | .23 |
| Size, inches, | ¾ | ⅞ | 1 | 1¼ | 1½ | 1¾ | 2 |
| Price, each, | $0.26 | .28 | .33 | .40 | .53 | .63 | .75 |

No. 12846. Set of 9 of the above turning chisels, one each, size, ⅛, ¼, ⅜, ½, ¾, 1, 1¼, 1½ and 2 inch.
Per set..........................................**$2.85**

No. 12847. Set of 14 above turning chisels, one each, size from ⅛ to 2 inch.
Per set..........................................**$4.30**

## Buck's Turning Gouges.

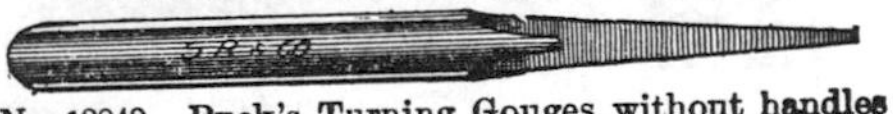

No. 12848. Buck's Turning Gouges, without handles; beveled on the outside. The 1 inch size is 10¼ inches over all.

| | | | | | | | |
|---|---|---|---|---|---|---|---|
| Size, inches, | ⅛ | 3/16 | ¼ | 5/16 | ⅜ | ½ | ⅝ |
| Price, each | $0.21 | .22 | .23 | .25 | .26 | .27 | .30 |
| Size, inches, | ¾ | ⅞ | 1 | 1¼ | 1½ | 1¾ | 2 |
| Price, each | $0.35 | .40 | .45 | .58 | .75 | .90 | 1.08 |

## Leather Capped Chisel Handles.

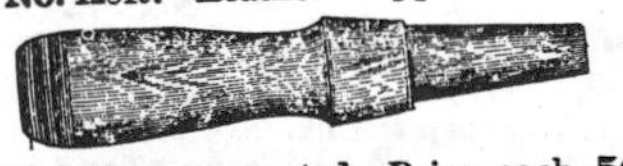

No. 12849. Leather Capped Hickory Chisel Handles for socket firmer chisels from ⅛ to 2 inches. When ordering give size of chisel for which they are wanted. Price, each, **5c**; per doz..**54c**

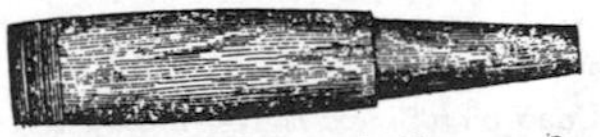

No. 12850. Leather Capped Hickory Chisel Handles, for socket framing chisels. When ordering give size of chisel for which they are wanted. Price, each, **6c**; per doz............**65c**

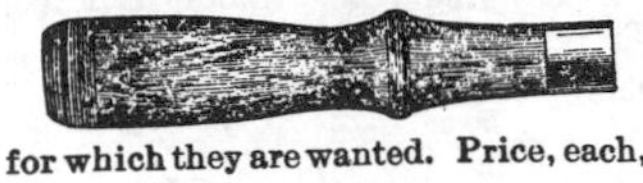

No. 12851. Leather Capped Hickory Chisel Handles with brass ferrules for tanged firmer chisels. When ordering give size of chisel for which they are wanted. Price, each, **8c**; per doz.**87c**

## Chisel Handles.

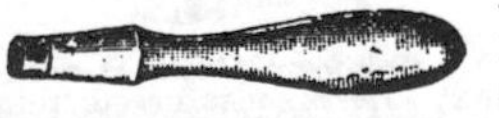

No. 12852. Handles for tanged chisels or gouges, polished hickory with brass ferrules. State for what size chisel wanted.
Each **2c**; per doz..........................................**20c**

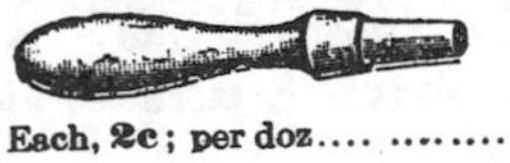

No. 12853. Handles for socket firmer or paring chisels or gouges, polished hickory. State for what size chisel wanted.
Each, **2c**; per doz.......................................**17**

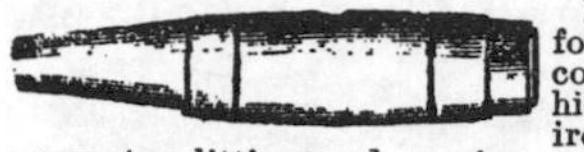

No. 12854. Handles for socket framing or corner chisels, polished hickory with malleable iron ferrule on end to prevent splitting and wearing away. State for what size chisel wanted. Each, 3c; per doz............23c

## Carving Tools.

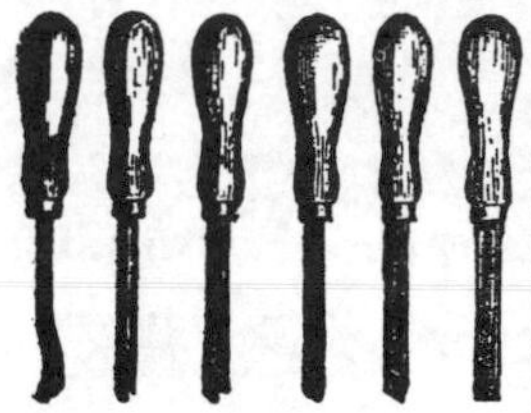

No. 12860. Set of Carving Tools consisting of 6 extra cast steel tools of various shapes and sizes as shown in cut, with rosewood handles. They are not intended for professionals, but they are just the thing for any one who but seldom has occasion to do carving. Full length of tool with handle, 5½ inches. Weight of set complete, 10 oz. Price, complete in a wood box........82c

We can furnish carving tools for professional carvers of any size or shape, but have not space to illustrate them here. Price will be cheerfully and promptly given on request. In asking for price make a drawing showing size and shape of end of blade, and if not wanted straight show shape of blade wanted.

## Chisel Grinder.

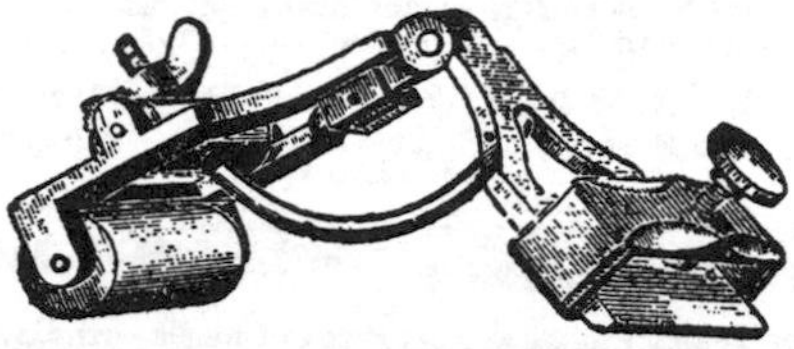

No. 12862. This is a new invention for holding chisels, plane irons, etc., while grinding them. When put in the holder and brought to the right bevel with the adjusting screw, nothing is left to do but to bear it on the stone, and it will grind all right without further care. Price, each..........62c

## Chisel Gauge.

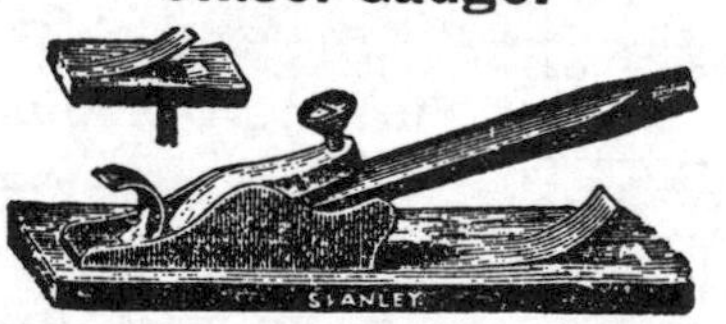

No. 12863. Chisel Gauge, used for blind nailing. Attach this to a ¼ inch chisel (with bevel edge up) and a shaving of any desired thickness can be raised, which, when glued down again, will leave surface of work perfectly smooth. Only one size made. Price, each (without chisel)..........13c

## Cold Chisels.

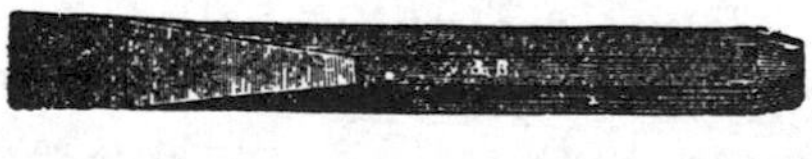

No. 12866. Cold Chisel, made from a superior quality octagon cast steel, ½ inch in diameter, with the cutting end drawn out wider, as shown above. Weight, 5 oz. Each..........8c

No. 12867. Cold Chisel. Same as above, made from ¾ inch octagon steel. Weight, 1 lb. 2 oz. Each....15c

## Screw Drivers.

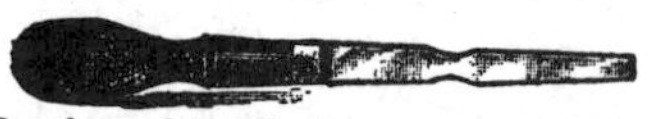

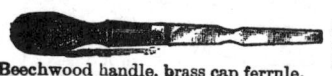

No. 12868. Screw Drivers. Cast steel forged blades. Beechwood handle, brass cap ferrule.

| | | | | | | |
|---|---|---|---|---|---|---|
| Size of blade, inches, | 1½ | 3 | 4 | 5 | 6 | 8 |
| Whole length, inches, | 5½ | 7¼ | 9 | 10¼ | 12¼ | 15 |
| Price, each, | $0.05 | .05 | .06 | .08 | .09 | .11 |

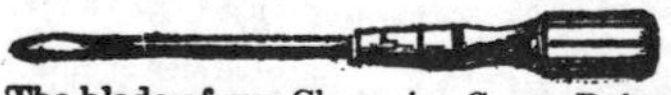

No. 12869. Champion Screw Driver. The blade of our Champion Screw Driver is forged from die steel, tempered and shrunk into a malleable bolster, heavy combined tang and ferrule, which prevents tang turning in handle or becoming loose. Handle is fluted, which is considered the best shaped handle made.

| | | | | | |
|---|---|---|---|---|---|
| Size of blade, | 3 | 4 | 6 | 8 | 10 |
| Whole length, inches, | 7½ | 9 | 12½ | 15 | 17 |
| Price, each, | $0.18 | .22 | .32 | .42 | .53 |

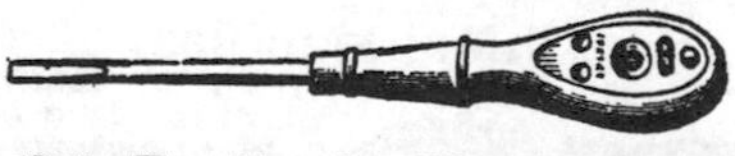

No. 12874. The old and well-known Gay's Double-Action Ratchet Screw Driver. The blade is forged from cast steel; used as a right or left hand ratchet or plain screw driver, ebony handle polished, steel plate.

| | | | | |
|---|---|---|---|---|
| Length of blade, inches, | 4 | 5 | 6 | 8 |
| Price, each, | $0.50 | .55 | .68 | .76 |

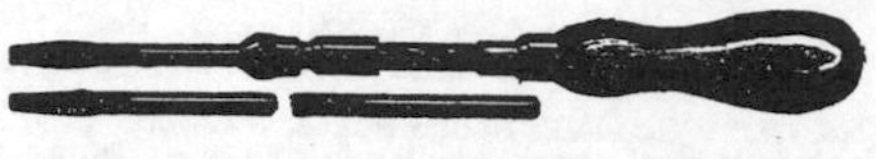

Goodell's Spiral Screw Driver can be used as a spiral ratchet or plain screw driver.

No. 12876. Goodell's Spiral Screw Driver, stained cherry handle. Length closed, 9½ inches; open, 14 inches, with 3 forged steel bits. Price, each........95c

No. 12877. Goodell's Spiral Screw Driver, stained cherry handle. Length closed, 11 inches; length open, 16 inches, with 3 forged steel bits. Price, each..$1.10

## Angular Boring Machines.

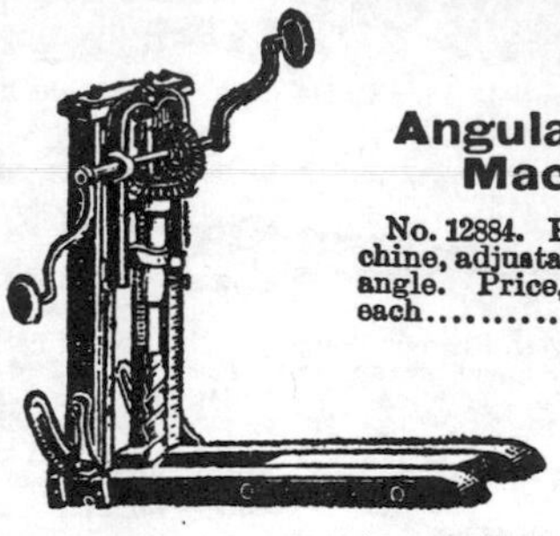

No. 12884. Patent Boring Machine, adjustable to bore at any angle. Price, without augers, each..........$2.65

## Boring Machine Augers.

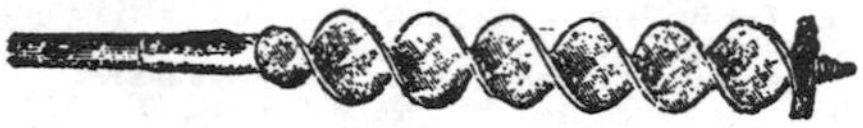

No. 12888. Extra quality augers for above or any other boring machine of standard make.

| | | | | |
|---|---|---|---|---|
| Size, inches, | 1 | 1¼ | 1½ | 2 |
| Price, each, | $0.30 | .35 | .43 | .60 |

## Mechanic's Auger.

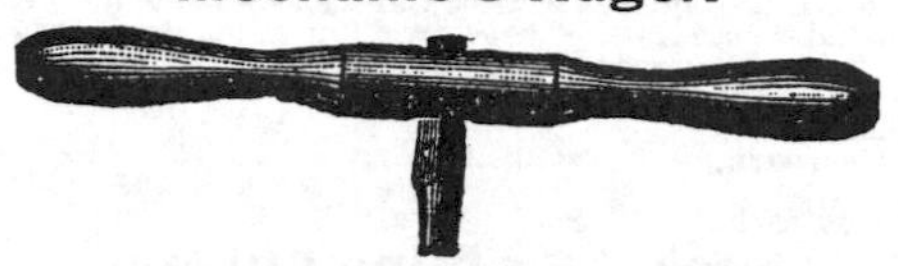

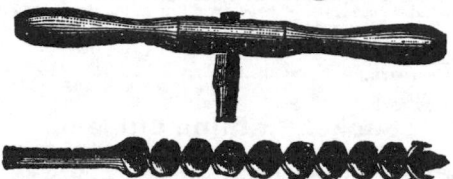

No. 12889. Extra quality carpenters' Auger, for cross handle of wood. Handle not included at price given. Extra cast steel, full polished; nut on end of shank.

| | | | | | |
|---|---|---|---|---|---|
| Size, inches, | 1 | 1¼ | 1½ | 1¾ | 2 |
| Price, each, | $0.32 | .35 | .42 | .48 | .60 |

## Adjustable Auger Handles.

No. 12890. Will fit any size auger, and is quickly removed, so augers can be easily packed in tool chest. Only one handle required for a full set of augers. Weight, 1 lb. Price, each..........17c

## Bit Braces.

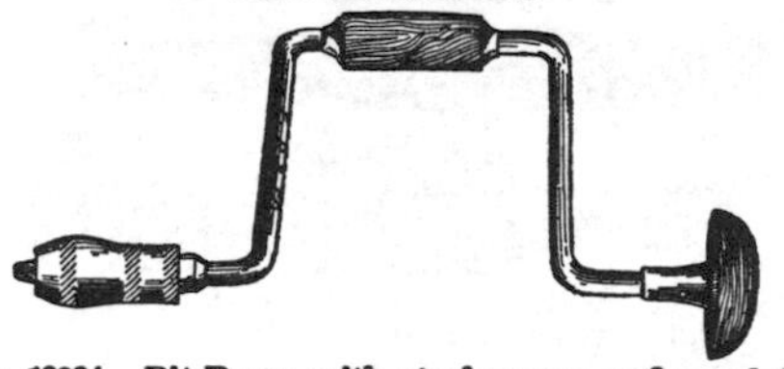

No. 12894. Bit Brace, with steel sweep and revolving head and handle. Sweep is made from $\frac{7}{16}$ cold drawn steel rod and head and handle are cherry or birch. We have two sizes; the 10 inch size is best for general work.
8 inch sweep. Price, each..........22c
10 inch sweep. Price, each..........25c

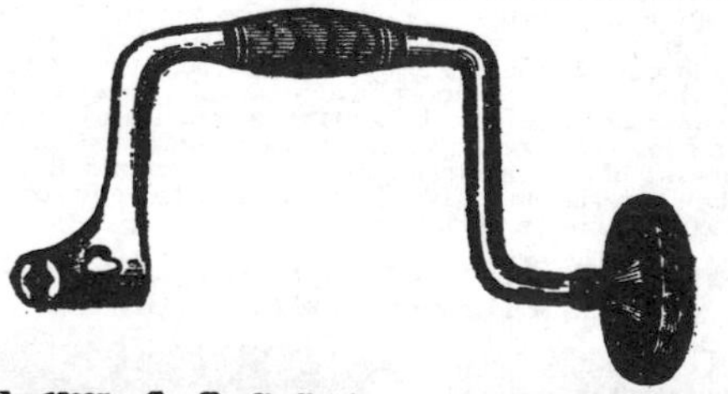

No. 12895. Spofford's Bit Brace has been in the market for years, and there is no doubt it will stand more rough usage and abuse than any other made. Will hold all sizes auger bits, gimlet bits, or bit stock drills. Bits are quickly fastened in and can't pull out. It's a great favorite with blacksmiths and carriage builders. Solid steel, nickel plated cocobolo head and handle, adjustable bit holder.
8 inch sweep. Each..........$1.05
10 inch sweep. Each..........$1.10

## Ratchet Brace.

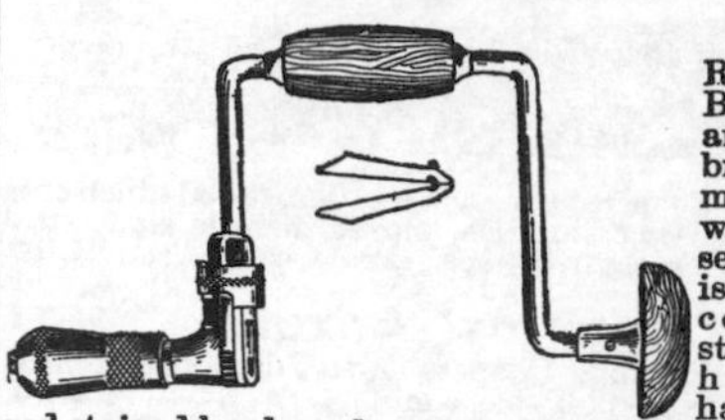

No. 12896. Ratchet Bit Brace. These are the best braces for the money that we have ever seen. Sweep is made of 7-16 cold drawn steel rod. The head and handles are red stained hardwood. The ratchet is same as shown in cut; jaws are same as shown in small cut and are the same pattern that's used in the most expensive bit braces made. The parts are accurately fitted. It is equal to our best brace except in finish. We have but one size of this brace—10-inch sweep—looks exactly like illustration above. Price, each..........55c

No. 12897. Ratchet Bit Brace. These braces are same as above in material and construction, but they are **finely polished and nickel plated** and have **cocobolo heads and handles**. We have three sizes of this brace:
8-inch sweep. Each..........73c
10-inch sweep. Each..........87c
12-inch sweep. Each..........90c

## Ball Bearing Ratchet Brace.

No. 12897½. Ball Bearing Ratchet Brace. These braces have same style ratchet and jaw as shown in cut of 12896. They are made from the best material and are finished in the very best possible manner. The head has ball bearings. Handles and head of cocobolo. All metal parts are elegantly and heavily nickel plated. We have this brace in three sizes:
8-inch sweep. Each..........$0.95
10-inch sweep. Each..........1.00
12-inch sweep, Each..........1.05

## Ratchet Brace with Ball Bearings.

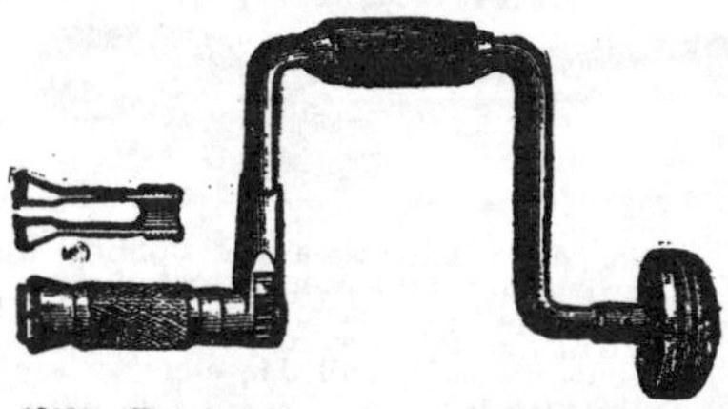

No. 12898. Ratchet Brace is a very strong brace, handsomely finished; will hold square or round shank bits ¼-inch and larger; lignum vitæ head strengthened by steel plate full size of head; steel bow nicely nickel plated; steel ball bearings.

| | | | |
|---|---|---|---|
| Sweep, inches.......... | 8 | 10 | 12 |
| Price, each.......... | $1.15 | 1.25 | 1.38 |

## Corner Brace.

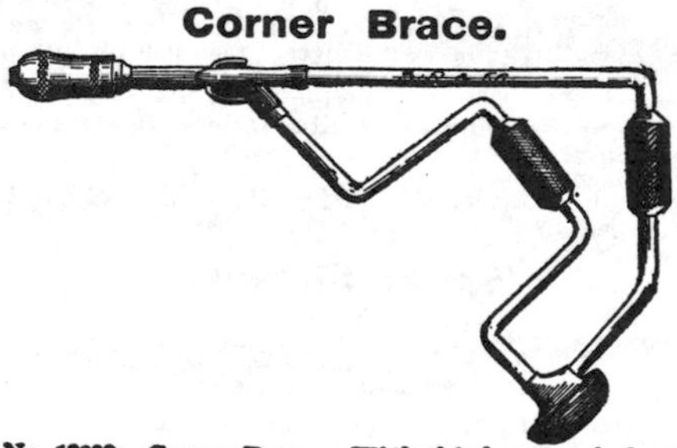

No. 12899. Corner Brace. With this brace a hole can be bored in a corner in places where no other brace can be used to advantage. It is a favorite with electricians, bell hangers, gas fitters, plumbers, cabinet makers, carpenters, and other mechanics. It is well made and finely finished. Steel rods, full nickel plated, with cocobolo head and handles. Made in two sizes,
8-inch sweep, price, each..........$2.10
10-inch sweep, price, each..........2.30

## Drill Brace.

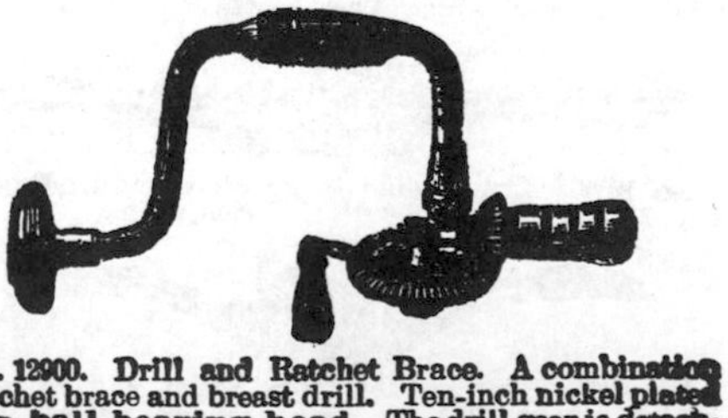

No. 12900. Drill and Ratchet Brace. A combination of rachet brace and breast drill. Ten-inch nickel plated sweep, ball bearing head. The drill gear is detachable and is easily and quickly adjusted. Jaws hold all kinds of bits and drills. Price, each..........$3.50

**You should find it easy to make up a club order among your neighbors, and by shipping everything by freight, save more than otherwise. See our club discounts.**

## Auger Bits.

No. 12912. Common Auger Bits. We call these common auger bits because this is the style to use for common work. They are not common in

**quality.** Every bit is made from extra cast steel with double spur and lip nicely finished. There are bits in the market which we could sell you much cheaper, but we know a **good bit** can't be made and sold (even with our one small profit) at less price than we offer below. This is **not** a bit made to sell and not to use. Its the kind you can use and use a good while and with satisfaction. Order No. 12912.

| | | | | | | | |
|---|---|---|---|---|---|---|---|
| Size, inches | 3/16 | 1/4 | 5/16 | 3/8 | 7/16 | 1/2 | 9/16 |
| Price, each | $0.10 | .09 | .09 | .10 | .10 | .10 | .11 |
| Size, inches | 5/8 | 11/16 | 3/4 | 13/16 | 7/8 | 15/16 | 1 |
| Price, each | $0.12 | .13 | .14 | .15 | .16 | .18 | .20 |

No. 12913. The above bits in sets of 13, one each size, from 1/4 to 1 inch. Price, per set........**$1.60**

No. 12914. The above bits (No. 12912) in sets of 7, one of each size, 1/4, 5/16, 3/8, 1/2, 5/8 and 3/4. Price, per set..**80c**

## Russell Jennings Bits.

No. 12916. **The Genuine Russell Jennings Extension Lip Auger Bits** are for first-class mechanics only. For ordinary work our common auger bits are the ones to buy. There are many imitations of this bit on the market called Jennings pattern or with the name Jennings used in some way with the purpose of working off inferior goods at high prices. These are the genuine double spur extension lip. You will always find our goods just as represented. When we sell an imitation of a well-known article we sell it for what it is, and at the right price. Order No. 12916.

| | | | | | | | | | | | | | |
|---|---|---|---|---|---|---|---|---|---|---|---|---|---|
| Size... | 1/4 | 5/16 | 3/8 | 7/16 | 1/2 | 9/16 | 5/8 | 11/16 | 3/4 | 13/16 | 7/8 | 15/16 | 1 |
| Each.. | $0.18 | .20 | .23 | .26 | .28 | .31 | .33 | .37 | .39 | .42 | .46 | .49 | .53 |

No. 12917. Set of 7 of the above bits, one each, 1/4, 3/8, 1/2, 5/8, 3/4, 7/8 and 1 inch........**$2.70**

No. 12918. Set of 13 of the above bits, one of each size, 1/4 to 1 inch. Per set........**$4.65**

## Car Bits.

No. 12920. Superior Cast Steel Extension Lip Car Bits with 12-inch twist. Same as cut 12912, except the twist is 12 inches long.

| | | | | | | | | |
|---|---|---|---|---|---|---|---|---|
| Size | 4/16 | 5/16 | 6/16 | 7/16 | 8/16 | 9/16 | 10/16 | 11/16 |
| Price | $0.26 | .28 | .30 | .36 | .41 | .45 | .51 | .53 |
| Size | | 12/16 | 13/16 | 14/16 | 15/16 | 16/16 | 17/16 | 18/16 |
| Price | | $0.62 | .66 | .71 | .75 | .82 | .96 | 1.08 |

No. 12921. Set of 15 of the above bits, one each size, from 4/16 to 18/16. Price, per set........**$13.38**

## Bit Sets in Boxes.

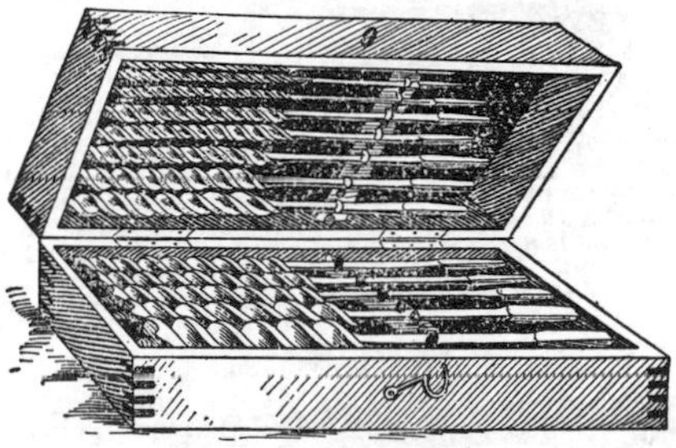

No. 12924. Set of 13 selected Auger Bits; one each size from 1/4 to 1 inch, put up in neat hardwood box with hinges and hook, same as illustrated above. Price........**$2.05.**

No. 12925. Set of 6 selected Auger Bits; one each size 1/4, 3/8, 1/2, 5/8, 3/4 and 1 inch, put up in a wood box similar to illustration of No. 12924 (only holding but 6 bits.) Price........**$1.15.**

## Bit Boxes.

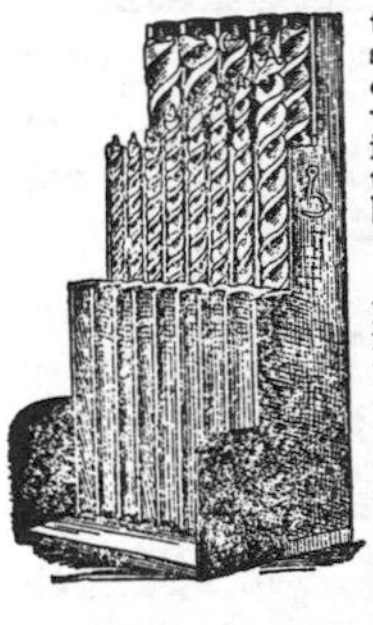

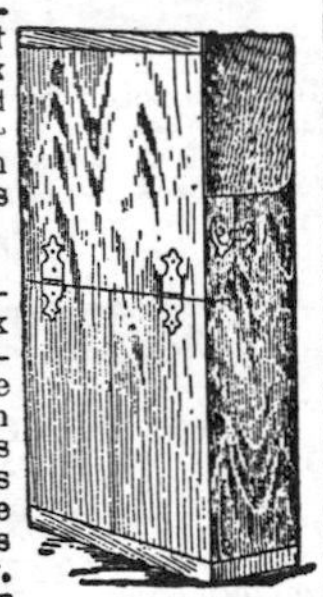

The illustration on the left shows box open and filled with bits. The illustration on the right shows box closed.

No. 12928. Bartlett's Improved Bit Box is much superior to the old style. When the cover is open it makes a large base which supports the box firmly. Short bits may be taken out easily. Holds 13 bits from 1/4 to 1 inch. Price, each, without bits........**35c**

## Gimlet Bits.

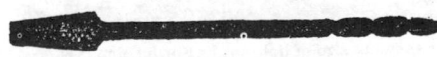

No. 12934. Double cut Gimlet Bits are best to buy if you are not a skilled mechanic. Extra quality cast steel, polished. No. 0 is about 1-16. The other numbers increase gradually up to No. 6, which is about 1/4 inch. Be sure to state what number is wanted.

| | | | | | | | |
|---|---|---|---|---|---|---|---|
| No. | 0 | 1 | 2 | 3 | 4 | 5 | 6 |
| Price each.... | $0.03 | .03 | .03 | .03 | .03 | .03 | .03 |

No. 12935. A set of Gimlet Bits, one of each size, weight, 10 oz........**19c**

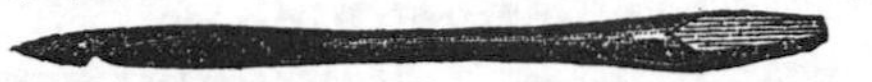

No. 12936. German pattern Gimlet Bits. Extra quality cast steel. Will bore with small risk of splitting. The small sizes are easily broken if not handled right, and should be used carefully. Draw the bit when you have bored to depth of pod, and you will have no trouble then to bore as deep as bit will go.

| | | | | | | | | |
|---|---|---|---|---|---|---|---|---|
| Sizes, | 1/16 | 3/32 | 1/8 | 5/32 | 3/16 | 7/32 | 1/4 | 5/16 |
| Price each... | $0.05 | .05 | .05 | .05 | .05 | .05 | .05 | .06 |

No. 12937. A set of the above bits, one of each size, weight, 10 oz. Price........**36c**

## Expansive Bits.

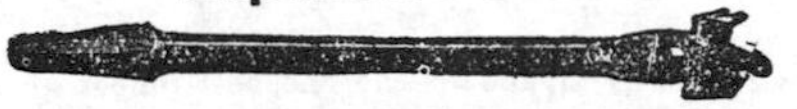

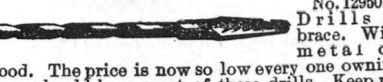

With this tool you can bore holes of any diameter between sizes mentioned. It is elegantly made and highly polished. Made in two sizes.

No. 12939. Clark's Improved Expansive Bit. Small size, with two cutters, one boring from 1/2 to 7/8 inch, the other, from 7/8 to 1 1/2 inch. Price, complete....**90c**

No. 12940. Clark's Expansive Bit. Large size, with two cutters, one boring from 7/8 to 1 3/4 inch, the other boring from 1 3/4 to 3 inches. Price, complete....**$1.30**

No. 12941. Extra cutters for Clark's expansive bits. For small size bit.

No. 1. Cuts from 1/2 to 7/8 inch. Price, each......**18c**
No. 2. Cuts from 7/8 to 1 1/2 inch. Price, each....**23c**
No. 12942. For large size bit.
No. 3. Cuts from 7/8 to 1 3/4 inches. Price, each..**32c**
No. 4. Cuts from 1 3/4 to 3 inches. Price, each...**36c**

## Twist Drills.

No. 12950. Twist Drills for bit brace. Will drill metal or bore wood. The price is now so low every one owning a bit brace should have a set of these drills. Keep point of drill well oiled when drilling metal.

| | | | | | | | | | |
|---|---|---|---|---|---|---|---|---|---|
| Sizes..... | 1/16 | 3/32 | 1/8 | 5/32 | 3/16 | 7/32 | 1/4 | 9/32 | 5/16 | 11/32 |
| Each..... | $0.05 | .05 | .07 | .08 | .10 | .12 | .13 | .15 | .17 | .20 |
| Sizes..... | 3/8 | 13/32 | 7/16 | 15/32 | 1/2 | 5/8 | 3/4 | 7/8 | 1 inch. | |
| Each..... | .23 | .27 | .33 | .36 | .40 | .50 | .60 | .70 | .90 | |

No. 12951. Set of 7 of the above bits, one each, size, 1-16, 1-8, 3-16, 1-4, 5-16, 3-8 and 1-2 inch. Per set...**$1.05**

No. 12952. Set of 11 of the above bits, one each, size, 1-16, 1-8, 3-16, 1-4, 5-16, 3-8, 1-2, 5-8, 3-4, 7-8 and 1 inch. Per set........**$3.50**

No. 12953. Set of 15 of the above bits, one each, size, 1-16 to 1-2 inch. Per set........**$2.45**

No. 12954. Set of 19 of the above bits, one each, size from 1-16 to 1 inch. Per set........**$4.88**

## Round Shank Drills.

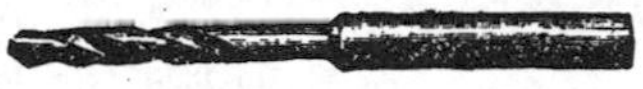

No. 12955. Twist Drill with round shank for drill presses. Will drill metal or bore wood. The shank of all sizes is 1/2 inch in diameter, 2 1/2 inches long.

| | | | | | | | | | | |
|---|---|---|---|---|---|---|---|---|---|---|
| Sizes, | 1/8 | 5/32 | 3/16 | 7/32 | 1/4 | 9/32 | 5/16 | 11/32 | 3/8 | 13/32 |
| Each... | $0.18 | .20 | .21 | .23 | .25 | .27 | .30 | .32 | .33 | .35 |
| Sizes, | | | 7/16 | 15/32 | 1/2 | 17/32 | 9/16 | 19/32 | 5/8 | 21/32 |
| Each | | | $0.36 | .38 | .39 | .40 | .41 | .42 | .43 | .45 |
| Sizes, | | | | | 11/16 | 23/32 | 3/4 | 25/32 | 13/16 | 27/32 |
| Each | | | | | $0.46 | .50 | .52 | .55 | .60 | .62 |
| Sizes, | | | | | 7/8 | 29/32 | 15/16 | 31/32 | 1 inch. | |
| Each | | | | | $0.63 | .65 | .70 | .72 | .75 | |

No. 12956. Set of 10 of the above drill bits, one each, size, 1-8, 3-16, 1-4, 5-16, 3-8, 1-2, 5-8, 3-4 inch. Price, per set........**$2.40**

No. 12957. Set of 29 of the above drills, one each, sizes from 1/8 to 1 inch. Price, per set........**$12.00**

## Screw Driver Bits.

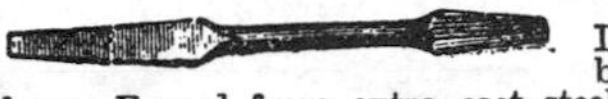

No. 12962. Screw Driver to use in bit brace is 5 1/2 inches long. Forged from extra cast steel. Not to be compared with cheap cast iron goods, of which there are too many in the market. Weight, 5 ounces. Price, each........**5c**

## Reamer Bits.

No. 12964. Square Reamer Bits. Forged from extra cast steel. Weight, 5 ounces. Each........**8c**

No. 12965. Octagon Reamer Bits. Forged from extra cast steel. Weight, 5 ounces. Each........**12c**

## Countersink Bits.

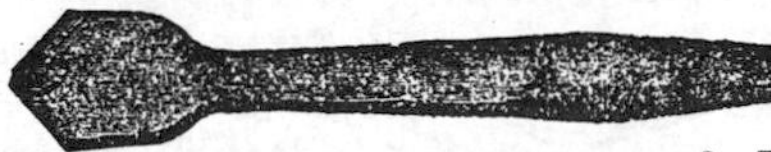

No. 12970. Flat Countersink Bit for metal. Forged from cast steel: polished. Weight, 5 ounces. Price, each........**7c**

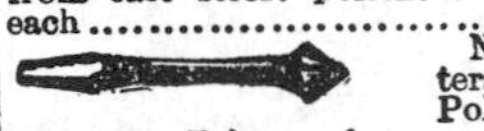

No. 12971. Rosehead Countersink Bit for metal or wood. Polished cast steel. Weight, 5 ounces. Price, each........**7c**

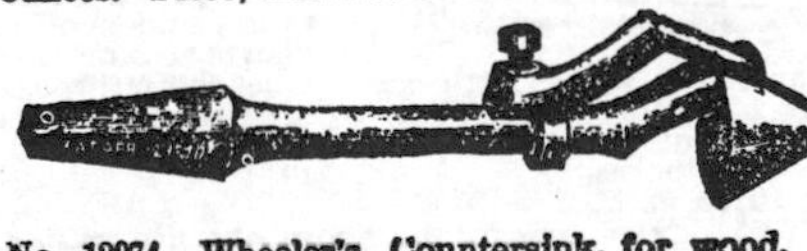

No. 12974. Wheeler's Countersink, for wood, with gauge. Weight, 5 ounces. Price, each........**16c**

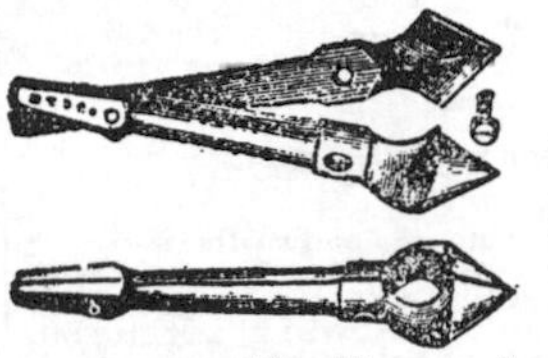

No. 12975. Clark's Countersink for wood. Without doubt the best countersink made for wood. Weight, 5 ounces. Price, each..**25c**

## Hollow Augers.

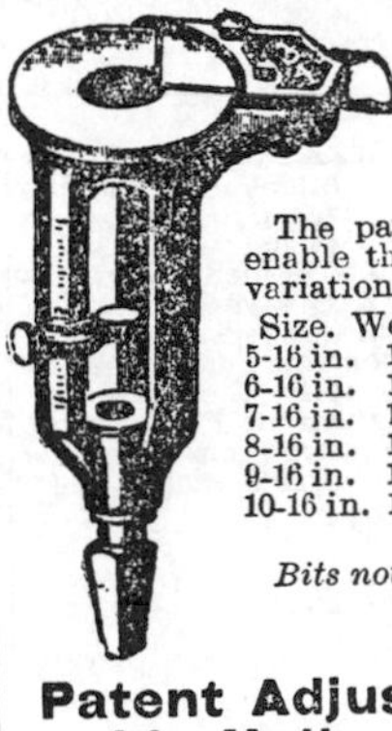

No. 12984. Stearn's Patent Hollow Augers, cutting but one size. The only single size hollow auger in which the length of tenon is regulated by an adjustable stop and graduated scale.

The patent adjustable cap and knife enable the user to overcome any slight variation in size of bits.

| Size. | Weight. | Each. | Size. | W'ght. | Each. |
|---|---|---|---|---|---|
| 5-16 in. | 12 oz. | $0.50 | 3/4 in. | 18 oz. | $0.55 |
| 6-16 in. | 12 oz. | .50 | 7/8 in. | 18 oz. | .82 |
| 7-16 in. | 12 oz. | .50 | 1 in. | 18 oz. | .83 |
| 8-16 in. | 12 oz. | .50 | 1 1/8 in. | 23 oz. | .88 |
| 9-16 in. | 12 oz. | .55 | 1 1/4 in. | 23 oz. | .90 |
| 10-16 in. | 15 oz. | .55 | 1 1/2 in. | 23 oz. | 1.00 |
| | | | 1 3/4 in. | 32 oz. | 1.00 |

*Bits not furnished.*

## Patent Adjustable Hollow Augers.

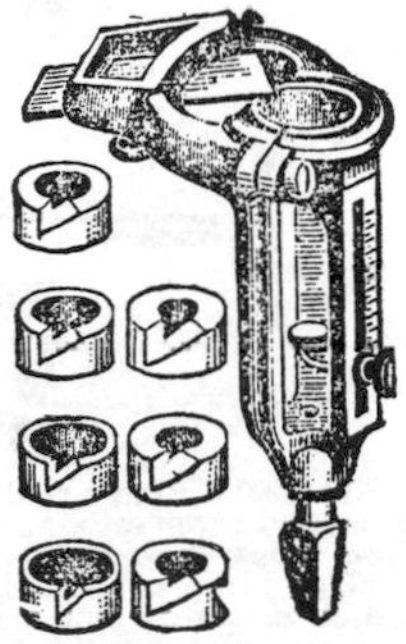

No. 12985. Stearn's Patent Adjustable Hollow Auger, made of malleable iron and nicely finished. The knife is made of the best tool steel, has adjustable stop, with scale for regulating length of tenon. It cuts eight sizes, as follows: 3/8, 7-16, 1/2, 9-16, 5/8, 3/4 and 1 inch. Weight, 1 lb. 9 oz. No. 1, complete. Price........**$3.15**

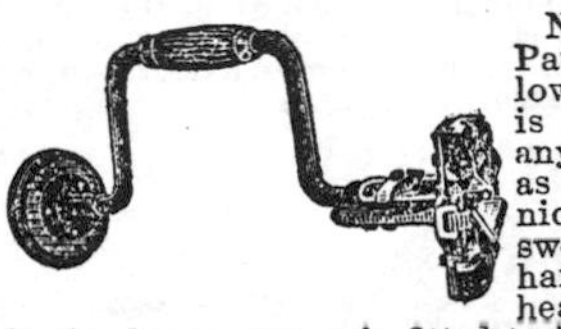

No. 12986. Goodell's Patent Adjustable Hollow Auger. This auger is an improvement on anything hitherto in use, as it has fitted to it a nickel plated bit brace sweep, with rosewood handle and lignum vitæ head; sweep, 14 inches. As the brace sweep is fitted to it, it will always work true, which is not the case when the ordinary kind is used in an ordinary bit brace; besides, it often happens that the bit brace on hand is not large enough to drive a spoke auger. The auger is adjustable to cut from 1/4 to 1 1/4 inches. Price, each, complete with sweep...**$3.35**

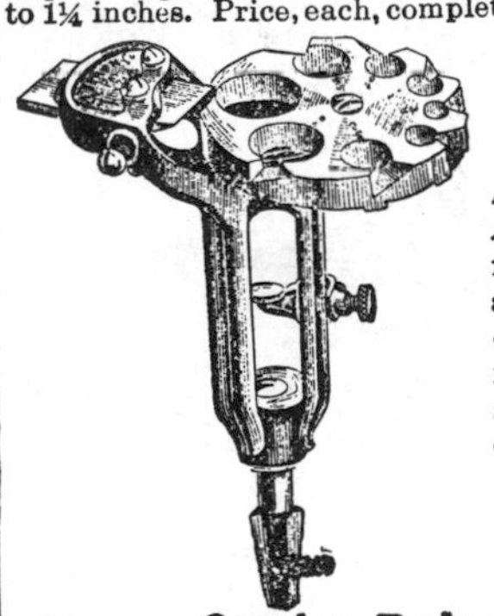

No. 12987. Bonney's Adjustable Hollow Auger is a tool that is first class in material and finish. Cuts 8 sizes of tenons from 3/8 to 1 inch. Has adjustable stop to regulate length of tenons. Price, each...**$1.75**

## Spoke Pointers.

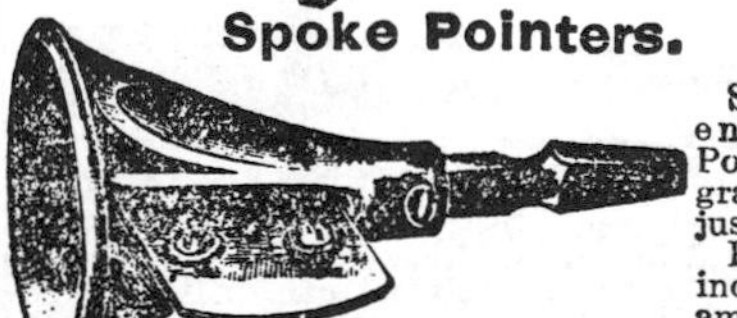

Stearn's Patent Spoke Pointer with graduated adjust'ble shank. Points, 1 7/8 inches in diameter.

No. 12990. No. 1, weight, 12 oz. Price, each......**56c**
No. 12991. No. 2, weight, 18 oz. (large). Price each. **94c**

## Angular Boring Attachment.

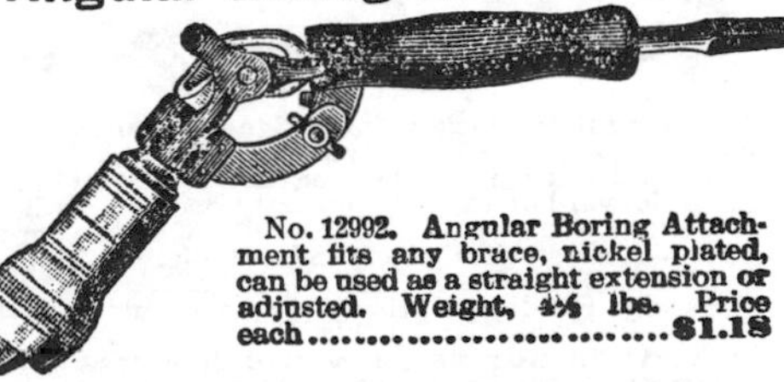

No. 12992. Angular Boring Attachment fits any brace, nickel plated, can be used as a straight extension or adjusted. Weight, 4 1/2 lbs. Price each........**$1.18**

**If you know anyone in Chicago, write to him and have him look us up. He can then be able to tell you as to our business and whether or not you will be safe in sending your order to us.**

## Bit Gauge.

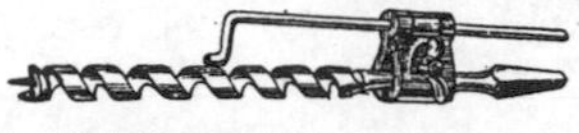

No. 12993. Bit Gauge. This cut shows the gauge in all of its parts. It will be seen that one bolt with thumb-screw tightens the clamps on the gauge spindle and auger bit at the same time. It will fit any size bit, and exactly gauge the depth of hole to be bored. Price, each .......... 25c

## Washer Cutter.

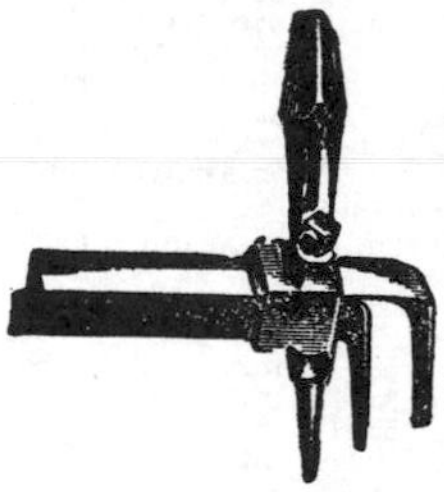

No. 12994. Washer Cutter for bit brace. Extra fine steel knives, polished. Cuts any size washer with any size hole up to 5½ nches in diameter. Will save its cost in one year. Besides, with this tool you can cut washers just exactly the size you want them and you can't always buy them the size wanted. Price, each.... 45c

## Breast Drills.

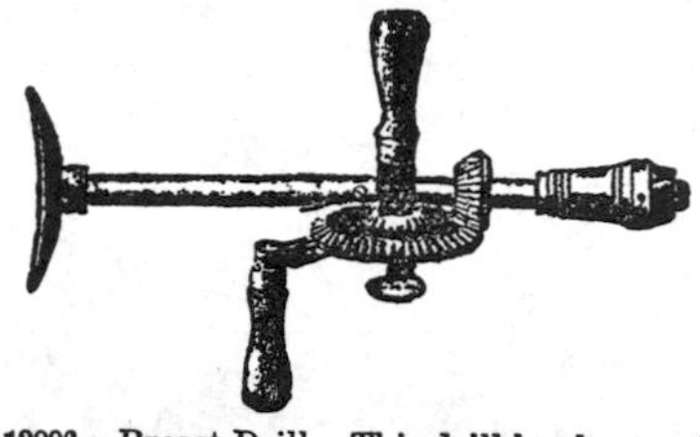

No. 12996. Breast Drill. This drill has been sold for years and given satisfaction to the user. Has malleable iron stock japanned rosewood handles, polished and plated. Improved chuck with recent improvement which makes it hold perfectly tools of all sizes and shapes. The gear is changeable—one even, the other three to one. A roller is placed under the large gear wheel which makes it practically equal to a double gear. Weight, 4 lbs. Price, each.......... $2.75

## Hand Drills.

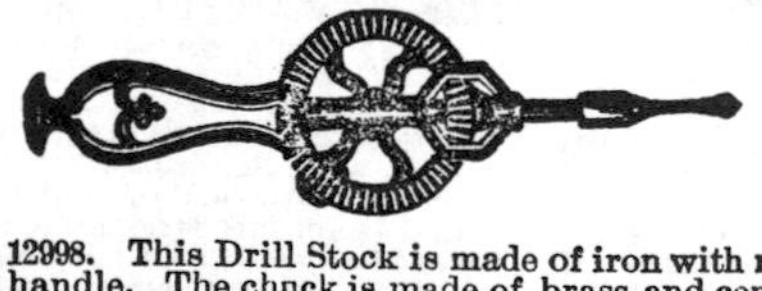

No. 12998. This Drill Stock is made of iron with rosewood handle. The chuck is made of brass and centers the drill perfectly and holds it securely. With each drill stock we furnish free of charge six superior drill points of various sizes. Weight, 8 oz. Price of stock and drills.......... 43c

No. 12899. Extra drill points, per set.......... 25c

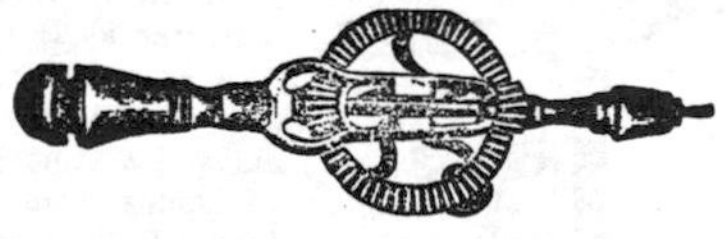

No. 13000. This Drill Stock is made of malleable iron with steel spindle and rosewood head and handle. The handle is hollow and contains six drill points of various sizes. The jaws are of forged steel and will hold perfectly drill shanks of any shape from 1-32 to ⅛ inch in diameter Price, each.......... $1.06

No. 13001. Extra drill points for above stock. Per set.......... 25c

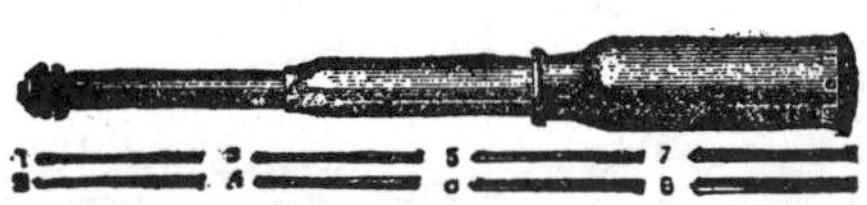

No. 13006 Automatic Drill, made of brass, nickel plated, with 8 drill points. There is a receptacle for each drill in the handle, and but one drill need be taken out and that the exact size wanted, as each receptacle is marked with size of drill contained. Price, each.......... $1.30

## Lightning Brace.

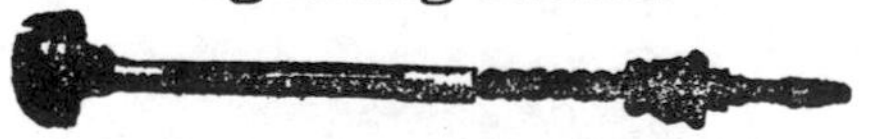

Lightning Brace, nickel plated, lignum vitæ and rosewood trimmings; is especially designed for light boring and screw driving; it may be used running the bit backward or forward or turn the bit only one way, as it is necessary; the movements are regulated by the head; very rapid in its work; strong and durable.

No. 13008. Like cut.......... $1.28

No. 13009. Small size, principle same as cut... 1.05

**A visit to our store would interest you. If you are ever in Chicago come and see us.**

## PINCERS AND NIPPERS.

### Carpenters' Pincers.

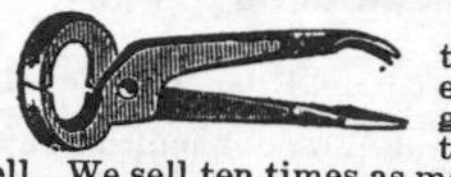

Did you ever see a Carpenters' Pincer that was good enough to suit you? We've got them. Some dealers say they are too high-priced to sell. We sell ten times as many of this grade as we ever could of the others. We like to sell this grade better than the cheaper ones. That's our plan, not how cheap, but how low-priced on good goods. Remember these pincers are not for cutting, but for pulling.

No. 13028. **Our best** Carpenters' Pincers, with claw on handle, forged from superior steel best adapted for the work.

| Size, inches, | 6 | 8 | 10 | 12 |
|---|---|---|---|---|
| Price, each, | $0.16 | .22 | .30 | .35 |

No. 13029. Carpenters' Pincers, as good as usually sold, and not by any means the cheapest pincer we can buy.

| Size, inches, | 6 | 8 | 10 |
|---|---|---|---|
| Price, each, | $0.14 | .18 | .25 |

### Pliers.

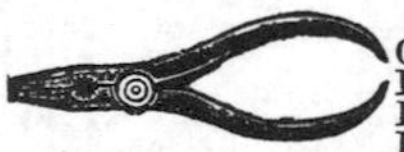

No. 13038. Family Plier and Cutter and Gas Burner Plier. It's a good one for the money. Length, 5½ inches. Weight, 7 oz. Price, each.......... 20c

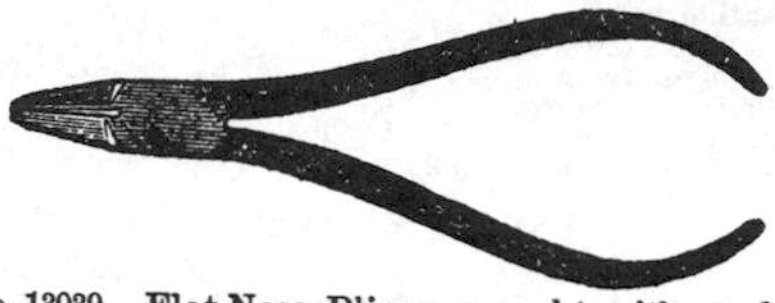

No. 13039. Flat Nose Pliers, wrought with steel face jaws. A good, cheap plier. Weight, about 7 oz.

| Size, inches, | 4 | 5 | 6 |
|---|---|---|---|
| Price, | $0.09 | .11 | .15 |

No. 13040. Flat Nose Pliers, solid extra cast steel. Good enough for anybody. Weight, 7 oz.

| Size, inches, | 4 | 5 | 6 |
|---|---|---|---|
| Price, | $0.13 | .15 | .20 |

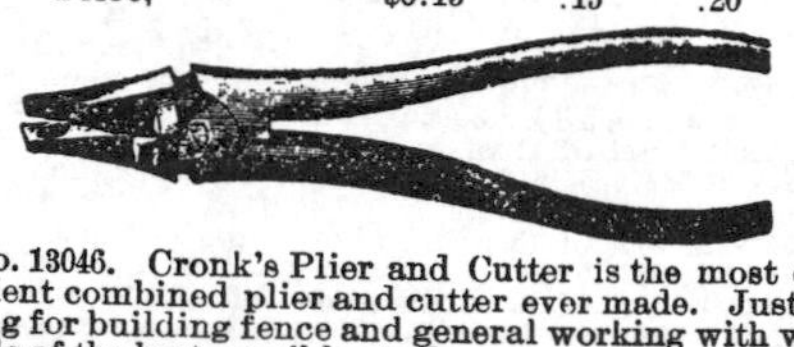

No. 13046. Cronk's Plier and Cutter is the most convenient combined plier and cutter ever made. Just the thing for building fence and general working with wire. Made of the best crucible steel.

| Size, inches, | 8 | 10 |
|---|---|---|
| Price, each, | $0.50 | 70 |
| Weight, ounces, | 17 | 23 |

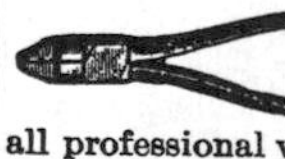

No. 13048. Solid steel Side Cutting Pliers, Stubb's pattern, with raised cutters. The plier used by electricians, bell hangers and all professional wire workers.

| Size, inches, | 4 | 5 | 6 |
|---|---|---|---|
| Price, each, | $0.40 | .45 | .50 |

### Round Nose Pliers.

No. 13049. Round Nose Pliers. Wrought with steel face jaws.

| Size, inches, | 4 | 5 | 6 |
|---|---|---|---|
| Price, each, | $0.15 | .20 | .25 |

No. 13050. Round Nose Pliers. Extra cast steel. Polished jaws. Don't pay more for same goods. Size, 6 inches. Price.......... 40c

### Cutters and Pliers.

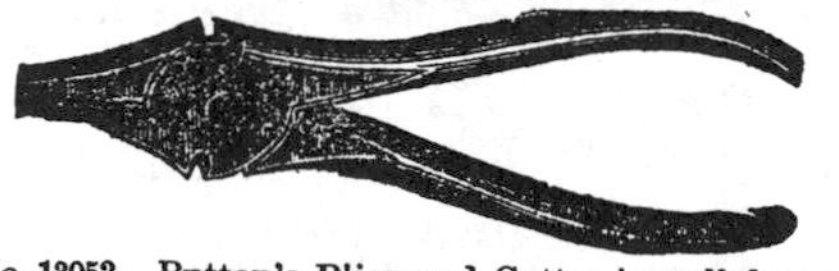

No. 13052. Button's Plier and Cutter is well known, Made from best quality of tool steel. We sell the genuine made by J. M. King & Co.

| Size, inches, | 6 | 8 | 10 |
|---|---|---|---|
| Price, each, | $0.28 | .38 | .48 |

### End Cutting Nippers.

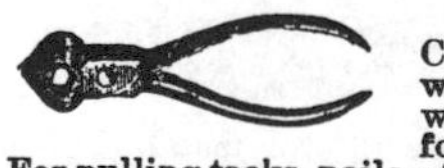

No. 13053. Solid steel End Cutting Nippers. Don't pry when cutting. If you do they will break if they are good for anything for cutting. For pulling tacks, nails, etc., use a carpenters' pincer.

| Size, inches, | 5 | 6 |
|---|---|---|
| Price, each, | $0.50 | .63 |

No. 13054. Wire Cutting Nippers, with removable jaws. The jaws can be taken off to be sharpened or new jaws can be replaced at little cost. A set screw through handles prevents jaws coming together too far, so one jaw cannot dull the other.

| Size, inches, | 8 | 10 | 12 |
|---|---|---|---|
| Price, each, | $0.65 | .75 | 1.00 |

No. 13055. Extra jaws for the above, any size wanted. Per pair.......... 25c

Send sample when ordering.

## Awls.

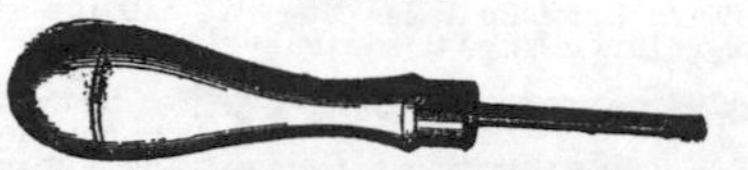

No. 13060. Handled Brad Awls, steel shouldered awl, polished handle with ferrule. Sizes small, medium and large. Weight, 6 oz. Price, each, 6c; per doz.......... 65c

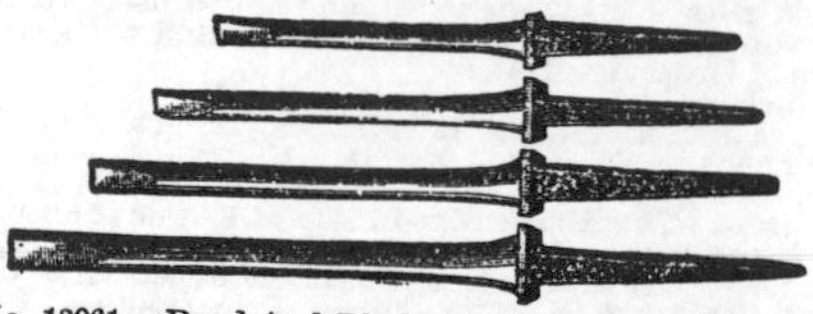

No. 13061. Brad Awl Blades, cast steel shouldered, no handles. Price, per doz., assorted sizes.......... 15c

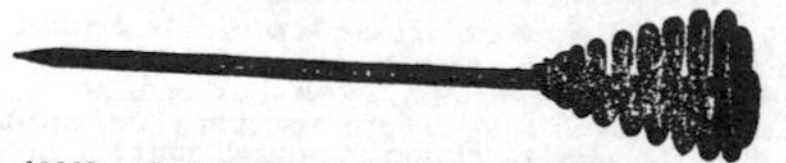

No. 13062. Solid Steel Scratch Awl. The blade and handles are made from one piece of **steel wire.** It is the strongest scratch awl made. Price, each.......... 6c

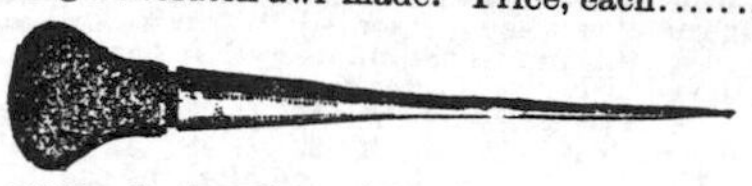

No. 13063. Socket Scratch Awl. Solid cast steel, polished beech handles. No danger of handle splitting and shank of awl being driven through your hand if you use this awl. Weight, 8 oz. Price, each.......... 10c

## Awl and Tool Sets.

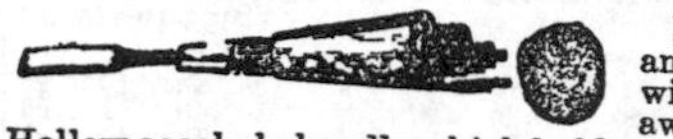

No. 13066. Awl and Tool Sets, with forged steel awls and tools. Hollow cocobolo handle which holds tools when not in use. Very convenient and serviceable. Weight, 9 oz. Price, each.......... 32c

## Leather Tool Set.

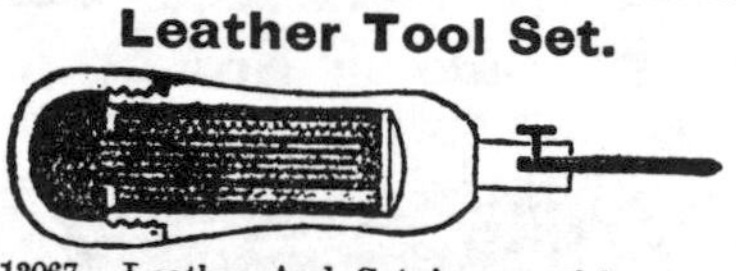

No. 13067. Leather Awl Set is something every one who has a harness should carry in his pocket when working on his farm, or in his buggy when driving on the road. It is a hollow handle, 5 inches long. Inside the handle is a spool holding 50 feet of best waxed linen shoe thread. Inside the spool are three awls and three needles of sizes commonly used. Awls are held in handle by a set screw. Weight, 6 oz. Price, each...... 18c

## Nail Sets.

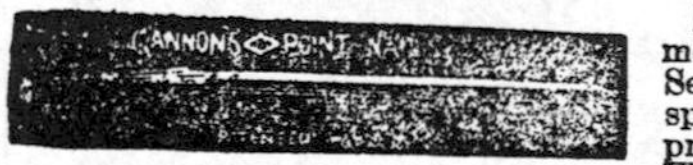

No. 13072. Diamond Point Nail Set, with sharp spur on point to prevent slipping. Weight, 4 oz. Price, each.......... 7c

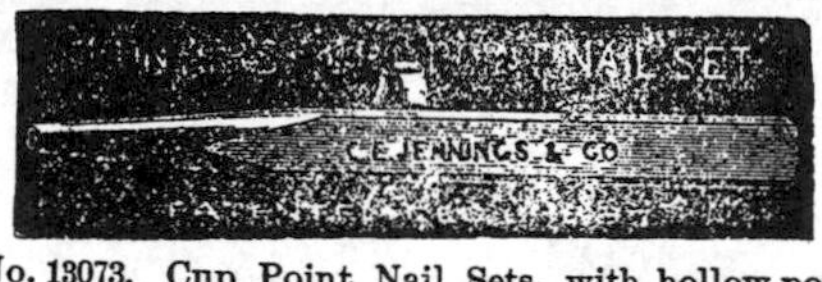


No. 13073. Cup Point Nail Sets, with hollow point. Just the thing for starting screws which are rusty or have broken heads. Weight, 4 oz. Price, each...... 5c

No. 13074. Forged Cast Steel Nail Sets. Octagon. Assorted sizes. Weight, 4 oz. Price, each, 4c; per doz. 38c

## Prick Punch.

No. 13075. Prick Punch, made of ⅜ inch octagon steel. Weight, 5 oz. Price, each.......... 5c

## Center Punch.

No. 13076. Center Punch, made of ⅜ inch extra octagon tool steel. Weight, 5 oz. Price, each.......... 5c

## Hollow Punches.

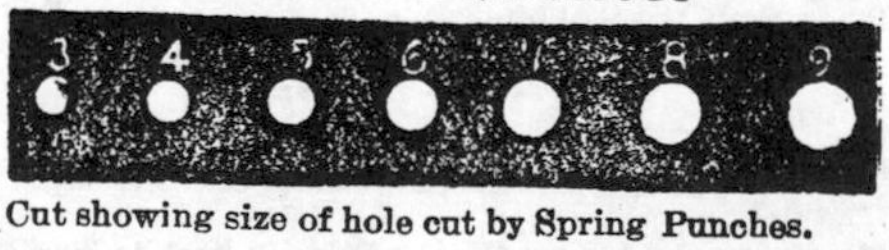


Cut showing size of hole cut by Spring Punches.

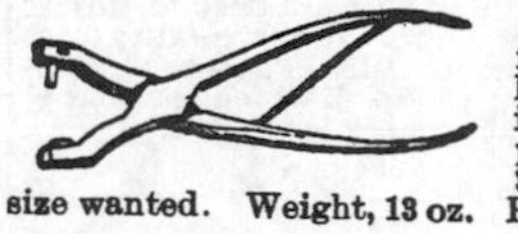

No. 13080. Spring Punch, for cutting holes in belts, harness, etc. Length, 6 inches; made of cast steel, polished. Tube sizes are 3, 4, 5, 6, 7, 8, 9. State size wanted. Weight, 13 oz. Price, each.......... 18c

**We ship Pianos and Organs subject to 20 days' trial. You can have a reputable music teacher give you a professional opinion as to whether the instrument is all that we represent.**

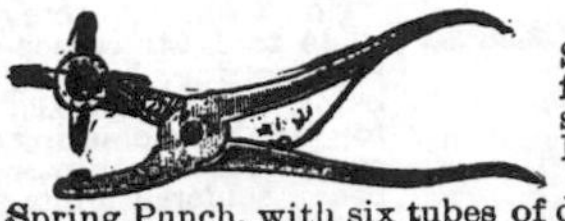

No. 13082. Revolving Spring Punch, with four tubes of different sizes. Weight, 14 oz. Price, each........**40c**

No. 13083. Revolving Spring Punch, with six tubes of different sizes. Weight, 14 oz. Price, each........**53c**

## Drive Punches.

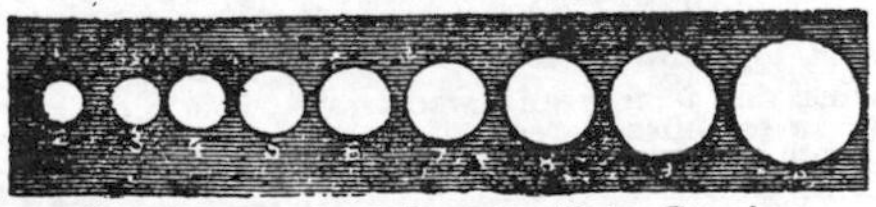

Cut showing size hole cut by Drive Punches.

No. 13084. Hollow Drive Punches. Sizes numbered from 1 to 9. Weight, 4 oz. Any one size, 1 to 5, price, **7c.** Any one size, 6 to 9, each, **8c.** Size 10, each...**10c**

## Conductors' Punches.

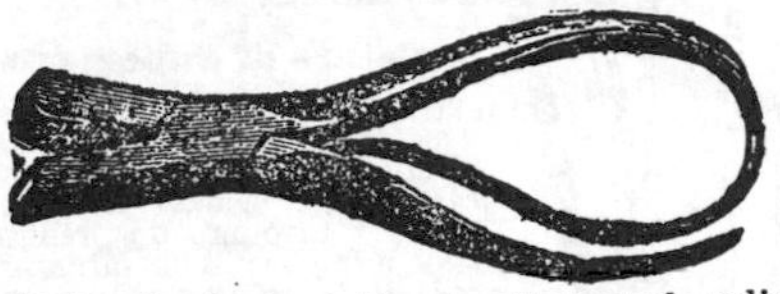

No. 13088. Conductors' Punch. Cast steel, polished and nickel plated, assorted holes, used for punching cards, tickets, etc. Price, each........**65c.**

No. 13089. Conductors' Punch. Made to order, to cut any letter. Hand made, nickel plated. Not sent C. O. D., and cannot be returned if sent as ordered. Price, each........**$2.00**

## Harness or Belt Rivets.

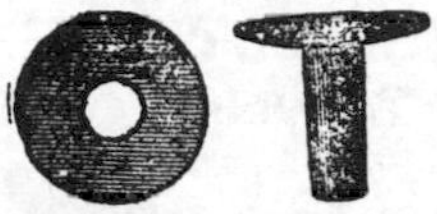

Size numbers refer to diameter, No. 8 being largest. There are more burrs than rivets in each package. We do not break packages.

No. 13090. Copper Rivets and Burrs. Size No. 8, either ⅜, ½, ⅝ or ¾ inches long. Only one length in a package. Price, per lb. package, **21c**; ½ lb. package........**12c**

No. 13091. Copper Rivets and Burrs. Size, No. 8. Lengths assorted from ⅜ to ¾ inches in each package. Price, per lb. package, **21c**; ½ pound package.....**12c**

No. 13092. Copper Rivets and Burrs. Size, No. 9. Either ⅜, ½, ⅝ or ¾ inch long. Only one length in a package. Price, per 1 lb. package, **22c**; ½ lb. package........**14c**

No. 13093. Copper Rivets and Burrs. Size, No. 9. Lengths assorted from ⅜ to ¾ inch in each package. Price, per 1 lb. package, **22c**; ½ lb. package........**14c**

No. 13094. Copper Rivets and Burrs. Size, No. 10. Either ⅜, ½, ⅝ or ¾ inch long. Only one length in a package. Price, per 1 lb. package, **24c**; ½ lb. package........**15c**

No. 13095. Copper Rivets and Burrs. Size, No. 10. Lengths assorted from ⅜ to ¾ inch in each package. Price, per 1 lb. package, **24c**; ½ lb. package........**15c**

No. 13096. Copper Rivets and Burrs. Size, No. 12. Either ⅜, ½, ⅝ or ¾ inch long. Only one length in a package. Price, per 1 lb. package, **26c**; ½ lb. package........**16c**

## Rivet Sets.

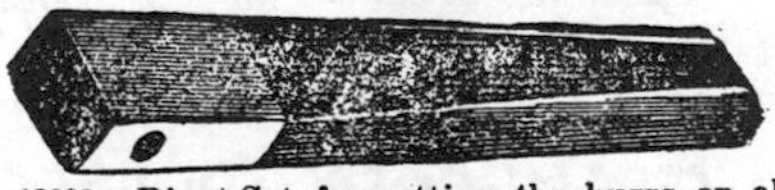

No. 13098. Rivet Set for setting the burrs on above rivets. No. 7 can be used for smaller rivets, but the No. 10 won't work on larger rivets. The sets are **just right** for the rivets of same number. Sizes either 7, 8, 9 or 10. Price, each........**12c**

## Slotted Rivets.

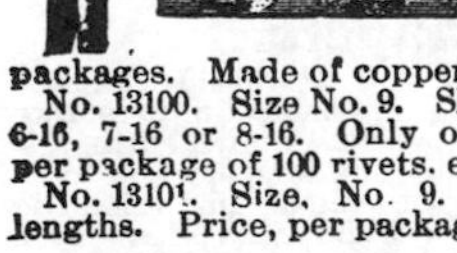

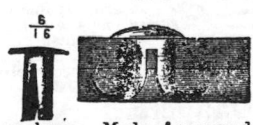

Slotted clinch Rivets are very popular, as no set or other tool is required except a common hammer. Put up in packages containing 100 rivets. We do not break packages. Made of coppered annealed steel.

No. 13100. Size No. 9. Slotted Rivets. Either 5-16, 6-16, 7-16 or 8-16. Only one size in package. Price, per package of 100 rivets, either size........**10c**

No. 13101. Size, No. 9. Slotted Rivets. Assorted lengths. Price, per package of 100 rivets........**10c**

## Steel Stamps.

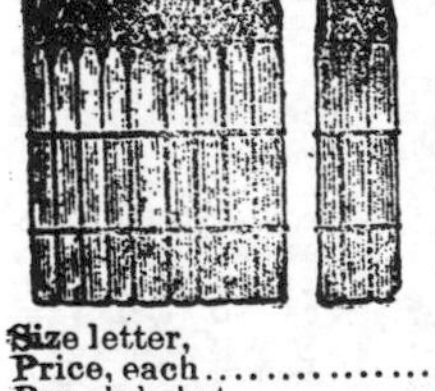

No. 13109. Steel letters and figures for stamping tools, etc. Mark your tools so you can always identify them. An alphabet consists of 26 letters, 1 period and 1 &. Sizes given indicate the length of letter which the stamp makes.

| Size letter, | ⅛ | 3/16 | ¼ | ⅜ |
|---|---|---|---|---|
| Price, each........ | $0.05 | .06 | .08 | .12 |
| Per alphabet........ | 1.30 | 1.70 | 2.20 | 3.50 |

No. 13110. Steel figures.

| Size, | ⅛ | 3/16 | ¼ | ⅜ |
|---|---|---|---|---|
| Price, each........ | $0.05 | .06 | .08 | .12 |
| Per set of 9........ | .40 | .50 | .65 | 1.00 |

No. 13111. We can furnish a number of letters in one stamp. These stamps are made to order, which requires three or four days' time in busy seasons. Be very careful in ordering these stamps, as they will not be taken back if sent as ordered.

⅛ inch letters, each letter costs........**20c**
3-16 inch letters, each letter costs........**25c**
¼ inch letters, each letter costs........**38c**

Cash in full must accompany orders for No. 13111 stamps.

## Stencil Sets.

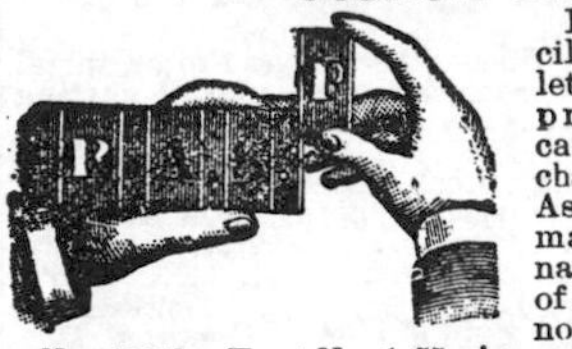

Interchangeable Stencils, put up in fonts of letters assorted by printers' rules. We cannot break fonts nor change the assortment. As put up they will make any ordinary name. They are made of spring brass and will not curl up.

No. 13112. Font No. 1, 55 pieces, consisting of letters, periods, etc.

| Size, inches, | ½ | ¾ | 1 | 1½ |
|---|---|---|---|---|
| Per font | $0.45 | .50 | .55 | .72 |

No. 13113. Font No. 2, 70 pieces, consisting of letters, periods, figures, etc.

| Size, inches, | ½ | ¾ | 1 | 1½ |
|---|---|---|---|---|
| Per font, | $0.60 | .65 | .70 | .93 |

## Bench Screws.

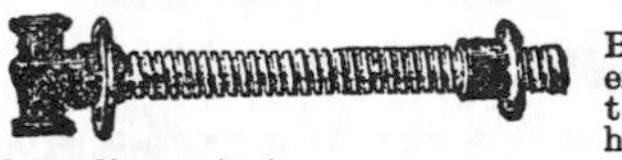

Wrought iron Bench Screw, patent collar, double thread, wood handle, length under collar, 15 inches.

No. 13118. Bench Screw, as above, 1 inch in diameter, weight 4¾ lbs. Price each........**25c**

No. 13119. Bench Screw, as above, 1⅛ inch in diameter, weight 6 lbs. Price each........**32c**

No. 13120. Bench Screw, as above, 1¼ inch in diameter, weight 7 lbs. Price each........**36c**

## Bench Stops.

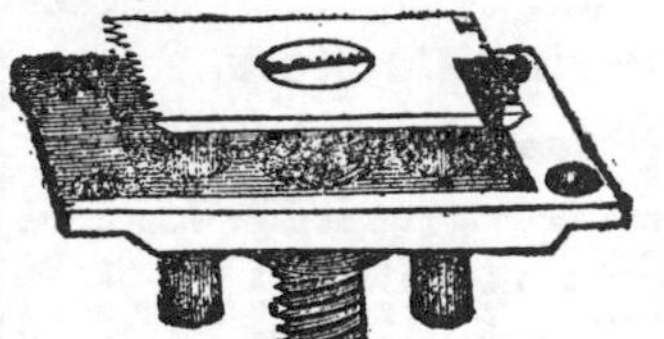

No. 13121. Bench Stop, reversible cast steel head, screw adjusting, weight 1 lb. Price each..**30c**

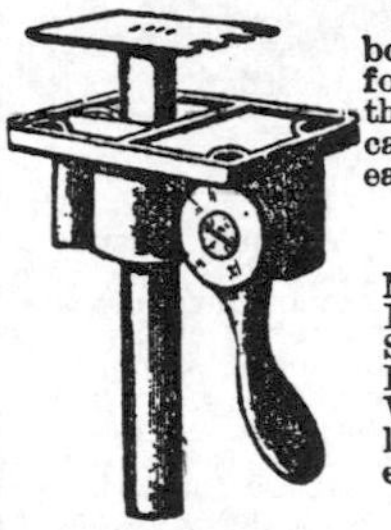

No. 13122. A ⅝ inch hole is bored through bench. The device for holding stop is fastened under the bench. The head is of solid cast steel. Weight 1¾ lbs. Price each........**48c**

No. 13123. Morrell's Patent Screw Set Bench Stop Weight, 1 lb. Price each...**43c**

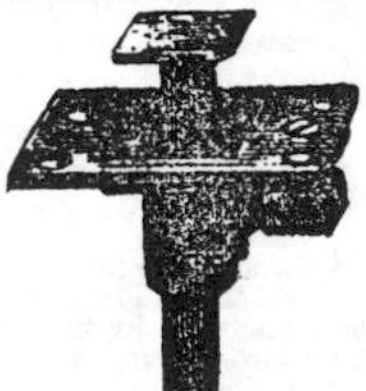

13123

## Eccentric Clamp.

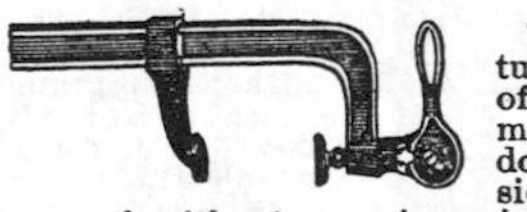

This Clamp is manufactured from the best quality of malleable iron; its main bar, or shaft, being double flanged upon each side, gives it the required strength without excessive weight.

The clamping arm, or jaw, is so adapted to the H shaft as to slide loosely upon it, or fasten immovably at any point the instant opposing pressure is brought to bear against it from the eccentric.

Thus, by placing the adjustable foot of the eccentric bolt against the work to be clamped, and moving the jaw up the shaft to oppose it, then simply raising the eccentric lever, the work is instantly clamped with all the power desirable, and with many advantages over the slow operating screw.

First, The work is accomplished with much greater facility, and with at least equal efficiency.

Second, The liability of slipping and displacement of the work by turning a screw against it is wholly obviated by the direct application of lever power.

Third, By the automatic adjustment of the foot, or bearing, it can be used upon beveled surface with the same facility as upon those that are square or right angular.

No. 13125. Eccentric Clamp.

No. 0 opens 2½ inches. Each........**18c**
No. 1 opens 4 inches. Each........**24c**
No. 2 opens 6 inches. Each........**33c**
No. 3 opens 8 inches. Each........**42c**
No. 4 opens 12 inches. Each........**52c**

## Long Bar Eccentric Clamp.

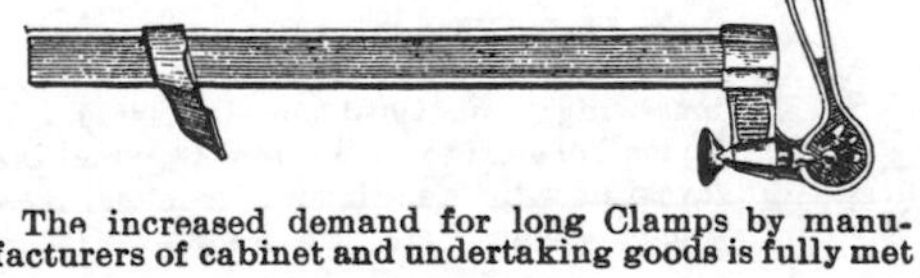

The increased demand for long Clamps by manufacturers of cabinet and undertaking goods is fully met by this Clamp. No other clamp made can equal it for strength, convenience and ease of adjustment, clamping instantly any width of work. Our Extra Heavy Clamp is exactly one-half heavier than our Heavy Clamp.

No. 13127. Cabinet Makers' and Builders' Heavy Clamp, each—

| | | | |
|---|---|---|---|
| 12-in., $0.54; | 24-in., $0.72; | 48-in., $1.08; | 72-in., $1.44 |
| 15-in., .58; | 30-in., .81; | 54-in., 1.17; | 78-in., 1.53 |
| 18 in., .63; | 36-in., .92; | 60-in., 1.26; | 84-in., 1.62 |
| 21-in., .67; | 42-in., 1.00; | 66-in., 1.35; | 90-in., 1.71 |

96-in., $1.80

No. 13128. Cabinet Makers' and Builders' Ex. Heavy Clamp, each—

| | | | |
|---|---|---|---|
| 12-in., $0.78; | 24-in., $1.06; | 48-in., $1.60; | 72-in., $2.16 |
| 15-in., .85; | 30-in., 1.19; | 52-in., 1.74; | 78-in., 2.29 |
| 18-in., .94; | 36-in., 1.33; | 60-in., 1.88; | 84-in., 2.44 |
| 21-in., .98; | 42-in., 1.47; | 66-in., 2.02; | 90-in., 2.57 |

96-in., $2.70

## Clamps.

No. 13133. Quilt Frame Clamps, japanned malleable iron, intended especially to hold quilt frames, but are convenient for many purposes; opens 2¼ inches. Price, each... **3c**; Per doz........**33c**

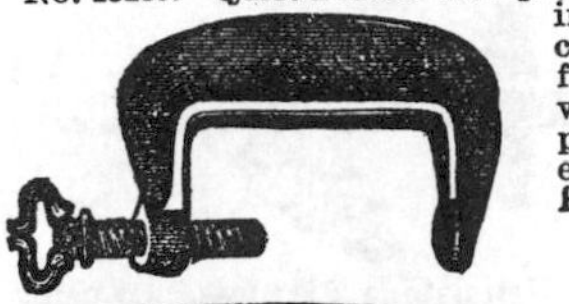

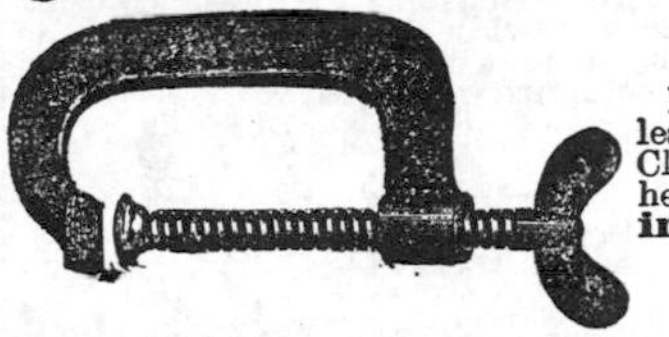

No. 13134. Malleable Iron Screw Clamps, swivel head, **wrought iron screw.**

| Opens, inches. | Weight, lbs. | Price, each. |
|---|---|---|
| 4 | 1½ | $0.16 |
| 5 | 1¾ | .19 |
| 6 | 2 | .24 |
| 7 | 3 | .29 |
| 8 | 3¼ | .32 |
| 10 | 5¼ | .41 |

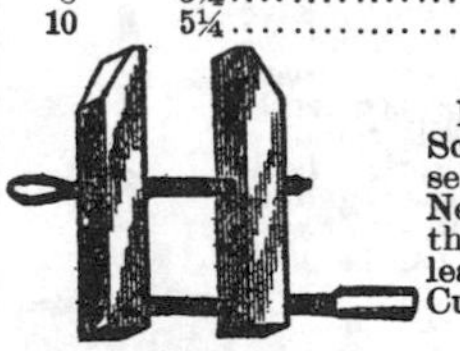

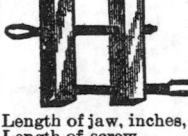

No. 13135. Wood Hand Screw Clamps, well made of seasoned hardwood stock. Never put oil of any kind on the screws; graphite or black lead is the proper thing to use. Cut shows complete set.

| | | | | | |
|---|---|---|---|---|---|
| Length of jaw, inches, | 8 | 10 | 12 | 16 | 20 |
| Length of screw, | 10 | 12 | 14 | 18 | 24 |
| Size of jaw, inches, | 1⅝ | 1¾ | 1⅞ | 2¼ | 2⅝ |
| Price, per set, | $0.16 | .20 | .23 | .33 | .43 |

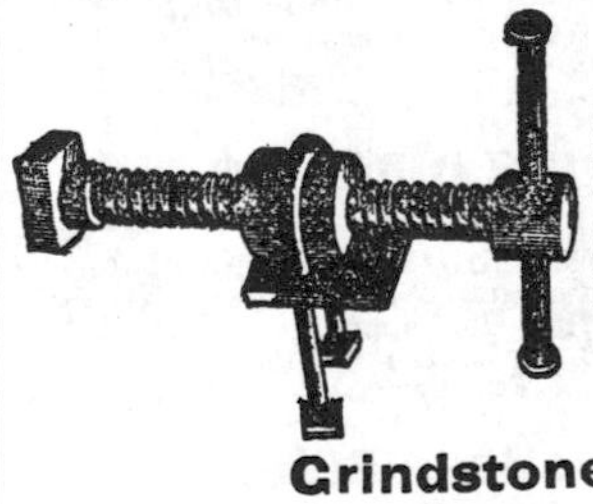

No. 13136. Clamp Head, wrought iron screw, revolving head, double thread, iron handles, diameter of screw 1 inch.
Price, each......**65c**
1⅛ inch......**90c**
1¼ inch....**$1.00**

## Grindstones.

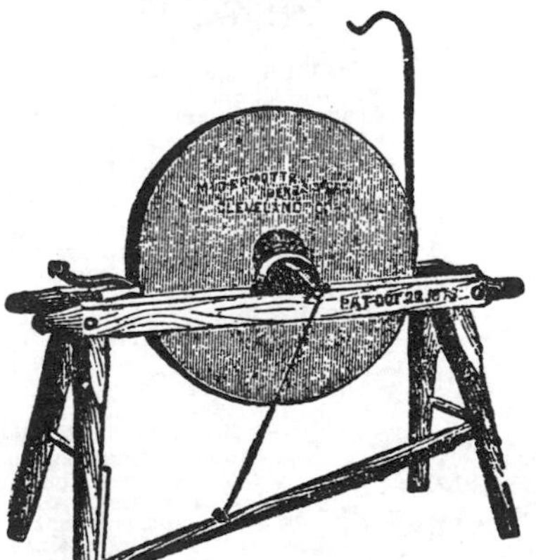

No. 13142. Grindstone, complete with oak frame, foot power, crank and fixtures, as illustrated. It is taken apart for shipping, but it is quickly and easily set up, as nothing but bolts are used. The usual thickness of stones is from 1¾ to 2¼ inches. Nothing but a select grade of first quality stones are used.

No. 1 stone weighs 100 to 110 lbs. Price, each..**$2.25**
No. 2 stone weighs 70 to 80 lbs. Price, each....**2.15**
No. 3 stone weighs 40 to 50 lbs. Price, each....**2.00**

No. 13143. Unmounted Grindstones of the best quality Berea or Huron grit, without frame or fixtures of any kind. Weights are from 40 to 200 lbs. Price, per lb........**¾c**

## Kitchen Grindstone.

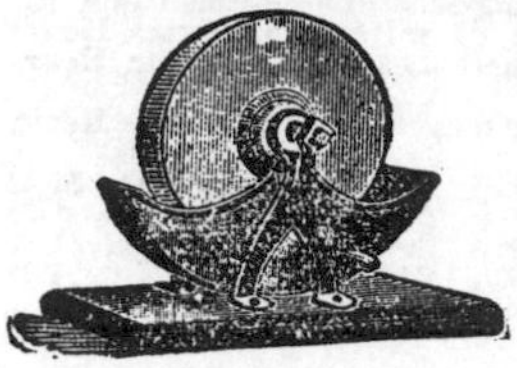

No. 13144. Kitchen Grindstone with water trough and frame as illustrated, solid stone, 8 inches in diameter; not a wood wheel covered with sand but a practical, serviceable tool that will put a keen edge on all kinds of tools.
Price, each.......**60c**

## Grindstone Fixtures.

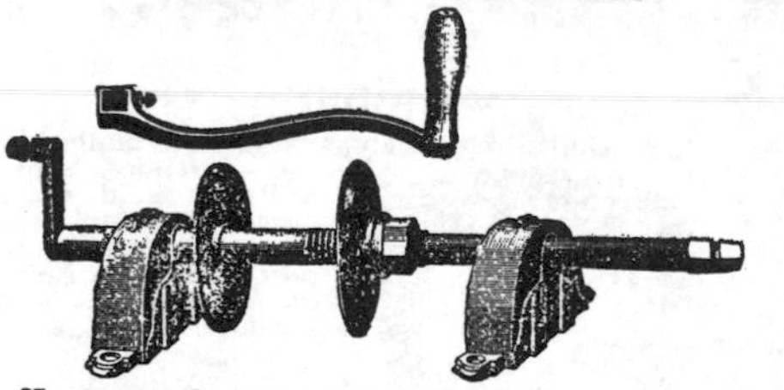

No. 13145. Cast iron Grindstone Fixtures. By using this fixture, stone is quickly centered and hung. No danger of splitting stone as is the case when a common shaft is used and held with wood wedges.

| | | | | |
|---|---|---|---|---|
| Shaft, inches long, | 15 | 17 | 19 | 21 |
| For lb., stone, | 40 | 60 | 80 | 100 |
| Price, each, | $0.25 | .28 | .30 | .35 |

## OIL CANS.

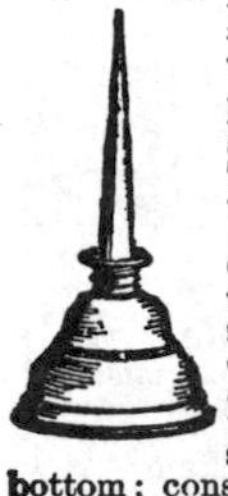

No. 13146.

| Size | 0 | 1 | 2 | 4 | 5 |
|---|---|---|---|---|---|
| Price, each........ | $0.04 | .05 | .06 | .08 | .10 |
| Price, per doz..... | .40 | .50 | .60 | .80 | 1.10 |

No. 0 is small, 2 inches across bottom and holds about ⅛ pint. No. 5 is 4¾ inches across bottom and holds about one pint. The others are graduated between. The weights vary from 4 to 7 oz.

No. 13146½. Automatic Zinc Oiler. This oiler cannot be tipped over like the ordinary zinc oiler. When accidently overthrown it will immediately resume an upright position because of the rounding shape of sides and very heavy bottom; consequently no oil can be accidently spilled from this oiler.

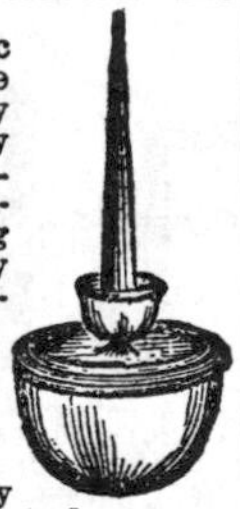

| Nos. | 1 | 2 | 3 |
|---|---|---|---|
| Holds, ounces ............ | 3 | 4 | 6 |
| Price, each................ | $0.15 | .17 | .19 |
| Price, per doz.............. | 1.62 | 2.16 | 2.38 |

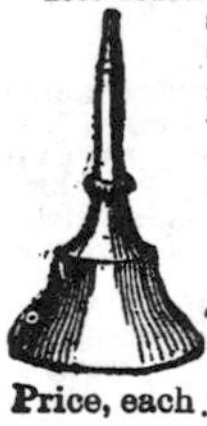

No. 13147. Malleable Iron Oiler; very strong; has patent elliptic steel spring. Weight 10 ounces.
Price, each.....................**25c**
Per doz...................**$2.70**

## Mowing Machine Oilers.

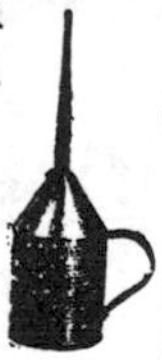

Mowing Machine Oilers, tin, bent or straight spout. Weight, 7 oz.
No. 13147½. Bent spout.
No. 13148. Straight spout.
Price, each...............**7c** Per doz..............**78c**

## Copperized Steel Oilers.

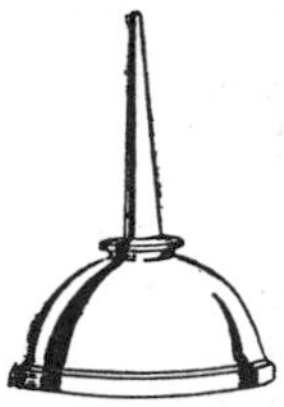

No. 13149. The Celebrated W. & H. Seamless Copperized Steel Oilers are cheap, durable and elegant. They are heavily electro-copper plated on the inside to prevent rust and to prevent the oil from becoming gritty. On the outside they perfectly resemble solid burnished copper. The 9-inch nozzles are bent, all the others are straight. Have clock steel spring bottoms.

| | | | | | | | |
|---|---|---|---|---|---|---|---|
| Diameter of bottom .... | 2¾ | 3⅜ | 3⅜ | 3⅜ | 3¾ | 4⅛ | 4⅛ |
| Length of nozzle, inches | 2½ | 3 | 5 | 9 | 3 | 3 | 9 |
| Price, each............ | $0.13 | .16 | .18 | .19 | .22 | .27 | .30 |

## OIL STONES.

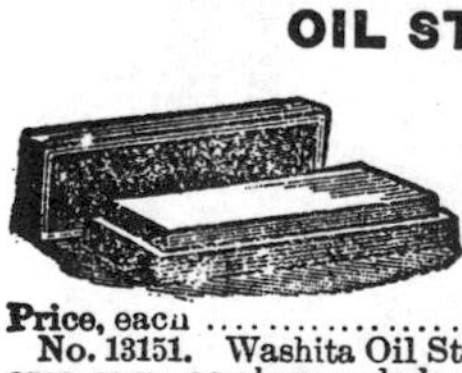

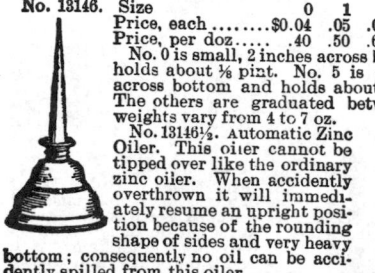

No. 13150. Washita Oil Stones, mounted in mahogany case, best quality selected stones, soft even grain and will not glaze if used properly; size, 6x1⅞x1; weight, 22 oz.
Price, each ..........................................**55c**

No. 13151. Washita Oil Stone, mounted in mahogany case, same as above only larger; size 7x1⅞x1; weight, 25 oz. Price, each..........................................**60c**

No. 13152. Washita Oil Stone, without case, same quality as above; weighing about 1 lb. Price, each.**30c**

No. 13153. Washita Oil Stone, without case, same quality as above, weighing about 1½ lbs.
Price, each ..........................................**45c**

No. 13154. Hindoostan Oil Stone, without case, weighing about 1 lb. Price, each..........................**10c**

No. 13155. Hindoostan Oil Stone, without case, weighing about 1½ lbs. Price, each........................**15c**

For emery stones, see emery goods department.

## Oil Stone Slips.

No. 13156. Round Edge Washita Slips, same quality as our Washita Oil Stones, from 3½ to 5 inches long.
Price, each..........................................**25c**

## Glass Cutters.

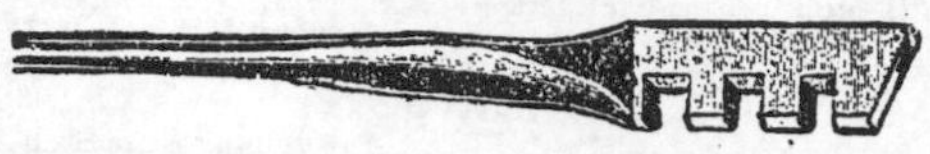

No. 13182. Revolving Steel Wheel Glass Cutter, metal handle polished and bronzed, extra quality cutting wheel. Price, each..............................**5c**
Per doz..........................................**50c**

No. 13183. Revolving Steel Wheel Glass Cutter, bronzed, with knife sharpener, cork screw and can opener combined. Price, each.....................**6c**
Per doz..........................................**60c**

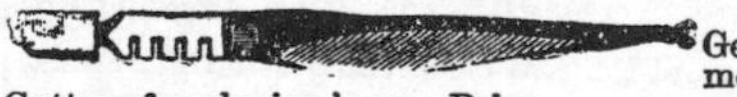

No. 13186. Genuine Diamond Glass Cutter, for glaziers' use. Price.............**$4, $5, $7** according to size and quality.

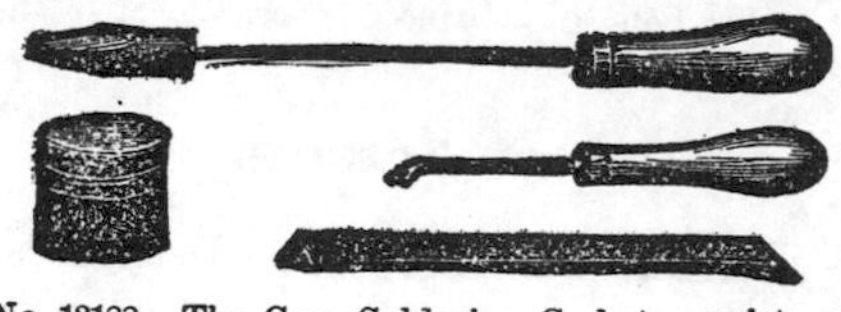

No. 13188. The Gem Soldering Casket consists of a small soldering copper, a scraper, a bar of solder and a box of rosin, all in a neat wood box with sliding cover. Weight, 1 lb. Price, each.........................**35c**

No. 13188½. The **Acme** Soldering Set consists of a small soldering copper, a piece of wire solder and a box of powdered rosin, packed in a paper box with full directions for use in mending tinware, etc. Weight, 5 oz.
Price..........................................**10c**

## Soldering Coppers.

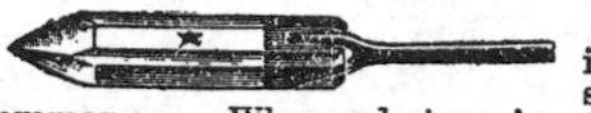

No. 13189. Soldering Coppers, with square points for common use. When ordering give number wanted, but **don't state weight.**

| No. | 1⅛ | 2 | 3 | 4 | 5 | 6 | 8 |
|---|---|---|---|---|---|---|---|
| Weight, lbs. each...... | ¾ | 1 | 1½ | 2 | 2½ | 3 | 4 |
| Price, each............ | $0.18 | .27 | .35 | .47 | .59 | .70 | .95 |

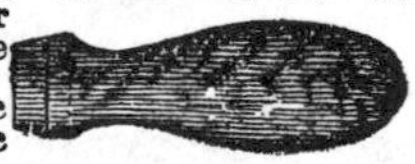

No. 13190. Soldering Copper Handles, Basswood, with wire ferrules.
Price, each..............................**3c**
Per doz..............................**25c**

## Tinners' Snips.

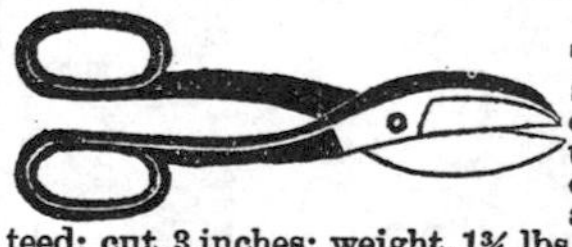

No. 13192. Cast Iron Tinners' Snips, are suitable for those who only occasionally have use for tin snips; they cannot be sharpened and are not guaranteed; cut 3 inches; weight, 1¾ lbs. Price, each.....**35c**

No. 13193. Tinners' Snips, good enough for anybody; same as used by tinners everywhere; no cast iron about these goods; cut 3 inches; weight, 1¾ lbs.
Price, each..........................................**$1.20**

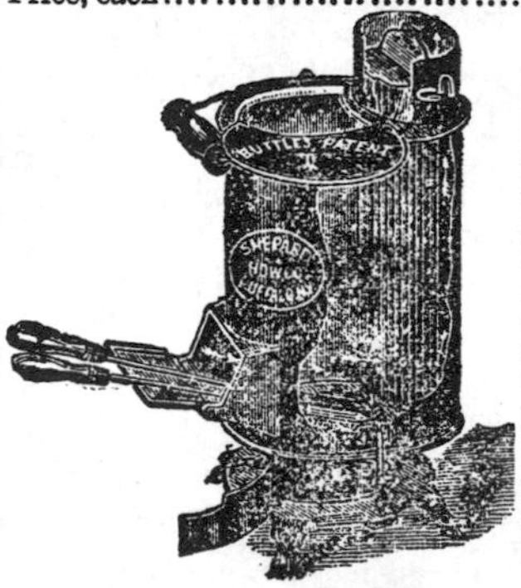

No. 13198. Tinners' Fire Pot, with shaking grate, hinged hearth door. The only double damper, reversible flue, tinners' stove made. When the fire is well started shut the front damper and open the back damper. This gives a downward draft directly on the coppers concentrating the heat where it is required.
Price, each. **$2.00**

## Solder.

No. 13199. Tinners' Solder, strictly half and half; bars weigh from 1¼ to 1½ lbs.; please notice a bar costs from 18 to 21c. Price, per lb...........................**14c**

Prices of metal are constantly fluctuating; we can't guarantee these prices on coppers and solder for the season. At all times we sell as cheap as possible, and should there be an extreme advance we should write you before filling order.

## Blow Pipe or Torch for Gasoline.

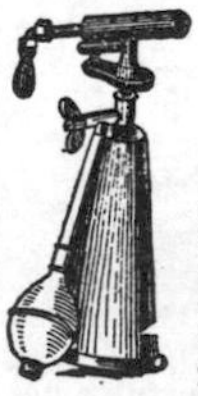

No. 13200. With this torch large or small flame can be used as desired. Made of brass, highly polished and lacquered. It is small enough to go in a tool bag, and is a favorite with electricians, painters, gas-fitters, plumbers, etc. Price, each....**$2.00**

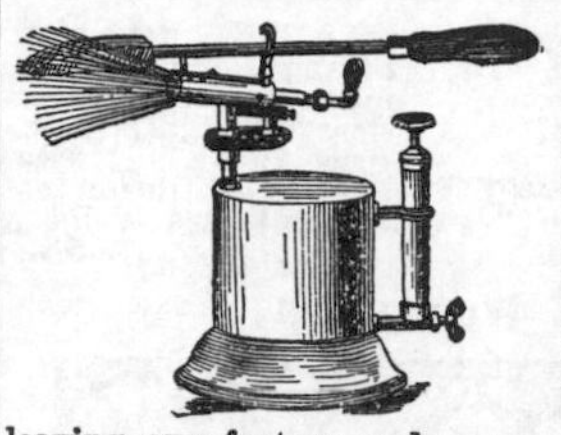

No. 13201. A complete tool for soldering, brazing, burning paint, melting metals; for heating soldering coppers, frozen pipes, heavy soldered joints, etc., etc.

A convenient, durable, reliable tool, adapted for a hundred purposes. Simple and safe in operation.

Each tested before leaving our factory and warranted. This Blow Pipe, with an established reputation, exceeds all others for strength, results and general excellence.
Price, each..........................................**$3.00**

## Hot Blast Brazer.

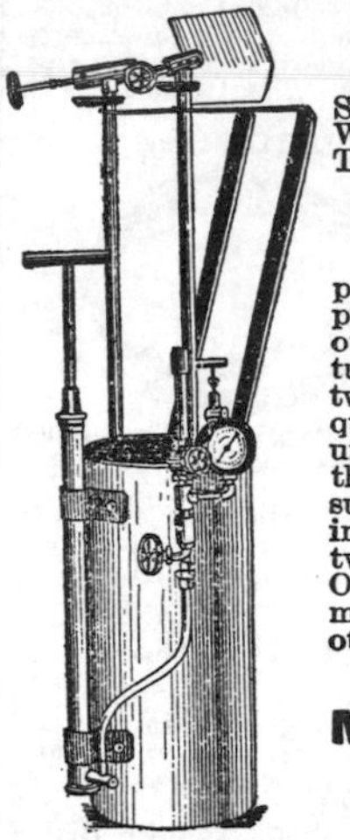

Most powerful machine made. Simple, durable, economical. Warranted to give satisfaction. Two burners.

**Points of Superiority.**

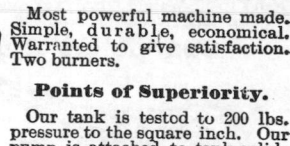

Our tank is tested to 200 lbs. pressure to the square inch. Our pump is attached to tank solid; others connected with rubber tube. Can pump up pressure in two minutes; five minutes required by others. Can work under 100 lbs. pressure. Can thereby braze under 100 lbs. pressure. Can braze with one flame in one minute; more time and two flames required by others. Our machine costs double to make, and sold at same price as others.

No. 13202. Price, each.**$18.75**

## MASONS' TOOLS.

### Trowels.

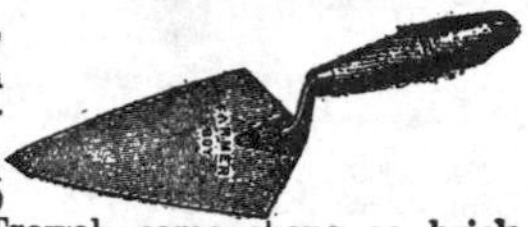

No. 13203. Masons' Brick Trowel, London pattern, cast steel polished.

| | | |
|---|---|---|
| Inches, | 10 | 11 |
| Price, each.... | $0.40 | .50 |

No. 13204. Pointing Trowel, same shape as brick trowel, only smaller, cast steel polished.

| | | | |
|---|---|---|---|
| Size, inches, | 4 | 5 | 6 |
| Price, each.................................... | $0.17 | .20 | .25 |

For other trowels see index.

### Plastering Trowels.

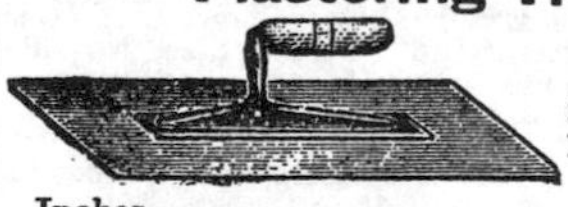

No. 13205. Plastering Trowel, cast steel polished.

| | | | |
|---|---|---|---|
| Inches, | 10 | 11 | 12 |
| Price, each.................................... | $0.40 | .50 | .65 |

### Corner Trowels.

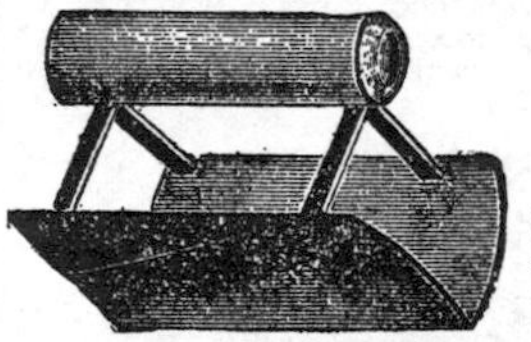

No. 13206. Corner Trowel, cast steel; length, 6 inches.
Price, each.........**50c**

## MACHINISTS' TOOLS.

### Spring Dividers.

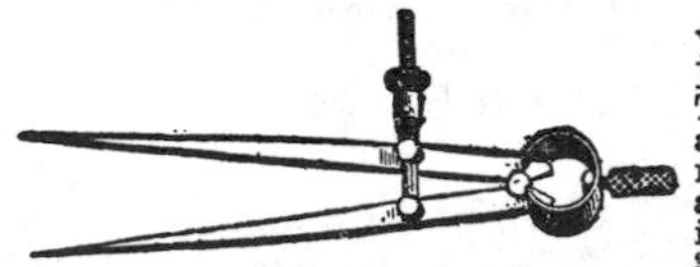

No. 13212. YankeeSpring Dividers. These dividers are very finely made goods and nicely finished. Length 3 inches, each **66c**; 4 inches, **70c**; 5 inches, **74c**; 6 inches, **76c**.

### Inside Calipers.

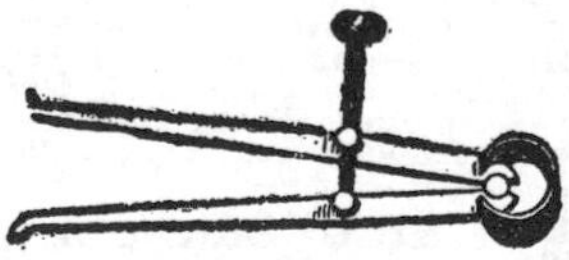

No. 13213. Yankee Inside Calipers, like the above spring dividers, are fine tools made on scientific principles, the spring being so applied that a firm joint is always maintained and an even tension is secured, whether the legs are closed or open to their full extent. Back lash in these calipers and dividers is impossible. Price, 4 inch, **58c**; 5 inch, **62c**; 6 inch, **67c**.

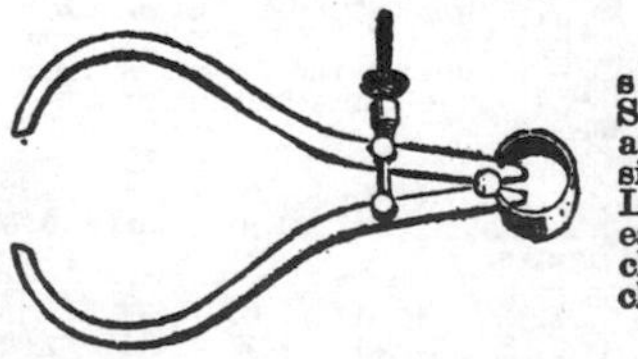

No. 13214. Outside Calipers. Same description as No. 13213. Inside Calipers. Length, 3 inches, each, **56c**; 4 inches, **60c**; 5 inches, **65c**.

**We have no salesmen, no accounts, no bad debts, none of this expense, and you don't have to pay for it. Do you see the point?**

## Bronze Dividers.

No. 13222. Starrett's Improved Bronze Divider. Nickel Plated.

The head and socket legs of this tool are made from drawn (not cast) bronze metal, and are hard, tough, strong, finely finished and nickel plated.

The joint is large and firm. Our patent locking nut between the arms, against which a spiral spring acts, is a valuable feature. After the fine adjustment is made, the nut may be turned back, locking spring and arms firmly, thus remedying the weak point in the common wing divider, which is only as stiff as the adjustable spring. The quadrant is fastened by our improved method.

A common pencil fits either socketed leg, while an auxiliary holder fits reversed end of either short point for an extension. The head, with short point, is eight inches long; may be extended two inches more; will caliper 10 inches outside and 12½ inside. With short points will scribe a 24-inch and with long points a 34-inch circle.

With short points only.....................$1.75
Set complete.............................. 3.25

## Caliper Square.

This cut represents an improved tool for both outside and inside measure. The beam is nicely graduated, 64ths on one side, 100ths on the other. For close work this is a reliable tool.

No. 13223. 4 inch, with adjustable screw.
Each..................................$3.60
No. 13224. 4 inch, without adjustable screw.
Each..................................$2.92

## Scriber.

No. 13226. Scriber for mechanics' use, made in three pieces, the center piece being heavily knurled, into which is screwed the two points which are made of fine steel, nicely tempered; is 7 inches in length. Each, 35c

## Depth Gauge.

No. 13228. Depth Gauge for machinists' use. The back is made from sheet steel, nicely polished; the edge is ground straight so that by removing the needle it may be used as a straight edge, as one edge of back is beveled and one side of needle is ground away, bringing the point of needle directly under edge of back; it may be rocked, thus determining the depth of hole or slot more accurately than can be done with a tool having a broad base. Price, each.......18c

## Double Square.

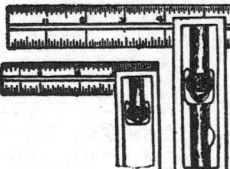

No. 13232. Patent Double Square. This Square is conceded the most practical one for machinists and fine tool makers' use ever offered. The sliding scale, shortened or extended full length, makes it more valuable than a full set of common kind, while with the extra bevel blade, shown in the following cut, we have both the hexagon and octagon angles.

The seat against which the blade is clamped being convex, should corners of the blade get injured, the accuracy of the square is not affected. 4 inch, each, $1.10; 6 inch .........................$1.80

## Bevel Blades.

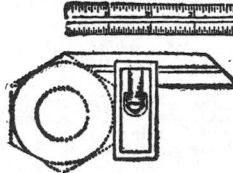

No. 13233. This cut represents the 4 inch and 6 inch double square, with hexagon end of blade applied. Reverse it and the octagon is in position for use. Bevel blades are made to fit only 4 inch and 6 inch sizes. These prices below are for the bevel blades only, and can not be used without the above square. 4 inch,

each, 32c ; 6 inch....................42c

## When Such Prices Are Named

— ON A —

**Violin, a Guitar, or a Mandolin**

Dealers say the goods are cheap. Don't be deceived.

Look at the goods and judge for yourself before paying.

## Starrett's Combination Square.

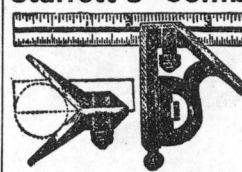

No. 13234. Patent Combination Square with the adjustable scale. Every tool warranted accurate. With the adjustable scale this forms one of the most convenient and useful tools ever devised for mechanics' use. One is a complete substitute for a whole set of common try-squares, and is one of the best gauges made for transferring exact measurements or laying out work. It is also convenient for a depth gauge, or to square in a mortise. For a mitre it is perfect, while with the auxiliary center head it forms a centering square, both inside and outside, which for convenience and accuracy has no equal. Made in three sizes with center head and level. Each, 6 inch, $1.55; 9 inch, $1.95; 12 inch, $2.32.

## Starrett's Combination Inclinometer.

No. 13235. Patent Inclinometer, Try-Square and Bevel Protractor Combined. This cut represents an Inclinometer, try-square and bevel protractor combined. It is compact, convenient and a complete and perfect substitute for several costly tools. It consists of a stock and disc, both slotted to receive the blade, which folds in the stock. The blade attached to the graduated rotary disc may be secured at any angle from 0 to 90 degrees, and by loosening the clamp screw it may be shortened or extended full length, or removed for a straight edge. The working face of the stock, extending both sides of the blade, admits of its being reversed, so that the same angle may be laid off in opposite directions **without changing** the angle in the tool, thus requiring but ¼ of a graduated circle to obtain all angles both ways. At 90 degrees, the blade brings up against a case hardened screw, accurately adjusted, thus forming a **try-square**; by holding the blade perpendicular (the level in the stock being at right angles), a **plumb**; by folding the tool, a **level**, length of blade. Open it to any degree, and work may be leveled to that incline. Each, 12 inch blade, $4.50; 18 inch, $5.40; 24 inch, $6.30.

## Bevel Protractor.

No. 13236. Improved Bevel Protractor. An adjustable rule, held firmly at any point by a thumb nut, passes through a revolving turret which is nicely graduated in degrees from 0 to 90, both right and left, and can be accurately adjusted to show any angle. A valuable auxiliary is made in the shape of a small level to be attached in place of the rule removed, forming an adjustable level to show any degree, thus greatly increasing the usefulness of the instrument. Each, 9 inch rule, 5 inch head, $2.33; 12 inch rule, 7 inch head, $2.52; 18 inch rule, 7 inch head, $3.10; 24 inch rule, 7 inch head, $3.49.

## Universal Bevel.

No. 13237. Improved features. The set-off in the blade increases its capacity and usefulness for bevel gear work, etc., so that any angle however slight, may be obtained. Another valuable feature is, one edge of the case being solid forms a rest directly under the blade, where thin templets may be placed and accurately fitted. Price, 3 inch...$1.30

## Screw Pitch Gauge.

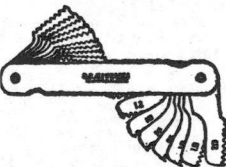

No. 13238. Improved Screw Pitch Gauge. This gauge has twenty pitches, viz: 9, 10, 11, 12, 13, 14, 15, 16, 18, 20, 22, 24, 26, 28, 30, 32, 34, 36, 38, 40. This is the only gauge made that can be used inside a nut as well as on the outside of a screw or bolt. A further improvement has recently been made in reducing the width of the leaves having the finer pitches, so that they will enter small nuts. Each......................75c

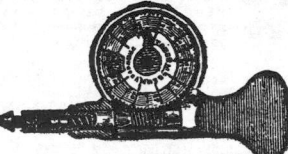

No. 13239. Speed Indicator. The Tabor Revolution Counter, with stop motion. A good, simple speed indicator. Each, 90c ; postage, 5c.

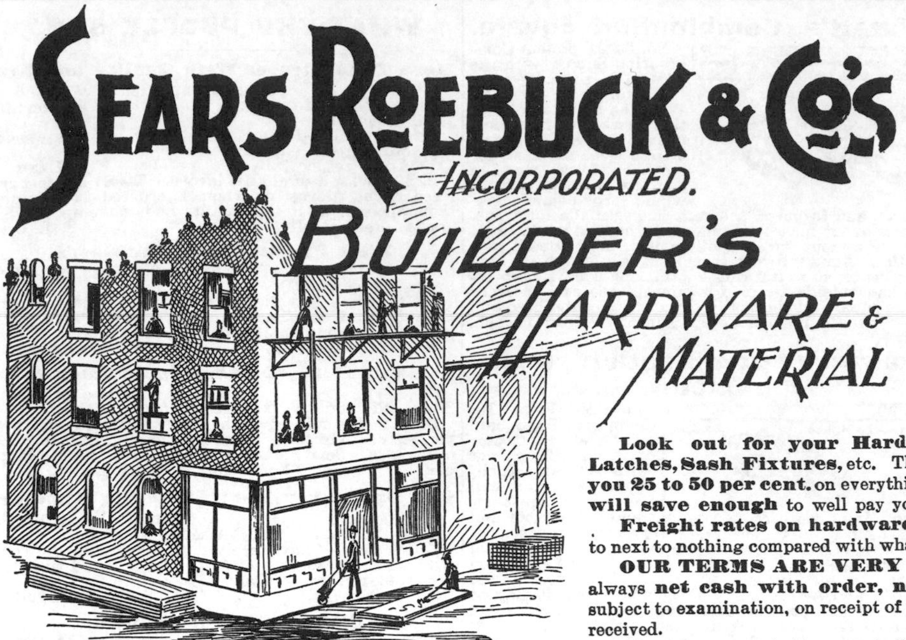
SEARS ROEBUCK & CO'S
INCORPORATED.
BUILDER'S
HARDWARE &
MATERIAL

**UNREASONABLE PROFITS** are usually asked on goods in this line.

**YOU WILL REQUIRE Doors, Sash, Building Paper, Paint, Lime, Hair, Cement, and Hardware,** when you get ready to build a house, and most of the articles named when building a barn or granary or other building.

**WE MAY NOT SELL YOU,** but if you will have your carpenter make out a bill of just what goods you will require in this line, **we will quote you a price, delivered at your nearest railroad station, and if we don't sell you,** we will compel your local dealer to lose money and **sell the cheapest bill he ever sold** and in either case **we will save you money.**

**LUMBER DEALERS** often sell lumber on a small margin and make it up by charging **unreasonably large** profits on **Doors, Sash, Building Paper and Paint. Look out for your Lumber merchant** on these lines.

**Look out for your Hardware merchant** on **Locks, Door Knobs, Hinges, Latches, Sash Fixtures,** etc. These are big profit goods with retail dealers. **We can save you 25 to 50 per cent.** on everything in this line, and no matter how little you wish to buy, **you will save enough** to well pay you for sending to Chicago for the goods.

**Freight rates on hardware and Building Material are low** and will amount to next to nothing compared with what you will save in price.

**OUR TERMS ARE VERY LIBERAL.** On all except **Doors and Sash,** which are always **net cash with order, no discount,** we will ship any goods by freight **C. O. D.,** subject to examination, on receipt of **one-fourth** the amount of the bill, balance to be paid when received.

**Three per cent. discount** allowed if cash in full accompanies your order.

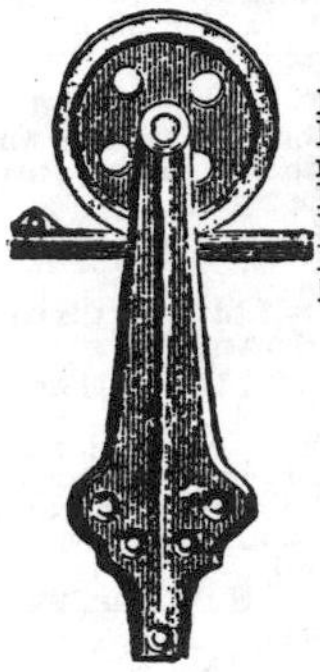

## Barn Door Hangers.

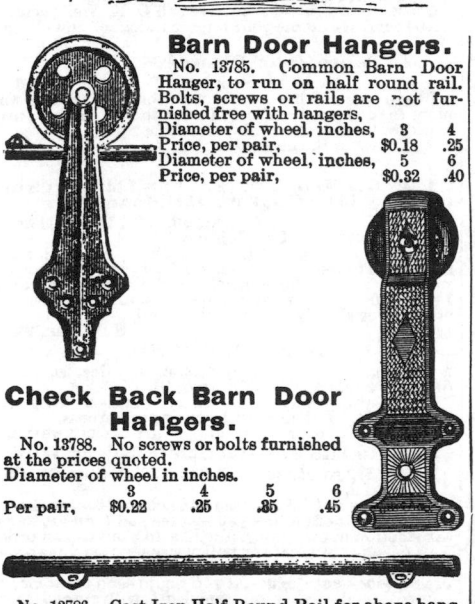

No. 13785. Common Barn Door Hanger, to run on half round rail. Bolts, screws or rails are not furnished free with hangers,

| | | |
|---|---|---|
| Diameter of wheel, inches, | 3 | 4 |
| Price, per pair, | $0.18 | .25 |
| Diameter of wheel, inches, | 5 | 6 |
| Price, per pair, | $0.32 | .40 |

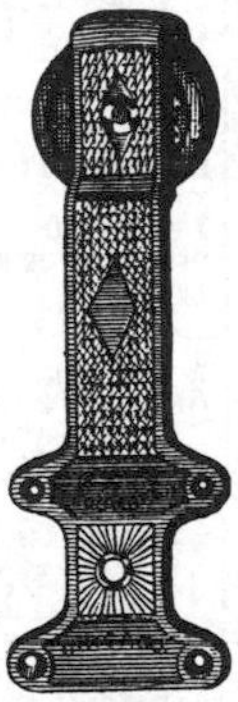

## Check Back Barn Door Hangers.

No. 13788. No screws or bolts furnished at the prices quoted.

| Diameter of wheel in inches. | 3 | 4 | 5 | 6 |
|---|---|---|---|---|
| Per pair, | $0.22 | .25 | .35 | .45 |

No. 13786. Cast Iron Half Round Rail for above hangers comes in pieces 2 feet long. Price, per foot, without screws.............................. **2c**

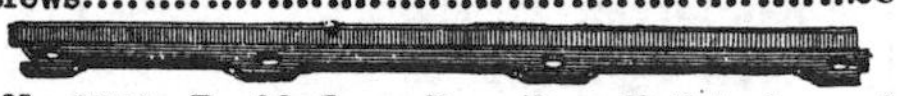

No. 13789. Double flange Barn Door Rail to be used with above hangers, No. 13788; comes in pieces 2 feet long. No screws furnished at prices quoted. Per foot.... **2½c**

## Cronk's Anti-Friction Steel Barn Door Hanger.

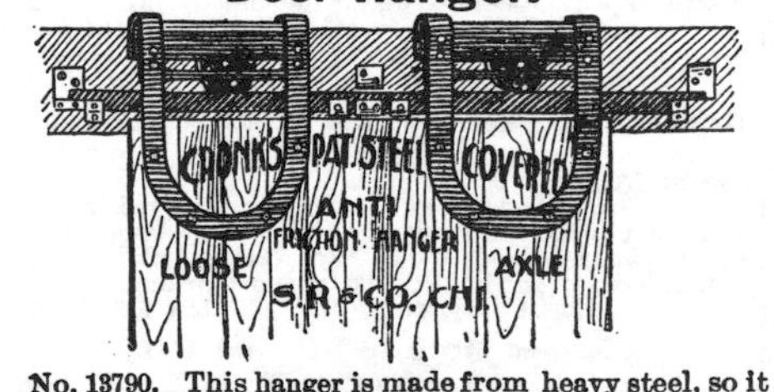
CRONK'S
PAT. STEEL
COVERED
ANTI
FRICTION HANGER
LOOSE
AXLE
S.R.&CO. CHI.

No. 13790. This hanger is made from heavy steel, so it will carry the door with perfect ease and no trouble. We make a round bearing at the ends of the run, so if used on wider doors than made for, the axle will not wear into the rider bar, and the round bearings also make it run much easier than it otherwise would, or than any other hanger will that is not made this way. The groove is U shape, so it will not touch or grind on the edges and create friction, and also having a deep groove, will not jump the track. These hangers are marked with a gauge to put them up by, which saves time and insures getting them up right, even if done by a man not posted in the business. No screws or bolts furnished at prices quoted.

| | | | Per pair. | Per doz. pair. |
|---|---|---|---|---|
| No. 1. | For 6 ft. run. | Price..... | .50c | $5.40 |
| No. 1½. | For 9 ft. run. | Price..... | .60c | 5.48 |
| No. 2. | For 10 ft. run. | Price..... | .70c | 7.90 |
| No. 3. | For 15 ft. run. | Price..... | .80c | 9.36 |

## Cronk's Double Braced Steel Rail.

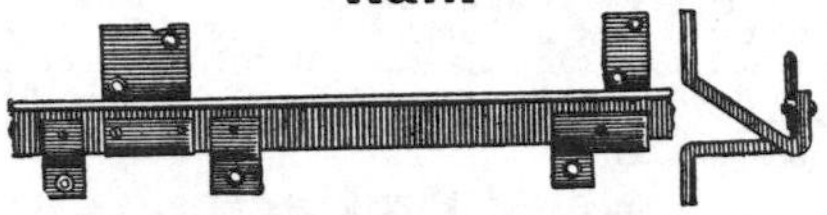

No. 13791. This rail, being double braced and double riveted, is the strongest rail in the market. Being braced both ways it will not sag. The joint is made so that it is perfectly solid. It can be used for any grooved wheel hanger, and a heavy door will not make it spring or tremble. Guaranteed to hold a door weighing 2,000 pounds, and used in connection with our Anti-Friction Hangers will work perfectly on large or small doors. If 1¼x10 screws or wire nails are used it will hold any door made.

Comes in pieces 6, 8 and 10 feet long. Price quoted does not include screws. Price, per foot.............. **3c**

## Barn Door Stay Rollers.

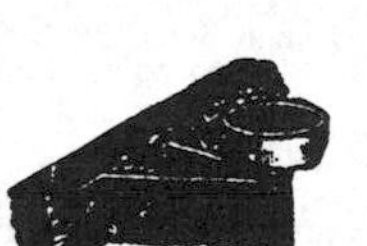

No. 13795. Barn Door Stay Rollers to screw, wrought iron shank. Weight, 14 oz. Price, each, **7c**; per doz........ **65c**

No. 13796. Barn Door Stay Rollers, adjustable to any thickness of door. Will always stay in the right position. Price, each, **8c**; per doz.................. **85c**

No. 13797. Barn Door Pulls, extra heavy japanned. Weight, 10 oz. Price, each, **4c**; per doz.................. **40c**

## Hinges.

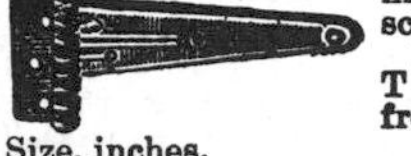

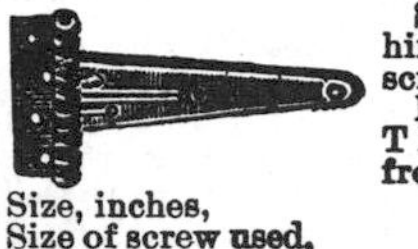

Screws are not furnished with hinges at prices quoted. For screws see index.

No. 13806. Light wrought steel T Hinges. Size given is measure from joint to end of hinge.

| | | | | |
|---|---|---|---|---|
| Size, inches, | 3 | 4 | 6 | 8 |
| Size of screw used, | 7 | 8 | 8 | 10 |
| Weight, pair, | 4 oz. | 5 oz. | 8 oz. | 12 oz. |
| Price, pair.......................... | $0.03 | .04 | .05 | .07 |
| Doz. pairs.......................... | .33 | .40 | .54 | .75 |

No. 13808. Extra heavy wrought steel T Hinges.

| | | | | | |
|---|---|---|---|---|---|
| Size, inches, | 6 | 8 | 10 | 12 | 14 |
| Price, pair............... | $0.09 | .13 | .20 | .27 | .33 |
| Price, doz. pairs......... | .98 | 1.40 | 2.20 | 3.12 | 3.65 |

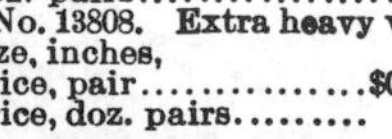

No. 13816. Light wrought steel Strap Hinges. Size given is measurement from joint to end of hinge.

| | | | | |
|---|---|---|---|---|
| Size, inches, | 3 | 4 | 5 | 6 |
| Price, per pair.................. | $0.03 | .04 | .05 | .06 |
| Price, doz. pairs.................. | .33 | .44 | .54 | .56 |

No. 13817. Heavy wrought steel Strap Hinges, without screws.

| | | | | |
|---|---|---|---|---|
| Size, inches, | 6 | 8 | 10 | 12 |
| Price, per pair.................. | $0.08 | .12 | .18 | .25 |
| Price, per doz. pairs............ | .80 | 1.26 | 1.92 | 2.83 |

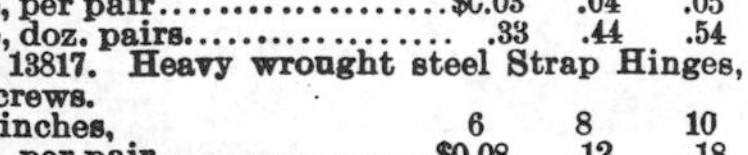

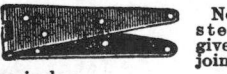

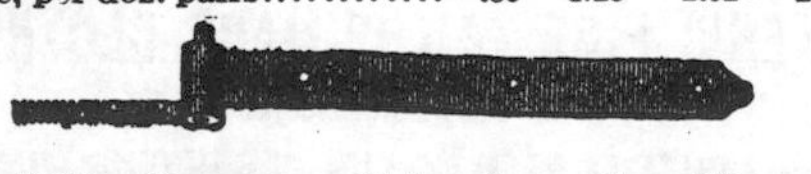

No. 13818. Heavy wrought iron Screw Strap Hinges.

| | | | |
|---|---|---|---|
| Size, inches, | 10 | 12 | 14 |
| Weight, per pair, lbs., | 3½ | 4½ | 5½ |
| Price, per pair.................. | $0.12 | .18 | .22 |
| Price, per doz. pairs............ | 1.28 | 1.75 | 2.00 |

**Screws not furnished.**

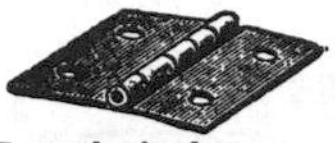

No. 13824. Narrow wrought steel Butts.

| | | | | | |
|---|---|---|---|---|---|
| Length. inches........... | 1 | 1¼ | 1½ | 2 | 2½ |
| Width, open............... | 1¼ | 1 5/16 | 1½ | 1¾ | 1⅞ |
| Size screw used.......... | 5 | 6 | 7 | 8 | 8 |
| Weight per pair, oz...... | 2 | 3 | 4 | 4 | 7 |
| Price, per pair......... | $0.02 | .02 | .03 | .04 | .04 |
| Price, per doz. pairs.... | .12 | .16 | .21 | .26 | .31 |

Screws are not furnished with Butts.

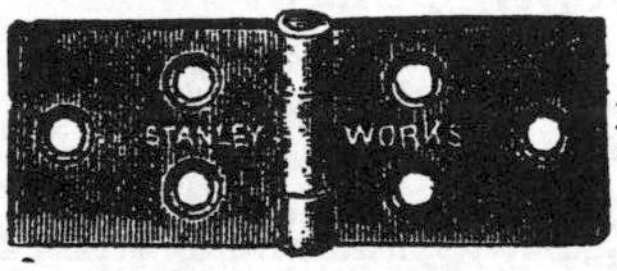
STANLEY
WORKS

No. 13825. Wrought steel Back Flaps.

| | | | | | | |
|---|---|---|---|---|---|---|
| Width, inches..... | ¾ | ⅞ | 1 | 1¼ | 1½ | 2 |
| Length, open...... | 2¾ | 2 13/16 | 2⅝ | 3 3/16 | 3 7/16 | 4⅜ |
| Size screw used... | 6 | 6 | 6 | 6 | 8 | 9 |
| Price, per pair... | $0.03 | .03 | .03 | .04 | .04 | .05 |
| Price, per doz. pairs | .20 | .22 | .23 | .29 | .35 | .49 |

Screws are not furnished with Butts.

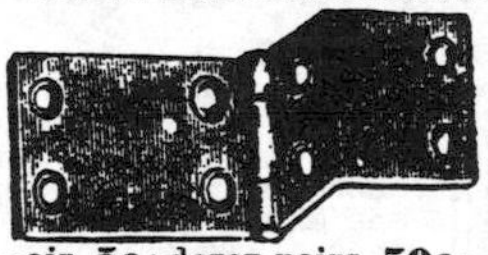

No. 13827. Wrought steel Chest Hinges. The 1½ inch size is 1½ inches wide and can be used on stuff ¾ inch thick. The 2 inch size is 2 inches wide and can be used on stuff ⅞ inch thick. 1½ inch, per pair, **5c**; dozen pairs, **50c**; 2 inch, per pair, **8c**; dozen pairs.................................. **70c**

## Hooks.

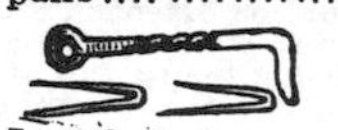

No. 13835. Wrought iron Hooks and Staples.

| | | | | |
|---|---|---|---|---|
| Length, inches.......... | 3 | 4 | 5 | 6 |
| Weight, oz............. | 3 | 4 | 4 | 5 |
| Price, each.............. | $0.02 | .02 | .03 | .03 |
| Price, per doz.......... | .12 | .16 | .19 | .22 |

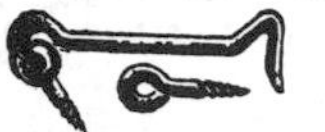

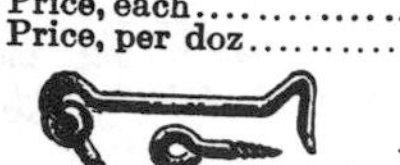

No. 13836. Bright iron Wire Hooks and Screw Eyes.

| | | | |
|---|---|---|---|
| Size, inches.................... | 2 | 3 | 4 |
| Weight, oz.................... | 2 | 2 | 3 |
| Price, each.................... | $0.02 | .03 | .03 |
| Price, per doz.................. | .15 | .18 | .22 |
| Price, per gross............... | 1.15 | 1.50 | 1.88 |

## Hasps.

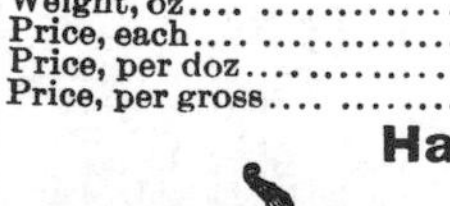

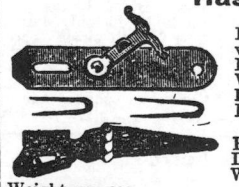

No. 13838. Wrought Iron Hasps and Staples complete with double hook.

| | | | | |
|---|---|---|---|---|
| Length, in., | 5 | 6 | 8 | 10 |
| Weight. oz., | 4 | 5 | 9 | 13 |
| Price, each., | $0.03 | .03 | .04 | .05 |
| Price, doz., | .24 | .28 | .36 | .50 |

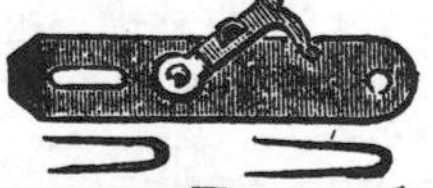

No. 13839. Wrought Iron Hinge Hasps, like cut.

| | | |
|---|---|---|
| Length of hasp, in., | 3 | 4½ |
| Whole length. in., | 5¾ | 7 |
| Weight, ounces, | 7 | 8 |
| Price, each, | $0.06 | .08 |
| Price, per doz., | .50 | .66 |

## Rings.

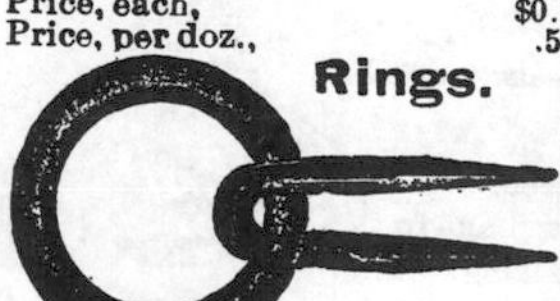

No. 13842. Wrought Iron Rings and Staples. Size given is diameter of rings.

| | | | |
|---|---|---|---|
| Size, inches, | 2 | 2½ | 3 |
| Weight, oz., | 2 | 3 | 4 |
| Each, | $0.02 | .03 | .03 |
| Doz. | .15 | .20 | .25 |

No. 13843. Wrought Iron Staples only.

## Staples Only.

| | | | | |
|---|---|---|---|---|
| Length, inches, | 2 | 2½ | 3 | 3½ |
| Weight, per doz., oz., | 5 | 8 | 10 | 14 |
| Price, per doz., | $0.03 | .04 | .05 | .06 |
| Price, per gross, | .23 | .32 | .43 | .50 |

No. 13844. Wrought Iron Staples, only **lengths assorted** from 1½ to 3 inches; 6 dozen in a box. Price, per box........................................**17c**

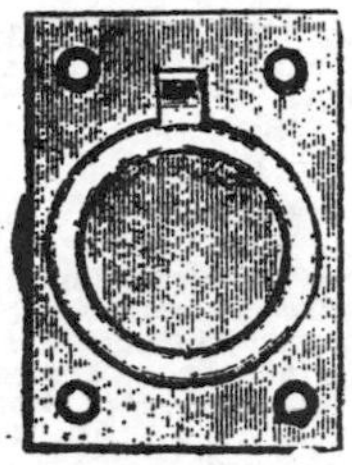

No. 13848. Flush Trap Door Ring. Japanned iron,

| | | |
|---|---|---|
| Size, inches, | 2¾ | 3 |
| Each, | $0.05 | .06 |
| Doz., | .54 | .65 |

**You will find it well worth your while to send for samples of Clothing.**

## Gate Hinges.

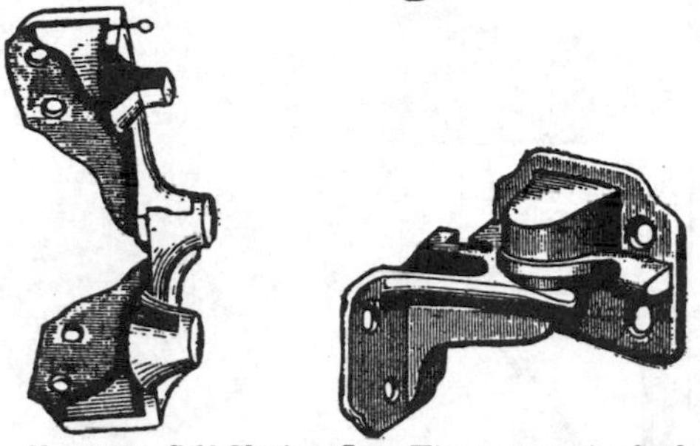

No. 13852. Self-Closing Gate Hinges, to swing both ways. No springs to get out of order. Weight, 2¼ lbs. Price, per set........................................**12c**

## Gate Latches.

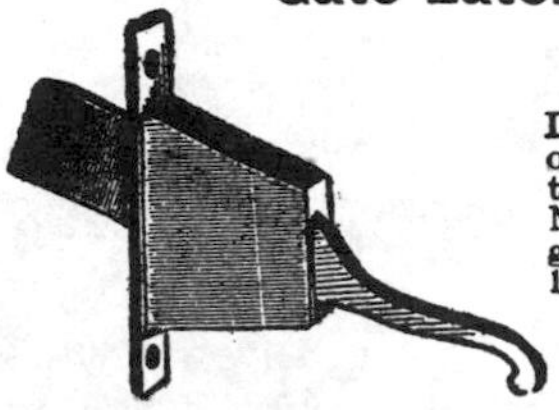

No. 13853. Gate Latches for either right or left hand gates, to swing both ways. No springs to break or get out of order; weight 1 lb. Price, each...**6c**

No. 13854. Gate Latch No. 13853 complete with hinges No. 13852. Price, per set........................... **17c**

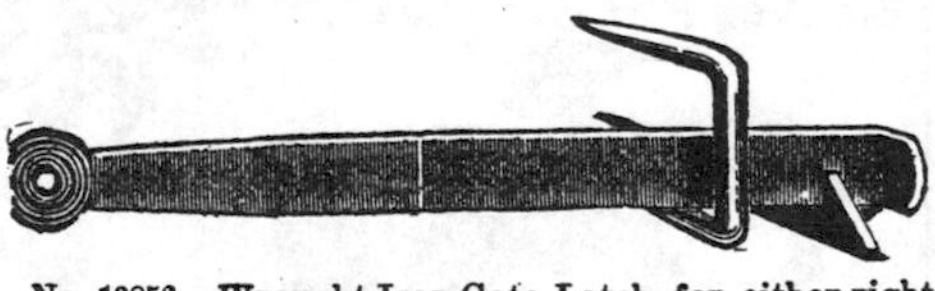

No. 13856. Wrought Iron Gate Latch for either right or left hand gates, to swing one way only.

| | | |
|---|---|---|
| Size, inches, | 8 | 10 |
| Weight, oz. | 10 | 12 |
| Price, each | $0.08 | .10 |

## Padlocks.

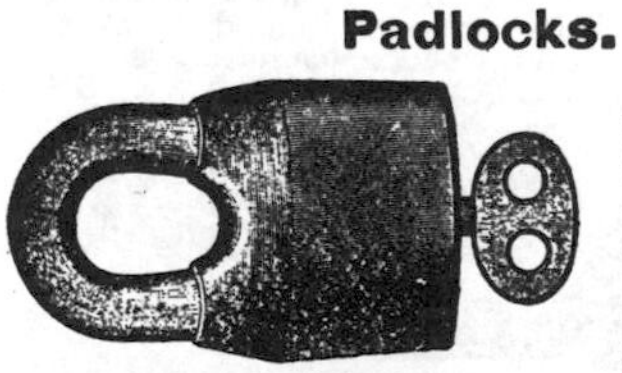

Include these goods in your order. You may as well save the retailers' 33⅓ per cent profit.

This padlock is so well known it needs no description. Painted red. Two keys with each lock.

No. 13876. Size, 2½x1½. Price, each, 7c; per doz., 50c; extra, if sent by mail, 7c each.

No. 13877. Size, 2⅞x1⅝. Price, each, 8c; per doz., 87c; extra, if sent by mail, 11c.

No. 13878. Size, 3¼x2. Price, each, 10c; per doz.,$1.08; extra, if sent by mail, 15c.

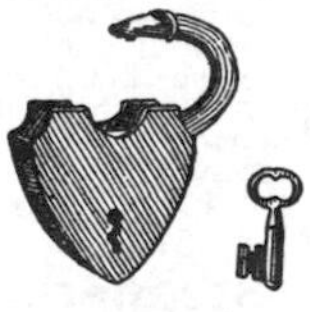

No. 13879. Wrought Iron Self-Locking Padlocks; size, 2 inches. Price, each........................................**5c**
Per doz........................................**55c**

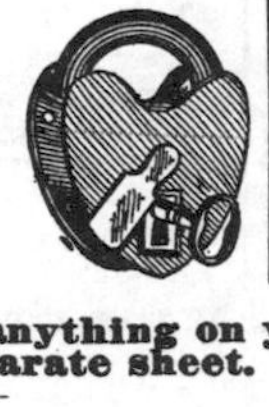

No. 13880. Wrought Iron Padlocks; size, 2¼ inches. Price, each........**10c**
Per doz..............................**$1.00**

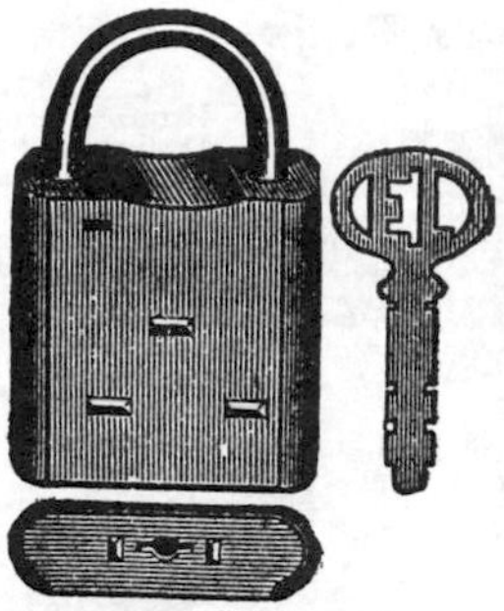

Eureka Padlock; self-locking spring shackle. Flat steel keys. Notice our full line of sizes. Suitable for any purpose for which locks are required. In giving size, length is stated first and the shackle is included in measurements.

No. 13881. Eureka Brass Padlock; size, 1½-x1 inches. Price, each.........**14c**

No. 13883. Eureka Brass Padlock; size, 1¾-x1¼ inches. Price, each.........**15c**

No. 13884. Eureka Brass Padlock; size, 2¼-x1½ inches. Price, each........................................**18c**

No. 13885. Eureka Iron Padlock: size, 2⅝x1¾ inches. Price, each........................................**10c**

No. 13886. Eureka Iron Padlock; size, 3x2 inches. Price, each........................................**12c**

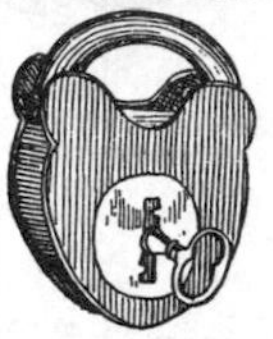

Wrought Iron Brass Bushed Padlock, solid brass wheel, side ward, double chamber, and double bitted keys. Extra fine finish.

No. 13887. Price, each............**15c**
Per doz..............................**$1.55**

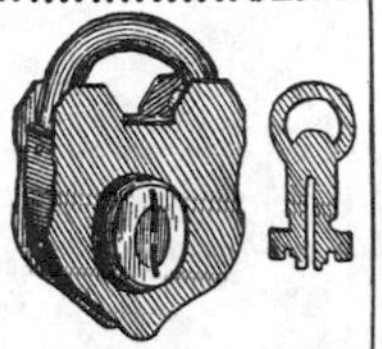

Wrought Iron Padlocks, brass bushings, double chamber, one wheel ward revolving key pin, 2 double, bitted flat steel keys, fine finish.

No. 13888. Price, each....**25c**
Per doz..................**$2.75**

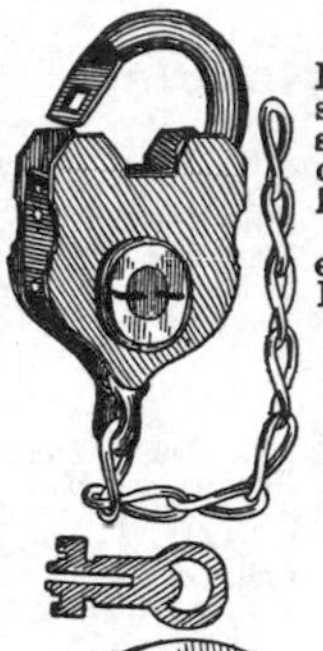

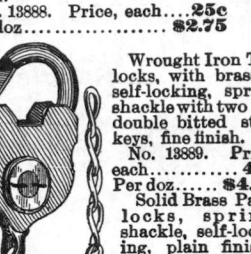

Wrought Iron Tumbler Chain Padlocks, with brass bushing on back, self-locking, spring shackle with two flat double bitted steel keys, fine finish.

No. 13889. Price, each..................**40c**
Per doz......**$4.50**

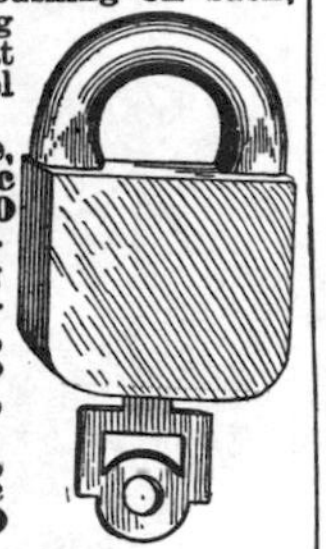

Solid Brass Padlocks, spring shackle, self-locking, plain finish, complete with two flat steel keys; size, 1½ inches.

No. 13890. Price, each...........**10c**
Per doz.....**$1.00**

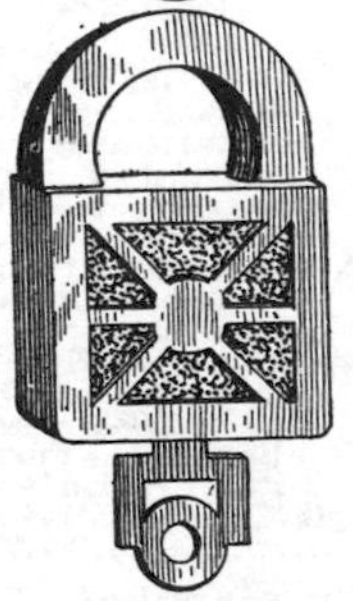

Cast bronze metal Padlocks, self-locking spring shackle. All inside work and springs are made of brass; extra quality and finish. Size, 2½ inches; measurement includes shackle. Two flat steel keys.

No. 13891. Price, each, **12c**; per doz......................**$1.15**

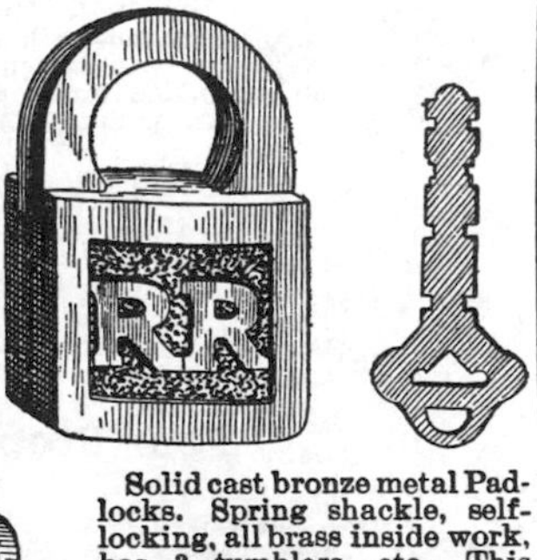

Cast solid bronze metal Padlocks. Dust-proof plunger. Spring shackle, self-locking, double locking bolts. Best padlock for the money ever sold. Size, which includes shackle, 2½ inches.

No. 13892. Price, each, **25c**; per doz..........**$2.85**

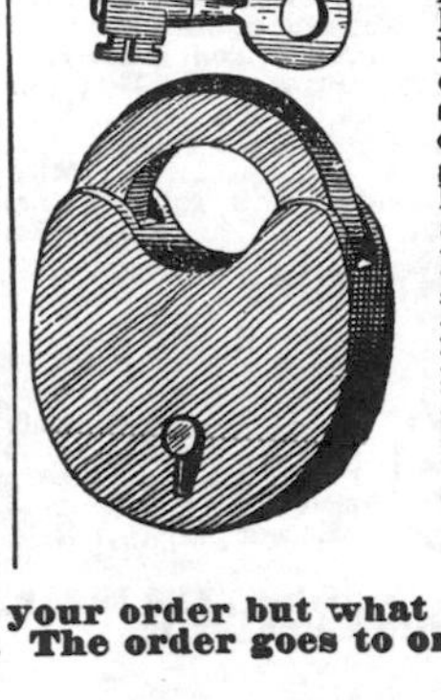

Solid cast bronze metal Padlocks. Spring shackle, self-locking, all brass inside work, has 3 tumblers, etc. This lock has our latest improved dust-proof plunger; the instant shackle is withdrawn the opening is covered by a spring guard from the inside which keeps out all dirt, cinders, ashes, etc. We recommend them as a strictly high grade lock; one of the most durable locks made; also one of the most difficult locks to pick made. Complete with 2 keys. Price, each..............**40c**
Per doz..........................**$4.50**

No. 13893. Same Lock as above, with 9 inch tinned chain. Price, each, **50c**; per doz...................**$5.00**

## Bronze Metal Padlocks.

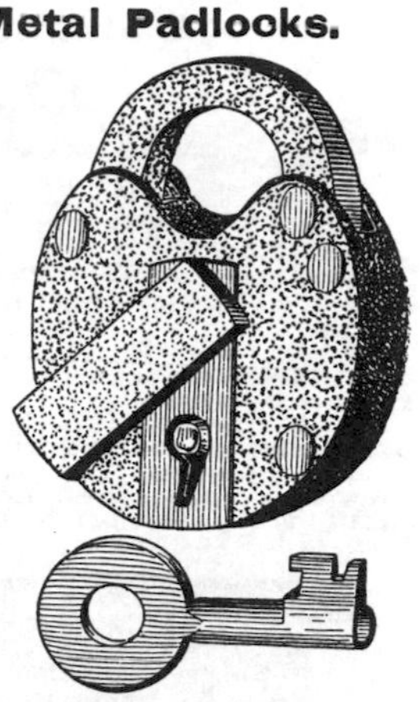

Solid cast bronze metal Padlocks, spring shackle, self-locking, spring drop over keyhole, rough finish; very heavy for railroads, jails, warehouses, etc. A strictly high-grade lock and of the highest type of perfection in durability, workmanship and material. Nothing better made. Size, which includes shackle, 3½ inches, two keys furnished with each lock. Price, each, **60c**; per doz..**$7.00**

No. 13894. Same lock as above with 10 inch japanned chain. Price, each, **75c**; per doz.........**$8.50**

## Lever Padlocks.

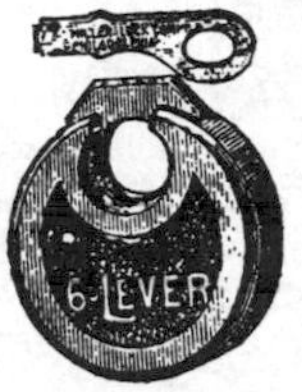

No. 13896. 6-Lever Padlocks are the finest, safest and most durable padlock sold at a reasonable price. Cast bronze outside. Brass inside. Phosphor bronze springs guaranteed not to rust or give out under the influence of any climate. Two nickel-plated flat steel keys with each lock. Size, 3½x2¼. Weight, 12 oz. Price, each........................................**35c**

No. 13897. Same lock as above, with tinned iron chain attached. Price, each........................**35c**

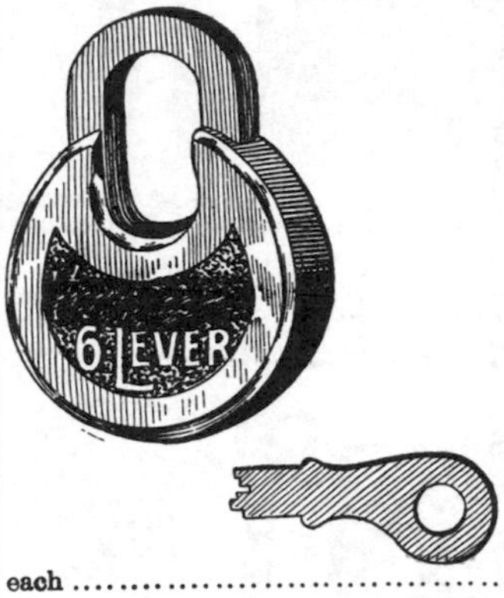

Special pattern 6-Lever Padlocks. Made of the same material as our 13896. Has heavy elongated shackle. Just the thing for gate or barn, as the long shackle will permit a chain or heavy staple being used. Complete, with two flat steel keys.

No. 13898. Price each..........**40c**

Same lock as above, with 9 inch tinned chain.

No. 13899. Price each........................................**50c**

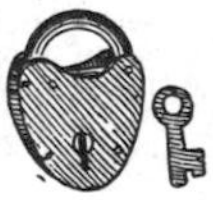

No. 13900. Nickel-Plated Brass Padlocks. Just the thing for small boxes, bags or dog collars. Size, 1⅛ inch. Price, each, **15c**; per doz..................................**$1.75**

No. 13901. 1¼ inch. Price, each, **20c**; per doz..................................**$2.15**

No. 13902. 1½ inch. Price, each, **22c**; per doz........................................**$2.40**

## Secure Lever Locks.

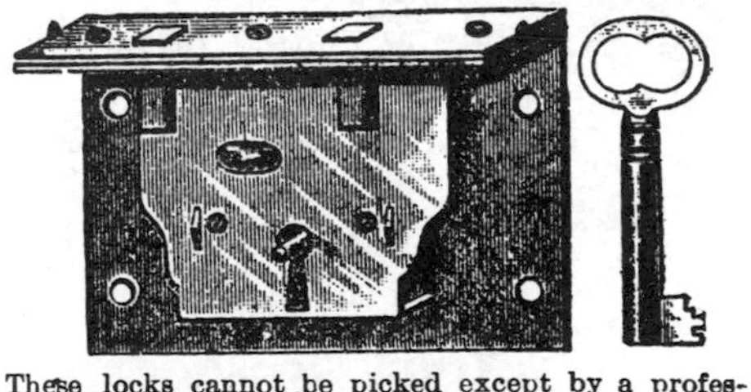

These locks cannot be picked except by a professional, and no key will unlock them unless it is like the original key. Each lock has **two secure levers**. We carry a full line of sizes. Note size carefully when ordering. Keys all different in a dozen.

No. 13925. Secure Lever Chest Lock. Double link, made of iron, size 1½x1⅛ inches, key pin ½ inch from top of lock. Price, each, **20c**; per doz..........**$2.16**

No. 13926. Secure Lever Chest Lock. Double link, made of iron, size 2x1¼ inches, key pin ⅝ inch from top of lock. Price, each, **21c**; per doz..........**$2.32**

No. 13927. Secure Lever Chest Lock. Double link, made of iron, size 2¼x1¾ inches, key pin ¾ inch from top of lock. Price, each, **22c**; per doz..........**$2.40**

No. 13928. Secure Lever Chest Lock. Double link, made of iron, size 3x2 inches, key pin ⅞ inch from top of lock. Price, each, **26c**; per doz..........**$2.94**

No. 13929. Secure Lever Chest Lock. Double link, made of iron, size 3½x2¼ inches, key pin 1 inch from top of lock. Price, each, **30c**; per doz..........**$3.42**

No. 13930. Secure Lever Chest Lock. Double link, made of iron, size 4x2⅜ inches, key pin 1¼ inches from top of lock. Price, each, **50c**; per doz..........**$5.37**

**Never ask questions or write anything on your order but what pertains directly to the order itself. Always write such matters on a separate sheet. The order goes to one department and your inquiries to anot' er.**

## Chest Locks.

No. 13920. Brass Box Lock for small boxes, cases, etc. Size, 1¼x¾ inch. Key pin, 5-16 inch from top of lock. Price, each, **5c**; per doz.............**54c**

No. 13921. Brass Box Lock, like cut of No. 13920. Size, 1½x⅞ inch. Key pin ⅜ inch from top of lock. Price, each, **5c**; per doz............**55c**

No. 13922. Brass Box Lock, like cut of No. 13920. Size, 1¾x1 inch. Key pin 7-16 inch from top of lock. Price, each, **6c**; per doz.............**65c**

No. 13923. Brass Chest Lock, double link. Size, 2x1¼ inches. Key pin 9-16 inch from top of lock. Price, each, **15c**; per doz............**$1.62**

No. 13924. Brass Chest Lock, double link. Size, 2½x1¾ inches. Key pin ¾ inch from top of lock. Price, each, **17c**; per doz.............**$1.84**

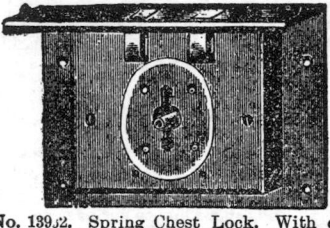

No. 13932. Spring Chest Lock. With double-bitted key, size 4x3 inches, key pin 1¼ inches from top of lock, brass key hole escutcheon. Price, each, **39c**; per doz.........................................**$4.32**

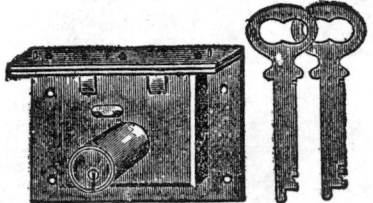

Brass Chest Lock. Size, 3x2 inches, 1 1-8 inches from top of lock to center of keyhole, two flat steel keys, **four secure levers.**
No. 13933. For 1 inch wood. Price, each.......**89c**
No. 13934. For 1¼ inch wood. Price, each.......**90c**
No. 13935. For 1½ inch wood. Price, each.......**91c**

## Drawer Locks.

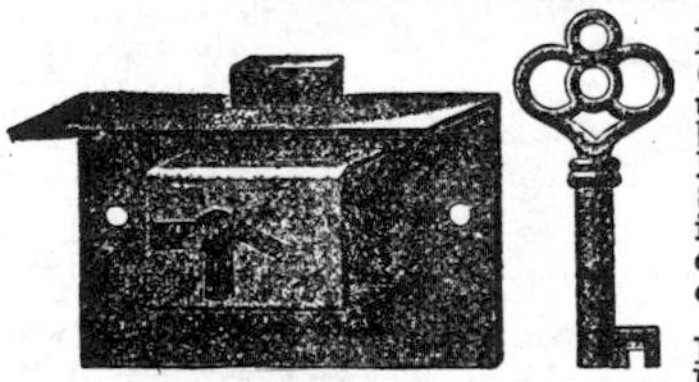

No. 13940. Drawer Lock (may also be used for cupboard lock). Made of iron. Size, 2¼x1½ inches. Price, each, **5c**; per doz........**45c**

No. 13941. Drawer Lock. Made of iron. Size, 2x1½ inches. Key pin, ⅝ inch from top of lock. **Three secure levers. Every key won't open** this lock. Price, each, **19c**; per doz............**$2.20**

## Cupboard Locks.

No. 13948. Cupboard Lock. Bolt shoots right or left. Made of iron. Size, 3x1¾ inches. For doors not more than 1⅜ inches thick. Common key. Price, each, **7c**; per doz.............**69c**

No. 13949. Cupboard Lock. Bolt shoots right or left. Made of iron. Size, 3 x 1¾ inches. For doors not more than 1⅜ inches thick. **Two secure levers.** Every key will not open this lock. Price, each, **21c**; per dozen.....................**$2.37**

## Trunk Locks.

No. 13954. Trunk Lock. Size, 4x3 inches. Heavy iron, patent hasp. A strong and durable lock, well made and well finished. Price, each.........**14c**

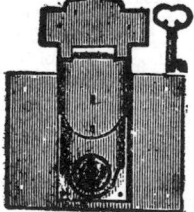

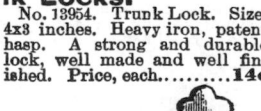

No. 13955. Excelsior Trunk Lock. Cast Brass. Two keys. Price, each, **50c**; per doz..**$5.40**

## Drawer Pulls.

No. 13975. Bronzed iron Drawer Pulls, packed complete with screws. Each weighs 4 oz. Price, each, **20c**; per gross..**$2.16**

No. 13975.

No. 13976. Drop Drawer Pulls. Ebonized wood, with gilt trimmings. Price, each, **4c**; per doz.....**35c**

No. 13978. Drop Ring Drawer Pulls. Gilt finish. Weight, per doz., 15 oz. Price, each, **3c**; per doz., **33c.**

No. 13976.

No. 13980. Flush brass Drawer Pulls. Sizes given indicate width across plate.

| Size, inches, | 1¼ | 1½ | 2 |
|---|---|---|---|
| Weight, oz., | 2 | 3 | 3 |
| Each | $0.08 | .09 | .15 |
| Doz | .80 | .90 | 1.62 |

## Fancy Furniture Handles.

No. 13981. Fancy Furniture Handles, gilt finish. Length, 4¼ inches. Price, each.... **3c** Per doz.......**25c**

No. 13982. Fancy Furniture Handles, gilt finished. Length, 4½ inches. Price, each.... **6c** Per doz........**60c**

No. 13983. Cast Brass Fancy Furniture Handles, polished and lacquered. Length, 3¾ inches. A heavy, strong, handsome drawer handle. Price, each, **$0.19** Per doz.... **2.00**

No. 13984. Cast Brass Fancy Furniture Handles, same as above, only smaller. Length, 2¾ inches. Price, each, **16c**; per doz........................**$1.73**

No. 13985. Fancy Keyhole Escutcheons, gilt finished. This pattern will match either No. 13981 or No. 13982 furniture handle. Price, each, **2c**; per doz.....................**15c**

No. 13986. Cast Brass Keyhole Escutcheons, polished and lacquered. This pattern will match No. 13983 or No. 13984 furniture handle. Price, each, **5c**; per doz............**42c**

## Door Stops.

No. 13988. Base Knobs to screw into base board to prevent door knob striking against the wall; bronzed iron, brass rim, rubber tip, wrought iron screw. Price, each, **3c**; per doz...................**25c**

No. 13989. Birchwood Base Knobs with rubber tips. Price, each, **2c**; per doz...............**20c**

No. 13990. Walnut Base Knobs with rubber tips. Price, each, **3c**; per doz................**25c**

## Lifting Handles.

No. 13994. Brass Lifting Handles for fiddle boxes, etc. Size, 2½ in.; weight, 5 oz.; price, per pair, **18c**; size, 3 in.; weight, 8 oz.; per pair.....**20c**

## Box Hooks.

No. 13995. Brass Hooks and Eyes for fiddle boxes, etc. Size, 1½ in.; weight, per doz., 5 oz.; price, each, **2c**; per doz., **9c**; size, 2 in.; weight, per doz., 6 oz.; price, each, **2c**; per doz............**15c**

## Door Bolts.

No. 13998. Door Bolts, japanned, with brass knobs.

| Size, inches, | 4 | 5 | 6 |
|---|---|---|---|
| Weight, each, ounces, | 8 | 10 | 12 |
| Price, each | $0.04 | .05 | .06 |
| Price, per doz | .37 | .50 | .65 |

No. 14005. Door Bolts, dark bronzed, packed with screws; 3 inch, each, **6c**; per doz. **65c**; 4 inch, each, **7c**; per doz. **75c**; 5 inch, each, **10c**; per doz. ............**90c**

## Cupboard Catches.

No. 14006. Cupboard Catch, japanned iron, porcelain knob, weight, 4 oz. Price, each, **4c**; per doz.....**44c**

No. 14008. Japanned Door Buttons on plates. Size, 1¾ inches; weight, 4 oz. Price, each, **2c**; per doz..........**22c**

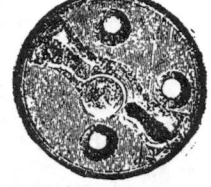

## Shelf Brackets.

No. 14012. Wire Shelf Brackets, japanned; are stronger and lighter than cast iron brackets.

| Size | 4x5 | 5x7 | 6x8 |
|---|---|---|---|
| Per pair | $0.04 | .06 | .08 |
| Size | 7x9 | 8x10 | 10x12 |
| Per pair | $0.10 | .12 | .15 |

No. 14013. Shelf Brackets, German bronzed, fancy design same as cut.

| Size | 4x5 | 5x7 | 6x8 | 8x10 | 9x12 |
|---|---|---|---|---|---|
| Per pr. | $0.07 | .10 | .12 | .18 | .23 |

## Flower Pot Brackets.

No. 14015. Flower Pot Brackets, iron antique verde finish; will hold four pots; one 12 inch arm and two 6 inch, diameter of dishes, three 5 inch, and one 5½ inch. Weight, 5 lbs.; price, each, complete, **68c**; per doz...................................**$8.00**

No. 14016. Japanned Iron, 5-inch arm, shelf 4 inches in diameter; weight, 12 oz. Price, each.............**7c** Per doz..................**75c**

No. 14017. Dark antique bronzed iron, 2 shelves, 12-inch arm, one 5½-inch shelf and one 4-in. shelf; weight, 25 oz. Price, each.... **35c** Per doz.... **$3.90**

## Foot Scrapers.

No. 14020. Iron, japanned, to screw on step; weight, 10 oz. Price, each.........**4c** Per doz.................**44c**

---

*If you want anything and do not happen to see it be sure to look in the index. If you shouldn't happen to find it in the index write us about it.*

No. 14022. Foot Scraper, fancy pattern, japanned iron. Price, each ..........8c
Per doz.............87c

## Clothes Line Hooks.

No. 14024. Clothes Line Hooks, japanned, heavy; weight. 6 oz. Price, each..3c
Per doz.................25c

## Line Cleat.

No. 14025. Line Cleats; length from tip to tip of horn, 2 inches; japanned. Price, each.........18c
Per doz.................18c
Galvanized; price, each.....5c
Per doz.................25c

## Clothes Line Pulleys.

No. 14026. Clothes Line Pulleys, jointed on plate. Japanned. Price, each........5c
Per doz.................54c
Galvanized, price, each.............7c
Per doz.........75c

## Bird Cages.

No. 14032. Square Cage: size, 8x8 inches; handsomely decorated and complete, with seed and water cup, perches and swing. Price, each.70c

No. 14033. Oblong Cage; size, 6½x9½ inches; nicely ornamented; a very pretty cage. Price, each...................82c

## Bird Cage Springs.

No. 14034. Bird Cage Springs. Each.... 5c
Per doz.............54c

## Bird Cage Hooks.

No. 14035. Bronzed Iron Bird Cage Hooks with wrought iron screw. Price, each..4c

No. 14036. Bronzed Iron Bird Cage Hook, to swing; length, 10 inches. Price, each......................9c

## Hat and Coat Hooks.

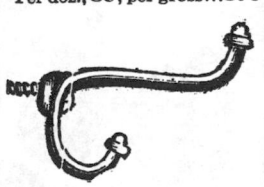

No. 14040. Wire Coat and Hat Hooks, with gimlet screw points. Will not break. No tools required to put them up. Lighter than cast iron hooks. Copper finished.

| Length, inches, | 2½ | 3 | 3½ |
|---|---|---|---|
| Per doz., | $0.06 | .07 | .09 |
| Per gross, | .62 | .75 | .96 |

No. 14041. Wire Coat and Hat Hooks, same as above, japanned finish.

| Length, inches, | 2½ | 3 | 3½ |
|---|---|---|---|
| Per doz., | $0.07 | .08 | .09 |
| Per gross, | .62 | .75 | .96 |

No. 14043. Iron japanned Hat and Coat Hook, 2½ inches. Weight per doz., 1¼ lbs. Per doz., 8c; per gross...87c

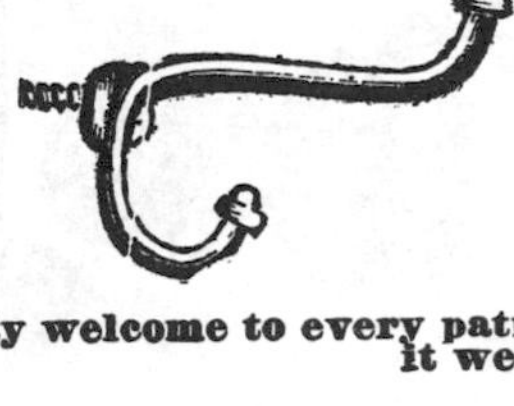

No. 14044. Iron japanned Hat and Coat Hook, 3½ inches. Weight, per doz., 1 lb. 5 oz. Per doz., 10c; per gross.........95c

No. 14045. Iron japanned triple Hat and Coat Hook, 4 inches. Weight, per doz., 1 lb. 13 oz.
Per doz.,10c; per gro..$1.05

No. 14046. Hat and Coat Hooks, bronzed iron, a very neat pattern. Weight per doz., 3½ lbs. Per doz., 30c; per gross $3.30

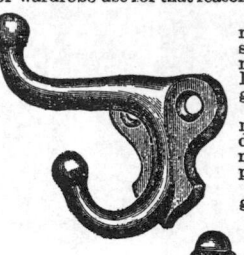

No. 14047. The Safety Coat and Hat Hook will safely hold a stiff, straw or soft hat of any kind without danger of its falling. Has short hooks for coat and umbrella; projects from the wall about 4 inches; whole length, 10 inches. We have it in two finishes.
Rough nickel plated, each, 6c; per doz...................65c
Polished and nickel plated, each, 10c; per doz.......$1.00

## Schoolhouse Hooks.

Schoolhouse Hooks are heavier and stronger than the ordinary hat or coat hooks and are sometimes preferred for wardrobe use for that reason.

No. 14048. Iron japanned Schoolhouse Hook, single hook, 2½ inches, no screws. Weight, 2½ lbs. Per doz., 15c; per gross..............$1.62

No. 14049. Iron japanned Schoolhouse Hook, double hook, 2½ inches, no screws. Weight per doz., 3 lbs. 13 oz. Per doz., 20c; per gross..............$2.00

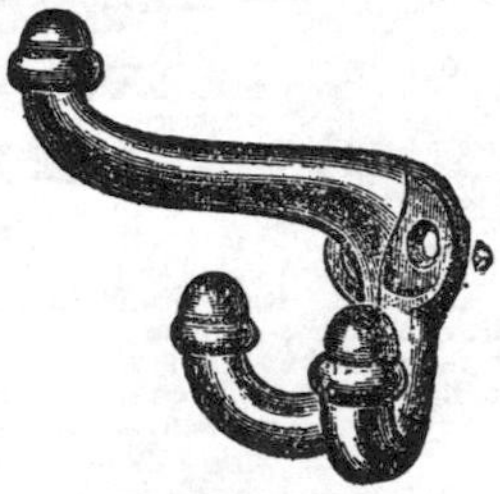

No. 14050. Iron japanned Schoolhouse Hook, triple hook, extra heavy, 2½ inches, no screws. Weight per doz., 3 lbs. 13 oz. Per doz., 25c; per gross,...........$2.50

## Hat Hooks.

No. 14055. Harness Hooks, japanned iron, 6 inches in length. Weight per doz., 6 lbs. Each, 4c; per doz., 45c;
No. 14056. Harness Hooks, braced, japanned iron, 8 inches long. Weight per doz., 10½ lbs. Each, 6c; per doz.....................65c

## Hat Racks.

No. 14058. Six-hook Hat Rack; sizes, 4x32 inches. Each, 8c; per doz.................86c
No. 14059. Four-hook Hat Rack; size, 4x21 inches. Each, 7c; per doz..................75c

No. 14062. Improved Hat Rack, will safely hold a stiff hat. Five hooks, each, 15c; per doz., $1.75; seven hooks, each, 20c; per doz.................$2.25

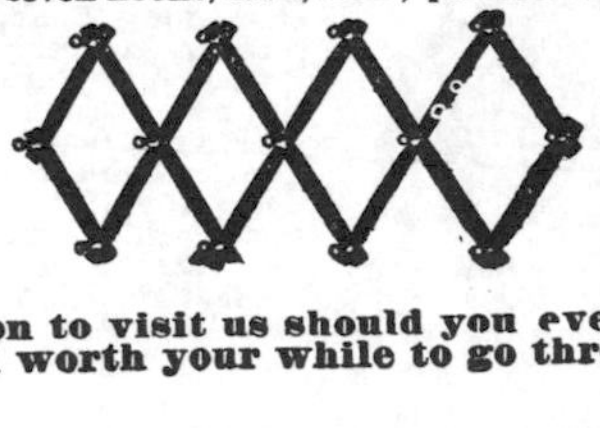

No. 14064. 13 Pin Folding Rack. The regulation folding pattern Hat Rack. Made of hardwood. walnut stain. Each................12c

## Sash Fasts.

No. 14068. Sash Lock, a neat pattern, enameled iron finish. Each..........4c
Per doz.............38c

14068.

## Ives' Sash Locks.

14069-14070.

Ives' Burglar Proof Sash Locks are pronounced by architects and builders to be the best in use. When locked they draw the two sashes tightly together, which prevents their rattling. They cannot be opened from the outside by putting a thin knife blade between sash and pushing the hook open, as is the case with common sash locks. They are ornamental and easily put on. Packed with screws.
No. 14069. Ives' Burglar Proof Sash Locks, Ogee tipped, ornamental iron. Each, 5c; per doz.......45c
No. 14070. Ives' Burglar Proof Sash Locks, ornamental iron, bronzed, with bronze metal knob. Each, 7c; per doz.................75c

14072-14074.

No. 14072. Ives' Burglar Proof Sash Locks, ornamental iron, bronzed bell tip. Each, 5c; per doz.............54c
No. 14074. Ives' Burglar Proof Sash Locks, ornamental iron, bronzed with bronze metal bell tip. Price, each, 10c; per doz.95c

## Window Spring Bolts.

No. 14078. Window Spring Bolts, japanned, silvered tip, tin case. Per doz., 10c; per gross......$1.18
No. 14079. Window Spring Bolts, japanned tip, tin case. Weight, per doz., 14 oz. Per doz., 8c; per gross.................88c

## Transom Plates.

No. 14084. Sash Centers or Transom Plates, iron, japanned.

| Length, | 1⅜ | 2¼ | 2⅞ |
|---|---|---|---|
| Weight, per set, ounces. | 3 | 7 | 10 |
| Per set of two..... | $0.03 | .04 | .05 |
| Per ½ doz. sets..... | .17 | .22 | .27 |

## Sash Cord.

Sash Cord is put up in bundles of 100 feet.

| No. | | Size. | Length Per lb. | Per lb. |
|---|---|---|---|---|
| No. 14086. | American Hemp Unbleached, | 8-32 | 38 ft. | $0.18 |
| No. 14087. | Indian Hemp Bleached, | 7-32 | 46 ft. | .20 |
| No. 14088. | Silver Lake Braided, | 7-32 | 55 ft. | .26 |
| No. 14089. | Silver Lake Braided, | 8-32 | 46 ft. | .26 |
| No. 14090. | Silver Lake Braided, | 9-32 | 40 ft. | .26 |
| No. 14091. | Silver Lake Braided, | 10-32 | 30 ft. | .26 |

7-32 weighs about 2¼ lbs. to the bundle.
8-32 weighs about 2½ lbs. to the bundle.
9-32 weighs about 2½ lbs. to the bundle.
10-32 weighs about 2¾ lbs. to the bundle.

## Sash Pulleys.

No. 14092. Common iron Sash Pulleys; 2 inch pulley. Per doz.........19c

## Sash Balances.

Sash Balance, for use instead of weights, can be applied to old houses where weights cannot be used; is easily put in and operates almost noiselessly. This style of balance is becoming very popular, is very neat in appearance, works smoother and lasts longer than sash cord. The tension or brake band is operated by an adjusting screw in face plate, which makes it adjustable to varying weights. If directions are fully carried out we will warrant the balance to work perfectly. Where there is not room enough to use a Side Balance we make a special balance for the top of the window, and can also be used in Mullen windows.

No. 14094. Side Balance.

| No. | Length. | Weight of each sash, | Per set of 4 |
|---|---|---|---|
| 0—for sash 30 in. | 4 to 5 lbs | | $0.75 |
| 1—for sash 30 in. | 5 to 7 lbs | | .76 |
| 2—for sash 30 in. | 7 to 9 lbs | | .80 |
| 3—for sash 38 in. | 9 to 11 lbs | | .85 |
| 4—for sash 46 in. | 11 to 13 lbs | | 1.00 |
| 5—for sash 46 in. | 13 to 15 lbs | | 1.10 |
| 6—for sash 46 in. | 15 to 17 lbs | | 1.15 |
| 7—for sash 46 in. | 17 to 19 lbs | | 1.30 |
| 8—for sash 46 in. | 19 to 21 lbs | | 1.50 |
| 9—for sash 48 in. | 21 to 24 lbs | | 1.60 |
| 10—for sash 48 in. | 24 to 27 lbs | | 1.70 |
| 11—for sash 48 in. | 27 to 30 lbs | | 1.80 |

No. 14095. Top Balance.

| No. | Length. | Weight of each sash, | Per set of 4 |
|---|---|---|---|
| 3—for sash 38 in. | 9 to 11 lbs | | $0.85 |
| 4—for sash 46 in. | 11 to 13 lbs | | 1.00 |
| 5—for sash 46 in. | 13 to 15 lbs | | 1.10 |
| 6—for sash 46 in. | 15 to 17 lbs | | 1.20 |

## Common Knobs, Locks, Etc.

The line of Common Locks which we sell is admitted to be the best line of low-priced goods in the market. The construction is such that they are durable and easy working. A lock is something you buy to wear out, and reliable good wearing locks cannot be sold at less than our prices. We could sell you cheaper locks. No one can sell these locks at less than our prices. Our constant aim is to raise the quality and lower prices; but not at the sacrifice of quality. On this basis we seek your trade.

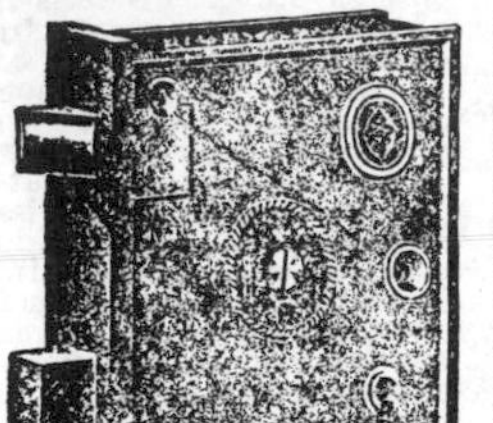

No. 14115. Upright Rim Knob Lock, for either right or left hand door, Size, 4x3¼, japanned, with stop, iron bolts, iron key, one tumbler, packed complete with screws and japanned keyhole escutcheons, without door knobs. If knobs are wanted order them separately; weight, 2¼ lbs.
Price, each ..........12c
Per doz ...........$1.20

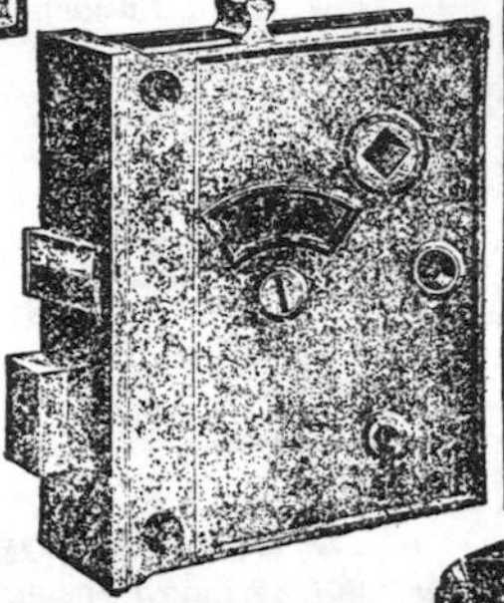

No. 14116. Upright Rim Knob Lock, for either right or left hand door; size, 4½x3¼, japanned with stop brass bolts, nickel plated steel key, japanned key hole, escutcheons, packed complete with screws, 1 tumbler, without door knobs. If knobs are wanted, order them separately. Weight, 2¼ lbs.
Price, each ........20c
Per doz....... ..$2.30

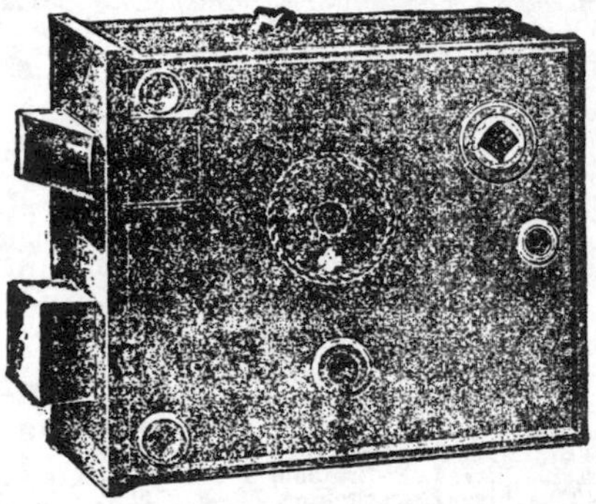

No. 14117. Horizontal Rim Knob Lock, for either right or left hand door; size, 3¼x 4, japanned, with stop, iron bolts, iron key, japanned key hole escutcheons, 1 tumbler, packed with screws, without door knobs. If knobs are wanted, order them separately. Weight, 2¼ lbs. Price, each ..........12c
Per doz ..........$1.25

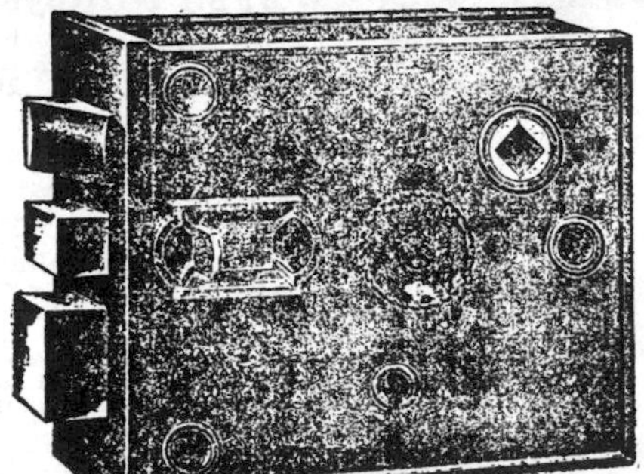

No. 14118. Horizontal Rim Knob Lock, for either right or left hand door. Size, 3¼x4¼, japanned, with stop, brass bolts, nickel plated steel key, one tumbler, japanned keyhole escutcheons, packed complete with screws. Without door knobs. If knobs are wanted, order them separately. Weight, 2¼ lbs.
Price, each, **25c**; per doz..........$2.50

## Rim Dead Locks.

These locks cannot be used with knobs. They are for closet doors, outbuildings, etc., and are cheaper and more convenient than a padlock and hasp and staples. All are for either right or left hand doors.

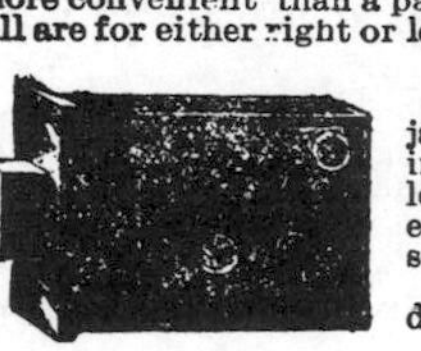

No. 14124. Rim Dead Locks, japanned case. Size, 2x2¾, iron bolt, iron key, one tumbler, japanned keyhole escutcheons, packed complete with screws.
Price, each, **10c**; per doz..........$1.00

No. 14125. Rim Dead Lock, japanned case. Size, 2½x3⅜, iron bolt, iron key, one tumbler, japanned keyhole escutcheons, packed complete with screws.
Price, each, **12c**; per doz..........$1.25

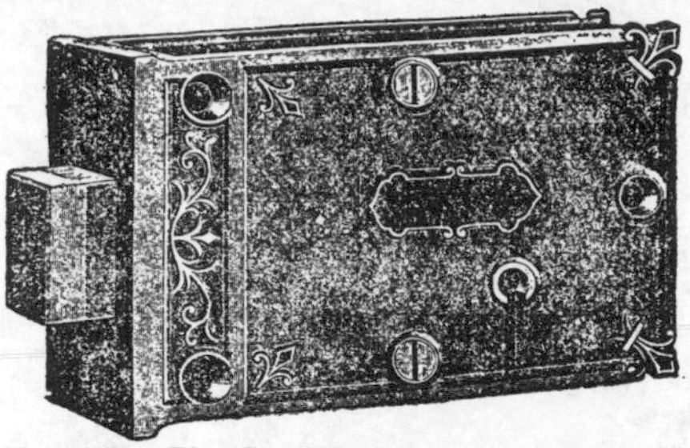

No. 14126. Rim Dead Lock, japanned case. Size, 2¾x4, iron bolt, iron key, one tumbler, japanned keyhole escutcheon, packed with screws.
Price, each, **15c**; per doz..........$1.65

No. 14127. Rim Dead Lock, japanned case. Size, 2½x3⅜, brass bolt, nickel plated, steel key, one tumbler, japanned keyhole escutcheons, packed with screws.
Price, each, **25c**; per doz..........$2.50

No. 14132. Rim Dead Lock, japanned case. Size, 2¾x4, **wrought iron inside work**, brass bolt, nickel plated steel key, **three tumblers**, japanned keyhole escutcheon. A lock which can't be picked.
Price, each, **35c**; per doz..........$3.50

## Rim Night Latches.

Rim Night Latches, cannot be used with door knobs. They are operated from the outside by key only and on the inside by the knob; the bolt may be fastened back at will by the spring catch on inside of case.

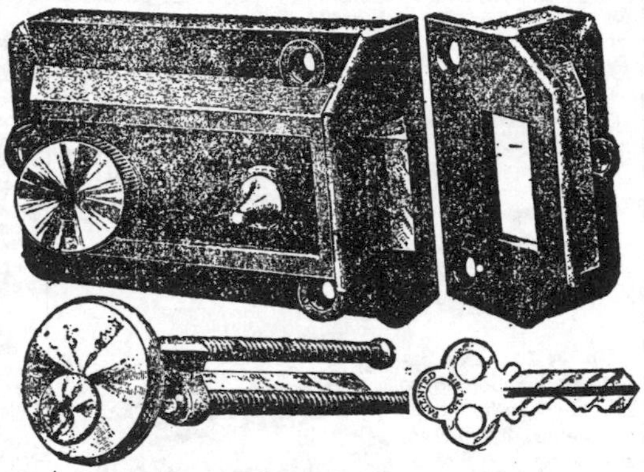

No. 14142. Rim Night Latch, plain japanned case. Size, 2½x3¾, bronze bolt, bronze escutcheon, three keys for either right or left hand doors, from ⅞ to 2¼ inches thick, packed complete with screws, safe and durable. Price, each..........$1.15

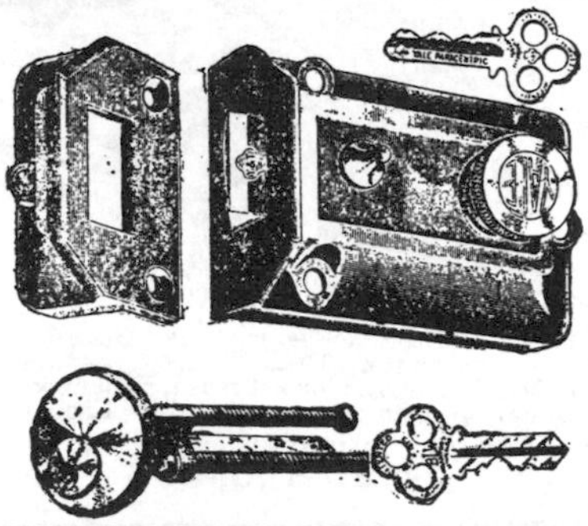

No. 14144. The **Genuine Yale** Paracentric Night Latch. This latch is so well known as the most perfect and secure lock made that our recommendation is unnecessary. Japanned iron case. Size, 2⅝x3⅝, bronze escutcheon, bronze knob, three paracentric keys, reversible and adjustable for doors from ⅞ to 2¾ inches thick. Price, each..........$1.35

No. 14146. Rim Night Latch (not illustrated). Size, 2½x3⅝, japanned iron case, two nickel-plated steel keys, iron bolt, brass knobs, one tumbler, for either right or left hand doors, not more than 1¾ inches thick, Price, each ..........30c

## Store Door Locks.

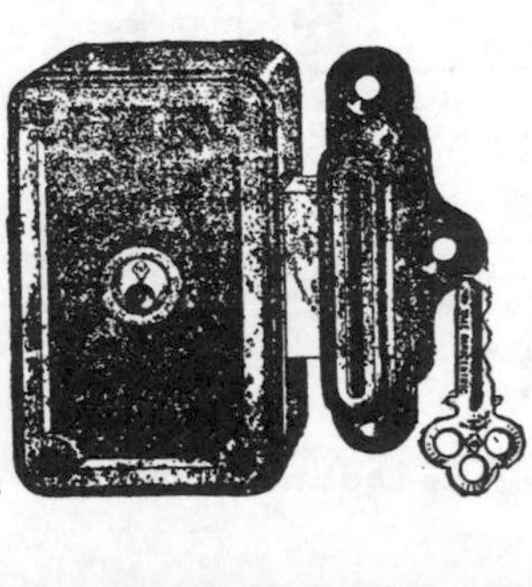

No. 14152. The **genuine Yale** store door Lock, Size 5x3, iron case, bronze bolts, plain bronze escutcheons, 3 paracentric keys, suitable for doors from 1⅛ to 4 inches thick, no two sets of keys made alike, weight 3¼ lbs. Price, each........$2.75

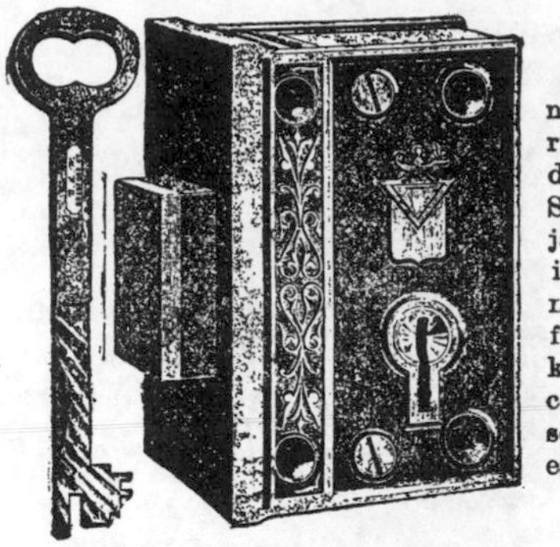

No. 14148. Ornamental Upright rim store door Lock. Size 5x3 inches, japanned case, iron bolt, 2 nickel-plated folding steel keys. Packed complete, with screws. Price, each ......50c

## Mortise Lock and Latches.

### Without Knobs.

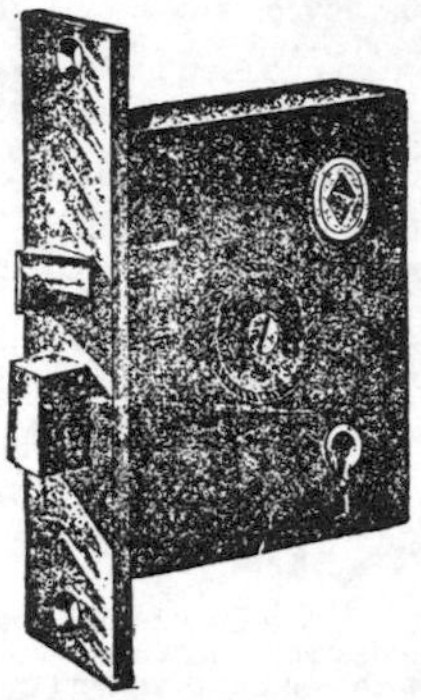

No. 14172. Reversible Mortise Knob Lock. Size, 3½x3¼; japanned iron case; lacquered iron front, strike and bolts; malleable iron keys, japanned escutcheons, one tumbler. Weight, 1¼ lbs.
Price, each, **12c**; per doz., $1.25.

No. 14173. Reversible Mortise Knob Lock. Size, 3½x3¼; japanned iron case, brass front and bolts; strike is wrought iron, brass plated; nickel-plated steel key, japanned escutcheons, one tumbler.
Price, each, **20c**; per doz. $2.20.

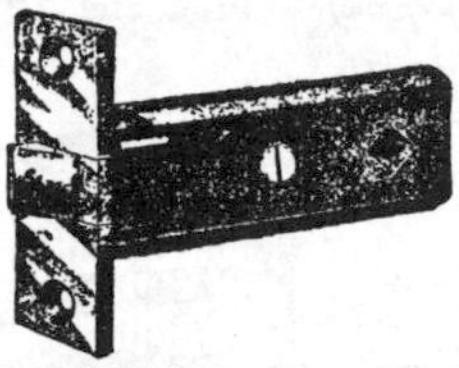

No. 14179. Mortise Knob Latches. Size, 1¼x3¼ inch; japanned iron case, iron front, bolt and strike, without knobs. Weight, 12 oz.
Price, each, **6c**; per doz., 60c.

No. 14180. Mortise Knob Latch, same as above, with brass front, bolt and strike.
Price, each, **15c**; per doz., $1.50.

**NOTICE.—Door knobs are not furnished with locks quoted above.** If knobs are wanted, order them separately.

## Door Knobs.

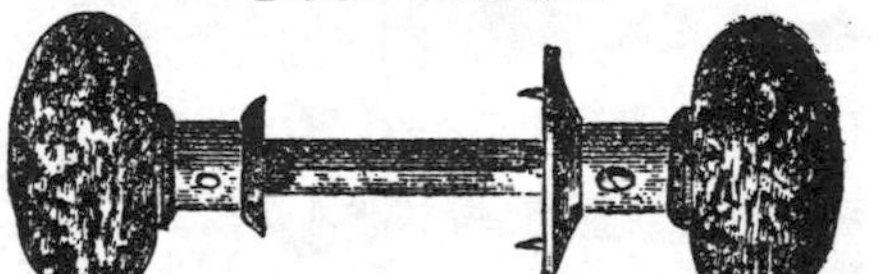

These Door Knobs will fit any standard make of lock and doors from ⅞ to 2¼ inches thick. The knob is 2¼ inches in diameter.

No. 14181. Mineral Rim Knob with japanned shanks and rose; fits rim knob locks; color, mottled brown; weight, 1 lb. Price, each, **6c**; per doz..........65c

No. 14182. Porcelain Rim Knobs with japanned shanks and rose; fits rim knob locks; color, white; weight, 1 lb. Price, each, **8c**; per doz..........87c

No. 14183. Jet Rim Knobs with japanned shanks and rose; fits rim knob locks; color, black; weight. 1 lb. Price, each, **8c**; per doz..........87c

No. 14184. Mineral Mortise Knobs with japanned shanks and roses; fits mortise knob locks; color, mottled brown; weight, 1 lb. Price, each, **6c**; per doz..65c

No. 14185. Porcelain Mortise Knobs with japanned shanks and roses; fits mortise knob locks; color, white; weight, 1 lb. Price, each, **8c**; per doz..........87c

No. 14186. Jet Mortise Knobs with japanned shanks and roses; fits mortise knob locks; color, black. Price, each, **8c**; per doz..........87c

## Thumb Latches.

No. 14189. Japanned Iron Thumb Latch with stop, suitable for doors ⅞ to 1½ inches thick. Price, each, **5c**; per doz..........50c

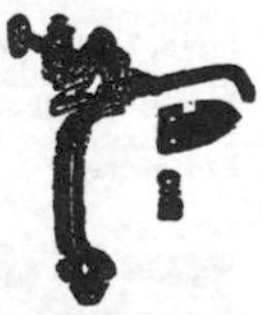

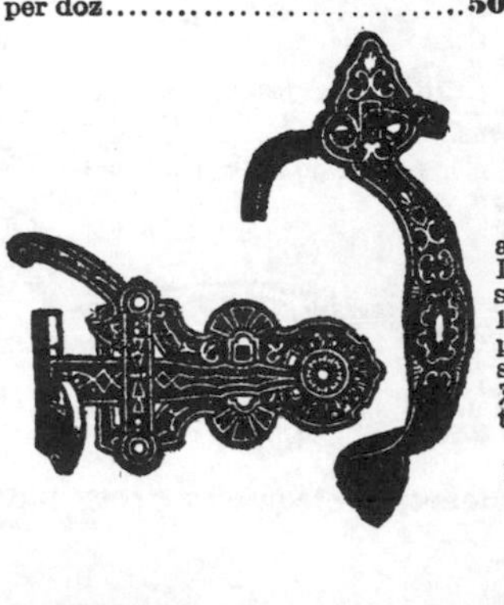

No. 14190. Enameled Thumb Latch; very handsome; weight about 1 lb. Packed complete with screws. suitable for doors ⅞ to 1½ inches thick.
Price, each, **8c**; per doz........65c

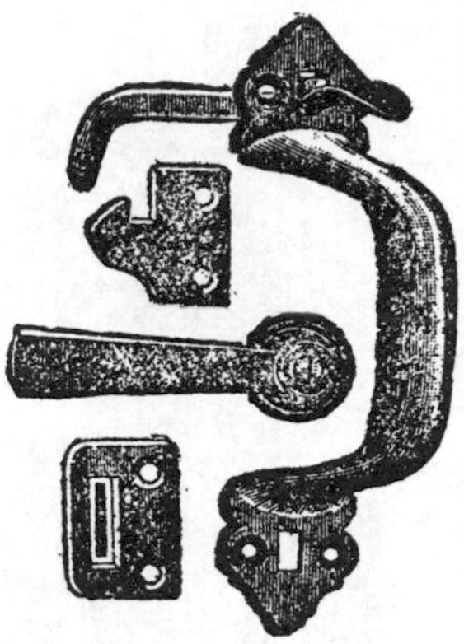

No. 14191. Japanned Store Door Latch, just the thing for barn doors hung on hinges or any heavy door subjected to rough usage.
Price, each, **8c**; per doz........**87c**

## Door Butts.

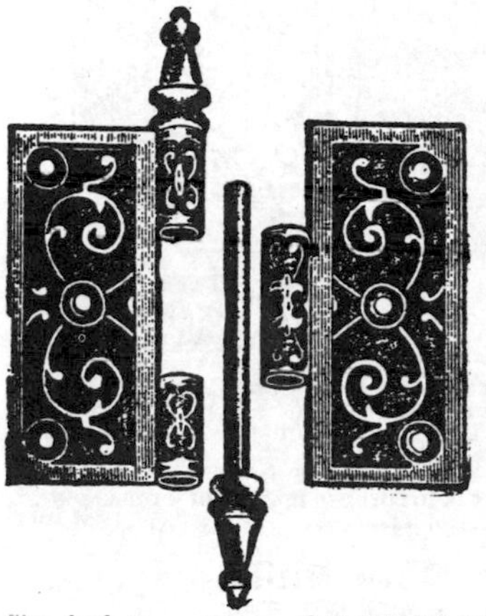

No. 14148. Loose Pin Cast Iron Butts, plain finish. The sizes given are measurements when butt is open, and **length is always given first.** Screws not included at prices quoted. For screws see index.

| Size, inches.......... | 2x2 | 2½x2½ | 3x3 | 3½x3½ | 4x4 |
|---|---|---|---|---|---|
| Weight, per pair, oz.. | 9 | 12 | 15 | 18 | 23 |
| Price, per pair........ | $0.03 | .05 | .06 | .08 | .09 |
| Price, per doz. pairs.. | .25 | .35 | .45 | .60 | .73 |

## Transom Lifters.

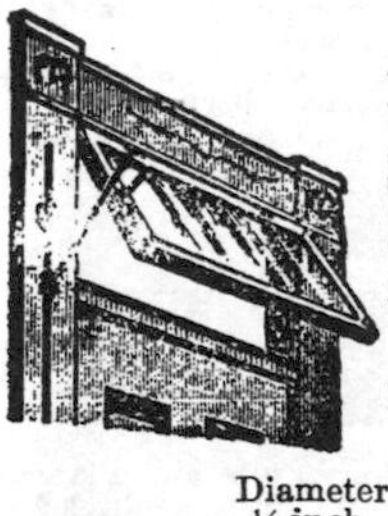

No. 14199. Transom Lifters. With this device transoms may be lowered or raised at will with great ease and locked in any position; no other fastenings required; when ordering give size of transom and whether hinged at bottom or top. They are made from round iron rods, bronzed and nicely finished.

For transoms hinged at top or hung in the middle.

| Length. | Diameter, ¼ inch. Bronzed iron | Diameter, 5/16 inch. Bronzed iron. | Diameter. ⅜ inch. Bronzed iron. |
|---|---|---|---|
| 3 feet. each.... | $0.15 | | |
| 4 feet, each.... | .15 | $0.30 | |
| 5 feet, each.... | | .40 | $0.50 |
| 6 feet, each.... | | .50 | .57 |
| 7 feet, each.... | | | .75 |

No. 14200. To hang on bottom.
4 feet, 5/16, iron, each....................................**40c**
5 feet, ⅜, iron, each....................................**60c**
6 feet, ⅜, iron, each....................................**70c**

## Ornamental Bronze Plated, and Solid Bronze Builders' Hardware.

**Bronze Plated Goods** are made of iron, heavily electro-plated with bronze, on the same principle used in plating table knives, forks and spoons with silver. They are handsome, cheap and durable. The most popular goods in the market to-day.

**Solid Bronze Goods** are made of **solid, genuine cast bronze,** and **will wear forever.** Cost of solid bronze goods is governed by weight. If weight is cut down, goods are cheaper, but not so strong. All our **solid bronze** goods are **full weight, full size** and **full value. No cheap stamped trimmings used on anything.**

**Ornamentation.** The background is finished in black enamel. The raised surfaces (which are shown by white lines in illustrations) are finely polished. The pattern is neat and popular.

We show in the following pages a **complete line** of builders' hardware, in both plated and solid bronze, and **all of same ornamentation.** This enables one to select solid bronze for better rooms, and plated for common rooms, and **all will match.** We claim this is the most complete line offered by any one, and the arrangement is such that an expert is not required to select the hardware for a house.

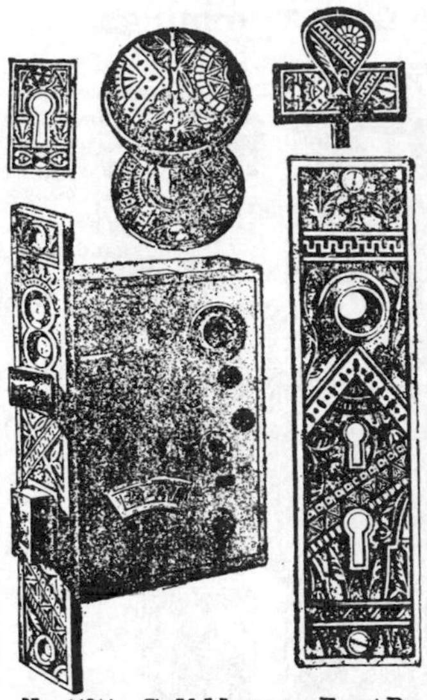

No. 14210. **Bronze plated** Front Door Lock Set, with night latch and stop. Lock is 4¾x3⅝ inches. Combined escutcheon is 7¼x1⅞ inch. Knobs, 2¼ inch in diameter. Lock has bronze bolts and one nickel plated steel key for dead bolt, and two for night latch. Dead bolt has one tumbler. Night bolt has one tumbler. Packed complete with screws. Price, per set..**$1.10**

No. 14211. **Solid bronze** Front Door Lock Sets, exactly same size and ornamentation as above. The lock, front, knobs, escutcheon, etc., are **real bronze** instead of bronze plated. Price, per set...........**$1.60**

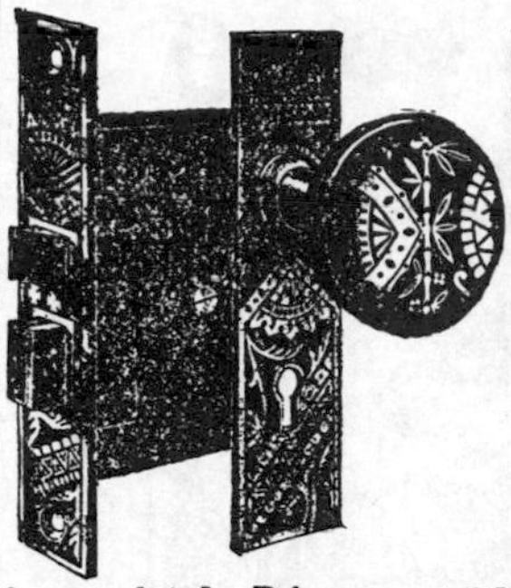

No. 14214. **Bronze plated** Inside Door Lock Sets. Lock is 3½x3¼ inches. Combined escutcheon, 5⅛x1⅛ inches. Knobs, 2¼ inches, nickel plated, steel key, for doors 1⅛x2¼ inches thick. Packed complete with screws. Price, per set..**$0.47**
Per doz. sets... **5.25**

No. 14215. **Solid bronze** Inside Door Lock Sets. Same size and ornamentation as above. The lock, fronts, knobs, escutcheons, etc., are real bronze instead of bronze plated. Price, per set, **83c**; per doz. sets **$9.34**

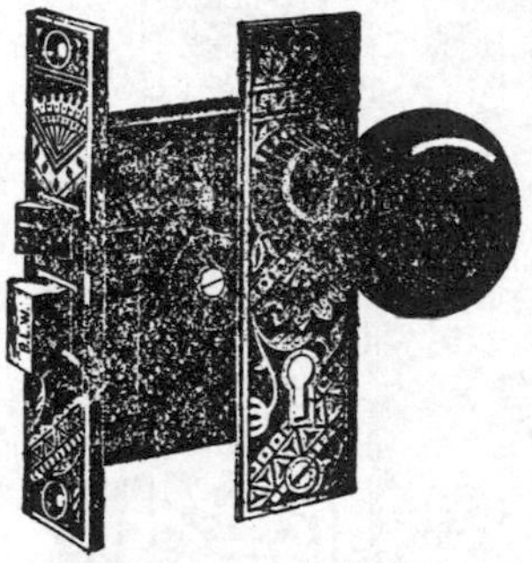

No. 14216. **Bronze plated** Inside Door Lock Sets. This lock and escutcheon, etc., is same size and description as 14214, except has jet knobs with bronze plated shanks. Is very popular. Price, per set, **35c**; per doz. sets....**$3.87**

No. 14217. **Solid bronze** Inside Door Lock Sets, same as above except the lock fronts. Escutcheons, strikes, etc., are solid bronze instead of bronze plated. Price, per set, **75c**; per doz. sets...........................**$8.40**

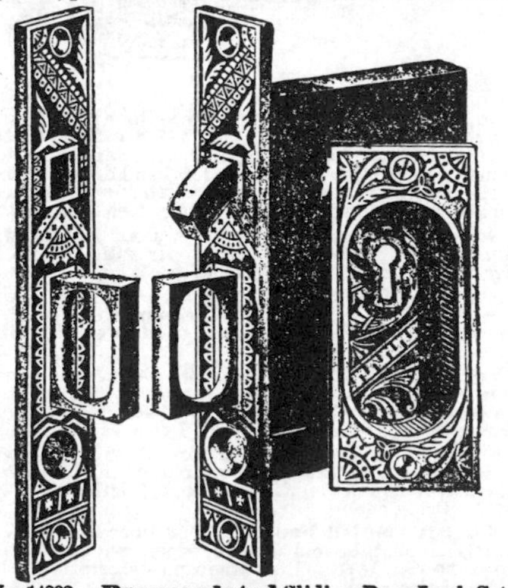

No. 14222. **Bronze plated** Sliding Door Lock Sets, for double doors. Lock, 5¼x3¼ inches. Set consists of 1 lock and box strike, 1 key, 4 cup escutcheons to match and stop. Packed with screws. Bolt and pull are bronze, all other exposed parts are bronze plated. Flat face. Price, per set...........................**$1.20**

No. 14223. **Solid bronze** Sliding Door Lock Sets, exactly like above except all exposed parts are solid bronze instead of bronze plated. Price, per set......**$2**

No. 14224. **Bronze plated** Sliding Door Lock Sets, exactly like No. 14222 except has astragal or rounding front. Price, per set...........................**$1.40**

No. 14225. **Solid bronze** Sliding Door Lock Sets, exactly like No. 14224 (astragal front) except all exposed parts are solid bronze instead of bronze plated. Price, per set...........................**$2**

No. 14226. **Bronze plated** Sliding Door Lock Sets for single door, flat front. Each set consists of lock and plate strike, 1 key and 2 cup escutcheons to match. Bronze bolt and pull, all other exposed parts are bronze plated. Price, per set...........................**85c**

No. 14227. **Solid bronze** Sliding Door Lock Sets, for single door. Same as No. 14226 except all exposed parts are solid bronze instead of bronze plated. Price, per set...........................**$1.25**

## Sliding Door Hangers.

No. 14237. Anti-Friction Parlor Door Hangers. Adjustable, noiseless. Each set will carry two doors, each 4½ feet wide (or smaller) without friction. One set consists of 4 hangers, 1 overhead stop, 4 lengths (7 feet each) of hard maple track. Full directions sent with each set hangers. Per set...........**$2.75**

If wanted for single door order ½ set, which we furnish for **$1.40.**

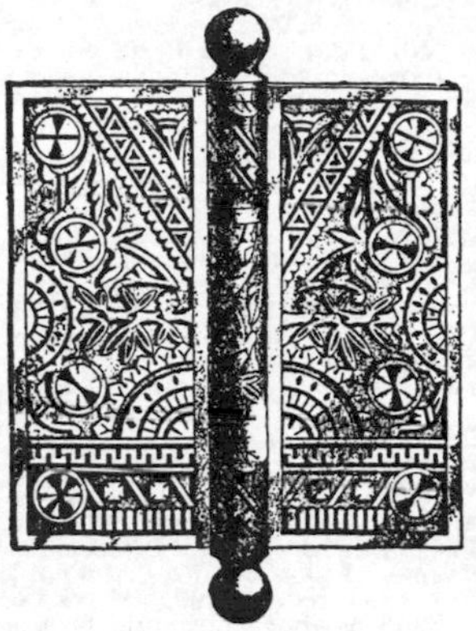

## Butts.

No. 14238. **Bronze plated** Butts, loose pin ball tips. For either right or left hand doors. In giving size, measurement is made when butts are open. Packed with screws.

| Size, inches, | 3x3 | 3½x3½ | 4x4 | 4½x4½ | 5x5 |
|---|---|---|---|---|---|
| Per pair, | $0.25 | .28 | .32 | .35 | .40 |

No. 14239. **Solid bronze** Butts, exactly like above, except are solid bronze instead of bronze plated.

| Size, inches, | 3x3 | 3½x3½ | 4x4 | 4½x4½ | 5x5 |
|---|---|---|---|---|---|
| Per pair, | $0.65 | .75 | .92 | 1.06 | 1.25 |

## Cupboard Turns.

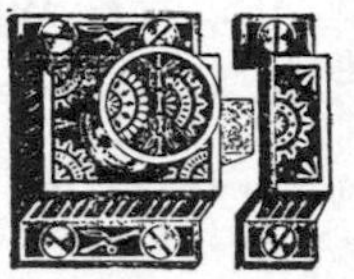

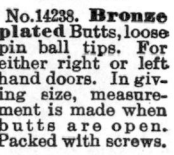

No. 14242. **Bronze plated** Cupboard Turns. Size, 2⅛x1⅛ inches. Packed with screws. Price, each, **15c**; per doz...**$1.68**

No. 14243. **Solid bronze** Cupboard Turns, exactly like above, except is solid bronze instead of bronze plated. Packed with screws. Price, each, **35c**; per doz...........................**$4.20**

## Cupboard Catches.

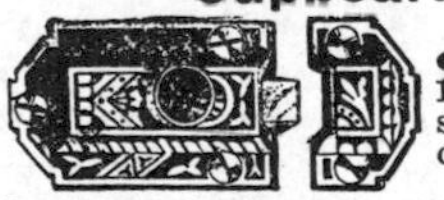

No. 14244. **Bronze plated** Cupboard Catch. Size, 1⅜x2¾ inches. Packed with screws. Price, each, **7c**; per doz...........................**75c**

No. 14245. **Solid bronze** Cupboard Catch, same as above, only solid bronze instead of bronze plated. Price, each, **20c**; per doz...........................**$2.16**

## French Window Catches.

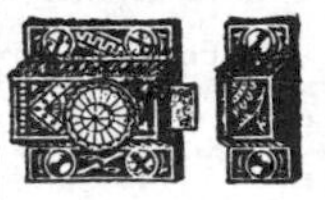

No. 14248. **Bronze Plated** French Window Catch. Size, 1⅜x1¼ inches. Packed with screws. Price, each, **7c**; per doz...............**75c**

No. 14249. **Solid bronze** French Window Catch. Same as above, only it is solid bronze instead of bronze plated. Price, each, **14c**; per doz...........................**$1.58**

## Shutter Bars.

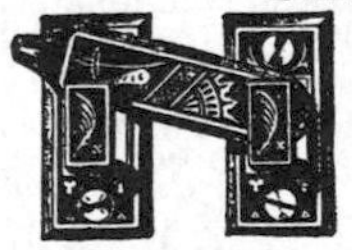

No. 14254. **Bronze plated** Shutter Bars. Length, 2 inches. Packed with screws. Price, each, **6c**; per doz...............**60c**

No. 14255. **Solid bronze** Shutter Bars. Same as above, only made of solid bronze instead of bronze plated. Price, each, **13c**; per doz...........................**$1.50**

## Sash Trimmings.

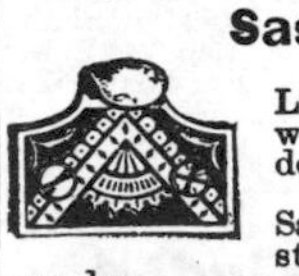

No. 14256. **Bronze plated** Sash Lifts. Size, 1½x1⅛ inches. Packed with screws. Price, each, **3c**; per doz...........................**25c**

No. 14257. **Solid bronze** Sash Lift. Same as above, only solid bronze instead of bronze plated. Price, each, **7c**; per doz...........................**70c**

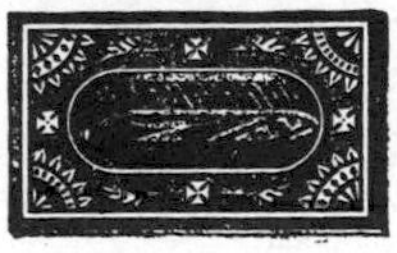

No. 14258. **Bronze plated** flush Sash Lift. Beveled edge. Size, 1¾x3 inches. Packed with screws. Price, each, **7c**; per doz...........................**78c**

No. 14259. **Solid bronze** flush Sash Lifts. Same as above, only solid bronze instead of bronze plated. Price, each **14c**; per doz ....**$1.60**

**The freight on 100 lbs. hardware will be very little when you consider the saving. If you don't need hardware to make 100 lbs., add enough groceries to make up the weight.**

### Door Bolts.

**No. 14260. Bronze plated** Sash Fasts. Size, 1½x2¼ inches. Packed with screws. Price, each, **13c**; per doz.....................**$1.35**
**No. 14261. Solid bronze** Sash Fasts. Same as above, only solid bronze instead of bronze plated. Price, each, **25c**; per doz..........**$2.70**

For other Sash Fasts see Index.

**No. 14266. Bronze plated** Sash Sockets. Size, 1x2 inches. Packed with screws. Price, each, **3c**; per doz......**28c**
**No. 14267. Solid bronze** Sash Sockets. Same as above, only solid bronze instead of bronze plated. Price, each, **6c**; per doz..........**60c**

**No. 14268. Bronze plated** Sash Hooks. Length, 2¾ inches. Packed with screws. Price, each, **7c**; per doz.....**75c**
**No. 14269. Solid bronze** Sash Hooks. Same as above, only solid bronze instead of bronze plated. Price, each, **20c**; per doz....**$2.16**

### Drawer Pulls.

**No. 14274. Bronze plated** Drawer Pulls. Size, 1¼x3¾ inches. Packed with screws. Price, each, **4c**; per doz.....**40c**
**No. 14275. Solid bronze** Drawer Pulls. Same as above, only solid bronze instead of bronze plated. Price each, **13c**; per doz.................**$1.40**

### Door Bolts.

**No. 14278. Bronze plated** Door Bolts. Length, 4 inches. Packed with screws. Price, each, **12c**; per doz.....**$1.32**
**No. 14279. Solid** bronze Door Bolts. Same as above only solid bronze instead of bronze plated. Price, each, **22c**; per doz....**$2.45**

### Screen Door Catches.

**No. 14286. Bronze plated** Screen Door Catches. Ornamentation to match this line of hardware. Size, 2¼x1⅞ inches. Packed with screws and knobs. Price, each, **20c**; per doz....................**$2.16**
**No. 14287. Solid bronze** Screen Door Catches. Same as above, only solid bronze instead of bronze plated. Price, each, **60c**; per doz..............**$6.40**

### Shelf Brackets.

**No. 14288. Bronze plated** Shelf Brackets. Packed with screws.

| Size, in., | 4x5 | 5x7 | 6x8 |
|---|---|---|---|
| Per pair, | $0.24 | .28 | .35 |

| Size, in., | 7x9 | 8x10 | 9x12 |
|---|---|---|---|
| Per pair, | $0.40 | .45 | .50 |

The above brackets are not made in solid bronze.

### Hat and Coat Hooks.

**No. 14294. Bronze plated** Hat and Coat Hooks. Packed with screws. Each......**5c** Per doz...........**55c**
**No. 14295. Solid bronze** Hat and Coat Hooks, same as above, except is made of solid bronze, instead of bronze plated.
Each....................**20c** Per doz...........**$2.16**

### Lamp Hooks.

**No. 14296. Bronze plated** Chandelier Hook. Length of screw, 3 inches. Price, each.......**8c** Per doz.. **87c** Not made in solid bronze.

### Postage Must be Included

*When goods are to be sent by mail.*

*Do not order heavy goods by mail.*

Always make up a freight order of Groceries, Hardware etc., and save all you can.

### Store Door Trimmings.

**No. 14298. Bronze plated** Store Door Lift Latch, with handle. Size of handle, 9½x2⅛ in. For right or left hand doors. Packed with screws.....**35c**

**No. 14299. Solid bronze** Store Door Latch, same as No. 14298, except is solid bronze instead of bronze plated. Price....**$1.10**

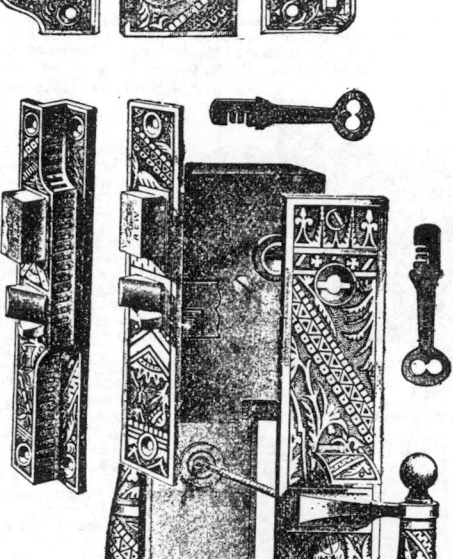

**No. 14306. Bronze plated** Store Door Handle, with mortise lock; flat face. **Anti-Friction Latch Bolt.** Size of lock, 4½x3 inches. Handles, 11½x2 inches. Reversible for right or left hand doors. Bronze bolts, two nickel plated steel keys, **three tumblers** packed complete with screws. Price, each......**$2.20**
**No. 14307. Solid bronze** Store Door Handle, with mortise lock, same as No. 14306, only solid bronze instead of bronze plated. Price, each..............**$3.50**
**No. 14308. Bronze plated** Store Door Handle, with mortise lock, **rabbeted face** for door, which **pushes open to the right**; otherwise same as No. 14306. Price, each..............**$2.70**
**No. 14309. Solid bronze** Store Door Handle, with mortise lock, **rabbeted face** for door which **pushes open to the right.** Same as No. 14308, except is solid bronze instead of bronze plated. Price, each....**$4.25**
**No. 14310. Bronze plated** Store Door Handle, with mortise lock, **rabbeted face** for door which **pushes open to the left**; otherwise same description as No. 14306. Price, each..............**$2.70**
**No. 14311. Solid bronze** Store Door Handle, with mortise lock, rabbeted face for door which **pushes open to the left.** Otherwise same description as No. 14310. Price, each..............**$4.25**

We can furnish any of the above Store Door Locks with **flat handle** (as illustrated in No. 14300) instead of **bar handle**, as shown above, for 50c less than above prices. The bar handle looks better, and we advise any one to buy it instead of the flat handle.

**No. 14300. Bronze plated** Store Door Handle, with mortise latch for either right or left hand doors. Size of latch, 3½x2¼ inches. Size of handles, 9½x2⅛ inches. Packed complete with screws. Price, each........**90c**
**No. 14301. Solid bronze** Store Door Handle, same as No. 14300, only solid bronze instead of bronze plated. Price, each.................**$1.90**

### Door Pulls.

**No. 14316. Bronze plated** Door Pulls. Size, 6x⅞ inch. Packed with screws. Price, each...........**7c**
**No. 14317. Solid bronze** Door Pulls. Same as No. 14316, except is solid bronze instead of bronze plated. Price, each..................................**20c**

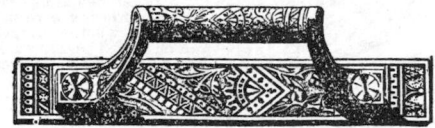

**No. 14318. Bronze plated** Door Pulls and Plates. Size, 7x1 inch. Packed with screws. Price, each..**12c**
**No. 14319. Solid bronze** Door Pulls and Plates. Same as No. 14318, except is solid bronze instead of bronze plated. Price, each........................**45c**

### Foot and Chain Bolts.

**No. 14324. Bronze plated** Foot Bolts. Size, 6x2¼ inches. Packed complete with screws. Price, each.**25c**
**No. 14325. Solid bronze** Foot Bolts. Same as No. 14324, except is solid bronze instead of bronze plated. Price, each.................................**75c**

**No. 14326. Bronze plated** Chain Bolts. Size, 6x2⅛ inches. Packed complete with screws. Price, each.....................................**25c**
**No. 14327. Solid bronze** Chain Bolt. Same as No. 14326, except is solid bronze instead of bronze plated. Price, each.................................**75c**

**By referring to the index, you will find hundreds of articles listed in this catalogue which you might overlook. See if you can't make up a freight order of Groceries and other needed articles each month**

## Flush Bolts.

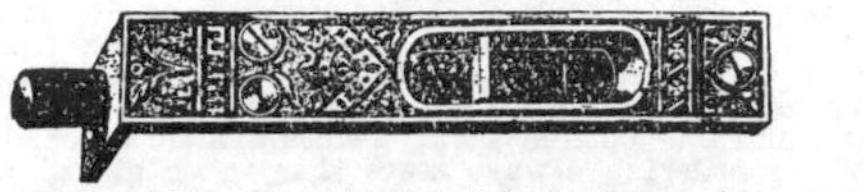

No. 14328. **Bronze plated** Flush Bolts. Size, 6x1 inch. Sunken thumb piece packed complete with screws. Price, each........................................**15c**

No. 14330. **Bronze plated** Flush Bolt. Size, 12x1 inch. Sunken thumb piece packed complete with screws. Not made in solid bronze. Price, each....**18c**

## Chain Door Fasteners.

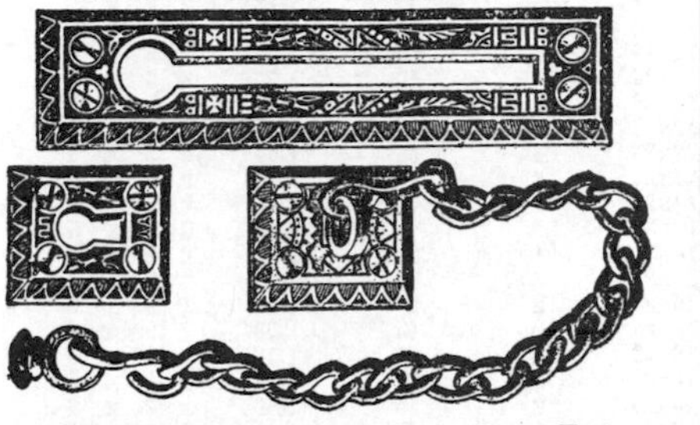

No. 14332. **Bronze plated** Chain Door Fasteners. Size, 1⅜x6 inches. Packed complete with screws. This allows the door to be opened a few inches and securely holds it there. A guard against tramps and other intruders. Price, each........................................**25c**

No. 14333. **Solid bronze** Chain Door Fasteners. Same as No. 14332, except is solid bronze instead of bronze plated. Price, each..............................**65c**

## Letter Drop Plates.

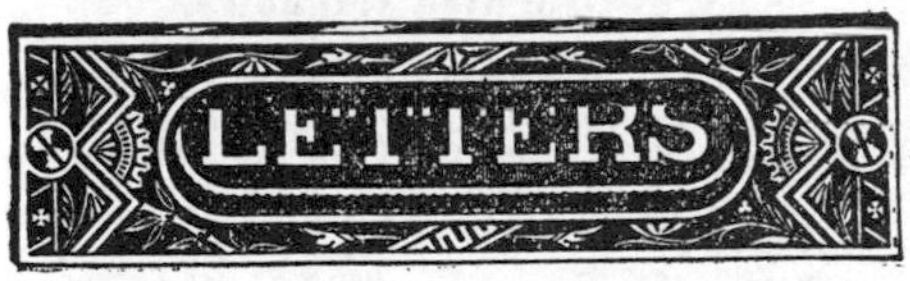


No. 14334. **Bronze plated** Letter Drop Plates. Size of plate, 2x7¼ inches. Size of opening, 1⅛x4¾ inches. Packed with screws. Price, each..........**20c**

No. 14335. **Solid bronze** Letter Drop Plates. Same as No. 14334, except is solid bronze instead of bronze plated. Price, each..............................**35c**

## Door Bells.

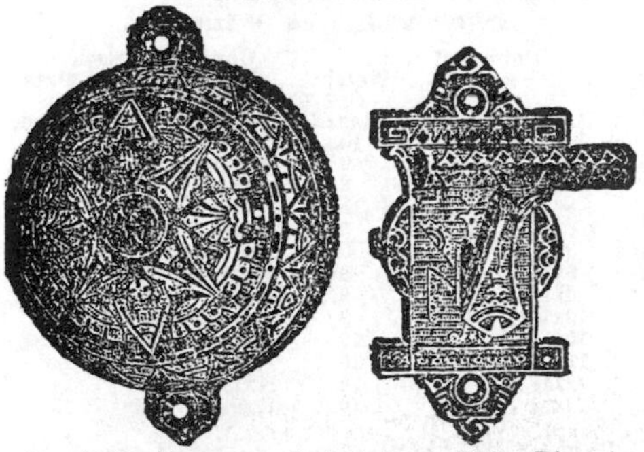

No. 14346. **Bronze plated** Door Bell. Diameter of bell, 4 inches. Pull down lever. Packed complete with screws. Weight, 2 lbs. 2 oz. Price, each, with pull........................................**45c**

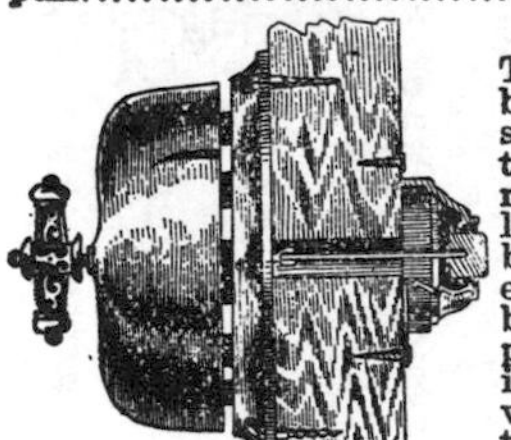

No. 14347. Door Bell. This door bell is wound up by turning the turn knob shown on bell. When button is pushed the bell rings. One winding will last six months. When bell is ringing it sounds exactly like an electric bell. One of the most popular bells made. Four inch nickel plated bell with real bronze push button and plate.
Price, each.........**$1.25**

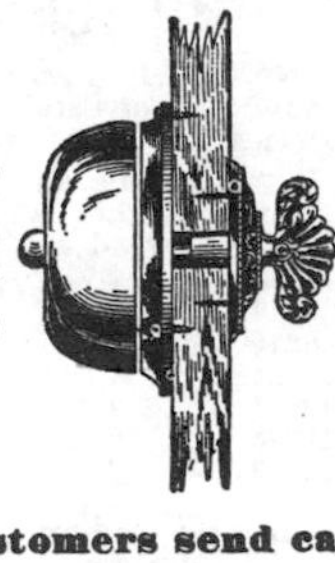

No. 14348. Door Bell. This door bell rings when knob is turned and has a ring similiar to an electric bell. Four inch bell with real bronze turn button and plate.
Price, each.................. **90c**

# BUILDERS' MATERIAL.

We illustrate a line of Builders' Material which we trust will meet all ordinary wants. We are prepared to make **anything** in this line, and will cheerfully and promptly give estimates on special mill work from architects' plans. **Don't wait until you are ready to use before ordering.** During the busy season it will sometimes be ten days before we can ship an order complete. Compare our prices with those of your local dealer. When you build let us furnish the doors, sash and blinds, as well as the hardware. We will save you enough to pay the painter or carpenter bill, possibly more. Freight amounts to nothing compared to what you save.

**We guarantee** a better grade of goods and an incomparably lower price.

**No matter** how large a house you are building, **order from this catalogue** or write us for an estimate on any special work.

## Outside Blinds with Roller Slats.

No. 14354. Outside Blinds measure same as check rail windows, with the addition of 1 inch to the bottom rail for sub sill window frames, which can be cut off if necessary. Outside blinds are 1⅛ inch thick, and prices are for a pair of blinds. **The size of glass and number of lights given below are to show what blinds to order for windows, with check rail sash.**

| Size of glass. | No. of lights. | Per pair. | Size of glass. | No. of lights. | Per pair. |
|---|---|---|---|---|---|
| 10x12 | 8 | $0.78 | 12x36 | 4 | $1.10 |
| 10x14 | 8 | .85 | 14x32 | 4 | 1.06 |
| 10x16 | 8 | .95 | 14x36 | 4 | 1.18 |
| 12x14 | 8 | .88 | 14x40 | 4 | 1.28 |
| 12x16 | 8 | .95 | 16x24 | 2 | .80 |
| 12x18 | 8 | 1.10 | 16x32 | 2 | 1.00 |
| 12x24 | 4 | .78 | 18x36 | 2 | 1.15 |
| 12x28 | 4 | .88 | 18x40 | 2 | 1.30 |
| 12x32 | 4 | .98 | 20x40 | 2 | 1.40 |

## Weights.

Blinds—Four-Lighted Windows.

| Size. | Thickness. | Weight. | Size. | Thickness. | Weight. |
|---|---|---|---|---|---|
| 12x24 | 1⅛ | 16 lbs. | 12x36 | 1⅛ | 23 lbs. |
| 12x28 | 1⅛ | 18 lbs. | 12x40 | 1⅛ | 25 lbs. |
| 12x32 | 1⅛ | 20 lbs. | 12x44 | 1⅛ | 29 lbs. |

Blinds—Eight-Lighted Windows.

| Size. | Thickness. | Weight. | Size. | Thickness. | Weight. |
|---|---|---|---|---|---|
| 9x12 | 1⅛ | 15 lbs. | 12x14 | 1⅛ | 18 lbs. |
| 9x16 | 1⅛ | 18 lbs. | 12x16 | 1⅛ | 20 lbs. |
| 10x14 | 1⅛ | 18 lbs. | 12x20 | 1⅛ | 25 lbs. |

Blinds—Twelve-Lighted Windows.

| Size. | Thickness. | Weight. | Size. | Thickness. | Weight. |
|---|---|---|---|---|---|
| 8x10 | 1⅛ | 14 lbs. | 10x14 | 1⅛ | 22 lbs. |
| 9x12 | 1⅛ | 18 lbs. | 10x18 | 1⅛ | 27 lbs. |
| 9x16 | 1⅛ | 23 lbs. | 10x20 | 1⅛ | 30 lbs. |

## Blind Fixtures.

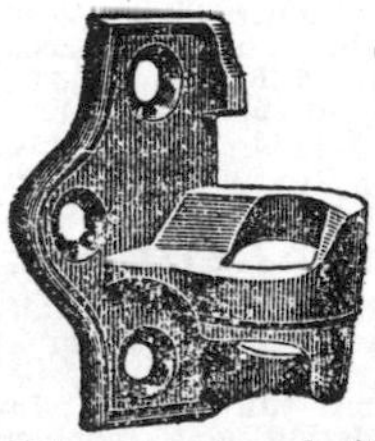

No. 14355. **Clark's or Shepard's Gravity Locking** Blind Hinges and Fasts for wood houses: throws the blind 1¼ in. from the casing.

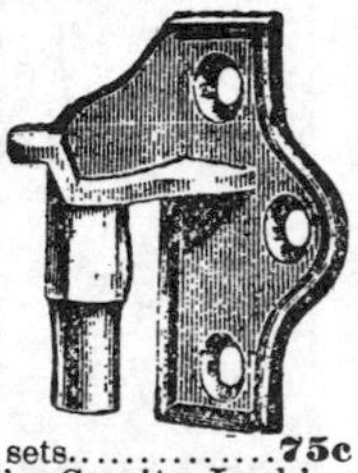

Price, per set, each, **10c**; per doz. sets..............**75c**

No. 14356. Clark's or Shepard's Gravity Locking Blind Hinges and Fasts for brick houses; throws the blind 3¼ inches from the casing. Price, per set, **12c**; per doz. sets.........................................**$1.25**

## Paints, Oils, Etc.

Prices on Paints, Oils, Putty, Varnish, etc., will be found on pages 20 to 23. If interested, send for our color card and prices on same. We can save you money on this class of goods.

## Window Glass.

Prices on Window Glass are constantly fluctuating, so we can not quote a price which will hold good for the season. Quotations will be found in our Grocery List, which will be sent free on request.

## Nails. (See page 38.)

## Lime, Hair and Cement.

See pages 22 and 23.

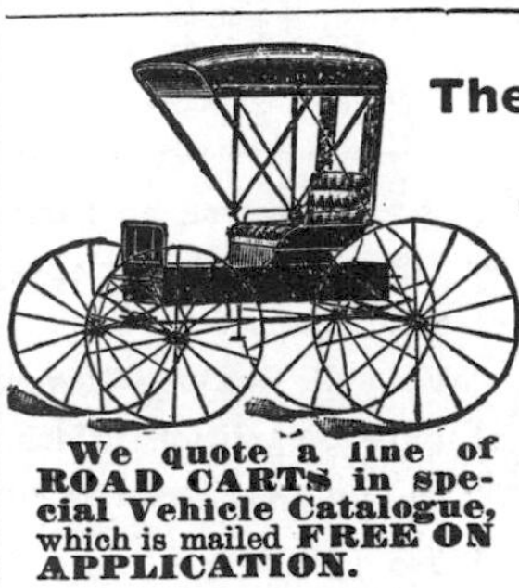

## The Columbus Buggy.

**The Buggy with a world-wide fame.** We sell it for.......**$39.90**

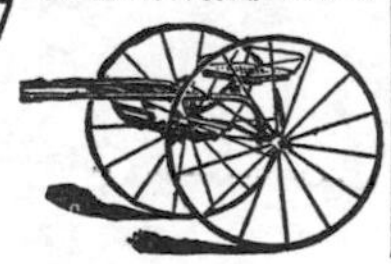

**We quote a line of ROAD CARTS in special Vehicle Catalogue, which is mailed FREE ON APPLICATION.**

## Doors.

No. 14359. O. G. Four Panel Door, raised panels on both sides.

| Size, ft. in. ft. in. | Thickness | Price, each, 1st q'lity. | Price, each, 2d q'lity. |
|---|---|---|---|
| 2 x6 | 1⅛ | $1.10 | $1.05 |
| 2 6x6 6 | 1⅛ | 1.35 | 1.30 |
| 2 6x6 8 | 1⅛ | 1.43 | 1.38 |
| 2 8x6 8 | 1⅛ | 1.49 | 1.42 |
| 2 10x6 10 | 1⅛ | 1.58 | 1.52 |
| 2 6x6 6 | 1⅜ | 1.61 | 1.45 |
| 2 8x6 8 | 1⅜ | 1.71 | 1.55 |
| 2 10x6 10 | 1⅜ | 1.97 | 1.80 |
| 2 6x7 | 1⅜ | 2.03 | 1.85 |
| 2 8x7 | 1⅜ | 2.17 | 1.96 |
| 3 x7 | 1⅜ | 2.25 | 2.05 |
| 3 x7 6 | 1⅜ | 2.52 | 2.30 |

Weights of Four Panel Doors.

| Size. ft. in. ft. in. | Thickness. 1⅛ lbs. | 1⅜ lbs. |
|---|---|---|
| 2 x6 | 22 | 27 |
| 2 6x6 6 | 28 | 33 |
| 2 8x6 8 | 30 | 35 |
| 2 10x6 10 | 33 | 37 |
| 3 x7 | 35 | 40 |
| 3 x7 6 | 37 | 42 |

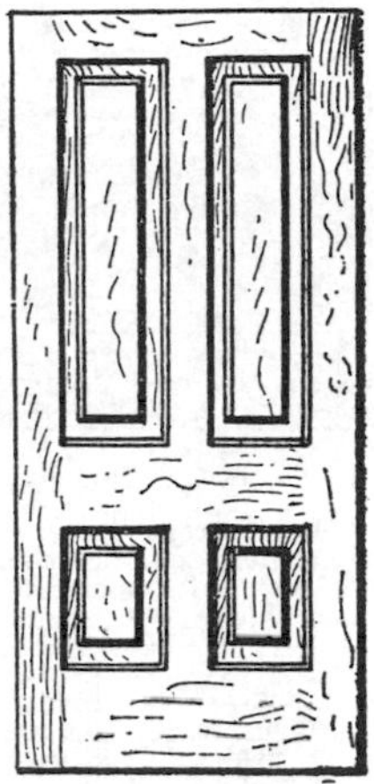

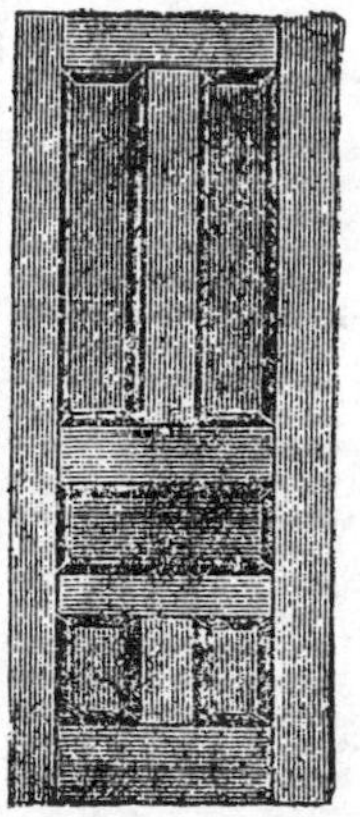

## O. G. Five Panel Doors.

No. 14360. First Quality.

| Size, ft. in. ft. in. | Thickness. in. | Price. |
|---|---|---|
| 2 6x6 6 | 1⅜ | $1.70 |
| 2 6x6 8 | 1⅜ | 1.75 |
| 2 8x6 8 | 1⅜ | 1.82 |
| 2 10x6 10 | 1⅜ | 2.07 |
| 2 6x6 6 | 1¾ | 3.09 |
| 2 8x6 8 | 1¾ | 3.14 |
| 2 10x6 10 | 1¾ | 3.53 |
| 2 6x7 | 1¾ | 3.41 |
| 3 x7 | 1¾ | 3.63 |
| 3 x7 6 | 1¾ | 4.10 |

## O. G. Sash Doors.

No. 14361. One light, double strength, plain glass; raised panel; thickness of door, 1⅜ inches; square corners, not molded, otherwise as shown in cut.

| Size, ft. in. ft. in. | Price, each, unglazed. | Price, each, glazed. |
|---|---|---|
| 2 6x6 6 | $1.70 | $3.12 |
| 2 8x6 8 | 1.90 | 3.40 |
| 2 10x6 10 | 2.15 | 3.90 |
| 2 6x7 | 2.20 | 3.80 |
| 3 x7 | 2.41 | 4.44 |
| 3 x7 6 | 2.70 | 5.20 |

We can furnish any size door. Prices quoted upon application.

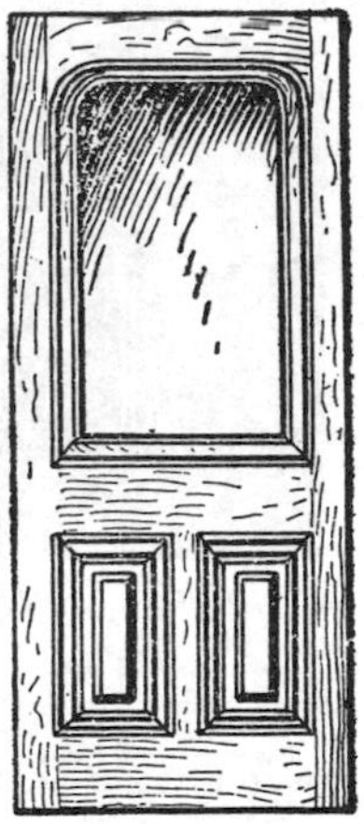

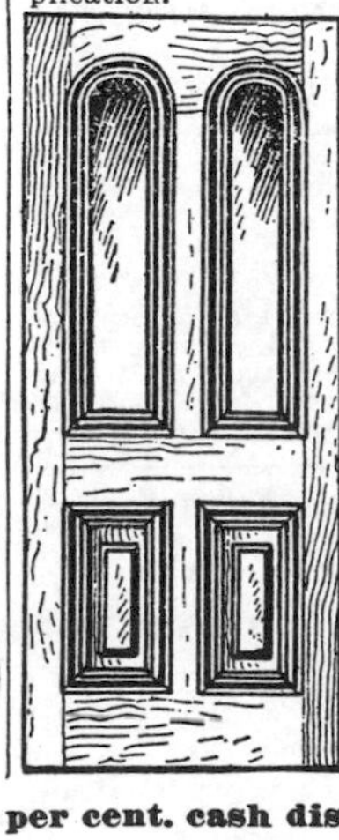

## O. G. Sash Doors.

No. 14372. Two lights, double strength, plain glass, raised panel on both sides. Thickness, 1⅜ inches.

| Size, ft. in. ft. in. | Price, each, unglazed. | Price, each, glazed. |
|---|---|---|
| 2 6x6 6 | $2.10 | $3.20 |
| 2 8x6 8 | 2.20 | 3.45 |
| 2 10x6 10 | 2.50 | 3.95 |
| 2 6x7 | 2.60 | 3.92 |
| 3 x7 | 2.77 | 4.35 |
| 3 x7 6 | 3.00 | 4.90 |

This door is not molded as shown in cut, otherwise the same.

## Front Doors.

No. 14373. Garfield.　　No. 14374. Jenny Lind.

These Front Doors are 1⅜ inches thick, glazed with plain, double strength glass. Can furnish doors 1¾ inch thick for $1.50 more than price of door 1⅜ inch thick, listed below.

|  | One light square top. Glazed, | | One light seg. top. Glazed, | |
|---|---|---|---|---|
| Size, ft. in. ft. in. | Price, unglazed. | D. S. plain. | Price. unglazed. | D. S. plain. |
| 2 8x6 8 | $2.90 | $4.32 | $3.30 | $4.80 |
| 2 10x6 10 | 3.20 | 4.75 | 3.60 | 5.30 |
| 2 8x7 | 3.30 | 4.90 | 3.75 | 5.50 |
| 2 10x7 | 3.40 | 5.25 | 3.85 | 5.85 |
| 3 x7 | 3.46 | 5.52 | 3.90 | 6.10 |

We can glaze the above doors with colored cathedral, enamel or chipped glass at an additional cost to the above prices of 75 cents to each door.

Write us for prices on any kind or size door you may want if not found here.

No. 14378. Garfield Marginal.　　No. 14379. Queen Anne.

These doors are 1⅜ inches thick, glazed, plain double strength glass.

|  | Garfield Marginal. | | Queen Anne. | |
|---|---|---|---|---|
| Sizes, ft.in. ft.in. | Price. unglazed. | Glazed, D.S. plain. | Price, unglazed. | Glazed, D.S. plain. |
| 2 8x6 8 | $3.80 | $5.65 | $4.60 | $6.25 |
| 2 10x6 10 | 4.20 | 6.10 | 4.90 | 6.80 |
| 3 x7 | 4.95 | 6.80 | 5.25 | 7.40 |

### Extras.

We can furnish the above doors, glazed, assorted colored border lights, with cathedral, enamel or chipped center light at an additional cost of 75 cents to the above price of each door. For doors 1¾ inches thick, add $1.50 to the above prices.

### Pages 20, 21, 22 and 23 for
### PAINTS, OILS, WHITE LEAD,
### LIME, CEMENT, VARNISHES,
### ETC., ETC.
**Quality unsurpassed.**
**Prices beyond competition.**

 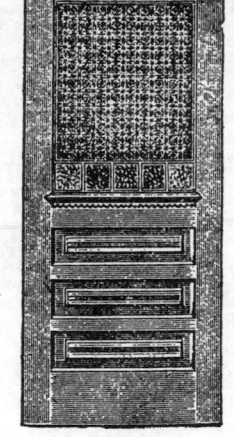

No. 14382. Quaker A.　　No. 14383. Quaker C.

Quaker Pattern Front Doors. The glass in Quaker A is cut by a new process, bringing out all the fine lines of the design. Something new, handsome and low priced. Quaker C is glazed with colored and enamel glass.

| Sizes, ft.in. ft.in. | No. 14382. Unglazed. | Glazed, Cut. | No. 14383. Unglazed. | Glazed, Colored and Enamel. |
|---|---|---|---|---|
| 2 6x6 6 | $2.45 | $3.70 | $2.75 | $3.60 |
| 2 8x6 8 | 2.65 | 3.80 | 3.00 | 3.70 |
| 2 10x6 10 | 2.80 | 4.15 | 3.05 | 4.00 |
| 3 x7 | 2.95 | 4.65 | 3.40 | 4.40 |

*For doors 1¾ inch thick add $1.50 to above. The above light of cut glass, which is cut by a new process, is of very handsome design and can be used in any of our front doors by adding $2.25 to the price of each door.*

No. 14384. Front Door, 1⅜ inches thick; glazed, with chipped center lights and colored border lights.

Quaker B style.
| ft. in. ft. in. | Glazed. |
|---|---|
| 2 6x6 6 | each, $3.60 |
| 2 8x6 6 | each, 3.70 |
| 2 10x6 10 | each, 4.10 |
| 3 x7 | each, 4.40 |

## Plain Rail Sash.

No. 14390. Plain Rail Sash are made 1⅛ inch thick and can not be hung with weights. In ordering give number and size of lights. A window consists of one top and one bottom sash. Prices are for a window. Be careful to see that size of your frames agree with sizes printed. Always state if open or glazed sash is wanted.

| Size of glass. | No. of lights in window. | Price per window, open. | Price per window, glazed. | Fits Frame ft. in. ft. in. |
|---|---|---|---|---|
| 7x 9 | 12 | $0.25 | $0.70 | 2 1 x 3 5½ |
| 8x10 | 12 | .31 | .75 | 2 4 x 3 9¼ |
| 8x12 | 12 | .37 | .91 | 2 4 x 4 6 |
| 8x14 | 12 | .38 | 1.04 | 2 4 x 5 2 |
| 8x16 | 12 | .45 | 1.19 | 2 4 x 5 10 |
| 9x12 | 12 | .39 | .97 | 2 7 x 4 6 |
| 9x13 | 12 | .42 | 1.07 | 2 7 x 4 10 |
| 9x14 | 12 | .43 | 1.08 | 2 7 x 5 2 |
| 9x15 | 12 | .48 | 1.13 | 2 7 x 5 6 |
| 10x12 | 12 | .44 | 1.03 | 2 10 x 4 6 |
| 8x10 | 8 | .34 | .57 | 1 8½x 3 9¼ |
| 9x12 | 8 | .37 | .72 | 1 10½x 4 6 |
| 9x14 | 8 | .41 | .78 | 1 10½x 5 2 |
| 10x12 | 8 | .40 | .76 | 2 0½x 4 6 |
| 10x14 | 8 | .43 | .86 | 2 0½x 5 2 |

It will do you no harm to understand the science of self defense.

We sell Boxing Gloves at anti-competition prices. A complete assortment on pages 593 and 594.

## Check Rail Sash.

No. 14391. Check Rail Sash are made 1⅜ inches thick, and are intended to be used with box frames and sash weights. See that sizes of your frames agree with sizes printed. A window consists of one top and one bottom sash. Prices are for a window. When ordering always state if open or glazed sash are wanted. State size of glass and number of lights in the window.

| Size of glass. | No. of lights in window. | Price per window, open. | Price per window, glazed. | Fits Frame ft. in. ft. in. |
|---|---|---|---|---|
| 10x12 | 8 | $0.40 | $0.88 | 2 1 x 4 6 |
| 10x14 | 8 | .45 | .98 | 2 1 x 5 2 |
| 10x16 | 8 | .50 | 1.15 | 2 1 x 5 10 |
| 12x14 | 8 | .47 | 1.18 | 2 5 x 5 2 |
| 12x16 | 8 | .52 | 1.30 | 2 5 x 5 10 |
| 12x18 | 8 | .55 | 1.40 | 2 5 x 6 6 |
| 12x24 | 4 | .40 | .95 | 2 5 x 4 6 |
| 12x28 | 4 | .46 | 1.10 | 2 5 x 5 2 |
| 12x32 | 4 | .46 | 1.43 | 2 5 x 5 10 |
| 12x36 | 4 | .53 | 1.60 | 2 5 x 6 6 |
| 14x24 | 4 | .43 | 1.12 | 2 9 x 4 6 |
| 14x28 | 4 | .46 | 1.40 | 2 9 x 5 2 |
| 14x32 | 4 | .51 | 1.65 | 2 9 x 5 10 |
| 14x36 | 4 | .55 | 1.84 | 2 9 x 6 6 |
| 16x24 | 2 | .39 | .78 | 1 8 x 4 6 |
| 16x32 | 2 | .47 | 1.11 | 1 8 x 5 10 |
| 18x28 | 2 | .43 | 1.08 | 1 10 x 5 2 |
| 18x32 | 2 | .45 | 1.16 | 1 10 x 5 10 |
| 18x36 | 2 | .51 | 1.35 | 1 10 x 6 6 |
| 18x40 | 2 | .53 | 1.50 | 2 10 x 7 2 |
| 20x28 | 2 | .40 | 1.15 | 2 0 x 5 2 |
| 20x30 | 2 | .42 | 1.20 | 2 0 x 5 6 |
| 20x32 | 2 | .45 | 1.35 | 2 0 x 5 10 |
| 24x28 | 2 | .42 | 1.30 | 2 4 x 5 2 |
| 24x30 | 2 | .43 | 1.40 | 2 4 x 5 6 |
| 24x34 | 2 | .50 | 1.65 | 2 4 x 6 2 |
| 24x38 | 2 | .55 | 1.90 | 2 4 x 6 10 |

### Weights.
#### Eight-Lighted Windows.

| | Plain Rail Sash. | | | Check Rail Sash. | |
|---|---|---|---|---|---|
| Size. | Weight, Glazed. lbs. | Weight, Unglazed. lbs. | Size. | Weight, Glazed. lbs. | Weight, Unglazed. lbs. |
| 8x10 | 12 | 5 | 9x12 | 17 | 8 |
| 8x12 | 12 | 5 | 9x14 | 18 | 9 |
| 8x14 | 14 | 7 | 10x12 | 18 | 9 |
| 9x12 | 14 | 6 | 10x14 | 19 | 11 |
| 9x14 | 17 | 7 | 10x16 | 22 | 12 |
| 10x12 | 15 | 8 | 12x14 | 23 | 11 |
| 10x14 | 18 | 8 | 12x16 | 24 | 12 |
| 10x16 | 20 | 9 | 12x18 | 27 | 13 |
| 12x14 | 19 | 9 | 12x20 | 32 | 14 |
| 12x16 | 22 | 11 | 14x20 | 35 | 15 |
| 12x18 | 25 | 12 | 14x24 | 40 | 17 |

#### Twelve-Lighted Windows.

| | Plain Rail Sash. | | | Check Rail Sash. | |
|---|---|---|---|---|---|
| Size. | Weight, Glazed. lbs. | Weight, Unglazed. lbs. | Size. | Weight, Glazed. lbs. | Weight, Unglazed. lbs. |
| 8x10 | 14 | 6 | 8x12 | 20 | 8 |
| 8x12 | 18 | 8 | 8x14 | 22 | 8 |
| 8x14 | 19 | 8 | 9x12 | 22 | 9 |
| 9x12 | 20 | 9 | 9x14 | 24 | 10 |
| 9x14 | 22 | 9 | 9x16 | 27 | 11 |
| 9x16 | 26 | 9 | 10x12 | 23 | 11 |
| 10x12 | 21 | 9 | 10x14 | 26 | 11 |
| 10x14 | 23 | 9 | 10x16 | 29 | 12 |
| 10x16 | 26 | 10 | 10x18 | 32 | 13 |
| 12x14 | 25 | 10 | 10x20 | 34 | 14 |
| 12x16 | 28 | 10 | 12x20 | 36 | 14 |
| 12x18 | 31 | 10 | 12x24 | 42 | 15 |

#### Two-Lighted Check Rail Windows.

| Size. | Thickness. | Glazed, Single Strength, lbs. | Glazed, Double Strength, lbs. | Size. | Thickness. | Glazed, Single Strength, lbs. | Glazed, Double Strength, lbs. |
|---|---|---|---|---|---|---|---|
| 20x24 | 1⅜ | 21 | 23 | 26x34 | 1⅜ | 27 | 31 |
| 20x28 | 1⅜ | 22 | 25 | 26x36 | 1⅜ | 28 | 32 |
| 20x32 | 1⅜ | 23 | 26 | 26x40 | 1⅜ | 30 | 34 |
| 20x36 | 1⅜ | 25 | 28 | 26x44 | 1⅜ | 32 | 36 |
| 20x40 | 1⅜ | 26 | 30 | 26x48 | 1⅜ | 34 | 39 |
| 24x30 | 1⅜ | 24 | 26 | 28x32 | 1⅜ | 29 | 32 |
| 24x32 | 1⅜ | 25 | 28 | 28x36 | 1⅜ | 30 | 34 |
| 24x36 | 1⅜ | 27 | 30 | 28x40 | 1⅜ | 32 | 36 |
| 24x40 | 1⅜ | 29 | 33 | 28x44 | 1⅜ | 34 | 38 |
| 26x30 | 1⅜ | 25 | 28 | 28x48 | 1⅜ | 36 | 40 |
| 26x32 | 1⅜ | 26 | 30 | | | | |

### Check Rail Pantry Sash.

No. 14396. Pantry Sash are only one light wide. Window consists of one top and one bottom sash. Prices are for a window.

| Size of glass. | Number of lights in window. | Price per window not glazed. | Price per window glazed. | Fits frame ft. in. ft. in. |
|---|---|---|---|---|
| 9x12 | 4 | $0.32 | $0.58 | 1 1⅛x4 6 |
| 9x14 | 4 | .35 | .63 | 1 1⅛x5 2 |
| 9x16 | 4 | .38 | .68 | 1 1⅛x5 10 |
| 12x14 | 4 | .35 | .75 | 1 4⅛x5 2 |
| 12x24 | 2 | .32 | .65 | 1 4⅛x4 6 |
| 12x28 | 2 | .35 | .73 | 1 4⅛x5 2 |
| 12x32 | 2 | .40 | .95 | 1 4⅛x5 10 |

**You may not find just what you want by glancing over this department. Refer to the index and you can't miss it. Our index, by the way, is worth reading over on general principles.**

## Oriel Front Window.

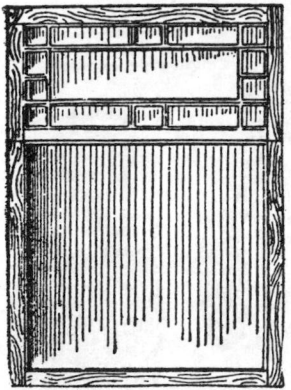

The lower sash is glazed with double strength AA quality glass. The upper sash is assorted colors in border lights of Venetian and opalescent glass. This makes a very handsome effect. Usual sizes made.

No. 14392. Made in two sashes.
No. 14393. Made in one sash. Either the same price.

| Size frame opening. | Large lower light glass measure. | Size top glass measure. | Price. top assorted colors, bottom plain, D. S. |
|---|---|---|---|
| 3 ft. 4 in. x5 ft. 10 in. | 36x48 | 36x16 | $4.44 |
| 3 ft. 8 in. x5 ft. 10 in. | 40x48 | 40x16 | 4.82 |
| 4 ft. x6 ft. 2 in. | 44x48 | 44x20 | 6.50 |
| 4 ft. x6 ft. 6 in. | 44x52 | 44x20 | 7.95 |
| 4 ft. 4 in x7 ft. 2 in. | 48x56 | 48x24 | 10.35 |

## Cellar Sash.

No. 14897. Cellar sash up to 10x14 are 1⅛ in. thick, above 10x14 are 1⅜ in. thick. Prices are for one sash only. Weight, from 7 to 15 lbs., glazed.

| Size of glass. | No of lights. | Price, each, open. | Price, each, glazed. | Size of Sash, ft. in. ft. in. |
|---|---|---|---|---|
| 8x10 | 3 | $0.14 | $0.30 | 2 4x1 2 |
| 9x12 | 3 | .15 | .38 | 2 7x1 4 |
| 9x14 | 3 | .16 | .39 | 2 7x1 6 |
| 10x12 | 3 | .17 | .40 | 2 10x1 4 |
| 10x14 | 2 | .17 | .36 | 2 1x1 6 |
| 12x14 | 2 | .18 | .40 | 2 5x1 6 |
| 12x16 | 2 | .19 | .46 | 2 5x1 8 |

## Transom Sash.

No. 14398. Transom sash are 1⅜ inches thick.

| Size of Sash, ft. in. in. | Price, each, open. | Price, 1 light, glazed. | Price, 2 light, glazed. |
|---|---|---|---|
| 2 6x12 | $0.18 | $0.39 | $0.32 |
| 2 6x14 | .19 | .42 | .34 |
| 2 8x14 | .20 | .44 | .37 |
| 2 10x14 | .21 | .45 | .38 |
| 2 10x16 | .23 | .50 | .44 |
| 3 x14 | .24 | .51 | .45 |

## Storm Sash.

No. 14399. Storm Sash (sometimes called outside windows or double windows) are made to fit frames of check rail sash. Storm sash, 1⅛ inches thick, are same prices as check rail sash of corresponding sizes. Compare sizes of your frame and see that they agree with dimensions given. If wanted with ventilators in top or bottom rail, add 10c to each window. If wanted with one light to swing on hinges, add 40c to each window. The window is made in one sash. When ordering give size of glass and number of lights in windows.

## Porch Trimmings, Etc.

No. 14410. Selected poplar Porch Columns, smooth turned (columns smaller than 4 inches are not bored). Bored center, avoids checking. Steam dried, prevents mildew.

| Size, in. | Length, ft. | Each. | Size, in. | Length, ft. | Each. |
|---|---|---|---|---|---|
| 4x4 | 8 | $0.69 | 5x5 | 10 | $1.19 |
| 4x4 | 9 | .75 | 6x6 | 8 | 1.44 |
| 4x4 | 10 | .82 | 6x6 | 9 | 1.50 |
| 5x5 | 8 | .94 | 6x6 | 10 | 1.60 |
| 5x5 | 9 | 1.05 | | | |

No. 14411. Brackets 1⅜ thick, 10x12 inch.
Each..........9c
Brackets 1⅜ thick, 12x14 inch.
Each..........11c
No. 14412. Brackets 1⅜ thick, 10x12 inch.
Each..........10c
Brackets 1⅜ thick, 12x14 inch; each..........13c

No. 14413. Baluster, made of pine, ⅞ inch thick, 6 inch wide, 18 to 20 inches long.
Each..........7c
No. 14414. Beaded Porch Rail. 2x2 inch.
Per foot..........2c

No 14415. Ball Spindles, 1¼ inch ball spindles, 8 to 10 inches long.
Each..........4c

No. 14416. Corner Bead, made of pine, 4 feet long, 1⅝ inch in diameter. Each..........7c
1⅜ inch in diameter. Each..........8c
1¾ inch in diameter. Each..........11c

No. 14417. Baluster, made from pine, 20 to 24 inches long, 1¾ inch diameter.
Each..........9c

---

No. 14418. Stair Baluster, 1¾ inch diameter, 20 to 24 inches long, made from oak or ash, each, 12c; made from walnut or cherry, each..........17c

No. 14419. Outside Newel, made from white wood, 4 feet long. Size, 4x4, each, 43c. Size, 5x5, each, 52c. Size, 6x6, each..........75c
No. 14420. Base Angle Bead, 1⅜ inches, 12 to 14 inches long (saves mitering base). Each..........3c
No. 14421. Spindle, 1¾ inches, 8 to 10 inches long. Each..........5c 
No. 14422. Spindle, 1¾ inches, 8 to 10 inches long. Each..........4c 

## Gable Ornaments, Adjustable.

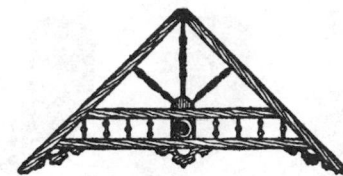

Block Pattern No. 14426.

Block Pattern extends 5 feet down the gable, furnished in either one-half or one-third pitch. These ornaments are neat and attractive designs, low in price, and are so constructed any carpenter can regulate to fit any pitch. Gable ornaments add ten times their cost to the appearance of any home.
No. 14426. Block pattern. Price, each..........$2.00
**When ordering state what pitch is wanted.**

Spindle Pattern No. 14428.
No. 14428. Spindle Pattern. Price, each..........$2.25

## Head and Base Blocks.

White or yellow pine.
Head Block.
Sizes:
4 x10x1⅛    5 x10x1⅛
4½x10x1⅛    5½x10x1⅛
No. 14432, Price, each..4½c

## Corner Block.

No. 14432.
White and yellow pine.
Sizes:
4 x4 x1⅛    5 x5 x1⅛
4½x4½x1⅛    5½x5½x1⅛
No. 14433. Price, each..2½c

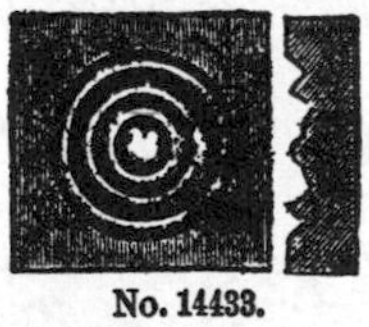

No. 14433.

## Base Block.

Sizes:
4 x11x1⅜    5 x11x1⅜
4½x11x1⅜    5½x11x1⅜
No. 14434. Price, each..4½c

## Casings and House Moldings.

White and yellow pine.

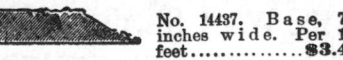

No. 14435.

| | Casing, in. wide, | 4 | 4½ |
|---|---|---|---|
| | Per 100 feet, | $1.80 | $2.00 |
| | Casing, in. wide, | 5 | 5½ |
| | Per 100 feet, | $2.25 | $2.40 |

No. 14436. O. G. Casing.

| | Wide, inch, | 4 | 4½ |
|---|---|---|---|
| | Per 100 feet, | $1.85 | 2.05 |
| | Wide, inch, | 5 | 5½ |
| | Per 100 feet, | $2.30 | 2.45 |

No. 14434.

No. 14437. Base, 7½ inches wide. Per 100 feet..........$3.40

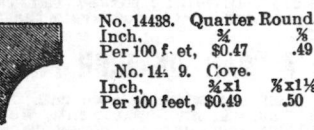

No. 14438. Quarter Round.

| Inch. | ¾ | ⅞ |
|---|---|---|
| Per 100 f. et, | $0.47 | .49 |

No. 14439. Cove.

| Inch. | ¾x1 | ⅞x1⅛ |
|---|---|---|
| Per 100 feet, | $0.49 | .50 |

No. 14439.                    No. 14438.

---

No. 14440. Parting Stop ½x⅝ inch, per 100 feet...40c

No. 14441.

No. 14441.  O. G. Stop.

| | Inch, | 1⅛ | 1¾ |
|---|---|---|---|
| Per 100 feet, | $0.45 | .50 | .65 |

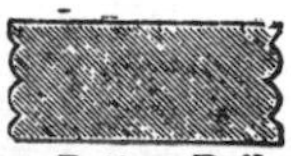

No. 14442.
Beaded Porch Rail, 1¾x3¾.
Price per foot......4½c

Top Rail.          Bottom Rail.

## Weights.

100 lineal feet of dry lumber, size, 1x1 inch, weighs about 15 lbs.

## Stair Posts and Rails.

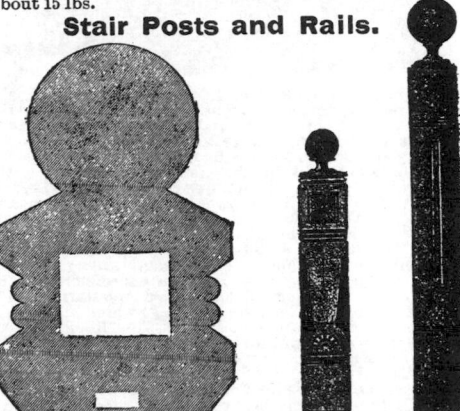

End View.
No. 14450. Front Stair Bottom Post, made of oak Size, 6x6; price, each..........$7.50
No. 14452. Front Stair Top Post, made of oak. Size, 5x5; price, each, $2.35. Size, 6x6; price, each..$2.65
No. 14454. Stair Rail. Size, 2½x4. Made of poplar, per foot, 12c. Made of oak, per foot..........14c

No. 14456. Oak Balusters, either 28 or 32 inches long, as desired. Each..........12c

No. 14457. Oak Balusters, either 28 or 32 inches long, as desired. Each..........12c
In ordering stair posts state if posts will stand on right or left hand as you go up the stairs.

## Building Paper.

We buy our Building Papers from the largest and most reliable makers in large quantities for spot cash, and sell them at our usual small profit. Samples sent free on request. Building paper is not intended to be exposed to the weather, but is intended to be used under shingles, clapboards, floors, etc.

The cost is very little, and can be saved in one season in your fuel bills, to say nothing of the comforts secured by its use.
No. 14488. **The genuine "Black Diamond" brand Red Resin Sized Sheathing** is a strong, smooth finish, durable, waterproof paper, put up in rolls of 500 square feet, 36 inches wide, weighing about 40 lbs. Clean to handle. Price, per roll..........$1.00
No. 14489. **The "Anchor" brand Red Resin Sized Sheathing** is the same grade as "Black Diamond" sheathing, but is not quite as heavy. Put up in rolls of 500 square feet, 36 inches wide, weighing about 35 lbs. Price, per roll..........80c
No. 14490. **The "Peerless brand Gray" Resin Sized Sheathing** is a fine grade of sheathing, strong and durable, waterproof, and clean to handle. Put up in rolls of 500 square feet, 36 inches wide and weighing about 35 lbs. Price, per roll..........70c
No. 14492. **The "Competition" brand Red Resin Sized Sheathing Paper.** A strong, clean paper, nearly waterproof, and lays smooth; better and cheaper than common strawboard. Put up in rolls of 500 square feet, 36 inches wide, and weighing about 25 lbs. Price, per roll..........45c
No. 14496. **Plain Strawboard Sheathing Paper** is put up in rolls weighing from 70 to 80 lbs., 32 inches wide, containing from 300 to 470 square feet. Price, per lb..........1c
No. 14497. **Tarred Strawboard Sheathing Paper** is put up in rolls weighing from 50 to 75 lbs., 32 inches wide. Price, per lb..........1¼c
No. 14498. **Blue Plaster Board** a strong, tough paper used on walls and ceilings in place of plaster. For cheap or temporary partitions it is used extensively. We have it in rolls of 250 square feet, and in rolls of 500 square feet. The 500 foot roll weighs 60 lbs. Price, per roll containing 500 square feet..........$2.65
Price, per roll containing 250 square feet..........$1.35
**We do not cut rolls of Building Paper.**

## S., R. & Co. Felt Roofing.

**When you build you will want roofing** (we will save you 33⅓ per cent. on it); **you will want hardware** (we will save you 33⅓ per cent. on it); you will want paint (we will save you 33⅓ per cent. on it); you will want paper (we will save you 50 per cent. on it); you will want doors, sash, moldings, blinds, etc. (we will save you 50 per cent. on it). Why not figure with us before you build?

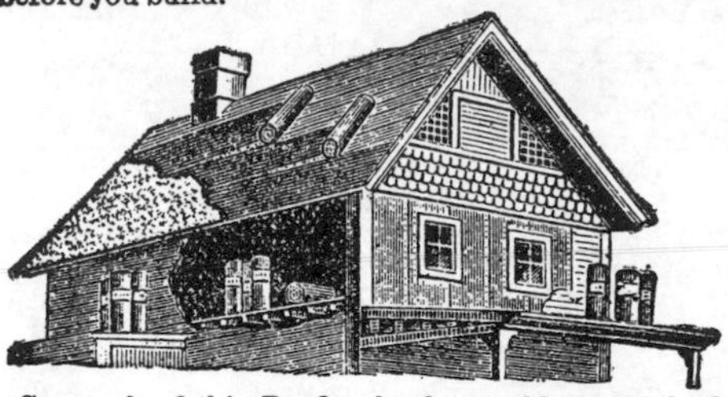

So much of this Roofing has been sold, we think almost everybody must be acquainted with its good qualities. It has been used in **all climates and has given universal satisfaction.** It is easily and cheaply applied, no tools being required except a jack-knife, hammer and brush. Complete directions with each roll. The Two-ply Roofing consists of two layers of Felt Roofing with a layer of waterproof asphalt cement between, the whole being united under great pressure. The Three-ply Roofing consists of three layers of Felt Roofing with two layers of asphalt cement between, the whole being united under great pressure. We have this roofing made for us in enormous quantities, by manufacturers of established reputation, and can offer our patrons all the advantage which large purchases for spot cash can secure. This Roofing is 32 inches wide, and is put up in rolls containing 108 square feet. Allowing for laps each roll will cover 100 square feet. The Two-ply Roofing weighs about 75 lbs. per roll; the Three-ply Roofing weighs about 100 lbs. per roll. If this Roofing is kept well coated with **our Roofing Cement** it is practically indestructible.

No. 14477. Two-ply Roofing **only**, per roll containing 108 square feet........ **87c**

No. 14478. Three-ply Roofing, **only**, per roll containing 108 square feet........ **$1.15**

No. 14479. Barbed Roofing Nails (1¼ lbs required for each roll of roofing. Per lb........ **4c**

No. 14480. Tin Roofing Caps (1 lb. required for each roll of roofing). Per lb........ **6c**

No. 14481. Roofing Cement (2 gals. required for each roll of roofing), in wood pails, kegs or barrels. Cost of package is included in these prices:

Two gals. or less, per gal........ **28c**
3 to 5 gals., per gal........ **23c**
6 to 10 gals., per gal........ **19c**
11 to 20 gals., per gal........ **17c**
21 to 40 gals., per gal........ **15c**
50 gals. or more, per gal........ **13c**

## Neponset Red Rope Roofing Fabric.

This is an air-tight and waterproof roofing paper, and makes a durable covering for roofs and sides of buildings at one-quarter the cost of shingles. A coat of good paint adds to its durability. It is also used extensively instead of plaster, being tacked to furring or laths and covered with wall paper. It is made in one grade only, and that is the best it is possible to produce. With each roll we furnish sufficient caps and nails to apply it to roof or siding.

No. 14485. Neponset Red Rope Roofing Fabric, in rolls of 250 square feet. Per roll........ **$2.55**

No. 14486. Neponset Red Rope Roofing Fabric, in rolls of 500 square feet. Per roll........ **$4.60**

## Steel Pressed Brick Siding.

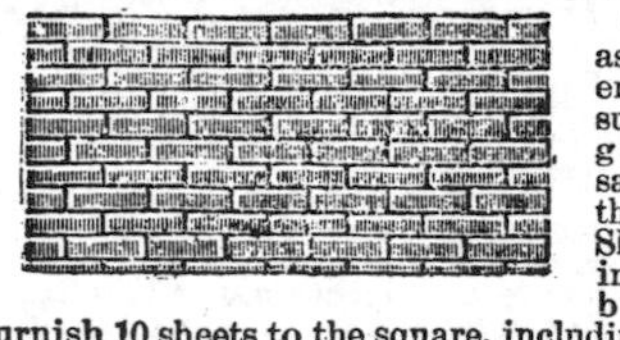

This has no equal as a handsome covering surface. Insurance companies generally give same rating for this as for stone. Sheets are 60x28 inches, painted on both sides. We furnish 10 sheets to the square, including nails to put it on, and sufficient dry paint for second coat. Weight, per square, 75 lbs.

No. 14502. Price, per square, for less than 5 squares, **$3.10**; price, per square, for 5 squares or more.. **$3.00**

We do not sell less than one square.

## V-Crimped Roofing.

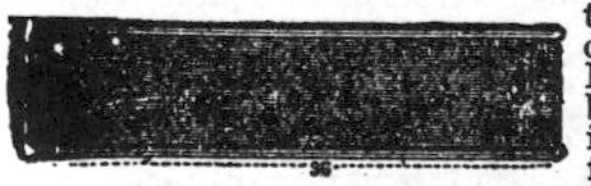

The popularity of this roofing is evidenced by the very large quantity sold by us continually. It is par excellence the farmer's roofing. It is the cheaper of all roofs offered and costs less to put it on the roof. Any person can apply it who can drive a nail. It is painted on both sides.

May be laid over sheathing, shingles, lath or direct to rafters placed 24 inches from center, on any roof having a pitch of more than two inches to the foot. The ends of sheets can either be lapped three inches or more, or put together with lock-joint.

For a square of this roofing we ship: 6¼ sheets, 24 inches to the centers, 8 feet long (or equivalent lengths); 1 lb. 1¾ inch, No. 10 barbed wire nails; 1 lb. dry mineral paint; 50 feet V sticks.

No. 14503. Price, per square, for less than 5 squares, **$2.85**; price, per square, for 5 squares or more.. **$2.70**

## Corrugated Iron.

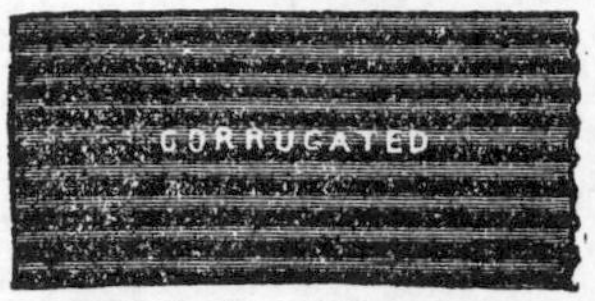


Corrugated Iron being used in such very large quantities, and for so many useful and varied purposes, it would seem useless to enter into any discussion concerning it. It is light, cheap, durable and fire proof. Used for roofing, siding, ceilings and partitions. When ordering state what it is to be used for, and give dimensions of space it is to cover, and we will send sizes that will cut and lay to best advantage and the proper corrugations.

Our iron roofing is put up in squares consisting of 6 sheets, 96 inches long by 26 inches wide (or its equivalent) with sufficient nails to put it on, and enough dry paint for second coat.

No. 14505. Price, per square, for less than 5 squares, **$2.80**; price, per square, for 5 squares or more.. **$2.60**

We do not sell less than one square.

## Galvanized Corrugated Expanding Conductor.

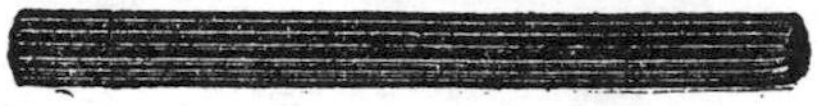

No. 14508. This pipe is made from galvanized iron and is a solid pipe 10 feet long without joints. We do not furnish cut lengths. It will **not** burst when full of ice.

| Size, inches, | 2 | 3 | 4 | 5 | 6 |
|---|---|---|---|---|---|
| Price, per foot, | $0.03 | .05 | .05½ | .07½ | .09 |

## Galvanized Iron Elbows.

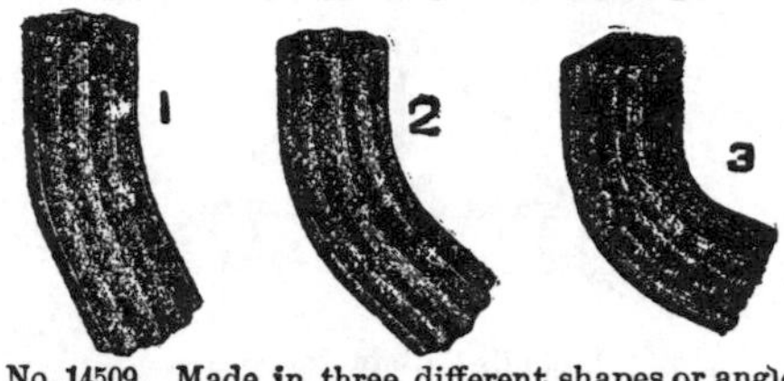


No. 14509. Made in three different shapes or angles. You must always state which angle is wanted.

| Size, inches, | 2 | 3 | 4 | 5 | 6 |
|---|---|---|---|---|---|
| Price, each round, | $0.09 | .11 | .15 | .18 | .22 |

## Galvanized Eave Troughs.

**"Slip Joint."**

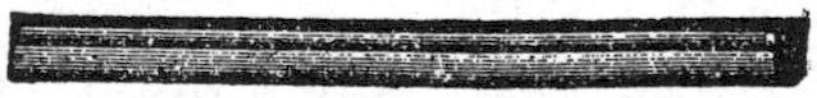

No. 14510. Made of galvanized steel in 10-foot lengths without cross seams, is much more durable than tin and easier to put up. It is made in 10-foot lengths, and we do not furnish cut lengths. Sizes are measured inside of bead.

| Size, inches, | 3½ | 4 | 5 | 6 |
|---|---|---|---|---|
| Price, per foot, | $0.03½ | .04 | .04½ | .06 |

## Galvanized Ridge Roll.

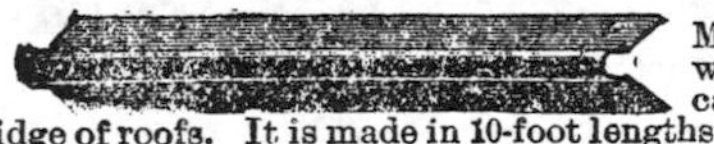

No. 14512. Makes a neat waterproof cap for the ridge of roofs. It is made in 10-foot lengths. We do not furnish cut lengths.

| Size of roll, inches, | 1¼ | 1½ | 2 | 2½ | 3 |
|---|---|---|---|---|---|
| Width of apron, inches, | 2 | 2 | 2½ | 2½ | 3½ |
| Girt, inches, | 7 | 8 | 10 | 12 | 15 |
| Price, per foot, | $0.04½ | .04½ | .05½ | .06½ | .07 |

## Galvanized Eave Trough Corners.

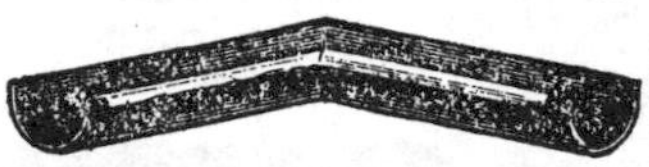

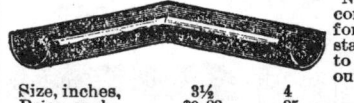

No. 14513. Made complete, ready for use. Always state if bead is to be inside or out.

| Size, inches, | 3½ | 4 | 5 | 6 |
|---|---|---|---|---|
| Price, each, | $0.23 | .25 | .27 | .30 |

## Wire Eave Trough Hangers.

| No. 14514. Size, inches, | 3½ | 4 | 5 | 6 |
|---|---|---|---|---|
| Per dozen, | $0.30 | .35 | .38 | .40 |

## Conductor Hooks, Tinned.

No. 14515. For fastening conductor to side of house.

| Size, inches. | 2 | 3 | 4 | 5 | 6 |
|---|---|---|---|---|---|
| Price, per dozen, | $0.12 | .25 | .35 | .50 | 1.00 |



## MISCELLANEOUS HARDWARE.

## Tackle Blocks.

Iron Strapped Tackle Blocks. Iron sheaves, steel pins. Remember that only the lower block requires a becket. Be careful to give the right order number.

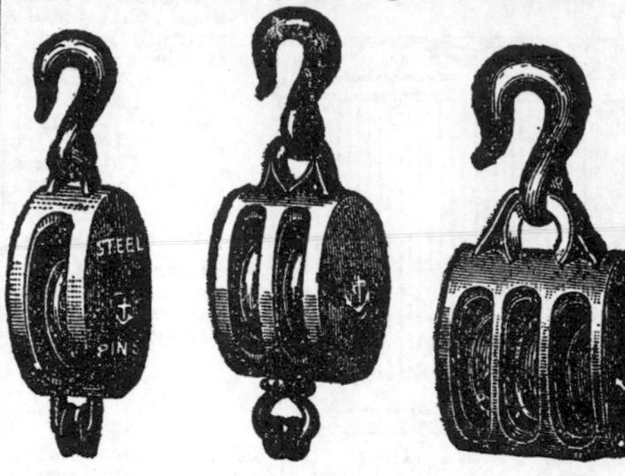


No. 14525. Tackle Block. **With Becket.**
No. 14526. Tackle Block. **Without Becket.**

| Size of shell. | For Rope. | Single pulley each. | Double pulley, each. | Triple pulley, each. |
|---|---|---|---|---|
| 3 | 5/16 in. | $0.19 | $0.35 | $0.48 |
| 3½ | ⅜ in. | .21 | .40 | .54 |
| 4 | ½ in. | .23 | .44 | .59 |
| 5 | ⅝ in. | .25 | .48 | .62 |
| 6 | ¾ in. | .30 | .54 | .79 |
| 7 | ⅞ in. | .35 | .65 | .95 |
| 8 | 1 in. | .45 | .78 | 1.15 |
| 10 | 1⅛ in. | .75 | 1.22 | 1.69 |
| 12 | 1¼ in. | 1.21 | 2.03 | 2.87 |

Single pulleys weigh from ¾ to 18 pounds. Double pulleys, from 1¼ to 32 pounds. Triple pulleys, from 2 to 64 pounds.

## Awning Pulleys.

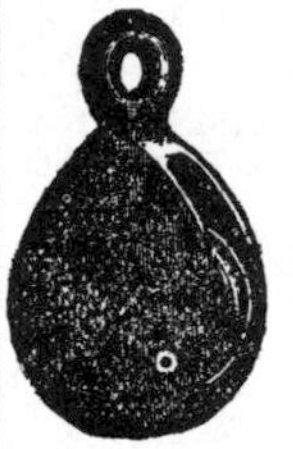

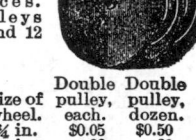

No. 14528. Galvanized Awning Pulleys. Will not take rope larger than 5-16 inch diameter. Single pulleys weigh 3, 5, and 8 ounces. Double pulleys weigh 6, 8 and 12 ounces.

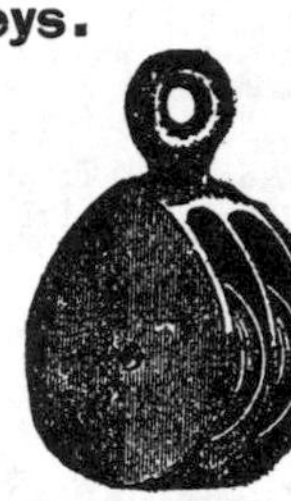

| Size of wheel. | Single pulley, each. | Single pulley, dozen. | Size of wheel. | Double pulley, each. | Double pulley, dozen. |
|---|---|---|---|---|---|
| ¾ in | $0.03 | $0.30 | ¾ in. | $0.05 | $0.50 |
| 1 in. | .04 | .40 | 1 in. | .06 | .60 |
| 1½ in. | .08 | .80 | 1½ in. | .11 | 1.15 |

## Screw Pulleys.

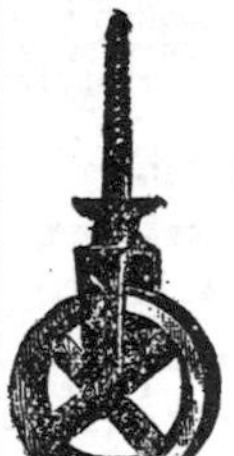

No. 14529. Screw Pulley, japanned iron; will not take rope larger than 5-16 inch.

| Size of wheel. | Weight. | Each. | Per doz. |
|---|---|---|---|
| 1½ inch. | 4 oz. | $0.03 | $0.20 |
| 1¾ inch. | 5 oz. | .03 | .28 |
| 2 inch. | 5 oz. | .04 | .35 |
| 2¼ inch. | 7 oz. | .05 | .45 |
| 2½ inch. | 8 oz. | .06 | .52 |
| 3 inch | 9 oz. | .07 | .65 |

## Hot House Pulleys.

Hot House Pulleys, japanned iron, takes small rope 5-16 or ⅜ inch. Single pulleys, 13 oz.; double pulleys, 1 lb. 2 oz.

No. 14530. Size of wheel, 2 inch. Single Pulley. Each. $0.08 Per doz. .80

No. 14531. Size of wheel, 2 inch. Double Pulley. Each. $0.12 Per doz. $1.25

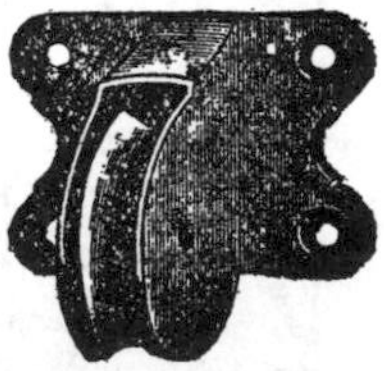

## Side Pulleys.

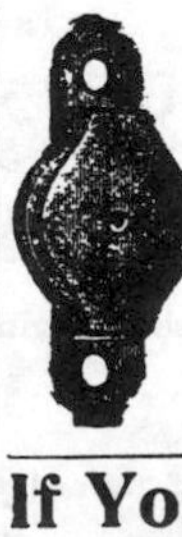

No. 14532. Japanned Iron Side Pulleys; will not take larger than 5-16 inch rope.

| Size of wheel. | Weight. | Each. | Per doz. |
|---|---|---|---|
| 1½ inch. | 5 oz. | $0.04 | $0.35 |
| 1¾ inch. | 7 oz. | .05 | .45 |
| 2 inch. | 10 oz. | .06 | .48 |
| 2½ inch. | 14 oz. | .07 | .70 |
| 3 inch. | 18 oz. | .10 | 1.00 |



**There is a chance of us not knowing exactly what you want if you fail to give Catalogue page and article number in your order. It is better to make everything plain and run no chances.**

## Jack Chain.

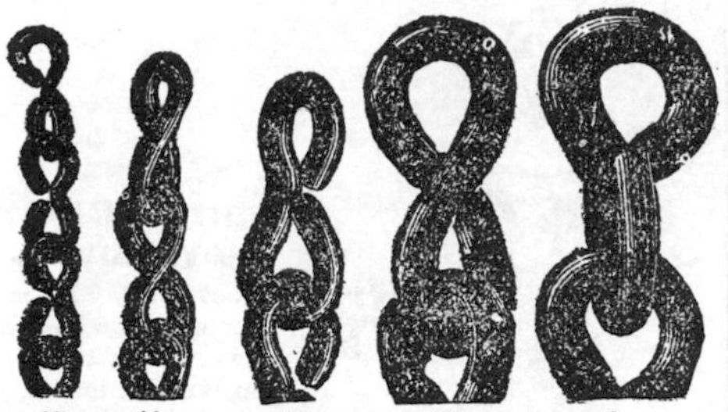

16 14 12 10 8

Cuts are exact size.

No. 14534. Iron Jack Chain. Cuts are exact size of chains.

| Nos. | 8 | 10 | 12 | 14 | 16 |
|---|---|---|---|---|---|
| Per yard, | $0.05 | .05 | .03 | .03 | .03 |
| Per doz. yards, | .40 | .30 | .20 | .18 | .15 |

No. 14535. Brass Jack Chain. Cuts are exact size.

| Nos. | 8 | 10 | 12 | 14 | 16 |
|---|---|---|---|---|---|
| Per yard, | $0.18 | .12 | .08 | .05 | .05 |
| Per doz. yards, | 1.90 | 1.27 | .75 | .48 | .35 |

## Log Chains.

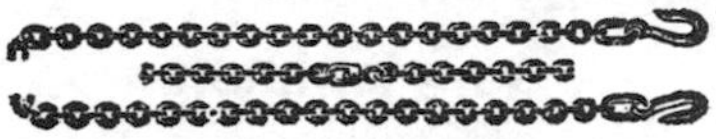

Cable Log Chains, made of self colored coil chain with hook on each end. The sizes given below indicate the size of iron from which the link is made. Made either 12 or 14 feet long, at same price.

No. 14538. Length, 12 feet.
No. 14539. Length, 14 feet.

| Size, inches, | ¼ | 5/16 | ⅜ | ½ |
|---|---|---|---|---|
| Price, | $1.00 | 1.25 | 1.50 | 2.00 |

## Cable Coil Chain.

No. 14542. **Straight link, hand made.** Size given indicates size of iron from which chain is made. **Note that price is per pound.**

| Size, | 3/16 | ¼ | 5/16 | ⅜ | 7/16 | ½ |
|---|---|---|---|---|---|---|
| Weight, per foot, | 8 oz. | 1 lb. | 1¼ lb. | 1½ lb. | 2 lb. | 2½ lb. |
| Price, per lb., | $0.10 | .08 | .07 | .06½ | .06 | .05½ |

## Repair Links.

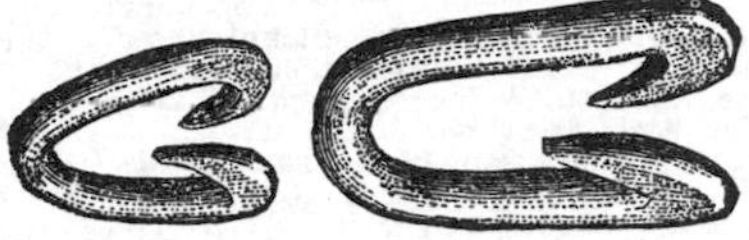

No. 14546. Repair Links for connecting or repairing chains. Size given indicates size of iron from which link is made.

| Sizes, | 3/16 | ¼ | 5/16 | ⅜ |
|---|---|---|---|---|
| Weight, per doz., | 12 oz. | 14 oz. | 1 lb. 7 oz. | 2½ lbs. |
| Price, per doz., | $0.12 | .20 | .25 | .28 |

For Trace Chains, Halter Chains, etc., see index.

## Manilla Rope.

No. 14548. We do not carry in stock Sisal Hemp or Jute Rope—Manilla is stronger and more durable and costs but very little more than the cheaper ropes. There are more feet in the pound, which nearly equals the difference in price per pound between Manilla and the cheaper ropes. Cash in full must accompany orders for rope, and rope once cut from the coil cannot be returned if sent as ordered. **Notice, price is per lb.**

| Diameter. | Number of feet in lb. | Price per lb. |
|---|---|---|
| ¼ inch. | 33⅓ ft. | 9½c. |
| 5/16 inch. | 25 ft. | 9½c. |
| ⅜ inch. | 20 ft. | 9 c. |
| ½ inch. | 13 ft. | 8½c. |
| ⅝ inch. | 7½ ft. | 8½c. |
| ¾ inch. | 6 ft. | 8½c. |
| ⅞ inch. | 4¼ ft. | 8½c. |
| 1 inch | 3½ ft. | 8½c. |

## Wire Rope.

No. 14549. Standard Hoisting Rope is composed of six strands, nineteen wires to the strand, laid about a hemp center. This construction makes a flexible rope, which can be used over drums and shafts of moderate size. Ropes of this kind are generally used for hoisting purposes in shafts, elevators, quarries and on inclined planes and slopes. We will not take back wire rope if sent as ordered.

| Diameter. | Size Sheave. | Price per foot. |
|---|---|---|
| ⅜ inch. | 1¼ ft. | 4½c. |
| 7/16 inch. | 2 ft. | 4¾c. |
| ½ inch. | 2 ft. | 5 c. |
| 9/16 inch. | 2½ ft. | 6½c. |
| ⅝ inch. | 3 ft. | 7½c. |
| ¾ inch. | 4 ft. | 10 c. |
| ⅞ inch. | 5 ft. | 12 c. |
| 1 inch. | 6 ft. | 16 c. |

Size of sheave given in above list is the **smallest** diameter of sheave over which this rope should be used. If used over sheaves larger than sizes given above it will be better.

Parties ordering wire rope for the first time should give full particulars of the work the rope has to do, the size of drums, pulleys, curves, etc., and if rope ordered is not suitable advice will be given.

## Wire Guy Rope.

No. 14550. This rope is composed of 6 strands (seven wires to a strand), laid about a hemp center. All the wires of each strand are coated with zinc so that the rope is proof against the action of the atmosphere. This rope is not suitable to be run over drums or pulleys, but is to be used for guys, etc.

| Circumference in inches, | ½ | ⅝ | ¾ | ⅞ | 1 |
|---|---|---|---|---|---|
| Price, | ¾c | ⅞c | 1c | 1¼c | 1½c |
| Circumference in inches, | 1¼ | 1½ | 1¾ | 2 | 2½ |
| Price, | 2¾c | 3c | 3½c | 4¼c | 5¾c |

**Notice, sizes given are not the diameter.**

## Wire Sash Cord.

No. 14551. Wire Sash Cord is a very flexible wire rope suitable to run over small pulleys. While it is used mainly for window sash, it is suitable for many purposes. Cut pieces cannot be returned if sent as ordered.

| Diameter, inches, | 3/16 | 5/32 | ⅛ | 3/32 |
|---|---|---|---|---|
| Price, per foot, | 3½c | 3¼c | 3c | 2½c |

## Wire Rope Clips and Clamps.

No. 14556. Clips and Clamps for wire rope are used to make an eye in the end of wire rope without splicing. Any one can put them on.

| Size, inches. | Price, each. | Size, inches, | Price, each. |
|---|---|---|---|
| ¼ | 25c | ⅝ | 35c |
| 5/16 | 25c | ¾ | 40c |
| ⅜ | 25c | ⅞ | 45c |
| ½ | 30c | 1 | 50c |

## Ice Skates.

All of our skates are carefully mated, inspected and packed. The material which we use is of the highest grade which can be obtained. Our aim is to retain the reputation of selling superior goods.

We guarantee all our skates to be equal to the very best goods made, and any not proving to be, may be returned to us.

When ordering skates, the best and surest way to obtain the right size skate is to always send us the length of boot or shoe in inches. Below we give the size of skates compared with the sizes of shoes by numbers:

| Skates, inches, | 7 | 7½ | 8 | 8½ | 9 | 9½ | 10 | 10½ | 11 | 11½ |
|---|---|---|---|---|---|---|---|---|---|---|
| Number of shoe, | 9½ | 11 | 12½ | 1 | 2½ | 4 | 5½ | 7½ | 9 | 10½ |

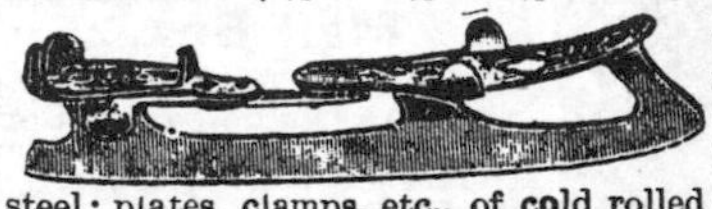

No. 14632. This skate runner is made from the best rolled cast steel; plates, clamps, etc., of cold rolled steel, bright finish. The runners are highly polished. The easy work and sure-grip lock-lever will fit large or small boot heels. Always give size of skate wanted in inches when ordering. Sizes 8 to 12 inches. Price, per pair....**25c**

No. 14633. This skate is the same as No. 14632, except that it is buffed and nickel plated. Price, per pair..........**47c**

No. 14636. This skate is of high grade material, with high toe runners of hardened steel, highly polished; plates, clamps, etc., of cold rolled steel, bright finish, sizes 9 to 12 inches. Always give size in inches when ordering. Price, per pair..........**65c**

No. 14637. This skate is the same as No. 14636, except that it is buffed and nickel plated. Price, per pair.**87c**

No. 14640. The runners of this skate are of hardened and welded steel of the same quality as that used for many years. It is buffed throughout and handsomely nickel plated. Sizes, 9½ to 12 inches. Always give size in inches when ordering. Price, per pair........**$1.50**

No. 14641. The runners of this skate are welded steel hardened. The heel and toe plates are made of the best crucible steel. All parts are highly polished and handsomely nickel plated. Sizes, 9 to 12 inches. Always give size in inches when ordering.
Price, per pair..........**$2.25**

## Racing Skates.

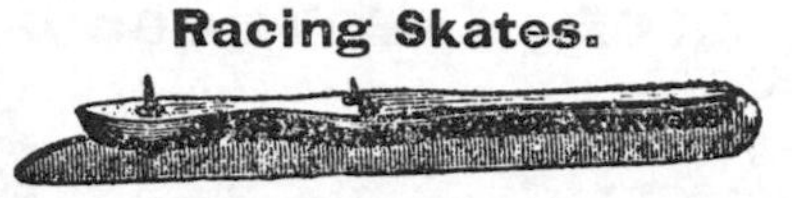

This skate is made under the personal supervision of Mr. Joseph F. Donoghue, world's champion skater, and is made of the highest grade of material, and by first class mechanics. Mahogany tops, hardened steel runners, nickel plated, russet harness leather straps, nickel tongue buckles. This skate was designed by Mr. Donoghue, and has been used for the past five years in winning all his great races and making his wonderful records, and his success is as much due to the perfection of these skates as to his own skill.

No. 14643. Made in three lengths, 14, 16, 18 inches. Price, per pair..........**$3.65**

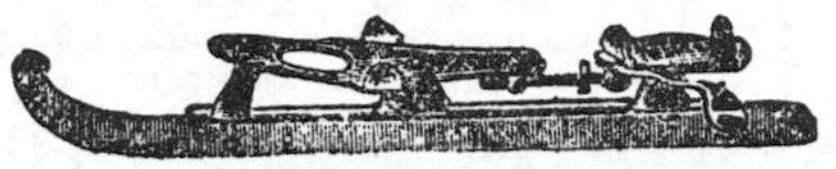

No. 14644. Racer Skate. Built entirely for speed and long distance skating. Sizes, from 10 to 12 inches. This is a very finely made skate, handsomely nickel plated. Price, per pair..........**$2.50**

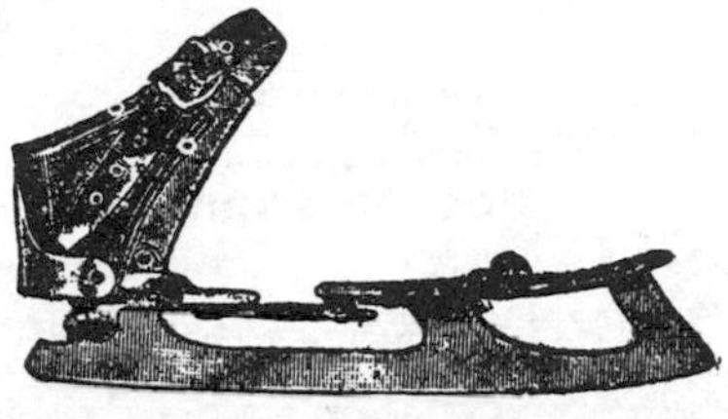

No. 14646. This skate has high toe runners of the best rolled cast steel, highly polished, with toe plate washer; plates and clamps are of cold rolled steel, bright finish; russet leather straps with nickel plated heel bands. Sizes, 8 to 10 inches. Always give size in inches when ordering. Price, per pair..........**85c**

No. 14647. The runners of this skate are made from hardened welded steel, nickel plated; plates, clamps, etc., are of cold rolled steel, buffed throughout and nickel plated; russet straps. The cheapest skate with absolutely first quality welded stock in the market. Sizes, 8 to 10½ inches. Always give size wanted in inches when ordering. Price, per pair..........**$1.75**

## Ladies' Skates.

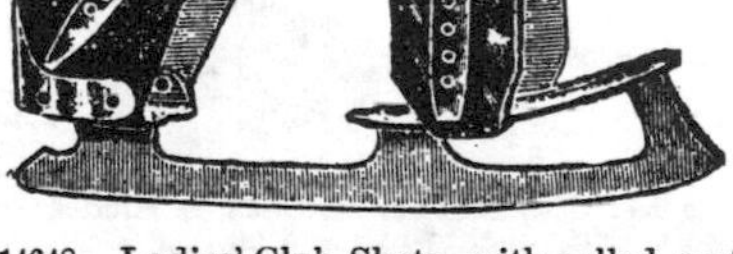

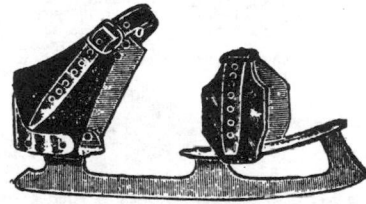

No. 14648. Ladies' Club Skate, with rolled cast steel polished runners, bright steel toe and heel plates, russet leather straps. Size, from 7 to 10 inches. Always give sizes in inches when ordering. Price per pair......**62c**

## STEEL SAFES

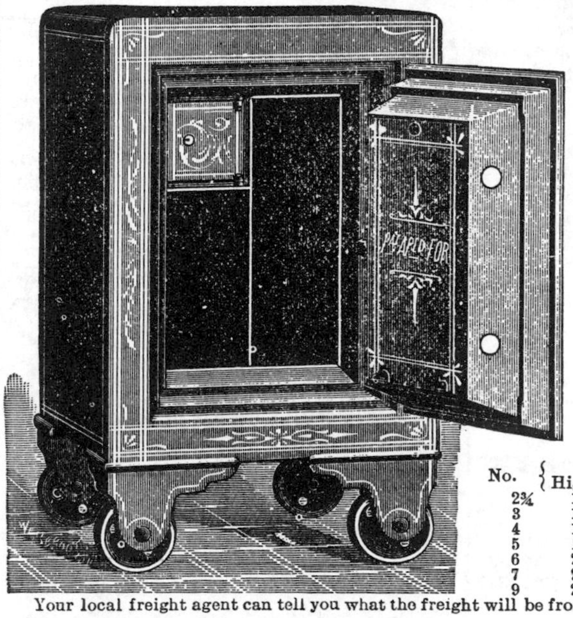

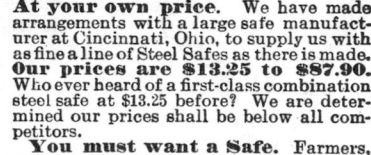

**At your own price.** We have made arrangements with a large safe manufacturer at Cincinnati, Ohio, to supply us with as fine a line of Steel Safes as there is made. **Our prices are $13.25 to $87.90.** Who ever heard of a first-class combination steel safe at $13.25 before? We are determined our prices shall be below all competitors.

**You must want a Safe.** Farmers, merchants and all business men require safes, and at our prices you can afford to buy. We save you one-half or more on any safe. Our Steel Safes are made of the best material, have finest combination locks, are handsomely decorated and are fire proof.

We ship them direct from the factory at Cincinnati, Ohio. Your name will be put on above the door, shaded in gold bronze, free of charge, when specified. Write name wanted on safe plainly, so no mistake will be made.

Order No. 14665.

| No. | Outside Measure. High | Wide | Deep |
|---|---|---|---|
| 2¾ | 24 | 15 | 15 |
| 3 | 28 | 18½ | 19 |
| 4 | 31 | 21½ | 21¼ |
| 5 | 34⅓ | 22¾ | 23¼ |
| 6 | 38¾ | 26 | 26 |
| 7 | 42½ | 29 | 29 |
| 9 | 46½ | 32 | 29½ |

| No. | Inside Measure. High | Wide | Deep | Appx. Wt. | Price. |
|---|---|---|---|---|---|
| 2¾ | 12 | 8 | 9 | 300 lbs. | $13.25 |
| 3 | 15 | 10 | 12 | 500 | 19.00 |
| 4 | 17 | 13¾ | 13½ | 650 | 25.00 |
| 5 | 19¾ | 14¼ | 14½ | 900 | 32.50 |
| 6 | 22 | 16 | 15½ | 1350 | 48.50 |
| 7 | 23½ | 17⅛ | 18 | 1800 | 54.00 |
| 9 | 27¾ | 21 | 18 | 2100 | 82.50 |

Your local freight agent can tell you what the freight will be from Cincinnati, Ohio, or we will on request.

**Our Sporting Goods Department includes everything for outdoor sports. The Bicycle Rider, the Foot Ball Player, the Base Ball Player, the Tennis Player, every sportsman will find complete outfits at Wholesale Prices.**

## MISCELLANEOUS GOODS.

15054

15055

### Lamp Chimney Cleaners.

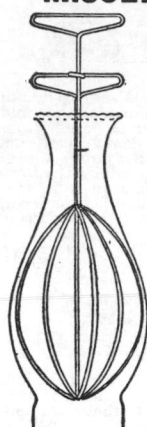

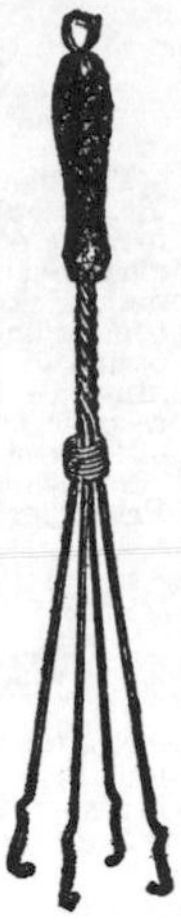

No. 15054. This article is useful for many purposes, but for cleaning lamp chimneys it is the best invention yet brought out. The illustration shows how it brings the wiping cloth in contact with every part of the chimney.
Each ................3c
Per doz............30c

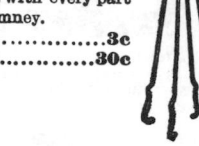

No. 15055. Wire Chimney Cleaner, Dish Cloth Holder, Cork Puller, etc.
Price each, 6c; per doz..........................56c

### Pot Cleaners.

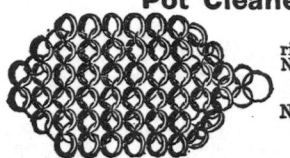

Pot Chain or wire ring Dish Cloth.
No. 15056. Small size.
Each ............5c
Per doz..........54c
No. 15057. Large size.
Each ..............7c
Per doz.........75c

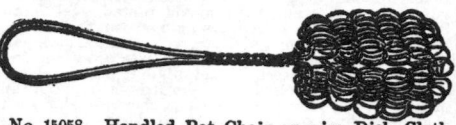

No. 15058. Handled Pot Chain or wire Dish Cloth. Turned wire handle, bright wire rings.
Price each, 8c; per doz..........................85c

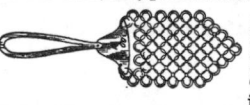

No. 15059. The Sensible Pot Chain and Scraper is a new and useful article, each ring is double, which makes it very durable. The handle is malleable iron; the blade is steel; the handle and scraper are tinned. Weight, 4 oz. Price, each, 10c; per doz..........................$1.08

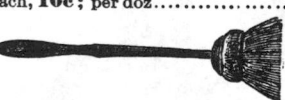

No. 15060. Wash your dishes without putting your hands into hot water. This dish mop is made of cotton and is securely fastened to handle. Length, 12 inches; weight, 4 ounces. Price, each, 8c; per doz..................87c

### Cork Screws.

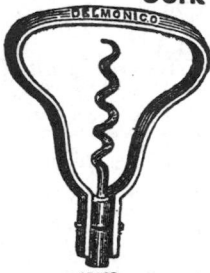

15062

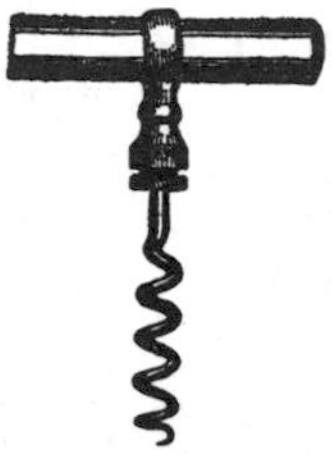

15061

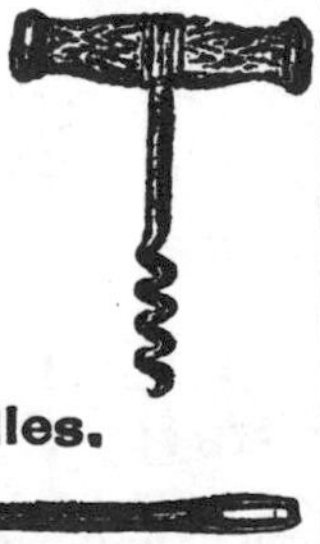

No. 15061. **Pocket Cork Screw.** Each in nickel case, case serving as handle, which is passed through ring in screw. Weight, 2 ounces. Each....................5c
No. 15062. Folding Pocket Cork Screw, nickel plated. Weight, 2 ounces. Price, each, 12c; per doz..........................$1.30
No. 15063. Extra heavy hand forged steel Cork Screw. Price, each ..............................20c

### Sacking Needles.

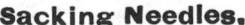

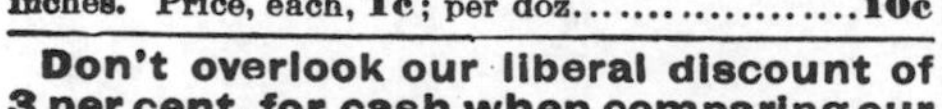

No. 15070. Sacking Needles. Length, 4, 4½, 5 and 5½ inches. Price, each, 1c; per doz..................10c

**Don't overlook our liberal discount of 3 per cent. for cash when comparing our prices. This discount will often pay the express or freight.**

### Hog Scrapers.

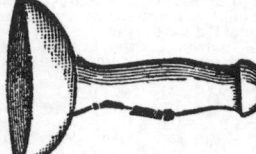

No. 15075. Hog Scraper. Will pay for itself the first time used. Wood handle with bolt extending through Scraper made of No. 18 sheet steel. Price, each..18c
No. 15076. Hog Scraper, made of No. 20 sheet iron. Price, each...............8c

### Pinking Irons.

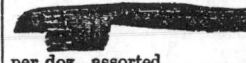

No. 15078. Pinking Iron, diamond tooth, ⅜, ½, ⅝, ¾, ⅞ or 1 inch. Price, each, 6c; per doz., assorted..................................65c

### Casters.

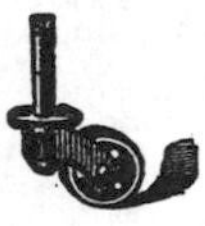

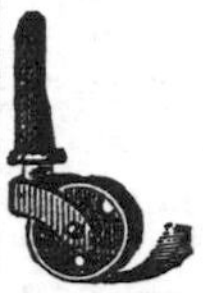

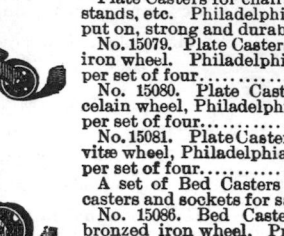

Plate Casters for chairs, tables, bureaus, stands, etc. Philadelphia pattern, easy to put on, strong and durable.
No. 15079. Plate Casters, ⅞-inch bronzed iron wheel. Philadelphia pattern. Price, per set of four.............................6c
No. 15080. Plate Casters, ⅞-inch porcelain wheel, Philadelphia pattern. Price, per set of four..........................7c
No. 15081. Plate Casters, ⅞-inch lignum vitæ wheel, Philadelphia pattern. Price, per set of four..........................8c
A set of Bed Casters consists of four casters and sockets for same.
No. 15086. Bed Casters with 1⅝-inch bronzed iron wheel. Price, per set complete..........................................8c
No. 15087. Bed Casters with 1⅝-inch porcelain wheel. Price, per set complete...........9c
No. 15088. Bed Casters with 2-inch lignum vitæ wheel. Price, per set complete...............................10c

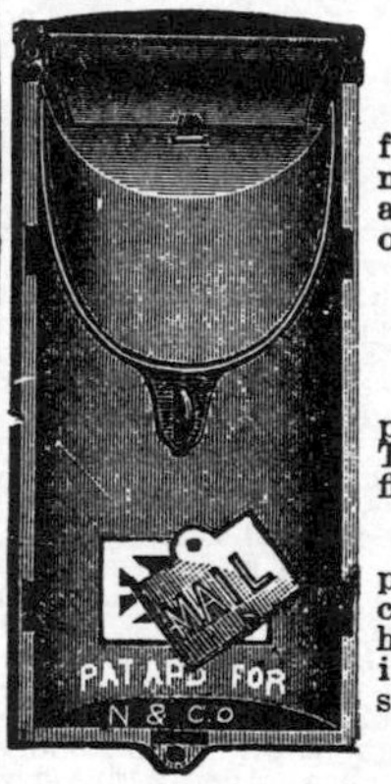

### Mail Box.

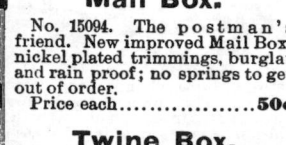

No. 15094. The postman's friend. New improved Mail Box, nickel plated trimmings, burglar and rain proof; no springs to get out of order.
Price each.................50c

### Twine Box.

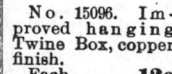

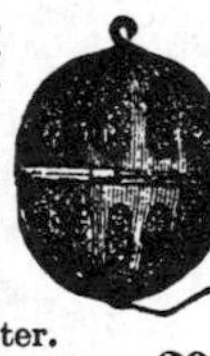

No. 15096. Improved hanging Twine Box, copper finish.
Each.........12c
No. 15097. Improved stand or counter Twine Box, has a base, and is intended to be screwed to the counter.
Price each..........................20c

### Nut Cracks.

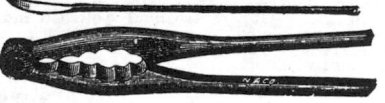

No. 15098. Nut Cracker and Pick, nickel plated; length, 5 inches.
Cracker and Pick..10c
Per doz..........$1.08
Nut Cracker only, lacquer finish, each.......5c
Per doz.............50c

### Broom Holders.

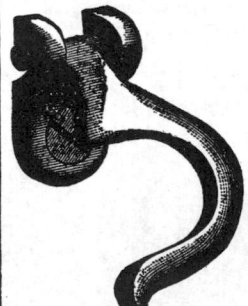

No. 15099. Broom Holder. A very simple and useful arrangement, which always keeps broom in good shape.
Each ....................4c
Per doz...............38c

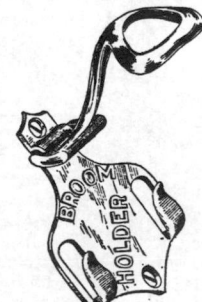

No. 15099½. The Acme Broom Holder is much superior to any that we have ever seen. It is handsomely nickel plated and has hooks to hang the dust pan and dust brush on. Projects 4 inches from the wall. Weighs 5 oz. Fastens to wall with two screws.
Each ...........................8c
Per doz.................87c

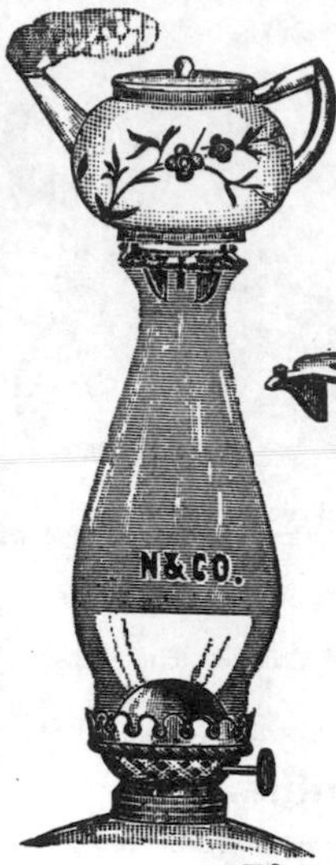

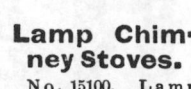

### Lamp Chimney Stoves.

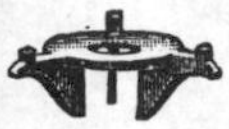

No. 15100. Lamp Chimney Stove, fits any ordinary crimped top lamp chimney, as shown in cut. Water may be boiled in a few minutes.
Each ............3c
Per doz.........35c

### Fire Kindler.

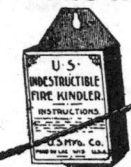

No. 15101. The Indestructible Fire Kindler and oil can is used for starting wood fires, burning brush and marshes, burning insects and worms from trees, thawing water pipes and many other purposes which will suggest themselves to the user. Length, 12 inches; weight, 5 oz. Price, each............................25c

### Can Openers.

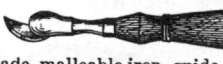

No. 15102. Star Can Opener, considered one of the best can openers made. Steel blade, malleable iron guide, nickel plated, antique oak handle with brass ferrule. A handsome and reliable article. Length, 6½ inches; weight, 3 oz.
Price, each, 10c; per doz..........................$1.08
No. 15103. Star Can Opener, same as above, with iron handle, all nickel plated. Length, 6½ inches; weight, 3 oz. Price, each, 8c; per doz ..........................87c

No. 15104. Can Opener, steel blade, cast handle.
Price, each..........4c
Per doz...........38c

No. 15105. Sprague Can Opener is without question the best can opener in the market at the price.
Price, each, 5c; per doz..........................54c

### Snip Snaps.

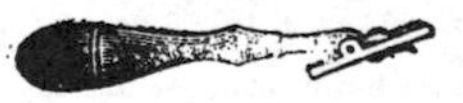

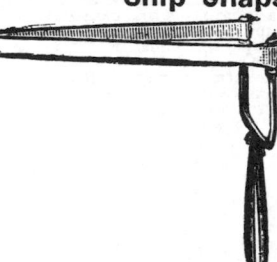

No. 15109. Snip Snap or Sling Shot. The boys can have lots of fun with this. Complete with rubber spri'g, as shown in illustration.
Price, each....7c
Per doz.....75c
No. 15110. Extra Rubbers for the above sling shot.
Each..........4c
Per doz......35c

### Steak Pounders.

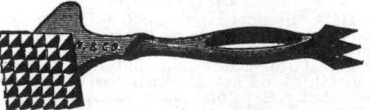

No. 15112. The Star Steak Pounder, Ice Pick and Shave. Malleable iron, plain finish.
Price, each, 5c; per doz..........................54c
No. 15113. The Star Steak Pounder, Ice Pick and Shave, **full nickel plated.**
Price, each, 10c; per dozen..........................1 08

### Lemon Squeezers.

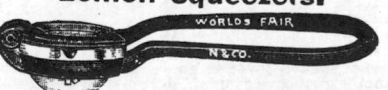

No. 15116. The World's Fair Lemon Squeezer. Bowls are made of malleable iron, nicely nickel plated; plunger from hard wood, and is detachable. The frame is of gray iron, japan finish; the handsomest and most complete lemon squeezer in the market.

**Do not fail to sign your name and give your address when you write us or send an order. Some careless people wonder why they get no answer to their letters.**

## Lemon Sqeezers.

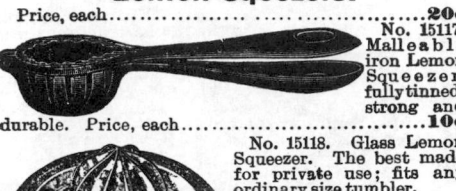

Price, each........................................20c

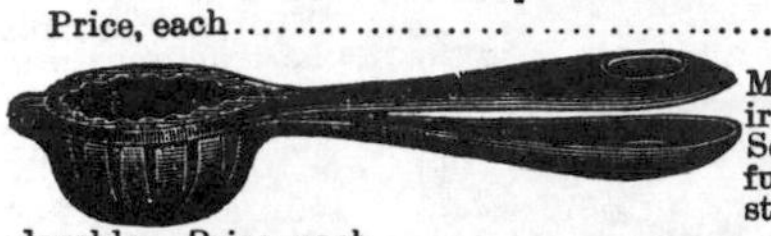

No. 15117. Malleable iron Lemon Squeezer, fully tinned, strong and durable. Price, each........................................10c

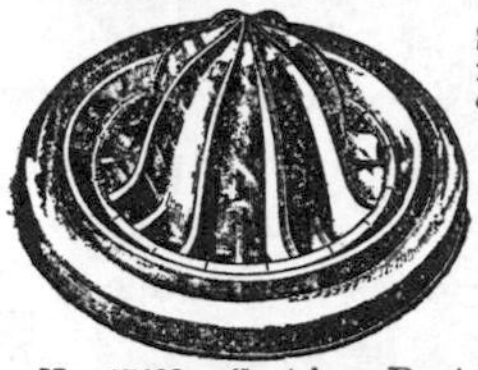

No. 15118. Glass Lemon Squeezer. The best made for private use; fits any ordinary size tumbler, Price, each............5c

## Boot Jacks.

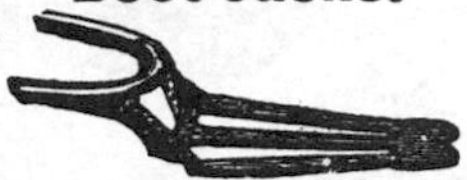

No. 15122. Cast iron Boot Jack, japanned, weighs 1¼ lbs. Price each........................................8c

## Fish Scalers.

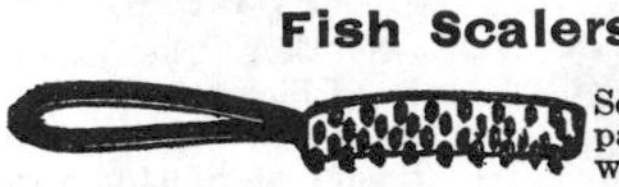

No. 15123. Fish Scaler, cast iron, japanned; length, 9 in.; weight, 9 oz. Price, each....5c

Per doz........................................54c

## Molasses Gates.

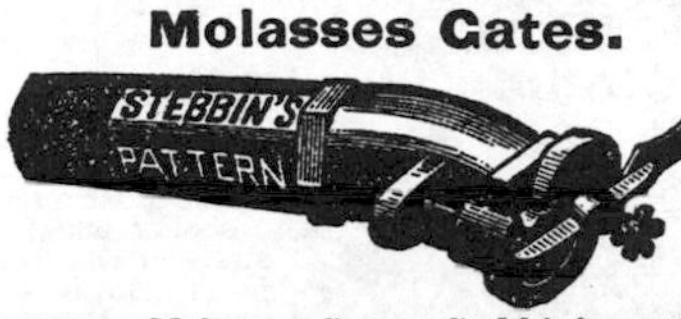


No. 15124. Molasses Gates, Stebbin's pattern. Size given indicates the size of hole which should be bored.

| Nos. | 1 | 2 | 3 | 4 | 5 |
|---|---|---|---|---|---|
| Size, inches, | 1 | 1⅛ | 1¼ | 1⅜ | 1½ |
| Each, | $0.12 | .13 | .15 | .17 | .20 |

## Oil Faucet.

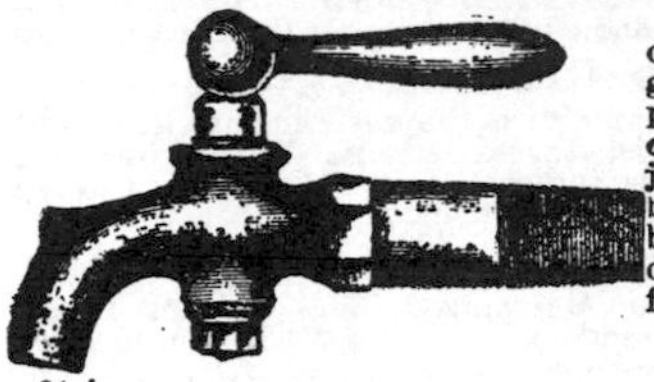

No. 15125. The original and only genuine Frary's patent Oil Faucet, made of iron, japanned, **key** bushed with brass, lever handle, screw **shank**; for oil barrel.

½ in.......**19c**
⅝ in.......**22c**
¾ in........................................**25c**
1 in........................................**32c**

## Chest Handles.

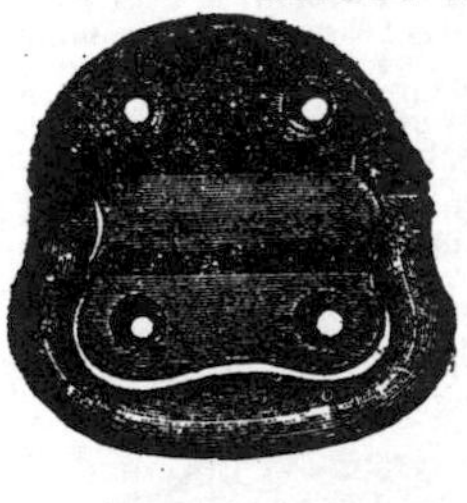

No. 15128. Chest Handles, 3½ inches, japanned, heavy; weight, per pair, 1 lb. 5 oz. No screws. Price, per pair.......**7c**

No. 15129. Chest Handles, 4 inches, japanned, heavy; weight, per pair, 1¾ lbs. No screws. Price, per pair.......**9c**

No. 15130. Chest Handles, 4½ inches, japanned, heavy; weight, per pair, 2 lbs. 6 oz. No screws. Price, per pair......**10c**

## Well Wheels.

Weight, 3 to 6 lbs.

No. 15131. Well Wheels, japanned.

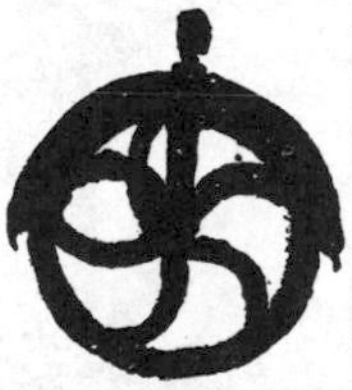

| Diameter, inches, | 8 | 10 | 12 |
|---|---|---|---|
| Each, | $0.18 | .22 | .27 |

## Well Wheel Hooks and Chains.

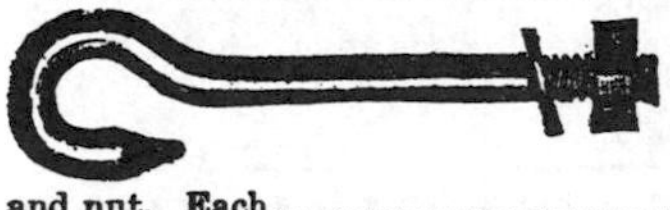

No. 15132. Well Wheel Hooks, ⅜ inch wrought iron; length 6½ in., with screws and nut. Each........................................**7c**

No. 15133. Well Chains, with hook and ring; length, 2 feet. Each........................................**10c**

## Iron Storm Threshold.

No. 15136. No matter how exposed your doors may be, or how severe the rain may beat against them, no rain will beat under them if you use this Iron Storm Threshold.

From 30 to 36 inches, inclusive, are cast in one piece; above 36 inches the sizes are made with a centerpiece, 30 inches in length and ends to make any size desired.

| Size, inches, | 30 | 32 | 34 | 36 | 38 | 40 |
|---|---|---|---|---|---|---|
| Price, each, | $0.75 | .75 | .95 | 1.00 | 1.20 | 1.20 |

Weights range from 7 pounds up, according to size.

## Screw Eyes.

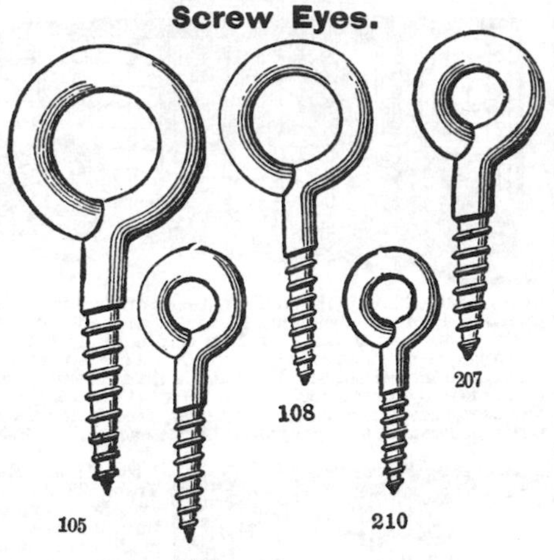

105 108 207 210 209

No. 15138. Screw Eyes, bright iron cut exact size.

| Nos. | 105 | 108 | 207 | 209 | 210 |
|---|---|---|---|---|---|
| Per dozen, | $0.05 | .05 | .05 | .03 | .03 |
| Per gross, | .39 | .25 | .25 | .20 | .20 |

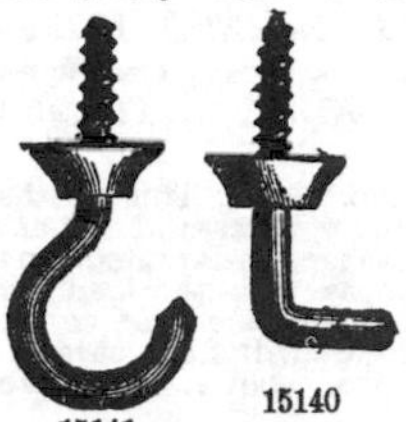

15141 15140

No. 15140. Brass Screw Hooks for bangle boards.

| Size, inches, | ½ | ⅝ | ¾ |
|---|---|---|---|
| Per doz., | $0.04 | .05 | .06 |

No. 15141. Brass Cup Hooks.

| Size, in., | ⅝ | ¾ | ⅞ | 1 |
|---|---|---|---|---|
| Per doz., | $0.06 | .07 | .08 | .09 |

## Money Drawers.

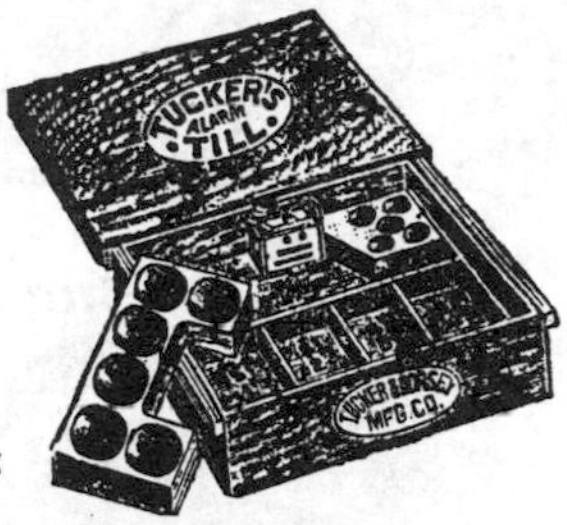


No. 15142. Patent Alarm Till Lock and Drawer; strongly made of hardwood. Combinations quickly changed. No keys required.

Price, each. **$1.35**

## House Numbers.

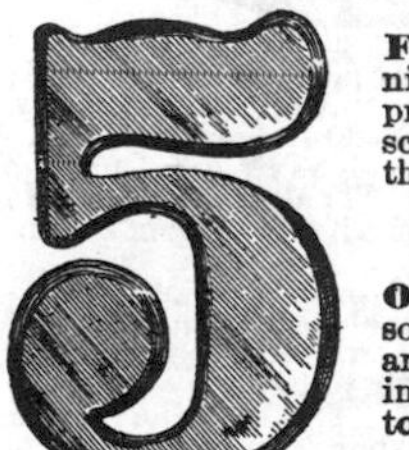

No. 15143. House Number **Flat**, made of iron polished and nickel plated; 3 inches long; provided with "spurs," so no screws are necessary to fasten them on.

Price, each........................**3c**
Per 100........................**$2.00**

No. 15144. House Number **Oval**, made of brass, handsomely designed, finely polished, and heavily nickel plated; 3 inches long; no screws required to fasten them on.

Price, each........................**7c**
Per 100........................**$5.50**

## Hay or Box Hooks.

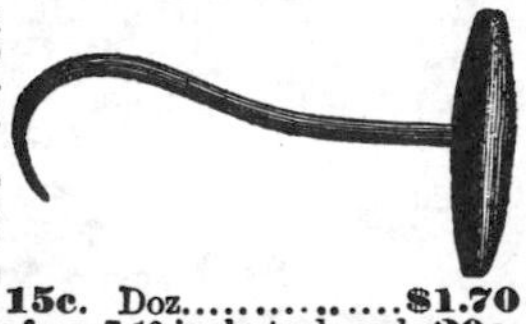

No. 15145. Hay or Box Hooks, forged from the best cast steel, and riveted through hardwood handle.

Length, 6 inches, made from ⅜-inch steel, each, **14c**. Doz.......**$1.50**

Length, 8 inches, made from ⅜-inch steel, each, **15c**. Doz.............**$1.70**

Length, 10 inches, made from 7-16-inch steel, each, **20c**. Doz........................................**$2.00**

## Toy Safes.

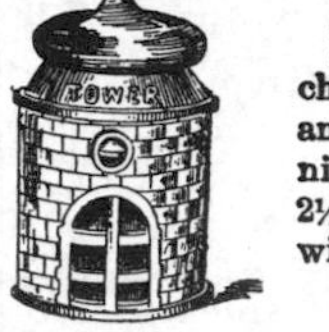


No. 15146. The Tower Safe is a fine cheap safe. The dome is polished and nickle plated, the base is rough nickel. Height, 4¼ inches; diameter, 2½ inches; weight, 10 oz. Fastens with a lock and key. Price, each..**10c**

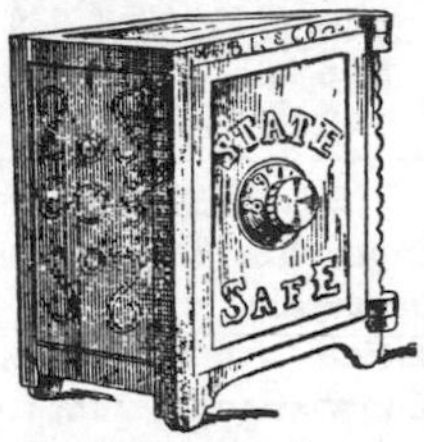


No. 15147. The State Safe is a neat safe. The raised ornamentations are polished and nickel plated. The ground work is rough nickel. Size, 2½x2¾x4 inches; weight, 1¼ lbs. Fastens with a two-tumbler combination lock. Price, each........................**25c**

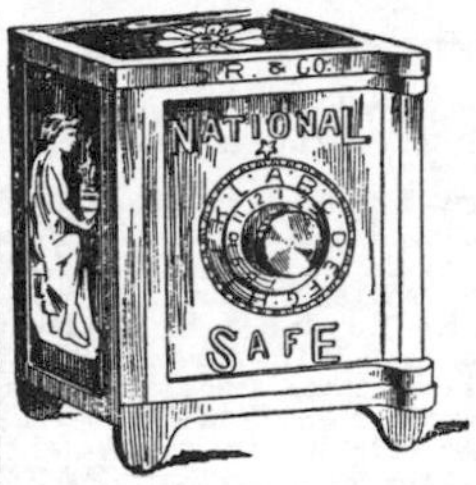


No. 15148. The National Safe is of the same handsome appearance and is finished like the **State** safe, only it is larger. Size, 3¾x3¼x4¾ inches. Weight, 2¼ lbs. Fastens with a 2-tumbler combination lock. Price, each.**35c**

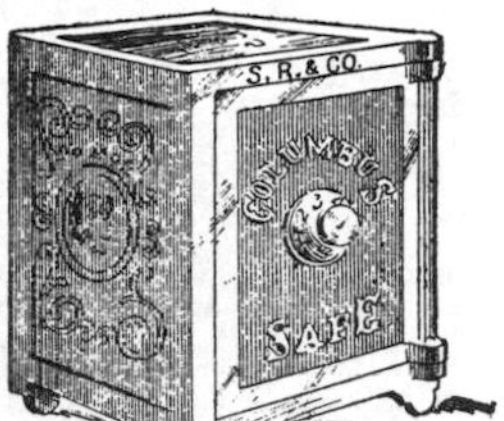


**No. 15149.** The Columbus Safe is finished same as the National, but is larger. Size, 3¾x4¼x5½ inches. Weight, 2 lbs. 10 oz. Fastens with a 2-tumbler combination lock. Price, each........................**50c**

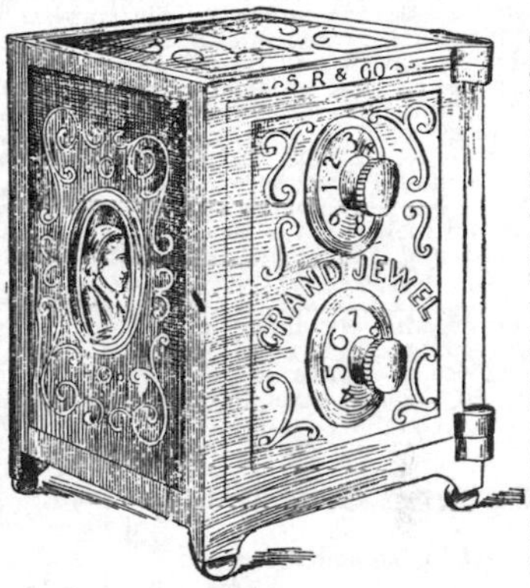


No. **15150.** The Grand Jewel Safe is the finest toy safe made. It is finished like the Columbus. Size 4x3¾x5¼ inches. Weighs 2¾ lbs. Fastens with **two 2-tumbler combination locks,** making it equal to a 4-tumbler lock. It can't be opened by any one not knowing the combination. Price, each......**75c**

## Toy Sad Irons.

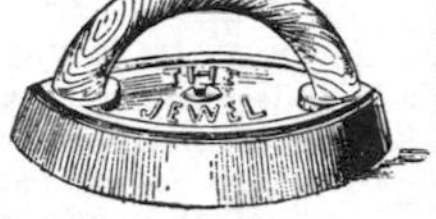


No. 15151. The Jewel Toy Sad Iron has a wood handle. The top of iron is bronzed. The body of iron is polished and nickel plated. Weighs 10 oz. Packed in pasteboard box with stand. Price for iron and stand..........**10c**

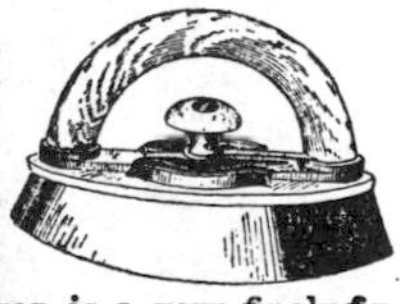

No. 15152. The Baby Sad Iron is a small size of the well-known Mrs. Potts pattern, (like cut) and has the same artistic finish. Has detachable wood handle. Weighs 12 oz. Packed in a pasteboard box with stand. Price for iron and stand... **17c**

No. 15153. The "Lace" Sad Iron is a very finely finished sad iron of the Mrs. Potts pattern (see cut). While it is sometimes sold for a toy, it is a great favorite with the ladies for doing fine work, such as laces, etc. Has one round end and is finely polished and nickel plated. Has detachable wood handle. Weighs 1½ lbs. Packed in a pasteboard box with stand. Price for iron and stand........................................**25c**

## Steel Traps.

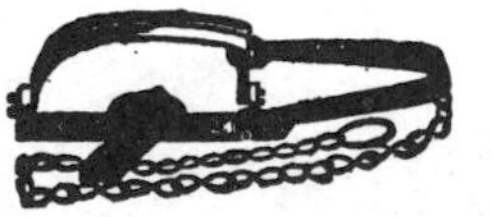

No. 15294. **Imitation Newhouse Traps,** 3½ inch jaw, with chain. Size No. 0, weight, 14 oz. Price, each........................**9c**
Per doz........................**$1.00**

No. 15295. **Imitation Newhouse Traps,** 4-inch jaw, with chain. Size No. 1, weight 14 oz. Price, each........................................**12c**
Per doz........................................**$1.20**

No. 15296. Imitation Newhouse Traps. Size No. 1½, mink trap; 4⅝-inch jaw; single spring, with chain. Price, each........................................**18c**
Per doz........................................**$1.80**

No. 15297. Imitation Newhouse Traps. Size No. 2, fox trap; 4⅞-inch jaw; double spring, with chain. Price, each........................................**22c**
Per doz........................................**$2.40**

No. 15298. Imitation Newhouse Traps. Size No. 3, the otter trap; 5½-inch jaw; double spring, with chain. Price, each........................................**34c**
Per doz........................................**$3.73**

No. 15299. Imitation Newhouse Traps. Size No. 4, the beaver trap; 6½-inch jaws; double spring, with chain. Price, each........................................**39c**
Per doz........................................**$4.40**

## GUNS AND SPORTING GOODS

*Of every desirable make quoted at trade producing prices on* *pages 562 to 610.*

**Our liberal C. O. D. Terms permit examination of any garment. We want our customers to be satisfied with what they buy. We allow 3 per cent. off when full cash comes with order.**

## Genuine Newhouse Traps.

The genuine Newhouse traps are branded on pan "S. Newhouse, Oneida Community." Traps not having this brand are imitations.

No. 15300. **Genuine Newhouse Traps.** Spread of jaws, 3½ inches, with chain. Size No. 0, weight 13 oz. Price, each, **20c**; per doz........................**$2.10**

No. 15301. Genuine Newhouse traps. Spread of jaws, 4 inches, with chain. Size No. 1. This is the size most used. Weight, 17 oz. Price, each, **25c**; per doz. **$2.45**

No. 15302. Genuine Newhouse trap. Spread of jaws, 4⅞ inches, with chain. Size, No. 1½. This is called the Mink trap. Is often used for catching foxes. Weight, 1 lb. 6 oz. Price, each, **35c**; per doz............**$3.70**

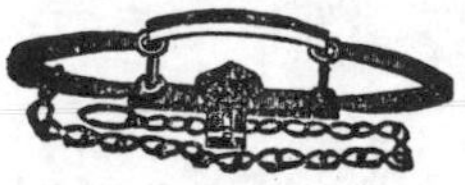

No. 15303. The genuine Newhouse trap, with double spring and chain, size, No. 2, the fox trap; spread of jaws, 4⅞ inches; weight, 1 lb. 10 oz. Price, each, **45c**; per doz. **$5.20**

No. 15304. The genuine Newhouse trap, with double spring and chain, size No. 3, the otter trap; spread of jaws, 5½ inches; weight, 2½ lbs. Price, each, **60c**; per doz..................**$7.00**

No. 15305. The genuine Newhouse trap, with double spring and chain; size No. 4, the beaver trap; spread of jaw, 6½ inches; weight, 3 lbs. 2 oz. Price, each, **70c**; per doz....................................**$8.25**

No. 15306. The genuine Newhouse trap, size No. 4½, especially adapted to catching wolves. This trap has 8 inch spread of jaws, with the other parts in proportion, and is provided with a pronged "drag," a heavy snap and and an extra heavy steel swivel and chain, 5 feet long, warranted to hold 2,000 lbs. The trap, complete with chain and "drag" will weigh about 9 lbs. Price, each, **$1.85**; per doz......................**$20.00**

No. 15307. The genuine Newhouse trap, No. 5 size, with offset jaws. This trap weighs 17 lbs. and has a spread of jaws of 11¾ inches. It is used for taking the common black bear, and is furnished with a chain and swivel sufficiently strong; double spring. Price, each...............................**$6.00**

No. 15308. The genuine Newhouse trap for grizzly bear. This is the strongest trap made; it will hold lion, cougar, tiger or moose, as well as the great grizzly bear. Spread of jaw, 16 inches; weight, 42 lbs. Price, each.......................................**$11.75**

## Setting Clamps.

No. 15309. For setting game traps.

| | Each. | Per doz. |
|---|---|---|
| No. 4 for setting No. 4 trap, | $0.12 | $1.20 |
| No. 5 for setting No. 5 trap, | .25 | 2.90 |
| No. 6 for setting No. 6 trap, | .45 | 5.00 |

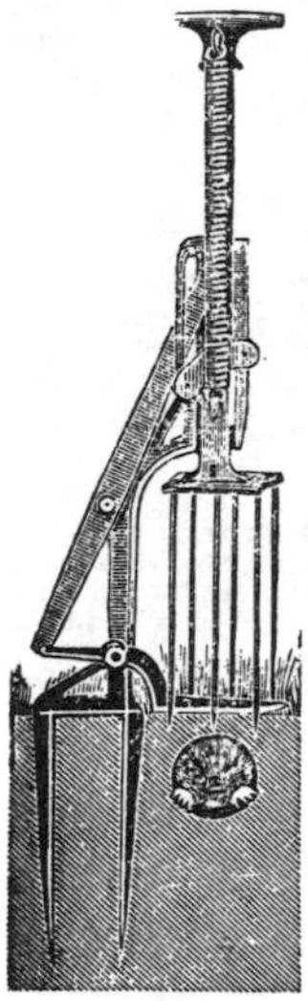

No. 15316. The S. R. & Co. Mole Trap. This is a decided improvement on all other makes; is more simple and less liable to get out of order. The principal feature is its self-setting device. Simply pulling up on the handle sets it.

## Directions for Setting.

Press the dirt down across the trail; push the trap down before setting, until the pan rests on the dirt; put foot on cross piece, and pull up on the handle a few times to loosen the dirt about the fork tines; then set it. Price, each, **70c**; per doz..........................**$8.00**

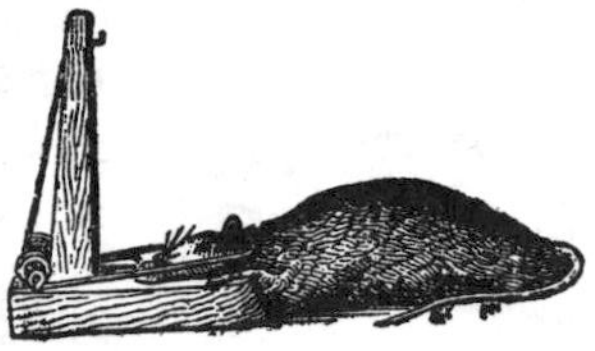

No. 15317. The Erie Rat Trap. This trap can always be depended on to catch rats every time. It kills them instantly without drawing blood, or otherwise scenting the trap; weight, 1½ lbs. Price, each..............**12c**

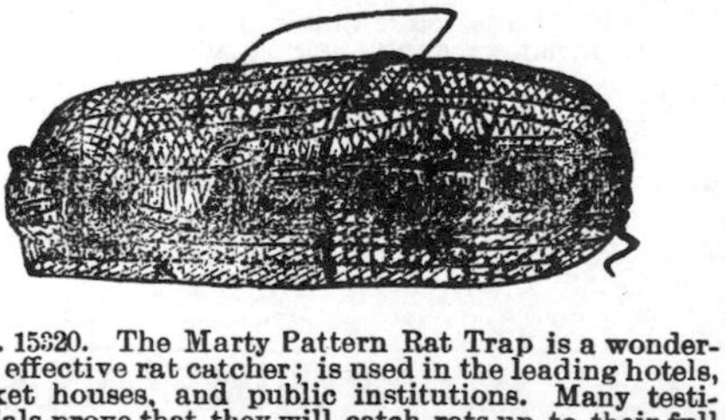

No. 15320. The Marty Pattern Rat Trap is a wonderfully effective rat catcher; is used in the leading hotels, market houses, and public institutions. Many testimonials prove that they will catch rats up to their full capacity night after night, as long as the rats hold out. No. 3, or family size, is 17 inches long; capacity, 20 rats. Price, each..................................**58c**

No. 15321. The Marty Rat Trap, No. 1, or hotel size, is 27 inches long; capacity, 50 rats. Price, each..**$1.45**

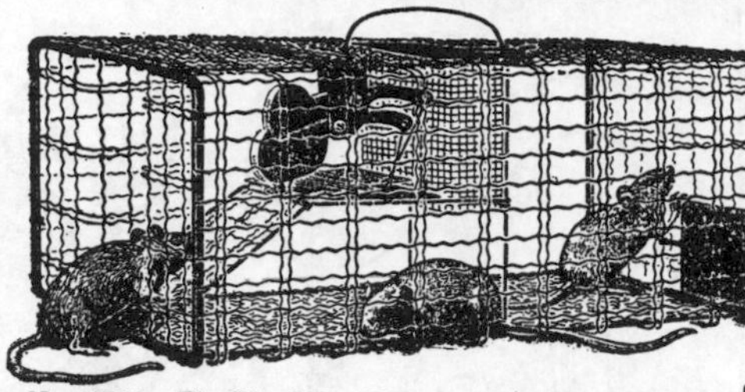

No. 15324. The Rival Rat Trap, made of steel wire, japanned. Size 15 inches long, 7½ inches wide, 6½ inches high. This trap is made with a self-locking, tilting, platform, so when a rat is once inside, he cannot escape. The bait holder is supplied through a lid at the top, and it displays the bait alluringly to rats. It is strong and has been proved a reliable rat catcher, free from all objections common to other traps. Price, each.........**72c**

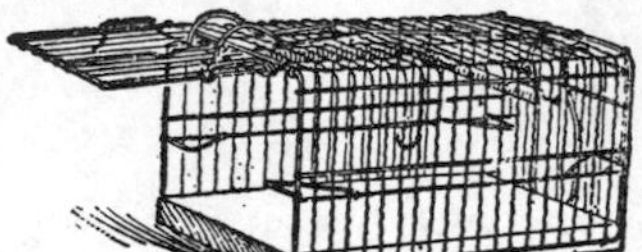

No. 15325. Rat Trap. This is an excellent trap, thoroughly well made from double tinned wire. Size, 6x11 inches. Each...**25c**

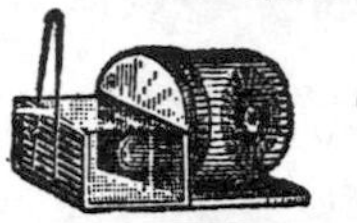

No. 15328. Revolving Mouse Trap, made of heavy steel wire. Each..................................**15c**

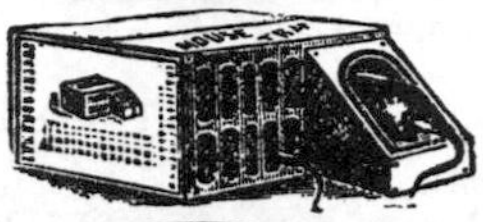

No. 15329. This is the most successful mouse catcher ever invented. One mouse sets the trap for the next one that comes along; will hold several. Price, each..........**10c**

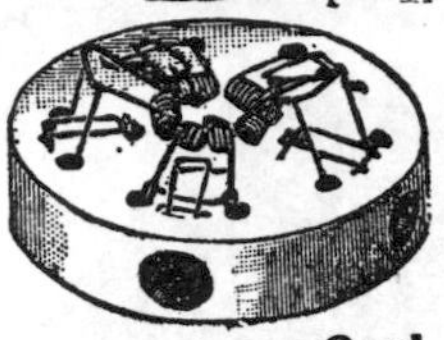

Choke Mouse Traps, round pattern.

No. 15331. 5 holes, each, **5c**; per doz........................**54c**

## Sad Irons.

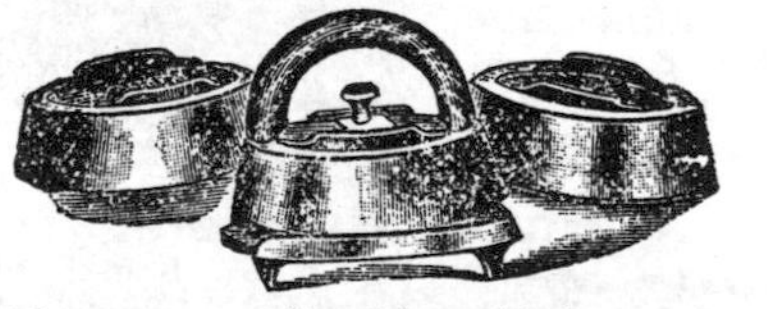

These irons are so well and favorably known, we only refer to a few points. There are three sizes in each set. No. 1 weighs 4 lbs. and has one end rounded for polishing; No. 2 weighs 5⅛ lbs., No. 3 weighs 5⅝ lbs. Only the No. 1 size has one end rounded. The detachable handle is of wood and fits naturally to the hand without straining the arm or wrist.

No. 15336. Potts' Pattern Sad Irons in sets of 3, as described above, with one detachable wood handle and one sad iron stand. Plain polished. Price, per set. **59c**

No. 15337. Same as 15336, nickel plated. Price, per set.......................................**64c**

No. 15338. Extra handles for above sad irons. Price, each.........................................**8c**

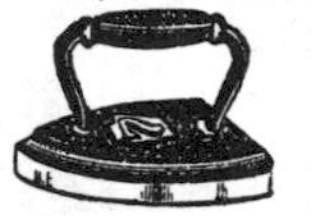

No. 15342. Common Pattern Sad Irons, with face finely polished. Weights given are not guaranteed exact. They are the manufacturers' weights (so-called), and are as near as it is possible to make them.

| Weight, lbs., | 5 | 6 | 7 | 8 | 9 |
|---|---|---|---|---|---|
| Price, each, | $0.13 | .15 | .18 | .20 | .23 |

## Sad Iron Stands.

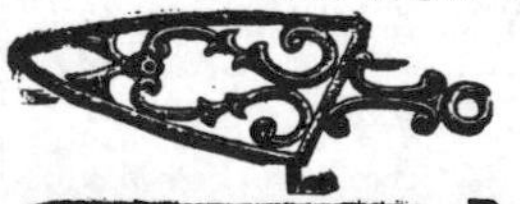

No. 15343. Sad Iron Stands. bronzed iron. Price, each......... **5c** Per doz.......... **54c**

## Polishing Irons.

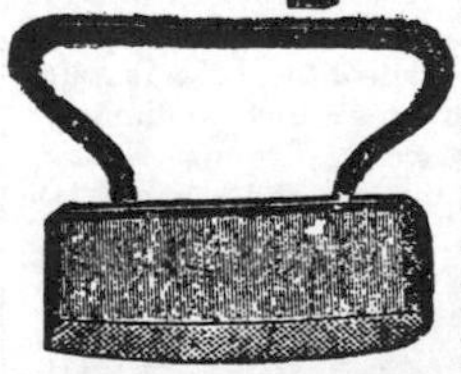

No. 15346. Troy Polishing Irons, with **perforated bottom**, nicely polished. Weight, 4 lbs. Price, each..............**30c**

No. 15347. Troy Polishing Iron with **smooth bottom**, nicely nickel plated. Weight, 4 lbs. Price, each............**35c**

DO NOT CUT descriptions or pictures from this book when you order. It is only necessary that you give Catalogue page, article number, price, size, etc., and we will know exactly what to send you.

## Charcoal Irons.

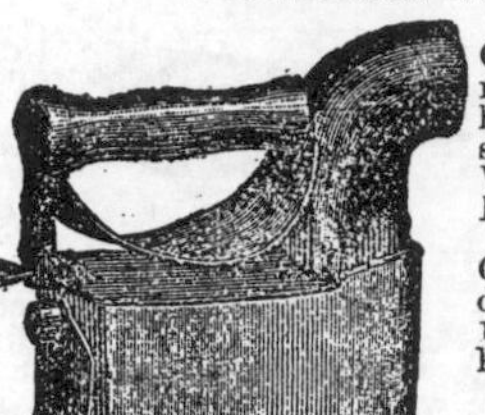

No. 15349. Family Charcoal Irons with removable top, wood handle with tin shield, one flue. Weight, 6½ lbs. Price, each......**75c**

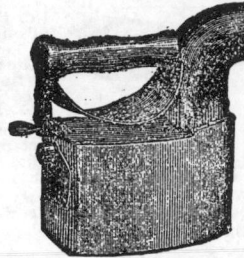

No. 15350. Tailors' Charcoal Irons, double flue. Weight, 17 lbs. Price, each...**$2.50**

## Tailors' Goose.

No. 15351. Tailors' Goose with extra polished face.

| Weight, lbs., | 16 | 18 | 20 | 22 |
|---|---|---|---|---|
| Price, each, | $0.56 | .63 | .70 | .77 |

## Fluters.

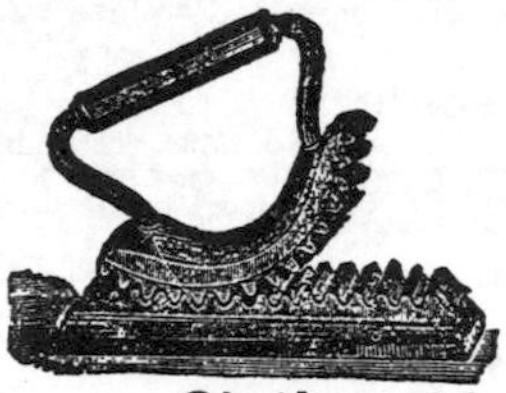

No. 15354. The Geneva Hand Fluter is the best known and most popular Hand Fluter in the market. Weight, 4¾ lbs. Price, each...........**80c**

## Clothes Line Reels.

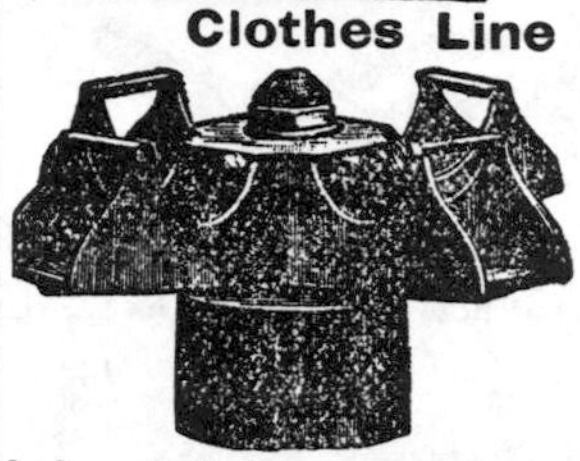

No. 15355. Clothes Line Reel or Clothes Dryer Casting. Has a socket which fastens over the top of a post. The reel revolves on this socket and is made for four bars. From 100 to 200 feet of line can be strung on bars (according to length of bars), and this can be hung full of clothes without moving basket or wading through deep snow in the winter. Price, each..**48c**

## Wire Clothes Lines.

No. 15358. Twisted Wire Clothes Lines in lengths of 100 feet each. Twisted from galvanized steel wire; will not rust. Size given indicates gauge of wire from which it is made. No. 18 is the size most used.

| Nos. | 18 | 20 |
|---|---|---|
| Price, each, | $0.20 | .17 |

No. 15359. Plain Galvanized Wire Clothes Lines. Made from one strand of No. 9 annealed wire, in coils of 100 feet. Price, each...................................**25c**

For other Clothes Lines see Grocery List.

## Wringers.

Our Wringers are manufactured by a firm who have been in this business for thirty years. The workmanship is of the highest order. All parts are closely matched, with no rough ragged or chipped edges. Even the under parts and inside of posts are finished smoothly. The rubber rolls are the vital part of the machine. The warranted rolls in our Wringer are made of **solid white rubber** and they are vulcanized immovably to the shaft. **We guarantee that should any warranted rolls turn on the shaft, become loose, bulge or give out because of defects within a year from time of being put into service, we will replace them free of charge.**

Wringers weigh about 10 lbs. each.

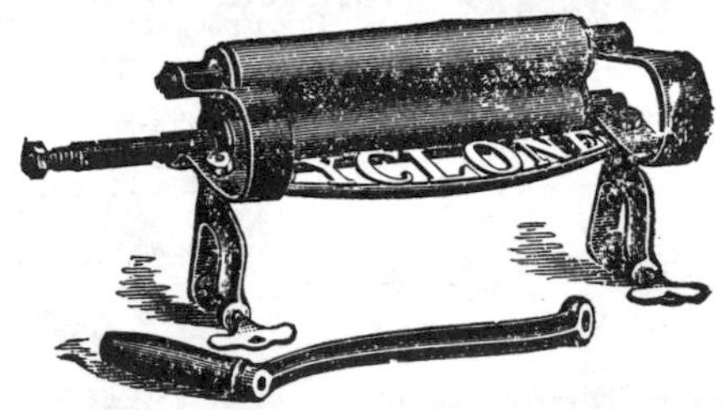


No. 15364. The Cyclone Iron Frame Wringer, with steel springs, galvanized malleable iron apron. Rolls, 10x1¾ inches. This wringer will give satisfaction for the price, and we have never seen its equal sold at anything like this price. Only...............................**$1.30**

*FOR FEAR YOU MIGHT FORGET IT,*

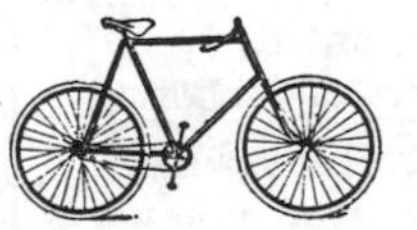

We direct your attention to our

# BICYCLES

(See pages 611 to 619).

If you couldn't afford a Wheel before, we now hang them within easy reach.

**We invite the most careful investigation of our reliability before you order. If you have any doubts about trusting your order and money with us, don't send it to us until you have been satisfied we are all that we claim.**

## The Cleveland Ball Bearing Wringer.

No. 15367. The Cleveland Ball Bearing Wringer. The greatest improvement yet applied to clothes wringers. Turns with half the strength required for others. This **ball** bearing must not be confounded with the roller bearing introduced some years ago. The arrangement of this bearing is almost identically the same as applied to bicycles. The cones and bearings are made of steel, hardened and tempered, and the balls of hardened steel, same as are used in bicycles. Has wood frame, steel adjusting spring, 2 adjusting screws; rolls, 10x1¾ inches. **warranted.** Price, each................$3.00

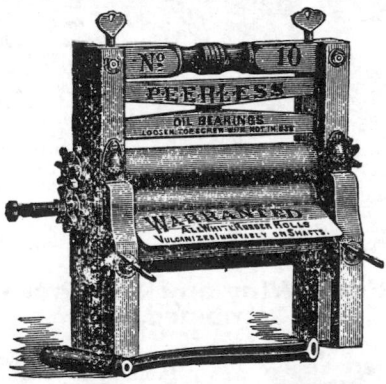

No. 15368. The Peerless Wringer is the most popular wringer with high class trade, and we can not recommend it too highly. The distinguishing feature of the Peerless is the clamping device which has recently been imitated by other makers, but comparison shows the imitation is only in general appearance and not in fine workmanship and finish which characterizes the Peerless. Has **guide roller, double gears** and rolls 10x1¾ inches; **warranted.** Price, each........$2.00

No. 15369. The Unrivaled Wringer. Desiring to give our customers a large variety of wringers to select from, we have added this first-class wringer to our line. The material for the frame is carefully selected from first-class lumber. Has guide roller, 2 top screws and swinging iron clamps. Rolls, 10x1¾ inches: **warranted.** Price, each......................$2.00

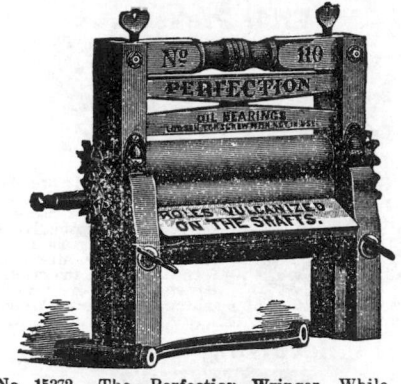

No. 15372. The Perfection Wringer. While this wringer will give excellent satisfaction for the price, and is as good as the first quality of some makers, the frame is not made from the same **selected** material as our other wood frame wringers. The frame is good and strong and the rolls of good material. Size, 10x1¾ inches; not warranted.
Price, each.....................................$1.50

No. 15375. The combination of Wringer and Bench combined is popular, and the Peerless is the best in the market. The bench is constructed on the principle of the truss bridge, and is exceedingly strong, though light. When folded for shipment or putting away when not in use it occupies but little space. With the ordinary tub wringer it is about as much work to hold the tub as to turn the wringer. The Bench Wringer does away with all this trouble. Rolls, 10x1¾ inches: warranted.
Price, each.....................................$3.00

### Carpet Sweepers.
**Something New. Cheap as a Broom.**

No. 15379. Bissell's Baby Sweeper is a toy that every parent will want. It is useful, durable, beautiful and cheap. The maker's name is a guarantee that it is first class in material and workmanship. It is 8 inches long, 4½ inches wide; has broom action, strongly made, and nicely finished. Price, each......40c

No. 15380. Bissell's Child Sweeper is a toy or a light small sweeper for practical use. Is 8 inches long, 5¼ inches wide, has broom action. Price, each......75c

**OUR CARPET SWEEPERS ARE NOT MERE CRUMB BRUSHES.** They do away entirely with the need of a broom on the carpet. They go into the nap and raise the dirt from where the broom never reaches. They will follow up a broom and remove more dirt than the broom did.
They sweep without dust or noise or wear on the carpet—almost without labor. They sweep any carpet.
The largest sweeper makers in the world make them. Sixty-five patents cover their devices.
And the price is low. Quantity makes it low.

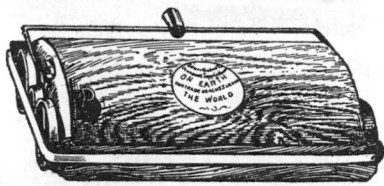

No. 15382. The Sears, Roebuck & Co.'s Sweeper is unquestionably the best low priced sweeper ever put on the market. It is a good sweeper and a good looker. It has the broom action—everlasting pure bristle brush—and spring dumping device.
The case is made with selected 3-ply veneer top, gracefully curved and attractively finished. Price, each.....................................$1.75

No. 15384. Bissell's "Grand Rapids." The best known and most widely sold carpet sweeper in the world.
Contains the famous Bissell broom action, and every other patented feature necessary in a first-class sweeper.
Made from the best selected cabinet woods in an assortment of attractive finishes.
Has rubber furniture protector encircling the case. Bissell's patent reversible bail spring, wheels outside the case, our everlasting pure bristle brush, both pans open at once by an easy pressure of the finger. Weight, 6 lbs. Price, each.....................................$2.30

No. 15385. Bissell's Prize Carpet Sweeper, the latest of the Bissell patterns, and differing in appearance from any other sweeper on the market.
A sweeper of the highest grade, with one of the handsomest patent case designs.
The case is hand polished. The bail, trimmings and iron end pieces are plated with nickel, brass, or antique copper, according to the finish of the case.
It contains our broom action, our patent reversible bail, and our pure bristle wire staple brush, adapted to be easily removed from the sweeper.
Its spring dumping device is convenient, opening one pan at a time. Length of case, 14 inches.
Its construction throughout is as perfect as care and skill can make it.
Price each.....................................$2.95

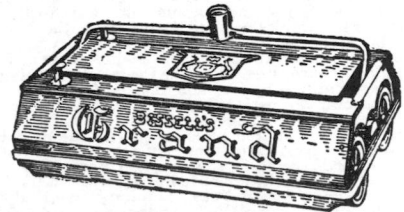

No. 15388. Bissell's Grand is constructed after one of the handsomest of our patented designs. The wheels do not project outside the case.
The bail and trimmings are nickeled, and the case is hand decorated.
The spring dumping device is one of the most convenient that we make.
This sweeper is made in natural walnut, maple with mahogany finish, and oak with the 16th century finish. Length of case, 17 inches.
Price each.....................................$3.90

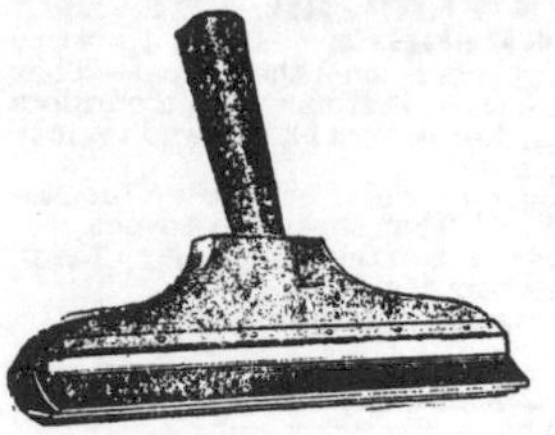

## Floor Scrapers.

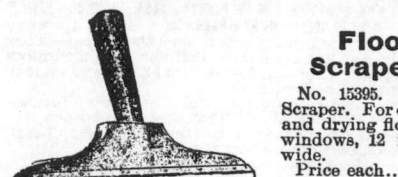

No. 15395. Rubber Scraper. For cleaning and drying floors and windows, 12 inches wide.
Price each......**30c**

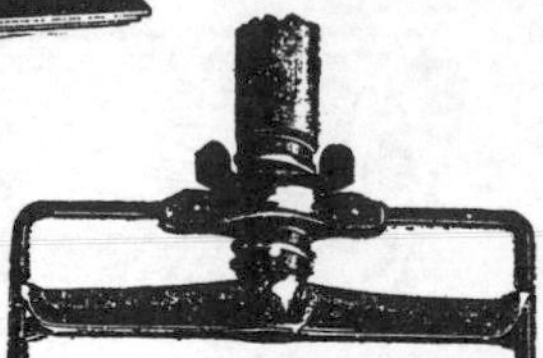

## Mop Heads.

No. 15396. Mop Head. Made of extra heavy wire with iron screw head, thumb screw to hold handle firm when screwed down upon rags.
Price each......**10c**

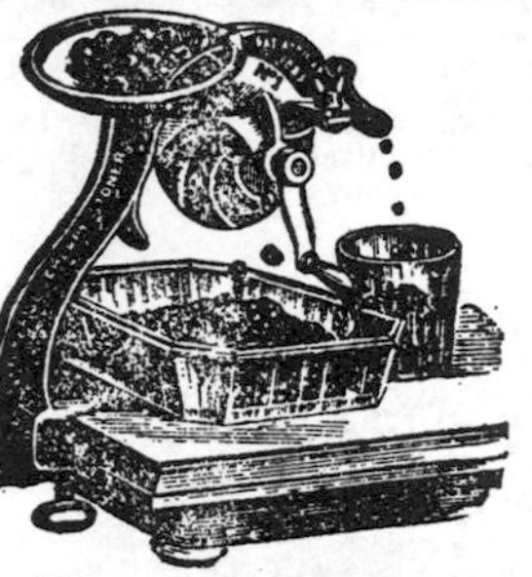

## Cherry Stoner.

No. 15397. The accompanying cut illustrates our Cherry Stoner, which is intended to stone cherries with rapidity. It is adjusted by thumb screws to adapt it to the different size cherry stones. It is nicely tinned to prevent rust.
Price each.....**60c**

## The Crown Raisin Seeder.

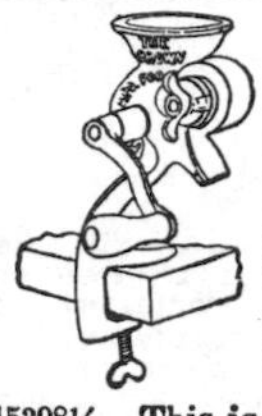

Patented October 26, 1896.

No. 15397½. Seeds one pound of raisins in five minutes with less waste than any machine made. Will not get out of order. Easily cleaned. Cannot become clogged. No pulp adheres to the seeds. Heavily tinned.
Price each..........................**50c**

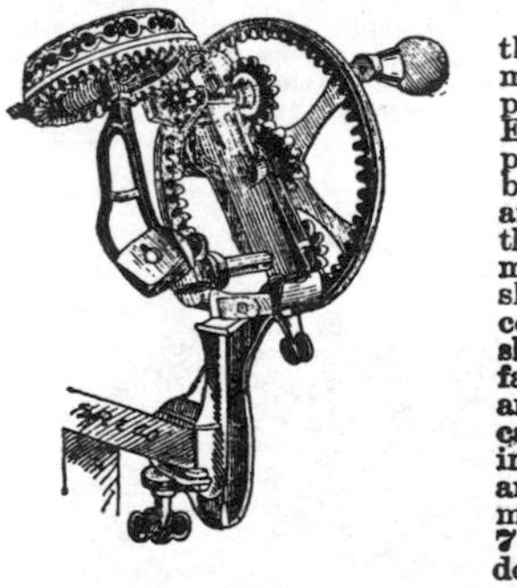

No. 15398½. This is the best known and most popular apple parer ever invented. Every machine works perfectly, all parts being accurately fitted and put together in the best possible manner. Machine should be fastened to corner of table, as shown in cut. Parings fall clear of machine and table. Gearing cannot clog with parings. Has curved knife and all latest improvements. Price, each, **75c.** Price per doz............**$8.00**

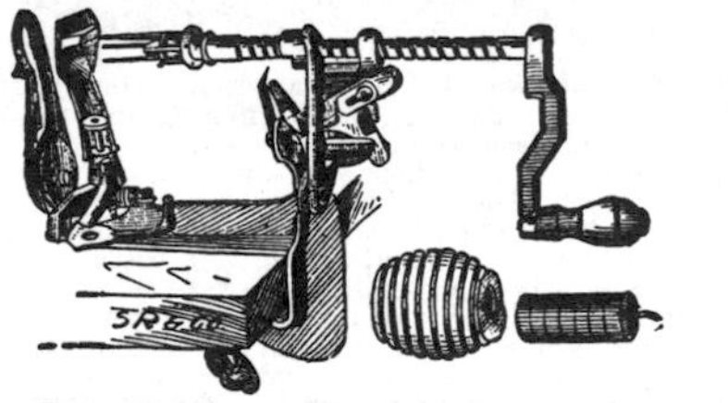

No. 15398¾. This is a strictly first-class machine at a low price, and is not intended to replace the inferior devices in the market. **With one hand you can pare, core and slice an apple, and withdraw the fork from the core. Directions**—Place the apple on the fork. By one turn of the crank the small knife pares the base of the apple—other machines require the base to be pared by hand. A few additional turns enables the machine to completely pare, slice and core the apple, leaving it perfectly smooth, unbroken and in a perfect coil. The shaft is then drawn back to release the apple, when the Automatic push-off removes the core from the fork, thereby requiring but one hand to operate the machine. By loosening the machine screw you can drop the coring and slicing knife down to the side, and pare only. The knives on this machine are of tempered steel, will retain their edge during constant use for a long time, and will not bend. Price, each, 40c. Per doz............**$4.50**

## THAT PICTURE ON THE BACK COVER.

**It is a fair representation of where your order comes from when you buy of us.**

From this, as a center, we have "strings out" to leading manufacturers in America and Europe, and by a perfect system are able to give you the best service and the best values you can get anywhere.

## Fruit Presses.

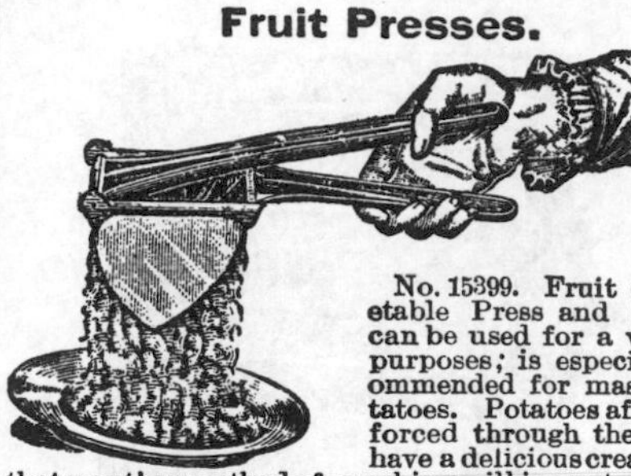

No. 15399. Fruit and Vegetable Press and Strainer; can be used for a variety of purposes; is especially recommended for mashing potatoes. Potatoes after being forced through the strainer have a delicious creamy taste that no other method of mashing will impart. Weight, 1 lb. 4 oz. Each..........................................**30c**

## Revolving Graters.

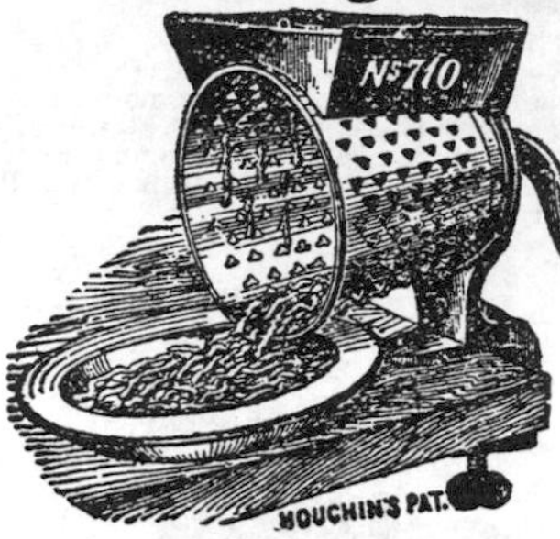

No. 15402. Revolving Grater for grating horseradish, cocoanut, pumpkins, squash, lemons, crackers, cheese, etc. The cylinder is 3 inches in diameter and 3 inches long. No family should be without one. Weight, 1 lb. 10 oz. Each..........................................**38c**

No. 15403. Revolving Grater, larger than No. 15402; has a cylinder 6 inches in diameter, 5 inches in length. Weight, 7 lbs. 7 oz. Each..........................**$1.20**

## Revolving Slicer.

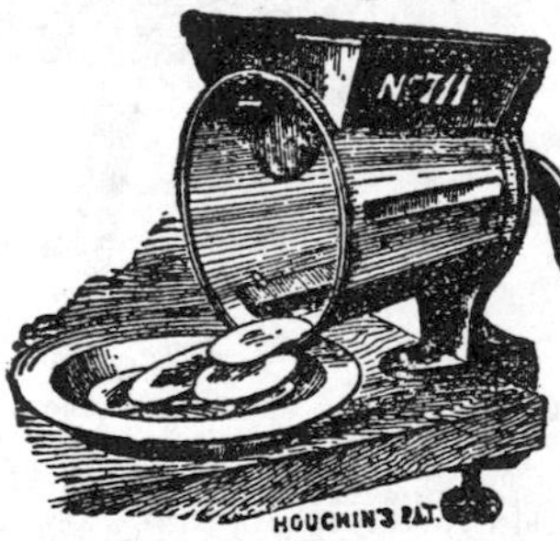

No. 15404. Revolving Slicer, for slicing apples, Saratoga potatoes, pumpkins, cucumbers and other vegetables. Weight, 1 lb. 13 oz. Each..........................**37c**

## Mincing Knives.

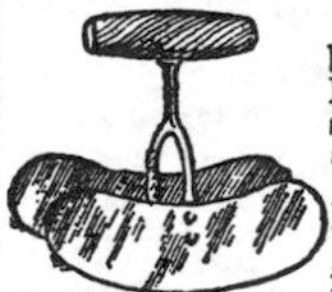

No. 15407. Double Mincing Knife. Polished steel blades, enameled handle. Weight, 8 oz.
Price, each....**5c**

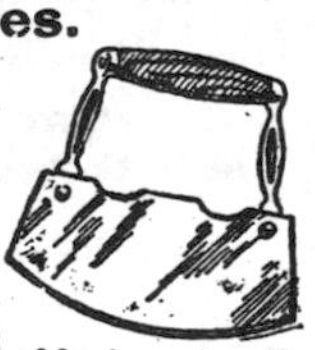

No. 15408. Mincing Knife, cast steel blade, ground sharp, solid malleable iron handle which can't split or get loose. Blade and handle nickle plated to prevent rusting. Price, each............**10c**

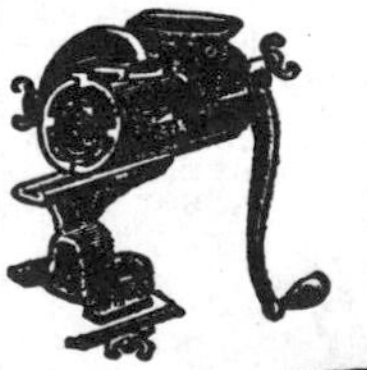

## Meat Choppers.

No. 15412. Triumph Meat Cutter. Cuts meats and vegetables equally well. Simple in construction, nicely tinned to prevent rust. Cutters are self sharpening.
Price, each..............**$1.35**

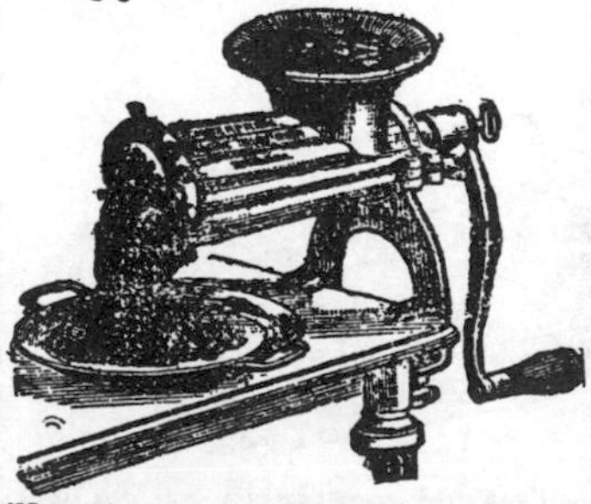

The Enterprise Meat Cutters cut the meat on the same principle as a pair of shears. By means of the stuffing attachment which we furnish at a small additional cost, they make excellent sausage stuffers.

No. 15416. Family size, with clamp (No. 10), same as illustration, chops one pound per minute. Price, each..........................**$2.35**

No. 15417. Stuffing attachment for No. 15416 chopper. Price each..........................................**30c**

No. 15417½. Extra knives for No. 15416. Each...**25c**

No. 15418. Family size, with legs to screw on bench or table; otherwise like illustration and of same capacity. Price, each..........................................**$2.00**

No. 15419. Stuffing attachment for No. 15418 choppr. Price, each..........................................**30c**

No. 15420. Extra knives for No. 15418 chopper. Price, each..........................................**25c**

No. 15421. Hotel size, with legs to fasten to table or bench. Chops two pounds per minute; weight, 12 lbs. Price, each..........................................**$3.10**

No. 15422. Stuffer attachment for No. 15421 chopper. Price, each..........................................**45c**

No. 15423. Extra knives for No. 15421 chopper. Price, each..........................................**45c**

## Sausage Stuffer.

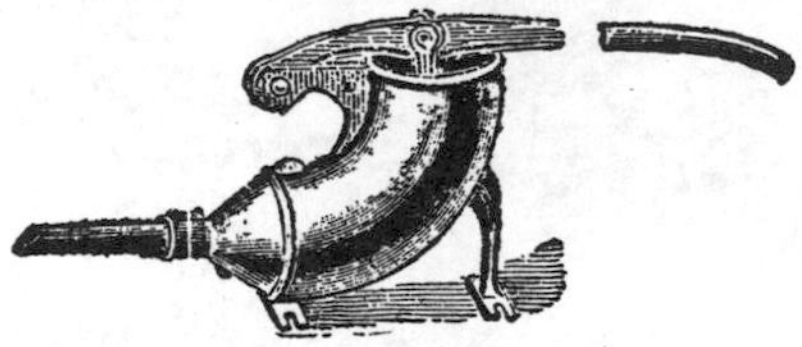

No. 15429. Lever Sausage Stuffer. Iron japanned. No. 0 for butchers' use; No. 1 for family use.
No. 0. Price, each..........................................**92c**
No. 1. Price, each..........................................**65c**

## Sausage Stuffer, Fruit and Lard Press Combined.

The Enterprise Combined Sausage Stuffer, Fruit and Lard Press; unexcelled for butchers' and farmers' use for stuffing sausages, and will be found useful for many purposes in every family. Directions will be found in catalogue that comes with each press.

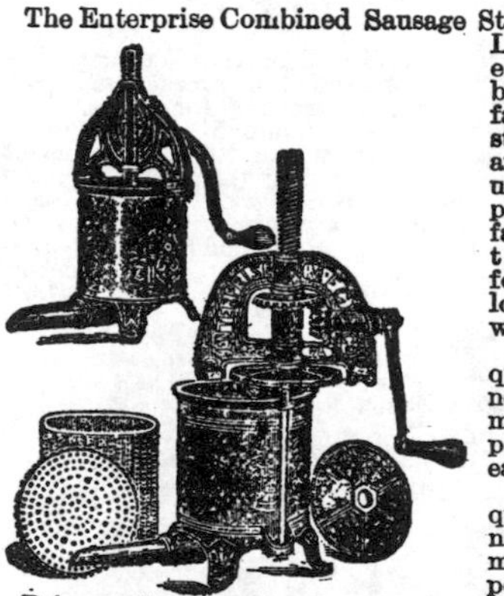

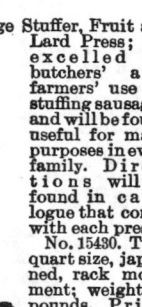

No. 15430. Two-quart size, japanned, rack movement; weight, 21 pounds. Price, each......**$2.40**

No. 15431. Four quart size, japanned screw movement; weight, 30 pounds.
Price, each..........................................**$3.90**

No. 15432. 8-quart size, japanned screw movement; weight, 44 lbs.
Price, each..........................................**$4.95**

## Fruit, Wine and Jelly Press Combined.

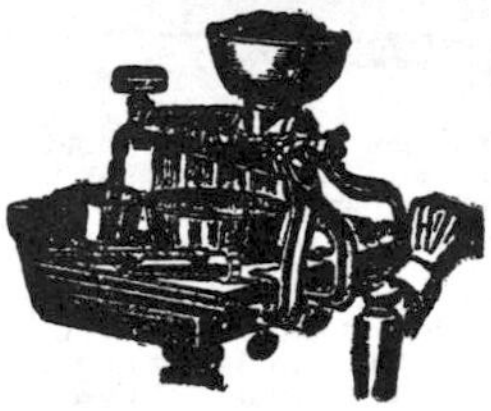

No. 15439. Combination Fruit, Wine and Jelly Press. Can be used for many purposes, such as making wines, jellies and fruit butter from fruits, the entire substance being extracted in one operation. Weight, 12½ lbs.
Price, each.......**$2.35**

## Meat Hooks.

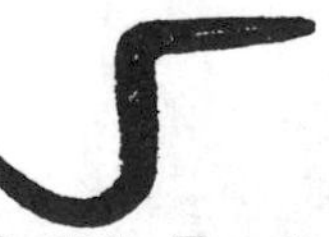

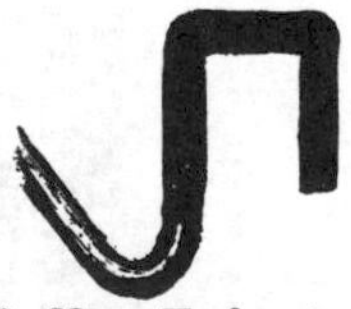

No. 15440. **Wrought iron** tinned Meat Hooks, to drive.

| | | | | | | |
|---|---|---|---|---|---|---|
| Nos.............. | 1 | 2 | 3 | 4 | 5 | 6 |
| Size of iron...... | ¼ | ¼ | 5/16 | ⅜ | ⅜ | ⅜ |
| Price, per doz.... | $0.10 | .12 | .16 | .21 | .25 | .35 |

No. 15441. Wrought iron tinned Meat Hooks, to screw in.

| | | | | | | |
|---|---|---|---|---|---|---|
| Nos.............. | 1 | 2 | 3 | 4 | 5 | 6 |
| Size of iron...... | ¼ | ¼ | 5/16 | ⅜ | ⅜ | ⅜ |
| Price, per doz.... | $0.10 | .12 | .16 | .21 | .30 | .35 |

No. 15442. Wrought iron tinned Mutton Hooks, for 2 inch bar, made of 5/16 square iron. Price, per doz....**45c**

No. 15443. Wrought iron tinned Beam Hooks, same shape as mutton hook, very heavy, for 2 inch bar, made of 7/16 square iron. Weight, per doz., 3 lbs. 15 oz. Price, per doz..........................................**70c**

No. 15444. Wrought iron tinned Beam Hooks, with large round bend, very heavy, for 2 inch bar, made of ½ inch iron. Weight, per doz., 9¾ lbs. Price, per doz..**80c**

**Our special discount of 3 per cent. for full cash with order is not overlooked by the careful buyer. This discount will often pay the freight or express.**

## Cleavers.

No. 15448. Family Cleavers, with improved malleable iron shanks riveted through handles into heavy iron caps, very strong and durable; 7 inch cast steel blades forged and hardened, is a very handy household article and should be in every one's kitchen. Price, each.............**32c**

## Butchers' Cleavers.

Extra cast steel, hickory handles.
No. 15449. Choppers, 7 inch cut, 1½ lbs.
Price, each..**60c**
No. 15450. Choppers, 8 inch cut, 1¾ lbs. Price, each.............**70c**
No. 15451. Cleavers, 9 inch cut, 3¼ lbs. Price, each.............**80c**
No. 15452. Cleavers, 10 inch cut, weight 4 lbs. Price, each.............**$1.15**
No. 15453. Cleavers, 12 inch cut, weight 5 lbs. Price, each.............**$1.45**

## Coffee Mills.

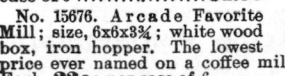

No. 15675. Arcade Side Mill, medium size, board back, crystallized metal hopper, japanned iron work. Each, 25c; per case of 6.............**$1.35**
No. 15676. Arcade Favorite Mill; size, 6x6x3¾; white wood box, iron hopper. The lowest price ever named on a coffee mill of any description. Each, 22c; per case of 6.............**$1.32**

No. 15677. Favorite (small size), raised hopper, no cover, japanned iron, hardwood box. Never before sold for less than 60 cents to our knowledge; usually retails at 75 cents. Best value for the money in the market. Each, 29c; per case of 6........**$1.57**
No. 15678. Arcade Favorite, same as No. 15677, only large size, 7x4¼ inches. Each, 35c; per case of 6.............**$1.89**
No. 15679. Arcade Favorite, retinned hopper, with patent shield, to prevent coffee from snapping out, new patent regulator and pulverizing burr, hardwood box, dove-tailed corners, polished, and finely made. Size, 7x7x4½ inches. Each, 45c; per case of 6.......**$2.43**
No. 15680. Arcade Favorite, wood top, with iron hopper and cover, similar to cut, hardwood box. Each, 43c; per case of 6.............**$2.20**
No. 15681. Arcade Favorite, with ornamental top and hinged cover; finely finished, patent regulator and pulverizing burr. Each, 45c; per case of 6..**$2.43**
No. 15682. Arcade Imperial, sunk hopper, all iron top, hinged cover, hardwood box, dovetailed, and finely finished; has patent regulator and pulverizing burr, largest size made, 7x7x5¼ inches. Each, 50c; per case of 6.............**$2.70**

No. 15683. Imperial, sunk hopper, hinged cover, iron, finished with French gold bronze, white walnut box. Each, 45c; per case of 6.............**$2.40**
No. 15684. Imperial, sunk hopper, hinged cover, nickel plated trimmings, white walnut box. Each, 58c; per case of 6........**$3.14**

## Ice Cream Freezers.

No. 15463. **Shepard's Lightning Ice Cream Freezers.** Lightning quadruple motion, automatic scraper, famous wheel dasher, combination hinge top gearing completely covered. Compared with other freezers we find: This **Tub** is cedar; competitors use pine; has round electric welded wire hoop, galvanized; competitors have flat hoops; can is full size and made from **one size heavier tin** than is used in other freezers; cast iron cover with drawn steel bottom; competitors have sheet tin cover and bottom; freezes as quickly as any other in the market, with much less effort. **All parts that come in contact with the cream heavily coated with pure block tin**; all other trimmings smoothly galvanized. **Uses 25 per cent. less ice and salt than any other Freezer.**

| Size, quarts, | 2 | 3 | 4 | 6 | 8 | 10 | 14 |
|---|---|---|---|---|---|---|---|
| Price, each, | $1.43 | 1.69 | 2.00 | 2.52 | 3.25 | 4.42 | 6.04 |

## Ice Tongs.

No. 15468. Ice Tongs. No. 1 opens 16 inches, steel point, family size. Each.........**48c**
No. 2 opens 18 inches, steel point. Each.............**60c**
No. 3 opens 24 inches, steel point, wagon size. Each.**70c** Weight, about 4 lbs.
No. 15469. Ice Tongs. No. 6, opens 14 inches, with bail top, family size. Weight, about 2¾ lbs. Each.............**40c**
No. 15470. Ice Chisel. 4 prongs, solid steel blade. The very best ice cutter that we know of. Will cut a much larger block than one would suppose. Weight, 9 oz.
Each.............**10c**

## Ice Shredder.

The operation of our shredder requires no explanation, being simply to draw the blade upon a piece of ice—the pressure applied producing fine or coarse pieces, as desired. To remove the finely cut ice from the cup, grasp the shredder firmly in the right hand and strike it, inverted, upon the left, at the same time being careful to keep the lid closed. Then scrape the ice into some convenient receptacle. It is not necessary to take the ice out of the refrigerator, as you may reach in and fill the cup from the side, end or top of a cake of ice without disturbing anything or wetting your hands. Its use will be appreciated for fruits, drinks, oysters and clams on the half shell, olives, celery, radishes, iced tea, sliced tomatoes, etc., and for many purposes in the sick room. It is also adapted for use in making "snow balls," which are variously flavored and sold to children on the streets and at their schools, also to the general public at fairs. Men engaged in making "snow balls" are making from $5 to $9 per day. No. 15475. Price, each, tinned.............**50c**

## Ice Chippers.

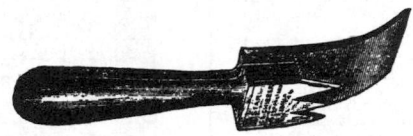

No. 15476. The Star Ice Chipper, iron handle. By the use of this chipper ice can be chipped into small and nearly uniform pieces. the guard projecting beyond the knife, making it impossible to cut off thicker pieces than the space between. Only a minute's time is required to reduce a 15 or 20 pound block of ice; cuts small pieces. Weight, 1¼ lbs. Each.............**25c**

## Combined Ice Hatchet, Pick and Chisel.

No. 15477. Combined Ice Hatchet, Pick and Chisel is one of the best combinations we have seen. Made of steel, finely polished and nickel plated, hardwood handle with heavy ferrule; entire length, 14 inches. Price, each.............**50c**

# OUR REFRIGERATOR DEPARTMENT.

We offer the Acme Refrigerators as the highest grade dry cold air refrigerators on the market.

**FROM THIS ILLUSTRATION WE ENDEAVOR TO SHOW** the construction of our Acme Refrigerator. The illustration shows the circulation of the air, arrangement of shelves and drip cup in position. It will be noticed that **the air after passing over the ice falls directly under** the provision chambers, displacing the warmer and lighter air and forcing it up the flues on either end, where by contact with the ice it is purified, cooled, and again falls, thus keeping up a constant circulation.

**PLEASE NOTE** that we do not have any condensation on exposed metal plates, but carry the air directly to the ice, which is the greatest purifier known to modern science.

**THESE REFRIGERATORS** are constructed with an inside case of **odorless and tasteless lumber**, matched and clamped together with nails and glue, and fastened to hardwood cleats, making it a thoroughly airtight, strong cabinet in itself. The insulator used is charcoal sheathing, which is odorless and tasteless and a perfect non-conductor.

**THE OUTSIDE CASE OF OUR CHEAPEST LINE IS SOLID ASH**, and on our finer grades it is of **solid antique oak, highly polished.** It is nailed and glued to the cleats which bind the inside case, thus making it one of the strongest and most durable refrigerators ever built.

**THE DRIP CUP IS SHOWN IN THIS CUT CLOSED.** To empty it, pull the wire and it will throw it over. The spring between the cup and loop will spring into position again. This is a very strong feature in our refrigerators, and is protected by U. S. patents.

**ALL THE WOOD IN THE PROVISION CHAMBER** is covered with metal, and there is no chance for it to become tainted or musty.

On all our Acme Refrigerators the foot-board is fastened with hinges instead of dowel pins; hence, if broken off can be quickly repaired by any one.

**DO NOT COMPARE** this Acme line of refrigerators with the many cheaper grades on the market, poorly constructed, often made of elm wood, and not built on scientific principles. We could furnish you a refrigerator for much less money, but could not guarantee it as we can the Acme.

**WE BELIEVE OUR CUSTOMERS** are entitled to the best, and we have carefully arranged with the manufacturers to supply us with as high grade a line of refrigerators as can be built. Every piece and part of the material used is of the very best, and the finish the very highest. Our refrigerators are paneled, top, sides, back and bottom, and finished as in no other make.

**OUR CHEAPEST REFRIGERATORS** have all the latest improvements that can be found in the highest grade of other makes; in fact, the Acme possesses all the good points of every refrigerator made, with the defects of none.

**OUR BINDING GUARANTEE: We guarantee every Acme refrigerator** to be made of the very best material throughout, to be constructed on the latest improved and most scientific principles, to be found exactly as represented in every respect, and to give universal satisfaction; and if found otherwise than as stated, we will cheerfully refund any money sent us and pay freight charges both ways.

**OUR LIBERAL TERMS:** We will ship refrigerators to **any address anywhere in the United States upon receipt of a sufficient deposit to cover freight charges both ways.** You can examine the refrigerator at your freight depot, and if found perfectly satisfactory and exactly as represented, pay the freight agent our prices and freight charges, less the amount sent with order.

**DISCOUNT FOR CASH.** We allow a discount of 3 per cent. if cash in full accompanies your order. If you send the full amount of cash with your order you may deduct 3 per cent. from our prices. Nearly all our customers send cash in full. Please consider the 3 per cent. cash discount when comparing our prices with others.

## Our Acme Hard Wood Ice Chest at $2.93 to $8.00.

We offer the best-made ice chest in the market at from **$2.93** to **$8.00**, and we would invite you to compare these prices with those of any other house, and if we can not save you money and furnish you a much better chest we will not ask you to send us your order.

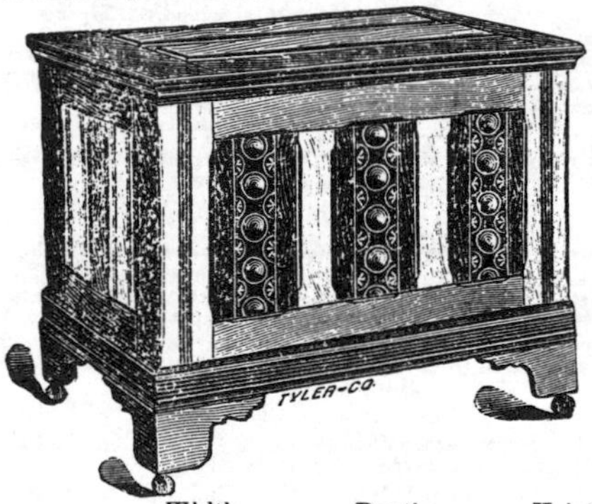


Please observe these chests weigh from 65 to 180 lbs., and when ordering to be shipped C. O. D. be sure to enclose enough to cover freight charges both ways. Balance and freight charges you can pay when the chest is received. Please note the 3 per cent. discount allowed if cash in full accompanies your order.

The Acme ice chest as illustrated is made of hard wood, has beautifully carved panels, is lined throughout with extra heavy metal, wooden slat rack on bottom for ice, heavy metal shelves. It is mounted on the very best anti-friction casters, and is offered to you as a first-class chest for little money. This chest has no circulation.

| No. | Width, inches. | Depth, inches. | Height, inches. | Weight, pounds. | Price. |
|---|---|---|---|---|---|
| 15495 | 25 | 17½ | 24 | 65 | $2.93 |
| 15495½ | 30 | 18 | 25 | 75 | 3.73 |
| 15496 | 32 | 18 | 26 | 100 | 4.53 |
| 15496½ | 30 | 21 | 30 | 120 | 5.07 |
| 15497 | 35 | 20 | 29 | 125 | 5.60 |
| 15497½ | 41 | 24½ | 36 | 180 | 8.00 |

The above dimensions are outside measurements.

Understand every refrigerator, every ice chest we sell, is guaranteed exactly as represented, and if not found so we will cheerfully refund your money.

## Our Acme Single Door Refrigerator at from $5.60 to $8.80.

For general description and construction of refrigerator see heading. Understand every refrigerator is guaranteed to be exactly as represented, to contain all modern improvements of every first-class refrigerator made, with the defects of none, and if not found so may be returned at our expense and your money will be cheerfully refunded

The illustration, engraved from a photograph, will give you some idea of the appearance of this beautiful single door refrigerator. As previously described it is manufactured of kiln dried ash lumber, beautifully finished antique, brass lock, fancy surface hinges, anti-friction casters.

All these refrigerators above $5.60 are fitted with two shelves and provision chambers.

| No. | Width, inches. | Depth, inches. | Height, inches. | Weight, pounds. | Price. |
|---|---|---|---|---|---|
| 15498. | 23½ | 16½ | 39 | 100 | $5.60 |
| 15498½. | 27½ | 17½ | 41 | 115 | 6.67 |
| 15499. | 29 | 19½ | 43 | 140 | 7.73 |
| 15499½. | 31 | 20½ | 45 | 150 | 8.80 |

We furnish the same refrigerator as above illustrated and described, but supplied with a very fine porcelain lined water cooler and faucet to match trimmings, at the following prices:

| No. | Width, inches. | Depth, inches. | Height, inches. | Weight, pounds. | Price. |
|---|---|---|---|---|---|
| 15500. | 23½ | 16½ | 39 | 110 | $ 7.20 |
| 15500½. | 27½ | 17 | 41 | 125 | 8.27 |
| 15501. | 29 | 19½ | 43 | 150 | 9.33 |
| 15501½. | 31 | 20½ | 45 | 160 | 10.93 |

## Our Extra High Upright Acme Refrigerators.

This refrigerator is made for the purpose of giving you a refrigerator of large capacity and still occupy small space in a room. We offer this refrigerator at **$10.40**, and invite a close comparison of the same with any refrigerator you can buy at $15.00 to $18.00; **$10.40** is the price when sent to any address by freight C. O. D. subject to examination on receipt of a sufficient deposit to cover freight charges both ways, balance and freight charges to be paid after refrigerator is received.

A discount of 3 per cent. allowed if cash in full accompanies your order. If you send the full amount of cash with your order you may deduct 3 per cent. from this price, when **$10.28** pays for it.

The above illustration engraved from a photograph will give you some idea of the appearance of this refrigerator. It is manufactured of the very best kiln dried ash lumber, beautifully finished antique, has solid brass locks, finest surface hinges, patent drip cup.

| No. | Width, inches. | Depth, inches. | Height, inches. | Weight, pounds. | Price. |
|---|---|---|---|---|---|
| 15502. | 28 | 18 | 54 | 180 | $10.40 |

## Our Acme Double Door Refrigerator at $11.73 and $15.47.

This is a very popular size refrigerator. The ice chest is very large, will hold artificial ice and is the only first-class refrigerator of this size made in which the chest will take in artificial ice.

The illustration shown will give you some idea of the appearance of this refrigerator. It is manufactured from the very best selected kiln dried ash lumber, handsomely carved, trimmed and polished. Our **$11.73** is made with no partitions between provision chambers. Our **$15.47** has partitions between provision chambers.

| No. | Width, inches. | Depth, inches. | Height, inches. | Weight, pounds. | Price. |
|---|---|---|---|---|---|
| 15502½ | 34½ | 22 | 49 | 230 | $11.75 |
| 15503 | 40 | 24 | 49 | 265 | 15.47 |

We furnish the same refrigerators as illustrated above except with a very fine porcelain lined water cooler attached at the following prices:

| No. | Width, inches. | Depth, inches. | Height, inches. | Weight, pounds. | Price. |
|---|---|---|---|---|---|
| 15503½ | 34½ | 22 | 49 | 240 | $13.87 |
| 15504 | 40 | 24 | 49 | 275 | 17.60 |

## Our Combined Acme Dry Air Refrigerator and Sideboard at from $11.47 to $18.67.

**O**ne of our very finest . .

### REFRIGERATORS

**It is made of solid oak.**

Finished antique, highly polished, heavily paneled on front, sides, back and bottom; is fitted with a sideboard attachment with a heavy beveled French plate mirror. The whole is beautifully carved and decorated with raised carved ornamentations. This is a very large refrigerator and one of the most popular styles we have. All but the two smaller sizes have an ice chest large enough to take artificial ice.

### Has lift-out Ice Reservoir.

### Ice Rack is made entirely of metal.

| No. | Width. | Depth. | Height of Refrigerator. | Height to top of Sideboard. | Weight. | Price. |
|---|---|---|---|---|---|---|
| 15504½ | 23½ in., | 16½ in., | 39 in., | 60 in., | 145 lbs., | $11.47 |
| | Same with water cooler attachment, | | | | | 13.07 |
| 15505 | 27½ in., | 17½ in., | 41½ in., | 62½ in., | 175 lbs., | 12.80 |
| | Same with water cooler attachment, | | | | | 14.66 |
| 15505½ | 30½ in., | 20 in., | 47 in., | 72 in., | 225 lbs., | 16.75 |
| | Same with water cooler attachment, | | | | | 19.20 |
| 15506 | 34 in., | 21½ in., | 49 in., | 74 in., | 265 lbs., | 18.67 |
| | Same with water cooler attachment, | | | | | 21.07 |

We can furnish the same refrigerator as described above complete without sideboard, otherwise exactly as above described, at the following prices:

| No. | Width. | Depth. | Height. | Weight. | Price. |
|---|---|---|---|---|---|
| 15506½ | 23½ in., | 16½ in., | 39 in., | 110 lbs., | $ 7.73 |
| | With porcelain lined water cooler attachment, | | | | 9.33 |
| 15507 | 27½ in., | 17½ in., | 41½ in., | 140 lbs.. | 9.07 |
| | Same with porcelain lined water cooler attachment, | | | | 10.93 |
| 15507½ | 30½ in., | 20 in., | 47 in., | 180 lbs., | 12.54 |
| | With porcelain lined water attachment, | | | | 14.93 |
| 15508 | 34 in., | 21½ in., | 49 in., | 220 lbs., | 14.40 |
| | Same with porcelain lined water cooler attachment, | | | | 16.75 |

## Our Acme Combined Dry Air Refrigerator and Sideboard for $22.93.

**$22.93** is our price when sent by freight C. O. D., subject to examination on receipt of sufficient deposit to cover freight charges both ways. Three per cent. discount allowed if cash in full accompanies your order. If you send cash in full with your order you may deduct 3 per cent., or **$22.24** pays for the refrigerator.

This refrigerator is an entirely new design for this season, and one of the handsomest and best we have to offer. It is made from the very best selected kiln dried oak, finished antique, highly polished, beautifully carved. It is trimmed with fancy heavy bronze trimmings throughout. The top is solid and makes a very useful sideboard, besides being a perfect refrigerator. As will be seen from the illustration the upper doors are arranged so that the ice can be placed in the chamber without the inconvenience of raising the upper lid, and when the ice does not fill the large chamber it serves as a place for storage around the ice.

The ice chamber of this refrigerator is made extra large, and will take artificial ice. It is constructed with a view to giving the greatest amount of room possible. We recommend this refrigerator either with or without sideboard above all others. It is the most popular size, is highly finished, and possesses the good points of every refrigerator made with the defects of none. We do not hesitate to guarantee it in every respect, and we are offering it at about one-half the price charged by retail dealers. We can only repeat that when comparing our prices with those of other houses, be sure that you are comparing ours with a high grade antique oak refrigerator, one which is made in the best possible manner from the very best material on the latest and most approved scientific principles.

| No. | Width. | Depth. | Height of Refrigerator. | Height to top of Sideboard. | Weight | Price. |
|---|---|---|---|---|---|---|
| 15508½ | 36½ in., | 22 in. | 50 in., | 77 in., | 295 lbs., | $22.93 |

No. 15509. We furnish this refrigerator without sideboard attachment at.................................................................**$17.60**

### Refrigerator Pans.

The Seamless Refrigerator Pans are made of the very best material, and galvanized after they are made, having no seams to break or leak. They are the most desirable pans to buy. We have 3 sizes:

| No. | Height, inches. | Depth, inches. | Price, each. |
|---|---|---|---|
| 15524 | 13½ | 4 | 18c |
| 15525 | 14⅝ | 4½ | 20c |
| 15526 | 16½ | 5 | 24c |

## Our Highest Grade Acme Dining Room Sideboard and Refrigerator Combined, $50.00.

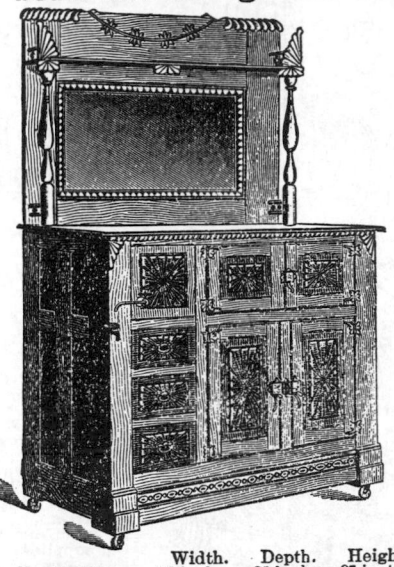

During the past several years our customers have asked us to make a combined sideboard and refrigerator suitable for a well furnished dining room, consequently we have designed and made one. as shown by the illustration. They are a combination of sideboard, refrigerator and water cooler. They are made of selected kiln dried quarter sawed oak, rubbed and polished. The refrigerator is entirely separated from the tank for ice water, and the drawers behind have a double partition lined with non-conducting material. It contains all the improvements of our celebrated Acme, and is one of the handsomest pieces of dining room furniture furnished in the country. It is not only highly polished but is heavily paneled, beautifully carved, decorated and ornamented. It is fitted with a very large beveled edge French plate mirror, trimmed throughout with heavy solid bronze trimmings, old copper finish, and is the handsomest thing in the way of a refrigerator ever produced.

| No. | Width. | Depth. | Height. | Shipping Weight. | Price. |
|---|---|---|---|---|---|
| 15509¼ | 56 inches. | 26 inches. | 27 inches. | 500 lbs. | $50.00 |

Please observe that our price of **$50.00** is the price for this refrigerator when shipped by freight C. O. D., subject to examination on receipt of a sufficient deposit to cover freight charges both ways. If you will send us your order with enough to cover freight charges both ways we will send the refrigerator to you by freight C. O. D. subject to examination. You can examine it at your freight depot, and if found perfectly satisfactory and exactly as represented, pay the freight agent the balance and freight charges, Three per cent. discount allowed if cash in full accompanies your order. If you send the full amount of cash with your order you may deduct 3 per cent., when **$48.50** pays for the refrigerator.

## Our Acme Grocers' Refrigerator.

We offer this refrigerator at from **$34.13** to **$37.33**, and would ask you to compare it with any refrigerator you can buy elsewhere for $50.00. We guarantee this the highest grade grocers' refrigerator made. The prices quoted are our regular prices when to be shipped by freight C. O. D. subject to examination on receipt of a sufficient deposit to cover freight charges both ways. A discount of 3 per cent. will be allowed if cash in full accompanies your order.

This refrigerator is made from selected kiln dried ash, highly polished and beautifully ornamented. Made with special hinges, adjustable shelves, very best improved insulation, perfect dry air circulation.

| No. | Width, in. | Depth. in. | Height, in. | Weight, lbs. | Price. |
|---|---|---|---|---|---|
| 15517 | 48 | 27 | 65½ | 500 | $34.13 |
| 15518 | 50 | 33 | 70 | 600 | 37.33 |

## Our Acme Grocers' Refrigerator at $49.07 and $61.33.

This Refrigerator is made from kiln dried ash; has adjustable shelves, antique finish, perfect dry air circulation. Our **$61.33** is made sectional, so that it may be taken down and passed through a narrow door or hallway, and set up again with comparative ease. Full directions for taking down and setting up accompany each refrigerator. In these refrigerators the rail between the upper and lower door, in the right hand partition chamber, is removable for the convenience of those who wish to put larger articles in than will go through the regular door, being arranged so that a quarter of beef, lamb, or other article can be placed in the refrigerator.

| No. | Width, inches. | Depth, inches. | Height, inches. | Weight, lbs. | Price. |
|---|---|---|---|---|---|
| 15522 | 61 | 37 | 81 | 1,000 | $49.07 |
| 15523 | 70 | 41 | 89 | 1,200 | 61.33 |

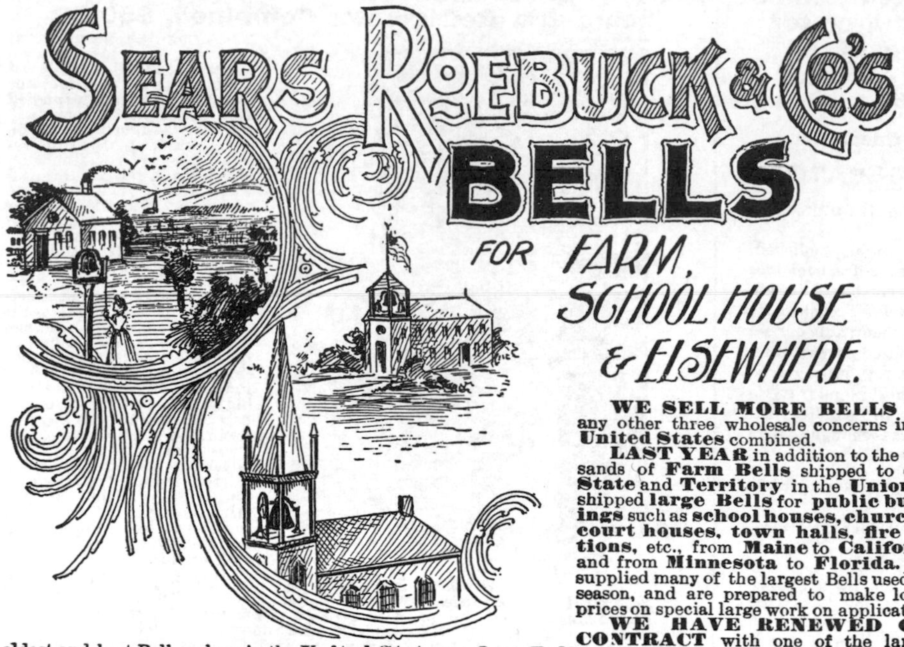
SEARS ROEBUCK & CO'S
BELLS
FOR FARM,
SCHOOL HOUSE
& ELSEWHERE.

**WE SELL MORE BELLS** than any other three wholesale concerns in the **United States** combined.

**LAST YEAR** in addition to the thousands of **Farm Bells** shipped to every **State** and **Territory** in the **Union**, we shipped **large Bells** for **public buildings** such as **school houses, churches, court houses, town halls, fire stations**, etc., from **Maine** to **California** and from **Minnesota** to **Florida**. We supplied many of the largest Bells used last season, and are prepared to make lowest prices on special large work on application.

**WE HAVE RENEWED OUR CONTRACT** with one of the largest, oldest and best Bell makers in the **United States. Our Bells this season** will be better than ever. They are made especially for us, and **for tone and finish** will be found superior to any other on the market, yet our prices are below all competition.

**OUR TERMS.** We will ship by freight **C. O. D.**, subject to examination, on receipt of **one-fourth** amount, balance and freight to be paid when received.

**Three per cent. discount allowed** if cash in full accompanies your order.

## Farm Bells.

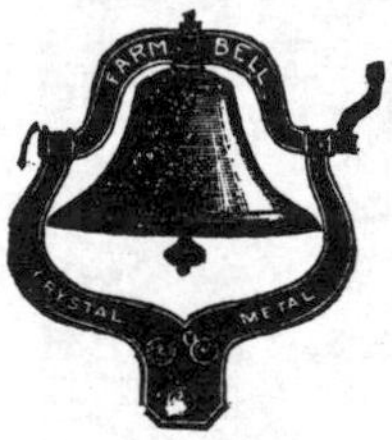
FARM BELL
CRYSTAL METAL

Nos. 1, 2 and 3.

This is one of the things that your dealer gets a big profit on. We buy direct from the maker, and when you buy from us you save the middleman's profit. The bells are so proportioned that they have a clear ring and a good tone. The bell is bronzed. The frame is iron, painted black. Bell Nos. 1, 2 and 3 have frame to go on post, as shown in cut. Bell No. 4 has frame to go on platform.

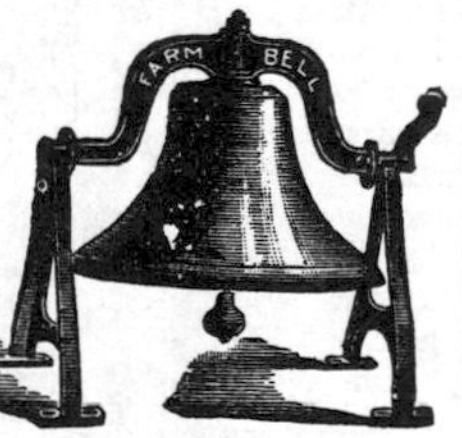
FARM BELL

No. 4.

| No. 14549. | Size, 1 | 2 | 3 | 4 |
|---|---|---|---|---|
| Diameter at mouth, inch. | 15 | 17 | 19 | 21 |
| Weight, with hangings, lbs., | 40 | 50 | 75 | 100 |
| Price, each, | $0.94 | 1.20 | 1.85 | 2.40 |

## Steel Alloy Bells.

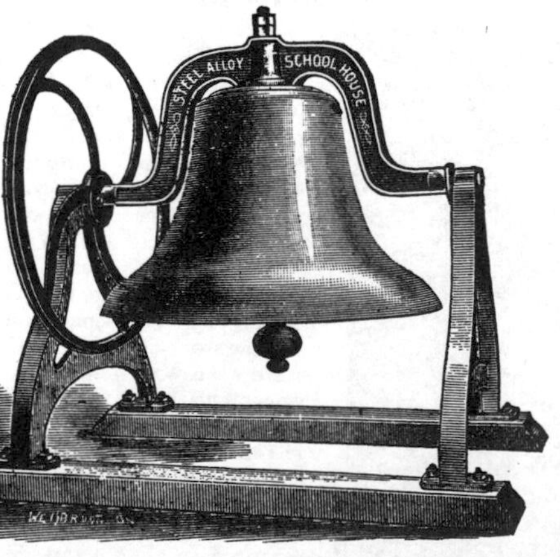
STEEL ALLOY
SCHOOL HOUSE

No. 14550. Steel Alloy Church Bells, made of an alloy of cast steel and crystal metal, and are of superior tone, finished and warranted against breaking with ordinary use for two years. For complete description send for our Special Bell Catalogue. Mailed free.

## School House or Factory Bells.

Bells are numbered by the diameter in inches.

| No. | Bell only, lbs. | Complete, lbs. | Price. |
|---|---|---|---|
| 20 | 105 | 150 | $ 7.20 |
| 22 | 125 | 175 | 9.00 |
| 24 | 155 | 225 | 11.25 |
| 26 | 220 | 325 | 18.00 |
| 28 | 255 | 425 | 22.90 |

## Church Bells.

No. 14551. Bells are numbered by the diameter in inches.

| No. | Bell only, lbs. | Complete, lbs. | Price. |
|---|---|---|---|
| 30 | 335 | 550 | $ 29.00 |
| 32 | 380 | 600 | 33.75 |
| 34 | 465 | 725 | 40.50 |
| 36 | 570 | 850 | 49.50 |
| 40 | 780 | 1,200 | 67.50 |
| 44 | 1,100 | 1,600 | 90.00 |
| 54 | 2,100 | 3,000 | 168.75 |

The weights and prices above named are for complete bells, and include wood sills, iron wheel: and for Nos. 30, 32, 34, 36, 40, 44 and 54, tolling hammer without extra charge.

Tolling hammers for Nos. 24, 26 and 28, when so ordered, **$3.00** each extra.

These bells are cast from an alloy of cast steel and crystal metal, and can be relied on under all circumstances and in all seasons. Nos. 20 to 28 are school or factory bells, and are not suitable for churches. Nos. 30 to 54, inclusive, are recommended for churches

## Hand Bells.

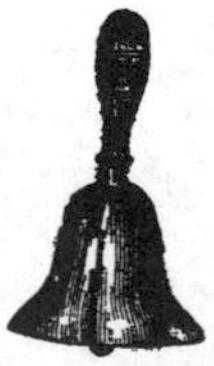

No. 14562.

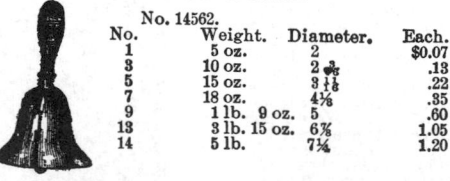

| No. | Weight. | Diameter. | Each. |
|---|---|---|---|
| 1 | 5 oz. | 2 | $0.07 |
| 3 | 10 oz. | 2⅜ | .13 |
| 5 | 15 oz. | 3 11/16 | .22 |
| 7 | 18 oz. | 4⅛ | .35 |
| 9 | 1 lb. 9 oz. | 5 | .60 |
| 13 | 3 lb. 15 oz. | 6⅞ | 1.05 |
| 14 | 5 lb. | 7¼ | 1.20 |

## Open Polished Bells.

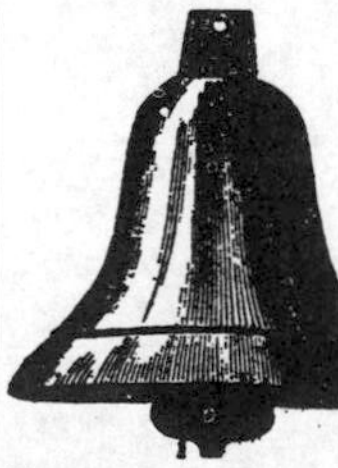

No. 14563. Open polished bells may be used for a variety of purposes; make good sheep bells, a harness bell for milk wagons, drays, etc.

| Nos. | 1 | 2 | 3 | 4 | 5 | 6 |
|---|---|---|---|---|---|---|
| Diameter of mouth in inches, | 2¼ | 2½ | 2¾ | 3 | 3¼ | 3½ |
| Price, each, | $0.06 | .07 | .8 | .12 | .15 | .19 |
| Price, per doz., | .62 | .75 | .85 | $1.20 | $1.63 | $2.00 |

## Sleigh Bells on Straps.

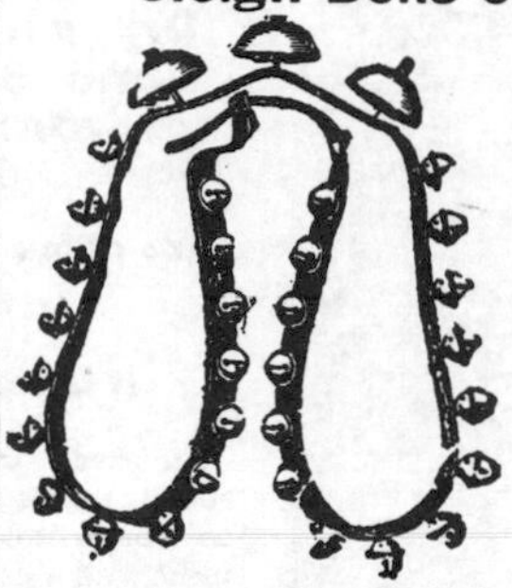

No. 14565. 30 round polished Bells, riveted on black leather strap, with chime, tinned. Per strap.....**$2.25**

No. 14566. Same as above, nickel plated. Per strap.....**$2.50**

Notice that price is for a single strap.

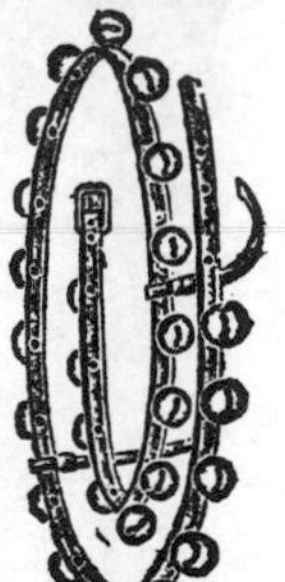

## Body Straps.

No. 14567. **24 common tinned Polar Bells.** No. 2 (1⅛ inch), riveted on russet or black leather strap. Price, per strap..................**80c**

No. 14568. **30 common tinned Polar Bells.** No. 2 (1⅛ inch), riveted on russet or black leather strap. Price, per strap............ **$1.20**

No. 14569. **30 extra white metal rim Bells.** No. 2 (1⅛ inch), riveted on russet or harness leather strap. Price, per strap.................................**$1.65**

No. 14570. **36 nickel plated Bells.** No. 2 (1⅛ inch), riveted on russet or harness leather strap. Price, per strap.............................................**$2.25**

## Assorted Sizes on One Strap.

No. 14574. 19 round polished Bells on leather strap, wire fastened; assorted sizes, from No. 2 to No. 8 bells. Price, per strap...............................................**$1.25**

No. 14575. 23 round polished Bells on leather strap, wire fastened; assorted sizes, from No. 1 to No. 8. Price, per strap...............................................**$1.40**

No. 14576. 23 round polished Bells, on leather strap, wire fastened; assorted sizes, from No. 5 to No. 13. Price, per strap........................... .......**$2.50**

## Neck Straps.

No. 14582. 9 round polished Bells on leather strap; assorted sizes, from No. 1 to No. 5. Price, per strap.............................................................**50c**

No. 14583. 15 round polished Bells, on leather strap, wire fastened; assorted sizes, from No. 2 to No. 9. Price, per strap............................................**95c**

## Loose Bells.

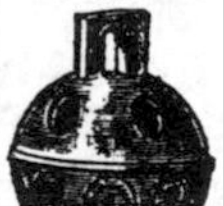

No. 14584. Common Loose Sleigh Bells, for the convenience of those who wish to make their own straps of bells.

| Nos. | 1 | 2 | 3 | 4 | 5 | 6 |
|---|---|---|---|---|---|---|
| Diameter, | 1⅛ | 1¼ | 1⅜ | 1 7/16 | 1⅝ | 1¾ |
| Per doz., | $0.23 | .31 | .41 | .49 | .58 | .66 |

| Nos. | 7 | 8 | 9 | 10 | 11 |
|---|---|---|---|---|---|
| Diameter, | 1⅞ | 2 | 2 3/16 | 2¼ | 2⅜ |
| Per doz., | $0.81 | .94 | 1.14 | 1.35 | 1.50 |

## Shaft Bells.

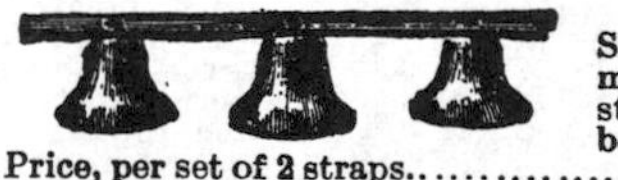

No. 14586. Open Shaft Bells. White metal on shaft straps. Three No. 1 bells on each strap. Price, per set of 2 straps...................................**31c**

No. 14587. Nickeled Gong Chime Sleigh Bells, extra finish, 3 bells on a strap, 6 bells to a set. Price, per set...............................................................**35c**

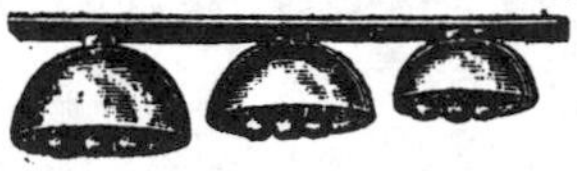

No. 14589. Nickel plated Swiss Shaft Chimes. Three bells on japanned iron straps. Six bells to set. Price, per set.........................................**65c**

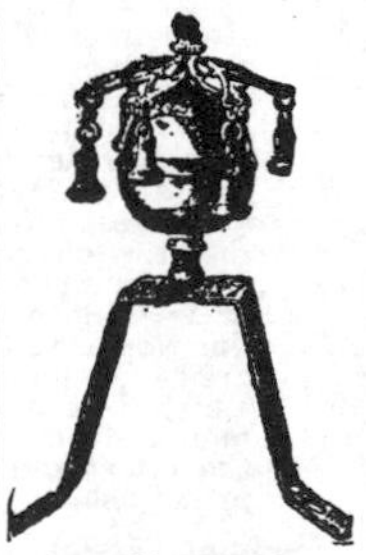

No. 14594. Harmonized Swiss Shaft Chimes. Nickel plated bells on japanned iron strap, 4 bells on a strap; 8 bells to set. Price, per set...........................................**$1.00**

No. 14595. Swiss Shaft Chimes. Tuned. Intervals, 1, 3, 5, 8; nickel plated bells, on japanned iron strap; 8 bells to set. Price, per set...........................**$1.65**

## Saddle Chimes.

No. 14601.

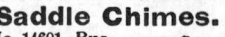

No. 14601. Russian Saddle Chimes. Price is for one only, as shown in cut. Price, each..**75c**

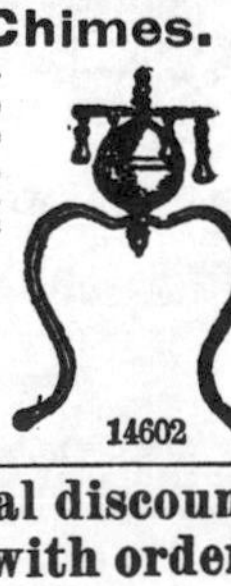

14602

No. 14602. Russian Saddle Chimes. Price is for one only, as shown in cut. Price, each.........................**$1.25**

For Cow Bells, Bicycle Bells, Electric Bells, Door Bells, and other bells see index. We sell them all.

**Don't overlook our special discount of 3 per cent. for full cash with order.**

**Don't be persuaded that you live so far that the freight will eat up the saving. When you buy at retail you pay the freight with a profit added. You don't see it in the price, but it's there.**

# TABLE CUTLERY.

Our Table Cutlery is selected from the stock of one of the most reliable and well known factories in this country. Our goods are the cleanest and best patterns possible to obtain. They are made of only the best steel; are fully warranted, and the workmanship cannot be excelled.

In this line, as well as in all others, we defy competition as regards quality and values. Should these goods not prove satisfactory, they can be returned at our expense, and money refunded.

**Our liberal terms offer** prevails on this line. Any cutlery will be sent by express C. O. D., subject to examination, on receipt of $1.00; balance and express charges payable at express office; 3 per cent. discount if cash in full accompanies your order.

**Don't overlook the advantages** of clubbing together, for on $100 we give a discount of 5 per cent.

**Try to make your order** 100 pounds in weight, even by adding sugar, so we can ship by freight at lowest freight rates.

Six knives and six forks constitute a set. Extra by mail, 25 to 40 cents per set.

No. 14668. Cocobolo handle Knives and Forks, no bolster. Per set, 6 knives and 6 forks, 40c; 1 doz. knives, only, 50c.

No. 14669. Iron handle Knives and Forks. Per set, 6 knives and 6 forks, 40c; 1 doz. knives, only, 50c.

No. 14670. White bone handle Knives and Forks, no bolster. Per set, 6 knives and 6 forks, 60c; 1 doz. knives, only, 70c.

No. 14671. Cocobolo handle Knives and Forks, single bolster. Per set, 6 knives and 6 forks, 70c.
No. 14672. Ebony handle Knives and Forks, single bolster. Per set, 6 knives and 6 forks, 75c.

No. 14673. White bone handle Knives and Forks, single bolster. Per set, 6 knives and 6 forks, 90c.

No. 14674. Fancy ring pattern, cocobolo handle Knives and Forks. Per set, 6 knives and 6 forks, 75c.
No. 14675. Same as No. 14674, with ebony handles. Per set, 6 knives and 6 forks, 80c.
No. 14676. Same as No. 14674, with bone handles. Per set, 6 knives and 6 forks, $1.15.

No. 14677. Fancy shape cocobolo handle Knives and Forks with one cross pattern, bolster. Per set, 6 knives and 6 forks, $1.00.
No. 14678. Same as No. 14677, with ebony handles. Per set, 6 knives and 6 forks, $1.35.
No. 14679. Same as No. 14677, with bone handles. Per set, 6 knives and 6 forks, $1.65.

No. 14680. Double bolstered cocobolo handle Knives and Forks. Per set, 6 knives and 6 forks, 75c.
No. 14681. Same as No. 14680, with ebony handles. Per set, 6 knives and 6 forks, 80c.

No. 14682. Double bolstered bone handle Knives and Forks. Per set, 6 knives and 6 forks, $1.05.

No. 14683. Double bolstered, sway back, Knives and Forks, cocobolo handles. Per set, 6 knives and 6 forks, 80c.
No. 14684. Same as No. 14683, with ebony handles. Per set, 6 knives and 6 forks, 95c.
No. 14685. Same as No. 14683, with bone handles. Per set, 6 knives and 6 forks, $1.15.

No. 14686. Double ring pattern Knives and Forks, cocobolo handles. Per set, 6 knives and 6 forks, 85c.
No. 14687. Same as No. 14686, with ebony handles. Per set, 6 knives and 6 forks, 95c.
No. 14688. Same as No. 14686, with bone handles. Per set, 6 knives and 6 forks, $1.20.

No. 14689. German style, cocobolo handles, Knives and Forks, sway back. Per set, 6 knives and 6 forks, 90c.
No. 14690. German style, same as No. 14689, ebony handle Knives and Forks, sway back. Per set, 6 knives and 6 forks, $1.00.

No. 14691. German style, bone handle Knives and Forks, sway back. Per set, 6 knives and 6 forks, $1.40.

No. 14692. Cross pattern, double bolstered, cocobolo handles, sway back Knives and Forks. Price per set, 6 knives and 6 forks, 95c.
No. 14693. Same as No. 14692, with ebony handles. Price per set, 6 knives and 6 forks, $1.05.
No. 14694. Same as No. 14692, with bone handles. Price per set, 6 knives and 6 forks, $1.50.

No. 14695. English pattern, double cross, bolstered, cocobolo handles, sway back Knives and Forks. Price per set, 6 knives and 6 forks, $1.25.
No. 14696. Same as No. 14695, with ebony handles. Price per set, 6 knives and 6 forks, $1.35.
No. 14697. Same as No. 14695, with bone handles. Price per set, 6 knives and 6 forks, $1.55.

No. 14698. Double bolster, sway back, cocobolo handles, Knives and Forks. Price per set, 6 knives and 6 forks, $1.20.
No. 14699. Same as No. 14698, with ebony handles. Price per set, 6 knives and 6 forks, $1.30.
No. 14700. Same as No. 14698, with bone handles. Price per set, 6 knives and 6 forks, $1.50.

No. 14701. French pattern bolster, cocobolo handle Knives and Forks. Price per set, 6 knives and 6 forks, $1.25.
No. 14702. Same as No. 14701, with ebony handles. Price per set, 6 knives and 6 forks, $1.35.

No. 14703. French pattern bolster, bone handle Knives and Forks. Price per set, 6 knives and 6 forks, $1.85.

No. 14704. Our latest style cross pattern, cocobolo handles, sway back. Price per set, 6 knives and 6 forks, $1.25.
No. 14705. Same as No. 14704, with ebony handles. Price per set, 6 knives and 6 forks, $1.35.
No. 14706. Same as No. 14704, with bone handles. Price per set, 6 knives and 6 forks, $1.85.

No. 14707. Swedish pattern bolster, cocobolo handles. Price per set, 6 knives and 6 forks, $1.75.
No. 14708. Same as No. 14707, with ebony handles. Price per set, 6 knives and 6 forks, $1.85.
No. 14709. Same as No. 14707, with bone handles. Price per set, 6 knives and 6 forks, $2.25.

No. 14710. Fancy double bolster, cocobolo handles, Knives and Forks, sway back. Per set, 6 knives and 6 forks, $1.70.
No. 14711. Same as No. 14710, with ebony handles. Per set, 6 knives and 6 forks, $1.90.
No. 14712. Same as No. 14710, with bone handles. Per set, 6 knives and 6 forks, $2.20.

**No. 14713.** Fancy double link bolster, cocobolo handles, Knives and Forks. Per set 6 knives and 6 forks, $1.65.

**No. 14714.** Same as No. 14713, with ebony handles. Per set 6 knives and 6 forks, $1.75.

**No. 14715.** Same as No. 14713, with bone handles. Per set 6 knives and 6 forks, $2.00.

**No. 14716.** Fancy shape blade, cocobolo handles, Knives and Forks, with fancy double bolster. Per set 6 knives and 6 forks, $1.65.

**No. 14717.** Same as No. 14716, with ebony handles. Per set 6 knives and 6 forks, $1.75.

**No. 14718.** Same as No. 14716, with bone handles. Per set 6 knives and 6 forks, $2.00.

**No. 14719.** Imitation stag handle, double bolster, Knives and Forks, sway back. Per set 6 knives and 6 forks, $1.75.

**No. 14729.** Hard rubber handles, Knives and Forks, medium blades. Per set 6 knives and 6 forks, $2.80.

**No. 14730.** Hard rubber handle, dessert Knives and Forks. Per set 6 knives and 6 forks, $2.50.

**No. 14731.** Hard rubber handles, Knives and Forks, medium blades. Per set 6 knives and 6 forks, $2.95.

**No. 14732.** Hard rubber handle, dessert Knives and Forks. Per set 6 knives and 6 forks, $2.65.

## CHILD'S SETS.

**No. 14737.** Child's Set, 1 knife and 1 fork, no bolster. A strong, well made set, best finish, cocobolo handle. Per set, 10c.

**No. 14738.** Child's Set, 1 knife and 1 fork, no bolster, bone handle. A set which will please any child. Per set, 14c.

**No. 14747.** Emery Knife Sharpener. A solid shaft of emery, secured in a handle by a steel rod extending the entire length. Each, 15c.

## CARVERS.

**No. 14748.** Celluloid handle Carvers. Blades of best steel, finely finished; a strong and neat design. Set consists of knife, fork and steel to match.

| Length of blade, inches, | 8 | 9 | 10 |
|---|---|---|---|
| Price, per set, | $2.30 | 2.50 | 2.65 |

**No. 14749.** Grained celluloid handle Carvers, with difficulty distinguished from ivory, which it will outlast. Blades of best steel, finely finished. Pair consists of knife and fork.

| Length of blade, inches, | 8 | 9 | 10 |
|---|---|---|---|
| Price, per pair, | $2.40 | 2.60 | 2.90 |
| Steel to match, extra, | .60 | .60 | .60 |

**No. 14750.** Celluloid handle Carvers, with German silver ferrule. A carver with best steel blade and every merit of beauty and finish. Pair consists of knife and fork.

| Length of blade, inches, | 8 | 9 | 10 |
|---|---|---|---|
| Price, per pair, | $2.85 | 3.15 | 3.45 |
| Steel to match, | .75 | .75 | .75 |

**No. 14756.** Stag handle Carver. Neat design, best steel blade, nickel plated capped end, finely finished, 9 inch blade. Pair consists of knife and fork. Price, per pair, $1.05; steel to match, 45c.

## BUTCHER KNIVES.

**No. 14760.** Cocobolo handle Butcher Knife, 6 inch steel blade, 3 rivets in handle. Price, each, 12c; per doz., $1.30.

**No. 14761.** Single bolster Butcher Knife, cocobolo handle, well riveted, 6 inch steel blade. Price, each, 28c.

**No. 14762.** Double bolster, cocobolo handle, Butcher Knife, 6 inch steel blade. Price, each, 20c; per doz., $2.15.

**No. 14763.** Butcher Knife, cocobolo handle, single bolstered and strongly riveted, best steel blade.

| Length of blade, inches, | 6 | 7 | 8 | 9 | 10 | 12 | 14 |
|---|---|---|---|---|---|---|---|
| Price, each, | $0.25 | .30 | .40 | .50 | .60 | .80 | 1.05 |

## GENUINE WILSON'S BUTCHER KNIVES.—Stamped I. Wilson.

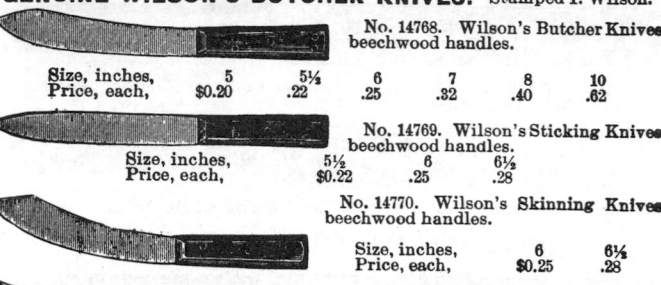

**No. 14768.** Wilson's Butcher Knives, beechwood handles.

| Size, inches, | 5 | 5½ | 6 | 7 | 8 | 10 |
|---|---|---|---|---|---|---|
| Price, each, | $0.20 | .22 | .25 | .32 | .40 | .62 |

**No. 14769.** Wilson's Sticking Knives, beechwood handles.

| Size, inches, | 5½ | 6 | 6½ |
|---|---|---|---|
| Price, each, | $0.22 | .25 | .28 |

**No. 14770.** Wilson's Skinning Knives, beechwood handles.

| Size, inches, | 6 | 6½ |
|---|---|---|
| Price, each, | $0.25 | .28 |

**No. 14771.** Wilson's latest pattern Boomerang Steak Knife. Beechwood handle.

| Blade, inches, | 10 | 11 | 12 |
|---|---|---|---|
| Price, each, | $0.65 | .80 | .95 |

## BUTCHERS' STEEL.

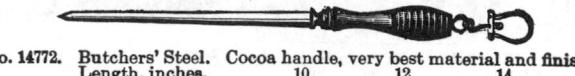

**No. 14772.** Butchers' Steel. Cocoa handle, very best material and finish.

| Length, inches, | 10 | 12 | 14 |
|---|---|---|---|
| Price, each, | $0.75 | .95 | 1.10 |

**No. 14773.** Butchers' Steel. Stag handle, finest quality, best finish. Length, 12 inches; price, $1.

## BREAD KNIVES.

**No. 14776.** Bread Knife. Cocobolo handle, best steel blade, finely finished. Each, 25c; per doz., $2.60.

**No. 14777.** Bread Knife. Polished steel blade, firmly set in hardwood handle. Each, 12c; per doz., $1.25.

## CRISTY PATTERN KNIFE SETS.

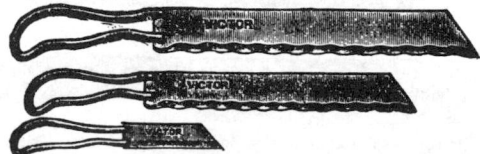

**No. 14778.** No crumbling. No grumbling. There are others but none so keen. Every blade warranted to be made of the best crucible steel, every one a cutter. Bread, Cake and Paring Knife. Per set of 3 knives, 25c; per doz. sets, $2.70.

**No. 14782.** Wire Handled Carving Sets. Blade of best steel firmly fastened to the handle. An excellent set for carving meats of all kinds. Per set, 30c; per doz. sets, $3.35.

## KITCHEN KNIVES.

**No. 14783.** Wood handle Paring Knife. Blade of best steel. Each, 8c; per doz., 80c.

**No. 14786.** Shoe Knife. Best steel blade, square point, brass ferrule, hardwood handle. Each, 10c; per doz., $1.10.

## PUTTY KNIVES.

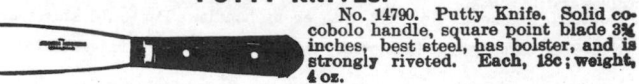

**No. 14790.** Putty Knife. Solid cocobolo handle, square point blade 3¼ inches, best steel, has bolster, and is strongly riveted. Each, 18c; weight, 4 oz.

## SHEARS AND SCISSORS.

We handle only the best quality of goods in this line and invite comparisons as to durability and workmanship. Weights vary from 3 to 20 ounces. Postage is 1 cent per ounce. All these goods go by express C. O. D., subject to examination, on receipt of $1.00; balance and express charges payable at express office. 3% discount for cash in full with order.

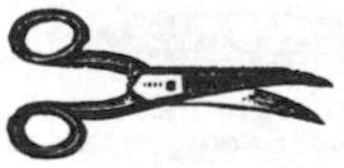

**No. 14796 Nail Scissors** for trimming nails on both hands and feet. Best cast steel, highly tempered, nickel plated, 4 inches. Each.............................**40c**

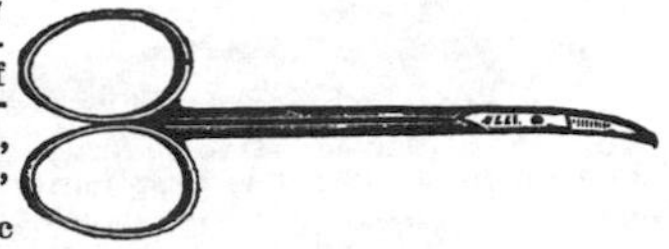

**No. 14797 Manicure Scissors,** made of best steel, highly tempered, nickel plated, curved ends. Each........**50c**

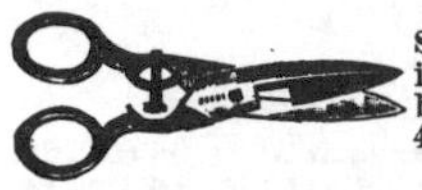

**No. 14798 Buttonhole Scissors,** nickel plated, with inside set screws to adjust blades for cutting, best steel, 4½ inches. Each.........**45c**

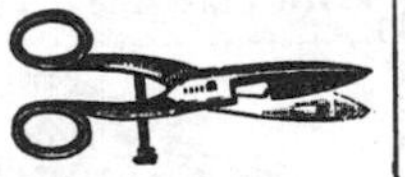

**No. 14799 Buttonhole Scissors,** with adjustable thumb screw, highly polished, fully warranted. Each...**33c**

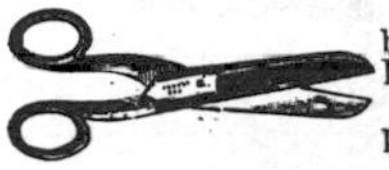

**No. 14803 Pocket Scissors,** best steel, polished, 4 inches. Each, 30c; 4½ inches.......**35c**

**No. 14804 Pocket Scissors,** polished, 4 inches. Each..**20c**

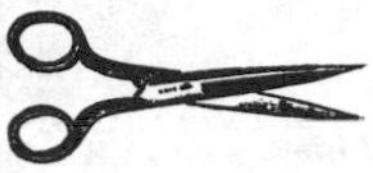

**No. 14805 Ladies' Scissors,** best steel, nickel plated, 4½ inches, each, 30c; 5 inches.**35c**

**No. 14806 Ladies' Scissors,** polished. 4½ inches. Each.**20c**

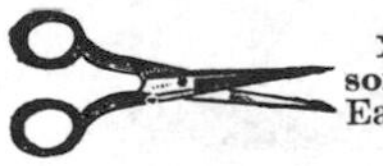

**No. 14807 Embroidery Scissors,** best steel, nickel plated. Each.........................**30c**

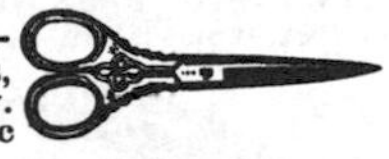

**No. 14808 Fancy Embroidery Scissors,** nickeled blades, gilt handles, best quality. Each......................**35c**

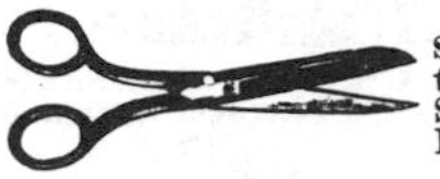

**No. 14809 Nickel Plated Scissors,** all steel blades of the best quality and finish.

| Size, inches | 4½ | 5 | 6 | 7 |
|---|---|---|---|---|
| Price, eaeh | $0.30 | .40 | .45 | .53 |

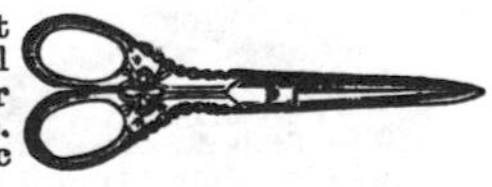

**No. 14810 Fancy Gilt Handle Scissors,** nickel plated blades, superior qaality and finish. Price, 5 inch, 35c; 6 inch....**38c**

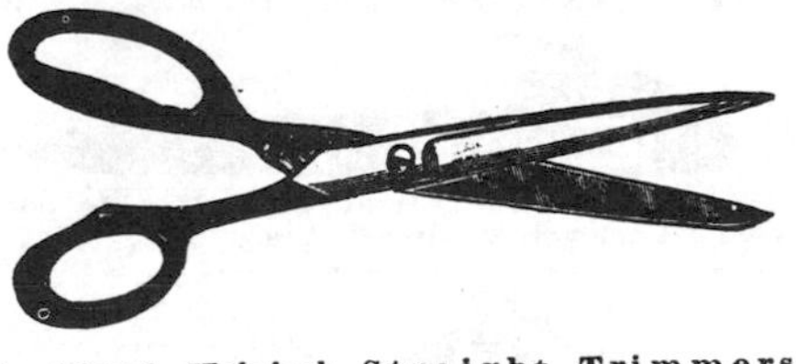

**No. 14816 Heinisch Straight Trimmers,** japanned haudles, finest laid steel blades. Fully warranted.

| Size, inches | 6 | 7 | 8 | 9 | 10 |
|---|---|---|---|---|---|
| Price, each | $0.35 | .38 | .42 | .48 | .70 |

**No. 14817 Straight Trimmers,** japanned handles. First class wearing quality.

| Size, inches | 6 | 7 | 8 |
|---|---|---|---|
| Price, each | $0.25 | .29 | .42 |

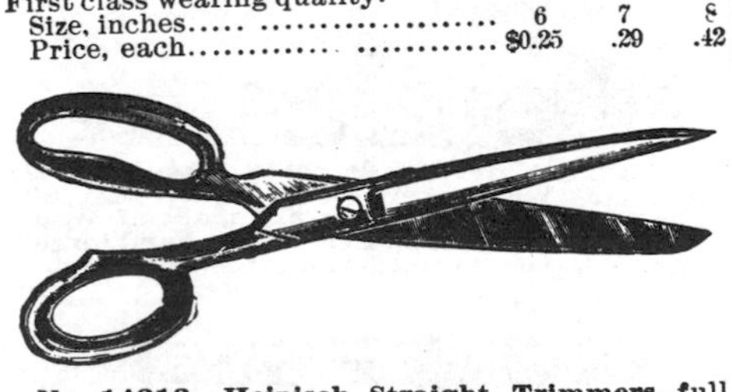

**No. 14818 Heinisch Straight Trimmers,** full nickel plated, fully warranted.

| Size, inches | 6 | 6½ | 7 | 7½ | 8 | 8½ | 9 |
|---|---|---|---|---|---|---|---|
| Price, each | $0.44 | .50 | .55 | 60 | .65 | .70 | .75 |

**No. 14819 Straight Trimmers,** nickel plated. Good wearing quality.

| Size, inches | 6 | 7 | 8 |
|---|---|---|---|
| Price, each | $0.35 | .38 | .42 |

**No. 14820 Left Hand Straight Trimmers,** nickel plated. Size, 8½ inches. Price, each.........**$1.00**

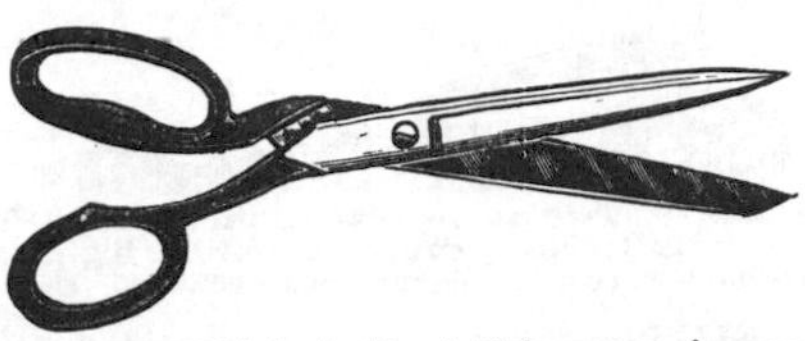

**No. 14821 Heinisch Bent Trimmers,** japanned handles, finest quality, Fully warranted.

| Size, inchcs | 8 | 9 | 10 | 12 |
|---|---|---|---|---|
| Price, each | $0.55 | .70 | .85 | 1.05 |

**No. 14822 Bent Trimmers,** japanned handles, good quality. Size, 10 inches. Price, each......**55c**

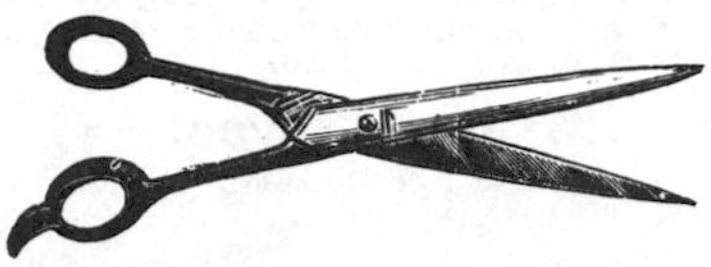

**No. 14825 Heinisch Barbers' Shears,** japanned handles. Best steel, warranted. Size, 8 inches. Price, each...............................**50c**

**No. 14826 Full Nickel Plated Barbers' Shears,** best quality, every pair warranted. Size, 8½ inches. Price, each...............................**65c**

**No. 14827 Left Hand Barbers' Shears,** best grade blades, japanned handles. Size, 9 inches. Price, each...............................**80c**

## Scissors Sharpener.

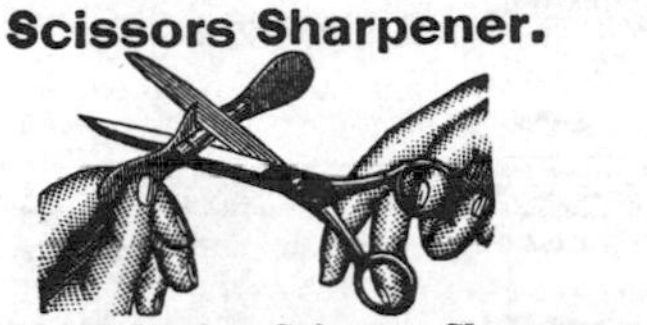

**No. 14832 Lightning Scissors Sharpener.** The only perfect scissors sharpener made. Will sharpen a pair of shears and scissors in ten seconds. Made of hardest steel. Finely finished and nickle plated. Price, each...............................**15c**

## Tracing Wheels.

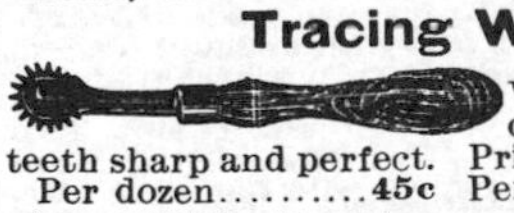

**No. 14833 Tracing Wheel,** hardwood handle, blue steel wheel, teeth sharp and perfect. Price, each..........**$0.05**
Per dozen..........**45c** Per gross............ **4.50**

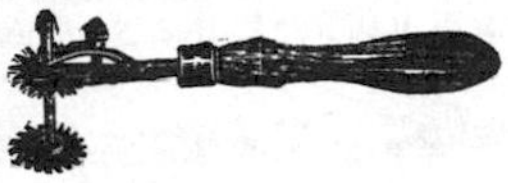

**No. 14834 Double Adjustable Tracing Wheel,** with set screw, enameled handle. Price, each, 10c; per dz., 95c; per gross, **$10**

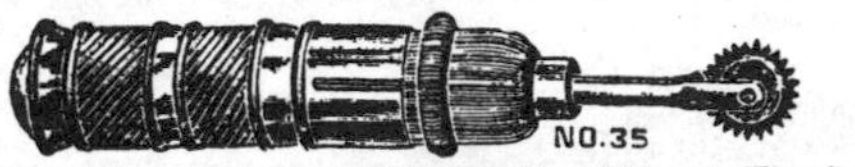


**No. 14835 Metal Handle Tracing Wheel.** Finely nickel plated and finished. Made reversible, so when not in use the wheel is entirely inclosed in handle. When lying in a work basket will not injure or become entangled with other articles. Price, each..... ....**10c** Per doz.......... ....**95c**

## POCKET CUTLERY.

For cutting quality, durability and finish our line of pocket cutlery has been selected with a view to meeting the wants of our customers. Our patterns are the latest, **w2rranted knives.** All knives which we warrant are guaranteed to be free from flaws and not too soft, and if found otherwise cau be returned at our expense and exchanged or money refunded. No knife can be returned, however, except it is clean and shows no evidence of abuse. A broken blade must show signs of flaw in the steel or will not be replaced. In this line also we save our customers from 25 to 75 per cent. on retail prices.

## Boys' Pocket Knives.

Postage, 4c extra.

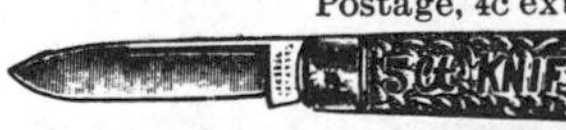


**No. 14842 Metal Handle Knife,** 1 blade, iron lined; a clipper; 2¾ inches. Each...............................**4c**

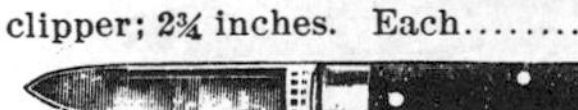

**No. 14843 Ebony Handle Knife,** 1 blade, iron lined; a good, strong knife, 2⅝ incher. Each......**7c**

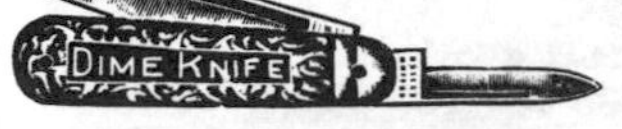


**No. 14844 Metal Handle Boys' Knife,** 2 blades, iron lined and capped, 2⅞ inches. Each..**8c**

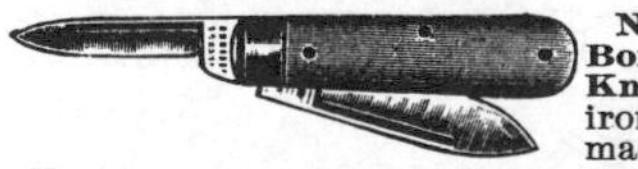

**No. 14845 White Bone Handle Jack Knife,** 2 blades, iron lined; a well made knife, 2¾ ins. Each...............................**12c**

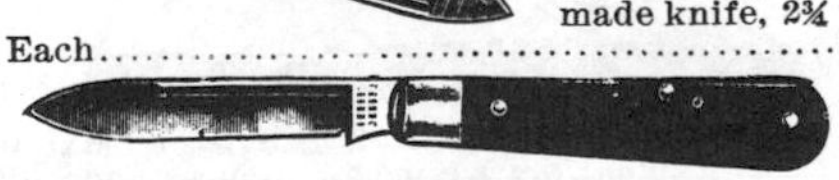

**No. 14846 Rosewood Handle Knife,** 1 blade, iron lined; a good knife, 3⅜ inches. Each.......**15c**

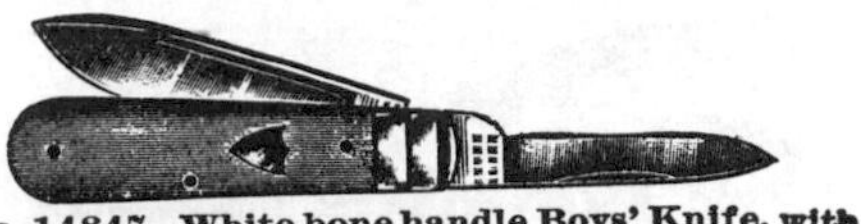

**No. 14847 White bone handle Boys' Knife, with** bolster. Two blades, iron lined, 3½ inches. Each...............................**18c**

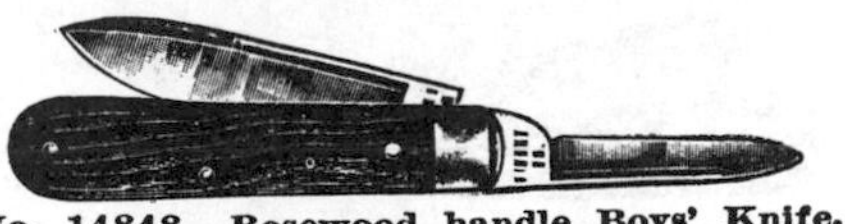

**No. 14848 Rosewood handle Boys' Knife, 2** blades, iron lined; a keen cutter, 3½ inches. Each...............................**25c**

## Men's Jack Knives.

**Postage, 5c extra.**

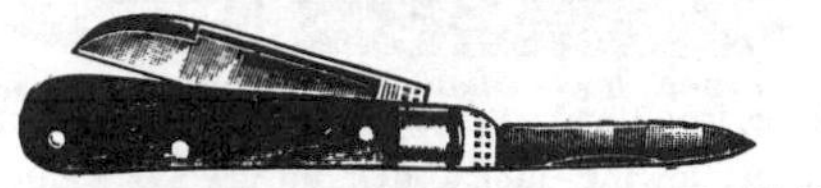

**No. 14854 Two blade, Rosewood Handle Knife,** ir n lined; a serviceable knife, 3¼ inches. Each...... ........ **17c**

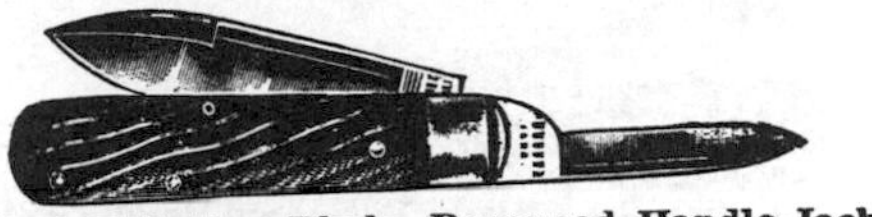

**No. 14855 Two Blade, Rosewood Handle Jack Knife,** iron lined, 3½ inches. Each..............**20c**

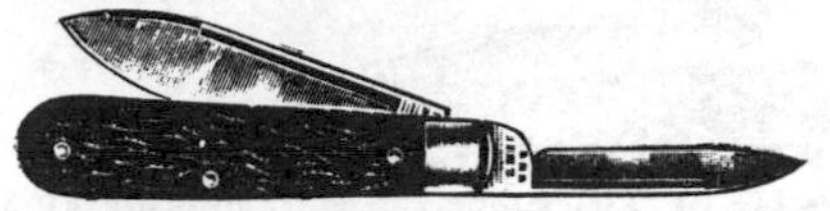

**No. 14856 Two Blade. Stag Handle Jack Knife,** iron lined, 3½ inches. Each.. ......................**22c**

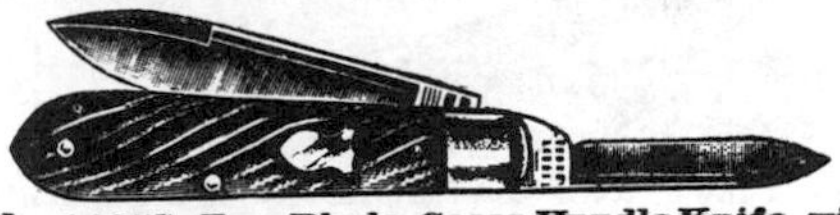

**No. 14857 Two Blade, Cocoa Handle Knife,** with bolster, iron lined, 3½ inches. Each.............**25c**

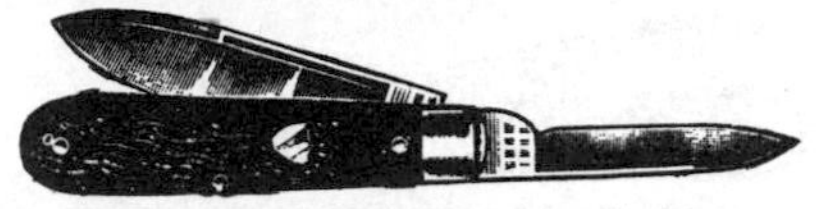

**No. 14858 Two Blade, Stag Handle Knife,** with bolster, brass lined, 3⅜ inches. Each............**25c**

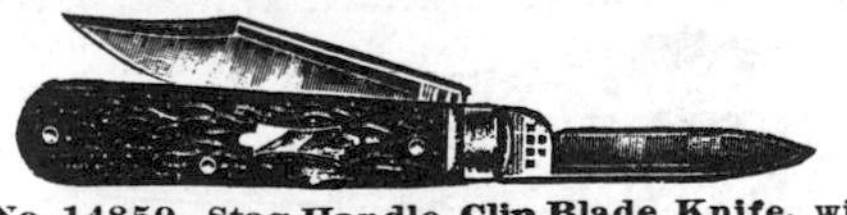

**No. 14859 Stag Handle, Clip Blade Knife,** with bolster, iron lined. 3⅜ inches. Each.............**25c**

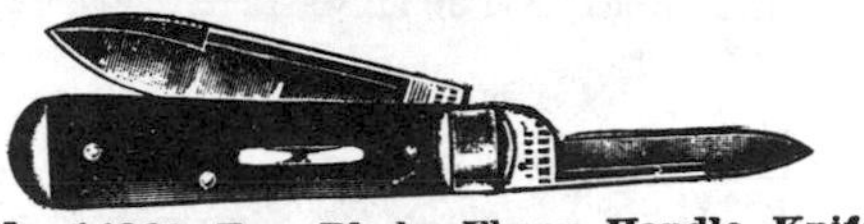

**No. 14860 Two Blade, Ebony Handle Knife,** with elongated bolstes, iron lined, 3½ inches. Each...............................**30c**

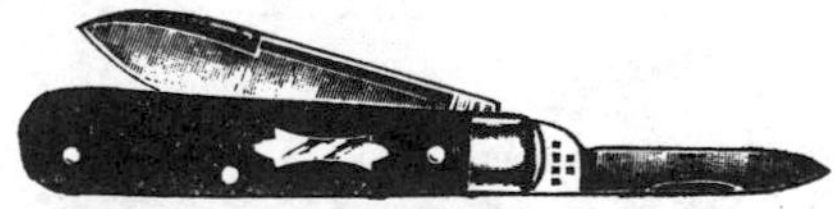

**No. 14861 Two Blade, Ebony Handle Knife,** with bolster, iron lined; a large knife, 4 inches. Each...............................**30c**

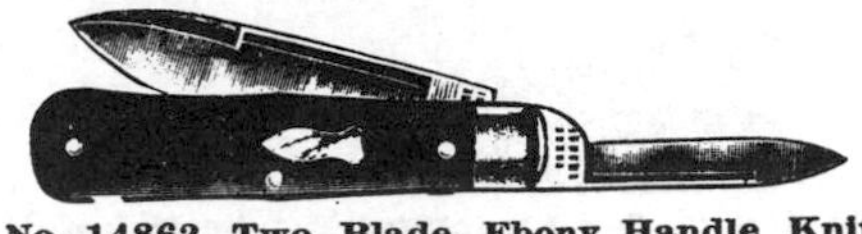

**No. 14862 Two Blade, Ebony Handle Knife,** with bolster, iron lined; a popular knife, 2¾ inches. Each...............................**32c**

**There is a Good Reason to Expect More Orders.**

OAKFORD, MENARD CO., ILL.

SEARS, ROEBUCK & CO.,

DEAR SIRS:—The gnn came to hand all O. K. and it is so much better than I expected I am well pleaeed with it; you may expect more orders from me before long. Yours respectfully,

W. O. EMERSON.

**DON'T FORGET TO GIVE EVERY NECESSARY BIT OF INFORMATION REGARDING ARTICLES WANTED. STATE NAME, PAGE IN CATALOGUE, ARTICLE NUMBER. ALWAYS GIVE SIZES, COLORS, ETC., WHEREVER NECESSARY.**

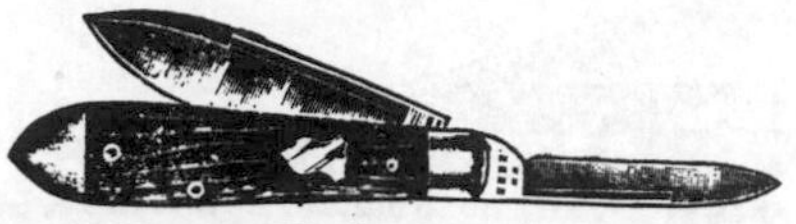

**No. 14863 Two Blade, Cocoa Handle,** iron lined, capped end; a durable knife, 3½ inches. Each, 33c

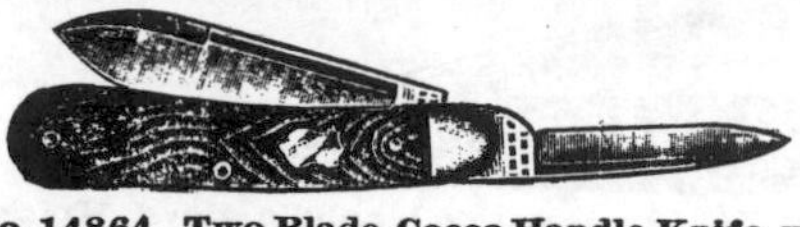

**No. 14864 Two Blade, Cocoa Handle Knife,** with bolster, iron lined, 3¾ inches. Each.............35c

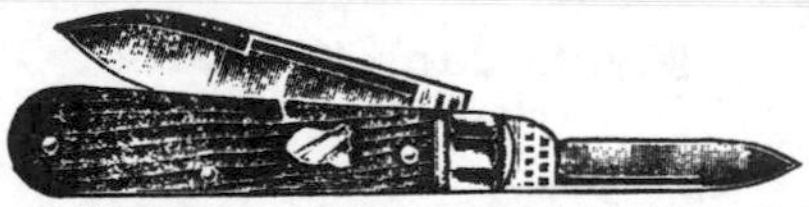

**No. 14865 Two Blade, Rosewood Handle,** with bolster, iron lined, 3⅝ inches. Each.............35c

**The following men's jack knives are made of Wardlow's fine English steel, every blade hand forged, finely tempered, finished, and fully warranted.**

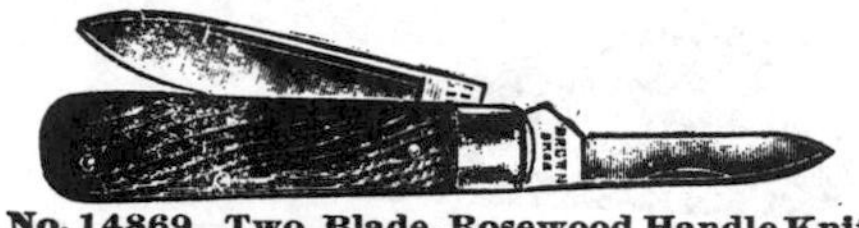

**No. 14869 Two Blade, Rosewood Handle Knife,** iron lined; a leader, 3¼ inches, warranted. Each, 25c

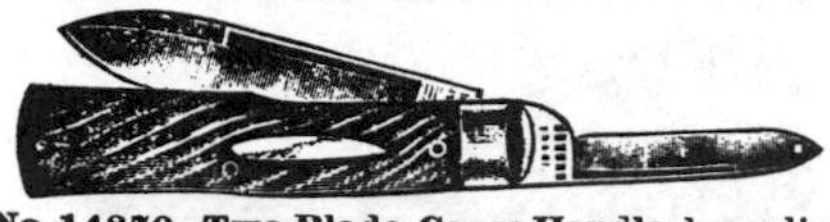

**No. 14870 Two Blade, Cocoa Handle,** brass lined, latest pattern, 3⅝ inches, warranted. Each.....40c

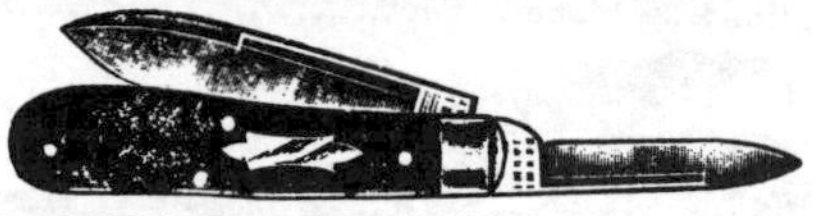

**No. 14871 Two Bladed, Ebony Handle Knife,** with shield, brass lined, warranted; best steel, 3¾ inches. Each..........................................40c

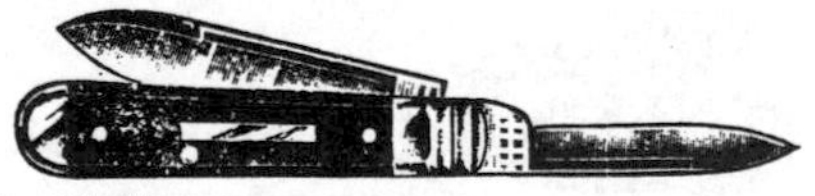

**No. 14872 Two Blade, Ebony Handle,** German silver bolster and capped, brass lined, 3½ inches, warranted. Each...................................45c

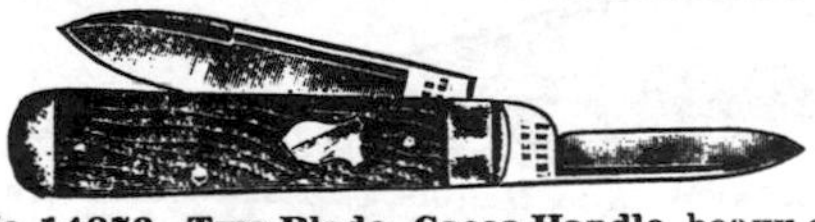

**No. 14873 Two Blade, Cocoa Handle,** heavy cap and bolster, brass lined, 3⅝ in., warranted. Each, 45c

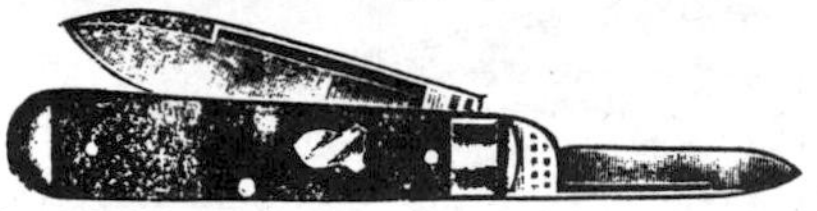

**No. 14874 Two Blade, Gray Buffalo Handle Knife,** bolster and cap, brass lined, 3⅝ inches, warranted. Each...................................55c

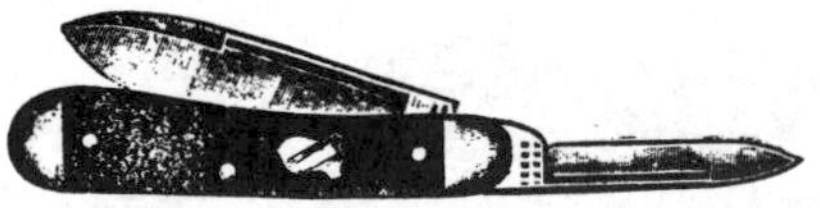

**No. 14875 Two Blade, Ebony Handle Knife,** with bolster and heavily tipped, brass liued, 3¾ inches, warranted. Each...........................60c

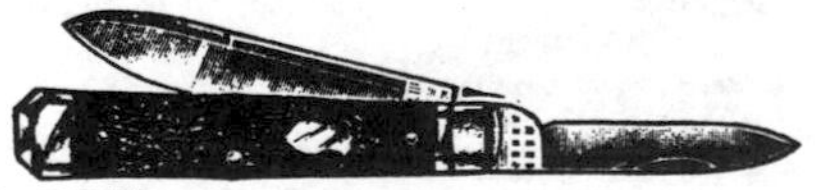

**No. 14876 Two Blade, Stag Handle Jack Knife,** German silver tipped and bolster, brass lined, 3⅝ inches, warranted. Each...........................60c

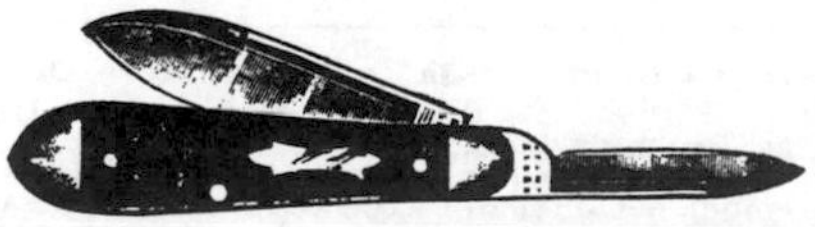

**No. 14877 Two Blade, Ebony Handle Knife,** brass lined, heavy cap and bolster, 3¾ inches; a decided leader, warranted. Each.........................60c

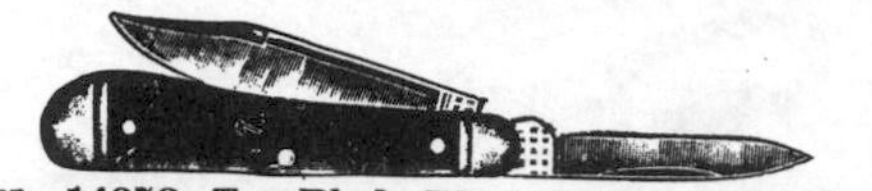

**No. 14878 Two Blade, Black Buffalo Horn Handle Jack Knife,** heavy cap, brass lined; a high grade knife n every respect, 3½ inches, warranted. Ea..65c

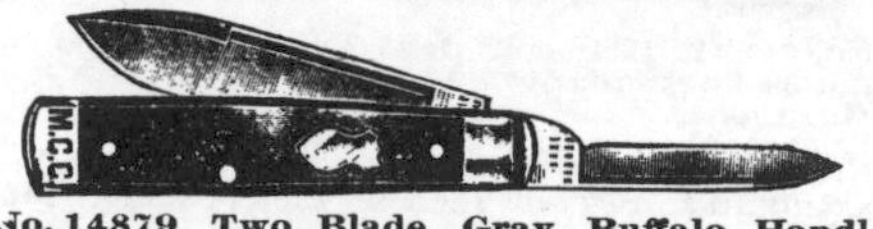

**No. 14879 Two Blade, Gray Buffalo Handle Knife,** brass lined cap and bolster, best material and finish, 3⅝ inches warranted. Each..........65c

## Ladies' Knives.

**Postage, 3c each.**

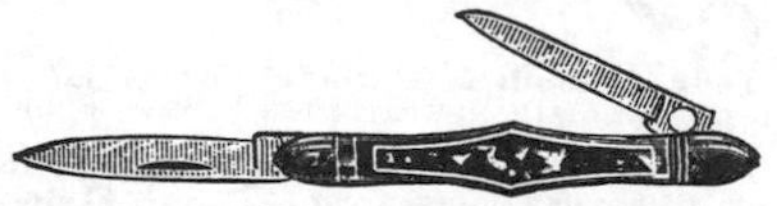

**No. 14884 Two Blade, Novelty Bolster, Ladies' Knife,** shell handle, strong pinned. Each.......12c

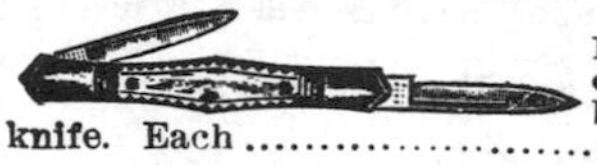

**No. 14885 Two Blade, Pearl Handle Ladies' Knife,** brass lined; a pretty knife. Each.............................................16c

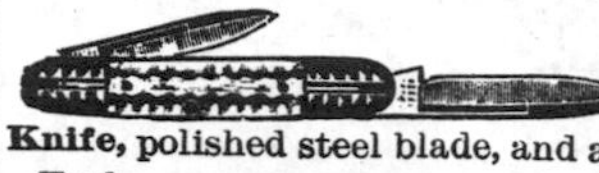

**No. 14886 Two Blade, Corrugated Pearl Handle Ladies' Knife,** polished steel blade, and a beauty, 2¾ inches. Each.............................................20c

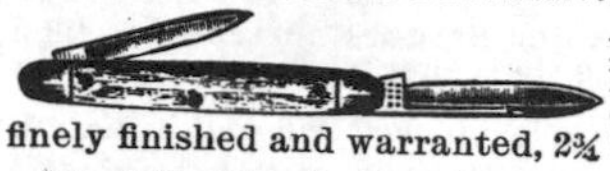

**No. 14887 Two Blade, Ladies' Knife,** pearl handle, brass lined, finely finished and warranted, 2¾ inches. Each, 35c

**The following Ladies' Knives are made of Wardlow's fine English steel, every blade hand forged, finely tempered, finished and fully warranted.**

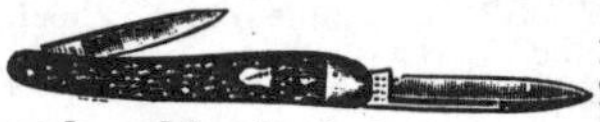

**No. 14892 Two Blade Stag Handle Ladies' Knife,** brass lined; a well made and fine knife, 2⅝ inches, warranted. Each, 35c

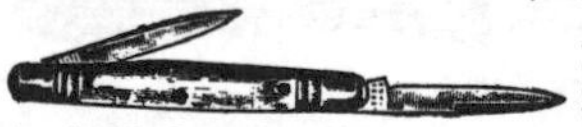

**No. 14893 Two Blade Pearl Handle Ladies' Knife,** brass lined; best steel blades, a favorite pattern, 2½ inches, warranted. Each.....................................40c

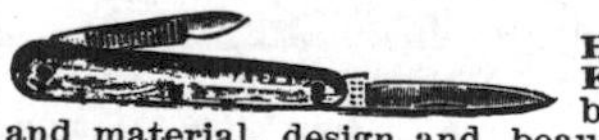

**No. 14894 Pearl Handle Ladies' Knife,** with nail blade; best finish and material, design and beauty unexcelled, 2⅛ inches, warranted. Each...........................46c

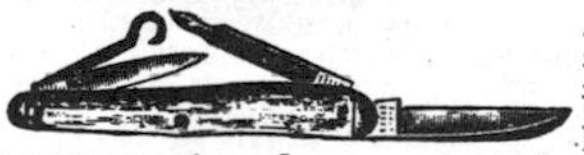

**No. 14895 Three Blade Ladies' Pocket Knife,** with button hook, pearl handle, brass lined, a very neat and convenient knife, 2¾ inches, warranted. Each...............................$1.00

## Men's Pen Knives.

**Postage, 5c extra.**

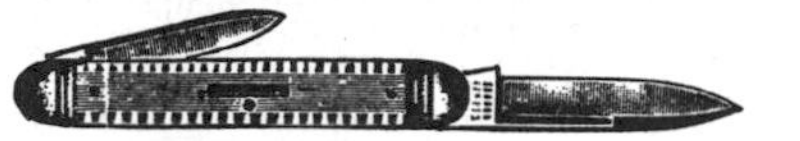

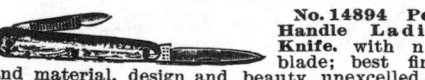

**No. 14899 Two Blade White Bone Handle Pen Knife,** brass lined, well finished, 3⅜ inches. Each, 25c

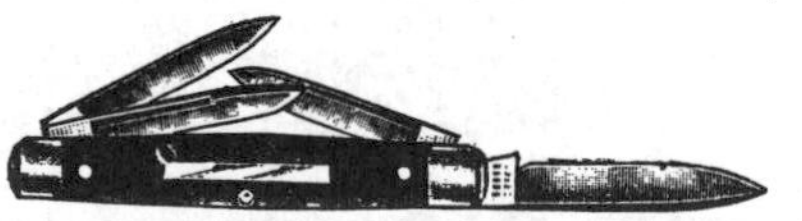

**No. 14900 Four Blade Ebony Handle Pen Knife,** elongated shield, brass lined, 3½ inches; a neat knife. Each......................................25c

**No. 14901 Same as No. 14900,** with stag handle. Each.............................................25c

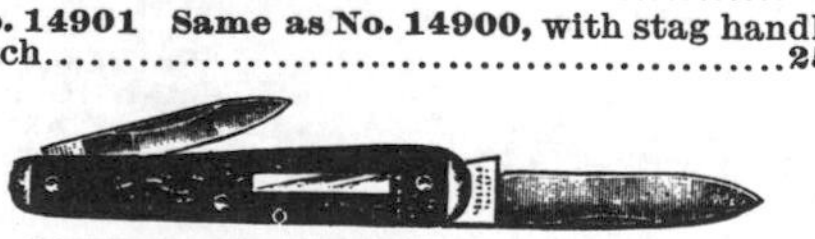

**No. 14901½ Two Blade Stag Hanfile Pen Knife,** with shield, brass lined, 3⅜ inches. Each........27c

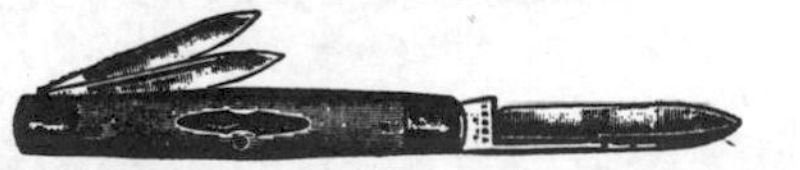

**No. 14902 Three Blade White Bone Handle Knife,** with shield, brass lined, 3½ inches. Each, 30c

**No. 14903 Same as No. 14902,** with stag handle. Each.............................................30c

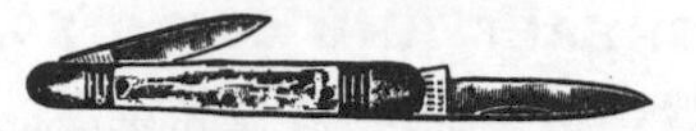

**No. 14904 Two Blade Pearl Handle Pen Knife,** fancy capped, brass lined, good material, 3 inches. Each.................................................35c

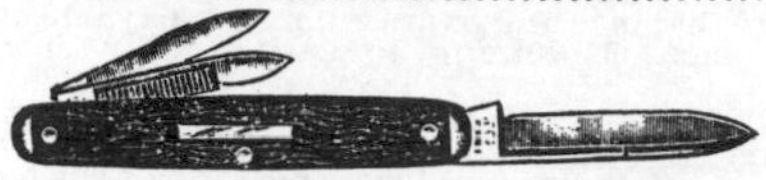

**No. 14905 Three Blade Stag Handle Pen Knife,** with shield, brass lined, 3½ inches. Each........40c

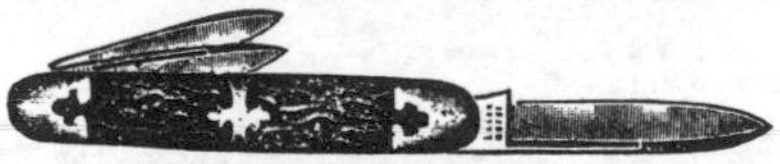

**No. 14906 Three Blade Stag Handle Knife,** fancy shield and capped; best material, 3½ inches. Each.................................................40c

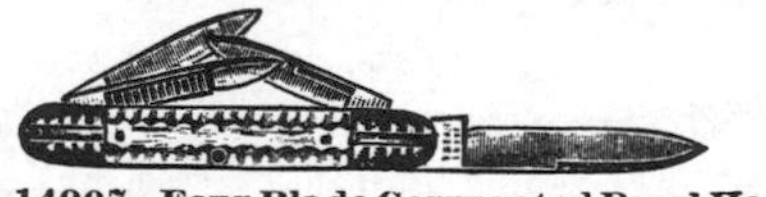

**No. 14907 Four Blade Corrugated Pearl Handle Knife,** brass lined; a serviceable article, 3⅛ inches. Each.................................................45c

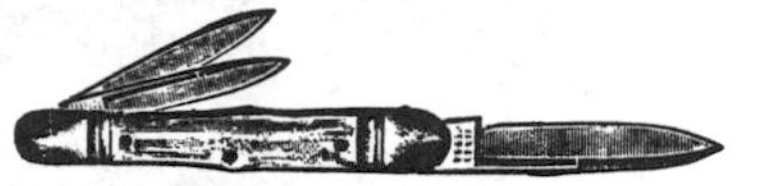

**No. 14908 Three Blade, Pearl Handle, Brass Lined Pen Knife,** 3¼ inches. Each..............45c

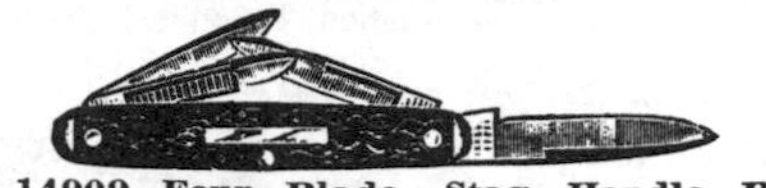

**No. 14909 Four Blade, Stag Handle, Brass Lined, a Neat Knife,** 3⅝ inches. Each........50c

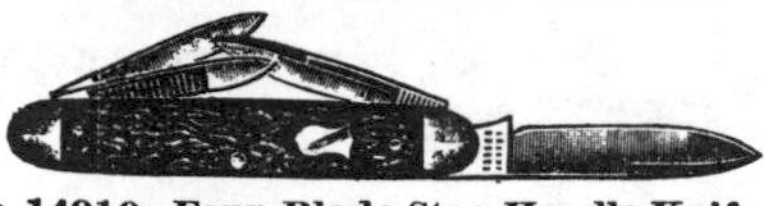

**No. 14910 Four Blade Stag Handle Knife** with bolster, brass lined, best finish, 3⅝ inches. Each 50c

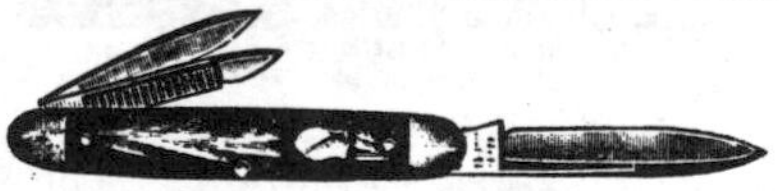

**No. 14911 Three Blade Gray Buffalo Handle Hnife** with bblster, brass lined, 3⅝ inches. Each 50c

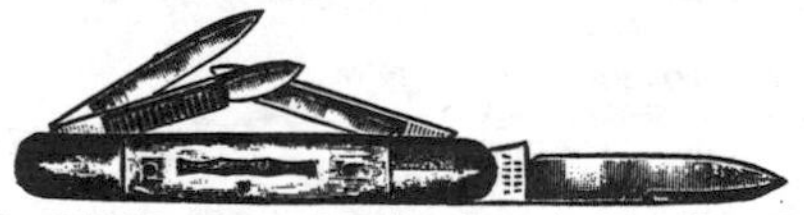

**No. 14912 Four Blade, Pearl Handle Knife,** with shield, brass lined, 3⅝ inches. Each........55c

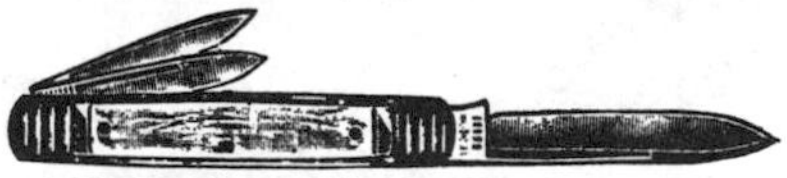

**No. 14913 Three Blade, Pearl Handle,** corrugated, German silver tipped, brass lined, 3¼ inches. Each.................................................60c

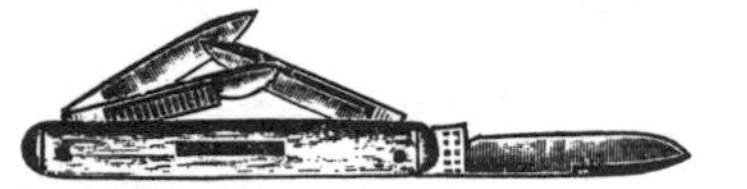

**No. 14914 Four Blade, Pearl Handle Pen Knife,** elongated shield, brass lined, 3⅜ inches. Each, 70c

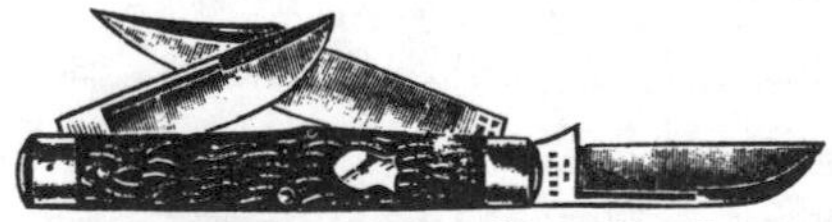

**No. 14916 Three Blade, Stag Handle, Cattle Knife,** brass lined, superior finish, 3¾ in. Each, 80c

**The following Pen Knives are made of Wardlow's fine English Steel, Every blade hand forged, finely tempered, finished and fully warranted.**

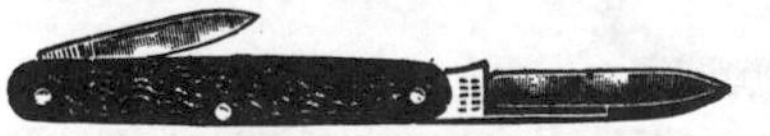

**No, 14918 Two Blade, Stag Handle, Pen Knife,** brass lined, our leading leader, 3¼ inches, warranted. Each.................................................25c

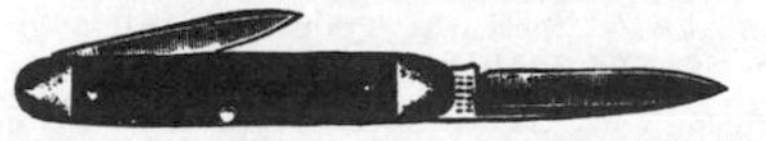

**No. 14919 TwoBlade, Ebony Handle Pen Knife,** brass lined, 3¼ inches, warranted. Each.........40c

**WHERE YOU FIND IT CONVENIENT TO SEND FULL CASH WITH YOUR ORDER, YOU CAN TAKE ADVANTAGE OF OUR 3 PER CENT CASH DISCOUNT AND ALSO SAVE THE ANNOYANCE OF C. O. D'S. WE POSITIVELY GUARANTEE SATISFACTION IN ALL CASES.**

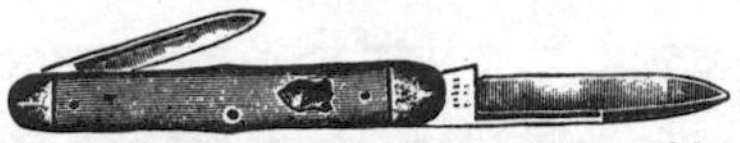

No. 14920. Two crocus polished blades, white bone handle Pen Knife, brass lined, best finish, best material, fully warranted, 3 inches. Each, 45c.

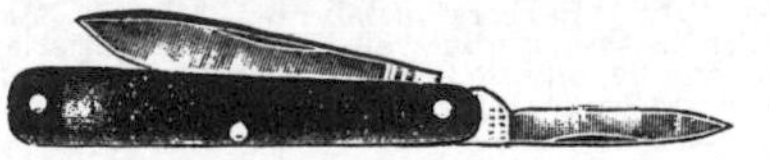

No. 14921. Two crocus polished blades, gray buffalo handle Knife, brass lined, fully warranted, 3⅜ inches. Each, 45c.

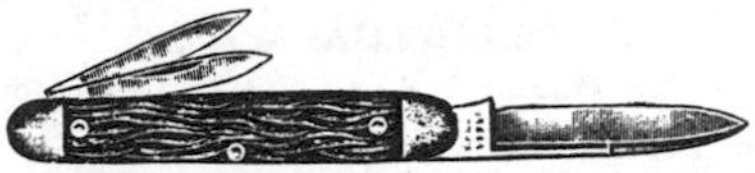

No. 14922. Three blade, stag handle Knife, brass lined, best steel blade and finish, 3⅜ inches, warranted. Each, 60c.

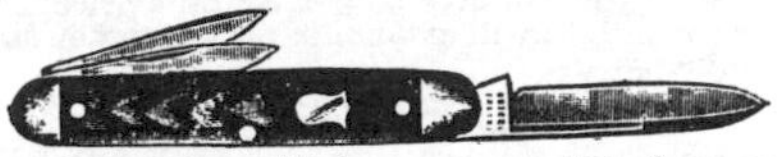

No. 14923. Three blade, crocus polished, gray buffalo horn handle Knife with bolster, brass lined, 3⅜ inches, warranted. Each, 75c.

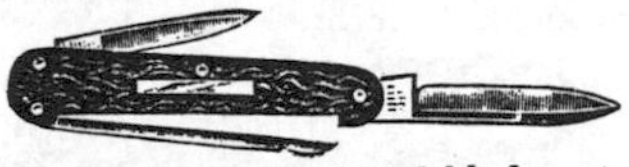

No. 14924. Two crocus polished blades, stag handle, with file on back, a neat pocket Knife, brass lined, fully warranted, 2¾ inches. Each, 80c.

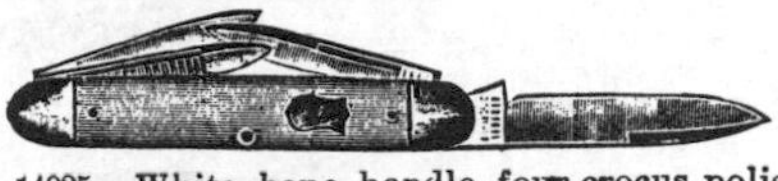

No. 14925. White bone handle, four crocus polished blades, with file blade, bolstered, brass lined, fully warranted, 3⅜ inches. Each, 85c.

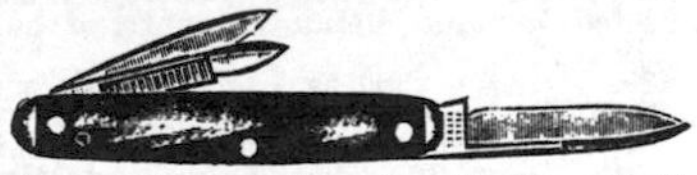

No. 14926. Gray buffalo handle Pen Knife, three blades, crocus polished, brass lined, fully warranted, 3 inches. Each, 85c.

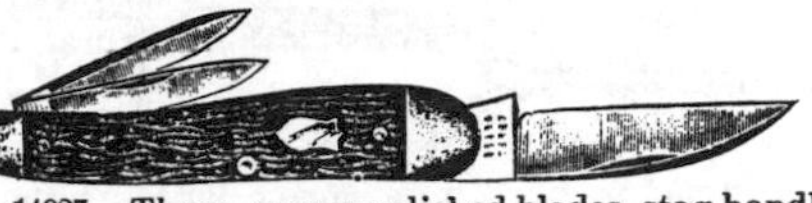

No. 14927. Three crocus polished blades, stag handle, heavy Pen Knife, with bolster, brass lined, fully warranted, 3¾ inches. Each, 90c.

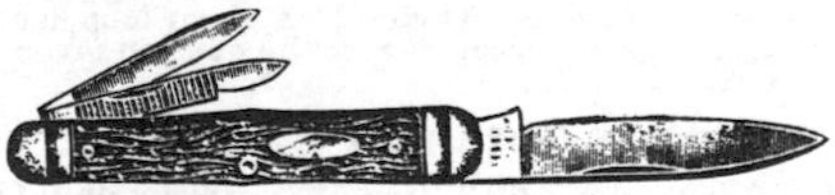

No. 14928. Three blade, stag handle Pen Knife, brass lined, warranted best material and finish, 3⅝ inches. Each, 90c.

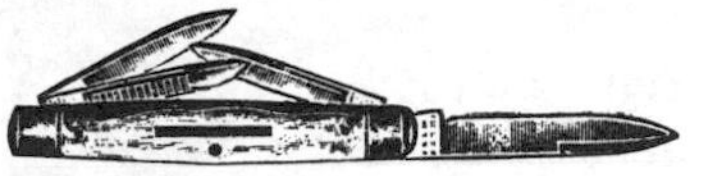

No. 14929. Four crocus polished blades, fine pearl handle Knife, German silver, tipped, brass lined, fully warranted, 3 inches. Each, 90c.

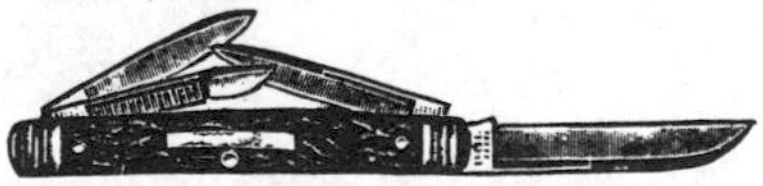

No. 14930. Four crocus polished blades, stag handle, congress Knife, brass lined, one of the neatest and best Pen Knives made, fully warranted, 3¼ inches. Each, $1.

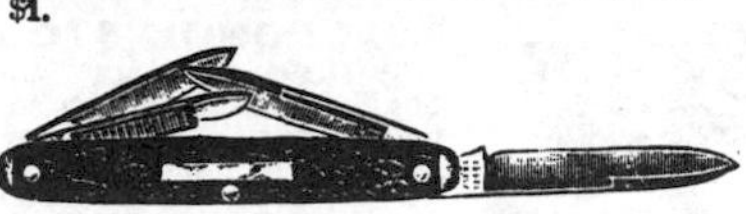

No. 14931. Stag handle Pen Knife with elongated shield, four crocus polished blades, brass lined, fully warranted, 3 inches. Each, $1.

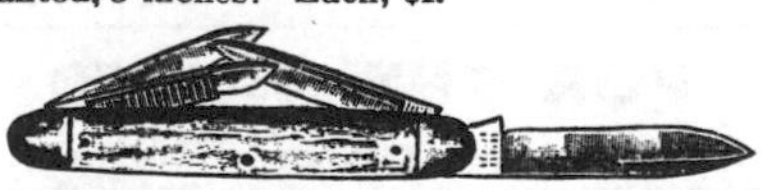

No. 14932. Four blade, fine pearl handle Pen Knife, brass lined, fully warranted, a neat and popular pattern, 3¼ inches. Each, $1.

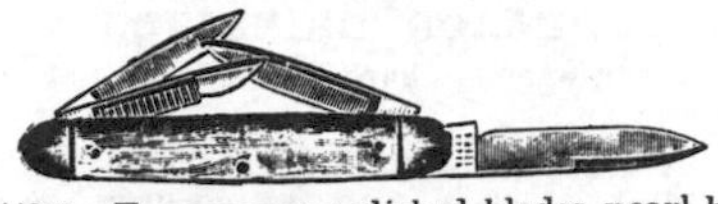

No. 14933. Four crocus polished blades, pearl handle Knife, brass lined, a well finished and neat pattern, fully warranted, 3 inches. Each, $1.

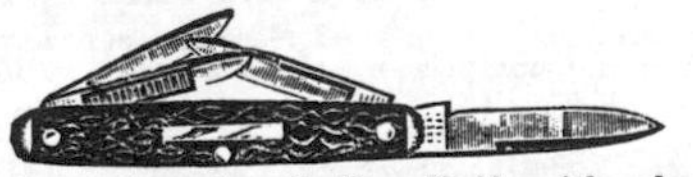

No. 14934. Stag handle Pen Knife with elongated shield, four crocus polished blades, brass lined, one of our best sellers, fully warranted, 3½ inches. Each, $1.20.

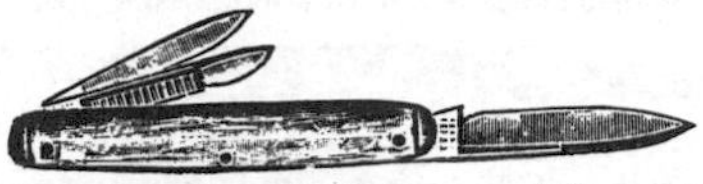

No. 14935. Pearl handle Knife, one of the neatest and most popular patterns made, three crocus polished blades, brass lined, fully warranted, 3 inches. Each, $1.40.

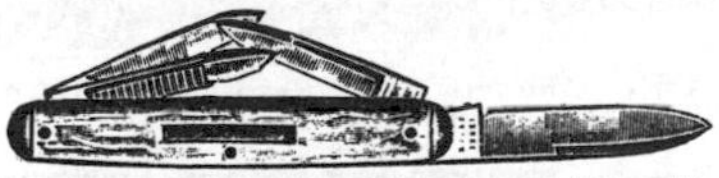

No. 14936. Our best Pen Knife, pearl handle with elongated shield, four fine crocus polished blades, brass lined, a prevalent pattern, fully warranted, 3⅛ inches, Each, $1.50.

## KNIFE HONE.

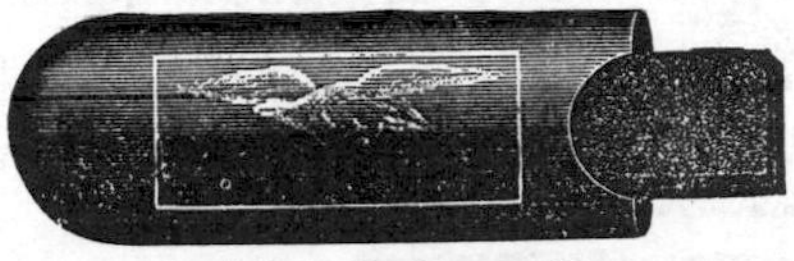

No. 14945. Pocket knife Hone. Why carry a dull knife? A fine emery knife hone in leather case. Each, 25c.

## KNIFE POCKETS.

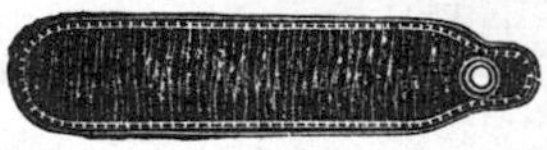

No. 14946. A good knife well kept will satisfy the owner. Leather Knife Pockets. Each, 8c.

## HAIR CLIPPERS.

We aim to carry a line of clippers from which can be made a selection either for family or for barbers' use. These goods are warranted to be fully up to descriptions, and if found in any way defective can be returned at our expense and exchanged or money refunded. Our liberal C. O. D. terms apply on these goods. Sent to any address C. O. D., subject to examination, on receipt of $1, balance and express charges payable at express office; 3 per cent. discount for cash in full with order.

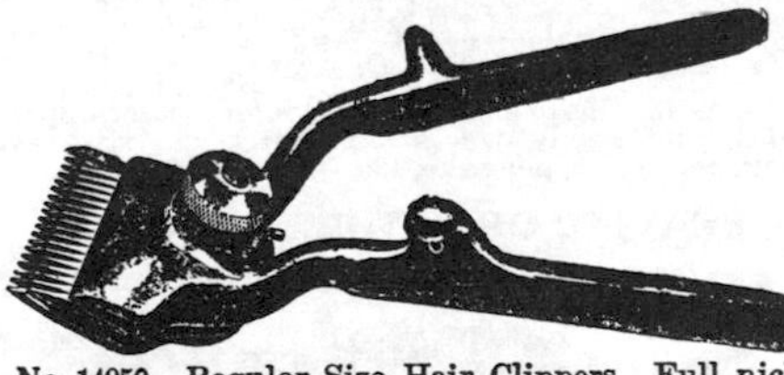

No. 14950. Regular Size Hair Clippers. Full nickel plated, best cast steel jaws, finely tempered and finished true, a wonderfully handy and economical clipper for family use. Per pair, $1.00.

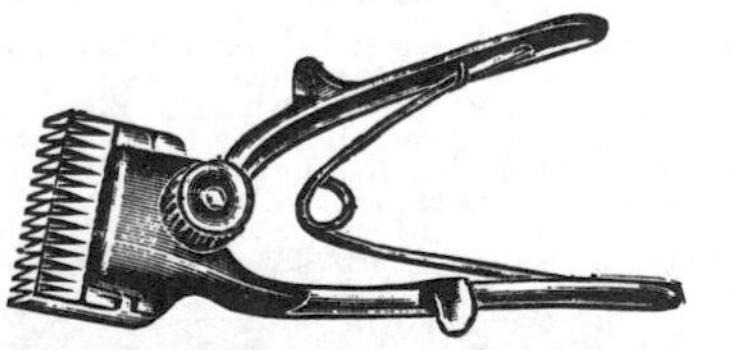

No. 14951. Toilet Hair Clipper. Nickel plated, has a single spring which can be easily removed and adjusted to different tension if desired. To cut ⅛ of an inch long. Each, $1.00.

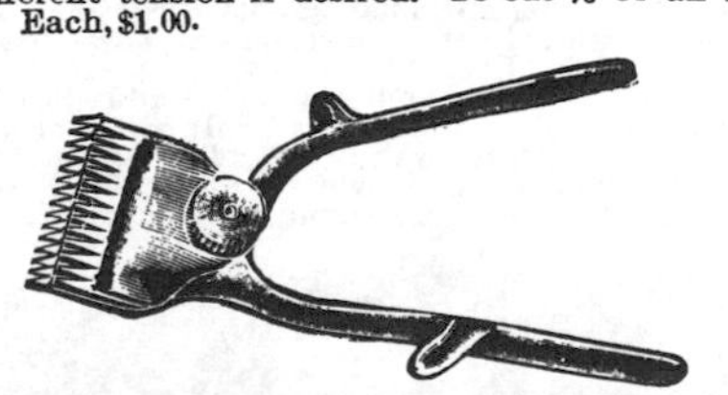

No. 14952. The Columbian Hair Clipper. Nickel plated, has detachable plates, all parts interchangeable, a high grade clipper, best material. Each, $1.65.

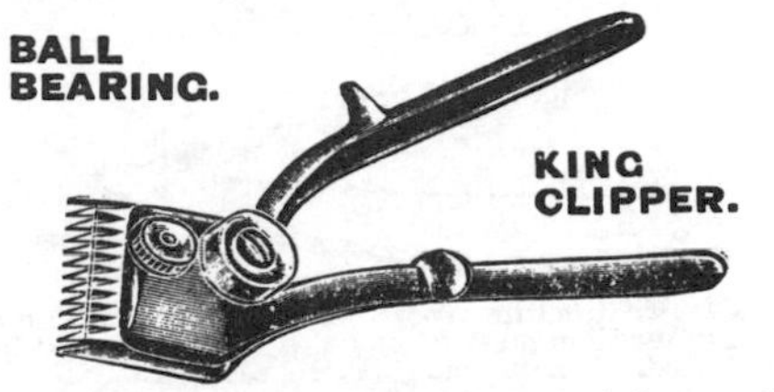


No. 14953. The King Hair Clipper. A first quality clipper for barbers' use, has detachable plates. Tension bolt is set forward of the lever spring directly over the teeth to insure the best cutting results; with Ball Bearings. Each, $2.25.

## BROWN & SHARP'S LATEST PATTERN HAIR CLIPPERS.

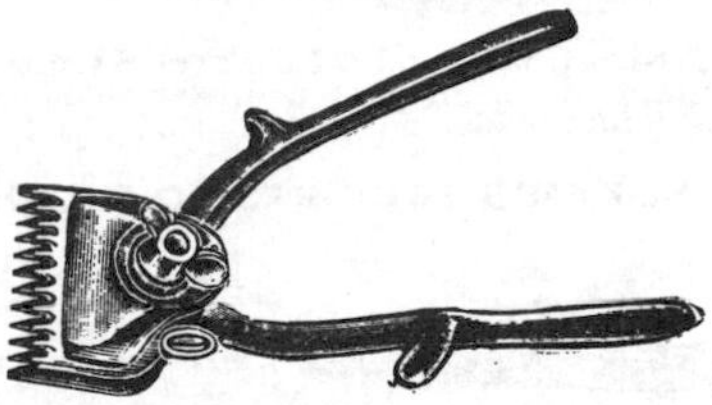

No. 14954. 0. B. & S., cuts 1/32 inch. Each, $2.74.
No. 14955. 1. B. & S., cuts ⅛ inch. Each, $2.76.
No. 14956. 2. B. & S., cuts ¼ inch. Each, $3.25.
No. 14957. 3. B. & S., cuts 5/16 inch. Each, $3.75.

## CLIPPER PARTS.

No. 14960. Repairs for No. 14950 Clipper Springs, each, 5c; top plate, each, 80c; bottom plate, each, 90c.
No. 14961. Repairs for No. 14951 Clipper Springs, each, 20c; top plates, each, 80c; bottom plates, each, 90c.
No. 14962. Repairs for No. 14952 Clipper Springs, each, 5c; top plates, each, $1; bottom plates, each, $1.25.
No. 14963. Repairs for No. 14953 Clipper Springs, each, 5c; top plates, each, $1; bottom plates, each, $1.50.
No. 14968. Adjustable Clipper Comb, with two adjustments. Will increase the cut of the clipper up to 5/16 in. Will fit Nos. 14953, 14954, 14955, 14956 and 14957 Clippers. State which clipper the comb is to be used on. Price, each, 68c.

## CLIPPER GRINDING.

We re-grind old clippers for 50 cents per pair. Express charges or postage both ways to be paid by customer. Read instructions for returning goods before sending us clippers. See page 2.

## RAZORS.

Our Razors are furnished from the lines of leading and well known manufacturers. They are made of only the best material and for private and barbers' use are unexcelled.

Sent by express C. O. D., subject to examination, on receipt of $1, balance payable at express office. Three per cent. discount for cash in full with order.

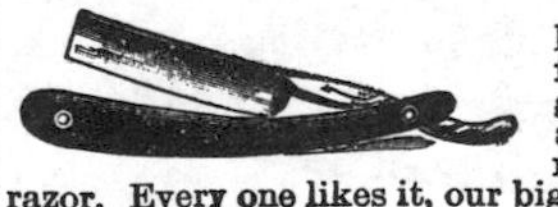

No. 14975. Wostenholm's new pipe ½ in., finest quality, hollow ground. A little gem and a dandy shaver, no better steel put in a razor. Every one likes it, our biggest seller, warranted. Each, $1.

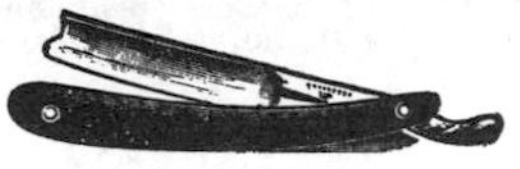

No. 14976. Black rubber handle, hollow point, a very finely made razor of serviceable quality. ⅝ inch. Warranted. Each, 60c.

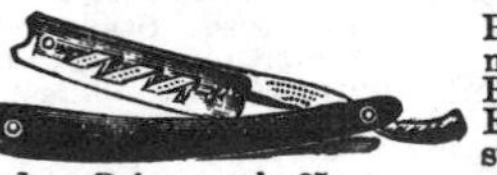

No. 14977. Wade & Butcher's hollow point, medium hollow ground, Razor, rubber handle. Fully warranted and a superior cutter. ⅝ inch blade. Price, each, 85c.

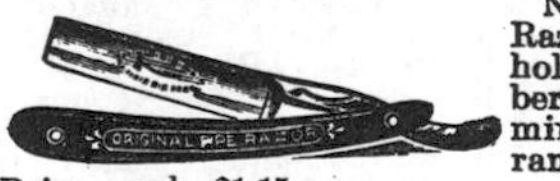


No. 14978. Original pipe Razor, square point, full hollow ground, black rubber handle, best steel, mirror finish. Fully warranted, ⅝ inch blade. Price, each, $1.15.

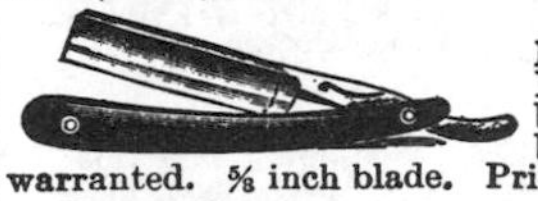

No. 14979. Full hollow ground Wostenholm Pipe Razor, black rubber handle, one of the best razors made. Fully warranted. ⅝ inch blade. Price, each, $1.50.

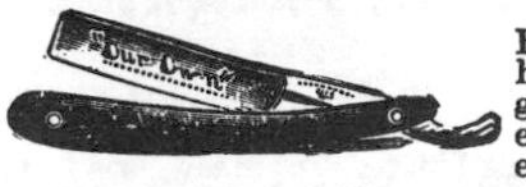

No. 14980. "Our Own" Razor, black rubber handle, medium hollow ground, very finely etched, ⅝ in. blade. Price, each, 95c.

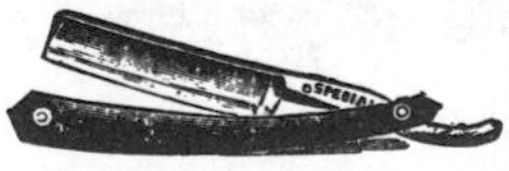

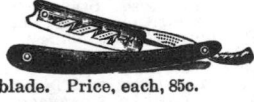

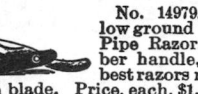

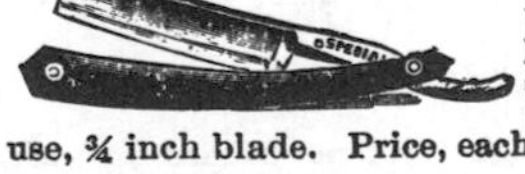

No. 14981. One of our best Razors, black rubber handle, blade full hollow ground, best steel, a superfine barbers' razor, set and ready for use, ¾ inch blade. Price, each, $1.50.

**All that a house can do, we promise to do in order to render your dealings with us satisfactory in every respect. You will find that your relations with us will be treated with the utmost consideration.**

**No. 14982.** Genuine ivory handle Razor, full hollow ground, medium weight, blade of best steel and fully warranted. ⅝ inch blade Price, each, $1.75.

**No. 14983.** Genuine John Engstrom Swedish Razor. A popular pattern, finely ground, warranted best steel blade. ⅝ inch blade. Price, each, $1.50.

### H. BOKER'S TREE BRAND RAZORS.

**No. 14984.** Fancy celluloid handle Razor, finely ground, set and ready for shaving, best steel blade. Fully warranted. Size, ⅝ inch. Price, each, $1.75.

**No. 14985.** Tree Razor, black rubber handle, hollow point, medium hollow ground. Fully warranted. If properly used will require no honing in private use. ⅝ inch blade. Price, each, $1.40.

**No. 14986.** Tree Razor, black rubber handle, square point, full hollow ground. Warranted best steel. The best barbers' razor on earth. ⅝ inch blade. Price, each, $1.75.

### FANCY HANDLE RAZORS.

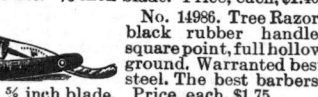

**No. 14987.** Fancy celluloid handle Razor. Best steel blade, hollow ground, finest finish. ⅝ inch blade. Price, each, $2.

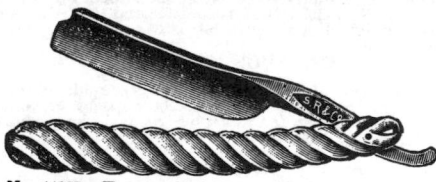

**No. 14788.** Fancy celluloid handle Razor. One of the best razors made for private or barbers' use. Full hollow ground, warranted best material. ⅝ inch blade. Price, each, $1.75.

### STAR SAFETY RAZOR.

**No. 14992.** Star Safety Razor. An invention which obviates all danger of cutting the face. It is especially adapted to old and young, and is indispensable to travelers, miners and persons camping out. Blades of best steel and full concave, which can be easily removed and placed in handle for stropping. Full nickel plated. Price, each, $1.50. Postage, 5c extra.

**No. 14993.** Stropping Machine for star safety razor. Price, each, $1.75.

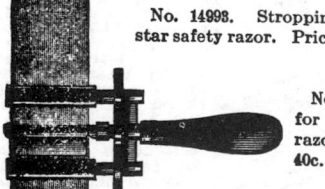

**No. 14994.** Strop for star safety razor. Price, each, 40c.

**No. 14995.** Extra Blades for star safety razor. Price, each, $1.

---

### RAZOR GRINDING.

Postage or express charges both ways to be paid by customer.
Plain ground, 35c.
Hollow ground, 50c.
Read instructions for returning goods before sending razor to us. See page 2.

### RAZOR STROPS.

Our strops are furnished strictly according to description and comprise the best goods for individual and for barbers' use.

**No. 14999.** Emerson's genuine, half round, elastic Strop, cushioned and well dressed. Each, 30c.

**No. 15000.** Combination Strop, four sides, double rods, with hone. Each, 40c.

**No. 15001.** German Belt Razor Strop, two sides, double rods, with paste box. Each, 45c.

**No. 15002.** White Horsehide Razor Strop, extra heavy, selected stock, surfaced, fashioned handle finished with eyelet, 2x24 inches. Each, 25c.

**No. 15003.** Oiled Horsehide Strop, extra heavy. Barbers' swinging Strop, selected stock, 2¼x24 inches. Each, 35c.

**No. 15004.** Genuine Russia Leather, single. Barbers' swing Strop, an extra fine strop, selected stock, with fashioned handle and eyelet, 2¼x24. Each, 40c.

**No. 15005.** White Satin Calf Razor Strop, with flat web, fashioned handles, solid metallic tip and swivel. A fine barbers' double swing strop, 2x23 inches. Each, 50c.

**No. 15006.** Razor Strop, size 2x25 inches. Combination boarskin and white satin. Boarskin for the first or roughing side and white satin for the finishing side. Boarskin takes the place of canvas, but is vastly superior, because of the increased frictional qualities of its surface. This strop is finished with leather handle attached to strop with nickel plated loop, and a single loop swivel. Each, 60c. Extra by mail, 5c.

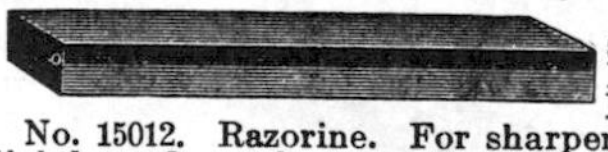

**No. 15009.** Extra superfine Belgian Razor Hones. Each, 75c.

**No. 15012.** Razorine. For sharpening razors, spread lightly and evenly over strop. Directions with each package. Price, per cake, 12c. Postage, 2c.

### SHAVING OR LATHER BRUSHES

Weight of each brush, 3 oz.

**No. 15018.** Black enameled handle Shaving Brush, medium size, all white stock. Each, 8c.
**No. 15019.** Black enameled handle Shaving Brush. A large brush, firmly set, all white bristles. Each, 15c.
**No. 15020.** Enameled handle Lather Brush, badger hair stock. Large size, well set and lasting. Each, 25c.

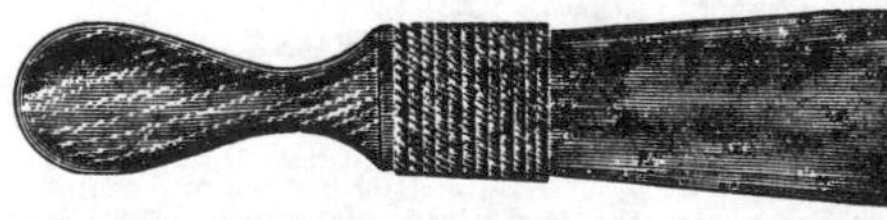

**No. 15021.** Black enamel handle wire-bound Lather Brush, all white bristles, medium size, a well made and durable brush. Each, 10c.
**No. 15022.** Cherry handle, twine-bound Lather Brush, medium size, all white bristles firmly set. Each, 15c.
**No. 15023.** Black walnut handle, barbers' Lather Brush, twine bound, all white bristles, firmly set, medium size, the best twine-bound brush made. Each, 15c.

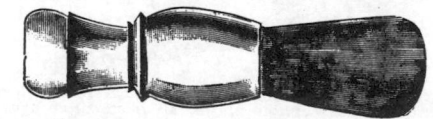

**No. 15024.** White bone handle Lather Brush, all white stock, medium size, well made, will give the best service. Each, 30c.

---

**No. 15025.** Barbers' celebrated "Trade Mark P" Lather Brushes, medium size, best white bristles, boxwood handle, buffalo horn ferrule, which will not crack like wood or rubber, the most durable brush made. Each, 35c.

### SHAVING SOAP.

**No. 15028.** Shaving Soap. Genuine Yankee Shaving Soap, a well known and reliable article. Per cake, 10c.

### POMATUM WAX.

**No. 15029.** Pomatum Wax. For waxing moustache, an unadulterated article which gives only the best results. Per bar, 7c.

### CURLING IRONS.

It will pay you to include all these small wares in your order; you can save 50 per cent. in price, and the express or freight will amount to nothing when shipped with other goods.

**No. 15035.** Made of polished steel, polished wood handles, medium size, better than any other made at this price; length, 7¼ inches. Each, 4c.

**No. 15036.** Duke moustache Curler, polished steel, nickel plated, antique oak handles; length, 6 inches. Each, 5c.
**No. 15037.** Medium size, or Little Princess Curler, same as No. 15036; length, 7¾ inches. Each, 6c.

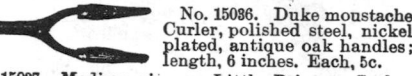

**No. 15038.** Full size, Princess Curler, polished steel, nickel plated, antique handles; length of curler, 9¼ inches. Each, 7c.
**No. 15039.** Paragon Curling Iron. This is a favorite curling iron. Having no pivot the jaws open practically parallel with each other, thus securing the hair at all points on the iron. The clasp being perfectly guided can not get out of line, and the spring is located where it can not be affected by heat. All parts fully nickel plated; antique handles; length, 8½ inches. Each, 9c.

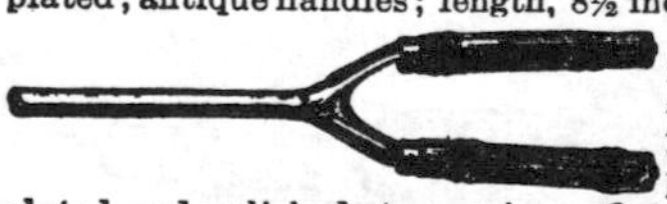

**No. 15040.** The Oxford Curling Iron is extra length and extra quality; heavy nickel plated and polished to a mirror finish. Handles of handsomely finished antique oak having ends ornamented with nickel plated tips; length, 10½ inches. Each, 10c.

**No. 15042.** National Waving Iron, shear loop handles, 5 prongs, gives a perfect wave to the hair; in favor with all users. Each, 15c.

### CURLING IRON HEATERS.

**No. 15046.** Tip-top Curling Iron Heater and Lamp Chimney Stove, a most popular heater. Can be used to heat a curling iron or heat a cup of water; made of bright brass, compact and ornamental. Each, 7c.

**No. 15047.** New Shield Curling Iron Heater to prevent curling irons from becoming soiled and blackened, thus doing away with wiping the iron. Ladies will appreciate this article. Each, 10c.

15047.

**No. 15048.** Always Ready Curling Iron Heater. Burns oil; an oblong flat metal lamp, when not in use is closed by brass screw cap. Hinged brackets for holding iron in place. Each, 10c.

### ALCOHOL STOVE.

**No. 15049.** Alcohol Stove. No possibility of danger, base tightly packed with cotton, cover extinguishes the flame, nicely finished, the whole neatly packed in box. An exceedingly useful article at all times. Each, 12c.

---

## FOR THE BABIES.

**Little carriages for the little ones. The handsomest on wheels. Our Baby Carriage Catalogue is free for the asking, and you will find that a $5 bill will get as much and as nice goods from this Catalogue as would a $10 bill spent over the counter.**

## BRUSHES.

In our Line of Brushes listed below we aim to give a list of Brushes such as are more commonly used. These goods are all of durable quality. We can furnish Brushes for less money, but when such is the case quality also must be sacrificed. On anything in this line which we do not list we will be pleased to furnish information if desired.

No. 15162. Camel hair Lettering Pencils. Rose bound, fine quality, hair ½, ¾, and 1 inch long.

| Nos. | 1 | 2 | 3 | 4 | 5 | 6 | 7 | 8 |
|---|---|---|---|---|---|---|---|---|
| Price, per doz., | $0.15 | .17 | .19 | .22 | .26 | .29 | .33 | .38 |

No. 15163. Superfine quality camel hair Lettering Pencils. Red and green silk and silver binding. Hair ½, ¾, and 1 inch long.

| Nos. | 1 | 2 | 3 | 4 | 5 | 6 | 7 | 8 |
|---|---|---|---|---|---|---|---|---|
| Price, per doz., | $0.18 | .22 | .30 | .33 | .41 | .48 | .54 | .60 |

No. 15164. Camel hair Striping Pencils. Rose bound, fine quality, hair 1¾ to 2 inches long.

| Sizes, | 1 | 2 | 3 | 4 | 5 | 6 | 7 | 8 |
|---|---|---|---|---|---|---|---|---|
| Price, per doz., | $0.15 | .17 | .21 | .26 | .31 | .36 | .40 | .44 |

No. 15165. Camel hair striping Pencils. Red and green silk and silver binding, superfine quality, hair 1¾ to 2 inches long.

| Sizes, | 1 | 2 | 3 | 4 | 5 | 6 | 7 | 8 |
|---|---|---|---|---|---|---|---|---|
| Price, per doz., | $0.17 | .23 | .27 | .32 | .40 | .47 | .55 | .63 |

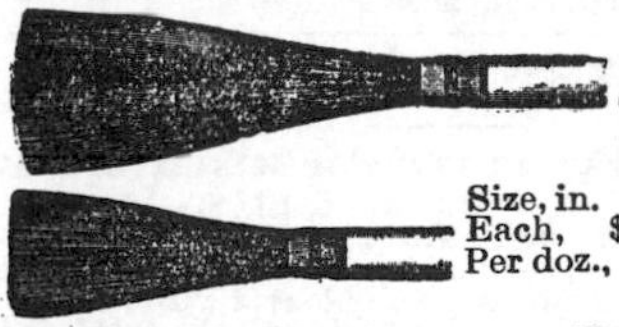

No. 15166. Camel hair swan quill Pencils for lettering.

| Size, in. | ½ | ¾ | 1 | 1¼ |
|---|---|---|---|---|
| Each, | $0.05 | .05 | .06 | .06 |
| Per doz., | .45 | .46 | .53 | .56 |

No. 15167. Camel hair, swan quill Pencils for striping.

| Size, inches, | 1½ | 1¾ | 2 | 2¼ |
|---|---|---|---|---|
| Price, each, | $0.06 | .06 | .07 | .07 |
| Price, per doz., | .59 | .62 | .65 | .70 |

No. 15168. Camel hair flat or Sword Stripers, square ends, tin ferrules, without handle, for carriage work. Hair 1½ to 2¼ inches long.

| Nos. | 1 | 2 | 3 | 4 |
|---|---|---|---|---|
| Price, each, | $0.06 | .06 | .07 | .08 |
| Price, per doz., | .60 | .64 | .75 | .90 |

No. 15169. Camel hair Dagger Stripers. Diagonal ends, copper wire bound, small cedar handles, for carriage work. Hair 1½ to 2¼ inches long.

| Nos. | 1 | 2 | 3 | 4 |
|---|---|---|---|---|
| Price, each, | $0.12 | .12 | .13 | .13 |
| Price, per doz., | 1.30 | 1.32 | 1.35 | 1.38 |

No. 15170. Camel hair Marking Brushes. Polished handles.

| Nos. | 1 | 2 | 3 | 4 |
|---|---|---|---|---|
| Price, each, | $0.04 | .05 | .05 | .07 |
| Price, per doz., | .40 | .46 | .50 | .64 |

No. 15171. Camel hair Lacquering Brushes. Polished handles, fine quality, round.

| Nos. | 1 | 2 | 3 | 4 | 5 | 6 |
|---|---|---|---|---|---|---|
| Price, each, | $0.04 | .04 | .06 | .08 | .10 | .12 |
| Price, per doz., | .41 | .43 | .55 | .77 | 1.00 | 1.25 |

No. 15172. Camel hair Lacquering Brushes. Polished handles, fine quality, flat.

| Size, inches, | ⅜ | ½ | ⅝ | ¾ | ⅞ | 1 |
|---|---|---|---|---|---|---|
| Price, each, | $0.06 | .07 | .08 | .10 | .12 | .15 |
| Price, per doz., | .60 | .72 | .85 | 1.10 | 1.32 | 1.50 |

No. 15173. Camel hair Lacquering Brushes. Superfine quality, flat.

| Size, inches, | ⅜ | ½ | ⅝ | ¾ | ⅞ | 1 |
|---|---|---|---|---|---|---|
| Price, each, | $0.06 | .08 | .10 | .11 | .14 | .16 |
| Price, per doz., | .65 | .88 | 1.08 | 1.15 | 1.45 | 1.65 |

No. 15174. Camel hair Mottling Brushes or Spalters. Short cedar handles, fine quality.

| Size, inches, | ½ | ¾ | 1 | 1½ | 2 | 2½ | 3 | 3½ | 4 |
|---|---|---|---|---|---|---|---|---|---|
| Price, each, | $0.07 | .11 | .14 | .21 | .28 | .35 | .42 | .49 | .56 |

No. 15175. Coach Painters' Color Brushes or double thick camel hair Mottlers. Short cedar handles, fine quality, tin bound.

| Size, inches, | 1 | 1½ | 2 | 2½ | 3 | 3½ | 4 |
|---|---|---|---|---|---|---|---|
| Price, each, | $0.19 | .29 | .38 | .48 | .57 | .67 | .76 |

No. 15176. Same as No. 15175. Brass bound.

| Size, inches, | 1 | 1½ | 2 | 2½ | 3 | 3½ | 4 |
|---|---|---|---|---|---|---|---|
| Price, each, | $0.21 | .32 | .42 | .53 | .63 | .74 | .84 |

No. 15177. Round badger hair Blenders or Softeners for graining and oil painting, polished handles.

| Nos. | 1 | 2 | 3 | 4 | 5 | 6 | 7 | 8 | 9 | 10 | 11 | 12 |
|---|---|---|---|---|---|---|---|---|---|---|---|---|
| Price, each, | $0.09 | .14 | .18 | .21 | .25 | .30 | .36 | .43 | .50 | .58 | .70 | .75 |

No. 15178. Flat knotted badger hair Blenders, polished handles, set in bone.

| Size, inch, | 2 | 2½ | 3 | 3½ | 4 | 4½ | 5 | 5½ | 6 |
|---|---|---|---|---|---|---|---|---|---|
| Price, each, | $0.56 | .72 | .87 | 1.00 | 1.15 | 1.94 | 2.16 | 2.38 | 2.60 |

No. 15179. Badger hair Flowing Varnish Brushes, for fine varnishing, carriages, pianos, etc. Single thick, chiseled.

| Size, inch, | 1 | 1½ | 2 | 2½ | 3 |
|---|---|---|---|---|---|
| Each, | $0.22 | .33 | .44 | .55 | .66 |

No. 15180. Same as No. 15179, only double thick.

| Size, inch, | 1 | 1½ | 2 | 2½ | 3 |
|---|---|---|---|---|---|
| Each, | $0.28 | .42 | .56 | .70 | .84 |

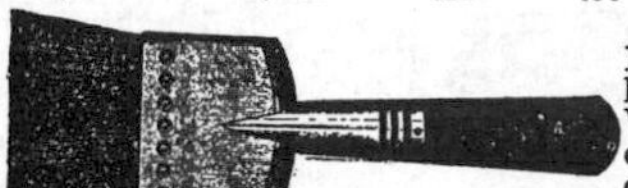

No. 15181. Fitch or bear hair Flowing Varnish Brushes, superfine quality, single thick, square.

| Size, inch, | ½ | ¾ | 1 | 1½ | 2 | 2½ | 3 |
|---|---|---|---|---|---|---|---|
| Each, | $0.08 | .12 | .16 | .24 | .32 | .40 | .48 |

No. 15182. Same as No. 15181, only double thick.

| Size, inch, | 1 | 1½ | 2 | 2½ | 3 |
|---|---|---|---|---|---|
| Each, | $0.20 | .30 | .40 | .50 | .60 |

No. 15183. Fitch or bear hair Flowing Varnish Brushes, superfine quality, single thick, chiseled.

| Size, inch, | 1 | 1½ | 2 | 2½ | 3 |
|---|---|---|---|---|---|
| Each, | $0.18 | .27 | .36 | .45 | .54 |

No. 15184. Ox hair Striping Pencils, superfine quality, in quills, hair, 1½ to 2½ inches long.

| Nos. | 1 | 2 | 3 | 4 | 5 | 6 | 7 | 8 | 10 | 12 |
|---|---|---|---|---|---|---|---|---|---|---|
| Price, each, | $0.03 | .04 | .04 | .05 | .06 | .07 | .09 | .10 | .17 | .20 |
| Per dozen, | .33 | .36 | .42 | .48 | .60 | .72 | .90 | 1.03 | 1.80 | 2.20 |

No. 15185. Ox hair Flowing Varnish Brushes, chiseled, superfine quality, polished cedar handles, nickel ferrules; for the finest varnish work; very durable.

| Size, inch, | 1 | 1½ | 2 | 2½ | 3 |
|---|---|---|---|---|---|
| Each, | $0.36 | .54 | .72 | .90 | 1.08 |

No. 15186. Same as No. 15185, only double thick.

| Size, inch, | 1 | 1½ | 2 | 2½ | 3 |
|---|---|---|---|---|---|
| Each, | $0.60 | .90 | 1.20 | 1.50 | 1.80 |

No. 15187. Thin, flat, bristle Varnish Brushes, white handles, tin ferrule.

| Size, inch, | 1 | 1½ | 2 | 2½ | 3 |
|---|---|---|---|---|---|
| Each, | $0.03 | .05 | .06 | .08 | .09 |

No. 15188. Common flat bristle Varnish Brushes, all bristles, cherry handles, in tin.

| Size, inch, | 1 | 1½ | 2 | 2½ | 3 |
|---|---|---|---|---|---|
| Each, | $0.04 | .06 | .08 | .10 | .12 |

No. 15189. Extra flat bristle Varnish Brushes, double thick, French bristles, cedar handles, lacquered tin.

| Size, inch, | 1 | 1½ | 2 | 2½ | 3 |
|---|---|---|---|---|---|
| Each, | $0.07 | .11 | .14 | .18 | .21 |

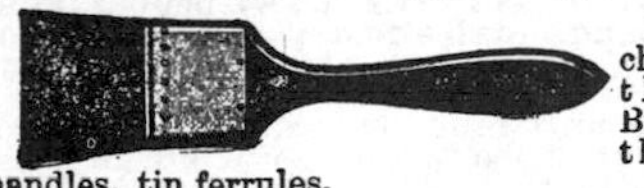

No. 15190. Extra chiseled, flat bristle Varnish Brushes, double thick, cedar handles, tin ferrules.

| Size, inch, | 1 | 1½ | 2 | 2½ | 3 |
|---|---|---|---|---|---|
| Each, | $0.09 | .14 | .18 | .23 | .27 |

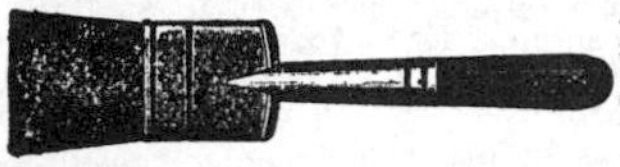

No. 15191. Bristle Flowing Varnish Brushes, black enamel handles, in tin, French bristles, chiseled.

| Size, inch, | 1 | 1½ | 2 | 2½ | 3 |
|---|---|---|---|---|---|
| Each, | $0.05 | .08 | .10 | .13 | .15 |

No. 15192. Same as No. 15191. Has Chinese black bristles.

| Size, inch, | 1 | 1½ | 2 | 2½ | 3 |
|---|---|---|---|---|---|
| Each | $0.06 | .09 | .12 | .15 | .18 |

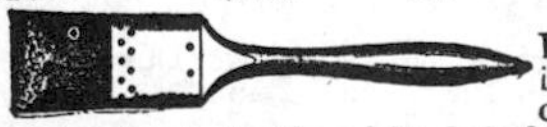

No. 15193. "Half Elastic" Bristle Flowing Varnish Brushes, cedar handles, tin ferrules, best elastic white bristles, chiseled.

| Size, inch, | 1 | 1½ | 2 | 2½ | 3 |
|---|---|---|---|---|---|
| Each, | $0.22 | .33 | .44 | .55 | .66 |

No. 15194. "Half Elastic" Brushes. Same as No. 15193, but has best elastic Chinese black bristles.

| Size, inch, | 1 | 1½ | 2 | 2½ | 3 |
|---|---|---|---|---|---|
| Each, | $0.22 | .33 | .44 | .55 | .66 |

### BRISTLE GRAINERS.

Width, 1 to 4 inches.

No. 15195. English Grainers. Price, per inch, 20c.
No. 15196. Knotted Grainers. Price, per inch, 23c.
No. 15197. Snake Grainers. Price, per inch, 20c.
No. 15198. Angular Grainers. Price, per inch, 20c.
No. 15199. Oak Grainers. Price, per inch, 23c.
No. 15200. Fan or Top Grainers. Price, per inch, 8c.

### PIPED OVER GRAINERS.

Width, 1 to 4 inches.

No. 15201. Bristle. Price, per inch, 19c.
No. 15202. Ox hair. Price, per inch, 36c.
No. 15203. Badger hair. Price, per inch, 36c.
No. 15204. Red sable hair, medium. Price, per inch, 47c.
No. 15205. Red sable hair, superfine. Price, per inch, 54c.

No. 15206. English Graining Combs. Best quality steel in sets of 12 assorted, 1 to 4 inches, in tin compartment case. Price, per set, $1.20.

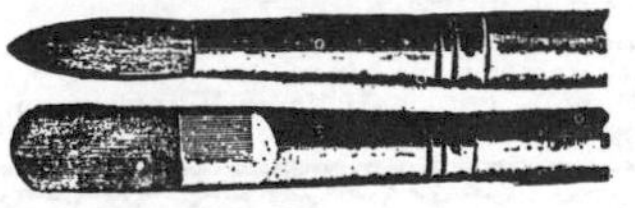

Bristle Marking Brushes, round or flat, polished handles.

No. 15209. Round.
No. 15210. Flat.

| Nos. | 1 | 2 | 3 | 4 | 5 | 6 |
|---|---|---|---|---|---|---|
| Price, each, | $0.02 | .02 | .03 | .03 | .04 | .05 |
| Price, per dozen, | .16 | .20 | .23 | .26 | .33 | .40 |

No. 15211. Ex-French Sash Tools. All white bristles, wire bound.

| Nos. | 1 | 2 | 3 | 4 | 5 | 6 | 7 | 8 | 9 | 10 |
|---|---|---|---|---|---|---|---|---|---|---|
| Price, each, | $0.03 | .04 | .05 | .06 | .07 | .10 | .11 | .13 | .15 | .20 |
| Price, per doz. | .32 | .40 | .47 | .58 | .68 | 1.02 | 1.20 | 1.38 | 1.68 | 2.16 |

No. 15212. Ex. Ex. French Sash Tools. All fine white bristles, wire bound.

| Nos. | 1 | 2 | 3 | 4 | 5 | 6 | 7 | 8 | 9 | 10 |
|---|---|---|---|---|---|---|---|---|---|---|
| Price, each, | $0.04 | .05 | .07 | .08 | .10 | .12 | .13 | .15 | .20 | 25 |
| Price, per doz. | .43 | .50 | .68 | .79 | 1.03 | 1.20 | 1.38 | 1.62 | 2.00 | 2.50 |

No. 15213. Flat chiseled Sash Tools. red polished handles, brass ferrules, all white bristles,

| Size, inch, | ½ | ¾ | 1 | 1¼ | 1½ |
|---|---|---|---|---|---|
| Each, | $0.07 | .11 | .13 | .16 | .20 |

No. 15214. Same as No. 15213, but has Chinese black bristles.

| Size, inch, | ½ | ¾ | 1 | 1¼ | 1½ |
|---|---|---|---|---|---|
| Each, | $0.07 | .11 | .13 | .16 | .20 |

### HEAD GLUE BRUSHES.

No. 15215. Glue Brushes, best gray Russian bristles, copper rings, riveted long handles,

| Nos. | 10 | 12 | 14 | 16 | 18 | 20 |
|---|---|---|---|---|---|---|
| Price, each, | $0.73 | .92 | 1.15 | 1.65 | 2.00 | 2.40 |

### HEAD STENCEL BRUSHES.

No. 15216. Improved Stencil Brushes, white bristles, zinc ferrules.

| Nos. | 1 | 2 | 3 | 4 | 5 | 6 | 7 | 8 |
|---|---|---|---|---|---|---|---|---|
| Price, each, | $0.07 | .08 | .09 | .10 | .11 | .12 | .18 | .20 |

### PAINT BRUSHES.

No. 15217. Round Paint Brushes, wire bound, white bristles outside, mixed center.

| Sizes, | 1-0 | 2-0 | 3-0 | 4-0 | 5-0 | 6-0 |
|---|---|---|---|---|---|---|
| Price, each, | $0.34 | .38 | .44 | .49 | .58 | .64 |

No. 15218. Round Round or oval Paint Brushes, wire bound. All best selected Russian bristles.

| Sizes, | 1-0 | 2-0 | 3-0 | 4-0 | 5-0 | 6-0 |
|---|---|---|---|---|---|---|
| Price, each, | $0.53 | .63 | .80 | .97 | 1.24 | 1.45 |

No. 15219. Chiseled oval Varnish Brushes, very elastic; best selected black Chinese bristles. Nickel plated rings,

| Sizes. | 1-0 | 2-0 | 3-0 | 4-0 | 5-0 | 6-0 |
|---|---|---|---|---|---|---|
| Price, each, | $0.39 | .43 | .62 | .61 | .67 | .79 |

No. 15220. Specially prepared white French bristles, chiseled oval Varnish Brushes, nickel plated rings; unequaled for fine work in varnishing.

| Sizes. | 1-0 | 2-0 | 3-0 | 4-0 | 5-0 | 6-0 |
|---|---|---|---|---|---|---|
| Price, each, | $0.44 | .49 | .60 | .64 | .79 | .90 |

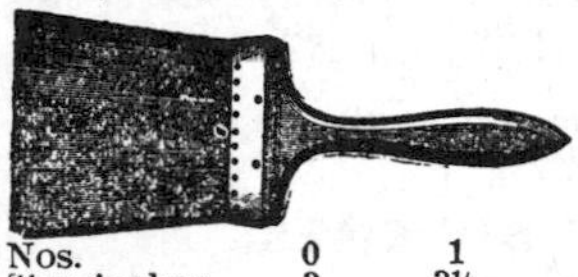

No. 15221. Extension Wall Paint Brushes. Long stock, best white Russian bristles; brass bound.

| Nos. | 0 | 1 | 2 | 3 | 4 |
|---|---|---|---|---|---|
| Size, inches, | 3 | 3¼ | 4 | 4½ | 5 |
| Price, each, | $0.37 | .43 | .63 | .84 | 1.30 |

No. 15222. Standard Wall Paint Brushes. All white Russian bristles, brass bound.

| Nos. | 25 | 30 | 35 | 40 | 45 |
|---|---|---|---|---|---|
| Size, inches, | 2½ | 3 | 3½ | 4 | 4½ |
| Price, each, | $0.32 | .39 | .51 | .64 | .82 |

No. 15223. Leather bound Wall Paint Brushes. All white Russian bristles.

| Size, inches, | 3 | 3½ | 4 | 4½ | 5 |
|---|---|---|---|---|---|
| Price, each, | $0.34 | .43 | .55 | .71 | .84 |

No. 15224. Stucco Paint Brushes. Extra long and very best selected white Russian bristles, leather bound.

| Nos. | 25 | 30 | 35 | 40 |
|---|---|---|---|---|
| Size, inches, | 3 | 3½ | 4 | 4½ |
| Price, each, | $0.99 | 1.21 | 1.58 | 1.95 |

### KALSOMINE BRUSHES.

No. 15225. Gray mixed center Kalsomine Brush. White bristles outside, imitation bound, excellent quality.

| Size, inches, | 6 | 7 | 8 |
|---|---|---|---|
| Price, each, | $0.48 | .58 | .67 |

No. 15226. Selected Russian white bristles Kalsomine Brushes, brass bound.

| Size, inches, | 6 | 7 | 8 |
|---|---|---|---|
| Price, each, | $1.45 | 1.87 | 2.38 |

No. 15227. New York style Kalsomine Brushes. Extra heavy, specially selected Russian bristles, gray center, white outside, finest workmanship, galvanized iron bands; will last a lifetime.

| Size, inches, | 6 | 7 | 8 |
|---|---|---|---|
| Price, each. | $2.12 | 2.63 | 3.00 |

REFER TO PAGES 21, 22, 23 & 24 FOR

**OILS, PAINTS, VARNISHES, ETC.**

**THE PUREST AND BEST ARE QUOTED.**

THE PRICES ARE RIGHT.

REFER TO THE INDEX WHENEVER YOU DO NOT SEE WHAT YOU WANT. THIS IS A BIG BOOK, AND YOU ARE LIABLE TO LOSE SIGHT OF SOME OF THE BARGAINS IF YOU HAVE NO GUIDE.

No. 15228. Whitewash Brushes. All white bristles, imitation brass bound

| Nos., | 1 | 3 | 5 | 7 |
|---|---|---|---|---|
| Size, inches, | 6½ | 7½ | 8½ | 9 |
| Price, each, | $0.38 | .50 | .63 | .85 |

No. 15229. Leather bound Whitewash Brushes. All white bristles.

| Nos., | 1 | 3 | 5 | 7 |
|---|---|---|---|---|
| Size, inches, | 5½ | 7½ | 8½ | 9 |
| Price, each, | $0.41 | 57 | .77 | .98 |

No. 15230. Painters' Dusters. All Russian bristles, long, and very heavy, gray center, extra white outside.

| Nos., | 15 | 17 | 19 |
|---|---|---|---|
| Price, each, | $0.38 | .74 |  |

No. 15231. Flat Painters' Dusters, black Russian bristles.

| Nos., | 40 | 45 |
|---|---|---|
| Size, inches, | 4 | 4½ |
| Price, each, | $0.45 | .51 |

No. 15232. Paperhangers' Brushes, best gray Russian bristles. "Popular."

| Size, inches, | 8 | 10 | 12 |
|---|---|---|---|
| Price, each, | $0.59 | .70 | .83 |

### Brick Liners.

No. 15233. Brick Liners, white or black hair.

| Size, inches, | 2 | 2½ | 3 | 3½ |
|---|---|---|---|---|
| Price, each, | $0.05 | .06 | .07 | .08 |

### Roofing Brushes.

No. 15234. Roof Paint Brushes, mixed center, gray bristles, outside round ferrules.

| Knots, | 2 | 3 | 4 |
|---|---|---|---|
| Price, each, | $0.46 | .68 | .86 |

### IDEAL SHINE CABINET.

This cabinet fastens to the wall or door casing, entirely out of the way but always ready for use—contents protected from dust and dirt. Foot rest will hold 150 pounds. Contents are: 1 brush, first quality bristle; 1 dauber, with nickel plated handle; 1 box blacking; 1 holder for bottle of ladies' shoe polish. (The bottle of ladies' shoe polish is not furnished.) Size, 6½x4½x15½ inches. When open for use it projects 16 inches from the wall. Weight, 7½ pounds.
No. 15239. Price, each, bronzed, $1.40.
No. 15240. Price, each, nickel plated, $1.87.
We can furnish same cabinet without contents.
No. 15241. Price, each, bronzed, $1.
No. 15241. Price, each, nickel plated, $1.40.

### SHOE BRUSHES.

No. 15245. Black and white fiber, solid black, a good cheap brush. Each, 10c; per doz., $1.10.
No. 15246. Black bristles, solid back, stock well set and selected. Each, 18c; per doz., $1.95.
No. 15247. All black bristles, solid back, a well made brush full and heavy. Each, 25c.
No. 15248. Mixed gray and black bristles, well set, large and full; our best one. Each, 35c; per doz., $3.90.

### SHOE POLISHERS.

No. 15249. Shoe polisher, all black bristles, hardwood back; a good brush for a small price. Each, 17c; per doz., $1.85.
No. 15250. Shoe polisher, walnut back, all black bristles, stock well set, and a good brush. Each, 25c; per doz., $2.25.
No. 15251. A remarkably fine all bristle Polisher, all black stock with black walnut back; our best polisher. Each, 40c; per doz., $4.50.

### DAUBERS.

No. 15252. Blacking Dauber, stencil brush style, made of pure black bristles, with metal ferrule, light hardwood handle; weight, packed, 4 oz. Each, 10c; per doz., $1.
No. 15253. Metal handle Dauber, heavily tinned, improved mud scraper on back; extra stiff solid bristles, will give the best of wear. Each, 14c; doz. $1.55

### BLACKING SETS.

No. 15254. Traveler's companion Blacking Set, consisting of polisher and dauber with box of blacking; hardwood back, all black bristles; a first-class set. Each, 20c; per doz., $2.25.

No. 15255. Three-piece Blacking Set, consisting of polisher, mud brush and dauber; all black bristles, oval back. Each 40c; per doz., $4.40.
No. 15256. Three-piece Blacking Set, consisting of polisher, mud brush and dauber, extra fine and well set black bristles, black walnut back; highly finished. Each, 70c; per doz., $7.00.
No. 15257. Three-piece blacking set, all Russia bristles; highly polished walnut back, oval shape. A strictly high grade set, will last a lifetime. Each, $1.25; per doz., $13.50.

### STOVE BRUSHES.

No. 15262. Straight hardwood back Stove Brush, white and black fibre; an excellent value. Each, 10c; per doz., $1.10.
No. 15263. Curved stock, solid back Stove Brush, best white and black fibre; a well made brush. Each, 12c; per doz., $1.35.
No. 15264. Curved hardwood back Stove Brush, mixed fibre and bristle; a staple article and one that cannot fail to give entire satisfaction. Each, 15c; per doz., $1.70.
No. 15265. Oval hardwood back Stove Brush, gray fibre; a brush for those who desire a first-class article. Each, 18c; per doz., $1.90.

### SCRUB BRUSHES.

No. 15270. Rice root Scrub Brushes; 2 row square, 10 inches, solid back. Each, 8c; per doz., 85c.
No. 15271. Rice root Scrub Brushes. 3 row, 10 inches long, solid back, well set. Each, 10c; per doz., $1.10.
No. 15272. Round end rice root Scrub Brushes, 10 inches long; a remarkably strong and durable brush. Each, 10c; per doz., $1.10.
No. 15273. Palmetto solid back Scrub Brush, medium size, similar to the "goose" scrub brush. Each, 12c; per doz., $1.35.
No. 15274. Corner Scrub Brush, all white fibre, 8 inches long. Each, 10c; per doz., $1.10.
No. 15275. White Tampica Scrub Brush, straight, solid back, 8 inches long. Each, 7c; per doz., 70c.
No. 15276. Our best scrub Brush, mixed white and black fibre; an excellent article, 11 inches long. Each 15c; per doz., $1.70.
No. 15277. Deck Scrub Brushes, gray and black fibre whole center, with rubber scraper on block; used for scraping floors. Each, 20c; per doz., $2.20.

### DUST BRUSHES.

No. 15280. Mixed, white and black fibre Dust Brush, red handle, 14 inches long; a good brush. Each, 12c; per doz., $1.35.
No. 15281. Standard, all gray bristle Dust Brush, enameled handle, 14 inches long. Each, 20c; per doz., $2.25.
No. 15282. Dust Brush, gray and white bristles, with snout; an extra fine brush. Each, 30c; per doz., $3.40.

### WINDOW BRUSHES.

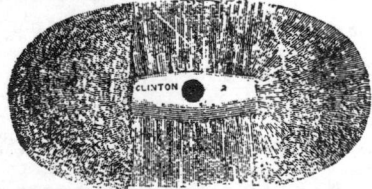

No. 15286. Pope's Eye or round window brush. Best black bristles, wire drawn. Each, 45c; per doz.. $5.00.

No. 15287. Oblong or spider Window Brush. All long black bristles. A very durable brush. Also suitable for use as a cob web or wall dust brush. Each, 50c; per doz., $5.50.

☞ FOR COMPLETE LINE OF HAIR AND TOOTH BRUSHES SEE NOTION DEPARTMENT, PAGES 327 & 328.

No. 15290. Hand or vegetable Brushes. Selected dressed fibre, solid hardwood block. Each, 3c; per doz., 33c.

### FLOOR BRUSHES.

#### For Schools, Halls, Stores and General Purposes.

No. 15291. English patent fibre Floor and Carpet Brushes are warranted to wear better than bristle brushes; will sweep anything from a common floor to a velvet carpet. *Wash and comb the brush when it appears to be clogged with dirt.* Can make larger sizes to order on short notice. Write for prices. Price includes handle 12 inches long, especially adapted for household purposes, each, 85c; 15 inches long, each, $1.50; 18 inches long, each, $1.88.

### WHAT THE PEOPLE SAY.

**Would Not Take $10.00 For His Overcoat.**
CORNELL, Ill., Dec. 28, 1896.
SEARS, ROEBUCK & CO., Chicago.
*Gentlemen:*—Enclosed find 27c. due you on order No. 308111. I can say I am very well pleased with the overcoat; it is a perfect fit and I would not take $10 for it if I could not get another like it. Accept my thanks for your fair and honorable dealings with me, and you can expect my future orders for goods. Yours truly,
H. W. McVAY.

**So Well Pleased, He Will Buy His Next Suit From Us.**
CANTON, O., Dec. 28, 1896.
*Dear Sirs:*—I will drop you few lines to let you know that I received the suit and is O. K. I am sure I got my money's worth. I expect to get another one in the spring. Yours truly,
R. S. GOUSER.

**No Complaint Can be Made of the Quality and Fit of the Suit.**
JEANERETTE, Iberia Co., La., Dec. 22, 1896.
SEARS, ROEBUCK & CO.
*Dear Sirs:*—I have received the suit and the goods and was perfectly satisfied and the suit is a perfect fit and I will try to send you an order in short. Please send me your clothing catalogue and samples.
MARY CASEMERE.
Direct MARY CASEMERE, Jeanerette, P. O. Box 20.

**Will Take Pleasure in Showing His Clothing.**
BELLEFLOWER, Mo., Dec. 28, 1896.
SEARS, ROEBUCK & CO.
*Sirs:*—An open confession is good for the soul, so I use a postal to inform you I am more than pleased with my $12.00 No. XXXX suit. I consider the $6.00 due bill a Xmas present from your firm. That mackintosh is immense, No. 4256. I will take pleasure in showing my clothes. Have my thanks, etc.
A. M. KIBLER.

**Always Pleased With Our Clothing.**
CONCORDIA, Mo., Dec. 28, 1896.
SEARS, ROEBUCK & CO., Chicago, Ill.
*Dear Sirs:*—Suit was received the other day and am well pleased with same. Many thanks.
Yours truly, F. W. VOGT.

**"I Have Never Had a Better Fit."**
MAGNOLIA SPRINGS, Tex., Dec. 24, 1896.
MESSRS. SEARS, ROEBUCK & CO., Chicago, Ill.
*Dear Sirs:*—The suit I just ordered has been received. It's O. K. I have never had a better fit. I will leave in a few days for Tuskegee, Ala. I wish I could have done you a better work but money matters have been such in this section that it has been almost impossible to secure orders. I aim to do you all the good possible in the way of commendation wherever I go. Yours truly,
W. W. BOOKER.

**"Will Do All I Can for Your Firm."**
ALVIN, Ill., Jan. 4, 1897.
SEARS, ROEBUCK & CO., Chicago, Ill.
*Dear Sirs:*—The suit of clothes received and found all O. K.; well satisfied with them; a thousand thanks; will do all I can for your firm. Yours, etc.,
JOHN DAVISON.
P. S.—No. of invoice 338067.

**We Can Please Every One The Same Way.**
RAY, N. Y., Dec. 24, 1896.
SEARS, ROEBUCK & CO., Chicago, Ill.
*Dear Sirs:*—I write to let you know that I am very much pleased with the suit you sent. It is a nice fit.
Yours truly, AMER GRISWOLD.

**Clothing Just as Represented and a Perfect Fit.**
KLAMATH FALLS, Dec. 15, 1896.
SEARS, ROEBUCK & CO.
*Dear Sirs:*—I received the suit of clothes and they are just as represented and a perfect fit. Every one that has seen the clothes says I got a good bargain. I think you will receive more orders from Klamath.
Very truly yours, C. W. BRANDON.

## GASOLINE STOVES.

The **Acme Gasoline Stove** is made especially for us and is **fully guaranteed** to be exactly as represented and to do everything we claim. **There is positively no danger in using the Acme Gasoline Stove. It cannot explode.** Stove should not be filled when there is a light or flame of any kind in the room, and gasoline should be kept in a perfectly air-tight can. If this is done it is **impossible to have an accident.** The **Acme Gasoline Stove is simple in operation.** Full directions for lighting and operating are with each stove. Nobody ever has any trouble with the Acme Gasoline Stove, and we challenge any one to produce a better stove than the **Acme.**

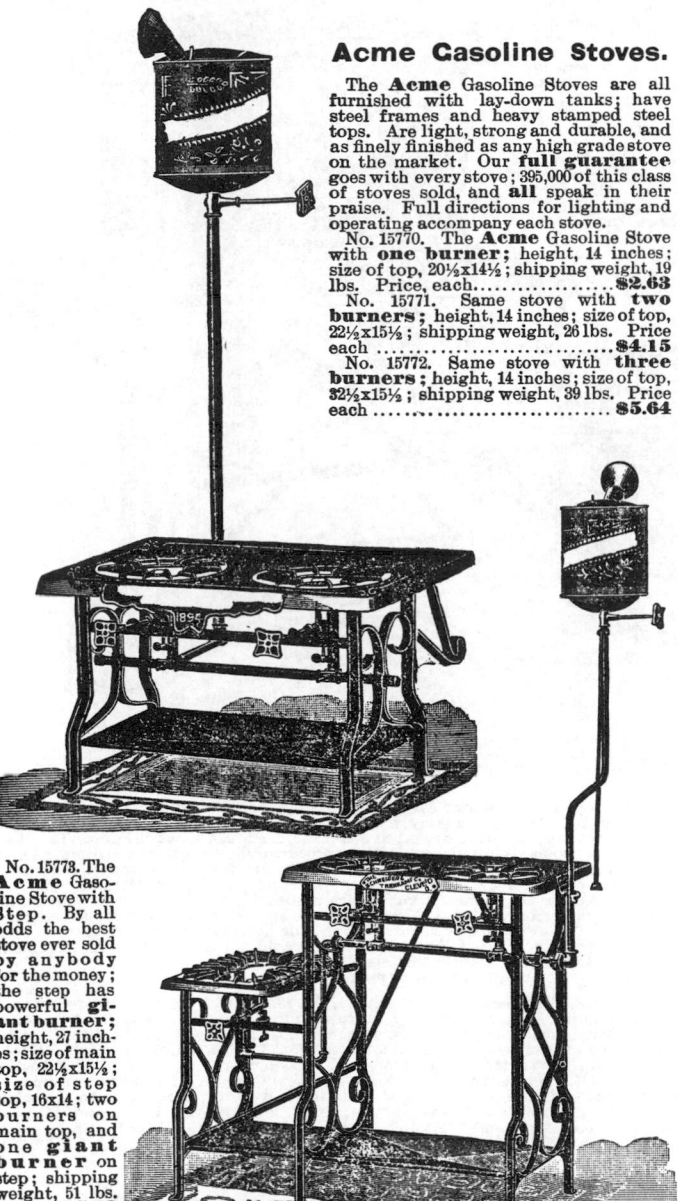

### Acme Gasoline Stoves.

The **Acme** Gasoline Stoves are all furnished with lay-down tanks; have steel frames and heavy stamped steel tops. Are light, strong and durable, and as finely finished as any high grade stove on the market. Our **full guarantee** goes with every stove; 395,000 of this class of stoves sold, and **all** speak in their praise. Full directions for lighting and operating accompany each stove.

No. 15770. The **Acme** Gasoline Stove with **one burner**; height, 14 inches; size of top, 20½x14½; shipping weight, 19 lbs. Price, each.....................**$2.63**

No. 15771. Same stove with **two burners**; height, 14 inches; size of top, 22½x15½; shipping weight, 26 lbs. Price each .................**$4.15**

No. 15772. Same stove with **three burners**; height, 14 inches; size of top, 32½x15½; shipping weight, 39 lbs. Price each ..................**$5.64**

No. 15773. The **Acme** Gasoline Stove with **Step.** By all odds the best stove ever sold by anybody for the money; the step has powerful **giant burner**; height, 27 inches; size of main top, 22½x15½; size of step top, 16x14; two burners on main top, and one **giant burner** on step; shipping weight, 51 lbs. Each.. **$7.13**

No. 15774. A **stove** exactly like above, except has three burners on main top; size main top, 32½x15½; size step top, 16x14; shipping weight, 60 lbs. Price each..........................**$8.63**

## Giant Acme Gasoline Stoves.
### THE BEST.

The **Giant Acme** Gasoline Stove, with lay-down tank, has latest, best and most perfect burner yet made; **lights and burns without smoke or odor, giving blue process flame** at great reduction in price. It is operated by **one valve, very simple; any child can operate it**; has loose grate; safety lay-down tank; when tank is filled it must be lowered and when lowered all fires are immediately extinguished. Beautifully ornamented with full nickel name plate. **Fully guaranteed, and can be returned at our expense if it does not do the work represented.**

No. 15775. The **Giant Acme** Gasoline Stove, with **two** burners, which give a process flame as described above; height, 14 inches; size of top, 25x17½ inches; shipping weight, 30 lbs. Price each....................**$4.88**

No. 15776. The **Giant Acme** Gasoline Stove, exactly like the above, except height, which is 24 inches; shipping weight, 40 lbs. Price each, **$5.63**

No. 15777. The **Giant Acme** Gasoline Stove, with **three** burners, which give a **process flame** as described above; height, 14 inches; size of top, 33x17½ inches; shipping weight, 43 lbs. Price each..........................**$6.38**

No. 15778. The **Giant Acme** Gasoline Stove, exactly like above, excepting height, which is 24 inches; shipping weight, 49 lbs. Price each.. **$7.13**

Full directions for operating with every stove.

No 15779. The **Giant Acme** Gasoline Stove, with step; two burners on top and one on step, all giving the process flame; height, 27 inches; size of main top, 25x17½ inches; size of step top, 13½x17 inches; shipping weight, 55 lbs. Price each.......................**$8.25**

No. 15780. The **Giant Acme** Gasoline Stove, with step; three burners on top and one on step; size of main top, 33x17½ inches; size of step top, 13½x17 inches; shipping weight, 64 lbs. Price each..........................**$9.75**

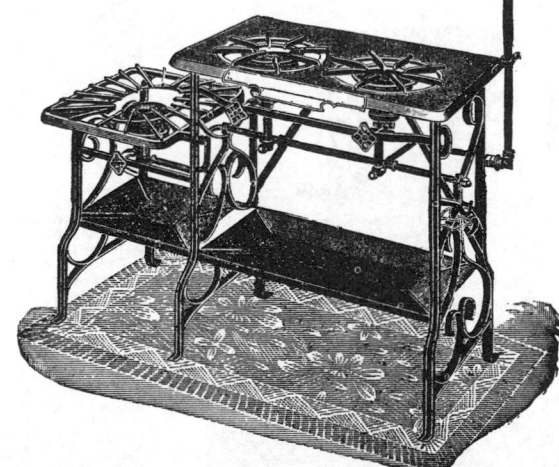

## The Acme Gasoline Ovens.

We have spared no trouble or expense to produce beautiful and perfect ovens. They are larger than any other ovens on the market, lots of room inside, wide space between grates. Will do the largest loaves of bread or roasts of meat without touching upper grate. They are full flued, tin lined, ventilated perfectly, air chamber in door, tastily designed, first-class in every particular. Anything done in them comes out sweet, clean and wholesome. When once used, preferred for baking to the best range ever made, and used the year round. The heat is evenly distributed, baking the tops of articles as thoroughly as the bottoms, without change of position. **All have decorated steel tops.**

No. 15786. **Small tin Oven**; size, 19x12½x13½ inches, full flued, steel top. Price each .........**$1.40**

No. 15787. **Large tin Oven**; size, 19x13x21 inches, full flued, steel top, end door. Price each .....................**$2.00**

No. 15788. **Small Russia Oven**; size, 19x12½x13½ inches, full flued, steel top, end door. Price each ......................**$2.05**

No. 15789. **Large Russia Oven**; size, 19x13x21 inches, full flued, steel top, end door. Price each ......................**$2.50**

No. 15790. **Large Russia Oven**; size, 19x13x21 inches, full flued, steel top, side door. Price each......................**$2.50**

## CARPETS *Direct from the Loom ...*

We command such prices on high grade Ingrains, Tapestry and Body Brussels Carpet that on our one-small-profit plan we can save you all the dealers' profits and give you better goods.

### *Fine Smyrna and Fur Rugs*

### *A Complete Line of Matting*

#### *SEE DRY GOODS DEPARTMENT.*

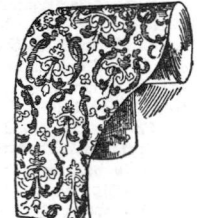

**Freight is but little on a stove, when you consider the great saving we effect for you. It is worth $2.00 to save $10.00.**

## Single Generator Gasoline Stoves.

No. 15781. The **Acme** Single Generator Gasoline Stove, No. 122, has two burners on top and one powerful double burner on step; a single generator serves all burners; every generator provided with a union joint coupling at bottom of stand pipe, and all generators have separate channels; size of main top, 20x27 inches; step top, 20x14 inches; high shelf, 7x22 inches; height to main top, 30 inches; height to top shelf, 44 inches; shipping weight, 105 lbs. **This is our Leader** in this class of stoves, and is as strong, handsome and durable a stove as any one could wish. Price, with tin oven, **$14.25**; with Russia oven....................**$15.00**
Full directions for operating with each stove.

**Acme Gasoline Stove.**

## 1897 Acme Process.

Finest on earth. Greatly improved for 1897. These improvements to be found only in the Acme.

**NOTE REDUCED PRICES.**

### Leading Points:

All Stoves are strongly and substantially built. All stoves are beautifully finished and elegantly designed. All competitors attest to the superiority of our stoves as regards finish and design. All hot air and vaporizing tubes are connected with removable cast iron elbows, easily taken apart, so that the vaporizers can be taken out and cleaned. All vaporizers are made of perforated brass and of the latest scientific construction. All burner drums are of the best sheet brass, and have

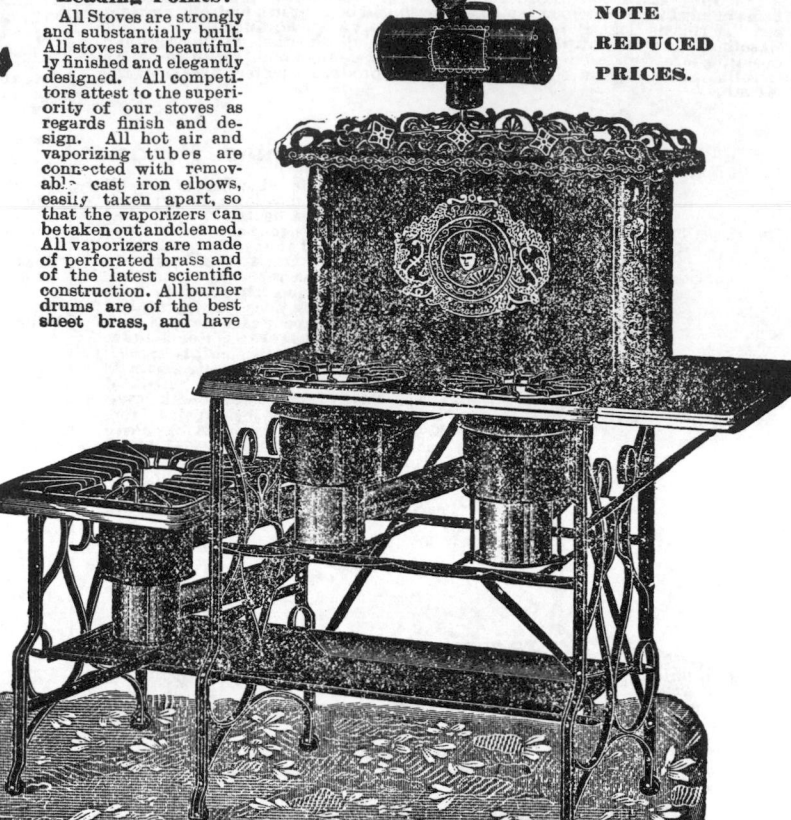

No. 15782. The **Acme** Gasoline Stove, No. 118, must be seen to be appreciated. For compactness, beauty and utility this stove is not surpassed. Single generator for all burners. Oven provided with improved slides and cast iron racks, broiler with XX tin pan, strong rack and improved slides. **Oven guaranteed to bake evenly top and bottom.** Flames on step are one foot apart; ovens and broilers each 17½x15x12 inches. **Two burners** on main top, **two** on step and two under the oven. Height to main top, 35 inches; size of main top, 21x28 inches; size of step top, 15x21 inches; height of high shelf, 49 inches; size of high shelf, 8x23 inches; floor space occupied, 23x28 inches. Shipping weight, 220 lbs. Price each............**$19.50**

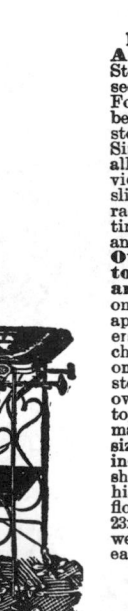

cast iron tops and bottoms. All cone seats are made of cast iron. All cone seats have large iron flanges so as to protect the drums from heat, grease and dirt, which have always caused burner drums to either burn or rust off at the top. This improvement makes all hot air conductors indestructible—a great improvement and one worthy of your consideration. All burners are fastened together with two bolts easily taken apart. All tanks for 1897 are simple, perfect and a proven success. All needle points on valves are made of German silver wire; they will never rust or corrode, and will always insure a steady drip. All tanks are so constructed that they cannot be removed for filling until all valves have been closed. All Acme Process Stoves will run perfectly in cold weather. All in all, the Acme Process is the king of evaporating stoves.

The most beautiful stoves ever manufactured.

No. 15783. The **Acme** Process Stove, No. 18, for 1897, with all improvements as noted above. Has two burners on top and one on step. Main top **in the clear**, 16x22 inches; shelf, 16x12 inches; step, 14x20 inches; height, 30 inches to main top and 54 inches over all; floor space, 38x22 inches; shipping weight, 146 lbs. Price with tin oven, **$15.75**; price, with Russia oven....................**$16.50**

No. 15784. The **Acme** Process Stove No. 19, for 1897, has all improvements noted above. Has three burners on main top and one on step. Main top **in the clear**, 36x16 inches; shelf, 16x12 inches; height, 30 inches to main top and 54 inches over all; shipping weight, 164 lbs. Price with tin oven, **$18.00**; price, with Russia oven.................................................................**$18.75**

No. 15785. The **Acme** Process Cabinet Stove, No. 113, is preferred by some, as it has large capacity and takes up little floor space. No. 113 has two burners on top, one on step and one under oven. Beautifully decorated, strongly constructed. Main top, 27x17; shelf, 16x12; step top, 21x15; height to top, 36 inches; height over all, 63 inches; shipping weight, 222 lbs.; floor space, 37x24.

Price each............**$21.00**

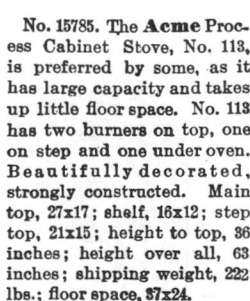

**We can save you money on these Stoves, and you know it by the price we name. If you are afraid to trust your order with us, send it to any express company in Chicago with instructions not to turn it over to us unless they know us to be reliable.**

No. 15791. One-Burner Lamp Stove. Height, 8½ inches; size of cast iron oil fount, 3½x5½ inches; one 4-inch brass burner soldered to fount; weight, per dozen, 50 lbs. Top tips back to light and trim the wick. The front is nicely nickel plated, and is so constructed that the mica frame can be easily removed to allow the user to replace broken mica or clean the old one after it becomes smoky or discolored. This stove is better than many lamp stoves that are being sold for considerably more money. Every stove warranted. Price each............**38c**

No. 15792. Two-Burner Lamp Stove (see cut). Height, 8¼ inches; size of cast iron oil fount, 5½x 5¾ inches; two 4-inch brass burners soldered to fount; weight per dozen, 80 lbs. The oil fount and top are nicely japanned; the mica front and swing doors are nickel plated, and the stove is thoroughly well finished throughout. This stove has swinging mica doors, so that the stove can be easily lighted without tipping back the chimney. Warranted not to leak. Price each......**75c**

No. 15793. Three-Burner Lamp Stove. Height, 8½ inches; size of cast iron oil fount, 5½x8½ inches; three 4-inch brass burners soldered to fount; weight per dozen, 120 lbs. Nickel plated front and swing mica doors, japanned top and oil fount. The combination nickel front and swinging mica doors are valuable features entirely original with us, and are covered by U. S. patents. Our lamp stoves never leak. Every stove is warranted. Price each..........**$1.15**

No. 15974. Wicks for above stoves, four inches wide. Each, **3c**; per doz., **30c**

## Summer Queen Oil Stoves.

No. 15795. It is the only stove made with a water pan, which, by our patented method, is hinged on the oil tank. This arrangement permits free access to any part of the stove.

Size No. 1 Single has one burner 3 inches wide. Price each..........**85c**
Size No. 2 Single has two burners 3 inches wide. Price each..........**$1.15**
Size No. 3 Single has two burners 4 inches wide. Price each..........**$1.60**
Size No. 3½ Single has three burners 4 inches wide. Price each..........**$2.00**

## Double Summer Queen Oil Stoves.

Size No. 2 Double has four burners 3 inches wide. Price each..........**$2.35**
Size No. 3 Double has four burners 4 inches wide. Price each..........**$3.27**
Size No. 3½ Double has six burners 4 inches wide. Price each..........**$4.15**

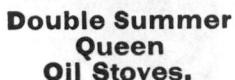

No. 15796.

## Reliance Oil Stoves.

No. 15797. The Reliance is a well made stove in every particular, and is the cheapest well made stove on the market, has three 4-inch burners. Price each..........**$1.35**

No. 103.

No. 15798. Reliance No. 102, Double Stove, has four burners 3 inches wide. Price each..........**$1.60**
Reliance No. 102½, Double Stove, has four burners 4 inches wide. Price..........**$2.20**
Reliance No. 103, Double Stove, has six burners 4 inches wide. Price..........**$2.80**

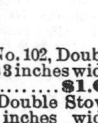

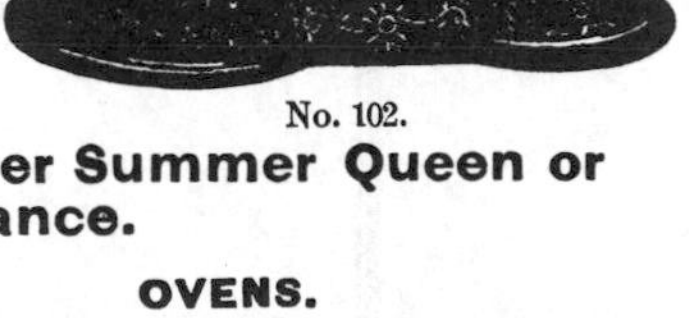

No. 102.

## Furnishings for Either Summer Queen or Reliance.

### OVENS.

No. 15799. No. 2 fits No. 2 Single or Double Stove, 11 inches wide, 12 inches long, 10 inches high. Price double casing..........**$1.55**
No. 3 fits No. 3 Single or Double Stove, 13 inches wide, 14 inches long, 12 inches high. Price double casing..........**$2.10**
No. 3½ fits No. 3½ Single or Double Stove, 14½ inches wide, 17½ inches long, 13¾ inches high. Price double casing..........**$2.60**

No. 15799.

### EXTENSION TOPS.

No. 15800. Queen Extension, fitting Nos. 3 and 3½ Single or Double Stoves. Price each........**$1.15**

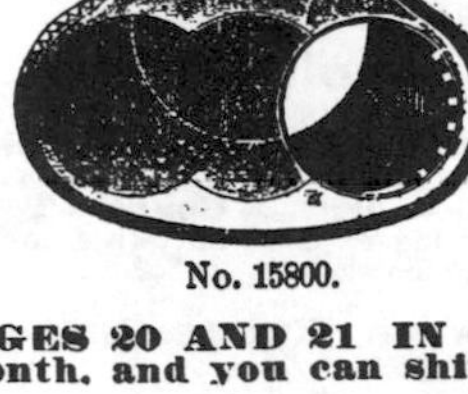

### SAD IRON HEATERS.

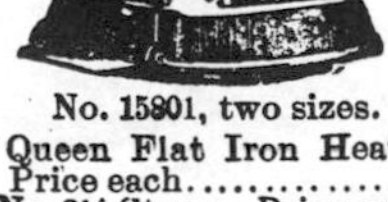

No. 15801, two sizes.

No. 15801. Queen Flat Iron Heater. No. 3 fits No. 3 Stove. Price each..........**50c**
No. 3½ fits No. 3½ Stove. Price each........**70c**

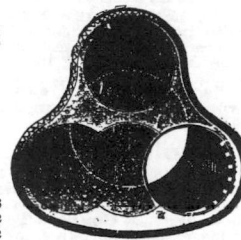

No. 15800.

No. 15802. Queen Upright. This style fits only No. 3½ Summer Queen. Price..........**70c**

No. 15802.

## The Acme Central-Draft, Round-Wick, Oil Cook Stove.

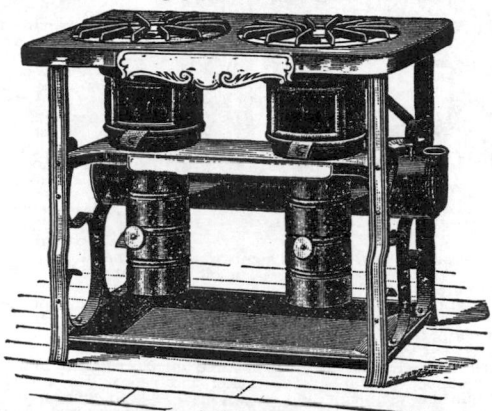

Our line of **Acme** Oil Cook Stoves is an embodiment of art and utility. They are modern in design, honest in construction, perfect in combustion. **Elaborately finished in nickel** and sure to give the best of satisfaction. We have spared neither labor nor money to make the **Acme** Cook Stoves the **finest finished, most durable** and **best operating** oil cook stoves in the world. Modern ideas and improvements make them the most convenient and economical stoves ever placed on the market. Our prices are always the lowest, quality considered.

No. 15803. One-Burner **Acme** Stove. Height, 17 inches; size of top, 14x14 inches; weight, crated, 20 lbs; **nickel trimmed, polished brass fount and burner,** 7½ inch circular wick. The fount holds one-half gallon and is located back of the burner at sufficient distance to keep it perfectly cool and prevent the oil from becoming heated. **The patent central draft burner is made entirely of brass,** and is a marvel of simplicity (any one can operate or rewick it). The chimney can be tipped back or quickly removed for lighting, trimming or putting in new wick; removable top grate, a big advantage in cleaning stove. Price each..........**$2.65**

No. 15804. Two-Burner **Acme** Stove (same as cut). Height, 17 inches; size of top, 15x24 inches; weight, crated, 30 lbs.; **nickel trimmed, polished brass fount and burners,** two 10-inch central draft burners, with circular wicks; give an even, white and intensely hot flame; the polished brass fount holds 1 gallon; is provided with patent automatic indicator, and is located back of the burners at sufficient distance to keep the oil perfectly cool; the **patent removable chimneys** and **top grates** are a great advantage in cleaning, also in lighting, trimming and putting in new wick. Price each..........**$4.20**

No. 15805. Three-Burner **Acme** Stove. Height, 17 inches; size of top, 15x34; weight crated, 35 lbs.; nickel trimmed, polished brass burners and founts, 10-inch circular wick, three powerful 10-inch central draft burners give an intensely hot flame, and will do all kinds of cooking and baking as well or better than any gasoline stove. The polished brass fount is provided with the Acme patent automatic indicator, has a capacity of 1½ gallons, and is located back of the burners at sufficient distance to keep the oil perfectly cool. Price each..........**$5.50**

No. 15806. **Acme** Cook Stove. Height, 30 inches; size of top, 20x45 inches; weight crated, 80 lbs.; mounted on rollers, **full nickel trimmed, polished brass fount and burners.** This stove is a three-burner step stove, resembling a gasoline stove in appearance. It has two 10-inch and one 16-inch powerful **patent central draft burner,** and will do more and better cooking and baking than most ranges or gasoline stoves. The polished brass founts have a capacity of 2½ gallons; are located back of the burners at sufficient distance to keep them perfectly cool and prevent the oil becoming heated, and are provided with our Acme patent automatic indicator; removable chimneys and top grates. The handsomest and most powerful oil cook stove ever produced.

Price each, without oven................................................**$12.00**
Price, with Russia oven..................................................**14.00**

A COMPLETE LINE OF OILS ON PAGES 20 AND 21 IN GROCERY DEPARTMENT. Make up a regular freight order of Groceries each month, and you can ship small goods along, with no extra expense.

## SOMETHING NEW.

**No. 15807. Acme Blue Flame Oil Cook Stoves;** clean and odorless, economical and efficient, safe and durable. They require no more care than an ordinary lamp. They are the embodiment of **art** and **utility.** Modern ideas and improvements make them the **most convenient, safe** and **economical** stoves ever placed on the market. Have the efficiency of the gasoline stove, and avoid the danger of having gasoline about the house. They were made first last year, and the makers could not fill their orders working day and night. Any cooking utensil can be placed directly in the flame. Will do better work than any gasoline stove ever made, and without the danger and disagreeable odor of gasoline. Acme Blue Flame Oil Cook Stoves lead—others follow. The Acme patent blue flame burners never get hot—all others do. The Acme patent check-stop, or lock and wick-raising device, is the acme of perfection and simplicity, any child can operate it. The services of a mechanical expert are never required by those who use Acme Stoves. No smoke, no odor, simple, novel, practical, perfectly safe, cannot explode. Elegantly finished in nickel and black, mounted on rollers, fount holds 1½ gallons oil. Height, 29 inches; weight, 60 lbs. Price......**$7.00**

Each stove is thoroughly tested before leaving factory, is warranted to be perfect and give absolute satisfaction.

No. 15808. Stove like No. 15807, with three burners; height, 29 inches; weight, 90 pounds; mounted on rollers, full nickel trimmed, polished brass fount and burners. Fount has a capacity of two gallons, and is so constructed that the oil never gets hot, as it does in other makes of blue flame stoves. **Acme patent central draft burners, automatic oil indicator and removable chimneys and top grates.** Price each......................................**$8.75**

No. 15809. Height, 17 inches; weight, 50 pounds; nickel trimmed; three powerful patent central draft burners, give an even blue and intensely hot flame, and will do all kinds of cooking and baking better than any gasoline stove, and without the unpleasant odor or danger of gasoline; fount holds 1½ gallons. Same as stove No. 15807, except has no tea shelf, and is 17 inches high instead of 29 inches. Price each...........................................**$7.00**

No. 15810. Height, 17 inches; weight, 40 pounds; nickel trimmed; polished brass fount and patent central draft burners, same as used on our large stoves; fount holds one gallon and is provided with our patent automatic indicator. Same as stove No. 15809, except it has only two burners. Acme stoves cannot explode, others can. Price each...........................................**$5.25**

No. 15811. Height, 17 inches; weight, 25 pounds; nickel trimmed; polished brass fount and burner; 10-inch circular wick; patent central draft burner; removable chimney and top grate. Same as stove No. 15810, except it has but one burner. Price each...........................................**$3.50**

**Acme** Blue Flame Burners are always cool, which is a very important feature possessed by no other blue flame stove.

**Acme** Blue Flame Oil Cook Stoves are the handsomest and most powerful blue flame oil cook stove ever made; have all the improvements embodied in our Acme Blue Flame Oil Cook Stove, with the advantage of the step. Height, 29 inches; length, 45 inches; top, 30x20 inches; step, 15x20 inches; weight, 120 pounds.
No. 15812. Price without Oven............................................ ........**$11.90**
No. 15813. Price with Russia Oven....................................... **14.00**

## The Choicest Parisian Novelties

..*IN*..

# Ladies' Capes

See full page Plates in Dry Goods
Department.

*Leaders in Style....Leaders in Price.*

## Oil Heaters.

**No. 15814. The Acme Oil Heater.**
No. 1775. Extreme height, 32 inches; diameter of lower Russia iron section, 7 inches; diameter of top section or heating drum, 6 inches; circumference of central draft wick, 5½ inches; circumference of pure white flame, 12 inches.

This is our smallest stove, and is a very powerful heater for its size, and is as well made in every way as our largest and most expensive stove. It was brought out expressly for heating bath rooms, sewing rooms and small bed rooms, and will be found far more desirable for these purposes than a large, heavy stove.

Being very light, it is easily carried from one room to another, and does not require casters. Price each, **$6.00**

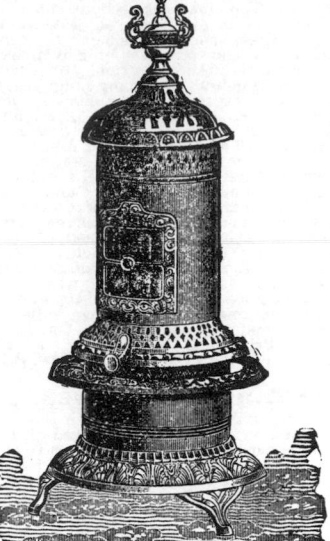

**No. 15815. The Acme Oil Heater.**
No. 1776. Extreme height, 36 inches; diameter of lower Russia iron section, 8 inches; diameter of top section or heating drum, 7 inches; circumference of central draft wick, 7½ inches; circumference of pure white flame, 15 inches.

This is our second size heater, and will be found one of the most desirable sizes for bedrooms, small offices and large bathrooms, and will throw more heat with corresponding size wick than any similar heater on the market.

The best proof of its merits is to test it.

This stove is fitted with hardwood casters in legs. Price each....**$7.33**
No. 15816. **Wicks for Acme Oil Heater.**
For No. 15814 stove, each, 6c; per dozen .............................**60c**
For No. 15815 stoves, each, 7c; per dozen .............................**70c**

## Gasoline and Oil Torches.

**No. 15816. The Acme Gasoline Torches,** for indoor or outdoor lighting; are not affected by wind, rain, cold or heat. They produce a large, brilliant, white flame, equal in volume to 10 gas jet flames. The reservoir holds nearly six quarts, and when filled will burn full flame for 9 hours. Price each.....................................**$1.25**
No. 15817. **The Acme Coal Oil Torch** is similar in general appearance to the gasoline torch with the exception of burner. When the reservoir is filled it will burn full flame for 15½ hours. Price each.....**$1.30**

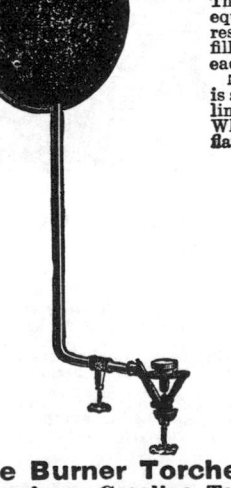

## Double Burner Torches.

No. 15818. **Acme Gasoline Torch,** with two burners, controlled by separate valves, so one only may be used if desired. The burners are 34 inches apart. Price each.....................................**$2.25**
No. 15819. **Acme Coal Oil Torch,** with two burners, same as above, except the burner. Price each....................**$2.30**

## Gasoline Torch Burners.

No. 15818½. **Gasoline Torch Burner,** same as used on our Acme Gasoline Torches. Price each.....................................**$1.00**
No. 15819½. **Coal Oil Torch Burners,** same as used on our Acme Coal Oil Torch. Price each.....................................**$1.05**

# STOVE DEPARTMENT.

In our stove department will be found a complete line of stoves, ranges and heaters in all the various sizes, styles, prices, etc., suitable for any kind of fuel. Notwithstanding the advance in cost of material and labor, we are able to make prices lower than ever before. Our sales have heretofore been phenomenal, but there is no limit to our ambition. We propose to sell twice as many stoves in 1896 as we did in 1895. Read our description carefully and notice many improvements. Note carefully the weights and size, and you will find no one can compete with us.

## ..GUARANTEE..

In each and every Sunshine Stove or Range sold by us will be found a fair, full, legal guarantee, engraved and printed on bond paper and signed by the manufacturers, warranting the stove to be perfect in manufacture and perfect in operation; that any defects in material or workmanship will be made good to the purchaser without charge. Never before has any stove manufacturer given any such liberal, broad, legal guarantee in black and white. It could only be done with the very best goods possible to be made.

**We can save you about 50 per cent.** on everything in this line, and you will also be sure of getting the highest grade goods on the market, goods made by one of the largest and most reliable manufacturers in America, a concern whose enviable reputation for the manufacture of strictly high grade stoves ought to be a guarantee for the quality.

**Freight is very low on stoves.** They are accepted by all railroad companies at third (3d) class freight rate, and you will see by weight of stove given under each description and third class freight rate to different states, as shown in front of book, that freight amounts to nothing compared with what you save in price.

**Our terms are very liberal.** We will ship any stove to any address within 1,000 miles of Chicago, by freight C. O. D., subject to examination, on receipt of $5.00 as a guarantee of good faith. You can examine it at the freight depot and if found perfectly satisfactory and exactly as represented pay the freight agent our price and freight charges, less the $5.00 sent with order.

**Three per cent. discount** will be allowed if cash in full accompanies your order. **You take no risk** for we will immediately refund your money, if you do not find goods perfectly satisfactory.

## DIRECTIONS FOR OPERATING STOVES.

To secure a good operation in all kinds of stoves and ranges, see—

First—That the flue stopper is in its place.

Second—That the chimney is clear and has a good draft at pipe hole. Many chimneys are made too low, and draw better when a "smoke stack" is put on them.

Third—That the pipe fits closely on the stove and in the chimney. No air should go in outside the pipe.

Fourth—That the pipe does not go too far in the chimney.

Fifth—That no ashes from chimney get into the end of the pipe.

Sixth—Avoid having the pipe telescope at the elbow. If you have all these parts properly adjusted and well arranged, open the direct draft damper and see if you can get a good fire in the stove, together with a strong draft. If the stove will not burn well then, the trouble is not in the stove but above it.

If the fire burns well on the above direct shaft, close the oven damper; then if it will not heat the oven and bake well, please examine the flues and damper, and see—

First—That all the flues are open and clear, so that the smoke can clearly pass through them. In cleaning flues, many do not clean all the flues and frequently push soot and ashes into back corners, and in that way stop them up.

Second—Examine all the dampers in the flues, and see that they open and close tightly and do not get out of place.

Third—Be sure that you know how they operate, so they may not be open when you think they are closed.

If you are trying a stove without a hot water reservoir, and have everything in good order as heretofore described, it cannot possibly fail in operation if you close the direct draft damper and throw all the heat around the oven. Time should be given to get the oven hot before trying to bake.

If you have a stove with a reservoir, be sure that the damper (if one is in the stove) to force the heat under the reservoir is closed, so that all the heat must go around the oven. Many reservoir stoves have two dampers, and in that case both should be closed.

We have known many persons who have tried to use such stoves with the damper under reservoir open when they thought it was closed. On that account the oven heated too slow, but worked fast enough when they closed the damper.

No pipe or utensils furnished with stoves at prices quoted. We can furnish repairs promptly for any stove we sell. We do not black stoves to make them "show up" better, but ship them just as we receive them from the foundry. Our prices are free on board cars, in Chicago.

### SIGNAL SUNSHINE.
#### For coal or wood, with Reservoir.

No. 15820. With coal fixtures.
No. 15821. With wood fixtures.
No. 15822. With both fixtures, add $1.00 to price quoted.

Our leading cheap coal or wood cook. With nickel panels; an entirely new and handsome dress, without burnished edges or tin lined oven doors. With portable outside oven shelf, flush swinging hearth plate, large fire box, nickel-plated knobs and pins, heavy covers with cut centers, very heavy sectional fire box and linings, oven door pedal attachment for opening oven door. Has 4 covers.

| Size. | Covers. | Size of Oven. | Weight. | Each. |
|---|---|---|---|---|
| 108 | 8 in. | 16x20 | 250 lbs. | $12.00 |
| 118 | 8 in. | 18x22 | 290 lbs. | 13.50 |
| 109 | 9 in. | 18x22 | 295 lbs. | 14.10 |

**Signal Sunshine** Cook **without Reservoir** or **Shelf** under reservoir, otherwise like cut above.

No. 15823. With coal fixtures.
No. 15824. With wood fixtures.
No. 15825. With both fixtures, add $1.00 to price quoted.

| Size. | Covers. | Size of Oven. | Weight. | Each. |
|---|---|---|---|---|
| 107 | 7 in. | 14x18 | 165 lbs. | $ 7.29 |
| 108 | 8 in. | 16x20 | 200 lbs. | 8.40 |
| 118 | 8 in. | 18x22 | 230 lbs. | 10.06 |
| 109 | 9 in. | 18x22 | 235 lbs. | 10.67 |

**No Stove Pipe or Stove Furniture goes with stoves at these prices. Make your own selection of furniture.**

## MERIT SUNSHINE.

### For hard or soft coal or wood, with Reservoir.

The Merit Sunshine is a substantial, well constructed stove of improved design, intended to meet the demand for a well made and attractive stove at a low price. The design is new and neat, and workmanship is equal to the best. The special features of this stove are: Cut top plates with heavy, deep edges; heavy rim covers and centers; heavy grate and fire box lining, dumping and shaking grates; nickel knobs and hinge pins; handsome nickel panel on oven door and on front doors; outside oven shelf; tin lined oven door; improved, nearly square oven, with broad rack.

No. 15826.  With hard or soft coal fixtures.

No. 15827.  With wood fixtures.

No. 15828.  With both fixtures, add $1.25 to prices quoted.

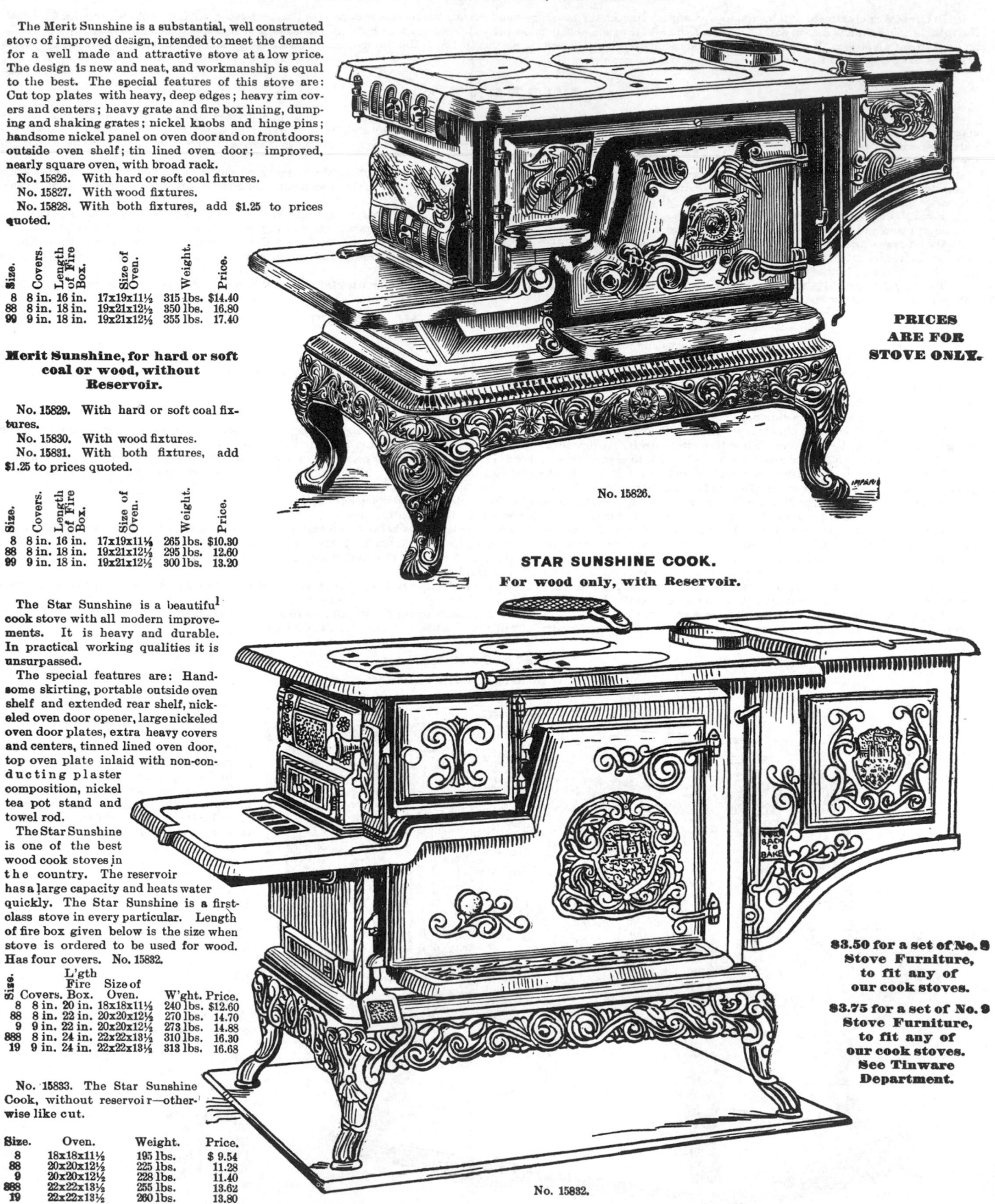

| Size. | Covers. | Length of Fire Box. | Size of Oven. | Weight. | Price. |
|---|---|---|---|---|---|
| 8 | 8 in. | 16 in. | 17x19x11½ | 315 lbs. | $14.40 |
| 88 | 8 in. | 18 in. | 19x21x12½ | 350 lbs. | 16.80 |
| 99 | 9 in. | 18 in. | 19x21x12½ | 355 lbs. | 17.40 |

### Merit Sunshine, for hard or soft coal or wood, without Reservoir.

No. 15829.  With hard or soft coal fixtures.

No. 15830.  With wood fixtures.

No. 15831.  With both fixtures, add $1.25 to prices quoted.

| Size. | Covers. | Length of Fire Box. | Size of Oven. | Weight. | Price. |
|---|---|---|---|---|---|
| 8 | 8 in. | 16 in. | 17x19x11½ | 265 lbs. | $10.30 |
| 88 | 8 in. | 18 in. | 19x21x12½ | 295 lbs. | 12.60 |
| 99 | 9 in. | 18 in. | 19x21x12½ | 300 lbs. | 13.20 |

**No. 15826.**

**PRICES ARE FOR STOVE ONLY.**

The Star Sunshine is a beautiful cook stove with all modern improvements. It is heavy and durable. In practical working qualities it is unsurpassed.

The special features are: Handsome skirting, portable outside oven shelf and extended rear shelf, nickeled oven door opener, large nickeled oven door plates, extra heavy covers and centers, tinned lined oven door, top oven plate inlaid with non-conducting plaster composition, nickel tea pot stand and towel rod.

The Star Sunshine is one of the best wood cook stoves in the country. The reservoir has a large capacity and heats water quickly. The Star Sunshine is a first-class stove in every particular. Length of fire box given below is the size when stove is ordered to be used for wood. Has four covers. No. 15832.

## STAR SUNSHINE COOK.

### For wood only, with Reservoir.

| Size. | Covers. | L'gth Fire Box. | Size of Oven. | W'ght. | Price. |
|---|---|---|---|---|---|
| 8 | 8 in. | 20 in. | 18x18x11½ | 240 lbs. | $12.60 |
| 88 | 8 in. | 22 in. | 20x20x12½ | 270 lbs. | 14.70 |
| 9 | 9 in. | 22 in. | 20x20x12½ | 273 lbs. | 14.88 |
| 888 | 8 in. | 24 in. | 22x22x13½ | 310 lbs. | 16.30 |
| 19 | 9 in. | 24 in. | 22x22x13½ | 313 lbs. | 16.68 |

No. 15833.  The Star Sunshine Cook, without reservoir—otherwise like cut.

| Size. | Oven. | Weight. | Price. |
|---|---|---|---|
| 8 | 18x18x11½ | 195 lbs. | $ 9.54 |
| 88 | 20x20x12½ | 225 lbs. | 11.28 |
| 9 | 20x20x12½ | 228 lbs. | 11.40 |
| 888 | 22x22x13½ | 255 lbs. | 13.62 |
| 19 | 22x22x13½ | 260 lbs. | 13.80 |

**$3.50** for a set of No. 8 Stove Furniture, to fit any of our cook stoves.

**$3.75** for a set of No. 9 Stove Furniture, to fit any of our cook stoves. See Tinware Department.

**No. 15832.**

**Prices named for Stove do not include Pipe or Stove Utensils.  Make your own selection from our catalogue.**

**PRICES ARE FOR
STOVE WITHOUT
FURNITURE OR
PIPE.**

**$3.50 for set of No. 8
Stove Furniture,
to fit any of our stoves
or ranges.**

**$3.75 for set of No. 9
Stove Furniture,
to fit any of our stoves
or ranges.**

No. 15834.

### SOUTHERN SUNSHINE COOK.

**For wood, with Reservoir.**

No. 15834. The Southern Sunshine with reservoir embodies every improvement that experience and ingenuity can suggest.

In style and selling points it surpasses its best competitors.

Though low in price it is a strong and durable stove. Length of fire box given below is the size when stove is ordered to be used for wood.

| Size. | Size of Covers. | Length of Fire Box. | Size of Oven. | Shipping Weight. | Price. |
|---|---|---|---|---|---|
| 8 | 8 in. | 20 in. | 18x18x12 | 216 lbs. | $10.38 |
| 88 | 8 in. | 22 in. | 20x20x12½ | 242 lbs. | 11.88 |
| 9 | 9 in. | 22 in. | 20x20x12½ | 245 lbs. | 12.18 |
| 888 | 8 in. | 24 in. | 22x22x13½ | 288 lbs. | 13.62 |
| 19 | 9 in. | 24 in. | 22x22x13½ | 295 lbs. | 13.80 |

15835. Southern Sunshine Cook, for wood. Plain square stove without reservoir. The length of fire box given below is the size when stove is ordered to be used for wood.

| Size | Size of Covers. | Length of Fire Box. | Size of Oven. | Shipping Weight. | Price. |
|---|---|---|---|---|---|
| 7 | 7 in. | 18 in. | 16x17x12 | 138 lbs. | $ 5.97 |
| 8 | 8 in. | 20 in. | 18x18x12½ | 175 lbs. | 7.35 |
| 88 | 8 in. | 22 in. | 20x20x12½ | 191 lbs. | 8.86 |
| 9 | 9 in. | 22 in. | 20x20x12½ | 197 lbs. | 9.00 |
| 888 | 8 in. | 24 in. | 22x22x13½ | 225 lbs. | 10.36 |
| 19 | 9 in. | 24 in. | 22x22x13½ | 230 lbs. | 10.56 |

### GLAD SUNSHINE RANGE.
**For hard or soft coal, with Reservoir.**

No. 15836.

No. 15836. Though low in price, quality has not been sacrificed to price in the construction of this range. It has all the latest improvements—ventilated oven, solid end hearth, duplex grate, patent pedal attachment, quick draft damper, etc. We are inclined to think that nothing so good and serviceable has ever before been offered for the money required to buy this range. This range has six holes.

| Size. | Size of Covers. | Size of Oven. | Shipping Weight. | Price. |
|---|---|---|---|---|
| 80 | 8 in. | 17x18x11½ | 306 lbs. | $19.00 |
| 18 | 8 in. | 19x20x12 | 345 lbs. | 21.60 |

No. 15836½. The Glad Sunshine Range, for hard or soft coal, without reservoir.

| Size. | Size of Covers. | Size of Oven. | Shipping Weight. | Price. |
|---|---|---|---|---|
| 80 | 8 in. | 17x18x11¼ | 270 lbs. | $14.00 |
| 18 | 8 in. | 19x20x12 | 302 lbs. | 16.75 |

Water-back and couplings, extra $4.00.

### TRUE SUNSHINE RANGE.

No. 15837. Hard or soft coal. The True Sunshine is the best type of this class of ranges that has ever been offered for sale. The flues are better constructed. The range is more attractive in appearance than any of its competitors. Has five holes; duplex grate.

| Size. | Size of Covers. | Size of Oven. | Shipping Weight. | Price. |
|---|---|---|---|---|
| 71 | 7 in. | 13x14x10 | 180 lbs. | $ 9.53 |
| 81 | 8 in. | 15x16x10½ | 225 lbs. | 10.80 |

Water-back and couplings, extra $4.00.

## HOME SUNSHINE RANGE.

**For hard or soft coal or wood, with Reservoir and High Shelf.**

No. 15838.   With hard or soft coal fixtures.
No. 15839.   With wood fixtures.
No. 15840.   With both fixtures, add $1.50 to price quoted.

Many people prefer a range to a cook stove. The Home Range is a desirable range with a good size square oven, large top, six holes, large flues, excellent fire box, flues ventilated, of first-class construction and ornamentation. It is sure to please in use. Can furnish this range without high shelf. Deduct from price when range is ordered without high shelf $1.80.

| Size. | Size of Covers | Size of oven. | Weight. | Price. |
|---|---|---|---|---|
| 80 | 8 in. | 17x18x11¼ | 290 lbs. | $19.42 |
| 18 | 8 in. | 19x20x12 | 336 lbs. | 21.75 |

Weight does not include high shelf, which weighs 30 lbs.

### Home Sunshine Range without Reservoir or High Shelf.

No. 15841.   With hard or soft coal fixtures.
No. 15842.   With wood fixtures.
No. 15843.   With both fixtures, add $1.50 to prices quoted.

| Size. | Size of Covers. | Size of Oven. | Weight. | Price. |
|---|---|---|---|---|
| 80 | 8 in. | 17x18x11¼ | 270 lbs. | $12.60 |
| 18 | 8 in. | 19x20x12 | 302 lbs. | 15.00 |

Water-back and couplings, extra $4.00.

We can furnish the range with high shelf. If ordered with high shelf, add $1.80 to prices quoted.

No. 15838.

No. 15850.

## OTHELLO RANGE, WITH EXTRA LARGE OVEN.

### For hard or soft coal or wood, with Reservoir and High Shelf and Skirting.

The Othello Range is made with special hard coal feature, yet has very large flues for soft coal; has brick linings. Our improved system of oven ventilation is a great feature of this range, with detachable end hearth as shown above. A hard coal fire in the Othello can be run constantly night and day and always be as good as a new fire. Handsomely ornamented with ground edges, nickel towel rod, nice castings and perfect mounting. The length of fire box given below is the size when stove is ordered to be used for wood. Has six hole top.

No. 15844.   With hard or soft coal fixtures.
No. 15845.   With wood fixtures.
No. 15846.   With both fixtures, add $1.50 to prices quoted.

| Size. | Size of Covers. | Length of Fire Box. | Size of Oven. | Weight. | Price. |
|---|---|---|---|---|---|
| 138 | 8 in. | 22 in. | 18x19x12½ | 417 lbs. | $25.73 |

We can furnish above range without high shelf. If ordered without high shelf deduct $2.93.

No. 15844.

**Othello Range, with extra large Oven. For hard or soft coal or wood, with Skirting.**

Without Reservoir or High Shelf.
No. 15847.   With hard or soft coal fixtures.
No. 15848.   With wood fixtures.
No. 15849.   With both fixtures, add $1.50 to prices quoted.

| Size. | Size of Covers. | Length of Fire Box. | Size of Oven. | Weight. | Price. |
|---|---|---|---|---|---|
| 138 | 8 in. | 22 in. | 18x19x12½ | 360 lbs. | $18.00 |

We can furnish the above range with high shelf. If ordered with high shelf add $2.98 to prices quoted.

## PERFECT SUNSHINE RANGE.

### For hard or soft coal or wood, with Reservoir and High Shelf.

The Perfect Sunshine Ranges have four holes, but are as large on the top as the general run of six-hole ranges. First-class in every respect. Has flues of such large capacity as to insure a quick, strong draft and perfect operation, even with the poorer qualities of coal. Has Read's patent check damper, which gives the user perfect control of the draft. Oven ventilating device, the most sensible and convenient arrangement in use for ventilating the oven. Heavy flat covers and cross pieces, which are far more durable than those deeply ribbed or fluted. Beautiful design and finish, which would alone give the Perfect Sunshine the lead over any of its competitors. The length of fire box given below is the size when stove is ordered to be used for wood. We can furnish this range without high shelf. If ordered without high shelf, deduct $2.95.

No. 15850.   With coal fixtures.
No. 15851.   With wood fixtures.
No. 15852.   With both fixtures, add $1.75 to prices quoted.

| Size. | Size of Covers. | Length of Fire Box. | Size of Oven. | Weight. | Price. |
|---|---|---|---|---|---|
| 8 | 8 in. | 20 in. | 18x20x11 | 382 lbs. | $25.43 |
| 8-20 | 8 in. | 22 in. | 20x21x12½ | 438 lbs. | 28.73 |
| 9-20 | 9 in. | 22 in. | 20x21x12½ | 445 lbs. | 29.33 |

Weights given do not include high shelf, which weighs 45 lbs.

### The Perfect Sunshine Range, without Reservoir or High Shelf. For hard or soft coal or wood.

No. 15853.   With coal fixtures.
No. 15854.   With wood fixtures.
No. 15855.   With both fixtures, add $1.75 to price quoted.

| Size. | Size of Covers. | Length of Fire Box. | Size of Oven. | Weight. | Price. |
|---|---|---|---|---|---|
| 8 | 8 in. | 20 in. | 18x20x11 | 331 lbs. | $16.80 |
| 8-20 | 8 in. | 22 in. | 20x21x12½ | 385 lbs. | 19.20 |
| 9-20 | 9 in. | 22 in. | 20x21x12½ | 392 lbs. | 20.40 |

We can furnish this range with high shelf. If high shelf is ordered, add $2.95 to prices quoted.

**PRICES ON STOVES DO NOT INCLUDE PIPE OR FURNITURE.**

## NEW SUNSHINE RANGE.
### For hard or soft coal or wood.

The New Sunshine is faultless in construction, containing every useful invention known to stove manufacturers. The duplex grate, quick draft damper and patent pedal attachments are all found on this range. Our oven ventilating device, first used by us in 1876 because of its simplicity and common sense, has reached a success and popularity not attained by any rival method of oven ventilation. Our device enables the user to change the range instantly, by simply operating a slide, from a ventilated oven to a tight oven range, and to regulate the volume of inflowing or outflowing air at will. Six hole top. The length of the fire box given below is the size when stove is ordered to be used for wood.

No. 15856. With hard or soft coal fixtures.
No. 15857. With wood fixtures.
No. 15858. With both fixtures, add to prices quoted $2.00.

| Size. | Size of Covers. | Length of Fire Box. | Size of Oven. | Weight. | Price. |
|---|---|---|---|---|---|
| 118 | 8 in. | 20 in. | 18x19x11 | 422 lbs. | $28.13 |
| 118-20 | 8 in. | 23 in. | 20x21x11¾ | 484 lbs. | 32.93 |
| 119 | 9 in. | 23 in. | 20x31x11¾ | 490 lbs. | 34.28 |
| 922 | 9 in. | 25 in. | 22x23x13½ | 528 lbs. | 38.75 |

Water-back and couplings, $4.00 extra.
Weights given do not include high shelf, which weighs 47 lbs.

If above stove is wanted in any size without high shelf, deduct $3.00.

The New Sunshine Range, for hard or soft coal or wood, without Reservoir or High Shelf.

No. 15859. With hard or soft coal fixtures.
No. 15860. With wood fixtures.
No. 15861. With both fixtures, add to prices quoted $2.00.

| No. | Size of Covers. | Length of Fire Box. | Size of Oven. | Weight. | Price. |
|---|---|---|---|---|---|
| 118 | 8 in. | 20 in. | 18x19x11 | 363 lbs. | $20.70 |
| 118-20 | 8 in. | 23 in. | 20x21x11¾ | 428 lbs. | 24.75 |
| 119 | 9 in. | 23 in. | 20x21x11¾ | 433 lbs. | 26.10 |
| 9-22 | 9 in. | 25 in. | 22x23x13½ | 453 lbs. | 29.50 |

We can furnish this range with high shelf.
If ordered with high shelf, add to prices quoted $3.00.

**Prices named here do not include stove furniture.**

No. 15856.

## THE STERLING SUNSHINE STEEL PLATE RANGE.
### With High Shelf.

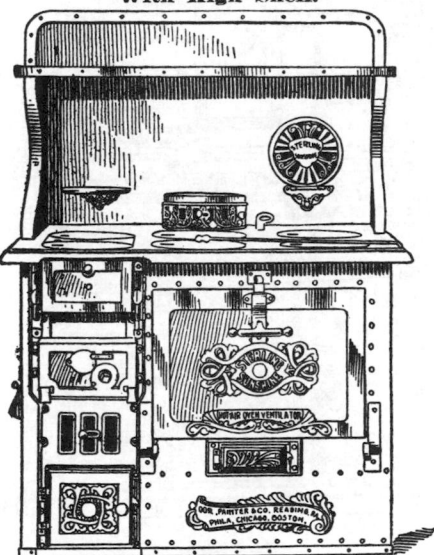

No. 15862.

No. 15862. With coal fixtures.
No. 15863. With wood fixtures.
No. 15864. With both fixtures, add $5 to prices quoted.
This range is constructed like No. 15865 (except it has no reservoir and has high shelf instead of high closet). Dimensions are the same.

| No. | Weight. | Price. |
|---|---|---|
| 68-18 | 500 lbs. | $33.30 |
| 68-20 | 522 lbs. | 37.20 |
| 69-20 | 530 lbs. | 37.80 |

## THE STERLING SUNSHINE STEEL PLATE RANGE.

With high closet and reservoir for hard or soft coal or wood. To meet the demand for a steel range we offer the **Sterling Sunshine**, in which is combined solidity, durability, efficiency and convenience. It has no devices for mere show and appearance, but it has **every good feature** that will promote **utility, convenience** and **durability. Special features:** The entire outer body is one piece of heavy, cold-rolled wrought steel. Inside the outer body there is a wall of asbestos (the best non-conductor known), and inside the asbestos a lining of sheet steel. All other parts of the range (except the oven) are also lined with asbestos. This method of construction concentrates the heat in the oven and secures an economy in fuel never heretofore attained. The top rim is cut in four sections. The slip plates, covers, and cross pieces are heavy and durable. The reservoir holds 15 gallons and the water is heated by a half-size water front by circulation, which does not interfere at any time with baking. Has six holes.

No. 15865. With coal fixtures.
No. 15866. With wood fixtures.
No. 15867. With both fixtures, add $5 to prices quoted.

We can furnish this range without reservoir. If ordered without reservoir, deduct $8 from prices quoted.

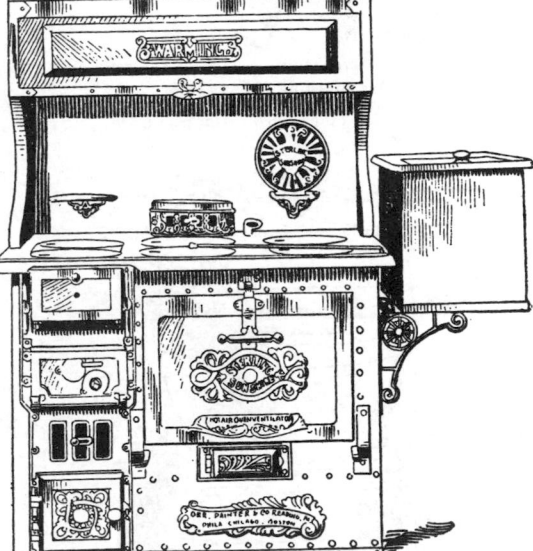

No. 15865.

| No. | Size of Covers. | Size of Oven. | Size of Top. | Weight. | Price. |
|---|---|---|---|---|---|
| 68-18 | 8 in. | 18x14x22 | 36x30 | 550 lbs. | $44.40 |
| 68-20 | 8 in. | 20x14x22 | 39x30 | 585 lbs. | 48.30 |
| 69-20 | 9 in. | 20x14x22 | 39x30 | 590 lbs. | 48.90 |

**Send for our Special Catalogue on Steel Ranges.**

## FAMILY SUNSHINE RANGE.

### With Reservoir and High Shelf and Low Closet.

No. 15868. For hard or soft coal. This is a large and superior range, with capacious ventilated oven, sheet flue, lower hot closet, large and well shaped fire box and the best sifter (patented arrangement) ever made, duplex grates. It is a complete kitchener in all its parts. The Family Sunshine is made with cut tops, and with the range and hot closet mounted separately. This range has six holes.

| Size. | Size of covers. | Size of oven. | Weight. | Price. |
|---|---|---|---|---|
| 80 | 8 | 20x20x12¼ | 618 lbs. | $35.90 |
| 90 | 9 | 20x20x12¼ | 628 lbs. | 36.50 |

No. 15869. This range with low closet and high shelf without reservoir.

| Size. | Weight. | Price. |
|---|---|---|
| 80 | 540 lbs. | $28.35 |
| 90 | 555 lbs. | 29.25 |

No. 15870. We can also furnish this range with low closet and high shelf **with a horizontal circulating boiler** above the high shelf, with connections all complete for the plumber to connect with the hot water delivery pipe and with the water system of the city or town. The boiler is out of the way and does not take up any floor space, and is near the water-back, which causes the water to heat rapidly, saves pipe and lowers the plumber's bills. Where there is no public waterworks system it may be connected with an elevated tank, placed at sufficient height to force the water to any part of the house where hot water is desired. **There must be a constant pressure of cold water into the boiler, either from a waterworks system or from a tank, or this range with circulating boiler cannot be used.**

| Size. | Weight. | Price complete. |
|---|---|---|
| 80 | 689 lbs. | $47.00 |
| 90 | 708 lbs. | 48.00 |

## LAUNDRY STOVES.

No. 15871.

No. 15871. Laundry Sunshine, No. 12, same as No. 15872, with two 8 inch boiler holes, and space on sides for nine irons. Weight, 96 lbs. Price, $6.00.

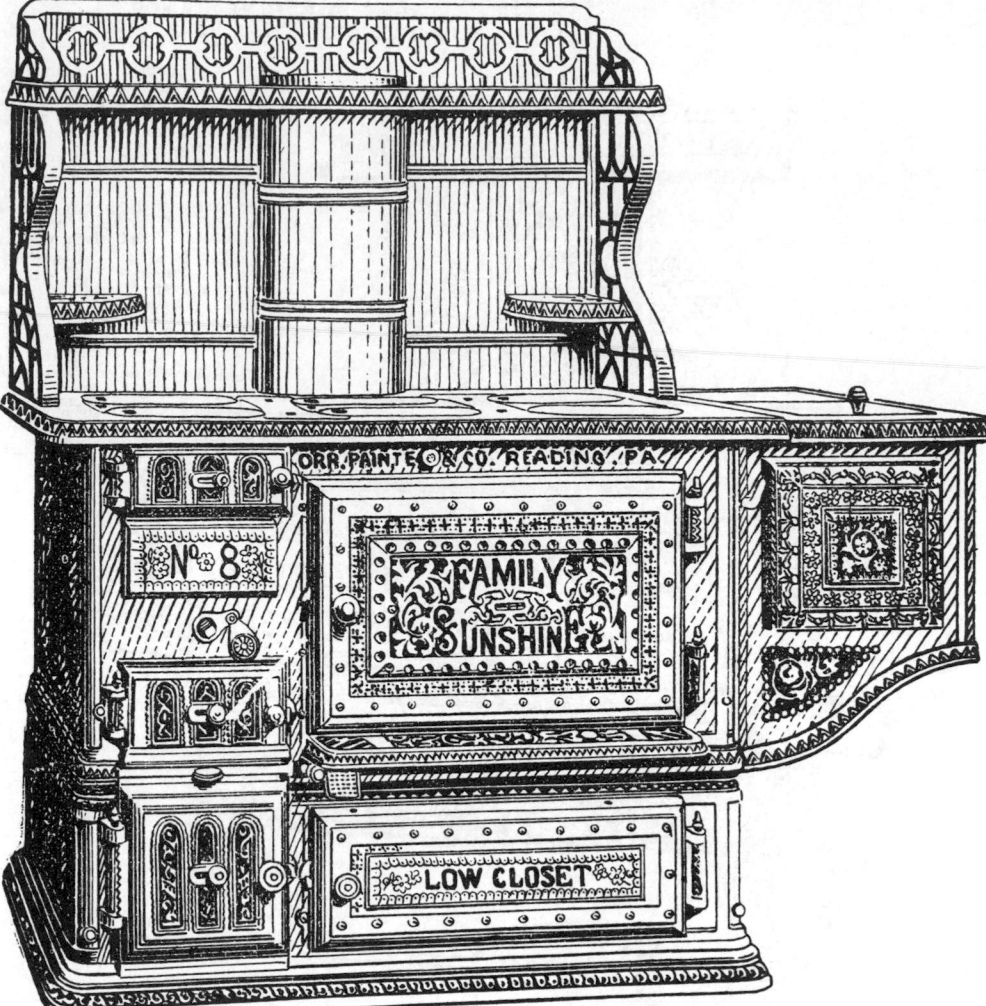

No. 15868.

## LAUNDRY STOVES.

No. 15872.

No. 15872. Laundry Sunshine, No. 11, a neat and durable laundry stove, with brick lined fire chamber, with ring covers from 8 to 12 inches, and space on sides for nine irons. Weight, 85 lbs. Price, $5.40.

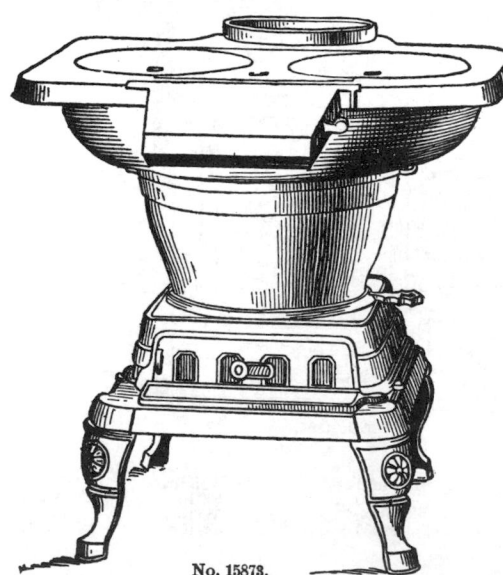

No. 15873.

## PUG LAUNDRY STOVE.

### Hard or soft coal.

No. 15873. A cheap, convenient and extremely popular laundry stove, with two covers, swing feed door and dumping grate.

| No. | Weight. | Price. |
|---|---|---|
| 7 | 67 lbs. | $2.82 |
| 8 | 80 lbs. | 3.60 |
| 18 | 70 lbs. | 3.00 |

No. 15874.

## DOMESTIC SUNSHINE RANGE.

### For hard or soft coal.

No. 15874. This handsome range is the leading kitchener of its class. In its construction is embodied every practical improvement and convenience. An effective sifter prevents the possibility of any waste of fuel. The ash pan is so wide and capacious that no ashes can fall outside of it. Made only in one size. Has six covers.

### Furnished with Duplex Grate.

| No. covers. | Size of oven. | Size of fire box. | Size of hot closet. | Weight. |
|---|---|---|---|---|
| 8 | 8 in. | 18x19½x10½ | 7¾x8x14½ | 19¾x22½x8 | 456 lbs. |

Price complete, with low closet and high shelf, $23.84.

If you want anything for any room in the house, be sure to write us before buying, if you don't see it in the Catalogue, or find it in the Index. We can quote selling prices on anything made, if it's in the market.

## BOX SUNSHINE.

Eight sizes, Nos. 18, 22, 25, 28, 30, 35, 37, 42.

### A new wood Box Stove.

No. 15888.

No. 15888. A handsome, durable heavy stove. The sides of the three largest sizes are made in two sections to prevent cracking.

No. 18, with one 6-inch boiler hole, 55 lbs..................................$ 2.58
No. 22, with one 7-inch boiler hole, 75 lbs................................. 3.48
No. 25, with two 7-inch boiler holes, 100 lbs.............................. 4.20
No. 28, with two 8-inch boiler holes, 125 lbs.............................. 5.40
No. 30, with two 8-inch boiler holes, 130 lbs.............................. 5.88
No. 35, with two 9-inch boiler holes, 180 lbs.............................. 7.50
No. 37, with two 9-inch boiler holes, 193 lbs.............................. 8.10
No. 42, with two 9-inch boiler holes, 260 lbs.............................12.90

## HEATING STOVES.

### Elwood.

No. 15889. The Elwood Heating Stoves, for wood only, a well made stove, mounted with sheet iron body. Has full nickeled foot rail and two cooking holes under swing top.

| Size. | Length of fire chamber. | Height. | Weight. | Price. |
|---|---|---|---|---|
| 19 | 19 in. | 45 in. | 87 lbs. | $6.00 |
| 22 | 22 in. | 47 in. | 105 lbs. | 7.20 |
| 25 | 25 in. | 49 in. | 134 lbs. | 8.40 |

No. 15889.

## DUKE CANNON STOVE.

### For hard or soft coal.

No. 15895. Four sizes. The Duke is the best and most complete cannon stove of its class in the market. It is a powerful heater at a very low price. It has a swing feed door and the top is arranged so that a drum can be attached if desired.

| No. | Diameter of fire pot. | Weight. | Height. | Price. |
|---|---|---|---|---|
| 3 | 8½ in. | 35 lbs. | 22 in. | $2.40 |
| 4 | 9½ in. | 48 " | 24 in. | 2.70 |
| 5 | 10½ in. | 55 " | 27 in. | 3.48 |
| 6 | 12 in. | 70 " | 30 in. | 3.90 |

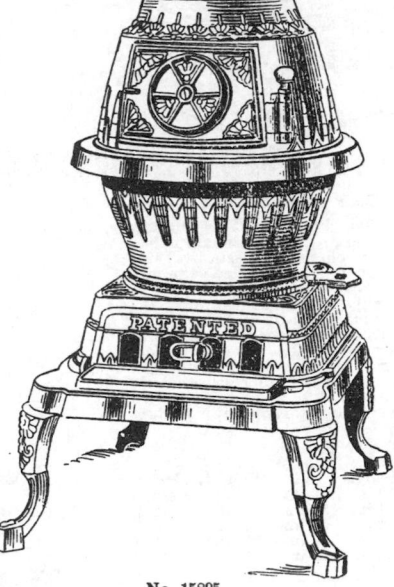

No. 15895.

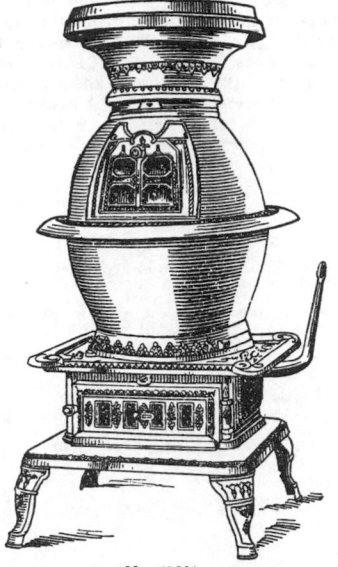

No. 15901.

## RADIANT SUNSHINE.

No. 15908. The Radiant Sunshine is the most beautiful, as well as the most complete and practical, of all the round fire pot Franklin stoves in the market. By closing the upper sliding mica doors, the stove can be used as an air-tight surface burner. These doors are so made that they never warp or stick. An efficient dust-flue carries away into the draft all the dust produced by cleaning the fire.

The center discharge grate as applied in this stove is unexcelled for effectiveness and convenience.

The design and ornamentation of the Radiant Sunshine are highly artistic. The skirt base, foot rail, dome plate and swing cover are nickel plated and the appearance of the stove is further enriched by six specially designed circular art tiles.

| No. | Size of fire pot. | Weight. | Price. |
|---|---|---|---|
| 24 | 12 in. | 147 lbs. | $12.60 |
| 28 | 14 in. | 171 lbs. | 13.30 |
| 32 | 16 in. | 205 lbs. | 14.85 |

## GLOBE LIGHTHOUSE.

### For hard or soft coal.

No. 15901. Four sizes, with plain grates. A strictly first-class Globe Stove of large size, adapted for bituminous or anthracite coal. The arrangement of the top permits a sheet iron section to be added without additional castings. It is provided with a clinkerless center discharge grate.

| No. | Weight. | Height. | Price. |
|---|---|---|---|
| 113 | 139 lbs. | 42 in. | $ 6.60 |
| 115 | 170 lbs. | 46 in. | 8.40 |
| 117 | 220 lbs. | 50 in. | 10.50 |
| 120 | 307 lbs. | 54 in. | 14.10 |

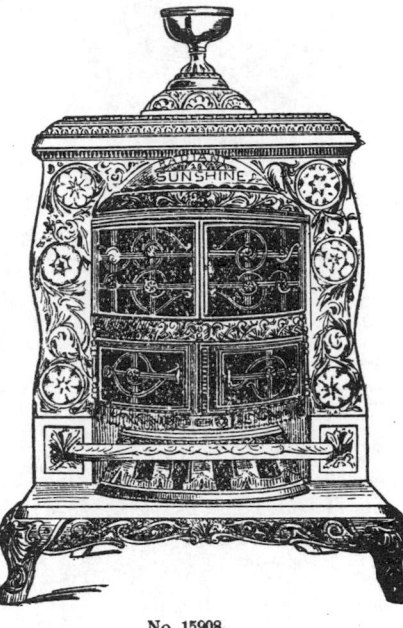

No. 15908.

No. 15912.

## THE OAK SUNSHINE.

### For hard or soft coal or wood.

No. 15912. With hard or soft coal fixture.
No. 15913. With wood fixture.
No. 15914. With both fixtures, add $1.00 to prices quoted.

This cut represents the finest and best "Oak" Stove yet made. Made of first-class material. Thoroughly mounted. Elaborately ornamented. It has full nickeled skirting and nickeled swing dome, an elegant and expensive urn, nickeled and tile door ornaments, nickel foot rails, nickel name plate, two check dampers in feed doors and one in collar. Vibrating grate with draw center, and sheet iron ash pan.

| No. | Weight. | Height. | Price. |
|---|---|---|---|
| 113 | 145 lbs. | 47 in. | $ 8.10 |
| 115 | 168 lbs. | 52 in. | 9.60 |
| 117 | 194 lbs. | 56 in. | 11.40 |
| 119 | 230 lbs. | 60 in. | 13.55 |
| 119½ | 245 lbs. | 72 in. | 16.20 |

If you want Furniture for parlor, library, hall, bedroom or office, send for our mammoth special Furniture Catalogue, mailed free on application. We have also a very select line of furniture in this Catalogue. Refer to index for what you want.

We would like to get one of our Stoves in your neighborhood as a sample to advertise our house. It doesn't take a neighbor long to find out that you are getting better bargains from us than he gets elsewhere, and hence we are sure to get more trade where our goods are once introduced.

In ordering Stoves, be sure to give the Catalogue page as well as the number of the stove. Do not fail also to give the size number and price of stove wanted. You cannot be too explicit, in order to avoid mistakes.

By referring to the index you can readily turn to the page of this Catalogue where we illustrate and describe a very select line of Carpets, Rugs, Oil Cloth, Lace Curtains, Portieres, Window Shades and Fixtures of all kinds; all quoted at prices so low that competition should stand not a shadow of show for your trade. You will learn to prize this Catalogue as a complete bureau of information on the great question of where, how and what to buy.

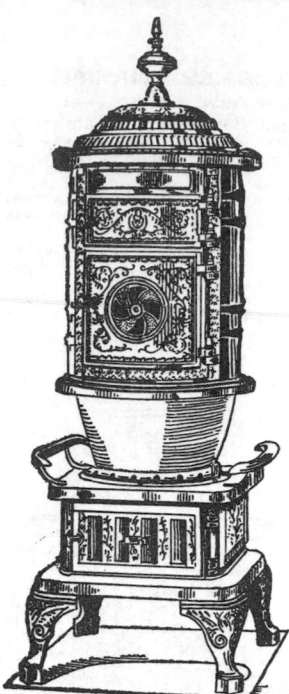

No. 15919.

## THE OAKLING SUNSHINE.
### For hard or soft coal.

No. 15919. This stove is made to meet the demand for an "Oak" at a moderate price, yet of fine form and perfect construction. Mounted with single fire pot. Feed door frame extends full width of the sheet steel from base to top.

Number indicates diameter of sheet iron cylinder.

| No. | Weight. | Height. | Price. |
|-----|---------|---------|--------|
| 12  | 98 lbs. | 46 in.  | $5.10  |
| 14  | 133 lbs.| 51 in.  | 6.00   |
| 17  | 181 lbs.| 58 in.  | 8.40   |

## OAKDALE SUNSHINE.
### For hard or soft coal or wood.

No. 15926. With hard or soft coal fixtures.
No. 15927. With wood fixtures.
No. 15928. With both fixtures, add 50 cents to prices quoted.

A new, handsome, low priced heater, mounted with heavy sheet steel, large extension feed door, spun brass nickel urn, nickel top ring, nickel swing top, nickel knobs and hinge pins, ash pan and cone grate of best form.

| No. | Diameter of body. | Weight. | Price. |
|-----|-------------------|---------|--------|
| 11  | 10 in.            | 65 lbs. | $5.70  |
| 14  | 13 in.            | 93 lbs. | 7.50   |
| 17  | 16 in.            | 125 lbs.| 9.60   |

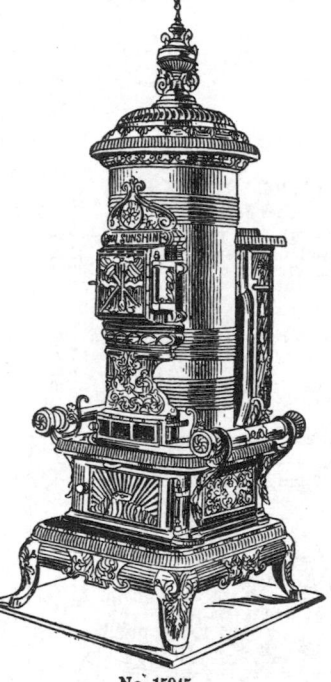

No. 15926.

## GEM SUNSHINE.
### For hard or soft coal.

No. 15940. We sell the Gem to those who want a good, durable, reliable heating stove for a small amount of money. Though very low in price, it has every essential feature of a good heating stove of this class. It does not, of course, have all the fancy frills and ornamental extras that are found on the highest priced goods of this kind, but nothing is lacking that will promote service and durability. And isn't it pretty? It costs no more to make a handsome stove than an ugly one.

Six sizes, Nos. 8, 9, 10, 11, 12 and 14. Which would you rather own?

| No. | Weight. | Price. |
|-----|---------|--------|
| 8   | 47 lbs. | $3.00  |
| 9   | 53 lbs. | 3.60   |
| 10  | 60 lbs. | 4.20   |
| 11  | 67 lbs. | 4.80   |
| 12  | 83 lbs. | 5.40   |
| 14  | 132 lbs.| 7.15   |

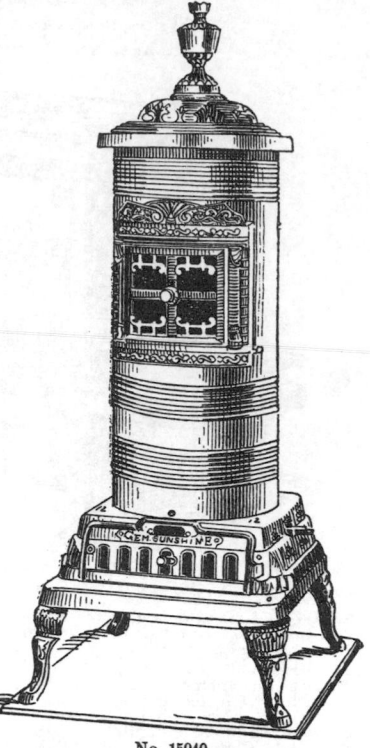

No. 15940.

## ROYAL SUNSHINE.
### Revertible Flue.

No. 15945. A new revertible flue surface burner, with Russia iron body, shaking draw center grate, cast iron revertible flue on the outside of the stove, thus giving a very much larger fire space to a given size of stove over the old style of construction. This flue stands clear of the stove, except at the upper and lower ends, allowing a greater radiation of heat from both the body of the stove and the cast iron column that forms the flue. We respectfully ask an impartial examination and test of this stove, as we believe it will fill the requirements of our patrons. With ornament on top, nickel plated name plate, foot rails, pins and knobs.

| No. | Inside diam. of fire pot. | Weight. | Price. |
|-----|---------------------------|---------|--------|
| 112 | 10 in.                    | 305 lbs.| $19.74 |
| 114 | 12 in.                    | 360 lbs.| 23.10  |
| 116 | 14 in.                    | 420 lbs.| 26.46  |

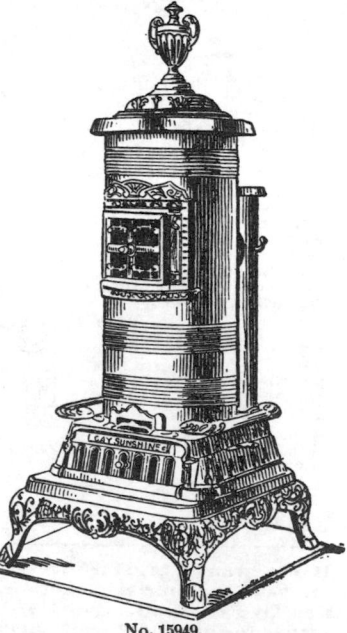

No. 15949.

No. 15932.

## LIVE OAK SUNSHINE.
### Will burn anything ever used for fuel.

The Live Oak Sunshine is a **GREAT BIG HEATER**, suitable for stores, school houses, halls, or any place where a powerful heater is required; mounted with Woods' celebrated sheet steel; constructed as nearly air tight as possible. The castings are heavy, smooth and well fitted. Diameter of body, 22 inches; height 7 feet; weight, 319 pounds.

No. 15932. With coal fixtures...... $20.40
No. 15933. With wood fixtures..... 20.40
No. 15934. With both fixtures...... 22.00

## GAY SUNSHINE.

No. 15949. Full revertible flue surface burner. The Gay Sunshine is a full revertible flue. Russia iron surface, burner of beautiful design and good proportions. This stove is thoroughly well made in every detail. It meets the demand for a durable, efficient and economical stoves at a very low price. The extra fuel consumed in one month in a straight draft cylinder or cannon stove would pay for the difference in price between such a stove and the Gay Sunshine.

| No. | Diam. of body. | Height floor to top. | Weight. | Price. |
|-----|----------------|----------------------|---------|--------|
| 110 | 10 in.         | 51 in.               | 110 lbs.| $10.40 |
| 111 | 11 in.         | 53 in.               | 115 lbs.| 11.40  |
| 112 | 12 in.         | 55 in.               | 135 lbs.| 12.25  |
| 114 | 14 in.         | 60 in.               | 154 lbs.| 14.40  |
| 116 | 16 in.         | 62 in.               | 212 lbs.| 16.50  |

If a Stove bought of us should not seem to give perfect service, read the complete instructions on first page of Stove Department. Nine out of ten cases of dissatisfaction with a really good Stove like ours is the fault of the chimney or ignorance.

**Consider our 3 per cent. discount for cash in full with order, when comparing our prices with those of other houses, and figure how much you can save.**

No. 15954.

### BRIGHT SUNSHINE.
#### Self-feed Base Burner.

No. 15954. Four sizes, Nos. 109, 110, 111, 112, straight draft. Three sizes, Nos. 120, 121, 122, base heaters.

A neat, attractive stove, complete in finish and operation but low in price. The Bright Sunshine has the Ransom duplex grate and all other improvements that can be applied to a stove of this class.

Fire pots: No. 109, 9 inch; 110 and 120, 10 inch; 111 and 121, 11 inch; 112 and 122, 12 inch.

Weight: No. 109, 120 lbs.; 110, 132 lbs.; 111, 151 lbs.; 112, 166 lbs.; 121, 167 lbs.; 122, 186 lbs.; 120, 150 lbs. Full nickel top.

Height from floor to top of ornament: No. 109, 47 inch; 110, 49 inch; 111, 50 inch; 112, 51 inch; 120, 49 inch; 121, 50 inch; 122, 51 inch.

| No. | Price. | No. | Price. |
|---|---|---|---|
| 109 | $ 9.25 | 120 | $11.40 |
| 110 | 10.20 | 121 | 12.30 |
| 111 | 11.10 | 122 | 14.40 |
| 112 | 12.30 | | |

### THE MERRY SUN-SHINE HEATER.

No. 15960. Revertible flue Parlor Stove. No better parlor stove has ever been produced for the price. Among all the heating stoves which have been placed on the market few have attained the popularity reached by the Merry Sunshine. Its admirable qualities have commended this heater to all who have used it, and one sold will cause the sale of several more. More points of merit are embodied in the Merry Sunshine than are found in any of its competitors. The nickel is elaborate and effective and so arranged as to display the graceful and artistic outlines of the stove to the best possible advantage. Stove has **full nickel top,** Ransom's improved duplex grate and shaking rings.

No. 15960.

| No. | Height to top of ornament. | Weight. | Price. |
|---|---|---|---|
| 12 | 54 in. | 235 lbs. | $17.40 |
| 13 | 56 in. | 263 lbs. | 19.68 |
| 14 | 58 in. | 285 lbs. | 22.32 |

### STOVE REPAIRS.

We can furnish repairs for any stove we sell. **We will not attempt to fill any orders** unless the following instructions are observed: Give name of stove, size, maker's name and dates. **Face the hearth** and state if repair goes on right or left hand side. Cash in full must accompany orders. Weigh up your old casting and you can tell about what the new one will cost. The average price is 9c per lb. If that price won't purchase the repair you order we will write you. If more than enough, we return balance.

### FARMERS' BOILERS.

No. 15970.

Four sizes, Nos. 15, 22, 30, 45. We invite attention to our new pattern Agricultural Furnace, and can assure our customers that there is none better made. We believe we are safe in saying that it will not require more than one-third of the amount of fuel to do the same work in these furnaces as it does in the old way, using the ordinary farmers' kettle. The prices are very reasonable.

Sizes of fire chambers for wood: No. 15, 18 inch; No. 22, 20½ inch; No. 30, 22½ inch; No. 45, 25½ inch.

No. 15. Will hold 15 gallons, with cover, for wood, $10.08; for coal, $12.40.

No. 22. Will hold 22 gallons, with cover, for wood, $12.60; for coal, $15.12.

No. 30. Will hold 30 gallons, with cover, for wood, $16.20; for coal, $19.32.

No. 45. Will hold 45 gallons, with cover, for wood, $21.84; for coal, $26.02.

## STEEL RANGES.

The price of Steel Ranges has always been too high. On account of the high price the sale was limited, and they were not made in large enough quantities to be made economically. We have contracted for a Steel Range to be made especially for us, and in quantities which reduce the cost of manufacturing to a reasonable basis. The material, workmanship, design and finish will be equal to the best in the market and the price lower than was ever before named for a Steel Range. We would rather sell 3,000 of these Steel Ranges and make only $1.00 on each sale than to sell 30 and make $10.00 on each sale. By selling 3,000 we make 3,000 friends and customers, and nearly every one who buys this range will induce his friends and neighbors to send to us for goods. These Ranges are now being made and will not be finished for two or three weeks. As soon as they are finished we shall get out a special circular on this Range, and any one wishing to purchase a fine Steel Range should not buy before sending to us for our prices and descriptions on this Range.

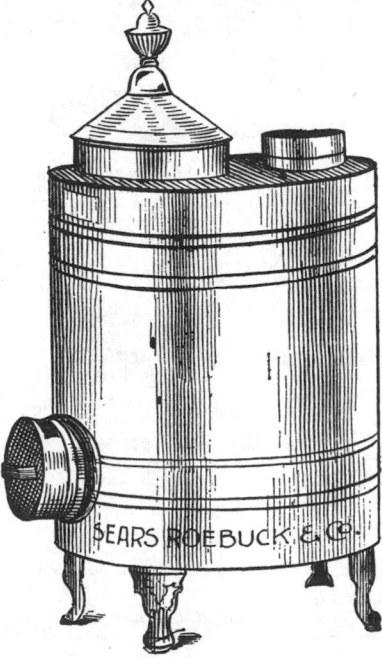

### AIR TIGHT STOVE.

No. 15961. The **Acme** Air Tight Heating Stove burns wood, chips or any offal. Will easily keep a wood fire over night. The most powerful heater for the least money. It is made strong, durable and neat. The ashes can be removed from the draft opening with an ordinary fire shovel. Put some ashes in bottom of stove when building first fire in stove, and always leave an inch or so of ashes in bottom of stove. We make it lined and unlined, and in smooth steel and planished iron (usually called Russia iron). We advise the use of the lined stove, as it is much more durable at little more cost.

| | Price Smooth Steel. | Price Planished Iron. |
|---|---|---|
| 20 inch, lined | $3 10 | $3 75 |
| 20 " not lined | 2 80 | 3 45 |
| 24 " lined | 3 35 | 4 67 |
| 24 " not lined | 3 00 | 3 95 |
| 30 " lined | 4 40 | 5 70 |
| 30 " not lined | 4 00 | 5 30 |

## STOVE FURNISHINGS.

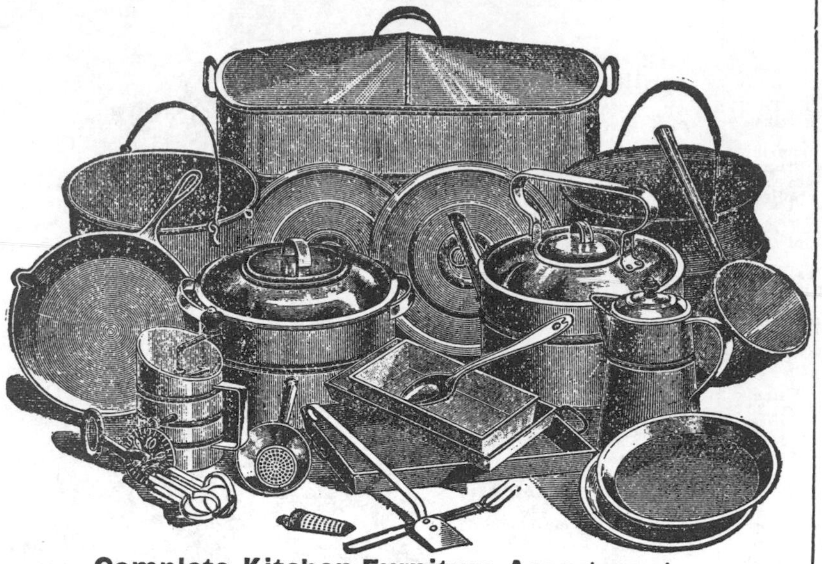

### Complete Kitchen Furniture Assortment.

Our facilities for furnishing all sorts of kitchen utensils are unequaled, and in the outfits named below we offer you an assortment which contains not a single article but what is a very necessary part of household furniture. **We handle no seconds.** All our utensils are first quality and guaranteed perfect. When you order your stove from this list be sure to include the assortment that goes with the size wanted.

We have quoted our stoves without furniture, for the reason that many people wanting a stove are already supplied with the necessary utensils.

Order from us and get more for your money than from any other house.

In ordering Stove Furniture be sure and buy same size as your stove.

No. 15984.

- 1 Copper bottom tin Wash Boiler.
- 1 Copper bottom tin Tea Kettle.
- 1 Cast iron Stove Kettle.
- 1 Cast iron Spider.
- 1 Wrought iron Fry Pan, 10 inch.
- 1 4-pint tin Tea Pot.
- 1 5-quart tin Coffee Pot.
- 1 10-quart retinned Dish Pan.
- 2 Black Dripping Pans, 10x12 and 10x14.
- 1 Tin Bread Pan, 5¾x10¾x3.
- 2 Common square Bread Tins, 7¾x11¾x1½.
- 1 Revolving Flour Sifter.
- 1 Box Grater.
- 1 Biscuit Cutter.
- 1 Dover Egg Beater.
- 1 Doz. 3-inch plain Patty Pans.
- ½ Doz. 9-inch tin Pie Plates.
- 1 14-inch tin Basting Spoon.
- 1 Cake Turner.
- 1 1-quart tin Cup.
- 1 Vegetable Fork.
- 1 Tin Dipper.
- 1 Flat handled Skimmer.
- 1 Fire Shovel.
- 1 Tin Wash Basin.
- 1 Tube Cake Pan, 10 inch.

Price above assortment, No. 7 or 8........................**$3.50**
Price above assortment, No. 9........................**3.75**

No. 15985.

- 1 Heavy 1X-tin copper bottom Wash Boiler.
- 1 Iron Stove Kettle.
- 1 Tin Cover to fit.
- 1 Iron Tea Kettle.
- 1 Iron Spider.
- 1 Fry Pan.
- 1 Stove Shovel.
- 1 Nickel plated copper 5-pints Coffee Pot.
- 1 Nickel plated copper 4-pints Tea Pot.
- 1 Retinned Preserving Kettle.
- 1 Cover to fit.
- 1 Retinned Saucepan.
- 1 Cover to fit.
- 1 Tin Muffin Frame, 12 cups.
- ½ Doz. tin Pie Plates, 9 inch.
- 1 Extra heavy retinned Dish Pan.
- 1 Pieced tin Cup, 1 pint.
- 1 Galvanized Water Dipper, 2 quarts.
- 1 Elat handled Skimmer.
- 1 Vegetable Fork.
- 2 Drip Pans (give size of oven).
- 3 Tin Bread Pans.
- 2 Tin Cake Pans.
- 1 Doz. assorted Patty Pans.
- 1 Basting Spoon.
- 1 Cake Turner.
- 1 Steamer.
- 1 Retinned Cullender.
- 1 Cake Cutter.
- 1 Biscuit Cutter.
- 1 Doughnut Cutter.
- 1 Nutmeg Grater.
- 1 Large Grater.
- 1 Patent Flour Sifter.
- 1 Dover Egg Beater.
- 1 Covered japanned Dust Pan.
- 1 Butcher Knife.
- 1 Paring Knife.
- 1 Mincing Knife, double blades.
- 1 Bread Board.
- 1 Rolling Pin.
- 1 Wood Potato Masher.
- 1 Oval hardwood Chopping Tray.
- 1 Set Mrs. Potts' Sad Irons.

Price above assortment, No. 7........................**$6.00**
Price above assortment, No. 8........................**6.25**
Price above assortment, No. 9........................**7.00**

### Stove Pipes.

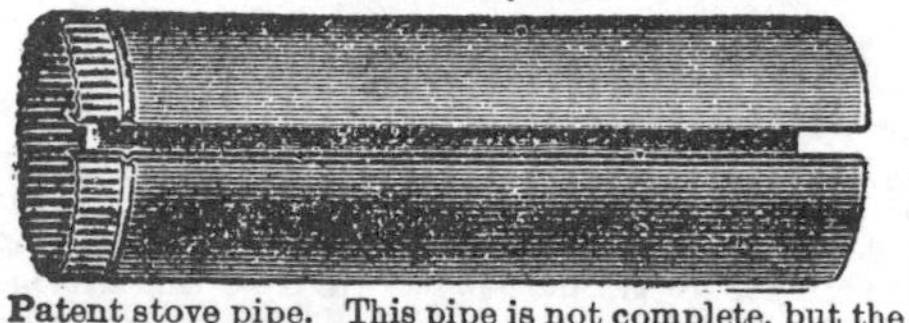

Patent stove pipe. This pipe is not complete, but the seam is made and edges turned over, and one with a mallet or hammer can put together in a few minutes' time. It is left this way to facilitate shipping, as a dozen joints do not occupy any more space than one joint put together; it is packed in crates of fifty joints, but we will sell any quantity ordered.

| | | |
|---|---|---|
| No. 15986. Diameter, inches, | 5 | 6 |
| Price, per length, | $0.10 | .12 |

Planished or American Russia pipe, made the same as No. 15986. Length, 28 inches.

| | | |
|---|---|---|
| No. 15987. Diameter, inches, | 5 | 6 |
| Price, per length, | $0.35 | .37 |

### Ready Made Stove Pipe.

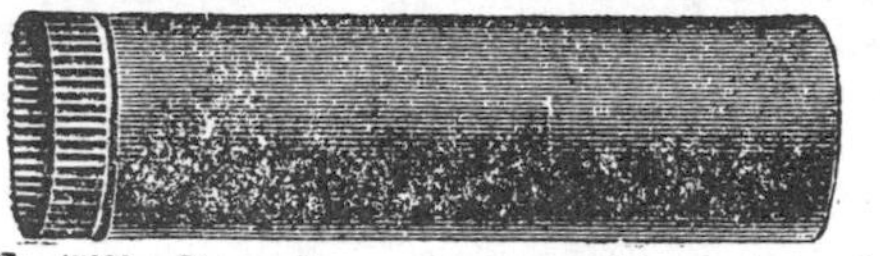

No. 15990. Stove pipe, made up complete, ready to adjust to stove. Pipe shipped this way takes up considerable room, and we would advise the purchase of the patent pipe when convenient, as it can be put together very quickly; can furnish in No. 27 iron only. Length, 24 inches.

| | | |
|---|---|---|
| Diameter, inches, | 5 | 6 |
| Price, per length, | $0.09 | .10 |

No. 15991. Planished or American Russia iron stove pipe, same style as No. 15990. Length, 28 inches.

| | | |
|---|---|---|
| Diameter, inches, | 5 | 6 |
| Price, per length, | $0.29 | .30 |

### Common Iron Elbows.

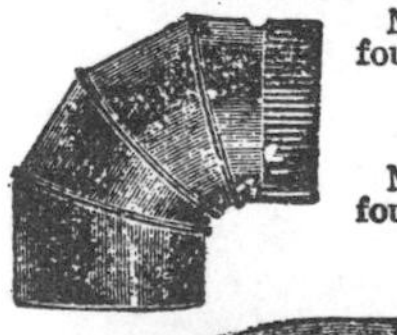

No. 15992. Common iron elbows, four pieces.

| | | |
|---|---|---|
| Diameter, inches, | 5 | 6 |
| Price, each, | $0.05 | .06 |
| Price, per doz., | .55 | .65 |

No. 15993. Planished iron elbows, four pieces.

| | | |
|---|---|---|
| Diameter, inches, | 5 | 6 |
| Price, each, | $0.16 | .18 |

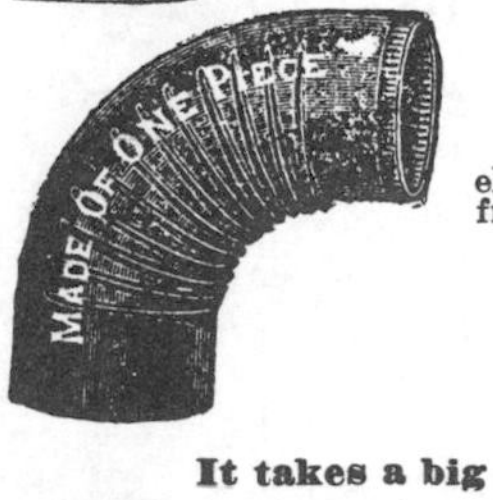


No. 15994. Planished iron elbows, corrugated, made from one piece of iron.

| | | |
|---|---|---|
| Diameter, inches, | 5 | 6 |
| Price, each, | $0.22 | .28 |

### Stove Pipe Shelf.

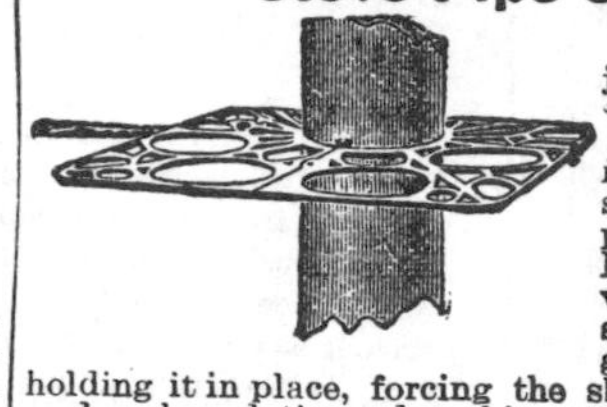

No. 15998. Cast iron japanned; is 18 inches square, made for 6 inch pipe. This shelf is very complete in itself and is easily applied or raised and lowered. A heavy weight upon it strengthens its grip grip and assists in holding it in place, forcing the shelf farther over the wedge shaped tin and making the grip on the pipe tighter. Price, each........................**48c**

### Chimney Thimbles.

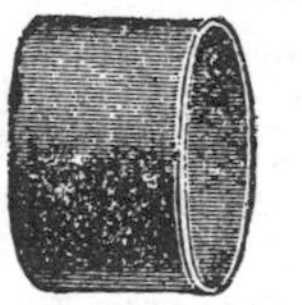

No. 15999.

| Diam. | | Length. |
|---|---|---|
| 6 inch | x | 4 inch. |
| 7 inch | x | 4 inch. |

Price, each....................**4c, 6c**
Price, per doz....................**45c, 60c**

### Stove Pipe Dampers.

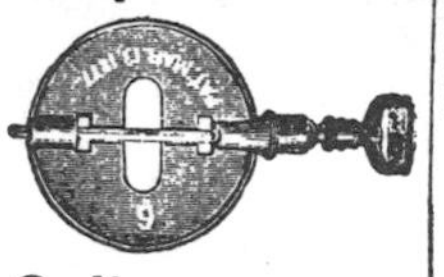

No. 16003. Stove Pipe Dampers—cool ventilated—Handle put in easily—weight, 12 oz.

5 inch. Price..........**6c**
6 inch. Price..........**7c**

### Stove Pipe Collars.

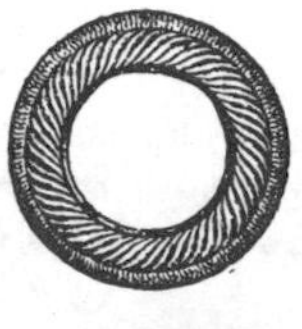

No. 16004. Stove Pipe Collars, plain, tin.

| | | |
|---|---|---|
| Size, inches, | 5 | 6 |
| Price, each, | $0.03 | .04 |
| Price, per doz., | .25 | .35 |

No. 16006. Stove Pipe Collars, lacquered.

| | | |
|---|---|---|
| Size, inches, | 5 | 6 |
| Price, each, | $0.04 | .05 |
| Priee, per doz, | .36 | .40 |

### Flue Stopper.

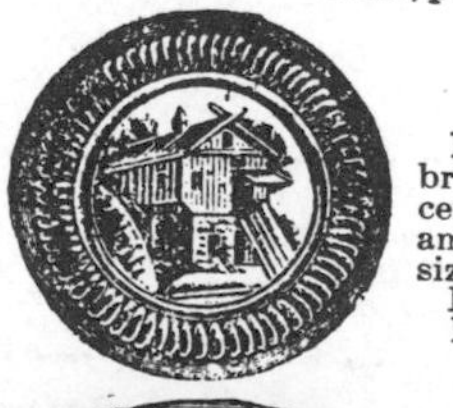

No. 16007. Flue Stopper, brass finished, with decorated centers; very handsome. Diameter, 8⅛ inches. Fits all size flues.

Price, each....................**4c**
Price, per doz....................**40c**

### Flue Stoppers, Common.

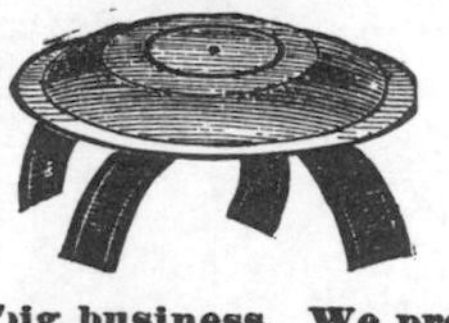

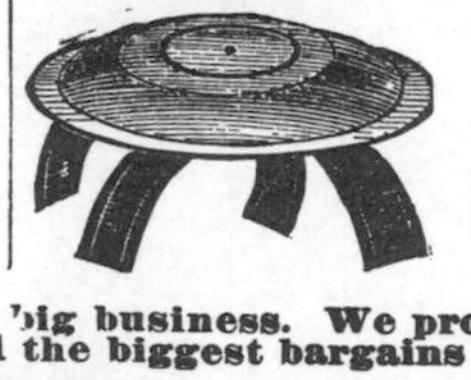

No. 16008. Size, 6 inch.
Each....................**4c**
Per doz....................**40c**

### Ventilators, Common.

| No. 16009. | Size. | Weight. | Each. |
|---|---|---|---|
| | 6x 4 | 2 lbs. 10 oz. | $0.25 |
| | 6x 6 | 2 lbs. 10 oz. | .30 |
| | 6x10 | 3 lbs. 4 oz. | .38 |

### Adjustable Thimble.

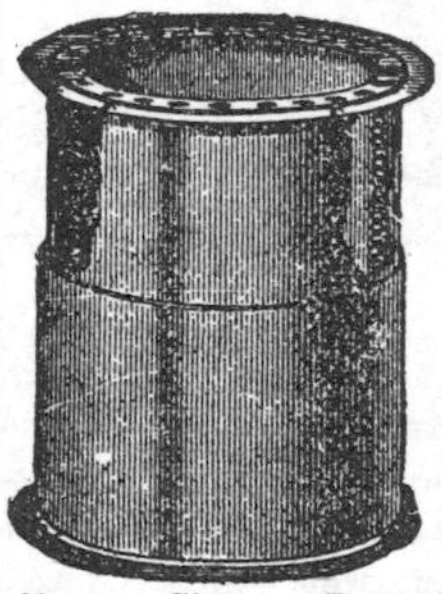

Adjustable Thimbles are perfect safeguards against fire from overheated stoves or furnace pipes passing through floors or partitions. The heads are connected by spiral steel springs, whose tension adjusts them to any thickness required. They can be used in connection with our double heating stoves for conducting heat overhead.

| No. | Size. | Extends from | Weight. | Each |
|---|---|---|---|---|
| 16010. | 5 inch | 4 to 8 inches | 2¼ lbs. | $0.31 |
| 16011. | 5 inch | 6 to 12 inches | 2¾ lbs. | .34 |
| 16012. | 6 inch | 4 to 8 inches | 2¼ lbs. | .35 |
| 16013. | 6 inch | 6 to 12 inches | 3¼ lbs. | .39 |
| 16014. | 7 inch | 4 to 8 inches | 2 lbs. 15 oz. | .43 |
| 16015. | 7 inch | 6 to 12 inches | 3¾ lbs. | .46 |

### Stove Shovels.

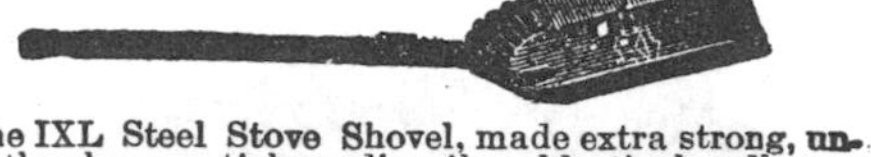

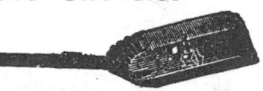

The IXL Steel Stove Shovel, made extra strong, unlike the cheap article ordinarily sold; the handle can not be broken; it is hollow and of an oval shape, and fits the hand nicely; it will outwear any other shovel.

No. 16022. The IXL Steel Shovel No. 0. Size of scoop, 5x7; full length, 15 inches. Each....................**6c**

No. 16023. The IXL Steel Shovel No. 1. Size of scoop, 5x7; full length, 20 inches. Each....................**8c**

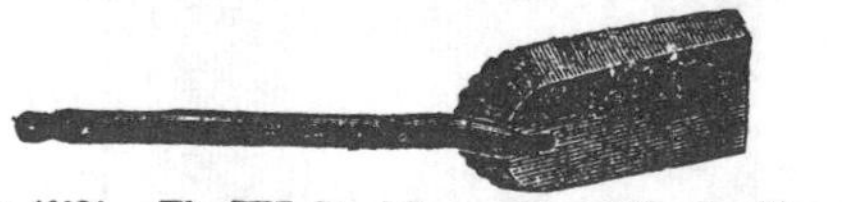

No. 16024. The IXL Steel Stove Shovel No. 2. Size of scoop, 5x8½: full length, 23 inches. Each..........**9c**

### Stove Lid Lifters.

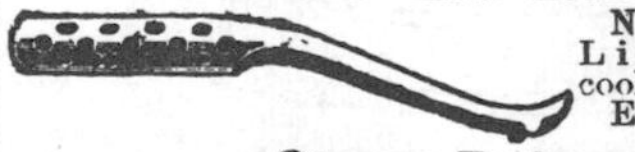

No. 16035. The Zero Lid Lifter, always cool, coppered iron. Each............**3c**

### Stove Pokers.

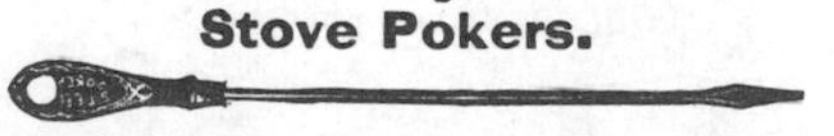

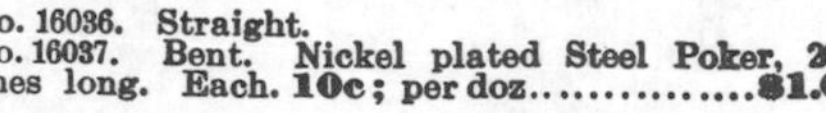

No. 16036. Straight.
No. 16037. Bent. Nickel plated Steel Poker, 20½ inches long. Each. **10c**; per doz..........**$1.08**

**It takes a big business block for a big business. We propose that you shall get the big end of every deal with us, and the biggest bargains you ever saw or heard of.**

## Adjustable Firebacks.

Readily adjusted to fit all sizes of cook stoves; made in two sizes. Send depth of fireback and fuel used. The only fireback that will adjust itself in both length and width. This fireback is so constructed that when contracted it will fit the smallest size cook stove, and when extended it will fit the largest size stove.
No. 16040. Length, 14½ to 21 inches; width, 5 to 6 inches; weight, 10 lbs.
Each................................................40c
No. 16041. Length, 17½ to 24 inches; width, 6½ to 7⅝ inches; weight, 15 lbs.
Each................................................75c

## Stove Lining.

No. 16049. Asbestos Plastic Stove Lining, composed of asbestos and other fireproof materials; is easily applied with a trowel, and makes a durable and economical lining for cook stoves; useful for repairing broken brick or iron lining. Put up in 5 and 10 lb. pails.
5 lb. pails, each, 40c; 10 lb pails, each.........58c

## Ash Sifters.

No. 16050. The Rival Ash Sifter. Frame is made of **hardwood.** The lid is hinged, and cannot be removed. More convenient than those made with lids to lift off. The sieve rests on iron rollers, reducing the friction and prolonging the life of the sifter. The wire is galvanized steel. The sifter is 13½x13½ inches, 3¾ inches high, and will hold a good big hod of ashes.
Price.........each 75c 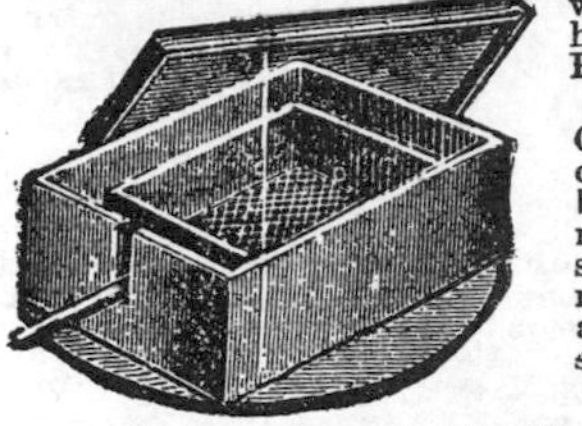
No. 16051. Barrel Cover Ash Sifter, with cover, will fit a sugar barrel. Inside box measures 12x12, outside box has cover; made of pine stained; a good serviceable sifter at a low price.
Each............27c

## Coal Hods.

No. 16055. Open Coal Hods, japanned.
16 inch, each................................................15c
17 " " ................................................18c
18 " " ................................................20c
No. 16056. Open Coal Hods, galvanized.
16 inch, each................................................20c
17 " " ................................................25c
18 " " ................................................27c
No. 16056. Funnel Coal Hods, japanned.
17 inch, each................................................22c
No. 16058. Funnel Coal Hods, galvanized.
17 inch, each................................................28c

## Stove Boards.

No. 16066. Crystallized Stove Boards, wood lined, square. The cut does not represent the exact pattern or finish, but only the general character.

| Size, inches. | Each. | Size, inches. | Each. |
|---|---|---|---|
| 26x26 | $0.54 | 30x30 | $0.72 |
| 26x32 | .60 | 33x33 | .75 |
| 28x28 | .62 | 30x38 | .77 |
| 28x34 | .70 | 36x36 | .80 |

### Range Stove Board.

No. 16067. 28x42 inches. Price, each..........$1.10

## Iron Tea Kettles.

No. 16074. Iron Tea Kettles, wood handle.
No. 7, weight, 8 lbs.
Each............28c
No. 8, weight, 9 lbs.
Each............36c
No. 9, weight, 11 lbs.
Each............41c

## Stove Kettles.

No. 16075, Iron Stove Kettle.

| No. | 7 | 8 | 9 |
|---|---|---|---|
| Weight, lbs. | 6 | 7½ | 9 |
| Price, each, | $0.26 | .28 | .34 |

## Scotch Bowl.

No. 16078. Iron Scotch Bowl.

| Size, in., | 10 | 11 | 12 |
|---|---|---|---|
| Each, | $0.18 | .20 | .24 |

## Spiders.

No. 16084, Iron Spider.

| Size, | 7 | 8 | 9 | 10 |
|---|---|---|---|---|
| Each, | $0.12 | .14 | .16 | .20 |

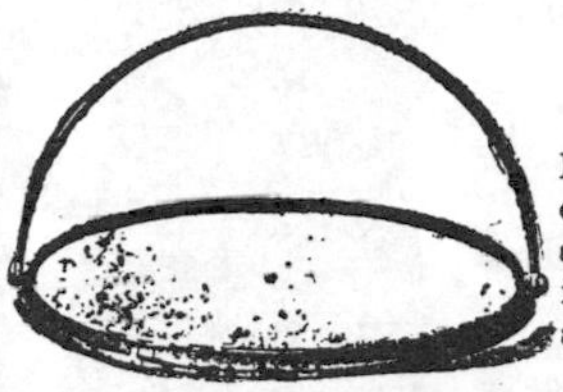

## Griddles.

No. 16085. Iron Round Cake Griddle, with bail. Diameter, 12 and 14 inches. Each, 30c. and................40c

## Flat Iron Heaters.

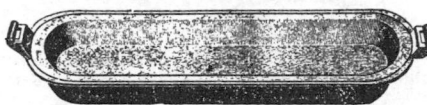

No. 16087. Iron Flat Iron Heaters or Long Griddle.

| Size, | 7 | 8 | 9 |
|---|---|---|---|
| Each, | $0.25 | .29 | .36 |

## Side Handle Griddles.

No. 16090. Iron Side Handle Griddle.

| Size, inches..... | 7 | 8 | 9 |
|---|---|---|---|
| Each ............ | $0.11 | .12 | .13 |

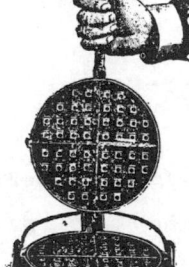

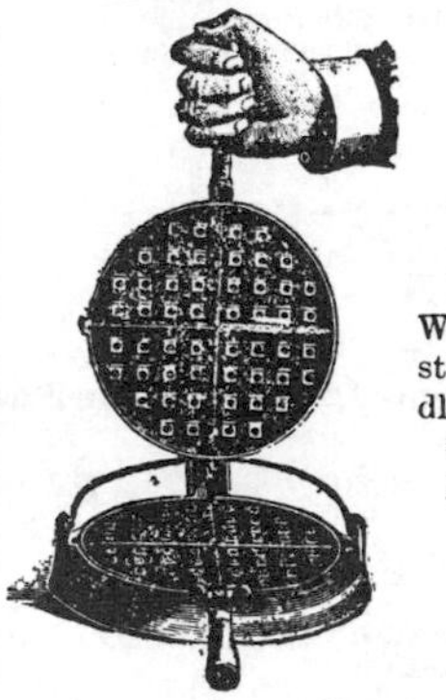

## Waffle Irons.

No. 16096. The American Waffle Iron. Simple in construction, convenient to handle, easy to clean.

| Size, No........ | 8 | 9 |
|---|---|---|
| Each............ | $0.65 | .68 |

## Gem Pan.

No. 16097. Iron Gem Pan, deep; weight, 5 lbs. Price, each, 17c.
No. 16098. Iron Gem Pan, oval pattern; weight, 3 lbs. 5 oz., 10 cups, shallow. Each, 14c.

## Pancake Criddle.

No. 16099. The Sun Pancake Griddle is made of wrought steel; is strong and durable, heats quickly and retains the heat, and is lighter than any other griddle made. All others are too heavy for convenience, absorb grease, are hard to clean and break easily, besides wasting fuel and time in waiting for a sufficiently hot fire.

The illustration above shows the Sun Pancake Griddle with its 3 hinged pans. The batter is first poured into the little round hinged pans. When done on the first side the round pans are turned over with a fork into the long pan, and while the cakes are finishing, the round pans are refilled and so on, thus baking at the actual rate of six cakes a minute. The cakes are served perfectly round, with smooth edges, are light and spongy and will tempt the most fastidious appetite. It is an absolute necessity in every household. Price, each, 35c; per doz., $3.75.

## Egg Poacher.

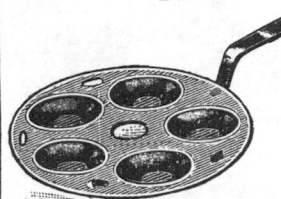

No. 16106. Egg Poacher; is designed to be placed within a spider or cooking vessel containing boiling water about one-half inch deep. Its merit is very evident. Each egg is of uniform size, perfectly cooked. "A round of white dotted with a firm golden center." Eggs are quickly and easily removed, etc. Adapted equally well for baking biscuit, gems, patty cakes, etc. Made of IX charcoal tin, without solder. Every joint and seam smooth and perfect. Price, each, 25c.

## Broilers.

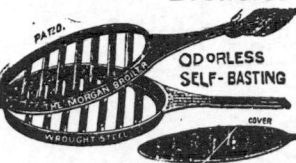

No. 16108. The illustration shows the two sections of the Broiler and the cover, the corrugated cross pieces being V-shaped into which the gravy drips during the broiling. It is thus self-basting and instead of the gravy falling into the fire, creating a suffocating smoke and disagreeable odor, it runs into the corrugations, is broiled into the meat, making an otherwise dry, tough steak tender and juicy.

The cover fits over the top, confining the appetizing flavor to the meat and prevents the escape of smoke into the room.

For toasting the Morgan Broiler is perfection. It makes no difference what kind of stove you use, gasoline, wood, coal, gas or oil, the Morgan Broiler is adapted to them all. Will not crack, warp or break; is easily cleaned, fits any stove; does not affect the draught nor deaden the fire. Price, each, 40c.

## Bake Oven.

No. 16112. Bake Oven, deep pattern, with bails, and covers. These ovens are designed for camp use; can be set in center of wood fire without injury to contents; cover fits down snug, so that nothing can get inside.
No. 0. 14-inch, weight, 27 lbs. Each............$1.15
No. 1. 12-inch, weight, 14 lbs. Each............ .90
No. 2. 11-inch, weight, 13 lbs. Each............ .71
No. 3. 10-inch, weight, 11 lbs. Each............ .65

## Asbestos Stove Mat.

### Diameter, 9 Inches.

No. 16115. A household necessity. This mat is made of asbestos of superior quality, and is scorch proof as well as fireproof. Any cooking utensil used upon it becomes absolutely scorch-proof.

| Price, each. | Per doz. | Per gross. |
|---|---|---|
| 3c. | 30c. | $3.50. |

## Brass Preserving Kettles.

Will not quite hold as much as represented.
No. 16118.

| 1½ gal., 10-inch.. | $0.75 |
|---|---|
| 2 gal., 11-inch.. | .90 |
| 3 gal., 13-inch.. | 1.25 |
| 4 gal., 14-inch.. | 1.50 |
| 5 gal., 15-inch.. | 1.95 |
| 6 gal., 16-inch.. | 2.25 |

**Scores of old customers visit our store daily. We are always glad to see them. If you ever happen in the city, do not fail to come and see us.**

9

## Porcelain Lined Cast Preserving Kettles.

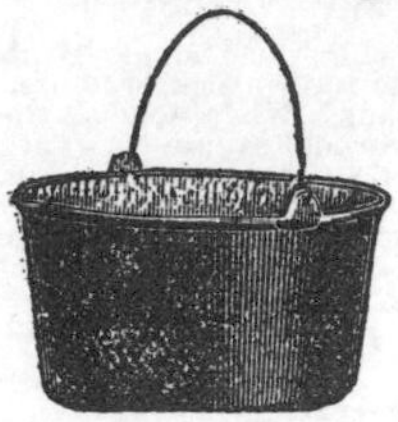

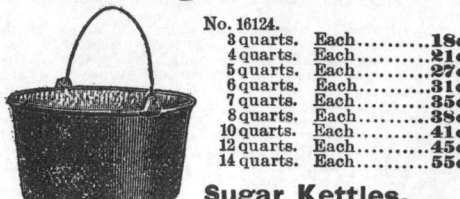

No. 16124.

| | | |
|---|---|---|
| 3 quarts. | Each | **18c** |
| 4 quarts. | Each | **21c** |
| 5 quarts. | Each | **27c** |
| 6 quarts. | Each | **31c** |
| 7 quarts. | Each | **35c** |
| 8 quarts. | Each | **38c** |
| 10 quarts. | Each | **41c** |
| 12 quarts. | Each | **45c** |
| 14 quarts. | Each | **55c** |

## Sugar Kettles.

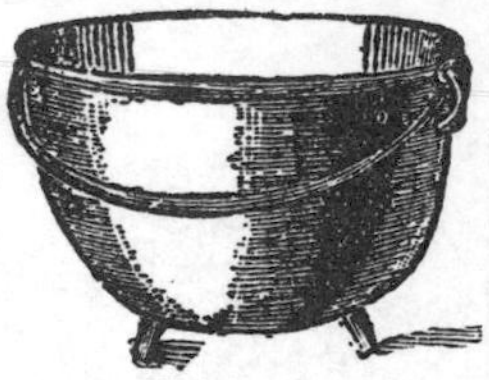

No. 16128. Sugar or Wash Kettles, with bails milled and painted. No. 7, 30-gal. kettle is the largest cast iron kettle, with bail, made. Average weights of kettles are given below.

| | Actual Measure. gallons. | Weight. pounds. | Each. |
|---|---|---|---|
| No. 1 | 8 | 25 | $0.88 |
| No. 2 | 10 | 30 | 1.12 |
| No. 3 | 15 | 42 | 1.40 |
| No. 4 | 18 | 48 | 1.80 |
| No. 5 | 21½ | 52 | 2.00 |
| No. 6 | 25 | 65 | 2.40 |
| No. 7 | 30 | 85 | 2.74 |

## Copper Kettles.

| | Size, gallons. | Weight, about, pounds. | Diameter on top inside, inches. | Deep, inches. | Price. each. |
|---|---|---|---|---|---|
| No. 16133 | 40 | 48 | 27 | 19¼ | $11.35 |
| No. 16133 | 36 | 46 | 26 | 19 | 11.00 |
| No. 16133 | 30 | 39 | 24½ | 17½ | 9.50 |
| No. 16133 | 25 | 32 | 23½ | 15 | 8.00 |
| No. 16133 | 20 | 29 | 22 | 14½ | 7.00 |

## Stamped Tinware and Enameled Ware.

Plain stamped tinware is formed from a sheet of tin plate. Retinned stamped ware is made in the same way and is given another coating of tin after being finished. Will last longer and looks better, but costs more to make than plain. Gray enameled ware is formed from a **sheet of steel** enameled, inside and outside, a gray color slightly tinged with blue, and presents a wave-like appearance which is very ornamental. For cleanliness, purity, durability and beauty this ware is unexcelled by any other gray enameled steel goods on the market. **It is entirely free from lead, arsenic and antimony**, metals so often used in enamels of this appearance. We buy all tin and enameled ware direct from the makers and are satisfied with our usual small profit. All goods are regular standard size. **No seconds or imperfect goods sold.** The market is just now flooded with cheap grades of enameled goods, many of which are not good as our tinware. Honest goods can not be sold for less prices than we name. We buy goods only from reliable manufacturers, who have an established reputation which is too valuable to them to be lost by sending out worthless goods. All tinware and enameled ware goods do not hold as much as represented. Sizes given are manufacturer's measure. Same as used by all manufacturers. Notice size given in inches, which is exact.

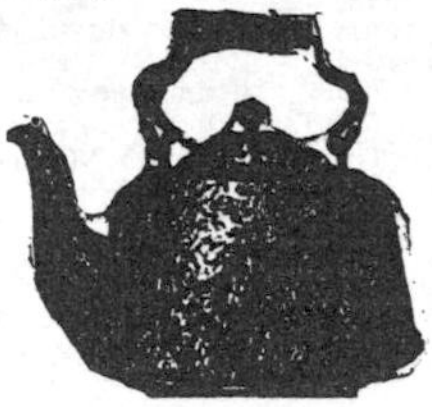

No. 16134. **Retinned tea kettles**, same shape as illustration.

| | | | | | | |
|---|---|---|---|---|---|---|
| Quarts, | 2½ | 3 | 4 | 5 | 7 | 9 |
| Diameter of bottom, inches, | 7 | 8¼ | 9 | 10 | 11 | 12 |
| Price, each, | $0.25 | .35 | .40 | .45 | .50 | .58 |

No. 16135. **Gray enameled** Tea Kettles, same shape as illustration above.

| | | | | | | | |
|---|---|---|---|---|---|---|---|
| Quarts | 2 | 3 | 4 | 5 | 7 | 8 | 11 |
| Diameter of bottom, inch. | 7¾ | 8¼ | 9 | 10 | 11 | 11¼ | 12 |
| Price, each | $0.50 | .56 | .64 | .75 | .86 | 1.02 | 1.23 |

No. 16136. **Gray enameled** Tea Kettle, with pit bottom.

| | | | |
|---|---|---|---|
| Fits stove Nos | 7 | 8 | 9 |
| Holds, quarts | 5 | 7 | 8 |
| Price, each | $0.75 | .86 | 1.02 |

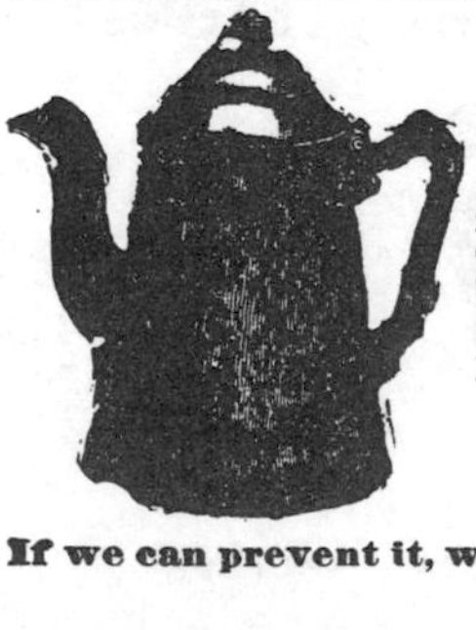

No. 16141. **Gray enameled** Tea Pots, like illustration, with retinned covers.

| | | | |
|---|---|---|---|
| Quarts | 1 | 1½ | 2 |
| Price, each | $0.32 | .36 | .40 |
| Quarts | 3 | 4 | 5 |
| Price, each | $0.46 | .52 | .58 |

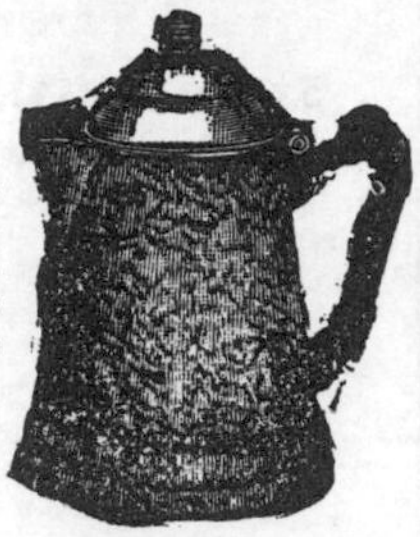

No. 16143. **Gray enameled** lipped Coffee Pots, like illustration, with retinned covers.

| | | | | | |
|---|---|---|---|---|---|
| Quarts | 1½ | 2 | 3 | 4 | 5 |
| Price, each | $0.36 | .40 | .46 | .52 | .58 |

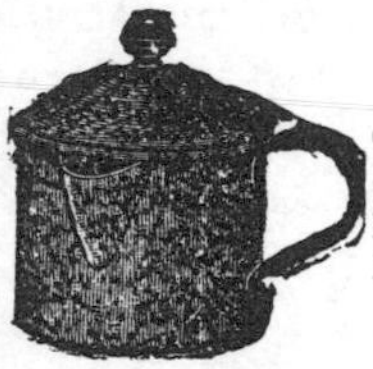

No. 16145. **Gray enameled** Tea Steeper, like illustration with retinned covers. Seamless.

| | | |
|---|---|---|
| Pints | 1½ | 2 |
| Price, each | $0.18 | .22 |

## Coffee Boilers.

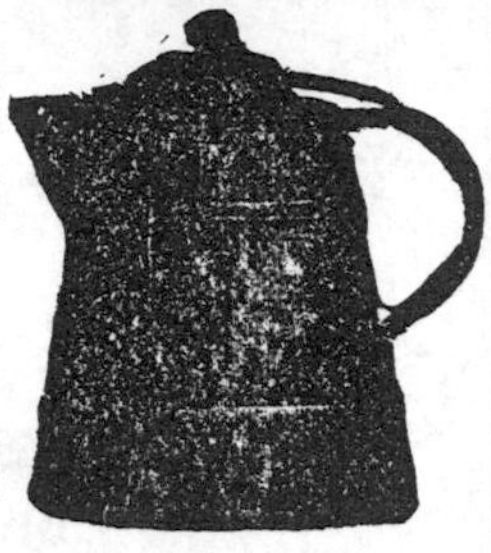

No. 16149. **Gray enameled** Coffee Boiler, flat bottom, with retinned cover.

| | | | |
|---|---|---|---|
| Quarts | 3½ | 4½ | 6 |
| Price, each | $0.56 | .64 | .72 |
| Quarts | | 8½ | 11½ |
| Price, each | | $0.80 | .96 |

No. 16151. **Gray enameled** Coffee Boilers, pit bottom, with retinned cover.

| | | | |
|---|---|---|---|
| Diameter of pits, inch. | 7 | 8 | 9 |
| Price, each | $0.72 | .80 | .96 |

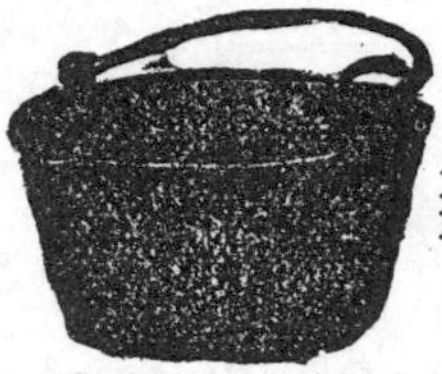

No. 16156. **Retinned** Lipped Preserving Kettles, like illustration.

| | | | |
|---|---|---|---|
| Quarts, | 2½ | 3 | 4 |
| Size, each, | 7¾x3½ | 8¼x3¾ | 9½x4 |
| Price, each | $0.08 | .09 | .11 |
| Quarts, | 5 | 6 | 8 |
| Size, inches, | 9¾x4¼ | 10¾x5 | 11¼x4⅞ |
| Price, each | $0.14 | .16 | .19 |

No. 16157. **Gray enameled** Preserving Kettles, same shape as above illustration, same measurements.

| | | | | | | | |
|---|---|---|---|---|---|---|---|
| Quarts, | 2 | 2½ | 3 | 4 | 5 | 6 | 8 |
| Price, each | $0.16 | .18 | .20 | .28 | .32 | .36 | .42 |

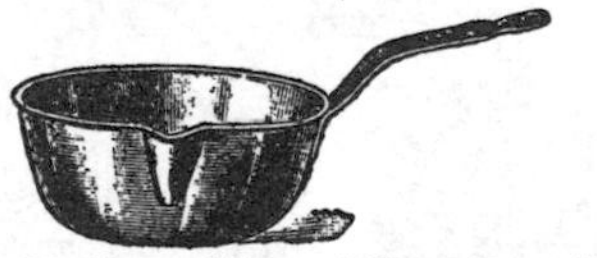

No. 16160. **Retinned** Lipped Sauce Pans, like illustration.

| | | | | |
|---|---|---|---|---|
| Quarts, | 1 | 2 | 3 | 4 |
| Size, inches, | 6x2½ | 7x3½ | 8½x3¾ | 9x4 |
| Price, each | $0.05 | .08 | .09 | .11 |
| Quarts, | 5 | 6 | 7½ | |
| Size, inches, | 9¾x4½ | 11x4½ | 11¼x4⅞ | |
| Price, each | $0.13 | .15 | .17 | |

No. 16161. **Gray enameled** Lipped Sauce Pan, same shape as above illustration.

| | | | | |
|---|---|---|---|---|
| Quarts, | 1 | 2 | 3 | 4 |
| Size, inches, | 6x2½ | 7x3½ | 8½x3¾ | 9x4 |
| Price, each | $0.12 | .16 | .24 | .28 |
| Quarts, | 5 | 6 | 7½ | |
| Size, inches, | 8¾x4¼ | 11x5 | 11¼x5½ | |
| Price, each | $0.32 | .36 | .42 | |

## Pot Covers.

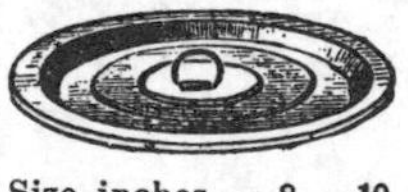

No. 16163. Hemmed Pot Covers, with rings made of tin.

| | | | |
|---|---|---|---|
| Size, inches, | 8 | 10 | 10½ |
| Each, | $0.03 | .04 | .04 |
| Per dozen, | .33 | .44 | .44 |
| Size, inches, | 11 | 12 | 13 |
| Each, | $0.05 | .06 | .08 |
| Per dozen, | .50 | .65 | .85 |

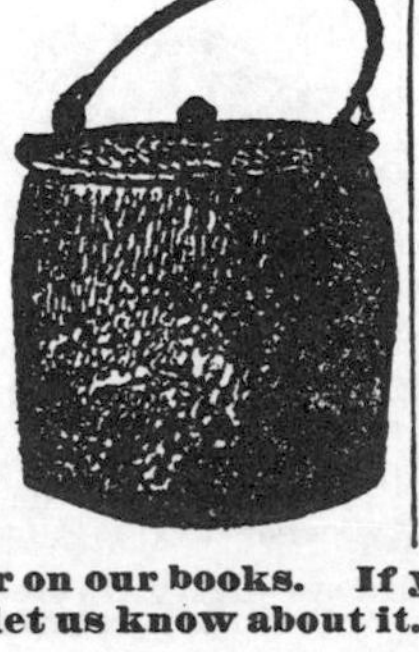

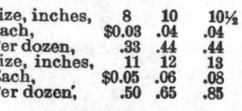

**Gray enameled** Stove Pot, with bail and retinned cover. Pit and flat bottom.
No. 16165. Flat bottom.
No. 16166. Pit bottom.

| | | | |
|---|---|---|---|
| Nos. | 7 | 8 | 9 |
| Quarts, | 9 | 14 | 18 |
| Inches, | 9½x9 | 10½x9¼ | 12x10 |
| Price, ea., | $0.72 | .92 | 1.12 |

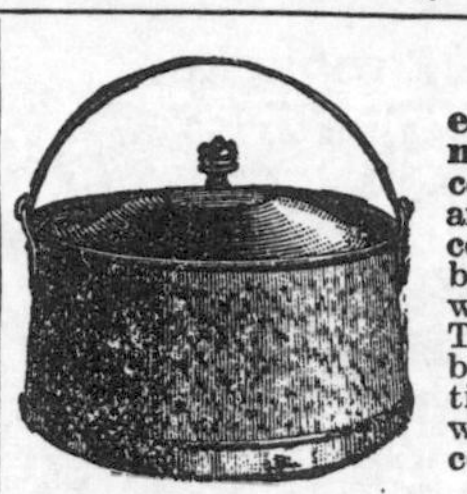

No. 16171. **Gray enameled** covered seamless **Climax** Cook Pot, with retinned covers. The Climax utensils are arranged with a heavy copper bottom attached to the body of the pot or sauce pan, with an air space between. This prevents scorching or burning and affords protection to that part of the vessel which in ordinary usage receives the most wear.

| | | | | |
|---|---|---|---|---|
| Quarts, | 2 | 3 | 5 | 7 |
| Size, | 6¾x4 | 8x4½ | 9x5 | 9⅝x6 |
| Price, each, | $0.44 | .52 | .60 | .68 |

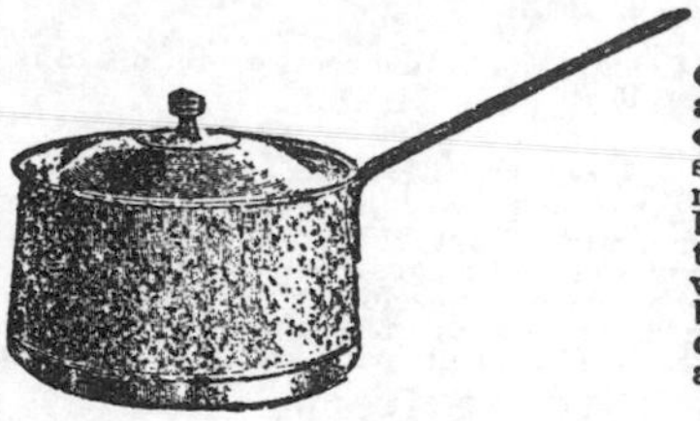

No. 16173. **Gray enameled covered** seamless Climax Sauce Pans, with retinned covers with **climax bottom**, as described above.

| | | | | |
|---|---|---|---|---|
| Quarts, | 2 | 3 | 5 | 7 |
| Size, | 6¾x4 | 8x4½ | 9x5 | 9⅝x6 |
| Price, each, | $0.44 | .52 | .60 | .68 |

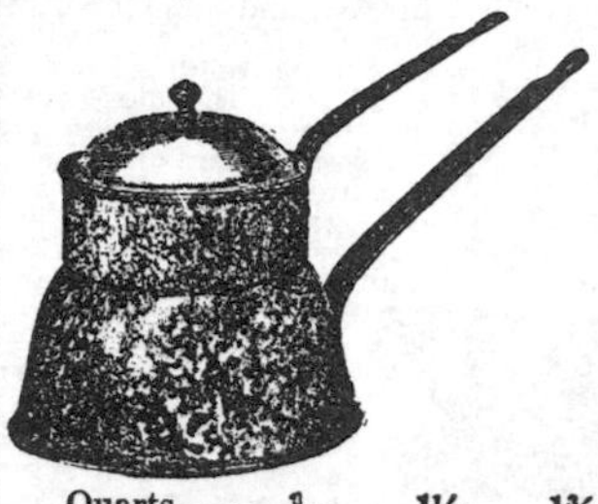

No. 16178. **Retinned Rice Boiler, seamless inside boiler.** For cooking rice, milk, oatmeal, farina, etc., without danger of scorching or burning. **Sizes given are for inside boiler.**

| | | | | | |
|---|---|---|---|---|---|
| Quarts | 1 | 1½ | 1¾ | 2 | 3 |
| Price, each | $0.42 | .48 | .54 | .66 | .72 |

No. 16179. **Gray enameled Rice Boiler**, with retinned covers. Same shape as above illustration. Sizes given are for inside boilers.

| | | | | | |
|---|---|---|---|---|---|
| Quarts | 1 | 1½ | 1¾ | 2 | 3 |
| Price, each | $0.40 | .45 | .50 | .70 | .90 |

## Bake Pans.

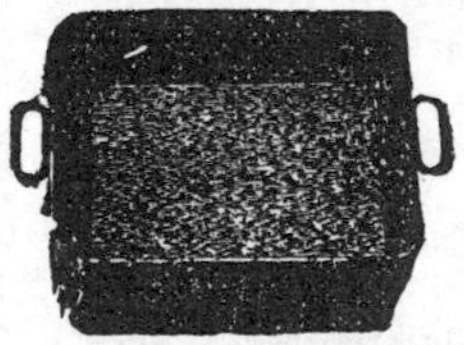

No. 16181. **Gray enameled** Bake Pans. Seamless. Price, each, 13x9x2¼ inches, **34c.** 14x9½x2½, **36c.** 15x10½x2½ inches, **40c.** 16x11x2½ inches, **48c.**

## Fry Pans.

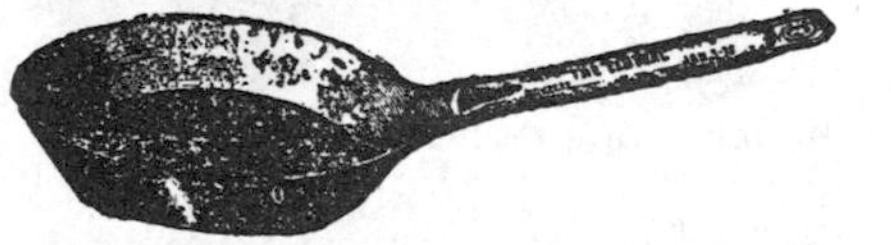

No. 16182. Stamped Seamless Lipped Frying Pans, polished, with patent handle. Always cool.

| | | | | |
|---|---|---|---|---|
| Nos | 3 | 4 | 5 | 6 |
| Inches | 9½ | 10 | 11 | 12 |
| Price, each | $0.12 | .14 | .15 | .17 |

No. 16183. **Gray enameled** Fry Pan, with patent handle. Always cool.

| | | | | |
|---|---|---|---|---|
| Diameter at top, inches | 9½ | 10 | 11 | 12 |
| Each | $0.36 | .40 | .44 | .48 |

## Milk or Dairy Pans.

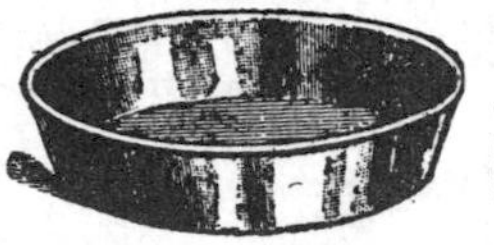

**Retinned.**

Dairy Pans, stamped ware, flat edge. They will not hold as much as represented. We sell any quantity at dozen prices.

No. 16184.

| Quarts. | Inches. | Weight, per doz. | Price, per doz. |
|---|---|---|---|
| ¼ | 5¼x1⅜ | 1 lb. 10 oz. | $0.27 |
| ½ | 6x1⅜ | 2 lbs. 2 oz. | .31 |
| 1 | 7x1⅝ | 2 lbs. 14 oz. | .39 |
| 1½ | 7½x1¾ | 3 lbs. | .45 |
| 2 | 8½x2 | 3 lbs. 6 oz. | .49 |
| 3 | 9¼x2¼ | 4 lbs. 10 oz. | .57 |
| 4 | 10⅝x2½ | 6 lbs. 3 oz. | .72 |
| 6 | 12⅝x2¾ | 7 lbs. 11 oz. | .92 |
| 8 | 13¼x2⅞ | 8 lbs. 12 oz. | 1.05 |
| 10 | 14¼x3 | 9 lbs. 8 oz. | 1.20 |
| 12 | 15x3½ | 11 lbs. 9 oz. | 1.35 |

Dairy Pans, holding 8, 10 and 12 **quarts**, are made of heavier tin than the smaller sizes.

No. 16185. **Gray enameled** straight Milk Pans. We sell any quantity at dozen rates. Will not hold as much as represented.

| | | | | | | |
|---|---|---|---|---|---|---|
| Quarts, | ¼ | ½ | 1 | 1½ | 2 | 3 |
| Per dozen, | $0.80 | .90 | 1.00 | 1.20 | 1.40 | 1.60 |
| Quarts, | 4 | 5 | 6 | 8 | 10 | 12 |
| Per dozen, | $2.00 | 2.20 | 2.40 | 2.70 | 3.20 | 3.80 |

**If we can prevent it, we do not propose to have a dissatisfied customer on our books. If you ever have cause for complaint, we ask it as a favor to us, that you let us know about it.**

## Pudding Pans—Extra Deep.

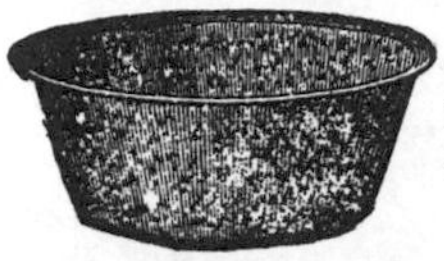

No. 16186. Extra deep plain Pudding Pan, made of I. C. tin, stamped ware.

| Size. quarts. | Actual capacity. | Each. | Per doz. |
|---|---|---|---|
| 1 | 1 quart | $.04 | $0.31 |
| 2 | 2 quarts | .05 | .40 |
| 3 | 2½ quarts | .06 | .50 |
| 4 | 3 quarts | .07 | .60 |
| 5 | 3¾ quarts | .08 | .75 |

No. 16187. **Gray enameled** Pudding Pans, flat edge extra deep.

| Size quarts. | Actual capacity. | Inches | Price each. |
|---|---|---|---|
| 1 | 1 quart | 7⅛x2½ | $0.12 |
| 2 | 1¾ quarts | 8⅝x3 | .15 |
| 3 | 2 quarts | 9⅝x3¼ | .17 |
| 4 | 2¾ quarts | 10¼x3¾ | .19 |
| 5 | 3½ quarts | 11 x3½ | .20 |
| 6 | 4½ quarts | 11⅞x3⅝ | .24 |

## Tubed Cake Pans.

No. 16189. Scalloped Tubed Cake Pans, plain tin. Size, 8 inches. Each............**3c**
10 inches. Each............**5c**

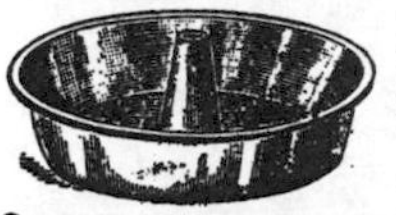

No. 16190. Retinned tubed Cake Pans. Size, 9¼x2¼, each, **7c**; 11x2⅝, **8c**; 8¾x3¾, **9c**; 11⅝ x2⅝............**10c**

No. 16191. **Gray enameled** tubed Cake Pans, extra deep.

| Quarts, | 2 | 3 | 4 | 5 | 6 |
|---|---|---|---|---|---|
| Size, inches, | 8½x3 | 8¾x3¼ | 9¾x3⅝ | 10½x3½ | 11¼x3¾ |
| Price, each, | $0.22 | .25 | .30 | .34 | .38 |

## Scalloped Cake Pans.

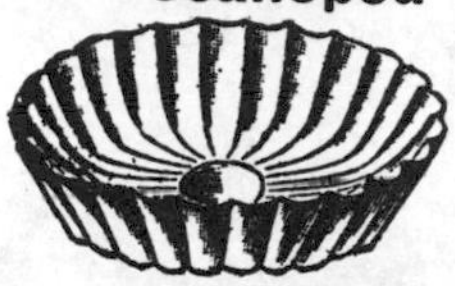

No. 16193. Scalloped Cake Pans, plain tin.
8 inch, each.......... **3c**
Per doz............**3?c**
10 inch, each......... **4c**
Per doz............**45c**

## Muffin Pans.

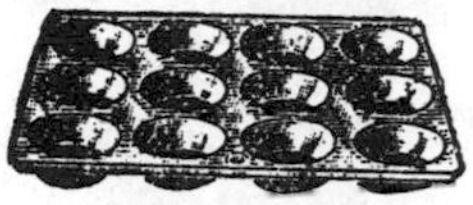

Plain stamped tinware, shallow.
No. 16194. 8 cups in frame, cups, 3x1 inches, per frame, **11c**; 12 cups in frame, cups, 3x1 inches, per frame............**15c**
No. 16195. Muffin Pans, deep, stamped tinware, same style as No. 16194. 8 cups in frame, cups 3x1¼ inches, per frame, **13c**; 12 cups in frame, cups 3x1¼ inches, per frame...............**19c**

## Turk's Head Pans.

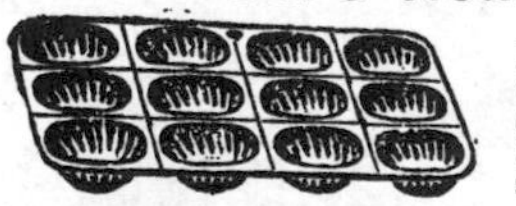

No. 16196. Turk's Head Pans, plain stamped tinware. 8 heads on frame, size, 3¼x1½ inches, each, **12c**; 12 heads on frame, size 3¼x1½ inches. Each............**18c**

## Patty Pans.

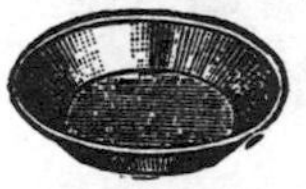

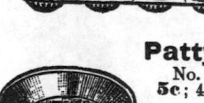

No. 16197. Plain, 3 inch, per doz., **5c**; 4 inch, per doz............**8c**

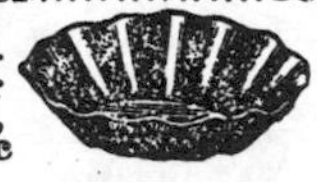

No. 16198. Scalloped, 3 inch, per doz., **7c**; 4 inch, per doz.......**10c**

No. 16199. Star. Per doz.........**7c**
No. 16200. Heart. Per doz........**7c**

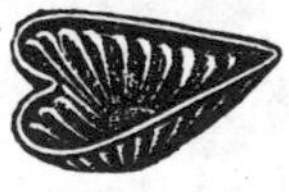

No. 16201. Assorted, two of each size. Per doz.....................**8c**

## PLATES.

## Pie Plates—Plain Tin.

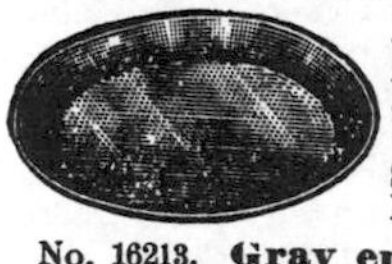

No. 16212. Plain tin pie plates. We sell any quantity at dozen prices.

| Size, inches, | 6x⅝ | 7x⅝ | 8x⅝ |
|---|---|---|---|
| Per doz., | $0.18 | .21 | .23 |
| Size, inches, | | 9x⅞ | 10x⅞ |
| Per doz. | | $0.28 | .37 |

No. 16213. **Gray enameled** pie plates. We sell any quantity at the dozen price.

| Size, inches, | 7x⅝ | 8x⅝ | 9x⅞ | 10x1 | 11x1 |
|---|---|---|---|---|---|
| Per doz., | $0.95 | 1.08 | 1.22 | 1.49 | 1.75 |

## Pie Plates—Extra Deep—Plain Tin.

| No. 16214. | Size, | 9x1⅛ | 10x1⅛ |
|---|---|---|---|
| | Per doz., | $0.30 | .40 |

## Dinner Plates.

No. 16215. **Gray enameled** dinner plates, round bottom. Size, 9x1 inch. Per doz..............**$1.30**

## Lettered Plates.

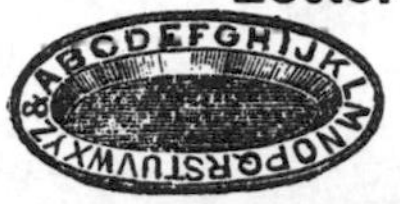



No. 16217. Size, 6 inches. Each, **2c**; per doz........................**20c**

## Jelly Cake Pans—Plain Tin.

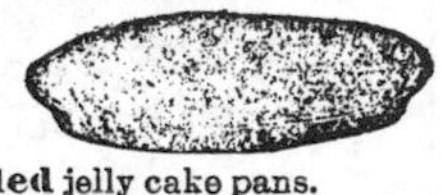

| No. 16218. | | |
|---|---|---|
| Size, inches, | 9x½ | 9x¾ |
| Per doz., | $0.30 | .45 |

No. 16219. **Gray enameled** jelly cake pans.

| Size, inches, | 9x½ | 10x½ | 9x¾ | 10x1 |
|---|---|---|---|---|
| Per doz., | $1.20 | 1.40 | 1.40 | 1.60 |

## Cups and Saucers.

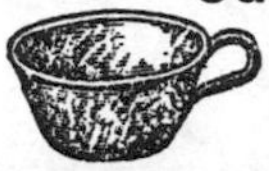

No. 16221. **Gray enameled** cups. Size, 4½x3. Price, ea., **10c**; per doz. **$1.00**

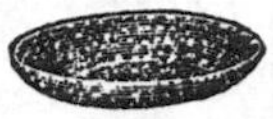

No. 16223. **Gray enameled** saucers, to match No. 16221 cups. Size, 6¾x1 inch. Price, each, **8c**; per doz.......................................**88c**

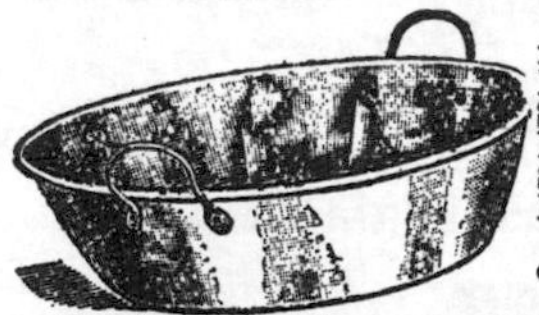

No. 16230. **Retinned** Dish Pans. Extra Heavy. Flat edge.

| Size, qts., | 10 | 14 |
|---|---|---|
| Each, | $0.20 | .26 |
| Size, qts., | 17 | 21 |
| Each, | $0.30 | .34 |

No. 16231. **Gray enameled** Dish Pan.

| Quarts, | 10 | 14 | 17 | 21 |
|---|---|---|---|---|
| Size, inches, | 14¼x5 | 15¾x5½ | 17¾x5¾ | 19¼x6 |
| Each, | $0.50 | .60 | .70 | .80 |

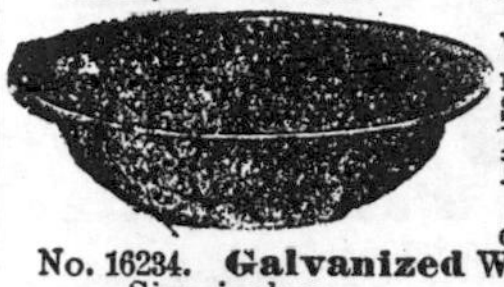

No. 16232. Plain tin Wash Bowls (not retinned.)

| Size, | 10¼x2¾ | 11½x2⅞ |
|---|---|---|
| Each, | $0.06 | .07 |
| Dozen, | .65 | .75 |

Size, 13x3. Each, **8c**; dozen...........................**85c**

No. 16234. **Galvanized** Wash Bowls.

| Size, inches, | 9½ | 10½ |
|---|---|---|
| Price, each, | $0.06 | .10 |

No. 16235. **Gray enameled** Wash Bowls.

| Size, inches, | 10⅜x2⅞ | 11⅝x2⅞ | 12¼x3⅛ | 13x3⅜ |
|---|---|---|---|---|
| Price, each, | $0.17 | .19 | .23 | .27 |

No. 16238. **Retinned seamless** Water Buckets. Flat bottom.

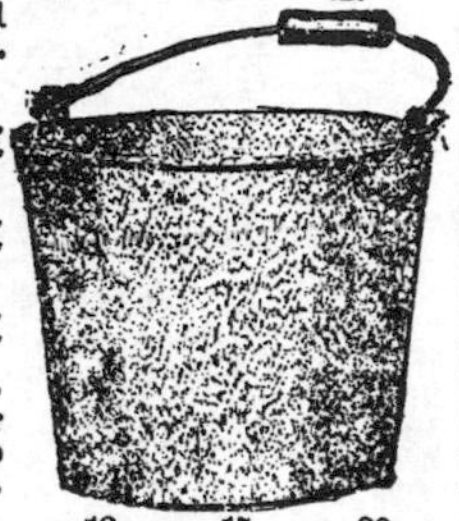

| Quarts, | 6 | 8 |
|---|---|---|
| Sizes, | 9x6½ | 9½x6¾ |
| Each, | $0.40 | .47 |
| Quarts, | 10 | 12 |
| Sizes, | 10¼x7¾ | 11½x8¾ |
| Each, | $0.56 | .64 |
| Quarts, | 15 | 20 |
| Sizes, | 12x9¾ | 13x10¾ |
| Each, | $0.72 | .86 |

No. 16239. **Gray enameled** seamless Water Buckets. Flat bottom, same shape as above illustration.

| Quarts, | 6 | 8 | 10 | 12 | 15 | 20 |
|---|---|---|---|---|---|---|
| Sizes, | 9x6½ | 9¼x6¾ | 10½x7¾ | 11½x8¾ | 12x9¾ | 13x10¾ |
| Each, | $0.42 | .50 | .60 | .72 | .84 | .90 |

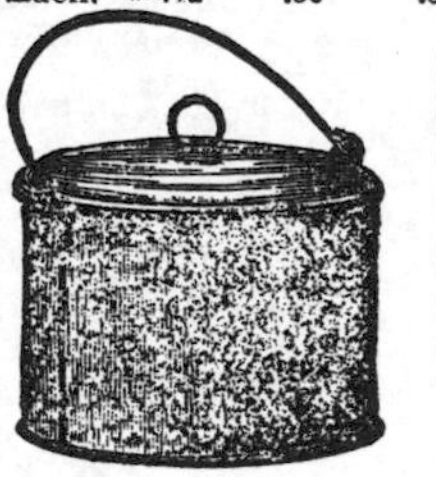

No. 16241. **Gray enameled** straight-seamed covered Buckets, with tin cover.

| Size, quarts, | ½ | 1 | 2 |
|---|---|---|---|
| Actual capacity, | ¾ | 1 | 1¾ |
| Price, each, | $0.16 | .20 | .24 |
| Size, quarts, | 3 | 4 | 6 |
| Actual capacity, | 2¾ | 4¼ | 6¼ |
| Price, each, | $0.30 | .36 | .40 |
| Size, quarts, | 8 | 10 | 12 |
| Actual capacity, | 8¼ | 9¾ | 12 |
| Price, each, | $0.54 | .64 | .76 |

## Drinking Cups.

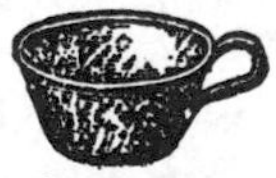

No. 16242. Stamped ware, light **retinned** seamless Cup.

| Sizes, | 3¾x2 | 4x2½ | 4⅜x3½ | 5x2⅝ |
|---|---|---|---|---|
| Each, | $0.03 | .04 | .05 | .06 |
| Per doz., | .35 | .40 | .45 | .55 |

No. 16243. **Gray enameled** Drinking Cup, seamless.

| Nos. | 14 | 16 | 18 |
|---|---|---|---|
| Size, inches, | 3½x2¼ | 4⅜x2⅝ | 5¼x2½ |
| Price, each, | $0.07 | .09 | .12 |

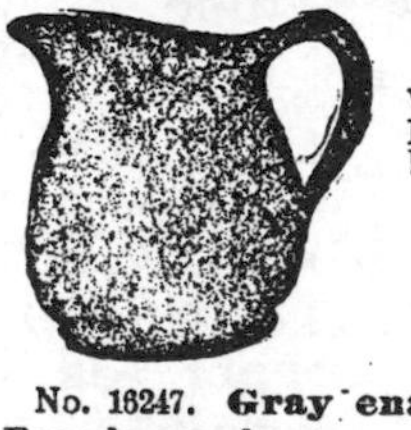

## Water Pitchers.

No. 16245. **Gray enameled** Water Pitchers, seamless.

| Pints, | 2 | 3 | 4 | 5 |
|---|---|---|---|---|
| Price, each, | $0.37 | .43 | .48 | .54 |

## Funnels.

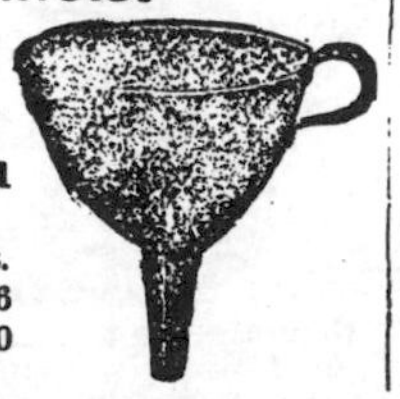

No. 16247. **Gray enameled** Funnels, seamless.

| Capacity, | ½pt. | 1pt. | 1qt. | 2qt. | 4qt. |
|---|---|---|---|---|---|
| Nos., | 102 | 103 | 104 | 105 | 106 |
| Price, each | $0.14 | .16 | .21 | .27 | .40 |

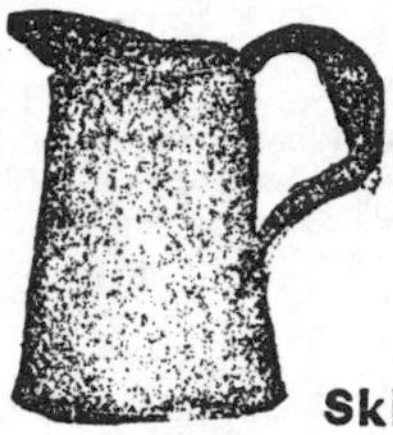

## Measures.

No. 16249. **Gray enameled** Measures.
½ pint..................**18c**
1 pint..................**23c**
1 quart..................
½ gal....................**29c**
1 gal....................**54c**

## Skimmers.

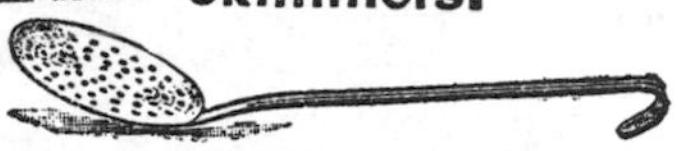

Flat Handles—Retinned.

| No. 16250. | | | |
|---|---|---|---|
| Size, inches, | 4 | 5 | 5½ |
| Each, | $0.04 | .05 | .06 |
| Per doz., | .44 | .54 | .65 |

## Milk Skimmers.

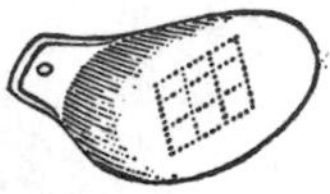

No. 16251. 5⅝x5 inches, plain, each, **3c**; per doz...........**30c**
No. 16252. Milk Skimmers, pierced, 5⅝x5 inches. Price, each, **4c**; per doz...........**45c**
No. 16253. Round Pierced Milk Skimmer, with handle. Size, 4⅝ inches in diameter. Each, **5c**; per doz..........................................**54c**
No. 16254. Round Solid Milk Skimmer, with handle. Size, 4⅝ inches in diameter. Each, **5c**; per doz....**54c**

## Kitchen Forks.

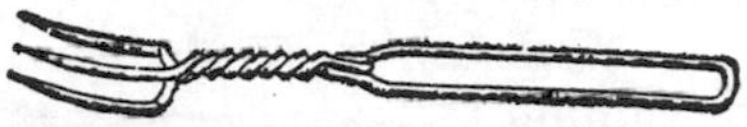

No. 16256. Steel Wire Kitchen Fork. Three prongs, tinned. Lengths, 12½ inches. Each, **3c**; per doz..**33c**

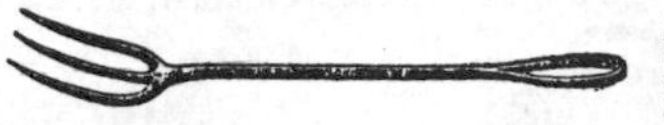

No. 16257. Extra heavy tinned iron Kitchen Fork. Three prongs. Length, 15 inches. Each, **6c**; per doz.... ..........................**65c**

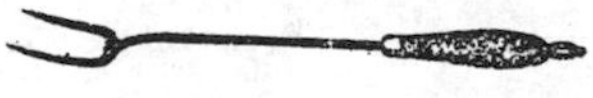

No. 16258. Extra heavy tinned iron Kitchen Fork. Two prongs, with ebonized wood handle. Length, 15 inches. Price, each, **5c**; per doz.........................................**54c**

## Tea and Table Spoons.

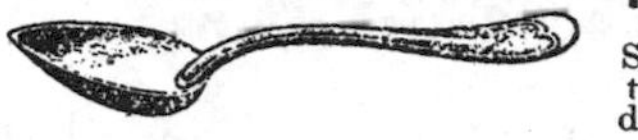

No. 16260. Tea Spoons, tin, retinned. Per doz..............**7c**

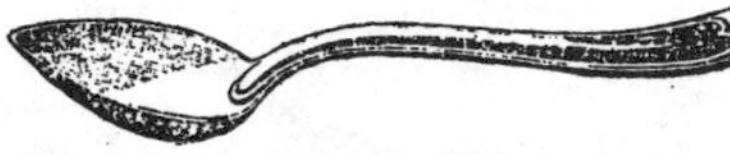

No. 16261. Table Spoons, same pattern. Per doz....**9c**

## Basting Spoons—Retinned.

| No. 16270. Inches | Weight per doz. | Each. |
|---|---|---|
| 10 | 1 lb. 7 oz. | $0.03 |
| 12 | 1 lb. 15 oz. | .04 |
| 14 | 2¼ lbs. | .05 |
| 16 | 2½ lbs. | .06 |
| 18 | 4½ lbs. | .07 |

## Basting Spoons—Gray Enameled.

No. 16271. Ten inches; each, **7c**; 12 inches, **8c**; 14 inches, **9c**; 16 inches, **12c**; 18 inches............**14c**

## Ladles.

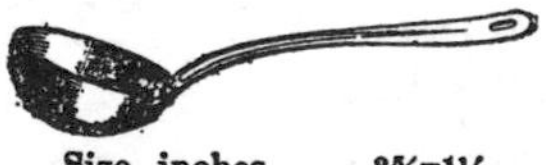

No. 16272. Retinned Ladles.

| Size, inches, | 3⅝x1½ | 4⅜x1¾ | 4⅝x2 |
|---|---|---|---|
| Each, | $0.04 | .05 | .06 |

No. 16273. **Gray Enameled** Ladles. Size, 3½x1⅝ inches. Each ......................................**10c**

## Soup Ladles—Retinned.

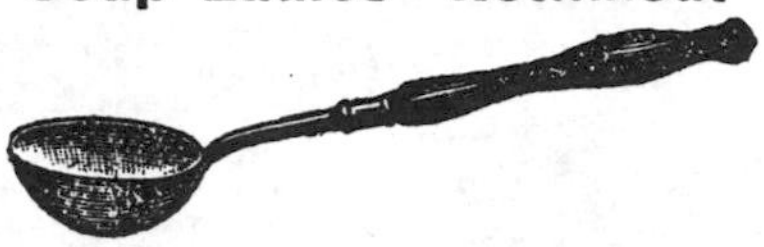

No. 16274. Soup Ladles, retinned, with black enamel wood handles.

| Size, inches, | 3¾x1¼ | 4x1½ |
|---|---|---|
| Each, | $0.05 | .07 |

## Pierced Ladles.

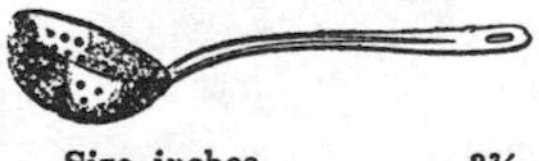

No. 16278. Deep retinned Pierced Ladles.

| Size, inches, | 3¾ | 4¼ | 5 |
|---|---|---|---|
| Each, | $0.05 | .06 | .07 |

**You may not find just what you want by glancing over this department. Refer to the index and you can't miss it. Our index, by the way, is worth reading over on general principles.**

## Water Dippers—Stamped—Tin.

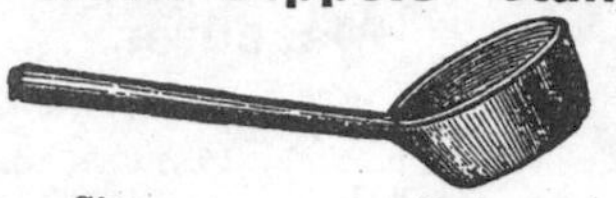

No. 16280. Will not hold as much as represented; bossed handles.

| Size. | Each. | Per doz. |
|---|---|---|
| 1 pint, | $0.04 | $0.36 |
| 1 quart, | .05 | .45 |
| 2 quarts, | .06 | .56 |

No. 16281. **Gray Enameled** Water Dippers, with round handle.

| Size, | 5x2½ | 5½x3 | 6½x3¼ |
|---|---|---|---|
| Each, | $0.16 | .20 | .24 |

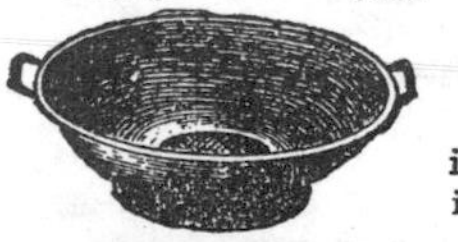

## Milk Strainers.

No. 16282. Size, 9¼x2⅝ inches. Each, **10c**; 9¾x3 inches......................**13c**

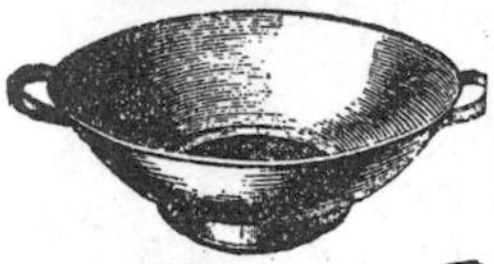

## Colanders—Tin.

No. 16283. Retinned. Size, 10 inch, **12c**; 11¼ inch......................**15c**

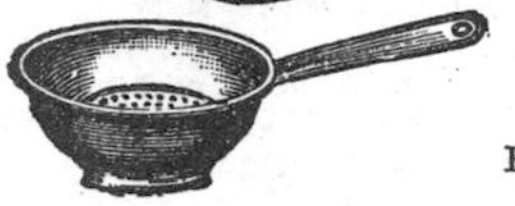

## Gravy Strainers.

Seamless—Retinned. No. 16284. 4⅜x1⅝ inch. Each......................**7c**

## Vegetable Strainer.

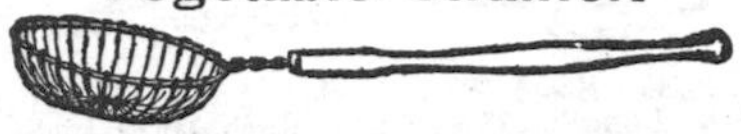

No. 16285. Wire handled Vegetable Strainer. Each, **5c**

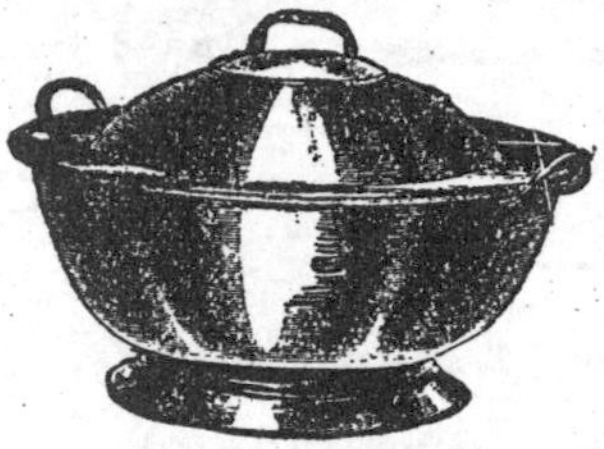

## Bread Raisers.

No. 16286. Bread Raisers, stamped, retinned.

| Qts. | Weight. | Each. |
|---|---|---|
| 10 | 2½ lbs. | $0.40 |
| 14 | 3 lbs. | .52 |
| 17 | 3½ lbs. | .60 |
| 21 | 4 lbs. | .85 |

## Divided Sauce Pans.

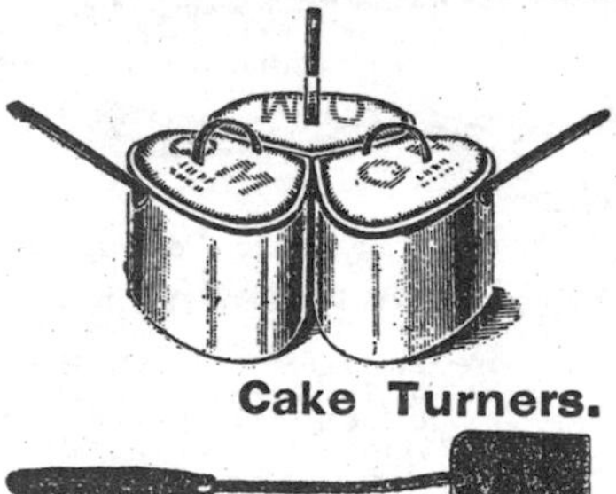

No. 16287. Divided Sauce Pans, made of tin. Three pans. Price, per set......**75c**

## Cake Turners.

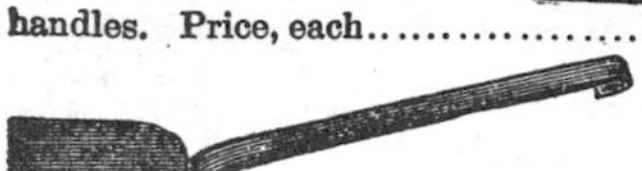

No. 16298. Russia iron Cake Turners with wood handles. Price, each......................**5c**

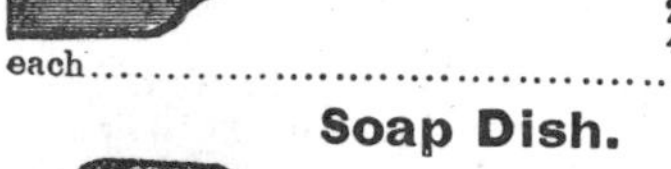

No. 16299. Retinned Cake Turner, with flat handle. Size, 2¾x3¾ in., each, **4c**; 3¼x4½ in., each......................**5c**

## Soap Dish.

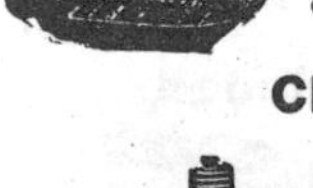

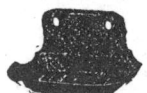

No. 16301. **Gray enameled** Soap Dish. Size, 6½x4x1½ inches. Price, each......................**16c**

## Chamber Pail.

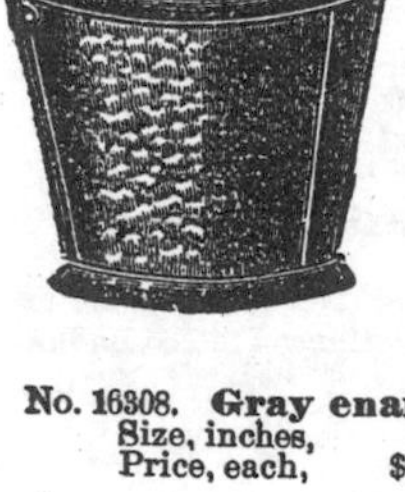

No. 16305. **Gray enameled** Chamber Pail. Size, 11¼x11½. Price, each. **$1.16**

## Chambers.

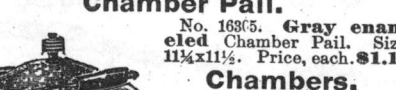

No. 16307. **Gray enameled** Chambers, without covers.

| Sizes, in., | 7x4⅛ | 8½x4⅞ | 9¾x5¼ |
|---|---|---|---|
| Each, | $0.30 | .38 | .46 |

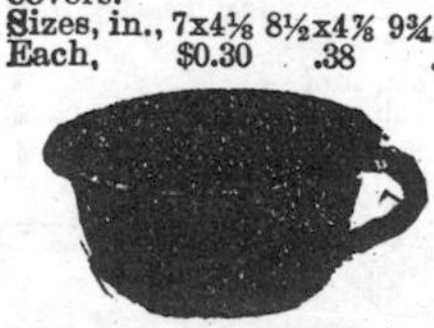

No. 16308. **Gray enameled** Covers for above.

| Size, inches, | 7 | 8½ | 9¾ |
|---|---|---|---|
| Price, each, | $0.10 | .14 | .18 |

## Bed Pans.

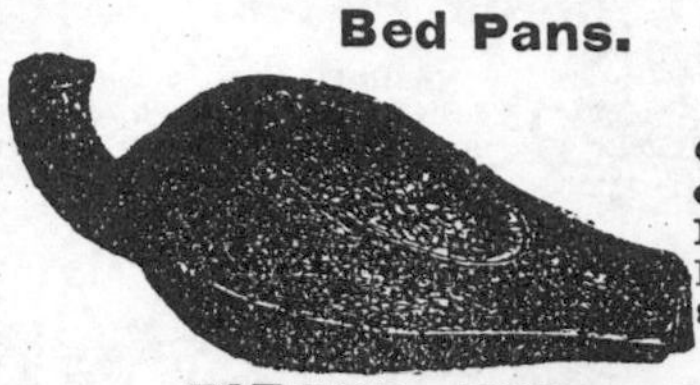

No. 16311. **Gray enameled** Bed Pans, like cut. Price, each, **$1.60.**

## PIECED TINWARE.

## Wash Boilers.

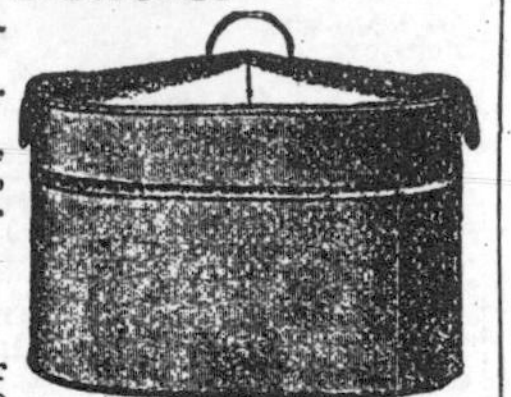

Heavy IX tin, with copper bottom, **full size.**
No. 16340. Flat bottom.
No. 16341. Pit bottom.
No. 7, each, **78c**; No. 8, each, **82c**; No. 9, each, **93c.** Weight, 5¼ to 7 lbs.

## All Copper Wash Boilers.

We guarantee all of our Copper Boilers to be made of 14 oz. copper and full size.
No. 16342. Flat bottom.
No. 16343. Pit bottom.
No. 8, each, **$1.75**; No. 9, each, **$1.90.** Weight, 6¼ to 8½ lbs.

## Copper Rim Wash Boilers.

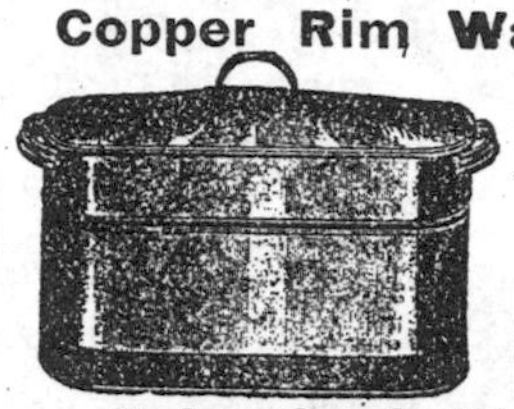

Heavy IX tin Wash Boilers, with copper bottom and rim.
No. 16344. Flat bottom.
No. 16345. Pit bottom.
No. 8, each, **$1.00**; No. 9, each, **$1.12.**

## Galvanized Wash Tubs.

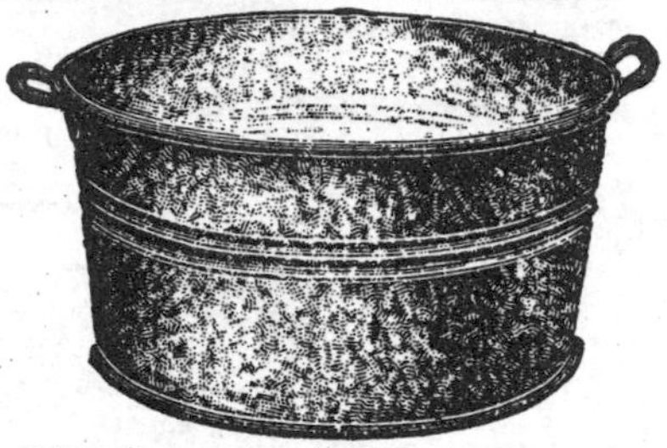

No. 16354. Heavy galvanized Wash Tubs; no leaking, no hoops to fall off, strong and durable.

| No., | 1 | 2 | 3 |
|---|---|---|---|
| Size, | 20x17¾x10⅝ | 22x17½x10¾ | 24⅛x21¾x10¾ |
| Each, | $0.60 | .70 | .80 |

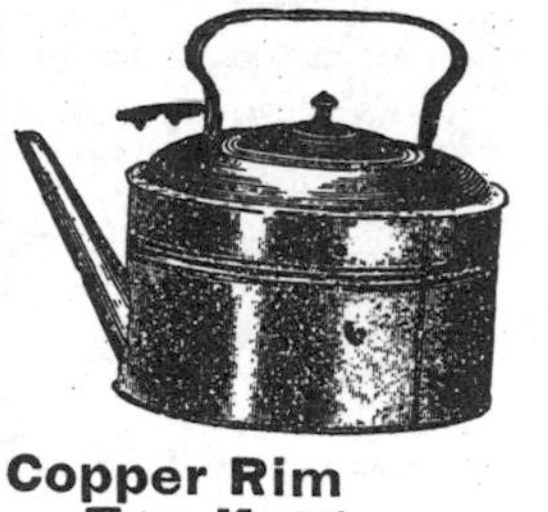

## Tea Kettles.

Tin, with copper bottom. Weight, from 1¼ to 2 lbs.
No. 16356. Flat bottom.
No. 16357. Pit bottom.
No. 7. Each, **26c**; No. 8, each, **30c**; No. 9, each............**35c**

## Copper Rim Tea Kettles.

Tin, with copper bottom and rim. Weight, 1¾ to 2¼ lbs.
No. 16358. Flat bottom.
No. 16359. Pit bottom.
No. 7. Each, **40c**; No. 8, each, **49c**; No. 9, each................**55c**

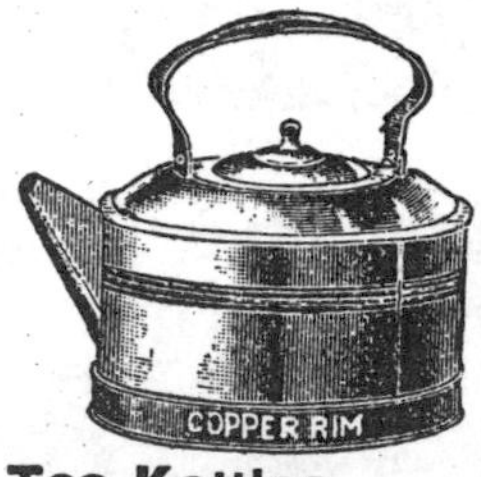


## All Copper Tea Kettles.

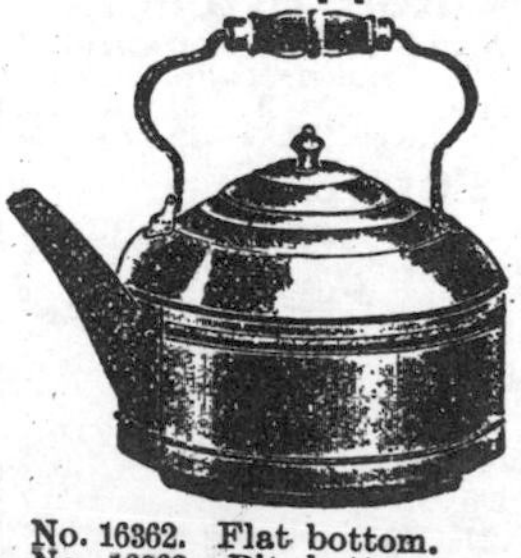

No. 16360. Flat bottom. Weight, 2 to 3 lbs.
No. 16361. Pit bottom.
No. 7. Each, **60c**; No. 8, each, **69c**; No. 9, each......**75c**

## Nickel Plated Copper Tea Kettles.

All copper, nickel plated, same style as No. 16360.
No. 16362. Flat bottom.
No. 16363. Pit bottom.
No. 7, each, **68c**; No. 8, each, **75c**; No. 9, each **85c**

## Tea Pots and Coffee Pots.

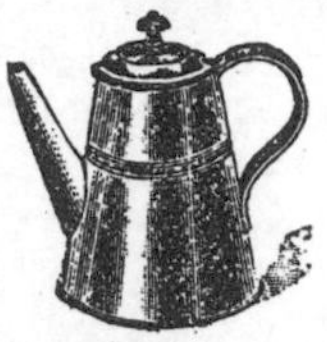

No. 16366. Common tin Teapots, made of IC tin.

| Pints, | 2 | 3 | 4 | 5 |
|---|---|---|---|---|
| Price, each, | $0.10 | .12 | .15 | .20 |

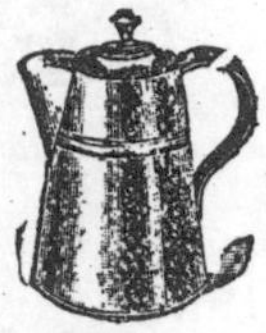

No. 16367. Common Coffee Pots, made of IC tin.

| Quarts, | 2 | 3 | 4 | 5 |
|---|---|---|---|---|
| Price, each, | $0.09 | .11 | .13 | .16 |

## Octagon Tea Pots.

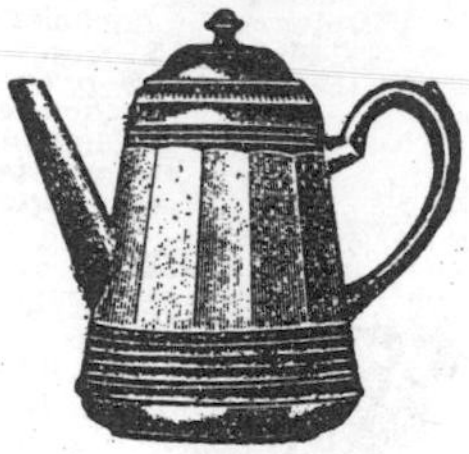

Tin Fluted Spouts, will not hold as much as represented.
No. 16368. 3 pints, each, **15c**; 4 pints, **18c**; 5 pints, **20c**; 6 pints, **22c.**

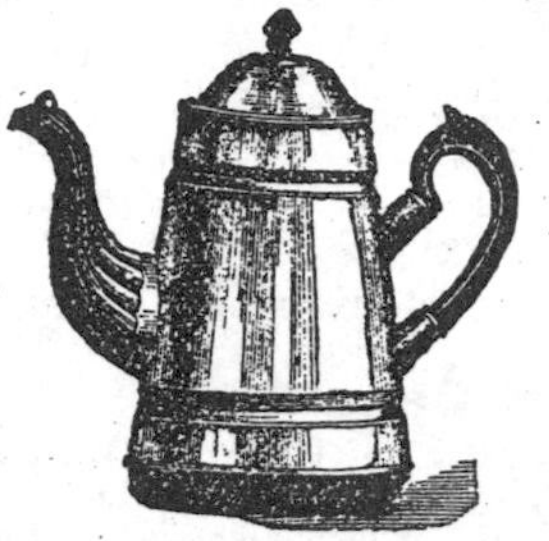

## Planished Tea Pots.

Will not hold as much as represented, with copper bottom.
No. 16369. 3 pints, each, **22c**; 4 pints, **25c**; 5 pints, **28c**; 6 pints, **32c.**

## Planished Coffee Pots.

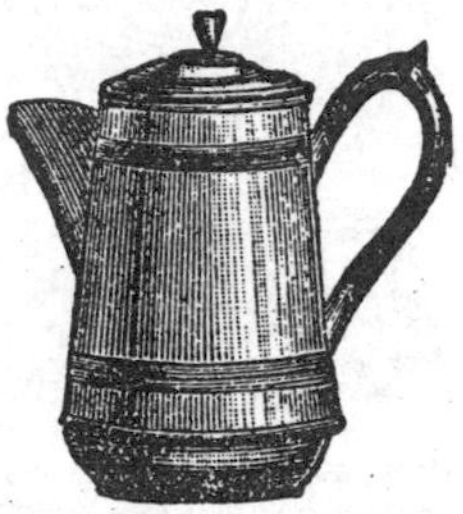

No. 16370. Planished Coffee Pots with copper bottom, same as above, except has a lip spout.

| Pints, | 3 | 4 | 5 | 6 |
|---|---|---|---|---|
| Each, | $0.15 | .19 | .21 | .25 |

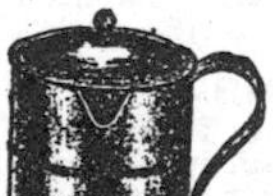

## Tea Steeper.

No. 16376. Pieced tin Tea Steeper. Size, 1 qt., each......................**8c**

## Solid Lip Coffee Pot.

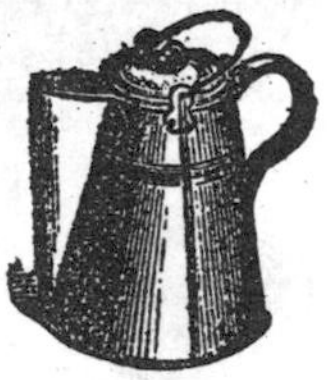

Heavy tin, for lumbermen and miners' use. The body and lip being in one piece the latter will not drop off when heated.
No. 16378. 2 quarts, each **18c**; 3 quarts, **23c**; 4 quarts, **26c**; 6 quarts..............................**32c**

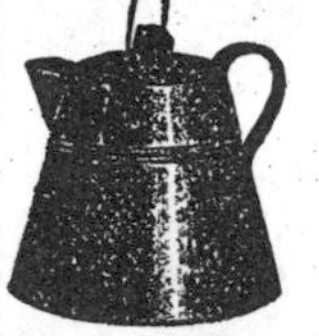

## Coffee Boilers.

No. 16380. Flat bottom with bail.

| Nos., | 7 | 8 | 9 |
|---|---|---|---|
| Each, | $0.27 | .31 | .38 |

## The Chicago Tea and Coffee Pot.

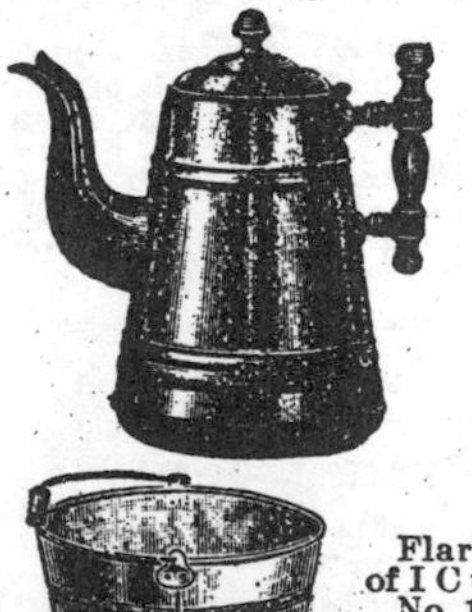

Nickel plated on polished copper Something very handsome.
No. 16386. Tea Pots, nickel plated, 3 pints, each, **45c**; 4 pints, **50c**; 5 pints................**52c**
No. 16387. Coffee pots, nickel plated, 3 pints, each, **46c**; 4 pints, **49c**; 5 pints, **53c**; 6 pints, **56c**

## Tin Pails.

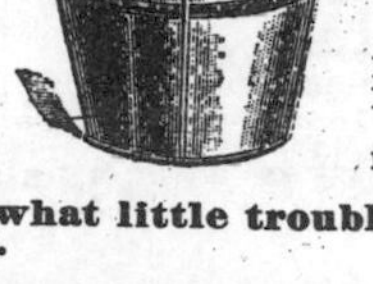

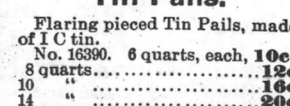

Flaring pieced Tin Pails, made of I C tin.
No. 16390. 6 quarts, each, **10c**;
8 quarts......................**12c**
10 " ......................**16c**
14 " ......................**20c**
They will not hold as much as represented.

**We urge care to be taken in making out your orders. We believe that nine-tenths of what little trouble occurs in filling orders is the result of utter carelessness in ordering.**

## Galvanized Iron Water Pails.

No. 16394. Made of heavy galvanized iron.
10 quarts, each........................................**20c**
12 " " ........................................**22c**
14 " " ........................................**26c**

## Strainer Pails, Tin.

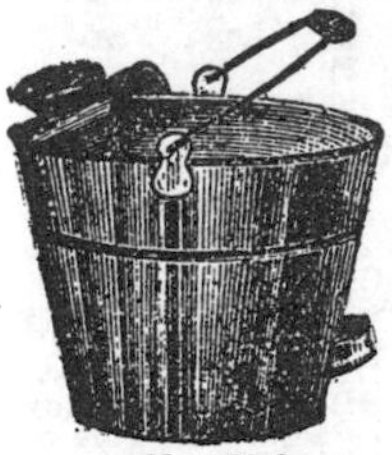

Will not hold as much as represented.
No. 17032. Price, 10 quarts, each........**20c**
Price, 14 quarts, each..**28c**

No. 17032.

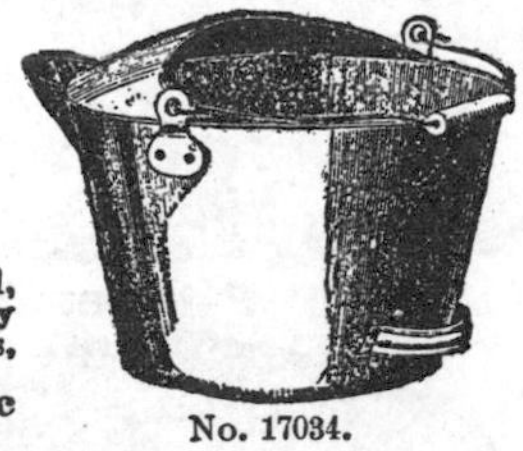

No. 17034. Milk Pail, with strainer, extra heavy tin, stamped seamless, holds 12 quarts.
Price, each........**90c**

No. 17034.

## The Dairyman's Favorite.

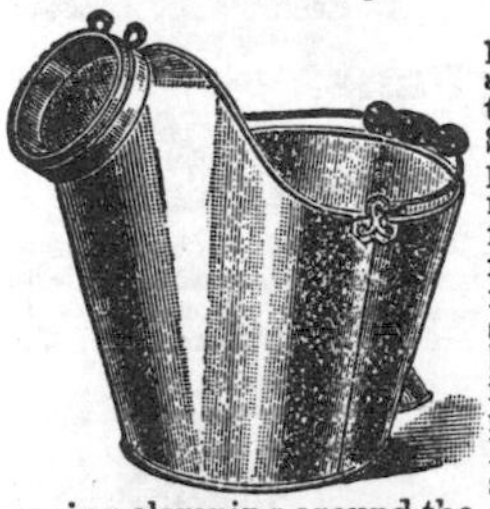

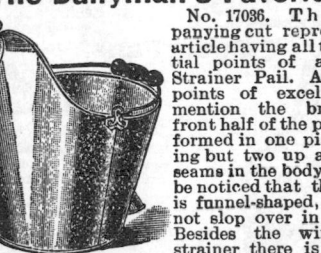

No. 17036. The accompanying cut represents an article having all the essential points of a perfect Strainer Pail. Among its points of excellence we mention the breast and front half of the pail being formed in one piece, making but two up and down seams in the body. It will be noticed that the breast is funnel-shaped, and will not slop over in pouring. Besides the wire gauze strainer there is a brass spring clamping around the mouth to hold a cloth, thus making a double strainer without extra labor or loss or time. Another important feature is, there is no part but what can be thoroughly washed, and no rough and unsoldered seams in which dirt can accumulate and sour.
Price, 12 quarts, each..............................**45c**
" 14 " " ..............................**51c**

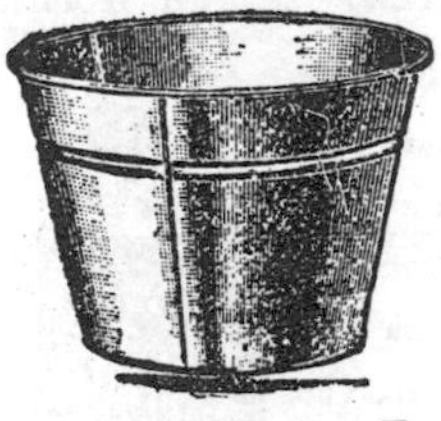

## Sap Pails.

No. 16395. Sap pails made from I C tin.

| Quarts. | Per doz. | Per gross. |
|---|---|---|
| 10 | $1.25 | $13.15 |
| 12 | 1.40 | 14.38 |

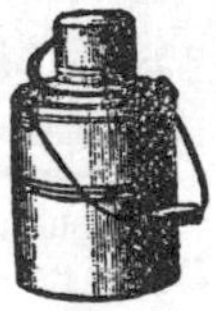

## Dinner Pails.

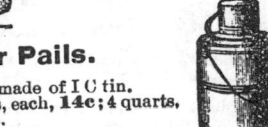

Round, with cup, made of I C tin.
No. 16398. 3 quarts, each, **14c**; 4 quarts, **16c**; 5 quarts, **23c**.

## Square Dinner Pails.

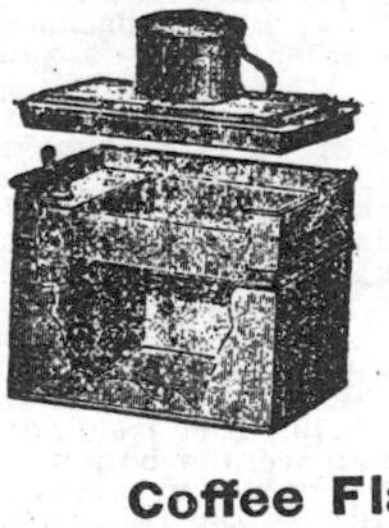

No. 16399. With cups, tray and coffee flask. 2 qts., 4⅞x7¾x5⅓, each, **25c**; 3 qt., 5⅜x7¾x5⅝, each, **27c**; 4 qt., 6¼x8¾x6½, each.........**30c**

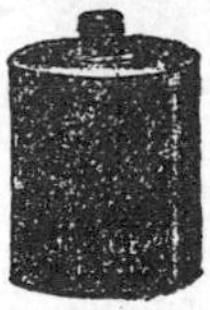

## Coffee Flasks

Tin, screw top.
No. 16403. 1 pint, each, **5c**.
No. 16404. 1½ pint, each, **6c**.

## Covered Pails—Tin.

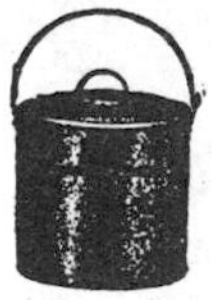

No. 16405. They will not hold as much as represented.

| Quarts. | Each. | Quarts. | Each. |
|---|---|---|---|
| 1 | $0.05 | 6 | $0.12 |
| 2 | .06 | 8 | .15 |
| 3 | .07 | 10 | .20 |
| 4 | .08 | | |

## Lunch Boxes.

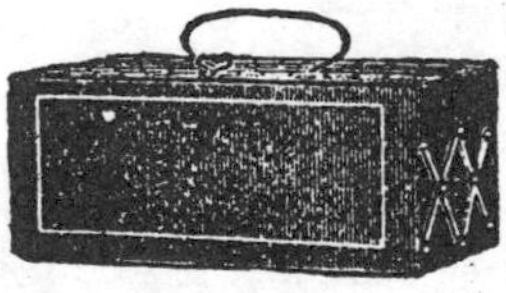

No. 16412. Folding Lunch Box, made of tin, nicely japanned, with handle.

| | Size, when opened. | Size, closed. | Each. |
|---|---|---|---|
| Small, | 7½x3¾x3¾ | 7½x3¾x½ | $0.17 |
| Large, | 9x4x4 | 9x4x½ | .38 |
| Large, with flask, | 9x4x4 | 9x4x1 | .57 |

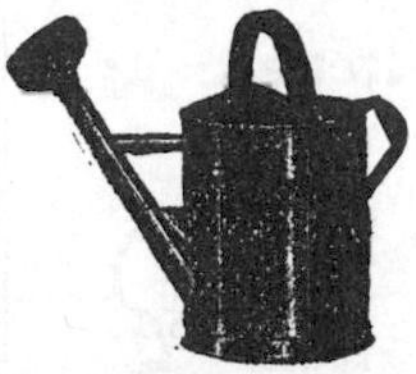

## Sprinklers.

No, 16413. Watering Pots made from I C tin.

| Quarts, | 1 | 4 | 6 | 8 | 10 |
|---|---|---|---|---|---|
| Inches, | 4⅜x4⅝ | 6¼x6½ | 7¼x7¾ | 8¼x8¾ | 8¾x10½ |
| Price, each, | $0.12 | .15 | .20 | .30 | .36 |

No. 16414. Galvanized Watering Pots.

| Size, quarts, | 6 | 8 | 10 | 12 |
|---|---|---|---|---|
| Price, each, | $0.30 | .33 | .36 | .50 |

## Funnels.

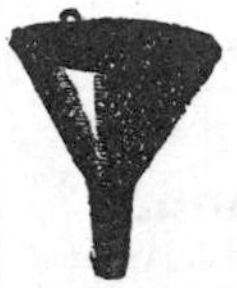

No. 16415. ½ pint, each, **3c**; 1 pint, **4c**; 1 quart, **5c**; 2 quarts, **6c**.

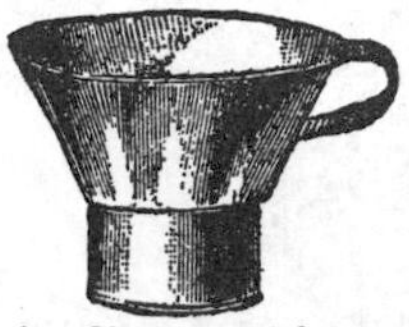

## Jar Funnels.

No. 16418.

Fruit Jar Fillers, made of tin. No one putting up fruit should be without one of these. Measures across lower end 2 inches; weighs, 5 oz. Price, each.......**5c**

## Measures—Tin.

### For Liquids.

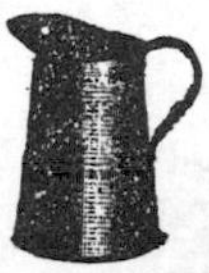

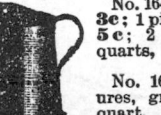

No. 16419. ½ pint, each **3c**; 1 pint, **4c**; 1 quart, **5c**; 2 quarts, **9c**; 4 quarts, **16c**.

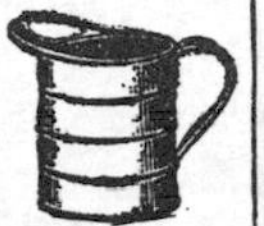

No. 16420. Milk Measures, graduated, tin. 1 quart. Each ..........**8c**

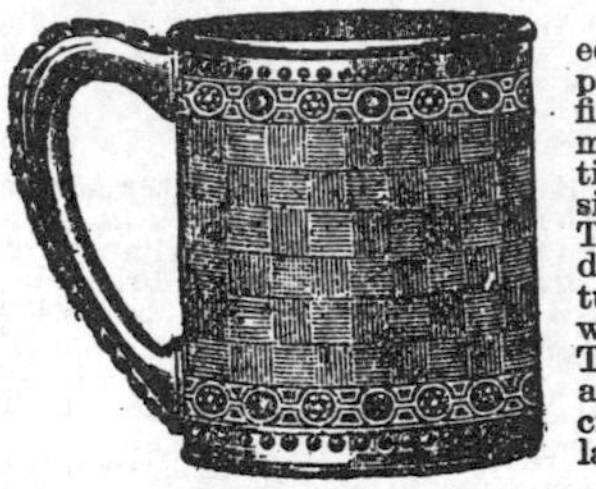

No. 16421. Embossed tin Mug, basket pattern. See cut. At five feet away this mug cannot be distinguished from a silver plated mug. The tin is heavy and double, with strong tubed handle that will not come off. This mug is made on an entirely new principle, and is made to last. Each.......**6c**

## Vegetable Boilers.

I C Tin—Pit.

No. 16430. Copper bottoms. Size 7, **25c**; size 8, **31c**; size 9, **35c**.

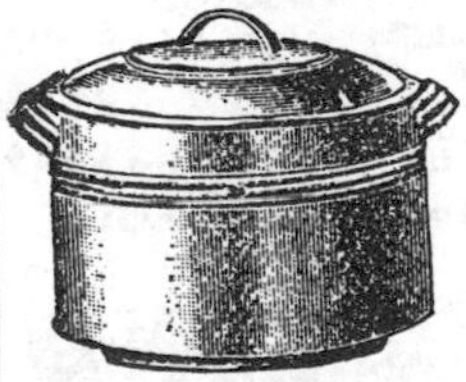

No. 16430.

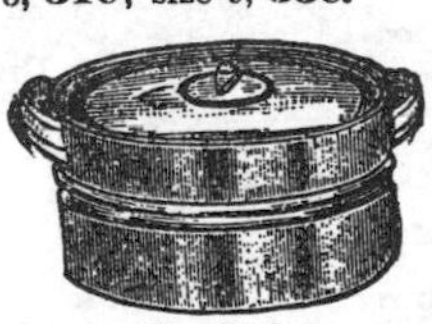

No. 16432.

## Steamers.

I C Tin.

No. 16432. Size 7; each, **15c**; size 8, **17c**; size 9, **22c**.

## Tin Cups.

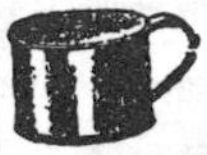

No. 16438.

| Size, | ½ pt. | 1 pt. | 1 qt. | 2 qt. |
|---|---|---|---|---|
| Each, | $0.02 | .03 | .04 | .06 |
| Per doz. | .20 | .25 | .45 | .60 |

## Lemonade Shakers.

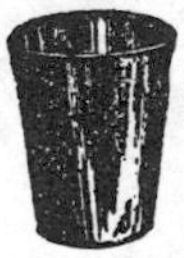

No. 16440. Liquor Mixers, or Lemonade Shakers, of tin. Size, 5⅛x2¾; weight, 5 oz. Price, each, **4c**; per doz......**50c**

## Deep Bread Pans.

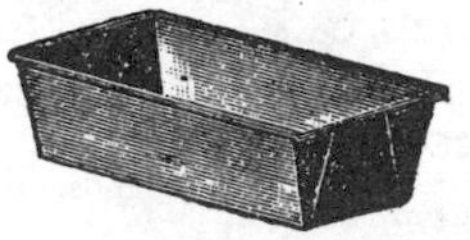

No. 16444—Tin.

| Sizes. | Each. | Per doz. |
|---|---|---|
| 9¼x5x3 | $0.07 | $0.70 |
| 10¼x6¼x¾ | .09 | .80 |
| 12 x6¼x3¼ | .10 | .90 |

## Common Square Pans.

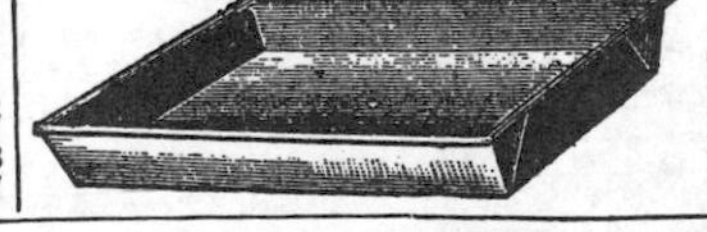

No. 16445—Tin. Size, 7¾x11¾x1⅜. Price, each, **6c**; per doz...**60c**

## Dripping Pans.

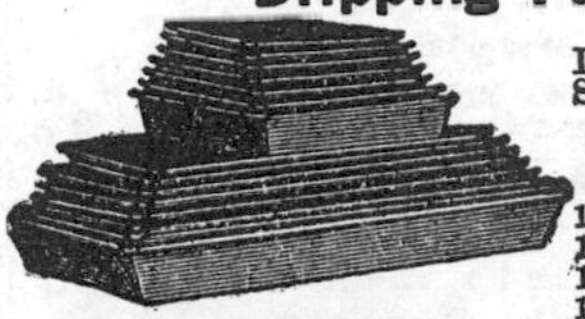

No. 16446. Sheet iron Dripping Pans.

| Size. | Each. | Per doz. |
|---|---|---|
| 7x10 | $0.07 | $0.75 |
| 7x14 | .08 | .80 |
| 8x12 | .09 | .95 |
| 10x12 | .10 | 1.05 |
| 10x14 | .12 | 1.25 |
| 10x16 | .13 | 1.35 |
| 12x19 | .14 | 1.57 |
| 14x17 | .15 | 1.69 |

## Roasting Pans.

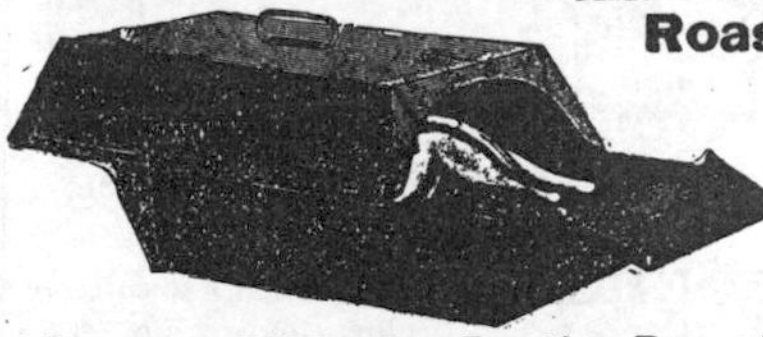

No. 16447. Self-basting Roasting Pan, with sliding cover and open end, the only first-class roaster and baker on the market, having a grate to keep the roast from the bottom of the pan, and a door at the end for browning to any desired extent a person may wish, and can be looked into without removing from the oven, as the cover slides on the pan. Made from the best iron, will last, if properly cared for, ten years or more.

| No., | 2 | 3 | 4 | 5 |
|---|---|---|---|---|
| Length, | 13 | 15 | 16 | 18¼ |
| Width, | 9 | 10 | 11 | 13 |
| Height, | 7 | 8 | 9 | 10 |
| Price, each, | $0.50 | .75 | .81 | 1.05 |

No. 16448. The Acme Roasting Pan is the strongest and best roasting pan in the market. The bottom is strengthened by two ribs. Has a heavy rack which keeps the meat out of the gravy. It is made of a fine grade of smooth steel. Try the pan for baking bread and you will never use anything else. Notice the very low prices. They are sold by agents at more than twice our price.

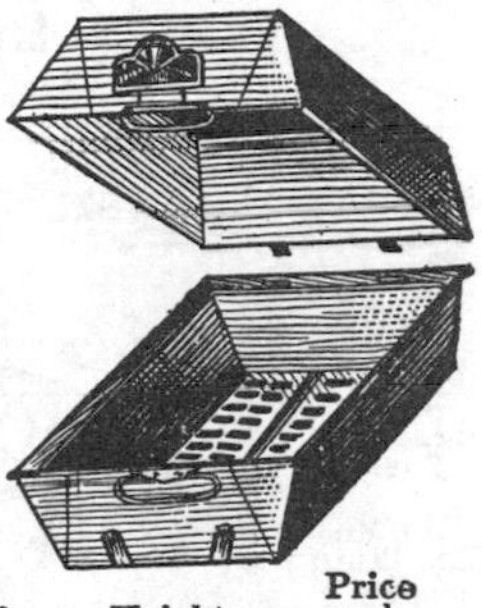

| No. | Width. | Length. | Height. | Price each. |
|---|---|---|---|---|
| 1 | 9 | 13 | 7½ | 50c |
| 2 | 10 | 15 | 7½ | 60c |
| 3 | 11 | 16 | 8½ | 70c |
| 4 | 13 | 18 | 9½ | 85c |

## Pieced Water Dippers.

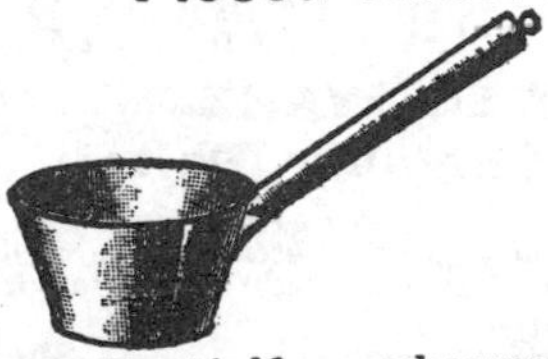

No. 16454. Pieced tin Water Dippers, with copper bottom. Size, 2 quarts. Price, each ............**9c**
Per doz............**$1.00**

## Galvanized Iron Dippers.

Manufacturers' measure will not hold as much as represented.
No. 16455. Price, each, 1 quart, **7c**; 2 quarts, **10c**; 3 quarts..............................................**11c**

## Biscuit and Cake Cutters.

No. 16459. Biscuit Cutters. Size, 3x1 in.
Each...........................................**3c**
Per doz......................................**28c**
No. 16460. Doughnut Cutters. Size, 3x1 in.
Each...........................................**4c**
Per doz......................................**40c**

16460

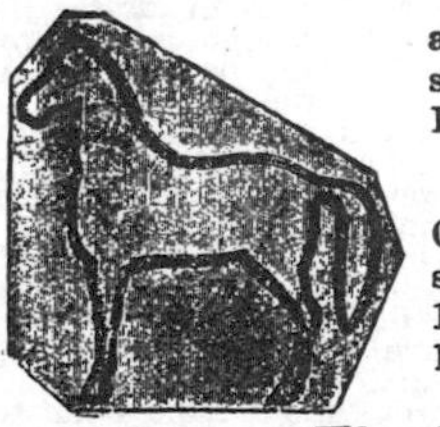

No. 16462. Cake Cutters, animals and birds, assorted styles. Each...............**4c**
Per doz..................**36c**

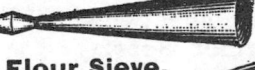

No. 16463. Cake Cutters, fancy, assorted styles.
Each.............**4c**
Per doz.........**40c**

## Tin Horns.

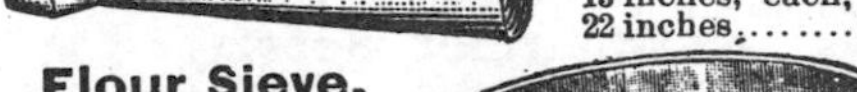

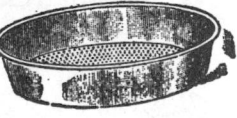

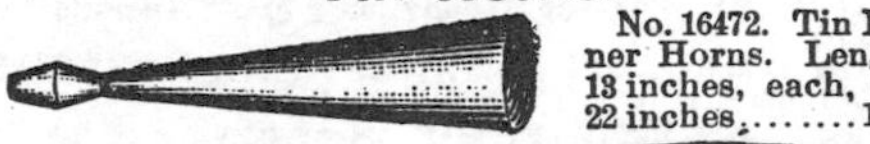

No. 16472. Tin Dinner Horns. Length, 13 inches, each, **6c**; 22 inches.........**15c**

## Flour Sieve.

No. 16476. Tin rim Sieve, 12½ inches diameter, well put together, made of heavy tin.
Each..............**12c**

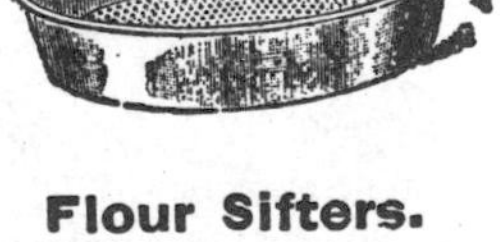

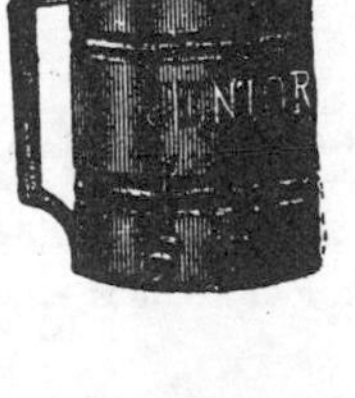

## Flour Sifters.

No. 16477. Rotary Flour Sifter, also serves as a scoop. Full size, well made.
Each...........................**9c**

**Nearly all our customers send cash in full with their orders and thus save 3 per cent. cash discount. Read our liberal terms before ordering.**

## Apple Corers.

No. 16465. Price, each............3c
Per doz....................30c

## Box Graters.

No. 16466. Patented Nutmeg Grater, japanned.
Each, 2c; per doz............20c

## Radish Graters.

No. 16467.

| Size, | 3x6½ | 4x9½ | 6x12 |
|---|---|---|---|
| Each, | $0.03 | .04 | .07 |
| Per doz., | 39 | .45 | .75 |

16467.                                  16466.

## The Improved Edgar Nutmeg Grater.

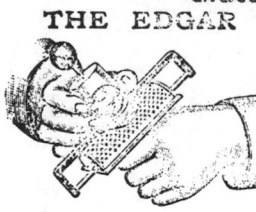

THE EDGAR

Nutmeg Grater.

No. 16468. It will not clog, tear the fingers, nor drop the nutmeg. It grates the nutmeg very fine, distributes it evenly, and grates it all up, leaving no pieces. It is simple and durable.
Price, each.......10c
Per doz........$1.00

## Egg Beaters.

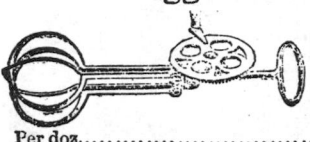

No. 16480. Dover Egg Beater. Celebrated as the best beater made; perfect action, strongly made, duplex iron frame.
Each..........9c
Per doz....................$1.00

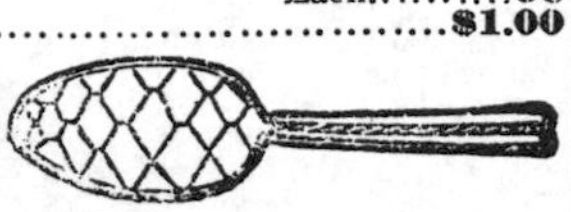

No. 16481. Surprise Egg Beater, retinned.
Each....................2c

No. 16482. Spoon Egg Whip, with wood handle.
Each............3c

## Scoops.

No. 16485. Tin Scoops, retinned. Weight, from ½ to 2 lbs.

| Size, | 6¾x4¾ | 8x5½ | 10x6½ | 11¼x7 |
|---|---|---|---|---|
| Price, each, | $0.08 | .11 | .13 | .16 |
| Per doz., | .88 | 1.14 | 1.37 | 1.76 |

## JAPANNED WARE.

### Chamber Pails.

No. 16494. Slop Pail. Full size, elegantly painted outside and in, with double gilt band, tight fitting top or tray.
Each....................30c
No. 16495. Galvanized iron Chamber Pail, made of heavy iron, will not rust.
Each....................40c

## Challenge Odorless Commode and Slop Bucket Combined.

No. 16495½. Beats everything of the kind on the market. It is impossible for the foul air to escape, when the lid is removed, as there is inside the lid a receptacle that holds a deodorizer and which neutralizes all gases inside the commode. The disinfectant (2 tablespoonfuls of chloride of lime) needs only to be renewed once in two weeks at a small cost.
It is indispensable in the sick room, especially in cases of contagious diseases and fevers. Does not have to be emptied until filled, no matter how long it stands.
Made of heavy galvanized iron, and has no paint to hold stench or disease germs. Has removable seat, etc. It needs only to be seen to convince you of its wonderful merit.
Price, each....................$3.25
Try one.

## Chamber Sets.

No. 16496. Chamber Sets. Full size, nicely finished in different styles, as follows: Oak, walnut, red and blue.
Price, per set of 3 pieces....................$1.30

## Bowl and Pitcher.

No. 16497. Decorated Bowl and Pitcher. Beautiful and artistic designs, elegant workmanship, high, rich colors. Price, per set....................84c
No. 16498. Bowl and Pitcher. Very heavy tin, painted in assorted colors; pretty set. 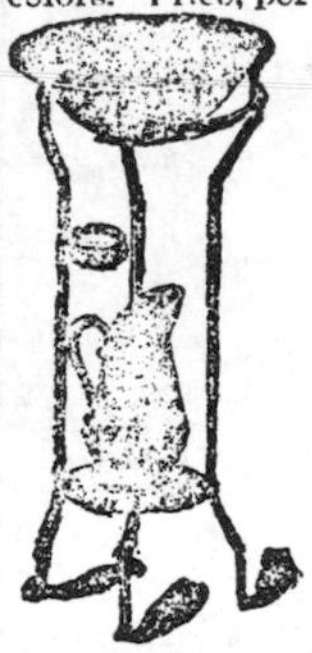
Price, per set....................50c

## Toilet Stand.

No. 16499. Toilet Stand, japanned. 30½ inches high, with japanned tin wash bowl and pitcher and soap cup; assorted colors; weight, 2¾ lbs.
Each, complete....................$1.40

## Bath Tubs.

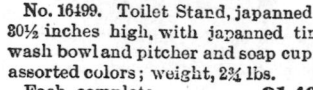

No. 16504. Plunge Baths; same shape as cut, made of heavy tin, with wooden bottoms and handles at each end; japanned, blue inside, drab outside, trimmed in black, blue and gilt stripes; weight, 50 lbs. Prices include crating. Each, 4 feet, $3.73; 6 feet....................$5.00

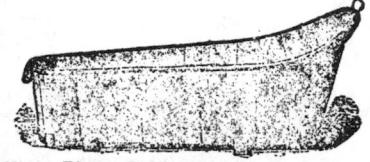

No. 16505. Infants' Bath Tub; weight, 10 to 25 lbs.; japanned tin.

| Size, 27 inches | $0.80 |
| 30 inches...... | .90 |
| 33 inches...... | 1.10 |
| 36 inches...... | 1.30 |

## Hip Baths.

No. 16506. Japanned Hip Baths. Diameter, 22½ inches.
Each....................$3.25
Diameter, 27 inches.
Each....................$4.00

## Japanned Foot Tubs.

No. 16508.

| Size. | Weight. | Price, each. |
|---|---|---|
| 17x13½x7½ | 2 lbs. | $0.40 |
| 18½x14½x8¼ | 2 lbs. | .45 |

## Spittoons.

No. 16512. Spittoons, japanned, assorted colors.
Each....................16c
No. 16514. Gilt Decorated Cuspidor. Handsome gilt decoration.
Price, each....................16c

## Protection Cuspidors.

No. 16518. Handsomely ornamented and secured to a mat 12 inches in diameter; cannot be tipped over; can be detached from the mat for cleaning. Three colors, blue, green and red; japanned.
No. 1, each....................24c

## Nickel Plated Cuspidors.

No. 16519. Cuspidor, nickel plated, full size.
Each....................35c

## Crumb Pans and Brush.

No. 16524. Crumb Tray and Brush. Handsomely decorated; brush made of pure bristles.
Price, per set....................20c

No. 16525. Brass Crumb Tray and Brush. Each...65c

No. 16526. Polished brass, nickel plated. Each..75c

## Tea Tray.

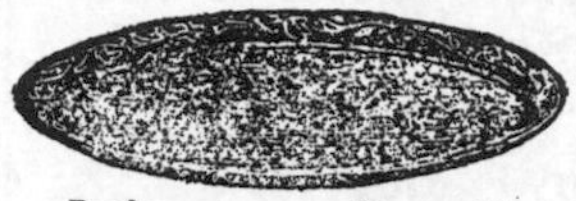

No. 16530. Tea Trays, oval, japanned.

| Inches, | 12 | 14 | 16 | 18 | 20 |
|---|---|---|---|---|---|
| Each, | $0.10 | .13 | .16 | .18 | .20 |
| Inches, | 22 | 24 | 26 | 28 | |
| Each, | .28 | .34 | .44 | .52 | |

## Child's Tray.

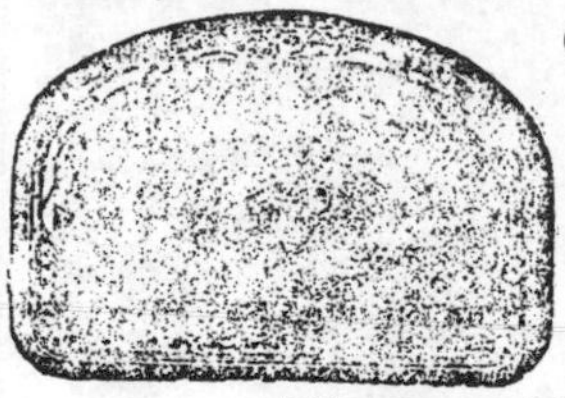

No. 16531. The Crown Child's Tray, silver finish, the best and cheapest child's tray made; complete with springs. Ready to adjust to table or high chair.
Price, each.....17c

## Pitcher Tray.

No. 16534. Round solid brass Tray, 13-inch fancy hammered brass tray, pretty pattern, beaded edges, highly polished.
Each............25c

## Dust Pans.

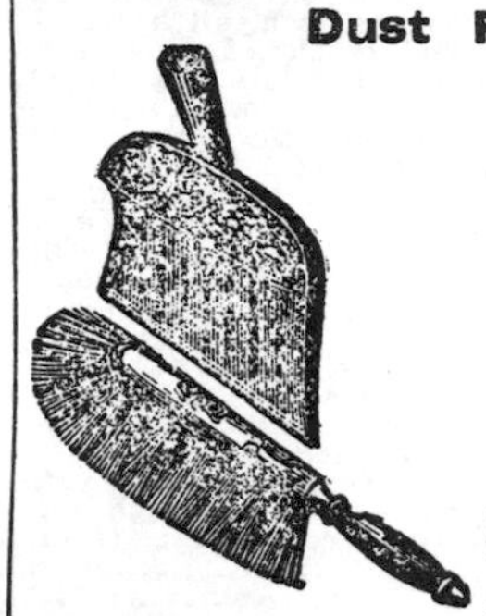

No. 16538. Whole sheet Dust Pan, Japanned; handle well braced, good, strong pan. Each......7c

No. 16540. Dust Pan, plain brown, covered. Each............10c
No. 16541. Dust Pan, fancy assorted colors, with brush. Each....................30c

## Canisters.

Tea and Coffee Canisters, japanned tin, with hinged covers. These canisters are preferable to the ordinary kind, as the covers can not get lost.
No. 16552. Tea Canisters.
No. 16553. Coffee Canisters.
To hold 2 lbs., each, 10c; doz........$1.08
To hold 4 lbs., each, 15c; doz....................$1.50

## Cream City Flour Bin and Sifter.

No. 16560. Made of I X tin, japanned and nicely ornamented. Packed one in a veneer package.

The sifter proper is protected from pressure by the flour in the bin by our new shield which enables the reels to work easily and smoothly, and obviates all grinding through of foreign substances. The flour is protected from coming in contact with the iron crank by an annular tin sleeve, and a tin skirt below the sifter prevents the flour from scattering all over the bottom of the bin, but instead directs it into the proper receptacle. The sifter rests on a strong ring which extends all around the inside of the bin, holding it securely in place, and still allowing it to be easily removed for cleaning.

| Pounds, | 25 | 50 | 100 |
|---|---|---|---|
| Inches, | 10¼x23 | 13x27¼ | 15½x33¼ |
| Price, each, | $1.10 | 1.45 | 2.00 |

## Pepper Boxes.

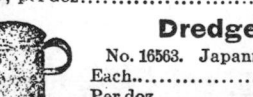

No. 16562. Japanned pepper boxes. Each, 4c; per doz....................42c

## Dredge Boxes.

No. 16563. Japanned, large size, 2½x3¼.
Each....................4c
Per doz....................44c

## Clothes Sprinkler.

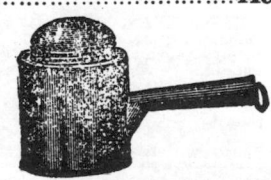

No. 16566. Clothes Sprinkler, with screw cover and handle. This is a new and very convenient article, used for sprinkling clothes before ironing.
Each............12c

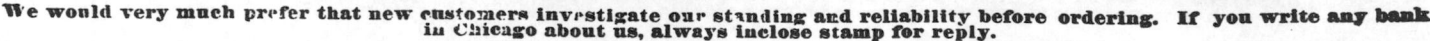

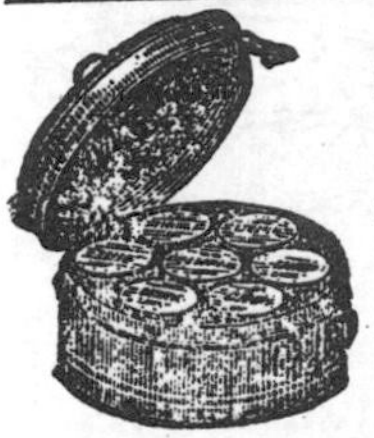

## Round Spice Boxes.

Japanned, containing five small boxes and grater.

No. 16568. Size, 6¼x3½ inches. Price, per set..................35c

## Bread Boxes.

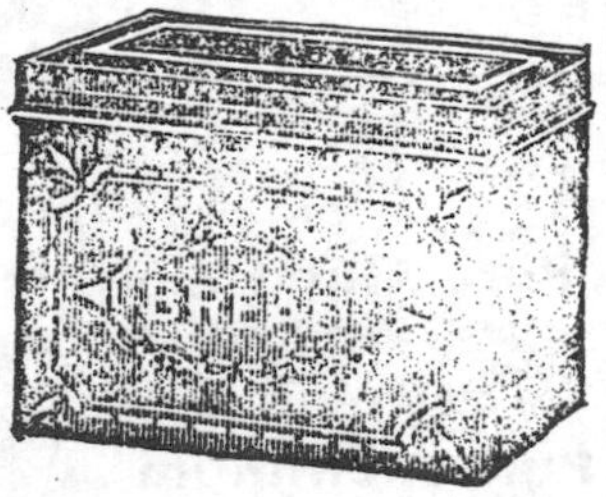

**Japanned.**

No. 16570. Medium; size, 15x11½x10¼; weight, 4¼ lbs. Each..........50c

No. 16571. Large; size, 19x13½x10½; weight, 4¾ lbs. Each..........70c

## Cash Boxes with Lock and Key.

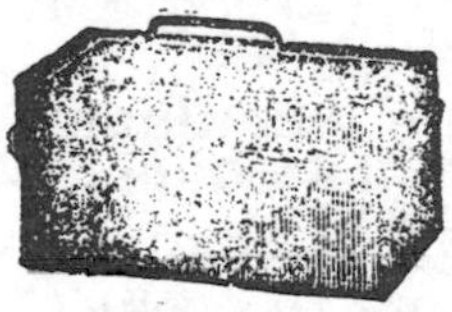

Weighs 1¼ lbs., 1½ lbs., 2 lbs.; japanned.

No. 16574. Size, 8½x5½x4. Each..................50c

No. 16575. Size. 10½x7x4½. Each..................60c

No. 16576. Size, 11⅛x8x5½. Each..................68c

## Deed Boxes.

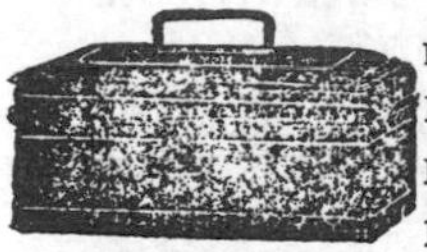

Weighs 1¼ to 2 lbs., japanned.

No. 16580. Size, 8½ inches. Each..................30c

No. 16581. Size, 10½ inches. Each..................40c

No. 16582. Size, 11 inches. Each..................45c

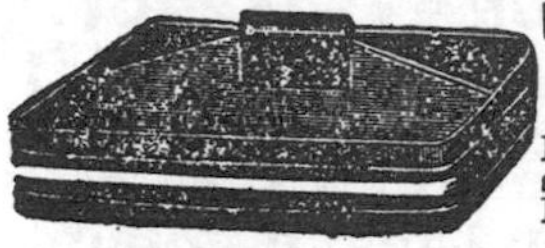

## Knife and Fork Boxes.

No. 16585. Knife and Fork Boxes, open top, size, 12x8. Each..................35c

## Water Coolers.

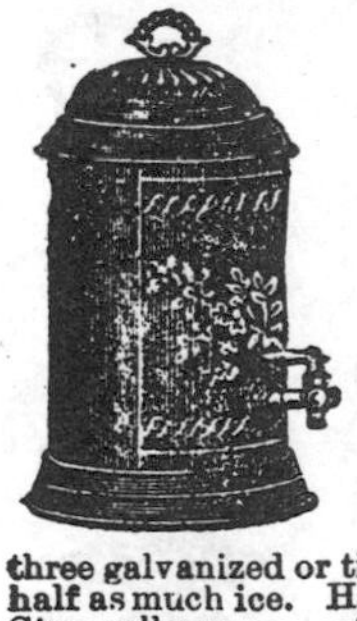

No. 16590. Japanned Water Coolers, wrought iron body and base, stamped tin breast, stamped tin plate cover, galvanized iron reservoir, plated faucet, charcoal filled, assorted colors, artistic decoration.

| Size, gallons, | 2 | 3 |
|---|---|---|
| Price, each, | $1.55 | 1.80 |
| Size, gallons, | 4 | 6 |
| Price, each, | $2.00 | 2.50 |

No. 16591. Enameled Reservoir Water Cooler, double walled. Inside lined with enamel or porcelain, nickel plated, self-closing or telegraph faucet, will outwear three galvanized or tin lined coolers. Does not require half as much ice. Handsomely decorated.

| Size, gallons, | 2 | 3 | 4 | 6 | 8 | 10 |
|---|---|---|---|---|---|---|
| Price, each, | $2.70 | 3.10 | 3.95 | 5.30 | 6.95 | 8.35 |

## Match Safes.

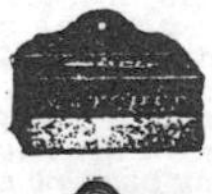

No. 16595. Square Match Safe, self-closing; size, 3⅜x2¼x1½ inches. Price, each, 4c; per doz..................40c

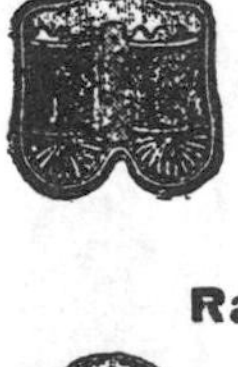

No. 16596. Twin Match Safe, with two receptacles for matches; size, 4½x5 inches. Price, each, 3c; per doz....30c

## Rattle and Whistle.

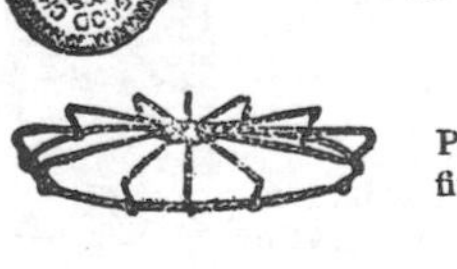

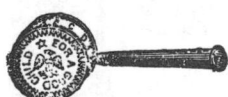

No. 16599. Rattle and Whistle, for the baby. Each, 3c; per doz....30c

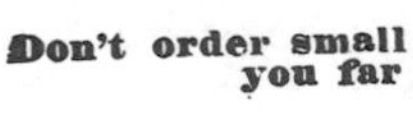

No. 16600. Tea or Coffee Pot Stand, made of bright finish wire. Each.........5c

## Wire Broilers.

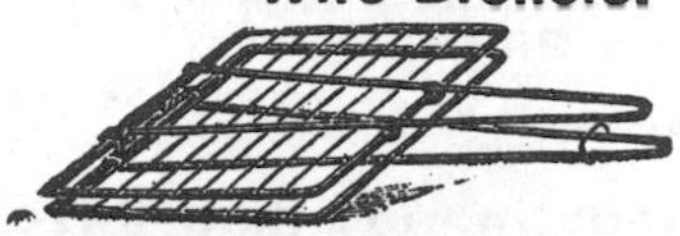

No. 16608. Heavy retinned Wire Broilers.

Size, 9x6 inches. Price, each..........................7c
Size, 9x7½ inches. Price, each..........................8c
Size, 9x9 inches. Price, each..........................9c
Size, 9x10½ inches. Price, each..........................10c
Size, 9x12 inches. Price, each..........................12c
Size, 9x13½ inches. Price, each..........................16c

## Wire Comb and Hair Brush Cases

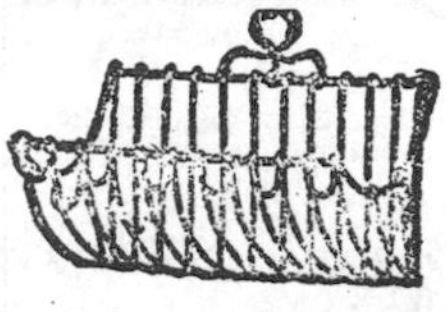

No. 16638. 6 inch, each, 10c; 9 inch..........16c

## Wire Sponge Basket.

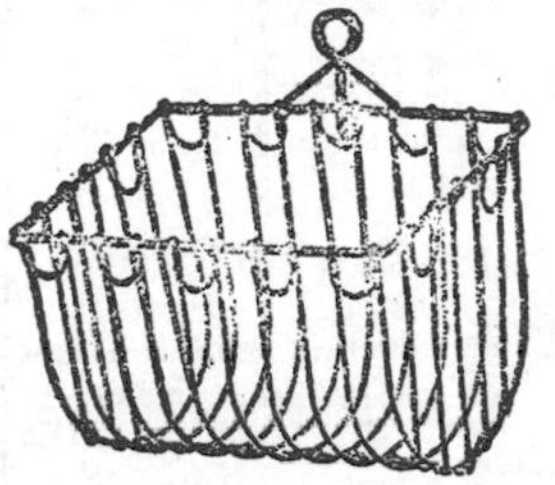

No. 16639.

| Size. | Each. |
|---|---|
| 5x3 | $0.15 |
| 7x4 | .18 |
| 8x5½ | .22 |
| 10x6½ | .26 |

## Wire Brush Broom Holders.

## Wire Soap Brackets.

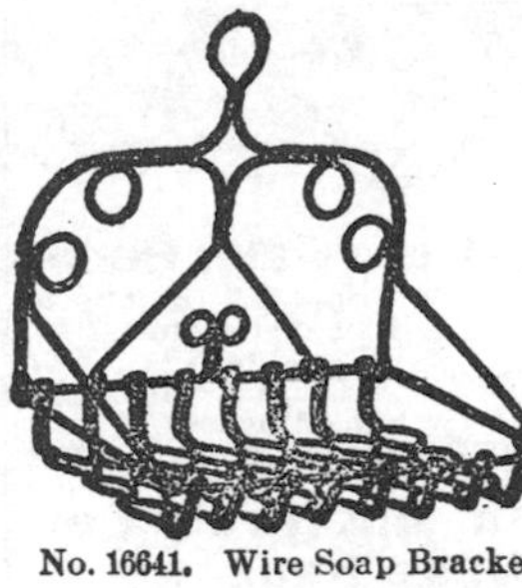

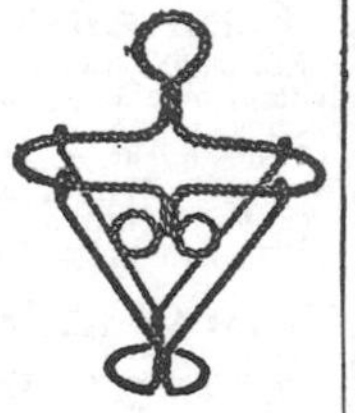

No. 16640. Adapted to all varieties of small brooms and brushes. Each..........12c

No. 16641. Wire Soap Bracket. Each .... ....14c

## Coat Hanger.

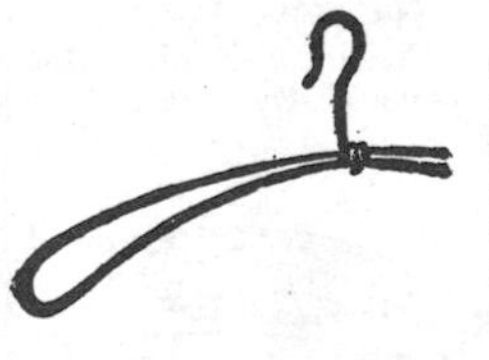

No. 16645. Wire Coat or Garment Hanger, 17 inches. Garments when hung on this device do not lose their shape as when hung on hook or nail. Price, each, tinned, 4c; per doz..................45c

## Corn Popper.

No. 16648. Corn Popper, tin top, 1 quart. Each...8c
No. 16649. Corn Popper, wire top; 2 quarts. Each.14c

## Oil Cans.

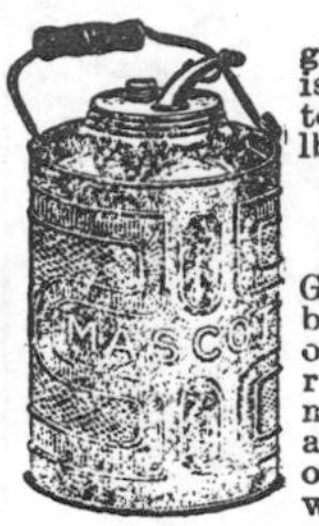

No. 16670. The body of this Can is glass, protected by a jacket of tin. It is well made and will not leak where top is attached. Weighs about 4¼ lbs. Price, each..................18c

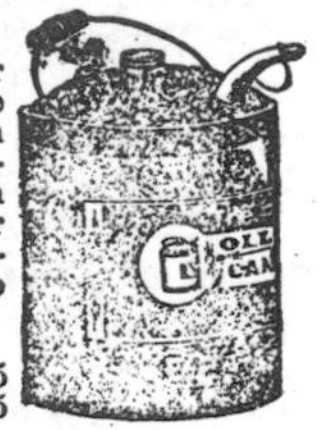

No. 16671. Oil or Gasoline Can. The body and bottom of this Can is corrugated, which makes it stiffer and stronger without adding to weight.

| Size, gal.......... | 1 | 2 | 3 | 5 |
|---|---|---|---|---|
| Price, each........ | $0.20 | .33 | .40 | .45 |

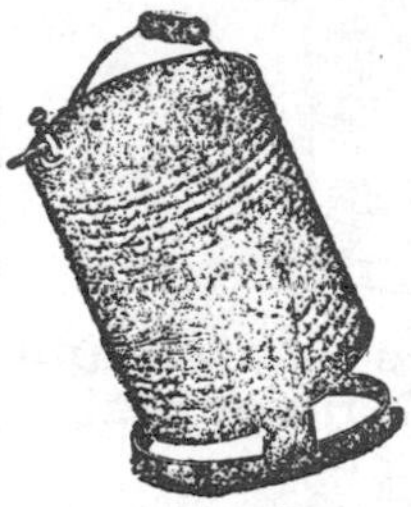

No. 16672. The Mazeppa Tilting Oil Can surpasses all others in appearance and strength. The body and bottom are corrugated, which is a great improvement. Made 5 gallon size only. Price, each..................80c

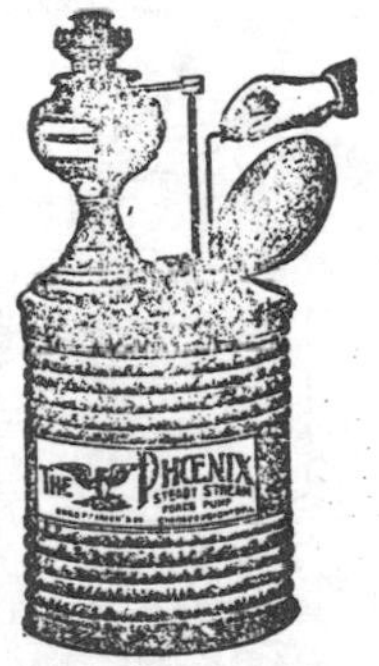

No. 16673. The Phoenix. A steady stream pump can, made of corrugated, galvanized iron in 5 gallons size only. Removable pump. Depressed safe to receive all drip and a strong hinged cover to keep out dust and protect parts; weight, about 7 lbs. Price, each..................80c

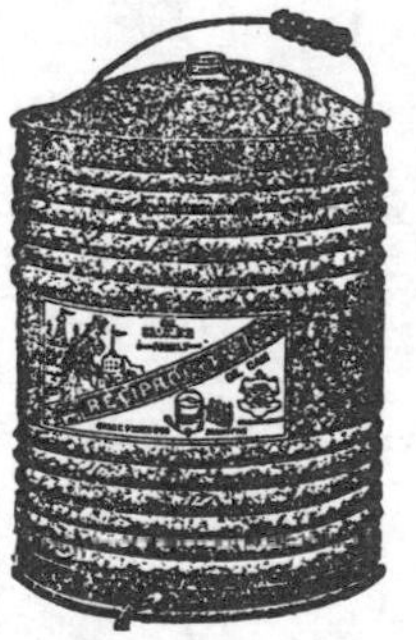

No. 16675. The Reciprocity Faucet Oil Can. The body and bottom of the can are made of corrugated galvanized iron, having a bright nickel finish angle faucet. Warranted not to leak. Made in two sizes.

| Size, gallons, | 5 | 10 |
|---|---|---|
| Price, | $0.50 | 1.00 |

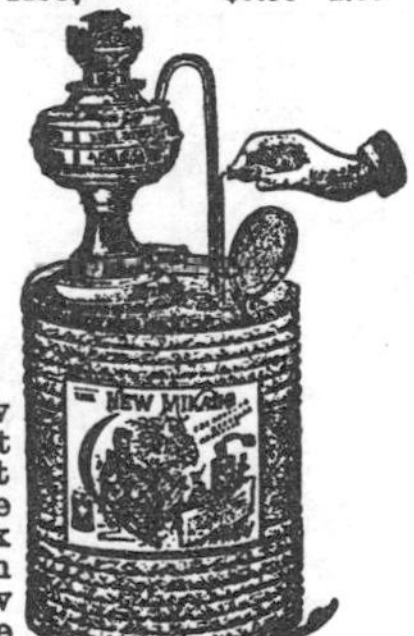

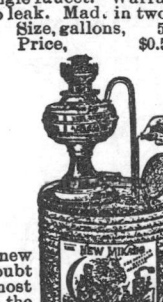

No. 16676. The improved new Mikado Oil Can is without doubt the best, strongest and most durable pump oil can in the market. We have the Phoenix can for those who want medium price goods. We offer the new Mikado to those who want the best possible goods. We sell both at the lowest possible price. Has removable syphon pump. Depressed safe to receive all drip. Milled hinged covers to keep out dust and protect parts. Corrugated body and bottom. Made of galvanized iron.

| Size, gallons, | 5 | 10 |
|---|---|---|
| Price, each, | $1.00 | 1.45 |

## PURE ALUMINUM WARE.

**Beautiful as Silver—Pure as Gold.**

Aluminum being now nearly as cheap as copper, no one who has consideration for purity, cleanliness, durability, and the other peculiar quality of aluminum ware, should use any thing else. There are several reasons why this metal is so well fitted for kitchen utensils, among which are its lightness, its absolute purity (it is entirely free from all poisonous elements, no verdigris, or salts of tin), its remarkable heat-conducting and retaining properties. The fact that it will not rust, and that it will not corrode under the conditions usually met with in cooking; that there is no enamel to flake off, and that vinegar and fruit acids have no effect upon it, and last but not least, its beauty and its durability (being pure solid metal all the way through, it is practically everlasting), render it most desirable.

As we have made special arrangements with one of the largest aluminum ware producers to use their entire output, we are enabled to give you prices never before heard of for pure aluminum ware. Compare our prices with other concerns and be convinced.

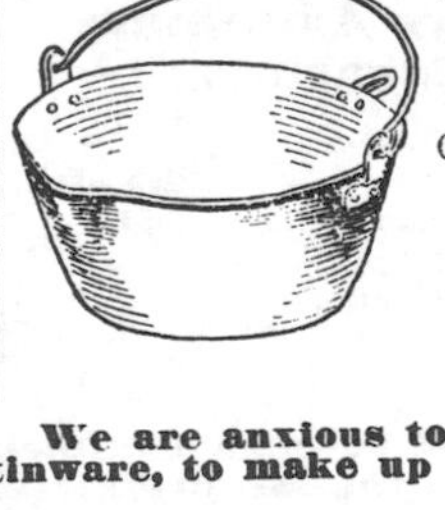

### Preserving Kettles.

No. 19000.

| Quarts. | Size across top. Inches. | Price, each. |
|---|---|---|
| 3 | 8¾ | $0.52 |
| 4 | 9¼ | .60 |
| 5 | 9⅞ | .71 |
| 6 | 10½ | .80 |
| 8 | 11⅞ | .96 |
| 10 | 12 | 1.05 |

### Sauce Pans.

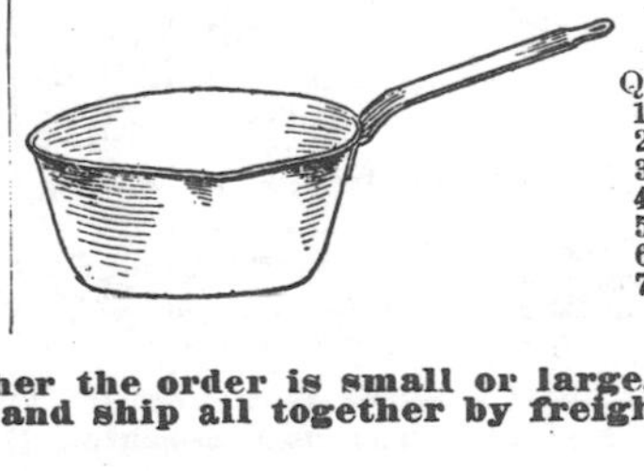

No. 19001.

| Qts. | Size across top. In. | Price, each. |
|---|---|---|
| 1 | 6⅛ | $0.30 |
| 2 | 7¼ | .41 |
| 3 | 8¾ | .54 |
| 4 | 9¼ | .63 |
| 5 | 9⅞ | .75 |
| 6 | 10½ | .84 |
| 7½ | 11⅞ | 1.02 |

**Don't order small items alone by express. We are anxious to serve you well whether the order is small or large, but it pays you far better, when you want tinware, to make up an order of groceries and ship all together by freight.**

## PURE ALUMINUM WARE—Continued.

### Pure Aluminum Bellied Sauce Pans.

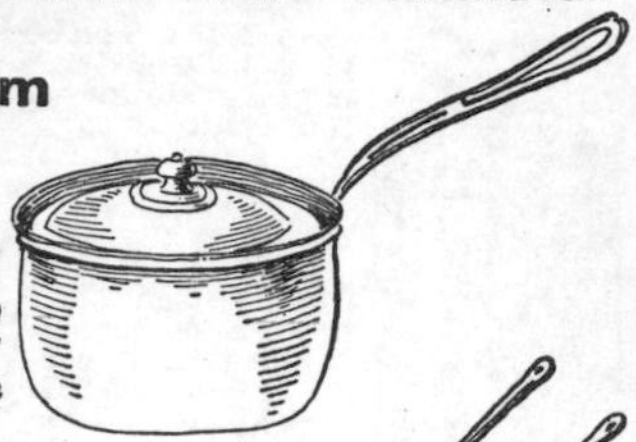

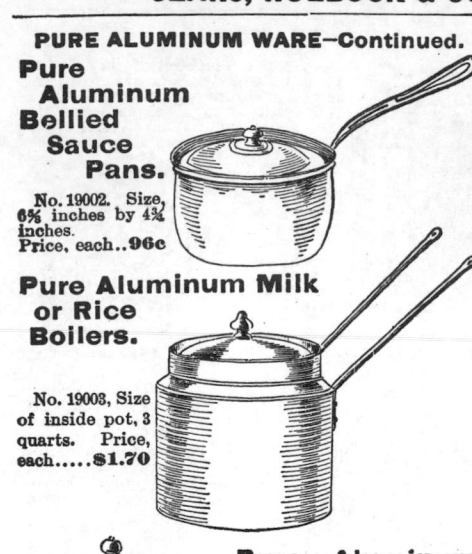

No. 19002. Size, 6¾ inches by 4¾ inches.
Price, each..**96c**

### Pure Aluminum Milk or Rice Boilers.

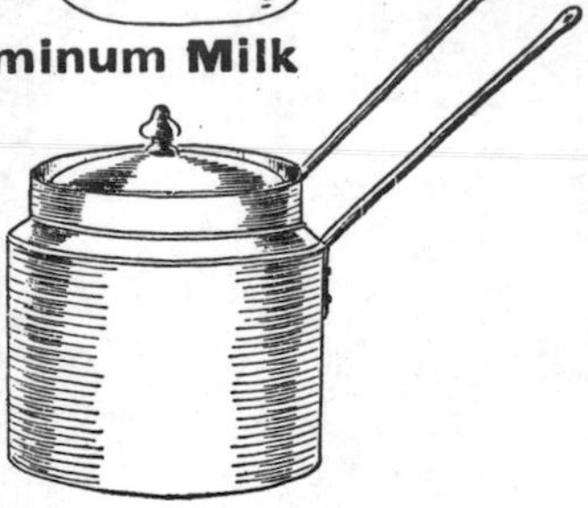

No. 19003, Size of inside pot, 3 quarts. Price, each.....**$1.70**

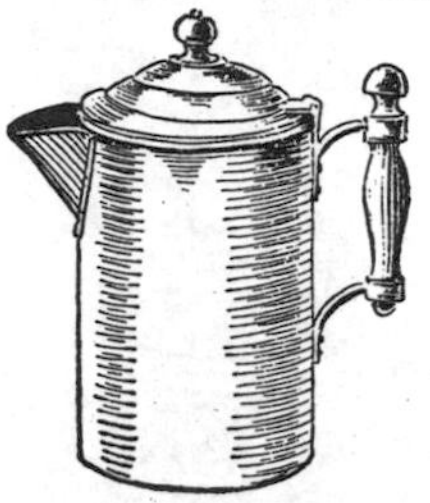

### Pure Aluminum Coffee Pots.

No. 19012.

| Size, pints, | 4 | 5 | 6 | 8 |
|---|---|---|---|---|
| Price, each, | $1.50 | 1.60 | 1.75 | 2.05 |

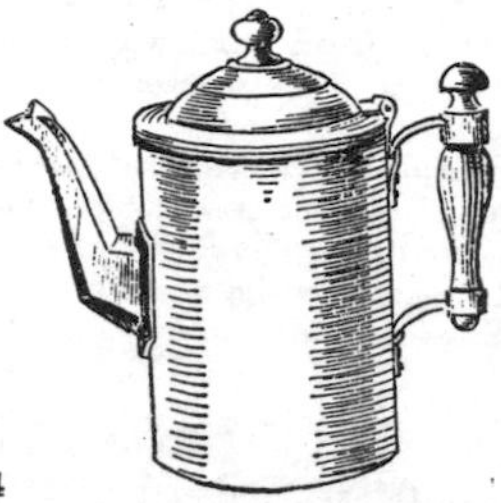

### Pure Aluminum Tea Pots.

No. 19013.

| Size, pints, | 4 | 5 | 6 |
|---|---|---|---|
| Price, each, | $1.69 | 1.75 | 1.94 |

**Special Notice.** We will furnish an improved pattern of above aluminum tea and coffee pots which are tapering, and have a bead around the bottom adding much to their appearance and are very much handsomer than cut.

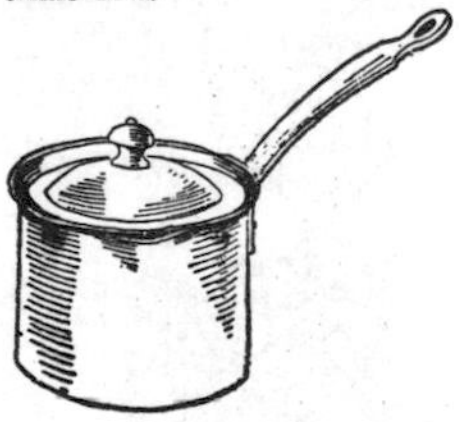

### Pure Aluminum Tea Steepers.

No. 19016. Size, 4¼x4 inches. Price, each..**40c.**

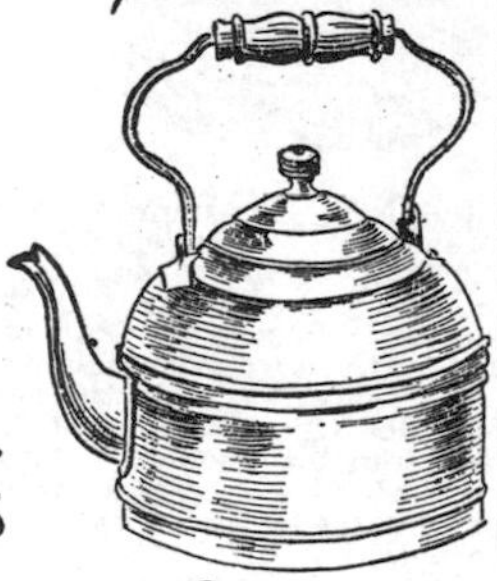

### Pure Aluminum Tea Kettles.

No. 19017. Pit bottom.
No. 19018. Flat bottom.
Size, No. 8. Price, each...............**$2.80**

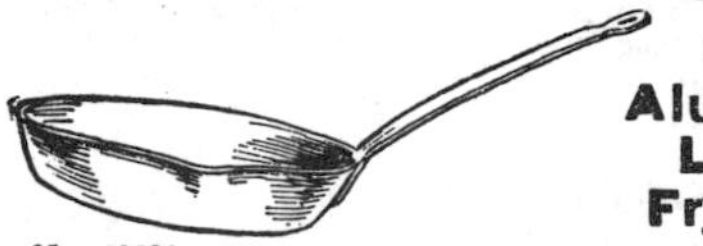

### Pure Aluminum Lipped Fry Pans.

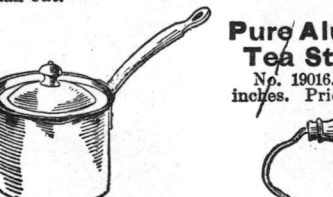

No. 19020.

| Size, inches.............. | 8½ | 9¼ | 10 | 10⅞ |
|---|---|---|---|---|
| Price, each............... | $0.51 | .60 | .84 | .96 |

### Pure Aluminum Dripping Pans.

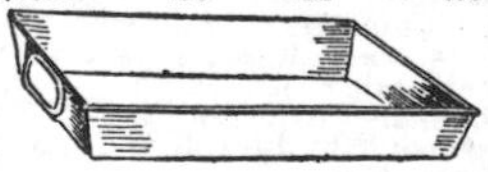

No. 19022.

| Size, inches............... | 8x10 | 9x14 | 10x15 | 12x17 |
|---|---|---|---|---|
| Price, each............... | $0.49 | .69 | .72 | .96 |

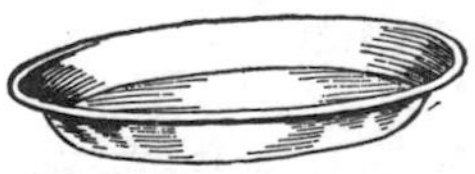

### Pure Aluminum Deep Pie Plates.

No. 19024. Size, 10 inches. Price, each, **21c**; per doz. ................**$2.35**

### Pure Aluminum Jelly Cake Pans.

No. 19025. Size, 9 inches; ¾ inch deep. Price, each, **21c**; per doz.....**$2.35**

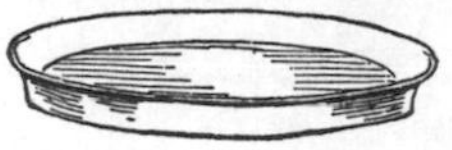

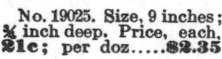

### Pure Aluminum Straight Pie Plates.

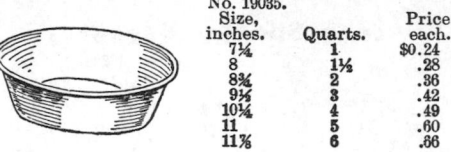

| 1 inch deep. | | Price, each. | Per doz. |
|---|---|---|---|
| No. 19026. | Size....... 9 inch. | $0.20 | 2.30 |
| No. 19027. | Size.......10 inch. | .26 | 3.15 |

### Pure Aluminum Mountain Cake Pans.

| ¼ inch deep. | | Price, each. | Per doz. |
|---|---|---|---|
| No. 19028. | Size........ 9 inch. | $0.20 | 2.30 |
| No. 19029. | Size.........10 inch. | .26 | 3.15 |

### Pure Aluminum Handy Dippers.

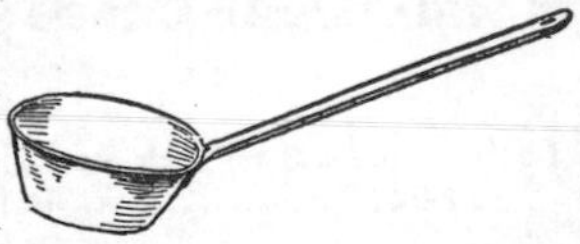

Flat Aluminum Handles.
No. 19030.
Size, 4¾x2¼ inch.
Price, each......**20c**

### Pure Aluminum Pudding Pans.

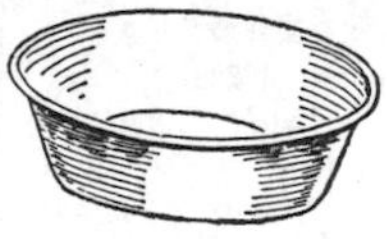

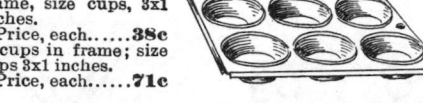

No. 19035.

| Size, inches. | Quarts. | Price, each. |
|---|---|---|
| 7¼ | 1 | $0.24 |
| 8 | 1½ | .28 |
| 8¾ | 2 | .36 |
| 9½ | 3 | .42 |
| 10¼ | 4 | .49 |
| 11 | 5 | .60 |
| 11⅞ | 6 | .66 |

### Pure Aluminum Bread Pans.

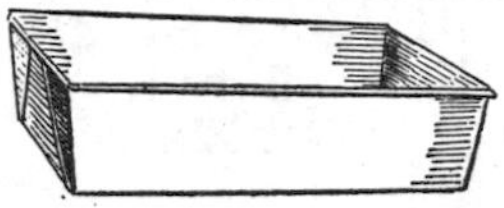

No. 19038. Size 5½x9½x2¾ inches.
Price, each.......**37c**

### Pure Aluminum Muffin Pans.

No. 19040. 6 cups in frame, size cups, 3x1 inches.
Price, each......**38c**
12 cups in frame; size cups 3x1 inches.
Price, each......**71c**

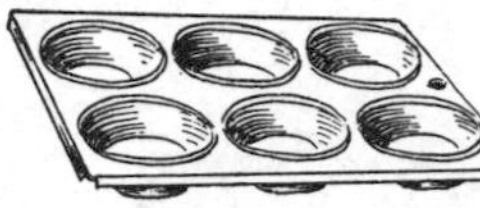

### Pure Aluminum Corn Cake Pans.

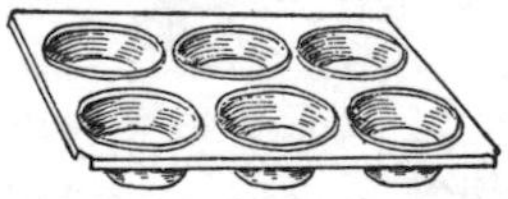

No. 19041. 6 cups in frame; size cups, 3 in.
Price, each......**42c**
12 cups in frame; size cups, 3 inches.
Price, each......**78c**

### Pure Aluminum Improved Perfection Cake Pans.

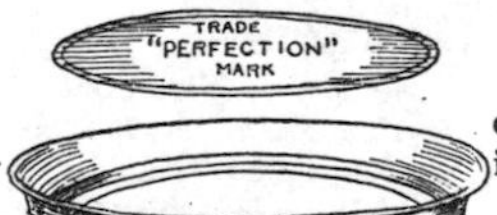

TRADE "PERFECTION" MARK


No. 19048. For layer cakes and pies. Size, 9¼x1 inch. Price, each....**39c**

No. 19049. For deep cakes. Size, 10¼x2⅞ in.
Price, each.........**65c**

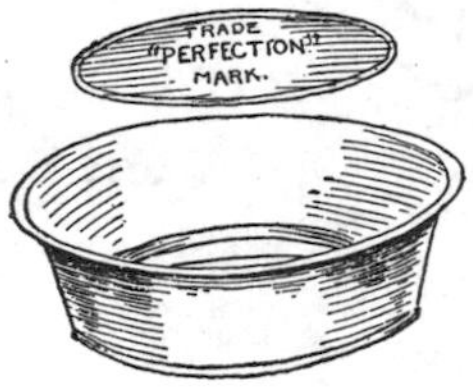

TRADE "PERFECTION" MARK.


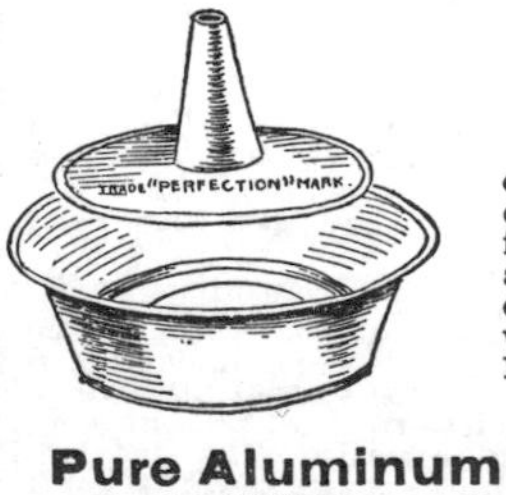

TRADE "PERFECTION" MARK


No. 19050. For deep cakes. No breaking of cakes when removing from pans. The removable bottom supports the cake, and is lifted out with the cake on it. Size, 10¼x2⅞ inches.
Price, each.........**69c**

### Pure Aluminum Wash Bowls.

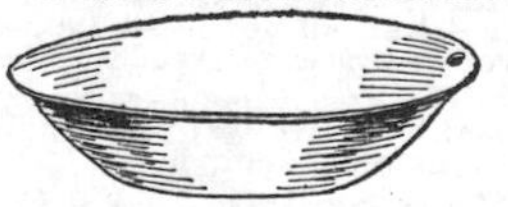

No. 19054.

| Size. | Price, each. |
|---|---|
| 10½ in. | $0.49 |
| 11⅜ in. | .51 |
| 12⅛ in. | .60 |
| 12⅞ in. | .69 |

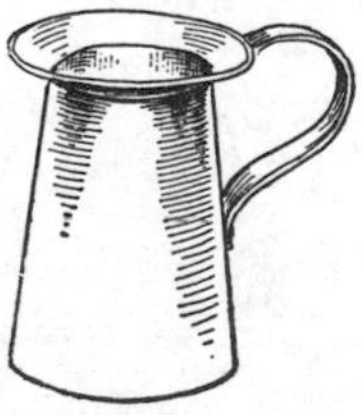

### Pure Aluminum Measures.

No. 19056.

| Size. | Price, each. |
|---|---|
| ½ pt. | $0.30 |
| 1 pt. | .39 |
| 1 qt. | .65 |
| 2 qt. | .90 |
| 4 qt. | 1.40 |

### Pure Aluminum Funnels.

No. 19057.

| Size. | Price, each. |
|---|---|
| 5¼x4⅜ in. | $0.29 |

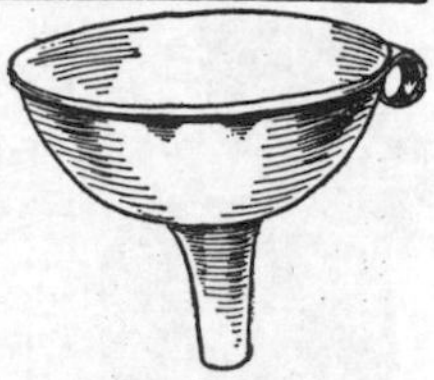

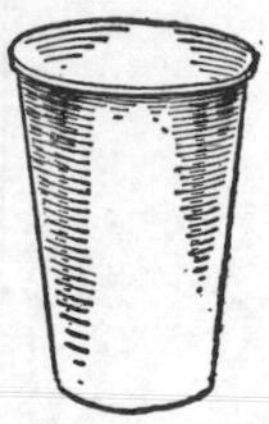

### Pure Aluminum Liquid Mixers or Lemonade Shakers.

No. 19065.

| Sizes. | Price, each. |
|---|---|
| 3¼ in. | $0.20 |
| 5¼ in. | .27 |
| 6 in. | .37 |

### Pure Aluminum Picnic Cups.

No. 19068. Round handles.

| Size. | Price, each. |
|---|---|
| 3⅜x3¼ in. | $0.36 |

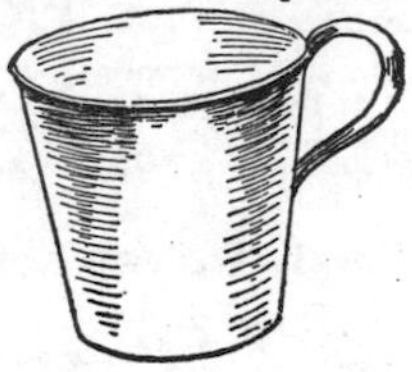

### Pure Aluminum Tumblers.

No. 19069. Same as Picnic Cups. Without handles.

| Size. | Price each. |
|---|---|
| 3⅜x3¼ in. | $0.19 |

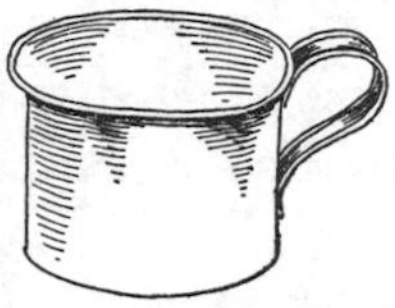

### Pure Aluminum Buffalo Cups.

No. 19072.

| Size. | Price, each. |
|---|---|
| 4 x2¾ | $0.18 |
| 4⅞x3½ | .36 |

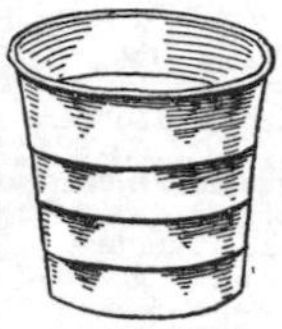

### Pure Aluminum Tourist Cups.

No. 19075. Telescope. These cups are made in sections which close into each other, making a compact package.

| Size. | Price, each. |
|---|---|
| 3x2¾ in. | $0.30 |

## LANTERNS FOR EVERYBOBY.

In selecting a lantern you should aim to secure the safest and best. Remember there are some makes of cheap lanterns that cause much annoyance as well as damage. The difference in price between our lanterns—the very best—and inferior makes is but a few cents.

### Tubular or Barn Lantern to Burn Kerosene.

No. 19280. Side Lift or Victor Tubular Lantern, for kerosene; No. 1 burner, ⅝-inch wick, No. 0 globe.

This is the most popular lantern on the market today.

The crank at the side raises and lowers the globe and locks the burner in place when down.

A late improvement on this lantern consists of a bend on the guard wire over which the crank moves, thus perfectly locking the globe frame and burner down. Price, each ...............................**40c**

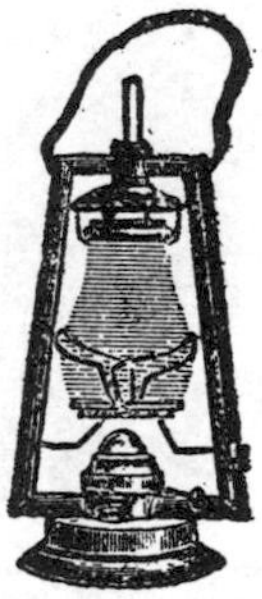

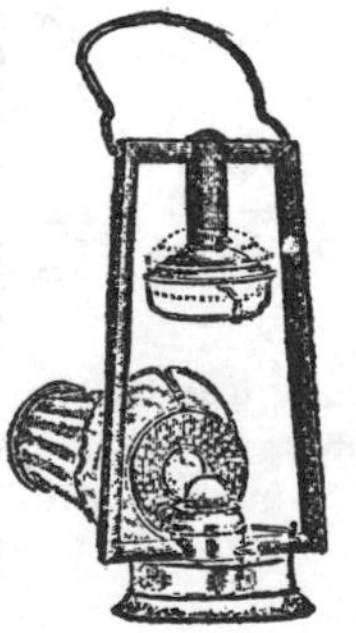

No. 19281. O. K. Tubular Lantern, for kerosene; No. 1 burner, ⅝-inch wick, No. 0 globe.

We consider this the best low-priced lantern on the market, and advise those in want of a cheap, reliable lantern to give it a trial.

The globe and frame are easily moved out of the way for lighting and trimming, tipping back on a hinge.

This is far ahead of any other hinge lantern on the market for ease of operation and safety, Price, each.................**40c**

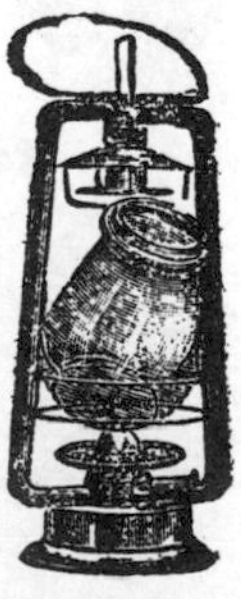

No. 19282. Square Lift, or Star Tubular Lantern, for kerosene; No. 1 burner, ⅝-inch wick, No. 0 globe.

This is the old reliable Square Lift Lantern.

We have sold it for years, and it gives universal satisfaction.

One of our most popular lanterns.

The globe is raised by the thumb piece on top. Price, each...................**40c**

**We shall esteem it a favor if customers will notify us promptly of any errors in their orders. We do not claim to be infallible, and an error may occasionally occur. When such is the case we are only too anxious to adjust it.**

## Brass Tubular Lantern.

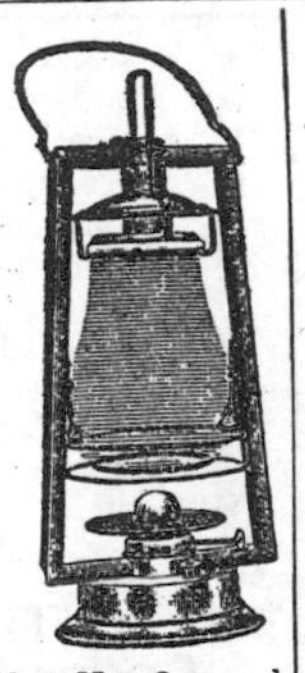

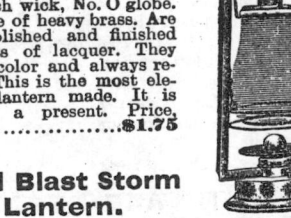

No. 19286. Star Brass No. O square lift tubular lantern, for kerosene. No. 1 burner, ⅝-inch wick, No. O globe. They are made of heavy brass. Are handsomely polished and finished with two coats of lacquer. They will hold their color and always remain bright. This is the most elegant tubular lantern made. It is suitable for a present. Price, each ........................ **$1.75**

## Cold Blast Storm Lantern.

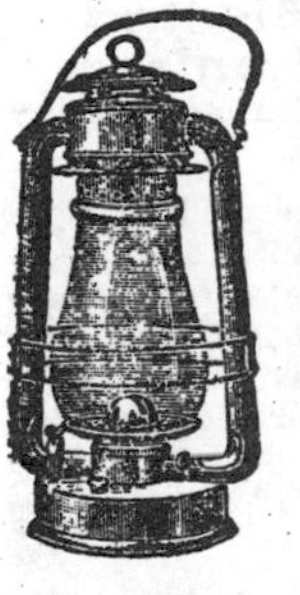

No. 19288. Cold Blast No. 2 round tube, bottom lift, tin tubular lantern; No. 2 burner, 1-inch wick No. O globe. Globe removable without taking off the guard. This lantern being made on the same principle as a street lamp, with **wind break**, makes it a superior lantern in its burning qualities—very desirable for use in places where there are strong drafts of wind. It is especially adapted for use in mills and other places where is considerable dust, as the burner will not clog up. The tubes are made from one piece, without elbows or joints. Gives a fine light. We have noticed when one of these lanterns goes to a town we get more orders from the same locality.
Price, each ........................ **85c**

## Lantern Holders.

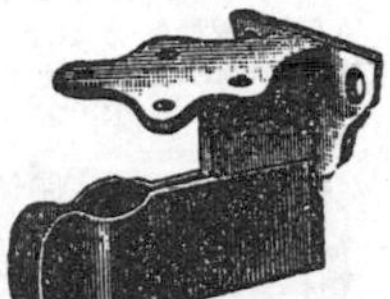

No. 19293. Warner Tubular Lantern Holder. For holding a tubular lantern under the body of a wagon for night driving. Price, each..... **20c**

## Bull's-Eye Lens.

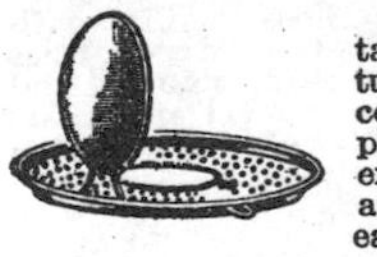

No. 19294. Bull's-eye Lens. Attached to perforated plate; for all tubular lanterns taking No. O (the common size) globe. Takes the place of bull's-eye globes at little expense; no danger of breakage and better in every way. Price, each ........................ **15c**

## Tubular and Railroad Lantern Burners.

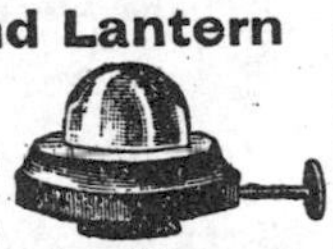

No. 19295. Tubular Lantern Burners will fit all regular tubular lanterns taking ⅝-inch wick.
Each ........................ **8c**

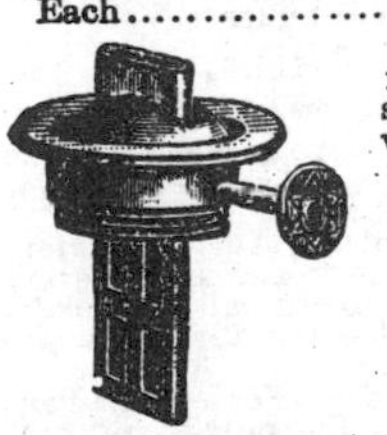

No. 19296. Rachet Burner for railroad lanterns, will burn kerosene or sperm oil, takes ⅝-inch wick.
Each ........................ **10c**

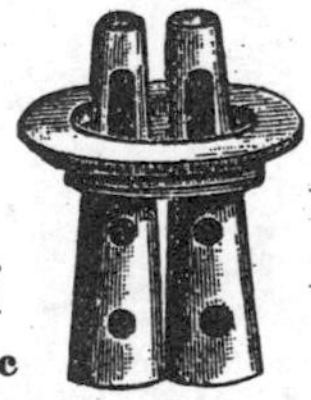

No. 19297. Two-Tube Burner for railroad lantern, will burn lard oil.
Each ........................ **6c**

## LAMP BURNERS.

### Sun Burners (Not Hinged.)

Sun Burners (not hinged) for sun chimneys.
This burner takes an ordinary straight bottom chimney and cannot be used with any other.

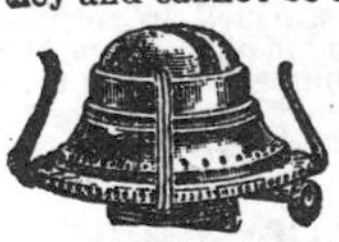

No. 19298. No. 0, brass, weight, 1 oz.
Each, **5c**; per doz ........ **50c**
No. 19299. No. 1 brass, weight, 1½ oz.
Each, **5c**; per doz ........ **55c**
No. 19300. No. 2 brass, weight, 1½ oz.
Each, **8c**; per doz ........................ **87c**

## Sun Hinge Burners.

This burner takes a Sun hinge chimney, which has flange on the bottom and cannot be used with any other.
No. 19310. No. 1 Brass Sun Hinge Burners for Sun-hinge chimneys. Weight, 2 oz.
Each, **7c**; per doz ........................ **75c**
No. 19311. No. 2 Brass Sun Hinge Burners. Weight, 2½ oz.
Each, **12c**; per doz ........................ **$1.30**

## Jumbo Burners.

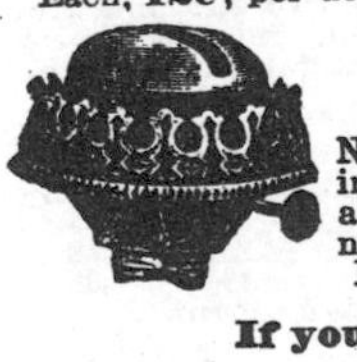

No. 19316. Jumbo Burner, fits No. 2 or No. 3 lamp collar; takes 1½-inch wick, gives a powerful light and takes an ordinary No. 2 chimney.
Each. **10c**; per doz ........ **$1.10**

## Duplex Burner.

This burner takes a special chimney, and cannot be used with any other.

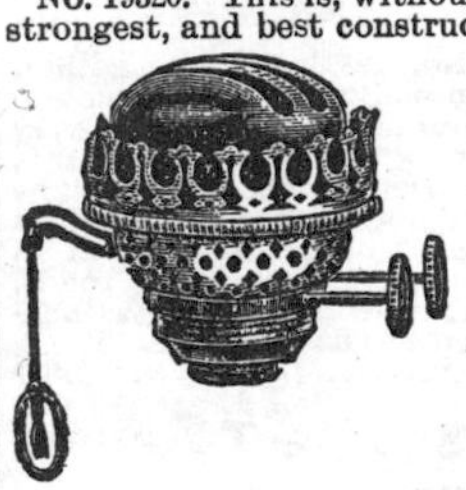

No. 19320. This is, without doubt, the most complete, strongest, and best constructed burner now in use. It takes 2 wicks; has a patent extinguisher to put out the light; emits a large, brilliant, and steady light, and is suitable for fine parlor, vase, or library lamps.
Price, with extinguisher, reducing collar, and ring for globe. Each...... **80c**
No. 19321. Extra chimney for No. 19320. Duplex Burner; weight, 12 oz.
Each, **8c**; per doz .... **87c**

## La Bastie Lamp Chimneys.

La Bastie Chimneys, not hinged, plain tops, patented process, very tough, can be thrown across a room without breaking. We will sell any quantity of these chimneys.
No. 19322. No. 1 Sun La Bastie Chimneys. Each, **12c**; per doz ........................ **$1.30**
No. 19323. No. 2 Sun La Bastie Chimneys. Each, **15c**; per doz ........................ **$1.62**

## Lamp Wicks and Candle Wicking.

No. 19325. Candle Wicking. Per lb ........ **22c**
No. 19326. Lamp Wicks, No. 0, ⅝ inch. Per doz... **3c**
No. 19327. Lamp Wicks, No. 1, ⅝ inch. Per doz... **4c**
No. 19328. Lamp Wicks, No. 2, 1 inch. Per doz... **5c**
No. 19329. Lamp Wicks, No. 3, 1½ inch. Per doz... **8c**
No. 19330. Lamp Wicking, No. 0, ⅜ inch. Roll, 32 yds ........................ **27c**
No. 19331. Lamp Wicking, No. 1, ⅝ inch. Roll, 32 yds ........................ **35c**
No. 19332. Lamp Wicking, No. 2, 1 inch. Roll, 32 yds ........................ **60c**
No. 19333. Lamp Wicking, No. 3, 1½ inch. Roll, 32 yds ........................ **80c**

For Lamps see Index.

## Railroad Lanterns.

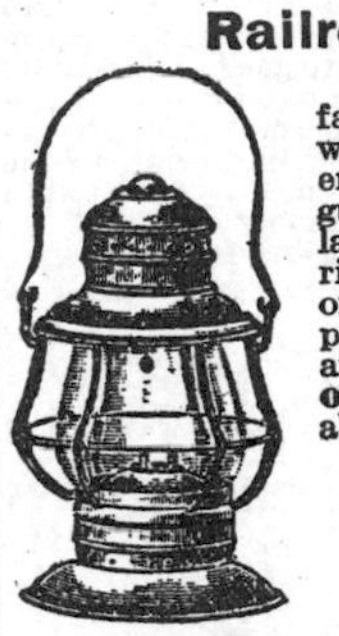

No. 19344. This style lantern is the favorite with railroad men everywhere and makes an excellent farmer's lantern. Bail is attached to the guard, frame is so arranged that when lantern is in use the bail stands upright. The bail can be thrown down on base of lantern if required. Oil pot fastens with catch, hinged top and removable globe. **Burns lard oil.** Made of heavy tin. Weighs about 2¼ lbs.
Price, each ........................ **50c**

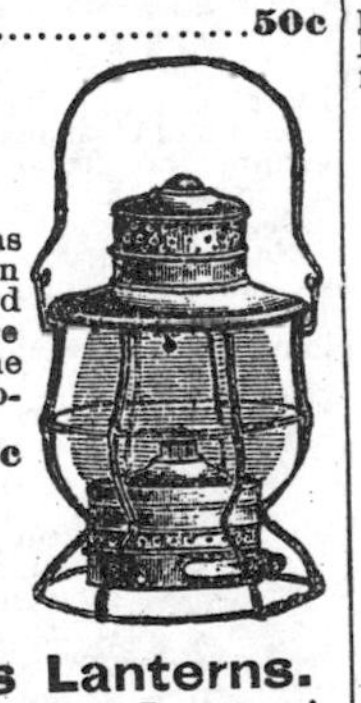

No. 19345. This lantern is same as above except it has a wire bottom which casts no shadow. The guard wires on both of these lanterns are securely locked together, making one of the strongest lanterns ever produced. Weighs about 2¼ lbs.
Price, each ........................ **49c**

## Conductor's Lanterns.

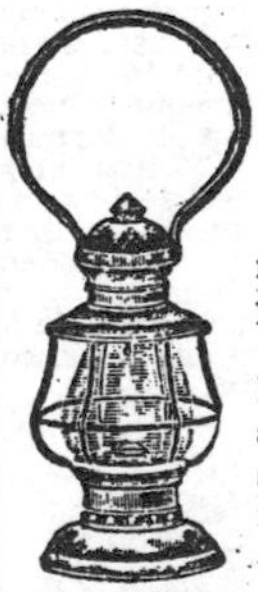

No. 19346. Conductor's Lantern is made of brass, finely finished and nickel plated. Has hinge top, removable globe, ⅝-inch ratchet burner. It is the favorite lantern with conductors everywhere, and any one wishing a handsome, strong and serviceable lantern will make no mistake in purchasing this one.
Price, with plain globe ........ **$3.35**

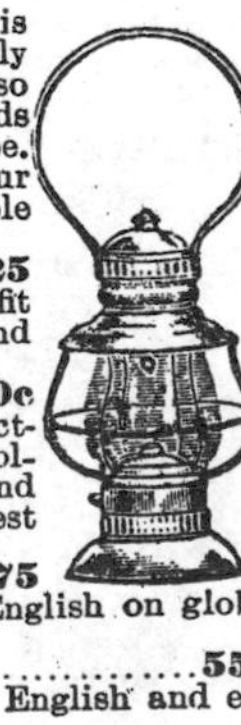

No. 19347. Conductor's Lantern, is standard size, made of brass heavily nickel plated. The bails are made so when lantern is put down the bail stands up. Has hinged top and removable globe. This lantern is not as finely finished as our No. 19346 but, it is a strong and durable lantern and is used extensively.
Price, with plain globe ........ **$2.25**
No. 19348. Plain crystal Globe to fit above conductor's lantern; they are hand made, from the best lead glass.
Each ........................ **50c**
No. 19349. Globes to fit above conductor's lanterns in any of the following colors: Half green and white, half blue and white or half red and white; the very best quality made.
Price, each ........................ **$1.75**
No. 19350. Engraving name in Old English on globe to fit above conductor's lantern.
Price, per name ........................ **55c**
No. 19351. Engraving name in Old English and encircling it in fancy engraved wreath.
Price, per name and wreath ........................ **80c**

## Car Inspector's Lantern.

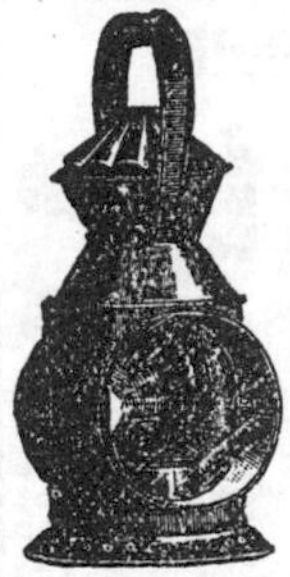

No. 19355. Car Inspector's Lantern. This lantern is used by car inspectors. It throws a powerful light to a distance. It has a 5-inch silvered glass reflector which will never tarnish, and a 5-inch beveled glass bull's-eye. Takes 1-inch wick, burns kerosene. It is an excellent lantern for rough usage. Price, each ........................ **$2.25**

## Fireman's Lantern.

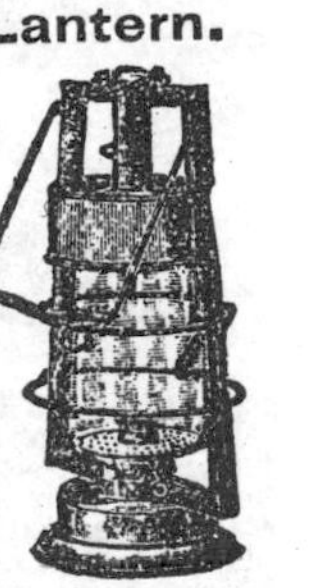

**Square Tube Brass Fire Department Lantern.**

No. 19356. Our Solid Brass Fire Department Lanterns are made of heavy material and are handsomely polished. While made especially for fire departments they are bought by those who desire a handsome, strong and durable lantern. Has No. 1 burner with ⅝ in. wick, takes the common tubular lantern globe, weighs nearly 3 lbs. Price, each, polished brass, **$2.35**; Price, each, nickel plated ........................ **$2.75**

## Dash Lanterns.

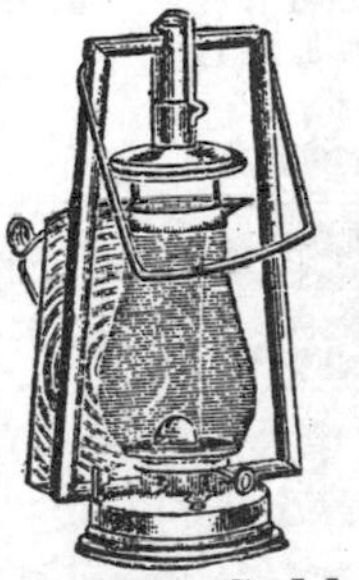

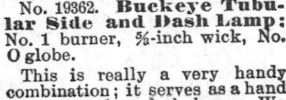

No. 19362. **Buckeye Tubular Side and Dash Lamp;** No. 1 burner, ⅝-inch wick, No. O globe.
This is really a very handy combination; it serves as a hand lantern and a dash lamp. We furnish it japanned blue. The lamp can be fastened under the body of the vehicle by means of a Warner holder. We furnish this lamp with our new bull's-eye lens—a bull's eye attached to the perforated plate. It is superior in every way to the bull's-eye globe.
Price each ........................ **65c**

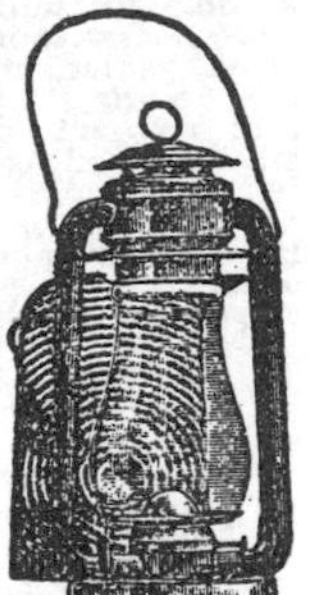

No. 19365. **Cold Blast Dash Lamp.** No. 2 burner, 1-inch wick, No. O globe. This lamp is intended for use when a very powerful light is required. It will not blow out in the strongest wind, and does not "flicker" as much as a lantern without windbreak. We furnish this lantern japanned blue—and with bull's-eye lens, which is attached to the perforated plate.
Price, each ........................ **$1.15**

## The Gem Driving Lamp.

**Improved.**

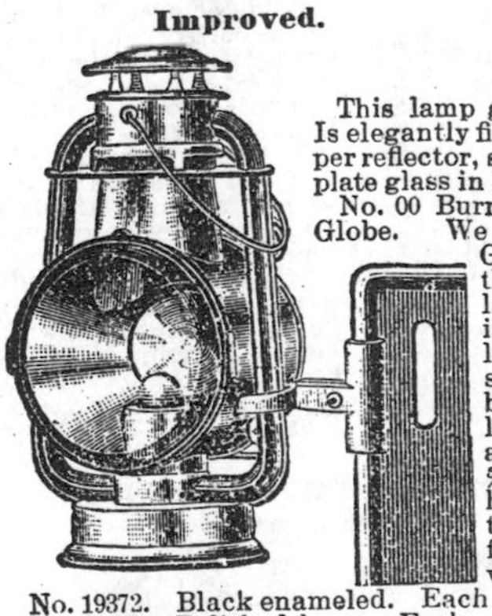

This lamp gives a fine light. Is elegantly finished. Has copper reflector, silver plated, bevel plate glass in door.
No. 00 Burner, ½ wick; Gem Globe. We claim for the Gem Driving Lamp that it is a perfect lantern in its burning qualities. The light produced is stronger and brighter than the light produced by any lantern using a ⅝-inch burner. We have this lamp in three finishes. We furnish dash clamp with each lantern.
No. 19372. Black enameled. Each ........ **$2.65**
No. 19373. Polished brass. Each ........ **$2.70**
No. 19374. Nickel plated. Each ........ **$3.20**
No. 19375. Extra globes for Gem Driving Lamps. Each, **6c**; per doz ........................ **65c**

## Tubular Side Reflector Lamps.

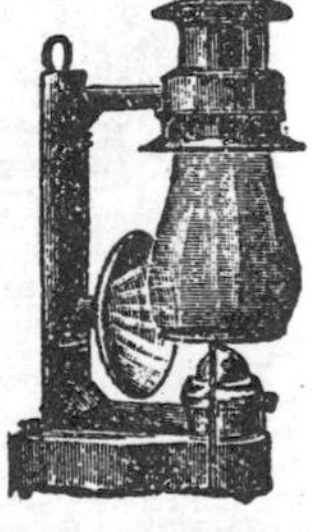

No. 19380. Tubular side lamp. These lamps operate on the same principle as our tubular lanterns and are not affected by wind, never heat, and are perfectly safe. Can be lit, filled and regulated without removing the globe. They are japanned blue and are unsurpassed for use in shops, halls and factories. No. 2 burner, 1-inch wick, No. O globe. Has a 6-inch silvered glass reflector; gives a large light; can be exposed to the wind and will not smoke or blow out. Can be filled, lighted and trimmed without removing the globe. Lamp is japanned blue. An excellent lamp for use in stores, warehouses, barns, engine rooms or any place which is exposed to drafts and where a brilliant light is required. Price, each.. **$1.45**

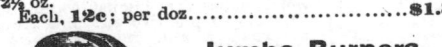

**If you have been well pleased with your dealings with us, we hope you will do us the favor of recommending us to your neighbors and urge them to send for our catalogue.**

## Tubular Driving Lamp.

**"Dietz."**

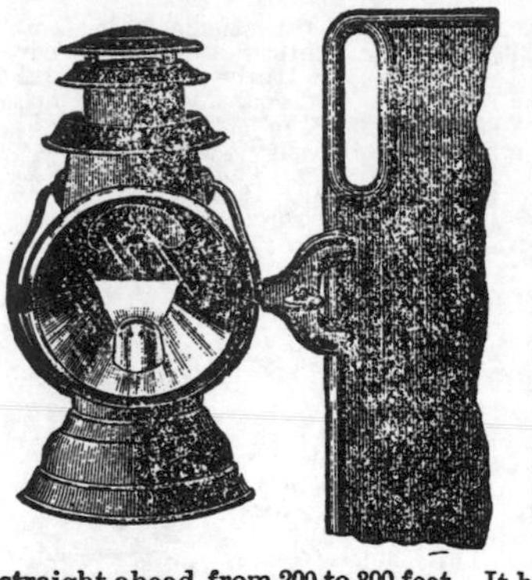

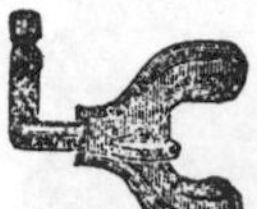

It is the only practicable and perfect Driving Lamp ever made. It will not blow out or jar out. It gives a clear, white light. It looks like a locomotive headlight. It throws all the light straight ahead from 200 to 300 feet. It burns kerosene.

By means of a spring on the back, the lamp can be instantly placed on the front of dash. By means of the holder, which we furnish with each lamp, it can be attached to either side of the dash. It can also be placed on the bracket of a carriage. 11 inches high; 6 inches in diameter; weight, 2½ lbs.

No. 19366. Price, each, japanned.............. **$2.40**
No. 19367. Price, each, nickel plated.......... **3.20**

## Tubular "Search Light."

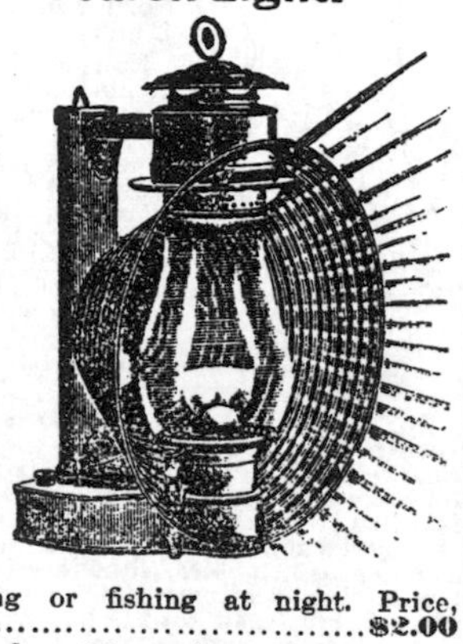

No. 19382. This light has No. 2 burner, 1-inch wick and takes No. 0 globes. It will not blow out in the strongest wind and is equally good for indoor use. It has a bright tin reflector 12 inches in diameter and 7 inches deep which spreads the light over a large surface. It is suitable for mills, ware houses, work shops, stables, summer resorts, or in fact any place where a good light is required. Makes an excellent "jack lantern" for hunting or fishing at night. Price, each.......................................... **$2.00**

## "Dietz Tubular Hunting Lamp."

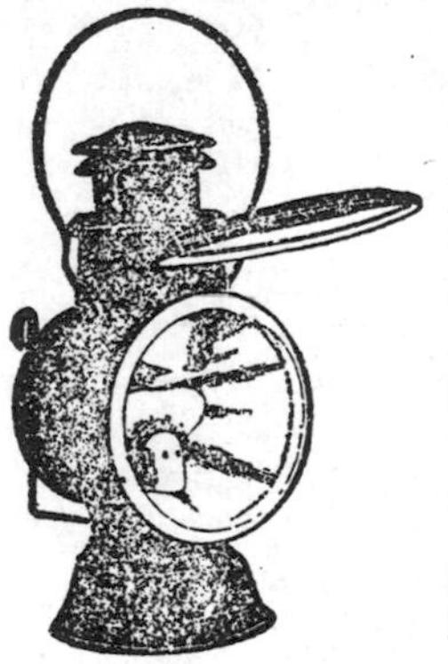

No. 19384. Looks like a locomotive headlight.

It will not blow or jar out.

The hood over the front works perfectly and without noise. When the hood is down no light escapes.

It will throw a powerful light 200 feet.

It burns kerosene oil, and will burn ten hours without refilling, 11 inches high; 6 inches in diameter; weight, 2¼ lbs.

It is compact and handsome. Has a bail and can be used as a hand and wall lantern in camp. Gives a brilliant light and is absolutely safe. Price.............. **$3.40**

## Dark or Police Lanterns.

Burns Sperm Oil.

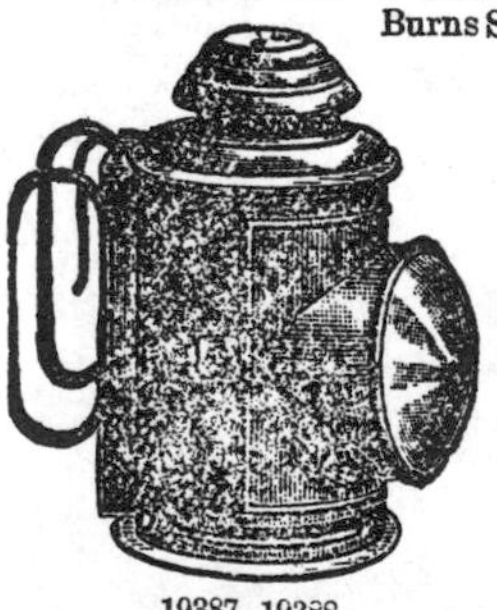

19387, 19388.

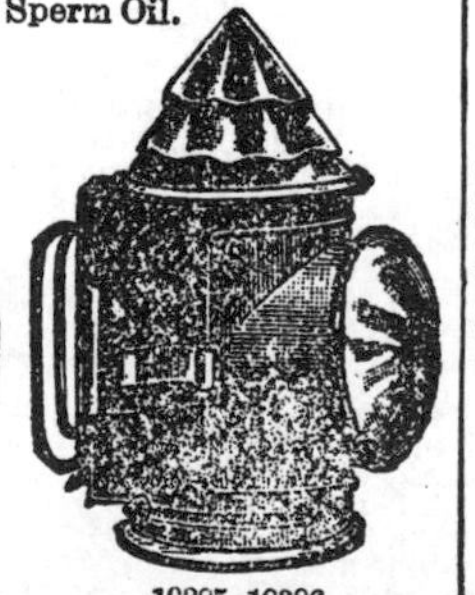

19385, 19386.

No. 19385. Police or Dark Lanterns, 2¼-inch bull's-eye; weight, 22 oz. Each.............................. **45c**

No. 19386. Police Lanterns, 3-inch bull's-eye; weight, 26 oz. Each.............................. **60c**

No. 19387. Special quality dark lanterns, made of heavy tin, nickel plated. These are considered the finest finish and strongest in the market; each lamp is furnished with the best quality fire polished lens. With 2¼-inch lens, each **90c**; with 3-inch lens, each... **$1.15**

No. 19388. Same as No. 19387, but is made of polished brass. With 2½-inch lens, each, **$1.90**; with 3-inch lens, each.............................. **$2.45**

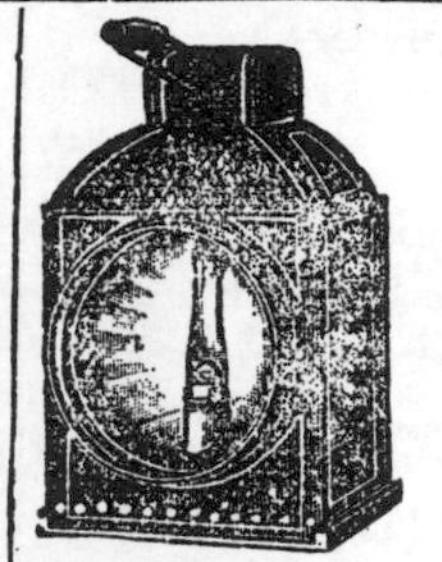

## Ten-inch Square Traction Engine Headlight.

No. 19390. This headlight especially adapted for traction engines, as it gives a very strong light and the draft is so arranged that the flame will not smoke or blow out in high winds, nor jar out in passing over rough roads. Packed complete with attachments to fit to engine. Price, each.............................. **$9.00**

## New Improved Square Tubular Lamp.

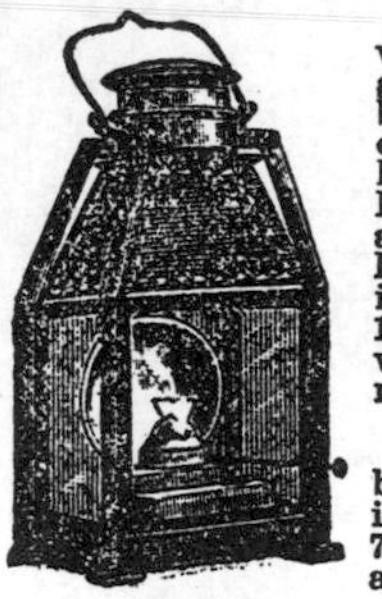

No. 19395. This lamp gives a very bright light, equal to the best gas jet, and will not smoke or blow out in strongest wind; especially adapted for use in warehouses, packing houses, saw mills, lumber yards, freight yards, or in any place where a good, strong light is required. Height, 22½ inches; width, 11¼ inches; depth, 10¼ inches; burner takes 1½-inch wick. Has an 8-inch silvered glass reflector. Weight, boxed, 22 lbs.

Price, each.............................. **$4.45**

No. 19396. Same as No. 19395, but is smaller. Measures 16¾ inches high, 8¾ inches wide and 7½ inches deep; takes No. 2 burner and 1-inch wick.

Price, each.............................. **$3.75**

## STREET LAMPS.

## Globe Tubular Street Lamp.

**Patented.**

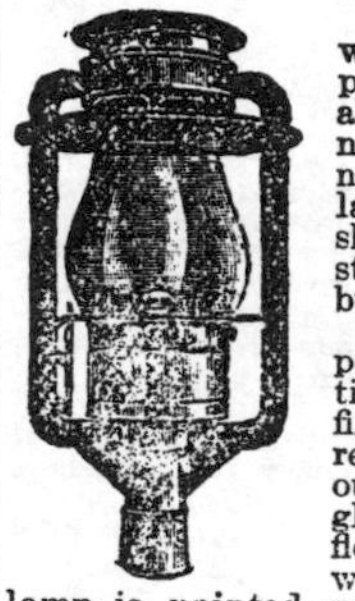

No. 19399. No. 3 burner, 1½ inch wick, No. 3 globe. Warranted to give perfect satisfaction; more sold than all other makes combined; no chimney; light equal to gas at a less cost; new globe lifter; outside wick regulator; does not smoke; casts no shadow; will not blow out in the strongest wind; can be regulated to burn a certain number of hours.

This lamp never fails to give perfect satisfaction. It can be filled, lighted and regulated without removing the globe. The reflector is painted white and the lamp is painted green. With our iron bracket it makes a useful and ornamental fixture. Packed 1 in a case. Average weight, with case, 30 lbs.

Each.............................. **$4.10**

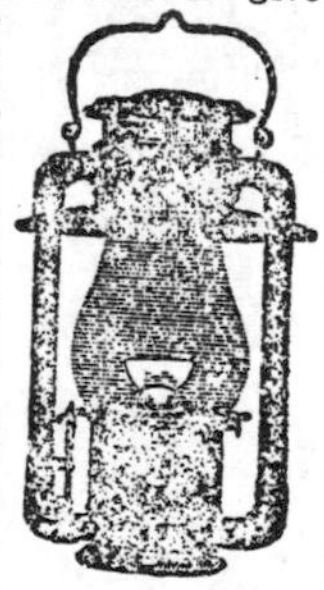

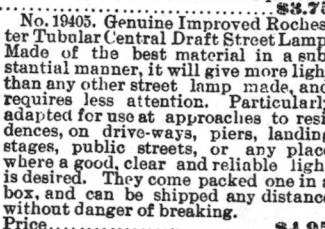

No. 19400. Globe Tubular Hanging Lamp is the same as our globe street lamp, but is intended to hang by the bail instead of fitting on post. It will be found very convenient, as it can be moved from time to time as occasion requires.

Each.............................. **$3.75**

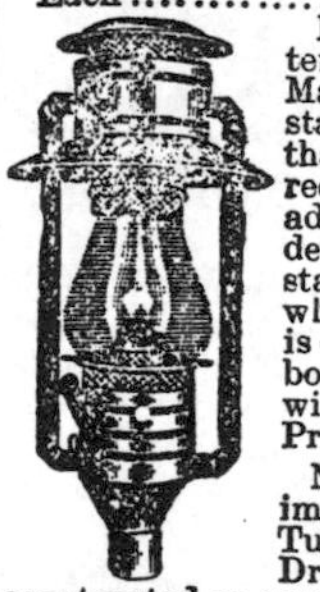

No. 19405. Genuine Improved Rochester Tubular Central Draft Street Lamp. Made of the best material in a substantial manner, it will give more light than any other street lamp made, and requires less attention. Particularly adapted for use at approaches to residences, on drive-ways, piers, landing stages, public streets, or any place where a good, clear and reliable light is desired. They come packed one in a box, and can be shipped any distance without danger of breaking.

Price.............................. **$4.95**

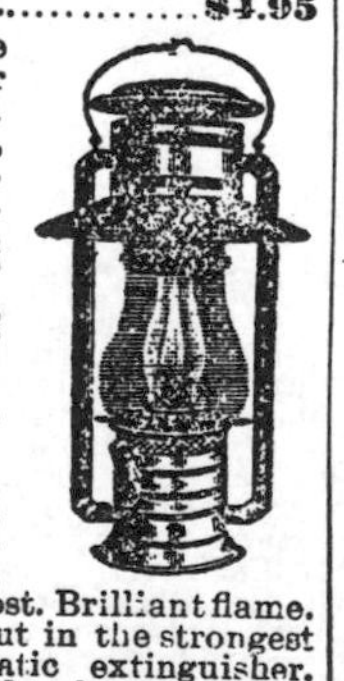

No. 19407. Genuine improved Rochester Tubular Central Draft Street Lamp, constructed on same principle as No. 19405, but is to be hung by the bail. Packed securely one lamp in box. Price.............................. **$4.95**

## Square Tubular Street Lamp.

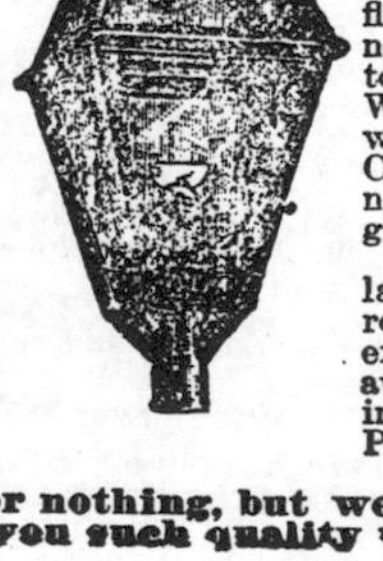

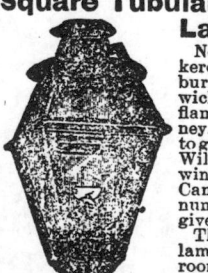

No. 19410. For kerosene. No. 3 burner. 1½-inch wick. 3-inch flame. No chimney. Light equal to gas at a less cost. Brilliant flame. Will not blow out in the strongest wind. Automatic extinguisher. Can be regulated to burn a certain number of hours. Warranted to give satisfaction.

This is a very large and handsome lamp. For lamp in front of lodge room, store or church it can not be excelled. Packed one each in a case; average weight with case, 43 lbs.; 36 inches high, 15½ inches square. Price, each.............................. **$5.45**

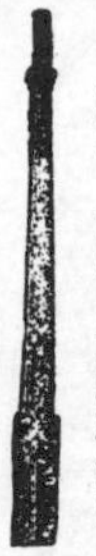

No. 19412. Turned Wood Posts for above lamps.

Price, each..... **$1.50**

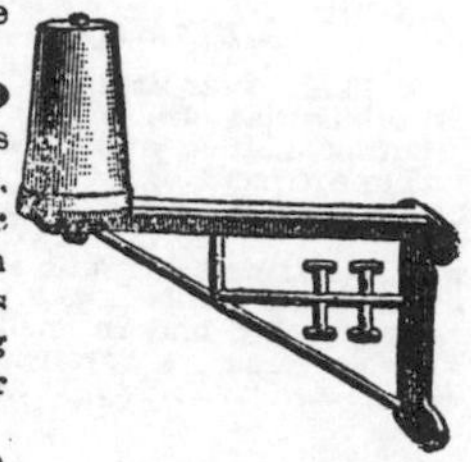

No. 19413. Iron Cross Bars for posts. Price, each........ **40c**

No. 19414. Iron Brackets, 24 inches long, for fastening lamp to buildings or posts.

Price, each.... **$1.00**

## WOODENWARE DEPARTMENT

## Cedar Ware, with Electric Welded Hoops—Galvanized,

**No wood known to man will resist decay equal to Virginia white cedar.**

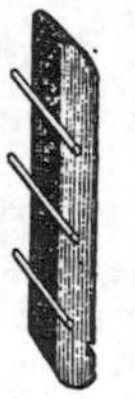

The Electric Welded Hoops used on this ware are sunk in grooves, and are three to four times as strong as a flat hoop, and consequently do not stretch when the wood expands, as is the case with a flat hoop, and therefore do not fall off when the tub or pail dries out. These hoops are **"too strong to break and can't fall off."**

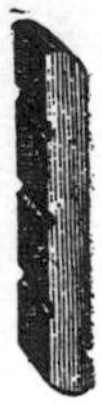

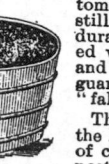

## Cedar Tubs.

**With Electric Welded Hoops.**

Made from the best Virginia white cedar. These tubs have met with wonderful success among our many customers. They are light, still very strong and durable, and are painted with the best oils and paint. They are guaranteed never to "fall down."

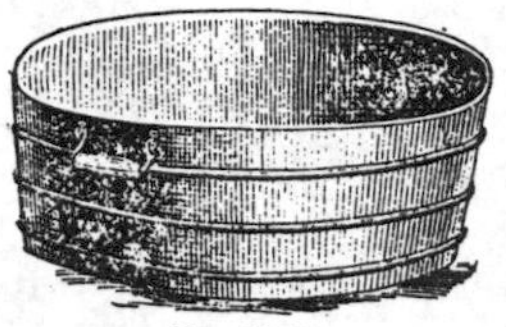

No. 16700.

Those familiar with the lasting qualities of cedar shingles and posts will appreciate the value of this material when used in tubs and pails. We have four sizes.

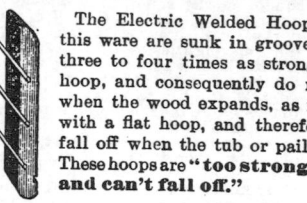

No. 16700.

| Size, No. | Diameter at Top. | Diameter at Bottom. | Depth. | Holds Gallons. | Price. |
|---|---|---|---|---|---|
| 0 | 23⅞ | 21⅝ | 12⅜ | 21 | $0.89 |
| 1 | 22⅝ | 19 | 11 5/16 | 16 | .70 |
| 2 | 20⅜ | 17⅝ | 10⅜ | 13 | .63 |
| 3 | 18½ | 16⅜ | 9⅛ | 9½ | .50 |

Sizes given above are inside measurements.

## Cedar Water Pails.

**With Galvanized Electric Welded Hoops.**

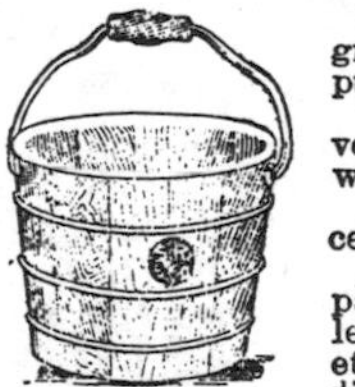

These pails have proven to be the greatest selling article we have ever put on the market.

They are **impervious** to water; very light and strong, and in every way superior to any pail ever made.

Made of the best Virginia white cedar.

No. 16705. Two-Hoop Cedar Pail, painted with the purest and best lead and oil on the outside. Diameter inside of top, 11¼ inches; diameter inside of bottom, 8⅞ inches; depth inside, 8 inches; holds 2¾ gals. Price, each, **15c**; per doz.............................. **$1.68**

No. 16706. Three-Hoop Cedar Pails, painted with the purest and best lead and oil on the outside. Diameter inside of top, 11⅝ inches; diameter inside bottom, 9½ inches; depth, 9⅝ inches; holds 3¾ gals. Price, each, **18**; per doz.............................. **$1.92**

No. 16707. Three-Hoop Cedar Pail, made of the best selected Virginia white cedar, and finished in natural wood. **Nickel plated** electric welded hoop, smoothly finished; a very handsome pail. Diameter inside top, 11¼ inches; diameter inside bottom, 8⅞ inches; depth inside, 8 inches; holds 2¾ gals. Price, each, **22c**; per doz.............................. **$2.50**

## Cedar Water Can or Sugar Bucket.

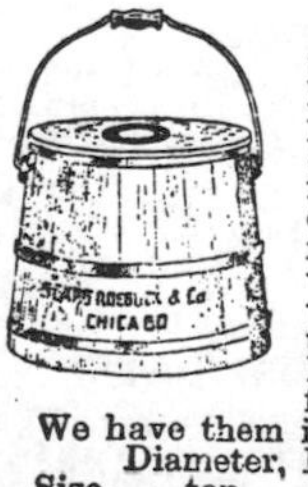


No. 16710. This is one of the most useful articles we sell. It has a handsome knob cover to lift off. Especially adapted for drinking water, as it keeps all dust and trash out. It is a well-known fact that the oil of cedar is death to nearly all forms of insect life. This property of the wood makes this bucket especially valuable to preserve anything from the attacks of ants and other insects. Finished in natural wood, with 3 flat brass hoops.

We have them in three sizes.

| Size. | Diameter, top. | Diameter, bottom. | Depth. | Holds, gallons. | Price, each. |
|---|---|---|---|---|---|
| 1 | 9 | 11 | 8½ | 3 | .55 |
| 2 | 8½ | 10½ | 8 | 2½ | .48 |
| 3 | 7⅛ | 9 | 7⅜ | 1½ | .38 |

The measurements above are inside measure.

**We do not pretend to give you something for nothing, but we always give a great deal for little money. We are careful to give you such quality that you will stay pleased.**

## PAILS.

**Standard Ware.**

No. 16716. 2 hoop, pine. Each, **12c**; per doz..................**$1.35**

No. 16717. 3 hoop, pine. Each, **15c**; per doz..................**$1.62**

## Stable Pails.

No. 16718. The J I C Oak Stable Pail has a strap ear running down sides of bucket that laps under the staves at the bottom. Has flush bottom so if horse gets his foot in the pail he can't break the pail. Considered by all horsemen the best stable pail made. Price, each, **45c**; per doz.....**$4.95**

## Well Bucket.

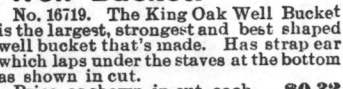

No. 16719. The King Oak Well Bucket is the largest, strongest and best shaped well bucket that's made. Has strap ear which laps under the staves at the bottom as shown in cut.

Price, as shown in cut, each....**$0.32**
Per doz..................**3.60**

No. 16720. The King Oak Well Bucket, same as above with swivel on bail.

Each..................**$0.36**
Per doz..................**4.00**

**For Well Wheels, Well Chains, etc., see index.**

## Sugar Buckets.

**With Wood Hoops.**

No. 16721. Holds 10 lbs.
Each..................**$0.28**
Per doz..................**2.75**

No. 16722. Holds 25 lbs.
Each..................**.32**
Per doz..................**3.50**

No. 16723. Holds 50 lbs.
Each..................**.36**
Per doz..................**4.00**

## Tubs.

**Standard Ware—Pine.**

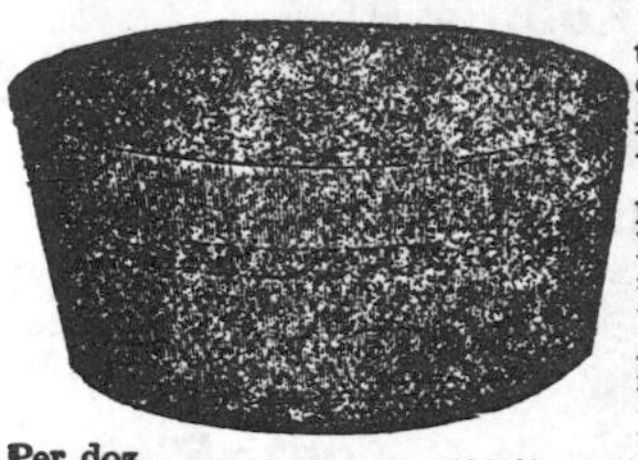

No. 16724. Extra large, 27 inches diameter at top.
Each.......**$0.80**
Per doz....... **8.80**

No. 16725. No. 1, pine. Diameter at top 24½ inches.
Each......**$0.65**
Per doz.... **7.25**

No. 16726. No. 2, pine. Diameter at top 23½ inches.
Each......**$0.58**
Per doz..................**6.25**

No. 16727. No. 3, pine. Diameter at top 20 inches.
Each..................**$0.50**
Per doz..................**5.25**

## Wash Boards.

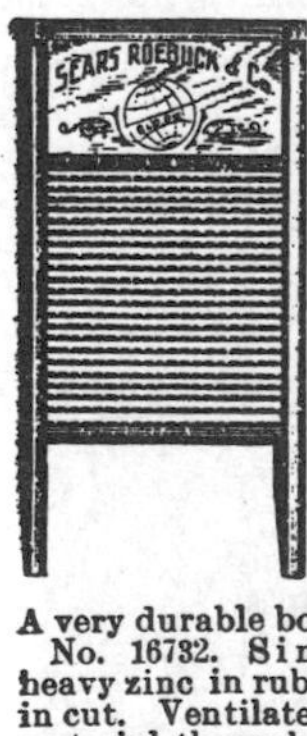



Our Wash Boards are made for us by the manufacturer who has the reputation of making the best wash board in the market. The frames are all hardwood, and the construction is the strongest and finish the best possible to produce. The rubbing surface is heavy zinc, and has the deep Globe crimp, as shown in cut.

No. 16730. Double Wash Board—plain crimp on one side, Globe crimp (which is shown in cut) on the other. Rubbing surface is 11 inches wide, 11½ inches long. A full size well made board. Price. each........**20c**

No. 16731. Single Washboard—Globe crimp, same as shown in cut. Best selected frame, heavy zinc in rubbing surface. Best material throughout. No better board made. A very durable board. Price, each..................**18c**

No. 16732. Single Washboard, hardwood frame, heavy zinc in rubbing surface. Globe crimp as shown in cut. Ventilated back and drainage dowel. Good material throughout. Price, each..................**15c**

No. 16733. Full size board with hardwood frame, solid back, Globe crimp. Price, each..................**12c**

## Eclipse Wash Bench.

No. 16734. Made of high grade oak lumber, with varnish finish; workmanship first-class. Has no castings to break or get out of order. Folds up compactly and can be packed away when not in use. Something the neat housekeeper has been looking for. Price..................**98c**

## Clothes Pins.

No. 16735. Hoyt's spring clothes pins are made of white basswood and the spring is one continuous piece of galvanized spring wire. Simple and convenient and the cheapest when durability is considered. Price, per doz. **5c**; Per gross..................**38c**

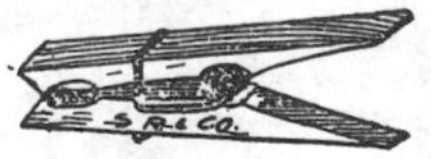



No. 16736. U. S. clothes pins, patent spring, 12 doz. in box. Price, per doz., **8c**; per box..........**85c**

No. 16737. Clothes pins, standard goods, full count. Price, per gross, **15c** price, per box containing 5 gross..................**50c**

No. 16738. Metallic Spring Clothes Pin. **Will never split or fall off in the severest storm or freeze to the clothes in the greatest frost.** It is easily applied and removed. It goes on any thickness of clothes and no baskets are necessary to carry them in. You can carry as many pins as are required for your entire wash in one hand by placing them on your fingers. They are applied to the clothes line the same as any other clothes pin. **They are made of wire heavily galvanized**, so that it is **impossible for them to rust.** They have been tested in all sorts of weather and found to be all we claim. Per doz., **7c**; per gross..................**80c**

## Washing Machines.

**Warrantee.**

The Anthony Wayne and the Western Star and the Electric Washers are warranted to be well made out of good, dry, sound material, and to do good work better, easier and quicker than can be done on a washboard; they will wash clean and will not tear the clothes. This warrantee is good only when the machines are used according to directions.

## The Anthony Wayne Washer.

No. 16744. The Improved Anthony Wayne Washer No. 2. This machine is of the same capacity as the No. 2 Western Star. Made out of white pine, painted and grained an ash color. The staves and bottom are corrugated. Wringer can be attached. Shipping weight, 46 lbs. Price each..................**$2.50**

### DIRECTIONS.

**How to Use Either the "Anthony Wayne" or "Western Star" Washer and Do a Quick and Clean Washing Without the Use of a Washboard.**

On the evening before wash-day place all the clothes you wish to wash in a tub, fill the same up with water (rain water preferred), so that they may be thoroughly soaked over night. On the following morning fill your wash boiler three-fourths full of rain water, put the same to boiling and cut into it one-half bar of hard soap and one teacupful of washing fluid, the recipe of which is found below. When boiling put in your clothes and boil from 10 to 15 minutes, after which wring them out, place them in the machine, work them from 5 to 10 minutes in the same, wring your clothes into the basket, rinse them through clear water, blue and hang on the line.

Do not put over five shirts or four sheets at a time into the machine, and see that the same is kept well filled with soap suds; the more water you can put in your machine and the freer the clothes will work in the machine, the easier the machine will work.

We warrant, if these directions are followed closely, that the washing will be as clean as any lady can desire them. Proceed with all the rest like above and the largest washing can be done in two or three hours. The suds need not be removed every time, but can be used until they become too dirty; but always add hot water, soap and compound in proportion and keep the machine well filled.

**Recipe for the Anthony Wayne Washing Fluid.**—Take 1 pound of potash, 1 ounce of salts of tartar, 1 ounce of ammonia, place the potash into a large crock or earthen vessel and pour a gallon of hot water slowly into this vessel. Wait until this cools, then add the salts of tartar and the ammonia, and when all is fully dissolved bottle the fluid for use. All the ingredients can be bought at any drug store at a cost not to exceed 25 cents.

Send for our special washing machine circular. It is free for the asking.

## The Western Star Washer.

No. 16742. Western Star Washer No. 2 is the popular family size washer. Inside dimensions, 17¾x23½x10½ inches; capacity, 5 shirts or its equal in bulk. This machine is too well known all over the country to require any extended remarks in regard to its utility. It has been in the market so long that it is known by thousands of housekeepers to be the standard family machine. The construction, material and finish of our Western Star Washer will be held to the same high grade as heretofore and will not be excelled by any other make. We wish to call attention to the fact that we do not use any nails in this washer below the water line, and that all iron parts that can come in contact with the clothing are heavily tinned, so that there is absolutely no danger of rust spots on the clothes. Shipping weight, 61 lbs.

Price, each, only..................**$2.49**

No. 16743. The Western Star Washer No. 3 is made same as the No. 2, only it is larger. Inside dimensions, 19¼x25¼x11½ inches; capacity, 7 shirts or its equivalent in bulk. This machine is made to meet the demand for a Western Star Washer of larger capacity. Suitable for large families, small hotels, etc. Weight, 68 lbs.

Price, each..................**$2.75**

## Electric Washer.

No. 16745. Made of the best Virginia white cedar, electric welded wire hoops. Price..................**$3.50**

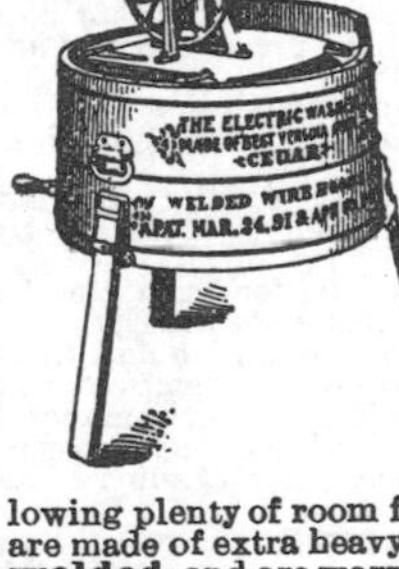



The cut shows the exterior of our celebrated **Electric Washer.** This machine is constructed of the **best Virginia white cedar,** and is stronger, more nicely finished, and is larger than any round machine on the market. It is supplied with our improved gearing, fully galvanized. The inside of the machine is fully corrugated, similar to a washboard, there being no nails or blocks of any kind on the inside. The machine is made with large end of tub down, allowing plenty of room for water and clothes. The hoops are made of extra heavy galvanized wire, are **electric welded**, and are warranted not to break or fall off.

Instead of using a square wooden post to work the dolly, we use a square galvanized iron rod, making it impossible to tear the most delicate fabric, as the dolly and standard are automatically adjusted to the quantity of clothes contained in the machine, so it offers nothing in which the clothing can catch.

The **electric** closes tight and retains the heat in the water for a long time, and prevents the odor of foul steam from the clothes. The Washer can be used on a carpet without soiling the same. It has a large, convenient place for holding the wringer, which need not be moved while using the machine. Our Electric Washers are guaranteed to be perfect in every respect. All we ask is a trial. Guaranteed to do the work and give satisfaction.

## Cline's Improved Steam Washer.

No. 16747. Cline's improved Steam Washer has several new features that others do not have. Has a corrugated cylinder, sliding cover and a faucet attached to the boiler for removing the water without lifting the boiler from the stove, which is a decided advantage. Weight, 32 lbs. Price, each..................**$5.50**

**When you buy at home, you think you save the freight, but you don't. The freight, with a big profit added, is in the price.**

## Mangles.

Hand power mangles have been in universal use in European countries for many years, and are considered as much a household necessity as a sewing machine. **Fully two-thirds of the week's washing** can be put through these mangles, such as table and bed linens, towels, handkerchiefs, spreads, blankets, underwear and all plain articles. (They are not suitable for starched shirts or clothes with hard buttons.) These mangles will save 20 per cent. of the household labor, and in hotels and institutes where our machines are used they enable the proprietors to save the wages and board of from 1 to 5 helpers in the laundry.

**The work is done by pressure.** And they give a **gloss** and **finish** to linens and all plain articles far superior to that possible to attain by any other method. Laces of all kinds are finished beautifully on these mangles.

They not only produce a smooth and uniform finish throughout the surface of the goods mangled, but bring out the figure and design on table linens, etc., and cause the goods to always retain their **pure whiteness**, having the same appearance as when new.

As an ordinary ironing can be done on these mangles in one-sixth the time required by flat irons and without heat or fuel, their great economy is at once apparent, and as they do not discolor the goods or destroy the fiber, as is done where heat is applied by hot irons or heated rolls mangles, the goods will wear at least twice as long.

It requires but little experience to become thoroughly familiar with the operation of these mangles and how to properly prepare the goods for them, and when well understood the results obtained are so superior and satisfactory that they would not be dispensed with for many times their cost.

No. 16748. Table Mangle; designed for small families and particularly where economy in room is to be considered. This machine is made sufficiently strong to sustain the necessary pressure to do good work. It is light and easily handled and takes up about the same space as a wringer. It is constructed with strong coil springs at the ends of the rolls, the pressure being adjusted by the thumb screws.

The shaft of the upper roll revolves in sliding journals so that the rolls adjust themselves to the varying thicknesses of the goods.

This mangle is made so it can be readily attached to any table; is reversible, so it can be operated by either right or left hand.

It will do all plain work much better than can be done with flatirons and in one-quarter the time.

Heretofore the price of mangles has kept many from purchasing; this objection has now been removed and we offer here a mangle first-class in every particular and at a price within the means of all. It will last for years and more than save its cost each year. Made in one size.

No. 15638. Table Mangle, rolls 23x3½ inches. Price........................................**$11.25**

No. 16749. These mangles are adapted for families, small hotels and laundries, restaurants, barber shops, etc. They do good work and will endure a ton pressure.

They are furnished with our patent automatic table adjustment, mounted on casters, are double geared with gear guard and have our combiuation driving gears, causing them to turn easy under great pressure. The pressure is obtained by heavy coil springs at the ends of the rolls and is easily regulated. Made in 2 sizes.

| Size of Rolls. | Floor Space. | Ship'ng Wgt. | Price. |
|---|---|---|---|
| 28x6 inches | 21x34 inches | 250 lbs. | $28.12 |
| 24x6 inches | 21x30 inches | 240 lbs. | 24.75 |

We can furnish these machines with tight and loose pulleys for power in place of hand wheel if desired, at $12.00 extra. Where power is used the machines are bolted to the floor.

**BEST MADE LAUNDERED SHIRTS ON PAGE 207.**

## Hotel Mangle.

Indispensable to the economical management of any hotel or public institution.

No. 16750. These are our heavy machines, and are especially adapted for use in hotels, laundries and institutes. They are built to sustain great pressure and are reinforced in all parts exposed to wear or strain. They are double geared, making the action of the rolls positive, and, being fitted with our combination driving gears, are very light running. The machines are mounted on casters, and can be easily moved from place to place, and when not in use are readily set out of the way, occupying but little more room than a sewing machine.

The gears are covered with a handsome guard, preventing the possibility of any danger to the operator.

**Our patent automatic table adjustment** (furnished only with our mangles) is a very desirable feature in a machine of this kind, being convenient and secure for shipping, and makes the machines always ready for use. The tables, being permanently attached to the machine, are not knocked about and marred or misplaced when needed.

For use it is only necessary to raise the tables parallel with the rolls, and our device automatically secures them firmly into that position. In lowering them they are raised about ten degrees, which releases the lock and they can be lowered to the side of the machine.

**Made in Two Sizes.**

| | Floor space. | Shipping weight. | Price. |
|---|---|---|---|
| Rolls 28 in. long, 6 in. diam. | 23x34 in. | 275 lbs. | $37.50 |
| Rolls 24 in. long, 6 in. diam. | 23x30 in. | 260 lbs. | 31.50 |

We can furnish these machines with tight and loose pulleys for power in place of hand wheel if desired at $12.00 extra. Power machines bolted to the floor.

## Schmuck's Mop Wringer.

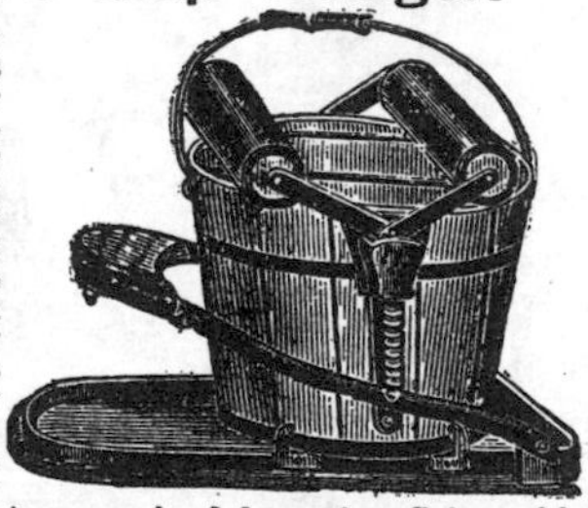

No. 16754. The Schmuck Patent Mop Wringers, for simplicity, durability, dry wringing and adaptability, have no equal. They are manufactured of wrought iron, the rollers made of hard maple, chemically treated, and will fit any size pail. Every wringer "warranted." Space permits us to mention only a few of the advantages gained by using Schmuck's Mop Wringers. 1.—Boiling hot water can be used to mop up the floor, which will cause the floor to dry quickly. 2.—Grease stains and dirt can be loosened with concentrated lye, potash or soda, and floor then mopped with Schmuck's Mop Wringer. 3.—Schmuck's Mop Wringer, by means of the wooden rolls, wrings the mop dry, and the water forces the dirt downward into the pail, leaving the mop clean and free from dirt, while all other mop-wringing devices and hand-wringing, twist the mop, wring out the water, leaving dirt in center of mop. 4.—Schmuck's Mop Wringer is a self-wringing mop, and while mopping, gloves can be used, as the hands do not come in contact with water. In fact, what has heretofore proven the dirtiest work in and about a house, is now made the easiest and cleanest by the use of Schmuck's Mop Wringer. Price for wringer with pail, each........................................**$2.25**

No. 16755. Self-Wringing Mop. The mop is made of cotton coils, large and full size. As the hands do not come in contact with the water, chapped, scalded and sore hands are avoided. The mop being wrung at arm's length, there is no stooping or straining of the back or shoulders. The hands are not soiled or disfigured by the wringing of a filthy, greasy cloth. As the clothing is not drenched or disfigured as in ordinary mopping, no special preparation is required. A silk dress can be worn with impunity. The floor can be mopped in case of need and other duties resumed as though no interruption had taken place.

The use of scalding water is another important advantage impossible with the ordinary hand-wringing mop. The floor washes easier, cleaner and quicker, and dries more readily. The grease and dirt being cut out by scalding waters, it saves soaps and alkalies. Price, each........................................**25c**

## Chopping Bowls.

Extra quality, with heavy rims, prevents checking. No. 16757. Chopping bowls.

| Inches, | 13 | 15 | 17 | 19 |
|---|---|---|---|---|
| Each, | $0.08 | .14 | .21 | .26 |
| Per doz., | .87 | 1.50 | 2.20 | 2.80 |

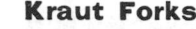

No. 16758. Hardwood patent oblong Chopping Trays.

| 11x22 | | 10x20 | | 9x18 | |
|---|---|---|---|---|---|
| Each. | Per doz. | Each. | Per doz. | Each. | Per doz. |
| $0.40 | 4.00 | .28 | 3.00 | .25 | 2.50 |

## Steak Mauls.

No. 16760. Steak Mauls. Each, **6c**; per doz......**60c**

## Lemon Squeezers.

No. 16762. Hardwood Lemon Squeezers. Each, **10c**; per doz.......**$1.00**

## Kraut Forks.

No. 16763. Kraut Forks. Each, **8c**; per doz..............**75c**

## Potato Mashers.

No. 16765. Potato Mashers, small. Each, **3c**; per doz..........**35c**

No. 16766. Potato Mashers, large. Each, **4c**; per doz...............**44c**

## Spoons.

No. 16767. Wood Kitchen Spoons, 14 inches long. Each, **6c**; per doz......**55c**

## Rolling Pins.

No. 16768. Rolling Pins, revolving handles. Each, **6c**; per doz..............**60c**

## Napkin Rings.

No. 16770. Napkin Rings, plain hardwood in assorted designs, finely polished. Price, each, **14c**; per doz............**$1.50**

## Tooth Picks.

No. 16771. Wood Tooth Picks, double points; 2,500 in a box, 100 boxes in case. Price, per box, **4c**; per case..............**$2.40**

No. 16772. Quill Tooth Picks, 40 bunches in package. Price, per bunch, **3c**; per package........**$1.00**

## Bread or Pastry Boards.

No. 16775. Bread or Pastry Boards made of poplar wood.

| Size. | Weight. | Each. |
|---|---|---|
| 16x22 | 4½ lbs. | $0.28 |
| 18x24 | 5¼ lbs. | .33 |
| 20x27 | 5¾ lbs. | .42 |
| 20x30 | 6½ lbs. | .46 |

## Slaw Cutters.

No. 16780. Slaw Cutters, one knife. Each......**22c**

## Adjustable Knife Kraut Cutters.

No. 16781. Kraut Cutters, 8 x 26 inches, 3 cast steel knives, with slide box. Each........................**$1.00**

No. 16782. Kraut Cutters, 30x9 inches; 3 cast steel knives, with slide box. Each..................**$1.75**

**The climax of perfection is reached in our fine Tailor Made Clothing. The best workmanship, the highest grade goods, and the lowest prices prevail.**

## Spice Cabinets.

No. 16783. Spice Cabinet, neatly constructed, an ornamental cabinet for holding and preserving spices. Eight drawers marked for contents. Very handsome for any use to which a cabinet can be put. Made of ash, oil finish; size, 12x18; weight, 6 lbs. Each......................60c

## Medicine Cabinet.

No. 16784. Medicine or Handy Cabinet, 12x16, made of ash, nicely trimmed, for holding medicine bottles or anything that necessity or convenience may suggest. Every family should have one. Weight, 3 lbs. Each..........60c

## Salt Box.

No. 16785. Salt Box, made of nice clear wood, is 6 inches square and will hold 2 small bags of salt. Each.......12c

## WOODEN MEASURES.

### Iron Bound.

No. 16790. ½ Bushel, iron bound. Each......................23c
No. 16791. Peck. Each...... 20c
No. 16797. ¼ Peck. Each.....18c
No. 16793. 2 qts. Each........15c
No. 16794. 1 qt. Each.........14c
No. 16795. Set of the above measures, one of each size, per set...80c

## Oat Sieves.

N o. 16800. Oat Sieves. Used to sift dust and dirt from oats. They can be marked to answer the purpose of a measure. Every owner of a horse should have one. Made in two sizes.

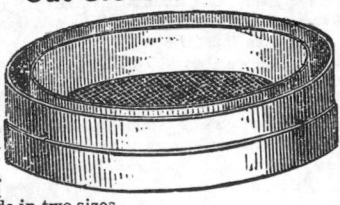

14-inch diameter. Price, each....................27c
16-inch diameter. Price, each....................32c

## Egg Cases and Fillers

Cases to hold 30 dozen.
No. 16802. No. 1 white pine, with fastener, no fillers.
Each....$0.23
Per doz. 2.63
No. 16803. No. 2 white pine, without fastener, no fillers.
Each....$0.14
Per doz. 1.60
No. 16804. No. 1 Fillers, 10 sections, 8 division boards.
Per set..$0.15
Per doz. 1.62
No. 16805. No. 2 Fillers, 10 sections, 8 division boards. Per set, 10c; per doz................$1.10
When large quantities of these cases are wanted we can ship "knocked down" which saves freight charges. We also make special prices on "knocked down" cases. If you are going to buy write us for prices stating how many you want. We can save you money on these goods.

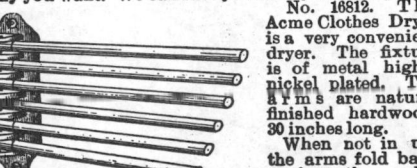

No. 16812. The Acme Clothes Dryer is a very convenient dryer. The fixture is of metal highly nickel plated. The arms are natural finished hardwood, 30 inches long.
When not in use the arms fold back against the walls.
Made in two sizes.
6 arms, each, 20c; 10 arms, each................35c

## Eureka Adjustable Clothes Bar.

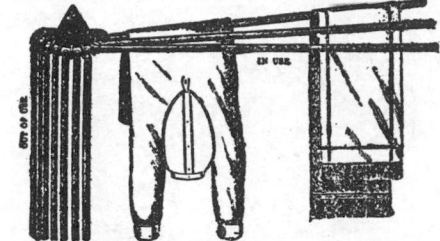

No. 16813. Eureka Adjustable Clothes Bar, intended to fasten to the wall. When not in use takes the space of an ordinary broom. The bars are 3 feet in length, with gilt tips; a very convenient household article; weight, 4 lbs. Each................39c
No. 16814. Same as No. 16813, with 6 bars, 2 feet long. Each................25c

## Folding Clothes Bar.

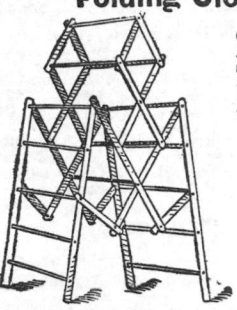

No. 16816. Folding Clothes Bar, all hardwood, has 54 lineal feet drying surface. Light, strong, and durable. Folds into a small space when not in use; stands 5¼ feet high. Each................60c

## Ironing Boards.

No. 16818. Ironing Boards, made of poplar wood.

| Length, feet. | Weight, lbs. | Price, each. |
|---|---|---|
| 4 | 6 | $0.33 |
| 4½ | 7 | .37 |
| 5 | 7½ | .42 |
| 5½ | 9 | .46 |
| 6 | 11 | .50 |

## Folding Ironing Boards.

No. 16819. This convenient household article is in great favor wherever shown. It has basswood top, 16x60 inches in size, with a sad-iron holder at one end. The legs are of hardwood, and the table may be easily and quickly adjusted to three different heights. When not in use occupies but little more space than the common ironing board. Price, each................60c

No. 16820. Combination Folding Ironing Board, has a steel wire tension at the bottom, which acts as an automatic folder; when set upright it can be used as a stepladder.

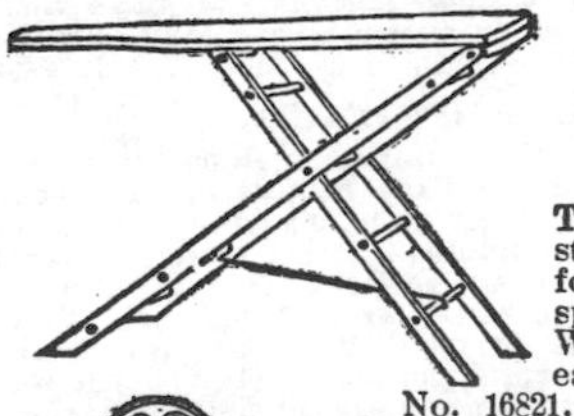

Top is 54 inches long, stands 29 inches high; folds into a small space when not in use. Weight, 18 lbs. Price, each..........$1.00
No. 16821. The Champion Bosom Board and Stretcher; the most complete in the market; with this board any lady can "iron" a white shirt equal to the best laundry work.
Price, each.................40c

## Lap Cutting Boards.

No. 16823. Lap Cutting Board, striped, oil finished and polished, with yard measure stamped on it. Size, 20x36 inches; weight, 4½ lbs.
Each.........65c
No. 16824. Lap Cutting Board, same shape as No. 16823, made of white wood, plain, 20x36. Each....52c
No. 16825. Folding Striped Lap Board, hard oil finish, can be rolled up and put into small space, and be put out of the way. It measures 20x36 inches, and has a yard measure printed on the edge. Price, each.........85c

## Folding Tables.

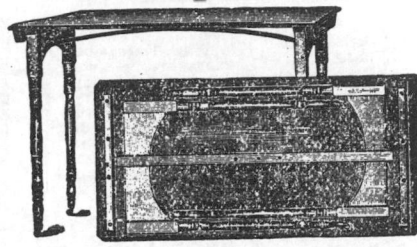

No. 16826. Folding Table, hardwood top, with a yard measure neatly stamped on the same. The cheapest light, strong, serviceable folding table made; indispensable to families where considerable sewing is done; also makes a nice card table. Weight, about 10 lbs.
Price, only...........................66c
For other folding tables see index.

## Wood Faucets.

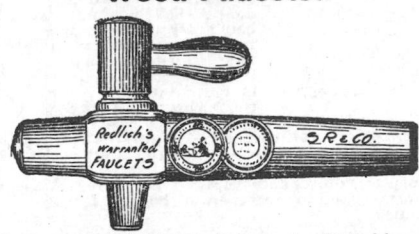

No. 16829. Redlich's Wood Faucets. Boiled in gutta percha, and fully warranted.

| No. | 1 | 3 | 5 | 6 |
|---|---|---|---|---|
| Length, inches, | 7 | 8½ | 10½ | 11¼ |
| Price, each, | $0.06 | .08 | .10 | .12 |
| Per doz., | .50 | .75 | .87 | 1.12 |

## Metal Keyed Faucets.

No. 16830. Metal Keyed Faucets. Maple wood, sole leather lined.

| No. | 0 | 1 | 2 |
|---|---|---|---|
| Length, inches, | 7½ | 9 | 12 |
| Price, each, | $0.13 | .15 | .18 |
| Price, per doz., | 1.40 | 1.65 | 2.00 |

## Step Ladders.

No. 16836. Patent Step Ladder, has wrought iron connecting bands. This prevents the ladder from spreading without the useless appendage of strings or braces. These ladders are all made from selected lumber, and put together for constant service.

| Weight. | Length. | Each. | Weight. | Length. | Each. |
|---|---|---|---|---|---|
| 9 lbs. | 3 foot | $0.30 | 27 lbs. | 10 foot | $0.90 |
| 10 lbs. | 4 foot | .40 | 37 lbs. | 12 foot | 1.00 |
| 11 lbs. | 5 foot | .50 | 50 lbs. | extra heavy | 2.00 |
| 14 lbs. | 6 foot | .60 | | 14 foot | |
| 18 lbs. | 7 foot | .70 | 65 lbs. | 16 foot | 2.35 |
| 21 lbs. | 8 foot | .80 | | | |

No. 16837. The Excelsior Step Ladder, designed for outdoor and where ladders are used roughly. It is made of the best seasoned Norway pine, braced with iron at the intersection of every piece. This is considered the very best ladder made.

| Weight. | Length. | Each. | Weight. | Length. | Each. |
|---|---|---|---|---|---|
| 15 lbs. | 5 foot | $1.89 | 35 lbs. | 10 foot | $3.00 |
| 18 lbs. | 6 foot | 2.16 | 40 lbs. | 12 foot | 3.95 |
| 22 lbs. | 7 foot | 2.35 | 60 lbs. | 14 foot | 4.95 |
| 26 lbs. | 8 foot | 2.50 | 75 lbs. | 16 foot | 5.50 |

## Step Ladder, with Shelf Attachment.

No. 16838. Step Ladder with shelf attachment. The shelf is so adjusted as not to interfere with the spread of the ladder; folds up readily when not in use; costs but a trifle, and is a valuable adjunct to the ladder

| Weight, lbs. | Feet. | Each. | Weight, lbs. | Feet. | Each. |
|---|---|---|---|---|---|
| 10 | 3 | $0.42 | 23 | 8 | $0.90 |
| 12 | 4 | .45 | 29 | 10 | 1.00 |
| 13 | 5 | .60 | 34 | 12 | 1.25 |
| 16 | 6 | .70 | 35 | 14 | 2.05 |
| 20 | 7 | .80 | 65 | 16 | 2.40 |

## Extension Ladders.

No. 16389. Extension Ladders are made from selected Norway pine and hickory rungs. Put together with screws; gotten up in a tasty manner; of sufficient strength for safety, and not too heavy to carry. Extension ladders all lengths. Per foot. 15c

## Extension Step Ladder.

No. 16840. Cut shows ladder extended; upper part can be instantly lowered, making an ordinary step ladder. When in position as a step ladder, two persons can work on it at the same time; being very strong and well braced, does not require strings to keep it from spreading. It is easily adjusted to the position as a long ladder and often of great convenience in reaching high ceilings and skylights. Can also be used as a trestle, and in the several positions can readily be appreciated by the carpenter, painter and fruit grower. It recommends itself to everyone who has use for a ladder.

| Length. | Weight. | Each. |
|---|---|---|
| 6 ft. step, extended, 11 ft. | 20 lbs. | $1.50 |
| 7 ft. step, extended, 12 ft. | 23 lbs. | 1.65 |
| 8 ft. step, extended, 15 ft. | 26 lbs. | 1.90 |
| 9 ft. step, extended, 17 ft. | 30 lbs. | 2.15 |
| 10 ft. step, extended, 19 ft. | 35 lbs. | 2.35 |
| 11 ft. step, extended, 21 ft. | 40 lbs. | 2.55 |
| 12 ft. step, extended, 23 ft. | 46 lbs. | 2.90 |

## Chair Seats.

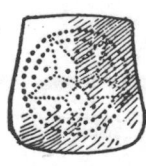

No. 16849. Ball Top Chair Seats.
No. 16850. Square Chair Seats.
**Cut shows shape of ball top seat.**
These chair seats are made from 3 pieces of birch veneer with grains crossing glued together under great pressure. They can not split. Sizes given are measurements across the widest place.

| Size in in., | 10 | 11 | 12 | 13 | 14 | 15 | 16 | 17 | 18 | 20 | 22 | 24 |
|---|---|---|---|---|---|---|---|---|---|---|---|---|
| Price, ea, | $0.04 | .04 | .05 | .05 | .06 | .06 | .07 | .07 | .08 | .10 | .14 | .17 |
| Per doz., | .40 | .45 | .50 | .55 | .60 | .65 | .70 | .75 | .90 | 1.10 | 1.20 | 1.90 |

No. 113. Brass Head Nails to fasten these seats to chairs, large size, per 100, 10c; small size, per 100...7c

## Oak Creek Splint Corn Baskets.

No. 16855. This basket is stronger and can be used for more purposes around a farm than any other on the market; we carry it in a full line of sizes and shall be glad to have your order for any quantity you may desire.

| Size, bushels, | ¾ | 1 | 1½ | 2 |
|---|---|---|---|---|
| Price, each, | $0.40 | .50 | .62 | .78 |
| Price, per doz. | 4.56 | 5.70 | 7.05 | 8.90 |
| Size, bushels, | | 3 | 4 | 6 |
| Price each, | | $1.00 | 1.35 | 1.65 |
| Price, per doz., | | 11.40 | 15.39 | 18.81 |

## Measuring Baskets.

No. 16856. Racine corn Basket, patent stave, ½ bushel with handle.
Each........18c
Per doz..........$1.35
No. 16857. Racine Corn Basket, patent stave, 1 bushel.
Each.............22c
Per doz..........$2.20
No. 16858. Racine Corn Basket, patent stave, 1½ bushels.
Each.............25c
Per doz..........$2.60
No. 16859. Racine Corn Basket, patent stave, 2 bushels.
Each, 33c; per doz..........$3.25
No. 16860. Splint, 1 bushel. Each.......35c
Per doz..........$4.00
No. 16861. Splint, 1½ bushels. Each.......40c
Per doz..........$4.50

## Clothes Baskets.

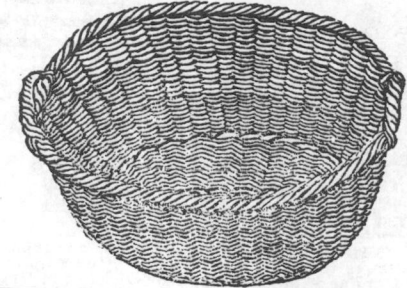

No. 16862. Clothes basket, willow, small. Each, 65c
Per doz..........$7.00
No. 16863. Clothes basket, willow, medium. Each, 75c
Per doz..........$8.00
No. 16864. Clothes basket, willow, large. Each, 85c
Per doz..........$9.50

## Market Baskets.

No. 16869. Market basket, willow, small. Each....27c
Per doz..........$3.00
No. 16870. Market basket, willow, medium. Each....32c
Per doz..........$3.50
No. 16871. Market basket, willow, large. Each....38c
Per doz..........$4.00

## Market Baskets.

No.16872. Market, woven splint, oval, small.
Price, each....25c
Per doz..........$2.50
No.16873. Market, woven splint, oval, medium.
Price, each....27c
Per doz..........$2.75
No.16874. Market, woven splint, oval, large.
Price, each....28c
Per doz..........$3.00
No.16875. Market, common elm.
Price, each, 5c; per doz..........50c
No. 16876. Market, extra elm. Price, each, 10c; per doz..........$1.00
No. 16877. Market, elm, covered, medium. Price, each, 20c; per doz..........$2.00
No. 16878. Market, elm, covered, large. Price, each, 22c; per doz..........$2.25

## Baby Swings.

No. 16889. Baby Swing has hardwood seat, 11 inches square, upholstered in cretonne; intended to be hung in a doorway; furnished with cotton rope and 2 hooks to hang it on; has no springs.
Price, each..........38c
No. 16890. Springs for Baby Swings; made of heavy steel spring wire 15 inches long. By adding a pair of these springs to above swing you have a baby jumper. Many people buy these springs and make their own jumper. Springs come in pairs; price for springs only per pair..........40c

## Baby Jumpers.

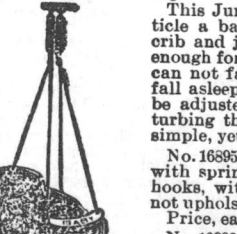

This Jumper combines in one article a baby swing-reclining-chair-crib and jumper; strong and large enough for a child 6 years old; child can not fall out. Should the baby fall asleep while in the chair it can be adjusted to a crib without disturbing the child. It is light and simple, yet substantial and perfect.
No. 16895. Baby Jumper complete, with springs and cotton rope and hooks, with veneer seat and back, not upholstered.
Price, each..........$1.50
No. 16896. Baby Jumper, complete with springs, rope, and hooks, upholstered in cretonne; like cut.
Price, each..........$2.00

## Improved Child's Lawn Swings.

They are strong and durable and made of the best material. They are well painted in bright colors. The chair and frame are put together with bolts.
No. 16899. Child's Lawn Swing, stands 6 feet high. Price, each..........$4.75

## Lawn Swings.

For ease and comfort they cannot be excelled, and with the canopy over the chair there is solid comfort in our Lawn Swing. They are very strong and made of the best material. The chairs are made of hardwood and are well painted in bright colors. The chair and frame are put together with bolts.
They are so constructed that it is impossible for even the smallest child to get hurt. Prices are for swing without canopy.
No. 16900.

| Height, feet. | Width of chair seat, inches. | Price, each. |
|---|---|---|
| 8 | 20 | $ 7.50 |
| 10 | 22 | 9.00 |
| 12 | 24 | 10.75 |
| 14 | 26 | 14.25 |
| 16 | 28 | 17.00 |

No. 16901. Sun shade or canopy to fit any of the above swings if ordered with swing $2.00 extra.

## Hammock Chair.

No. 16902. Cut represents Hammock Chair, as used when suspended from ceiling of porch or limb of tree.
This chair automatically adjusts itself to any desired position by the slightest effort of the occupant; has an adjustable foot rest, which can be easily and quickly adjusted to suit people of different heights. Has adjustable web seat, which can be so adjusted as to keep the seat in a comfortable and firm position. In fact, no Hammock Chair can be complete without this patent web seat. Finished in natural wood oiled, and vermilion. All weighing but 14 lbs., and folding as completely as a camp stool.
Price, each..........$3.20

No. 16903. Our Hammock Chair, shown in cut, is, with the following exceptions, the same as No. 16902, shown above. In this, rope hangers are used instead of wood, and it is made from a cheaper, but at the same time durable duck. The woodwork is finished in oil only.
Price, each..........$2.70

## Patent Swing Horses.

No. 16905. Swing Horse, 18 inches high from floor to saddle, nicely trimmed has hair mane and tail.
This horse requires very little strength to operate, and for that reason is a decided improvement over the old style rocking horse.
Each.....$1.80
No. 16906. Swing Horse, 21 inches high from floor to saddle, otherwise same as No. 16905. Each....$2.65
No. 16907. Swing Horse, 22 inches high from floor to saddle, and trimmed in a superior manner.
Each..........$3.25

## Patent Swinging Shoo-Fly Rockers.

No. 16909. Swinging Shoo-fly, easy to operate, no danger of child falling out; nicely upholstered in cretonne and painted dapple gray.
Each ...$1.80

## Shoo-Fly Rockers.

No. 16912. Shoo-fly, 12x40 inches; painted and dappled, has painted hardwood seat, bent rocker and hair tail. Price.............**75c**
No. 16913. Shoo-fly, same as No. 16912, but is upholstered in cretonne. Price............**90c**
No. 16914. Shoo-fly, 12x44 inches, neatly painted and dappled, has box in front to hold a child's toys, and is upholstered in cretonne; hair tail, bent rocker. Price............................**$1.10**

## Boys' Wagons.

Boys' Steel Wagons. The best and strongest cheap wagon made; finely painted and ornamented, steel box, malleable iron gear, tinned steel wheels.
No. 16925. Body 12x24 inch, wheels 10 and 14 inch. Price, each..................**$1.15**
No. 16926. Body 13x26 inch, wheels 10 and 14 inch. Price, each..................**$1.30**
No. 16927. Body 14x28 inch, wheels 12 and 16 inch. Price, each..................**$1.50**
No. 16928. Body 15x30 inch, wheels 12 and 16 inch. Price, each..................**$1.65**

No. 16929. Iron axles: body, 14x28 inches; wheels, 12 and 16 inches. Hardwood paneled body, landscape painting, scrolled and varnished, hub caps, high seat and dashboard. Iron braced, heavy iron axles in iron thimble skein, oval tires welded and shrunk on. Same as cut. Price, each.....................**$2.00**

No. 16930. Boys' Farm Wagon, with pole and shafts. Body, 18x36 inches, with hardwood frame. The sides and ends can be taken off, leaving bed with stakes. The gearing is made like a farm wagon, having bent hawns and adjustable reach; all parts are strongly ironed and braced; wheels are 14 and 20 inches; heavy welded tires; sand boxes and hub caps; has seat, handle and a pair of hardwood shafts for dog or goat. It is handsomely ornamented with landscapes and scroll work. This wagon is the best in the market. Price, each....**$6.75**
For Goat or Dog Harness see index.

## Dairy Supplies.

The goods which are most commonly used by dairymen are illustrated and described in the following pages. We will be pleased to give information and quote prices on anything not found here, and are in a position to give our patrons very low prices.

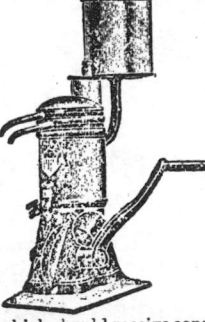

No. 16920. The Young America Cream Separator, for hand or power; capacity, 300 lbs. per hour. This is a departure from anything of its kind on the market in construction, style and finish. The frame is very compact and simple, with no movable lugs or parts to get out of order. The bowl is of special design, the result of years of experiment, and is made of the best steel obtainable, of the greatest tensile strength. The wings are simple in construction, easy to clean, as they may be quickly removed. All parts are interchangeable, which is a point which should receive consideration. For workmanship, material, finish, ease of cleaning, ease of turning, this separator cannot be excelled. It will give you an improved quality of butter, smoothest of cream and bluest of skim milk.
Price, each.....................**$97.00**
Single pulley for power, extra.............**2.00**

## First Prize Dog Power.

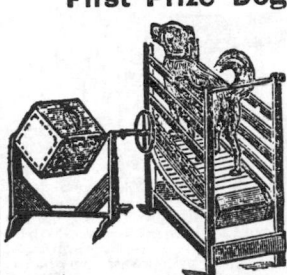

No. 16924. This power can be operated by a dog, goat or sheep; yields 25 per cent. more power from a given weight of animal than any other, and with adjustable bridge to regulate the required power and motion, a 30 pound animal will do the churning; if you keep a dog, make him "work his passage." The power can be connected to any churn sold by us.
Price....................**$15.00**

The illustration above shows how the double dog power can be used in operating a cream separator. When the separator is not in use and you desire to churn, connect it to tumbling rod sent with machine. A corn sheller, fan mill or sawing machine can be connected by belt from balance wheel. Separators require a high gear, and for this purpose we recommend our steel pulley, 3½x36 inches. This we can furnish at $6 extra. If iron coupling rod and coupling as shown in illustration are desired to connect and run cream separator, we can furnish them at $3 extra.

## The Peerless Creamery.

No. 16928. The Peerless Creamery is more especially intended for water alone. The cans are oblong, 14 inches long, 5 inches wide and 14 inches deep, thus giving larger cooling surface. We have a large ice space in rear of and also between the cans. In the No. 4 we have the space between the two middle cans, 7 inches; also, in all the other sizes we have a large space between the second and third, fourth and fifth, and sixth and seventh. In these, as in the round can creamers, we use a straight faucet underneath, which is easily cleaned.

The class to observe the cream is in the nut, and not in the can, so is easily repaired if accidentally broken. In the No. 3 and larger sized creameries the faucet for drawing water from the tank is placed outside of creamery, as shown in illustration. Where ice is not used, we would suggest emptying tank of water about a half hour after milk has been placed in cans, and refilling tank with cold water. This will save a few hours time in the gathering of cream. Furnished complete, with cream pail, strainer and dairy thermometer.

PRICE LIST.
Capacity of cans, 18 quarts each.

| No. | No. of cans. | No. of cows. | Height, inches. | Length, inches. | Width, inches. | Weight, pounds. | Price. |
|---|---|---|---|---|---|---|---|
| 2 | 2 | 4 to 6 | 35 | 25 | 23 | 100 | $17.85 |
| 3 | 3 | 7 to 9 | 35 | 34 | 23 | 125 | 21.80 |
| 4 | 4 | 10 to 12 | 35 | 41 | 23 | 160 | 26.40 |
| 5 | 6 | 13 to 18 | 35 | 61 | 23 | 220 | 34.82 |
| 6 | 8 | 19 to 24 | 35 | 77 | 33 | 280 | 42.65 |
| 7 | 10 | 25 to 30 | 35 | 80 | 23 | 320 | 49.40 |
| 8 | 12 | 31 to 36 | 35 | 96 | 24 | 440 | 56.30 |

Our prices on these creameries are 40 per cent. below factory prices.

## Sturges' Steel Churn.

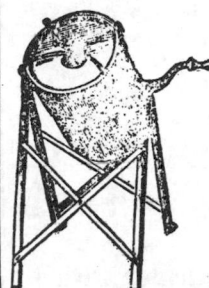

The latest and best thing out. It is exceptionally well made, being heavily coated inside with chemically pure tin, while the stand, which is also steel, is tastefully decorated in colors to brighten the home of the housewife.
An important feature, and one that can not but be appreciated by those desirous of keeping their churn sweet and clean, is the diameter of this churn's mouth, which is full size. The inside of the churn is perfectly smooth, making it as easy to clean as a crock. The cover has a half-inch cork lining around the edge, which prevents any possibility of a leak. A glass vent and peep hole adorns the cover for the purpose of determining when butter comes and also to let off the gases.
No. 16932. Five gallon Sturges' Steel Churn, for one to four gallons of cream. Price..............**$5.00**
No. 16933. Nine gallon Sturges' Steel Churn, for four to seven gallons of cream. Price..............**$8.00**

## The Star Barrel Churn.

This style of churn is old, tried and reliable, easy to operate and keep clean; it is absolutely impossible for this churn to leak, as the wear can be taken up as simply as any one can turn a thumb nut. The fastenings are attached to the outside of the churn, and it will be seen from the cut that the bail and cover fastening is a compound leverage which increases the pressure ten times more than any other make of churn.

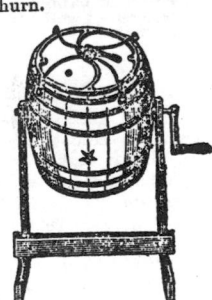

No. 16934. Five gallon Barrel Churn, for 1 or 2 gallons of cream. Each..........**$2.85**
No. 16935. Nine gallon Barrel Churn, for 1 to 4 gallons of cream. Each.......**$3.05**
No. 16936. Fifteen gallon Barrel Churn, for 2 to 7 gallons of cream. Each.......**$3.30**
No. 16937. Twenty gallon Barrel Churn, for 3 to 9 gallons of cream. Each......**$3.75**
No. 16938. Twenty-five gallon Barrel Churn, for 4 to 12 gallons of cream. Each......**$4.40**
No. 16939. Thirty-five gallon Barrel Churn, for 5 to 16 gallons of cream. Each..**$5.60**

## Curtis' Improved Square Box Churn.

No. 16945. Its compactness, durability and efficiency make it very desirable for a dairy of one cow or fifty. It is a great favorite and has been improved in many respects, until it is believed to be absolutely the most perfect box churn to be found anywhere. The cover is of heavy tin and securely fastened. The corners are protected with iron caps and are so constructed that when the buttermilk is drawn out and cleansed it will drain perfectly dry.

| Holds, gallons, | 7 | 10 | 12 | 20 |
|---|---|---|---|---|
| Churns, gallons, | 1 to 3 | 2 to 4 | 2 to 6 | 3 to 9 |
| Price, | $3.50 | 4.05 | 4.35 | 4.80 |
| Holds, gallons, | 26 | 40 | 60 | 80 |
| Churns, gallons, | 4 to 12 | 6 to 20 | 8 to 30 | 10 to 40 |
| Price, | $6.00 | 12.80 | 18.80 | 20.80 |

The three largest sizes are adapted to large dairies. They have a crank on one side, a long gudgeon for pulleys on the other; strong bands and rods running around the churn make them very substantial. Tight and loose pulleys are worth $6 extra.

## Rectangular Churns.

No. 16940. The Rectangular Churn works the easiest and quickest of any churn on the market. At the Dairy Fair, held in Chicago, December, 1878, it received the highest award, a cash premium and diploma in competition with the world. Wisconsin butter won five medals at the Centennial Exhibition at Philadelphia, and four of these were awarded to butter made in the Rectangular Churn.

| No. | Gallons. | Price. | No. | Gallons. | Price. |
|---|---|---|---|---|---|
| 0 | 7 | $3.50 | 3½ | 26 | $ 6.00 |
| 1 | 10 | 4.00 | 4 | 40 | 12.80 |
| 2 | 12 | 4.35 | 5 | 60 | 18.40 |
| 3 | 20 | 4.80 | | | |

## Union Churn.

The Union Churn. You can make, gather, work and salt your butter without removing from the Union Churn, or without touching the butter with your hands. It churns with ease by the extra power and motion gained by gear wheels.

No. 16948. Union Churn, holding 5 gallons. Each.....**$3.20**

No. 16949. Union Churn, holding 7 gallons. Each.....**$3.75**

No. 16950. Union Churn, holding 10 gallons. Each.....**$4.65**

## Improved Cedar Cylinder Churn.

No. 16951. White Cedar Cylinder Churn. We use a double dasher, and the crank is locked to the churn with a clamp and thumb screw, which prevents leakage. Lock cannot break. The top is large, and dasher easily removed. The hoops are galvanized iron, and will not rust. The best churn in use.

| No. | 1 | 2 | 3 | 4 |
|---|---|---|---|---|
| Will hold, gallons, | 3 | 4 | 7 | 10 |
| Will churn, gallons, | 2 | 3 | 4 | 5 |
| Price, | $1.50 | 1.90 | 2.25 | 2.50 |

## Dash Churn.

Common Dash Churns. A long handle goes through the cover at the top, with a dasher at the bottom which is worked up and down inside the churn.

| | Price, each. | Per doz. |
|---|---|---|
| No. 16952. 3 gallon dash churn.... | $0.56 | $6.00 |
| No. 16953. 4 gallon dash churn.... | .70 | 7.56 |
| No. 16954. 5 gallon dash churn.... | .85 | 9.18 |
| No. 16955. 6 gallon dash churn.... | .96 | 10.37 |

## Dash Churns, Striped Cedar, With Brass Hoops.

| | | |
|---|---|---|
| No. 16957. 4 gallons. Price, each.... | **$1.30** |
| No. 16958. 5 gallons. Price, each.... | 1.45 |
| No. 16959. 6 gallons. Price, each.... | 1.59 |

*IF WE FAIL TO PLEASE YOU,*

*It is not because we did not do our best.*

If you will follow our explicit instructions on first pages of catalogue and will use your **GOOD JUDGMENT IN ORDERING, WE CAN RENDER YOU BETTER SERVICE THAN ANY OTHER HOUSE ON EARTH.**

## Reid Butter Workers.

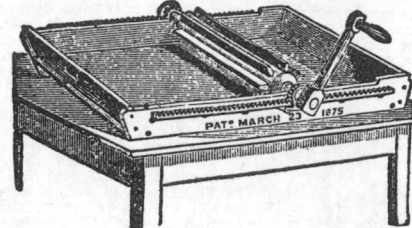

No. 16964. Size, 14x23 inches, to work 8 lbs. of butter. Price, each.................**$3.60**
No. 16965. Size, 17x27 inches, to work 18 lbs. of butter. Price each..................**$4.25**
No. 16966. Size, 20x36 inches, to work 25 lbs of butter. Price, each..................**$4.80**
No. 16967. Size, 23x36 inches, to work 50 lbs. of butter. Price, each..................**$5.75**

## Improved Butter Worker. Dairy Size.

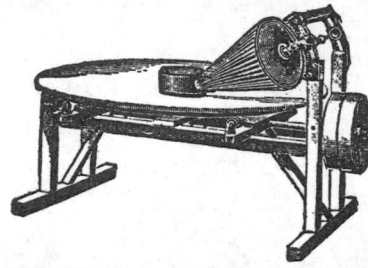

No. 16968. The increase of the use of the small separators in the dairy has created a demand for hand or power workers of smaller capacity than those generally used; we are now prepared to fill orders for them, suitable for farm or dairy use. It is sent out complete, as shown in cut, and can be used with power or by hand; 8-foot table. Price.................**$21.85**

## Lever Butter Workers.

No. 16972. The Lever Butter Worker; its simplicity, saving of time, ease of operation and very low price commend it as an indispensable adjunct to every dairy. No. 0 size, 20 inches wide, works 15 lbs. Each...........**$3.50**
No. 16973. No. 1 size, 30 inches wide, works 25 lbs. Each .............**$4.15**
No. 16974. No. 2 size, 40 inches wide, works 35 lbs. Each.............**$4.85**

## Cottage Butter Workers.

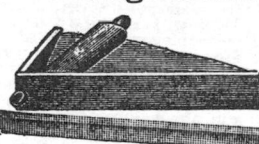

No. 16974. A convenient low priced worker that is placed upon a table when in use. The end is placed over the side of the table, and the drip falls into a vessel upon the floor. For 1 or 2 cows.

Each, $2.50; 2 or 3 cows, $3.00; 4 or 5 cows....**$3.50**

## Tank for Deep Setting Cans.

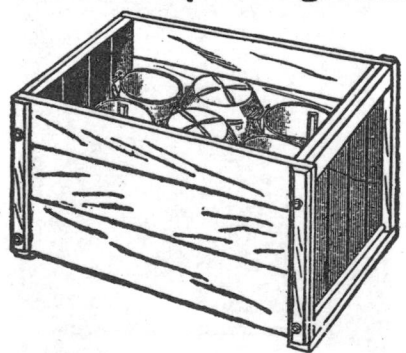

No. 16984. These tanks are made from 2-inch lumber, the ends securely clamped and fastened with rods, and have a hinged cover not shown in cut. It is fitted with an inlet and overflow. Painted both outside and inside. It is made strong and substantial, and will hold Cooley or any deep setting can.

| Size. | Price. | Size. | Price. |
|---|---|---|---|
| To hold 4 cans, | $5.50 | To hold 8 cans, | $7.50 |
| To hold 6 cans, | 6.65 | To hold 10 cans, | 8.45 |

## Boyd's Automatic Cream Vat and Fermenting Can for Farm Use.

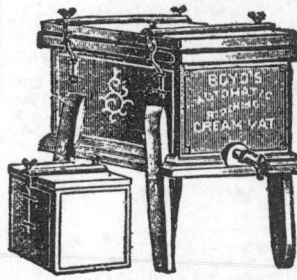

No. 16987. This cut represents Boyd's Automatic Cream Vat, for farm use, and it can truthfully be said that no other known process will produce as much and as good butter from a given amount of cream. It accomplishes for butter making what has never been done before. It enables the butter maker to work to a given rule every day in the year, and produces absolutely uniform results. It does away entirely with the necessity of coddling the cream around the stove. This vat is so constructed that when the cream is put into the vat the temperature of the cream will scarcely vary over three or four degrees in twenty-four hours. It is a perfect refrigerator vat with a cover. Quotations are for ripening vats only. Fermenting cans are quoted separately.

| Size. | Price. | Size. | Price. |
|---|---|---|---|
| 10 gallon vat, | $15.10 | 100 gallon vat, | $35.30 |
| 15 gallon vat, | 17.65 | 150 gallon vat, | 40.35 |
| 20 gallon vat, | 20.10 | 200 gallon vat, | 45.30 |
| 30 gallon vat, | 22.68 | 250 gallon vat, | 50.40 |
| 50 gallon vat, | 25.20 | 300 gallon vat, | 55.45 |
| 75 gallon vat, | 30.25 | 400 gallon vat, | 63.00 |

## Boyd's Automatic Fermenting Can.

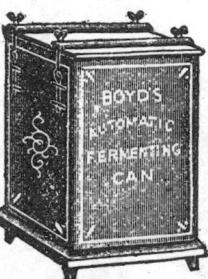

No. 16990. The Boyd process of fermenting is very simple, yet more scientific than appears at first sight. It consists of making a lactive ferment from sweet skimmed milk, divested of its butter fat, taken from a fresh cow or cows. The milk is treated to a warm water bath and brought to a certain required temperature. when it is placed in the fermenting can and the vessel closed tightly. In a given time the lactive ferment is ready for use. A small percentage of this ferment is placed in the cream at a required temperature, and the cream vat is closed in the same manner as the fermenting can. In so many hours the result is ripe cream that is, cream of one chemical condition. The operation is uniform; so also is the result. If the rules are strictly obeyed, the operator is at all seasons master of the situation. He has perfect control over the conditions, consequently his work is all down to rule, nothing being left to chance or good luck. The automatic fermenting can and automatic ripening cream vat are sold only in connection with each other, and are essential to the process.

| | | |
|---|---|---|
| Fermenting cans holding 1 gallon. | Price...... | **$3.80** |
| Fermenting cans holding 2 gallons. | Price...... | 4.20 |
| Fermenting cans holding 3 gallons. | Price...... | 4.65 |
| Fermenting cans holding 4 gallons. | Price...... | 5.10 |
| Fermenting cans holding 5 gallons. | Price...... | 5.50 |
| Fermenting cans holding 6 gallons. | Price...... | 5.90 |
| Fermenting cans holding 8 gallons. | Price...... | 6.35 |

## Small Cream and Cheese Vats. Curtis' Improved Channel.

No. 16992. These vats are made to meet the wants of a large class of dairymen who make up their own milk on the factory or creamery plan. The bottom of this vat inclines toward the center channel or groove, which gradually increases in depth throughout its entire length to the outlet, draining the contents from the vat completely. The channel or groves, being swaged in the bottom tin, stiffen the vat bottom, thus rendering it less liable to move up and down as steam is applied, breaking the joints and causing the vat to leak. The water space underneath the tin vat will be appreciated by everyone who has had any experience in cooling or warming up vats of cream or milk. They are made in a superior manner. Perfection gates are used, and no expense is spared to make them the best vats the dairy public has seen. Price 25-gallon vat, with ice box on end, **$18**; price 50-gallon vat with ice box on end, **$21**. We can quote prices on large vats, same as above, holding from 100 to 800 gallons.

**REFER TO THE INDEX**
When you don't see what you want. Anticipate your wants and order your supplies by freight.

As the recognized leaders in mail order merchandising we are bound to make lower prices than can be obtained elsewhere. Try us once and you will buy in no other way.

## Curtis' Improved Self-Heating Cheese Vats.

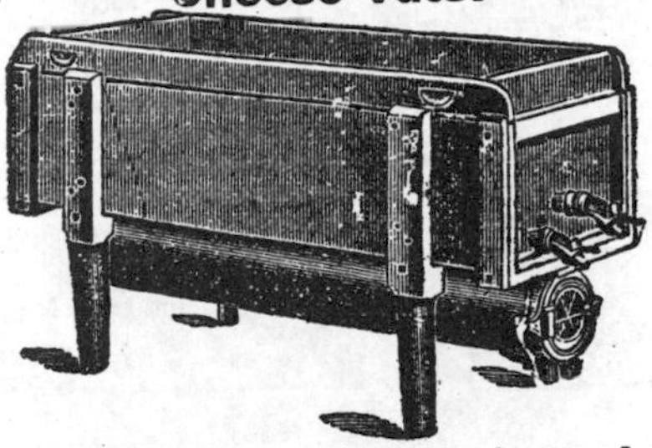

No. 16993. This vat is designed for large and small dairies. It is built same as No. 16992 vat. Price, 25-gallon, **$21.00**; 50-gallon, **$24.50**. We can quote prices on self-heating cheese vats holding from 75 to 600 gallons.

## Family Cheese-Making Apparatus.

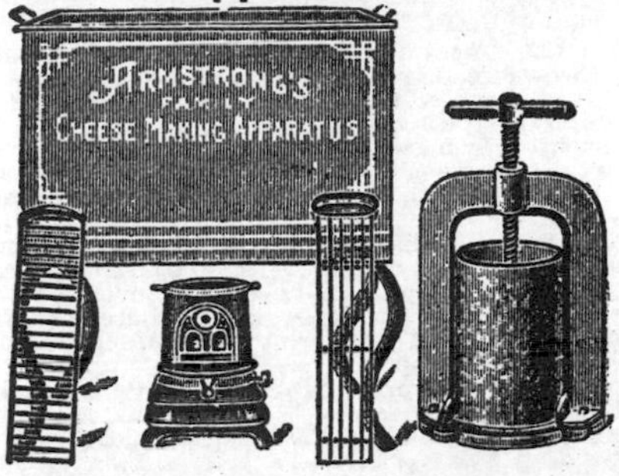


No. 16994. This is a very simple apparatus, adapted to the wants of all farmers or dairymen who keep from 2 to 10 cows, or more. It will make from 2 to 10 lbs. of cheese each operation, according to the quantity of milk; so simple that any boy or girl of average intelligence can learn the process in a very few operations. It makes a perfect cheese each time, whether 2 lbs. or 10 lbs.

You will admit that 2 cows give at least 6 quarts at a milking, making 6 gallons a day. A gallon of milk will make a pound of cheese; 6 gallons make 6 lbs; for 30 days is 180 lbs. of cheese, which at 10 cents per lb. is $18 for 1 month. This is a low wholesale price. The milk is heated by a coal oil lamp, which is easily kept under control. The heating vat is so constructed that the lamp gives all the heat that is necessary. The management of the heat is the secret of success in making good cheese. The entire apparatus is so light in weight that a lady can move it from one place to another with ease. It does not take up quite as much room as an ordinary kitchen table. A lady can make cheese in the kitchen or pantry, and carry on her household work at the same time. With each machine we send simple and full instructions how to make cheese successfully. Each apparatus is complete with heating vat, press, curd knives, lamp, and thermometer, made of good material, strong, and well finished. The apparatus is guaranteed to do the work exactly as represented. We also include sufficient rennet tablets, bandages, and cheese color to make a nice little batch of cheese.

| No. | Holding gals. | Weight lbs. | Price. |
|---|---|---|---|
| 1 | 10 | 100 | $12.00 |
| 2 | 20 | 155 | 20.00 |
| 3 | 30 | 160 | 25.60 |

## Flat Side Curd Pail.

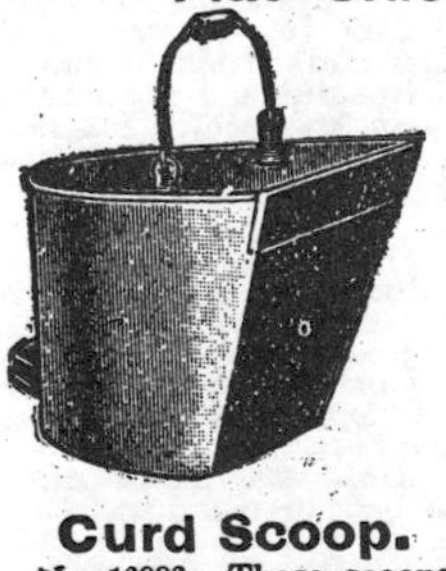

No. 16995. This is a strongly built pail from the best 4X tin used for lifting the curd from the vat. Price, each.....**95c**

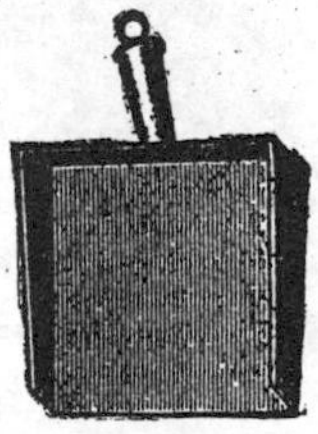

## Curd Scoop.

No. 16996. These scoops are made of heavy tin and all seams and wire carefully soldered. Price, each..................**50c**

## Improved Curd Knives.

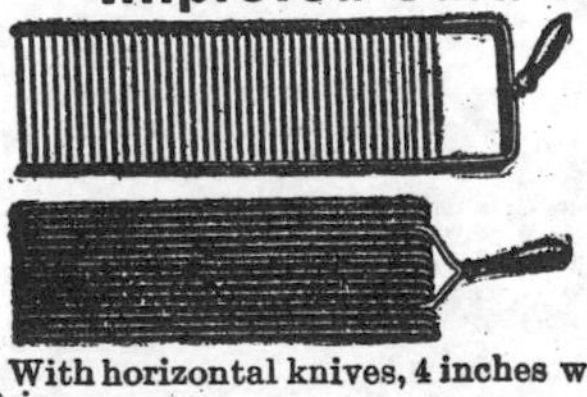

No. 16998. These knives have no wood about them except the handles. The blades are of steel, ground to an edge, and tinned over to prevent rusting.

With horizontal knives, 4 inches wide, 20 inches long. Price..........**$3.75**
With horizontal knives, 6 inches wide, 20 inches long. Price..........**$4.75**
With horizontal knives, 8 inches wide, 20 inches long. Price..........**$5.75**
With horizontal knives, 10 inches wide, 20 inches long. Price..........**$7.00**
With horizontal knives, 12 inches wide, 20 inches long. Price..........**$8.50**
No. 16999. With perpendicular knives, 4 blades, 20 inches long. Price..........**$2.35**
With perpendicular knives, 6 blades, 20 inches long. Price..........**$2.85**
With perpendicular knives, 8 blades, 20 inches long. Price..........**$3.35**
With perpendicular knives, 10 blades, 20 inches long. Price..........**$3.65**
With perpendicular knives, 12 blades, 20 inches long. Price..........**$4.40**
With perpendicular knives, 14 blades, 20 inches long. Price..........**$4.95**
With perpendicular knives, 15 blades, 20 inches long. Price..........**$5.40**
With perpendicular knives, 20 blades, 20 inches long. Price..........**$6.00**

## Standing Press for Cheese.

The illustration shows the method of making a good standing press for cheese factory or private dairy. The construction is so simple that any person familiar with the use of saw and hammer can make it. It consists of a frame, which is supported on legs, and the loose boards on which the hoops stand, and which are grooved to allow the whey to run off. For making a 4-hoop press, as shown, it takes 5 sets of rods and saddles, 4 heavy press screws, and 4 hoops and followers. The rods pass up one side and over the iron saddles, shown on the top of the press, and down on the other. Holes are bored through the top timber to allow the screws to project up through when raised to allow the removal of the hoops. The divisions between the hoops are made of 2-inch plank, and support the upper timber when the screws are raised. The presses can be made any length desired. Explanation: A set of screws consists of 1 screw and 1 washer; a set of rods, saddles, and washers means 1 bent rod, with nuts and washers for fastening same.

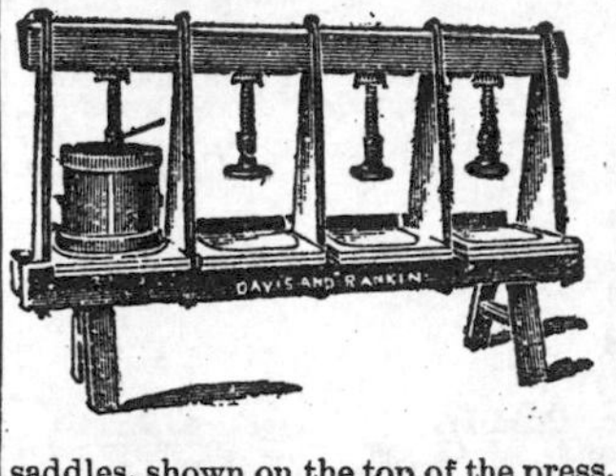


No. 17006. Rods, saddles, and washers. Per set. **$1.50**
No. 17007. Screws, 1¾ by 20 inches long. Per set. **2.75**
Prices quoted on all sizes of hoops and followers.

## Curtis Babcock Farm Tester.

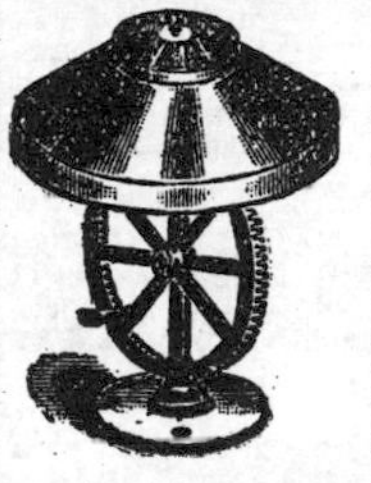

No. 17024. Every dairyman or farmer who keeps a half dozen cows ought to provide himself with one of these milk testers, if he cares the snap of his finger to know whether he has a cow in the herd that is worth keeping. (More than one cow "eats her head off" every year she is kept.) This tester is designed expressly for farm use, and so low a price put on it that every man who owns two cows can have a 4-bottle machine. Price, 4 bottle Tester complete, **$5.00**; 6 bottle Tester, complete, **$6.00**; 8 bottle Tester, complete, **$7.00**. With each machine there is a pipette acid measure, a bottle of acid and directions for operating.

## Babcock Milk Test.

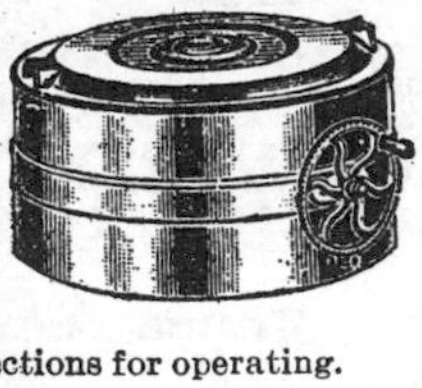

With Roe's Improved swinging heads.

No. 17025. Price 4 bottle Tester, complete, **$8.00**; 8 bottle Tester, complete, **$10.00**; 12 bottle Tester, complete, **$14.00**; 24 bottle Tester, **$21.00**. With each machine is included testing bottles, pipette acid measure and acid for 50 to 200 tests according to size, and full directions for operating.

## Cooley Creamer.

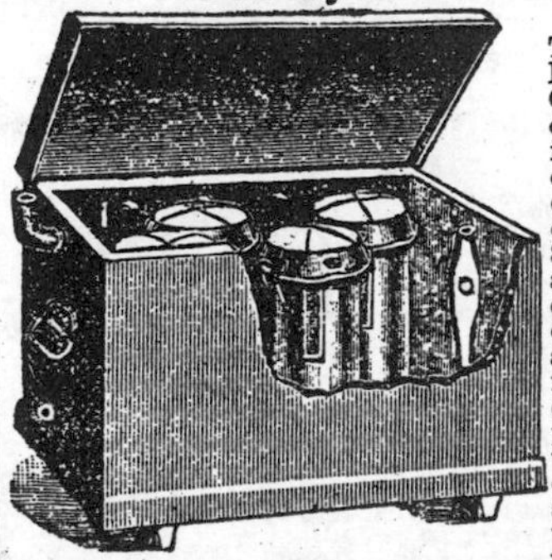

No. 17010. This is an illustration of the Cooley system of setting milk in submerged cans. These cans are 20 inches deep and 8½ inches in diameter; the covers are fastened down, and the air under the rims of the covers prevents the passage of any water into the cans. The cans are set in the water coolers, which are lined with metal and fitted with inlet and overflow for using flowing spring water. A thermometer is inserted in the front of each cooler, in order that the temperature can be ascertained without raising the cover. This apparatus is very simple, dispensing with costly milk rooms, as but little room is required.

If the temperature of the water in the cooler is kept at 45 to 50 degrees in spring and summer, and at 40 degrees or below in winter, the cream will rise in 12 hours, in which time the water is changed three times. No ice is required. By this system of setting milk we have sweet cream from sweet milk, raised in the shortest possible space of time. Prices include cans with bottom faucet and glass panel in the side of can, showing depth of cream.

No. 0, for 1 can, milk of 1 cow, 28 qts. Price..**$15.16**
No. 00, for 2 cans, milk of 2 to 4 cows, 36 qts. Price..........**$21.00**
No. 1, for 3 cans, size 25x32 inches, milk of 6 to 9 cows, 51 qts. Price..........**$23.50**
No. 2, 4 cans, size 28x38 inches, milk of 9 to 12 cows, 68 qts. Price..........**$25.20**
No. 3, for 6 cans, size 28x49 inches, milk of 12 to 18 cows, 102 qts. Price..........**$33.60**
No. 4, for 8 cans, size 28x61 inches, milk of 18 to 24 cows, 136 qts. Price..........**$42.00**
No. 5, for 10 cans, size 28x72 inches, milk of 24 to 30 cows, 170 quarts. Price..........**$50.00**
No. 6, for 12 cans, size 28x84 inches, milk of 30 to 36 cows, 204 quarts. Price..........**$58.80**

In connection with the Cooley Creamer, if Boyd's Automatic Fermenting Can and Automatic Ripening Cream Vat are used, nothing can be more simple for making prime butter every day in the year. It is making butter by rule. No process in the world like it.

## Cream Setter.

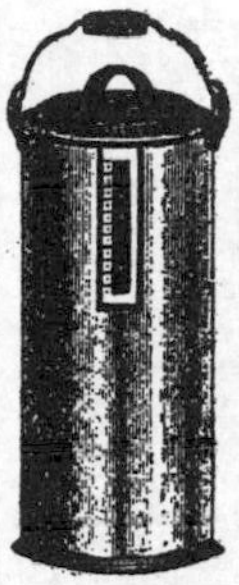

No. 17040. This cream setter has tinned iron bottom, glass panel in graduate case. The glass panel in can is graduated so that if parties are buying cream two degrees will make one pound of butter. Thousands of them are in successful and satisfactory operation. They are easily cleaned and raise as much cream and as quickly as any other cream setting can in the market. The can has a bail on it so that a man can carry two of them at a time. Size, 8¼x20 inches; weight, 4¼ lbs. Price, each..........**60c**
Per doz..........**$6.48**

No. 17041. Cream Setters, same as above, without gauge. Price, each..........**55c**
Per doz..........**$5.95**

For Dairy Thermometers see index.

## Plain Cooley Can.

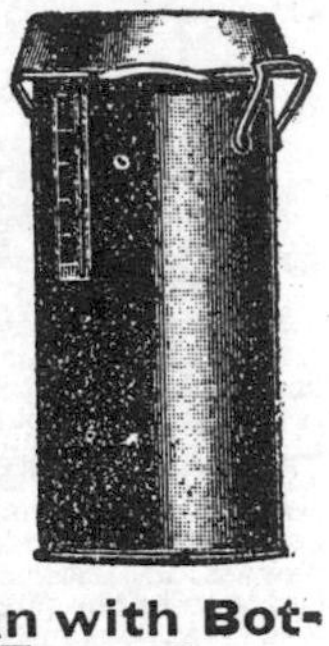

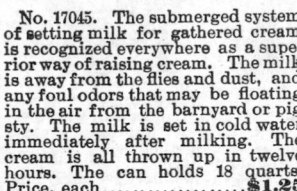

No. 17045. The submerged system of setting milk for gathered cream is recognized everywhere as a superior way of raising cream. The milk is away from the flies and dust, and any foul odors that may be floating in the air from the barnyard or pig sty. The milk is set in cold water immediately after milking. The cream is all thrown up in twelve hours. The can holds 18 quarts. Price, each..........**$1.25**

## Cooley Can with Bottom Faucet.

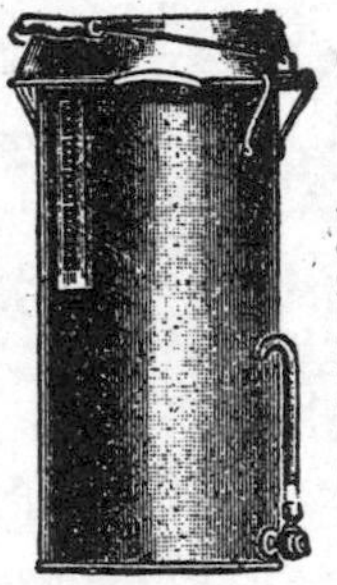

No. 17046. For private dairies this can has no equal. The milk is drawn off through the bottom faucet, leaving the cream in the can to be poured into the cream pail. (We do not furnish bail on can as shown in cut). The value of sweet skim milk over sour milk for feeding purposes will more than pay for the cans every three months. All of the Cooley cans are made from the best tin obtainable. They hold 18 quarts. Price, each..........**$1.75**

## The Common Sense Milk Jar.

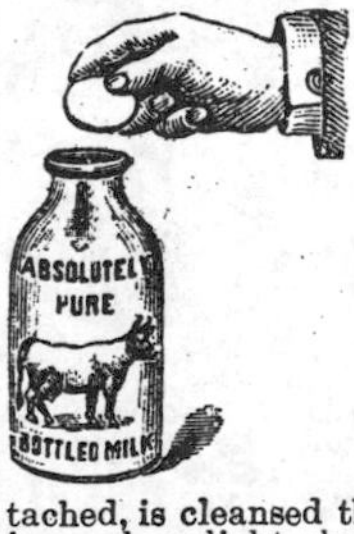


No. 17048. This milk jar is giving the best of satisfaction, as it combines economy of time, labor and expense of materials; it discards the use of glass or metal tops, wire bails or other fastenings which render the ordinary milk jar so difficult to keep clean and in good order, and reduces the cost of manufacture and breakage to the smallest degree possible, and requires no washer; the old style attached cover interferes to a considerable extent with washing the jars; this jar having no cover, either attached or detached, is cleansed thoroughly and with dispatch, having only a slight shoulder within the neck of the jar which serves to hold the cap or cover in position when adjusted, and is all glass without separate parts; the cap or cover is made of heavy wood fibre prepared so as to resist the moisture from within and without, and when pressed into the neck of the jar to the shoulder with the thumb or finger it forms a tightly fitting cover; the operation of capping is quickly and easily accomplished, and when completed is perfectly tight and can be handled in any position and transported without danger of leakage; the disc can be removed when the milk is required for use by inserting the blade of a penknife or any other sharp instrument and lifting the cap out; the cap can again be used and will seal the jar reasonably tight, but their nominal cost allows the dealer to discard them after using them once; large dealers or milk depots can stamp the cap with date, etc., giving the producer a number that will enable them to keep a thorough record of milk, and trace the same to the producer when the milk proves unsatisfactory.

Price, quarts, per doz., **$1.25**; per gross, **$13.50**
Pints, per doz., **$1.00**; per gross.......... **10.80**

No. 17049. Fibre Stoppers for both sizes common

## Instruments for Testing Milk.

**No. 17050.** These instruments are used very largely by factory men to find out who puts the most water in his milk. They are very good detectives. Directions showing how to operate sent with each set.
Price, per set.....................$1.90

## Cheese Factory Milk Cans.

**No. 17060.** Genuine steel.

| Holds gallons, | 15 | 20 | 30 | 40 |
|---|---|---|---|---|
| Price, each, | $3.90 | 4.32 | 4.92 | 5.76 |

### Weighing Cans

**No. 17062.** Made of heavy tin with 3 inch perfection gate and sloping bottom.

| Holds gallons, | 40 | 60 | 80 |
|---|---|---|---|
| Price, each, | $6.00 | 7.20 | 8.40 |

## Milk Cans.

The Improved Breast.     New Seamless Neck.

The illustrations above show the improved breast used on all our milk cans; the most important feature is to make a breast that is proof against being "jammed in." Our heavy half oval hoop accomplishes this; the hoop is forced on the breast in the block, securely fastened and afterwards retinned, which makes it absolutely safe against being knocked off. We have also adopted a new seamless neck on all our cans; this, you will observe, is drawn in one piece. The advantages of the new seamless neck, as compared with the old style bowl and neck in two pieces, are many. There are no seams to come unsoldered, no edges or joints to rust, no bowl to work loose. Adds to weight of your can, being heavier material. Strengthens the weakest part of your can. Is perfectly smooth inside and out.

**No. 17064.** Sturges' or Teet's Pattern Railroad Milk Can, with improved breast and new seamless neck.

| | Weight. | Each. | Per doz. |
|---|---|---|---|
| 8 gallons, | 15½ lbs. | $1.56 | $17.78 |
| 10 gallons, | 17½ lbs. | 1.68 | 19.16 |

**No. 17066.** Elgin Pattern. All steel Railroad Milk Can with improved breast and new seamless neck.

| | Weight. | Each. | Per doz. |
|---|---|---|---|
| 8 gallons, | 18 lbs. | $1.92 | $21.89 |
| 10 gallons, | 22 lbs. | 2.16 | 24.62 |

**No. 17068.** Iowa or Dubuque Pattern Railroad Milk Can, with improved breast and new seamless neck.

| | Weight. | Each. | Per doz. |
|---|---|---|---|
| 8 gallons, | 18 lbs. | $1.50 | $17.10 |
| 10 gallons, | 21 lbs. | 1.62 | 18.47 |

**No. 17070.** Chicago Pattern. All Steel Railroad Milk Can, with improved breast and new seamless neck.

| | Weight. | Each. | Per doz. |
|---|---|---|---|
| 8 gallons, | 18 lbs. | $2.25 | $25.65 |
| 10 gallons, | 22 lbs. | 2.40 | 27.36 |

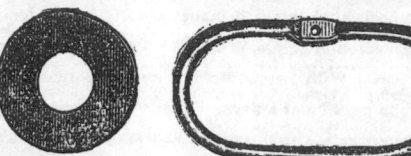

**No. 17078.** Milk Can Links and Washers. We always use this washer to strengthen can and prevent its wearing. We can fit any of our milk cans with link and washer at an additional charge of 5 cents per can.

**No. 17079.** Brass or Copper Milk Can Letters; size 1⅝ inches, soldered onto can at 1½ cents per letter; when ordering state which is desired, otherwise copper letters will be used.

**No. 17080.** The illustration shows ⅝ inch brass faucet fitted to milk can for delivery purposes.

When desired it can be put on any of our cans at an additional cost, "including price of faucet and labor," for.....................$1.50

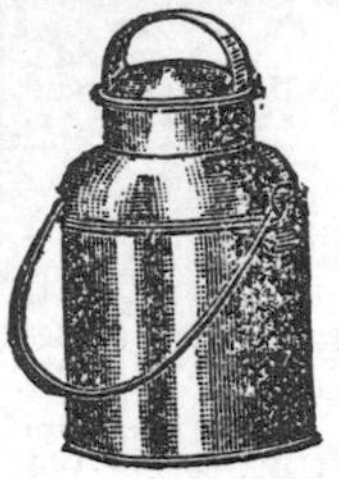

**No. 17085.** Milk or Cream Pails, tin, with bails.

| Quarts | 1 | 2 | 3 | 4 |
|---|---|---|---|---|
| Each, | $0.10 | .13 | .15 | .20 |
| Per doz. | .95 | 1.28 | 1.63 | 1.86 |

**No. 17086.** Milk Peddling Cans. They are made of 4X tin, with heavy brass, hoop on top and bottom, spout tipped with brass; a very strong and serviceable article. Capacity, two gallons. Each....$1.56

**No. 17090.** Milk Measure, graduated, made of good quality tin and holds 1 quart. Each.......8c

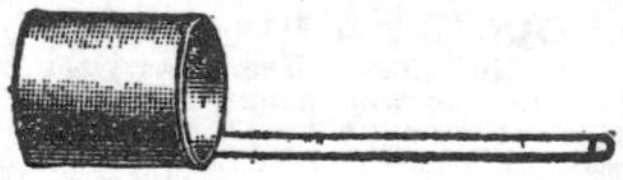

**No. 17092.** Milk Dippers, made of tin, with long handle. Price, each 1 pint, 10c; 1 quart......15c

**No. 17094.** Conical Milk Skimmer, well made of good stock. Each, 8c; per doz.90c

**No. 17095.** Extra heavy 4X tin Milk Dippers; capacity, 1 gallon. Each.................45c

**No. 17099.** Milk Can Strainer. It is made of heavy tin and has a 4 inch brass wire strainer; it will fit a milk can. Cooley, or our regular cream setters. Each.............80c

## Cheese and Butter Triers.

**No. 17072.** Cast steel nickel plated.

| Inches, | 4 | 6 | 12 | 18 | 21 | 24 |
|---|---|---|---|---|---|---|
| Each, | $0.22 | .25 | .35 | .42 | .50 | .55 |

## Fancy Square and Round Butter Molds.

Made from selected maple wood, and every one guaranteed perfect.

| No. | Mold lb. | | Per doz. | Each. |
|---|---|---|---|---|
| 17105 | 2 | Fancy carving, round, | $2.16 | $0.20 |
| 17106 | 2 | Jersey cow, round, | 3.40 | .30 |
| 17107 | 1 | Fancy carving, round, | 1.70 | .13 |
| 17108 | 1 | Jersey cow, round, | 2.85 | .26 |
| 17109 | ½ | Fancy carving, round, | 1.35 | .12 |
| 17110 | ½ | Jersey cow, round, | 2.60 | .22 |
| 17111 | 1 | Fancy carving, square, | 2.85 | .26 |
| 17112 | ½ | Fancy carving, square, | 2.60 | .23 |

| No. | | Per doz. | Each. |
|---|---|---|---|
| 17118 | Individual mold, fancy carving, round, | $0.75 | $0.08 |
| 17119 | Individual mold, fancy carving, with any initial letter, round, | .85 | .10 |
| 17120 | Individual mold, fancy carving, square, | 1.55 | .14 |

## California Butter Molds.

**No. 17122.** This cut represents a very popular mold, and is used very extensively in all parts of the country. Made in 2-lb. size only.
Price, each.............$0.25
Per doz. ... 2.16

## BUTTER MOLD.

**No. 17129.** These celebrated molds are made of selected white wood, and only brass hooks and screws are used throughout, so that there is no possibility of rust and consequent discoloration of the wood. The bottom is prevented from warping by strong wooden cleats, while the sides are grooved sufficiently deep to allow for swelling when in use, and are "lock-cornered" together, thus securing the utmost possible rigidity. One great advantage of these molds over most other patterns on the market is that the prints are released by a single motion and in perfect shape instead of being pushed forcibly through a form by a plunger, which injures the grain.
Price, half pound size, print 5 inches long, 2¾ inches wide, 1¼ inches deep.......................75c
One pound size, print 5 inches long, 4½ inches wide, 1¼ inches deep.......................90c
Two pound size, 10 inches long, 4½ inches wide, 1¼ inches deep.......................$1.20

## Reid's Butter Mold.

**No. 17180.** Fig 1 represents the butter as being in the mold, and the hands of the operator in the act of pressing.

Fig 2 shows the butter molded on the print, ready to be taken and turned on to a tray or elsewhere, when it will show the printed face. With this mold very firm butter may be printed.

Fig 1.

As shown in Fig 1, the operator can not only put his entire weight on the print, but at the same time he may clasp the base with his fingers, thus add the power of the grip; and, further, by giving the print block a rocking motion by pressing alternately with each hand. The mold with the butter in it may be quickly turned the other side up by lifting it with a finger of each hand in the small depressions in ends of box, when the base may be removed and the butter pushed out, as shown in Fig 2.

Fig 2

Price, half pound size, each.... $1.25
One pound size, each.......................1.35
Two pound size, each.......................2.10

## Mrs. Bragg's Butter Fork.

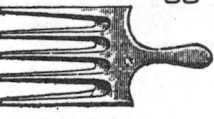

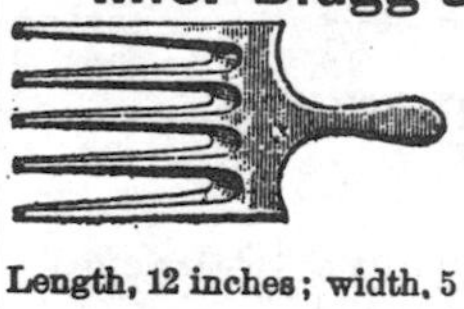

**No. 17186.** A useful and convenient article to remove butter from the churn. In general use throughout the country in creamery and dairy, and considered almost indispensable. Made of hard maple and well finished.
Length, 12 inches; width, 5 inches. Price, each....15c

## Butter Tray.

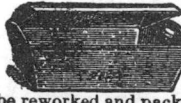

**No. 17138.** The Butter Tray here illustrated is believed to fill the vacant place in nearly every creamery and dairy. It is designed to hold the butter when taken from the churn to be reworked and packed for market. The oval cover, which increases the capacity of the tray one-third, is made to fit tight, to exclude bad air and dust. It is strong and durable.
To hold 20 lbs., price, $1.87; 40 lbs., $2.32; 60 lbs., $2.80; 75 lbs., $3; 125 lbs., $3.65; 175 lbs....$4.65

## Lee's Shipping Box for Print Butter.

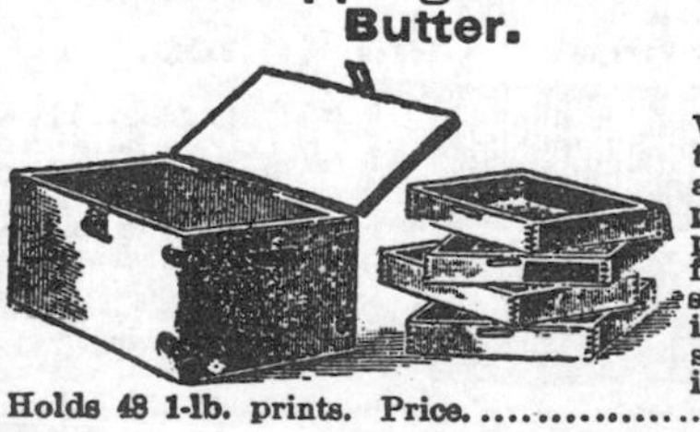

**No. 17144.** We offer the above as a low priced shipping box for large shippers; it is made strong and is durable.
Holds 48 1-lb. prints. Price.....................$1.20

When you need some small articles, you will always find it will pay you to make an order for our fine Groceries, and have

## Curtis' Shipping Box for Print Butter.

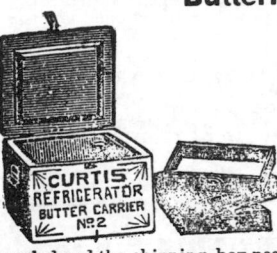

No.17142. This shipping box is made with two dead air spaces around the box, doing away with the can of ice and water in center of the box that causes such a muss when tipped partly over by careless shippers, often injuring the sale of butter. The butter being thoroughly protected, no ice is needed and the shipping box need not be so large and cumbersome. In these days of questionable butter, parties who buy are glad to get it direct from the farmer or creameryman, put up in nice prints. A little attention in this matter secures a good customer the year around. The boxes are made in the most substantial manner, the trays being dovetailed together, and all inside work being of white wood, which is free from taint or smell. Chest handles are put on the ends for convenience in handling. A shipping box will many times pay for itself in three or four shippings. Capacity, 15 lbs., price. **$3.25**; 20 lbs., **$4.20**; 30 lbs., **$5**; 45 lbs., **$6.00**; 60 lbs., **$6.75**; 80 lbs. . . . . **$7.65**

## Wooden Butter Spades and Ladles.

| No. 17146. | No. 17147. | No. 17148. |
| No. 1. | No. 2. | No. 3. |
| 8c each. | 8c each. | 8c each. |
| Per doz....85c | Per doz....85c | Per doz....85c |

## Maple Butter Plates.

No. 17150. Oblong Butter Plates, maple.

| Size. | ½ lb. | 1 lb. |
| Price, per 1,000, | $2.00 | $2.10 |
| Size, | 2 lbs. | 3 lbs. | 5 lbs. |
| Price, per 1,000, | $2.25 | $2.53 | $3.07 |

## Butter Packages.

Bradley Butter Boxes.

No. 17151. 2 lbs., 24 in crate......95c
No. 17152. 3 lbs., 16 in crate......72c
No. 17153. 5 lbs., 12 in crate......69c
No. 17154. 10 lbs., 6 in crate......69c

## Bail Butter Boxes.

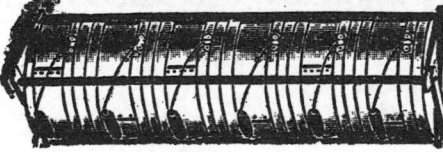

Six boxes in a crate.

No. 17158. 8 lb. bail butter boxes, 50c per crate.
No. 17159. 9 lb. bail butter boxes, 50c per crate.
No. 17160. 10 lb. bail butter boxes, 50c per crate.

## Creamery Butter Tubs.

No. 17161. Butter, Tubs, spruce, 10 lbs. Price......15c
No. 17162. Butter Tubs, spruce, 20 lbs. Price......18c
No. 17163. Butter Tubs, spruce, 30 lbs. Price......22c
No. 17164. Butter Tubs, spruce, 50 lbs. Price......23c

## Ash Butter Tubs.

No. 17172. 60 lbs., 5 hoop. Price......24c
No. 17173. 40 lbs., 4 hoop. Price......22c
No. 17174. 25 lbs., 4 hoop. Price......19½c
No. 17175. 10 lbs., 4 hoop. Price......15c

## Preservaline.

This is the only article that can be used by creameries, dairies, milkmen, farmers, ice cream manufacturers, and all those requiring pure, sweet milk and cream. Preservaline is a harmless substance, which, when added to milk or cream in accordance with directions accompanying each package, will keep milk and cream for weeks in an absolutely perfect and wholesome state in any kind of weather—even through thunder storms—without requiring ice or any refrigerator; absolutely tasteless, odorless, simple and cheap to use; does not affect the flavor or qualities of the milk; for preserving composite samples of milk for test purposes. Preservaline is unsurpassed; if used in the manufacture of butter Preservaline will hold the fine, natural flavor of the butter and prevent it from spoiling; butter put up with Preservaline will never get rancid, and can be held years or exported anywhere. We furnish two kinds of preservaline for the use of creameries and dairies.
No. 17190. BB Preservaline is used to keep milk and cream which is intended to be made into butter and cheese, and for keeping butter and cheese. Price, 1 lb. boxes, **26c**; 5, 10 and 25 lb. boxes, per lb., **23c**; 50 to 100 lbs., per lb . . . . . . **21c**
No. 17191. M Preservaline is used to keep milk and cream for drinking, and which is made into ice cream; also buttermilk. Price, 1 lb. boxes, per lb., **33c**; 5, 10 and 25 lb. boxes, per lb., **30c**; 50 and 100 lb. boxes, per lb . . . . . . **28c**

## Ozaline.

No. 17194. The finest disinfectant for creameries and dairies. Has no smell and gives out none. Removes every offensive smell at once. Positively marvelous in its actions. The only perfect disinfectant for creameries, dairies, stables, pig-pens, outhouses, etc. Cheap and reliable. Prevents flies in creameries. Its use in creameries and dairies is of untold advantage, as it kills all germs in the air, gives off oxygen and thus keeps the air pure, and by this means helps to keep butter, milk and cream sweet. Positively odorless and ever active. Contains no carbolic acid or chloride of lime. In use by hundreds of creameries. A small quantity of Ozaline sprinkled on dung heaps and in manure pits, and on offal in outhouses, and on anything having a bad odor, will remove all smell at once and for good. A great advantage of Ozaline is that it is a valuable fertilizer. If used alone it is equal to the highest grades of fertilizers. It will also prevent chicken lice. Price, in small quantities, **6c** per lb.; in 100 lb. sacks, **5c** per lb.; in 250 lb. sacks, per sack . . . . . . **$10.25**

## Feverine.

A Safe and Sure Cure for Milk Fever.
No. 17196. Dairymen should ever have a bottle of this remedy on hand, and upon the first appearance of the malady follow the directions closely. There is not a dairyman in the country who has not lost valuable cows with milk fever. At last science has come to our aid and given us Feverine, a positive cure and an infallible preventive. Price, per bottle . . . . . . **90c**

## Hansen's Butter Colors, Rennet, Cheese Colors, Etc.

No. 17200. Hansen's Rennet Extract, 1 gallon bottles. Each . . . . . . **$2.00**
No. 17201. Rennet Tablets, per box of 100, No. 1 tablets . . . . . . **$3.75**
No. 17202. Rennet Tablets, per box of 200, No. 2 tablets . . . . . . **$2.00**
No. 17203. Sample boxes, containing 50 No. 2 tablets. Per box . . . . . . **70c**
No. 17204. Sample boxes, containing 24 Rennet Tablets, No. 2 size. Per box . . . . . . **45c**
No. 17205. Hansen's Household Rennet Tablets, for making junket, or curd and whey, 12 tablets in glass. Each, **15c**; per doz. . . . . . . **$1.20**
No. 17206. Bavarian Rennets, dry. Each, **12c**; per doz . . . . . . **$1.20**
No. 17207. Hansen's Cheese Color, 1 gallon bottles. Each . . . . . . **$1.90**
No. 17208. Hansen's Cheese Color 4 oz. sample bottle. Each, **16c**; per doz . . . . . . **$1.90**

## Hansen's Danish Butter Color.

| | Per doz. | Each. |
| No. 17210. 4 oz. bottles | $1.80 | $0.16 |
| No. 17211. 9 oz. bottles | 3.75 | .35 |
| No. 17212. 20 oz bottles | 8.10 | .75 |
| No. 17213. Gallon square jacket cans, | 2.90 | |

## Wells, Richardson's Improved Butter Color.

No. 17214. Large, $1.00 size. Price......75c
No. 17215. Medium, 50c size. Price......37c
No. 17216. Small, 25c size. Price......18c

## Butter Paper.

No. 17228. Waxed Butter Paper, grease proof, 9x12 inches, 480 sheets, **20c**; 12x18 inches, 480 sheets....**40c**

## Parchment Dairy Paper.

Cut in the sizes as quoted and put up in packages of 1,000 sheets.

| No. 17229. Size. | Price, 1,000 sheets. | Price, 5,000 sheets. |
| 12x12, | $1.30 | $6.28 |
| 10x10, | .96 | 4.47 |
| 9x12, | 1.05 | 4.99 |
| 8x11, | .92 | 4.37 |
| 9x9, | .87 | 4.13 |
| 8x8, | .70 | 3.33 |
| 6x6, | .35 | 1.67 |

## Parchment Paper Circles.

No. 17234.

| Diameter. | Price, per 1,000. | Diameter. | Price, per 1,000. |
| 4 inches | $0.30 | 11 inches | $1.88 |
| 5 inches | .40 | 12 inches | 2.22 |
| 6 inches | .53 | 13 inches | 2.58 |
| 7 inches | .72 | 14 inches | 3.00 |
| 8 inches | .97 | 15 inches | 3.45 |
| 9 inches | 1.25 | 16 inches | 3.95 |
| 10 inches | 1.50 | 17 inches | 4.28 |

½ inch sizes between can be furnished at 10 cents per 1,000 extra. Write for our prices on large lots.

## Cloth Circles.

We guarantee count and every one to be a perfect circle.

No. 17238.

| Diameter. | Price, per 1,000. | Diameter. | Price, per 1,000. |
| 4 inches | $0.59 | 11 inches | $3.91 |
| 4½ inches | .70 | 11½ inches | 4.33 |
| 5 inches | .91 | 12 inches | 4.78 |
| 5½ inches | 1.07 | 12½ inches | 4.95 |
| 6 inches | 1.20 | 13 inches | 5.36 |
| 6½ inches | 1.35 | 13½ inches | 5.77 |
| 7 inches | 1.65 | 14 inches | 6.19 |
| 7½ inches | 2.06 | 14½ inches | 6.47 |
| 8 inches | 2.27 | 15 inches | 6.60 |
| 8½ inches | 2.47 | 15½ inches | 7.01 |
| 9 inches | 2.77 | 16 inches | 7.42 |
| 9½ inches | 3.10 | 16½ inches | 7.84 |
| 10 inches | 3.46 | 17 inches | 8.25 |
| 10½ inches | 3.71 | | |

## Butter Cloth, Best Grade.

No. 17239.
28 inch, per piece 120 yards, 3c per yard.
36 inch, per piece 120 yards, 3 1-2c per yard.
42 inch, per piece 120 yards, 3 3-4c per yard.
45 inch, per piece 120 yards, 4c per yard.

## Butter Cloth, Medium Grade.

No. 17240.
36 inch, per piece 120 yards, 3c per yard.
42 inch, per piece 120 yards, 3 1-2c per yard.
45 inch, per piece 120 yards, 3 7-8c per yard.

# SEARS, ROEBUCK & CO.'S AGRICULTURAL IMPLEMENT DEPT.

**THE GROWTH OF OUR AGRICULTURAL IMPLEMENT DEPARTMENT** the past few years has been phenomenal. It has grown until it now ranks among our largest departments. Our sales of agricultural implements of every kind are very great in number and extend into every state and territory in the Union.

**THERE IS NOTHING IN THE LINE OF STRICTLY HIGH GRADE AGRICULTURAL IMPLEMENTS** that we can not furnish and at a saving of from 25 to 50 per cent. in price.

**BIG PROFITS TO MANUFACTURER, WHOLESALER AND RETAILER** have heretofore compelled the farmer to pay two prices for everything in the implement line, and our farmer customers know too well that the excessive prices asked for agricultural implements are responsible for many a mortgage which industrious farmers are laboring under.

**THE OLD SYSTEM OF HANDLING AGRICULTURAL IMPLEMENTS** is very expensive, and works great injury to the farmer. The actual cost of producing an implement seems to have had no bearing whatever on the price that would be finally asked by the retailer. The manufacturers have made enormous profits, often sold to dealers whose credit in many cases was none too good, and in addition to adding their exorbitant profits they have added a large percentage to cover the risk of loss.

The dealer has, as a rule, sold these goods on time, adding a large percentage for risk of loss, also a large profit, and the result has been that even though a farmer paid cash he has paid his proportion of two, three or four exorbitant profits and the percentage of loss calculated by three or four dealers.

**WE CHANGE ALL THIS. BY CONTRACTING WITH THE MANUFACTURERS DIRECT FOR LARGE QUANTITIES AND ON A SPOT CASH BASIS,** we reduce the cost of the agricultural implements we offer to actual cost of material and labor, with only a small manufacturing profit allowed. To this we are not compelled to add anything for loss, for we make no losses. We add simply our one small percentage of profit, ship the goods to you direct from the factory, and as a result our customers can own anything in the agricultural implement line, which we are able to offer at much less than the same goods are sold by the manufacturer to the retail dealer in quantities.

**EVERY IMPLEMENT WE OFFER IS GUARANTEED.** We guarantee every agricultural implement to be exactly as represented, and if not found perfectly satisfactory we will refund your money.

**EVERY IMPLEMENT WE OFFER IS MADE BY A MANUFACTURER OF ESTABLISHED** reputation for only the highest grade goods, and on this class of goods we invite a close comparison of our prices with those of any other house in the land.

**WE WOULD CALL YOUR SPECIAL ATTENTION TO OUR LINE OF PLOWS.** We show a complete line of high grade plows, suitable for all sections of the country, and all classes of soil. No matter where you live we can supply you with a plow that we will guarantee to scour, guarantee to give the best satisfaction, and at a price about one-half that charged by retail dealers.

**WIND MILLS. We have made arrangements with two of the best manufacturers in America,** and are this season able to offer a line of wind mills which we believe are equal to anything on the market at any price, and by a comparison of our prices you can see for yourself the saving to be gained by placing your order in our hands.

**OUR LINE OF GRINDING MILLS CAN NOT BE EXCELLED.**

**WE OFFER THE BEST LINE OF HARROWS THAT** have ever been shown, and our prices can not be met even by any wholesale house.

**TERMS: Our terms are very liberal.** We will send agricultural implements to any address anywhere in the United States by freight, C. O. D., subject to examination on receipt of a sufficient deposit to cover transportation charges both ways. You can examine the goods at your freight depot, and if found perfectly satisfactory and exactly as represented, pay the freight agent our price and freight charges less the amount sent with order.

**DISCOUNT FOR CASH.**

**PLEASE NOTE THAT WE ALLOW A DISCOUNT OF 3 PER CENT.** if cash in full accompanies your order. If you send the full amount of cash with your order you can deduct 3 per cent. from our prices.

**IN COMPARING OUR PRICES WITH THOSE OF ANY OTHER HOUSE** do not overlook this 3 per cent. cash discount. It means a saving to you of 30c on every $10 purchase, and is quite an item when figuring profit on the basis we do, and should be carefully considered when comparing our prices with others.

**ABOUT THE FREIGHT.** You pay the freight, but you will find the freight will amount to next to nothing as compared with what you will save in price. As a rule we give the weight of the different implements under the different descriptions, and by referring to the freight classification in front of book you can calculate very closely what the freight will amount to on any implement. Add the approximated freight to our net cash price, and you will see we are saving you at least 25 to 33⅓ per cent.

**DO NOT HESITATE TO SEND YOUR IMPLEMENT ORDERS TO US.** Don't allow the local dealer to deceive you. He may endeavor to make you believe he offers a better grade of goods, but we will guarantee, we will stake our reputation, such is not the fact. On the contrary, our goods are the best that are made, there is nothing better on the market, and the chances are two to one that notwithstanding the great difference in price in our favor the implements you buy from us will be better than the ones you would buy at home.

**NO MATTER WHAT YOU MAY BE IN THE MARKET FOR, A WIND MILL, HORSEPOWER, SAW, FEED MILL, HARROW, SEEDER, PLOW, CULTIVATOR, HAY RAKE, HAY PRESS, OR OTHER AGRICULTURAL IMPLEMENT,** send us your order and see how much money we can save you. We are more than anxious to receive your orders for agricultural implements, not so much for the little profit there is in them to us, for these goods are sold on the smallest kind of a margin, but for the good it will do us as an advertisement.

**THERE ARE MILLIONS OF DOLLARS INVESTED IN IMPLEMENTS EVERY YEAR,** and the amount of money farmers needlessly throw away in the way of exorbitant profits, as before explained, is enough to go far towards paying off the mortgages resting on thousands of farms. If we could only get one implement sale in each township we know that the purchaser would be so well pleased with the goods received, and the big saving in price would be so apparent, that it would soon become generally known throughout his neighborhood. The result would be that our implement trade would be trebled in volume, and a large part of this money now needlessly thrown away could be saved by the farmers and thus divert the trade into legitimate channels, which would compel manufacturer and dealer to sell on legitimate margins.

**WE REPEAT, DO NOT OVERLOOK THE 3 PER CENT. CASH DISCOUNT WHEN COMPARING OUR PRICES WITH OTHERS. DO NOT OVERLOOK OUR BINDING GUARANTY. DO NOT OVERLOOK** the fact that we guarantee all implements are the highest grade made, and do not wish them compared with inferior goods, which are offered by many.

## Our Celebrated Acme Power Wind Mill.

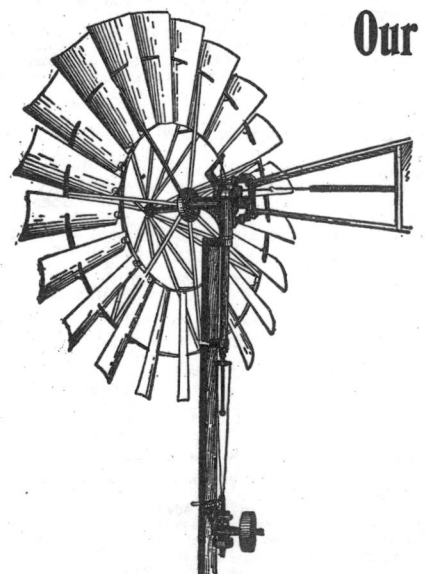

These mills are made for driving machinery, such as shelling, grinding, cutting feed, sawing wood, churning, etc., also for pumping water. We believe we offer the best power wind mill on the market at anything like the price. The prices quoted are for the mills delivered on board the cars at Kalamazoo, Mich., where the mills are made for us under contract, and from which point you must pay the freight. You will find the freight will amount to next to nothing, as compared with what you will save in price.

In the illustration herewith we show the mill, also the gearing and manner in which it is attached to the grinder.

No. 18003. Galvanized steel power mill, with upright shafting, for 50 foot tower; mill 13 feet in diameter. Price, for mill without tower...................$60.00

Our celebrated Acme grinder, for 13 foot steel mill, with foot gear, pulley, and short piece of line shafting, complete, for $16.00. Foot gears, pulley, and short piece of line shafting. Our price................$12.00

No. 18004. Wood wheel, geared, 16 feet in diameter. Our price...............................................$155.00

No. 18005. Wood wheel, geared, wheels 18 feet in diameter. Our price..................................$190.00

The prices of wood wheel wind mills include upright shafting and jack, 5 feet of horizontal shafting and boxes for same, 1 double pulley and 1 single pulley.

| | |
|---|---|
| No. 18006. Pump attachment.............. | $10.00 |
| No. 18007. Horizontal shafting, per foot...... | .25 |
| No. 18008. Pump attachment shafting, per foot | .15 |
| No. 18009. Boxes for horizontal shafting, per set | .60 |

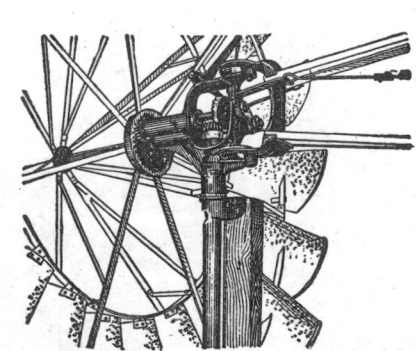

We will be pleased to furnish further information regarding our power mills on application. We are in a position to save you at least 25 per cent. on anything in the line of power mills, and shall be pleased to quote you anything special you may desire. On our power mills the shaft makes 4½ revolutions to 1 revolution of the wheel. The pulley on the grinders is 14 inches in diameter.

If you want more complete information about our mills, write us and we will send specially illustrated pamphlet giving a more detailed description.

## The Celebrated Acme Galvanized Steel Wind Mill at $19.00 to $28.00.

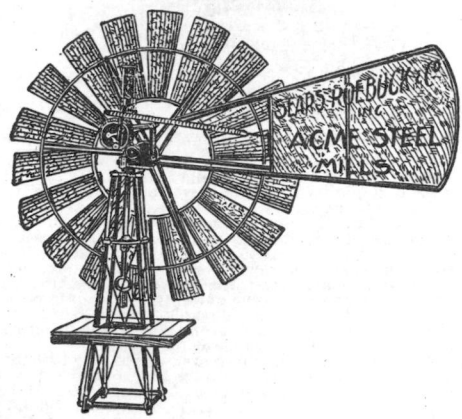

No. 18000. 8-foot mill.............................$19.00
No. 18001. 9-foot mill............................. 25.75
No. 18002. 10-foot mill............................ 28.00

The Acme Steel Mill is the best mill on the market at anything like the price. There are in this mill many points of superiority over any other. Among the most important are the following: The mill is manufactured to do good service and last for years, instead of cheap affairs made only to sell which blow to pieces in the first storm. It has a long spring to govern the mill, which governs much more easily and evenly than a short spring and with less strain. The tension of this spring can be regulated at will to hold the mill in either light or heavy winds as desired. The gearing is fully covered, making it proof against sleet, ice, etc. We use self-oiling brass oiler on pitman, carrying three months' supply of oil, which is too expensive to be put on cheaper mills made to sell at a less price. We have a positive brake which effectually prevents the mill from turning when thrown out of gear. We use ten to twenty pounds more steel in the wheel alone than is used in any other mill; also 10 to 15 pounds more in the vane, making it light and strong. The wheel of this mill makes 2½ revolutions to one stroke of the pump. When thrown in gear it will head to the wind instantly. When thrown out of gear it instantly turns edgeways to the wind and remains perfectly still. Every mill is guaranteed, and can be used either on patent tubular steel tower, angle tower, or wood tower. When ordering be sure to state what kind of tower mill is wanted to be used on.

At our special prices of $19.00, $25.75, and $28.00 we will hope to receive your order. The prices quoted are for the mills delivered on board the cars at Kalamazoo, Mich., from where they are made for us under contract, and from which point you must pay the freight. We will accept any orders for these mills on receipt of sufficient deposit to cover transportation charges both ways. You can examine the mill at your freight depot when received, and if found perfectly satisfactory and exactly as represented, pay the agent our price, less the amount sent with order, and the mill is yours. Three per cent. discount allowed if cash in full accompanies your order.

## Our Solid Wood Wheel $24.00 Wind Mill.

$24.00 is our price when sent by freight C. O. D. subject to examination on receipt of a sufficient deposit to cover freight charges both ways. Such a mill as this was never before offered at anything like the price. The manufacturer has sold these mills to dealers in quantities at 25 and 30 per cent. above the price we offer.

Three per cent. discount allowed if cash in full accompanies your order, in which case $23.58 pays for the mill.

Please note our price for this mill net cash with order is $23.28 when comparing our prices with those of other houses.

Do not buy a wind mill from your local dealer and pay his long profit price when you can get one of the best wind mills made for $23.28.

This illustration, which our artist engraved from a photograph, will give you a slight idea of the appearance of this mill. It is a solid wood wheel with the proper dish to secure strength; maintained by iron rods. To put the mill out of motion the vane is swung around parallel with the wheel which turns the edge to the wind, and it remains firm and motionless.

The main casting is perfect in its design, and all parts are simple and will not get out of order.

We furnish the wind mill complete with long bolts to secure the top of the tower and 40 feet of pump rod. The purchaser makes the material for and erects his own tower, which can be done by any good carpenter in a short time at from $10.00 to $15.00. We furnish printed instructions for the erection, by means of which any one can put it up. These instructions are very complete, giving full description of the work from beginning to end. The mill is so simple that no one could possibly have any trouble in putting it in working order.

This is the best mill made for a simple pumping mill, or to grind feed by means of a shaft or power connected to pumping rod.

No. 18010. Price for this mill complete with 10-foot wheel.....................................$24.00
No. 18011. 12-foot wheel........................... 30.00
No. 18012. Price for tower for 10-foot wheel, per foot...................................................40c
No. 18013. Price for tower for 12-foot wheel, per foot...................................................50c

The shipping weight of this mill is 575 lbs. You will find the freight will amount to next to nothing as compared with what you will save in price.

## Sears, Roebuck & Co.'s Royal Grinder Wind Mill for $23.00.

$23.00 is our regular price when sent by freight C. O. D., subject to examination on receipt of the necessary deposit.

Three per cent. discount allowed if cash in full accompanies your order, in which case $22.30 pays for the mill. In comparing our prices with those of other houses, please note our 3 per cent. cash discount.

An all steel mill, the best steel wind mill ever offered at anything like the price.

The manufacturer of this mill has been building wind mills for the last twenty years, and his experience has enabled him to build a steel wind mill which is second to none and superior to many, a mill embodying new patents, new and valuable features not found in other mills. The six sections of this mill when bolted together and strongly braced in front as shown in the illustration, make a very rigid, strong and safe wheel. The wheel shaft having its two bearings 8 inches apart in the drive pinion just inside the outer bearing, is extremely well arranged for effective work and durability. An effectual brake is applied as the mill is pulled out which absolutely holds the wheel still against weather and wind. The vane is a single sheet of steel riveted to a bow shaped bar of angle steel, the two ends hinging on the pivot casting. The construction of the wheel, which is all steel, is such as to give the mill a light, airy appearance, yet make it strong and most substantial.

The arms, double bolted to the spider casting, are made from angle steel, being the strongest possible form for the weight of the material employed. The outer girths are made of channel steel bent on a circle. They are so shaped as to form a bearing the full width of the sail, thus strengthening the same and holding its curved form securely.

We guarantee this mill to stand the test of all kinds of weather and to equal in power any other mill of a similar size. It is put together in the most substantial manner, nicely painted throughout by hand, and fully guaranteed. The mill complete weighs about 300 lbs.
No. 18014. 8-foot steel mill. Our price........$23.00
No. 18015. 9-foot steel mill. Our price........ 26.00
For Tower. With this mill we furnish any angle steel tower at 60c per foot. Anchor posts, per set of four.................................................$3.00
In ordering the mill be sure to order a tower of the height wanted. The price is 60c per foot.
We believe we offer you a first-class mill which, when put up with one of our very best steel towers, will mean a saving to you of from $15.00 to $25.00.

## The Celebrated Acme Wind Mill Grinders for $18.00.

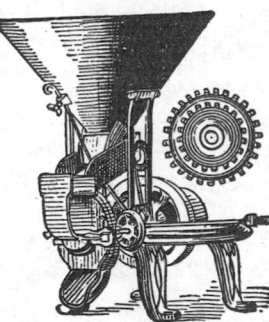

The illustration shows this mill with the pulley attachment and the smaller illustration shows the sprocket wheel attachment. The sprocket grinder was gotten up especially for chain wind mills and is adapted to 12 to 14 feet geared wheels. It is furnished with a double sprocket wheel by which the speed of the mill can be changed to correspond with the speed of the wind mill. The sprocket wheels are 6 and 10 inches in diameter fitted with link chain and belting. We can also furnish the link belting and driving sprocket with spring clutch complete for line shaft on wind mill, which taken together makes a complete outfit at a very reasonable price. Capacity, 8 to 15 bushels per hour according to the velocity of the wind and size of wheel used. In ordering this kind of a mill be sure to give the diameter of the line shaft if driving sprocket and spring clutch are wanted.

The pulley grinder is similar in all respects to the sprocket grinder as described above, only it is furnished with a 6 or 9 inch pulley with a 6 inch face. Both of these mills have adjustable slots in the standard or legs whereby the belt or chain can be tightened without being taken off, which is a great advantage. Both these mills are shipped with right hand burrs unless otherwise ordered.

## ACME WIND MILL GRINDERS—Cont.

No. 18016.
Price, 3 sets 6 inch burs.........................$18.00
Price of 6-inch burrs, per set..................... 1.00
Price of 20 feet of link chain belting.............. 5.00
Price for 6 and 10 inch double driving sprocket with spring clutch complete with line shaft for wind mill................................................ 3.00

## Our $12.75 Pumping Wind Mill Attachment.

No. 18017. This attachment is used very largely for churning.

The above illustration represents a device for transmitting the perpendicular motion of a pumping wind mill to a rotary. By using the same device that operates our wind mill grinder we are able to get a continuous forward motion. By the use of a heavy balance wheel we are able to produce a rotary power driven by the perpendicular stroke of the pumping wind mill. For driving light machinery, like churning, turning a

## PUMPING WIND MILL ATTACHMENT—Continued.

grindstone, shelling corn, this machine will be found very useful. Size of pulley, 12½ inches, 2½ inch face; size of balance wheel, 28 inches. Full instructions for setting up are furnished with each machine.
Price............................................$13.00

## Pumping Jacks.

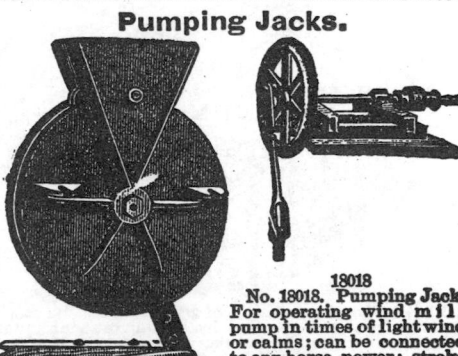

18018
18019

No. 18018. Pumping Jack. For operating wind mill pump in times of light wind or calms; can be connected to any horse power; stroke 4 to 16 inches; balance wheel, 300 pounds, complete. Jack weight, 600 lbs.
Price..............................$18.00

No. 18019. Our $10.00 Wind Mill Grinder. We furnish an elbow to connect this mill to the pump rod. Adapted to a large farm with 50 head of cattle. Weight, 75 lbs.
Price.....................................$10.00
No. 18020. Tallerdey Automatic Wind Mill Regulator. Weight, 50 lbs. Price.........................$4.00

## Big Giant Improved Grinding Mills.

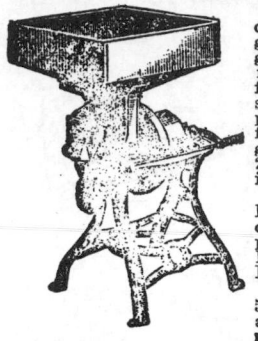

A mill with the greatest capacity and most even grinding of all kinds of grain ever offered to the farmer. Automatic in feeding, simple in construction, scientific in principle, looked upon by feeders as the gem of all grinders; requires from 2 to 10 horse power, according to size and speed.

No. 18020½. The No. 1 size Belt Mill; 5¾ inch burrs; capacity, 10 to 20 bushels per hour; weight, 175 lbs.
Price of mill .... **$20.75**
Extra burrs, set.. 1.00

No. 18021. The No. 2 size, 5¾ inch burrs, geared for attachment to tumbling rod; capacity, 10 to 20 bushels per hour; weight, 225 lbs.
Price of mill ................................ **$23.75**
Extra burrs, per set .................. 1.25

No. 18021½. The No. 3 size Belt Mill, 7¼ inch burrs; weight, 200 lbs; capacity, 20 to 30 bushels per hour.
Price of mill ................................ **$30.00**
Extra burrs, per set .................. 1.25

No. 18022. The No. 4 size, geared for attaching to tumbling rod; 7¼ inch burrs; capacity, 20 to 30 bushels per hour; weight, 225 lbs.
Price of mill ................................ **$32.75**
Extra burrs, per set .................. 1.25

No. 18022½. No. 5 Double Mill, has just double the capacity of No. 3 belt mill; 2 sets of 7¼ inch burrs in operation at one time, 1 on each end of shaft; weight, 300 lbs.
Price of mill ................................ **$45.50**
Extra burrs, per pair .................. 1.25

Nos. 2 and 4 have 12 inch pulley to connect with corn sheller; 3 sets burrs furnished with each of above mills.

## The Kelly Duplex Mill.

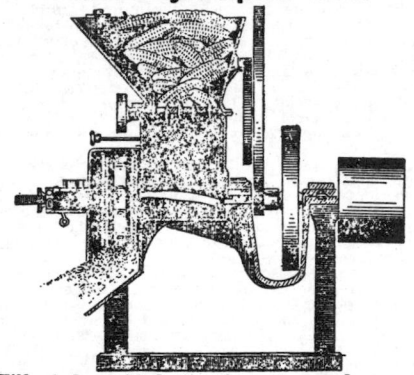

Will grind any kind of grain, cotton seed, corn and cob and corn with shucks on equally well and in grist of any quality. Will grind meal with an evenness that no other mill can approach, and in the hands of an ordinary operator will do more work better and easier than any other mill made.

This mill is a general favorite and is well known all over the country.

| No. 18023. | Approximate Weight, lbs. | Horse Power. | Price. |
|---|---|---|---|
| No. 1 | 320 | 4 to 6 | **$32.00** |
| No. 2 | 500 | 6 to 8 | **41.00** |
| No. 3 | 550 | 8 to 10 | **45.00** |
| No. 4 | 750 | 10 to 15 | **65.50** |

## The Genuine Monarch Corn and Cob Mill.

No. 18023½. The question of grinding food for stock has been practically settled by the almost unanimous adoption of ground feed among our largest stock raisers and most successful farmers; the one important point now seems to be to secure the best mill for the purpose, the mill that will grind the largest quantity with the least power, the most durable and the least complicated—one that will grind corn and cob, shelled corn, oats and other small grain, and also make family meal. We have no hesitation in saying we have that mill. Our mills have met with a success far exceeding our most sanguine expectations.
Weight, 540 pounds. Price ................ **$18.75**
Extra burrs, per pair ..................... 3.90

## Our New Improved Acme Sweep Grinder for $19.00.

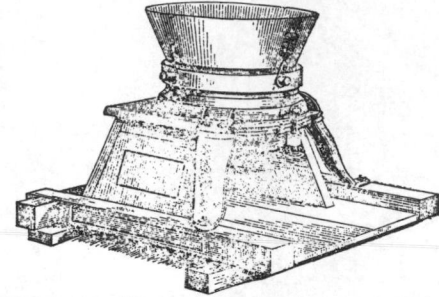

This is one of the best grinders on the market. Grinds ear corn, new or dry, shelled corn alone or mixed with other grain for chopped feed, oats, etc., and is so arranged that the interior parts of the mill revolve with the revolutions of the team. The power is applied directly to the grinding parts, thereby making the draught very light.

Our grinder rings or burrs have a peculiar dress by means of which the broken pieces of cob and hull grains are gradually reduced to the fineness desired, so that we produce a better quality of feed with less work to the team. We make two sets of grinding rings, one for coarse and one for fine grain. The capacity for fine grains is: Corn in the ear, 12 bushels of feed per hour. Shelled corn, 15 bushels of feed per hour. Corn and oats (chopped feed), 10 bushels of feed per hour. To grind very fine the amount will of course be reduced. With coarse plates the mill can grind: Shelled corn, 15 to 20 bushels of feed per hour. This mill is warranted not to choke on new or old corn, wet or dry. A perfect sweep mill of large capacity.
No. 18024. Price of mill complete, with one set of plates ................................................ **$19.00**
Extra grinders, additional .................... 2.50

## Our $3.65 Grist Mill.

To any one who has use for a hand mill this machine will pay for itself a dozen times over in a single season.

This machine is well adapted for grinding corn meal, hominy, split peas, cracked wheat, Graham flour, fine table or butter salt; in fact, everything that is ground at a custom mill, except fine bolted family flour. In these mills the grinding plates are removable, and can be changed in a moment's time. They are of the hardest cast steel. This hand mill will grind just as much in proportion to its grinding surface as any larger mill, ½ lb. to 1 lb. per minute being the average, according to the grain and fineness. We warrant these mills to be equal to any of the same size made. Weight, 36 lbs.
Price ............................................ **$3.65**
No. 18024½. Extra burrs, per pair ........... .60

## Our Acme Overhead One Horse Power for $18.00.

No. 18025. **$18.00** is the price when sent by freight

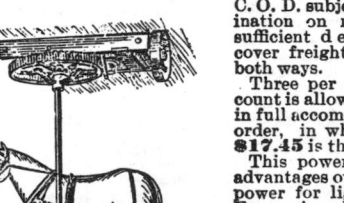

C. O. D. subject to examination on receipt of a sufficient deposit to cover freight charges both ways.

Three per cent. discount is allowed if cash in full accompanies your order, in which case **$17.45** is the price.

This power has many advantages over a down power for light work. For use in a barn where several horses are kept or in small livery stables it is excellently adapted. When not in use the center shaft can be set one side. When it is desired to run, set the shaft in place, hitch the horse to the power and go ahead. No jack is required with this power. Length of sweep levers is 8 feet. The horse makes therefore a circle of 16 feet. The upright shaft is wood and can be cut off to suit the height from floor to ceiling. The height of stake as furnished is 10 feet. This power makes about 125 revolutions per minute. Unlike any other sweep power, the tumbling rod is overhead and the gear out of the way of snow in winter and mud and dust in summer. Weight, 400 lbs. Price of power complete ................................ **$18.00**

## The Genuine Carey Pitts Horse Power for $46.50.

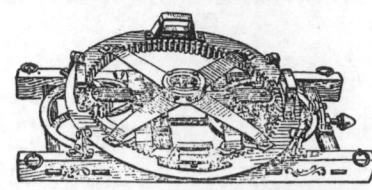

The Pitts horse power as illustrated above is too well known to require much comment from us. It is made of the best quality air seasoned white ash, charcoal iron gears, the frame is of steel and the gear is heavier than in any other power of the same horse power made. The weight is so distributed as to give the greatest possible strength. This power is especially adapted for farm work, such as wood sawing, cider making, etc. The height of the main gear wheel is 4 feet. Measurement across power from one end of sweep to end of opposite sweep, 24 inches. Number of revolutions, 50 to one turn of the wheels. Two sweeps, one 16 foot tumbling rod and a 24 inch pulley go with each power.

Please remember that this power weighs only 1,150 lbs., hence we do not recommend it for the work of a 6 or 8 horse power which should weigh from 1,500 to 2,000 lbs.
No. 18025½. Price ............................ **$46.50**

We can furnish horse powers of any size and will be glad to quote special prices on special sizes upon application.

## Our $95.00 Tread Power.

We offer these tread powers to the public with entire confidence in their being superior to any other line of treads ever manufactured. This power is made upon purely scientific principles and is constructed of the very best materials. The rods are of best Bessemer steel, the trucks are bored to a perfect fit and have the end center guide instead of pressing against the rim of the truck. Our end circles are large, allowing the roller to pass without any jerking or back lashing motion. The rear circle is adjustable to take up wheel. Full directions for operating this tread accompany every machine.
No. 18026. One horse, weight 1,200 lbs., with governor ................................................ **$ 95.00**
No. 18026½. Two horse power, 2,000 lbs., price **115.00**
No. 18027. Three horse power with governor, weight 2,400 lbs ................................. **130.00**

## Speeding Jacks.

No. 18028. Bevel Jacks used only in connection with a horse power to increase the speed. Is connected to end of tumbling rod and transmits motion in the same direction. Furnished with 15-inch pulley, made in one size, for 2 or 4 horse power only; weight, 100 lbs.
Price ........................................... **$9.00**

## Spur Jack.

No. 18029. Spur Jack; transmits motion at right angles to the tumbling rod to which it is attached, for 2 or 4 horse power only; weight, 100 lbs.
Price ........................................ **$9.00**

## Bevel Jack.

No. 18030. Bevel Speeding Jack for 4 to 8 horse power, iron frame, bearings all on one casting, a strong, durable Jack furnished with slip knuckle; particularly recommended for 4 to 8 horses; geared 2¾ to one turn of tumbling rod; any size pulley furnished up to 24 inches; state size of hole in coupling wanted; this jack adapted to our Carey Pitts power; weight, 185 lbs.
Price ........................................ **$12.00**

## Can't You Find What You Want?

Look in the INDEX; it's there.

## We Are Headquarters for Engines and Boilers.

**The past year has developed such inquiry from farmers, mechanics, manufacturers, and others** for medium low priced boilers that we have set about to make satisfactory arrangements—in fact, such arrangements as will enable us to meet this demand, and at a saving to our customers of the profit of the retail dealer and a portion of the profit of the manufacturer.

That we can save you this profit our prices and descriptions we feel sure will clearly demonstrate.

**The engines and boilers that we handle are made by one of the largest and most reliable manufacturers in this state, and are guaranteed in every respect.** If not found exactly as represented, we will pay the freight both ways and cheerfully refund your money.

**The prices are net cash. There is no discount whatever from the prices quoted on these goods.** We have succeeded in getting the manufacturer down in price to practically the cost of material and labor and to this we have added but a few dollars on each outfit for ourselves and can not give a percentage of discount for cash without depriving us of all our profit.

We are prepared to furnish almost any kind and any size of engines or boilers, and will be very glad to quote special prices on application.

## Our $125.00 Two-Horse Power Engine and Boiler.

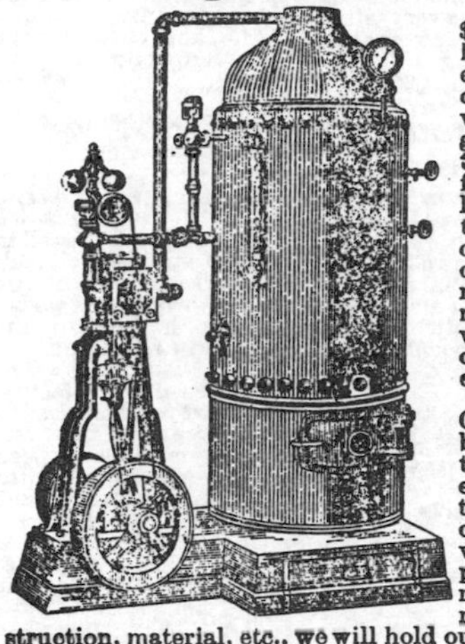

We offer for $125.00 a 2-horse power boiler and engine complete, which we believe is greater value than has ever before been sold at less than $160.00 to $175.00. It is one of the best outfits that are made and should not be compared with a cheap class of machinery.

A Binding Guarantee. A binding guarantee goes with every outfit by the terms and conditions of which if any piece or part is not perfect in mechanical construction, material, etc., we will hold ourselves responsible to make the deficiency good.

The above illustration of our 2-horse power boiler and engine is engraved direct from a photograph. In comparison with many motors seeking recognition at the hands of the public our Acme engine and boiler occupies a position far in advance. An examination into its construction will convince any reasonable person that it is the lowest priced good medium power on the market, the best small engine now offered. The engine is constructed on exactly the same principle as the larger engines we build, except that the cylinder of steam chest and crank shaft bearings are all made of one solid piece, hence can not get loose or out of line.

No. 18031. Our special net spot cash with order price for the engine and boiler complete is .........**$125.00**

## Our $135.00 Four-Horse Power Boiler and Engine Combined.

We furnish a 4-horse power boiler and engine combined for $135.00, and larger engines up to 10-horse power boiler and engine for $235.00. The above prices are net spot cash with order, and we believe are fully 25 to 30 per cent. lower than any other on the market.

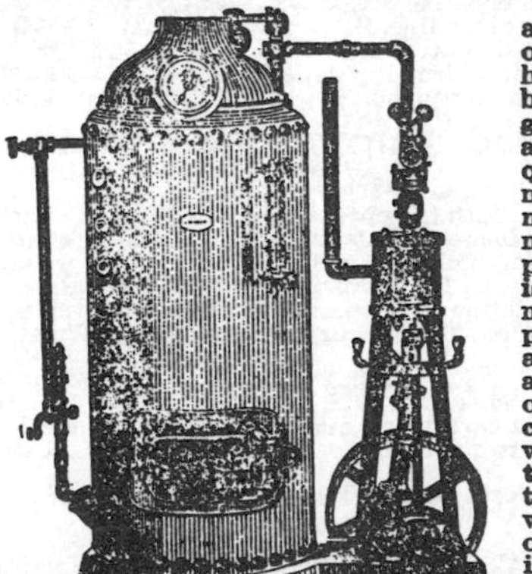

The above is an illustration of our 4-horse power boiler and engine which we are able to quote at $135.00 net cash. To meet the demand for a plain, well finished, reliable, moderate priced boiler and engine we are able to offer our trade a combination which fulfills these conditions, and which we call our Acme. It is made in four sizes, 4, 6, 8 and 10 horse power, and at the price includes all the attachments that go with the boiler and engine, including even an injector for feeding the boiler, pipe connections for same with valves. The price at which we are offering this is lower than any boiler and engine of equally good quality has ever been offered before. The boilers we offer are made of homogenous plate steel, 60 thousand lbs. tensile strength to the square inch, with best lap welded wrought iron flues, and include the following fittings; safety valve, blow off valve, steam gauge, water gauge and three compression gauge cocks, injector fitted to boiler with pipes and valves. The shells of these boilers are made of ¼ inch steel, fire box of 5-16th inch steel, heads ⅜ inch steel. The engines furnished with this combination are center crank engines of the very best grade and are guaranteed in every respect.

| | | | | | | |
|---|---|---|---|---|---|---|
| Weight of | 4 H. P. outfit, | 1000 lbs. | Height, | 5 ft. | 6 in. |
| " | 6 " " | 1350 " | " | 6 " | 4 " |
| " | 8 " " | 1650 " | " | 6 " | 4 " |
| " | 10 " " | 1850 " | " | 7 " | 10 " |

No. 18032. Price of 4 horse power engine and 4 horse power boiler on combination base............**$135.00**

No. 18033. Price of 4 horse power engine and 6 horse power boiler on combination base............**$155.00**

No. 18034. Price of 4 horse power engine and 8 horse power boiler on combination base............**$170.00**

No. 18035. Price of 4 horse power engine and 10 horse power boiler on combination base............**$180.00**

No. 18036. Price of 6 horse power engine and 6 horse power boiler on combination base............**$175.00**

No. 18037. Price of 6 horse power engine and 8 horse power boiler.......................................**$190.00**

No. 18038. Price of 6 horse power engine and 10 horse power boiler on combination base............**$200.00**

No. 18039. Price of 8 horse power engine and 8 horse power boiler on combination base............**$200.00**

No. 18040. Price of 8 horse power engine and 10 horse power boiler on combination base............**$220.00**

No. 18041. Price of 10 horse power engine and 10 horse power boiler on combination base.......**$235.00**

**Further information concerning the engine above illustrated** and described will be cheerfully furnished on application, and we would again state that we can furnish any size boiler and any size engine, or will be pleased to submit prices on anything special on application. We feel perfectly safe in assuring our customers of a saving of from 25 to 50 per cent. on anything in this line.

## Hay Presses.

**We are headquarters for Hay Presses,** and have arranged with one of the **largest and most reliable manufacturers in this country,** a concern located at **Ann Arbor, Mich.,** who, we believe, make more presses than all other manufacturers combined, and the reputation they have gained for the manufacture of **the best hay presses on the market** has warranted us in making our contracts with them.

**Limited space prevents our giving a lengthy and detailed** description of these machines; but we shall be pleased to furnish any special information desired upon application, and we would say before you buy a hay press elsewhere communicate with us.

**Whether you finally buy from us or not,** we believe we can be the means of saving you from **$25.00 to $75.00 on your machine.**

## Our $195.00 Half Circle Baler.

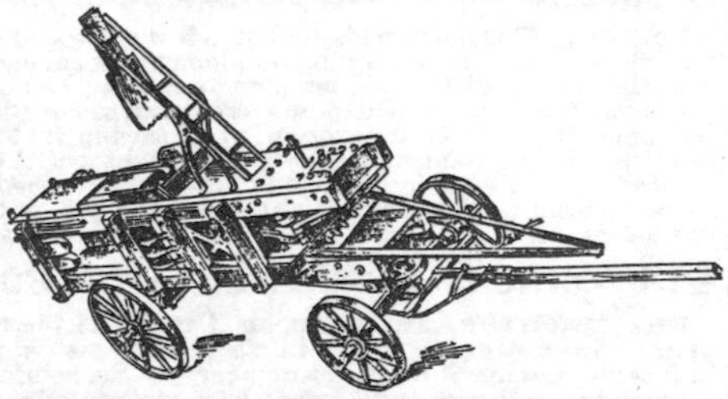

No. 18042. **We furnish this machine at $195.00 net cash with order,** and guarantee it to be exactly as represented and the best press ever made at the price. If it is not found as represented you can return it and we will refund your money. For more particulars concerning this machine, or for larger sized balers, communicate with us.

The principle of power used in this machine is nearly the same as that in the full circle presses, and is just as effective. Two horses can do the work easily on a 4 foot sweep. The leverage increases in proportion as the pressure increases. It is simple in construction, having but few parts. Not a link, chain or pulley. Nothing but a crank, pitman and lever. It is made as strong and substantial as any machine on the market. The frame is of the very best seasoned hard wood and is well bolted together with Norway iron bolts. The castings are very heavy. The bale chamber is lined with the very finest Bessemer steel. It is otherwise the same in construction as that of the steam and full circle presses. The tension rods are similar to those in all our presses. Size 17x22. **Our price, $195.00 net cash with order.**

Other sizes made to order.

## Our $225.00 Advance Full Circle Baler.

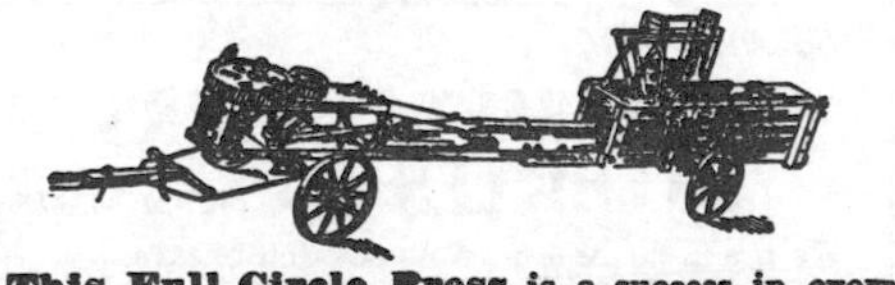

**This Full Circle Press** is a success in every respect. It has been in use for the past three years and we have not heard a complaint from them, nor have we had a call for repairs. It is what every man wants in a baler, large capacity, light draught, simple construction, durability, ease and safety, and is easily transported. It is well constructed of the best seasoned hardwood, Norway iron and Bessemer steel. Its power is centered and accumulated. As the pressure of the hay increases the fulcrum of the lever moves towards the center, thus increasing the power in proportion as the pressure increases. Two horses can do the work easily and make heavy bales. The plunger is all Norway iron. Two 12-foot sweeps. Bale chamber is lined with the best Bessemer steel. Two feeds to each round of the horse. Bale indicator. Chaff grate in bottom of bale box. Large feed table, wrench, and everything complete. In this machine as in any other the capacity depends upon the men and horses doing the work. Actual results vary from 10 to 15 tons per day. We make this press in two sizes.

No. 18043. Size 17x20, price.........................**$225.00**
No. 18044. Size 17x22, price.........................**240.00**

## Our $235.00 Belt Power Hay Press.

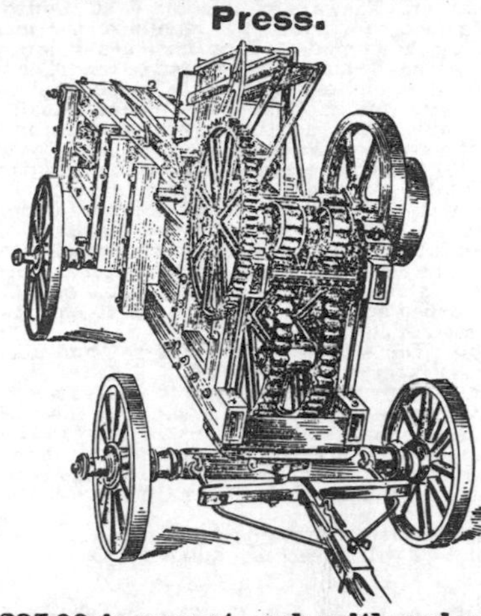

**$235.00 is our net cash with order price,** the price from which there is no discount to any one under any circumstances. The price quoted is for the hay press delivered on board the cars at Ann Arbor, Mich., from which point you must pay the freight. We can offer no discount for cash. For a more complete description of this hay press please correspond with us. We know we are headquarters on this line of goods and can save you so much money that you can not afford to buy elsewhere.

The power of this press is the most simple and direct that can be adopted. It consists of two crank wheels between which a pitman is pivoted and connected direct to the plunger block. It is driven by two pinions on an intermediate shaft to which the belt and balance wheel are geared, thus securing rapid momentum to the balance wheel and requiring but a small, light belt. Steady motion and power are obtained by the momentum of the balance wheel, the balance wheel being secured by friction so that if the belt is overcharged or abused the wheel will slip and avoid accident or breakage.

The castings are made of the best iron we can buy, thus securing strength. The frame is entirely of hardwood, which, as every press man knows, is better than iron. Heavy ¾ and ⅞ inch rods put through the frame both ways hold it together. A wooden frame is preferable to iron or steel because for the same strength hard wood is lighter than iron, and also because it is impossible to keep bolts tight on an iron or steel frame, as there is no give to these metals, and bolts furthermore are liable to be cut in two in a heavy metal hay press. The shafting is of heavy 2¼ and 3⅞ inch cold rolled iron, and very tough iron. The boxes are strongly babbeted, well bolted to frame and double nutted. The top boxes are in one casting and main box is separate, so that if you break one box you do not have to buy a whole hay press nearly as you do in many machines. The plunger block is in one casting. It moves on ways that are oiled like those of a steam engine, thus less power is needed to push it. The pitman is wrought iron and is just as long as can be used. The longer pitman is the longer lived will be the machine and the less power used. The arms of the feeder are of wrought iron and gears are all 2⅝ inch face, very widest used, with heavy round cogs. Baling chamber is lined with steel. The feeder is perfect. There is not the slightest danger in dropping the divide oars in without stopping the press if dropped when the blade of the feeder is in the feed chamber going down. At this time the boards can not get out of position. A bell, which can be easily moved to lengthen or shorten the bale, rings when it is time to drop in a board. The tension is obtained by means of heavy bolts put through, up and down and crosswise. The ball box also condenses some. Every part performs its work to perfection and makes a nice looking bale.

A hay press is a machine subjected to very great strain, greater than any other machine on a farm, so it must be very heavy to have strength to stand the strain. Our machine has a heavy wood frame, the best made, that will stand up to business. The capacity of a hay press depends upon the men who handle it. Ours will do as much as any other of the same size on the market. Our larger sizes will press from 4 to 10 tons per hour. The weight of bale is governed by the tension of the bale chamber. 14x18, 17x20 and 17x22 are our sizes, these sizes loading the car best. Either iron or wood wheels furnished.

No. 18045. Price for press for bale size 14x18..**$235.00**
No. 18046. Price for press size 17x20..........**236.50**
No. 18047. Price for press size 17x22..........**237.25**

**Refer to our Harness and Saddle Department for the best bargains you ever heard of. See and examine the goods before paying in full.**

## Our Eclipse Self-Feed Drag Saw for $56.00.

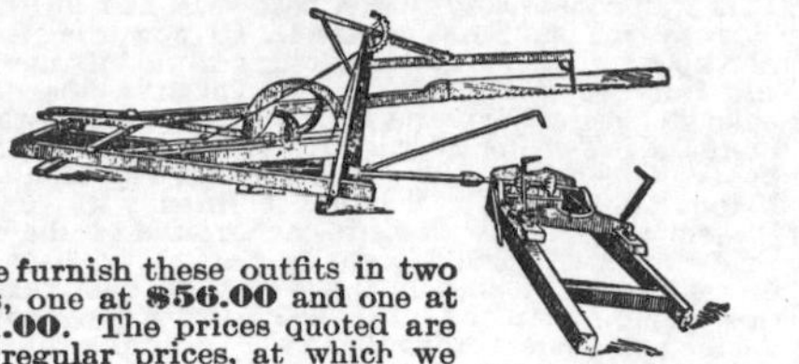

We furnish these outfits in two sizes, one at **$56.00** and one at **$61.00.** The prices quoted are our regular prices, at which we will ship the outfit by freight C. O. D., subject to examination, on receipt of sufficient deposit to cover transportation charges both ways. Three per cent. discount allowed if cash in full accompanies your order, in which case you may deduct 3 per cent. from our prices.

The Eclipse self-feed drag saw machines are the best on the market. They are manufactured at Manitowoc, Wis., by a concern which has a reputation for making the best drag saws made. They have heavy hardwood frames, steel shafts and well babbeted boxes. The large fly wheel has weighted balance to perfectly offset the weight of saw pitman, thus giving an easy, steady motion. Occupies less space than any other machine, thus making it convenient for staking or fastening for work. Each pulley is easily detached and belt can be used to run a circular saw or other machine when you have more power than is required to run drag saw alone. Pitman boxes are so arranged that they are easily adjusted to compensate for any wear that may occur. Strokes of saw can be adjusted to either 16, 20 or 24 inches; 20 feet of log carriage, trucks, rollers, boxes, etc., are always furnished as extras. Can be geared to fit any style, sweep, tread or steam power.

No. 18048. Our **$56.00** machine is recommended for all ordinary farm and timber work.

No. 18049. Our **$61.00** machine has extra heavy shafts and boxes, otherwise the same as the **$56.00** outfit. Is recommended where extra heavy work is required or if the machine is to be driven by steam power. The outfit weighs about 1,000 lbs. and the price quoted is for the same delivered on board the cars at Manitowoc, Wis.

We can furnish everything in the line of sawyer's goods and we will cheerfully quote prices on application.

## Our Celebrated Eclipse Circular Saw Machine

**Complete with the Best Disston Circular Saw, Guaranteed in every respect, at from $23.45 to $27.75.**

**If you desire the machine without saws** we can quote you special prices.

Please consider the price is complete with saws in comparing our prices with others; also please observe our 3 per cent. discount. We allow a discount of 3 per cent. if cash in full accompanies your order. At our regular prices we will ship these machines by freight C. O. D., subject to examination, on receipt of a sufficient deposit to cover freight charges both ways, balance and freight charges to be paid after machine is received. If cash in full accompanies your order you may deduct 3 per cent. from our prices.

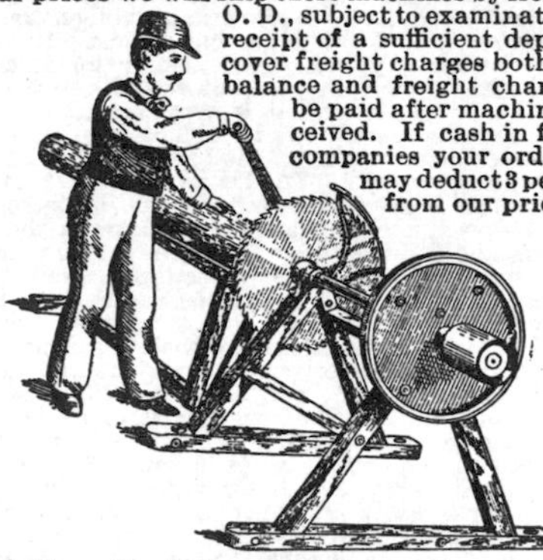

We believe the Eclipse circular sawing machine is superior to any other made. The frame is of hardwood, strongly mortised, the joints fastened by iron bolts at both top and bottom. The shaft of saw or mandrel is steel, and is not weakened by being turned down at the bearings. The chain rests in well babbeted long bearing boxes. The boxes or bearings are extra long to insure steadiness. The feed frame holds long or short timber with equal facility. The feed frame returns to position automatically by means of a suitable mechanical device, not, as on most machines, being pulled to position by the operator. The lever holds the timber, thus avoiding any danger of the operator's hands coming into contact with the saw. The pieces as cut fall to the ground and do not require as on many machines an extra man to remove them. The saw blade itself is the very best procurable, and is not furnished by the manufacturer simply because it can be purchased at a bargain. The machine is warranted to give satisfactory results in actual trial. Most machines possess some of the features described above, but we make the assertion and with no fear of successful contradiction, that the Eclipse saw is the only saw on earth which possesses all of them, and it stands without a rival as a successful general purpose farm saw machine. Our prices are as follows:

| | | | |
|---|---|---|---|
| No. 18056. | Weight, 350 lbs., 20 inch saw. | Price, | **$23.45** |
| No. 18057. | Weight, 360 lbs., 22 inch saw. | Price, | **24.25** |
| No. 18058. | Weight, 370 lbs., 24 inch saw. | Price, | **25.20** |
| No. 18059. | Weight, 380 lbs., 26 inch saw. | Price, | **27.55** |
| No. 18060. | Weight, 390 lbs., 30 inch saw. | Price, | **27.75** |

## Our Battle Creek Circular Saw Mill at from $23.45 to $27.75.

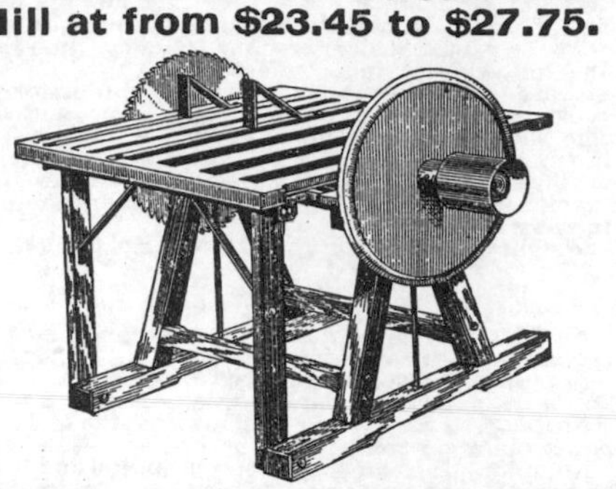

**The prices quoted are for the mill when shipped by freight C. O. D.,** subject to examination, on receipt of sufficient deposit to cover freight both ways. Three per cent. discount will be allowed if cash in full accompanies your order, in which case you may deduct 3 per cent. from our prices.

The Battle Creek circular saw mill has been made for years, and is too well known to require any special comment. It is furnished with any size saw, 20 to 30 inches at the different prices named, and has feed table with pulley and weight attached, which returns the table automatically as soon as the cut is made.

Prices as follows;

| | | |
|---|---|---|
| No. 18050. | With 20 in. saw; weight, 350 lbs...... | **$23.45** |
| No. 18051. | With 22 in. saw; weight, 360 lbs...... | **24.25** |
| No. 18052. | With 24 in. saw; weight, 370 lbs...... | **25.29** |
| No. 18053. | With 26 in. saw; weight, 370 lbs...... | **26.45** |
| No. 18054. | With 28 in. saw; weight, 380 lbs...... | **27.55** |
| No. 18055. | With 30 in. saw; weight, 390 lbs...... | **27.75** |

**Three per cent. discount from the above prices if cash in full** accompanies your order.

**We can furnish any kind of saw wanted.**

**We guarantee to meet any prices made by** any concern for any reliable make of saws on the market.

Our prices are complete with Disston's high grade circular saw fully warranted.

## Sawing Machine.

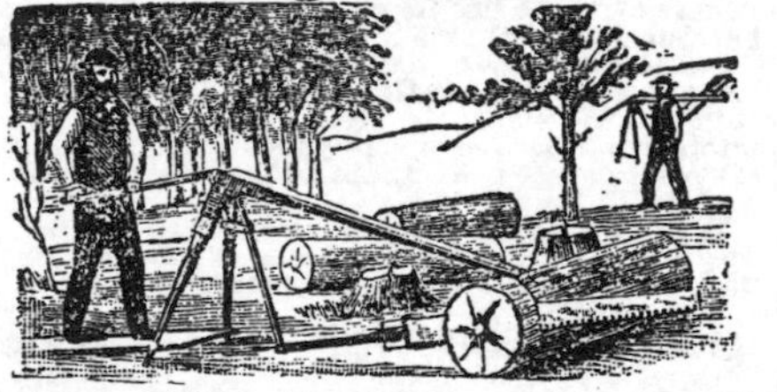

No. 18061. This machine is sold at a low price and is an efficient and easy running implement; furnished with the very best Disston Champion tooth saw; has all the advantages of any hand power cross cut saw made; the uncomfortable bent position when sawing in the usual way is overcome and a natural upright position secured, enabling the full force and weight of the body to be thrown on the saw; weight, 44 lbs. Price, with one 5-foot saw........................................**$7.50**

## Our Acme Lever Cutter for $2.80.

**Our trade the last year on these Cutters was enormous,** so large, in fact, that we were induced to arrange for a large number for the coming season, and while the Acme lever cutter last season was equal to anything on the market of its kind, we have materially improved it for this year. It is stronger and heavier, and in every way is, we believe, much more durable than any other cutter on the market.

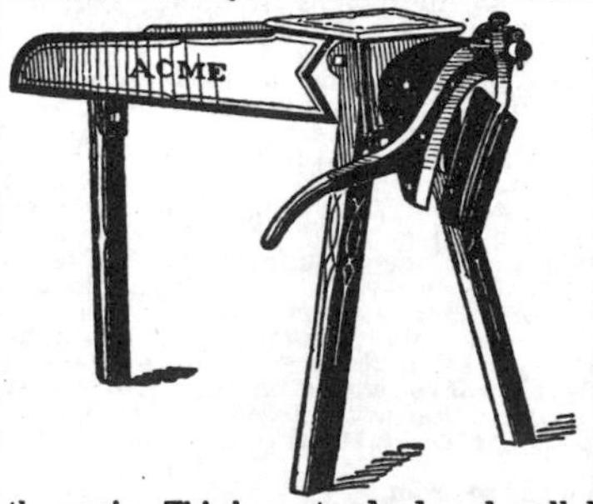


This cutter is made on the most approved manner with adjustable gauge to regulate the length of cut. Has the best steel knife, which can readily be ground, and a double tension nut with which to set the blade close up to the work. This is a standard and well known implement and one of the best of its kind made.

| | | |
|---|---|---|
| No. 18062. | Weight, 60 lbs.; price.............. | **$2.80** |
| No. 18063. | Extra knives, each.................. | **1.00** |

*WE ARE THE*

**LARGEST DEALERS IN VEHICLES IN THE UNITED STATES**

We are in the best possible position to save you money on a Buggy, Cart or Wagon.

**Mammoth Special Catalogue Free**

## $8.10 for Our High Grade Acme Root Cutter.

No. 18064. **$8.10 is our price when sent by freight C. O. D. subject to examination** on receipt of sufficient deposit to cover freight charges both ways. **Three per cent. discount allowed** if cash in full accompanies your order, when **$7.86 pays** for the implement. When comparing our prices with those of other houses do not overlook the cash discount.

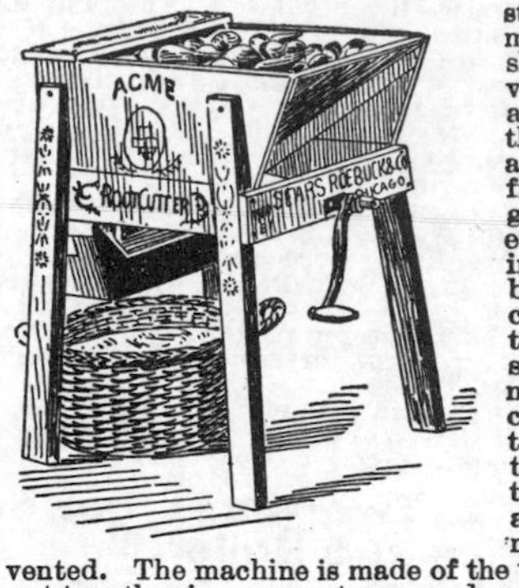


This is a good, strong and durable machine, which slices roots and vegetables quickly and effectively, at the same time separating the feed from any clay, gravel or other foreign matter by an iron grate at the bottom of the feed chute. We guarantee these cutters to satisfy even the most critical purchasers, and claim that they will do the work set out for them as quickly and neatly as any machine ever invented. The machine is made of the very best material, put together in a very strong and substantial manner, nicely finished and guaranteed the best cutter for the size at anything like the price. Capacity, 30 to 50 bushels. Weight, 125 lbs. Price.........................**$8.10**

## High Grade Cummings Feed Cutter for $14.75.

**We offer you for $14.75 a feed cutter that your retail dealer would ask $20.00 to $25.00 for.** The manufacturers have arranged to furnish us these goods on the basis of but a very small profit above actual cost to manufacture, and to this we add only our one small percentage of profit, and we believe we are entitled to your orders on the basis of the best goods on the market at prices below all others.

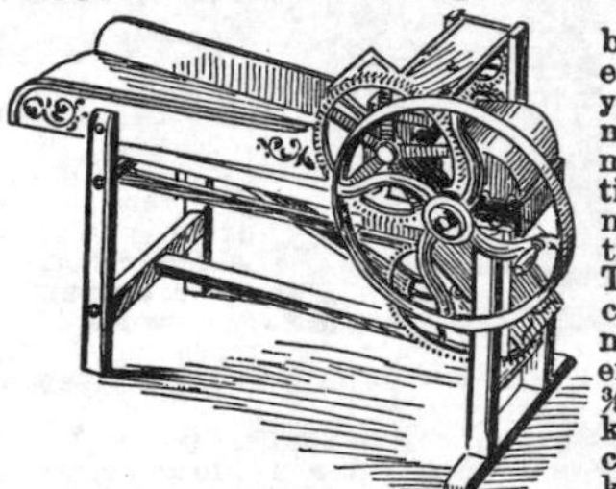

This cutter has been manufactured for the past 25 years. Improvements have been made from time to time until now the machines are practically perfect. This is a hand machine only and is not used with power. This cutter has ⅜ and ¼ inch knives and will cut material of all kinds easily and rapidly. For a hand feed cutter it is the most suitable size for all purposes. It is heavy, strong and durable in all its parts and very easy working. Nothing has as yet been made to equal it. The power is applied direct to the knife shaft without any intermediate gearing. It has an upper cut and a regulating feed roller. Length of cut ⅜ and ⅝ inch. Weight, 200 lbs. Capacity, 400 lbs. per hour.

| | |
|---|---|
| Price.................................................. | **$14.75** |
| No. 18068. Extra knives, 2¼ inch............ | **1.00** |

## Improved Cummings Cutter, No. 2.

No. 18068A. This cutter has four 10-inch knives, is intended for hand and power and has no equal; used in either way. Length of cut, ⅜ and ⅝ inch. Power required, two-horse. Capacity, about 2,000 lbs. per hour of dry feed. Speed, 400 to 600 revolutions per minute. Weight, 300 lbs.

| | |
|---|---|
| Price as hand machine, A.............................. | **$16.00** |
| Price as power machine, B............................. | **19.00** |
| Price with crusher attachment, C..................... | **30.00** |
| Price of carrier, 12 feet and under, D............. | **16.00** |
| Over 12 feet, extra per foot, E........................ | **1.00** |

## Improved Cummings Cutter, No. 3.

No. 18068B. With the patent safety fly wheel. Length of knives, 12 inches. Cuts four lengths—¼, ½, ¾ and 1 inch. Size of pulley, 14 inches, diameter 5½ inches face. Any size pulley furnished when ordered. Speed, 400 to 600 revolutions. Power required, two-horse tread power. Capacity, 3,000 lbs. dry feed per hour. Weight, 500 lbs.

| | |
|---|---|
| Price............................................................ | **$37.00** |
| Price, with crusher.......................................... | **52.00** |
| Price of 12 foot carrier (or under)................... | **16.00** |
| Over 12 feet, extra per foot............................ | **1.00** |

## Improved Cummings Cutter, No. 4.

No. 18068C. Capacity about 5 tons per hour. Weight, 800 lbs. Length of knives, 16 inches. Number of knives, 3 or 4; size of pulley, 14 inches in diameter, 5½ inches face.

| | |
|---|---|
| Price............................................................ | **$62.00** |
| Price, with crusher.......................................... | **80.00** |
| Carrier, 12 feet long or under.......................... | **16.00** |
| Over 12 feet long, extra per foot...................... | **1.00** |

Carriers for all sizes are made to angle right or left or straight-away. State which is wanted.

## Our Special $9.50 Cutter.

No. 18065. **We believe we have the best cutter on the market at the price.** Last year we handled a cutter almost identical in design to this, which we offered at the same price, but for this season we have materially improved the machine. The frame is stronger and the general workmanship is better. We guarantee this cutter equal to any cutter made, regardless of price.

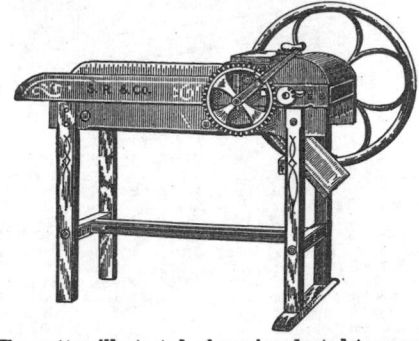

The cutter illustrated above is adapted to general work on hay, straw, etc. For rapid and easy cutting, large capacity, hand power, simplicity of construction, strength and durability, at a moderate cost, this cutter cannot be excelled. It is not intended to do the work of the largest horse-power cutter, but will do more work than any other cutter of its size. It has one spiral knife geared to make four cuts to one turn of the crank, giving it a splendid cut at the least expense of power. Length of knife, 10 inches. Gears are few and strong. Workmanship and material both are equal to that of the most expensive cutter made. Weight, 150 lbs.

No. 18065½. Price.................................$9.50
Extra knives, each...............................1.00

## Our $10.00 and $13.25 Acme Cutters.

**We believe the Acme Cutters at $10.00 and $13.25 are the best cutters on the market regardless of price.** The prices quoted above are for these cutters when shipped by freight C. O. D., subject to examination, on receipt of sufficient deposit to cover freight charges both ways, balance and charges to be paid after cutters are received.

Three per cent. discount allowed if cash in full accompanies your order, in which case you may deduct 3 per cent. from our prices.

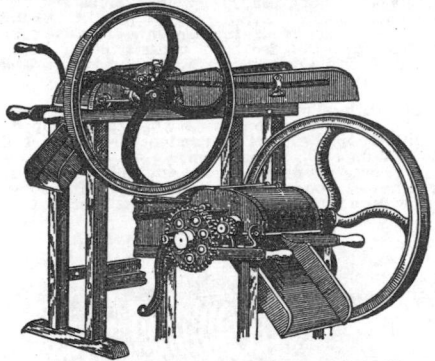

The cutter above illustrated has been used for 25 years and it will continue to lead. Beauty of design, simplicity of mechanism, superiority of construction, strength and easy running qualities are the features which have gained for it the reputation it enjoys, and which associates it in the minds of dairymen and farmers with all that is best in ensilage and fodder cutting machines. It is made with strong hardwood frame, heavy balance wheel, one knife, which makes three revolutions to each turn of the crank, and which can be adjusted to cut any length from ¼ to 1 inch, a handsome low priced machine for hand use only.

For poultrymen we build the same machine, with two knives instead of one, designed especially for cutting clover and feed extra short for poultry.

The illustration above shows the wheel both with the fly wheel side and with the crank side, and from the illustration you can get some idea of the appearance of the cutter.

No. 18066. Price for medium size.............$10.00
No. 18067. Price for large size................13.25

## $10.75 BUYS A $20.00 GUN

Opportunities to be found nowhere else are offered in our Gun and

## SPORTING GOODS DEPARTMENT.
### PAGES 562 TO 610.

## Bone Mills at Manufacturers' Prices.

**We Lead All Others on these Mills.**
### OUR $3.45 HAND BONE MILL.

Poulterers who have never fed bone meal will be surprised at the increase of eggs where ground bone is supplied. By furnishing the material for egg shells in ground bone you increase the production of eggs at once. Feed only corn and you induce the production of fat. Bone meal retails for 4c per lb., and is worth three times its cost for fowls on any farm. With this machine we reduce the cost of the meal to merely the labor, and as the capacity is large and the power required comparatively slight you will find yourself handsomely rewarded by the use of this machine. It has been advertised by many at from $5.00 up. We reduce the price to $3.45. The teeth of this mill are very strong and coarse and will not grind corn for family use. Allow fresh bones to dry before grinding; will not grind green bones. Weight, 35 lbs. Our special price.....................$3.45

No. 18069. Patent bone mill same as above, but on iron legs. Weight, 65 lbs. Our special price.....$5.75

## Our $6.95 Bone Cutter.

No. 18070. We believe this is the best bone cutter on the market at any price, and no farmer should be without one. Our price, $6.95, is for the cutter when sent by freight C. O. D. subject to examination on receipt of sufficient deposit to cover freight charges both ways. A discount of 3 per cent. allowed if cash in full accompanies your order, in which case $6.74 pays for the machine. This is the strongest, easiest operated and best cutter of its size manufactured. There is no better mill on the market. The knives and cutting parts are very carefully made and will never give out. Our special price.......................$6.95

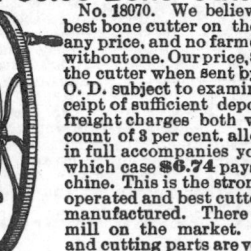

## Our $16.50 Bone Cutter.

This is the genuine Mann's green bone cutter, and we believe the best on the market at any price.

This is a thoroughly practical machine for cutting green bones either by hand or power. Simple in construction, with nothing to get out of order, and easy to operate. They cut fast and fine. The knives are made of the finest steel, can be taken out when dull, sharpened, and replaced in a few minutes.

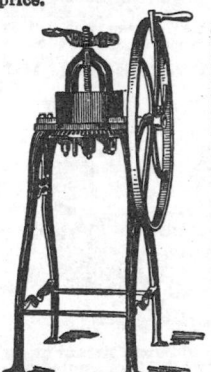

No. 18071. Price for hand cutter like illustration; weight, 142 lbs........$16.50

No. 18072. Price for small power cutter, tight and loose pulleys, 2 balance wheels; weight, 147 lbs.........$23.50

No. 18073. Large power cutter; weight, 426 lbs. Price...................$68.00

No. 18074. Largest power cutter; weight, 730 lbs. Price.................$200.00

## Corn Shellers.

We believe we offer the best corn sheller made and at a saving in price of at least 33⅓ per cent. to the purchaser.

**We guarantee every sheller** in every respect, to be made of the very best material and to do as good or better work than any other sheller of equal size.

**Our shellers are made by a reliable maker,** who has established a reputation for the best sheller made.

**Our Terms are Liberal.** Any sheller will be sent to any address by freight C. O. D. subject to examination on receipt of a sufficient deposit to cover freight both ways.

**Three per cent. discount** allowed if cash in full accompanies your order. Nearly all our customers send cash in full.

Please consider the cash discount when comparing our prices with other houses.

## Our 95 Cent Corn Sheller.

No. 18075. This is the most simple and effective arrangement for corn shelling made. There are only six pieces in the entire machine, main frame, shell disc, shaft, tension, ring and crank. This sheller separates the corn from the cob, and deposits the corn in the box on which it is mounted and the cob outside. It has a perfect tension that can

be adjusted instantly, will shell all sized ears, popcorn to the largest southern dent. Weight, 12 lbs. Price, 95c

## Patch's $2.30 Corn Sheller.

No. 18075½. We offer this corn sheller at $2.30, about one-half the price charged by retail dealers. We have sold a vast number of these machines and the universal satisfaction they have given everywhere prompts us to say that we will guarantee the machine to give the best of satisfaction, and if it does not you can return it at our expense and we will refund your money.

This machine is made from the best malleable iron. It is almost impossible to break it with any ordinary usage. It will shell all sizes of corn easily and rapidly. It is considered to be one of the best hand shellers made and is thoroughly covered by patents.

Weight, 15 lbs. Price......................$2.30

## Our Great Acme $4.80 Combined Corn Sheller and Grinder.

This is the strongest, most perfect, easiest running and best combined machine ever made at anything like the price.

This machine is designed to shell and grind corn and does it perfectly. The shelled corn or meal passes into the receptacle below. The sheller is the most perfect implement of its kind and does not scatter the corn. The cobs are thrown out at the rear of the machine and do not mix with the shelled corn.

B is corn sheller hopper and A is grinder hopper. The entire sheller is built of iron, being put up in a machine shop by men of good mechanical training, and then carefully finished. It is nicely painted.

No. 18076. Not mounted, weight, 53 lbs., price....$4.80
No. 18077. Mounted on heavy strong iron stand, weight 100 lbs............................7.25
No. 18078. Extra burrs for above, per pair........ .60

## S., R. & Co. Corn Shellers.

No. 18079. The S. R. & Co. "Sheller" is the best one hole corn sheller in the market. Has the largest balance wheel put up on any sheller, being 27 inches in diameter and weighing 35 lbs.; is a right hand sheller with end delivery. One hole Sheller, with fan and feed table. Right hand sheller. Weight, 150 lbs.

Price .............$5.40
Pulley, extra..... .50

No. 18079A. S. R. & Co. two-hole Sheller, with fan, feed table and pulley. Weight, 225 lbs.........$10.80

No. 18079B. S.R.& Co. two hole Sheller, complete with fan, feed table, pulley and cob carrier. Weight, 225 lbs.........................$18.75

## Our Great $10.80 Two Hole Corn Sheller.

No. 18080. This corn sheller is equal to those that are being sold at retail at from $15 to $20. Our special price is $10.80. This two hole corn sheller is made of the very best material throughout. The frames are handsomely striped and varnished, and finished in natural wood color so that the quality of the lumber is open to inspection. The castings are of the very best grade of charcoal iron, making repairs for breakage very seldom if ever necessary. They are put together by skilled mechanics and guaranteed in every respect. Whether the ears of corn are large or small it will shell perfectly clean without breaking the grain or throwing any out with the cobs. Such a thing as choking is unknown. We warrant this corn sheller in every respect. We always furnish it complete with feed table, fan, belt, pulley and handle. Weight, 220 lbs. Price, $10.80

## Our Special $14.90 Two Hole Corn Sheller with Cob Carrier.

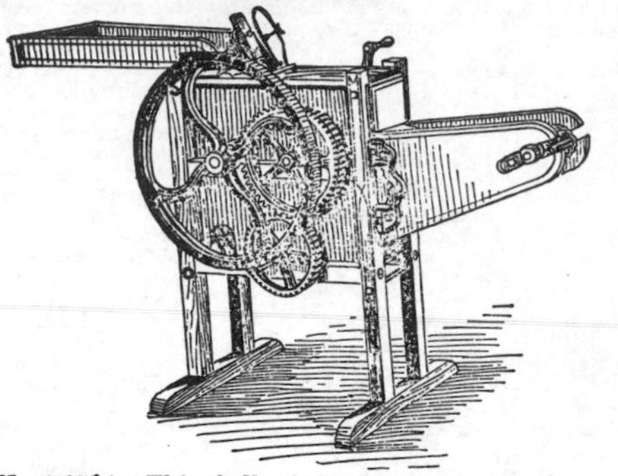

No. 18081½. This sheller is built with a square frame to support the cob carrier.

We are able to offer this machine at **$14.90** only by reason of large and favorable contracts with the manufacturer, which makes it possible for us to get the price down to the basis of actual cost of material and workmanship. This machine has a belt and pulley for power connection or a handle for hand power. Weighs 250 lbs. Our price complete..........**$14.90**

## The Celebrated Hutchinson Cider and Wine Mill for $7.50.

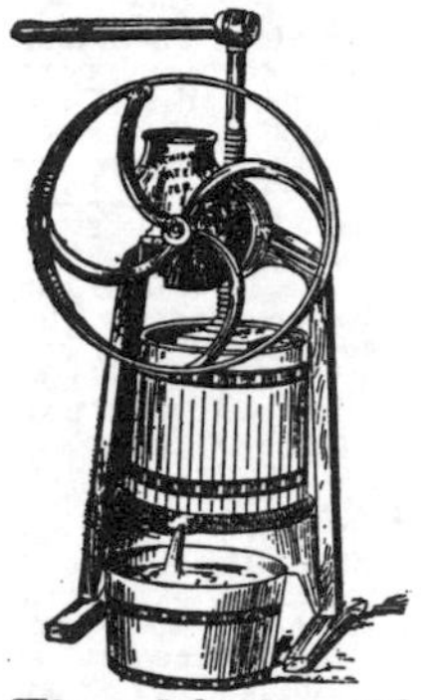

No. 18082. **$7.50** is our price to be shipped by freight C. O. D. subject to examination on receipt of sufficient deposit to cover transportation charges both ways.

Three per cent. discount allowed if cash in full accompanies your order, in which case **$7.27** pays for the mill.

This is a well known implement, one of the most economical and useful cider mills manufactured. Thousands of these mills are in use. Warranted to do fine work. Capacity, 2 to 3 barrels of cider per day.

No. 18082. Weight, 105 lbs. Price..........**$7.50**

## The Little Giant Cider Mill for $7.65.

No. 18083. This is a strong, serviceable, and handy machine, the smallest, lightest, and cheapest made. The cutter is made of tinned steel, and by its motion it cuts the fruit and carries off the cut apple before it touches any portion of the hopper or other metal, from which it might be stained. By the operation of the press the fruit is brought up with a screw and away from the cider. The Little Giant is not intended for extensive cider making, but distinctively for family use, though its capacity is quite sufficient for making large quantities. Considering that it is operated by one person, its results will compare favorably with larger mills.

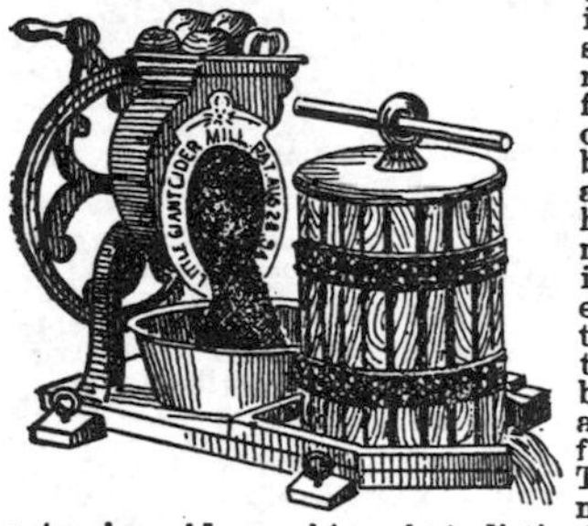

No. 18083. Weight, 95 lbs. Price..........**$7.65**

## Our Improved Cider Mill at $13.75.

These mills have hardwood frames strongly bolted together; the beams are of heavy cast iron, screws are of wrought iron, capable of standing the most severe pressure applied by the lever or the crushing roller. Made in three sizes:

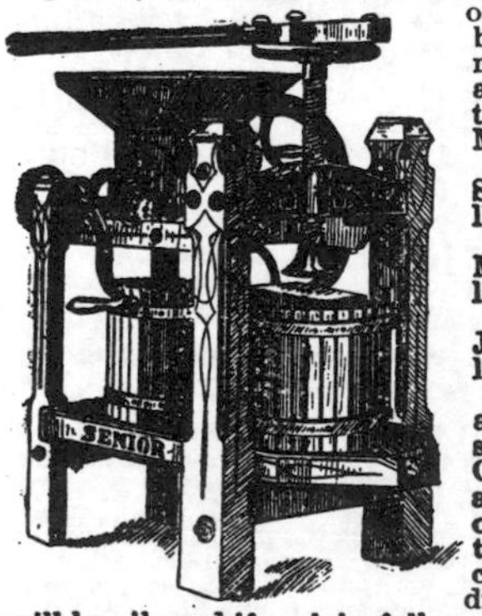

No. 18084. Price of Senior; weight, 410 lbs..........**$20.50**

No. 18085. Price of Medium; weight, 230 lbs..........**$17.50**

No. 18086. Price of Junior; weight 165 lbs..........**$13.75**

The prices quoted are for the mills when shipped by freight C. O. D., subject to examination, on receipt of a sufficient deposit to cover freight charges both ways. A discount of 3 per cent. will be allowed if cash in full accompanies your order.

## Our $16.00 Cane Mill.

We offer cane mills at from **$16.00** to **$48.00** according to size and weight, and if you are in the market for anything in this line we hope you will favor us with your order. By a careful comparison of our prices with those of other houses we feel sure you will see where we can save you at least 25 per cent. We have succeeded in bringing the prices of cane mills down to about one-half the prices at which they are usually retailed. This we have been able to do by contracting with the manufacturers for quantities and compelling them to figure on the cost of material and workmanship, eliminating the exorbitant profits heretofore asked and any percentage of allowance for loss, of which we know nothing in our method of dealing direct with the user on our manufacturer to consumer one small profit plan.

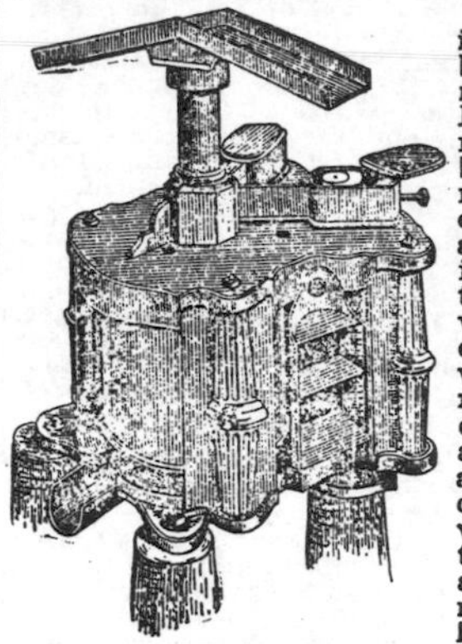

The Acme cane mill as illustrated here is, we believe, the best cane mill on the market. It has the best turned rolls, steel shafts, brass bearings, gearings and rollers of the very best cast steel, cast separate. The cog gearing is cast separately from the rollers and made very heavy with two clutches on each wheel which fit into two corresponding ones in each roller, thus doing away with all screws and the consequent danger of splitting the wheels when driven too tight, also enabling any one to take up the mill. These wheels have steel shaft with turned bearings, rollers turned and serrated. The main rollers are flanged at top and bottom, preventing the cane from passing either up or down. We can furnish these mills in the following sizes:

No. 18087. One horse power, weight 400 lbs., capacity 40 to 50 gallons per hour..........**$16.00**

No. 18088. One horse power, capacity 50 to 60 gallons, price..........**$20.00**

No. 18089. Two horse power, weight 625 lbs., capacity 60 to 75 gallons per hour..........**$25.00**

No. 18090. Two horse power, weight 800 lbs., capacity 75 to 90 gallons per hour, price..........**$31.00**

No. 18091. Two horse power, weight 850 lbs., capacity 90 to 100 gallons per hour, price..........**$35.00**

No. 18092. Heavy two horse power, weight 1150 lbs., capacity 100 to 120 gallons per hour, price......**$40.00**

No. 18093. Extra heavy two horse power, weight 1250 lbs., capacity 120 to 140 gallons per hour, price.**$48.00**

## Cook's Portable Evaporator for $14.63.

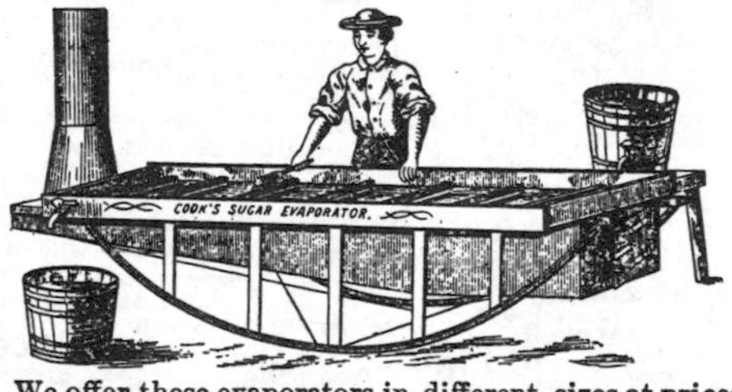

We offer these evaporators in different sizes at prices ranging from **$14.63** to **$21.56**. Please note carefully the descriptions and illustrations and compare our prices with others before placing your order elsewhere.

Our special descriptive circular of cane mills and evaporators is free. If interested send for it.

These evaporators are made of galvanized sheet steel or copper, heavily bound and riveted, strongly made, and the whole mounted upon rockers of angle iron, thus furnishing a complete portable furnace of iron and brick combined in one with all the advantages of both, and yet so light that it can be easily moved by two men. This is the most convenient arrangement for small house operation, and for custom work it is well-nigh indispensable. With it the operator can move from field to field, from farm to farm, and thus avoid the labor and expense of hauling the cane. The evaporator pan is made of galvanized sheet steel or copper of a thickness proportionate to the length of the same.

To avoid mistakes in ordering please notice that the evaporator means to include both pan and furnace. Our prices are for furnace, pan, grate, chimney and two skimmers complete.

No. 18094. Size, 44x72; weight, 300 lbs., galvanized steel pan..........**$14.63**
Copper..........**20.46**

No. 18095. Size, 44x90; weight, 360 lbs.; galvanized steel pan..........**$16.94**
Copper..........**24.20**

No. 18096. Size, 44x108; weight, 400 lbs.; galvanized steel pan..........**$19.25**
Copper..........**27.98**

No. 18097. Size, 24x126; weight, 450 lbs.; galvanized steel pan..........**$21.56**
Copper..........**30.50**

**REFER TO THE INDEX.**

**You can learn the exact page on which to find the goods you want.**

## Cook's Pan for Brick Arch.

**Our price. $4.40 to $26.40**, according to size and quality. Our price includes copper pan or galvanized iron pan complete with two skimmers.

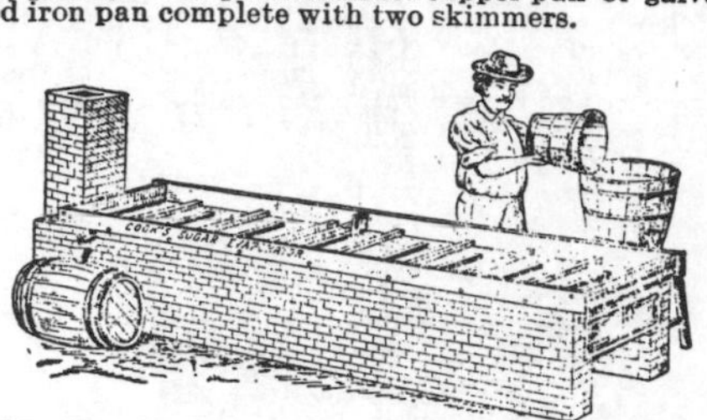

No. 18098. Size of pan, 44x66. Price, galvanized iron, **$4.40**; copper..........**$9.90**

No. 18099. Size of pan, 44x72. Price, galvanized iron, **$4.75**; copper..........**$10.56**

No. 18100. Size of pan, 44x90. Price, galvanized iron, **$5.94**; copper..........**$13.20**

No. 18101. Size of pan, 44x108. Price, galvanized iron, **$7.15**; copper..........**$15.88**

No. 18102. Size of pan, 44x126. Price, galvanized iron, **$8.36**; copper..........**$18.48**

No. 18103. Size of pan, 44x144. Price, galvanized iron, **$9.46**; copper..........**$21.12**

No. 18104. Size of pan, 44x180. Price, galvanized iron, **$11.80**; copper..........**$26.40**

## Our $25.00 Ohio Fruit Dryer.

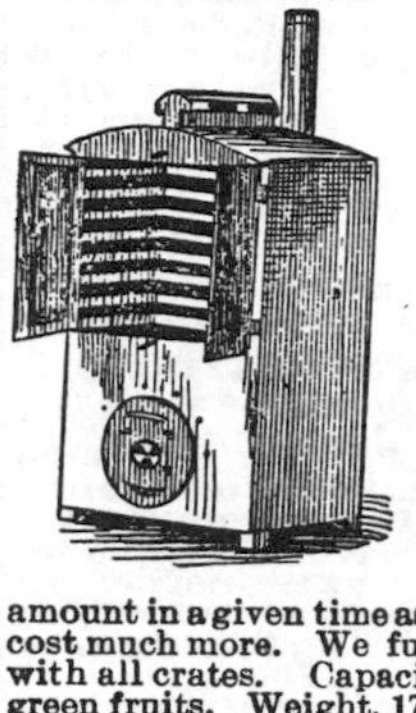

$25.00 is the price when sent by freight C. O. D. subject to examination on receipt of a sufficient deposit to cover freight charges both ways. A discount of 3 per cent. will be allowed if cash in full accompanies your order, when $24.25 pays for the dryer.

This size evaporator is mostly used by farmers, has 16 trays, 12x24 inches, with all the latest improvements; made of the best galvanized iron with galvanized wire cloth trays. These evaporators are warranted to produce as nice white fruit as any evaporator made and to produce the same amount in a given time as others of equal capacity which cost much more. We furnish the evaporator complete with all crates. Capacity, 3 to 4 bushels per day of green fruits. Weight, 175 lbs.

Price..........**$25.00**

No. 18105. Larger size, 20 trays 24x36, capacity 4 to 5 bushels per day of green fruit, weight 225 lbs.

Price..........**$30.00**

No. 18106. Larger size intended for extensive work, size 31x38 inches, 6¼ feet high, capacity 6 to 8 bushels of green fruit per day, weight 390 lbs., price....**$39.50**

## Our $11.55 Hay Rake.

$11.55 with wooden wheels, $13.00 with steel wheels. The above prices are our prices when to be shipped by freight C. O. D. subject to examination on receipt of a sufficient deposit to cover transportation charges both ways. Three per cent. discount allowed if cash in full accompanies your order. If you send the full amount of cash with your order you may deduct 3 per cent

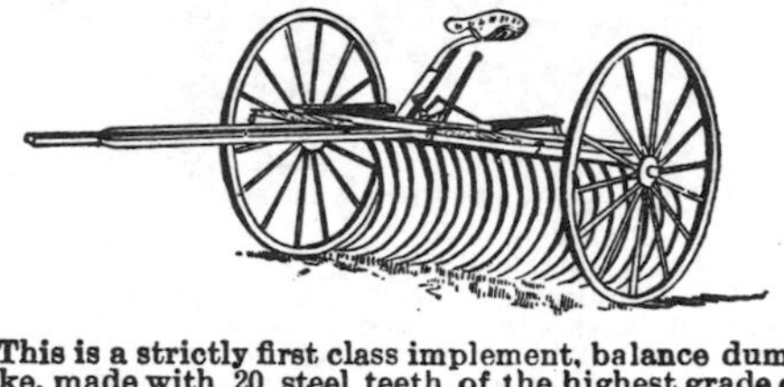

This is a strictly first class implement, balance dump rake, made with 20 steel teeth of the highest grade of steel, carefully tempered. It has wrought iron wheel spindles and the axle is stiffened by a truss rod, which prevents any sagging. In operative qualities it will meet the requirements of the farmer, being a perfect lock lever which can be operated with great ease while teeth can not raise except when required to dump. The workmanship is first class. 20 teeth 4¾ inches apart. Weight, 200 lbs.

No. 18107. Price, with wood wheels..........**$11.55**

No. 18108. Price, with steel wheels..........**13.00**

## Our $13.25 Acme Hand Dump Rake.

No. 18109. **$13.25** for rake with wood wheels, **$14.50** for rake with steel wheels. This rake possesses a number of excellent features that are not found in any other make. It is built of the very best material and will wear as long as any rake on the market. Its dumping arrangement is so simple and unique that it is practically a self-dump rake. It only needs the slightest movement of the lever to break the lock, which can be done with the foot or hand, and after this is done the operation becomes automatic. The lever is convenient to right hand of the driver, and when the moment for dumping has arrived he has only to take hold of the lever and raise it up, or rather start it up. It requires no power to do this. The throw or sweep of the lever is very short, and the smallest movement upward breaks the lock. The foot or hand may then be removed from the lever and the rake will dump itself.

Price, with wood wheels..........**$13.25**

Price, with steel wheels..........**14.50**

## Our Celebrated Acme Self Dump Rake for $16.50.

No. 18110. $16.50 is the price for this 20-tooth rake with wood wheels; $17.75 with steel wheels.

We believe this is the best self dump rake on the market. The mechanical device for effecting the dumping is a most ingenious yet simple and effective arrangement, and operated as follows: When the driver wishes to dump he places his foot gently on the chain which is connected to the trip, thereby releasing the pauls, which immediately engage with the teeth of the revolving ratchet wheel on the axle. The rake head is thus connected with the revolving axle and turns with it until the end of the trip lever strikes against the stop. The rake teeth are thus raised up, permitting the hay or whatever the material may be to drop off. As soon as the teeth have reached the proper height the trip lever coming against the stop forces it back into its former position, thus withdrawing the pauls and locking them away from the ratchet wheels, permitting the rake head to turn on its axles, by which the teeth are restored to their raking position. The rake can thus be automatically dumped at any time by simply tripping the lever. It may be dumped when either wheel is in motion. It is a perfect self-dump rake, obviating the usual side draught or jar. The teeth are made of the best steel and are thoroughly tested before leaving the factory. Weight, 200 lbs. Price, $16.50 and............$17.75

## The Acme Hay Tedder.

No. 18111. We offer at $21.00 the celebrated Acme hay tedder.

The main frame of this tedder is constructed in the simplest and most substantial manner, thoroughly bolted together with angle brackets to prevent racking and is arranged for either shafts or combination pole and shafts. The tedder forks are made of the very best quality crucible spring steel on our peculiar pattern, and the shape and sweep of the fork are just right to do perfect work. The chain drive is effected by means of sprocket wheels connected to the main crank shaft and the use of sprockets and chains dispenses with the cumbersome cog gearing, materially reducing the draught of the tedder. The shifting device is very simple and located within convenient reach of the operator. The driver's seat is adjustable and may be secured at any height to suit a small boy or a tall man. The height of the fork is controlled by lever with ratchet stand located within convenient reach of the driver. You can by the use of this lever set the forks to run close to or any distance from the ground. These tedders are furnished complete with shafts, pole attachments, double trees, single trees and neck-yoke. Weight, 490 lbs. Our special price......................$21.00

## The Acme Hay Loader for $41.00.

No. 18112. $41.00 is the price when sent by freight C. O. D., subject to examination, upon receipt of sufficient deposit to cover freight charges both ways. Three per cent. discount allowed if cash in full accompanies your order, when $39.75 pays for the loader.

We offer this Hay Loader with the assurance that its possession will place its owner in the best position for taking care of his hay crop in the most economical manner. The Hay Loader, as illustrated above, we offer to our customers with the assurance that it will in every particular do its work as well, if not better, than any other now in use. It is offered with the further guaranty that it is constructed of better material, is better made, and more handsomely finished than any other now on the market. It is intended particularly as a swath loader, but will work very satisfactorily in windrows, in fact, where the hay is light it is better to rake it in small windrows first. Weight, 800 lbs.
Our price............................$41.00

## Mowers.

No. 18113. The S., R. & Co. iron Mower. Weight, 500 lbs. Price, 4 ft. cut, $36.00; 4 ft. 6 in. cut, weight, 540 lbs, $37.00.
No. 18114A. Wide cut Mower, with bar carrying spring. This is a heavier and wider cut machine than above. Pressure of bar on ground relieved by spring. It has many advantages. Weight, 675 lbs. Price, 4 ft. 6 in. cut, $40.00; 5 ft. cut, $42.00; 6 ft. cut, $45.00.

## Our $7.00 Wheelbarrow Grass Seeder.

No. 18114. The best machine ever made to sow clover and timothy. machine, light, strong and durable. No gearing, no friction; more accurate than a general machine. An all iron wheel, 30 inches in diameter, with broad rim made like a bicycle rim; always runs true on hollow axle. Weight, 40 lbs. Our price......................$7.00

## Our $8.50 Niagara Broadcast Seeder.

This is a positive force feed end gate seeder.

The Niagara combines all the latest improvements in sowers. The machine is attached to an end gate that fits any wagon. Attach sprocket to left hind wheel, put on link chain and go ahead. Save grain and seed by sowing it evenly. The machine throws the seed evenly and sows two acres to every half mile covered by the team. The Niagara has all the good qualities of all other broadcast seeders.
No. 18114½. Weight, 120 lbs., price............$8.50

## Our $14.75 11 Foot Broadcast Seeder.

No. 18115. We offer a broadcast seeder at $14.75 which is equal to anything you can buy in your local market at $25.00.

$14.75 is our regular price when sent by freight C. O. D. subject to examination on receipt of a sufficient deposit to cover freight both ways. Three per cent.

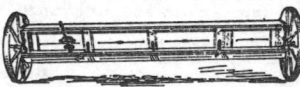

discount will be allowed if cash in full accompanies your order. If you send the full amount of cash with your order you may deduct 3 per cent. from our price. This is a broadcast seeder made extra wide, 11 feet, to cover a large amount of ground, and is used very generally in the west and northwest, especially in the Dakotas, Minnesota, Kansas and Nebraska. We believe it is the best seeder on the market at anything like the price. Weight, 350 lbs.
Price.............................$14.75

## The Little Giant Broadcast Hand Seed Sower.

No. 18116. With this seeder, when properly used, you can distribute wheat 56 feet to a round, flax-seed 36 feet, clover seed 36 feet, timothy 27 feet, oats 36 feet. It will also sow rye, barley, millet, Hungarian corn or any grain or seed that can be sown broadcast. This seeder has a light centrifugal wheel at the bottom 11 inches in diameter, that is revolved rapidly in opposite directions by means of a bow, scattering the seed with great velocity. Weight, 3 lbs. Price, each.................$1.50

## The Granger Seeder.

No. 18117. The Granger Broadcast Hand Seeder, for sowing all kinds of grain and grass seed, sows on an average of 6 acres per hour at a common walking gait. The bag and hopper will hold about 22 quarts. Weight, 5½ lbs. Price......$3.25
No. 18117½. The Improved Cahoon Broadcast Hand Seeder. Weight, 5½ lbs. (Retail price, $5.) Our price, each..$3.00

## The Cyclone Hand Seeder.

No. 18118. This is somewhat simpler and cheaper made than the Granger, but works on the same general plan. It will sow with ease to the operator 60 acres of grain or grass seed per day. Has a shake feed, and sows perfectly accurate. Weight, 4 lbs. Price........$2.25

## The New Five-Hoe One-Box Grain Drill.

No. 18119. The New Five-Hoe One-Box Grain Drill. Used principally for drilling between corn rows or putting in grain with one horse. Part of the holes can be stopped, which makes it an excellent corn, bean or pea drill; also for beets and other coarse seed. Weight, 140 lbs.
Price.............................$14.00

## Corn Planter.

No. 18119½. Triumph Hand Corn Planter; can be used on any plowed ground. Weight, 4½ lbs.
Price, each.........................75c

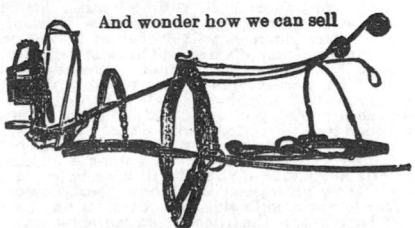
**Don't think you live too far away to order goods. The more the freight the more the dealer charges.**
**When you buy at home you pay a profit on the freight.**

# PLOWS.

**We are headquarters for everything in the line of plows. We have spared no pains in selecting a line of goods that we can guarantee in every respect,** plows that are suitable to all sections of the country and for all purposes. **Our line of riding and walking plows is for quality,** durability, draught and all requirements second to none. Our plows are made for us under contract by several of the largest and most reliable makers in the country, concerns who have devoted their life's work to the manufacture of this class of goods and are turning out the highest grade of work that can be produced. **Our line of riding and walking plows for the western prairies is, we believe, without exception the best on the market. There is nothing superior to our prairie breaking plows, if indeed there is anything on the market that will equal them. Our Texas and southern style plows are designed and** made especially for that territory, and guaranteed to scour in any soil. **Every plow we sell is fully guaranteed for two years. We issue a binding guaranty with every plow,** by the terms and conditions of which if it fails to scour and is not found exactly as represented, or if any piece or part gives out by reason of defect in material or workmanship within two years, we will replace it free of charge. **Do not pay your local dealer long retail prices for a plow when** we can save you 33⅓ to 50 per cent. We can sell you a plow for as little or less money than your local dealer can buy in quantities.

## Our $4.75 Cotton King Plow.

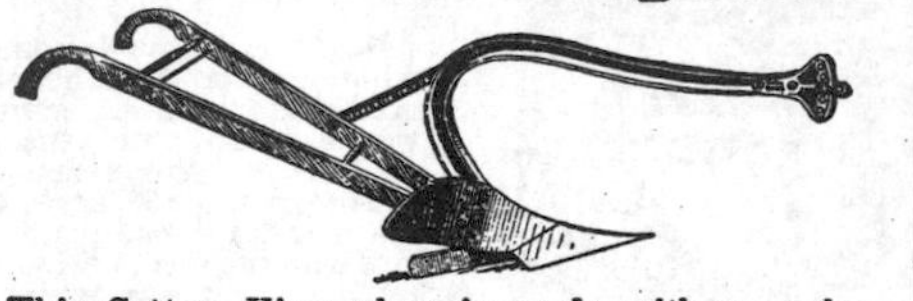

This Cotton King plow is made with new shape boards, adopted after a thorough investigation of the requirements of a plow for the blacklands of Texas and the south.

No. 18120. 7 inch cut, weight 54 lbs., wood beam.. **$4.75**
Steel beam, weight 73 lbs. ........ **6.25**
No. 18121. 8 inch cut, weight 62 lbs., wood beam.. **5.50**
Steel beam, weight 80 lbs. ........ **7.15**
No. 18122. 9 inch cut, weight 79 lbs., wood beam.. **6.25**
Steel beam, weight 94 lbs. ........ **8.00**
No. 18123. 10 inch cut, weight 82 lbs., wood beam, **$7.15.** Steel beam, weight 97 lbs. ........ **$9.54**
No. 18124. 12 inch cut, wood beam, weight 100 lbs., **$9.52.** Steel beam, weight 110 lbs. ........ **$11.75**

## Our $9.75 Walking Plow.

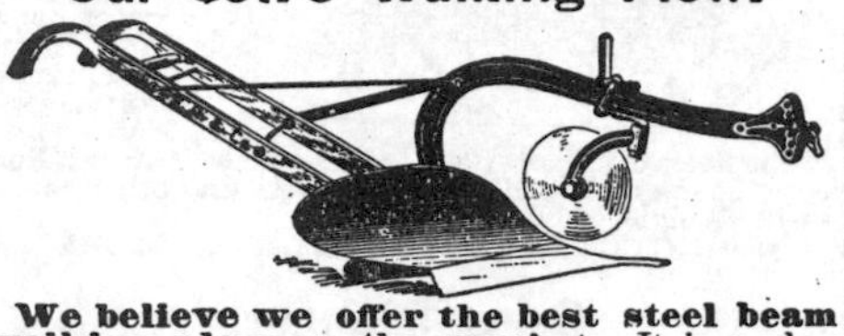

**We believe we offer the best steel beam walking plow on the market.** It is a plow that we guarantee to scour in any soil. It is especially adapted to the prairies of Kansas and Nebraska, Minnesota and the Dakotas, but is used in every state.

We illustrate this plow with rolling coulter, but the prices quoted are without coulter. We will furnish 13 inch rolling cast coulters at $2.00 extra when desired. This plow is made with a very heavy solid steel point and extra wide shares, warranted to scour in any soil—to scour where all others fail. Remember we guarantee to use a one-half inch wider share than any other manufacturer.

These are our double board plows, made from a solid wedge-shaped piece of steel which is as thick again at the front or wearing side as it is at the rear, extending with a true taper throughout in thickness to the wing of the moldboards. This is by far the most durable and economical method. The plow will wear just twice as long, and the moldboard can be tempered more uniformly throughout.

No. 18125. 12-inch plow, weight 90 lbs. ........ **$ 9.75**
No. 18126. 14-inch plow, weight 100 lbs. ........ **9.95**
No. 18127. 16-inch plow, weight 110 lbs. ........ **12.50**

## Double Moldboard Plow.

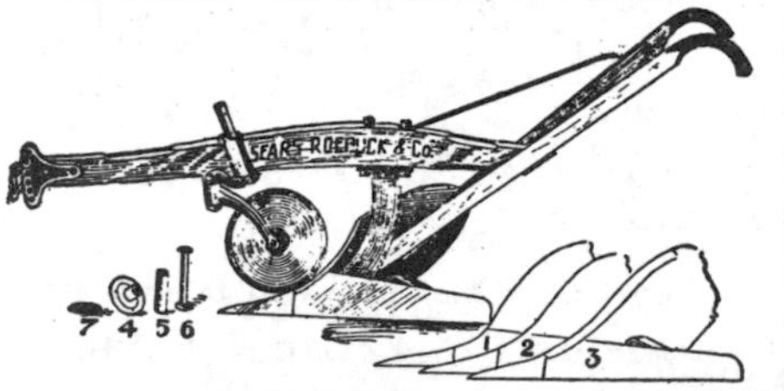

No. 18128. Price for 12-inch Plow ........ **$10.00**
No. 18129. Price for 14-inch Plow ........ **10.25**
No. 18130. Price for 16-inch Plow ........ **12.75**

We show this Plow with rolling coulter attached, but the prices quoted are for the plow without the rolling coulter, which we will furnish at **$2.00** extra. This is our double moldboard and bent standard plow. The advantages of the bent standard are apparent to any one. We warrant the double moldboard to wear twice as long as the ordinary single shin, or the welded double shin made by other manufacturers. It is well understood by all practical farmers that a patch welded on the shin of a plow is an actual damage to the board. Any farmer that will examine our double moldboard plow will be convinced that it will wear twice as long as any of the other styles. It is the cheapest plow on the market; has a double thickness of steel on the face of the boards. In the illustration we show our new patent cutter and cutter hub. Other cutters attach to the round part of the beam, and so far forward that they do not do good work, and lift the plow out of the ground. Our cutters are attached to the square part of the beam, and nearly over the cutter blade; have a perfect crank adjustment, and made for either wood or steel beam plows. Price of cutter, **$2.00.** Figure No. 1 shows sectional view of plow; Fig. No. 2 shows sectional view of plow, with patched or welded shin; Fig. No. 3 shows sectional view of plow, without double moldboard; Fig. No. 4 shows our cutter hub proper, that can not break, and never wears out; Fig. No. 5 is the hub center, or thimble, that works in the hub; Fig. No. 6 is the steel pin, on which the thimble turns, and if kept well oiled it will last for years. The thimble and pin are the only parts that can wear out, and are cheap and easily replaced. The new hub can be put on any of our old cutters without trouble, as well as on most other kinds in the market.

## Our $3.95 Wood Beam Plows.

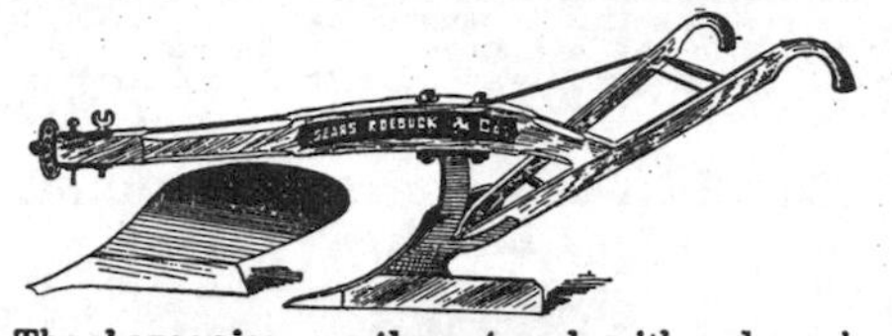

The above prices are the net cash with order prices for these plows delivered on board the cars at Alton, Ill., from which point you must pay the freight. The prices quoted are net cash. There is no discount to any one under any circumstances. These plows are designed to scour in all kinds of soil, they are made by a manufacturer whose reputation for the manufacture of strictly high grade plows is second to none, and they are guaranteed in every respect. There is nothing better on the market at any price. Made with curved standard, best land side, bar or slip share as desired, right or left hand, as desired, very finest hardened board.

No. 18131. Single board, 6 inch cut, corn plow, weight, 42 lbs., price ........ **$3.95**
No. 18132. Single board, 7 inch cut, corn plow, weight, 45 lbs., price ........ **$4.10**
No. 18133. Single board, 8 inch cut, corn plow, weight, 45 lbs., price ........ **$5.25**
No. 18134. Single board, 10 inch cut, corn plow, weight, 65 lbs., price ........ **$6.10**
No. 18135. Single board, 11 inch cut, corn plow, weight, 70 lbs., price ........ **$6.40**
No. 18136. Single board, 12 inch cut, corn plow, weight, 70 lbs., price ........ **$6.75**

We invite a close comparison of the above prices with those of any other concern. If you do not conclude we can save you money we will not ask you to place your order in our hands.

## Our $7.75 Brush Plow.

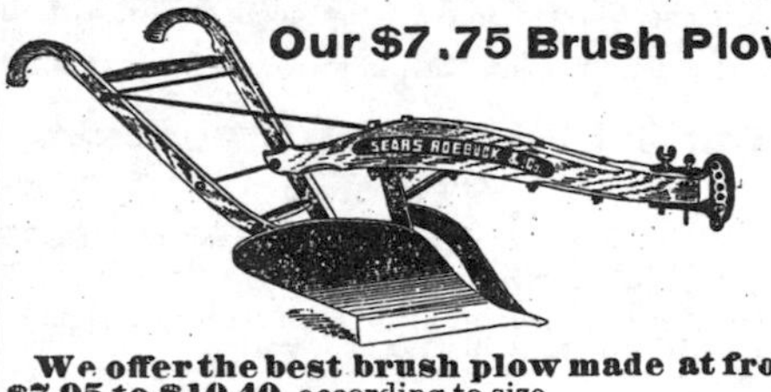

**We offer the best brush plow made at from $7.95 to $10.40,** according to size.

No. 18137. 10-in. with Quincy cutter and iron strap **$7.95**
No. 18138. 11-in. with Quincy cutter and iron strap **$8.50**
No. 18139. 12-in. with Quincy cutter and iron strap **$8.95**
No. 18140. 14-inch with Quincy cutter and iron strap ........ **$10.40**

The above illustration engraved from a photograph will give you some idea of the appearance of this, the best brush plow on the market. It comes complete with cutter and iron strap under beam. This plow is intended for new and brushy land, where there are stumps and roots. It is very strong and does its work perfectly in all kinds of land. It is also generally used for a road plow, and as such gives universal satisfaction. Weight, 80, 85, 90 and 100 lbs., according to size.

## Our $7.00 Stubble Plows.

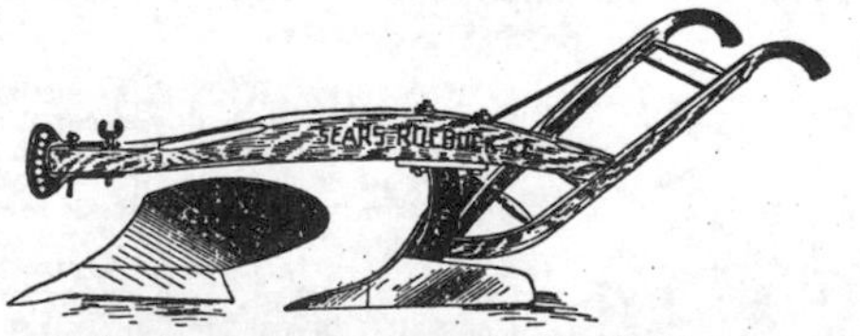

**We believe these are the best all purpose stubble plows** on the market, and we are satisfied our prices are below any competition.

This is a very strong substantial plow with 3-horse clevis, adjustable heavy wrought iron standard with extra hardened land side share and moldboard, material used being the best in the market. Is nicely constructed and is furnished with wrought iron frog. Extra shares can be furnished which we guarantee to fit. Points are made heavy and strong. Beams and handles are made of the best southern white oak, well braced, and the plow is finished in a very attractive manner. They are made throughout of soft center steel, extra hardened. Made for either right or left hand, as desired. This is a very popular plow throughout the central and western states, made especially for the west and northwest, and guaranteed to scour in any soil.

| | Size, inch. | Weight, lbs. | Single share. | Double share. | Extra share. |
|---|---|---|---|---|---|
| No. 18141. | 12 | 76 | $7.00 | $ 8.00 | $2.00 |
| No. 18142. | 14 | 90 | 8.40 | 9.40 | 2.25 |
| No. 18143. | 16 | 100 | 9.50 | 10.50 | 2.75 |

## Our Steel Beam Rod Breakers at from $6.50 to $7.70.

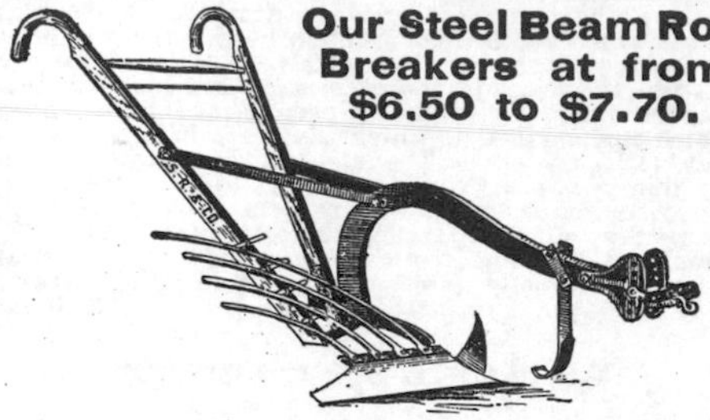

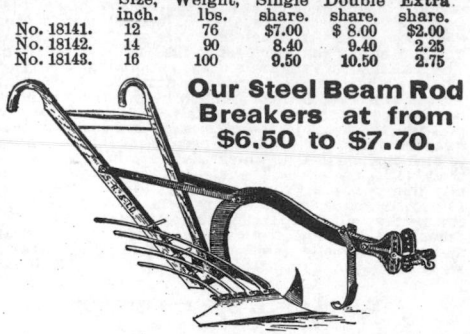

No. 18144. 12-inch with Fin cutter and extra share, weight 750 lbs. Price ........ **$6.50**
No. 18145. 14-inch with Fin cutter and extra share, weight 80 lbs. Price ........ **$7.10**
No. 18146. 16-inch with Fin cutter and extra share, weight 85 lbs. Price ........ **$7.70**

We guarantee this the best rod breaker on the market. It is made of the very best material throughout, put together in a very strong and substantial manner and guaranteed in every respect. It comes with the very best steel land side, best steel Fin cutter and extra share.

## The Prairie Breaking Plow at $10.90.

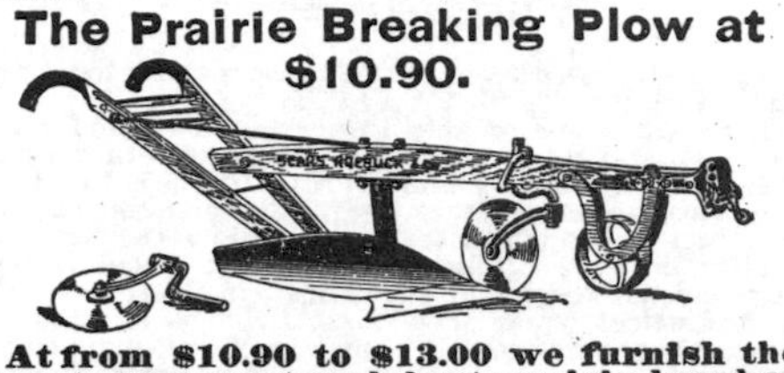

**At from $10.90 to $13.00 we furnish the finest, strongest and best prairie breaker made, complete with rolling coulter, gauge wheel and extra share.**

No. 18147. 10-inch plow complete with rolling coulter, gauge wheel and extra share. Weight, 125 lbs.. **$10.90**
No. 18148. 12-inch plow complete with rolling coulter, gauge wheel and extra share. Weight, 130 lbs.. **$11.40**
No. 18149. 14-inch plow complete with rolling coulter gauge wheel and extra share. Weight, 150 lbs.. **$12.10**
No. 18150. 16-inch plow complete with rolling coulter, gauge wheel and extra share. Weight, 155 lbs.. **$13.00**

## Our $21.00 Mountain Plow.

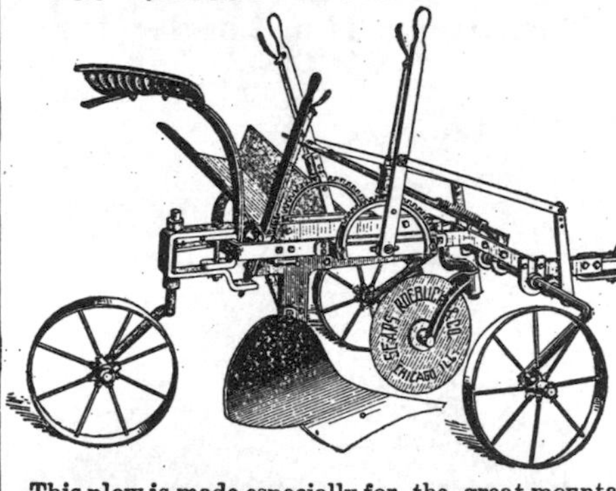

This plow is made especially for the great mountain wheat fields of Washington and other mountainous states, and our price is about one-half the price charged by the ordinary local dealer in those sections.

While this plow is made especially for mountainous country, it is equally adapted for loose and level countries, and especially desirable where the farmer does not want his field cut up with dead furrows or back furrows. It is arranged so that one movement of the lever changes it from a right hand to a left hand plow; at the same time the rear wheel is automatically changed from behind the plow so that it is raised and placed behind the plow that is to do the work. The side levers are so arranged that the wheel can be raised and lowered 12 inches, so that the plow can be run level on any hill side or set to run with the hill to suit the wishes of the operator. You will find with this plow on a hill side you can turn a furrow down 24 inches wide, and not only do the work well but with less draught than a narrower furrow on level ground. There is a perfect adjusting lever to throw the draught where wanted without the driver leaving his seat as the plows are changed. It is perfect in every respect, thoroughly tried, and has two complete plows. It is the cheapest riding plow on the market.

No. 18152. Our price, 14-inch ........ **$21.00**
No. 18153. Our price, 16-inch ........ **$24.00**

## The Best Sulky on the Market.

**No. 18154. Your choice of 14 or 16 inch.**
**Our net cash with order price is $29.00,** and the price quoted is for the sulky delivered on board the cars.

The above illustration represents our new tongueless three wheel sulky with cast wheel in the furrow both at rear and in front of plow, and which is warranted to turn a square corner better than any other sulky made. It is light draught, simple in construction, very easily handled, and made of the very best material, and at the price we quote is the cheapest sulky on the market. Is made with best Bessemer steel wheels with movable boxes and has steel rolling coulter. In turning at end or moving about the doubletrees rise off the ground and the brake keeps the plow from running into the horses' heels.

## Our Gang Plow for $42.00.

**$42.00 is our net cash with order price for this plow. There is no discount.** At $42.00 we furnish this plow complete with land lever, wide shares, steel seat, double board, two large rolling coulters, weed hooks and four horse evener. It turns a square corner to perfection.

The above illustration represents our new tongueless gang plow which works perfectly with four horses abreast or strung out, the off horse in all cases walking in the furrow. It has the best steel wheels, spring lift, large rolling coulters, leveling lever, adjusting land lever and perfect lifting lever, which gives it an advantage over all other wheel plows. It is also made without riding attachment when desired. Plows are made with double boards and steel seats. We can furnish it with arch or moldboard breaker bottom when desired. All our tongueless gang plows and sulkies are provided with a device for holding the plow from running into the horses' heels when the plows are out of the ground. This is a valuable improvement over all others. Weight of plows, about 500 lbs.
No. 18155. Our price for gang with 2 12-inch plows..............................................$42.00
No. 18155½. Price for plow with 2 14-inch plows. 45.00

## The King of Gang Plows.

**$43.00 net cash with order, no discount.** We do not make any discount on plows, but we make you the price of $43.00 for this gang plow delivered on board the cars at the factory from which point you must pay the freight.
No. 18156. Our price with 2 12-inch plows complete..............................................$43.00
No. 18157. Our special price with 2-14-inch plows complete..............................................$46.00
The above illustration shows our improved old reliable gang, which works perfectly with 4 horses abreast, or 2 ahead of 2. Has steel wheels, spring lifts, 2 cutters, 4 horse evener and neckyoke. Beams are very strong. It is very easy to handle, easily carried on three wheels, and is guaranteed to be lighter on the team than any other walking plow in proportion to the work done, and lighter with driver than any other wheel plow made. Plows are made with double board and chilled cast shares. We recommend cast shares for hard or sandy ground. Rods or moldboard breaker bottoms can be furnished for our sulkies, gangs, etc., when desired. Special prices on application.

## Our $13.00 Subsoil Lister with Wood Beam Complete with Runners.

**No. 18158.** We furnish this lister in either 14 or 16 inch as desired. We guarantee this lister will scour in all soils. The only lister on the market furnished with runners, easy to handle and will almost run alone. Weight of lister, 100 lbs.
Price..............................................$13.00

## Our $13.00 Subsoil Lister.

**No. 18159.** Complete with steel beam and runners. Our price of **$13.00** is the net cash price, from which there is no discount, and the price quoted is for the lister delivered on board the cars at the factory in Alton, Ill., from which point you must pay the freight.
This is a 14 inch subsoil lister complete with steel beam and runners. Weight, 100 lbs. Made with wide or narrow boards as desired; is very light and perfect in every respect. We claim for it the following advantages over any other lister made. It has patent double runners, which carry the plow in an upright position. It has patent frog, which enables us to use a lister lay much cheaper than any other. It has covering shovels so arranged that they rise up with the wheel in turning around, and with the aid of the covering shovels the furrow is made highest in the middle, and the corn comes up in the highest place and is much less liable to be washed out by sudden rains. This lister is high under the beam and will not clog up with trash. We guarantee this the best lister on the market regardless of price, and earnestly solicit your orders.

## Our $22.95 Lister, with Runners.

We can furnish this lister in both 14 and 16 inch.
No. 18160. 14 inch, with both wheels; weight, 175 lbs. Price..............................................$22.95
No. 18161. 16 inch, both wheels; weight, 180 lbs. Price..............................................$23.95
We furnish this lister, with either sprocket or solid wheel, or both, as desired. When solid wheel is used, a spring scraper is attached. Deduct **$1.00**, if only one wheel is wanted. We claim for this lister the following advantages over any other lister on the market: It has double runners, which carry the plow in an upright position. Farmers who have handled a lister without runners will appreciate this; has new patent triple cut off dropper box, which rarely ever misses, and is guaranteed not to cut the corn, the only perfect drop on the market; has our new patent frog, which enables us to use a lister lay much cheaper than any other; is less liable to break, and is more easily sharpened; has covering shovels, so arranged that they rise up with the wheel when turning around, and with the aid of the covering shovel the furrow is made high in the middle, the corn comes up in the highest place, and is much less liable to be washed out by a heavy rain; it is also much easier to cultivate when the corn comes up in the highest part of the ditch; has a subsoil drill separate, and can be adjusted to break up the ground and plant at any required depth; that is, corn may be deposited one-half as deep as your subsoil, placing the seed in the soft ground instead of the hard, cold bottom. Practical farmers will readily appreciate the advantages of this plan. The lister is high under the beam, and will not clog up with trash. The rear wheel can be raised up when turning, and when raised throws the dropper out of gear. The drill is made substantial, and the plates can be changed in a moment without the use of a wrench. It has 3 dropper plates, with different holes, and can be adjusted to drop 12, 16, or 20 inches apart, as desired. Is warranted not to cut the corn, and we furnish sorghum or broom corn plates when desired, at **$1.50** extra.
Prices on riding listers furnished on application.

## Our 14-inch Sulky Lister Complete with Covering Shovels for $36.00.

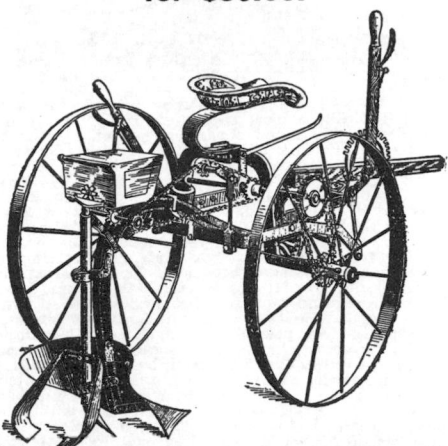

**Our 16-inch sulky lister complete with covering shovels at $37.00.** This is an old reliable lister and the only successful riding lister on the market. New triple cut off, spring lift and all the latest improvements. It has exactly the same frame as our old reliable sulky, and any farmer that has that sulky can obtain an attachment to convert it into a listing sulky at **$23.00** for 14-inch, **$22.50** for 16-inch, which includes triple trees, drill and fixtures. Weight of this sulky lister complete is 450 lbs. Price quoted is for the sulky lister delivered on board the cars at Alton, Ill., from which point you must pay the freight.

## Our Channel Steel Harrows at from $7.90 to $12.75.

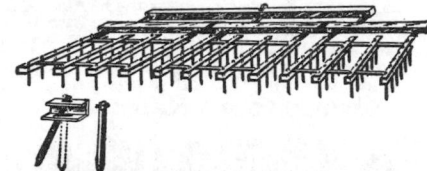

No. 18162. 48 teeth, 2 sections. Price........$ 7.90
No. 18163. 72 teeth, 3 sections. Price........ 11.00
No. 18164. 96 teeth, 4 sections. Price........ 12.75
We consider our channel steel harrow the best harrow on the market of any kind. It is simple and durable. It has no bolts and nuts to work loose. The teeth reverse automatically and it does perfect work in all kinds of soil. Has hinged drawbar and same steel rail as on our lever harrows. We have put our prices below any competition and we shall hope to be favored with your orders.

## Our $9.25 Steel Lever Harrow.

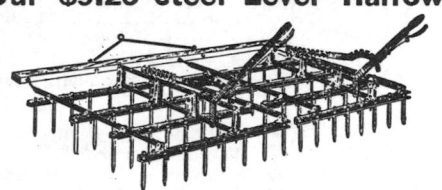

No. 18165. Price with 64 teeth, 2 sections, flexible harrow..............................................$ 9.25
No. 18166. Same harrow with springs......... 10.00
No. 18167. 96 teeth, 3 sections, flexible harrow. 13.00
No. 18168. Same harrow with springs........ 14.50
We make these harrows with both light and heavy rails, and guarantee the heavy harrow in any work; will furnish new rails free if you break them. We make these harrows in 2 sections, 64 teeth, and in 3 sections, 96 teeth. We make these harrows with flexible or rigid frame as desired, the flexible frame having cross or truss bars only on the top, while the rigid have the cross or truss bars across both top and bottom. The rails are made of channel steel, very light and very strong, with a square hole at the bottom and a round hole at the top, enabling us to get the full strength of the teeth, which are fastened in by a hexagon nut on top of the rail. This harrow is a great improvement over any other harrow made and has features covered by our patent that no farmer will do without when once understood. The illustration above of our flexible harrow shows the spring device which we can put on either style harrow at an additional expense of 50c a section. The spring gives the teeth a vibrating or dancing motion which keeps them from gathering trash, causes them to pulverize the ground more thoroughly and prevents the teeth from being injured or bent when striking an obstruction. The springs can be changed to the ordinary style by changing the pin from the hole in front of the casting to a hole through the casting, and thus giving the operator both styles of harrow in one. This is the easiest harrow on the market to set up, the castings being fastened to the rails and the cross bars attached with bolts.

---

**If there is any way we can serve you on any purchase whatsoever, do not hesitate to write us. We can save you money on almost anything that is made.**

## The $7.70 Harrow.

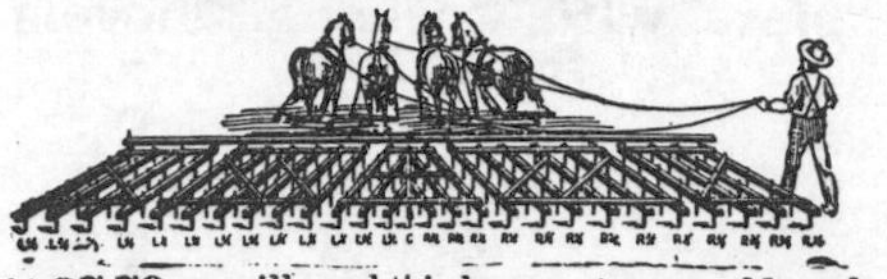

At **$7.70** we will send this harrow to any address by freight C. O. D., subject to examination, on receipt of sufficient deposit to cover transportation charges both ways. Three per cent. discount will be allowed if cash in full accompanies your order, in which case **$7.46** pays for the harrow. Please observe our 3 per cent. discount in comparing prices with other houses.

Made at St. Paul. This harrow is made at St. Paul by one of the largest manufacturers there, and the price quoted is for the harrow delivered on board the cars at St. Paul, from which point you must pay the freight. This harrow is intended especially for northwest and western trade. For Minnesota, the Dakotas and Iowa there is perhaps no more popular harrow made. This harrow is constructed to accomplish the greatest amount of work in the least possible time, and in such a manner that the farmer can have two or more harrows by purchasing one, the changes being made by adding or taking off the sections as a narrow or wide harrow is wanted. The bars are made 2 by 2½ inches, eveners 2 by 4 inches, of the very best seasoned oak. Each bar is insured against splitting by long double clinchers on either side of each tooth. Teeth are ½ inch square, steel with dagger point or square center point. The sections are independent and connected with evener by eye-bolts so as to secure a perfect hitch, allowing the sections flexibility and vibration without permitting the teeth to drag or follow each other. Each tooth cuts its own way. To insure deep cutting and thorough pulverization, dagger teeth are used. The two-horse harrow consists of center section and two next sections. The three-horse harrow of center section and three sections adjoining. The four-horse harrow consists of all the sections shown. We furnish draw bars to match number of sections ordered.

No. 18169. Two-horse harrow, 78 teeth, cuts 13 feet; weight, 190 lbs. Price........................ **$7.70**

No. 18170. Three-horse harrow, 82 teeth, cuts 16¼ feet; weight, 240 lbs. Price........................ **$9.95**

No. 18171. Four-horse harrow, 150 teeth, cuts 26 feet; weight, 360 lbs. Price........................ **$14.00**

Remember the prices quoted are for the harrow delivered on board the cars at St. Paul, Minn., and we allow a discount of 3 per cent. if cash in full accompanies your order. If you live within a thousand miles of St. Paul, either east, west or northwest, you will save 25 per cent. in price by ordering this harrow from us.

## Spring Tooth Harrow.

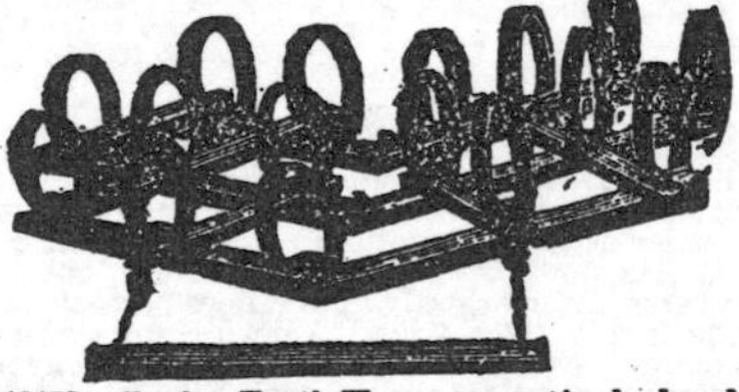

No. 18172. Spring Tooth Harrow, particularly adapted to stony and stumpy ground or tough sod. The spring tooth will cultivate the ground thoroughly. Now furnished with steel frame in place of wood. Average weight, 200 lbs. Price, 16 tooth........................ **$11.50**
Price, 18 tooth........................ **12.50**

## Harrow Teeth.

No. 18173. Steel Harrow Teeth, square, plain head. Give length when ordering.

| Sizes, inches. | Wt. per doz. lbs. | Per doz. |
|---|---|---|
| ½x8, 8½ or 9 | 6 to 7 | **25c** |
| 9-16x8½ or 9 | 8 to 9 | **30c** |
| ⅝x8½, 9, 9½ or 10 | 10 to 12 | **40c** |
| ¾x10 or 11 | 17 to 21 | **90c** |

## Plow Shares.

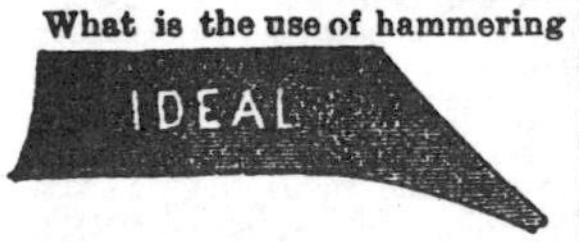


What is the use of hammering out your shares when you can get shares drawn, shaped and polished, ready to weld? They are made of the best soft center and solid crucible cast steel. They are the best shape; have an upset edge, and can be easily fitted to any plow

No. 18174. No. 1 Shares, double shinned, for old ground plows, made from soft center steel, 12, 14 or 16 inch cut. Each........................ **$1.32, $1.62, $1.85**

No. 18175. No. 1 Shares, single shinned, for old ground plows, made from soft center steel, 12, 14 or 16 inch cut. Each........................ **$1.11, $1.28, $1.45**

No. 18176. No. 2 Shares, double shinned, for old ground plows, made from solid crucible cast steel, 12, 14 or 16 inch cut. Each........................ **90c, $1.13, $1.20**

No. 18177. No. 2 Shares, single shinned, for old ground plows, made from solid crucible cast steel, 12, 14 or 16 inch cut. Each........................ **88c, $1.05 $1.18**

We guarantee every share to be as represented.

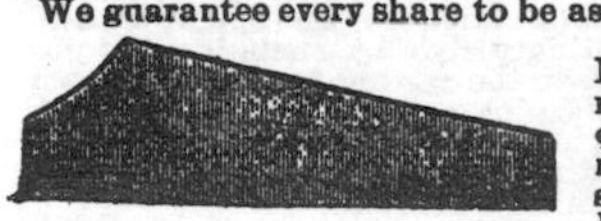

No. 18168. No. 1 Landside Plates, ready for use for 14 or 16 inch plow, made of soft center steel. Each..... **80c, 90c**

No. 18178. No. 2 Landside Plates, ready for use for 14 or 16 inch plow, made of crucible cast steel. Each........................ **45c, 55c**

## Steel Beam Double Shovel Plow for $2.50.

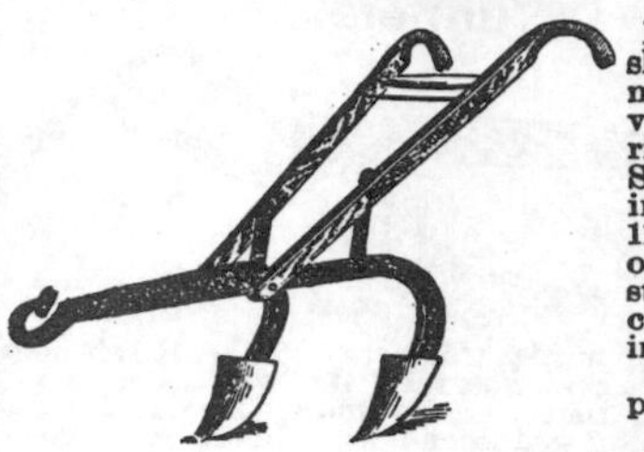

No. 18180. This shovel plow is made of the very best material throughout. Shovels are 6 inches wide and 11 inches long, of hardened steel. Width of coulter, 20 inches.

Our special price.... **$2.50**

## Five Tooth Steel Frame Cultivator at $2.60.

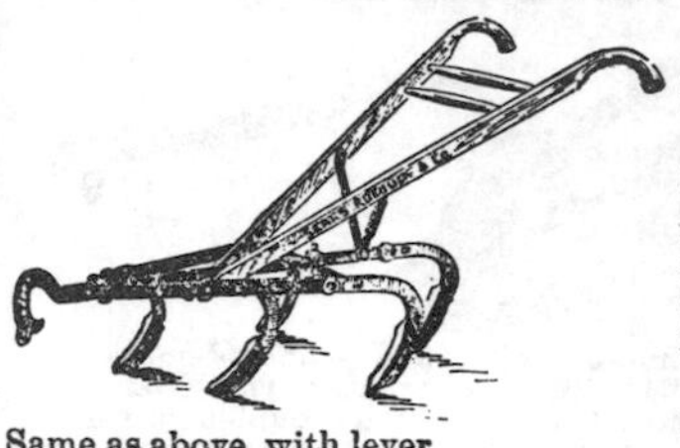

No. 18181. 10 inch shovels. This is the strongest, cheapest and best 5-tooth cultivator made. Adjustable teeth to suit all kinds of soil.

Our special price ... **$2.60**

Same as above, with lever........................ **3.10**
Same, with wheel and lever........................ **3.45**

## Our Boys' Cultivator at from $12.00 to $14.00.

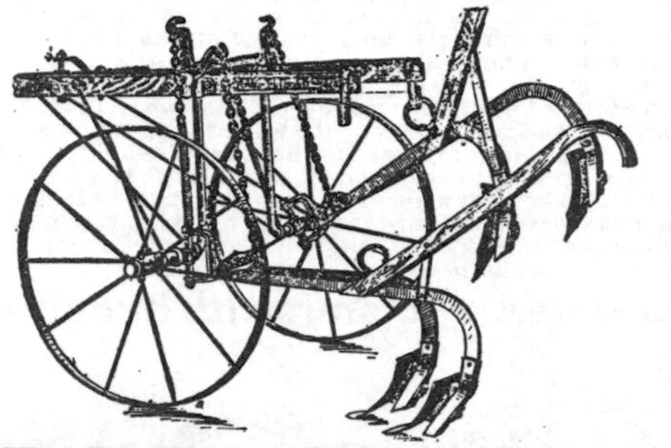

**We offer at from $12.00 to 14.00 a strictly high grade cultivator** which we can guarantee in every respect, and that can not be equaled by any other in the market at less than $20.

The illustration above represents what we have named our "Boys' Cultivator," because it works so easily and is so easily adjusted that the boys all like it. We claim it has the best and most perfect spring in the world, one that needs no fixing and does all that you want a spring to do. In the work there is no lift. The shovels run naturally by the hitch when started. The swinging chain is so arranged that there is no tendency to draw the shovels together or to swing apart, the chain always being straight over the load. We use the finest steel wheels with chilled boxing, and the casting is A No. 1. We believe in making the best regardless of cost. Do not buy a steel wheel cultivator without movable boxes. Weight of cultivator, 210 lbs.

No. 18182. Price for Boys' Cultivator with steel beam........................ **$12.00**

No. 18183. Price for Boys' Cultivator, with "eagle claw"........................ **$13.00**

No. 18184. Price for Boys' Cultivator, with spring tooth........................ **$11.00**

No. 18185. Price for Boys' Cultivator, with parallel beam........................ **$14.00**

## Our Tongueless Cultivator at $12.00.

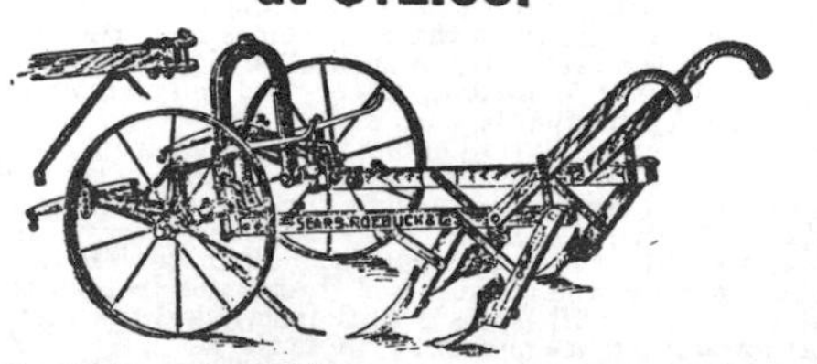


No. 18186. **$12.00** is our net cash with order price, from which there is no discount. All orders for this cultivator must be accompanied by cash in full. We offer for **$12.00** a cultivator which you could not duplicate for less than **$20.00**. The price quoted is for this cultivator delivered on board the cars at Alton, Ill., from which point you must pay the freight.

We guarantee this the best tongueless cultivator on the market, regardless of price.

Your choice of wood beam or steel beam, as desired. The price is the same.

The above illustration, engraved from a photograph, will give you some idea of the appearance of this perfect, high grade cultivator. It has a perfect lateral, or vertical adjustment; has hang-up hooks, which can be turned out of the way when at work; runners, which can be put in a carrying position quickly without the use of a wrench; has the same device for taking up slack or wear as our regular tongue cultivators; has an arch that does not fall down when turning at the end of the row; has shovels on a gang, shaped so as to turn the earth the same way, and throw it over like a plow, and yet, when both are set to turn the same way, they perfectly follow the line of draught, and do not swing off to one side, and when pushed out to dodge the corn will instantly swing back; has a tongue attachment, by which it can be changed into a perfect tongue cultivator, and when used as a tongue cultivator there is no vibrating or swinging of the tongue to fret or wear the horses—has the very best malleable break pin—the highest grade movable boxes over wheels. Weight, 171 lbs. Our special price........................ **$12.00**

## Our Acme Wood or Steel Beam Cultivator for $12.95.

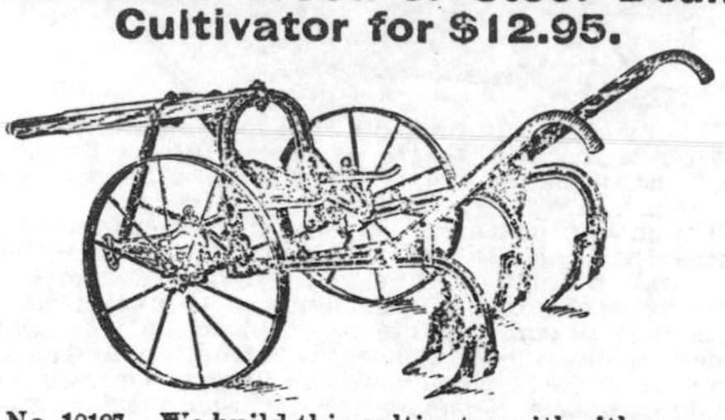

No. 18187. We build this cultivator with either wood or steel beam, as desired. The price is the same.

The above illustration represents our new Acme cultivator, which is a great improvement over all others of its class, being a perfect tongue cultivator, and can be changed to the best tongueless cultivator on the market in a few minutes. The wheels, being hinged to the frame or arch, are always in line with the draught of the team and turn easily and naturally; it makes no difference in what position the team may be. Other cultivators having the vibrating movement and the wheels attached rigidly to the frame or arch are always parallel to the frame, and when the team is turning and one horse stands ahead of the other the wheels must scrape or slide sidewise, thus making it hard on the team and liable to break the wheels or axle. This hinging of the wheels to the axle is a feature that belongs to the Acme exclusively, and puts it ahead of all others of its class. Examine the Acme carefully and you will at once see its advantages over all others. Has malleable break pin and low hitch. The wheels have movable boxes, making them wear resisting.

We can furnish the Acme cultivator with "Eagle Claw" beam or "Spring Tooth" beam at 50c extra when so desired. The prices quoted are for the cultivator delivered on board the cars at Alton, Ill., from which point you must pay the freight. This is one of the most popular cultivators on the market, and there are more of them in use in Iowa, Kansas, Nebraska, Missour and Illinois than any other three cultivators made.

## Our Celebrated Riding Vibrating Hitch Cultivator for $22.00.

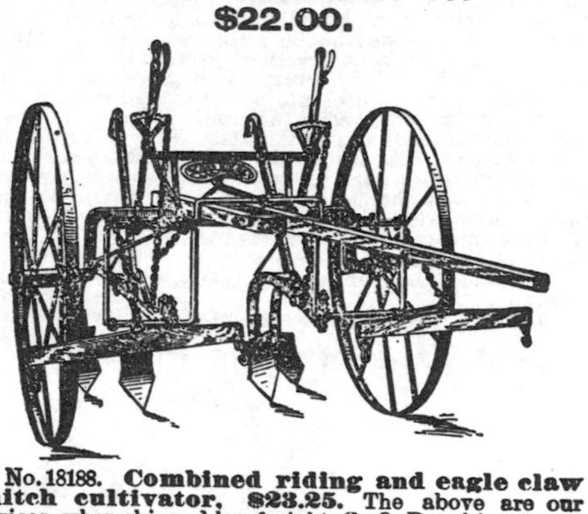

No. 18188. **Combined riding and eagle claw hitch cultivator, $23.25.** The above are our prices when shipped by freight C. O. D. subject to examination on receipt of a sufficient deposit to cover freight charges both ways.

**Three per cent. discount** will be allowed if cash in full accompanies your order.

These cultivators have been thoroughly tested the past eight years by practical farmers and pronounced an entire success. With this cultivator the team is hitched close to the work and practically direct to the shovel beams. Each horse is made to pull his own gang or shovels and it entirely does away with the vibrating or swinging of the tongue. Has patent double hitch which perfectly controls the tendency of the tongue to rise up when the operator rides, and takes the weight off the horse's neck when he walks. Has springs which can be adjusted to carry the shovels to any desired lift or to be non-acting when at work. By the use of these springs the combined riding cultivator can be changed into a perfect walking spring cultivator. Has a perfect foot lift, which enables the driver to raise the shovels with his foot in turning. When the cultivator is used as a rider, the shanks or beams can be carried on a stationary chain in the usual way or allowed to work free, and the depth of the shovels can be changed while the team is in motion. We furnish twisted or straight shovels as ordered, but where no special orders are given we send them with two twisted and two straight shovels and shields. Bull tongues and moldboard shovels furnished extra when desired. Can also be changed to an eagle claw or spring tooth cultivator. Price, **$22.00**, or **$23.25** when furnished with a combined eagle claw.

**When you order your Cultivator or Plow you can have small articles, such as Clothing, Dry Goods, Notions or Books, sent along at no extra expense.**

## Our Single Row Two Horse Riding Corn and Cotton Stalk Cutter for $22.00.

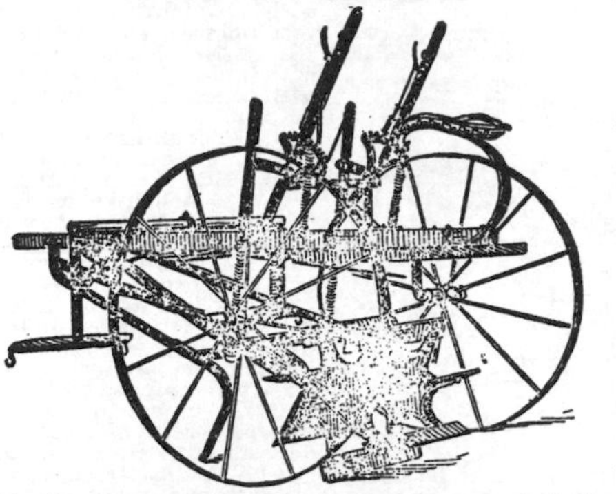

The illustration above shows the new patent single row corn and cotton stalk cutter. The double row has two revolving discs and the machine is just double the width of the single row cutter. Has double pole to use three horses. The plan is different from all others. Instead of cutting by the weight of the cutter head and machine, the power comes entirely from springs. The combination of lever and springs enables the operator to apply any force to the knives that may be necessary to do the work, and when raised from the ground to turn the same springs raises the cutter head, making the easiest cutter to handle in the world. The seat and wheels are high and the driver well up out of the dust. The wheels running into low places have no effect on this cutter, as the frame never rides the cutter head, which has always plenty of room to work, and the knives are never crushed into the ground as with all other cutters, making them do poor work and over-straining the horses. The steel wheels have malleable boxes, which are bored and fitted as perfectly as those on a buggy. The axles are also turned upon a lathe and are protected by a hub nut instead of a hole in the axle fitted with a pin to keep the wheel on. The machines are made of the very best material, elegantly finished wheels with adjustable hubs and perfect in every respect.

No. 18189. Single row cutter for two horses, shipping weight, 750 lbs. Price.......................... **$22.00**

No. 18190. Double row cutter for three horses, shipping weight, 650 lbs. Price........................ **$40.00**

## Our Acme New Riding Disc Cultivator at from $19.00 to $25.00.

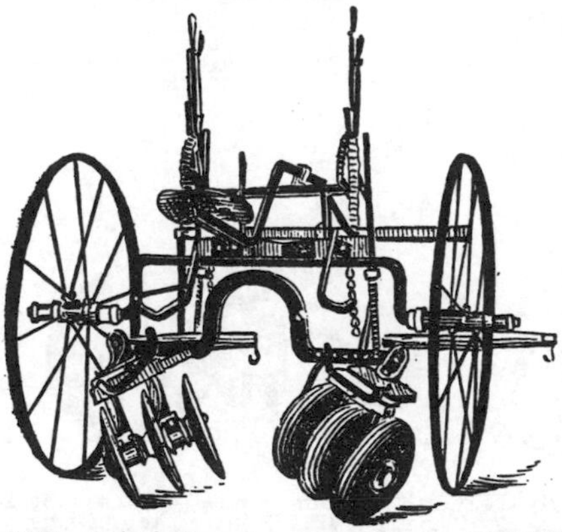

No. 18191. 14-inch discs, 3 on each side....... **$19.00**
No. 18192. 16-inch discs, 3 on each side....... **$21.00**
No. 18193. 14-inch discs, 4 on each side....... **$24.00**
No. 18194. 16-inch discs, 4 on each side....... **$25.00**

This cultivator possesses all the advantages of all other riding cultivators, and has in addition cultivating discs that can be set at any angle and any distance apart. They can be reversed so as to turn the ground up or away from the corn. Has light hitch. Each horse pulls his own side of the cultivator. No swinging of the tongue. The wheels and gangs work parallel and are thrown sidewise by simply bearing down on the foot pedal, leaving both hands free to handle the team. This makes plowing of the crookedest rows very easy, overcoming a great fault with all other discs. We hitch the drag to the front end of a beam with a clevice and are able to gauge the depth just the same as on a walking plow. Made with 3 or 4 discs on each side. When 4 discs are put on the implement can be used in place of a disc harrow, and it is but a moment's work to change from 3 to 4 discs and vice versa. Weight 450 lbs.


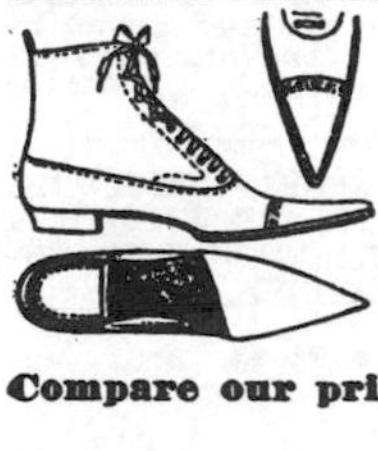

**Never Such Bargains**

As are offered in our

**SHOE DEPARTMENT.**

**See Pages 180 to 205.**


## Our New Style Steel Frame Disc Harrow, at $22.00 and Upwards.

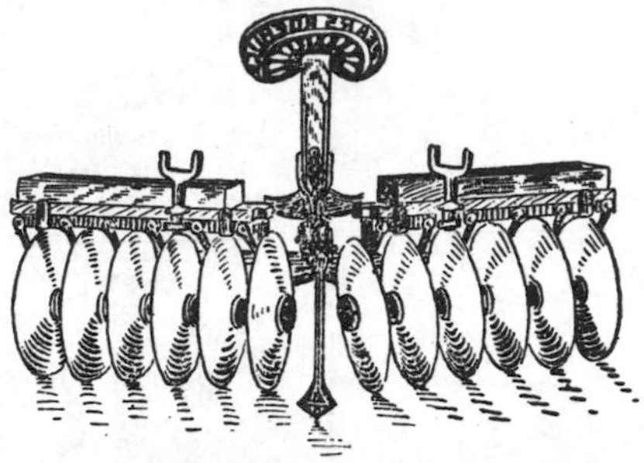

**We furnish this Harrow either with sections** close together or spread apart, with center shovel, if desired, complete, with 4 horse evener.

No. 18195. Price for harrow, with 12-16 inch discs, cut 6¼ foot, no center shovel .................. **$22.00**
Same harrow, with center shovel............ **24.00**
No. 18196. Price for harrow, with 14-16 inch discs, cut 7½ foot, with no center shovel ............ **$23.00**
Same, with center shovel ..................... **25.00**
No. 18197. Price for harrow, with 16-16 inch discs, cut 8½ feet, no center shovel.................. **$26.00**
Same harrow, with center shovel............. **28.00**
No. 18198. Price for harrow, with 12-20 inch discs, cut 6¼ feet, no center shovel .................. **$23.50**
Same harrow, with center shovel............. **25.50**
No. 18199. Price for harrow, with 14-20 inch discs, cut 7¼ feet, no center shovel.................. **$25.50**
Same harrow, with center shovel............ **27.50**
No. 18200. Price for harrow, with 16-20 inch discs, cut 8½ feet, no center shovel.................. **$29.00**
Same with center shovel, cut 9 feet........... **31.00**

At the above prices we furnish this harrow, delivered on board the cars at Alton, Ill., from which point you must pay the freight.

We believe this to be the best disc harrow in the world. The gangs are set the proper distance apart for cultivating corn, while with others the machines have to be taken apart to get the inside discs off, and when they are off they are too far apart to do good work. Cuts 6 inches deeper than any other of the same size on account of leaving a space between the sections. The space left is cut by the shovel, which leaves the earth behind the machine, while others leave a little ridge in the center with a ditch on either side, and do not pulverize the center. The center shovel can be raised with the foot when turning or passing an obstruction. The center shovel can be taken out and sections put close together for cutting sod. The box which bears the pressure of the side dish of the gangs is made of the same hard material that is used in our moldboards, is guaranteed to wear longer than any other, and the wearing parts can be replaced for 50 cents. All our harrows are arranged to work with 2, 3 or 4 horses, but we furnish combined 2, 3 and 4 horse evener that works perfectly either way. There is no side or gang draft. We can furnish our harrows with 16 discs, and you can reduce the size to any number of discs desired by simply taking them off. This is a great advantage, as it enables the farmer to enlarge or reduce his disc to suit his team or work. We make all sizes, so that the sections can be set close together for cutting sod or spread apart and used with the center shovel. The advantage of the center shovel is so apparent that no one who investigates the matter will use any other, as it does better work, cutting out the center left untouched by other harrows, and adds 6 inches to the amount cultivated every round.

## Our Special $36.50 Side Throw Disc Harrow.

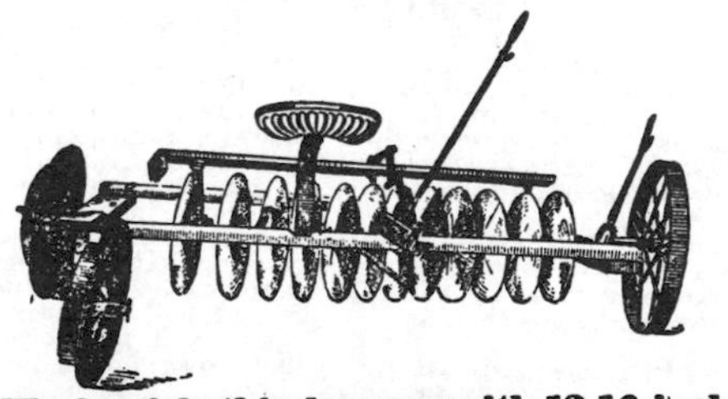

**We furnish this harrow with 12 16-inch discs and 6¼-foot cut, for $36.50.**

**Price with 12 20-inch discs and 6¼-foot cut, $40.50.**

**The prices quoted are for the harrow when shipped** by freight C. O. D. subject to examination on receipt of a sufficient deposit to cover freight charges both ways, balance and freight charges to be paid after the harrow is received. Three per cent. discount will be allowed if cash in full accompanies your order. We feel safe in saying that we are quoting this harrow at least 33⅓ per cent less than it can be had at retail.

With discs throwing all one way; is carried on wheels and with a flexible tongue. We claim the following points of superiority over all others: The discs being in one gang and turning the earth in one direction, there is no ditch left in the middle or any ridge made where the earth laps or comes together. All farmers who have used the old style discs will see the advantage of this point. It being carried on wheels, the depth can be perfectly controlled, as the discs will run at full angle without running so deep the team cannot pull it. The old style disc when set at full angle in soft ground ran too deep, and when the angle was changed to keep them out of the ground did not do good work.

It can be raised off the ground to move about the farm or to turn around at the end of the land. The discs can be raised or lowered in an instant without stopping the team, and from the driver's seat. The rear wheel being a cast wheel, the machine is very easy to turn at the ends when it is unlatched. Our disc boxes are oiled through the top of the standards, the oil going just where wanted, and the oil holes being where no dirt can get in them. If it is necessary to move the discs over rocky ground, the flanges or knives on the wheels can be esily taken off by removing 4 bolts. The disc harrow is a perfect cultivator and weed killer and the best machine for cultivating summer fallow.

No. 18201. Price for 12 16-inch discs, 6½-foot cut............................................. **$36.50**

No. 18202. Price for 12 20-inch discs with 6½-foot cut............................................. **$40.50**

## Our Combination Disc Harrow and Grain Drill.

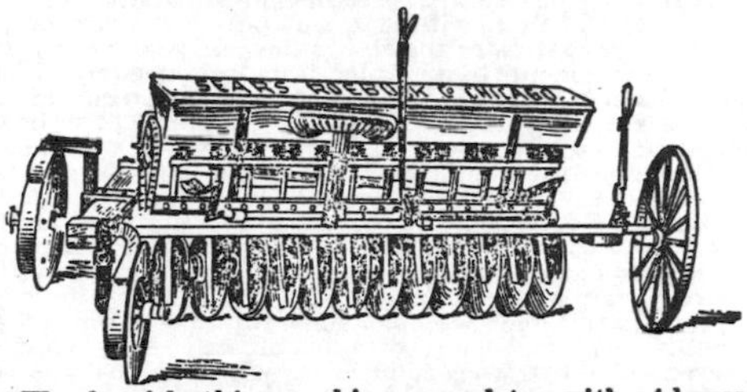

We furnish this machine complete with 4-horse evener and polished discs at from $44.00 to $51.00 according to size.

No. 18204. Machine complete with 12 20-inch polished discs............................................. **$44.00**

No. 18205. Machine complete with 14 20-inch polished discs............................................. **$47.00**

No. 18206. Machine complete with 16 20-inch polished discs............................................. **$51.00**

There are many advantages in this machine over all others. The disc drill when polished will cut through sod and trash, and run where no other drill can go. Drills in rows over 6½ inches apart, so that the grain is more perfectly distributed and less likely to grow with a line of weeds alternating with a row of grain. The discs perfectly cleave the ground at the time of putting in the grain and leave it in better condition. The grain is deposited in the bottom of trench behind the discs, put in at a uniform depth and covered perfectly, and thus needs no wheel behind to cover the grain. The wheels make a furrow over the rows of grain and may cause it to be blown away by a strong wind or washed out by rain. The drill devices are adjustable so that the grain can be discharged at any height, which is an important point, as when cutting in sod the drill must discharge the seed near the ground or it will scatter and not fall in the furrow, and be left on top of the ground. Do not forget this point when selecting a drill. In our drill the driver at all times can see the cups or drill spouts, and know that they are working perfectly. We guarantee our seeding apparatus to be as good as any made, and to sow from one-half to four bushels to the acre perfectly. All our drills are furnished with broadcast seeder attachment and the drill can be changed to a broadcast seeder and vice versa in a few moments' time. This disc harrow is a perfect cultivator and weed killer, and the best machine made for summer fallow. The drill or seeder attachment can be removed, and then you have a perfect disc harrow, giving you the use of two machines in one.

## Our $2.15 Little Giant Disc Sharpener.

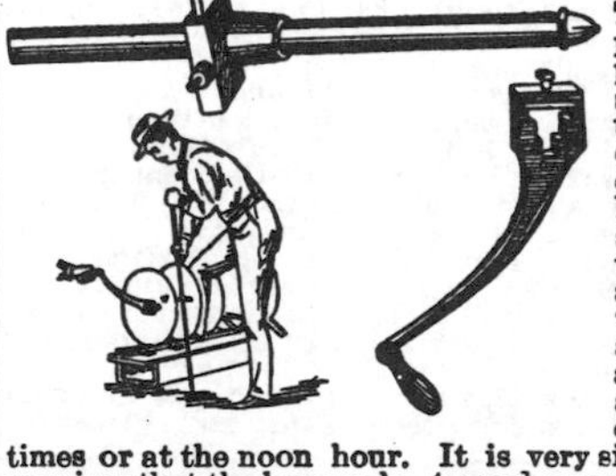

No. 18207. This is the most practicable, portable disc sharpener manufactured. Any disk harrow or cultivator can be thoroughly sharpened without taking apart in less than an hour, and practically at no expense, as it can be done at odd times or at the noon hour. It is very simple and only requires that the harrow be turned upon its back disc upwards and the crank attached to end of shaft as shown in illustration. The crank is made to fit any shaft, any size, round or square.

The sharpener is all iron and will last a lifetime. The plate or chisel is made of Mushat steel hardened, which will bring the disc to a sharp keen edge without destroying the temper and without the use of water. The iron stand which holds the sharpening disc is made adjustable so that it will slide up and down in the bar in order to get the desired distance from the ground. The sharpening chisel is also adjustable and can be extended as it wears away and thus one chisel will last many years. One set screw operates both adjustments. Rolling coulters can also be sharpened nicely by taking them out of the bracket and passing them through the posts the proper height from the ground. Attach the coulter to post and attach the crank same as to harrow. Weight, 7½ lbs. Price............................................. **$2.15**

**Compare our prices if you will with those of any other Mail Order House, and if you don't find our prices the lowest and our terms the most liberal, don't buy of us.**

## Our Combination Disc Harrow and Grain Drill Complete with Four Horse Eveners and Polished Discs at $44.00 to $51.00.

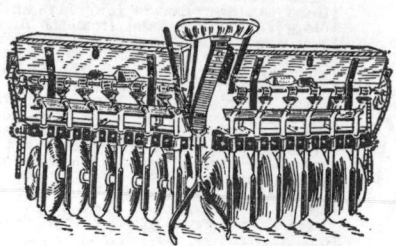

No. 18208.  Price with 12 20-inch polished discs complete ................**$44.00**
No. 18209.  Price with 14 20-inch polished discs complete ................ **47.00**
No. 18210.  Price with 16 20-inch polished discs complete ................ **51.00**

The above illustration shows the drill ready for operation.  It can be changed in a few moments to a regular broadcast seeder, which you can work anywhere a disc harrow will go.  Please note the following advantages:  The drill device can be set up or down to suit the operator; the boxes are set apart so that they will not strike together when at work; we use 12 seed cups, or double the number others do, and thus the grain is distributed evenly regardless of wind or side hills; the covering plates in the center not only cover the grain but level the ground; the drill deposits the grain at a uniform depth where it is well covered, and can be set to sow any depth as deep as the discs run; can be thrown out of gear on one side, leaving the other to work and enabling the operator to sow a narrow strip or finish the land when running near a fence; it has an adjustable chain tightener which enables you to take off and put on the chain without trouble.  The drill can be taken off and discs used separately.  The shields prevent the dirt from interfering with the driving sprocket wheel.  It has a perfect index, showing the quantity sown to the acre.  It has a perfect force feed.  We warrant our improved drill to work in as many kinds and conditions of work as any drill made, and to do good work in places where no shoe or hoe drill will work, but there are places and conditions where it will not work, and in such cases the broadcast seeder attachment, which goes with the drill, covers the case, making a machine that the farmer can always work with, wet or dry.  We guarantee the drill to sow perfectly ½ bushel to the acre, or any larger quantity, and not clog or cut the ground.  The seat is so arranged that the operator sits comfortably on a good spring seat, and back of the drill so that he can see that the seed cups are properly discharging.

## Our Improved Disc Harrow with Seeder Attachment.

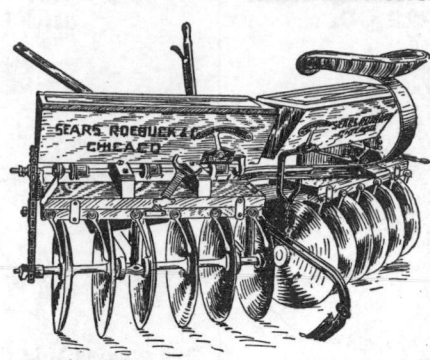

No. 18212.  Price of harrow with 12 16-inch discs complete, with 4-horse evener ..**$34.00**
No. 18213.  Price of harrow with 14 16-inch discs complete, with 4-horse evener ..**$40.00**
No. 18214.  Price of harrow with 16 16-inch discs complete, with 4-horse evener ;..**$46.00**
No. 18215.  Price of harrow with 12 20-inch discs complete, with 4-horse evener..**$36.00**
No. 18216.  Price of harrow with 14 20-inch discs complete, with 4-horse evener ..**$41.00**
No. 18217.  Price of harrow with 16 20-inch discs complete, with 4-horse evener ..**$48.00**

The above are our prices when to be shipped by freight C. O. D., subject to examination, on receipt of sufficient deposit to cover freight charges both ways; balance and freight charges to be paid after harrow is received.  Three per cent. discount will be allowed if cash in full accompanies your order.

The prices quoted are for the harrows delivered on board the cars at the factory at Alton, Ill., from which point you must pay the freight.  You will find the freight will amount to next to nothing as compared with what you will save in price.

This improved disc with seeder attachment has the same features as our drills, except that the seed is scattered broadcast in front of the blades where it is covered.  We claim for it the following advantages over all other machines of the same character:  It has a perfect force feed, which is a very essential feature; it is driven from both sections, and the drive chain is always in line; it is provided with a spring chain tightener, which enables you to take the chain off or put it on without removing the wheels and preventing it coming off; either side can be thrown out of gear; the driver sits where he can see at all times whether the seeds are discharged properly; it has a perfect index, showing the quantity sown to the acre; it is nicely and substantially put up in every way.  We have a center shovel which covers the grain sown in the middle, which no other has, and they not only leave a ditch, which we do not, but they leave grain in the center which is not covered.  It can be used without a shovel if desired.  It has shields which prevent the dirt from interfering with the driving chain sprockets.  This machine is made of the very best material, and is guaranteed to give the most perfect satisfaction when properly operated.

Please note that the seeder can be taken off and the disc used as a separate machine, giving you two perfect machines in one.

## "PLANET JR." GARDEN TOOLS FOR 1897.

We issue a Special Catalogue of "Planet Jr." Garden Tools, which is mailed free on application.

### The "Planet Jr." No. 5 Hill Dropping Seeder.

No. 18211.  This beautiful new tool will be a delightful surprise to every gardener who tries it.  We all know that a garden seed sower that does not drop in hills is fast becoming a thing of the past, for there are but few now who do not wish to plant beans and corn, spinach and salsify, carrots and turnips, parsnips and beets, in hills.  All crops that are to be grown from seed and then thinned to a regular stand, should be planted in hills and at just the distance apart the plants are desired; for in drilling, unless the seed is sown unnecessarily thick, there will not always be a plant at the proper spot, and the crop is therefore irregular.  This means that nowadays a seed sower should drop in hills and at almost every distance apart.  The new No. 5 "Planet Jr." drops at 5, 6, 8, 10, 12, 16, 24 and 48 inches apart, and also beautifully in a continuous row.  It drops without injury, can be changed from hill to drill or from one distance to another very quickly, and without any changing of bolts, and without any loose wheels or parts so easily lost or mislaid; and a neat, clear index with brass screw regulator and quick cut-off is arranged most conveniently just at the top of the handle.

The newcomer is a great favorite, too, because it is unusually large, holding three quarts, yet very light running; and it is also a model of simplicity, strength and durability.  Its large capacity will suit all large growers, and yet it works so perfectly that it will sow a single paper of seed or drop it in hills accurately, to the very last grain.

In a word, no seeder has ever been made that compares with this newly perfected No. 5 "Planet Jr."—the 1897 surprise.  Price........................**$12.00**

## The "Planet Jr." No. 4 Combined Hill Dropping Seeder and Single Wheel Hoe, Cultivator, Rake and Plow.

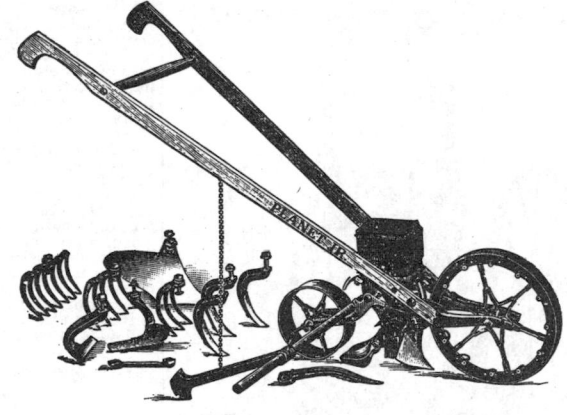

No. 18218.  This is exactly the same fine strain of blood that has proven such a marvelous success in the No. 5 "Planet Jr." Hill Dropper.  As a drill, the points of difference are:  First, that it is smaller in capacity, though still of good size, holding three pints, and that it does not drop at so many different distances apart; however, it drops at all the most important distances, at 6, 9, 12, 18 and 36 inches.  The index is just as fine and accurate and plain, though being a combined tool it is not placed at the top of the handle, but at the side.  It is like No. 5 in dropping in just the same way, just as accurately, and in handling the smallest paper of seed perfectly and to the last grain; has no loose parts, and is simple, durable and very light running.  The drill is quickly detached and the tool frame substituted.  It then becomes the most admirable Single Wheel Hoe of the "Planet Jr." family.  Has a fine garden plow, two elegantly shaped, new-style hoes, three delightful cultivating rakes, made new form and specially to fit 6, 9, 12, and, using two at once, 14 and 16 inch rows; and a practical leaf guard.  Price, complete, **$10.00**; as a drill only ................................................**$7.00**

### The "Planet Jr." No. 2 Seed Drill.

No. 18219.  This tool is used the world over, and with the exception of the "Planet Jr." Hill Dropping Drills, is the most perfect drill known.  It holds two and one-half quarts.

The sowing cylinder is a drum of spring brass, set between the driving wheels.  Around this drum is a brass band, drawn tight to the drum by a cam which joins the ends.  In both drum and band are corresponding diamond-shaped discharge openings; by loosening the cam and sliding the outer band the discharge may be regulated to suit any kind or thickness of seed.  The index contains the names of the principal seeds, and when the name wanted appears through the index slot, it is set right for that seed.  The drill sows in an even, regular stream, whether there is much or little in the hopper.  The opening plow, being directly between the wheels, follows all irregularities of the ground, is adjustable, and once set, opens the furrow at a uniform depth, and the seeds are deposited in a very narrow line.  The machine is extremely simple; having no agitators, belts or gearing, the seed cannot be injured, even if sprouted.  It received the highest award at the World's Fair at Chicago.  Price ................................................**$6.50**

**We guarantee our goods of every description to be fully up to representation or they may be returned to us at our expense and money refunded.**

## The "Planet Jr." No. 3 Hill Dropping Seeder.

Sows either in Hills or Continuous Row.

No. 18220. Until recently there was no such thing as a Hill Dropping Seeder, modern drills sowing continuously only. This drill will sow in a continuous row, in the ordinary way, with the greatest regularity; but its distinctive feature is that it will drop neatly in hills, either 4, 6, 8, 12 or 24 inches apart. It opens the furrow, drops in hills, or drills, covers, rolls down and marks the next row, all at one operation. The hopper holds three quarts. The wheel is 15 inches high, with a broad face. It is changed in a moment from hill dropping to drill work. It has a rubber force feed, sows equally well whether the hopper is full or contains only a paper of seed, and will not injure delicate seeds, such as radish, cabbage, etc., which are so often peeled or crushed by drills having agitators or metal feed wheels. It is nicely adapted to all conditions of land, working especially well in fresh ground or when planting on a ridge. The plow is adjustable and opens a very narrow furrow, which is a great advantage for after-cultivation.

1896 was the first year that this machine was sold widely by the manufacturers of the celebrated line of "Planet Jr." goods, but the machine was bought very largely by careful gardeners and nurserymen during the season, and gave entire satisfaction. Price ................................................ **$9.00**

## The "Planet Jr." No. 1 Combined Drill and Wheel Hoe.

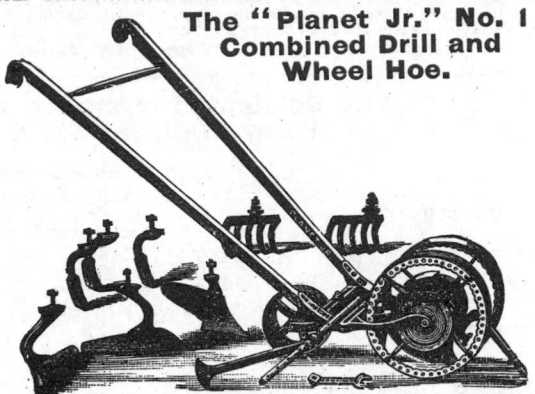

No. 18221. This is the most popular combined tool known, and its friends have been gained by substantial merit alone. It won the highest and only award at the Chicago Exposition. As a seed sower it is identical with the No. 2 "Planet Jr." Drill, except in size, and has all its merits, its strength, durability, ease of operation and perfection of work.

This combined tool has a complete set of cultivating tools, and all its operations are rapid, easy, perfect and delightful. When used as a drill the seed is sown with great regularity and at uniform depth, regulated at pleasure. The hopper holds one quart. The door, when opened, forms a convenient spout for filling with seed. From a drill it is changed to its other uses by unscrewing but two bolts, when any of the attachments shown in the cut can be instantly attached. In short, every purchaser of this machine will find it an excellent seed sower; a first-class double wheel hoe, for use when plants are small; a first-class single wheel-hoe; an excellent furrower; an admirable wheel cultivator; a capital garden rake; a rapid and efficient wheel garden plow; and that it is without an equal in variety of tools, easy adjustment, lightness, strength and beauty. Price .............................................................. **$9.00**

## The "Planet Jr." Double Wheel Hoe.

No. 18222. Thousands of farmers and gardeners who own this tool save its cost one or more times every year, for in an onion field and among many other crops one can do more and better work with it than six men with ordinary hoes. It is invaluable for all market garden crops. The wheels are only ten inches high, as a high wheel is wrong for a Wheel Hoe, since the wheels are simply depth regulators, not load carriers.

The "Planet Jr." Double Wheel Hoe will straddle plants eighteen inches high, and finish rows from six to eighteen inches apart at one passage. One hoe sets slightly ahead of the other, to prevent dragging out young plants. The new frame permits the changing of attachments without removing the nuts. All the tools shown in the cut go with the machine for the price; and all the blades are steel, hardened in oil and polished. The wheels are adjustable to make the work shallow or deep, as required, and to adapt the machine to all width rows. The tool is charming in every style and kind of work, the admiration of all who see it in operation, and is the acknowledged standard the world over. Price.. **$6.00**

To accommodate those who have little work but hoeing, we offer the above machine, with hoes only, under the name of "Planet Jr." Plain Double Wheel Hoe, at .........................................................................**$3.50**

The other parts can be added at any time, and will be found to fit.

## The "Planet Jr." 12-Tooth Strawberry Cultivator and Harrow.

No. 18223. This comparatively new tool has rapidly grown into favor with market gardeners and strawberry growers. It is carefully made and finished, has a high frame and the chisel shape teeth cut an inch wide each, and may be worn down three inches before that width is lessened or the teeth worn out; even then they are cheaply replaced.

It may be set with teeth trailing, by simply changing one bolt in each tooth.
The foot lever pulverizer is a capital addition for preparing ground for the seed drill or for plant setting. Hand levers regulate both width and depth while in motion; it contracts to 12 inches, and may be further reduced in width by taking off the outside teeth; it expands to 32 inches. It cultivates deep without throwing earth upon the plants, and the smooth, round-throated teeth turn strawberry runners without injuring them. Price, plain, **$4.90**; with wheel, **$6.15**; complete. ...........................................................................**$7.50**

## The "Fire-Fly" Wheel Garden Plow.

No. 18225. This tool is invaluable for those who have small gardens. The moldboard is tempered and polished steel. The depth may be changed very quickly. The low price brings it within the reach of all. Price............**$2.00**
Very useful to plow up the chicken yards.

## The "Planet Jr." Grass Edger.

No. 18226. The grand secret of attractiveness in grounds surrounding a house is extreme neatness. The "Planet Jr." Grass Edger assists wonderfully in producing this effect. It will do either straight or curved edging at a speed of a mile an hour. It should be the constant companion of the lawn mower.
Strawberry growers will find the Grass Edger, with the hoe removed, a rapid and perfect tool for cutting off surplus runners. Price......................**$5.00**

## The "Planet Jr." No. 8 Horse Hoe.

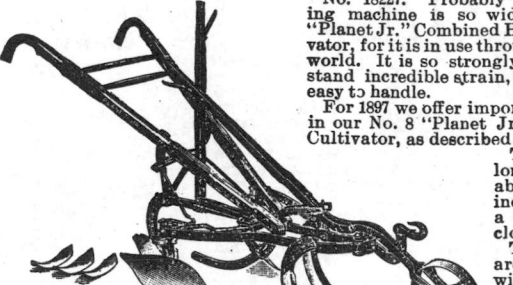

No. 18227. Probably no other cultivating machine is so widely known as the "Planet Jr." Combined Horse Hoe and Cultivator, for it is in use throughout the civilized world. It is so strongly built as to withstand incredible strain, yet it is light and easy to handle.

For 1897 we offer important improvements in our No. 8 "Planet Jr." Horse Hoe and Cultivator, as described below:

**The Frame** is longer than usual and about one and a half inches higher, making a tool that will not clog easily.

**The Standards** are formed up hollow with round throats of stiff steel; they polish quickly and free themselves readily from obstructions, and they clasp the frame and strengthen it.

**The Depth** is under perfect control by means of a new lever wheel and the new patented depth regulator, which are moved instantly in unison by a single lever, making exact work, steadying the machine and relieving the operator.

**The Expander.** This is an entirely new pattern, superior to all other forms; exceedingly strong, simple, accurate and positive in all positions.

**Handle and Braces.** These are also absolutely new and the most effective stiffest combination known, at once making the tool rigid, yet allowing adjustment of handles in height and sidewise.

Every part is perfected to make the tool acceptable to the intelligent farmer, who knows the best is always the cheapest. Price, **$7.50**; without Depth Regulator ......................................................................**$7.00**

## The "Planet Jr." No. 5 Horse Hoe.

No. 18228. This tool is similar to the No. 8 Horse Hoe, but it has a plain wheel instead of one operated by a convenient lever. It has the same standards and teeth, but is made in other respects like the popular 1895 pattern. It does not have the improved depth regulator and the expander and braces of the No. 8, yet it is strong and serviceable and will give full satisfaction. Has an excellent expander and handles adjustable, both perpendicularly and sidewise. Price.......**$6.25**

**We quote a complete assortment of Garden, Grass and Flower Seeds on Page 25. Profits of dealers are very large on these goods, and you can save these profits by buying of us.**

## The "Planet Jr." No. 15 Single Wheel Hoe, Cultivator, Rake and Plow. Price, Complete, $6.00.

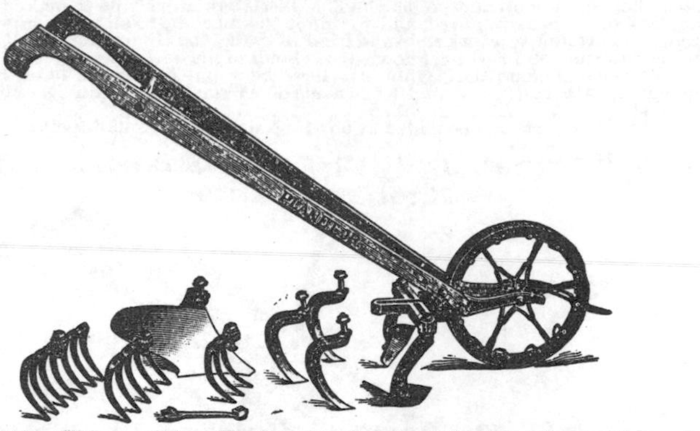

No. 18229. This new Wheel Hoe has the advantage of a high wheel with broad face, of a convenient arrangement of the frame, and a very full set of tools, most of them being of new, special design, such as have been found to perform wheel hoe work in the very best manner. It also has the great advantage of being convertible into a hill dropping and row seeder, by buying the seeder attachment. Price........ **$4.50**

The tools are: A well-shaped garden plow, for plowing, marking out, covering and late cultivation; a pair of neat shield hoes, just right for hoeing in rows 9 to 12 inches, and with the assistance of a cultivator tooth or rake, rows up to 16 inches; a set of three hoes, cutting 3½, 7 and 10 inches wide, respectively, just right for 6, 9 and 12-inch rows, and, two together, for rows up to 16 inches. With two arranged side by side, the rakes are just the thing for preparing ground for the seed drill. It has also a practical leaf guard for fallen plants, such as peas, and for wide spreading plants. It raises the leaves and allows perfect cultivation without injury or increased labor.

It is also sold without rakes and leaf guard. Price........ **$5.00**

Also plain, having only one pair of hoes and one pair of rakes. Price.. **$4.00**

The seeder attachment is quickly exchangeable for the wheel hoe frame; it is identical with the "Planet Jr." Hill Dropping Seeder No. 4, and drops at 6, 9, 12, 18 and 36 inches apart. Price........ **$4.50**

## The "Planet Jr." Single Wheel Hoe.

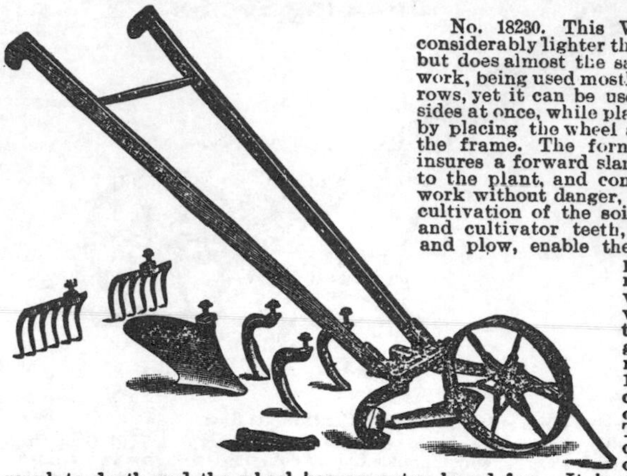

No. 18230. This Wheel Hoe is considerably lighter than the double, but does almost the same variety of work, being used mostly between the rows, yet it can be used to hoe both sides at once, while plants are small, by placing the wheel at one side of the frame. The form of the hoes insures a forward slanting cut next to the plant, and consequent close work without danger, and thorough cultivation of the soil. The rakes and cultivator teeth, and the hoes and plow, enable the operator to perform almost every variety of work, either in the field or garden. All rows from 6 to 18 inches apart can be hoed at one passage. The frame is quickly raised or lowered to regulate depth, and the wheel has an extra broad face. It is pronounced by practical men without an equal in design and finish, ease of operation, variety of adjustment and perfection of work, and we feel confident that every one who tries this tool will be glad that he did so.

Price........ **$4.50**

To supply a demand for a cheap Single Wheel Hoe, we offer the above machine (plain, with the hoes only) at **$2.75**, and the other attachments can be added at any time and will be found to fit.

## The "Fire-Fly" Single Wheel Hoe, Cultivator and Plow.

No. 18231. This popular tool is exactly the same as the "Planet Jr." Single Wheel Hoe, excepting that it does not have the rakes or leaf lifter. The attachments are a pair of hoes that can be set to work to or from the row, a set of three reversible cultivator teeth, and a large garden plow. The whole tool is light and strong, and capable of standing hard usage for years. Price........ **$3.75**

**Send for Our Special Catalogue of "Planet Jr." Garden Tools.**

## Our $25.00 Western Potato Bug Sprinkler.

No. 18232. $25.00 is our regular price when sent by freight C. O. D., subject to examination, on receipt of a sufficient deposit to cover freight charges both ways. Three per cent. discount allowed if cash in full accompanies your order. If you send the full amount of cash with your order $24.25 pays for the sprinkler.

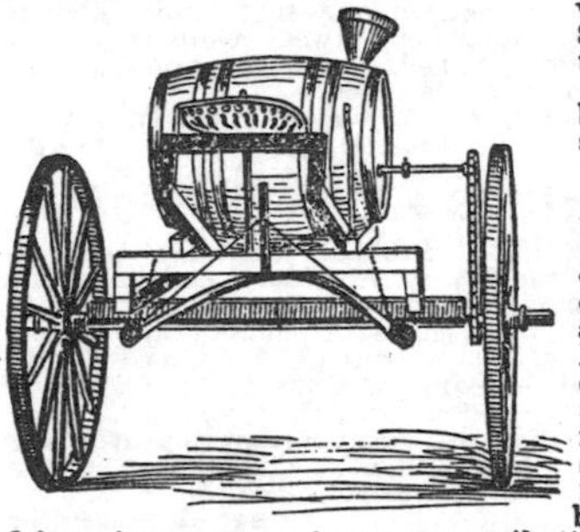

This is the best potato bug sprinkler on the market. It applies the poison upon two rows at once, and will cover 12 to 15 acres per day. It is the cheapest, simplest and most perfect potato bug sprinkler ever invented. Any boy that can drive a horse can perform more easily the same amount of work it heretofore required 12 men to perform in the same time. You have complete control over the quantity of water you wish to throw, opening or closing the valve with the lever.

The wheels run on tubular axles and can be shifted to any width of rows desired, 2 to 3 feet. Weight, 450 lbs. Price........ **$25.00**

## Our $5.50 Knapsack Spray Pump.

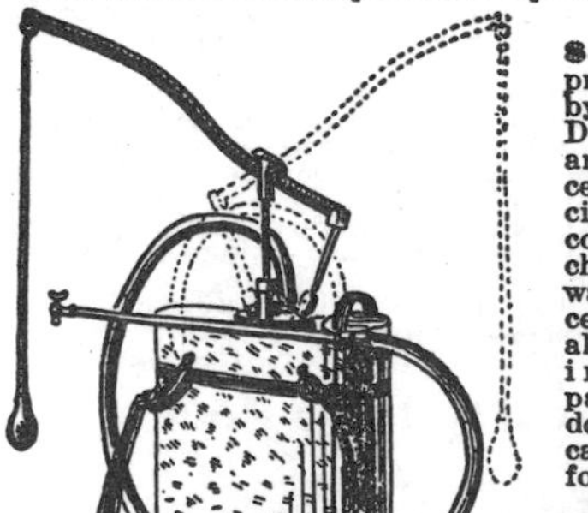

No. 18233. **$5.50** is our price when sent by freight C. O. D. subject to examination on receipt of a sufficient deposit to cover freight charges both ways. Three per cent. discount allowed if cash in full accompanies your order, in which case **$5.35** pays for the pump.

This is a thoroughly first-class outfit, designed for orchard, vineyard or general use. Four to six acres of vines can be covered in one day. The tank holds five gallons and is fitted with lid and strainer which can be removed. It is a brass bucket spray pump with air chamber, ball valves, solid plunger and agitator. We wish to call attention to the fact that this is the only knapsack spray pump on the market with an agitator. It is so arranged that no water can drip on the operator.

*Our House is the*

# CENTER

***From which great bargains emanate.***

The pump can be removed easily. It can be carried by hooking snap in staple on opposite side provided for the purpose, as shown by dotted lines. The handle lever can be shifted from right to left shoulder at will. Price........ **$5.50**

## $15.00 for the Celebrated Sherwin Patent Adjustable Field Roller.

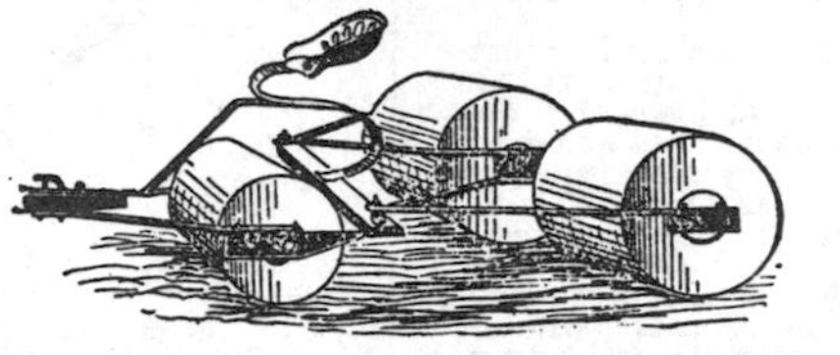

The rollers are made from 18 to 22 inches in diameter, and 3 feet in length, covering 8½ feet of ground. They are turned from solid oak logs and painted. The gudgeons are cased with a flange, and bolted to the rollers, not driven in.

The weight is in the rollers, and rests directly on the ground, not in a box on top of the bearings to produce friction. Weight, 1,200 to 1,700 lbs., according to the size of rolls. When the rollers are to be shipped a long distance parties ordering can save by ordering the frame and seat only, and supplying the log sections themselves.

No. 18234. Price, without rolls........ **$15.00**
Price, complete, with rolls........ **20.00**

## Our $16.75 Land Roller.

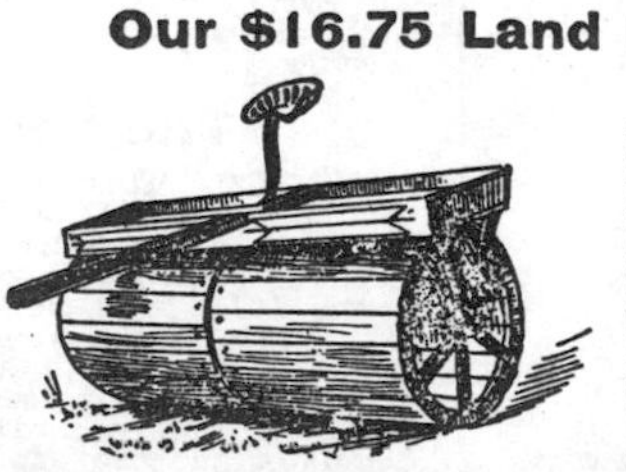

No. 18235. This is the best Land Roller on the market, at anything like the price. It is a light-running, easily balanced roller. Each drum turns independently of the other. The drums are 3 feet 8 inches long, and 30½ inches in diameter. The stays are of white oak, bolted to strong, cast heads. The box is 22 inches wide by 8 feet long, supported by heavy brackets in the center and at both ends, to an axle 1¼ inches in size, running through both drums. Weight, 700 lbs. Price... **$16.75**

## The Celebrated Myers Knapsack Spray Pump at $2.75.

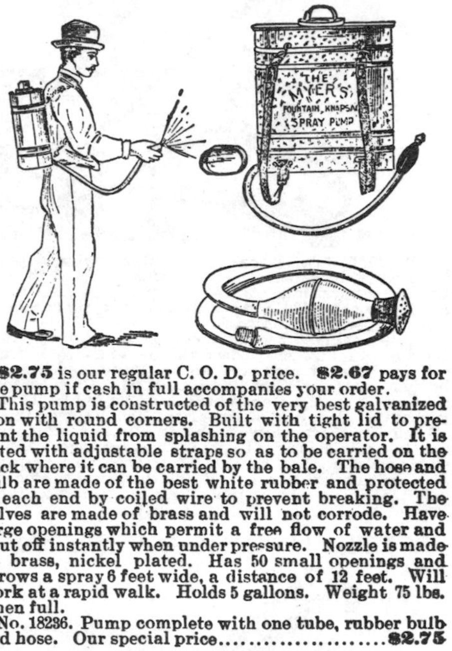


**$2.75** is our regular C. O. D. price. **$2.67** pays for the pump if cash in full accompanies your order.

This pump is constructed of the very best galvanized iron with round corners. Built with tight lid to prevent the liquid from splashing on the operator. It is fitted with adjustable straps so as to be carried on the back where it can be carried by the bale. The hose and bulb are made of the best white rubber and protected at each end by coiled wire to prevent breaking. The valves are made of brass and will not corrode. Have large openings which permit a free flow of water and shut off instantly when under pressure. Nozzle is made of brass, nickel plated. Has 50 small openings and throws a spray 6 feet wide, a distance of 12 feet. Will work at a rapid walk. Holds 5 gallons. Weight 75 lbs. when full.

No. 18236. Pump complete with one tube, rubber bulb and hose. Our special price........ **$2.75**

## Paris Green Sprinkler.

No. 18237. Every one that raises potatoes should have one of these sprinklers.

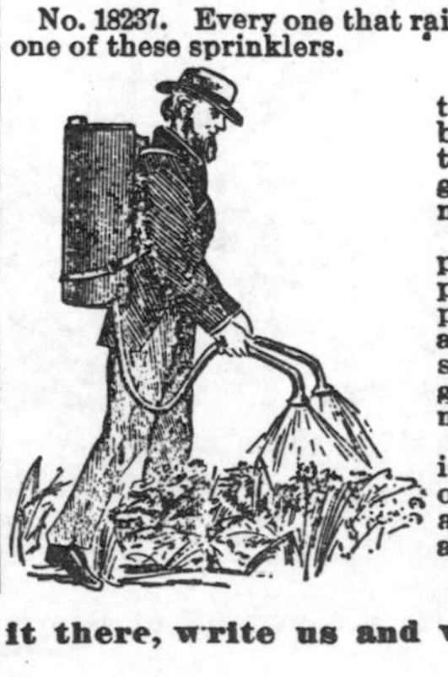

It enables you to protect your potatoes from bugs. Requires only ½ the amount of Paris green used by any other method.

Will sprinkle 1 acre per hour and not wet the person carrying it. Is painted inside and out, and has an apparatus inside by which the Paris green and water is kept mixed constantly.

The quantity to be used is regulated by pressure of the fingers on the hose at the connection of hose and tin pipe.

Price, each...... **$3.50**

**Should you fail to find what you want, refer to the index. If you don't find it there, write us and we will name you a price that will save you money.**

## $11.90 for an Acme Fanning Mill.

$11.90 is our regular price when shipped by freight C. O. D., subject to examination, upon receipt of a sufficient deposit to cover freight charges both ways. Three per cent. discount allowed if cash in full accompanies your order, when $11.54 pays for the fanning mill. Please consider our net cash with order price when comparing our prices with those of other houses.

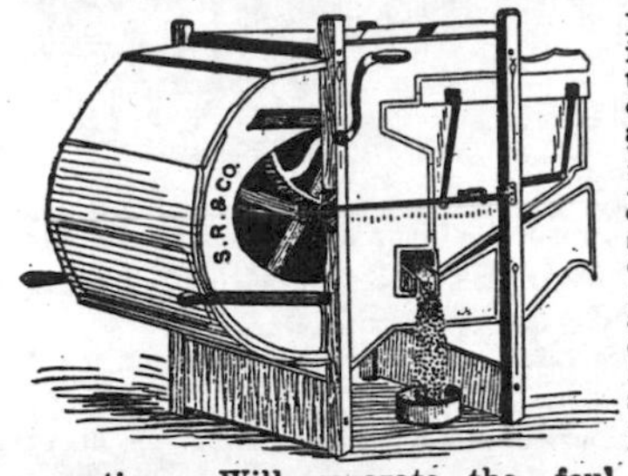


The Acme Fanning Mill is we believe the best mill on the market at anything like the price. It has plenty of wind and shake and carries more screen than any other mill on the market. Will separate wild seed from wheat in one operation. Will separate the foul seeds, such as mustard, pigeon grass, etc., from flax on once going through the mill. Is a perfect cleaner of clover and timothy. We ship all mills knocked down so as to secure the lowest freight rate possible, and you will find the freight will amount to next to nothing as compared with what we can save you in price. We furnish this mill with one wire wheat hurdle, three sieves, wheat screen, wheat grader, corn and oat sieve and barley sieve. This is a fanning mill that is being retailed everywhere by implement dealers at $20.00 to $25.00. When we are able to offer you such a mill at **$11.90** and send it to you by freight C. O. D., subject to examination, we believe we are entitled to your order.

No. 18238. No. 1 Farm Mill, weight, 120 lbs., sieves 24 inches wide, capacity 60 to 90 bushels per hour. Price.................................................**$11.90**

No. 18239. No. 2 Farm Mill, weight, 125 lbs., sieves 30 inches wide, capacity 100 to 125 bushels per hour. Price.................................................**$15.85**

No. 18240. No. 2 Warehouse Mill, weight, 175 lbs., sieves 40 inches wide, capacity 200 to 300 bushels per hour. Price.................................................**$34.00**

No. 18241. No. 3 Warehouse Mill, weight, 200 lbs., sieves 48 inches wide, capacity 300 to 400 bushels per hour. Price.................................................**$43.50**

We can furnish these mills with any special attachment when desired.

## Square Wood Watering Tanks.

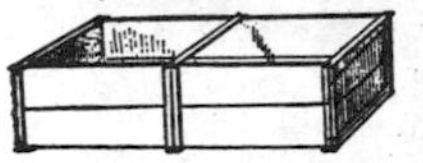

Our prices are from **$10.15** to **$19.00.** These tanks are made of the very best seasoned hardwood, thoroughly well ironed and stayed and guaranteed not to leak.

| | Capacity. | Weight. | Size. | Price. |
|---|---|---|---|---|
| No. 18242....... | 11 barrels | 450 lbs. | 11 foot | $10.15 |
| No. 18243....... | 13 barrels | 500 lbs. | 12 foot | 12.25 |
| No. 18244....... | 18 barrels | 575 lbs. | 13 foot | 14.75 |
| No. 18245....... | 20 barrels | 650 lbs. | 15 foot | 17.10 |
| No. 18246....... | 22 barrels | 700 lbs. | 16 foot | 19.00 |

## Farmers' Round Wood Tanks.

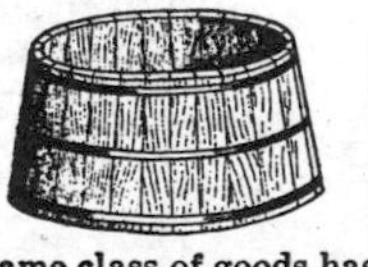

There is nothing more economical on the farm than one of these round wood tanks for watering stock, and we have succeeded in offering a thoroughly substantial tank, one that can be guaranteed in every respect, at prices lower than the same class of goods has ever been sold before.

| | Stave. | Bottom. | Weight. | Capacity. | Price. |
|---|---|---|---|---|---|
| No. 18247. | 2 foot, | 5 foot, | 200 lbs., | 8 barrels, | $ 7.50 |
| No. 18248. | 2 foot, | 5½ foot, | 250 lbs., | 11 barrels, | 8.12 |
| No. 18249. | 2¼ foot, | 5½ foot, | 300 lbs., | 11 barrels, | 8.75 |
| No. 18250. | 2½ foot, | 5½ foot, | 325 lbs., | 14 barrels, | 9.35 |
| No. 18251. | 3 foot, | 5½ foot, | 350 lbs., | 16 barrels, | 10.75 |
| No. 18252. | 4 foot, | 5½ foot, | 400 lbs., | 22 barrels. | 13.50 |
| No. 18253. | 2¼ foot, | 6 foot, | 350 lbs., | 14 barrels, | 10.00 |
| No. 18254. | 2¼ foot, | 7 foot, | 450 lbs., | 22 barrels, | 13.00 |
| No. 18255. | 2¼ foot, | 8 foot, | 470 lbs., | 30 barrels, | 14.25 |

No. 18256. Covers for round wood tanks, 5 feet.................................................**$2.00**

No. 18257. Covers for round wood tanks over 5 feet.................................................**$2.50**

The capacity of these tanks in barrels is based on 50 gallons to the barrel.

## Galvanized Riveted Steel Tanks.

These tanks are durable, will not shrink, swell, leak or fall down, will weigh only one-half as much and are very much stronger than the wood tanks. Capacity, ¼ more, because the sides are straight and the bottom is the bottom. No soaking required, for they never leak. A fire box of either stone or brick can be built under this tank, forming an excellent tank heater.

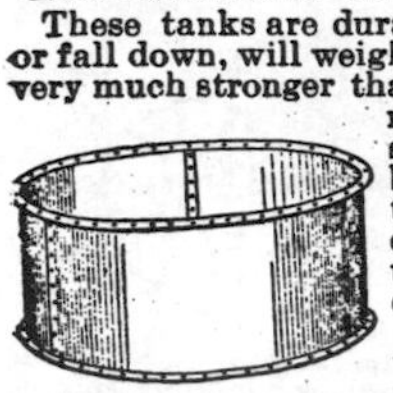

These tanks are made of the very best quality 17 gauge galvanized steel.

$8.00 buys a 6 barrel capacity galvanized steel tank.
$25.00 buys a 25 barrel galvanized steel tank.

| | Capacity. | Price. |
|---|---|---|
| No. 18258. | 6 barrels................................ | $8.00 |
| No. 18259. | 7 barrels................................ | 9.00 |
| No. 18260. | 9 barrels................................ | 11.00 |
| No. 18261. | 12 barrels................................ | 13.00 |
| No. 18262. | 14 barrels................................ | 15.50 |
| No. 18263. | 17 barrels................................ | 19.00 |
| No. 18264. | 20 barrels................................ | 20.00 |
| No. 18265. | 27 barrels................................ | 25.00 |

## Oblong Galvanized Steel Tanks at from $10.00 to $27.00.

Our **$10.00** tank has a capacity of 7½ barrels; our **$27.00** tank has a capacity of 29 barrels. These tanks are made of the very best quality 17 gauge steel, galvanized and warranted not to rust. They are absolutely indestructible.

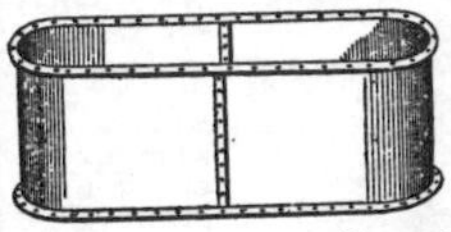

| | Capacity. | Weight. | Price. |
|---|---|---|---|
| No. 18266............ | 7½ barrels. | 80 lbs. | $10.00 |
| No. 18267............ | 9½ barrels. | 109 lbs. | 11.50 |
| No. 18268............ | 12 barrels. | 132 lbs. | 13.25 |
| No. 18269............ | 15 barrels. | 165 lbs. | 16.50 |
| No. 18270............ | 18 barrels. | 200 lbs. | 19.50 |
| No. 18271............ | 24 barrels. | 265 lbs. | 24.00 |
| No. 18272............ | 29 barrels. | 295 lbs. | 27.00 |

## Galvanized Riveted Steel Square Tank.

**We offer these tanks at $11.00** for a **7½ barrel tank, $29.20** for a **29** barrel tank.

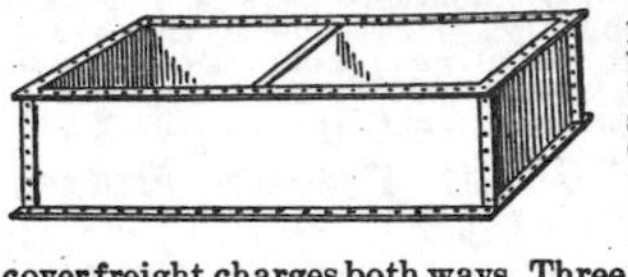

Consider these prices are our regular prices when tanks will be shipped by freight C. O. D. subject to examination on receipt of sufficient deposit to cover freight charges both ways. Three per cent. discount allowed if cash in full accompanies your order. Deduct 3 per cent. from our prices before comparing them with the net prices of other houses.

| | Capacity. | Price. |
|---|---|---|
| No. 18273. | 7½ barrels................................ | $11.00 |
| No. 18274. | 9½ barrels................................ | 12.65 |
| No. 18275. | 12 barrels................................ | 14.30 |
| No. 18276. | 15 barrels................................ | 18.15 |
| No. 18277. | 17 barrels................................ | 20.90 |
| No. 18278. | 23 barrels................................ | 25.30 |
| No. 18279. | 24 barrels................................ | 26.40 |
| No. 18280. | 29 barrels................................ | 29.70 |

## Our $4.75 Improved Acme Tank Heater.

No. 18281. This tank heater is used for warming water in stock tanks. Five cents worth of soft coal per day and the Acme Tank Heater will heat the water for 50 head of stock. This heater can not possibly be burned out, as it is entirely surrounded by water. No trouble to keep it cleaned out, as the fire box can be taken out by a ten-year-old boy; has an adjustable draft, by means of which it can be heated to any desired temperature. The cover is hinged in the center, giving ready access to ash chamber, making it easy to remove the ashes or replenish the fuel. The partition can also be withdrawn—grate can be removed—and the entire contents of the heater cleaned out in a few moments' time; can be located at such a place in the tank as is most convenient; can be secured in place, or removed as pleasure without injury to the tank. The heater is oblong in shape, as shown in cut; is made of galvanized iron; has a cast iron slide, which partitions the ash chamber from the other chamber; removable grate, with ample space beneath for ashes; cover is of cast iron, fitted closely, and not liable to warp, as is the case with sheet iron. A draft regulator is provided in the cover. The heater is fastened to the tank bottom by means of rod and wood screws. A poker and shovel accompany each heater. Size, 24 inches deep, 24 inches long and 13 inches wide. Weight, 113 lbs.

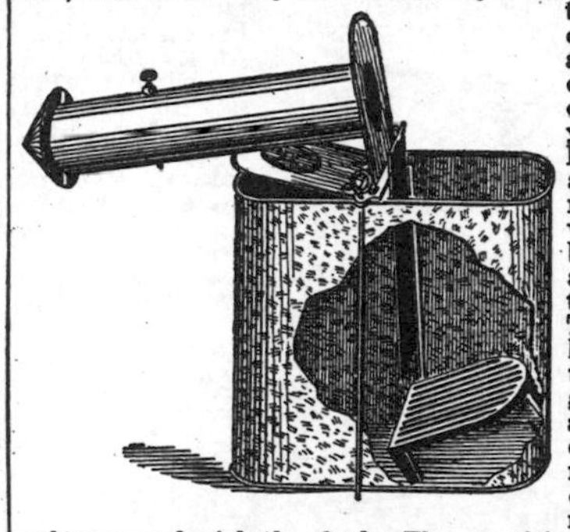

Price.................................................**$4.75**

## The Acme Feed Steamer for $19.75.

No. 18282. **$19.75** is the price if sent by freight C. O. D., subject to examination, on receipt of a sufficient deposit to pay freight charges both ways. Three per cent. discount allowed if cash in full accompanies your order, in which case **$19.16** pays for the machine. This steamer, as illustrated above, has a large and convenient fire-box, the whole length of the boiler—40 inches—being covered with water entirely over the top and down both sides to the bottom, which gives the full benefit of all the heat from the fuel, and making it of greater capacity than all other steamers. It is easily and simply filled. Made of best boiler plate steel with heavy cast iron heads put together with bolts that pass through the flanges on the heads; therefore there is not a single hole in the steel inside the fire-box. There is water over the thin sheet down both sides of the fire-box, which gives it the same capacity as a flue boiler without any of the disadvantages. No clogging up or leaking. They are easily and quickly filled with an apparatus furnished with each steamer and can be filled when steaming. There is a stopper on each side of the pump on the bottom to open and insert a rod to loosen any and all sediment, and which will clean it out in five minutes. They are also used for letting the water out. The steamer is mounted on large wheels, and is easily moved to any place where needed. The fire-box is 3 feet long, 10 inches deep, 12 inches wide, has an adjustable partition, and can be used for coal, wood, or cobs. As many as six barrels can be steamed without moving either barrels or steamer. Will steam sufficient to cook two to three barrels with only one filling. Is very useful for heating water for slaughtering, for making soap, and for laundry and dairy purposes. Will get up steam in 10 to 20 minutes, and will cook up a barrel of turnips or potatoes in 15 to 20 minutes. We furnish this steamer equipped with a small hand pump for putting water in the boiler, which is a great improvement. Boiler is 40 inches long. Weight, 350 lbs.

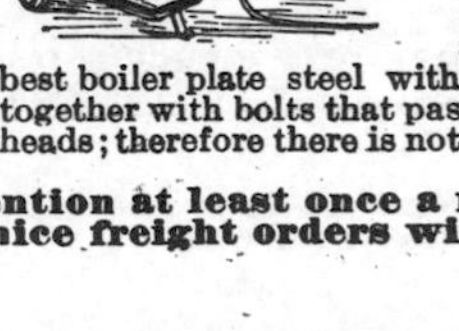

Price.................................................**$19.75**

## Our $4.90 Cast Iron Pig Trough.

No. 18283. **$4.90** is the price when sent by freight C. O. D. subject to examination on receipt of a sufficient deposit to cover freight both ways. Three per cent. discount allowed if cash in full accompanies your order, in which case **$4.75** is the price. Please consider our price of **$4.75** cash in full with order, when comparing our prices with those of other houses.

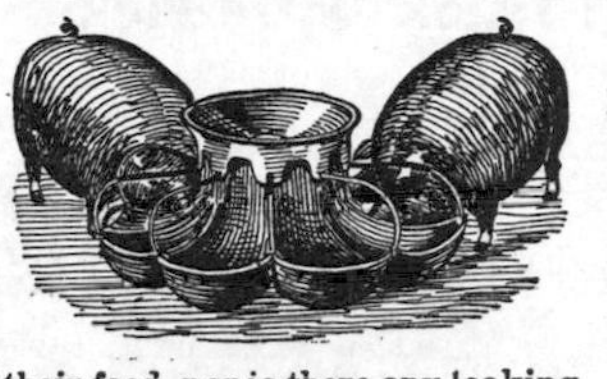

In each trough there are 8 separate compartments; 8 large hogs can eat at one time. Different kinds of feed can be fed at the same time, the bowls preventing them mixing. Hogs cannot upset the trough and waste their feed, nor is there any leaking. There is very great economy and satisfaction in using these troughs. Made of cast iron they will not break; in fact are indestructible. Height, 24 inches; width, 32 inches; weight, 120 lbs.

Our special price on regular terms.................................................**$4.90**

## The Little O. K. Stock Fountain.

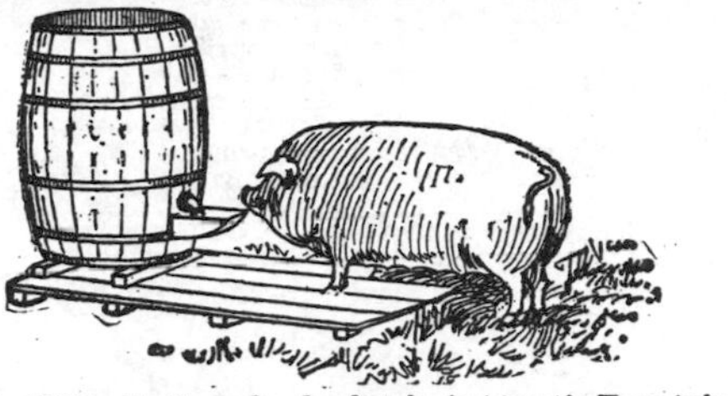

No. 18284. Is the only absolutely Automatic Fountain made. Can easily be placed in operation by anybody who knows how to bore a hole in the side of a barrel or tank. Simply bore a hole and then screw the pipe (which is part of the fountain) into the barrel, and it is ready for use, requiring no further attention.

It is simply a watering trough made of metal, with a pipe shank to screw into the barrel or tank, with automatic valve, furnishing water as fast as consumed; one that will easily supply water each day to one hundred animals. No part is operated by springs, floats or "nose pressure," but simply a positive equipoise valve. This fountain is all iron, except valve. It will last a generation.

Sheep, calves and chickens, as well as hogs, always find the drinking bowl of the fountain full of fresh water, and as fast as it is consumed more flows in to take its place without any pressing down of the animal with his nose to open the valve.

This fountain has no working parts in the drinking bowl to get detached, lost or stolen by mischievous boys, or under which corn cobs or sediment may lodge and prevent its operation. Nothing can obstruct it, and it is always in order and full of fresh water. It has no working part except the valve, which is beyond the reach of the stock and located where dirt or sediment cannot lodge. Weight, about 11 lbs.

Our price, complete.................................................**$1.75**

## Forges for Farmers.

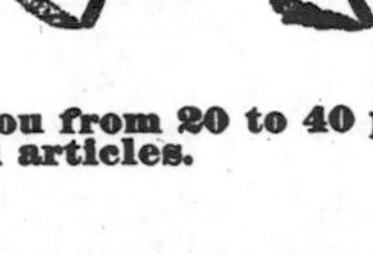

A SPLENDID RELIABLE FORGE FOR

**$7.95.**

**Regular $12 Value**

SEE PAGE 64.

**Complete outfits for Blacksmiths and Repair Shops.**

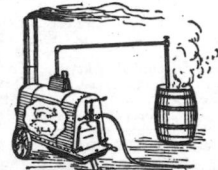

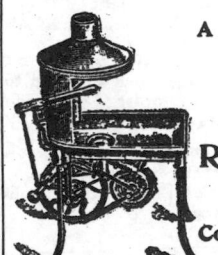

**Our Grocery Department deserves your attention at least once a month. We can save you from 20 to 40 per cent., and besides they make up nice freight orders with which to ship small articles.**

## Our $3.50 Boss Sickie Grinder.

No. 18285. If you pay us **$3.50** for this grinder you will save more than the cost of it in time the first season, to say nothing of the amount of satisfaction in doing the work in the field with greater comfort. **$3.50** is our regular price; 3 per cent. discount allowed if cash in full accompanies your order, in which case **$3.40** pays for the grinder.

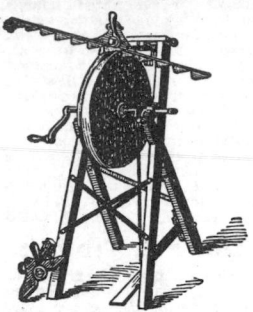

This implement comprises a first-class grind stone with a sickle grinder attachment, and as either is worth double its cost, the cost of it is a trifle more than the ordinary grind stone, and it will answer for all purposes. The stone is accurately centered, hung true, and does perfect work. The height of the stone is 18 inches; it is 2¾ inches thick, and the complete outfit weighs 123 lbs. Our special price, **$3.50** on regular terms; **$3.40** if cash in full accompanies your order.

## Our $3.25 Truck with Sack Holder.

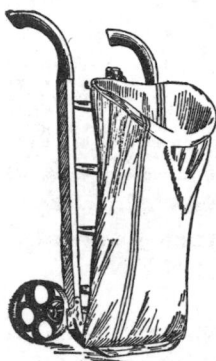

No. 18286. This is an implement that is almost indispensable on the farm. It is worth its cost a dozen times over every season. We believe it is the best combination truck and sack holder made. We can guarantee it superior to those offered by many at from $3.50 to $5.00.

The illustration represents the sack placed on the holder and truck ready for filling. The holder is composed of a semi-circular malleable casting, to which is hinged a steel spring bar. The casting has a flange on the outside over which the sack is placed. The spring bar is then brought over the top of the flange and placed directly under it. This holds the sack firmly and cannot injure it in the least. Our price for truck with combination sack holder, complete ............ **$3.25**

## Trucks.

No. 18287. Warehouse Truck (like cut). Hard wood, well ironed, neatly finished. Axles turned and wheels bored. **Steel nose, side straps, axles and legs.**

We guarantee this the best truck on the market, and, quality considered, 20 per cent. cheaper in price than any other.

| No. | Length Handle. | Width. | Weight. | Price. |
|---|---|---|---|---|
| 1 | 3 ft. 11 in. | 19 inches | 44 lbs. | $2.80 |
| 2 | 4 ft. 4 in. | 20 inches | 56 lbs. | 3.55 |
| 3 | 4 ft. 8 in. | 22 inches | 77 lbs. | 4.95 |

No. 18288. **Daisy Truck,** with steam bent handles. Length of handle, 46 inches; width at nose, 12 inches; at upper cross-bar, 17½ inches. Weight, 30 lbs. Price, each ............ **$1.65**

**Our special price of $1.65** ought to induce you to give us your order if you are in the market for a light truck.

**The man who makes** these trucks has the reputation of making the best trucks sold in Chicago.

## Our $3.25 Wood Frame Barrel Cart.

No. 18289. **$3.25** is our price on regular terms. Three per cent. discount if cash in full accompanies your order, when **$3.15** pays for the cart. Consider our discount when comparing prices, and note the cash with order price is **$3.15**.

We furnish the trucks only, which can be attached to any barrel. Very useful for gardening and feeding purposes. Large flanges to fit any barrel. Two of these barrels will be found very convenient, one kept near the kitchen door to be filled with skim milk or other slops, while the other is to be kept at the piggery. The patent device to be attached to different barrels costs more, and is not as convenient as a set of wheels, and handles to each barrel. Please note that we do not furnish the barrel, but any good molasses or kerosene barrel will answer. Weight, 65 lbs.

Price ............ **$3.25**

## Our $3.30 Steel Frame Barrel Cart.

No. 18290. **$3.30** on our regular terms; **$3.20** if cash in full accompanies your order.

This cart is made entirely of steel, no wood being used in its construction. The frame, wheels, and all are made of the very best Bessemer steel, all made extra strong, and will stand any kind of usage. We do not furnish the barrel, but only the frame, wheels, and iron to attach to barrels. It will fit to any kind of a barrel, kerosene, molasses, or vinegar barrel. Weight, 49 lbs.

Price ............ **$3.30**

## Our Combination Barrel and General Utility Cart.

This is a combination implement that is almost indispensable on any farm. At the low price we offer it will pay for itself a dozen times over every year. We sold so many of these combination outfits last year that we have arranged for the coming season for a large number. We are having them better made than ever before. The manufacturer has agreed to put in better material and so construct them that they will be practically indestructible. While there are similar combination carts on the market we believe there is nothing that will compare

with ours in quality of material, strength, durability, finish.

Complete combination for **$6.00**; without box, **$4.25**.

These prices are subject to 3 per cent. discount if cash in full accompanies your order, making the prices **$5.82** and **$4.12**. Always consider this discount when comparing our prices with those of other houses.

The two illustrations above show this combination barrel and general utility cart used as a hand cart with box, the dotted lines in the illustration showing the manner in which the box can be dumped, also as a barrel cart with the barrel removed, which can be done in an instant. The attachment to barrel and the attachment for the automatic dumping of the box are also shown in one of the illustrations. The barrels have iron gudgeons bolted to each side. The cart will pick up the barrel or box in a moment. One cart answers for any number of barrels required. We furnish everything here shown (except the barrel) for **$6.00**. Wheels are 30 inches high. Box is 4 feet long, 2 feet 6 inches wide, 6 inches deep; weight, 100 lbs. Please note that we do not furnish the barrel, but any kerosene, molasses or vinegar barrel will answer.

No. 18291. Our price for cart with box as here illustrated, with irons for 1 barrel ............ **$6.00**
No. 18292. Without box ............ 4.25
No. 18293. Irons for each additional barrel. Per pair ............ 75c
No. 18294. Cart box iron. Per pair ............ 70c
No. 18295. Axle irons. Per pair ............ $1.00

**FIGURE UP the retail cost of what Implements** you have. COMPARE THE PRICES you paid with those we quote here. THE DIFFERENCE is just the amount we would have saved you. Think of that in the future.

## Our $4.90 Cart.

No. 18296. **$4.90** is the price for this cart on regular terms. Three per cent. discount allowed when cash in full accompanies your order, in which case **$4.75** pays for the cart.

This is a very useful implement on the farm about the barns, stable or garden. Has 36-inch wheels, box is 24x36 inches in size, 10 inches deep; weighs 85 lbs. Has removable end boards, bent handles, iron foot rest, iron hubs, is well painted and striped, in every respect a first class job. Price, **$4.90**.

## The Best All Steel Road Scraper Made for $4.40.

For **$4.40** we offer a road scraper that you could not buy elsewhere within 50 per cent. of the price. Guaranteed the best made. Made from heavy plates of steel specially hardened and stamped from one sheet without joints, seam or rivet. It

is superior to any other drag scraper on the market. The bowl being made of thicker and harder steel enables it to scour where all other scrapers fail, and owing to the sharp rounded nose will enter the ground more readily than any other scraper. Bowls are steel, perfect working, handles are best hardwood. Will guarantee this scraper in every particular. Is made in three sizes.

No. 18297. Carries 4 feet of earth, weight, 90 lbs.; price each ............ **$4.40**
No. 18298. Carries 5½ feet of earth, weight, 100 lbs.; price ............ **$4.90**
No. 18299. Carries 7 feet of earth, weight, 110 lbs.; price ............ **$5.40**

All our scrapers are furnished with runners on bottom without charge. The runners increase the durability and materially lessen the draught in hauling.

## Barrows.

This wheelbarrow is well made. Has full sized tray. Wheels 16 inches in diameter. When packed for shipment wheel is bolted on inside of tray and legs are folded on side of handle. Can be easily set up by any one.
No. 18300. Half bolted railroad Wheelbarrow, with wood wheel. Each ............ **$1.00**
No. 18301. Half bolted railroad Wheelbarrow, with steel wheels. Each ............ **$1.10**

No. 18302. Clipper garden Wheelbarrow is strong, well made and nicely painted and striped. With steel wheel. Price .. **$2.50**

No. 18303. Tubular steel miners' Barrow. Size No. 6. Tray made of No. 14 steel. Capacity, 3 cubic feet of dirt. Weight, 80 lbs. Price, each ............ **$5.82**
We can give you rock bottom prices on mining or contractors' supplies. Send us your specifications for prices.

## Our $2.10 Handsome Lawn Wheelbarrow.

No. 18304. This is the handsomest and best Lawn Wheelbarrow made. This wheelbarrow has finely shaped handles, braced with steel; two coats of brightest and best vermillion paint; one coat of high grade varnish; sideboard staples are riveted, non pull out. It is the best mortised wheelbarrow on the market. These barrows are fitted with the neatest steel wheels, 18 or 20 inches. In this feature they are incomparable. There are few barrows on the market having wheels larger than 16 inches. These wheels are constructed on the latest improved model of the bicycle, and are remarkably light and substantial broad tired wheels. Our special price for this wheelbarrow ............ **$2.10**

---

**Our prices are low, but the quality of the goods does not suffer. It does not take high prices to make good goods. Don't be fooled by your local dealer.**

## The Acme Shoveling Board for $1.60.

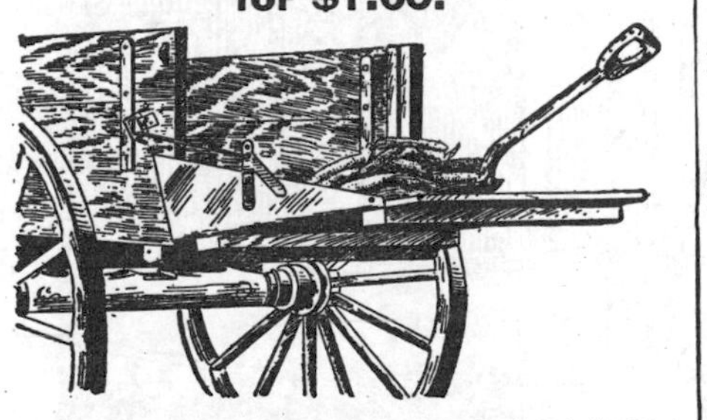

No. 18305. No loose parts to be detached or to be lost. The rods do not extend below the box to catch or get bent. It is not attached to the box, making it more substantial. It can be thrown on top of the box without detaching. Very useful in dumping grain or shelled corn, or on hog or sheep racks. Weight, 45 lbs. Price.......................................**$1.60**

## Jack Screws.

No. 18306. Jack Screws, wrought iron screws, cast iron stands. We do not furnish levers with these screws.

| Diam. of screw. | Height of stand. | Height over all. | Price each. | Price per doz. |
|---|---|---|---|---|
| 1½ in. | 8 | 12 | $1.12 | $12.00 |
| 1½ in. | 10 | 14 | 1.27 | 14.25 |
| 1½ in. | 12 | 16 | 1.40 | 15.75 |
| 1¾ in. | 10 | 14 | 1.50 | 17.25 |
| 1¾ in. | 12 | 16 | 1.67 | 18.00 |
| 1¾ in. | 14 | 18 | 1.80 | 20.00 |
| 2 in. | 8 | 12½ | 1.60 | 18.00 |
| 2 in. | 10 | 14½ | 1.80 | 20.00 |
| 2 in. | 12 | 16½ | 2.00 | 22.00 |
| 2 in. | 16 | 20½ | 2.40 | 27.00 |

## Press Screws.

No. 18307. **For pressing cider, wine, tobacco, lard, cloth, etc.** These Screws are made of wrought iron, with cast iron nuts and caps.

| Diameter of Screws | 24-in. long Price each. | 30-in. long Price each. | 36-in. long Price each. | 40-in. long Price each. |
|---|---|---|---|---|
| 2 inches | $2.25 | $2.55 | $2.90 | $3.10 |
| 2½ inches | 3.20 | 3.60 | 4.00 | 4.30 |
| 3 inches | 5.10 | 5.80 | 6.40 | 6.85 |

## Hay Pitching Tools.

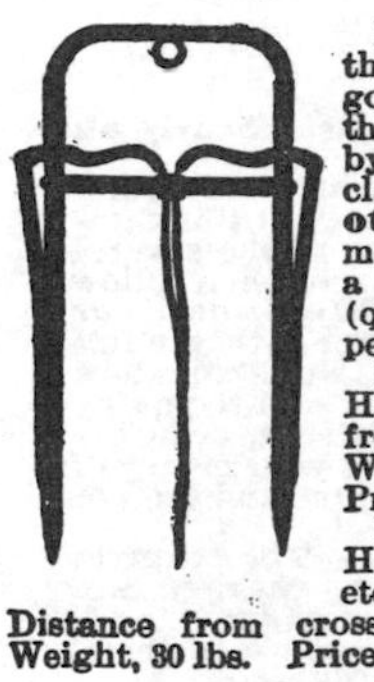

Hay tools are now so well known that it is hardly necessary for us to go into detail in description of them. The goods we sell are made by one of the largest makers of this class of goods, and **under another name** are sold at much more than our prices. We list here a full line and at prices which (quality considered) are below competition.

No. 18326. The Double Harpoon Hay Fork, for general use. Made from best quality iron and steel. Weight, about 18 lbs. Price each.......................**63c**

No. 18327. The Long Time Double Harpoon Hay Fork, for loose straw, etc., made in same quality as above. Distance from cross-bar to end of tines, 32 inches; Weight, 30 lbs. Price each.......................**$1.30**

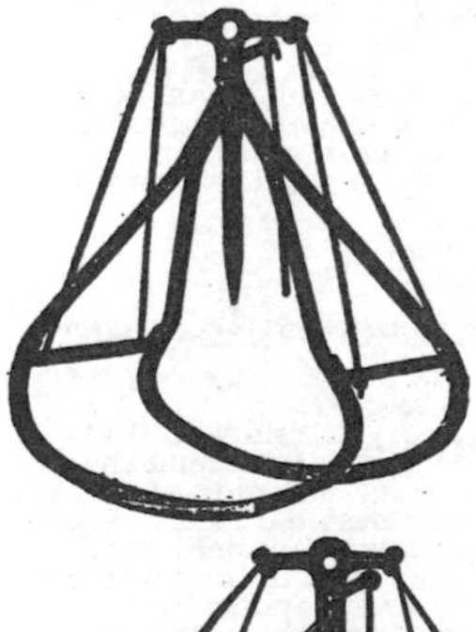

No. 18328. Grapple Horse Hay Fork, with four tines. Weight, about 40 lbs. Price each.......**$4.25**

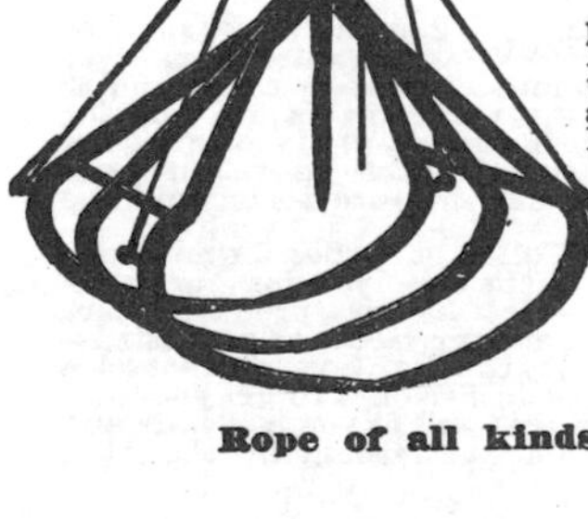

No. 18329. Grapple Horse Hay Fork, with six tines. Weight, about 55 lbs. Price each, **$5.25**

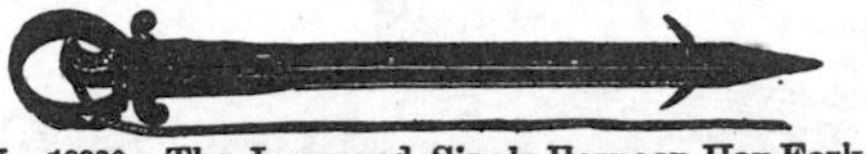

No. 18330. The Improved Single Harpoon Hay Fork. Full regular size. Weight, about 7 lbs. Price each, **$1.25**

## Wagon Sling.

No. 18333. The Standard Wagon Sling is used to take the place of a horse hay fork. Place one of these slings on bottom and another in the middle of load, and load may be removed in two hoists. Most people prefer to

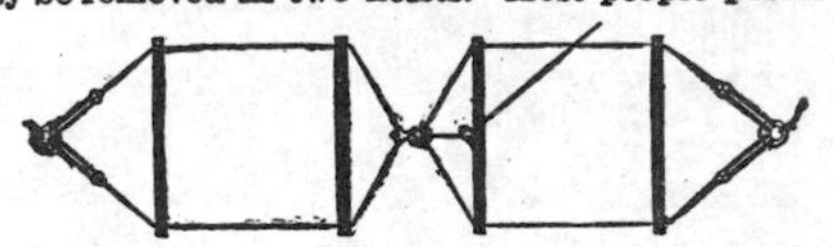

use three slings and make three hoists of the load. Is made adjustable to suit any length of rack. Cut shows hoist with four spreaders. Two may be used to make the sling lighter. Weight, about 18 lbs. Price each.......................**$2.25**

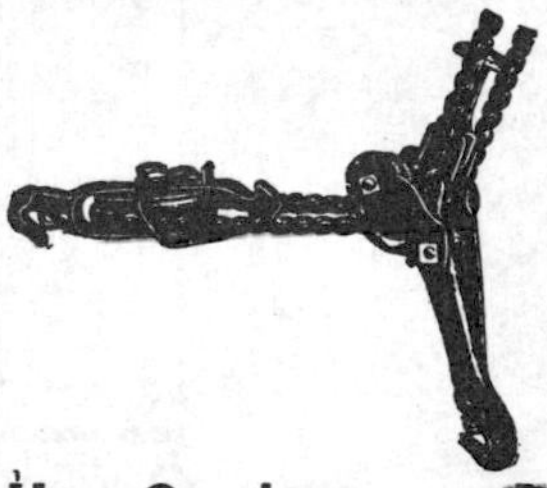

No. 18334. This Sling Pulley is to be used in connection with our Standard Wagon Sling and either of our carriers. Weight, 10 lbs. State which carrier the pulley is to match. Price for pulleys as shown in cut (no rope included)......**$2.00**

## Hay Carriers.

No. 18336. The Sears, Roebuck & Co. Reversible Hay Carrier for wood track. Has **positive dead lock.** Made of the best malleable iron and does the best of work. Very simple, strong and durable. The travelers and rope pulley revolve on **turned iron bushings.** Will work on ordinary 4x4 or 3x4 wood track. Weight, 27 lbs. Price each..........**$3.00**

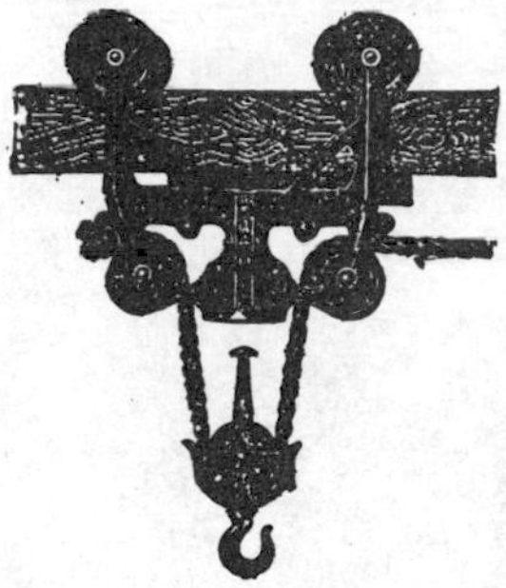

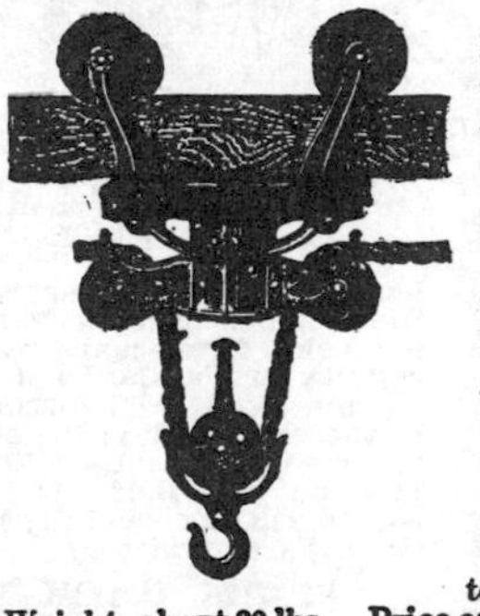

No. 18338. The Sears, Roebuck & Co. Swivel Hay Carrier for wood track. The merits of this carrier are many—Strength; **positive dead lock; large flanged wheels.** Ready adjustment to the stop on the track and the ease and perfection of its entire operation make this the most desirable carrier in the market. Is made from the best malleable iron. Works on track 4x4 (which should always be dressed), and reverses by swivel without having to pull the rope through. Weight, about 30 lbs. Price each.......................**$3.50**

No. 18339. **Extra stops for wood track carrier.** Price, each.......................**25c**

No. 18340. **Extra trip pulleys.** Weight 4 lbs. Price each.......................**75c**

No. 18342. Our new Reversible Rod or Cable Hay Carrier. Is simple in construction, and will work either way from the stop without changing on the track. Strong and well made, and will give satisfaction if properly used. Weight, 20 lbs. Price..........**$3.00**

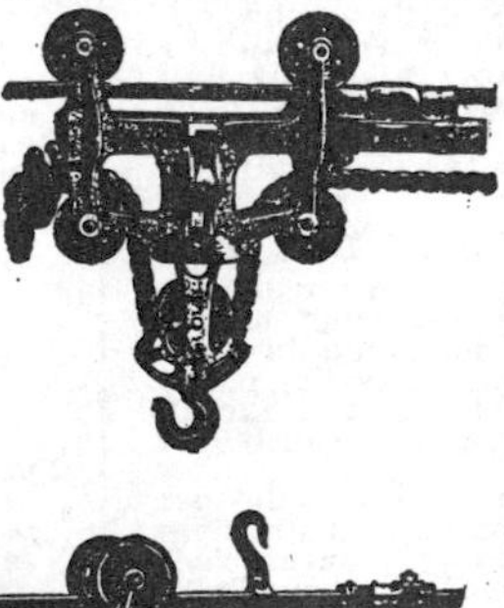

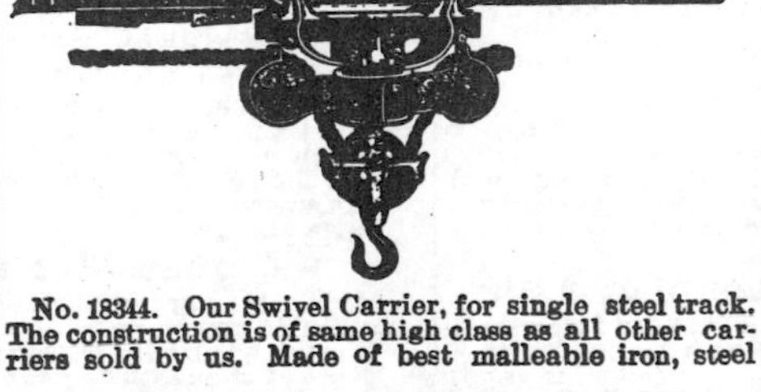

No. 18344. Our Swivel Carrier, for single steel track. The construction is of same high class as all other carriers sold by us. Made of best malleable iron, steel turned bushings, and thorough workmanship. Every carrier fully warranted. Weight, about 27 lbs. Track is furnished in lengths of 6, 8, 10 and 12 feet each, so track can be furnished for any length barn without cutting. Price of Carrier only.......................**$3.00**

No. 18345. Track for above Carrier, including couplings and bumper. Per foot.......................**12c**

No. 18346. Hanger Hook, with rafter irons. Per set, 1 hook and 1 rafter iron.......................**11c**

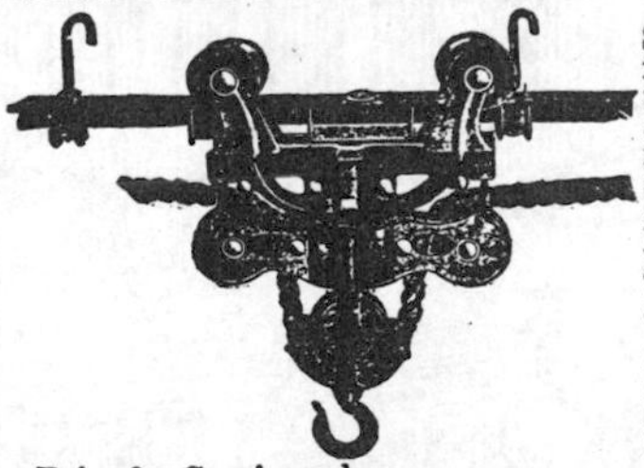

No. 18348. Our Swivel Carrier for double steel track possesses all the **good** features described in our wood track hanger. Guaranteed in every respect. Weight, about 30 lbs. Track furnished in lengths of 6, 8, 10 or 12 feet. Price for Carrier only.......................**$3.50**

No. 18349. Track for above Carrier, including couplings and bumper. Per foot.......................**12c**

No. 18350. Hanging Hook and Rafter Iron. Price for one of each...!.......................**11c**

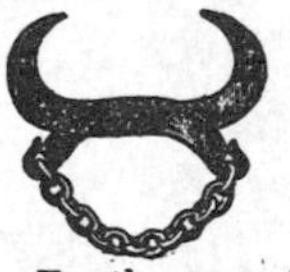

No. 18356. Solid Steel Grapple Hook, for hooking into rafter or beam where holes cannot be bored. Weight, 4½ lbs. Price each.......................**75c**

For the convenience of our customers we show below what constitutes a complete outfit for the various carriers quoted by us.

No. 18358. Outfit for Wood Track Carrier for 40-foot barn; everything except wood track, which we do not furnish. 1 carrier, **$3.00**; 1 fork, **63c**; 13 rafter irons, **65c**; 13 hanging hooks, **65c**; 6 floor hooks, **42c**; 5 knot passing pulleys, **$1.25**; 110 feet manilla rope, ¾-inch, **$2.20**; 50 feet check rope, **50c**. Complete outfit, **$9.30.**

If wanted for barn longer than 40 feet, add 8c to this price for each additional foot in length of barn.

No. 18359. Outfit for Steel Track Hanger for 40-foot barn, complete with track. 1 carrier, **$3.00**; 1 fork, **63c**; 40 feet steel track, **$4.80**; 13 rafter irons, **65c**; 13 hanging hooks, **65c**; 6 floor hooks, **42c**; 5 knot passing pulleys, **$1.25**; 110 feet manilla rope, ¾-inch, **$2.20**; 50 feet check rope, **50c**. Complete outfit, **$14.10.**

If wanted for barn longer than 40 feet, add 19c to this price for each additional foot in length of barn.

No. 18360. Outfit for Cable Carrier for barn 50 feet in length. 1 carrier, **$3.50**; 1 fork, **63c**; 50 feet cable with clamps and eye bolts, ready to hang, **$2.50**; 5 knot passing pulleys, **$1.25**; 120 feet ¾-inch manilla rope, **$2.40**; 75 feet check rope, **40c**; 6 floor hooks, **42c**; 2 hanging hooks rafter irons, **30c**. Complete outfit, **$10.90.**

For barn more than 50 feet in length, add to this price 6c for each additional foot in length.

**Cable will not be cut for lengths less than 50 feet.**

Any parts listed above furnished at prices quoted.

No. 18361. Outfit for Cable Carrier for stack using 50 feet of cable. Stack poles and end stakes not furnished. 50 feet cable clamps and eye bolts, ready to hang, **$2.50**; 2 knot passing pulleys, **50c**; 120 feet ¾-inch manilla rope, **$2.40**; 75 feet check rope, **40c**; 1 fork, **63c**; 1 cable carrier, **$3.00**; 2 50-foot guys with loops and clamps, **$2.47.** Outfit complete, **$11.90.**

Outfit for Cable Carrier to be used for either stack or barn, or for both as desired. Price, complete, **$13.47.**

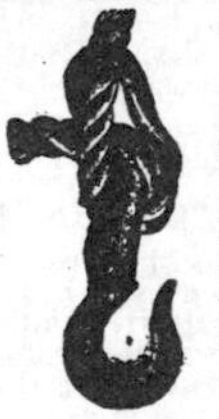

No. 18365. The places where this device can be used to advantage are only known to those who have had them on their farm. One on each end of a piece of rope often takes the place of a log chain, and is much lighter and better to handle. For hay carrier outfit they do away with twisting of rope. Take up can be made in a minute's time. They are made of the best malleable iron. Weight, about 1 lb. Price each.......................**20c**

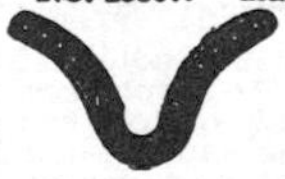

No. 18367. Rafter Irons for use in hanging track. Weight each, ¾ lb. Price each.......................**5c**

No. 18368. Straight, Hanging Hooks for use in hanging wood track to above brackets. Each..............**5c**

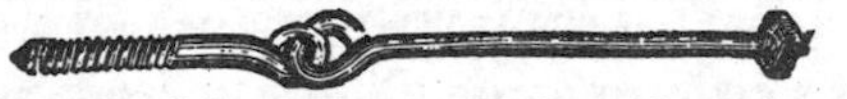

No. 18369. Jointed Hanging Hooks, with wood screw thread on one end for use in hanging wood track to beam without using bracket. Price each.......................**10c**

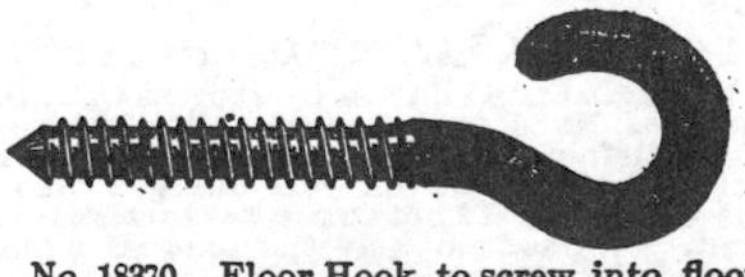

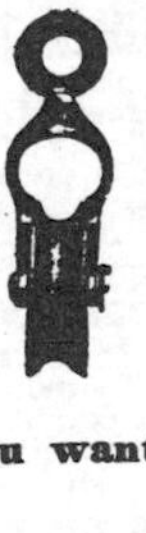

No. 18370. Floor Hook, to screw into floor to hold pulley. Price each..................**7c**

No. 18371. Knot Passing Hay Fork Pulley, will take ¾ to 1 inch rope. Malleable iron frame, wood sheave. Price each.........**25c**

**Rope of all kinds quoted on another page. Refer to index. Anything you want about the farm can be furnished at prices to suit.**

# CLOTHING DEPARTMENT OF SEARS·ROEBUCK &·CO·

**South Wing.** · OFFICE · **North Wing.**

**Above we show an interior view of our Clothing department,** as drawn by our artist. For want of space we can only show a portion of the north and south wings, but from this you may be able to form some idea of the extensive scale on which this portion of our business is conducted.

**The Clothing Department** occupies the entire sixth floor, from where we ship more clothing direct to the consumer than any other five concerns in the United States combined.

**For the coming season** we have made far more extensive preparations than ever before. We have contracted with some of the largest and most reliable woolen mills for their entire product of certain fabrics, and in doing so have been able to get prices lower than ever before, and prices that will enable us to make the goods up in the very best manner and offer them direct to our customers at lower prices than merchants can buy in quantities.

## HOW OUR CLOTHING IS MADE.

**Every garment we offer is cut on the** very latest style patterns by expert cutters and by the latest perfect fitting process. **They are made by first class tailors,** the linings, fittings and general finish are strictly first class, and those on all suits we offer above $6.00 will compare favorably with the trimmings and general finish of any custom tailor work. The cheaper suits will be found far superior to ready made goods offered by the average retail dealer.

**We recognize no competition whatever in this line,** We operate directly in connection with the woolen mills, and our customers own the garments they buy from us at the actual cost of producing the raw material and putting it together with only our one small percentage of profit added, with no allowance whatever to be made for bad debts, traveling men's expenses, collections, and the various other expenses which go to make up the regular wholesaler's calculation of cost, to say nothing of the exorbitant profit usually added by retail dealers.

**If you buy your Clothing from us** you will own it cheaper than any one who does not buy from us. **You will be sure to have the very latest styles,** no carried-over stock, and goods that are made up by manufacturers of established reputation and manufactured by mechanics who are exclusive men's clothing tailors.

**Terms—Our terms are very liberal.** Any regular sized suit or garment will be sent to any address by express C. O. D. subject to examination on receipt of $1.00. **You can examine it at the express office,** and if found perfectly satisfactory and exactly as represented, pay the express agent our advertised price and express charges, less $1.00 paid in advance, and the goods are yours. If not found perfectly satisfactory and exactly as represented, you need not pay the express agent a cent and the goods will be returned at our expense.

**Cash Discount.—We allow a cash discount of 3 per cent** if cash in full accompanies your order. If you send cash in full with your order you may deduct 3% from our price. **You take no risk in sending cash in full,** for if the goods do not suit you in every particular you can return them at our expense and we will cheerfully refund your money. The best way is to send cash in full with your order. You not only save the 3% discount but you also save return charges on money to us. **Nearly all our customers send cash in full.**

**How to Order.** Select the garment or suit wanted by number as described on following page of this catalogue; see that it is furnished in the style wanted as shown in the several illustrations or in our fashion plate, the style being noted by number, follow our rules for measurement closely as given on page 158 **or fill out one of our regular order blanks if you have it,** and send to us either with the full amount less 3% cash discount or with a deposit of not less than $1.00; allow us three to five days to get the goods ready, and they will be sent to you by express C. O. D. subject to examination if only a deposit is sent, or by express not C. O. D. if cash in full accompanies your order, and your money of course will be cheerfully refunded if the goods do not fit you and are not perfectly satisfactory.

**Do not think you live too far away.** The express charges are very low. See full information concerning express rates on pages 5 and 6. A suit of clothes, nicely packed in a strong paper box as we ship them, weighs about 5 lbs., and the express charges range about as follows:

For 200 miles or less.................................................25c.
For 500 miles or less.................................................50c.
For 1000 miles or less................................................75c.

**So you see you have but little express charges to pay,** and if you send cash in full the 3% discount will usually nearly or quite pay all express charges, and you have the satisfaction of not only saving one-half on your suit, but of getting a better suit than you could possibly buy in the average retail store.

## ABOUT FREE SAMPLES.

**We can furnish cloth samples of everything we catalogue,** and we will at all times take pleasure in sending free of charge any samples our customers may ask for.

**We issue a special card of cloth samples** and would recommend that you ask for our special sample card rather than ask for samples of any particular number, for this card is arranged to show our best bargains. **We have made the selection with a view to showing our customers cloth samples of such goods we catalogue as are special leaders with us, and which we can recommend above all others.** Drop us a postal card saying, "Please send cloth samples of men and boys' suitings and pants," and this card will be mailed to you post paid at once.

**20 Per cent. extra for extra sizes.** Regular sizes run for men's suits from 34 to 42 inches chest measure, and for pants 30 to 40 inches waist measure and 30 to 35 inches leg measure. Any size above these is termed extra size, and for which we charge 20 per cent. extra on all suits $10.00 or upwards; on all suits less than $10.00, $2.00 per suit extra. Please consider this in taking your measurement, and if you require an extra size suit be sure to include the extra charge.

**We guarantee a perfect fit.** Follow our rules for measurement closely, using our regular clothing order blank and following the rules for measurement there given if you have a blank. If not, give the measurements as per instructions given on page 158, and if you have a sample of the cloth be sure to attach a piece of the cloth to your order, allow us three to five days to get your suit ready, and we will guarantee to ship you suits that will fit you perfectly and of such value as were never seen in your section at anything like the price.

SEE PAGE 158 FOR FULL INSTRUCTIONS HOW TO TAKE YOUR MEASURE.

## RULES FOR MEASUREMENT

**FOLLOW THESE..**

unless you have one of our regular clothing order blanks, in which case fill out the blank according to he rules there given.

### If You have no Regular Order Blank,

please observe the following rules: Give your **HEIGHT, WEIGHT, AGE,** and say whether you have sloping or square shoulders. **Be sure to give your correct height and weight.**

**FOR COAT** measurement to be taken over vest. Be sure to take measure under your coat, not over it. Chest measurement, take the measurement at Fig. 1 in cut, giving the number in inches around the body, also length of sleeves to elbow, 7 to 8, per cut, and from elbow to hand, 8 to 9, per cut. (Be sure to take measure under your coat, not over it.)

**FOR VEST** Chest measure at Fig. 7 only required.

**FOR PANTS** measure around the body over vest for the waist measure, Fig. 2, per cut. At Fig. 3 for hip measure, per cut, and for measure of inside seam from 4 to 5 per cut, tight in crotch at 4 to heel at 5.

**FOR OVERCOAT** measure to be taken exactly the same as for coat, always over vest under coat.

**Be sure to take measure under coat, not over it.** We will make the necessary allowance.

**FOR BOYS' LONG PANTS SUITS.** For boys from 10 to 19 years of age, measurement should be taken the same as for men's suits. **FOR CHILDREN'S KNEE PANTS SUITS.** State age of boy and say whether large or small of his age. **No further measurement will be necessary.**

**MEN'S $2.98 SUITS**

## No. 4300, Men's $2.98

**Suits** in styles 1 or 2, round cut sack or square cut sack. This suit is made from a fair grade of domestic Satinett with cotton chain. It is a good weight goods suitable for year around wear. They come in a variety of neat shades and plaids, medium and dark colors. The coats are lined with cotton lining, and at $2.98 are such bargains as were never before offered.

**WHILE WE OFFER AT $2.98** such a suit as was never sold at any such a price, we **CAN NOT** recommend so low a priced suit, and we would advise our customers to select a suit at $4.75 or upwards. We offer a line of suitings at $2.98 to $4.50 in competition with dealers who sell, under glowing descriptions at big prices the poorest goods that can be made. **WE SELL THEM FOR WHAT THEY ARE** and give values that can not be had elsewhere; BUT TAKE OUR ADVICE, select a suit at from $4.75 upwards, a suit we can **guarantee,** one that will give you wear and satisfaction and bring us your future trade and good will. **Our Special Price for Suit 4300, Style 1 or 2..........$2.98**

**No. 4301. MEN'S $3.50 CASSIMERE SUIT.** These suits are made from a wool and cotton mixed cassimere. The goods are good weight, suitable for year around wear. They come in a variety of neat checks, stripes and small plaids, in light, medium and dark shades. They are lined throughout with cotton lining. They come in Styles 1 or 2, as desired, and only in regular sizes 34 to 42 inches chest measure.

**Our Special Price......................$3.50**

**MEN'S $3.98 SUITS**

## Samples of Cloth Free on Application. Your Choice of Styles;

round cut, style 1, or square cut, style 2. Be sure to state size wanted. Regular sizes run from 34 to 42 inches. Extra sizes are $1.50 extra.

**Remember Our Liberal Terms.** Any clothing sent to any address C. O. D., subject to examination on receipt of $1.00, balance and express charges payable at express office. Three per cent discount allowed if cash in full accompanies your order.

**Our $3.98 Line of Men's Suits** is without exception the greatest value for the money ever offered. There is nothing made that will in any way compare with them at the price.

**Our $3.98 Line of Men's Suits** is made of good weight, strong, closely woven domestic cassimere (part cotton). The goods will wear well and look neat and dressy.

**REMEMBER, OUR PRICE IS $3.98.** While we furnish you with a far better suit than you can buy elsewhere for the price, we would urge you to select a suit at $4.75, or upwards, and get a suit we can guarantee and one that will give you wear and perfect satisfaction.

They come in the following patterns:

**No. 4302. Gray Mixed Pin-check effect,** a very neat pattern, this season's production, goods that make up dressy.

**Price for Men's Suit, Style 1 or 2...............$3.98**

☞ Samples of cloth free on application.

**No. 4303. Dark Brown Mixture,** a neat small check effect. This pattern is the very latest production of the mill, and we know will please you. At the price $3.98, we know you will wonder how we can produce such goods.

**Price for Men's Suits, Style 1 or 2...............$3.98**

☞ Samples of cloth free on application.

## Men's $4.75 CHEVIOTS BLACK AND NAVY BLUE.

### OUR $4.75 WONDERS

**We guarantee these suits superior in quality,** make and style to any black cheviot suit on the market at within 50% more than our price.

**Regular sizes run from 34 to 42 inches** chest measure. Extra sizes are $2.00 extra.

Styles:—
- Round cut sack, style 1.
- Square cut sack, style 2.
- Double breasted, style 3 at 50 cents extra.

**BLACK CHEVIOTS ARE A LEADER WITH US.** We cut up more black cheviot cloth than any other manufacturer in America, and as a result we are able to buy our material at the lowest possible price.

**Order your Black Cheviot Suit from us,** and if you do not say we have furnished you a better suit for less money than you could possibly buy elsewhere, return it to us and we will refund your money.

**Our Black Cheviot Suits are all tailor made,** the trimmings and finish in quality and workmanship depending on the price.

**Our $4.75 suit is the greatest value ever shown for the money.**

**Our $5.75 suits are better made,** and somewhat better made.

**Our cheviot suits which range in price from $7.00 to $10.00** illustrated and described in the following column are equal to anything your local tailor can produce at two to four times our price.

**Don't forget our very liberal terms.** Any suit will be sent to any address anywhere in the United States by express C. O. D. subject to examination on receipt of $1.00 as a guarantee of good faith. You can examine the goods at the express office, and if found perfectly satisfactory and exactly as represented, pay the express agent our price and express charges less the $1.00 sent with order.

A discount of 3 per cent. allowed if cash in full accompanies your order. Nearly all our customers send cash in full.

**Cloth samples of black cheviot furnished free on application.**

**You will also find them in our special card of samples.**

**OUR $4.75 BLACK CHEVIOT SUIT.**

**No. 4304.** This suit comes in Style 1, round cut sack, or Style 2, square cut sack, or Style 3, double breasted. Made from a good quality domestic cheviot in black or navy blue, goods generally sold for all wool. There is a small cotton thread running one way, but you can not tell it from all wool goods. It is a material that will wear well and not fade. It makes up very neat and dressy. We cut them perfectly, they are made by good tailors, well lined and trimmed and guaranteed in every respect. Sample of cloth free.

**Our Challenge Price, Style 1 or 2..........$4.75 Style 3........$5.25**

**OUR $5.75 BLACK CHEVIOT SUIT.**

**No. 4305.** These suits are made from good strong closely woven black wool cheviot cloth, a material used in tailors' regular $10.00 and $12.00 suits, a soft smooth goods that will wear well and look neat and dressy. They are cut in the very latest styles, made by good tailors, lined with genuine black, Italian cloth, well sewed and trimmed.

**Our Challenge Price, Style 1 or 2.......$5.75 Style 3..........$6.25**

## OUR $4.85 BROWN TWILLED MELTON SUIT

**4305½** This suit is made from a very nice imported German wool twilled Melton, comes in light and dark shade of brown. It is a goods that is often sold for all wool though there is a slight cotton mixture in the wool, just enough to give it strength. It is made by an old reliable German maker, goods that are closely woven and guaranteed to give excellent wear. It is a very stylish shade of brown and will make up very dressy. We make these suits in either Style 1, 2 or 3, round cut sack or square cut sack, as desired. They are cut by expert cutters and made by first-class tailors, lined throughout with a good quality Italian cloth lining, coats are satin piped throughout, fancy arm shields under sleeves, well padded, stayed pockets, sewed throughout with linen and guaranteed in every respect. There is no suit on the market in a brown Melton that will compare with it at anything like our price.

**Style 1.** Round Cut Sack Suit.

**Style 2.** Square Cut Sack Suit.

**Our Special Price, Style 1 or 2..........$4.85 Style 3.........$5.35**

**No. 4306. MEN'S $5.15 BROWN MELTON SUIT.** These goods are also imported German twilled Melton in medium and dark brown, but are better quality than **No. 4305.** They are very closely woven, have a very soft surface, guaranteed for wear, very stylish shade, will make up very dressy. They are cut to fit perfectly, fine tailor made, coats are lined throughout with an extra quality Italian cloth, satin piped throughout, velvet arm shields under sleeves, nicely padded, stayed pockets, each garment sewed throughout with silk and linen and guaranteed in every respect. They come in Style 1, 2 or 3. Sample of cloth free on application.

**Our Special Price.........$5.15 Style 3............$5.65**

# Men's $5.50 WORSTEDS
## BLACK AND NAVY BLUE.
### OUR $5.50 WONDERS

This is the first time a Genuine Worsted Suit of this character was ever offered at anything like the price.

We have arranged with the manufacturer for his entire product of these goods in two certain patterns, which will be all the style for the coming season.

They closely resemble the expensive Genuine French Worsteds which first-class tailors use in their finest $40.00 and $50.00 suits, in fact, made up, at a short distance you can not tell one cloth or one suit from the other.

**No. 4306½. THIS IS A WOOL AND COTTON MIXED WORSTED,** extra heavy, a very closely woven goods, and a goods that there is practically no wear-out to.

They come in Black or Navy Blue, as desired. We are able to make the exceptionally low price of $5.50 only by reason of our very favorable contract with the mill that makes the cloth, and our very economic method of manufacturing and handling. Samples of cloth will be furnished free on application.

Price for Suit Style 1 or 2 .....................$5.50  Style 3......$6.00

**No. 4307. NAVY BLUE MUMMIE CLOTH WORSTED.** These goods have a very delicate roughed raised effect, the same as the genuine Mummie Cloth, and in appearance cannot be told from the genuine Mummie Cloth.

Our Special Price in Blue, Style 1 or 2.... $5.50  Style 3......$6.00
**No. 4308.** Same in Black, Style 1 or 2 ......$5.50  Style 3......$6.00

**No. 4310. NAVY BLUE BASKET WEAVE WORSTED.** This is the genuine basket weave, a pattern that has been so very stylish in all suits of the finest German Worsteds, and in appearance these suits can not be told from the genuine German Worsted goods.

Our Special Price Style 1 or 2 .................$5.50, Style 3......$6.00
**No. 4311.** Same in Black, Style 1 or 2 ......$5.50, Style 3......$6.00

# MEN'S $4.75 SUITS

## The very latest patterns in Men's $4.75 all wool cassimere suits.

In offering men's all wool cassimere suits for the coming season at $4.75 we feel confident we are selling direct to the consumer at at least $1.25 less than the same goods could be bought in dozen suit lots by dealers, and we know where one suit goes others are sure to follow. This is a suit that your local dealer would charge you double our price for. It is made from a medium weight, all wool, domestic cassimere, in a very neat, stylish, medium brown with good, modest plaid. It is a goods that will wear well, and for a gentleman's business suit there is nothing more desirable. **Fine Tailor Made.** These suits are made by first class tailors, they are lined throughout with a good quality serge lining, color to match the cloth, coats are satin piped throughout, fancy arm shields under sleeves, well padded, pockets stayed, sewed throughout with silk and linen and guaranteed in every respect. They come in round cut sack or square cut sack as desired.

**No. 4311 1-2.** Our Special Offer Price for this Suit Style 1 or 2...$4.75

**No. 4312. MEN'S $5.50 ALL-WOOL CASSIMERE SUITS.** We have bought over 3000 yards of these goods, enough to make a thousand suits. We bought the cloth under value, and for this reason we can offer you at $5.50 a better suit than you could possibly buy in your local market for $10.00. We have these suits in a variety of patterns, light, medium and dark gray, light, medium and dark brown, in small checks, plaids and stripes. The goods are guaranteed all wool, they are good weight, suitable for year around wear, guaranteed for service. They are made by a very reliable mill, the suits are cut by expert cutters, made by first class tailors, lined throughout with a very nice Italian cloth, coats are satin piped throughout, have fancy velvet arm shields under sleeves, nicely padded, pockets are stayed, each garment sewed throughout with silk and linen, and every piece warranted.

Our Special offer price, Style 1 or 2.............$5.50  Style 3......$6.00

**No. 4312 1-2. MEN'S $5.75 ALL-WOOL CASSIMERE SUITS.** These suits are made from a good quality all-wool Cassimere cloth. They come in light, medium and dark shades. We have over 20 patterns, including small checks, plaids and stripes. If you will give us an idea of the color and pattern wanted we will guarantee to please you. The goods are good weight, suitable for year around wear. They are gotten up in the very latest styles for this season. They are made by first-class tailors, coats lined throughout with Italian cloth in colors to match the goods, satin piped throughout, fancy velvet arm shields under sleeves, and guaranteed to give first-class satisfaction. We furnish these suits in Style 1, 2 or 3. In ordering be sure to state style wanted.

Our Special offer price for suit, Style 1 or 2.....$5.75  Style 3....$6.25

# CHALLENGE PRICES IN MEN'S BLACK AND BLUE CHEVIOTS SUITS.

$5.75  $6.50  $7.00  $7.50  $8.00  $9.00  $10.00

## PRICES GUARANTEED BELOW ALL OTHERS.

We repeat that we are Headquarters for All Kinds of Cheviot Suits, and we cut up more black and blue cheviot cloth than any other maufacturer in America.

Our output of Black Cheviot enables us to dictate terms by which we can market the goods made up in fine styles at far less money than dealer can buy in quantities.

There is no such thing as any firm being able to compete with us on black cheviots; in fact, we recognize no competition in the clothing line, but on black cheviots and clay worsteds we are not only headquarters, but you will find our prices in many cases even less than one-half the price charged by others.

Black Cheviots are leaders with us and we show a very big line with prices ranging from $4.75, as previously quoted, to $10.00. Every Black Cheviot suit listed below is cut on the very latest style patterns by the latest patent perfect fitting process—we employ only first-class cutters—they are made by the very best tailors we can employ, every garment is lined throughout with a fine imported Italian cloth, coats are satin piped throughout, have fancy velvet arm shields under sleeves; they are well padded, every pocket stayed, every garment sewed throughout with silk and linen and guaranteed in every respect.

They come in style 1, 2, 3 or 4. Styles 3 and 4 will be 50c extra. We can furnish any size wanted. Sizes over 42 inches will be $1.50 extra. Samples of cloth will be furnished on application. The choicest will be found on our regular sample card.

**No. 4313. MEN'S $5.75 BLACK MANCHESTER CHEVIOT SUITS.** We can also furnish this in navy blue. This is a very good medium weight, all-wool domestic black or blue cheviot, is made by a first-class maker and guaranteed for wear.

Our price.................................................$5.75

**No. 4314. MEN'S $6.50 BLACK CHESTER CHEVIOT SUITS,** also furnished in navy blue. This is a very fine all wool Washington black or navy blue cheviot, a good weight suitable for year around wear, a soft finished closely woven goods, makes up very neat and dressy, and we guarantee it in every respect.

Our Special Price.........................................$6.50

**No. 4315. MEN'S $7.00 BLACK STERLING CHEVIOT SUITS.** Also furnished in navy blue. This is an extra fine all wool black or navy blue cheviot, made in Pennsylvania by one of the most reliable makers, a closely woven wear-resisting goods which makes up very neat and dressy.

Our Special Price.........................................$7.00

**No. 4316. MEN'S $7.50 BLACK SHEFFIELD CHEVIOT SUITS.** Very similar to our $7.00 suit but of a finer weave, and we make the price to you the exact difference in cost to us. Also furnished in navy blue.

Our Special Price.........................................$7.50

**No. 4317. MEN'S $8.00 BLACK PICADILLY CHEVIOT SUITS.** This is a very fine imported all wool English black or navy blue cheviot cloth, one of the best cheviots made in England, a very closely woven goods, very soft finish, and there is nothing more stylish for a dress or business suit. The same class of goods as is used by the best merchant tailors in the cities, which they make up at three and four times our price. Also made in navy blue.

Our Special Price. .......................................$8.00

**No. 4318. MEN'S $9.00 BLACK LUZERNE CHEVIOT SUITS.** These suits are made from a very fine inported, all wool French black or navy blue Thibet Cheviot Cloth, one of the very finest French weaves. For a very stylish, dressy, serviceable suit we would recommend this fine cheviot. Also made in navy blue.

Our Special Price.........................................$9.00

**No. 4319. GENUINE VICUNA BLACK CHEVIOT SUIT FOR $10.00.** These goods are genuine imported, all wool German Vicuna cheviot cloth which come in black or navy blue, one of the very finest cheviots imported to this country, good year around weight, very closely woven, very smooth, soft surface, a goods that will wear until you are tired of it. This is our finest cheviot suit, we make it up without regard to expense, and produce as fine a cheviot suit as can be turned out.

Your tailor can make you nothing better at even three times the price. Nothing has been left undone to make this suit a big advertisement for us, and we especially recommend to your consideration this extra fine cheviot suit. Also made in navy blue.

Our Special Price.........................................$10.00

ANY SUIT ON THIS PAGE FURNISHED IN EXTRA SIZE AT $1.50 TO $2.00 EXTRA. SEE PAGE 156 REGARDING EXTRA SIZE.

# SEND FOR OUR LARGE CARD OF CLOTH SAMPLES.

It will be mailed to any address free. This card of cloth samples includes THE MOST DESIRABLE FABRICS WE HAVE. You will avoid any possible delay by sending for sample card in preference to sending for samples of any special numbers. The large sample card is already prepared and ready for mailing. It covers the most desirable numbers in the entire line of Men's, Boys' and Children's Clothing, we have used our best judgment in making the choicest selection, and we recommend that you SIMPLY SEND A POSTAL CARD, SAYING: "Please send me your full Sample Card of Cloth Samples of Men's, Boys' and Children's Clothing."

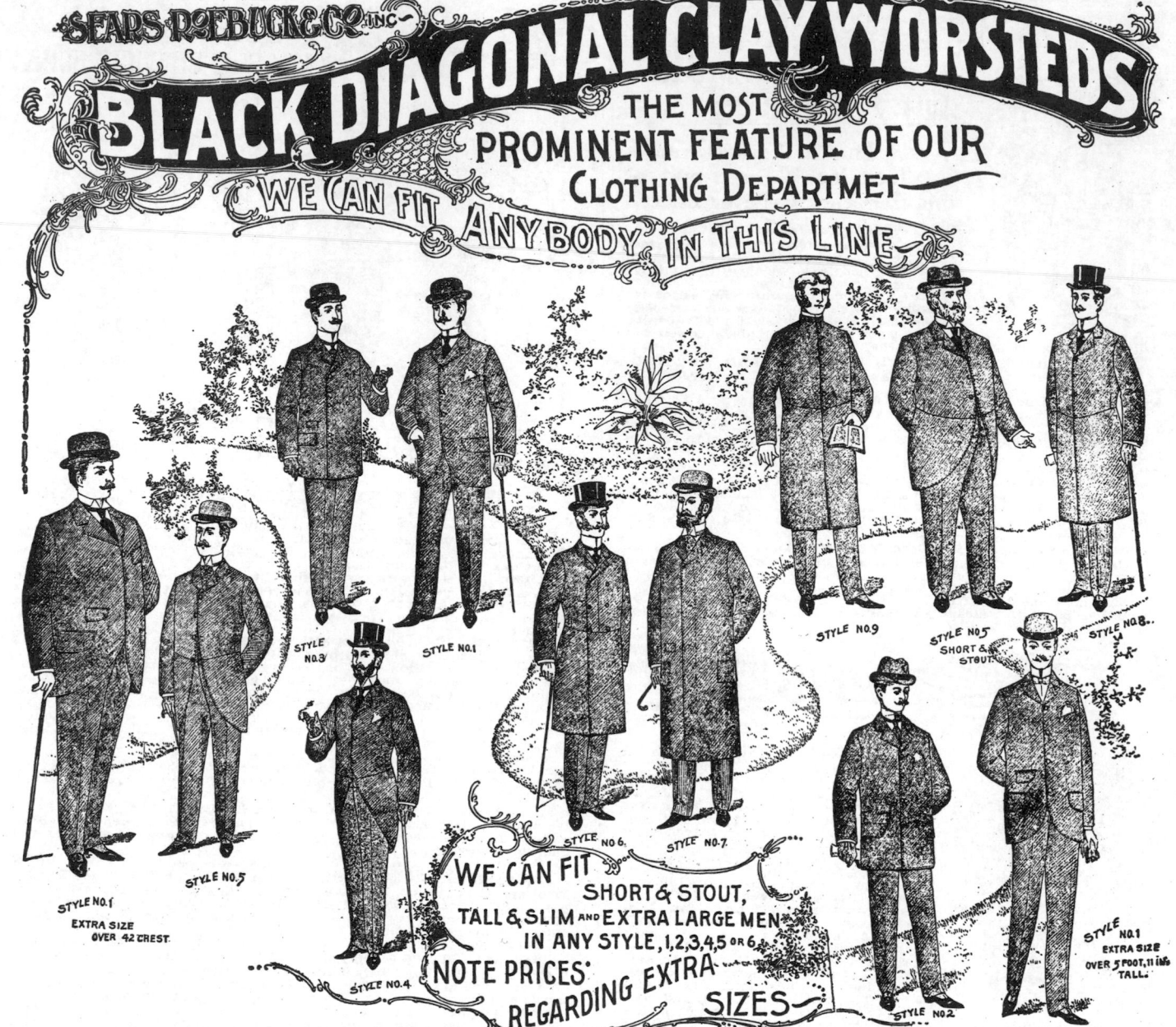

# SEARS ROEBUCK & CO. INC. BLACK DIAGONAL CLAY WORSTEDS

### THE MOST PROMINENT FEATURE OF OUR Clothing Departmet

### WE CAN FIT ANYBODY IN THIS LINE

STYLE NO.3

STYLE NO.1

STYLE NO.5

STYLE NO.1 EXTRA SIZE OVER 42 CHEST.

STYLE NO.4

STYLE NO.6

STYLE NO.7

WE CAN FIT SHORT & STOUT, TALL & SLIM AND EXTRA LARGE MEN IN ANY STYLE, 1, 2, 3, 4, 5 or 6

NOTE PRICES REGARDING EXTRA SIZES

STYLE NO.9

STYLE NO.5 SHORT & STOUT.

STYLE NO.8.

STYLE NO.2

STYLE NO.1 EXTRA SIZE OVER 5 FOOT, 11 IN. TALL.

---

**If you do not find our prices on Clay Worsted Suits** not only lower, but far lower, than you could possibly buy elsewhere, return the goods to us at our expense, and we will refund your money and pay any expenses you have been put to.

**We are headquarters for Clay Worsted Suits.** We import the goods from England direct, and our contracts are always so large as to insure the very lowest prices. Last year we cut up over 70,000 yards of black worsted goods, 40 miles of cloth. Imagine a piece of black cloth 54 inches wide, and 40 miles in length and you can form some idea of what our Clay Worsted business amounts to.

**We have no competitors in this line.** Select the Clay Worsted suit wanted, follow our rules for measurement, and we will send you such a suit as was never seen in your section at anything like the price.

**Our best tailors handle this work**, every garment is cut on the very latest style patterns by expert cutters to fit perfectly and is guaranteed in every respect. Sizes run from 34 to 42. Extra sizes are $2.00 extra on suits $10.00 or under, 20% extra on suits over $10.00.

**Any style wanted.** You can have these suits in any style wanted, 1, 2, 3, 4 or 5. For styles 6, 8 and 9 see quotations on Prince Albert and Professional Men's suits. ☞ Styles 3, 4 and 5 are 50 cents to $1.00 extra. Samples of cloth free on application. A selection of our Clay Worsted cloth, samples will be found on our regular sample card.

**No. 4328. MEN'S $6.50 BLACK CLAY WORSTED SUITS.** A genuine imported all-wool English Black Clay Worsted suit was never before offered at anything like $6.50.

Our $6.50 suits are made from 14 oz. black all-wool Clay Worsted. They are lined throughout with a good quality Italian cloth, the coats are satin piped throughout, have fancy velvet arm shields under sleeves, they are well padded, every pocket stayed, every garment sewed throughout with silk and linen, and will compare favorably with any Clay Worsted suit you can buy in your local market at from $10.00 to $12.00.

Our Special Price, Style 1 or 2.....$6.50    Styles 3, 4 or 5.....$7.00

**No. 4329. MEN'S $7.50 BLACK CLAY WORSTED SUITS.** These suits are made from good quality all-wool imported English Clay Worsted cloth in 15 oz. weight. A good weight for year round wear. It is a closely woven, wear resisting material which we guarantee will not wear shiny. They are made by our very best tailors. Coats are lined throughout with fine black Italian cloth, satin piped throughout, fancy velvet arm shields under sleeves, nicely padded, every pocket stayed, sewed throughout with silk and linen, and guaranteed in every respect.

Our Special Price, Style 1 or 2.....$7.50    Style 3, 4 or 5.....$8.00

**No. 4330. MEN'S $8.50 BLACK CLAY WORSTED SUITS.** These suits are made from a 16 oz. all-wool imported English Clay Worsted Cloth, the product of one of the very best English mills, a closely woven, wear resisting all-wool worsted, guaranteed in every respect. The coats are lined throughout with fine imported Italian cloth, satin piped throughout, fancy velvet arm shields under sleeves, nicely padded, every pocket stayed, sewed throughout with silk and linen, every garment guaranteed.

Special Price, Style 1 or 2.....$8.50
Special Price, Style 3, 4 or 5.....9.00

**No. 4331. MEN'S $9.50 BLACK CLAY WORSTED SUITS.** Also furnished in navy blue. These goods are guaranteed 18 oz., a weight suitable for year round wear, the product of one of the oldest and most reliable woolen mills, closely woven, soft surface, wear-resisting fabric. This is a beautiful suit. There is nothing more desirable for dress or business wear. It is made up in the highest style of the art, lined throughout with fine imported black Italian cloth, coat is satin piped throughout, fancy velvet arm shields under sleeves, sewed throughout with silk and linen and guaranteed in every respect.

Price, Style 1 or 2.....$9.50
Price, Style 3, 4 or 5.....10.00

**No. 4332. MEN'S $10.50 BLACK CLAY WORSTED SUITS.** These suits are made from one of the very finest imported all-wool 18 oz. black or navy blue German Clay Worsted cloths, such goods as are used by the very best tailors in their made-to-order suits at $25.00 to $40.00. The coats are lined throughout with very fine imported all-wool Italian cloth, satin piped throughout, fancy velvet arm shields under sleeves, nicely padded, every pocket stayed, every garment sewed throughout with silk and linen and guaranteed in every respect. Also furnished in navy blue.

Our Special Price, Style 1 or 2.....$10.50
Our Special Price, Style 3, 4 or 5.....11.00

**No. 4333. MEN'S $11.50 BLACK CLAY WORSTED SUITS.** This is one of the very finest imported all wool 18 oz. black or navy blue German worsted cloths, the product of one of the very best German mills and one of the best worsteds that comes to this country. It is a goods that will wear like iron, never wear smooth or shiny, and there is nothing more desirable for a dress or business suit. Your tailor would charge you two or three times our price for such a suit, and no such goods will be found in any ready made stocks. The coats are lined throughout with fine imported all wool Italian cloth, satin piped throughout, velvet arm shields under sleeves, every pocket stayed, every garment sewed throughout with silk and linen, guaranteed in every respect. Also furnished in navy blue.

Our Special Price, Style 1 or 2.....$11.50    Style 3, 4 or 5.....$12.50

# Mens Black Prince Albert Suits

We make and sell more Prince Albert Suits direct to the consumer than all other mail order houses combined and we are prepared to offer values that will mean a saving to you of 25% to 50%. We can furnish you a double breasted Prince Albert suit, perfect fitting and equal to anything your local tailor can make, at a saving to you of at least 50%. We are anxious to get your order for one of these suits to show you that it is possible for us to furnish the highest class goods at prices within easy reach of all. Our Prince Albert suits are made in the very highest style of the art on the latest patterns, cut by expert cutters to fit perfectly, and made by the best tailors we can employ. The linings and trimmings are all of the very finest, and we guarantee every suit to give the best satisfaction. Sizes run regularly from 34 to 42 inches chest measure, but larger sizes can be furnished at 20% extra.

Our terms are liberal. Any suit will be sent to any address on receipt of $1.00 as a guarantee of good faith, balance and express charges payable at express office. A discount of 3% allowed if cash in full accompanies your order. ☞ Samples of cloth will be sent free on application.

Men's tailor made Clay Worsted Double Breasted Prince Albert Suits at $9.80 surely should interest all careful buyers, for a Clay Worsted Prince Albert suit was never before offered at anything like the price.

We offer a line of Double Breasted Prince Albert Suits at $9.80, $12.00, $14.00, $16.00, $18.00, and $20.00, and we know that the sale of one suit in a neighborhood will result in the sale of many more.

No. 4342. Our $9.80 Men's Black Clay Worsted Prince Albert Suit, a suit that would retail at nearly double our price. Made from a good quality imported All Wool Black Clay Worsted Cloth, well lined, trimmed and finished and guaranteed in every respect. Our Special Price........ $9.80

No. 4343. Our $12.00 Men's Clay Worsted Prince Albert Suit, made from 14 oz. imported all wool black English clay worsted cloth, guaranteed for wear, nicely lined, trimmed and finished and guaranteed in every respect. Our Special Price.................................$12.00

No. 4344. Our $14.00 Black Clay Worsted Prince Albert suit, made from an imported all wool 16 oz. black English clay worsted cloth, finely lined, trimmed and finished and guaranteed in every respect. Our Special price..$14.00

No. 4345. Our $16.00 Black Clay Worsted Prince Albert Suit, made from 18 oz. imported all wool black English clay worsted, coat lined throughout with fine imported Italian cloth, elegantly trimmed and finished, and guaranteed in every respect. Our Special Price.........................$16.00

No. 4346. Our $18.00 Black Clay Worsted Prince Albert Suit, made from a very fine imported all wool English 18 oz. black clay worsted cloth. This is one of our finest Prince Albert suits. The coat is lined throughout with fine imported black Italian cloth, nicely trimmed and finished, and gotten up first-class in every respect. Our Special Price.............. $18.00

No. 4347. $20.00 for our very finest Black Clay Worsted Prince Albert Suit. The suit is made from our 19 oz. imported all wool black English clay worsted, one of the best English weaves, a goods that we guarantee will never wear smooth, has a very nice soft surface finish. Every suit is made by expert tailors, the coats are lined throughout with fine imported black Italian cloth, nicely trimmed and guaranteed in every respect. Our Special Price.......................................$20.00

# PROFESSIONAL MENS SUITS
### FOR MINISTERS DOCTORS LAWYERS ETC.

The demand the past season from professional men such as clergymen, doctors, lawyers and the other professions, for something we could guarantee, and sell at a price in keeping with our general rock bottom prices, has induced us to make quite extensive preparations for the coming season. We have contracted for quite a quantity of extra fine material for this class of goods, have arranged for special cutters and special tailors, and will be able to furnish these suits in Styles 8 or 9 as illustrated above made up thoroughly first class, and at less than one half the price charged by local tailors. Regular sizes will run from 34 to 42 inches chest measure. Extra sizes can be had at 20 percent. extra. Orders will be accepted the same as for any other suits on receipt of $1.00 as a guarantee of good faith, balance and express charges to be paid at the express office. A discount of 3 per cent. allowed if cash in full accompanies your order. Sample of cloth free on application.

No. 4548. Our $18.00 Clerical or Professional Suit, made in either style, single breasted Prince Albert or standing collar clerical, as desired. Made from a very fine quality imported English clay worsted, one of the finest English weaves, elegantly lined, trimmed and finished, and warranted in every respect. Our Special Price, Style 8 or 9......................$18.00

No. 4549. Our $22.00 Professional Suit, in either style. These suits are made from the very finest imported black clay worsted, one of the finest English weaves, in weight suitable for year around wear, elegantly lined, trimmed and fully warranted. Our Special Price, Style 8 or 9..$22.00

No. 4350. Our $23.00 Broadcloth Professional Suit in either style, just the suit for ministers, physicians and other professional men. Your tailor would charge you $40.00 for such a suit. Made from fine imported smooth finished black broadcloth, elegantly trimmed with the finest material made, and made by the best workmen. Every garment fully warranted. Our facilities for furnishing these suits are second to none, and if you will favor us with an order we will convince you that we can give you such values as can be had from no other concern.

# MENS SIX-DOLLAR CASSIMERE SUITS.

Our $6.00 line is a leader this season. Very Fine, Stylish, All-wool Fabrics. All fine tailor made. You would pay others $10.00 to $12.00 for such Suits, and then consider you had a rare bargain. We only ask that you send us $1.00 with your order, balance, $5.00, and express charges to be paid at your express office when received. One quality of material in our $6.00 line. They differ only in the color and pattern. The cassimere is the product of one of the oldest and most reliable woolen mills in America, a manufacturer with a reputation for the production of only first-class goods. The cloth is closely woven, good weight, guaranteed strictly all-wool and unexcelled for wearing qualities. Very latest in style for this season, guaranteed fine tailor made, made only by our best tailors and cut by expert cutters to fit perfectly. Coats are lined throughout with fine Italian cloth in shades to match the cloth, satin piped as shown in cut. Fancy velvet arm shields under sleeves. Sewed throughout with silk and linen, nicely padded, trimmed and finished. Sizes run from 34 to 42. Extra sizes, $2.00 extra. They come in Styles 1, 2 or 3, round cut sack, square cut sack or double breasted square cut sack, as desired. Style 3 is always 50 cents extra. Samples of cloth free on application.

No. 4360. This beautiful $6.00 all-wool Cassimere Suit is made in a medium gray with very neat hair line stripe and invisible cross weave. It is very stylish and will make up very dressy.
Our price, Style 1 or 2..................$6.00 Style 3................$6.50

No. 4361. This $6.00 tailor made suit comes in a very neat brown and gray check with invisible plaid, the very latest thing for this season and a goods that will make up very stylish.
Our price, Style 1 or 2..................$6.00 Style 3................$6.50

No. 4362. This $6.00 tailor made suit comes in a gray and white check invisible whip cord stripe, one of the latest patterns for this season.
Our price, Style 1 or 2..................$6.00 Style 3................$6.50

No. 4363. This $6.00 tailor made suit comes in a very neat medium brown with very small check and large modest invisible plaid effect.
Our price, Style 1 or 2..................$6.00 Style 3................$6.50

No. 4364. This $6.00 tailor made suit comes in a brown with small white check and large modest invisible plaid, a very stylish pattern.
Our price, Style 1 or 2..................$6.00 Style 3................$6.50

# MENS $6.95 CASSIMERE SUITS.

### Our Guarantee.

On receipt of $1.00 we will ship one of these suits to any address anywhere in the United States by express C. O. D. subject to examination, balance, $5.95, and express charges payable at express office, guaranteeing it lower in price than is sold by any Other House on Earth, agreeing if you will prove to disinterested parties that such a suit is sold by any other firm at anything like our price, that we will make you a present of as nice a pair of pants as our tailoring department can produce.

Our $6.95 price can not be met by any one. There is no such thing. We control this bargain. We have the entire output of cloth of the mill. At $6.95 such an offer was never known before.

All the latest things of the season, a great line of all wool fancy cassimeres, such goods as tailors will use in their $15.00 to $25.00 suits this season, the same class of goods as you will find in $12.00 to $18.00 ready made suits.

Quality all alike and all at $6.95 per suit, the only difference in the suits listed is the color and pattern. Quality and make are all the same.

These beautiful wool cassimeres are good weight, closely woven all wool goods, make up very dressy and stylish, goods that will give excellent wear, and the price will astonish you when you see the suit. They come in Style 1, round cut sack, Style 2, square cut sack. Style 3, double breasted square cut sack, or Style 4, 3 button cutaway frock as desired. They are all cut on the latest style patterns for this season by expert cutters to fit perfectly, and made by our best tailors. Coats are lined throughout with fine imported Italian cloth in colors to match the cloth, satin piped throughout, fancy velvet arm shields under sleeves, well padded, every pocket stayed, sewed throughout with silk and linen. Regular sizes run from 34 to 42.

Extra sizes are $2.00 extra.
☞ Samples of cloth will be furnished free on application. You will find them in our regular sample card.

No. 4365. THIS MEN'S $6.95 TAILOR MADE SUIT comes in a neat gray check, one of the latest weaves, makes a very modest dressy suit.
Our Price, Style 1 or 2..................$6.95 Style 3 or 4.........$7.45

No. 4366. THIS MEN'S $6.95 TAILOR MADE SUIT comes in a beautiful brown and white mixture with modest invisible stripe effect. Nothing more dressy or more stylish.
Price, Style 1 or 2..................$6.95 Style 3 or 4.........$7.45

No. 4367. THIS MEN'S $6.95 TAILOR MADE SUIT comes in a beautiful medium dark brown with small check and invisible large plaid effect, a very stylish fabric.
Price, Style 1 or 2..................$6.95 Style 3 or 4.........$7.45

No. 4368. THIS MEN'S $6.95 TAILOR MADE SUIT comes in a very small dark gray and white check with large invisible plaid effect. Nothing

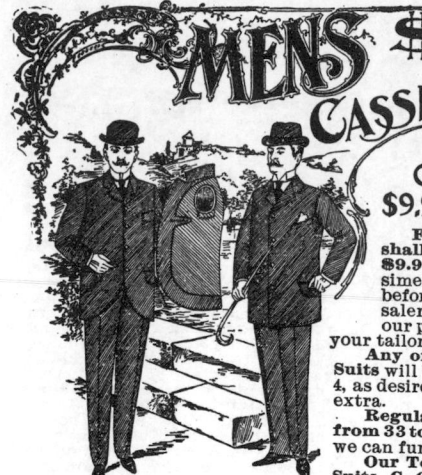

# MEN'S $7·95 CASSIMERE SUITS.

## Our $7.95, $8.95 and $9.95 Cassimere Suits.

For the coming season we shall offer at $7.95, $8.95 and $9.95 men's very fine all wool cassimere suits such as were never before offered by any dealer, wholesaler or retailer, at within 50% of our price, and equal to anything your tailor will make at $20.00 to $30.00.

Any of our $7.95, $8.95 or $9.95 Suits will be furnished in styles 1, 2, 3 or 4, as desired. Styles 3 and 4 are 50 cts. extra.

Regular Sizes in these suits run from 33 to 42 inches chest measure. but we can furnish extra sizes at $2.00 extra.

Our Terms are the same as on all Suits, C. O. D. subject to examination on receipt of $1.00, balance and express charges payable at express office. 3% discount will be allowed if cash in full accompanies your order.

☞ Samples of cloth will be sent free on application. If you will send for our Special Card of Cloth Samples it will include some desirable numbers in this line.

**No. 4375. MEN'S $7.95 ALL WOOL CASSIMERE SUITS.** These suits are made from a good quality domestic all wool cassimere, good medium weight, the product of one of the best western woolen mills. They come in light, medium and dark shades, gray check or brown check, neat stripes and plaids. If you will give us an idea of the pattern wanted we will guarantee to please you. They are fine tailor made, coats are lined throughout with good Italian cloth in colors to match the goods. satin piped throughout, with fancy velvet arm shields under sleeves as shown in illustration above, sewed throughout with silk and linen and guaranteed in every respect.

Our Special Price, Style 1 or 2 ......................$7.95
Our Special Price, Style 3 or 4 ......................8.45

**No. 4376 MEN'S $8.95 ALL WOOL CASSIMERE SUITS.**
This line includes a great variety of the choicest and latest style fabrics, goods that have been made expressly for this season's wear by the best mills in the country; closely woven, smooth surface, wear-resisting materials.

We have them in all shades and patterns, light, medium and dark, small checks, narrow and wide stripes and fancy plaids. Give us an idea of the color wanted and we will guarantee to please you.

Our Special Price, Style 1 or 2 ......................$8.95
Our Special Price, Style 3 or 4 ......................9.45

**No. 4377 MEN'S ALL WOOL $9.95 CASSIMERE SUITS.** These suits will compare favorably with anything your tailor would make at two to three times our price. They are made from the very finest all wool domestic cassimeres, and include all the very latest and most stylish patterns on the market.

There is not a pattern in this $9.95 line that is not exceedingly desirable. They come in light, medium and dark shades, very neat small checks, small and wide stripes, small, medium and large plaids. Give us an idea of color and pattern wanted and we will guarantee to please you.

Our Special Price, Style 1 or 2 ......................$9.95
Our Special Price, Style 3, 4 or 5 ......................10.45

## Our Very Finest Men's Suits. Fancy Cassimeres, Worsteds, Black and Blue Vicunas, Thibets, Tricot Longs, etc., etc.

**Our Line of Men's High Grade Tailor Made Suitings** is so very large and extensive that want of space in this catalogue prevents our listing it complete. It covers almost everything on the market that is desirable in foreign and domestic fabrics, including the best of everything.

**As to the Make of the Goods Listed Below,** they are their finest goods, made by our very best tailors, in fact nothing but the very best trimmings are used.

**We Guarantee Every Garment** to be sewed with silk and linen; coat linings are all genuine Italian cloth; coats are satin piped throughout, are well padded, all pockets stayed, in fact, every garment is guaranteed.

**Sizes run regularly from 34 to 42 inches** chest measure, but extra sizes will be furnished at 20% extra. We furnish these different suits in all styles, viz: 1, 2, 3, 4 and 5. Samples of cloth will be sent free on application.

The choicest selection will be found on our regular sample card, which we would recommend you to send for in preference to selecting any certain number or numbers.

**Our Terms are the Same on all Clothing.** Any suit will be sent to any address by express, C. O. D., subject to examination on receipt of $1.00, balance and express charges payable at express office. 3% discount allowed if cash in full accompanies your order.

---

**No. 4378. MEN'S $9.80 TRICOT LONG SUITS.** This is a plain, medium dark gray cassimere, nothing more suitable on the market. It is woven by the Springfield, Ill., mill. There is practically no wear out to the goods. It is especially desirable as an old man's suit in Style 5. They are well lined and tailored, and guaranteed in every respect.
Our Special Price for Style 1 or 2..................$9.80
Other styles, 50c extra.

**No. 4379. OUR SPECIAL $10.55 CASSIMERE LINE.** This line cludes a large variety of the very finest fabrics offered this inseason, beautiful invisible small plaids in brown, light gray, dark gray and brown and gray mixed. No finer made garments on the market.
Our Special Price in Style 1 or 2..................$10.55
Extra for Styles 3, 4 or 5, 50c.

**No. 4380. OUR $12.50 CASSIMERE LINE.** These goods are all fine all wool imported French cassimeres, medium weight, suitable for year around wear, very soft, closely woven, wear resisting material. They come in a variety of shades and patterns, all the very latest effects, light, medium and dark, in checks, invisible stripes, large and small plaids. There is nothing finer on the market this season, and for make they cannot be excelled.
Price in Styles 1 or 2..................$12.50
Other Styles 50c extra.

**No. 4381. OUR FINEST CASSIMERE LINE FOR $14.00.** We offer a line of men's suits made from the finest all wool cassimeres that are brought to this country at the exceptionally low price of $14.00. These goods are all of French and German make, all fine wool, good weight, and the latest and most stylish effects, including a beautiful steel gray, very rich brown boucle cloth, some very beautiful modest plaids in brown and gray, gray and white, brown and black, neat checks, invisible plaids, light medium and dark shades. They are fine tailor made; no tailor can make better.
Our Special Price in Style 1 or 2.................. $14.00
Other Styles 50c extra.

## CHALLENGE PRICES IN MEN'S FANCY WORSTED SUITS

### Our Fancy Worsted Line.

**No. 4382. OUR $10.00 LINE OF MEN'S FANCY WORSTED SUITS.** We have these suits in black, navy blue, or brown; Wide Wale Worsted in black or navy blue; French back Worsted in gray pincheck hair line; Barrington Worsted in black or navy blue; imported French Worsted, also in a great variety of fancy English Worsteds, including a beautiful dark gray hair line, a beautiful silk mixed Worsted, black background and blue and red silk mixed thread, in a genuine mumie cloth Worsted black or navy blue, a goods with a raised surface effect, a black or navy blue Worsted with invisible raised pinhead stripe, also a line of dark gray and dark brown invisible small plaid Worsted, and in very popular steel gray, Oxford gray and brown plain Washington clay Worsted.

**We have everything made in Worsted** in our $10.00 line. Simply give us an idea of the color wanted, whether plain or a pattern, and if so what pattern, and we will guarantee to please you.

**These suits come in any style** 1, 2, 3, 4 or 5. All styles other than 1 and 2 are 50c extra, or $10.50 per suit. Regular sizes run from 34 to 42 inches chest measure. Extra sizes will be $2.00 extra.

**These suits are cut by expert cutters** on the very latest patent perfect fitting process, and made by the best tailors we can employ. Coats are lined throughout with fine imported Italian cloth, satin piped throughout, fancy velvet arm shields under sleeves, every garment well padded, pockets stayed, each garment sewed throughout with silk and linen. We honestly believe we offer the finest line of worsteds that was ever shown at the price, viz: $10.00.

Sample of cloth will be sent on application. The more desirable patterns will be found on our regular sample card. Simply send us a postal saying: "Please send your card of cloth samples of men's clothing," and you will see the most desirable fabrics.

**No. 4383. MEN'S $12.50 FANCY WORSTED LINE.** We offer at $12.50 the same line of goods as quoted in our $10.00 line excepting they are slightly heavier in weight and have a finer finish. The same patterns, same shades, same makes. The patterns are of a better quality, in fact, this $12.50 line is offered in competition with anything your local dealer can make for you at any price. If you will send us your order for one of our $12.50 Worsted Suits, telling us the color, pattern and style wanted, we will send it to you by express, and if you do not find it equal to anything your tailor can make to your measure and order at from two to three times our price we will not ask you to accept it; you can return it at our expense and we will cheerfully refund your money. Samples of cloth will be furnished free on application.

---

**EXTRA SIZE SUITS** include all suits over 42 in. chest measure or for men over 5 feet 11 inches tall.

**DON'T OVERLOOK THE EXTRA CHARGE** for all extra size suits.

**YOUR CORRECT WEIGHT and HEIGHT** are absolutely necessary for a correct fit. **DON'T FAIL IN THIS.**

**SEND FOR OUR REGULAR SAMPLE CARD OF CLOTH SAMPLES. IT INCLUDES ALL THE BIG BARGAINS.**

# BLUE FLANNEL
# GRAND ARMY OF THE REPUBLIC

## SUITS
### HEADQUARTERS FOR G.A.R. SUITS

Nº 1       Nº 2

**Our trade on Grand Army Suits** the past two seasons has been so large and increased so rapidly that we have decided to make much more extensive preparations this year than ever before, and at $6.50 to $8.00 we will furnish Grand Army suits in sizes from 34 to 42, or at $2.00 extra in larger sizes wanted, that can not be produced by a tailor at 50% advance.

**Don't compare our G. A. R. Suits** with those offered by the average clothing merchant. There is absolutely no comparison.

**Our G. A. R. Suits** are made up in a thoroughly first-class manner, cut by expert cutters and made by first-class tailors. The linings, trimmings and general finish are far superior to those used in ready-made stock.

**The old soldiers** all over the United States are patronizing us by the thousands, and in honor to them and the G. A. R. we have cut our per centage of profit on G. A. R. suits lower than on anything else we handle.

**Almost cost, is the way we sell G. A. R. Suits.** Yet we are anxious for your trade, we appreciate it just the same, builds up our business and makes many new customers for us.

**Many G. A. R. Posts** join in a body and give us their orders for 20 to 100 suits for the entire post, but the price is the same whether you buy one suit or 100 suits. You will find our prices on G. A. R. Suits far below the price charged by retail dealers. As before explained, you will find there is no comparison in the goods or make.

**We furnish these Suits** in either style 1, 2 or 3, round cut sack or square cut sack, as illustrated above, or double breasted square cut sack style 3 at 50 cents extra. We also furnish an extra set of G, A. R. brass buttons with each suit. The buttons are detachable and can be easily removed.

☞ Samples of cloth sent free on application.

**No. 4386. Our $6.50 Blue Flannel G. A. R. Suit.** We guarantee this suit to be equal to anything your local tailor can offer at $12.00, and is better value than those carried by the average clothing store. It is made from a Fine Indigo Blue Flannel, fast color, warranted not to fade. If one fades we will send you a new suit. Nearly all wool, a very small cotton chain one way of the weave to make it firm and wear resisting, in fact, goods that will wear like iron. It is a suit that is generally sold for all wool.
Our Special Price..................................$6.50

**No. 4387. Our $7.50 Blue Flannel G. A. R. Suit.** This suit is made from a finer and closer woven material than our $6.50 suit, the trimmings are somewhat better and it is well worth the difference in price.
Our Special Price..................................$7.50

**No. 4388. Our $8.90 Blue Flannel G. A. R. Suit,** made from an extra fine all wool pure indigo blue flannel, warranted not to fade.
The finest all wool fast color G. A. R. goods made. These goods are made by one of the largest and most reliable mills in America, a concern whose reputation for the manufacture of high grade G. A. R. flannel is second to none.
Our Special Price..................................$8.90

**No. 4389. Our $9.00 All Wool Blue Flannel G.A.R. Suit.** This suit is made from a finer and closer woven blue flannel than the $8.90 suit, the trimmings are somewhat better, in all it is worth the difference in price.
Our Special Price..................................$9.90

## BARGAINS IN MENS COATS & VESTS

### With Odd Pants to Match.
### Wonderful Values in Men's Coats and Vests and Mixed Suits,
coat and vest of one pattern and pants of another pattern. **Handling, as we do, over a thousand suits a day** in the season, we get an accumulation of broken suits. Among a lot of a thousand suits of one pattern which are made up, after 900 or 950 are sold from the lot, we find we have left a broken lot of goods. **The pants are not the size to fit the coats and vests.** We then throw them into what we call our "Odd Lots," or mixed suits, offering the coats and vests alone or as mixed suits, coat and vest of one pattern and pants of another, always, however, as a very desirable pants pattern.

As mixed suits are now very stylish and are worn everywhere, and especially in large cities, the coat and vest of one pattern and pants of a special pants pattern, there is nothing in which you can get such value and general satisfaction as from this lot. We do not expect any profit on our coats and vests, single coats, single vests or mixed suits.

We are willing to sustain a loss, and for that reason we feel that this offering will interest you.

As described under the different numbers, we have these goods in all shades, in all the most desirable patterns, in all weaves and all styles, but we can not furnish cloth samples as we close the lots as fast as possible, and if we furnished you a sample, by the time you were ready to order the exact

pattern might be sold. **Sizes run from 34 to 42 inches** chest measure. **Extra-sizes $1.00 extra.** We can furnish these coats and vests in styles 1, 2, 3 or 4. Styles 3 and 4 will be 50c extra.

**No. 4399. GOOD QUALITY WOOL AND COTTON MIXED CASSIMERE** in light, medium or dark shade, in checks, stripes, plaids, good weight goods, suitable for year around wear.
Price for Coat and Vest.............................$2.00

**No. 4400. Price for Complete Suits,** including a pair of neat striped cassimere pants.............................$2.75

**No. 4401. EXTRA QUALITY CASSIMERE, WOOL AND COTTON MIXED,** cannot be told in appearance from all-wool. Good wearing goods, good weight for year around wear, light, medium or dark shade, in stripes, checks or plaids.
Price for Coat and Vest.............................$3.00

**No. 4402. Price for Complete Suit,** including pair of neat striped cassimere pants.............................$4.25

**No. 4403. BLACK OR NAVY BLUE WOOL CHEVIOT CLOTH,** very good weave, closely woven, nicely made and finished.
Price for Coat and Vest.............................$2.50

**No. 4404. Price for Suit,** including neat striped cassimere pants.$3.50

**No. 4405. ALL WOOL MEDIUM WEIGHT WISCONSIN CASSIMERE** in light, medium or dark shades, neat checks, stripes and plaids.
Price for Coat and Vest.............................$4.00

**No. 4406. Price for Complete Suit,** including pair neat narrow stripe, all wool cassimere pants.............................$5.65

**No. 4407. GENUINE OGDEN ALL WOOL CASSIMERE,** medium weight, suitable for year around wear, one of the best American weaves, light, medium or dark shades, neat checks, stripes and plaids.
Price for Coat and Vest.............................$5.00

**No. 4408. Price for Complete Suit,** including pants of good weight, all wool cassimere, any shade.............................$6.75

**No. 4409. VERY FINE ALL WOOL ENGLISH CASSIMERE,** good weight, suitable for year around wear, light, medium or dark, in checks, stripes or plaids.
Price for Coat and Vest.............................$6.00

**No. 4410. Price for Complete Suit,** including pair of English cassimere pants in any shade.............................$7.90

**No. 4411. VERY FINE IMPORTED ALL WOOL ENGLISH WORSTED CLOTH** in black or navy blue. This includes the very finest worsted fabrics we use. The garments are elegantly made up.
Our Price for Coat and Vest.............................$7.00

**No. 4412. PRICE FOR COMPLETE SUIT** including a pair of fine English Worsted or Cassimere Pants in any shade..............$9.90

☞ The prices quoted above are about one-half our regular prices for complete suits out of regular stock. We make these prices so very low only with a view to interesting you to place your order for these goods to assist us in keeping our broken stock cleaned up.

**Special offer of only $1.00 additional for extra sizes on mixed suits.**

## BARGAINS IN MENS COATS

### In our made up stock of Clothing
there are constantly accumulating odd pieces where a big lot of a thousand or more suits will not run out even. We find we are left with Coats and Vests with no pants to match in size, or with vests where the coats do not match, and coats where neither the vests nor pants will match; and where we have used all the piece goods we are unable to cut any garments to match the suits and are therefore compelled to sell the odd garments at any prices they will bring.

**Having arrived at a price** that we know they will bring, and will advertise our house and give our customers such value as was never seen or heard of before, we fix the price regardless of value, profit or cost.

**We do not expect to make any profit** on these broken lots, we are willing to sacrifice a big percentage of loss. We have these coats in all styles and in all regular sizes, in all shades, all patterns, in all qualities of material and all qualities of make.

**If you will give us an idea** of what you want in the way of material, shade, weight, pattern and style, we will guarantee to please you in every respect, and as for price we will furnish you a thorough surprise.

No cloth samples can be furnished of these garments. The piece goods have all been consumed.

The lots, while very large in the aggregate, are very small to each pattern. You will have to leave it to our judgment to give you the most desirable goods we can.

**No. 4423. WOOL AND COTTON MIXED CASSIMERE,** good weight for year around wear, light, medium or dark shade, neat check.
Price of Coat in any style.............................$1.50

**No. 4424. EXTRA QUALITY WOOL AND COTTON MIXED CASSIMERE,** light, medium or dark brown shade, neat check, stripe or plaid.
Our price for Coat.............................$2.00

**No. 4425. GOOD QUALITY BLACK WOOL CHEVIOT,** well lined and trimmed, very good coat.
Our Special price.............................$2.25

**No. 4426. VERY FINE ALL-WOOL BLACK CHEVIOT,** Italian lined, nicely trimmed and finished, an extra fine garment.
Our Special price for Coat.............................$3.50

**No. 4427. GOOD QUALITY ALL-WOOL WISCONSIN CASSIMERE,** good weight for year around wear, light, medium or dark shade, in check, stripe or plaid.
Our Special price.............................$3.25

**No. 4428. EXTRA QUALITY IMPORTED ALL-WOOL ENGLISH CASSIMERE CLOTH,** in good weight for year around wear, light, medium or dark pattern, neat check, stripe or plaid.
Special price for Coat only.............................$4.00

**No. 4429. VERY FINE ALL-WOOL IMPORTED ENGLISH CLAY WORSTEDS,** in black or navy blue, also fancy patterns; fine all-wool English Cassimeres in light, medium and dark shades, very good patterns.
Our Special price for Coat only.............................$4.50

---

**EXTRA SIZES** in Suits on all sizes over 42 inches chest measure, or for men over 5 ft. 11 in. high.

**DON'T FAIL** to allow for extra charge if you use an extra size suit.

**REMEMBER** if over 42 in. chest or over 5 ft. 11 in. tall, you require an extra size.

**LOOK AT OUR MIXED SUIT BARGAINS. WE CAN FURNISH LIGHT COLORED PANTS WITH DARK OR BLACK COAT AND VEST WANTED**

# BARGAINS IN MEN'S CORDUROY SUITS

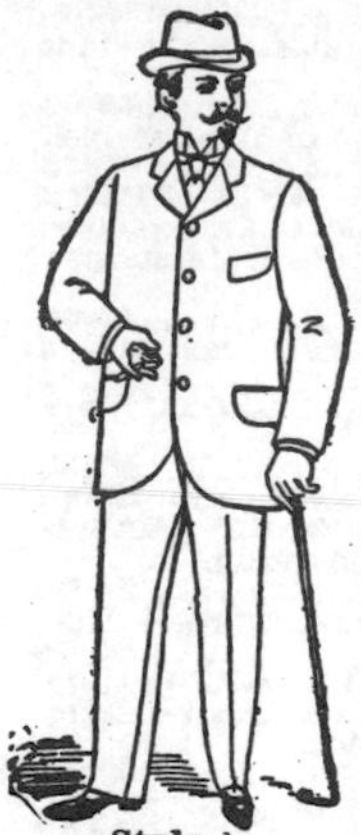

Style 1. Round Cut Sack Suit.

**The great demand for Corduroy Suits** has induced us to arrange with one of the largest mills for a line of Corduroys, which for quality is second to none, and we have secured the piece goods at a price which will enable us to make prices against which none can compete. **Such Corduroys as we sell** made up in the ordinary way retail at from $10.00 to $18.00.

**We offer you a line of Corduroy Suits,** which for quality of material, style and workmanship can not be excelled by your local tailor if made to your measure and to your order. **We offer these suits** at prices against which we have no possible competition, and our terms are very liberal.

**Any suit will be sent to any address C. O. D.** subject to examination on receipt of $1.00. You can examine it at the express office, and if found perfectly satisfactory and exactly as represented, pay the agent the balance and express charges and the suit is yours. **Sizes run from 34 to 43 inches chest measure.** Larger sizes are $2.00 extra. We can furnish these suits in style 1 or 2, round cut sack or square cut sack. ☞ Samples of cloth will be sent free on application.

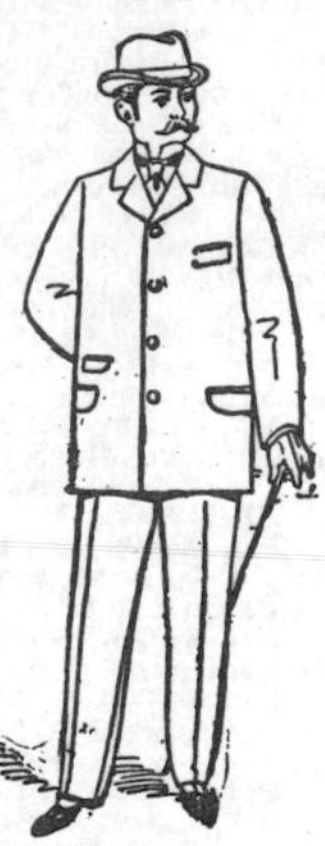

Style 2. Square Cut Sack Suit.

**No. 4440. SPECIAL BARGAIN AT $7.95.** We offer a Corduroy Suit at $7.95 which cannot be duplicated within 50% more than our price. It is a genuine imported French Corduroy in gray only, goods that are simply wear resisting, is nicely lined, trimmed and finished, and at $7.95 must surely prove a good seller. **Our Special Price**..........**$7.95**

**No. 4441. OUR $9.95 CORDUROY.** This is one of the best imported English pure dye gray corduroys, made by one of the largest and most reliable mills in England. It is elegantly lined, trimmed and finished, and every suit is fully warranted. If you are in need of a Corduroy Suit we know that this one will not only please you but will lead to more sales in your neighborhood. **Our Special Price**..........**$9.95**

**No. 4442. OUR $10.50 CORDUROY.** This is one of the very finest pure dye imported brown English Corduroys on the market. It is a corduroy any first class tailor would make up into a suit at not less than $25.00. We are able to make a special price on this suit which surely will interest any intending buyer. The suit is made in the highest style of the art, elegantly lined, trimmed and finished. **Our Special Price**..........**$10.50**

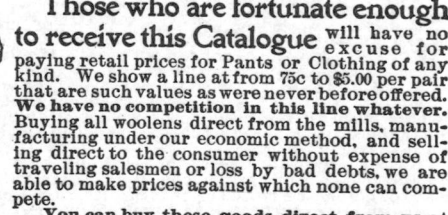

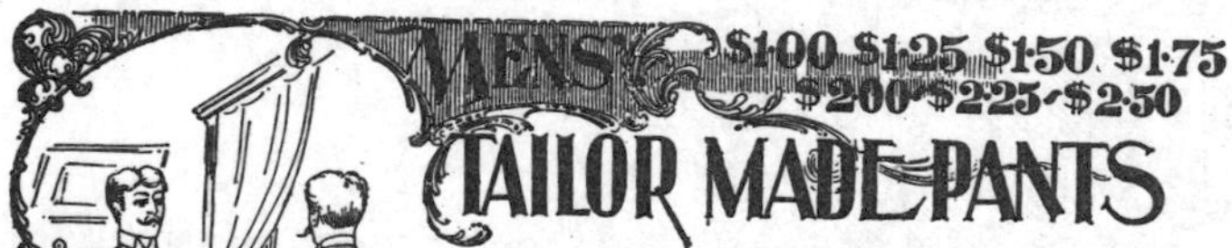
MENS' $1.00 $1.25 $1.50 $1.75 $2.00 $2.25 $2.50
TAILOR MADE PANTS

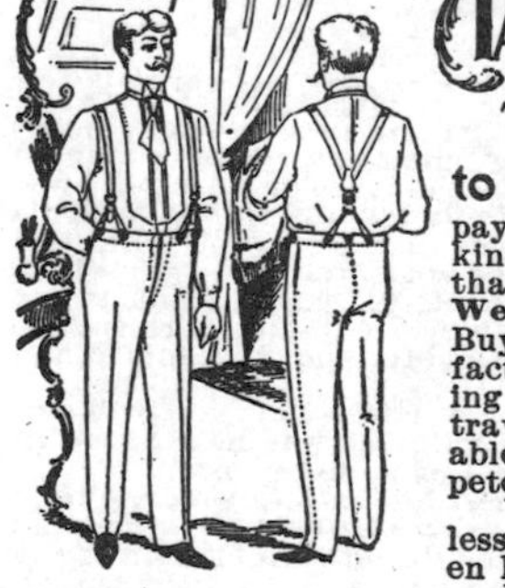

**Those who are fortunate enough to receive this Catalogue** will have no excuse for paying retail prices for Pants or Clothing of any kind. We show a line at from 75c to $5.00 per pair that are such values as were never before offered. **We have no competition in this line whatever.** Buying all woolens direct from the mills, manufacturing under our economic method, and selling direct to the consumer without expense of traveling salesmen or loss by bad debts, we are able to make prices against which none can compete.

**You can buy these goods direct from us** at less money than your local dealer can buy in dozen lots.

**Every pair from the cheapest to the best guaranteed** fine tailor made. Made on the very latest style patterns, cut by expert cutters, made by first-class tailors, and superior to the goods commonly carried by retail clothiers.

**Our terms are very liberal.** Any of these goods will be sent to any address by express C. O. D. subject to examination, on receipt of $1.00, balance and express charges payable at express office. 3% discount allowed if cash in full accompanies your order.

**ABOUT MEASUREMENTS.** Give your height, weight and age, state number of inches around body at waist, number of inches around body at hips, length of inside seam from tight in crotch to heel, and we will guarantee a perfect fit.

**No. 4461. MEN'S 75c PANTS.** Our 75c line is made from good, strong, closely woven wool and cotton mixed cassimere in plain dark gray. The goods have all the appearance of wool and can not be told from all wool except by a very close inspection. **Our Special price**..........**75c**

**No. 4462. MEN'S $1.00 PANTS.** Our $1.00 line is made from a good weight black wool cheviot, also a good weight dark gray wool cheviot. There is a small thread of cotton running one way in these goods but they are guaranteed to wear. **Our Special price**..........**$1.00**

**No. 4463. MEN'S $1.25 PANTS.** Our $1.25 line is made of good strong wool cassimeres, good weight, in very neat dark gray and brown hair line stripes, the most desirable patterns for this season's wear. We also have them in heavy strong black wool cheviot. **Our Special Price**..........**$1.25**

**No. 4464. MEN'S $1.50 PANTS.** Our $1.50 line is made from a good weight wool cassimere, in light gray and brown hair line stripes, also an extra quality black wool cheviot. Very good wearing goods and wonderful values. **Our Special Price**..........**$1.50**

**No. 4465. MEN'S $1.75 PANTS.** We have a very large variety in the $1.75 line. Extra strong, good weight, special wool cassimere pants goods in dark patterns with invisible stripe and red and blue silk thread, also dark gray hair lines, and in light, medium and dark plaids and invisible stripes. We have over 50 patterns in our $1.75 line, and if you will give us an idea of what is wanted we will guarantee to please you. **Our Special Price**..........**$1.75**

**No. 4466. MEN'S $2.00 PANTS.** Our $2.00 pants consist of a variety of the most desirable all wool cassimere pants fabrics in small hair lines, dark gray and dark brown; also some very fine all wool cheviots in black and dark gray. Give us an idea of the pattern wanted and we will send you a pair of pants for $2.00 which cannot be duplicated in your local store for less than double the money. **Our Special Price**..........**$2.00**

worsted goods, a very fine imported all wool closely woven black Thibet cheviot, a very fine black worsted pants with invisible hair line. Retailers' regular $4.00 pants. Also a very fine line of closely woven wear resisting dark gray, light gray and brown tricot long pants. Give us an idea of the pattern wanted and we will guarantee to please you. **Our Special Price. $2.25**

**No. 4468. MEN'S $2.50 PANTS.** We offer a line of pants at $2.50 which are equal to those that retail at $5.00. They include a very fine imported all wool black English clay worsted, a very fine all wool imported closely woven genuine Vicuna black cheviot goods, a very fine neat dark gray and bluish striped worsted, small striped dark gray worsted, wide striped black worsted with invisible blue stripe effect. This $2.50 line is such value as has never been offered at anything like the price. **Our Special Price. $2.50**

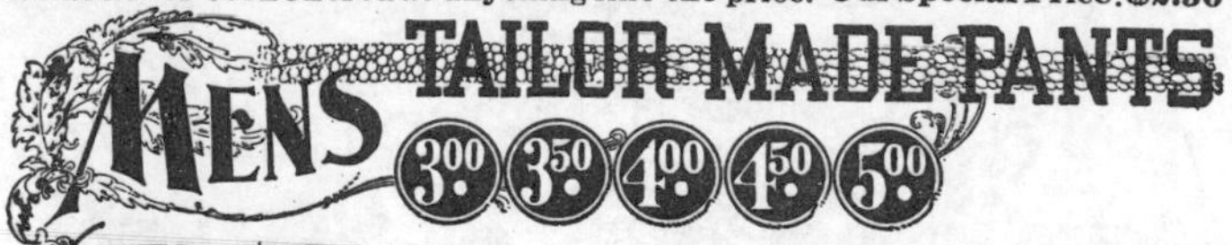
MENS TAILOR MADE PANTS
3.00 3.50 4.00 4.50 5.00

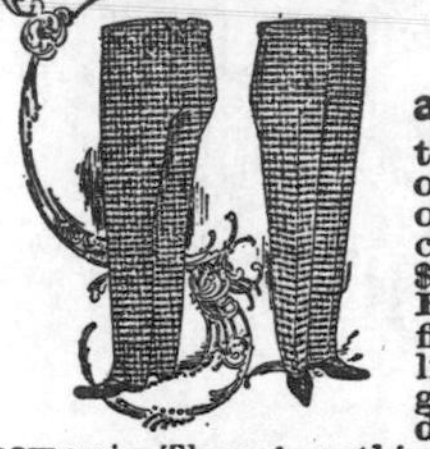

**Our very finest Tailor made Trousers are offered at from $3.00 to $5.00,** and we invite the closest comparison of these goods with those offered by retail dealers at double the price. We offer at $3.00 a pair of pants which cannot be duplicated by your local tailor at less than $6.00, and our $5.00 pants cannot be duplicated for less than $10.00. **Every pair is cut by an expert** cutter, made by a first-class tailor, sewed throughout with silk and linen, gotten up in the very latest style, and we guarantee if a pair rips or a button comes off through defective material or to replace the pants with a new pair. There is nothing on the market that will compare with this line within 50% more than our price.

**No. 4479. MENS' $3.00 PANTS.** This lot consists of about 25 different patterns, including a very fine heavy all wool imported English clay worsted, a very fine imported all wool genuine Vicuna black cheviot, a very fine imported French cassimere in neat narrow black stripe with raised effect—a very stylish fabric—a very fine imported English cassimere with narrow gray and black hairline stripe, very stylish goods, a very fine all wool English cassimere, dark color, almost black, with invisible mixed silk effect in dark stripe, a very fine black English worsted goods with fancy black satin stripe. **Our special price for this line**..........**$3.00**

**No. 4480. MEN'S $3.50 PANTS.** This line comprises about 25 patterns, including a very fine imported all-wool black English clay worsted, a very fine imported all-wool genuine Vicuna black cheviot; a very fine imported all-wool cassimere in dark brown and gray effect with very fine invisible black stripe, a very fine imported all-wool black silk raised stripe. **Our Special price**..........**$3.50**

**No. 4481. MEN'S $4.00 PANTS.** This line comprises about 25 patterns, including a very fine imported all-wool black English clay worsted; a very fine imported all-wool black Vicuna cheviot; our very finest all-wool English hairline with black background and neat narrow gray stripe, a very stylish pants pattern; a fine gray and black invisible narrow stripe French worsted; a very fine black French worsted with narrow neat raised stripe effect; a fine all wool black French worsted with raised black silk effect stripe. **Our price**..........**$4.00**

**No. 4482. MEN'S $4.50 PANTS.** This line comprises about 20 patterns, including a very fine imported French black worsted with raised black silk stripe effect; fine French worsted with bluish cast and brown and gray invisible stripe, a very stylish goods; a dark French worsted with invisible blue and gray stripe on black background, a very stylish medium or light pattern with light gray and brown mixed, wide invisible stripe effect, one of the most stylish pants patterns for this season. **Our Special price**..........**$4.50**

**No. 4483. OUR VERY FINEST LINE AT $5.00.** At $5.00 we offer the finest line of trouserings we make, and this line includes the finest imported fabrics that we can buy. Every pair is made as well as it is possible to manufacture, employing only the best tailors and using the best material that we can buy. Our $5.00 line is made only from imported French and German worsteds. We have a black or dark navy blue French worsted with very fine raised black or blue silk stripe effect; dark gray narrow striped French worsted; a brown and white mixed stripe German worsted; a bluish gray and black striped German worsted. We have the fancy patterns in light, medium and dark shades. Give us an idea of the pattern and shade wanted and we will guarantee to please you. **Our Special price**..........**$5.00**

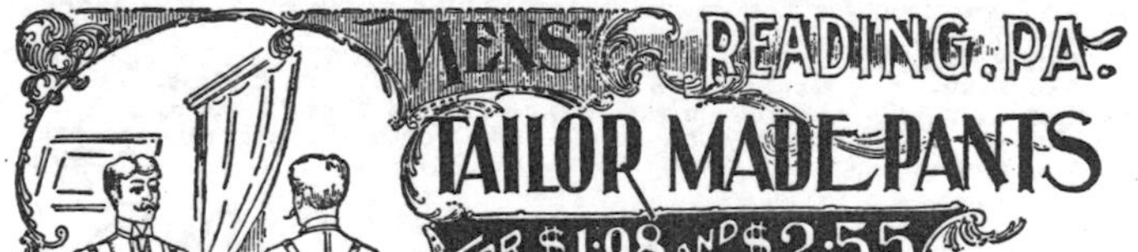
MENS' READING, PA.
TAILOR MADE PANTS
FOR $1.98 AND $2.55

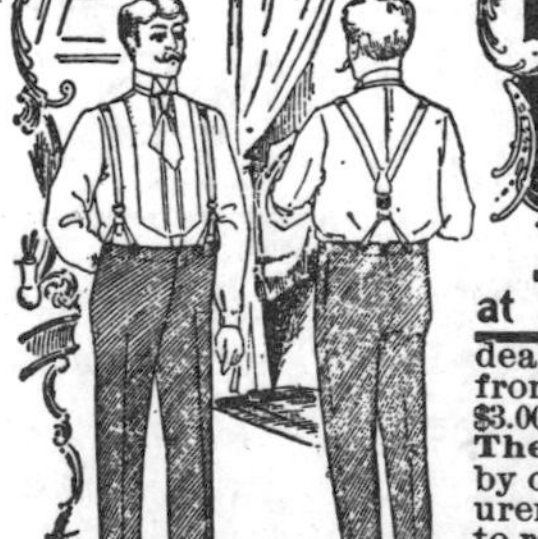

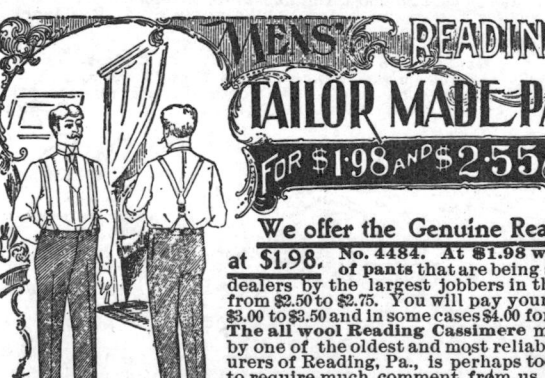

**We offer the Genuine Reading Pants at $1.98.**

**No. 4484. At $1.98 we offer a line of pants** that are being sold direct to dealers by the largest jobbers in the country at from $2.50 to $2.75. You will pay your retail dealer $3.00 to $3.50 and in some cases $4.00 for these pants. **The all wool Reading Cassimere** manufactured by one of the oldest and most reliable manufacturers of Reading, Pa., is perhaps too well known to require much comment from us. There is no better wearing material made. It will wear until you are tired of it. These pants are ready made. They are made by the mill. The manufacturer of the cloth does not figure one penny profit on the manufacturing. **We buy the pants from him in thousand lots** at the lowest manufacturer's price for the cloth, with the actual cost of manufacturing added, and they guarantee that if a pair rips or a button comes off, or when the garment is found defective, they will replace it free of charge, and we extend the same guarantee with any pair you may buy. They are all wool and extra good weight. They are closely woven and there is practically no wear out to the goods. They come in a medium dark gray with a fine hairline stripe effect and there is nothing more desirable nor more stylish for pants material.

**When we offer them to you at $1.98,** we feel that we have done our part towards encouraging your orders, for our price is based on the smallest percentage of profit possible, and the price is about one-half the price you have been in the habit of paying for similar goods.

**No. 4485. GENUINE READING PANTS FOR $2.55.** This mill makes only two grades of cassimere, and we offer you this, the very best grade they make, which is somewhat heavier, finer and closer woven than our $1.98 pants. Like the $1.98 they are guaranteed in every respect. If a pair rips or a button comes off, return them to us and we will replace them with a new pair. They come in the same pattern, a dark gray narrow stripe. **$2.55**

## MEN'S OVERCOATS FOR SPRING, SUMMER AND FALL.

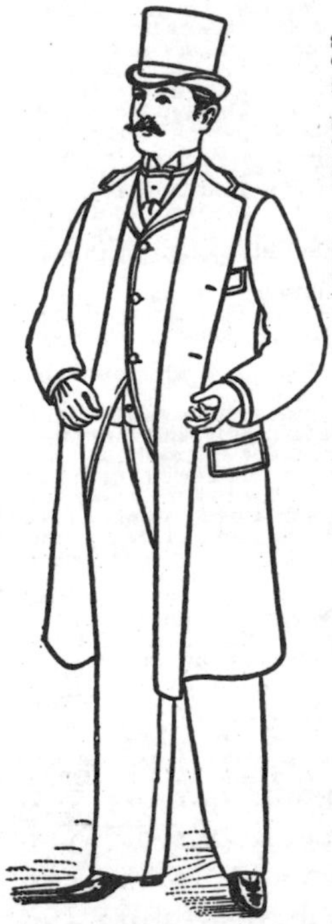

**This Line of Overcoats** is intended for spring, summer and fall wear, yet all our coats are made of a good medium weight material and are suitable in southern climates for year around wear. We offer you a line of spring overcoats which for style, general appearance and price can not be equaled, a line of fine tailor made garments at from $6.95 to $12.75 that retail in first-class establishments at from $10.00 to $25.00.

**We make our terms very liberal.** Any coat will be sent to any address by express C. O. D. subject to examination on receipt of $1.00. You can examine it at the express office and if found perfectly satisfactory and exactly as represented pay the express agent the balance and express charges.

**A discount of 3 per cent will be allowed if cash in full accompanies your order.**

**Samples of cloth free on application.**

**Give your size as follows:** Chest measure only is necessary, state number of inches around body at chest taken over vest under inside coat, and in making we will allow for the outside coat.

**No. 4486. OUR $6.95 SPRING OVERCOAT.** Made of a very fine quality all wool gray cheviot, a weave from one of the best American mills, made expressly for overcoating, and such material as will be found in first-class tailoring establishments for spring overcoats. These goods are made in the very latest styles as illustrated, elegantly lined, trimmed and finished and every garment is fully warranted.
**Our price**........$6.95

**No. 4487. OUR $7.10 SPRING OVERCOAT.** Made from a dark gray all wool cheviot overcoating cloth, very fine, overcoat of the latest shade for spring and summer, elegantly lined, trimmed and finished.
**Our Special Price**........$7.10

**No. 4488. OUR $8.95 SPRING OVERCOAT.** Made from a very fine imported all wool medium brown Melton cloth, goods woven expressly for overcoats and such goods as will be found only in first-clasf tailoring establishments. Made in the highest style of the art by the best tailors we can employ, elegantly lined, trimmed and finished and fully warranted.
**Our Price**........$8.95

**No. 4489. OUR $9.50 SPRING OVERCOAT.** Made from a very fine quality all wool black cheviot cloth, one of the very finest weaves made. Nothing makes a more dressy or stylish appearing overcoat. It is elegantly lined, trimmed and finished and we guarantee it equal to anything your local tailor can furnish at double the price.
**Our Special Price**........$9.50

**No. 4490. OUR $9.45 SPRING OVERCOAT.** Made from a very fine all wool tan color Melton cloth. This tan shade will be very popular for the spring and summer season and makes a very neat and dressy appearing overcoat. This coat is elegantly lined, trimmed and finished and guaranteed in every respect.
**Our Special Price**........$9.45

**No. 4491. OUR $9.90 SPRING OVERCOAT.** Made from a very fine stylish light tan all wool Melton, a goods that is made by one of the best French mills and expressly for overcoats. We offer you this overcoat at less than half the price charged by local tailors, and we trust to receive a trial order. No description we can give of these garments will do them justice. You must see them to appreciate their value.
**Our Special Price**........$9.90

**No. 4492. OUR $10.20 SPRING OVERCOAT.** Made of a light olive all wool Melton, one of the finest imported all wool overcoat goods on the market, makes a very stylish garment and we make them up in the highest style of the art with best trimmings. It will compare favorably with anything your tailor can produce at double the price.
**Our Price**........$10.20

**No. 4493. OUR $10.95 SPRING OVERCOAT.** Made from a very fine imported Oxford English clay worsted, almost black. It makes a very dressy neat appearing garment, elegantly lined, trimmed and finished and fully warranted.
**Our Price**........$10.95

**No. 4494. OUR $10.90 ENGLISH CLAY WORSTED,** a fancy new gray shade made expressly for spring overcoats. Understand in ordering from us you have the advantage of not only securing a garment made in the very latest style and pattern by the best tailors we can employ, but you also get all the latest shades, the equal of which you would not be likely to get from your local tailor at three times our price.
**Special Price**........$10.90

**No. 4495. OUR $11.75 SPRING OVERCOAT.** Made from a very fancy tan imported English clay worsted material. Makes a neat, stylish garment. Elegantly lined, trimmed and finished and fully warranted.
**Our Price**........$11.75

**No 4496. OUR $12.75 BLACK ENGLISH CLAY WORSETD OVERCOAT.** We can furnish you an English clay worsted overcoat for much less, but we have decided to offer our very finest worsted only. This is the very finest 18 oz. English clay worsted on the market. There is nothing better at any price. The coat is made in the highst style of the art, elegantly lined, trimmed and finished and fully warranted. It is heavy enough for year around wear in all central and southern localities and as a dress coat it is worn in every state throughout the year.
**Our Special Price**........$12.75

## MEN'S FANCY SILK VESTS.

**No. 4497. MEN'S $2.50 SILK VESTS.** A fancy vest made from a very nice imported silk worsted vest material, in all shades, with invisible silk stripes, dots or checks.
**Our Special price, Single Breasted**........$2.50
**Double Breasted**........$2.75

**No. 4498. MEN'S $3.00 FANCY SILK VESTS.** Made from a very fine imported silk worsted in fancy light, medium and dark shades, beautiful raised effects, with invisible colored silk mixtures.
**Our Special price for Single Breasted**........$3.00
**Double Breasted**........$3.25

**No. 4499. OUR FINEST FANCY SILK VESTS FOR $3.00.** These vests are made from very fine imported French silk mixed worsted in beautiful raised effects, light, medium and dark shades with beautiful invisible silk mixed neat dots, checks or stripes.
**Our Special price, Single Breasted**........$2.50
**Double Breasted**........$3.75

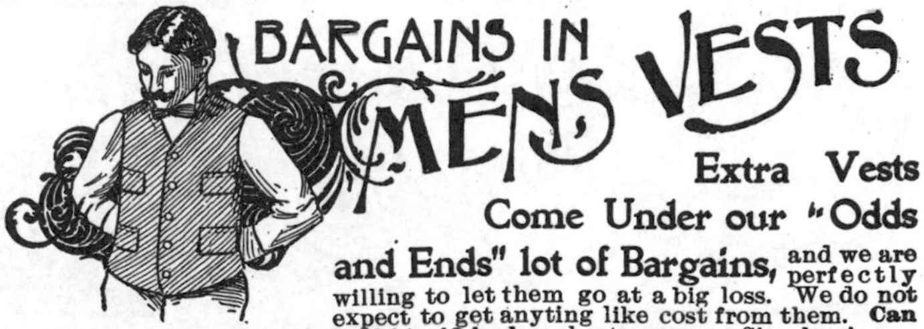


**Extra Vests Come Under our "Odds and Ends" lot of Bargains,** and we are perfectly willing to let them go at a big loss. We do not expect to get anyting like cost from them. **Can be furnished in any size from 34 to 42 inches** chest measure. Simply give us your chest measurement, enclose the price named, less 3% discount for cash, and the vest will be sent you.

**No. 4500. MEN'S DOMESTIC CASSIMERE CLOTH,** good weight, medium, light or dark shade, neat check, stripe or plaid.
**Price for Vest Only**........65c.

**No. 4501. MEN'S DOMESTIC WOOL CASSIMERE,** light, medium or dark, neat checks, stripes or plaids. **Price for Vest Only**........90c.

**No. 4502. MEN'S BLACK OR NAVY BLUE WOOL CHEVIOT CLOTH VESTS. Price of each**........$1.25.

**No. 4503. MEN'S EXTRA FINE IMPORTED ALL WOOL ENGLISH CASSIMERE,** in light, medium and dark, neat checks, stripes and plaids.
**Price for Vest Only**........$1.50

**No. 4504. VERY FINEST ALL WOOL ENGLISH CASSIMERES,** in light, medium and dark shades; also English worsteds in black, blue and fancy patterns, very finest goods, the very finest make.
**Price for Vests Only**........$1.75

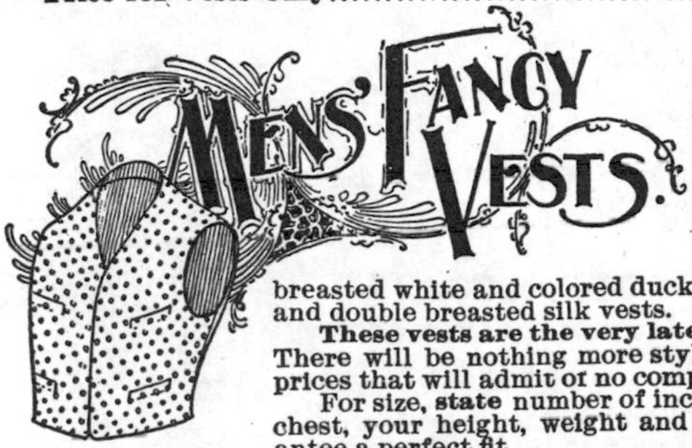


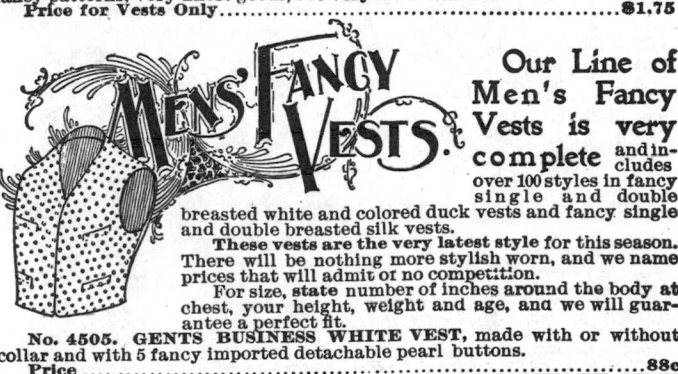

**Our Line of Men's Fancy Vests is very complete** and includes over 100 styles in fancy single and double breasted white and colored duck vests and fancy single and double breasted silk vests.

**These vests are the very latest style for this season.** There will be nothing more stylish worn, and we name prices that will admit of no competition.

For size, **state number of inches around the body at** chest, your height, weight and age, and we will guarantee a perfect fit.

**No. 4505. GENTS BUSINESS WHITE VEST,** made with or without collar and with 5 fancy imported detachable pearl buttons.
**Price**........88c

**No. 4506. MEN'S HEAVY WHITE COTTON BARNESLEY DUCK VEST,** with or without collar, fancy pearl detachable buttons.
**Our Special Price**........$1.25

**No. 4507. MEN'S WHITE LINEN BASKET WEAVE VESTS,** with or without collar, fancy detachable pearl buttons. **Our Special Price**....$1.75

**No. 4508. MEN'S NEAT POLKA DOT SINGLE BREASTED FANCY DUCK VESTS.**
**Our Special Price**........$1.05

**No. 4509. Same, Double Breasted**........$1.25

**No. 4510. MEN'S NEAT STRIPED SINGLE BREASTED FANCY DUCK VESTS.**
**Our Special Price**........$1.10

**No. 4511. Same, Double Breasted**........$1.35

**No. 4512. MEN'S BASKET WEAVE AND WEB DUCK WOOLZER FACING VESTS,** with or without collar, fancy detachable buttons.
**Our Special Price, Single Breasted**........$2.25

**No. 4513. Same, Double Breasted**........$2.50

**No. 4514. MEN'S VERY NOBBY STRIPED DUCK FANCY VESTS. Single Breasted, Our Special Price**........$2.95

**No. 4515. Same, Double Breasted**........$3.25

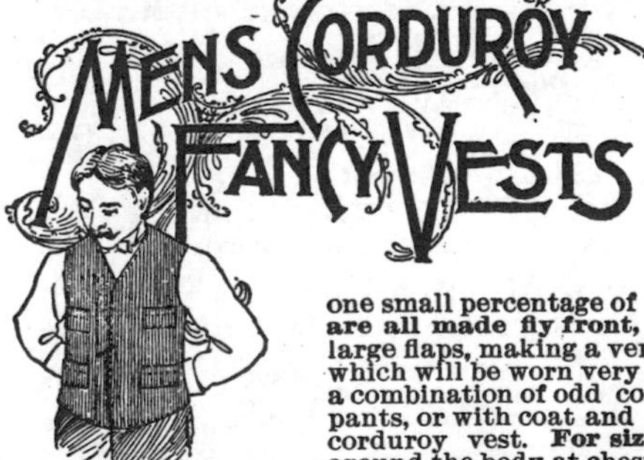


**Men's fancy fly front corduroy vests** will be all the style for the coming season. **We have a very large line of these goods,** and can offer them to you at actual cost of material and making, with only our one small percentage of profit added. **These vests are all made fly front,** four outside pockets with large flaps, making a very stylish garment, and one which will be worn very largely by good dressers in a combination of odd coat, corduroy vest and odd pants, or with coat and pants of one pattern and corduroy vest. **For size,** state number of inches around the body at chest, taken over vest under inside coat; also state height and weight and we will guarantee a perfect fit.

**Terms are the same** on these as on all other goods, C. O. D. subject to examination on receipt of $1.00, or a cash discount of 3 per cent. if cash in full accompanies your order. Samples of cloth free on application.

**No. 4516. OUR $2.25 CORDUROY VESTS.** Made of a very fine pure dye gray imported silk finished English Corduroy. Made expressly for fancy fly front vests as above described. **Our Special Price**........$2.25

**No. 4517. MEN'S $2.50 FANCY CORDUROY VESTS.** These vests are made from an extra fine imported silk finished English corduroy in dark gray; fly front, as illustrated. **Our Special Price**........$2.50

**No. 4518. MEN'S $2.75 FANCY CORDUROY VESTS.** Made from a fancy brown, pure dye silk finished, imported English corduroy.
**Our Special Price**........$2.75

**No. 4519. MEN'S $3.00 FANCY CORDUROY VESTS.** These vests are made from a very fine imported pure dye silk finished, English corduroy either in a rich brown or gray, as desired. **Our Special Price**........$3.00

**No. 4520. MEN'S $3.90 FANCY CORDUROY VESTS.** These vests are made from a pure dye Swiss silk embroidered gray corduroy. The vest is fancy embroidered throughout, is made up in the very finest style with fly front and 4 pockets, with large lapel. **Our Price**........$3.90

**No. 4521. MEN'S $4.00 FANCY CORDUROY VESTS.** Made from seal brown or gray pure dye imported Swiss silk embroidered fancy corduroy, the finest embroidered corduroy that is on the market.
**Our Special Price**........$4.00

**SEND FOR OUR REGULAR FREE SAMPLE CARD OF CLOTH SAMPLES. IT CONTAINS SAMPLES OF ALL DESIRABLE THINGS.**

## SEARS, ROEBUCK & CO. INC. SUMMER CLOTHING

WE OFFER THE MOST AT-TRACTIVE LINE OF SUMMER CLOTHING that has ever been shown, and we believe you will be interested in some of our offers. Our line of light coats, vests and suits, white duck pants, vests, fancy vests, etc., etc., is very complete, and embraces everything desirable in wearing apparel for all summer outing occasions. We offer only strictly high grade goods made from the best domestic and imported fabrics, and every garment is tailor made and cut on the latest style patterns for this season's wear. This department we are sure will interest a great many customers, for it will afford them an opportunity to get just what they want for summer wear, an opportunity to make your own selection from everything the market affords. whereas in your local market you are compelled to take what is carried in stock even though inferior goods or the style of a year or more ago.

**TERMS. THE SAME TERMS APPLY ON SUMMER GOODS** as on all other clothing. We will accept orders to be sent by express C. O. D. subject to examination on receipt of $1.00. The goods can be examined at the express office, and if found perfectly satisfactory and exactly as represented, pay the express agent our price and express charges, less the $1.00 sent with order.

**A DISCOUNT OF 3 PER CENT.** if cash in full accompanies your order. Nearly all our customers send cash in full.

**ABOUT SIZES.** Sizes to be the same as for any other clothing. Always be sure to give height and weight. For coats and vests, state number of inches around the body at chest taken over vest under coat. For pants, number of inches around the body at waist, around the body at hips, and length of inside seam from tight in crotch to heel.

**NO SAMPLES CAN BE FURNISHED.** We have found it very difficult to furnish samples of summer clothing and then be sure of filling orders that might come in later for certain patterns that are sold out from time to time, and many a customer is disappointed and we are unable to fill the order when received. We will therefore ask you to order from the descriptions we have given, and if we are unable to send the exact pattern we will reserve the right to send you as near the pattern described as possible, always guaranteeing to send you equally as good or better goods, never poorer.

## MEN'S SUMMER COTTON COATS.

**No. 4522** BLUE PINCHECK COTTON COAT, very latest style. Size, 34 to 42......35c

**No. 4523** BLUE STRIPED COTTON COAT, 4 button. Sizes, 34 to 42......45c

**No. 4524** MEN'S LIGHT BLUE AND WHITE STRIPED 4 BUTTON COTTON COAT, Sizes 34 to 42......45c

**No. 4525** MEN'S BLACK AND WHITE STRIPED 3 BUTTON COTTON COAT, extra heavy, a good grade of goods......65c

**No. 4526** MEN'S BLUE AND WHITE 4 BUTTON COTTON COAT, one of the finest cotton coats made for summer wear. Price......95c

## LINEN COATS.

**No. 4527** MEN'S BROWN LINEN SUMMER COAT, well made, quality guaranteed. Sizes 34 to 42. Each......95c

## MEN'S BLACK ALPACA COATS.

There is nothing more durable for summer wear. Our black alpaca coats are fine tailor made, sewed throughout with linen and guaranted in every respect. They are made in the very latest style for this season's wear, and will compare favorably with anything you can buy at double the price.

**No. 4528** MEN'S BLACK ALPACA 1 BUTTON COAT, 3 pockets. Price......95c.

**No. 4529** MEN'S BLACK ALPACA COATS, 1 button, 3 pockets, extra quality......$1.25

**No. 4530** MEN'S FINE BLACK ALPACA COATS, 3 button, 4 pockets, well made and finished. Our special price......$1.35

**No. 4531** MEN'S VERY FINE BLACK ALPACA SUMMER COATS, made with 4 buttons in front, 4 pockets. Our price......$1.60

**No. 4532** MEN'S FINE BLACK ALPACA SUMMER COATS, made with 4 buttons in front, 4 pockets. Our special price......$1.95

**No. 4533** VERY FINE BLACK ALPACA COAT, fine French faced and double front, made with 4 buttons, 4 pockets. Our special price...$2.50

**No. 4534** OUR VERY FINEST BLACK ALPACA COATS, 4 buttons in front, made French faced and double front, 4 pockets. Our special price......$3.20

The above coats are furnished at the prices named in regular sizes, 34 to 42. Extra sizes, over 42 chest measure, or extra lengths, 35c extra.

## MEN'S BLACK ALPACA VESTS.

**No. 4535** BLACK ALPACA VESTS to match coats described above, well made, latest style for this season. Our special price......95c

**No. 4536** MEN'S BLACK ALPACA VESTS to match coats above described, well made and guaranteed. Our special price......$1.20

**No. 4537** VERY FINEST BLACK ALPACA VEST, to match coats above described. Our special price......$1.65

## MINISTERS' EXTRA LONG BLACK ALPACA COATS.

**No. 4538** FINE BLACK ALPACA COAT, extra long. Price.....$1.90

**No. 4539** FINE BLACK ALPACA COAT, made extra long. Price.$2.35

**No. 4540** VERY FINE BLACK ALPACA COAT, made extra long, buttons to neck. Price......$2.75

## MEN'S MOHAIR COATS AND VESTS.

WE OFFER THE FINEST LINE OF MOHAIR COATS AND VESTS on the market. They are all the very latest style for this season, are cut on the latest style patterns to fit perfectly and guaranteed in every respect. Every garment is fine tailor made and sewed throughout with linen. You will find these goods far superior to those offered by the average dealer. They come in regular sizes, 34 to 42 inches chest measure.

Follow our regular rules for measurment in ordering.

**No. 4541** MEN'S BLACK AND WHITE STRIPED MOHAIR COAT AND VEST. Our price......$3.25

**No. 4542** MEN'S BLACK AND WHITE FINE MOHAIR COAT AND VEST, made double front. Our price......$4.50

**No. 4543** MEN'S DARK GRAY MOHAIR COAT AND VEST. Price......$2.95

**No. 4544** MEDIUM GRAY SILK MIXED MOHAIR COAT AND VEST. Price......$3.75

**No. 4545** DARK GRAY MOHAIR, coat only......$1.95

**No. 4546** LIGHT TAN STRIPED MOHAIR, coat only......$2.10

**No. 4547** BLACK CASHMERE COAT AND VEST, French faced. Special price......$4.95

**No. 4548** PONGEE SILK COAT AND VEST, double front, straw color. Price......$6.23

**No. 4549** BLACK SILK COAT AND VEST......$7.50

## MEN'S SERGE COATS AND VESTS.

**No. 4550** BLACK OR BLUE SERGE COAT AND VEST, 4 pockets, fine tailor made, sewed throughout with silk and linen. Our Special Price $3.95

**No. 4551** MEN'S BLACK OR NAVY BLUE SERGE COAT AND VEST. Our Special Price......$4.50

**No. 4552** MEN'S BLACK OR NAVY BLUE SERGE COAT AND VEST. Our Price......$5.25

**No. 4553** MEN'S FINE BLACK OR NAVY BLUE SERGE COAT AND VEST. Price......$5.95

**No. 4553½** MEN'S BLACK OR BLUE COTTON SERGE COAT AND VEST, 3 button front. Our Special Price......$1.50

**No. 4554** MEN'S DOUBLE BREASTED BLACK OR NAVY BLUE SERGE COAT. Only......$3.50

**No. 4555** MEN'S FINE BLACK OR NAVY BLUE CLAY WORSTED SUMMER COAT. Unlined, fine tailor made. Only......$4.95

## MEN'S CRASH OR LINEN SUITS.

COMPLETE SUITS, COATS, VESTS AND PANTS. There is nothing more desirable for summer wear, nor more stylish for outing purposes.

**No. 4556** MEN'S LINEN SUIT, made from good quality imported linen thoroughly shrunk, coat with 4 button front. Price for Complete Suit......$2.95

**No. 4557** MEN'S LINEN SUIT, made from extra quality light grey linen. Our Special Price......$3.50

**No. 4558** MEN'S LINEN SUITS, fancy linen with neat pincheck. Price for Suit......$4.25

**No. 4559** MEN'S VERY FINE IMPORTED IRISH LINEN SUITS, fancy piping and and extra fine suit. Price......$5.50

**No. 4560** MEN'S VERY FINE IMPORTED DIAGONAL FANCY IRISH LINEN SUITS. Price for Suit......$5.95

**No. 4561** MEN'S HEAVY RUSSIAN LINEN SUITS. These suits are made from a heavy rough surface imported Russian linen. Wonderful values. Our Price......$6.25

## MEN'S LINEN DUSTERS.

OUR LINE OF LINEN DUSTERS is very complete and includes the finest goods in the market. They are cut very long for driving or traveling. A comparison of the goods we offer with those carried by the average retail dealer will convince you of the extraordinary values we are giving. FOR SIZE state number of inches around the body at chest taken over vest, under inside coat.

**No. 4562** GOOD QUALITY GRASS CLOTH DUSTER. Price......$0.85

**No. 4563** EXTRA QUALITY PLAIN LINEN DUSTER. Price......$1.25

**No. 4564** BETTER QUALITY LINEN DUSTER, Price......$1.35

**No. 4565** BETTER QUALITY LINEN DUSTER. Price......$1.75

**No. 4566** BLACK ALPACA DUSTER. Price......$2.95

**No. 4567** LIGHT GRAY SERGE DUSTER. Price......$1.95

**No. 4568** DARK OR MEDIUM GRAY MOHAIR DUSTER. Price......$2.95

## BOYS' SUMMER WEAR.

Our line of Boys' Summer Wear is very complete. Want of space prevents our quoting but a few special bargains. When ordering, be sure to state age of boy and say whether large or small of his age, and a perfect fit will be guaranteed. Sizes run from 12 to 18 years.

**No. 4569** BOYS' BLACK AND WHITE STRIPED ONE BUTTON SUMMER COATS. Price......$0.30

**No. 4570** BOYS' BLACK AND WHITE STRIPED SATEEN COATS, 3 button front. Price......$0.65

**No. 4571** BOYS' BLUE STRIPED FLANNEL COAT AND VEST. Price......$0.75

**No. 4572** BOYS' DARK GRAY MOHAIR COAT AND VEST. Price......$2.35

**No. 4573** BOYS' BLACK ALPACA COATS ONLY. Price......$0.90

**No. 4574** BOYS' BLACK ALPACA COAT ONLY, made 3 button front. Price......$1.35

# Men's Smoking Jackets.

3.25  5.50  8.50  9.50

## To Supply a demand for Men's Smoking Jackets

we have arranged to make up a limited quantity of these goods in the very latest style with the finest quality of material, and offer them to our customers at about one-half the prices they have been in the habit of paying. If you are interested in anything in this line it will pay you to consider the prices quoted.

**No. 4575. SMOKING JACKET A.** See illustration marked A. Smoking jacket of English plaid in striped and checked patterns, silk cord binding on edge, pockets and sleeves.

**Our Special Price**................ $3.25
Other grades according to quality at $4.25, $5.00 and $5.25.

**No. 4576. SMOKING JACKET MARKED B.** Made of fine Matelasse with double stitched satin binding on pockets and sleeves, fine Italian lining in fancy figured effects.

**Our Special Price**........................ $9.50
Others at $10.50, $11.50, $12.50 and $13.50 according to quality.

**No. 4577. SMOKING JACKET MARKED C.** Made of fancy blanket with fancy collars and cuffs, satin binding on edge and sleeves, the latest thing in smoking jackets.

**Our Special Price**........................ $8.50
Others at $9.50, $10.50 and $11.50.

**No. 4578. OUR SMOKING JACKET MARKED D.** Made from very fine imported all wool tricot in navy blue, black or garnet color, with quilted satin collar, double stitched satin bound pockets and sleeves, and quilted throughout with fine Italian cloth.

**Our Special Price**........................ $5.95

# Bicycle Suits

$2.95  $3.50  $4.50  $5.50
$3.25  $3.75  $4.75  $6.00

## Our line of Bicycle Clothing is very extensive.

We have made arrangments with one of the largest manufacturers of Bicycle Clothing in America to supply us, and for the coming season we can offer you such bargains as were never offered before. The great craze for bicycles has induced one of the largest clothing manufacturers in America to turn his attention to the manufacture of bicycle clothing exclusively and he has gotten out a line that is without an equal in the market, and under our arrangments we are prepared to furnish you these goods at less money than your local dealer can buy them in large quantities. Our bicycle suits are all fine tailor made throughout, cut on the latest style patterns by expert cutters to fit perfectly; they are elegantly trimmed and finished, and in every way they make a first class suit.

**RULES FOR MEASUREMENT.** Measurements should be taken exactly the same as for other suits. See our "Rules for Measurement" on another page.

**OUR SPECIAL TERMS.** Bicycle Suits, like all other clothing, will be sent C. O. D. by express, subject to examination, on receipt of $1.00 as a guarantee of good faith. You can examine the suit at the express office, and if found perfectly satisfactory and exactly as represented, pay the express agent the balance and express charges and the suit is yours. Three per cent discount allowed if cash in full accompanies your order.

**No. 4579 OUR $2.95 BICYCLE SUIT.** This suit is made of a light tan diagonal suiting, good wearing goods and consists of one bicycle coat and one pair of bicycle pants. Coat is made with 4 buttons, sack style. It is the best bicycle suit for the money that has been offered.

Price...........................$2.95
Separate Bicycle Pants Only, price........................$1.50
Bicycle Cap to match, price........................ 0.35

**No. 4580 MENS' DARK OXFORD MIXED BICYCLE SUITS.** This is a very firmly woven fabric and will give first-class service.

Price for suit including bicycle coat and bicycle pants...........$3.25
Price for separate bicycle pants............................ 1.50
Price for bicycle cap to match............................ 0.35

**No. 4581 MENS' BLACK CHEVIOT BICYCLE SUITS.** These suits are made from a very nice imported wool black cheviot cloth. The suit consists of one sack coat and one pair of bicycle pants.

Price for suit...........................$3.95
Price for separate pants............................ 1.75
Price for bicycle cap to match............................ 0.40

**No. 4582 BROWN PINCHECK WOOL CASSIMERE BICYCLE SUIT,** consisting of one bicycle coat, sack style, and one pair of bicycle pants.

Price for suit...........................$4.25
Price for separate bicycle pants............................ 1.85
Price for bicycle cap to match............................ 0.45

**No. 4583 MENS' FANCY BROWN INVISIBLE PLAID WOOL CASSIMERE.** These goods are woven expressly for bicycle suits. The suit consists of one bicycle coat, sack style, one bicycle pants. Coat has cash pocket, pump pocket and inside pocket, also four outside pockets.

Price for suit...........................$4.60
Price for separate bicycle pants............................ 1.90
Price for bicycle cap to match............................ 0.40

**No. 4584 EXTRA QUALITY LIGHT GRAY SMALL CHECK WOOL CASSIMERE BICYCLE SUITING.** These goods are woven expressly for bicycle suits, and it is a cloth that will give the best service.

Price for bicycle suit, including bicycle coat, sack style, and bicycle pants........................$4.65
Price for separate bicycle pants............................ 1.90
Price for bicycle cap to match............................ 0.40
The above suit will also be furnished in light brown invisible plaid at the same price.

**No. 4585 MEN'S BROWN CHECK IMPORTED SCOTCH SUITING CLOTH,** one of the best fabrics woven for bicycle suits, will give excellent wear, and the suit will compare favorably with those that retail at double the price.

Price of suit, including bicycle coat and bicycle pants...........$5.50
Price for separate bicycle pants............................ 2.25
Price for bicycle cap to match, made with satin lining.......... 0.50

**No. 4586 MEN'S LINEN CRASH BICYCLE SUIT.** Suit is made from an extra quality imported Irish linen crash, fine tailor made.

Price for complete bicycle suit, including bicycle coat, sack style, and separate bicycle pants........................$4.25
Price of extra bicycle pants............................ 1.85
Price of bicycle cap to match............................ 0.40

Want of space prevents our illustrating or quoting but a portion of our line of bicycle clothing, but above we give you the descriptions and prices of the most desirable goods, and on these suits we are able to make prices against which we can have absolutely no competition.

---

# WHAT THE PEOPLE SAY.

### I Thank You for Your Promptness and Honesty.
CROTON, N. C.

SEARS, ROEBUCK & CO.
DEAR SIRS:—The clothes are at hand and are perfectly satisfactory. I thank you for your promptness and honesty, and will do all I can for you.
Yours truly, GEO. DANCER.

### Suit Wears as Well as it Looks.
NEWTON, N. C.

MESSRS. SEARS, ROEBUCK & CO., Chicago, Ill.
GENTLEMEN:—I received the suit of clothes invoiced No. T 22903 and like it very well. If it wears as well as it looks it will be all right.
Yours truly, J. B. LEONARD.

### Clothes Perfectly Satisfactory and Wants More.
ALBERTVILLE, WIS.

SEARS, ROEBUCK & CO., Chicago, Ill.
DEAR SIRS:—Please send me one or two order blanks, I would like to send and get another suit of clothes. Also find fifteen cents for which please send me your big catalogue. I wish you would send the order blanks at once—no rush about the catalogue. The clothes you sent reached me the 25th. I found them perfectly satisfactory, both regarding fit and quality, for which please accept my thanks. Yours truly, A. LARSEN.

### More Than Pleased and Will Hear from Him Again.
SAN JACINTO, CAL.

SEARS, ROEBUCK & CO., Chicago, Ill.
GENTS:—I received the clothes the 28th, O. K. They are a good fit. I am more than pleased with them. I think you will hear from me again.
Yours in haste, W. R. HUILL.

### I Received More Value for My Money Than I Expected.
ELLSWORTH, KAS.

GENTLEMEN:—
I received goods in good order, the 31st day of December. They have given perfect satisfaction. I received more value for my money than I expected. I shall try and sell some more suits if possible.
Yours truly, FRED H. SCHULTZ.

### Everybody Pleased With Everything.
LEWISTOWN, O.

SEARS, ROEBUCK & CO.
I received goods and was well pleased with them. Boys' suit fits to perfection. Dr. Akey was well pleased with his pants; he said he could not get such pants for less than five dollars, and I could not get handkerchiefs for less than 12½ cents like those I got. Thanking you for promptness in filling my order. I will probably send you another order in the near future, as some others wants some articles. I remain, Yours truly,
ANNIE CLAY.

### The Suit Fits Neat.
STEWARKAN, ILL.

SEARS, ROEBUCK & CO., Chicago, Ill.
DEAR SIRS:—I received my clothing O. K. They fit neat and I was well pleased with them. Yours truly, T. F. RICKETTS.

### "Your House Shall Always Have Our Preference."
BRUNSWICK, GA.

MESSRS. SEARS, ROEBUCK & CO.
Your extreme favor received with gladness. I took out the suit on the second inst. at $5.95 and was well pleased with it. We examined it and found it to be all that was recommended. Your house shall always have our preference. Yours respectfully, J. E. JONES.

### The Clothes Are a Perfect Fit.
HARRISVILLE, O.

SEARS, ROEBUCK & CO., Chicago, Ill.
DEAR SIRS:—I have received invoice No. 329951, and will say that I am perfectly satisfied with same. The clothes are a perfect fit and splendid as to quality. Yours truly, GEO. W. CRUMLEY.

### Well Pleased With Color, Fit and Quality.
CONCORD, MICH.

SIRS:—
Overcoat came to-day; all is satisfactory. I am well pleased with the color, fit and quality of goods and make.
Yours respectfully. N. L. GIBBS.

### The Suit Keeps Him Warm and is Admired by His Neighbors.
OHIOPYLE, PA.

SEARS, ROEBUCK & CO., Chicago, Ill.
The XXXX suit is keeping me warm today, is a perfect fit and admired by my neighbors. It's an advertisement that may make you many customers in this section. Wishing you a prosperous new year, I am,
Yours very truly, ISAIAH L. COLLINS.

### Could Not Duplicate the Suit for Less than Twice He Paid Us.
ACKLEY, IA.

SEARS, ROEBUCK & CO.
DEAR SIRS:—I received the suit of clothes and will say that I am highly pleased with it. I do not think I could duplicate the same for less than twice what I paid you in this place. Respectfully,
F. E. WATTERS.

### Pants Fit Better Than Any He Ever Had.
SHUSHAN, N. Y.

SEARS, ROEBUCK & CO., Chicago, Ill.
DEAR SIRS:—I received my goods I ordered of you last night, everything was just as you represented it and much better than I expected, the pants fit me better than any I ever had, you could not have done better if I had been there. I thank you very kindly for sending by freight, as it did not cost half as much as by express, everything suits me to my entire satisfaction. I will thank you once more for your honorable dealing with me and await my further orders. Yours respectfully,
W. D. STEWART.

---

IF YOU DOUBT OUR RELIABILITY, WRITE WITH STAMP ENCLOSED, TO METROPOLITAN NATIONAL BANK, CHICAGO.

# OVERALLS, JUMPERS AND DUCK COATS.

## THE SURVIVAL OF THE FITTEST

Garments that stand the Search Light of Investigation. Garments that are built "on Honor." Garments that are Practical, Strong, Comfortable and Dependable. We are not given to Boasting, but we really believe that we have the Very Best Goods in this Line that Ever a Manufacturer Turned Out. If you are in search of something Absolutely and Undeniably Good, you cannot possibly make a mistake in ordering any of the following garments. • • •

## MEN'S OVERALLS.

### AT 35c MEN'S DENIM OVERALLS.

**No. 21810  WE OFFER THESE AS A LEADER.** They are made from medium weight dark blue denim; made with two pockets and two ply flaps. Sizes, 30 to 42 waist and 29 to 35 in seam. Made plain without bib.
Price, per pair...................35c

**No. 21812  MEN'S OVERALLS,** same as above, but made from fancy striped denim. Also gray mixtures.
Price, per pair...................35c

### 40c APRON OVERALLS.

**No. 21814  MEN'S MEDIUM WEIGHT DARK BLUE DENIM OVERALLS.** Made with two pockets, reinforced crotch and two ply bands. Sizes, 30 to 42 waist, 29 to 35 in seam.
Price, per pair...................40c

**No. 21815  FANCY STRIPED APRON OVERALLS,** same as above but made in neat striped patterns. Also gray mixtures. Price, per pair.....40c

### 50c NEVER RIP OVERALLS.

Sizes, 30 to 44 waist, 29 to 36 in seam.
**No. 21816  THE VERY BEST 50c OVERALLS EVER MADE.** These overalls are made from heavy weight blue denim. Two front, one hip and one watch pocket, sewed with double lock stitch all through and warranted not to rip; made plain without apron; heavy riveted undestructible buttons. Price, per pair...................50c

### 58c SPECIAL BRAND APRON OVERALLS.

**No. 21817  SPECIAL BRAND NEVER RIP OVERALLS.** Made from heavy blue denim, with large bib apron and shoulder straps; cut full size; double lock stitch seams warranted never to rip; patent riveted indestructible buttons; front and hip pocket and rule pocket; felled seams; double reinforced crotch. Guaranteed to give thorough satisfaction in every way.
Price, per pair...................58c

### OUR 65c CARPENTERS' SPECIAL.

**No. 21818  CARPENTERS' AND MECHANICS' SPECIAL BRAND NEVER RIP OVERALLS.** Made from heavy 9 oz. brown duck; extra well made and warranted not to rip; double reinforced crotch; large bib apron; front, hip, rule and pencil pockets; patent riveted buttons; full of real goodness. Price, per pair.....65c

### GENUINE YORK DENIM APRON OVERALLS 80c.

**No. 21819  THERE IS A VAST AMOUNT OF REAL SATISFACTION** in buying overalls of this sort. They are so thoroughly good in every way that it is a great pleasure for us to quote them. They are made from the genuine extra heavy weight York blue denim with large bib apron and straps; front, hip and rule pockets; patent riveted buttons and double reinforced crotch; warranted not to rip. You will make no mistake in ordering these garments. Price, per pair...............80c

**No. 21821  MEN'S EXTRA HEAVY GENUINE YORK BLUE DENIM OVERALLS.** Made plain without apron; sewed all through with double lock stitch and warranted never to rip; two front, one hip and one watch pocket; patent riveted buttons; double reinforced crotch, and flat felled seams. Particularly adapted for hard service. Guaranteed in every way. Price, per pair...................75c

### OUR 85c RIDING OVERALLS.

**No. 21822  EXTRA HEAVY RIDING OVERALLS.** Made with double seat and crotch; extra strong, heavy weight, Oxford gray, twilled denim; the toughest made; three pockets and watch pockets; felled seams and patent riveted buttons; especially desirable for horseback riding as well as working; plain, without apron. Price, per pair...................85c

### THE BLACK HUSSAR AT 71c.

**No. 21824  MEN'S BLACK HUSSAR OVERALLS.** Made from jet black 9 oz duck, with felled seams. Riveted buttons set in pants pockets. 2 front, 1 hip and watch pocket. Pantaloon style. Made plain without apron.
Price, per pair......... .........71c

### THE BLACK CROOK APRON OVERALLS 79c.

**No. 21825  THE BLACK CROOK OVERALLS** are made from extra heavy 9 oz fast black duck with large bib apron and straps. Front, hip and rule pockets, and best riveted buttons. Double stitched and felled seams. Thoroughly well made and will stand the hardest kind of service. Built "on honor" and guaranteed to satisfy.
Price, per pair...................79c

**No. 21826  MEN'S 9 OZ. BLACK DUCK OVERALLS** with apron. Same as the Black Crook but made with double knees and front. Extra heavy and extra strong. Price, per pair...................90c

---

## THE S. AND R. BLACK GIANT. THE STRONGEST OVERALLS IN THE WORLD. 95c.

**No. 21827  THE S. & R. BLACK GIANT.** Our great specialty. These overalls are made of specially prepared, extra heavy, super stout, 10 oz. black duck, with double seat, double knees and front; patent never break brass riveted buttons; three pockets and watch pocket; double felled seams. The strongest overalls in the world. Made plain, without apron.
Price, per pair.......................95c

### COW BOYS' RIDING OVERALLS. THE SADDLE KING 98c.

**No. 21828  COW BOYS' SADDLE KING OVERALLS.** Made from extra heavy 9 oz. brown duck; two front, one hip and one watch pocket; double seat and made double all the way down inside of legs; double lock stitched seams; riveted buttons and double stays. Always popular and always to be depended upon for hard service. Plain, without apron.
Price, per pair.......................98c

### "THE TEXAS RANGER" THE HEAVIEST AND STRONGEST OVERALLS MADE. PRICE, $1.15.

**No. 21829  "THE TEXAS RANGER," COW BOYS' RIDING OVERALLS.** Made from heaviest denim; plain blue, with riveted brass buttons; double seat and double in-seam all the way down; four pockets with flaps that button down, and watch pocket; double lock stitch, felled seams; made for the very hardest kind of wear. Words cannot express their goodness. The world has never produced their equal. Made plain, without apron. Price, per pair.............$1.15

### PAINTERS' WHITE OVERALLS.

**No. 21830  PAINTERS' WHITE DRILL OVERALLS,** made with apron and shoulder straps, two pockets and knife pocket. Double stitch never rip seams.
Price, per pair....... 42c; Per ½ doz.............$2.38

### BOYS' OVERALLS.

**No. 21832  BOYS' MEDIUM WEIGHT DENIM OVERALLS.** Plain blue or fancy striped, good reliable garments. Size 26 to 30 inch waist and 26 to 31 inseam. Made plain, without apron. Price, per pair.............38c

### BOYS' BLACK OVERALLS.

**No. 21833  BOYS' EXTRA HEAVY JET BLACK PANTALOON OVERALLS.** Front and hip pockets; patent riveted buttons; extra well made and fast color; felled seams and extra fine finish; warranted to thoroughly satisfy in every way. Sizes same as above. Made plain without apron. Price, per pair.............50c

### MEN'S WAISTS AND JUMPERS. Sizes, 34 to 44 Chest Measurement.

**No. 21834  MEN'S PLAIN BLUE GENUINE YORK DENIM JUMPERS.** Single breasted with riveted buttons and felled seams; extra well made and warranted not to rip. Price, each.............48c

**No. 21835  MEN'S DARK OXFORD MIXED OR STRIPED JUMPER WAISTS.** Single breasted with riveted buttons and pocket; very strong and tough; unexcelled for wear.
Price, each...................50c

**No. 21836  PAINTERS' AND PAPER HANGERS' WHITE DRILL WAISTS OR JUMPERS.** Medium weight, very strong and easy to wash. Extra well made and finished.
Price, each...................40c

### ENGINEERS' ...JACKETS.

Sizes 34 to 46

AT 35c.

**No. 21837  ENGINEERS' BLUE AND WHITE CHECK OR PLAID GINGHAM JACKETS** with neat collar and pocket. Price, each 35c; 3 for $1.00

**No. 21838  AT 45c. ENGINEERS' BEST QUALITY BLUE AND WHITE CHECKED JACKETS.** Genuine Amoskeag. Single breasted with neat collar and pockets. Extra well made and warranted to give better service than any other jacket of this kind ever manufactured.
Price, each...................45c

**No. 21839  EXTRA QUALITY TWILLED DENIM JUMPERS.** Dark blue mixed, with neat collar and pockets. Better made garments are not to be found in any market. The wearing qualities of twilled denim are unexcelled. Every one of these garments guaranteed first class in every respect. Each......75c

## MEN'S DUCK COATS.

For Miners, Teamsters, Farmers, Prospectors, Fishermen, Hunters, Trappers, Etc., Etc.

**No. 21840  MEN'S 8 oz. TAN DUCK COAT.** Single breasted; plaid lining; flap pockets; patent buttons; not a cheap coat, but a good coat at a cheap price. Size 36 to 46.
Each...................$1.25

**No. 21841.  MEN'S 8 oz. BROWN DUCK COATS.** Heavy blanket lining; patent riveted buttons; three outside pockets; corduroy collar. Sizes 36 to 46. Each.........$1.45

**No 21842  MEN'S BLACK DUCK COATS.** Made from fast black, 10½ oz. U. S. Y. duck; double breasted; heavy gray blanket lining throughout; wide corduroy collar; rubber interlining; two outside flap pockets and inside pocket; patent riveted buttons. A coat that gives thorough satisfaction. Sizes 36 to 46. Each...................$2.65

### DUCK VESTS.

**No. 21850  MEN'S 10 oz. BROWN DUCK VESTS.** Lined with gray striped blanketing; cut high in neck; four patch pockets. Sizes 36 to 46. Each...................85c

**No. 21851  MEN'S DUCK VESTS.** Same as above, in black. Our price, each...................85c

### OUR $2.10 HUNTING COAT.

**No. 21852  FOR SPRING AND SUMMER SHOOTING.** Made of dead grass color; specially prepared waterproof duck; five pockets outside; large game pockets inside; straps on sleeves. Sizes 36 to 48. Each...........$2.10

### DUCK PANTS.

**No. 21854  MEN'S 10 oz. BROWN DUCK PANTS.** Heavy gray blanket lining. Sizes 30 to 40 waist, 30 to 45 inseam. Price, per pair...$1.48

**No. 21856  SAME AS ABOVE IN BLACK 10 oz. DUCK.** Pair.$1.48

---

# SEARS ROEBUCK AND CO. INC.
# BOYS CLOTHING DEPARTMENT

### EVERYTHING IN CHILDRENS CLOTHING

## OUR BOYS' AND CHILDREN'S DEPARTMENT HAS DEVELOPED INTO ONE OF THE LARGEST IN THIS COUNTRY,

and we have facilities for supplying the very finest wearing apparel at prices that will mean a saving to our customers of from 25 to 50%.

FOR THE COMING SEASON WE WILL SHOW A LARGER LINE OF JUVENILE CLOTHING THAN EVER BEFORE. It includes everything desirable in Boys' Long Pants Suits for boys from 10 to 19 years of age, Boys' Long Pants, Children's Knee Pants Suits, Four-Piece Combination Suits, Reefer Suits, Sailor Suits, Kilt Suits, Head-to-Foot Combinations, Children's Knee Pants, in fact, everything that goes to make up a thoroughly complete JUVENILE CLOTHING DEPARTMENT.

WE OFFER YOU EVERY ADVANTAGE, EVERY INDUCEMENT TO PLACE YOUR ORDER WITH US. Different from buying in the average retail clothing store where you must confine your selection to the limited stock carried, often made up of goods one, two and three years old and consequently out of style, we offer you an opportunity to select only the very latest styles and that from an endless variety and almost unlimited stock.

EVERY GARMENT IN OUR CHILDREN'S DEPARTMENT IS GUARANTEED THE VERY LATEST STYLE, cut on the latest style patterns by expert cutters to fit perfectly, cut by the latest perfect fitting process to insure a perfect fit, every garment fine tailor made, made by tailors who are employed exclusively on juvenile clothing.

## OUR JUVENILE CLOTHING DEPARTMENT IS A BIG DEPARTMENT

in itself. With few exceptions the cloth is woven expressly for juvenile clothing, goods that are designed for wear, and the same care is given to the manufacture of these garments as is given to our regular clothing for men.

DO NOT OVERLOOK OUR JUVENILE CLOTHING DEPARTMENT when making up your spring or summer order. Include a Suit, Pair of Pants or a Combination Outfit for the boy. It will add next to nothing to the transportation charges if to be shipped with other goods by freight or express.

**TERMS.** OUR TERMS ON JUVENILE CLOTHING ARE EXACTLY THE SAME AS ON ALL OTHER CLOTHING. Any goods will be shipped by express C. O. D., subject to examination on receipt of $1.00 as a guarantee of good faith. You can examine the goods at your nearest express office, and if found perfectly satisfactory and exactly as represented pay the express agent our price and express charges, less the amount sent with order, and the goods are yours.

A DISCOUNT OF 3 PER CENT. will be allowed if cash in full accompanies your order. Nearly all our customers send cash in full.

**ABOUT SIZES.** BOYS LONG PANTS SUITS ARE MADE IN SIZES FROM 10 TO 19 YEARS OF AGE. IN ORDERING, STATE AGE OF BOY, STATE HEIGHT AND WEIGHT, also number of inches around body at chest over vest, under inside coat, number of inches around body at waist, and length of leg from tight in crotch to heel.

FOR BOYS' LONG PANTS, FOR BOYS FROM 10 TO 19, state age of boy, weight, also number of inches around body at waist, and length of leg inside seam from tight in crotch to heel.

FOR CHILDREN'S TWO-PIECE SUITS, FOR CHILDREN FROM 4 TO 14 YEARS OF AGE, state age of boy and say whether large or small of his age.

FOR REEFER SUITS, FOR CHILDREN FROM 3 TO 8 YEARS OF AGE, state age of child, and say whether large or small of age.

FOR SAILOR SUITS, FOR CHILDREN FROM 3 TO 10 YEARS OF AGE, state age of child and say whether large or small of age.

FOR CHILDREN'S KILT SUITS, FOR CHILDREN 2, 2½, 3, 3½ AND 4 YEARS OLD, state age of child and say whether large or small of age.

FOR BOYS' SEPARATE KNEE PANTS, FOR BOYS FROM 4 TO 14 YEARS OF AGE, state age of boy, and say whether large or small of age.

**ABOUT FREE CLOTH SAMPLES.** We can, as a rule, send Cloth Samples of any of the goods quoted in this book, but we would advise you to send for our regular card of 20 samples which includes the most desirable goods in Boys' and Children's Clothing. Simply send us a postal card Saying: "Please send Cloth Samples of Boys' and Children's Clothing."

## BOYS LONG PANTS SUITS.
### For Boys from 10 to 19 years of age.

GUARANTEED FINE TAILOR MADE, every suit cut and made by first class tailors with the same care as given our men's tailor made clothing.

IN ORDERING state size wanted by following our regular rates for measurement for men's clothing, viz: HEIGHT, WEIGHT, Measurements as instructed.

TERMS. Any suit will be sent to any address by express C. O. D. subject to examination on receipt of $1.00, balance and express charges payable at express office.

DISCOUNT. THREE PER CENT. DISCOUNT allowed if cash in full accompanies your order.

No. 4587. OUR BOYS' $2.25 SUIT. This is the cheapest suit we handle and a suit equal to those retailed in country stores at four or five dollars. It makes a good, strong, serviceable, every day suit, made from a cotton worsted material that is wear resisting. It comes in very dark gray striped effect, lined throughout with good cotton serge, lined flaps on all pockets and comes in Style 1.

Many of our customers wonder how it is possible to get out a suit in good workmanlike manner for boys from ten to nineteen years of age at $2.25, but with our facilities we are only paying for the raw material, the actual cost to produce and our one small profit, and on this basis we are able to offer you such values as have never been offered before. We have every confidence in holding your trade if we get your first order. We would only ask that you compare our $2.25 suit with any suit you can get elsewhere at 50 per cent. advance, and if you do not pronounce ours the best you can return it at our expense and we will cheerfully refund your money.

Our special price........................................$2.25

No. 4588. YOUTHS' $2.25 SUIT comes in Style 1 only, as shown in above illustration. Made from a good quality of wool finished cassimere, dark corkscrew effect, lined throughout with good lining, lined flaps on all pockets and a suit that would retail at double the price, while we offer this at the extraordinary low price of $2.55. You will find it equal to suits that retail at nearly double the price.

No. 4589. ONE OF OUR FIRST BARGAINS IS A YOUTH'S $2.95 LONG PANTS SUIT, made from a good quality strong wool surface cassimere, good year around weight. It comes in assorted patterns, light, medium and dark and all with neat check effects. We can furnish these suits in Styles 1 and 2 only. In ordering be sure to state style wanted, and also shade and we will guarantee to please you.

Special price........................................$2.95

No. 4590. OUR $3.25 YOUTHS' SUIT. This suit is made from an extra quality of cotton and wool mixed cassimere, the surface is nearly all wool, and in fact can only be told from wool by an expert. It comes in an assortment of patterns ranging from light gray to dark with neat check effects. The suit is well lined throughout, lined flaps on all pockets and comes in Styles 1 and 2; the price is the same. In ordering be sure to state style wanted and also give us an idea of the shade wanted and we will guarantee satisfaction.

No. 4591. YOUTHS' $3.55 SUIT. We furnish this suit in Styles 1, 2 and 3. No. 3 comes 50c extra. In ordering be sure to state the style wanted. This suit is made from a good quality brown and gray mixed all-wool cheviot. It is lined throughout with good serge lining, lined flaps on all pockets and well made in every respect. A suit we are selling at one-half the price charged by retail dealers.

Our special price........................................$3.55

No. 4592. OUR $3.95 BLACK AND BLUE CHEVIOT SUIT. We furnish this suit in either navy blue or black as desired. In ordering be sure to state color wanted. It comes in Styles 1, 2 and 3. Style 3 at 50 cents extra. It is made from a good quality all-wool cheviot, nicely lined throughout with Italian lining, coat is piped throughout with same material, lined flaps on all pockets and makes a very neat and dressy suit.

Our special price........................................$3.95

No. 4593. OUR $4.05 DARK GRAY ALL WOOL CHEVIOT SUIT, made from a very good quality of dark gray wool cheviot and comes in Styles 1, 2 and 3. Style 3 is 50 cents extra. In ordering be sure to state style wanted. It is lined throughout with a good quality serge lining, lined flaps on all pockets, comes in

Our Special Price........................................$4.05

DON'T FORGET OUR THREE PER CENT. DISCOUNT FOR CASH IN FULL WITH ORDER. IT NEARLY ALWAYS AMOUNTS TO ENOUGH TO PAY ALL EXPRESS CHARGES.

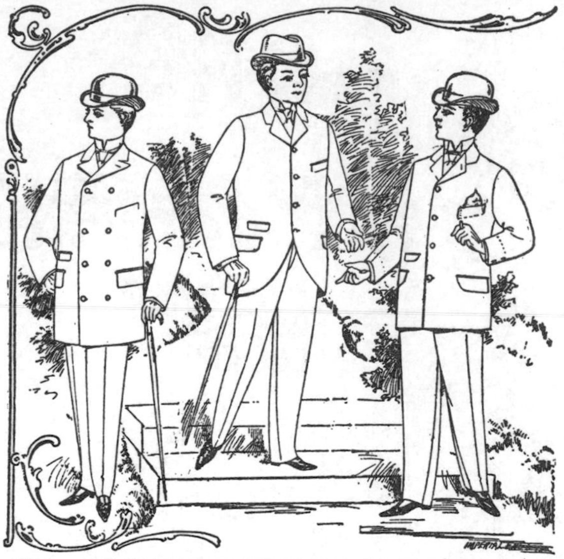

**No. 4594. OUR $4.10 BROWN MELTON SUIT IN STYLES 1, 2 and 3. Style 3 comes 50c extra.** This suit is well made, lined throughout with a good quality of serge lining, lined flaps on all pockets, and we are offering it at a price that will make you a saving of 33⅓ to 50%.

**Our special price** ........................................ **$4.10**

**No. 4595. OUR $4.55 YOUTHS' BLACK CHEVIOT SUIT, MADE FROM AN EXTRA QUALITY OF FINEST ALL-WOOL CHEVIOT.** Good weight, suitable for year around wear. It makes up very neat and dressy and we can furnish it in Styles 1, 2 and 3. **Style 3 is 50c extra.** It is lined throughout with good quality of serge lining, piped throughout with same material, nicely finished and pressed and a special bargain at our price.

**Our special price** ........................................ **$4.55**

**No. 4596. OUR $5.40 LINE OF YOUTHS' HIGH-GRADE CASSIMERE SUITS. This line is a special leader with us;** such suits as retail at $8.00 and $9.00. They are made from an excellent quality of all-wool Michigan Cassimere, one of the best weaves made, and we have them in about twenty shades, running from very light to medium and dark, in gray, brown and bluish shades, with small check and invisible plaids and stripes. Styles 1, 2 and 3. **Style 3 is 50c extra.** These suits are lined throughout with an extra quality of serge lining, flaps on all pockets and lined throughout. They are all fine tailor-made, gotten up in the very latest style by first-class tailors and are bargains that are sure to please.

**Our special price** ........................................ **$5.40**

**No. 4597. OUR $5.95 LINE HIGH-GRADE ALL-WOOL BLACK CHEVIOT SUITS. We furnish these suits in either the plain finished goods or the unfinished rough effect as desired,** and in Styles 1, 2 or 3 as desired. **No. 3 is 50c extra. This is one of the best black cheviot suits in the market;** it is nicely lined throughout with a good quality of serge lining, fancy piped throughout, well padded, nicely lined flaps on all pockets and gotten up in first-class style by the best tailors and such suits as retail in first-class stores at nearly double the price we ask. They come in very good weight, making them suitable for year around wear. **They are very popular as a dress or Sunday suit, to be worn on occasions every month of the year.**

**Our special price** ........................................ **$5.95**

**No. 4598. OUR $6.10 YOUTHS' ALL-WOOL TRICOT SUIT,** made from **navy blue all-wool tricot. This class of goods is so well known that** it is unnecessary for us to comment on its wearing qualities and dressy appearance in which the suit makes up. **It is fine tailor made,** lined throughout with an extra **quality of lining, fancy piped throughout, serge lined flaps** on all pockets, and comes in style 2 only.

**Our special price** ........................................ **$6.10**

**No. 4599. OUR $6.35 YOUTHS' SUIT, MADE FROM A VERY FINE GRADE OF ALL-WOOL OREGON CASSIMERE.** A small check light gray goods, lined throughout with a good quality of lining to match. Flaps on all pockets lined throughout. This suit comes in Styles 1, 2 and 3. **Style 3 is 50 cents extra.** Be sure to state style wanted

**Our special price** ........................................ **$6.35**

**No. 4600. OUR $6.65 YOUTH'S TRICOT-LONG,** either **dark gray** or **brown** as desired. **Be sure to state color wanted.** It comes in Style 1 only. **There is no better wearing goods made.** It is all-wool tricot that will **wear** like iron. Lined throughout with a very good quality of Italian lining, lined flaps on all pockets. **Our special price is** .................... **$6.65**

**No. 4601. OUR $7.50 FANCY WORSTED LINE. This class of goods is seldom seen made up in youths' suits.** It is a very fine quality of imported English all-wool worsted, such as is used in men's high-grade clothing, and will be found in all first-class establishments where men's suits are made to order at from $25.00 to $30.00 **We guarantee these suits to be fast color, all-wool worsted.** They come in a variety of shades, **gray, slate, blues** and **drab.** They are **lined throughout with a very fine quality of imported Italian lining,** wide satin piping throughout, very fancy striped sleeve lining, shoulders are well padded, lined flaps on all pockets. **These suits are gotten up in the highest style of the art** and with the same care as is bestowed on our highest grade men's suits. **There is nothing better in the market at the price.** For a real dressy, stylish, well-wearing garment for spring, summer or fall, we would recommend this line above all others. We have so much confidence in these goods that we have placed an order for 5,000 suits in men's sizes, and we therefore own the yardage cheaper than any other concern, and offer you these suits, made in boys' Style 1 and 2 at the heretofore unheard of price of ........................ **$7.50**

**No. 4602. OUR $7.60 YOUTHS' ALL-WOOL IMPORTED WORSTED SUITS.** Black or navy blue, as desired. Styles 1 or 2. as desired. These suits **are** made from **a very fine grade of medium weight imported English wide wale diagonal worsted. No neater, better wearing or more stylish** garment made at any price. **They are gotten up in the highest style** of the **art** by first-class tailors. Styles 1 and 2, lined throughout with fine quality of imported Italian lining. wide satin piping throughout, nicely padded and **finished.**

**We offer these suits at $7.60,** in competition with suits that retail in the finest stores in the land at double our price.

**No. 4603. OUR $7.95 YOUTHS' SUIT. Is made of very fine all-wool worsted in dark pin head checks,** rolling collar, wide flaps on all pockets, **nicely** lined, very handsomely finished throughout, lined with the very best **Italian** cloth, plain lining, fancy striped sleeve lining, satin piped, shoulders **are extra** well padded and stayed, hand-made buttonholes. This is, indeed, **a very beautiful suit,** one of the handsomest designs in worsted, and finest weave, **giving** a very genteel appearance, and we can **guarantee** that it will be very satisfactory in regard to wear and style.

# BOYS' BLACK CLAY WORSTED SUITS.

## FOR BOYS 10 TO 19 YEARS OF AGE.

**WE CHALLENGE COMPETITION** in this line. We cut up more Black and Navy Blue Clay Worsted cloth than any other **Five Concerns in America combined.**

**OUR BARGAINS** are bargains such as can be had from no other house.

**WE SELL A FINE TAILOR MADE SUIT** for less than one-half the price charged by local tailors. **Much less** than any retail clothier can sell at.

**BOYS' CLAY WORSTED SUITS** are made in the same manner as any Men's Clay Worsteds. **All the very latest style.** All cut by expert cutters, and made by the very best tailors we can employ.

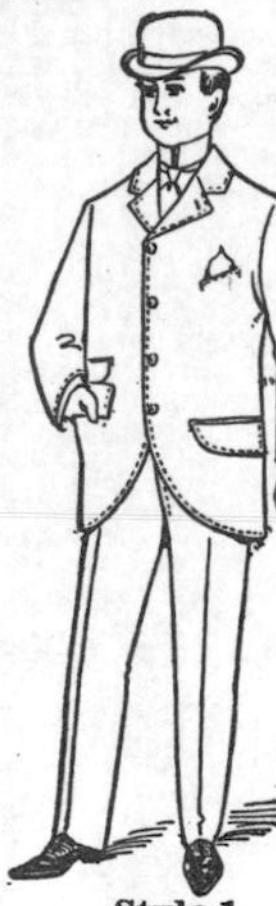

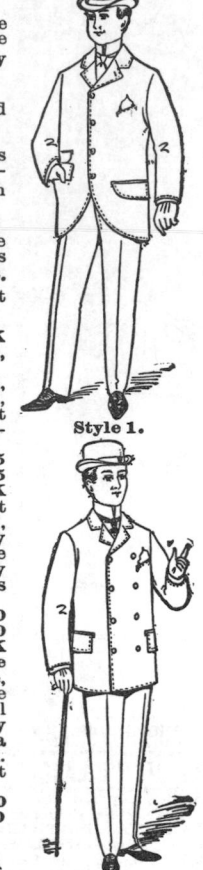

Style 1.

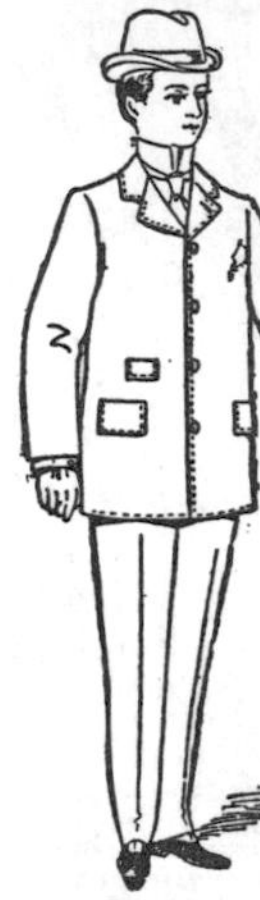

Style 2.

**No. 4604 BOYS' $5.95 BLACK CLAY WORSTED SUIT.** Style 1, 2 or 3. Style 3, 50 cents extra.

This suit is made from a good, light weight, imported, all wool, Black Clay Worsted cloth; coat lined with black Italian cloth, nicely trimmed and finished.

**Our price, Slyle 1 or 2** ........ **$5.95**
**Our price, Style 3** ............ **6.45**

**No. 4605 BOYS' $6.50 BLACK CLAY WORSTED SUIT.** This suit is made from a 14 ounce, all wool, imported Black English Clay Worsted Cloth, lined with a fine imported black Italian cloth, nicely trimmed and finished, and at $6.50 is a wonderful bargain.

**Price, Style 1 or 2** ............ **$6.50**
**Price, Style 3** .................. **7.00**

**No. 4606 BOYS' $7.50 BLACK CLAY WORSTED SUIT.** The Finest Clay Worsted Suit we make, **no tailor would make better.** Made from a good, year round weight, all wool, imported Black English Clay Worsted Cloth; coat lined with a fine imported black Italian cloth. Every garment sewed throughout with silk and linen.

**Price for boys suit, Style 1 or 2** .................. **$7.50**
**Price for boys suit, Style 3** ....................... **8.00**

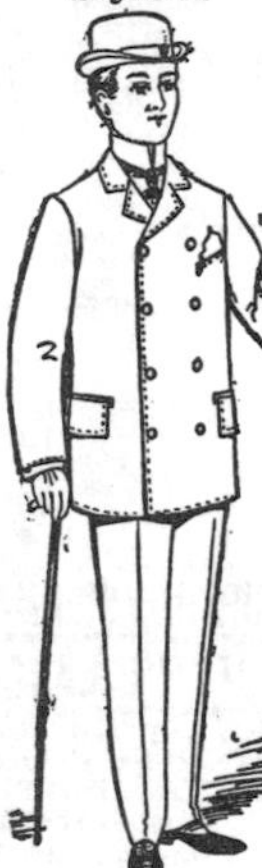

Style 3.

**Order by Catalogue Number, and don't fail to give sizes and styles wanted**

# BOYS' LONG PANTS.

**Our clothing department is so extensive** that we can safely say there is nothing made in the line of clothing, either in men's, boys' or children's that cannot be had from our establishment at from a saving of 33⅓ to 50 per cent over any prices you can possibly get elsewhere. **If you are in want of clothing send your orders to us.** We believe we can say without fear of contradiction that we are prepared to serve you in this line as no other concern can. **We have earned a reputation of being the largest dealers in clothing in America** and our facilities for purchasing these goods are second to none. **All the garments we handle are made by first-class tailors, all cut on the latest style patterns and every garment is fully warranted.**

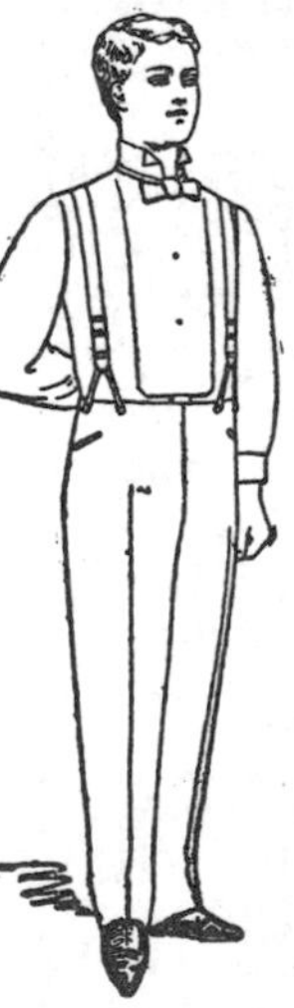

**We contract with the mills both in this country and in** Europe for large quantities of clothing and with our facilities for cutting and making them up we are prepared to furnish you the goods direct at less money than your dealer can buy. **We have boys' long pants in endless variety,** but for want of space we quote you only our special leaders, and it will pay you to consider them before placing your orders elsewhere.

**RULES FOR MEASUREMENT.**

**Boys' pants are made to fit boys 10 to 19 years of age,** and measurements should be taken exactly the same **as** for men. See our rules for measurement.

**We have boys' pants in waist measure ranging from 27 to 31 inches;** also state inside seam, number of inches from tight in crotch to heel. **(See rules for measurement.) We have boys' pants ranging in size 26 to 31 inches inside seam. Also state number of inches around body at hips,** as per rules for measurement. **Boys' pants will be shipped to any address on the same terms as our other clothing.** Send us $1.00 as a guarantee of good faith and we will send you the pants by express, C. O. D., subject to examination. **You can examine them** at the express office and if found perfectly satisfactory and exactly as represented, pay the express agent the balance and express charges and the pants are yours.

**In placing orders for clothing or other merchandise** we would advise you to include such goods in this line as are needed; also all other light merchandise; in so doing you reduce the express-charges to next to nothing. We call your attention to the following special bargains:

**No. 4607. 75 CENTS BUYS BOYS' $1.50 PANTS.** These pants are made of a very good grade of wool and cotton mixed cassimere. They come in a variety of shades ranging from light to dark. Give us an idea of the shade wanted and we will guarantee to please you. Understand, they are nicely made, trimmed and finished, and are warranted in every respect.

**No. 4608. $1.00 BUYS A REGULAR $2.00 PANTS. These pants are made of a very good quality of western cassimere,** they are regular wear-resisting goods, nicely made and trimmed, reinforced in every respect. They come in a variety of colors, ranging from medium and dark shades. Give us an idea of the shade wanted and we will guarantee perfect satisfaction.

**No. 4609. BOYS' BLACK CHEVIOT PANTS FOR $1.75.** These pants are made from a very good grade of all-wool imported black cheviot, cut on the latest style patterns for the season of 1896, nicely trimmed and finished and tailor-made throughout. We offer these pants in competition with those that retail at even double the money.

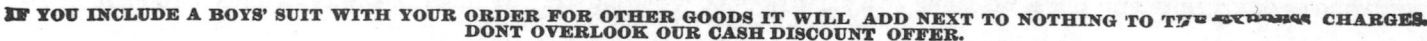

**IF YOU INCLUDE A BOYS' SUIT WITH YOUR ORDER FOR OTHER GOODS IT WILL ADD NEXT TO NOTHING TO THE EXPRESS CHARGES. DONT OVERLOOK OUR CASH DISCOUNT OFFER.**

## BOYS' LONG PANTS.—Continued.

**No. 4610. OUR $1.95 LINE. We have a very fine line of boys' $1.95 pants,** a line of pants that would retail at from $3.00 to $4.00; in fact, goods that are equal to anything a local dealer would make at $5.00 to $7.00. We have these $1.95 pants in endless variety and patterns, made specially for the spring, summer and fall wear and for the season of 1896, but they are heavy enough for year-around wear. They are cut on the latest style patterns by experienced cutters to fit perfectly, fine tailor-made throughout; in fact, you cannot get a better pair of pants if you go to your local tailor and pay $6.00 or $7.00. They are reinforced in every respect, nothing but silk and linen thread used in the sewing, hip pockets reinforced, both side pockets reinforced, made from a very fine quality of all-wool Wisconsin cassimere and regular wear-resisting material. Makes up very neat and dressy, and give the appearance of pants that would cost double the price. We have this line of $1.95 goods in endless variety, as above explained, including light gray with small pin check, gray with small plaid, dark gray, gray pin check, light brown pin check, light, medium and dark stripes; in fact, if you will give us an idea of what is wanted in the shade and color we will take pleasure in sending you such a pair of pants as was never seen in your section at anything like the price.

**No. 4611. OUR $2.95 CLAY WORSTED LINE. We offer at $2.95 a fine tailor-made worsted pants that no local dealer would make at less than $6.00.** These pants will be sent to any address by express, C. O. D., subject to examination, on receipt of $1.00. They are made from a fine grade of 16 oz. all-wool imported black English clay worsted, one of the highest grade clay worsteds made. Made by a mill in England whose reputation for the manufacture of high grade worsted is so well known that no comment from us is necessary. They are elegantly lined, trimmed and finished, and we offer them at $2.95 in competition with anything that you can get made at double the price.

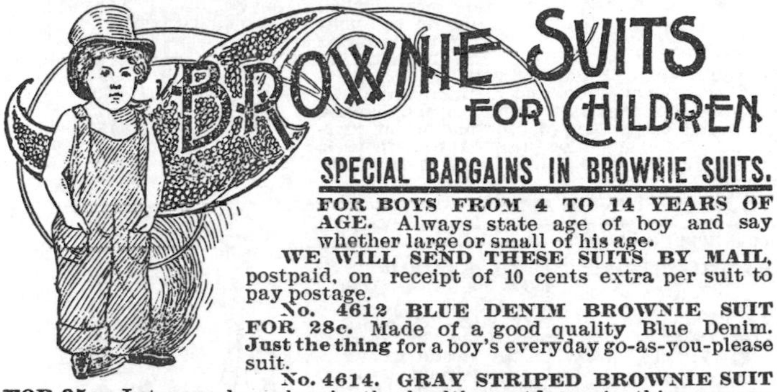


**SPECIAL BARGAINS IN BROWNIE SUITS.**

**FOR BOYS FROM 4 TO 14 YEARS OF AGE.** Always state age of boy and say whether large or small of his age.

**WE WILL SEND THESE SUITS BY MAIL,** postpaid, on receipt of 10 cents extra per suit to pay postage.

**No. 4612 BLUE DENIM BROWNIE SUIT FOR 28c.** Made of a good quality Blue Denim. **Just the thing** for a boy's everyday go-as-you-please suit.

**No. 4614. GRAY STRIPED BROWNIE SUIT FOR 35c.** Let your boy play in the healthy outdoor air this summer dressed in a Brownie Suit. **They are all the style this season.**

**No. 4616. EXTRA QUALITY DENIM.** In blue, gray and striped Extra heavy wear-resisting.

**OUR BROWNIE SUITS** will delight your boy, they are worn everywhere this season. Our price per suit, 50c.

## WHAT THE PEOPLE SAY.

**Would Not Take $8.00 for His $4.98 Suit.**

SUBLIME, TEX.

SEARS, ROEBUCK & CO., Chicago, Ill.

DEAR SIRS:—The suit of clothes you sent have arrived. I am well pleased. I would not take $8.00 for it. Paid $4.98. Please accept thanks.

Yours truly, S. W. ADAMS.

**Better Satisfied Than Expected.**

MILAN, GA.

SEARS, ROEBUCK & CO., Chicago, Ill.

GENTLEMEN:—I have received my clothes; am better satisfied than expected. Will do all in my power for you in the future.

Very respectfully yours, WORTEZ JOINER.

**Neighbors Hardly Believe Him When He Tells The Price.**

SEARS, ROEBUCK & CO., Chicago. BURR OAK, MO.

DEAR SIRS:—I received the suit of clothes I ordered from you and it is a very fine one. I could not have got a better fit if I had been there. I would have written to you sooner but have been very sick and could not try them on. If I ever need another suit I will remember you. I am very well pleased with it. I have showed it to some of my neighbors and they hardly believe me when I tell them what I paid for it.

Yours truly, GEO. HAFER.

**Suit Would Have Cost Him $10.00 There.**

MCGONIGLE, OHIO.

SEARS, ROEBUCK & CO.

DEAR SIRS:—I received the suit in good order and am confident it would have cost me ten dollars at our local clothiers. I will do all in my power to promote your interests in this vicinity. Please send me one of your Gun and Sporting Goods catalogues for 1897, as I expect to buy something in that line later on.

Yours hastily, CLARK D. NELSON.

**Suits Better Than Expected.**

MORLEY, MICH.

SEARS, ROEBUCK & CO.

DEAR SIRS:—I received the suits in good condition and are better than expected. I would have to pay $6 per suit here.

I remain, Yours truly. OTTO PLATH.

**Pleased With Suit as Well as With Everything Ordered.**

RUSSELLVILLE, KY.

GENTLEMEN:—I received the blue tailor-made suit I ordered from you, and was greatly pleased, and we were with everything ordered from your house. Will you please mail me your catalogue of books? Wishing you all success, and thanking you for your kindness, I am

Respectfully yours. MISS ELOISE WHITAKER.

**Mr. McKinney is so Well Pleased With His Goods that He Sends These Testimonials of His Neighbors.**

CLEAR SPRING, S. C.

SEARS, ROEBUCK & CO.

GENTLEMEN:—The suit that I ordered a few days previous has arrived, and am well pleased. I have showed it to my friends, and I give a few of their testimonials below. Yours truly, THOS. F. MCKINNEY.

SEARS, ROEBUCK & CO. SIMPSONVILLE, S. C.

GENTLEMEN:—The suit of clothes that Thos. F. McKinney bought of you is worth twice the money he gave for it. Sears, Roebuck & Co.'s is the cheapest supply house in the world. Yours truly, R. M. LEAGUE.

SEARS, ROEBUCK & CO. CLEAR SPRING, S. C.

GENTLEMEN:—I don't see how you can sell such fine suits for the money. I have seen the suit you sent Thos. F. McKinney and I think it is a magnificent suit. Sears, Roebuck & Co. must be the cheapest bargain house in the world. Respectfully yours, T. D. WOOD.

# CHILDREN'S DEPARTMENT

# JUVENILE CLOTHING.....

**The Most Stylish, Best Wearing, and Cheapest ever Sold.**

**We dress the boy from 3 to 19 years of age, HEAD TO FOOT. EVERYTHING FOR SPRING AND SUMMER OF 1896.** All the latest styles, all the novelties for the season. **OUR FANCY JUVENILE SUITS** will make the **BOY'S HEART GLAD.** It will make the **proud mother happy and SURPRISE THE FATHER,** for at last he can clothe his boys in the nobbiest of suits at a cost **NEXT TO NOTHING.**

**DON'T FORGET THE BOYS this summer.** The suit you buy him now he is likely to remember the longest day he lives, one of those tender recollections we are wont to look back into our childhood days as the much-appreciated, never-to-be-forgotten gift of a generous parent. **DON'T BE STINGY WITH THE BOY. We have 2-piece suits, 4-piece combination suits, sailor suits, reefer suits. SUCH A COMPLETE LINE** as can be had nowhere else.

**WE CAN FIT YOUR BOY.** State age of boy and say whether large or small for age and we will guarantee a fit.

**OUR TERMS** are so reasonable we will send any suit by express, C. O. D., subject to examination on receipt of $1.00. You can examine the suit at the express office and if found perfectly satisfactory, and exactly as represented, pay the express agent the balance and the express charges and the pants are yours.

**It will pay you to order several suits at a time.**

**By so doing you will save transportation charges.** A boy's 2-piece combination suit weighs but very little, for the express company will charge from 25 to 35 cents for transportation, according to the distance, no matter how small or light the package may be, and by adding two or three suits in making your order you do not increase the express charges. **We would, therefore, advise you to influence your neighbors to join with you in making a club order and thus reduce the express charges on a single suit to next to nothing.**

**Where it is practicable to send by mail** we have quoted the postage rate and on all garments weighing 24 ozs. or under, we would recommend shipping by mail, the rate being 1 cent per oz., in which case enough extra should accompany your order to prepay postage.

**You will observe many of our 2-piece suits can be sent by mail at from 8 to 15 cents, thus saving you from 17 to 25 cents express charges and delivering the goods directly at your nearest postoffice.**

**In making up your order for clothing do not omit any item you may be likely to need,** for understand the addition of one or two items adds nothing to the transportation charges when it is to be shipped by express or freight; but when ordered separately it is quite expensive, and to this end we would urge you to make up a club order when possible, getting as many of your friends and neighbors to join with you in sending their order. **You can examine the goods at the express office,** and any that are not perfectly satisfactory can be returned at our expense; those that are satisfactory will be delivered and the agent will collect the same.

**Understand, you take no risk in ordering** from this department whether you send cash in full or order the goods shipped C. O. D., subject to examination. **Every garment is guaranteed to be exactly as represented** and if not found so and perfectly satisfactory and a perfect fit, you can return it at our expense and we will cheerfully refund your money.

**The encouragement we have received that the past season has induced us to make the Juvenile Department** one of the leading features of our business and no pains have been spared in selecting a line of staple and novelties, which in variety, style, finish and price cannot be equaled by anything in the market. We have selected only the very latest styles for the season of 1896; everything is strictly modern, up to date in every respect. **Our goods are all made by first-class tailors,** cut by experienced cutters and gotten up in the highest style of the art.

**You will find a distinctiveness in our juvenile clothing** which is not seen in goods carried by the average retail dealer. Such goods as we offer are gotten up specially for city trade and will be found in the representative clothing stores in large cities, for on our system of one small profit direct from manufacturer to consumer, under the terms and conditions of our contract for this line of goods for the season of 1896, we are able to offer you the highest grade of juvenile clothing made and at prices against which our competitors will not be able to compete even on the cheap commonplace goods with which the market is always flooded.

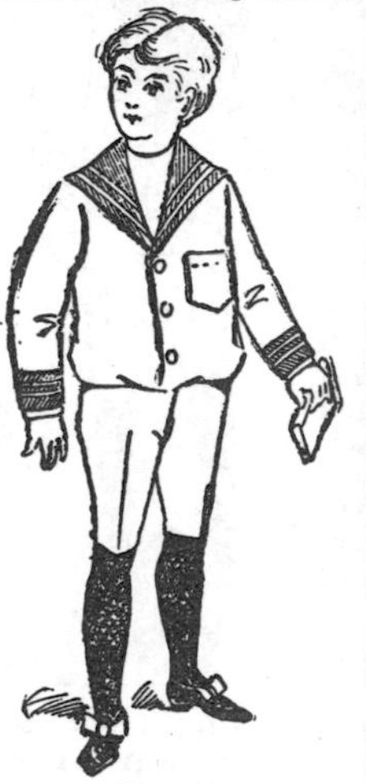

No. 4185.

**First in this line** we would call your attention to our wash goods suits, a line of high class children's novelty suits; gotten up by one of the largest and most reliable manufacturers in New York, a concern whose reputation for the manufacture of high-class juvenile clothing is second to none. **Every garment is fine tailor made,** of the latest style, made to fit perfectly and such goods as are sure to meet with the approval of the buyer.

**No. 4184. OUR 75 CENT LINE. We offer here a line of children's two-piece suits at 75 cents** which cannot be equaled in your local market at less than $1.25. **We are extremely anxious to receive your trade,** anxious to receive your order for one of these suits, not for the little profit there is in it to us, but for the good it will do us as an advertisement; for we know you will be so well pleased with the suit that you will show it to your friends, tell them where you bought it and what you paid for it, and in that way we will get many more orders in your neighborhood.

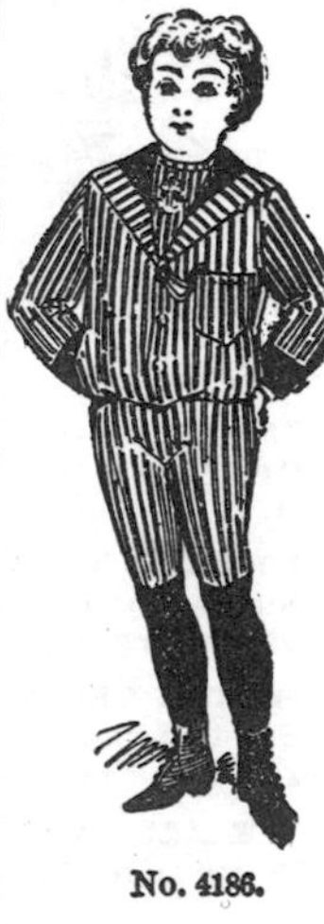

No. 4186.

**These suits run in sizes from 3 to 10 years of age.** Be sure to state age of boy and whether large or small of his age.

**No. 4185. TWO-PIECE SAILOR SUIT.** Wash goods, consisting of one light blue sailor blouse and one pair of knee pants. This suit is made of striped pique, warranted fast color. It is good weight and a good wearing material, nicely made with large, square back sailor collar, lapel front. Collar, cuffs and lapel made of plain blue pique to match stripe in the garment. Collar and cuffs trimmed with two rows of fairy stitch braid, one outside pocket in blouse, with ivory buttons. Each suit is furnished with a whistle and cord. Price, per suit, 75 cents. The postage 10 cents per suit extra.

**No. 4186. BOYS' TWO-PIECE WASH GOODS SUIT,** made of heavy navy blue with pencil stripe, square sailor collar, lapel front and cuffs of plain navy blue, trimmed with two rows of pique braid, ivory buttons and surplice front, one outside pocket. Price per suit 75 cents. The postage 10 cents per suit extra.

**OUR SPECIAL DISCOUNT OF 3 PER CENT. FOR CASH WILL OFTEN PAY THE EXPRESS ON A SUIT.**

**No. 4187. BOYS' TWO-PIECE SUIT,** made of twilled tan color nankeen, one outside pocket, square sailor collar, lapel front with surplice, handsomely embroidered with a red anchor, ivory buttons down the front, with pants to match. Price per suit, 75 cents.

The following suits ranging in prices from $1.05 to $1.25 for boys' two-piece suits are the latest style and goods that are sure to give the best of satisfaction. We specially refer these suits to your favorable consideration, and we feel confident that if you favor us with an order as a trial, will result in our getting many more orders from your neighbors. We would advise you to place your order as early as possible, for our stock, although very large, is moving rapidly and will be sold out before the season is very far advanced.

In ordering these goods to go by mail be sure to enclose the necessary amount to pay postage.

Understand, any garment that does not fit, does not give perfect satisfaction, can be returned at our expense and your money will be cheerfully refunded. We offer you this special line of children's two-piece wash suits as special leaders, bargains against which we recognize no competitors.

No. 4187.

**No. 4188. BOYS' TWO-PIECE BLOUSE SUIT** made of navy blue wash duck, thoroug. made throughout, double stitched, outside pocket, square sailor collar with lapel front, handsomely embroidered with white anchor and two embroidered stars in the back of the square collar, pearl buttons, with pants to match, price per suit, $1.05. Postage 10 cents extra.

**No. 4189. BOYS' TWO-PIECE SUIT** made of extra heavy twilled navy blue duck with pencil stripe, blouse suit, plain navy blue, square sailor collar with surplice, embroidered with white anchor and two stars in back, striped border all around the collar, ivory buttons, outside pocket, thoroughly made throughout. Price per suit, $1.10. Postage 10 cents extra.

No. 4189.

No. 4188.

**No. 4190. BOYS' TWO-PIECE SUIT** made of narrow light blue striped twilled duck, outside pocket, square sailor collar with lapel front, with surplice and cuffs made of plain light blue duck, to correspond with the stripe, collar and surplice handsomely trimmed with two rows of white galloon braid, white ivory buttons. This garment is handsomely made throughout. Price per suit, $1.15. Postage 10 cents extra.

**No. 4191. ONE OF THE NOBBIEST SUITS CREATED** this season, made of heavy cream sateen, with navy blue duck square collar and cuffs, cream surplice, handsomely embroidered anchor in center, pearl buttons, outside pocket, extra well made. Price, $1.25 per suit. Postage 10 cents extra.

No. 4190.

No. 4191.

**No. 4192. BOYS' $1.25 SAILOR SUIT.** Nothing finer within 50 per cent of the price. You will find no such goods in an ordinary retail store, and if you are interested in buying goods direct from the manufacturer at the lowest wholesale prices, surely these goods will interest you. This suit is made of an extra heavy quality striped wear-resisting duck, made especially for boys' sailor suits, has a very large square fancy collar, nicely trimmed with braid. These suits are well-finished in every respect, and there is nothing better for boys from 3 to 8 years of age.

No. 4192.

**No. 4193. $1.10 BUYS A BOYS' REGULAR $2.00 SAILOR SUIT** for boys from 3 to 8 years of age. At 10c. extra we will send this suit by mail, postage prepaid. It is made from an extra quality, wear-resisting duck, nicely trimmed and finished, with very fancy large square collar, and is one of the most stylish suits on the market for this spring and summer. We offer you a line of children's clothing such as has never been shown before and at prices which we feel sure will interest all economic buyers. We are anxious to receive your order for one of our juvenile suits, not so much for the little profit there is in it, but for the good it will do us as an advertisement.

We know you will be so well pleased that you will favor us with future orders; also influence your friends in our behalf.

**No. 4194. BOYS' FANCY SAILOR SUIT FOR $1.15.** This suit is made up in the very latest style for boys from 3 to 8 years of age, made from a heavy, strong, wear-resisting duck, with very fancy large square collar, nicely embroidered and finished. Each suit comes with a cord and whistle. At 10c. extra we will send the suit by mail, postage paid.

**No. 4195. BOYS' $1.45 TWO-PIECE SUIT.** This suit is made from a very fine quality flannel, in either navy blue, tan, slate, or brown, as desired, well made and trimmed and guaranteed in every respect. It is the latest style for the spring and summer of 1896, fine tailor-made throughout and one of the very latest patterns. There is nothing more stylish for a boy from 3 to 8 years of age. At 15c. extra we will send this suit by mail, postage prepaid.

No. 4193.

No. 4195.

No. 4194.

**No. 4196. $1.25 BUYS A BOYS' TWO-PIECE SUIT,** which cannot be duplicated in any store within 50 per cent of our price. These suits are made for boys from 3 to 8 years of age. Made of a very fine quality heavy tricot flannel, in blue, tan, slate, or brown, as desired, nicely trimmed and finished, and a suit we can guarantee in every respect.

**No. 4197. BOYS' FANCY TWO-PIECE SAILOR WASH SUIT FOR $1.12.** A suit that would retail in any first-class store at double our special offer price. This suit will be sent by mail for 12c. extra to pay postage. These suits are made for boys from 3 to 8 years of age. In ordering, be sure to state age of boy and say whether large or small of his age. This suit is made from a very large strong blue and red stripe duck, has a very large square collar, scalloped, and nicely bound with white binding, large scalloped front, large scalloped cuffs, one fancy trimmed pocket.

No. 4196.

No. 4197.

**IF YOU ONLY WANT ONE SUIT** we recommend ordering it sent by mail; enclose enough extra to pay postage, but when packed with other goods it will add nothing to freight or express charges.

**BE SURE TO STATE AGE OF BOY** in ordering clothing, and always remember the larger your order the less the transportation charges will be in proportion.

**BY EXPRESS 25 cents** will pay the charges on 4 or 5 suits to most any point. It will pay you to get your neighbors to join with you in ordering these goods.

**WE RECOMMEND 100 POUND** orders to go by freight. This can be easily arranged by adding the needed groceries to your order.

**REMEMBER** you always get your goods from us at lowest wholesale prices. No one can buy cheaper.

**INCLUDE YOUR BOY'S SUIT WITH YOUR OWN. IT WILL ADD NOTHING TO THE EXPRESS CHARGES.**

**No. 4198. EXTRA GOOD VALUE, HEAVY PIN STRIPE,** with fancy navy blue square sailor collar, bordered with a wide stripe revere, inside border to match, with navy blue surplice, trimmed to match collar and cuffs. Outside pocket and pearl buttons, making a very attractive and serviceable garment, something that we can recommend and guarantee to give extra good satisfaction. Price $1.25. Postage, 10c. extra.

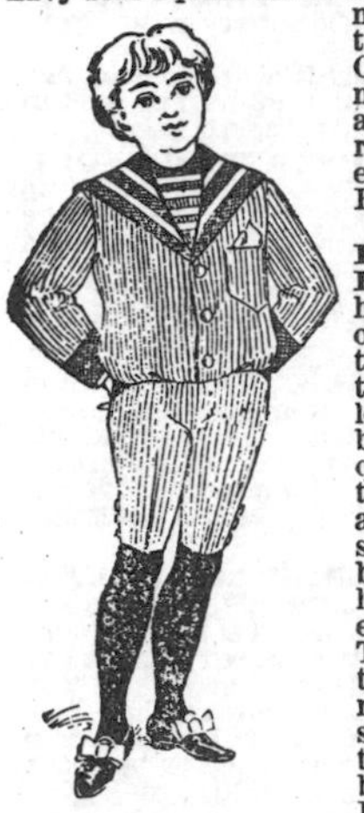

No. 4198.

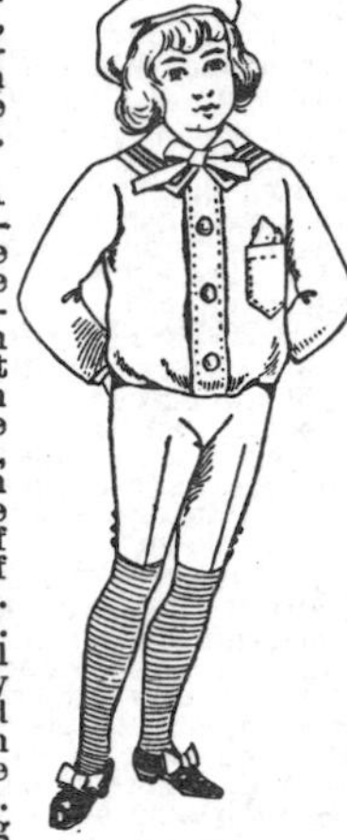

No. 4199.

**No. 4199. $1.15 BUYS A REGULAR $2.00 BOYS' TWO-PIECE SUIT.** A garment to be had from no other concern. We are offering these suits direct to our customers on our one small profit from the factory to the consumer plan, at less money than the same goods can be bought by retail dealers in large quantities. They come in navy blue, tan, slate, or brown, as desired, in ages 3 to 10 years. In ordering, be sure to state color wanted and age of boy, and whether large or small of his age. If to be sent by mail, 10c. extra should accompany your order. These suits are made of all-wool tricot, double stitched and thoroughly made throughout, outside pocket and square sailor collar, trimmed with three rows of three cord soutache braid and silk ribbon bow in front. Ivory buttons, heavy elastic gathering string at waist. The pants are extra well made, with felled seam, three small ivory buttons at the bottom to match the blouse, extra well-made bands and finely finished.

**No. 4200. OUR SPECIAL $1.95 FOUR-PIECE COMBINATION SUIT,** consisting of one jacket, two pairs of knee pants and one cap; sizes run from ages 3 to 10 and in navy blue, brown, tan and drab. If to be sent by mail, send 15 cents extra to pay postage. The suits are exactly the same as our No. 4199, with the exception of the extra pair of pants and cap which constitutes the four-piece combination suit.

We are offering you at $1.95 a special leader, and we would urge you to place your order immediately, as the demand will surely exhaust the supply before the season is very far advanced. There is nothing on the market that will begin to compare with these, either for style, quality or finish at anything like the price. Give us a trial order; let us send you one suit, and if you do not pronounce it the greatest bargain you have ever seen in a boys' four-piece combination, all-wool, tailor-made sailor suit, return it at our expense, and we will cheerfully refund your money. Understand, we are offering these goods to you as strictly up-to-date, high-art, tailor-made novelty suits for children, and the goods should not be compared with those handled by the average retail dealer.

Under the old system of a long chain of profits from manufacturer to your local dealer, it has been impossible to get these goods at anything like our price; but bridging all this unnecessary cost and offering goods to you direct from the factory, we are able to put you in possession of strictly high-grade novelty suits at prices that will admit of your getting the best. We have the cheaper and more common children's suits in the different styles in combination and at correspondingly low prices, as hereinafter illustrated.

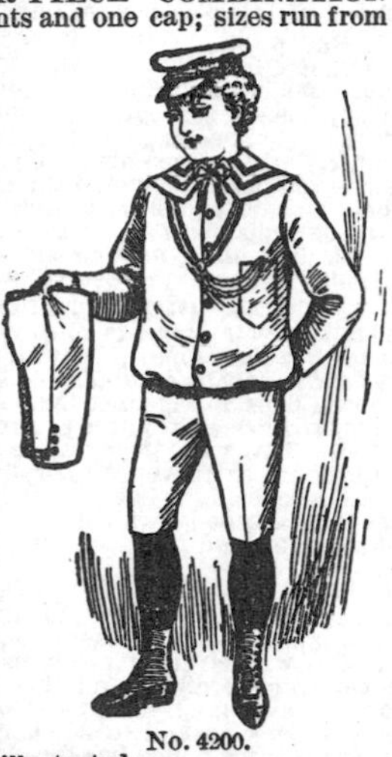

No. 4200.

**No. 4201. OUR $2.25 TWO-PIECE BROADCLOTH SAILOR SUIT,** in navy blue, slate color, or tan, as desired. These suits come in sizes, ages 3 to 10. Be sure to state the age of boy and whether large or small of his age, and also state color desired. If you wish the suit sent by mail enclose 18 cents extra to pay postage. Understand, any of these goods will be sent by express C. O. D., subject to examination, on receipt of $1.00, but if ordering only one suit, you will save transportation charges by enclosing the additional amount to cover postage and have the suit come by mail. It will pay you handsomely to order several suits at a time, as the express charges on three or four suits will not amount to over 25 or 30 cents to any point in the United States. Order one of these suits at $2.25, examine it at the express office or in your home, and if you do not say it is a bargain worth more than the price asked, as we are saving you at least 33⅓ per cent., return it at our expense and we will cheerfully refund your money. These $2.25 suits are high-art garments, made by one of the best and most reliable makers in New York, a concern that employs none but skilled tailors. The garments are cut on the latest patterns for the season of 1896 and such as will be found only in high-class clothing stores in cities. On our system we put you in a position to own the best at prices heretofore paid for inferior goods. These suits are made of good weight, serviceable broadcloth, large square back sailor collar, with lapel front and cuffs, handsomely trimmed with hercules braid, one inch wide, surplice fronts, with anchor, handsomely embroidered and underlined, outside pocket, double stitched and extra well-made throughout, heavy elastic gathering-string at waist, rubber buttons. The pants are extra well-made, with a felled outside seam and continuous band, small buttons to match the blouse. This is indeed a very stylish garment and something we can recommend to give perfect satisfaction.

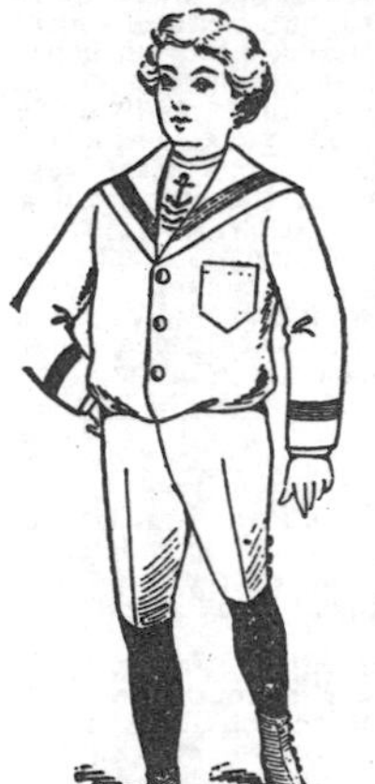

No. 4201.

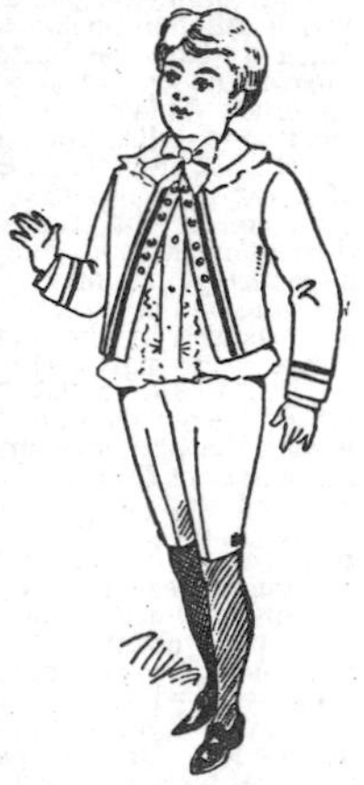

No. 4202.

**No. 4202. OUR $2.25 TWO-PIECE CHILDREN'S JUNIOR SUIT,** in sizes ages 3 to 8. Be sure to state age, and say whether boy is large or small of his age. If to be sent by mail, enclose 15 cents extra to pay postage. This garment is made of a fine gray mixed cheviot cassimere, handsomely bound neck, front and cuffs trimmed with a fine galloon braid and very small silk buttons, finely lined, with inside pocket, extra well-made pants, continuous band, extra well-made button holes and the bottom ornamented with small nickelplated buckle. Something very neat and pretty for the junior.

**No. 4203. OUR HIGH-ART $2.30 EXTRA FINE QUALITY NAVY BLUE WOOL CHEVIOT** children's junior suits, age 3 to 8. Be sure to state age and say whether the boy is large or small of his age. If to be sent by mail enclose 15 cents extra to pay postage; but the better way is to order several suits and have them come by express and thereby reduce the transportation charges. We offer this suit at $2.30 in competition with two-piece junior suits that retail at clothing stores from $3.50 and upwards. If, upon examination you do not find the suit equal to those sold by retail dealers at $3.50 you are at liberty to return the suit at our expense and we will cheerfully refund your money. This suit is handsomely cut in a new design, round sailor collar and lapel front, which is handsomely trimmed with silk braid and two rows of silk ball buttons, with cuffs to match; slashed on each side of the back and trimmed with soutache braid, with pants to match.

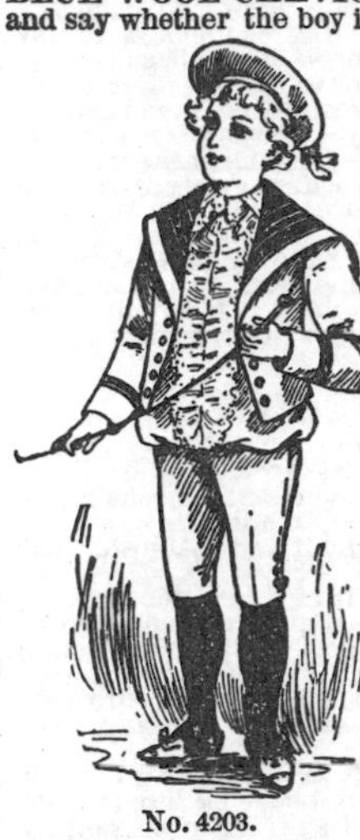

No. 4203.

**No. 4204. OUR SPECIAL $3.40 FANCY ZOUAVE CHILDREN'S SUIT,** ages 3 to 10. Be sure to state age of boy and say whether large or small of his age. If to be sent by mail enclose 16 cents extra to pay postage. This is one of the finest two-pieced suits we make, and would retail at any first-class house for nearly double our price. If you will send us $1.00 and allow us to send you this suit by express subject to examination we feel confident that you will not only accept it and be well pleased with your bargain, but we think it will be the means of our selling more goods of this department in your neighborhood. This suit is made of a fine brown pin stripe cassimere, neck handsomely bound and stitched, large lapels, beautifully trimmed with five rows of soutache braid and small silk ball buttons, slashed on each side of the back and trimmed with soutache braid, cuffs handsomely trimmed with three-quarter inch braid and one row of soutache braid, ornamented with two little silk ball buttons to match the front. Very handsomely lined with one outside pocket bound with silk braid. Pants are extra well-made, double stitched, continuous band, extra well made buttonholes, one hip pocket and ornamented with buckle and bow at bottom of each leg. This makes a very stylish and dressy little suit.

## CHILDREN'S TWO-PIECE REEFER SUITS.

**OUR LINE OF REEFER SUITS IS VERY COMPLETE** and we are prepared to furnish you these goods in endless variety at prices that will admit of no competition. **We present for your consideration four special bargains** selected from our stock, bargains such as have never been before offered. They are made by a concern whose reputation for the manufacture of high-art juvenile goods ought to be a sufficient guarantee for their quality, and on the basis of the highest grade of goods at prices that will save you from 33⅓ to 50 per cent we earnestly request the privilege of sending you at least one suit to examine and if not found perfectly satisfactory and exactly as represented, you can return it at our expense and we will cheerfully refund your money. These suits run in sizes, ages 3 to 8. **Be sure to state age of boy and say whether large or small of his age.**

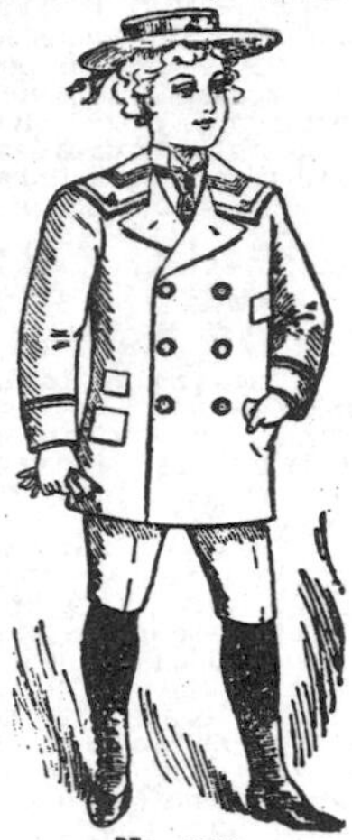

No. 4205.

**No. 4205. A TWO-PIECE REEFER SUIT AT $1.58,** made of a good grade of all-wool imported navy blue cheviot is a suit that is sure to please you, as it is one that cannot be equaled in your local market within 50 per cent of our price. It is nicely lined throughout with serge lining and fancy sleeve lining, well sewed throughout, full-sized flaps on pockets, lined throughout, three outside pockets to coat, large square sailor collar nicely finished with three rows of soutache braid all around, collar lined throughout with good quality serge lining, sleeves trimmed with three rows of soutache braid and finished with two buttons on each sleeve. Knee pants well made with continuous reinforced band, three buttons at bottom of each pant leg, two pockets in pants.

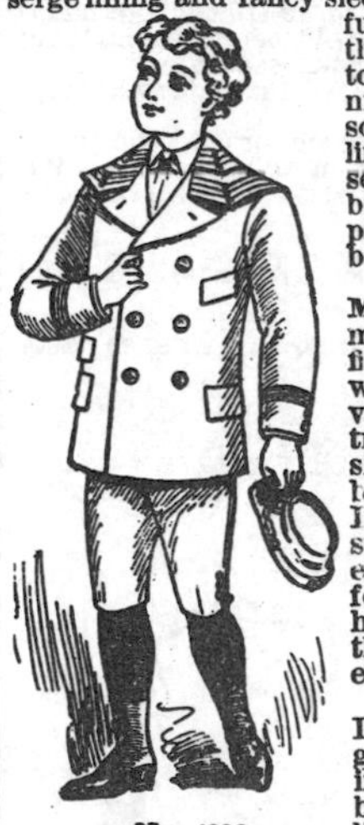

No. 4206.

**No. 4206. OUR $3.35 FINE ALL-WOOL CASSIMERE REEFER SUIT** for boys from ages 3 to 8. By mail 25 cents extra to pay postage. This is one of the very finest all-wool reefer suits, made of an extra quality of all-wool cassimere gray mixed basket pattern, made up in a very dressy manner, square back sailor collar, handsomely trimmed with two wide and four narrow braids, three outside pockets and cuffs trimmed to match the collar, double-breasted and slashed lapel front, beautifully lined with fine Italian cloth, one inside pocket, sleeves lined with fine striped silecia, extra well made pants with reinforced bands, extra well made buttonholes; also having the elastic loops for the back buttons, extra well stayed at crotch, with one hip pocket and side pockets, each leg ornamented with three satin bows with steel buckle, making something extra fine and desirable.

**No. 4207. OUR $4.35 REEFER.** If you can afford to pay $4.35 for a high-grade reefer suit we will take pleasure in sending you such a suit as has never been seen in your section at anything like the price; a better suit no doubt than has ever been seen in your market. At least if you do not find it so upon examination, you are at liberty to return it at our expense and we will cheerfully refund your money. It runs in sizes ages 3 to 8, and when ordering be sure and state age of boy and say whether large or small of his age. If you wish the suit sent by mail, enclose 22 cents extra to pay postage. We are exceedingly anxious to get your order for some of our higher grade suits, not that there is any more profit in it for us; but they are works of art, strictly first-class tailor-made; nothing has been spared or left undone to make them the best that can be had at any price, and such suits as are sure to advertise us wherever they go; in fact the best advertisement we can possibly have is a well-pleased customer, and these are suits that are made to satisfy.

This suit is made of a very fine imported all-wool dark gray and brown mixed cassimere. It is regular wear-resisting goods and will outwear three of the ordinary suits such as you will see every day in the local clothing stores. Cut on the latest pattern of 1896 it presents a very stylish appearance, lined throughout with a good quality of serge lining in a suitable color to match, very good grade of sleeve lining, very large square sailor collar, lined throughout with high-grade Italian lining, large fancy lapel lined with material same as the suit. It is finished with

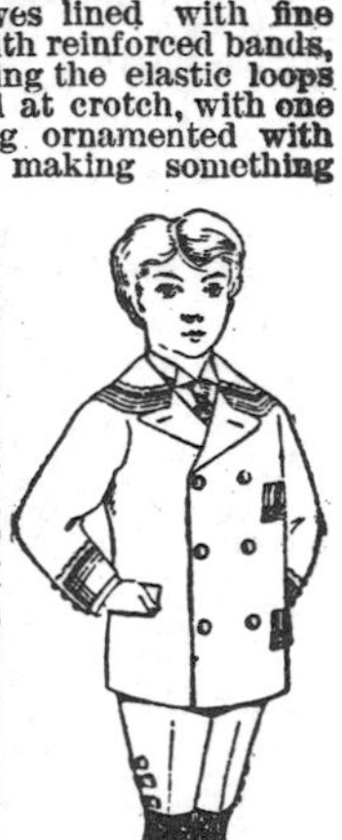

No. 4207.

**IF TO BE SENT BY MAIL, DON'T FORGET TO ADD ENOUGH TO PAY POSTAGE, AND NEVER FORGET TO STATE AGE OF BOY AND SAY WHETHER LARGE OR SMALL OF AGE.**

**No. 4223. OUR $3.45 BOYS' TWO-PIECE SUIT FROM 4 TO 14 YEARS OF AGE.** No. 3818. In ordering be sure to state age of boy and say whether large or small of his age. If to be sent by mail send 24 cents extra to pay postage. Understand, any of these suits will be sent by express C. O. D., subject to examination, on receipt of $1.00, balance and express charges to be paid after goods are received. We hold you under no obligation to take the goods if not found exactly as represented, a perfect fit and every other way satisfactory. This is a suit which is fine tailor-made, manufactured by one of the largest and most reliable makers in this country, made from a very fine quality of all-wool cassimere of dark gray mixed invisible check, comes in the latest style, double-breasted as shown in cut, lined throughout with a very good quality of serge lining, good sleeve lining, four pockets on coat with full length flaps, lined throughout. Knee pants are well made, reinforced waistband, good button holes on waistband; also elastic loops on the back to prevent the buttons pulling off the waist. Two side pockets and one hip pocket, nicely finished, three buttons on each side of pants leg at bottom. This makes a very stylish suit and one that is sure to please and bring us more business.

## BOYS' $3.50 CORDUROY SUIT.

**No. 4224. THIS $3.50 CORDUROY SUIT is one on which we are making a special run,** a suit that retails at $5.00 in first-class stores, a thoroughly well-made suit in every respect, guaranteed tailor-made throughout and by one of the best makers in this country. Sizes from 4 to 14 years of age. In ordering be sure to state age of boy and say whether large or small of his age, and if you desire suit sent by mail enclose 24 cents extra to pay postage.

**Made of an excellent quality of dark brown corduroy,** two side pockets, one top pocket and one ticket pocket, with full-sized square flaps, brown buttons to match the goods, first-class button holes, lined with a good quality black serge, rolling collar, wide lapels, double-breasted square front. Knee pants, extra well-stayed crotch, waistband with button holes; also elastic loops on the back, two side and one hip pocket. all handsomely finished, making a very rich, as well as a very durable, suit. It will give perfect satisfaction.

**No. 4225. OUR BOYS' $2.95 CORDUROY SUIT, in two pieces, with choice of colors,** brown or slate color, as desired. In ordering be sure to state color wanted, price the same. Sizes run from 4 to 14 years of age. If to be sent by mail, enclose 29 cents extra to pay postage. We offer these suits in competition with suits that retail at $4.00 and $5.00. We believe if you will examine one of these suits you will be so well pleased with it that you will recommend our house to your friends and we can sell you all the clothing you buy, your neighbors as well.

**No. 4226. OUR $2.90 CORDUROY SUIT,** made of a very good quality of corduroy, three outside pockets, full square flaps, rolling collar, wide lapels, with buttons to match the goods. Double-stitched edges, thoroughly made in every way. An excellent serge lining to match the goods, handsomely-finished button holes. Knee pants, extra well stayed in every way; waistband with button holes and elastic loops on the back to ease the buttons on waist, two side and one hip pockets, finished with three little buttons on the bottom of each leg. This is positively the best wear-resisting suit for the money ever put upon the market, besides being very genteel.

## SPECIAL BARGAIN OF FINE IMPORTED ALL-WOOL CHEVIOT SUIT IN EITHER BLACK OR NAVY BLUE, AS DESIRED, FOR $2.35.

**These suits are made from an extra quality of all-wool cheviot goods,** made by one of the best cheviot makers in the country, guaranteed fast color and regular wear-resisting material. In ordering be sure to state whether black or navy blue is desired; the price is the same. Sizes run from 4 to 14 years of age. Be sure to state age. If to be sent by mail, 22 cents extra should accompany your order to pay the postage.

**No. 2227. Our $2.35 Suit.** These suits are fine tailor made, cut on the latest pattern for the season of 1896, made by one of the best and most reliable makers in this country. They are lined throughout with a very nice quality of serge lining, fancy sleeve lining, four pockets to coat with flaps on each pocket, lined throughout with good serge, have large lapel collar, nicely made and pressed, sleeves are finished with buttons on each cuff. The suits come double-breasted as shown in cut. The knee pants are nicely made, reinforced throughout, reinforced waistband with hand-worked button holes. In fact, this is a suit we have never sold before at anything like the price; but by reason of the large contract for the coming season, we are for the first time able to offer you for $2.35 a suit which will compete favorably with anything you can buy at your local market for double the money.

We are extremely anxious to receive your order, not so much for the little profit there is in a single suit to us, as for the good it will do us as an advertisement. We feel confident that if we get your order for one of these suits at $2.35 it will result in our getting further orders for our various departments.

## CHILDREN'S COMBINATION KNEE PANTS SUITS.

**These suits consist of the following 4 pieces:** 1 jacket, 2 pair knee pants and 1 cap.

**WE RECOMMEND** the four-piece combination suit, for jacket will outwear two pairs of pants, and by buying the four pieces the boy has a whole suit as good as new twice the time he would a two-piece suit.

**OUR COMBINATION SUITS** are all fine tailor made, made by one of the largest and most reliable manufacturers in New York, a concern which employs only skilled tailors; all are cut by expert cutters on the latest patterns for 1896, and every garment warranted. **SIZES RUN FROM 4 TO 14 YEARS.** Be sure to state age of boy and say whether large or small of age.

**We will send all combination suits by mail, post paid,** on receipt of 35c extra to pay postage.

The best way is to have them sent by express, and you will save money by ordering several suits at a time.

As above stated, all combination suits will be sent by mail, postage prepaid, on receipt of 35c extra to pay postage. We recommend ordering one or more suits by express. The express charges on from one to four suits will range from 25c to 40c, according to the distance. It pays to make a club order and save on transportation charges.

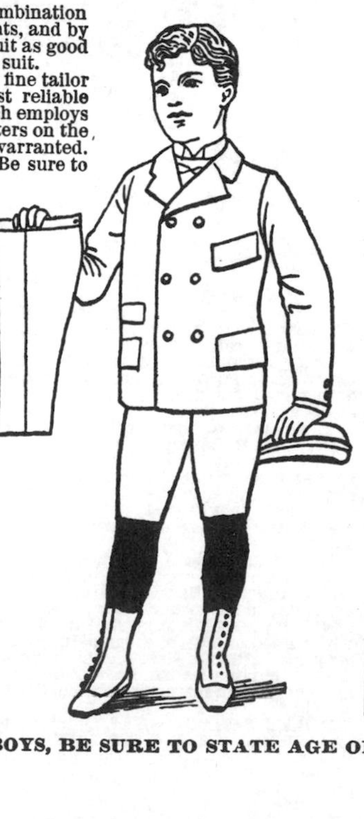

**No. 4228. THIS FOUR-PIECE SUIT AT $2.25** consists of one double-breasted coat, one cap and two pairs of pants, exactly as illustrated. The suit is made of a very good quality dark gray wool cheviot, from one of the best Michigan mills. It is a material that will wear, always look neat and dressy, and sure to give the best of satisfaction. The coat is lined throughout with a good quality of serge, fancy striped sleeve lining, large collar lined with serge, large well-made lapels, producing a very nice effect. Two pockets to coat, with flaps on both pockets. Both pants are well made, with side pockets, reinforced waistband, button-holes worked in waistband, reinforced crotch, finished with buttons at bottom of each pants leg. We offer these suits for $2.25 in competition with suits that retail at $3.00 and upwards. We have only to get your first order to be sure of getting your future orders.

Situated as we are, and in a position to furnish you goods direct from manufacturers on the basis of actual cost to produce, with our one small profit added, we can supply you with staple merchandise at prices that will admit of no competition.

**No. 4229. OUR $2.45 FOUR-PIECE SUIT FOR BOYS FROM FOUR TO FOURTEEN YEARS OF AGE** as above described. The suit consists of the following four pieces: one coat, two pair of pants, and cap. The suit is made in the very latest style for the season of 1896 and, as above illustrated, comes in double breasted with full-sized collar and lapels, four large pockets to coat, with flaps on all pockets, lined throughout with good serge lining. Pants are all thoroughly well made, reinforced waistband, reinforced crotch, finished with buttons at bottom of each leg. Every piece is guaranteed.

**No. 4230. OUR $3.00 FOUR-PIECE COMBINATION SUIT** made from a light gray check wool and cotton mixed Michigan cassimere, wear-resisting goods. Something your boy can wear for a whole season, and that your boy may wear his suit the season through, we recommend by all means that you buy a combination suit, as the one coat will outwear two pants. This suit as made like others above described, with good serge lining throughout, reinforced in every respect and a suit that is sure to please.

**No. 4231. OUR SPECIAL LEADER BOYS' FOUR-PIECE COMBINATION SUIT, blue or black, all-wool cheviot, for $3.25.** We put this suit in competition with suits retailed at $5.00 and upwards. It makes a very dressy suit, suitable for Sunday or everyday wear; coming as it does with two pair of pants, a boy has a good suit for the whole season. Like our other suits, it is made same as above described, four pockets, with large lined flaps on all pockets, double-breasted as illustrated, two pair of pants, the pants thoroughly well made and stayed as heretofore described. In ordering this suit be sure to state whether you wish black or blue, the price is the same, and also state age and say whether large or small of his age.

**No. 4232. OUR $3.40 BOYS' FOUR-PIECE COMBINATION SUIT** as illustrated above. This suit is made in the very latest style, double-breasted, lined throughout with serge lining, reinforced in every particular. Nothing has been left undone to make this a strictly first-class suit. Made from a good weight dark-gray check Michigan wool cassimere.

**No. 4233. OUR $3.50 FANCY BROWN BROADCLOTH FOUR-PIECE COMBINATION SUIT.** A suit that you would pay your local retail dealer double the money for. Made of a fine, medium weight, dark brown broadcloth, nicely finished throughout, rolling collar, lined lapels, four outside pockets with wide flaps nicely lined and stitched, lined with a good heavy serge, fancy striped sleeve lining, finely finished button holes, rubber buttons. Having two pair of pants nicely made with a felled outside seam with the Peerless waistband, which has the elastic loops on back as well as the button holes, wide hemmed bottom, each leg finished with two small buttons. Cap to match, very handsomely made and finished exactly as per illustration, making one of the most stylish and durable suits on the market, suitable for Sunday or everyday wear.

**No. 4234. OUR $3.75 COMBINATION SUIT,** consisting of double-breasted coat, two pair of pants and cap, all to match, is undoubtedly a "world-beater;" made of a handsome quality all-wool cheviot, in brown mixture, No. 2429. The coat is handsomely made, rolling collar, wide lapels, four outside pockets, all having wide square flaps, nicely lined and finished, lined throughout with a good twilled serge, fancy striped sleeve lining, handfinished button holes with buttons to match the goods. Two pair of pants nicely made, felled outside seam, two side pockets, one hip pocket, extra well stayed, finished with the Peerless waistband, which has the elastic loops on the back as well as the button holes, which gives ease to every movement of the body, with a Stanley cap made of the same material and color, with a silk cord around front, all complete, making one of the nobbiest suits produced in this line.

**No. 4235. OUR $3.85 ALL-WOOL CHEVIOT COMBINATION SUIT** is another special bargain, made of good weight all-wool gray cheviot, rolling collar, wide lapels, double-breasted square cut coat with buttons to match, four outside pockets with large square flaps nicely lined and finished, handmade button holes, edges stitched all around, lined throughout with a fine serge to match the goods, fancy sleeve lining. The two pair of pants are extra well made and finely finished, outside felled seam, two side and one hip pocket, which is extra well stayed, Peerless waistband, which has the elastic loops as well as the button holes, wide hemmed bottom, and finished on the leg with three small buttons; also a cap to match the suit in the very latest style.

**No. 4236. OUR $3.90 COMBINATION SUIT** is decidedly one of the greatest bargains ever produced. Is made of pepper and salt tweed, fine texture, and in every way substantially made throughout, rolling collar, handmade button holes, buttons to match the goods, double-breasted square front, lined throughout with a good serge lining, fancy striped sleeve lining. Two pair of pants substantially made in a thorough workmanlike manner, felled outside seam, two side pockets and one hip pocket, having the Peerless waistband, which has the elastic loops on the back as well as the button holes, preventing the buttons from coming off the waist, which is certainly an advantage to every mother, nicely finished with three small buttons at the bottom of each leg, nicely hemmed at bottom; also having a cap made in the latest style.

**No. 4237. OUR $4.25 COMBINATION SUIT** is a wonder, consisting of a stylish double-breasted coat, two pair of pants and cap made of all-wool cheviot, either in navy blue or black. Be sure to mention the color wanted, they are both the same price. The coat is handsomely made with a rolling collar, large lapel, handmade button holes, rubber buttons, having four outside pockets with wide square lapels nicely lined; also an inside dress pocket lined throughout with an excellent quality of serge, fancy striped sleeve lining. The two pair of pants are extra well made, double-stitched pocket and extra well stayed, two side pockets and one hip pocket, finished with three buttons at the bottom of the leg. Excelsior waistband which has the elastic loop as well as the button holes, extra stayed crotch, with cap of the same material. This suit, we are sure, will give you undoubted satisfaction and it certainly has a very stylish appearance.

**No. 4238. OUR $4.00 COMBINATION SUIT** is exceedingly nobby, made of a very fine imported Harris cassimere, light gray pin stripe, with double-breasted coat, square cut front, rolling collar, wide lapel, handmade button holes, lined throughout with a serge lining, fancy sleeve lining, four outside pockets with square flaps nicely lined and stayed, one inside pocket. The pants are extra well made, two side and one hip pockets, extra well stayed, Excelsior waistband, having the elastic loops as well as the button holes and finished with three small buttons at the bottom; also a cap to match, the same color and material.

**No. 4239. OUR $5.50 FOUR-PIECE COMBINATION SUIT,** the highest grade combination suit we make; you cannot buy better at any price. If you want something very fine, we will advise you to order one of our $5.50 suits. They come in sizes four to fourteen and like the others consist of the following four pieces: one coat, two pair of pants and the cap. These suits are finest tailor made, cut on the latest style patterns and made up very nobby, double-breasted, exactly as illustrated above. You can have these suits in either gray or brown mixture, made of a fine guaranteed all-wool cassimere, double-breasted coat, rolling collar, wide lapel, handmade button holes, having four outside pockets, one inside pocket, lined with a fine quality of farmer's satin, fancy sleeve lining. The two pair of pants are extra well made, two side pockets, one hip pocket; extra well stayed having the Peerless waistband, which has the loops as well as the button holes on the back; also having nickel plated buttons for suspenders. Finished with three small buttons at bottom of each leg. In ordering do not fail to mention which color you want, gray or brown mixture; both are the same price.

**INCLUDE A SUIT FOR YOUR BOY WITH YOUR OWN SUIT. IT WILL ADD NOTHING TO THE EXPRESS CHARGES.**

**IN ORDERING SUITS FOR BOYS, BE SURE TO STATE AGE OF BOY AND SAY WHETHER LARGE OR SMALL OF HIS AGE.**

three rows of fancy gold and black mixed soutache braid, with fancy corner ornamentation in each corner of the sailor collar, double-breasted, as shown in cut, large square lapel on pockets, lined throughout with serge lining, four full-sized pockets in coat. Attached to coat on inside are four extra buttons of assorted sizes. Pants made of the same material, extra strong reinforced waist band, pants reinforced throughout. Attached to pants is a piece of cloth 4 by 5 inches for patch. The legs are finished with fancy brass buckles and three buttons on each side. At our special price of $4.35 you will be more than pleased, and we believe it will be the means of adding more customers to our list.

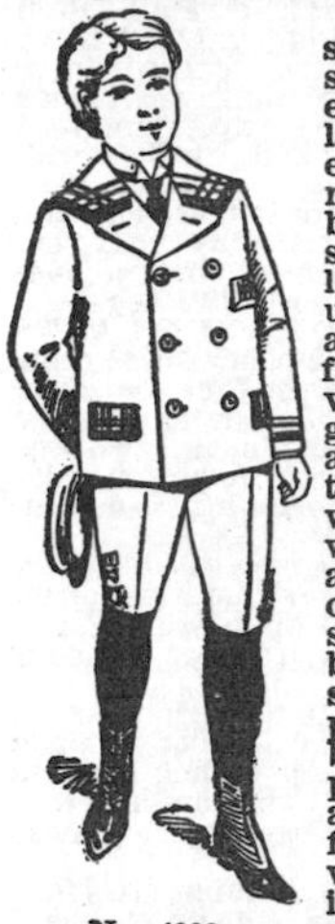
No. 4208

**No. 4208. OUR $4.95 TWO-PIECE REEFER SUIT,** sometimes called the Military Reefer, is the most sightly reefer suit made regardless of price. It comes in sizes ages three to eight. In ordering be sure to state age of boy and say whether large or small of his age. If to be sent by mail enclose 28 cents extra to pay postage. This suit is made from a black and blue mixed imported wool cassimere; the background is black with blue mixture in very small dots which gives it a very neat and stylish appearance. It is of the latest patterns from a very reliable woolen mill and wear-resisting cloth. The coat is gotten up very stylish with a large square sailor collar bound all around with wide military black braid and with one row of fancy gilt soutache braid, one row of black braid, making a very handsome effect. The collar is lined throughout with a good quality imported Italian lining, has large lapel nicely made and pressed, lined throughout with the same material as suit, two pockets on one side one pocket on the other, each covered with flaps. The three flaps are very nicely finished and bound with fancy wide military black braid, then with one row of gilt and one row of black soutache braid. Sleeves are finished with one row of wide black military braid, one row of narrow gilt soutache and one of narrow black soutache braid. Double breasted, six very fancy polished gilt buttons. Pants made of same material, to match the coat, with reinforced waistband, pants reinforced and well stitched throughout, ornamented at bottom of leg with three fancy satin bows and buckles. The pants are finished with three pockets, viz.: Two side pockets and one hip pocket nicely bound and finished, as well made and finished as a $10.00 tailor-made man's pants. The back of the waistband is finished with elastic loops to prevent buttons coming off the waist.

## CHILDREN'S KILT SUITS FOR CHILDREN,

### AGES, 2½, 3, 3½ AND 4 YEARS.

**In ordering these suits be sure to state age of boy and say whether large or small of his age. Our line of Kilt Suits is very complete and embraces about fifty styles;** but for your consideration we present to you two special bargains selected from all the suits that we are offering at a price that is sure to bring orders from those in need of this class of goods.

**No. 4209. FIRST AMONG THIS LOT OF BARGAINS IS OUR $1.45 KILT SUIT,** which we furnish in navy blue, brown, slate and tan, as desired. In ordering, be sure to state color wanted, and if to be sent by mail enclose 15 cents extra to pay postage.

Want of space prevents our showing even a small portion of the line we carry; but we do offer you the two biggest bargains we have, and we know that if we receive your order, you will be so well pleased that you will favor us with your orders for other departments.

This garment is made of good weight broadcloth, blouse waist cut in the most approved manner, large square back sailor collar, with white anchors in each corner of the back, handsomely embroidered with silk floss, round front, ornamented with little bow, rubber buttons. Full-plaited kilt, box front, ornamented on each side with four small rubber buttons to match the waist. Continuous waistband with extra well-made button holes and finished with a hem one inch wide, double-stitched and extra well-made throughout.

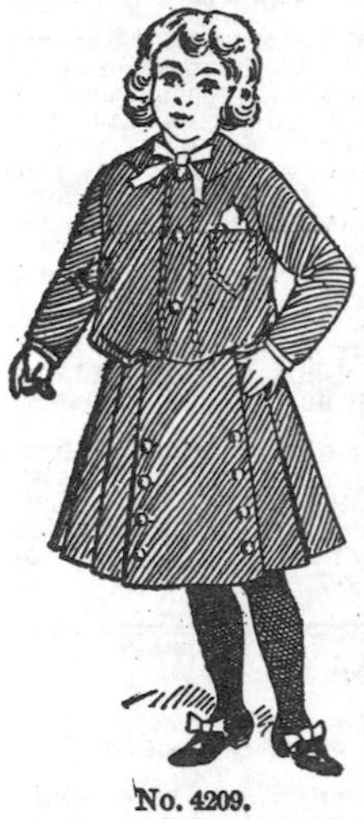
No. 4209.

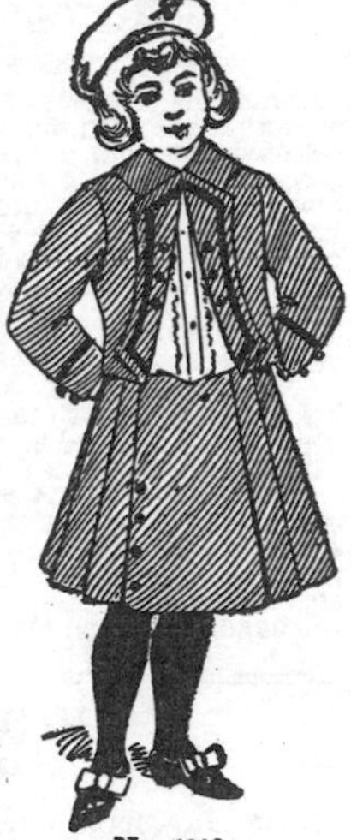
No. 4210.

**No. 4210. OUR $2.60 ALL-WOOL NAVY BLUE CHEVIOT KILT SUITS,** for boys 2½, 3, 3½ and 4 years of age. Be sure to state age of boy and say whether large or small of his age. If sent by mail enclose 25 cents extra to pay postage. If by express C. O. D., subject to examination, send us $1.00, the balance and express charges can be paid after suit is received. Coat made with round sailor collar, lapel front, similated vest, trimmed with silk braid, one-half inch wide, and silk ball buttons, lined throughout with serge, the sleeves lined with striped silesia, slashed on each side of the back and trimmed with soutache braid. Kilt skirt with nine plaits and box front, trimmed on each side with four silk ball buttons to match coat, continuous band, extra well-made and finished with button holes, wide hem on the bottom. This makes a very dressy and stylish little suit.

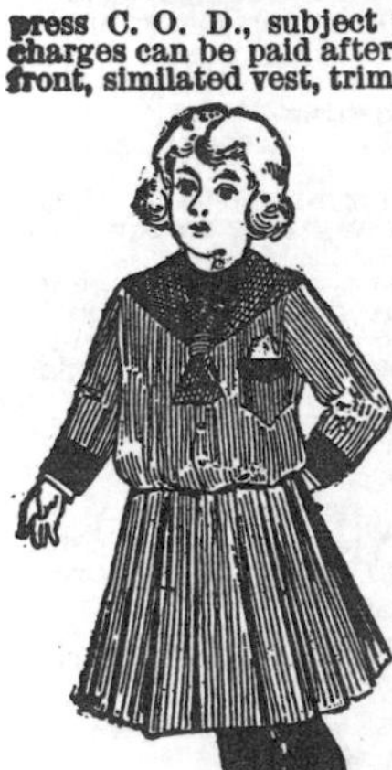
No. 4211.

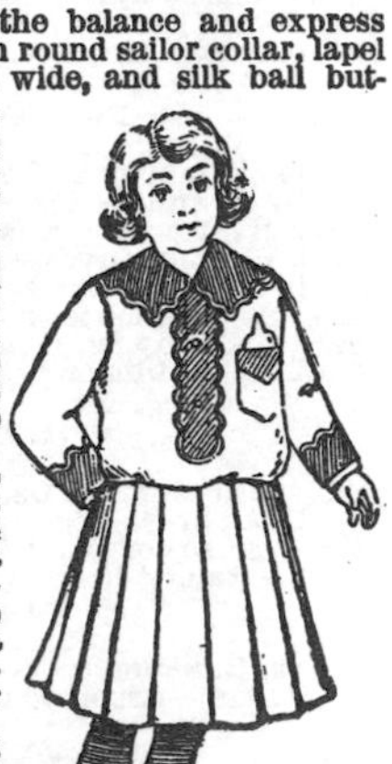
No. 4212.

**No. 4211. OUR SPECIAL 75c. KILT SUIT.** This suit is made for children from 2½ to 4 years of age. It is made of a heavy blue and white stripe duck-ing, with very large square blue collar, fancy cuffs, fancy tie, a suit that would retail in any first-class store at nearly double our special offer price.

**No. 4212. OUR $1.15 KILT SUIT.** We offer for $1.15 a very fine kilt suit, one that cannot be duplicated in any retail store within 50 per cent of our special offer price. These suits are made for children 2½, 3, 3½ and 4 years of age. In ordering be sure to state age. At 15 cents extra we will send these suits by mail, postage paid. When ordering by mail be sure to enclose the 15 cents to pay postage. This suit is made from a heavy blue and red stripe duck, has a very large fancy square red collar, scalloped and nicely bound, large red scalloped cuffs and front.

**WE CALL YOUR ATTENTION TO OUR REGULAR LINE OF CHILDREN'S TWO-PIECE AND FOUR-PIECE COMBINATION SUITS.** You have but to glance at the prices we name to convince yourself that we are offering prices against which no dealers can compete. **Armed with the advantages possessed by no other concern, viz: the largest output of clothing** of any firm in existence, selling our clothing direct to the **consumer for cash,** thereby making no bad debts, buying our goods in large quantities from the mills, making them up by the thousands, we are prepared to make you prices that will admit of no argument, no dispute in comparison and we would advise you by all means to get up a club order, **ordering three or four, or better still a dozen suits at a time,** let us send them to you by express and thus reduce the charges on one suit to but a very few cents at the most. We are filling a great many club orders, thereby reducing the cost to the purchaser, which is our sole aim. We are anxious for you to co-operate with us with reference to the club order system and by so doing you will own the goods at 25 per cent less than your local dealer can buy in large quantities.

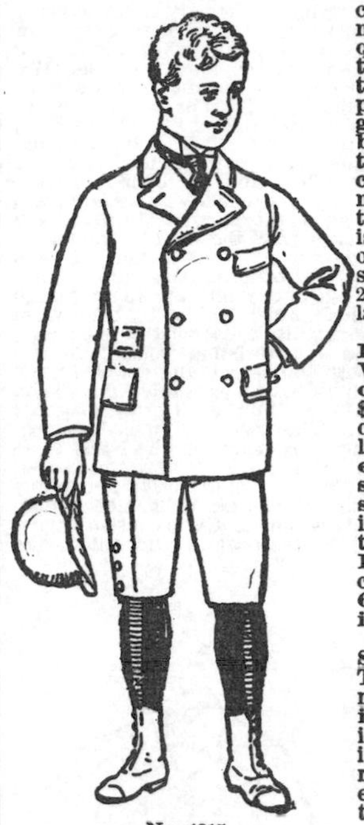
No. 4215.

**No. 4213. OUR FIRST SUIT, A TWO-PIECE BOYS' SUIT FOR 65 CENTS IS A WONDER. We are offering this suit at 65** cents in competition with suits that retail at from $1.25 to $1.50. **They come in ages 4 to 12.** In ordering be sure so state age of boy and say whether large or small for his age. **If to be sent by mail, enclose 16 cents extra to pay postage. These suits are made from a very fair quality of** satinette, a dark gray mixture and good wearing material, lined throughout with cotton serge, two pockets to coat, single-breasted, round collar. **Pants are well made,** two pockets, stayed crotch, button holes worked in waistband. **At 65 cents we challenge any concern in existence to show the equal.**

**No. 4214. OUR $1.05 TWO-PIECE BOYS' SUIT FOR BOYS 4 TO 12 YEARS OF AGE.** This suit is made of a heavy dark brown satinette, made in exactly the same style as our No. 4213. **It is a good weight, well-wearing material,** coat is lined throughout with a good quality cotton lining, two pockets on coat with flaps on pockets, round collar. Pants are well made, drilling pockets, button holes worked in waistband, two buttons on each side of pants leg at bottom.

**No. 4215. OUR $1.45 TWO-PIECE BOYS' SUIT FROM 4 TO 14 YEARS OF AGE. In ordering be sure to state age of boy and say whether large or small of his age.** If you wish suit send by mail send 30 cents extra to pay postage. **Two, three or even four suits can be sent by express** to any address, at a cost of from 25 to 30 cents; for that reason we would advise ordering several suits at a time and having them shipped by express and thus reduce the express charges. **This $1.45 suit is thoroughly** well-made two-piece suit; good enough for any boy for everyday wear. It is made from an extra quality of **dark mixed diagonal goods,** a regular wear-resisting garment, lined throughout with a good quality of serge lining, good sleeve lining, **double breasted as shown in cut,** large collar with large lapels, three pockets to coat, flaps on all pockets, pockets made of good quality of silesia. Pants are well made throughout, reinforced waistband, button holes worked in same, two side pockets, finished with two buttons on bottom of each pants leg. These pants are extra well stayed in crotch.

**No. 4216. OUR $1.55 TWO-PIECE BOYS' SUIT.** Sizes from 4 to 14 years of age. In ordering be sure to state age of boy and say whether large or small for his age. If to be sent by mail, enclose 25c extra to pay postage. This suit is made from a good quality dark gray wool cheviot, medium weight, double breasted, square front with rubber buttons, two outside pockets with flaps, round collar, lapel front, well made button holes, lined throughout with good quality of serge lining and fine striped sleeve lining. Pants are well made, continuous waistband, extra well stayed and well finished.

**No. 4217. OUR $1.70 BOYS' SUIT. Made of fine all-wool serge,** having a very genteel appearance, in dark mixed colors. In ordering be sure to state age of boy and say whether large or small for his age. If to be sent by mail, enclose 25c extra to pay postage. This suit is nicely made, finely finished buttonholes and rubber buttons, three outside pockets with flaps, lined with fine black serge, fine striped sleeve lining. The pants are extra well made, extra stayed crotch, extra stitched waistband, two small buttons on the bottom of each leg to match the buttons on the coat.

**No. 4218. OUR $1.85 BOYS' TWO-PIECE SUIT. For boys from 4 to 14 years of age.** Be sure to state age of boy and say whether large or small for his age. If to be sent by mail, add 25c extra to pay postage. We offer you in this a regular $2.50 suit at $1.85. No. 910. Made of a heavy gray mixed cheviot, extra wear-resisting material, handsomely made, round collar with wide lapels, finely finished buttonholes, with single front. Three outside pockets with flaps, lined throughout with a good black serge and fine striped sleeve lining. Extra well made pants, felled outside seam, two buttons at bottom of the leg, waistband extra stitched and good button holes, two drilling pockets, bottom hemmed and nicely finished.

**No. 4219. OUR $2.20 TWO-PIECE BOYS' SUIT. From 4 to 14 years of age.** If to be sent by mail enclose 25c extra to pay postage. No. 1073 Made of a heavy gray cheviot, double breasted, square front, round collar and wide lapels, black rubber buttons, lined throughout with a good quality of serge, fine striped sleeve lining, three outside pockets with flaps. Pants are extra well stayed, drilling pockets and handsomely finished. This we consider extra good value and very stylish.

**No. 4220. OUR $2.55 TWO-PIECE BOYS' SUIT. For boys from 4 to 14 years of age.** Be sure to state age of boy and say whether large or small for his age. If to be sent by mail enclose 25c extra to pay postage. No. 1071. Made of a very fine, heavy, all-wool brown mixed cheviot, double-breasted front, round collar, wide lapels, three outside pockets with flaps, extra well made throughout, lined with black serge, fine striped sleeve lining, with buttons to match goods. The pants are extra well stayed and stitched throughout, handsomely finished with buttons at the bottom of each leg to match coat, waistband extra well stitched and good buttonholes. This is a very nobby and handsome suit.

**No. 4221. OUR $2.75 BOYS' TWO-PIECE SUIT FROM 4 TO 14 YEARS of age.** Be sure to state age of boy and say whether large or small of his age. If to be sent by mail enclose 25 cents extra to pay postage. No. 1040 made of fine all wool gray mixed cassimere with an indistinct check, double-breasted, round collar, wide lapels, lined with good quality of farmer's satin, handsomely finished buttonholes and rubber buttons, three pockets with flaps. The pants are very nicely finished extra well stayed in crotch, patent waistband with extra elastic loops at the back to prevent the pulling off of the buttons from the waist. One hip pocket and two side pockets, outside felled seam, each leg finished with three small buttons to match coat. You will find this a very stylish and well-made garment, suitable for the most fastidious.

**No. 4222. OUR $2.95 BOYS' TWO-PIECE SUIT FOR BOYS FROM 4 TO 14 years of age.** Be sure te state age of boy and say whether large or small of his age. If to be sent by mail enclose 25 cents extra to pay postage. Made of a select fine checked all wool cassimere, brown and white predominating, double-breasted, round collar, wide lapels, brown buttons, lined with a fine brown farmer's satin and extra well finished. The pants are extra well made and finished with a felled outside seam, extra stayed crotch, one hip and two side pockets. Finished with three small buttons to match the coat. Patent waistband with button holes and extra elastic loops. This is indeed a very fine genteel suit, nice enough to wear to church or any other place.

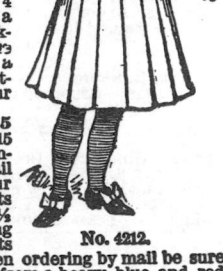

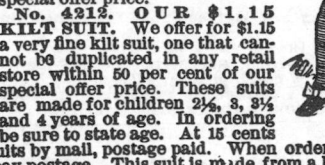

**No. 4240. OUR SPECIAL $5.25 HEAD-TO-FOOT DRESS FOR BOYS FROM 4 TO 15 YEARS OF AGE.**

At $5.25 we offer you an outfit which cannot be duplicated in any retail store within 50 per cent of the price; in fact, this is an outfit which you will find in very few retail stores. If you wish to dress your boy in the very latest style for the spring and summer of 1896, give him an outfit which is as stylish as anything turned out for the coming season. We recommend this head-to-foot dress at $5.25. Send us $1.00 as a guarantee of good faith, and the outfit will be sent to you by express C. O. D., subject to examination. You can examine it at the express office, and if found perfectly satisfactory and exactly as represented, pay the agent the balance, $4.25 and express charges and the outfit is yours. If not found perfectly satisfactory you can return it. In ordering this suit be sure to state age of boy and say whether large or small of his age. This suit is made from genuine Michigan hard twist cassimere, a regular wear-resisting goods. Pants are made with double seat and double knees, patent buttons and warranted not to rip. Comes in medium dark gray diagonal pattern. The coat is double-breasted, and the suit is made on the latest style pattern for the spring and summer of 1896, cut by expert cutters and fine tailor-made, made to fit perfectly, nicely lined, trimmed and finished, and consists of one double-breasted coat, as illustrated, one

**No. 4240.**

fancy cap of material to match suit, and two pairs of knee pants; also a very neat shirt waist, nicely trimmed and finished, a handsome Windsor tie, one pair good substantial hose and a pair of extra quality serviceable lace shoes. Our sale on these special outfits has been enormous, and by reason of this enormous sale we have been able to make such arrangements with the manufacturers that we can offer you the outfit at less money than your local dealer can buy in quantities. We know if we get your order for this boys' head-to-foot combination suit outfit, it will mean the sale of a great many more outfits in your neighborhood.

☞ **BE SURE TO GIVE SIZE OF SHOES WANTED.**

**No. 4241. OUR $4.98 BOYS' CONFIRMATION SUITS.** Sizes ages 5 to 11 years. Do not forget to give size and say whether boy is small or large of his age.

Boys' very dark blue two-piece Confirmation Suit, made of the celebrated Slater tricot, which is strictly all-wool, with a beautiful finish, good weight, for all-the-year-around wear, positively wear-resisting and always looks nice for all occasions. All seams are felled in first-class style, double-breasted coat with rolling collar, wide lapels, full square flaps on all pockets, lined with the best imported Italian lining, fancy striped sleeve lining, very handsomely finished. Hand-made button holes. Parents having a boy about to make his confirmation should order this special suit at our special price, $4.98.

We guarantee every suit to give perfect satisfaction as to fit and quality, and not retailed for less than 50 per cent more than we ask. If to be sent by mail, enclose 20 cents extra to pay postage.

**No. 4241.**

## BOYS' KNEE PANTS.

We have them, and from 15 cents to $1.00.

Our prices are right, we can save you so much you can't afford to buy at home.

OUR BARGAINS in knee pants will surprise you, for the reason they are made from remnants of fine woolens, used in our men's clothing, and in this way much better value can be had from us in this line than from any other concern.

We can fit any boy from 4 to 14 years of age, state age, and say whether large or small of his age.

Our knee pants are all well made, well sewed throughout, reinforced seats and waistbands, every pair warranted.

Sent by mail on receipt of 8 cents additional to pay postage.

IT WILL PAY YOU to order several pairs at a time, or get your neighbors to join with you and make up an order for several pairs and let us send by express, which will bring the transportation charges down to next to nothing.

**No. 4241½. BOYS' 15 CENT KNEE PANTS.** These knee pants are made of a good quality striped cottonade, a good wearing material and will give excellent satisfaction. Only from us can you get them at 15 cents per pair.

**No. 4242. OUR 22 CENT KNEE PANTS.** If you can match it anywhere for double the money, we won't ask you a cent for the goods. By mail 8 cents extra to pay postage. We recommend ordering these in half dozen lots, in which case we will give them to you in assorted patterns. In this way we can deliver half dozen paid by express for 25 cents. No. 6843. These pants are made from a very fair quality of cottonade, black ground, small colored stripe, reinforced waistband, buttons worked in waistband, two side pockets.

**No. 4243. OUR 30 CENT KNEE PANTS** equal to anything in the market at double the price. These knee pants run in sizes 4 to 14, sent by mail on receipt of 8 cents extra to pay postage. They are made of a very good quality of wool and cotton mixed cassimere, a good wearing material, well made throughout, reinforced waistband, button holes worked in waistband, two side pockets, and we are able to get them at 15 cents per pair.

**No. 4241½.**

**No. 4244. ANOTHER 35 CENT BARGAIN,** sizes 4 to 14, made of very good quality brown mixed invisible satinette, well made in every respect, reinforced waistband, button holes worked in waistband, side pockets; offered in competition with pants that sell at twice the money; our special price, 35 cents.

**No. 4245. OUR 38 CENT PANTS** to fit boys from four to fourteen years, extra by mail 8 cents to pay postage. Made of an extra good quality well woven cottonade, regular wear-resisting material, wool finish, dark gray invisible stripe. Reinforced waistband, button holes worked in waistband, side pockets; our special offer price, 38 cents.

**No. 4246. OUR 45 CENT LINE. WE OFFER THESE PANTS** in competition with those which retail as high as $1.00. They are thoroughly well made in every respect; sizes run from four to fourteen years of age; 8 cents extra if to be sent by mail. These pants are good enough for any boy for everyday wear, made from a good quality of wool and cotton mixed cassimere, dark gray stripe, reinforced waistband, with button holes worked in waistband, side pockets, finished with buttons at bottom of each leg.

**No. 4247. A BARGAIN AT 48 CENTS** for boys from four to fourteen years of age. Here is a pair of pants your boy won't wear out in a year, made from a very strong, well woven, wear-resisting check goods. Reinforced waistband, button holes worked in waistband, side pockets, finished with buttons on bottom of pant legs.

**No. 4248. BLACK AND BLUE ALL-WOOL CHEVIOT KNEE PANTS FOR 48 CENTS.** We furnish a very neat all-wool cheviot knee pants for 48 cents in either black or blue as desired. In ordering be sure to state whether you desire black or blue. They come in sizes four to fourteen years of age. Be sure to state age of boy. By mail 8 cents extra to pay postage. These pants are made with two side pockets and one hip pocket, nicely finished, reinforced waistband, with button holes worked in waistband. Finished with two buttons on bottom of each leg. You cannot match these pants in your retail stores for double the money.

**No. 4249. OUR 50 CENT LINE.** These pants are made from a good quality, well woven, wear-resisting cotton mixed cassimere, dark gray, small invisible plaid. Side pockets, reinforced waistband, with button holes worked in waistband; two buttons at bottom of each leg. It will pay you to order four or five pairs at a time if they come by express, and thus reduce the express charges.

**No. 4250. BOYS' 58 CENT KNEE PANTS,** sizes four to fourteen years of age. Made of a very good quality of gray wool cheviot, good wearing goods. Made of a fine medium-weight cheviot, felled outside seam, side and hip pocket, Peerless waistband, which has the elastic loops as well as button holes to button the waist, extra well stayed, and finished with two little buttons at the bottom of each leg, making a very dressy little pant.

**No. 4251. BOYS' 75 CENT KNEE PANTS,** regular $1.25 value, sizes four to fourteen years of age; 8 cents extra if to be sent by mail. Made of an excellent quality medium-weight cheviot, assorted select patterns in dark mixtures, extra well stayed and finished, with Peerless waistband, which has the elastic loops as well as the button holes, having two side pockets and one hip pocket, nicely finished in every way, and having three small buttons at the bottom of each leg, which is nicely hemmed and bound.

**No. 4252. THE BEST WE MAKE,** and the price is $1.10, by mail 8 cents extra, ages 4 to 14 years of age. The best we make is the best that money can buy. Made of a pin stripe fine imported Harris cassimere, extra well made and finished with a felled outside seam, two side and one hip pocket, which is extra well finished, with the Excelsior waistband, extra stayed crotch, making one of the finest and most desirable pants in the market.

## BOYS' CORDUROY KNEE PANTS.

OUR LINE OF CORDUROY PANTS IS VERY COMPLETE and we embrace the products of all the best makers in the country. We have made up in endless variety, but for want of space we are only able to show three special bargains selected from our entire stock, one at 58 cents, one at $1.00 and one at $1.10. We recommend these to your favorable consideration as goods that make up very nice, always look neat and dressy and something your boy can never wear out. They run in sizes 4 to 14 and at 8 cents extra we will send by mail postpaid. Our 58 cent corduroy pants, is made of a good quality stone color corduroy, well made throughout, with the Peerless waistband, which has the elastic loops as well as the button holes, two side pockets and one hip pocket, finished with two buttons on each leg, hemmed at the bottom, extra well stayed at crotch, with drilling pockets, making a very sightly as well as durable pants.

**No. 4253. OUR $1.00 QUALITY** is made of a very excellent quality dark brown corduroy with the Excelsior waistband, extra well finished, two side and one hip pocket, hemmed bottom. The front of the knee is nicely lined to keep it in place. The bottom of each leg is finished with three small buttons.

**No. 4254. OUR $1.10 CORDUROY PANTS** made of a superior navy blue corduroy, very good weight, extra well made throughout and extra well stayed, with the Excelsior waistband, handsomely finished with two side and one hip pocket, made very substantial, hemmed bottom and lined in front of the knee as an extra stay to keep the knee in shape. Finished with three rubber buttons, making one of the handsomest and most durable pants that any one can buy.

**CONSIDER OUR LIBERAL C. O. D. TERMS AND 3 PER CENT. CASH DISCOUNT ON CLOTHING.**

# MEN'S MACKINTOSHES.

**SPECIAL NOTICE!**—MEN'S MACKINTOSHES MADE ONLY IN SIZES FROM 36 TO 48 INCH BREAST MEASURE. Sizes larger than 48 inch breast measure will have to be made to order at our eastern factory and will cost from $1.50 to $2.00 extra to make. It usually requires about three weeks to have special size mackintoshes made to order and WE REQUIRE THE FULL AMOUNT OF CASH WITH THE ORDER. Special or extra size mackintoshes cannot be returned or exchanged, unless we are clearly at fault. We guarantee to make them exactly according to the measurements you send us. The measurements required for garments to be made to order are chest measure, waist measure, length of sleeve from center of back, and length of garment from collar seam to length desired. ALSO GIVE HEIGHT AND WEIGHT. Do not forget this; it is important.

**SPECIAL NOTICE**—THE ONLY MEASUREMENT REQUIRED FOR MEN'S READY MADE MACKINTOSHES IS CHEST MEASUREMENT.

## Our $2.95 Special Bargain Coat.

**Men's Double Texture . . .**

**. . . Mackintosh Rain Coats.**

**No. 21870** Made from good quality diagonal cloth, with large detachable cape and handsome plaid lining. A most desirable coat for any climate. Made up in first class manner and suitable to wear in place of an overcoat. Made in latest style and cut full size. Thoroughly well sewed and carefully tailored. Sizes 36 to 48 only. Colors black and navy blue. Average length, 52 inches.
Price each.............. **$2.95**

**No. 21871 Men's Cape Mackintosh** with velvet collar and detachable cape. Made from fine black diagonal serge. This is a double texture coat and is lined throughout with fancy plaid linings. One of the neatest and dressiest waterproof coats we have ever offered. All seams are waterproof and each garment is correct in size and carefully tailored. Size 36 to 48 breast measure. Length 52 inches. Color plain black. Price each.............. **$3.89**

**No. 21872 Men's Velvet Collar Mackintosh.** Same as above but made in plain navy blue.
Price each.............................. **$3.89**

**Special Notice.** The only measurement required for mackintoshes is chest measurement.

**No. 21874 Men's Heavy All-wool Double texture Black Diagonal Cashmere Mackintosh Coat.** With double sewed welt seams throughout. Detachable cape which is made with seamless back. This is a handsome coat and can be used in place of an overcoat. Lined throughout with handsome plaid lining. Carefully tailored and perfect fitting. Cape is full size and the coat has large velvet collar. Sizes 36 to 48. Length 52 inches. Price each, **$4.85**

**No. 21875** Same coat as above in plain navy blue. Very handsome and stylish. Price each.... **$4.85**

**No. 21876 A Double Texture Mackintosh Coat** of surpassing goodness, full of real merit and excellent wearing qualities; made from medium weight, very fine black diagonal all wool cashmere; lined throughout with black serge; large full size detachable cape and velvet collar; made with sewed, strapped and cemented seams, and warranted thoroughly waterproof; extra fine workmanship and finnishings; cemented facings and pockets. No need of an overcoat when you own a garment of this sort. Made in sizes 36 to 48; length 52 inches.
Price each.............................. **$5.10**

**No. 21877 Men's Double Texture All Wool Cashmere Mackintosh Overcoat,** same as above but made in navy blue. Price each................ **$5.10**

**No. 21878 Men's Heavy Double Texture Mackintosh.** Made from all wool tricot cloth. Fine soft finish. Heavy plaid lining throughout. Handsomely made up in the very latest style. With large full size detachable cape. Very warm and comfortable and can be worn in place of an overcoat. Double sewed welt seams. A wonderful coat for the money. Your local dealer would ask you $7.00 for an inferior garment. Made in sizes 36 to 48 breast measure, and cut full size. Length 52 inches. Color plain black.
Price each.............. **$4.95**

**No. 21879** Same Mackintosh as above made in dark blue. Warranted fast color. Very handsome and thoroughly reliable. Price each........ **$4.95**

**No. 21880 Men's Double Texture Mackintosh Coats;** with large full size cape and velvet collar. Made from strictly high grade all wool heavy weight imported tricot cloth. Seams are sewed, strapped and cemented. Patent cemented facings and strapped cemented pockets. Finely made and carefully tailored; one of the very best wearing Mackintosh Coats on the market. Cape is made with seamless back and is detachable. Heavy weight, extra quality fancy plaid lining throughout. Made up in the latest style and handsomely finished throughout. Guaranteed to be thoroughly waterproof and to give perfect satisfaction in every way. Sizes 36 to 48 in. breast measure; average length 52 to 54 inches. Color plain black. Price, each............ **$6.79**

**No. 21881 Men's Double Texture, all Wool Tricot Mackintosh Coats.** Exactly same description as the above in every way, excepting that same is made in dark navy blue color. Warranted fast color and absolutely waterproof. Price, each....... **$6.79**

**No. 21883 Men's Strictly High Grade Double Texture Cape Mackintosh Coat.** This garment is made from the finest all wool imported dark Oxford gray mixed covert cloth. Inside lining is a very handsome white and black pin check. Very latest pattern, and very nobby and fashionable this season. Seams are sewed, strapped and cemented; cemented facings and pockets. These are strictly high grade in every respect. Will give better wear, and hard service, than any coat ever sold for double the price we ask for them. Capes are made with seamless back, and are detachable. The garments are finished with wide velvet collars; carefully tailored and perfect in fit, and finely finished throughout. Full of real genuine goodness, and guaranteed strictly waterproof, and dependable in every way. We offer them at a remarkably low price. Sizes 36 to 48 breast measure; average length 52 inches. Largest sizes, however, will run about 54 inches in length. Price, each.................. **$8.40**

**No. 21884 This is Exactly the Same as No. 21883,** but comes made up in a rich and beautiful shade of brown, slightly tinged with gray, and has a fancy plaid lining. These coats are very fashionable this season, and will give great satisfaction.
Price............................................. **$8.40**

## A Combination Coat.

**Two styles in one. Something strictly new and up-to-date.**

**No. 21885 Men's Extra Fine Combination Mackintosh Coats.** This is something entirely new, and one which we are sure will meet with popular favor. It is made in the regulation Box Coat style, double breasted, with large full shaped detachable cape, and can be worn either as a box or cape coat as desired. These garments are made from extra selected all wool tricot cloth, with fine heavy weight fancy plaid lining. Large fine silk velvet collar. Silk stitched button holes. Seams are sewed, strapped and cemented. Ventilated arm holes. Perfect in fit and workmanship, and absolutely waterproof. Pockets are sewed, strapped and cemented, and in fact these garments are made up in the very finest style. Sizes run from 36 to 48 breast measure, and the average length of the garments is about 54 inches. We can furnish these in plain black or dark blue. In ordering, be sure to give breast measure and color desired. The retail value of this garment is $10.00.
Our price............................................. **$6.98**

## Men's Fashionable Box-Style Mackintosh Coats.

**The latest and most popular style mackintosh coats made. Don't let this season go by without supplying yourself with one of these handsome and thoroughly dependable garments. Our prices will enable you to secure one of these strictly high-grade coats at a price which will clearly prove to you that we are masters of the mackintosh business in this country.**

**No. 21886 Men's Latest Style Double-texture, Double-breasted Box Style Mackintosh Coats.** Made from fine all-wool cashmere. Seams are sewed, strapped and cemented; large velvet collar; strapped and cemented pockets; ventilated armholes; silk sewed buttonholes; first-class material and workmanship throughout. This is a strictly up-to-date garment, very new and dressy, and can be worn as an overcoat. Has a fancy plaid lining throughout Box coats will be very much in demand this season, and this is an exceptionally nice one at a very low price. We have them in plain black or navy blue. Sizes run from 36 inches to 48 inches breast measure; average length is 54 inches.
Price, each...... **$5.25**

**A Wonderfully Cheap Line of**

## Umbrellas and Parasols

**Farther Along in this Catalogue. ——See Index.**

**No. 21887 An Up-to-date Thoroughly Dependable High-Grade Double Breasted Mackintosh Box Coat.** Large velvet collar Seams are all sewed, strapped and cemented; also facing; made with ventilated armholes. Fancy plaid lining throughout. Made from fine all wool imported Tricot cloth; double texture; good weight, and a splendid garment for all year around wear. Carefully tailored, and guaranteed to be a perfect fit, and unexcelled in finish. Warranted absolutely waterproof.

We have these in plain black or navy blue, as desired. Sizes run from 36 to 48 inches breast measure. Average length 54 inches. These coats are made with a deep cut or slit in back, which buttons, and will be very useful in horseback riding or walking. These garment are extra finely finished throughout, and buttonholes are silk sewed. Our price,.... **$5.79**

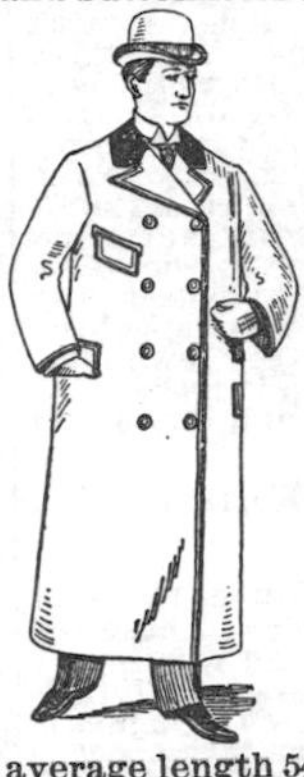

**No. 21888 Men's Light Colored Double Texture Double Breasted Box Mackintosh Coat.** A very swell shade of light tan mixed English Covert cloth, with a very wide velvet collar to correspond. Handsome broken plaid lining throughout. Sewed, strapped and cemented seams; ventilated under armholes; silk sewed button holes. Deep slit up in back, which can be buttoned or not as desired. This is a very swell coat in every respect. Strictly up-to-date in style, finely made and finished, double texture goods, guaranteed absolutely waterproof, and thoroughly dependable in every respect. Invest in one of these coats, this season, and you will never regret it. We will cheerfully refund your money if this garment proves unsatisfactory. Sizes run from 36 to 48 in. breast measure; average length 54 inches. Retail value of this garment is $7.50. Our Special Price.................. **$4.98**

**No. 21889 Men's Double Breasted Latest Style Box Mackintosh Coats.** Made from the finest grade of imported handsome brown mixed all wool English Covert cloth. Sewed, strapped and cemented seams. Wide brown silk velvet collar. Ventilated armholes; fancy plaid twilled lining. These are good weight double texture garments, all wool and strictly waterproof. Made with deep buttoned slit in back. This is an extremely popular shade of cloth and will be worn very extensively this season. Sizes run from 36 inch to 48 inch breast measure; average length 54 inch. Retail value, $12.00.
Our Special Price.................................. **$7.90**

**No. 21890 Men's High Grade Double Breasted Box Style Mackintosh Coats,** double texture goods, and large velvet collar. Outside cloth is all wool imported melton, with fancy plaid lining throughout. Seams are sewed, strapped and cemented; ventilated under the armholes; silk sewed buttonholes; cemented and strapped pockets. Large, deep buttoned slit in back; very useful for both horseback riding and walking. These are strictly high grade goods in every respect, and can be used to good advantage in place of an overcoat in any climate. They are guaranteed to be absolutely waterproof, and perfectly satisfactory. They are made up with the same careful attention to every detail as goods retailed as high as $20.00. Made of positively the best goods ever put into a mackintosh sold at anywhere near the price at which we offer it. We furnish these garments in either plain black or navy blue, in sizes from 36 to 48 breast measurement; average length 54 in. Always mention size desired, and color, in ordering. Our price .............. **$7.95**

## Boys' Mackintosh Coats.

**Sizes 26 to 36-inch Chest Measure.**

**No. 21891 Boys' Double Texture Mackintosh Coat,** made from good quality diagonal cloth, with large cape, and handsome plaid lining. Well made and finished, and will give excellent satisfaction. Colors plain black or navy blue. Sizes 26 to 36 chest measure. Always give size and color.
Price, each............................................ **$2.75**

**No. 21892 Boys' Extra Quality Double Texture Mackintosh Coats,** made from fine all wool tricot. with large detachable cape and handsome plaid lining. Extra well made and finished. Can be used in place of an overcoat. Sizes 26 to 36 only. Plain black only. Sewed, strapped and cemented seams, and warranted waterproof. Price, each....... **$4.95**

**We are Leaders in Ladies Fashions**

The Very Latest Styles IN Tailor-Made Suits

**THE NEWEST PARISIAN NOVELTIES**

**$8.00 to $15.00**

**LADIES' Tailor-Made SUITS**

**At $4.50, $6.75, $7.50 and $8.50.**

——SEE FULL PAGE PLATES——

**IF PRICES AND QUALITY CAN ACCOMPLISH OUR OBJECT, WE WILL HOLD YOUR TRADE. OUR LIBERAL C. O. D. TERMS MAKE IT POSSIBLE FOR YOU TO SEE THAT WHAT WE SAY IS SO, BEFORE YOU PAY.**

## Ladies' Mackintoshes.

**Ladies' Mackintoshes are made in the following sizes only.**

**Bust measure—32, 34, 36, 38, 40 and 42 inches.**
**Length measure—52, 54, 56, 58, 60 and 62 inches.**

**SPECIAL NOTICE.** If you are built out of proportion and cannot use regular sizes as quoted above, we can have extra or special sizes made to order for you. It usually requires about three weeks to have special garments made to order, and the additional cost would be from $1.50 to $2.00 more than our regular selling price according to the size and quality of garment desired. The full amount of cash must be sent when garments are to be made be to special order.

**HOW TO MEASURE.** Give bust measure taken close up under the arms, stating number of inches around the entire bust. For length measure take same from the collar seam to the bottom or hem of garment or length desired. For a 32 bust order 52 length, for 34 bust order 54 length, for 36 bust order 56 length and so on, according to the scale of sizes noted above. If you are short and stout and cannot find your size in ready made garments and do not care to pay the extra price for having a special size made to order, we would suggest that you order a longer garment than you wish but of the desired bust measure. You can in a very few minutes cut it off or hem it up to the desired length. This will save you quite a little expense and cause you but very little trouble.

## Ladies' Double Cape Mackintoshes.

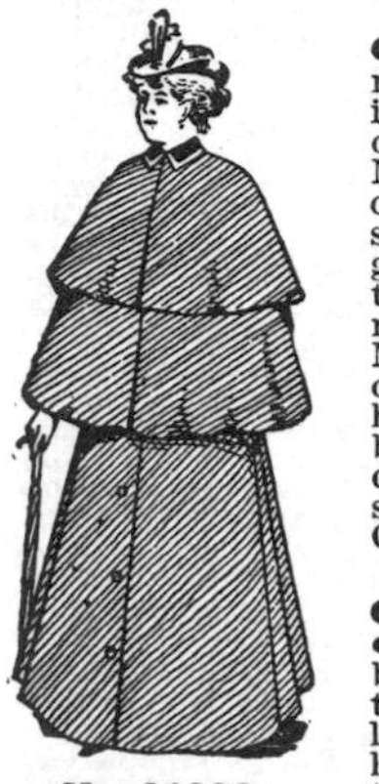

No. 21893.

**No. 21893 Ladies' Double Cape Mackintoshes.** These are made from a good quality of imported diagonal mackintosh cloth, rubber lined throughout. Made up in very latest style, cut full size; well made and sewed; carefully tailored and guaranteed to be very satisfactory. Sizes 32 to 42 in. bust measure, and 52 to 62 in. length. Made in accordance with scale of sizes as noted above. We have these garments in plain black and navy blue. In ordering always state color and size desired.
Our Special Price.........**$2.95**

**No. 21894 Ladies' Two Cape Light Tan Colored Covert Cloth Mackintoshes.** Double texture goods, lined throughout with fancy plaid lining. Detachable cape with handsome set in velvet collar to match. Handsomely made and trimmed, and will give good satisfaction; full sweep detachable cape. This is the first time we have been able to offer a really good light colored ladies' mackintosh at anywhere near the price we can furnish these. The goodness of these garments at the low price we offer them will certainly surprise and please you. Made in all regular sizes.
Our Special Price..............................**$3.95**

**No. 21895 Ladies' Two-Cape Inverness Double Texture Mackintosh.** Made from fine wale diagonal serge, with fancy plaid lining throughout. Full sweep double detachable cape, with velvet collar. Cape is made seamless, and seams in the garment are all felled. This mackintosh is elegantly made up, and trimmed in a strictly first-class manner. We have them in plain black and navy blue, in all regular sizes. When ordering please be sure to state size and color desired. Our special price......**$4.69**

**No. 21896 A Very Handsome and Stylish Ladies' Double Texture Inverness Mackintosh.** Made of a fine, imported, all wool, diagonal serge cloth. Large, full, seamless detachable double cape, with set in velvet collar. This mackintosh is trimmed and made in exactly the same careful manner as the highest class of mackintoshes. Has double felled seams, and silk string ties at waist. Inside pocket, also inserted apperture, with pinked flap, which will be found very handy in raising up dress skirts. Strictly high grade in every respect, and thoroughly waterproof. We can furnish these mackintoshes in plain black and navy blue as desired. All regular sizes. In ordering, state color and size desired.

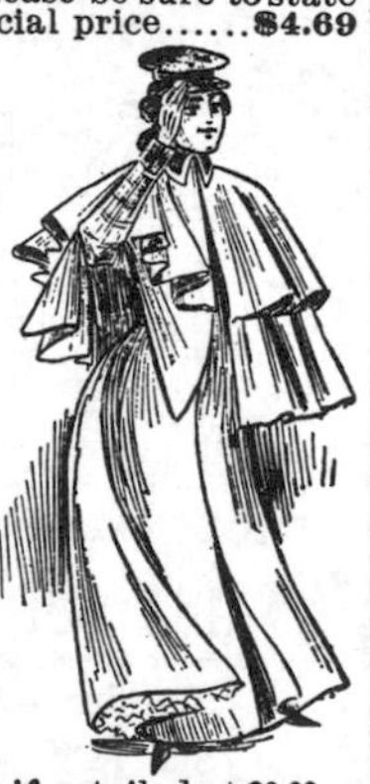

These garments would be cheap if retailed at $6.00.
Our special price..............................**$4.75**

**No. 21897 Ladies' Double Texture Two Cape Inverness Mackintosh.** Made from all wool fine diagonal English cashmere. Detachable cape, with deep, set in velvet collar. Lined throughout with fancy plaid lining; felled seams; extra selected stock; made up in strictly first-class manner throughout. Guaranteed to give perfect satisfaction in every respect, and to be absolutely waterproof. Capes are detachable and have 110-inch sweep. Made in all regular sizes, in plain black and navy blue. In ordering please state size and color desired. Our Special price.................... **$5.29**

**SAVE ALL YOU CAN WHEN YOU ECONOMIZE. REMEMBER OUR DISCOUNT FOR CASH.**

**No. 21898 Ladies' Two-Cape Double-Texture Inverness Mackintosh.** Made from strictly all-wool imported cashmere. An extra fine selected fabric and specially imported by us. Guaranteed to give long and lasting satisfacfion. This is positively the best cashmere ever put into mackintosh goods. It is very fine and soft in finish, and the colors are perfectly fast, and guaranteed waterproof. These garments have large double detachable capes, with full 110-inch sweep, set in velvet collar. Are made up in a strictly first-class manner throughout. Body of mackintosh is lined throughout in a very fancy plaid. The cape is seamless, and is lined throughout with a very handsome changeable silk. These are exceptionally fine garments, and are guaranteed to give perfect satisfaction in every sense of the word. We can furnish them in all regular sizes in plain black and navy blue. In ordering, please state color and size desired. Retail value of these garments is $10.00. Our special price..................**$6.95**

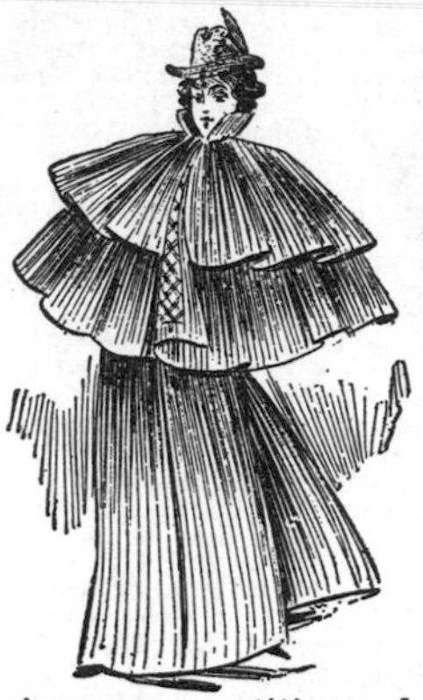

**No. 21899 Ladies' Double Texture Inverness Mackintosh Coat.** This is certainly one of the handsomest ladies' mackintoshes ever made up. It is made of strictly all wool imported English cashmere, fine diagonal twill, with worsted finish. Large full sweep double cape, detachable, with set in collar of velvet. Fancy plaid lining throughout the body of the garment. Cape is made seamless, and is lined throughout with a rich fancy brocaded silk, presenting a most charming and beautiful effect. Your retailer would ask you from $10.00 to $15.00 for a garment like this one. We have them made up in immense quantities, and offer them at a price so low that every one can take advantage of it. We guarantee the garments to be strictly first-class in every way. Thoroughly up-to-date, stylish, dressy, and dependable. Made in all regular sizes, in plain black and navy blue. Our special price, each.**$7.69**

**No. 21900 Ladies' Extra Quality Two-Cape Inverness Mackintosh.** This is an exceptionally fine garment, and is made from finest imported all wool English mackintosh serge. Heavily lined with silk throughout. Capes are made detachable and seamless, and have set in collars of velvet. Full 110 sweep cape. These garments are finely tailored, strictly up-to-date in style and finish. These are actually worth double the price we are asking for them. Made in all regular sizes, in plain black and navy blue. Always state size and color desired.
Our special price ..............................**$7.98**

## The New Military Cape Mackintoshes.

**The Most Up-to-date and Handsome Ladies' Mackintosh Made.**

**No. 21901 Ladies' Military Cape Mackintosh.** The very latest style out. Made with a 27 inch Military Cape, full 150 inches sweep, with Watteau back, and handsome velvet collar to match. This cape is made detachable, and is very useful and can be worn either with or without the mackintosh. These garments are made from the finest all wool English serge with handsome plaid lining throughout. Handsomely made up, and carefully tailored, and finished in the finest possible manner. Single cape mackintoshes, such as here described, will be very popular this season. The are rapidly taking the place of the double cape garments. We have these in plain black and navy blue, in all regular sizes. When ordering, be sure to state size and color desired. Our Special Price .............**$5.87**

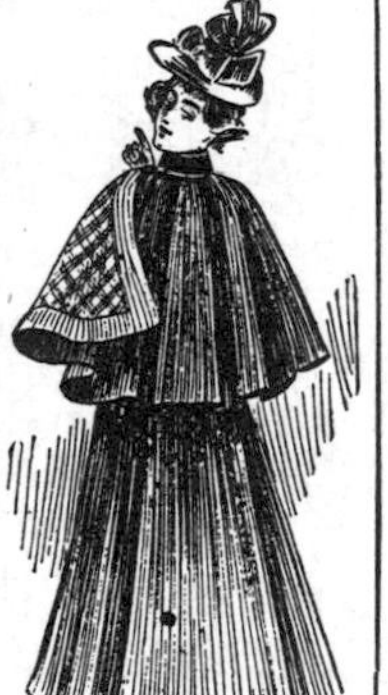

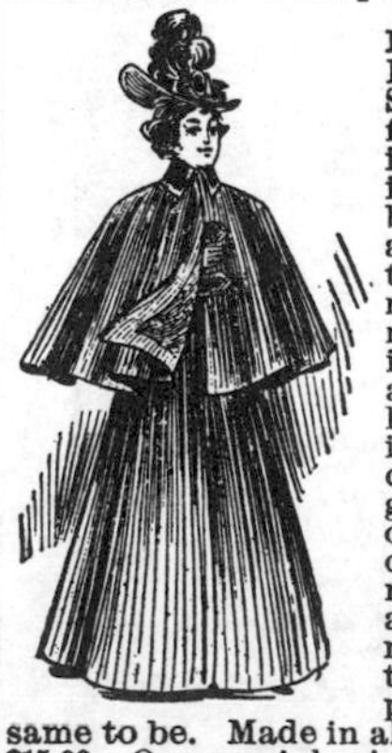

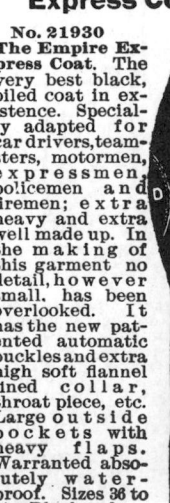

**No. 21902 Ladies' Single Military Cape Mackintosh.** Made from extra fine all wool Scotch mixed cheviot, with fine soft dressy finish, such as is found only in the best quality goods. The pattern is a beautiful blending of light and dark olive and white mixture, forming a very neat novelty combination. Being neither too light nor too dark, it strikes the Happy Medium, and will, therefore, please the large majority of ladies. Cape is full 150 inch sweep and detachable, with a handsome green velvet collar, which corresponds with the dark color in the fabric of the garments. Cape is full seamless and 27 inches long. Your money cheerfully refunded if this mackintosh does not prove exactly as we represent same to be. Made in all regular sizes. Retail value, $15.00. Our special price..............................**$9.40**

## Misses' Mackintoshes.

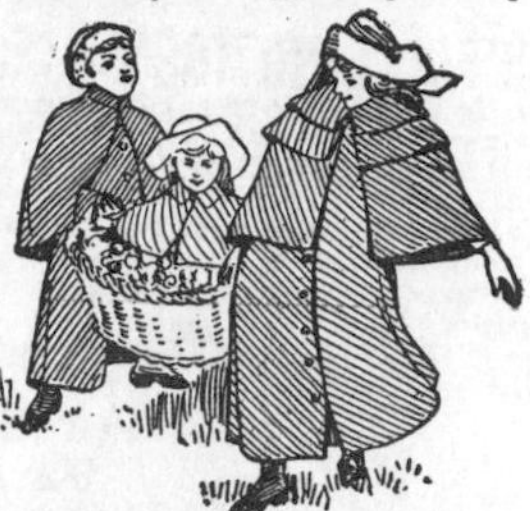

**No. 21903 Misses' Extra Fine Quality Navy Blue Fine Diagonal Serge Mackintosh.** Double texture with double detachable cape and handsome plaid linings. These are strictly first class garments in every respect and are handsomely made up and artistically finished and perfect fitting. The handsome double cape gives extra protection to the throat and lungs, besides giving the garment a nobby and stylish appearance. In ordering give length from collar seam to bottom of garment or length desired. Made in lengths from 36 to 52 inches. Always measure back of garment, not the front. Retail value of these garments $5.00.
Our price, each..............................**$3.90**

## Men's Slickers and Oil Clothing

**Guaranteed Absolutely Waterproof. The Slickest Line of Slickers on Earth.**

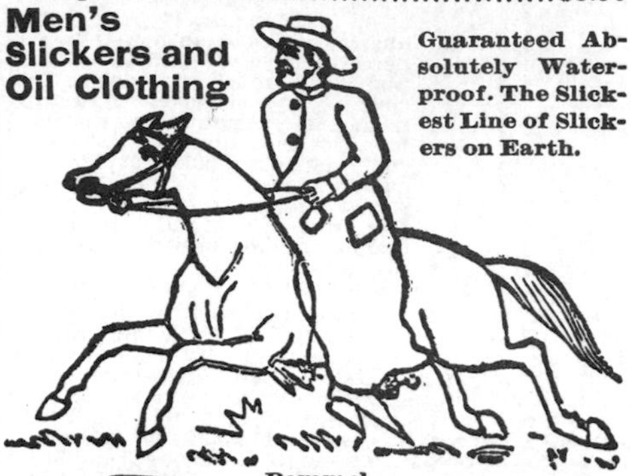

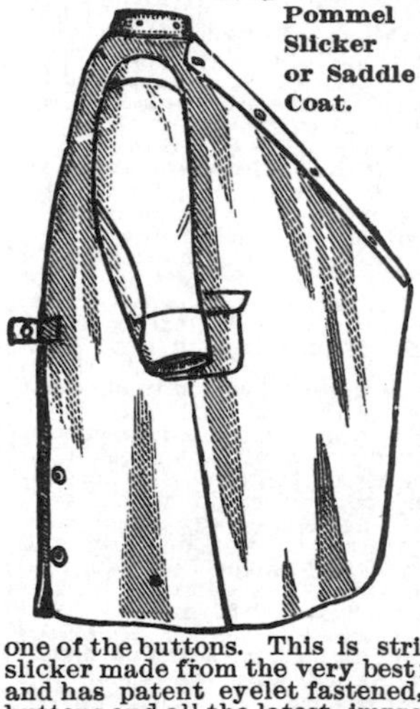

**Pommel Slicker or Saddle Coat.**

**No. 21925 Men's Yellow Oil Pommel Slicker or Saddle Coat.** This coat is patented and is the most perfect rain coat ever invented for the use of horsemen. It is a decided improvement over earlier productions covering the entire saddle as well as the rider, thus ensuring a perfectly dry seat while the lower part of the coat is wide enough to go all around the legs of the wearer. This coat is also a combination coat and can be immediately changed from a riding to a walking coat by simply adjusting one of the buttons. This is strictly a high grade slicker made from the very best material obtainable and has patent eyelet fastened, non-corrosive zinc buttons and all the latest improvements. Guaranteed to be the very best oil coat made. Sizes 36 to 44. Cut full and large. Price each..............**$2.85**

**No. 21927 Pommel Slicker or Saddle coat,** made exactly same as above in black. Price each...**$2.95**

## The Empire Express Coat.

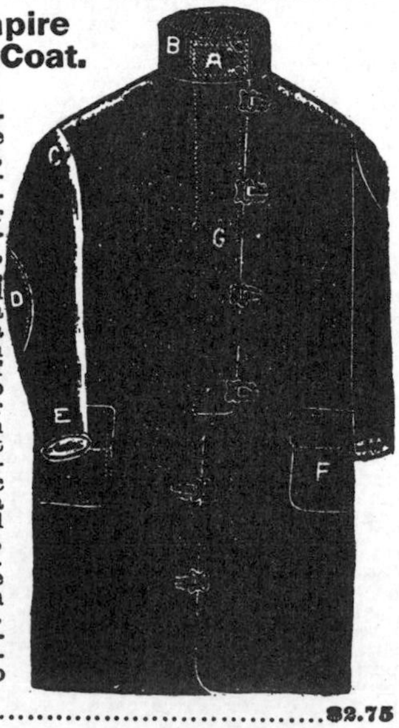


**No. 21930 The Empire Express Coat.** The very best black, oiled coat in existence. Specially adapted for car drivers, teamsters, motormen, expressmen, policemen and firemen; extra heavy and extra well made up. In the making of this garment no detail, however small, has been overlooked. It has the new patented automatic buckles and extra high soft flannel lined collar, throat piece, etc. Large outside pockets with heavy flaps. Warranted absolutely waterproof. Sizes 36 to 44. Black only.
Price each..............................**$2.75**

**IF WE PLEASE YOU IN FILLING YOUR ORDER SATISFACTORILY AND WITH MONEY SAVING, AS WE INTEND IT SHALL BE, WE HOPE YOU WILL SPEAT OKIND WORD FOR US TO YOUR FRIENDS,**

## The Manhattan Cape Coat.
### Black Only.

No. 21931 The Manhattan Black Oiled Cape Coat is exactly the same quality as the Empire Express coat and is made with large shoulder cape as shown in the adjoining illustration. This coat is particularly adapted for motor and grip men, drivers, teamsters, miners and farmers, and is constructed with cape overlapping and fastened in front leaving the arms unobstructed and giving perfect freedom of action. No binding or girting in any part of the coat. Warranted absolutely waterproof, made with large high collar, lined with soft flannel. Sizes, 36 to 44. Made in black only. Price, each....**$2.90**

## Plain Oil Slickers.
**MEN'S LONG YELLOW OILED SLICKERS.**

21932 Well made and finished with eyelet fastened zinc buttons. Sizes, 36 to 44, warranted waterproof.
Price, each ... .........**$1.85**
21933 Men's Long Black Oiled Slicker, same style as above, warranted waterproof.
Price, each.............**$1.95**

No. 21932.

## Oiled Jackets.
**MEN'S DOUBLE YELLOW OILED JACKETS.**

No. 21934 Made same as adjoining illustration, and warranted waterproof. Sizes, 36 to 44. Average length, 30 inches.
Price, each..............**$1.00**
No.21935 Men's Double Oiled Short Jackets. Same as above, but made in black.
Price, each.................**$1.10**

## Squam Sou'westers.
No. 21936 Men's Yellow Squam Sou'wester Oiled Hats. Made up same as adjoining illustration, and warranted waterproof. Sizes, 6⅝ to 7½. Price, each............**$0.25**
No. 21937 Squam Sou'wester. Same as above, in black.
Price, each... .. ..........**$0.25**

## Oiled Pants.

No. 21938 Men's Yellow Oiled String Pants. The best ever made. These pants are made double and are doubly reinforced in crotch and waist, with riveted zinc buttons on fly. Warranted absolutely waterproof. Full sizes.
Price, per pair .........**$0.95**

No. 21939 Men's Double Oiled String Pants, same as above in black.
Price, per pair .........**$1.00**

No. 21938.

## Oiled Apron Pants.
No. 21940 Men's Heavy Double, Yellow Oiled Pants, with apron and shoulder straps. Extra well made up and thoroughly reliable in every way. Large full sizes. Warranted waterproof.
Price, per pair .........**$1.00**
No. 21941 Men's Heavy Double Apron Pants, exactly same as above but made in black. Price, per pair ...**$1.10**
SPECIAL NOTICE.—The above lines of oiled clothing are the very best manufactured and cannot be compared with the cheap inferior grades on the market. If you want the cheaper grades we can furnish them, but we cannot recommend them. **Buy the best and you will not have to buy so often. There can be but one best. Remember the line we quote is the best. Our guarantee is back of every garment.**

No. 21940.

## Boys' Rubber Coats.
No. 21942 Boys' Rubber Coats, on heavy sheeting, black, luster finish. Sizes 24 to 34 chest measure.
Price.......................................**$1.47**
No. 21943 Boys' Rubber Coats, on heavy sheeting, black, dull finish. Sizes 24 to 34 chest measure.
Price.......................................**$1.85**

## RUBBER BOOTS OF ALL DESCRIPTIONS
On Page 195.......

## Men's Rubber Coats.
### Sizes 36 to 44 Chest Measure.
### High Grade, Finely Finished Garments.

No. 21944 Men's Medium Weight Fine Black Rubber Coats, fancy plaid back, 50 inches long, double breasted. Price.....................**$2.15**
No. 21945 Men's Medium Weight Coats, wine color, velvet collar, fancy plaid back, double breasted. Price.....................**$2.50**
No. 21946 Men's Medium Heavy Black Rubber Coats, fancy plaid back, double breasted. Price.................**$2.75**
No. 21947 Men's Medium Weight Black Rubber Coats, fancy plaid back, double breasted. Price.................**$3.00**
No. 21948 Men's Medium Heavy Black Rubber Coats, fancy plaid back, double breasted. Price.................**$3.25**
No. 21949 Men's Medium Weight Black Rubber Coats, patent ventilated epaulet shoulders, fancy plaid back, double breasted. Price.................**$3.50**
No. 21950 Men's Heavy Black Rubber Coats, fancy striped twilled back, double breasted. Price.....**$3.50**
No. 21951 Men's Medium Heavy Black Rubber Coats, double back, fancy sateen back, double breasted, velvet collar. Price**$3.60**

No. 21953 Men's Medium Weight Black Rubber Coats, extra long double back, fancy striped lining double breasted. Price.....................**$4.00**
No. 21954 Fireman's Regulation Rubber Coats, double coated, extra wide fly front, with snaps and rings, straps and buckles on sleeves and neck. Price.......................................**$4.00**
No. 21956 Policeman's Regulation Rubber Coats, fancy plaid back, double back, patent ventilated shoulders, patent ball and socket buttons, straps on sleeves, pocket for billy and shield for star. Price.......................................**$4.90**

## Men's Heavy Rubber Clothing.
Weight of Rubber Clothing, 3½ to 5½ pounds, according to size and quality.
Sizes on men's clothing are as follows:

| Size | 3 | 4 | 5 | 6 | 7 |
|------|---|---|---|---|---|
| Chest | 36 | 38 | 40 | 42 | 44 |

No. 21956 Rubber Coats, on heavy sheeting, black luster finish; officers' length.............**$1.60**
No. 21957 Rubber Coats, on heavy sheeting, dull finish; officers' length......................**$2.00**
No. 21958 Rubber Coats, on heavy sheeting, dull finish; mountaineers' length, extra long.......**$2.75**
No. 21959 Rubber Coats, on heavy drill, dull finish; officers' length......................**$2.25**
No. 21960 Rubber Coats, on heavy drill, dull finish, mountaineers' length, extra long; can be buttoned around legs and made a riding coat if desired. Price...............................................**$3.00**

---

# WHAT THE PEOPLE SAY:

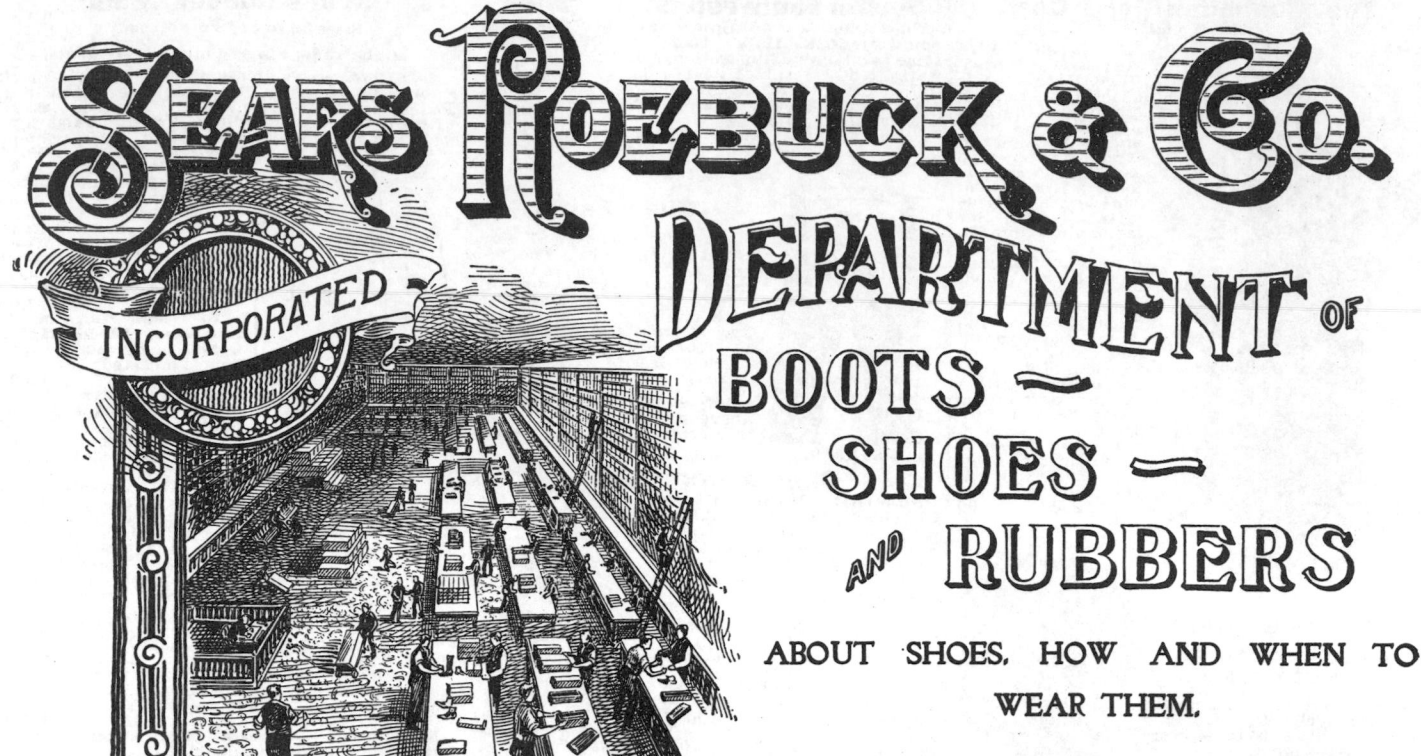

## ABOUT SHOES, HOW AND WHEN TO WEAR THEM.

**TO THE MEN:** Shoes to wear well should be adapted in make, material and weight to the kind of use to which they are to be subjected. For instance: A good many men buy a fine calf or kangaroo shoe and expect it to give the same service as a plow shoe. A fine shoe is not intended for heavy wear any more than a top carriage is intended to carry a load of wheat. Following are a few things which should not be done: **Don't** wear a thin shoe for street or rough wear. **Don't** wear shoes too narrow for your feet. **Don't** fit your shoes short; especially the ones with the pointed toes. On the contrary, they should be fitted very long. Make your foot much more stylish in appearance. **Don't** put your shoes on the stove, steampipe or register, especially if they are damp. Leather will burn, if damp, even where you can hold your hand.

**HOW TO CARE FOR THEM.** If your shoes are wet they should never be dried quickly, but allowed to dry slowly and then a little oil or vaseline should be carefully rubbed into the leather. This will keep them soft and prevent their cracking. Mud or dirt should always be carefully removed before the shoes are put away. If your feet perspire, the same pair of shoes should never be worn two days in succession. You should have two pairs, wearing one pair one day and the other the next, thus allowing the shoes to dry out during the alternate days. Your shoes will last much longer by doing this, and your feet will not get sore. Perspiration or sweaty feet will always cause shoes to crack sooner or later, particularly if the shoes are light weight. We would recommend tan shoes for such feet, particularly during the summer, as the tan stock is porous and consequently much cooler. The blacking for men's shoes is not injurious for calf skin, but is for kid or kangaroo.

**A WORD TO THE LADIES.** Ladies often complain that the soles of their shoes do not wear well. This is undoubtedly because they wear a light hand-turned shoe, when they really should have a Goodyear Welt or a McKay sewed shoe. The hand-turned shoe has a very thin sole and is designed principally for indoor and dress wear. The McKay sewed shoe has a heavier sole, and consequently will wear longer. Use as little blacking as possible, as it will do your shoes more harm than good. Tan shoes, however, should be cleaned and polished often, as the preparations used for this purpose nearly always act as a preservative to tan and Russian leathers.

**ABOUT RUBBERS AND OVERSHOES.** We will handle this season both first and second quality of rubber goods. We have always handled strictly first quality, but owing to the fact that a great many dealers handle only seconds and sell them at about the same price that firsts are worth, we have decided to handle both, so that our patrons, who wish the cheaper grade can be supplied at wholesale price. For the benefit of those who are not familiar with these goods, we will say that every rubber factory makes two grades of goods. They are termed firsts and seconds. The firsts are made from the pure Gumrubber and consequently cost more and will wear longer than the seconds. The second quality which we handle, however, is of extra quality and come in all the latest and most desirable styles. Below we name some of the best known Firsts and Seconds. These are firsts, and if genuine every pair should be stamped. "Boston Rubber Shoe Co.," "Woonsocket Rubber Co.," "Wales Goodyear Rubber Co.," "Candee Rubber Co.," "American Rubber Co." and "New Brunswick."

Below are seconds:

"Bay State Rubber Co.," "Rhode Island Rubber Co.," "Connecticut Rubber Co.," "Federal Rubber Co." and "Essex."

Note the above very carefully and don't let your dealer sell you second quality goods and make you believe they are just as good as firsts.

Rubber loses its wearing qualities when old, hence it is to your advantage to buy from a firm who always have fresh stock. Our output is so large that we are constantly receiving fresh goods. **DON'T WAIT UNTIL IT SNOWS**, and then pay your dealer a big profit, but order your rubbers and overshoes when you buy you shoes or other goods, then you will be prepared, and besides you will get them at the regular wholesale price. **Just as cheap** as any retail dealer can buy them.

**ABOUT GUARANTEED GOODS.** We wish to call special attention to those goods marked "Warranted." If at any time a pair of warranted boots or shoes give out without just cause, report the fact to us, and we will repair them, replace them with others, or refund the amount paid for them according to the circumstances of the case, if shoes are sent to us to show where the fault lies.

**IF YOU ARE DISSATISFIED** with any shoes, or if any mistake is made in filling your order, don't hesitate to notify us at once. We sell such a large quantity of shoes that we may make a few mistakes. We are only too glad to rectify them, however, if given an opportunity.

**WE THANK OUR MANY PATRONS** for past favors and we assure you that it is your liberal patronage which has made success possible and placed our Shoe Department in a position where we can offer you reliable footwear lower than it can possibly be obtained elsewhere.

**WHEN ORDERING** be sure to state size you want, when you know it; otherwise send us the length and shape of your foot, drawn with a pencil while standing on a piece of white paper. Instep, ball and other measurements not necessary. From length and shape of outline we can determine from our knowledge of measurements what size and width will fit your feet best.

**THE WIDTHS RUN** AA, extremely narrow; A, extra narrow; B, very narrow: C, narrow; D, medium; E, wide; EE, very wide.

**OUR TERMS ARE VERY LIBERAL.** We will ship Boots or Shoes C. O. D. subject to examination, on receipt of 50 cents per each pair, as a guarantee of good faith balance and express to be paid at express office, provided they are exactly as represented and better value than you can possibly obtain elsewhere. Otherwise they can be returned at our expense, and the amount paid will be promptly refunded, or you can have it applied on other goods.

**A SPECIAL DISCOUNT** of 3 per cent. will be allowed if **CASH IN FULL** accompanies your order (except on rubber goods, which are net), in which case you can deduct the three per cent. from our prices. You not only save the 3 per cent. by so doing, but also the return charges on money sent to us.

**NEARLY ALL OUR CUSTOMERS SEND CASH IN FULL, AND WHY NOT?** If you are not perfectly satisfied, we immediately refund your money.

**IT IS CHEAPER** to send ladies' shoes, slippers, etc., by mail than by express. The postage rate is **ONE CENT** for each ounce. When you wish goods sent by mail always send cash in full, deduct 3 per cent. discount, and include enough extra to pay postage, and we will ship by mail, postpaid. Be sure to inclose enough extra to pay postage; if you send too much we will promptly return what is over.

**POSTAGE NECESSARY** is given under each description, that you may know the amount necessary to send.

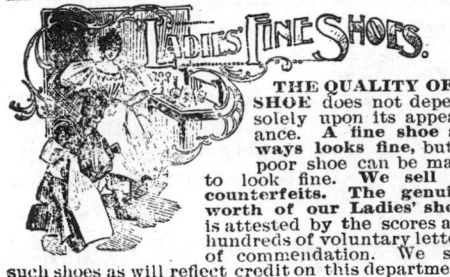

## LADIES FINE SHOES.

THE QUALITY OF A SHOE does not depend solely upon its appearance. A fine shoe always looks fine, but a poor shoe can be made to look fine. We sell no counterfeits. The genuine worth of our Ladies' shoes is attested by the scores and hundreds of voluntary letters of commendation. We sell such shoes as will reflect credit on this department, such goods as will stand the test of wear.

Our Terms: Send 50 cents with your order, and we will send any pair of shoes C. O. D. subject to examination. 3 per cent discount when cash in full accompanies order. If you wish your order delayed, forget to state size wanted.

## Ladies Fine Coin Toe Lace or Button.

The accompanying cut represents our Ladies' Coin Toe Lace Shoe, which for style and fit is not excelled by any shoe on the market. We carry this shoe in both Lace and Button and guarantee it to wear as well as any hand turn shoe ever sold, no matter what the price. It is cut from the very finest Vici Kid stock, hand turn soles, very flexible, newest fancy heel foxing, patent leather tips, and the tops are faced with the very best of black silk. We recommend this shoe to those who wish the very latest style, together with ease and the best of wearing qualities. Sizes 2½ to 8, widths AA, A, B, C, D, E, and EE. Weight 17 ounces.

No. 3546  Hand turn lace, per pair..........$2.98
No. 3547  Hand turn button, per pair....... 2.98

## Fine Needle Toe Lace.

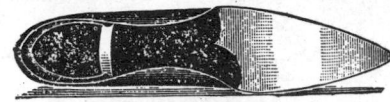

No. 3545  Ladies' Paris Kid Lace, made from selected stock, with long drawn out needle toe, hand turn flexible sole and long, narrow patent leather tip. This shoe has medium heel, fancy patent leather lace stays and the new heel foxing, making a shoe which will be very popular the coming season, and one which will wear fully as well as those usually sold at from four to four and one-half dollars. Sizes, 2½ to 7; widths, AA,A, B, C, D, E and EE; weight, 15 oz.  Price, per pair....................$2.98

## Ladies' Cloth Top Lace or Button.

BE IN STYLE.

No. 3537  Ladies' Fine Vici Kid Lace Shoe, made with long drawn out needle toe, long narrow patent leather tip, hand turn soles, medium heel and a very fine black cloth top. The shoe has fine colored satin top facing, fancy patent leather lace stays and makes a very handsome dress shoe. It is made by one of the best manufacturers in the west, hence we have no hesitancy in recommending it to our patrons. Sizes, 2½ to 7; widths, C, D, E and EE; weight, 16 oz.  Price per pair.............$2.70
No. 3537½  Same as above in button. Sizes, 2½ to 7; widths, C, D, E and EE.  Per pair.........$2.70

## Fine Needle Button.

No. 3544.  Ladies' Paris Kid Button, very finest selection, long drawn out needle toe, with narrow patent leather tip, which gives the foot a neat slender appearance. The shoe has a medium heel, fancy stitched heel foxing, hand turn soles, and for serity, style and fitting qualities compares very favorably with shoes usually sold for a good deal more money. Sizes, 2½ to 7; widths, AA,A,B,C,D,E and EE. Weight, 16 oz.  Price, per pair......... ...$2.98

## Goodyear Welt Lace.

No. 3550.  Made from a Fine Vici Kid Stock, Goodyear welt bottoms, imperial toe, with long patent leather tip. patent leather lace stays, fancy foxed heel, and the soles being cut from the best of stock and sewed on by the Goodyear process make it a very durable shoe for general wear. This shoe would be especially desirable for skating. Sizes, 2½ to 7. Width, B, C, D, E and EE. Weight, 17 oz.  Price per pair......................$2.75

## Goodyear Welt Button.

No. 3552.  Ladies' Genuine Goodyear Welt Button, made from same quality vici kid as the one preceeding; imperial toe with patent leather tip, foxed heel, and being manufactured here in Chicago by one of the largest houses in the west, we do not hesitate to recommend it to our patrons as being first-class in every particular. Sizes, 2½ to 7; widths, B, C, D, E and EE. Weight, 17 oz. Price per pair..$2.75

## Sears' Special Goodyear Welt Lace.

A GREAT BARGAIN FOR $3.00.

No. 3565  Ladies' Goodyear Welt, (lace, made from the finest selection of vici kid, with the long, drawn out needle toe, with patent leather tip). The bottoms are cut from No. 1 oak sole leather; it has fancy patent leather lace stays, foxed heel, and having the long, drawn out toe gives the foot a slender appearance. We have this shoe made especially for our own trade, and can recommend it as being first class in every particular. Sizes, 2½ to 7; widths, A, B, C, D, E and EE; weight, 16 oz.  Price, per pair...............................$3.00

## Sears' Special Goodyear Welt Button.

A $5.00 SHOE FOR $3.00

No 3566  This shoe, like the one preceding, is manufactured especially for our house, hence we know positively just what goes into it. We have it made from the best of vici kid, with a fine satin finish long, drawn out needle toe. patent leather tips foxed heel, Goodyear welt bottoms, which are cut from the best of oak tan sole leather, and will wear like iron. This particular style of toe is very popular, and it gives the foot a very stylish appearance. We can thoroughly recommend this shoe to those of our patrons who wish something up-to-date, good fitting, and suitable for general wear. Sizes, 2½ to 7; widths, AA, A, B, C, D, E and EE. Weight, 16 oz.  Price, per pair..................................$3.00

Our assortment of Mackintoshes is very complete. We invite a close comparison of price on the same quality which other houses furnish.......

SEE PAGE 177.

## Our New Trilby.

**No. 3578** The accompanying cut is an exact reproduction of our new Trilby Shoe. Cut from the same fine Vici kid stock which has made our No. 3579 shoe so popular. The shoe is made over the latest coin toe last, with patent leather tip, finest imported cloth top, patent leather lace stays and handsome inside top facing. It is McKay sewed, very flexible and as we have it made especially for our own trade, we do not hesitate to recommend it as being the most stylish and durable shoe ever sold for this price. Sizes, 2½ to 8; widths, C, D, E and EE; weight, 15 oz. Price per pair................**$2.00**

## Our Trilby.

**No. 3579.** This Shoe is Made the Same as Our Last Season's Trilby.

**McKAY TURN, BEST VICI KID FOXING. FRENCH SERGE CLOTH TOP.**

Columbia toe, with long patent leather tip and lace stays. 1 inch heel, and we do not hesitate to say that it is the most handsome shoe ever placed on the market for the money. Sizes, 2½ to 7; widths, C, D, E and EE. Weight, 14 oz. Per pair.. **$2.00**

## Ladies' Fine Lace Spring Heel.

**No. 3583.** The styles this season more than ever are running into Lace Shoes, and to meet the growing demand for them in a fine spring heel shoe we have had this shoe made especially for us. With the exception of the heel it is made after the same style as our finest shoes.

The stock is a very fine selection of vici kid; it has the new coin toe with beautiful patent leather tips, best oak tanned soles, McKay turn, which renders it as flexible as the hand turn and much more durable. This shoe also has fancy patent leather lace stays and the new foxed heel, making it altogether the most handsome and up-to-date spring heel shoe ever placed on the market. Sizes 2 to 6; widths, A, B, C, D and E. Weight, 14 oz. Per pair..............**$2.48**

## Ladies' Fine Big Ankle Shoe.

**No. 3584** Owing to the Large Demand for a Fine Fat Ankle Shoe, which would not have a cheap appearance, we have had this shoe manufactured especially for our trade. It is made from best vici kid, McKay sewed, 3½ inch vamps, 1 inch heel, medium opera toe and with beautiful patent tips. Sizes, 3 to 9; width, F only. Weight, 16 oz. Per pair.........**$2.45**

## Ladies' Big Ankle Shoe.

**No. 3586.** This Shoe we also have made to meet the wants of those who do not wish so fine a shoe as No, 3584. It is made from a good grade of dongola, low heel, medium toe, and is cut extra wide at the ankle. Sizes, 3 to 8; width, EE only; weight, 19 ounces. Per pair..**$1.85**

## Ladies' Medium Spring Heel Patent Tip. Lace or Button.

This shoe is made especially for those of our customers who do not like the regular heeled shoe, and to give the wearer the most comfort and the best wear possible in a medium priced shoe. We feel sure that it will meet with success. Made from a good dongola kid stock, all solid. McKay sewed, medium weight sole, new coin toe with patent leather tip, fancy foxed heel, and for appearance it compares favorably with shoes sold for a good deal more money. Sizes, 2½ to 6; widths, D. E and EE; weight, 16 oz.

**No. 3588.** Coin toe, button. Price per pair. **$1.75**
**No. 3589.** Coin toe, lace. Price per pair.... **1.75**

## Old Ladies' Congress.

**No. 3590** Old Ladies' Congress Shoe, is made from genuine dongola, over a common sense last, and is specially designed for comfort. Requires no lacing or buttoning, and at the same time has a very neat appearance. Sizes 3 to 9; widths, E and EE only; weight 20 oz. Price per pair................. **1.40**

## Ladies' Button or Lace New Coin Toe.

**Our $1.68 Bargain.**

**Ladies' Dongola Kid,** button or lace, made from good stock over the new Coin last, which is the very newest style worn in the large cities. Some call it the quarter toe, as it is round and about the width of a 25 cent piece. This shoe is made with medium weight sole, long patent leather tip, foxed heel, kid top facing, and we can recommend it as being the best shoe we have ever seen for the price. Weight 17 ounces. Size 2½ to 7. Width D, E, and EE.

**No. 3592 Button Coin Toe.** Price, per pair.**$1.68**
**No. 3593 Lace Coin Toe.** Price, per pair. **1.68**

**Our $1.68 Line.**

SPECIAL NOTICE.—We wish to call special attention to numbers 3594, 3596 and 3599. These shoes are made to our order, by one of the largest manufacturers in the west and for style, fit and wearing qualities are equal to most $3.00 shoes.

## Solid Comfort.

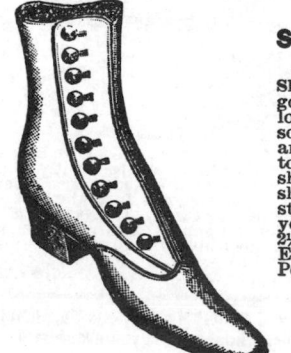

**No. 3601.** This Shoe is made from good dongola stock, low heel, broad toe, soft and pliable sole, and we guarantee it to be as easy as any shoe ever sold. This shoe is always in style and suitable for young and old. Sizes, 2½ to 8; widths, E and EE; weight, 20 ounces. Per pair........**$1.50**

## Ladies' Square Toe Button.

THIS SHOE IS DESIGNED FOR THOSE WHO CANNOT WEAR THE NEEDLE TOE LAST AND STILL WISH A NEAT APPEARING SHOE.

**No. 3604.** It is made from a good grade dongola medium heel, and square toe, with patent leather tip. Sizes, 2½ to 8; widths, D, E, and EE; weight, 20 oz. Per pair..**$1 50**

## Ladies' Serge Congress.

**OUR 98 CENT CONGRESS SHOE.**

**No. 3606** This shoe is made from a good quality of serge, leather soles and counters, common sense last, and is not only a very cool and comfortable shoe, but will give excellent service. Sizes, 3 to 8; width, EE only. Price, per pair.................**$0.98**

## Our Queen Spring Heel.

**LACE OR BUTTON.**

We have been compelled to add these shoes on account of the large demand for a ladies' spring heel shoe which could be sold at a low price and still give a reasonable amount of wear. Our Queen line is so well and favorably known that it is only necessary to say that these shoes are made from the same grade of genuine dongola stock with opera toes, patent leather tips, and come in button or lace as desired. Weight 18 oz. Always order by number.

**No. 3612 Ladies' Lace,** Sizes 2½ to 6, width E. Per pair................**$1.35**
**No. 3613 Ladies Button,** Sizes 2½ to 6, width E. Per pair................**$1.35**

## Our "Queen" Button.

**No. 3614.** Made from a splendid quality of genuine dongola kid, our own selection. Has solid one piece counter, solid one piece insole, best outer sole, needle toe with beautiful patent leather tip, is flexible, and is certainly "Queen" of all shoes under $1.75. They will give good service, and if you try them once you will want them again. Sizes, 2½ to 7; widths, D, E and EE. Weight, 17 oz. Price, per pair.......**$1.35**

## Our "Queen" Lace.

**No. 3615** This Shoe, like the one preceding, is made from a good selection of genuine dongola, machine sewed, flexible sole, steel shank, solid leather counter, one piece leather inner sole and the best outer sole. It is made on the new needle last, with beautiful patent leather tip, has patent leather lace stays. We claim it to be "Queen" of all shoes sold under $1.75. Sizes, 2½ to 7; widths, D, E and EE; weight, 17 oz. Price per pair, **$1.35**

**Don't Forget** Our Liberal Terms. Shoes Sent D. O. D. on 50 Cents Deposit, or 3 Per Cent Off For Full Cash With Order.

# OUR $1.98 LINE.

**SPECIAL NOTICE.**—We wish to call special attention to numbers 3594, 3596 and 3599. These Shoes are made to our order by one of the largest manufacturers in the west, and for style, fit and wearing qualities are equal to most $3.00 shoes.

## The Footlight.
**Ladies' Fine Vici Kid Lace.**

**No 3594** Long, drawn out needle toe, patent leather tip and lace stays, McKay sewed flexible soles, fancy heel foxing, and without a doubt the most handsome shoe ever sold for the money. Sizes, 2½ to 8. Widths, C, D, E and EE. Weight, 16 oz. Price, per pair.. ................................$1.98

## Ladies' Vici Kid Lace.

**No, 3596** This Shoe is made from the same fine Vici kid stock as the one preceding, over the new coin toe last, with handsome patent leather tip and lace stays, new style heel foxing, McKay sewed. very flexible and to those who wish a stylish, durable and good fitting shoe at a medium price, we recommend it. Sizes, 2½ to 8; widths, C, D, E and EE; weight, 16 oz. Price per pair......... ...........$1.98

**LADIES INTERESTED IN FANCY WORK** will find a tasty assortment in our Notion Department. See Index.

## Ladies' Vici Kid Button.

**No. 3599.** Ladies' Vici Kid Button Shoe, cut from selected stock, new needle toe, with patent leather tip, McKay sewed flexible soles, and medium heel. The shoe has the new fancy heel foxing and we recommend it as being one of the best shoes we have ever been able to offer at this price. Sizes, 2½ to 8; widths, C, D, E and EE. Weight, 16 oz. Price per pair.................................$1.98

---

## Our Leaders in Lace or Button.

These shoes are made from good plump **India Kid**, have good bottom stock, opera toe with patent leather tip, and are as neat in appearance as any $1.50 shoe. We do not warrant these shoes but claim them to be extra value for the price. Sizes 2½ to 8, widths D, E and EE. Weight 20 oz.
**No. 3616** Ladies' Lace Patent Tip, per pair, net...............$1.00
**No. 3618** Ladies' Button Patent Tip, per pair, net...............$1.00

## Ladies' Kangaroo Calf Shoes.

**There is no leather which for wet weather and general wear is equal to Kangaroo Calf.**

**No. 3619** This shoe is not so heavy as the calf shoes are, is more pliable, made with medium heel, narrow square toe, patent leather tip, and for actual wearing qualities has no equal Sizes, 2½ to 8; widths, E and EE; weight, 20 oz. Per pair.. ........$1.75

WE HAVE BROKEN THE ICE IN THE SALE OF PHONOGRAPHS. You will now find them within your reach. See the line we quote and note the prices. Refer to index.

## LADIES' HEAVY SHOES.
### Ladies' Oil Grain Button.

**No. 3633.** This shoe is made from Genuine Oil Grain Leather, with solid bottoms and counter. It is designed principally for rough wear, and still is not real heavy or clumsy. This leather is always soft and pliable, and when wet will always dry soft Sizes, 2½ to 8; widths, E and EE. Weight, 27 oz. Price per pair.......$1.25

### Our Special Oil Grain Button.

**BEST EVER SOLD**

**No. 3634** This shoe is made same style as above, but from the very best Milwaukee oil grain stock. and we guarantee it to be as good as any oil grain shoe ever sold. Warranted. Sizes, 2½ to 8; widths. D, E and EE. Weight, 26 oz. Price per pair......$1.50

### Ladies' Glove Grain Button.

**No. 3636** Ladies' Glove Grain Button, strictly custom made, oil tanned for wet weather, half double sole, worked button holes, pegged or screwed, warranted. Sizes, 2½ to 8; widths, D, E and EE; weight, 25 oz. Price, per pair, $1.65
**No. 3637** Ladies' Glove Grain Button. made from good stock solid sole leather counter, (and inner soles, and the best of bottom stock. A shoe which will give excellent wear and we can thoroughly recommend it. Weight, 27 oz.; sizes, 3 to 8; full width. Price per pair...............$1.20

## Ladies' Bright Grain Button.
**No. 3639.** Ladies' Bright Grain Button Shoe; worked buttonholes, half double sole, solid leather counter and insole, and the best shoe on the market for the price. Sizes, 2½ to 8; full width. Weight, 27 oz. Per pair......$1.25

## Ladies' Lace Shoes.

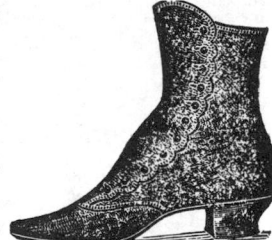

**No. 3641.** Ladies' Calf Polish, made from the best all calf stock, half double soles and hand pegged. This is a strictly western custom made shoe, and there is nothing better for heavy wear at any price. Warranted. Sizes, 3 to 8; weight, 26 oz. Price per pair.............$1.76
**No. 3642.** Ladies' Calf Polish, half double soles, pegged, and a good serviceable shoe. Sizes, 3 to 8; weight, 26 oz. Price per pair. $1.40
**No. 3643.** Ladies' Oil Grain Polish, all solid, half double soles. A great shoe for wet weather. Sizes, 3 to 8; weight, 28 oz. Price per pair...............................$1.20

## Ladies' Best Glove Grain Polish.
**No. 3646.** This Ladies' Glove Grain Lace Shoe is made from the best stock procurable, half double sole, machine sewed and being strictly custom made, will give the best of service. Warranted. Sizes, 3 to 8. Weight 26 oz. Price, per pair.............$1.45
**No. 3647.** Ladies' Glove Grain polish, made from good stock, all solid, machine sewed, and will give more service than shoes usually sold at this price. Sizes, 3 to 8. Weight 26 oz. Price, per pair. $1.20

WE GUARANTEE THAT IF YOU ARE NOT ENTIRELY SATISFIED with the value we give you, you can return any article to us and we will exchange or refund money.

OUR 3 PER CENT. DISCOUNT FOR CASH IN FULL WITH ORDER MUST NOT BE FORGOTTEN. OUR C. O. D. TERMS ARE ALSO VERY LIBERAL. SEE FIRST FOUR PAGES OF CATALOGUE.

## Misses' and Children's Shoes.

Misses' and Children's Shoes, Made from a very fine selection of Vici Kid, spring heel, lace, and over the new Dime toe last. This shoe has beautiful patent leather tip and lace stays, fancy foxed heel, very best white oak soles, McKay sewed, flexible, and we recommend it to those who wish the very latest style, together with a first class fit and good wearing qualities. Weight, 12 to 16 ounces.

No. 3648 Misses' Sizes, 11½, 12, 12½, 13, 13½, 1, 1½ and 2 widths, C, D, E and EE. Per pair.......$1.55
No. 3649 Child's Sizes, 8, 8½, 9, 9½, 10, 10½ and 11, widths, C, D, E and EE. Per pair..............$1.30

## Misses' and Childs' Button.

This shoe is made from a very fine selection of Vici Kid, with spring heel, new Dime toe last with patent leather tip, McKay sewed, flexible, and the bottoms being cut from the very best of oak sole leather, will give excellent service. This shoe will fit right, wear right, and the price is right. Weight, 12 to 16 oz.

**$1.55.**

No. 3650. Misses' Sizes, 11½, 12, 12½, 13, 13½, 1, 1½ and 2. Widths, C, D, E and EE. Per pair..............$1.55
No. 3651. Childs' Sizes, 8, 8½, 9, 9½, 10, 10½ and 11. Widths, C, D, E and EE. Per pair..............$1.30

## Misses and Children's Lace.

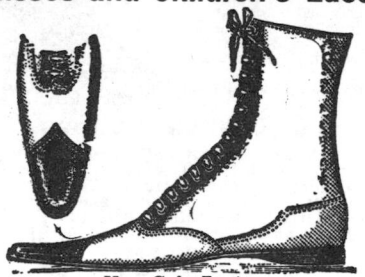

**New Coin Last.**

This shoe is made from a good Dongola Kid stock, over the new coin last, with spring heel, and patent leather tip toe. It is the very latest style, and will give excellent wear. Weight 12 to 15 oz.
No. 3661 Misses Sizes, 11½, 12, 12½, 13, 13½, 1, 1½ and 2; widths, D, E and EE. Per pair..........$1.30
No. 3662 Child's Sizes, 8, 8½, 9, 9½, 10, 10½ and 11; widths, D, E and EE. Per pair..............$1.15

## Misses' and Children's Cloth Top Shoes.

Misses' Lace Shoes, made from good grade of dongola kid, spring heel, needle toe, with long patent leather tip, black cloth top, and patent leather lace stays. The soles are of medium weight, with fair stitch on outside edge, making in all a very neat and serviceable shoe. Weight 15 oz.
No 3686 Misses' sizes, 11½, 12, 12½, 13, 13½, 1, 1½ and 2. Price per pair..............$1.60

## Misses' Oil Grain Button.

No. 3700. Made from best Milwaukee Oil grain stock, all solid, and suitable for general wear. Sizes 12 to 2, full width.
Price per pair.........$1.20

Made from Milwaukee Grain stock.

**$1.20.**

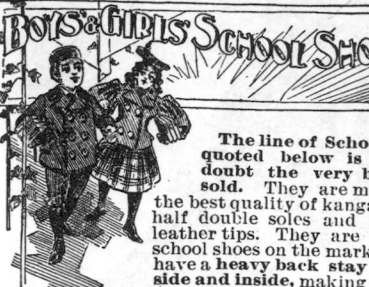

## BOYS & GIRLS SCHOOL SHOES.

The line of School Shoes quoted below is without doubt the very best ever sold. They are made from the best quality of kangaroo calf, half double soles and box sole leather tips. They are the only school shoes on the market which have a heavy back stay on outside and inside, making them the strongest yet produced. They also have an extremely low heel, and bottoms cut from the finest oak sole leather. The stock from which these shoes are made is much more tough than either dongola or pebble grain stock, is as near water proof as leather can be made, and the shoe, as a whole, is without a doubt the best ever produced. We quote elsewhere a cheaper school shoe, but recommend these as the very best that money can buy. Every pair warranted.

This shoe, like the one preceding, is made from best kangaroo stock, sole leather box tip, and has the new improved back stay. For complete description see above. We guarantee every pair of these shoes to give entire satisfaction, also to be the best school shoe ever produced, no matter what the price.
No. 3713. Sizes, 1, 1½, 2, 2½ and 3. Per pair.$1.60
No. 3714. Sizes, 11, 11½, 12, 12½, 13 and 13½. Per pair..............$1.45
No. 3715. Sizes, 8, 8½, 9, 9½, 10 and 10½. Per pair..............$1.30
No. 3716. Sizes, 5, 5½, 6, 6½, 7 and 7½. Per pair..............$1.05

## S. R. & Co.'s School Shoes.

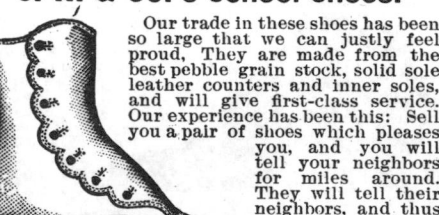

Our trade in these shoes has been so large that we can justly feel proud. They are made from the best pebble grain stock, solid sole leather counters and inner soles, and will give first-class service. Our experience has been this: Sell you a pair of shoes which pleases you, and you will tell your neighbors for miles around. They will tell their neighbors, and thus we will have a large trade from your vicinity. We cannot afford to sell poor goods. Order a pair of school shoes and be convinced of their value. Postage, 10c to 20c. Price.
No. 3718. Sizes, 5, 5½, 6, 6½, 7 and 7½........$0.75
No. 3719. Sizes, 8, 8½, 9, 9½, 10 and 10½...... .98
No. 3720. Sizes, 11, 11½, 12, 12½, 13 and 13½.. 1.18
No. 3721. Sizes, 1, 1½ and 2...................... 1.28

## We Sell Saddles

As cheap as many Retail Dealers buy at.
We make it pay you when you buy of us

## Child's Pebble Grain School Shoe.

Button, Double sole, low flat heels, sole leather box tip toes, worked button holes. All solid.

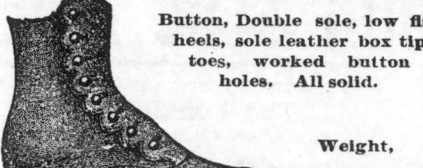

Weight, 12 to 20 Ounces.

No. 3722. Sizes, 5, 5½, 6, 6½, 7, 7½, pair.......$0.75
No. 3723. Sizes, 8, 8½, 8, 9½, 10, 10½, pair...... .98
No. 3724. Sizes, 11, 11½, 12, 12½ 13, 13½, pair.. 1.18
No. 3725. Sizes, 1, 1½, 2, pair.................... 1.28

No. 3744 Child's Bright Grain Button, made from good stock, with heels and box tip. A serviceable shoe for little money. Sizes, 5 to 8.
Price per pair..........$0.65

## Fat Baby Shoes.

No. 3748. Child's Fat Baby Shoes, made from fine quality of kid skin, spring heel, patent leather tip, and cut with extra wide soles and full ankles. The soles are hand turn, flexible, and it has worked buttonholes and silk tassel to top. Sizes, 4 to 8. EE only
Price per pair..........$0.72

## Child's Paris Kid Button.

No. 3749. Child's Fine Shoes, spring heel, made from best selection of Paris kid, worked buttonholes, hand turn, fancy foxed heel, square toe with patent leather tip, and suitable for fine dress wear. Sizes, 4, 4½, 5, 5½, 6, 6½, 7, 7½ and 8. Widths, C, D and E.
Price per pair.......$0.85

## Fat Baby.

No. 3752. Infants' Domestic Kid Fat Baby Shoes, button, no heels, very light and fine and cut large at ankles, especially for thick, fat feet. Sizes 2 to 5.
Price per pair..........$0.58
No. 3750 Child's Kid Button Spring Heel, patent leather tip, flexible soles, all solid and a good wearing shoe, sizes 5 to 8; weight 6 oz. Per pair.....................$0.60

## Infants' Leader.

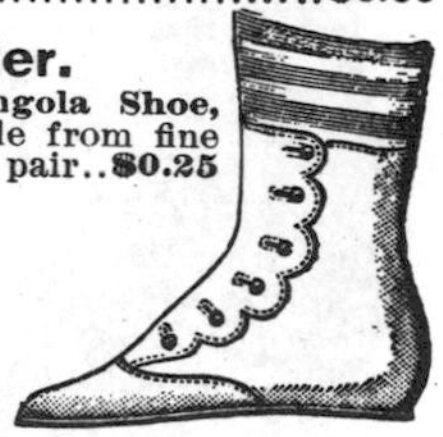

No. 3756. Infants' Dongola Shoe, no heel, flexible sole, made from fine stock; sizes, 2 to 5. Price, per pair..$0.25

## Infants' Fine Shoes.

3758 Infants' Glazed Dongola Kid Button, very good stock, turn soles, no heel, narrow square toe, with patent leather tip and neat tassel at top. A very dressy shoe. Weight, 4 oz. Sizes 2, 2½, 3, 3½, 4, 4½ and 5. Per pair.............$0.55
No. 3762 Infants' Dongola Shoe, turn sole, no heel, and neat patent leather tip. Weight, 4 oz. Sizes, 2, 2½, 3, 3½, 4, 4½ and 5. Per pair.......$0.50
3763 Infants' Kid Button, turn sole, patent leather tip, no heel, a neat and well-made shoe. Weight, 5 oz. Sizes, 2, 2½, 3, 3½, 4, 4½ and 5. Per pair........................$0.40

## Infants' French Kid Button.

No, 3765 This Shoe is made from a choice selection of genuine kid fancy stitched, has kid sole, and is a very pretty shoe for an infant. Cut very full so you will have no trouble to put them on. Color, tan. Sizes, 1, 2, 3 and 4.
Per pair..........$0.40
No. 3766 The same style, in dongola kid. Black only. Sizes, 1, 2, 3 and 4.
Per pair,........$0.25

FREIGHT IS A VERY SMALL ITEM OF EXPENSE WHEN COMPARED WITH WHAT WE SAVE YOU. IF YOU DON'T NEED ENOUGH GOODS TO MAKE A FREIGHT ORDER, PERHAPS YOUR NEIGHBOR DOES, AND YOU CAN SEND TOGETHER.

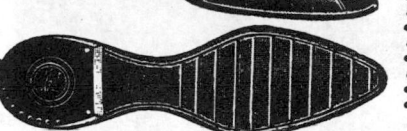

# MEN'S RUSSIA CALF AND COLORED VICI KID SHOES...
## LATEST STYLES—LATEST COLORS.

**WEAR THE LATEST** and keep up with the procession. **ORDER NOW** and lead the fashion for your neighborhood.
OUR HARD CASH line of Colored Shoes are the top notch of fine shoemaking.

## THEY FIT LIKE A GLOVE AND WEAR LIKE IRON.

**THEY ARE GUARANTEED** to be equal in every respect to any Colored Shoe ever sold for $5.00—strong assertion, but we are here to make it good. **Order a pair** and see them talk for themselves. **Every pair** made especially for us, after our own designs, and under our personal supervision. **We know what's in them**—you will, if you wear a pair. **Money back,** together with express charges, if they are not exactly as represented in every way. Below we show exact colors and styles as reproduced from the shoes by our artist.

### MEN'S VICI KID HAND SEWED LACE.

#### COLORED FEEL EZY.

**No. 3574.** Men's Hard Cash Lace, best vici kid, dark chocolate color, hand sewed. Made with plain toe of medium width, medium heel, desirable for tender feet. Fast color eyelets and fancy colored inside top facing. You never saw its equal under $5.00. Sizes, 6 to 11; widths, D, E and EE.

**SPECIAL PRICE, PER PAIR, $2.98.**

### MEN'S RUSSIA CALF LEADER.

#### NEW COIN LAST.

**No. 3575.** Made from a good grade of Russia calf, dark wine color, McKay sewed, New Coin Last with long perforated tip. The last is exactly like our Hard Cash line and we can honestly recommend the shoe as the best ever seen for the price. Sizes, 6 to 1'; widths, D, E and EE. Weight, 32 ounces.

**SPECIAL PRICE, PER PAIR, $1.98.**

### MEN'S OX BLOOD LACE.
#### Chocolate Cloth Top—Hand Sewed —Needle Toe.

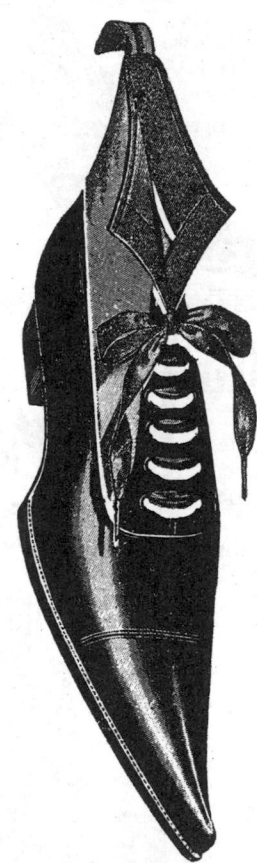

**No. 3576.** This Shoe is one we have made after our own peculiar style and we consider it one of the neatest colored shoes out this season. Made from the very finest Russia Calf; the new Ox Blood (dark wine) color, long drawn out Needle Toe with corded imitation tip. The tops are made from a very fine Chocolate colored cloth which, together with the wine colored vamps, produces a striking contrast. The shoe is strictly hand sewed, has fast color eyelets, fancy colored top facing, and we recommend it as being firstclass in every particular. The height of fashion and very durable. Sizes, 5 to 11; widths; B, C, D, E and EE.

**PRICE, PER PAIR, $2.98.**

### Men's Ox Blood Calf Lace—Hand Sewed.

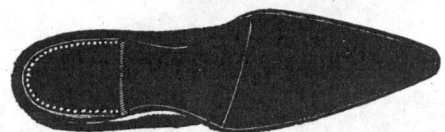

#### NEW COIN LAST.

**No. 3577.** Men's Hard Cash Lace, best Russia Calf, latest Ox Blood (dark wine) color, strictly hand sewed, agatine eyelets, fancy colored calf top facing, soles cut from best oak tan sole leather and finished in black which together with the wine uppers makes one of the handsomest shoes we have ever seen. This shoe retails at $5 everywhere. Sizes from 5 to 11; widths, B, C, D, E and EE.

**SPECIAL PRICE, PER PAIR, $2.98.**

### MEN'S VICI KID LACE—HAND SEWED.

**No. 3585.** Men's Chocolate Vici Kid Shoe, best selection of stock and latest Coin Toe Last, fancy stitched tip, strictly hand made, kid inside top facing, fast color eyelets, bottoms cut from the best California oak sole leather. If you wish a shoe thoroughly up-to-date, soft and durable, order this one. Sizes, 5 to 11; widths, A, B, C, D and EE. Weight, 32 ounces.

**SPECIAL PRICE, PER PAIR, $2.98.**

# LADIES' COLORED SHOES.

**W**E HAVE THIS SEASON HAD ALL OF OUR LADIES' COLORED GOODS MADE ESPECIALLY TO OUR ORDER, and we propose to sell them to you at prices never before heard of. The demand for Tan Shoes was never so great as at the present time, and we realize the fact that by offering these **SHOES AT AN EXTREMELY LOW PRICE** we will gain many new customers for our shoe department, and after a trial order we feel sure you will always buy your shoes from us. We never before were in a position to sell

## ━━━ THOROUGHLY HIGH GRADE FOOTWEAR ━━━

AT SUCH EXTREMELY LOW PRICES. ORDER EARLY AND LEAD THE STYLE in your town. Money back on any pair not satisfactory.
**ALL SHOES SHIPPED C. O. D.** SUBJECT TO EXAMINATION, upon receipt of **50 cents** per each pair, as a guarantee of good faith. 3 PER CENT. CASH DISCOUNT if money is sent with the order.

## LADIES' EXTRA FINE VICI KID LACE.
### COLORED PATENT LEATHER TRIMMED.

**No. 3531** The accompanyng cut is a very good representation of our best Ladies' Tan Shoe. It is made from the very finest selection of Vici kid, which is as soft as a glove, chocolate color, hand turn soles, new coin last with tan patent leather tip. The shoe has fancy colored patent leather heel foxing and lace stays, handsome inside top facing, and it is the very latest style out. We guarantee it to be equal to any colored shoe ever sold up to $5.00, and to those who wish the very latest production in fine footwear, and a shoe that fits like a glove we recommend it. Sixes, 2½ to 7. Widths, AA, A, B, C, D and E. Weight, 16 ounces.

### PRICE, PER PAIR $3.50.

## LADIES' TAN CLOTH TOP.

**No. 3541** This shoe is made from a good grade of genuine Dongola, chocolate color, and with a fine tan cloth top; needle toe with tip, solid sole leather counter and insoles, good bottom stock, and is without a doubt the very best colored shoe we have ever seen at the price. Weight, 16 ounces. Sizes, 2½ to 8. Widths, D, E, and EE.

### PER PAIR, $1.65.

## OUR PRICES
### $1.45, $1.98, $2.15, and $3.50....
### GUARANTEE YOU A SAVING
.....OF.....
**33⅓ PER CENT** TO **40 PER CENT.**

## LADIES' TAN VICI KID.
### CLOTH TOP.

**No. 3539** This Shoe is made from a very fine selection of tan Vici kid, chocolate color, new coin toe, which is round and about the width of a half dollar, with fancy tip toe, genuine McKay sewed, very flexible and has the very best of oak tan bottom stock. It has a very fine tan cloth top, fancy kid lace stays and colored kid inside top facing. We have had this shoe made especially for our trade and to meet the demand for a colored shoe with cloth top, medium price and durable. We recommend it as being the very best, and most handsome tan shoe we have ever seen for the price. Sizes, 2½ to 8. Widths, C. D. E and EE. Weight, 18 oz.

### PER PAIR, $2.15.
**No. 3539½** Same in spring heel. Misses' sizes, 12 to 2.

### PER PAIR, $1.75.

## LADIES' CHOCOLATE LACE.

**No. 3535** The above cut represents a Ladies' Vici Kid Shoe, chocolate color, McKay sewed, flexible soles, long drawn out needle toe with tip, new scroll heel foxing, and as easy and durable as any hand turn shoe we have ever seen. The shoe has all the style of the $4.00 and $5.00 shoes and at the same time is very durable. Sizes, 2½ to 7. Widths, C, D, E and EE.

### PER PAIR, $1.98.

## LADIES' TAN BUTTON.

**No. 3543** Ladies' Button Shoe, made from a good chocolate color Dongola, all solid, needle toe with tip, new style heel foxing, and a shoe which we honestly believe will wear as well as any $2.00 colored shoe ever sold. Weight, 16 ounces. Sizes, 2½ to 8. Widths, D, E and EE.

### PER PAIR, $1.45.

# OUR LATEST SPECIALTIES IN COLORED GOODS.

HAVING quite a number of Shoes to show and only a limited amount of space, we make the descriptions short as possible, but the cuts are in every instance an exact reproduction from the shoe. We wish to state that every shoe shown on this page is a LEADER, made especially for our own trade, and positively cannot be equaled anywhere for the price.

### Ladies' Dark Wine Oxford.

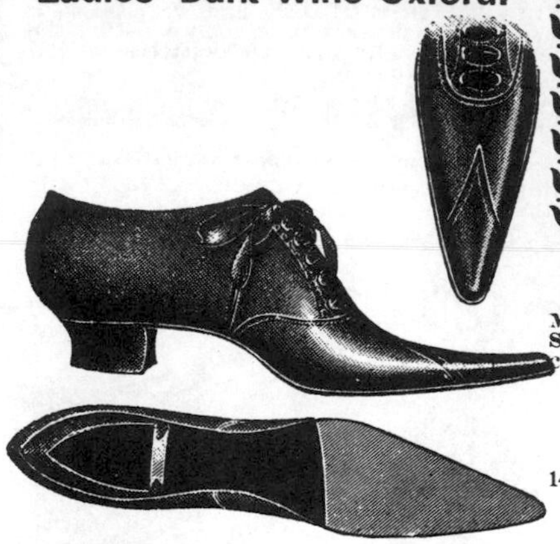

**No. 3553 This Oxford is Made from Genuine Goat Skin,** dark wine (ox blood) color, machine sewed, medium narrow toe with tip, and will give you splendid wear for the money. Sizes, 2½ to 8. Widths full. Weight, 14 ounces.
Per pair..............**$1.00**

### Ladies' Oxford Vici Kid Lace.

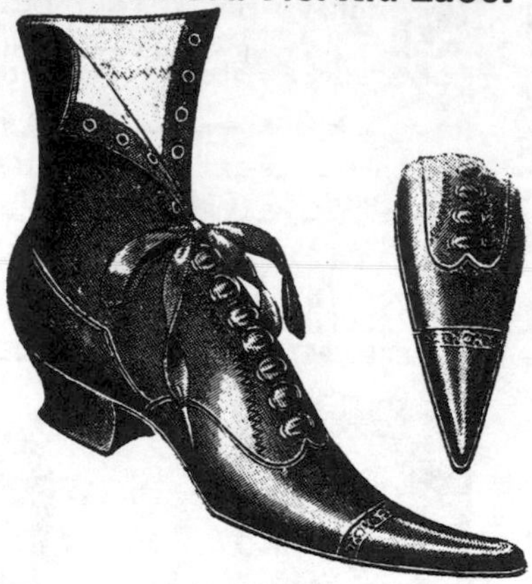

**No. 3534 Made from Finest Selection of Vici Kid,** dark wine (ox blood) color, long drawn out needle toe and tip. The shoe is McKay sewed, very flexible sole, and to those who wish a first class and stylish shoe for little money, we recommend it. Sizes 2½ to 7. Widths, B, C, D and E. Weight, 17 oz.
Per pair..... .......**$2.35**

### Boys' and Youths' Tan Shoes.

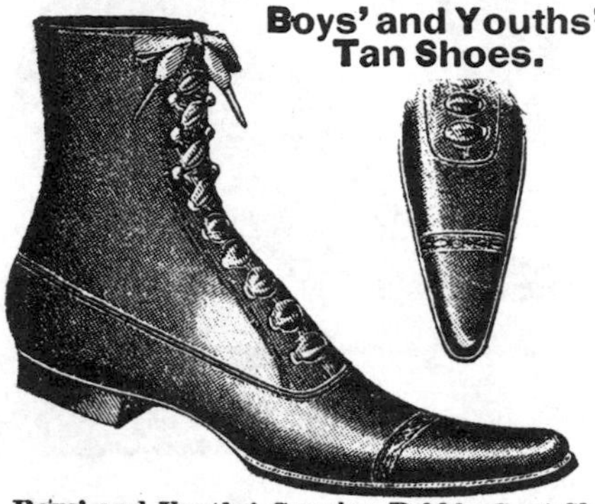

**Boys' and Youths' Genuine Pebble Goat Shoes,** chocolate color, made over the new coin toe last, with tip, best of soles, all solid, and besides being very stylish in appearance; a splendid wearing shoe. Weight 15 to 20 oz. Widths, D, E and EE.
**No. 3555** Boys' sizes, 2, 2½, 3, 3½, 4, 4½, 5 and 5½. Per pair..............**$1.75**
**No. 3556** Youths' sizes, 11, 11½, 12, 12½, 13, 13½, 1 and 1½. Per pair..............**$1.50**

### Misses' and Childrens' Tan Button.

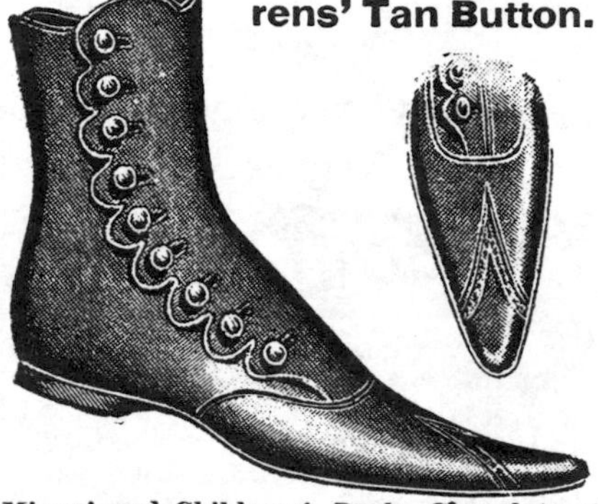

**Misses' and Childrens' Dark Chocolate Goat Button,** made with spring heel, new opera toe with tip, all solid, and a splendid shoe for the price. Weight, 12 to 15 oz.
**No. 3707** Sizes, 11½, 12, 12½, 13, 13½, 1, 1½ and 2. Per pair..............**$1.10**
**No. 3709** Sizes, 8, 8½, 9, 9½, 10, 10½ and 11. Per pair..............**$1.00**

### Ladies' Tan Kid Oxford.

**No. 3551 Ladies' Fine Chocolate Vici Kid** Oxford, made over the new Coin last, with long perforated tip toe.

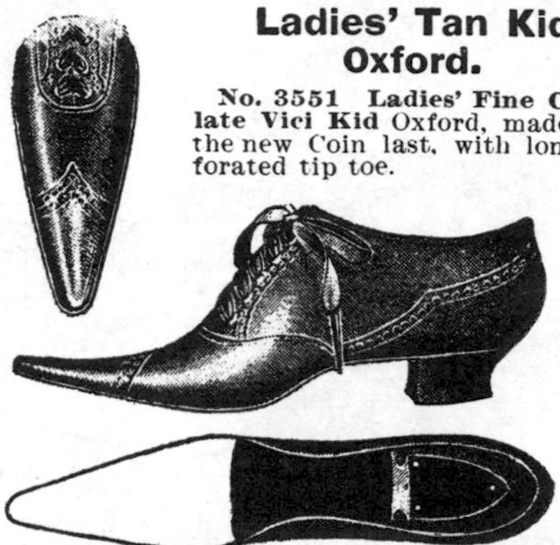

The shoe is McKay sewed, very flexible, is suitable for dress or every day wear, and we consider it one of the neatest low shoes out this season. We can recommend it as being first class in every particular. Sizes 2½ to 7. Width, C, D, E and EE. Per pair, **$1.50**

### Childs' Tan Button.

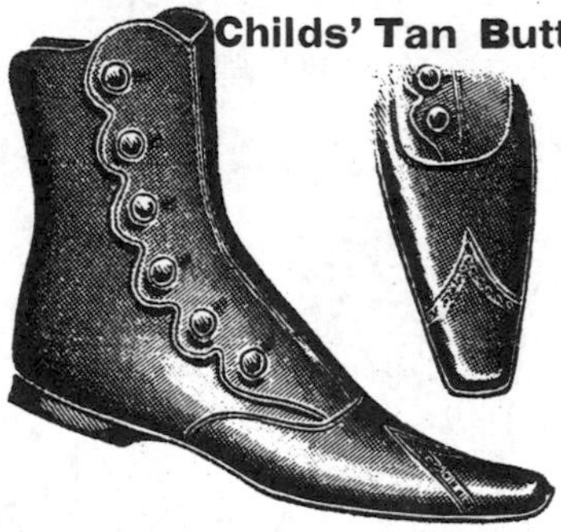

**No. 3753 Child's Genuine Chrome Tanned Dongola Kid Button,** latest dark wine (ox blood) color, hand sewed, flexible soles, narrow square toe with tip, spring heel with silk tassel at top. A very dressy and durable shoe. Sizes, 5, 5½, 6, 6½, 7, 7½ and 8. Weight, 7 oz. Per pair..............**$0.80**

### Infants' Tan Button.

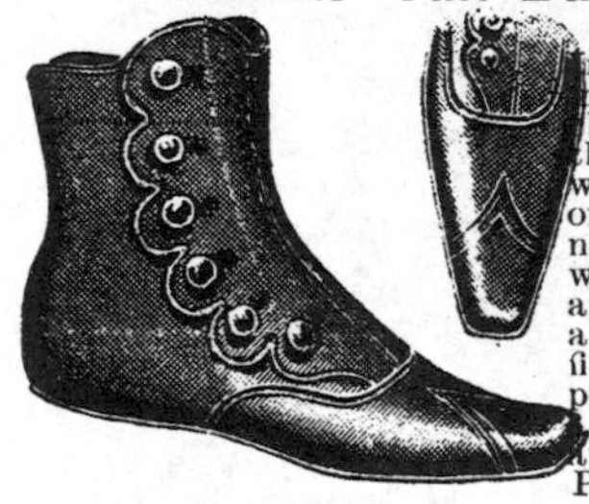

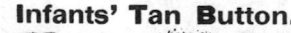

**No. 3755 This Infant's Shoe** is made from fine chrome tanned kid the latest dark wine (ox blood) color, hand sewed, narrow square toe with tip, no heel, and with silk tassel at top. Nothing finer made at any price. Sizes, 2, 2½, 3, 3½, 4, 4½, 5, 5½ and 6. Weight, 6 oz.
Per pair.....**$0.60**

### Misses' and Childrens' Tan Sandals.

**No. 3554 Misses' and Children's Vici Kid Strap Sandals,** the latest dark wine (ox blood) color, spring heel, needle toe, hand turn flexible soles, kid quarter lining and fancy satin bow and strap over instep.

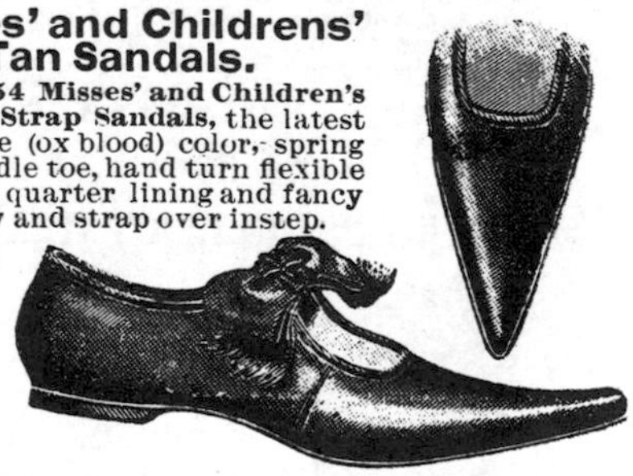

This is a very beautiful sandal for dress wear and is the latest style and color. Weight 6 to 12 oz. Widths, D, E and EE.
Sizes, 11, 11½, 12, 12½, 13, 13½, 1, 1½ and 2. Pair, **$1.35**
Sizes, 8, 8½, 9, 9½, 10 and 10½. Per pair ....... **1.20**
Sizes, 5½, 6, 6½, 7 and 7½. Per pair..... ...... **1.05**

### Ladies' Elastic Front Slippers.

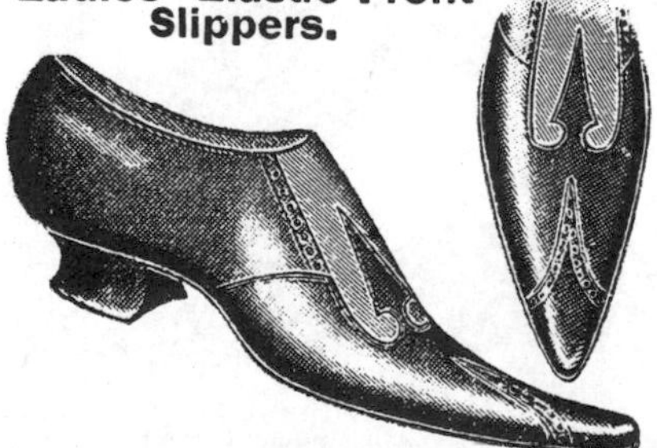

**No. 3789 Chocolate Color.** This is one of the leading novelties in low shoes, out this season. Made from a good selection of Vici Kid, chocolate color, hand turn, flexible sole and elastic front, which conforms to the shape of the foot whether high or low instep. The shoe is made over the new Dime Toe Last, with tip, kid lined, and is one of the most popular low shoes we have ever presented. Weight, 11 oz. Sizes, 2½ to 8. Widths, D, E and EE.
Per pair..............**$1.50**

### Misses' and Child's Tan Button.

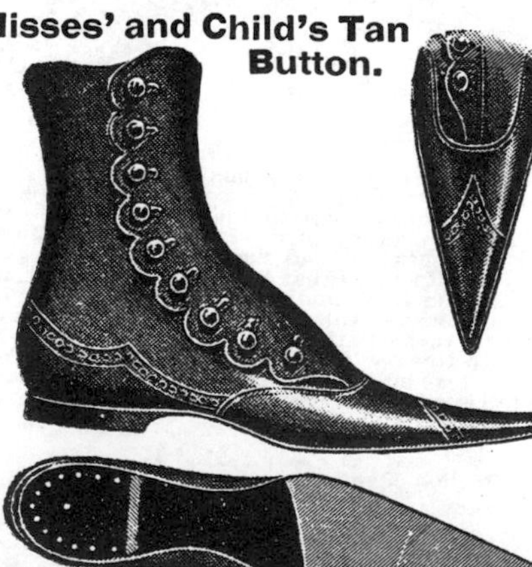

**Misses' and Child's Dark Chocolate Vici Kid Button,** made from selected stock, spring heel, McKay sewed, needle toe with tip, and fancy foxed heel. This shoe is suitable for dress wear and can also be worn every day as it is very durable. We never saw its equal for the price.
**No. 3557** Sizes, 11, 11½, 12, 12½ 13, 13½, 1, 1½ and 2. Per pair..............**$1.45**
**No. 3558** Sizes, 8, 8½, 9, 9½, 10 and 10½. Pair. **1.30**

### Misses' and Childrens' Tan Lace.

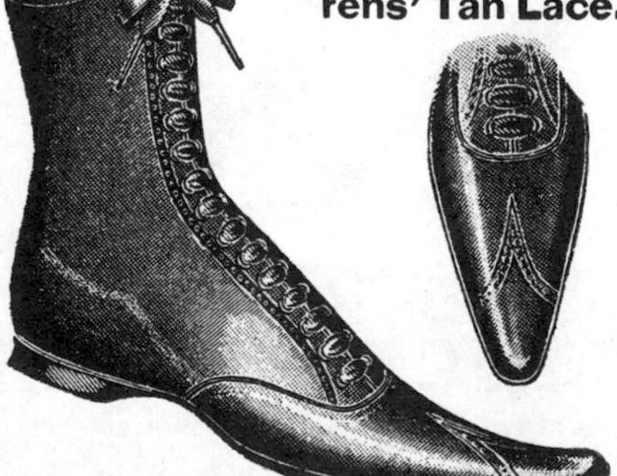

**This Shoe is made from a good grade of Goat Skin,** color dark chocolate, with spring heel and opera toe with tip. The shoe is all solid, and a good thing for the price. Weight 12 to 15 oz.
**No. 3703** Sizes, 11½, 12, 12½, 13, 13½, 1, 1½ and 2. Per pair..............**$1.10**
**No. 3705** Sizes, 8, 8½, 9, 9½, 10, 10½ and 11. Per pair..............**$1.00**

### Infants' "Princess."

**No. 3774** This is one of the leading novelties in infants' wear for the coming season. It is made from the finest kid, kid sole, handsomely trimmed with silk ribbon and has silk ribbon tie at ankle which holds it in position. (See cut.) There is nothing nicer for the baby than this shoe. **Colors, tan and wine. Sizes 1 to 4. In single carton.**
Per pair,..........................$0.45

### Our Special Infants' Moccasin.

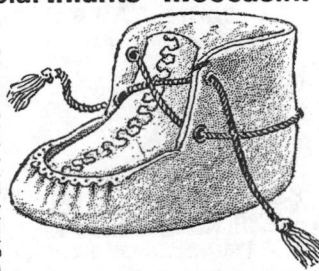

**No. 3776** This Infants' Moccasin is one we have made for our own trade, and we guarantee that it is unequaled for price and quality by any concern in existence. It is made from soft dongola stock, very full, so you will have no trouble putting them on. Sateen lined, silk stitched and handsome silk cord laces. Colors, tan and wine. Sizes, f, 2, 3 and 4. Weight, 2 oz. Sold by other houses at 35c. Our price, per pair................**19c**

### Ladies' Dongola Oxfords.

**No. 3782.** Made from good plump dongola kid, McKay turn sole, opera toe, with patent leather tip, all solid and a very sightly shoe. In this shoe we give extra good value. Sizes, 2½ to 7. Full width. Weight, 12 oz. Price, per pair,........**$0.95**

### Ladies' Fine Dongola Oxfords.

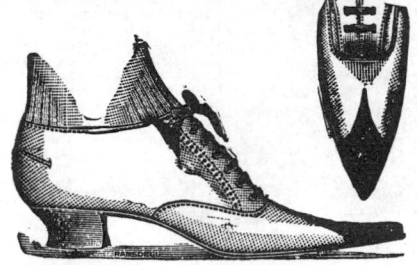

**No. 3783** This Oxford is made from the finest selection of dongola kid, McKay turn, flexible sole and needle toe with patent leather tip. The soles are made from the very best material, it has fancy patent leather trimming up the front, and fine kid lining. This is certainly a very beautiful and dressy shoe. Sizes, 2½ to 7. Widths, C, D and E. Weight, 12 ounces. Price, per pair,......................**$1.45**

### Ladies' Vici Kid Oxford.

**No 3784. Ladies Vici Kid Oxford**, made from fine selected stock, McKay turn flexible sole, and new coin toe, with patent leather tip. This Oxford is one of the latest out this season, and will give excellent service. Sizes 2½ to 7. widths B, C, D, E, and EE; weight 12 oz.
Per pair..........................**$1.45**

### Black Prince Alberts.

**No. 3798** Made from the very best vici kid, hand turn flexible sole, needle toe, patent leather tip and fancy double stitched front stay. It has fine silk elastic sides, medium heel and kid lining. If you want something dressy, comfortable and durable, order this shoe. Sizes, 2½ to 7; widths, C, D and E. Weight, 12 oz. Price, per pair..............**$1.90**

### Ladies' Elite.

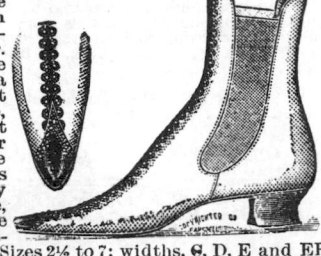

**No. 3804** One of the most stylish things for ladies' wear. Made from the best dongola kid, very soft and pliable, turn sole, neat patent leather stay up the front, and is not only a very pretty shoe, but saves the bother of buttons or laces. Sizes 2½ to 7; widths, C, D, E and EE.
Per pair (Postage, 18c.)......................**$2.40**

### Ladies' Vici Kid Strap Slippers.

**No. 3810** Strap Sandals made from selected dongola kid, hand turn, needle toe, medium high heel, fancy beaded toe and strap, and a shoe which will give splendid wear and always look neat. Sizes, 2½ to 7; widths, A, B, C, D and E. Weight, 12 oz. Per pair......................**$1.58**

### Ladies' Vici Kid Strap Sandals.

**No. 3814** Made from the finest selection of vici kid, hand turned, very flexible sole, has the new needle toe and handsome satin strap at the instep, with elegant silver buckle. The heel is medium high. We can assure you that this is one of the most handsome slippers for house or dance wear ever put on the market. Sizes, 2½ to 7; widths, A, B, C, D and E.
Per pair (Postage, 12c.)......................**$1.60**

**No. 3815 Ladies' kid strap sandals**, made from fair quality of stock, hand turn flexible soles, medium narrow toe, and satin strap at the instep, with metal buckle ornament. This slipper is excellent value for the price. Size 2½ to 7; widths full. Weight, 12 oz Price, per pair......................**$1.00**

### Misses' and Children's Dongola Oxfords.

Made from good quality vici kid, hand turn, spring heel, patent leather tip, and a good durable shoe.
**No. 3824** Sizes, 12, 12½, 13, 13½, 1, 1½ and 2. Per pair......**$1.20**
**No. 3825** Sizes, 8, 8½, 9, 9½, 10, 10½, 11 and 11½. Per pair....**$1.10**
**No. 3826** Sizes, 5, 5½, 6, 6½, 7 and 7½. Per pair....................**$0.95**

### Misses' and Children's Tan Colored Oxfords.

Made from the Best Tan Colored Vici Kid, hand turn, flexible sole, and a very neat Oxford; will give excellent wear.
**No. 3828.** Sizes, 12, 12½, 13, 13½, 1, 1½ and 2. Per pair......**$1.05**
**No. 3829.** Sizes, 8½, 9, 9½, 10, 10½, 11 and 11½. Per pair....**90c**
**No. 3830.** Sizes, 5, 5½, 6, 6½, 7, 7½ and 8. Per pair....**75c**

### Ladies' Satin Slippers.

**No. 3835.** Made from Fine Heavy Satin, light, hand turned sole, opera toe, very flexible, French heel, with satin strap buttoning across instep. A very handsome slipper for party wear. We have them in the following colors: Black, blue, pink, red, white, Nile green, lavender, lemon, canary and brown. Sizes, 1 to 7; widths, A, B, C, D and E. Per pair......**$1.98**

### Ladies' White Kid Strap Sandals.

**No. 3840** Made from very best quality white kid, narrow opera toe, hand turn soles, opera heel, kid lined and with handsome satin strap and oxydized buckle over instep. Nothing better at any price. Size 2 to 7. Widths A, B, C, D and E. Weight, 10 oz. Price, per pair......................**$1.65**

**No. 3841** Ladies' white kid Sandals, good quality, hand turn soles, opera toe and heel, fancy satin bow and buckle at instep. Sizes, 2½ to 7. Widths, B, C, D and E. Price, per pair....**$1.35**

### Ladies' White Kid Opera Slippers.

**No. 3850** Made from good selection of white kid, hand turned flexible sole, narrow opera toe, fancy bow, medium high heel, and one of the most beautiful slippers ever put on the market. Sizes, 2½ to 7; widths, C, D and E only. Wt. 10 oz. Per pair..**$1.10**

### Ladies' Dongola Opera Slippers.

**No. 3855.**

### LADIES' DONGOLA OPERA SLIPPERS.

Made from finest quality of Dongola Kid, needle toe, hand turn soles, soft and pliable. The kind that usually sells for $2.00. Size, 2½ to 7; widths, B, C, D and E. Wgt. 10 oz. Price, per pair..**$1.35**

### Ladies' Kid Opera Slippers.

**No. 3856.**

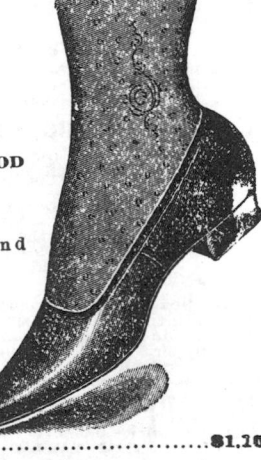

### LADIES' KID OPERA SLIPPERS.

MADE FROM A GOOD SELECTION OF DONGOLA KID.

medium opera toe and medium heel. The soles are hand turned and very flexible. This is a very comfortable house shoe and one which will look well and wear well. Weight, 12 oz. Sizes, 2½ to 7. Widths, D, E and EE. Per pair......................**$1.10**

No. 3858 Ladies, Common Sense Oxford, made from good dongola kid stock, with wide plain toe, low broad heel and McKay sewed sole. The shoe is very neat and comfortable for house wear. Sizes, 2½ to 8. Weight 12 oz. Widths, full. Per pair.....$1.00

## Ladies' Paris Kid Oxfords,--Common Sense Last.

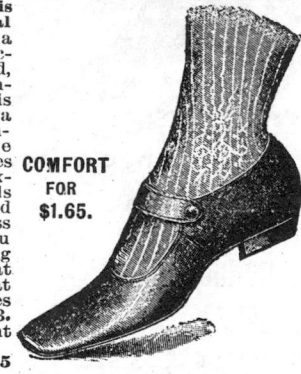

**EXTRA VALUE.**

No. 3860 This Oxford is made from a fine selection of Paris kid, with broad, plain toe and sensible heel. The soles are hand turn, very flexible, and we can recommend it as being a very neat, comfortable and durable house shoe. Sizes, 2½ to 8. Widths, B, C, D, E and EE. Weight 12 oz. Per pair, $1.40

## Ladies Common Sense Sandals.

No. 3862 This one strap Sandal is made from a very choice selection of Paris kid, over a common-sense last, and is designed for a thoroughly comfortable house slipper. The soles are hand turn, flexible, and the heels are very low and broad. Do not pass this Sandal if you wish something comfortable and at the same time neat and durable. Sizes 3 to 8; widths, B. C, D and E. Weight 14 oz.

**COMFORT FOR $1.65.**

Per pair...$1.65

## Pebble Grain Newport Tie.

No. 3870. Ladies' Pebble Grain Newport Tie. All solid and well made for rough wear. Sizes, 2½ to 8; regular width; weight, 10 oz. Price per pair.....$0.85

No. 3871. Ladies' Grain Slippers, damp proof, sewed, strong and durable, for out or indoor wear. All solid. Sizes, 3 to 8; full widtth; weight, 15 ounces. Price per pair.....$0.70

No. 3874. Ladies' Serge Buskin Slippers, turn soles, low, flat heels, fine quality. Sizes, 3 to 8; full width; weight, 8 oz. Price per pair.....$0.85

No. 3878. Ladies' Serge Buskin Slippers, medium grade. Sizes, 3 to 8; full width. Price per pair.....$0.60

## Ladies' Carpet Slippers.

No. 3879. Made from Brussels Carpet, leather sole and heel, good quality, bound and stayed. Sizes, 3 to 8. Price per pair.....$0.24

## Ladies' Felt Slippers, Leather Sole

No. 3907 Made from good felt, velvet bound, flannel lined, with good leather sole and heel, also leather side patches. A comfortable and very popular slipper. Sizes, 3 to 8; no half sizes. Price per pair.....$0.90

**THE LADY** Is Hard to Please who does not find from our Dry Goods deoartment just the fabric that suits her. We take care that the PRICES ARE RIGHT.

## Ladies' Fine Felt Nullifier, Fur Trimmed.

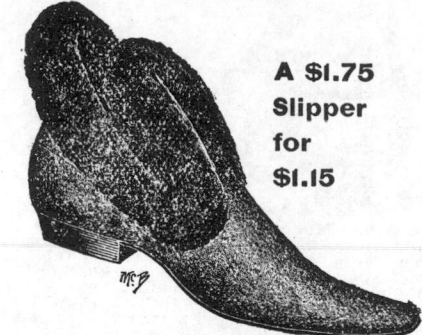

**A $1.75 Slipper for $1.15**

No. 3909. Made of Finest Toilet Felt, with hand turn leather sole, also leather heel. This shoe is trimmed with a very fine, soft fur, flannel lined, and being cut high in front and behind protects the ankles from the cold air; is very soft, light and comfortable, and will give good service. Color, black; size, 2½ to 8; widths. D and E. Price per pair.....$1.15

## Ladies' All Felt Slippers.

No. 3914 Ladies' all felt slippers, flannel lined, felt sole from ½ to ⅝ in. thick, no heel, and a good warm house slipper. Sizes, 3 to 8. No half sizes. Weight 13 oz. Price, per pair.....$0.75

## Ladies' and Misses' Fur Trimmed Felt Slippers.

No. 3916 Ladies' slippers made from best toilet felt, flannel lined throughout and genuine fur trimmed. It has the best hand turn leather sole, which is light and flexible, leather heel, opera toe, and makes a very handsome and comfortable house slipper. Sizes, 3 to 8; weight 11 oz. Price per pair.....$1.15

No. 3918 Misses' Slipper, felt, flannel lined, hand turn sole, spring heel, fur trimmed, opera toe, very neat, easy and warm. Sizes 11 lo 2; weight 9 oz. Price per pair.....$1.00

## Misses' and Children's Beaver Button Leather Foxed.

Misses' and children's button. made from good beaver felt, flannel lined throughout, leather foxed, leather sole, patent leather tip and spring heel, just the thing for cold weather.

No. 3920 Misses' sizes, 12 to 2. Per pair.....$1.30
No. 3921 Child's sizes, 9 to 11. Per pair.....1.15
No. 3922 Child's size, 4 to 8. Per pair.....85

## Infant's Beaver Button.

No. 3924 Infant's Beaver Button, same as one preceding. leather sole, no heel. Sizes, 3 to 5. Price, per pair.....$0.60

## MEN'S AND WOMEN'S WARM SHOES.
## The Motorman's Best.

No. 3882 Men's best beaver felt shoe, lace, medium width toe, solid comfort felt insole. This shoe has a very fine and soft leather foxing, long tip toe, and, while it is fully as warm as the all felt shoe, it is more desirable on account of the leather sole and foxing which enables the wearer to go in the snow the same as if he wore a full leather shoe. Sizes, 6 to 11. Per pair.....$2.15

## Men's All Felt Shoes.

No. 3884 This Shoe is mae from the very best beaver felt throughout. The sole is made from one heavy piece of felt and is very much superior to the two-piece soles which are put on the cheaper grades of felt shoes. We guarantee this shoe not only to be warm and comfortable but to be the best ever offered for the money. Sizes, 6 to 11. Per pair...$1.98

## Ladies' All Wool Felt Shoes.

No. 3896 Uppers, soles and heels of all wool felt, soles ¼ to ⅜ inch thick, black worked buttonholes, felt heels. This shoe we guarantee to wear longer than any shoe in the catalogue. If you wear Felt Shoes in cold weather, do not forget to order this shoe, as we warrant every pair. They fit as neat as any dongola shoe, and are very light. Weight, 20 oz. Sizes 2½ to 8. Price, per pair, $1.50

## Ladies' All Felt Lace.

No. 3897

**Ladies' All Felt Front Lace Shoes.**

Made from good quality of wool felt, soles and heels all felt, plush trimmed, light and serviceable: sizes, 3 to 8; no half sizes; weight 20 oz. Per pair $1.30

No. 3899.

**Womans' All Felt Lace.**

Felt sole ⅝ inches thick, plush bound top; flannel lined; sizes, 4 to 8, no half sizes. Price per pair... $0.90

## Ladies' Beaver Foxed Lace.

No. 3900. Ladies' Beaver Felt Shoe, lace, with fine Dongola Kid foxing around the lower part, and leather sole and heel. This shoe is flannel lined throughout, has leather lace stay, velvet bound and is very comfortable for cold weather, also very neat in appearance. Sizes, 2½ to 8; weight, 20 oz. Per pair.....$1.40

## Ladies' Beaver Button, Leather Foxed.

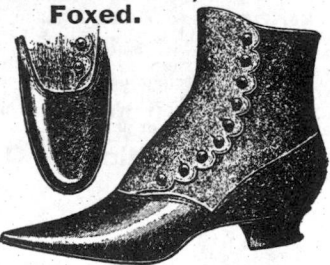

No. 3905 Made from good grade beaver felt, with fine leather foxing, leather sole and heel. This shoe is as warm as the all felt. and will give excellent service Sizes, 3 to 8. Per pair, .....$1.60

## Ladies' Beaver Congress, Leather Sole.

**Solb by others at $1.50, Cur Price, $1.00.**

No. 3906. Ladies' Beaver Congress, felt lined throughout, with leather sole and heel; also leather side patches. This shoe has the best of elastic goring, can be removed or put on quickly, and is very durable. Size, 4 to 8; no half sizes. Price per pair.....$1.00

**THE SAFEST WAY TO SEND MONEY IS BY EXPRESS MONEY ORDER. NEVER SRND COIN BY OPEN MAIL. IT IS LIABLE TO WEAR THROUGH THE ENVELOPE AND BE LOST.**

## MENS SHOES.

### Men's Custom Calf Bals.

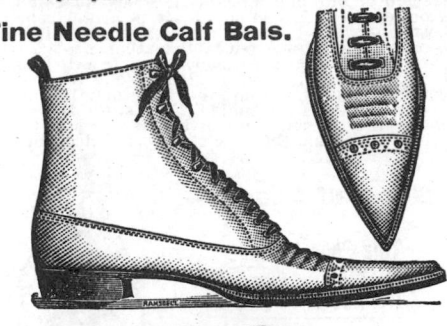

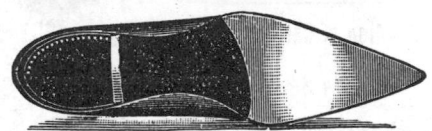

**No. 3942 Men's Custom Calf Bals,** made from the finest selected calf skin, hand sewed with the best linen waxed thread; made over the new opera last, which will be very popular this season, fine kangaroo tops, and bottoms cut from the best oak tan sole leather. If you wish a shoe thoroughly up to date, and as good as can be made, do not pass this one. Warranted. Sizes, 6 to 11; widths, A, B, C, D, E and EE. Weight 33 oz.
Price, per pair,..... ........................$3.75

### Fine Needle Calf Bals.

**No. 3944 Men's custom made Calf Lace Shoes.** The stock in this shoe is of the very best selection, and is of such weight as to give the best possible service. The shoe is made over the long drawn out needle last, with tip, has the finest topping, and the bottoms are cut from the best oak tan sole leather, and sewed on by thoroughly experienced shoemakers. Warranted. Sizes, 5 to 11; widths, A, B, C, D, E and EE. Price, per pair........................$3.75

### Men's Shell Cordovan Shoes.

**No. 3946 Men's Cordovan or Horse Hide Shoes** are made from the very finest selection of Cordovan, lace, plain medium toe, best oak tan bottoms, hand sewed, and for style, fit and wearing qualites is equal to any $7 shoe ever sold. The cordovan leather is made from certain portions of horse hide and has long been known as the best wearing leather ever sold. It is very light and tough, and as the texture is much finer than any calf skin it is much easier to polish. Every pair guaranteed. Sizes, 5 to 11; widths, C, D, E and EE.
Price, per pair .....................$4.50
**No. 3947 Men's Cordovan Congress,** made over same last as the one preceding, hand welt, best oak bottoms, and a shoe which we can recommend as being first class in every particular. Horse hide shoes will keep their original shape much better than the ordinary calf skin. Sizes, 5 to 11. Widths, C, D, E and EE. Price per pair..................$4.50

### Our Crack Proof Shoe.

**No. 3950.** The best tanners in America have been experimenting for years, trying to discover a leather which would be crack proof. One at least has been successful, and has discovered a new method of tanning calf skin which not only makes it absolutely crack proof, but improves its looks. The stock has a heavy pebbled surface, is very soft and pliable, and will take a polish much better than the ordinary calf skin. The shoe is made over the Bull Dog last, which is the newest thing out, is a Goodyear welt, and the bottoms are the best oak sole leather with extended edges. It has a calf back stay and top facing, and we can recommend it to those who want one of the latest shoes out. Every pair warranted crack proof. Sizes, 6 to 11; widths, C, D, E and EE. Price per pair....$3.45

### Men's Cordovan Lace, Opera Toe.

$6 VALUE FOR $4.50

**No. 3952 Men's Shell Cordovan Bals.** made from finest selection of cordovan, or horse hide. This shoe has the new opera toe, which is between the needle and the Yale toes, and a great many prefer it to any other style. The bottoms are cut from the best oak sole leather and sewed on by hand, making it a very handsome and durable shoe. The horse hide leather being very tough will retain its shape much better than any other leather. Sizes, 6 to 11; widths, C, D, E and EE; weight, 32 oz. Price, per pair..................$4.50

### Bankers' Shoes.

**No. 3962. We** have decided this season to have this shoe made from llama skin, as we believe it will give much better service than kangaroo and at the same time is fully as soft and pliable. The stock has a **fine pebbled surface,** looking exactly like the kangaroo stock, and is as tough as horsehide. The shoe is made with Adelphia last with tip, **genuine Goodyear welt bottoms** and there is nothing easier for bankers, lawyers and others who are doing office work. Sizes, 5½ to 11; widths, C, D, E and EE; weight, 32 oz. Price, per pair... $3.25

### Men's Kangaroo Lace, Plain Toe.

**No. 3965.** This Shoe is made from the genuine Kangaroo skin, which is very soft and glovelike and at the same time tough, which will wear equally as well as stock much heavier, and will give much more comfort to the wearer. We can thoroughly recommend this shoe, and for a light, comfortable and dressy shoe it has no equal. Sizes, 6 to 11. Widths, D, E and EE. Weight, 31 oz.
Per pair ...............$2.95

### OUR HARD CASH LINE.

**SPECIAL NOTICE.**—We wish to call the attention of our patrons to the fact that our hard cash line of shoes is fully equal in style, fit and wearing qualities to most shoes retailed at from $4.00 to $5.00. This line is one of our best sellers and we have spared no pains to put everything into it which would increase its wearing qualities. If a pair gives out without just cause send them back and get another pair, for they are fully warranted.

### Hard Cash Needle Bals.

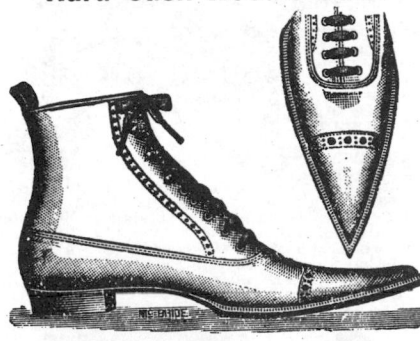

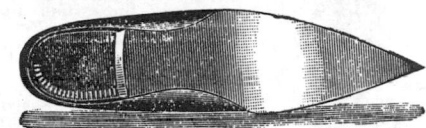

**No. 3967. Men's Selected Calf Bals,** made over the needle toe last, with tip, Goodyear welt bottoms, fine dongola top, and a shoe which is suitable for dress wear and will give splendid service. We warrant every pair. Sizes, 5 to 11. Widths, A, B, C, D, E, EE; weight, 32 oz. Price, per pair ......$2.98

### Hard Cash Plain Congress.

**No. 3968.** This shoe, like the one preceding, is made from selected calf skin, Goodyear welt bottoms, and has the plain Adelphia toe, which is medium square and very popular. It has the best Dongola topping and genuine Hub goring; warranted; sizes, 5 to 11; widths, B, C, D, E and EE; weight, 32 oz. Price, per pair...$2.98

### Hard Cash Bals, Jewel Toe.

**No. 3970 Men's Hard Cash Bals,** made from selected calf skin and over the Jewel last, which has the latest narrow round toe and is at the present in great demand. We have the soles made quite heavy and with the edges slightly extended, which gives the shoe a better appearance and also makes it very durable. Genuine Goodyear welt, best dongola tops and fully warranted. Sizes, 5 to 11; widths, B, C, D, E and EE; weight, 32 oz. Price, per pair.......$2.98

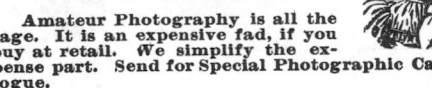
**DO NOT LOSE SIGHT OF THIS CATALOGUE; IF YOU DO NOT HAPPEN TO NEED ANY GOODS AT ONCE, LAY IT ASIDE CAREFULLY IT WILL BE USEFUL TO YOU LATER ON.**

## Our Corn Cure Shoe.

No. 3973. This Shoe we made for our own trade. This stock is a first-class selection of calfskin, with dongola top, Goodyear welt bottom. The chief feature of this shoe is the toe, as it runs extra wide, being about the same width as it is across the ball of the foot, giving the toes abundance of room to lie in their natural shape without being cramped as they are in a narrow toe shoe. This shoe will create no corns or ingrowing nails, but on the other hand will cure them if you wear a pair of these shoes. Very neat in appearance, and made of the very best material. If you are after a comfortable and at the same time serviceable shoe, order this one. Sizes, 6 to 11; widths, D, E and EE; weight, 35 ounces. Price, per pair, $2.98.

## Invisible Cork Sole Calf Lace.

No. 3982 This Shoe has been very popular the past season, from the fact that it has the same appearance as an ordinary shoe, and at the same time is absolutely water-proof. It is made from selected calf-skin, Goodyear welt, has the new opera toe with tip, and has a genuine cork sole between the outer and inner soles, making it very warm and thoroughly water-proof. When you want a cork sole shoe do not overlook this one. Sizes, 5 to 11; widths, C, D, E and EE. Weight 38 oz. Per pair..............$3.25

## Men's Calf Lace, Case Cork Soles.

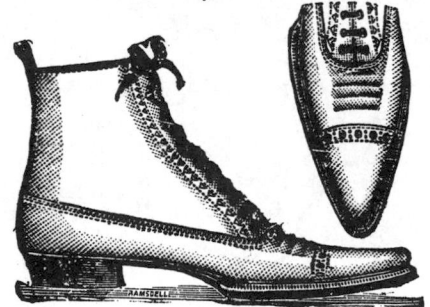

No. 3985. Made from Satin Calf, opera toe with tip, glove top, machine sewed and has the case cork sole, made from genuine sheet cork, but is visible. This shoe, while not quite so sightly as the one preceding, will give good service. Sizes 5 to 11; widths, D, E and EE. Weight 38 oz. Per pair.........$2.00

## Men's Satin Calf Lace, Cork Sole

We have this Shoe made from the finest selection of Satin Calf, with Needle Toe and Tip.

No. 3986    The soles are made extra heavy and with extended edges, which give it the appearance of a much higher priced shoe. It has fine Dongola tops and a genuine cork sole placed between the outer and inner soles, thereby making it very warm and damp proof. We can recommend it as the best cork sole shoe we have ever seen for the price. Sizes, 6 to 11; widths, D, E and EE. Weight 38 oz. Price per pair..............$2.50

## Imported Russia Colt Skin Shoes.

No. 3990 The Stock in this Shoe is Imported directly from Russia, and tanned here in Chicago. Our house has not secured all of the skins, but have been fortunate enough to secure such a quantity as will supply our patrons. The stock is thoroughly crack proof, very soft, and has a fine grain surface, similar to a kangaroo, and is very tough. We warrant each pair not to crack, and if they do, without just cause, we will replace them with new ones. The shoe has the long, drawn out needle toe, with tip, McKay sewed bottoms, and we can recommend it as being a first-class shoe. Sizes, 6 to 11; widths, D, E and EE. Weight 32 oz. Price, per pair............$2.60

## A Good Thing.

No. 3991. This Shoe we have called "A Good Thing," because the name signifies just exactly what we believe the shoe is.

It is made from genuine Russia colt skin, which is very soft and pliable, and has a fine grain surface, similar to a kangaroo.

It is also said to be crack proof. This shoe is made with plain, medium toe (congress), and has the best of bottom stock. We can commend it as being first-class in every particular. Sizes, 6 to 11; widths, D, E and EE. Weight 32 oz. Price per pair......$2.60

No. 3992 The accompanying cut represents our imported Russia colt skin plain toe lace shoe. The stock is same as the one preceding, and will give excellent service. The shoe has all of the style and finish found in the higher priced shoes. Sizes, 6 to 11; widths D, E, and EE. Weight 32 oz. Price, per pair.........$2.60

## Russian Colt Lace New Coin Toe.

No. 3993 This shoe is cut from the same stock as the one preceding. Imported direct from Russia and tanned here in Chicago. The style of last is the very latest out, the shoe has the best of bottom stock and we recommend it as being first class especially for spring and summer wear. This stock is as soft as a kangaroo and will wear much better. Sizes 6 to 11; widths, D, E and EE; weight, 35 oz. Per pair..............$2.60

## Fine Kangaroo Congress.

No. 3995 Men's Kangaroo Congress Gaiter, Goodyear welt, opera toe last which is a medium width and rather square, with long tip. The stock is very pliable and soft and contains the required amount of toughness to have it wear well. A great shoe for those troubled with tender feet; medium weight sole, perfectly solid, and will give excellent wear. Sizes, 5 to 11; widths, C, D, E and EE; weight, 27 oz. Price per pair..............$3.75

## Men's Seal Calf Shoes.

WEARS LIKE IRON.

No. 3997. The accompanying cut is a good illustration of our men's Seal Calf Shoe, and as an all around shoe it has no equal. It is made from the best seal calf, which has a rough pebble finish, and is one of the most serviceable leathers on the market. We have the soles made heavy, so as to be practical for all kinds of wear. It has solid insoles and counters, medium square toe, with long tip, and for heavy wear it is unequaled. The stock is as near waterproof as leather can be made. Sizes, 6 to 11. Widths, D, E and EE. Weight 45 oz. Price, per pair..............$2.35

## Our Calf Leaders.

This Shoe is made from a good selection of Caska Calf, McKay Sewed . . .

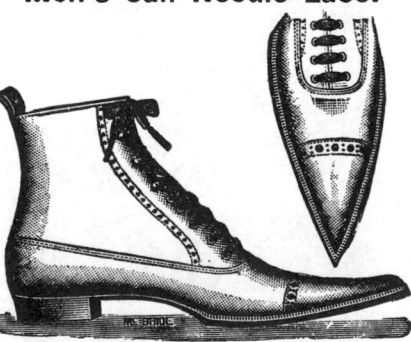

No. 31009.    This Shoe is Made From a Good Selection of Caska Calf, McKay Sewed, and the bottoms are cut from best oak leather. Made over the new coin last, with tips, and besides being the latest style is very serviceable; sizes, 5 to 11, widths, B, C, D, E, and EE. Weight, 36 oz. Per pair..............$2.10

## Men's Calf Needle Lace.

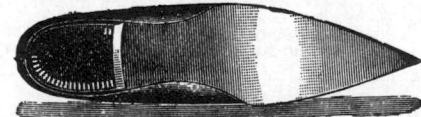

No. 31019. This shoe is made from genuine caska calf-skin, McKay sewed, flexible sole, needle toe, with tip, and we honestly believe it is the cheapest genuine calf shoe ever offered. Understand, they are guaranteed to be fine calf-skin and McKay sewed, which is as flexible as the hand turn. Sizes, 5 to 11; widths B, C, D, E and EE. Price, per pair..............$2.10

## Men's Calf Lace, Square Toe.

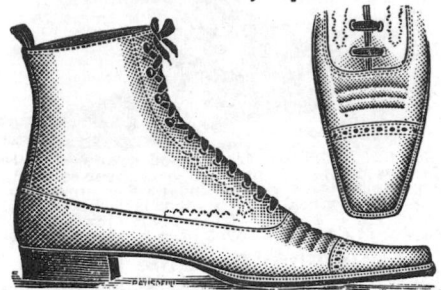

**No. 31011. Made from Genuine Caska Calf-Skin**, McKay sewed, flexible sole, all solid, narrow square toe, with long perforated tip, and in appearance compares favorably with any of our high grade shoes. This is the cheapest genuine calf shoe ever offered. Sizes, 5 to 11; widths, B, C, D, E, EE; weight, 38 oz. Per pair...................**$2.10**

## Men's Police Lace.

*Men's Extra Heavy Satin Calf Police Shoes.*

**No. 31012** Made from selected stock, heavy dongola tops, broad toes with tip. Full double soles which are cut from No. 1 stock. We can recommend this shoe as being first class in every particular, and for hard wear it cannot be duplicated at the price. Sizes 6 to 11. Full width; weight, 40 oz. Price per pair........**$2.45**

## Men's Police Congress.

**No. 31013.** Men's Extra Heavy Police Shoes, made from selected satin calf stock, heavy dongola tops, hub goring, and the soles are made extra heavy so as to be practical for hard wear. This shoe will give you entire satisfaction. Size, 6 to 11. Full width; Weight, 40 oz. Price per pair..........**$2.45**

**No. 31014** This Shoe we have made especially for our trade and to meet the demand for an extra wide shoe which will not be so heavy and clumsy as those usually sold. It is a genuine calf skin congress, Goodyear welt, 9 wide, with wide toe, and at the same time has a very neat appearance. If you have a wide foot don't overlook this shoe. Sizes, 6 to 11; warranted. Per pair, **$2.90**
**No. 31015** Same Style in Lace. Sizes, 6 to 11. Warranted. Per pair.............**$2.90**

## OUR SPECIAL SATIN CALF LINE.

**NOTE: Nearly 8000 Pairs of these Shoes Sold in 1896, and all Gave the Best of Satisfaction.**

## Satin Oil Lace, Razor Toe.

**No. 31026** Made from the best Satin Oil Stock, new style toe, machine sewed, medium heel, fine dongola top, and for wearing qualities and neat appearance it is unequaled at this price. Sizes 5 to 11; widths, D, E, and EE; weight, 38 oz. Per pair...........**$1.75**

## Satin Oil Lace.

**No. 31028.** Men's Satin Oil Bals, plain Adelphia toe, machine sewed, dongola top, and a shoe which is sold everywhere at from $2 to $2.50. For every day wear, satin oil stock gives excellent service, and at the same time has the appearance of a fine shoe. By placing a very large order we have been able to reduce the price 20 cents below that of last season. Sizes, 5 to 11; widths. D, E & EE; weight, 32 oz. Pair........**$1.75**

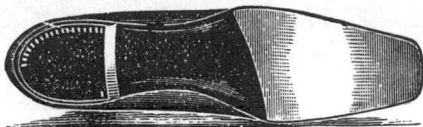

## Satin Oil Congress.

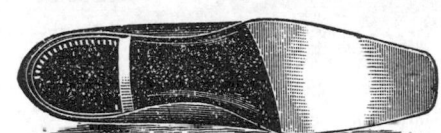

**No. 31029.** Men's Satin Oil Congress, plain Adelphia toe, Dongola tops, Hub goring, and one of the most handsome shoes we have ever been able to offer at this price. It has the appearance of a much finer shoe, and will give good service. Sizes, 5 to 11; widths, D, E and EE. Per pair.................**$1.75**

## Satin Calf Lace, Coin Toe.

**No. 31030** We have this Shoe made especially for us from the best Milwaukee Satin Calf. New Coin toe with tip, and Dongola top. The bottoms are cut from first-class stock, sewed, and for appearance fit and wearing qualities this shoe is equal to many $3.00 shoes. Sizes, 5 to 11; widths, D, E and EE. Weight, 37 ounces. Per pair........**$1.75**

## S. R. & Co.'s Rock Bottom Line.

**Every Pair Warranted.**

**No. 31034.** Men's "S" Calf Lace, broad plain toe, extra wide double sole with heavy tap nailed. These shoes are made for hard and heavy wear, and we guarantee them to be the best shoes ever sold at this price. Warranted. Sizes, 6 to 12; full width. Price, per pair .................................**$1.75**

## S. R. & Co.'s Rock Bottom Congress.

**Every Pair Warranted.**
**No. 31035.** This Shoe is made from Heavy "S" Calf, plain broad toe, heavy double sole with nailed tap extra. Has the best Hub gore, and for hard wear you cannot beat it. Warranted. Sizes, 6 to 12; full width. Price per pair....
**$1.75**

## Men's Satin Calf Lace.

*MEN'S SATIN CALF LACE SHOES*

**No. 31038** Made with Yale tip toe, which is a medium narrow square. The stock is well oiled and suitable for every day wear. This is not a handsome shoe, but we can recommend it as splendid value. Sizes, 6 to 11; full width. Price, per pair, **$1.50**

## Men's Plain Buff Lace.

**REGULAR $2.00 VALUE**

**No. 31041** Made from good Buff Stock, plain medium toe, solid sole leather counters and inner soles, glove grain top, and a shoe which usually sells for more money. Sizes, 6 to 11. No half sizes. Price, per pair....................................**$1.25**

## Men's Buff Congress.

**YOU SAVE HALF THE PRICE OF THIS SHOE**

**No. 31042** Men's Buff Congress, made with plain medium toe, solid leather counters and inner soles, Hub goring, and being all solid leather will wear much better than shoes usually sold at this price. Sizes, 6 to 11; full width. No half sizes. Price, per pair....................................**$1.25**

## THE MOST STUPENDOUS SALE OF TAN SHOES IN THE HISTORY OF SHOE SELLING.

**WE BOUGHT BY CARLOADS; not by dozens. We have the goods and we have the prices.**

See Special Colored Pages in this Department.

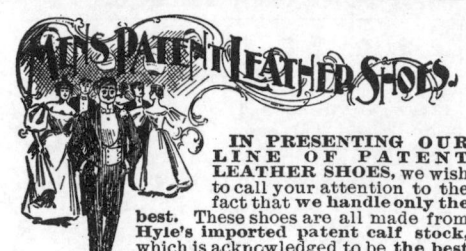

## MEN'S PATENT LEATHER SHOES.

IN PRESENTING OUR LINE OF PATENT LEATHER SHOES, we wish to call your attention to the fact that we handle only the best. These shoes are all made from **Hyle's imported patent calf stock**, which is acknowledged to be the best ever produced. Patent leather is apt to crack when cold, hence should always be warmed by rubbing briskly with the hand before putting on. Understand, every pair we sell is made from best French stock. We do not warrant them not to crack if not properly cared for. Be sure to give correct size and widths.

### Men's Patent Leather Bals, New Opera Toe.

**No. 31054.** Men's Imported Patent Calf Bals, made with the new opera toe, with tip, hand sewed bottoms, which are cut from the best oak tan stock, and are as hard as flint. This shoe has fine vici kid top, kid top facing and back stay, and being made over the latest last will undoubtedly be very popular this season. To those who wish a very fine dress shoe we can recommend it as being thoroughly first-class in every particular. Sizes, 5 to 11; widths, AA, A, B, C, D, E and EE. Weight, 28 oz. Price per pair.....................**$3.75**

### Men's Patent Leather Lace.

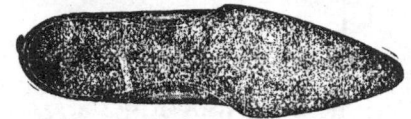

◆◆◆◆◆◆◆◆◆◆
**OUR MOST STYLISH $3.75 SHOE.**
◆◆◆◆◆◆◆◆◆◆

**No. 31055** This shoe, like all the rest of our patent leather shoes, is made from **Hyle's imported patent calf**, hand sewed, square plain toe, finest cloth top, has selected vici kid back and lace stays, and for those who wear a plain toe shoe there is nothing finer. A regular $7 shoe. Sizes, 5 to 11; widths, C, D and E. Weight, 28 oz. Per pair.........**$3.75**

### Men's Patent Leather Lace.

**No. 31056.** Made from Hyle's Imported Patent Calf, machine sewed, new opera toe, with long perforated tip, fine dongola top, and a very fine dress shoe. Sizes, 5 to 11; widths, AA, A, B, C, D and E. Weight, 27 oz. Price, per pair................**$3.25**

### Men's Common Sense Dongola Oxford.

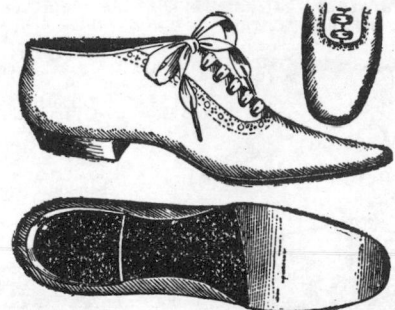

**No. 31064.** This Dongola Oxford is more especially designed for those who wish a cool and comfortable shoe for summer wear. It is made from **Genuine Dongola**, common sense last, which is broad toe and low heel; handsomely stitched front, and is all solid. It is without a doubt the best shoe of its kind ever offered for the money. Sizes, 6 to 11; full width. Weight, 20 oz. Price, per pair..........**$1.45**

### Men's Dongola Nullifiers.

**No. 31066** Men's Dongola Nullifiers, made from good quality of dongola kid, light flexible soles, medium heel and toe, the best elastic or gore, and a slipper which will be very comfortable, and can also be worn on the street if desired. Sizes, 6 to 11. Weight, 20 oz.
Price per pair .............................**$1.60**

### Men's Embroidered Slippers.

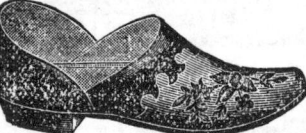

**No. 31067.** Men's Silk Plush Chenille embroidered Slippers, fancy shades, opera cut, extra fine quality and finish, hand sewed, turn soles. These are decided novelties in the slipper line and cannot fail to please. Sizes, 6 to 11; weight, 13 oz. Per pair.......................**$1.30**

### Men's Velvet Slippers, Opera Cut.

**No. 31068.** Men's Velvet Embroidered Slippers, opera cut, good style and quality; sewed. Sizes, 5 to 11. Per pair.................................**$0.89**

### Men's Oil Grain Slippers.

**No. 31073.** Men's Oil Grain Slippers, machine sewed, damp proof, all solid, and will give good service. Sizes, 6 to 11. Per pair.................**$0.88**

### Men's Carpet Slippers.

**No. 31074.** Men's Brussels Carpet Slippers, good quality, with leather sole and heel, sewed. Sizes, 6 to 11. Per pair.... .......... ................**$0.32**

### Men's Fine Dongola Oxfords.

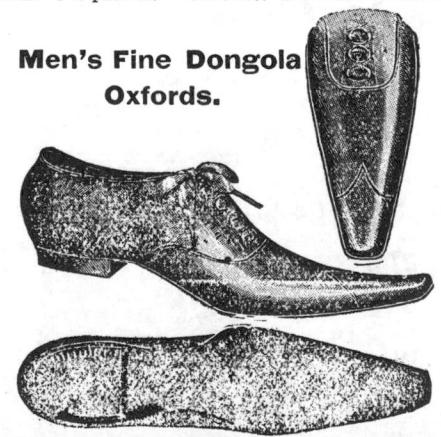

**No. 31075.** This Oxford is made to our order from a fine quality of Dull Dongola, over the new narrow Yale last with tip, and when on the foot it has the appearance of a fine shoe. The bottoms are the very best stock, sewed on by the McKay process, and besides being a very neat shoe, it will give the wearer a great deal of wear and solid comfort. Sizes, 6 to 11; widths, D, E and EE. Weight, 18 oz.
Per pair.................................**$1.65**

### Men's Patent Leather Oxfords.

**No. 31076** Made from good grade of patent leather, medium hand turn or slipper sole, and a shoe which is very neat and at the same time is easy and serviceable. This shoe is used principally for dancing and for dress wear. Sizes, 5 to 11; widths, D, E and EE. Weight, 20 oz. Per pair.**$1.75**

### Men's Fine Dongola Oxfords.

**No. 31080** This shoe is made from a fine dongola kid, light sole, which is very flexible, medium heel, medium opera toe, and is very durable. Nothing cooler or more comfortable for summer wear. Sizes, 6 to 11; widths, D, E and EE. Weight, 20 oz. Per pair.......................**$1.50**

### Men's Nullifiers, Tan Colored.

## $1.65.

**No. 31082** The Nullifier is fast becoming the most popular slipper on the market, and it certainly deserves to be. Made from a very fine selection of tan or russet goat, medium toe, soft pliable sole and thoroughly solid; being high cut, it protects the ankles from any drafts, and will thus save the wearer many colds. It can also be worn on the street. Sizes, 6 to 11. Weight, 20 oz. Per pair.**$1.65**

### Men's Velvet Embroidered Slippers.

**No. 31084.** Men's Embroidered Slippers, Everett cut, patent quarter, and a very pretty and serviceable shoe. Sizes, 6 to 11; full widths.
Per pair....................................**$0.69**

### MEN'S HEAVY PLOW SHOES, MINING SHOES, LUMBERMAN'S PACS, ETC.
### Sears' Cotton King.

**No. 31095.** This Shoe is Made From the Best Milwaukee Oil Grain Leather, medium low cut, lace with bellows tongue or dirt excluder. It has solid sole leather counters and inner soles, and the very best of bottom stock. We guarantee it to be the best wearing shoe on earth for the money. Sizes, 6 to 11; no half sizes; weight, 35 oz. Price, per pair.................net, **$1.25**

### Oil Grain Creole.

**No. 31096** We take pleasure in presenting our best Oil Grain Creole, and we honestly believe it to be the best Creole ever put on the market. It is made from the best Milwaukee oil grain stock, is very soft and pliable, has sole leather counter and inner sole, and a good heavy outer sole cut from the best of stock. We believe that it is impossible to produce a more serviceable shoe at any price. Warranted. Sizes, 6 to 12; no half sizes; weight, 42 oz. Price, per pair....**$1.40**

**PEOPLE FORGET TO SEND POSTAGE FOR MAIL SHIPMENTS AND THEN THEIR ORDER IS DELAYED, MUCH TO THEIR ANNOYANCE, AS WELL AS OURS. YOU WILL BE SURE TO REMEMBER IT**

**No. 31097. Men's Oil Grain Congress Plow Shoes**, made from all solid leather, and will give excellent wear. Sizes. 6 to 11; no half sizes; weight 40 ounces. Price. per pair, $1.20.

## Oil Grain Dom Pedro.

**No. 31098.** This shoe is made from best Milwaukee oil grain stock, has sole leather counters and insole, is soft and pliable and will not get hard when wet. It has bellows tongue, which makes it dirt proof. Sizes. 5 to 12; no half sizes. Weight, 42 oz. Per pair ..... $1.28

## "Our Own" Custom Creedmore.

**No. 31100.** Made from Grade "S" Calf-Skin, sole leather counter and inner sole, Blucher style lace, with bellows tongue, making it dirt proof, and has extra tap fastened on with best standard screws. It will wear like iron. Sizes, 6 to 12; no ½ sizes. Per pair ....... $1.90

## Men's Spring Heel Plow.

**No. 31101** Men's Two-Buckle Oil Grain Plow Shoes, dirt excluder, spring heel and a very easy shoe for plowing or harrowing in soft ground; very comfortable on the foot and will give good service. Don't forget that each pair of our plow shoes is fully warranted. Sizes. 6 to 11; no half sizes. Per pair.. .... $1.28

## Oil Grain Two Buckle Plow.
### —Men's—
### Oil Grain Two Buckle Plow Shoes.

**No. 31107** Made from best Milwaukee oil grain stock, dirt excluding, half double soles and all solid leather. Warranted. Sizes, 6 to 11; no half sizes. Per pair, $1.25

## Mining Shoes.

**No. 31110 Men's Whole Stock Kip Mining Shoes**, high cut, lace with bellows tongue or dirt excluder. It has extra heavy soles, cut from the best of stock, and both soles and heels are thoroughly hob-nailed. If you want a shoe that will wear like iron do not pass it; warranted. Sizes, 6 to 11; no half sizes. Price, per pair........ $1.98

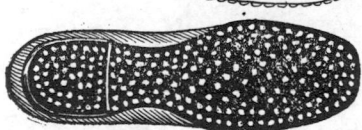

## Men's River Shoes.

**No. 31120. Men's River or Driving Shoe**, made from best calfskin, with double sole, which is sewed on, extended edges, also an extra tap put on with pegs and brass screws. **The seams are all riveted so it cannot rip**, and it has a heavy rawhide outside counter, also a calf outside back stay sewed and riveted. Extra high cut, bellows tongue with four rings and strap lace to buckle at top. A Chicago made shoe and **every pair warranted**. Sizes. 6 to 11; no half sizes; wt., 59 oz.

Price. per pair....................$3.75

## Men's River Shoes.

**No. 31121.** This Shoe is made from Genuine Calfskin, extra high cut, lace with bellows tongue making it very warm and practically waterproof. It has a heavy double sole, which protects the uppers, also an extra tap extending nearly to the heel. The shoe being a lace. fits very closely about the ankles, and is one of the neatest river shoes yet produced. **Every pair western made and warranted.** Sizes, 6 to 11; no half sizes; weight, 55 oz. Price, per pair.........$3.85

## Lumberman's Pacs.

Note Reduced Prices in Pacs and Moccasins.
**No. 31124** The accompanying cut represents our best hand sewed pac with 10 inch leg of oil grain leather and oil tan pac leather uppers; the soles are double, sewed and inserted with round cone-headed Hungarian nails, which add to the wearing qualities. The sole is light and flexible, and very easy to walk in, and does not slip; weight, 41 oz.; sizes, 6 to 12. Per pair........$2.10

## Shoe Pacs.

**No. 31125** This pac is made from an oil tanned pac, leather uppers and soles with low flat heels, making a very light and serviceable shoe for all kinds of wear; weight, 29 oz.; sizes, 6 to 12. Per pair..... .....$1.45

## Moose Hide Moccasins.

**No. 31128.** This moccasin is made from the genuine moose skin, smoke-tanned by the Indians, which gives it that peculiar toughness and also thickness not found in other grades of chemically tanned leather. The same we have made running heavier on the bottom than on any other part of the shoe. The seams are genuine hand-stitched and guaranteed not to rip like the ordinary machine sewed. Nicely embroidered vamp and bellows tongue. A great shoe for hunting or snowshoeing. Sizes, 6 to 11. Weight, 11 oz.

Per pair........................$2.25

**No. 31129. This moccasin is an exact reproduction of the above**, with the exception of being a trifle lighter and with a plain vamp. The seams are genuine hand sewed, and it has all the good qualities of the above It will wear like iron. Sizes, 6 to 11. Weight, 11 oz. Per pair. $2.00

## High Cut Fine Shoe.

**No. 31135.** This Shoe is so Constructed as to be Practical for All Kinds of Wear. Made from selected calf skin of medium weight, with fine Puritan calf top eleven inches high. This kind of a top is very desirable, from the fact that it is very soft and pliable and fits much better about the ankle than does the heavier leather. Made with bellows tongue to top, half double sole with extended edges, fair stitched, plain medium toe and when on the foot looks as neat as a dress shoe. It is suitable for hunting, log driving and would be very desirable for deep snow or wet weather. Warranted. Sizes, 6 to 11; no half sizes; weight, 45 oz. Price per pair....................$4.15

## Light Weight Creedmoor.

**No. 31136** This extra light shooting Creedmoor weighs only 2 pounds. In putting this Creedmoor on the market we have endeavored to make a shoe which would be extra light, have the wearing qualities of the heavier shoes, and above all at a price which would be in the reach of every sportsman. After having samples submitted by all the leading manufacturers of this class of goods we have at last succeeded in securing a shooting Creedmoor which meets all of the requirements, and we honestly believe is without an equal; made from the finest oiled black kip, which has a pebbled surface; cut 11 inches high and with bellows tongue to top, making it practically waterproof. It has a medium weight oak tan sole, sewed on by hand, (old army shoe style), making it as flexible as a ladies' shoe and as noiseless as a moccasin. It is not clumsy as are most shooting creedmoors, and considering the extra light weight (2 pounds) it is certainly **a very desirable shoe. Money back on any pair not satisfactory.** Sizes, 6 to 11; widths, D, E and EE. Price, per pair........................$4.25

*$6.00 WORTH FOR $4.25.*

## The Dress Parade.

**No. 31151 Men's Opera Cowboy Boots**, made from an extra fine selection of dongola kid, which is of medium weight and will give a fair amount of service. It has a 19 inch leg, handsomely quilted, 2 inch opera heel, medium shank, is extra light, and, while not intended for real hard wear, is one of the most handsome riding boots we have ever seen. Sizes, 5 to 9, no half sizes; weight 44 ounces.
Price, per pair........ $4.75
Remember our discount of 3 per cent. for cash.

ALWAYS
ORDER
BY
NUMBER.

### The Western.

No. 31153. This Boot is Made of Genuine Calf Skin, is all solid and one of the most popular "cowboy" boots we have ever sold. It has extra high heel, medium toe, and is an extremely durable boot for all kinds of wear. Every pair warranted to be better value than can possibly be obtained elsewhere. Note reduction. Size, 5 to 10; no half sizes: weight, 56 oz.
Price per pair.... $2.95

### Blue Ribbon Cowboy.

No. 31152. Men's Calf Cowboy Boot, made from an extra fine selection of domestic calfskin, 16 inch leg, half double sole and 2 inch heel. The bottoms are cut from the best of oak tan sole leather, extra heavy shank and the boot will give splendid service. This boot was awarded the blue ribbon at the World's Fair in Chicago, which is sufficient guarantee as to its good qualities. Warranted. Sizes, 5 to 11; no half sizes. Price, per pair, $3.50.

### Men's Calf Opera Boots.

No. 31154 Men's Selected Calf Opera Boot, fine goat leg, hand welt, half double sole, low broad heels and a boot suitable for fine dress wear. Warranted. Sizes, 6 to 11; no half sizes. Weight 42 oz.
Price per pair,... $4.60
No. 31155 Men's Selected Calf Opera Boot, fine goat leg, machine sewed, half double sole, low broad heel and very durable. Sizes, 6 to 11; no half sizes. Weight 42 oz.
Price per pair,... $3.90

### Men's Calf Dress Boots.

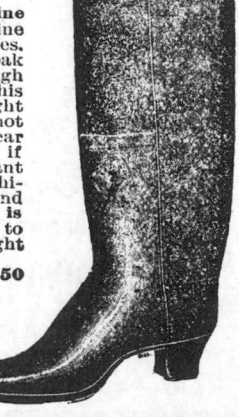

No. 31158. Men's Fine Calf Boot, made from fine light stock, double soles, cut from best of white oak sole leather, medium high heel, medium toe. This boot having light weight calf fronts and back is not intended for the same wear as the stoga boot, but if properly used we warrant it thoroughly. It is a Chicago custom made boot, and for its weight there is nothing better. Sizes, 6 to 11; no half sizes. Weight 45 oz.
Price per pair....... $3.50

### River Boots.

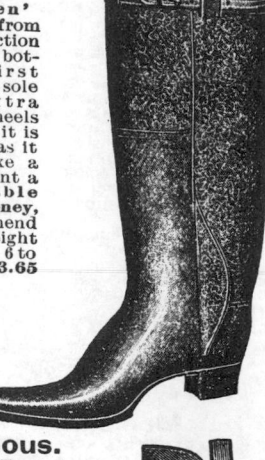

No. 31165. Men' River Boot, made from the very best selection of oil grain stock, bottoms cut from first quality of oak tan sole leather, with extra heavy tap. The heels are low and broad, it is as near waterproof as it is possible to make a boot, and if you want a thoroughly reliable boot for little money, we would recommend this one. Sizes. Weight 45 oz. no half sizes. 6 to 11; Price, per pair $3.65

### The Famous.

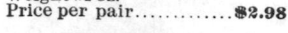

No. 31166. This Boot is one which we have Made Specially for Our Own Trade, and a great many of our customers will have nothing else. It is made from the best California kip, medium weight, half double sole, medium toe and heel, and has absolutely solid counters and inner soles. This boot is made for hard wear, and we can recommend it as being first-class. Warranted. Sizes, 6 to 11. No half sizes. Weight 54 oz.
Price per pair............ $2.98

### Oil Grain Plow Boot.

No. 31170. This Men's Plow Boot is made from the best of Milwaukee oil grain stock, single or half double sole as desired, solid sole leather counters and inner soles. It is especially designed to give good hard wear, and is sold at a price which will meet the desired wants of a great many. Sizes, 6 to 12. No half sizes. Weight 48 oz. Price,.... ..per pair $2.35

### Special Value.

No. 31168 Men's Best Kip Boot, first quality front and back, half double sole, low flat heel, and we can assure our many patrons that it is the best value we have ever seen in a strictly custom boot. Chicago made and warranted. Sizes, 6 to 12; no half Sizes. Weight 54 oz. Price per pair....... $3.40
No. 31169 Men's Flesh Split Boot, made from best flesh split stock, half double sole, low broad heels, hand pegged and serviceable. Sizes, 6 to 11; no half sizes. Weight 54 oz.
Price per pair, .......... $2.10

### Sheep Lined Boots.

No. 31171. This Boot Has Been Out of the Market for Years, but on account of the many inquiries we have had for a boot of this description and knowing that it is a very warm and durable boot, we have had them made up especially for our own trade. It is made from the best Milwaukee oil grain leather, is thoroughly water-proof and lined throughout with the natural wool sheep-skin. A boot which takes the place of a felt, leather and rubber boot combined. Sizes, 6 to 11. Weight 57 oz. Per pair..... $3.40

### Russet Hunting Boot.

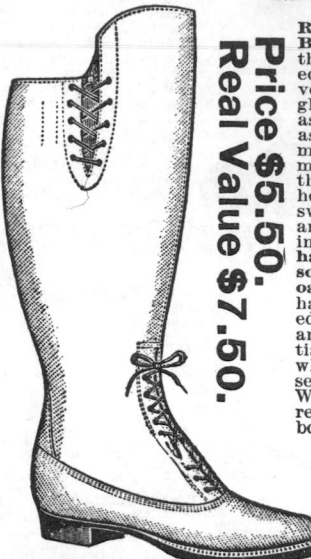

**Price $5.50. Real Value $7.50.**

No. 31173 This Russet Hunting Boot is made from the best russet oiled kip, which is very soft and glove-like and is as near waterproof as leather can be made. The boot is made to lace over the instep and is held up over the swell of the calf by an adjustable lacing at the top. It has half double soles cut from best oak tan stock, is handsomely stitched with red silk, and has a substantial back stay which protects the seams at the heel. We can thoroughly recommend this boot as the most handsome, most durable and most comfortable hunting boot we have ever sold. Order a pair and if they are not better value than you ever had, send them back and get your money. Every pair warranted. Sizes, 6 to 11. No half sizes. Price, per pair.............. $5.50

### Felt Boots.

No. 31180. This Boot is Made from Fine Quality of All-Wool Felt, light color; has genuine calf front, back and side stays, and we guarantee it to be unequaled for the money. Sizes, 6 to 12.
Per pair..... ........$0.85
Per doz., net.... 9.25

### Men's Medium Felt Boots.

No. 31181 These Boots are Made from Good Quality All-Wool

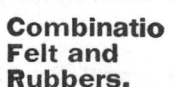

Felt, dark gray color, calf stays, and a boot which will give good service. Sizes, 6 to 12.
Per pair....... $0.55
Per doz., net... 6.00

### Combinatio Felt and Rubbers.

No. 31186. This combination is composed of all wool felt boot, calf stays, splendid quality and the lumberman's rubber ankle boot of first quality. You can save considerable by buying them together. Remember this combination is first quality and guaranteed to give service. Sizes, 6 to 12; weight, 90 oz.
Price per pair... $1.98
Per doz., net.....23.50

## Boys' Felt Boots

31182, Boys' All Wool Felt Boots, extra quality, gray color, calf back and front stays and heel strap for removing. Will give splendid service. Sizes, 1 to 5. Per pair, 55c; per dozen, net.......... **$6.50**

## LUMBERMAN'S SOCKS.

Lumberman's Socks, if first quality, are superior to felt boots in many respects and a great many prefer them.

They are always soft and easy on the feet, will not break at the ankle as felt boots are liable to do, and if wet they can be turned inside out and dried as quickly as an ordinary stocking. Ours are all first class in every respect, have strap and buckle at the top and are warranted to give entire satisfaction.

No. 31190 This Lumberman's Sock is made from the best of pure black wool by one of the best knitting mills in the west. The leg is full 20 inches long; it has heavy tufted lining throughout, reinforced feet, and is as good as a sock can possible be made. It is really worth more than we ask for it. Money back if not satisfactory. Price, per pair, $1.00 Price per doz.......... **$11.25**

No 31192 Lumberman's Knit Socks, strictly pure wool color, dark gray mixed; heavy tufted foot lining, 18 inch leg with leather strap and buckle at top, reinforced heels and toes and thoroughly reliable. Price, per pair, 75c; per dozen, net.......... **$8.50**

No. 31194 Lumberman's Knit Socks, dark gray heavy wool, 18 inch leg, tufted foot lining, reinforced feet and extra value. Price, per pair, 50c; per dozen, net.......... **$5.50**

## Boys' German Socks.

No. 31196. Boys' Knit German Socks, heavy all wool, black tufted foot lining, reinforced heels and toes and a sock which is first class in every particular. Price, 50c; per doz., net.......... **$5.50**

## Boys' and Youths' "B" Calf Narrow Square Toe.

Boys' Machine Sewed Lace, half double sole, medium square toe, with tip. A very durable shoe, and for the price certainly has no equal.

No. 31209 Boys' sizes, 2½ to 5; widths full. Price per pair.......... **$1.30**

No. 31210 Youths' sizes, 11 to 2; widths full. Price per pair.......... **$1.20**

## Boys' and Youths' Square Toe Bals.

This Shoe is made from a fine selection of satin calf, narrow square toe, with tip, half double sole, fine dongola top, and will wear and look equal to shoes often sold for a great deal more money.

No. 31212. Boys' sizes, 2½ to 5; widths, D, E and EE. Price, per pair.......... **$1.65**

No. 31213 Youth's sizes, 11 to 2; widths, D, E and EE. Price, per pair.......... **$1.45**

---

## Boys' and Youths' "B" Calf Shoes.

This Shoe is made from good, plump stock, half double sole, new opera toe, with tip, fine tops, and will give good service. This makes a splendid school shoe.

No 31218. Boys' sizes, 2½ to 5; widths, E and EE. Price, per pair.......... **$1.45**

No 31219. Youths' sizes, 11 to 2; widths, E and EE. Price, per pair.......... **$1.25**

## Boys' and Youths' "Hard Knock" Shoes.

No. 31230. We have this Shoe made special for Boys and of an Extra Quality of Light Kip, with bellows tongue, hook lace, seams all riveted, which makes a shoe thoroughly reliable and one to give good solid service. Weight, 33 oz. No half sizes; sizes, 1 to 5. Per pair.......... **$1.25**

No. 31231. We have this shoe made exactly as the one preceding as it has always been a hard matter for customers to get a good solid heavy shoe for a youth. This one will give excellent service. Made from light kip skins. Riveted seams; will not rip. No half sizes; sizes, 10 to 13. Per pair.......... **$1.15**

## Boys' and Youths' Plow Shoes.

No. 31233. Boys' Oil Grain two buckle plow Shoes, pegged, strong and heavy; warranted. Sizes, 1 to 5; weight, 32 ounces.

Per pair.......... **$1.20**

## Boys' Oil Grain Creole.

No. 31235. Made from the Best Milwaukee Oil Grain Stock, all solid, half double sole. Being elastic top, it is impossible for the dirt to get in. Sizes, 2 to 5. Per pr. **$1.20**

## Boys' and Youths' Kip Boots.

No. 31245. Boys' Best Kip Boots, whole stock, pegged, double sole, all hand made, warranted. Sizes, 1 to 5. Price per pair.......... **$2.40**

No. 31246. Boys' Whole Stock Kip Boots, half double sole, pegged, well made and solid throughout. Sizes, 1 to 5; weight, 48 oz. Price per pair.......... **$1.98**

No. 31247. Boys' Best Kip Boots, whole stock, pegged, double sole, all hand mand, warranted. Sizes, 1 to 5; weight, 29 oz. Price per pair. **$1.85**

No. 31248. Youths' Whole Stock Kip Boots, half double sole, pegged, well made and solid throughout. Sizes, 10 to 13; weight, 29 oz. Price per pair.......... **$1.60**

## Little Men's Shoes.

No. 31251— Made from good quality of stock, all solid, square toe with tip, spring heel and durable. Sizes, 9 to 13½; widths, E and EE. Price, per pair.... **$0.90**

---

## Men's Base Ball Shoes.

No. 31252 Men's Heavy Canvas Base Ball Shoes, calf trimmed solid leather soles, and counters, extra quality. Sizes 6 to 11; weight, 22 oz. Per pair.......... **$1.15**

No. 31253 Boys' Heavy Canvas Base Ball Shoes, calf trimmed, all solid. best grades. Sizes 1 to 5; weight, 20 oz. Per pair. **$1.00**

No. 31254. Men's Heavy Canvas Shoe; leather sole and counters, calf trimmed, medium quality. Sizes, 6 to 11. Per pair.......... **$0.95**

## Black Tennis Shoes.

No. 31256. Men's Black Satteen Tennis Bals. Corrugated soles with leather insoles. Sizes 6 to 11; weight, 20 oz. Per pair, net.......... **$0.75**

No. 31257. Boys' Black Tennis Bals, corrugated rubber soles with leather insoles. Sizes, 1 to 5; weight, 17 oz. Per pair, net.......... **$0.70**

No. 31258. Ladies' Black Tennis Bals, corrugated rubber soles, with leather insoles. Sizes, 2½ to 7; weight, 17 oz. Per pair, net.......... **$0.70**

## Back Tennis Oxfords.

No. 31259 Men's Black Satteen Tennis Oxford, corrugated rubber soles with leather insoles. Sizes, 6 to 11. Per pair.......... **$0.60**

No. 31260 Boys' Black Tennis Oxford, corrugated rubber soles, with leather insoles. Sizes, 1 to 5; weight, 15 oz. Per pair.......... **$0.57**

## White Tennis Bals.

No. 31261. Men's White Duck Tennis Bals Corrugated rubber soles and solid leather insoles. Also used for yachting, base ball and gymnasium, strictly first quality; sizes 6 to 11. Weight 20 ounces. Per pair, net.......... **$1.00**

No. 31262 Ladies' White Duck Tennis Bals. Corrugated rubber soles, solid leather insoles and suitable for gymnasium, Yachting, Tennis, etc. A very neat shoe and strictly first quality. Sizes 2½ to 6; weight 15 oz. Per pair, net.......... **$0.90**

## White Duck Oxfords Rubber Sole.

No. 31263 Men's White Duck Oxford with corrugated rubber soles and solid leather insoles. Strictly first quality and a very cool and dressy shoe for all kinds of summer sports. Sizes, 6 to 11; weight, 16 oz. Price, per pair.......... **$0.80**

No. 31264 Ladies' White Duck Oxford with corrugated rubber sole and solid leather insole. A very neat tennis, gymnasium, or yachting shoe, and strictly first quality. Sizes, 2½ to 6; weight, 15 oz. Per pair, net.......... **$0.75**

## Men's Gymnasium Shoes.

No. 31265 Men's Low Cut Canvas Pumps, canvas sole, and a very popular shoe at the price. Sizes, 6 to 11. Per pair.......... **$0.46**

---

## RUBBERS AND OVERSHOES.

We have always handled strictly first quality of Rubbers and Overshoes, and will continue to do so this season. For the benefit of those of our patrons who wish something a little cheaper, however, we have decided to quote also one of the best brands of second quality rubbers on the market. They are fully as good as a great many so-called firsts. It will be to your interest to order your rubbers early, then when you need them you will not be obliged to pay a big profit to your local dealer. We quote all rubber goods at wholesale prices. Your dealer can't buy 1000 pairs any cheaper than you can buy one pair from us.

ALL RUBBER GOODS ARE NET.

### Styles of Toes in Men's Shoes.

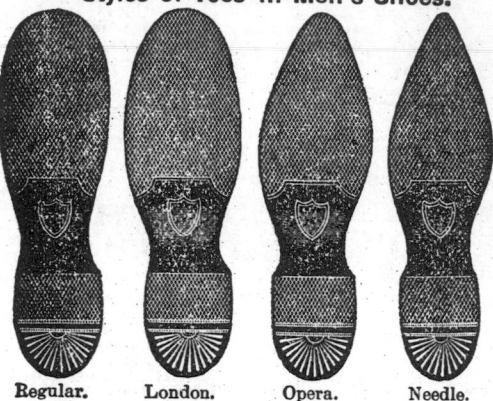

Regular.    London.    Opera.    Needle.

### Styles of Toes in Ladies' Shoes.

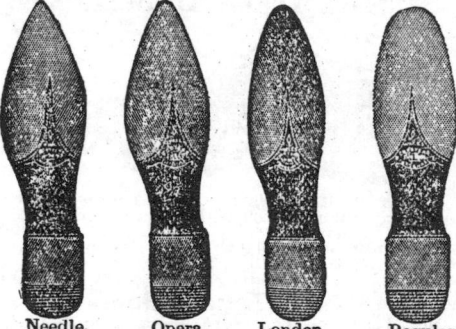

Needle.    Opera.    London.    Regular.

## MEN'S AND WOMEN'S ARCTICS.

No. 31270. Men's one buckle arctic, extra heavy, dull finish, heavy cloth top, wool fleece-lined, first quality. Sizes, 6 to 13; full width; weight, 39 oz.; regular toe only. Price, per pair, $1.28.

No. 31271. Men's good quality one buckle arctics, extra heavy, wool fleece lined, heavy cloth top. Sizes, 6 to 13; full width; weight, 39 oz.; regular toe only. Price, per pair, $1.15.

No. 31272. Women's first quality one buckle arctics, heavy cloth top, wool fleece lined, made for heavy wear; full width. Sizes, 3 to 8; weight, 20 oz. Price, per pair, 98c.

No. 31273. Women's good quality one buckle arctics, made same as above, for heavy wear; full width. Sizes, 2½ to 8; weight, 20 oz. Price, per pair, 90c.

## BOYS' AND YOUTHS' BUCKLE ARCTICS.

No. 31274. Boy's first quality buckle arctics, heavy, cloth top, wool lined. Sizes, 2 to 5; weight, 24 oz. Price, per pair, $1.05.

No. 31275. Boys' good quality buckle arctics, same as above. Sizes, 2 to 5; weight, 24 oz. Price, per pair, 95c.

No. 31276. Youths' first quality buckle arctics, heavy, cloth top, wool lined. Sizes, 10 to 1; weight, 20 oz. Price, per pair, 95c.

No. 31277. Youths' good quality buckle arctics, same style as above. Sizes, 10 to 1; weight, 20 oz. Price, per pair, 85c.

## MISSES' BUCKLE ARCTICS.

No. 31282. Misses' first quality buckle arctics, wool fleece lined. Sizes, 11 to 2; weight, 16 oz. Heel or spring heel. Price, per pair, 77c.

No. 31283. Misses' good quality buckle arctics, wool fleece lined. Sizes, 11 to 2; weight, 16 oz. Price, per pair, 70c.

## CHILD'S BUCKLE ARCTICS.

No. 31268. Child's first quality buckle arctics, wool fleece lined. Sizes, 5 to 10½; weight, 10 oz. Price, per pair, 56c.

No. 31287. Child's good quality buckle arctics, wool fleece lined. Sizes, 5 to 10½; weight, 10 oz. Price, per pair, 50c.

## MEN'S SNOW EXCLUDERS.

No. 31290. Men's first quality buckle snow excluders, wool fleece lined, heavy, for hard wear. Sizes, 6 to 12; full width; weight, 40 oz. Price, per pair, $1.39.

No. 31291. Men's good quality buckle snow excluders, wool lined, heavy. Sizes 6 to 12; full width; weight, 40 oz. Price, per pair, $1.25.

## WOMEN'S SNOW EXCLUDERS.

No. 31294. Women's first quality buckle snow excluders, wool fleece lined. Sizes, 2½ to 8; full width; weight, 24 oz. Price, per pair, $1.09.

No. 31295. Women's good quality snow excluders, wool fleece lined. Sizes, 2½ to 8; full width; weight, 24 oz. Price, per pair, 98c.

No. 31298. Boys' first quality buckle snow excluders, wool lined. Sizes 1 to 5. Price, per pair, $1.12.

No. 31299. Boys' good quality snow excluders, wool lined. Sizes 1 to 5. Price, per pair, 93c.

## MEN AND WOMEN'S EXTRA LIGHT BUCKLE ARCTICS, FIRST QUALITY ONLY.

No. 31300. Men's extra light buckle arctics, made from first quality of pure gum rubber, light Jersey cloth top, and suitable for fine wear. We have it in regular, London, piccadilly and needle toes. Sizes, 6 to 11; widths, M and F; weight, 24 oz. In carton. Price, per pair, $1.39.

No. 31302. Women's light Jersey arctics, made from first quality of pure gum rubber, fine Jersey cloth top, and suitable for fine wear. Comes in regular, London, Piccadilly and needle toes. Sizes, 2½ to 8; widths, S, M and F. Price, per pair, $1.08.

## MEN'S HEAVY ROLLED EDGE ARCTICS.

No. 31304. Men's extra heavy buckle Arctic, wool lined with heavy rolled edge protecting the uppers, and extra heavy sole and heel. First quality only. Sizes, 6 to 13; full width. Price, per pair, $1.45.

## MEN'S 3-BUCKLE SNOW EXCLUDER.

No. 31306. This three buckle shoe is cut extra high, snow excluding to the top, and being impervious to the water over half way up makes it a very dry and warm shoe. It is made from first quality of rubber, fine cloth top, medium weight, and we can furnish both medium and needle toes. This is certainly a very comfortable shoe, and having the fine cloth top, looks as dressy as the light arctic. Sizes, 6 to 11; weight, 42 oz. Per pair, $1.95.

## LADIES' STORM ALASKAS.

No. 31308. This Storm Alaska differs from the ordinary Alaska, as it is cut high in front, and protects the front of the foot more. It is made from first quality of rubber, has fine cloth top, wool fleece lined, and makes a very desirable shoe for cold weather. We have it in broad, medium opera and needle toe. Sizes, 2½ to 8; weight, 12 oz. Per pair, 86c.

No. 31310. Misses' Storm Alaska, made as above, with spring heel, first quality. Sizes, 11 to 2; weight, 9 oz. Per pair, 70c.

## LADIES' EMPRESS

No. 31312. Ladies' high cut Buckle Gaiter, made from first quality pure gum, Jersey cloth top, and wool fleece lined. This is without a doubt one of the most comfortable overshoes ever worn. We have it in regular, opera and piccadilly toes. Sizes, 2½ to 8; weight, 17 oz. First quality only. Price, per pair, $1.79.

## LADIES' PEERLESS.

No. 31314. Ladies' first quality high cut Button Gaiter, made from pure gum, fine Jersey cloth top and wool fleece lined. Comes in regular, opera, or piccadilly toes. Sizes, 2½ to 8; widths, S, M and F; weight, 17 oz. Per pair, $1.62.

## LADIES' SPRING HEEL PEERLESS.

No. 31316. Ladies' High Button Gaiter, made especially for spring heel shoes, same as above; all style toes. First quality. Weight, 16 oz.; sizes, 2½ to 7. Price, per pair, $1.62.

No. 31318. Misses' Spring Heel Peerless, made same as the one preceding. Regular, opera, or piccadilly toes. Sizes, 11 to 2; weight, 12 oz. Price, per pair, $1.39.

No. 31320. Child's Spring Heel Overshoes, high cut, button. First quality. Sizes, 8 to 10½; weight, 10 oz. Price, per pair, $1.15.

## MEN'S EXTRA LIGHT ALASKA.

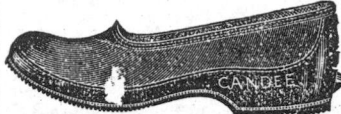

No. 31324. Men's extra light self-acting Alaska, Jersey cloth covered, fine wool fleece lined, best quality pure gum, and suitable for fine wear. We carry this shoe in the following toes: Glace, regular, London, Piccadilly, and needle. Sizes, 6 to 12; widths, S, M, F and W. Per pair, in carton, $0.95.

## MEN'S MEDIUM HEAVY ALASKA.

No. 31326. Men's first quality self-acting Alaska, cloth covered, wool fleece lined. Regular toe only. Sizes, 6 to 12; full width. Price, per pair, $0.89.

No. 31327. Men's good quality self-acting Alaskas, cloth covered, wool fleece lined. Regular toe only. Sizes, 6 to 12; full width. Price, per pair, $0.79.

## MEN'S STORM ALASKAS.

No. 31328. This is wool lined, first quality. The style is very desirable, as it protects the foot more than the ordinary warm-lined Alaska. They are not clumsy on the foot. We have them in the broad, medium and needle toes. Remember they are the best made. Sizes, 6 to 12; weight, 16 oz. Price, per pair, $1.07.

## MEN'S STORM RUBBERS.

(First Quality.)

No. 31330. This is one of the most popular rubbers ever sold, as it has a very neat appearance, and coming up high in back and front, insures dry feet on stormy days. It is made from light first quality rubber, net lined, and comes in medium, piccadilly and needle toes. Sizes, 6 to 11. Price, per pair, $0.68.

No. 31331. Men's Storm Rubbers, good quality, same style as above. Sizes, 6 to 11. Price, per pair, $0.60.

## MEN'S AND BOYS' RUBBERS.

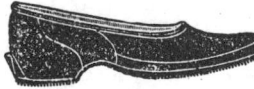

No. 31334. Men's first quality self-acting Rubbers, put up in the finest style, come in regular, London Piccadilly and needle toes. Widths, S, M and F; made especially for fine wear; sizes, 6 to 11. Price, per pair, 70c.

No. 31335. Same as above, medium quality. Per pair, 60c.

No. 31338. Men's self-acting Clog or Toe rubber, made from strictly first quality rubber, regular, London, Piccadilly, or needle toes. Sizes, 6 to 11; widths, M and F. Price per pair, 69c.

No. 31339. Men's self-acting clog, good quality; same style as above. Sizes, 9 to 11; widths, F and M. Price, per pair, 59c.

## MEN'S AND BOYS' EXTRA HEAVY OVERS.

Made from pure gum, extra heavy, dull finish, medium high cut, net lined, first quality and a splendid rubber for good hard service.

No. 31340. Men's sizes, 6 to 12; weight, 25 oz. Per pair, 78c.

No. 31341. Men's plain heavy Overs, good quality, same style as above. Regular toe only. Sizes, 6 to 13. Price, per pair, 68c.

No. 31346. Boys' plain heavy Overs, first quality, regular toe only. Sizes, 1 to 5. Price, per pair, 55c.

No. 31347. Boys' good quality plain heavy Overs. Sizes, 1 to 5. Price, per pair, 46c.

## MEN'S AND WOMEN'S FOOTHOLDS.

No. 31350. Men's improved Footholds, made from first quality of rubber, regular or Piccadilly toes. Sizes, 6 to 11. Price, per pair, 55c.

No. 31352. Women's improved Footholds, first quality, regular and Piccadilly toes, extra light weight, net lined, and just the thing for fine wear. Price, per pair, 34c.

## LADIES' AND MISSES' STORM RUBBERS.

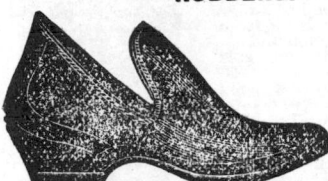

No. 31354. Ladies' fine light Storm Rubbers, first quality, cut high in front and back, and afford good protection for the ankles. Come in regular, opera, Piccadilly, and needle toes. Sizes, 2½ to 8; width, S, M and F; weight, 10 oz. Price, per pair, 48c.

No. 31355. Ladies' good quality Storm Rubbers, same style as one preceding, regular, opera and Piccadilly toes. Sizes, 2½ to 8; widths, M and F; weight, 10 oz. Price, per pair, 42c.

No. 31356. Misses' first quality Storm Rubbers, spring heel. Sizes, 11 to 2; regular and opera toes. Price, per pair, 38c.

No. 31360. Women's first quality Croquet Sandals, made in regular, opera, Piccadilly and needle toes, net lined and very dressy. Sizes, 2½ to 8; widths, S, M and F. Price, per pair, 44c.

No. 31361. Women's good quality plain Croquet Sandals, light weight, net lined, comes in regular, opera, and Piccadilly toes. Sizes, 2½ to 8; widths, M and F. Price, per pair, 35c.

No. 31362. Misses' spring heel plain Croquet Sandals, first quality, light weight, net lined, regular, opera or Piccadilly toes. Sizes, 11 to 2. Price, per pair, 30c.

No. 31363. Misses' good quality Croquet Sandals, regular or opera toes. Sizes, 11 to 2. Price, per pair, 26c.

No. 31365. Children's good quality plain Croquet Sandals, light weight, spring heel, regular or opera toes. Sizes, 5 to 10½. Price, per pair, 22c.

## LADIES' CROQUET ALASKA.

No. 31368. Made from first quality rubber, extra fine and light weight, fine cloth top, wool fleece lined, and an excellent shoe, either for dress or every-day wear. We have both wide, medium and needle toes. Sizes, 2½ to 8, weight, 12 oz. Per pair, 73c.

Same in Misses', spring heel. Sizes, 11 to 2. Price, per pair, 58c.

No. 31369. Ladies' good quality Croquet Alaska, cloth top, wool fleece lined, regular and opera toes. Sizes, 2½ to 8. Price, per pair, 65c.

## RUBBER BOOTS.

In ordering rubber boots be sure to state whether wool or net lining is wanted. We always send cotton lining unless otherwise ordered.

## IMPROVED EXTRA LIGHT VACATION BOOT.

No. 31410. This boot is a favorite among sportsmen, from the fact that it can be rolled up closely and takes up little room in a satchel. It is made extra light, weighing only a little over three pounds; net lined, first quality, thigh leg, and is a cool summer boot. Sizes, 6 to 10. Price, per pair, $3.95.

## MEN'S, BOYS' AND YOUTHS' PEBBLE LEG SHORT BOOTS.

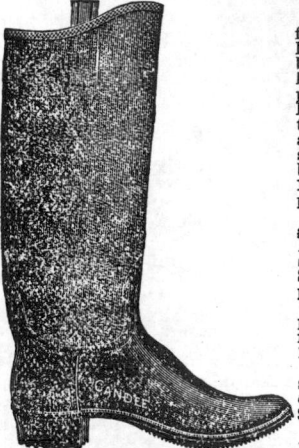

No. 31380. Men's first quality pebble leg short rubber boots, bright finish, handsome 16 inch pebble leg, very light and neat fitting, wool net lined, and will give good service. Nothing better. Sizes, 6 to 11; F. or W. Per pair, $2.60.

No. 31381. Men's good quality pebble leg boots, same style as above. Sizes, 6 to 11. Per pair, $2.35.

No. 31382. Boys' pebble leg boots, first quality. Sizes, 1 to 5. Per pair, $2.15.

No. 31383. Boys' same as above, good quality. Per pair, $1.95.

No. 31384. Youths' pebble leg rubber boots, first quality. Sizes, 10 to 13½. Price per pair, $1.55.

No. 31385. Youths', same, good quality. Sizes, 10 to 13½. Price per pair, $1.40.

## THE OLD RELIABLE SNAG PROOF BOOTS.

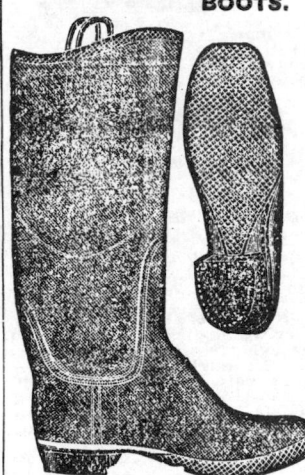

No. 31388. The accompanying cut represents the old reliable snag proof rubber boot which we have handled ever since we opened our shoe department, except for the spring season, which has just past. We were led to believe that the boot we quoted would give better service than this one. After giving the new boot a fair trial we are thoroughly convinced that there is no rubber boot made which will give as much wear as the old reliable. Made from heavy imported snag proof duck, covered with the very best of rubber, thoroughly waterproof, with heavy sole and tap, heavy rolled edge, which protects the uppers to a great extent, and altogether makes a boot which cannot be excelled. Every pair is warranted for a fair and reasonable amount of service and also warranted not to crack or snag. Sizes, 6 to 12, Short boot, $3.50. Hip boot, $4.50.

## SPECIAL COMBINATION.

No. 31389. Men's felt boot and perfection combination. Consists of a good felt boot, and Lumberman's one buckle perfection of second quality. We do not claim this to be a first quality combination, but we do claim it to be equal to many combinations which are sold and claimed to be first quality. It will give good service. Sizes, 6 to 12. Price per pair, net, $1.85. Price, per doz. pairs, net, $21.00.

## MEN'S HIP BOOTS.

No. 31390. Men's hip leg Boots, made from pure gum, first quality only, wool or net lined. Every one knows how a pure gum boot will wear. Sizes, 6 to 12. Per pair, $4.50.

No. 31392. Men's dull finish hip Boots, first quality, wool or net lined, and a good serviceable boot. Sizes, 6 to 12. Per pair, $3.83.

No. 31393. Men's dull finish hip Boots, good quality, wool or net lined. Sizes, 6 to 12. Per pair, $3.40.

No. 31394. Men's dull finish rubber Boots, thigh leg, wool or net lined, first quality. Sizes 6 to 12. Weight, 90 ounces. Per pair, $3.83.

No. 31395. Men's dull finish rubber boots, thigh leg, wool or net lined, good quality. Sizes, 6 to 12. Weight, 90 ounces. Per pair, $3.40.

No. 31400. Men's pure gum rubber boots, short 16 inch leg, wool or net lined. Sizes, 6 to 13; weight, 81 oz. Price, per pair, $3.25.

No. 31402. Men's dull finish rubber boots, short 16 inch leg, wool or net lined, first quality. Sizes, 6 to 12; weight, 81 oz. Price, per pair, $2.55.

No. 31403. Men's dull finish rubber boots, short 16 inch leg, wool or net lined, good quality. Sizes, 6 to 12; weight, 81 oz. Price, per pair, $2.30.

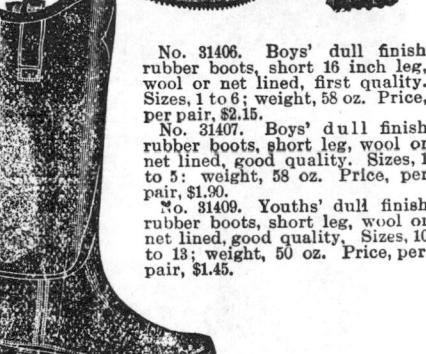

## BOYS' RUBBER BOOTS.

No. 31406. Boys' dull finish rubber boots, short 16 inch leg, wool or net lined, first quality. Sizes, 1 to 6; weight, 58 oz. Price, per pair, $2.15.

No. 31407. Boys' dull finish rubber boots, short leg, wool or net lined, good quality. Sizes, 1 to 5; weight, 58 oz. Price, per pair, $1.90.

No. 31409. Youths' dull finish rubber boots, short leg, wool or net lined, good quality. Sizes, 10 to 13; weight, 50 oz. Price, per pair, $1.45.

## LADIES', MISSES' AND CHILD'S PEBBLE LEG BOOTS.

No. 31412. Women's first quality rubber boots, bright finish, fleece lined, pebble leg, will fit well and give good wear. Sizes 2½ to 8. Price, per pair, $1.55.

No. 31413. Woman's good quality, same as above. Sizes, 2½ to 8. Price, per pair, $1.40.

No. 31415. Misses' good quality, pebble leg boot, bright finish. Sizes, 11 to 2. Price, per pair, $1.15.

No. 31417. Child's good quality rubber boot, same style as one preceding. Sizes, 6 to 10. Price, per pair, $1.05.

## RUBBER PAC ROLLED EDGE.

No. 31420. This Lumberman's over is made from first quality rubber, dull finish, extra high cut lace, and is snow excluding to the top. Made with heavy rolled edge (see cut), and will give the best of wear. Width, F only, for German socks. Sizes, 6 to 12. Price, per pair, $1.95.

## Lumberman's Two Buckle Captain Rolled Edge.

**No. 31424.** This Shoe is one which we have made special for for our own trade. It has rubber vamp, extra heavy sole and solid heel. The heavy rolled edge is very popular from the fact that it protects the sides. Heavy cloth top, wool lined, snow excluding, and has two adjustable buckles. A good shoe for rough wear. Width F, for German socks, width W, for wool boots. Sizes, 6 to 12; weight, 58 oz. Price, per pair.........$1.85

## Lumberman's Two Buckle Captain

**No. 31426** First quality rubber, heavy sole, heavy cloth top, snow excluding, wool lined, two buckles, rubber vamp, extra high cut and a very popular shoe for lumbermen. Width F, for German socks, width W, for wool felt boots. Sizes. 6 to 12; weight 54 ounces. Price per pair.......$1.70

### Lumberman's Erie.

**No. 31428.** This Lumberman's Over is made from first quality pure gum, over a heavy imported duck, making it one of the most durable shoes ever sold. It has extra heavy sole, solid heel, front lace, fleece lining, and is snow excluding to the top. Width, F for German socks only. Sizes, 6 to 12. Price, per pair.............................$2.15

### Men's Hurons.

**First Quality.**

**No. 31430.** This ankle boot is made from all rubber, first quality, and can be worn over wool boots or German socks. The top is clasped over the instep by an adjustable buckle, and the tongue and gusset make it snow excluding. Width F for socks; width W for wool boots. Sizes, 6 to 12. Price, per pair.............................$1.28

### Boy's Hurons—First Quality.

**No. 31432** This Boys' Ankle Boot is made same as the men's first quality. F for socks; W for wool boots. Sizes 1 to 5. Price per pair.............$1.09
**No. 31433** Boys' Ankle Boot, same style as above. Good quality; widths, F and W. Sizes, 1 to 5. Price per pair.............................$0.98

### Lumberman's Overshoes.

**Our Buckle Perfection.**

**No. 31436.** Men's First Quality Ankle Boot, made with water-tight fold, and to buckle closely around the ankle, can be put on or taken off quickly. When ordering be sure to state width, F for German socks, W for wool boots. Sizes, 6 to 13. Price, per pair.............................$1.53
**No. 13437.** Men's Good Quality One Buckle Perfection, same style as above. Width. F for German socks; W for wool boots. Sizes, 6 to 13. Price, per pair.........$1.38

## Lumberman's Bootees.

**First Quality.**

**No. 31438** Lumberman's Two Buckle Bootees, all rubber, first quality, tap sole and heel, net lined, are strongly constructed, and water-tight to the top. Width, W for wool boots only. Sizes, 6 to 13. Price, per pair............................................$1.91

**No. 31441.** Lumberman's favorite two buckle Bootee, all rubber, heavy tap sole, solid heel, net lined, and water tight to the top. Width, W for wool boots only. Sizes, 6 to 12. Price, per pair.........$.170

**No. 31443.** Lumberman's Friend. Made from all rubber, one buckle, heavy sole and heel, one bubkle over instep, net lined and will give good service. Width F for socks; width W for wool boots. Sizes 6 to 12. Price per pair......................$1.15

## McIntosh Wading Pants.

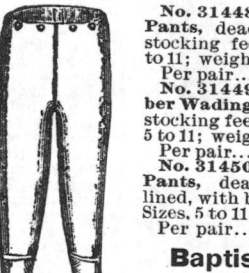

**No. 31448.** McIntosh Wading Pants, dead grass color, with stocking feet, net lined. Sizes, 5 to 11; weight, 70 oz. Per pair.....................$9.00
**No. 31449.** Dull Finish Rubber Wading Pants, on drill, with stocking feet, best quality. Sizes, 5 to 11; weight, 72 oz. Per pair.................$5.00
**No. 31450.** McIntosh Wading Pants, dead grass color, net lined, with boots, extension edge. Sizes, 5 to 11; weight, 101 oz. Per pair.................$10.00

## Baptisimal Pants.

**No. 31452. Made the Same Style as the Accompanying Cut,** a very light weight; black, with bright finished boots, neat and dressy; then there is a fine cashmere pants made same as an ordinary pants to be worn over same, making a **practically water-proof outfit.** When ordering give size of boots only, as no other measurement is required. Sizes, 5 to 10; weight, 110 oz. Per pair......................$11.00

## Running Shoes.

**No. 31491. Made from selected calfskin,** lace nearly to the toe, genuine sewed, five spikes, very light and extremely well made. Sizes, 6 to 10. Price per pair...................................$2.65

## XXX Professional Clog Shoes.

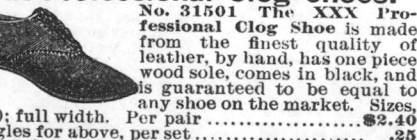

**No. 31501** The XXX Professional Clog Shoe is made from the finest quality of leather, by hand, has one piece wood sole, comes in black, and is guaranteed to be equal to any shoe on the market. Sizes, 6 to 10; full width. Per pair..........$2.40
Jingles for above, per set.................$.25
The Original Fargo Ball Bearing Bicycle Shoes quoted on colored pages.

## Ladies' Bicycle Leggins.

**No. 31514.** Ladies' Canvas Bicycle Leggins, very fine, in fact, look like a fine black button, knee length, with 9 buttons and buckle at top. Sizes, 2½ to 7; weight, 7 oz. Colors, black or brown. Per pair.......$0.40

## Men's Bicycle Shoes, Medium Grade.

**No. 31516** Men's Bicycle Shoes, made from a good grade of Kangaroo calf, which isvery soft and glove like, best bottom stock and eual to those usually sold for $2.25. Sizes 6 to 11. Widths full. Per pair, $1.60

## Ladies' Jersey Bicycle Leggins.

**Latest Style.**

**No. 31517.** The accompanying cut represents our latest production in Ladies' bicycle leggins. Made from the very finest imported all wool Jersey cloth, cut golf style, the tops being turned over, and of fancy figured patterns. The Jersey Leggin fits like a stocking, and is the coolest and most comfortable bicycle leggin made. Colors black with gray mixed top, blue with fancy top, and brown with fancy figured top. Sizes, 1 to 7. Weight, 6 oz. Per pair............$0.85

## Ladies' Plain Jersey Leggins.

**No. 31518.** Ladies' Bicycle Leggins, made from finest imported all wool Jersey cloth, with 10 buttons and buckle at top. This leggin comes just below the knee, fits like a stocking, conforms to every movement of the muscles and was one of our best sellers astl season. Colors, black, blue and brown. Sizes, 1 to 7; weight, 6 oz. Per pair.........$0.75
**No. 31519.** Ladies' Corduroy Bicycle Leggins, made from imported corduroy, and finished in the best possible manner. We have this leggin in brown, blue and black. A very handsome and durable leggin. Sizes, 2 to 7; weight, 7 oz. Per pair.........$0.85

## Ladies' Overgaiters.

**No. 31521** Ladies' Fine Black Overgaiters made heavy, for fall and winter wear. Shoe sizes, 1 to 7. Ladies' 7 button black melton, extra heavy, and the best we have ever seen for the price. Per pair, 25c; per doz. pairs......................$2.50
**No. 31522** Ladies' 7 Button Black Cheviot, very fine, fancy ribbon trim; med, usual price, 50c. Per pair, 35c; per doz. pairs..................$3.75
**No. 31523** Ladies' 7 Button English Beaver, extra heavy. Per pair, 45c; per dozen pairs..............$4.50
**No. 31524** Ladies' 7 Button Imported Kersey Silk Ribbon Top Facing, the nobbiest and unexcelled. Price, per pair, 65c; per dozen...................$7.25
**No. 31525** Ladies' 9 Button Overgaiters, made from good quality of English melton, very heavy and warm. Sizes, 1 to 7. Price, per pair, 40c; per dozen.....$4.25
**No. 31526** Ladies' 9 Button Overgaiters, made from heavy imported doe skin; very neat and one of the most popular overgaiters out this season. Sizes, 1 to 7. Price, per pair, 85c; per doz.....$9.00

**WE WANT YOUR ENTIRE CONFIDENCE, FOR WE CAN SERVE YOU BETTER IF YOU WILL TRUST MANY THINGS TO US. HOWEVER, IF YOU HAVE ANY DOUBTS, WE DON'T WANT YOUR ORDER TILL YOU ARE SATISFIED OF OUR INTEGRITY.**

## Combination Thigh Leggin.

### Ladies, Misses and Children.

No. 31530. This cut is a very good illustration of our Combination Leggin and Overgaiters. It is without a doubt the best fitting, warmest and most comfortable leggin that can be produced. Being made from a fine black Jersey cloth it fits as closely as a stocking and conforms to every movement of the limb. Has 7 buttons up side and elastic top.

Ladies' sizes, 1 to 7.
Price per pair .......... $1.45
Misses' sizes, 12 to 2.
Price per pair .......... $1.20
Child's sizes, 8 to 11.
Price per pair ........ $0.80

## Men's Overgaiters.

Men's Heavy Overgaiters, made from fine black cloth and just the thing for winter wear. Give size of shoe when ordering.
No. 31540. Heavy 5-Button Melton. Per pair ............. $0.25
No. 31541. Heavy 8-Button Melton. Per pair ............. $0.45
No. 31542. Heavy 5-Button Beaver. Per pair ............. $0.45
No. 31543. Heavy 5-Button Imported Kersey. Per pair ....... $0.65
No. 31544. Heavy 5-Button Imported Kersey. Per pair ............. $0.65
No. 31545. Heavy 8-Button Imported Kersey. Per pair ............. $0.85

## Heaton's Patent Button Machine.

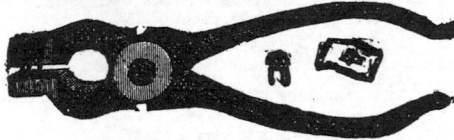

No. 31555. This is one of the Most Useful Machines Ever Invented. It is very simple and most any child can fasten the buttons on his own shoes. Every family should have one. Price each, 55c; 1 gross fasteners for above, 10c; 1 great gross. $0.85

### Black Shoe Buttons.

No. 31556. Ordinary Size first quality black shoe buttons. Price per gross, 4c; per great gross. $0.40

### Colored Shoe Buttons.

No. 31557. Best quality Shoe Buttons, medium size, in red, brown or russet.
Per gross, 15c; per great gross ............. $1.25

## Shoemaker's Hammers.

No. 31560. Best Steel Shoemaker's Hammer. No. 0 or 1; weight, 15 or 17 oz. Each.. $0.30
No. 31561.
Shoemaker's Hammer No. 2. Each.......... $0.35
No. 31562. Shoemaker's Hammer No. 3.
Each.......................... $0.40
No. 31563. Cheap Shoemaker's Hammer, medium size only. Each.......... $0.15

## Shoemaker's Rasps—Best Quality.

No. 31564. 8 inch half round; weight, 6 oz.
Each.......................... $0.25
No. 31565. 9 inch half round; weight, 8 oz.
Each.......................... $0.30
No. 31566. 10 inch half round; weight, 11 oz.
Each.......................... $0.35

## Awl Handles and Blades.

No. 31570. Shoemaker's Peg Awl Handles. Each.................... $0.10
No. 31571. Shoemaker's Sewing Awl Handles. Each.................... $0.03
No. 31572. Sewing Awl Blades, assorted sizes. Per dozen.......... $0.15
31573. Peg Awl Blades, assorted sizes. Per dozen.......... $0.08

## Shoemakers' Needles.

No. 31580. Shoemaker's Needles, for sewing leather; any size. Per paper.......... $0.08

## Shoemakers' Pinchers.

No. 31585. Timmons No. 1. Each........$0.50
No. 31586. Timmons No. 2. Each........ 0.60
No. 31587. Timmons Vo. 3. Each........ 0.65
No. 31588. Timmons No. 4. Each........ 0.75

---

# FAMILY COBBLER, HARNESS MENDER
## —AND TINKER—

No. 31550 THIS OUTFIT IS ONE WHICH EVERY FAMILY SHOULD HAVE, as it contains all the necessary tools for repairing almost anything, and will pay for itself many times in a single year.

### ...CONTENTS...

1 Iron Stand for lasts.
1 Iron Last for men's work.
1 Iron Last for boy's work.
1 Iron Last for women's work
1 Iron Last for children's work.
1 Shoemaker's Hammer.
1 Shoemaker's Knife.
1 Patent Peg Awl Handle.
1 Peg Awl.
1 Sewing Awl Handle.
1 Sewing Awl.
1 Harness Awl Handle.
1 Harness Awl.
1 Wrench for Peg Awl Handle.
1 Bottle Leather Cement.
1 Bottle Rubber Cement.
1 Bunch Bristles.
1 Ball Shoe Thread.

1 Ball Shoe Wax.
1 Package Shoe Pegs.
1 Package Heel Nails.
1 Package Half-soling Nails
1 Package Half-soling Tacks
4 Pairs Heel Plates.
½ dozen Shoe and Harness Needles.
1 Saw and Harness Clamp.
1 Box Harness and Belt Rivets.
1 Harness and Belt Punch.
1 Soldering Iron with Handle
1 Bar Solder.
1 Box Rosin.
1 Bottle Soldering Fluid.
1 Copy Directions for Soldering etc.
1 Copy Directions for Half-soling etc.

Securely packed in wooden box with hinged lid; weight, 25 pounds. Price.......................... $1.95

Special Discount on ½ Dozen Lots.

---

## Sears, Roebuck & Co.'s Shoe Repair Outfit No. I.

No. 31551
Weight, 18½ lbs.

No. 31551. This Outfit of Shoemaker's Tools is the most complete ever offered. We have placed an order for a large quantity to be put up especially for us, and of the very best material. Every family should have one. We quote below a list of articles contained in the outfit.

### CONTENTS.

1 Large Iron Last.
1 Medium Iron Last.
1 Small Iron Last.
3 Pairs Mens' Good Tap Soles.
2 Papers Cobblers' Nails.
1 Peg Awl Handle.
3 Sewing Awl Blades, best quality.
3 Peg Awl Blades; best quality.
1 Bottle Rubber Cement, best quality.

1 Reversible Iron Stand.
1 Shoe Hammer, best quality.
12 Best Heel Plates.
1 Sewing Awl Handle.
1 Best Shoemaker's Knife.
1 One Bottle Leather Cement, best quality.
1 Piece Shoemakers' Wax.
1 Bunch Bristles.
1 Ball Shoe Thread.
36 pieces in all.

Remember that these tools are all of the very best material.

Price, complete in wood box, with hinged lid.......... $1.45

Special Discount on Half Dozen Lots.

## The "Economical" Cobbler.

No. 31552 The Economical Cobbler contains all the tools necessary for shoe repairing, is cheap, good, and a great time and money saver.

### CONTENTS.

1 Iron Stand, for Lasts.
1 Last for Men's work.
1 Last for Boys' work.
1 Last for Children's work.
1 Shoemaker's Hammer.
1 Shoemaker's Knife.
1 Patent Peg Awl Handle.
1 Peg Awl.

1 Sewing Awl Handle.
1 Sewing Awl.
1 Harness Awl Handle.
1 Harness Awl.
1 Paper Heel Nails.
1 Paper Half Soling Nails.
1 Wrench for Peg Awl Handle.
1 Copy Directions for Half Soling.

Securely packed in wooden box with hinged lid.

WEIGHT, 14 LBS.          Per Set, $0.68.

Special discount on 1 dozen lots.

---

## SpringPunches.

No. 31589. Punches, No. 6, for B long eyelets. Each... $0.40
No. 31590 Punches, Nos. 8 and 10, for large eyelets. Each.... $0.40
No. 31591. Revolving Punch, 4 size tubes. Each... $1.40
No. 31592. Revolving Punch, 6 size tubes. Each... $1.60

## Iron Shoe Lasts and Stand.

No. 31593. Reversible Iron Stand,15 inches high, with three lasts, small, medium and large.
Per set, complete.......... $0.35

**BE STYLISH FOR $1.98**   ...SEE...
Colored Sheets

---

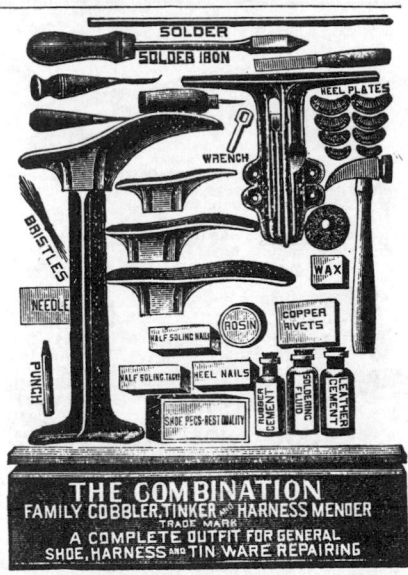

THE COMBINATION
FAMILY COBBLER, TINKER AND HARNESS MENDER
TRADE MARK
A COMPLETE OUTFIT FOR GENERAL SHOE, HARNESS AND TIN-WARE REPAIRING

---

## Witham's Patent Hand-Made Boot Calks.

| | No. 00. | No. 0. | No. 1. | No. 2. | No. 3. | No. 4. | | |
|---|---|---|---|---|---|---|---|---|
| No. 00. | Extra small ball. | | | Per doz. | 7c | Per 100, | $0.50 |
| No. 0. | Small ball. | | | Per doz. | 7c | Per 100, | .50 |
| No. 1. | Small ball. | | | Per doz. | 7c | Per 100, | .50 |
| No. 2. | Medium ball. | | | Per doz. | 7c | Per 100, | .50 |
| No. 3. | Large ball, or small heel. | | | Per doz. | 7c | Per 100, | .50 |
| No. 4. | Large heel. | | | Per doz. | 7c | Per 100, | .50 |

Put up 100 in packages.

Calk Set, and punch for setting calks, 4 inches long, each, 25c. Per doz.......................... $2.65

---

## IRON LAP LASTS.

Made of iron and very handy to have in the house.
No. 31594. Men's large, 30c.
No. 31595. Men's razor toe, 30c.
No. 31596. Men's medium, 25c.
No. 31597. Ladies' medium, 20c.
No. 31598. Ladies' razor toe, 20c.

## ROYAL RUBBER SOLES.

No. 31600. This sole is made of best rubber and is made to cement on the sole. If the sole of your shoe is thin this is a splendid thing for damp weather.
Price, per pair, 25c.

## WOOD SHOE STRETCHERS, "HOLD FAST."

No. 31602. "Hold Fast" Shoe Stretcher (see cut) is the best, from the fact that it can be fastened in place, and will not slip. Every family should have one. Comes in 4 sizes: No. 1, Men's large; No. 2, Men's small; No. 3, Ladies'; No. 4, Child's. Price, each, $1.15.

## WOOD SHOE STRETCHER, COMMON.

No. 31603. Wood Shoe Stretcher, made medium size, so it can be used for ladies' or gentlemen's shoes. Has corn and bunion attachments, and is an article which every family should have in the house. Weight, 30 oz. Price, each, 75c.

## STAR STEEL PLATES.

No. 31608. Star Heel Plates, to prevent boots and shoes from wearing off at the heels. No nails or screws required: No. 1 for Child's heels, No. 2 for Ladies' heels, No. 3 for Boy's heels, No. 4 for Men's heels. Per pair, 2c; per dozen pairs, 20c.

## HAND PEG BREAK.

No. 31610. A very handy article for every family. If you buy a pair of boots or shoes, and the pegs are not all taken out, you can easily make them comfortable with the Hand Peg Break. Price, each, 40c.

No. 31611. Same as above, reversible. Price, each, 60c.

## SHOE PEGS AND NAILS.

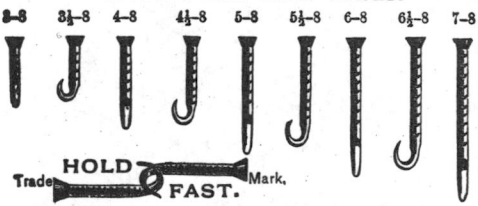

No. 31613. Latest improved brass clinching Nails. Sizes, 3-8, 3½-8, 4-8, 4½-8, 5-8 and 6-8. Price, per lb., 24c.
No. 31615. Baker's patent wire clinch Nails, 3-8 and 3½-8, 17 wire. Price, per lb., 17c.
No. 31617. Baker's patent wire clinch Nails, 4-8, 4½-8, 5-8, 5½-8 and 6-8. Price, per lb., 12c.
No. 31619. Common iron Shoe Nails, ⅜, 4-8, 5-8 and 6-8. Price, per lb., 6c.
No. 31620. Hungarian Nails, for bottom of miners' boots and shoes. Sizes, 3-8 stout, 3-8 fine. Price, per lb., 15c.
No. 31621. Shoe Pegs. The famous "Blue Star" peg, made from best hardwood; nothing better. Sizes, 3-8, 4-8, 5-8, 6-8. Price, per quart, 5c.

## REVOLVING EYELET SET AND PUNCH.

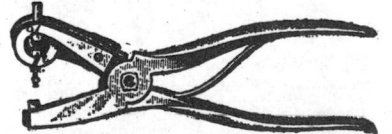

No. 31623. This combination is composed of a Revolving Eyelet Set and Punch, used for B long eyelets, making almost an indispensable tool in any household; will last a lifetime properly used; eyelet set and punch combined. Weight, 12 ounces. Price, each, 90c.

## FISHER'S HEEL STIFFENERS.

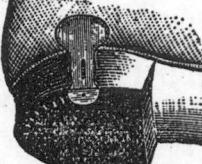

No. 31622. The best in the world. Fisher's Heel Stiffeners are easily put on, and will fit any shoe. Per pair, 10c; per doz., 75c.

## MEN'S, WOMEN'S AND BOYS' TOP LIFTS.

No. 31624.

| Grade. | Height, per dozen, | Price. |
|---|---|---|
| Fine, men's top lifts, | 5¾ inches, | $0.85 |
| Fine, men's top lifts, | 5½ inches, | .75 |
| Fine, men's top lifts, | 5 inches, | .65 |
| Fine, men's top lifts | 4½ inches, | .60 |
| Fine, men's top lifts | 4 inches, | .55 |
| Fine, boys' top lifts,, | | .60 |
| Fine, women's top lifts, | | .45 |

## MEN'S JUMBO OAK BLOCKS.

These pieces are cut from best oak sole leather and will cut four different size taps.

| Grade. | Lbs., per doz. | Price, per doz. |
|---|---|---|
| No. 31628. Extra fine quality, | 9 to 11 | $5.50 |
| No. 31629. Good quality, | 8 to 10 | 4.50 |
| No. 31630. Medium quality, | 7 to 8 | 4.00 |

## HEMLOCK TAP SOLES.

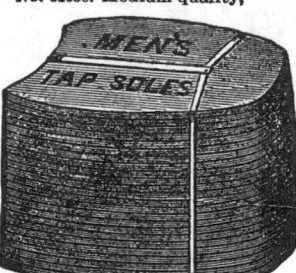

No. 31631. Men's tap soles. Sizes, 6, 7, 8, per pair, 19c; sizes, 9, 10, 11, per pair, 20c. Per doz., assorted, $2.10.
No. 31632. Boys' tap soles. Sizes, 1 to 5, per pair, 17c; per doz., assorted; $2.00.

No. 31634. Women's hemlock Tap Soles, fine quality. Per pair, 15c; per dozen pair, $1.50.
No. 31635. Women's medium fine hemlock Taps. Height, per doz., 4½ inches. Price, per doz., only $1.35; per single pair, 13c.

## HEMLOCK SOLE LEATHER.

### BUFFALO'S "CELEBRATED" SLAUGHTER SOLE LEATHER.

**Rumsey's, Howard's, & Gaenslen's.**
Subject to Market Change.

No. 31640. Best Buffalo Sole, 17 to 30 lbs., single side, 25c.
No. 31641. Best Buffalo Sole, 17 to 30 lbs. (spready) single side, 24c.
No. 31642. Good Buffalo Sole, 17 to 30 lbs. (one brand to each side), single side, 24c.
No. 31643. Best Buffalo Sole, 14 to 16 lbs., all clear, single side, 24c.
No. 31644. Good Buffalo Sole, 14 to 16 lbs. (one brand to each side), single side, 23c.
No. 31645. No. 2 Buffalo Sole, 20 to 30 lbs. (two brands to each side), single side, 22c.
No. 31646. Extra Best Buffalo Sole, 20 to 30 lbs. (extra plump, clear of brands and cuts), single side, 26c.

### HEMLOCK BACKS.

Heads and bellies trimmed off. No flanks or offal. Cheapest stock for tapping.
No. 31647. Best Buffalo Slaughter Backs, 14 to 19 lbs., single side, 30c.
No. 31648. Good Buffalo Slaughter Backs, one brand, 14 to 19 lbs., single side, 29c.

## MATAMORA SOLE LEATHER.

No. 31649. No. 1 Matamora Sole, plump and clear, 16 to 29 lbs., single side, 22c.
No. 31650. No. 1 Matamora Sole, one brand, 16 to 29 lbs., single side, 29c.

## CHICAGO SLAUGHTER SOLE LEATHER.

Tannage and Selection Equal to Any.
No. 31651. Chicago Slaughter, No. 1, plump and clear 18 to 26 lbs., single side, 25c.

## OAK SOLE LEATHER.

We only sell the best tannages of Oak Sole Leather made from "Packer's Hides."
No. 31652. Philadelphia, extra choice, 17 to 29 lbs., single side, 29c.
No. 31653. Philadelphia A, one brand, 17 to 26 lbs., single side, 28c.
No. 31654. Philadelphia B, two brands, 17 to 26 lbs., single side, 27c.
No. 31655. Philadelphia, extra choice, 14 to 16 lbs., single side, 28c.
No. 31656. Scoured Oak, extra choice, 17 to 20 lbs., single side, 30c.
No. 31657. Scoured Oak, extra choice, 14 to 16 lbs., single side, 29c.
No. 31658. Louisville Oak, extra choice, 20 to 26 lbs., single side, 30c.
No. 31659. Louisville Oak, extra choice, 17 to 19 lbs., single side, 29c.
No. 31660. Baltimore Star, extra choice, 22 to 28 lbs., single side, 30c.

## WAX UPPER LEATHER.

No. 31661. Union Upper, 12 to 14 feet, fine and light, single side, per foot, 18c.
No. 31662. Union Upper, 15 to 18 feet, medium and fine, single side, per foot, 18c.
No. 31663. Union Upper, 18 to 20 feet, heavy, but fine, single side, per foot, 18c.
This celebrated stock is the best and finest for fine calf or kip boot backs, much finer and less flanky than oak, but same light colored grain.

## GRAIN LEATHER.

No. 31664. English Oil Grain, 14 to 20 feet, No. 1, single side, per foot, 18c.
No. 31665. Milwaukee Oil Grain, 18 to 24 feet, single side, per foot, 17c.
No. 31666. German Oil Shoe Grain, 16 to 18 feet, single side, per foot, 15c.
No. 31667. Light Oil Shoe Grain, single side, per foot, 14c.
No. 31668. Polish Grain, for shoes or boot legs, 12 to 16 feet, single side, per foot, 15c.

## CHAMOIS SKINS—Imported Best.

No. 31669. Best and large, per skin, 75c.

## DONGOLA KID—Glazed Finish.

No. 31670. Extra for ladies' shoes, 3 to 5 feet. Per skin, per foot, 35c.
No. 31671. Good for patching. Per skin, per foot, from 22c to 24c.

## RUBBER SOLING.

No. 31672. Rubber Soling, for boots and shoes. Per lb., 45c.

## FRENCH CALF SKINS.

Price on calf skins subject to change without notice. These skins run in weight from 2 to 3½ lbs. each.
No. 31673. Simon Ullmo, first choice, 2 to 3½ lbs. Each, per lb., $1.80.
No. 31674. Mercier's, first choice, 2 to 3½ lbs. Each per lb., $1.80.

## OAK TANNED CALF SKINS.

No. 31675. Crown, extra choice; weight, 2 to 2½ lbs. Each, per lb., $1.25.
No. 31676. Crown, extra choice; weight, 2½ to 3 lbs. Each, per lb., $1.20.

## HEMLOCK CALF SKINS.

No. 31677. Chicago, a calf, extra selection, 2 to 2½ lbs. Each, per lb., $1.00.
No. 31678. Chicago, a calf, spready, 3½ to 4 lbs. Each, per lb., 75c.
No. 31679. Chicago, a runner, for boot backs, 4 to 5 lbs. Each, per lb., 70c.

## ALLIGATOR SKINS.

No. 31680. Large size, $5.50; medium size, $5.00.

## ELASTIC GORING.

No. 31681. Hub Goring, 5 inch, per yard, 50c; Hub Wool Goring. 5-inch, per yard, 60c.

## KNIVES AND SKIVERS.

No. 31682. Square point, T. Harrington's best; each, 15c; per doz., $1.25. Curve point, T. Harrington's best, each, 15c; per doz., $1.25. Lip or fore part, T. Harrington's best, each, 15c; per doz., $1.25. Thin kid Skivers; T. Harrington's best, each, 25c; per doz., $2.50. Sole leather Skivers, T. Harrington's best, each, 25c; per doz., $2.50.

## LEATHER CEMENT.

We carry only the best cements, and they are all fully guaranteed. For cementing all kinds of leather.
No. 31683. 1 oz. bottle; weight, 3 oz. Price each, 7c; per doz., 80c.
No. 31684. 2 oz. bottle; weight, 6 oz. Price each, 13c. per doz. $1.40.

## RUBBER CEMENT.

Rubber Cement is used for repairing rubber boots and shoes.
No. 31685. 2 oz. bottle, guaranteed the best. Price each, 12c; per doz., $1.20.
No. 31686. 4 oz. bottle, guaranteed the best. Price each, 18c; per doz., $2.00.

## The Nightingale Shoe Lace.

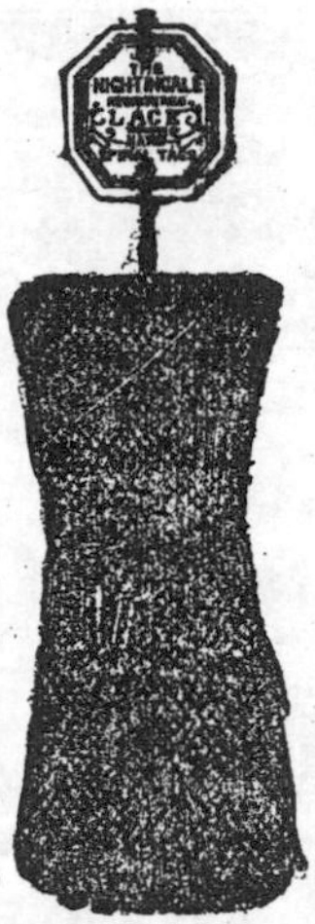


**No 31711 This lace is made from the best of linen woven very close,** is about ⅛ inch wide, 1 yard long, with brass spiral tags. It is without a doubt the best lace ever made for men's shoes, as it has the strength and wearing qualities of the porpoise lace. Try them. Per pair 2c; per gross...... **$1.30**

## Best Porpoise Laces.

No. 31714 **Best English Porpoise Laces,** 36 inches long, with brass spiral tags. The strongest and best made at any price. Per pair. 4c; per dozen pairs, 45c; Per gross......... ............**$2.50**

No. 31715 **Medium Porpoise Laces,** 36 inches long, with spiral tags, very strong and the kind usually sold for 5c per pair. We can recommend them. Per pair, 3c; per dozen pair 35c.
Per gross.................... **$1.90**

## Round Leather Laces.

**No. 31716. Men's Very Best Round Leather Laces,** 36 inches long, cut from straight leather, plain, without tags. One end unsplit, so you can see how they are cut.
Price per 2 pairs, **5c**; per doz. pairs..........**$0.27**
**No. 31717. Round Leather Laces,** good grade, with spiral tags on each end. They are as strong as a good many so-called porpoise.
Price, 2 pairs, **5c**; per doz. pairs...............**$0.27**
**No. 31718. Men's Linen Laces,** extra heavy ⅛ inch wide, 1 yard long, made for heavy wear.
Price, per 2 pair, **3c**; per doz. pairs, **15c**; per gross. **$0.80**

## Lamb's Wool Slipper Soles.

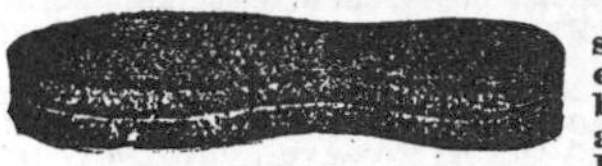

Cork slipper soles, leather covered bottoms, bound with braid and heavy fleece lamb's wool facing. **Used with crocheted uppers.**
**No. 31720.** Men's sizes, 6 to 11. Per pair...**$0.20**
**No. 31721.** Women's sizes, 3 to 7. Per pair. **0.18**
**No. 31722.** Misses' sizes, 13 to 2. Per pair. **0.15**
**No. 31723.** Child's sizes, 8 to 12. Per pair.. **0.12**

## Leather Insoles.

**Gummed insoles, cemented on the bottom, make a smooth and comfortable shoe.**
**No. 31724. Men's Gummed Insoles.** Sizes, 6 to 11. Per pair........................................**$0.08**
**No. 31725. Women's Gummed Insoles.** Sizes, 3 to 7. Per pair..........................................**$0.06**

## Cork Insoles.

**No. 31726 Men's Cork Insoles.** Sizes, 6 to 11. Per pair....................................**$0.06**
**No. 31727 Women's Cork Insoles.** Sizes, 2 to 7. Per pair..........................................**$0.05**

## Sheep-Skin Slippers.

**For Inside of Rubber Boots.**

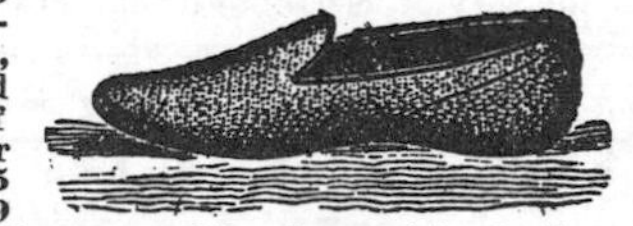

**No. 31728 Men's Sheep-Skin Slippers,** first quality, used to wear inside of rubber boots. Per pair...... ..**$0.15**
**No. 31729 Men's Canvas Slippers,** with sheep-skin bottom, used for same purpose as above. Per pair.....**$0.10**

## Colored Shoe Laces.

**No. 31730. Ladies' Tan, Black or Wine Oxford Lace,** best quality, ¾ yard long. Per 3 pairs..**$0.05**
**No. 31731. Ladies' Shoe Lace,** 6-4 long, brown or Oxblood, best quality. Per pair.................**$0.02**
**No. 31732. Mens' Dark Wine Shoe Laces,** 4-4 long, best quality. Per 2 pair.....................**$0.05**

## Button Hooks.

**No. 31735. Wire Button Hooks,** 3 inches long.
Per dozen, **2c**; per gross........................ **$0.20**
**No. 31736. Fancy Button Hook,** 6 inches long, with plain rosewood handle. Each,............ **3c**;
per dozen, **30c**; per gross....................... **$3.25**

## Shoe Threads.

| | Per ball. | Per lb. |
|---|---|---|
| **No. 31697. Barbour's Irish Flax,** No. 12.. | **18c** | **$1.25** |
| **No. 31698. Barbour's Irish Flax,** No. 3.. | **15c** | **1.00** |
| **No. 31699. Barbour's Irish Flax,** No. 1.. | **13c** | **.90** |
| **No. 31700. Barbour's American Flag,** No. 10 | **10c** | **.60** |

## Rubber Patching, Repair Cloth and Rubber Soling.

**No. 31687. Light Patching,** dull or luster.
Price per square..................................**$0.45**
**No. 31688. Medium Patching,** dull or luster.
Price per square..................................**$0.50**
**No. 31689. Heavy Patching,** dull or luster.
Price per square..................................**$0.60**
**No. 31690. Rubber Repair Cloth.**
Price per square, **25c**; per yard...............**$2.50**
**No. 31691. Rubber Soling,** heavy, heavy medium and medium. Price per lb.......................**$0.40**

## Shoemaker's Wax.

**No. 31692. Shoemaker's Wax,** black or yellow.
Price per ball, **1c**; per doz.......................**$0.10**

## Bristles.

**No. 31693. Russian Bristles, XXXX.**
Price per oz..........................................**£1.10**
**No. 31693. Russian Bristles. XXX.**
Price per oz.......................................... **.95**
**No. 31693. Russian Bristles, XX.**
Price per oz.......................................... **.80**
**No. 31693. Russian Bristles, X.**
Price per oz.......................................... **.65**
**No. 31693. Fitting Bristles.** Price per oz.. **.50**

## Eyelets.

**No. 31694. Eyelets,** black or yellow, B long, put up 1,000 in box. Weight, 2 oz. Price per box ..**$0.10**

## Eyelet Sets.

**No. 31695. Eyelet Sets,** common, Weight, 10 oz.
Price..................................................**$0.45**
**No. 31696. Eyelet Sets,** with spring. Weight, 10 oz.
Price..................................................**$0.55**

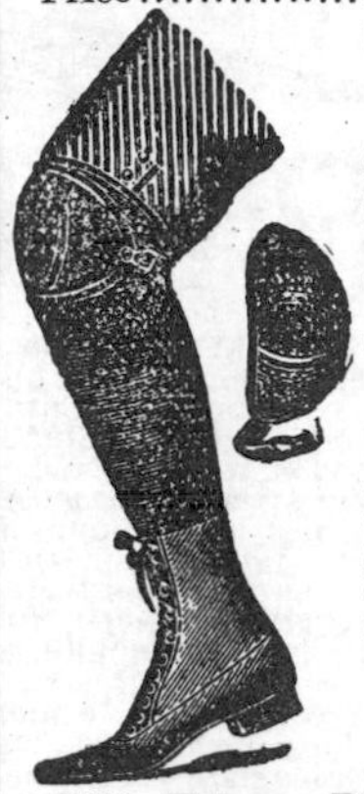

## Knee Protector or Stocking Shields.

A good thing for the boys and girls who wear their stockings out at the knee. Sizes, medium and large.
**No. 31745** Made from heavy Jersey cloth. Each.........**$0.20**
**No. 31746** Made from good grade of leather. Each..**$0.25**

## Stocking Heel protector.

**No. 31747 This article will save many times its cost every month.** Made from best quality lamb's skin. Come in men's, boys' and women's. Per pair, **10c**; per dozen pairs .......................**$1.10**

## Gilt Edge Dressings.

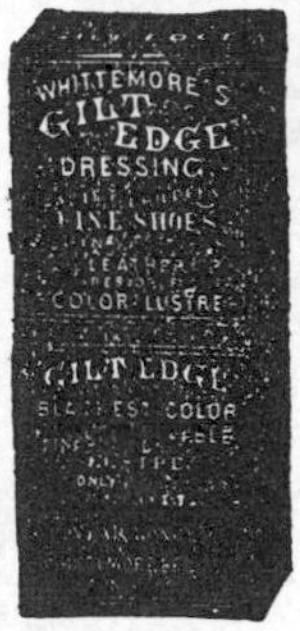


**No. 31756. Ladies' Gilt Edge Shoe Dressing** is very useful for a great many things besides shoes. It will make your old rubbers, shopping bags, and black kid gloves, **look equal to new.** Many use it to dye straw hats and as a stove polish, thus saving time and labor, dust and brushes, as it requires no rubbing. **You will find it a necessity in your family.** Sold everywhere for **25c**. Weight, 14 oz. Price per bottle..........**$0.18**
Per dozen .................. **1.90**

## SHINE 'EM UP.

We quote below our famous **B. C. French Blacking,** which is acknowledged to be the **best in the world, the Gilt Edge,** finest thing for ladies' shoes, and many others which are absolutely first-class.

## The Famous B. C. French Blacking

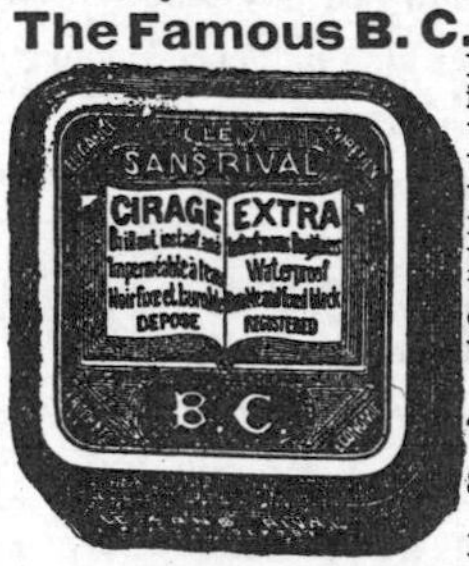


**No. 31749. This Blacking** is known all over the world and acknowledged to be the best. It prevents the leather from becoming hard and will quickly produce a polish even when the boot or shoe is damp. Every box guaranteed.
No. 0. Small, per box. **4c**; per doz. . ...... **$0.45**
No. 1. Medium, per box, **8c**; per doz..........**$0.85**
No. 2. Large, per box, **12c**; per doz...........**$1.40**

## Smith's Patent Leather Polish.

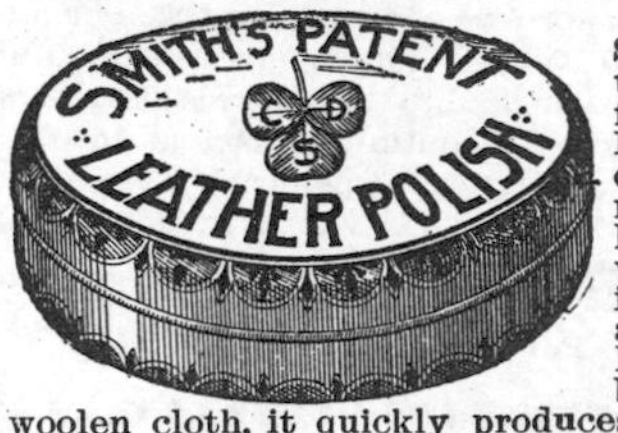


**No. 31752 Smith** manufactures perhaps the finest **Patent Leather Polish** ever sold. It will not injure the leather in any way, and by cleaning the shoes well and applying the Polish, then rubbing with a soft woolen cloth, it quickly produces a brilliant and waterproof luster. Price, per box. **7c**; per doz.,**$0.75**

## Smith's Russet Paste.

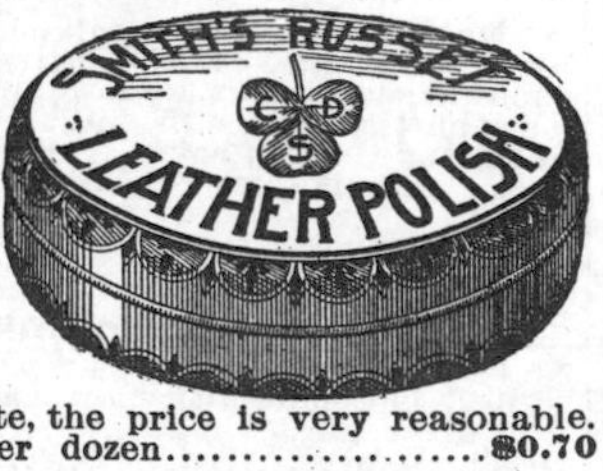


**No. 31753 Smith's Russet Leather Polish** is manufactured in Chicago, and is sold and recommended by all first-class shoe stores in this and other large cities. We have no hesitancy in saying that it is equal to any made and as you will note, the price is very reasonable. Price per box **7c**; per dozen....................**$0.70**

## Smith's Combination Russet.

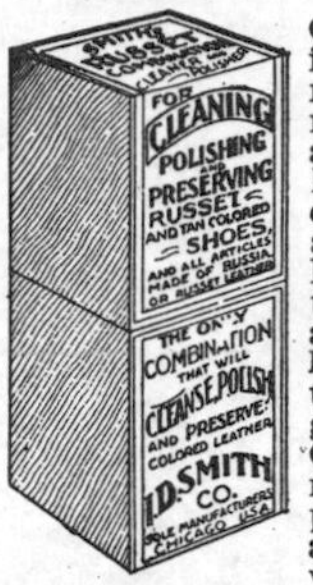


**No. 31755. Cleaner and Polish.** Contains a full size bottle of dressing for polishing, cleansing and removing stains from all kinds of russet or tan colored shoes. Also a decorated tin box of Polishing Paste. For giving russet and tan-colored shoes a brilliant, durable and water-proof polish as follows: First remove the stains and cleanse the leather with our dressing, then apply a thin coating of our "**Yellow Polishing Paste**" (according to directions on box), and you will get an elegant and lasting polish. On new shoes, or those that do not need cleansing, only the polishing paste need be used. Try them once and you never will be satisfied with any other polish. This is a regular **25c** package. Our price, each.........**$0.15**
Per dozen ........ . .......................... **1.60**

## Smith's Russet Combination.

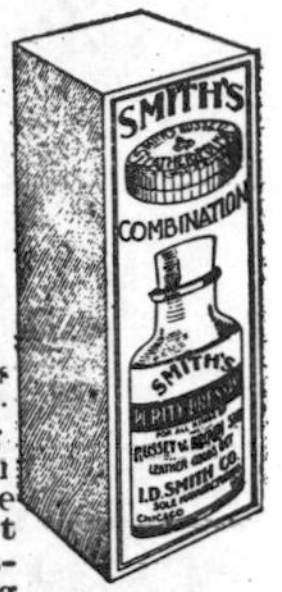


Same as above, put up in smaller package. Regular 15c. size.
Price, each............ .........**$0.08**
Per doz........................... **.80**

## Boston Waterproof Polish.

**For Men's and Boys' Shoes**

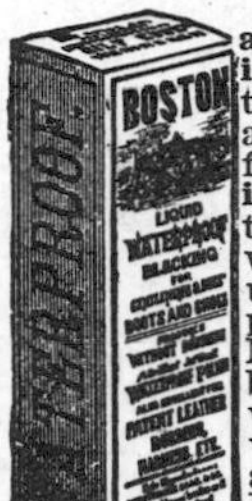


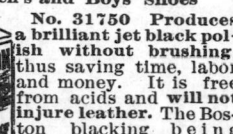

**No. 31750 Produces a brilliant jet black polish without brushing** thus saving time, labor and money. It is free from acids and **will not injure leather.** The Boston blacking being waterproof in rain or snow, is largely used in winter to keep the feet dry **thus preventing colds and rheumatism.** Men or boys who dislike to wear rubbers should use Boston, as it sheds water like a rubber. It is a favorite with gentlemen, as it will not rub off and ruin their pants or soil their hands. Do not fail to keep the rubber boots and shoes of your family looking like new by the use of Boston. Apply with sponge attached to cork.
Per bottle, **20c**; per doz........................**$2.10**

## Foerderer's Tan Kid Dressing.

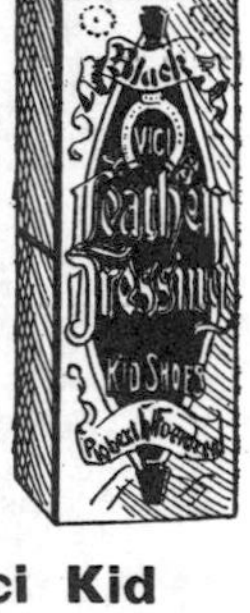


**31794 Foerderer's Vici Kid** is known all over the civilized world, and this dressing is used on every skin before it leaves his factory. **It is the only tan dressing which produces a lasting and brilliant lustre without rubbing,** and the factthat Mr. Foerderer uses it on all of his Kid stock is sufficient guarantee as to its good qualities. It is applied with a sponge and **makes tan shoes look like new.** Is suitable for all tan Kid shoes. This Dressing is sold everywhere at 25 cents Weight 13 ounces.
Price each........................**$0.16**
Price per doz. net...............**$1.75**

## Foerderer's Black Vici Kid Dressing.

**No.31795 Best Dressing ever used,** can be applied with a sponge, produces a brilliant lustre without rubbing, and the fact that all of Foerderer's Vici Kid stock is finished with it assures us that it does not in any way injure the leather. It is the best ever sold at any price. Weight 13 oz; regular **25c** size. Price per bottle...........................**$0.16**
Per doz., net .............................. **1.75**

## The Gem Shoe Polisher.

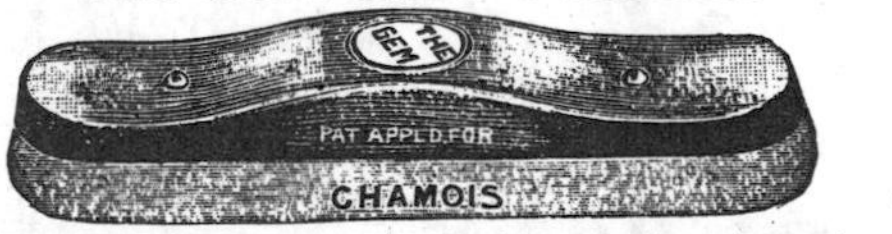


**No. 31797. The above cut is a good representation of Our Gem Shoe Polisher,** for tan, patent leather, enamel, box calf, and all kinds of kid shoes. It is made with oxidized metal back and with chamois face. This polisher is especially adapted for polishing tan shoes, and will pay for itself many times each season. Packed in neat leatherette box. Weight, 7 oz. Price each, **23c**; per doz.........**$2.60**

**THE MOST EXQUISITE AND MOST FASHIONABLE STYLES IN WRAPPERS AND WAISTS.**

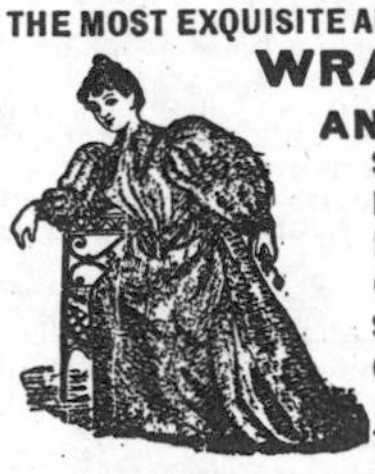

See full Plate Pages of Our most Stylish Goods. REFER TO INDEX.

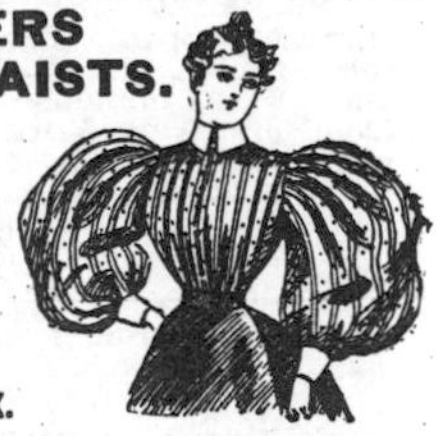

**OUR BEST CUSTOMERS ARE STEADY CUSTOMERS. MORE AND MORE PEOPLE ARE GETTING INTO THE HABIT OF ANTICIPATING THEIR WANTS, AND THUS MAKING UP ORDERS SUFFICIENTLY LARGE TO GO BY FREIGHT.**

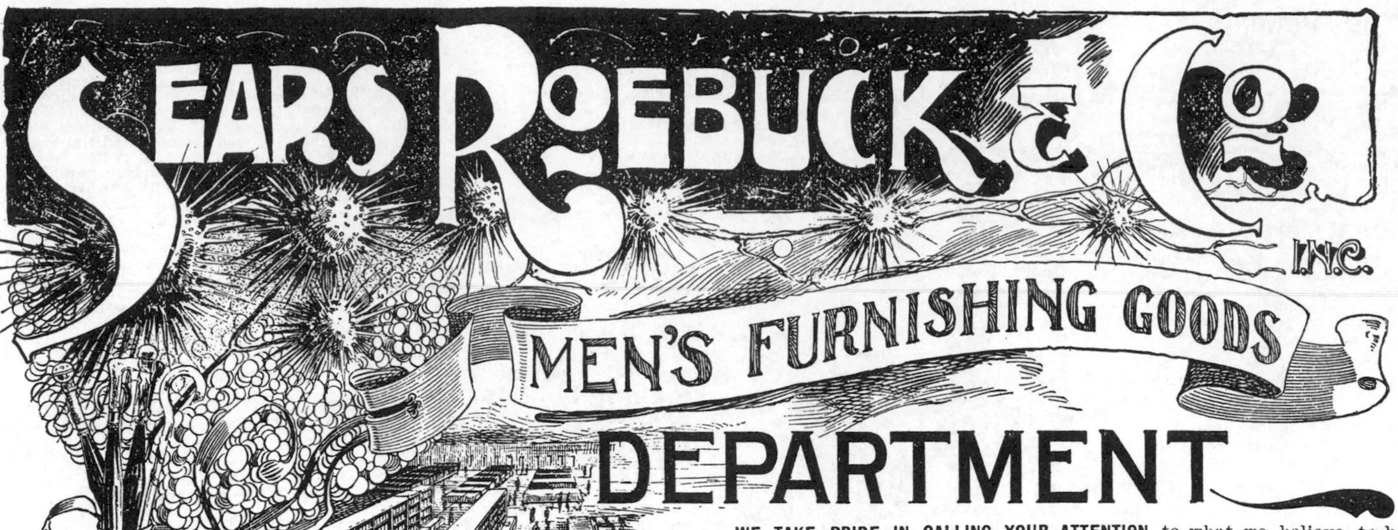

# SEARS ROEBUCK & Co INC

## MEN'S FURNISHING GOODS DEPARTMENT

**WE TAKE PRIDE IN CALLING YOUR ATTENTION** to what we believe to be the most complete and up to date Furnishing Goods Department ever placed before the buying public in Catalogue form.

**AMONG THE DESIRABLE GOODS IN FURNISHINGS FOR 1897** we do not think there is an item omitted. Our professional buyers have been in the market constantly since the new styles began being made, and neither time nor expense has been spared in our efforts to give our customers an opportunity of securing the very latest and most desirable merchandise and at the very minimum price as well as on liberal terms of shipment.

**AGAIN, WE INVITE YOU TO A CLOSE COMPARISON OF OUR PRICES WITH THOSE OF ANY OTHER CONCERN.** We would ask you to carefully study our Catalogue, our descriptions, illustrations and prices, to compare them with others, and then send your order where, in your judgment, you can get the most desirable goods and the greatest value for your money. We are perfectly willing that our goods, our descriptions, illustrations and prices should stand on their merits, and on their merits alone we anticipate the largest trade in this line we have ever enjoyed.

**OUR PREPARATIONS FOR THE COMING SEASON HAVE BEEN FAR MORE EXTENSIVE** than ever before. Every item we have listed has been contracted for direct with the manufacturer on the basis of large quantities for Spot Cash, and to this we have added only our one small conservative percentage of profit, which alone enables you to buy the goods for even less than dealers can buy in quantities, and on this basis we earnestly speak for your trade.

**OUR GUARANTEE.** We guarantee every article quoted to be exactly as represented, and if not found so you are at liberty to return it and we will cheerfully refund your money.

**OUR TERMS.** Our Terms are very Liberal. Any goods will be sent to any addree by freight or express C. O. D., subject to examination, on receipt of a sufficient deposit to cover transportation charges both ways. As a rule $1.00 deposit with order is sufficient with express shipments. Where goods are sent C. O. D. you examine them at your nearest railroad station, and if found perfectly satisfactory and exactly as represented, pay the express agent our price and charges, less the amount sent with order.

**DISCOUNT FOR CASH.** We allow a Discount of 3% if cash in full accompanies your order. If you send the full amount of cash with your order you may deduct 3% from our price. Nearly all our customers send cash in full. You take no risk, for if the goods are not perfectly satisfactory you are at liberty to return them to us and we will cheerfully refund your money.

**WE ARE EXTREMELY ANXIOUS TO RECEIVE YOUR ORDER FROM THIS DEPARTMENT,** not so much for the little profit there is in the goods to us for they are sold on a very small margin, but for the good it will do us as an advertisement. We know we carry a much better line of merchandise than is carried by the average dealer, and yet we are able to sell it to you at far less than inferior goods can be had at home, and if we get one order from you we know you will be so well pleased that you will not only favor us with your future orders but will use your kind influence among your friends in our behalf.

**THIS DEPARTMENT IS IN CHARGE OF A MAN WHO HAS MADE FURNISHING GOODS HIS LIFE'S BUSINESS.** He is assisted by a large number of able clerks, and nothing is allowed to come in or go out of this department unless it passes a very critical inspection. No goods are bought except those that are manufactured by concerns of established and well known reputation.

**WE THANK YOU IN ADVANCE IN ANTICIPATION OF YOUR ORDER,** at the same time assuring you of such values and service as cannot be had elsewhere.

## ...MEN'S UNLAUNDERED WHITE SHIRTS...

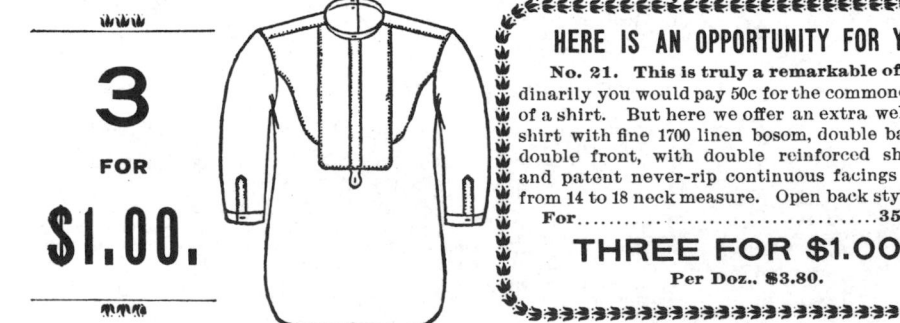

**3 FOR $1.00.**

**HERE IS AN OPPORTUNITY FOR YOU.**

**No. 21.** This is truly a remarkable offer. Ordinarily you would pay 50c for the commonest kind of a shirt. But here we offer an extra well made shirt with fine 1700 linen bosom, double back and double front, with double reinforced shoulders and patent never-rip continuous facings in sizes from 14 to 18 neck measure. Open back style.

For.................................................35c each.

**THREE FOR $1.00.**

Per Doz., $3.80.

**GOOD WEAR.**

**GOOD FIT.**

**FULL SIZE.**

### Our Great 50c Line.

**No. 22.** An unlaundered, **open back shirt** made expressly for us. You cannot buy as good a shirt at retail for less than 75 cents. We use the entire product of one immense factory. This shirt is made from fine New York mills muslin, with four ply warranted linen bosom, patent continuous never-rip facings and gusseted all over. Sizes 14 to 18. Hand made button holes.

Price each..........................$ 0.50
Six for.............................2.85

**No. 23.** Same as above, open either front or back.

Price each..........................$ 0.50
Six for.............................2.85

### 69c For a Dollar Shirt.

**No. 24.** This line of unlaundered shirts is made up with the same care and attention to details as if each garment was made to order. Made from New York muslin with finest all linen bosom and hand made button holes. Double front and double back. Long bosoms. Open back style only. Sizes 14 to 18.

Price each..........................$ 0.69
Three for...........................2.00

### Short Bosom Shirts 69c.

**No. 25.** Same shirt exactly as the one above described, but made with short bosoms.

Price each..........................$ 0.69
Three for...........................2.00

### 89c For the Best Shirt Made.

**No. 26.** Better shirts than these cannot be made. The very best of muslin is used which insures durability, and the bosoms are made from the finest Irish linen. Extra reinforced at every vital point. Full dress finish throughout. Double back and front. Extra high grade, and warranted to fit perfectly. Sizes 14 to 18. Open back style only.

Price each..........................$ 0.89
Six for.............................5.00

### Boys' White Unlaundered Shirts.

**No. 27.** Boys' unlaundered shirts made of New York mills muslin. Double front and back. Linen bosom. Sizes 12 to 14.

Price Each..........................$ 0.45

**WE CAN FIT YOU OUT FROM THE CROWN OF YOUR HEAD TO THE SOLE OF YOUR FOOT FOR LESS MONEY THAN YOUR DEALER WILL CHARGE YOU FOR A SUIT ALONE.**

# MENS' FINE DRESS SHIRTS

## FINELY FINISHED
## ....EXQUISITELY LAUNDERED....
## THOROUGHLY GOOD.

In these garments we have attained the highest grade of excellence. They possess every improvement known to modern shirt manufacturers, and every shirt we quote is a work of perfection—a finished product, beautiful in appearance, desirable because of its completeness and distinctly **A TRIUMPH OF THE SHIRT MAKERS' ART.** **THE PRAISE OF OUR PRICES, LIKE THE PRAISE OF OUR QUALITIES** comes to us in multitudes of unsolicited testimonials from thousands of satisfied customers from every quarter of the globe.

AN ERA OF VERY LOW PRICES

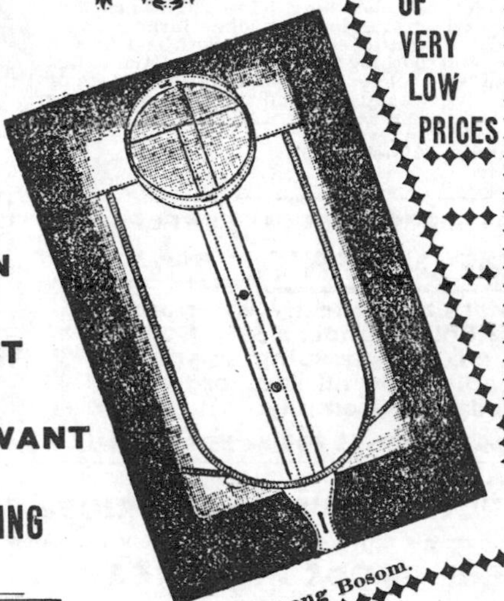

SHIRTS THAT FIT BUT DO NOT RIP

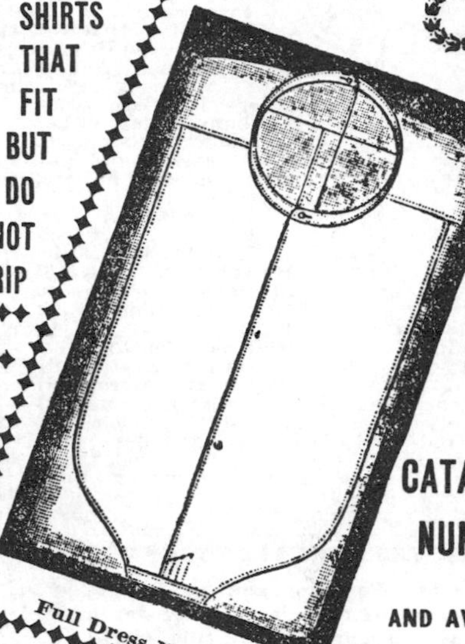

**ALWAYS MENTION THE EXACT SIZE YOU WANT**

**WHEN ORDERING SHIRTS.**

Long Bosom.

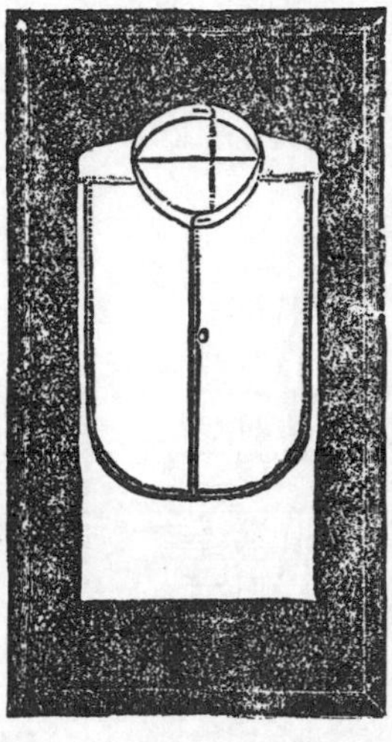

Short Bosom.

Full Dress No. 227.

**ORDER SHIRTS BY CATALOGUE NUMBER**

AND AVOID ALL POSSIBLE MISTAKES.

## SHIFTLESS HE WHO SHIRTLESS GOES.

**No. 221. OUR 50c LONG BOSOM SHIRT.** Men's finely laundered white dress shirts. Made from the famous Dwight Ancnor muslin; gathered back and double reinforced bosoms. Open back style only. Long bosoms. Sizes 14 to 17.
Price, each................................$ .50
Six for...................................... 2.80

**No. 222. OUR 50c SHORT BOSOM SHIRT.** The quality of this shirt is exactly the same as the preceding number. It is made in open back style and has the new short bosom. Finely finished and laundered. Sizes 14 to 17.
Price, each................................$ .50
Six for...................................... 2.80

**No. 223. THE S. & R. SPECIAL 73c.** A perfect fitting, finely laundered and beautifully finished white dress shirt. Made from extra selected muslin, noted for its superior wearing qualities. All linen, 4-ply bosom and bands, double stitching, reinforced front and back. A wonderful shirt at a wonderful price. Open back style with long bosom. Sizes 14 to 18.
Price, each................................$ .73
Six for...................................... 4.00

**No. 224. THE S. & R. SHORT BOSOM SPECIAL. 73c FOR THIS STYLISH SHIRT.** This is indeed a truly handsome shirt. Nothing more comfortable made in dress shirts. Made of same quality goods as the preceding number. Made with the new short bosom. All sizes from 14 to 18, open front or back, or front and back as desired.
Price, each................................$ .73
Six for...................................... 4.00

**No. 225. 95c FOR THIS $1.25 SHIRT. SIZES 14 TO 18.** Men's long bosom, highest grade laundered white dress shirts. Made from finest New York Mills muslin with 4-ply 2.000 linen bosom and bands. Barred buttonholes and eyelets, open front or back or front and back as desired, single or box pleat. Warranted absolutely faultless in fit and construction. Nothing equal ever before sold for less than $1.25. Note our special price.
Price, each................................$ .95
Three for.................................. 2.75
Six for..................................... 5.10

**No. 226. 85c FOR THIS SHORT BOSOM SHIRT. FAULTLESS IN FIT, HANDSOME IN FINISH.** The Boston short bosom laundered white dress shirt. Made from finest Fruit of the Loom muslin with 2100 all linen 4-ply bosom and bands. Open front and back with hand barred buttonholes and eyelets. Highest grade custom finish throughout. Reinforced wherever a shirt should be. Absolutely perfect in every detail. Sizes 14 to 18. Always state size wanted.
Price, each................................$ .85
Six for..................................... $4.75

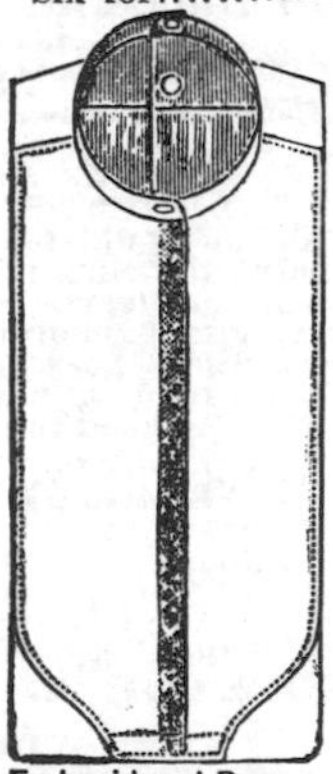

**No. 227. MEN'S FULL DRESS SHIRTS, EXTRA, WIDE, LONG BOSOMS. SIZES 14 TO 17½.** A very swell shirt for weddings, balls, parties and other functions where full dress apparel is required. **Made in very latest full dress style.** Open front and back. Extra wide and long bosom of the very finest linen. The body of this shirt is made from the very finest grade muslin, thoroughly reinforced at all vital points. Hand-barred buttonholes and eyelets. Shaped neckband and the very highest grade laundered finish. Nothing finer ever produced. Always state size desired.
Price, each................................$1.50
Three for.................................. 4.20

**No. 228. FANCY EMBROIDERED BOSOM WHITE DRESS SHIRTS.** Men's laundered white dress shirts. Open front and open back. Made from extra Pepperal A muslin with imported hand made linen embroidered bosom; new and neat designs. Very popular. Sizes 14 to 17.
Price, each................................$ .95
Three for.................................. 2.65

**No. 229. PLEATED BOSOM SHIRTS.** Men's finest laundered white dress shirts with full pleated linen bosoms. Wide or narrow pleats. Artistically finished, thoroughly well made and very much in demand for summer wear. Sizes 14 to 17½.
Price, each................................$1.00
Three for.................................. 2.80

Embroidered Bosom.
Open front or back.

### Boy's Laundered White Shirts.
#### Sizes 12 to 14 only.

**No. 230.** Boy's fine laundered white dress shirts. All linen bosom; superior quality muslin; high grade finish. Guaranteed to give good service. Sizes 12 to 14 only.
Price, each................................49c

**No. 231.** An extra fine quality boy's laundered white shirt, made from specially selected muslin with all linen bosom. Thoroughly well made and reinforced. Fine dress finish. Sizes 12 to 14 only.
Price, each................................73c

## DON'T DELAY YOUR ORDER
### BY NEGLECTING TO MENTION SIZE
### WHEN YOU ORDER SHIRTS..............

ALWAYS GIVE SIZE, STYLE AND CATALOGUE NUMBER and your orders will have prompt attention, and be filled correctly, and to your entire satisfaction.

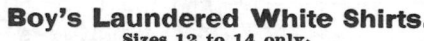

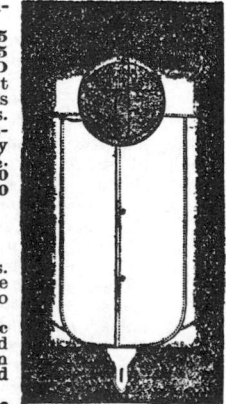

## Collar and Cuff Yourself
### AT HALF PRICE.
SEE OUR ELEGANT LINE OF NECKWEAR.

THE FACT THAT WE SELL LOWER THAN ANY OTHER HOUSE IS BECAUSE OUR BUSINESS IS CONDUCTED ON CLOSER MARGINS. WE BUY CHEAP BECAUSE WE BUY BIG. WE SELL CHEAP BECAUSE THAT'S THE WAY WE DO BUSINESS.

# MEN'S NIGHT SHIRTS

## Comfortable ∾ Wear Well Garments of the Better Sort ∾ Dependable Qualities ∾ Artistic Styles and Soul Satisfying Prices.

**No. 235. MEN'S PLAIN WHITE, BLEACHED MUSLIN NIGHT SHIRTS.** Cut full large throughout. Double yoke back. Nicely made and finished. Large collar and cuffs. Sizes 14½ to 17

Each.................................... 49c

**No. 237. MEN'S FANCY FRONT NIGHT SHIRTS.** Made from superior quality white muslin. Tastefully embroidered on collar and down the front in beautiful contrasting colors. Double yoke back. Perfect fitting. Full size and very durable. All new handsome patterns. Sizes from 14½ to 17.

Price each............50c. 6 for........$2.75

**No. 239. MEN'S EMBROIDERED NIGHT SHIRTS.** Fine Utica mills muslin. Yoke back and patent facings. New improved stitching. Cut full large and very richly embroidered in contrasting colors on collar, front and cuffs. Breast pocket embroidered to match. Dainty colorings of light blue, pink, cardinal, etc. Sizes 14½ to 18.

Price each.... 73c
6 for.........$4.15

**No. 241. MEN'S SUPERFINE NIGHT SHIRTS** made of finest Utica mills muslin with full yoke back. Finest white pearl buttons and patent facings. Cut full length and extra well made throughout. Front, collar and cuffs all handsomely trimmed with insertion and richly embroidered in silk of contrasting shades. Cardinal, baby blue, rose pink, opal, lavendar, etc. An artistic success and one of our specially good things. Sizes 14½ to 18.

Each . ..........95c. 3 for...........$2.65

No. 241.

No. 235.

> **NOTE.** You save money by buying your Shirts of us in ½ dozen or dozen lots. We want you to know this. It will do your pocket book good.

## MEN'S FLANNEL NIGHT SHIRTS.

### Here's Real Comfort for you.
### ☞ 98c FOR A $1.50 SHIRT.

**No. 243. MEN'S EXTRA FINE FRENCH FLANNELETTE OR TEASELDOWN CLOTH NIGHT SHIRTS.** Try them once and you will never wear any other kind. They are made in the best manner possible and possess all the improvements and essential points found only in strictly up-to-date garments. These night shirts are cut full 54 inches long, have yoke back, five white pearl buttons, breast pocket, large roll collar and double stitched seams. Soft and fine in texture and soothing to the most sensitive skins. Made in light colors, neat combination stripes or checks. Very handsome and the best value ever offered in a night shirt. Sizes 14½ to 17½. Healthful, durable and warm.

Our Special price each................. 98c
3 for................................$2.75

The price of these **SHIRTS** is so low and the quality so good that you really cannot afford to overlook them.

No. 245.

> **IMPORTANT.** Always state just what size you desire, when ordering Shirts, Underwear, Collars, Cuffs, etc. By doing so you will enable us to fill your order correctly and promptly.

### SIMPLY BECAUSE OUR PRICES ARE LOW

Is no reason why you should buy from us. Some people prefer to buy **WHERE GOODS ARE CHEAP.**

The same people want good goods. **WE HAVE NOTHING ELSE.**

---

# MEN'S FANCY BOSOM LAUNDERED SHIRTS.

## FASHION'S LATEST EDICT.

To be Thoroughly Up-to-date You Must Wear Up-to-date Shirts. We have Up-to-date Shirts for Up-to-date People, at Up-to-date Prices.

☞ Our QUALITIES were Never so Good. Our PRICES Never so Low.

### ALWAYS MENTION SIZE WHEN ORDERING SHIRTS.

### 49c FOR A $.75 SHIRT. THE ENTIRE PRODUCT OF ONE IMMENSE FACTORY AT YOUR SERVICE.

This line of Shirts is made by one of the largest shirt factories in this country. A specialty is made of this particular line, no other style or quality being made in the factory. These garments possess more points of excellence than any other shirts ever put upon the market. They are unsurpassed for style, quality, fit and general make-up. You will get more than your money's worth in these garments. We have contracted for the entire output of the factory for the season. And just by way of showing what we can do in bargain giving we are going to sell them at the heretofore unheard of price of 49C EACH, OR 6 FOR $2.75. Read the following description carefully. Order early and state the size you desire.

### No. 251. OUR GREAT SPECIAL SHIRT OFFER. MEN'S ELEGANT FANCY BOSOM LAUNDERED DRESS SHIRTS. Open back style. Fine white muslin body with fast colored percale bosom, including fine pin stripes. Beautiful Persian patterns, fancy figured effects in red, tan, blue pink mode, black, etc., etc. All bright up-to-date patterns, and not a single unsightly garment among them. Beautifully laundered. Artistically made and absolutely correct in fit. Sizes 14 to 17 only. All admirers of fashionable shirts will appreciate this wonderful offer.

**NOTE OUR GREAT CUT PRICE.** ☞ Each.....................49c. 6 for...................$2.75

Stripe.    Fancy Figure.    Persian.
The handsomest combination of colors in the world.

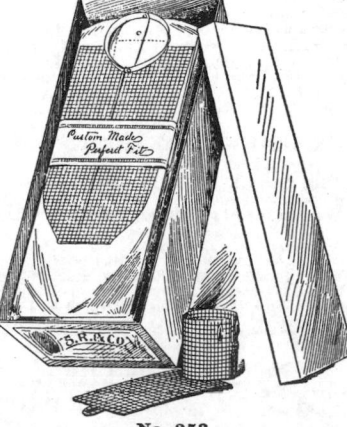

No. 253

**No. 253.** Perfect fitting, solid comfort Laundered Dress Shirts. Finest white muslin bodies with short bosom of colored Madras cloth. New and handsome striped and check patterns. Detachable link cuffs to match. Open front and back, with 4-ply band and hand barred buttonholes, and stud holes. A large assortment of new patterns in blues, pinks, browns, blacks, etc. Absolutely high grade. Sizes 14½ to 17.

Each...................90c
3 for............ $2.55

## A PRINCELY SHIRT FOR PRINCELY MEN.

### 95c FOR THIS EXQUISITE GARMENT.

**No. 255.** Absolutely high grade in every particular. Fashionable, handsome, exclusive and effective. Finest white muslin body with fancy colored bosom and detachable cuffs of either English woven madras or finest French percale. Stripes, plaids, checks and broken stripe pattern in all the new colorings, delft blue, opal, lavender, cadet and Yale blue, pink, turquoise, etc. The turquoise and Yale blues relieved with small threads of black or garnet and white are particularly new and effective. Sizes 14 to 17. Open front and back with hand barred button and stud holes.

Each...................95c. 3 for.................$2.75

### 73c. One of our Strongest Shirt Values.

**No. 256.** An exceptionally fine finished laundered dress Shirt made from the famous cast iron brand white muslin with entirely new design fronts of Garnes' best percale. Cuffs to match. Absolutely fast colors. New plaid and check patterns, also large, medium and small stripes in beautiful colorings of blue, opal, pink, lavendar, garnet and other fashionable shades. Open back. 4-ply bosom. Artistic, stylish and thoroughly well made. Sizes 14 to 17.

Each...................73c. 3 for.................$2.05

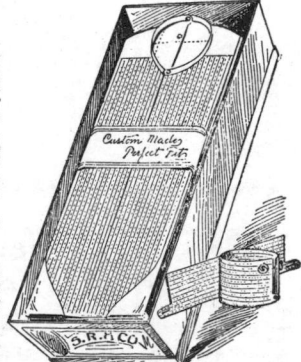

No. 256.

**WE WILL NOT BE UNDERBID FOR YOUR TRADE—BUT WE WILL NOT STOOP TO ANY CATCH-PENNY SCHEMES TO GET IT. HONEST REPRESENTATIONS, HONEST GOODS AND HONEST PRICES ARE THE BEST INDUCEMENTS FOR HONEST TRADE.**

# BOYS' FANCY DRESS SHIRTS.

## SIZES 12 TO 14 NECK MEASURE.

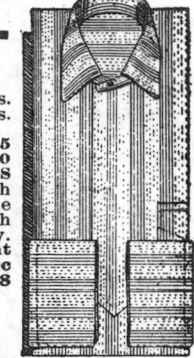

**No. 257. BOYS' FINE FANCY LAUNDERED DRESS SHIRTS,** white body with fancy colored percale bosom. Open back style with 4 ply bands. Beautiful striped and checked patterns, blacks, blues, pinks, browns, etc. Sizes 12 to 14 only. Always mention size when ordering.

Price, each...............................$0.48
Three for............................... 1.35

**No. 258. BOYS' PENANG SHIRTS.** Boy's extra fine quality imported Penang Laundered Shirts, fancy stripes, checks and figures in a rich assortment of the newest and best patterns out this season. Nothing finer made in boys' fancy shirts; made with attached collar and cuffs. Extra fine dress finish. If you are looking for something particu-

larly nice and dressy, don't overlook these garments. They will give you perfect satisfaction in every way. Sizes 12½ to 14 only.

Price, each.............................$0.75
Three for.............................. 2.00

**No. 259. BOYS' LAUNDERED NEGLIGEE SHIRTS** made from fancy colored French Percale, open front with attached turn down collar and cuffs. New and fashionable stripes, figures, plaids and pin checks; white ground with colorings of black, red, pink, blue, etc. Sizes 12 to 14 only. Fine dressy finish. **Always mention just what size you want**

Price, each............................50c
Three for.............................$1.38

No. 257.

No. 259.

## Men's Laundered Fancy Dress Shirts.

### Sizes 14½ to 17. Detachable Collars and Cuffs.

A magnificent assortment of the season's newest and best productions; made by America's greatest manufacturers. Every garment made and trimmed in fine custom style and guaranteed to give perfect satisfaction. Every design is new—not an old or unsightly pattern in our shirt stock this season. Our prices will appeal to all shrewd buyers.

### IMPORTED PERCALES 95c.

**No. 260.** We offer these excellent shirts at just about one-half what your local dealer can sell them. They are made from Finest French Percale, fast colors and fine custom finish. One turn down and one standing collar and one pair cuffs are included with each shirt. New and nobby patterns in neat stripes and checks, white ground relieved with black, red, blue or pink figures. Sizes 14½ to 17.

Each............................$0.95
Three for... .................. 2.65

No 260.

No. 261.

### $1.25 FOR A FRENCH PENANG SHIRT.

**No. 261.** Men's Finest Quality Penang Laundered shirts, white ground with fancy stripes, checks or fancy figures of red, blue, black, brown, etc. Open front and back. One standing and one turn down collar, and one pair cuffs to match are included with each shirt. Quality, style and workmanship unsurpassed. Sizes 14½ to 17.

Each............$1.25    Three for......$3.60

### PAR-EXCELLENCE FANCY SHIRTS $1.45.

**No. 262.** These shirts are noted particularly for their fine finish and exclusive patterns. They are the handsomest, best fitting and most comfortable shirts that can be made. The fabric is the finest French Percale. Perfectly fast colors in beautiful up-to-date shadings of blue, pink, mode, etc. Assorted patterns. Two detachable collars and detachable link cuffs. High class in every respect. Sizes 14½ to 17. Regular retail price, $1.75.

Our price each..........$1.45
Three for............... 4.00

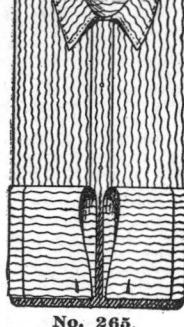

# MEN'S LAUNDERED NEGLIGEE SHIRTS.

## SIZES 14½ TO 17.

### STRICTLY HIGH-GRADE, UP-TO-DATE GARMENTS. MADE FOR FINE TRADE. THEY ARE THE IDEAL NEGLIGEE SHIRTS AND ALWAYS GIVE COMPLETE SATISFACTION.

### OUR 45c TRUE MERIT SHIRT.

**No. 263.** Men's fine laundered Percale Negligee Shirts. Attached collars and cuffs and detachable buttons. Assorted striped and checked patterns, white ground with contrasting colors of black, red, blue, etc. Sizes 14½ to 17. Finely made and finished.

Each.............................$0.45

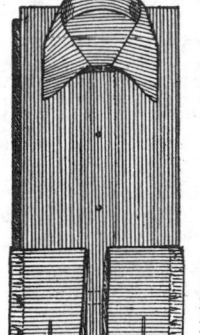

No. 263.

### OUR GREAT 75c SPECIAL.---A WONDERFUL BARGAIN.

**No. 264.** Men's high grade French Penang Shirt, cut full 36 inches long with yoke back, pearl buttons, flat felled seams, reinforced and gusseted. Attached collar and cuffs, white ground with new and handsome contrasting stripes, plaids, checks and Persian patterns, in all staple colorings.

Our Special Price, Each.................$0.75
Three for..... ...................... 2.10

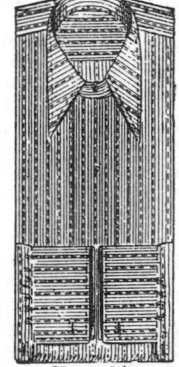

No. 266.

### 58c FOR A $1.00 SHIRT.

**No. 265. HANDSOMEST OF PATTERNS.** Men's laundered French Percale shirts, attached collar and cuffs, fast colors in new and novel effects, pin checks, broken and hair line stripes. Double yoke and hand barred buttonholes. Equal to any $1.00 shirt made. Light colors, blues, pinks, browns, etc., predominating. Sizes 14½ to 17.

Each..................................$0.58

No. 265.

### 95c FOR THIS $1.50 SHIRT.

**No. 266.** This finely laundered negligee shirt will at once appeal to the tastes of all lovers of high class garments. It is made from finest imported woven cheviot. The colors are not printed, but woven through the fabric, and are absolutely fast. Made in light colors fancy plaid and check patterns and combination stripes, the predominating colors being white, blue, red, brown and black. One of the best wearing shirts ever made, and sold at retail usually at $1.50.

Our Special Price, each.......................$0.95
Three for........ . ..................... ......... 2.60

### THE PICK OF THE FLOCK.

#### SIZES 14½ TO 17.

**No. 267.** Our extra high grade laundered Negligee Shirts with attached collar and cuffs. Nothing better made. These shirts are made from very best grade light weight imported Madras cloth, sometimes called zephyr cloth. It is fine in texture, very light in weight, and extra strong and durable. These shirts have attached collar and cuffs, breast pocket and double yoke back, white background with dainty contrasting stripes of light or dark blue, brown, pink and cadet. Beautifully finished and laundered. A line of shirts heretofore handled only by high priced haberdashers and sold at fancy prices, such as $2.50, $2.75 and $3.00. Note our special prices.

Each..............................$1.50
Three for.......................... 4.25
Six for............................ 8.10

No. 267.

### MEN'S EXTRA SIZE LAUNDERED SHIRTS.

#### SIZES 17½, 18, 18½ ,19.

**No. 268. MEN'S LAUNDERED NEGLIGEE SHIRTS.** Made from fine French Penang. Fast colors. Very fine blue and white or cadet and white stripes. Open front with attached turn down collar and cuffs. Detachable buttons, large breast pocket. Extra well made. Sizes, 17½ to 19 only.

Price, each..........................$0.98
Per half doz.......................... 5.25

### OUR FAT MEN'S SPECIAL, $1.25.

**No. 269.** Men's extra selected laundered Percale Shirts, made extra large for fat men. A handsome assortment of new and fashionable patterns in beautiful stripes, checks and fancy figures. Open fronts with attached collar and cuffs; extra well made and finely finished. Thoroughly good and dependable in every way. Sizes 17 to 19 only.

Price, each.................................$1.25
Three for....... ...................... ... 3.50

# FORGETFULNESS

## IS A HABIT WITH MOST OF US.

**THAT'S THE REASON** we are constantly reminding you that **YOU MUST NOT FORGET TO MENTION YOUR SIZE** when you order shirts, underwear, collars, cuffs, etc.

**ALWAYS MENTION SIZE** And your order will have prompt and satisfactory attention.

## THE TRUTH EVERY TIME.

That's what sensible people want now-a-days. Men who want good, stylish, perfect-fitting shirts, the kind that cannot be found in ordinary stocks, the dependable, wear well, fit well, feel well sort, will be interested in the above quotations. Remember, clever values is one of our strong points.

**WHILE WE HAVE A MOST PERFECT SYSTEM OF HANDLING OUR ENORMOUS BUSINESS, AN OCCASIONAL MISTAKE CANNOT BE ABSOLUTELY PREVENTED. WE PAY ALL EXPENSES WHERE THE FAULT IS OURS.**

# MEN'S IDEAL OUTING SHIRTS.

**A GREAT BIG SUCCESS.** The new Outing Shirts, such as we illustrate below, have won the highest praise from men who have long wished and longed for something really **comfortable** as well as dressy, and strictly Up-to-Date. These are the Shirts that will win the pennant for popularity this season. Correct Dressers will all Wear Them.

## THE IDEAL SHIRT FOR BICYCLING, BOATING, FISHING AND GENERAL WEAR.

**NOTICE.** White Collars and Cuffs are worn with these Shirts but are not included with them. See our Up-to-Date line of Collars and Cuffs which are listed on another page.

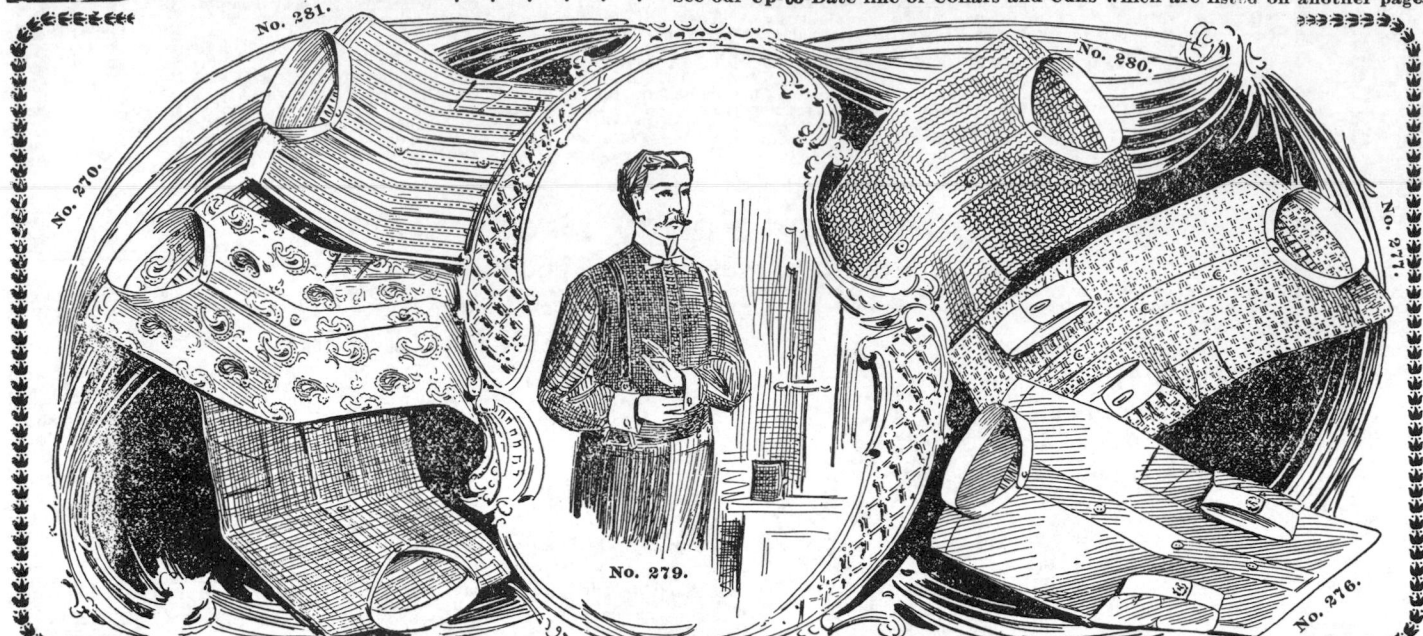

No. 281.    No. 270.    No. 280.    No. 277.    No. 279.    No. 276.

No. 274.

### Our 50c. Percale.

**No. 270. IDEAL OUTING SHIRT.** Made from fast colored imported percale in a specially selected and handsome assortment of new and fashionable colorings and patterns, light colors predominating. Neat stripes, checks and figures. Yoke back, pearl buttons, soft bosom with laundered 4-ply white neck band and wrist bands. Sizes, 14½ to 17; desired. Price each, 50c; 6 for..........**$2.65**

**No. 272. IDEAL OUTING SHIRT.** Made same style as above from plain natural linen grass cloth, with yoke, breast pocket and all improvements. Open front with white 4-ply bands. Sizes 14½ to 17. Price each, 75c; 3 for.....................**$2.05**

**No. 274. IDEAL OUTING SHIRT.** Same as above in fancy plaid woven madras cloth, light colors, assorted patterns; warranted to wash and wear beautifully. Sizes 14½ to 17. Price each, 79c; 3 for.....................**$2.25**

### 90c. For the Ideal Black Sateen Shirt, The Wheelman's Delight.

**No. 275. IDEAL OUTING SHIRT.** Made from extra fine heavy fast black sateen with laundered 4-ply white linen neck and wrist bands, open front with yoke back, white pearl buttons and breast pocket. You will get value in this shirt such as you have never had before. Sizes 14½ to 17. Price each, 90c; 3 for.....................**$2.50**

### Our $1.00 Linen Crash Shirt.

**No. 276. IDEAL OUTING SHIRT.** Same as above but made from finest quality linen crash, natural linen color, with white linen bands. Price each, $1.00; 3 for.....................**$2.75**

### Our 95c. Chelsea Cloth Shirt.

**No. 277. IDEAL OUTING SHIRT.** Made from imported Chelsea cloth, similar to French penang but heavier and better. Fancy broken striped and figured designs; blue, pink and tan are the leading shades. Yoke back, pearl buttons and white linen neck and wrist bands, large breast pocket; strictly up-to-date nobby patterns. Sizes 14½ to 17, Price each, 95c; 3 for.....................**$2.65**

### $1.25 for a $2.00 French Madras.

**No. 279. FINEST FEATHER WEIGHT FRENCH WOVEN MADRAS CLOTH SHIRT.** Made in Ideal Outing style, with one pair of detachable link cuffs to match included. The pattern is a small blue and white pin check and is the handsomest and neatest design out this season. Made with all improvements, yoke back, pocket, pearl buttons, etc. Sizes 14½ to 17. Price each.....................**$1.25**

**No. 280.** Same as above in beautiful English plaids, assorted colorings, blues, olives, pinks, etc. Very swell. Price each.....................**$1.25**

**No. 281. SILK STRIPED FEATHER WEIGHT FRENCH MADRAS CLOTH IDEAL OUTING SHIRTS.** Laundered white 4-ply collar band and wrist bands. gathered yoke back, breast pocket and white pearl buttons, medium colors, cadet blue predominating; handsome woven silk stripes. Sizes 14½ to 17. Price each.....................**$1.35**

No. 285.    S.R.&Co.INC. WHITE HOUSE SHIRT    S.R.&Co.INC. WHITE HOUSE SHIRT    No.288.    No.287.

..THEY'LL.. ...WIN... THE ..PENNANT..

....TREAT...., ..YOURSELF.. .....TO..... .SOMETHING. .....GOOD.....

## THE WHITE HOUSE SHIRT.

### The Swellest Line of Shirts Ever Shown.

**PEOPLE LIKE GOOD THINGS.**

These are good things and there is a vast amount of comfort and soul satisfying freshness about them. The style, the fit and the workmanship, combined with the finest materials obtainable make this the most exquisite and fashionable line of Shirts ever made up. Make yourself a present of a couple of these Shirts and get such value as you never had before in your life. All orders filled promptly and correctly. Always state size wanted.

**No. 285. GENTLEMEN'S WHITE HOUSE SHIRT.** Made from finest white muslin. With wide pleated puff bosom of snow white dotted Swiss. Open front with patent facings, barred button holes and stud holes. Exquisitely laundered and strictly up-to-date. Sizes 14½ to 17. Price each..........**$1.25**

**No. 286. SILK BOSOM SHIRT.** Same as above but made with all pure white silk bosom, pleated and puffed with white pearl buttons in front. Price each.....................**$1.50**

**No. 287. THE WHITE HOUSE SHIRT.** Made from finest imported linen grass cloth, with wide pleated puff bosoms. Open front with patent facings, barred button holes and stud holes. Natural linen color with small white polka dots embroidered on bosom. A perfectly charming effect. White linen neck and wrist bands. Sizes 14½ to 17. Price..**$1.25**

**NOTE.** White Linen Collars and Cuffs are to be worn with these Shirts. For money saving prices on up-to-date Collars and Cuffs see quotations on another page.

**No. 288. THE WHITE HOUSE SHIRT.** White body with wide pleated puff bosom of fancy colored feather weight French Organdie lawn. In new and strictly original design, combinations of rose color, golden brown, tan or Cadet blue. White laundered neck and waistbands. Open front with hand made button holes and stud holes. 14½ to 17. Each..**$1.25**

NOTHING TOO NEW FOR US.........
We have the most Up-to-date
... FURNISHING GOODS DEPARTMENT IN THE WORLD.

# MEN'S SOFT NEGLIGEE SHIRTS

## UNPRECEDENTED VALUES.          PRICES THAT RULE THE WORLD.

No. 290.

and will wash and wear beautifully. Size 14½ to 17 only.
low price.

**Our Special Price..............$0.48.**

### TEN TONS
### OF OVERSHIRTS

**THE GREATEST SHIRT DEMONSTRATION EVER ATTEMPTED BY ANY ONE CONCERN IN THE WORLD.**

**At 48c.** We offer you these shirts. Your local dealer would ask you double this amount for an inferior shirt. This line of shirts we have had made up for us in vast quantities, our first shipment from the factory weighing more than ten tons. We expect to duplicate this shipment inside of 60 days, so as to have enough on hand for all possible orders. Orders for 6 or more shirts will be filled at dozen rates. This is by far the greatest overshirt offer we have ever made. Read carefully the following description of these shirts. No. 290. OUR GREAT 48c. SHIRT. Made in the way that we think a shirt ought to be made to give perfect satisfaction. The material is a light colored madres cloth, spring weight with colors woven clear through (not printed). The length of the shirt is full 36 inches, not 30 or 32 inch, like most cheap shirts. This shirt has double yoke back, fine white pearl buttons, patent extension neck band, shaped sleeves and is cut full size, made in light plaid and fancy stripe patterns, fast color and will wash and wear beautifully. Size 14½ to 17 only. A remarkably good shirt at a remarkably low price.

**Per Dozen....................$5.26**

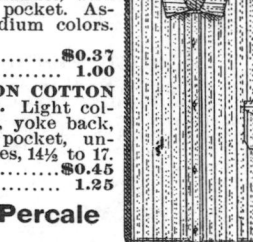

No. 292.

lar 50 cent quality, extra well made and finished. Sizes, 14½ to 17 only.

Our price, each ..................$0.37
3 for ................................. 1.00

**No. 293 MEN'S NEGLIGEE SHIRTS.** Made from fine soft finished fancy striped flannel, with yoke back and breast pocket. Assorted light and medium colors. Sizes, 14½ to 17.

Each.......................$0.37
3 for.......................... 1.00

**No. 294 CAST IRON COTTON NEGLIGEE SHIRTS.** Light colored striped patterns, yoke back, felled seams, breast pocket, unequaled for wear. Sizes, 14½ to 17.

Each.......................$0.45
3 for.......................... 1.25

### Fine French Percale

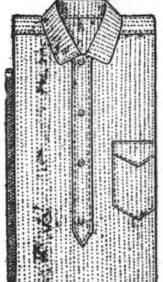

### Shirts.

No. 293

**At 50 Cents We Offer This One.**

**No. 295 A Neglige Shirt of surpassing excellence.** Made from fine fast colored French percale. In fine light colored stripes and checks; made with double yoke back, pearl buttons, extension neck band and breast pocket cut full 36 inch. long, can be starched and laundered if desired. Sizes, 14½ to 17, assorted patterns.

Each.......................$0.50
6 for.......................... 2.75

**No. 291 MEN'S SUMMER NEGLIGEE SHIRTS.** Made from standard grade cotton, well made and finished, medium and light colors, fancy stripes, checks and figures, will give good substantial service. Sizes, 14½ to 17.

Each.... ..$0.25
Per Doz... 2.70

**OUR 3 FOR $1.00 LINE.**

**No. 292 MEN'S WOVEN COTTON CHEVIOT OVERSHIRTS.** Medium weight, blue mixtures, checks and stripes. medium dark colors. Regular 50 cent quality, extra well made and finished.

## French Domet Flannel Shirts.

**The Shirts that Satisfy.**

**No. 296 A 50 CENT WONDER.** French Domet Flannel Shirts are popular because they are dependable; these in particular are popular, because they are the best made. They possess all the new improvements, known to the modern shirt makers. Including patent extension neck band, shaped shoulders, yoke back and fine pearl buttons. They are cut 36 inch. long, are made in light and medium colors, stripes and plaids, all neat modest patterns. Sizes 14½ to 17. There is a world of durability in these garments as well as good looks and solid comfort.

Each.....................................$0.50
6 for.......................................... 2.75

No. 296.

## Fine French Sateen Shirts.

**ALWAYS POPULAR FOR SUMMER WEAR.**

No. 297.

No. 297 Men's Fine Twilled Sateen Negligee Shirts, light colors fine pin stripes, checks broken stripes and figures, cream colored grounds with black, blue, pink, etc. as contrasting colors, very handsomely made up with yoke back and extension band; cut 36 inches long. Sizes 14½ to 17.

Each.........$0.43
Per doz.........4.75

## Our 50 Cent Special Twill.

No. 298 A Negligee Shirt possessing many points of excellence. Made from extra fine French Twilled Sateen, cream ground, with black contrasting stripes and checks of pink, black, blue, brown, etc. These shirts have flat felled seams, pearl buttons, yoke back, extension bands and shaped shoulders. They are 36 inches long and guaranteed to be the equal of any 75 cent shirt in the market. Sizes, 14½ to 17.

Our special price, each........................$0.50
6 for........................................................ 2.75

## Our 47c. Blue Chambray Never Rip Shirt.

No. 2001. Men's Plain Dutch Blue Chambray Overshirt. Good solid woven fabric known the world over for its excellent wearing qualities. Made with yoke back, breast pocket, extension neck band, double shoulders, shaped to fit and warranted full 36 inches long. Sizes 14½ to 17.

Price each, $0.47; 6 for...................... 2.68

## Corded Front Overshirts.

**50c. for a 75c. Shirt.**

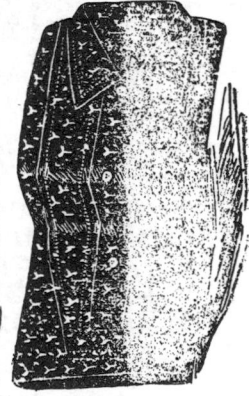

No. 2003. Men's Fancy Corded Front Overshirt. Made from heavy fast colored percale. Neat blue and white or black and white striped patterns. Patent extension neck band, yoke back and double shoulders, gusseted and warranted 36 inches long. Sizes 14½ to 17 only; light colors.

Price each...$0.50
6 for........... 2.75

## Indigo Blue Shirts.

**New Style Shield Front.**

No. 2005. Men's Shield Front Overshirts. Made from good heavy indigo blue cotton, with neat white figures. Box pleat, felled seams, cut full size and one of the very best shirt values ever made. Sizes 14½ to 17. Guaranteed to give the best of satisfaction. Always mention just what size you want when you order.

Price each...... $0.49
6 for.............. 2.70

## 58c. for this Handsome Shirt.

**Sizes 14½ to 17.**

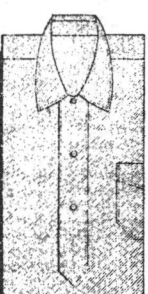

No. 2007. This is one of the very best overshirts we have ever offered. It is made from heavy twilled Georgia cotton, plain black with small white polka dots, soft smooth finish, sateen effect. Made with double yoke back, patent extension band and double shoulders. Cut full 36 inches long, warranted perfect in fit, workmanship and wearing qualities, nonshrinkable neck band and all modern improvements are to be found in this shirt. Our guarantee stands back of every one of them.

Price each.....................$0.58
3 for............................. 1.65

## Men's Black Sateen Overshirts.

**Unprecedented Values in these Garments.**

**We offer you herewith** a chance to buy black **sateen** overshirts of the **dependable wear well sort,** that are without any exception the best values in all America. We make no exceptions whatever. **These are the best.** Every garment fully warranted. Your money back if not satisfied.

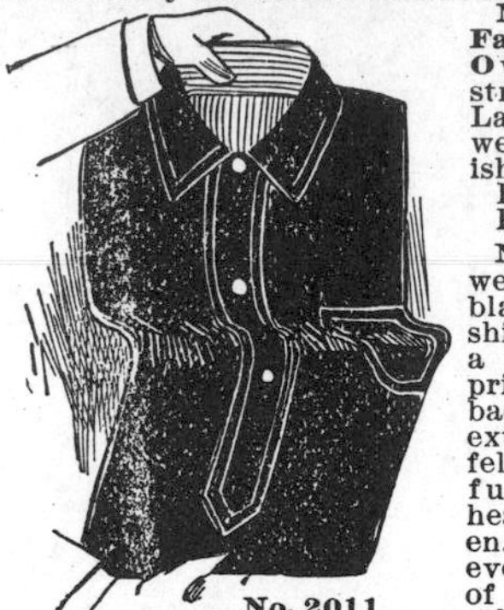

No. 2011.

**No. 2010. Men's Fast Black Sateen Overshirts,** extra strong and durable. Large breast pocket; well made and finished. Sizes 14½ to 17.
Price, each...$0.45
Per dozen.... 5.20

**No. 2011.** At 58c we offer you this fast black sateen overshirt. It is positively a wonder at this price. It has yoke back, pearl buttons, extension collar band felled seams, and is full finished, soft, heavy and close woven. Guaranteed in every way the equal of any 75c shirt ever sold. Sizes 14½ to 17.
Price. each.......$0.58 Six for...........$3.20

**No. 2012.** An extra fine quality fast black sateen overshirt, well made and dependable. Double yoke back, pearl buttons, felled seams, extension neck band. Heavy weight and full size. Finely made-up and finished. Breast pocket and large collar. Sizes 14¼ to 17. Price, each......$0.75 Six for.......$4.20

**No. 2014. S. & R. Special.** The S. & R. Special black sateen shirt, made with every known improvement, including double yoke and neck band, extension collar band, flat felled seams, gussets and sleeve facings, shaped shoulders, etc. Made from a specially prepared absolutely fast black heavyweight sateen, cut full 36 inches and warranted in every way. Sizes 14½ to 17. Price each..$0.87
Three for........ 2.50

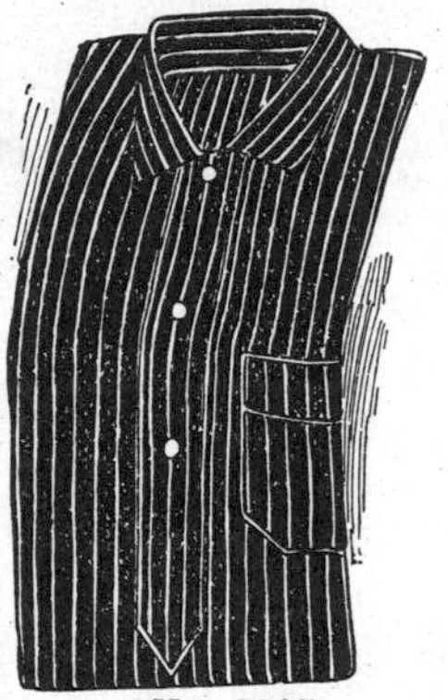

No. 2015.

**No. 2015.** Men's black and white striped sateen overshirts. Full length well made and finished, and warranted fast color. Sizes 14½ to 17. Always mention size wanted. Price ea..$0.43
Per dozen........ 5.00

**No. 2016.** Men's extra quality black and white striped sateen overshirts, 36 inches long with yoke back, pearl buttons and double neck band. Large well shaped collar. First class in every respect, and a wonder at the price. Sizes 14½ to 17. Price, each$0.50 Per doz....$5.40

## Men's Extra Strong and Durable Overshirts.

**Strong Men require Strong Shirts. The strength of these shirts is wonderful. They are made up expressly to meet the requirements of men who are hard on shirts. They are also made to fit and look neat as well. The price, too, is made to fit the pocketbooks of the shrewdest buyers. Ours are money saving prices.**

## Buckskin Cloth Overshirts.

**The strength and wearing qualities of buckskin cloth is something wonderful. There is real merit in these garments.**

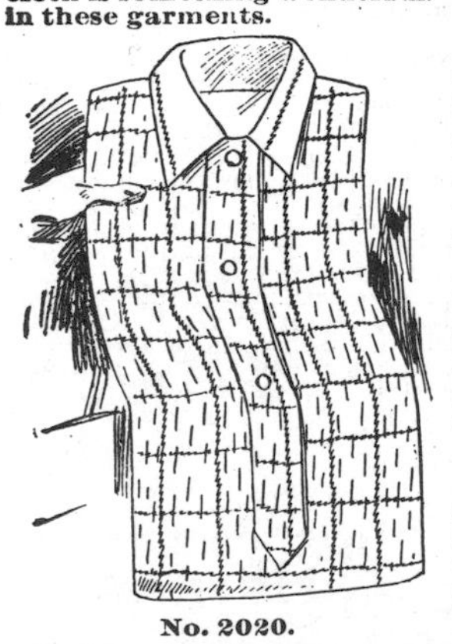

No. 2020.

**No. 2020. Men's Heavy Weight Buckskin Cloth Overshirts.** Solid and firm goods of unquestionable wearing qualities, thoroughly well made and sewed. Yoke back and improvedfelled seams. Cut full size and guaranteed to wear like iron. Sizes 14¼ to 17 only. Tan colored plaid and striped patterns.
Price each. $0.47
Six for...... 2.66

**No. 2021. Genuine Buckskin Cloth Shirts.** Same as above in neat black and white stripes. Sizes 14½ to 17 only.
Price each. $0.47
Six for........................................ 2.66

**No. 2022. Genuine Buckskin Cloth Shirts.** Same as above in neat slate colored stripes, very desirable and wont show dirt. Sizes 14½ to 17 only.
Price each...............$0.47 Six for.....$2.66

**No. 2023. Genuine Buckskin Cloth Overshirts.** Same as above plain indigo blue color, always a favorite, warranted fast color and full size. 14½ to 17 only. Price each........$0.47 Six for......$2.66

## Reflect on These Values.

**No. 2024. Men's Extra Quality Heavy Woven Cotton Overshirts.** Black with neat small white stripes double stitched yoke, patent extension collar band, shaped shoulders, cut full size and guaranteed to wear long and well. Sizes 14½ to 17. The wearing qualities of these shirts are unexcelled. You will certainly like them if you buy them.
Price each.................$0.48
Six for......................... 2.65

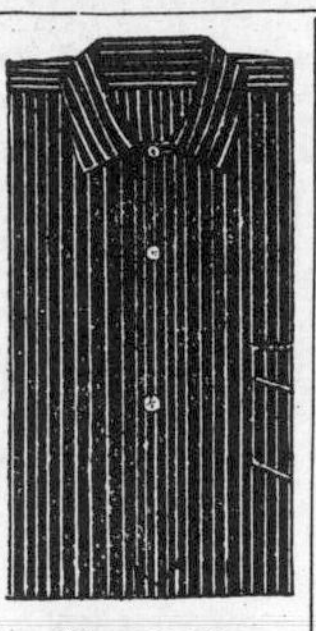

No. 2018.

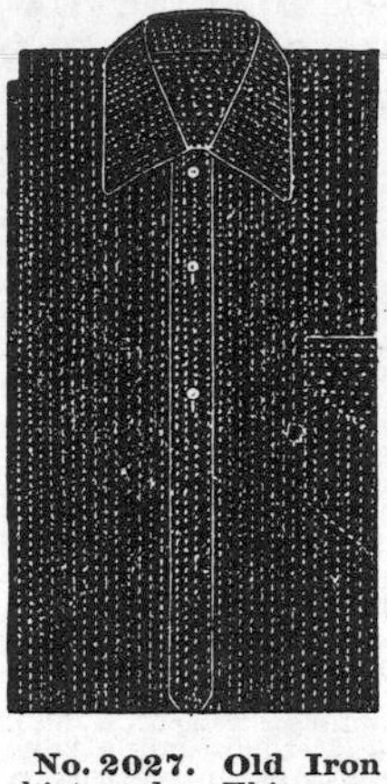

## Moleskin Shirt at 74c.

**Extraordinary Values.**

**No. 2025. Moleskin Shirts.** $1.25 value, a heavy twilled cloth, positively fast black ground with white pin stripe a quarter of an inch apart; extra well made with pointed double yoke, double stitched, long pointed collar, pearl buttons, wide cuffs, outside pointed pocket, made very full, and 36 inches long; this is one of the best wear-resisting shirts made at any similar price, and has a nice genteel appearance.
Price, each ..........$0.74
Three for ........... 2.00

**No. 2027. Old Iron Sides.** The strongest over shirt made. This garment is made from dark blue mixed 9 oz. denim. The same as used in making men's overalls. It is made with yoke back, felled seams and has breast pocket. It is cut full large and 36 inches long. Two of these shirts will last longer than 6 shirts of any other kind ever made. Sizes 14½ to 17 only.
Price, each..................................$0.75
Three for.................................... 2.10
Per Dozen................................... 7.50

## Men's High Grade Outing Shirts.

**For Summer Wear.**

**Fine Soft Finish. Fast Colors and Full Sizes.**

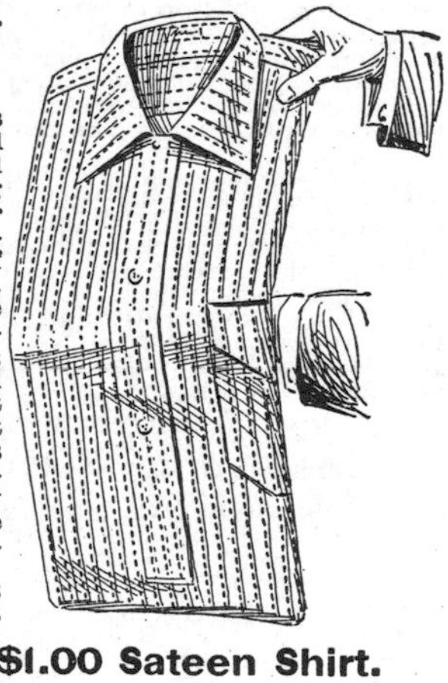

No. 2028. **Men's Fine Light Colored Bedford Cord Summer Outing Shirt.** Cream color with dainty contrasting stripes of black, blue or red. Yoke back, fine white pearl buttons, breast pocket, flat felled seams and gussetts. Patent extension band. Cut full length. Sizes 14¼ to 17. A handsome and dressy shirt that will give the best of satisfaction.
Price, each..$0.58
Six for..... 3.25

## 69c for a $1.00 Sateen Shirt.

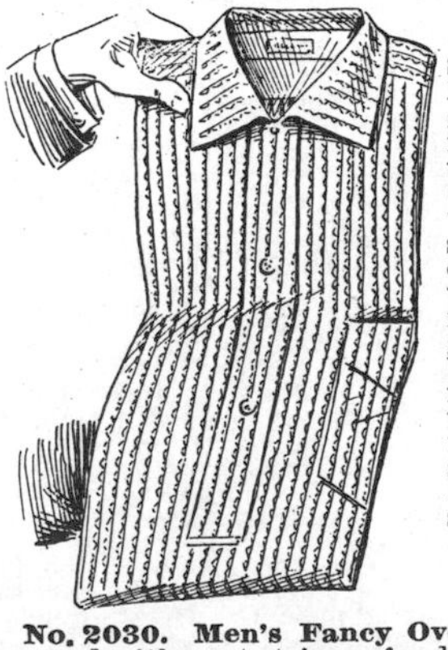

**No. 2029. This Shirt we offer as an Exceptional Bargain.** It is made from finest heavy twilled Sateen, light colors, cream ground with neat broken stripes in contrasting colors. Made with all the newest improvements including gathered back, pearl buttons, double yoke, felled seams, etc. Better workmanship was never put into a shirt. Sizes 14½ to 17. Always state size desired.
Price, each...$0.69
Three for..... 1.95
Six for........ 3.80

**No. 2030. Men's Fancy Overshirts,** light cream ground with neat stripes of red, black or blue. Made from heavy pique Bedford cord. Yoke back, pearl buttons, pocket, etc. Unexcelled for wear and a perfectly handsome garment. Sizes 14½ to 17.
Price, each.................................$0.87
Three for.................................... 2.45

......SEE OUR STOCK SADDLES......

## French Madras Cloth Shirts.

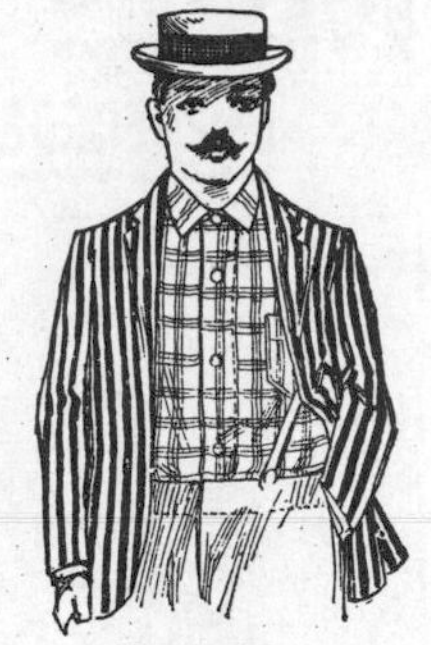

No. 2032.

**French Madras** is a fine soft finished fabric with the colors woven through. It is noted for its superior wearing qualities. It is the best wearing, light weight shirt fabric known. It is handsome and stylish as well, hence its great popularity with all admirers of neat, stylish and serviceable garments. Our prices put these beautiful shirts within the reach of all. **French Madras Shirts will give you perfect satisfaction. Try them for the service that is in them.**

**No. 2032. Men's Genuine Woven French Madras Shirts.** Light colors, plaids or stripes. Made with yoke back, fine pearl buttons, felled seams, and gussets breast pocket and extension neck band. All the latest and best improvements. Warranted to wear well and fit perfectly. Sizes 14½ to 17, assorted light colors.
Price, each...............................................$0.75
3 for........................................................ 2.16

## Our Special 87c Outing Shirt.

**Men's Extra Fine Imported WOVEN FRENCH.... ....MADRAS CLOTH OUTING SHIRTS.**

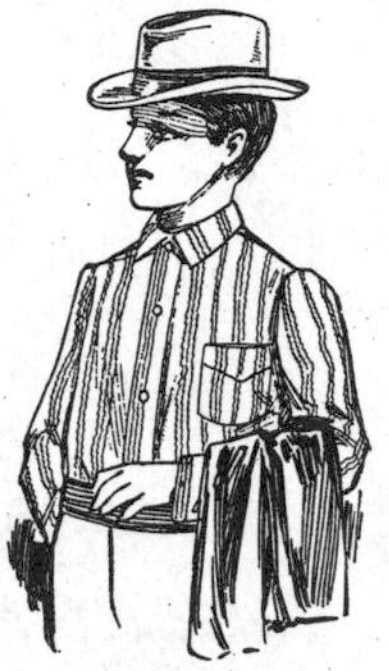

No. 2033.

**No. 2033.** Light colors, stripes or plaids. Patent double extension band. Yoke back, finest pearl buttons, felled seams. Sleeve facing and gussets, shaped shoulders and full length. A most excellent and trustworthy garment. Handsome new pattern. Everyone a beauty. Sizes, 14½ to 17.
Price, each...... ...$0.87
3 for................ 2.44

## 98c. for a $1.50 Silk Striped Madras Shirt.

**COMFORT.... ......AND...... ....ELEGANCE ...COMBINED...**

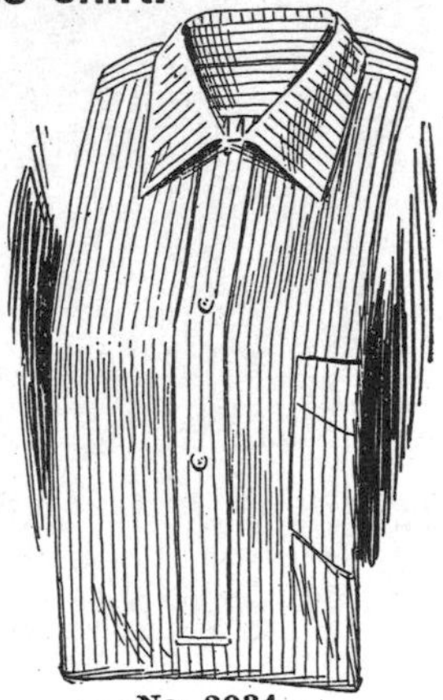

No. 2034.

**No. 2034. Finest Imported Madras Cloth Outing Shirts.** Light in weight, but very strong and durable. Light blue and white, and goblin blue and white stripes and plaids with beautiful silk stripes. Full yoke back, pearl buttons, pocket, felled seams and in fact every known improvement. One of the season's handsomest effects. Sizes 14½ to 17.
Price, each...$0.98
3 for......... 2.75

## French Flannel Shirts.

**No. 2035. Men's Fine Summer weight French Wool Flannel Shirts.** White ground with neat colored, contrasting pin stripes and dots. Pointed yoke back, white pearl buttons, extension band and breast pocket. Light and cool. Sizes 14½ to 17.
Price each..............................................$1.25
3 for........................................................ 3.50

## Feather Weight Wool Shirt.

**THE LIGHTEST.... WOOL SHIRTS MADE.**

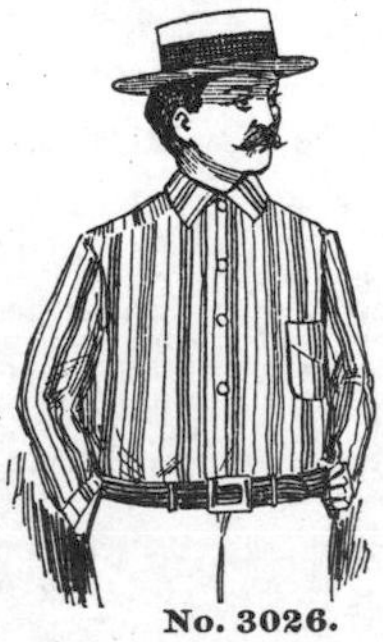

No. 3026.

**No. 2036. Men's Feather Weight Wool Outing Shirts.** With beautiful silk stripes in contrasting colors, all handsome light colors, perfect beauties. Light strong and cool for summer wear. Made up in very best manner with yoke back, pearl buttons, felled seams, etc. Sizes 14½ to 17 only.
Price each..........$1.50
3 for................ 4.20

**WHEN YOU ORDER GOODS TO BE SENT BY MAIL, ALWAYS INCLUDE THE NECESSARY POSTAGE. IT IS CHEAPEST FOR YOU TO ORDER ENOUGH GROCERIES TO MAKE UP A FREIGHT ORDER, AS FREIGHT IS VERY SMALL COMPARED WITH POSTAGE.**

## Men's Extra Size Overshirts.

### Sizes 17½, 18, 18½ and 19 only.

**No. 2037. Extra Size Overshirts.** Made from fine twilled sateen. Cream color ground contrasted with neat fancy colored stripes, yoke back, pearl buttons and breast pocket. Made full large throughout and warranted to wear. Made in extra sizes only.

Price each...**$0.75**
3 for.......... 2.15

**No. 2038. Extra Size Overshirts.** Made from best quality fast colored per-

No. 2037.

cale, light colors. Can be laundered if desired. Yoke back, pearl buttons, breast pocket and all improvements. Sizes 17½ to 19; assorted patterns.

Price each, 75c; 3 for.........**$2.15**

## Men's Heavy Weight Overshirts.

**For Fall and Winter Wear. Men's Fancy Jersey Shirts.**

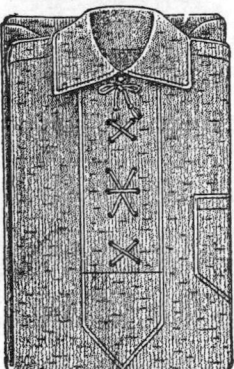

**No. 2040. Men's Heavy Knit Jersey Overshirts.** Random mixed dark colors, lace front buttoning underneath the lacing, assorted patterns, sizes 14½ to 17.
Each.......... **$0.39**
6 for.......... 2.00

**No. 2041. Men's Extra Heavy Knit Overshirts,** dark mixed colors with lace front buttoning underneath, very strong and durable.
Retail value..**$0.75**
Our price...... 0.59
3 for.......... 1.55

Jersey Shirt.

## Heavy Cassimere Overshirt.

**Nothing Better for Hard Wear.**

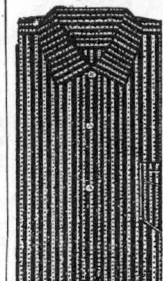

**No. 2042. Men's Heavy Winter Weight Cassimere Cloth Overshirts,** 80 per cent wool, plain front with pocket and shaped arm holes, very neat check, plaid or striped patterns and mixtures, dark or medium colors, all sizes from 14½ to 17. Actually worth $1.25.
Our special price each......**$0.90**
3 for.......... 2.48

### Plain Melton Over-Shirts.

**Sizes 14½ to 17.**

No. 2042.

**No. 2043. Men's Heavy Winter Weight Melton Overshirts,** made same as above in plain colors, shades, Oxford gray, brown mixed, etc., splendid for wear, sizes 14½ to 17. Price each......**$0.87**
3 for.......... 2.40

## Men's Blue Flannel Shirts.

**Sizes 14½ to 17.**

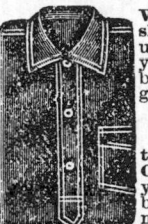

**No. 2044. Men's Heavy Winter Weight Navy Blue Flannel Overshirts,** made from best twilled union flannel single breasted with yoke back, curved armholes and breast pocket, pearl buttons and guaranteed to satisfy..
Price each......**$0.95**
3 for.......... 2.75

**No. 2046. All Wool Heavy Winter Weight Navy Blue Flannel Overshirts,** single breasted with yoke back, pearl buttons and breast pocket, an excellent garment in every way.
Price each......**$1.48**
2 for.......... 2.85

No. 2044.

## Double-Breasted Blue Flannel Shirts.

**Sizes 14½ to 17.**

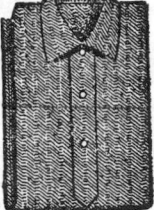

**No. 2047. Men's Heavy Weight Navy Blue Union Flannel Overshirts.** Double breasted with white pearl buttons and double yoke.
Price each, 98c; 3 for....**$2.75**

**No. 2048. Men's Heavy Winter Weight Navy Blue Flannel Overshirts.** All wool with fine white pearl buttons and double yoke; large collar and cuffs, double breasted.
Price each. **$1.45;** 2 for....**$2.80**

**No. 2049. Men's Extra Fine and Heavy All Wool Navy Blue Flannel Overshirts.** Double breasted, with large white pearl buttons,

No. 2049.

non-shrinkable band, full size and length, large collar and cuffs. Price each, **$1.98;** 2 for.......**$3.90**

## Boy's Overshirts.

**Sizes 12 to 14 only.**

**No. 2050. Boys' Fancy Striped Cotton Overshirts.** Assorted patterns, medium and light colors, very good values, sizes 12 to 14 only; for summer wear. Price each..**23c**

**No. 2052. Boys' Fancy Striped Flannelette Overshirts.** Soft and fine, will wash and wear beautifully, extra well made, assorted light and medium colors, good weight, suitable for all seasons; sizes 12 to 14. Price each........**39c**

No. 2050.

**No. 2054. Boys' Fast Black Sateen Overshirts.** Finely made and finished, yoke back and breast pocket; reliable in every way. Sizes 12 to 14.
Price each......................**43c**

## Boy's Percale Shirts.

**No. 2056. Boys' Fancy Striped French Percale Shirts.** New and handsome patterns, assorted light colors, finely made and trimmed. Can be starched and laundered if desired; sizes 12 to 14.

No. 2056.

Price each, 50c; 3 for......**$1.35**

---

# MEN'S AND BOYS' SWEATERS.

**OPEN THE PORES.**

**WE SELL SWEATERS GOOD ONES TOO....**

Nothing Will open them quite so well as a SWEATER. No garment in the whole world has ever attained such universal popularity as the SWEATER of to-day. All sorts and conditions of mankind are numbered among its devotees.

They are the very best that human skill can devise. Our sweaters have more special features and are made from finer yarns than any other line of sweaters known. Its never wise to be boastful and we try to be modest about our sweaters, but we cannot help feeling enthusiastic over the pleasant surprise that awaits a purchaser of one of these garments. Every garment we quote is strictly up-to-date and will give thorough satisfaction. Our prices are based on the lowest possible percentage, and you will find them from 25 to 40% lower than you can possibly purchase the same grade of goods for elsewhere.

## Men's Cotton Sweaters.

**Sizes 34 to 44.**
**25c Sweaters.**

**No. 2061. Men's Medium Weight Cotton Sweaters,** ecru or cream colors. Sizes 34 to 40.
Price, each...**$0.25**

**Pure Cotton Worsted Sweaters at 47c.**

**No. 2062. Men's Heavy Weight Pure Cotton Worsted Sweaters.** Finely fashioned neck, cuffs and skirt. Absolutely fast colors. Wine, black, navy or golden tan.
Price, each...**$0.47**

**Lace Front Sweaters at 50c.**

**No. 2064. Men's Lace Front Cotton Worsted Sweaters.** Made same as above, with large collar. Nothing better for wear and service. Colors, black, navy, maroon or tan. Always mention color desired. Price, each...**$0.50**

## Men's Wool Sweaters.

**Sizes 34 to 44.**
**At 85c.**

**No. 2066. Men's Heavy Ribbed Wool Sweaters.** Double neck, ribbed cuffs and tail, 80 per cent. pure wool. Handsome in appearance and well knit. Usually retails at $1.25. Colors, black, maroon, navy or golden tan. Price, each......................**$0.85**

**At $1.25.**

**No. 2067. Extra Heavy Full Fashioned Wool Sweaters.** Heavy ribbed and close knit. A great favorite owing to its superior wearing qualities. Colors, black, maroon, navy or tan. Extra good value. Price, each......................**$1.25**

**Our Scorcher at $1.75.**

**No. 2068.** The greatest value ever offered in a sweater. Extra heavy ribbed and made from all pure Australian wool. Fancy ribbed neck and elas-

tic ribbed cuffs and tail. Plain colors, black, navy, maroon or golden tan. The golden tan is an entirely new shade of tan and very popular this season. You will make no mistake in buying one of these garments. Price. each....................**$1.75**

**$2.10 for an Extra Heavy Worsted Sweater.**

**No. 2069. Pure, Heavy Weight, Extra Heavy Ribbed, all Wool, Worsted Sweaters.** Fancy ribbed neck and tail, fine elastic ribbed cuffs. Full fashioned and seamless. Soft and fine and guaranteed in every way. If you are looking for something extra good, handsome and dependable, don't overlook this number. Retail value, $3.00. Black, navy or maroon. Our special price, each..............**$2.10**

## Men's Sailor Collar Sweaters.

**No. 2070. Heavy Ribbed, Lace Front, Sailor Collar Sweater.** Heavy domestic union wool. Guaranteed to give long and lasting service and prove satisfactory in every way. Made with large sailor collar, ribbed cuffs and tail. Two contrasting stripes on collar. Black, tan, navy and maroon colors. Sizes, 34 to 44.
Price, each........**$1.25**

**No. 2072.** Same style Sweater as above, but made from extra quality Australian wool. Soft, thick and fine. Excelent value. Colors, black, maroon, wine, navy or tan. Sizes, 34 to 44. Price, each.........**$1.89**

## Pure Worsted Sweaters.

**Fine Ribbed, with Sailor Collar.**

**No. 2073. Men's Fine Worsted Sweaters.** Extra heavy weight, made from the very finest Australian lambs' wool, with large, square sailor collar. Fine ribbed double cuffs, silk lace front; contrasting stripes on collar, cuffs and skirt in the following combinations: Black and orange, green and white, maroon and white, and navy and white. Full, regular made, and finely fashioned; the best sweater made. Sizes, 34 to 44. Price each............**$3.10**

## The New "Bike" Sweater.

**No. 2074. Men's New "Bike" Sweaters.** Heavy all-wool, soft and fine; heavy ribbed and full fashioned; new style shirt collar, the most popular sweater of the season. Leading wheelmen all use this style in preference to any oher. Made in solid colors with white stripes on collar, cuffs and skirt. Colors, black, wine, maroon or navy. Sizes, 34 to 44. Price each..................**$1.50**

**No. 2075. Men's New "Bike" Sweater,** made from purest Australian wool; heavy weight and heavy ribbed; full fashioned solid colors, with white stripes on collar, cuffs and skirt; new style shirt collar; unexcelled for wearing qualities, actually worth half a dozen ordinary sweaters. Colors: Black, maroon, wine or navy. Sizes, 34 to 44. Price each....................**$3.10**

## Turtle Neck Sweater.

**EXTRA HEAVY KNIT, ALL WOOL, TURTLE NECK ....SWEATERS. ..**

**No. 2076.** Full regular made and very elastic. Silk cord lacing, elastic ribbed cuffs and tail; extra heavy weight, soft and fine; one of the very best sweaters ever made. Made up either with or without contrasting stripes on collar. State which you prefer. Sizes 34 to 44. Price each.....**$3.25**

No. 2076.

## Boys' Sweaters.

Sizes 26-28-30-32, Chest Measure.

**No. 2077. Boys' Plain Ecru or Dark Cream Colored Cotton Sweaters.** Plain roll collar; extra good value. Price each................**$0.23**

**No. 2078. Boys' Full Fashioned Heavy Weight Cotton Worsted, Ribbed Sweaters.** Plain roll collar, elastic ribbed cuffs and skirt. Plain colors, black, navy, maroon, wine or golden tan. Cannot be beat for wear. Price each................**$0.42**

**No. 2079. Boys' Extra Heavy Union Wool Ribbed Sweater.** Full fashioned, with fancy ribbed roll collars, elastic ribbed cuffs and tail, 80 per cent wool, and warranted to give extra good service. Plain colors, black, maroon, navy or tan. Sizes 26 to 32. Price each................**$0.85**

**No. 2080. Boys' Extra Heavy Ribbed Wool Sweaters.** Full fashioned, fancy ribbed roll collar, cuffs and skirt. One of the very best wearing sweaters made. Plain colors, black, maroon, wine and navy. Sizes 26 to 32. Price each................**$0.98**

## Boys' Lace Front Sweaters.

**No. 2082. Boys' and Children's Heavy Wool Mixed Worsted Sweaters,** made with lace front and large sailor collar, elastic ribbed cuffs and skirt, white stripe on collar; extra good value. Sizes 24 to 32, chest measure. Colors, maroon or navy blue. Price each....**$0.75**

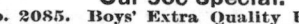

**No. 2083. Boys' and Children's Heavy Wool Sweaters,** with large sailor collar, elastic ribbed cuffs and skirt. Full fashioned. 80 per cent wool, will wear better than all-wool and will not shrink. Colors, black, navy blue or wine, with white stripes on collar. Sizes 24 to 32. Price each................**$1.00**

No. 2083.

**No. 2084. Boys' Extra Fine All Wool Sweater, Lace Front and Large Sailor Collar.** Full fashioned, with elastic ribbed cuffs and fancy ribbed skirt, handsome silk lacing, heavy ribbed pattern; the handsomest boys' sweaters made. Colors, navy blue, wine or maroon, with handsome white stripes on collar, cuffs and skirt. Sizes 26 to 32. The best value ever offered, Price each................**$1.45**

### Our 50c Special.

**No. 2085. Boys' Extra Quality Heavy Cotton Ribbed Worsted Sweaters,** with lace front and small collar, Plain colors only, navy or maroon. Sizes 26 to 32. Price each................**$0.50**

## Mens' Bicycle and Golf Hose.

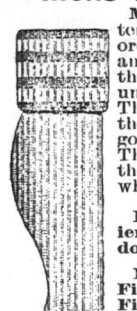

Made without feet and intended to be worn over ordinary cotton half hose and retained in place by a thin knitted strap passing under the ball of the foot. The only practical, and therefore the most sensible golf and bicycle hose made. They have met with the very highest favor wherever used.

In ordering Bicycle Hosiery always state predominating colors desired.

**No. 2086. Fancy Colored Fine Ribbed Worsted Finish Bicycle Hose.** Fancy ribbed turnover tops. Assorted colors and patterns, greens, blues, tans, and wines with black mixtures predominating. No plain or solid colors. Made without feet.

No. 2086.     No. 2087.

Price................per pair, **$0.42**

**No. 2087. Medium Weight, Fine Ribbed Fancy Scotch Plaid Wool Hose,** very fine and soft, medium and dark Scotch mixtures with roll tops. Brown mixtures predominate in this assortment and the patterns are very neat. They will go well with almost any color suit or sweater. Made without feet. Price................per pair, **$0.50**

**No. 2088. Heather Brown and Olive Mixed Heavy Ribbed Footless Bicycle Hose.** Made from selected domestic wool, and warranted to give excellent satisfaction. Plain roll top. Price................per pair, **$0.50**

**No. 2089. Our 58c Special mens' footless bicycle hose,** heavy weight wool. Plain colors, black, maroon, brown or navy with fancy plaid roll tops of contrasting colors. Very popular with wheelmen of all classes. Price................per pair, **$0.58**

**SEE INDEX FOR WHAT YOU DON'T FIND.**

---

**No. 2090. The Best 75c Bicycle Hose on Earth.** Made from extra heavy domestic wool. Heavy fancy rib stitch with double roll over tops. Plain color with striped tops, black with orange stripes, navy blue with white stripes, or maroon with white stripes, made without feet and guaranteed to give better service than any other hose on earth for the same price. Price..per pair, **$0.75**

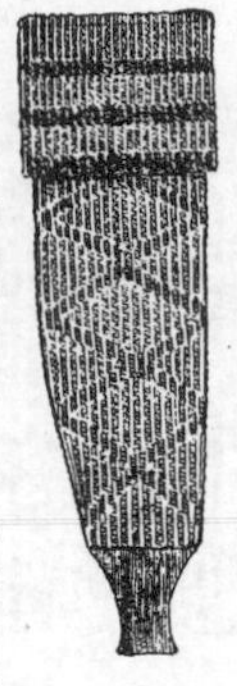

**No. 2091. Same Hose as above** but made in fancy mixtures. Beautiful Scotch and English designs in browns, olives, heathers, grays, cardinals, wines and other desirable colorings. All fancy mixtures with roll tops, No plain colors. Price.. per pair, **$0.75**

No. 2090.     No. 2091.

### Our 79c Worsted Hose.

**No. 2092. Medium Weight Pure Worsted Bicycle or Golf Hose.** Made expressly for those who do not desire heavy or coarse ribbed hose. Made in plain staple colors, with roll over tops striped with contrasting colors. Very neat, modest patterns. Fine ribbed, light and strong. Price................per pair, **$0.79**

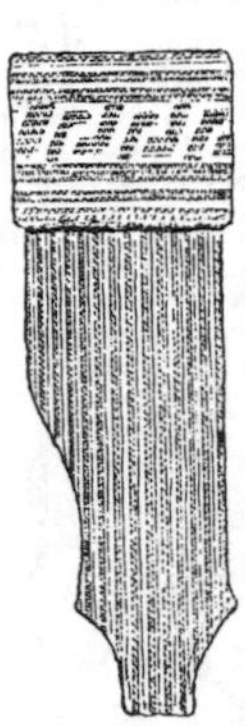

**No. 2093. Mens' Fancy Top Golf or Bicycle Hose.** Extra heavy, all wool. Wide ribs in plain colors, black, navy or maroon, with fancy colored roll tops, of contrasting colors. Very rich and effective in appearance. Made without feet. One of our most excellent values. Price..per pair, **$0.87**

**No. 2094. Extra Heavy All Wool Scotch Bicycle or Golf Hose.** Made without feet and with heavy double roll tops. Fancy patterns and fancy mixed colorings. All the new and desirable combinations. Brown, myrtle, olive, heather, blue, tan, etc., all mixed colors. No plain or solid colors. In ordering state predominating colors desired. Price, per pair................**$1.10**

Fo. 2093.     No. 2094.

## Men's Plain Black Bicycle Hose.

**Special Bargain 21c.**

**No. 2096. Men's Guaranteed Fast Black Bicycle Hose.** Extra heavy ribbed cotton. Heavy spliced knee and heel, and double toe. The best wearing stocking ever made. Just the thing for base ball, bicycling and out-door sports. Sizes, 10, 10½ and 11. Special price, per pair....**$0.21**

### Boy's Bicycle Hose.

Sizes, 7, 7½, 8, 8½, 9.

**No. 2097 Boy's Extra Heavy Fast Black, Heavy Ribbed Cotton Hose.** Double knit knee, spliced heel and double toes. Full seamless. Specially desirable for school wear as well as bicycling. Warranted to give iron-clad service. Don't overlook this number if you want something thoroughly dependable. Price................**$0.25**
6 pairs for................**1.39**

### A Rare Bargain.

**75c for $1.50 Bicycle Hose.**

**No. 2098 Our entire stock of men's fancy colored wool bicycle hose with feet.** We want to close them out, as the footless hose are more popular. We offer the entire lot in fancy Scotch mixtures, plaids, etc. All of our $1.00, $1.25 and $1.50 qualities. Here is your chance for a big bargain. Price, per pair........**75c**

---

## Men's Belts.

**BELTS ARE POPULAR.** More so this season than ever before.

They are used by all classes of people. The styles this season are the handsomest ever manufactured. In ordering belts, state number of inches around waist. Always order by catalogue number. Sizes, 30 to 42 Waist Measure.

No. 2099.

**No. 2099. The Wheelmen's Favorite Belt.** Made from fine smooth finish, russet leather, 1½ inches wide, with enameled rings and buckle, and solid leather match or coin pouch with patent snap fastener. Strong and very handy. Price. each.**$0.37**

**No. 2102. Men's Aligator Belts.** Made from fine russet leather, 1½ inches wide. Alligator finish, with the new harness buckle and nickeled eyelets. Very popular, Retails at 75c. Our price, each.**$0.45**

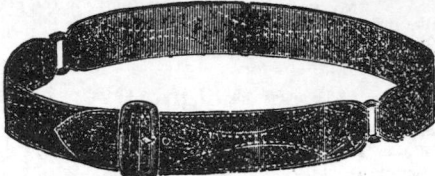

No. 2103.

**No. 2103.** This is a 2 inch all leather Belt. Russet or tan color, with large leather covered buckle and leather covered rings. Sewed throughout with silk thread. Plain fine smooth finish. Price, each................**$0.47**

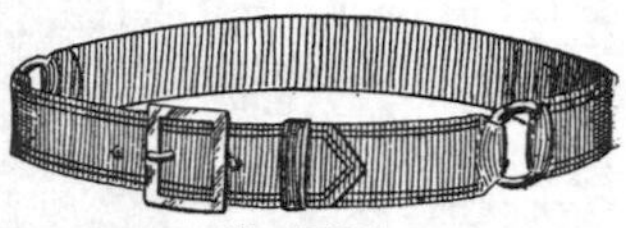

**No. 2104. Men's Solid Russet or Tan Colored Belts,** 1⅜ in. wide with enameled square buckle and enameled rings. Silk stitched throughout. A great bargain. Price, each....**$0.21**

No. 2104.

**No. 2106. The Swellest Belt out.** Don't judge from the price that the material is cheap. We bought an immense quantity at a big bargain direct from the makers. These belts are made from finest jet black patent leather, with finely nickeled harness buckle and eyelets. Sewed throughout with silk thread. One inch wide, and the neatest and most dressy belt made. Our special price, each................**$0.25**

**No. 2107. Light Tan Colored Solid Leather Belts.** 1⅛ inch wide, with heavy nickel harness buckle and nickeled eyelets. Silk sewed throughout. Very fine soft finish. Price, each........**$0.43**

**No. 2108. The Prince of Wales Belt.** The very latest. Fine soft russet leather, 1½ inch wide, with two large nickel plated buckles. Very strong and thoroughly dependable. Price, each...........**$0.50**

No. 2110.

**No. 2110. A very Handsome and Fashionable Belt,** made from fine embossed leather 1⅜ inch wide. Handsome dove color or light drab, with new design nickel buckle and rings and nickel eyelets. Sure to please, and therefore, sure to satisfy. Price each................**$0.75**

### The Latest Duck Belts.

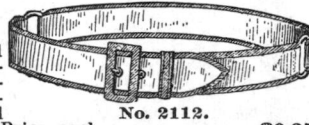

No. 2112.

**No. 2112. Men's Fine White Duck Belts.** Bound all around with russet leather. Russet leather covered buckles and rings to match. Price, each................**$0.25**

No. 2112.

**No. 2113. Men's Belts.** Made from the new linen crash or grass cloth. Natural linen color. Leather bound, with russet leather covered buckle and rings. Strictly up-to-date for outing purposes. Price, each................**$0.25**

**No. 2114. An Odd Lot of Men's and Boys' Canvas Belts,** with neat hook clasp. Just the thing for base ball clubs. Price until sold. each, 8c; per dozen..........**$0.75**

---

**IF YOU HAVE ANY TROUBLE ABOUT YOUR ORDER, DON'T KEEP IT TO YOURSELF AND GRUMBLE, BUT LET US KNOW, AND YOU MAY BE SURE THAT WE WILL TAKE PAINS TO RECTIFY ANY MISTAKE. ALWAYS GIVE INVOICE NUMBER.**

# MEN'S LINEN COLLARS AND CUFFS.

## THE NEWEST, NOBBIEST AND BEST STYLES OF THE SEASON.

**HOW TO ORDER COLLARS AND CUFFS.** We furnish any of the following shapes shown in Collars in three different qualities, as described below at 9c., 13c. and 18c.. and Cuffs at 18c and 25c per pair. Price governs quality. Order the quality you wish by catalogue number and the style or shape you desire by the letter designating the style, and always mention size wanted. which should be half size larger than size of shirt worn.

**OUR FAMOUS 9 CENT COLLAR.** **No. 2116 Our Famous 4-ply Linen Collars.** Guaranteed perfect in workmanship, correct in style and fit, excellent for wear. Sizes 14 to 17½. Retail value, 15c. Our price. each. 9c.; per doz........................**$1.00**

### Our Great 13c Line--All Linen Collars.

**No. 2117. Perfect Fitting, All Linen, 4-Ply Collars.** Extra Fine Irish linen, unequealed for wear. Made in all the styles shown below. Regular retail value, 20c. Sizes, 14 to 17½. Our price, each........................**$0.13**
Per dozen........................1.40

### 25c All Linen Collars for 18c.

**No. 2118.** This is a line of collars sold under a famous manufacturer's name, all over the country, at 25c. They are made from extra fine 2100 linen, 4-ply, with hand-made button holes and double stitching. Better linen collars cannot be made. Sizes 14 to 17½. Made in all the styles shown below.
Our special price, each........................**$0.18**
Per dozen........................1.95

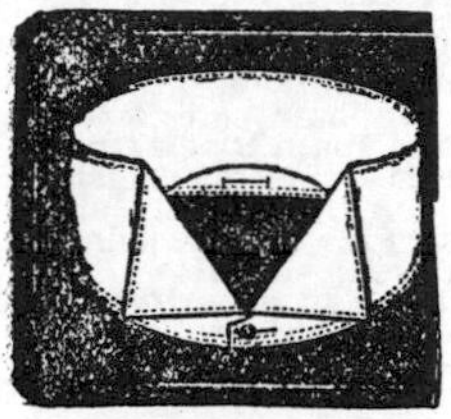
**STYLE A.** Front 2¼ in., Back 2 in.

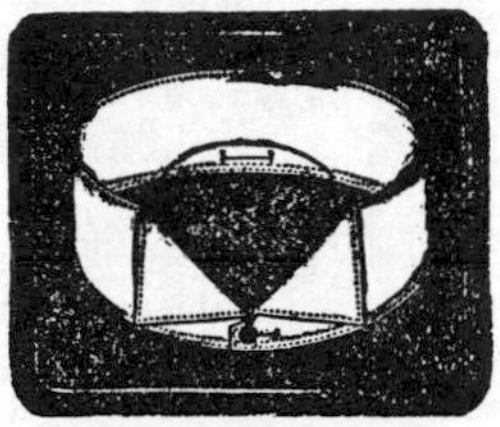
**STYLE B.** Front 1¾ in., Back 1⅝ in.

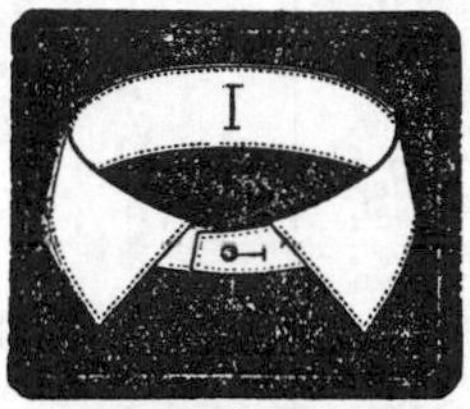
**STYLE C.** Space 1 in., Points 2¼ in,

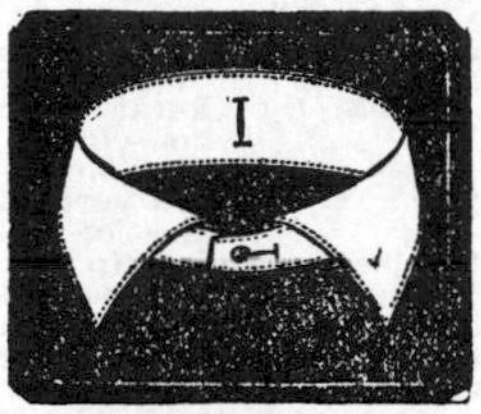
**STYLE D.** Roll Front. Points 2¾ in.

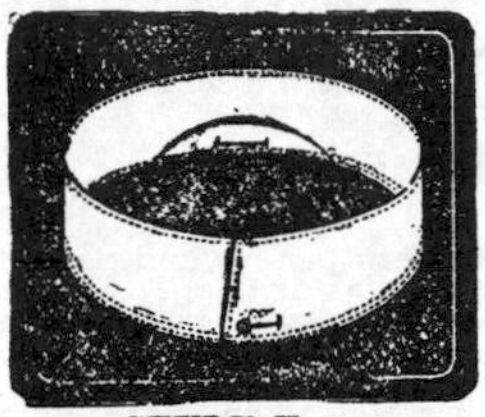
**STYLE E.** Front, 1⅝ in., Back, 1½ in.

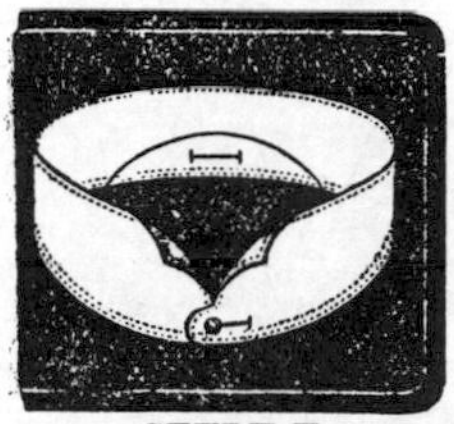
**STYLE F.** Frt. 1⅞ in., Bk. 1½ in., Sp. 1 in.

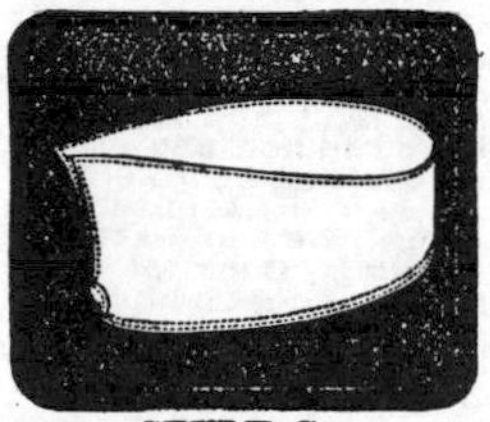
**STYLE G.** Front 2⅛ in., Back 2 in.

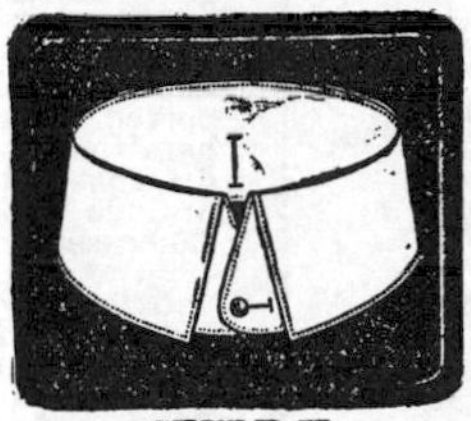
**STYLE H.** Points 2⅛ in., no space.

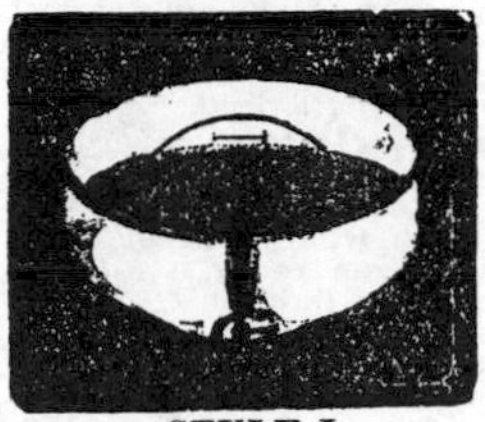
**STYLE I.** Front 2¼ in., Back 1⅞ in.

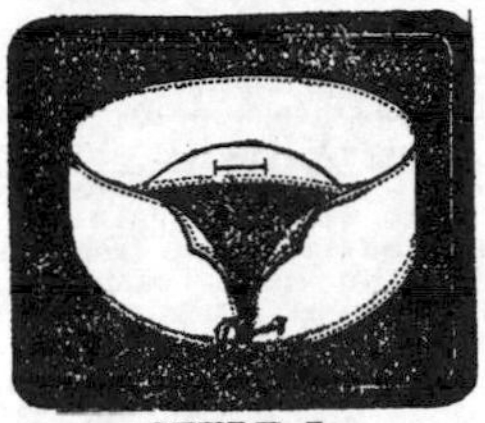
**STYLE J.** Front 1⅞ in., Back 1⅝ in.

**No. 2120. Boys' All Linen 4-Ply Collars.** Extra fine finish, made only in sizes 12, 12½, 13, 13½ and 14. Style **B, C, E** or **F.** Always mention size wanted. Each 13c; per dozen........................**$1.40**

# MEN'S HIGH GRADE LINEN CUFFS, THE VERY LATEST STYLES.

## SIZES, 10, 10 1-2 AND 11.

**No. 2123. Men's High Grade All Linen Cuffs,** made from a special grade of Irish linen, which will take an extra high polish. Made in all the styles shown below. Always mention size and style desired. Price per pair...**$0.18**
Six pairs for........................1.00

**No. 2125. Men's Finest Quality 4-Ply All Linen Cuffs.** Hand-made button holes and extra fine, full dress finish. Positively the finest cuffs that can be made. Made in all shapes as shown below. Don't forget to mention style and size desired. Price per pair 25c; six pairs for........................**$1.35**

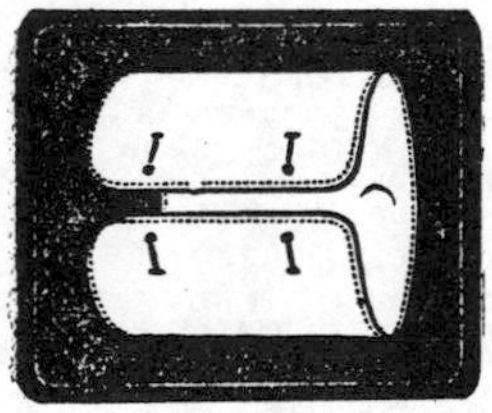
**STYLE K.** Width 4 in.

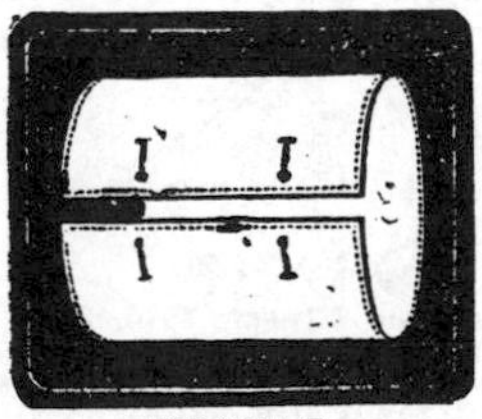
**STYLE L.** Width 3¾ in.

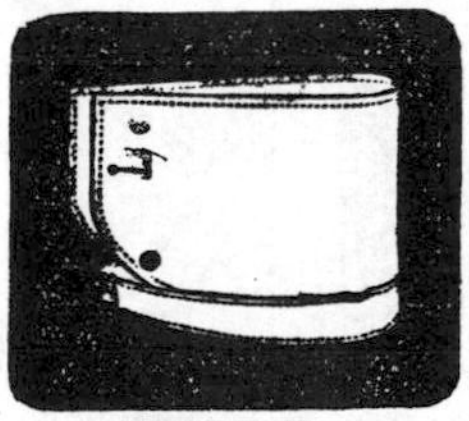
**STYLE M.** Width 3¾ in.

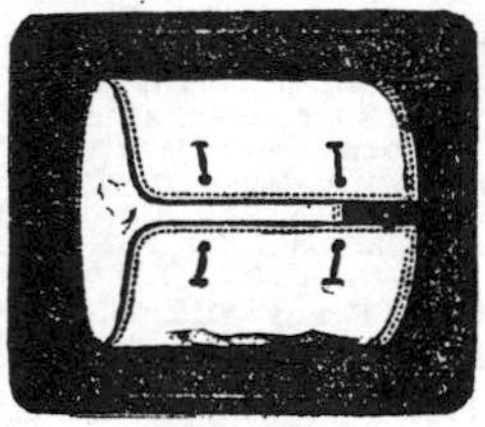
**STYLE N.** Width 3¾ in.

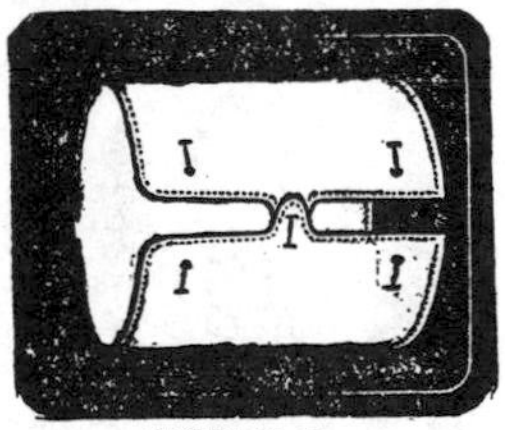
**STYLE O.** Double Link. Width 4½ in.

# CELLULOID COLLARS AND CUFFS.

## THE "INTERLINED" BRAND, THE VERY BEST IN THE WORLD.

**The following are by far the best line of Waterproof Collars and Cuffs ever manufacturned. They retain their shape and color and are unexcelled for wear and comfort. They positively will not break or tear at button holes. Order by name and catalogue number, and always mention size wanted which should be one-half size larger than that of shirt worn.**

**NOTE.—Dozen rates apply where half dozen or more of the same kind of collar or cuffs are ordered.**

**No. 2126 Genuine Interlined Celluloid Collars,** any of these styles. Price, each, 14c.; doz........**$1.60**

**No. 2128 Genuine Interlined Celluloid Cuffs,** Excelsior style. Price, per pair........................**28c**
Per dozen pairs........................**$3.00**

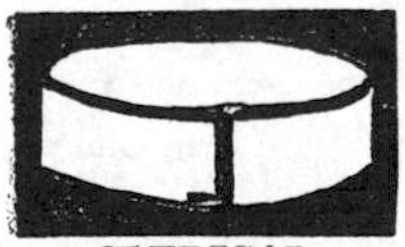
**CLERICAL.** Sizes, 12 to 19½ in. Front 1½, back 1⅝in.

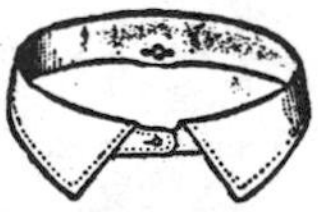
**ROYAL.** Sizes. 12½ to 20 in. Front, 1⅞ in.

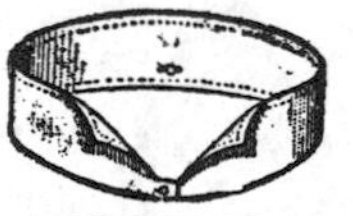
**IMPERIAL.** Sizes, 13½ to 18½ in. Front 2, back 1¾ in.

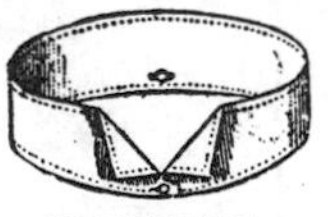
**STERLING.** Sizes, 12 to 18½ in. Front 2, back 1¾ in.

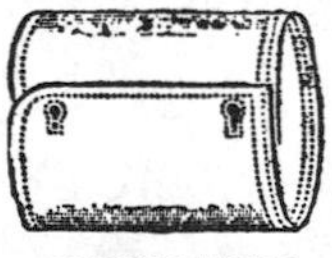
**EXCELSIOR.** Sizes, 8 to 11½ in. Width, 3½ in.

## THE FAMOUS VICTOR BRAND WATERPROOF COLLARS AND CUFFS FOR MEN AND BOYS.

**Splendid for wear, unequaled for comfort, perfect fitting and warranted to retain their shape and color. Order by catalogue number and name and always state size wanted.**

**No. 2129 Victor brand waterproof collars,** any of these styles or sizes. Each........................**$0.09**
Per dozen........................1.00

**No. 2130 Victor brand waterproof cuffs,** Albert style. Price, per pair, 20c.; per dozen pairs...**$2.20**

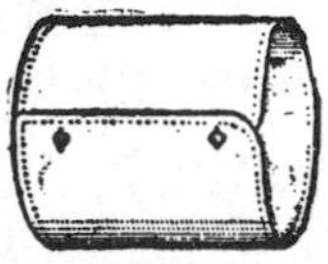
**ALBERT.** Sizes, 9½ to 11½ in. Width 3¼ in.

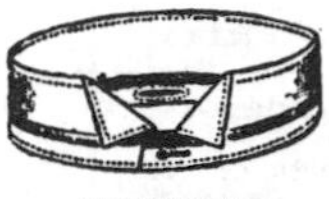
**EDMUND.** Sizes, 12½ to 18 in. Front 2, back 1¾ in.

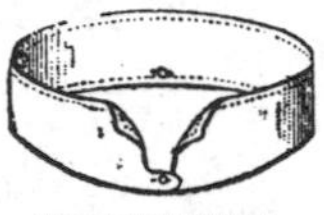
**MORTIMER.** Sizes, 13½ to 18 in. Front 2, back 1¾ in.

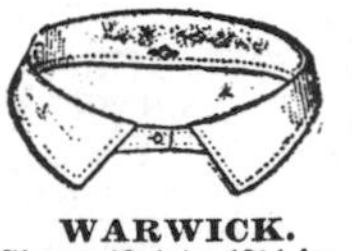
**WARWICK.** Sizes, 12½ to 18½ in. Front 2¼. back 1⅝ in.

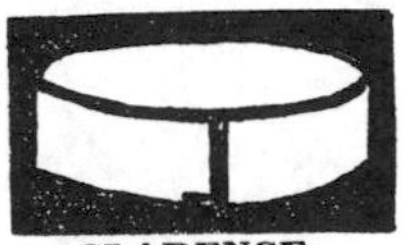
**CLARENCE.** Sizes, 14 to 18 in. Front 1⅝, back 1⅝ in.

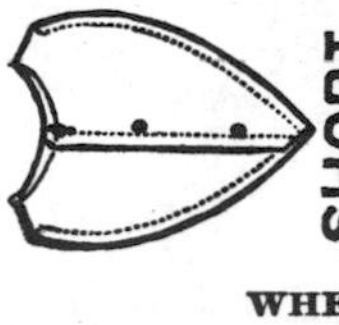
**SHORT. Front 7 In. Width 6 3/4 In.**

### Celluloid Shirt Front.

**No. 2131 Extra Quality Celluloid Shirt Front, interlined.**
Each........................**$0.35**
Per dozen........................3.75

### Celluloid Shirt Front.

**No. 2132 Long Shirt Front,** made of extra quality celluloid, interlined.
Each........................**$0.60**
Per dozen........................6.00

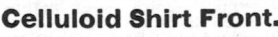

**LONG. Front 13 In. Width 6 7/8 In.**

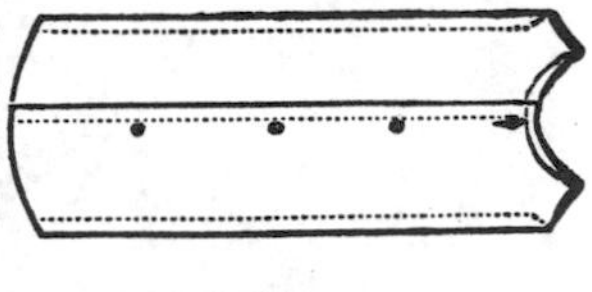

**WHEN COLLARS AND CUFFS ARE ORDERED SENT BY MAIL, ALWAYS INCLUDE ENOUGH EXTRA FOR POSTAGE.**

# SUSPENDERS AND BRACES.

## UNPRECEDENTED VALUES.

A MATCHLESS LINE OF MODERN SUSPENDERS AND SHOULDER BRACES made from best materials obtainable and possessing every new and modern improvement known to the best manufacturers of this class of goods. Every pair guaranteed absolutely perfect in every way and exactly as represented. All new, clean and fresh goods direct from the manufacture, at prices that discount all possible competitors.

Anything in this line will be sent C. O. D., subject to examination on receipt of ONE DOLLAR, balance and express charges payable at the express office. A 3 per cent. Discount will be allowed if cash in full accompanies your order. ☞ Nearly all our customers send cash in full with order.

**NOTE.** When ordering Suspenders sent separately by mail allow from 4 to 6c for postage.

## BRETELLE'S UNIVERSELLES.—THE FAMOUS FRENCH SANITARY SUSPENDERS.

**No. 2135.** The Finest Sanitary Suspenders in the world. Made in France and imported by us direct. They are very light in weight, yet possessing remarkable strength and durability; made from the finest French lisle web, non-elastic, except the back pieces which contain the very highest quality elastic webbing. French sliding adjusters and patented self-adjusting ends. No rollers or pulleys to get out of order; no buckles to break; no heavy harness to wear; no colors to fade. Instead you will find these the most comfortable, most serviceable, neatest looking and most healthy suspenders ever made. Wear them once and you will never use any other kind. Made in plain solid colors, black, white, tan, slate, navy, pearl, yellow or flesh. The ideal dress suspender. You will like it; remember that. Price per pair................50c

**No. 2136** Bretelle's Universelles, French Sanitary Suspenders. Made same as above in a very fine assortment of dainty figured patterns, light and dark colors, black, cream, blue, green, etc., with very fine pin head dots of contrasting colors. Very much admired by gentlemen of quiet refined tastes. Always state color desired. Price per pair.....50c

## Non-Elastic Web Suspenders,
### WITH WOVEN ELASTIC ENDS.

**No. 2137** Men's Superior Non-Elastic Web Suspenders. Made from fine 1 inch web with gold sliding buckle and cast-off. Seamless woven round elastic ends. Very neat, dressy patterns, light or dark colors, with small polka dots, stripes or figures. Price per pair........................18c

## All Silk Suspenders.
### THE FINEST LIGHT WEIGHT SUSPENDERS MADE.

**47c for a pair of $1.00 Suspenders.**
**No. 2138** Men's Non-Elastic Silk Web Suspenders. Made from finest imported silk. Made with silk woven elastic ends, embossed kid trimmings and handsome ornamental gold sliding buckles. The rarest of bargains; do not hesitate; get them of us while you can. Others ask $1.00 for them. Assorted light colors and the daintiest of patterns. Our special price per pair ................47c

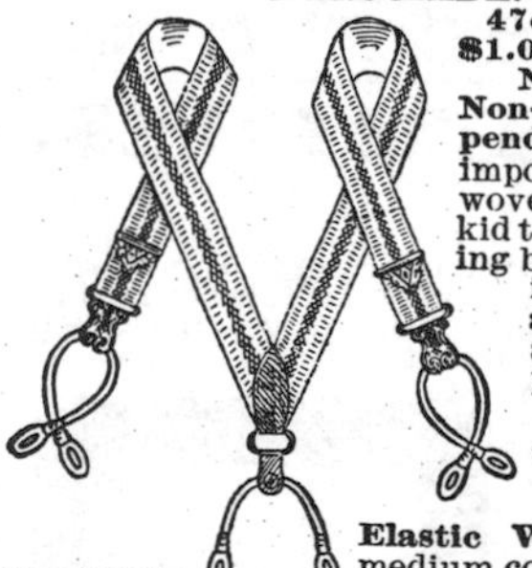

**No. 2137**

**No. 2138.**

## Men's Elastic Web Suspenders.

**No. 2139** Men's 1¼ inch Elastic Web Suspenders. Dark or medium colors, fancy patterns, metal grip back, braided ends and strong wire buckles. Per pair, 8c; Per dozen Pairs.....................90c

**No. 2140** Men's Fancy Silk Embroidered Suspenders. Made from strong 1⅜ inch elastic web, medium colors, with russet leather trimmings' and braided ends and drawer supporters. Nickeled cast off buckles. Handsomely embroidered with silk in assorted patterns. Price per pair, 15c; per dozen pairs ...........................$1.60

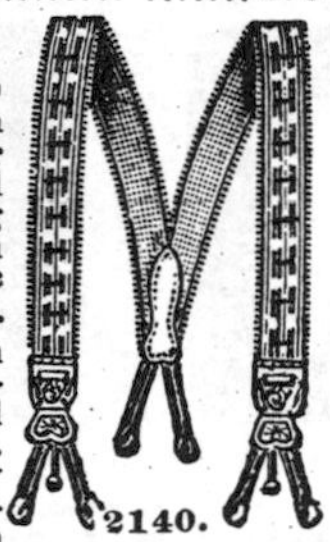

**No. 2142** Same as above, but made with the ever popular wire buckles. Per pair, 15c; per doz. pairs $1.60

**No. 2143** Fancy Wire Buckle Suspenders. 1⅜ inch heavy elastic web, dark or light ground with handsome variegated silk scroll embroidery work. Fine braided ends and drawers supporters, new metal clinch back very strong and durable. Per pair, 20c; per dozen pairs.............$2.00

**No. 2145** Men's Fine Woven Ribbed Elastic Web Suspenders. 1½ inch imported web. A very handsome assortment of new designs in vine or scroll pattern embroidery work, rich contrasting colors, russet leather trimmings, fine braided mohair ends and drawer supports, new automatic gold buckles and cast off, sewed with linen thread and warranted not to rip, light and medium colors. Price per pair, 25c; Per dozen pairs ...................$2.70

**No. 2139.**

**2140.**

**No. 2145.**

## Men's Plain White Elastic Web Suspenders.

**No. 2147** Men's Plain White Suspenders, 1⅜ inch elastic web, embossed kid trimmings, white braided mohair ends and drawers supports, metal sliding buckles and clasps. Strong, dressy and very desirable. Price per pair, 23c; per doz. $2.50

**No. 2148** Men's Plain White Elastic Web Suspenders, 1⅜ inch very strong web. Cross back with white kid patent glove snap fasteners, fine white braided lisle ends, and drawers attachment. Neat and dressy and guaranteed to give long and lasting service. Full regular length. Price per pair.$0.33
6 pair for........................... 1.75

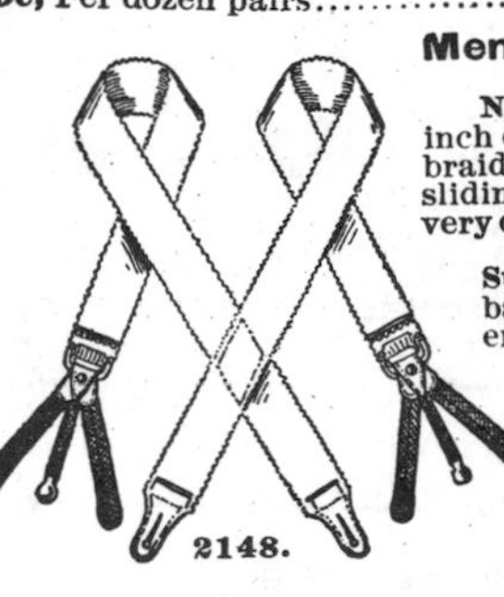

**2148.**

---

---

**No. 2147** Men's Plain White Dress Suspenders, 1⅜ inch fine woven elastic web. Handsomely embossed kid trimmings, very close woven white mohair ends and drawers supporters. Fancy gold slide buckles, and new automatic cast off. Extra well made and finished. Retail value, 65c. Our price per pair...... ..$0.40; Per dozen$.....4.30

*Our 40c White Dress Suspenders.*

## Rialto Dress Suspenders.

**50c for 75c Suspenders.**
**No. 2150** The Rialto Fine Dress Suspenders, 1⅜ inch close woven imported white elastic web, cross back with fine finished kid ends, new design ornamental slide buckles and improved automatic castoff. Handsome dressy and durable. High grade in every respect. Don't overlook this Number. Price per pair $0.50; Doz. $4.50

## Men's Plain Black Suspenders.

**No. 2149.**

**No. 2152** Men's Fine Plain Black Suspenders close woven 1¼ inch elastic web. Embossed kid trimmings. Beautiful ornamental sliding buckles and clasps. Fine black braided mohair ends, and drawers supporters. One of our exceptionally good values. Price per pair.$0.25; Per dozen pairs.$2.70

**No. 2153** Men's Fine Plain Black Dress Suspenders, made from imported elastic webbing, 1½ inches wide. Handsomely embossed kid trimmings. Fine braided black mohair ends with drawers supporters attachment. Entirely new and beautiful design, gold sliding buckles and clasps. Extra fine dress finish. Retail value 75c. Our price per pair..............$0.43; Per dozen pairs.............$4.65

**No. 2152.**

## Wear Jewell Suspenders.

**25c for the Richest, the Handsomest and Most Attractive Novelties.**
**No. 2154** A Handsome Novelty in Men's Fine Dress Suspenders, made from 1⅜ inch fancy imported elastic web. In light and medium colors, handsomely embroidered in new and attractive designs in beautiful contrasting colors. Fine braided mohair ends, and drawers supportors. Embossed kid trimmings. New and artistic ornamental Gold Sliding Buckles; each buckle set with handsome large sized jewel. Imitation of amethyst emerald, topaz, etc. Try a pair of these if you want something attractive as well as strong and serviceable. Regular 50c quality. Our Special Price, per pair.$0.25; 6 pairs for..$1.40

## 37c Silk Embroidered Suspenders.

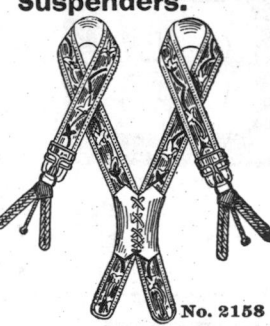

**No. 2154.**

**No. 2156** Men's Extra Fine Silk Embroidered Suspenders, with handsome ornamental gold slides and cast off. Braided lisle ends and drawers supporters. New and exclusive patterns made up at the factory expressly for us, and warranted high grade in every respect. Light medium and dark colors with artistic and elaborate silk embroidery, Presenting charming and effective contrasts. Per pair .....$0.37
6 pair for........................ 2.10

## Comfortable Lace Back Suspenders.

**No. 2156.**

**No. 2158** Men's Fine Elastic Web Suspenders, with self-adjusting lace back braided mohair ends and Sandow wire buckle. Medium colors, with fancy silk embroidered designs in contrasting bright colors. Drawers supporters with new patent grip ends. Per pair, 25c; per dozen...........$2.70

**No. 2158**

**No. 2161** Extra Fine Lace Back Suspenders, 1⅜ inch imported elastic web. Very strong and wear resisting. Fine white kid back piece, white kid trimmings fancy braided silk ends and drawers supporters attachment. New Patented Gold Slide Buckles and cast off. Medium, light and dark colors. A magnificent assortment of patterns. Persians, Orientals, Dresdens, floral and scroll work, beautifully and heavily embroidered, in finest silk floss, actually worth nearly double our asking price.
**No. 2160.** Per pair, 55c; 6 pairs for..............$2.96

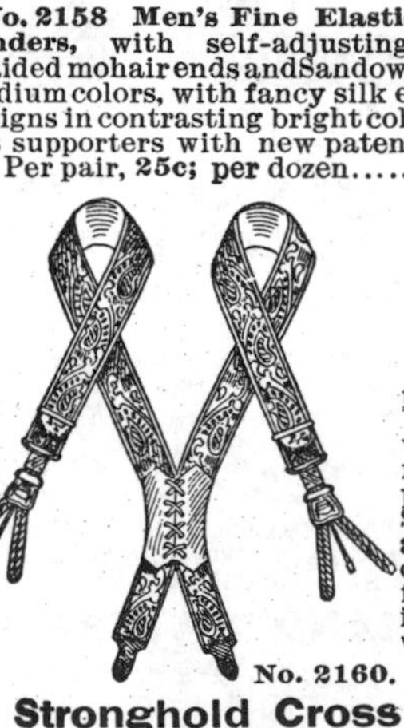

## Stronghold Cross Back Suspenders.

**No. 2162.** Men's Heavy and Strong Elastic Web Cross Back Suspenders, 1⅜ inch heavy leather trimmings and leather ends. Strong buckles. High colored stripes. Per pair, 19c; per dozen................$2.10

**No. 2163** Men's Extra Heavy and Strong Cross Back Suspenders. Assorted dark and medium colored stripes, extra heavy wide elastic web, real cow hide ends. Heavy leather trimmings. Sandow wire buckles. The strongest and best web suspender ever made. Retail value, 35c. Per pair, 28c; per dozen pairs........$3.20

*No. 2162.*

**No. 2165** A great success. **The Self Adjusting, One Piece Berlin Back Suspenders.** Made from heavy and strong 1½ inch elastic web. Heavy cushioned back. Assorted fancy colored patterns. Extra strong, non-breakable clasp and buckels. Leather ends.
Per pair...25c; per dozen .......................... $2.70

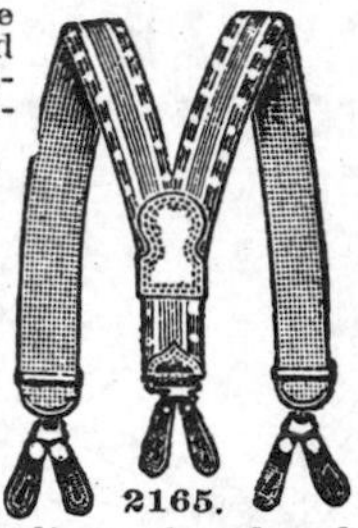

2165.

## Men's Extra Length Suspenders.

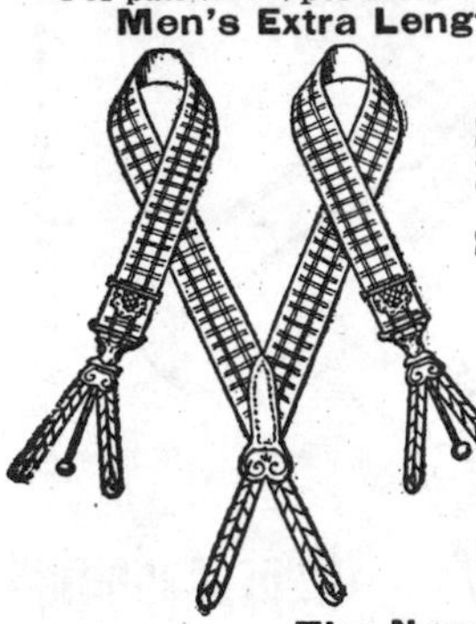

No. 2166.

**No. 2166 Men's Extra Long, Elastic Web Suspenders.** Suitable for very tall men. Assorted medium colors, neat patterns. Fine ornamental metal sliding buckles and leather trimmings. Fine braided mohair ends, sewed with heavy linen thread and will not rip. Price, per pair.......... $0.25

**No. 2167 Men's Fine 1½-inch Elastic Web Suspenders.** Extra long, and suitable for very tall men. Dark colors with neat contrasting stripes and figures. Handsome gold sliding buckles and improved cast off. Fine braided lisle ends and drawer supporters. Kid trimmings. Sewed with heavy linen thread and will not rip.
Price, per pair......... ............$0.40

## The New Glove Snap Fastener.

**No. 2168 Handsome Silk Embroidered Suspenders.** Made with the **new patent Glove Snap Fastener.** Cross back style with fine kid trimmings. Fancy silvered ornamental slide buckles. Fine braided mohair ends, and drawers supporters. Medium colors with beautiful contrasting silk embroidery work. A most excellent wearing and fine looking suspender.
Price, per pair, 27c; per doz.. $2.80

**No. 2169 Plain Black Suspenders,** with white kid glove snap cast off and trimmings. Fine 1½-inch elastic web. Fancy metal sliding buckles. Black braided mohair ends and drawers supporters. Plain black woven web. **Heavy, strong and very dressy. Cross back style.** Price, per pair....... $0.25
Per dozen ..................... 2.70

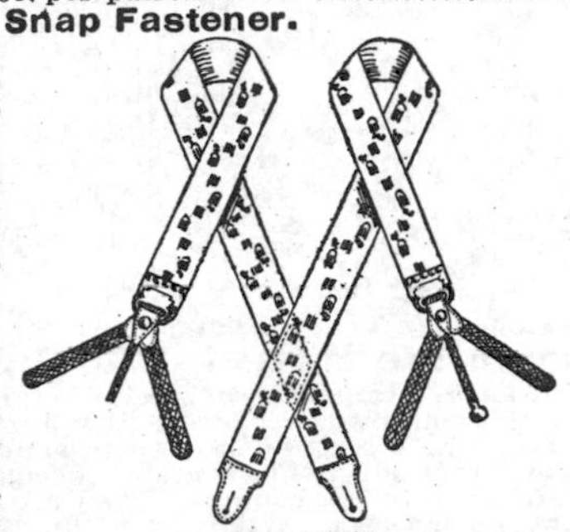

No. 2168.

## The Elite Kid End Suspenders.

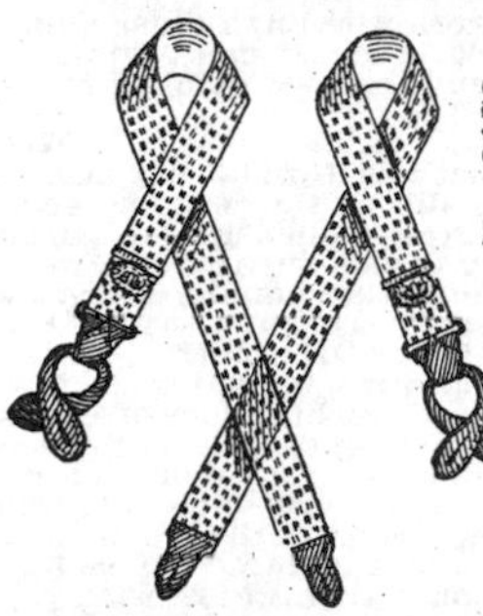

No. 2170.

**No. 2170 Elite Kid End Suspenders,** with patent glove snap cast off. Cross back style. Made from extra imported 1⅜-inch elastic web. Very artistic new colorings and designs and handsome ornamental gold sliding buckles. Medium colors, with neat and very rich embroidery work in contrasting effects. No loud or unsightly patterns. All new, clean goods, direct from the largest and best suspender factory in this country. Regular retail value, 85 cents.
Our special price, per pair.......... $0.50
Per dozen pairs...................... 5.40

**No. 2172 A Most Artistic and Handsome Pair of suspenders.** Made from the finest French elastic web. 1⅜ inches wide. Cross back style, with white kid trimmings and **glove snap fasteners.** Handsome silvered slide buckles, silver gray braided lisle ends and drawers supporters. A particularly neat striped pattern of silver gray with narrow white silk stripes. A highly artistic effect.
Price, Per pair, 58c; 6 pair for. $3.20

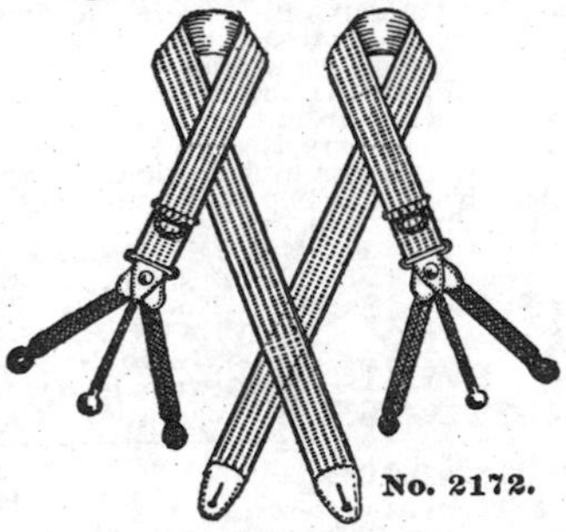

No. 2172.

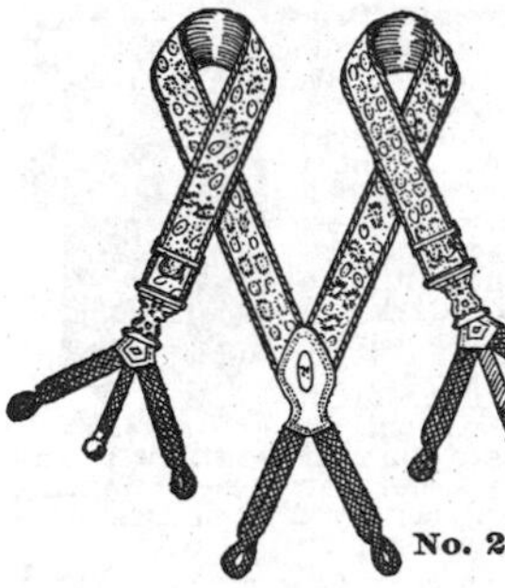

No. 2173.

## DRESDEN BUCKLE SUSPENDERS...

**PERFECT BEAUTIES, EVERY PAIR OF THEM.**

**No, 2173 High Grade Imported Elastic Web Suspenders.** Embossed white kid trimmings, braided silk ends, and drawers supporters. Double kid cushioned back piece and handsome enameled Dresden pattern buckles and Dresden cast off. Very neat, small figured silk embroidery in new and artistic colorings. Medium and light shades. Beautiful, dependable and comfortable. Price per pair.... $0.60
6 pairs for.......... .......... 3.25

## The Eureka Leather Suspenders.

**No. 2174 The Eureka Leather Suspenders** are made from fine, soft and pliable oak tanned, russet belt leather and are guaranteed to adjust themselves to any position instantly and without strain. They are more comfortable than elastic suspenders and possess more than double the wearing qualities. They will keep in place not fall from the shoulders, pull off buttons or pull the trousers up when bending over or sitting down. **This is the original and only practical all leather suspender ever produced. The most economical and comfortable suspender in the world.** Price per pair. 35c; 3 pairs for $1.00; per dozen pairs.................. $3.75

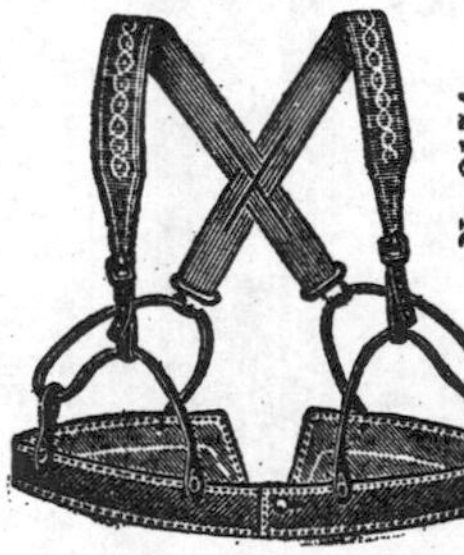

No. 2174.

## Boys' and Youths' Suspenders.

**No. 2175 Boys' Elastic Web Suspenders.** Made from good substantial web, fancy striped patterns, leather trimmings and ends. 1 pair, 5c; 1 doz. pairs. $0.50

**No. 2176 Boys' and Youths' Suspenders.** Fancy striped patterns, metal grip back, strong elastic web, woven ends and good strong buckles.
Price, per pair, 10c; per dozen pairs.......... $1.00

**No. 2177 Boys' and Youths' Fancy Silk Embroidered Elastic Web Suspenders.** Woven ends and non-breakable wire buckles. All new handsome designs.
Price per pair, 15c; 6 pairs for...... .......... $0.65

No. 2177.

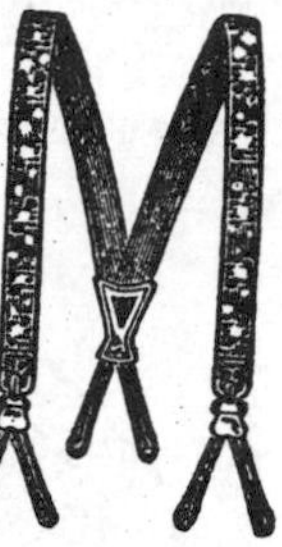

## SHOULDER BRACES.

**BRACE UP!** **Don't be round shouldered. THE GAMBLE SHOULDER BRACE will straighten your shoulders, throw out your chest and strengthen your lungs. Positively the best shoulder brace ever made.**

## The Gamble Brace for Men.

**A GUARANTEED CURE FOR ROUND SHOULDERS.**

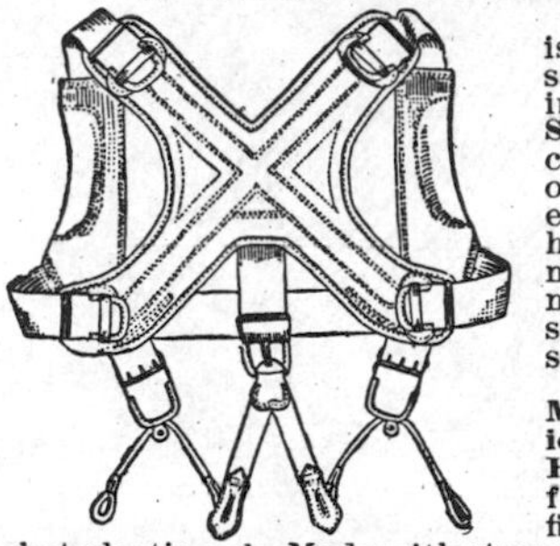

**No. 2178 The specialty of this Brace** is two light steel springs which acts the same as if you gently press your thumbs in one's shoulder blades. **It is the only Shoulder Brace made** on the right principle. They are handsomely made throughout, perfectly adjustable, fine roll leather ends, patent cast-off snaps, the best made hair pads, leather lined in front of arms, making it the most comfortable brace made and will brace a man up in a good shape so he will grow fat and healthy; sizes, 32 to 40. Each.................. $1.50

**No. 2179 Men's Superior Shoulder Braces,** made from fancy figured overshot elastic web. Made with straps to brace the shoulders and straighten the back. Suspender attachment with fine braided lisle ends and drawers supporters. Light and medium colors. This is a splendid brace and one which we have handled for years and never had a complaint.
Price per pair ........................... $0.50

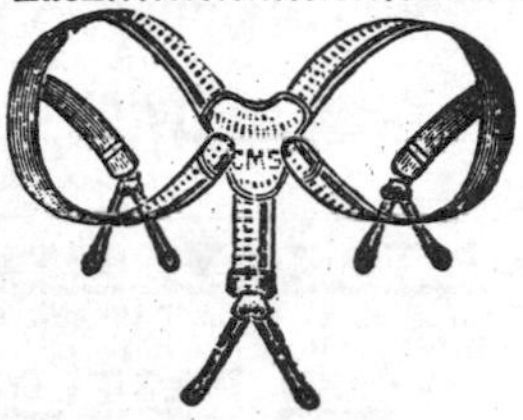

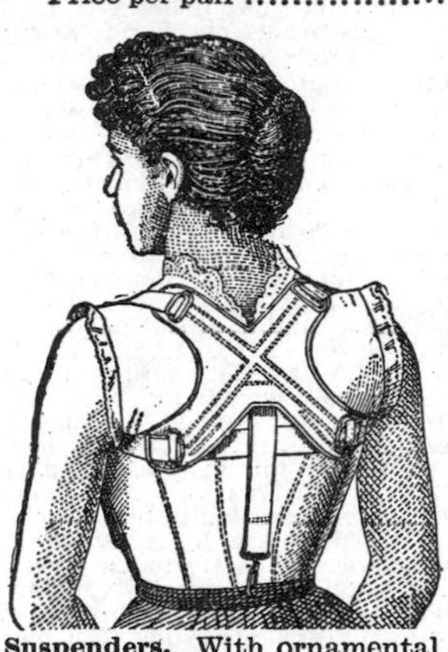

## The Gamble. Ladies' and Misses' Shoulder Brace.

**A Perfect Shoulder Brace and Skirt Supporter Combined.**

**No. 2180. The Gamble Shoulder Brace for Ladies.** A perfect shoulder brace in every sense of the word. Made from fine light drab jeans. Perfectly adjustable to any position; finest hair padding; leather lined in front of the arms, soft and pliable and will not chafe or irritate the skin. The principle is the same as in the men's brace, No. 2178, the specialty of which is two finely tempered steel springs which act the same as if you gently press your thumbs or one's shoulder blades, throwing the chest out and the shoulders back. The most comfortable and effective brace made. Sizes 26, 28, 30, 32, 34, and 36 inch bust measure. Take measure close up under the arms and above the breasts. Each... $1.00

## Suspenders for Gifts.

**Each Put up in a Fancy Box.**

**No. 2184 Men's Fancy Silk Embroider Suspenders.** With ornamental sliding buckles. Fine 1⅜ inch imported web. Soft kid trimmings. New patent glove snap cast off. Fine braided lisle ends, and drawers supporters. All new handsome patterns. Attractive designs. Medium, dark, or light shades. No plain colors. Guaranteed first class in every respect. Put up 1 pair in box. Price, per pair .............. $0.65
3 pairs for.................................... 1.75

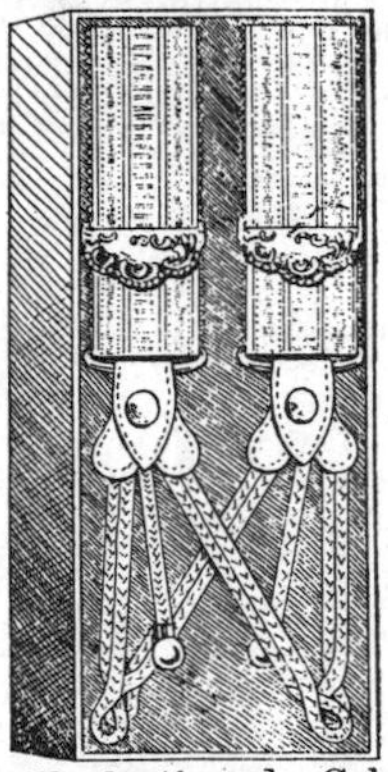

No. 2184.

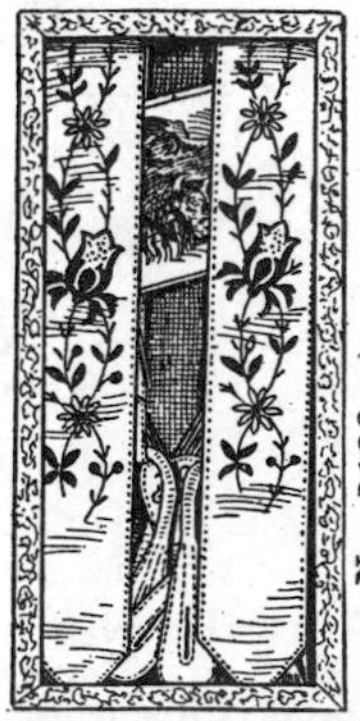

No. 2186

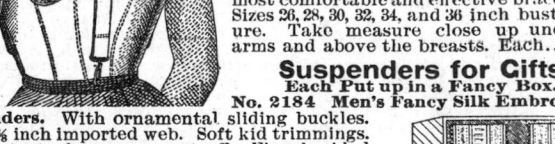

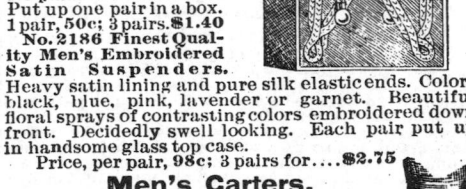

**No. 2185 Men's Fancy Silk Embroidered Suspenders.** Made from fine imported elastic web. Richly embroidered in attractive and beautiful designs. Ornamental sliding buckles. Fine braided ends. Light or medium colors. No plain or solid colors. Put up one pair in a box. 1 pair, 50c; 3 pairs. $1.40

**No. 2186 Finest Quality Men's Embroidered Satin Suspenders.** Heavy satin lining and pure silk elastic ends. Colors black, blue, pink, lavender or garnet. Beautiful floral sprays of contrasting colors embroidered down front. Decidedly swell looking. Each pair put up in handsome glass top case.
Price, per pair, 98c; 3 pairs for.... $2.75

## Men's Garters.

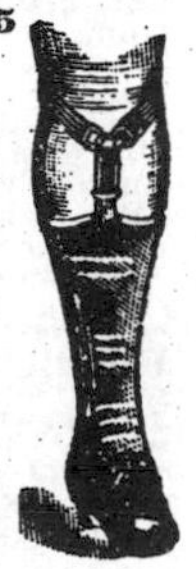

**No. 2187.** Men's Elastic Web Garters, made in neat fancy striped patterns. Assorted colors. See adjoining illustration for style. Price, per pair.......... $0.10 Per doz. pairs.......... $0.95

**No. 2188.** Men's fine Silk Web Garters. Made same style as adjoining illustration. Put up one pair in box. Pure silk, very fine. Black, white, old gold, blue, etc.
Price, per pair............ $0.18 Per dozen pairs.............. $2.00

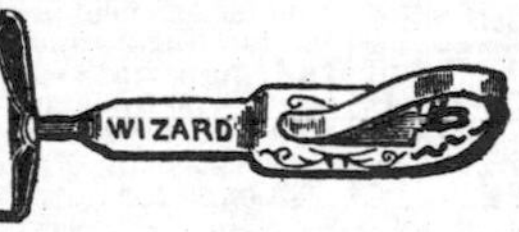


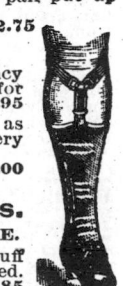

## Wizard Cuff Holders.

**THE MOST POPULAR MADE.**

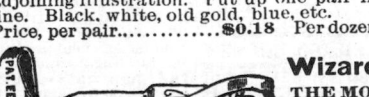

**No. 2189.** The Wizzard Cuff Holders, improved nickel plated.
Per pair, 8c; perdoz...... $0.85

**THE MOST MARVELOUS BARGAINS IN COLORED SHOES EVER OFFERED ARE HANDSOMELY ILLUSTRATED IN COLORS ON THE SPECIAL PAGES OF OUR SHOE DEPARTMENT.**

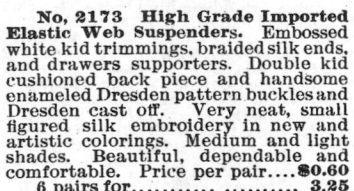

# MEN'S NECKWEAR DEPARTMENT.
## FIVE MAGNIFICENT NECKWEAR LEADERS.

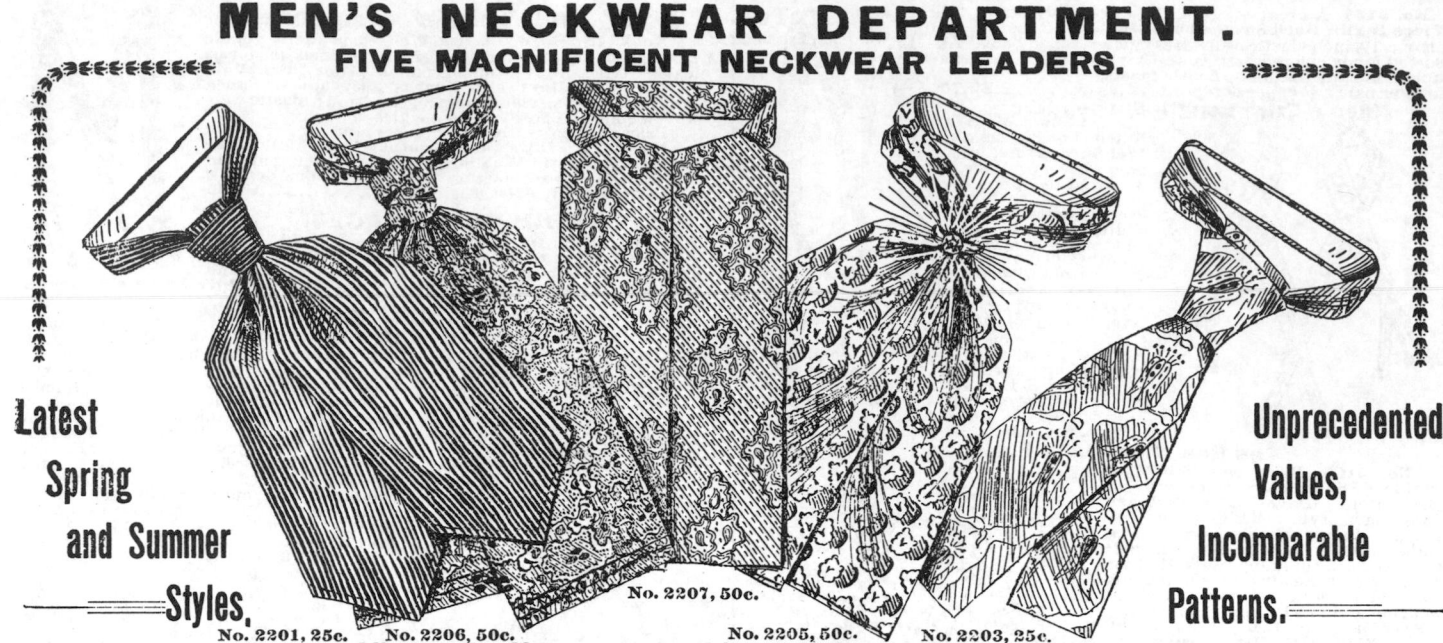

**Latest Spring and Summer Styles.**

**Unprecedented Values, Incomparable Patterns.**

No. 2207, 50c.

No. 2201, 25c.  No. 2206, 50c.  No. 2205, 50c.  No. 2203, 25c.

**All that is New and Fashionable We Have in Stock.**

**UP-TO-DATE STYLES AT UP-TO-DATE PRICES.** We are the Largest importers of Neckwear Silks in America. Our shelves are loaded down with rich and novel Brocades, Satins, Japanese Silks, Persian Novelties, French Fancies, Kai, Kais, Taffetas, and many others too numerous to enumerate. We import the silks direct and have them made up into the latest shapes, in Tecks, De Joinvilles, Four-in-hands, Puffs, Bows, Club Ties, etc. Our prices are in many instances lower than your local merchant could buy the same qualities at wholesale.

**OUR PATTERNS** are far ahead of anything ever shown in this line of goods in this country. They are really superb. You will be more than pleased if you place your order with us for neckwear this season. Aside from the fact that we save you all middlemen's profits and sell you the goods at less than wholesale prices, the fact is worthy your consideration that we carry the largest assortment of neckwear of any one concern in this country, perhaps in the world. There is hardly a style or shape manufactured but what we can supply it.

**No. 2201. FLOWING END TECK SCARF.** Made from fine imported silks in an immense assortment of new and beautiful patterns; neat stripes, handsome brocades, fancy figures, dots and all sorts of pretty effects in all sorts of colorings, **except plain white and black.** Always in style and always neat and dressy; handsomely made up and finished; pointed or square ends; pure silk and worth at retail 50c each. Our price, each, 25c.; half doz..$1.30

**No. 2203. BROCADED FOUR-IN-HAND SILK SCARF.** The illustration shows the scarf tied. The knot can be tied large or small, to suit the wearer. The quality is the finest for the price ever sold in this country. The patterns are superb, and embrace many rich and effective designs in foreign novelties; thousands of patterns in checks, plaids, floral patterns, Oriental figures, etc. Price each, 25c.; per half dozen..$1.30

**No. 2205. THE FAMOUS DE JOINVILLE SCARF.** The most popular and swellest gentleman's scarf ever produced. These scarfs are 6 inches wide and 38 inches long, and are made from purest woven silk specially imported by us, and without any exception they are the handsomest line of silks ever brought to this country. We have an immense assortment, comprising more than three hundred different designs; all light and medium colorings in nearly every color and shade ever thought of. They consist mostly of combination colors, just a few of which are, blue, lavender, light green, cherry, strawberry, olive, myrtle, moss green, torquoise, opal, red, etc., all combined with light contrasting shades of cream, white, bright sunshiny yellow, pale blue and a host of other beautiful shades; handsome brocade patterns in Persian effects, Oriental figures, Dresden fancies, Chameleon grotesques, Roman novelties, Scotch and Highland checks, and an almost endless variety of artistic and fashionable designs; our own special importations and not to be found elsewhere in this country. The De Joinville scarf is popular with fashionable gentlemen, because of its exclusiveness and because it can be tied into several different shapes.

llustration No. 2205 shows the De Joinville as worn with an ordinary finger ring. No. 2206 shows it tied in Prince of Wales knot. It can also be tied into shapes like illustrations No. 2201 and 2203 and into beautiful puffs similar to No. 2207. Retail value of these scarfs, $1.00.

Our price, each, 50c.; three for..$1.40

**No. 2206. THE DE JOINVILLE SCARF,** same as No. 2403, but made in rich, dark combination colors. All pure woven silk of the very finest sort. Artistic colorings of cardinal, navy, myrtle green, wine, black, purple, dahlia, etc., with delicate tintings of contrasting shades, such as gold, pearl, lemon, lettuce green, scarlet, lavender, violet and other equally attractive shades. Uuapproachable in richness and style. Price each, 50c.; 3 for..$1.40

**No. 2207. GENTLEMEN'S FINE SILK BROCADE PUFF SCARFS,** made in dark and light shades; entirely new patterns, including the fashionable Persian and Dresden designs in all sorts of combinations of colors; handsomely made up and artistically finished; thoroughly correct in every detail. In ordering, state whether you wish light or dark color, and give predominating colors desired. We do not have these scarfs in plain or solid colors. They are all made in combination colors. Some of the predominating colors are myrtle, olive, garnet, brown, blue, lavender, red, green, light blue, etc. Extra high grade in every way. We offer them at less than your local dealer can buy the same goods at wholesale.

Price each, 50c.; three for..$1.40

**No. 2209 FINE PUFF SCARF,** same style as above, but made from extra heavy plain black satin; silk lined and very dressy. Price each..$0.50

**A 25c EVENT.**

**No. 2209. A RARE BARGAIN. MEN'S FINE PLAIN BLACK SATIN PUFF SCARFS.** Similar in style to No. 2407; nicely made and finely finished. Always in style and always neat and dressy. Regular 50c quality. Our price, each..$0.25

## Silk Four-in-hand Scarfs.
Newest and Best Patterns. Exceptional Values.

**No. 2210. Fancy Silk Four-in-Hand Ties.** Very attractive and nobby patterns in dark and medium colors. New designs in fancy checks, oriental figures, floral designs and a large assortment of fresh and tastefully arranged designs, combination colorings in all the popular colors. Special bargain price, each..$0.18

Per dozen..1.98

## Our 25c Four-in-hands.

**No. 2211. Read this Astonishing Offer.** We offer you herewith, four-in-hand ties at 25c that are unquestionably fine. The quality of the silk is astonishing. The patterns are simply superb. It is possible that you may have purchased ties as good as these at 50c or 75c, but certainly never for less money. They are made from specially imported silks and satins and we have them in a large and varied assortment of designs. Persians, plaids, checks, brocades, dots, floral and in fact a vast array of new and fashionable patterns. All finely made and silk lined. All sorts of colors. Always mention the predominating colors which you wish. Your money's worth here and more too.

No. 2210.

Our special price, each..$0.25

6 for..1.30

**THE HIGHEST REFERENCES IN CHICAGO AND NEW YORK.** IF YOU DOUBT OUR RELIABILITY, SEND YOUR ORDER AND MONEY TO THE METROPOLITAN NATIONAL BANK, CHICAGO, WITH INSTRUCTIONS NOT TO TURN IT OVER TO US UNLESS THEY ARE SATISFIED WE WILL DO AS WE AGREE.

## Reversible Four-in-Hands.

**No. 2212.** These ties are made from pure China Silk, alike on both sides and reversible. The patterns are all new and very nobby. Light and medium colors; various shades of green, blue, olive, etc. Rich and tasty Persian effects. Oriental figures. Handsomely made up and finished. All pure silk.

Price..$0.23  6 for..$1.20

**No. 2214. Extra Fine Black Brocaded or China Silk Reversible Four-in-Hand Ties,** with pointed ends. Price, each..$0.23

6 for..1.20

## Four-in-Hands in Fancy Boxes.
Made expressly for gift purposes.

**No. 2213.** These are exceptionally handsome Scarfs, and never fail to please. Each one is packed in a handsome box. We have them light, medium or dark colors, in a large and beautiful assortment of new designs in imported silks and satins. All satin lined and made up in the finest manner possible. Retail merchants never charge less than $1.00 for scarfs of this sort. Our price is far different and will surely interest you. Price, each..$0.58

3 boxes for..1.55

## 43c Four-in-hands.

**No. 2214. Heavy French Brocade Silk Novelties,** assorted colors, very neat and modest patterns, square or pointed ends. Heavily silk lined. An endless variety of patterns. All are neat and modest. If you should like a black tie with neat red, blue, white, wine, gold or lavender figures, we have it in this lot. We also have dark blue or dark red back grounds, with neat contrasting figures. Then, too, we have thousands in light and medium shades of all kinds. We will be glad to have you compare one of these ties with any 75c tie you have ever seen. Give predominating colors desired and we will send you a handsome up-to-date scarf that will certainly please you.

No. 2212.

Price, each..$0.43

## Black Silk and Satin Four-in-Hands

**No. 2215. Heavy Black Silk or Satin Four-in-Hand Scarfs.** Finest imported quality, lined with heavy silk or satin. Rich and dressy. Regular 75c quality. Price, each..$0.50

3 for..1.37

No. 2216.

**SEE PAGE 4** AND LEARN HOW IT PAYS TO SEND CLUB ORDERS. YOU GET AN EXTRA DISCOUNT, WHICH IS AN OBJECT. YOU WILL FREQUENTLY NEED SOME SMALL ARTICLES, AND YOU CAN HAVE THEM SENT ALONG WITH YOUR NEIGHBORS' FREIGHT ORDER AT NO EXPENSE. THAT'S AN OBJECT. EVERY CENT YOU CAN SAVE IS THAT MUCH LAID UP FOR A RAINY DAY.

**WHEN YOU ARE IN NEED OF ORDER BLANKS DROP US A POSTAL CARD AND WE SHALL SEND A SUPPLY. WE WOULD MUCH RATHER HAVE ALL ORDERS MADE OUT CAREFULLY ON OUR REGULAR BLANKS.**

## Black Teck Scarfs.

**No. 2220. Men's Fine Black Silk or Satin Teck Scarfs,** with flowing ends. Our own special importation, and we offer them at just one-half their regular retail value. All made up first-class and guaranteed to satisfy. Price, each....................25c

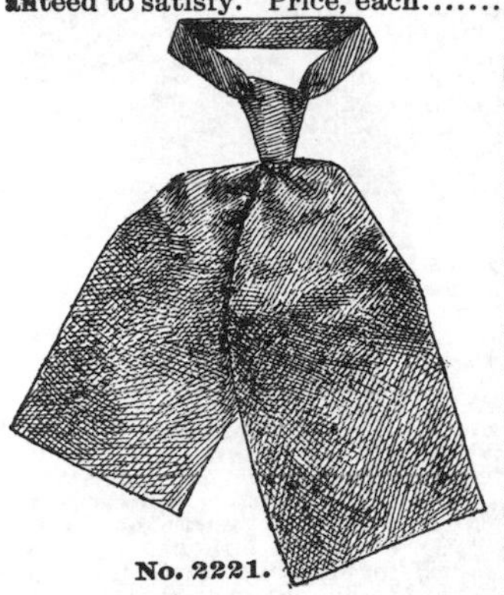

No. 2221.

**No. 2221.** If you are in search of a rich jet black silk or heavy satin teck scarf, something that you usually pay a dollar to get but do not feel like paying it this season, order one of these scarfs at 50c and if you do not think it a bargain return it to us at our expense and we will cheerfully return you your money. These scarfs are made from extra heavy and fine black satin or silk, as desired, and heavily silk lined. They are elegantly made up in full teck shape, some with pointed and some with square ends. All are first quality in every way. Price, each..................50c; 3 for.......... .....$1.35

## Our 35c All Silk Tecks.

**A SUPERB BLENDING OF PRICE AND QUALITY.**

**No. 2222.—Men's Handsome Silk and Satin Fancy Teck Scarfs,** made in latest style with square or pointed ends and medium sized knot. Made from specially imported silks and satins in a large and particularly choice assortment of artistic designs, medium, light and dark colors, in stripes, checks, Persians, floral and polka dots; also fancy vine and figured patterns. All beautifully made up and warranted to give the very best of satisfaction. State predominating colors. Price, each...35c; 3 for....$$1.00

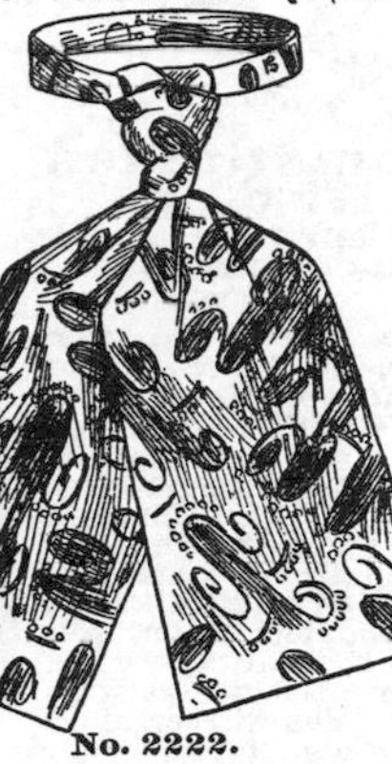

No. 2222.

## AT 50C. Our Price Poultice for Tired ...Pocket Books...

**A PLEASING ARRAY AT A PLEASING PRICE....**

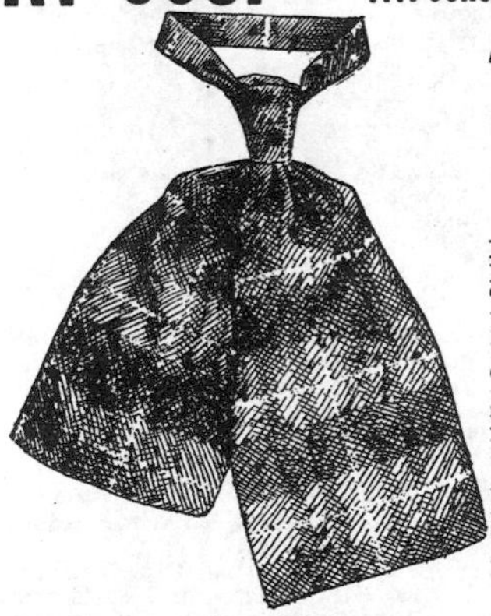

No. 2223.

**No. 2223. Strictly High Grade Teck Scarfs.** The kind that you often long for but don't feel that you can afford to invest a dollar in purchasing. We solve the problem for you by cutting the price in half. The quality remains the same. We offer you these handsome scarfs at a price that will enable you to purchase two of them for what you have been paying your retail dealer for one. The richest and handsomest assortment of neckwear ever shown by any concern on earth. We have thousands of dozens of these scarfs, all made up from the finest imported silks and satins. Made with flowing or square ends, as desired. We have them in rich Persian or Dresden effects; French brocades, English plaids and checks, Scotch and Highland plaids, polka dots, pin stripes, small figures, and a vast array of every conceivable shade and color, all made in combinations of rare beauty. Finished in the very finest manner. Regular retail value, $1.00.
Our price, each.............................................50c
3 for.........................................................$1.35

**THE NEWEST PARISIAN NOVELTIES.... IN LADIES' COLLARETTES**
**WILL BE FOUND IN OUR DRY GOODS DEPARTMENT**
**REFER TO THE INDEX.**

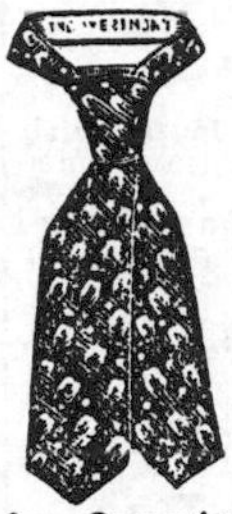

## Silk Teck Scarfs.

**An Extraordinary Offering.**

**At 19c WE OFFER YOU THESE MAGNIFICENT TECK SCARFS.**

**See our special half-dozen offer. It will pay you to lay in a supply for yourself and friends.**

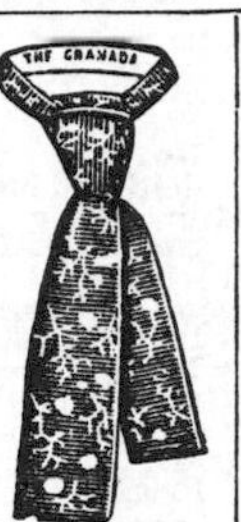

**No. 2224. Men's Fine Fancy Silk Teck Scarfs.** The kind that you usually pay 35c, 45c, and 50c for. Our price is a revelation. We buy these goods direct, thousands of dozens at a time, and all the year around. These scarfs are made from fine quality imported fancy silks. We have them in checks, stripes, dots, neat figures, and imperial designs, medium and dark combination colors. **No plain black or white.** All nicely made and trimmed. Surprising values, every one of them. Our special price, each..........19c; Six for......$1.00

## Silk Folding or String Ties.

**Fancy Figured Silk String Ties.**

**No. 2225.** Medium width, assorted, dark or medium colors, nicely made and finely finished folded string ties.
Per dozen.... 2.50 Price, each.... $0.23

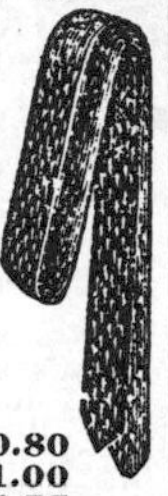

## Black Silk Folded Ties.

Known as string ties, made of pure gros grain silks, extraordinary values in each number; this is a tie that can be worn on all occasions, and especially suitable for elderly gentlemen.

No. 2226. ⅝ inch wide...14c each...6 for $0.80
No. 2227. ¾ " " ...18c each..6 for 1.00
No. 2228. ⅞ " " ...22c each..6 for 1.25
No. 2229. 1 " " ...27c each..6 for 1.55
No. 2230. 1⅛ " " ...30c each..6 for 1.75

## Hot Weather Neckwear.

An untied man is ever an untidy man. No chance for untidiness here. Ours is a tide of low prices and should be taken at the flood.

## Gentlemen's Silk Bow Ties.

**For turn-down Collar.**

**No. 2232. Fancy Silk Bow Ties for 6 cents,** with shield for turn-down collar. Any of this lot of ties would cost you a quarter in any retail store. There is nothing old or off-color; everyone is as handsome as can be; all full size, pretty fancy colors; made of remnants of silks. We have contracted to take all the largest manufacturer of neck ties in New York will have for the entire season. They are made from remnants left from high grade ties, and are a bargain.
Each........................6c
½ doz., assorted............30c

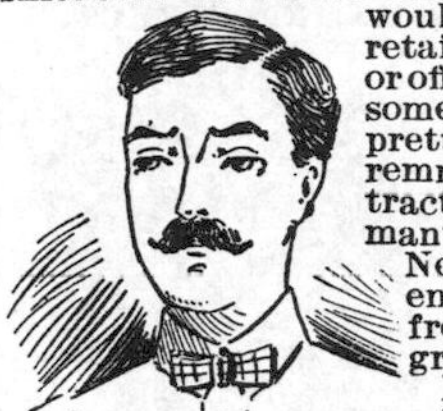

**No. 2246. Black Silk Bows,** with shield and elastic loop for turn-down collar.
Each..........10c; ½ dozen, for.....50c

**No. 2250. Men's Fine Black Satin Bows,** with shield and elastic loop, for turn-down collars. Extrafine selected stock. Price, each........10c; 6 for..........................................50c

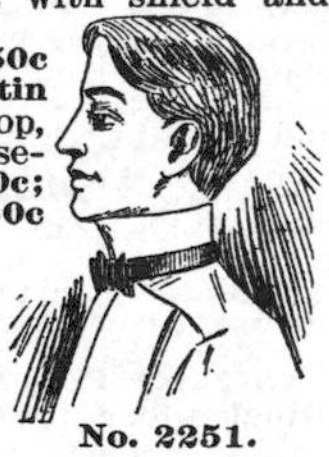

No. 2251.

## Black Band Bows.

**For Standing Collar.**

**No. 2251. Black Bow.** Popular wedding tie, fine grade satin and silk. Each.... .. 15c
Half doz........................80c

**No. 2252.** Same as above, only pure white. Each. ..15c Half doz........80c.

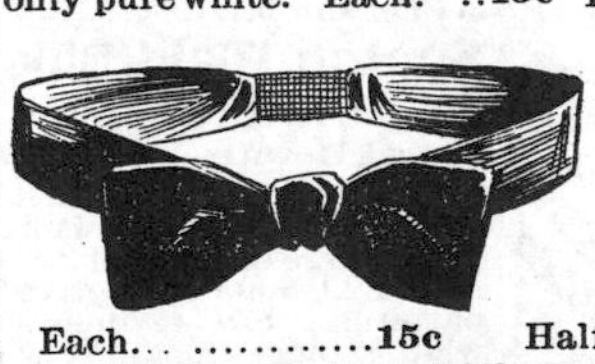

**No. 2254. Senator Band Bow.** Extra quality silk or satin, latest shape, with patent band clasp at back so it can be worn with standing collar. Plain black only.
Each... ............15c Half dozen..........80c

## White China Silk Band Bows.

**No. 2255. Men's Extra Fine Pure White China Silk Band Bows** for standing colars.—The daintiest white bow tie ever made. Very fine elastic band in back. An excellent bow for parties, weddings, etc.
Price each .........23c. Six for............$1.25

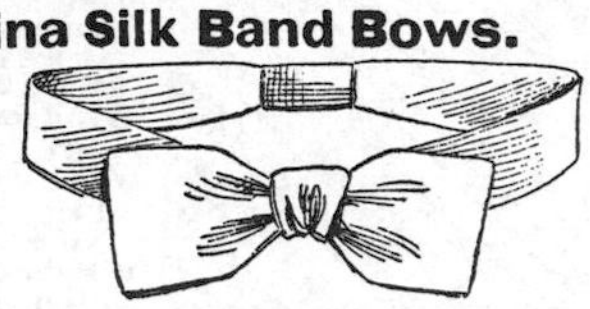

No. 2255.

## Fancy Silk Band Bows.

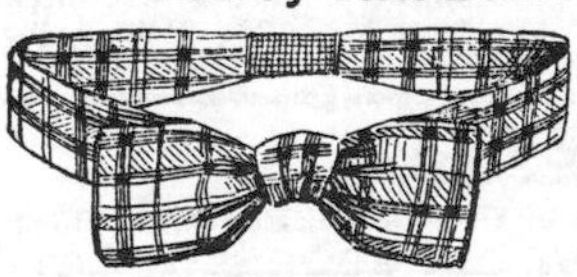

No. 2256.

**No. 2256. Fine China Silk Fancy Band Bows,** made with elastic adjustable strap in back. Rich Persian and Dresden designs in new and artistic colorings. Combinations of olive, myrtle, mode, blue, red, green and a host of other new and staple shades. Also made in floral and fancy figured patterns, checks, etc. Rich and dressy; square or pointed ends.
Price each..........18c.; Six for.........$0.90

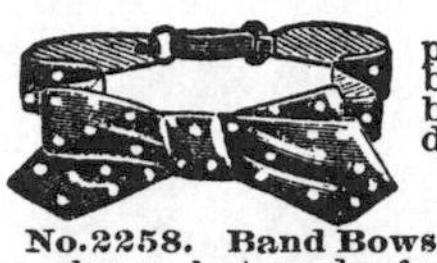

**No. 2257. Band Bow** patent adjustable neck band, will fit any size collar, best of silk, in light and dark colors.
Price each............12c.
Six for..............60c.

**No. 2258. Band Bows** for standing collars. Same as above, but made from heavy fancy imported silks in medium light or dark colors. New and handsome patterns. Square or pointed ends; stripes, checks, dots; Persian patterns. Oriental fancies and beautiful floral patterns. All sorts of colorings. Strictly up-to-date. Every fashionable man will wear them this summer.
Price each...............25c. Six for............$1.30

**No. 2259.** The handsomest and richest **Band Bows** that we could possibly secure this season. We can assure you that they are beauties. We have them in a large and rich variety of fashionable colorings. Square or pointed ends as desired. Dark and medium colors. Beautiful and attractive combinations in endless variety. Nobby Dresdens, Persians, Romans, Scotch plaids and checks, fancy figures and dots in greens, olives, browns, blues, reds, wines, all intermingled with dainty contrasting shades. Actually worth double our asking price. Don't overlook these if you want the swellest tie of the season. Price each..............................38c.

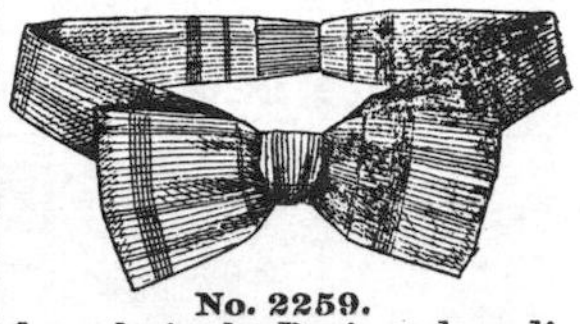

No. 2259.

## Madras Pull Band Bows.

**Uery Popular for Outing Wear.**

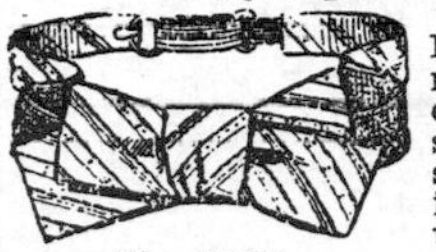

No. 2260.

**No. 2260. The New Pull Band Bow,** made of French madras or cheviot, in 50 different patterns, checks, stripes, etc., light and dark shades, rubber elastic band in back with movable ends, that can be lengthened or shortened as desired. The newest, the nobbiest, the coolest looking, neatest appearing summer tie ever made. Order ½ dozen assorted patterns; they will please you. Pointed or square ends as desired.
Price each..................14c. Per ½ dozen........75c.

## New Lawn Dress Bows.

**With Band for Standing Collar.**

**No. 2261. Fancy Figured Band Bows.** Fine quality figured lawn in silk effect, entirely new and very pretty goods. Light and medium colors, 100 different patterns. Every one a beauty.
Each................12c. Per half dozen......65c.

## Embroidered Pique Teck Scarfs.

**Something New and Beautiful.**

**No. 2262. This is a most beautiful white corded pique teck scarf.** Elaborately embroidered in Silk down the entire front, finely made and finished, very nobby and rich looking, new and handsome patterns. Sure to please you.
Price each..................$0.25
Six for.......................1.30

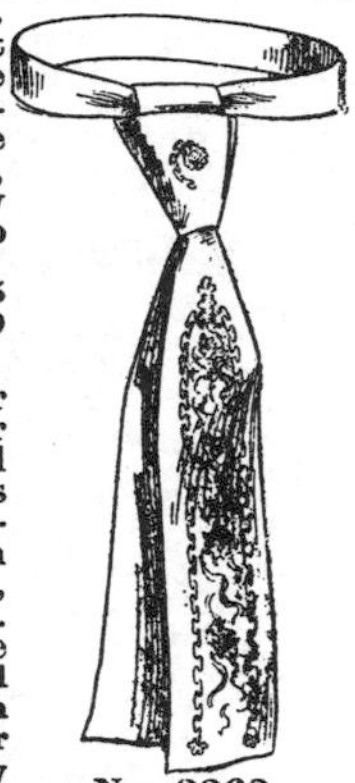

No. 2262.

## Club House Ties.

In the history of the neckwear business probably no tie has ever attained the popularity reached by the **Club House Tie.** It is neat, genteel and dressy, and furthermore very stylish. They can be worn with any style of collar, and are suitable for all occasions. They are particularly desirable for wear with our famous **Ideal Outing Shirts and Fancy Bosom Shirts as shown on another page.** Ladies wear them too, they are just the thing for shirt waists.

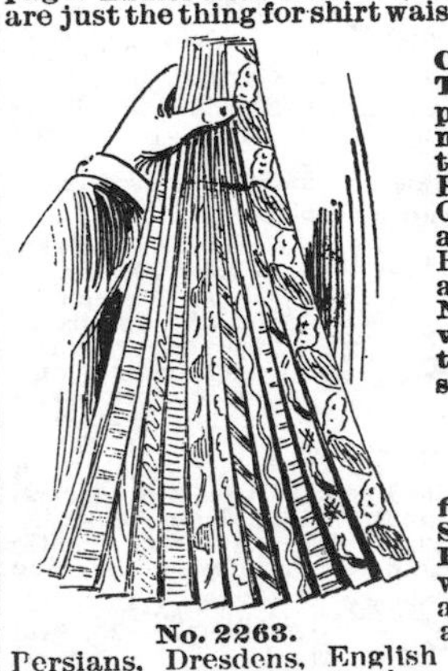

No. 2263.

**No. 2263. Pure China Silk Club House Ties.** Entirely new patterns, including many novel and attractive combinations. Persians, Dresdens. Checks, fancy figures and Oriental designs. Hundreds of charming and effective styles. **No plain blacks or whites. Remember these ties are pure silk.**
Price each.....$0.14
Six assorted patterns..... .75

**No. 2264. Extra fine quality imported Silk and Satin Club House Ties,** one inch wide, 36 inches long, in almost every conceivable pattern. The Persians, Dresdens, English Checks and Scotch Plaids are the most popular. We also have an immense assortment of stripes, dots and neat small figures, all sorts of colorings in the richest of combinations, beautiful Chamelon blendings, garnet and black or green and gold, with black, green and black in all shades. Olive, myrtle, blue, wine, crimson, tan, brown, lavender, fawn, in all their different shades and combined with rich contrasting colors. Light, medium or dark as desired.
Price each....$0.25 Six assorted patterns...1.30

No. 2265. Finest quality plain black or white Silk or Satin Club House Ties. Elegantly made up for ladies and gentlemen.
Price each.........$0.25

No. 2266. Washable Club House Ties. Made from extra fine madras or zephyr cloth, a woven fabric of superior wearing qualities. New and fashionable colorings. Light and medium shades, fancy stripes, checks, plaids, etc.
Price each.........$0.09
Six for.............. .50

**No. 2265.**

## White Lawn Folded Ties.

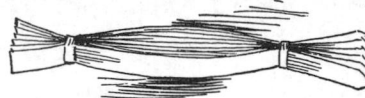

No. 2267. White Lawn Ties, one inch wide, regulation length, good quality. Per doz.............10c
No. 2268. White Lawn Ties, one inch wide, regulation length, fine quality. Per doz.............15c
No. 2269. Very Fine Quality White Lawn Ties, with silk stitched square ends, regulation length and width. Per doz.............20c
No. 2270. Extra Fine Quality White Lawn Ties, with silk stitched square ends, 1¼ inches wide, full length. Per doz.............25c

## Fancy Percale Folded Ties.

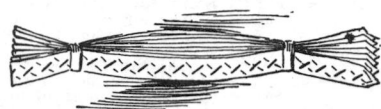

No. 2271. Excellent Quality Fancy Figured Percale Ties, regulation size and length.
Price per doz.............$0.10
Per gross.............1.00
No. 2272. Fine French Figured Penang or Chelsea Cloth Ties, fast colors and new and beautiful patterns. Regular 25c. quality.
Price per doz.............18c

## Washable String Ties.

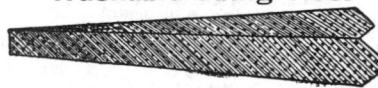

No. 2273. New effects, very fine silk designs, white or light ground figured or plain, reversible, can be worn on either side, the colors are woven in, and the tie is generally sold as linen for 15 to 25 cents each. Our price, each.............$0.07
Half doz. for.............. .35

## White Lawn Dress Bows.

No. 2274. Men's White Lawn Dress Bows for standing collars. Very neat. Price, per dozen ties..50c

No. 2275. Fine White French Lawn Full Dress Bows, with silk elastic adjustable bands for standing collars. Pointed or square ends. Two in a box. Price per box of two, 28c; price per doz. bows.$1.50

No. 2276. Fine White Lawn Dress Bows, square or pointed ends, with elastic bands in back, and silk stitched ends. Extra fine finish. Price each.............$0.10
Per dozen.............1.10

**No. 2276.**

## Silk Embroidered Band Bows.
### For Standing Collars.

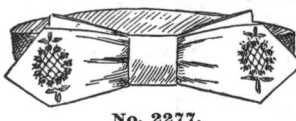

No. 2277. Men's Fine White Lawn Band Bows, with elastic in back, square or pointed ends, richly embroidered. Assorted patterns.

**No. 2277.**
3 in a box. Price per box of 3.............$0.28
Per dozen bows.............1.10
No. 2278. Fine White French Lawn Band Bows, embroidered ends, in new and handsome designs. Square or pointed ends. Silk adjustable elastic band in back. Price each, 15c; per box of 3......40c

No. 2279. White Lawn Bows, large full dress size, beautiful shape, extra fine quality, elegantly embroidered ends, with fine silk floss adjustable band for standing collar; in fact, this is the handsomest white bow made and it is very pretty.
Each, 25c; box of 2 for.............45c

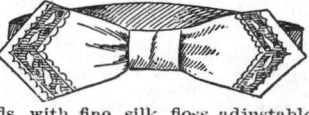

## White Lawn Bows.
### For Turn Down Collars.

No. 2280. Men's Fine White Lawn Bows, with shield and elastic loop for turn down collars. Medium shape. Price per dozen.............25c
No. 2281. Extra Fine White French Lawn Bows, with shield and elastic loop at back; pointed or square ends; silk stitched; very neat.
Price per dozen.............40c
No. 2282. Extra Fine White French Lawn Dress Bows, with shield and elastic loop at back, for turn down collars only. New shape, square or pointed ends. Silk Stitched. Extra fine high grade finish.
Price each, 10c; per ½ dozen.............50c

## Washable Four-in-Hand Ties.

No. 2283. Men's Washable Four-in-Hand Ties, made from fine imported zephyr madras. New and artistic patterns, very neat, and can be washed and laundered. Blues, pinks, tans, browns, lavender, etc., in plain mixtures; also stripes and checks. Very stylish and strictly up-to-date. Retail value, 20c.
Our price each.............7c
6 assorted for.............35c

**No. 2283.**

No. 2284. Reversible Four-in-Hand Scarfs, made of fine imported Percale, medium and light colors, newest effects, very pretty patterns, stripes, checks, mixture crepes and figures; proper styles for young men. Each.............10c
Half-dozen assorted for.............50c
No. 2285. Pure White Pique Four-in-Hand Scarfs, made reversible; alike on both sides and will wash and wear nicely. Price each.............10c
6 for.............50c
No. 2286. Reversible Pure White Corded Pique Four-in-Hand Scarfs. Can be worn on either side. Finest French Cord. Always neat and dressy and always in style. Price each, 19c; 6 for........$1.00

## Windsor Ties.

Windsor Ties are used by men, ladies and children. They are always popular for summer wear. Nothing is nicer for negligee shirts, ladies' waists or children's blouses. They never go out of style and always look cool and comfortable. OUR PRICES ON WINDSOR TIES ARE LESS THAN WHOLESALE. WE IMPORT THEM DIRECT.

No. 2287. The biggest bargain we have ever offered in neckwear. Fine imported French Sateen Windsor Ties. Beautiful, soft, silky finish. In stripes and fancy figures. Light and medium colors. Blue, pink, red, ecru, etc., in fancy combinations. Regular retail value, 10c.
Our price each.............4c
Per dozen.............40c

No. 2288. Fine French Sateen Windsor Ties. Plain black, with handsome lace insertion stripes. Very rich and effective. Price each, 6c; per dozen.........65c

**No. 2287.**

## 12c Pongee Silk Windsors.

No. 2289. Pure Pongee Silk Windsor Ties, 5 inches wide and 36 inches long. Cardinal, light blue, lavender, cream, pink, etc., with neat dots or figures of contrasting shades. Soft and fine.
Price each, 12c; per dozen.............$1.38
No. 2290 Pure Silk Windsor Ties, 5 inches wide, 36 inches long, made in plain colors, cardinal red, light blue, pink, navy blue, black, cream, lavender lemon, lavender or nile green.
Price each.............$0.13. Per dozen.............$1.40

## Scotch Plaid Silk Windsors.
### Real Beauties at 19c.

No. 2291. Fine all Silk Scotch Plaid Windsor Ties. Large or small plaids in bright and attractive patterns. Size, 5 inches wide, 36 inches long. Very fashionable colorings.
Price each.............$0.19
No. 2292. Fine all Silk Windsor Ties. Same as above in neat black and white checks or stripes.
Price each.............$0.19
No. 2293. Fine all Silk Windsor Ties. Extra selected stock. Heavy and soft. We have them in a large assortment of rich and new colorings. Neat, small checks and figures. Light, medium or dark colors. Regulation size and warranted all pure silk. Price each.............$0.19

## Our 25c Windsors.
A Quarter of a Dollar Works Wonders Here.

No. 2294. Extra fine Heavy all Silk Scotch Plaid Windsor Ties. 5 inches wide, 36 inches long. Dark colors with bright attractive plaids, large and medium. Rich and beautiful contrasts. Superb color combinations. Thoroughly good in every way.
Price each.............$0.25
No. 2295. Extra Heavy all Silk Windsor Ties. Same as above in plain black, fine and soft.
Price each.............$0.25
No. 2296. Extra Heavy all Silk Windsor Ties. Same as above in cream white. Price each.............$0.25

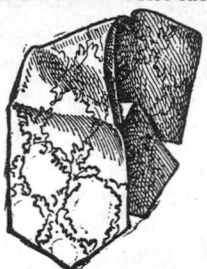

**No. 2294.**

No. 2297. Finest Imported Persian Silk Windsor Ties. 5 inches wide, 36 inches long. Beautiful brocaded patterns in a choice assortment of colorings. Persian, Dresden and Oriental designs. Rich and tasteful combinations, including among hundreds of others the following special popular shades: Claret, Cardinal, Ruby, Navy, Myrtle, Sapphire and Bottle Green.
Price each.............$0.25

## Hemstitched Windsors.
Specially Desirable for Ladies, Misses and Children.

No. 2298. This is a Line of Neckwear of Which we cannot Speak too Highly. We import these goods direct from France and guarantee them to be first-class in every respect. They are made from extra fine quality twilled silk. The dependable, wear well sort that always gives such perfect satisfaction. You will certainly like them if you order them. Made in plain colors, Black, Navy Blue Celestial or Sky Blue, Garnet, Lemon, Cream, etc.
Price each.............$0.19. Six assorted for.....$1.05

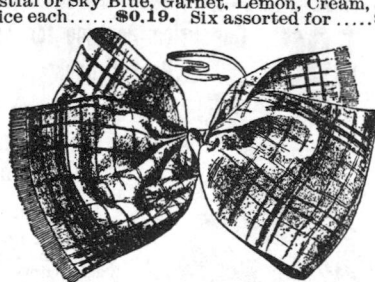

**No. 2298.**

2299 Children's Large Fancy Plaid Bow Ties in dark and bright colors, made of a soft woven silk ribbon, 6½ inches wide, with elastic to go around the collar and fasten with a hook behind the bow. Can be worn with either turn down or stand up collar. Each.............$0.24

## Ladies' Four-in-Hand Scarfs.
Just the tie to wear with Shirt Waists.

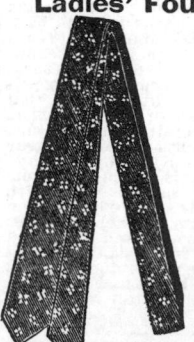

2300 Ladies' Fine Japanese Silk scarfs in handsome light colors and tints, pretty figures and handsome combinations, sure to please.
Each.............$0.18
2301 Newest and prettiest Brocade Silk Effect in high colors, pearl, lilac, robin's egg blue and other pretty shades. Each.. $0.20
2305 Rich Persian Effects is a very swell and handsome four-in-hand scarf, made of fine silk, satin lined, light and medium colors; this is the latest novelty shown.
Each.............$0.43

**ALWAYS ORDER BY NUMBER.**

# Save Money on Handkerchiefs.

**WE IMPORT ALL OUR OWN HANDKERCHIEFS** and offer them to you for about one-third their regular retail value.

**WE HAVE AN IMMENSE ASSORTMENT** of new and handsome patterns. Qualities were never so good and prices never so low. Send us your orders for handkerchiefs and we will give you better value than you have had before.

**ALLOW 7 CENTS POSTAGE** for a dozen handkerchiefs. You can't afford to pay retail prices for handkerchiefs. Our Prices on these goods will be found about one-half the regular retail price, and our customers will do well to lay in a supply at our cut prices. Anything in this line will be sent C. O. D. subject to examination, on receipt of $1.00, balance and express charges payable at the express office. **A 3 PER CENT DISCOUNT will be** allowed if cash in full accompanies your order. ☞ Nearly all our customers send cash in full.

## MEN'S HANDKERCHIEFS.
### Genuine Martha Washington Turkey Red Handkerchiefs.

These are the Old Reliable, Fast Colored Standard Quality Goods, known the entire world over. Do not accept the imitations sold by many dealers. These handkerchiefs we quote below will outwear any other known make.

No. 2306 Men's Genuine Turkey Red Martha Washington Handkerchiefs:

Size,
18x17 inches; per doz....$0.43
21x20 inches; per doz.... .55
24x23 inches; per doz.... .65
28x26 inches; per doz.... .90

### Indigo Blue Handkerchiefs.

The Best Ever Manufactured
No. 2307 Men's Hemmed Handkerchiefs. Genuine indigo blue with white figures and dots. Warranted absolutely fast color. Assorted patterns.

| Size, | Price, |
|---|---|
| 21 inches; per doz..... | $0.60 |
| 24 inches; per doz..... | .85 |

Note:—Where Handkerchiefs are quoted at dozen rates we sell any quantity from half dozen up at dozen rates.

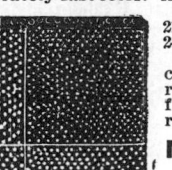

No. 2307.

### Men's Plain White Cambric Hand'fs.

Extraordinay Values, Record Breaking Prices. No. 2309 S. and R. Special Value. Men's fine plain white linen finish cambric handkerchiefs. Plain hem with rib effect border medium size. Price, each.....................$0.05
Per dozen............................ .54

No. 2310 Men's Extra Fine White Cambric Handkerchiefs, large size, linen finish, rib effect border; our own importation, and we guarantee them equal to any 15c handkerchief on the market, Price, each.$0.07
Per dozen... .74
No. 2312 Men's extra large size plain white, linen effect, cambric handkerchiefs. Size 24 x 24 inches. The largest and best cambric handkerchief ever made. Ribbed pattern borders. Regular 25c quality. Our price, each............................$0.10
Per dozen...........................1.00

### Men's Hemstitched Handkerch's.

No. 2313 Men's fine white Cambric Handkerchiefs. Linen finish. One inch hem. Medium size and the quality is exceptionally good.
Price, each............$0.08
Per dozen............ .80

No. 2314 This is certainly the best handkerchief ever offered for the money. We import them ourselves and make a specialty of this particular quality. Retail dealers get 25c for the same goods. Made from finest white Cambric with 1 inch hemstitched borders. Full size.
Price, each..........$0.10
Per dozen...........1.00
No. 2315 Same as

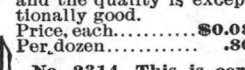

above, with ½ inch hemstitched borders. Very neat.
Price, each ..........$0.10
Per dozen...........1.00

---

No. 2316 Finest quality men's white Cambric Handkerchiefs. Linen effect. Our own special importation. Full size, will wash and wear beautifully. Extra wide, 1½ inch hem.
Price, each....$0.12
Per dozen...... 1.25
No. 2317 Same as above, but made with 1 inch hem. Very fine, soft finish.
Price, each ....$0.12
Per dozen...... 1.25
No. 2318 Same as above, with very fine neat ½ inch hemstitched border.
Price, cash....$0.12
Per dozen...... 1.25

### Men's Pure Irish Linen Handkerchiefs.

Made from the purest and best linen in the world. Every handkerchief we quote, is imported by us direct from the mills. Our prices are less than wholesale and about one half retail price.

No. 2319 Men's pure Irish linen handkerchiefs. Plain white. Large size with finished borders. The best value in the market. You can't beat it, anywhere on earth.
Price, each ..$0.14
Per dozen............1.46

### Pure Linen Hemstitched Hand'fs.
#### Our Own Importation.

No. 2320 Men's fine Irish Linen White Handkerchiefs, with one inch hem. Heavy and strong; size 18x18, warranted extra value, and the same handkerchief that retailers sell at 25 cents.
Price, each......$0.15
Per doz.......... 1.50
No. 2321 Extra quality Pure Irish Linen White Handkerchiefs, one inch hem, size 19x19, fine hand finish, excellent for wear and fine and soft to the touch. True merit in these goods. Try them and you will be well satisfied. Price, each........$0.20

No. 2320.

Per doz............2.25
No. 2322 Same as above with narrow ½ inch hem. Very popular this season. Price, each..$0.20
Per doz............2.25
No. 2323 This is one of our specialties. Imported direct from the mills. Made from extra selected pure Irish linen. Plain white with 1½ inch hem. Extra fine soft hand finish, full size and the equal in wear and finish to any 50c. handkerchief ever sold. Price, each.......................$0.25
Per doz............2.66
No. 2324 Same as above, with very neat one-half inch hem. Price, each........$0.25
Per doz............2.66

#### 35c. 3 for $1.00.

No. 2325 Our own special importation. One of the finest white linen handkerchiefs ever offered for sale at any price. Made from purest stock Irish linen, fine soft hand finish, with wide 1½ inch hem. Full size. One of our very best values.

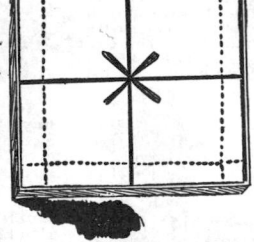

No. 2325.
Retail value, 65c. Our special price, each.....$0.35
3 for...........1.00
Per doz............3.80

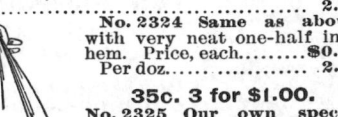

---

### Men's Colored Border Handkerchiefs.

Allow 9 cents extra for postage on a dozen Men's Handkerchiefs when you wish them sent separately by mail.

No. 2326 Men's Hemmed Colored Border Handkerchiefs. Fine soft finish. White center, with fancy colored borders. Assorted colors and patterns.
Price per doz.$0.35

No. 2328 Men's Hemmed Colored Bordered Handkerchiefs, with woven borders. Colors woven in, not printed. White center, fine French finish, soft and fine and excellent for wear. Assorted colors. Full size.
Price, each ..$0.05
Per doz....... .55

### An Extraordinary Bargain.

No. 2329 Fancy plaid Woven Color Handkerchiefs. White, with neat stripes running through entire handkerchief, both ways, forming handsome plaid. Full size. Assorted colors. One of the very best wearing handkerchiefs ever made.
Price, each.. ...$0.07
Per doz.......... .64

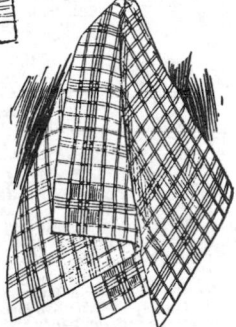

### Fancy Border Hemstitched Handkerchiefs.

No. 2330 New Design Fancy Colored Bordered Cambric Handkerchiefs. White center with one-inch colored border hem. Handsome assorted patterns and colors. Full size.
Price, each... ..$0.06
Per doz.......... .60

#### 10c. For These Beauties.

No. 2331 Men's Fine Cambric Handkerchiefs. White center with particularly handsome colored borders. Hemstitched and soft

No. 2330

and fine in finish. Fast colors in more than 300 different patterns of the seasons, newest and best effects. All colors. Full size. Price, each..............$0.10
Per doz....................1.00

#### 13c. For These Imported Novelties.

No. 2332 Our own special importation. Men's Finest Cambric Hemstitched Handkerchiefs. Colored centers and borders, in the largest and choicest assortment of patterns ever brought to this country. Every design is new, every combination of colors superb. You will like the quality. You will like the patterns. And best of all you will like the price. Price, each.$0.13
6 for........... 0.70
Per doz........... 1.35

No. 2333 Gentlemen's Extra Fine Lawn Handkerchiefs; white center with very neat and pretty hemstitched colored borders. New and handsome patterns. Very latest colorings, 250 different patterns. Fine, light and soft.
Price, each... ..$0.20
Per dozen............2.25
No. 2334 Pure Linen Hemstitched Handkerchiefs, with fancy colored borders and white centers. Newest patterns, handsomest effects. The season's best novelties. Warranted fast colors and thoroughly dependable.
Price, each, 18c; 6 for............................$1.00

**No. 2335 Pure Linen Hemstitched Handkerchiefs**, white centers with handsome and artistic fancy colored borders. Full size. Beautiful as well as thoroughly good. Soft and fine. All kinds and colors. New effects and combinations. Warranted in every way. Perfectly fast colors.
Price, each......$0.25
Per dozen........ 2.66

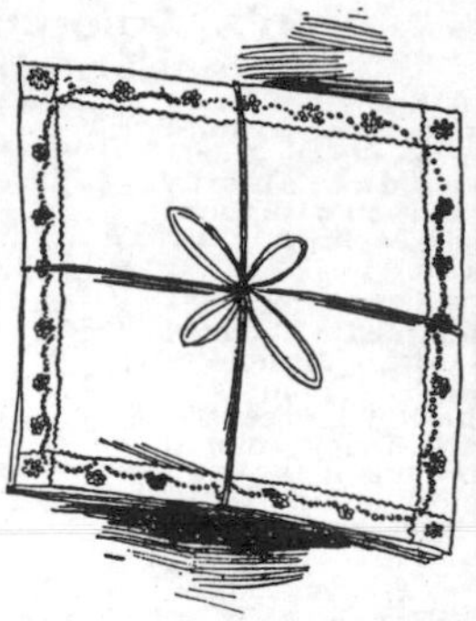

**NOTE.—We sell ½ dozen or more handkerchiefs at dozen rates. It will pay you to buy these goods in dozen lots.**

**SAVE MONEY wherever you can, even on handkerchiefs.**

## Men's Initial Handkerchiefs.

SPECIAL NOTICE—Initial Handkerchiefs come in all letters of the alphabet except I, O, Q, U, V, X, Y and Z.

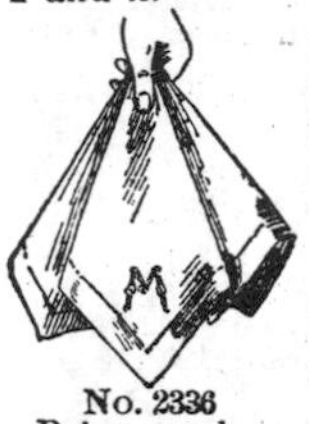

No. 2336

**No. 2336 Japanette Inital Handkerchiefs**, looks and feels almost the same as real Japanese Silk, fine and soft with 1 inch hem, cream white with handsome silk embroidered initials.
Price, each..................$0.15
6 for.................... .75

**No. 2337 Men's Pure Irish Linen Handkerchiefs**, plain white with handsome embroidered initial, full size with 1 inch hem. **Put up ¼ dozen in box.**
Price, each..........................$0.25
Per box of ¼ dozen.......................... 1.45

## Men's Silk Initial Handkerchiefs.

**No. 2338 Pure White Japanese Silk Initial Handkerchiefs**, full size with neat hemstitched border, and silk embroidered initial.
Price, each..................$0.39
6 for...................... 2.10

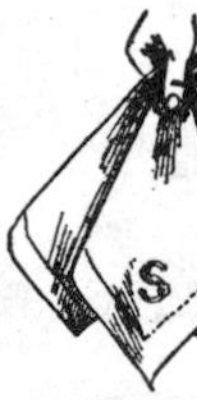

**No. 2339 Men's Extra Quality Very Heavy White Japanese Silk Initial Handkerchiefs**, with wide 1½ inch hem, full size 21 inches, richly embroidered silk initial. Excellent for gifts. Price each..$0.58
3 for....$1.60 Per doz..... 6.25

## Men's Imported Sateen Handkerchiefs.

**IMITATION SILK Fine and Serviceable.**

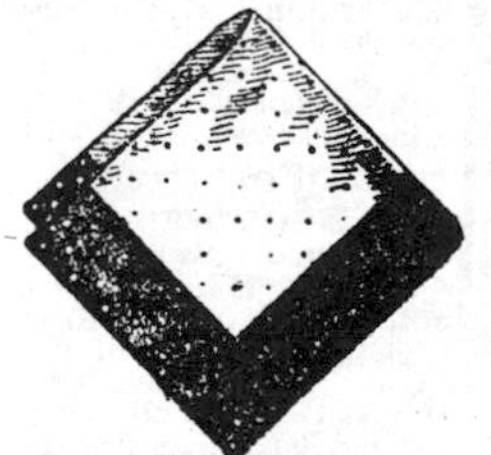

**No. 2340 Imported French Sateen Handkerchiefs.** A good imitation of silk, full large size, fine soft finish, fancy wide navy blue and white dotted, and figured borders and figured centers, warranted fast colors. Very handsome and dressy.
Price, each.......$0.08
Per dozen....... .90

**No. 2341** Same as above in handsome red and white effects. Price, each..........................$0.08
Per dozen.......................... .90

## Men's Japanette Handkerchiefs.

**No. 2342 Men's Cream White Imitation Silk Japanette Handkerchiefs**, size, 19x19, with 1½ inch hemstitch. Price, each..........................$0.13
Per dozen.......................... 1.45

## Silk Handkerchiefs.

We sell Silk Handkerchiefs at lower prices than any dealer in America, we except none, retailer wholesaler, or importer.

We import our goods, buy in large quantities for spot cash, and on our one small profit basis, with no allowance for bad debts, no traveling men's expenses, our prices will astonish and please our customers.

Look carefully at the following bargains and don't fail to include a few of our silk handkerchiefs with your first order.

## Men's Plain White Silk Handkerchiefs.

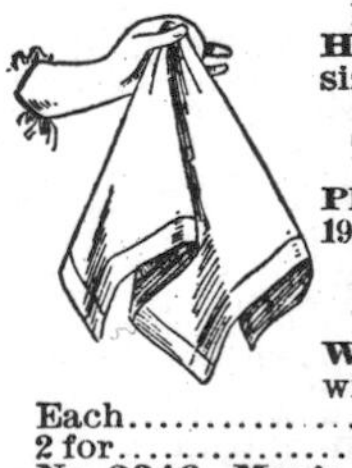

**No. 2343 Men's Plain White Hemstitched Silk Handkerchief**, size, 19x19, with ½ inch hem.
Each..........................$0.25
6 for.......................... 1.40

**No. 2344 Extra Heavy Men's Plain White Silk Handkerchief**, 19x19, regular 50c. goods.
Each..........................$0.35
3 for.......................... 1.00

**No. 2345 Men's Extra Heavy White Silk Handkerchief**, 20 inch, with 1 inch hemstitched border.
Each..........................$0.48
2 for.......................... .90

**No. 2346 Men's Extra Heavy and Extra Fine Pure Japan Silk Handerkchiefs**, with wide hem, large full size, made up expressly for fine trade. Retails at $1.25.
Our special price, each..........................$0.98
3 for.......................... 2.80

## Men's Plain Black Silk Handkerchiefs.

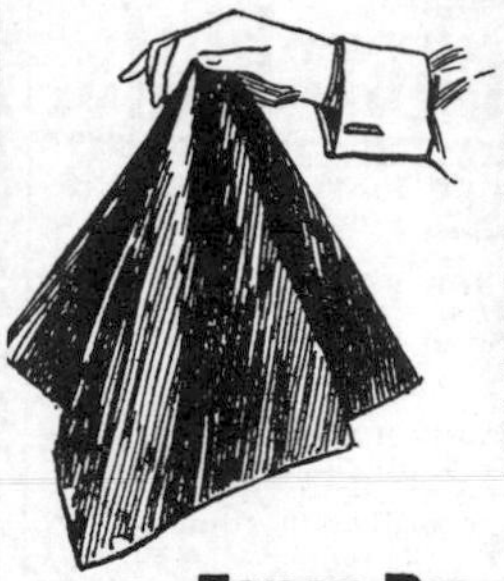

**No. 2347 Men's Plain Black Silk Handkerchiefs.** 22 inch, with neat hemstitched border. These handkerchiefs are our own special importation, we buy them direct from the manufacturers in immense quantities and offer them to you for less than half their regular retail value. Such handkerchiefs have never before been sold for less than $1.00
Our price, each..$0.47
3 for.............. 1.25

## Fancy Brocaded Silk Handkerchiefs.

**For Ladies and Gentlemen.**

**No. 2348 Handsome brocaded silk handkerchiefs.** Ladies' size, assorted colors and patterns. Good quality. Price each, $0.22
Per doz.......................... 2.14

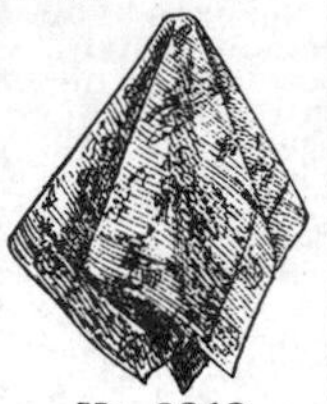

No. 2348

**No. 2349 Fancy brocaded pure silk handkerchiefs.** Rich combinations of colors and attractive patterns, size about 19x19. Black, cream and all staple colors. Most of them have two or more colors beautifully blended. **For ladies or gentlemen.**
Price, each..$0.40 6 for..$2.25
Per doz.......................... 4.35

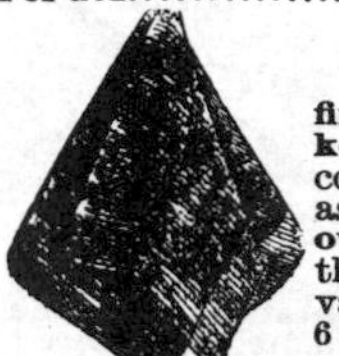

**No. 2350 Men's or ladies' extra fine heavy weight pure silk handkerchiefs.** Large size, very latest colorings, richly brocaded all over, assorted patterns and colors. **Our own importation**, and we offer them at just one-half their retail value. Price, each.........$0.50
6 for..........................$2.75

## MENS MUFFLERS.

On mufflers we have figured our prices lower than ever. No wholesale house can sell dealers at the prices we make to you, and on the basis of more value for your money than you can possibly get elsewhere. We shall hope to receive your orders.

## Special Bargain at 23c to Close Them Out.

**No. 2351** An odd lot of mens extra fine dark colored cashmere mufflers, large size handsome plaid patterns. Regular 50c value, we offer this lot until sold at less than half price. All bright new clean goods, an odd lot we bought from a retiring manufacturer at a sacrifice. Your choice of the lot.
Price, each...$0.23
Per dozen.... 2.60

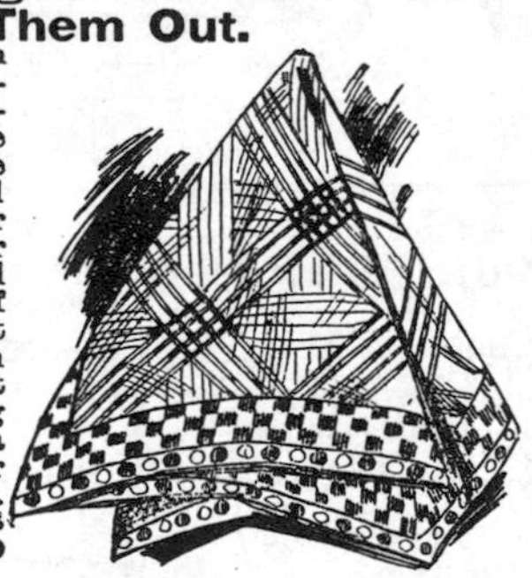

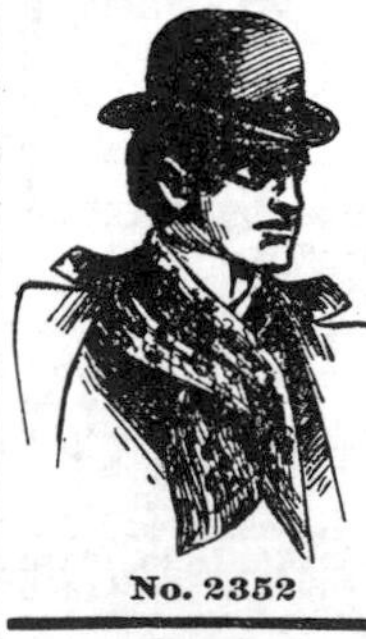

No. 2352

**No. 2352 Imported Saxony Wool Mufflers.** Fine Saxony wool, soft as silk, good weight goods, fancy stripe and check patterns.
Price, each..........$0.35

**No. 2353 All Pure Silk Mufflers.** Best silk goods, rich brocaded patterns, large assortment of colors.
Each..........................$0.60

**No. 2354 Pure Silk Mufflers.** For ladies or gentlemen, handsome brocaded patterns of pure silk, in a variety of designs; size 28x28.
Each..........................$0.80


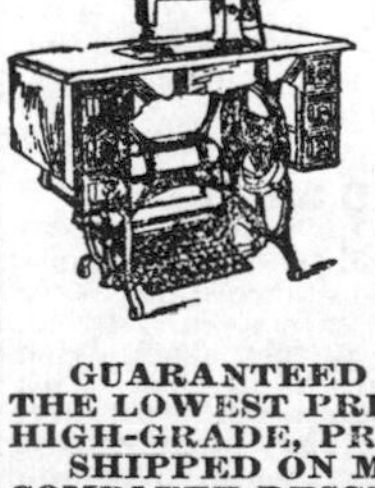

FOR HEMMING......

Ruffling and all kinds of Plain or Fancy Sewing.

Our Minnesota Sewing Machine is Unrivalled

GUARANTEED FOR 10 YEARS, SOLD AT THE LOWEST PRICE EVER KNOWN FOR A HIGH-GRADE, PRIZE WINNING MACHINE.
SHIPPED ON MOST LIBERAL TERMS, SEE COMPLETE DESCRIPTIONS ON PAGES 697 TO 705, or send for SPECIAL FREE CATALOGUE.


## LADIES' HANDKERCHIEFS....

**THE BEST PRODUCTS of leading manufacturers at home and abroad are listed here.** Our stock is selected by an **expert buyer**, a gentleman fully acquainted with values and styles. We are hence in a position to offer the **best**, and with our ability to make net spot cash deals, **we name prices that no dealer can possibly compete with.**

**YOU HAVE OUR GUARANTEE** that any goods not fully up to our representation may be returned.

**REMEMBER** our liberal discount of **3 per cent. off for full cash with order.**

☞ **When Handkerchiefs are quoted by the dozen, the** dozen rate will be allowed on ½ dozen or more of one kind.

## Special Bargain at 5c.

**No. 2355 Ladies' Cambric Handkerchiefs**, with narrow hemstitched fancy colored borders. Assorted patterns and colors, neat and dainty.
Price, each...$0.05
Per doz....... 0.50

**No. 2356 Ladies' fine hemstitched cambric handkerchiefs**, medium size, fancy colored borders, all new choice patterns, assorted colors and designs.
Price, each...$0.08
Per doz....... 0.75

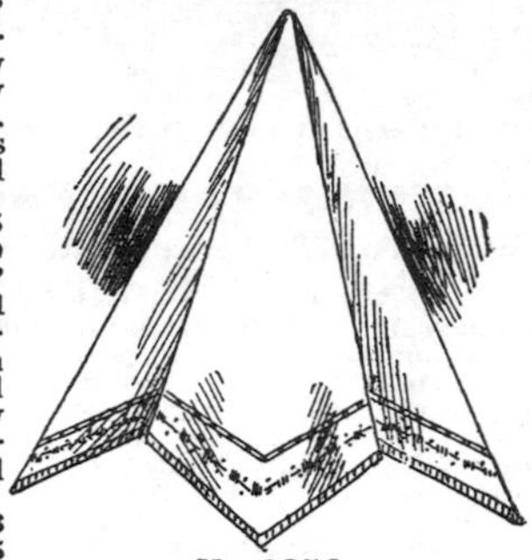

No. 2356

**No. 2357 Ladies' fine imported cambric handkerchiefs**, with ¾ inch hemstitched border, very pretty and neat colored borders Nearly one hundred different patterns. Sure to please.
Price, each..........................$0.10
Per doz.......................... .90

## At 12c Our Own Importation.

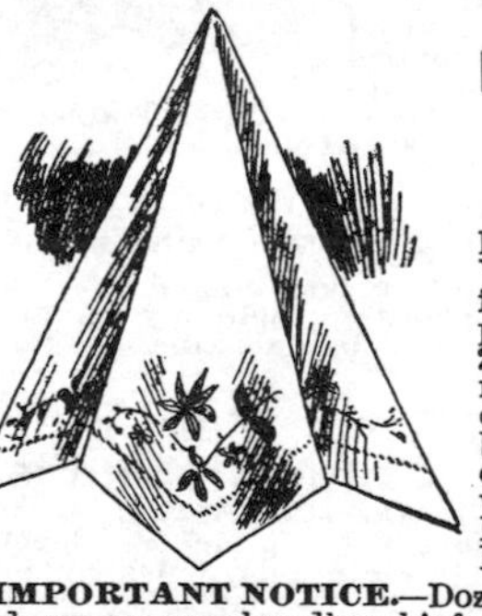

**No. 2358**

**Ladies' Extra Fine Colored Border Handkerchiefs,**

With one inch hemstitched borders. Very dainty patterns in blue, lavender, pink, etc. Regular 25c quality. We have more than 200 different patterns in these beautiful handkerchiefs. Every one a work of art.
Price, each.....$0.12
Per doz......... 1.25

**IMPORTANT NOTICE.**—Dozen rates apply where ½ dozen or more handkerchiefs of the same kind **and** catalogue number are ordered. **It will pay you to buy at dozen rates. Save a few cents wherever you can, even on handkerchiefs.**

**No. 2359**

**Ladies' Fine Imported Lawn Handkerchiefs.**

With very neat narrow hemstitched colored borders, very small dainty patterns in all the new colorings.
Price, each............$0.13
Per doz............ 1.30

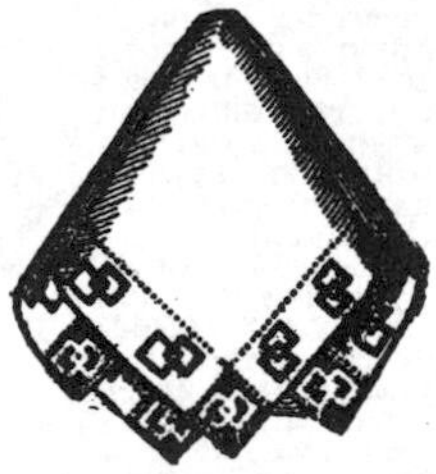

## Mourning Handkerchiefs.

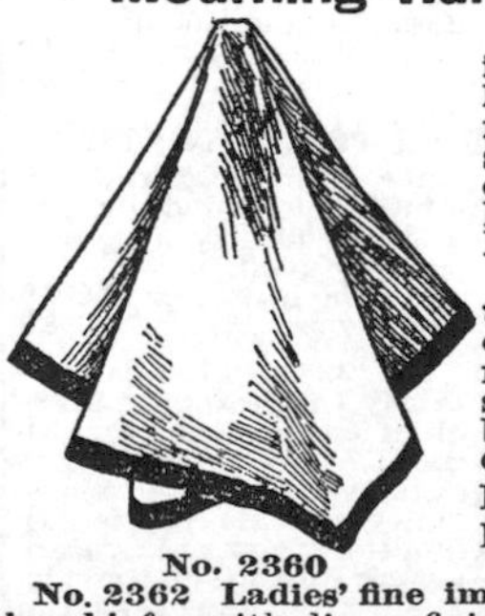

No. 2360

**No. 2360 Ladies' fine imported cambric handkerchiefs**, with neat fast black hemstitched borders. Our own importation.
Price, each.........$0.10
Per doz.......... 1.00

**No. 2361 Ladies' extra fine lawn handkerchiefs.** Genuine British manufacture, fine and soft, with one inch fast black hemstitched borders. Excellent quality.
Price, each........$0.19
Per doz.......... 1.94

**No. 2362 Ladies' fine imported cambric handkerchiefs**, with linen finish, one inch fast black hemstitched borders. Excellent for wear.
Price, each..........................$0.21
Per dozen..........................$2.25

**No. 2363 Ladies' fine imported linen handkerchiefs**, with neat ½ inch fast black borders. Fine soft finish.
Price, each..........................$0.25
Per doz.......................... 2.70

**ONE OF THE ILLS THAT FLESH IS HEIR TO, IS THE LIABILITY TO MAKE A MISTAKE. OUR EMPLOYES ARE MOST CAREFUL, BUT AN ERROR WILL OCCUR, DESPITE THE UTMOST PAINS TO PREVENT. IF WE MAKE A MISTAKE GIVE US A CHANCE TO CORRECT IT.**

## Plain White Hemstitched Handkerchiefs.

**No. 2364** Ladies' Fine White Cambric Handkerchiefs with neat, narrow, hemstitched borders, imported goods and qualities that retail at 10c.
Price each.....$0.05
Per doz........ .50

**No. 2365** Ladies' Fine Imported White Cambric Handkerchiefs, with one inch hemstitched border. Regular 15c quality.
Price each.....$0.08
Per doz....... .75

**No. 2364**

**No. 2366** Our Special Value Imported White Lawn Handkerchiefs, fine and soft, with ½ inch hemstitched border. A positive bargain and one that will surely please you.
Price each.................$0.10
Per dozen................... 1.00

**No. 2367** Ladies' White Lawn Handkerchiefs. Same as above but made with one-inch hemstitched border.
Price each.................$0.10
Per dozen................... 1.00

**No. 2368** Extra Fine Plain White Imported Lawn Handkerchiefs, with one-inch hemstitched border. Very dainty and fine; always sold by retailers for 25c.
Price each.................$0.14
Per dozen................... 1.40

**No. 2369** Same as above, with very neat one-half inch hemstitched border.
Price each.................$0.14
Per dozen................... 1.40

**No. 2368**

### These Beautiful Importations for 9c

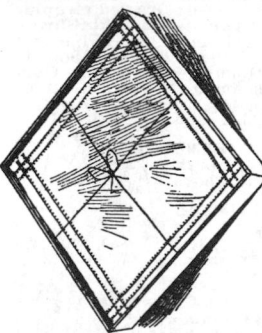

**No. 2370** Ladies' Extra Fine Quality White Linen Finish Cambric Handkerchiefs, with ¾ inch hemstitched border and fancy white, corded design inside of the border. These are our own special importation and are surprisingly hand-same. The finish is extra fine and the quality will certainly please and surprise you. Order half a dozen and we guarantee that you will be well satisfied.
Price each.....$0.09
Per doz......... .90

**No. 2370**

NOTE. Dozen rates apply where half a dozen or more of the same kind of handkerchiefs are ordered. Save money by purchasing handkerchiefs at dozen rates.

### Pure Irish Linen Handkerchiefs.
**Every One Warranted.**

**No. 2371** Ladies' Pure Irish Linen White Handkerchiefs, with narrow hemstitched borders. Regular 20c quality when bought at retail. Price each...........$0.10
Per dozen................... 1.00

**No. 2372** Ladies' All Linen White Hemstitched Handkerchiefs, warranted pure Irish linen, one-inch hem. Our own importation. They usually retail at 25c.
Our price each.................$0.14
Per dozen................... 1.40

**No. 2371**

**No. 2373** Fine Irish Linen Handkerchiefs, plain white, with neat, one-half inch hemstitched borders, warranted all pure linen, soft and smooth.
Price each.................$0.20
Per dozen................... 2.10
**No. 2374** Fine Irish Linen Ladies' Handkerchiefs. Same as above with one-inch wide hemstitched borders. Price each.................$0.20
Per dozen................... 2.10

**No. 2375** Ladies' Extra Selected Pure White Irish Linen Handkerchiefs, with one-half inch hemstitched borders, fine and soft, high-class finish, warranted first-class in every particular. We import them direct and offer them at less than regular wholesale price.
Price each.................$0.25
Per dozen................... 2.70
**No. 2376** Ladies' High-Class Irish Linen Handkerchiefs. Same as above with one-inch hemstitched borders. Price each.................$0.25

**No. 2375**
Per dozen................... 2.70

### At 35c or 3 for $1.00.

**No. 2377** Our Own Special Importation Ladies' Pure White Extra Superfine Irish Linen Handkerchiefs, with one-half inch fine hemstitched borders. These handkerchiefs are the best value we have ever offered. They are fine and soft as silk and are warranted all pure linen of the very best kind. There is real satisfaction in buying handkerchiefs of this sort. Retail merchants ask and get 65c for the same goods.
Our price, each.............$0.35
3 for....................................... 1.00
Per dozen................... 3.75

**No. 2377**

### Ladies' Embroidered Handkerchiefs.

**No. 2378** Ladies' Scalloped Swiss Handkerchiefs. Neat chain stitch edge with silk embroidered corner. Very neat designs.
Price, each......$0.06
Per dozen...... 0.58
**No. 2379** Ladies' Extra Fine White Chiffonette Handkerchiefs, with neat one-inch hemstitched borders. Beautiful floral designs embroidered in corner in handsome colored silk.
Price, each......$0.10
Per dozen........ 1.00

**No. 2378**

**No. 2380** Ladies' Fine Imported Hemstitched White Lawn Handkerchiefs, with rich silk embroidery all around inside of hem. Specially neat designs and new and dainty colorings. Regular 25c quality.
Price, each.....$0.14
Per dozen....... 1.40
**No. 2381** Ladies' Fine Swiss Handkerchiefs. Plain white with scalloped edges and embroidered borders. All pure white, soft and fine. Price, each..$0.15
Per dozen...... 1.58

**No. 2380**

**No. 2382** Very Fine Sheer Scalloped Edge Snow White Swiss Handkerchiefs. New design borders and very dainty embroidered borders. Our own special importation direct from Switzerland. Retail value, 35c.
Our price, each $0.18
Per dozen...... 1.90

ALWAYS GIVE CATALOGUE NUMBER WHEN ORDERING HANDKERCHIEFS

### 19c. Lace Border Handkerchiefs.

**No. 2383** Ladies' Extra Quality Fine Imported Cambric Handkerchiefs. White with one-inch scalloped edge lace borders. Entirely new designs and very pretty effects.
Price, each....$0.19
3 for.......... 0.50
Per dozen..... 1.90

Buy Your Handkerchiefs in dozen lots. It will pay you to do it.

### Ladies' Fine Snow White Swiss Handkerchiefs.

**No. 2384**

Beautifully embroidered in dainty patterns Scalloped edges with fine open work designs. Hundreds of charming patterns. Our own special importation.
Price, each.....$0.25
6 for.......... 1.35
Per dozen........ 2.64

---

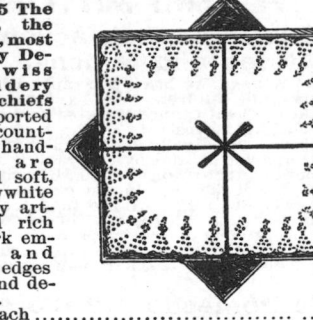

**No. 2385** The Prettiest, the Daintiest, most Delicately Designed Swiss Embroidery Handkerchiefs ever imported into this country. These handkerchiefs are fine and soft, pure snow white with very artistic and rich open work embroidery and scalloped edges. Dainty and dependable.
Price, each............................$0.35
Three for................................. 1.00

### Ladies' Initial Handkerchiefs.

NOTICE.—Initial Handkerchiefs are made with all letters of the alphabet except I, O, Q, U, V, X, Y and Z.

**No. 2386** Pure White Irish Linen Initial Handkerchiefs, hemstitched border with white embroidered initial in corner. Always state just what letter you wish. Price, each....$0.23
Six for.............. 1.30

**No. 2387** Ladies' Pure Cream White Japanese Silk Handkerchiefs, with hemstitched border and silk embroidered initial in corner. Soft and fine.
Price, each..................$0.25
Six for...................... 1.35

### Ladies' Fancy Silk Embroidered Handkerchiefs.

**No. 2388** Fine Imported White Silk Handkerchiefs, with scalloped edges and handsome contrasting colored silk embroidery, pink, blue, lilac, olive, cardinal, etc. Very neat and dainty.
Price, each..................$0.12
Per doz.................... 1.40

**No. 2389** Ladies' Extra Fine Imported Pure Silk Handkerchiefs, cream white with scalloped and embroidered borders, delicately tinted colorings, and rich floral designs. Size, 11x11 inches. We import these handkerchiefs direct from Japan, and offer them at an extremely low price. Assorted patterns and colors, Price, each...$0.18
Three for............ .50

**No. 2390** Very Rich and Attractive Pure Silk Handkerchiefs. Cream white with beautiful fancy colored silk embroidery and scalloped edges and artistic open work designs. The handsomest colorings ever brought to America. Fine and soft, and high class in every respect. Retail value never less than 50 cents.
Our price, each......$0.25
Six for.............. 1.35

### Childrens' Handkerchiefs.

**No. 2392** Childrens' Fancy Bordered Cambric Handkerchiefs. Very neat hemmed borders. A choice assortment of new and novel colorings and pretty designs. We make a specialty of these handkerchiefs and sell them at less than your retail merchant can buy them. Owing to the remarkable low price we make on these goods, we cannot sell less than one dozen of them.
Price per dozen................$0.17

### The Greatest of All Bargains

**No. 2394** A B C HANDKERCHIEFS 18c PER DOZEN. Childrens' Cambric Handkerchiefs, with neat hemmed border. Complete alphabet printed in center with fancy pictorial designs around the border. Useful as well as instructive.
Price per dozen................$0.18

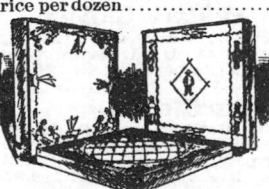

**No. 2395** Little Beauties for Little People. Fancy Hemmed Cambric Handkerchiefs in a large assortment of new and beautiful patterns. Handsome pictorial patterns, new Brownie figures, maps, fancy figures, etc., etc. Always sure to please the children as well as instruct them. Rich and attractive colorings, including some new and charming patterns just imported from Europe. Order a dozen assorted patterns, you will be sure to like them and want more of them. Price per dozen.................$0.25

## GLOVES AND MITTENS.

### We Guarantee Satisfaction in Gloves and Mittens.

In this department we have a complete line for men women and children. We have everything from the cheapest oil tanned working gloves to the finest imported kid gloves.

We buy these goods direct from the manufacturers, in immense quantities, and by contracting for the entire output of a factory on a spot cash basis, which we often do, we get the very lowest possible figures at which they can be sold. We are thus enabled to offer them to you at prices heretofore unheard of. We guarantee every pair of gloves or mittens to be just as they are represented in the quotation. **Your money back** if you are not satisfied.

### Men's Domestic Kid Gloves.

**Sizes, 8 to 10½ Only.**

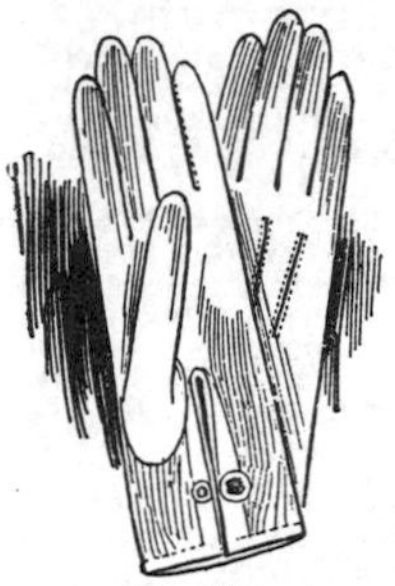

No. 2401.

**No. 2400 Men's standard quality unlined domestic kid gloves.** Smooth carefully selected stock, stitched backs and patent buttons, sizes 8 to 10½ only, dark brown colors only.
Price, per pair.........**$0.48**

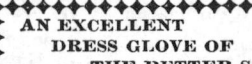

**Special Men's Stock Domestic Kid Glove.**
**No. 2401**
One button with soft dress finish, stitched backs. Good weight and very durable. Black or brown, sizes 8½ to 10½ only.
Price per pair..........**$0.75**

### Men's Fine Kid Dress Gloves.

**Sizes 7¼ to 10½.**

**No. 2402 Men's Imported Stock Kid Gloves,** fine dress finish, medium weight with new welt stitched backs and patent buttons. Silk sewed throughout. **All the new shades,** browns, tans and English reds. Sizes, 7¼ to 10½. Price per pair........**$0.95**

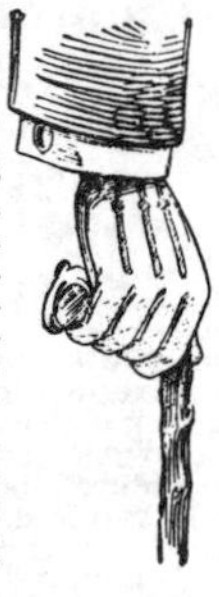

**AN EXCELLENT DRESS GLOVE OF THE BETTER SORT.**
**No. 2403** These gloves are made from real kid, handsomely finished and are very dressy. Made with patent buttons and gusseted between the fingers; stitched backs; beautiful shades of brown, tan, ox blood, black or white. Sizes, 7 to 10½. Always state size and color desired.
Price per pair..........**$1.25**

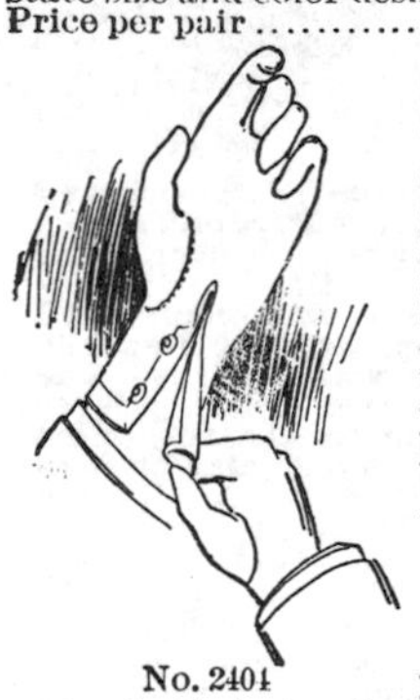

No. 2404

**No. 2404 Men's Extra Selected Real Imported Kid Gloves.** Made from the best cape stock, fine and soft; very handsome and guaranteed to be the equal of any $2.00 kid glove on the market. Made and finished in the very best manner possible, stitched with silk throughout; neatly stitched backs. Colors, brown, h ox tan, mode or Englis snap blood red. Two patent buttons. Sizes, 7 to 10.
Price of pair..........**$1.45**

### Light Weight Driving Gloves.

**No. 2405 Men's Mocha Driving Gloves** similar to castor buck but softer and smoother. Made with one button and out seams. Sizes 7½ to 10½. Browns and tans only. **Warranted genuine Mocha.**
Price per pair..........**$0.95**

**No. 2406 Finest Quality Velvet Finish Genuine Mocha Driving Gloves;** unlined, with two patent snap buttons; silk sewed throughout and silk covered seams on backs. These gloves are noted particularly for their excellent wearing qualities and soft fine finish. They have long been **the most popular Driving Glove on the market.** They are light weight and fit as perfectly as the finest kid glove. Made in browns and tans only. Sizes 7½ to 10½.
Price per pair..........**$1.25**

### White Cotton Military Gloves.

**No. 2407 Men's regular made, set in thumb, White Cotton Military Gloves.** Good weight, very durable and neat fitting. Price per Pair.......**$0.12**
Per dozen pairs..........1.35

### Black Berlin Gloves.

**No. 2408 Men's Black Berlin Cotton Gloves.** Good weight; neat and very durable; elastic adjustable wrists. Price per pair..........**$0.08**
Price per dozen pairs..........0.85

### Men's Unlined Leather Gloves.

**We undersell all competition on this class of goods. We will sell you better made and better wearing gloves for less money than any concern on earth. Our prices are shining marks showing the true road to economy in glove buying.**

### Mule Skin Gloves.

**Here's value for you that will open your eyes. Your pocket book too, if you're wise.**

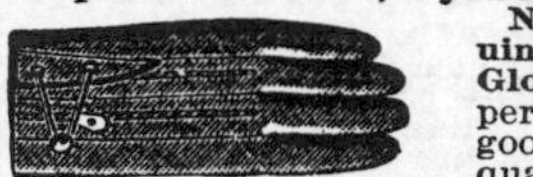

**No. 2420 Men's genuine unlined Mule Skin Gloves.** Not very pretty, perhaps, but full of real goodness and wearing qualities. Tough and strong yet not stiff or clumsy. Warranted to wear long and wear well. Made with string fastener.
Price per pair........**$0.23** Per dozen pairs.**$2.45**

**No. 2421 Mens' Yellow, Oil Tanned, Heavy, Unlined, Grained Leather Gloves,** with cord fasteners. Full size and excellent value. Price, per pair.**$0.25**
Per dozen pairs..........2.70

### Mens' White Napa Goat Gloves.

**No. 2422 Mens' Genuine Unlined White Napa Tanned Goat Skin Gloves,** light weight, soft and pliable and very tough. Price, per pair........**$0.25**
Per dozen pairs..........2.70

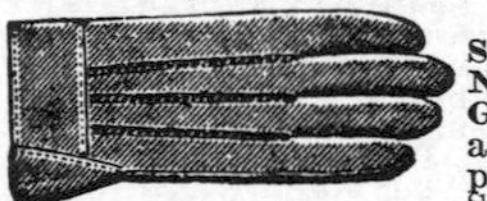

**No. 2423 Mens' Extra Selected White Unlined Napa Tanned Goat Skin Gloves,** extra well made and sewed, cord backs and patent string fasteners. Soft and pliable, wide band tops. Price, per pair..........**$0.35**
Per dozen pairs..........3.90

### Olive Napa Tanned Goat Gloves.

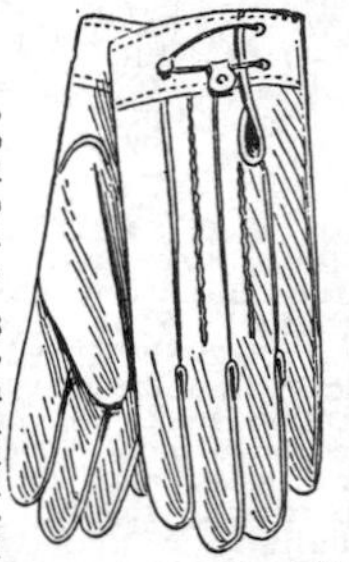

**No. 2424 The Real Thing. Men's Medium Heavy, Olive Color, Genuine Napa Tanned Goat Skin Gloves.** Unlined, made with stitched backs, wide band tops and patent cord fasteners. Soft and pliable and fire proof.
Price, per pair..........**$0.48**

**No. 2425 Men's Heavy Unlined Oil Tanned Yellow Grain Leather Gloves,** full size with cord stitched backs and band wrists; extra well made and sewed. Patent back string fastener. Clear stock and warranted to wear. Price per pair..........**$0.39**

**No. 2426 Men's Extra Selected Stock Yellow Oil Tanned Unlined Grain Leather Gloves.** Heavy weight, strong and dependable. Overstitched welt backs, and broad band wrists. Patent back string fasteners. Price, per pair..........**$0.45**

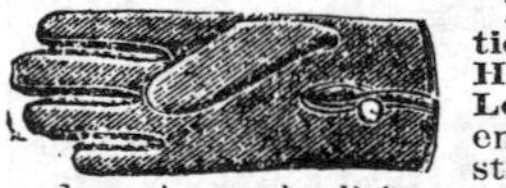

**No. 2427 An Exceptional bargain. Men's Heavy Oil Tanned Grain Leather Gloves,** with patent button fastener, stitched backs, extra well made and sewed. Price per pair..........**$0.50**

### Genuine Calfskin Gloves.

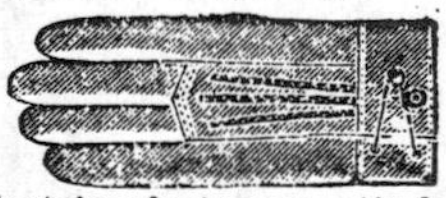

**No. 2429 Men's Genuine Oil Tanned Heavy Weight CalfskinGloves.** The sort that have never failed to give real satisfaction. Extra well made and sewed. Patent string fasteners, stitched backs and band wrists. Warranted genuine calfskin. Unlined and clear stock. Price per pair.......**$0.69**

### Matamora Hogskin Gloves, 70c.

**No. 2430 These Gloves are made from genuine imported Matamora hogskin.** Heavy weight and unlined, with patent string fasteners. They are extra well sewed and finely finished and have attained a world wide reputation for durability. They are rapidly taking the place of genuine buckskin. We recommend them very highly.
Price per pair..........**$0.70**

### Genuine Peccary Hogskin Gloves.

**They Never Wear Out.**

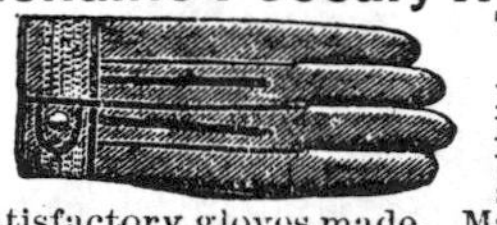

**No. 2431 Genuine Imported Peccary Hogskin Gloves.** The toughest, best wearing and most thoroughly satisfactory gloves made. Made with patent back snap buttons and stitched wrists. Heavy weight and unlined. Actually worth half a dozen pairs of ordinary gloves. Price per pair..........**$0.98**

### Real Unlined Calfskin Gloves.

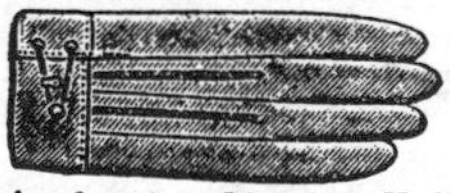

**No. 2432 Men's Real Calfskin Gloves.** Heavy weight, unlined and oil tanned. Made with patent back string fastener and out seams. Guaranteed all solid calfskin, front and back. Full of goodness and will give a vast amount of satisfaction. Price per pair..........**$0.74**

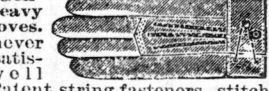

### Men's Super Stout Driving Gloves.

**A line of driving gloves unequalled anywhere on earth.** Every pair is made from first quality prime leather and our guarantee stands back of them. You will make no mistake in selecting any of the following numbers. They are positively the best driving gloves made.

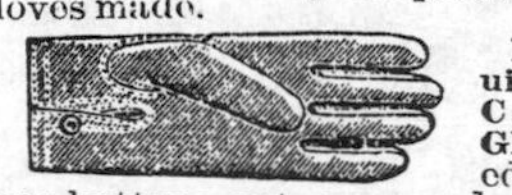

**No. 2433 Men's Genuine Medium Weight Cape Goat Driving Gloves,** with silk stitched welted backs, patent snap buttons, cut seams and silk sewed throughout. Sizes, 8 to 10½. Tan color. Price per pair.....**$0.50**

**No. 2434 Men's Genuine California Tanned Olive Colored Napa Goat Gloves.** Silk stitched, welted backs, set in thumbs, and patent snap buttons. Sewed throughout with silk. Medium weight and unexcelled for wear. **You will line them.** Sizes, 8 to 10½. These are the real olive Napa goat gloves that have given such excellent satisfaction for years. Retail value, $1.00. Our price per pair..........**$0.75**

**No. 2436 The Best Driving Gloves Made.** These gloves are made from the choicest patent dressed cape goat, with welt seam backs, patent snap buttons, out seams and French thumb. Medium weight and sewed throughout with silk. Made ni handsome tan color. Sizes, 8 to 10½. Price per pair.....**$1.00**

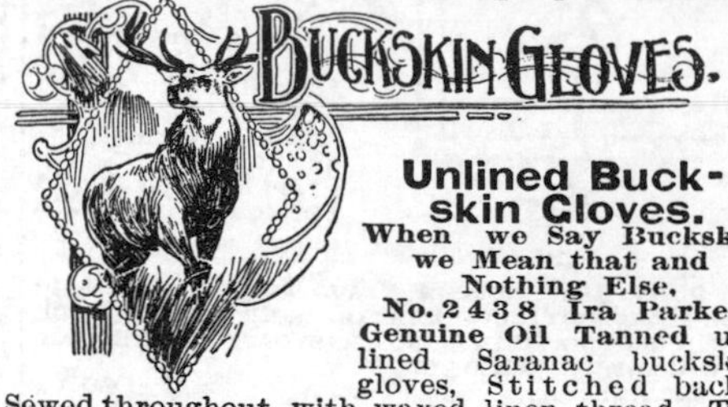


### Unlined Buckskin Gloves.

**When we Say Buckskin we Mean that and Nothing Else.**

**No. 2438 Ira Parker's Genuine Oil Tanned** unlined Saranac buckskin gloves, Stitched backs. Sewed throughout with waxed linen thread. The best buckskin gloves ever made anywhere. Patent Porter string fastener. The best fastener known. Price per pair...**$0.95**

No. 2438

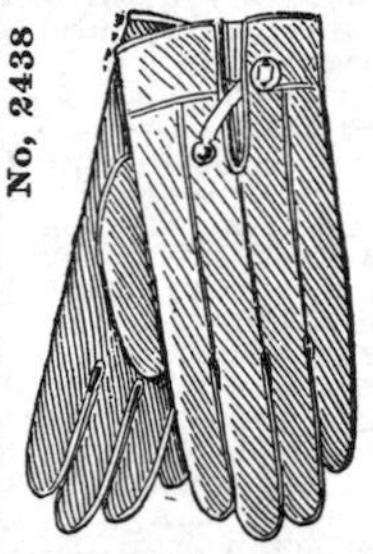

**No. 2439 Ira Parker's Steam and Waterproof** genuine Saranac buckskin gloves. Heavy weight, and very strong. Sewed with waxed linen thread and fitted with the Porter string fastener. Price per pair.... **$0.89**

### Plymouth Buckskin Unlined Gloves.

**No. 2440 Men's Heavy-weight Genuine Plymouth Buckskin Gloves.** Heavy corded stitched backs and patent back snap fastener. Clear stock and the best value ever offered. Price per pair**$0.78**

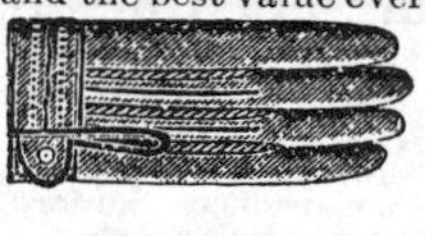

No. 2440

**No. 2441 Men's Extra Fine Soft-dressed Genuine Plymouth BuckskinGloves.** Medium weight. Fine welt stitched backs. Set in thumbs and patent front snap buttons. Genuine table cut, soft and pliable and warranted in every way.
Price per pair..........**$0.98**

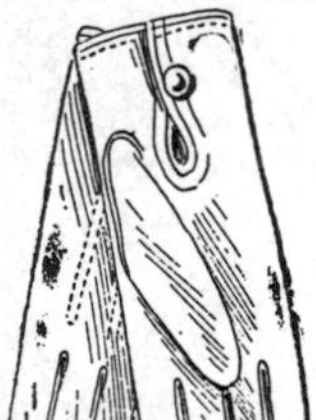

**No. 2442 Men's Plymouth Buckskin Gloves.** Same as above but made in heavy weight.
Price per pair.......... **$1.15**

### Our $1.00 Indian Tanned Buckskin Gloves.

**The Best Dollar's worth on earth.**

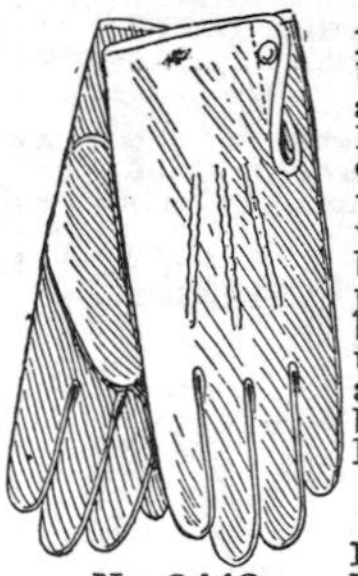

No. 2443

**No. 2443 Men's Genuine Unlined Indian Tanned Buckskin Gloves.** Heavy weight with welt stitched backs and patent back snap buttons. Smooth clear prime selected stock. You can't beat it anywhere on earth. Made under our own special directions and warranted to give the very best of satisfaction.
Price per pair.......... **$1.00**

No. 2441

### Fire Proof Gloves.

**Unexcelled for Wear and Proof aginst Fire, Steam and Water.**

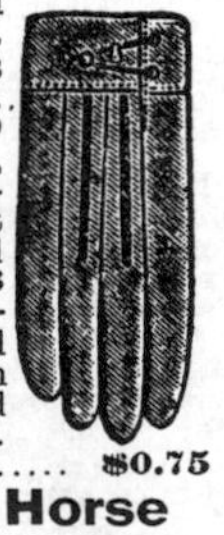

**No. 2445 Men's Unlined Asbestos Tanned Fire and Waterproof Glove.** Light gray color. Soft, smooth kid finish. Stitched backs and patent back cord and hook fastener.
Price per pair.......... **$0.50**

**No. 2446 Genuine Ibex Glove.** Fire, water and steam proof. Yellow asbestos tan with stitched backs and patent cord and hook fastener. Band wrists and extra well sewed. Price per pair **$0.58**

**No. 2447 Genuine Asbestos Cordovan** horsehide gloves. Specially adapted for railroad men. Fire, water and steam proof. Heavily stitched backs and patent back cord and hook fastener. Heavy and tough. Price per pair..........**$0.75**

### The Asbestol Cordovan Horse Hide Gloves.

**The Best Fire-proof Glove in the World.**

**No. 2448 Genuine Asbestol Cordovan Horsehide Gloves.** Special tannage. Guaranteed to remain soft and pliable, and to be proof against heat, steam, boiling water and cold water. Specially desirable for railroad work and mining, as well as farming, driving and all pursuits requiring superior wearing qualities. Sewed throughout with waxed thread. Stitched backs, banded wrists, and patent cord and snap fasteners. There is but one genuine asbestol cordovan horsehide fire-proof glove in the market.
Price per pair..........**$0.85**

OUR CATALOGUE IS ISSUED REGULARLY IN MARCH AND SEPTEMBER. WE MAKE NO CHARGE FOR THE BOOK WHICH IS ABSOLUTELY FREE. WE REQUEST YOU TO SEND 15 CENTS TO PARTLY PAY POSTAGE. SEND IN YOUR APPLICATION EARLY.

## Small Size Gloves.
**For Youths and Men with Small Hands.**

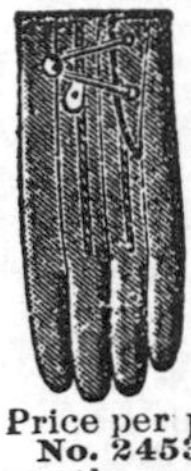

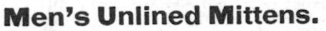

**No. 2450 California** white napa tanned goat unlined gloves. Patent dressed. Plain backs and wrists. Small size. Price per pair .................. **$0.25**

**No. 2451 California napa tanned unlined Gloves,** for youths and men with small hands. Heavy stitched backs banded wrists and patent cord and snap fasteners. Price per pair........ **$0.42**

**No. 2452 Asbestos Railroad Fire Proof Gloves.** Unlined with corded backs, banded wrists and patent back string fastener. Strong and tough. Price per pair........................... **$0.50**

**No. 2453 Olive Colored Driving Gloves** for youths and men with small hands. Genuine Napa goat, stitched, welted backs, banded wrists and patent cord and hook fastener. An excellent glove in every way. Price per pair................ **$0.50**

**No. 2454 Same style glove as above** but made from genuine Plymouth buckskin. Medium heavy weight. For youths and men with small hands. Price, per pair........................... **$0.85**

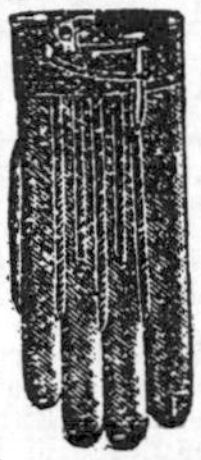

**No. 2455 Genuine Ira Parker Saranac Buckskin Gloves.** Fine oil tan, stitched backs. Banded wrists and Porter's patent string fastener, sewed throughout with waxed thread, every pair stamped and warranted genuine. Small and medium sizes for youtns and men with small hands. Price, per pair...... **$0.89**

## Men's Unlined Mittens.
**FOR CHOPPERS, HEDGE CUTTERS. LUMBERMEN, ETC.**

**No. 2456 Men's Fine Oil Tanned Grain Leather Choppers' Mits.** Large, full size, made from best quality selected stock and sewed with waxed thread. Patent cord loop fastener. Price, per pair........................... **$0.47**

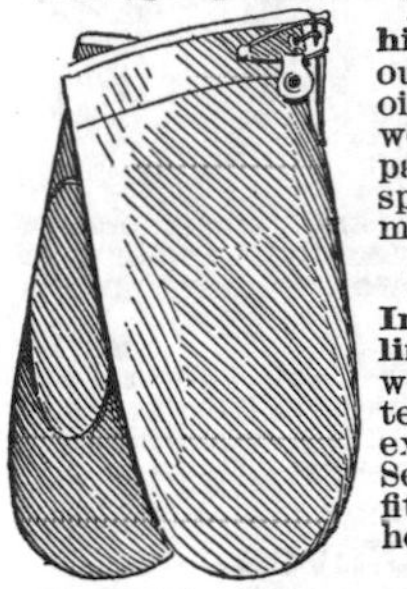

**No. 2457 Unlined Horse-hide Mitten.** Made throughout from splendid quality of oil finished horse-hide leather, welted and wax thread sewed, patent loop fastenings; made specially to wear over a woolen mitten for wood chopping, etc., Price, per pair......... **$0.55**

**No. 2458 Men's Genuine Indian Tanned Buckskin Unlined Choppers' Mittens.** The wearing qualities of these mittens are un excelled. They are exceptionally tough and strong. Sewed with waxed thread and fitted with patent cord and hook fastener at wrists. Price, per pair......... **$0.85**

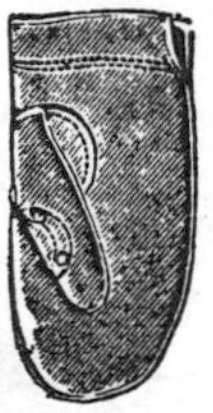

**No. 2459 Extra Super, Stout, Heavy and Thick Indian Tanned Buckskin Choppers' Mittens.** Heavy welt seams and riveted thumbs. Sewed with waxed thread and warranted genuine Indian tan and real buckskin. Price, per pair............... **$1.00**

**No. 2460 Genuine Jack Buckskin Mitten.** Strictly No. 1 selected stock, light yellow tan, double stitched and double thumb, made-out seam riveted thumb. The best in the world. Price, per pair.......................... **$1.10**

## Tile Handler's Gloves.
**With Woven Wire Palms.**

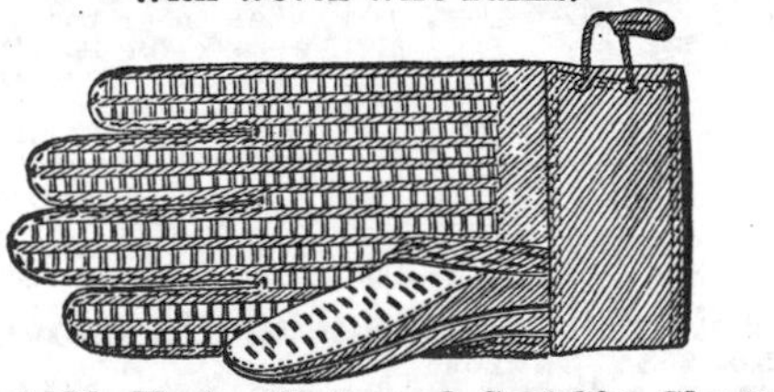

**No. 2462 Men's Oil Tanned Goatskin Gloves.** Steel wire quilted palm and thumb, used by tile handlers and lumbermen. Patent string fasteners; unlined. Per pair.......................... **$0.85**
Per doz ................................. 9.00

**No. 2463 Men's Genuine Oil Tanned Calfskin Gloves.** Steel wire quilted palm and thumb, patent string fastener unlined. Per pair............ **$1.10**
Per doz.......................................... 12.00

## Men's Gauntlet Gloves—Unlined.

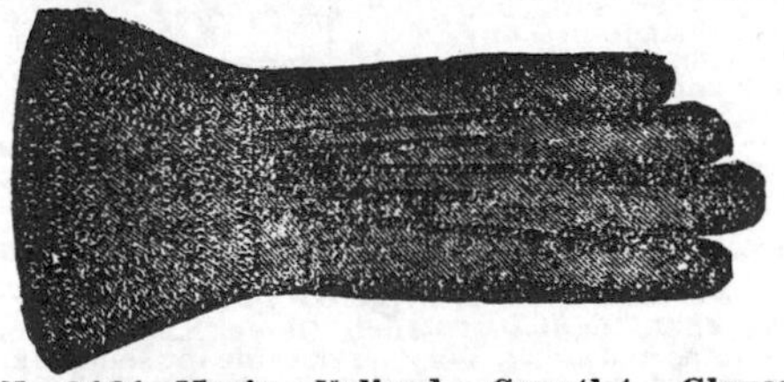

**No. 2464 Men's Unlined Gauntlet Gloves.** Genuine Napa tanned goatskin, medium weight, soft, smooth stock. Fancy overstitched backs, wide gauntlet wrists. Excellent for driving and Bicycle riding. Price, per pair........................ **$0.48**

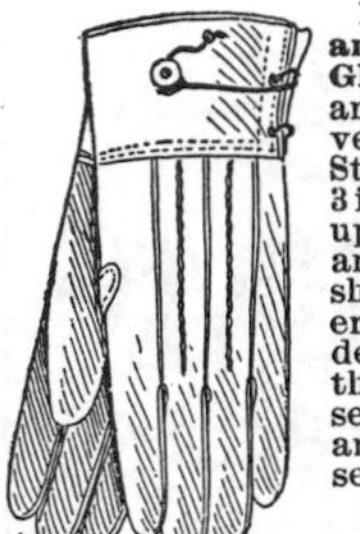

**No. 2465 The Phoenix Fire and Waterproof Gauntlet Gloves.** Real asbestos tan, soft and smooth. Heavy weight and very desirable for railroad men. Stitched backs and welt seams, 3 inch gauntlet wrists that lace up the outer side, can be laced and fastened over the sleeve of shirt or coat. Patent cord fastener. These are exceptionally desirable gloves and are something entirely new. They are sewed with waxed linen thread and are warranted to give good service.
Price, per pair.......... **$0.75**

**No. 2466 Fire-proof Asbestos Tan Horse-hide.** Also waterproof, heavy, yet very soft and pliable, and they will retain their softness; wide gauntlet. All seams wax thread sewed and welted; fancy over-stitched backs. Reinforced thumbs and in fact made up first class in every way. These are the genuine **Asbestos** tan. The process is patented and every pair of the gloves is stamped "Asbestol Cordovan Horse-hide" and is fully warranted. An extraordinary glove. Price, per pair.................... **$0.90**

**No. 2467 Men's Heavy Unlined Plymouth Buckskin Gauntlet Gloves.** Solid and smooth; over-stitched backs and fancy stitched gauntlets. Thoroughly well made and warranted to give satisfactory service. Price, per pair.......... **$1.00**

## Cow Boys' Gauntlets
**The Very Best Made.**

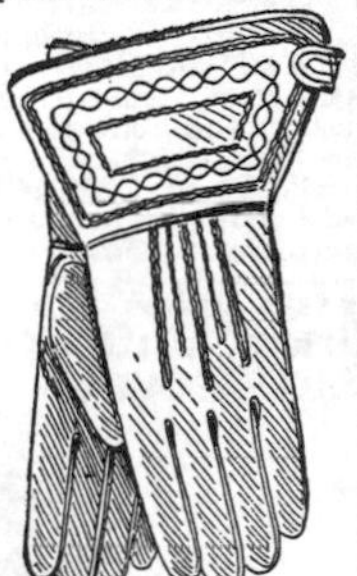

**No. 2468 Cow Boys' Buckskin Gauntlet Gloves,** made from prime selected jack buck, medium weight and unlined. Soft and smooth, made with wide gauntlet wrists. Heavily silk stitched backs and richly embroidered silk gauntlets. One of the finest looking, as well as best wearing gloves ever made. A great favorite with cow boys, ranchmen and cattle men. Also popular for horse-back riding in all parts of the country. Price, per pair. **$1.50**

## The Lone Star Gauntlet.

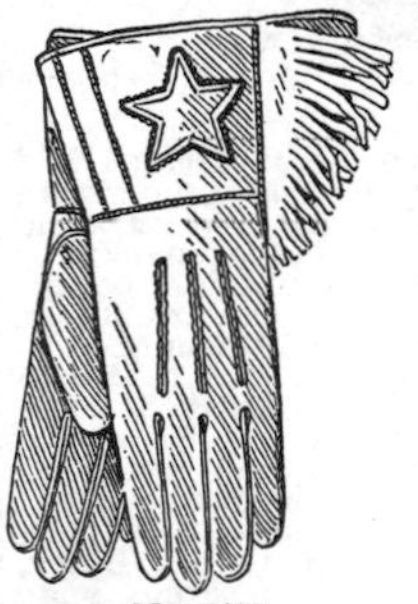
No. 2469.

**The Most Popular Glove Ever Manufactured.**

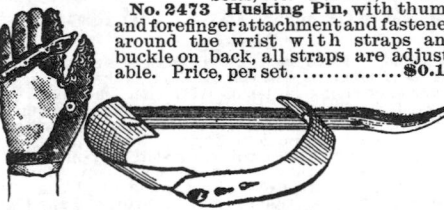

**No. 2469 The Lone Star Gauntlet Gloves,** made from the finest quality table cut Plymouth buckskin. Light yellow color, soft and fine. Fine welt seams, three rows of heavy red embroidery on backs. Fancy embroidered gauntlets, with large five point star embroidered in red in center. Trimmed with buckskin fringe, and finished in very best manner throughout. Price, per pair....... **$1.75**

**No. 2682 Silver Stars** for decorating the above gloves, also for decorating hats, belts, etc. Per doz,...... **$0.70**

**No. 2473 Husking Pin,** with thumb and forefinger attachment and fastened around the wrist with straps and buckle on back, all straps are adjustable. Price, per set.............. **$0.19**

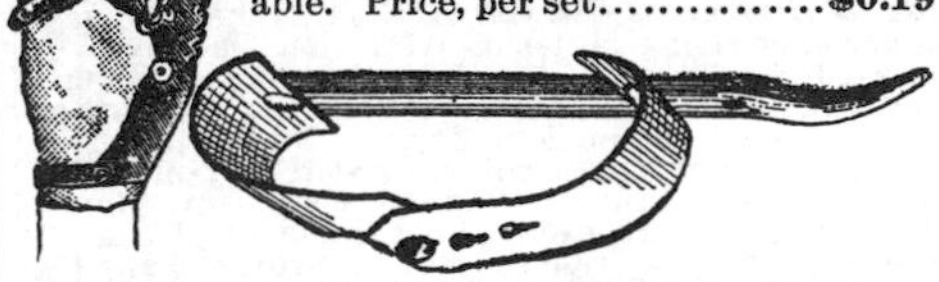

**No. 2474 Husking Pin,** single point with strap. can adjust to any size hand. Price, each...... **$0.05**

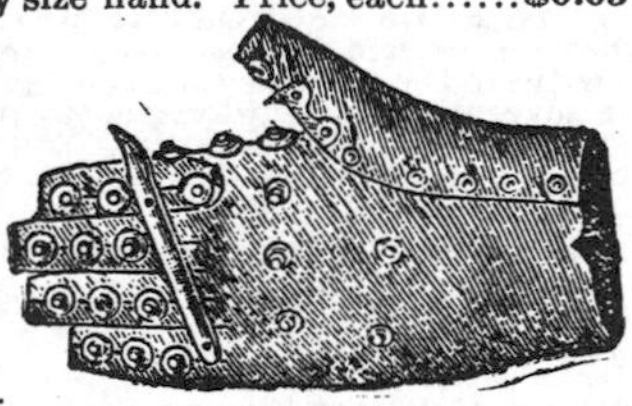
No. 2475.

**No. 2475 Husking Glove,** made of heavy oil-tanned grain leather, soft and easy to the hand; specially tanned leather for this trade. Price, per pair........ **$0.40**

**No. 2476 Men's Best Quality Oil Tanned Calfskin Husking Gloves,** riveted palms and patent husking pin attached. Price, per pair................ **$0.95**

## Husking Mitten.

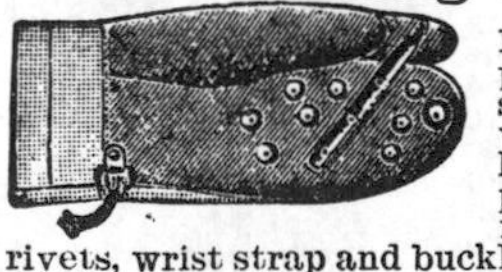

**No. 2478 Made of Heavy Canvas** and palmed with good calf skin, fingers protected with metal plates, steel husking band and metal plates on thumb piece, fastened with copper rivets, wrist strap and buckle.
Price, per pair........................... **$0.36**

**WE SAVE 1-3 ON AGRICULTURAL IMPLEMENTS.**

## Men's Lined Leather Gloves.

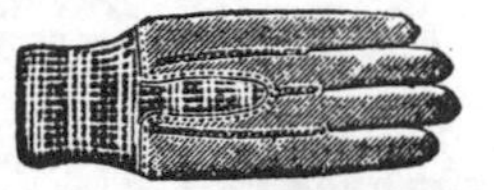

**No. 2479 Is a Man's Fleece Lined Leather Glove,** made with a fancy elastic wrist, double stitched, heavy oil tanned stock. Per pair **$0.25**

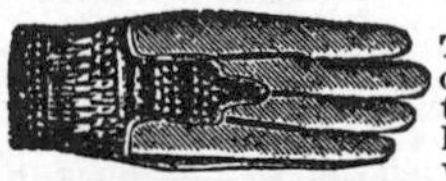

**No. 2480 Lined Oil Tanned Glove,** made of oil grained leather, welted throughout, fancy back and heavy fleece lined, long wool wrist. Per pair. **$0.35**

**No. 2481 Is a Fireproof Arabian Goat,** heavily fleece lined throughout, back sewed seams, patent loop fastenings and a good, warm. durable glove. Per pair.................................. **$0.50**

**No. 2482 Men's Fxtra Heavy Oil Tanned Goat Gloves,** fleece wool lined, string fasteners, thoroughly reliable, wool ribbed wrists and full sizes. Price per pair .................................. **$0.75**

**No. 2484 Same as above in best oil tanned calf-skin.** Price per pair............................ **$0.95**

**No. 2485 Genuine Asbestoe Cordovan Gloves,** warranted fire and steam proof, heavy wool knit ribbed wrists and fleeced wool lining, one of the very best wearing gloves ever made. Price per pair **$0.95**

**No. 2486 Same as above in Plymouth Buckskin** (not fireproof), but will give good substantial service. Price per pair................................ **$0.75**

**No. 2487 Same as above in best grade genuine Napa Tanned Buckskin.** Price per pair. ..... **$1.00**

## Men's Fleece Lined Kid Gloves and Mittens.

**No. 2488 Men's Domestic Kid Glove;** heavy fleece lined, with patent button fasteners; fancy stitching on back. Price per pair.............. **$0.48**

**No. 2489 Is a heavy Fleece Lined Kid Glove;** three rows of fancy stitching on back; patent button fastener. Price per pair.............. **$0.74**

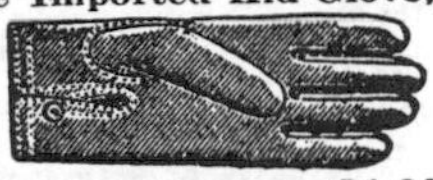

**No. 2490 Is an extra fine Imported Kid Glove;** heavy fleece lined, fancy double stitched back, patent button fastener, is a dressy, warm glove; comes in light and dark brown. Price per pair.................................. **$1.00**

**No. 2491 Mocha Kid, two patent button fasteners,** heavy fleece lined, fancy silk stitched back; comes in dark brown and is a very popular and dressy glove. No better glove made. Price per pair.................................. **$1.25**

**No. 2492 Is a fine Imported Kid Glove;** heavy fleece lined, two button, fancy silk embroidered back, made out of soft and fine stock. A glove that retails in large cities in big stores at $1.75. Our special price per pair...................... **$1.48**

## Men's Leather Mittens.

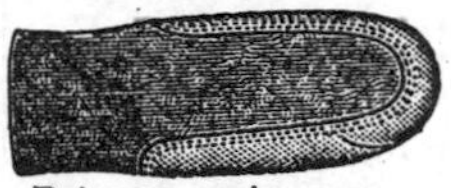

**No. 2493 Is a Leather Faced Mitten,** made of the best quality of wool stock, faced with grain leather; it is as soft and smooth as calf.
Price per pair.................................. **$0.24**

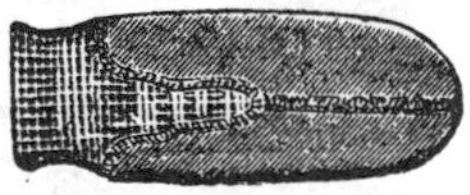

**No. 2494 Is a Lined Mitten,** extra grade, oil stock, heavily fleece lined throughout; knit wrists. Price per pair...**$0.26**

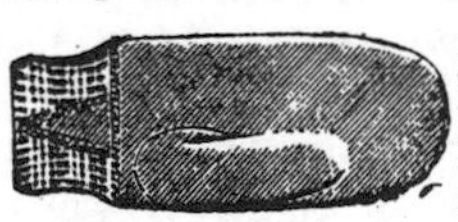

**No. 2496 Is a Horse-hide Mitten,** made of heavy tanned, soft smooth stock, has welted seams and all wool corded wrists; all wool heavily fleece lined. Price, per pair.................................. **$0.40**

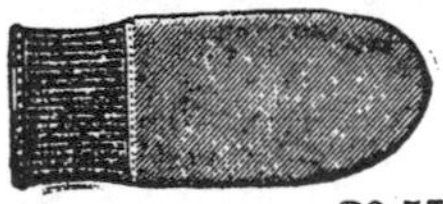

**No. 2497 Men's Buckskin Mittens,** heavily fleece lined, with a fancy all wool wrist, welted seams, durable and warm mittens. Price per pair.................................. **$0.55**

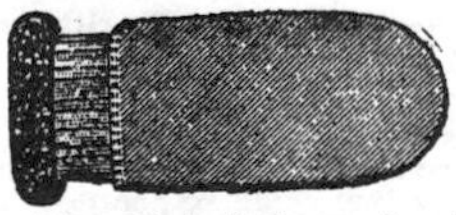

**No. 2498 Extra fine Buckskin Mitten,** comes in extra large sizes, made out of the choicest buckskin stock, has a long all wool wrist with a fancy knit roll top, double stitched throughout. Price per pair... **$0.74**

**No. 2499 Is an extra heavy Mitten.** make out of the finest oil tanned stock lined with pure lamb's wool; no warmer mitten made, has patent loop fastenings and a fancy stitched back. Price per pair.................................. **$0.80**

## Men's Wool Mittens.

**No. 2500 Wool Mitten,** knit of heavy all wool yarn, fulled outside, striped patterns. Per pair.................................. **$0.13**

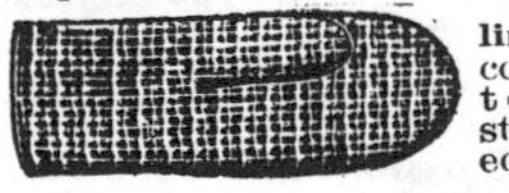

**No. 2502 Is a heavy lined All Wool Mitten;** comes in assorted patterns and fancy stripes, is fancy stitched on the end. Per pair....... **$0.25**

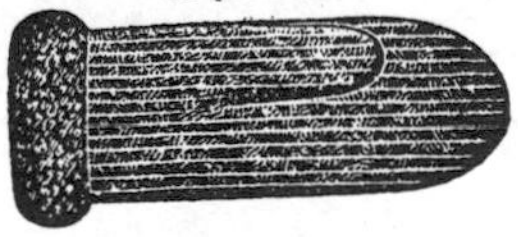

**No. 2503 Is an all Wool mitten;** heavily fleece lined; fancy knit roll top; assorted colors and stripes. Per pair....... **$0.31**

**SHOULD YOU CHANGE YOUR RESIDENCE, BE SURE TO NOTITY US, GIVING BOTH OLD AND NEW ADDRESS, THAT WE MAY BE ABLE TO CONTINUE KEEPING YOU INFORMED ON MARKET PRICES.**

## Kumfort Brand Mitten.

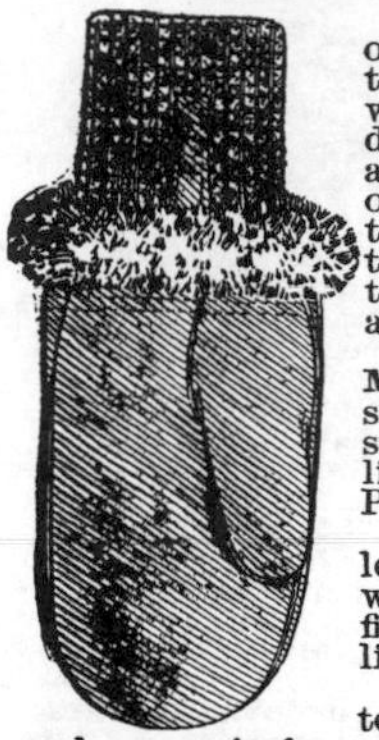

The "Kumfort" Brand Mittens overcome all objectionable features of the old styles. The wrists are made with an elastic double knit web. fitting closely, and giving freely to the action of the hand; this combined with the fringe, serving as a protection against the wind and cold, the most complete and practical article ever made.

**No. 2504 Kumfort Brand Mittens,** made out of fine buckskin, fine welted seams, double stitched and heavily all wool lined, fancy wrists as per cut. Per pair........................ **$0.90**

**No. 2505** Is an oil tanned leather Kumfort brand mitten with fancy wrist as per cut, has fine welted seams heavily fleece lined. Price per pair...... **$0.51**

**No. 2506** Kumfort Brand mittens, made out of a fine Scotch wool, comes in fancy plaids and checks in variety of colors; has fancy wrists as per cut, comfortable and warm mitten. Per pair.................... **$0.46**

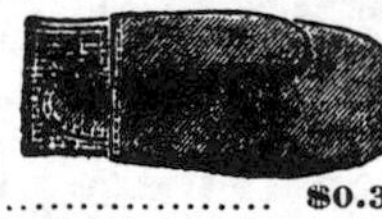

**No. 2507 Boys' Leather Mittens,** extra quality of yellow oil-tanned stock, welted and double-stitched, fleece lined with long T-shaped wrist.
Price per pair...... ........................... **$0.38**

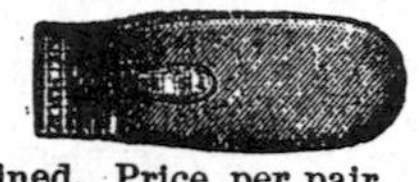

**No. 2508 Boys' Horsehide Mittens,** made of fine tan colored horsehide, all-wool knit wrist, extra long, fancy stitched and fleece lined. Price, per pair................................ **$0.59**

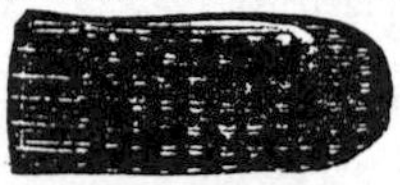

**No. 2509 Boys' Wool Mittens,** all-wool goods, fancy colors, fine fleece lined throughout. Price, per pair............ **$0.24**

## Men's Lined Kid Mittens.

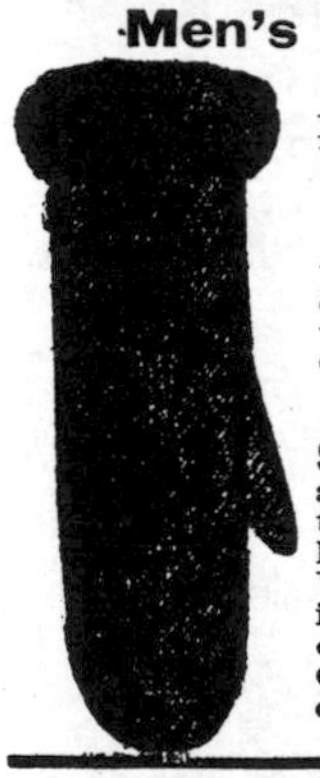

**No. 2510 Is a Men's Fleece Lined Domestic Kid Mitten,** rubber wrist and embroidered back. Price. per pair.............. **$0.48**

**No. 2512 Is a Man's Imported,** wool lined, kid mitt, with fancy embroidered black and spring wrist, trimmed with fine sheared Coney Fur. Price, per pair... **$0.98**

**SPECIAL NOTICE. For a complete line of Fall and Winter Gloves and Mittens of all kinds, see our large Fall and Winter Catalogue, which will be issued early in September. We can save you more money on Gloves and Mittens than any other concern in the country.**

## What the People Say:

**Well Pleased With Groceries.**

ALTON, ILL.

SEARS, ROEBUCK & CO., Chicago, Ill.

DEAR SIRS:—Please find enclosed fifteen cents in stamps for watch. Please send me your large catalogue of all of your goods, and oblige.

Yours truly, C. S. LEHR.

P. S. I received the bill of groceries and am well pleased with them.

**Pleased with Buggy.**

CANTON, ILL.

SEARS, ROEBUCK & CO., Chicago, Illinois.

DEAR SIRS:—My buggy came all O. K., and am well pleased. Yours truly. W. H. JOHNSTON.

**Recommends Our Goods as Best in the World for the Money.**

HILLSBORO, IND.

MESSRS. SEARS. ROEBUCK & Co., Chicago, Ill.

SIRS:—The goods I ordered of you some time ago arrived all right, and were better than expected. I will recommend your goods to my friends to be the best in the world for the money.

Yours respectfully,
LEVI BEVER.

**Wife More Than Pleased With Sewing Machine.**

WILA, MO.

SEARS, ROEBUCK & CO.

Please find enclosed 25c, balance on sewing machine. Sewing machine was received the 16th. My wife is more than pleased with it. Two neighbors have said they will send for one.

Yours truly.
W. T. HEADY.

**"Suit Fits as Neat as Any I Ever Tried On."**

UNIONTOWN, PERRY CO., ALA.

SEARS, ROEBUCK & CO.

GENTLEMEN:—The suit which I ordered of you reached me in perfect safety, and am glad to say that I was perfectly satisfied. It fit me as neat as any suit I ever tried on. I am representing you among my friends every day.

Yours,
ROBERT FINCH.

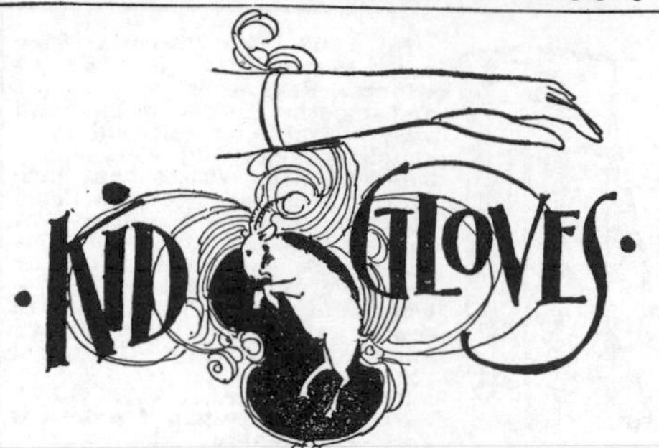


## For Ladies and Misses.

**In this Department** we have selected for the coming season a line of gloves of exceptional quality, rare beauty, and of surpassing excellence in finish, and absolute correctness as regards style. We are strictly up-to-date on ladies' gloves, as you will see by the quotations below. Perfection in fit is one of our strong points. Every glove we send out we guarantee to be the exact size it is marked. Our gloves all run true in size. In ordering always be careful to state the exact size you wish, you will then secure a perfect fit.

**Ladies' Sizes** are 5½ to 8 only.
**Misses' Sizes** are 4¾ to 6½ only.

The size is determined by drawing a tape line around the fleshy part of the hand, close to the knuckles. The number of inches around the hand determines the size of gloves required. Draw tape medium tight.

**SPECIAL NOTICE:—We cannot furnish Ladies' Kid Gloves larger than size 8. They are not manufactured.**

## The New Snap Button Kid Gloves.

**The Most Popular Gloves Made.**

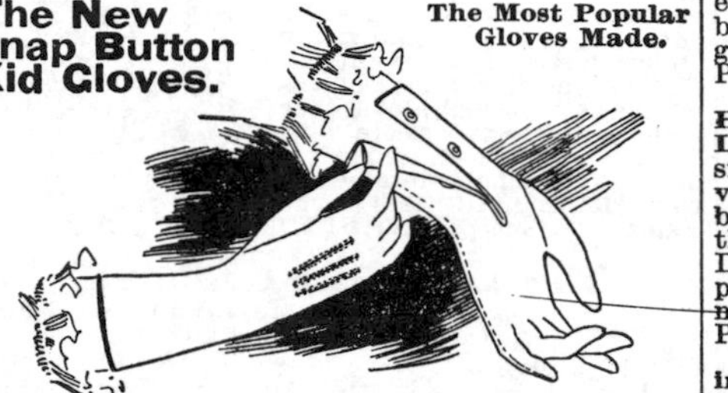

**No. 2520 Ladies' Blenda,** fine dressed Kid Gloves. Extra selected prime stock. Medium weight with three rows of heavy silk stitching on back. Smooth fitting set in thumb. Two patent snap fancy metal enameled buttons. No trouble to fasten. Fine dressy glove and very popular. Colors, Black, White, Tan, Brown or Red. Sizes, 5½ to 8 only.
Price, per pair...................................... **$0.95**

**No. 2521 The Davenport,** ladies' extra fine imported Kid Gloves. Three rows of heavy silk stitching on back. Pique stitched seams. Gusseted thumbs. Silk sewed throughout. Medium weight for street wear. French set in thumbs. Perfect fitting and thoroughly dependable. Colors, Black, Brown or Tan. Sizes, 5½ to 8. Two patent snap enameled metal buttons. Price, per pair.... **$1.15**

## $1.29 For Real Imported Mocha Gloves.

**No. 2522 Here is a glove that is as fine and soft as a piece of silk velvet,** yet it is the strongest and best wearing ladies' glove made. These gloves are made from the very finest grade imported Mocha, Similar to undresed kid but much finer and softer and will wear 50 per cent. better. Made with three rows of very fine needle point silk stitching on backs. French gusseted thumbs and silk sewed throughout. Strictly up-to-date and a glove that will please all who purchase it, Colors, Black, Brown, Tan, Ox Blood Red or Grey. Sizes, 5½ to 8.
Price, per pair..................................... **$1.29**

**SOME FOLKS FORGET to Mention Size When They Order Kid Gloves.** When they do so we have to write to them for size, thus delaying their order for several days. Always see to it that you put down just what size you desire. Your order will then have prompt attention and be filled correctly and to your entire satisfaction.

## Ladies' 4 Button Kid Gloves.

**Sizes, 5½ to 8.**

**No. 2523 The Apollo** Ladies' Fine Dressed Kid Gloves with 4 large pearl buttons. Handsomely made and finished and of a stock that can be relied upon for good service. Sizes, 5½ to 8. Colors, Black, Brown, Tan and English Red. Plain backs. Price, per pair. **$0.69**

**No. 2524 Ladies' Emergo** fine dressed imported kid gloves with 4 large white pearl buttons and three rows of heavy silk stitching or embroidery on back. French gusseted thumbs. Fine smooth soft finish. High grade and thoroughly dependable. Colors, Black, Brown, Tan, English Red or White. Sizes, 5½ to 8. Price, per pair.......... **$0.85**

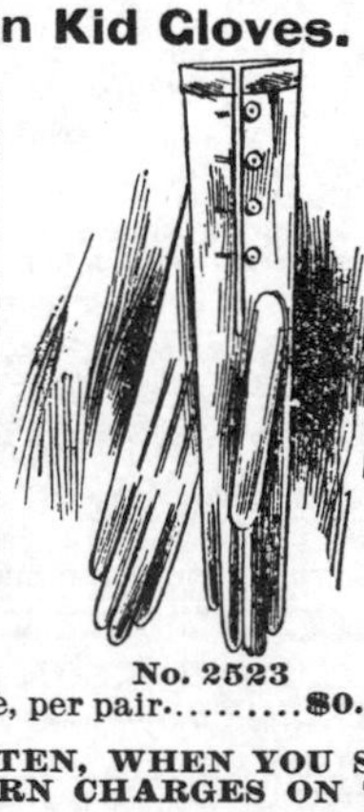

No. 2523

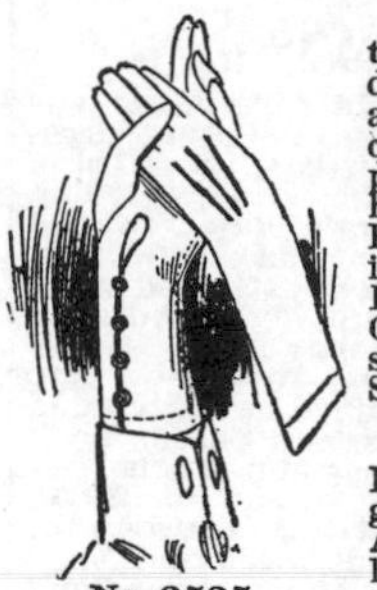

No. 2525

**No. 2525 Ladies' Four Button Neptune.** An imported dressed kid glove of rare beauty and fineness. Made from first quality prime kid. Four large pearl buttons and three rows of heavy embroidery on backs. French gusseted thumbs. Made in all the popular colors, Black, Brown, Tan, Mode, Grey, Navy, Green, Red and White. Always state color and size you wish. Sizes, 5½ to 8.
Price, per pair.......... **$1.38**

**No. 2526 Ladies' Marcean.** Finest dressed imported kid gloves. Extra selected prime A No. 1 stock. Made with four large pearl buttons. French set in gusseted thumbs and new pattern fancy embroidered backs. Gloves that retail in many places at $2.50. Colors, Black, Brown, Tan, Mode, Red, Navy and Green. Sizes, 5½ to 8.
Our price, per pair................................. **$1.75**

## Ladies' Hook Gloves.

**The New Foster Lacing. Four Large Hooks.**

**No. 2527 Genuine Four Hook Foster Lacing Glace Kid Gloves.** Made and finished in the same manner as many of our finest gloves. Fine cord stitching on back, and gusseted thumbs. Sizes 5¾ to 8. Colors black, brown or tan only. Retail value $1.00. Our price per pair.. **$0.85**

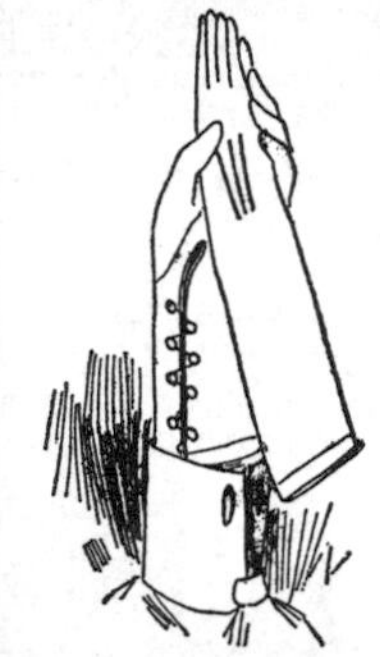

**No. 2528 Ladies' New Style Four Hook Shiller Glove,** genuine Foster lacing. Fine selected dress kid, with embroidered backs and French gusseted thumbs. Perfect in fit and extra fine finish. Colors, black, brown, tan, mode, grey, navy, green and white. Sizes, 5½ to 8.
Price, per pair......... **$0.95**

**No. 2529 The New Four Hook Goethe Genuine Foster Lacing Kid Gloves.** Fine, smooth, soft, dress finish, with very fine narrow silk stitched backs, and patent gusseted thumbs. First grade material and workmanship. Dependable and beautiful; perfect in fit and sure to please. Colors, black, tan, brown, red, navy, green, mode and white. Sizes, 5½ to 8.
Price, per pair.......................................... **$1.15**

**No. 2530 The Zenabia Four-Hook Foster Lacing Glace Kid Gloves.** Finest imported stock, made same as above, with three rows of heavy embroidery on backs. Same colors as above. Sizes, 5½ to 8.
Price, per pair........................................ **$1.47**

## Misses' Kid Gloves.

**Sizes, 4½ to 6½.**

**No. 2532 Misses' Four-Hook Etelka Dressed Kid Gloves.** Genuine Foster lacing, plain, silk stitched backs and gusseted thumbs. Colors, brown, tan or red. Always give size and color when you order. Price, per pair........................ **$0.89**

## Misses' Four-Button Kid Gloves.

**Sizes, 4½ to 6½.**

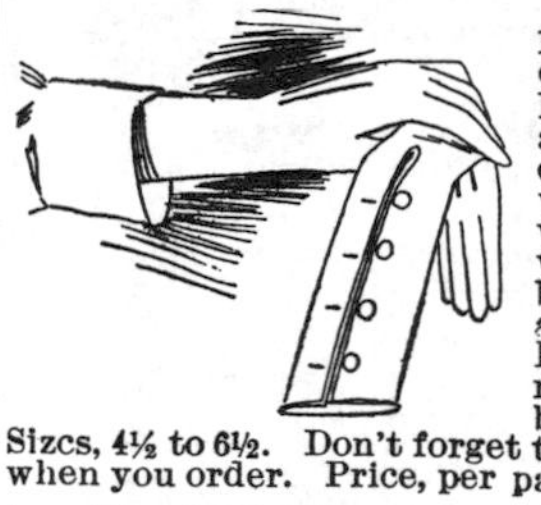

**No. 2533 Misses' Four-Button Bertha Glace Kid Gloves.** Fine imported stock and the very best glove ever offered at anywhere near the price we ask for it. Made with four large pearl buttons, plain backs and gusseted thumbs. Perfect in fit and workmanship. Colors, brown. tan and red. Sizes, 4½ to 6½. Don't forget to state size and color when you order. Price, per pair............... **$0.75**

## Ladies' Undressed Suede Gloves.

**No. 2534 Ladies' Minerva Undressed Suede Mousquetaire Gloves.** Our own special importation and the finest gloves of the kind ever brought to this country. They are made eight button length, open at wrists, with three small pearl buttons. Very soft, fine finish. Made in the following beautiful colors: tan, brown, mode, gray, black and white. High class in every respect. Sizes, 5½ to 8. Price, per pair............................. **$1.69**

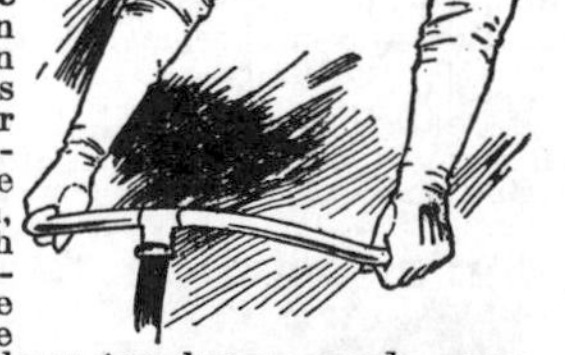

**No. 2535 Chamois Mousquetaire Gloves,** with two large buttons at wrist. Very desirable for spring and summer wear. Known as six-button length. Made in white or yellow. Sizes, 5¾ to 7½.
Price, per pair........................................... **$0.75**

## A Special Bargain for 89c.

**No. 2536 Ladies' 12-Inch Glace Kid Gloves.** Fine imported stock. Very serviceable for shopping, driving, bicycle riding and general wear. Handsomely made and finished. Thoroughly dependable in every way. Our own importation. Colors, black, tan, brown, mode, slate, grey, etc. Sizes, 5¾ to 7½ only. Price, per pair............................ **$0.89**

**OUR DISCOUNT OF 3 PER CENT. FOR CASH MUST NOT BE FORGOTTEN, WHEN YOU SEND CASH IN FULL, YOU NOT ONLY SAVE THE DISCOUNT, BUT ALSO THE RETURN CHARGES ON THE MONEY.**

## Ladies' Gauntlet Gloves.

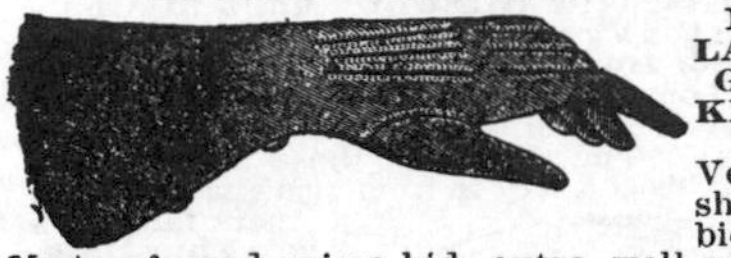

**No. 2537 LADIES' GAUNTLET KID . . . . GLOVES.** Very nice for shopping or bicycle use. Made of good prime kid, extra well made, pretty three point stitched backs, cuffs fastened with one patent catch button. Colors: tan, brown or dark red. Per pair...... **$0.95**

**No. 2538 Ladies' Fine Imported Gauntlet Kid Gloves.** Wide gauntlet, two patent catch button fastenings, made of prime stock Arabian goat, table cut, handsomely made and finishsd, three point fancy stitched backs. Colors, brown or dark red. Per pair...... **$1.25**

## The New Chamois Gloves.

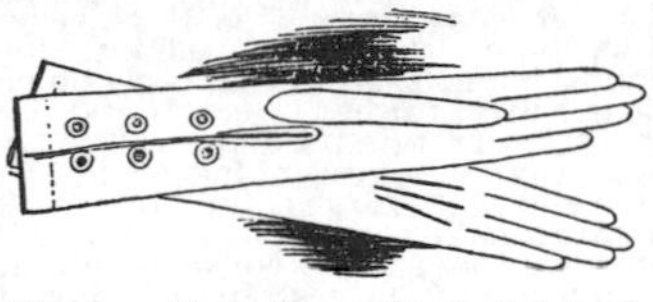

**No. 2539 Ladies' Extra Selected Chamois Gloves.** Made with the new three patent snap button fasteners. Very handy and serviceable. Extra well made and finely finished. Made in white only. Sizes, 5¾ to 7½. Price, per pair...... **$0.75**

## Ladies' Silk and Cotton Gloves.

**Sizes 6 to 8.**

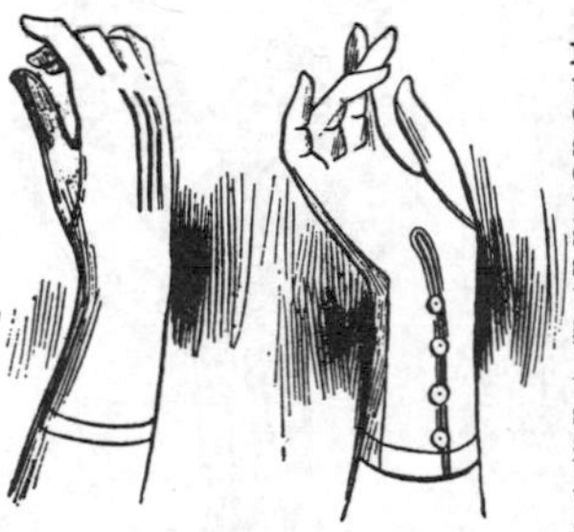

**No. 2540 The New Four-Button Pure Silk Glove.** The handsomest ever made Guaranteed all pure Milanese silk. Real "Amsterdam" double tipped. These gloves are plain black, with three rows of white silk stitching on back and have four large white pearl buttons. The finest silk glove ever produced. Price, per pair...... **$0.75**

**No. 2541 Ladies' Fine Viennesse Thread Gloves.** Specially desirable for spring and summer wear. Made same style as above with four buttons and three rows of stitching. Sizes 6 to 8. Colors, black or tan. Price, per pair...... **$0.25**

## Ladies' Fabric Gloves.

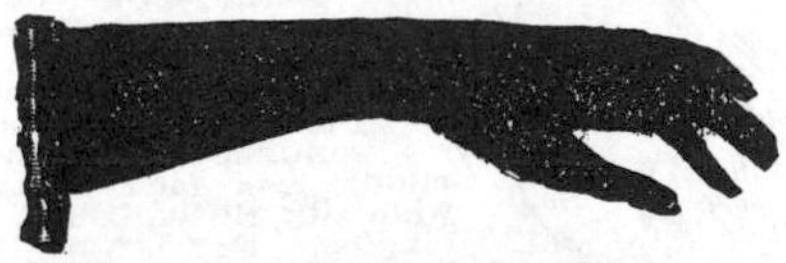

**No. 2542 Ladies' Black Berlin Gloves,** very fine quality, handsome color, three point back set-in-thumb. Length, 11 inches; sizes, 6 to 8. Per pair...... **$0.09**

**No. 2543 Ladies' Light Weight Black Silk Gloves.** Three rows silk stitching on back, French set-in thumbs. Very fine finish and warranted all pure silk; sizes, 5¾ to 8. Price, per pair...... **$0.25**

**No. 2544 Ladies' Medium Weight Pure Black Silk Gloves.** Three rows of stitching on back and French set-in thumbs. Warranted to give excellent service; sizes, 5¾ to 8. Price, per pair...... **$0.38**

## Ladies' Silk Mitts.

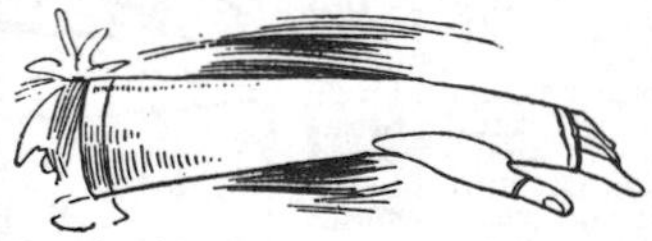

**No. 2545 Ladies' Black Pure Silk Jersey Mitts,** with plain back; length. 10 in. very fine quality, and equal to any retailed for double the money. Price, per pair...... **$0.10**

**No. 2546 Ladies' Black Pure Silk Jersey Mitts,** with three rows of embroidery on the back; length, 10 inches; very fine material and handsomely finished. Price, per pair...... **$0.15**

**No. 2547 Ladies' Black Pure Silk Jersey Mitts,** hand point; full regular made; set-in French thumb; of the finest silk to be had; length, 11 inches. Price, per pair...... **$0.19**

**No. 2548 Ladies' Pure Black Jersey Silk Mitts,** three point embroidered backs; French set-in perfect fitting thumb; wide hem at top; length. 11 in. Price, per pair...... **$0.25**

**No. 2550 Black Milanese Silk Mitts,** the softest, finest and most durable of all silks; French set-in thumb; three row embroidered backs, with wide hem at the top; length, 11 inches. Price, per pair...... **$0.35**

**No. 2551 Extra Quality Black Milanese Silk,** exceedingly fine and heavy; we will guarantee this mitt will outwear any other made; handsomely finished, with three row hand pointed back; wide hem top; length, 11 inches. Price, per pair...... **$0.45**

**DON'T FORGET THE POSTAGE . . . . FOR MAIL SHIPMENTS.**

## Extra Size Black Silk Mitts.

**For Ladies with Large Hands.**

**No. 2552 Ladies' Extra Size Black Silk Jersey Mitts.** with three row embroidered backs; warranted all pure silk. Price, per pair...... **$0.19**

**No. 2553 Ladies' Extra Size Black Silk Jersey Mitts,** very fine and soft; warranted all pure silk. Three rows narrow silk stitching on back. French set-in thumbs; handsome and durable. Price. per pair...... **$0.25**

## The New Silk Mitt With Kid Palms.

**Just the Thing for Driving.**

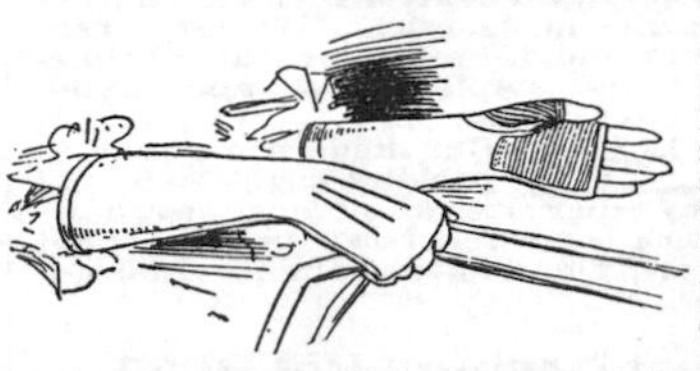

**No. 2554 Ladies' Extra Fine Quality Pure Silk Driving Mitts,** three rows of narrow silk embroidery on back. French set-in thumbs; black kid palms and thumb facings. Finely made and finished. An excellent mitt for driving and bicycle riding. Price, per pair...... **$0.50**

## Silk Mitts In Extra Lengths.

**No. 2555 Very Fine Black Silk Jersey Mitts,** full regular made, and two inches longer than the usual length. being 13 inches long; very nice weight, and handsomely finished, with three rows of neat embroidery on the back. Price, per pair...... **$0.39**

**No. 2556 Ladies' Black Jersey Pure Silk Mitts,** extra heavy and fine quality; length, 15 inches; hand pointed back, French set-in thumb, wide hem top. This length is very stylish, and known as the elbow length. Price per pair...... **$0.48**

**No. 2557 Eighteen Inches in Length,** and reaches above the elbow, made of beautiful quality, thread silk; very heavy and elegant for wear, three row, hand pointed silk backs, wide hem top, and comes in the following colors: Black, cream, white, tan, mode, slate, pink, sky blue, lemon, straw, cardinal, heliotrope, and nile green. These mitts are worn for evening dress purposes, and are as stylish as kid gloves which cost $3.00 per pair. Our price, per pair...... **$0.60**

**No. 2558 Twenty-two Inches in Length,** and reaches nearly to the shoulder; is also made of beautiful quality, pure thread silk, which is the best wear resisting mitt made, handsomely finished, three point back and French set in thumb, and come in black or cream. Price, per pair...... **$0.75**

## Misses' and Children's Mitts.

**No. 2559 Misses' Pure Silk Black Jersey Mitts,** three row pointed back. Length, 8 inches. Price, per pair...... **$0.15**

**No. 2560 Misses' Jersey Silk Mitts.** Superior quality, fine and heavy, set-in thumb, three row dainty silk embroidered backs. Length, 9 inches. None better or prettier. In street or opera colors, also in black. Price, per pair...... **$0.23**

## LADIES' MISSES' AND CHILDREN'S FALL AND WINTER GLOVES AND MITTENS.

**SPECIAL BARGAINS. BUY NOW AND YOU BUY CHEAPLY.**

## Ladies' Lined Gloves and Mittens.

**No. 2561 Is a Ladies' Domestic Kid Glove,** with fine white fleece lining, fancy stitching on back. This is a dressy and durable glove. Price, per pair...... **$0.45**

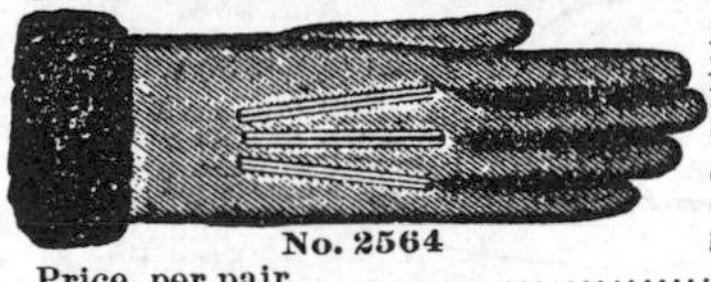

No. 2564

**No. 2562 Is a Ladies' Undressed Kid Mitten,** rubber wrist and fancy back, heavily fleece lined. Price, per pair...... **$0.59**

**No. 2563 Ladies' Very Fine Kid Mitten,** with rubber wrist, fancy embroidery back, heavily fleece lined with fur top. Price, per pair...... **$0.74**

**No. 2564 Ladies' Fur Top Kid Gloves,** heavy fleece lined and elastic rubber wrist. Price. per pair...... **$0.49**

**No. 2565 Is a Ladies' Fancy Back Kid Glove,** heavy wool fleece lined, spring wrist and trimmed with sheared coney fur. Price, per pair...... **$0.95**

## Misses' and Children's Fleece Lined Mittens.

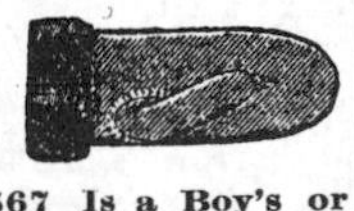

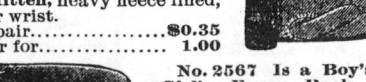

**No. 2566 Is a Girl's or Boy's Kid Mitten,** heavy fleece lined, rubber wrist.
Per pair...... **$0.35**
3 pair for...... **1.00**

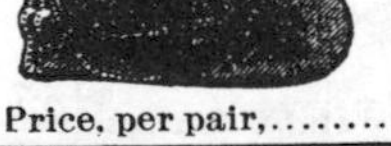

**No. 2567 Is a Boy's or Girl's Fancy Back Kid Mitten,** rubber wrist, heavy fleece lined. Price, per pair,...... **$0.48**



## Ladies' Plain Knit Wool Mittens.

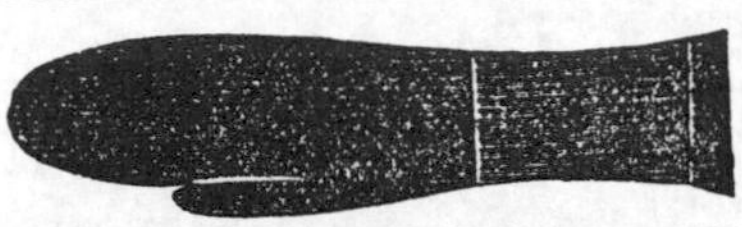

**No. 2568 Is a Ladies' Plain Knit wool Mitten,** derby ribbed wrist, well finished thumb (black only.) Price, per pair...... **$0.09**

**No. 2569 Is a Ladies' Heavy Wool Knit Mitten,** with a double wrist and regular made. Price, per pair...... **$0.14**

**No. 2570 Is a Ladies' Double Knit Mitten,** with extra long wrist and fine soft wool, Price, per pair...... **$0.24**

**No. 2571 Is a Ladies' fine Cashmere Knit Mitten,** with a fancy double knit wrist, silk bow on back. Price, per pair...... **$0.26**

**No. 2572 Is a Ladies' Extra Fine Double Knit Cassimere Mitten,** with silk cord and tassel on back, derby wrist. Price, per pair...... **$0.35**

**No. 2573 Is a Ladies' Fine Australian Wool Mitten,** with heavy ribbed wrist, lined with grey Angora wool; nothing better and warmer made. Price. per pair...... **$0.45**

## Ladies' Fancy Wool Knit Mittens.

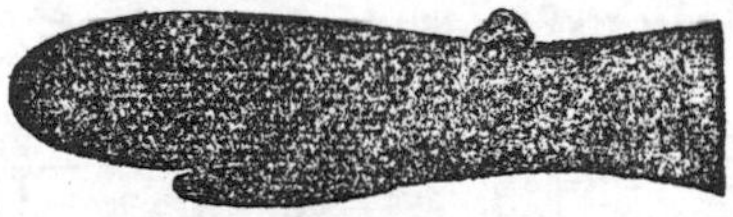

**No. 2574 Is a Ladies' Double Knit Cassimere Wool Mitten,** fancy open work on back. Price, per pair...... **$0.24**

**No. 2575 Ladies' Double Saxony Wool Knit Mitten.** fancy open work on back and satin bow. Price, per pair...... **$0.34**

**No. 2576 Ladies' Double Knit Mitten,** made of finest Saxony, has a fancy open work back and fancy wrists with satin bow on back. Price, per pair...... **$0.45**

**No. 2577 Ladies' Wool Knit Mitten,** made out of the very finest Saxony yarn, with three rows of colored silk embroidered on back, satin bow on back, Bichelieu ribbed wrist. Price, per pair...... **$0.52**

## Ladies' Silk Mittens.

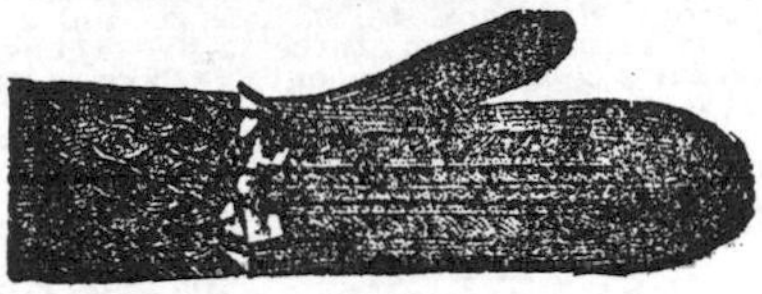

**No. 2578 Ladies' Richelieu Ribbed Silk Mitten,** with satin bow on back. Price, per pair...... **$0.39**

**No. 2579 Ladies' Spun Silk Mitten,** wool lined, with four rows of fancy open work on back. Price, per pair...... **$0.52**

**No. 2580 Ladies' Double Silk Mitten,** with a fine black Angora wool lining, fancy back. Price, per pair...... **$0.67**

**No. 2581 Ladies' Spun Silk Double Knit Mitten,** lined with fine wool, fancy back, with tassels on back; extra long wrist. Price, per pair...... **$0.58**

## Infants' Knit Mittens.

**No. 2582 Made out of Fine Quality Saxony Yarn,** nicely finished; comes in light blue, pink, red, and green. Sizes, 0, 1 and 2. Price, per pair...... **$0.08**

**No. 2583 Made out of Finest Quality Saxony Yarn,** with fancy elastic wrist, comes in light and dark shades. Price, per pair...... **$0.14**

## Children's Wool Knit Mittens.

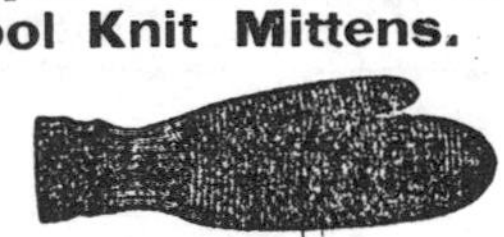

**No. 2584 Good Quality Wool Saxony Yarn,** comes in black only. Sizes, 3, 4 and 5. Price, per pair... **$0.07**

**No. 2585 Misses' Derby Ribbed Double Kntt Mitten,** with a very fine elastic wrist. Price, per pair...... **$0.14**

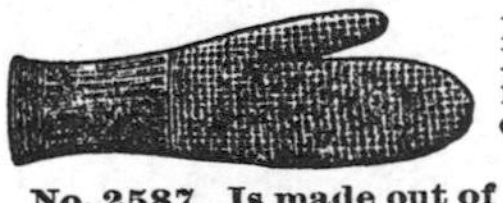

**No. 2586 Misses' Pure Saxony Wool Double Knit Mitten,** made extra heavy, black only. Price, per pair... **$0.17**

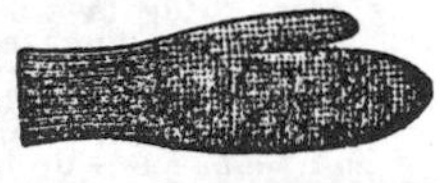

**No. 2587 Is made out of a very fine Saxony Yarn,** with very fine elastic derby ribbed wrist, double knit throughout. Price, per pair...... **$0.24**



**YOJ CANNOT AFFORD TO PAY YOUR LOCAL MILLINER TWICE OUR PRICE FOR A SPRING HAT, ANY MORE THAN YOU CAN AFFORD TO SELL BUTTER AND EGGS AT HALF MARKET PRICES.**

# HAT AND CAP DEPARTMENT

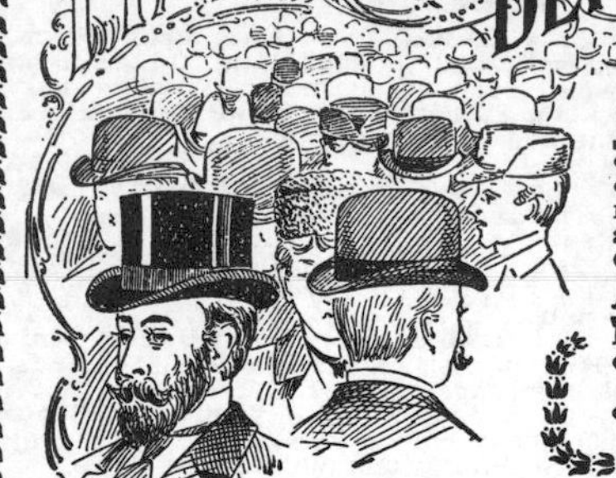

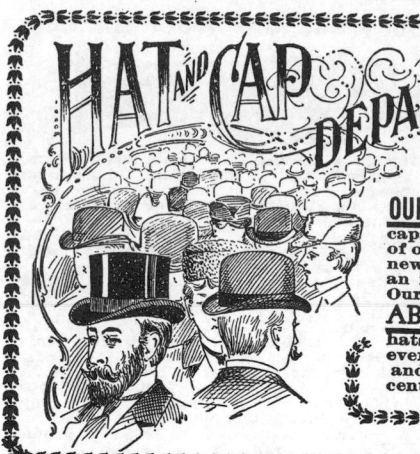

## MANY MEN HAVE MANY NOTIONS.

We have a notion that you will like our hats if you will but try them. Other people have tried them and like them. We have satisfied thousands of customers in this respect.

**OUR FACILITIES THIS SEASON** are better than ever. We now buy all of our hats and caps direct from the factory, and control the entire output of one of the largest factories in America. We have every new style hat, that is out and keep in stock at all times an immense stock of all the staple Shapes and Styles. Our prices will certainly interest you.

**ABOUT PACKING HATS.** Our modern methods in packing, enable us to ship hats of all kinds with any other class of merchandise, however heavy or bulky, with perfect safety. Include a hat and cap with your next order and save from 40 to 50 per cent. retailer's profit.

## How to Measure for a Hat.

| Head size | Inches Around head. | Head size | Inches Around head. | Head size | Inches Around head. |
|---|---|---|---|---|---|
| 5⅞ | 18¾ | 6⅝ | 21 | 7⅜ | 23⅜ |
| 6 | 19 | 6¾ | 21¼ | 7½ | 23¾ |
| 6⅛ | 19⅜ | 6⅞ | 21⅝ | 7⅝ | 24 |
| 6¼ | 19¾ | 7 | 22¼ | 7¾ | 24½ |
| 6⅜ | 20⅛ | 7⅛ | 22½ | 7⅞ | 25 |
| 6½ | 20¾ | 7¼ | 23 | 8 | 25¼ |

**Men's Sizes** are 6¾, 6⅞, 7, 7⅛, 7¼, 7⅜, and 7½.
**Boys' Sizes** are 6½, 6⅝, 6¾, 6⅞ and 7.
**Children's Sizes** are 6¼, 6⅜, 6½, 6⅝ and 6¾.

**If you no not have a tape measuse at hand, use a string or strip of paper for measuring and attach same to your order.**

**N. B.: Sizes 7⅝, 7¾, 7⅞ and 8** are extra large sizes and cannot usually be found in ready-made stocks. Any of our customers requiring any of these sizes can obtain prices for having same made to order, upon application. In making inquiries of this nature, always state style, size and color wanted. It requires from three to five weeks to have special size hats, and about five days to have special size caps made to order, and the full amount of cash must accompany same. We guarantee perfect satisfaction in every instance.

## Men's Latest Style Stiff Hats.

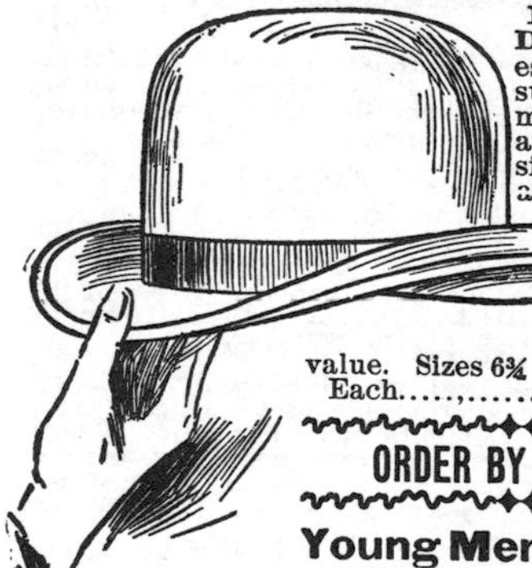

**No. 2600 Men's Derby,** The newest shape, black stiff, fur felt hat, medium crown and brim. Black silk ribbon band and binding. fancy satin lining, very nob by in appearance. extra good value. Sizes 6¾ to 7½, Each.......................$0.98

**ORDER BY NUMDER.**

## Young Men's Derby.

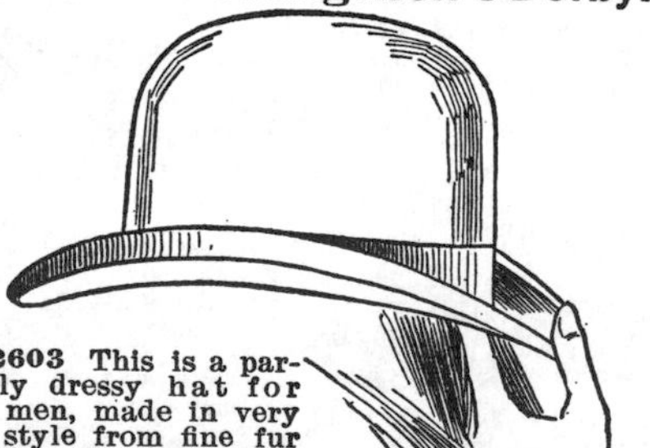

**No. 2603** This is a particularly dressy hat for young men, made in very latest style from fine fur stock. Fine silk ribbon band and binding. Elegantly made and trimmed. We have had them made up in plain black and golden brown in sizes from 6¾ to 7⅜. Improved leather sweat band. Each.....$1.50

**Dishes a Bargain at Even More Than the Price Paid.**

REGINA, WIS.

SEARS, ROEBUCK & Co., Chicago, Ill.

DEAR SIRS:—A mistake was made in the amount of money sent you in payment for dishes. Please find enclosed 25 cents with the assurance that it was not a mistake made on purpose, for the dishes are a bargain at even more than the price you set.

Yours respectfully.
EDWIN LANE.

## Our Great Danbury Hat $1.69.

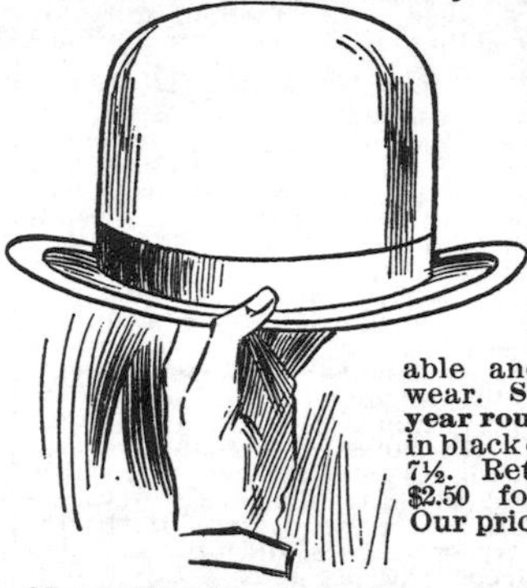

**No. 2605 Our Great Danbury Stiff Fur Hat.** Medium shaped crown and brim. Fine black silk ribbon band and binding. Improved leather sweat band. Self conforming to the head. Easy, comfortable and excellent for wear. **Standard all the year round style.** Made in black only. Sizes 6¾ to 7½. Retail dealers ask $2.50 for this quality. Our price each.. **$1.69**

**Always Mention Size when ordering Hats.** This will save us the trouble of writing to you for size and thus delaying your order.

## Knox and Dunlap Styles.

**Always Correct in Shape. A $3.00 Hat for $2.00.**

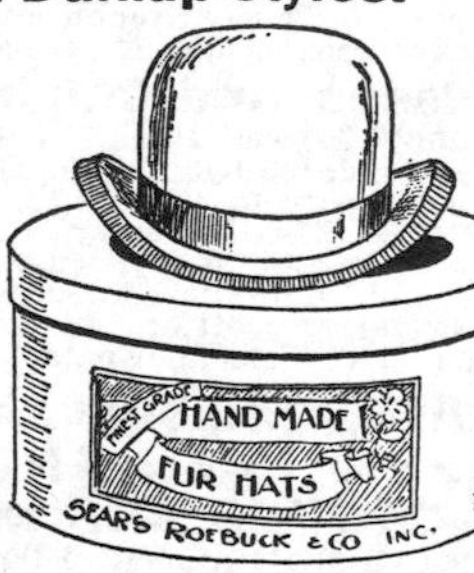



**No. 2607 Men's Fashionable Up-to-Date Black Stiff Fur Hats.** Made up in the very latest Knox or Dunlap style. Heavily satin lined, with finest leather sweat band, black silk ribbon band and binding. Self-conforming to the head. **Regular $3.00 quality, when bought at retail.** Sizes, 6¾ to 7½.
Our price, each........................................$2.00

## $2.39 for a $4.00 Dunlap Style Hat.

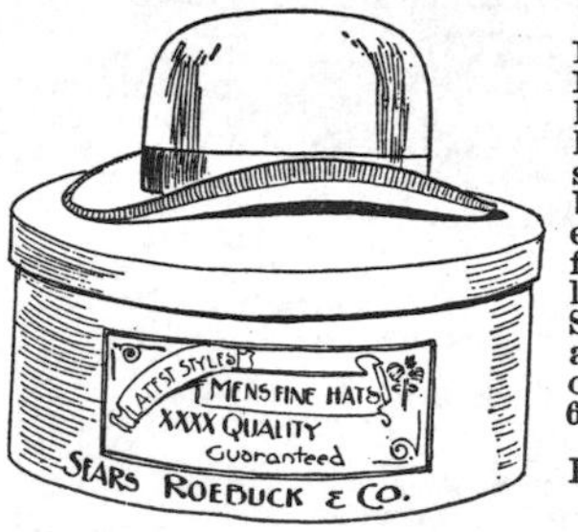



**No. 2609 The Prince of all Derby Hats.** A strictly high grade stiff fur hat. Latest Dunlap style. Silk ribbon band and binding, extra fine hand finish. Finest goat leather sweat band. Self-conforming and thoroughly comfortable. Sizes, 6¾ to 7½.

Price, each...**$2.39**

## French Pocket Hats.

**Sizes, 6¾ to 7⅜ Only.**

**No. 2610 The Finest, Softest, Lightest Weight Pocket Hat ever produced.** Made from finest French fur felt, with satin lining and ribbed silk sweat band. Roll brim, raw edge and narrow silk ribbon band. Color dark navy blue.

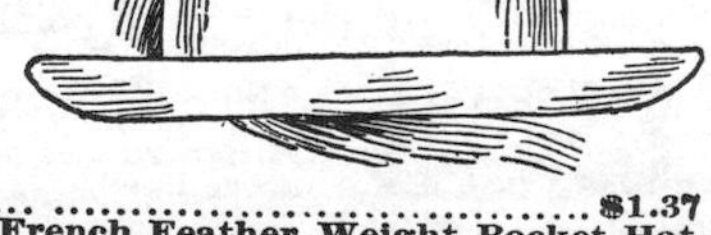

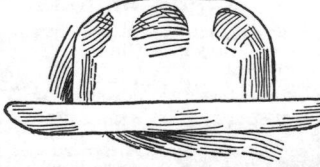

Price each.......................................$1.37
**No. 2611 French Feather Weight Pocket Hat.** Same as above in seal brown. Price each......**$1.37**
**No. 2612 Same as above in black. Always mention size wanted.** Price each..............**$1.37**

**REFER TO INDEX** WHEN YOU WANT ANY-THING YOU DON'T SEE.

## Nutria Fur Hats.

**The Finest Hats in the World are Made in America, and the Finest American Hats are Made from Clear Nutria Fur.**

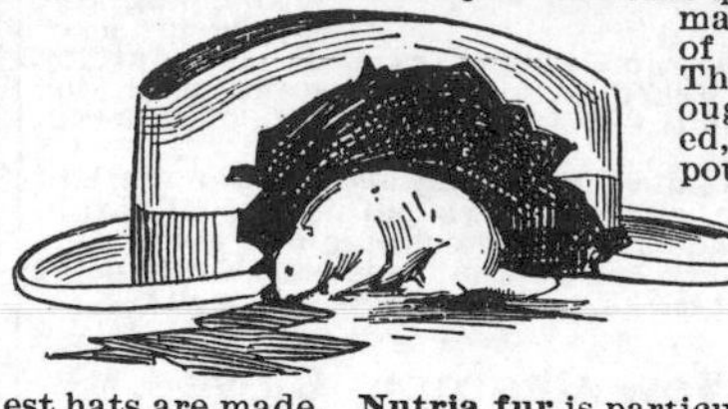

**Nutria Fur** comes from a small South American animal, greatly resembling the beaver, but much more plentiful. The skins of these animals are imported into this country in immense quantities by manufacturers of **Fine Hats.** The fur is thoroughly cleaned, combed and pounced, being finally transformed into felt, out of which the finest hats are made. **Nutria fur** is particularly desirable for this purpose, as it is very fine, soft and silky, and when prepared into felt contains no lumps, impurities or other objectionable matter. A clear Nutria fur hat is as soft and smooth as a piece of silk, will retain its shape and color and will outwear any other kind of hat made. Our connections with one of the largest fur hat manufacturers in this country make it possibla for us to sell these **Nutria fur hats** direct to the consumer at about one-third ordinary retail prices. **In ordering always mention catalogue number, size and color desired.**

## Our Great $2.25 Fedora Hat.

**Made from Clear Nutria Fur. We Challenge the World to Beat It.**

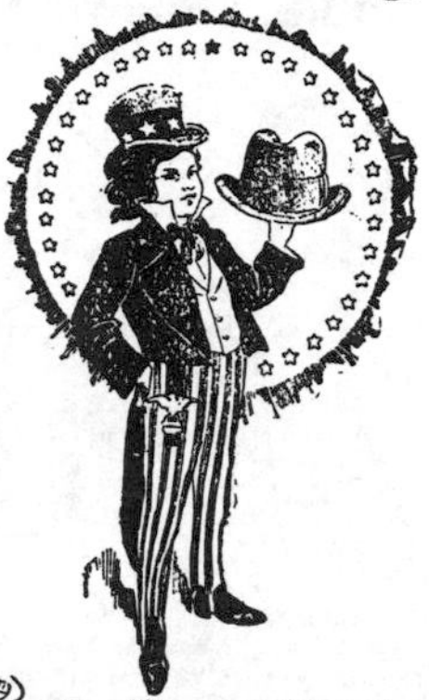

**No. 2613 Men's Clear Nutria Fur Fedora Hats.** Finest quality. Medium shaped brim and crown. Suitable for all men. Wide corded silk ribbon band and binding, Finest improved leather sweat band and best quality satin lining. Absolutely high grade and warranted to wear. A fine dressy up-to-date hat. In plain colors, black, brown or grey. Sizes 6¾ to 7½. Retails at $4.00. Our price.....**$2.25**

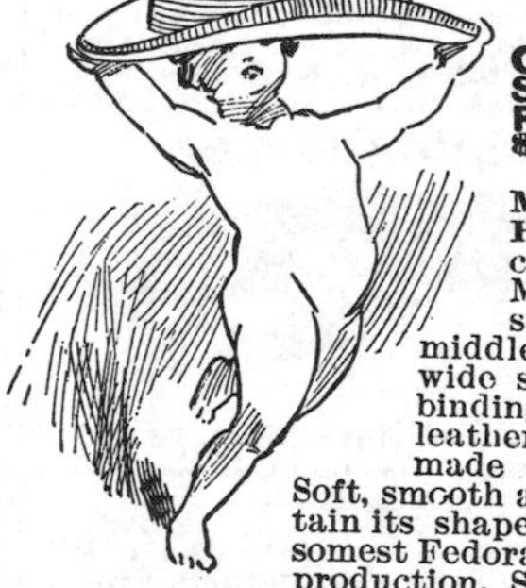

## Our Young Men's Special Nutria Fur Fedora.

**$1.88 for a $3.00 Hat.**

**No. 2614 Our Young Men's Special Fedora Hat.** An excellent clear Nutria fur hat. Medium small, shape suitable for young and middle aged men. Heavy, wide silk ribbon band and binding. Finest quality leather sweat band. Hand made and kettle finished. Soft, smooth and guaranteed to retain its shape. One of the handsomest Fedora hats of this season's production. Sizes, 6¾ to 7½. Black, brown or grey. Our special price, each.......**$1.88**

## $1.50 for this Clear Nutria Fur Hat.

**The Most Popular Hat Made.**

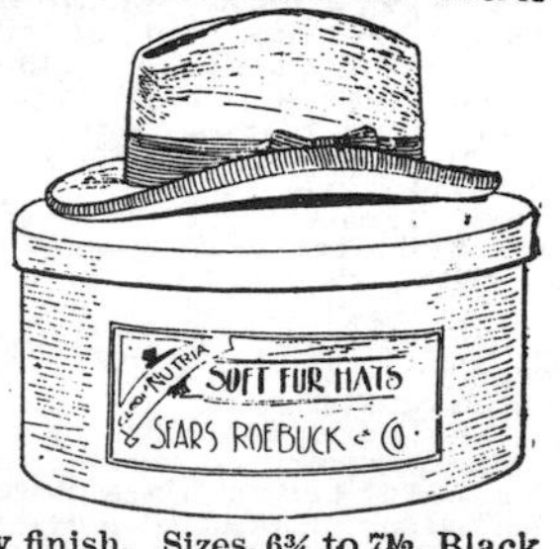



**No. 2615 Men's Full Shaped Fedora Hat.** Made from clear Nutria fur. Wide silk ribbon band and binding. Improved leather sweat band. Standard shape and weight. Suitable for all the year around wear. We make a specialty of this hat and guarantee it to give perfect satisfaction. Very fine dressy finish. Sizes, 6¾ to 7½. Black or brown. **Satin lined or unlined, as desired.**
Price, each..............................................**$1.50**

## Our $1.25 Nutria Fur Fedora.

**No. 2616 Men's Medium Shape Nutria Fur Fedora Hat.** Wide silk ribbon band and binding, and fancy satin lining. Leather sweat band. Sizes, 6¾ to 7½. Black, brown or grey. Nine soft finish.
Price, each..............................................**$1.25**

## A 98 Cent Wonder.

**No. 2618 Men's Fine Nutria Fur Fedora Hat.** Medium shape. Good heavy stock, suitable for wear all the year round. Wide silk ribbon band and binding. Heavy satin lining. A most excellent hat in every way. Made in black or brown. Size, 6¾ to 7⅛.
Price, each..............................................**$0.98**

## 60c for a Saxony Wool Fedora Hat.

**No. 2619 Men's Extra Fine Black Saxony Wool Fedora Hat.** Medium shape, with leather sweat band and wide black ribbon band. An excellent wearing and fine looking hat. Sizes, 6¾ to 7⅜ only.
Price, each..............................................**$0.60**

**OUR MILLINERY DEPARTMENT IS IN CHARGE OF A MANAGER OF WIDE EXPERIENCE AT HOME AND ABROAD. WE ARE OFFERING THE NEWEST PARISIAN NOVELTIES AT HALF RETAIL PRICES.**

## Men's Crusher Hats.

Sizes 6¾ to 7½.

**73c.** CLEAR NUTRIA FUR

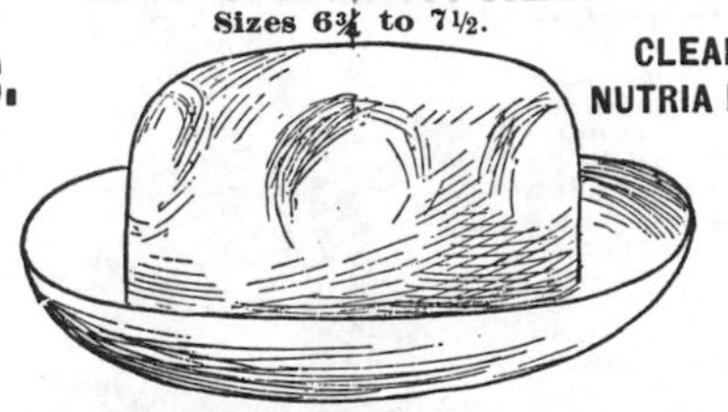

**No. 2620 Men's Medium Shaped Nutria Fur Crusher Hat.** Fancy narrow silk ribbon band and flexible leather sweat band; fine soft stock. Sizes 6¾ to 7½. Colors black, blue or brown. Each.....**$0.73**

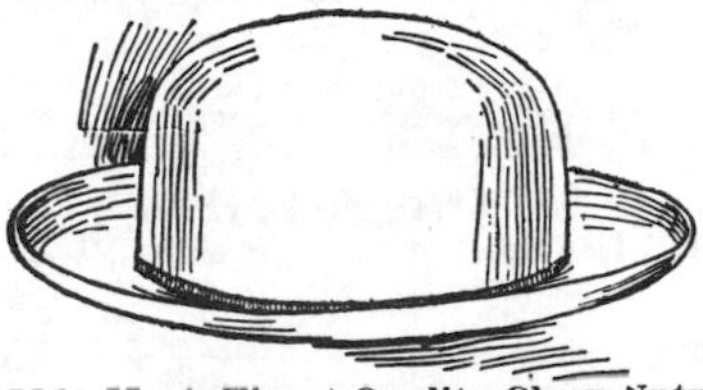

**No. 2621 Men's Finest Quality Clear Nutria Fur Crusher Hat.** Medium shape with curled brim and raw edge, very narrow silk ribbon band and heavy satin lining. Sizes 6¾ to 7½. Made in black, blue or seal brown. Very nobby and extra fine finish. Each.......................................**$0.95**

## A Great Drive in Driving Hats.

**750 Dozen Finest Fur Driving Hats** which we closed out from an Eastern hat factory at 40c on the dollar. For your choice ............................**$0.79**

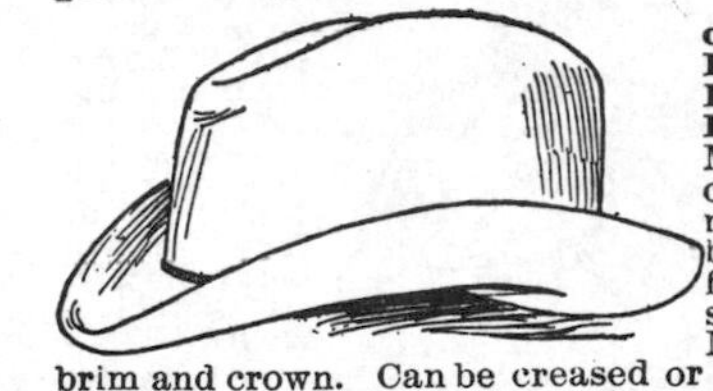

**No. 2622 An odd lot of Men's Finest Soft Fur Felt Crusher Driving Hats.** Made up in first class style with narrow silk ribbon band and finest leather sweat band. Medium shaped brim and crown. Can be creased or not as desired. Made up to retail for $1.50. Sizes 6¾ to 7⅜ only. Made in navy blue color. Order at once as we will have no more when this lot is closed out.
Our special price, each..........................**$0.79**

**No. 2623 Men's Full Shape Black Saxony Wool Hats.** 6 inch crown, 2⅝ inch brim. Fine leather sweat and silk ribbon band. Sizes 6¾ to 7⅛.
Price each...........................................**$0.50**

## 48c. For a Fine Wool Crusher.

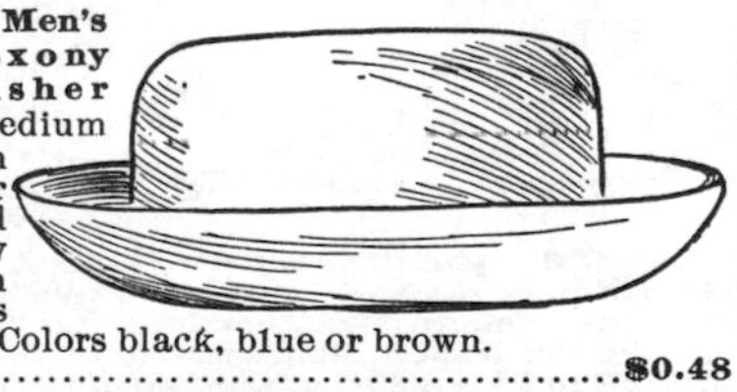

**No. 2624 Men's Pure Saxony Wool Crusher Hats.** Medium shape with leather sweat band and narrow silk ribbon band. Sizes 6¾ to 7⅜. Colors black, blue or brown.
Each.................................................**$0.48**

## Men's Full Shape Crusher Hats.

HAND MADE — CLEAR STOCK.

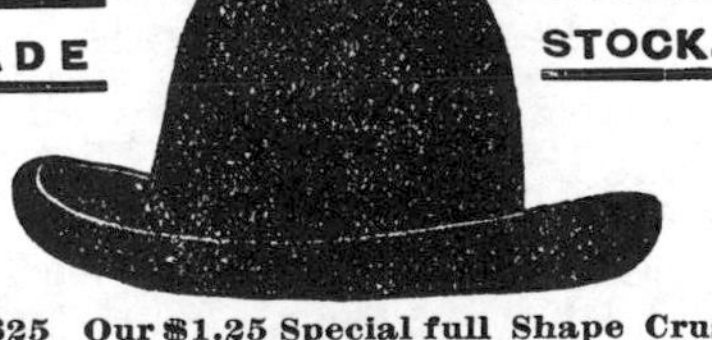

**No. 2625 Our $1.25 Special full Shape Crusher Hat.** Made from clear Nutria fur. Extra fine soft finish, medium weight. Fine leather sweat band; large full shaped crown that can be creased; full shape brim: made in black or blue only. **A decidedly popular and durable hat.** Sizes 6¾ to 7½.
Each.................................................**$1.25**

## The Railroad Hat.

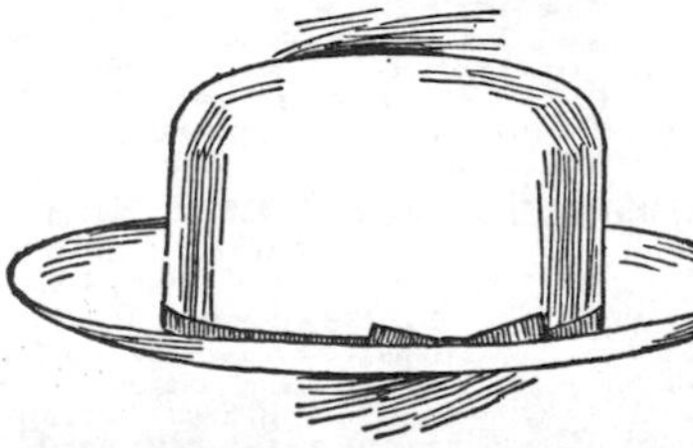

**No. 2626 Men's fine Saxony Wool Railroad Hat.** Raw edge with cord band, 4 inch crown and 2½ inch brim. Guaranteed to give excellent service. Made in black only. Sizes 6¾ to 7⅜. Price. each....**$0.55**

## $1.45 for a Clear Fur Railroad Hat.

**No. 2627 Men's Clear Fur Railroad Hat.** 2½ inch brim, 4 inch crown, silk cord band, raw edge and fine leather sweat band. Black, brown or drab. Sizes 6¾ to 7½. Each.......................................**$1.45**

## Our Famous $2.00 Railroad Hat.

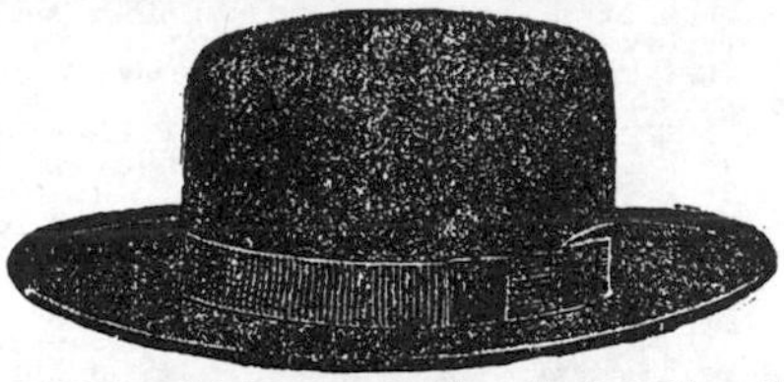

**No. 2628 This is an exceptionally fine Clear Nutria Fur Hat.** Finished in extra fine style with finest leather sweat band, silk ribbon band and binding. Regulation railroad style. 4 inch crown, 2½ inch brim. Sizes 6¾ to 7½. Black. brown or grey. Price, each..................................................**$2.00**

## Grand Army Hats.

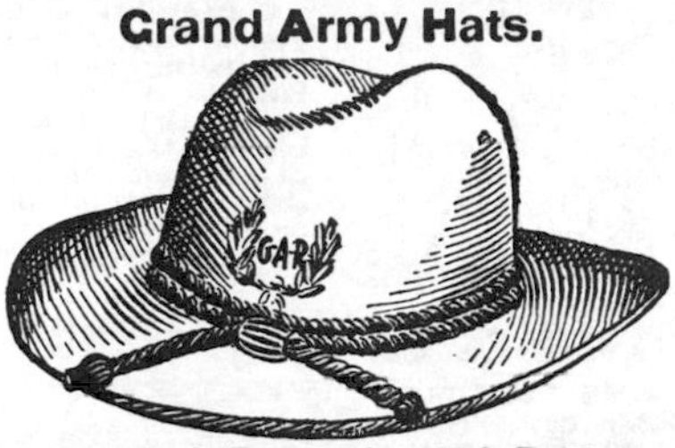


**No. 2630 Men's Regulation G. A. R. Hats,** made from best fine Saxony wool with gold cord and G.A.R. wreath. Leather sweat band. Black only. Size 6¾ to 7⅜ only. Price, each..........................**$0.78**
Per dozen..................................................**8.75**

**No. 2631 Men's Clear Fur G. A. R Hat,** full regulation shape with gold cord and G. A. R. wreath and leather sweat band. The best wearing Grand Army hat made. Black only. Sizes 6¾ to 7½,
Price, each..........................................**$ 1.37**
Per dozen..................................................**15.00**

## U. S. A. Cavalry Hats.

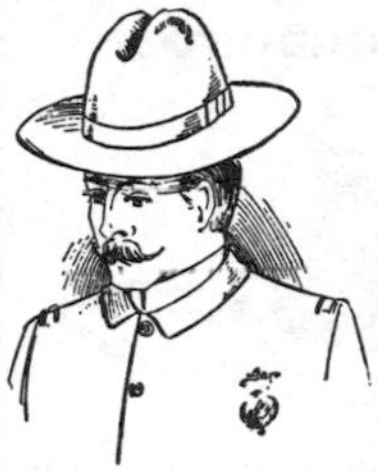

**Adopted by the Government.**

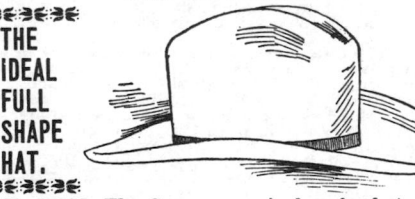

**No. 2632 U.S.A. Regulation Cavalry Hats.** The same as used by the government troops and militia. Made from fine soft fur and intended for hard service. Narrow silk ribbon band, leather sweat band and raw edge. Side nutria or drab color. Sizes 6¾ to 7½.
Our price. each..........**$ 1.37**
Per dozen ...............**15.00**

## The Governor.

THE IDEAL FULL SHAPE HAT.

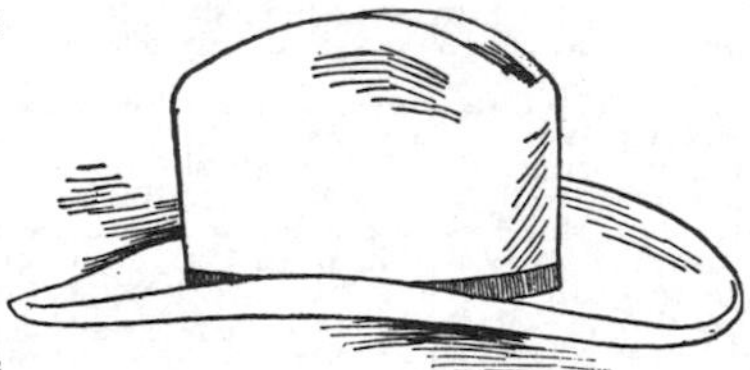

**No. 2633 The Governor.** A clear fur hat with full shape 6 inch crown and 3½ inch brim. Fine silk ribbon band and improved leather sweat band, raw edge, fine finish. Made in black only. Sizes 6¾ to 7½, Price, each.........................................**$1.45**

**No. 2634 The Governor.** An ideal full shaped hat, made from clear nutria fur stock, 6½ inch crown and 3½ inch brim. Finest leather sweat and narrow silk ribbon band, raw edge. Sizes 6¾ to 7½. Made in black. Price, each.....................................**$2.00**

**No. 2636 The Governor.** Same as above, in drab. Sizes 6¾ to 7½. Price, each.............................**$2.00**

## J. B. Stetson Hats.

The Finest Hats ... in the World.

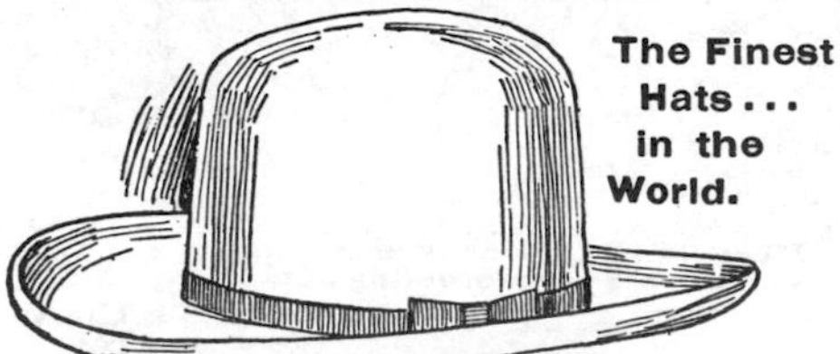

The Dakota.

**No. 2637 J. B. Stetson's Dakota Men's Fine Black, Soft Fur Hats,** 5½ inch crown, 3½ inch raw edge brim, finest quality leather sweat band, narrow silk ribbon band, sizes 6¾ to 7½. Price, each..**$3.90**

**No. 2638 J. B. Stetson's Dakota,** same as above in belly nutria color. Always state size desired.
Price, each...................................................**$3.90**

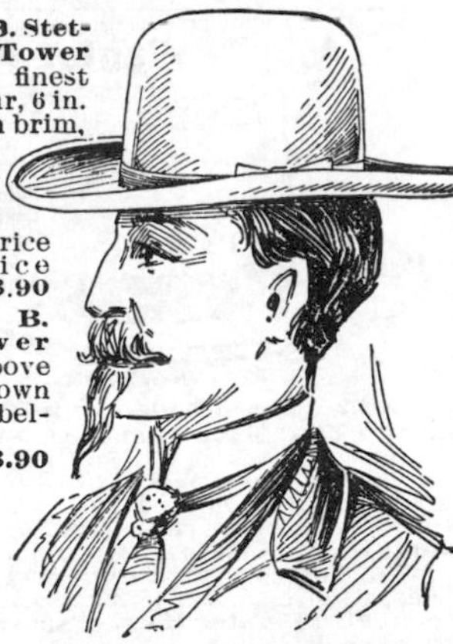

J. B. Stetson's Tower.

**No. 2640 J. B. Stetson's Famous Tower Hat,** made from finest quality nutria fur, 6 in. crown and 3 inch brim, narrow silk ribbon band and raw edge. Sizes 6¾ to 7⅜, black only. Retailer's price $5.00. Our price
Each.........**$3.90**

**No. 2641 J. B. Stetson's Tower Hat,** same as above with 6 inch crown and 3 inch brim, belly nutria color.
Each.........**$3.90**

## The Citizen's Hat.

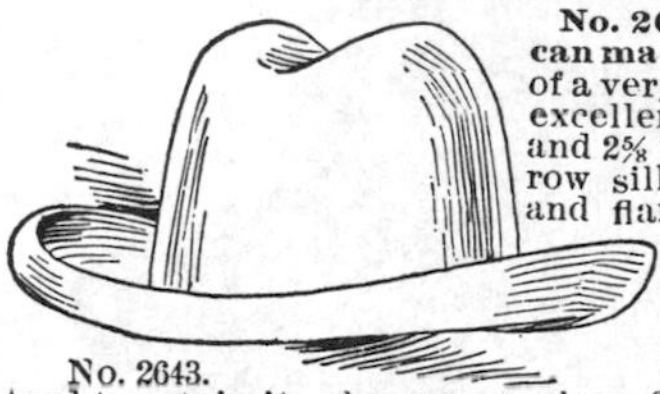

No. 2643.

**No. 2643 An American made Soft Fur Hat** of a very high degree of excellence, 6 inch crown and 2⅝ inch brim, narrow silk ribbon band and flange brim with raw edge, finest goat leather sweat band, soft and easy on the head, guaranteed to retain its shape and color. Sizes, 6¾ to 7½, color black. Each.......................................**$2.25**

**No. 2644 Same Hat as above,** made in side nutria or drab color. Each..............................**$2.25**

## Young Men's Pasha Hats.

LATEST STYLE SOFT HATS.... Sizes, 6¾ to 7⅜

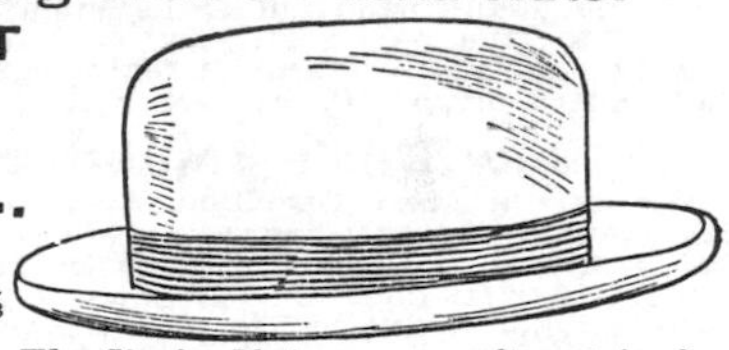

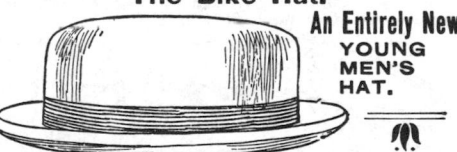

**No. 2645 The Pasha Hat.** a new soft nutria fur felt hat, made same shape as above illustration, with silk ribbon band, raw edge and curling flange brim; colors, black or brown. Very dressy.
Price, each ......................................................**$1.25**

**No. 2646 The Pasha Hat, Extra Fine** high grade soft fur, medium shape crown and brim, finest silk ribbon band, raw edge and flange brim. Sizes, 6¾ to 7⅜. Black, brown or nutria. Price, each...**$2.15**

## The Bike Hat.

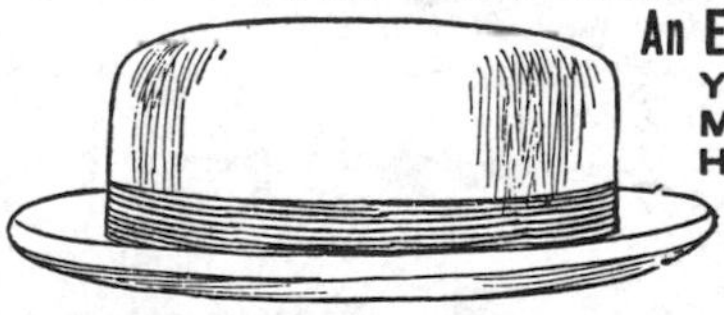

An Entirely New YOUNG MEN'S HAT.

**No. 2647 The New Bike Hat,** made from finest clear nutria fur felt, fine soft finish, medium low crown and curled brim, silk ribbon band and binding. Colors, black or brown. Sizes, 6¾ to 7⅜ only.
Price, each..........................................................**$1.50**

## Linen Crash Hats.

**The coolest, lightest and most comfortable Summer hats in the world. Order early as there will be an immense demand for these hats.**

**No. 2648 Men's Genuine Natural Linen Crash Hats,** full shape fedora style, linen band with stitched brim and ventilated crown. Sizes 6¾ to 7⅜ only. **Solid comfort in these hats.** You will surely like them. Made in natural linen color.

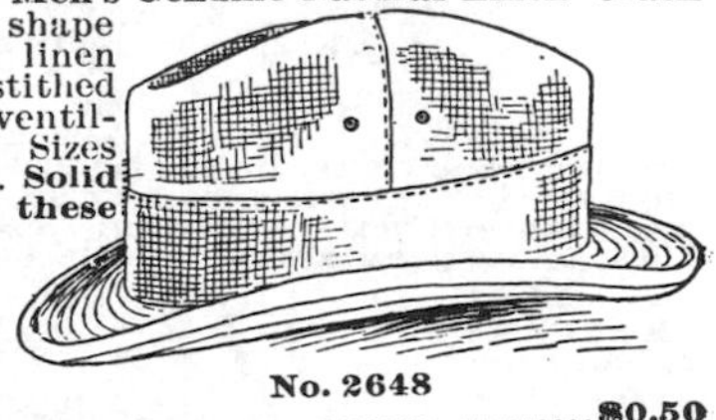

No. 2648

Price, each.............................................**$0.50**
Per dozen...................................................**5.40**

**No. 2650 Men's Natural Linen Crash Stiff Hats.** Medium shape crown and brim, fine leather sweatband, ventilated crown, serge lining, narrow silk ribbon band. Very cool and easy on the head. Light in weight and light in price. Sizes 6¾ to 7⅜ only. Natural linen color.

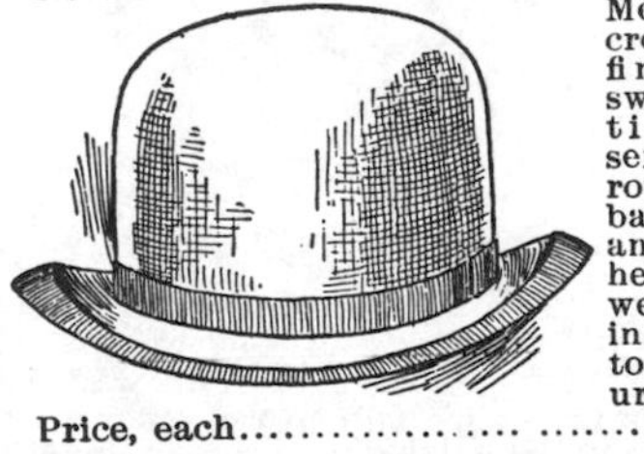

Price, each...................................................**$0.79**

**BETTER ORDER SHRITS, UNDERWEAR, SHOES ETC. WHEN YOU ORDER YOUR HAT, AND SHIP ALL TOGETHER. BETTER STILL, MAKE UP A FREIGHT ORDER OF GROCERIES AND SHIP FURNISHING GOODS ALONG AT NO EXPENSE.**

## Men's Planter Hats.

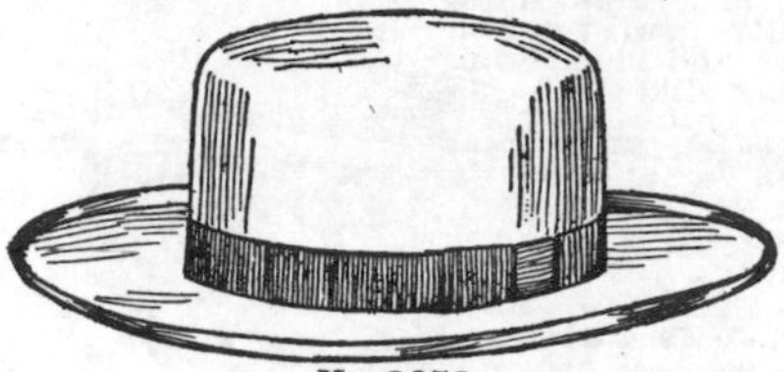

No. 2652

No. 2652 **Men's Wide Brim Plain Black Wool Planter Hats.** Made from fine quality Saxony, soft and smooth. Sizes 6¾ to 7⅜. Price, each......**$0.75**

No. 2653 **Men's Wide Brim Planter Hats.** Same as above in drab color. Each..................**$0.75**

No. 2654 **Men's Best Quality Saxony Wool Planter Hats.** Wide brim with ribbon band and binding. Guaranteed to give good service. Color, black. Price, each...................................**$0.95**

No. 2655 **Planter Hats.** Same as above in drab. Price, each.. ...................................**$0.95**

## Ranch Hats.

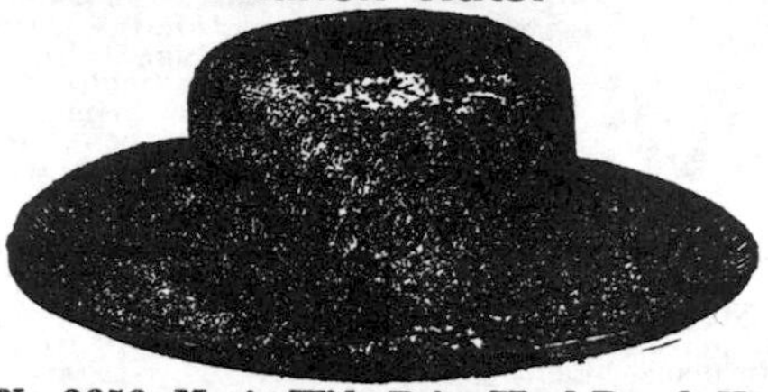

No. 2656 **Men's Wide Brim Wool Ranch Hats.** Cord band and leather sweatband. Nutria or tan color. Sizes, 6¾ to 7⅜ only. Each..............**$0.50**

No. 2657 **Ranch Hats.** Made of fine Saxony wool, with fancy cord band and leather sweat band, warranted to give good solid service. Sizes, 6¾ to 7⅜. Nicely made and trimmed. **A real bargain. Colors,** light nutria or tan. Price, each................**$1.00**

## Cow Boy's Sombreros.

**We have a Most Excellent Line of Cow Boy Hats and Sombreros.** They are made from the very best materials; all hand finished with the very best quality of trimmings, and warranted to give perfect satisfaction. Every hat has been made with the strict understanding that it must give real and lasting satisfaction to the wearer. We quote only the standard shapes, but can at any time have special hats or special sizes made to order. **Special Attention** however is directed to the fact that it requires about three weeks to have a special hat made to order. If you desire to have a special hat made to order always write to us first describing fully the kind of hat wanted, being sure to state size, color, width of brim, height of crown, etc. **The following Hats are made in sizes 6¾, 6⅞, 7, 7⅛, 7¼, 7⅜, 7½.** Other sizes would have to be made specially to order and cost from 75 cents to $1.50 extra.

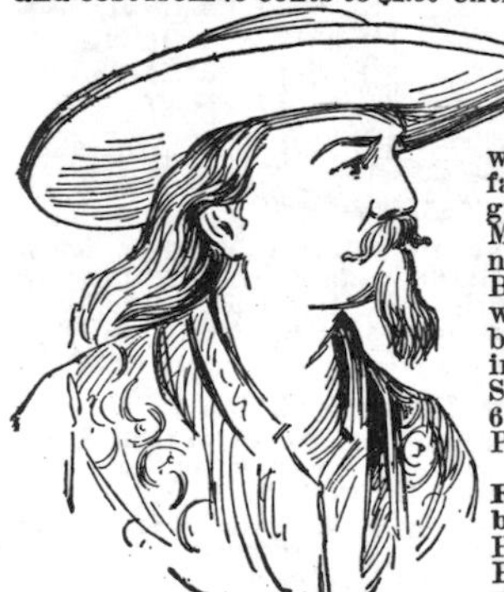

**No. 2658 The World famous J. B. Stetson Sombrero Hat,** worn by the most famous scout and guide in the world. Made from finest nutria fur stock. Belly nutria color with silk band and binding. Crown 4½ inch; brim 4 inch. Sizes 6¾–7½; weight 6 oz. Price each.. **$5.00**

**No. 2660 The Reservation Sombrero,** or Cow Boy's Hat; clear fur stock. Belly nutria color, with silk ribbon band and binding; 4½-inch crown; 4-inch brim; fancy satin lining; heavy leather sweat band; weight 7 oz.; soft smooth finish; will hold its shape and give good solid wear. Sizes 6¾ to 7½. **Always state size desired.** Price each.........**$3.00**

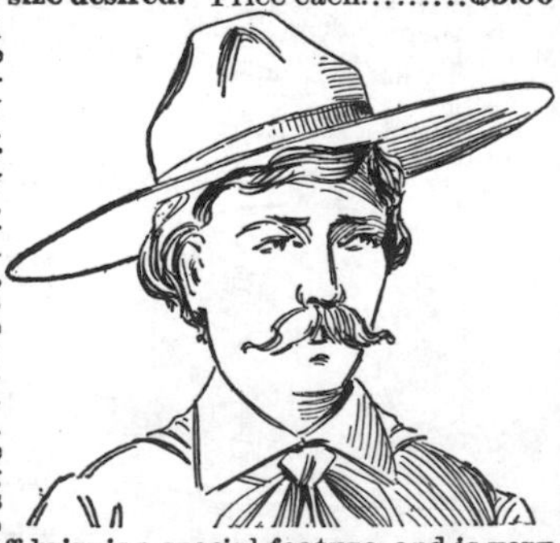

**No. 2661 The Pine Ridge Sombrero,** or Cow Boy's Hat. **Clear Fur Stock.** Belly nutria color, with silk ribbon band; 4½-inch crown, and 4 inch flat stiff knife blade brim; raw edge, improved leather sweatband. One of the best wearing cow boy hats made. The never flop stiff brim is a special feature, and is very popular. Sizes 6¾ to 7½; weight 6 oz. Price, ea..**$3.00**

No. 2663 **Boss of the Plains,** Cow Boy's Sombrero. Made from pure Belgian nutria fur; 4½-inch crown; 4-inch brim, with raw edge; 1 inch silk ribbon band; fancy satin lining; weight 8 oz.; sizes 6¾ to 7½. Belly nutria color. Price. each..... ..........**$3.25**

No. 2664 **Cow Puncher's Sombrero,** clear fur stock; 4½-inch crown; 4-inch brim, with raw edge; silk ribbon band and heavy satin lining; weight 6 oz.; sizes 6¾ to 7½. An excellent hat in every respect. Belly nutria color. **Always state size desired.** Price, each.......................................**$2.85**

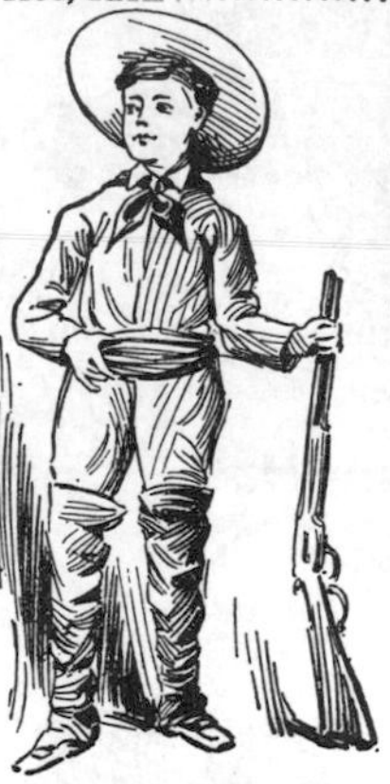

**No. 2665 Pride of the Platte.** A fine soft fur sombrero hat with 4-inch crown and 3½-inch brim with raw edge, and fine 1-inch silk ribbon band. Very popular with cow boys, herdsmen, hunters, vanqueros and planters. Belly nutria color. Sizes 6¾ to 7½. Price each.**$2.75**

**WRITE TO US**

**Concerning anything you do not undurstand regarding COW BOY HATS. We can supply you with any kind of hat in the market at prices that are lower than any other concern on earth.**

## The Cattle King, $2.50

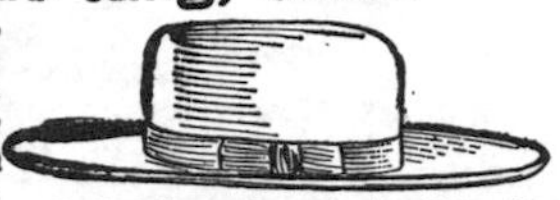

**No. 2667 The Cattle King, cow boys' sombrero. Clear nutria fur stock. Belly nutria color. 4½-inch crown; 4-inch brim, with raw edge.** Fine soft finish. One inch silk ribbon band. Sizes 6¾ to 7½. **One of our specially good things.** Guaranteed to give satisfaction. Weight 6 oz. Price, each .................................**$2.50**

No. 2668 **The Cattle King Sombrero.** Same as above, with silk band and binding; weight 6 oz.; sizes 6¾ to 7½. Belly nutria color. Price, each ......... .........................**$2.75**

## Buckskin Felt Sombreros.

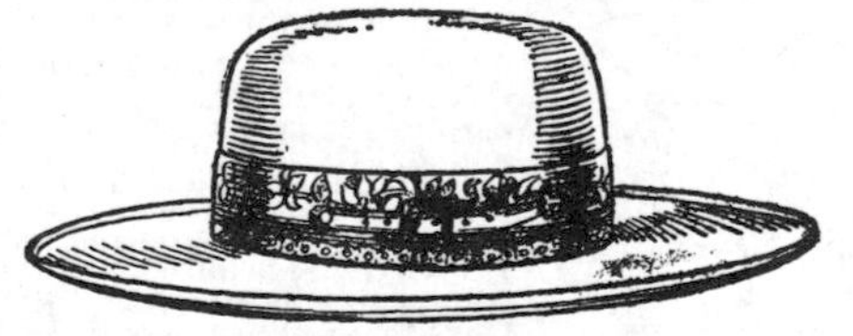

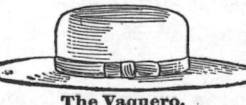

Nos. 2669–2670.

No. 2669 **Cow Boys' Buckskin Felt Sombreros.** 4½-inch crown; 4-inch brim, and 1⅜-inch leather band. Belly nutria or buckskin color. Raw edge and fine leather sweat band. Sizes 6¾ to 7½. Weight 8 oz. Price, each...................................**$2.25**

No. 2670 **Cow Boys' Extra Fine Heavy Weight Saxony Wool Sombreros,** with 4½-inch crown and 4-inch brim, with wide single buckle embossed leather band and leather binding. The leather band on this hat is a handsome and desirable feature; it is embossed in beautiful floral and novelty patterns in variegated colors; very attractive and handsome. Sizes 6¾ to 7⅜ only. Color belly nutria or light calfskin. Price, each.................**$1.69**

## The Mustang Hat.

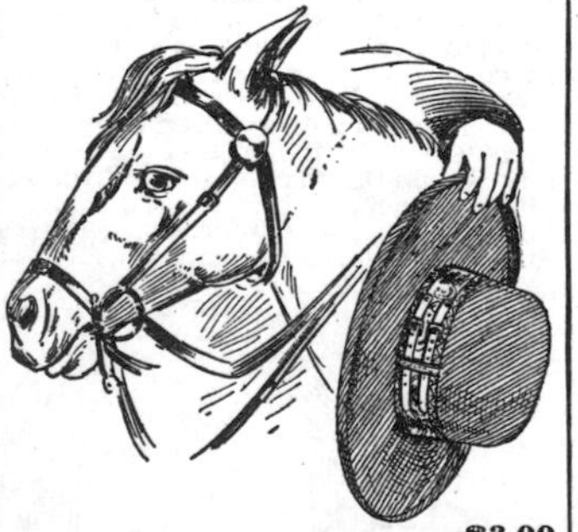

**No. 2672 The Mustang. Cow Boy's Buckskin Felt Sombrero.** 4½ inch crown, 4 inch brim and 2 inch embossed double buckle; leather band and leather binding, and fancy satin lining. Sizes. 6¾ to 7½. Color, calfskin or buckskin. Weight, 8 oz. **Always state size desired.** Price, each.......................................**$3.00**

**IMPORTANT.—Always mention size and Catalogue number when ordering hats of any kind.**

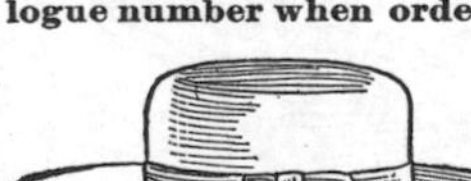

The Vaquero.

**No. 2674 The Vaquero.** An ideal sombrero. Made from clear nutria fur. Belly nutria color. 4½ inch crown, and 3¾ inch flat air splitting brim. Improved leather sweat band and raw edge. Made without lining and with one-inch, silk ribbon band. Silk, elastic cord and eyelet, which can be attached to the coat, thus avoiding trouble and "cuss words" in case the hat should blow off. Sizes, 6¾ to 7½. Weight, 6 oz. Price, each.......................**$3.00**

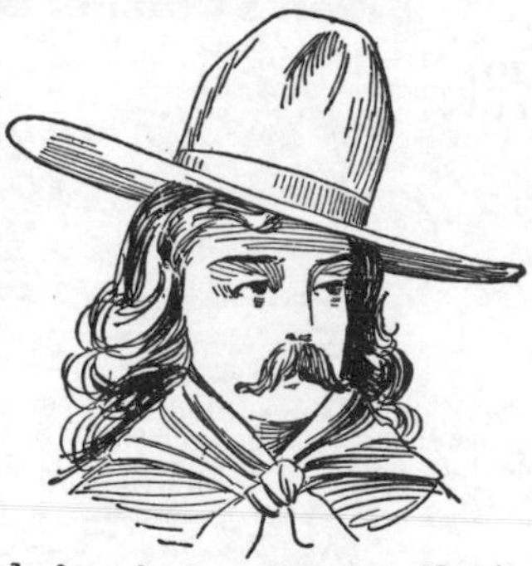

**No. 2675 Texan Chief Cow Boys' High Crown Mexican Style Sombrero Hat,** five-inch brim and 6½ inch crown; fine leather sweat band and handsome satin lining. One-inch silk ribbon band and flat. Never-flop brim with raw edge. One of the very best as well as the most popular Sombreros ever made. Sizes, 6¾ to 7½. Color belly nutria. Made from best quality clear Nutria fur. Full of real goodness and will give excellent satisfaction. Price, each...............................**$5.25**

## An Old Favorite.

**Hand Made. Kettle Finish.**

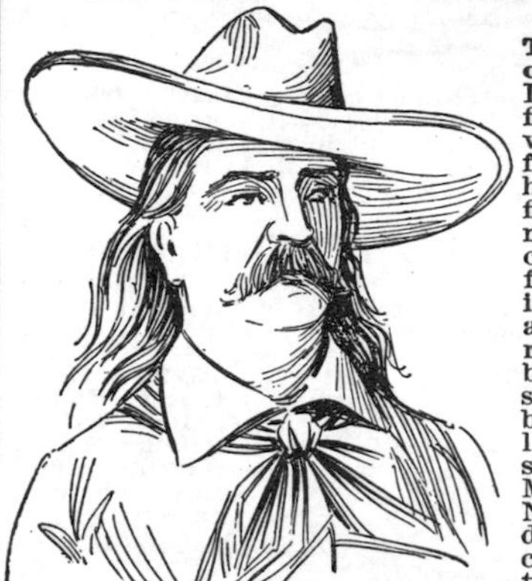

**No. 2676 This hat is an old favorite.** It has that fine soft velvety finish found only in hats of the finest grade, made from clear nutria fur, with 6½ inch crown and 3½ inch raw edge brim. Narrow silk ribbon band and fine leather sweat band. Made in Belly Nutria or dark cream color. Sizes 6¾ to 7½. Price, each....**$2.75**

No. 2677 **Same hat as above,** but made in jet black. Warrented to wear and prove satisfactory in every respect. Price. each...................**$2.75**

## The Sportsman's Hat.

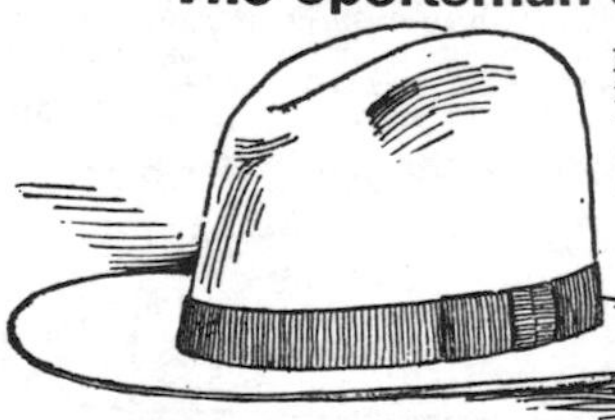

**An entirely new hat and one that is largely used by wheelmen, tourists, hunters, horsemen, and for general wear. Its popularity is unquestioned. It is comfortable dependable and dressy.**

No. 2678 **Sportsman's Soft Felt Hat** made from clear Nutria stock, 6-inch crown, 3-inch brim with raw edge. Improved leather sweat band. One inch silk ribbon band. Handsome fawn brown color. Sizes 6¾ to 7½. Light, soft and comfortable. Price, each.......................................**$1.50**

No. 2679 **Sportsman's Hat,** same as above, but made in drab color. Sizes 6¾ to 7½, **Always state size wanted.** Price, each.......................**$1.50**

## Leather Hat Bands.

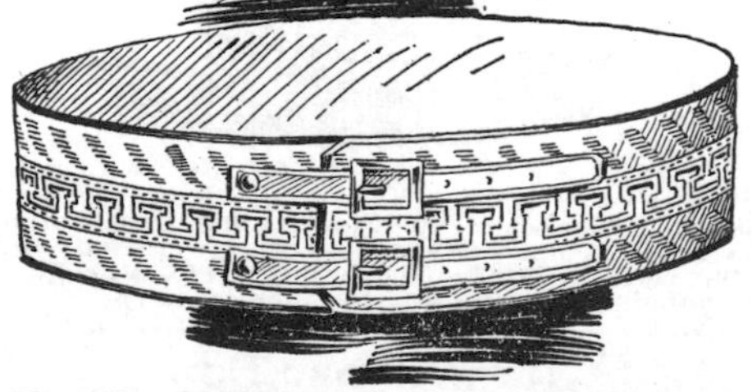

No. 2680 **Cow Boy's** 2-inch all leather hat bands. Embossed russet leather, with double straps and two small buckles, will fit any hat. Each.....**$0.39**

No. 2681 **Russet Leather Embossed Hat Bands,** 1½ inches wide, with single strap and buckle. All solid leather oak tanned. Price, each.........**$0.25**

## Imported Silver Tinsel Stars.

**For Decorating Cow Boys' Hats, Gloves, Etc.**

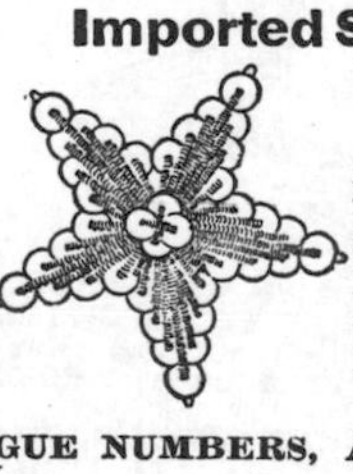

No. 2682 **Extra Fine Quality Imported Silver Stars.** Largely used for decorating sombreros, gauntlet gloves, masquerade costumes. etc., etc. We import these stars direct and guarantee the quality to be first-class in every respect. Per do..**$0.70** Per gross.**$7.50**

## MEN'S STRAW HATS.

**Sizes 6¾, 6⅞, 7, 7⅛, 7¼ and 7⅜ Only.**

We Positively cannot furnish sizes larger than 7⅜ in straw hats. **They are not manufactured.**

**ORDER STRAW HATS EARLY. The season for this class of goods is short. We cannot guarantee to fill orders for straw hats later than Sept. 1st.**

### Canton Straws, 25c.

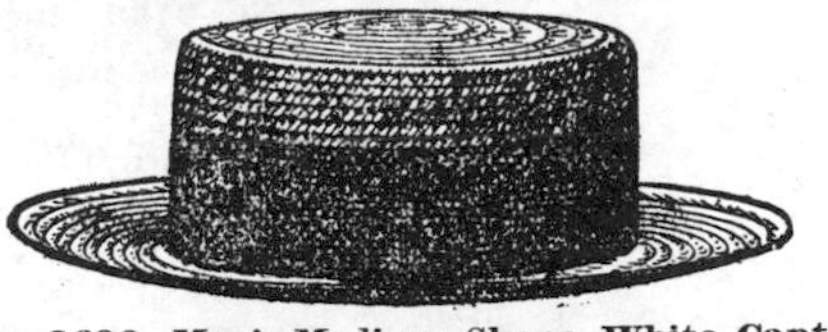

**No. 2690 Men's Medium Shape White Canton Straw Hats,** with wide ribbon band, soft braided straw; sizes 6¾ to 7⅜ only. Price each........**$0.25**

**No. 2691 Men's Extra Quality Fine Braided White Canton Straw Hats,** medium shape brim and crown, wide ribbon band. Special price each..**$0.45**

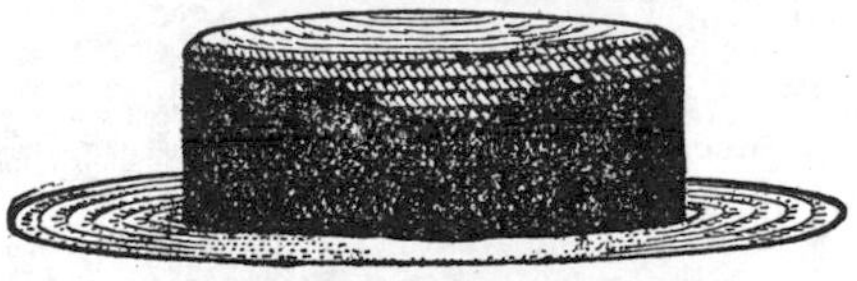

**No. 2692 Young Men's Extra Quality White Braided Straw Hats,** with flat brim and wide ribbon band; very popular, nobby shape. Sizes 6¾ to 7⅜. Price each............**$0.50**

**No. 2693 Young Men's Finest Quality White Braided Straw Hats,** same style and shape as above; sizes 6¾ to 7⅜. Price each............**$0.75**

### Full Shape Canton Hats.

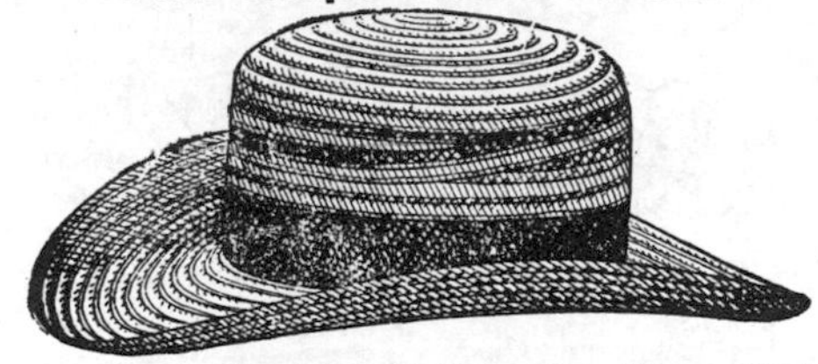

**No. 2694 Men's Braided Canton Straw Hats.** Full shape with roll brim and ribbon band; ventilated crown; sizes 6¾ to 7⅜. Each............**$0.21**

### Harvest Hats.

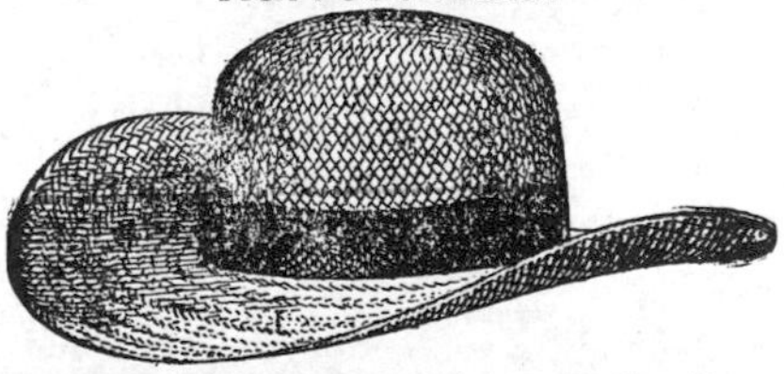

**No. 2695 Men's Full Shape India Panama Harvest Hats,** 3-inch brim. Also a very desirable hat for fishing and rusticating.
Price each.........**$0.05** Per dozen.........**$0.50**

### Boys' Straw Hats.

**Sizes 6½ to 7 Only.**

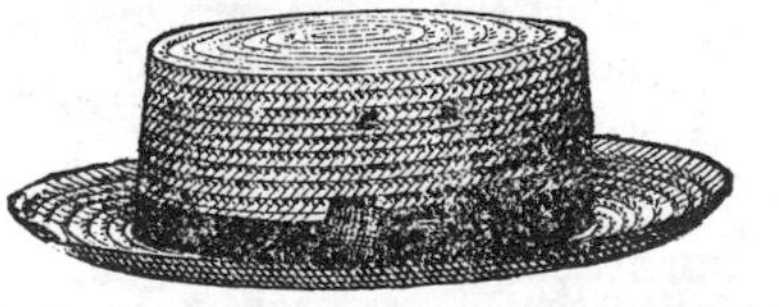

**No. 2696 Boy's Medium Shape Braided Straw Hats,** with ribbon band; good standard quality.
Price each............**$0.25**

**No. 2697 Boys' Extra Quality White Braided Canton Straw Hats,** medium shape with black ribbon band; sizes 6½ to 7. Price each........**$0.45**

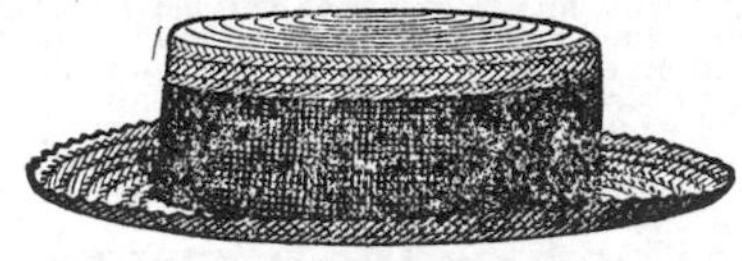

**No. 2698 Boys' Fine White Braided Straw Sailor Hats,** with wide ribbon band; very nobby; sizes 6½ to 7. Price each..........**$0.47**

**Suit a Perfect Fit.**

BENAN, IOWA.

SEARS, ROEBUCK & CO., Chicago.

GENTLEMEN:—I received the suit of clothes O. K. A perfect fit and a much better suit than I expected to get. Thanks. Yours respectfully,

T. J. BUTRICK.

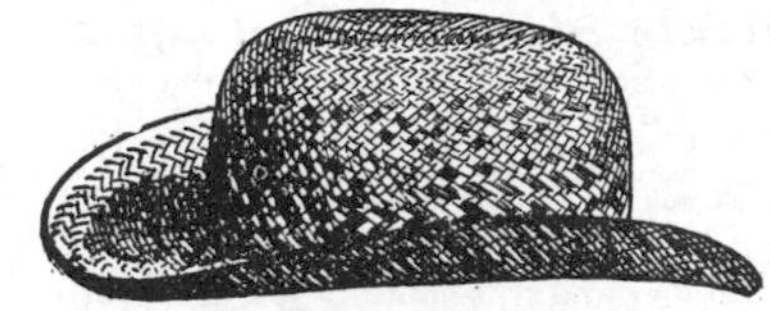

**No. 2699 Boys' Indian Panama Hats,** with curl brim; cheap and durable; extra good value.
Price each............**$0.05** Per dozen........**$0.50**

### Children's Straw Hats.

**Sizes 6 to 6¾ Only.**

**Made expressly for little children and not made in large boys' sizes.**

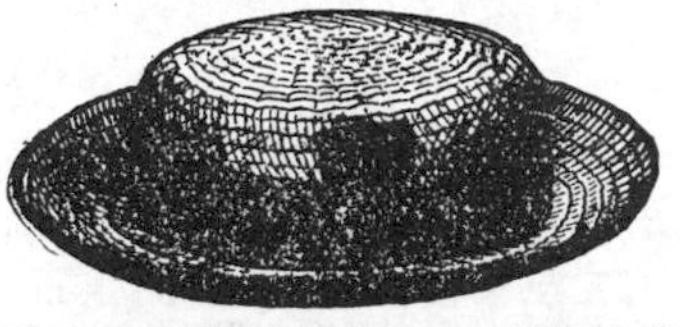

**No. 2700 Children's White or Mixed Braided Straw Turban Hats,** with ribbon band; very nobby and extra quality. Prize each............**$0.24**

**No. 2701 Children's Fancy Braided Straw Turban Hats,** white, brown or fancy mixtures; ribbon band and bow. Price each............**$0.37**

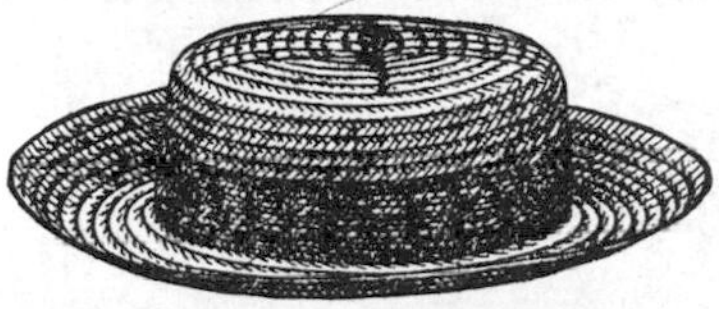

**No. 2702 Children's Extra Fine White Braided Straw Hats,** with fancy colored satin ribbon bands; one of the nobbiest made; sizes 6 to 6¾.
Price each............**$0.50**

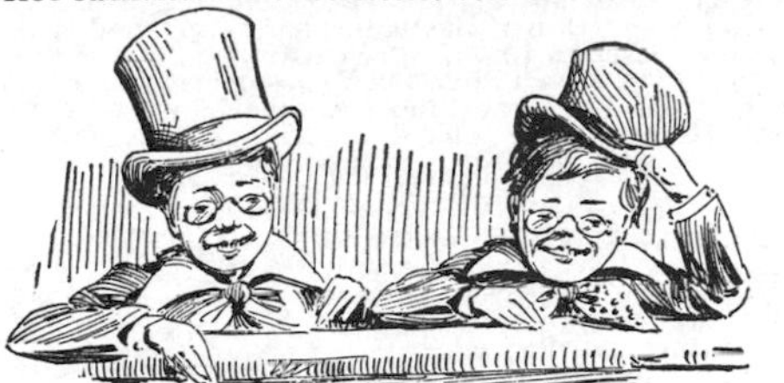

### Boys' Hats.

**Sizes 6½, 6⅝, 6¾, 6⅞ and 7. Always state size desired.**

**No. 2705** Boys' School Hats, made from staple wool felt. Turban style, with neat band and leather sweat Sizes 6½ to 7. Black only. Price, each.........**$0.25**

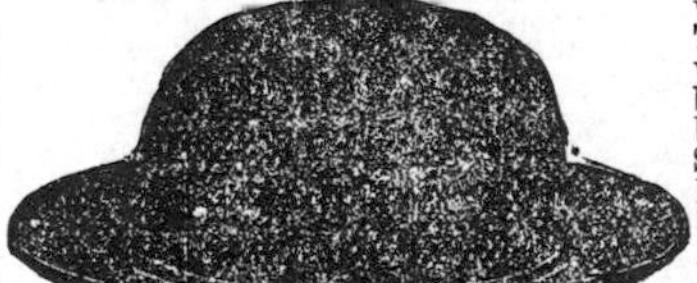

**No. 2706 Boys' and Youths fine Saxony wool Hats,** medium shape crown and brim. Colors, **black, blue** or **brown.** Always state size and color wanted. These hats will give excellent service. They are fine in finish and very durable. Made with ribbon band and leather sweat band. Price, each............**$0.45**

**OUR SCHOOL SPECIAL.**

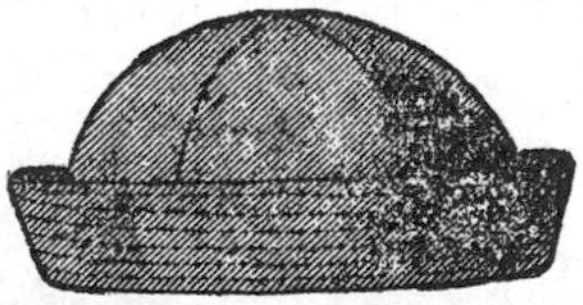

**No. 2708 The best Boys' School Hat ever made.** We have these hats made up from fine navy blue wool worsted suitings. Made in turban style with heavily stitched brim and 6 piece top. Sizes 6½ to 7. Price, each............**$0.47**

### Boys' Crushers.

**No. 2709 Boys' and Youths Fine Saxony Wool Crushers.** Curling brim and round crown. Made from extra selected stock. Colors black, blue or brown. Finely made and finished. Leather sweat band and raw edge. Price, each............**$0.50**

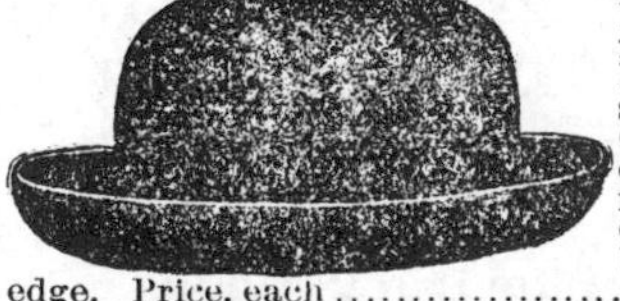

**Always state size and color desired.**

**No. 2710 Boys' and Youths Fine Soft Fur Felt Crushers.** Raw edge, with curling brim and round crown. Fine soft finish, narrow ribbon band and fine leather sweat band. Sizes 6½ to 7 only. Colors, black, brown or blue. Price, each............**$0.75**

**Always state size and color desired.**

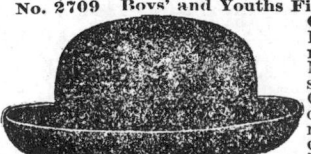

### Boys' Fedora Hats.

**No. 2711 Boys' latest style Fedora Hats.** Made from fine Saxony wool, with band and binding and leather sweat band. Sizes 6½ to 7. Color black. Price, each......**$0.47**

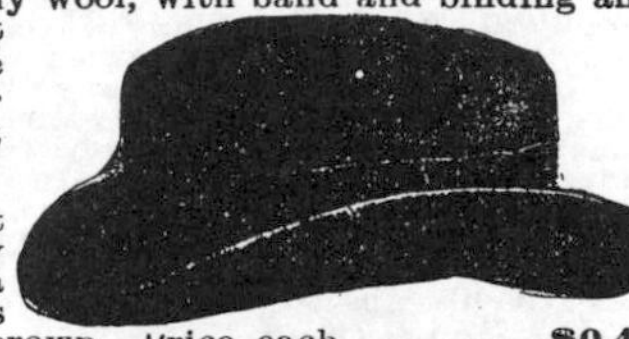

**No. 2712 Boys' latest style Saxony Wool Fedora Hats.** Same as above, in dark brown, Price, each............**$0.47**

**No. 2713 Boys' handsome Clear Fur Felt Fedora Hats.** Wide silk ribbon band and binding. Latest and nobbiest style. Sizes 6½ to 7. Color black, Price, each............**$0.95**

**No. 2714 Boys' Clear Fur Felt Fedora Hats.** Same as above, in dark brown. Price, each....**$0.95**

**No. 2715 The handsomest Boys' Hat made.** Very latest Fedora style, with heavy satin lining, wide silk ribbon band and binding and fine leather sweat band. Soft and fine and very dressy. Sizes 6½ to 7 only. Color black. Made from finest fur felt. Price, each............**$1.25**

**No. 2716 Same hat as above,** made in a beautiful shade of seal or golden brown. Price, each....**$1.25**

**THE SIZE OF A HAT is very important, therefore when you make out your order don't forget to state just what size you want. We can then fill your order promptly and to your entire satisfaction.**

### Men's Spring and Summer Caps.

**"He that hath no head needs no Cap,"** But he that hath a wise head will readily appreciate the wonderful values we are offering this season in this line of goods. Every Cap we quote is exactly as we represent it. Order the Cap you wish by catalogue number, always being sure to state size wanted and we will guarantee to fill your order correctly and give you such satisfaction as you have never had before. **Always mention size wanted.**

**MEN'S SIZES 6¾, 6⅞, 7, 7⅛, 7¼, 7⅜ and 7½.**

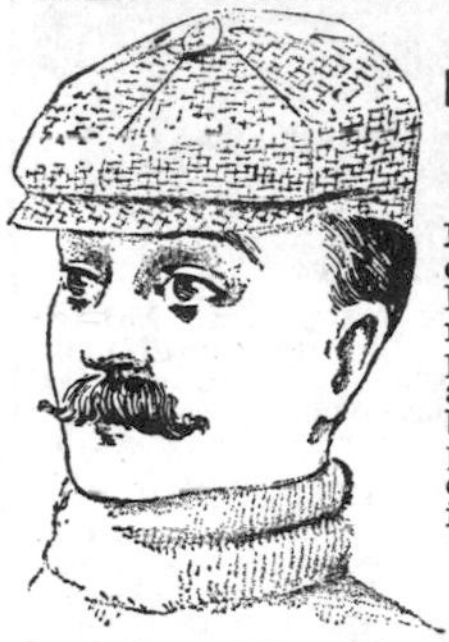

### Men's Fancy Golf Caps at 21c.

**No. 2718 Men's Fancy Mixed Cassimere Golf Caps,** extra well made and nicely lined; assorted dark and medium colors. This is positively a great bargain and one that we know will be appreciated by every person securing one of these caps. We have them made in all sizes from 6¾ to 6½.
Price each............**$0.21**
Per doxen............**2.35**

### At 25c.-The Fourth Part of a Dollar.

**No. 2719 One of our specially good values, Men's Navy Blue Broadcloth Golf Caps.** Six piece top; extra well made and nicely lined. Sizes 6¾ to 7½. Price each............**$0.25**
Per dozen............**2.70**

**No. 2720 Men's Navy Blue Fine Ribbed Corduroy Golf Caps.** Six piece top, well made and lined throughout. Very popular for summer wear. Sizes 6¾ to 7½. Price each............**$0.25**
Per dozen............**2.70**

**No. 2721 Men's Corduroy Golf Caps;** same as above in beautiful drab shade.
Price each..........**$0.25** Per dozen.. ......**2.70$**

**No. 2722 Men's Handsome Golden Brown Corduroy Golf Caps;** same style and quality as above, Sizes 6¾ to 7½. Price each............**$0.25**
Per dozen............**2.70**

### Fancy Corduroy Caps.

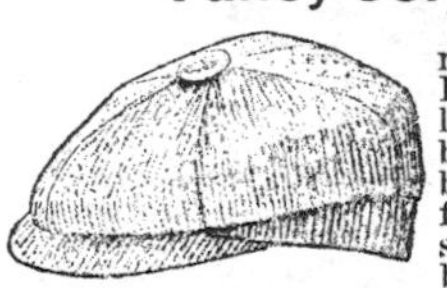

**No. 2724** Men's fancy mixed Corduroy golf caps. Extra fine quality, with leather sweat bands and beautiful silk lining. Dark blue with an artistic silver fawn mixture of small specks, forming a truely beautiful combination. Sizes 6¾ to 7½. Price, each............**$0.45**

**No. 2725** Men's fancy mixed Corduroy golf caps, same as above, in handsome golden brown mixtures. Price, each............**$0.45**

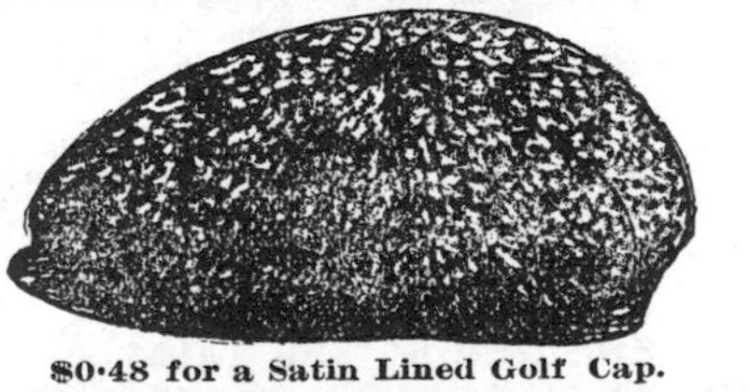

**$0.48 for a Satin Lined Golf Cap.**

**No. 2726 Men's Extra Quality** all wool gray mixture cheviot golf caps. Six peice top and hook down front. Fine leather sweat band. All neat dressy patterns. Sixes 6¾ to 7½, Price, each. .......**$0.48**

**No. 2727 Same Cap** as above in handsome brown mixed all wool cassimers. Full satin lined,
Price, each............**$0.48**

**IT ISN'T BECAUSE WE HAVE NOT TRIED, IF WE DO NOT PLEASE YOU BEYOND YOUR EXPECTATIONS. IF ANY MISTAKE SHOULD OCCUR IN YOUR ORDER, WE ARE AS ANXIOUS TO REMEDY IT AS YOU ARE. WRITE US.**

## $0.50 for a Satin Lined Broadcloth Golf Cap.

**No. 2728** This is certainly a remarkable offer. These caps are made from an extra fine quality navy blue broadcloth, with heavy satin lining and hook-down front. Six piece top with double stitched seams and extra fine finish. **They would be cheap in large retail stores at $0.75.** Sizes 6¾ to 7½.
Our price, each....................................$0.50

**THE SIZE OF A CAP is very important. Do not neglect to state size when making out your order,** Men's caps are made in the following sizes, 6¾, 6⅞, 7, 7⅛, 7¼, 7⅜, 7½.

## Linen Crash or Grass Cloth Caps.

**The Coolist Caps in the World.**

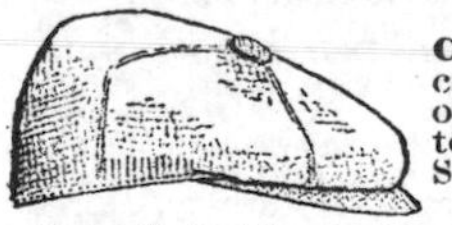

**No. 2729 Men's Linen Crash** or grass cloth golf caps. Regulation golf or outing style, with 6-piece top and light sateen lining. Sizes 6¾ to 7½.
Price, each..........$0.23

**No. 2730 Men's Superior Quality** plain white duck golf caps—very popular for all outing purposes. Sizes 6¾ to 7½. Price, each............$0.23

**No. 2731 Men's Extra Quality** linen crash yacht caps with leather sweat band. Light and cool, and very much in demand among men of fashion and lovers of solid comfort. Natural linen color. Sizes 6¾ to 7½. Price, each............$0.21

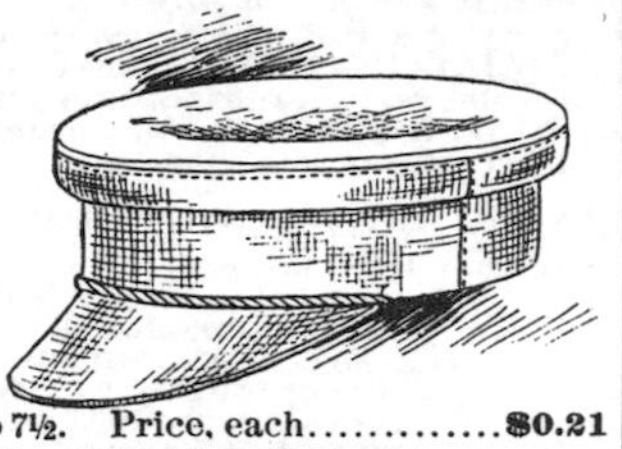

## Men's Yacht Caps.

**Extraordinary Bargains.**

**No. 2739 Men's Extra Quality Navy Blue Cloth Yacht Caps** with wide Hercules braid and cord in front; nicely made up and lined. The best value ever offered. Take advantage of this offer if you want a real bargain. Sizes 6¾ to 7½.
Price each.... ..$0.22

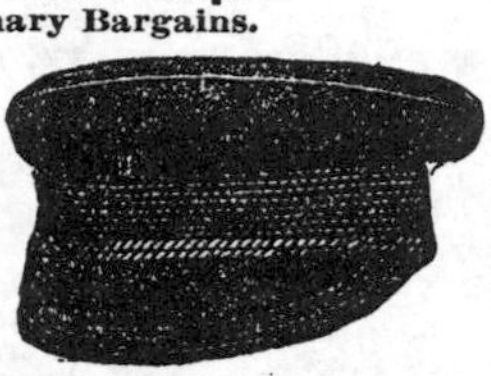

**No. 2740 Men's Imported Navy Blue Broadcloth Yacht Caps,** with wide Hercules braid band and silk cords; fine leather sweat band. One of the very best yacht caps made this season.
Price each....................................$0.45

## Men's Summer Helmets.

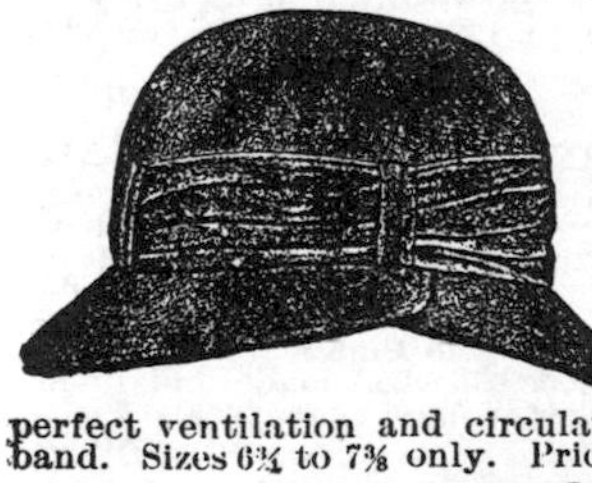

**No. 2741 Solid comfort in these hats; no mistake about that.** They have fine braided straw body, covered with fine slate or dead grass colored selisia with sash to match. Patent ventilated sweat band, allowing perfect ventilation and circulation around entire band. Sizes 6¾ to 7⅜ only. Price each .......$0.49

## Conductor Caps.

**MADE WITH PATENT WIRE FRAME. NEVER GETS OUT OF SHAPE.**

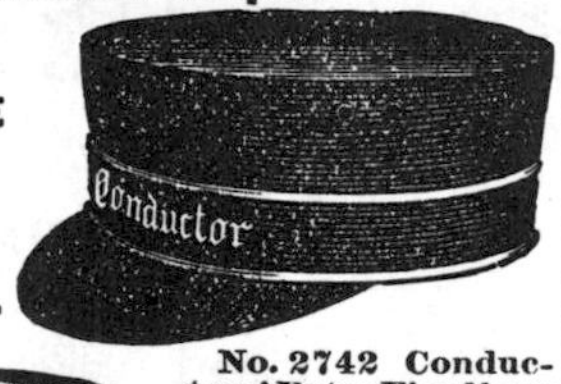


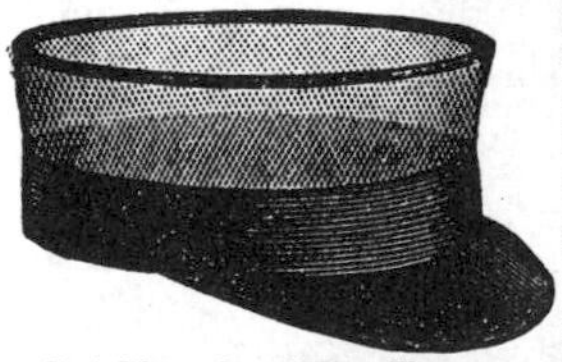

**Cut Showing Wire Frame.**

**No. 2742 Conductors' Extra Fine Navy Blue Broadcloth Caps,** with patented wire frame and fine leather sweat band. These are the same quality caps for which conductors, news agents, trainmen and others who use them are usually obliged to pay from $2.50 to $3.00. We guarantee them to be the most practical as well as best wearing caps of this kind made. Send us your orders direct and **save a dollar or a dollar and a half.** Money refunded if not exactly as represented. Sizes 6¾ to 7½. Price each.......................$1.45

**This price is for plain cap without lettering. Gold wire block embroidered letters will cost 10c. per letter extra.**

## Engineers' Silk Caps.

**Sizes, 6¾ to 7⅜.**

**No. 2743 Engineers' Fine Black Silk Caps,** with extra wide visor to protect the eyes. Handsomely satin lined.
Price, each.. ....$0.69

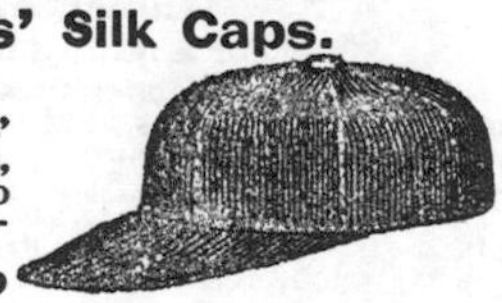

## Nickel Plated Cap Badges.

The following badges are made from the finest German silver handsomely nickel plated.

These badges are made to order with any lettering desired. **The full amount of cash must be sent with the order. We do not send these goods C. O. D.,** and they cannot be returned or exchanged unless we are clearly at fault. Always order by catalogue number and state plainly just what lettering you desire and your orders will receive prompt attention and be filled correctly.

**No. 2744 Nickel Plated German Silver Badge,** size ¾ x3 inches. Conductor, Baggageman, Porter, News Agent, Expressman or any words not exceeding fifteen letters. Made to order.
Price, each........ 0.60 Per dozen..........$6.50

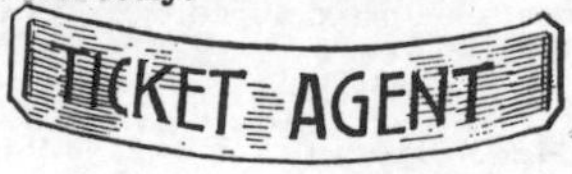


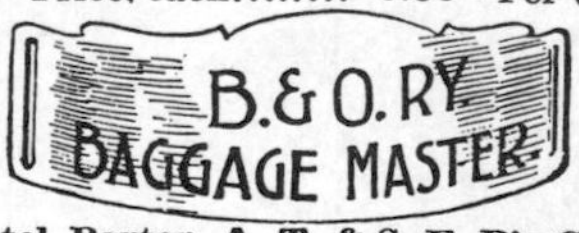


**No. 2745 Nickel Plated German Silver Badge,** with fancy oval. 1 inch wide by 3 inches long. Suitable for such words as **Hotel Porter, A. T. & S. F. R'y Conductor, City Expressman, B. & O. Baggageman** and similar words not exceeding twenty-two letters **Always state what letters you want.**
Price, each....... 0.80 Per dozen. .........$8.90

**NOTE.**—Larger badges made to order at from $1.25 to $2.50 according to size and lettering. It requires about 5 days to have these badges made to order.

## The Paddock Cap.

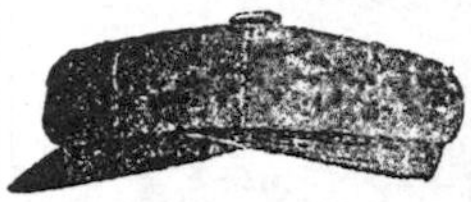

**No. 2746 The New Paddock Cap,** with eight piece puff top and visor made from fine navy blue broadcloth. Nicely lined and finished. Strictly up-to-date. Sizes 6¾ to 7½.
Price each....................................$0.34

## Our 50c. Paddock Cap.

**No. 2747 Men's New Paddock Cap,** made from strictly all wool fancy grey mixed English Cheviot suiting, with fine leather sweat band and heavy satin lining. One of the handsomest caps made this season. Sizes 6¾ to 7½. Price each. ..........$0.50

**No. 2748 Men's Paddock Cap,** same as above but made from fine navy blue broadcloth, with heavy satin lining. Price each..........................$0.50

## Boys' Summer Caps.

**Sizes, 6½, 6⅝, 6¾, 6⅞, 7.**

**No. 2749 Boys' Fancy Mixed Cassimere Golf Caps,** neat grey and brown mixtures, nicely lined and well made up. Always state size desired.
Price, each..............$0.20
Per doz.......................2.25

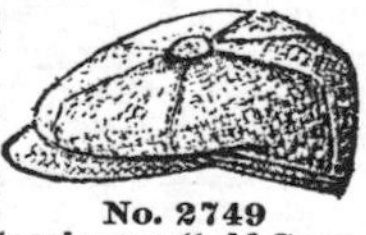

No. 2749

**No. 2750 Boy's Fine Wool Cassimere Golf Caps,** with six-piece top. Fancy plaid and checked patterns and neat mixtures of brown and grey. Fancy lining. Very nobby. Sizes 6½ to 7.
Price, each........ 0.25 Per dozen..........$2.70

**No. 2751 Boy's Plain Navy Blue Broadcloth Golf Caps.** Six piece top with sateen lining.
Price, each......... 0.25 Per dozen..........$2.70

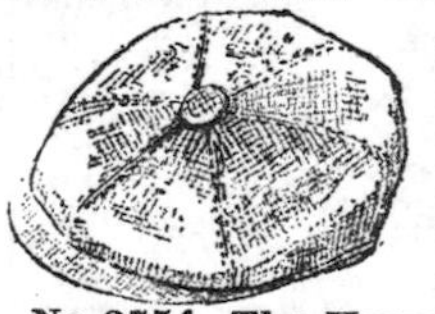

**No. 2752 The Most Stylish** as well as most comfortable summer cap made. These caps are made from imported linen crash, natural linen color, with six piece top, nicely made and sure to please. Sizes, 6⅛ to 7.
Price, each............$0.23
Per dozen.............. 2.58

**No. 2754 The Harvard Golf Cap.** Made from fine all wool fancy grey mixed cheviot suitings. Heavy satin lining and patent hook down front. Sizes, 6⅛ to 7.
Price, each...........$0.45

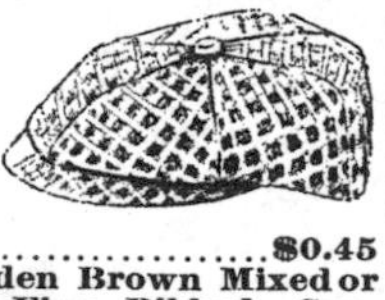

**No. 2755 The Harvard Golf Cap.** Same as above in rich brown mixtures.
Price, each....................................$0.45

**No. 2756 Boys' Fancy Golden Brown Mixed or Drab Fine Ribbed Curduroy Golf Caps.** Nicely made up and lined. One of the most popular caps of the season. Sizes, 6½ to 7.
Price, each..........$0.33

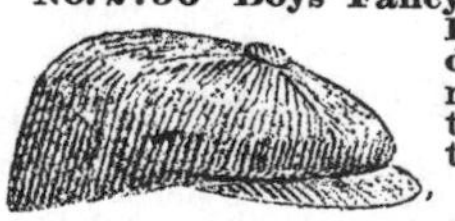

## Boys' Yacht Caps.

**Sizes, 6½ to 7.**

**No. 2757 Boys' Navy Blue Flannel Yacht Caps.** With cord band. Well made and lined.
Price, each, 18c; per dozen..........................$1.65

**No. 2758 Our Special 25c Yacht.** Made from fine quality navy blue broadcloth, with wide Hercules braid and silk cord trimming. Serge lining. Price, each..................$0.25
Per dozen................................................ 2.70

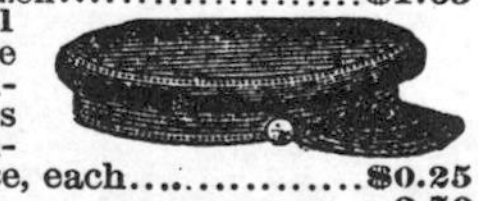

## Boys' White Duck Caps.

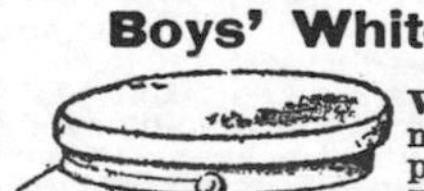

**No. 2759 Boys' Fine White Duck Caps.** Nicely made and finished. Very popular for general wear as well as outing purposes.
Sizes, 6½ to 7. Price, each........$0.23
Per dozen.................................................. 2.60

## The New University Cap at 50c.

**No. 2761 Boys' Finest Navy Blue Broadcloth University Caps.** Similar to the golf style, but fuller in the crown, and does not hook down in front lined with satin. Sizes, 6½ to 7. Warranted first class in every way. Price, each, 50c; per dozen.......$5.40

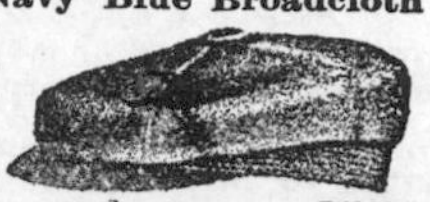

## Boys' Military Caps.

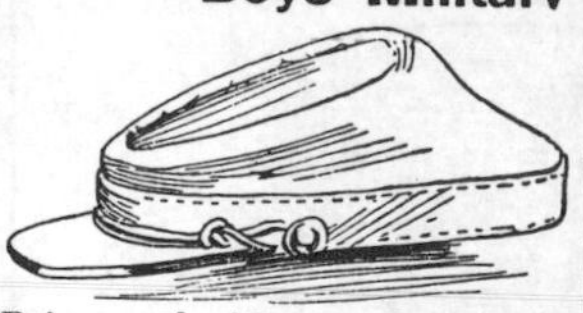

**No. 2763 Boys' Fine Navy Blue Cadet or Military Cap.** Made from regulation uniform cloth, with gilt cord and buttons. Always a great favorite with the boys. **Sizes, 6⅝ to 7⅛.**
Price, each, 48c; per dozen..............................$5.35

## Children's Caps.

**A Specially Selected Assortment of Strictly Up-to-date Styles, at Prices Calculated to Make Your Pocket Book Feel Good.** Made in the following sizes, 6⅛, 6¼, 6⅜, 6½, 6⅝, 6¾ and 6⅞

**No. 2765 Children's Navy Blue Broadcloth Golf Cap.** Silk lined throughout and handsomely embroidered on front of crown in gold and silver. Fancy designs. One of the handsomest and swellish caps we have. **Sure to please.** You will like it if you order it. Price, each....$0.47

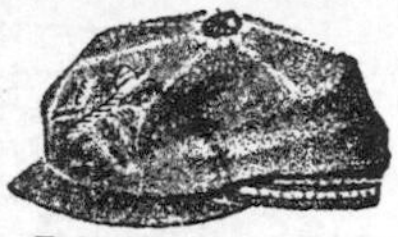

## The Midshipman Cap. at 50c.

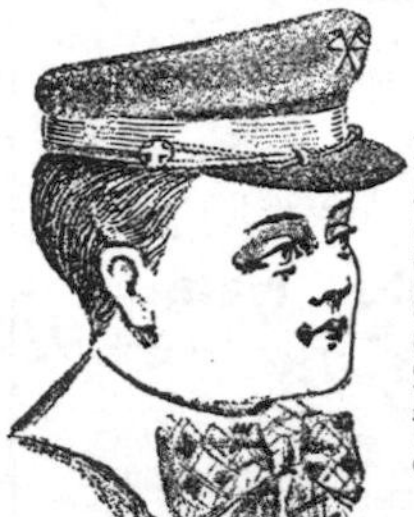

**No. 2766 Children's Fancy Midshipman Yacht Cap.** Made from imported navy blue broadcloth, with fine leather sweat band and silk lining, one-inch gold band and heavy double gold cord and buttons. Handsome gold embroidery on front of crown. Rich and dressy. Nothing but fine materials used in this cap. Sizes, 6⅛ to 6⅞.
Price, each.................................$0.50

## Washable Sailor Caps.

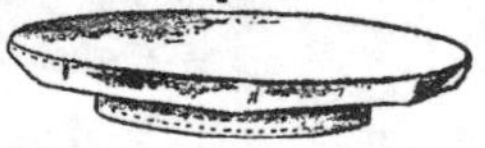

**No. 2767 Children's and Misses' Washable Sailor Caps.** Made of plain white duck. Unlined, with removable bands that can be taken out when the cap is washed. Sizes, 6⅛ to 6⅞. Price, each..............................$0.25

**No. 2768 Washable Sailor Cap.** Same as above in plain cadet blue duck. Price, each.........$0.25

**No. 2769 Washable Sailor Cap.** Same as above in white duck with small black dots. Very neat.
Price, each............................................$0.25

**No. 2770 Washable Sailor Cap.** Same as above but made from pure linen crash cloth. Plain natural linen color. Very fashionable and unexcelled for wear. Washes beautifully. Price, each........$0.25

## Sailor Caps.

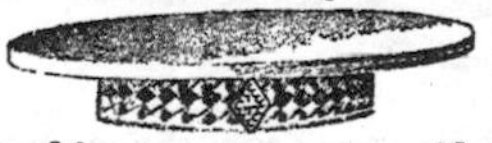

**No. 2771 Children's and Misses' Broad Crowned Sailor Caps.** Fine all wool flannel, with fine selisia lining and fancy braided bands and fancy ornament on side. Sizes, 6⅛ to 6¾. Navy blue color. Each.......................................$0.33

**No. 2772 Sailor Cap.** Same as above in cardinal red, Price, each.......................................$0.33

## Evangeline Sailors.

**The Neatest Ever Made.**

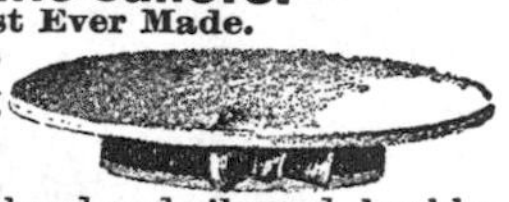

**No. 2774 Children's and Misses' Broad Crown Evageline Sailor Caps.** Plain navy blue or gornet yacht cloth, with black silk ribbon band and silvered buckle; nicely lined and extra well made, very dressy. Sizes, 6⅛ to 6¾. Price, each......................$0.48

## Saratoga Corduroy Caps.

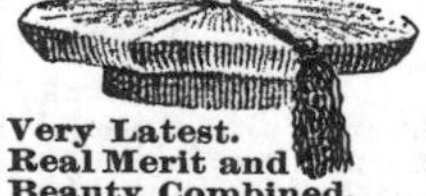

**Very Latest. Real Merit and Beauty Combined.**

**No. 2776 The Saratoga Cap.** The most sensible and practical, as well as handsomest, children's and misses' cap made. These caps are made from specially imported birds-eye fancy corduroy, fine and soft as velvet; dark blue color, with fine sprinkling of silver gray birds-eye dots, handsomely made and lined. Octagonal shape crown with black silk cord and tassel. Sizes. 6⅛ to 6¾. Price, each.......................................$0.50

**No. 2777 The Saratoga Corduroy Cap,** same as above but made in one of the most beautiful shades of golden brown ever shown. Price, each......$0.50

## The Primrose Tan O'Shanter.

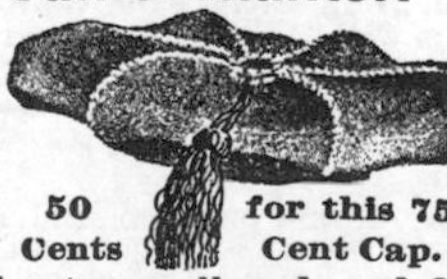

**50 Cents for this 75 Cent Cap.**

**No. 2778 The Primrose Tam O'Shanter,** made from fine all wool navy blue yacht cloth, large broad crown tastefully trimmed with white silk gimp cord, ornamented in center of crown. Silk cord and tassels, fancy lining and extra well made and finished, Sizes, 6⅛ to 6¾. Always state just what size you want. Price, each.....................................$0.50

**WE HAVE IN STOCK AN ENDLESS VARIETY OF CHILDREN'S CLOTHING. REFER TO PAGES 171 TO 176. OUR PRICES ARE THE LOWEST AND OUR C. O. D. TERMS ARE MOST LIBERAL.**

## Our Famous 25c Tam O'Shanter.

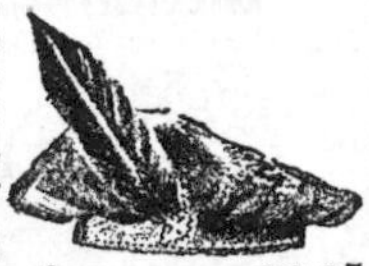

**No. 2779.** We offer these caps at about one half what your local dealer could sell them for. They are made from fine navy blue wool cloth, nicely lined and trimmed with narrow tinsel braid around band; fancy buckle and feather at side. Very nobby looking and sure to please. Sizes 6⅛ to 6¾. Price, each...........**$0.25**

**No. 2781 Tam O' Shanter Cap.** Same as above; made in garnet color. Price, each.............**$0.25**

## The Paris Novelty Tam O'Shanter.

### 45c.

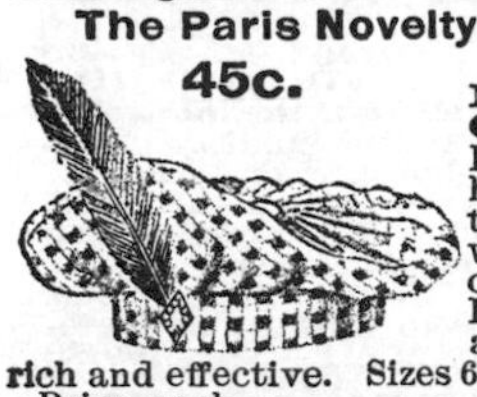

**No. 2782 The Paris Novelty Tam O' Shanter Cap,** made of imported French novelty cloth, in handsome plaid combinations of navy blue and white, with full gathered crown and button on top. Fancy buckle and feather at side; fancy lining; very rich and effective. Sizes 6⅛ to 6¾.
Price, each ..................................... **$0.45**

**No. 2783 The Paris Novelty Tam O' Shanter Cap.** Same as above, in rich golden brown and white checks and plaids. **Truly beautiful.**
Price, each....................................... **$0.45**

## The Baltimore Middy Cap.

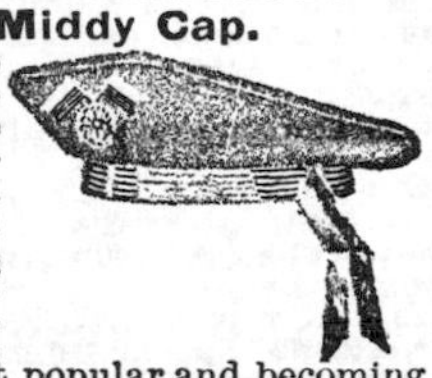

**No. 2784 The Baltimore Middy Cap,** absolutely correct sailor shape. Made from finest imported broadcloth, plain navy blue, with one inch imported gold band and finest gold embroidered marine ornament in front of crown. Full silk lined throughout, with ribbons on side. This is one of the most popular and becoming sailor caps ever made up. Heretofore they have only been handled by exclusive and high-priced retailers. We have had them made up for us in immense quantities and will sell them at a price within the reach of all. Sizes 6⅛ to 6⅞. Here is your chance to get something really fine at your own price.
Our special price, each........................ **$0.75**

## The Priscilla Cap, 85c.

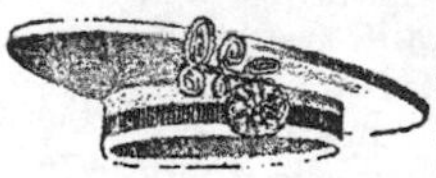

**No. 2785 The Priscilla Cap,** something entirely new and strictly up-to-date. Made from finest imported French ladies' cloth, with extra wide spring edge crown. Wide black ribbon band and large black fancy braid ornament on side; silk lined throughout; navy blue or garnet color. Sizes 6⅛ to 6¾.
Price, each ......................................... **$0.85**

## The Princess Cap, $1.00.

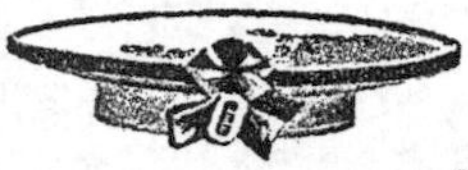

**No. 2787 The Princess Cap,** made from finest imported navy blue broadcloth, with wide crown and flange edge, with spring running around entire outer edge to keep it in shape. Bound around edge with heavy corded black silk, with black silk ribbon and pearl buckle ornament at side. Lined throughout with extra heavy satin. Nothing but the very finest materials used. Regular retail value anywhere, $1.50. Our Special price each. **$1.00**

## Misses' and Children's Silk Caps.

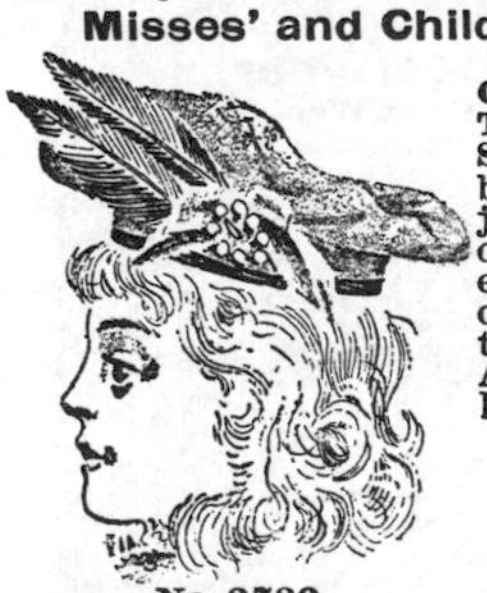

No. 2789

**No. 2789 Misses' and Children's Fine Heavy Trimmed Silk Tam O' Shanter Caps.** Silk ribbon bow and beautiful jeweled imperial buckle on side with jaunty feather to correspond with color of cap. Pleated puff top with button in center. Assorted colors.
Price each.......... **$1.00**

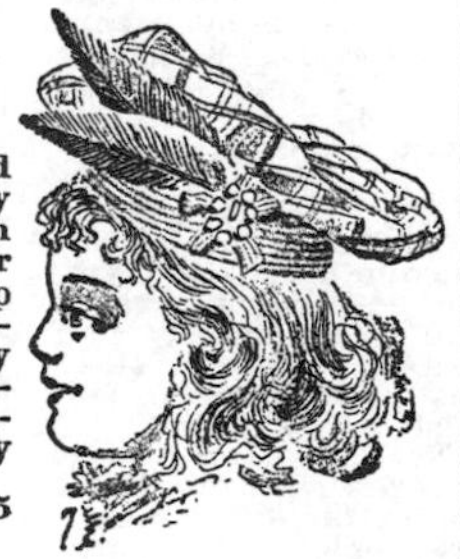

**No. 2790 Misses' and Children's Extra Quality Bright Colored, Scotch Plaid, Silk Tam O'Shanter Caps** with gathered Puff top and heavy silk or satin lining, wide silk corded fancy ribbon band, jeweled buckle and feathers at side. Elegantly made up and finely finished throughout.
Price each............**$1.45**

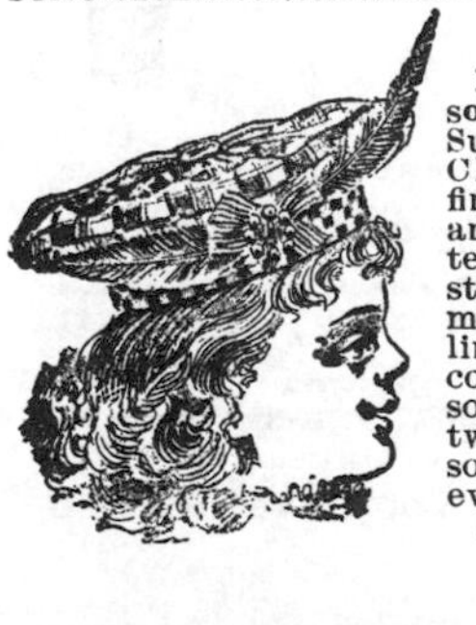

**No. 2791 The Handsomest Cap of the Season.** Suited alike for Misses and Children. Made from finest taffeta silk in rich and beautiful plaid patterns, in a choice and strictly up-to-date assortment of colors. Full satin lined, with heavy fancy corded ribbon band, hand some jeweled buckle and two feathers on side. Absolutely high grade in every respect.
Price each..........**$1.69**

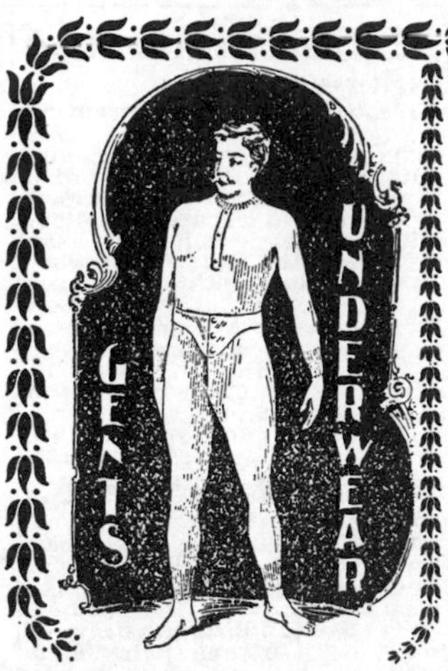


# MEN'S UNDERWEAR.

**ASTONISHING TEMPTATIONS FOR ALL MANKIND.**

**QUALITIES THAT WILL SURPRISE YOU,**

**PRICES THAT WILL CONVINCE YOU.**

MAKE A CHANGE. **Off with the Old, on with the New. Prudence suggests it, your health demands it. Our prices protect you from over profit paying. We handle more Underwear and Hosiery than any one concern in the World. We save you nearly 50 per cent. on your purchases and give you better values than you could possible obtain anywhere else either wholesale or retail. Every garment we quote is guaranteed to be exactly as represented or money refunded. EVERY PRICE WE QUOTE IS A REVELATION.**

OUR TERMS ARE LIBERAL. All goods sent C. O. D., subject to examination, on receipt of $1.00, balance and express charges payable at express office. **Three per cent. Discount allowed if cash in full accompanies your order.**
**Nearly All Our Customers Send Cash in Full.**

## MEN'S SUMMER UNDERWEAR.

**Shirt Sizes: 34, 36, 38, 40, 42 and 44, Chest Measurement.**
**Drawers Sizes: 30, 32, 34, 36, 38, 40 and 42, Waist Measurement.**
**Always mention size when ordering underwear.**

## A Balbriggan Shirt for 25c.

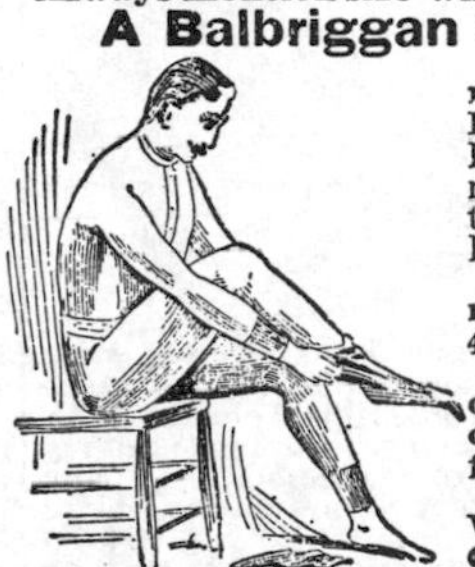

**No. 2801 Men's Summer Weight Unbleached Balbriggan Undershirts.** Fancy stitch collarette neck, ribbed cuffs and taped front. Sizes, 34 to 44. Price each............**$0.25**

**No. 2802 Drawers to match above.** Sizes, 30 to 42. Price, per pair..**$0.25**

**No. 2803 Three suits of the above shirts and drawers,** six pieces. Price for three suits.......**$1.40**

**No. 2804 Men's Spring Weight, Soft Finished, Cotton Merino Undershirts.** Camels hair color, collarette neck, taped front and ribbed cuffs. Sizes, 34 to 44. Always state size desired.
Price, each........................................... **$0.25**
Per dozen............................................. **2.70**

**No. 2808 Men's Drawers to match above.** Sizes 30 to 42 only. Price, per pair................. **$0.25**
Per dozen pairs.................................... **2.70**

## Derby Ribbed Balbriggans for 38c.

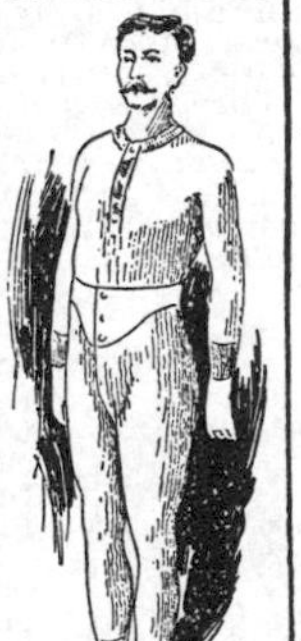

**No. 2809 These are handsome garments. Fine Derby Ribbed Balbriggan Shirts.** Made from fine, soft finished, combed cotton yarn, silk taped front, pearl buttons, French collarette neck and, in fact, made up same as all high priced garments. Ecru or dark cream color. Sizes 34 to 44. **Always mention size wanted.** Good summer weight goods and guaranteed to satisfy in every particular. Price each..**$0.38**

**No. 2810 Derby Ribbed Balbriggan Drawers** to match above. Sizes 34 to 42. Price per pair.........**$0.38**

**No. 2812 Three Full Suits** of the above underwear, shirts and drawers, six pieces in all. Price...... ..**$2.00**

## Light Blue Mixed Balbriggans, 38c.

**No. 2814 Light Blue Mixed Derby Ribbed Balbriggan Shirts.** Made exactly same as above. Very handsome, soft and fine. Price each..................................**$0.38**

**No. 2215 Light Blue Mixed Balbriggan Drawers** to match above. Elastic and form fitting.
Price per pair........................................**$0.38**

**No. 2816 Three Suits** of the above underwear, shirts and drawers. Price............................**$2.00**

## French Balbriggan Summer Underwear At 39c.

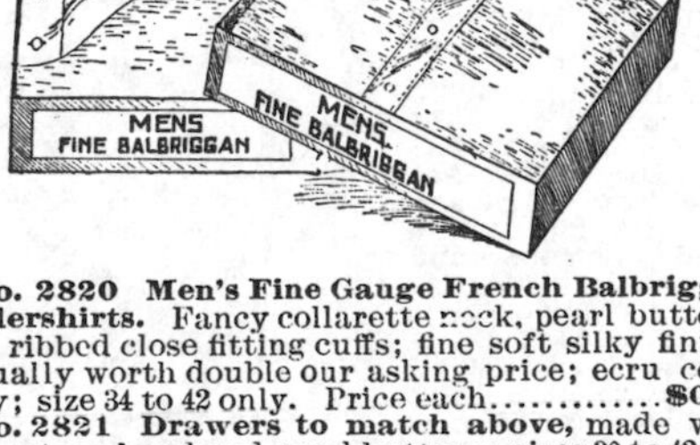


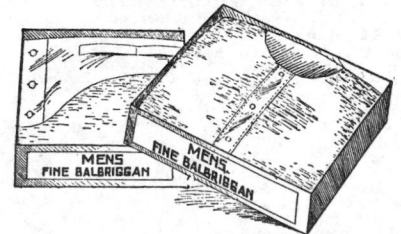

**No. 2820 Men's Fine Gauge French Balbriggan Undershirts.** Fancy collarette neck, pearl buttons, and ribbed close fitting cuffs; fine soft silky finish; actually worth double our asking price; ecru color only; size 34 to 42 only. Price each............**$0.39**

**No. 2821 Drawers to match above,** made with fine sateen band and pearl buttons; sizes 30 to 42.
Price per pair.........................................**$0.39**

**No. 2822 Three full suits of the above underwear, Special price** ..........................**$2.05**

## 50c for an 85c Imported Garment.

**No. 2824 Men's Extra Fine Quality Genuine French Balbriggan Undershirts,** very fine gauge, light weight and soft as silk; made with fancy French collarette neck, white pearl buttons and silk finished front; fine close fitting ribbed cuffs; sizes 34 to 44. **Always state size** when ordering.
Price each.................................................**$0.50**

**No. 2825 French Balbriggan Drawers** to match above; made with sateen band, pearl buttons, ribbed ankles and reinforced crotch; sizes 30 to 42.
Price per pair.........................................**$0.50**

**No. 2826 Three full suits** of the above underwear, shirts and drawers. Special offer price..**$2.75**

**No. 2827 Men's Spring and Summer Weight Balbriggan Shirts.** Made from pure Egyptian combed yarn, fine gauge, good weight and very durable natural balbriggan color, **Ribbed Cuffs,** collarette neck and pearl buttons; sizes 34 to 44.
Price each..................................................**$0.48**

**No. 2828 Drawers to Match above,** sateen waist band, ribbed ankles and adjustable waist straps; sizes 30 to 42. Price per pair...........................**$0.48**

**No. 2829 Three suits** of the above, shirts and drawers. Special offer..................................**$2.65**

## Ventilated Health Underwear.

**Summer Weight Balbriggan.**

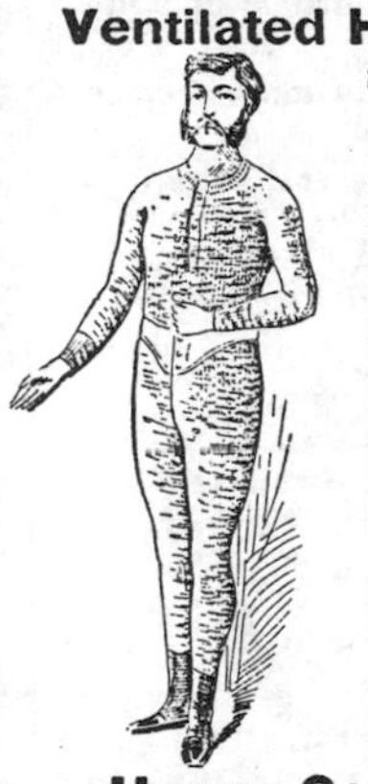

**No. 2830 Men's Ventilated Natural Gray Mixed Summer Undershirts.** The most comfortable as well as the most healthful balbriggan underwear ever made; fine gauge and soft finish; fancy collarette neck, pearl buttons and ribbed cuffs; ventilated all over with small drop stitch openings. Highly recommended by the best physicians as conducive to good health. Sizes 34 to 42 only. Price each..**$0.58**

**No. 2832 Drawers to Match** above; sizes 30 to 40 only.
Price each......................**$0.58**

**No. 2094 Special Offer. Three full suits** of the above underwear, shirts and drawers.
Price.......................**$3.10**

## Honey Comb Balbriggans.

**No. 2836 Men's Summer Weight Honey Comb Balbriggan Shirts.** Collarette neck, pearl buttons, ribbed cuffs and taped front; very fine honey comb pattern; plain ecru or dark cream color; sizes 34 to 42. Price each ..........................................**$0.49**

**No. 2837 Men's Honey Comb Balbriggan Drawers** to match above; sizes 30 to 40.
Price per pair..............................................**$0.49**

**No. 2838 Special Offer.** Three full suits of the above underwear, shirts and drawers. Price..........**$2.70**

## Form Fitting Derby Ribbed Underwear.

**For Spring and Summer Wear.**

### At 45c.

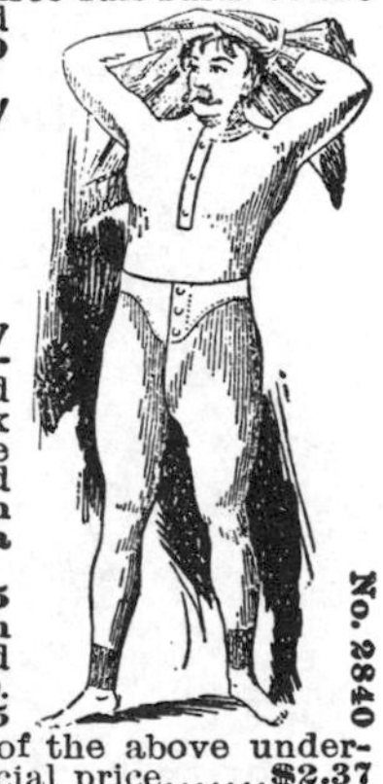

No. 2840

**No. 2840 Men's Derby Ribbed Form Fitting Undershirts,** made from fine combed Egyptian cotton, ecru or dark cream color; French collarette neck, pearl buttons and finished seams. **Knit to fit the form perfectly and not show a wrinkle.** Sizes 34 to 42.
Price each.................**$0.45**

**No. 2842 Drawers to match above.** Fine sateen front and reinforced crotch; sizes 30 to 40.
Price per pair.............**$0.45**

**No. 2843 Three full suits** of the above underwear, shirts and drawers. Special price.......**$2.37**

**SPECIAL NOTICE.**—When you wish to take advantage of our special prices which we offer **for Three Suit Lots** of underwear, always order from the catalogue number under which we make this offer. **Give Catalogue Number, Size of Shirts and Size of Drawers.** We will then fill **your order** promptly and correctly.

## Cadet Blue Fancy Ribbed Underwear.

**No. 2844** Men's Fancy Ribbed Balbriggan Undershirts. Handsome shade of cadet blue with fancy collarette neck, pearl buttons, taped front and ribbed cuffs, soft silky finish, fast color, light weight and very durable. Beautiful and trustworthy garments. Sizes, 34 to 42 only. Price, each......**$0.50**

**No. 2845** Cadet Blue Fancy Ribbed Drawers to match above, extra well made and finished. Sizes, 30 to 40 only. Price, per pair.................**$0.50**

**No. 2846** Special Offer. Three full suits of the above underwear, shirts and drawers for......**$2.75**

### A Special 34c. Bargain.

**No. 2848** Men's Fine Summer Weight, Fancy Mixed Striped Undershirts, made from fine combed cotton yarn, soft smooth finish and fine guage, neat two toned shades, silver gray predominating. Handsomely made up and trimmed, collarette neck, ribbed cuffs. Sizes 34 to 42 only. Price, each......**$0.34**

**No. 2849** Men's Fancy Striped Drawers to match above. Sizes, 30 to 40 only. Price per pair.........**$0.34**

**No. 2850** Special Offer. 3 full suits of the above underwear, shirts and drawers. Price.......**$1.85**

### Rainbow Balbriggans at 50c.

**No. 2854** Men's Rainbow Balbriggan Undershirts. Made from finest combed Egyptian yarn, in beautiful subdued rainbow colored mixtures. French collarette neck, pearl buttons and fancy ribbed cuffs etc. Fine guage, summer weight, soft and silky; fast colors. Sizes 34 to 42 only. Each...**$0.50**

**No. 2855** Men's Rainbow Balbriggan Drawers, to match above. Sizes 30 to 40 only. Price per pair..................**$0.50**

**No. 2856** Special Offer—Three full suits of the above beautiful underwear. Price.............**$2.75**

### Fancy Striped Balbriggan.
**Beautiful as well as Good and Oh So Cheap!**

**No. 2857** Men's Extra Fine Cadet Blue and White Striped French Balbriggan Undershirts. Good spring and summer weight, handsomely finished neck, silk finished front and fine white pearl buttons. Full of real goodness and beauty. Fast colors and perfect in fit and finish. Sizes 34 to 42 only. Price each...................**$0.50**

**No. 2858** Fancy Striped Drawers to match above. Fine sateen band and ribbed ankles. Sizes 30 to 42. Price per pair...................**$0.50**

**No. 2859** Special Offer. Three full suits of the above underwear, shirts and drawers. Price..**$2.75**

### Men's Fancy Random Figured Underwear.

**No. 2860** Gentlemen's High Grade English Underwear. Made from finest selected Egyptian cotton. Light Summer weight. Silk finished, English style, silk front and fine white pearl buttons and ribbed cuffs. Colors blue and white or tan and cream mixtures. Sizes 34 to 42 only. Price each..........**$0.57**

**No. 2861** Fancy Mixed Drawers to match above. Finely made and finished, Sizes 30 to 40 only. Price per pair.......**$0.57**

**No. 2862** Special Offer. Three full suits of the above underwear, Shirts and drawers. Price......**$3.10**

No. 2860

**IMPORTANT!** Always mention just what sizes you want when ordering underwear. Give chest measurement for shirts and waist measurement for drawers. Your order will then be filled promptly and correctly.

## Men's Fancy Striped Form Fitting Underwear.

**No. 2864** We take special pride in presenting these undershirts to your notice. They are made from finest combined Egyptian cotton, soft and smooth as silk. Spring and summer weight with beautiful light blue and ecru alternating stripes. Finest Satin Front with white pearl buttons, collarette neck and silk finished cuffs and tail. Very Fine Ribbed, perfectly form-fitting and thoroughly dependable. Sizes 34 to 44. Always state size wanted. Price each....................**$0.48**

**No. 2865** Fancy Striped Drawers to match above. Fine sateen band and pearl buttons. Sizes 30 to 42 inch waist measure. Price per pair.........**$0.48**

**No. 2866** Special Offer. Order three suits of the above underwear, shirts and drawers, under this catalogue number, and get them at our special 3 suit rate. Price for three suits.................**$2.65**

### Special Silk Finish Balbriggans.

**No. 2867** Men's Summer Weight cadet blue mixed balbriggan undershirts. English style, silk taped front and neck. Pearl buttons and ribbed cuffs. Fine guage and high class finish. Sizes 34 to 42. Excellent value. Price each..................**$0.45**

**No. 2868** Cadet Blue Mixed Balbriggan drawers to match above. Sizes 30 to 42. Price per pair...**$0.45**

**No. 2869** Special Offer, Three full suits of the above underwear, shirts and drawers, (don't forget to state size.) Price..................**$2.37**

### Finest French Balbriggans.

**No. 2870** Men's High Grade Real French Balbriggan Undershirts. Finely fashioned and elegantly made up. Pearl buttons, ribbed elastic cuffs, and all improvements, ecru color. We particularly recommend these garments to gentlemen requiring light weight underwear of very fine texture. Sizes 34 to 44. Price each....................**$0.75**

**No. 2871** Real French Balbriggan Drawers to match above. Handsomely made and shaped. Sizes 30 to 42. Price per pair.................**$0.75**

**No. 2872** Special Offer. Three full suits of the above underwear, shirts and drawers, price, **$4.10**

### Men's Pure Lisle Thread Underwear at 95 Cents.

**No. 2874** Pure English Lisle Thread Undershirts. Finest made for summer wear. Light, durable and healthy. Finest silk front with pearl buttons, collarette neck and elastic ribbed cuffs. Sizes 34 to 42., ecru color. Price each..............**$0.95**
Three for....................2.70

**No. 2875** Men's Pure English Lisle Thread Drawers to match above. Finely made and finished, elastic ribbed ankles, pearl buttons, etc.; sizes 30 to 40 inches waist measurements. Price per pair **$0.95**
Three pairs....................2.70

### Men's Extra Size Underwear.

Shirts, Sizes 44 to 52. Drawers, Sizes 42 to 52.
**No. 2880** Men's Extra Size Balbriggan Shirts. French collarette neck, pearl buttons and ribbed cuffs. Ecru or dark cream color. Fine soft finish. Made full large throughout.

Price, each, 58c; 3 for.........**$1.60**

**No. 2881** Men's Extra Size Balbriggan Drawers to match above. Sizes, 42 to 52 waist measure.
Price, per pair, 58c; 3 pairs for. **$1.60**

**No. 2882** Men's Extra Size French Balbriggan Undershirts. Fine gauge soft silky finish. Fancy collarette neck, pearl buttons and ribbed cuffs. Full large. Sizes, 44 to 52-chest measure. Ecru color.
Price, each, 79c; 3 for......**$2.25**

**No. 2883** Men's Extra Size French Balbriggan Drawers to match above. Sizes, 42 to 52 waist measure.
Price, per pair, 79c; 3 pairs for.............**$2.25**

### Fish Net Undershirts.
**Hot Weather Specialties.**

**No. 2884** Men's Fish Net Undershirts. Sateen front with pearl buttons. Made with short sleeves. Fine soft finsh netting. Sizes, 34 to 44. Ecru or cream color.
Price each.........**$0.25**
Per dozen........2.75

**No. 2885** Men's Extra Quality Fish Net Undershirts. Cream color, with fine white covered buttons and front. Short sleeves. The coolest undershirts made. Sizes, 34 to 44.
Price, each....**$0.43**
Per dozen........4.65

**SPECIAL NOTICE.—** The above fish net garments are made in shirts only. We cannot furnish drawers to match.

No. 2884.

## Bleached Jean Drawers.

**No. 2886** Scriven's Famous Elastic Seam Bleached Jean Drawers. The strongest, best wearing and most comfortable drawers that have ever been made. Wide set in elastic balbriggan seams in back and sides. Self-adjusting, easy and comfortable. Ribbed elastic balbriggan ankles. Sizes, 30 to 44 waist and 30 to 34 inseam measurements.
Price, per pair.........**$0.95**

**No. 2887** Finest White Pepperell Jean Drawers. with elastic ribbed ankles. Absolutely high class garments.
Price, per pair.........**$0.45**

**No. 2888** Bleached Jean Drawers, with ribbed elastic ankles. Extra good value. Sizes, 30 to 42 waist measurements. Price, per pair.........**$0.39**

## Men's Medium Weight Underwear
**For Spring and Fall Wear at 50c.**

**No. 2890** Fine Soft Finish Fancy Striped Merino Undershirts. Fancy collarette neck. Satin front pearl buttons and elastic ribbed cuffs. Fast colors and warranted to wear. Light blue and white stripes. Very handsome and thoroughly good. Usually retail for 75c. Our price, each...... ..**$0.50**

**No. 2891** Drawers to match above. Sizes, 30 to 40 waist measurements, Price, per pair..........**$0.50**

**No. 2892** Special Offer. 3 full suits of the above merino underwear. Price....................**$2.75**

**No. 2894** Men's Medium Weight Merino Undershirts. Same as above, in handsome fawn and cream stripes. Price, each..........**$0.50**

**No. 2896** Drawers to match above. Fawn and white stripes. Price, per pair..........**$0.50**

**No. 2897** Special Offer. Three full suits of the above beautiful fawn and cream striped merino underwear. Price....................**$2.75**

No. 2890.

## Our 45c Grey Merino Underwear.
**Extra Fine Quality.**

**No. 2898** Men's Medium Weight Natural Grey Merino Undershirts. Soft wool finish, silk taped and trimmed neck and front and ribbed cuffs. Fine pearl buttons. Sizes, 34 to 44.
Price, each........**$0.45**

**No. 2899** Men's Grey Merino Drawers to match above. Sizes, 30 to 42 waist measure.
Price, per pair..........**$0.45**

**No. 2900** Our Special Offer. 3 full suits of the above merino underwear, Shirts and Drawers. Price....................**$2.45**

## Light Weight Wool Underwear.

The demand for Light Weight Wool Underwear becomes more popular every season. It is more healthful than cotton or silk, as it always keeps the pores open and absorbs all perspiration, and is proof against the ill effects of cold, heat and dampness. Wool gently stimulates the skin and co-operates with it to regulate the temperature of the body. We have a specially selected line of light weight and medium weight wool underwear which we can highly recommend. Order from the following quotations and you will get such values as you have never had before. **Always state just what sizes you wish.**

**No. 2901** Men's Light Weight Natural Wool Undershirts. Sanitary grey color, silk taped front and neck, pearl buttons and ribbed cuffs. Sizes 34 to 46. 80 per cent. pure wool. Price, each............**$0.75**

**No. 2902** Natural Wool Drawers to match above. Sizes 30 to 42. Price, per pair.................**$0.75**

**No. 2903** Three Full Suits of the above underwear—shirts and drawers. Price..............**$4.10**

**DON'T** FORGET POSTAGE FOR MAIL SHIPMENTS.

**DO** MAKE UP CLUB ORDERS. SHIP BY FREIGHT AT ABOUT ONE-SIXTEENTH OF COST OF POSTAGE.

## Camel's Hair Wool Underwear At 75c.

**NO. 2905.** Men's Extra Fine Quality Camels Hair Wool Undershirts, light weight, soft, smooth and very fine finish, Finely finished throughout, pearl buttons, ribbed cuffs, etc. First class workmanship and materials. Will please the most skeptical, non-irritating and non-shrinkable. Sizes, 34 to 44. 80 per cent wool. Price, each............$0.75

**No. 2906** Men's Camel's Hair Drawers to match above. Sizes, 30 to 42. Price, per pair.........$0.75

**No. 2907** Our Special offer. Three full suits of the above underwear, shirts and drawers. Price............................$4.10

## Dr. Reihl's Health Underwear.
### Light Weight Sanitary Wool.

This Famous Health Underwear is made from the finest uncolored Australian lamb's wool, natural grey color. It is a non-conductor of cold and moisture. It opens the pores of the body, absorbs all perspiration and the vaporous exhalations of the skin, and regulates the temperature of the body, keeping the skin always dry, even when perspiring freely.

Dr. Reihl's Health Underwear is exceedingly fine and soft and will not irritate or scratch the most tender skins. The best medical authorities in Europe and America have pronounced it the most healthful underwear ever made.

**No. 2909** Dr. Reihl's Light Weight Natural Grey Sanitary Wool Shirts, fine, soft, silky finish, handsomely made and trimmed, pearl button front, ribbed cuffs and high grade finish throughout. Light, serviceable, healthful, and handsome. Sizes, 34 to 44. Price, each...........................$1.10

**No. 2910** Dr. Reihl's Sanitary Drawers to match above. Handsomely made and finished. Sizes, 30 to 42. Price, per pair..........................$1.10

**No. 2912** Special Offer. Three full suits of the above Dr. Reihl's underwear. Price............$6.00

**No. 2914** Dr. Reihl's Finest Grade Medium Weight Health Undershirts. Fine and soft as silk. Made from purest and best quality Australian lamb's wool. Same style as above, but heavier and finer. Natural sanitary grey color. Sizes, 34 to 44. Price, each............................$1.50

**No. 2916** Medium Weight Sanitary Drawers to match above. Sizes, 30 to 42. Price, per pair...$1.50

**No. 2917** Special Offer: Two full suits of the above Dr. Reihl's famous underwear, Price..$5.50

## Feather-weight Pure Wool Underwear.

**No. 2918** Men's Natural Sanitary Wool Undershirts, all pure lamb's wool of the very finest quality. Very fine guage and light weight, no heavier than summer weight balbriggan, English style neck, fine white pearl buttons, royal ribbed cuffs and ribbed tail. The most healthful summer underwear in the world. Sizes, 34 to 44. Price, each...$1.25
Three for...............................3.50

**No. 2919** Men's Feather-weight All Wool Drawers to match above. Pearl buttons, ribbed ankles and reinforced crotch. Sizes, 30 to 42. Price, per pair,.........................$1.25
Three pairs for.........................3.50

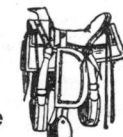

## Men's Winter Weight Underwear.
### Always State Just What Size You Want.
Shirt Sizes, Chest Measurements........34 to 44.
Drawers Sizes, Waist Measurements....30 to 42.

**No. 2920** Men's Heavy Winter Weight Natural Grey Mixed Merino Undershirts. Collarette or taped neck and ribbed cuffs. Excellent wearing garments and guaranteed to give perfect satisfaction, Price. each...........................$0.45
Three for..............................1.25

**No. 2921** Heavy Merino Drawers to match above. Sizes, 30 to 42. Price, per pair..........$0.45
Three pairs for.........................1.25

**No. 2922** Men's Natural Grey Heavy Weight Wool Undershirts. Very fine soft finish. Ribbed cuffs and tail and fine pearl button front. Regular retail value $1.25. Sizes, 34 to 44. Price, each...$0.95

**No. 2924** Men's Extra Fine Natural Wool Drawers, to match above. Extra well made. Sizes, 30 to 42.
Price, per pair.....$0.95

**No. 2926** Special Offer. Two full suits of the above underwear, shirts and drawers, Price....$3.65

**No. 2928** Men's Heavy Winter Weight Derby Ribbed Wool Shirts. Natural color. Finely finished and form fitting. Two-thirds wool and excellent for wear and warmth. Non-shrinkable Sizes, 34 to 42.
Price, each.........$0.87
Three for.........7.45

**No. 2930** Men's Derby Ribbed Drawers, to match above. Sizes, 30 to 40 only. Price, per pair.....$0.87
Three pairs for.....2.45

**No. 2924**

## Australian Lamb's Wool Underwear.
### Extra Heavy Winter Weight.
### Special Bargain until Sold. 98c.

**No. 2931** Three Hundred Dozen Men's Extra Heavy Winter Weight Australian Lamb's Wool Undershirts. Olive brown or dark tan color. All pure wool of the very finest kind. Handsomely made and trimmed. We bought these garments late in the season at a great bargain and will close them out for 98c per garment. The regular value is $1.75. We have all sizes from 34 to 42 chest measure. Send in your orders early and make first and second choice as to size. This is a rare bargain and shrewd buyers will take advantage of it at once.
Special price, each...........................$0.98

**No. 2932** Pure Australian Wool Drawers to match above. Sizes 30 to 40 only.
Price, per pair..........................$0.98

**No. 2933** Special Offer. Three full suits of the above underwear, shirts and drawers. Price..$5.25

## Fleece Lined Wool Underwear.
### The Warmest Underwear in the World.

**No. 2934** Men's Extra Heavy and Fine All Wool Natural Grey Undershirts, with wool fleece inside; finely made and finished; non-shrinkable and absolutely dependable; made from purest Australian wool. Sizes 34 to 44. Price each...............$1.37
Three for..............................$3.75

**No. 2936** Men's Australian Fleece Lined Wool Drawers to match above. Sizes 30 to 42.
Price per pair.....$1.37 Three pairs for....$3.75

## Dr. Wright's Health Underwear.

**No. 2937** Dr. Wright's Health Undershirts for men; non-shrinkable and very fine gauge; pure lamb's wool fleece; seamless shoulders and pearl buttons; very warm and healthful. Sizes 34 to 42; camels' hair color. Price each...................$0.95

**No. 2938** Drawers to match above, extra long woven elastic ankles and pearl buttons. Sizes 30 to 42, Price per pair...........................$0.95

**No. 2939** Special offer—Three full suits of the above Health Underwear, shirts and drawers, Price.................................$5.50

## Dr. Wright's Best Fleeced Underwear.

**No. 2940** Dr. Wright's Best Quality Non-shrinkable Health Undershirts. Extra heavy soft and warm. Pure lambs' wool fleece lining. Silk stitched and silk bound. Guaranteed to give perfect and lasting satisfaction. Price each.................$1.75

**No. 2942** Dr. Wright's Best Quality Non-shrinkable Drawers to match above. Extra fine finish throughout. Price per pair...................$1.75

**No. 2943** Special Offer. Two full suits of the above health underwear. Price.............$6.75

### Here is a Chance for You at 23c.
Take Advantage of it While You Can. Sizes, 38, 40, 42 and 44 Only.

**No. 2944** An Odd Lot of 250 dozen men's heavy weight merino undershirts, natural grey or camel's hair color. Regular 45c, 50c and 65c values, left over from last season. We want to close them out and offer the entire lot until closed out at 23c each. Sizes, 38, 40, 42 and 44 only. It will pay you to buy them even if the sizes are not just what you require. The price and quality is certainly an object. Order at once if you wish to take advantage of this offer.
Price each...................$0.23
Six for...................1.25

**No. 2946** Men's Heavy Merino Drawers. Natural grey and tan mixtures, odd sizes and shades, same grades as shirts quoted above. We cannot, however, guarantee to match same in colors. Sizes 38, 40 and 42 only. Until sold, price per pair................................$0.23
6 pairs for..............................1.25

## Men's Cardigan Jackets.
### Sizes 36 to 44 Chest Measurements.

All these goods go C. O. D., subject to examination on receipt of $1.00. balance and express charges payable at express office. Discount of 3 per cent. allowed if cash in full accompanies your order.

**No. 2947** Men's Knit Cardigan Jackets. Medium heavy ribbed. Heavy weight. Two pockets nicely made and trimmed. Two-thirds wool. Colors plain black. Single breasted. Price, each...........$1.15

**No. 2948** Good Heavy Weight Wool Jackets. Ribbed patterns with elastic ribbed wrists and fancy knit front. Two pockets, Taped all around. Colors black or brown, Single breasted.
Price, each...$1.75

**No. 2949** Men's Double Breasted Knit Cardigan Jackets. Fine ribbed raised stitch, with satin faced lapels, and ribbed elastic wrists. Colors black or brown. All wool. Price, each...........................$2.75

## AN UP-TO-DATE LADIES' UNDERWEAR DEPARTMENT.

**Form Fitting, Dependable Underwear** — AT — **Purse Fitting, Non-irritating Prices.**

Soft, skin-soothing garments that wear well and fit well. Garments that in style, texture and finish show the masterful hand of the expert. Garments that are perfect in every way.

Elastic and self conforming, and equally adapted to the slightest as well as the most perfectly developed figures. **Never in the History of Our Underwear Business** have we ever been able to offer such **EXCELLENT GARMENTS** FOR SO LITTLE MONEY AS WE QUOTE THIS SEASON.

It is a downright pleasure to handle underwear that we know beyond the shadow of a doubt is PERFECTLY TRUSTWORTHY, and to be able to offer it at a price so low that even persons in the humbler walks of life can easily afford to buy it.

We know that our customers will appreciate these remarkably low prices and take advantage of them.

## WE FULLY GUARANTEE EVERY GARMENT TO BE EXACTLY AS REPRESENTED.

**Money Cheerfully Refunded if You are not Satisfied.**

## LADIES' SUMMER UNION SUITS.
### IN UNION THERE IS STRENGTH.

No. 2953.    No. 2954.    No. 2950.

| Sizes | 3 | 4 | 5 |
|---|---|---|---|
| Bust Measure | 32 to 34 | 36 to 38 | 40 |

### 43c for a Princess Union Suit.
No. 2950 Ladies' Princess Jersey Ribbed Union Suit. Knit-to-fit from fine imported Egyptian cotton; ecru color, low neck, short sleeves and knee length; open down front; taped and crocheted all around neck and front; shaped waist; fine white pearl buttons and silk crochet edging; sizes 3, 4 and 5, 32 to 40 bust measure. Always give size when you order. Price per suit, 43c.; three suits for....$1.20

### 50c For the Empress Union Suit.
**Fine Lisle Finish.**
No. 2952 Ladies' Empress Lisle Finish Summer Jersey Ribbed Union Suit, beautiful ecru color, square neck and sleeveless, silk ribbon finished neck and armholes and silk crochet edging all around neck and armholes. Open down front all the way, shaped form fitting waist, knee length. This suit's finished in high grade manner throughout and is a wonder at the price we offer it. Sizes 3, 4 and 5. Price, per suit, 50c.; three suits for....$1.40

### A Snow White Venus, At 75 cents.
No. 2953 The Venus Jersey Ribbed Union Suit. Snow White, Pure Lisle Finished. One of the handsomest union suits we have ever seen. And we have seen nearly every style ever manufactured. The Venus Suit has curved silk crocheted neck trimmed with white silk ribbon, shaped form fitting waist and short wing sleeves. This suit opens all the way down front, and is easily put on and off. finished down front with fine white pearl buttons and fancy silk crochet edge, an air of refinement and durability pervades every feature of it. **Comfortable as can be made.** Sizes, 3, 4 and 5 knee length. Price, per suit, 75c.; 3 suits for................$2.00

### 50c for a 75c Oneita Union Suit.
No. 2954 The Oneita Form Fitting Union Suit. Pure snow white, with short sleeves and silk crochet edging all around neck and across the front. Knee length and silk finish sleeves and silk edging. Silk ribbon at neck. Form fitting shaped waist, buttoned across the chest, and enables the wearer to wear smaller corset than usual. Sizes 3, 4 and 5. Always give size when you order. Price per suit, 50c.; three for................$1.40

No. 2955 The Oneita Union Suit, similar to above but made in ecru color, a very light shade of tan. Price per suit, 50c.; three for..................$1.40

### The Trilby Lisle Union Suit, 85c.
No. 2956 A Pure Lisle Union Suit of surpassing beauty and goodness. Low neck, short sleeves, and knee length. Silk ribbon trimmed all around neck and armholes and edged with silk crochet work; white pearl buttons to waist line only. Soft and fine with close-fitting shaped waist and silk overstitching on all edges. Ecru color only. Sizes 3, 4 and 5. One of the most perfect fitting union suits made. Price, per suit.....$0.85. Two suits for.....$1.60

No. 2957 Ladies' Spring and Fall Weight Natural Grey Union Suits. Fine merino yarn, two-thirds wool. Long sleeves and ankle-length. Open down front. Fine white pearl buttons; shaped waist, and knit to fit the form perfectly. Good weight, and suitable for wear all the year around. Sizes 3, 4 and 5. Price, per suit..................$1.25

### Children's and Misses' Union Suits

| Sizes | B | C | D | E | F |
|---|---|---|---|---|---|
| Years | 2 to 4 | 4 to 7 | 7 to 9 | 9 to 12 | 12 to 14 |

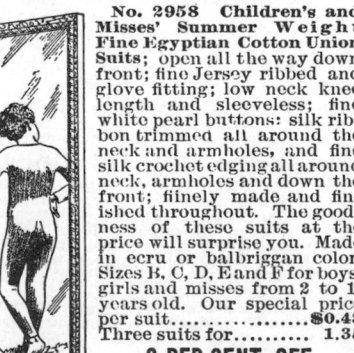

No. 2958 Children's and Misses' Summer Weight Fine Egyptian Cotton Union Suits; open all the way down front; fine Jersey ribbed and glove fitting; low neck knee length and sleeveless; fine white pearl buttons: silk ribbon trimmed all around the neck and armholes, and fine silk crochet edging all around neck, armholes and down the front; finely made and finished throughout. The goodness of these suits at the price will surprise you. Made in ecru or balbriggan color. Sizes B, C, D, E and F for boys, girls and misses from 2 to 14 years old. Our special price per suit................$0.48
Three suits for.........1.35

### 3 PER CENT. OFF
FOR FULL CASH WITH ORDER.

## Ladies' Spring and Summer Vests.
### Sizes, 3, 4 and 5.

Size 3 is for 32 and 34 bust; size 4 is for 36 and 38 bust; size 5 is for 40 inch bust. For sizes larger than 40 inch bust, see our quotations on extra size garments. Nos. 2985 and 2986.

No. 2959 Ladies' Sleeveless Summer Vests, ecru or cream color, elastic derby ribbed. Sizes 3, 4 and 5. Price, each......$0.06
Per doz..........60

No. 2960 Ladies' Fancy Ribbed Sleeveless Summer Vests, V shaped neck, crochted armholes and taped neck, ecru or cream color. Sizes 3, 4 or 5. Price, each.....$0.12
Per doz......1.30

No. 2961 Ladies' Fine Ribbed Seamless Vests, square neck and taped all around neck and armholes, crochet edge, ecru or cream color. Very soft smooth combed cotton, and vests that will give most excellent service. Sizes 3, 4 and 5. Price, each....$0.15
Per dozen..............1.55

No. 2962 Ladies' Sleeveless Summer Vests, V shaped neck, taped and crocheted, fine derby ribbed ecru cotton. Always mention size wanted when ordering. Sizes, 3, 4 and 5. Price, each......$0.15
Per dozen..............1.55

No. 2961.

No. 2962.

### LADIES' ECRU OR CREAM ....COLORED....
## EGYPTIAN COTTON VESTS.

No. 2964 With curved crocheted neck. taped and crocheted armholes and neck. Shaped form fitting waist. Sizes 3, 4 and 5. Price, each....$0.13
Per dozen..............1.40

## Our Knit-to-Fit Egyptian Vests.
No. 2965 Ladies' Fine Jersey Ribbed Egyptian Vests. Knit from very fine combed yarn, soft and smooth. Fancy crocheted and taped curved neck, and crocheted arm holes, taped all around. Shaped at waist to fit the form perfectly. **One of our very best values.** Sizes, 3, 4 and 5. Ecru color or dark cream. Each......$0.25
Per dozen..................2.68

No. 2966 Ladies' Fine Jersey Ribbed Vests. Same as above in snow white. Price, each....$0.25
Per doz.....2.68

No. 2965

## Ladies' Fancy Swiss Ribbed Vests.
**Soft and Soothing to the Skin.**
No. 2967 Ladies' Fancy Ribbed Real Egyptian Cotton Sleeveless Vests. Knit from fine, soft finished, combed yarn, with fancy crocheted V-shaped neck, and taped and fancy crocheted arm holes. Ecru or dark cream color. Exceptionally good value. Sizes, 3, 4 and 5. Price each.... ............$0.18
Per dozen..................1.75

No. 2968 Ladies' Fancy Ribbed Vests. Same as above in pure snow white. Price, each.......$0.18
Per dozen..............1.75

No. 2967

## Our Magnificent 25c Line.
We Challenge the World to beat us on This Line of Goods.

No. 2970 The Empress jersey ribbed summer vests. Low neck and no sleeves. Square front richly crocheted in silk with silk ribbon tape. Broad silk crocheted arm holes, silk tape all around. Shaped bust. Very fine combed Egyptian cotton, soft as silk. Fine ribbed and very durable. Real skin comfort in these garments. Ecru or cream color. Price each...........$0.25
Per dozen..............2.70

No. 2971 The Empress jersey ribbed form fitting vests. Same as above in pure snow white. Price each...........$0.25
Per dozen..............2.70

No. 2970

# SEARS, ROEBUCK & CO., (Incorporated), Cheapest Supply House on Earth, Chicago.

241

**No. 2972** A Beautiful Snow White Vest of the finest silk finished Egyptian cotton. Fancy Swiss ribbed with silk ribbon laced front and silk ribbon trimmed armholes. Silk open work all around neck and down front. Handsomely crocheted and beautifully finished. Regular 50c quality. Low neck and no sleeves.

Our price, each................$0.25
Per dozen.................. 2.70
**No. 2973** Same Vest as Above but made in ecru or cream color.
Price each................$0.25
Per dozen... ............ 2.70

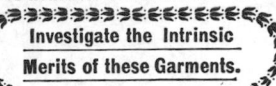
Investigate the Intrinsic Merits of these Garments.

No. 2972

## Swiss Tinted Vests. Beautiful and Dependable. At 25 Cents.

**No. 2974** Ladies' Extra Fine Swiss Ribbed Summer Vests. Made from fine silk finished Egyptain Cotton, soft and smooth. Low neck and no sleeves. Lace insertion and silk ribbon trimmed all around front neck and armholes. Made in beautiful shade of sea shell pink. Sizes, 3, 4 and 5.
Price, each....................$0.25
Per dozen........................ 2.70
**No. 2975** Ladies' Swiss Tinted Fancy Ribbed Vests. Same as above in beautiful shade of light blue, very fine and delicate.
Price, each ....................$0.25
Per dozen........................ 2.70
**No. 2976** Ladies' Superfine Swiss Ribbed Summer Vests. Made from fine combed silk finished Egyptian Cotton, ecru color, with low neck No. 2974 laced up front with silk ribbon, trimmed, elaborately with fancy open work crocheted lace patterns, silk finished; armholes trimmed with fine pure silk ribbons. One of the handsomest vests made.
Price, each.............................$0.35
3 for................................ .95

## Wing Arm Vests 18c.

**No. 2977** Ladies' Fine Jersey Ribbed Summer Vests. New fancy ribbed Egyptian cotton with square fancy crocheted neck and short wing arms. Ecru color. Sizes, 3, 4 and 5. These are very desirable garments and usually retail for 25c. Our price is different.
Price, each.............$0.18
Per dozen.............. 2.00

## Snow White Vests 25c.

**No. 2978** Ladies' Extra Fine Snow White Egyptian Cotton Summer Vests, with short or wing arms. Fine jersey ribbed with high neck. Sateen front and pearl buttons. Crocheted and silk ribbon trimmed neck. Very fine ribbed garments and sure to please. Very close ribbed, shaped waist, insuring a perfect fit.
Price, each.....................................$0.25
Per dozen...................................... 2.70

No. 2977

## Silk Trimmed, Wing Arm Vests at 30c.

**No. 2979** Ladies' Finest Imported Egyptian Cotton Summer Vests. Fancy Swiss ribbed, with rich silk crochet and open work, fancy V-shaped front and short sleeves or wing arms. White silk ribbon running all around the entire neck and front. Made in ecru or cream color. Soft and soothing to the skin; very durable and comfortable. You will like them—no mistake about that. Price, each...$0.30
Three for................... 0.79

## Ladies' Lisle Vests.

**No. 2980** Ladies' Ecru or Cream Colored Fine Lisle Summer Vests. Fine Swiss ribbed, with low neck and no sleeves. Artistically finished on neck and armholes with silk ribbon and fancy crochet stitching. Perfectly form fitting, dependable and positively high-grade throughout. Sizes 3, 4 and 5. Price, each....$0.46
Per dozen.......................... 5.25

## Ladies' Silk Vests.

**No. 2981** Ladies' Extra Quality Fine Ribbed Summer Silk Sleeveless Vests. Fine soft texture and fast colors. Silk ribbon trimmed neck. Colors black, salmon, white, or apricot. Perfectly form-fitting and finely finished. Sizes 3, 4 and 5. Price, each................$0.48
Three for.......................$1.35
**No. 2982** Ladies' Extra Fine Swiss Ribbed Pure Summer Weight Silk Vests. Silk ribbon finished neck. Low neck and no sleeves. Colors black, salmon, apricot, white and light blue. Sizes 3, 4 and 5.
Price, each................$0.87
Three for....................... 2.45

## Ladies' Long Sleeve Vests.

### Summer Weight.

**No. 2983** Ladies's Fine Soft Finished Combed Egyptian Cotton Vests, with high necks and long sleeves. Shaped at waist to fit the form perfectly without showing a wrinkle. Silk ribbon trimmed and crocheted neck. Sateen front with pearl buttons. Elastic ribbed cuffs. Sizes 3, 4 and 5.
Price, each................$0.25
Three for....................... .68
**No. 2984** This is a Regular 50c Vest and has never before been sold for less money. Made from extra selected fine combed Egyption cotton, very soft and smooth and will not irritate the most tender skin. Fine silk ribbon trimmed neck, crocheted all around; sateen front and fine white pearl buttons; high neck and long sleeves with elastic ribbed cuffs; sizes 3, 4 and 5; ecru color. Price each.........$0.37
Three for.......................... 1.00
**SPECIAL NOTICE.**—Size 3 corresponds with 32 or 34 bust, size 4 with 36 and 38 bust, and size 5 with 40 inch bust. For ladies requiring larger size than 40-inch bust measure we quote the following extra large sizes.

## Ladies' Extra Large Vests.

**No. 2985** Ladies' Extra Large Size Summer Weight Egyptian Cotton Vests, ecru or cream color, square shape, taped neck, no sleeves; sizes 6, 7 and 8, for bust measure 42, 44 and 46; fine ribbed.
Price, each................$0.25
Three for...................... .70
**No. 2986** Ladies' Extra Large Size Summer Weight Egyptian Cotton Jersey Ribbed Vests, ecru color with low cut taped neck and crocheted and tape trimmed arm holes; sizes 6, 7 and 8.
Price each................$0.45
Three for...................... 1.25

No. 2985.

## Ladies' Summer Drawers and Tights.

**No. 2988** Ladies' Fine Swiss ribbed form fitting Egyptian Cotton Drawers. Knee length with sateen band and shaped waist. Sizes 3, 4 and 5. Ecru color.
Price, per pair.$0.25
3 pairs for...... .70
**No. 2989** Ladies' Extra Fine Soft finished Swiss ribbed Egyptian Cotton Drawers. Knee length with fine sateen band and shaped waist. Sizes 3, 4 and 5. Very soft smooth finish and perfectly form fitting. Ecru color.
Price, per pair.$0.43
3 pairs for...... 1.20
**No. 2990** Pure lisle form fitting jersey ribbed Summer Drawers. Knee length with shaped waist and legs and fine sateen band. Sizes 3, 4 and 5. Very fine high class garments.
Price, per pair.....................................$0.48
3 pairs for...................................... 1.35

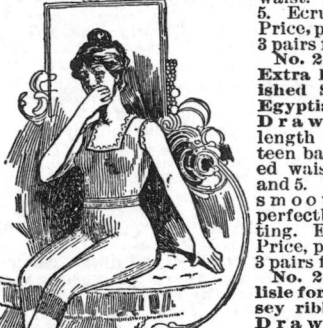

## Black Cotton Summer Tights.

**No. 2991** Ladies' Fine Jersey ribbed Fast Black Open Summer Tights. Finely made and finished. knee length. Sizes 3, 4 and 5. Price, per pair,.$0.68

## Bicycle Tights.

**No. 2992** The Oneita Bicycle Tights. A specialty that is meeting with marked approval by all ladies who ride bicycles or on horseback. Made with heavy seat and gusset. Ecru color only. Made from Swiss ribbed, combed Egyptian cotton. Sizes, 3, 4 and 5. Price, per pair.........................$0.73

## INFANTS' AND CHILDRENS' SUMMER UNDERWEAR.

### THE RUBEN'S INFANT'S SHIRT.

No Buttons to Bother You.

**No. 2993** The Ruben's Shirt is simplicity itself, Is made without any buttons whatever, and is so constructed that double protection is given to the vital parts—the chest, lungs and abdomen. This is by all odds, the most sensible and practical infant's shirt ever made. The highest medical authorities pronounce it healthful and as being particularly desirable for delicate infants. They are made from fine, white merino and lamb's wool, and contain about 40% pure wool. Cream white, with double stitched edges to prevent raveling. The straps fasten at back with small safety pin, and can be adjusted almost as quick as a cat can wink her eye.

| Length, inches.... | 10 | 12 | 14 | 16 | 18 | 20 |
|---|---|---|---|---|---|---|
| Sizes ...... ...... | 1 | 2 | 3 | 4 | 5 | 6 |
| Price, each........ | 20c | 25c | 30c | 33c | 36c | 39c |

**No. 2994** The Ruben's Shirt. Same as above, but made of all pure, soft, cream white Saxony wool. Fine derby ribbed.

| Length, inches.... | 10 | 12 | 14 | 16 | 18 | 20 |
|---|---|---|---|---|---|---|
| Sizes ...... ...... | 1 | 2 | 3 | 4 | 5 | 6 |
| Price, each... ....... | 32c | 35c | 38c | 42c | 46c | 50c |

## Infants' Wool Vests.

**No. 2995** Infants' Fine Derby Ribbed Cream White Merino Vests, buttoned all the way down front, with overcast stitching on neck, cuffs and tail. Soft and comfortable and non-shrinkable.

| Length, inches...... | 10 | 12 | 14 | 16 | 18 |
|---|---|---|---|---|---|
| Sizes ...... | 1 | 2 | 3 | 4 | 5 |
| Price, each............ | 14c | 17c | 20c | 23c | 25c |

**No. 2996** Infants' Fine Derby Ribbed Cream White Saxony Wool Knit Vest. Button all the way down the front. Very easily put on and taken off. Neck, front and tail all overcast with silk cross-stitch embroidery. Very fine and soft and non-irritating.

| Lengths, inches ......... | 10 | 12 | 14 | 16 | 18 |
|---|---|---|---|---|---|
| Sizes..................... | 1 | 2 | 3 | 4 | 5 |
| Prices, each............ | 20c | 25c | 30c | 35c | 40c |

## Child's Ribbed Seamless Waist and Shirt Combined.

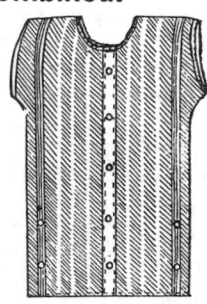

**No. 2997** This is a Combination Waist and Shirt Combined, and can be worn either with or without regular undershirt. It is made from fine jersey ribbed seamless Egyptian cotton, ecru or dark cream color. Made with taped stays running all the way down front and back and over the shoulders and has two rows of waist buttons for fastening on the underclothes. A complete, healthful and comfortable garment. Strong and durable. For children from 1 to 12 years of age. Give age of child when ordering. Price, each......................$0.20

## Children's Derby Ribbed Summer Vests.

### Sizes, 1 to 7 Years Only.

**No. 2998** Children's Ecru Egyptian Cotton Derby Ribbed Summer Sleeveless Vests. Taped crocheted neck and sleeves. Soft and smooth and non-shrinkable. For children from 1 to 7 years. Give age of child when ordering.
Price. each. .....................$0.10
Per dozen........................ 1.00

## Children's Fine Derby Ribbed Egyptian Cotton Vests.

**No. 2999 Children's Fine Derby Ribbed Egyptian Cotton Vests.** Ecru or balbriggan color. Made with long sleeves and high neck. Overstitched cuffs and tail, fancy crocheted neck and sateen front. Sizes 1 to 7 years. Always give age of child when ordering. Very soft and non-shrinkable.
Price each............**$0.12**
Per dozen............ **1.35**

## Misses' Summer Underwear.

| Sizes | B | C | D | E |
|---|---|---|---|---|
| Years | 8 to 10 | 10 to 12 | 12 to 14 | 15 |

**No. 21001 Misses' Fine Jersey Ribbed Summer Vests**, ecru color, sleeveless, square front, full finished. Each..........**$0.14**
Per doz.......... **1.50**
**No. 21002 Misses' Fine Lisle Summer Vest**, ecru color, V-shaped front, silk taped. Each.....**$0.25**
Per doz.......... **2.70**
**No. 21004 Misses' High Neck and Long Sleeved Summer Vests**, fine Swiss ribbed, ecru color.
Each..........**$0.25**
Per doz.......... **2.70**
**No. 21006 Misses' Swiss Ribbed Summer Drawers**, to match above.
Price, per pair..........**$0.25**
Per doz.......... **2.70**

## Children's White Gauze Vests.

**Sizes 16 to 34 Inch Bust Measure.**

### Children's Fine Summer Weight White Gauze Vests.

**No. 21007 Children's Fine Summer Weight White Gauze Vests.** High neck and short sleeves. Finely bound neck and front, and hemmed tail. These are most excellent garments, and we warrant them to give good satisfaction.

**We make a special feature of these Gauze Vests, they are full of real old fashioned goodness and will not shrink or irritate the skin.**

| Sizes | 16 | 18 | 20 | 22 | 24 | 26 | 28 | 30 | 32 | 34 |
|---|---|---|---|---|---|---|---|---|---|---|
| Price, each | 8c | 10c | 12c | 14c | 16c | 18c | 20c | 22c | 24c | 26c |

**No. 21008 Children's Fine White Gauze Summer Vests or Shirts**, same as above but made with high neck and long sleeves.

| Sizes | 16 | 18 | 20 | 22 | 24 | 26 | 28 | 30 | 32 | 34 |
|---|---|---|---|---|---|---|---|---|---|---|
| Price each | 9c | 11c | 13c | 15c | 17c | 19c | 21c | 23c | 25c | 27c |

## Children's Fine Balbriggan Shirts.

**Sizes 22 to 34 Inch Bust Measure.**

**No. 21010 Children's Fine Soft Finished Balbriggan Shirts**, extra well made and finished, taped neck and front and hemmed tail. Natural grey color. Sizes 22, 24, 26, 28, 30, 32 and 34 bust measure. All sizes at same price. Price each..........**$0.19**

**No. 21012 Children's Fine Balbriggan Shirts.** Same as above in ecru or dark cream color. Sizes 22 to 34. Price each.... ..........**$0.19**

## Children's Medium Weight Shirts and Drawers.

**For all the year around wear. White Merino Underwear.**

**No. 21014 Children's Fine White Merino Undershirts.** Nicely taped front and ribbed cuffs. Non-shrinkable and warranted to give good service. Suitable for nearly any climate.

| Sizes | 16 | 18 | 20 | 22 | 24 | 26 | 28 | 30 | 32 | 34 |
|---|---|---|---|---|---|---|---|---|---|---|
| Price, each | 12c | 15c | 18c | 21c | 24c | 27c | 30c | 33c | 36c | 39c |

**No. 21015 Children's White Merino Pantalets to match above.**

| Sizes | 16 | 18 | 20 | 22 | 24 | 26 | 28 | 30 | 32 | 34 |
|---|---|---|---|---|---|---|---|---|---|---|
| Price, each | 12c | 15c | 18c | 21c | 24c | 27c | 30c | 33c | 36c | 39c |

**No. 21016 Children's Natural Grey Medium Heavy Weight Undershirts.** Fine finished neck and taped front, elastic ribbed cuffs. Excellent for wear all the year around.

| Sizes | 16 | 18 | 20 | 22 | 24 | 26 | 28 | 30 | 32 | 34 |
|---|---|---|---|---|---|---|---|---|---|---|
| Price, each | 12c | 15c | 18c | 21c | 24c | 27c | 30c | 33c | 36c | 39c |

**No. 21017 Children's Fine Natural Grey Mixed Merino Pantalets**, to match above.

| Sizes | 16 | 18 | 20 | 22 | 24 | 26 | 28 | 30 | 32 | 34 |
|---|---|---|---|---|---|---|---|---|---|---|
| Price each | 12c | 15c | 18c | 21c | 24c | 27c | 30c | 33c | 36c | 39c |

## Children's All Wool Underwear.

**The Best All Wool Children's Underwear Manufactured. We Guarantee Every Garment to be Exactly as Represented.**

**No. 21018 Children's Extra Fine Quality All Wool Camel's Hair Shirts**, collarette neck and ribbed cuffs, heavy weight, well made and finely finished garments.

| Sizes | 16 | 18 | 20 | 22 | 24 | 26 | 28 | 30 | 32 | 34 |
|---|---|---|---|---|---|---|---|---|---|---|
| Price, each | 25c | 30c | 35c | 40c | 45c | 50c | 55c | 60c | 65c | 70c |

**No. 21019 Children's Pantalets**, to match above.

| Sizes | 16 | 18 | 20 | 22 | 24 | 26 | 28 | 30 | 32 | 34 |
|---|---|---|---|---|---|---|---|---|---|---|
| Price per pair | 25c | 30c | 35c | 40c | 45c | 50c | 55c | 60c | 65c | 70c |

**No. 21020 Children's Shirts**, same as above in natural grey.

| Sizes | 16 | 18 | 20 | 22 | 24 | 26 | 28 | 30 | 32 | 34 |
|---|---|---|---|---|---|---|---|---|---|---|
| Price | 25c | 30c | 35c | 40c | 45c | 50c | 55c | 60c | 65c | 70c |

**No. 21021 Pantalets** to match above, natural grey color.

| Sizes | 16 | 18 | 20 | 22 | 24 | 26 | 28 | 30 | 32 | 34 |
|---|---|---|---|---|---|---|---|---|---|---|
| Price, per pair | 25c | 30c | 35c | 40c | 45c | 50c | 55c | 60c | 65c | 70c |

**No. 21022 Children's Pure Natural Grey Lamb's Wool Heavy Weight Undershirts**, fancy collarette neck, ribbed cuffs and pearl buttons, extra fine and soft, strong and durable. These garments will give perfect satisfaction.

| Sizes | 16 | 18 | 20 | 22 | 24 | 26 | 28 | 30 | 32 | 34 |
|---|---|---|---|---|---|---|---|---|---|---|
| Price, each | 30c | 35c | 45c | 55c | 65c | 75c | 85c | 95c | $1.05 | $1.15 |

**No. 21023 Pantalets to match above, extra well made and finished.**

| Sizes | 16 | 18 | 20 | 22 | 24 | 26 | 28 | 30 | 32 | 34 |
|---|---|---|---|---|---|---|---|---|---|---|
| Price per pair | 30c | 35c | 45c | 55c | 65c | 75c | 85c | 95c | $1.05 | $1.15 |

## Boys' Underwear.

**No. 21024 Boys' Natural Grey Merino Undershirts**, with fancy collarette neck and ribbed cuffs; well made and finished and warranted good.

| Sizes | 24 | 26 | 28 | 30 | 32 | 34 |
|---|---|---|---|---|---|---|
| Price, each | 22c | 24c | 26c | 28c | 30c | 32c |

**No. 21025 Boys' Drawers**, to match above; open front.

| Sizes | 24 | 26 | 28 | 30 | 32 | 34 |
|---|---|---|---|---|---|---|
| Price, per pair | 22c | 24c | 26c | 28c | 30c | 32c |

## Great Bargains in Ladies' Fall and Winter Underwear.

**NOW IS THE TIME TO BUY.**

### Ladies' Derby Ribbed Underwear.

**Sizes, 32 to 40 Bust Measure.**

**No. 21026 Ladies' Heavy Weight Natural Grey Derby Ribbed Vests.** Perfectly form fitting and excellent for wear. Made from specially prepared combed cotton and warranted non-shrinkable.
Price each.......**$0.24**
Three for........ **.69**
**No. 21027 Ladies' Form Fitting Derby Drawers** to match above.
Price per pair....**$0.24**
Three pairs for.. **.69**

**No. 21028 Ladies' Extra Quality Derby Ribbed Non-Shrinkable Vests.** Made from heavy weight Egyptian yarn, natural grey color; fine pearl buttons; silk taped and crochet neck; elastic form fitting shaped waist; thoroughly well made; sizes 32 to 40 bust, Price each..........**$0.47**
Three for.......... **1.35**
**No. 21029 Ladies Extra Quality Ankle Length Drawers**, to match above. Price per pair.....**$0.47**
Three pairs for.......... **1.35**
**No. 21030 Ladies' Natural Sanitary Grey Wool Ribbed Undervests**, with fancy crocheted neck and and front; pearl buttons and shaped waist, perfectly form fitting; nearly all wool; just enough cotton in them to keep them from shrinking. They are excellent value and usually retail for $1.25; sizes 32 to 40 bust measure. Our special price each.......**$0.75**
Three for.......... **2.10**
**No. 21031 Ladies' Fine Sanitary Derby Ribbed Drawers**, to match above. Price, per pair....**$0.75**
Three pairs for.......... **2.10**

**SKIN COMFORT IN THESE GARMENTS. They Will Sooth the Skin and Warm the Flesh. Please the Eyes as Well as Fit the Form.**

**No. 21032 Ladies' Pure Worsted Ribbed Vests**, heavy weight, knit from fine Australian all wool worsted yarn, shaped to fit the form, collarette neck, pearl buttons, full fashioned cuffs. The sort of garments that give supreme satisfaction. One of them will outwear three ordinary vests at the same price. Exceptionally well made and finished. Natural grey color. Made full sizes. Price, each......**$1.20**
**No. 21033 Ladies' All Wool Pants**, to match above. Fine sateen band, ankle length. form fitting and perfect. Price, per pair..........**$1.20**

## Fine White Merino Vests for 40c.

**Sizes 28 to 40 Only.**

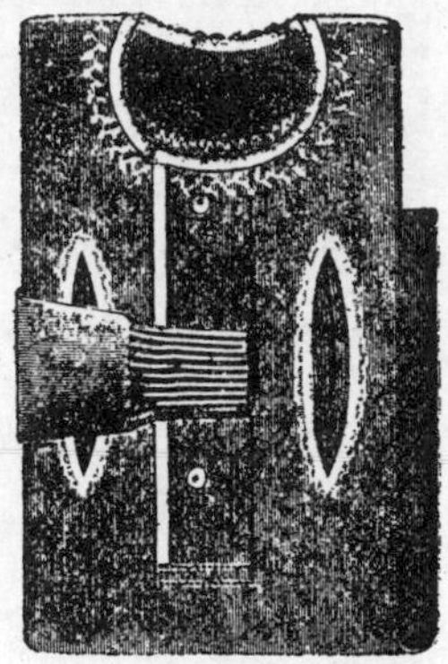

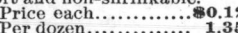

**No. 21035 Ladies' Heavy Fine White Merino Undershirts or Vests.** Silk taped and finely finished. White pearl buttons and elastic ribbed cuffs Never before sold for less than 50c. Many merchants ask 75c for them.
Price, each......**$0.40**
Three for........ **1.10**
**No. 21036 Ladies' Fine White Merino Drawers** to match above.
Price, per pair...**$0.40**
Three pairs for.. **1.10**
**No. 21037 Ladies' Heavy Winter Weight Natural Grey Mixed Merino Vests.** Made in first-class manner nicely taped and finished, with ribbed cuffs and fine pearl buttons. Positively the best garments ever offered at the price. Strong and durable, soft and fine. Sizes, 28 to 40.
Price, each..........**$0.45**
Three for.......... **1.25**
**No. 21038 Ladies' Natural Grey Mixed Merino Drawers** to match above. Price, per pair.....**$0.45**
3 pair for.......... **1.25**
**No. 21039 Ladies' Heavy Winter Weight Undervests.** Same as above in camel's hair mixture. Sizes 28 to 40. Price, each..........**$0.45**
**No. 21040 Ladies' Camel's Hair Mixed Drawers**, to match the above vests. Price, per pair, **$0.45**

## 73c. for Natural Wool Vests.

**No. 21041 Ladies' Fine Natural Sanitary Grey Wool Undervests.** Heavy winter weight. Contain 80 per cent. pure wool and are warranted not to shrink. Finely taped with silk and furnished with elastic ribbed wrists and pearl buttons. Full of real goodness and wearing qualities. Retail value **$1.00**
Our price, each.......... **.73**
3 pairs for.......... **2.10**
**No. 21042 Ladies' Non-Shrinkable Sanitary Wool Drawers** to match above. Sizes 28 to 40.
Price, per pair.......... **$0.73**
3 pairs for.......... **2.10**

## Sanitary Health Underwear.

**No. 21043 Ladies' Health Undervests.** Made from pure natural grey sanitary wool. Specially adapted to persons requiring heavy and warm underwear. Soft and fine, nicely finished and finely made up, white pearl buttons, ribbed cuffs. etc. There is real satisfaction to be had from wearing garments of this sort. Sizes 28 to 40.
Price each.......... **$1.00**
Three for.......... **2.75**
**No. 21044 Ladies' Sanitary Health Underdrawers** to match above.
Price per pair.......... **$1.00**
Three pairs for.......... **2.75**

## Ladies' Medicated Scarlet Underwear.

**No. 21046 Ladies' Fine Soft All Wool Medicated Scarlet Undervests.** Highly recommended by physicians for persons troubled with rheumatism. These are exceptionally fine garments and are not to be compared with the cheap inferior scarlet underwear with which the market is flooded. Sizes 28 to 44.
Price each.......... **$1.20**
Three for.......... **3.45**
**No. 21048 Ladies' Scarlet Medicated Drawers** to match above. Sizes 28 to 40.
Price per pair.......... **$1.20**
Three pairs for.......... **3.45**

**WE SELL LADIES' AND MENS' WATCHES**

**AT PRICES THAT LEAVE NO ROOM FOR COMPLAINT.**

**THE GOLD CURE**

**FOR POVERTY CAN ONLY BE EFFECTED WITH THE AID OF ECONOMY. TAKE REGULAR DOSES FROM THIS CATALOGUE AND BE**

**WELL HEALED.**

**Capes, Wraps AND Waists**

**For the Proper Season BUY... WHEN YOU DO BUY**

**AT PRICES THAT PERMIT OF YOUR BUYING SOMETHING ELSE.**

**YOU CAN'T DO HALF SO WELL ELSEWHERE AS YOU CAN WITH US.**

**See Full Plate Engravings**

**IF YOU DOUBT THAT WE WILL DO AS WE AGREE, SEND YOUR ORDER TO THE METROPOLITAN NATIONAL BANK OF CHICAGO, AND TELL THEM NOT TO TURN IT OVER TO US UNLESS THEY KNOW WE ARE RELIABLE.**

# HOSIERY DEPARTMENT.

THE LARGEST STOCK OF HOSIERY
EVER UNDER ONE ROOF.

## PROGRESS IS THE WATCHWORD OF THE HOUR.

Ours is a progressive Hosiery Department. It is the largest exclusive hosiery department in the world. Our warerooms are full to overflowing and are full of good things, too. Never in the history of hosiery buying have we ever before been able to offer our customers such exceptionally good values as we hold out to them this season. We control the entire output of three of the largest and best hosiery and knitting mills in the world. Two in America and one in Europe. The products of these mills have attained a lasting reputation throughout two continents. We believe that the great majority of the people appreciate good hosiery and we are going to give them a chance to buy the best hosiery made at prices that will at once appeal to shrewd and economical buyers.

## Men's Half Hose at Half Price.

Scale of Sizes.

Shoe size .5   6   7   8   9   10
Sock size .9  9½ 10  10  10½ 11

Men's Cotton Half Hose.
No. 21050 Men's Full Seamless Knit Half Hose in assorted gray mixtures. Good weight; suitable for wear all the year around. Extra good value. Weight per dozen, 3 pounds.
Price, per dozen .... $0.55
No. 21051 Men's Very Strong Fine Knit Gray Mixed Cotton Socks. Full seamless foot; neat elastic ribbed top. The best light weight cotton socks ever offered for the money.
Price, per pair...... $0.08
Price, per dozen ...... 0.90
No. 21052 The Nelson Knitting Co's Seamless Rockford Socks. Blue or brown mixed. Heavy double heel and toe and fine finished ribbed tops. Every pair warranted.
Price, per pair................$0.08
Price, per dozen ........ ..... 0.90
No. 21054 Men's Extra Fine Full Seamless Half Hose in new and handsome brown and olive mixtures, also neat grey mixtures; extra fine quality, with finely finished foot and elastic ribbed tops. The equal of any 25c half hose in the market.
Price per pair................$0.13
Per dozen ................... 1.40
No. 21055▢ Men's Fine Gauge French Mixed Half Hose. Full seamless and knit from soft smooth cotton yarn; made with shaped feet and ribbed elastic tops; very neat grey and olive brown mixtures; easy on the feet and easy on the pocket book.
Price per pair....$0.15  Four pairs for.....$0.50

### Genuine British Socks.

No. 21056 Men's Genuine Cream Brown British Seamless Socks. Fine elastic ribbed tops, double heels and toes; knit to wear long and well and guaranteed to do so.  Price per pair................$0.15
Per dozen pairs ........................... 1.45
No. 21057 Men's Genuine Cream Brown British Socks. Same a above but finer in texture; very easy on the feet; extra durable.
Price, per pair ........................$0.19
Per dozen pairs ......................... 2.14
No. 21058 Our Great 40 Gauge Genuine British Socks. Medium weight; full seamless, with elastic ribbed tops and spliced heels and toes; ecru or cream brown color; strong and dependable.
Price per pair......$0.23  Per dozen...........$2.66

### Men's Fancy Silk Embroidered Half Hose.

No. 21059 Men's Fast Black Seamless Cotton Half Hose. Very fine gauge, soft finish with fancy silk embroidered stripes running down the front. Handsome patterns and fast colors. Always sell for from 25c. to 40c. at retail.
Our price, per pair........$0.18
Three pairs for............ .80

### Fancy Lisle Socks.

No. 21060 Men's extra fine guage, light weight, pure Lisle Thread Socks. Black, with fancy colored cross stripes. The handsomest striped half hose ever made. Full seamless and perfect fitting.  Price, per pair....$0.35
3 pairs for ................... 1.00

No. 21061 Men's Fancy Silk Embroidered Socks. Full seamless, perfect fitting and very fine gauge. Assorted colors with neat fancy figures and dots embroidered in silk. All fast colors and strictly high grade goods. Sizes, 9 to 10½.
Price, per pair...............$0.35
Three pairs for........................

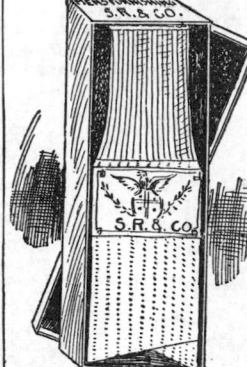

No. 21063.

### Men's Fine Balbriggan Socks.

No. 21062 Men's Extra Quality Fine Soft Finished Balbriggan Socks. Double heels and toes. Guaranteed real two-thread extra super stout cotton, ecru or cream brown color. Finely shaped foot and long elastic ribbed tops. Sizes 9 to 11.  Price, per pair.........$0.15
Four pairs for,..$0.50
No. 21063 Men's Extra Fine Cream, Brown or Ecru Colored Balbriggan Socks. Our own special importation, made in neat fancy rib or drop stitch patterns, with seamless finely shaped foot, spliced heels and toes, and long elastic ribbed tops. Very fine gauge, close knit, firm and to be depended upon for hard service. Neat and dressy as well as good. Sizes 9 to 11. Price, per pair....$0.19
Three pairs for........................$0.50

### Men's High Grade Half Hose.

SOOTHING SOCKS FOR TIRED FEET.
Black Cotton Socks.
No. 21064 Men's Fast Black Cotton Half Hose. Full seamless, fine quality with spliced heels and toes. Fine elastic ribbed tops. Extra good value.
Price, per pair..........$0.09
Per dozen............ .98
No. 21065 Men's Fine Gauge, absolutely Fast Black Seamless Cotton Socks. Knit from fine combed Egyptian cotton, double heels and toes. Very soft and comfortable on the feet. Strong and full of good wearing qualities. Sizes 9 to 11.
Price, per pair...........$0.12
Per dozen pairs,........ 1.30

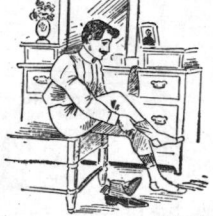

No. 21076

No. 21066 Men's Solid Colored Fast Black Seamless Socks, with high spliced heels and toes. Medium weight and fine gauge. Fine elastic ribbed tops. High grade, soft finish. Sizes, 9 to 11.
Price, per pair...$0.15
Four pairs for... .50
No. 21068 Men's Pure Domestic Lisle Half Hose, with three ply heels and toes and fine elastic ribbed tops. Strictly high grade in every respect. Regular retail value 25c. Sizes, 9 to 11. Plain fast black.
Price, per pair......$0.18
Per doz. pair.... 1.70
No. 21069 Men's Extra Fine Real Two-Thread Maco Cotton Socks. The very best made. Plain black, with double heels and toes and spliced soles. Long, elastic ribbed tops. Absolutely fast color. Sizes. 9 to 11. Price, per pair.....$0.25
Per dozen pairs .................................. 2.70

## Men's Fine Silk Half Hose.

No. 21070 Our Own Special Importation. Men's Extra Quality Plain Fast Black Silk Seamless Half Hose. Very fine soft high grade finish, light weight and thoroughly good; sizes 9 to 11.
Price per pair.............$0.75
No. 21071 Men's Pure Silk Seamless Half Hose. Extra quality imported stock; absolutely fast black and stainless; sizes 9 to 11.  Price per pair.....$0.98
Three pairs for ............. 2.75

## Black Hose With White Feet.

No. 21072 Men's Medium Weight Fast Black Cotton Half Hose, with white heels and toes and white soles; double heels and toes and fine ribbed elastic tops; made from extra fine real maco cotton; our own importation; sizes 9 to 11.
Price per pair ..... $0.24
Per dozen.... 2.66
No. 21073 Men's Extra Quality Imported Cotton Half Hose. Warranted real Maco; soft fine finished; plain black with all white foot; full seamless with double heels and toes; sizes 9 to 11. Price per pair..$0.35
Per dozen pairs.... 2.70

## Black Lisle Thread Socks.

No. 21074 Men's High Grade Pure Lisle Thread Socks. Our own special importation. Very fine and thin. Full regular made and seamless. It's downright refreshing to put on a pair of socks of this sort. Nothing finer for summer wear. Sizes, 9 to 11.
Price, per pair.....................$0.45

## Men's Tan Colored Half Hose.

No. 21075

Sizes, 9 to 11.
No. 21075 Men's Fine Tan Colored Half Hose. Full seamless with spliced heels and toes and long elastic ribbed tops. Extra good value. Sizes, 9 to 11.
Price, per pair.... $0.09
Per dozen................ .98
No. 21076 Fine Gauge Seamless Cotton Half Hose. Knit from fine combed Egyptian yarn. Made with double heels and toes. Soft and fine and very easy on the feet. Plain tans and browns.
Price, per pair.........$0.12
Per dozen................ 1.30
No. 21077 Men's Extra Quality Seamless Cotton Half Hose, with double heels and toes, medium weight and fine gauge. Long elastic ribbed tops. High class finish. Made in light and dark tan colors. Price per pair...$0.15
Four pairs for...........................50
No. 21078 Men's Fine Domestic Tan Color Lisle Half Hose. Medium weight with 3-ply heels and toes and elastic rib tops. High grade and fine gauge. Retail value, 25 cents.
Our special price, per pair.....................$0.18
Per dozen pairs............................. 1.70

## Something New Under the Sun.

Men's Ribbed Cotton Half Hose.
No. 21079 Men's Seamless Cotton Half Hose. Handsome shades of brown and tan. Spliced heels and toes. Fine elastic ribbed tops and full derby ribbed, close fitting legs. Fine gauge and thoroughly reliable. Sizes 9 to 11.
Price, per pair...............$0.15
Three pairs for............... 0.40

### SAVE MONEY By Buying your —HOSIERY— in dozen lots.

No. 21080 Men's Plain Extra High-Grade Genuine Maco Cotton Half Hose. Handsome shades of tan and brown. Fine soft finish combed yarn with double heels and toes and long elastic ribbed tops, full seamless and fast color. Finely shaped foot and the most perfect fitting half hose made. Sizes, 9 to 11. Price, per pair.....................$0.25
3 pair for ......................................... 0.68

## Men's Fine Merino Half Hose.

No. 21082 Men's Fine Soft Finished Merino Half Hose, tan and gray mixtures, medium weight suitable for wear all the year around. Seamless and perfect fitting. Sizes, 9 to 11.
Price, per pair, 15c; 2 pairs for $0.25
No. 21083 Men's Extra Fine Skin Soothing Merino Half Hose. Medium weight, fine close knit and made with double soles, high spliced heels and toes. Very strong and durable. Specially adapted to persons who cannot wear all wool hosiery. Handsome shades of mode and tan and reddish brown mixture. Sizes, 9 to 11. Full seamless. Price, per pair, 24c; 3 pairs for $0.65

### Men's Fine Cashmere Socks.

**No. 21085** Men's Fast Black Medium Weight Seamless all Wool Cashmere Half Hose. Spliced heels and toes and long elastic ribbed tops. Fine soft finish and very easy on the feet. Warranted fast color. Sizes 9 to 11. Price, per pair.....$0.24
Per dozen pairs.................. 2.65
**No. 21086** Men's Fine Wool Cashmere Half Hose, same as above in handsome tan and brown shades.
Price per pair.................. $0.24
Per dozen pairs.................. 2.65
NOTE.—Dozen rates apply where a half dozen or more of the same kind of hosiery is ordered. It pays to buy your hosiery at dozen rates.

### MEN'S HIGH CLASS
### FAST
## BLACK SEAMLESS CASHMERE SOCKS.

**No. 21088** Our own special importation. Fine gauge, soft and full of comfort and durability, medium heavy weight with double heels and toes and elastic ribbed tops. Regular 50c quality. Sizes 9 to 11.
Price per pair.................. $0.37
Three pairs for.................. 1.00

**No. 21089** Men's Heavy Weight All Wool Imported Cashmere Socks. Fine and soft and non-shrinkable and will not irritate the feet. Made with double heels and toes and elastic ribbed tops. These are the very best cashmere socks ever sold for anywhere near our asking price. We know they will please you. Made in plain black color and warranted absolutely fast black and stainless. Sizes 9 to 11. Price per pair.................. $0.48
Three pairs for.................. 1.35

### Men's Wool Half Hose.
#### For Fall and Winter Wear.

**No. 21090** Men's all-wool natural gray mixed half hose. Full seamless. Finely shaped foot and elastic derby ribbed tops. Sizes 9 to 11. Full seamless. Price per pair.................. $0.18
Per dozen.................. 1.80
**No. 21091** Men's Extra Heavy Weight All-wool Socks. Light or medium gray mixtures. Well shaped foot and long elastic tops. Very strong and reliable. Full seamless.
Price per pair.................. $0.20
Per dozen pairs.................. 2.25
**No. 21092** Men's Extra Heavy All-wool Socks. Blue mixed color. Same quality as above. Full seamless.
Price per pair.................. $0.20
Per dozen pairs.................. 2.25
**No. 21093** Men's Heavy All-wool Blue Gray Mixed, seamless Shaker socks. Double heels and toes. Extra strong and dependable. Price per pair.................. $0.25
Per dozen.................. 2.75

**No. 21094** Men's Extra Heavy All Wool Seamless Shaker Socks. knit from pure lamb's wool; heavy and soft and guaranteed to satisfy. Gray mixed or scarlet. Price per pair.................. $0.35
Three pairs for.................. 1.00

### Lumbermen's Wool Socks.
#### Extra Heavy Soft Wool.

**LUMBERMEN'S**
**EXTRA HEAVY, ALL WOOL....**
## RIBBED SOCKS.

**No. 21096** Double heels and toes. Knit from extra fine soft wool, specially selected for this class of hosiery. Long legs and full sizes. Colors red, gray or cream. Regular 50 cent quality.
Our price per pair.. $0.25
Per dozen pairs..... 2.70

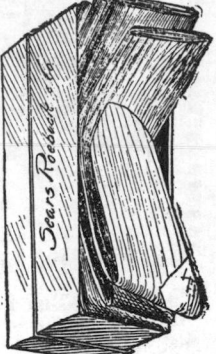

Lumbermen's Extra Fine and Extra Heavy
## LAMB'S WOOL SOCKS.

**No. 21097** With ribbed legs and double spliced soles. Colors natural gray, blue mixed, scarlet or cream.
Price per pair...... $0.28
Per dozen pairs.... 2.95

No. 21096

---

# LADIES' HOSIERY.

## THE DAWN OF BETTER TIMES IN HOSIERY BUYING BEGINS HERE.

You cannot afford to pay tribute to the retail merchant in the shape of large profits, when we can give you better values for decidedly less money. Then, too, our assortment is unlimited. We have Ladies' Hosiery of every description. Read our descriptions carefully. They point out the right path, and show you the true road to economy in hosiery buying.

**SAVE MONEY WHEREVER YOU CAN.**

**SAVE IT ON HOSIERY**
**AND YOU SAVE DOUBLY WELL.**

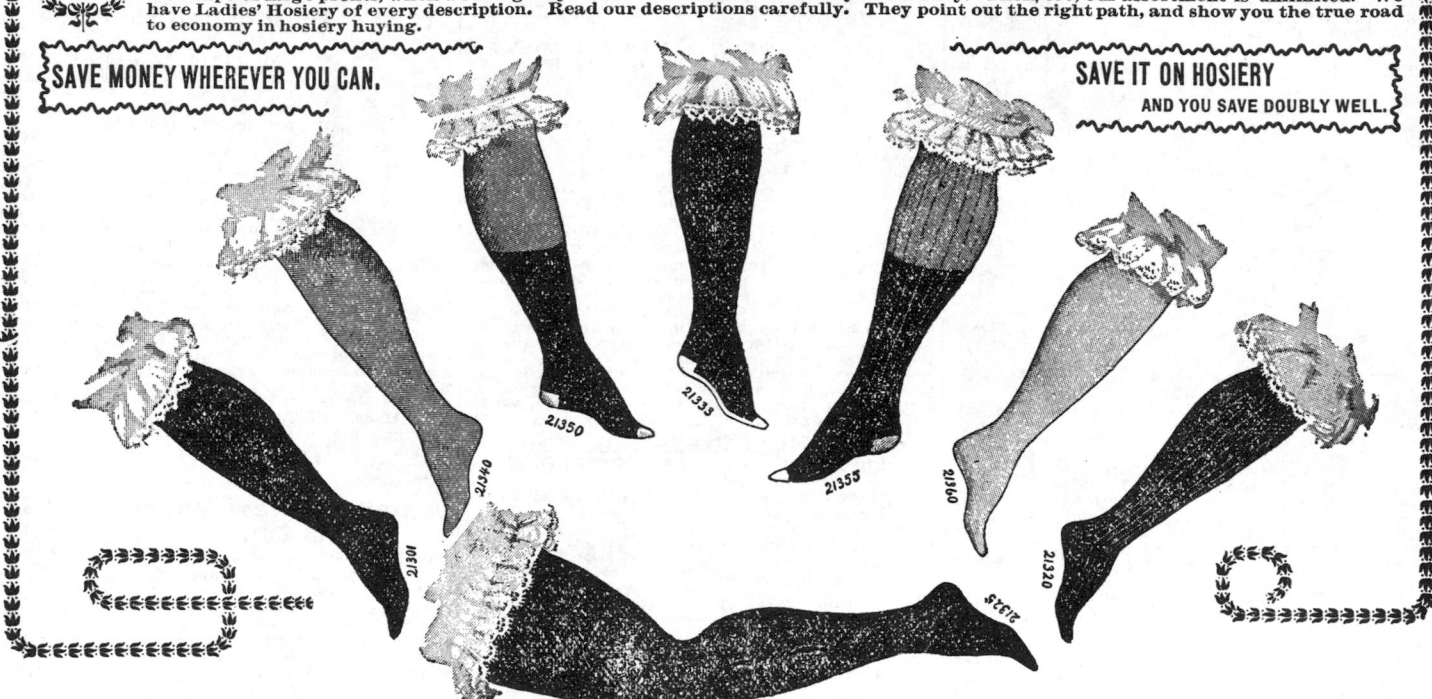

---

**SPECIAL NOTICE.**—In ordering Ladies' Hose, please refer to the following scale of sizes:
#### SCALE OF SIZES.
No. 1      Ladies' Shoe takes about 8 inch hose.
No. 2      Ladies' Shoe takes about 8½ inch hose.
No. 3 and 4 Ladies' Shoe takes about 9 inch hose.
No. 5 and 6 Ladies' Shoe takes about 9½ inch hose.
No. 7      Ladies' Shoe takes about 10 inch hose.

### Ladies' Fast Black Cotton Hose.
Every Pair Warranted Fast Black and Stainless.
**No. 21300** Ladies' Fast Black Cotton Hose with patent finished seams, 24 gauge. Fast color and stainless. Price per pair.................. $0.05
Per dozen pairs.................. 0.55
**No. 21301** Ladies' Good Grade Fast Black Cotton Hose. Better quality than above and finer gauge. Will give excellent satisfaction. Price per pair.................. $0.08
Per dozen.................. 0.90
**No. 21302** Genuine Laurence Mills Fast Black Cotton Hose. Seamless with high spliced heels and double toes. Made full size and length. Medium weight. Very Strong and reliable. Price per pair.................. $0.10
Per dozen.................. 1.00
**No. 21303** Ladies' Fast Black Cotton Hose. Same as above in heavier weight. Very durable and sure to satisfy. Price per pair.................. $0.14
Per dozen.................. 1.50

**No. 21305** Full Seamless Hose. Warranted absolutely fast black and stainless. Made from fine two thread Egyptian cotton, 40 gauge. Soft smooth finish with elastic hemmed tops, double heels and double toes. Regular 25 cent quality when bought at retail. Price per pair.................. $0.18
Three pairs for.................. 0.50

### Our Famous 25c Hose.
#### Unequalled Anywhere on Earth.

**No. 21307** Extra Fine Silky Finished Real Maco Cotton Hose. Plain black with three thread heels and toes. Made from extra selected combed yarn, fine and soft as silk. Full seamless finely shaped and handsomely finished. Guaranteed absolutely fast black and stainless. Easy on the feet and easy on the purse. Nothing as good ever sold for less than 40c. Medium weight.
Price per pair, 25c.; per dozen pairs.........$2.68

### 35c for Pure Lisle Hose.

**No. 21309** Pure Two Thread Fast Black Lisle Hose. Fine gauge soft finish, handsomely shaped and full seamless. Reinforced heels and toes. Medium weight. An excellent wearing hose and one that fits to perfection. Tired feet will find a vast amount of real comfort in these goods.
Price, per pair, 35c; 3 pairs for.................. $1.00

**No. 21320** The Illustration of this Hose is shown above. It is an exceptionally nice Richelieu ribbed fast black cotton hose. Genuine Hermsdorf dye, fast black and stainless; fine 40 gauge; full fashioned and full regular made seamless. High spliced heels and toes and finely shaped foot. Handsome and full of goodness.
Price, per pair, 25c; per dozen pairs.......... $2.68

### Opera Length Black Hose.

**No. 21325** Ladies' Extra Long or Opera Length Hose, as shown in the illustration above. Full seamless with high spliced heels and toes and elastic hemmed tops. Warranted absolutely fast black and stainless. An extra long hose for a very short price. Always mention size when ordering.
Price, per pair, 25c; per dozen pairs.......... $2.68
**No. 21326** Ladies' Fast Black, Real Maco, Opera Length Cotton Hose; leg is full 32 inches long, full regular made, finely gusseted and handsomely shaped, double heels and toes. This stocking is extra heavy and 40 gauge fine; soft, smooth, silky in finish and very easy on the feet. Per pair.......... $0.35
Three pairs for.................. 0.98

## FOR FINE SHOES.
We are Without Competitors in the Matter of Prices.
**➤➤➤ SEE SHOE DEPARTMENT.**

---

REFER TO THE VOLUMINOUS INDEX IN THE BACK PART OF CATALOGUE FOR ANYTHING YOU DON'T SEE IN THE BOOK.
ABOUT EVERYTHING YOU WANT IS QUOTED.

**No. 21327 Ladies' Opera Length Hose;** positively fast black, made of finest Maco yarn, full fashioned and full regular made; extra elastic hemmed tops; the leg is fully 34 inches long; very finely finished foot and handsomely shaped, high spliced heel and French finished toe; an exceedingly handsome stocking.
Per pair..........**$0.50**

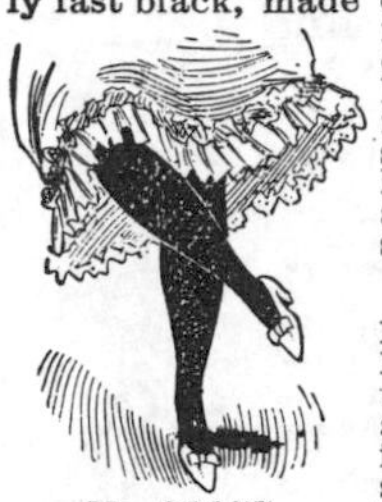

No. 21357

**No. 21328 Ladies' Extra Fine Quality Opera Length Hose;** full regular made; lisle thread; warranted fast black and stainless. Our own special importation. They are full seamless and extra fine gauge; full opera length, with wide elastic hemmed tops. Price per pair..........**$1.00**

**No. 21333 Fast Black Hose,** with cream colored unbleached heels, toes and soles. Spliced heels and toes. Made from extra selected real maco cotton, soft and smooth and very strong and durable. Absolutely fast black and stainless. Can be used with slipper, as the white sole will not show above the top of slipper. Regular 40c quality.
Price, per pair....**$0.28** Three pair for....**$0.75**

**No. 21335 Fast Black Real Egyptian Cotton Hose,** with unbleached and uncolored heels, toes and soles. Same style as above, but heavier and finer. Regular 50c quality when bought at retail.
Per pair..........**$0.39** Three pairs for..........**$1.05**

## Ladies' Plain Tan Colored Hose.

**No. 21340 Ladies' Plain Tan Colored Cotton Hose.** Good weight and full seamless, with spliced heels and toes. Nicely finished and finely shaped. Elastic hemmed tops. Assorted light and dark shades of tan.
Per pair..........**$0.12**
Per dozen pairs..........1.38

**No. 21342 Fine 40-gauge Tan Colored Hose.** Finely shaped and handsomely finished, extra high spliced heel and toes and double soles, medium weight and full seamless; guaranteed absolutely fast color and thoroughly dependable. Price per pair..........**$0.18**
3 pairs for..........45

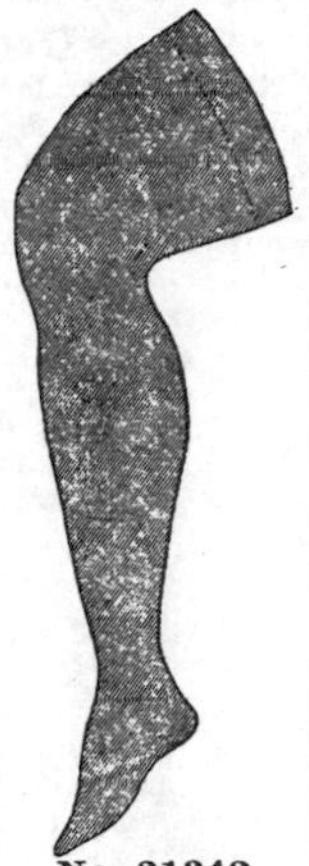

No. 21342

**No. 21344 Extra 40 gauge Tan Colored Hose,** 35 cent quality. Real two-thread Maco cotton, extra high spliced heel, double sole, French finished toe, full regular made very elastic hemmed top. Per pair, **$0.25**
One-half dozen for..........1.35

**No. 21345 Ladies' Tan Cotton Hose.** Made of the finest Maco yarn, silk finish; full regular made and fashioned; extra gusseted leg and foot; extra spliced heels and toes. This is really a beautiful stocking. Per pair..........**$0.35**
3 pairs for..........1.00
Per dozen pairs..........3.80

## Ladies' Fancy Boot Top Hose.

**No. 21350 Ladies' Fancy Boot Top Hose.** Fast black with white tipped heels and toes and plain bright colored tops. Cardinal, pink, lavender, light blue, heliotrope and yellow. These are extra fine guage close knit hose and must not be compared with the cheap inferior grades which are dear at any price. We guarantee this line of hosiery to be strictly high grade and dependable, absolutely fast colors and soft fine silky finish. Regular 50c quality. Price per pair..........**$0.25**
6 pairs assorted in box..........1.40

## Richelieu Ribbed Boot Top Hose.

**No. 21355 Fast Black Boot Pattern,** colored tops with fancy Richelieu ribbed leg, full regular made and handsomely finished double white tipped heels and toes; come in the following shades: Pink, tan, pale blue, yellow, nile, heliotrope and red, making a very pretty stocking, which, to all appearances and wear, are as good as Lisle thread.
Per pair..........**$0.25**
Put up in boxes of six pairs of assorted colors, per box..........1.40

**No. 21356 Ladies' Imported Lisle Thread Boot Top Hose.** Same style as above but made with fancy striped boot tops in slate, tan, brown, gray mode and other desirable shades. White tipped, double heels and toes. Warranted absolutely fast colors, strictly high grade. Price, per pair..........**$0.48**
3 pairs for..........1.35

## Ladies' Balbriggan Hose.

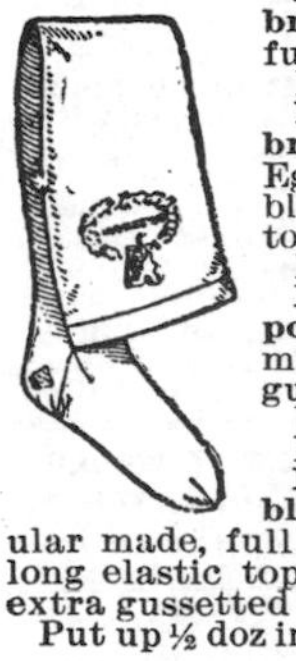

**No. 21360 Ladies' Unbleached Balbriggan Hose;** extra long, elastic top, full seamless foot. Per pair....**$0.11**
Per dozen..........1.20

**No. 21362 Full Regular Made Balbriggan Hose;** made of fine combed Egyptian yarn; high spliced heel, double toe and sole, extra long and elastic top. Per pair..........**$0.19**
Per dozen..........2.10

**No. 21363 Extra Fine Quality Imported Balbriggan Hose;** full regular made and full fashioned to fit; extra gusseted; high spliced heel and toe.
Per pair..........**$0.25**
Put up ½ doz in a box, per box..1.40

**No. 21364 Fancy Ribbed Top Unbleached Balbriggan Hose;** full regular made, full shaped and finely finished; extra long elastic tops, high spliced heel and double toe; extra gussetted foot. Per pair..........**$0.25**
Put up ½ doz in box, per box..........1.40

## Long Ribbed Top Hose.

### LADIES' FAST BLACK UPPER LENGTH HOSE.

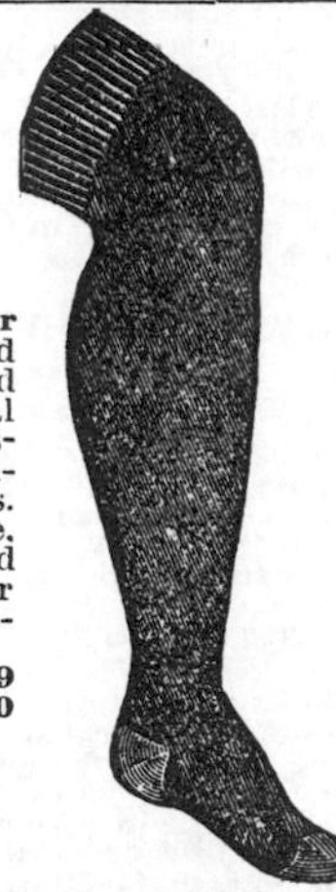

No. 21365.

**No. 21365 Ladies' Upper Length Hose.** With long ribbed tops; full seamless with spliced heels and toes. Our own special importation and a grade of hosiery that possesses exceptionally good wearing qualities. They are thoroughly well made, finely fashioned and are of good medium weight. Order a pair of them for trial and you surely will want more of them.
Price, per pair..........**$0.19**
3 pairs for..........0.50

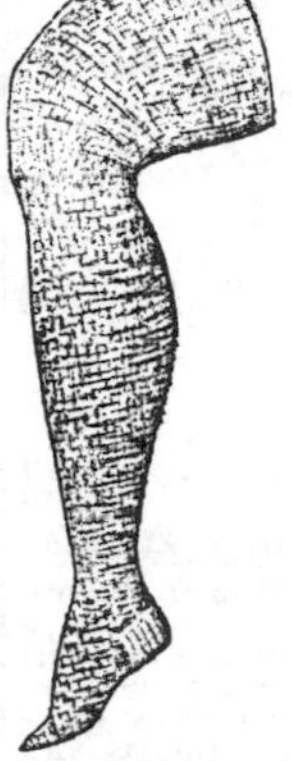

## Ladies' Oxford Mixed Hose.

TRUE MERIT IN THESE GOODS.

### LADIES' EXTRA QUALITY DARK OXFORD GRAY MIXED SEAMLESS COTTON HOSE.

**No. 21368** Fine gauge and good medium weight for all the year around wear. We make a specialty of this line of hose. We sell tons of them every year and have never had a single complaint in regard to them. They are soft and close knit, very strong and durable and will give long and lasting satisfaction.
Price, per pair..........**$0.10**
Per dozen pairs..........1.00

## Ladies' Extra High Grade Hose.

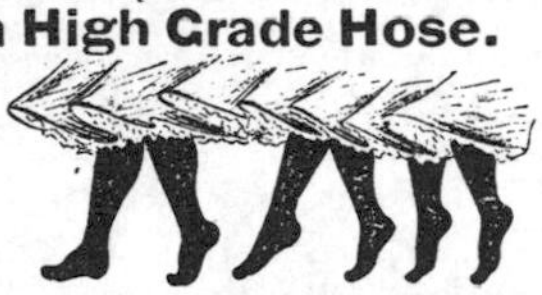

**Soft skin soothing stockings. A sure cure for that tired feeling in the feet. Extra fine, handsome and dependable. You cannot help but like them.**

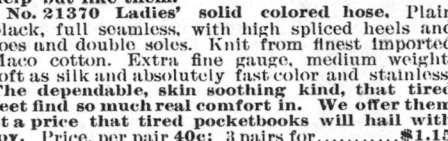

**No. 21370 Ladies' solid colored hose.** Plain black, full seamless, with high spliced heels and toes and double soles. Knit from finest imported Maco cotton. Extra fine gauge, medium weight, soft as silk and absolutely fast color and stainless. **The dependable, skin soothing kind, that tired feet find so much real comfort in. We offer them at a price that tired pocketbooks will hail with joy.** Price, per pair 40c; 3 pairs for..........**$1.15**

## White Tipped Lisle Hose.

THE KIND THAT SATISFY.

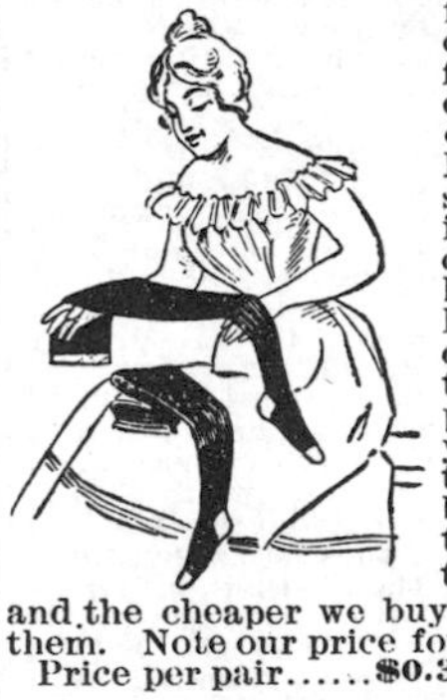

**No. 21371 Ladies' absolutely fast black lisle hose,** with snow white tipped, double heels and toes, full seamless, with wide elastic hemmed tops. Extra fine gauge. Very soft and easy on the feet. **Real foot comfort in these goods.** Medium weight and very strong, insuring lasting satisfaction in the wearing qualities. We offer these hose at a price that is far lower than your local merchant could afford to sell them. We use the entire product of one factory and you know as well as we do that no retail merchant ever buys hosiery in such quantities. The more we buy the cheaper we buy them, and the cheaper we buy them the cheaper we sell them. Note our price for this season.
Price per pair......**$0.37** Three pair for....**$1.00**

**No. 21374 Extra quality good weight lisle hose,** absolutely fast black and warranted stainless. Full seamless with double heels and toes, the heels, toes and soles are light unbleached balbriggan or cream color. This is an extra fine gauge hose, and one of the most durable ever made, they are soft and easy on the feet, warranted to give lasting satisfaction in looks and wear, trustworthy, dependable and comfortable stockings.
Price, per pair..........**$0.50**
Three pair for..........1.35

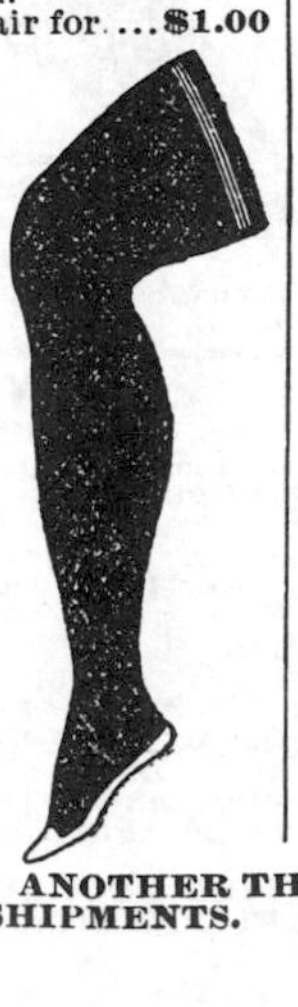

**ALWAYS STATE JUST WHAT SIZE YOU WANT when ordering hosiery. This will save us the trouble of writing to you for size, and will always insure your order being filled promptly and correctly.**

## Richelieu Ribbed Pure Lisle Hose.

**Guaranteed 4 Thread Lisle.**

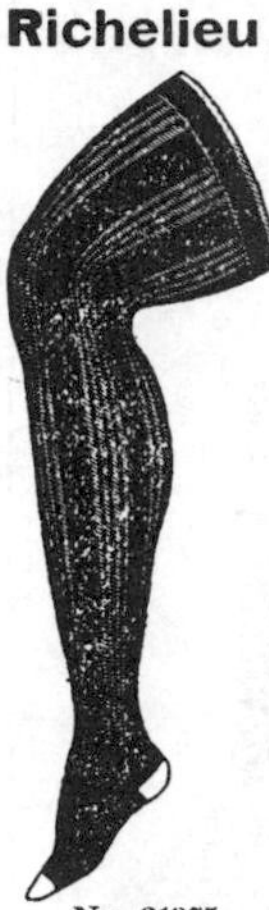

No. 21375

**No. 21375 If you buy a pair of these stockings** you will not only get something fine and dependable but you will get the handsomest pair of black stockings ever sold for less than $1.00 a pair. These are pure 4 thread lisle genuine Hermsdorf dye and warranted absolutely fast black and stainless. They are full seamless and have extra high spliced heels, white tipped heels and toes and tops. Fancy drop stitch Richelieu ribbed pattern. Perfect beauties and thoroughly high grade and fine gauge. Note our extraordinary low prices on these goods. We import them direct.
Price per pair..........**$0.43**
Three pairs for..........1.20

**No. 21376 Ladies' Heavy Weight Fast Black Lisle Hose,** seamless and perfect fitting; fine gauge, spliced heels and toes and double soles. High class in every respect.
Price per pair..........**$0.73**

**No. 21377 Ladies' High Grade Fast Black Hose,** same as preceding number but made in light weight.
Price, per pair..........**$0.73**

**No. 21378 Ladies' Silk and Lisle Mixed Hose,** extra high grade, high-spliced heels and toes and double soles, absolutely fast black and stainless, made for high-class trade. One of our specially good things. Price, per pair..........**$0.95**

## Ladies' Silk Hose.

**No. 21380 High Grade Silk Plait Hose,** full seamless, perfect fitting, spliced heels and toes, absolutely fast black, very fine and soft and easy on the feet.
Price, per pair..........**$0.98**

**No. 21382 Ladies' All Silk Hose,** high-class stock, full seamless and perfect fitting, spliced heels and toes, warranted absolutely fast black, one of our specially good values, full of real goodness and superior wearing qualities. Price, per pair..........**$1.48**

**No. 21384 Ladies' Fine Silk Hose,** made of finest and purest silk ever produced. Made same style as above. Warranted fast black and stainless. Extra fine gauge and the softest and smoothest ladies' hose ever made. All regular sizes.
Price, per pair..........**$2.47**

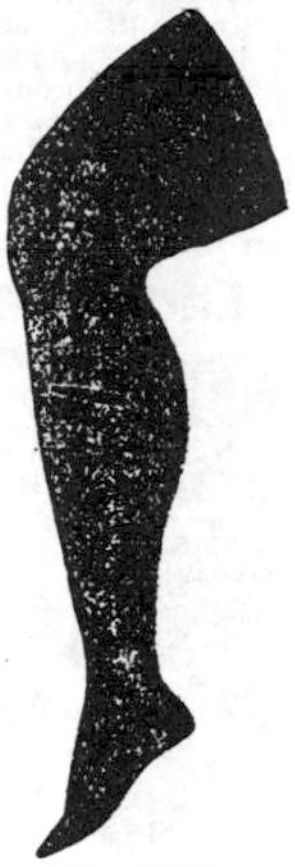

No. 21380.

## Ladies' Out Size Hose.

**Made with Extra Wide Legs.**

**No. 21385 Ladies' Out Size Hose,** made with extra wide legs. Fast black heavy cotton, with double heels and toes. Weight, 2½ lbs. to the dozen. Thoroughly well made and warranted to give perfect satisfaction in every way.
Price, per pair..........**$0.17**
Six pairs for..........**.90**

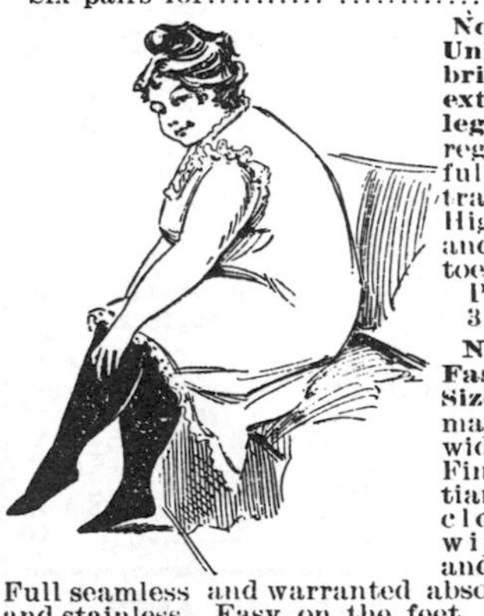

**No. 21386. Ladies' Unbleached Balbriggan Hose, with extra large wide legs and tops.** Full regular made and full fashioned. Extra fine finished foot. High spliced heel and French finished toe, ecru color.
Price, per pair, **35c**
3 pairs for.....**98c**

**No. 21387. Ladies' Fast Black, Out Size Cotton Hose,** made with extra wide legs and tops. Fine 40 gauge, Egyptian Cotton, soft and close knit made with spliced heels and double soles. Full seamless and warranted absolutely fast black and stainless. Easy on the feet, and easy on the pocket book.
Price, per pair..........**25c**
6 pairs for..........**$1.35**

**No. 21388 Ladies' Out Size Hose,** fast black, very good weight, made of the very best selected Maco cotton which is very soft and will be appreciated by fleshy patrons, as the feet remain much cooler and will not burn while wearing this make; full regular made, with extra finished foot, high spliced heel, French finished toe. Per pair..........**$0.37**
Three pairs for..........1.00

**WE DON'T WANT YOUR ORDER**
**If we can't save you money.**
**BUT WE CAN SAVE YOU MONEY.**

# LADIES' FALL AND WINTER HOSIERY.

## Ladies' Wool Hosiery.

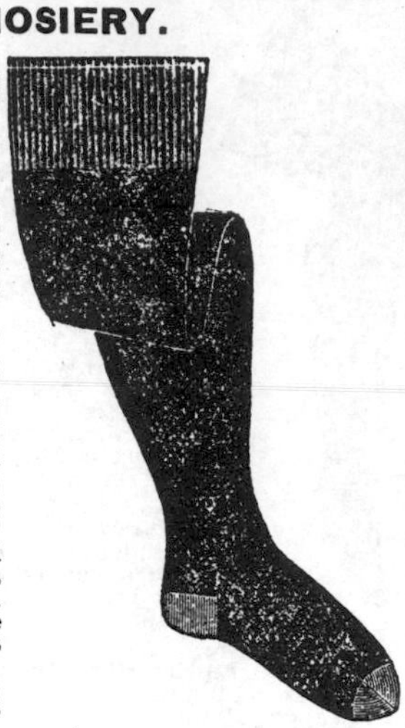

**No. 21390 Ladies' Fast Black Wool Hose,** full seamless merino heel and toe.
Per pair......$0.19
Six pairs for 1.00

**No. 21392 Ladies' All Wool Full Seamless Hose,** extra length, double heels and toes, elastic ribbed top, regular 35-cent goods, black only. Our price per pair..........$0.25
Six pairs for 1.40

**No. 21393 Ladies' Pure Lamb's Wool Hose,** full seamless double heel and toes. This is an extra fine hose usually sold at 50 cents a pair.
Per pair.....$0.35
Six pairs for 1.85

## Ladies' All Wool Ribbed Hose.

**No. 21394 Ladies' All Wool Hose,** heavy weight, ribbed, full seamless. double heel and toe. Black only. Per pair 19c; 3 pairs for.................$0.50

**No. 21398 Ladies' Fine All Wool Hose,** heavy ribbed, full seamless, with double heel and toe; fine, soft and warm goods. Extra long, black only.
Per pair 25c; six pairs for.....................$1.40

**No. 21396 Ladies' Extra Heavy Fancy Ribbed Wool Hose,** made of choice wool, with double soles, high spliced heel, very soft and durable.
Per pair 35c; three pairs for.................. $1.00

## Ladies' Fine Cashmere Hose.

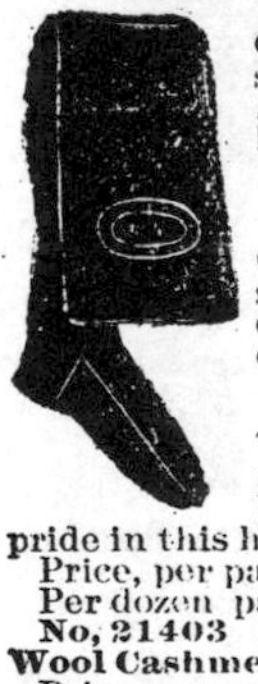

**No. 21400 All Wool, fine soft finish Cashmere Hose,** absolutely fast black, specially prepared yarn, full seamless. Another of our specially clever values, heavy weight.
Price, per pair....................$0.25
Per dozen pairs.................... 2.68

**No. 21401 All Wool Heavy Weight, Cashmere Hose,** absolutely fast black, soft and fine, full seamless and thoroughly well made. Knit to fit. Fine derby ribbed. Price, per pair...$0.25
Per dozen pairs.................... 2.68

**No. 21402 All Wool Medium Heavy Weight Cashmere Hose,** double heels and toes, seamless, perfect in fit, absolutely fast black. We take a just pride in this hose, there is a world of goodness in it.
Price, per pair...............................$0.34
Per dozen pairs.............................. 3.60

**No. 21403 Same as above, in Fancy Ribbed All Wool Cashmere.**
Price, per pair, 34c; per dozen pairs..........$3.60

**No. 21405 Ribbed Top all Wool Cashmere Hose,** very fine and soft, seamless and guaranteed fast black. Specially prepared stock.
Price, per pair, 45c; per dozen pairs..........$4.90

**No. 21406 Extra Fine Gauge all Wool, Medium Weight, Cashmere Hose,** double heels and toes, guaranteed absolutely fast black and stainless. We have made a specialty of this hose for years and it has always given great satisfaction.
Price, per pair, 50c; per dozen pairs.........$5.40

**No. 21407 Extra Fine Gauge All Wool Black Cashmere Hose,** heavy weight, double heels and toes, soft and fine, knit to satisfy the best trade. We warrant them to be absolutely fast black and stainless, seamless and perfect fitting.
Price per pair.................................$0.64
3 pairs for....................................1.80

**No. 21408 Ladies' Extra Selected Cashmere Hose,** same quality as the preceding number. Extra wide legs. Price per pair......................$0.64
3 pairs for.................................... 1.80

**No. 21409 Ladies' Extra Fine Selected All Wool Cashmere Hose.** These stockings are smooth and soft and extra fine gauge. They are soft and flexible, soothing to the skin and absolutely fast black, made with double heels and toes, medium weight.
Price per pair.................................$0.75
3 pairs for.................................... 2.10

# IT IS SURPRISING

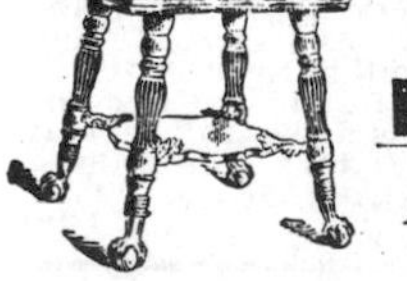

HOW CHEAP WE DO SELL

**FURNITURE**

AND GOOD FURNITURE AT THAT.

☞ You'll never know what bargains we have until you order

Give our Furniture Department a trial.

## Boys' and Misses' Hosiery.

**MAKE A NOTE OF IT that you are going to buy your boys' and misses' hosiery of us this season, you will profit by it if you do. Other lines of hosiery may be good, ours is better. Better in many ways, better in fit, in finish, and best of all, better in wearing qualities.**

## Boys' Cotton Ribbed Hose.

Sizes 6 to 9½.

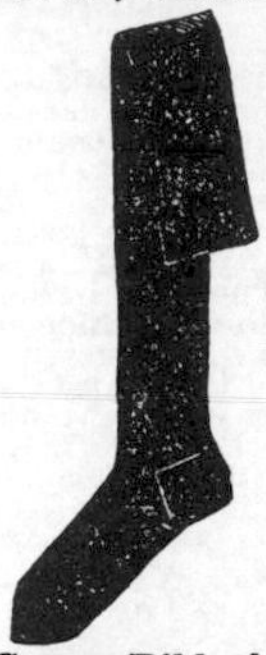

**No. 21410 Boys' heavy ribbed cotton hose,** full seamless with long legs and nicely shaped foot, warranted fast black and stainless, good strong stockings. Sizes, 6 to 9½ only.
Price, per pair.... ........$0.10
Per dozen pairs..... ...... 1.00

**NOTE: Buy your hosiery at dozen rates.** Dozen rates apply only where ½ dozen or more stockings of the same kind and price are ordered. You will save money if you order ½ dozen or more at one time.

**No. 21412 Boys' or Misses Fine Gauge Ribbed Cotton Hose.** Extra well made with double heels and toes. Warranted absolutely fast black and stainless. The best cheap hose ever made. Sizes 6 to 9½. Always state size. Price per pair.... $0.15
Per dozen pairs........................... 1.64

**No. 21413 Boys' or Misses' Special Wear-Well Stockings.** Heavy ribbed legs and full seamless feet. Warranted absolutely fast black and stainless. Knit from specially prepared Egyptian cotton. Soft and smooth and very dressy and perfect fitting. Finely shaped and made with double spliced knees, and three thread heels and toes full of goodness. Sizes 6 to 9½. Price per pair..................$0.19
Six pairs for................................. 1.00

## Boys' Special Iron Ribbed Hose.

**No. 21415 Boys' Special Iron Ribbed Cotton Hose.** Extra heavy two-thread maco yarn, with heavy ribbed legs, 3-thread heels and toes and double spliced knees. Made especially for boys who are hard on stockings. These stockings are very elastic and fit perfectly. They are full seamless and smooth finish, not coarse and unshapely like many manufacturers produce. These are thoroughly dependable in every way and absolutely fast black. Sizes 7 to 9½ only. Price per pair........... $0.23
Per dozen pairs.............................. 2.45

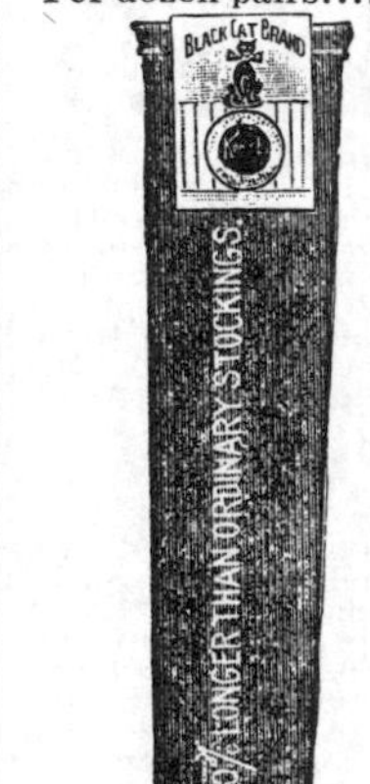


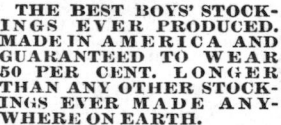

## Boys' Leather Stockings, with Triple Knees.

**THE BEST BOYS' STOCKINGS EVER PRODUCED. MADE IN AMERICA AND GUARANTEED TO WEAR 50 PER CENT. LONGER THAN ANY OTHER STOCKINGS EVER MADE ANYWHERE ON EARTH.**

**No. 21419 Leather stockings for boys,** so called not because they are made from leather, for they are not, they are made from cotton yarn, but because **they wear like leather.** These are the genuine triple knee leather stockings, made from the finest, softest and smoothest Egyptian cotton, with triple knees, heels and toes, making them the strongest, heaviest, most elastic, perfect fitting and cheapest boy's stockings in the world. Buy them once and you will never buy any other kind. There is a vast amount of real satisfaction in buying boys hosiery that you know is thoroughly good. You will never know what a vast amount of satisfaction you can get out of these stockings until you try them. Include a pair of these stockings in your next order and learn where true economy lies in stocking buying. Sizes 7 to 10. Always state size. Price, per pair......$0.25
Per dozen pairs.......... 2.70

**ALL HOSIERY...**

**Quoted by the dozen pair may be obtained at the same rate when a half dozen pairs are ordered. If less than ½ doz. pairs are ordered the price will be at the single pair rate.**

## Boys' Wool and Merino Hose.

**No. 21420 Boys' Extra Heavy Merino Hose,** with long ribbed legs. An excellent school stocking and will give good service. Warranted fast black. Sizes, 7, 7½, 8, 8½, 9, 9½ and 10. Always state size when you order. Price, per pair, 19c; 3 pairs for..........$0.50

**No. 21421 Boys' and Misses' Extra Heavy Wool Hose,** with long ribbed legs, double heels and toes, and full seamless feet. Fast black. Only sizes, 6 to 9½. Price, per pair, 27c; per ½ dozen pairs....$1.50

**No. 21423 Boys' Extra Heavy Ribbed Fine and Dressy Imported Cashmere Hose,** high spliced heel, double knee and soles; come in extra large sizes, can also be worn for bicycle hose. Sizes from 7 to 10. Per pair...................................$0.48

## Misses' and Children's Hose.

**HIGH GRADE STOCKINGS FOR SPRING AND SUMMER WEAR.**

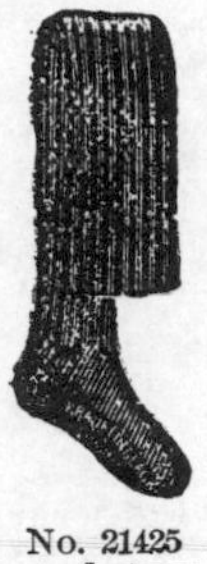

No. 21425

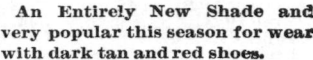

**No. 21425 Misses' Fine Single Ribbed Black Cotton Hose;** extra well made and finely finished. Perfectly shaped and correct in fit. Sizes 7 to 8½ only. Warranted fast black.
Price per pair..................$0.08
Per dozen.......................... 0.80

**No. 21426 Misses' and Childrens' Fine Single Ribbed Fast Black Cotton Hose.** Finely shaped and full seamless. Warranted absolutely fast black and stainless. Sizes 6 to 8½ only.
Price per pair..................$0.10
Per dozen.......................... 1.00

**No. 21427 Children's Tan Colored Cotton Hose;** long, fine ribbed legs; full seamless with extra spliced heels and toes, elastic and perfect fitting. Good weight and warranted to give good service. Sizes 6 to 7½.
Price per pair........$0.15 Per dozen pairs...1.65

**No. 21428 Misses' Tan Colored Cotton Hose.** Same as above but made in larger sizes, 8, 8½, 9 and 9½. Price per pair..........................$0.19
Per dozen pairs.................................. 2.16

**No. 21429 Children's Fine Ribbed Cotton Hose.** Same as above in black, warranted fast color and seamless. Your choice of sizes, 6, 6½, 7 and 7½.
Price per pair....................................$0.15
Per dozen pairs.................................. 1.65

**No. 21430 Misses' Fine Ribbed Cotton Hose.** Same as above in larger sizes. Your choice of sizes, 8, 8½, 9 and 9½. Price per pair...................$0.19
Per dozen pairs........................... ..... 2.16

## Our 25c Special.

**No. 21432 Misses' and Children's Extra Fine Fast Black Cotton Hose.** Very fine ribbed and close knit, made from finest combed Maco yarn with double sole, high spliced heels and toes. Full seamless elastic and perfect fitting. All sizes from 6 to 9. Your choice of any size. Price per pair.......$0.25
Per doz pairs..................... ........ 2.70

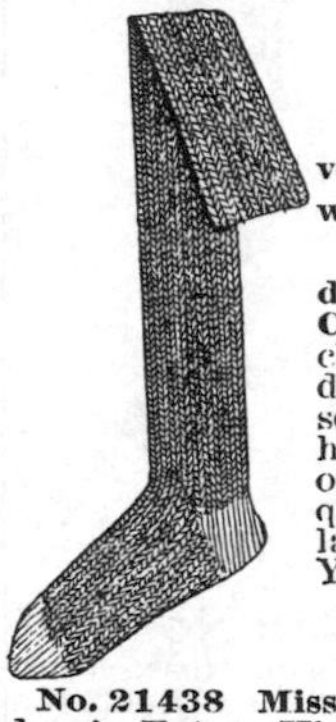

## Oxblood Hose.

**An Entirely New Shade and very popular this season for wear with dark tan and red shoes.**

**No. 21435 Misses' and Children's Extra Fine Oxblood Red Cotton Hose.** Very fine ribbed close knit and extra strong and durable. Made with long legs, full seamless and has double sole and high spliced heels and toes. Full of real goodness and wearing qualities. Very stylish and popular this season. Sizes 6 to 9½. Your choice of any size.
Price per pair................$0.25
3 pairs for..................... .68

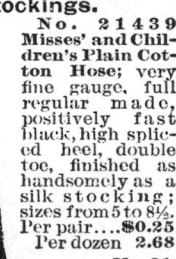

**No. 21438 Misses' and Children's Extra High Grade Fine Ribbed Cotton Hose;** full seamless with unbleached heels, soles and toes. Guaranteed real maco: two thread heels, toes and soles; unexcelled for wear. Sizes, 6 to 9½. Warranted fast black and stainless. Price, per pair.........$0.35
3 pairs for.....................0.98

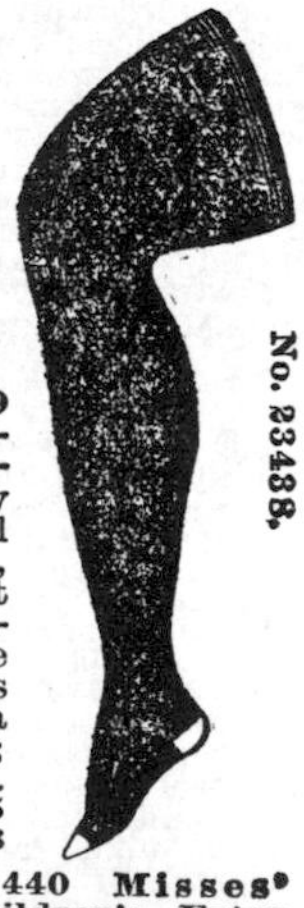

No. 23438.

## Misses' and Children's Plain Stockings.

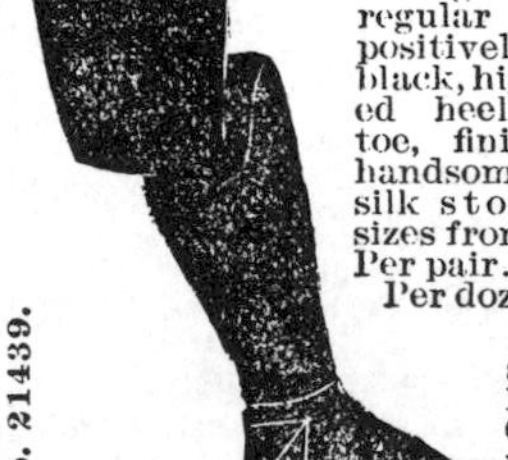

No. 21439.

**No. 21439 Misses' and Children's Plain Cotton Hose;** very fine gauge, full regular made, positively fast black, high spliced heel, double toe, finished as handsomely as a silk stocking; sizes from 5 to 8½.
Per pair....$0.25
Per dozen 2.68

**No. 21440 Misses' and Children's Extra High Grade Seamless Cotton Hose;** plain black with double spliced heels and toes; extra fine gauge; soft finish maco yarn; finely shaped with wide elastic hem at top. One of the most satisfactory hose we have ever handled. Sizes, 6 to 9½.
Price, per pair......$0.35; 3 pairs for.........$0.98

**No. 21443 Misses and Children's Fast Black Plain Fine Gauge Egyptian Cotton Hose,** with cream white unbleached balbriggan heels, soles and toes. Full seamless, strong and dependable, and finely shaped. One of our extra good values. All sizes from 6 to 9½. Price per pair 30c; per doz. prs $3.10

**A HALF DOZEN STOCKINGS BY FREIGHT WOULD NOT PAY.**

**Our experienced customers are careful to anticipate their needs, and make up combination freight orders of groceries and all needed supplies.**

**....THEN IT PAYS....**

**YOU WILL HAVE LITTLE DIFFICULTY IN GETTING UP A CLUB ORDER FROM YOUR NEIGHBORS. WHEN YOU SHOW THEM OUR CATALOGUE AND WONDERFUL PRICES. READ OUR LIBERAL TERMS TO CLUBS ON PAGE 4.**

## MISSES' AND CHILDRENS'

### ...PLAIN BLACK...

## CASHMERE HOSE.

No. 21445. Misses' and Childrens' Extra Quality Plain Black Fast Colored Cashmere Hose. Our own special importation and the best value ever offered at anywhere near our selling price, full seamless, double knee, double heel and toe, regular 40 cent value.
Our special price, per pair.... $0.25
Six pair for..................... 1.40
No. 21446 Misses' and Children's Extra Fine Imported Fast Black Cashmere Hose, made of very choice Australian wool, high spliced heel, double soles. Sell in large retail stores in big cities at 50c per pair. Our Special price for all sizes 6 to 8½.
Per pair......................... $0.35
Three pair for.................. 1.00

### ...INFANTS'...

FANCY RIBBED,
=====FAST BLACK,

## COTTON HOSE.

No. 21450 Extra spliced heels and toes. Fine soft finish, close knit and seamless. Sizes 4, 4½, 5 and 5½.
    Price, per pair........... $0.15
    Per ½ dozen pairs......... .80
No. 21542 Infants' Fast Black Cotton Hose. Same as above, but plain knit (not ribbed). Full fashioned and finely shaped. Sizes, 4, 4½, 5 and 5½.
    Price, per pair........... $0.15
    Per ½ dozen pairs......... .80
No. 21453 Infants' extra fine Ribbed Cotton Hose, with extra spliced heels and toes. Full seamless, warranted fast black and stainless, very soft and fine gauge. Sizes, 4, 4½, 5 and 5½.
Price, per pair............ $0.17
Per ½ dozen pairs ......... .90

### Infants' Silk Tipped Hose.

No. 21454 Infants' extra selected tan Colored cotton Hose, very fine elastic ribbed legs. Full seamless with pure silk heels and toes. These stockings are made from the finest imported Maco yarn and are the equal of any genuine lisle thread hose made, in looks, and are much better for wear. Sizes, 4, 4½, 5 and 5½. Price, per pair............ $0.23
    Per ½ dozen pairs......... 1.30
No. 21455 Infants fine gauge Silk Tipped Heel and Toe Hose, same as above in fast black.
    Price, per pair........... $0.23
    Per ½ dozen pairs........ 1.30

### Infants' Wool Hose.

No. 21456 Infants' Cashmere Hose, made of pure wool, come in black only, with ribbed legs. Sizes, 4, 4½, 5, 5½. Per pair................ $0.15
Six pairs for...................... .75
No. 21458 Infants' Fine Imported English Cashmere, made of fine soft wool, very warm and will not shrink. Sizes, 4, 4½, 5, 5½. Regular 35c value.
Our price, per pair............... $0.20
Three pair for................... .50
No. 21460 Infants' Extra Fine Imported Cashmere Hose, made of very choice Australian lamb's wool, with colored silk heel and toes and ribbed legs.
Per pair.......................... $0.24
Three pair for................... .70

## BOYS' WAISTS AND BLOUSES.

Sizes 4 to 14 years.

All New Spring and Summer Patterns.

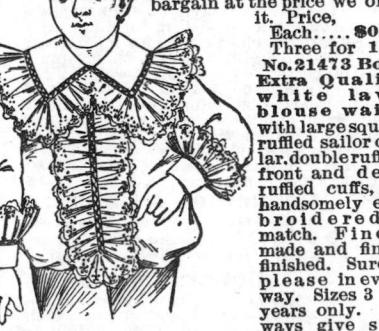

No. 21465 Boys' Medium Color Fancy Figured Shirt Waists, pleated front and back with large collar. Small neat figured patterns. Sizes 4 to 14 years.
    Price each..... $0.20
    3 for ........... .55
No. 21466 Boys' Extra Quality Dark Colored Fancy Percale Shirt Waists, neat handsome patterns, pleated front and back with large collar. Sizes 4 to 14: assorted colors.
    Price each..... $0.25
    3 for ........ .68

No. 21465.

No. 21467 Boy's extra quality Indigo blue shirt waists with neat white figured designs. Pleated front and back and large collar. Sizes, 4 to 14 years. Extra well made and finished. Price. each.... $0.30
Three for............. .78

## Boys' Laundered Waists.

Sizes 4 to 13 Years.
A Handsome Tie with each one.

No. 21468 Boys' Extra Fine Laundered Percale Shirt Waists, pleated front and back with large collar and removeable buttons, assorted light and medium colors in handsome and stylish patterns, thoroughly well made and dependable. We give a handsome sateen windsor tie with each one of these waists. Sizes, 4 to 13 years.
Price, each... $0.50
Three for...... 1.40

No. 21469 Boys' Laundered Shirt Waists. Same as above in handsome cadet blue and white mixtures. We make you a present of a handsome Windsor tie with each of these waists. Each... $0.50
3 for...........$1.40

### Plain White Laundered Waists.

Sizes 4 to 12 only.
No. 21470 Boys' Extra Fine White Laundered Shirt Waists, with fine pleated front and pleated back. Fine white pearl buttons, large collar and finely finished cuffs. Exceptionally well made and finished. Warranted high grade in every respect. A handsome Windsor tie with each one.
Price each............................... $0.75

### Boys' Blouse Waists.

Sizes 4 to 12 Years.
EVERY ONE A GREAT BARGAIN. New and Handsome Patterns; Nobby Effects and Rich Colorings. You cannot afford to overlook them.

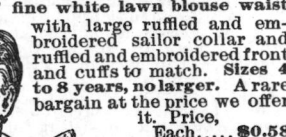

No. 21471 Boys' Extra Quality Fast Colored Percale Blouse, with large ruffled sailor collar, ruffled front and cuffs. Assorted colors and patterns; pinks, blues, etc. All combination colors. Sizes 4 to 12 years.
    Price each...$0.43
    Three for.... 1.20

### Boys' White Lawn Blouse Waists.

SIZES 3 TO 8 YEARS ONLY.
No. 21472 Boys' fine white lawn blouse waist with large ruffled and embroidered sailor collar and ruffled and embroidered front and cuffs to match. Sizes 4 to 8 years, no larger. A rare bargain at the price we offer it. Price,
    Each..... $0.58
    Three for 1.60
No. 21473 Boys' Extra Quality white lawn blouse waists with large square ruffled sailor collar, double ruffled front and deep ruffled cuffs, all handsomely embroidered to match. Finely made and finely finished. Sure to please in every way. Sizes 3 to 8 years only. Always give size when you order. Price, each. 75c. Three for.$2.15
No. 21474 The Little Prince. Made from extra fine white French lawn, with large square sailor collar, ruffled and embroidered all around with rich open work loop edging. Double ruffle front and cuffs all embroidered to match. All pure white Retail merchants never sell garments like these for less than $1.50. Sizes, 3 to 8 years.
    Our price, each.$0.98    Three for............$2.85

## A 50c Wonder

No. 21475 This is a Blouse that will please any mother in looks, fit and wearing qualities. The style and pattern is superb. Made from extra quality indigo blue French percale, with random white stripes, forming a handsome and very swell contrast. Made with full ruffled sailor collar. Double ruffled front and ruffled cuffs. A blouse of this sort and quality has never before been sold for less than 75c. It is the nobbiest, swellest looking and most becoming blouse made this season. You cannot help but like it. Made in sizes from 4 to 12 years only.
Price, each............................ ....$0.50

### Our 50c. Black Sateen Blouse.

No. 21476 If you are looking for something thoroughly well made and dependable in a black sateen blouse you will find this number interesting. This blouse is made from an extra heavy absolutely fast black sateen fine soft twilled finish, with very large full ruffled sailor collar double ruffled front and ruffled cuffs. Extra well made and finely finished throughout. Full of the kind of goodness that counts. The best blouse ever made for every day wear. Don't overlook it if you want something extra good. Size 4 to 12 years.
Price each......................................$0.50

### Our 50c Combination.

Handsome Blouse and Windsor Tie.

No. 21477 Boy's Extra Fine Fast Colored French Percale Blouse. Handsome dark blue and white stripes; also fancy figures; light and dark colors in new and beautiful shades and nobby and dressy patterns. Blues, pinks, tans, garnet, etc. Made with large full ruffled collar, ruffled front and cuffs. We give a handsome windsor tie with each one of these garments, in light medium or dark colors as desired. Sizes 4 to 12 years.
Price, each................ $0.50
3 for.................... 1.40

### 79c for a Real Chelsea Cloth Blouse.

No. 21478 Boy's Extra High Grade Blouse; made from finest Chelsea cloth, a new fabric similar to fine French penang but heavier and closer woven and has very fine, soft, smooth finish. Made in beautiful light Cadet blue with neat white and black figures. Entirely new and stylish patterns. Made up in the very finest manner with large deep ruffled collar, double ruffled front and deep ruffled cuffs. Sizes, 4 to 12.
Price, each......$0.79
3 for............. 2.25

IF YOU ARE IN A HURRY FOR YOUR GOODS AND WANT THEM TO COME JUST AT YOU EXPECT THEM, DON'T FAIL TO GIVE CATALOGUE NUMBERS AND PRICES OF ARTICLES WANTED.

# UMBRELLAS, CANES AND PARASOLS.

RAINY DAYS WILL COME AGAIN.

**Be prepared for them in time. Include an umbrella in your next order to us. We offer you herewith a chance to buy the very best umbrellas ever made in this country at prices so low that you cannot afford to overlook them. We guarantee every umbrella we quote to be exactly as represented in the quotation. All orders will be filled promptly and correctly. We'll trade back, too, if you are not thoroughly satisfied, remember that.**

## Men's Umbrellas.

**Fast Black Ginghams.**

**No. 21490 Fast Black Gingham Umbrellas.** 8 ribs, hook or straight handles. Size, 28 inch............$0.70
Size, 30 inch.. .75 Size, 32 inch.. .85

**No. 21492 Fast Black Gingham Umbrellas.** 10 ribs, hook or straight handles.
Price each, size, 28 inch ........$0.79
Size, 30 inch.. .84 Size, 32 inch.. .94

**No. 21493 Men's Extra Fine Quality Black Sateen Umbrella;** paragon frame; natural hook wood handles; made in a thoroughly first-class manner throughout. Sure to be satisfactory. Prices, size, 26 inch........$0.60
Size, 28 inch.. .75 Size, 30 inch.. .85

**No. 21495 Men's Fine Black Gloria Silk Umbrella;** eight rib Paragon frame; natural oak hook **handles.** This is guaranteed absolutely fast color, **and is an umbrella that will give good satisfaction.**
Price size 26.......................... $0.79
Price size 28.......... .87 Price size 30...... 1.00

**No. 21496 Men's Fine Black Gloria Silk Umbrella.** With eight rib Paragon frame and steel rod. Extra fine imported natural Congo crook handles. Guaranteed absolutely fast black.
Price size 28....... $1.18 Price size 30..... 1.35

**No. 21497 An exceptionally fine black twilled silk Umbrella.** Fine paragon frame and steel rod. Extra fine imported natural Congo hook handles; handsome silk case and silk cord and tassel with each one of these umbrellas. This is a very handsome and serviceable umbrella, and will give perfect satisfaction.
Size 26 inch.......................... $1.35
Size 28 inch.... 1.55 Size 30 inch. 1.85

**No. 21498 An exceptionally fine black twilled silk Umbrella.** Fine paragon frame and steel rod. Extra fine imported natural Congo hook handles, fancy silver trimmed; handsome case and silk cord and tassel. Guaranteed to give perfect satisfaction. Retail value $2.25 to $2.50.
Prices, Size 26 inch................$1.85

**No. 21498** Size 28 inch.. 1.98 Size 30 inch.. 2.15

**No. 21500 Men's Extra Fine Genuine Black Taffeta Silk Umbrella;** made with genuine paragon frame and steel rod; natural English Congo hook handles; silk case and silk cord and tassel. Made up in strictly first-class manner throughout, and guaranteed to be satisfactory in every respect.
Size 26 inch 2.10 Size 28 inch. $2.25

No. 21501

**No. 21501 Men's Extra Fine Fast Black Imported Twilled Silk Umbrella,** with genuine paragon frame, and steel rod; handsome case and silk cord and tassel; medium heavy polished horn hook handles. A thoroughly reliable, fine looking and excellent wearing umbrella. These will give perfect satisfaction. **Horn handles are very fashionable this season.**
Prices, Size 26 inch.... 2.15 Size 28 inch....$2.45

21502

**No. 21502 Men's Extra Fine Fast Black Taffeta Silk Umbrella.** Genuine paragon frame and steel rod; handsome case and silk cord and tassel; handsome natural imported Congo hook handles. Very fine and dressy, and thoroughly dependable in every way. size 26 inch. 2.25 Size 28 inch. $2.49

**No. 21503 Men's Extra Selected Imported Fast Black Taffeta Silk Umbrella.** Genuine paragon frame and steel rod, with handsome case and silk cord and tassel. Extra fine imported natural Congo hook handles, with silver trimmings. Very neat and popular, and thoroughly dependabl in every way. All new beautiful pattern handles.
Price, size 26 inch..........$2.58
Size 28 inch ............... 2.85

**No. 21504 Men's Extra Quality Fast Black Gloria Silk Umbrellas,** with genuine paragon frame cord and tassels. Large handsome dog head handles of imitation ivory, handsomly polished and beautifully finished. Guaranteed to give excellent service.
Size 26 inch.....2.37 Size 28 inch. $2.65

## The New Detachable Handle Umbrella.

**A LONG FELT WANT FILLED AT LAST.**

**No. 21505 Men's Fast Black Twilled Silk Umbrella,** with detachable handle. Seven rib paragon frame, and tempered steel rod. Natural imported Congo hook handle, which is made detachable so that the umbrella will fit into any ordinary sized trunk. This is a handsome and serviceable umbrella, and is guaranteed to give perfect satisfaction in every respect.
Price, size 26 inch............. $1.48
Price, size 28 inch............ .. 1.70

**No. 21506 Mens's Extra Fine Quality Fast Black Twilled Silk Umbrellas,** made with genuine paragon frame, and steel rod. Finest quality imported natural Congo hook handle, made detachable, so as to fit into any ordinary sized trunk. Handsome case and silk cord and tassel. A handsome and dependable umbrella, which is guaranteed to give entire satisfaction. Extra well made throughout.
Price, size 26 in.......... ...... $2.10
Price, size 28 in.......... 2.25

**No. 21507 Men's Extra Selected Imported Fast Black Taffeta Silk Umbrella.** Genuine paragon frame, and steel rod, Handsome silk cord and tassel, and handsome silk case. Extra fine imported Congo hook handle, made detachable so that it will fit into any ordinary size trunk. A very dressy umbrella which is guaranteed to give perfect satisfaction in every way.
Price, size 26 in.......3.15 Price, size 28 in....$3.40

## Combination Umbrella and Cane.

**The latest novelty out and very swell consists of a Tight Roll Umbrella with Leather Cover.**

**No. 21508 Fine Quality Black Gloria Silk Umbrella,** steel rod, natural wood hook handle; and genuine 8 rib paragon frame, tight roll with russet leather case and tassel.
Size, 26 inch.... 2.25 Size, 28 inch......$2.75

**No. 21510 Men's Fine Black Taffeta Silk Umbrella,** 7 rib paragon frame, steel rod, fine imported Congo or Weichsel handle, Prince of Wales hook style, leather case with long steel ferrule on the bottom and patent spring catch button at the top. Something very swell, can be used for a cane or umbrella and makes a handsome present.
Size, 26 inch......................$4.00
Size, 27 inch...................... 4.50
Size, 28 inch............ .. 5.00

## Cane and Umbrella Sets.

**A novelty of the season.** We meet the popular demand for combinations of cane and umbrellas to match, at less than half the regular retail prices. Compare our special prices with those of any retail dealer even on inferior goods. In fact, few but the most fashionable retail stores in large cities keep these goods. You get a cane and umbrella from us at less than the retail price of the umbrella alone.

**A Handsome Present for any Gentleman.**

**No. 21512 Cane and Umbrella Set.** The umbrella is of fine twilled silk on a substantial 7 rib paragon frame, and has case and tassel. The cane is of fine Congo wood with handle to match umbrella. Both are strapped together for convenience in carrying. Price complete,
26 inch umbrella..........................$2.35
28 inch umbrella.......................... 2.70

**No. 21513 We offer this handsome combination set consisting of Cane and Umbrella to match at less than half retail price.** The umbrella is of very choice quality of black twilled silk, on paragon 7 rib frame, either 26 or 28 inch. Handle is of genuine Congo wood, and cane is made of same with handle to match. Both are elegantly trimmed with solid silver, strapped with two leather straps.
Price 26 inch umbrellas..............$3.40
Price, 28 inch umbrella................ 3.75

## Gentlemen's Canes.

**A Strictly High Grade Assortment of Staple and Fancy Canes at less than wholesale prices.**

## Hickory Canes.

**No. 21515 Natural clear stock genuine hickory canes with crook handles.** Fine shellac finish, medium and small sizes.
Price, each.......................$0.25
Per doz............................ 2.65

**No. 21516 Men's Extra Selected Fine Quality Genuine Hickory Canes,** natural color, with fine shellac finish. Large size, heavy and strong. Large hook handles.
Price, each............................$0.39
Per doz.................................. 4.20

**No. 21517 Men's Extra Fine Quality Ebonized Hickory Canes,** jet black and highly polished. Medium heavy weight, very strong and dependable, large hook handle and steel tipped ferrule.
Price, each.................................$0.69

**No. 21518 Medium Size Straight Natural Wood Canes,** nicely varnished, strong and reliable.
Price, each................................$0.08
Per dozen........................................ .75

**No. 21519 Good Heavy Weight Natural Wood Straight Stick Canes,** extra selected stock, with fine shellac finish, extra strong and thoroughly dependable, usually retail for 25 cents.
Our price, each..............................$0.17
Per dozen..................................... 1.75

**No. 21520 Straight Natural Hickory Canes** nicely varnished, medium weight and extra strong.
Price, each...... ...............................$0.10
Per dozen................................................ 1.00

**No. 21521 Genuine Imported Bamboo Canes** with bulb tops and long ferrules. We sell these canes in dozen lots only. Our price on them is so low that we cannot afford to sell less than one dozen. Just the thing for picnics, marching clubs, etc.
Price per dozen.... ......$0.45

## Loaded Canes.

**No. 21523 Genuine Steel Rod Canes** with loaded heads, spun worsted covered. The old reliable steel rod canes that have always proved satisfactory.
Price each, 12c; Per dozen.........$1.25

**No. 21524 Natural polished Wood Canes** with extra heavy spun covered loaded heads. Good heavy weight and thoroughly reliable. Price each....$0.19
Per dozen............................ 1.75

**No. 21525 Extra Heavy Genuine Rattan Canes,** large size, highly polished sticks, with large spun covered loaded heads. An excellent cane in every respect and an admirable weapon.
Price, each.......................................$0.25
Per dozen........................................ 2.50

## Fancy Metal Handle Canes.

**A SPECIAL LOT OF CANES.**

**No. 21527** Our New York buyer picked the lot up from a large manufacturer at 50 cents on the dollar. We have about five hundred dozen of these canes and will offer them until sold at less than one half their real value, assorted handles, all new and desirable patterns, nickle finish, large and medium sized crooks. Fine polished sticks, assorted styles, all bright, new goods just from the factory. Everyone guaranteed a bargain.
Price, each.... ........................$0.19
Per dozen.... .................. 2.39

## High Grade Fashionable Walking Sticks.

**No. 21530 Natural Imported Congo Walking Sticks,** long steel tipped ferrules. Natural color and finish. Medium size, crook handles. Our own special importation. Price, each..............$0.43

**No. 21531 Natural Imported Congo Walking Sticks.** Same as above, in large size, heavy weight; large crook handles.
Price, each...........................$0.75

**No. 21532 The greatest of all bargains. Genuine Imported Congo Walking Sticks.** Medium size with large Prince of Wales hook handles, with heavy silver plated tip at end of hook. Long steel tipped ferrule. Note our record breaking price on this walking stick. Price, each.......$0.54

## Silver and Gold Trimmed Congo Canes.

**No. 21533 Extra Fine Imported Real Congo Canes,** with Prince of Wales hook handles, trimmed with solid sterling silver, handsomely engraved. Extra fine selected sticks, none better ever imported. Made with long steel tipped ferrules. Medium size. Price each............$1.15

**No. 21534 Extra Fine Best Selected Imported Weichsel Wood Walking Sticks.** Medium large size with large Prince of Wales solid sterling silver trimmed crook handles and long steel tipped ferrules. Very handsome and fashionable. Retail value, $2.00.
Price each.............. ..........$1.35

**No. 21535 This is a particularly handsome and fashionable Walking Stick,** and one which retail furnishing goods dealers and fashionable jewelry stores sell for $2.50 to $3.50. It is made from finest imported Congo with large Prince of Wales crook handle which is trimmed with heavy engraved 14k gold; handsome and artistic patterns. This cane makes a handsome and sure-to-be-appreciated gift to any gentleman. Our price each, $1.69

WE ARE NOT INFALLIBLE. WE EMPLOY 600 PEOPLE TO ATTEND TO YOUR ORDERS. MISTAKES WILL OCCUR, BUT WE ARE ANXIOUS TO CORRECT THEM. SHOULD ANY MISUNDERSTANDING OCCUR, WRITE US FULLY.

## Ladies' Umbrellas.

**No. 21537 Ladies' Extra Fine Quality Fast Black Twilled Sateen Umbrella,** with 8 rib paragon frame; handsome Dresden china hook handles, handles decorated in a large assortment of designs. This is an exceptionally fine umbrella for the price at which we offer it to you. Size 26 inch.
Our special price..................$0.69

**No. 21539 Ladies' No. 1 Quality Fast Black Twilled Sateen Umbrella.** Finely made, with genuine paragon frame. Handsome natural oak, tied or loop handles. A very reliable umbrella at a very low price. Size 26 inch.
Price..................$0.75

**No. 21540 Ladies' extra fine quality fast black Union Twilled silk umbrella;** good weight, strong, and reliable. Eight rib paragon frame, silk cord and tassel. Handsome decorated Dresden china heads. We have these heads either hook or ball shape, as desired, all decorated in the newest and most fashionable design. A thoroughly reliable umbrella in every way. Size 26. Price..................$0.98

**No. 21541 Ladies' fine black twilled silk umbrella.** Seven ribbed paragon frame. Handles made of handsomely carved imported black rubber, in loops or ties. Made up first class in every way. Size 26. Warranted first class in every way. Price..................$1.35

No. 21541

**No. 21543 This is an exceptionally handsome fine quality fast black twilled silk umbrella with steel rod.** Genuine seven rib paragon frame, and case, with silk cord and tassel. Beautifully decorated dresden china handles; these come in hook or ball shapes. (In ordering please state which shape you prefer.) These umbrellas are very stylish this season, and are thoroughly well made, strong and reliable. Size 26.
Our special price each..................$1.75

**No. 21545 A Handsome and Dependable Ladies' Umbrella.** Extra quality imported fast black twilled silk; made with seven rib paragon frame, with steel rod. Handsome case and silk cord and tassel. Extra fine natural English Congo handles, loop or tied, neatly trimmed in silver. Handsome and reliable in every way. One of our specially clever values. Size 26 inches.
Special price, each..................$1.75

**No. 21546 Ladies' Fine Pearl Handle Umbrella.** Made from an extra fine imported fast black twilled silk; with genuine seven rib paragon frame and steel rod. Handsome case and silk cord and tassel. Has a beautiful small white pearl hook handle, which is very dainty and dressy. Size 26 inches. Warranted to please and satisfy in every particular
Special price..................$2.10

No. 21545.

**No. 21548 Ladies' Extra Fine Fast black Imported Silk Umbrella.** Seven rib paragon frame, and steel rod. Handsome silk case and silk tassel and cord. Made with neat natural Congo or imported Bamboo, loop or tied handles. Handsomely trimmed in silver. Strictly up-to-date and sure to give perfect satisfaction. Size, 26 inches.
Price..................$2.18

**No. 21550 Ladies Extra fine Imported fast black Taffeta silk umbrella;** seven rib paragon frame and steel rod. Handsome case and silk cord and tassel. Made with finest quality Imported English Congo loop or tied handles. An excellent umbrella in every particular, and especially adapted for hard wear. Size 26 inch.
Price..................$2.35

**No. 21552 Ladies' extra fine Imported black Taffeta silk umbrella;** Seven rib paragon frame, with steel rod. Handsome silk case and silk cord and tassel. Assorted natural wood handles, with sterling silver trimming. A handsome umbrella with latest style designs in handles and guaranteed to give exceptional service. Size, 26 inch.
Price..................$2.69

**No. 21553 Ladies' Extra Fine Fast Black Imported Taffeta Silk Umbrella.** Made with seven rib paragon frame, and steel rod; handsome silk case, and silk cord and tassel. Handsome gold plated handles, hooks or straights as desired. One of the best wearing umbrellas made. Size 26 inches.
Price..................$3.25

**No. 21554 Ladies' Fast Black No. 1 Gloria Silk Umbrella.** Made first class throughout; seven rib paragon frame, and **very** handsomely polished celluloid loop handles. Steel rod running all the way through. Warranted to give good satisfaction in every way.
Our special price each..................$1.25

No. 21537

No. 21543

**No. 21555 Ladies' Detachable Handle Umbrellas.** Made from imported fast black twilled gloria silk; made up strictly first-class in every way. Seven rib paragon frame, natural Congo hook handles, neatly trimmed with silver; handles are made detachable, so that the umbrella can fit into any ordinary sized trunk, a special feature and one which is sure to prove a pleasure to the purchaser. Full 26 inch, and a bargain at our price; warranted every way. Special price..................$1.65

**No. 21557 Ladies' Extra Fine Fast Black Gloria Silk Umbrella.** Paragon frame, steel rod, handsome natural Congo tied or loop handles, made detachable, so that the umbrella will fit in any ordinary sized trunk, same as described in preceding number. These are made of specially selected silks, and will give exceptional service. Size 26 inch. Price, $2.05

## Spring Parasols

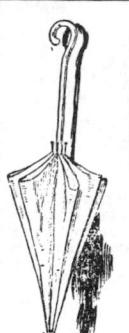

**No. 21558 An Entirely New Design in Ladies' Parasols.** Made from natural Linen Grass Cloth. Natural linen color, with variegated black stripes and natural wood handles. Finely made and finished throughout. Grass cloth parasols will be all the rage during the coming season, and we here with give you a chance to secure an exceptionally fine one at a very low price. Our price..................$0.98

**No. 21559 Ladies' Fine Black Silk Serge 22 in. Parasol.** Genuine paragon frame, and neat black fancy crooked handles. This is a splendid parasol for the money, and will give substantial service, and prove satisfactory in every way.
Special price..................$1.00

No. 21558. No. 21559.

**No. 21560 Ladies' Extra Quality 20 Inch Parasol.** Plain black silk, with genuine Paragon frame; silk puff top; extra quality; natural black English sticks in assorted patterns. Fine black silk cord and tassel to match. All plain black with black handles. Will give No. 21560 excellent satisfaction and is thoroughly good and dependable in every way.
Our special price..................$1.65

**No. 21562 This is an exceptionally nice 20 inch Ladies' Black Silk Parasol,** with two 6 inch flounces, puff top and horn tip; fancy black ebonized carved handles, assorted styles and designs. One of the very best parasol values we offer this season; fine looking and very strong and dependable. Price ea..$2.37

**No. 21564 A very strong and therefore very desirable plain, heavy black Taffeta Silk Parasol.** Finely made and finely finished Japanned frame. Fancy No. 21562 black carved and No. 21564 polished hook handles, and puff at top. Fine silk cord and tassel. Made up in first-class manner and sure to please. Price each..................$2.10

**No. 21565 An Elegant and Strictly High Grade Parasol** in every way. Made from finest jet black China silk with two handsome flounces of purest sewing silk veilings. Finest black enamelled frame, and black ebonized crook handles. Large full puff at top and black horn tip. Beautiful, stylish and thoroughly dependable. Retails for $3.25.
Our price each..................$2.79

**No. 21566 China Silk Parasol,** same as above exactly but made in beautiful snow white with white enamelled ribs and white handles. Price, each..................$2.79

### A Wonderful Line of
## Late Style Mackintoshes
On Pages 177 to 179. **PRICES TO SUIT.**

**No. 21567 Ladies' Beautiful Pure White China Silk Parasol.** Handsome white enameled ribs; white hook and loop handles. Made up in the finest manner possible; has beautiful white puff top, with white cord and tassel. This is a full 22-inch parasol, and at our price is a rare bargain. The retailers cannot sell a parasol made of equal materials for less than $2.00.
Our special price, each..................$1.37

No. 21567.

**No. 21568 Ladies' Pure White China Silk Parasol,** with large fancy flounce and puff top. Beautiful pure white enameled ribs, with white horn tip. White enameled loop handles to match. These are our own special importation, and are extra fine, finished throughout in a strictly high-grade manner. Nothing cheap about them whatever, excepting the price. We guarantee these parasols to give perfect satisfaction in every way. Retail everywhere at $2.50. Our special price..................$1.98

No. 21568.

**No. 21569 This is a truly Handsome Plain Colored Silk Parasol.** Genuine paragon frame, silk puff top, and handsome horn tips, natural English handles, in large assortment of new hook styles, assorted plain colors. Fine silk cord and tassel to match. This is a very handsome and durable parasol, and we guarantee it to give excellent satisfaction. These usually retail at $2.00.
Our special price....$1.65

**No. 21570 Ladies Changeable Silk Parasols,** with fancy border. Made of fine imported silk, in a large assortment of colors, wine, navy, cardinal, brown, etc. Changeable silk parasols are always very popular, and will be even more so this season than ever before. These No. 21569. are exceptionally fine, of our own importation, and we assure you that they will give splendid satisfaction in every respect. These parasols usually retail at $3.50. No.21570.
Our special price, each..................$2.25

**No. 21572 Ladies's Extra Fine Imported, Embossed Dresden Parasols,** in a large and handsome assortment of entirely new patterns and combinations of colorings Red, green blue, pink, garnet, etc. combined with cream white and other light contrasting shades. Made with natural English hook or loop handles. Fine puff at top, and beautiful horn tips, and handsomely enameled ribs. Strictly Up-TO-Date in every way and a rare bargain at the price at which we offer it. These usually retail at $3.75. Size, full 22 inches.
Our special price..................$2.69

**No. 21574 An Entirely New Parasol of our own Special Importation.** This is a 20 inch ladies' parasol made of the very finest quality China silk in a beautiful assortment of Dresden patterns and artistic floral designs. Among the many beautiful combinations we have in this parasol are green grounds with red flowers, cream and blue flowers, pale lavender with lilac combinations, etc.; also many other choice and artistic effects. These are made with fine silk puff tops, handsome polished horn tip with beautiful white silk cord and tassel; natural Congo wood loop handles. The ribs are handsomely enameled and the parasol is made up throughout in the finest manner possible. It is equal to any $4.00 parasol on the market.
Our special price..................$2.95

**THE INDEX IS ON THE LAST PAGES OF THE CATALOGUE AND IS VERY COMPLETE. CONSULT IT FREQUENTLY TO FIND WHAT YOU WANT.**

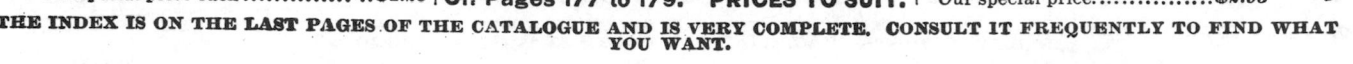

**Children's Parasols**

**No. 21575** Children's Fancy Parasols. Made in new and beautiful patterns; light colors, like pink, blue, etc. Size, 10 inch..**$0.17**

Size, 12 inch............................. .22
Size, 14 inch............................. .33

**No. 21576** This is an exceptionally nice Misses' Sateen Parasol; 14 inch., plain solid colors, with ruffle, fancy stained and polished handles; colors, pink, cardinal, white, or blue.

We offer this at an exceptionally low price, and guarantee it to give perfect satisfaction.
Our special price.....................**$0.48**

## Misses' Fancy Foulard Pattern Parasol.

**No. 21577** Large choice assortment of handsome patterns; floral and dresden designs, etc., new and beautiful colorings. Nicely made and finely finished throughout; natural wood handles. Our special prices,

14 inch.....................................**$0.50**
16 inch..................................... .76

**THIS IS A VERY HANDSOME**

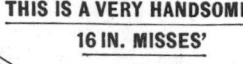

**16 IN. MISSES'**

## FANCY FOULARD... PATTERN PARASOL.

**No. 21578** with a beautiful star ruffle of satin, corresponding in color to that of the parasol. Handsome shades of light blue and pink. Newest fancy patterns; natural wood handles; nicely made and finished.
Our special price.....................87c

**THIS IS AN**

**EXCEPTIONALLY FINE....**

**MISSES' PURE ..SILK..**

## PARASOL.

**No. 21579** Has deep flounce and puff. Extra fine quality natural wood sticks. Size 14 inch. Made in plain colors only; pink, blue and cardinal. Extra made and nicely finished. Guaranteed to please the most sceptical.
Our Special Price.....................**$1.10**

**IF THE COST OF THE BOY'S CLOTHING**

Has Troubled You, Your Troubles are over.

## LEARN

**HOW MUCH, TOO MUCH**

YOU HAVE BEEN PAYING BY TURNING TO PAGES 169 TO 176.

## WONDERFUL VALUES.

## WONDERFUL PRICES.

## TRUNKS AND BAGS.

**DON'T PAY TWO PRICES FOR A TRUNK OR BAG.** By sending your order direct to us you will be supplied at a very small percentage above actual cost to manufacturers. Our trunks and Bags are made by one of the largest factories in this city and it is the best line on the market. We are prepared to furnish anything in the line; our stock embraces several hundred styles, so if you don't see illustrated what you want, write for it; we are prepared to supply you.

When ordering trunks and bags be particular in giving catalogue number and sizes.

When ordering duplicate keys give catalogue number of trunk or bag, also number of letter on key, or impression of keyhole.

Duplicate keys furnished at 5 cents each.

To secure lowest freight rates, we suggest to customers that they order bags or other goods with trunks, to pack inside.

Trunks will be sent by express C. O. D. subject to examination on receipt of $1.00, balance and express charges to be paid after received.

**Order a trunk** and we will pack the balance of your order in the trunk and make entire shipment as one package.

## Capacious Packing Trunk.

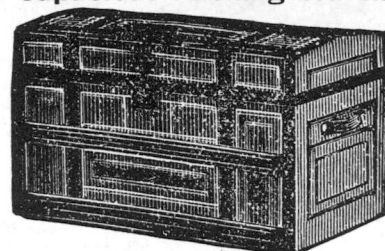

**No. 21601.**

**No. 21601** Imitation Leather; extra well made; iron bands, valance, hinges, hasp lock, long hardwood slats,

| 24 inch | $0.48 | 32 inch | $1.68 |
| 26 inch | .68 | 34 inch | 1.8g |
| 28 inch | .88 | 36 inch | 2.08 |
| 30 inch | .98 | | |

## Crystallized Metal Covered Trunks
### FLAT TOP.

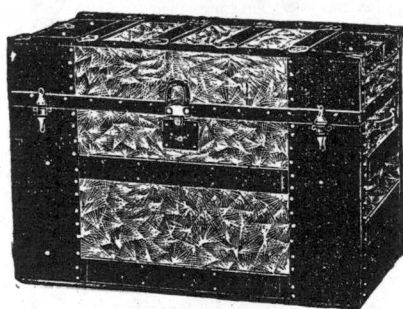

**No. 21604** This is a handsome and durable trunk, thoroughly well made with flat top, iron bound with cross bar slats on the top and body slats. Set up tray and bonnet box. Iron bottom.

| 26 inch | $1.70 | 32 inch | $2.48 |
| 28 " | 1.98 | 34 " | 2.75 |
| 30 " | 2.25 | 36 " | 2.95 |

## Crystallized or Fancy Metal Covered Trunk.
### Cross Bar Slats. Iron Bottom.

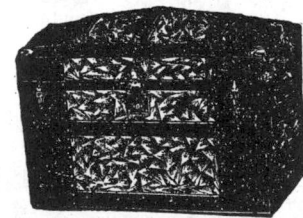

**No. 21605.**

**No. 21605.** Very substantially made; barrel stave top; iron bound, cross bar slats on top; body slats; set up tray with covered bonnet box; iron bottom.

| 26 inch | $1.75 | 32 inch | $2.50 |
| 28 inch | 2.00 | 34 inch | 2.75 |
| 30 inch | 2.25 | 36 inch | 3.00 |

**WHAT WE SAVE YOU** on a Trunk will pay for part of **THE GOODS YOU PUT INTO IT.**

**IT'S WELL TO WATCH YOUR EXPENSE ACCOUNT.**

## GREAT BARGAIN $2.25 TRUNK.

**No. 21607.**

**No. 21607.** Extra quality Crystallized Metal Trunks. Full finished cross-bar slats, iron bottom, barrel stave top, cross-bar slats on top, an upright on front, iron clamps, flat steel key lock, patent bolts, rollers, hinges, etc.; covered tray with bonnet box and side compartments; fall in top. This is a handsome trunk, very wide and high and extra well made.

| Sizes. | | Sizes. | |
| 26 inch | $2.25 | 32 inch | $3.00 |
| 28 inch | 2.50 | 34 inch | 3.25 |
| 30 inch | 2.75 | 36 inch | 3.50 |

## New Shape Up-to-Date Trunk.
### Cross Bar Slats, Iron Bottom.

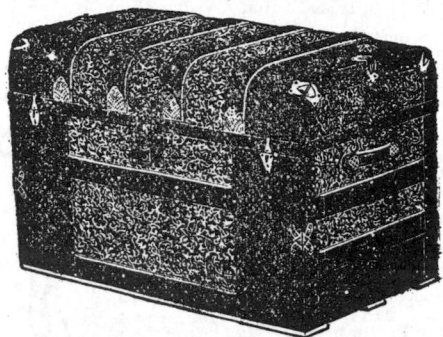

**No. 21608.**

**No. 21608.** Fancy Metal Covered, flat top, with front and back rounded, hard wood reverse bent slats, metal corner bumpers, clamps, bottom rollers, etc.; **Monitor lock and patent bar bolts, heavy strap hinges, tray with bonnet box. Fall-in Top and Side Compartments, all Separately Covered and Four Slats on size 34 and 36 inches.** Without a doubt this is the handiest and most substantial trunk ever built for twice the money.

| Sizes | 28 | 30 | 32 | 34 | 36 |
| Price | $3.00 | $3.25 | $3.50 | $3.75 | $4.00 |

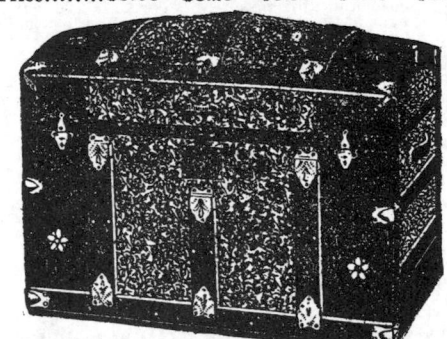

**No. 21609.**

**No. 21609.** Large full-sized trunk. Eugene finish with parasol case, hinge tray, malleable iron corners, dress tray, iron bottom, with barrel stave top, with fancy metal covering, extra wide iron bound, cross slats on top and upright on front; corners protected with very heavy malleable iron bumpers that are warranted not to break under any circumstances; hasp lock, bolts, hinged, covered tray with bonnet box, fall in top and other compartments, beside parasol case and dress tray.

| 26 inch | $3.20 | 30 inch | $3.45 |
| 32 inch | 3.70 | 34 inch | 3.95 |

**DON'T BUY YOUR CLOTHING, AND DRY GOODS, AND HARNESS AND SHOES AT HOME, AND SEND TO US FOR A CURLING IRON. IF ECONOMY IS WORTH PRACTICING, IT'S WORTH PRACTICING THOROUGHLY.**

## Crystallized Metal Covered Trunk.

No. 21610.

**No. 21610. Cross Bar Slats, Hinge Tray, Iron Bottom, Full Finish, with Parasol Case.** Barrel stave top, wide iron bound, five cross bar slats on top and upright on front, end slats, malleable iron corners and shoes, etc., stitched leather handles. Excelsior lock, patent bolts, fancy skeleton work, covered tray with bonnet box, parasol case and side compartment, fall in top.

| | | | |
|---|---|---|---|
| 28 inch | $3.40 | 34 inch | $4.15 |
| 30 inch | 3.65 | 36 inch | 4.40 |
| 32 inch | 3.90 | 38 inch | 4.80 |

No. 21612.

**No. 21612. Cloth Finish Cross Bar Slats, Hinge Tray, Parasol Case, Iron Bottom, Large Barrel Stave Top,** crystallized metal covered, extra heavy iron-bound, cross bar slats on top and upright on front, end slats, malleable iron corner bumpers, rollers, etc., heavy stitched leather handles, **large brass Monitor lock,** patent side bolts, fancy skeleton work on top, covered tray with bonnet box, parasol case, side compartment, fall-in-top, cloth finish.

| | | | |
|---|---|---|---|
| 28 inch | $4.00 | 34 inch | $4.90 |
| 30 inch | 4.30 | 36 inch | 5.20 |
| 32 inch | 4.60 | 38 inch | 5.75 |

## Charter Oak Special.
### IRON BOTTOM AND OAK FINISH.

**No. 21613 High, Wide Trunk,** covered with heavy iron, enamelled and finished in handsome imitation of quarter sawed oak. Flat top, iron bottom, round corners. Harwood bent slats over entire top upright on front and end slats. All protected with heavy metal clamps and bumpers, cross strip clamps and fancy skeleton iron work on ends. Heavy brass lock and side bolts, stitched leather handles, heavy hinges, covered tray, with bonnet and parasol compartments. Handsomely finished and one of the very best values we have ever offered.

| | | | |
|---|---|---|---|
| 28 in. $3.70 | 30 in. $3.98 | 32 in. $4.25 |
| 34 in. 4.67 | 36 in. 4.79 | 38 in. 5.18 |

## The Black Hussar.

No. 21615

**No. 21615 A Handsome and Reliable Flat Top Black Iron Covered Trunk.** Hardwood slats over entire top, body and end slats, metal corner bumpers, clamps, bottom rollers, etc. Heavy iron bottom, **Patent Monitor Lock** and patent bar bolts, heavy hinges, tray with bonnet box fall in top and side compartment. All seperately covered and finely finished. Note on special low prices:

| | | | |
|---|---|---|---|
| 28 inch | $3.25 | 34 inch | $4.00 |
| 30 inch | 3.48 | 36 inch | 4.25 |
| 32 inch | 3.75 | | |

No. 21617

**No. 21617 Black enameled iron,** round top trunk, large size box covered with black enameled iron, flat top, with rounded corners, four hardwood bent slats on top with one extra slat in center full length of trunk, fancy clamps, rollers, leather handles, brass Monitor lock, patent bolts, full covered hinged tray, with bonnet box, fall-in top, all fancy trimmed. Iron bottom,

| Sizes, inches | 28 | 30 | 32 | 34 | 36 |
|---|---|---|---|---|---|
| Price | $3.75 | $4.05 | $4.35 | $4.65 | $4.95 |

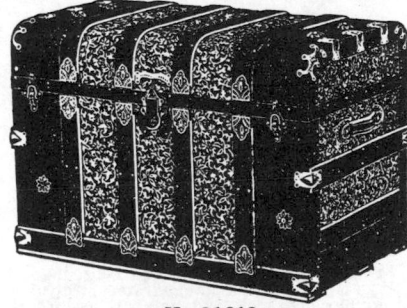

No. 21619.

**No. 21619 Large full sized iron bottom, crystal covered trunk;** flat top with rounded corners and hardwood reverse slats over entire top, upright on front, end slats and bar bolts, mallable iron bumpers and skeleton work covered tray with bonnet box and side compartment fall in top, parasol case, 4 slats on 34 and 36 inch sizes. monitor lock. handsomely made and finished. **A real bargain.**

| | | | |
|---|---|---|---|
| 28 inch | $3.45 | 34 inch | $4.25 |
| 30 inch | 3.70 | 36 inch | 4.50 |
| 32 inch | 3.98 | | |

No. 21620.

**No. 21620 Canvas covered, iron bottom, square top,** corners double iron bound, four hardwood slats full length of trunk, two slats all around body, japanned steel bumpers and clamps, large brass plated Monitor lock, heavy bolt locks, extra wide iron center band on top and body, tray containing hat box and packing compartment, fall-in top, all covered.

| Sizes, inches | 28 | 30 | 32 | 34 | 36 |
|---|---|---|---|---|---|
| Prices | $3.75 | $4.00 | $4.25 | $4.50 | $4.75 |

**No. 21621 Flat top, heavy duck cover trunk.** Double wide iron bound, two center bands, hardwood slat on top and body end slats all protected with heavy iron bumpers, corner shoes, etc. Excelsior lock and patent buckle bolts, heavy hinges, rollers, etc., stitched leather handles. high combination tray, hat box with removable frame hinged shirt box on side and compartment underneath, all covered, linen finish, iron bottom.

| | | |
|---|---|---|
| 30 inch | $5.25 | 34 inch | $6.25 |
| 32 inch | 5.75 | | |

**No. 21625 Canvas Covered, Iron Bottom, Cloth Finish, Excelsior Lock.** High and wide trunk, covered with heavy canvas duck, flat top, with front and back rounded, hardwood bent slats over entire top, upright on front end, slats all protected with tinned clamps, bumpers, cross strip clamps, fancy skeleton iron works on ends, etc., heavy brass locks, patent side bolts. stitched leather handles, heavy hinges, set-up tray, cloth faced.

| | | | |
|---|---|---|---|
| 28 inch | $4.35 | 34 inch | $5.25 |
| 30 inch | 4.65 | 36 inch | 5.55 |
| 32 inch | 4.95 | | |

## Canvas Covered Trunks.

### No. 21631

**No. 21631 An Unquestionable Bargain.** Square Trunk, with heavy iron bottom. Painted canvas covering, heavy and strong, as well as neat in appearance. This trunk has hardwood slats on top and body, and is protected with heavy malleable iron clamps and bumpers.

| | | | |
|---|---|---|---|
| 28 inch | $2.50 | 32 inch | $2.95 |
| 30 inch | 2.75 | 34 inch | 3.25 |

**No. 21632 Sole leather straps, canvas covered,** heavy Japanned steel clamps and corners. We have here an article to meet the demand of a cheap 3 trap trunk, **large box covered with heavy canvas,** painted, wide iron bound, heavy hardwood slats full length of trunk, body and end slats, heavy bumpers and steel clamps, rollers, etc., and **brassed Excelsior lock,** with heavy bolts, iron bound, all protected with **two heavy sole leather straps,** high set-up tray with hat box, and side compartments all separately covered and cloth faced, **extra dress tray.**

| | | | |
|---|---|---|---|
| 28 inch | $5.50 | 34 inch | $7.00 |
| 30 inch | 6.00 | 36 inch | 7.50 |
| 32 inch | 6.50 | 38 inch | 8.00 |

## Canvas Covered Stateroom Trunks

### No. 21633

**No. 21633 Iron center band, steel trimmings.** Made to go under berth of any steamship. This is a very convenient trunk for short journeys; japanned iron trimmed; bumpers, clamps, and corner shoes; large flat steel key, lock, side pockets, and set up tray.

| | | | |
|---|---|---|---|
| 28 inch | $3.00 | 32 inch | $3.50 |
| 30 inch | 3.25 | 34 inch | 3.75 |

**No. 21635 Leather bound brass excelsior lock** steel trimmings, covered tray. Cheapest leather bound trunk made, canvas duck covered, edges bound with heavy leather, and leather center band, best steel bumpers, clamps, corner shoes, valance clamps, hinges, etc., excelsior lock, full covered tray, linen lined throughout.

| | | | |
|---|---|---|---|
| 30-inch | $6.25 | 34-inch | $7.25 |
| 32-inch | 6.75 | 36-inch | 7.75 |

## Toy Trunks.

**No. 21635 Square top, good lock, handles, set up tray.**

| SIZE. | PRICE. |
|---|---|
| 12 inch | $0.40 |
| 14 inch | .50 |
| 16 inch | .60 |

**No. 21636 Paper Saratoga.** Barrel stave top, good lock, set up tray with covered bonnet box.

| SIZE. | PRICE. |
|---|---|
| 14 inch | $0.65 |
| 16 inch | .75 |
| 18 inch | .85 |

**No. 21637 Crystal Saratoga.** Fancy metal cover, barrel top, fancy stripe, with clamps, bottom rollers, set up tray and covered hat box.

| SIZE. | PRICE. |
|---|---|
| 16 inch | $1.00 |
| 18 inch | 1.15 |
| 20 inch | 1.35 |

## Traveling Bags.

No better selection of Club Bags, Satchels, Gladstones, etc. can be found anywhere than the assortment shown herein. Our line comprises the best products of three leading factories, and we offer the goods with **our guaranty** that if they are not fully up to our representation, and if you do not think you have gotten your money's worth, and more, you can return goods to us and we will refund amount paid. Remember our **special discount of 3% for full cash with order.**

**No. 21638 Alligator Cloth Club Bag,** alligator finish, top push lock, cloth lined Chestnut.

| | |
|---|---|
| 10 inch | $0.35 |
| 11 inch | .40 |
| 12 inch | .45 |
| 13 inch | .50 |
| 14 inch | .55 |
| 15 inch | .60 |
| 16 inch | .65 |

**No. 21640 Club Sac,** selected pebble leather, large nickel lock and side catches, leather handles with rings, cloth lined.

**Brown and Orange.**

| | |
|---|---|
| 10 inch | $0.60 |
| 11 inch | .70 |
| 12 inch | .80 |
| 13 inch | .90 |
| 14 inch | 1.00 |
| 15 inch | 1.10 |
| 16 inch | 1.20 |

**No. 21641 Fine Alligator Club Bag,** made of selected goat skin, double flange frame, large nickel plated double hasp lock and side catches, English handle with ring attachments, linen lined.

| | | | |
|---|---|---|---|
| 10 inch | $0.70 | 15 inch | $1.20 |
| 11 inch | .80 | 16 inch | 1.30 |
| 12 inch | .90 | 17 inch | 1.40 |
| 13 inch | 1.00 | 18 inch | 1.50 |
| 14 inch | 1.10 | | |

## Rubber Pellissier.

**No. 21642 Pebble and alligator finish,** japanned frame, flat steel key lock and tinned iron trimmings, strong iron handle.

**Black.**

| | |
|---|---|
| 14-inch | $0.35 |
| 16-inch | .40 |
| 18-inch | .45 |
| 20-inch | .50 |
| 22-inch | .55 |
| 24-inch | .60 |

**Brown.**

| | | | |
|---|---|---|---|
| 14-inch | $0.60 | 20-inch | $0.75 |
| 16-inch | .65 | 22-inch | .80 |
| 18-inch | .70 | 24-inch | .85 |

## Alligator Rubber Gladstone.

**No. 21643 Alligator finish, strong lock and** catches, straps all around, linen lined. Chestnut.

| | | | |
|---|---|---|---|
| 14-inch | $0.85 | 20-inch | $1.15 |
| 16-inch | .95 | 22-inch | 1.25 |
| 18-inch | 1.05 | | |

**No. 21644 Made of heavy selected sheep skin,** with heavy japanned frame, nickel lock and trimmings. English handle, cloth lined, a very cheap and durable bag.

| | | | |
|---|---|---|---|
| 12 inch. Each | $2.25 | 16 inch. Each | $3.25 |
| 13 inch. Each | 2.50 | 17 inch. Each | 3.50 |
| 14 inch. Each | 2.75 | 18 inch. Each | 3.75 |
| 15 inch. Each | 3.00 | | |

**No. 21645 Best selected grain leather, leather** covered frame, large nickel lock, with combination ring handle and top catches, full leather lined, inside pockets.

**Brown.**

| | | | |
|---|---|---|---|
| 12 inch. Each | $3.75 | 16 inch. Each | $4.75 |
| 13 inch. Each | 4.00 | 17 inch. Each | 5.00 |
| 14 inch. Each | 4.25 | 18 inch. Each | 5.25 |
| 15 inch. Each | 4.50 | | |

**No. 21646 Grain Leather Gladstone.** One of the most serviceable and best grain leather bags in the market, made of fine selected full stock grain leather, heavy grain leather straps all around, double flange frame, nickel plated long flat key lock, with handle combined, heavy nickel side catches, linen lined.

**Brown and Orange.**

| | | | |
|---|---|---|---|
| 14 inch, Each | $2.85 | 20 inch. Each | $3.60 |
| 16 inch. Each | 3.10 | 22 inch. Each | 3.85 |
| 18 inch. Each | 3.35 | | |

**No. 21647 Grain Leather Gladstone.** This bag is made from the very best full stock grain leather, double strong frame, nickel corner protectors, large nickel lock, with combination handle, heavy English snap catches, grain leather straps, full leather lined.

**Brown and Orange.**

| | | |
|---|---|---|
| 14 inch. Each....$3.75 | 20 inch. Each.....$4.88 |
| 16 inch. Each..... 4.12 | 22 inch. Each..... 5.25 |
| 18 inch. Each..... 4.50 | |

**No. 21650 Leather Gladstone.** Very fine pebble leather, grain leather straps all around, double flange frame, large nickel flat key lock, heavy nickel catches, double stitched leather handle, heavy rings, linen lined.

**Brown.**

| | | |
|---|---|---|
| 14 inch. Each......$1.55 | 20 inch. Each......$2.45 |
| 16 inch. Each...... 1.75 | 22 inch. Each...... 2.65 |
| 18 inch. Each... 1.95 | |

**No. 21652 Alligator Leather Gladstone.** Made of selected goatskin leather, heavy double flange frame, nickel double hasp lock and side catches, heavy English handle, with ring attachment, cloth lined, portfolio. Tan and chestnut.

| | | |
|---|---|---|
| 14 inch. Each......$1.70 | 20 inch. Each......$2.30 |
| 16 inch. Each...... 1.90 | 22 inch. Each...... 2.50 |
| 18 inch. Each...... 2.10 | |

## Canvas Gladstone.
### Strong, Serviceable and Popular.

**No. 21655 This is an exceptionally Fine Gladstone Bag.** Made from extra heavy canvas with morocco leather corners, grain leather straps all around and large handsomely nickel-plated lock. Finely japanned frame and heavy stitched grain leather handle. Full linen lined. **One of our specially good values.**

| | | |
|---|---|---|
| 14 inch.......... $1.37 | 20 inch............$1.90 |
| 16 inch.......... 1.50 | 22 inch............ 2.25 |
| 18 inch.......... 1.67 | |

## Canvas Cabin Bag.

**The Handsomest Bag ever Made.**
**No. 21657** The **Famous Canvas Cabin Bag.** Made from extra strong heavy weight canvas. Opens at top with spring clasps.

| | |
|---|---|
| 14 in., price ..$0.74 | |
| 16 in., price.. .85 | |
| 18 in., price.. .98 | |
| 20 in., price.. 1.05 | |
| 22 in., price ..$1.25 | |

## Canvas Telescope Cases.

**No. 21658.** Riveted leather corner and bottom tips, heavy stitched handle; two straps.

| | | |
|---|---|---|
| 14 inch. Each......$0.35 | 20 inch. Each......$0.65 |
| 16 inch. Each...... 0.45 | 22 inch. Each...... 0.75 |
| 18 inch. Each...... 0.55 | 24 inch. Each...... 0.85 |

**No. 21659** Heavy canvas, leather bound, hand sewed, heavy leather tips, grain leather straps all around.

| | | |
|---|---|---|
| 16 inch. Each......$1.10 | 22 inch. Each......$1.75 |
| 18 inch. Each...... 1.25 | 24 inch. Each...... 1.98 |
| 20 inch. Each...... 1.50 | 26 inch. Each...... 2.23 |

With patent lock strap, 50 cents extra.

**No. 21660 Extra Heavy Canvas;** edges bound all around with wide leather; very heavy corner protectors; two and three sole leather straps; best handle made.

| | | |
|---|---|---|
| | 16 in., each ...$2.00 |
| | 18 in., each ... 2.50 |
| 20 in., each........$2.85 | 22 in., each.......... 3.25 |
| 24 in., each........ 3.60 | |

## Dress Suit Case.

**No. 21662**

**No. 21662 Dress Suit Case.** Plain Canvas, telescope style, heavy collar, leather straps and handles.

| | | |
|---|---|---|
| 20 inch. Each......$0.90 | 24 inch. Each......$1.10 |
| 22 inch. Each...... 1.00 | |

## Shoulder or Sling Straps.

**No. 21663 Solid Grain Leather Shoulder or Sling Straps,** for use on club bags, ½ inch wide with spring snaps. Price each....................$0.18

## Shawl Straps.

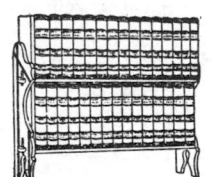

**No. 21665 Grain leather,** spring snaps, ½ inch. Each.......................$0.18

**No. 21667 Good Solid Shawl Straps** with heavy stitched handles and rings with 2 straps 2 feet long. Price, each.............................. ..........$0.25

## Fibre Lunch Boxes.
### Warranted Water-Proof.

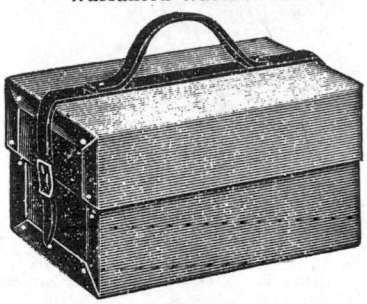

**No. 21669.**

**No. 21669 This is Something Entirely New,** and it is certainly the very best thing in lunch boxes ever produced. These boxes are made from a specially prepared fibre. Leather color and thoroughly water-proof. They are very strong and tough, and will stand the very hardest kind of service. Each box has neat attached leather strap and handle. Made in three sizes, as follows:

| | |
|---|---|
| Size, 4½x6½x4 in. deep. Price, each........$0.15 | |
| Size, 5½x7½x4 in. deep. Price, each........ 0.20 | |
| Size, 6x9x4¾ in. deep. Price, each........ 0.25 | |

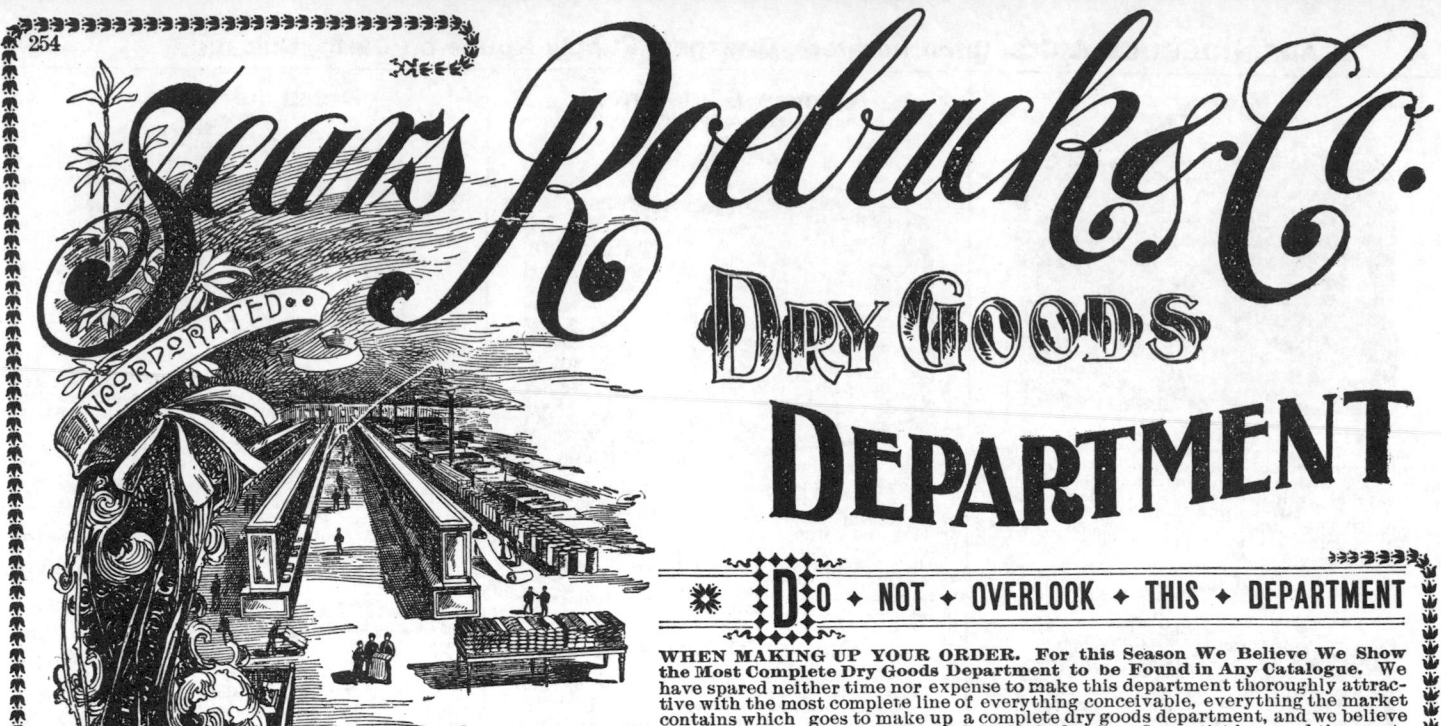

# Sears Roebuck & Co. Dry Goods Department

## Do + NOT + OVERLOOK + THIS + DEPARTMENT

**WHEN MAKING UP YOUR ORDER.** For this Season We Believe We Show the Most Complete Dry Goods Department to be Found in Any Catalogue. We have spared neither time nor expense to make this department thoroughly attractive with the most complete line of everything conceivable, everything the market contains which goes to make up a complete dry goods department, and we believe there is nothing wanting in any of the details. Our artist has used the greatest care to clearly and correctly illustrate all the different articles quoted, and in such a way that you can order from us almost as intelligently as if you were in our store selecting the goods from stock.

**ABOUT PRICES.** We are Determined in Every Department to Maintain Our Well Earned Reputation of The Cheapest Supply House on Earth, and that our prices may be below all others our dry goods buyers have made this season's purchases direct from mills and manufacturers on the basis of very large quantities for spot cash. The Department is so Organized that it can be run very Economically, and to the actual cost to produce we add simply our one small percentage of profit, and offer you your choice of this great collection on our one small profit manufacturer-to-consumer plan. Compare Our Prices With Those of Other Houses Before Making up Your Order. We Claim to be the Cheapest Supply House on Earth; we would like for you to make the comparison. If we are not the cheapest house we will not expect your order. If Everyone Before Ordering Would Look Over the Different Catalogues, inquire of their home markets and ascertain the financial standing and reputation of the house to whom they are about to send an order, they would be very sure of placing their orders in the hands of people whose reputation is unquestioned whose ability to make the lowest prices is the best, and where they would get the greatest satisfaction. We always urge our customers to this precaution, and we think this alone is a guarantee for our ability to save you money.

**OUR SPECIAL TERMS.** We will Ship Any Goods from this Department (except cut piece goods) by Freight or Express C. O. D., subject to examination on receipt of a sufficient deposit to cover freight or express charges both ways. You can Examine Goods at Your Nearest Railroad Depot, and if found to be perfectly satisfactory and exactly as represented, pay the agent our price and charges less amount sent with order, and the goods are yours. Three Per Cent. Discount Allowed if Cash in Full Accompanies Your Order. If you send the full amount of cash with your order you may deduct 3 per cent. from our price. Nearly all our customers send cash in full. In Comparing Our Prices with Those of Other Houses, please consider this THREE PER CENT. CASH DISCOUNT. It makes quite a difference in the price of the goods and will nearly always more than pay the freight or express charges

**ABOUT FREE SAMPLES.** When Requested We will Furnish Cloth Samples of Dry Goods, Carpets, etc., but we would consider it a special favor if you would confine your requests to the exact styles interested in. We are Anxious that You Should Have the Samples Needed to make up your order, but as a matter of economy of time we are compelled to urge our customers to Confine Themselves Strictly to the Exact Number, Kind and Price of Goods Wanted, and not ask for samples which would be of no use to you and considerable expense to us. The time used in supplying one applicant with samples amounts to very little, but in supplying several thousand daily it is very great; in order to prevent delay we trust you will adhere as closely as possible to this request. Furthermore, the cost of material used in supplying several thousand requests for samples daily is considerable, and you will be benefited by preventing the necessity for advancing the prices of the goods, as the cost of samples very materially increases the cost of the goods. At the Same Time, We Assure You We will Deem it a Privilege to Supply You with the Needed Samples, and would thank you in advance for this privilege as well as for your consideration in making your requests for samples as inexpensive for us as possible.

**WE OFFER YOU THE FOLLOWING ADVANTAGES.** By Selecting the Goods Wanted from this Department you are sure of getting the very Latest Styles. Everything We Offer is brand new, Manufactured Expressly for this Season's Use, the very latest styles direct from the largest and most reliable American and European manufacturers. There is Nothing Old, no last season's goods, nothing that is shop-worn. When You Send Your Order to Us you are assured of getting the very latest, and that at a SAVING OF FROM 25 TO 50 PER CENT. IN PRICE. You Have the Benefit of Selecting from One of the Largest Assortments in the country, and you have our Guarantee that if the goods are not exactly as represented, if they are not satisfactory in every way, you can return them at our expense.

**IF YOU ARE UNACQUAINTED WITH US** AND HAVE ANY DOUBTS as to our responsibility, you are at liberty if you choose to send your order and money to any Express Company in this city, to the Metropolitan National Bank or the National Bank of Commerce of this city, with instructions not to turn it over to us unless they know us to be thoroughly reliable. Your Attention is also Called to the Two Bank Letters in the front of this book, reproduced from photographs and the testimonials shown on several of the pages in this book from customers of ours who have, of their own free will, written us saying how much they have saved and what advantages they have gained by sending their orders to us.

**IF YOU HAVE NEVER ORDERED DRY GOODS FROM US,** We are More Than Anxious to receive an order if ever so small, not for the little profit there will be in it for us, for these goods are sold on very close margin, but for the good it will do us as an advertisement. We will endeavor to send you such goods as have never been seen in your section at anything like the price, send you so much value for your money that you will of your own free will recommend our house to your friends, and in this way increase our sales of dry goods in your neighborhood.

---

## Colored Imported and Domestic Serges, Cashmere and Henriettas.

**No. 22100** Single Fold Alpaca, 22 inches wide, comes in the following colors: Black, brown, navy, and wine. Price per yard.....................$0.08½

**No. 22101** Double Fold English Cashmere, worsted, suitable for spring or summer, 28 inches wide. Comes in navy, seal and light brown, myrtle, garnet, tan and black. Per yard.............$0.12½

**No. 22103** Double Fold Henrietta, partly wool, fine finish, will give excellent service and look well; comes in the following colors: black, brown, slate, myrtle green, tan, garnet. 34 inches wide.
Per yard....................................$0.15

**No. 22104** Heavy Extra Fine Finish Henrietta, with all-wool filling, and a very serviceable cloth, 36 inches wide; comes in the following staple colors: black, slate, seal and light brown, myrtle, tan, navy, garnet, and slate. Price, per yard.............$0.20

**No. 22105** Very Fine All Wool Filled Henrietta. This is a splendid wearing cloth and will hold its color and give much better satisfaction than an all wool Henrietta at same price. Comes in the following colors: navy, black, seal and light brown, tan, myrtle, slate, olive and garnet; 36 inches wide.
Price per yard....................................$0.25
Or a dress pattern of 9 yards.................2.10

**No. 22106** Is a strictly All Wool French Henrietta, 36 inches wide; makes up a rich, serviceable dress. This goods usually retails at 45 cts. per yard.
Our special price per yard...................$0.29
Or a full dress pattern of 9 yards..............2.50

**No. 22107** This is a very fine strictly All Wool Imported Henrietta. Very fine weave, 38 inches wide and a good substantial cloth which we can highly recommend. Comes in the following colors: garnet, black, myrtle and olive green, light and dark brown, tan, navy and slate. Price, per yard..$0.35
Or a dress pattern of 9 yards for.............2.98

**No. 22109** This is a fine German Henrietta, extra wide, 45 inches. Strictly all wool. This is one of our popular and best sellers and usually retails at 65c. Comes in all staple shades, such as navy, dark and light brown, tan, myrtle, green, olive, slate, gamet and black.
Our special price, per yard..................$0.50

**No. 22110** This is one of our Special Leaders. Extra Fine Silk Finished German Henrietta, has a very rich appearance, 46 inches wide and is well known for its sterling wearing qualifications. Comes in all staple shades, such as black, navy, wine, golden, brown, myrtle and slate. Per yard.....$0.65

**No. 22112** Fine Imported French Henrietta, with an extra heavy warp, and a very silky fine finish, is as handsome as any silk wrap, and will last you for years. Comes in all staple shades, such as myrtle, navy, black, wine, slate, and light and dark brown. 46 inches wide. Per yard.............$0.75

## Domestic and Imported Serges.

Serges are known for their durability and weight; for being the best wearing cloth, and are getting more popular every day. Give us a trial order in these goods and you will be a regular customer of ours.

**No. 22114** 36 inch Imported All Wool Serge, with a nice fine twill. We sell an enormous lot of this line of goods, positively All Wool. Comes in all staple shades, such as myrtle, wine, dark and light brown, black, navy and slate.
Price per yard...$0.25
Or a dress pattern of 9 yards 2.10

**No. 22116** 38 Inch Fine Imported All Wool Serge. This has a beautiful finish to it, and we can guarantee it to give entire satisfaction to the wearer. Colors, wine, black, navy, dark and light brown, myrtle and slate. Price per yard.....$0.35
Dress pattern of 9 yards for...................2.98

**No. 22118 46 Inch Very Fine French Serge.** Very closely woven and has a waterproof finish. For a good, serviceable dress there is nothing better, as it will retain its appearance to the last. Colors, black, brown, navy, myrtle and wine.
Price, per yard........................$0.45

**No. 22119 Extra Value. Our 46 Inch French Waterproof Serge.** Very fine weave, has a silk finish, and will wear for years. This cloth comes only in navy and black. Per yard..........$0.55
Dress pattern of 8 yards for.............. 4.15

**22121 This is Extra Superfine,** strictly rain and mud proof French serge with a good firm twill, and is very popular for ladies' suits and skirts, 46 inches wide. Colors navy, black, myrtle, golden brown, wine and tan. Price, per yard..............$0.69

## Evening or Light Shades of Henrietta, Cashmere and Albatross Dress Goods.

**The New Swell Creations for 1897 will all be Found Here.**

**No. 22122 36-inch Wool Filled Henrietta,** colors cream, pink, old rose, nile green and sky blue.
Per yard..............................$0.25

**No. 22124 36-inch All Wool Albatross,** colors cream, pink, old rose, nile green, cardinal and lemon color. Per yard..........................$0.35

**No. 22126 38-inch Silk Finish Henrietta,** colors cream, pink and blue. Per yard.............$0.50

## Special Bargains in Sicilian Cloth to Close Out.

**Take Advantage of Bargains While They Last.**

**No. 22128 100 Pieces Only.** 56 inch fine imported Sicilian cloth (3 yards make a skirt), worth fully $2.00 per yard; colors, brown, navy and black only. Our special bargain price per yard.....$1.10
Skirt pattern of 3 yards ........................ 3.10

## Ladies' Cloth and Broadcloth Department.

**We Have Made Extraordinary Preparations to Do a Large Business in This Line.**

**We are the recognized headquarters for these cloths, and by our liberal method of selling can SAVE our CUSTOMERS much money and give them better values than are obtainable from any other house. Our broadcloths are 50 inches wide, and a nice full cape can be made of from 1½ to 2½ yards of the material.** Save money and order your dress goods of Sears, Roebuck & Co.

**No. 22130 A 50 inch Ladies' Strictly All Wool Broadcloth;** colors, black, navy, seal and medium brown, tan, green, cardinal and grey. A suit can be made from five yards of broadcloth this width; regular retailers ask 60c for these cloths.
Our special price per yard..................$0.43

**No. 22131 Extra Quality Superb Finish Broadcloth,** much heavier than the preceding number; 50 inches wide; very suitable for ladies' capes and jackets; colors, black, navy, seal and medium brown, tan, green, cardinal and grey.
S. R. & Co.'s special price per yard...........$0.60

**No. 22132 Extra Heavy-weight Broadcloth,** 50 inches wide, this is a cloth that has great wearing qualities and will look well after years of wear. Suitable for ladies' wraps, capes and suits. Colors black, navy, seal and medium brown, tan, green, cardinal and grey. Per yard....................$0.85

**No. 22134 A Very Fine Imported English Broadcloth,** (Prince of Wales) style, waterproof, a heavy fabric of excellent quality. Can be used for wraps, capes, suits and for men's wear. A great bargain at the price we quote. Colors black, navy, seal and medium brown, tan, green, cardinal and grey. Per yard...........................$1.10

## Covert Cloth.

**A nice cloth,** that wears well and has the advantage of not showing the dirt. This cloth can be washed. Very fashionable for skirts and dresses.

**No. 22138 A 34-inch covert cloth,** wears better than many of the higher grades of cloth; makes up pretty in tailor-made skirts; blue mixed, tan mixed, and gold and green mixed. Per yard..........$0.25

**No. 22140 A 36-Inch Covert Cloth,** imported; this cloth is noted for its wearing qualities, and has a changeable or two-toned effect; makes up into elegant ladies' tailor-made suits. Blue mixed, tan mixed, and gold and green mixed, per yard....$0.50

**No. 22142 A 50-Inch Genuine Imported Covert Cloth,** with a very fine lustre finish; a very beautiful cloth with a very firm weave; always looks neat and pretty. The correct thing for a high-grade tailor suit. Colors drab mixture, tan mixture, and blue-grey mixture. Cloth like this is usually sold at retail for $2.00 per yard. Sears, Roebuck & Co.'s special price, per yard. ..................$1.00

## De'Beige Cloth.

This class of cloth is gaining in popularity of late, as it retains its very nice appearance a great while. It is the same on both sides, and does not spot or show the dust; strictly all wool. A French fabric that is admired by all who see it.

**No. 22144 38 Inch Strictly All-Wool Fine French De'Beige Cloth.** Colors, blue, grey and tan only.
Per yard.......................................$0.50

**No. 22146 A Genuine Worsted Diagonal,** strictly all wool. This class of cloth is very popular for ladies' skirts and is one of the newest ideas; it will make up as rich as a silk skirt; 44 inches wide; colors, **Navy Blue Only.** Price per yard..........$0.55

**No. 22148 38 inch Mohair Stripe Novelty,** one of the newest and most popular cloths for dress goods for the season of 1897. Our own importation and sold at a price unapproachable by any other house; colors, navy blue only. The stripe in these goods has a very pretty dot. Per yard.........$0.69

## Seven Special Bargains in Dress Goods

**THE LIKE OF WHICH HAVE NEVER BEEN SEEN.**

**One of the largest eastern mills found itself with 2,250 pieces of dress goods on its hands. They were new and desirable goods, but the mill owners wanted to realize the ready cash. Sears, Roebuck & Co.'s buyers as usual were on hand and bought the entire stock at 47c. ON THE DOLLAR. We quote these goods at the same rate as bought, and our customers can procure a great big bargain while they last. Send for these goods soon, as the best styles are sure to sell rapidly.**

## One of Our Big Bargains.

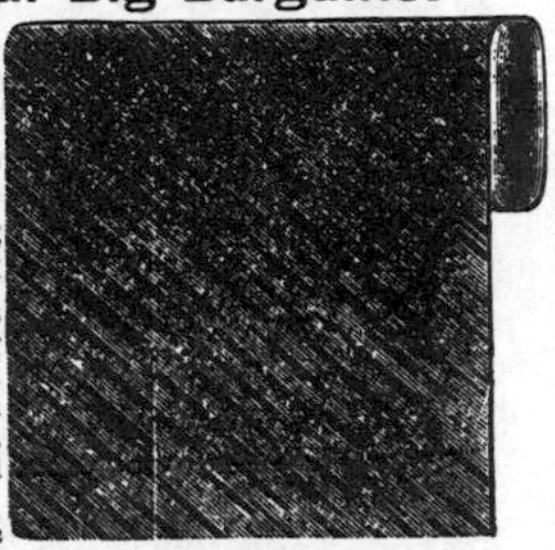

**No. 22150 28 inch Novelty Dress Goods** half wool; comes in both light and dark shades; these goods come in natty checks, small plaids and a combination of stripes and fancy mixtures; the goods come in the following colors: gray mixture, tan mixture, brown mixed, blue mixture, red mixture and black.
Per yard.....$0.12½

## A Big Dress Goods Bargain.

**No. 22152 28 inch Reversible Suiting,** can be worn the entire year, as it is of medium weight nearly all wool, will wear much better than an all all wool at the same price. One dress like this in a a locality makes friends for our dress goods department. This cloth comes in checks only; colors, navy blue and red mixed, green and red mixed, navy blue, white and red mixed. Per yard..........$0.25

## Read About This Extra Good Value.

**No. 22154 34-Inch Novelty Boucle Checks,** with raised effects. These goods resembles the imported goods, costing many times as much. The colors are green and black mixed, red and black mixed, brown and black mixed. **Don't pay your retail dealer 50c** a yard for goods no better than this.
Per yard.........................................$0.25
A dress pattern of 9 yards..................... 2.10

## Sheppard Plaids at Bargain Prices.

**No. 22156 36-Inch Strictly All Wool Sheppard Plaid.** Colors brown and white, blue and white, and black and white. We handle only the good wearing Sheppard plaids, and do not keep any shoddy goods. These plaids will be used very much for ladies' skirts. Per yard..........................$0.32

## Serges at a Bargain Price.

**Extraordinary Values.**

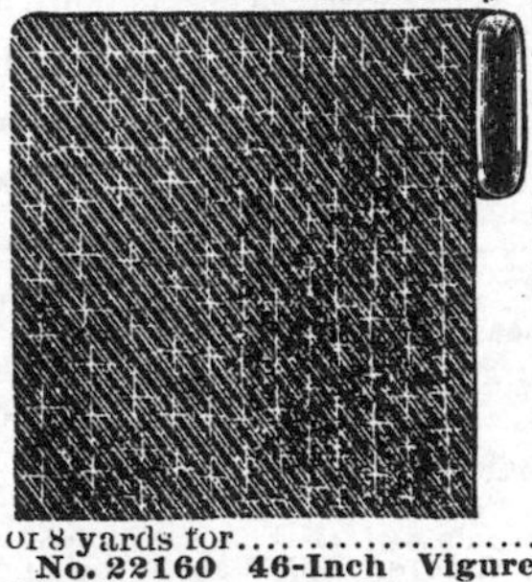

**No. 22158 46-inch Twill Serge,** same on both sides, both water and dust proof; will wear as well as goods costing $1.50 per yard. This cloth is used for ladies' skirts or entire suits and is one of the handsomest cloths we have ever been able to procure. Colors black and navy only.
Per yard.....$0.45
A full dress pattern or 8 yards for.........................$3.50

**No. 22160 46-Inch Vigureaux Suiting,** something similar to a French serge, but of a much prettier weave, a swell up-to-date kind of dress goods that will be worn largely by fashionable dressers, this spring and summer. The value is good and is rarely obtainable. Colors are grey, tan and brown mixture. Per yard.................$0.69

**No. 22161 46 Inch Fine Double Warp Serge,** has a very pretty weave. This cloth has a silk finish and makes up beautifully. The price we sell it at is very low, and it will give our customers great satisfaction and help to make our dress goods department popular. Colors, black, navy, wine and golden brown. Per yard....................$0.55

**No. 22161½ 28 Inch Novelty Dress Goods,** comes in large and medium plaids, also in medium broken checks, colors are light and dark, such as red, green and white, navy, gold and white, navy, gold and red, green and red, green and white and red and blue mixed. A fine quality of dress goods at a very low figure. Per yard...............................$0.09

## Remnants of Dress Goods.

**Can You Use a Remnant of Dress Goods at a Bargain Price?**

In a business as large as ours, short lenghts and remnants will accumulate. In order to sell these remnants rapidly and give our customers great big bargains, we will take all of our short lengths of dress goods and divide them into three lots, no matter what the former price was. Lot No. 1 consists of wool mixed dress goods, short lengths of cashmere, serges and henriettas, from 1 to 5 yard pieces, formerly sold up to 25c. per yard, at 7½c. Lot No. 2 consists of goods that formerly sold up to 35c. per yard, at 12½c. per yard. Lot No. 3 consists of remnants of all of our best dress goods, at 25c. per yard.

**No. 22162** Remnants of dress goods, consisting of **Serges, Cassimeres, Henriettas** and mixed goods in various colors and patterns. Lengths, from one to five yards. Some of these goods worth 25c.
Remnant price, per yard.......................$0.07½

**No. 22164** Remnants of Dress goods, consisting of **Cassimeres, Henriettas, Serges** and mixed suitings of all kinds, in nearly any color, dark and light shades. Lengths, one to five yards. Sold at from 15c to 35c per yard.
Remnant price, per yard..........................$0.12½

**No. 22166** Remnants of dress goods, consisting of high grade novelty goods of all descriptions, also an accumulation of fine **Serges, Henriettas, Mohairs,** and fancy suitings of all descriptions. Lengths, one to five yards. Some of these goods worth 50c, 75c, and $1.00 per yard.
Remnant price, per yard...........................$0.25

**REMEMBER that remnants come in short lengths only; one to five yards.**

## All Wool German Novelty Dress Goods.

**No. 22168 46 Inch Strictly All Wool German Novelty Dress Goods,** comes in very pretty scroll and floral figured designs. This is a very substantial and well wearing cloth and always looks rich and neat. Colors are black and red, black and green and black and navy. Well worth 75c. Per yard....$0.55

## Sheppard Plaids.

**These plaids will be greatly used this coming season and we can save our customers a great deal of money on these goods.**

**No. 22170 28 Inch Sheppard Plaids.** Colors, black and white, brown and white and blue and white. Per yard..............................$0.12½

**No. 22172 34-Inch Wool Mixed Sheppard Plaid.** Colors as above. Per yard........................$0.25

**No. 22174. 36-Inch All Wool Sheppard Plaids.** Colors as above. Per yard........................$0.35

**No. 22176 42-Inch Fine All Wool Sheppard Plaid.** Colors as above. Serge effect, a very handsome, stylish and durable plaid. Retailers get as high as 65c per yard for these goods.
Our price, per yard.................................$0.45

## Fancy Dress Plaids.

**For Children's Dresses and Ladies' Waists.**

**ENGLISH PLAIDS, HALF WOOL.**

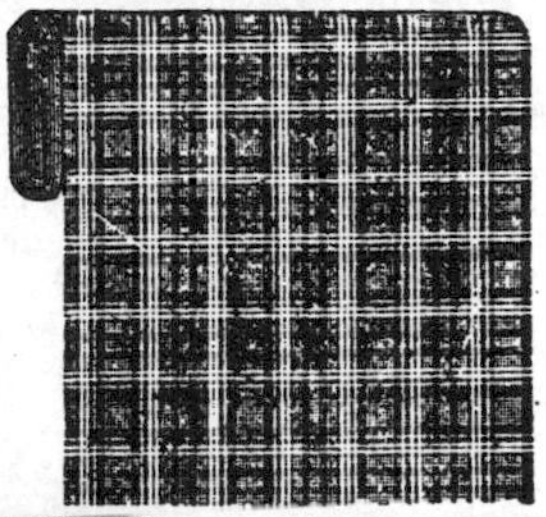

**No. 22180** Width 32 inches, fine close wove serge plaid, a good wearing cloth and come in all the fashionable combinations.
Per yard...$0.25

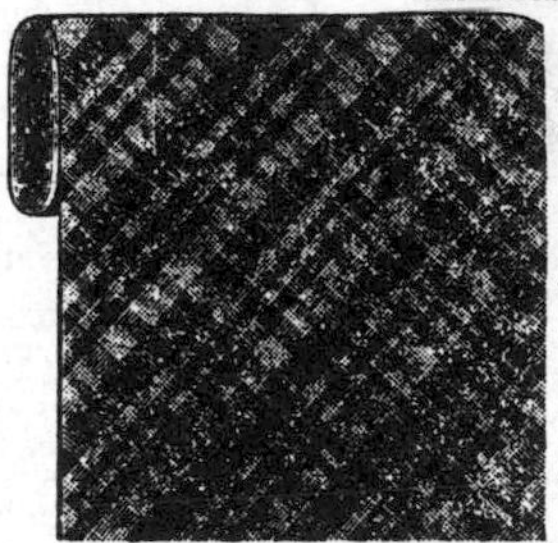

**No. 22181 Scotch Wool Plaids.** Width, 32 inches, a good substantial cloth, made in many pretty plaids of the different clans of Scotland. The following are some of the best sellers: Navy and brown, red and brown, green, blue and white, red, blue and white, red, blue and black, green, blue and brown. All combinations are striped with narrow stripes, contrasting colors. Per yard.......................$0.29

**No. 22182 Imported Worsted Plaids, 55 cents per yard.** Real English pure worsted Highland plaids. Width, 38 inches. Coming from one of the largest manufacturers in Manchester, whose reputation is second to none in the world, this class of goods is only found in first class stores in very large places like Chicago and New York City, and retail for 85 cents per yard as a bargain. We simply mention this fact as a demonstration to show the advantage of ordering nice goods of us. These plaids come in many handsome plaid combinations of red, blue or green. Medium or large plaids. Per yard....$0.55

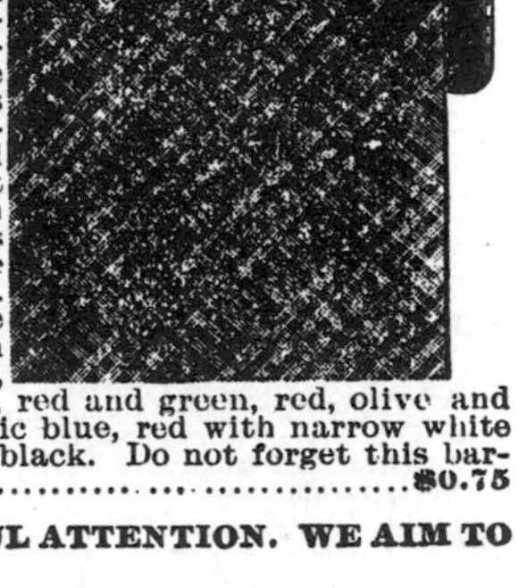

**No. 22184 Fine Imported All Wool Plaids.** Beautiful French colors, Persian effects, all narrow silk, striped, the handsomest plaids imported, and generally cost $1.00 per yard to land. We will not say how we got them as our competitors would learn how; we will let them wonder. The following are the combinations: Tan and electric blue, green and red, blue, red and green, red, olive and ecru, red and electric blue, red with narrow white and blue or red and black. Do not forget this bargain. Per yard.................................$0.75

**WHETHER YOU BUY A YARD OF SERGE OR A $75.00 SURREY, YOUR ORDER WILL RECEIVE THE MOST CAREFUL ATTENTION. WE AIM TO GIVE THE MOST PERFECT POSSIBLE SERVICE TO EVERYONE ALIKE.**

## Plain Black Dress Goods Department.

Black Dress Goods is one of our strongest departments. We handle only the best makes in both domestic and foreign goods. We guarantee every yard to be perfect and fast black.

**No. 22188  22 inch Black Alpaca.**
Per yard.............................................$0.08½
**No. 22190  Black Cashmere, part wool, 28 inch.**
Per yard.............................................$0.12½
**No. 22191  Black Henrietta, half wool, 34 inch.**
Per yard.............................................$0.15
**No. 22192  Black Fine Finished Wool Filled Henrietta, 32 inch.** Per yard..............$0.20
**No. 22193  Best Black Domestic Henrietta,** all wool filling, good and strong; will give good wear; 36 inch. Per yard........................$0.25
Or dress pattern of nine yards for..........2.10
**No. 22194  This is a Beauty, Strictly All Wool French Henrietta.** Positively fast black. This number is a genuine bargain. 36 inches wide.
Per yard.............................................$0.29
Or a dress pattern of 9 yards for...........2.50
**No. 22195  Black Imported Henrietta,** strictly all wool, 38 inches wide. Has a very rich finish and makes up a very rich dress. Per yard........$0.35
Or a dress pattern of 9 yards for...........2.98
**No. 22196  Extra Wide Black German Henrietta,** width 45 inches. This cloth is getting very popular. Has a very rich appearance and will make a good serviceable garment. Per yard................$0.50
Or a dress pattern of 8 yards for...........3.90

### Here is Your Opportunity.

**No. 22198  46-inch Black Silk Finish German Henrietta;** this goods you much see to appreciate, will outwear anything in the dress goods line and usually retails at $1.00 per yard.
Our special price..............................$0.69
Or a dress pattern of 8 yards for .........5.25
**No. 22199  38-inch Black Silk Warp Henrietta,** with a rich silk finish and splendid wearing quality, will wear for years. Price, per yard.........$0.90
**No. 22200  46-inch Black Double Silk Warp Sublime Quality Henrietta.** Will outwear and look far better than a silk dress. Price, per yard..$1.00
Or a dress pattern of 8 yards for...........7.50
**No. 22201  38-inch Black Sebastapol Cloth,** this is one of the newest styles in black dress goods, having a small pretty corduroy twill and about same weight as a waterproof serge. Price, per yard.$0.75

## Black, Domestic and Imported Serges.

**No. 22202  36 inch All Wool Serge French Twill.** Positively All Wool. Good substantial and wearing cloth. Per yard...............................$0.25
Or a dress pattern of 9 yards for..........2.10
**No. 22203  38 inch All Wool French Serge;** very fine weave and makes up a rich, serviceable dress.
Price per yard...................................$0.35
Or a dress pattern of 9 yards for..........2.98
**No. 22204  46 inch French Serge,** waterproof finish. This is a very fine, firm and substantial cloth, and will give good satisfaction to the wearers.
Price per yard...................................$0.45
Or a dress pattern of eight yards for........3.45
**No. 22205  46-Inch Very Fine French Serge,** has an excellent finish. This is one of our great leaders in black dress goods, and actually retails for 75c per yard. Our special price......................$0.55
Or a dress pattern of 8 yards for...........4.25
**No. 22206  46-Inch Water-Proof Highest Quality French Serge.** This is a very recommendable cloth; has a fine finish and is very durable.
Price per yard...................................$0.69
**No. 22208  46-Inch Black Vuas Serge.** Positively none better. Fast black. Very fine weave.
Price per yard...................................$0.90
**No. 22210  Black French Storm or Coating Serge,** the correct thing for ladies' skirts; 46 inches wide; regular 75c. value. Our price, per yard......$0.45
**No. 22211  Black Extra Heavy Storm Serge,** 48 inches wide; the proper thing for light-weight capes or ladies' suits or skirts. Per yard...........$0.98

## Plain Black Mohairs or Alpacas.

**No. 22212  38 inch Black Mohair,** strictly all wool; this is a fine imported cloth and for wear there is nothing better. Per yard..............$0.35
**No. 22213  38 inch Black English Mohair,** all wool; these goods make up pretty in skirts and can be worn any season. Per yard..............$0.42½
**No. 22214  38 inch Black Silk Finish Pure English Mohair.** This cloth is getting very popular and cannot be outclassed for wear. Per yard..$0.48
**No. 22216  58 inch Black Imported Sicilian,** same make of goods as above, but much heavier; having a magnificent lustrous appearance; these goods will be very much worn in skirts the coming season. Price per yard..................$1.10

## Velveteens.

Our velveteen department contains only the better grades of these goods, as cheap velveteens do not wear well. The colors and shades of our velveteens are perfect and the cloth of good quality. We at all times guarantee our prices to be away down, and money will be saved by buying velveteens of this house.

### Black Velveteen.

**No. 22217**  18 inches wide. Per yard........$0.22
**No. 22218**  18 inches wide. Per yard........ .35
**No. 22220**  22 inches wide. Per yard........ .50
**No. 22222**  24 inches wide; super quality.... .75
**No. 22223  Our Specialty, the velveteen we recommend;** 22 inches wide; a good quality cloth, of good heavy weight. We have bought a large manufacturer's entire output of this quality, and can offer a **much superior article than usual at the price.** People wishing a high-grade velveteen at the usual price of cheap, **shoddy goods,** should be very particular to order this number. The quantity is large, but we expect a big run on this number, so we would suggest that orders oe sent in early. Usual price of this velveteen, 75c. per yard.
Sears, Roebuck & Co's special price per yard.$0.45

### Colored Velveteens.

We do not carry light colors in the lowest grade of of velveteens as years of experience has taught us that light colors in this grade of velveteen will not wear.
**No. 22224  Colored Velveteen,** 18 inches wide, comes in brown. navy, cardinal and green only.
Per yard...........................................$0.22
**No. 22225  Colored Velveteen,** 22 inches wide, comes in brown, navy, cardinal, green, yellow, tan, grey, olive, myrtle, sky blue, royal blue, slate, gobelin and peacock blue, old rose, sapphire blue, purple, cream and white. Per yard.................$0.50
(NOTE. — These 50c velveteens are reliable and trustworthy and are recommended by us.)

### Black Silk Velvet.

We are the recognized headquarters in this market for silk velvets and whenever the importers are short of funds and want to realize on a quantity, they always look to S., R. & Co. In this way we often buy velvets away below the market and our customers get the benefit every time.
**No. 22226**  18 inches wide. Per yard........$0.75
**No. 22227**  18 inches wide, good quality.
Per yard............................................ .98
**No. 22228**  18½ inches wide, fine quality.
Per yard.............................................1.25
**No. 22229**  18½ inches wide, extra quality.
Per yard.............................................1.50
**No. 22230**  24 inches wide, suitable for capes.
Per yard.............................................2.00
**No. 22231**  24 inches wide, much better quality.
Per yard.............................................2.50

### Colored Silk Velvet.

**No. 22232  Lyons Colored Silk Velvet.** We can match any color; 18 inches wide. Per yard..$0.75
**No. 22234  Lyons Colored Silk Velvet,** in any color. A fine quality, 18 inches wide.
Per yard...........................................$0.98
**No. 22236  Croise Back Colored Velvet.** An excellent velvet, 19 inches wide. All colors.
Per yard...........................................$1.25
Our special $0.98 Black and Colored Velvets cannot be surpassed by any house in the U. S. We make a special feature of this number.
**No. 22238  Corduroy Velvet,** all colors, 18 inches wide, for ladies' waists and gentlemen's vests. Corduroys will be worn largely this season.
Per yard...........................................$0.80

### Cape Plush.

**No. 22240  Silk Finish Cape Plush.** Black only, 24 inches wide, short pile. Per yard..........$2.15

## Silk Department.

An important and growing department in our vast establishment. We import our silks direct, and buy those of domestic manufacture direct from the factory. We sell dress silks to our customers for less money than the retailer pays for these goods. Silks will be very popular this spring and summer. Samples of silks mailed upon application. Remember that we can furnish anything desired in silk.

### Novelty Silks.

**No.22261  Union Figured Silk,** comes in small pretty designs, beautiful changeable effects, colors, drabs and gold, blue and gold, green and red, pale blue and pink, also plain black; 19 inches wide. Per yard,$0.29
**No. 22263  19 inch Silk,** with cotton back, changeable effects in pretty designs of scrolls and floral figures, combination of colors are wine and gold, blue and red. green and gold, redand blue, and red and black, also plain black. Per yard........$0.35
**No. 22264  Changeable Silk,** 19 inches wide, very pretty, and comes in the newest and most fashionable styles and patterns. Colors are black and green, gold and blue, wine and green, wine and navy, red and green, gold and green, drab and green, black and red; also plain black. Per yard....$0.48
**No. 22265  Pointelle Changeable Silk.** This is one of the richest things procurable in a medium price silk. We can match any color as we carry a vast assortment of all combination of colors. This silk has a satin stripe, divided by a pretty pin dot, in contrasting color with ground work; principal colors are drab and pink, blue and pink, old rose and gold, drab and green, drab and helliotrope, drab and yellow, also plain black, 19 inches wide.
Per yard...........................................$0.50
**No. 22267  Carnelle Changeable Pure Silk,** 19 inches wide, can be used on either side, has a two toned effect, regular summer weight, one of the newest and most nobby things for waists shown this season. Floral design and figure of contrasting colors, so arranged as to give the silk a beautiful and very rich effect. Colors, green and blue, red and black, grey and gold, pink and green, and drab and green. Our special price. per yard.......$0.75
**No. 22268  Changeable Taffeta Silk,** 19 inches wide; waists made of this handsome silk can be worn with any skirt; silk has a two toned effect; medium weight, fine texture and pure silk; the principal and leading colors are, a new shade of green, dark red and a medium shade of blue.
Per yard...........................................$0.85
**No. 22269  19 inch Changeable Surah Silk,** has a two toned effect, quiet colors and very suitable for people of quiet tastes, who prefer quality to show and style. This silk is very soft and makes up beautifully; colors, navy blue and red mixed, green and black mixture and drab and red mixture.
Per yard...........................................$0.75
**No. 22271  Florentine Silk,** 21 inches wide, the ground work of this silk is similar to a gross grain silk, but much finer. This silk comes only in the combined of black with black satin and white silk dot. A beautiful swell piece of silk that will please everyone. Any one wishing a stylish novelty silk, will find this number just the thing. Per yard.$0.98

### Wash Silks.

**No. 22273  Kai-Kai Wash Silk,** 19 inches wide. A new and very stylish silk for ladies' summer waist. The price we sell this Kai-Kai Wash Silk at enables you to have a silk waist for the price of a cotton one. Come in very handsome stripes and checks. Colors, blue and white, pink and white, green and white, brown and white, grey and white, and drab and white, and salmon and white.
Per yard...........................................$0.25
**No. 22274  Shautong Wash Silks;** they come in natural color (ecru) only; very much used for traveling dresses and waists; the correct thing for men's summer coats and vests and negligee shirts; 19 inches wide. Per yard.........................$0.20
Full piece of 18 yards.........................3.35
**No. 22275  Shautong Wash Silk,** same as above, but in a very much better quality; 26 inches wide.
Per yard...........................................$0.35
Full piece of 14 yards.........................4.65
**No. 22276  Fancy Wash Silk,** 27 inches wide, comes in a navy blue ground only. The real China silk. Colors, navy blue ground and white dots, navy blue ground and white lace scrolls. Per yard,$0.67
**22278  Dresden Washable China Silk,** 23 inches wide, a beautiful silk of good quality that we import direct. The new Dresden effects are very handsome and are sure to be popular this spring; this silk comes in a cream ground with lavender and green and lavender and red design. Just the thing for silk waists. Per yard.........................$0.72

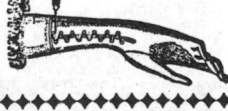
**MAKE NO MISTAKE IN YOUR ORDER. DO NOT BLAME US FOR ERRORS WE DO NOT MAKE. IF WE MAKE A MISTAKE WE WILL CORRECT IT WITHOUT EXPENSE TO YOU.**

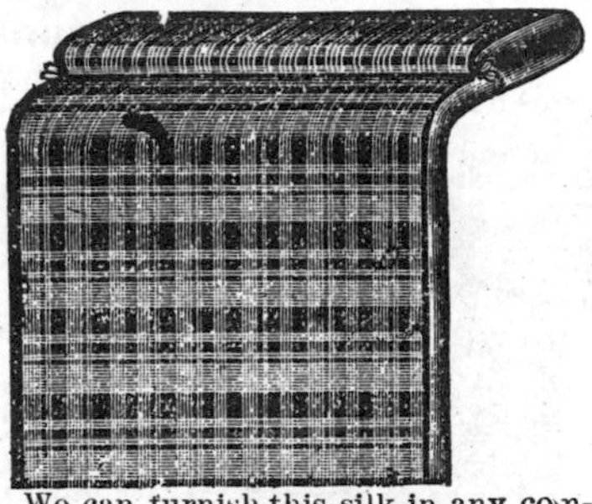

**No. 22280 A Novelty Plaid Silk,** a beautiful combination of colors, 21 inches wide. This is a genuine taffeta, plaid silks are going to be used a great deal and by buying this class of merchandise of us you are assured of a big saving. We can furnish this silk in any combination of colors. Worth $2.00 per yard, and sold at that figure by most retailers. Always mention predominating colors wanted.
Per yard.......................................**$0.98**

## Colored Lining Silks.

**No. 22282 Colored Cashmere Glace Silk,** 19 inches wide; used extensively for lining capes; will also make very pretty waists, as it looks as rich as an expensive silk. When ordering, please mention color you wish to predominate. Colors, red and black, green and black, gold and red, etc.
Per yard.......................................**$0.25**

**No. 22284 Changeable Surah Silk,** 19 inches wide. A much finer grade of silk than the above; used for lining capes; will also make neat and pretty waists. Colors both light and dark shades. We can match any combination of colors in this silk.
Per yard.......................................**$0.35**

## Plain Surah Silks.

**We Sell Only Fabrics that are All Silk.**

**No. 22286 Plain Surah Silk,** 19 inches wide; this silk is very much used for waists, dresses and trimmings; colors, black, navy, brown, green, yellow, red, purple, tan, olive, myrtle and apple green, heliotrope, cardinal, scarlet, sapphire, peacock, white, cream and ecru. Per yard.......................**$0.25**

**No. 22288 Superior Quality of Surah Silk,** 19 inches wide, strictly all silk. These silks are used a great deal for waists, dresses and trimming. Colors, black, navy, brown, green, yellow, red, purple, tan, olive, myrtle and apple green, heliotrope, sapphire, cardinal scarlet, peacock, white, cream and ecru. Per yard.......................**$0.50**

## Plain Colored China Silks.

**No. 22289 All Silk** and comes in all shades of every color from white to black, about forty shades in all and is used chiefly for decorative art purposes, lamp shades, linings, etc.; width 18 inches.
Per yard.......................................**$0.22**

**No. 22290 Best Quality China Silks,** much used for waists and the best linings and decorations. Come in all colors, the same as above; width, 22 inches. Per yard.......................**$0.37½**

**No. 22292 Habutai Silk,** very fine quality and very durable, will wash like a piece of linen. Colors—black or white only. Width 22 inches.
Per yard.......................................**$0.50**

**No. 25294 Colored Faille Silks.** Complete assortment of colors and shades; always in demand, but only in good quality; width 19 inches.
Per yard.......................................**$0.95**

## Cream White Habutai Silks.

In extraordinary demand for spring and summer, for party, evening and confirmation dresses, and for underwear and night robes.

| | | |
|---|---|---|
| **No. 22296** | 20 inch per yard | **$0.35** |
| **No. 22298** | 24 " " | **42½** |
| **No. 22299** | 27 " " | **50** |
| | Heavier and Better Quality. | |
| **No. 22300** | 20 inch per yard | **40** |
| **No. 22301** | 24 " " | **50** |
| **No. 22302** | 27 " " | **60** |

## Colored Japanese Silks.

**These Silks Will Be Worn a Great Deal and Are Very Popular. They Are Especially Adapted for Ladies' Waists.**

**No. 22303 Colored Japanese Silk,** 20 inches wide; plain or solid colors only. Colors blue, pink, nile green, red, black, white, cream, yellow, brown and tan. Per yard.......................**$0.40**

**No. 22304 Colored Japanese Silk,** 27 inches wide; plain or solid colors only. Colors blue, pink, nile green, red, black, white, cream, yellow, brown and tan. This silk is well worth 75c per yard.
Our very special price, per yard.......................**$0.50**

## Black Silk Department.

**Black China Silk.**

**No. 22306 Black China Silk.** 18 inches wide.
Per yard.......................................**$0.22**

**No. 22308 Black China Silk.** 20 inches wide.
Per yard.......................................**$0.30**

**No. 22309 Black China Silk.** A very good quality. 22 inches wide. Per yard.......................**$0.40**

**No. 22310 Black China Silk.** Extra fine quality. 24 inches wide. Per yard.......................**$0.50**

**No. 22311 Black China Silk.** The very best quality procurable. 27 inches wide. Per yard.....**$0.75**

## Black Japanese Silk.

**No. 22312 Black Japanese Silk,** much heavier than a China silk, all pure silk; these silks make very pretty waists; 20 inches wide. Per yard.......**$0.40**

**No. 22312½ Black Japanese Silk,** same as above quality, 27 inches wide. Per yard.......**$0.50**

**No. 22313 Black Japanese Silk,** very heavy, 24 inches wide. Per yard.......................**$0.75**

## Black Gros Grain Silk.

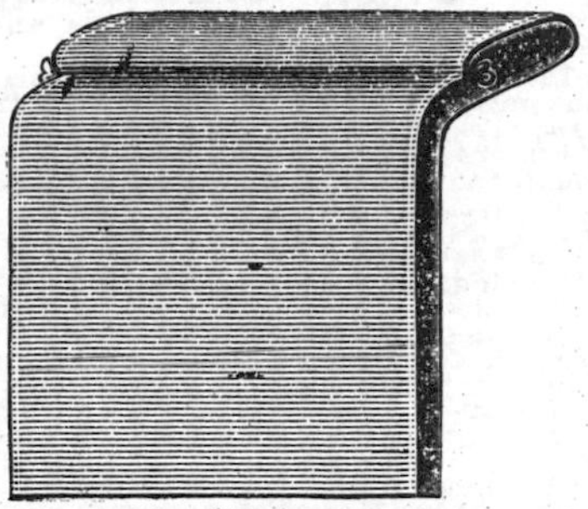

**No. 23314 Black Gros Grain Silk.** Positively the best black in the world. **Our Make of** Gros Grain silks is not only controlled by us but is absolutely warranted for good wear. They are bright, soft andlustruos.

**No. 22314 Black Gros Grain Silk,** a very nice quality, the same on both sides, 18 inches wide.
Per yard.......................................**$0.60**

**No. 22316 Black Gros Grain Silk,** excellent quality, 19 inches wide. Per yard.......................**$0.85**

**No. 22318 Black Gros Grain Silk,** fine quality, 23 inches wide. Per yard.......................**$0.95**

**No. 22319 Black Gros Grain Silk.** Superior quality. 24 inches wide. Per yard.......................**$1.25**

**No. 22320 Black Gros Grain Silk.** Extra heavy and one of the best qualities. 24 inches wide.
Per yard.......................................**$1.75**

## Black Taffeta Silks.

This is very nice, soft silk, with a beautiful black. For wear, it gives excellent satisfaction, and is very popular for skirting and dress purposes.

**No. 22322 Black Taffeta Silk.** Width, 24 inches.
Per yard.......................................**$0.73**

**No. 22324 Black Taffeta Silk.** Width, 27 inches.
Per yard.......................................**$0.95**

## Black Surah Silks.

All silk, and very desirable for waists and dresses where softness and good service is wanted.

**No. 22325 Black Surah Silk,** 19 inches.
Per yard.......................................**$0.25**

**No. 22326 Black Surah Silk,** Per yard...**$0.45**

**No. 22328 Black Surah Silk,** extra quality, 19 inches. Per yard.......................**$0.60**

**No. 22330 Black Surah Silk,** extra super., 22 inches. Per yard.......................**$0.73**

**No. 22332 Black Surah Silk,** sublime quality, 24 inches. Per yard.......................**$1.00**

## Black Satin Duchess, all Silks.

The popular black silk of the present time, celebrated for good wear and elegance of appearance.

**No. 22333 Black Duchess Silk,** 19 inches.
Per yard.......................................**$0.58**

**No. 22334 Black Duchess Silks,** good quality, 19 inches. Per yard.......................**$0.85**

**No. 22336 Black Duchess Silks,** fine quality, 20 inches. Per yard.......................**$0.98**

**No. 22338 Black Duchess Silks,** fine quality; 24 inches. Per yard.......................**$1.05**

**No. 22340 Black Duchess Silks,** fine quality, 27 inches. Per yard.......................**$1.20**

## Black Peau de Soie.

Reversible, both sides alike, and can be turned to advantage. This weave is noted for good wear and challenges the Duchess silks in popularity. Each number is all silk.

**No. 32342 Black Peau de Soie,** 19 inches.
Per yard.......................................**$0.75**

**No. 22344 Black Peau de Soie,** 21 inches.
Per yard.......................................**1.20**

**No. 22346 Black Peau de Soie,** 24 inches.
Per yard.......................................**$1.35**

## Black Silk Rhadames.

This older satin face weave is always popular and sold largely for skirtings in the wide widths, as well as full costumes. Each number is all silk.

**No. 22350** Black Silk Rhadames, fine, 19 inch.
Per yard.......................................**$0.68**

**No. 22352** Black Silk Rhadames, extra good value. 24 inch, per yard.......................**$0.90**

**No. 22354** Black Silk Rhadames, sublime quality, 24 inch, per yard.......................**$1.25**

## Fancy Black Silks.

The new patterns and the new weaves are all here. These silks are just the thing for ladies' skirts and dresses. In placing our orders for these silks, we were very careful to select only the most reliable manufactures. Dealing, as we do, with A1 concerns that have a world wide reputation, and buying, as we do, large quantities of silk for spot cash, enables us to offer our customers values that are unapproachable by any other house. **Save money and buy your silks of Sears, Roebuck & Co.**

## Fancy Black Silks.

**No. 22355 Black Fancy Satin,** 19 inches wide, has a medium size scroll figure, cotton back.
Per yard.......................................**$0.50**

**No. 22356 Fancy Figured Gros Grain Silk,** 19 inches wide with very pretty and neat designs; this silk is of medium weight and is very suitable for summer waists, we have purchased a large quantity of this silk at a very low figure, and in turn sell it to our customers at a big bargain price.
Per yard.......................................**$0.65**

**No. 22358 19 inch black figured gros grain silk.** The designs are neat, medium and large scroll figures. This handsome silk is one of our great specialties and we can assure our customers that it will give great satisfaction; the price is away down low and any one wanting a big bargain in silk should select this number. Per yard.......................**$0.75**

**No. 22359 24 inch Black Figured Gros Grain Silk.** The designs are very swell and artistic. We have made preparations to sell a great deal of this silk, and have made the price very low in order to accomplish this end. It will pay people wanting a 24 inch silk, at a rock bottom price to order this number. Per yard.......................**$0.85**

**No. 22360 21 inch Black Fancy Figured Gros Grain Silk,** with satin scroll or lizard patterd, extra heavy. This is a very rich silk and is just the thing to make those handsome stylish skirts of. This number is well worth $1.50 and is sold at this price by the retail stores right here in Chicago. Per yard. **$0.98**

**No. 22362 20 inch Figured or Brocaded Satin,** comes in very pretty large scroll figure and floral effects. A very rich and nobby satin, and one of the swellest things of the season. This class of silk is only retailed by large high grade stores and brings them great big profits. People desiring a high grade silk at a rock bottom price should order this number. Per yard.......................**$1.00**

**Oo. 22364 20 inch Figured or Brocaded Satin,** in the latest design and patterns, all the new novelties in the fine qualities. A saving and a big one every time for our customers on these silks.
Per yard.......................................**$1.35**

**No. 22366 22 inch Figured or Brocaded Satin,** one of the finest qualities made. All the new patterns. Per yard.......................**$1.75**

## Black Silk Grenadine.

**No. 22368 43 inches wide Black Silk Grenadine** makes up beautifully in skirts and waists, and being of a transparent nature, looks rich and stylish when a lining of colored goods is used under the grenadine silk. This is the way in which the new grenadine silk skirts are made up and the effect is both striking and beautiful. **This is just the material for warm weather wear' being of very light weight.** Our special price per yard.......................**$0.80**

## Black Moire or Watered Silk.

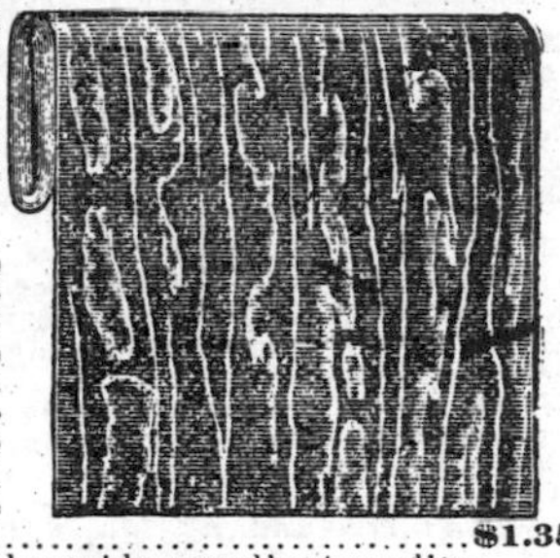

**Very much used for skirts, waists and trimming. A good reliable silk that will not crack and always looks rich and handsome.**

**No. 22369** 19 inches wide. Per yard.......**$0.90**

**No. 22370** 20 inches wide, better quality. Per yard.......**$1.10**

**No. 22371** 21 inches wide, fine quality. Per yard.......................**$1.35**

**No. 22372** 21 inches wide, excellent quality.
Per yard.......................................**$1.50**

## Black Moire Silk.

**Antique Designs.**

**No. 22374** 21 inches wide, extra fine quality.
Per yard.......................................**$1.35**

**No. 22376** 21 inches wide, extra super quality.
Per yard.......................................**$1.65**

## Black Satins.

**No. 22378 19 inches wide, medium quality.**
Per yard.......................................**$0.50**

**No. 22379 19 inches wide, all silk satin.**
Per yard.......................................**$0.75**

**No. 22380 27 inches wide. Satin is used largely this season for ladies' skirts,** and this number being a very heavy satin of good quality, is a great bargain at the price we offer it at. We have closed out the entire stock of a leading manufacturer and are in a position to give our customers a big bargain in the number. Per yard.......................**$0.98**

## Colored Satins.

**There is a Large Quantity of Low Grade Satins on the Market,** but we do not quote them because a cheap satin is not satisfactory. The face wears off in a short time. We have a good quality and all the shades in the following colors, sixty-three shades in all: White, cream—all shades between scarlet and dark cardinal—lightest blue to dark navy blue, fifteen shades of green, twenty shades of tan and browns, canary, orange, purple, heliotrope, steel gray, drab, old rose, etc. **We can match almost any color or shade.** Width 18 inches.

**No. 22381 A Fine Quality satin** 18 inches wide in the above shades. Per yard.......................**$0.37½**

**No. 22382 Extra Quality Satin** 18 inches wide in the above colors and shades. Per yard......**$0.50**

## Drapery Silks.

**Used largely for Sash Curtains,** draperies of all kinds, coverings for sofa pillows, and various other purposes.

**Drapery Silks in Solid Colors.**

**No. 22384 30 inches wide Drapery Silk,** colors gold, yellow, nile, cardinal, old rose, olive, mahogany.
Per yard.......................................**$0.33**

**No. 22385 Figured Drapery Silk,** 30 inches wide, large artistic designs that harmonize with ground work. Come in the following grounds, old rose, nile green, old gold, olive, blue, ecru and red.
Per yard.......................................**$0.39**

**WE CAN SAVE** YOU ENOUGH MONEY ON A SILK DRESS, .. TO BUY A NICE SUIT .... OF CLOTHES **FOR YOUR HUSBAND.**

IF YOU ORDER GOODS TO BE SENT BY MAIL AND FAIL TO ENCLOSE SUFFICIENT POSTAGE, WE ARE COMPELLED TO HOLD YOUR ORDER UNTIL WE HEAR FROM YOU IF YOU SEND TOO MUCH, WE WILL REFUND BALANCE.

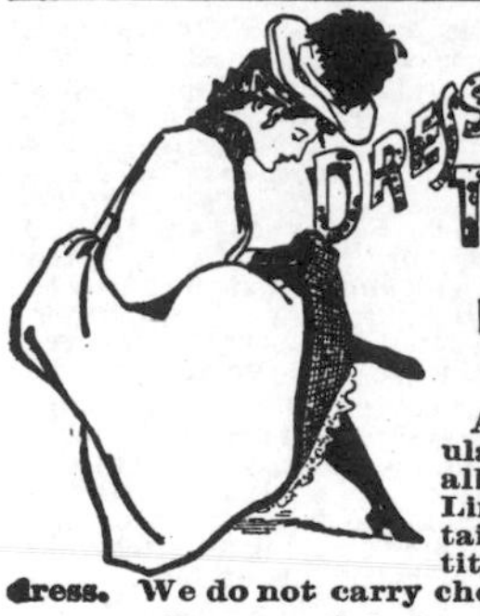
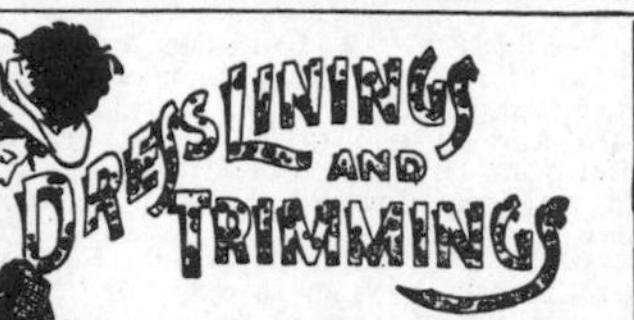


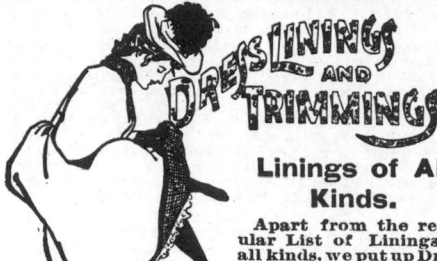

## Linings of All Kinds.

Apart from the regular List of Linings of all kinds, we put up Dress Linings in sets, each containing the regular quantity of material for a dress. We do not carry cheap, unreliable linings.

## Dress Linings in Sets.

**No. 22410 Lining Set,** put up in black, drab, slate and brown, contains 6 yards kid finished cambric, 2 yards corset, jean or waist lining and 1 yard wigan for stiffening. Price per set............$0.40

**No. 22411 Lining Set,** put up in black, drab, slate and brown, contains 6 yards kid finished cambric; 2 yards good Silesia waist lining; 1 yard French elastic canvas for skirt stiffening. Price per set ..............................$0.55

**No. 22413 Lining Set,** put up in black, drab, slate or brown, contains 6 yards good kid finish cambric; 2 yards silk finished percaline waist lining, and 1½ yards best imported linen canvas for skirt stiffeing. Price per set.........................$0.65

**No. 22415 Lining Set,** put up in black, drab or brown, contains 6 yards Taffeta or Rustle skirt lining; 2 yard Fancy Silesia waist lining and 1½ yards of best French canvas. Per set................$1.00

## Waist Linings.

**No, 22417 Rockford Sateen Finished Twilled Waist Lining** 27 inches wide, colors black, slate drab and brown and white. Price per yard...... $0.05

**No. 22417 Best Sateen Twilled Waist Lining** 27 inches wide; colors same as above. Price per yard......................................$0.07

## Silesias.

**For Waist Lining and Tailor's Use, Width 36 in.**

**No. 22420 Ascot Silesia,** very fine and closely woven, colors black, brown, slate and white. Per yard.........................................$0.08

**No. 22421 Columbia Silesias.** Very strong and firm. Comes in black and all staple colors. Per yard..........................................$0.10

**No. 22422 Roman Silesias.** Extra fine twill. Comes in black and all staple colors. Price per yard..........................................$0.15

**No. 22424 Fine Satin Finish Sarah Silesia.** Comes in fast black only. Price per yard.... $0.20

**No. 22425 Fancy Silesias,** come in stripes and figures both light and dark colors. Per yard $0.15

**No. 22426 Fancy Silesias.** Black one side, figured the other. This is a spendid quality and has a satin finish. Per yard.......................$0.20

**We do not send samples of linings or domestics.**

## Percalines.

**A Soft Waist Lining now Much Used.** While light in weight, it is firm and does not stretch, and is preferred to any other lining by ladies who have their dresses tightly fitted. Owing to its light silky texture it does not make bluky seams or enlarge the size of the dress waist.

**No. 22427 Percaline, Moire Silk Finished,** all colors, 36 inches wide. Per yard.............$0.12½
Full piece of about 55 yards. Per yard......... .12

**No. 22429 Madras Fast Black Percaline,** 36 inches wide. Per yard.........................$0.12½

**No. 22430 English Percaline,** extra fine quality, fast black and all colors. Per yard........$0.18

## Cambric or Skirt Linings.

**No. 22431 Best Soft Kid Finished Cambric;** colors; slate, drab, gray; light, medium or dark brown; black, tan myrtle, navy or wine; all dark. staple shades; 27 inches wide. Per yard...............$0.03½
Full piece of about 55 yards, no less.

**No. 22432 Soft Kid Finished Cambric;** 27 inches wide, high colors; cream, white, pink, light blue, scarlet, yellow, etc. Per yard...................$0.04¼
Full piece of about 55 yards ........................ .04¼

**No. 22433 Fast Black Cambric,** warranted perfectly fast dye; 27 inches wide. Per yard....$0.06
Full piece of about 49 yards........................0.05¾

**No. 22434 Soft Finished Cambric,** black one side, white the other; 25 inches wide. Per yard...$0.07
Full piece of about 50 yards.......................... .06¾

**No. 22435 Paper Cambric,** double fold, in black, brown, drab or slate; 36 inches wide.
Per yard.......................................................$0.07
Full piece of about 53 yards.......................... .06¾

**No. 22437 Paper Cambric,** double fold, in high colors; red, pink, white, light blue, dark blue, or green and orange; 36 inches wide. Per yard, $0.08
Full piece of about 54 yards........................ .07¾

## A New Skirt Lining.

**No. 22439 Taffeta or Rustle Lining** is an improved skirt lining, universally used by first class dress makers; it is of a fine texture, light weight, watered, and highly finished. It has just enough stiffness, and makes a pleasing rustling sound when worn, resembling silk; is a superior skirt lining in every way. The colors are: tan, medium brown, seal brown, light grey, medium drab, dark slate, black or white; width 27 inches. Per yard.. $0.08

**No. 22440 Morocco Rustle Lining;** width, 36 inches; extra quality, and very nice; comes in all colors, and also fast black. Per yard........ $0.12

## Linings for Stiffenings.

**For bottoms of dresses, collars and cuffs and tailors' use.**

Linings of this class are in great demand, owing to the present styles of wide bottom, flared or bell-shaped skirts.

**No. 22442 Wiggan, black, grey brown or white,** similar to crinoline, but stiffer, with less body than canvas; 33 inches wide. Per yard........... $0.07
Full piece of about 55 yards. Per yard....... .06¾

**No. 22444 Grass cloth,** a very light weight wiry stiffening much used for skirts and interlinings for large sleeves now so fashionable. It keeps the latter in shape without noticeably increasing the weight. Colors: Gray, brown, black, white or natural tan. Per yard.........................................$0.08

**No. 22446 Padding,** a stiff glazed lining for bottom of dresses, in black, cream, brown or slate; 27 inches wide. Per yard..............................$0.12
Full piece of about 66 yards. Per yard....... .11½

**No. 22448 Elastic canvas,** good quality, used for skirt stiffening. Black, brown or grey; width, 25 inches. Per yard.......................................$0.09

**No. 22449 Linen Canvas,** French elastic, the best lining for bottoms of dresses; it retains its stiffness longer than any other lining; no dress can set well without it. Colors, white, natural linen, brown grey or black. Medium grade. Per yard......$0.15
Full piece of about 50 yards, Per yard......... 0.13

**No. 22450 Linen French Elastic Canvas,** better quality than the above. Per yard...................$0.20
Full piece of about 50 yards. Per yard......... 0.19

**No. 22452 Crinoline,** 20 inches wide, for lining collars, cuffs, skirts, sleeves, etc., in black, brown, slate or white. Per yard.............................$0.07
Full piece of 12 yards. Per piece............... 0.75

**No. 22454 Crinoline;** width, 33 inches, black, brown, slate or white; extra heavy. Pr. yd....$0.10
Full piece of about 30 yards. Per yard........ 0.09¾

**No. 22456 Black Barred Crinoline.** 33 inches wide. Per yard......................................$0.10
Full piece of about 30 yards. Per yard........ 0.09¾

**No. 22458 Tailors' Canvas,** natural color only. Per yard..........................................$0.15

**No. 22460 Tailors' Canvas,** natural color only, better than above. Per yard.....................$0.18

**No. 22462 Imitation Hair Cloth,** grey striped; width, 17 inches; for skirt stiffening. This is a new, light-weight stiffening, made of elastic cotton, in exact imitation in color and texture of the imported hair cloth, and costs very much less.
Per yard...............................................$0.25
Full piece of about 45 yards. Per yard....... .23½

**No. 22463 Imitation Hair Cloth,** grey striped; width, 16 inches; used for stiffening skirts where something cheaper than real hair cloth is wanted. Per yard...............................................$0.15
Full piece of about 45 yards. Per yard......... .14

**No. 22464 Imported Grey Hair Cloth,** 16 inches wide. Per yard......................................$0.50
Full piece of about 65 yards. Per yard......... .47½

**No. 22465 Buckram,** similar to wiggan; 24 inches wide; put up in rolls; in black or white only.
Per yard...............................................$0.12
Full piece of about 8 yards. Per piece.......... .85

**No. 22467 Linen Scrim,** for stiffening sleeves, etc.; black, slate, brown, tan, cream or white; 27 inches wide. Per yard..............................$0.12½

## Oriental Fibre Lining.

**No. 22468 Special Fibre Interlining,** 64 inches wide; good weight and answers every purpose; colors, black, slate or natural. Per yard......$0.10

**No. 22469 Fibre Interlining,** made by the same process as Fibre Chamois, to supply a demand for something at a lower price and equally as good; 64 inches wide, in slate, natural or black. Cut lengths. Per yard...............................................$0.20

## Serge Coat Lining.

**No. 22470 Mohair Serge Lining,** 32 inches wide, black or brown only. Per yard....................$0.55

## Farmers' Satin and Italian Cloth.

**No. 22472 Farmers' Satin,** black; 27 inches wide. Per yard...............................................$0.25
Full piece of about 50 yards, per yard........ .23½

**No. 22474 Farmers' Satin,** black; 27 inches wide. Per yard...............................................$0.50
Full piece of about 50 yards per yard........... .48

**No. 22476 Farmers' Satin,** black; 54 inches wide. Per yard...............................................$1.00
Full piece of about 54 yards, per yard........... .95

**No. 22478 Farmers' Satin,** black; 54 inches wide. Per yard...............................................$1.25
Full piece of about 50 yards, per yard......... 1.14

**No. 22480 Farmers' Satin,** black; 54 inches wide. Per yard...............................................$1.40
Full piece of about 40 yards, per pard........... 1.30

**No. 22482 Farmers' Satin,** 27 inches wide, fine quality. Colors, navy blue, bottle green, old gold, wine, tan, golden brown, light blue, medium blue, dark brown and scarlet. Per yard............$0.40
Full piece of about 28 yards, per yard........... .37

## Fine Fancy Sateen Linings.

**No. 22484 Fancy Sateen Lining,** 36 inches wide, made in drab or slate, with small fancy figures printed in fast colors. Per yard...............$0.19
Full piece of about 50 yards, per yard............ .18

**No. 22486 Extra Fine Sateen Lining,** 38 inches wide, black on one side, tan and drab on the other, over which is printed neat designs in fast colors. This class of linings is now much used.
Per yard...............................................$0.24
Full piece of about 50 yards, per yard............ .23

Special Baby Carriage Catalogue

MAILED FREE ON APPLICATION.

## Flannel Department.

**Outing Flannel.**

This flannel is suitable for ladies' wrappers, waists, night robes, childrens' cloaks, also men's and boys' shirts and night shirts. We have a choice stock of stripes, checks, and soft mixtures.

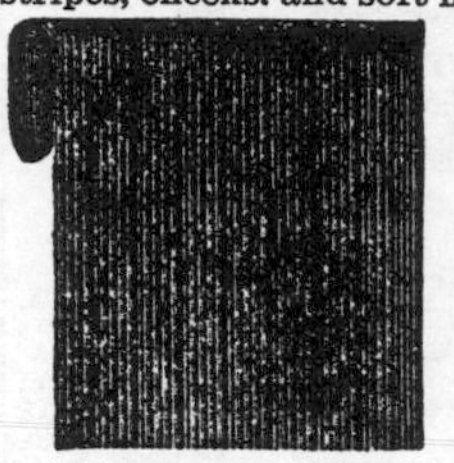

**No. 22488 Outing Flannel,** 27 inches wide; comes in stripes, both light and dark shades.
Per yard..........$0.05¼
Full piece of about 45 yards............ 0.05

**No. 22490 Outing Flannel,** soft and fleecy, superior quality of goods, in stripes only. Colors, grey, light blue, cream, light brown and and tan; 27 inches wide.
Per yard...........$0.06¾
Per piece of 45 yards, per yard............ 0.06

**No. 22496 Outing Twilled Flanellette,** comes in a beautiful assortment of stripes and plaids; has the appearance of an all-wool flannel worth 35c per yard. Colors blue, pink and tan stripes and plaids. This number is a special bargain, and the patterns are controlled by us; 29 inches wide.
Per yard...............................................$0.09
Full piece of 45 yards. Per yard.............. 0.08½

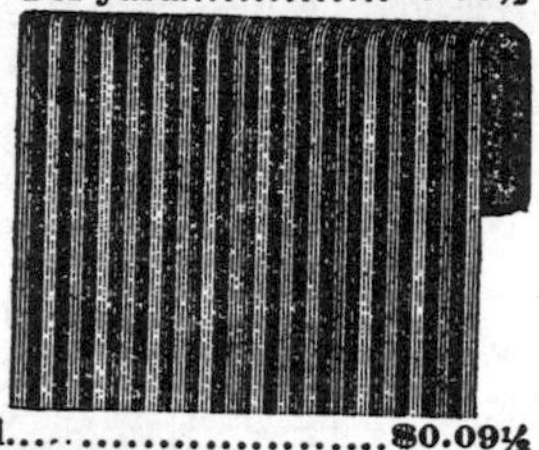

**No. 22498 The well known Amoskeag Teazle Down Outing Flannel.** This is a spring novelty; comes in an assortment of stripes and checks and lace stripe effects; in all colors of grounds, such as blue, pink, tan, red, green; stripes to match; 29 inches wide. Per yard..............................$0.09½

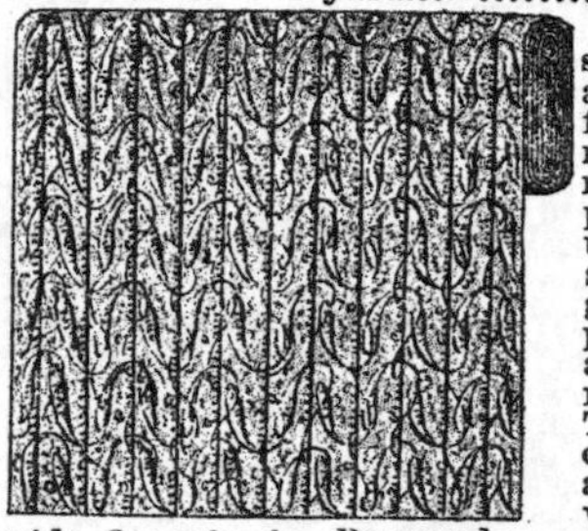

**No. 22499 Persian Flanellette,** an entirely new fabric, comes in a magnificent assortment of Persian patterns and is used very extensively for tea gowns and wrappers. The colors are light blue, old rose, green and red. This is a fabric of exceptional beauty and is very good value; 28 inches wide, fleece back. Per yard...... $0.12½

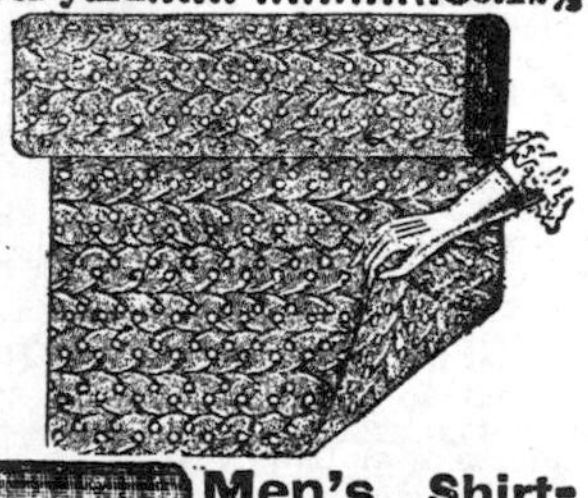

**No. 22500 Dresden Flannelette,** a very stylish and late material; this cloth makes up pretty in wrappers and tea gowns; the colors are blue, green, brown, red and black; fleece back; 28 inches wide.
Per yard...$0.12½

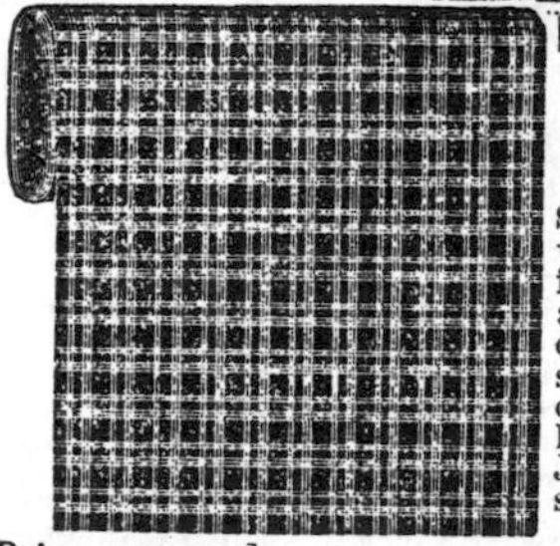

## Men's Shirting Twilled Flannel.

**No. 22501 Men's Shirting Flannel,** very fine twill; comes in very nice medium and light stripes and checks and lace stripes in the staple colors, also plain light and dark grey. Just the thing for summer shirts. Width, 28 inches.
Price, per yard.........................................$0.18

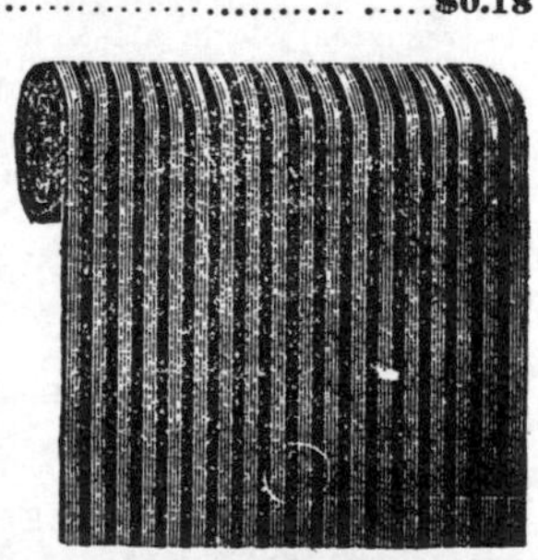

**No. 22502 All Wool Shirting Flannel** comes in a nice assortment of checks and stripes, fast colors, non-shrinkable and one of the latest patterns in the market, Width 28 inches.
Per yard...$0.25

NOTE—We were very fortunate in being able to obtain these goods at a figure that enables us to sell them at $0.25.

WE PUBLISH the most elaborate Organ and Piano Catalogue ever issued. More valuable hints on prices and value than any other house dare give.

LEAVE NOTHING FOR US TO GUESS AT WHEN YOU SEND YOUR ORDER. REMEMBER THAT THE ONLY WAY WE CAN KNOW THE SIZES, COLORS, &C., YOU WANT IS FOR YOU TO TELL US. MAKE YOUR ORDER PLAIN.

# BLACK DRESS GOODS DEPARTMENT

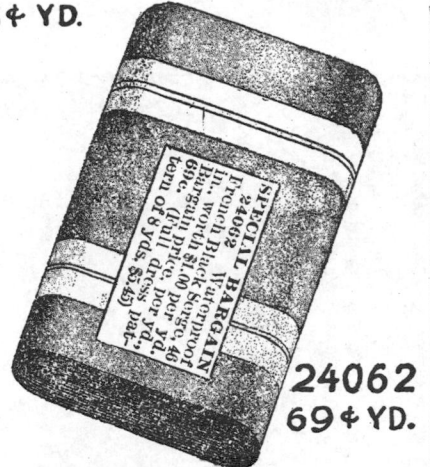

**24061** 45¢ YD.

**24060** 69¢ YD.

**24062** 69¢ YD.

SPECIAL BARGAIN 24061 Black French Serge, 46 inch. Per yard.... 45c (8 yd. dress pattern $3.50)

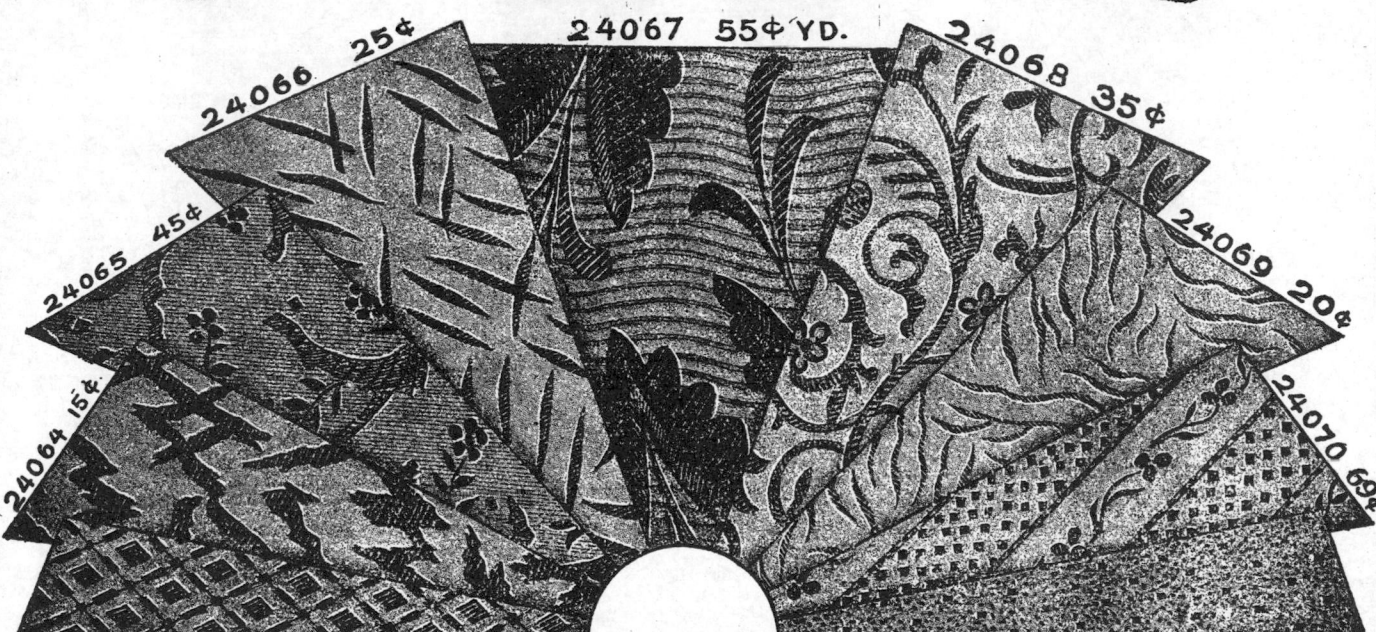

24067 55¢ YD. 24066 25¢ 24068 35¢ 24065 45¢ 24069 20¢ 24064 15¢ 24070 69¢

**24063** 12½¢ YD. **24071** 50¢ YD.

### Novelty Black Goods.
**24063** Novelty Black Goods, very popular now for skirts, comes in a great variety of patterns such as scrolls, dots, squares and leaf patterns. Price, per yard .................$0.12½

### Half Wool Black 27-inch Novelty Goods.
**24064** Half Wool Black 27-inch Novelty Goods, comes in a variety of floral and scroll designs. Some of the designs in this number, are very exclusive and are obtainable only from Sears, Roebuck & Co. Per yard.................$0.15

### Black Jacquared Cloth.
**24065** Black Jacquared Cloth, 37 inches wide, with a very fine twill, strictly all wool, very pretty patterns in small scroll effects, makes up beautifully in ladies skirts and can be worn the year round. Retailers usually ask 69 cents for this class of goods. Our very special price, per yard.................$0.45

### Black Mohair Brilliantine Dress Goods.
**24066** Black Mohair Brilliantine Dress Goods, 36-inches wide. Comes in a large variety of desirable patterns suitable for skirts and dresses. This cloth is a serviceable fabric and is a great big bargain at the price we sell it. Per yard.................$0.25

### Black Lizard Cloth.
**24067** Black Lizard Cloth, this is one of the novelties of the season, width 38 in., comes in handsome floral and raised designs. A very high grade of black goods which makes up into beautiful skirts, that can be worn with the nicest of silk waists, also a very nice material for entire suits. Regular value of cloth like this is 95 cents per yard, but it is only

because our European dress goods buyer closed out the entire lot of a leading French manufacturer that we are able to make this special price. Per yard.................$0.55

### Black Mohair Sicilian Dress Goods.
**24068** Black Mohair Sicilian Dress Goods, has the appearance of silk. This cloth makes up beautifully into skirts. A very large line of exclusive designs, some of which are to be obtained only from our house, width 38 inches, regular retail price 50 cents. Per yard.................$0.35

### Half Wool Black 34-inch Novelty Goods.
**24069** Half Wool Black 34-inch Novelty Goods, comes in a large variety of designs such as floral and scroll patterns. This is a very fair specimen of black goods and it is only through our system of cash buying, direct from the factory in large quantities, that we are enabled to offer such values. Per yard.................$0.20

### Black Satin Striped Novelty Goods.
**24070** Black Satin Striped Novelty Dress Goods, 38 inches wide, one of the richest things obtainable for skirts and ladies suits. comes in a very exclusive weave, that is only obtainable in high class stores in our foremost cities. A trial order of this goods will convince you of its merit and a dress pattern of these goods shown in any locality will sell hundreds of dresses for us. Per yard.................$0.69

### Black English Novelty Goods.
**24071** Black English Novelty Goods, 40 inches wide, with silk finished floral and scroll designs; a handsome thing for skirts. Per yard.................$0.50

# Sears, Roebuck & Co's INC

## BARGAINS IN DRESS GOODS.

24042 25¢ YD.  24043 12½¢ YD.

24040 12½¢ YD.  24041 12½¢ YD.  24044 12½¢ YD.  24045 20¢ YD.

24046 25¢ YD.  24047 35¢ YD  24050 50¢ YD.  24051 50¢ YD.

24048 48¢ YD.  24049 75¢ YD.

**24040 Novelty Dress Goods,** 28 inches wide, blue, red, brown and green ground, with black figure, a very stylish and handsome thing for children's dresses; this quality and pattern of goods is well worth 16 cents per yard. Our special price, per yard....................$0.12½

**24041 Scotch Plaids,** in green, tan and red, crepe effects; 28 inches wide, used largely for ladies' waists and children's dresses; this class of plaid is often sold as high as 18 cents at retail. S., R. & Co's price, per yard..............$0.12½

**24042 Novelty Boucle Plaid,** with raised effects, colors red, green and brown mixtures, 34 inches wide, this is a beautiful and very stylish pattern and well worth 39 cents per yard. Our special price per yard. $0.25

**24043 The Old Reliable Sheppard Plaids,** come in blue and white, black and white, and brown and white checks, used largely for skirts, 28 inches wide. Per yard....................................$0.12½

**24044 Novelty Plaids,** a beautiful raised effect, comes in all combinations of colors, 28 inches wide. When made up, this material will look better than goods retailers ask 18 cents for. Our special price per yard.....$0.12½

**24045 Novelty Effect,** this cloth looks a great deal like the imported goods; colors, blue, brown, red and green ground, with a black figure, a beautiful and handsome piece of dress goods, one that has a rich, fine effect when made up. Width 34 inches. Per yard...........................$0.20

**24046 A 40-inch Jacquard Cloth,** comes in light and dark blue, red, green and brown ground with black or colored figures of contrasting colors, makes into pretty skirts or dresses  Our price, per yard..............$0.25

**24047 Novelty Dress Goods,** raw silk and wool, 32 inches wide, colors, brown or green mixed, this is a handsome piece of dress goods and makes up very nicely. Per yard.....$0.35

**24048 All Worsted Novelty Dress Goods,** colors, green mixed with black and red mixed with black only, is 40 inches wide and a nobby stylish piece of goods, goods like these are obtainable in our large cities only and from dealers of fine goods, who ask as high as 75c for these goods. Our price per yard..................$0.48

**24049 Pure Silk and Wool Mixed Dress Goods,** colors, blue and gold mixed, red and black mixed, 40 inches wide; goods like these are only sold by dealers in high grade goods in the larger cities like Chicago and New York and these houses get big prices, often $1.25 per yard. Our price, per yard......................................$0.75

**24050 A Fancy Novelty All Wool Dress Goods,** comes in the following mixtures, brown and green, red and black, blue and gold 38 inches wide, a high grade of dress goods that will wear well and always look rich and grand, goods not nearly as showy as this are often sold at 75 cts per yard. Our price per yard..................$0.50

**24051 Wool and Silk Suiting,** 36 inches wide, colors, blue and white and green and white, makes up very handsomely into bicycle or walking suits, also makes very beautiful skirts and dresses, goods like these are usully sold by retailers at from 75 cents to 85 cents per yard. S., R. & Co's price per yard................................$0.50

# NOVELTIES IN SILK DRESS GOODS

**24340** — 25¢ YD.

**24341** — 85¢ YD.

**24342** — 72 ¢ YD

**24343**

**24344** — 50¢ YD

75¢

**24345** — 50¢ YD

**24346** — 45¢ YD

**24347** — 68¢

**24348** — 29 ¢ YD

**24349** — 90¢ YD

**24351** — 35¢ YD

**24350** — 67¢ YD

## SILK DEPARTMENT.

**24340** A 20-inch Imported China Silk, colors, blue and pink, white and pink, and salmon and white checks.
Our special price, per yard................................$0.25

**24341** A very stylish Black Brocaded Silk, of a high grade. 24 inches wide.
Per yard.........................................$0.85

**24342** Dresden Washable Silks, tinted patterns cream ground, combinations pink and cream, old rose and green and heliotrope and green. All silk and very stylish and pretty for waists; 23 inches wide.
Per yard.........................................$0.72

**24343** Good Quality Black Brocaded Satin, 19 inches wide.
Per yard...........................................$0.50

**24344** Cannelle, All Silk, Changeable, Pretty Floral Designs, 19 inches wide; colors, red and black, blue and green, gray and gold, pink and green, drab and green.
Our special price...................................$0.75

**24345** Plain Black Crystal Silk, 19 inches wide.
Per yard.........................................$0.50

**24346** A Novelty Silk, changeable floral designs; colors, saphire blue with gold, black with green, green with blue, red with blue, drab and green, drab and blue and red with black, 19 inches wide.
Our price, per yard................................$0.45

**24347** A Black Gros Grain Silk, 19 inches wide, has a figured design, large and small pattern.
Per yard.........................................$0.68

**24348** Fancy Cotton Back Silks, 19 inches wide, beautiful mixtures of blue and gold, red and green, drab and red and also black.
Per yard.........................................$0.29

**24349** Black Brocaded Silk, a very fine quality, makes up beautifully in skirts, 21½ inches wide. Per yard...............$0.90

**24350** A very nice Imported Washable China Silk, (all silk) navy blue ground, with white lace effects, large and small designs, 27 inches wide.
Per yard.........................................$0.67

**24351** Fancy Illuminated Novelty Silk, 19 inches wide and has a floral figure. The colors are red and gold, drab and gold, green and red and also plain black.
Per yard .........................................$0.35

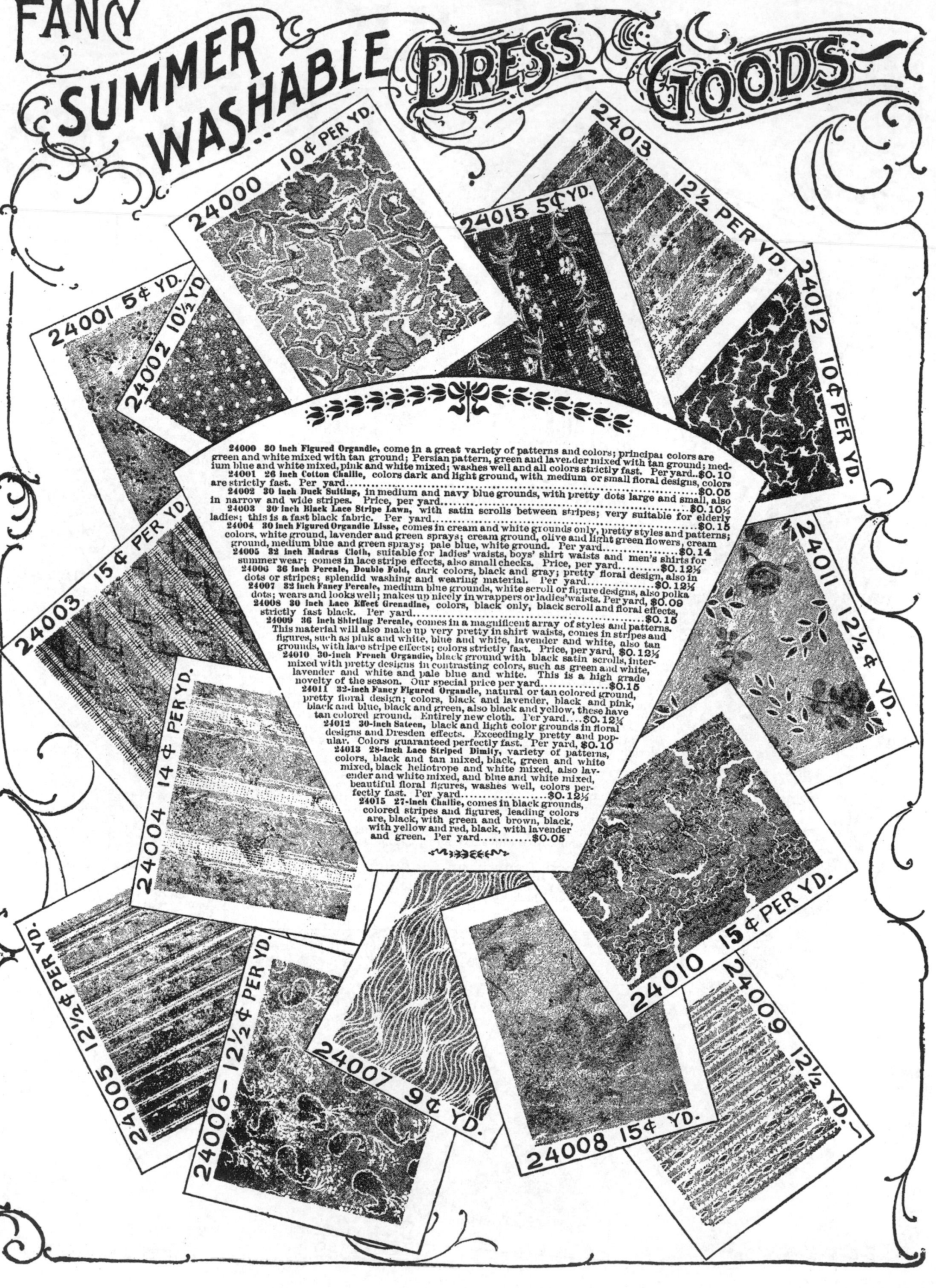

# FANCY SUMMER WASHABLE DRESS GOODS

**24000** 10¢ PER YD. — **24013** 12½ PER YD. — **24015** 5¢ YD. — **24012** 10¢ PER YD. — **24001** 5¢ YD. — **24002** 10½ YD. — **24003** 15¢ PER YD. — **24011** 12½¢ YD. — **24004** 14¢ PER YD. — **24005** 12½¢ PER YD. — **24006** 12½¢ PER YD. — **24007** 9¢ YD. — **24008** 15¢ YD. — **24009** 12½¢ YD. — **24010** 15¢ PER YD.

**24000** 30 inch Figured Organdie, come in a great variety of patterns and colors; principal colors are green and white mixed with tan ground; Persian pattern, green and lavender mixed with tan ground; medium blue and white mixed, pink and white mixed; washes well and all colors strictly fast. Per yard..$0.10

**24001** 26 inch Cotton Challie, colors dark and light ground, with medium or small floral designs, colors are strictly fast. Per yard.................................................................$0.05

**24002** 30 inch Duck Suiting, in medium and navy blue grounds, with pretty dots large and small, also in narrow and wide stripes. Price, per yard..........................................$0.10½

**24003** 30 inch Black Lace Stripe Lawn, with satin scrolls between stripes; very suitable for elderly ladies; this is a fast black fabric. Per yard.............................................$0.15

**24004** 30 inch Figured Organdie Lisse, comes in cream and white grounds only, pretty styles and patterns; colors, white ground, lavender and green sprays; cream ground, olive and light green flowers, cream ground, medium blue and green sprays; pale blue, white ground. Per yard.........$0.14

**24005** 32 inch Madras Cloth, suitable for ladies' waists, boys' shirt waists and men's shirts for summer wear; comes in lace stripe effects, also small checks. Price, per yard..........$0.12½

**24006** 36 inch Percale, Double Fold, dark colors, black and gray; pretty floral design, also in dots or stripes; splendid washing and wearing material. Per yard...........................$0.12¾

**24007** 32 inch Fancy Percale, medium blue grounds, white scroll or figure designs, also polka dots; wears and looks well; makes up nicely in wrappers or ladies' waists. Per yard, $0.09

**24008** 30 inch Lace Effect Grenadine, colors, black only, black scroll and floral effects, strictly fast black. Per yard..........................................................................$0.15

**24009** 36 inch Shirting Percale, comes in a magnificent array of styles and patterns. This material will also make up very pretty in shirt waists, comes in stripes and figures, such as pink and white, blue and white, lavender and white, also tan grounds, with lace stripe effects; colors strictly fast. Price, per yard, $0.12½

**24010** 30-inch French Organdie, black ground with black satin scrolls, intermixed with pretty designs in contrasting colors, such as green and white, lavender and white and pale blue and white. This is a high grade novelty of the season. Our special price per yard................$0.15

**24011** 32-inch Fancy Figured Organdie, natural or tan colored ground, pretty floral design; colors, black and lavender, black and pink, black and blue, black and green, also black and yellow, these have tan colored ground. Entirely new cloth. Per yard....$0.12½

**24012** 30-inch Sateen, black and light color grounds in floral designs and Dresden effects. Exceedingly pretty and popular. Colors guaranteed perfectly fast. Per yard, $0.10

**24013** 28-inch Lace Striped Dimity, variety of patterns, colors, black and tan mixed, black, green and white mixed, black heliotrope and white mixed, also lavender and white mixed, and blue and white mixed, beautiful floral figures, washes well, colors perfectly fast. Per yard..................$0.12½

**24015** 27-inch Challie, comes in black grounds, colored stripes and figures, leading colors are, black, with green and brown, black, with yellow and red, black, with lavender and green. Per yard...........$0.05

SEARS, ROEBUCK & CO'S. INC

# RIBBON DEPARTMENT.

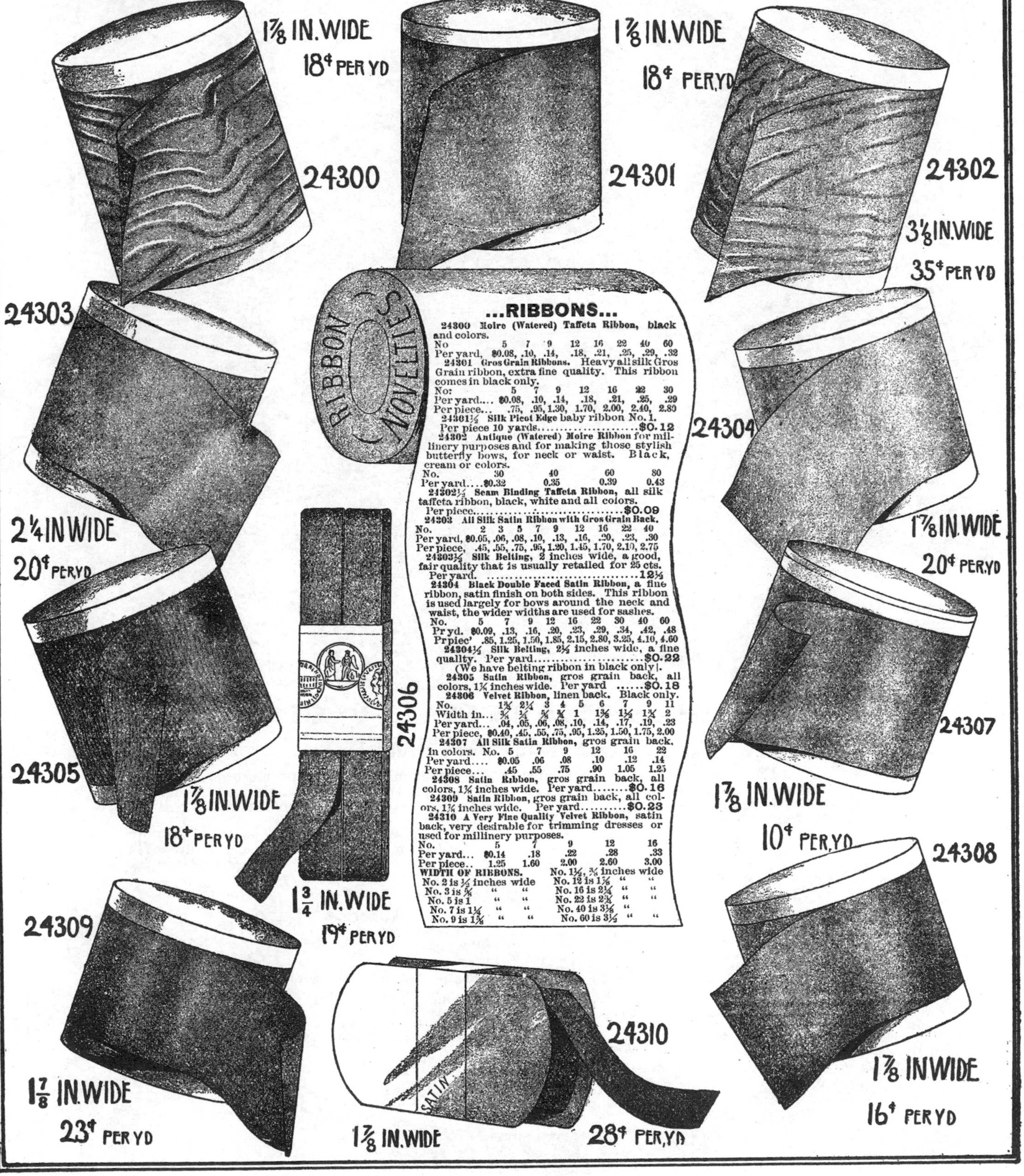

1⅞ IN. WIDE
18¢ PER YD
24300
1⅞ IN. WIDE
18¢ PER YD
24301
24302
3⅛ IN. WIDE
35¢ PER YD
24303
2¼ IN WIDE
20¢ PER YD
RIBBON NOVELTIES
24304
1⅞ IN. WIDE
20¢ PER YD
24305
1⅞ IN. WIDE
18¢ PER YD
24306
1¾ IN. WIDE
19¢ PER YD
24307
1⅞ IN. WIDE
10¢ PER YD
24308
24309
1⅞ IN. WIDE
23¢ PER YD
24310
SATIN
1⅞ IN. WIDE
28¢ PER YD
1⅞ IN WIDE
16¢ PER YD


## ...RIBBONS...

**24300 Moire (Watered) Taffeta Ribbon,** black and colors.

| No | 5 | 7 | 9 | 12 | 16 | 22 | 40 | 60 |
|---|---|---|---|---|---|---|---|---|
| Per yard, | $0.08, | .10, | .14, | .18, | .21, | .25, | .29, | .32 |

**24301 Gros Grain Ribbons.** Heavy all silk Gros Grain ribbon, extra fine quality. This ribbon comes in black only.

| No: | 5 | 7 | 9 | 12 | 16 | 22 | 30 |
|---|---|---|---|---|---|---|---|
| Per yard.... | $0.08, | .10, | .14, | .18, | .21, | .25, | .29 |
| Per piece... | .75, | .95, | 1.30, | 1.70, | 2.00, | 2.40, | 2.80 |

**24301½ Silk Picot Edge** baby ribbon No. 1. Per piece 10 yards........................$0.12

**24302 Antique (Watered) Moire Ribbon** for millinery purposes and for making those stylish butterfly bows, for neck or waist. Black, cream or colors.

| No. | 30 | 40 | 60 | 80 |
|---|---|---|---|---|
| Per yard.... | $0.32 | 0.35 | 0.39 | 0.43 |

**24302½ Seam Binding Taffeta Ribbon,** all silk taffeta ribbon, black, white and all colors. Per piece...............................$0.09

**24303 All Silk Satin Ribbon with Gros Grain Back.**

| No. | 2 | 3 | 5 | 7 | 9 | 12 | 16 | 22 | 40 |
|---|---|---|---|---|---|---|---|---|---|
| Per yard, | $0.05, | .06, | .08, | .10, | .13, | .16, | .20, | .23, | .30 |
| Per piece, | .45, | .55, | .75, | .95, | 1.20, | 1.45, | 1.70, | 2.10, | 2.75 |

**24303½ Silk Belting,** 2 inches wide, a good, fair quality that is usually retailed for 25 cts. Per yard. ...............................12½

**24304 Black Double Faced Satin Ribbon,** a fine ribbon, satin finish on both sides. This ribbon is used largely for bows around the neck and waist, the wider widths are used for sashes.

| No. | 5 | 7 | 9 | 12 | 16 | 22 | 30 | 40 | 60 |
|---|---|---|---|---|---|---|---|---|---|
| Pr yd. | $0.09, | .13, | .16, | .20, | .23, | .29, | .34, | .42, | .48 |
| Pr piec' | .85, | 1.25, | 1.50, | 1.85, | 2.15, | 2.80, | 3.25, | 4.10, | 4.60 |

**24304½ Silk Belting,** 2½ inches wide, a fine quality. Per yard.........................$0.22

(We have belting ribbon in black only).

**24305 Satin Ribbon,** gros grain back, all colors, 1⅞ inches wide. Per yard ......$0.18

**24306 Velvet Ribbon,** linen back. Black only.

| No. | 1½ | 2¼ | 3 | 4 | 5 | 6 | 7 | 9 | 11 |
|---|---|---|---|---|---|---|---|---|---|
| Width in... | ⅜ | ¼ | ⅝ | ¾ | 1 | 1⅜ | 1½ | 1¾ | 2 |
| Per yard... | .04, | .05, | .06, | .08, | .10, | .14, | .17, | .19, | .23 |
| Per piece, | $0.40, | .45, | .55, | .75, | .95, | 1.25, | 1.50, | 1.75, | 2.00 |

**24307 All Silk Satin Ribbon,** gros grain back, in colors.

| No. | 5 | 7 | 9 | 12 | 16 | 22 |
|---|---|---|---|---|---|---|
| Per yard.... | $0.05 | .06 | .08 | .10 | .12 | .14 |
| Per piece... | .45 | .55 | .75 | .90 | 1.05 | 1.25 |

**24308 Satin Ribbon,** gros grain back, all colors, 1⅞ inches wide. Per yard........$0.16

**24309 Satin Ribbon,** gros grain back, all colors, 1⅞ inches wide. Per yard..........$0.23

**24310 A Very Fine Quality Velvet Ribbon,** satin back, very desirable for trimming dresses or used for millinery purposes.

| No. | 5 | 7 | 9 | 12 | 16 |
|---|---|---|---|---|---|
| Per yard... | $0.14 | .18 | .22 | .28 | .33 |
| Per piece.. | 1.25 | 1.60 | 2.00 | 2.60 | 3.00 |

**WIDTH OF RIBBONS.**

| | |
|---|---|
| | No. 1½, ⅜ inches wide |
| No. 2 is ½ inches wide | No. 12 is 1⅞ " " |
| No. 3 is ⅝ " " | No. 16 is 2¼ " " |
| No. 5 is 1 " " | No. 22 is 2¾ " " |
| No. 7 is 1¼ " " | No. 40 is 3⅛ " |
| No. 9 is 1⅝ " " | No. 60 is 3½ " " |

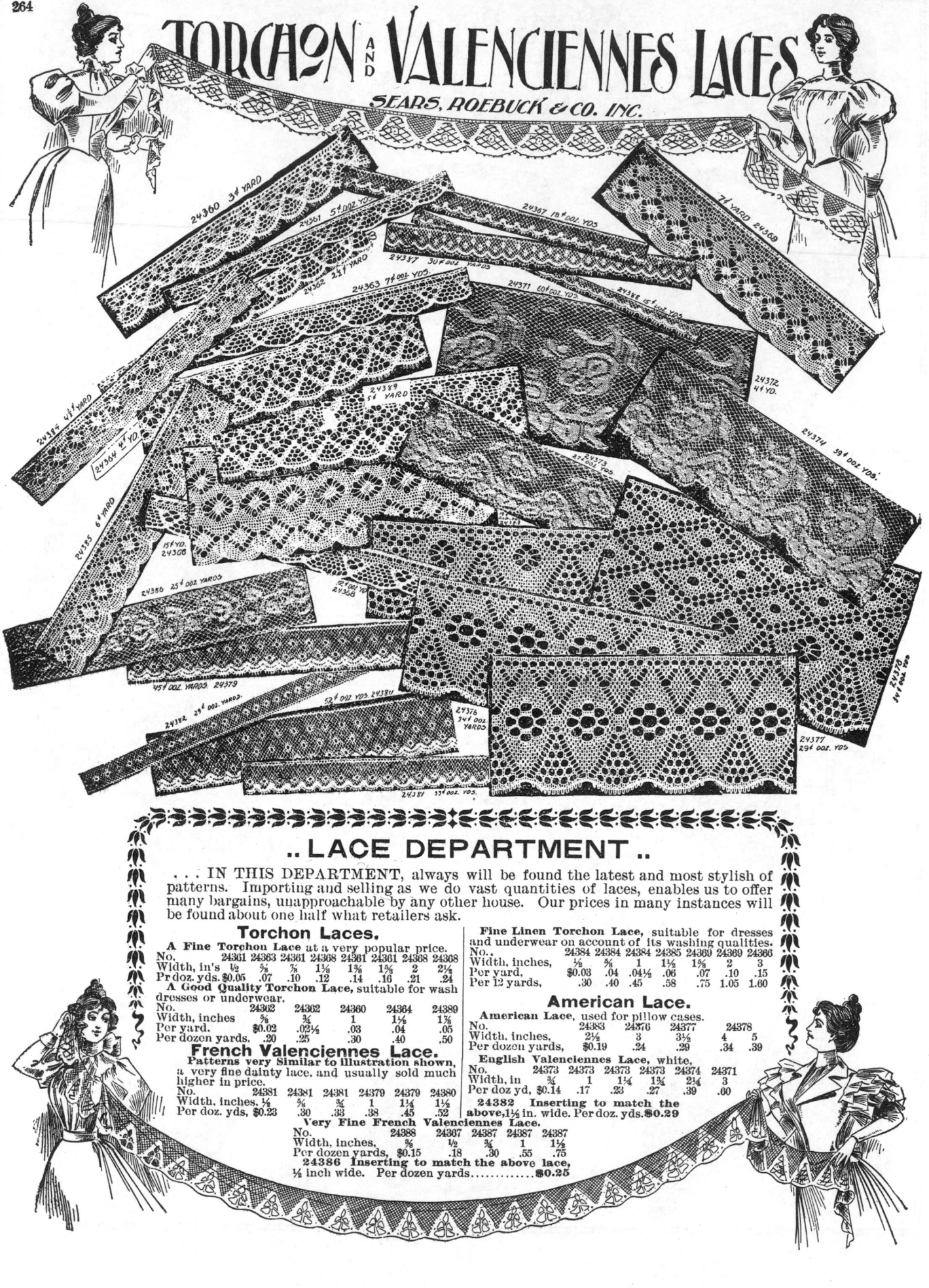

# TORCHON AND VALENCIENNES LACES

SEARS, ROEBUCK & CO. INC.

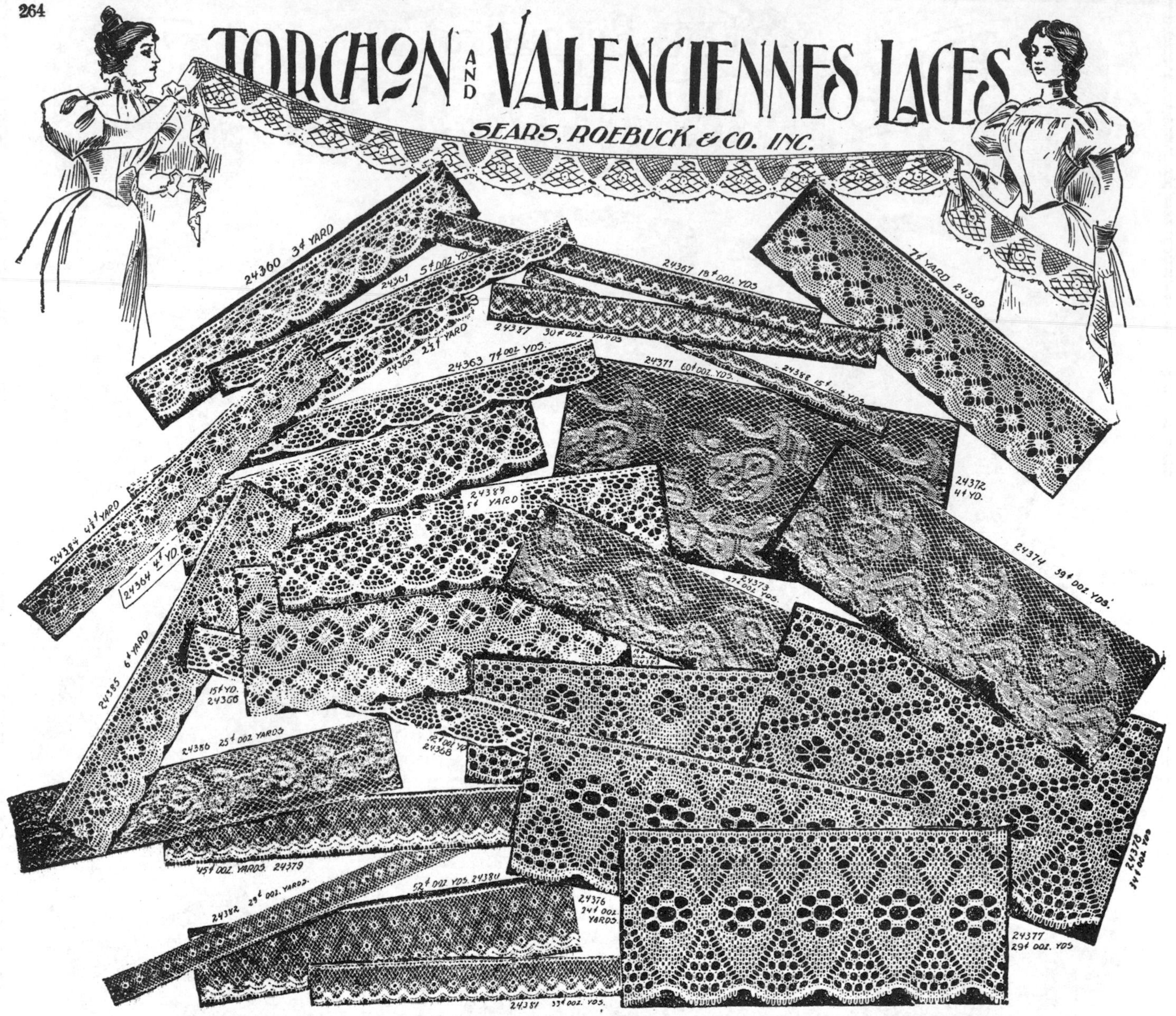


## .. LACE DEPARTMENT ..

. . . IN THIS DEPARTMENT, always will be found the latest and most stylish of patterns. Importing and selling as we do vast quantities of laces, enables us to offer many bargains, unapproachable by any other house. Our prices in many instances will be found about one half what retailers ask.

### Torchon Laces.

**A Fine Torchon Lace** at a very popular price.

| No. | 24361 | 24363 | 24361 | 24368 | 24361 | 24361 | 24368 | 24368 |
|---|---|---|---|---|---|---|---|---|
| Width, in's | ½ | ⅝ | ⅞ | 1⅛ | 1⅜ | 1⅝ | 2 | 2½ |
| Pr doz. yds. | $0.05 | .07 | .10 | .12 | .14 | .16 | .21 | .24 |

**A Good Quality Torchon Lace,** suitable for wash dresses or underwear.

| No. | 24362 | 24362 | 24360 | 24364 | 24389 |
|---|---|---|---|---|---|
| Width, inches | ⅝ | ¾ | 1 | 1½ | 1⅞ |
| Per yard. | $0.02 | .02½ | .03 | .04 | .05 |
| Per dozen yards. | .20 | .25 | .30 | .40 | .50 |

### French Valenciennes Lace.

**Patterns very Similar to illustration shown,** a very fine dainty lace, and usually sold much higher in price.

| No. | 24381 | 24381 | 24381 | 24379 | 24379 | 24380 |
|---|---|---|---|---|---|---|
| Width, inches. | ⅛ | ⅝ | ¾ | 1 | 1¼ | 1½ |
| Per doz. yds, | $0.23 | .30 | .33 | .38 | .45 | .52 |

**Fine Linen Torchon Lace,** suitable for dresses and underwear on account of its washing qualities.

| No. | 24384 | 24384 | 24384 | 24385 | 24369 | 24369 | 24366 |
|---|---|---|---|---|---|---|---|
| Width, inches, | ½ | ⅝ | 1 | 1¼ | 1⅝ | 2 | 3 |
| Per yard, | $0.03 | .04 | .04½ | .06 | .07 | .10 | .15 |
| Per 12 yards, | .30 | .40 | .45 | .58 | .75 | 1.05 | 1.60 |

### American Lace.

**American Lace,** used for pillow cases.

| No. | 24383 | 24376 | 24377 | 24378 | |
|---|---|---|---|---|---|
| Width, inches, | 2½ | 3 | 3½ | 4 | 5 |
| Per dozen yards, | $0.19 | .24 | .29 | .34 | .39 |

**English Valenciennes Lace,** white,

| No. | 24373 | 24373 | 24373 | 24373 | 24374 | 24371 |
|---|---|---|---|---|---|---|
| Width, in | ¾ | 1 | 1¼ | 1¾ | 2¼ | 3 |
| Per doz yd, | $0.14 | .17 | .23 | .27 | .39 | .60 |

**24382 Inserting to match the above,** 1½ in. wide. Per doz. yds. **$0.29**

**Very Fine French Valenciennes Lace.**

| No. | 24388 | 24367 | 24387 | 24387 | 24387 |
|---|---|---|---|---|---|
| Width, inches, | ⅜ | ½ | ¾ | 1 | 1½ |
| Per dozen yards, | $0.15 | .18 | .30 | .55 | .75 |

**24386 Inserting to match the above lace,** ½ inch wide. Per dozen yards............**$0.25**

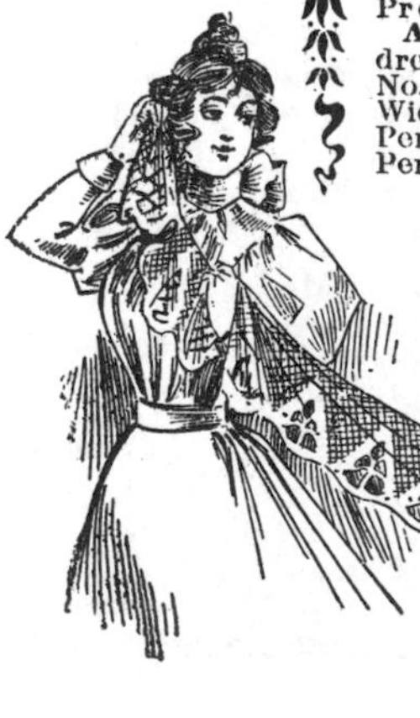
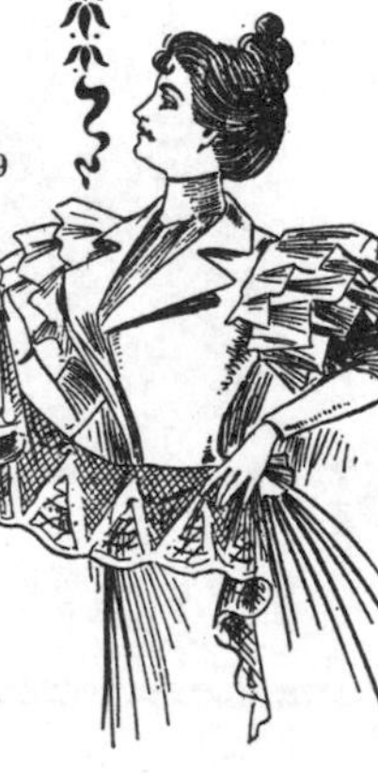
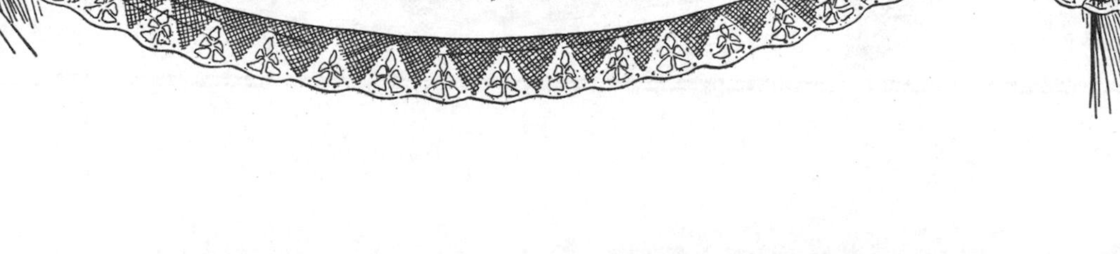

# CREAM, BUTTER-COLOR AND BLACK Oriental, Chantilly and Spanish Laces

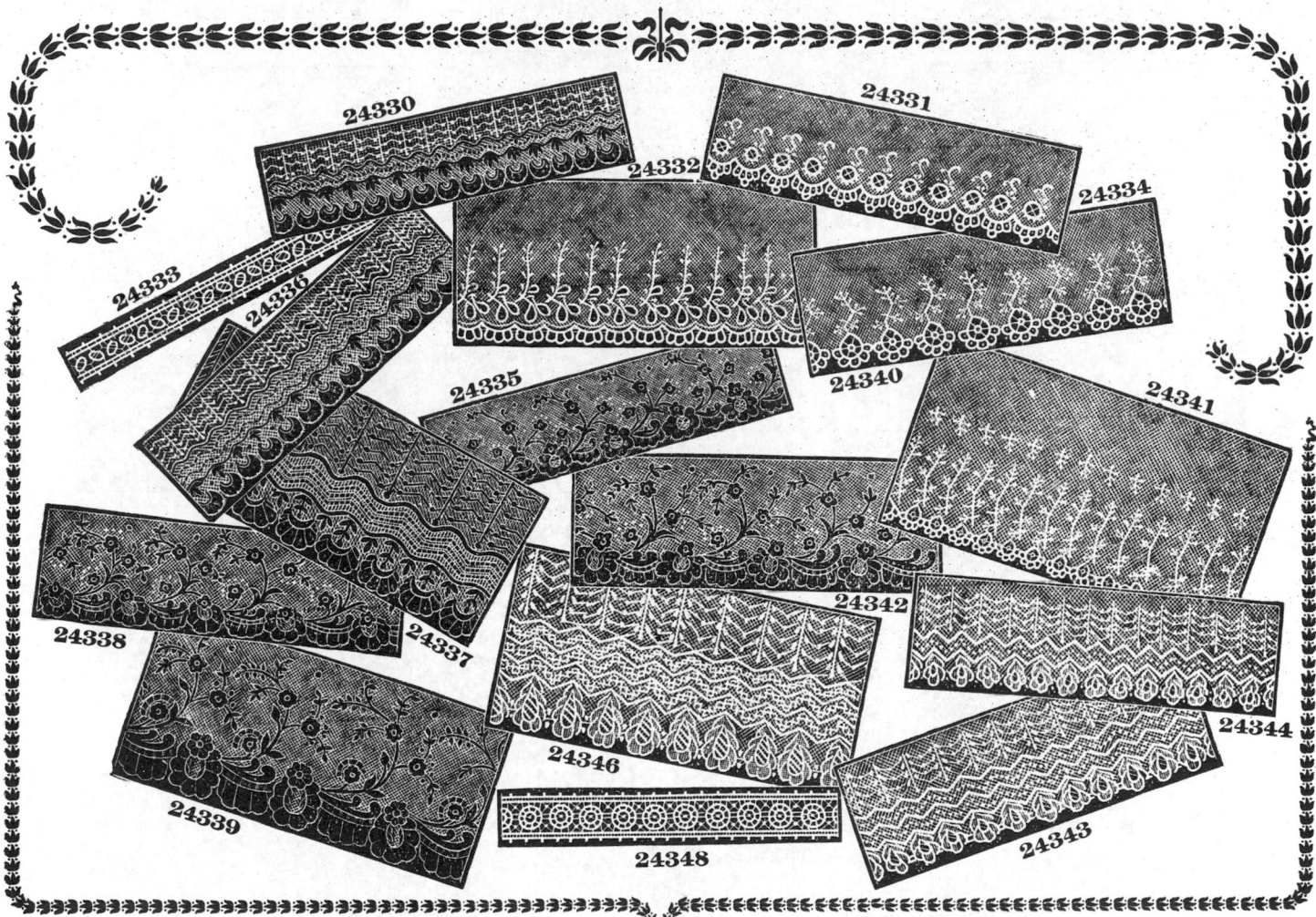

## White Oriental Lace.

| Nos | 24334 | 24334 | 24334 |
|---|---|---|---|
| Width, inches | 4 | 5½ | 7½ |
| Per yard | 7c | 11c | 15c |

## Black Silk Chantilly Lace.

Nice Quality Chantilly Lace, usually sold at a much higher price.

| Nos | 24330 | 24336 | 24337 |
|---|---|---|---|
| Width, inches | 3 | 4 | 6 |
| Per yard | 8c | 10c | 12c |

Good Quality Silk Chantilly Laces, black or cream, pattern about like illustration.

| Nos | 24332 | 24332 | 24332 | 24332 |
|---|---|---|---|---|
| Width, inches | 3 | 4 | 5 | 6 |
| Per yard | 15c | 17c | 21c | 26c |

This Handsome Black Silk Chantilly Lace is of a very fine quality and has a rich and beautiful effect.

| Nos | 24335 | 24335 | 24335 | 24342 |
|---|---|---|---|---|
| Width, inches | 3 | 4 | 5 | 6 |
| Per yard | 28c | 38c | 46c | 55c |

A Very Pretty White Silk Lace Chantilly, patterns about like illustration.

| Nos | 24344 | 24340 | 24346 |
|---|---|---|---|
| Width, inches | 4 | 4½ | 6 |
| Per yard | 8c | 9c | 10c |

## Butter Color Oriental Laces.

Very Handsome Butter Color Oriental Laces, very stylish and handsome, novelty edge, beautiful patterns.

| Nos | 24343 | 24332 | 24332 | 24341 |
|---|---|---|---|---|
| Width, inches | 3 | 4 | 8 | 9 |
| Per yard | 7c | 10c | 16c | 19c |

Inserting for the above laces, butter color.
24333  1 inch wide, per yard.........................8c
24348  1½ inch wide, per yard.........................15c

## Raised Valenciennes Lace.

### CREAM OR BUTTER COLOR.

A Very Handsome Raised Valenciennes Lace, entirely new and will be largely used this season.

| Nos | 24331 | 24331 | 24331 | 24331 |
|---|---|---|---|---|
| Width, inches | 2 | 2½ | 4½ | 5½ |
| Per yard | 9c | 11c | 15c | 25c |

## Spanish Lace.

Black Silk Spanish Guipure Lace, for dress trimming.

| Nos | 24338 | 24339 | 24339 |
|---|---|---|---|
| Width, inches | 3½ | 4½ | 6 |
| Per yard | 14c | 19c | 24c |

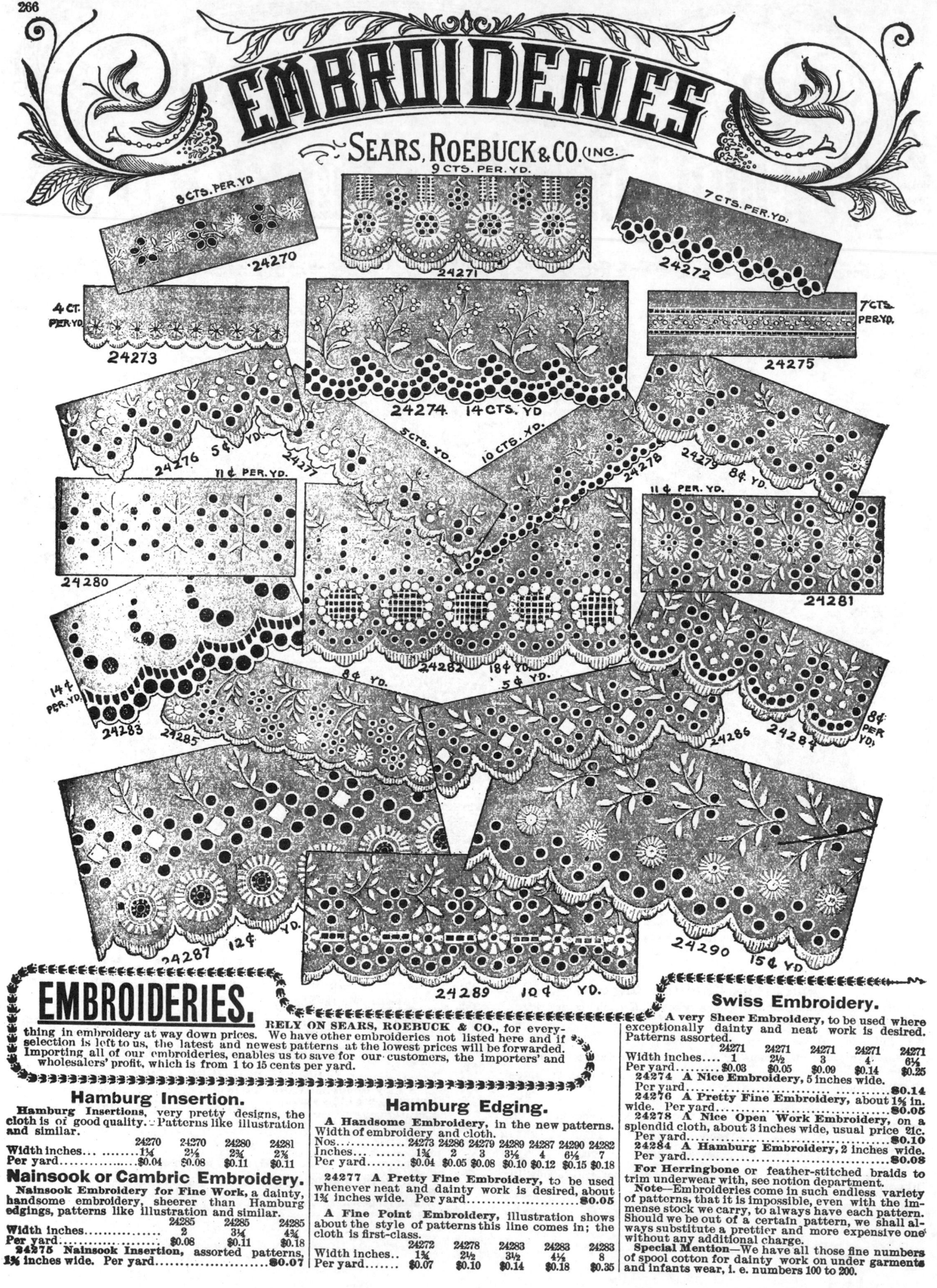

# EMBROIDERIES

SEARS, ROEBUCK & CO. (INC.

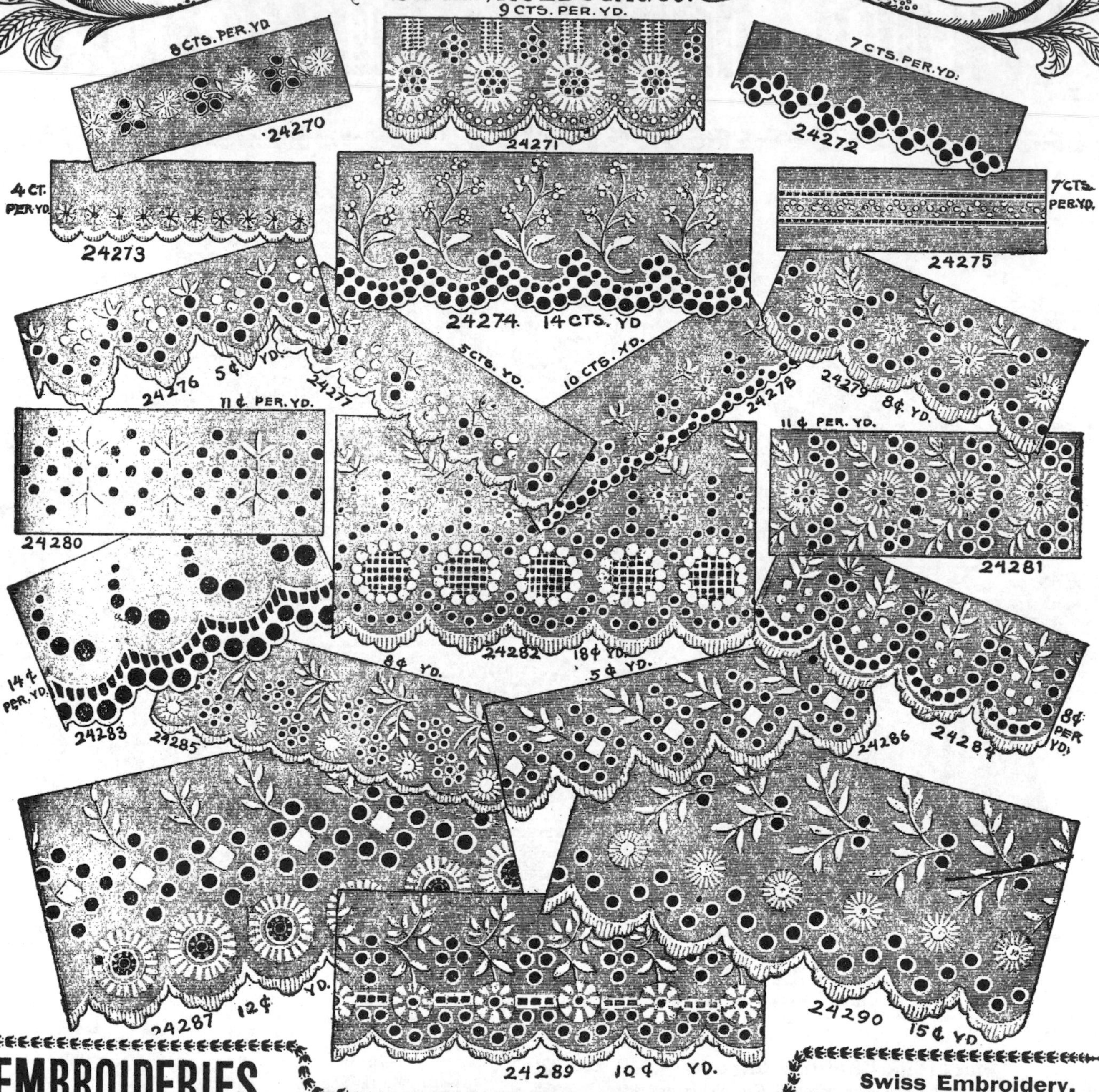
9 CTS. PER. YD.
8 CTS. PER. YD.
24270
24271
7 CTS. PER. YD.
24272
4 CT. PER. YD.
24273
24274 14 CTS. YD
7 CTS. PER. YD.
24275
24276 5¢ YD.
5 CTS. YD.
24277
10 CTS. YD.
24278
24279 8¢ YD.
11¢ PER. YD.
24280
11¢ PER. YD.
24281
24282 18¢ YD.
8¢ YD.
5¢ YD.
14¢ PER. YD.
24283
24285
24286
24284
8¢ PER YD.
24287 12¢ YD.
24290 15¢ YD.
24289 10¢ YD.

## EMBROIDERIES.

**RELY ON SEARS, ROEBUCK & CO.**, for everything in embroidery at way down prices. We have other embroideries not listed here and if selection is left to us, the latest and newest patterns at the lowest prices will be forwarded. Importing all of our embroideries, enables us to save for our customers, the importers' and wholesalers' profit, which is from 1 to 15 cents per yard.

### Hamburg Insertion.

**Hamburg Insertions**, very pretty designs, the cloth is of good quality. Patterns like illustration and similar.

| | 24270 | 24270 | 24280 | 24281 |
|---|---|---|---|---|
| Width inches........... | 1¼ | 2½ | 2¾ | 2⅞ |
| Per yard.................. | $0.04 | $0.08 | $0.11 | $0.11 |

### Nainsook or Cambric Embroidery.

**Nainsook Embroidery for Fine Work**, a dainty, handsome embroidery, sheerer than Hamburg edgings, patterns like illustration and similar.

| | 24285 | 24285 | 24285 |
|---|---|---|---|
| Width inches................ | 2 | 3¼ | 4¾ |
| Per yard.................... | $0.08 | $0.11 | $0.18 |

**24275 Nainsook Insertion**, assorted patterns, 1⅜ inches wide. Per yard........................**$0.07**

### Hamburg Edging.

**A Handsome Embroidery**, in the new patterns. Width of embroidery and cloth.

| Nos.............. | 24273 | 24286 | 24279 | 24289 | 24287 | 24290 | 24282 |
|---|---|---|---|---|---|---|---|
| Inches........... | 1¾ | 2 | 3 | 3½ | 4 | 6½ | 7 |
| Per yard........ | $0.04 | $0.05 | $0.08 | $0.10 | $0.12 | $0.15 | $0.18 |

**24277 A Pretty Fine Embroidery**, to be used whenever neat and dainty work is desired, about 1¾ inches wide. Per yard.........................**$0.05**

**A Fine Point Embroidery**, illustration shows about the style of patterns this line comes in; the cloth is first-class.

| | 24272 | 24278 | 24283 | 24283 | 24283 |
|---|---|---|---|---|---|
| Width inches.. | 1¾ | 2½ | 3½ | 4½ | 8 |
| Per yard....... | $0.07 | $0.10 | $0.14 | $0.18 | $0.35 |

### Swiss Embroidery.

**A very Sheer Embroidery**, to be used where exceptionally dainty and neat work is desired. Patterns assorted.

| | 24271 | 24271 | 24271 | 24271 | 24271 |
|---|---|---|---|---|---|
| Width inches.... | 1 | 2½ | 3 | 4 | 6½ |
| Per yard......... | $0.03 | $0.05 | $0.09 | $0.14 | $0.25 |

**24274 A Nice Embroidery**, 5 inches wide. Per yard...................................**$0.14**

**24276 A Pretty Fine Embroidery**, about 1⅝ in. wide. Per yard...................................**$0.05**

**24278 A Nice Open Work Embroidery**, on a splendid cloth, about 3 inches wide, usual price 21c. Per yard...................................**$0.10**

**24284 A Hamburg Embroidery**, 2 inches wide. Per yard...................................**$0.08**

**For Herringbone** or feather-stitched braids to trim underwear with, see notion department.

**Note**—Embroideries come in such endless variety of patterns, that it is impossible, even with the immense stock we carry, to always have each pattern. Should we be out of a certain pattern, we shall always substitute a prettier and more expensive one without any additional charge.

**Special Mention**—We have all those fine numbers of spool cotton for dainty work on under garments and infants wear, i. e. numbers 100 to 200.

# Ladies' Ready-to-Wear Clothing

## FOR SPRING AND SUMMER OF 1897.

For the Spring and Summer of 1897 we offer a line of Ladies' Waists, Skirts, Wrappers, Cloaks and Dresses, which for style, quality of material and make cannot be equalled elsewhere at anything like the price. We have made our preparations for the coming season's business on such an extensive scale that we have been able to reduce the cost of production to the very lowest mark, and by adhering strictly to our one small profit plan we are prepared to supply our customers with anything in this line for even less money than the average dealer is compelled to pay when ordering in quantities.

## STYLES GUARANTEED THE VERY LATEST FOR SPRING AND SUMMER.

The garments we offer in the following pages are cut on the very latest style patterns and made up in the best possible manner. The quality of material used is of the very latest. We have made our selections with great care and with a view to insuring perfect satisfaction in every case. We employ only the most skilled cutters and tailors and make a class of goods that will compare favorably with the lines handled by the most fashionable tailors in large cities where fancy prices are always secured.

## DO NOT PAY RETAIL PRICES

For this class of merchandise. With our facilities for securing material at first cost to produce, and being in position to manufacture the same at the minimum cost and always in the very latest style, we can supply you with any garment wanted for spring and summer at about what the material alone would cost you if bought of your local dealer.

## YOU CAN NOT AFFORD

To buy the material and make a waist, skirt, wrapper, dress or other garment, nor can you afford to pay a dressmaker for making such garments, when you can buy from us the finished garments for the price of the material alone in your own market.

### You will Find our Garments Distinctively Different from those Carried by the Average Retail Dealer.

They will not only be made of the very latest material, fabrics which have been woven expressly for this season's wear, but they will be cut on the very latest style patterns, the same as are used by the best tailors in metropolitan cities. They will be made up in the finest style and best possible manner, and as a rule you will get a better fitting, more stylish and better made garment and always at the price you would have to pay for material alone if you were to have it made by your local tailor or dressmaker. Look at the grand array of bargains in Ladies' Waists on the two fashion plates following at from 25c to $3.98, which for style, quality of material and workmanship can not be equalled elsewhere at anything like the price.

We would ask you to carefully compare our prices, descriptions and illustrations on this line with anything offered by others at anything like the price, and if you do not conclude that we can save you money and furnish you more stylish garments than you could get elsewhere we will not expect your order.

We will send any waist by mail postage prepaid where cash in full accompanies your order at 12c extra to pay postage. Please observe this in ordering, and by sending cash in full with your order you can deduct 3 per cent from our price.

To insure a perfect fit when ordering a waist, state your height and number of inches around body at bust and waist. We furnish waists in all sizes ranging from 32 to 42 inches bust measure. Extra sizes will be made to order at 20 per cent extra. (Note our special C. O. D. terms as given below.)

## ☐ Look at our Bargains in Ladies' Spring and Summer Skirts on the Following Pages

We show a line of ladies' spring and summer skirts in the very latest styles at prices ranging from $1.19 to $9.25, skirts that you can not buy elsewhere at anything like the price. We wish to say that we have selected the materials for these skirts with great care, and we feel confident we can supply you a more stylish, better made and better fitting skirt for less money than any other house in existence. Every skirt we carry from the cheapest to the best is thoroughly well made and guaranteed in every respect, and as for the price, we would ask you to carefully compare our prices with those of any other house and favor us with your order only if you find our prices lower.

When skirts are ordered we must know the number of inches around the body at waist, lenght of skirt from waist to bottom, and weight. With this information we can guarantee to furnish a perfect fitting garment. We furnish skirts in lengths from 38 to 44. Larger size will be made to order and are 20 per cent extra. Please note our 3 per cent discount for cash, which will nearly cover express charges. (Note our special C. O. D terms as given below).

## OUR SEVEN BIG BARGAINS IN LADIES' WRAPPERS

will be found on the following plate. We show a line of ladies' wrappers in the very latest style for spring and summer of 1897 at prices ranging from 69c to $1.75, wrappers that you can not buy elsewhere at anything like the price. We wish to say that these goods are made from the very latest style fabrics, they are nicely tailored, well trimmed and finished, and are far superior to the goods carried by the average retail dealer. We would only ask that you carefully compare the illustrations, descriptions and prices with those of any other concern, and if you do not conclude we can save you money we will not expect your order. We guarantee every garment to be exactly as represented and more value for the money than you can possibly get elsewhere. These wrappers come in sizes, 32 to 42 bust, and in lengths 54 to 58 inches. Larger sizes will be made to order and furnished at 20 per cent extra.

In ordering, state number of inches around the body at bust, your height and and weight, and we can guarantee a perfect fit.

Wrappers will be sent by mail postpaid when cash in full accompanies your order and 25c extra to pay postage. When you send the full amount of cash with your order you may deduct 3 per cent from our prices which will help you to pay the postage (Note our special C. O. D. terms as given below.)

## LOOK AT OUR LINE OF INFANT'S, CHILDREN'S, MISSES' AND LADIES' SPRING AND SUMMER CLOAKS AND WRAPS,

We show all the Latest Styles and most desirable goods and the greatest value ever offered. Compare our prices on these goods with those of any other concern and judge for yourself as to the money saving argument we give in every price quotation.

In ordering infant's long cloaks no size is necessary. In ordering children's reefer jackets, state age of child, and say whether large or small of age. In ordering children's summer jackets, state age and say whether large or small of age. In ordering ladies' or misses' spring or summer wraps, viz. cloaks and capes, follow our rules for measurement as given below, or if bust measure and weight is given us we can guarantee a perfect fit.

We wish to say that our cloaks and capes are of the very latest style for spring and summer. They are cut by expert cutters on the very latest style patterns, made by the very best tailors we can employ and such goods as you will find only in the finest retail houses in large cities. We are extremely anxious to receive your order for one of these garments, not so much for the little profit there will be in it to us as for the good it will do us as an advertisement. We know that you will be so well pleased that you will favor us with your orders for other goods. (Note our special C. O. D. terms below.)

## GREAT BARGAINS IN LADIES' TAILOR MADE SUITS.

For the spring and summer of 1897 we offer a line of ladies' strictly high grade tailor made suits, which for style, quality and price will not be equalled elsewhere. Every garment is of the very latest style, cut on the latest style patterns by expert cutters, made by the very best tailors and such goods as you will find only in the largest cities and there in the most fashionable stores.

We have figured our prices on the basis of actual cost of material bought direct from the mills and labor, with our one small profit added, and on this basis we can furnish you a tailor made suit for about the cost of the material alone if bought from your local dealer.

We will call your attention especially to the three plates shown in this catalogue which show a line of ladies' suits at from $2.75 to $18.00, which are equal to anything you can buy at retail for double the money.

In ordering suits, it is only necessary for us to have your bust measure, your waist measure, length of skirt from waist to bottom, your height and weight, and we can guarantee a perfect fit; or, if you will follow our rules for measurement as given below it will be preferred. (Note our special C. O. D. terms as given below.)

## OUR SPECIAL C. O. D. TERMS.

We will send any garment illustrated in this catalogue, fill any order for ladies' waists, skirts, wrappers, cloaks, dresses, etc., shipped by express C. O. D. subject to examination on receipt of $1.00 as a guarantee of good faith. You can examine the goods at the express office, and if found perfectly satisfactory, exactly as represented and such value as you have never seen before at anything like the price, pay the express agent our price and express charges less the $1.00 sent with order, and the goods are yours.

## DISCOUNT FOR CASH.

We allow a discount of 3 per cent if cash in full accompanies your order. If you send the full amount of cash with your order you can deduct 3 per cent from our price. The best way is to send cash with your order, for you not only save the three per cent cash discount, but you also save return charges on money to us. You take no risk whatever, for we will immediately refund your money if you are not perfectly satisfied.

## HOW TO ORDER.

Select the style wanted by number, follow our rules for measurement closely, enclose the necessary remittance of $1.00 as a guarantee of good faith, or our advertised price, less 3 per cent discount, and we will send the goods to your nearest express office by express, and if sent C. O. D. your agent will allow you to examine the garment and satisfy yourself in every way before paying the balance.

### HOW TO TAKE A MEASURE FOR A CLOAK, CAPE, WAIST, SKIRT OR DRESS.

BUST MEASURE—All around under the arms over fullest part in front and well up over the shoulder blades in back is.............inches.
WAIST—Around smallest part of waist at Fig. 6 is...............inches.
HIP—Fullest measure around the hips, about 6 inches below the waist line (See Fig. 7) is..........inches.
ACROSS BACK—From shoulder seam to shoulder seam (No. 1 to No. 2) is.............inches.
LENGTH OF WAIST IN BACK—Measure from colar seam to waist line in back 9 to 10 is........inches.
SLEEVE LENGTH—Exact measure of the inside sleeve seam from arm hole (3) to wrist bone (4) with arm extended is.............inches.
ARM HOLES—Around shoulder where sleeve is sewed in.............inches.
NECK—All around neck over dress collar at bottom of collar, not too tight, is.............inches.
LENGTH OF SKIRT—From waist line (6) to bottom of skirt is............inches.
FOR CHILDRENS GARMENTS, state age of child and say whether large or small of age.

## OUR BINDING GUARANTEE.

We guarantee every article to be exactly as represented, to be greater value than can be had elsewhere, every garment to fit perfectly, if our rules for measurement are carefully observed, and if not perfectly satisfactory in every respect

### WE WILL CHEERFULLY REFUND YOUR MONEY.

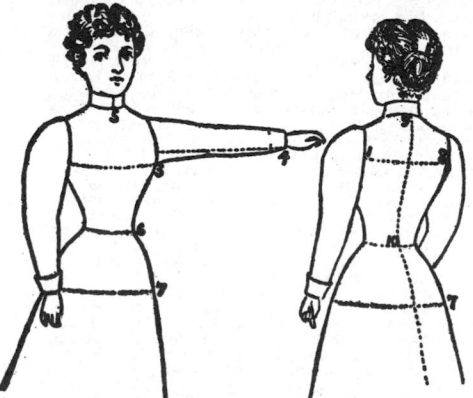

# LADIES WAISTS

SEARS ROEBUCK & CO. CINC.

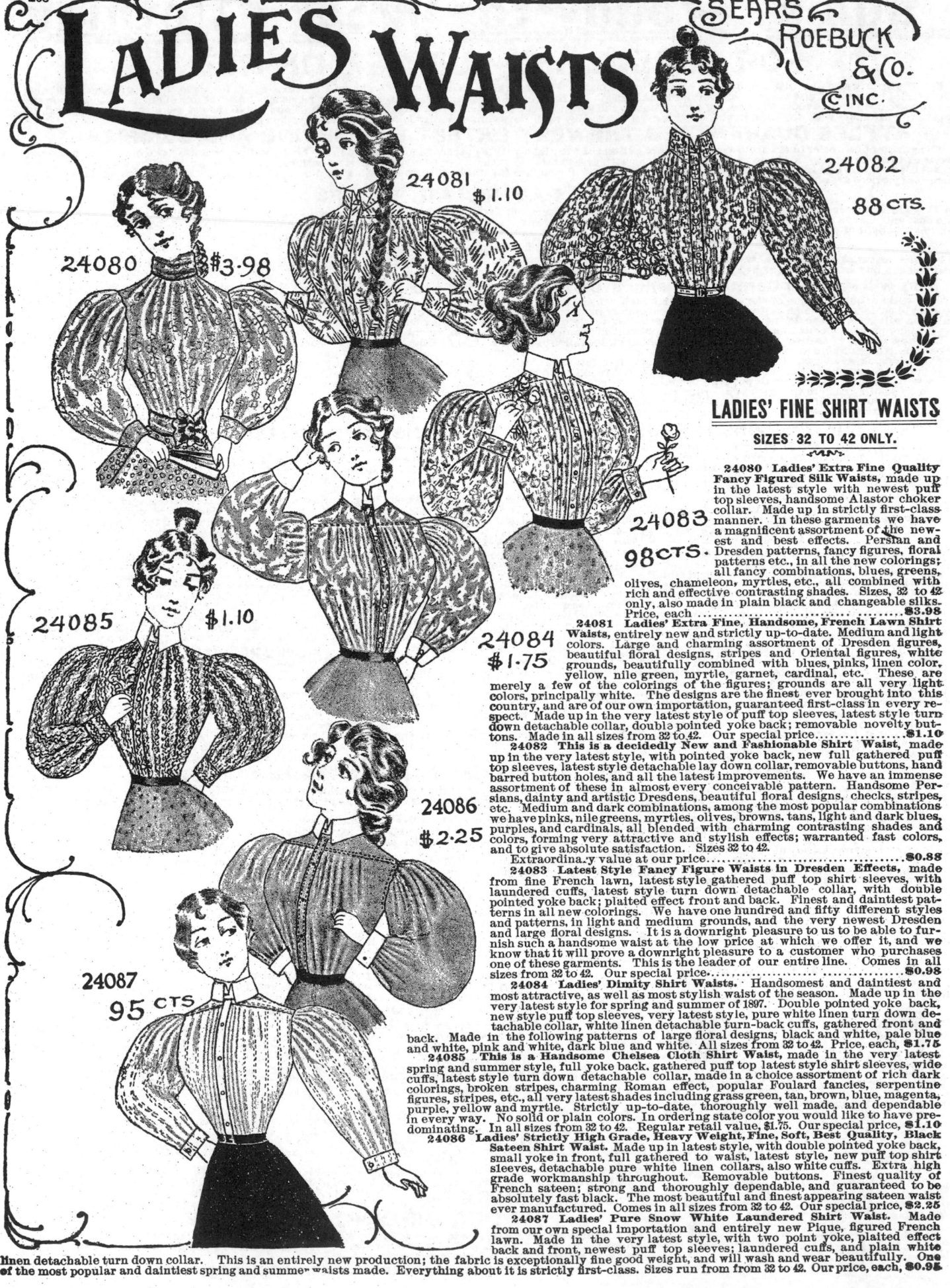

24080 $3.98

24081 $1.10

24082 88 CTS.

24083 98 CTS.

24084 $1.75

24085 $1.10

24086 $2.25

24087 95 CTS.

## LADIES' FINE SHIRT WAISTS

### SIZES 32 TO 42 ONLY.

**24080 Ladies' Extra Fine Quality Fancy Figured Silk Waists,** made up in the latest style with newest puff top sleeves, handsome Alastor choker collar. Made up in strictly first-class manner. In these garments we have a magnificent assortment of the newest and best effects. Persian and Dresden patterns, fancy figures, floral patterns etc., in all the new colorings; all fancy combinations, blues, greens, olives, chameleon, myrtles, etc., all combined with rich and effective contrasting shades. Sizes, 32 to 42 only, also made in plain black and changeable silks. Price, each ............................................$3.98

**24081 Ladies' Extra Fine, Handsome, French Lawn Shirt Waists,** entirely new and strictly up-to-date. Medium and light colors. Large and charming assortment of Dresden figures, beautiful floral designs, stripes and Oriental figures, white grounds, beautifully combined with blues, pinks, linen color, yellow, nile green, myrtle, garnet, cardinal, etc. These are merely a few of the colorings of the figures; grounds are all very light colors, principally white. The designs are the finest ever brought into this country, and are of our own importation, guaranteed first-class in every respect. Made up in the very latest style of puff top sleeves, latest style turn down detachable collar, double pointed yoke back; removable novelty buttons. Made in all sizes from 32 to 42. Our special price.................$1.10

**24082 This is a decidedly New and Fashionable Shirt Waist,** made up in the very latest style, with pointed yoke back, new full gathered puff top sleeves, latest style detachable lay down collar, removable buttons, hand barred button holes, and all the latest improvements. We have an immense assortment of these in almost every conceivable pattern. Handsome Persians, dainty and artistic Dresdens, beautiful floral designs, checks, stripes, etc. Medium and dark combinations, among the most popular combinations we have pinks, nile greens, myrtles, olives, browns, tans, light and dark blues, purples, and cardinals, all blended with charming contrasting shades and colors, forming very attractive and stylish effects; warranted fast colors, and to give absolute satisfaction. Sizes 32 to 42. Extraordinary value at our price..........................................$0.88

**24083 Latest Style Fancy Figure Waists in Dresden Effects,** made from fine French lawn, latest style gathered puff top shirt sleeves, with laundered cuffs, latest style turn down detachable collar, with double pointed yoke back; plaited effect front and back. Finest and daintiest patterns in all new colorings. We have one hundred and fifty different styles and patterns, in light and medium grounds, and the very newest Dresden and large floral designs. It is a downright pleasure to us to be able to furnish such a handsome waist at the low price at which we offer it, and we know that it will prove a downright pleasure to a customer who purchases one of these garments. This is the leader of our entire line. Comes in all sizes from 32 to 42. Our special price.........................................$0.98

**24084 Ladies' Dimity Shirt Waists.** Handsomest and daintiest and most attractive, as well as most stylish waist of the season. Made up in the very latest style for spring and summer of 1897. Double pointed yoke back, new style puff top sleeves, very latest style, pure white linen turn down detachable collar, white linen detachable turn-back cuffs, gathered front and back. Made in the following patterns of large floral designs, black and white, pale blue and white, pink and white, dark blue and white. All sizes from 32 to 42. Price, each, $1.75

**24085 This is a Handsome Chelsea Cloth Shirt Waist,** made in the very latest spring and summer style, full yoke back, gathered puff top latest style shirt sleeves, wide cuffs, latest style turn down detachable collar, made in a choice assortment of rich dark colorings, broken stripes, charming Roman effect, popular Foulard fancies, serpentine figures, stripes, etc., all very latest shades including grass green, tan, brown, blue, magenta, purple, yellow and myrtle. Strictly up-to-date, thoroughly well made, and dependable in every way. No solid or plain colors. In ordering state color you would like to have predominating. In all sizes from 32 to 42. Regular retail value, $1.75. Our special price, $1.10

**24086 Ladies' Strictly High Grade, Heavy Weight, Fine, Soft, Best Quality, Black Sateen Shirt Waist.** Made up in latest style, with double pointed yoke back, small yoke in front, full gathered to waist, latest style, new puff top shirt sleeves, detachable pure white linen collars, also white cuffs. Extra high grade workmanship throughout. Removable buttons. Finest quality of French sateen; strong and thoroughly dependable, and guaranteed to be absolutely fast black. The most beautiful and finest appearing sateen waist ever manufactured. Comes in all sizes from 32 to 42. Our special price, $2.25

**24087 Ladies' Pure Snow White Laundered Shirt Waist.** Made from our own special importation and entirely new Pique, figured French lawn. Made in the very latest style, with two point yoke, plaited effect back and front, newest puff top sleeves; laundered cuffs, and plain white linen detachable turn down collar. This is an entirely new production; the fabric is exceptionally fine good weight, and will wash and wear beautifully. One of the most popular and daintiest spring and summer waists made. Everything about it is strictly first-class. Sizes run from 32 to 42. Our price, each, $0.95

# Ladies New Spring and Summer Shirt Waists

24390
50¢

24391
50¢

24392
85¢

24393
58¢

24394
47¢

24395
75¢

24396
75¢

24397
25¢

## Very Latest Styles

**24390 Ladies' Fast Black, Twilled Sateen, Unlaundered Shirt Waists.** Good heavy weight goods, made up in the latest style for coming spring and summer season, with gathered puff top sleeves, pointed cuff, and small attached turn-down collar, with belt to match. This is an exceptionally fine sateen, guaranteed to be absolutely fast black. Comes in all sizes from 32 to 42. Our special price.......................................................$0.50

**24391 Ladies' Fast Color Percale Laundred Waists,** very neat black and white stripe patterns, warranted fast colors, made up in the latest 1897 styles, with new plaited puff top shirt sleeves, latest style turn-down detachable collar. This is a very neat and durable garment, which is always stylish, and is sure to give perfect satisfaction. Made in sizes 32 to 42 only. Would be cheap at retail at 75 cents. Our special price.......................$0.50

**24392 Ladies' Extra Fine Quality French Penang Shirt Waist.** This is an entirely new effect, and comes in combinations of dark back grounds with white, yellow, garnet, pink, green, and all other light colors, in choice Persian and Oriental patterns. Strictly first-class make, with double pointed yoke back, gathered puff top sleeves, latest style detachable turn-down collar. All striking colorings and handsome combinations. No plain or solid colors. In all sizes from 32 to 42. In ordering please state color you desire to predominate. Retail value $1.25. Our special price.................$0.85

**24393 Ladies' Laundered Percale Shirt Waists.** Made from the new and popular Foulard pattern percale. Very latest design, with gathered puff top sleeves, deep cuffs, and detachable turn-down collars. Come in handsome combinations of navy blue and white, and black and white; always state which you prefer. This is a very handsome and attractive waist, and the pattern is strictly new this season. In all sizes from 32 to 42.
Our special price.......................................................$0.58

**24393½ Ladies' Extra Fine Percale Laundered Shirt Waist,** same as preceding number. In a choice assortment of new and novel patterns, embracing the season's latest and most choice effects. We have them made up in medium and dark patterns. Persians, stripes, checks, fancy designs etc., in a large assortment of colors, including blue, green, garnet, cardinal, pink, etc., combined with handsome contrasting colors and shades. Guaranteed to give good satisfaction. Sizes, 32 to 42. Price, each.............$0.58

**24394 Ladies' Latest Style Laundered Persian Percale Waists.** Made with the newest style of detachable turn-down collar, plaited front, with removable buttons. Plaited puff top sleeves, with cuffs. Made in the latest spring style. We have these in a very large assortment of new and fashionable patterns, medium and light colorings. Persian patterns, no plain or solid colors, in placing your order, please state color you desire to predominate. Sizes run from 32 to 42. Regular 75 cent value.
Our special price.......................................................$0.47

**24395 Ladies' Light Weight, Fine Laundered Shirt Waist,** made from special selected French percale, in a handsome assortment of choice colors, also combinations of black and white and blue and white. Made up in first-class style in every respect, with laundered cuffs, and latest style detachable collars, gathered puff top sleeves, pointed double yoke back, and removable novelty buttons. Made in a very large assortment of light colors, in Persian effects, floral designs etc. All charming effects which are sure to please. In placing your order, please state color you desire to predominate. In all sizes from 32 to 42. Our special price.............$0.75

**24396 Ladies' Extra Fine Quality, Heavy Weight, Fast Black Percale Laundered Shirt Waist,** made with new style turn-down collar, detachable, full gathered puff top sleeves, with attached cuffs. Plaited front and back. Guaranteed absolutely fast color, and will give long and lasting satisfaction. This is one of the very best grades, plain black percale ever manufactured, which would be cheap at $1.00. Sizes 32 to 42.
Our special price.......................................................$0.75

**24397 Ladies' Fancy Figured Shirt Waist,** an exceptional fine garment at a remarkably low price, made with neat lay down collar, ruffle front, plaited puff top sleeves, detachable belt to match. Made in a choice assortment of medium colors, natural linen color with red, black or blue figures with white combinations. Sizes 32 to 42, we cannot furnish larger sizes. Regular retail value 50 cents. Our special price.................$0.25

# LADIES SPRING AND SUMMER SKIRTS

## SEARS, ROEBUCK & CO. INC.

$2.95  24140

24141  $1.95

24142  $2.50

24143  $5.95

24144  $1.19

24145  $1.50

24146  $4.98

## ...LADIES' READY MADE SKIRTS...

**NO CHEAP SKIRTS HERE....
But Good Serviceable Skirts Cheap.
Don't Forget to Mention Size Wanted.**

Our business in skirts during the fall and winter season was immense, in fact the largest business ever done by us in this line, during our business career. On every hand our skirts gave great satisfaction, people who ordered one, when they saw what stylish and good values we sent ordered 3 and 4 more, and each mail brought letters from pleased customers, telling us how agreeably they were surprised in the values sent. We buy the latest, most stylish and most durable piece goods in the market direct from the mills, and use only the best of trimmings. We control the making of our skirts and employ only the best and most skilled hands obtainable; this enables us to offer our patrons skirts of a high standard at prices that cannot be approached by any other house. Retail merchants can positively not furnish goods like these for double the money.

**HOW TO MEASURE A SKIRT.** Give the number of inches around at body at waist, length required in front and we will send you a perfect fit. Selling as we do several thousand skirts weekly enables us to fit everybody perfectly.

**WE ARE OFFERING WONDERFUL BARGAINS IN OUR SILK DEPARTMENT.**

Skirts come in any size of waist measure from 21 to 3 inches.

Skirts come in any size of length measure from 39 to 44 inches, larger size are 50 cents higher.

**24140 $2.95 Will Purchase a $5.00 Skirt.** A black grenadine skirt, has beautiful floral designs, is lined with red, blue, pink, green or yellow taffeta. The goods themselves being of a transparent fabric, showing colored lining, thus producing a handsome and very stylish effect, full 4½ yard sweep, velvet bound. This beautiful garment would sell in any retail store for $5.00. Save dollars and buy your skirts of S., R. & Co. Each..............$2.95.

**24141 A Plain Black Henrietta Skirt,** velvet bound, rustle lined and interlined with canvas, full four yard sweep. This skirt is very desirable for elderly people, who prefer quality to show. This skirt would be considered cheap if bought for $3.50 at retail. S. R. & Co's special price, each..............$1.95

**24142 $2.50 for a Skirt worth $4.00.** This is a wool twilled Jaquard cloth skirt, scroll figured, mixed with dots, full four yard sweep. rustle lining, velvet piped, well made and a beautiful garment that will far surpass the expectation of any one. Each..............$2.50

**24143 This Number is a Lizard Cloth Skirt,** all wool, very new and stylish. Large patterns, full 4½ yard sweep, lined with very fine fancy stripe rustle taffeta, faced half way up with canvas, velvet bound, covered seams. A fine grade of skirt at the price we offer it at. Each..............$5.95

**24144 This Skirt is Our Leader,** made of black figured goods, rustle lining, velvet bound, has a 3½ yard sweep; the actual value of this skirt is $2.25. Our price..............$1.19

**24145 For $1.50 We Offer a $2.75 Skirt.** Sheppard plaid, black and white, or brown and white full 4 yard sweep, rustle lined, velvet bound, very stylish and nobby. Each..............$1.50

**24146 $4.98 Will Buy a Very Fine Taffeta Silk Skirt.** This skirt is made of silk, that has a beautiful pattern, is lined and interlined, has full sweep of four yards and has fine velvet binding. Ladies ordering this skirt will get one of the biggest bargains ever known in the skirt line, everybody can now have a silk skirt. We succeeded in closing out the entire fabric stock of a large silk manufacturer and are thus enabled to offer a fine silk skirt, away below the cost of a woolen skirt, order quick; the quantity is large but big, big bargains like this go fast. This fine silk skirt only..............$4.98

# Ladies SPRING AND SEARS, ROEBUCK SUMMER & Co. INC. SKIRTS

**24150**   $7.00

**24151**   $9.25

**24152**   $2.85

**24153**   $3.75

**24154**   $1.69

**24155**   $3.25

**24156**   $2.35

### Extra Heavy Gros Grain Silk Skirt.

**24150** An Extra Heavy Gros Grain Silk Skirt, very large, beautiful and stylish patterns of floral and scroll designs, has a fine rustle taffeta lining, interlined throughout with canvas, full 4½ yard sweep, velvet bound, covered seams. This skirt would be excellent value at $11.50.
Our special price...................$7.00

### Handsome Silk Moire Skirt.

**24151** This is one of the Handsomest Silk Moire Skirts Made, lined with silk finished taffetta, interlined throughout with canvas, very wide sweep, extra fine velvet binding. Skirts not nearly as nice as this skirt have been and are sold as high as $15.00.
Our price, each..................$9.25

### Black Serge Skirt.

**24152** $2.85 Buys a $3.95 Skirt. A black serge skirt has a four yard sweep, rustle lining, velvet bound.
Each................................$2.85

### Plain Black Brilliantine Skirt.

**24153** A Plain Black Brilliantine Skirt, fine quality, full 4½ yard sweep, lined with full rustle taffeta, half interlined with canvas, fine velvet binding. This skirt has every appearance of a fine silk skirt and is fashionable and very durable, good value at $6.50.
Each...................... .........$3.75

### Black Figured Moire Skirt.

**24154** $1.69 Buys a $3.00 Skirt, such great big values at S., R. & Co's only. A black figured mohair skirt, rustle lined and canvas interlined on bottom, has a full 4 yard sweep, velvet bound. In appearance this skirt looks as well as the finest and most stylish garments in the market. Our special price.....$1.69

### All Wool Sheppard Plaid Skirt.

**24155** All Wool Sheppard Plaid Skirt, black and white, brown and white, sweep 4½ yards, velvet bound, interlined with canvas, lining matches color of plaid. This is great value and a skirt that would be called cheap at $5.00.
Our price, each......................$3.25

### Black Figured Brilliantine Silk Skirt.

**24156** A Black Figured Brilliantine Silk, skirt full 4 yards sweep, rustle lining, velvet bound. Each......................$2.35

# SEARS, ROEBUCK & CO. INC. LADIES WRAPPERS.

**24120** 98¢

**24121** 69¢

**24123** $1.50

**24124** 85¢

**24122** $1.15

**24125** $1.75

**24126** $1.39

**24120** An entirely new and handsome Persian Percale Wrapper, made in the very latest style, with large puff top sleeves, full Watteau back, full gathered front, with girdle belt and large ruffled sailor collar. We have these wrappers in a large assortment of colorings in entirely new patterns and shades. Beautiful Persian effects only, no plain colors, all medium colors, exceedingly popular and sure to please you. Sizes, 32 to 42 inch bust. Our special price..**$0.98**

**24121** Ladies' Wrapper, made from fast color genuine Simpson print. Watteau back, and full gathered front, with girdle belt, latest style puff top sleeves. Well made throughout, and comes in steel gray mixtures, half mourning and blue with small white figures and dots. The best cheap wrapper ever made up. Made in all sizes from 32 to 42 inch bust measures. Our special price.......**$0.69**

**24122** Latest Style Foulard Percale Wrapper, black or blue ground, with novel designs in white figures. Made with latest style puff top sleeves, neat turned down collar, three rows of fancy serpentine braid across bust and back forming yoke; back with plaited effect from yoke to waist; girdle belt, collar, sleeves and belt trimmed with serpentine braid. An exceptionally attractive and handsome wrapper, very finely made throughout; full skirt with wide hem. Sizes 32 to 42 inch bust. Our special price.........................**$1.15**

**24123** Extra-fine French Chelsea Cloth Wrapper, made in new and handsome designs, neat turn down collar, and latest style puff top sleeves, yoke back and butterfly epaulets extending over sleeves. Yoke effect made in front by two rows of narrow ribbon, epaulets, collar, belt and sleeves trimmed to match. A large assortment of patterns in entirely new colorings. Beautiful combinations of black, olive, green, myrtle, brown, white and blue, and other desirable shades forming a charming blending of colors in artistic effects, medium shades, no plain colors. In ordering state what colors you wish to predominate. Sizes from 32 to 42 inch bust.
Price.....................................................................**$1.50**

**24124** Ladies' Fine Percale Wrapper, full Watteau back, neat turn down collar, braided around collar, front and back in yoke effect with serpentine braid. Neat ruffle around yoke in front and back, finely made and finished, lined to waist, full skirt with wide hem, girdle yoke in front. Large and medium sized figured patterns, black and white, half mourning, and navy blue and white mixed, guaranteed fast color. Sizes 32 to 42 inch bust measure, retail for $1.25. Our price each......................................................**$0.85**

## Ladies' Black Sateen Wrappers.

**24125** Ladies' Superior Quality, Fast Black Sateen Wrapper, made with new puff top sleeves and cuffs trimmed with narrow black serpentine braid, gathered front and Watteau back; neat turn down collar and belt trimmed with narrow black serpentine braid, wide skirt with deep hem at bottom. An excellent garment in every respect. Sizes, 32 to 42 only. Price, each.............................**$175**

**24126** An Extra-fine Imported Chelsea Cloth Wrapper, a new fabric, similar to French Penang, but heavier and finer. These wrappers are made in a large assortment of medium colors, large figures, Persian effects, floral designs, etc. Leading colors, greens, browns, wine and blue, with combinations of beautiful contrasting shades; no plain colors. These wrappers are made up same as shown in illustration, new puff sleeves, front and back gathered on a square yoke; yoke, belt and sleeves handsomely trimmed with novelty braid. Sizes 32 to 42 inch bust. Price...... .........................**$1.39**

# Ladies Spring and Summer Wraps.
## Sears, Roebuck and Co. Inc.

24934 $11.00.

24910 $3.98

24913 $4.85

24912 $4.50

24935 $13.50

24933 $11.50

24914 $6.00

24911 $4.12

24936 $14.75

**24910** Very Stylish Ladies' Cape, braided all around with soutache braid, lined throughout with fancy lining, satin ribbon, rouching around collar and long streamers in front. Colors, black, blue, green or Havana. Well worth $6.00. Our price only...................................................$3.98

**24911** Sicilian Silk, Ladies' Cape, elaborately embroidered with jet, lined throughout with changeable taffeta silk, lace trimming on collar and gros grain satin ribbon around collar and down front.
A very nobby garment for................................ ....$4.12

**24912** A Neat, Full Sweep Ladies' Cape, of very fine imported black, clay worsted richly beaded and braided with jet and tinsel all around bottom, lace around collar and satin ribbon streamers in front, collar and fronts faced with silk serge. Would be cheap at $8.00.
Our price..................................................$4.50

**24913** This is the Exact Copy of a Parisian Cape, made of fancy silk brilliantine, lined throughout with changeable silk, very full sweep, collar trimmed with very fine black lace and satin ribbon. Can not be duplicated for less than $7.50. Our price..................................................$4.85

**24914** A Very Nobby Ladies' Cape, made of fine tan broadcloth, entire cape overlaid with straps and trimmed with small pearl buttons, two bows in front and one in back, stitched all around with silk. An exquisite $10.00 cape for.................................. ... ..........$6.00

**24933** Fine Tan Kersey Jacket Tailor Made, fly front, trimmed with fancy pearl buttons, fronts lined with plaid taffeta silk, entire jacket stitched with silk, sleeves and lapels are of the very newest style.
Our price..................................................$11.50

**24934** A Very Genteel Double Breasted Reefer Jacket, made of tan imported covert cloth, four white pearl buttons in front and eight on sleeves, lined throughout with fancy figured silk. A real $15.00 jacket for.....$11.00

**24935** Imported English Covert Cloth Jacket, in either gray or tan, fly front, coat back, very newest lapels and sleeves, two rows of silk stitching all around, six rows around sleeves, lined throughout with plaid taffeta silk. A very nobby jacket. Our price.................................$13.50

**24936** Ladies' Tailor Made Jacket, very latest style made of fine Kersey, in black, tan, blue or green lapels; and sleeves are the very newest shape, pointed cuffs, fancy pocket flaps, lined throughout with brocaded silk, stitched all around with silk. Any retailer would ask at least $22.00 for this jacket, we sell it for...................................$14.75

# LADIES SPRING & SUMMER WRAPS

**24930**
**$6.50**

**24906**
**$3.35**

**24932**
**$9.00**

**24907 $3.75**

**24931**
**$7.75**

**24909**
**$3.35**

**24908**
**$4.12**

**24929**
**$5.25**

**24905**
**$2.75**

**24905** You could not get anything more appropriate for an elderly lady. It is made of imported black repellant cloth, trimmed with lace around collar and jet and lace around yoke. You may compare this cape (not picture) with any $4.00 cape and shall find it an excellent value. Only $2.75

**24906** Black Sicillian Silk, lined all through with fancy lining, satin ribbon streamers in front and satin ribbon rouching around the collar, very full sweep. Very rich....................................................$3.35

**24907** A Very Handsome Circular Cape, of fine quality, ladies' cloth in tan, blue or black, lined all through with changeable taffeta silk, soutache braiding as shown in illustration, satin ribbon rouching around collar. Very rich and stylish cape for................................................$3.75

**24908** Velvet Cape, very full sweep, lined throughout with changeable silk, the entire cape heavily braided as shown in picture, jet trimming and satin ribbon rouching around collar. A really elegant cape for only...$4.12

**24909** Ladies' Double Cape made of fine black broadcloth, deep rolling collar and very wide facing of silk serge. It is also suitable for an elderly lady. Price only...........................................................$3.35

**24929** Ladies' Extra Quality, Black Clay Worsted Jacket, double breasted, latest shape cuffs, sleeves and lapels, four large smoked pearl buttons in front, ripple back. A very serviceable jacket, and cannot be duplicated for less than $7.50 Our price.........................................$5.25

**24930** An Extremely Pretty Fly Front Ladies' Coat, of finest quality, tan colored broadcloth lined throughout with beautiful figured changeable serge, newest sleeves and coat back, two large pearl buttons in front and eight on back. An ideal spring jacket for only..................$6.50

**24931** Ladies' Tailor Made Jacket, made of English covert cloth double breasted, four fancy horn buttons in front and ten on the back, silk stitching all around, strap seams in back, fronts lined with figured silk. A good $12.00 jacket for only.....................................................$7.75

**24932** Stylish Ladies' Jacket, tailor made, double breasted, of fine broadcloth in black, navy, green or tan, fancy pearl buttons in front and on cuffs, coat back, fronts lined with fancy brocaded silk.
Our price only.............................................................$9.00

# Ladies and Misses Spring and Summer Wraps

**24917 $10.00**

**24919 $12.75**

**24916 $7.75**

**24918 $11.00**

**24915 7.25**

**24946 $4.75**

**24948 $6.50**

**24945 3.25**

**24947 5.75**

**24915** Ladies Single Full Sweep Cape, of very fine black broadcloth, front handsomely trimmed with soutache braid ornaments. Queen Ann collar trimmed with satin ribbon, two bows in front and a large one in back, lined all through with best plaid silk. It would not look dear at double the price...........................................................$7.25

**24916** A Very Handsome Vest Front, Full Sweep Ladies' Cape of high grade tan Kersey, bottom of cape overlaid with same material and heavily stitched, eight fancy horn buttons on front, satin ribbon rouching around collar and two stylish streamers in back. A remarkable value for only...................................................$7.75

**24917** This Cape is made of Fine Tan Broadcloth in the Very Latest Style, elaborately embroidered with brown silk cord and gold beads, lined throughout with figured silk, muslin de soi and gros grain satin ribbon around collar and in front. Words cannot describe the beauties of this cape, it must be seen. Our price only.................$10.00

**24918.** Heavy Broadcloth, made in the very Latest Style in tan or olive green, embroidered all around with white silk cord and tinsel to match cape. Lined all through with figured silk. Another $18.00 cape for.........................................................$11.00

**24919** Ladies' Cape of Finest Quality Gros Grain Silk, wide plait in center of back, bow in back and on sides, heavily beaded panels of same material trimmed all around with jet, lined throughout with excellent quality changeable silk, full lace rouching around collar. Very rich and nobby. Price............................................$12.75

## ... MISSES' JACKETS ...

**Sizes from 14 to 18. Just State Age and Inches around Bust.**

**24945** Double Breasted Misses' Jacket made of imported repellant in black, navy or tan, six fancy horn buttons in front, very newest sleeves and cuffs. Excellent value for the money. Price..........$3.25

**24946** Very Nobby Misses' Jacket, made of twilled cloth in navy, tan or green, fly front, velvet collar, very similar to 24948. Price only..$4.75

**24947** Misses' Jacket of Fancy Scotch Mixture, double breasted, six large buttons in front, ripple back, latest style sleeves and cuffs. A very nobby coat for..........................................$5.75

**24948** Stylish Misses' Jacket, made of fancy Scotch mixture, fly front, velvet collar to match material, side pocket and also a watch pocket as shown in picture. This garment sells everywhere for $10.00. Our price only...........................................$6.50

# Ladies' Spring and Summer Wraps

**24902 $1.75**

**24901 $1.48**

**24903 $2.35**

**24927 $5.00**

**24900 $.98**

**24928 $3.85**

**24925 $2.98**

**24904 $2.75**

**24926 $5.00**

**24900  Ladies' Single Cape,** elaborately braided all around, made of imported repellant cloth in black, blue and tan.  This cape is good and stylish enough for anybody and is worth at least double of what we charge for same........................................................................$0.98

**24901  A Very Stylish Looking Ladies' Cape,** made of "Henrietta" cloaking, mohair braid all around, fancy velvet trimming in front.  You can not duplicate this cape in any retail store for less than $3.00.  We make this in black, blue and tan for...........................................................$1.48

**24902  This Beautiful Cape** is made of fine ladies' cloth in the very latest shades, very full sweep, deep rolling collar, three rows of soutach braid around the cape, as shown in illustration, satin ribbon streamers in front, and excellent value for...........................................................$1.75

**24903  A Ladies' Cape** like this was never put on the market for such a low price.  It is made of black velvet with a very full sweep, trimmed around neck with satin ribbon and lace.  The entire cape is lined all through with fancy lining.  This description cannot give justice to the cape, it must be seen to be appreciated.   It would be cheap at $4.75.
Our price only..............................................................$2.35

**24904  Tailor Made Ladies' Cape,** made of ladies' fine cloth in black, blue or tan lined all through with changeable silk serge, full sweep.  Elegantly trimmed with two rows of mohair braid, and three rows around the bottom, ribbon streamers as shown in illustration.  A $5.00 cape for....$2.75

**24925  A Very Nobby Ladies' Jacket,** made in the very latest style, newest sleeves as shown in illustration, double breasted, four large and ten small pearl buttons, wide cloth facing of same material.  A splendid $6.00 jacket for only................................................................$2.98

**24926  Ladies' Fine Jacket,** of high grade, tan colored ladies' cloth, rolling collar and very latest lapels and back.  Extra wide cloth facing, fronts half lined with changeable silk, trimmed in front with four handsome pearl buttons.  A very rich and nobby $10.00 garment for........$5.00

**24927  Ladies' Stylish Jacket,** made of twilled cloth in black, blue or tan, newest sleeves and back, fly front and pointed cuffs.  A most remarkable value at only............................................................$5.00

**24928  Ladies' Coat Shaped Jacket** of excellent quality, black ladies' cloth, the sleeves are the exact copy of an imported jacket, coat back, very wide facing of same material, fronts lined with changeable silk, two large pearl buttons in front.  It would be cheap at $5.50, only.................$3.85

# CHILDREN'S SPRING AND SUMMER JACKETS

1897

24957
$5.25

24954
$3.65

24956
$4.75

24952
$2.48

24953
$3.00

24951
$1.98

24955
$4.15

24950
$1.35

## CHILDREN'S JACKETS SIZES FROM 4 TO 12.

### State Age and number of Inches around bust.

**34950  Very Neat Childs' Jacket,** in either navy or dark red, large sailor collar, trimmed with fancy buttons.
Our leader for only.................................................$1.35

**24951  Childs' Jacket,** handsomely gotten up in navy, red or tan, large sailor collar trimmed with white braid.  Would be cheap at $3.00.
Our price....................................................$1.98

**24952  This Beautiful Childs' Jacket** is made in either navy and white trimming or red and black trimming, the contrast of shades shows off very nicely.  Fancy anchor buttons in front and on sailor collar.  Price................................................. $2.48

**24953  An Extremely Nobby Child's Jacket** of fancy green mixture, large sailor collar and cuffs, inlaid with green broadcloth, three rows of white mohair braid all around collar, six pretty pearl buttons in front.  For the low price of. ..............$3.00

**24954  Newest Style Child's Jacket** of fine heliotrope ladies' cloth reefer front and empire back, yoke and cuff trimmed in white mohair braid and tinsel, satin ribbon streamers, six large pearl buttons in front.  Very rich at...........................................$3.65

**24955  High Grade Child's Jacket,** made of fine imported Scotch mixture, large sailor collar, trimmed with silk cord and small pearl buttons, six large fancy horn buttons in front, cuffs to match collar. Others sell it for $6.00, we sell it for...........................$4.15

**24956  A Very Stylish Child's Jacket,** made in empire style, either red or navy, trimmed elaborately with white braid (as shown in illustration) very latest sleeves.  Fancy anchor buttons.
Can't be beat, only ..............................................$4.75

**24957  Fancy Child's Jacket,** made of imported Scotch mixture red, gold braid trimming on collar and cuffs, newest shape sleeves and collar, four fancy buttons in front, very wide facing of same cloth.  An elegant $9.00 jacket for............................................................... $5.25

# CHILDREN'S · REEFER · JACKETS
## SEARS ROEBUCK & CO., INC.

$1.98

24170

85¢

24171

$1.50

24172

$2.75

24173

$2.10

24175

98¢

24174

**REEFER JACKETS** FOR CHILDREN FROM 1 TO 5 YEARS OLD.

Do not forget to mention age and color desired when ordering.

Reefer Jackets for little toddlers, from one to four years, nobby, stylish little coats at little bits of prices. As usual S. R. & Co. will save you money on these goods.

**24170** A very nobby and swell Double Breasted Reefer Jacket, has a very wide sailor collar, trimmed with two rows of Hercules braid, in fancy designs, sleeves trimmed with two rows of Hercules braid. Colors brown, tan, navy and red. This beautiful and durable garment is well worth $2.50 at retail but by buying a large quantity of the material at a forced sale, we are enabled to offer them at, each........................$1.98

**24171** Reefer Jacket, Empire style, pleated back, made of fancy Scotch plaid cloth, trimmed with two rows of fancy plaid braids in contrasting colors. This is a gem at the price we offer it at. Sizes 1 to 5 years. Each.........$0.85

**24172** A Handsome Little Coat, for tots from 1 to 5 years old, new empire shape, collar. Waist and sleeves trimmed with gold and colored soutache braid, put on in fancy designs, fine full puffed sleeves. This garment is equal in appearance to jackets usually sold at retail for $2.25. Colors, tan, brown, red and navy. Our price each.........................$1.50

**24173** The Swellest Reefer of the Season, is a very fine novelty. Fine check cloth, colors, black, navy and green checks, V shaped back, small plaited skirt very full, has collar and shoulder capes of solid colored Broadcloth, handsomely trimmed with gilt and colored soutache braid in fancy designs, a coat at $5.00 would look no better. Each..................$2.75

**24174** This Reefer Jacket, is made of all wool cloth, large sailor collar, trimmed with three rows of Hercules Braid, double breasted, handsome buttons, come in red, navy, brown and tan, a very nobby little coat. Each.........$0.98

**24175** This Tony Little Jacket, is made of the latest cloth in fancy wool checks, colors, brown, blue, green and black checks, has a wide sailor collar of fine contrasting shade of cloth, thus producing a fine and stylish effect, collar trimmed with one row of wide and one row of narrow Hercules braid, sleeves trimmed with braid, has handsome buttons. This coat is double breasted, a winner anywhere at $2.65. Each.................................$2.10

---

## CHILDREN'S SHORT WHITE CAMBRIC DRESSES.

**For Children from 6 months to 4 years old.**

| Sizes, | A 6 months to 1 year. | 1 1 to 2 years. | 2 2 to 3 years. | 3 3 to 4 years. |
|---|---|---|---|---|

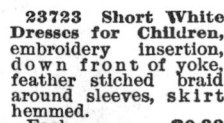

**23723** Short White Dresses for Children, embroidery insertion, down front of yoke, feather stiched braid around sleeves, skirt hemmed. Each.............$0.33

No. 23723.

No. 23724.

**23724** Child's Short White Cambric Dress, large full cambric collar, embroidered yoke and trimmed with two rows of feather stitched braid. One row of feather stitched braid around sleeves, skirt hemmed. A little dress like this usually sells for 85c. Our Special price, each...................$0.55

No. 23725.

**23725** Child's Short White Cambric dress, a nobby stylish garment, has 3¼ inch English embroidery around bottom of skirt, two tucks in back, plain collar, embroidered yoke, leeves trimmed with feather stitched braid; a real nice little dress, that is easily recognized as the $1.00 kind. Our price, each, $0.68

---

## INFANTS' FLANNEL SHAWLS.

**23745** Infant's Flannel Shawl, 28 inches square, pretty floral design worked with silk in one corner, silk stitching all around, hem stitched. Each.............................$0.55

**23747** Infant's Flannel Shawl, 28 inches square, has beautiful heavy silk embroidery in one corner, plain hem all around, the usual $1.10 kind. Our price....................$0.80

**23749** Infant's Flannel Shawl, 30 inches square, has a very heavy floral design worked in two corners, hem stitched with silk all around, sold at retail at $1.65. Our price....................$1.18

**23751** Infant's Flannel Shawl, inches square, elaborate hand worked design is two corners, the flannel is of very fine quality, scalloped edges all around worked with silk. Our special price each.........$1.65

---

A COMPLETE LINE OF CHILDREN'S ROCKERS, HIGH CHAIRS, CRADLES AND CRIBS IN FURNITURE DEPARTMENT. REFER TO INDEX.

# LADIES TAILOR MADE SUITS

## STYLE 1897

**24959 $4.50**

**24965 $6.75**

**24966 $7.50**

**24961 $4.50**

**24960 $4.50**

**24967 $8.50**

**24959**
**24960  24961**
Very fine ladies' suit made of imported repellant cloth in black, navy or tan. We make the suit 24959 Bolero, 24960 Blazer, 24961 Reefer styles. The skirt is very full; lined throughout with rustling taffeta and bound with velvet. $4.50
**24962** Same style as 24959 made of fine serge in black, blue or green. Jacket all lined with fine fancy serge. Price..........................$5.50
**24963** Same style as 24960 made as 24962. Price...$5.50
**24964** Same style as 24961 made as 24962. Price.......$5.50
**24965** Smart Blazer suit made of imported ladies cloth, in either black or navy, trimmed with braid and small buttons, full skirt, lined throughout with rustling taffeta, bound with velvet, $6.75
**24966** A magnificent Eaton style ladies suit of fancy Scotch mixture, trimmed with fine Hercules braid around bottom of waist and on sleeves, fancy horn buttons in front, waist lined with changeable silk serge, full sweep skirt interlined with crinoline and lined with rustle taffeta, bound with velvet. A fine $15.00 suit for.........$7.50
**24967** Very Stylish Ladies' Suit, Bolero style, made of blue or black serge cheviot, newest sleeves, outer jacket trimmed all around with black mohair and silk, mixed gimp and lined with changeable silk. Very full skirt trimmed as illustrated. Skirt lined with rustling taffeta and interlined with crinoline, bound with velvet. Very rich. Price..........................$8.50

### SPECIAL OFFER.

WE WILL SEND ANY of these fine tailor-made suits C. O. D., **SUBJECT TO EXAMINATION**, on receipt of $1.00, balance with express charges to be paid upon examination and approval.

**3 PER CENT. OFF** for full cash with order.

## SOLD ONLY BY SEARS ROEBUCK & CO. incorporated Chicago.

# LADIES TAILOR MADE SUITS

24968
$9.00

24969
$10.50

24972
$14.50

24973
$18.00

24974
$2.90

24971
$13.25

24970
$12.25

**24968  Ladies' Suit, Blazer Style**, made of green and gray mixed goods, velvet inlaid rolling collar, newest sleeves, waist lined with changeable silk serge.  Extra full sweep skirt, lined with rustling taffeta and interlined with crinoline.  None better made in this style for.................................................................$9.00

**24969  Newest Style, Empire Suit**, made of black, blue or green ladies' cloth, jacket lined throughout with fancy figured silk and trimmed with small pearl buttons, very full skirt, lined throughout with rustling taffeta, bound in velvet.  Would be cheap at $15.00.
Price, only .................................................................$9.00

**24970  Ladies' Eaton Suit**, made of imported Scotch mixture, front of jacket and cuffs appliqued with broadcloth to match, jacket lined all through with fancy silk.  Very full skirt lined all through with rustling taffeta and bound with velvet.  This is one of the finest productions of the season.  Only..........................$12.25

**24971  Very Handsome Combination Suit**, jacket made of either green or blue cheviot to match skirt and edged with gimp, the skirt very full, made of imported checked goods and inlaid of same material as jacket, lined with rustling taffeta and bound with velvet, style and general appearance cannot be excelled.
Price.................................................................$13.25

**24972  This Elegant Ladies' Suit**, is made of imported black cheviot, jacket fly front, small lapels, newest sleeves and cuffs, lined all through with black silk serge, trimmed with small pearl buttons, full skirt lined with taffeta and bound with velvet all around.
Nothing nicer made for..........................................$14.50

**24973  An Extremely Beautiful Ladies' Suit**, in Bolero cape style, of very fine quality, brown and gold mixture.  Collar and lapels appliqued and very elaborately embroidered, four rows of soutach braid all around cape, waist lined with best quality silk, trimmed with green moire ribbon.  Very full skirt, lined throughout with rustling taffeta and bound with velvet.  Absolutely perfection in every respect.  Price................................................$18.00

**24974  Another Beautiful Combination Suit**, skirt is made of fancy Scotch mixture, very full, lined all through with rustling taffeta, and bound with velvet.  Detachable belt and Chatelain bag made of same material as skirt.  You must have one of these to be in style.  Dresden pattern, French lawn waist, with detachable collar and attached cuffs.  Large assortment of beautiful patterns in light and medium shades.  The price of this stylish suit is only......$2.90

We also furnish the skirt **without the waist** for..............$2.00

We make the same style skirt as 24974 **without the waist**, in three grades.  All fancy Scotch mixed goods as follows:

| | |
|---|---|
| 24975 | $2.75 |
| 24976 | 3.25 |
| 24977 | 3.75 |

# 1897

# TAILOR MADE WALKING AND BICYCLE SUITS

**24993 $6.75**

**24990 $3.75**

**24980 $3.15**

**24982 $4.25**

## SUITS FOR HIGH SUMMER WEAR.

**24980 Made of Washable Linen Crash,** Blazer style with newest sleeves and cuffs, very finest skirt. Price..................$3.15

**24981 Very Stylish,** made of high grade plaid washable linen crash, big sailor collar fancy front. Our price, only............$4.00

**24982 This Beautiful Summer Suit,** is made of fancy checked washable linen crash. sailor collar and fronts of white linen, newest sleeves and cuffs. Very rich. Price...........................$4.25

**24983 $10.00** Would not be too much for this Elegant Suit, made of fancy washable linen crash, big sailor collar, front and cuffs of blue linen, making a very pretty combination.
Price only....................................................$5.00

## BICYCLE SUITS.

**24989 Consists of five pieces,** Jacket, Skirt, Bloomers, Leggins and Cap, made of Austrian covert cloth in brown or gray mixtures. Blazer Jacket very nobby. Price.................................$3.75

**24990 This Nobby Suit** (illustrated) is made of five pieces in double breasted Reefer style, full skirt in either tan or gray mixed Austrian covert cloth. Would be cheap at $7.50.
Only.......................................................$4.00

**24991 Very Similar to 24993,** made of very stylish novelty cloth, in five pieces consisting of cap, jacket, skirt, leggins and bloomers. Only .....................................$4.25

**24992 Blazer Style made of Imported Tiger Cloth,** consisting of five pieces. Material durable and will outwear any material. Others sell it for $8.00, we sell it for...........................$4.75

**24993 This Handsome Suit** (illustrated) is made of brown or blue Repellant cloth, bound in leather all around and consists of five pieces, jacket, half lined with silk. Can't be beat..............$6.75

**24983 $5.00**

**24981 $4.00**

# LADIES WHITE MUSLIN NIGHT GOWNS.

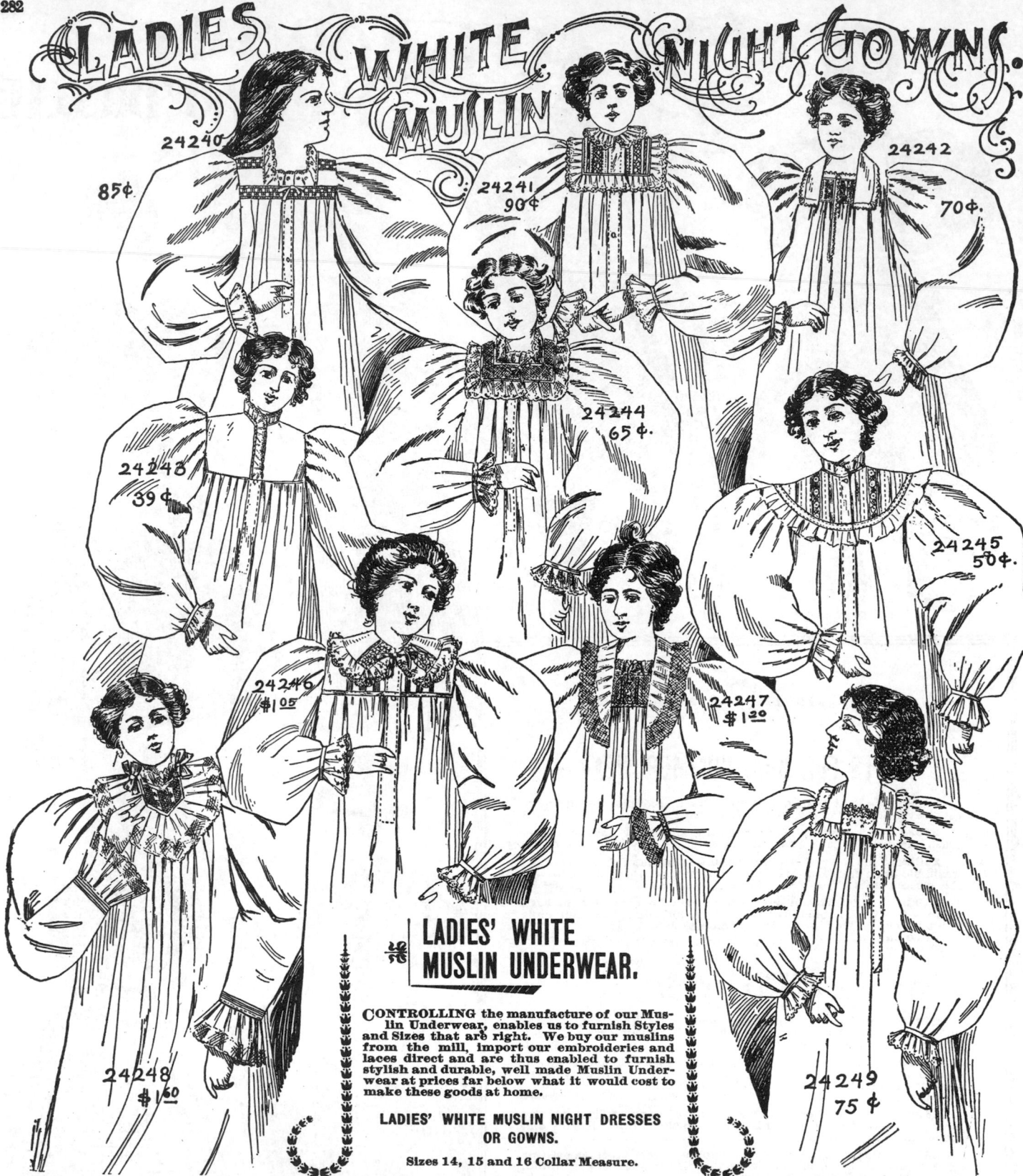

24240   85¢

24241   90¢

24242   70¢

24244   65¢

24243   39¢

24245   50¢

24246   $1.05

24247   $1.20

24248   $1.60

24249   75¢

## LADIES' WHITE MUSLIN UNDERWEAR.

**CONTROLLING** the manufacture of our Muslin Underwear, enables us to furnish Styles and Sizes that are right. We buy our muslins from the mill, import our embroideries and laces direct and are thus enabled to furnish stylish and durable, well made Muslin Underwear at prices far below what it would cost to make these goods at home.

### LADIES' WHITE MUSLIN NIGHT DRESSES OR GOWNS.

Sizes 14, 15 and 16 Collar Measure.

**24240  Marlborough Mother Hubbard Night Gown,** square neck, two rows fine open work, embroidered across front, neck and sleeves trimmed with 2 inch point open work embroidery, finished with ribbon bows. Each, 85c; two for.................................................$1.60

**24241  A Fine Cambric Ladies' Night Gown,** mother hubbard front, eight tucks, two insertions of embroidery, 2½ inch point open work embroidery, around neck front and sleeves. Each, 90c; two for.........$1.75

**24242  This is one of the New Patterns. Ladies' Empire Night Gown,** made of good muslin, gown has a collar, four rows embroidery insertion, embroidery edge around collar, neck and sleeves. Each, 70c; two for.................................................$1.30

**24243  Ladies' Muslin Gown,** mother hubbard yoke, cambric ruffle, trimmed with torchon lace around neck and sleeve. Each, 39c; two for..76c

**24244  One of our Best Styles. Ladies Fine White Muslin Night Gown or Dress,** Malborough style, square neck, bosom trimmed with torchon insertion, edged up and down with torchon lace, finished with bow of ribbon, sleeves trimmed with torchon lace. Each, 65c; two for....................$1.25

**24245  Ladies' Muslin Night Dress,** twelve tucks, two insertions of embroidery, cambric ruffle around yoke, neck and sleeves; good quality muslin. Each, 50c; two for.................................................$0.97

**24246  Ladies' Night Dress,** mother hubbard style, raised shoulders, thirty tucks in front, round collar trimmed with insertion and edging, sleeves nicely trimmed, finished with ribbon bows. Each, $1.05; two for......$2.00

**24247  Ladies' Cambric Night Dress,** empire style, trimmed around neck and sleeves with fine lawn ruffle. The ruffle is trimmed with 2 inch medici lace, sleeves headed with herringbone trimming. Bosom has two rows of medici lace insertion and one open applique embroidery insertion, edged with 1 inch medici lace, finished with ribbon bows. Each, $1.20; two for.................................................$2.30

**24248  Ladies' Bridal Night Gown,** Victoria shape, made of fine cambric, large bows of satin ribbon on shoulder, white lawn, ruffle edged with 2 inch valenciens lace around bosoms and sleeves. Front has three rows of valenciens lace insertion. Headed around neck with 2 inch valenciens lace Neck V shape, sleeves headed with eight tucks. Back yoke has three box pleats. Each, $1.60; two for.................................................$3.00

**24249  Ladies' Empire Stylish Muslin Night Gown,** with collar and sleeves trimmed with cambric, ruffle and finished with embroidery, bosom trimmed with fine embroidery. Each, 75c; two for....................$1.42

# INFANT'S · LONG · CLOAKS
## SEARS ROEBUCK & CO. INC.

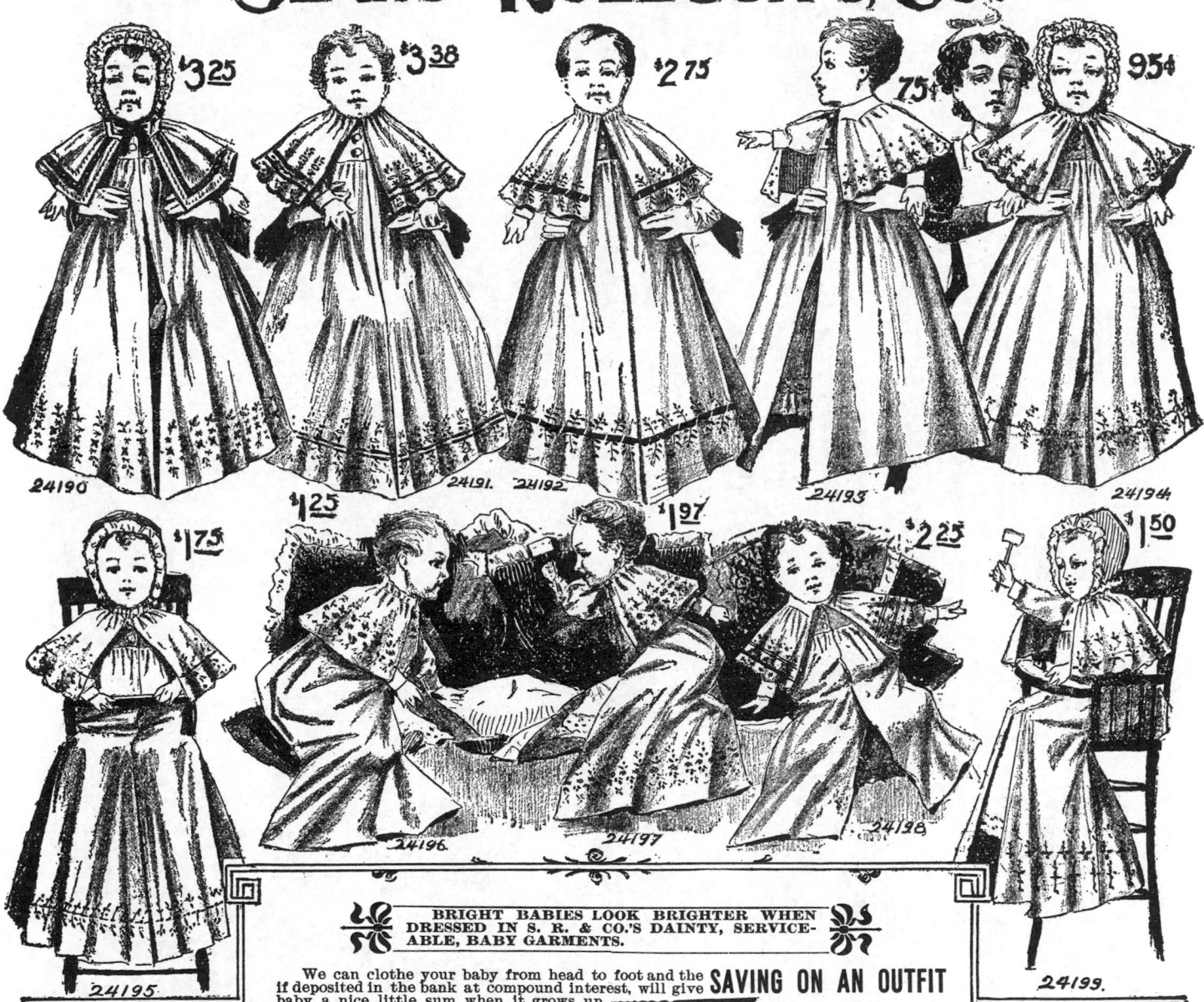

**BRIGHT BABIES LOOK BRIGHTER WHEN DRESSED IN S. R. & CO.'S DAINTY, SERVICE-ABLE, BABY GARMENTS.**

We can clothe your baby from head to foot and the **SAVING ON AN OUTFIT** if deposited in the bank at compound interest, will give baby a nice little sum when it grows up.

## INFANTS' LONG EMBROIDERED CASHMERE CLOAKS.
### (AT SHORT PRICES.)

**24190** The Late Parisian Novelty Cloak, is made of all wool cashmere, has the new style double split cape, trimmed with fancy, satin ribbon and one row of fancy silk gimp on each side of ribbon, sleeves nicely trimmed with satin ribbon and silk gimp, skirt is nicely embroidered with wide heavy silk embroidery, lined with the finest quality of sateen. A cloak like this always retails for $4.25, (cream or tan).
Our price.................................................$3.25

**24191** An All Wool Cashmere Cloak, large full cape, heavily embroidered and trimmed with two rows of ribbon, skirt heavily embroidered and has two rows of satin ribbon around bottom, large full puff sleeves, sateen lining. Each...................................$3.38

**24192** A Handsome All Wool Cashmere Cloak, skirt and cape embroidered with handsome silk embroidery, cape very full, ribbon drawn through, embroidered on cape and also on skirt, lined with a superior quality of sateen, puff sleeves. This cloak is made after the latest Parisian styles and is a handsome, stylish garment. Looks as well as the $5.00 cloaks. Our price, each....................................$2.75

**24193** Infants' Long Cashmere Cloaks, nicely lined, has silk embroidered cape, full length and width, puff sleeves, colors, tan or cream. Each.................................................$0.75

**24194** Infants' English Cashmere Cloak, nicely lined, skirt embroidered, and cape embroidered with silk embroidery, full puff sleeves, 35 inches long and 50 inch sweep in skirt. This cloak is sold by most retailers at $1.50; colors, tan and cream. Our price, each............$0.95

**24195** A Handsome Infants' Cloak, made of English cashmere, cape and skirt heavily embroidered with silk embroidery, cape scalloped: this cloak is lined with good quality sateen, is full 36 inches long, full width, extra large puff sleeves, stylishly made. A cloak like this easily retails for $2.50. Our special price, each...........................$1.75

**24196** This Handsome Cashmere Cloak, has a beautiful embroidered cape, 2 rows of silk ribbons drawn through the embroidery, nice full puff sleeves, sateen lined. This handsome garment retails everywhere for $2.00. Each.................................................$1.25

**24197** This Number is a very Nobby Infants' Good Quality Cashmere Cloak, both the cape and skirt embroidered with heavy embroidery in the latest and most stylish patterns, new Berlin collar. Cloak lined throughout with a nice quality sateen, good length and width; this handsome cloak is well worth $2.75, and in fact is sold for that price at retail in the city of Chicago. Our price, each....................$1.97

**24198** A Fine All Wool Cashmere Cloak, One of Our Novelties, cape handsomely embroidered and scalloped, made very wide, collar is trimmed with five rows of ribbon, producing a very handsome and stylish effect, large sleeves, nicely puffed. cloak lined throughout with a sateen of good quality, a cloak of this quality usually retails for $3.50; colors, cream or tan. Our very special price, each....................$2.25

**24199** This Handsome Infants' Cloak, is made of good quality cashmere, both cape and skirt are handsomely embroidered with silk, lined throughout with good quality sateen, full length and width, has five large puff sleeves; taken in all, this is a garment that retails everywhere at $2.00; colors, cream or tan. Our price.........  .............$1.50

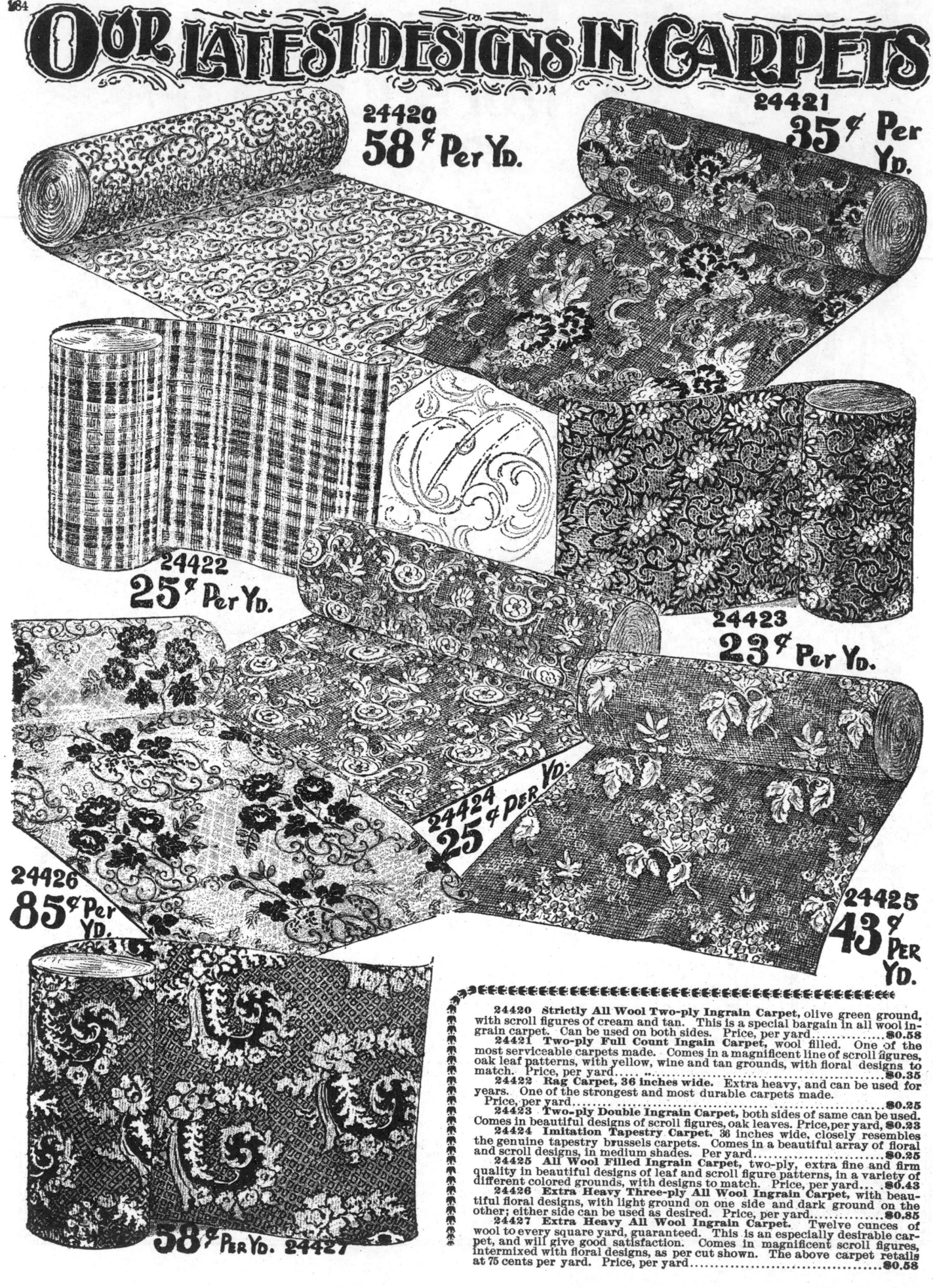

# OUR LATEST DESIGNS IN CARPETS

184

**24420**
**58¢ Per Yd.**

**24421**
**35¢ Per Yd.**

**24422**
**25¢ Per Yd.**

**24423**
**23¢ Per Yd.**

**24424**
**25¢ Per Yd.**

**24426**
**85¢ Per Yd.**

**24425**
**43¢ Per Yd.**

**58¢ Per Yd. 24427**

**24420** **Strictly All Wool Two-ply Ingrain Carpet,** olive green ground, with scroll figures of cream and tan. This is a special bargain in all wool ingrain carpet. Can be used on both sides. Price, per yard..............$0.58

**24421** **Two-ply Full Count Ingain Carpet,** wool filled. One of the most serviceable carpets made. Comes in a magnificent line of scroll figures, oak leaf patterns, with yellow, wine and tan grounds, with floral designs to match. Price, per yard..............$0.35

**24422** **Rag Carpet, 36 inches wide.** Extra heavy, and can be used for years. One of the strongest and most durable carpets made. Price, per yard..............$0.25

**24423** **Two-ply Double Ingrain Carpet,** both sides of same can be used. Comes in beautiful designs of scroll figures, oak leaves. Price, per yard, $0.23

**24424** **Imitation Tapestry Carpet.** 36 inches wide, closely resembles the genuine tapestry brussels carpets. Comes in a beautiful array of floral and scroll designs, in medium shades. Per yard..............$0.25

**24425** **All Wool Filled Ingrain Carpet,** two-ply, extra fine and firm quality in beautiful designs of leaf and scroll figure patterns, in a variety of different colored grounds, with designs to match. Price, per yard.....$0.43

**24426** **Extra Heavy Three-ply All Wool Ingrain Carpet,** with beautiful floral designs, with light ground on one side and dark ground on the other; either side can be used as desired. Price, per yard..............$0.85

**24427** **Extra Heavy All Wool Ingrain Carpet.** Twelve ounces of wool to every square yard, guaranteed. This is an especially desirable carpet, and will give good satisfaction. Comes in magnificent scroll figures, intermixed with floral designs, as per cut shown. The above carpet retails at 75 cents per yard. Price, per yard..............$0.58

# OUR LATEST DESIGNS IN CARPETS

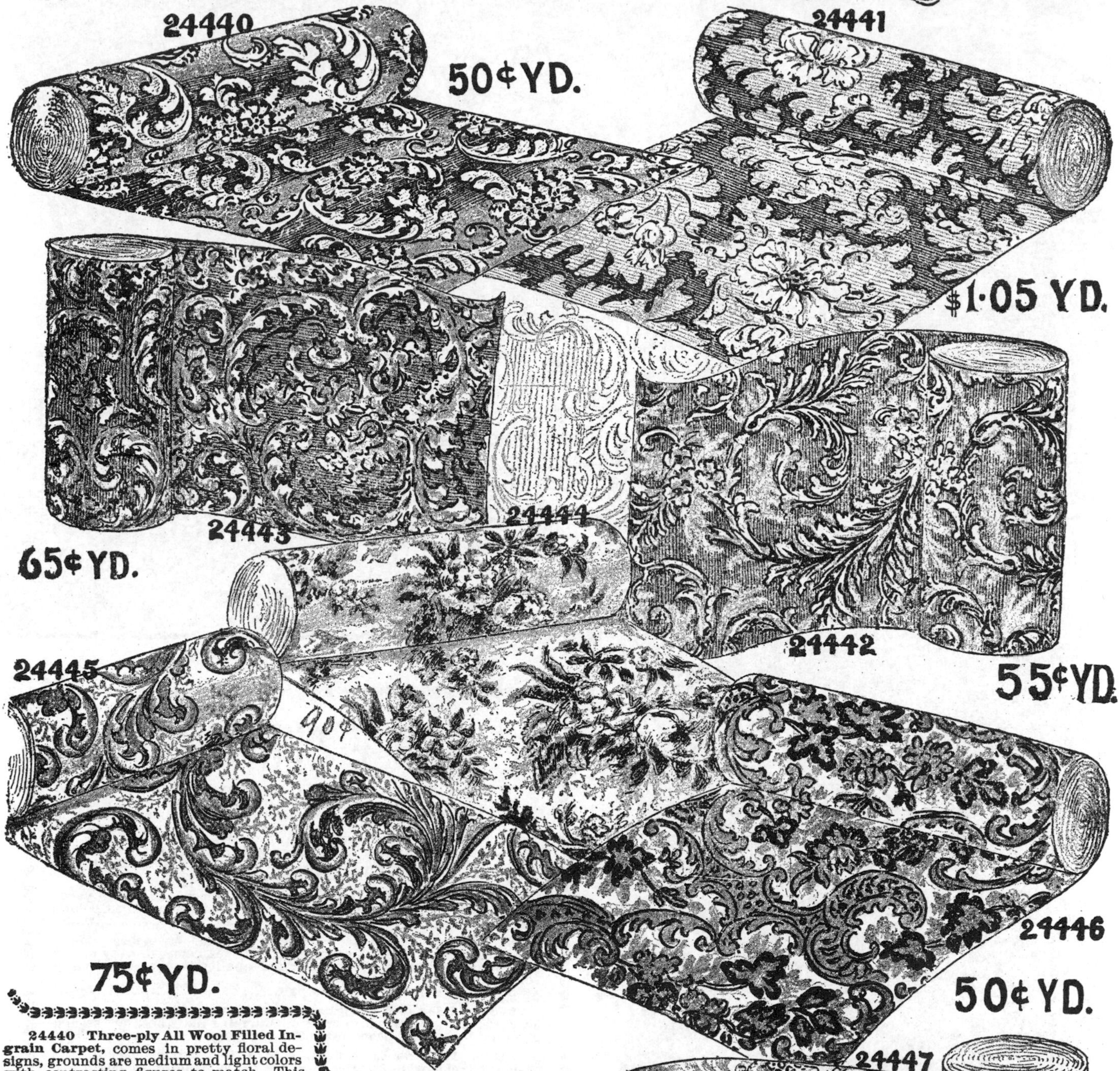

24440

24441

50¢ YD.

$1·05 YD.

24443

65¢ YD.

24444

24442

55¢ YD.

24445

24446

75¢ YD.

50¢ YD.

$1·25 YD.

24447

**24440   Three-ply All Wool Filled Ingrain Carpet,** comes in pretty floral designs, grounds are medium and light colors with contrasting figures to match. This carpet will wear well and is almost as good a carpet as money can buy. Per yard..**$0.50**

**24441   27-inch Body Brussels Carpet,** a good firm carpet, that will wear like iron. Comes in medium and light grounds, and has very pretty designs of contrasting colors. We can furnish nearly any combination of colors in this carpet. Per yard............................**$1.05**

**24442   A Tapestry Brussels Carpet,** 27 inches wide in light and medium colored grounds in the latest up to date patterns, we can send almost any combination of colors in this handsome carpet. Per yard............**$0.55**

**24443   Tapestry Brussels Carpet,** 27 inches wide, a beautiful carpet, colors all fast, comes in medium and light colors in some of the newest and swellest designs of the season. This is a carpet that will please all. Per yard............................**$0.65**

**24444   Velvet and Mouquette Carpets.**   A rich velvet carpet, 27 inches wide, comes in medium and light grounds with nice floral designs in pretty contrasting colors, this handsome carpet is admired by all who see it. Per yard............................**$0.90**

**24445   27-inch Tapestry Brussels Carpet.**   This number is a beauty, comes in the medium and light grounds in the newest patterns. The quality is superior to most carpets at this price and it is considered a big bargain by all who see it. Per yard............................**$0.75**

**24446   Tapestry and Body Brussels Carpets.**   Tapestry Brussels Carpet 27 inches wide, a carpet that will wear well and give satisfaction, comes in pretty designs in light, medium and dark colors. Per yard............**$0.50**

**24447   A Swell Moquette Carpet,** 27 inches wide, long pile, which makes a soft carpet, light and medium grounds, pretty floral designs in nice colors, a carpet that is a beauty and very cheap at the price we sell at. Per yard............................**$1.25**

# LACE CURTAINS

24601 $0.55

24602 $0.95

24600 $1.50

24606 $1.25

24607 $0.75

24608 $1.35

24609 $1.95

24603 $0.98

24604 $1.75

## ...LACE CURTAINS...

**WE SELL CURTAINS IN PAIRS ONLY.** Our lace curtain department is one of the most important in our vast establishment. We sell thousands of pairs of curtains weekly. Our immense sales in this department enable us to often take the entire production of foreign mills. Our buyers are always on the alert for values. We can, and do save our patrons much money on curtains. In buying a bill of curtains of us, the amount saved over retail merchant prices, is often enough to buy a handsome piece of furniture.

**24600 Nottingham Lace Curtain,** 50 inches wide, 3½ yards long, comes in pretty patterns, similar to illustration, taped, colors, cream and white. Per pair............................................**$1.50**

**24601 Nottingham Lace Curtain,** imported, 40 inches wide, 3 yards long; colors, cream or white, taped edges, comes in very pretty designs and is equal in appearance and quality to curtains usually sold by retail merchants at $1.00.
S., R. & Co's special price, per pair...................................**$0.55**

**24602 A Large Nottingham Lace Curtain,** 54 inches wide and 3½ yards long; colors, white or ecru. Curtains like these are selling right in the city of Chicago for $1.50. Per pair.. ................**$0.95**

**24603 The New Lace Curtain Fish Net Patterns,** (small neat design) 36 inches wide, 3 yards long. This very handsome curtain has a beautiful border, and in general appearance is equal to curtains usually sold by regular retail merchants at $2.00; colors, cream or white. Our special price, per pair............ ................ **$0.98**

**24604 Medium Heavy Nottingham Lace Curtain,** 54 inches wide, 3½ yards long, various patterns similar to illustration, taped, comes in white and ecru. Per pair....................... ...........**$1.75**

**24606 Nottingham Lace Curtain,** 46 inches wide, 3½ yards long, a beautiful curtain like illustration, has a handsome wide border and comes in cream or white. Per pair.................................**$1.25**

**24607 Imported Nottingham Lace Curtain,** 46 inches wide, 3 yards long, taped edges, colors, cream or white, new and fashionable patterns. These curtains are similar to illustration shown.
Per pair......................................................................**$0.75**

**24608 Handsome Nottingham Lace Curtains,** 46 inches wide, 3½ yards long, has a beautiful floral pattern, taped; colors, cream and white. Per pair...........................................**$1.35**

**24609 A 54-inch Nottingham Lace Curtain,** similar to illustration, 3½ yards long; a beautiful floral design of leaves and flowers, comes in cream or white. Per pair............... .. .........**$1.95**

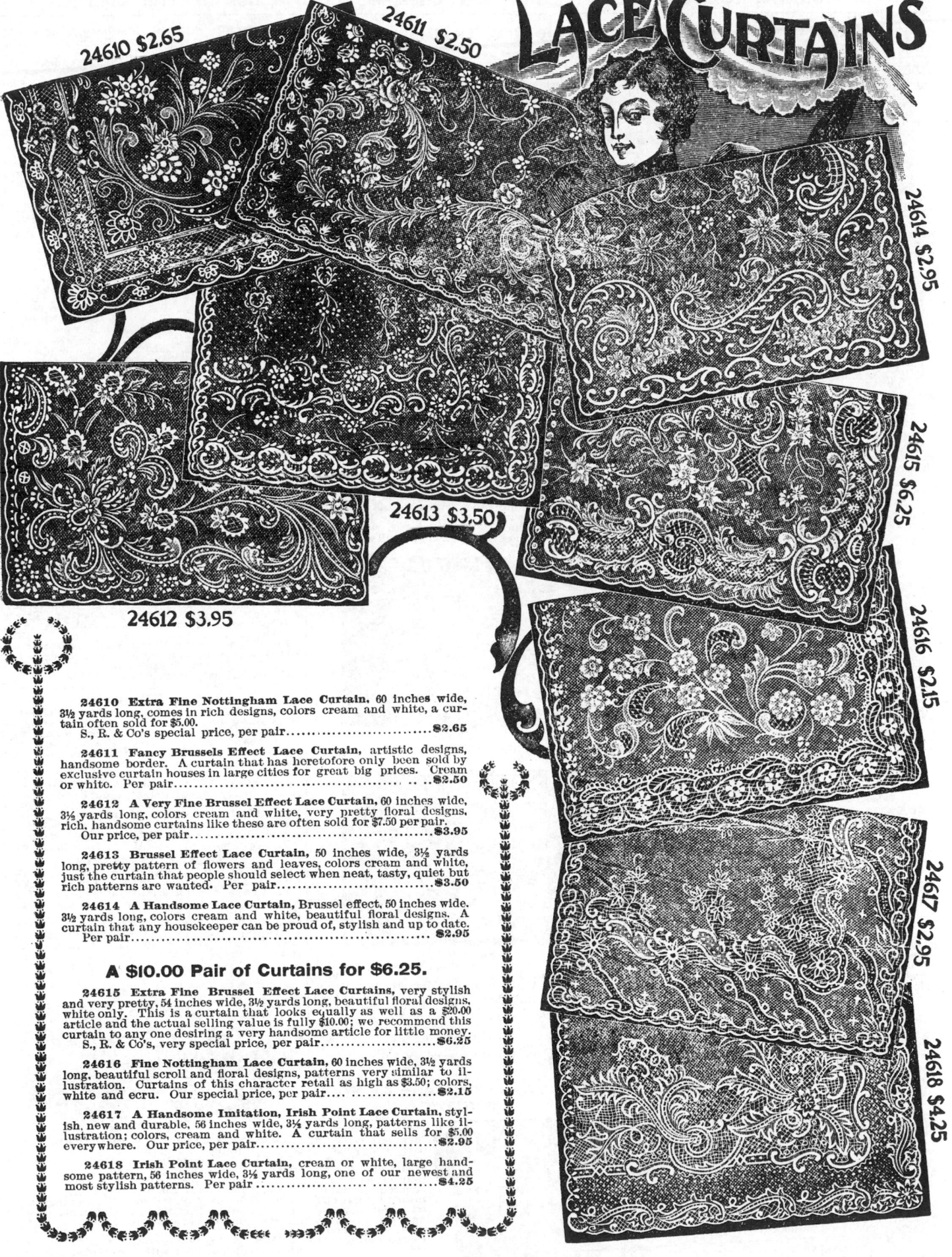

# LACE CURTAINS

24610 $2.65

24611 $2.50

24614 $2.95

24615 $6.25

24612 $3.95

24613 $3.50

24616 $2.15

24617 $2.95

24618 $4.25

**24610  Extra Fine Nottingham Lace Curtain**, 60 inches wide, 3½ yards long, comes in rich designs, colors cream and white, a curtain often sold for $5.00.
S., R. & Co's special price, per pair..............................$2.65

**24611  Fancy Brussels Effect Lace Curtain**, artistic designs, handsome border. A curtain that has heretofore only been sold by exclusive curtain houses in large cities for great big prices. Cream or white. Per pair..............................................$2.50

**24612  A Very Fine Brussel Effect Lace Curtain**, 60 inches wide, 3½ yards long, colors cream and white, very pretty floral designs, rich, handsome curtains like these are often sold for $7.50 per pair.
Our price, per pair................................................$3.95

**24613  Brussel Effect Lace Curtain**, 50 inches wide, 3½ yards long, pretty pattern of flowers and leaves, colors cream and white, just the curtain that people should select when neat, tasty, quiet but rich patterns are wanted. Per pair..............................$3.50

**24614  A Handsome Lace Curtain**, Brussel effect, 50 inches wide. 3½ yards long, colors cream and white, beautiful floral designs. A curtain that any housekeeper can be proud of, stylish and up to date.
Per pair.......................................................... $2.95

## A $10.00 Pair of Curtains for $6.25.

**24615  Extra Fine  Brussel Effect Lace Curtains**, very stylish and very pretty, 54 inches wide, 3½ yards long, beautiful floral designs, white only.  This is a curtain that looks equally as well as a $20.00 article and the actual selling value is fully $10.00; we recommend this curtain to any one desiring a very handsome article for little money.
S., R. & Co's, very special price, per pair.....................$6.25

**24616  Fine Nottingham Lace Curtain**, 60 inches wide, 3½ yards long, beautiful scroll and floral designs, patterns very similar to illustration.  Curtains of this character retail as high as $3.50; colors, white and ecru.  Our special price, per pair.... .................$2.15

**24617  A Handsome Imitation, Irish Point Lace Curtain**, stylish, new and durable, 56 inches wide, 3½ yards long, patterns like illustration; colors, cream and white. A curtain that sells for $5.00 everywhere.  Our price, per pair...................................$2.95

**24618  Irish Point Lace Curtain**, cream or white, large handsome pattern, 56 inches wide, 3½ yards long, one of our newest and most stylish patterns.  Per pair............................. .............$4.25

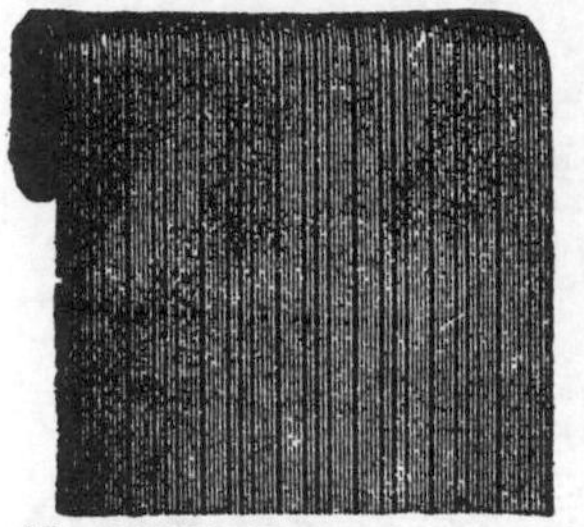

**No. 22504 All Wool Shirting Flannel,** 28 inch wide, has a silk stripe, colors blue, red and pink. This flannel makes up into very handsome shirts and is also a very desirable fabric to make ladies' shirt waists; suitable for cool summer evenings.
Per yard...$0.25

**No. 22506 Extra heavy All Wool Farmers' Shirting Flannel,** stripes and small and large checks; colors, blue and black, red and black and gray and blue stripes; 28 inch wide. This flannel can be used for shirts, children's dresses or ladies' skirts. A very desirable and useful flannel.
Per yard....................................$0.25

## Shaker Flannel.

**No. 22507 White Shaker Flannel,** 25 inches wide.
Per yard.................................................04
Full piece of 50 yards, per yard...............$0.03¾
**No. 22508 White Shaker Flannel,** 28 inches wide.
Per yard.............................................$0.06
Full piece of 50 yards, per yard.................0.05¾
**No. 22509 White Shaker Flannel,** 30 inches wide.
Per yard.............................................$0.08
Full piece of 50 yards, per yard.................0.07½
**No. 22511 White Shaker Flannel,** extra heavy, 30 inches wide. Per yard...........................$0.10
Full piece of 50 yards, per yard.................0.09½

## Unbleached Cotton Flannel.

**Our Cotton Flannels are the Nashua Brand,** which are noted for having a longer nap and firmer back than any other line made. They cost less of us than others ask for ordinary grades.

**Revised List.**

**No. 22546 Unbleached Cotton Flannel,** cheapest made, width, 25 inches. Per yard...............$0.04
Full piece of about 60 yards, per yard..........03¾
**No. 22548 Unbleached Cotton Flannel,** width 25 inches. Per yard.................................$0.05
Price for full piece of about 58 yards,
Per yard.............................................$0.04¾
**No. 22550 Unbleached Cotton Flannel,** width 25 inches. Per yard.................................$0.06½
Price for full piece of about 58 yards.
Per yard.............................................$0.06¼
**No. 22551 Unbleached Cotton Flannel,** width, 28 inches. Per yard.................................$0.08½
Price for full piece of about 58 yards.
Per yard.............................................$0.08¼
**No. 22552 Unbleached Cotton Flannel,** width, 31 inches. Compare this with 10c quality others sell.
Per yard.............................................$0.10
Price for full piece of about 67 yards.
Per yard.............................................$0.09¾
**No. 22553 Unbleached Cotton Flannel,** heavy weight; width, 31 inches. Per yard...............$0.12
Price for full piece of about 55 yards.
Per yard.............................................$0.11½
**No. 22555 Unbleached Cotton Flannel,** width, 32 inches, extra heavy twilled back and thick napping.
Per yard.............................................$0.15
Price for full piece of about 55 yards.
Per yard.............................................$0.14½

## Bleached Cotton Flannel.

**No. 22556 Bleached Cotton Flannel,** 24 inches wide, per yard.............................$0.06½
Price for full piece of about 58 yards, per yd. .06¼
**No. 22558 Bleached Cotton Flannel,** 26 inches wide, per yard.................................08½
Price for full piece of about 58 yards, per yd. .08¼
**No. 22560 Bleached Cotton Flannel,** 26 inches wide, per yard.................................10
Price for full piece of about 57 yards, per yd. .09½
**No. 22561 Bleached Cotton Flannel,** 28 inches wide, per yard.................................12
Price for full piece of about 55 yards, per yd. .11¼
**No. 22563 Bleached Cotton Flannel,** heavy weight, 30 inches wide, per yard....... .14
Price for full piece of about 55 yards, per yd. .13¼
**No. 22565 Bleached Cotton Flannel,** 31 inches wide, extra heavy, per yard.............15½
Price for full piece of about 54 yards, per yd, .15

## Half Wool, Twilled Flannel.

**No. 22512 White Twilled Flannel,** half wool, 27 inches wide. Per yard..........................$0.18
**No. 22514 White Twilled Flannel,** half wool 27 inches wide, extra heavy. Per yard...........$0.25

## White Wool Flannel.

**No. 22516 White Flannel,** 26 inches wide.
Per yard.............................................$0.15
**No. 22517 White Flannel,** wool with cotton warp, non-shrinkable, 27 inches wide, per yd.. .19
**No. 22519 White Flannel,** all wool, 27 inches wide, per yard.................................25
**No. 22521 White Flannel,** all wool, 28 inches wide, per yard.................................35.
**No. 22523 White Flannel,** all wool, extra fine 36 inches wide, per yard........................50

## Heavy Blue Flannels.

| No. 22525 | Per Yard. |
|---|---|
| 23 inches wide, good value | $0.15 |
| 23 inches wide, good value | .20 |
| 23 inches wide, good value | .26 |
| 27 inches wide, good value | .28 |
| 27 inches wide, good value | .33 |
| 27 inches wide, good value | .39 |
| 27 inches wide, good value | .49 |

## Blue Gray Twill Flannels.

| No. 22527 | Per Yard. |
|---|---|
| 27 inches wide, part wool | $0.15 |
| 27 inches wide, part wool | .25 |
| 27 inches wide, all wool | .29 |
| 27 inches wide, extra fine, all wool | .39 |

## Pure Wool Scarlet Twill Flannels.

| No. 22529 | Per yard. |
|---|---|
| 23 inches wide, good value | $0.15 |
| 23 inches wide, good value | .20 |
| 23 inches wide, good value | .26 |
| 27 inches wide, good value | .28 |
| 27 inches wide, good value | .33 |
| 27 inches wide, best value | .39 |
| 27 inches wide, best value | .49 |

## Best California Scarlet Flannels.

| No. 22530 | Per yard. |
|---|---|
| 28 inches wide, pure wool, 5 oz | $0.31 |
| 28 inches wide, pure wool, 6 oz | .35 |
| 28 inches wide, pure wool, 7 oz | .41 |
| 28 inches wide, pure wool, 8 oz | .53 |
| 28 inches wide, pure wool, 9 oz | .65 |

## Mackinaw or Blanketing Flannel.

**Comes in Navy Blue Only,**

**No. 22531 Mackinaw Flannel,** navy blue only; width, 52 inches; 20 ounces to the yard.
Per yard.............................................$0.85
**No. 22533 Mackinaw Flannel,** navy blue only; 52 inches wide, extra heavy. Per yard.........$1.05
**No. 22534 Extra Heavy All Wool Shirting and Lumbermen's Coat Flannel,** weight 8 ounces to the yard 28 inches wide, colors, blue with black stripe, gray with blue stripe, red with black stripe. This fabric can also be used for skirts.
Per yard.............................................$0.39

## Silk Embroidered Flannels.

**New Designs. Note Reduced Prices.**

**Embroidery is done with a smooth twisted silk, giving more service and is more showy than the flat silk usually used.** The work is all done on a specially selected cream white 36-inch all wool flannel, with 2-inch folded edge. Designs are all new and are handsomer and greater width embroidery than can be found elsewhere at the same price.

**It is not customary to sample embroidered flannels,** as very accurate descriptions are given and expense of sampling is great. However, where selections cannot otherwise be made, we will send samples upon request.

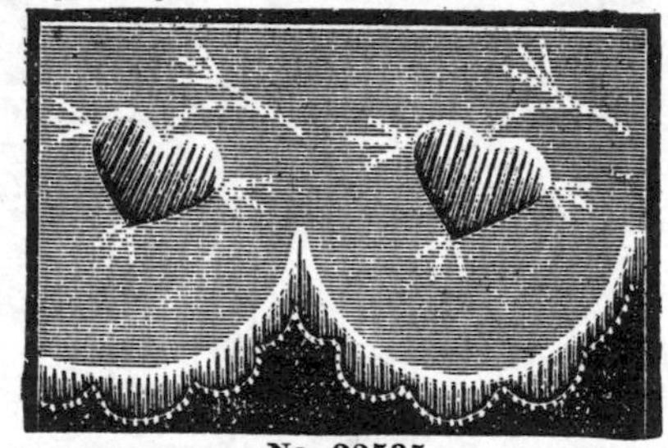

No. 22535.

**No. 22535** Width of embroidery 1½ in; small neat spray designs. Per yard.........................$0.59

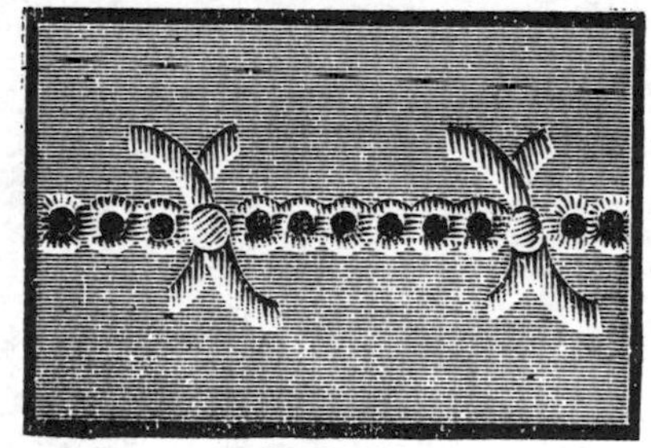

No. 22357.

**No. 22537 Hem Stitching Embroidery,** olive branch design. Per yard...........................$0.68
**No. 22538 Width of Embroidery** 3 inches, double crescent design, detached pattern. Per yard ..$0.79
**No. 22540 Width of Embroidery** 3½ inches, snow ball and vine pattern, very pretty.
Per yard.............................................$0.85
**No. 22542 Width of Embroidery,** 4½ inches, artistic design, vine and crescent. Per yard....$0.87
**No. 22544 Width of Embroidery,** 5 inches, floral scroll design.
Per yard.............................................$0.90

## Cotton, Wool Mixed and All Wool Eiderdown.

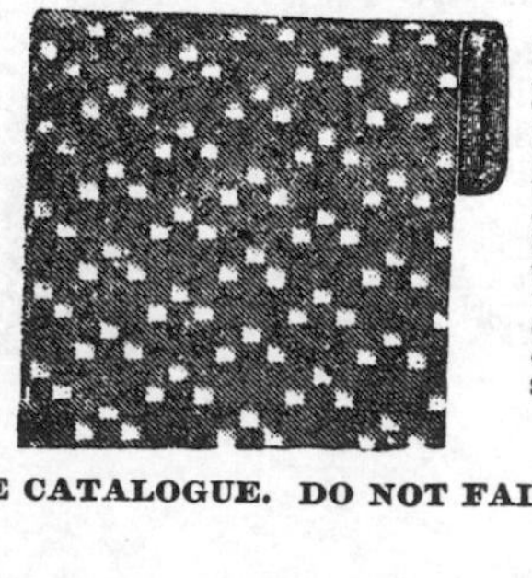

**No. 22569 Cotton Eiderdown,** 28 inches wide, has an extra heavy fleece, and closely resembles a genuine all wool eiderdown; comes in the following colors, red with white dots and tan with white dots; these goods can be used on both sides.
Price, per yard
..........$0.18

**No. 22569½ All Wool Eiderdown,** 28 inches wide; light and dark grey, pink and blue; also in stripes.
Per yard.............................................$0.38
**No. 22570 Cotton Teazledown,** 28 inches wide; colors, light and dark gray, pink and tan.
Per yard.............................................$0.07
**No. 22571 Extra Heavy Teazledown,** 28 inches wide, fleeced on both sides and is used extensively for underwear, skirts, men's shirts, and infants' cloaks; colors, tan, light and dark gray, light blue and pink. Per yard.................................$0.12½

## BLANKET DEPARTMENT.

**THIS IS ONE OF THE LARGEST AND MOST RAPIDLY GROWING DEPARTMENTS IN OUR ESTABLISHMENT. OWING TO THE LATENESS OF THE SEASON, WE WERE ENABLED TO PURCHASE THE ENTIRE STOCK OF A LARGE BOSTON JOBBER AT A VERY LOW FIGURE AND CAN OFFER OUR CUSTOMERS BLANKETS AT A GREAT DEAL LESS THAN THE USUAL PRICE.**

## Blankets.

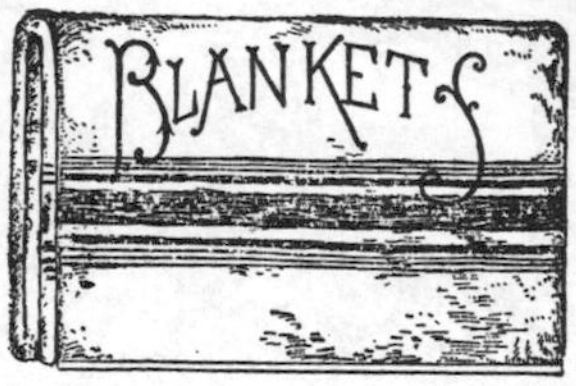


**No. 22573 Full fleeced,** good quality, bound edges, with fancy borders, regular 10-4 size, gray or white.
Per pair....$0.55
**No. 22574 White, gray or blue-gray,** with combination border, heavy fleeced, regular 10-4 size, regular $1.00 value.
Per pair....$0.70
**No. 22575 Extra heavy, large sized blankets,** size about 64x80 inches, comes in light and dark gray, also white, with heavy long fleecing, bound ends and fancy borders. Retail price, $1.50.
Our special price, per pair.........................$0.98

## White Blankets.

**No. 22577 Extra White Twilled Bed Blankets** soft and warm, with fancy border, size 76x65 inches.
Special price per pair..............................$1.65
**No. 22578 Extra Heavy Wool-Filled Blanket,** weight about 4 lbs. size 64x80 inches. Special price per pair.............................................$2.25
**No. 22579 Strictly All-Wool White Bed Blanket,** colored border, regular 10-4 size, weight about 4 lbs. Regular value about $4.00. Our special price. Per Pair......................................$2.95
**No. 22580 Extra Heavy All-Wool Blankets,** Made out of pure Australian wool, mohair bound, with a combination blue and pink border. This is a splendid wearing and warm blanket. Large size.
Price.................................................$3.65
**No. 22581 Strictly Finest Wool California Bed Blanket,** made of the finest selected wool, extra large size, very soft and downy, silk bound with fancy borders, full size. Regular value, $6.50.
Price per pair.......................................$4.75

## Gray Blankets.

**No. 22583 Heavy Wool Filled Silver Gray Blankets,** weight, about 5 lbs., with fancy border and bound ends. Regular 10-4 size. Price per pair, $1.65
**No. 22584 Extra Heavy Gray Wool Mixed Blankets,** extra large size, with combination border, bound edges, positively the best value ever offered.
Price, per pair.......................................$2.35
**No. 22585 All Wool Blankets,** with fancy stripe border, nicely bound; weight, about 5 lbs. Size, 11-4.
Price, per pair.......................................$3.75
**No. 22587 All Wool Gray Blankets,** extra fine quality pure Australian wool, new ingrain border, silk bound. Regular value, $7.50. Regular 11-4 size.
Price, per pair.......................................$4.75

## Scarlet Blankets.

**No. 22588 All Wool Bed Blankets,** weight, about 4 lbs. Regular 10-4 size. Price, per pair.......$2.98
**No. 22589 Scarlet Blankets,** made out of pure Australian wool, medicated dye, silk bound. Regular 10-4 size. Price, per pair............................$3.95
**No. 22590 Scarlet Blankets,** made out of finest Australian lamb's wool, medicated dye, fancy borders, silk bound, best grade blanket made. Regular 11-4 size. Price, per pair..............................$4.98

## Bed Quilts or Comforters.

**At prices to meet the stringency of the times.**

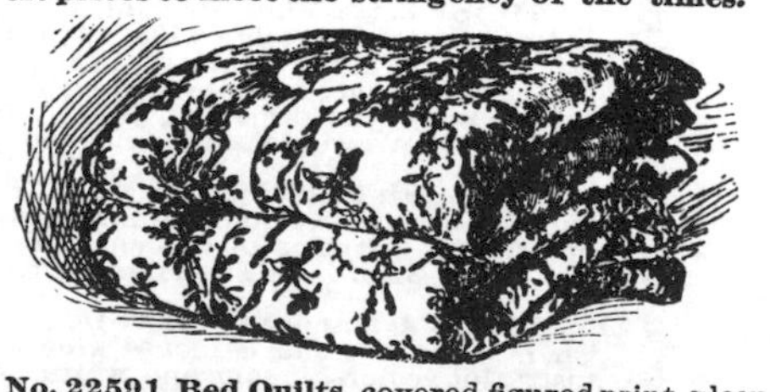

**No. 22591 Bed Quilts,** covered figured print, plain or figured lining. Each, $0.48; 6 for.............2.70
**No. 22593 Bed Quilts** covered with fancy figured sateen, red figured lining; weight about 7 lbs.; good full size; regular $1.25 value.
Special price, each, $0.90; 3 for..................2.60
**No. 22594 Bed Quilts** covered with fancy figured drapery cloth on both sides; good full sizes; weight about 7½ lbs. Our special price, each..........$1.20
2 for...................................................2.35
**22595 Bed Quilts** covered with handsome figured silkolene, filled with fine carded cotton; full size and extra weight; regular $2.25 value.
Bargain price, $1.75; 2 for..........................3.40

THE INDEX IS ON THE LAST PAGES OF THE CATALOGUE. DO NOT FAIL TO LOOK THERE FOR SUCH GOODS AS YOU CAN'T FIND.

## White Bed Spreads.

We buy all our spreads direct from the mills in such large quantities that enables us to sell them cheaper to you than your local dealer would have to pay for them in wholesale dry goods houses.

**No. 22596 White Crochet or Honey Comb Spreads,** full size 70x75, with Marseilles patterns; this is excellent value; regular retail price 75c.
Our Price, each.................................$0.50
Per doz.........................................5.75
Above number is hemmed ready for use.

**No. 22597 Extra Quality White Crochet Spread,** very large size 75x82; full Marseilles pattern, with raised diamond pattern centre; hemmed ready for use. Price.......................................$0.75
Or three for......................................2.10

**No. 22598 Our Well Known "Triumph" Bed Spread** leads them all; made of domestic long combed stock with beautiful raised diamond patterns. This spread usually retails at $1.50.
Our Special Price.............................$0.98
Size 83x83. Hemmed ready for use.

**No. 22599 Very Fine Quality Honey Comb Bed Spread,** has a very pretty raised pattern in center and a handsome border all around; would be considered good value at $2.00. Size, 72x86 inches. Hemmed ready for use. Each.................$1.25

**No. 22600 Extra Heavy White Mitcheline Bed Spread,** will wear as well as a genuine Marseilles spread, costing a great deal more money, full bed size, A good spread that looks well, wears well and is cheap at the price we sell it at. Hemmed ready for use. Each.................................$1.50

**No. 22601 White Marseilles Bed Spread,** full size, has a pretty center pattern with a combination diamond border all around. We can recommend this spread for general use, a spread most retailers would ask $2.50 for. Our special price, each...$1.69

**No. 22602 A Good Quality White Marseilles Bed Spread, Full Regular Size.** Come in pretty patterns and has a nice border all around. We can recommend this spread as being of extraordinary value. Our price, each.........................$1.98

**No. 22603 A White Marseilles Bed Spread,** full bed size, satin damask finish, pretty raised patterns nicely embossed. A very handsome spread that is admired by all who see it. It is only in the great commercial centers that such goods as these can be had. Each.........................................$2.50

**No. 22604 A Very Fine White Marseilles Bed Spread,** with a satin damask finish. Full regular size, beautiful patterns, floral border. Money can procure but few handsomer bed spreads than this one; it's a spread that is well worth a great deal more than the money we ask for it.
Sears, Roebuck & Co's special price...........$3.75

## Colored Bed Spreads.

**No. 22605 A Fancy Colored Bed Spread,** full bed size, colors, blue and red only. These spreads come in a great variety of scroll and floral designs, colors are fast, both sides are different and spread can be used on either side, has a pretty center and border to match. Each...............................$1.25

**No. 22606 A Fancy Crochet Colored Bed Spread,** full regular double bed size, has a heavy knotted fringe, colors, brown, red and blue, has a pretty center, with a heavy deep border to match. Can be used on either side. Each....................$1.50

**...MAMMOTH FURNITURE CATALOGUE FREE...**

## SUITINGS AND PANTS GOODS.

**Extraordinary inducements for Shrewd Buyers.**

### Kentucky Jeans, 27 inches wide.

**No. 22607 Kentucky Jeans,** a very fair quality, 27 inches wide, colors dark and light gray and brown. Per yard...............................$0.10

**No. 22608 Kentucky Jeans,** a firm, heavy cloth, 27 inches wide, colors dark and light gray and brown. Per yard...............................$0.12

**No. 22609 Very Heavy Kentucky Jeans.** This is the very best quality manufactured in cotton goods, 27 inches wide. These are Southern jeans and they excell all others, colors light and dark gray and brown, also black. Per yard.................$0.16

**No. 22610 Wool Filled Kentucky Jeans,** the Triumph brand, 27 inches wide, a good firm cloth and will give utmost satisfaction to the wearer, colors light and dark gray, medium brown and black. Per yard............................................$0.21

**No. 22611 Wool Mixed Kentucky Jeans,** extra heavy, firmly woven, no better wearing goods made, strictly all wool fillings, 27 inches wide, colors, light and dark gray, medium brown and black.
Per yard...........................................$0.30

**No. 22612 27 inch Cotton Worsted Cassimere,** comes in a very fine assortment of stripes suitable for men's and boys' pants. This is a good grade of cloth and a great deal of money can be saved by buying it at our great bargain prices. Colors are blue and black mixture, brown and blue mixture and red and blue mixture; usually sold at 25 cents per yard. Our special price, per yard.........$0.16

### Extra Heavy Cotton Worsted Cassimere.

**No. 22613 Can be had in a very choice assortment of stripes.** This cloth is just the the thing for men's working pants, and **wears like iron.** Colors, brown and blue, blue and black, brown and white and brown and black. 27 inches wide.
Our price per yard................................$0.20

**No. 22614 27 Inch Cottonade.** This class of goods is lighter weight than a cassimere, but of a finer texture. A splendid thing for boys' pants. Garments made of this cloth look well and there is no wear out to them. We save our customers considerable money on this class of goods. Colors blue and black mixed in small neat stripes; gray and black mixed; brown and black mixed; black and gray check. Per yard.........................$0.18

**No. 22615 27 Inch Wool Mixed Tweed or Suiting,** for making men's and boy's suits, also for ladies' and children's dresses, for every day wear. It is a good heavy and serviceable material and looks fully as well as the more expensive goods. The colors are blue and gray mixture, tan mixture, red and gray mixture; also come in neat decided patterns in gray

## WASH DRESS GOODS.

**This rapidly growing Department is one of the foremost in our establishment.** We buy all of our Wash Dress Goods in case lots direct from the mills. Our customers can save a great deal of money by buying Wash Dress Goods of us. Shirt waists will be largely worn this season, and we have made preparations to do an extensive business in shirt waist materials. We have all the new patterns and styles and the prices are away down.

We send samples of all Wash Dress Goods FREE upon application, provided they are more than 7½c per yard. However, if a full description is sent regarding price and color, and you allow us to use our own judgment, we will take the utmost pains to select the very best values obtainable, and in nearly every instance will please you.

**◆◆◆ SAMPLES OF WASH DRESS GOODS FREE. ◆◆◆**

### Wash Goods.

**Four Special Bargains in Summer Wash Goods.** We have closed out an immense lot of Summer wash goods from the "World's Famous Mulhouse Mills," and can offer you the following four numbers at prices which your local dealer would have to pay 25 per cent more.

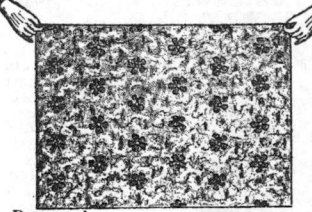

**No. 22625 31 inch Grass Linen Figured Lawn in Dresden Patterns.** They are just the thing for Children's dresses and Ladies' waists; light effect grounds Special bargain prices.
Per yard.....................................$0.07

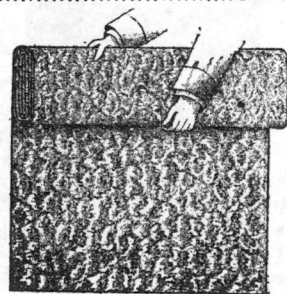

**No. 22626 Linen Figured Lawn.** Same grade of goods as above, in navy, light blue and tan effects, 31 inches wide. We have purchased a big lot of these goods at a very low figure and therefore can sell them so cheap. Price, per yard.....$0.07

or tan mixed. This is a special bargain at the price we offer it. Per yard......................$0.14

**No. 22616 27 Inch Tweed or Fine Cassimere,** strictly all wool filled; comes in both dark and light shades, plain or striped. **Used for men's pants, boy's and men's suits.** A very handsome, durable cloth, that will give the wearer a great deal of satisfaction. Colors, blue and black mixed stripes; gray and black mixed stripes; brown and mixed stripes; also plain blue and gray. Per yard...............$0.35

**No. 22617 Strictly All Wool Fine Tweed Suiting,** 27 inches wide, one of the nobbiest and newest fabrics of the season. Very pretty for men's or boy's suits, **or will make very fine bicycle suits.** Small checks and broken plaids, colors are brown and white mixed, blue and gray mixed, brown and grey mixed, black and gray mixed. Per yard..$0.42

**No. 22618 Strictly All Wool Suiting,** 27 inches wide, very fine quality, a handsome cloth for men's pants or suits, very firm texture. A trial suit or pants order of this material will convince the most skeptical of its value and merit. Colors gray and brown mixed, blue and gray stripe mixed, also steel gray and brown mixture, also plain navy blue.
Per yard..........................................$0.55

### Corduroy.

**No. 22619 Imported Corduroy,** 27 inches wide, for men's pants, colors drab, brown or black; very good quality. Per yard.........................$0.70

**No. 22620 Imported Corduroy,** 27 inches wide, for men's pants; colors, drab, brown or black, best quality made. Comes in a heavy cord, will wear like iron. Per yard...............................$0.85
NOTE—Cheap Corduroys will not wear. We do not keep them; we can recommend the above corduroys for their fine appearance and wearing qualities.

### Colored Cheviots, Cassimere and Worsteds for Men's Clothing.

The cloth is double widths, 54 inches only.
**No. 22621 Cheviot Suitings,** rough finish, medium and dark mixtures, 54 inches wide. Per yard..$1.45

**No. 22622 Cheviot Suitings,** fine imported goods, comes in stripes, checks and pretty mixture; colors are brown mixed, gray mixed and blue mixed; 54 inch wide. Per yard...........................$1.95

**No. 22623 Fine Cassimere Suitings,** fine imported goods, come in the latest styles for the coming season; this is one of the finest qualities procurable, colors are neat brown mixture, tan mixture, gray mixture, also a fancy weave in black and navy blue mixtures, 54 inches wide. Per yard.........$3.25
(Note. These cloths also make up very pretty in pants.)

**No. 22624 Black Clay Worsted,** weight about 12 ounces to the yard, diagonal weave, a splendid cloth for mens's suits; 54 inches wide. Per yard.....$1.25

### A New Wash Fabric.

**No. 22627 This is one of the newest wash fabrics,** has the appearance of a high grade Persian silk. Comes in a magnificent combination of colors, such as light blue, pink, old rose and lavender to harmonize with ground color. Width 30 inch.
Price per yard...........$0.09

### A New Wash Fabric.

**No. 22628 Comes** in the following colors: blue, pink, old rose and lavender. Same grade of goods as above, in beautiful spray and scroll effects. 30 in. wide. Price, per yard...........$0.09

**☞ SAMPLES OF MEN'S CLOTHING FREE**
....ON APPLICATION....

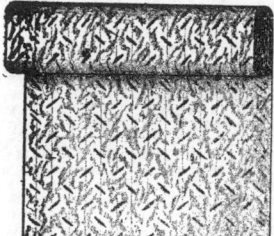

## Wash Dimity.

**No. 22629** Is a pretty **Wash dimity**. Comes in a magnificent combination of colors, such as white ground with navy effect, tan and white, blue and white and black and white. 30 inches wide. Per yard...**$0.10½**

## Wash Dimity.

**No. 22630** We call special attention to this number because we know it to be a big bargain. Same as above in light tints, such as tan and white, pink and white and green and white. 30-inches width. Per yard, **$0.10½**

**No. 22631** High-grade of fine Imported Paris Organdies, with lace effects, with colored roses, buds and leaves to match grounds. Make up very handsome waists and dresses. This is one of the highest grade novelties of the season, can be obtained only in the large cities. 28 inches wide. Per yard.....................**$0.15**

**No. 22633** Serpertine Crepe or Cotton Crepon, 28 inches wide; this makes up very pretty for evening wear, colors are strictly fast and the material will retain the crinkles after washing. Colors are white, cream, lemon, light pink, dark pink, pale blue, nile green, cardinal and black. Per yard, **$0.13½**

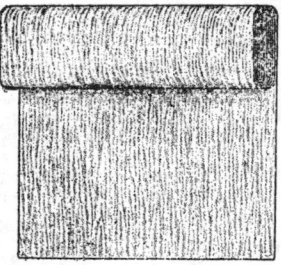

## Percales.

**No. 22634** One of our Special Numbers. Mulhouse Percales, 36 inches wide, warranted fast colors, dainty little figures, linen effects on white ground, blue on white, pink on white or black figures on white ground, very pretty and neat for any purpose. Per yard....**$0.07**

**No. 22636** Mulhouse Percales, 36 inches wide, warranted fast colors, fine, neat diagonal check effects with light blue or pink ground, very finely checked with white and white diamond spots about a half inch apart. Very pretty for waists or whole suits. Per yard.....**$0.07**

**No. 22640** Mulhouse Percales, 36 inches wide. Hair line stripes. Warranted fast colors. light blue, medium blue or pink. The prettiest, neatest patterns in cambric. Per yard.....**$0.07**

---

**No. 22638** Mulhouse Percales, 36 inches wide, warranted fast colors, in the popular black and white stripes. Such values were never seen before. The white stripe is nearly twice as wide as the black stripe; this is what every one wants, it's all the rage! Small, medium, or wide stripe. Per yard.........................**$0.07**

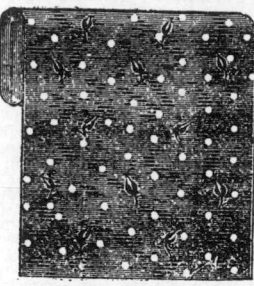

**No. 22642** Westbrook Percales, 36 inches wide, 9 cents per yard. Extra good value and would advise our customers to buy early what they may want this season. We have secured the product of this mill, which is large, but at the above price will not last very long. They come with white or clouded ground, figured or striped; pretty new styles. Per yard.....**$0.09**

**No. 22644 Minerva Percales,** width 36 inches, 12½ cents per yard. This is the most popular cambric we have and comes in the largest assortment of styles and is not excelled for quality, beauty and variety. Colors guaranteed absolutely fast. We have them in white, light blue, yellow, linen or pink ground, small, medium and large figures, plain and fancy, wide and narrow, straight and serpentine, tape and hair-line stripes, in all the fashionable colors, and latest Persian and clouded effects. New, neat scroll designs; also a nice assortment of checks, stripes, anchors, horseshoe, etc., for shirting and boys' waists. A complete assortment that cannot be surpassed for originality and taste of designs and exquisite beauty of coloring at any price. Per yard........................**$0.12½**
Full piece of 40 to 50 yards. Per yard.... ................. .11¾

**No. 22646** Imperial cotton duck, 30 inches wide, 12½ cents per yard. A very stylish and fashionable fabric, one of the best wearing cloths manufactured for late spring and summer wear. Comes in light ground with plain and fancy stripes of various colors, or with small set figures or polka dots, also with black or navy blue ground with white polka dots, stripes or figures of various sizes. We have also the linen colored ground, with white figures, stripes or dots; also in plain solid colors—black, navy, cream, tan, white or cardinal. Per yard.............................**$0.12½**

## A 39-Inch Double Fold Lawn.

**A Bargain that is Obtainable only from S., R. & Co.**

**No. 22648** A 39-inch Double Fold Lawn, white and tinted grounds; fast colors. A closely woven cloth that will laundry well. Just the thing for a summer waist. We have it in plain stripes of various sizes in black, navy blue, light blue, pink, heliotrope and green; and in fancy designs, we have a large assortment of set figures and floral designs in same colors as the plain stripes. The quantity of this lot is large, but it is such a bargain that we suggest that orders be sent in early, as there is sure to be a big run on this number, Per yard.....................**$0.09½**
Full piece of 45 yards, per yard, .09

## Sateens.

**No. 22649** Simpson's Sateens, 27 inches wide, 9 cts. per yard. Black ground with a large variety of floral designs in colors; also black ground with stripes and dots in various sizes. This is an American production, but we guarantee the colors positively fast and as good as any made in the world. Per yard.....**$0.09**

---

**No. 22650 Fine Henrietta Finished Sateens, 12 Cents Per Yard.** Width, 31 inches, beautiful floral designs in their natural colors on black ground, small medium and large figures, also in white spots or stripes on black ground. Colors are guaranteed absolutely fast. Per yard.. **$0.12**

### Imported Sateens

At Special Bargain Prices. **No. 22651** Imported Sateens, Henrietta finish, 16 cents per yard. Black ground artistically printed with small and medium floral figures in colors, handsome designs, positive fast colors; 31 inches wide. Per yard...**$0.16**

### Black Dress Sateens.

**The Best in the World. Warranted Absolutely Fast Black.** These goods are warranted full dyed Aniline Black, and will not change by washing, age or exposure to the sun, and guaranteed not to crock. Acid and Perspiration Proof.
**No. 22652 Fast Black Sateen,** width 28 inches. Per yard.......................**$0.08½**
**No. 22654 S. B. Fast Black Sateen,** cashmere finish, and just as handsome as wool cashmere; 30 inches wide. Per yard......................**$0.10**
**No. 22656 J. S. B. Fast Black Sateen.** Henrietta finish, the best weight and best wear resisting sateen in the market and looks as handsome as the wool goods costing 50c. per yard; width 30 inches. Per yard.............................**$0.12**
**No. 22658 G. B. Very Fine Henrietta Finished Sateens.** Absolutely fast black, guaranteed, beautiful quality, as fine as any imported for double the money, and will make up as handsome as wool goods costing 55c. per yard; width, 31 inches. Per yard.............................**$0.14**
**No. 22659 Sublime Quality Fast Black Sateens.** This is a handsomer quality than any produced last year in weight, fineness of weave and finish. There is nothing to equal this number in the market at any price; width 31 inches. Per yard..........**$0.16**
**No. 22659½** Extra fine silk finish best black sateen. This is one of the finest qualities made, 32 inches wide. Per yard........................**$0.23**

### Colored Dress Sateens.

**No. 22660** Extra fine plain colored Sateens, 12 cents per yard. Absolutely fast colors, 31 inches wide. Colors—cream, light, medium and dark tan, cardinal or pink, navy blue, medium blue and light blue. Per yard.......................**$0.12**
**No. 22661** French Sateens, plain colors, 19 cents per yard. This is the best made in the world and generally retailed for 35 cents per yard. Width 31 inches. Colors—cream, tan, brown, light blue navy, scarlet or pink. Per yard....................**$0.19**

### Black Wash Dress Goods.

**COLORS GUARANTEED STRICTLY FAST.**
**No. 22663** Black checked dimity, similar to cut, also comes in small neat stripes, 28 inches wide. Per yard...**$0.10**

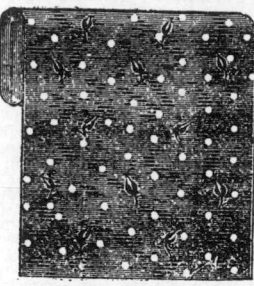

**No. 22664.** Black lace stripe India lawn, both in wide and narrow stripes, with a black pin dot between the stripes; this dot gives the goods a beautiful appearance, used largely for waists, width 28 inches. This number also comes in even checks. Per yard, **$0.12½**

**No. 22665** Black lace stripe lawn, with a wide satin stripe; this number is a beauty and is one of the most handsome and stylish things procurable in black wash dress goods. Colors are perfectly fast black. We make a great leader of this number for the reason that it is of such good value that it pleases all and sells goods for us wherever shown. The regular retail value is 25 cents, 32 inches wide. Our special price, per yard ...................**$0.16**
**No. 22666** Black Stripe Dimity, 30 inches wide, colors are strictly fast, comes in medium and very narrow stripes, used for ladies' waists and dresses, and is just the thing for warm weather, being light and cool. Per yard.......................**$0.15**
**No. 22667** Black Satin Check Lawn, 30 inches wide; this also comes in broken plaid. A very pretty fabric and one that will please everybody; positively fast black and will stand the most severe test, being a genuine aniline black. Per yard........**$0.16**

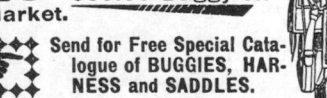
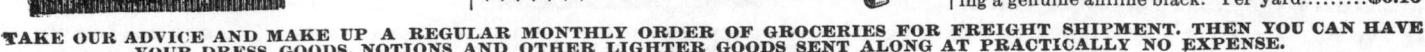

**TAKE OUR ADVICE AND MAKE UP A REGULAR MONTHLY ORDER OF GROCERIES FOR FREIGHT SHIPMENT. THEN YOU CAN HAVE YOUR DRESS GOODS, NOTIONS AND OTHER LIGHTER GOODS SENT ALONG AT PRACTICALLY NO EXPENSE.**

**No. 22668 Black French Grenadine,** 30 inches wide, comes in pretty lace stripes, with a pretty satin figure between the stripes; this is a light transparent fabric and is to be used with a colored lining underneath, which produces a very striking effect; used largely for ladies dresses, skirts and waists. Just the thing for summer wear.
Per yard....................$0.16

## Plain Black Lawns—Positively Fast Black.

**No. 22669 Fine Quality Fast Black Lawn;** width, 29 inches. Per yard..........$0.10½
**No. 22771 Very fine,** with a high grade finish; width, 29 inches. Positively fast black......$0.12½
**No. 22773 Extra Fine Quality Fast Black,** superior finished lawn; width, 29 inches. Per yard..$0.16

## Black India Linon.

**Positively Fast Black** and will not crock or fade by exposure to the sun. This fabric is generally called India linen, which is misleading, as it is made of select sea island cotton, very fine and sheer, with a smooth, silky finish, is very popular and durable. Extra good values guaranteed in each number. Width, 32½ inches.
**No. 22774 India Linon,** positive fast black.
Per yard....................$0.10
**No. 22776 Finer Quality India Linon,** positive fast black. Per yard..........$0.12½
**No. 22778 Fine India Linon,** positive fast black.
Per yard....................$0.15
**No. 22779 Very Fine Quality India Linon,** positive fast black. Per yard..........$0.18
**No. 22780 Extra Fine Quality India Linon,** positive fast black. Per yard..........$0.20

## Ginghams.

**Apron Checks.**

**No. 22790 27 inch Apron Ginghams,** comes in small and large checks, such as blue and white, green and white, pink and white, brown and white.
Price, per yard....................$0.03½
Full piece of 45 to 50 yards, per yard same price.
**No. 22791 27 inch Amoskeag Apron Ginghams;** these are the most reliable ginghams made.

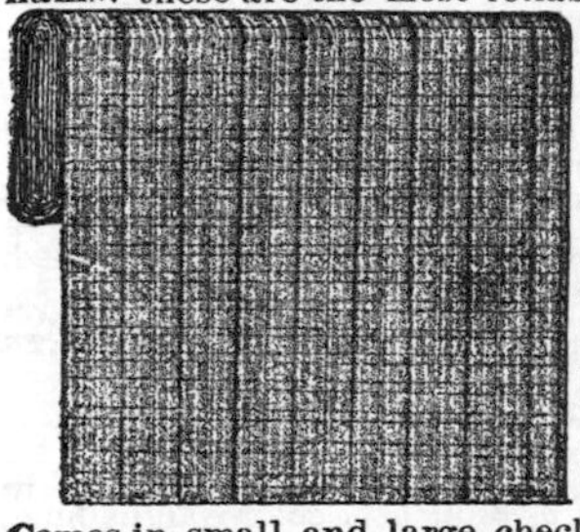

Comes in blue and white, back and white, and brown and white.
Per yard...$0.05
Full piece of 45 to 50 yards same price.
**No. 22792 27 inch Turkey red and white checks Apron Ginghams.** This is a well known make and well recommended for its wearing qualities. Colors perfectly fast. Comes in small and large checks.
Price per yard..........$0.07¼
Full piece 45 to 50 yards, per yard.......... .07

## Dress Ginghams.

**No. 22794 Aurania Dress Ginghams,** comes in a beautiful line of colors, small and large plaids. The combination of colors are, blue and red, pink and blue, brown and green, brown and black, medium blue and black and lavender and blue. This is a good quality of cloth and fast colors.
Per yard....................$0.05
Full piece of 50 yards, per yard.......... 0.04¾
**No. 22795 Amoskeag Dress Ginghams,** comes in a beautiful assortment of broken plaids, with lace stripe effects. The colors are brown and white mixed, gold and brown with green, pink and blue, red and green and pale blue and brown mixed; guaranteed strictly first-class.

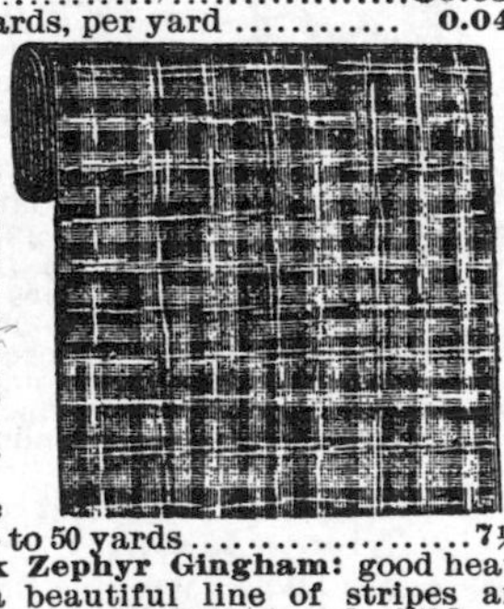

Price per yard 7¼c
Or a full piece of 45 to 50 yards.......... 7¼c
**No. 22796 York Zephyr Gingham:** good heavy cloth; comes in a beautiful line of stripes and checks; makes up pretty in ladies' and children's dresses, in the following colors: blue and white, pink and white and tan and white: 27 inches wide.
Price per yard....................$0.09

## The Famous Toile Du Nord.

**Toile Du Verd.**

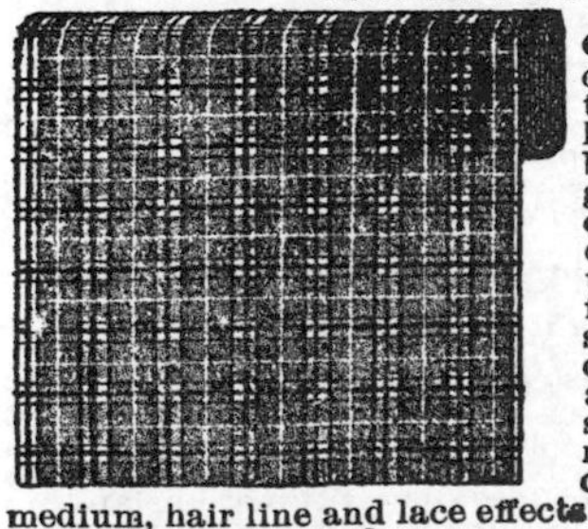

**No. 22797 Dress Gingham** is the cheapest gingham to buy, as it lasts longer and washes better than any gingham made. It comes in exclusive designs and patterns, colors are fine bright colored scotch plaids for children's dresses, also beautiful small checks in all new colors and combinations; medium, hair line and lace effects stripes. 27 inches wide. Price per yard....................$0.09
**Full piece of 45 to 50 yards, no less.**

## Fine French Veronese Dress Gingham.

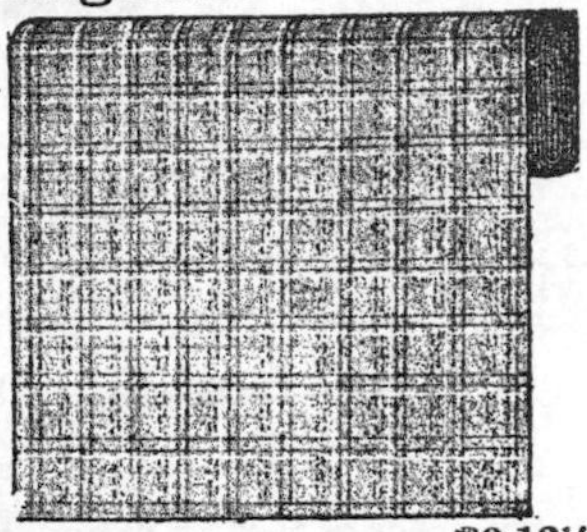

**No. 22798 Fine French Veronese Dress Ginham** has the appearance of a silk fabric, comes in medium open check only in the following colors: white, blue and tan combination. Tan green and black combination. Pink blue and tan combination and green red and black combination, 27 inches wide. Colors strictly fast. Per yard....................$0.12½
**No. 22799 Fancy "Precesi" Dress Gimgham.**

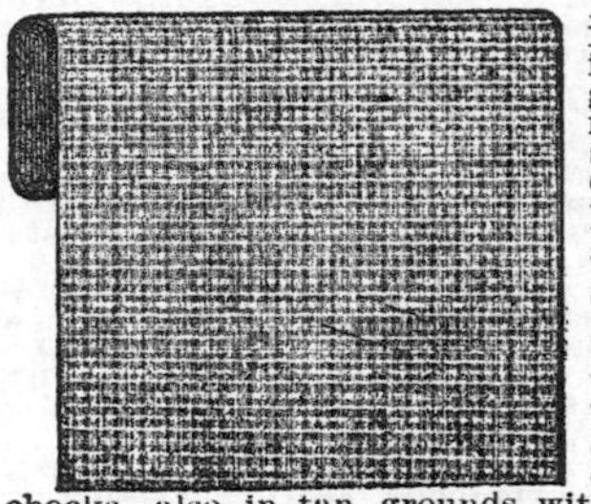

Is the novelty of 1897 season, comes in light and dark grounds, intermixed with raised stripes and checks. This is very pretty and has to be seen to be appreciated. Colors are olive ground with white, red and black checks, pale blue with white checks and lavender and white checks, also in tan grounds with different color checks, in tan, golden brown and navy blue checks, 27 inches wide. Per yard....................$0.15

## The New Kingston Gingham.

**No. 22800**

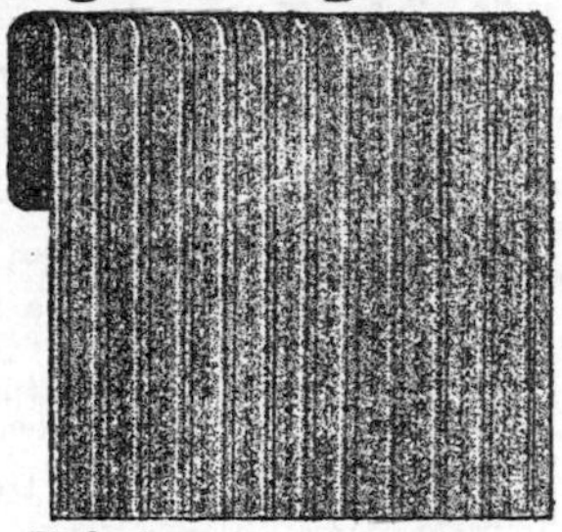

This is one of the novelties of the season. Lace stripe zephyr gingham comes in pretty designs in pink and white, blue and white, black, blue, and white mixed. Colors strictly fast. Will make up pretty in children's and ladies' dresses. 30 inches wide.
Price, per yd. $0.15
**ORDER BY NUMBER**

## Prints.

**Novelties in Dress Styles, Novelties in Waist Styles, Novelties in Mourning Prints, Pinks, Purples and Shirting Styles.** We are in position to furnish any combination of colors at each price quoted.
**Special. We often have opportunities to buy stand prints, old, or what is known as off styles,** undersirable patterns at about half the market price. Short lengths, too, are sold very cheap—to parties that are not particular as to style or lengths; we can give some good bargains. Send in your order, name your price, and we will give you the best bargain possible. We recommend the regular quoted style up-to-date patterns; straight goods are more satisfactory to every one.
**No. 22801 Belgian Fancy Styles,** 27 inches wide, worsted effects, mixtures, stripes or figures; also chambray effects suitable for waists or dresses.
Per yard....................$0.05
**No. 22802 Merrimack Prints,** 27 inches wide, full standard in pretty chambray stripes, checks or figures; also polka dots in medium or light colors; also red ground with small gold or white figure or stripe.
Per yard....................$0.05½
**No. 22803 Hamilton Prints.** Some very beautiful styles have been brought out in this line called silverette mohair dress goods. Effects come in mixtures, stripes or plaids; also black ground with red figure, stripe or dot; also zephyr effects in blue, figured or striped. Per yard....................$0.06
**No. 22804 Windsor Epatant.** Beautiful new effects. New designs in dress styles, dark and medium colors, floral patterns, mixtures and stripes; also Venetian Foulard dress goods effects. Hazel brown dress goods effects, specially pretty for dresses, Per yard....................$0.06½
**No. 22805 Shirting Prints.** Cambric. Styles nice for waists. White or tinted ground with neat figure, stripe or checks of black, red, blue, pink, brown; also combinations of colors in a great variety of styles. Per yard....................$0.04½
**No. 22806 Simpson's Mourning Prints.** Novelties in grays, worsted mixture effects, stripes and figures; also black ground with white figures, or striped in a great variety of patterns, also plain black. Per yard....................$0.06
**No. 22807 Pacific Mourning Prints,** similar to Simpson's styles; also in plain black. Per yd.. $0.05
**No. 22308 Indigo Blue Prints or Dutch Blue** as they are usually called, come in solid blue ground, white figures, stripes or dots. Width, 24 in.
Per yard....................$0.06
**No. 22809 American Dutch Blue,** 28 inch wide. White figure, stripes or dots on a solid navy blue ground. Per yard....................$0.08
**No. 22810 Extra Quality German Blue,** 32 inches wide, solid dark blue ground with white figure, stripes or bars. Per yard....................$0.10
**No. 22811 Turkey Red Print** with blue or white figures or bars. Per yard....................$0.05½

**No. 22812 Plain Turkey Red Calico,** oil colors. Width, 24 inches. Per yard....................$0.05
**No. 22813 Extra quality Turkey Red Calico.** Width, 24 inches. Per yard....................$0.07
**Same as above.** Width, 27 inches. Per yard $0.09½

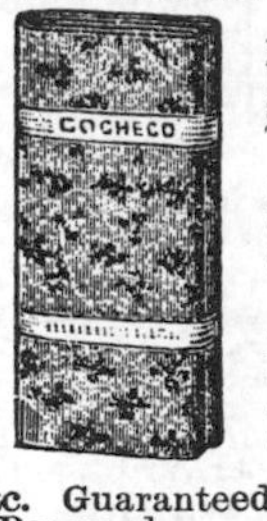


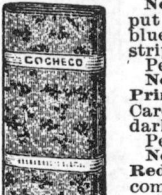

**No. 22814 Simpson Dress Prints,** put up same as above; come in blue grounds with white figures or stripes.
Per pattern of 10 yards.....$0.65
**No. 22815 Plain Solid Colored Prints** in the following fast colors. Cardinal, orange, green, brown, dark blue, scarlet or black.
Per yard....................$0.06
**No. 22817 Best Quality Turkey Red Cambric,** 31 inches wide, comes in black or white figures or stripes, also a splendid assortment of sporting patterns for boys' waists, anchors, horseshoes, whips, etc. Guaranteed strictly fast colors.
Per yard....................$0.10

## Drapery Prints.

**No. 22819 Allen Twill Drapery Print,** 25 inches wide, in large handsome designs or smaller flowers on the following colored grounds: Cream, ecru, sapphire, wine, navy, light blue or brown.
Per yard....................$0.06
Full piece of about 20 yards, per yard...... .05¾
**No. 22820 Purdah Rep Drapery,** 29 inches wide, similar weave to the imported English cretonne. They come in the following color grounds, with large harmonizing floral designs: Gray, ecru, cream, wine, navy, black. Per yard....................$0.12
Full piece of about 40 yards, yer yard........ .11
**No. 22821 Cameo Drapery,** 30 inches wide, in handsome patterns and rich colorings. Cloth is good and strong, and woven in twilled effects. They will drape beautifully. Designs are medium or large, and highly artistic in shadings. Colors of ground work: Tan, black, brown, navy, wine, cream, light blue or slate. Per yard....................$0.12
For full piece of about 50 yards, per yard.... .11

## DOMESTICS.

Quantity regulates the price of everything, but more so in staple domestics than in anything else. **These goods come to us in car load lots and we are** enabled to save our customers money on every yard they buy. Should prices decline our patrons get the benefit; **should prices advance we must advance them,** but in all probability these prices will hold good all season.

## Sheeting—Heavy Unbleached.

**No. 22832 Special Atlanta Heavy Sheeting.** 36 inches wide, 3¾ yards to pound, direct from the mill. A nice clean even weave, and a much better made cotton than some sold on the market at 1 cent more a yard. Per yard....................$0.05
**No. 22834 Augusta A No. 1 Heavy Sheeting.** 36 inches wide 40x44 count, is another special brand we recommend. Coming as it does direct from the Atlanta mills under favorable circumstances to us we are in a position to sell them to our customers ½ cent per yard less than your local dealer can buy them for in case lots.
This is a nice, clean, even cotton, with extra good wear resisting qualities, with a soft twisted thread that will make it wash easy. Per yard.......$0.06
We quote the following well known brands and prices per yard.

| | | Per yard. |
|---|---|---|
| No. 22835 | Aurora L. L. | $0.04½ |
| No. 22836 | Aurora C. | .04 |
| No. 22837 | Badger State | .05 |
| No. 22838 | Cabot, A. | .06 |
| No. 22839 | Cabot, W. | .05½ |
| No. 22840 | Great Falls | .06¼ |
| No. 22841 | Indian Head | .06½ |

## Sheeting, Fine Unbleached.

**No. 22852 Special Brand Argyle Fine Unbleached Cotton,** 36 inches wide, made of select first picking of domestic cotton; nice, clean and even woven soft round thread. This is something we can recommend to wear well, wash easy, and bleaches out nice and white; comes in 25 yard pieces, or we will sell a yard at the same price. Per yard...$0.06
**No. 22853 Lockwood Very Fine Unbleached Cotton,** 36 inches wide. This is another make we get under very favorable circumstances direct from the south; this is really one of the prettiest cottons made, very clean, nice and smooth, with an even round thread. The advantage of using a round threaded cotton is apparent to all housekeepers; it is easier worked and washes and wears better.
Per yard....................$0.06½
**No. 22854 S. & R. Special,** a fine and heavy unbleached cotton, 3½ yards to the pound, 68x72 count, considered by all old judges of cotton to be the best wearing fine cotton made. Comes from one of the largest and most reliable manufacturers in this country, specially made and guaranteed every piece perfect throughout. Per yard....................$0.07
The following brands are well known makes of fine unbleached cottons.

| | | Per yard. |
|---|---|---|
| No. 22855 | Aurora B. | $0.05 |
| No. 22857 | Pepperell | .05½ |
| No. 22859 | Dwight Star | .06½ |
| No. 22860 | Cast Iron | .07 |
| No. 22861 | Pocahontas | .06½ |

## Wide Sheetings—Unbleached.

**Pepperell, a well known make specially good for pillow cases and wide sheets.** Made of a good clean cotton with the round thread which makes a cotton look better and softer, easier to make up and washes easier and is much better to wear.

| | Width, | | | Per yard. |
|---|---|---|---|---|
| No. 22862 | Width, 39 inches. | 9-8 | | $0.07½ |
| No. 22864 | " 45 | " 5-4 | " | 0.10 |
| No. 22866 | " 54 | " 6-4 | " | 0.12½ |
| No. 22867 | " 68 | " 8-4 | " | 0.15½ |
| No. 22868 | " 80 | " 9-4 | " | 0.17 |
| No. 22869 | " 88 | " 10-4 | " | 0.19½ |

READ WHAT WE SAY ON PAGE 4 ABOUT CLUB ORDERS, AND OUR SPECIAL DISCOUNTS. YOU WILL HAVE NO TROUBLE IN INTERESTING YOUR NEIGHBORS IN OUR CATALOGUE WHEN YOU SHOW THEM THE 30 OR 40 % SAVING ON ALL CLASSES OF GOODS.

## Pequot Wide Sheeting.

**Extra quality sheeting and pillow case cotton,** heavier than Pepperell, with a nice, fine, even thread. The best made cotton on the market.

**No. 22869½** Width 42 inches. Per yard. $0.10½
**No. 22870** Width 45 inches 5-4 Per yard. 0.11½
**No. 22871** Width 54 inches. 6-4 Per yard. 0.14
**No. 22872** Width 68 inches. 8-4 Per yard. 0.17½
**No. 22874** Width 80 inches. 9-4 Per yard. 0.19
**No. 22876** Width 88 inches. 10-4 Per yard. $.20

## Pepperell Bleached Wide Sheeting and Pillow Case Cotton.

**No. 22877** Width 42 inches per yard......$0.10
**No. 22878** Width 46 inches per yard....... .11
**No. 22879** Width 50 inches per yard........ .12½
**No. 22880** Width 54 inches 6-4 per yard.... .14
**No. 22881** Width 68 inches 8-4 per yard.... .17
**No. 22882** Width 80 inches 9-4 per yard.... .18½
**No. 22983** Width 88 inches 10-4 per yard... .20½

## Twilled Bleached Sheetings.

**22984 Bleached Pepperell Twilled Sheeting** (9-4) 81 inches wide. Best Sheeting made for wear. Per yard......................................$0.24

## Bleached Cottons.

**No. 22885 Special Dauntless Bleach, Soft Finished Cotton,** full 36 inches wide, the best cotton on the market for the money. Per yard...........$0.05

**No. 22886 Rutledge Bleached Cotton,** 36 inches wide; another special brand we can recommend as extra good value; it has a good round thread, soft finish and a good wearing cotton.
Per yard..........................................$0.05½

**No. 22887 Harvest E,** a specially good brand selected for its handsome appearance and wear resisting qualities, soft finish and good weight.
Per yard.........................................$0.05¾

**No. 22888 Fitchville Bleached Cotton,** extra good value, as good as any cotton on the market costing a half cent more a yard; we receive this cotton direct from the mill in very large lots and we are in position to offer this brand less than the market price. Per yard...........................$0.07½

**No. 22889 Androscogun Bleached Cotton for General Use,** there is no cotton on the market to compare with it, having a nice fine even round thread, handsomely made and excellent to wear.
Per yard.........................................$0.07½

**No. 22890 Golden Wedding Bleached Cotton,** very fine, put up in 25 yard lengths or half price.
Per yard.........................................$0.08

**No. 22891 Dwight Anchor,** the best wearing cotton made, soft finish, round soft twisted thread, a little heavier than most cottons; for skirts it is excellent, takes the starch well and extra good for night gowns and all purposes requiring wear resisting qualities. Per yard..........................$0.08

**No. 22892 Fruit of the Loom,** a fine cotton, not quite as heavy as the above number, but finer and heavier than any other cotton, excellent for shirts and ladies' underwear. Per yard..............$0.07

## Jones' White Cambric.

**No. 22893 Very Fine** and a little heavier than Nainsook; 36 inches wide. Per yard...........$0.16
**No. 22894 Berkley White Cambric;** 36 inches wide. Per yard......................................$0.10
**No. 22895** Extra quality Berkley Cambric; 36 inches................................................. .12

## Cheese, Butter and Dairy Cloth.

**No. 22843 Unbleached, 36 inches, Nabob Royal Cheese Cloth.** Per yard.......................$0.02¾
Full piece of about 65 yards, about 2,000 yards to a bale.................................................$0.02½
**No. 22845 Unbleached Cheese Cloth,** East Hampton, 36 inches wide, extra good value.........$0.03¼
Full piece of about 50 yards............................ .03¼
**No. 22847 Unbleached Cheese Cloth,** Persian, 36 inches wide, extra fine quality. Per yard...$0.04
Full piece of about 65 yards............................ .03¾
**No. 22849 Bleached Butter Cloth,** Jersey, 36 inches wide. Per yard..........................$0.03½
Full piece of about 60 yards............................ .03¼
**No. 22850 Bleached Dairy Cloth,** 45 inches wide.
Per yard...................................................$0.04½
Full piece of about 120 yards........................ .04¼

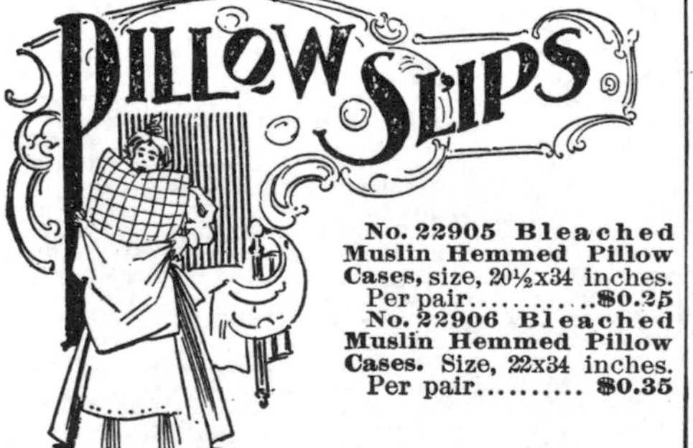


**No. 22905 Bleached Muslin Hemmed Pillow Cases,** size, 20½x34 inches.
Per pair............$0.25
**No. 22906 Bleached Muslin Hemmed Pillow Cases.** Size, 22x34 inches.
Per pair........... $0.35

## Ready Made Sheets.

**No. 22902 Bleached Hemmed Sheets,** made from cotton manufactured by the **Celebrated Mohawk Valley Cotton Mills.** Size 2 yards by 2½ yards. Each..........................................$0.48

**No. 22903 Bleached Hemmed Muslin Sheets,** made of the same quality muslin as above number. Size, 2¼ yards by 2½ yards. Each................$0.55

**No. 22904 Bleached Hemmed Muslin Sheets,** made of the same quality muslin as the foregoing. Size, 2½ yards by 2½ yards. Each...............$0.60

## Unbleached Drilling.

**No. 22919 Unbleached Drilling** used for linings, pockets, boat sails, etc., 29 inches wide.
Per yard.............................................................$0.06
Full piece of about 40 yards, per yard............ .05½
**No. 22920 Unbleached Drilling,** extra heavy and strong; a splendid wearing cloth, 29 inches wide.
Per yard..............................................................$0.07
For full piece of about 40 yards, per yard.. .06¼
**No. 22921 Unbleached Boat-Sail Drilling,** weight 6 to 7 oz. to the yard, a very fine linen twill 29 inches wide, per yard..........................................$0.08
For a full piece of 40 to 45 yards, per yard. .07¼

## Bed Ticking.

These goods are made blue and white stripe only.
**No. 22922 Straw Ticking, Oakland B,** 27 inches, Per yard................................................$0.05
Full piece of about 55 yards. Per yard..... .04¾
**No. 22924 Straw Ticking, Swift River,** 30 inches. Per yard ..................................................... .06
Full piece of about 55 yards, Per yard....... .05½
**No. 22926 Straw Ticking, Amoskeag H,** 30 inches. Per yard.......................................................... .07
Full piece of about 55 yards. Per yard....... .06½
**No. 22928 Ticking, Amoskeag G,** 31 inches.
Per yard.......................................................... .08
Full piece of about 55 yards. Per yard..... .07½
**No. 22930 Amoskeag D,** new improved, 31 inches.
Per yard.......................................................... .10
Full piece of about 55 yards. Per yard..... .09½
**No. 22932 Feather Ticking, Amoskeag A,** new improved, 31 inches. Per yard........................... .11
Full piece of about 55 yards. Per yard..... .10½
**No. 22933 Feather Ticking, Amoskeag ACA,** best plain tick made, new improved. 32 inches... .12½
Full piece of about 55 yards. Per yard..... .11¾
**No. 22934 Herringbone Feather Ticking,** 31 inches wide, blue and white striped only, very heavy and firm. Per yard................................... .15
Full piece of about 55 yards. Per yard..... .14
**No. 22936 Amoskeag Tick, ACA,** 36 inches wide. Per yard......................................... .18
Full piece of about 55 yards. Per yard..... .17
**No. 22937 Conestoga Ticking,** 60 inches wide, double fold, blue and white narrow stripes. Tick can be made with sewing but two seams. Heavy cloth, fast colors.
Per yard....... ................................................ .32½

## Denims.

**SPECIAL.** We have made very favorable arrangements with one of the largest and most reliable manufacturers of denims, that will enable us to sell to our customers a superior quality of denim at the same price your local dealer pays for inferior goods on the long-dating and credit system.

**No. 22938 Oakland Blue Denim;** a good, fair quality. Per yard..............................$0.07½
**No. 22939 Blue Denim;** 300 quality; very good. Per yard................................................$0.10
**No. 22940 Blue Denim;** 250 quality; heavier. Per yard................................................$0.12
**No. 22941 Blue Denim;** 220 quality; excellent. Per yard................................................$0.13½
**No. 22942 Blue Denim;** 9 oz; extra heavy twill. Per yard................................................$0.15
**No. 22943 Brown Denim;** 300 quality; very good. Per yard................................................$0.10
**No. 22944 Brown Denim;** 250 quality; very good. Per yard................................................$0.12
**No. 22945 Brown Denim;** 9 oz.; extra heavy twill. Per yard..........................................$0.15
**No. 22946 Fancy Striped Denim;** good fair quality. Per yard.........................................$0.10
**No. 22947 Fancy Tricot Denim;** 8 oz. to the yard. Per yard................................................$0.12½
**No. 22948 Fancy Striped Denim;** 8 oz.; extra quality. Per yard......................................$0.15
**No. 22949 Brown Duck;** XX quality; extra good weight. Per yard.......................................$0.10
**No. 22951 Drab Duck;** XX quality; extra good weight. Per yard.......................................$0.10

## Fancy Cheviot Shirtings.

Novelties in stripe and check shirtings; new select pattern, as well as the staples; we can recommend every number as a specially good thing for the money. Each item was selected with the idea of giving extra good value to our customers and friends that they might take pleasure in recommending our firm as a money-saving institution.

**No. 22955 Holly Shirting.** A good weight, sightly shirting; comes in fine mixtures; stripes, checks or plaids in blue and white, or brown and white; width, 27 inches. Per yard...............................$0.07

**No. 22956 Defender Shirting,** 30 inches wide; splendidly made; good weight; comes in fine mixtures, checks, stripes and plaids, blue and white, brown and white, or red and blue. Per yard...$0.08

**No. 22958 Extra Quality Amoskeag Shirting;** 28 inches wide; good weight; twill finely wove; comes in new, select stripes and checks.
Per yard.....................................................$0.10

## Fine Cheviots—Linen Effects.

**No. 22960 Ashbyrne Cheviots,** linen effects; light and medium colors, in pretty small and medium broken checks and stripes; an excellent quality.
Per yard.....................................................$0.10

**No. 22961 Oakland Fine Cheviots,** new linen effects; light and medium colors; choice select small broken checks and fine mixtures. Per yard...$0.12

**No. 22962 Newport Extra Fine Cheviots,** linen effects; the latest styles imported, come with white ground and small checks or stripes, also shaded stripes and checks. Each style is as pretty as can be. Per yard...........................................$0.14

## Cotton Batting.

**Almost all dealers sell Cotton Batting** by the roll, and while nothing may be said regarding their weight, people suppose they are getting 16 ounce rolls, as they have always been put up in that way. **Almost all dealers have their batts put up to-day with but 12 ounces, or three-fourths of a pound to the roll,** which makes comparisons of prices by the roll obviously unfair, unless weight is taken into consideration.

**All our rolls weigh about 16 ounces—1 pound each** (except the cheapest), We say about 16 ounces, as they are as near that uniform weight as can be put up; some may exceed that while others may be a trifle under; the average is one pound each. Our batts are Patent folded, and are not simply a wad of cotton to be repicked and put into the quilt in bunches; each batt is nicely papered, is folded, and will open up all the same thickness; 36 inches wide and 7 feet long.

**Cotton batting** is put up 50 pounds to the bale, and if sold in that quantity an extra discount of 5 per cent will be allowed.

**No. 22964 Cotton Batting, S., R. & Co., E.,** 12 ounces, 67 rolls to the bale. Per roll...........$0.07
**No. 22965 Cotton Batting,** fair quality, D.
Per roll.....................................................$0.08
**No. 22966 Cotton Batting,** good quality.
Per roll.....................................................$0.09
**No. 22967 Cotton Batting,** fine quality.
Per roll.....................................................$0.12½
**No. 22968 Cotton Batting,** clean white.
Per roll.....................................................$0.15
**No. 22969 Snow White Cotton Batting,** 16-ounce roll, used for medical purposes, baby quilts, etc.; extra long staple, no specks. Per roll....$0.25

## Mosquito Nets.

**Mosquito Net is about 63 inches wide and comes 8 yards to the piece.**

**No. 22970 Mosquito Net,** in white, black, blue, green, drab, yellow or brown.
Per piece of 8 yards.................................... $0.35
**No. 22971 Mosquito Net,** in pink and red.
Per piece of 8 yards.................................... $0.40
**We do not cut pieces of Mosquito Net.**

## Cotton Wadding.

**No. 22972 Cotton Wadding,** slate color only, good cotton, nicely glazed; size, about 32x36 inches.
Per sheet...............................................$0.03
Per dozen sheets........................................ .20
**No. 22974** Cotton Wadding, white, nicely finished, clean and white; size, about 28x39 inches.
Per sheet...............................................$0.03
Per dozen sheets........................................ .25

## Tinted Wadding.

**For Fancy Work.**

**No. 22976** Fancy French Tinted Wadding, in sheets; size, about 28x36 inches; colors—light blue, pink, Nile, yellow, lavender or white.
Per sheet ..............................................$0.05
Per dozen sheets........................................ .50

## Carpet Warp.

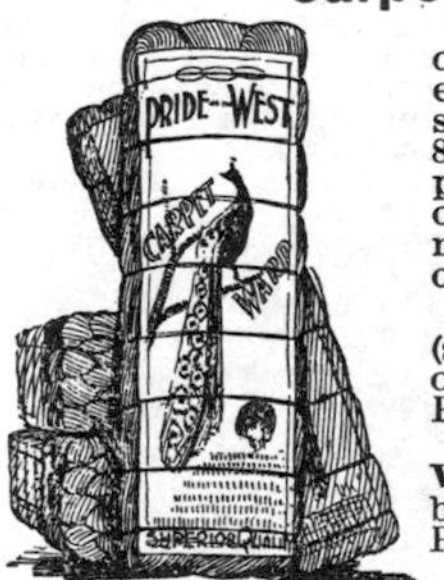


Our warp is carefully made of good cotton, hard and evenly twisted, of uniform size and long reel; 4 ply No. 8½ yarn, 90 inch reel; five pounds will make 25 yards of yard-wide carpet. We do not sell less than 5 pounds of white or any one color.

**No. 22978 White Warp** (sold in five-pound bundles only) net weight.
Per pound .........................................$0.14

**No. 22980 Colored Cotton Warp** (sold in five-pound bundles only), net weight.
Per pound ..........................................$0.16

Colored carpet warp comes in brown, orange, red, green, black or medium blue; one color in each bundle. Special prices will be given on quantities of 300 pounds or more.

## Weaving Cotton or Cotton Yarn for Hand Looms.

**No. 22981 White Weaving Cotton,** single thread, numbers 8, 10 and 12. We do not sell less than 5 pounds, one bundle, Per pound...................$0.16

**No. 22982 Colored Weaving Cotton, No. 10,** only size. Colors brown, red, blue, green, old gold, yellow, orange or black, sold in 5-pound bundles of one color only. Per pound..................................$0.25

## Bibb Carpet Warp on Spools.

**These Spools are Ready for the Warper.** They save the weaver tedious hand winding. Put up in 5-pound boxes. 20 quarter-pound spools. Exclusive selling agents in Chicago.

**No. 22984** Price, colored, per pound........$0.21
**No. 22986** Price, white............................ 0.19

## Burlap Sacking.

**No. 22996** Weight per yard.

| 7 oz. | 8 oz. | 9 oz. | 10 oz. | 11 oz. | 12 oz. |
|---|---|---|---|---|---|
| $0.03¾ | $0.04 | $0.04¼ | $0.05 | $0.05¼ | $0.06 |

Prices for full pieces of about 225 yards, ¼ cent less per yard than for cut length. Above is 40 inches wide, about 225 yards in each piece, Special prices will be furnished on large quantities of Burlap.

If you use any amount you should certainly write us.

**OUR DISCOUNT OF 3 PER CENT. FOR FULL CASH WITH ORDER MUST NOT ESCAPE YOUR NOTICE, AND IT MUST BE CONSIDERED WHEN YOU COMPARE OUR PRICES WITH THOSE OF ANY OTHER CONCERNS.**

## Grain Bags and Sacks.

**(No discount on Grain Bags.)**

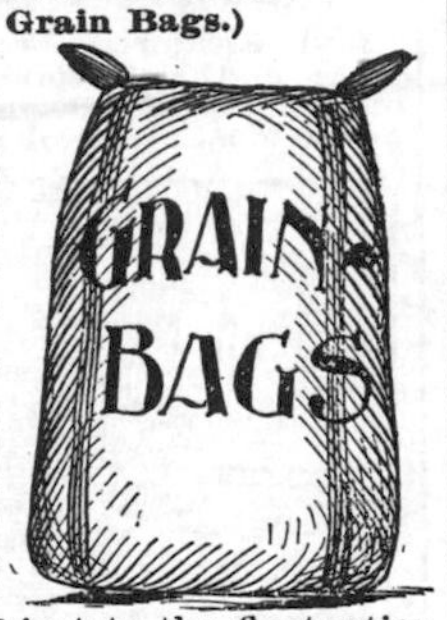


**No. 22987 Harmony Grain Bags,** 2 bushels, 16 oz. seamless. Strong and good in every way. Our last quotation on this bag was $14.00 per bale; a big purchase enables us to turn them over to you now at $10.37½ per bale, or 12c each when bales are broken.

**No. 22988 Grain Bags,** 2 bushels, American A.
Each.............. $ 0.13
Per bale........... 12.00

**No. 22989 Stark A Bags,** 2 bushels. Each... $ 0.14½
Per bale........ 14.00

Grain bags are put up 100 to the bale. We sell any quantity. Bags are sold subject to the fluctuation of the market.

**No. 22990 Wool Sack,** size, 90x40 inches, weight, 3¼ pounds. Each.......... $ 0.28
Per bale.......... 25.00

Prices herewith quoted are not guaranteed. We shall charge market value the day the order is filled. Burlaps fluctuate every day in price, 1-16 to ¼ cts.

**No. 22992 Burlap Wheat Bags,** 2 bushels.

| 8 oz. | 10 oz. | 12 oz. |
|---|---|---|
| $0.05 | $0.06 | $0.07 |

**No. 22964 Burlap Wheat Bags,** 4 bushels.

| 8 oz. | 10 oz. | 12 oz. |
|---|---|---|
| $0.07 | $0.08 | $0.09 |

## The National Flag.

**Made of All Wool Bunting.**

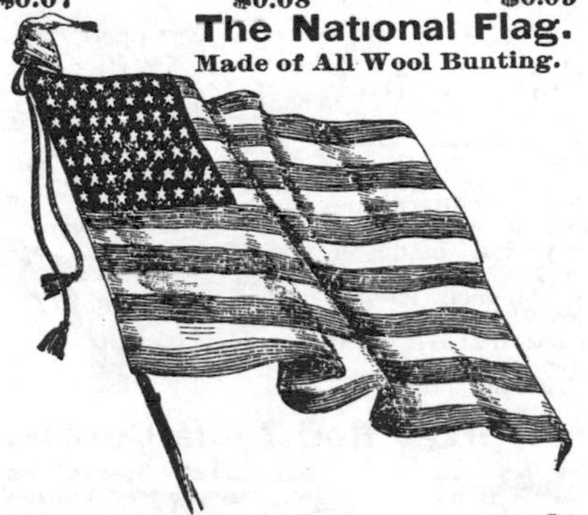

| | | | | |
|---|---|---|---|---|
| 23005 | Length, 5 feet, | Each........... | $1.25 |
| | Length, 6 feet, | Each........... | 1.50 |
| | Length, 7 feet, | Each........... | 2.00 |
| | Length, 8 feet, | Each........... | 2.50 |
| | Length, 10 feet, | Each........... | 3.50 |
| | Length, 12 feet, | Each........... | 4.50 |
| | Length, 14 feet, | Each........... | 5.50 |
| | Length, 16 feet, | Each........... | 7.00 |
| | Length, 18 feet, | Each........... | 8.50 |
| | Length, 20 feet, | Each........... | 10.00 |

The combination list on a 20 foot flag equal to ours is $18.40

## National Decoration Bunting.

Entertainment and decoration committees will save money by sending to us for their supplies.

**No. 23007 Print Cloth,** similar to bunting, printed in red, white and blue stripes, with stars. 21 inches wide. Per yard.......... $0.04½
Price for full piece of about 65 yards, per yd.. .04¼

**No. 23008 Red, White or Blue Bunting,** 25 inches wide, plain solid colors for festooning or draping. In ordering always specify the colors wanted.
Per yard.......... $0.04
Full piece, about 55 yards, per yard.......... .03⅞

**No. 23009 Tri-color Bunting;** width, 25 inches; striped in wide bands of red, white and blue; plain, no stars. Per yard.......... $0.05
Full piece, about 50 yards, per yard.......... .04¾

**No. 23010 Flag Bunting,** 28 inches wide, made with two or four flags to the yard.
Price, per yard.......... $0.06
Price for full piece of about 53 yards, per yd. .05¾

**23011 Muslin Flags,** mounted on sticks.

| | | | |
|---|---|---|---|
| Size.......2 x 3 | inches. | Per gross.......... | $0.18 |
| Size.......2½x 4 | inches. | Per gross.......... | .23 |
| Size.......4 x 6 | inches. | Per gross.......... | .38 |
| Size.......4½x 7 | inches. | Per gross.......... | .50 |
| Size.......6 x 9½ | inches. | Per gross.......... | .90 |
| Size.......9 x14 | inches. | Per gross.......... | 1.75 |

## Wide Duck or Canvas.

**No. 23012 Extra Heavy Ducks** of the best quality used for tents, awnings, stack covers, harvester aprons, etc. The table below gives widths and weights of those most used.

| Width. | No. 4. Weight per Square Yard about 20 oz. Price, per yard. | No. 6. Weight per Square Yard about 18 oz. Price, per yard. | No. 8. Weight per Square Yard about 15 oz. Price, per yard. | No. 10. Weight per Square Yard about 13 oz. Price, per yard. |
|---|---|---|---|---|
| 30 inch.. | $0.28 | $0.25 | $0.21 | $0.19 |
| 36 inch.. | .35 | .31 | .26 | .23 |
| 40 inch.. | .39 | .35 | .29 | .27 |
| 44 inch.. | .43 | .39 | .32 | .30 |
| 48 inch.. | .47 | .42 | .34 | .31 |
| 52 inch.. | .51 | .45 | .37 | .35 |
| 56 inch.. | .54 | .49 | .41 | .39 |
| 60 inch.. | .59 | .53 | .44 | .42 |
| 66 inch.. | .64 | .57 | .48 | .46 |
| 72 inch.. | .70 | .62 | .52 | .50 |
| 84 inch.. | .81 | .72 | .61 | .58 |

Full pieces of 100 yards are sold at 5 per cent less than the above prices.

## White Goods Department.

This department is **always forging ahead**; why? **Because** we sell the same goods for less money than any other house. Having recently purchased several large stocks of **desirable white goods** at about **one-half** their value, will enable us to offer some extraordinary inducements this coming season. We only carry reliable goods, and not the cheapest, trashy goods made.

## Natural Dress Linens.

**No. 22027 Natural Dress Linen,** will be very much used the coming season. Is very appropriate for picnic and traveling dresses; will wash and match up beautifully. Comes in natural (or Dark-ecru) color only. 30 inches wide. Per yard.... $0.14

**No. 23029 Natural Dress Linen,** same class of goods as above, but much finer quality. 30 inches wide. Per yard.......... $0.20

## Long Cloths.

**Long Cloths** are very much used for ladies' and children's underwear. They are nice, soft goods, and much finer than muslin.

**No. 23031 White Long Cloth,** 36 inches wide.
Price, per yard.......... $0.09½
Or a full piece of 12 yards for.......... 1.08

**No. 22033 White Long Cloth,** 36 inches wide, much finer than above. Per yard.......... $0.12½
Or a full piece of 12 yards for.......... 1.40

**No. 23035 White Long Cloth,** extra superfine quality, very firm, 36½ inches wide. Per yd.. $0.14
Or a full piece of 12 yards for.......... 1.50

## White Apron Novelties.

**No. 23037 40-inch White Apron Lawn,** with lace stripe border on one side, consisting of five or six stripes, ¾ to 1¼ inches apart.
Price per yard.......... $0.10

**No. 23039 Fine White Lawn,** with a fancy lace border on one side for aprons, skirts and dresses; width, full 40 inches. The border consists of five or six lace stripes in different widths, about ¾ to 1½ inches wide, very neat effects, style and quality that usually retails for 25 cents per yard.
Our price, per yard.......... $0.14

**No. 23041 Apron Novelty** of very fine quality white lawn with a high grade satin stripe border on one side. The border consists of five or six satin stripes, different widths, in one group; something very handsome and would retail for double the money we ask. Width, full 40 inches.
Our price.......... $0.16

**No. 23043 Apron Novelty,** with hemstitched satin stripe border; the stripes are different widths; the lawn is very fine, a much better quality than is usually to be had of local dealers, and is only found in large cities, and sold at a bargain at 35 cents per yard. Our price.......... $0.18

**No. 23044 Apron Novelty,** with a beautiful border of satin and lace stripes in combinations, and dainty hem stitching for bottom hem; altogether a very handsome border and newest effects. Extra fine quality. Per yard.......... $0.20

## White India Mull.

Very fine and sheer; width 32 inches; smoother and more durable than Swiss.

**No. 23045 India Mull,** a good fair quality, $0.16
**No. 23046 India Mull,** finer.......... .19
**No. 23048 Very Fine India Mull**.......... .24
**No. 23049 Extra Fine India Mull**.......... .30

## Cream India Mull.

**No. 23050** The same qualities and prices as the white India Mull.

## White Swiss Mull.

**No. 23051** Width, 25 inches; extra good value.......... $0.09

**No. 23053 Very Fine White Swiss;** 29 inches wide.......... .12½

**No. 23055 Extra Fine Quality White Swiss;** 33 inches wide; superior finish.......... .19

## Tarletan.

**No. 23056 Tarletan.** Colors: pink, pale blue, white, black, yellow and all colors. 50 inches wide. Per yard.......... $0.10

**No. 23057 Tarletan.** 60 inches wide. Colors same as above. Per yard.......... .12

## Dimity.

**No. 23058 White Checked Dimity,** extra fine and strong. A much better wearing goods than Nainsook. Comes in small, medium and large checks, 31 inches wide. Per yard.......... 0.11

**No. 23059 White Dimity.** Comes in pin-head checks and hair line stripes; 31 in. Per yard. 0.15

**No. 23061 White India Dimity.** Nothing finer made. This comes in pretty stripes and checks; both large, medium and small; 31 inches wide.
Per yard.......... 0.20

## White Heavy Corded Pique.

**Called Welt Pique,** the cords running across the cloth, not lengthwise. Very pretty and durable for children's wear and ladies' dresses.

**No. 23063 White Welt Pique,** fine cord; width, 27 inches. Per yard.......... 0.14

**No. 23065 White Welt Pique,** fine and heavy cords in groups; width, 27 inches. Per yard... 0.20

## White Check Nainsook.

**No. 23066 White Check Nainsook,** 24 inches wide; comes in small medium and large check.
Per yard.......... $0.04½

**No. 23067 25-inch Wide Nainsook,** comes in different checks, small, medium and large.
Per yard.......... $0.06

**No. 23068 27-inch Wide Nainsook,** with satin finish checks, in small, medium and large.
Per yard.......... $0.08

**No. 23069 25-inch Satin Check Nainsook.** This is an exceedingly fine quality; don't fail to include some of this in your order; comes in pin head, medium and large check. Per yard.......... $0.10

**No. 23070 Extra Fine Satin Finish Check Nainsook,** comes in pin head and small checks; 25 inches wide. Per yard.......... $0.12½

**No. 23071 Extra Quality Check Nainsook,** very firm and close weave and will give excellent wear; comes in pin head and small checks; 27 inches wide. Per yard.......... $0.15

## Plain White Nainsook.

**Plain White Nainsook is a soft fabric, well finished; used extensively for infants' and childrens' dresses and underwear.**

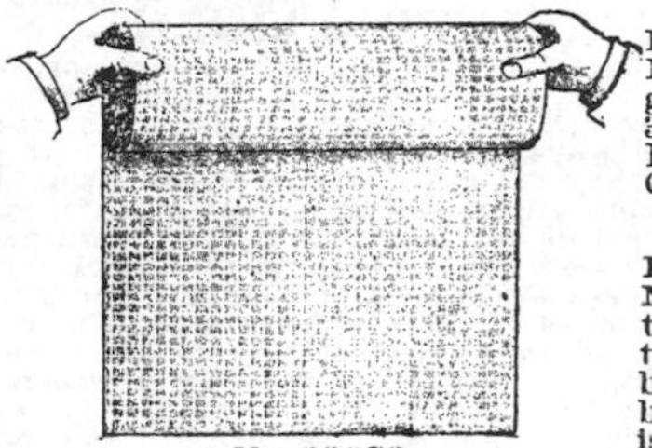

No. 23072

**No. 23072 Plain White Nainsook;** good quality; 31 inches wide. Pr yard $0.09
Or full piece of 20 yds. $1.75

**No. 23073 Plain White Nainsook;** this is an extraordinary bargain; has a beautiful finish, and usually retails in large stores in big cities for 20 cents per yard.
Our special price, per yard.......... $0.12½
Or a full piece of 20 yards.......... 2.30

**No. 23074 Extra Superfine Quality Plain Nainsook;** 36 inches wide. Price per yard.......... $0.18

**No. 23075 Finest Imported English Nainsook,** which only can be obtained in big cities at fancy prices; we sell it at a small profit price. 36 inches wide. Per yard.......... $0.25

## White Victoria Lawns.

**No. 23076 White Victoria Lawn,** 26 inches wide. Per yard.......... $0.07
Full piece of 24 yards, per yard.......... .06¾

**No. 23077 White Victoria Lawn,** much better than above, being very fine and sheer finish. Per yard.......... .10
Full piece of 24 yards for.......... 2.20

**No. 23078 Superior Quality Victoria Lawn,** which retails at 20c per yard; we have bought a big lot of these goods at a great bargain. Special price, per yard.......... .12½
Full piece of 24 yards for.......... 2.75

**No. 23079 White Victoria Lawn.** Extra fine quality, very close weave, with satin finish. Per yard.......... .15
Full piece of 24 yards, per yard.......... .14

**No. 23080 Very Highly Finished Victoria Lawn,** with an even and perfect surface, nothing finer made. Per yard.......... .18
Full piece of 24 yards, per yard.......... .16

## Colored Dotted Swisses.

**No. 23098 Colored Dotted Swiss,** with hair line stripes between dots, which are of medium size. Colors are light blue, pink, cardinal, corn color, nile green, cream and navy blue; 26 inch. Per yard. $0.22

## White India Linon.

**We Are Headquarters for India Linon.**

**No. 23099 White India Linon,** 30 inches wide; good quality. Per yard.. $0.07½
Or full piece of 24 yard.
Per yard.......... 0.07

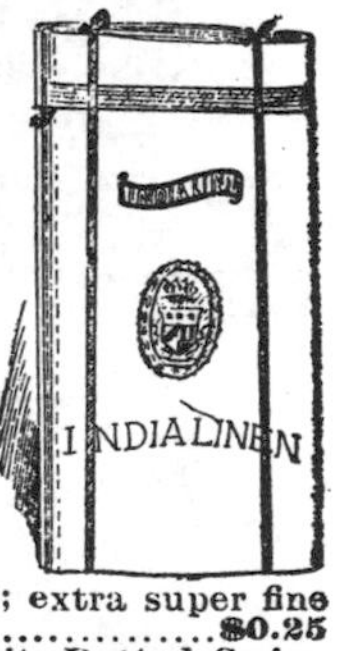


**No. 23100 White India Linon,** very fine and sher 30 inches wide. Per yard. $0.10
Or a full piece of 24 yds.
Per yard.......... 0.09½

**No. 23101 White India Linon,** 30 inches wide; extra fine and sheer per yard..... $0.12½
Or a full pice of 24 yds. 2.75

**No. 23102 White India Linon,** much better and finer than above; 30 inch.
Per yard.......... $0.15

**No. 23103 White India Linon;** superfine quality; 30 inch. Per yard.......... $0.20

**No. 23104 White India Linon;** extra super fine quality. Per yard.......... $0.25

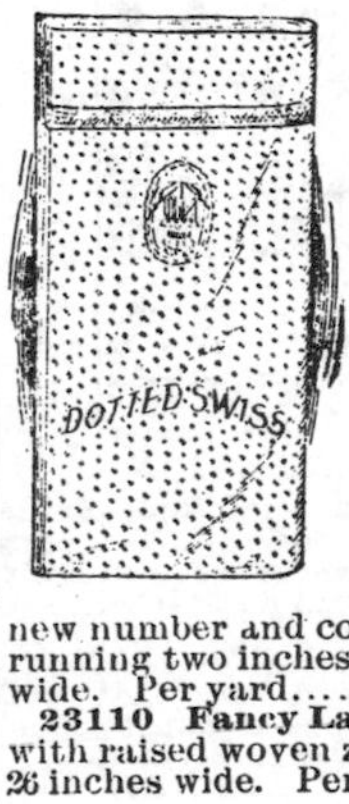


**23106 White Dotted Swiss,** 25 inches wide with pin head dots, very fine and sheer.
Per yard.......... $0.15

**23107 White Dotted Swiss,** 26 inches wide, comes in small medium and large dots, much finer than above number and is extra value. Per yard.......... $0.20

**23108 Extra Fine Dotted Swiss,** this is one of the best number, and is sold in large retail stores at 35c. and 40c. per yard, comes in a very fine sheer cloth with pin head dots, also medium and large size dots. 26 inches wide. Per yard.......... $0.25
Or full piece of 25 yards, Per yard.......... $0.23

**23109 Fancy Lace Stripe Dotted Swiss.** This is an entire new number and comes in lace stripe effects, stripes running two inches apart between the dots. 26 inch wide. Per yard.......... $0.15

**23110 Fancy Lace Stripe Swiss,** 26 inches wide with raised woven zagzag stripes running between. 26 inches wide. Per yard.......... $0.25

## White Dotted Swisses.

**No. 23111** White Dotted Swisses, 25 inches wide, genuine imported goods. Comes in three styles of dots, small, medium and large. Per yard....**$0.08**
Full piece of 24 to 25 yards. Per yard......**.07¾**
**No. 23112** White Imported Swiss, 25 inches wide. Comes in three styles of dots, large, medium and small, and has a nice, sheer finish.
Per yard.........................**$0.10**
Full piece of 24 to 25 yards. Per yard ....**.09½**
**No. 23113** White Imported Dotted Swiss, 25 inches wide. Finer and better quality than above number. Makes up pretty for ladies' and childrens' dresses. Per yard........................**$0.12½**

## HOUSKEEPING LINENS.

Our linen department is one of the foremost in our vast establishment, and is presided over by one of the most expert linen buyers in the United States. Our aim is always to give our customers better values than they can get elsewhere; doing this at all times has built up an immense linen business for us. Buying all of our linens from the manufacturer direct, whether he is located in America or Europe, enables us to offer the consumers linens at prices few wholesalers are able to make the retailer. What woman does not take pride in her linens? What woman is not a judge of linen? The more they know about linen the better for us, because such bargains as we give pleases them and they tell the whole community of the great big bargains in linens to be had of Sears, Roebuck & Co.

## Turkey Red Table Damask.

**No. 23120** Turkey Red Table Damask; 52 inches wide, strictly fast colors; same as your local dealer would ask 25c per yard for; splendid for wear and very neat patterns.
Per yard.....**15c**
**No. 23121** Exceptionally Good Value. Finest quality fast colored Turkey Red Damask Table Cloth; 58 inches wide; fine satin finish; dice patterns; regular 45c value.
Price per yard, **35c**
Four great big bargains in linen. Read them over carefully if you are interested in big linen bargains.

No. 23120.     No. 23121.

**No. 23122 Our Pride.** 58-inch fast colored Turkey Red Table Damask; oil boiled and extra fine finish. Your choice of the four beautiful patterns, as shown above; dice and floral designs; all new and handsome. Price per yard.....**24c**

No. 23123     No. 23124

**No. 23123 Handsome Green and Red Table Damask** in rich floral and fruit designs. 58 inches wide. Warranted strictly fast colors. An entirely new style of Damask with beautiful floral borders to match centers. Price per yard................**37½c**
**No. 23124** 58 Inch Table Damask in handsome check patterns of red and white. A very pretty and new style Damask of our own special importation. Extra heavy and the colors are absolutely fast.
Price per yard.......................**35c**

## Half Bleached Table Damask.

**No. 23125** Imported Satin Finished Turkey Red Table Damask. Perfectly fast colors, and a handsome assortment of new patterns with fancy borders. Width 60 inches.
Price, per yard.....**50c**

## ...BARGAINS...
## —IN—
## LINEN TABLE DAMASK.

**No. 23126** Half Bleached Linen Table Damask, 54 inches wide, new and beautiful patterns. Splendid value and excellent for wear. Price per yd... **27½c**
**No. 23127** Extra Quality Half Bleached Table Damask. Made in new and beautiful floral patterns. Width, 58 inches. One of our specially good values.
Price, per yard........**35c**

## Bleached and Half Bleached Table Damask.

**No. 23128** Extra fine Cream Bleached Table Damask, 60 inches wide; made in handsome assortment of new patterns; unexcelled for wear and looks.
Price per yard...........**45c**
**No. 23129** Purest Linen Half Bleached Table Damask. Nothing better made for wear. Handsome patterns, all new and freshly imported; 64 inches wide. Thoroughly dependable in every way.
Price per yard........**55c**

No. 23120     No. 23127

No. 23128.     No. 23129.

## Full Bleached Table Damask.

No. 23130.    No. 23131.    No. 23132.

**No. 23130 Full Bleached Linen Table Damask** very fine, smooth finished and durable. 57 inches wide, and very even texture. Price, per yard ...**35c**
**No. 23131** Full Bleached and Genuine Pure Linen German Damask, woven in an assortment of beautiful and new patterns, with plain borders. Extra good value. 58 inches wide.
Price, per yard.......... ................**48c**
**No. 23132** This is a Very Heavy, Full Bleached, All Linen Table Damask, of exceptional quality. Extra fine satin finish; pretty floral designs in assorted patterns. 66 inches wide. One of our very good things. Price, per yard................**59c**
**No. 23133** 70-inch All Pure Linen Table Damask; warranted high quality and unexcelled for service. Made in new and handsome designs, assorted patterns; regular $1.25 quality.
Price per yard...........**78c**
**No. 23134 Genuine White Satin Table Damask.** Made from finest selected linen. The wearing qualities of this Damask have never been equaled. Retailers never sell it for less than $1.50 per yard. Made in beautiful Dresden patterns; width 72 in. Price per yd.**98c**

No. 23133.       No. 23134.

## Ready-To-Use Table Cloths.

**Red Bordered Loom Damask Table Cloths.** These cloths are immense sellers with us and we offer them this season at a price within easy reach of the most economical buyers.

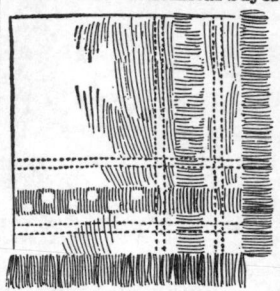

**No. 23135** This is an All Linen Half Bleached Table Cloth with neat red border. Perfectly fast color, and exceptionally good value. Size 50 x 60, with fringed borders.
Price each......**45c**
**No. 23136** Same cloth exactly as above, but made size 50x70. Price each, **55c**
**No. 23137** Same cloth exactly as above, but made size 50x78. Price each, **65c**
**No. 23138** Same cloth as above exactly, but made in size 50x94.
Price each.... . ..................**85c**

## White Hemmed Bleached Damask Table Cloths.
**With Dotted Center and Floral Borders to Match. Finest Imported Goods.**

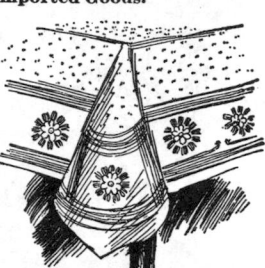

**No. 23139** This is an exceptionally fine, satin finished, all linen Table Cloth. Snow white, bleached, with hemmed borders. Size, 68x68.
Price, each...**$1.75**
**No. 23140** Same cloth as above, exactly, but made in size 68x90.
Price, each. .**$2.25**
**No. 23141** Napkins to match above table cloth. Size, 19x20.
Price per doz. **$1.10**

## Turkey Red Table Covers.

**No. 23142 Special Bargain Real Turkey Red Table Cover.** Fine imported goods, oil boiled and warranted not to fade. Good, heavy quality, fine finish, made in handsome floral designs, with fringed borders to match. Size, 58x70.
Price, each............**55c**
**No. 23143** Same as above. Size, 58x79. Price. each......**75c**
**No. 23144** Same as above. Made in size 58x88.
Price, each.................**90c**

**No. 23145 Our Own Special Importation Extra Fine Turkey Red Table Cloths,** extra high grade satin finish. Beautiful floral design, center with deep fringed borders to match. Very heavy quality goods, oil boiled and warranted absolutely fast color. Nothing finer made. Size 67x85.
Price, each......**$1.85**
**No. 23146** Same Table Cloth as above exactly but made in size 68x98.
Price each.......**$2.20**

## Bleached Fringed Linen Table Cloths.

**No. 23147** This is a Handsome White Cloth, of fine German linen with satin damask finish, and has handsome colored borders of blue, pink, salmon and white. Handsomely designed and fringed. Size, 60x62.
Price, each....**$0.95**
**No. 23148** Same quality and style cloth as above, but made in size 69x82 inches.
Price, each....**$1.55**
**No. 23149** A beautiful Snow White Damask Cloth, with fine satin finish. Deeply fringed all around. This is a table cloth that will be the pride of any woman who takes special interest in her table linens. Made with handsome floral center and border to match. All pure white. Size, 66x66. Price, each..........**$1.35**
**No. 21350** Same Cloth as above exactly, but made in size 59x82. Price, each..............**$1.69**

No. 23147.

## Linen Lunch Cloths.

**Also Largely Used as Covers for Small Tables.**
**No. 23151** An artistic and beautiful white brocaded Damask linen lunch cloth. Size 37x37 inches. This cloth has a beautiful floral design center with border to match and is fringed all around. Made from an exceptionally good grade of linen. All white and very dainty in effect.
Price each........ $0.50
Per dozen........ 5.70
**No. 23152** A special importation of our own. You can never know what handsome and dependable lunch cloths these are until you order one of them and see for yourself. They are made from the finest satin finish German linen with beautiful knotted fringe and open work borders. It is only in the better class of large stores in our large cities that cloths of this quality are obtainable and at very high prices. The size of these cloths is 44x44 inches. Retail value: $2.25.
Our price each .......................... $1.59

No. 23152

## MATCHED TABLE SETS.

**EACH SET CONSISTS OF ONE TABLE CLOTH AND 12 NAPKINS TO MATCH.**

### Our $1.95 Princess Set.

**No. 23153** Our Princess Table Set consists of one handsome 56x56 inch all linen table cloth with beautiful colored borders, fringe all around and 12 fringed napkins size 15x15 to match. We make a specialty of these sets and import them direct in very large quantities. The patterns for this season are particularly choice and pretty. The designs are all new and the colorings are specially attractive. We have them with the following colored borders, gold, light blue, red, blue, pink and white. Regular retail value of these suits, $2.50.
Our price per set............................. $1.95

### Our $2.90 Duchess Set.

**No. 23154** This is positively the handsomest, most durable, and thoroughly dependable table set we have ever imported. The cloth is of the finest pure linen with colored borders, heavily fringed all around in the newest and most up-to-date patterns made this season. Beautiful brocaded center. The size of the table cloth is 63x84, and the set includes 12 handsome fringed napkins, size 15x15 with colored borders to match the cloth. The colors are red, light blue, pink, gold and plain white. Guaranteed strictly high grade in every respect. Order a Duchess set and you will get a table set your local dealer could not sell you for less than $3.75 or $4.00.
Our price, per set............................. $2.90

## Linen Napkins.

This department is a very important branch of our business. We import all of our napkins direct and save our customers the importers' and wholesalers' profits. We handle only thoroughly good and reliable grades of linens. The kind that always satisfy. Include what napkins you need in your next order to us and get such value as you could not possibly get elsewhere. Save money wherever you can.
**No. 23155** Standard Quality Bleached Linen Napkins, size 15x15 inches. Price per dozen......50c

---

**No. 23156** Superior Quality Bleached Linen Napkins, handsome floral patterns in new designs, size 17x17 inches. Price, per dozen........... 75c
**No. 23157** S. & R's Special Value, extra quality, bleached linen napkins, new and very handsome floral designs, size 17x17 inches. We make a special feature of these napkins and have imported them in vast quantities for the coming season. They are handsome in pattern and finish and are dependable in every way. We warrant them to give satisfaction in every way. Price per dozen................98c
**No. 23158** Extra Fine Silver Bleached All Linen Imported Napkins, size 21x21 inches, with charming floral designs, good heavy weight, close woven and extra fine finish Price, per dozen,$1.50
**No. 23159** Real German Bleached Linen Napkins, with extra fine satin finish, size 22x22 inches, heavy weight, very closely woven and durable as well as beautiful in appearance.
Price, per dozen..........................$1.95
**No. 23160** Real German Bleached Satin Finished Napkins, size 24x24, heavy weight and closely woven. All pure linen and thoroughly dependable; handsome floral patterns, one of our specially clever values. Price, per dozen..........................$2.50
**No. 23162** Our Special Importation, Extra large size Dinner Napkins, made from the very finest imported linen, in new and handsome designs, size 27x27 inches. Extra fine finished, heavy and strong.
Price, per dozen..........................$2.85

### Fringed Napkins.

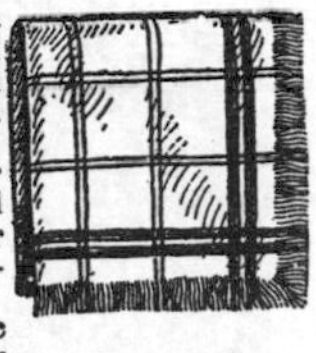

**No. 23163** Bleached Linen Napkins. Handsome pink and blue checked patterns, fringed borders. Size, 11½x11½ inches. Splendid value.
Price per dozen................25c
**No. 23164** Bleached Fringed Linen Napkins. Beautiful red or blue checked patterns, with borders to match. Size 14x14 inches.
Price per dozen..............35c

No. 23163.

**No. 23165** Handsome red or blue checked Linen Napkins. Sizes 16x16 inches. Fringed all around. Extra heavy quality. Price per dozen..........................43c
**No. 23166** Extra Selected Bleached Linen Napkins. Plain centers with pink or blue borders, fringed all around. Sizes, 16x16 inches. Specially good value. Price per dozen..........................55c

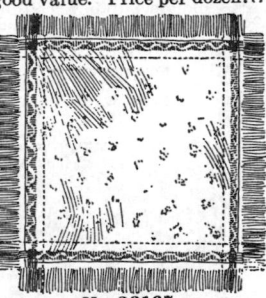

**No. 23167** Half Bleached extra fine All Linen Napkins with plain floral pattern center and pretty red figured borders, fringed all round. Size, 15½x15½ inches. One of our specially good values. Price per dozen..........75c

No. 23167.

**No. 23168** Full Bleached extra fine Imported Napkins, warranted all pure linen. Made in plain white only. Beautiful floral designs with fringed borders. Size 14x14 inches. Heavy and fine and extra good value. The sort of napkins that you can point to with pride.
Price per dozen..........................95c

### Fringed Linen Doylies.

**No. 23169** Extra Selected Turkey Red Doylies, warranted absolutely fast color. Size, 14x14 inches. Fringed border all around.
Price per dozen..........50c

No. 23169.

**No. 23170** Extra fine quality Real Turkey Red Doylies. Fine satin Damask finish. Absolutely fast colors. Size, 16x16 inches. Fringed borders all around. Price per dozen..........80c

### Cotton Crash Toweling.

**No. 23171** Unbleached Twilled Cotton Crash Toweling, 15 inches wide, linen finish.
Price, per yard............................. $0.04
Per bolt of 25 yards................ .93
**No. 23172** Bleached Cotton Crash Toweling, 17 inches wide. Price, per yard............$0.04½
Per bolt of 25 yards................ 1.00
**No. 23173** Cream Half Bleached Glass Toweling, small red and blue checks; width, 14 inches.
Price, per yard..........................$0.05

---

## Bleached and Unbleached Crash.

**No. 23174** All Linen Unbleached Crash, 15 inches wide, standard quality. Price, per yard.......$0.05

**No. 23175** Brown All Linen Crash, extra selected stock, fully warranted, 15 in. wide.
Price, per yard....6¼c
**No. 23176** An Extra Fine Quality All Lined Unbleached Crash, 17 inches wide.
Price, per yard....7c
**No. 23177** All Linen Unbleached Crash, very heavy and closely woven; width, 19 inches, extra good value.
Price, per yard....9c
**No. 23178** Cream Bleached Linen Crash, 16 inches wide, with colored border.
Price, per yard..........................6½c
**No. 23179** Cream Bleached All Linen Crash Toweling, 17½ inches wide, extra fine weave, with fancy border, thoroughly good. Price, per yard..9c
**No. 23180** Extra Heavy Bleached Huckaback Toweling, all pure linen, 18 inches wide, fully warranted. Price, per yard..........................12c
**No. 23181** All Linen Checked Glass Toweling, in blue and red checks, 17½ inches wide. Our own special importation. Price, per yard.............10c

## Cotton Diapers.

**Cotton and Linen Diapers** put up in 10 yard pieces, we do not sell less than a piece, our Sanitary Diaper cloth is chemically pure and absorbent. The very best manufactured.
**No. 23182** 18 inch Cotton Diaper, in 10 yard pieces, per piece, 45c; 20 inch, 55c; 22 inch, 65c; 24 inch, 70c; 27 inch, 75c.

## All Linen Diapers.

**No. 23183** 18 inch Linen Diapers, 10 yard pieces, per piece, $1.25; 20 inch, $1.40; 22 inch, $1.60; 24 inch, $1.95.

## Irish Butcher Linen.

**No. 23184** Bleached Pure Linen, 36 inches wide, per yard.............25c
**No. 23185** Better and Finer Quality, 36 inch, per yard..........................35c
**No. 23186** Heavy Grade Linen, 40 inch, per yard..........................35c
**No. 23187** Better Quality Finer and Heavier, 40 inch, per yard..........................45c

Never before in the history of our business have we been able to offer such extraordinary values in towels. Our towel department is stocked to overflowing with tons upon tons of the very finest towels ever imported into this country. We import them direct and purchase them in immense quantities on a strictly spot cash basis and we therefore buy them for less money than any other concern on earth. That is why we sell better towels for less money than any other house in this country.

## Loom Damask Towels, Half Bleached.

**No. 23188** A World Beater. Pure Linen Half Bleached Damask Fringed Towels, with centre patterns and fancy colored borders. Worth fully 10c each. Size, 14x27.
Our price, each...... 6c
Per dozen......65c

No. 23188.

**No. 23189** All Linen Half Bleached Damask Fringed Towels, with fancy centre and colored border. Size, 16x32.
Price, each.......... 9c
Per dozen.............98c

---

No. 23190.

**No. 23189.**

**No. 23190 Loom Damask Fringed Towel.** Comes in a beautiful assortment of centre patterns and colored borders. Extra heavy quality. Size, 18x38.
Price, each............$0.12
Per dozen............1.35

**No. 23191 Extra Large Bleached Fringed German Damask Towel,** with beautiful fancy centre and colored border. Size, 19½x42.
Price, each............$0.20
Per dozen............2.35

No. 23191.

No. 23192.

**No. 93192 Extra Large Loom Damask Fringed Towel.** Very heavy, with beautiful floral centre and 4½ inch colored border on each end. Cannot be worn out. Size, 24x49.
Price, each............$0.29
Per dozen............3.25

## Bleached Damask Linen Towels.

**No. 23193 Bleached Damask Linen Towels,** knotted fringe, fancy colored border, with floral center, good heavy quality of linen. Size 15x35.
Price, each...$0.13
Per doz......1.50

**No. 23194 Bleached Damask and Linen Knotted Fringed Towels,** with floral center and very pretty assorted colored borders. Size, 17x35 inches.
Price each...........$0.16
Per doz............1.85

**No. 23195 Our Leader.** This is a beauty. Fine satin Damask Bleached Linen Towels, knotted fringe with pretty borders, such as pink blue and salmon, also plain white. Size, 15½x38.
Each......$0.20
Per half doz 1.00
20x44.

## FOR BATH BRUSHES
### SEE PAGE 327.

---

**No. 23196 Fine Bleached Satin Finished Damask Towel,** with beautiful leaf pattern center, and fancy colored border heavy knotted fringe. Size, 20x42.
Price each........$0.25
Per half doz......1.40

**No. 23197 Extra Large Size Bleached Satin Damask Towel.** Made of very fine quality linen, very heavy knotted fringe, comes in plain white only.
Price each...........$0.27
Per half doz...........1.50

## Bleached Damask Towels With Open Work Borders.

## Extra High Grade, Finest All Linen Bleached Damask Towels

**No. 23198 Extra High Grade, Finest All Linen Bleached Damask Towels.** Size 25x51 inches. Very heavy knotted fringe; fancy vine and floral figured center and very deep fancy colored borders of pink and red, salmon and blue. Warranted extra fine quality.
Price, each....$0.30
Per doz........3.50

## Good Quality Bleached All Linen Damask Towels

**No. 23199 Good Quality Bleached All Linen Damask Towels.** Fancy red or blue border with open work on each side. Long knotted fringe. Very handsome figured centers in new designs. Size 17x36 inches.
Price each.....$0.17
Per doz........2.00

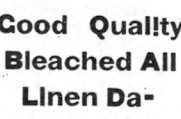

## Bleached Satin Damask Towels.

**No. 23200 Bleached Satin Damask Towels.** All linen with heavy knotted fringe and hand tied open work at each end. Beautiful floral figured center and handsome colored borders. Size 20x42 inches.
Price, each....$0.25
Per doz........2.85

---

**No. 23201 Extra Fine All Linen Satin Damask Towels** with two rows of open work on each end. Beautiful pearl pattern center and fancy colored and heavy knotted fringe. Size 22x44. Colors, pink, blue, salmon, red, etc.
Price, each............$0.35
Per doz...............2.00

## Huckaback Towels.

**No. 23202 A Special Bargain Fine Bleached Linen Huckaback Towels,** with neat hemmed borders, extra heavy and regular 20 cent quality. Size, 17½ x35½. Price each.12½c.
Per doz.........$1.45

**No. 23203 Extra Large and Heavy all Linen Huckaback Towels.** Size 22 x 42 with fancy borders, neatly hemmed ends. The very best towel ever offered for this price. Price each, 20c.
Per doz.........$2.30

## Cotton Towels.

**No. 23204** Selected quality white duck towels, for barbers' and kitchen use. With neat colored borders and fringed ends; size 14x29. Price per dozen........45c

**No. 23205** Fancy half bleached honeycomb towels; fancy striped on both sides; specially good value; sizes 15x40 inches. Price each.......5c
Per dozen........48c

**No. 23206** Extra heavy cotton half bleached honeycomb towels; with handsome red borders and fringed ends. Size 20x40.
Price each........6c. Per doz....58c

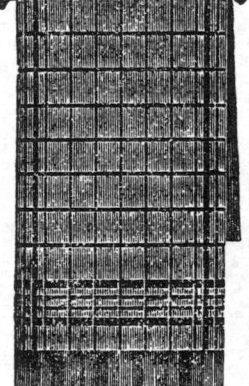

**No. 23207 Special value.** Extra heavy full bleached fancy cotton towels, crepon effect, with beautiful raised figures. Regular retail price 15c. Special price each....$0.10
Per dozen........1.00

**No. 23208 Fine white glass towels,** with blue and pink checks. Size 15 x 28. A specially good towel at a very low price.
Each.........$0.10
Price per dozen....1.00

**No. 23209 Extra fine glass towel;** same as preceding number; made of pure linen; size 18x38.
Price each...$0.10
Per dozen....1.00

## TURKISH TOWELS

A good rubbing down with a Turkish towel after a refreshing bath, will put new life and vigor into your system. Nothing will dry the skin so quickly or create such a ruddy glow to the skin and quicken the circulation quite so well. Turkish Towels were never quite so good or so remarkably cheap as they are with us this season.

**No. 23210** Genuine Turkish towels, cream color; size 16x30; good heavy weight and specially good value. Price each, 5c
Per dozen...........55c

**No. 23211** Genuine Turkish towels; cream or unbleached; extra heavy weight. Size 19x42. Specially good value. Price, each....9c. Per doz.....98c

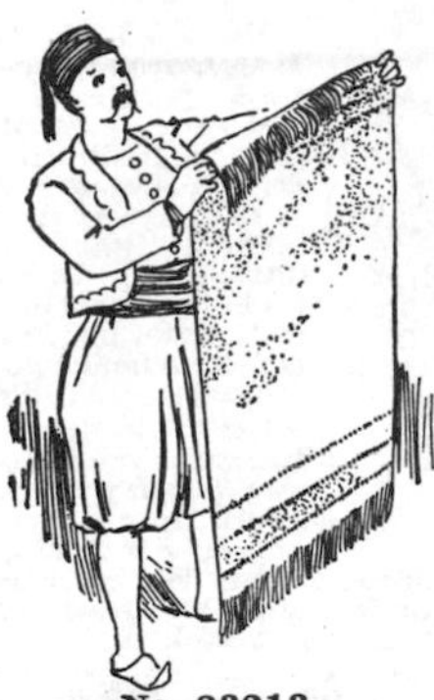

No. 23213.

**No. 23212 This is an Exceptionally Fine Towel,** extra heavy, large sized unbleached turkish towel. Your local dealer asks at least 20 cents for a towel of this quality. Handsomely made towel with red border; full size 22x44. We make a specialty of this particular grade of Turkish towels, guaranteed to give exceptional satisfaction.
Special price ea..$0.12½
Per dozen....... 1.40

**No. 23213 Extra Fine Quality of Unbleached Turkish Towels,** extra heavy, and large sized; fancy border; size 24½x47. Exceptionally well made, and a thoroughly dependable towel in every respect Price, each....$0.16
Per dozen.... 1.80

## Bleached Turkish Towels.

**No. 23215 Extra Selected Pure White Bleached Turkish Towels;** heavy and very soft and very absorbent. Made with neat red border and fringed ends. Size, 16½ by 38. Price each....$0.09
Per dozen.... 1.00

**No. 23216 Extra Selected Fine Bleached Turkish Towels;** sizes, 17x39; very soft and fine; handsomely made and finished, and will give excellent satisfaction in every respect. You will never know what a good towel this is, until you have tried it.
Price each.... $0.12½
Price per dozen.... 1.40

**No. 23217 Extra Heavy Fine Snow White Turkish Towel.** Very soft and absorbent; fancy made and finished, with fringed edges and fancy colored border. An exceptional bargain.
Price each.... $0.17
Per dozen.... 1.90

## Turkish Tidies.

**No. 23218 Fancy colored Turkish Tidies,** figured center and border in variegated colors, long knotted fringe. Size, 16x35 inches. Price each....11c

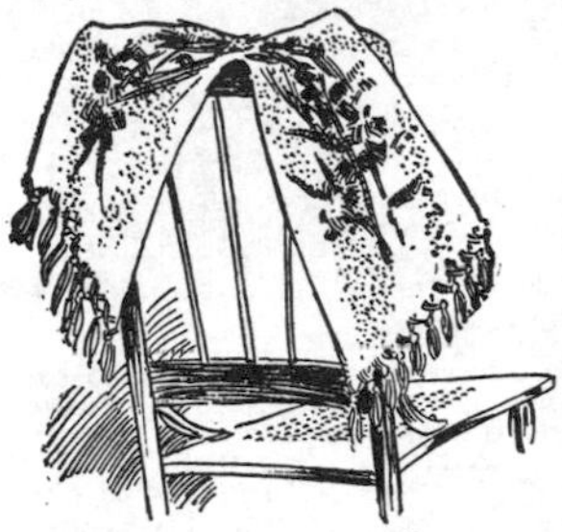

### Very Handsome Turkish Tidies.

**No. 23219 Very Handsome Turkish Tidies,** fringe on both ends, with very fancy and attractive center. Very pretty and will give excellent satisfaction. Size 15½ by 40.
Price each..$0.15
Per dozen.. 1.70

### Genuine Marseilles Turkish Tidy.

**No. 23220 Genuine Marseilles Turkish Tidy,** made in new and beautiful raised patterns; choice assortment of strictly up to date designs. With double knotted fringe; size 19½x41.
Price, each..25c
½ dozen...$1.40

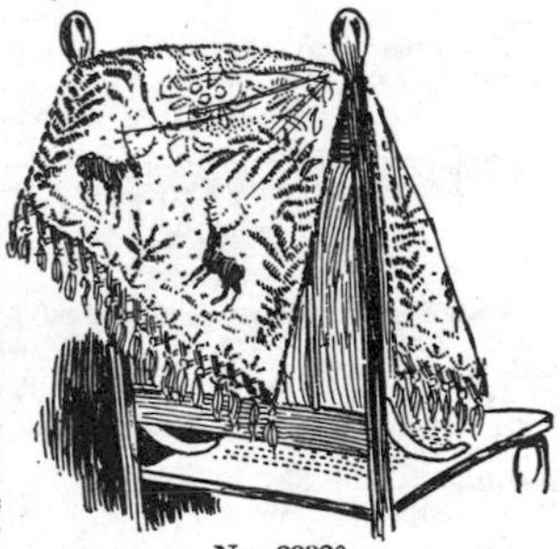

No. 23320.

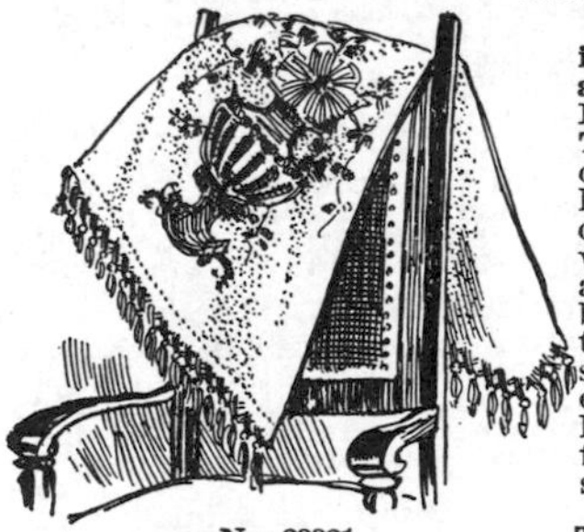

No. 23321.

**No. 23222 This is an exceptionally heavy and Fine Genuine Turkish Tidy,** comes in the following beautiful colors, pink, white, nile green and canary, with beautiful contrasting floral designs on both ends; handsomely finished with fringe at ends, size 18x60.
Price each, 35c
Three for...$2.00

**No. 23222 This is a beautiful Turkish Stand Cover;** comes made with white centers, and beautiful bright colored borders, finished with knotted fringe all around. Never before sold at less than 60c. Price each....$0.35; Three for....$1.00

## Turkish Face Cloths.

**No. 23223 Bleached Face Cloth.** Size, 15x15, full bleached, plain white or with stripe.
Price.... 5c; Per dozen....56c

**No. 23225 Fancy Pattern Face Cloth.** Size, 16x16, full bleached goods fancy block pattern center with striped border.
Each.... 9c; Per dozen....80c

# CHENILLE PORTIERES.

**Heavy Chenille Curtains.** We have made every effort to make this one of the foremost departments of our establishment. Being firmly convinced that cheap shoddy portieres are expensive at any price, **we have excluded cheap unreliable curtains from our list.** Our line consists of nice curtains with soft, dainty effects and the prices we sell them at are away down. We sell a great many hundred chenille portieres each week buy them in large quantities direct from the manufacturer. **We are sure that we can save our customers a great deal of money on Chenille Portieres.**

## Our Chenille Portieres at $2.15.

**No. 23271 A Very Pretty Chenille Curtain,** 3 yards long and 36 inches wide. This curtain has a handsome border on the bottom 15 inches wide, the border being a work of art in floral designs, in beautiful shaded colors. A 5 inch border on top matching the lower border. A very neat and new fringe 5 inches wide on top, and the bottom is finished with 2½ inch chenille tassels. The following colors are to be had: peacock, red, bronze, olive, blue, terra-cotta, rose and brown. We are not inclined to do any boasting, but we know it is just **like thowing money away** for people to buy chenille curtains outside of our house. Our special price, pair....$2.15

## A $5.00 Chenille Curtain at $2.95.

**No. 23272 This Number is a very handsome Chenille Curtain,** 3 yards long and 40 inches wide; it has a handsome 16½ inch border on the bottom. This border is a triumph in the art of curtain making. Border of a handsome floral design in mixed colors. A 5 inch border on top to match the lower one. Has a handsome 7 inch Chenille fringe on top and 2½ inch Chenille tassels on the bottom. The following colors can be had: peacock, red, bronze, olive, blue terra cotta, rose and brown. This curtain is a winner every time at the price we sell it. Such values as these are obtainable only from Sears, Roebuck & Co. Each....$2.95

## A $6.00 Tapestry Curtain for $3.25

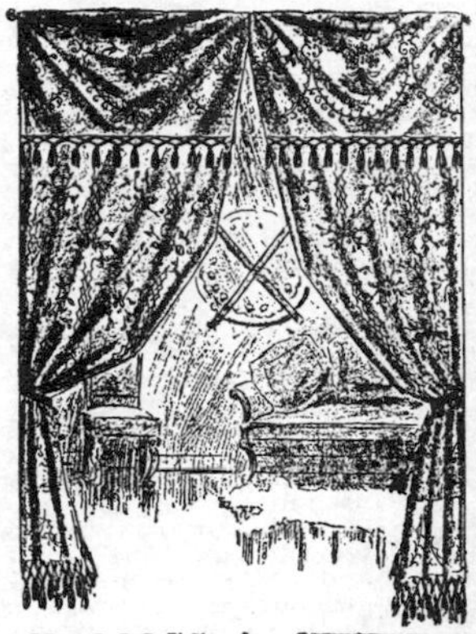

**No. 23274 It's bargains like these that make us friends.** A handsome tapestry curtain, 3 yards long and 36 inches wide, a beautiful floral design, has a 6 inch knotted fringe at the top and a 4 inch fringe at the bottom; this curtain comes in the new and very fashion'ble changeable effects and is a great big bargain at the price we sell it. Don't pay $6.00 but send to S. R. & Co., and save your money. Colors are terra cotta, olive and cardinal.
Perpair.. $3.25

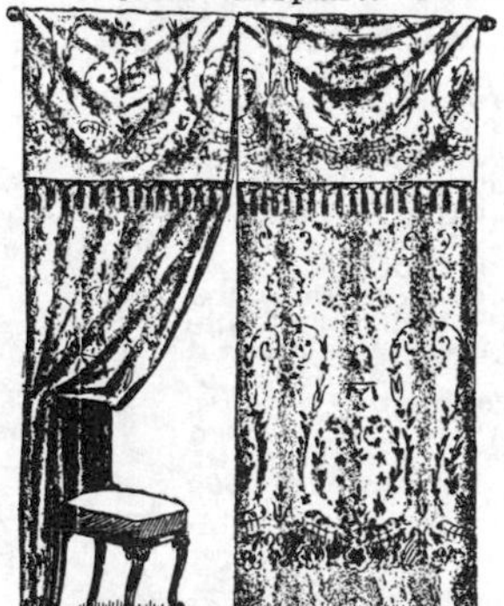

**No. 23275 A Rich Appearing Tapestry Curtain,** 3 yards long and 36 inches wide, comes in solid colors interwoven with a gold tinsel thread producing an effect that is very pleasing to the eye; floral pattern, 6½ inch fringe on top with very heavy tassel, a light 5 inch fringe on the bottom; colors, terra-cotta, olive and cardinal. This is a curtain we can recommend to all lovers of nice tapestries. The price is as low as retail merchants ask for cheap shoddy goods. Don't pay $7.00 for curtains like these.
Sears', Roebuck & Co's. price, per pair....$4.25

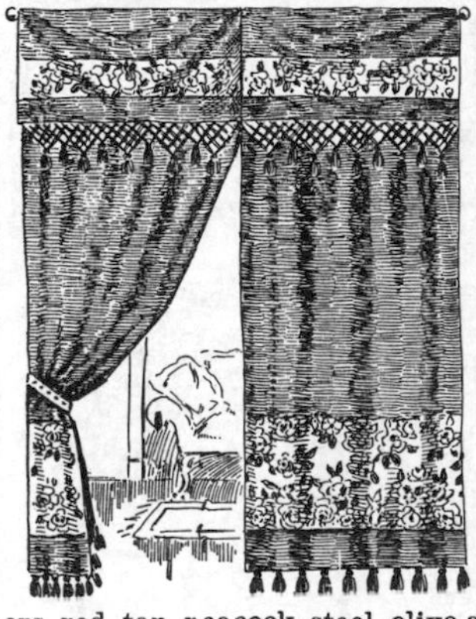

**No. 23276 A Very Heavy Chenille Curtain,** of a very fine quality, 3 yards long and 46 inches wide; has a 26 inch pretty floral border on the bottom and a 7 inch border to match on top; a new and handsome fringe 10 inches wide on top, and a 2 inch tassel fringe on the bottom. A curtain like this is an ornament to any home, and it is only by our method of buying and selling that such values are obtainable. Colors, red, tan, peacock, steel, olive and rose.
Per pair....$4.69

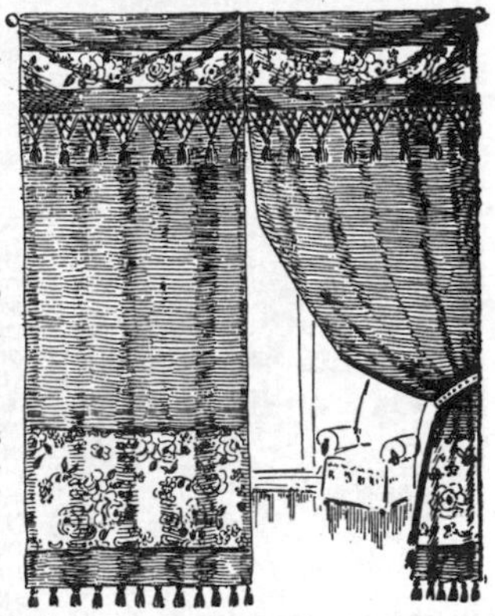

**No. 23278 A Very Fine Quality Chenille Curtain,** 3 yards long and 46 inches wide, has a handsome 27 inch floral border of variegated colors on bottom and a 5 inch border to match on top; has a very new 9 inch fringe on top and a 2 inch tassel fringe on the bottom. This very rich curtain comes in red, slate, bronze, nile and rose.
Per pair....$5.25

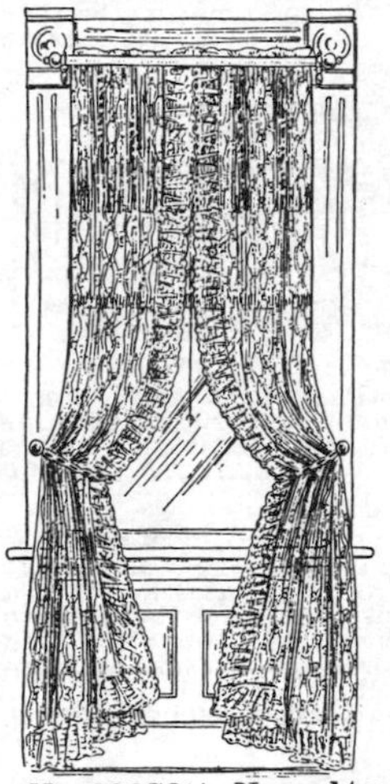

## Novelty Lace Curtains.

**No. 23279 Novelty Fancy Fish Net Lace Curtain,** 40 inches wide, 3½ yards long. This curtain has a fancy ruffle lace border and comes in ecru or cream only, loop pattern. This curtain is very desirable for bed rooms, or dining rooms. This is an entirely new curtain and is very popular just now.
Our special price, per pair....$1.68

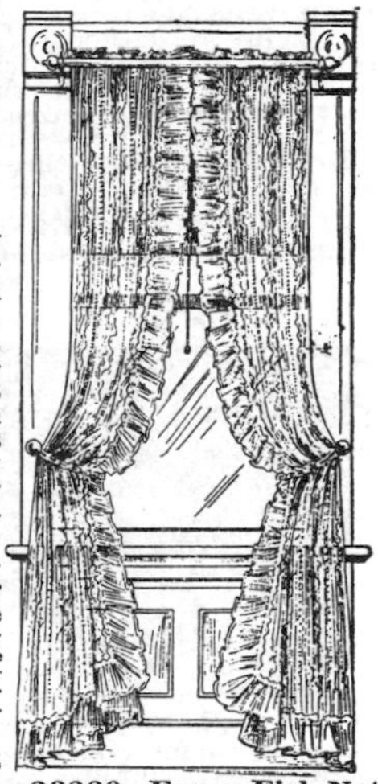

**No. 23279½ Novelty Fancy Lace Striped Figured Mull Curtain,** 41 inches wide, 3½ yards long, has a mull ruffle border, made of a fancy mull fabric, with a lace stripe, a very useful and stylish curtain and one that is being used very largely for bed rooms and dining rooms and parlors, a curtain that has become very popular of late and in appearance is much nicer than the old style lace curtain. Don't pay fancy prices for these goods of the retailer, but take advantage of our extremely low price.
Per pair....$1.95

**No. 23280 Fancy Fish Net for shades, curtains or shams spreads, etc.** Colors cream or white, the new designs are here and the prices were never as low. Width 43 inches.
Per yard....15c

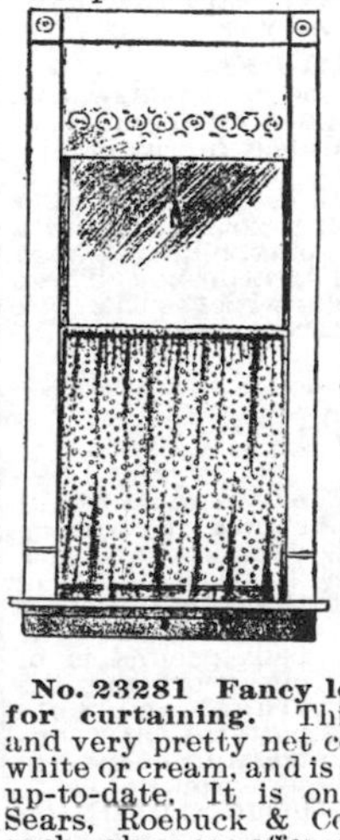

Fancy Fish Net for Sash, Curtains, Shams, Spreads, Etc., Etc.

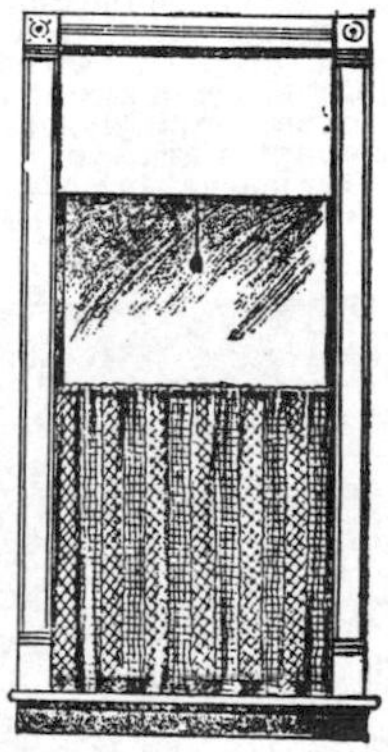

**No. 23281 Fancy loop net for curtaining.** This new and very pretty net comes in white or cream, and is strictly up-to-date. It is only from Sears, Roebuck & Co., that such values are offered at the price. Per yard....25c

**No. 23282** A Lace Lambrequin, made of Nottingham lace, size, 56x38 inches. This handsome lambrequin can be used over chenille curtains or in connection with lace curtains. These lambrequins, although not new, are staple, and are largely used by those lovers of the practical, sensible things we used in the home long ago,
Our very special price, each......................50c

## Lace Bed Sets.

Beautiful to look at, wear well, wash nicely and cost little when bought of Sears, Roebuck & Co.

**No. 23283** Three Piece Lace Bed Set consisting of spread large enough for full size bed and two pillow shams. Nottingham lace in handsome floral designs, perfectly matched. Irish point finish, colors, cream or white. This is a handsome set and would be considered a bargain if bought in the regular way for $2.50. Our method of selling goods enables you to buy this handsome set at bargain Per set..................$1.50

**No. 23284** Three Piece Lace Bed Set, white only, handsome floral patterns; consists of a spread and two shams; spread is large enough for a full size bed. Nottingham lace with Irish point effect. Set is perfectly matched. A set like this at the price is a treasure and a bargain plum long talked of. One set sold in a neighborhood sells dozens and dozens for us. Per set....................$2.25

## Draperies.

**No. 23285** Novelties in draperies, even the price is a novelty, it's so low. You have every advantage in buying these goods from our catalogue that a resident of a large city has. You have the styles to select from and you get the rock bottom prices. In fact the large retail concerns ask a great deal more for these goods than we sell them at.
Draperies for chair throws, sofa cushions, curtains, art work and coverings for furniture.

## Silkoline.

A handsome Silkoline 36 inches wide, at 10c per yard.

**No. 23286** Handsome Silkoline, has a fine silk-like finish, in every day use for draperies of all kinds. Used for sofa cushions, chair drapes, etc. Beautiful floral designs in colors and tints. The ground comes in the following colors; Cream, light blue, pink, yellow and terra cotta, and the floral design is of a contrasting color. The effect of these combinations is very pretty and the goods themselves appear to be worth very much more money. Our Special price per yard.........10c
Full pieces of 50 yards 9½c per yard.

## Gobelin Silkoline.

The New Art Drapery, and the price is new, too, in lowness. 36 inches wide at 12½c per yard. A stylish and exceedingly handsome fabric, rich in appearance and low in price when bought of S. R. & Co. In finish this cloth is made to appear like a very handsome silk. The cloth comes in a plain ground, in cream, yellow, pink, blue and terra cotta, decorated with beautiful floral designs. These designs are in a contrasting color with the the back ground, producing an effect rarely seen except in the higher grade of materials.
Our special price, per yard........ ...12½c.

## Tinsel Drapery.

29 inches wide, 10 cents per yard.

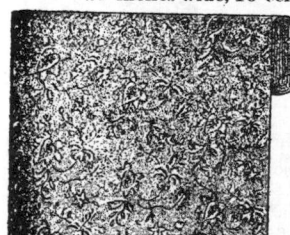

**No. 23288** One of the most handsome drapery cloths yet produced, a beautiful thing for draperies of all kinds. The back ground is of one color and the tinsel and floral patterns of contrasting colors are so arranged as to make this cloth closely resemble the Japanese silk crepe. Colors: rose,

green, pink, yellow and blue. It is just like burning money to buy cloth like this of a retail merchant; why pay the same amount for 10 yards, as S. R. & Co. sell 20 yards for. It is not using one's self right. Per yard, 10c; full pieces, 50 yards, 9½c.
**No. 23289** Tinsel Drapery. It is like finding money to buy goods like these at the prices we quote. A Tinsel Drapery 31 inches wide, 12½c per yard. This drapery comes in Parisian and Dresden patterns, back ground of rose, pale blue and pink colors; the tinsel and contrasting colors are in the form of scroll and floral designs and are interwoven in such a manner as to give the cloth a very rich and handsome effect. The cloth is very fine for sofa cushion covers. Per yard.........12½c

## Satin Damask Drapery.

THE MOST ECONOMICAL DRAPERY MADE, DOUBLY SO WHEN BOUGHT OF SEARS, ROEBUCK & CO. ORDER SOME AND TRY MAKING A FANCY TABLE COVER, THE CLOTH AND A FEW YARDS OF FRINGE WILL DO IT. THOUGHTFUL, SENSIBLE AND ECONOMICALLY INCLINED PEOPLE OFTEN PROFIT BY THESE SUGGESTIONS.

**No. 23290** Satin Damask Drapery. This cloth is 50 in. wide and is just the thing for furniture covers, and making fancy table covers; it also makes up into rich curtains. Colors, cardinal, terra-cotta and olive back grounds, interwoven with scroll and floral designs of contrasting colors producing a very rich and up-to-'97 appearance. This damask is liked and admired by all, and never do we hear of a complaint.
Our very special price, per yard. ............39c
**No. 23291** Satin Damask Drapery, similar to the above, but of a finer quality, 50 inches wide. Comes in cardinal, terra-cotta, olive and brown back ground, with scroll and floral designs interwoven. The interwoven designs are of a contrastive color and produce a swell effect, with that up-to-date newness which every person likes. Per yard, 48c

## Denim for Fancy Work.

**No. 23292** 36 inches wide; 15c per yard. A wearing fabric; a popular fabric, a well known fabric, at Sears, Roebuck & Co.'s well known low prices. This denim is used for drapery and fancy work purposes; colors terra cotta, blue olive and Nile green back ground; has an empire or Louis XV pattern woven into it, of a contrasting color. Per yard.......15c

**No. 23293** 36 in. Denim, 25c per yard. The same denim as described above only of a much superior quality. Used for drapery and all kinds of fancy work. Colors, terra cotta, blue, olive and Nile green. Has a scroll and floral design of contrasting colors, which adds much beauty to the cloth. Per yard..... 25c

## Chenille Table or Stand Covers.

**No. 23294** A Very Pretty Chenille Stand Cover, size, about 34x34 inches, including fringe, has a pretty fancy floral border. Each..............35c
**No. 23295** A Handsotte Chenille Stand Cover, size, about 38x38 inches, including fringe, has a very pretty fancy floral border. Each......45c

**No. 23294.**

**No. 23296** A Very Nice Chenille Table Cover, size, 54x54 inches, including fringe, has a very pretty center in a fancy design, woven in colors. Each, 78c
**No. 23297** A Beautiful Chenille Table Cover, size, 54x 54 inches, including fringe, fancy design in colors all over cover. This very handsome cover at Each........$1.25

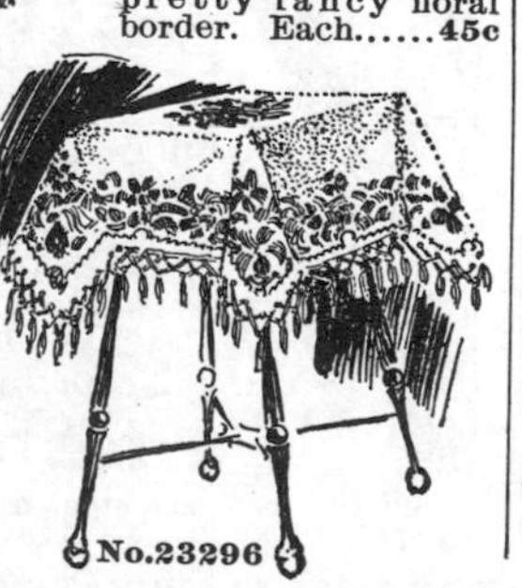

**No. 23296**

**No. 23299** A Handsome Tapestry Table Cover, 54 x 54 inches, including fringe, beautiful floral designs, come in light and dark blue, light and dark green, red, rose, brown, tan and peacock. Each........98c
NOTE.—Nothing adds more to the beauty of a room than a nice stand or table, nicely covered with a handsome cover. We handle only reliable fancy table covers, and sell them at prices that bring them within the reach of all.
**No. 23300** A very handsome Tapestry Table Cover. Comes in pretty fancy designs, interwoven with fine tinsel thread, producing a very fine effect; size, 54x54 inches, including fringe. Colors black, green, blue, red, olive and peacock.
Each.................$1.45

## Curtain Loops, Chains and Hooks.

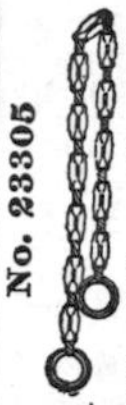

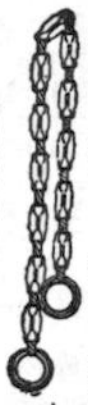

**No. 23301** A White Cotton Curtain Loop, (cord and tassels. Per pair. ........8c
**No. 23303** Curtain Loops, cord and tassels, to be used with tapestry curtains. Per pair................15c
**No. 23304** Heavy Chenille Curtain Loops, cord and tassels. Per pair....19c
**No. 23305** Brass Curtain Chains, a good strong chain usually sold for very much more money. Per pair................7c
**No. 23306** Brass Curtain Chains, better quality than the above. Per pair................8c
**No. 23308** Spiral Curtain Chains, pretty and strong and durable. Per pair................14c
**No. 23309** Brass Tassel Hooks, polished, each. 5c

**No. 23301**

## Rug Fringes.

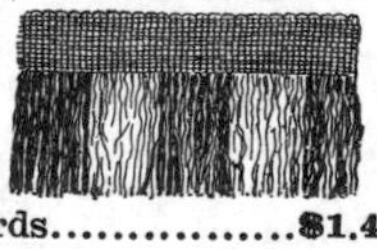

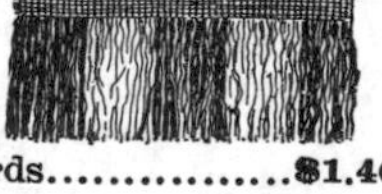

**No. 23310** Wool Rug Fringe, with gimp heading 3 inches deep; tan, olive or red combinations.
Per yard.... ..........5½c
12 yards.................64c
**No. 23312** Knotted Rug Fringe, 4¼ yards wide, tan, olive or red.
Per yard, 12c; per dozen yards..............$1.40

## Fringes.

For window shades, curtains, stand covers and all kinds of fancy work. Always mention predominating color wanted, or if practical send a sample.

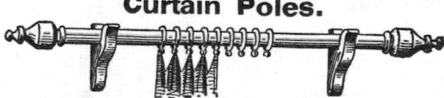

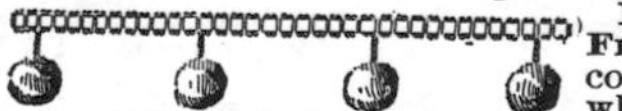

**No. 23314** Ball Fringe, cotton; comes red, olive white, cream, pink and white, and blue and white. Full width 1½ inches. Per yard, 3c; 12 yards ................35c

## Curtain Poles.

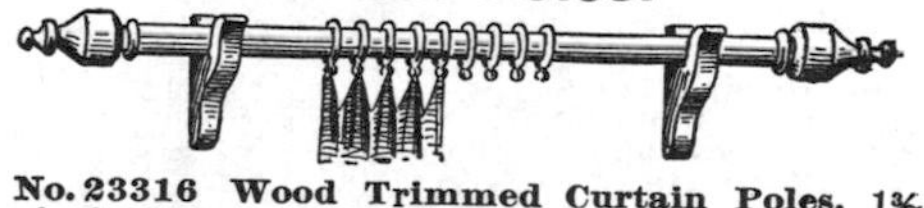

**No. 23316** Wood Trimmed Curtain Poles, 1⅜ inch furnished in California walnut, mahogany, oak and ebony. Price includes two turned wooden ends, two brackets for ends and two rings for each foot of pole. Don't fail so mention kind of finish wanted.

| Length, | 5ft. | 6ft. | 7ft. | 8ft. | 9ft. |
|---|---|---|---|---|---|
| Price, each.. | 25c | 29c | 32c | 36c | 40c |

**No. 23318** Brass Trimmed Curtain Poles, 1⅜ inch poles, finished in oak, mahogany, walnut and ebony, complete with two brass ends, two brass brackets and two brass rings to each foot of pole.

| Length, | 5ft. | 6ft. | 7ft. | 8ft. | 9ft. |
|---|---|---|---|---|---|
| Price, each.. | 19c | 23c | 26c | 29c | 32c |

## Furniture Gimp.

**No. 23320** Furniture Gimp, cotton ½ inch wide in all staple colors. Per yard.....................1c
Twelve yards.................12c
**No. 23321** Furniture Gimp, silk mixed ½ inch wide in all staple colors. Per yard.................2c
Twelve yards.................20c
**No. 23322** Furniture Gimp, extra quality silk mixed ½ inch wide in all staple colors. Pr yard.. 3c
Twelve yards.................30c
**No. 23324** Adjustable Brass Extension Brackets for 1⅜ inch wood or brass poles; these brackets are the proper thing when you wish your lace curtains to hang away from the window and especially so if there are inside blinds. Brackets adjust 4 to 7 inches. Per pair. ................16c
**No. 23326** Brackets that adjust from 7 to 12 inches. Per pair ........................21c

**SPECIAL**
**BABY CARRIAGE CATALOGUE...**
**....FREE ON APPLICATION....**

YOU WILL GAIN THE LASTING GRATITUDE OF YOUR NEIGHBOR IF YOU WILL PERSUADE HIM TO SEND FOR OUR CATALOGUE. SEE PAGE 4 FOR SPECIAL CLUB DISCOUNTS.

## Telescope Vestibule Rods.

**No. 23328 Suitable for Sash Curtains.** The rods come with brackets complete, that can be adjusted inside or outside. The rods are made of two brass tubes, one sliding closely and will fit any window from 24 to 44 inches wide. Each..............15c

**No. 23229 Brass Nickel Plated Solid Vestibule Rods,** ¼ inch diameter, cut any length. Per foot, 2½c

**No. 23330 Outside Brass Vestibule Brackets,** for ¼ inch rods. Per pair..........................10c

**No. 23331 Inside Brass Vestibule Brackets,** for ¼ inch rods. Per pair..........................6c

**No. 23332 Brass Rings for Vestibule Rods,** ⅜ inch in diameter. Per dozen..........................17c

**No. 23333 Brass Sockets for all kinds of Poles,** 1½ inch. Per pair..........................7c

**No. 23334 Brass Finish Picture Hooks,** will fit any 1 or 1½ inch moulding. Per dozen..........19c

**No. 23335 Gilt Furniture Nails or Tacks,** small, per hundred..........................7c

**No. 23336 Gilt Furniture Nails or Tacks,** large, per hundred..........................10c

**No. 23337 Picture Cord;** colors are scarlet, green or blue. Per ball of 36 yards..................25c

**No. 23338 Bright Tinned Picture Wire;** fine, 25 yards in piece. Per piece..........................5c

**No. 23339 Bright Tinned Picture Wire;** coarse. 25 yards in piece. Per piece..........................12c

## Window Shades.

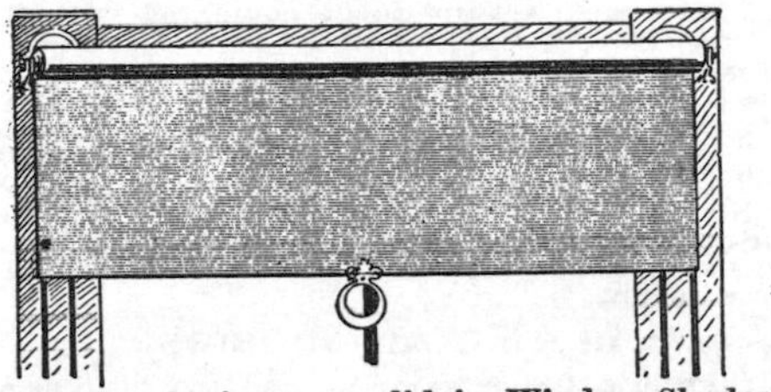

**The large business we did in Window Shades** the last year has greatly encouraged us to make an extra effort in securing novelties and enlarging the department considerably. We now control many special designs and makes at far below their market value, and can furnish any style in the window shade line in any quantities.

**All Window Shades are made** 3 feet wide and 6 feet long. Larger than this size will cost a little extra in proportion to size wanted.

**No. 23340 Felt Window Shades,** made of a good substantial paper and looks like opaque cloth; very durable and looks as well as any; length, 6 feet by 3 feet wide; colors, olive, green, pea green, stone and terra-cotta. Price, each, including good spring roller and all necessary fixtures.............**$0.16**
Per doz..........................**1.50**

**No. 23341 Ontario Window Shades,** a good durable cloth mounted on an extra quality spring roller, with all fixtures needed. Colors, olive green, stone, pea green and ecru; length, 6 feet.
Each..........................**$0.25**
Per doz..........................**2.80**

□**No. 23342 Seneca Window Shades,** a strictly lead and **oiled cloth shade;** warranted not to fade or curl in the hottest sun. No better made. Mounted on best quality spring roller with all fixtures needed. Colors, olive green, pea green, terra-cotta, olive or ecru; length 6 feet. Each**$0.30**
Per doz..........................**$3.35**

## Fringed Window Shades.

**No. 23344 Seneca Fringed Window Shades,** with best spring roller and all fixtures; handsome deep fringe to match shade; colors, olive green, pea green, ecru or light olive and terra cotta. Length, 6 feet. Each..........................**$0.32**
Per dozen..........................**3.70**

**No. 23345 Ontario Fringed Shades,** with best spring roller and all fixtures; heavy deep fringe; colors, olive green, stone, pea green, ecru and terra cotta. Length, 6 feet. Each..............**$0.27½**
Per dozen..........................**$3.15**

## Dado Shades.

**No. 23346 Felt Plain Shades,** with handsome dado at bottom, 6 feet long, with spring roller and all fixtures needed; colors same as No. 23345.
Each, **25c**; per dozen..........................**$2.80**

**No. 23347 Ontario Plain Shades,** with an elegant dado border, like cut, best spring rollers and all fixtures. Colors the same as No. 23345.
Each, **32c**; per dozen..........................**$3.65**

**No. 22348 Seneca Window Shades,** complete with fixtures; plain with a beautiful dado at bottom; colors, pea green, slate and terra cotta, olive or ecru.
Each, **35c**; per dozen..........................**$3.80**

**No. 23349 Extra Width Shades** furnished on short notice in best grade of cloth only. Write for estimate giving size and quantity wanted.

**Sample Book** of colors of any of the above goods sent free of charge upon application.

## Window Curtain Holland and Opaque Cloth by the Yard.

Weight of Holland, per yard, 4 oz; Opaque cloth, 8 oz.

**No. 23350 Window Curtain Holland,** best grade, 36 inches wide only. colors, olive, pea green, brown, slate or ecru. Per yard..........................**10c**

**No. 23351 Window Curtain, Opaque Cloth,** best grade, 38 inches wide only; colors, light, olive, greenish tint, light slate, brown or stone. Per yard..**15c**

**No. 23352 The "Hartshorn" Patent Spring Rollers,** complete with fixtures and slats, adjustable to fit any window, except unusually wide ones.
Each, **15c**; per doz..........................**$1.52**

**No. 23353 Patent Spring Rollers,** complete with fixtures and slats. Each. **10c**; per doz..........**$1.08**

## Fringes and Laces for Shades.

**Fringes and Laces are in demand** for the rich and elegant finish they give to window shades. Put on any grade and style of shade at a nominal cost.

**No. 23355 This is a very nice number of Fringe,** which adds to the beauty of any shade. Per yard, **3c**

**No. 23357 Shade Lace** to put on the bottom of shades; beautiful patterns. Per yard..........**25c**

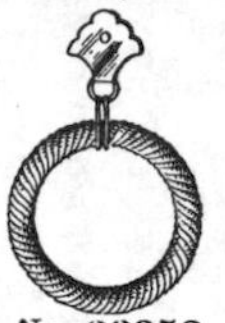

**No. 23358 Shade Pulls;** brass, copper or silver. Each, **5c**; per doz...**52c**

**No. 23359 Bar Shade Pulls;** spiral bar; silver, brass or copper.
Each.......... **5c**
Per dozen...**54c**

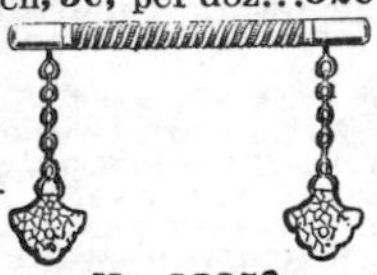

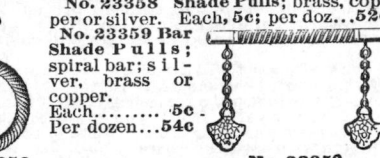

No. 23358 No. 23359

## Special Order Shade Department.

**An extra department under our personal supervision,** adopted to supply the great demand for shades in extra widths and lengths, and for those who desire less than one dozen of one color and size. We use nothing but the very best hand made, oil painted cloth in this department. The following colors are always carried in stock: dark green, olive, terra cotta, stone, pea green, Spanish olive, ecru.

**State whether width given is cloth or roller measure.** Roller measure means from end to end of tips. Say whether inside or outside brackets. Add to length of window 6 inches to cover cloth in hem and one turn around roller. Shade cloth 48 inches and wider is made of heavier fabrics and will not always be a perfect match in color.

**Unless otherwise ordered,** shades will be cut six inches longer to allow for hemming and charged accordingly. **Prices are for Single Shades.**

| Length in feet | Width in inches. | | | | | | | | | |
|---|---|---|---|---|---|---|---|---|---|---|
| | 38 | 42 | 45 | 48 | 54 | 63 | 72 | 81 | 90 | 104 |
| 4 ft. | $.45 | $.70 | $ .75 | $ .98 | $1.26 | $1.84 | $2.10 | $2.40 | $2.75 | $3.04 |
| 5 ft. | .55 | .80 | .85 | 1.12 | 1.43 | 2.04 | 2.32 | 2.70 | 3.08 | 3.50 |
| 6 ft. | .60 | .90 | .95 | 1.27 | 1.56 | 2.24 | 2.54 | 2.94 | 3.40 | 3.87 |
| 7 ft. | .70 | 1.00 | 1.05 | 1.42 | 1.76 | 2.44 | 2.77 | 3.20 | 3.72 | 4.25 |
| 8 ft. | .76 | 1.10 | 1.20 | 1.56 | 1.93 | 2.64 | 2.98 | 3.47 | 4.04 | 4.63 |
| 9 ft. | .84 | 1.20 | 1.35 | 1.71 | 2.10 | 2.84 | 3.20 | 3.74 | 4.36 | 5.00 |
| 10 ft. | .95 | 1.30 | 1.43 | 1.86 | 2.26 | 3.04 | 3.43 | 4.00 | 4.68 | 5.39 |
| 11 ft. | 1.00 | 1.40 | 1.54 | 2.00 | 2.43 | 3.24 | 3.64 | 4.27 | 5.00 | 5.76 |
| 12 ft. | 1.08 | 1.50 | 1.66 | 2.15 | 2.60 | 3.44 | 3.87 | 4.54 | 5.32 | 5.94 |

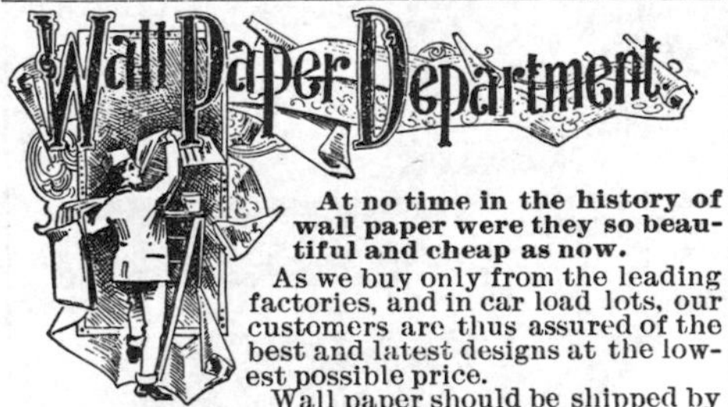


**At no time in the history of wall paper were they so beautiful and cheap as now.**

As we buy only from the leading factories, and in car load lots, our customers are thus assured of the best and latest designs at the lowest possible price.

Wall paper should be shipped by freight. Small shipments should be included with other goods, thereby effecting a saving.

We do not ship wall paper by express. C.O.D.

Wall paper is manufactured in 16 yard lengths, which are put up in one double roll.

Our prices are for double rolls of 16 yards each.

## Hints on Hanging.

New ceilings and walls should be first given a coat of glue size before hanging paper.

Dissolve one pound of ground glue in one bucket of hot water. This makes a strong glue size.

Should the ceilings and walls be calcimined or whitewashed, wash off old calcimine or whitewash and size as above.

To make paste:—Use wheat flour made into a paste with cold water, then scald with boiling water, stirring same until the proper consistency is reached. Never boil paste.

Paste the length of paper you wish to hang, fold each end toward the center, being careful to have the edges exactly even, then trim. This insures paste up to the extreme edge, makes a better job and takes half the time, as you cut two thicknesses at once.

Full piece of about 50 yards..........................11½c
Full piece of about 50 yards..........................9½c

## Samples.

Always state what price paper you want. We will send samples of wall paper on request. We desire orders to be sent in as soon as possible, on receipt of samples, as we are unable to keep in stock very long any one pattern. If possible, send a first and second choice. Should you wish to us to send you wall paper at any time, without first selecting same, please state price, what room it is for, and whether light, dark or medium shades are desired.

## Rules for Measuring a Room.

Measure the length and breadth of the room, then multiply by two; multiply the result by the height of the room in feet. To allow for doors and windows, multiply the height of each by the width; add same together and deduct from amount. Then divide by 60. The result is the number of double rolls required for side walls. This rule makes all necessary allowance for waste and matching.

EXAMPLE. Room 15 feet long, 12 feet wide, 9 feet high. One window, 6x4 feet; one door 7x4 feet; one window, 3½x4 feet:

15 plus 12 x 2 = 54 x 9 = 486
1 window 6 x 4 = 24
1 door 7 x 4 = 28 — 66
1 window 3½ x 4 = 14 — 60) 420
66
7 d'b'l rolls.

The number of rolls required for ceiling is ascertained the same way, dividing the number of square feet by 60.

EXAMPLE. Room 15 feet long, 12 feet wide.
15 x 12 = 180 60) 180
3 double rolls.

Wall paper weighs about 1¼ pounds per double roll.

Always state what room paper is for.

We do not trim wall paper because the edges being exposed, if damaged in transit, would render perfect matching impossible.

## Our Prices are for Double Rolls.

Wall paper is usually sold by the single roll.

All papers have match borders and ceilings.

We do not sell paper by the single roll nor sell half double rolls.

## Color Papers and Borders.

**No. 23368 White Back Papers Printed in Colors,** silver illumination, in scroll, floral, stripes and geometrical designs. All colors: blue, tan, light yellow, buff, green, pink, olive, terra cotta, ecru, delft blue, etc.

The above are of a good grade, easily hung, and all the latest shades and designs.

Price per double roll..........................**9c**

**White Back Ceiling Paper,** same quality to match the above. Price per double roll..........**9c**

**No. 23369 18-in. Border to match.** Per yard, **4c**
**No. 23370 9-in. Border to match.** Per yard, **2c**
**No. 23371 6-in. Border to match.** Per yard, **1c**

## Gilt Paper.

**No. 23372 These papers we recommend** for those wishing a higher grade paper than above. They are printed on heavier stock and are ornamented with bronze gilt. They are suitable for parlors, dining-rooms, halls, etc. The designs are leaf, floral, scroll, stripes colonial, empire, etc., in the latest shades of tan, light blue, nile green, yellows, reds, pink, ecru, etc. Price per double roll..........................**16c**

**No. 23374** Gilt ceiling to match. Per double roll, **16c**
**No. 23375** 18-inch border to match. Per yard, **5c**
**No. 23376** 9-inch border to match. Per yard, **2½c**

## Gold Parlor Paper.

**Our gold parlor papers** are positively the best ever manufactured for the money. They are of high grade in quality and design and make very handsome rooms. All the latest shades and blendings are represented here, the colorings being in the new blues, greens, lilacs, reds, tans and terra cottas.

We wish to draw particular attention to our blended 18-inch borders. This is the latest novelty, shading from the side wall paper to a lighter ceiling, thus making a blended contrast of perfect harmony.

**No. 23377** Price per double roll..................**24c**
**No. 23378** Ceiling to match, per double roll...**24c**
**No. 22379** 18-inch border to match per yard.. **7c**
**No. 22380** 9-inch border to match, per yard, **3½c**

## Gilt Embossed Papers.

**Our Gilt Embossed Papers** are very popular, being very rich and heavy. They come in all shades, colorings and designs, and are suitable for halls, parlors, drawing rooms, libraries and dining rooms. Price, per double roll.......................... **25c**

**No. 23383** Ceiling to match, per double roll **25c**
**No. 23384** 18-inch border to match, per yard **07c**
**No. 23385** 9 inch border to match, per yard.**3½c**

## High Grade Embossed Papers.

**No. 23387 This is the best grade paper made;** the most artistic designs, the latest colorings, newest shades and finest stock only being used in above. The most beautiful and decorative effects are obtained by the use of these papers. Only 18 inch borders are made with same.

Price, per double roll..........................**30c**

**No. 23388** Ceiling to match, per double roll...**30c**
**No. 23389** 18 inch border to match, per yard.. **8c**

## Embossed Leatherettes.

**No. 23390 These papers are very clever imitations of embossed leather.** The colorings are very rich and the paper is very durable. They are suitable for halls, dining rooms and libraries, and come in tan, blue and green shades.

Price per double roll..........................**50c**

**No. 23392** Ceiling to match, per double roll...**50c**
**No. 23393** 18 inch border to match (the only width made), per yard..........................**10c**

## Varnished Tile Paper.

**No. 23394 Varnished or Washable Wall Paper.** This paper is 22 inches wide and is the best varnished paper in the country. We only use the imported paper. Years of experience have taught us that the English varnished paper is highly preferable both in quality and design. These are finished in imitations of tiling and are used for bath rooms, kitchens, halls, etc. Can be washed. This imported paper comes 12 yards to the roll. Price, per roll.......................... ....**45c, 60c and 70c**

# CARPET AND RUG DEPARTMENT.

**IF YOU HAVE ANY DOUBT ABOUT OUR SAVING YOU MONEY ON CARPETS, SEND FOR SAMPLES AND COMPARE QUALITY AND PRICE.**

**OUR CARPET DEPARTMENT** is now recognized as one of the best in the west, and is fast growing better. Greater sales give us greater purchasing power, experience teaches us how to avoid errors, how to present the matter plainer to you and also how to fill your orders more to your liking. Nearly all manufactured goods have advanced in price within the last two months, **and Carpets are sure to follow.** We have bought a very large stock of all grades for the spring trade, and are quoting them lower than the same grades were ever sold before. **Shrewd buyers will please take note of the above.** Carpets will not be sent C. O. D.

**SAMPLES** Our experience of several years teaches us it is not necessary to send for samples before ordering to be satisfied with your carpet; your giving quality, color, size of design, what the room is used for that it is to cover, etc., being all that is necessary to get what will suit, **(we have never failed to please our customers when the above instructions were given)**, but in some cases samples seem necessary; to such we say: We will send you small samples of carpet from which you can judge quality, color, etc., free upon request. Should larger samples be wanted we will send you ¼, ½ or one yard samples as ordered, to cover the amount of money you allow for their payment, in the design, coloring or quality wanted, and refund you what you paid upon their return if the transportation charges are paid. **We must know what price carpet you want sample of, also of design and color.** Make these points clear.

**SEWING CARPETS** **It will usually require a day or two longer to fill an order when carpet is ordered made.** Our charges for sewing carpets are: Ingrain and all yard wide carpet 3 cents per yard; Brussels and all ¾ yard carpet 5 cents per yard; fitting borders, 5 cents per yard extra; sewing borders, 5 cents per yard. When you want carpets sewed, write **"Make"** on the order and allow from one to two yards (according to size of room) for waste in matching. We always cut carpets to match with as little waste as possible. All ingrain carpets are sewed by professional carpet sewers with the herringbone stitch, which makes a flat, turnable, elastic seam. Brussels and all ¾ wide carpets are sewed with a machine made for the purpose. It sews them much better than can be done by hand, and then the seams are all ironed. All ¾ yard goods, especially, should be ordered sewed here, as it is often difficult to make them by hand so they will lie smooth. **In ordering** mention the predominating color wanted, and state whether a plain and fancy pattern is preferred, or whether you want large or small figure. We will use our best judgment in making selections. **Carpets cut and sewed to order cannot be returned if sent as ordered.**

**RULES FOR MEASURING CARPETS** Ascertain the **width of room** in inches; divide that product by the width of carpet (27 or 36 inches); the answer will give the number of breadths required. Multiply the number of breadths by the **length** of room (allowing 12 to 18 inches on each breadth for possible waste in matching), the answer will give approximate number of feet required. Divide that number by 3 to find the number of yards. Measures for bordered carpets must be very exact. Give diagram of all odd shaped rooms.

## Stair Carpets.

**No. 23401 Hemp Stair Carpet,** medium or bright colors, 18 inches wide. Per yard....................11c

**No. 23401½ Hemp Stair Carpet,** medium or bright colors, 22½ inches wide. Per yard........15c

## Brass Stair Rods.

⅝ inch wide, 22 inches long, per doz.................$0.54
¾ inch wide, 24 inches long, per doz.................. .66
¾ inch wide, 26 inches long, per doz.................. .73
¾ inch wide, 30 inches long, per doz.................. .87

## Hemp Carpets.

**Hemp Carpets are too well-known to require any introduction.** We have all grades of them.

**No. 23402 Hemp Carpet, 32 inches wide,** nice mixed colors, with stripes of red, green or yellow. Per yard....................10c

**No. 23403 36 inch Hemp Carpet,** handsome woven colors. Per yard....................12c

**No. 23404 Hemp Carpet 36 inches wide,** a fine quality carpet, that comes in a nice variety of stripes and mixtures. Per yard....................17c

**NOTE—Mention what color you would like most prominent in your carpet and you will get it.**

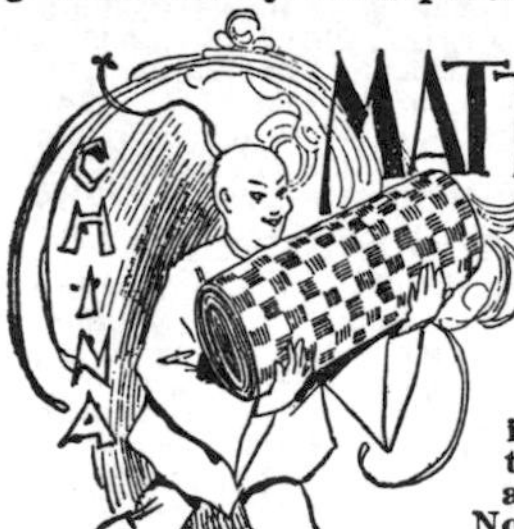

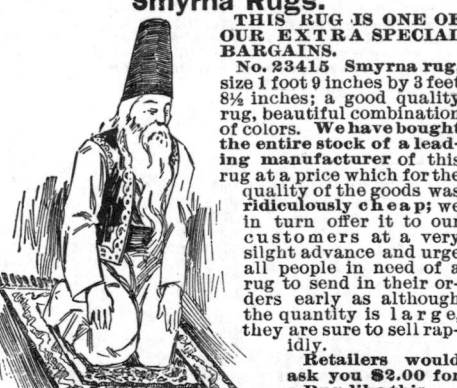

## MATTING CHINA STRAW Matting.

**Straw matting is being largely used and at the prices we sell them at, money can be saved.**

**No. 23405 Plain Straw Color and Check Straw Matting,** 36 inches wide. Per yard....................10c
Full piece 40 yards..... 9½c

**No. 23406 Fancy Check Matting,** very pretty and durable; 36 inches wide, color medium. Per yard 15c; full piece 40 yds. $5.20

**No. 23407 Fancy Check or Plain Straw Color Matting,** fine quality; one of the best grades made; 36 inches wide, medium coloring. Per yard...$0.22
Full piece 40 yards.................... 7.60

## Japanese Straw Matting.

**23408 This Matting Has a cotton Warp, Which Makes it very durable.** Fancy Japanese matting, with a cotton warp which makes it flexible and durable, medium light and dark colors. 36 inches wide. Per yard....$0.20 Full piece 40 yards $7.60

**No. 23409 Japanese Fancy Matting,** with a cotton warp running through it, 36 inches wide, comes in medium, light and dark colorings. Per yard...22c
Full piece, 40 yards.................... $8.00

## Carpet Linings.

**No. 23410 Felt Carpet Lining** or paper in rolls of 50 yards (weight about 31 lbs). Per roll........52c
We do not cut rolls.

**No. 23411 Sewed Carpet Lining,** filled with jute, 36 inches wide, keeps the floor nice and warm and protects the carpet. Per yard....................2c
Full bale of 200 yards.................... $3.50

## Carpet Binding.

**Cotton and Wool Carpet Binding,** 1 inch wide, 36 yard rolls, the colors are assorted. Per roll....11c

## Smyrna Rugs.

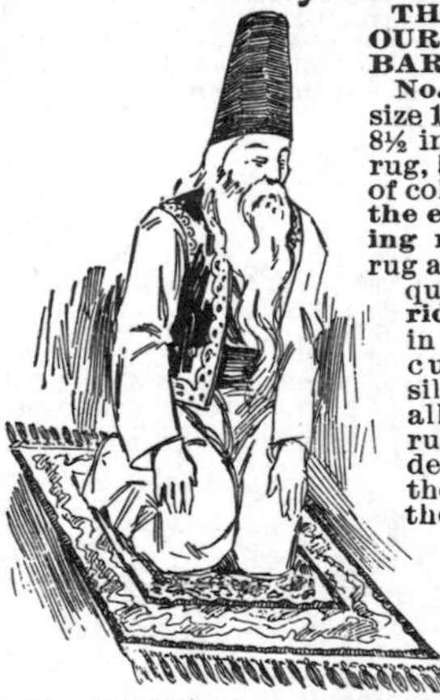

**THIS RUG IS ONE OF OUR EXTRA SPECIAL BARGAINS.**

**No. 23415 Smyrna rug,** size 1 foot 9 inches by 3 feet 8½ inches; a good quality rug, beautiful combination of colors. **We have bought the entire stock of a leading manufacturer of** this rug at a price which for the quality of the goods was **ridiculously cheap;** we in turn offer it to our customers at a very slight advance and urge all people in need of a rug to send in their orders early as although the quantity is large, they are sure to sell rapidly.

**Retailers would ask you $2.00 for a Rug like this. Our special price, each..........$1.08**

**No. 23414 A Very Pretty Smyrna Rug,** artistic combination of colors, fringed, size 16x31 inches. Each........$0.62

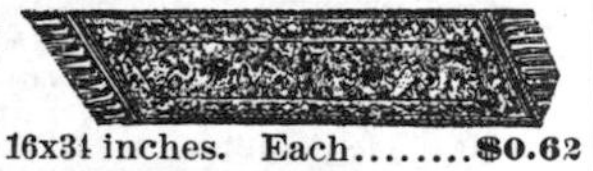

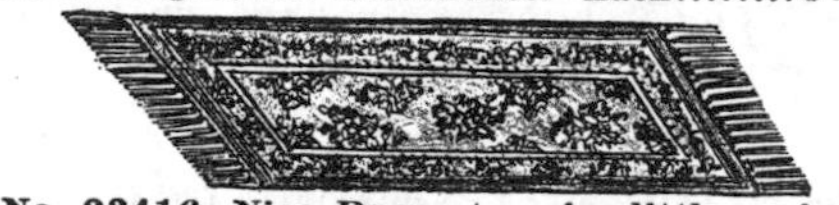

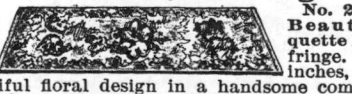

**No. 23416 Nice Rugs** at a nice little saving if bought here. Smyrna rugs of a good quality, the combination of colors are beautiful, nothing flashy or loud about them, but so gotten up that they look rich and handsome.

Sizes, 1 foot 10 inches x 3 feet 9 inches, each..$1.15
Sizes, 2 feet 2 inches x 4 feet 6 inches, each.. 1.63
Sizes, 2 feet 6 inches x 5 feet, each.......... 1.90
Sizes, 3 feet x 6 feet, each.................. 2.90
Sizes, 4 feet x 7 feet, each.................. 4.75

## Moquette Rugs.

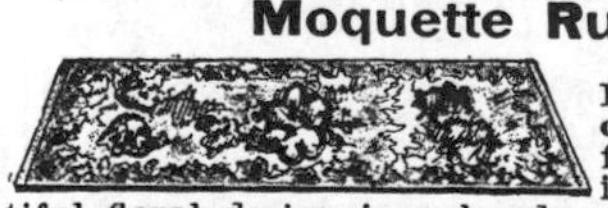

**No. 23417 A Beautiful Moquette Rug,** has no fringe. Size 18x36 inches, has a beautiful floral design in a handsome combination of colors. A rug that usually retails for double the money we ask. Each....................$0.85

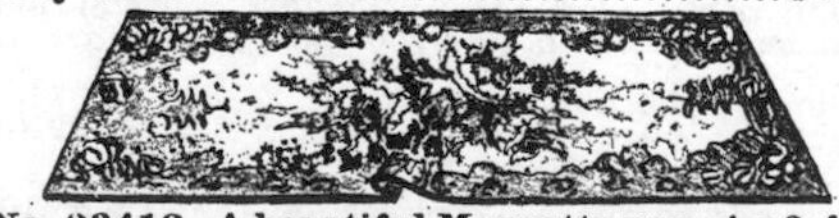

**No. 23418 A beautiful Moquette rug,** size 2 feet 3 inches by 5 feet 3 inches; has no fringe. A swell up-to-date pattern, and the combination of colors can not be surpassed. This rug has that rich appearance that is only obtained where rug making has become a fine art, **that's where our rugs are made.** Don't pay retail dealers double, if you need a rug save your money by ordering of S. R. & Co. Price, each....................$1.95

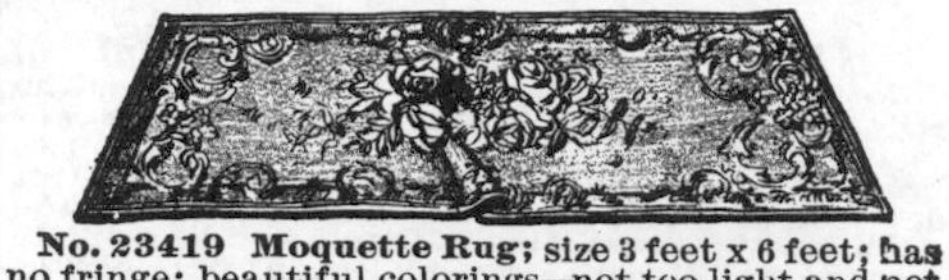

**No. 23419 Moquette Rug;** size 3 feet x 6 feet; has no fringe; beautiful colorings—not too light and not too dark, just the pretty floral design in a medium combination of colorings, that are pronounced **O. K.** A rug like this will satisfy anybody. It will surpass anything at the price ever seen or heard of. Price, each....................$3.20

## Axminsters Rugs.

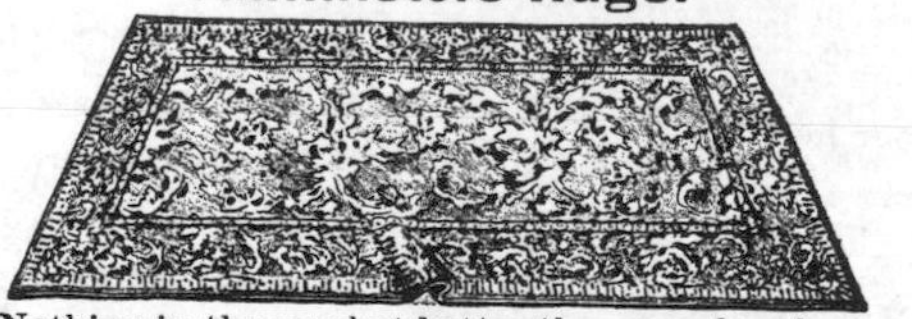

Nothing in the market better than our **Axminster Rugs,** rich in appearance and wear like iron. They come in medium colorings, fringed on both ends, floral and scroll designs. When a real fine rug is desired the **Axminster fills the bill.**

**These rugs are not to be compared with the cheap trashy goods now on the market.**

Size, 4 feet 6 ins. by 6 feet 4 ins. Each.........$7.50
" 6 " 9 " " 9 " 9 " " .........15.00
" 8 " 3 " " 10 " 6 " " .........21.00
" 9 " 3 " " 12 " 6 " " .........26.00
" 11 " 3 " " 14 " 3 " " .........40.00

**NOTE.—We guarantee our Axminster Rugs to be of a superior quality and worth twice as much as the inferior quality that is being sold at a trifle less money.**

## Ingrain Art Squares.

**Ingrain Art Squares** are woven the same as an ingrain carpet. They have a nice fringe on two edges; they also have a border all around and look just like a rug. **These art squares are all wool, perfectly fast colors, and will wear three times as long as the cheap so-called one-fourth wool filled rugs on the market.** Medium colors.

**No. 23421 All Wool Ingrain Art Squares.**

| Size.. | 7½x9 ft. | 9x9 ft. | 9x10 ft. | 9x12 ft. | 9x13½ ft. | 12x15 ft. |
|---|---|---|---|---|---|---|
| Each, | $4.50 | $5.65 | $6.75 | $7.75 | $9.00 | $13.50 |

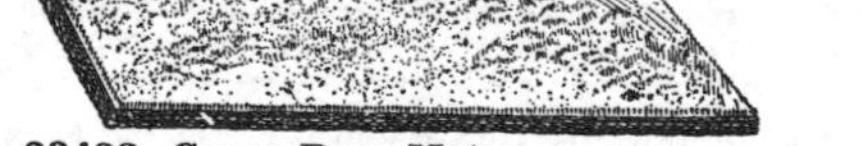

**No. 23422 Cocoa Door Mats.**

| Sizes, inches............ | 14x25 | 16x27 | 18x30 | 20x33 |
|---|---|---|---|---|
| Price, each............ | 32c | 39c | 53c | 75c |

## Floor Oil Cloth.

**Direct from the largest manufacturer of these goods.** Made of a high grade of hemp burlap, which is prepared with a body or filling of oil and mineral, then painted and printed in the different patterns. We only quote the best grades, the very cheap quality does not prove satisfactory to any one.

**Colors** are dark or bright block patterns or medium light stone colors, small, medium or large patterns as desired.

**No. 23434** Weight, 2 pounds per square yard.

| Width.............. | 1 yd. | 1½ yds. | 2 yds. |
|---|---|---|---|
| Price, per yard..... | 20c. | 30c. | 40c. |

**Floor Oil Cloth—Better Quality.**

**No. 23435** Weight, 3 pounds per square yard.

| Width.......... | 1 yd. | 1¼ yds. | 1½ yds. | 2 yds. |
|---|---|---|---|---|
| Price, per yard, | 24c. | 30c. | 36c. | 48c. |

**Floor Oil Cloth—Best Quality.**

**No. 23436** Weight, 3½ pounds per square yard.

| Width.......... | 1 yd. | 1¼ yds. | 1½ yds. | 2 yds. | 2½ yds. |
|---|---|---|---|---|---|
| Price, per yard, | 36c. | 45c. | 54c. | 72c. | 90c. |

## Table Oil Cloth.

**Best Quality, Body Pure Paint and Oil Face.**

**No. 23437 Marble Oil Cloth,** 45 inches wide. Per yard....................16c

**No. 23439 Oak Pattern,** 45 inches wide. Per yard....................15c

**No. 23441 Reversible Table Oil Cloth,** something new, marble face and turkey red damask patterns printed on the back, 45 inches wide. Per yard....................30c

**No. 23443 Shelf Oil Cloth,** white or fancy wood patterns, 12 inches wide, scalloped edge, printed with pretty lace effects. Per piece of 12 yards...60c

## Linoleum.

**Linoleum** is very like oil cloth except that there is ground cork in its composition, which makes it much heavier, more durable; also, very much softer to walk on.

**No. 23445 Linoleum,** 2 yards wide. Per square yard....................88c

**No. 23446 Linoleum,** 2 yards wide; a better quality. Per square yard....................$1.25

**No. 23447 Linoleum,** 2 yards wide; the best quality. Per square yard....................$1.68

## Hassocks or Foot Rests.

**No. 23448 Hassocks Round** are made from short lengths of carpets, which enables us to sell them away down: 8½ inches in diameter, 3½ inches high; on cloth bottom. Each....................25c

**No. 23449 Hassocks Square.** 10½x10½ inches; 4 inches high; oil-cloth bottom. Each....................50c

# MILLINERY DEPARTMENT

**WE TAKE PLEASURE** IN DIRECTING THE ATTENTION OF OUR CUSTOMERS TO THIS VERY COMPLETE DEPARTMENT, including as it does a line of trimmed and untrimmed hats patterned after the latest novelties imported from Europe. Our buyers have been unusually fortunate in securing for the coming season a selection of millinery that has no equal in any ordinary retail store in the country. By importing in very large quantities, securing our goods from the leading manufacturers at home and abroad and selling on our one small profit plan direct to the consumer, we are able to in most cases sell to you a better class of goods than you can find in local retail stores, at about half the ordinary retail price. The illustrations in no instance do the goods justice, and we can only urge our customers to take advantage of our liberal terms and inspect any of the goods which they desire. We have every reason to believe that they will be delighted with the purchase and will be so well pleased with the goods that they will take pleasure in telling their friends where they have secured them and the unusually low price paid.

**OUR LIBERAL TERMS.** ON RECEIPT OF $1.00 WITH ORDER we will send any trimmed or untrimmed hat C. O. D. subject to examination. You can examine it at the express office, and if found exactly as represented, pay the express agent the balance with express charges and the goods are yours; otherwise return them at our expense and we will cheerfully refund your money. Three per cent discount allowed if cash in full accompanies your order. This discount will in many cases be sufficient to partially pay the express. It is well to consider the extra saving that may be affected by anticipating your wants, making up a freight order, and including millinery desired with other goods, and have them all shipped together by freight.

### The Louette.

No. 23471 The cut shows one of the loveliest creations of the season. A very pretty fancy straw, trimmed full around front and on sides with gathered lace, wired wings of lace and two pretty bunches of wild flowers on right and left sides, ribbon finishing lace and flowers turned up in back and finished with two large rosettes of satin ribbon. This is a hat that is rarely seen in a retail store at less than $3.50, and is only obtainable at this price from Sears, Roebuck & Co. Black, brown and navy, each...........................$1.99

### A Nobby Hat.

No. 23472 A Lace Straw Hat, new and stylish, with a pleating of silk net around crown, coils of ribbon and net around edge; trimmed with two loops of good quality satin ribbon, large bunch of violets, turned up in back, finished with bunch of violets and coil of ribbon. Violets will be very stylish this coming season and this hat will be right in the style; colors black, brown and navy.
Each.......$2.49

No. 23460 A new and very swell "Made Hat." Straw crown, wire rim covered with pleated chiffon, trimmed with ribbon loops and a beautiful steel buckle, has two tips and a bunch of "American Beauties," turned up slightly in back, finish with foliage. The cut shows one of the most stylish hats shown this year, very handsome and well worth double as much as we sell it for. Comes in black, tan and navy blue.
Each......$6.95

### $1.95 Buys a $3.25 Hat.

### The Evette.

23465 A Regular $3.25 Trimmed Hat for $1.95. Economical Lovers of Stylish Hats Save just $1.30 when they buy this hat.
This hat is made of a fancy rough straw and is trimmed with a ruffle of ribbon and lace around crown and band of jet, loop of lace and plume on side, finished with large rosette of lace, turned up in back and finished with rosette of ribbon. People wanting a fine hat cheap, should order this hat; it is a bargain rarely seen. Each...$1.95

No. 23474 The Susanne, a swell stylish trimmed, a triumph of millinery art. A fine Milan straw hat, lace around rim, trimmed on right side, with standing plume, finished with roses and lace, on left side with very full and pretty wing of lace, bunch of flowers, large rosette of ribbon and finished with two pretty stick pins, turned up in back and finished with rosette of ribbon and lace. A very pretty hat at a price within the reach of all. Black only.
Each.........$2.49

### The Florence.

No. 23461 A $2.50 Trimmed Hat for $1.25. Milliners say these hats ought to sell for $2.50; we say $1.25 buys them. A beautiful rough straw turban, with a hair braid crown, with fold ribbon and velvet around crown; trimmed with 3 quills and fancy rosettes of ribbon and knots of velvet; very pretty twist of ribbon on right side. This is a swell hat at a very low price. Take advantage of this great bargain while you can. Colors, black, brown and navy.
Price, each........$1.25

### A $3.50 Trimmed Hat for $2.20.

No. 23467 A hat that makes friends for our Millinery Department. Save $1.30 if you value money. A swell made hat, straw crown, wire rim, covered with lace finished with straw braid, has a beautiful ruffle of lace around crown, band of ribbon and fancy buckle in front, trimmed on right side with a very pretty plume and on left with loops of satin ribbon and bunch of violets, turned up in back and finished with large bunch of violets. **Colors cream and black.**
Our very special price. Each...............$2.20

### The Swell Evangeline Hat.

$1.50 Easily Saved by Buying This Hat.

No. 23474½ A hat very suitable for young ladies, Milan straw, fancy shape, trimmed in the latest style, with ruffles of ribbon running from left to right, very large bunch of flowers and laces on right side, trimmed on left side with a double loop and 5 points of heavy satin ribbon, turned up side back and finished with two rosettes. This hat comes in black only,
Each.....$2.75

23463 The Illustration Shows a "Bon Ton" Hat that will be seen much on the fashionable boulevards of our chiefs cities this summer. Hair braids, Milan edge straw shape, trimmed with a pretty silk net in beautiful contrasting colors, one handsome plume, two bunches of roses also two pretty stick pins, turned up in back and finished with very full rosettes of silk net. Everybody that sees this hat pronounces it the "sweetest ever seen;" color black, tan and navy. Each........$3.50

### Our $1.99 Leader.

No. 23469 A style made Hat, one of the lovely productions of '97. Wire frames entirely covered with handsome lace, finished with a jet edge and a very pretty jet crown, trimmed on right side with loops of lace and on left side with a handsome bunch of flowers and loops of wired lace band underneath of pleated ribbon, finished with two fancy buckles. Colors black and tan. Each, $1.99

WHEN YOU BUY OF US YOU ARE SURE OF THE LATEST STYLES, SUCH AS PREVAIL IN LARGE CITIES. THE LOCAL MILLINER DOES THE BEST SHE CAN, BUT THE PRICES ARE DOUBLE THOSE WE NAME.

## A Hat Like This for $2.99.

### LACE AND MILAN BRAID MIXED.

**No. 23475** Is trimmed with latest chiffon ribbon, with satin edge, pleated and coiled around crown and rim, trimmed with two loops of satin ribbon and bunch of roses and buds, finished with large rosette and foliage, caught up twice in back with rosettes of satin ribbon. A hat that is stylish, fine and becoming, and is obtained at this ridiculous low price from Sears, Roebuck & Co., only, Black only. Each.........$2.99

## The Latest Star Shaped Hats.

**No. 23475½** "Knowing people" pay less money and have nicer hats than others by sending to S., R. & Co. The new star shaped hat, hair braid straw, fancy edged, has a ruffle underneath on edge, has a ruffle silk net and band of ribbon around crown, trimmed with two loops of ribbon and two ends of ribbon, finished on rim with large rosette of silk net and foliage running around to right side with two ribbon ends, turned up slightly in back and finished with foliage and silk net. Colors: black, brown, navy and ecru. This hat is only obtainable from dealers in large cities at a very high figure. Each.................................$3.25

## ...A VERY... STYLISH HAT.

**No. 24476** Of our own creation at our own peculiar style of price—low. A made hat, wire frame covered with lace, straw crown and straw edge; trimmed with ruffle around crown; loops of ribbon in front and two sides; two pretty bunches roses; steel ornament; has a band underneath, with chiffon ribbon, finished with buds. Black only. Price, each.....$2.95

**No. 23477** Fancy Rough Straw; open straw crown; trimmed on right side, with plume finished with a large rosette of dotted net, trimmed on left side with 3 loops of net and fancy straw braid; rosette of straw braid and dotted net; large bunch of flowers, turned up in back; finished with rosette of dotted net and large bunch of flowers. This is a hat we recommend as being stylish and very pretty. Colors, black and brown. Price, each. $3.50

## A Made Bonnet Suitable For Elderly Ladies.

### THIS BONNET IS OF EXTRAORDINARY VALUE

**And a Big Bargain at ....the Price....**

**No. 23478** This Bonnet is Made of Fancy Rough Straw, has a facing gathered chiffon, two rosettes of chiffon ribbon, foliage on left side and trimmed in back with three loops of satin ribbon, ties of satin ribbon. Each.........$2.95

### LADIES' MOURNING BONNET.

**No. 23479** We show in this illustration a very handsome Bonnet and Mourning Veil. It is made exactly like the cut, of extra quality material. We offer it as an especial bargain and its actual value is at least 50 per cent. above our prices if bought in retail stores. Our special price.......$2.98

**NOTE.—**When ordering trimmed hats kindly mention color that is wanted.

## Untrimmed Hats.

Our Line of Untrimmed Hats was never more complete at the beginning of a season than it is now. We have everything that is new and stylish, and the prices are lower than ever. It is well to remember that many a dollar can be saved by buying your hats of Sears, Roebuck & Co.

**No. 23481 Children's Straw Sailor Hats,** ribbon around band and ribbon streamers in the back. Colors, navy, brown, cardinal and black. This hat is usually sold by retail merchants at from 30c. to 35c. Our special price, each................... ..........19c

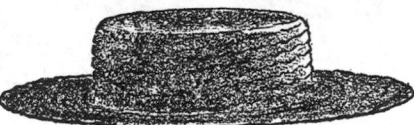

**No. 23483 Charlotte,** a new straw shape like cut, but made of a rough straw; this hat will be very fashionable this spring. Colors, black, white and tan. Each.................................................25c

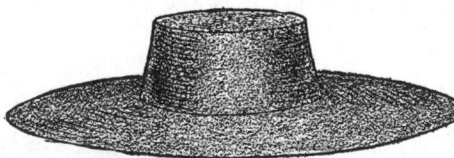

**No. 23484 Ladies' Black or White "Leghorn Flats" Straw Hats.** Like illustration. Each...25c
**No. 23486 The Murray Hill Ladies' Black or White Leghorn Flat Straw Hats.** A good quality of this ever staple and popular shape. Each.....39c
**No. 23488 A Very Stylish Leghorn Flat Straw Hat.** Reliable quality. Colors, black or white. Each.................................................50c
**No. 23490 Misses' "Leghorn Flats" Straw Hats.** Each......................................50c

**No. 23492 The Climax,** Lace Straw Turban, comes in black only; a new and very stylish shape for the spring season. Each... ...........45c

**No. 23494 A new and very fashionable Ladies' open straw dress hat** (The Olympia), with a fancy chip edge. Comes in black only. Each........ 50c

**No. 23496 Lace and Hair Braid Mixed,** a shape that is bound to be a success in '97. This is a new stylish straw hat. (See cut.) Each..............50c

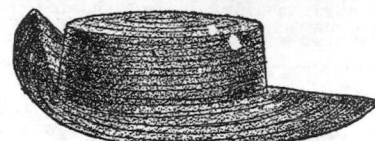

**No. 23498 This cut shows the Benwood,** a swell, new spring hat. Imitation hair and braid mixed. comes only in black. Each...............50c

**No. 23499 The Irma.** A black, hair braid, straw edge turban, like illustration. This number is exceptionally good value. Each.......................75c

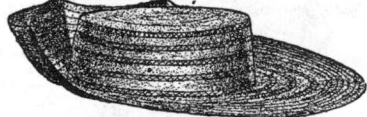

**No. 23500** Ladies' Neopolitan Dress Hat, with a Milan edge. This is a fine, new style of a fancy straw shape. Black only. Price, each...........75c

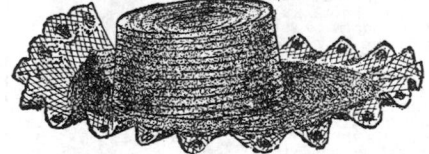

**No. 23501 Ladies' Neopolitan Hat.** Fancy lace edge. A straw hat that is bound to be very popular this season. Comes in black only. Price, each..98c

### FINE CROCHET LACE STRAW ..BONNET..

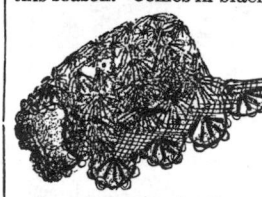

**No. 23502** A Fine Crochet Lace Straw Bonnet, comes in black only. This is a bonnet of very nice quality and one that will give the wearer satisfaction. Each .........................$1.45

**No. 23504 Old Ladies' Bonnets,** shape like cut; in black only; good quality straw. Each............50c Better qualities at 75c, $1.00, $1.25 and $1.75.

23504

**No. 23505 The Boston.** A very fine quality and extremely stylish ladies' tape sailor straw hat. Colors, black, brown, navy, cream and white. Trimmed with ribbon band around crown. Each.......$1.95

**No. 23509** A Child's Fancy Shape Untrimmed Straw Hat. New spring style, made of good material, staple colors. Each..........................39c

**No. 23511** Child's Straw Tam O'Shanter. Satin ribbon and quill trimming, plain staple colors or mixed colors. Each..................................59c

## Ostrich Tips.

**No. 23512** A very fashionable style of Hat Trimming is the very handsome 9-nine Demi-Plume, similar to the illustration. It is made of very fine quality of ostrich feather and makes a very elaborate trimming for any hat. Such plumes as we carry in our stock are seldom sold in retail stores, as they do not carry them from the fact that the prices which they are accustomed to receive are so large that they would have no trade in these articles. In the select retail stores of large cities these plumes are sold at twice our regular price. Our special price, each......39c
Three for.......$1.00
**No. 23513** This is a very choice 10-inch Demi-Plume, made of very fine curly stock and warranted to keep its curl for a long time. This is an especially choice style of hat trimming, and the demand for these goods will be very large during the coming season. Our special price, each.....59c
Two for...................................$1.00
**No. 23514** A Very Beautiful Demi-Plume, 12 inches in height, made of the choicest quality of ostrich feather stock. This is a quality that can be very easily cleaned and can readily be brought back to original shape after being worn for several years. Such a purchase as this will last quite a number of years, and it is a very inexpensive style of hat trimmings which is extremely popular.
Our special price, each ...........................95c
**No. 23515** A Very Choice Bunch of Princess Plumes that can only be offered at our importer's price by securing them in very large quantities and furnishing to our customers at a very narrow margin of profit. These Princess Plumes are a very excellent quality of ostrich feather, and consists of three beautiful tips. This is a class of goods on which retailers make a very large profit.
Our special price, each............................$1.25
**No. 23517** We can save you a very large proportion on millinery goods. The tips which we show in above illustration are no exception in the general rule of fashionable goods at low prices. They are made of very fine quality of stock, and cannot be duplicated for less than 75c.
Our price per bunch ............................39c
Three bunches for ................................$1.00
**No. 23519** The Very Beautiful Princess Tips make a very handsome style of hat trimming, and are composed of extra choice stock. These trimmings, as stated above, are decidedly in style for the coming season, and we offer them at about half the ordinary retail price. Our price, per bunch...$0.59
Two bunches for ..................... 1.00
**No. 23520** A Very Handsome Bunch of Three Princess Tips, and offered as an extremely rare bargain. Made of very fine curly stock. Can be readily cleaned and the original shape renewed after being worn a long time. Our price, per bunch..95c
**No. 23521** One of the Finest Bunches of Princess Tips that can only be offered at double our price. Made of a very choice quality of ostrich feathers, and consists of three beautiful tips. Bought by us in large quantities, and sold on very narrow margin, hence our ability to offer at the exceedingly low price named below. Our price, per bunch.....$1.25

**IF YOU FEAR IT ISN'T SAFE**

## Flowers.

Our flower department was never more complete than it is now. Never did we show so many new and stylish things at so small a price. We have any and everything in flowers, whether illustrated here or not. We ask our friends and customers to send us a description or a cut of any flower they want and we will be sure to please them.
**No. 23522** Violet Bouquet. Each bunch contains 20 violets.
Per bunch.........................4c

32522

**No. 23524** Silk and Velvet Roses. Three roses and three buds in each bunch; rubber covered stems. Colors, jack. yellow, light blue, white, cardinal, geranium, moose, heliotrope, Nile green, pink and lilac. These roses are sold in bunches only.
Per bunch............ .....12½c

23524

**No. 23526** A Large Velvet Rose, with a muslin center, two large roses in a bunch and two buds. Sold in bunches only. All colors.
Per bunch..12½c

23526

**No. 23528** American Beauty Rose, with foliage. A very pretty and popular flower, (see illustration). Pink and Jack shades. Each....18c

23528

**No. 23530** Violets in bunches, about 25 flowers to each bunch.
Each bunch..........10c
Three bunches for ..25c

23530

## Rose Foliage.

**No. 23532** Rose Foliage, has four pretty buds and leaves, a very handsome spray. Each.................38c

## VERY....
## ...PRETTY...
## ....ROSES.
## WITH FOLIAGE.

**No. 23534** Four roses in each bunch, with leaves.
Each spray.....29c
Three sprays.....75c

23534

## VERY FINE
## SILK...
## ...VELVET...
## ...VIOLET.
## WITH LEAVES.

**No. 23536** One of the finest flowers made. Per dozen..40c

23536

**No. 23538** A Handsome Satin Violet, nicely made and very popular. Per doz .........10c

23538

**No. 23540** Silk and Velvet Variegated Roses, 6 roses in each bunch, rubber stems. Each bunch..........45c
Silk and Satin Black Roses, for mourning, 6 roses in a bunch.
Per bunch..........45c

23540

## Mourning Sprays.

The Prices are Right.

The Styles Correct.

**No. 23544** Mourning Spray, black satin flower, with jet center.
Each spray .................29c
Three spray for ...........80c

23544

**No. 23546** Blossom Wreath, very full and well made; used for trimming children's hats. Each..............15c

**No. 23548** A Mourning Glory Wreath; very pretty and nicely made; just the thing for trimming children's hats. Each.... ...............29c

**No. 23550** Bridal Wreath, with brooch and bouquet, made of wax and orange blossoms. Each...............................89c
**No. 23551** A Very Fine Bridal Wreath, including brooch and bouquet; rubber stemming; made of wax and orange blossoms. Each...............$1.25

# CHILDRENS' AND MISSES' x x x x x x x READY MADE DRESSES.

**NO NEED TO BOTHER ABOUT MAKING YOUR CHILDREN'S DRESSES.** We offer them to you all ready made in the very latest styles at prices considerably cheaper than you could possibly make them.

**EVERY GARMENT IS MADE UP IN STRICTLY FIRST CLASS MANNER,** and guaranteed to be exactly as represented.

**A PLEASANT SURPRISE AWAITS THE PURCHASER** of one of these garments. They are all so handsome and dependable; so thoroughly well made and so strictly up-to-date in style that you cannot help but be pleased with them.

**IT IS A DOWNRIGHT PLEASURE** for us to quote garments of this sort. They are so full of real genuine goodness and we offer them at such remarkably low prices that they cannot help but win the highest praise from every purchaser.

**ORDER BY CATALOGUE NUMBER AND ALWAYS STATE SIZE DESIRED.**

**No. 22001 Children's Ready Made Fancy Mixed Cotton Cheviot Dresses.** Large epaulet collar, trimmed with neat rick-rack braid. We have these dresses in a large assortment of colors, light and medium, in three sizes only, 22, 24 and 26 inch, for children from 1½ years to three years of age. These garments are all extra well made, with newest baby dress sleeves, wide skirts and deep hems, and will give the greatest satisfaction. Our special price, each...37c

**No. 22002 Children's Extra Quality Fine Chambray Dress.** Comes in neat pink and blue mixtures. Full gathers from yoke, and fancy epaulet collar, trimmed with fancy novelty braid; fancy insertion trimming down center of yoke. Newest style puff-top baby dress sleeves; well made with full skirt, and deep hem; will wash and wear beautifully, and at our price is an exceptional bargain. Comes in three sizes only, 22, 24 and 26 inch, for children from 1½ to 3 years of age. Our special price, each...............50c

**No. 22202**

**No. 22003 Children's Extra Fine Fancy Figured Woven Madras Cloth Dresses.** Made in medium and light colors, pinks and blues, etc. Full gathers from square yoke, plaited standing collar, with fancy epaulets, edged all around with neat, small pattern white embroidery. Neatly made dresses, finely finished, full skirt with deep hem, and latest style puffed top baby-dress sleeves. Will wash and wear beautifully, and are guaranteed to give good satisfaction in every way. Come in three sizes only, from 1½ to 3 years. Special price, each ... ..58c

**No. 22004 This is an entirely new design in Children's Dresses,** made from fast color fancy figured percale, in a handsome assortment of light colors, pinks, blues, etc. Yoke, with full blouse effect to waist, neat narrow standing collar, large epaulets, shoulder straps in back extending to waist, full ruffle cuffs; collar, cuffs, epaulets, straps, all finished with a pretty piping of contrasting color, making a very pretty and novel effect. Thoroughly well made throughout, with full skirt, with deep hem, latest style baby-dress sleeves, and is a garment which is sure to give perfect satisfaction in every particular. A great bargain at our very low price. Comes in three sizes only, 22, 24 and 26 inch, for children from 1½ to 3 years of age. Our special price, each...............79c

**No. 22005 A Decidedly Handsome Children's Ready Made Dress.** Something entirely new. This dress is made of a new fabric, known as pique flannel; this is a very closely woven pique figure cotton cloth, with fleeced back, suitable for wear all year around. Made with a finely tucked square yoke of white, with a fancy open work embroidery trimmed collar, large epaulets over shoulder and neat cuffs; collar, epaulets and cuffs all trimmed in open work embroidery to match. You can never know what a handsome dress this is until you have seen it, and we can assure you that it will more than please you. It is well made, with full skirt, latest style puff top sleeve, and comes in pretty shades of pinks and blues. We have these in three sizes only, 22, 24 and 26 inch, for children from 1½ to three years of age. Our Special Price, each.............89c

**No. 22007 Children's Lawn Dresses.** Made from extra selected grade, heavy weight lawn. Our own special importation, and one that we guarantee will give perfect satisfaction. These garments are made up with yoke, full gathered skirt from yoke, latest style puff top baby sleeves, with wide cuffs, standing collar, shoulder straps and fancy epaulets, all neatly trimmed with handsome open work embroidery, forming a very pretty as well as most stylish effect. Made in light colors, pinks and blues, in four sizes, 22, 24, 26 and 28 inches. One of the handsomest and best wearing garments of the season. Our price, each..98c

**No. 22009 Children's and Misses' Fancy figured, Close Woven Cotton Cheviot Dresses** unexcelled in appearance and wear. Made upin a neat assortment of medium and light colors, in fancy figures, plaids, etc. Large split circular collar, edged all around with fancy novelty braid, newest style large puff top sleeves. Finely made throughout, with full skirt and deep hem. Will give absolute satisfaction as to washing and wearing qualities. Comes in all sizes from 4 to 14 years of age. (In ordering, always be sure to state what size you wish.) An exceptional bargain. Price......58c

**No. 22010 Children's and Misses' Fancy Figured Ready made Dresses,** made from extra fine imported Madras cloth. Fine and soft fabric which will wash and wear beautifully. Large butterfly collar. newest style large puff top sleeves, collar and cuffs neatly trimmed with fancy novelty braids. Large full sized skirt with extra deep hem. Patterns are particularly choice, and we have them in a large variety of assorted light and medium colors, in fancy figures, plaids, checks, etc. All desirable light shades, blues, pinks, etc. Come in all sizes for from four to fourteen years of age. Finely made and finished and a great bargain at our special price, each...............75c

**No. 22012 Children's and Misses' Extra Fine Ready Made French Percale Dresses** handsomely made with extra large circular collar, fancy braided V shaped front and back, latest style plaited puff top sleeves neat cuffs, neatly braided, white pearl buttons. Large full skirt with deep hem at bottom. We have these dresses made up in a choice assortment of handsome light colors, no plain or solid colors. Sizes from 4 to 14 years of age. Our special price, each .............87c

**No. 22014 Childrens' and Misses' High Grade Ready Made Dresses.** Made from an extra fine quality Zephyr cloth, with colors woven through and through, (not printed.) Made with a ruffled standing collar, wide epaulets over shoulder, and three wide straps running upward from waist to shoulder; large puff top sleeves and cuffs. Epaulets. straps, etc., trimmed with a very pretty fancy open work white embroidery edging, making a very attractive garment. These are beautifully made and finished, have a full skirt, with a very deep hem, and we feel confident will more than please you in every respect. Come in all sizes from four to fourteen years. Our special price, each.........................98c

**No. 22015 Children's and Misses' Scotch Plaid French Madras Cloth Dresses.** These garments are made from exceptionally heavy fabric, with colors woven through and through. Colors are guaranteed fast, and are unexcelled for wash and wear. Made up with a very fancy new design of full blouse effect front. Plain colored V shapes yoke, with four rows of fancy braid. New effect Bolero fronts. with braided lapels; new style puff top sleeves, with fancy ruffled cuffs, braided to match collar, large full shirt with deep hem. This is one of the seasons' newest and fanciest dresses, and a garment which cannot fail to please. Sizes, 4 to 14 years. Our Special Price, ....$1.33

**No. 22021 Misses' and Children's Fancy Ready Made Dresses.** The swellest dress of our entire line. Made of heavy and very best quality of Chelsea cloth; an entirely new fabric, similar to French penang, closer woven, and will wear much better. Made in assorted light colors, with large floral or Dresden designs, fancy figures, etc. Newest style full puff Marlborough sleeves; blouse effect front, with fancy embroidery trimmed bolero; shirred around neck, collar and cuffs trimmed with a deep edge of fancy open work embroidery; two rows of embroidery in back running from shoulder to waist line. Very full skirt, with deep hem. Come mostly in pinks, blues and tans. The nobbiest dress of the season. Made in all sizes from four to fourteen years of age. Our special price......$1.75

**No. 22017  Children's and Misses Up-to-date Fancy Sailor Suit.** Large rolling sailor collar, fancy edged, with pretty braided box plait front; extra large plaited puff top sleeves; full width skirt and deep hem. All braided with novelty braid, which makes the garment very attractive and stylish. It is made of first quality Imported English Chelsea Cloth, which is guaranteed fast color and will wash and do up handsomely. Sizes 4 to 14 years, Colors light blue, pink, etc. Our special price.......**$1.58**

**No. 22019  Misses' and Children's Novelty Dresses, Made From Genuine Kingston Mills Chelsea Cloth.** Made in a large and handsome assortment of rich and attractive patterns. Principally light colors, pinks, blues, etc., contrasted with neat white mixtures. Made with blouse effect front, Bolero jacket effect, ruffled cuffs, all trimmed with white novelty braid, 2-inch belt braided to match. Bolero, collar, cuffs, etc., trimmed with fancy open worked embroidery edging, and fancy stripes running across front. Latest style puff top sleeves. A very handsome and attractive garment; guaranteed fast colors, and one which we feel sure will more than please you. Comes in all sizes from 4 to 14 years of age. Our special price, each.......**$1.62**

## Ladies' and Misses' Fascinators.

A very comfortable style of headwear. Our fascinators are made of good quality of yarn and well knit. Low prices prevail in this as well as other departments.

**No. 23560  Ladies' Fascinator,** made of good quality yarn, comes in black only. Each.......**24c**

**No 23561  Ladies' Fascinator,** made of good quality Shetland yarn, warm, yet handsome. Cheap, yet of good quality colors, pink and white. Each.... **35c**

**No. 23562  A handsome Ladies' Fascinator,** made of Shetland wool, comes in white and pink. This is a nice warm fascinator. Each.......**55c**

**No. 23564  Ladies' very heavy Wool Fascinator,** made of good quality yarn. Colors, black, cardinal, pink and white. This is of extraordinary value. Each.......**74c**

**No. 23566  A Nice Warm Fascinator,** made of soft all-wool yarn, large and handsome, nice tassels on each end. Colors, pink, blue and white. Each..**85c**

## Ladies' and Misses' Hoods.

**High Grade Warm Hoods Sold Only by Us.**

**No. 23568  Ladies' or Misses' Double Knit Hood,** made of fine yarn, soft and warm, has a 3½ inch cape. Colors, black, brown and navy. Each.......**45c**

**No. 23569  Ladies' or Misses' Knit Wool Hoods,** made of a fine grade of all-wool yarn, has a 5 inch cape, and a silk ribbon bow on top and on back, tied with silk ribbon strings. Colors, black and white. Each.......**85c**

**No. 23570  Ladies' or Misses' Knit Wool Hoods,** with weaves of fine silk floss, which adds greatly to the appearance; heavy knit wool lining, tufted top, silk bow in the back. This is as good a hood as money will buy, as far as appearance and wearing qualities are concerned. Each.......**$1.40**

## SHAWL DEPARTMENT.

**Every Shawl We Quote is a Great Big Bargain.**

### Beaver Shawls.

**No. 23578  This is a Square Beaver Shawl,** comes in plain or plaid centers, the colors are brown and gray. Each.......**$1.20**

**No. 23579  Reversible Shawl,** with knotted fringe; a good sized shawl, heavy weight; colors, black, gray and brown. Each.......**$2.05**

**No. 23580  A Very Heavy Beaver Shawl,** is of a very good quality, knotted fringe and fancy border. This shawl is very large; colors, black, gray and brown.

**No. 23581  A Reversible Beaver Shawl,** made of a material of choice quality; knotted fringe; and a very handsome fancy border. This shawl can be worn on both sides. Each.......**$4.95**

### Shoulder Shawls.

**Always Mention Color Wanted.**

**No. 23582  Misses' and Children's Wool Shoulder Shawls;** medium and bright colors; size, 37x37 inches. Each.......**35c**

**No. 23584  Misses' and Children's Wool Shoulder Shawls** in plaids and checks; medium and bright colors; size, 42x42 inches; wool fringe. Each....**50c**

**No. 23585  A very fine grade of Misses' and Children's Shoulder Shawls,** dark, medium or bright colors; size, 42x42 inches; wool fringe. Each....**70c**

**No. 23586  Misses' and Children's Fine Wool Shoulder Shawls;** best grade; dark, medium and bright colors; wool fringe; size, 40x40 inches. Each.......**90c**

### Cashmere Shawls.

**No. 23588  Cashmere Shawls** for ladies, twilled, wool fringe. Size, 58x58 inches. Colors, black or cream; all wool. Each.......**95c**

**No. 23589  Cashmere Shawls** for ladies, all wool, twilled, wool fringe. Size, 60x60 inches; black or cream white. Each.......**$1.20**

**No. 23590  Cashmere Shawls** for ladies, a very fine quality all-wool twilled shawl, wool fringe. Size, 60x60 inches; black or cream white. Each.......**$1.85**

**No. 23591  Black Cashmere Shawl for Ladies,** has a handsome 5-knot silk fringe, five inches deep, alike on all sides. Size, 56x56 inches. This shawl is all wool. Each.......**$2.10**

**No. 23592  Black Cashmere Shawl,** made of all wool material, has a 5-knot silk fringe 7 inches deep, alike on all sides. Size, 62x62 inches. Each.......**$2.85**

**No. 23594  Black Cashmere Shawl for Ladies,** material all wool. This handsome shawl has 5-knot silk fringe, 7 inches deep, alike on all sides. Size, 62x62 inches. Each.......**$3.60**

**No. 23596  Ladies' Black Cashmere Shawl,** made of an A1, all wool material. This very beautiful shawl has a 5 knot silk fringe 8 inches deep, alike on all sides, size 66x66 inches. Each.......**$4.75**

**No. 23597  Black Cashmere Shawl for Ladies;** this is a handsome all wool shawl, wool fringe, size 72x144 inches. Each.......**$6.25**

**No. 23598  Black Cashmere Shawl,** wool fringe, a very fine shawl, size 72x144 inches. Each....**$7.75**

### Ladies' Double Wool Shawls.

**No. 23599  Ladies' All-Wool Shawl;** size 67 x 135 inches. This shawl has plain and plaid centers; the colors are grey mixed and brown mixed only. Price, each.......**$1.80**

**No. 23600  Ladies' All-Wool Shawl;** size 67 x 135 inches. This number has plain or plaid centers. Comes in black, gray or brown. Price, each...**$3.10**

**No. 23601  Ladies' Double Shawl;** size 72 x 144 inches. This shawl has plain or plaid centers. Colors black, grey and brown, also mourning. Price, each.......**$4.35**

**No. 23602  Extra Quality All Wool Shawl,** size 72x144, the colors that this shawl come in are black, gray, brown and mourning. Each.......**$4.85**

**No. 23603  This Number is a Very Fine All Wool Shawl,** comes with plain or plaid centers. Colors black, gray mixed and brown mixed, size 72x144 inches. Each.......**$6.00**

## Shetland Shawls.

**Knit Shetland Wool Shawls.**

**No. 23604  Shetland Wool Shawl,** 28x28 inches; made of good quality yarn. Colors black, blue and cardinal. Each.......**24c**

**No. 23605  Imported Shetland Wool Shawl;** size, 36x36 inches; made of a high grade imported yarn; comes in black and white only. Each.......**35c**

### Ice Wool Shawls.

**No. 23606  Ice Wool Shawl,** imported, size 26x26 inches, warm and nice and soft. These shawls are usually sold at a much higher rate by retail dealers. Colors black or white. Our special price, each.......**35c**

**No. 23607  Ice Wool Shawl,** size 30x30 inches, colors black or white, made of good quality and very serviceable. The regular price of these goods is 75c. Our price, each.......**50c**

**No. 23608  Ice Wool Shawl,** size 36x36 inches; colors black or white. This shawl is made of a high grade imported yarn and is worth a great deal more money than we ask. Each.......**65c**

### Ladies' Underskirts.

**No. 23612  Ladies' Black Sateen Underskirt,** has a 2½-yard sweep, a 6-inch ruffle, made of fast black sateen; a good skirt that will wear. Each.......**50c**

**No. 23613  Ladies' Black Sateen Underskirt,** has a 3-yard sweep and a 12-inch double ruffle. This skirt is made of a high grade of fast black sateen and is exceptionally good value at the price we quote it. Each.......**75c**

**No. 23614  Ladies' Black Sateen Underskirt,** has a 3-yard sweep and 12-inch ruffle, with four rows of piping, made of the finest quality fast black sateen and a skirt that pleases all who see it. This number is a bargain at the price offered. Each.......**97c**

### Flannelette Underskirts.

**No. 23616  This skirt is made of a fine outing flannel,** comes in a variety of colors, such as gray and drab. Has a border, consisting of three stripes. Each.......**22c**

### Rustle Taffeta Underskirts.

**No. 23618  Black Rustle Taffeta Underskirts,** 14 inch flouncing and velvet bound, has a 3 yard sweep. This is a skirt we can recommend as being exceptionally good value. Each.......**75c**

### Moreen Underskirts.

**No. 23620  Ladies' Moreen Underskirts,** made of a good quality moreen. Has a yoke band, and a six inch skirting ruffle. A very good skirt for the money. Each.......**$1.35**

## Unfinished Skirt Patterns.

**These Skirt Patterns** are put up in pieces just the right amount to make a skirt. They are sold at very close prices, and are listed by us for the benefit of those who have the time or inclination to do the work at home.

**No. 23621** This is an All Wool Skirt Pattern, of ample material to make a skirt of any size wanted. Comes in red and black, blue and black, or gray and black, with narrow and wide stripes. We can furnish it in plain brown if desired. Comes full 40 inches wide. It is made of very choice quality of material, and after the skirt is made up at home, it would equal anything that you could secure at a retail store at from $1.50 to $2.00.
Our special price, per pattern..............**69c**

**No. 23622** This is an All Wool, Strictly Non-Shrinkable Skirt Pattern. It is very closely woven, and is a quality that is very durable and warm. Comes in red and black, blue and black, or grey and black, with narrow and wide stripes.
Our special price, per pattern..................**78c**

**No. 23623** This is an extra quality, very fine All Wool Skirt Pattern, and we can furnish it in a variety of combinations, such as blue and black, red and black, or black and white, with narrow and wide stripes; or, if so desired, we can furnish it in large checks. This skirt after made up would equal anything your local dealer would ask $2.00 for.
Our special price..................**95c**

**No. 23624** We offer a very excellent quality of Mixed Flannel Skirting, with neat woven border of same goods in stripes. This when made up makes an exceedingly warm and durable skirt. The goods are all closely woven stuff, and we consider the pattern one of the choicest bargains we offer.
Our special price, per pattern. ..................**90c**

## CORSET DEPARTMENT.

**A Corset Weighs about 15 Ounces.**

Our efforts to make the corset department one of the foremost departments of our vast establishment have not been in vain. We now sell several thousands of corsets weekly. Taking care to sell nothing but good corsets that we can guarantee, no matter how low the price, and at all times selling corsets at prices way down, has built up our business in this line.

We directly control the manufacture of a great many of the corsets we sell, and are in a position to see that the material is good, the fit perfect and the corset durable.

If you want to buy one Corset as cheap as your local dealer buys one or more dozens, send your order to Sears, Roebuck & Co.

Please order corsets by waist measure only. Corsets are numbered by actual waist measure. If measure is taken outside of dress, deduct two inches for dress, and this will give you the correct size to order. **Do not order by bust measure.**

## Dr. Warner's Four-in-Hand Corsets

**No. 23631** Boned with Coraline. High Hip for ladies with large hips whose corsets break down at the sides. Just the corset for such people. It is worth four times the price to any one so troubled. It is easy fitting and adds grace to the figure. Comes in drab only. Sizes 18 to 30. Per pair......**75c**

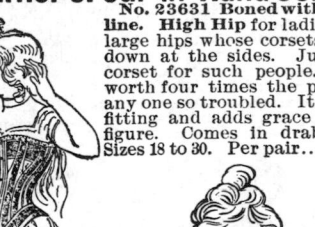

## Warner's 333 Corset.

**No. 23632** Boned with Coraline. Extra long waist, medium form. A very popular corset, made of heavy jean with three boned strips of fine sateen. Beautifully shaped and a very comfortable, easy fitting corset. Colors drab or black. Sizes 18 to 30.
Price..................**75c**

## Dr. Warner's Health Corset.

**Boned with Coraline.**
**No. 23633** Made in Two Lengths, medium and long waist; adapted to ladies deficient in bust fullness, and those desiring bust support. For both slim and stout figures. The special features of this corset are the Coraline busts, which are light and flexible, and give to any lady an elegant figure, and assure a well fitting dress. This corset, with constant improvements, has been before the public for seventeen years, and has been worn by over six millions of ladies, a success never attained by any other corset. Colors: white, drab or black. Sizes 18 to 30. Price..............**$1.00**

---

S R

**No. 23634** Extra Long Waist 6 Hook Corset made of the best quality satin handsomely embroidered, a corset that will give satisfaction and one of the best corsets that we handle; drab or black.
Price, per pair........ **90c**

## BALL'S STYLE B.

**No. 23635** The Most Comfortable Corset Ever Made. They need no "breaking in," has a coiled wire elastic section which yields to every movement of the wearer. Ball's corsets are boned with Kabo, made of fine quality jean; white and drab only. Sizes 18 to 30.
Price..........**75c**
Extra sizes 31 to 36. Price..**$1.00**

## KABO STYLE 110.

**No. 23636** A Corset of Perfect Form that will not stretch, break, roll up or pucker; extra long waist; made in white, French drab and black sateen. Sizes 18 to 30. Price..........**75c**
Extra sizes 31 to 36.
Price..............**$1.00**

**NOTE—If you require a corset larger than size 30, order from those we quote in extra sizes. Ordinary corsets are made in sizes 18 to 30 only.**

**Kabo Style 110.**

## Dr. Warners' Coraline Corsets.

**No. 23637** Made in Medium Length Waists. Adapted to ladies of average figure. This corset has been before the public for fifteen years, has the largest sale and gives the best value and best service of any dollar corset ever manufactured. Made in two thicknesses of fine corset jean, heavily boned with coraline in a manner that prevents the corset from losing its shape, and makes it absolutely unbreakable. The hip is extra stayed with clock spring side steels. Colors; drab or black. Each .... **$0.75**
Extra large sizes, 32 to 36, 25 cents extra.

## Dr. Warners' Abdominal Corset.

**No. 23638** Boned with Coraline. Adapted to ladies with either full or slender figure desiring a corset long below the waist, to give abdominal support. Made with extension steels, side lacings and elastic gores on each side. Colors, drab or black. Sizes 18 to 30.
Price..................**$1.25**
Extra large sizes, 31 to 36 inches. Each........**$1.50**

**Special Sewing Machine Catalogue Free.**

---

## Nursing Corset.

**No. 23639.** Nursing Corset. The most sensible, convenient and comfortable nursing corset made, well stayed on the sides, but very pliable over the sensitive parts of the body; the opening permits the use of nipple without the least inconvenience; made of fine jean. Colors, white or drab; size, 18 to 30. Price....**85c**

**No. 23641** Ladies' Perfection Waist; made of fine sateen; soft puffed busts; clasp front. Colors white, black or drab. Sizes 18 to 30.
Price..................**90c**

### ALWAYS GIVE WAIST MEASURE WHEN ...ORDERING... CORSETS.

**No. 23642** Young Ladies' Corsets, suitable for girls 13 to 17 years of age; made of good jean; nicely corded; with shoulder straps. Colors, white or drab; sizes 18 to 26 waist measure. This corset in appearance and durability is equal to goods that retailers sell at a very much higher figure. Each........**40c**

**No. 23644** Warner Corsets, No. 65. Boned with rust proof, made of fine corset jean striped with sateen. The bust is flexible, but sufficiently rigid to give form to the figure. Silk embroidered white, drab or black.
Price..................**75c**

**No. 23646** Best Quality Jeans Corset, striped with sateen, bone bust, two side steels, 6-hook clasp, embroidered at top and bottom; in shape, appearance and durability equal to any $1.00 corset; unquestionably the best corset ever produced for the money we ask. Colors; white, drab or black..................**50c**

**No. 23648** Exposition, perfectly shaped and a fine fitting Corset, equal to any retailed at 80c; made of heavy jean, striped with sateen, wide zone, double bust, two side steels. Colors: white, drab, cream or gold..................**40c**

---

**TENNIS AND CROQUET SETS AT POPULAR LOW PRICES IN SPORTING GOODS DEPARTMENT. REFER TO INDEX.**

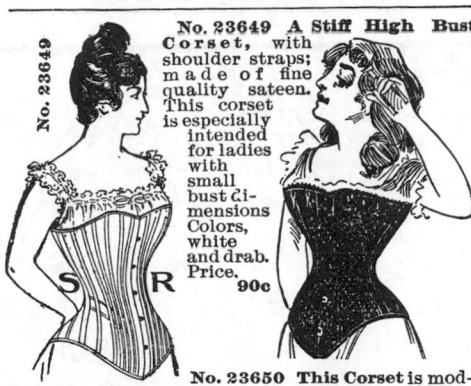

**No. 23649 A Stiff High Bust Corset**, with shoulder straps; made of fine quality sateen. This corset is especially intended for ladies with small bust dimensions Colors, white and drab. Price. **90c**

**No. 23650 This Corset** is modeled after the finest French shapes and will fit any lady of average proportions; it is made with soft busts and stayed with unbreakable French wire. Colors, black or drab. Size 18 to 30. Price........**75c**

**No. 23651 Comfort and elegance,** a summer corset made of improved netting; striped with satin; reinforced front steels, two side steels, and extra heavy back wire; six hook clasp; as perfectly fitting as any of the highest price corsets. Colors: white or drab; size 18 to 30. Price................**45c**

**No. 23652 A well** made summer corset, with double bust; two side steels; wide zone; in white only; size 18 to 30. Price................**39c**

**No. 23653 French Coutel Corset;** extra long waisted; sateen striped; fitted with unbreakable French wire; trimmed with handsome silk embroidery and heavily flossed, and produces an elegant appearance equaled only by corsets costing double the money. Colors: White, drab or black. Sizes, 18 to 30 only. Price........**95c** Extra size in black only; size 31 to 36. Price............**$1.20**

**No. 23654 The Very Latest Improved French Corset,** very highest grade workmanship and material; made of finest Zanella cloth, extra long waisted, medium size bust and hips, cross boned, high back, beautifully embroidered and finished in every way equal to any corset retailing for $2.65 each; colors, drab or black; size 18 to 30........**$1.89**

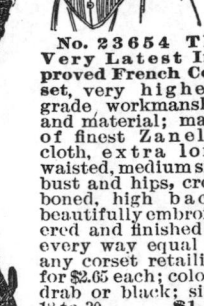

**No. 26655 High Grade Special Corset,** in every way equal to the best imported corset that retails for $2.50; made of the best quality improved sateen, long waisted, high back, extra heavy clasp, elegantly embroidered and silk trimmed. Colors: white, drab or black; sizes 18 to 30...........,.....**$1.25**

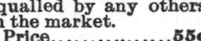

**No. 23656 Ball's Child's Waists,** with patent tape buttons and buttonholes; sizes, 18 to 28. A perfect fitting waist; colors white and drab. Price..........**38c**

**No. 23657 Ball's Misses' Waist,** white and drab; sizes, 18 to 28. Ball's waists are unequalled by any others in the market. Price................**55c**

**No. 23658 Young Ladies' Corset,** with soft expanding bust; made of fine sateen with shoulder straps; clasp front; tape fastened buttons for skirt. Colors: white, drab or black; sizes, 19 to 28 waist measure; just the corset for growing girls ....**75c**

**No. 23658.**

**No. 23659 Corset waist for girls** from 8 to 12 years of age; button front; lace back; made of fine quality silesia; well corded; shoulder straps; tape fastened buttons for skirts. Colors: white or drab; size 19 to 28..................**69c**

**No. 23659.**

**No. 23660. Bust Pads,** the kind that usually sell for 50 cents. Our price............................**25c**

**No. 23662. Ladies' Genuine Haircloth Combination Hip Pad Bustle,** padded with curled hair, very light in weight, comes in black, drab and white, the usual retail price, $1.00. Our price, each, ................**56c**

## Ladies' White Skirts.

Lengths 36, 38, 40, 42 inches. Our skirts are three yards around the bottom, never less, often wider. Please give size when ordering.

**No. 23670 Ladies' White Muslin Skirt,** lawn ruffle 6½ inches wide, trimmed with embroidery, good width, patent facing. Each...**$0.50** 2 for....  .95 3 for....  1.40

**No. 23671 Muslin Skirt,** umbrella style, 3 yards around bottom, lawn ruffle 6½ inches wide finished with fine linen torchon lace, a regular $1.00 skirt. Each 65; 2 for $1.25; 3 for...................... **$1.85**

**No. 23672 Ladies' White Umbrella Skirt,** 3 yards around bottom, lawn ruffle 6½ inches wide finished with open work embroidery, a regular $1.25 skirt. Each..... **$0.79** 2 for......  1.52 3 for......  2.20

**No. 23673 Ladies' White Skirt** made of good muslin, 3 yards wide, 2 lawn ruffles 1½ inches wide, finished with torchon lace, 3 inches wide. Retailers ask $1.50 for goods like these. Each 90c; 2 for $1.70; 3 for $2.50

**No. 23674 Ladies' Fine White Skirt,** 3½ yards wide, has 9-inch lawn ruffle finished with very handsome open work embroidery; regular price $2.00. Each, **$1.25.** 2 for..  2.40 3 for..  3.30

**No. 23675 A very Handsome Ladies' Skirt** of good quality, 3½ yards wide. 16-inch lawn ruffle, finished with fine Hamburg embroidery; well worth $2.50. Each......... **$1.65** 2 for........  3.10 3 for......  4.50

**No. 23676 An exceptionally fine white underskirt for ladies.** Umbrella pattern, 3½ yards wide. English open work embroidery; width of ruffle and embroidery 15 inches. This skirt is well worth $3.75.

Each, **$1.85** 2 for..  3.50 3 for..  5.00

## LADIES' MUSLIN SKIRTS—Continued.

**No. 23677** A Pretty Skirt made of a cotton embroidery 9 inches wide 4 cloister tucks, a skirt that would be good value at $1.25 This skirt is made like the good old fashioned skirts made for wear more than for show, a good skirt for ladies' wanting value and durability.

Our special price, 82c; 2 for.................$1.58

**No. 23678. A Skirt built for wear,** of a fine quality muslin, the embroidery is 10 inches wide and is headed by a cloister of five tucks. The pattern of embroidery is neat and quiet, but nevertheless rich in appearance. Realizing that there are a great many women who still want the class of reliable merchandise on the market years ago, we make a special feature of this skirt. If you want a well wearing skirt order this number. Each........$1.20
Two for...............................2.30

## Ladies' White Muslin Corset Covers.

Sizes 32, 34, 36, 38 and 40 Bust Measure.

**No. 23679 Ladies' Corset Covers,** made of good quality muslin. Each........ .. ...15c
2 for ............................28c
3 for ............................41c

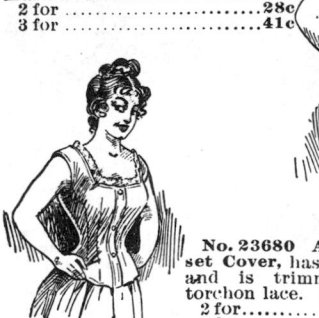

**No. 23680 A very fine Corset Cover,** has a square neck and is trimmed with real torchon lace. Each.........25c
2 for.........................48c
3 for.........................71c

**No. 23682 A Corset Cover** of good quality. V shaped neck trimmed with Valenciennes lace. Actual value 60c
Our price each ........$0.35
2 for ...................... .68
3 for ...................... 1.00

## Ladies' White Muslin Drawers.

Lengths 25, 27, 29 inches. Specify open or closed.

**No. 23683 Ladies' White Drawers;** good quality muslin; 1½ in. hem, cloister 3 tucks.
Per pair...........20c
Two pair.........38c
Three pair.......56c

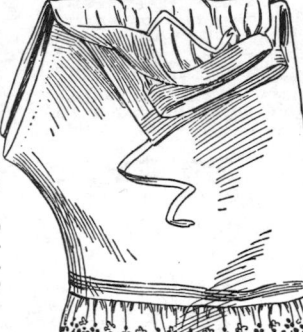

**No. 23684 Ladies' Fine White Drawers;** three tucks and 2½ inch cambric hem at bottom.
Per pair......25c
Two pair....47c
Three pair....69c

**No. 23685 Ladies' Drawers,** made of fine quality muslin, finished with five tucks and 1½ in. point embroidery.
Per pair... 35c
Two pair...68c
Three pair..99c

**Always give length measurement when ordering ladies' drawers.**

**No. 23686 Ladies' fine quality muslin drawers;** five tucks and finished with fine open work embroidery 2¾ in. wide.
Per pair, $0.45
Two pair, .85
Three pr. 1.25

**No. 23687** These Exceptionally Fine Ladies Drawers are full width, have 5 tucks and are trimmed with real hand made torchon lace.
Per pair 50c
2 pair.. .95c
3 pair, $1.40

No. 23688

## FINE... CAMBRIC DRAWERS

**HAS 7 TUCKS, IS FULL WIDTH**
...and...
FINISHED WITH
**Open Work Embroidery 2¼ Inches Wide,**

**GOOD VALUE AT $1.25 PER PAIR**

Per pair............65c
2 pair........ ...$1.20
3 pair......... 1.75

**No. 23689** A Regular $1.50 Drawers, made of very nice cotton, full regular width, neat open embroidery 3½ inches wide, has 9 tucks.
Per pair. ........80c
2 pair.... ..... $1.50
3 pair.. ..... $2.15

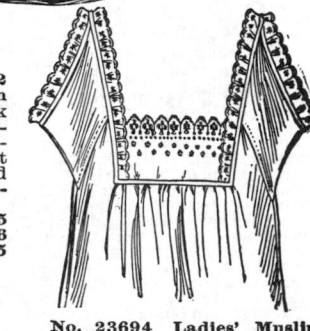

## Ladies' White Muslin Chemise.

**No. 23690 Ladies' Chemise,** trimmed with torchon lace, good quality muslin.
Each..........25c
2 for............48c
3 for............70c

**No. 23692 Ladies' Muslin Chemise,** neck and sleeves trimmed with embroidery, bosom set with one solid piece of embroidery.
Each.....$0.45
2 for...... .86
3 for.. .. 1.25

**No. 23694 Ladies' Muslin Long Chemise,** (skirt chemise), good quality muslin, 2½ inch hem, 4 tucks round, neck trimmed with full Valenciennes lace. Each, 78c; 2 for $1.50
3 for.................. ........ 2.20

**No. 23695 Ladies' Fine Washable Lawn Chemise,** long skirt chemise, trimmed with flounce, 5-inch ruffle, finished with 1½-inch hem, 5 cluster tucks, sleeves and neck trimmed with 3-inch Valenciennes lace. Each, $1.00; 2 for $1.92; 3 for........................$2.80

**No. 23696 A Matched Set of Ladies' White Muslin Underwear.** This set consists of a handsome night gown empire style, trimmed with fine Hamburg embroidery, one corset cover, one pair good drawers, and one long white skirt, wide and full trimmed with beautiful embroidery. Everything matches. **Retail price of this set, $5.00.** Our price per set.... . .................................$2.15

## Ladies' Aprons.

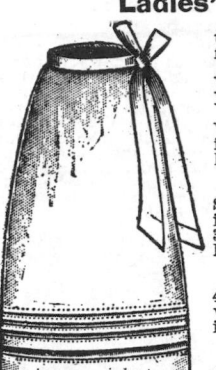

The material costs more than our price for the finished product.

**No. 23697** Ladies' Plain White Aprons, 2 inch hem. Each, 12½c; 4 for.......45c

**No. 23698** Ladies' White Victoria Lawn Apron, 40 inches wide, has a 2 inch hem and 3 tucks. Each, 15c; 4 for.......55c

**No. 23699** Extra Large Sheer Lawn Apron, three 1 inch tucks, 40 inches wide, 39 inches long, good wide long string. Each, 35c; 3 for....$1.00

**No. 23700** Lawn Apron, 40 inches long and 40 inches wide, 10 inch hem, strings 4 inches wide. Each, 25c; 4 for.......92c

**No. 23701.** This is an Apron 60 inches wide, has a 6 inch hem, 3 tucks, strings 5½ inches wide and 40 inches long. Apron made of sheer lawn and is 39 inches long. 2½ inch hem on strings. Each, 45c; 3 for.......$1.20

**No. 23703** Ladies' good Gingham Aprons. Each.......$0.10 12 for.......1.15

**No. 23704** Gingham Apron, 50 inches wide, 36 inches long, 2 inch hem, long side string. Each..25c 4 for.......95c

**No. 23705** Ladies' Black Sateen Aprons, with pocket; 36 inches wide, 36 inches long. Each.....25c 4 for.......96c

## Infants' Long Cambric Slips.

These dress robes are made up of good material and in the latest and swellest of style.

**No. 23716** Infants' Long White Cambric Slip, sleeves and neck trimmed with wash lace, skirt hemmed string bow around waist. Each.......22c

**No. 23717** Infants' Cambric Slips; has a plain collar, sleeves trimmed with feather stitched braid and skirt hemmed. Each.......27c

**No. 23718** Infants' Long Cambric Slips, collar trimmed with embroidery, sleeves nicely finished with embroidery of good quality, yoke has solid piece of three inch embroidery, skirt hemmed. Retailers get 60c for these garments. Our price, each.......38c

**No. 23719** Infants' Long Cambric Slips, of good quality cambric, collar trimmed all around with nice feather stitched braid, yoke has one and one half inch embroidery all around front skirt hemmed neatly, a very pretty garment. Each.......45c

**No. 23720** A very handsome Infants' Long Cambric Slip, made of a fine quality of cambric, has embroidery 2½ inches wide at bottom of skirt. Sleeves nicely trimmed with embroidery; large circular collar and yoke, trimmed with embroidery 1½ inches wide around front, feather stitched braid and three plaits. Each.......65c

No. 23719

No. 23720    No. 23721

**No. 23721** Infants' Long Cambric Slips; this number is a beauty, well made, pretty and made up in the latest style embroidery 2¼ inches wide around bottom, headed with three tucks, sleeves trimmed with feather stitched braid, and finished with handsome embroidery. Embroidered yoke with 4 rows of tucks on each side, large full round collar with handsome embroidery all around. Each.......95c

---

**No. 23726** Infants' long flannelette skirt, 1½ yards wide. Each.......25c

**No. 23727** Infants' long flannelette skirt, made of very heavy material, 1½ yards wide. Each.......35c

23726.    23727.

23729

**No. 23729** Infants' flannelette sacque, pinked edges, gathered cuffs, tied with silk bow, colors, pink and blue. Each.......18c

**No. 23730** Infants' sacque very handsome, made of fleeced French flannelette, crochet edges, pink and blue gathered cuffs with crochet edges, collar also has a crochet edge. Each.......42c

23730.

**No. 23731** Infants' Gilbert flannel sacque, white, has nice silk feather stitching down front, around the bottom and around collar and cuffs, a very neat and handsome garment. Each.......58c

**No. 23733** Infants' hand crochet bootees, made of good quality zephyr yarn. Colors: White, blue and pink. Per pair.......8c

**No. 23734** Infants' hand crochet booties in better qualities. Per pair.......15c

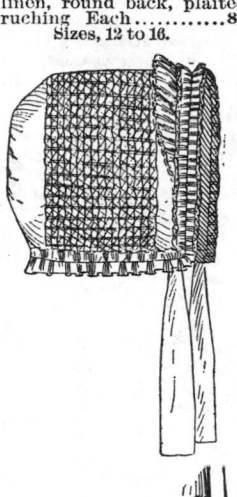

**No. 23735** Infants' fine hand crochet sacques, made of a fine all wool yarn, in the latest and most popular manner. Colors: Pink, blue and white. Each.......22c

**No. 23736** Infants' fine hand crochet sacques in the better grade. Colors: Pink, blue and white. Each.......35

**No. 23737** Honey-comb bib, made of white honey comb cloth and trimmed with lace. Each.......3c Per dozen.......30c

**No. 23739** Honeycomb bib, large sized, taped; has pet name such as "baby," "darling," etc., in center. Each.......5c Per dozen.......55c

23739.

23737.

**No. 23740** Waterproof Bibs for children. Each.......4c Per dozen.......42c

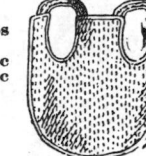

**No. 23731** Quilted Bib, made of fancy quilted cloth, neatly trimmed with lace; a pretty little bib. Each, 7c; per dozen.......78c

**No. 22743** Lace Trimmed Honey Comb Cloth Bib. Has a stamped medallion pocket to hold a celluloid teething ring which is attached with a narrow ribbon. Each, 9c; per dozen.......98c

## SPECIAL FOR THE BABIES.

...SEND FOR CARRIAGE CATALOGUE...

---

## Oil Cloth Mats For Children.

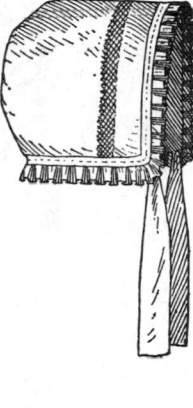

**No. 23753** Handsome Little Mats made of oilcloth used beneath children's dishes on the table protecting the linen. They come in a great many pretty designs and besides having a picture in the center, have the alphabet and a series of numerals around the border. Size, 13 by 16 inches. Each 5c per doz.......55c

## Infant's and Children's Headwear.

Postage on Hats, 8c.

In this important and growing department will be found the latest and most stylish goods in the market. No old styles here; our business in this branch is so large and our stock turns itself so rapidly, that old styles cannot accumulate. Manufacturers knowing of our large output and cash method of buying always look up S. R. & Co., if they want to realize on a large lot. In this way we buy goods cheap. We stand ready to sell you new desirable headwear for less money than the local dealer pays for job lots.

## Infants' White Lawn and Embroidery Bonnets or Caps.

**No. 23760** Infants' Caps made of good quality India linen, round back, plaited ruching Each.......8c Sizes, 12 to 16.

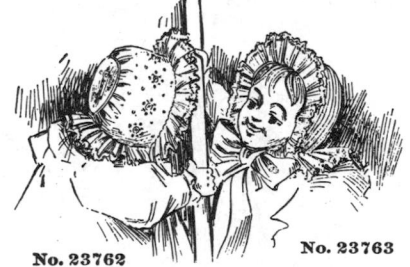

**No. 23761** This Cap is made of fine white lawn corded, double ruching all around, wide ties. Each.......12c

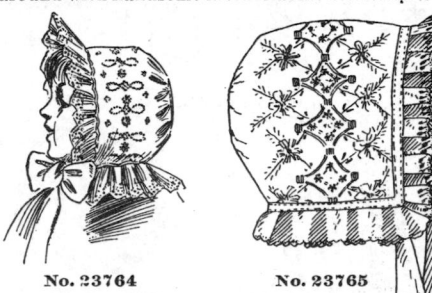

No. 23762    No. 23763

**No. 23762** New Style French Poke Bonnet with cape made of nice soft washable material trimmed with lace all around, bonnet faced with full ruch. A swell up-to-date cap. Each.......25c

**No. 23763** Pretty Poke Style Bonnet, made of stylish washable embroidery, has a cape nicely trimmed with lace, new double front, trimmed all around with handsome lace. Each.......25c

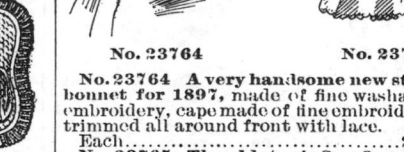

No. 23764    No. 23765

**No. 23764** A very handsome new style bonnet for 1897, made of fine washable embroidery, cape made of fine embroidery trimmed all around front with lace. Each.......25c

**No. 23765** The old staple San Quentin Pattern Poke Bonnet, always just as pretty as the latest; made of Swiss embroidery, plaited ruffle of dainty embroidery all around, wide ties. Each.......30c

**No. 23766 Round Shaped Cap.** Made of very fine revere open work. Swiss embroidery. New style Chicago Ruching and a very prety ponpon of point lace and netting. Each.................40c

**No. 23767 Washable Sun Bonnet**, made of white pique, full puff crown, and cape of sheer lawn trimmed with zig-zag braid and made with draw string, so that they can readily be laundered. Each......................15c
**No. 23767½ Gingham Sun Bonnets**, made up like above number, blue and white check, brown and white and pink and white. Each..................15c

**No. 23768**
**Pique Sun Bonnet**, With wide flaring top edge with fancy lace, extra long cape with draw string to be let out when washed.
Each.................25c

**No. 23769 New Style Poke Shaped Cap**, made of very fine Irish point embroidery in late and pretty patterns; front of cap made in the latest design, cape trimmed with Irish point embroidery, edge wide lawn ties and full handsome ruch.
Each..........68c

**No. 23770 Washable Poke Shaped Bonnet**, made with cords so that it can be readily laundered, handsome Irish point insertion new style open work edge, wide ties, full ruching of lace, materials of the very best quality.
Each....82c

**No. 23771 Shirred lawn hat** with bow, pink, blue or white. Each..........12½c

**No. 23773 Infants' Cream Silk Bonnets**, made of Japanese silk, nicely embroidered with silk floss, silk cord all around. Nice Ponpon, ruch.
Each..... ..............25c

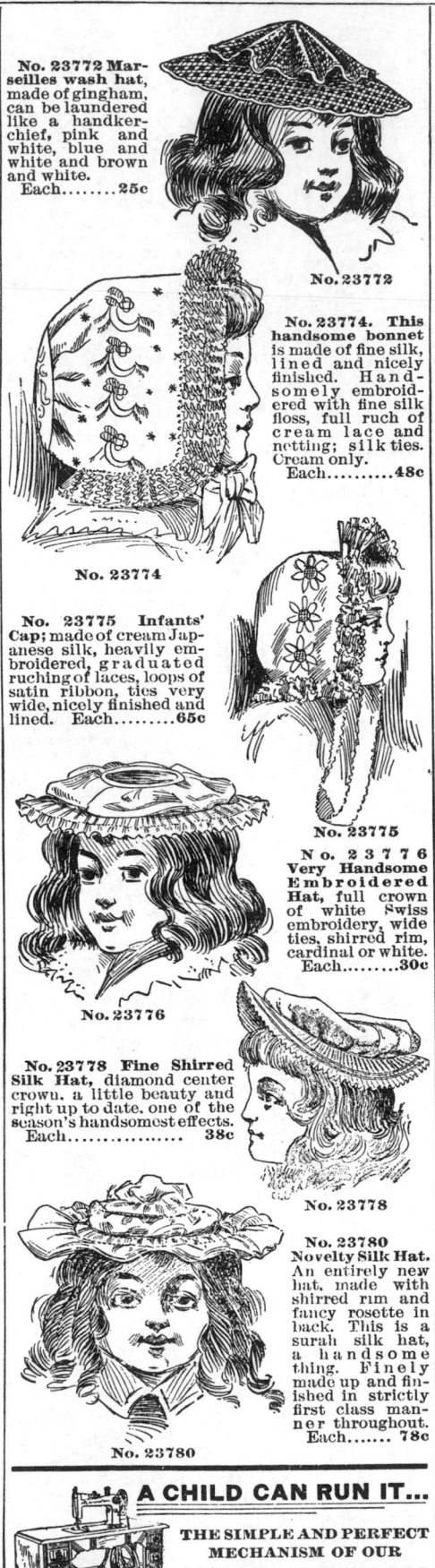

**No. 23772 Marseilles wash hat**, made of gingham, can be laundered like a handkerchief, pink and white, blue and white and brown and white.
Each........25c

No. 23772

**No. 23774. This handsome bonnet** is made of fine silk, lined and nicely finished. Handsomely embroidered with fine silk floss, full ruch of cream lace and netting; silk ties. Cream only.
Each..........48c

No. 23774

**No. 23775 Infants' Cap;** made of cream Japanese silk, heavily embroidered, graduated ruching of laces, loops of satin ribbon, ties very wide, nicely finished and lined. Each..........65c

No. 23775

**No. 23776 Very Handsome Embroidered Hat**, full crown of white Swiss embroidery, wide ties, shirred rim, cardinal or white. Each..........30c

No. 23776

**No. 23778 Fine Shirred Silk Hat**, diamond center crown, a little beauty and right up to date, one of the season's handsomest effects. Each.................38c

No. 23778

**No. 23780 Novelty Silk Hat.** An entirely new hat, made with shirred rim and fancy rosette in back. This is a surah silk hat, a handsome thing. Finely made up and finished in strictly first class manner throughout.
Each....... 78c

No. 23780

**A CHILD CAN RUN IT...**
**THE SIMPLE AND PERFECT MECHANISM OF OUR**
**SEWING MACHINES**
**Gives them Superiority over all others.**
*IN ONLY ONE POINT IS THERE ANY INFERIORITY*
**...THAT'S IN THE PRICE...**
Special Catalogue Free.

## Ladies' Neckwear.
### Swell Novelties for 1897.

Novelties in Neckwear will be worn by everybody this season. We have all the new and nobby things and the prices are right. We have these goods manufactured for us, by one of Americas' foremost neckwear manufacturers. These goods are the exact counterpart of the fine French collarettes costing several times as much. The illustrations are copies of photographs of the goods themselves, they give at least a faint idea of the stylish appearance of these goods. On goods like these the retailer makes his largest profit. Save your money and buy your neckties of S. R. & Co.

**No. 23781 A Fine White Embroidered Collar**, the new three cornered shape sailor collar, yoke made of alternate rows of very fine wide inserting and lawn, edged all around with Irish point embroidery, a regular $1.00 collar. Our price.......50c

**No. 23782 One of our novelties in neckwear.** Made of satin and oriental lace, yoke made of alternate rows of satin and butter color insertion, very full edge of oriental lace. The satin comes in all colors; this collar is well worth $1.25. Each..........58c

**No. 23783 The latest and most stylish collar out.** Has a new style square yoke, bands of satin and fine oriental lace, edged with wide handsome oriental lace, butter color. This is a regular $1.50 collar. Each.............81c

**No. 23784 A New Style Lace Collar**, large and full "V" shaped, yoke satin band; 8 inch oriental lace, butter color, full gathered; a handsome stylish collar. Each..........$1.18

**No. 23786 A $2.50 Collar for $1.40.** A nobby new swell collarette, new shape collar, square yoke, has alternate rows of satin and butter colored insertion, edged with 5½ inch open work oriental lace, made very full. Great value for............$1.40

**No. 23787 A very Novel Piece of Neckwear**, fancy five cornered yoke, made of extra quality satin alternated with fine butter colored inserting, edged with 4½ in. duoble chiffon. Comes in all colors. A $3.00 collar. Our price....$1.95

**No. 23789 A Handsome New Collar** made of fine black chantilly lace band of colored silk covered with lace bourdon band producing a novel and rich effect. The cut gives but a faint idea of what this beautiful collar is like. Each..........$2.25

# WONDERFUL BARGAINS IN LADIES' NECKWEAR.

**No. 23791 New Bolero Front**, the latest, the swellest and the most stylish of the year. Made of alternate rows of fine, wide satin ribbon and oriental bands, reaching to waist, elaborate bows on neck piece. A regular $2.50 article. Each...........$1.65

**No. 23793 New Puff Bolero Front** made of fine Japanese silk, three rows of butter color val lace across front, collar trimmed with butter color val lace. Each............$1.89

**No. 23795.** Large white embroidered collar; new style, sailor shape, narrow and wide Irish point insertion, edged with pretty patterns of Irish point embroidery. A handsome collar that is always retailed at $2.00. Each..........$1.38

**No. 23797** This beautiful collar is made of fine Habutai silk, ornamented with alternating rows of shirred silk and point Venice insertion, very wide lace border in butter color all around. Silk comes in popular shades; a very showy collar. Regular retail value $2.75. Each...........................$1.95

**No. 23801** The new white Bolero shaped collar; the latest novelty, reaching to waist; full shoulder pieces; the finest qualities and patterns of Irish point embroidery is used in the making of this collar. This collar is a gem and retails at $2.75. Our price, Each.......$1.89

## Collars and Cuff Sets.

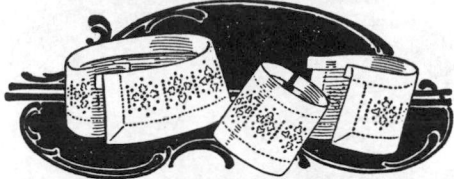

**No. 23803** Ladies' Collar and Cuff Sets, made of fine Swiss embroidery, both collar and cuffs hemstitched all around; these sets are to be very stylish this spring and summer; width of collar 2½ inches, width of cuffs, 3¼ inches. Per set.............60c

**No. 23805** Ladies' Collars and Cuffs, both collar and cuffs headed with a colored linen lawn and finished with a handsome Swiss embroidery; this combination is very new, stylish and pretty, width of collar, 2¼ inches, width of cuffs, 3¼ inches. Our special price for this grand set, colors of lawn, pink, white, cream, blue and tan. Per set.............85c

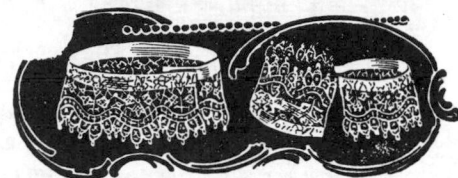

**No. 23807** Ladies' Collar and Cuff Set, Point-de-ernee lace; this lace has a beautiful serpentine or wave pattern running through it, width of collar 2½ inches and width of cuffs 3¾ inches. We make a leader of this number and offer the set at.....$1.25

# LATEST STYLES IN LADIES' CHEMISETTES, COLLARS AND CUFFS.

## Ladies' Chemisettes.

The Style, the finish of our collars, the material used in them, compares very favorably with goods at twice the price.

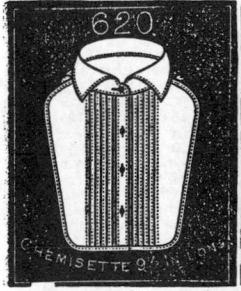

**No. 23809** Fine Quality White Linen Chemisettes, handsomely finished. Sizes, 12½ to 15. Each.................23c

Postage, 4 cents.

Sensible thinking women are assured of stylish, up-to-date collars cheap, when they buy of S. R. & Co.

## Ladies' High Grade Linen Collars.

There is the good collar that wears and the cheap collar that don't. We sell our good collars cheap.

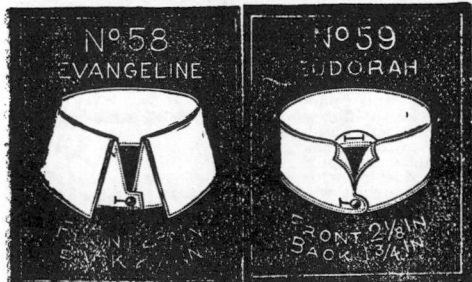

**No. 23811** Sizes, 12½, 13, 13½, 14, 14½. Each......................12½c

Our expert buyers in this as well as other departments always aim to have the newest and latest for less money than others sell out of date stuff for.

## Ladies' High Grade Linen Cuffs.

Any of these three styles, per pair, 20c. Always give style, number of collars and cuffs in addition to regular numbers. No back numbers here, we haven't got room for them.

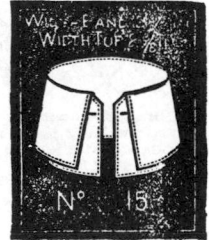

**No. 23813** Ladies' 4-ply Linen Cuffs to match collar. Sizes, 7½, 8, 8½. Per pair.......................................................20c

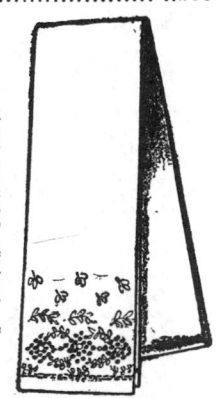

## White Mull Ties.

**No. 23815** Fine Sheer Mull Ties, 6 inches wide, scalloped and embroidered ends 3½ inches deep. Each.................10c

**No. 23817** A Beautiful White Mull Tie 4½ inches wide, hemstitched ends with fine open work embroidery. Each.................18c

**No. 23819** Fine White Mull Tie 4½ inches wide, with handsome open work. Guipure embroidered end 3¼ inches deep. Each..................20c

No. 23817.                    No. 23819.

## ....A MORE COMPLETE LINE OF LADIES' TIES....

ON PAGE 224. WE ARE **HEADQUARTERS** FOR THE NEWEST AND **MOST DESIRABLE** PATTERNS.

**DON'T FORGET THE EXTRA POSTAGE THAT IS ABSOLUTELY NECESSARY WHEN GOODS ARE TO BE SENT BY MAIL. IF YOU SEND TOO MUCH, WE REFUND BALANCE.**

## VEILING DEPARTMENT.

Our buyer has been unusually fortunate in securing for the season some of the **very latest styles** for **veilings**, and by reason of our unusually large purchases we are enabled to offer the best goods the market affords at about half the usual retail prices. Only the **very latest and most desirable patterns** are handled by us, and should you place your order with us for anything in this line we can guarantee that you will not only be pleased with the quality of the goods and their handsome appearance, but also with the great saving which we are able to effect for you.

### Our 19c Silk Veiling.

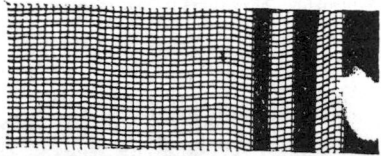

**25000** As shown in above illustration this is **a very desirable pattern of silk veiling** 14 inches **wide**, and comes in such popular colors as black, cream, navy blue and brown.
Our special price per yard.................$0.19

### Our 20c Veiling.

**25002** A **27 inch Maline net veiling**, similar to the illustration of No. 25000 above. A very popular veiling which always has a large sale and gives entire satisfaction from the fact that it is very well made of the best material, and furthermore it is unusually cheap. It comes in black, brown, cream or navy blue.
Our special price, per yard.................$0.20

### Our 13c Veiling.

**25003** A most desirable pattern of coarse net **Tuxedo veiling** 18 inches wide. As shown in illustration it has chenille dots and presents a very neat and striking appearance.
Our special price, per yard.................$0.13

### Our 19c Tuxedo Veiling.

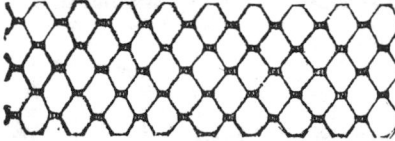

**25004** The illustration shows another pattern of **the coarse net Tuxedo veiling.** We secure this veiling in large quantities from leading manufacturers, and are able to offer the quality which we illustrate above at about half the retail price. It is 18 inches wide, very handsome and durable.
Our special price, per yard.................$0.19

### Our 22c Veiling.

**25005** A **48 inch Maline net veiling** with chenille dots about one-half inch apart. This is very finely made of the best material, and is one of the best veilings that we carry in our stock. It has a very large sale, which is evidence of its unusual popularity.
Our special price, per yard.................$0.22

## Dress Trimmings.

We take pleasure in presenting to the attention of our customers the newest popular designs in dress trimming, patterns that have just been put on the market and which will not be found in any retail stores at the present time, as the manufacturers have just brought out the styles.

These are an **inexpensive** line of ornamentation, and will be exceedingly popular for the season of 1897. We desire that our catalogue shall contain not only goods that are serviceable, but such as are strictly up-to-date and which we can offer at **very reasonable prices.** These are exceedingly **stylish trimmings** and such

**Fashion A.**

as will be found later on in the season only in the most fashionable retail stores. We buy them in large quantities and hence are able to offer them at **exceedingly low prices. All the new Parisian novelties** will be found below, stylish Braids, handsome Beleros and tasty Jets. **We import direct from Europe from first hands,** and thus save our customers all the profits of importers, wholesalers and retailers. The illustrations will give you some idea of the handsome appearance of these trimmings. Fashion A shows the elegant appearance of one of our handsome Boleros, Fashion B shows a striking effect of our up-to-date Loop Sets.

**Fashion B.**

### Our $2.56 Black Boleros.

**25006** We show in illustration a very handsome and decidedly stylish black Bolero.

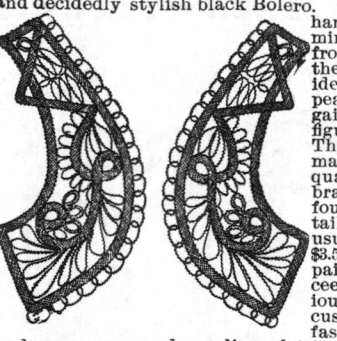

This is a very handsome trimming for waists from the neck to the waist. An idea of its appearance can be gained from the figures above. This Bolero is made of a choice quality of silk braid and when found in any retail store will usually cost from $3.50 to $4.00 per pair. We are exceedingly anxious to please our customers in new fashioned goods, and can recommend our line of trimmings without reservation as the best the market of the world affords. On our factory to consumer system we are able to bring the prices down within the reach of the most limited means.
Our special price per pair.................$2.56

### A $2.50 Bolero at $1.25.

**25008** An up-to-date black jet Bolero. The illustration will give you some idea of the appearance of this handsome Bolero, which is 12 inches long, and will seldom if ever be found in the ordinary retail store.

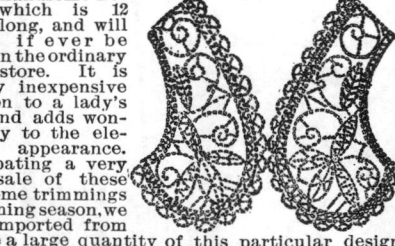

It is a very inexpensive addition to a lady's dress and adds wonderfully to the elegant appearance. Anticipating a very large sale of these handsome trimmings the coming season, we have imported from Europe a large quantity of this particular design, and shall be able to fill all orders promptly, and give better value in this line than can be secured from any other house.
Our special price, per pair.................$1.25

### A $2.50 Bolero at $1.29.

**No. 25010** Fancy Cut Beaded Jet Bolero. This Bolero for trimming dresses from neck to waist is beyond a doubt one of the most stylish and desirable patterns that will be sold. We are fortunate in securing a large bulk of the output of this particular pattern, and it is for this reason that we are able to make the price so exceedingly low. This trimming is made of fine cut beaded jet, a handsome pattern that presents an elegant appearance and adds very greatly to the richness of any dress. It will be all the rage for the coming season, and the pattern which we show in the illustration is one of the most stylish importations from Paris. By our one small profit plan we place our poorest customer upon the same footing as the one with much greater means, and enable him to secure new and stylish fabrics at an exceedingly low price.
Our special price.................$1.29

### A Stylish Black Silk Military Cord Loop Set.

**25014** The Loop Set shown in the accompanying illustration consists of 5 loops of graduated sizes and is used very largely for dresses.

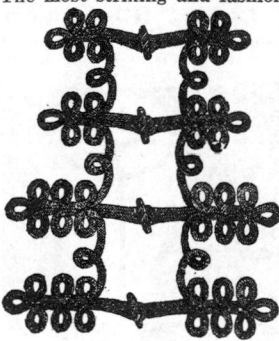

The fashion cut B shown above will give you some idea of the elegant appearance that this loop set presents, and at our low price of 90 cents we enable the customer with limited means to take advantage of the most desirable and fashionable patterns in dress trimmings which the market affords. These can be sent by mail at a very small expense, the postage being only 12 cents.
Our special price.................$0.90

### A $2.75 Loop Set for $1.18.

**25016** Our Special 4 Piece Mohair Loop Set. The most striking and fashionable article of dress trimming which you could possibly secure would be one of these handsome Parisian novelties which we have just secured from France. It is made of very fine mohair after a most desirable and beautiful pattern and is well worth the ordinary retail price of $2.75. It is such an article as you will seldom if ever see in the small retail stores. By our one small profit method we put you on the same footing as your local dealer and furnish you these goods at about what he himself would have to pay.
Our special price per set.................$1.18

### Our $1.75 Loop Set.

**25018** A Most Stylish Four-Piece Silk Military Loop Set. We guarantee that if you order one of these loop sets such as we show in the illustration you will be so well pleased with it that you cannot help recommending us to your friends and neighbors. We look for increased trade by the values which we give old customers, and hence we take pride in showing this handsome military set, and urge the purchase of it, knowing the pleasure it will give you. It is one of the most handsome pieces of dress

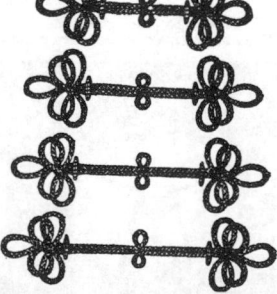

trimming that could be bought, and being made of silk cord with four graduated loops, it is especially rich and durable. We furnish this set at about half the retail price, and we feel sure that it could not be purchased even in the finest retail stores where it would be carried at less than $3.00.
Our special price, per set.................$1.75

## Silk Dress Loop.

**25019** We have very handsome black silk dress loops which are not illustrated, but which are excellent value and on which we guarantee satisfaction. Our special price each .................... **$0.09**

**25020** Black silk dress loops. much better quality, much more handsome than the ones quoted above. Our special price each .................... **$0.16**

**25021** Black silk dress loops, very best quality, finest in our stock. made of very fine silk. the choicest that you would desire. Our special price each .................... **$0.25**

## Bead Garniture.

**25022 A Beautiful Bead Garniture for 47c.** The garniture which we show in illustration is such as you would expect to pay at least $1.00 for. It is a very handsome waist garniture and the style is one of the newest novelties which is on the market, in fact it is a pattern you will very likely not find in any retail store. It is made of fancy flat and round cut beads. The illustration can give you but a slight idea of its beautiful appearance. We recommend this article as one of the most desirable and best purchases which you can possibly make in the line of dress trimmings. Our special price each .................... **$0.47**

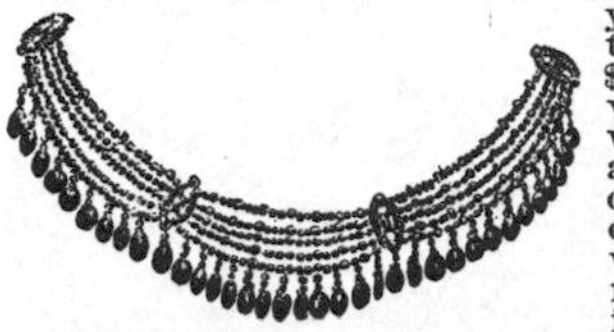

**25023** We have a **very beautiful Black Silk Foregier or Waist Garniture** after a design similar to the Boleros illustrated on page 318. These foregiers are very handsome decorations and will be sold very largely during the coming season. Our special price .................... **$1.18**

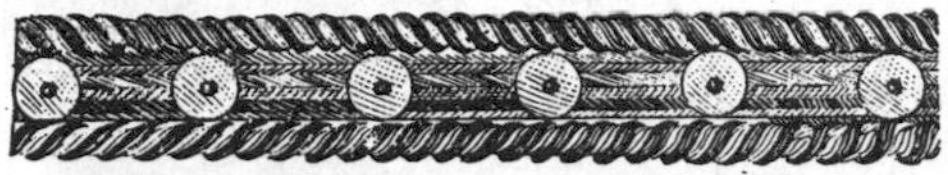

**25024 A Handsome New Novelty Spangle Trimming** like illustration. Cut shows exact size. Comes in red, navy blue, green, brown and black. Regular retail value 40c .................... per yard **19c**

**25026 This is a Pretty Staple Spangle Trimming.** Colors same as above. Value 20c .................... per yard **9c**

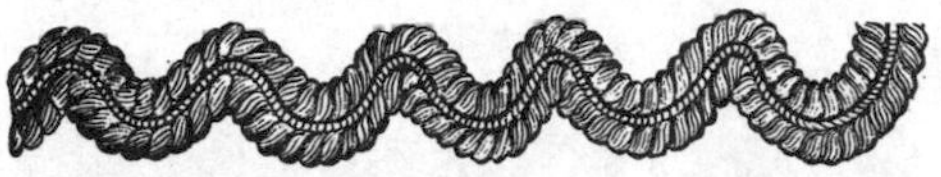

**25028 A Beautiful Silk Gimp.** Exact size and style of illustration. Very stylish and nobby. A regular 18c gimp. Colors, cardinal, navy blue, green, brown, tan and black. Per yard .................... **10c**

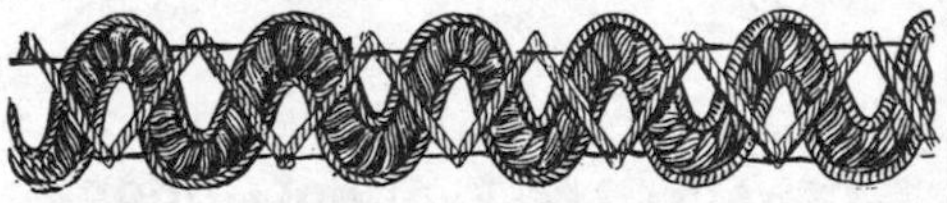

**25030.** The cut shows exact size and pattern of a handsome silk and tinsel mixed gimp. Worth 23c per yard. Colors as above. Per yard .................... **12c**

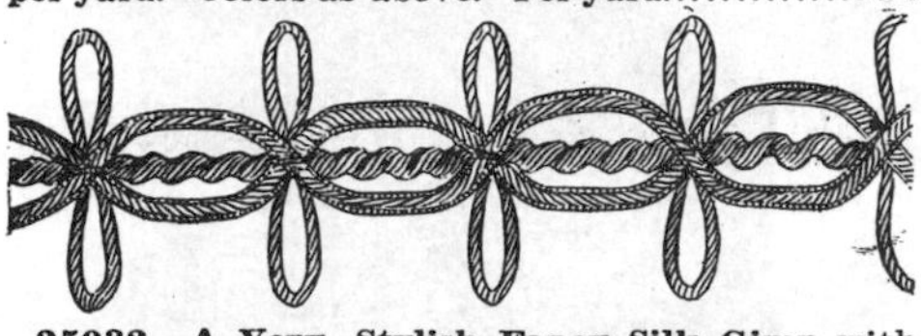

**25032. A Very Stylish Fancy Silk Gimp** with loop edges. The picture shows pattern and size exactly. Comes in staple colors and black. Value 35c per yard. Per yard .................... **18c**

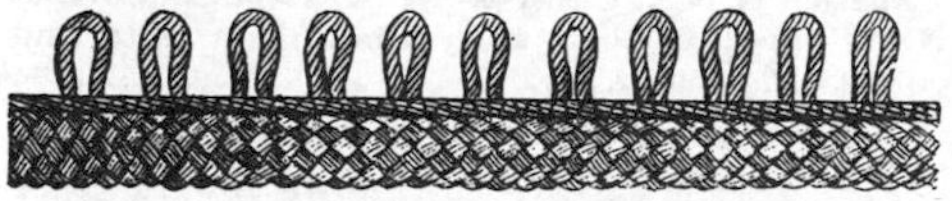

**25034. Novelty Mohair Edging,** Comes in black only, has a handsome loop edge, is very new and popular. The cut shows size and pattern but does not do the edging justice, goods showing up very much nicer. Per yard .................... **15c**

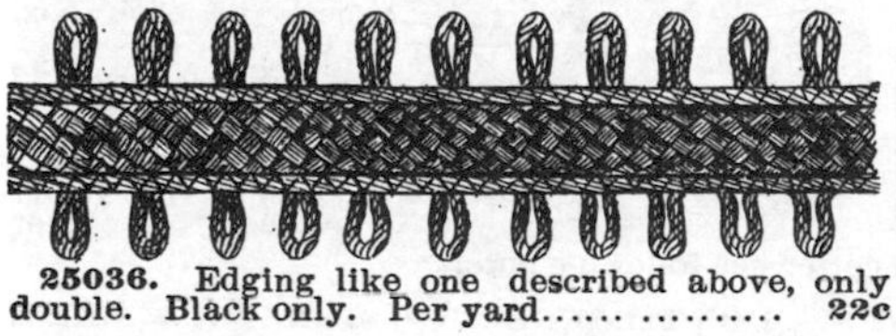

**25036.** Edging like one described above, only double. Black only. Per yard .................... **22c**

## Black Beaded Trimmings.

**The new and stylish creations are here. Big money saved by buying of us.**

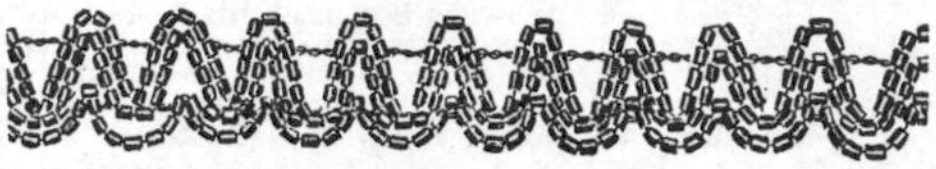

**25038 Beaded Edging,** ½ inch wide. One of the latest ideas. Illustration shows pattern and size. Per yard .................... **7c**

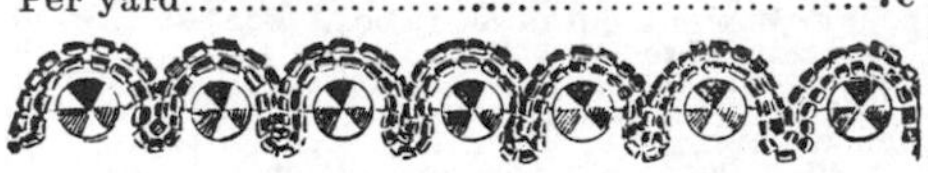

**25040 A handsome new beaded gimp,** ½ inch wide, serpentine pattern (see cut). Per yard ...... **8c**

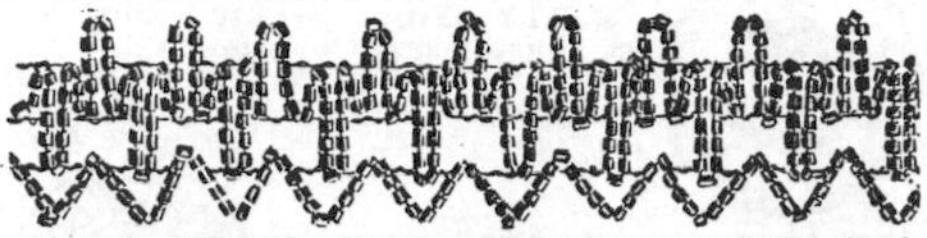

**25042 The illustration shows a pretty ⅜ inch** cut bead edging. The goods look much nicer than the cut. Value, 20c. Per yard .................... **13c**

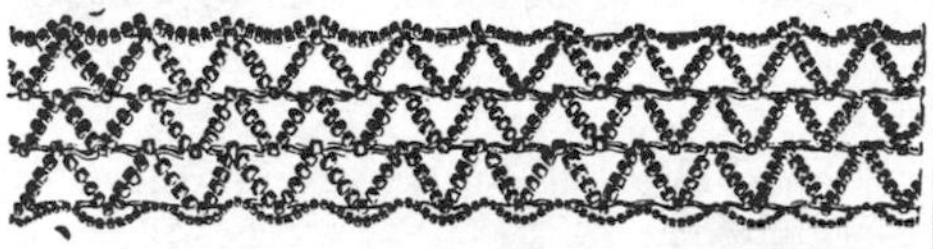

**25044 A fine beaded gimp,** one inch wide, handsome and stylish, in fact a regular 25c trimming. **Our special price,** per yard .................... **14c**

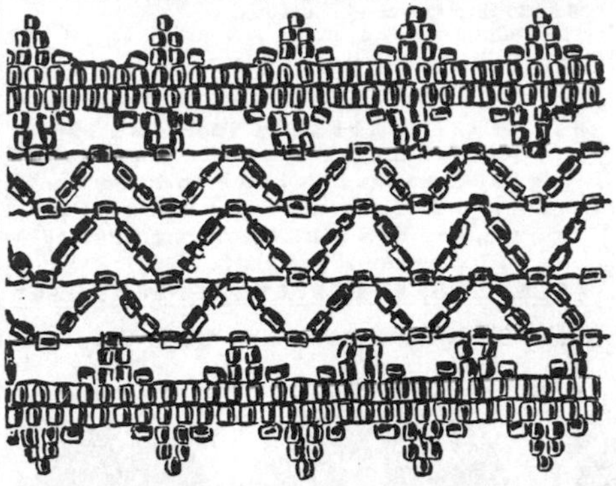

**25046 This stylish gimp** is often retailed as high as 50c. It is 2 inches wide, has a jet band (see illustration). Our price, per yard .................... **23c**

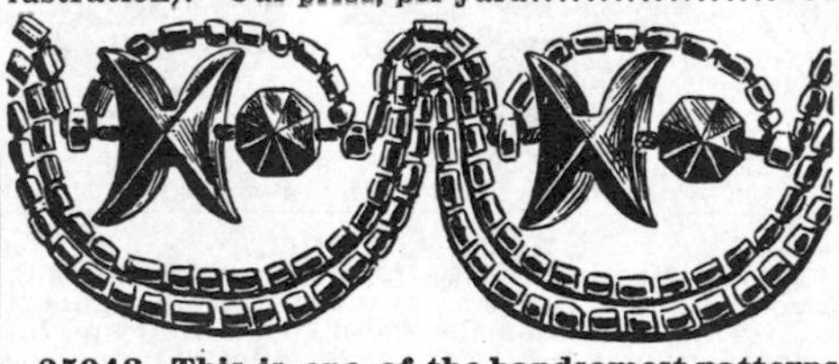

**25048 This is one of the handsomest patterns** we have seen. A ¼ inch fancy jet gimp, made of cut beads. Per yard .................... **25c**

## Soutache and Tubular Braid.

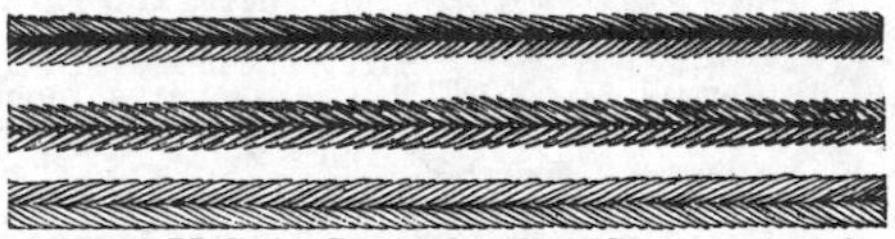

**25054 Mohair Soutache Braid,** for trimming, black and staple colors. Per yard, **1c**; 12 yards, **11c**

**25056 Silk Soutache Braid,** for trimming, black and colors. Per yard, **4c**; 12 yards .................... **43c**

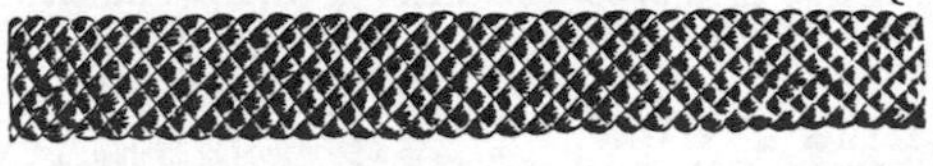

**25058 Silk Tubular Braid,** for dress trimmings. ¼-inch wide, see illustration for size and pattern, Black and colors. Per yard .................... **9c**

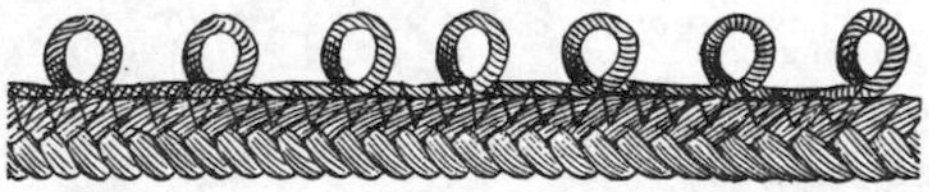

**25060 A very pretty Picot edge trimming braid,** mohair, ⅜-inch wide. Black and colors. Per yard .................... **10c**

## Gold Tinsel Braid.

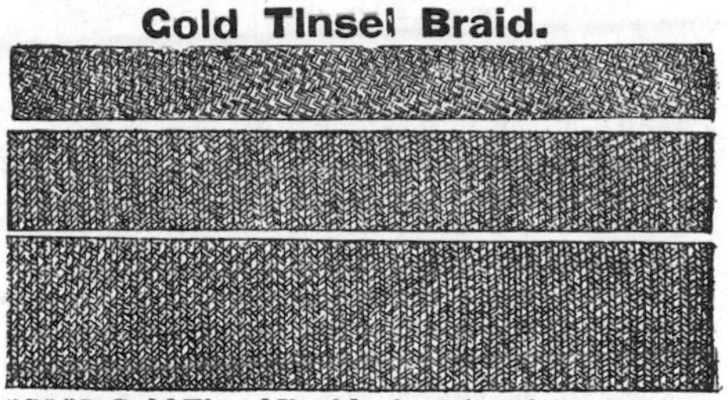

**25062 Gold Tinsel Braids,** for trimming purposes.

| | | | | | |
|---|---|---|---|---|---|
| Line | 2 | 3 | 4 | 5 | 8 |
| Width, inches | 1-16 | ⅛ | ¼ | ⅜ | ½ |
| Per yard | **2c** | **2½c** | **3c** | **4c** | **8c** |

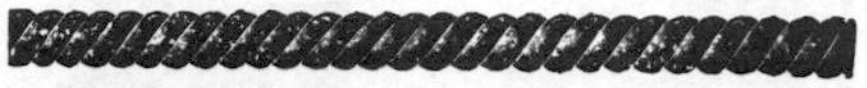

**25064 Lacing Cord Silk,** black and colors. Silk lacing cord in black and all colors. Per yard ...... **2c**
Per dozen .................... **17c**

**25066 Silk Cable Cord,** size of illustration, black and colors. Per yard, **6c**; 12 yards .................... **68c**

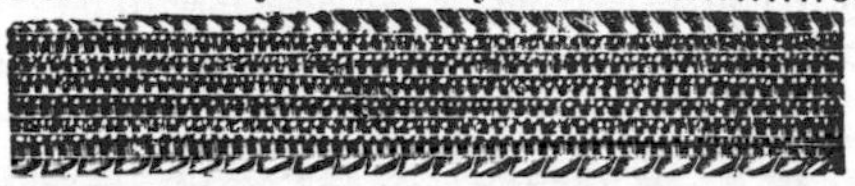

**25068 Black and Silk Gimp, or Trimming Braid.** Fancy cord edge raised, stylish and lasting trimming.

| | | | | | |
|---|---|---|---|---|---|
| Width inches | ¼ | ⅜ | ⅝ | ¾ | 1 |
| Per yard | **4c** | **6c** | **9c** | **10c** | **12c** |
| Per dozen yards | **39c** | **58c** | **90c** | **1.00** | **1.30** |

**25070 Hercules Braids, black and cream only.**

| | | | | | | | |
|---|---|---|---|---|---|---|---|
| Width, inches | ¼ | ½ | ⅝ | ⅞ | 1⅛ | 1¼ | |
| Per yard | **1c** | **1½c** | **2c** | **2½c** | **3c** | **4c** | |
| Per dozen yards | **7c** | **11c** | **19c** | **26c** | **30c** | **38c** | |

## BUTTON DEPARTMENT.

**Button Scale.** Showing size of buttons.

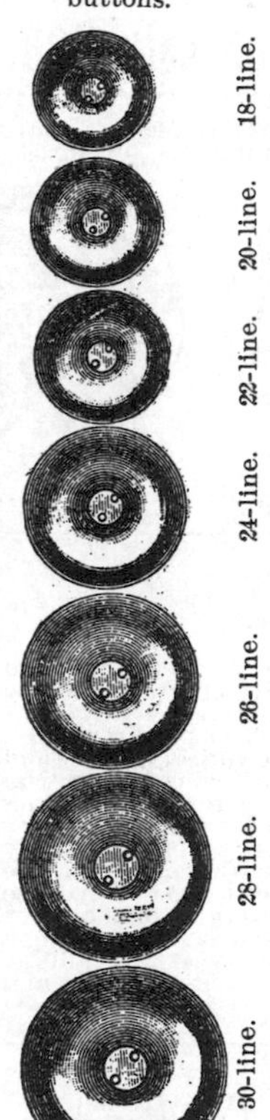


### White Pearl Buttons for Cloaks, Jackets, Dresses, Etc.

**25072.** White Pearl Buttons, 4 holes.

| | | | | | |
|---|---|---|---|---|---|
| Size line | 24 | 36 | 45 | 55 | 60 |
| Per doz | $0.20 | .50 | .75 | .90 | 1.25 |

### Imitation Pearl Buttons.

**25074.** Polished Horn, imitation smoked pearl buttons; flat.

| | | | |
|---|---|---|---|
| Size line | 20 | 22 | 24 |
| Per doz | $0.04 | .04 | .04 |
| Per gross | .45 | .45 | .45 |

**25076.** Polished Horn, imitation white pearl buttons; flat,

| | | | |
|---|---|---|---|
| Size line | 20 | 22 | 24 |
| Per doz | $0.04 | .06 | .06 |
| Per gross | .45 | .60 | .60 |

### Pearl Dress Buttons.

**25078.** White Pearl Dress Buttons; flat; 2 holes.

| | | | | | | |
|---|---|---|---|---|---|---|
| Line | 18 | 22 | 24 | 26 | 28 | 30 |
| PrDoz. | $0.08 | .09 | .10 | .12 | .12 | .12 |
| Gross | .79 | .95 | 1.05 | 1.25 | 1.25 | 1.25 |

**25080.** Smoked Pearl Dress Buttons.

| | | | | | | |
|---|---|---|---|---|---|---|
| Line | 18 | 22 | 24 | 26 | 28 | 30 |
| PrDoz. | $0.05 | .07 | .09 | .11 | .15 | .15 |
| Gross | .50 | .75 | .90 | 1.10 | 1.65 | 1.65 |

**25082.** Superfine Clear White Pearl Buttons; flat; 2 holes; nice quality.

| | | | | | | |
|---|---|---|---|---|---|---|
| Line | 18 | 20 | 22 | 24 | 26 | 28 |
| Prdoz. | $0.10 | .12 | .15 | .16 | .18 | .20 |
| Gross | 1.10 | 1.20 | 1.40 | 1.60 | 1.85 | 2.20 |

**25084.** Super White Full Ball Pearl Button, with holes to sew through. Size line .......... 18
Per doz .................... $0.25
Per gross .................... 2.70

### Bone or Vegetable Ivory Dress Buttons.

**25086.** Full Ball Bone Buttons, self shank; in white, cream, black and colors. Nice for wash goods. Per doz .................... **4c**
Per gross .................... **40c**

**25088.** Plain Vegetable Ivory Buttons; in colors white, rose, drab, slate, tan, light blue, ecru, mode cardinal, red, brown, purple, wine, light brown, navy myrtle and black; 22 line; plain, with self shank and stud back. Per doz .................... **5c**
Per gross .................... **50c**

**25090.** Fancy Oval Vegetable Ivory Buttons; fine finish; assorted color. Per doz .................... **5c**
Per gross .................... **50c**

**25091 Ball Pearl Buttons,** with holes to sew through. (See button scale for sizes.) Size 16 per doz., **15c**; size 14 small, **12½c**; size 8 very small, **12c.**

**POSTAGE MUST ALWAYS BE INCLUDED FOR ORDERS TO GO BY MAIL. IF YOU DO NOT SEND POSTAGE, WE HOLD ORDER UNTIL WE HEAR FROM YOU. IF YOU SEND TOO MUCH, WE RETURN BALANCE.**

## Pant Buttons.

25092  Black Metal Buttons, small or fly size.
Per gross........................................5c
Per great gross................................55c
25094  Black Metal Buttons, suspender size.
Per gross........................................6c
Per great gross................................65c
25096  Black Solid Metal Suspender Buttons.
Per gross.......................................9c
Per great gross................................85c
25098  Brass Fly Buttons, best quality.
Per gross........................................8c
25100  Brass Suspender Buttons, best quality.
Per gross........................................9c
Pant buttons are put up in one gross boxes. We do not sell less than one box.

## Button and Drawers Supporter.

25102  Chapman's Button and Drawer Supporter. Can replace a button at a moment's notice; nicely nickel plated, convenient and substantial.
Each.............................................4c
Per dozen.......................................40c

**BUY YOUR SHOES AND** Small notions at one time, have them all shipped together and save expenses.

See our Shoe Dep't on page 180.

## Hand Snap Buttons.

By the use of these buttons the traveling man, the farmer, the laborer, the mechanic, the growing boy and his father, of any profession, can instantly replace his missing buttons.
25104  Black, Gold or Silvered Metal Snap Fly Buttons, one dozen in box. Per box.....$0.05
Per dozen boxes...............................50
Per gross boxes...............................5.75
25106  Black, Gold or Silvered Metal Snap Suspender Buttons, one dozen in box. Per box..$0.06
Per dozen boxes...............................65
Per gross boxes...............................7.25
25108  Bone collar buttons. Per dozen.....03
Per gross........................................30
25110  Pearl collar buttons. Each...........04
Per dozen........................................40

## Agate Buttons.

25112  White Agate Buttons, (see button scale for size).

| Size | 16 | 20 | 24 | 28 | 30 |
|---|---|---|---|---|---|
| Per gross | 3c | 7c | 8c | 9c | 10c |
| 12 gross | 23c | 70c | 80c | 90c | $1 00 |

25114  Fancy Pearl Agate Buttons, White.

| Size | 16 | 20 | 24 | 28 |
|---|---|---|---|---|
| Per gross | 7c | 12c | 14c | 19c |

25116  Pearl Shirt Buttons.
Per doz. 7c; gross................................80c
25136  Silk Covered Buttons.
Vest size, per doz..............................8c
Coat size, per doz.............................12½c
Over Coat size...................................17c

Our Reading Tailor-Made Pants on page 164 are the best in the world for the money. We guarantee the buttons to stay on, and if a pair rips through defect we will give you a new pair.

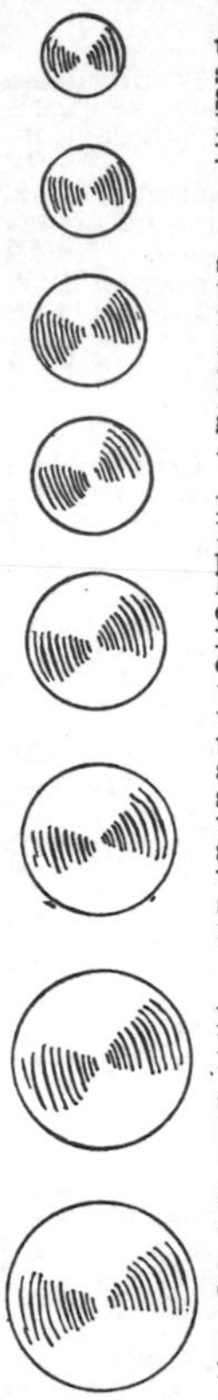

## 25138 Flat Gold or Silver Buttons.

25138  Flat Gold or Silver Buttons. Gilt or Silver Buttons with shank. (See cut for exact sizes.)

| Sizes.. | 10 | 12 | 14 | 16 | 18 | | 20 | 22 | 24 |
|---|---|---|---|---|---|---|---|---|---|
| Per doz | 5c | 6c | 6c | 7c | 8c | | 10c | 12c | 15c |
| 12 doz.. | 55c | 65c | 65c | 75c | 90c | $1.00 | $1.30 | $1.65 |

## Fancy Dress Buttons.

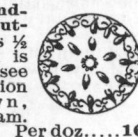

25140  A very Handsome Fancy Dress Button, has a shank, is ½ inch in diameter, rim is gilt of fancy design (see cut) centre of imitation pearl, colors, brown, green, drab and cream.
A regular 35c button. Per doz.....16c

25142  A Larger Button, pattern just like above description 1¼ inches in diameter, these buttons can be used when a large and small button of the same pattern are desired. A big bargain at the price we mention. Regular value 85c.
Per doz.............................47c
25144  A Fancy Jet Button, with a shank ½ in. in diameter Black only. A button that is always sold at 15c per dozen. 
Per doz.....10c; 3 doz. for.....25c

25146  The same as button described above. Size 1¼ inches in diameter. Good value at 40c.
Per doz.............................25c
25148  A larger button than the above, but of the same pattern. Size 1⅝ inches in diameter. A regular 75c button.
Per doz.............................40c

---

| Anchor Brass Button. Vest Size. | G. A. R. Oval Top Republic Button. Coat Size. | Officer's Plated Buttons. | Brass | Black Horn Over Coat Button. | Black Horn Coat Button. | Black Horn Vest Buttons. | Black Mohair covered Buttons. |
|---|---|---|---|---|---|---|---|

| **25120.** doz. | **25122.** doz. | **25124.** | **25126.** | | **25128.** | **25130.** | **25132.** | **25135.** |
|---|---|---|---|---|---|---|---|---|
| Vest..... 8c | Vest..........13c | Vest, per doz.......13c | | | | | Over Coat Size, per doz...... 10c | |
| Coat......10c | Cont..........19c | Coat, per doz.......19c | Per doz......15c | Per doz......5c | Per doz....4c | | Coat size, per doz.....5c | |
| Over Coat 12c | Over Coat.....21c | | | | | | Vest size per doz.....3c | |

---

## NOTIONS.

### Small Wares.

**Little necessities,** things that everybody needs and everybody must have. They seemingly amount to but little, but people buy them every day. Now it is a paper of pins, again it is a spool of thread, or a paper of collar buttons, or a dozen dress buttons, and so on down the list. You pay a few cents more on each article in buying from the retail merchants and these few cents thrown away daily in a year's time amount to a great deal—perhaps enough to buy a new dress, an overcoat or a sewing machine. **Do you want to throw your money away?** Of course not. Look through our list, carefully compare our prices, and notice the amount you save by buying a little quantity at a time. Below we give you a little illustration of the difference between our prices and retail merchants' prices.

| | Retailers price. | Sears, Roebuck & Co.'s price. | Saving. |
|---|---|---|---|
| Clark's O. N. T. Spool Cotton, per spool.................... | $0.04 | $0.03 | $0.01 |
| Hooks and eyes, per card........ | .03 | .01 | .02 |
| Pins, per paper................... | .03 | .01 | .02 |
| Sewing silk, Corticelli, 100 yards per spool.................... | .08 | .06½ | .01½ |
| | .18 | .11½ | .06½ |

It is seen by the above that 6½ cents is saved on a 18 cent purchase, or 33 cents on a purchase of $1.00, $3.30 saved on $10.00 worth. Do you use $10.00 worth of small wares a year?
**NOTE**—$3.30 buys two pairs of very good shoes.

## Spool Cotton.

25150  Basting Cotton, (200 yards on each spool), a very superior cotton; the retail merchant gets 24 to 36 cents per dozen for these goods. Our special price, per dozen, 17c; 3 dozen for 49c; 12 dozen for..............................$1.90
25152  J. O. King's Machine Spool Thread, nice and smooth, will run on any machine, full length, 200 yards on each spool, made from the best of selected cotton yarns, black and white, all numbers, colors in No. 50 only. Retail merchants ask 5 cents per spool for thread that in many cases is not as good. Our price per spool, 2c; per dozen, 19½c; 12 dozen for..........................$2.25
Note the saving in buying one or more dozens.
25154  500 yard sewing thread. Per spool, 4c; 12 spools........................................43c
A 500 yard spool contains 2½ times as much as an ordinary spool.

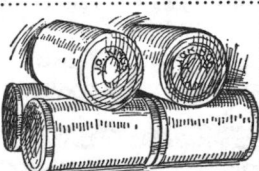

25156  J. O. King's Giant Thread, 100 yard spools, stronger than linen, smoother than silk, for all kinds of heavy sewing. Nothing better for sewing carpets, buttons, etc., made. Black, white and staple colors.
Per spool.....5c
Per dozen.....48c

## Clark's O. N. T. Spool Cotton.

25158  Geo. A. Clark & Bros.' Best Six Cord O. N. T. Spool Cotton, 200 yards, black white and colors. Per spool.........................03c

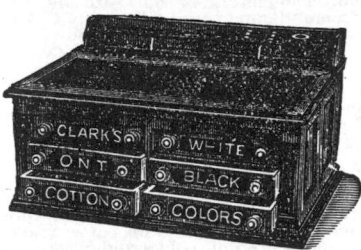

Staples as well as novelties away down low in price here.
25159  J. O. King's Best Crochet Cotton. 200 yard balls, white and colors. 10 balls to each box.
Per ball.........03½c
Per box.........33c

**Merchants** ask 5c for cotton no better than this.

For colors and numbers for cochet cotton see following note.

---

**USE CARE IN MAKING OUT YOUR ORDER. STYLES, COLORS, ETC., MUST ALWAYS BE GIVEN. DON'T FORGET TO SIGN YOUR NAME TO YOUR ORDER.**

**25160 Clark's O. N. T. Crochet Cotton.** 200 yard balls, white and colors. 10 balls to each box. Per ball, 4c; per box........40c

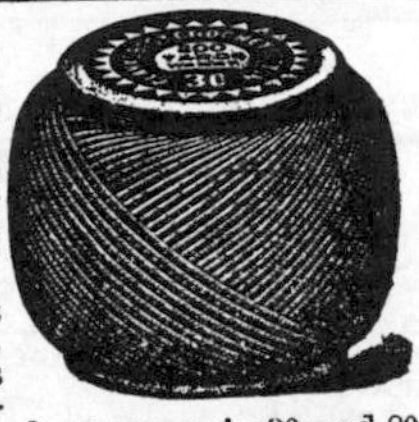

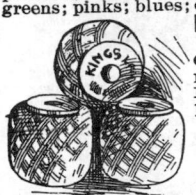

For colors and numbers of crochet cotton see following note.

**Colors and Numbers that Crochet Cotton comes in.** White Crochet Cotton comes in 25, 30, 40, 50, 60, 70, 80; Colored Crochet Cotton in solid colors comes in 30 and 80 only and in the following colors. Cream ecru, pink, salmon, mahogany, moss green, navy, fast red, fast black, blues, yellow, orange, heliotrope, nile green, lilac, olive green, lavender, peacock, old gold, rose and old rose. Colors that Shaded Crochet Cotton comes in, numbers 30 and 50 only. White and blues; white and pinks; white and yellows, white and lilacs; white and nile green; white and moss green; white, blue and pink; white, yellow and pink; white, green and pink; white, blue and yellow; white and cream; white and salmon; white and ecrus; shaded yellows; shaded creams: red, white and blue; olive green; peacock; lilacs; old golds; old rose; heliotropes; moss greens; pinks; blues; ecru.

## Embroidery Cotton.

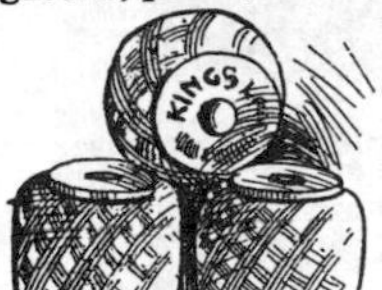

**25162 King's Embroidery Cotton** on spools. fast turkey red. Numbers, 8, 10, 12, 14, 16, 18, 20, 22, 24. Per spool, 1½c; per dozen, 17c; per gross, $1.75

## Darning Cotton.

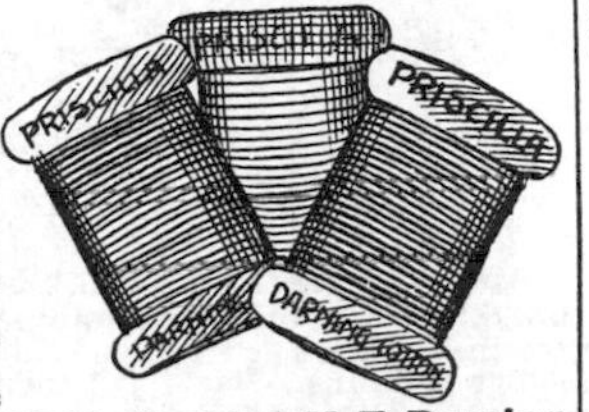

**25164 Priscilla Darning Cotton,** 30 yards on each card. In all staple plain colors, and brown and white, red and white, black and white and mixed blue and white. Per doz., 6c; per gross.....60c

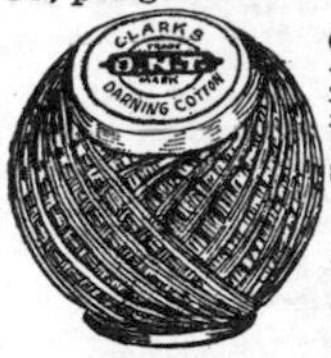

**25166 Clark's O. N. T. Darning Cotton.** Diagonally wound 45 yards on each spool. The black is fast and will stand washing and boiling. Also come in all the staple colors. Per box of 12 spools. ........19c

**25168 Dorcas Darning Worsted.** Black, white and plain colors. Per card, 2c; per doz., 20c

## Knitting Cotton.

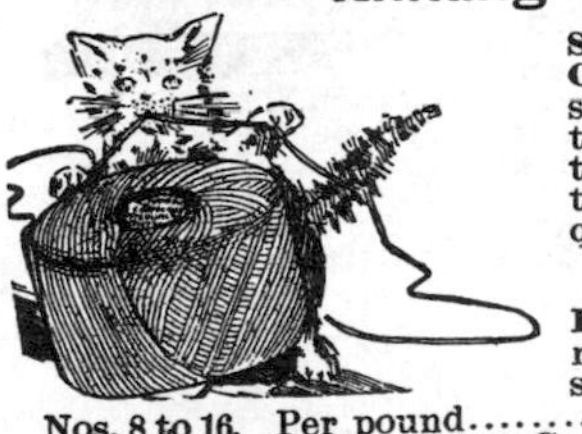

**25170 White Sterling Knitting Cotton,** full weight, superfine, four (4) thread, put up 8 balls to pound, 2 pounds to box. Order any quantity. Nos. 6 to 24. Ball, 5c.; lb... 35c

**25172 Sterling Knitting Cotton,** navy blue, same description as above Nos. 8 to 16, Per pound........$0.40

**25174 Sterling Knitting Cotton,** blue and white mixed, Nos. 8 to 16. Per pound........$0.40

**25175 Egg Darners,** with handle, dark finish. Each........$0.04 Per doz........0.35

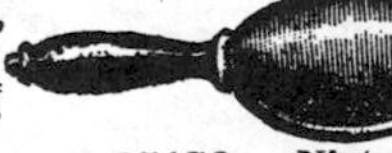

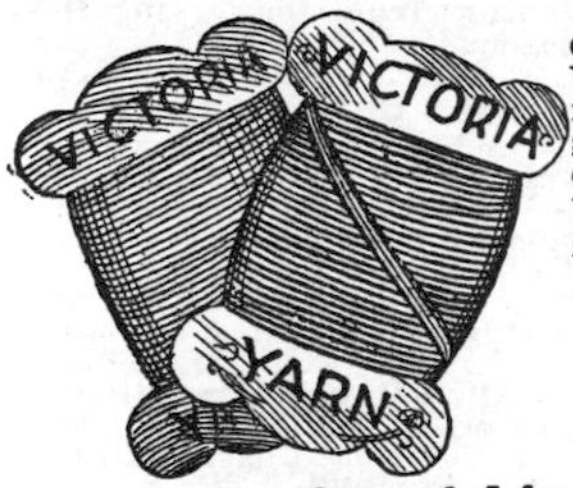

**25176 Nictoria Cashmere Mending Yarn, manufactured from the very finest grade of wool.** A crowning success in the yarn maker's art; black and navy, brown, gray, tan and white.
Per card.....$0.03
Four for.......10
Per doz.......29

## Spool Linen.

**25178 Marshall's Linen Thread.** (100 yd. spools. black only.) Coarse and fine numbers. Per spool, 3c.; 6 spools, 17c.; 12 spools........$0.32

**25180 Barbour's (200-yd. spools) Best Linen Thread.** Numbers run from No. 25 (coarse) to No. 100 (fine), black, white, drab, and whitish brown. Per spool........$0.07

**25182 Carpet Thread,** black, brown, green, red, drab, slates, whitey brown. Per lb. (40 skeins) 70c.; ¼ lb. (10 skein)........$0.18

## Sewing Silk and Twist.

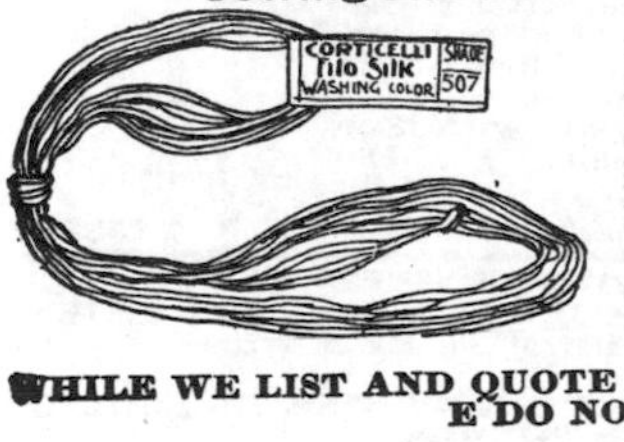

Corticelli silk is warranted full size and full length. Black spool silks are marked OO, O, A, B, C and D, No. OO being the finest. Colored spool silks come in letter A only.

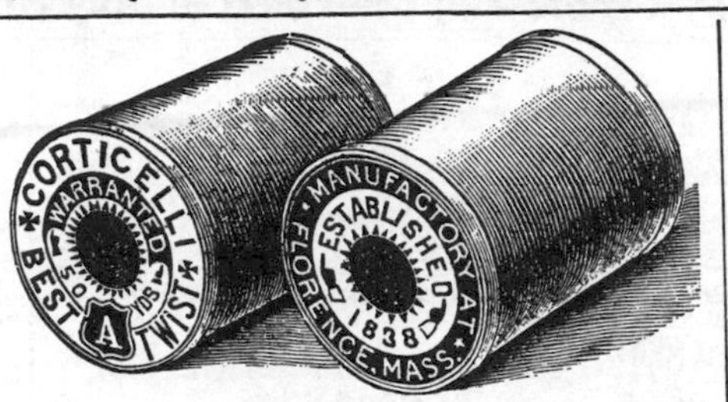

## Corticelli Sewing Silk.

**Less than dozens will not be filled at dozen prices.**

**25184 Corticelli Sewing Silk,** 50 yard spools, black, white and all colors. Per spool........$0.03

**25186 Corticelli Sewing Silk,** 100 yard spools, black, white and all colors. Per spool........$0.05½

**25190 Corticelli Button Hole Twist,** 10 yard spools, black, white and all colors. Spool....$0.01½

## Corticelli Embroidery Silk on Spools.

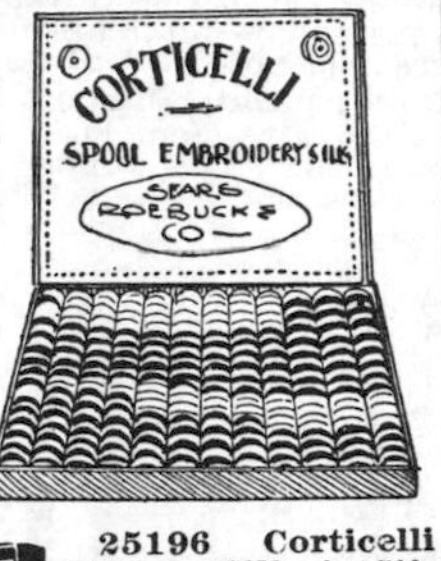

**25193 Corticelli Embroidery Silk** on spools, 3 yards, size EE, all colors.
Per spool........$0.01
Per doz........ .08
Per 100........ .70

**25194 Skein Embroidery Silk.** 18 skeins of assorted colors to each bunch.
Per bunch........$0.08
Three for........ .21
Per doz........ .80

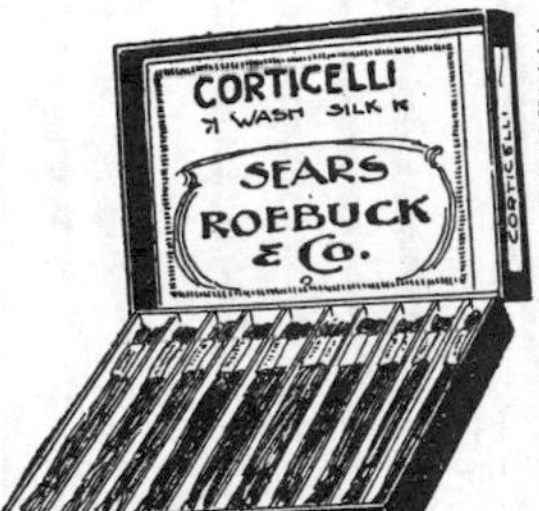

**25196 Corticelli Etching Silk,** size 500, positively a fast dye silk, medinm size for outlining work and etching, 10 yards to the skein.
Per skein....$0.03
12 skeins for. .35

**25198 Corticelli Twisted Embroidery Silk.** Size EE. This size is the regular wash embroidery silk; fast color, pure dye, 10 yds. in skein.
Per skein....$0.03
12 skeins for. .35

**25200 Corticelli Rope Embroidery Silk,** washing colors. A course silk, for bold designs either in outline or solid embroidery on heavy material, when rapid work is desired. Per skein, 3c.; 12 for...$0.35

**25202 Corticelli Filo Floss.** This is a fine size, slack twist wash silk and is used for embroidery purposes of all kinds, but is especially desirable for embroidering on stamped linens, comes in black, white and all colors. Per skein, 3c.; doz........$0.35

**25204 Corticelli Waste Embroidery Silk,** assorted colors, odds and ends. Just the thing for fancy work. One oz. in pkg. Per pkg........$0.37

## Corticelli and Florence Knitting and Crochet Silks.

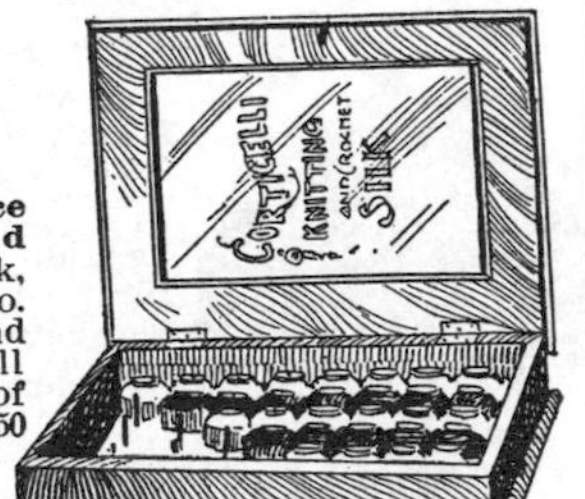

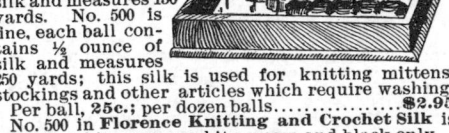

**25206 Florence Knitting and Crochet Silks,** black, white and colors. No. 300 is used most and is coarse; each ball contains ½ ounce of silk and measures 150 yards. No. 500 is fine, each ball contains ½ ounce of silk and measures 250 yards; this silk is used for knitting mittens, stockings and other articles which require washing. Per ball, 25c.; per dozen balls........$2.95

No. 500 in **Florence Knitting and Crochet Silk** is made in white, cream white cream and black only.

**25208 Corticelli Knitting and Crochet Silk,** for embroidering, knitting and crocheting, made in size 300 only, comes in black, cream and white. Per ball, 35c.; 12 balls for........$4.15

Quantity of silk on Corticelli spools same as Florence.

## Interesting to all Needle Workers.

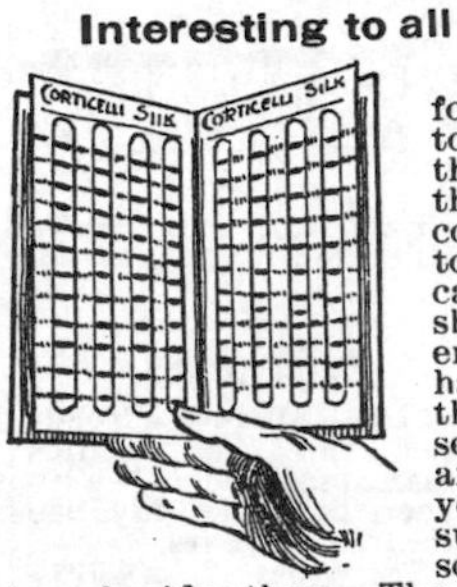

**25210** It is very difficult for people using wash silk to order the exact shade they want by mail unless they send a sample. To overcome this we have arranged to have a number of color cards made showing over 200 shades of Corticelli wash embroidery silks, (each shade has a number) by selecting the shade you want and sending us the number, you are sure to get just what you want. We have also issued "a flower book" describing 70 flowers and how to embroider them. The two books for........$0.05

## Ladies' Dress Shields.

**25212 Stockinet Dress Shields.** Good shields for little money.

| Size, | 1. Small. | 2. Medium. | 3. Large. |
|---|---|---|---|
| Per pair, | $0.05 | .06 | .07 |
| Per dozen, | .55 | .65 | .75 |

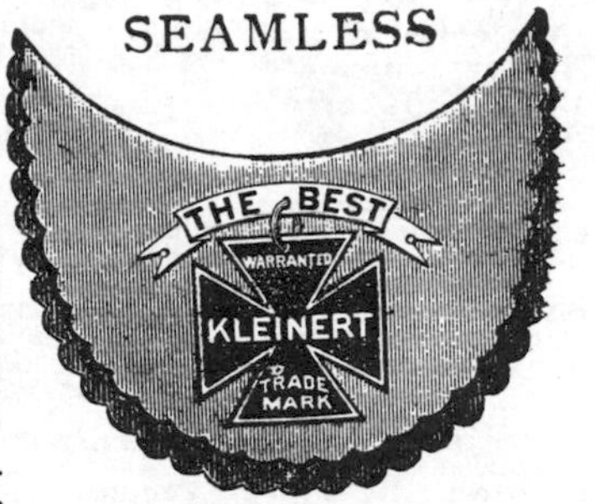


**25214 Kleinert's Seamless Stockinet Dress Shields. Every pair warranted.** Kleinert pays for the dress if it is ruined by perspiration while his shields are used in it, and Kleinert is responsible for what he says.
Size 2, medium, per pair, 14c; per dozen....$1.45
Size 3, large, per pair, 15c; per dozen........$1.70

**25216 Pure Gum Dress Shield.** A good cheap shield.
Size 2, medium, per pair, 10c; per dozen......$1.10
Size 3, large, per pair, 12c; per dozen........1.15

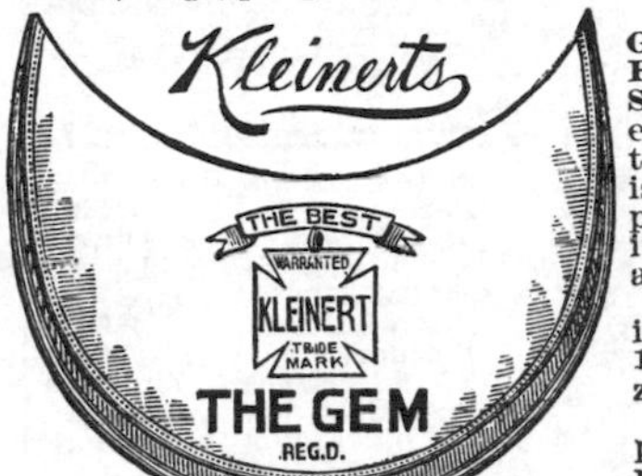


**25218 The Gem Pure Rubber Dress Shield.** Kleinert pays for the dress if it is ruined by perspiration, if his shields are used in it.
Size 2, medium, per pair, 14c; per dozen.....$1.45
Size 3, large, per pair, 15c; per dozen......$1.70

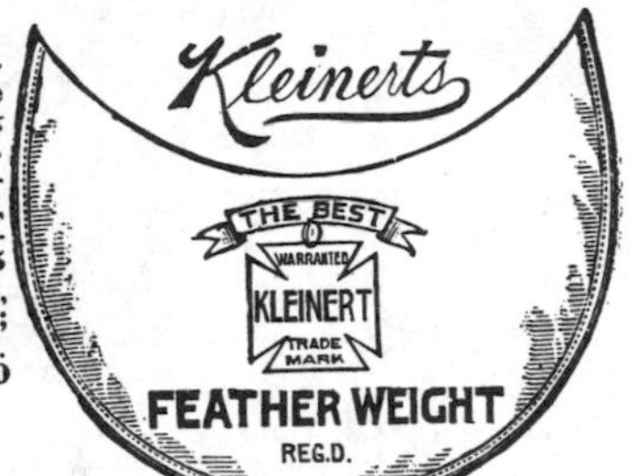


**25220 Feather-weight Fine Nainsook Dress Shields.**
Size 2, medium, per pair, 13c; per dozen.....$1.35
Size 3, large, per pair, 14c; per dozen.......$1.60

## Shoe Laces.

| | | Per Doz. | 12 Doz. |
|---|---|---|---|
| 25222 | Round Shoe Laces, short, | $0 03 | $0 30 |
| 25224 | Round Shoe Laces, medium, | 04 | 37 |
| 25226 | Round Shoe Laces, long, | 05 | 42 |
| 25228 | Flat Shoe Laces, short, | 05 | 58 |
| 25230 | Flat Shoe Laces, medium, | 06 | 70 |
| 25232 | Flat Shoe Laces, long, | 07 | 80 |

**25234 Real Porpoise Leather Shoe Laces,** twist wire ends, per pair, 5c; per dozen........$0.42

## Corset Laces.

**25236 Round Cotton Corset Laces, short,** per dozen........$0.06

**25238 Round Cotton Corset Laces, medium,** per dozen........$0.08

**25240 Round Cotton Corset Laces, long,** per dozen........$0.09

**25242 White Cotton Elastic Corset Laces,** length 2½ yards, 12 for........$0.28

## Key Chains.

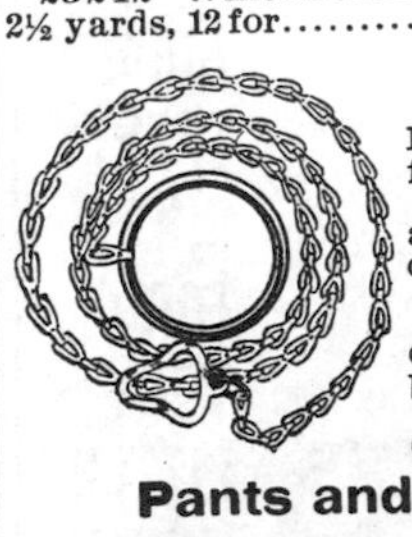

**25244 Key Chain with Key Ring and Loop End.** 3 for 11c; per dozen....$0.40

**25246 Steel Key Chain,** as described above, better quality. Each 7c; per dozen...$0.75

**25248 Aluminum Key Chain,** light, strong and durblea, each........12½c

**25250 German Silver Key Chains,** each........12½c

## Pants and Vest Buckles.

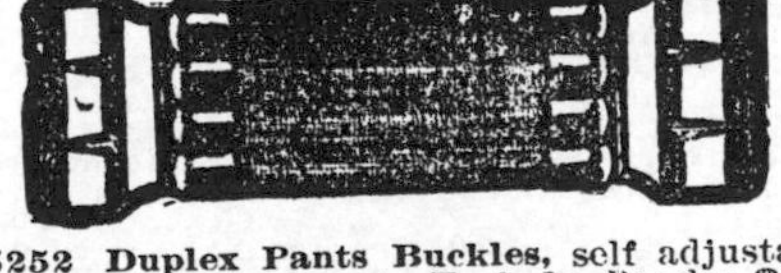

**25252 Duplex Pants Buckles,** self adjustable, 4 strand for vests and pants. Each, 7c. Per doz. $0.70

**25254 Duplex Pants Buckles,** 6 springs. Each, 8c. Per doz........$0.80

**25255 Black or White Pants Buckles.** Per doz........0.14

**WHILE WE LIST AND QUOTE AT WHOLESALE PRICES, A COMPLETE LINE OE NOTIONS AND SUCH VERY NECESSARY LITTLE ARTICLES, E DO NOT ADVICE ORDERING THEM ALONE. ANTICIPATE YOUR WANTS IN GROCERIES, ETC., AND MAKE UP A FREIGHT ORDER, IF POSSIBLE.**

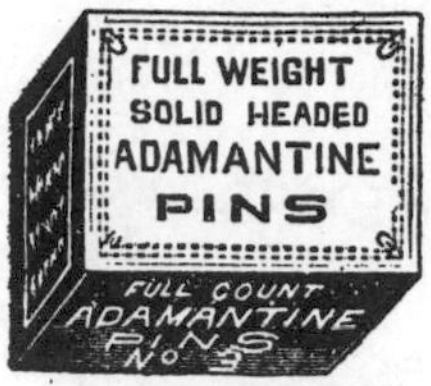


## Pins.

**25256 Pins** are put up, one dozen papers to the package. Adamantine pins per package.
2 large, 3 medium, 4 small.
**$0.16 $0.14 $0.12**

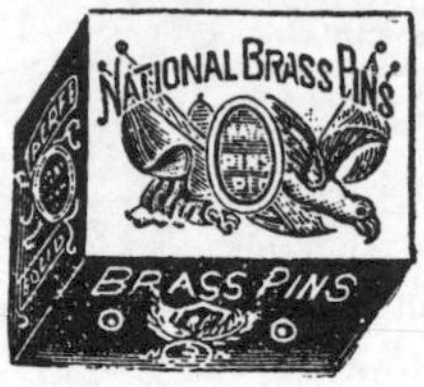


## Brass Pins.

**25258 Brass Pins,** 360 pins to each paper.
2 large, 3 medium, 4 small.
**$0.30 $0.28 $0.25**
Single papers of brass pins **3c.** or **4 for 10c.**

## Book Pins.

**25260 Toilet Pin Book,** contains 150 solid head black pins, assorted sizes.
Per paper........**$0.02** Per doz............ 0.22

## A Special Bargin in Pin Books

**25262 Book Pins,** 9 rows of 26 pins each, 234 pins, one row of black; all ne plus ultra high grade brass pins. Three sizes in book.
Per book.....**$0.04**
Per doz. 0.40

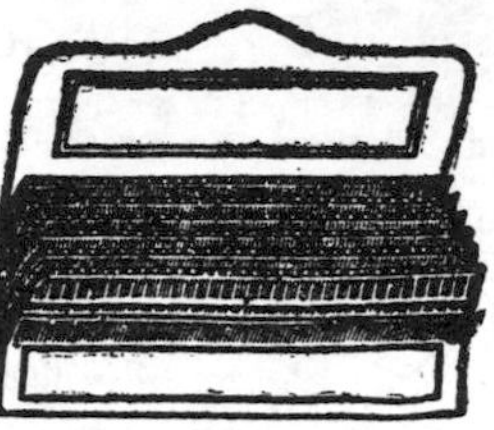

**25264 Black Pins.**
Per box of 50.........**$0.03**
**25265 Jet Black Mourning Pins,** solid heads, assorted sizes. 200 in box.
Per box..............**$0.03**
Per doz 0.32
**25266 Fancy Chromo Pins.** Card contains 25 jet head black pins and 25 small fancy head black pins.
Per card.............**$0.04**
Per doz 0.32
Per gross 3.65

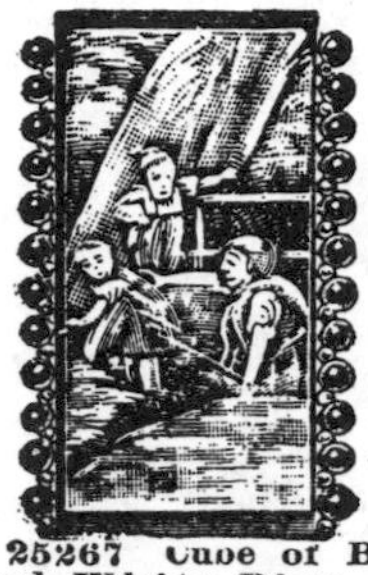

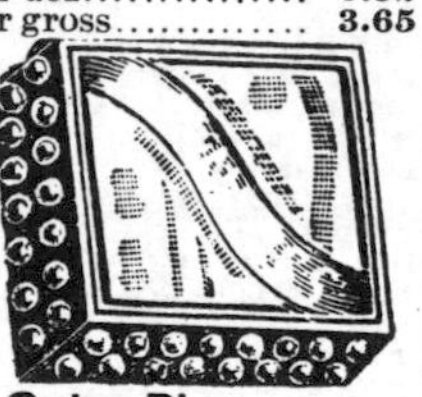

**25267 Cube of Black and White Pins,** with black, white and assorted fancy heads. Each **$0.04**
Per doz............ 0.45
Per gross.......... 4.75

## Cube Pins.

**25268 Cube Pins Assorted Colors.** Is a cube containing 200 pins; black, white and fancy colored heads.
Each.......................**$0.09**
Per doz. ... ............ 0.90

## Black Pins Good Quality.

**25270 Black Pins,** Brass box of black pins, with bright jet heads; **why pay the retailer 100 per cent profit on these little things?** Each. **$0.03**
Per doz ........0.30

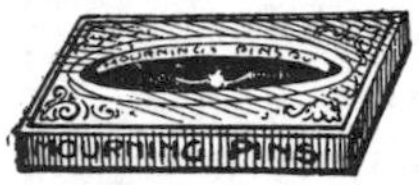

**25271 Box of Jet Black Mourning Pins,** about 50 pins in each box. The usual retail price of these goods is **5c.** per box.
Each, **2c.** Per doz. **$0.22**

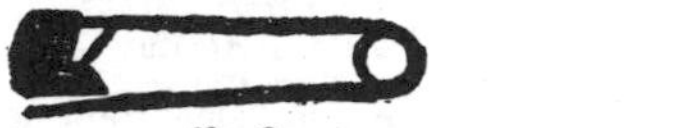

No. 2

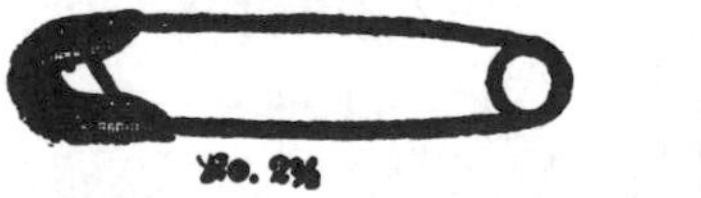

No. 2½

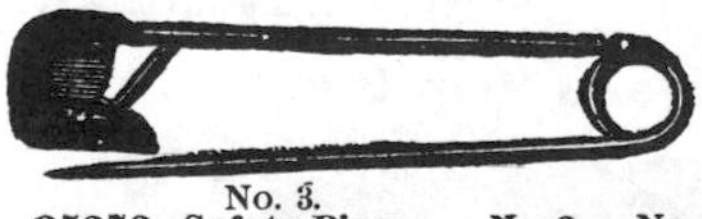

No. 3.

**GOOD SAFETY PINS FOR VERY LITTLE MONEY.**

| **25272 Safety Pins.** | No. 2 | No. 2½ | No. 3 |
|---|---|---|---|
| Per doz | **$0.02** | **$0.02½** | **$0.03** |
| 12 doz | 0.22 | 0.28 | 0.31 |

**25273 Large Safety Blanket Pins.** 4 inches, long the most substantial and practical pin made.
Each ........................................................ **$0.03**
6 for.............. 0.16 Per doz...................... 0.30
**25274 Hat and Shawl Pins.** Hat pins, with black heads, 5 or 6 inches long.
Per doz...........**$0.03** 12 dozen for............ 0.25
**25275 Hat Pins,** white heads, 5 inches long.
Per doz...........**$0.05** 12 dozen for........... 0.50
**25276 Shawl or Belt Pins,** large black heads.
Per doz...........**$0.03** Per gross............... 0.24

## Hair Pins.

**25278 Hair Pins, Straight or Crimped,** 8 papers to roll; here is where 5 cent values are given for less than half.
Per roll..**$0.02**
10 rolls for **0.11**

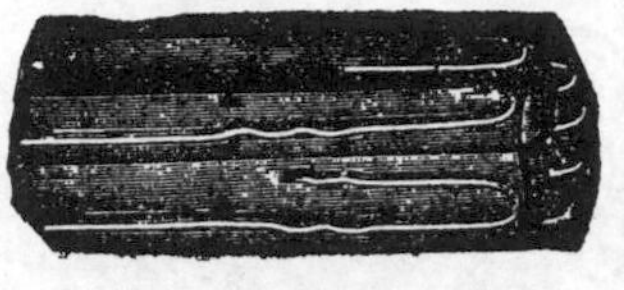

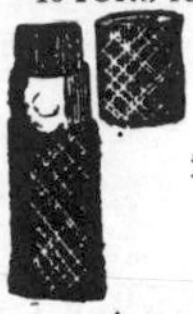

## Invisible Hair Pins Made of Good Wire.

**25279 Invisible Hair Pins,** about 50 in each box.
Per box ................................**$0.02**
12 boxes for.......................... 0.19

## Hair Pin Cabinets, A handy way to buy Hair Pins.

**25280 Hair Pins in Wood Boxes,** assorted sizes, handy and useful to have around; you get all the sizes in one box. Per box, 4c. Per doz.......**$0.35**
**25281 Hair Pins in Cabinets,** made of good quality wire, four sizes, crimped or straight. 100 pins in box. This number retails for 10c. In most retail stores. Per box **$0.05** Per doz........ 0.53

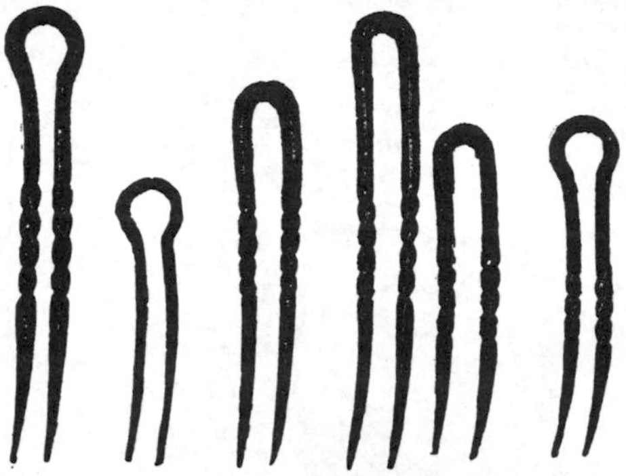

## Rubber Hair Pins.

25282 Rubber Hair Pins polished, 3½ inches long.
Each..............**$0.03** Per doz..........**$0.25**
25283 Rubber Hair Pins polished, 4¼ inches long.
Each..............**$0.03** Per doz..........**$0.30**
25284 Rubber Hair Pins polished, 5 inches long.
Each..............**$0.04** Per doz..........**$0.39**
25285 Fancy Rubber Hair Pins, 3¼ inches long.
Each..............**$0.02** Per doz..........**$0.20**
25286 Fancy Rubber Hair Pins, 4½ inches long.
Each..............**$0.04** Per doz..........**$0.37**
25287 Fancy Rubber Hair Pins, 5¼ inches long.
Each..............**$0.04** Per doz..........**$0.39**
25288 Rubber Hair Pins, (1 doz. pins in each box), straight or crimped.
Per box..............................**$$.08**
Per doz.............................. 0.85

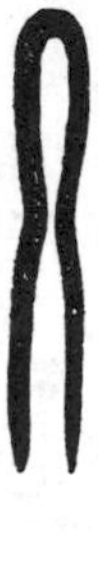

## Thimbles.

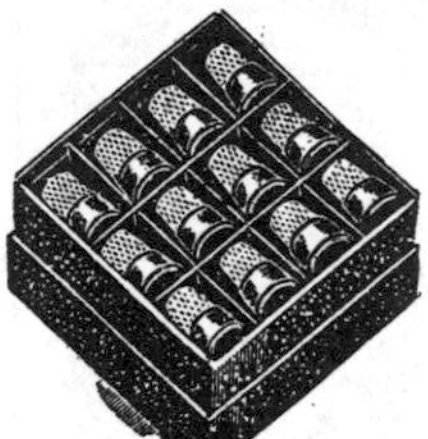

**25289 Aluminum Thimbles,** all sizes.
Each.........**$0.01**
Per doz....... 0.11
Per gross..... 1.30
**25290 German Silver Thimbles,** closed top.
Each.........**$0.03**
Per doz...... 0.25

## Hair Crimpers.

**25292 Common Sense Hair Crimpers,** made of lead with woven covers. 2 inch. 3 inch.
Per package...............**$0.03** **$0.04**
Per doz.................. 0.28 0.37
**25293 Duplex Hair Crimpers,** nickel plated.
Per doz...........**$0.05** 12 doz for..........**$0.50**

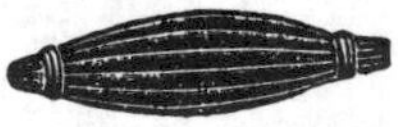

**25286 Kid Hair Crimpers,** 12 in package.
Length inches, 3¼ 4 4½
Per package...**3c. 5c. 7c.**

## Tape Measures.

**25294 Tape Measure,** printed on both sides, double stitched (60 inches long), fine heavy cloth. **This grade of Tape Lines is suitable for Tailors or Dressmakers' use.**

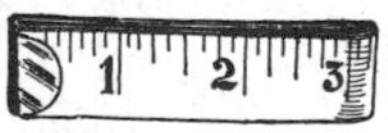


Each ............**$0.04**
Per doz.......... 0.40

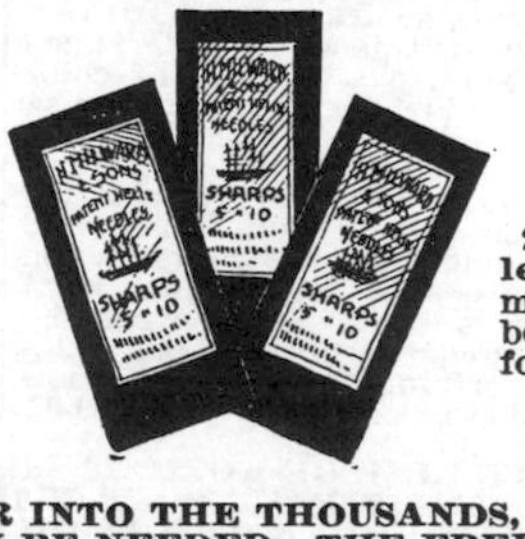

## Needles.

**25296 Millard's Needles,** the best needles manufactured. Have been in every day use for over 70 years.
Per paper......**$0.04**
3 papers for.... 0.11
12 papers for.... 0.44

**25297 Steel Crochet Needles,** all sizes, coarse or fine.
3 for.....................**$0.04**
12 for..................... 0.16
**25298 Steel Knitting Needles,** coarse or fine.
5 needles for..............**$0.04**
**25299 Darning Needles,** each paper contains 25 needles, coarse or fine.
Per paper..................**$0.04**
3 papers.................... 0.10
Per doz..................... 0.39

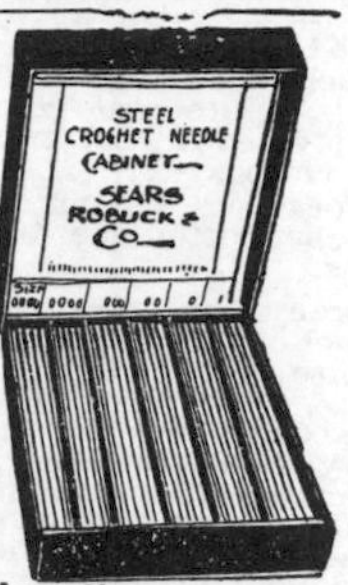


## Sewing Machine Needles.

**25300 Sewing Machine Needles,** for any machine made.
Per paper of 3 needles...... ...........**$0.04**
Per dozen needles.......................... 0.16

## Needle Cases.

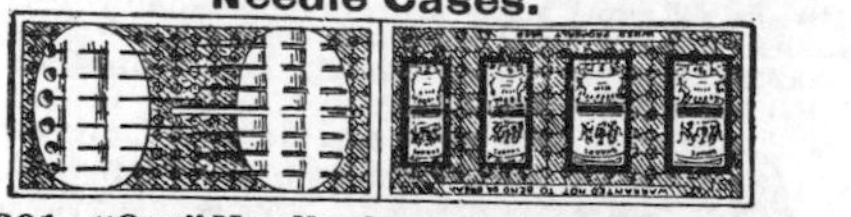

**25301 "Our" Needle Case** contains 4 papers of needles, also other needles and pins. **These cases are usually retailed for 10c.** Each **4c**; per doz.,**$0.39**

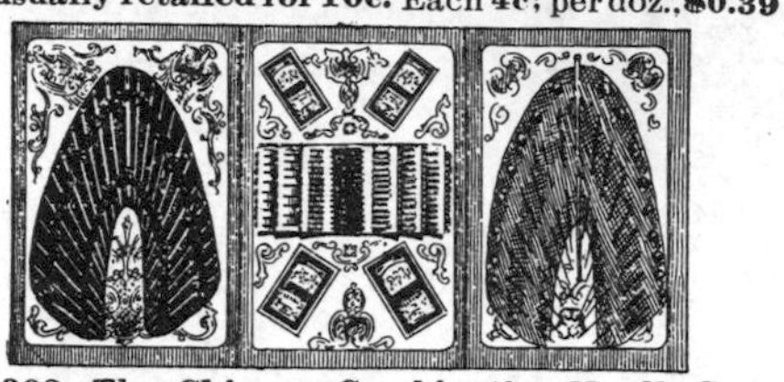

**25302 The Chicago Combination Needle Case,** contains 4 papers of needles and a large variety of needles and pins. Size 4½x7 inches when closed, 3 fold. Each **12c**; per dozen......................**$1.18**

## Curling Irons.

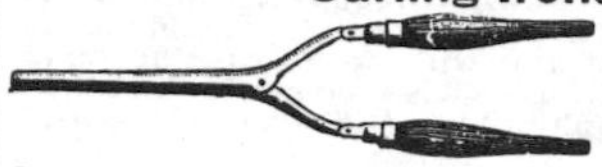

**25304 Curling Iron** 7½ inches long, has two wooden handles. Each, **4c**; per dozen...........................**$0.35**
**25306 Curling Iron,** 9 ins. long, has two wooden handles, a good spring, iron nicely polished. Each, **7c**; per dozen...**$0.65**

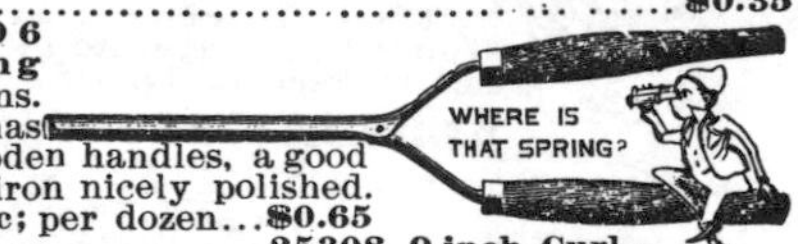


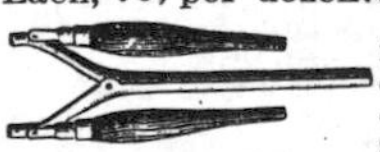

**25308 9 inch Curling Iron,** wooden handles, which can be folded. (see cut) handles can be placed in such a position that iron can be heated over a lamp chimney without holding iron.
Each, **8c**; per dozen.............................**$0.85**

**Waving Irons.**

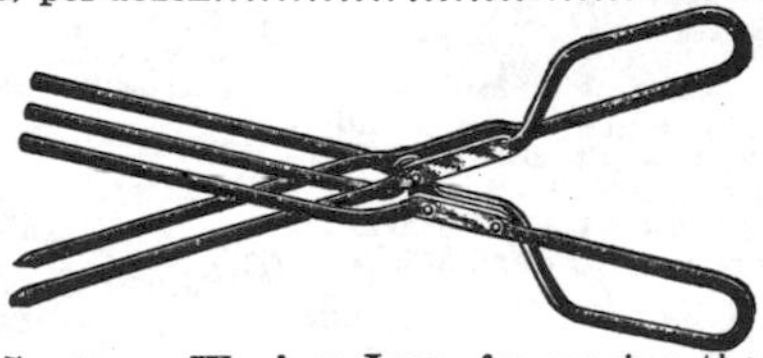

**25310 5 prong Waving Iron,** for waving the hair, made of good quality metal. Each, **12c**; per dozen........................................**$1.25**

## Button Clasp Hose Supporters.

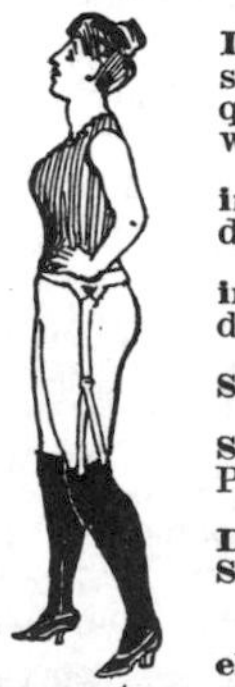

**The Button Fastener is very simple. It does not tear the stocking;** cannot slip. Our Supporters are made of good quality elastic. Colors black and white.
**25312 Babies' Single Strap Stocking Supporters.** Per pair, **5c**; per dozen............................**$0.55**
**25314 Child's Double Strap Stocking Supporters.** Per pair, **6c**; per dozen............................**$0.63**
**25316 Misses' Double Strap Hose Supporters.** Per pair, **8c**; per doz **$0.85**
**52318 Young Ladies' Double Strap Stocking Supporters.** Per pair, **9c**; Per dozen......**$0.95**
**25320 Ladies' Double Strap Hose Supporters.** Pair, **10c**
Dozen..........**$1.00**

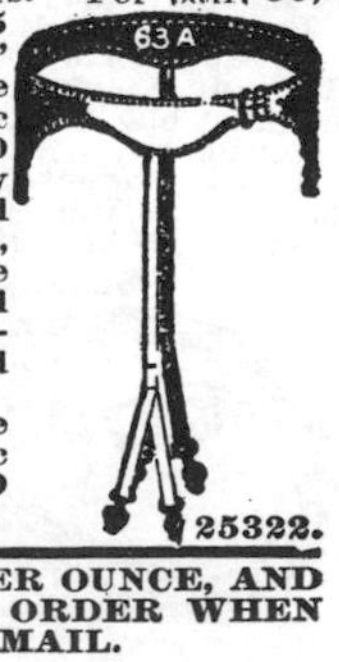


**NOTE.—Ordinary elastic when used for garters or hose supporters, binds and is injurious, stops the circulation. People having used our button fastener hose supporters are never without them. Send for some with your next order.**
**25322 Ladies' Belts with hose supporters.** Per pair...... ....18c
Per dozen...................**$1.90**

**25322.**

**POSTAGE IS ONE CENT PER OUNCE, AND MUST BE ENCLOSED WITH ORDER WHEN GOODS ARE TO BE SENT BY MAIL.**

**OUR REGULAR CUSTOMERS, NUMBERING FAR INTO THE THOUSANDS, MAKE MONTHLY ORDERS USUALLY OF GROCERIES, INCLUDING SUCH OTHER ITEMS AS MAY BE NEEDED. THE FREIGHT IS VERY LITTLE ON A HUNDRED POUNDS.**

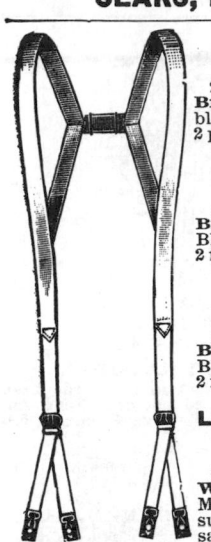

### Ladies' Shoulder Braces.

**25324** Ladies' Shoulder Braces with hose supporters, black or white. Per pair, 23c; 2 pair for 45c; per dozen, $2.35

### Misses' Shoulder Braces.

**25326** Misses' Soulder Braces with hose supporters. Black or white. Per pair, 18c; 2 for 35c; per dozen......$1.90

### Children's Shoulder Braces.

**25328** Children's Shoulder Braces with hose supporters. Black or white. Per pair, 16c; 2 for 31c; per dozen......$1.70

### Ladies' Black or White Combination Belt.

**25330** Ladies' Black or White Combination Belt. Made of good sateen, with hose supporters and points for safety belt. Sizes 22 to 36.

Each 25c; per dozen......................$2.55

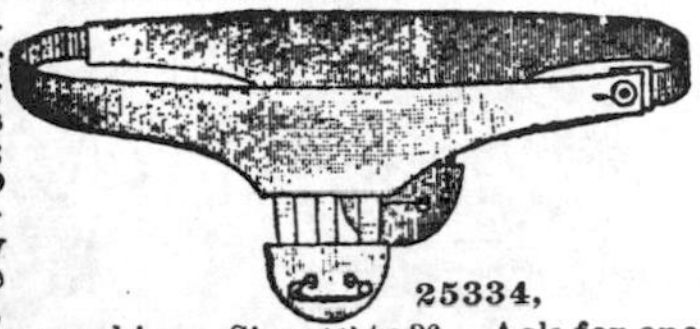

**25332** Suspenders for supporting Ladies' Skirts Per pair, 10c; per doz. $1.00
**25334** Ladies' Safety Belts, made of sateen, rubber band across hips. Sizes 22 to 36. Ask for one inch larger than your exact waist measure. (Sizes every inch). Each 21c; per doz...$2.45

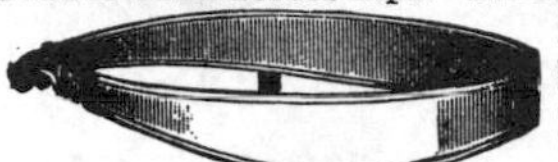

**25334,**

### Ladies' Satin Belt Hose Supporters.

**25339** Ladies' Satin Belt Hose Supporters; well made. Comes in colors; yellow, blue, pink, red and black. A regular 50c supporter. Per pair, 25c; 2 pair for 45c; per dozen......$2.70

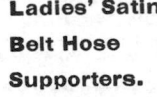

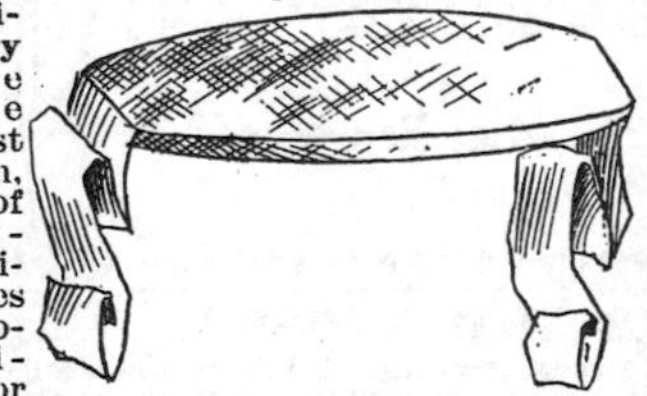

**25338** "Serviette" Saintary Cloth. These Serviettes are made of the finest absorbent cotton, with a layer of absolutely impervious material, which insures cleanliness. Absolutely antiseptic, ready for instant use. These Serviettes possess from three to four times the absorbent qualities of the best toweling. Recommended by the medical profession as indispensible in every ladies wardrobe.
Each, 4c.; per dozen......................$0.40

### The Common Sense Diaper.

Can be adjusted to the baby's hips and limbs so as to fit perfectly, and give absolute ease and comfort. These diapers are made of the best absorbent flannel, which protects the child's clothing, bedding, etc. Children do not become ruptured or bow-legged when these diapers are used.
**25344** Infants' Common Sense Diaper or Absorbent Cloths. Manufactured of the best quality absorbent flannel, bound edges; small, medium and large sizes; safety pin with each diaper.
Each, 15c; per dozen......................$1.60

---

### The Model Hose Supporter.

**25350** The Model Hose Supporter for children, a combination as a shoulder brace, waist and hose supporter. Waist band has two rows of buttons to attach garments to. Colors black and white. Sizes 2 to 14 years. Each, 25c; per doz........$2.85

REMEMBER OUR LIBERAL DISCOUNT FOR CASH.

### Ladies' Fancy Garters.

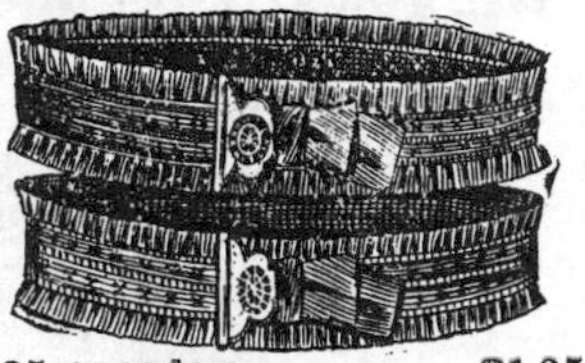

**25346** Our Fine Garters for Ladies; made of fancy elastic, good plated adjustable buckles, nice ribbon bows; each pair in a fancy box; all colors and black; regular retail price, 35c.
Our special price per pair, 13c; 2 for 25c; per dozen......$1.25
**25348** Our Handsome Garters for Ladies; fancy silk elastic; heavily plated adjustable buckles; elegant silk ribbon bows; each pair in a fine glass top box; regular price, 75c.
Per pair, 25c; 2 for 40c; per dozen ......$2.40
**All Colors.**

### Dress Stays.

PERFECTION DRESS STAY

**25349** The Victoria Dress Stay. A first class stay in every respect; worth 12½c.
Per set, 7c; 12 sets......$0.80
**25350** The Perfection Dress Stay (a perfect stay) has stood the test of years; will not rust or break through the ends; retailed as high as 15c per set. Our special price, per set, 10c; per dozen......$1.10
Each set contains nine steels of assorted lenghts (just enough for a dress); colors, black, drab, white, cardinal, blue, pink and brown.

### Whalebone Casing.

**25352** Whalebone Casing (9 yard pieces); black, white and drab.
Per piece, 7c; per dozen......$0.80

### Corset Clasps.

**25354** Corset Clasps, (re-enforced); double steel; covered with good material; 5 hooks; black, white and drab.
Per pair 5c; per doz. $0.55

### Hooks and Eyes.

**25356** Hooks and Eyes. Black and white; Nos. 3 and 4; 2 dozen on a card.
Per card, 1½c; 6 cards, 6c; 12 cards. $0.12
**25358** Hooks and Eyes, with a hump, secure and safe, cannot become unfastened.
Per card of 2 dozen, 4c; per box of 12 dozen......$0.20
**25369** DeLong's Hooks and Eyes, acknowledged to be the best hook and eye made, the original hump; cannot become unfastened; black or white; 2 dozen on a card.
No. 3—per card, 8c; per gross, 45c; per great gross......$5.60
No. 4—per card, 9c; per gross, 50c; per great gross......$5.70

See that Hump.

### Skirt Braid.

**25360** Star Skirt Braid. Per piece, 4c; doz. 41c
**25361** The Well Known Goff's Skirt Braid. "The braid that is known the world around." black, white and colors. Per roll, 5c; per dozen rolls......50c
**25362** No. 29 Alpaca Trimming Braid, ¼ inch wide, made in black, white and colors. Per piece of 24 yards, 15c; per dozen......$1.68
We do not sell less than one piece.

---

### DON'T BE DECEIVED....

Just because our prices are low, retailers try to make you believe they are inferior. If they could buy in as large quantities, buy as low and sell as close as we do, their prices would be just as low as ours.

---

### Velveteen Skirt Binding.

**25364** Velveteen Dress Binding, 3 yard pieces, black and colors. Per piece......6c
**25366** The Well Known "Monarch Brand" Velveteen Skirt Binding, 4 yard pieces, 2 inches wide, black and colors. Per piece, 12c; per dozen...$1.40
**25368** The "Belle" Velveteen Skirt Binding, 4 yard pieces, 2 inches wide. Per piece......25c
We keep this superior brand of Belle Velvetine in black only.
**25370** Velveteen Skirt Binding by the yard. The most economical way to buy it; order any quantity, 2 inches wide, black and all colors.
Per yard......4c
12 yards for......43c

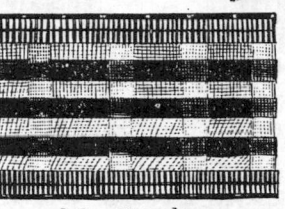

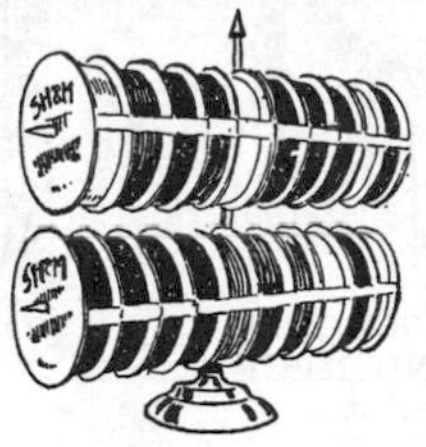

### Plain Garter Elastics.

**25372** Plain Black or White Garter Elastic, good quality.

| | Per yard | 12 yards |
|---|---|---|
| ⅜ in | $0.03 | $0.30 |
| ½ in | .04 | .35 |
| ⅝ in | .04 | .40 |
| ¾ in | .04 | .45 |

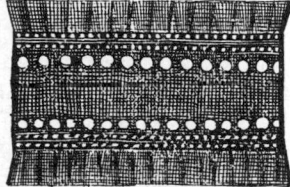

**25378** Plaid and Staple Fancy Garter Web, a great variety of patterns. This is a good reliable quality and the price cheaper than trashy goods are sold at by retail merchants.
Per yard, 3c; 12 yards......25c
**25380** Elastic Garter Web, fancy frill edge, 1 inch wide, very heavy and well worth 10 cents per yard, comes in a great variety of colors.
Per yard....5c
Per piece 10 yards.. ......45c

### Feather Stitch Braid.

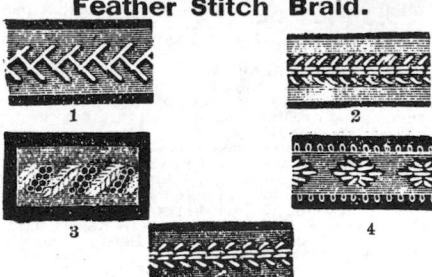

1    2

3    4

5

**25382** Feather-Stitched Braid, comes in pieces of six yards, used for trimming underwear, etc., pattern 1 can be had in black, blue pink and white; Other patterns in white only. Per piece, 6c; 3 pieces, 16c; 12 pieces......63c

### Non-Elastic Webbing.

**25384** White Non-Elastic.

| | ½ in. | ⅝ in. | ¾ in. | 1 in. |
|---|---|---|---|---|
| Per yard | 2c | 2c | 2c | 2c |
| 12 yards | 14c | 14c | 16c | 18c |

**25386** Black Non-Elastic.

| Width | ½ in. | ⅝ in. | ¾ in. | 1 in. |
|---|---|---|---|---|
| Per yard | 2c | 2c | 2c | 2½c |
| 12 yards | 15c | 16c | 18c | 22c |

### Elastic Truss Webs, Heavy.

**25387** Heavy Elastic for Trusses, Artificial Limbs, etc.

| Width | ¾ in. | 1 in. | 1½ in. | 2 in. |
|---|---|---|---|---|
| Per yard | 7c | 10c | 16c | 25c |

A special discount of 12½ per cent allowed if full pieces containing 30 to 50 yards are ordered.

### Hat Elastic.

Per piece
**25388** Hat Elastic Cord, fine, black or white, 12c
**25390** Hat Elastic Cord, medi'm, black or white, 15c
**25392** Hat Elastic Cord, heavy, black or white, 18c
24 yards to each piece; we do not sell less than one piece.

Per piece.
**25394** Hat Elastic braid, narrow, black or white, 18c
**25396** Hat Elastic braid, medium, bl'ck or white, 25c
**25398** Hat Elastic braid, wide, black or white, 29c
24 yard pieces; we do not cut pieces.

---

**IF YOU SHOULD NEED SMALL ARTICLES ALONE AND WANT THEM SENT BY MAIL, YOU MUST NOT FORGET THE NECESSARY POSTAGE. IF YOU FORGET THIS, WE HOLD YOUR ORDER FOR THE AMOUNT.**

# SAVE YOUR MONEY AND BUY

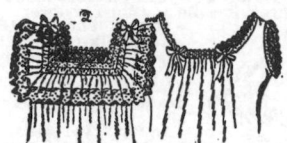

**THE NEW IDEA PATTERN**

**No. 25400 Any Pattern 10 cents.**

**821**
LADIES' CHEMISE WITH SQUARE OR ROUND NECK.
Sizes 32, 34, 36, 38, 40, 42, 44.

**This Pattern 10 cents.**
Any style or size of any pattern designed (we have over 1000 kinds) sent at the uniform price of 10 cents.

**801**
LADIES' FIVE GORED SKIRT.
Sizes, 22, 24, 26, 28, 30.

**ANY PAPER PATTERN 10 CENTS.**
These and 1000 other Paper Patterns can be had for 10c each. Catalogue showing several hundred patterns to select from 4c. Send for it.

**946**
LADIES' NIGHT GOWN.
Sizes 32, 34, 36, 38, 40, 42, 44

**This Pattern 10 cents.**
Guaranteed as perfect in fit as the best known or highest priced pattern. Send for our pattern catalogue, price 4 cents. 500 patterns to select from.

**879—LADIES' WRAPPER.**
Sizes, 32, 34, 36, 38, 40, 42
This Pattern 10 cts.

**944**
GIRLS' DRESS.
Sizes 2, 4, 6, 8 years.
This Pattern 10 cts.

**1042—LADIES' BLOUSE or Shirt Waist.**
Sizes 32, 34, 36, 38, 40, 42.
This Pattern 10 cts.

**1044—Girl's Dress.**
Sizes 6, 8, 10, 12, 14 years.
This Pattern 10 cts.

Have Your garments made up in the latest style. You can do this by ordering the "New Idea" paper pattern. Send 4 cts. to help pay postage for our Pattern Catalogue showing several hundred styles. Each pattern sold at the uniform price of 10 cents. Always mention Pattern Number,

---

## Findings for a Dress.

Our popular finding sets; these sets contain everything needed in the making of your dress. SAVE A DOLLAR or more by ordering one.
**25401 Finding Set for a medium priced dress.**

2 yards Selisia waist lining.   1 spool silk.
6 yards Cambric skirt lining.   1 yard wigan.
2 spools button hole twist.   1 dozen dress steels.
1 pair dress shields.   1 spool cotton thread.
1 piece 4 yds. Velveteen skirt   1 card hooks and eyes.
   binding.     Retail price......$1.75
Our price for entire set.........................82c
NOTE—Linings, silk and thread can be had in any color.
**25402 Finding Set for a good quality dress.**
Retail value, $3.00   Our price, $1.32
2 yards fine quality Selisia waist lining.
6 yards good quality Cambric skirt linings.
1½ yards good quality canvas.
1 set sateen covered dress stays.
1 pair Kleinert's warranted dress shields.
1 spool Corticelli 100 yard sewing silk.
2 spools Corticelli button hole twist.
1 spool Clark's O. N. T. best spool cotton.
1 piece 4 yard S. H. & M. best velveteen skirt binding.
1 card hump hooks and eyes.   Retail price, $3.00
Our price for this set.......................$1.32

### The Magic Darner.

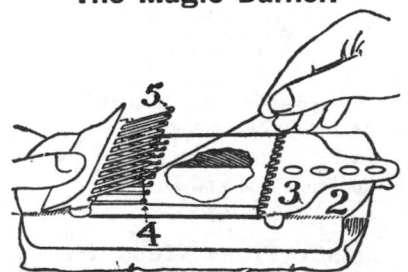

**25404 The Magic Darner** is a machine recently invented and patented for mending hosiery, silk, wool or cotton, all kinds of underwear, napkins, table linens and in fact everything in the household that needs darning. It is a boon to the overworked women, is an ornament to her work basket, is a time, labor and eye saver, is so simple in operation that children can do the darning, and it proves such a pleasure that they tease mamma for that which of all things mamma hates doing the most. One does not have to be an expert needle worker to mend lace curtains and other fine fabrics, the Magic Darner does it for you and saves you one-twentieth of your time. You can take 20 stitches on the machine while you take one in the old way. Well worth $2.50. Price each, 35c; 2 for 65c; 12 for...............$3.75

## POCKET BOOKS AND PURSES.

On this and the next page, we quote a line of **Purses, Pouches, Pocketbooks, Bill Books, etc., etc.,** that is unequalled in its variety, and in the **value it represents.** The goods are **very profitable for the retailer to sell,** and hence, are very profitable for you to buy from us, where you can save 50 per cent on the price. You can include a pocketbook in your order for other goods and the express or freight will be no more. 3 per cent discount on all orders where cash in full is sent.

### Bill Book and Draw String Pouches

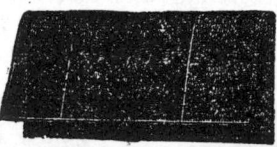

**25406 Fancy Embossed Colored Leather Bill Book.** Size 3½x8 inches. Cloth lined, canvas faced, four regular pockets. Would be considered fair value at 60 cents. Each... ....$0.27

**25408 Leather Bill Book.** Fancy colored, embossed. Size, 3½ x 8 inches. Leather faced, cloth lined, large coin pocket with fancy nickeled frame. Four regular pockets. Each..........$0.50

**25400 Finest English Finish Bill Book.** Bound and stitched, all leather. Size, 3¾x8¼ inch. Three regular and two smaller pockets. Light, durable and flexible. Each.....$0.58

**25412 Leather Coin or Tobacco Pouch, with draw strings.** 4x3½ in. Each,........................$0.05

**25414 A Very Good Oozed Leather Tobacco or Coin Pouch.** Draw strings. 5x4 inches. Each..........$0.08 Per dozen.... .75

**25416 Prussian or Maltster's Pouch.** An excellent pouch for tobacco or coin. An inside pocket for gold. This pouch is manufactured from one solid piece of leather. A shining star at 25c. Our price....................$0.13

**25418 The Genuine Buckskin Pouch.** Made of six pieces, light and dark alternating. Securely stitched with silk, buckskin top, draw strings. 5½ inches deep, 5 inches wide. Each...........$0.20

**No. 25520 Raleigh Velvet Rubber Tobacco Pouch.** Self-closing, tan color. Diameter, 3¾ inches. Keeps tobacco moist, clean and sweet. Each..........................$0.17

---

SOME PEOPLE ARE VERY CARELESS. WE HAVE OVER $5,000.00 IN THE BANK AWAITING CLAIMANTS. THIS MONEY WAS SENT IN BY PEOPLE SO THOUGHTLESS THAT THEY GIVE NO NAME AND ADDRESS. THIS MEANS THAT YOU MUST BE CAREFULL.

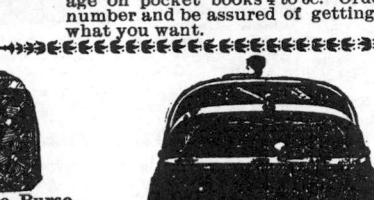

# LADIES' POCKET BOOKS.

CHICAGO, the greatest leather market in the world; SEARS, ROEBUCK & CO., the foremost dealers in leather goods in that greatest market. This means a great deal; we are right in it on pocket books and our prices are so far down, that it makes the retailer sick to read them. Big money saved by buying of us. Postage on pocket books 4 to 6c. Order by number and be assured of getting just what you want.

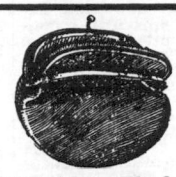

**25457 A Fine Black and Colored Calf Purse,** 3 ball catch, with inside partition. A good 10c book. Size 2½x2½ inches. Each..............5c

**25458 A Fine Black and Colored Kid Purse,** Size 2¾x3 inches, three ball catch, fine nickeled frame, inside partition. A 18c book. Each......................9c

**25459 A Very Handsome Grain Purse,** size 3x3 inches, three ball catch, inside partition, kid lining, interlocking frame, money can't drop out. A 25c book. Each..12½c

**25460 A Square Purse,** 2x3 inches, nickel frame, ball catch, kid lined, embossed leather. A good bargain at retail for 20c, a 10c possibility here at each,
................................10c

**25461 Fine Buck Purse,** with gusseted bottom and welts, riveted frame with partition, three ball catch, chamois lined, two pockets, size 3x3¼. Each..................21c

**25462 Fine Alligator Purse,** nickel frame, ball catch, kid lined, inside pocket with catch. Size 2½ x3¼ inches. A regular 50c purse. Each..............25c

**25463 A Fine Grain Leather Purse,** kid lined, nickeled frame, ball catch, has inside pocket. Size 2½ x3¾ inches. Each........20c

**25464 Seal Grain Leather Pocket Book,** outside card pocket and inside card pocket with flap, two regular pockets and coin pocket with snap. Size 3x4½ inches. Each..............25c

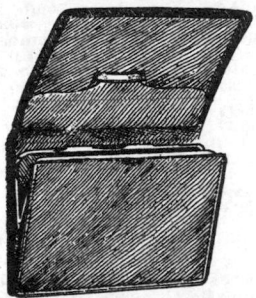

**25465 Fine Grain Leather Pocket Book,** inside card pocket with flap, smooth kid lining, two regular and one coin pocket with snap. Colors, black, brown and tan. Size 3x4½ inches. Good value at 75c. Each...35c

**25452 Morocco Grained Leather Pocket Book,** silvered catch, metal corners, four regular pockets and coin pocket, with snap frame. A regular 65c pocket book. Size 2¾x4 inches. Our low price, each...........25c

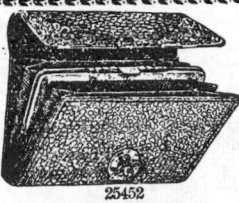
25452

**25453 Fine Grain Leather Purse,** size 2½x4 inches, nickeled, riveted frame, ball catch, kid lined, two outside pockets. Good value at 38c. (Without handkerchief.) Our special price, each..............19c

**25467½ Morocco Grained Leather,** with genuine Sterling silver corner ornament, faced with same leather, regular card pocket, coin pocket with snap frame, two regular pockets, size 3¼x4½ in. Each........78c

**25466 A Fine Alligator Pocket Book,** 3x4 inches, calf lined, inside card pocket with flap, two regular and one coin pocket with snap. Each....50c

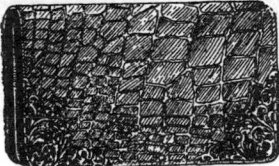

**25454 This Handsome Embossed Leather Ladies' Pocket Book** is 2½x4 inches, riveted frame ball catch, coin pocket with catch, lined throughout with kid, has leather attachment on outside for holding handkerchiefs. A bargain in any store at 50c. (Without handkerchief.) Our leader at, each..................25c

### 4 BIG BARGAINS SURROUND THIS SQUARE.

25455

25454

25453

**25455 Ladies' Beautiful Grain Leather Pocket Book,** silvered corners, has two regular pockets, and coin pocket with nickeled snap frame, card pocket with flap and tuck strap. A book that always has sold for 60c. Size 3x4½ inches. A special feature at, each.
.............................25c

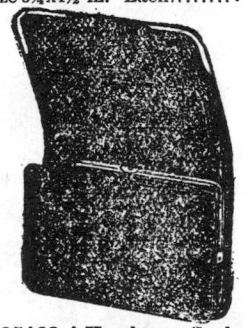

**25468 A Handsome Grained Goat Leather,** faced with same, regular card pocket and one with flap and tuck, coin pocket with polished snap frame, and two regular pockets, size 3x4½ inches. Each................92c

## ..MENS' POCKET BOOKS..

**25467 A Beautiful Alligator Pocket Book,** 2½x5 inches, metal corners, four pockets, coin pocket with snap, kid lined, card case inside with snap. A $1.25 bargain. Each.......75c

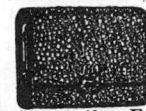

**25469 The Midget,** a perfect miniature pocket book, 1¾x2⅝ in. Has 4 regular pockets and coin pocket with snap, clasps on outside handy and cute for small change or for children's use. Good value at 40c. Each...................25c

25470

**25470 Mens' Patent Box Flap Book,** seal grain, outside card pocket, five regular and four smaller pockets. Size 2¾ x 4 inches. Each...........50c

**25472 Mens' Strap Book,** sheep leather stamped. Size 2¾x4¾ inches. 3 pockets and bill fold. Each.............16c

25472

**25482 Hip Pocket Book,** a nice seal grain book with a button lock, 3x6½ inches, canvas faced, four regular and three small canvas pockets, bound and stitched. Each,
................................23c

**25474 Mens' Strap Books,** heavy sheep, calf finish, stitched all round, leather faced, cloth lined, 3 pockets and bill fold. Size 2¾x 4¾ inches. Each
................................25c

25476

**25476 Mens' Strap Book,** size 2½x 4½ inches, calf finish, sheep stitched all around, leather faced, buck lined, four large and three small pockets, bill roll with flap. A winner for $1.00. Each, 38c

**25478 Mens' Strap Book,** good leather, size 2⅝x4½ inches, leather faced 3 small and 4 regular all leather pockets, bill fold, bound and stitched. A beauty at $1.15. Each...53c

25478

25480

**25480 Our Very Fine English Finest Calf Pocket Book,** firmly stitched, faced with kid, three small and four regular pockets, bound and stitched, drop bill fold, with flap and strap. Size 2¾x4¾ inches. Each................72c

25482

**25484 A Nice Bill Book,** grain leather, size 3½x8 inches, cloth faced and lined, three pockets. Each............................17c

**IF YOU ORDER A POCKET BOOK SENT BY MAIL, ALWAYS INCLUDE FROM 2 TO 6 CENTS FOR POSTAGE.**

## COMBS.
### THE COMBS WE SELL DO NOT BREAK EASILY.

A word about combs; unreliable combs are expensive at any price. We handle only such combs as we can recommend (no matter how low the price); we are very large buyers of combs and are thus enabled to sell these goods for less than the average retailer pays for them. Note the inducements we make to purchasers of three or more combs at one time. The money you can save by buying a few at a time, more than pays the transportation charges.

**25510 Horn Dressing Combs,** 7 in. long, nickel plated backs. Each 10c; 3 for 25c; per doz...**$0.95**

**25511 Horn Dressing Combs,** 7 in. long, nickel plated eyelet to which a chain can be attached. Each 10c; 3 for 25c; per doz.................**$0.95**

**25512 A First Class Rubber Dressing Comb,** 7 inches long. Each, 5c; 6 for 25c; per doz.........**$0.48**

**22513 A Handsome, Substantial, 8-inch Dressing Comb,** Goodyear rubber, ornamental fancy back. Each 8c; 3 for 21c; per doz............**$0.80**

**25514 A Good Heavy 8-inch Rubber Dressing Comb,** well made, perfectly finished, (combs not as good are often retailed for 15c). Each 10c; 3 for 25c; per doz..................**$0.92**

**25515 A Very Handsome and Durable 8-inch Dressing Comb,** well worth 25c. Each 14c; 2 for 25c; 12 for....................**$1.40**

**25516 A Regular 30c. Comb,** Goodyear rubber, 8 inches long, very heavy. Each 16c; 2 for 30c; per doz........**$1.65**

**25517 A Heavy unbreakable Rubber Dressing Comb,** (this comb can also be had with **all coarse teeth**). Each 18c; 2 for 33c; per doz.........**$1.75** The above comb will be replaced by a new one if broken within 12 months in fair use. (See illustration.)

**25518 A Very Heavy Ladies' Unbreakable Rubber Comb,** good value at 35c. Each 23c; 2 for 40c; per doz....................**$2.25**

### Aluminum Combs.

**25519 Aluminum Dressing Combs,** 7 in. long, 1¼ in. wide, fine and coarse teeth. Each 23c; 2 for....................**$0.40**

**25520 Pure Aluminum Combs,** for ladies, fine and coarse teeth, 7½ in. long, 1½ in. wide, as light as a feather, will not tarnish. Each.............**$0.38**

**25521 Aluminum Barber or Gentlemen's Comb,** 7 inches long, ¾ inches wide, fine and coarse teeth. Each....................**$0.18**

### CHILDREN'S GOOD QUALITY ROUND COMBS.

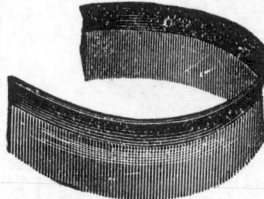

**25522 A Handsomely Finished Circular Rubber Comb.** Child's round comb. Each 6c; 3 for 16c; per doz.......**$0.55**

**25523 Beautiful Unbreakable Circular Rubber Comb.** About like cut. One dozen round combs weigh about 10 ounces. Each 9c; 3 for 25c; per doz....................**$0.95**

**25524 Rubber Pocket Combs** in leatherette cases, usually sold at 10 cents. Each 6c; 3 for 15c; per doz....**$0.48**

**25525 Rubber Pocket Combs** in cases, good value at 15c. Each 10c; 3 for 25c; per doz....**$0.95**

**25526 Folding Pocket Comb,** made of unbreakable hard rubber. Each 11c; per doz...**$1.05**

**No. 25527.**
**25527 Aluminum Pocket Comb,** fine and coarse teeth, 5 inches long, straight backed. Durable, and will not tarnish. Each 8c; per doz..........**$0.90**

**No. 25526.**

**25529 A Heavy Comb,** all coarse teeth, just the thing for ladies having long and heavy hair; has a good strong handle. (See cut) Each 32c; per doz.**$3.35**

**25531 Rubber Barber Comb,** nicely finished, 7½ inches long. Usually sold for 10 cents. Each 5c; 6 for 25c; per doz....................**$0.48**

**25533 A Very Fine Rubber, Barber or Gentleman's Comb.** Always sold by retailers at 25 cents. Each 8c; per doz....................**$0.80**

**25535 Rubber Fine Tooth Combs,** the regular 10 cent kind. Each 5c; 6 for 25c; per doz.........**$0.48**

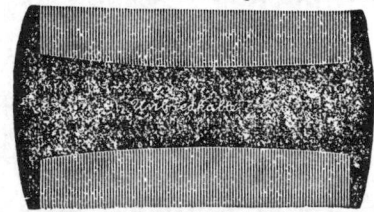

**25537 A Hard Rubber Fine Tooth Comb,** good quality. Usual price 15 cents. Each 7c; 3 for 18c; per doz....................**$0.70**

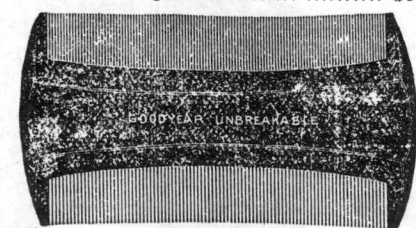

**25539 An Unbreakable Goodyear hard Rubber Fine Tooth Comb.** Each 9c; 3 for 25c; per doz....................**$0.92**

## CELLULOID COMBS.
See our quotations of rubber and horn combs.

Celluloid dressing combs, nothing is nicer than combs made of celluloid, pretty to look at and they are serviceable too. Our prices are away below the retailers cost.

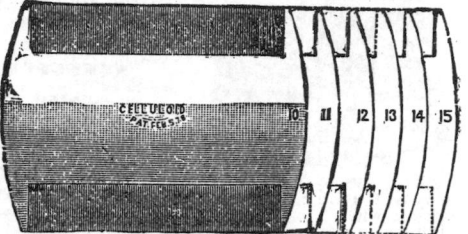

**25541 A 7 inch White Celluloid Dressing Comb.** Regular retail price 25 cents. Each.**$0.10**

**25543 The same Comb** as described above, in Amber. Retailers ask 25 to 30 cents. Each...**$0.13**

**No. 25545 A Beautiful 7½ inch beaded black Celluloid Amber Dressing Comb,** coarse and fine teeth, druggists ask as high as 35 cents for these combs. Each....................**$0.19**

**25547 A very handsome 7½ inch rope back White Celluloid Dressing Comb,** good heavy weight. This comb is easily worth 40 cents. Each 25c; 2 for 45c; per doz..........**$2.60**

**25549 This pretty Imitation Tortoise Shell Celluloid Barber's Comb** (gentlemen's combs), 7 inches long, is really worth 25 cents. Each....................**$0.15**

### Celluloid Fine Tooth Combs.

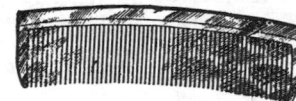

These combs are imitation ivory, look and last as long as goods costing four and five times as much. 10, 12 and 14 are the best sizes.
**25551 White Celluloid Fine Tooth Comb,** 2½ inches long (style 10). Each....................**$0.08**
**25553 White Celluloid Fine Tooth Comb,** 3 inches long (style 12). Each....................**$0.10**
**25555 White Celluloid Fine Tooth Comb,** 3½ inches long (style 14). Each....................**$0.13**

### Celluloid Pocket Combs.

**25557 White Celluloid Pocket Comb** in case, 3½ inches long; regular retail price 20 cents. Each....................**$0.09**

### Celluloid Round Combs.

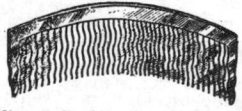

**25559 An Imitation Tortoise Shell Pocket Comb,** each in a neat case, made of celluloid, 4½ inches long; regular value 35 cents. Each....**$0.25**

**25561 Is a Celluloid, Child's Round Comb,** comes in blue, red or tortoise shell. A regular 15 cent comb. Each..........**$0.08**

### Ladies' Side Combs.

**25563 Ladies' Side Combs,** curved, come in tortoise shell; size, 3½ inches, made of celluloid. Per pair, 8c; 3 pairs for....................**$0.20**

**25565 A fine 3¾ inch Ladies' Side Comb,** made of celluloid, imitation tortoise, fancy back. Per pair, 10c; 3 pairs for....................**$0.28**

**25567 This handsome side comb** is 3¾ inches long, made of celluloid, imitation tortoise shell, crimped teeth, which prevent comb from slipping out of the hair. Per pair, 15c; 2 pairs....................**$0.25**

**25571 A beautiful 4-inch Side Comb,** made of celluloid, imitation tortoise shell, has a fancy ornamental back, graduated teeth, longest at center and tapering toward each end. A regular 35c comb. Per pair, 21c; 2 for.........**$0.40**

**25573 A Handsome Back Comb,** celluloid, imitation tortoise shell, fine fancy top; size, 2½ and 3 inches. Each 13c; 2 for......**$0.23**

## Hair Brushes.
### Wood Back Hair Brushes.

**ALL of our Wood Back Hair Brushes,** the cheapest number up, are made of one solid piece of wood. (Solid Back Hair Brushes.) Most hair brushes are made of two pieces of wood glued together, which, when wet, warps and comes apart. A **Solid Back Hair Brush** will outwear three ordinary hair brushes. We sell our solid back hair brushes at less than the price usually asked for ordinary goods. (Remember that a solid back hair brush will last two or three times as long as an ordinary brush.) Hair brushes weigh from 6 to 8 ounces.

**25580 Is a seven-row Hair Brush,** made of mixed stock—a brush that usually retails for 15c.
Price, 3 for....**25c**
Per doz........**85c**

**25582 A Medium Sized, Square Back Hair Brush.** Black Russian bristles; would be considered good value at 25c. Each **15c**; 2 for....**25c**
25583    25584    25586

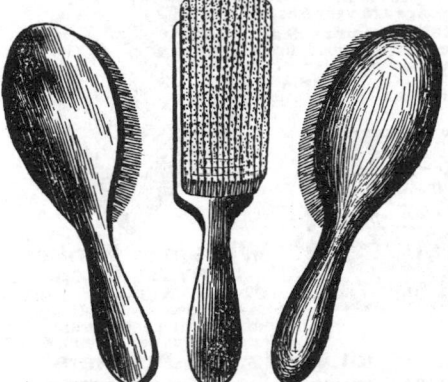

### Three Great Brush Bargains.

Get a supply of these splendid hair brushes while you can. Every one made to sell for 50c. Genuine Russian bristle, with solid one piece back, highly polished. Each one absolutely perfect and fully warranted. We purchased the entire stock of a leading manufacturer at 50c on the dollar and divided it into three lots.
WE OFFER THESE 50c BRUSHES FOR 25c. Send in your orders early and make first and second choice as to style. We expect an immense sale on these brushes and may run out of some styles before the season is over. Order two or three while you can get them. Lots of ½ dozen or more will be sold at dozen rates.
**25583 Highly Polished 11-row Hair Brush.** Fine black penetrating Russian bristles, handsome oval shaped backs. medium size, solid one piece backs. A handsome, durable brush; every one worth 50c. Our great special price, each....**25c**
**25584 A Fine, Choice Assortment of 9-row White Bristle Hair Brushes.** Highly polished square backs, medium shapes, solid one piece backs, particularly desirable for ladies' use. Finely made and finished. Our great special price, each....**25c**
**25586 A splendid Assortment of Finely Finished Oval Back Hair Brushes.** Solid one piece backs with 12 rows of fine white Russian bristles. Our great special price, each....**25c**

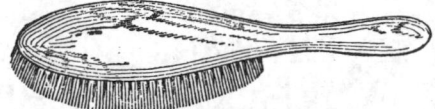

**25588 This Handsome Brush** is made of nine rows of white Russian bristle, oval back, nicely polished (solid back). Each....**38c**

A FULL LINE OF
## PAINT, VARNISH AND OTHER BRUSHES
IN OUR HARDWARE DEPARTMENT.
SEE INDEX.

**25589 This is a Handsome 13-row Hair Brush.** White bristles, nicely polished back. A regular $1.00 hair brush. Each....**50c**

### Wire Hair Brushes.

**25590 Small Size Metallic Wire Hair Brush,** nicely polished wood backs.
3 for 28c; per dozen....**$1.10**
**25592 10 Row Metallic Wire Hair Brush,** straight or twist handles, nicely polished and decorated backs. Each, 25c; per dozen....**$2.50**

### Florence Hair Brushes.

**25594 All Black Bristle Hair Brush** (Florence); rubber backs; a regular 40c brush.
Each....**22c**
**25596 Is a Nine Row White Bristle Hair Brush,** Florence; (rubber backs.)
Each....**29c**; Per dozen....**$3.00**
**25598 A Very Fine Russia White Penetrating Bristle Hair Brush.** Florence. (Rubber back) nicely figured, good value at $1.00. Each....**48c**

### The Ideal Hair Brush.

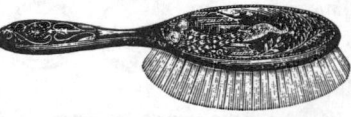

**25609 It is a Genuine Siberian Bristle Brush,** with a single bristle substituted for the ordinary tuft, the bristle being set in an **elastic air-cushioned base.** This construction enables it to penetrate the most luxuriant growth of hair without effort.
It also prevents the possibility of injuring the hair or scalp.
It will effectively **remove dandruff** without irritating the scalp.
It is **clean, light and durable.**
**25601 Ideal Hair Brush,** as described above. Medium size, cherry wood back. Each....**$0.60**
**25602 Ideal Hair Brush,** as described above. Large size, cherry wood back. Each....**$0.72**

### The Cosmeon Hair Brush.
**25603 A Pure Aluminum Hair Brush.** This brush will not tarnish like Sterling silver, is not as heavy, and has no plating to wear off. Should it become soiled it can be cleaned with pure soap and water. Good Russian bristles. In appearance this brush is equal to a $7.50 silver brush.
**Our special price....$0.90**

### Flesh and Bath Brushes.

**25604 Is a Seven Row Bath Brush,** curved handles, white bristles, made of one solid piece of wood. Cannot split or warp when wet. (A 40c brush.) Each....**18c**

**25608 Is a Long Curved Flesh Brush,** (for either dry use, or use in water). Length of brush, 17½ in. 6 rows of black and white mixed bristles. Light satin wood back. Weight, 10 ounces.
Each....**38c**

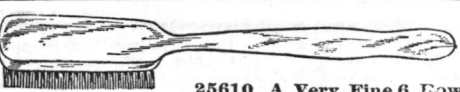

**25610 A Very Fine 6 Row Russian Bristle Bath Brush.** Black and white bristles. Made of one solid piece of wood. Length of brush 19 inches. Each....**45c**

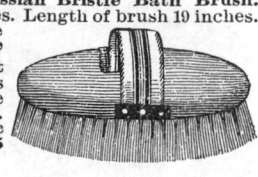

**25611 An Excellent Flesh Brush.** 5½ inches long, with strap. Can be used dry or in the bath.
Each....**25c**
Per doz........**$2.75**

**25612 9 rows all Bristle Bath Brush,** with detachable handles, length of brush with handle attached (16 inches)—This brush has a strap and when handle is detached can be used dry as a friction brush.
Each....**85c**

### Beauty Complexion Mitten.

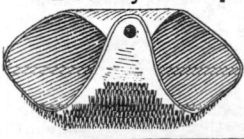

**25613 Beauty Complexion Mitten,** made of rubber will not irritate the skin, soft and flexible, this is really a toilet luxury once used always used. Each....**48c**

**25614 Bailey's rubber hand brush with handle;** an indispensible toilet article. Each....**25c.**

### Rubber Hand Brush.

**25615 Rubber Hand Brush,** size 1¾ by 3 in.
Each....**$0.20**
Per dozen....**2.00**
It's worth six times the price, at least that is what people say who use it.

### Hand Brushes.

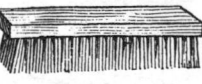

Little, useful, inexpensive brushes, nothing nicer made to keep the hands clean.
**25616 Is a 4 row Hand Brush,** 5 inches long, square back. 4 for 10c; per doz..**25c**

**25618 A nicely finished 6 row Hand Brush,** oval back, nicely polished. 2 for....**12c**
Per dozen....**70c**

### Cloth Brushes.
**25620 A good 6 row cloth or clothes brush,** black or white, mixed stock, 8 by 2½ inches, good value at 15c. Each, 9c; per dozen....**90c**

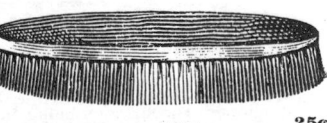

**25622 A very fine cloth brush,** made of black and white Russian bristles, nicely polished red wood backs. Each....**25c**

**25624 A Regular 60c Cloth Brush,** made of very fine black Russian bristles, fancy backs, nicely polished, size 8½x2 inches. Each, 38c; per doz..**$3.75**

**25626 Is a Cloth Brush,** black and white mixed bristles, usually sold by retail dealers at 90c. Size, 8½x2 inches, back made of heavy wood, nicely finished. Each....**50c**

## Shoe Brush Sets.

**15254** This is a two piece Shoe Set, consisting of a good dauber and a good shoe brush, put up in a handsome box. Per set............ ...... **20c**

**15255 S. R. & Co. Leader.** A handsome 3 piece shoe set, consisting of one mud brush, one dauber and one good shining brush, put up in a handsome box. Regular price, 75c; per set................**40c**
These sets are very handy and useful to have around, a place for everything and everything in its place; for travelers' use they are just the thing.

## Shaving or Lather Brushes.

Do not forget that we handle shaving soap and sell it cheap.

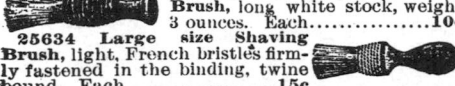

**25632 Medium Size Shaving Brush,** long white stock, weight 3 ounces. Each................**10c**
**25634 Large size Shaving Brush,** light, French bristles firmly fastened in the binding, twine bound. Each................**15c**
**25636** Shaving Brush, medium size, rosewood handle, fine light French bristles, oval cut; a 50 cent brush. Each....................**25c**
**26638** Is a Shaving Brush that will last, fine French bristles, firmly fastened rubber ferrule, usually sold for 65 cents. Each........**35c**

## Tooth Brushes.

Good Tooth Brushes cost but very little, even our cheap numbers are of good quality. Note the reductions we make when two and three are purchased at one time. It will pay you to order this way, for the amount you save will more than pay the postage. Remember we sell tooth powders and tooth soaps at less than one-half drug store prices.

**25640 Is a small White Bristle Tooth Brush,** white handles. Each, 3c; 4 for 10; doz., 25c
**25642** A good 4 row Tooth Brush, good bristles, nice white handles. Each, 5c; 4 for............**18c**
**25644 A very large, good quality Tooth Brush,** pure white French bristles, worth 20 cents and usually sold at that price. Each, 10c; 3 for...............**25c**
**25646 A very fine Imported Tooth Brush,** our own importation, superior quality, usually sold by retail dealers at from 30 to 35 cents. Each, 15c; 2 for.......**25c**
**25648 Fine Imported Badger Hair Tooth Brush,** very fine and very soft, for tender or sore gums. Each, 17c; 2 for.......**32c**

FLORENCE DENTAL PLATE.

**25650** Florence Dental Plate Tooth Brushes, for cleaning artificial teeth. Each...............**28c**

**25652** Prophylactic Tooth Brush, a perfect cleanser of the teeth, constructed upon principles of dental science, the bristles being in separate and distinctly pointed tufts, that they may be forced between the teeth as well as cleanse the surface; directions for use are given with each brush. Each...............**28c**
**25654 Folding Pocket Tooth Brush,** good imported French bristles. Each, 25c; 3 for...............**65c**
**25656 Extra Fine Nail Brush,** 5 rows of imported bristles, white bone handles; a brush that druggists and retail dealers usually ask 15 cents for. Each, 8c; three for...............**20c**
**25658** Is a very fine 8-row, Winged Nail Brush, with nail cleaner and scourer; dealers ask 50 cents for brushes of this quality. Each, 25c; 2 for...............**45c**

A COMPLETE ASSORTMENT OF . . .
**MIRRORS, CABINET WARE, COMB and BRUSH CASES** . . IN OUR FURNITURE DEPARTMENT. SEE INDEX.

## Hand Mirrors.

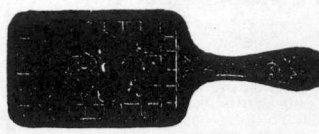

**25660** A Fine Rubber Back Hand Mirror, black, length of glass and handle combined 10 inches, good, clear glass. Each,....**19c**

**25662** A Beautiful Beveled Glass Rubber Back Hand Mirror, black, length 9 inches. This is a regular 50 cent mirror. Each,...............**25c**
We have Hand Mirrors from 10c up to $1.25.

## Whisk Brooms.

**25663** A Good Whisk Broom well sewed, a broom that sells at retail for 10c. Each.........**5c**
**25664** Heavy Whisk Brooms, made of good quality corn, double sewed. A regular 18c broom. Each..................................**10c**
**25666** A very fine 3 sewed Whisk Broom, made of fine quality corn, (would be considered a bargain in any retail store at 25c.) Each....................**15c**

## Celluloid Soap Boxes.

**25670** Celluloid Soap Boxes, white. Sizes 3½ x 2½ inches. Each....**25c**

**25672** Same as above in amber and colors. Retailers get 50c for these boxes. Each...................**35c**

## Celluloid Baby Rattles and Rings.

**25674** Celluloid Rattle, with teething ring, comes in assorted colors (ring pure white). Each....................**25c**

**25676** Celluloid Rattle, (with whistle) 6 inches long comes in very pretty assorted colors. Each........................**25c**

## Celluloid Teething Rings.

**25678** Celluloid Teething Ring, pure white. Far superior to rubber. Each...........**13c**

## Teething Rings.

**25680** Rubber Teething Rings, best black or white rubber. Each...................**3c**

## Toilet Soaps.

**25690** Cocoanut Oil Soap is is now so well known, that little need be said about it. Can be used in very hard water, also in soft water. Just the thing when there is alkali in the water. 12 cakes in a box.
Per cake, 3c; 12 cakes for....**28c**

**25692 Swiss Buttermilk Soap,** packed 3 cakes in a handsome box, a first-class complexion soap. Per cake, 3½c; 3 cakes, 10c; 12 cakes,.......**35c**

## Medicated Soaps.

We sell Medicated for less than half the price drug stores ask.

**25693** Tarlo, a large cake of medicated tar soap. Per cake, 5c.; 6 cakes, 25c; per dozen............**48c**

**25694** The above soaps are all regular 10c toilet soaps highly perfumed, honestly made, and are first-class complexion soaps. Choice of Brown Windsor, Elder Flower, Oat Meal, Summer Bouquet, Winter Bouquet. State which you want. 3 cakes for 14c; 12 cakes for 48c.
When ordering state what brand is desired.

## Complexion Soap.

**25696** Our Complexion Soap contains Benzoin, Buttermilk and Glycerine, highly perfumed. 6 cakes for 20c; 12 cakes for 35c; per gross...............**$3.75**
We make a special feature of this celebrated soap and put the price way down. We cannot fill orders for less than six cakes.

## Sulphur Soap.

**D1022** Sulphur Soap, a remedy for skin diseases. Per cake, 8c; 3 cakes for 22c; per dozen............**80c**

## Carbolic Soap.

**D1022** Carbolic Soap, a sanitary and healing soap. Per cake, 8c; 3 for 22c; per dozen, ......**80c**

## Castile Soaps.

**G2008** White or Mottled Castile Soap. ¼ lb. bars. Per dozen........32c; per gross.........**$3.20**
At this special price we cannot fill orders for less than 1 dozen cakes.
**25701½** Smyrna Imported White Castile Soap, 3½ ounce cakes. Per cake, 5c; per dozen, 50c; ten dozen.......**$4.50**

## Shaving Soaps.

Our prices on Shaving Soaps are very low.
**25702** Genuine Shaving Soap, a good first-class shaving soap. Per cake, 4c; 3 cakes 10c; per dozen..........**39c**

## Williams' Yankee Shaving Soap.

**G2029** Williams' Yankee Shaving Soap, so well known that nothing need be said of it. Per cake, 9c; per dozen...**$1.05**

## Tooth Soaps and Powders.

**D1045** Sanitary Tooth Soap, a perfect soap for the teeth; purifies the breath, hardens the gums and preserves the teeth. Per cake......**.12c**
12 cakes.......**$1.25**

## Standard Soaps.

Those well known staple soaps on which the retailer expects to make 100 per cent profit, note what we save you.
**G2024** Pear's Soap unscented per cake......**10c**
**G2025** " " scented, per cake.........**14c**
**G2028** Cuticura Soap, per cake......**18c**
**25709** Glycerine Soap, per cake......**14c**
**D1021** Tar Soap, per cake......**08c**
**25714** Kirk's Juvenile Soap, per cake......**17c**
**25716** Colgate's Cashmere Bouquet, per cake 21c
**25718** " " small size " **13c**
Drug Stores ask from 25c to 30c per cake for the above soap.

## JUVENILE CLOTHING DEPARTMENT....

PAGES 172 TO 174.

OUR LINE IS MOST COMPLETE AND VARIED.
OUR PRICES ARE TEMPTING.
IF YOU WANT TO GET WHAT YOU PAY FOR AND BETTER VALUE.
THAN ANY OTHER HOUSE CAN GIVE
SEND US YOUR ORDERS.

$1.15    $1.12

THE QUALITY OF GOODS WE HANDLE IS OF THE HIGHEST STANDARD OF EXCELLENCE. AS WITNESS OF OUR OWN CONFIDENCE IN THEIR DESIRABILITY, NOTE OUR LIBERAL C. O. D. TERMS AS EXPLAINED ON THE FIRST PAGES OF CATALOGUE.

## Perfume Leaders.

**Good Perfume Cheap.**

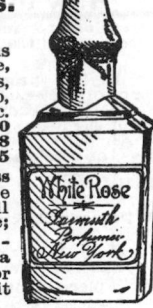

**25744** This bottle contains **nearly 1 ounce of good perfume,** lasting and refreshing, — odors, White Rose, Violet, Jockey Club, Lily of the Valley, Heliotrope, etc.
Per bottle ....................... $0.10
3 for ........................ .28
12 for ........................ 1.05

25744

**25746 Our two ounce Glass Stopped Bottle,** of high grade **Quadruple Perfume,** come in all the staple odors. Per bottle, 25c;

**25747 Imported Eau-de-Cologne Water. "Johann Maria Farina" Cologne;** for the bath, for the sick room or for the toilet, it has no superior.

25748

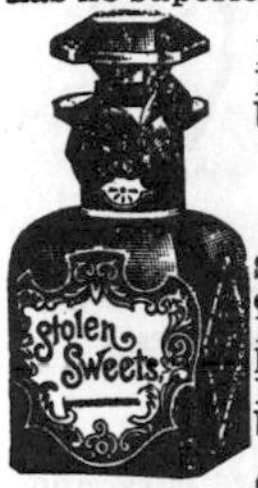

It has stood the test of seventy years. Regular retail price, 25c; our 1 ounce bottle, each ....................... $0.15
Per dozen ....................... 1.65
2 ounce bottle, each ....................... .25
Per dozen ....................... 2.90

**25748 The Famous "Stolen Sweets" Perfume,** known by all lovers of exquisite and lasting perfume. It's worth $1.00 an ounce, put up in a handsome glass stoppered bottle. Each bottle contains 1 ounce. Per bottle ....................... $0.35

**NOTE.—The leading theaters of Chicago were perfumed with this odor last winter.**

## Perfume Atomizers.

**25749 A regular 50c Perfume Atomizer,** pressed glass bottle, capacity 3 ounces. Each ....................... $0.19
3 for ....................... 0.55

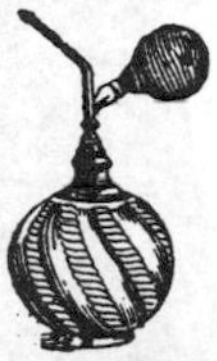

**25750 A fine pressed glass, Perfume Atomizer,** holds 3 oz. Good rubber bulb.
Each ....... $0.39
3 for ....... 0.80

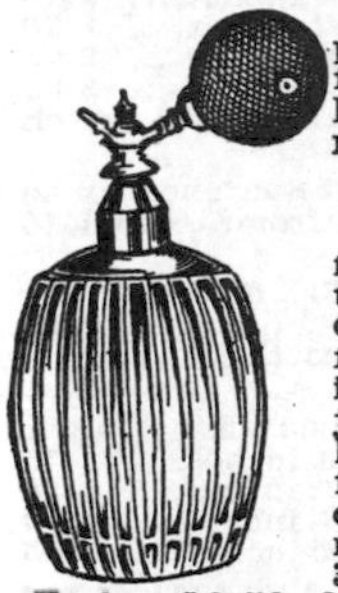

**25751 A fine Imitation Cut Glass Perfume Atomizer,** looks just like the kind that sell for $3.50. Bulb covered with net; capacity 3 ounces.
Each.... $0.50 3 for.... $1.04

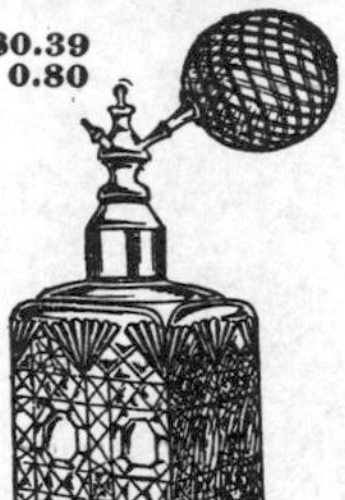

## Rubber Goods, Syringes etc.

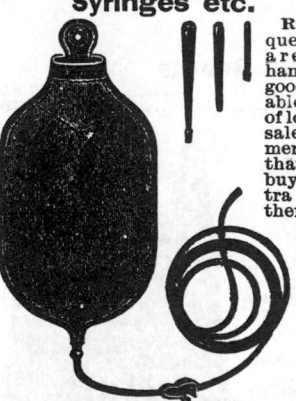

**Rubber Goods** of questionable quality are worthless. We handle only the best goods, made by reliable manufacturers of long standing. Our sales in this department are so large, that we are enabled to buy these goods in extra large quatities, thereby getting the lowest of prices. Turning over our stock often, leaves our goods always clean and fresh. Druggists pay a great deal more for rubber goods, than you can buy them for from us.

**25760 Columbia Fountain Syringe,** made from white rubber, with hard rubber fittings, 3 hard rubber pipes, in a neat box, long rubber pipes with patent shut off. Each, 2 quart ....................... $0.50
Each, 3 quart ....................... .60
Each, 4 quart ....................... .70

**25761 Pioneer Fountain Syringe,** in fine wooden box, made of extra quality rubber, extra long rubber pipe, patent shut off; five hard rubber pipes. Read our prices carefully. Drug stores charge twice as much. Each, 2 quart ....................... $0.78
Each, 3 quart ....................... 0.88
Each, 4 quart ....................... 0.95

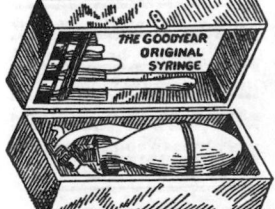

**25764 Goodyear Original Syringe,** in a handsome wooden box. A well-known, high-priced syringe; 3 hard rubber pipes —drug store price $1.25.
Each ......... 75c;
Per dozen .... $8.00

## Favorite Bulb Syringes.

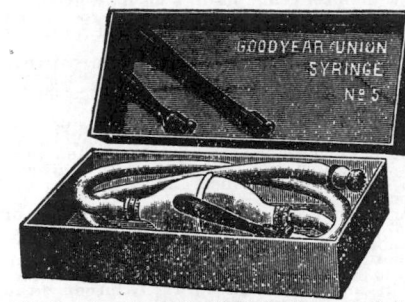

**25762 The Favorite Bulb Syringe,** made by the Goodyear Rubber Co. Two hard rubber pipes. Drug store price 50c. Each ....................... 25c;

## Union Syringe.

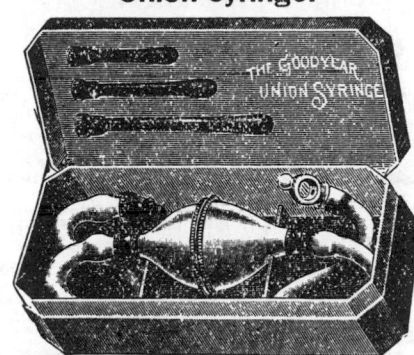

**25763 Goodyear Union Syringe,** with 3 hard rubber pipes, put up in a neat box. Druggists ask $1.00 for this syringe. Each ....................... 50c

## Ladies' Syringes.

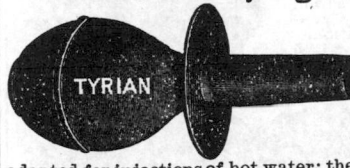

**25765—"Tyrian", female syringe** for cleansing vaginal passages of all discharges, especially adapted for injections of hot water; the liquid being driven from the syringe when the bulb is compressed and drawn back into it on relaxing the pressures, this giving an opportunity to thoroughly wash the diseased parts. Capacity, 8 ounces. Made of one piece of soft rubber, with removable hard rubber shield. Having no valves or connections, cannot get out of order. Weight, 13 onnces. Drug store price, $2.00. Each ....................... $1.25

## Ladies' Syringe.

**Patented, Feb. 8th, 1881.**

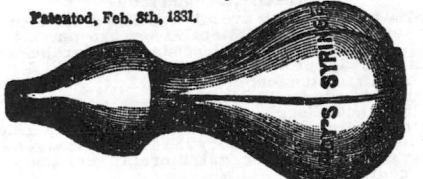

**25766** Constructed on the principle of **Injection and Suction.** A plan generally admitted by the medical profession as correct and efficient, it cleanses the passage of all discharges to perfection. It is easily cleaned. During the injections no fluid need be spilled on the clothing, etc. Consists of one piece of fine soft rubber. Weight, 17 ounces.
Each ........... $2.35

25766½ 25767 25768

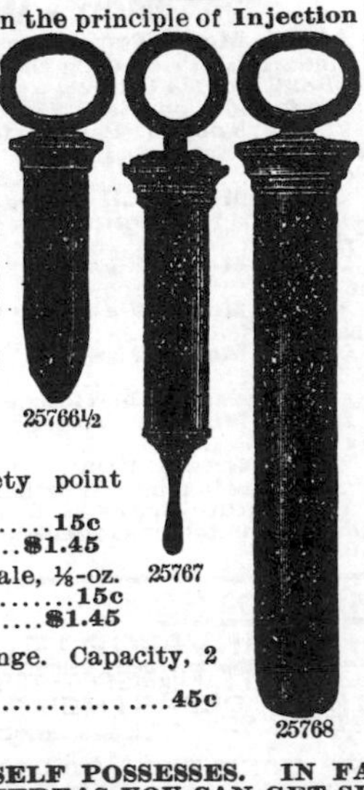

## Hard Rubber Syringes.

**25766½** ⅛ oz. safety point syringe.
Each ....................... 15c
Dozen ....................... $1.45

**25767** Urethal or male, ⅛-oz.
Each ....................... 15c
Dozen ....................... $1.45

**25768** Vaginal syringe. Capacity, 2 ounce.
Each ....................... 45c

## Hot Water Bottles.

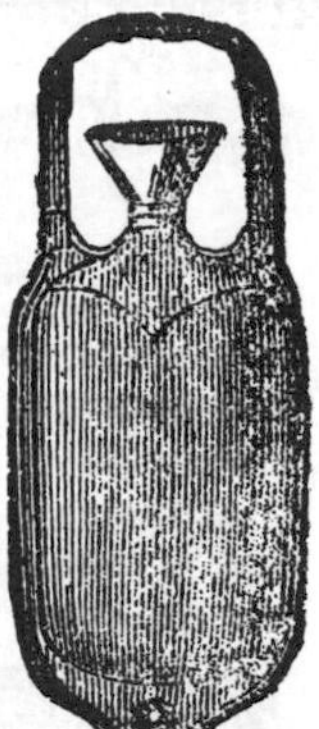

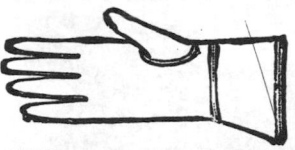

**25769** Goodyear's rubber hot water bottles, good quality, every one warranted. (Our prices are less than one-half of what retailers ask.)
2-quart, each ....................... 75c
3-quart, each ....................... 80c
4-quart, each ....................... 85c

**25770 Ladies' Short Rubber Gloves.** Colors tan or black. Sizes 6, 7, 8, 9. Per pair ........... $0.70

**25771 Ladies' Gauntlet Rubber Gloves.** Black or tan. Sizes 6, 7, 8, 9. Per pair ....................... $0.95

**25772 Men's Heavy Rubber Mittens.** Lined with sheeting. Black only.
Per pair ................. $0.95

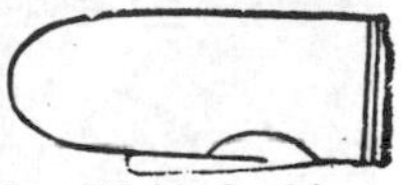

## Invalid Air Cushions

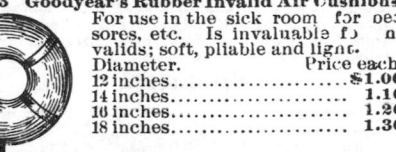

**25773 Goodyear's Rubber Invalid Air Cushions**

For use in the sick room for bed sores, etc. Is invaluable to invalids; soft, pliable and light.

| Diameter. | Price each. |
|---|---|
| 12 inches | $1.00 |
| 14 inches | 1.10 |
| 16 inches | 1.20 |
| 18 inches | 1.30 |

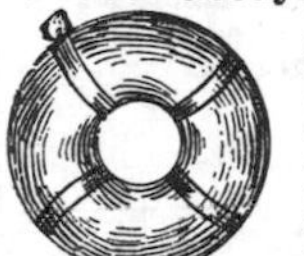

## Goodyear Plant Sprinkler.

**25774 Plant Sprinkler for Spraying Plants and Flowers** without injury. Useful and handy for sprinkling clothing in the laundry. Can also be used to spray carpets and clothing to prevent moths, spraying disinfectants in the sick room, etc. (A very useful and handy article to have, and should be in every household.) Far superior to a watering pot. Capacity, 6 ounces; weight, 8 ounces.
**Our exceptionally low price, each** ....................... 50c

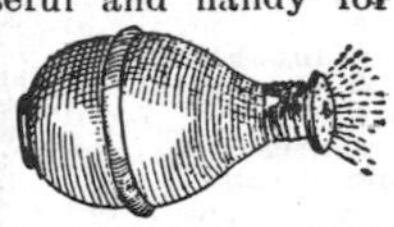

## Toilet or Medicinal Atomizers.

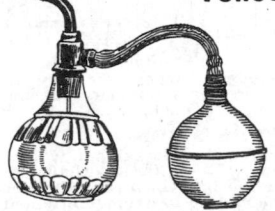

**25775 Atomizer, for either Toilet or Medicinal Use.** Hard rubber nozzle, rubber bulb of fine quality. Retailers ask as high as 75c for similar goods. Our price,
Each ......... $0.38
(Continuous spray.)

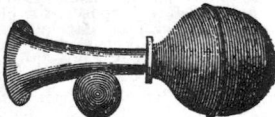

**25777 English Breast Pump,** white rubber bulb; one in box; weight 8 oz.
Each ......... $0.18
Per doz ....... 1.75

**25778 Rubber Diaper Drawers.** 3 sizes, large, medium and small; weight 6 ounces.
Each ....................... $0.23
3 for ....................... .60
Per doz ....................... 2.35

**25780 Good Quality Rubber Bibs.** Bound with tape all around, positively water proof. Length, 10, 11 and 12 inches. Measure bibs from chin to lower end.
Each ....................... 12c
Postage 3 cents.

## Rubber Nipples and Nursing Bottles.

**25781 Rubber Nipples,** white. Per doz.. $0.10

**25782 Rubber Nipple.** Will fit any bottle; made of pure gum rubber. Per doz..... $0.35

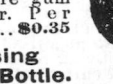

### Nursing Bottle.

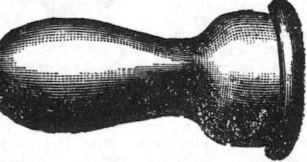

**25783 Nursing Bottle** complete with glass and rubber tube and nipple.
Each ....................... 8c

**ORDER BY NUMBER.**

**YOU WILL LESSEN THE EXPENSES OF TRANSPORTATION BY ORDERING ENOUGH GROCERIES TO MAKE UP 100 POUNDS, AND SHIP SMALL ARTICLES WITH THEM BY FREIGHT. THE ADVANTAGE IS SO OBVIOUS THAT IT NEEDS NO ARGUMENT.**

**WE OFFER YOU ALL THE PRIVILEGES THAT THE DEALER HIMSELF POSSESSES. IN FACT, YOU ARE IN A BETTER POSITION THAN HE, FOR THE RETAILER MUST BUY IN QUANTITIES, WHEREAS YOU CAN GET SINGLE ITEMS AT WHOLESALE PRICES.**

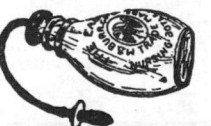

## Nursing Bottles, Etc.,—Continued.

**25784** Nursing Bottle Fittings. Rubber nipple and tubing, wood stopper and glass tube. Each................................ $0.05

**25785** Nursing Bottle. Extra good quality, fittings made of the very best rubber, contains brushes etc., for cleaning. Each................ $0.20

### Sponges.

**25790** Very Fine, "Small Eye" Sponge. For surgical and nursery use. Each.. $0.06
**25792** Small Size Toilet Sponge, for toilet use or can be used in shaving. Each 5½c;
**25794** Medium Size Sheeps' Wool Sponges, tough and durable. Each............ 9c;
**25795** Large Toilet Sponge, suitable for the bath. Each...15c;
**25796** Large Size Sheeps' Wool Sponges. A very durable sponge. Each..........................22c
**25798** Cleaning Sponges. When wet they are about 15 to 24 inches in circumference. Suitable for carriage, wood work. etc. Each................8c

### Chamois Skins.

We are headquarters for chamois skins; buy them in large quantities and sell them for less than a retail druggist or dealer can buy them for. Chamois are very useful and should be in every household. Chamois skins are used as follows: Ladies use them for toilet purposes, for cleaning glass, woodwork of all kinds, carriages, silverware or any metal; lining pockets and for chest protectors.
**25799** Our Very Fine Toilet Chamois, for applying powder, etc., to the face. Size about 5x6 inches. Each................................... $0.05

**25801**

| Style, | A | B | C | D | E | F |
|---|---|---|---|---|---|---|
| Size (inches) | 9x6½ | 12x9 | 14x11 | 20x16 | 26x23 | 33x25 |
| Each, | .05 | .10 | .16 | .32 | .52 | .70 |
| 1 doz. for | .52 | .95 | 1.60 | 3.50 | 5.50 | 7.50 |

NOTE.—If a chamois about size 14x11 inches is wanted, order as follows: No. 25801......Style C.

### Shaving Sets.

**25801½** A Very Special Offer. We have just purchased a very large quantity of Shaving Sets, like cut, at less than one-third the regular wholesale prices. We can thus offer them at a great deal less than the merchant buys them for—probably for ½ what the retailer pays. Set consists of one Sears 1865 warranted razor, "The Clean Shaver," regular retail price $1.25, one fine razor strop, leather handle, patent swivel end, one good shaving cup, one fine shaving brush and one cake of shaving soap. Price of entire set...75c

**25803**

Retail Price.
Sears' Razor........................$1.25
Razor Strop........................ .40
Shaving Cup........................ .20    Our price 75c
Shaving Brush..................... .20    for the entire
Shaving Soap ..................... .10    set.
                                 $2.15

**RAZORS** IN GREAT VARIETY AND AT SMALL PRICES IN OUR HARDWARE DEPARTMENT. SEE INDEX.

## Human Hair Goods.

Allow about 5 cents postage on hair goods. Please do not forget to inclose a good-sized sample of the exact shade wanted, and cut it out as near to the roots as possible.

The prices quoted of waves, bangs and switches are for ordinary shades only, and on the basis of a 3-inch parting in the center. Gray and extra shades on larger foundations will cost additional.

There is a great diversity in the styles of hair dressing, according to the tastes of individuals, but none is more in demand than curly bangs, and when used in connection with a nice switch the hair can always be made to look nice, and suitable for any occasion.

There are a great many kinds and styles of "pieces" for the hair, designated by different names. We cannot show or describe them all in our limited space, but if there is any hair work, not here shown, which you may want, please send a description picture of it, and we will guarantee to produce the article for you at the shortest notice.

Any of the goods sent C. O. D., subject to examination, on receipt of $1.00, balance and express charges payable at express office.

Three per cent. discount for cash in full with order.

### Our $3.00 Puff Bang.

**25820** Puff Bang. Parted in the latest style, made for fine trade, on ventilated foundation, with hair lace part. See cut. Each... .........$3.00

### Parisian Bang.

**25822** Parisian Bang. Ladies who do not require large heavy front will find this a little gem; light and fluffy, ventilated foundation. Each........ .$1.25

### Alice Wave.

**25823** Alice Wave, invisible hair lace; foundation natural, curly hair; 3 inch part, 12 inches from side to side. Each.........................$3.00
Better qualities, $4, $5, $6, $8, and $10.

### Ladies' Wigs.

**25824** These wigs are all ventilated on a delicate open mesh foundation. They are perfect in fit. having a graceful and natural appearance not found in wigs of other manufacture. Each.
Short hair, cotton foundation....................$10.00
Short hair. silk foundation...................... 12.00
Hair, 18 inches long............................ 15.00
Hair, 24 inches long............................ 18.00
This is only for ordinary shades; light and half gray are worth 25 per cent. more; if very gray, 50 per cent. more.

### Men's Wigs.

**24825** Men's Toupee, weft foundation. Price each **$5.50**
**25826** Men's Toupee, ventilated foundation. Each **$10.00**

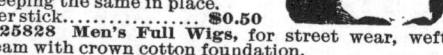

**25827** Toupee Paste, for keeping the same in place. Per stick.........................$0.50
**25828** Men's Full Wigs, for street wear, weft seam with crown cotton foundation. Price each.................................... $8.00
**25829** Men's Wigs, silk foundation. vegetable net seam. Price each.................... $12.00
**25830** Men's Wigs, silk foundation, gauze net seam. Price each.............................. $15.00
**25831** Men's Wigs, silk foundation, hair lace. Price each.................................... $21.00
Extra shades will be charged according to color.
**25833** Minstrel Wigs, or plain black negro wigs. Each ........................................ $0.75
**25835** Grease Paint, for make-up purposes; eight colors in a box. Per box................$0.70
We can furnish any kind of a wig for ladies or gentlemen for masquerade, stage or character purposes.

**HAIR DYES**
**HAIR INVIGORATERS**
AND A GREAT VARIETY OF TOILET PREPARATIONS IN DRUG DEPARTMENT. PAGES 26 TO 35—WHICH SEE.

## How to Measure a Wig.

Directions for measuring the head for a wig to insure a good fit, and mention number of inches.

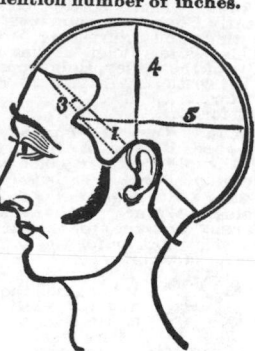

No. 1. The circumference of the head.
No. 2. Forehead to nape of the neck.
No. 3. Ear to ear. across the forehead.
No. 4. Ear to ear, over the top.
No. 5. Temple to temple, around the back.

**To Measure for a Toupee.**

Cut a piece of paper the exact size and shape of the bald spot, also the measure around the head, and mention which side the parting is on.

### Extraordinary Values in Human Hair Switches.

**No. 25836** Short Stem Hair Switches, in all ordinary and medium shades; extra shades will cost from 25 to 50 per cent. extra.

| Weight About. | Length About. | Price. Each. |
|---|---|---|
| 2 ounces | 20 inches | $0.65 |
| 2 ounces | 20 inches | 0.90 |
| 2 ounces | 22 inches | 1.25 |
| 3 ounces | 22 inches | 1.50 |
| 3 ounces | 24 inches | 2.25 |
| 3½ ounces | 26 inches | 3.25 |

Note—The above 65c. switch has long stem.

French Hair Switches can be made to order from $5.00 to $10.00 each.

**No. 25837.** Gray Hair Switches, fine quality, short stem. Be sure to send sample of hair.

| Weight. | Length. | Each |
|---|---|---|
| 2 ounces | 18 inches | $1.75 |
| 2¼ ounces | 22 inches | 2.50 |
| 3 ounces | 23 inches | 4.00 |
| 3 ounces | 25 inches | 5.45 |

Note.—The above prices are for medium shades of gray. Where extra white is ordered it will cost ½ or 50 per cent. more.

### Full Beards.

**25838** On wire..............................$0.80
**25839** Ventilated........................ 1.75

**25840** Mustashe on wire spring, common.
Each.............$0.10
Per dozen............. .75
**25841** Mustache, ventilated.
Each.............$0.20
**25842** Imperials.
Each.............$0.10
**25843** Goatees.
Each .............$0.10
**25844** Whiskers, side. Each........$0.75

The above come in dark and medium shades only.

### The Imperial Hair Regenerator.

**25845** No matter how gray your hair is, or how Bleached or how spoiled by dyes, makes it beautiful, natural, healthy. Restores gray hair to color of youth. Gives the hair new life.

PRICE PER BOTTLE $1.25

## Ladies' Belts.

Belts are going to be largely worn this spring and summer. We have them in large variety and sell them cheap. If new styles appear, after this book goes to press, we are prepared to furnish them. If you do not see what you want among our large assortment, or have some particular style in mind, send us an OPEN ORDER as follows: ("Send me the best belt you can for 25c, 50c or $1.00, latest style.") And you will be well pleased. (Sizes of belts, 20 to 40, waist measure.)

**25850** Ladies' Black Silk Belts; good fancy plated buckles, gilt, silver or black; belting 2 inches wide.
Each................21c

**25851** Ladies' Black Silk Belts; fine quality belting; heavily plated buckles, black, silvered or gold plated.
Each................35c

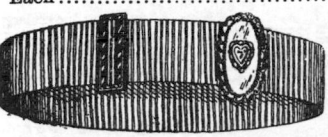

**25852** Our "Special Belt" is an exceptionally fine black silk belt for ladies; 2½ inches wide; handsome heavily plated buckle, black, silver or gold plated.
Each................50c

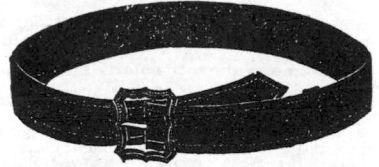

**25853.** Leather Belts for women, in tan and black. Each................10c
**25854.** Stitched leather belts for women, tan or black. Each................15c
**25855.** A fine highly polished leather belt, in black, tan or brown, 1¼ inches wide. Good value at 35c; each................20c
**25856.** Same as above, 1½ inches wide. Each, 22c

**25857** A very handsome alligator Belt, 1½ inches wide, well made and durable, a regular 50c belt. Colors black, brown and tan. Each, $0.25;

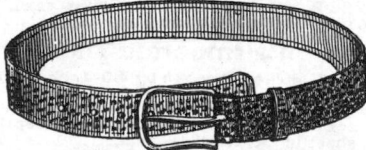

**25858** A very fine Leather Belt, bound with black patent leather. Colors, black, tan and brown. The latest style harness buckle. See cut. Each, 20c

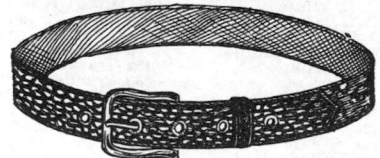

**25860** A Handsome Belt, with a harness buckle stitched all around, lined and well made; colors, tan and brown. Each................25c

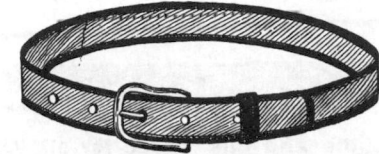

**25862** A Fine Pressed Leather Belt, with harness buckle, good strong loops; colors, orange, tan, grey, green. Each, 25c; 2 for 45c; per doz....$2.50

**25864.** A Fine Embossed Leather Belt, 1½ inches wide, nicely lined, new style harness buckles; colors green, black, tan, orange. Each............$0.50
Two for............$0.95  Per dozen............$5.50

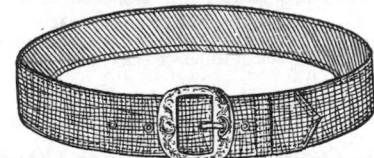

**25866.** A Fine Seal Belt, lined, with handsome plated buckle; comes in tan, olive, orange and black. Each............$0.60
Two for... ............$1.10  Per dozen............6.00

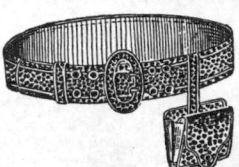

**25868** A Fine Belt, made of leather with pocket book attached. Worth 50 cents. Colors, black, tan or brown. Each............25c
**25870** A regular $1 Belt, with pocket book attached. Colors, black, tan or brown. Each............50c

### Belt Holder for Leather Belts.

**25872** Our new belt holder holds the belt in place and prevents the band of the skirt from showing. Universally used last season, and ladies who have used it would not be without it at any cost. Gilt, silvered and black. The belt won't slip and the band won't show if you wear our belt holder. Each............$0.04
Three for............10

### Belt Pins.
**For Holding Ladies' Silk Belts in Place.**

**25876** A Good Silvered or Gilt Pin. 3 for 5c; Per doz............$0.15
**25877** Fancy Ornamental Belt Pins. Each, 4c;
**25878** Nice Heavy Belt Pins, nicely cut, looks like sterling silver, fancy loop edge. These pins are really worth 25 cents each. Each............10c

**25880** Ladies' Fine Plated Belt Buckle, either in gilt or silver, complete with slide.
Each............11c
**25882** A Beautiful Buckle for ladies' belts, good heavy plate in gold or silver. New and extremely pretty designs. A buckle that every retail merchant sells for 50c. Each............25c

### Silk Belting by the Yard.
**25884.** Silk Belting, 2 inches wide; a good fair quality and one that usually sells for 25c.
Per yard............12½c
**25886** Silk Belting, 2½ inches wide; a fine quality. Per yard............22c
Add ¼ yard additional to waist measure when ordering belting.

### Stamped Cotton Duck Tidies—White.
**25890** White Duck Tidies, 7 inches square, stamped (just the thing for children to practice on).
Per dozen............$0.10
Three dozen for............0.28
Per gross............1.05
**25892** Same as above, in the following sizes:

| Size (inches) | 9x9 | 12x12 | 18x18 | 24x24 | 18x27 |
|---|---|---|---|---|---|
| Each | $.02 | $.03 | $.07 | $.12 | $.10 |
| Dozen | .15 | .25 | .70 | 1.30 | 1.00 |
| Gross | 1.75 | 2.85 | 7.50 | 14.00 | 11.00 |

### Stamped Linen Squares.

**Stamped Linen Squares.**

**25894** Stamped on good quality linen; can be worked with any kind of wash silks. These squares are stamped in all the latest patterns.

| Sizes (inches) | 7x7 | 9x9 | 12x12 | 18x18 | 24x24 | 18x27 |
|---|---|---|---|---|---|---|
| Each | $.03 | $.04 | $.06 | $.12 | $.24 | $.20 |
| Dozen | .30 | .40 | .60 | 1.25 | 2.30 | 2.00 |

**25896** Linen Squares, fine quality, hemstitched, usually sold at more than twice the prices we ask.

| Size (inches) | 7x7 | 9x9 | 12x12 | 18x18 | 24x24 |
|---|---|---|---|---|---|
| Each | $0.08 | $0.13 | $0.18 | $0.34 | $0.45 |

Note.—This quality of linen worked with wash silks, size 18x18, has been sold as high as $8.00 in this market.
**25898** Linen Squares, hemstitched, open work in corners and on all four sides.

| Sizes (inches) | 12x12 | 18x18 | 24x24 |
|---|---|---|---|
| Price | $0.18 | $0.28 | $0.38 |

**28899** Dresser Scarfs, size 16x46, fringed, cotton cloth. Each............$0.12
**25900** Linen Dresser Scarf, 17x54 inches, stamped in newest design, hemstitched. Each............$0.40
**25902** Linen Dresser Scarf, good quality cloth, handsomely stamped, hemstitched, with open work all around. Each............$0.55

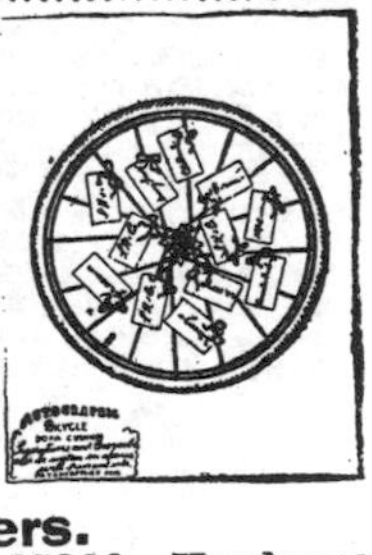

**25904** Autographic Bicycle Sofa Cushion, top made of sateen, 22x22 inches, bicycle wheel pattern, with cards attached to spokes. When these cards have been filled out with the autographs of your friends and cushion is worked, it has a handsome effect—entirely new. Each............$0.40
**25905** Denim Sofa Cushions, stamped; size, 18x18. Each............$0.16

### Table Covers.

**25906** Handsome Table Covers, 1 yard square, fringed all around, stamped and tinted in beautiful colors, center to be worked with silks or linen floss. Material, white cotton cloth. Each............$0.25
3 for............0.68
**25908** A Beautiful Denim Table Cover, 36 inches square, fringed with fine quality linen fringe, good value at $1.00 each.
Our price, each............$0.63
2 for............1.10

### D'Oyles.
**25910** Stamped Linen D'Oyles, fringed; a nice line of patterns. Size, 8x8 inches. Each............$0.05
6 for............0.25
**25912** Stamped Linen D'Oyles, fringed, large assortment of patterns. Size, 10x10 inches.
Each............$0.05
6 for............0.25

### Splashers.
**25914** Stamped Splashers, on white cotton duck cloth. Size, 18x27 (fringed on three sides).
Each............$0.10
3 for............0.28

### Stamped Tray Cloths.
**25916** Tray Cloth, stamped on art linen and 4 d'oyles. Size, 18x36 inches. Each............$0.22

## Shoe Pockets Stamped.

**25918** 2-Pocket Denim Shoe Pocket, nicely stamped, with brass eyelet (to hang up by). Each.......... $0.17
**25920** Same as above, with 4 pockets, each.. $0.25

## Laundry Bags.

**25922** Laundry Bags, made of good denim, stamped good, draw strings at top. Size, 16¾x31. Each...... $0.30

## Stamped Pillow Shams.

**GOOD QUALITY PILLOW SHAMS FOR VERY LITTLE MONEY.**

**25924** Muslin Pillow Shams, white, assorted patterns. Size, 32x32 in. Per pair.......... $0.19

**25926.** Muslin Pillow Shams—One stamped—" I slept and dreamt that life was beauty." The other stamped—"I awoke and found that life was duty." Per pair........ $0.23 (Other designs also.)

## Muslin Bibs.

**25928** Stamped Cotton Bibs, 10x13 inches—bound and fringed. Each........... $0.05 Six for........... 25
**25930** Heavy Duck Bib, stamped, bound and fringed. Each, 6c; 6 for....... $0.28

## Linen Fringe.

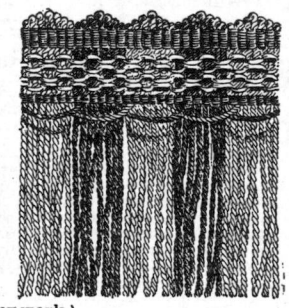

**25932** Linen Fringe, 4 inches wide, nice showy heading, plain colors, cream white and ecru, shaded colors, white and pink, white and yellow, white and red, white and green, blue and white, brown and white, pink and green.
Per yard... $0.05
Per dozen.. $0.52
(Note.—Linen fringe is used for edging table corners, cushions and for all kinds of fancy work.)

## Ornaments for Fancy Work.

**25934** Silk Chenille Balls for fancy work, about ¾ inch in diameter, can be used for finishing all kinds of fancy work. Colors, white, pink, rose, blue, green, red, yellow; shaded colors, pink and blue, pink and green, blue and white, heliotrope and white, yellow and white. Per dozen.................... $0.09
Three dozen for............ 0.25

**25936** Silk Tassels, about 2½ inches long, made in almost every color, good silk loops, can be used for all kinds of fancy work. Per dozen........... $0.06
Three dozen.............. .17

**25938** Silk Tassels, about 4 inches long, very full and heavy, comes in all colors, for fancy work.
Per dozen..................... $0.25

**25940** Silk Tassel Fringe, comes in nearly all colors (18 tassels to each yard), heading of silk ¾ inch wide, tassels nearly two inches long—for fancy work. This fringe is worth 15c per yard.
Per yard, 10c; 4 yards for..................... $0.35

## Fancy Cords.

### Chenille and Silk Cords for all Kinds of Art Work.

**25942** Chenille Cord, combined with tinsel, a very pretty cord for fancy work, comes in all standard colors.
Per yard........................ $0.05
12 yards......................... 0.55
**25944** A Very Nice Twisted Cord for fancy work, comes in all shades in popular use; good value at 15c per yard.
Per yard.......................... $0.07
12 yards.......................... $.75

## Materials for Art Embroidery.

**25946** Embroidery Hoops, wood, sizes 4 to 12 inches in diameter. Per pair................... $0.05

### Beads.

**25948** Steel Beads, cut. Per bunch....... $0.10
**25950** Gold Beads, cut. Per bunch....... $0.15

### Embroidery Linen.

**25952** Ideal Embroidery Linen Thread, for working all kinds of linen, comes in all staple shades. Per dozen skeins.......................... $0.28

### Washable Gold Thread.

**25954** Washable Gold Thread, for fancy work, 12 yards to each bunch. Per bunch........... $0.15

**FOR WASH EMBROIDERY SILKS SEE NOTION DEPARTMENT.**

## Honiton Lace Braids.
### (For fancy work.)

**25958** Honiton Lace Braid, like illustration.
Per yard.............................. $0.06
Per dozen............................ 0.60

**25960** Honiton Lace Braid, like illustration.
Per yard............................ $0.07
Per dozen............................ 0.75

**25962** Honiton Lace Braid, see illustration.
Per yard.............................. $0.08
Per dozen............................ 0.80

**25964** Honiton Lace Braid, see drawing.
Per yard.............................. $0.08
Per dozen............................ 0.80

**25966** Lace Braid, see illustration.
Per yard.............................. $0.08
Per dozen............................ 0.80

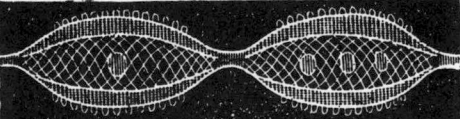

**25968** Honiton Braid, see drawing.
Per yard.............................. $0.09
Per dozen............................ 0.95

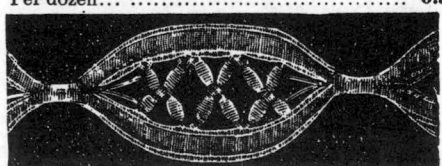

## Stamping Pattern Outfits.
### STAMP YOUR OWN LINEN.

Stamping Patterns Perforated, new and desirable patterns.

Send us a sketch or tell us what you want and we will design you any pattern for stamping. The cost is regulated by the size and amount of work on patterns. A pattern 5x5 inches is 5 cents, 15x25 inches is 25 cents, and so on.

**Our Outfits Contain the Following Articles.**

**25972** The "Quinette" Stamping Outfit consists of 26 full sized, new and pretty stamping patterns, one complete alphabet, one box black and one box white stamping powder and one pad.
Per outfit.................... $0.40
**25974** The "Loueve" Stamping Outfit consists of 75 full sized patterns, for stamping any and all kinds of linens and sofa pillows, one complete alphabet, one box white and one box black stamping powder and one pad. Price per outfit. $0.79
**25976** Stamping Powder, black, white or blue.
Per box..................... $0.10
**25978** Stamping Liquid, in blue and black.
Per bottle..................... $0.10

**Liquids are not Mailable.**

The pleasure of knitting is greatly enhanced by working with good material. The line of yarns we quote is the best, and we take pains to send out such quality that we will have no occasion to apologize, but, on the other hand, are sure to please our customers and gain their future trade.

**25980** Good Quality German Knitting Yarn, skeins to each pound. Black or white. Per lb. $0.55
5-lb. package............... 2.50
**25982** Same as above in colors. Per pound $0.60
5-lb. package............... 2.75
**25984** Our Best Imported German Knitting Yarn, very soft nice yarn; 4 skeins to each pound. Black, white or colors; usual value $1.25 per pound.
Per pound........ $1.05   5-lb. package...... $4.90
**25986** Our Best Imported Saxony Yarn, used for knitting fine goods. Black, white or colors. 20 skeins to pound; value, $1.50. Per pound... $1.10
**25988** Imported Spanish Yarn, (a little coarser than saxony); black, white and colors; 8 skeins to pound. Per pound........................ $1.05
**25990** The Best Germantown Yarn, Imported; 16 skeins to each pound. Black, white and colors. Per pound............................. $1.15
**25992** Single Zephyr. Black, white and colors; ours is the finest kind ever brought to this country; 40 skeins or laps to pound. Per pound....... $1.25
**25994** Split Zephyr. Half the thickness of single, none better imported; black, white and colors; 40 skeins or laps to pound. Per pound.... $1.30

### Ice Wool.

**25996** Small Boxes of Ice Wool, 8 balls to box, 16 boxes to pound; black and white. Per box.. $0.10
Per pound..................... 1.58
**25998** Ice Wool, colored. Per box....... $0.12
Per pound..................... 1.88
**26001** Angora Yarn, black, white or colors; the fine fluffy yarn, often called "Pussy yarn," 64 balls to each pound. Per ball..................... $0.12

## Denison's Imported Tissue Paper.

**26002** Size of Sheet 20 by 30 Inches. This paper is used for making artificial flowers, doll dresses and for all kinds of decorations and fancy work.
Price of Tissue Paper, All Colors Excepting Red.
Per sheet 1c; per dozen sheets............... $0.09
Red Tissue Paper, Per sheet 2c; 12 sheets.... $0.20

**Colors of Plain Tissue Paper.**

| No. | Color | No. | Color |
|---|---|---|---|
| G. B. | White | 017 | Olive Green |
| B. 1. | Pearl | 9b | " " med'm d'k |
| 30 | Blue, light | 9c | " " dark |
| 31 | Blue, medium | 8a | Blue Green |
| 35 | Blue dark | 15x | Grass Green |
| T4 | Apricot | 63 | Lavender, light |
| 70x | Brown, light | 120 | " med'm light |
| 72 | " medium | 123 | Purple, medium |
| 72a | " dark | 124 | " med'm dark |
| 90x | Cream | 68a | " dark |
| 20a | Yellow, light | 126b | " dark |
| 20 | " med'm light | 81 | Salmon, light |
| 21 | " medium | 86 | " medium |
| 22 | " dark | 87x | " dark |
| 22c | " dark | 48 | Pink, light |
| 98 | Orange light | 48½ | " med'm light |
| 94 | " med'm light | 48x | " medium |
| 96 | " medium | 40 | " " |
| 96x | " " dark | 41x | " med'm dark |
| 95a | " " dark | 45 | " dark |
| 95c | " dark | 55 | Red light |
| 095d | " darker | 55a | " medium |
| 111 | Black | 55b | " dark |
| 0 | Green, light | 53c | " dark |
| 12 | Green, medium | 155 | " very dark |

**26004 Crepe Tissue Paper.** This paper comes on rolls 20 inches wide; about ten feet in each roll. Crepe Tissue Paper is used for making lamp shades, dolls, photograph frames, fancy boxes, etc., etc. Comes in the following colors: Light Amber, Dark Amber, Apple, Moss, Grass, Nile and Sea Green; Light blush Pink, Dark blush Pink, Pale and Dark Coral, Celestial Blue, Heliotrope, Violet, Purple, Virgin White, Apricot, Ruby Red, Canary, Light Brown, Nut Brown, Black. Per roll........ $0.16

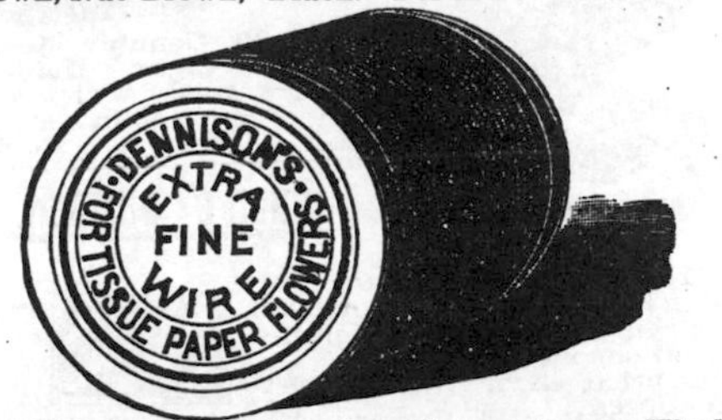


**26006 Spooled Wire for Tissue Paper Work.** Green and White Covered or Plain, per spool 4c. Per dozen.......... $0.45

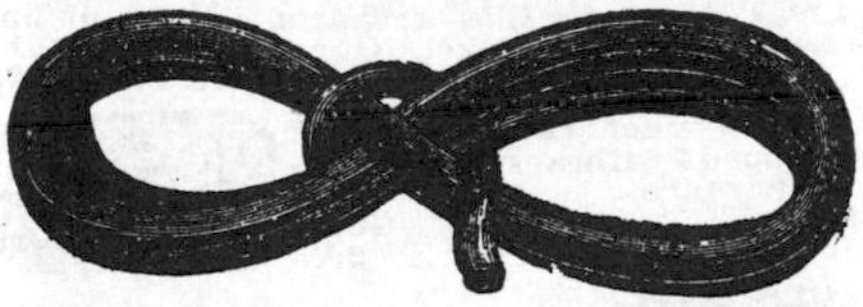

**26008 Rubber Tubing for Flower Stems.** Per Yard.......... $0.03

**26010 Paste for Tissue Paper Work,** Per Bottle.......... $0.07

## Tissue Paper Outfits.

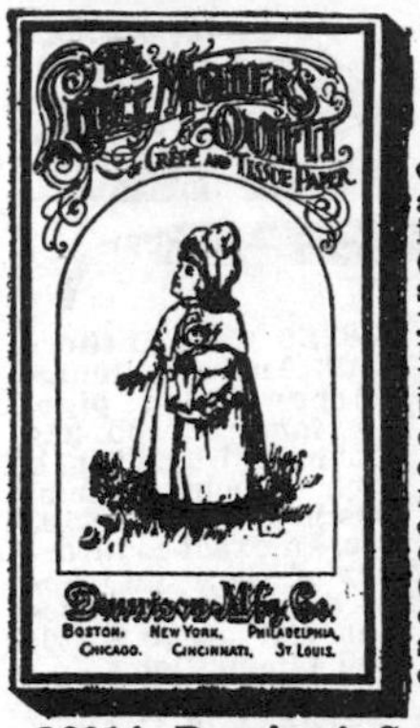


**26012 Little Mother's Outfit.** Put up in a very attractive box; size, 11x6 inches. Contains 5 sheets (5x10) assorted imported tissue, 2 pieces crepe paper, 2 jointed doll forms, 4 dress forms, gold and silver stars, 1 piece paper lace, 3 sheets lace paper, a "Little Mother's Fashion Book," showing designs and directions for making dolls' dresses, a copy of "Art and Decoration in Crepe and Tissue Paper," (144 pages), with 130 samples of tissue paper, and crepe sample card showing 30 colors. Each.......... $0.23

**26014 Dennison's Complete Outfit.** Size of box, 16x6 inches. 36 sheets (15x20) assorted imported tissue, 8 pieces crepe paper, 1 piece tubing each, small and large, 1 doz. each culots, cut sprays and natural moss, 1 spool hair and cotton covered wire, 1 doz. wire stems, 1 doz. leaves, ½ doz. each poppy centers, poppy buds, rose centers, daisy centers, 1 doz. daisy petals, 4 dolls' heads, 4 pairs legs, 4 body forms, 4 dress forms, lithographed sheet in colors, showing various styles of dolls' dresses, directions for making same, a copy of "Art and decoration in Crepe and Tissue Paper," with 130 samples of tissue paper and a sample card of crepe paper. Each.......... $0.70

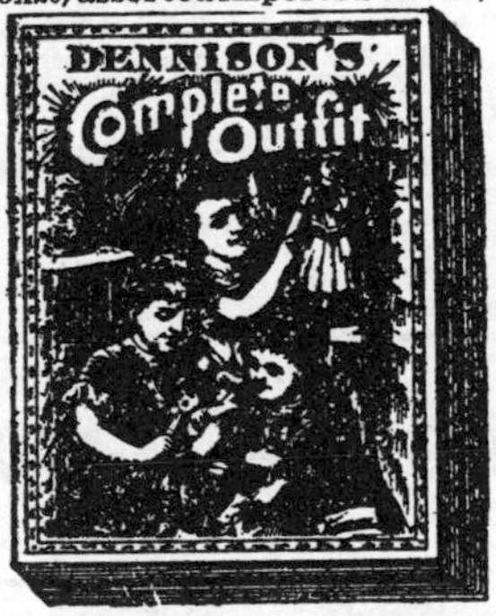


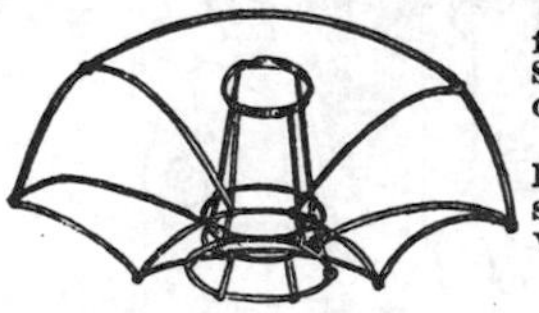

**26016 Wire Frames for making Lamp Shades.** 14 to 18 inches across. Each, 12c;

**26018 Asbestos Collars,** to be placed inside of shade to prevent it taking fire. Each.......... 3c

**26020 This book is worth a great deal of money.** Our little book "Art and Decoration in Crepe and Tissue Paper," tells how to make all kinds of tissue paper work from "A to Z." It contains samples of all the colors of tissue papers; 144 pages. Each.......... $0.07

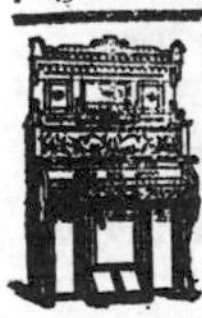

**WE SELL ORGANS ON LIBERAL TERMS....**

**YOU PAY ONLY WHEN SATISFIED THAT THE INSTRUMENT IS FULLY AS REPRESENTED.**

☞ SPECIAL CATALOGUE FREE.

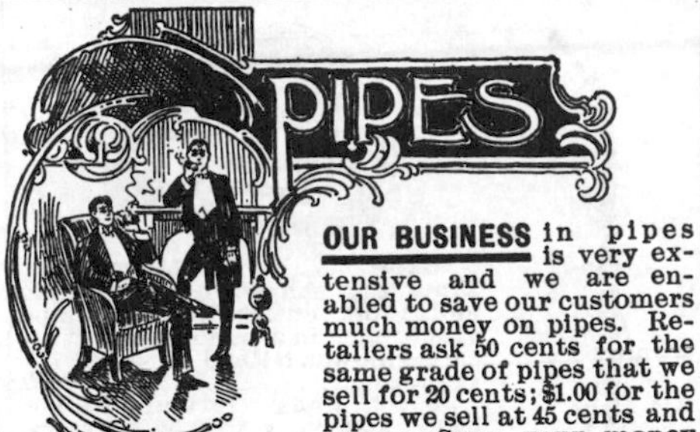


**OUR BUSINESS** in pipes is very extensive and we are enabled to save our customers much money on pipes. Retailers ask 50 cents for the same grade of pipes that we sell for 20 cents; $1.00 for the pipes we sell at 45 cents and so on. **Save your money and buy your pipes of Sears Roebuck & Co;** good pipes only, if cheap trashy goods are wanted we have not got them.

**26030 Polished Apple Wood Pipe,** with silver ferrule and with rubber stem, 2¼ inches long. This is a very handy pipe and well known as a 10 cent article. Our price, each.......... $0.04 Per doz.......... .45

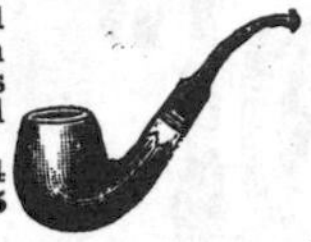

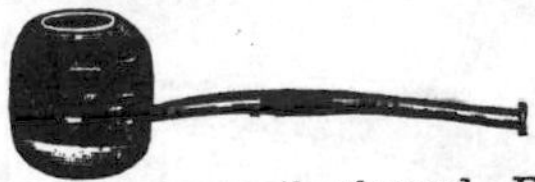

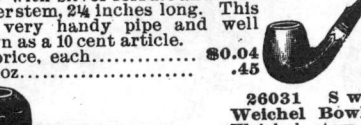

**26031 Sweet Weichel Bowl** and Weichel stem, very highly polished and gives a satisfactory smoke, very easily cleaned. Each.......... 7c

**26032 Good Sized Briar Bowl Pipe,** with a thin rubber shove bits 5¼ inches long. A very nice, convenient pipe and a novelty. Our price, each.......... 8c

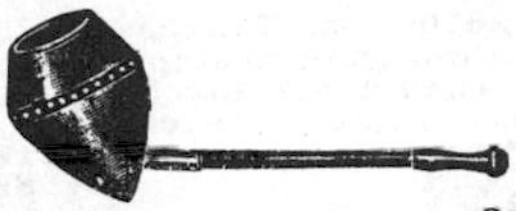

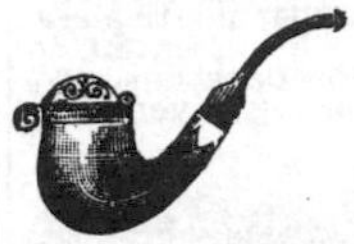

**26034 Handsomely Polished Apple Wood Pipe,** with a highly polished nickel covered spring attachment silver cap, and 2¼ inch rubber stem. A pipe that usually retails in any store for 25 cents. Our price, each.......... $0.10 Per dozen.......... 1.10

**26036 Straight Stem Apple Wood Pipe,** ebonized bowl, making it a very handsome, highly polished pipe; nickel band and 2¼ inch rubber stem. Each,.......... 12c

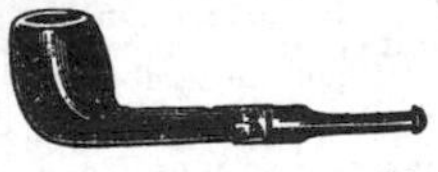

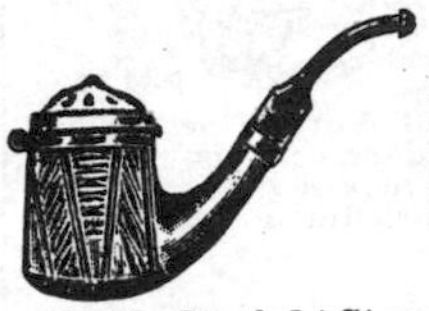

**26038 Fancy Carved Apple Wood Bowl Pipe,** polished nickel cover, with spring attachment, nickel ferrule and cap, 2½ inch rubber stem; an exceedingly handsome pipe. Our price, each.......... $0.15 Per dozen.......... 1.65

**26040 Straight Stem Apple Wood Pipe,** with a patent push cover and a 2-inch rubber stem. By putting your finger on the top and pressing down on the spring, you can push the ashes down in your pipe without lifting the cover. It is considered quite an advantage. Price, each.......... $0.18 Per dozen.......... 2.00

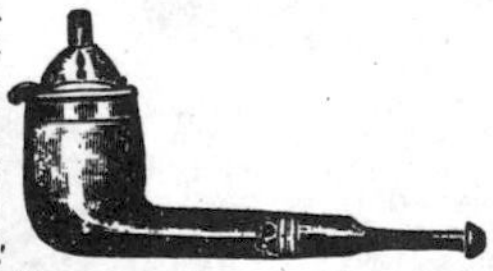

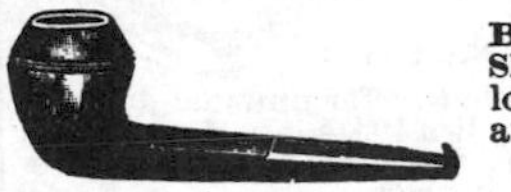

**26042 Real French Briar Pipe, Hayti Shape,** rubber stem 2 in. long, very finely finished and a nicely made pipe. Our price, each.. $0.18 Per dozen.......... 2.00

**26044 Genuine French Briar Pipe,** bulldog shape, square rubber stem and nickel band, an exceedingly handsome pipe and very durable. Our price, each.......... $0.20 Per dozen.......... 2.25

**26046 The New Ceylon Wood Pipe,** meerschaum lined bowl, large bit, rubber stem three inches long, very handsomely finished. Our price, each.. $0.20 Per dozen.......... 2.25

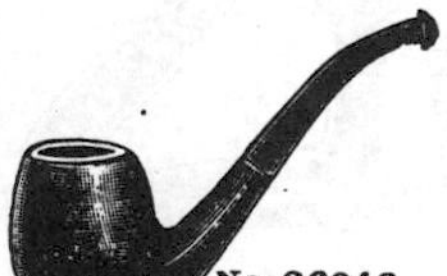

No. 26046

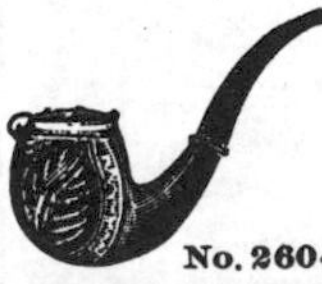

No. 26048

**26048 Beautiful Rosewood Pipe,** handsomely carved bowl, fine nickel cover and nickel cap, 2½ inch rubber stem. Our price each... $0.23 Per dozen.......... 2.50

**26050 Student's Favorite, Dark Colored French Briar,** English bulldog shape, handsome Chinese amber bit 2¼ in. long, square nickel ferrule. Full size, very handsomely finished and a self-cleaner. Price, each.......... $0.25 Per dozen.......... 2.75

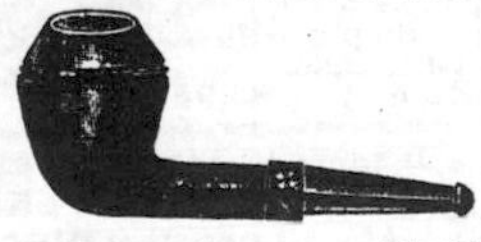

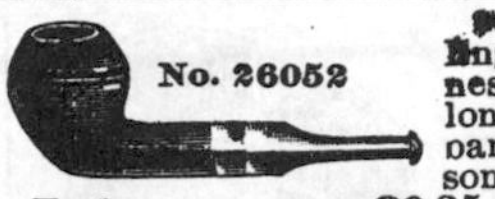

No. 26052

**26052 French Briar** English bulldog shape, Chinese amber bits about 5½ in. long, self-cleaner, nickel band, something very handsome and nicely finished. Each.......... $0.25 Per dozen.......... $2.65

**26054 Chip Meerschaum Pipe,** handsomely nickel mounted, Chinese amber mouthpiece, good sized bowl and looks like a $2.00 pipe. Our price, each.......... $0.25 Per dozen.......... $2.60

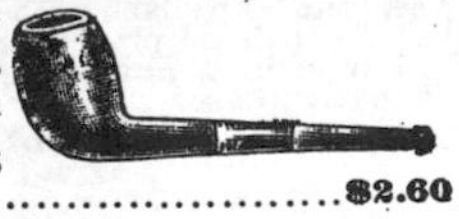

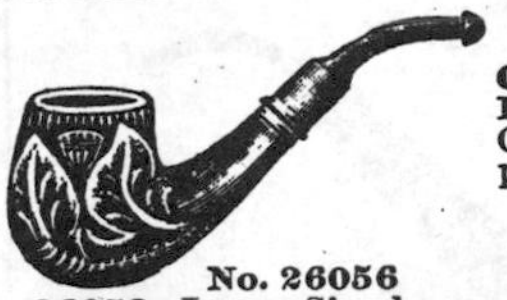

No. 26056

**26056 Handsome Colored Real French Briar Bowl,** bent stem, Chinese amber mouth piece. Each.......... $0.25 Per dozen.......... 2.75

**26058 Large Sized Dark Colored French Briar Pipe,** English amber mouth-piece; entire length of pipe 5 inches. An excellent pipe for anyone enjoying a good smoke. Our price, each.......... $0.30 Per dozen.......... 3.40

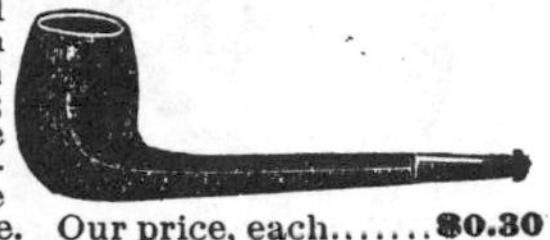

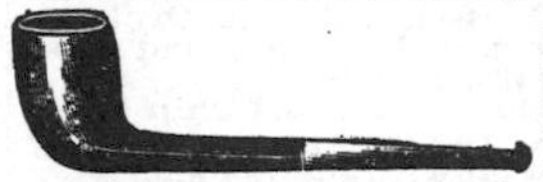

**26060 A Very Fine French Briar Pipe,** good sized bowl, 2½ inch amber stem. A very neat pipe and one that will give satisfaction. Our price each.......... $0.33 Per dozen.......... 3.60

**26062 Handsomely Carved Briar Bowl,** cherry stem, 3 inches long and rubber mouthpiece, entire length of pipe 7 inches. A pipe that is easily cleaned and kept in order and always gives satisfaction. Our price, each.. $0.35 Per dozen.......... 3.75

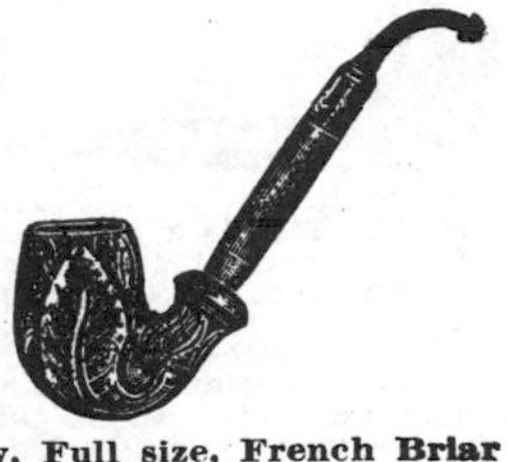

**26064 Extra Quality, Full size, French Briar Pipe,** English bull dog shape, Chinese amber bit, fancy decorated ferrule; gives a very sweet smoke and will be found a good, durable pipe; never retails less than 60 to 70 cents. Our price, each.......... $0.35 Per dozen.......... 4.00

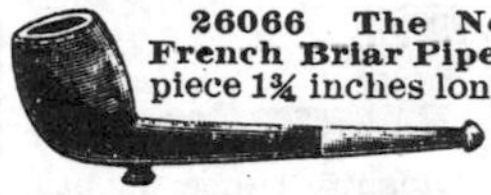

**26066 The New Egg-Shaped Bowl French Briar Pipe,** Chinese amber mouthpiece 1¾ inches long. A very neat pipe. Each.......... $0.35 Per dozen.......... 4.00

**26068 The Always Clean Briar Bowl,** long rubber stem, nicotine absorber, handsomely decorated cover; a pipe that can be taken apart in four pieces, and usually retails for $1.00. Our price, each.... $0.40

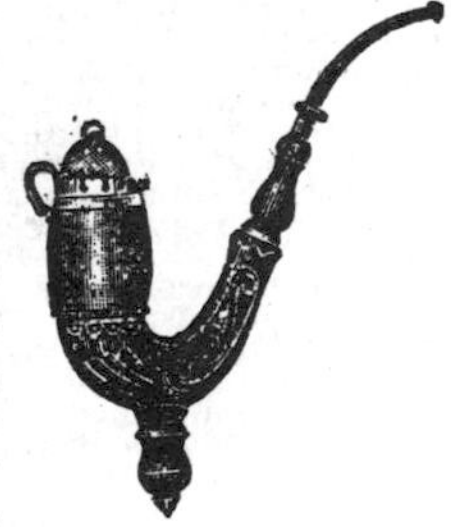

No. 26068

**26070 Genuine Briar Pipe,** fancy hand-carved bowl, 1¼ inch amber mouthpiece. A very handsome, as well as durable, pipe. Length of pipe is 5½ inches.

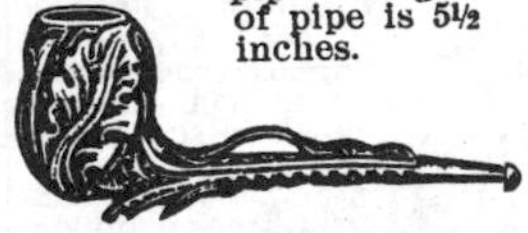

Price, each.......... $0.45 Per dozen.......... 5.00

**26071 A Very Swell French Briar,** known as the Manhattan; with a beautiful bowl, Chinese amber bit, twisted shape in the middle; length of bit, 3½ inches, with a good sized bowl, dark colored briar, making a very handsome pipe. Each, 45c; per dozen.......... $5.00

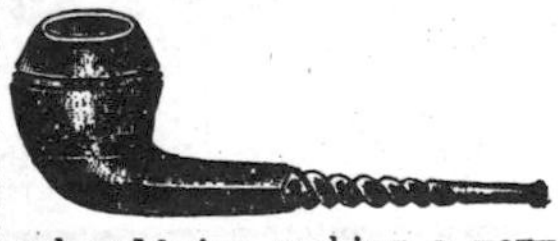

**THIS NUMBER IS A SPECIAL BARGAIN.**

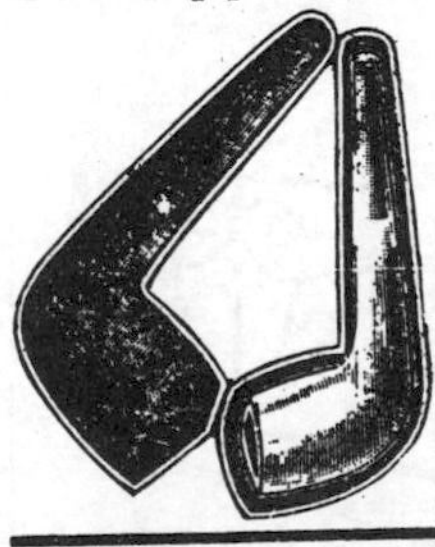

**26072 A Very Handsome Chip Meerschaum Pipe,** with amber mouthpiece 1½ inch long, good sized bowl. Entire length of pipe, 5 inches. Each pipe in a plush lined leather case. Price, each.......... $0.70

**MARVELS OF STYLE.** SEE THE FULL PAGE PLATES OF LADIES' CAPES.

OUR GROCERY DEPARTMENT QUOTES A COMPLETE LINE OF THE CHOICEST TOBACCOS. WE ARE VERY LARGE BUYERS OF TOBACCO AND CAN SAVE YOU FROM 20 TO 40 PER CENT. SEE PAGES 23 AND 24.

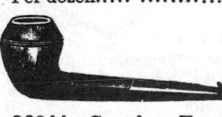

## Fine Chip Meerchaum Pipe.

**26074 Fine Chip Meerchaum Pipe,** bulldog shape, medium sized, with nickle band and English amber bit. Length of pipe, 5 in. Each pipe in a plush lined red leather case.
Price, each .......... $0.75

## Large Size Chip Meerchaum Bowl.

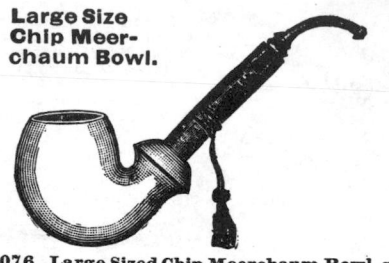

**26076 Large Sized Chip Meerchaum Bowl,** good sized egg shape, handsome cherry stem and Chinese amber bit, silk cord and tassel, entire length of pipe 8½ inches. Something very handsome and looks like a $5.00 article. Our price, each ............ $0.65

**26078 Fine Half Colored Oil Bowl Chip Meerchaum Pipe,** egg shaped, the same as above, cherry stem and Chinese amber bit with silk tassel. Price, each .................... $0.75

**20680 A Handsome French Briar Pipe,** straight stem, 5½ inches long, aluminum band and fine Chinese amber bit, a regular 50c pipe. Our price, each .................... $0.25

**26082 This is a beautiful French Briar Pipe,** straight stem 5½ inches long genuine amber mouthpiece; dealers ask 60c for pipes like these. Each .................... $0.32

**26084 A French Briar Pipe,** one of Sears, Roebuck & Co.'s winners), plain nickled band Chinese amber push bit, cannot get out of order, mouthpiece 2½ inches long; a 75c pipe everywhere; buy them of Sears, Roebuck & Co., at the special price of, each .................... $0.35

**26086 Army French Briar Pipe,** 5 inches long, bent amber mouth-piece; a regular 75c pipe. Each .................... $0.38

**26088 French Briar Pipe,** as per illustration. Has a glass chamber through which the smoke passes, nicotine remaining in the tube, pipe can be taken apart and cleaned, vulcanite rubber mouthpiece; length of pipe, 5 inches. A pipe that is healthful, pleasant and sweet at the same time. This pipe was made to sell at $1.00, but we have made a deal so that we can sell them at a price within the reach of all. Our special price .................... $0.46

**36090 A Fine French Briar Pipe** 5½ inches long, fancy rim of aluminum around top, also band of aluminum; a regular 75 cent pipe. Our price $0.35

**26092 French Briar Pipe,** with nickel band and horn mouth piece, bull dog shaped bowl, 5½ inches long, a regular 80c pipe. Our price, each .......... $0.37

**26094 This Beautiful, Swell, Little Pipe is** 4¼ inches long, briar, bull dog shape bowl, mouth piece of genuine clear amber. This is the pipe, when a real high toned pipe is wanted. Good value at $1.65. Our price .................... $0.78

**26096 A French Briar Pipe** 5½ inches, long aluminum rim around bowl, also aluminum band around stem, mouth piece of Chinese amber, twisted, put up in a fancy case. A pipe that is made to retail for $1.95.

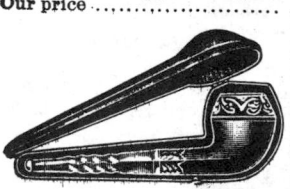

Our price, each .................... $0.96
**56098 The Same Pipe** as described above with a straight Chinese amber mouth piece. Each $0.96

## IRON BEDS AT HALF PRICE....

**SEE FURNITURE DEPARTMENT.**

---

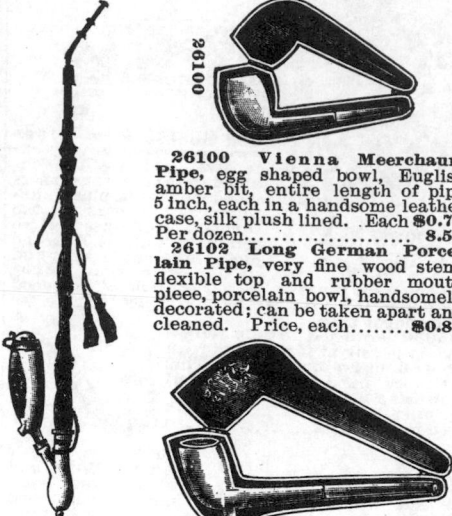

26100

**26100 Vienna Meerchaum Pipe,** egg shaped bowl, English amber bit, entire length of pipe 5 inch, each in a handsome leather case, silk plush lined. Each $0.75
Per dozen .................... 8.50

**26102 Long German Porcelain Pipe,** very fine wood stem, flexible top and rubber mouth piece, porcelain bowl, handsomely decorated; can be taken apart and cleaned. Price, each .......... $0.85

26102     26106

**26106 Chip Meerchaum Pipe.** Length, 6 inches, with an amber mouthpiece 2½ inches long, good sized bowl, warranted to color. Each pipe in a plush lined leather case. Price, each .................... $1.25

**26110 Extra Fine Quality Select French Briar Pipe,** English bulldog shape, 5½ inches in length, 3 inch genuine amber mouth piece. Each .................... $1.35

**26112 The same as above pipe** in dark finish, 2½ inches, genuine amber bit and sterling silver band, good sized bowl. Each .................... $1.35

**26114 Handsome French Briar,** Dublin shape, dark colored pipe; with genuine amber bit entire length of pipe, 5¼ inches, each in a fine leather case, plush lined. Each .................... $1.45

26114

**26116 Very Fine French Briar,** dark color bowl, 3 inch amber mouth piece, each in silk plush lined leather case. Each .................... $1.75

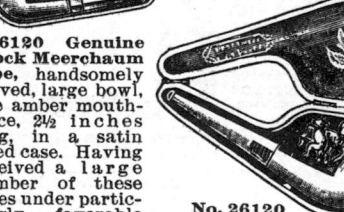

**26120 Genuine Block Meerchaum Pipe,** handsomely carved, large bowl, fine amber mouthpiece, 2½ inches long, in a satin lined case. Having received a large number of those pipes under particularly favorable circumstances, we are able to offer unusual inducements. The price we ask is a little less than what it costs to import them. It is a pipe that usually retails for at least $4.50. Our price .................... $2.50

No. 26120

**26122 Genuine Block Meerchaum,** with real Amber mouth-piece, 2½ inches long, good sized bowl, egg shaped, the very finest quality. Each in a velvet and satin lined leather case, and come in the following sizes:

| Nos. | 4 | 5 |
|---|---|---|
| Price | $2.25 | $3.25 |
| Nos. | 6 | 7 |
| Price | $3.95 | $4.50 |

**26126 Finest Quality French Briar Pipe.** English bulldog shape, three inch genuine amber mouth-piece with wide solid gold band; really the handsomest got up pipe made; each in a silk plush lined leather case. Each ...... $3.95

---

**26130 Twisted Rubber Cigar Holder,** something new, to give a nice cool smoke. Price, each .......... $0.10

**26134 Genuine Meerchaum Cigar Holder** with amber mouth piece, each in leather case. Price .................... $0.45

**26136 Genuine Meerchaum Cigar Holder,** fancy carved with real amber bit, each in leather case. Each ........ $0.69

## ORDER BY NUMBER.

**26138 The Handy Pocket Match Safe,** finely finished nickel, by pushing cover slightly it pushes out but one match at a time. Our price, each ............ $0.10
Per dozen .................... 1.00

**26140 The Charm Match Safe,** smooth top and bottom, rough sides, opens with a spring like a charm. Made of fine nickel. Our price, each .. $0.14
Per dozen .................... 1.25

**26142 Pocket Match Safe,** solid nickel, opens with a spring, something very nice. Each .................... $0.25
Per dozen .................... 2.75

**26144 Snuff Box,** oval shape, made of composition, inlaid, pearl top and tin lined. Each .................... $0.39

**26146 Handsomely Decorated Snuff Box,** pearl inlaid cover, flat shape, very convenient. Price, each .......... $0.25

**26150 "The Fatherland" Antique Vienna Meerchaum pipe,** bowl fancy carved, has a cover and long 8 inch bowl, wiechsel stem. This is a regular $5.00 pipe, an exact counterpart of those old fashioned German pipes that sell up to $25.00; bowl 4 inches long. Each .................... $1.35

**26152 2 in. straight rubber mouthpiece.** Each .................... 3c
**26154 2½ in. curved rubber mouthpiece.** Each, 5c
**26156 2 in. square rubber mouthpiece.** Each, 5c
**26158 2½ in. rubber mouthpiece,** with nickle ferrule. Each .................... 5c
**26160 6½ in. weichsel pipe stem,** with curved mouthpiece. Each .................... 15c
**26162 7 in. cherry pipe stem,** with curved mouthpiece. Each .................... 10c

## ♦♦♦♦ MEN'S ♦♦♦♦
# FINEST TAILOR-MADE CLOTHING.

**OUR MOST COMPLETE STOCK IS**
**PARTIALLY ILLUSTRATED AND DESCRIBED,**
ON PAGES 156 TO 176.

---

## >>> THE NEW FANS FOR 1897. <<<

WE IMPORT ALL OF OUR FANS DIRECT. Our fans are selected by competent buyers who chose the prettiest patterns from among thousands. The price we sell fans at are as in all of our lines, away down low.

### Japanese Folding Fans.

**No. 26300** Japanese Folding Fans, 12 inches long, made of a good quality paper. Beautifully decorated, strong split stick outside. Handsomely corded. Each........**$0.03**

**No. 26302** Full 13-inch Folding Fan, made of fine parchment paper, silver effects, handsomely decorated and illuminated, strong split stick outside, fine colored cord and tassel, a beautiful fan that would retail quick at 25 cents. Our price, each..**6c.**

### Black Folding Fans.

**No. 26304** Black fans, polished sticks, 10 in. Ea. **$0.18**
**No. 25306** Black satin folding fans, 10 inches, Each......**$0.45**
**No. 26308** Black silk gauze fans, 12 inches, carved stick, each..**$0.75**
**No. 25309** Black satin fans, polished, carved stick, 12 inches, Each................**$0.75**

**No. 26310** The New Empire Fan. 9 inches long made of satin, handsomely decorated, sticks nicely ornamented. This is the new swell theatre fan that all of the most stylish ladies of this and other large cities are using at present. Each..**$0.35**

**No. 26312** A Fine 10 Inch Silk Fan, handsomely decorated with buds and leaves on white or tinted ground; decorated sticks equal in appearance to fans that retail at a far higher figure. Each................**$0.66**

**No. 26313** Handsome Tinted Silk Fans, 12 in. long, decorated in handsome floral designs, such a fan as this is would be valued by most judges at twice the price we retail it at. Each................**$0.88**

NOTE—Send us a description of what you want in a fan if you do not see what you want in our list and we will send you better values by 30 per cent. than you expect.

**No. 26314** Coque Feather Fans, polished sticks; fan 12 in. Colors cream, blue and pink. A high grade popular fan for a very small price. Each......**$0.44**
**No. 26316** Genuine Ostrich Feather Fans, cream or black, good first-class stock, will always look nice and curly, fine polished sticks, full size. Each........**$1.25**
**No. 26318** A fine quality Ostrich Feather Fan cream or black, few better made; full large ostrich tips, handsome carved stick. A fan that in appearance looks swell and rich as though it cost much more money than we ask. Each................**$1.95**

## TOILET ARTICLE COMBINATION.

### 10 Useful Articles at the Usual Price of Three.

**EVERY LADY IN THE LAND** Knows what a Luxury it is to have these Little Toilet Articles Around Handy.

### $3.00 Worth of Useful Articles for the Toilet for 95c.

**No. 26338 THIS COMBINATION CONSISTS OF:**

**95 c. for the entire outfit**

1 bottle (8 oz.) Witch Hazel.
1 cake buttermilk soap.
1 bottle Petroleum Jelly (for burns, scalds, etc.)
1 box Swan Down Face Powder.
1 box Tooth Powder.
1 box Cold Cream (for freckles. sunburn, etc.)
1 box Toilet Powder.
1 Fancy Jug Shampoo (makes thirty shampoos.)
1 bottle Triple Extract Perfume (any odor.)
1 Face Chamois Skin.

The Entire Outfit for ....................... **95c.**

### Stamped Tidies and Wash Silk Sets

**No. 26340** A very special inducement, 6 tidies nicely stamped, 9x9 inches, made of duck and 6 skeins of Corticelli wash silk, any shade. The outfit for................**$0.23**
Note the saving.

## A Little Child

Can instantly Mend a rent in any garment. Mend your Clothing neatly and quickly without using needle and thread, by using

**MOSHER'S CELEBRATED....**

### Mending Outfits.

**26342** Outfit consists of 3 square pieces of tissue, about 7x7 inches square in an envelope. Lay the tissue under the rip or tear in the garment whether it be a pair of men's pants, a coat, or a ladies' dress, or a pair of boy's trousers, bring the ends of the cloth together, run a hot flat iron over it and the tear is mended instantly and neatly.
Price, per outfit................**$0.10**

If you tear your coat or dress, use Mosher's Mending Outfits and not needle and thread.

## MANY A WOMAN

Works hard and struggles greatly over a simple little job, when about her daily work, because she has not got the tools,

### TOOLS, TOOLS, TOOLS

That women use every day in the household and sewing room.

### Our Womans' Tool Set

**No. 26344.** Consists of one sewing machine screw driver, one tracing wheel, one machine oil can, one pinking iron, one darning egg, one emery bag, one piece of mending tissue, for mending tears without thread or needle, one pair wooden embroidery hoops, for fancy work, six crochet needles, one set knitting needles, one tape needle, one button hook, one pair button hole scissors, one box patent buttons, instantly attached without sewing.
Our special price for the entire outfit........**$0.75**

### Boston Shopping Bags.

**No. 26320** Boston Shopping Bags. 7x11 inches, has two handles, outside pocket, cloth top with draw strings. Each........ **$0.25**
**No. 26322** Boston Shopping Bags, 8x11 inches, has two handles, outside pocket with clasp, cloth top with draw strings, Each.. **$0.30**
**No. 26324** Boston Shopping Bags, 8x11 inches, two handles, outside pocket and pocket book, with clasp, cloth top with draw strings. Each................ **$0.48**

### Wire Sleeve Supporters, Arm Bands and Garters.

**No. 26328** Patent Duplex Ventilated Men's Arm Bands or Ladies' Garters; fine nickeled steel wire; one pair in box. Each................**$0.08**
Per doz..... .80
**No. 26332** Elastic Band Armlet. made of good, heavy web, assorted colors, sliding clasp. Per pair........................ **$0.04**
**No. 26334** Elastic Band Armlets. Elastic band in assorted colors, with patent sliding clasp to fit any arm. Per pair................ **$0.04**
**No. 26436** Men's Crown Arm Band. Solid rubber cable covered with yarn. strong and cheap. Per pair................**$0.03**

**DRESS IN STYLE.** Buy the New Idea Paper Patterns, any patterns 10c. Send for our pattern catalogue, price, 4c. Illustrations of 500 patterns,

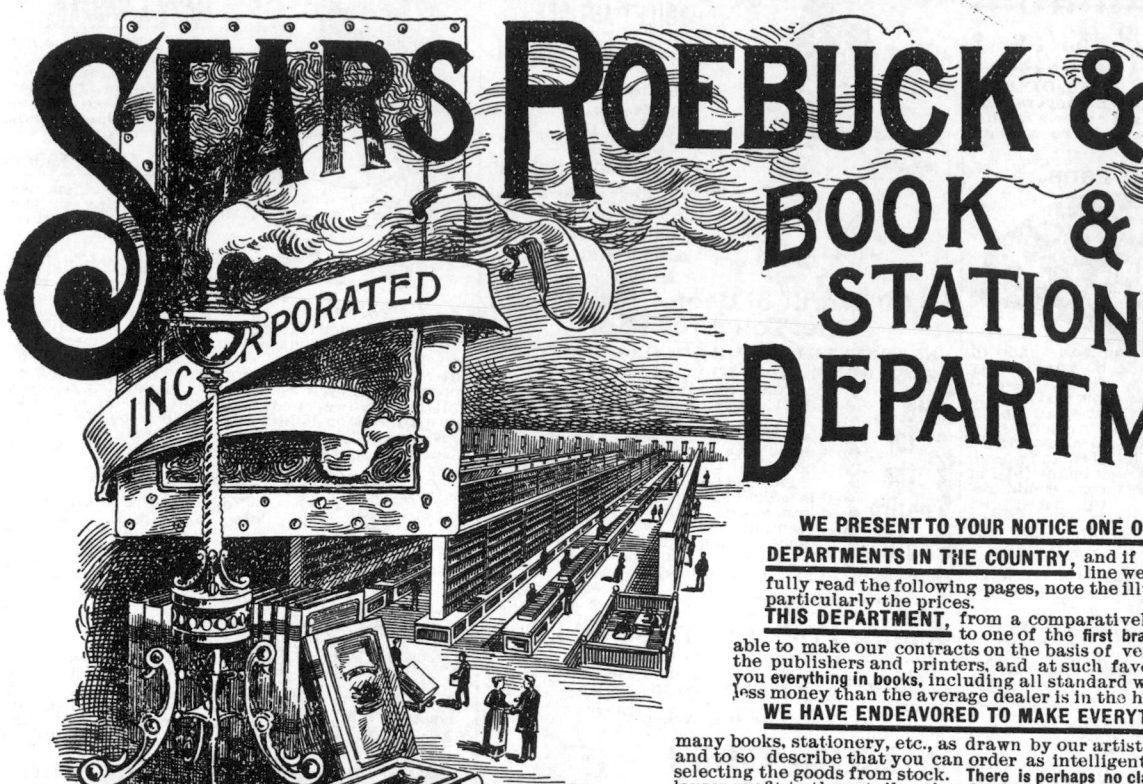

# SEARS ROEBUCK & CO. INCORPORATED BOOK & STATIONERY DEPARTMENT

**WE PRESENT TO YOUR NOTICE ONE OF THE MOST COMPLETE BOOK DEPARTMENTS IN THE COUNTRY,** and if interested in anything in this line we believe it will pay you to carefully read the following pages, note the illustrations and descriptions and particularly the prices.

**THIS DEPARTMENT,** from a comparatively small beginning, has grown to one of the **first branches of our business.** We are able to make our contracts on the basis of very large quantities direct with the publishers and printers, and at such favorable prices that we can offer you **everything in books,** including all standard works and publications, at even less money than the average dealer is in the habit of paying.

**WE HAVE ENDEAVORED TO MAKE EVERYTHING PLAIN** by showing small illustrations of many books, stationery, etc., as drawn by our artists direct from the photographs, and to so describe that you can order as intelligently as if you were in our store selecting the goods from stock. There is perhaps no class of merchandise which bears a larger profit to the retailer than books and stationery. What his profit is you can readily ascertain by comparing our prices with the prices charged by retailers. To save this profit it is only necessary to send your orders to us, and your order and your correspondence will have the prompt and careful attention of either the manager or one of his able assistants.

**TERMS.** We will **ship books** by express or freight C. O. D. **subject to examination,** when a sufficient amount accompanies the order to cover transportation charges both ways. You can examine the goods at your freight or express office, and if found satisfactory pay the agent our price and transportation charges, less the amount sent with order. **A DISCOUNT OF 3 PER CENT.** will be allowed if cash in full accompanies your order. **The best way** is to send cash in full, for you save express charges on return of money to us, and also the 3 per cent. cash discount.

**ABOUT MAIL SHIPMENTS.** When books are to be sent by mail be sure to enclose enough extra to pay postage. If you send too much we will immediately return the balance, but if you do not send enough we will be compelled to hold your order and write for the balance. **Do not** overlook the necessary postage in ordering books by mail.

**OUR CLUB ORDER SYSTEM** commends itself to book buyers, for you will observe in looking over this catalogue that we have been able to figure our prices so low on many of the books that we can quote them to you at but little more than the cost of postage. For example, **our Advance Series,** beautiful cloth bound books at 22c each, or 20c in lots of five; postage 10c per volume. It is therefore much cheaper to have books shipped by express or freight, freight being preferable. The transportation cost per volume is then reduced to next to nothing. **To take advantage of the lowest transportation rate** it is desirable to make up a freight order. This you can do by getting your friends and neighbors to join with you and make up a club order, which will also entitle you to our larger discount of 4 and 5 per cent. if the order is sufficiently large. See "Discounts for Cash" on page 3.

**WE ALWAYS ADVISE OUR CUSTOMERS** to make their book orders large enough that we may **ship by freight,** but if one or more books are wanted by mail the postage must be included.

---

## Harvard Book Holders.

An ornament to the home, office and library. No wood-work used in their construction. A holder we highly recommend. The sides are operated by double acting springs, the book being firmly clamped while closed, and resting upon a level surface when open. The adjustment to books of different sizes and the inclination to any angle or slant are effected by a single screw. They are adjustable to different heights, and are easily set up. They are warranted not to break or get out of order with ordinary use, and after years of proper use will be as good as new. **52000** Complete with casters and revolving book shelf. Nickel Plated and highly polished or antique copper. Price............$3.85

**52002** Complete with casters and Revolving Book Shelf and finished in rubber, Japan or bronze. Price...............$2.10

**52003** One same style as No. 52000 but no shelf or casters. Price...............$1.85

## Noyes' Dictionary and Book Holders.

Cannot be broken with ordinary usage. The edges of the covers are protected by felt-lined guards, and the rests are so made that the book cannot get out of shape.

**52008.** Noyes' adjustable Book Holder with book rest, bronze. Price...............$2.10

No. 52010.    No. 52008.

**52010** With Book Rack to hold two volumes, bronze. Price...............$3.25

---

## Globes.

For offices, homes, libraries, or the school room these globes **are the best in the country** at the price we offer them.

**It would be impossible** to place too much emphasis upon the fact that the covers used upon these globes, all sizes, **are from new plates.** Every improvement in engraving, printing, coloring and mounting the maps has received critical attention, and the latest geographical changes are correctly shown.

A copy of the Globe Manual will accompany each globe.

**The Manual Gives Explanations of the Terms Used in Geography and Astronomy,** and the phenomena of mathematical geography, including **temperature and ocean currents,** and forty-six problems on the use of globes, with rules and illustrative examples; also several valuable tables.

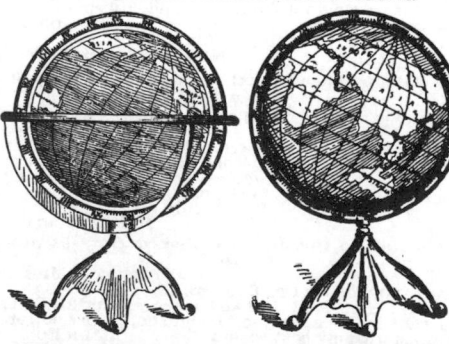

**52012. Full Mounted.**
(Order by number.)

12-in. (Terrestrial) $8.75
8-in. (Terrestrial) 6.25
12-in. (Celestial) 10.00

**52014. Meridian.**
(Order by number.)

12-in. (Terrestrial) $6.25
8-in. (Terrestrial) 4.38
12-in. (Celestial) 7.50

**With Plain Wood Stand.**
Full Mounted.

12-in. (Terrestrial) $4.00

Meridian.
8-in. (Terrestrial) $2.00
6-in. (Terrestrial) .85

---

## Rand, McNally & Co.'s Columbia Series of large scale school maps.

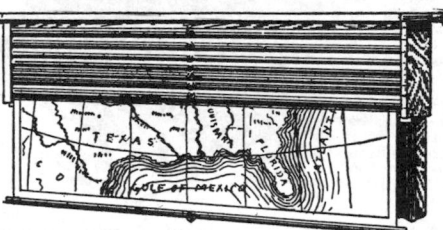

**52020.** This series is prepared in the light of the experience attained in the preparation of the Globe Series, and is intended to stand at the head as excelling in all essential points of merits every other school map published in this or other countries. Seven maps—United States, five continents and World on Mercator's Projection. Best series of educational maps published. Each map 66x46 inches in size. The maps are oil colored and finished and backed with heavy cloth.

| | Pub. price on common rollers. | Our price |
|---|---|---|
| United States | $6 00 | $3 40 |
| North America | 6 00 | 3 40 |
| South America | 6 00 | 3 40 |
| Europe | 6 00 | 3 40 |
| Asia | 6 00 | 3 40 |
| Africa | 6 00 | 3 40 |
| World on Mercator's Projection | 6 00 | 3 40 |

The above maps in Diamond case, publishers price each.........$9.00; our price each......$4.75

**THIS PICTURE** was taken with **THIS CAMERA.**

**WE SELL CAMERAS** at 90c and up. Large Special Catalogue Free on Application, or see our line in this book. Refer to index.

CAMERAS, at 90c and up.

---

**THREE THINGS TO REMEMBER.    POSTAGE MUST BE PREPAID.    EXPRESS IS USUALLY CHEAPER THAN MAIL.    FREIGHT SHIPMENTS ARE THE MOST ECONOMICAL.**

## Rand, McNally & Co.'s "Globe" Series of Wall Maps.

### On Common Rollers.

**52016. All the countries of the world** are shown in this series. Each map is oil colored and finished and backed with heavy cloth.

| | Pub. price | Our price |
|---|---|---|
| Western Hemisphere, size 41x58 inches.. | $5 00 | $2 45 |
| Eastern Hemisphere, size 41x58 inches.. | 5 00 | 2 45 |
| North America, size 41x52 inches........ | 5 00 | 2 45 |
| South America, size 41x52 inches........ | 5 00 | 2 45 |
| United States, Canada and Mexico, size 41x52 inches.......... | 5 00 | 2 45 |
| Europe, size 41x52 inches.............. | 5 00 | 2 45 |
| Asia, size 41x52 inches.................. | 5 00 | 2 45 |
| Africa, size 41x52 inches................ | 5 00 | 2 45 |

**52018.** Any one of the above maps in Diamond case. Publishers price, **$6.50**; our price, **$3.90**

## Rand, McNally & Co.'s Indexed Pocket Maps.

**52022.**

Alabama, 21x28.
Arizona Territory.
Arkansas, 21x28.
British Columbia.
California, County Map of, 21x28.
Colorado, County, 28x21.
Connecticut, 21x14.
Delaware and Maryland.
Florida, 28x21.
Georgia, 28x21.
Idaho.
Illinois, 21x28.
Indiana, 21x28.
Indian Territory, 34x26.
Iowa, 28x21.
Kansas, 28x21.
Kentucky, 28x21.
Louisiana, 28x21.
Maine.
Manitoba.
Maryland and Delaware.
Massachusetts, 28x21.
Michigan, 21x28.
Minnesota, 21x28.
Mississippi, 21x28.
Missouri, 28x21.
Montana.
Nebraska, 28x21.
Nevada.
New Hampshire.
New Jersey.
New Mexico Territory.
New York, County Map of, 28x21.
North Carolina, 28x21.
North Dakota, 24x18.
Nova Scotia, New Brunswick and Pr. Ed. Is.
Ohio, 28x21.
Ontario, Province of, Canada, 28x21.
Oregon, 28x21.
Pennsylvania, County of, 28x21.
Quebec, Prov. of Canada.
Rhode Island, 21x14.
South Carolina, 28x21.
South Dakota, 24x18.
Tennessee, 28x21.
Texas, 28x21.
Utah Territory.
Vermont.
Virginia, 28x21.
Washington, 21x28.
West Virginia.
Wisconsin, 21x28.
Wyoming, 24x18.

Without index. Maps are 14x21 inches, unless otherwise indicated.
Publisher's price, each.............................. **$0.25**
Our price, each................................... **.15**
**Postage, 2c. extra.**

## Map of the World.

**52024. A large map of the World,** with a special map of the United States, England and Wales, Germany, Norway and Sweden. Comprehensive diagrams of mountains and rivers, and alphabetically arranged compilation, describing every country in the world, and its location indexed. The only reversible map showing Rand, McNally & Co.'s latest general map of the United States, size 66x46. Bound with tape; sticks top and bottom, ready to hang on the wall.
Our special prepaid price........................ **$ 1.00**
Per dozen.......................................... **10.80**

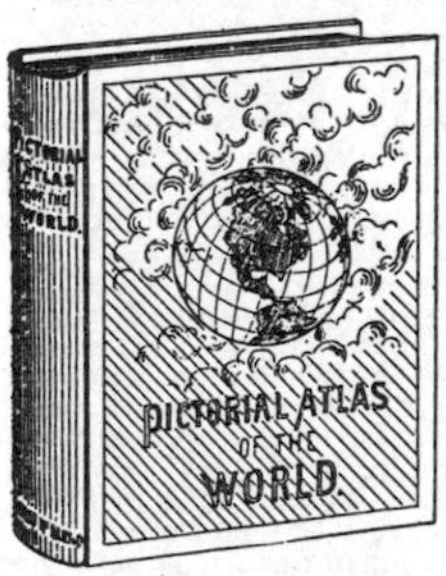


**52026 Rand McNally & Co's. New Pictorial Atlas of the World.** A voluminous description of the world of to-day. It gives correctly the area, population, resources, form of government, geographical position, climate, typography, every point of information of every country on the face of the globe, the world's people, their origin, historical and ethnological development; fully illustrated, showing each state and territory in the United States, Canada, the continents and their subdivisions, prepared with the utmost care, and attractively presented on a large scale in fine colors. A ready reference marginal index is shown upon the maps of every state, city and county. The complete work contains 320 pages, size 12x14½ inches, and is richly and substantially bound. English cloth, marble edges.
Publishers price.................................. **$5.00**
Our price............................................ **2.75**
Half leather, marbled edge, Pub's price.... **8.00**
Our price............................................ **3.60**
**Postage extra 54 cents.**

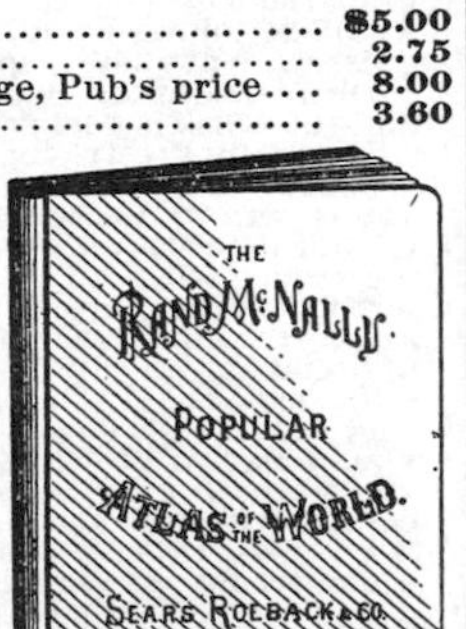


**55028 Popular Atlas of the World.** Rand McNally's Edition, containing large scale, colored maps of each state and territory in the United States, provinces of Canada, the continents and their subdivisions. A ready reference marginal index is shown upon each map: 159 pages, size 11¼x14 inches, cloth bound.
Publisher's price.. **$2.00**
Our price.......... **1.25**
**Postage extra 34 cents.**

## $19.95 Buys a Set of the Encyclopedia Britannica.

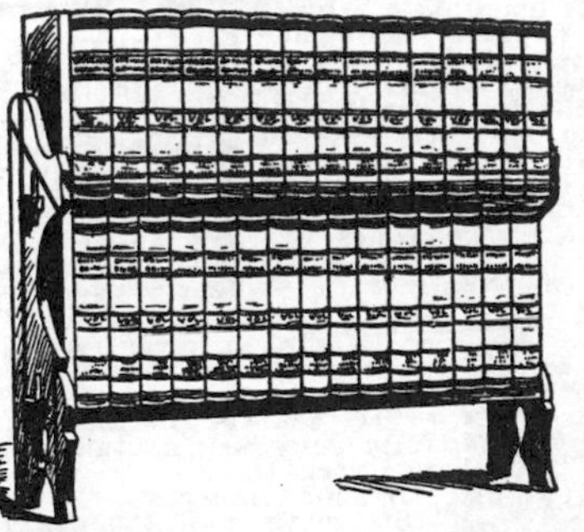

**52030. We have about 100 sets left** out of a lot of 500 complete sets which we purchased some time ago at a close out price. We have been selling them at $29.50, but to close out what we have on hand we have decided **to make a price of $19.95.** When these are gone there will be no more. **Those who order early** will get the benefit of this close out sale, those ordering later may be disappointed. **The above illustration will give you some idea** of the appearance of this set. **It is a complete library in itself.** The reprint edition of the **Encyclopedia Britannia** has sold at from $75.00 to $100.00. the original as high as $250.00. **This is the original Encyclopedia Britannica** reprinted by special arrangements with the publishers and to which has been added an up to date American supplement of five volumes. **This** edition contains exactly the **the same matter as is found** in the higher priced ones which retail at from **$85.00 to $250.00.** Not a syllable or word is missing. **Every map, illustration,** text, shoulder note and marginal reference, being, in fact, page for page, word for word, map for map, plate for plate and volume for volume of the original Edinburg edition. **Thirty large quarto volumes, 26,200 pages, 450 full page engraved plates, 750 full page maps, 14,000 illustrations,** each volume **11 inches long. 9 inches wide** and nearly 2½ inches thick and weighs over 5½ lbs. The volumes are very **handsomely and substantially bound** in heavy cloth, leather trimmed, and much more strongly than the Edinburgh edition. The paper is perfect, of excllent quality, the type is large and clear, while the binding and general appearance of each volume could **not be** more desirable.

**Our Special Terms Offer.** on receipt of $5.00 as a guarantee of good faith, we will send a set of the Encyclopedia Britannica to any address anywhere in the United States by freight C. O. D. subject to examination. You can examine it at the freight depot and **if found perfectly satisfactioy** and exactly as represented, pay the freight agent the balance, $14.95 and freight charges.

## Chambers Encyclopedia.

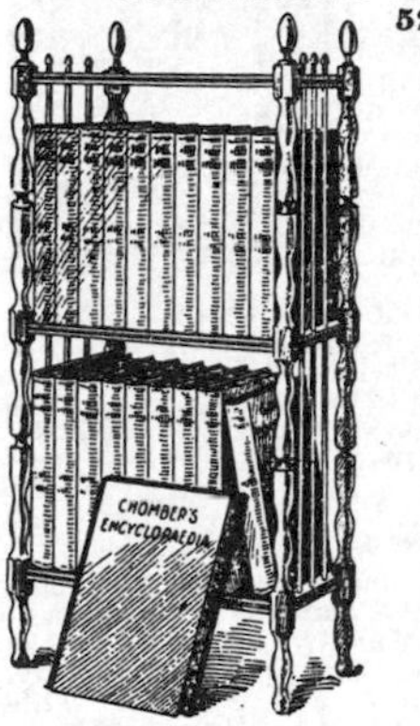


**52032. The popular and reliable Chamber's Encyclopedia,** entirely rewritten and revised; brought down to date in every particular, making a most thorough and complete work of reference on Art, Science, History, Literature, Music, Mythology, Fable, Biography, Geography and in fact all information embracing the entire circle of human knowledge and made especially valuable by the recent American additions on topics of special intrest to Americans. **The latest American census given in full,** in connection with other information of **national importance,** printed in clear type on good paper and bound in finest quality of English silk library cloth, 12mo. complete in 20 volumes.
Publishers price.......................................... **$18.00**
Our price................................................ **7.50**
12 large 12mo. vols., publishers price......... **15.00**
Our price............................................... **5.75**
We do not furnish book stand. See special furniture catalogue.

## The Unique Album Atlas of the World.

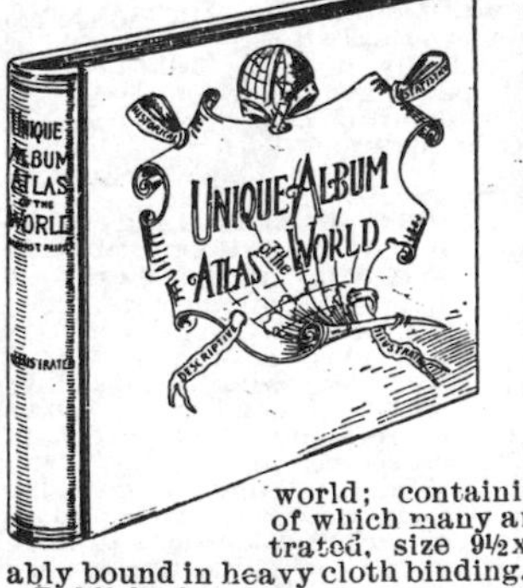


**52034 The World of To-day.** Astronomical, geographical, historical, political, statistical, chronological, financial, commercial, educational, diagrammatical, descriptive and illustrative, together with practical, useful and comprehensive information respecting all the nations and races of the world; containing over 700 pages of which many are profusely illustrated, size 9½x12½ inches, durably bound in heavy cloth binding, embossed in gold.
Publisher's price........................................ **$6.00**
Our price.. .............................................. **2.35**
**Postage 55 cents extra.**

## Webster's Unabridged Dictionary.

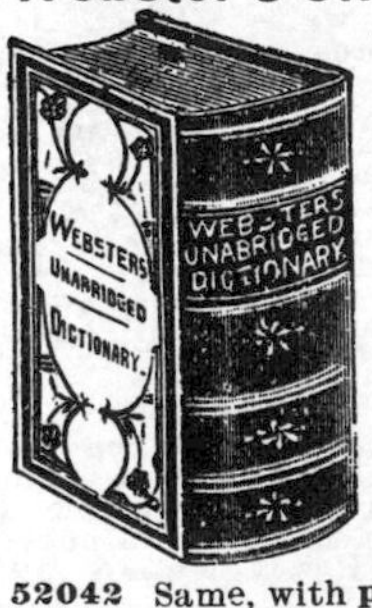


**52040 Original edition, revised and enlarged by Chauncey A. Goodrich, Professor in Yale College.** This Dictionary contains every word that Noah Webster ever defined and 10,000 additional words. **1708 pages; 1500 illustrations; an appendix of 10,000 words.** It also contains **Nine Special Dictionaries,** protected by copyright and not found in any other dictionary. Substantially bound in sheep, with embossed sides, marble edges.
Publishers' price........ **$5.00**
Our price.................... **$1.68**

**52042** Same, with **patent index.**
Publishers' price........................................ **$8.00**
Our Price ................................................ **$3.25**
**Postage extra, 68c.**

## Webster's Unabridged Dictionary.

**52044 Cheaper edition** containing over 1300 **pages,** a table of over 1200 synonyms and a full page portrait of the author, and his autobiography; **the** flags of all nations in their various colors; **size,** 8½x10¾x4 inches; printed on extra strong **paper** from new clear type; bound in heavy cloth **binding.**
Publishers' price ...................................... **$2.50**
Our price.................................................. **.87**
Sheep bound, Publishers' price.................. **3.75**
Our price.................................................. **1.48**
**Postage extra, 48c.**

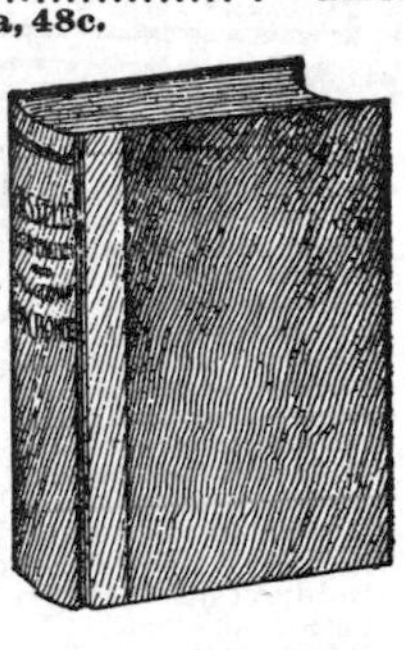

**52046 Cassell's German-English and Englist-German Dictionary.** 90th edition, revised and enlarged by Elizabeth Weir; substantially bound in heavy cloth, crown 8vo.
Publishers' price....... **$1.50**
Our price.... .......... **1.05**
**Postage extra, 18c.**

**52048 Cassell's French-English and English-French Dictionary.** Compiled from the best authorities of both languages. By Professors De Lolme and Wallace and Henry Bridgeman. Revised, corrected and enlarged. Crown 8vo., cloth.
Publishers' price ......................................... **$1.50**
Our price.................................................. **1.05**
**Postage extra, 17c.**

**52050 The Classic French-English and English-French Dictionary.** 8vo, half morocco.
Publishers' price ......................................... **$2.00**
Our price.................................................. **1.50**
**Postage extra, 20c.**

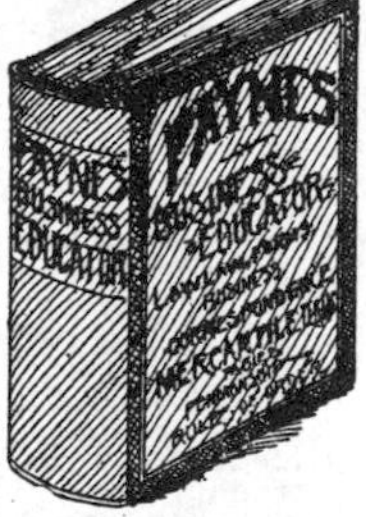


**52060. Payne's Business Encyclopedia and Practical Educator.** A complete Compendium of the knowledge necessary to business success. This great work is conceded to be the most comprehensive, thorough and exhaustive work of this kind ever published. It contains all the essentials of information that may be found in higher priced works, and much that cannot be found elsewhere; also a complete dictionary of mercantile terms, lessons in penmanship, illustrated specimens of pen lettering and brush marking, rules for punctuation marks, dictionary of synonyms. A full working library in one volume. Nothing lacking to its completeness; large 12mo., extra cloth, 600 pages, size 8¼x6 in., weight 2½ pounds.
Publisher's price.......................................... **$3.00**
Our price.................................................. **1.50**
**Postage 18c. extra.**

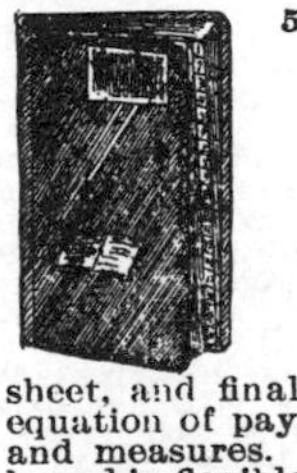

**52062. The Little Giant Book-keeper. Book-keeping at a glance.** By expert J. T. Brierley. A simple and concise method of practical book-keeping. With instructions for the proper keeping of books of accounts and numerous explanations and forms used in a commercial business, showing an entire set of books based upon actual transactions. How to take off a trial balance sheet, and finally close and balance accounts; equation of payments; metric system of weights and measures. Containing 144 pp.; size, 5x2¾ in., bound in flexible Russia, indexed.
Publishers' price.......................................... **70c.**
Our price.................................................. **40c.**
**Postage 4c. extra.**

**A MOST IMPORTANT PART OF THIS CATALOGUE IS THE INDEX. IT IS A GUIDE POST TO ALL THE BARGAINS THE MARKETS OF THE WORLD AFFORD. IF YOU DON'T SEE WHAT YOU WANT, LOOK IN THE INDEX.**

**52064. Brown's Business Correspondence and Manual of Dictation.** A new and desirable work of dictation for teachers and students of shorthand and typewriting, containing a collection of selected lotters representing actual correspondence in banking, insurance, railroad and mercantile business. A chapter on punctuation, spelling and use of capital letters, also special exercises for dictation, carefully graded, comprising selections from choice literature, addresses to jury, judge's charge and sentence, architects' specifications, etc. An important feature of this book, and one that will be appreciated, is the spelling list of over 25,000 words at the end of the book. In no other work, excepting a dictionary, can such a full and complete list be found, and to those who are occasionally uncertain whether "I comes before e," or vice versa, or whether there are two "l's" or only one in a word, this list will prove invaluable; containing over 368 pages; durably bound in cloth.
Publishers' price .......$1.50 Our price.......75c
**Postage extra 12c.**

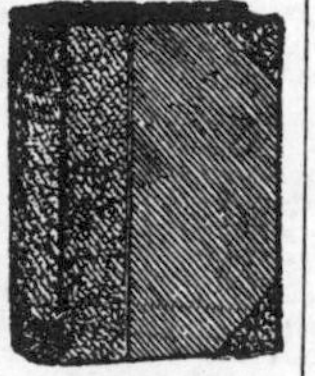

## Hill's Manual of Social and Business Forms.

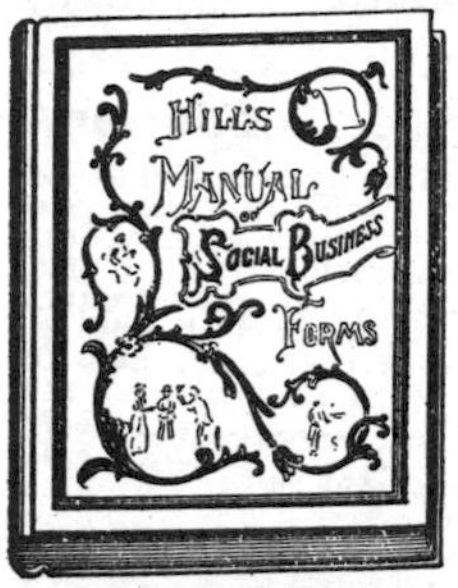


**52066.** This wonderful work has for the last twenty years out classed its imitators and proven its **superior excellence**, and it now stands acknowledged as the **best Manual of Social and Business Forms** before the public. Not only is it the best comprehensive general educator ever published, but it is the **most complete work of reference** that has yet been compiled. It will give the young men a better education than the most expensive set of Encyclopedia's. It is a complete and exhaustive manual of self-education in Penmanship, Elocution, Commercial Law, Parliamentary Law, Incorporation Law, Bookkeeping, Engraving, Courtship and Marriage, Commercial Forms, Sports and Games, Weights and Measures, Dress, Shorthand, Oratory, Banking, Etiquette, Legal Forms, Printing, Sign Writing, How to Write Poetry, Ready Made Speeches, Proof Reading, Rhetoric and Composition, Grammar, Common Law, Financial Law, Balls and Dances, Mortgages, Notes and Leases, Debating, Architecture, 200 Poetic Masterpieces, Historical Outlines, Reference Tables, Health, etc. Size 7½x9 inches; weight 5½ pounds. Sides and back stamped in black and aluminum; red edges; extra quality paper.
Publisher's price..............$3.00;Our price,1.75
Half Morroco, Publishers price 5.00;Our price,2.50
Full Morocco, Publishers price 8.00;Our price,4.25
**Postage extra, 45c.**

**52068. Law at a Glance, or Every Man His Own Counselor,** is a new epitome of the laws of the different states of our Union and those of the **general government of the United States,** and will be found invaluable to those who are forced to appeal to the laws, as well as to that class who wish to avoid it. The whole is alphabetically arranged so as to make reference to it easy. Condensed table of contents: acknowledgment, action, administrator, affidavit, agents, agreement, arbitration, assignment, attorneys, power of attorney, bailment, bankruptcy, bill of exchange, bill of lading, bill of sale, chattel mortgage, form of chattel mortgage, checks, common carrier, consideration, contract, form of contract, conveyance, co-partnership, corporations, damage, debt, deeds, quit-claim form deed, delivery, deposition, descent and distribution of descendents' estates, divorce, draft, easment, employer and employe, endorsement, executors and administrators, exemptions, fraud, guaranty, form of guaranty, guardian, hiring homestead, hotel husband and wife, injunction, injury, inn, insolvency, insurance, interest, judge, judgment, sales, satisfaction, stream, statute of frauds, suit, taxation, tenant, term, trade marks and copyrights, use and occupation, verification, warranty, watercourse, will. This is the most complete work of its kind ever published, containing 317 pages, bound in extra cloth.
Publisher's price......$1.50; Our price.......75
**Postage extra, 12c.**

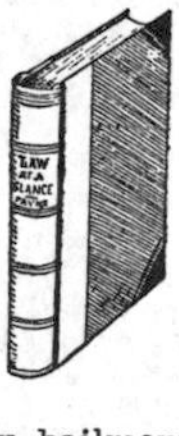

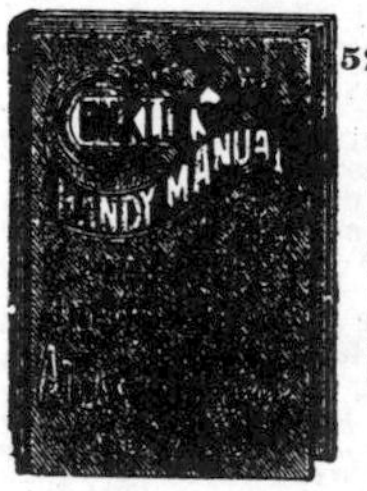


**52070. Conklin's Handy Manual of Useful Information, and Atlas of the World.** A compendium of reliable knowledge; contains 512 pages, 50 full page colored maps; the 1894 Tariff and the McKinley Bill compared; the new copyright law, etc.; strongly bound in extra silk cloth, fine paper, head banded, marbled edges.
Price..............................60c
**Postage 8c extra.**

**52072. Lee's Priceless Recipes.** Containing 368 pages; up to date in every particular; seven leading departments, each thoroughly indexed; recipes for the druggist, the chemist, toilet articles, the household, the farm and the dairy, all trades and professions, etc.; strongly bound in extra silk cloth, printed on fine paper, marbled edges.
Price ..............................60c
**Postage 8c extra.**

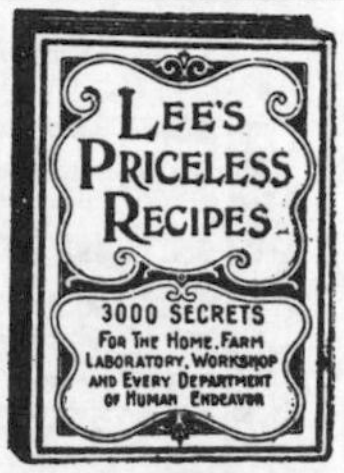


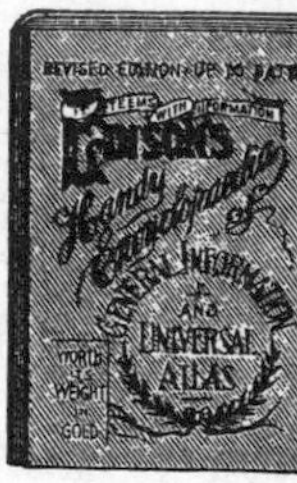

**52074. Edison's Encyclopedia of General Information,** containing 200 subjects of highest value to all, carefully classified; every country in the world fully described; contains over 520 pages.
Bound in limp cloth.......17c
Stiff cloth, gold stamp....35c
**By mail extra 6c.**

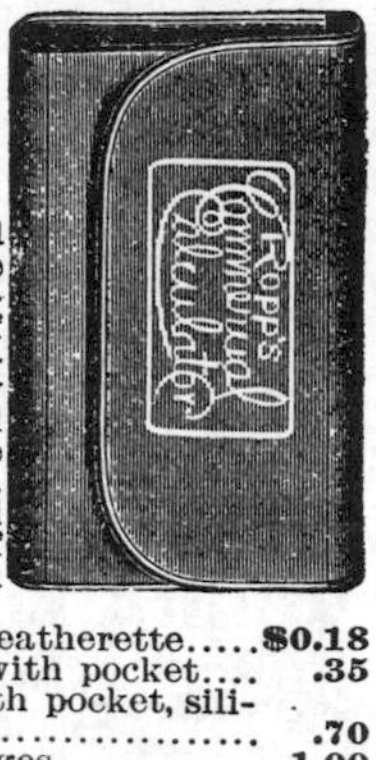


**52076. Ropp's Commercial Calculator.** Saves labor, time and money; simple, rapid, reliable; adapted to all kinds of business, trades and professions. It is unquestionably the most useful, complete and practical work on the science of arithmetic ever published. It is the only work of its kind that has survived the test of time and acquired a national reputation.
No. 1, bound in waterproof leatherette.....$0.18
No. 2, in fine colored cloth, with pocket.... .35
No. 3, in elegant leather, with pocket, silicate slate and account book.................. .70
No. 5, fine seal grain, gilt edges ............ 1.00

**52078. Vest Pocket Edition.** Bound in extra red linen cloth.................................. .18
Seal grain leather........................... .35
**Postage extra 5c each.**

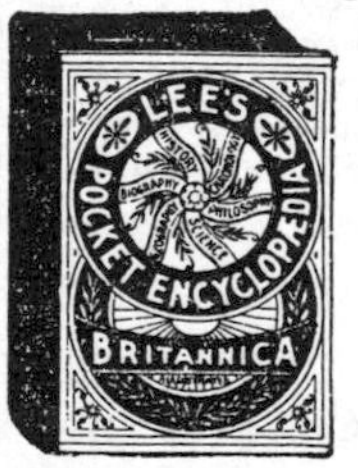


**52080. Lee's Pocket Encyclopedia Britannica.** Contains all the leading facts and dates in History, Biography, Geography, Philosophy and Science. This work will prove invaluable to readers, writers, mechanics and merchants; contains 84 portraits of celebrities and six keyed maps, 412 pages.
Strongly bound in heavy silk ..........60c
**By mail extra 8c.**

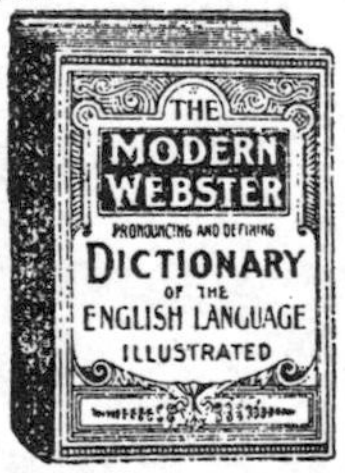


**52082. The Modern Webster, Pronouncing and Defining Dictionary of the English Language.** An entirely new book, illustrated, index cut on edges, contains 6000 definitions, 432 pages, size 8¾x4¼ inches.
Price .......................70c
**By mail extra 12c.**

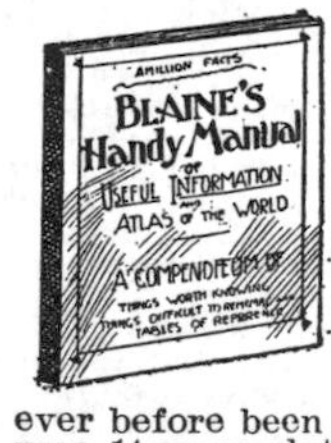


**52084. Blaine's Handy Manual of Useful Information and Atlas of the World.** A hand-book of ready reference useful to everyone, containing over a million things worth knowing, things difficult to remember and tables of reference. Compiled and corrected to date by Prof. Wm. H. Blaine. It contains an indexed and classified mass of information on a greater variety of subjects than has ever before been brought within scope of one volume, 14 maps, cloth, flexible covers..........$0.17
**Postage 5 cents extra.**

**52086. Vest Pocket Webster's Dictionary and Complete Manual of Parliamentary Pratice.** It contains a dictionary of over 40,000 words, as well as a vocabulary of Latin, French, Italian and Spanish words and phrases met with in English literature. It contains full and concise rules for spelling, punctuating and the use of capital letters. It contains a Complete Manual of Parliamentary practice not only giving the rules which govern the conduct of Legislative Bodies, Conventions, Societies, etc., in full, but also the celebrated Ford's Index, by means of which the proper rules in any instance may be ascertained at a glance, thus making it possible for anyone to preside without the embarrassment of making a misruling. It is the most valuable book ever published. Full Russia leather gilt edges.
Publisher's price......$0.50; Our price.... 0.30
Cloth red edges.................................. 0.18
**Postage, 3 cents.**

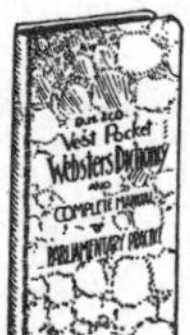

**52088. Electric Toy-Making, Dynamo Building and Electro-Motor Construction.** This work treats of the making at home of electric toys, electrical apparatus, motors, dynamos and instruments in general, and is designed to bring within the reach of young and old the manufacture of genuine and useful electrical appliances.
The work is specially designed for ameteurs and young folks.
This is a work in which the American boy will find explanations of the details of a great number of pieces of electrical apparatus which he may construct with his own hands and for his own amusement and pleasure. The nine chapters of the book treat respectively of batteries, permanent magnates, electro-magnates, electric motors, electric bells, miscellaneous toys, spark and induction coils, and allied subjects, the hand power dynamo and miscellaneous receipts and formulæ. The chapter on primary batteries will be found especially valuable. Illustrated 16 mo.—Electrical World.
Publisher's price .....$1.50; Our price..... .75
**Postage, 10c extra.**

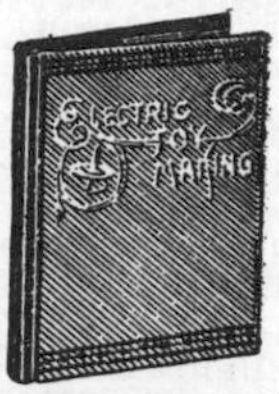

**52090. The Great Practical Work. Lawler's Hot Water Heating, Steam and Gas Fitting.** For Plumbers, Steam Fitters, Architects, Builders, Apprentices and Householders, containing practical information of all the principles involved in the construction of steam or ho water plant, and how to properly do gas fitting. The illustrations show the latest and best appliances used for all systems. Complete plans for different kinds of buildings, with regular working drawings—the principle of circulation of hot water in a heating system illustrated and explained in the most comprehensive way. How to properly estimate on steam and hot water work. How to set up a steam and hot water plant from the foundation of the boiler to the bronzing of the radiators and the starting of the fire. Noises in water and steam pipes explained and how to find and remedy them. The one and the two pipe system of steam heating illustrated. Gas fitting explained in all its branches, from the tapping of the main pipe in the street to the burners in the house. Everything explained in the most simple language, so that it will be impossible to misunderstand anything. The best illustrated work of the kind ever published, showing many new appliances and devices not illustrated in any other work. Containing 320 pages, large 12mo. cloth, elegantly illustrated. Publisher's price..$3.00; Our price... 1.50
**Postage, 12c extra.**

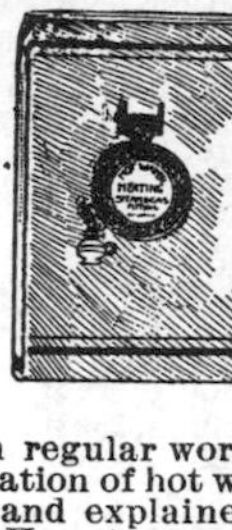

**52092. American Plumbing.** By Alfred Revill. For Master Plumbers, Architects, Builders, Apprentices and Householders. A complete compendium of practical plumbing from solder making to high class open work. The only work on plumbing containing a complete drainage system, elevation and plan, for use of architects and plumbers. This work tells how to make joints of all kinds; how to make traps; how to make bends; how to set fixtures; how to provide for varying head of water; how to run pipes; how to arrange vents; how to find defects; how to make repairs; how to test plumbing work; laws and rules governing plumbing; form of specifications. In short it gives in detail everything of importance great or small in modern plumbing. Antiquated or obsolete fixtures, etc., find no room in this work. 225 pages devoted to the very latest improved sanitary methods and appliances used in plumbing. Plumbing has hitherto been much of a mystery, "American Plumbing," by Alfred Revill, is so plain and lucid that no excuse exists for ignorance of the most vital system of fixtures in a house. Containing 225 large 12mo. pages, cloth, illustrated.
Publisher's price....$3.00; Our price...... 1.50
**Postage, 13c extra.**

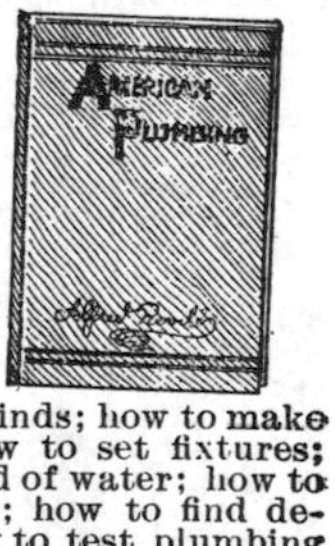


**52094. How to Become a Successful Electrician.** It is the ambition of thousands of young and old to become electrical engineers. Not every one is prepared to spend several thousand dollars upon a college course, even if the three or four years requisite are at their disposal. It is possible to become an electrical engineer without this sacrifice, and this work is designed to tell "How to Become a Successful Electrician" without the outlay usually spent in acquiring the profession. "Every young man who wishes to become a successful electrician should read this book. He will not be an electrician when he has mastered the book, but if he follows the advice there given he will become an electrician at some future time, if he is capable of becoming anything. It may be called a minimum book, for it tells the least that will be necessary, but it tells it in such a way that no worthy young man will be satisfied with the minimum, but will strive for that greater knowledge that will compel true and continually growing success. It is filled with good common sense, and is the clearest and most practical book on the subject we have ever seen."—Public Opinion.
Illustrated, 12mo.......................................70c
**Postage, 8c.**

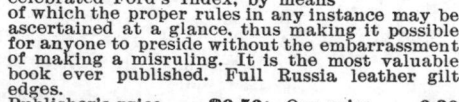

**52096. Briggs' American Tanner.** Containing improved quick methods for tanning all kinds of light skins, such as sheep, goat, dog, rabbit, otter, beaver, mink, muskrat, wolf, fox, etc., with or without the wool or fur; with hints how to cure skins, and color wool or fur. By N. R. Briggs. This is the work of a practical tanner and gives the latest instructions on the subject including a plain description of the necessary implements and their uses; illustrated by diagrams .......... **$0.20**
**Postage 3 cents.**

**52098. Fleischman's Art of Blending and Compounding Liquors and Wines.** Showing how all the **leading and favorite brands** of whiskies, brandies and other liquors and wines are prepared for the trade by rectifiers, etc., at the present time; with complete and correct recipes for making all the ingredients, flavorings, etc., employed in their manufacture, and the actual cost of each product as offered for sale. By Joseph Fleischman.
Publisher's price ........... **$2.50**
Our price ........................ **1.50**
**By mail 12c extra.**

**52100. The Bordeaux Wine and Liquor Dealers' Guide.** A Treatise on the Manufacture, Rectifying and Reduction of Liquors without the use of poisonous or deleterious ingredients, and on the preparation of Wines, Cordials, etc., for dealers' instruction. It includes also directions for Brewing Ales, Porter, etc., and for compounding Wines, Bitters and Punches, and Colorings and Beading for Liquors. 12mo.
Cloth, Publisher's price ........................ **$5.00**
Our price ................................ **2.00**
**By mail 12c extra.**

**52102. The Amateur Printer; or Type-Setting at Home.** A thorough instructor for the amateur in all the details of the Printer's art, giving practical information in regard to type, ink, paper and all the implements requisite, with **illustrated directions** for using them in a proper manner. The **practical instructions** given in this work are so plainly described that any amateur can become a good printer by studying and applying the information it contains.
Paper covers .............................................. **$0.20**
**Postage 3 cents.**

**52104. Pitman's Manual of Phonography.** This work contains all that is necessary for the application of Phonography to all ordinary requirements. It is a complete exposition of the system, with examples and exercises in both writing and reading. Over 800,000 copies of this book have been sold, affording sufficent evidence of its pre-eminence as in instructor in Shorthand. Although the "Manual" is complete in itself, a previous study of the "Phonographic Teacher" will aid greatly in mastering the lessons furnished in the "Manual" and render the students's progress easier.
Price ............................................... **$0.35**
**Postage, 3 cents.**

**52106. Key to Pitman's Manual of Phonography.** This is of great assistance to students; it gives in Shorthand, all the exercises contained in the Manual, thus affording the means of proving and correcting their performance without the aid of a teacher.
Uniform in size with the Manual ............. **$0.20**
**Postage 3 cents.**

**52108. Isaac Pitman's System of Phonography.** By special and exclusive arrangement with Isaac Pitman & Sons we are enabled to supply the very latest editions of the following Hand-Books of Phonography, printed by themselves at Bath, England. This system has been adopted as text-books by the New York board of education and other educational institutions, and is rapidly superseding and other methods of shorthand writing. It is beyond comparison the most practical, easy of acquirement, and obviates all needs of personal instruction.

**52109. Pitman's Phonographic Teacher.** This is an elementary work of instruction in Phonography, containing the first principles of the system and a series of progressive lessons. Although the acquisition of any art involves patience, practice and perseverance, the simplicity and arrangement of the lessons render progress easy and insure success.
Price ............................................... **$0.20**
**Postage, 3 cents.**

**52110. Donovan's Science of Boxing,** with Articles on **Training, Generalship in the Ring,** and kindred subjects. By **Prof. Mike Donovan, ex-Middle - Weight Champion of America,** and **Instructor in Boxing, New York Athletic Club.** It contains fifty-eight beautifully-executed halftone illustrations of the Professor and a skilled antagonist, photographed from life, showing exactly every movement described in the text, furnishing a series of object-lessons which completely replace personal instruction.
Cloth binding, Publisher's price ........... **$1.00**
Our price ........................................ **.75**
Paper covers ................................... **.40**
**By mail 6c extra.**

**52112. The Taxidermist's Manual.** Containing Complete Instructions in the Art of Taxidermy, with directions how to prepare, mount and preserve all kinds of birds, animals and insects. By Graham Allen. Profusely illustrated.
Large 16mo ........................................ **$0.20**
**Postage, 3 cents.**

**52114 Vest Pocket Webster's Manual for Readers, Writers and Speakers.** It contains a complete dictionary of 13,000 synonyms and furnishes full and concise information regarding the following particulars: How to write for the press. How to converse well in society. How to read, write, recite and impersonate. How to address public bodies. How to organize societies. How to prepare constitutions and by-laws. How to spell. How to punctuate. When to use Capital Letters. How to correct common errors of speech. Also contains a complete table of abbrevations, foreign words and phrases, etc. Full Russia Leather gilt edges.
Publishers price ........................................ **$0.50**
Our price ................................................ **0.30**
Cloth red edges ........................................ **0.15**
**Postage 3 cents, extra.**

**52116. Robert's Rules of Order.** For deliberative assemblies based on the rules and practice of congress, considered the standard with all literary and other societies connected with Universities, Colleges, Academies and High Schools. It contains a table which will aid a chairman to decide 200 questions of importance without turning a leaf.
Publishers price ...... **$0.75**
Our price ................ **0.52**
**Postage 6 cents, extra.**

**52118. Thimm's French Self-Taught.** A new system on the most simple principles, for universal self-tuition, with English pronunciation of every word. By this system the acquirement of the French language is rendered less laborious and more thorough than by any of the old methods.
By Franz Thimm ............................................ **20c**
**Postage, 2c.**

**52120. Thimm's German Self-Taught.** Uniform with "French Self-Taught," and arranged in accordance with the same principle of thoroughness and simplicity.
By Franz Thim ........................................... **20c**

**52122. Thimm's Spanish Self-Taught.** A book of self-instruction in the Spanish language, arranged according to the same method as the "French" and "German" by the same author and uniform with them in size. By Franz Thimm ............... **$0.20**
**Postage, 2 cents.**

**52124. Thimm's Italian Self-Taught.** Uniform in style and size with the three foregoing books. By Franz Thimm ............................................ **$0.20**
**Postage, 3 cents.**

**52126. How to Learn the Sense of 3,000 French Words in One Hour.** This ingenious little book actually accomplishes all that its title claims. It is a fact that there are at least three thousand words in the French language, forming a large proportion of those used in ordinary conversation, which are spelled exactly the same as in English, or become the same by very slight and easily understood changes in their termination. 16mo. illuminated paper covers ........................... **$0.20**
**Postage, 3 cents.**

## Pictorial History of the United States.

**52128.** This work has taken rank as the **standard History of the United States.** Contains a clear, vivid and brilliant narrative of the events of our history, from the discovery of the American continent down to the present time. It gives a most interesting account of the **Indians of North America** from the time of the coming of the white men. Every step of our **colonial history** is traced with patient fidelity, and the sources of those noble and, we trust, enduring institutions, which have made our country free and great, are shown with remarkable clearness. Then follows a clear and succinct account of our great struggle for independence, and the establishment of the Federal Union, the events of our career from the close of the revolution to the administration of Harrison. 960 pages, 500 fine engravings. Bound in silk cloth, marbled edges.
Publisher's price ........................................ **$3.50**
Our price .................................................. **$1.50**
**By mail 28c. extra.**

**IF YOU DO NOT SEND SUFFICIENT POSTAGE** where books are to be sent by mail, we will have to hold your order for balance.
**ALWAYS INCLUDE THE NECESSARY POSTAGE.** If you send too much we will return balance.

## Pictorial History of the Great Civil War.

**52130. Its causes, origin, conduct and results,** containing graphic descriptions of the heroic deeds achieved by armies and individuals, narratives of personal adventure, thrilling incidents, daring exploits, wonderful escapes, life in camp, field and hospital, adventures at sea, blockade life etc., by John Laird Wilson. It is printed from new clear type on fine calendered paper, made expressly for the work, and comprised in one royal octavo volume of 976 large double column pages. It is superbly embellished with numerous fine steel-plate engravings and with maps illustrative of the events recorded in the narrative, embracing battles and other historical scenes; portraits of the leading generals both north and south; maps and diagrams of battle-fields, etc. The work is bound in the most handsome and substantial manner.
Publisher's price ........................................ **$4.00**
Our price .................................................. **$1.50**
**By mail 28c. extra**

## Macaulay's History of England.

**52132.** Printed on good paper from large clear type, bound in heavy cloth, complete in 5 vols, 12mo. size. The period covered by each volume is as follows:
Vol. I. British under the Romans to the Persecution of the Protestant dissenters, 1685.
Vol. II. The Power of James at its Height to William and Mary proclaimed.
Vol. III. William and Mary proclaimed. The Battle of Fleurus.
Vol. IV. William in Belfast to the Funeral of Mary.
Vol. V. Effect of Mary's Death on the Continent to the Death of William.
Publisher's price ........................................ **$3.75**
Our price .................................................. **$1.00**
**Postage extra 45c.**

**Household Edition** with title stamped on leather label, gilt top, 5 vols. 12mo,
Publishers' price ........................................ **$5.00**
Our price .................................................. **$2.00**
**Postage extra 50c.**

**52150 Rev. J. S. Woods' Popular National History.** From entirely new electrotype plates, with 500 illustrations by eminent artists, attractively bound in heavy cloth. Illustrated cover, crown 8 vo. Price ........................... **$1.25**
**By mail 18 cents extra.**

**52152 History of Our Own Time.** From the accession of Queen Victoria to the general election of 1880. By John McCarthy. Library Ed., 2 vols. Price ................................................ **$1.15**
**By mail 25 cents extra.**

**52154 Conquest of Mexico.** Portraits and notes; durably bound in cloth; 3 vols.; 12 mo.
Price ................................................ **$1.00**
**By mail 33 cents extra.**

**52156 Conqnest of Peru.** Portraits and notes; bound in cloth; 12 mo. 2 volumes.
Price ................................................ **$1.00**
**By mail 25 cents extra.**

**52158 History of Rome by Edward Gibbon** with notes by Dean Milman, M. Guizot and **Wm. Smith;** illustrated with frontispiece, title on **leather label;** gilt top; 5 vols.; 12 mo. Price ................ **$2.10**
**By mail 45 cents extra.**

**52162 Abbott's Illustrated Histories.** Biographical Histories by Jabob Abbott and John C. Abbott. The volumes are printed and bound **uniformly,** and with numerous engravings. 16 mo.
Each ................................................ **75c**

| | |
|---|---|
| Alexander | King Philip |
| Alfred | Louis XIV |
| Charles I | Louis Philippe |
| Charles II | Madame Roland |
| Cleopatra | Margaret of Anjou |
| Cyrus | Marie Antoinette |
| Darius | Mary Queen of Scots |
| Elizabeth | Nero |
| Genghis Khan | Peter the Great |
| Hannibal | Pyrrhus |
| Henry I | Richard I |
| Hernando Cortez | Richard II |
| Hortense | Richard III |
| Joseph Bonaparte | Romulus |
| Josephine | William the Conqueror |
| Julius Cæzar | Xerxes. |

**Postage 12 cents per volume.**

**THREE PER CENT. CASH DISCOUNT.....**
**WHEN FULL CASH COMES WITH ORDER.** We guarantee satisfaction in all cases, and you may depend on our guaranty that money will be refunded where goods are not as represented.

**WHEN ORDERING BOOKS DO NOT FAIL TO GIVE NOT ONLY THE ARTICLE NUMBER, BUT BE SURE TO GIVE NAME OF BOOK AND PRICE. DO NOT EXPECT US TO GUESS AT WHAT YOU WANT.**

**52166. THE MOST WONDERFUL BARGAINS** in fine bound books. **Read the list of titles** as given below, and you will find the best known and most widely read works of popular authors. These books are **bound in handsome and durable silk finish cloth**, stamped with attractive designs in genuine gold. The paper used is of surprisingly good quality, while the **print is large and clear**, a feature that commends itself especally to those whose eyes will not stand reading the small type usually found in the very cheap books with which the market is flooded.

**THIS ENTERTAINING SERIES** includes the best **Fiction, Essays, Poetry, History and Travels.** Only such books as you will find in the **best home and school libraries.** We have **made the price exceedingly low** and at **22 cents** are selling such quality of the bookbinder's art as you will seldom, if ever, see sold at less than 50 cents.

**IT WILL PAY YOU** to get up a club among your **neighbors and order 22 or 30 of these books** sent all together by freight. **The freight will be little or nothing compared** with what we save you in **price. REMEMBER 3% DISCOUNT** when cash in full accompanies your order.

Publisher's price, each.......................... **$0.50**
Our price, each........................................ **.22**
5 books for................................................ **1.00**

**Postage 10c. extra per volume.**

Adam Bede. Geo. Eliot.
Adventures Among the Indians. W.H.G.Kingston
Æsop's Fables.
Allan Quartermain. H. Rider Haggard.
Andersen's Fairy Tales, Hans Christian Andersen
Arabian Night's Entertainment.
Ardath. Marie Corelli.
Autocrat of the Breakfast Table, The. Oliver Wendell Holmes.

Beyond Pardon. Bertha M. Clay.
Black Beauty. Anna Sewell.
Called Back. Hugh Conway.
Camille. Alexander Dumas, Fils.
Child's History of England, A. Charles Dickens.
Children of the Abbey. Regina Maria Roche.
Claribel's Love Story. Bertha M. Clay.
Cleopatra. H. Rider Haggard.
Count of Monte Cristo, The. Alexander Dumas.
Crooked Path, A. Mrs. Alexander.
Dark Days. Hugh Conway.
Dark Marriage Morn, A. Bertha M. Clay.
Deerslayer, The. J. Fenimore Cooper.
Diana Carew. Mrs. Forrester.
Dodo. E. F. Benson.
Donovan. Edna Lyall.
Dora Thorne. Bertha M. Clay.
Duke's Secret, The. Bertha M. Clay.
East Lynne. Mrs. Henry Wood.
Edmund Dantes. Alexander Dumas.
Egyptian Princess, An. George Ebers.
Emerson's Essays. (First Series.) R. W. Emerson.
Emerson's Essays. (Second series.) R. W. Emerson.
Felix Holt. George Eliot.
First Violin, The. Jessie Fothergill.
Five Years before the Mast. Hazen.
Foiled by Loving. Bertha M. Clay.
Forging the Fetters. Mrs. Alexander.
From Out the Gloom. Bertha M. Clay.
Frozen Pirate, The. W. Clark Russel.

Grimm's Fairy Tales. The Brothers Grimm.
Gulliver's Travels. Dean Swift.
Handy Andy. Samuel Lover.
Hardy Norseman, The. Edna Lyall.
Harry Lorrequer. Chas. Lever.
Her Only Sin. Bertha M. Clay.
House of the Wolf, The. Stanley J. Weyman.
House Party, The. Ouida.
Hypatia. Cearles Kingsley.
Imitation of Christ. Thomas A. Kempis.
Ivanhoe. Sir Walter Scott.
Jack in the Forecastle. Martingale.
Jane Eyre. Charlotte Bronte.
Jess. H. Rider Haggard.
John Halifax. Miss Mulock.
Kenilworth. Sir Walter Scott.
King Solomon's Mines. H. Rider Haggard.
Knight Errant. Edna Lyall.
Lamplighter, The. Maria Cummins.
Last Days of Pompeii. Lord Lytton.
Last of the Mohicans, The. J. Fenimore Cooper.
Legacy of Cain, The. Wilkie Collins.
Life's Remorse, A. The Duchess.
Lord Lynn's Choice. Bertha M. Clay.
Lover or Friend. Rosa B. Carey.
Love's Chain Broken. Bertha M. Clay.
Lucile. Owen Meredith.
Madcap Violet. William Black.
Mad Love, A. Bertha M. Clay.

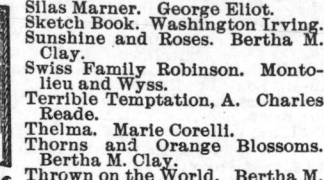

Mary St. John. Rosa N. Carey.
Natural Law of the Spiritual World. Henry Drummond.
New Magdalen, The. Wilkie Collins.
Old Mam'selle's Secret. B. Marlitt.
On Her Wedding Morn. Bertha M. Clay.
Only One Sin. Bertha M. Clay.
Pair of Blue Eyes, A. Bertha M. Clay.
Perilous Adventures by Land and Sea. Frost.
Pilgrim's Progress. John Bunyan.
Pioneers, The. J. Fenimore Cooper.
Pirate, The. J. Fenimore Cooper.
Prairie, The. Sir Walter Scott.
Robinson Crusoe. Daniel Defoe.

Romance of Two Worlds, A. Marie Corelli.
Saddle and Sabre. Hawley Smart.
Scarlet Letter, The. Nathaniel Hawthorne.
Scottish Chiefs. Jane Porter.
Sesame and Lillies. John Ruskin.
Shadowsand Sunbeams. Fanny Fern.
She. H. Rider Haggard.
Ships That Pass in the Night. Beatrice Harradan.

Silas Marner. George Eliot.
Sketch Book. Washington Irving.
Sunshine and Roses. Bertha M. Clay.
Swiss Family Robinson. Montolieu and Wyss.
Terrible Temptation, A. Charles Reade.
Thelma. Marie Corelli.
Thorns and Orange Blossoms. Bertha M. Clay.
Thrown on the World. Bertha M. Clay.
Tom Brown's School Days. Thomas Hughes.
Tom Brown at Oxford. Thomas Hughes.
Tour of the World in Eighty Days. Jules Verne.
Two Years Before the Mast. R. H. Dana, Jr.
Uarda. George Ebbers.
Vanity Fair. W. M. Thackeray
Vendetta. Marie Corelli.
Wee Wifie. Rosa N. Carey.
We Two. Edna Lyall.
When a Man's Single. J. M. Barrie.
Wide, Wide World, The. Elizabeth Wetherell (Susan Warner.)
Wife in Name Only. Bertha M. Clay.
Willy Reilly. Wm. Carleton.
Woman Against Woman. Mrs. M. E. Holmes.
Woman's Error, A. Bertha M. Clay.
Woman's Face, A. Bertha M. Clay.
Wooed and Married. Rosa N. Carey.
Wormwood. Mary Corelli.
Young Girl's Love, A. Bertha M. Clay.
Three Guardsmen. Alexander Dumas.
Louise de La Valliere. Alexander Dumas.
Viscount de Bragelonne. Alexander Dumas.
Sign of the Four. A. Conan Doyle.
Study in Scarlet. A. Conan Doyle.
Auld Licht Idylls. J. M. Barrie.
Widow in Thrums, A. J. M. Barrie.
Idle Thoughts of an Idle Fellow. Jerome K Jerome
Three Men in a Boat. Jerome K. Jerome.
Deemster. Hall Caine.

**52170 Willis J. Abbot's Works.** New Edition. Fully illustrated by W. C. Jackson, with original cover designs. Large 8vo. Per vol.......... **$1.40**

| | |
|---|---|
| Blue Jackets of '61 | Battlefields of '61 |
| Blue Jackets of '76 | Battlefields and Campfires |
| Blue Jackets of 1812 | Battlefields and Victory. |

**Postage 18 cents per volume.**

**52172 The Alger Series.** Uniform cloth binding. Illustrated; 12mo. Each................................ **55c**

Adrift in the Wilds. Edward S. Ellis.
Boy Cruisers, The. St. George Rathborne.
Boy Explorers, The. Harry Prentice.
Budd Boyd's Triumph. Wm. P. Chipman.
Captain Kid's Gold. James Franklin Fitts.
Captured by Apes. Harry Prentice.
Captured by Zulus. Harry Prentice.
Castaways, The. James Otis.
Dan the Newsboy. Horatio Alger, Jr.
Errand Boy, The. Horatio Alger, Jr.
Frank Fowler the Cash Boy. Horatio Alger, Jr.
Guy Harris the Runaway. Harry Castleman.
Island Treasure, The. Frank H. Converse.
Jaunt Through Java. Edward S. Ellis.
Joe's Luck. Horatio Alger, Jr.
Julian Mortimer. Harry Castleman.
Lost in the Canon. Alfred R. Calhoun.
Roy Gilbert's Search. Wm. P. Chipman.
Runaway Brig, A. James Otis.
Search for the Silver City. James Otis
Slate Picker, The. Harry Prentice.
Tom Temple's Career. Horatio Alger, Jr.
Tom Thacher's Fortune. Horatio Alger, Jr.
Tom the Bootblack. Horatio Alger, Jr.
Tom the Ready. Randolph Hill.
Tony the Hero. Horatio Alger, Jr.
Train Boy, The. Horatio Alger, Jr.
Treasure Finders, The. James Otis.
With Lafayette at Yorktown. James Otis.
Young Hero, A. Edward S. Ellis.
Young Scout. Edward S. Ellis.

**Postage 12 cents per volume.**

**52174 Louisa M Alcotts Works.** Little Women Series. 8 vols. 12mo. Per volume............ **$1.00**

| | |
|---|---|
| An Old Fashioned Girl. | Little Men. |
| Eight Cousins. | Little Women. |
| Jack and Jill. | Rose in Bloom. |
| Jo's Boys. | Under the Lilacs. |

**Postage 12 cents each.**

**52176 The Elsie Books.** By Martha Finley. Illustrated; 12mo. uniform. Price per vol..... **75c**

| | |
|---|---|
| Elsie Dinsmore, | Elsie's Girlhood, |
| Elsie's Holidays at Roselands, | Elsie's Womanhood, |
| | Elsie's Children, |
| Elsie's Motherhood, | Grandmother Elsie, |
| Elsie's Widowhood, | Elsie at Nantucket, |
| Elsie's New Relations, | Elsie's Kith and Kin, |
| The Two Elsie's | Christmas with Grandma Elsie, |
| Elsie's Friends at Woodburn, | Elsie's Yachting with the Raymonds, |
| Elsie and the Raymonds, | |
| Elsie's Vacation, | Elsie at Ion, |
| Elsie at Viamede, | Elsie at the World's Fair. |
| Elsie's Journey on Inland Waters. | |

**By mail 11 cents extra.**

**52178 Mark Twain's Works.** Attractively and durably bound in heavy cloth.

Innocence Abroad. Illustrated; 8vo...... **$1 05**
Gilded Age. Illustrated; 8vo.......... **1 95**
Life on the Mississippi. Illustrated; 8vo........ **1 85**
Roughing It. Illustrated; 8vo......... **1 95**
Tramp Abroad. Illustrated; 8vo......... **1 95**
A Connecticut Yankee in King Arthur's Court. Illust'd 8vo.. **1 80**
Huckleberry Finn. Illustrated; quarto.. **1 65**
Prince and Pauper. Illustrated; quarto.............................. **1 75**
Sketches. Illustrated; quarto........................... **1 70**
Tom Sawyer. Illustrated; quarto........................ **1 65**
The American Claimant. Illustrated; quarto **1 55**

**Postage 25 cents per volume.**

The American Claimant. 12mo..................... **1 05**
Sketches. 12 mo..................................... **70**
Prince and Pauper. 12mo........................... **70**
Tom Sawyer. 12mo.................................... **70**
Tom Sawyer Abroad.................................... **1 05**

**Postage 12 cents per volume.**

The Stolen White Elephant. 16 mo.............. **70**

**Postage 8c.**

**52180 Young American Series.** High class reading for young people. Four amusing, wholesome and instructive vols; beautifully illustrated and superbly bound in silk cloth; gilt top, with stamp in gold and colors on front, side and back.

Per set.............. **$3.00**
**Postage extra 40 cents.**

Separately per volume as follows:
Air Castle Don or From Greenland to Hard Pan; by Freeman Ashley.................. **80c**
Dick and Jack's adventure on Sable Island, by Freeman Ashley.................. **80c**
Ten Pile Jim; by Freeman Ashley............ **80c**
The Heart of a Boy; by Edmon Di Amics...... **80c**

**Postage extra, each 11 cents.**

**52182 Air Castle Don** or From Greenland to Hard Pan. The adventures of a manly little fellow left to fight his way up in one of the largest American cities. Bound in silk cloth; 12mo.
Price.......................... **80c**
**By mail 12 cents extra.**

**52184 Harry Castleman's Works.** Neatly bound in heavy cloth; illustrated. 12mo size.

Gunboat Series. 3 volumes. 12mo.... ........**$2.50**
**By mail, 35c extra.**
Sold separately. Per volume.................... **0.88**
**By mail, 12c per vol. extra.**
Frank on the Lower Mississippi.
Frank on a Gunboat.
Frank before Vicksburg.

Hunter Series. 3 volumes. 12mo............**$2.50**
**By mail, 35c extra.**
Sold separately. Per volume .................. **0.88**
**By mail, 12c per volume extra.**
Two Ways of Becoming a Hunter.
Oscar in Africa.
Camp in the Foot-Hills.

Lucky Tom Series. 3 volumes. 12mo ..........**$2.50**
**By mail, 35c extra.**
Sold separately. Per volume.................. **0.88**
**By mail, 12c per volume extra.**
Our Fellows.
Elam Storm, the Wolfer.
The Missing Pocket-book; or Tom Mason's Luck.

Sportsman Club Series. 3 volumes. 12mo.....**$2.50**
**By mail, 35c extra.**
Sold separately. Per volume.................. **0.88**
**By mail, 12c per volume extra.**
The Sportsman's Club in the Saddle.
The Sportsmun's Club afloat.
The Sportsman's Club Among the Trappers.

Boy Trapper Series. 3 volumes. 12mo........**$2.50**
**By mail, 35c extra.**
Sold separately. Per volume.................. **0.88**
**By mail, 12c per volume extra.**
The Buried Treasure.
The Boy Trapper.
The Mail Carrier.

Roughing It Series. 3 volumes. 12mo.........**$2.50**
**By mail, 35c extra.**
Sold separately. Per volume.................. **0.88**
**By mail, 12c per volume extra.**
George in Camp.
George at the Wheel.
George at the Fort.

Rod and Gun Series. 3 volumes. 12mo..........**$2.50**
**By mail, 35c extra.**
Sold separately. Per volume.................. **0.88**
**By mail, 12c per volume extra.**
Don Gordon's Shooting Box.
Rod and Gun Club.
The Young Wild Fowlers.

**52186 Peck's Bad Boy and his Pa, and Compendium of Fun.** Profusely illustrated with appropriate and original designs. Substantially bound in best English cloth. 544 pages, size 7½ by 9 inches.
Price........................................**$0.85**
**By mail, 14c extra.**

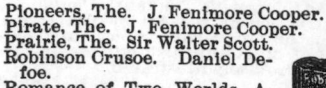

## HANDY VOLUME EDITION

**52220.** 18 Cents per volume is the price of the series of books listed below. It is simply impossible for a publisher to make these books at a profit, and sell them at such a price. We were fortunate to secure at a close out sale, about 8000 volumes at less than the actual cost to make, and in offering them at 18 cents each, we believe we are giving the best book bargain ever heard of. Think of it, there are just 68 different volumes in this series and the total cost at our bargain price would only be $12.24 or less money than agents or dealers will often ask for a single expensive book. **68 books at the price of one.** You can fill your library with the choicest works of the best authors, and the cost will be small. These books are bound in excellent quality of cloth, with neat silver stamping. The paper is uniformly good, while the print is large, clear and easily read. Remember we allow 3 per cent. for cash in full with order.

Publisher's price..........................$0.40
Our price......................................18

**Postage each extra 10c.**

The Abbe Constantin. Ludovic Halevy.
Alice's Adventures in Wonderland. Lewis Carroll.
The Autocrat of the Breakfast Table. Oliver Wendell Holmes.
Bacon's Essays. Francis Bacon.
Beyond the City. A. Conan Doyle.
A Bird of Passage. Beatrice Harradan.
Book of Golden Deeds. C. M. Young.
Black Beauty. Anna Sewell.
Browning's Poems. Robert Browning.
Burns' Poems. Robt. Burns.
Carlyle's History of the French Revolution, Vol. I. Thos. Carlyle.
Carlyle's History of the French Revolution, Vol. II. Thos. Carlyle.
The Coming Race. Lord Lytton.
The Confessions of an English Opium Eater. Thos. DeQuincey.
Crown of Wild Olive. John Ruskin.
Dream Life. D. G. Mitchell. (Ike Marvel).
Dreams. Olive Schreiner. (Ralph Iron).
Drummond's Addresses. Drummond.
Emerson's Essays. 1st Series.
Emerson's Essays. 2d Series.
Essays of Elia. Chas. Lamb.
Ethics of the Dust. John Ruskin.
Evangeline. H. W. Longfellow.
Half Hours with Great Authors.
Half Hours with Great Humorists.
Half Hours with Great Novelists.
Half Hours with Great Story Tellers.
Heroes and Hero Worship. Thos. Carlyle.
Heroes of Greek Fairy Tales, The. Chas. Kingsley.
House of Seven Gables, The. Nathaniel Hawthorne.
Ideala. Sarah Grand.
Idle Thoughts of an Idle Fellow, The. Jerome K. Jerome.
Imitation of Christ. Thos. A'Kempis.
John Halifax, Gentleman. Vol. I. Miss Mulock.
John Halifax, Gentleman. Vol. II. Miss Mulock.
Lady of the Lake, The. Sir Walter Scott.
Lalla Rookh. Thos. Moore.
Lays of Ancient Rome. Lord Macaulay.
Longfellow's Poems. W. H. Longfellow.
Lorna Doone. Vol. I. R. D. Blackmore.
Lorna Doone. Vol. II. R. D. Blackmore.
Love Letters of a Worldly Woman. Mrs. W. K. Clifford.
Lowell's Poems. James Russell Lowell.
Lucile. Owen Meredith.
Mill on the Floss. Vol. I. Geo. Eliot.
Mill on the Floss. Vol. II. Geo. Eliot.
Mosses from an Old Manse. Nathaniel Hawthorne.
Natural Law in the Spiritual World. Drummond.
Paradise Lost. Milton.
Poe's Poems. Edgar Allan Poe.
Representative Men. Ralph W. Emerson.
Reveries of a Bachelor. D. G. Mitchell.
Sesame and Lillies. John Ruskin.
Ships that Pass in the Night. Beatrice Harradan.
The Sign of the Four. A Conan Doyle.
Sketch Book. Washington Irving.
Tennyson's Poems. Vol. I. Lord Tennyson.
Tennyson's Poems. Vol. II. Lord Tennyson.
Treasure Island. Robt. Louis Stevenson.
Twice Told Tales. Nathaniel Hawthorne.
Uncle Tom's Cabin. Harriet Beecher Stowe.
Vanity Fair. Vol. I. W. M. Thackeray.
Vanity Fair. Vol. II. W. M. Thackeray.
Vicar of Wakefield. Oliver Goldsmith.
Wide, Wide World, The. Vol. I. Elizabeth Wetherell.
Wide, Wide World, The. Vol. II. Elizabeth Wetherell.
Wonder Book for Boys and Girls. Nathaniel Hawthorne.
Whittier's Poems. John Greenleaf Whittier.

**What You Want** is the best to be had for the money.
Look in the index and you will always find.. **What You Want**

## Handy Volume Classics.

**52212.** Very attractively bound in silk finish cloth, 16mo size. Order by name and number.
Elsie Dinsmore, by Martha M. Finley. Price, 35c; by mail 7c.
Border Sheperdess, by Amelia Barr. Price, 27c; by mail extra 7c.
Abbe Constantin, by Ludovic Halevy. Price 27c; by mail 7c extra.
Bow of Orange Ribbon, by Amelia Barr. Price, 27c; by mail 7c extra.
History of Three Burglars, by Stockton. Price, 30c; by mail 7c extra.
Jean Vedder's Wife, by Amelia Barr. Price, 30c; by mail 7c extra.
An Original Belle, by E. P. Roe. Price 27c; by mail 7c extra.
Bitter Sweet, by C. Holland. Price, 27c; by mail 7c extra.
Christie Johnstone, by Reade. Price, 27c; by mail 7c extra.
The Little Huguenots, by Pemberton. Price, 35c; by mail 7c extra.
Cycling for Health and Pleasure, by Porter. Price, 30c; by mail 7c extra.

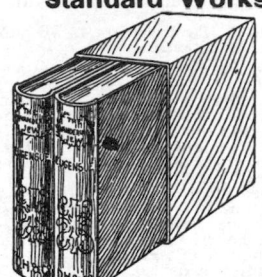

## Standard Works in Sets.

**52214.** Eugene Sue's Works. Wandering Jew, Library edition, printed on calandered paper from large clear type, bound in extra silk finish cloth, stamped in gold, uniform with Les Miserables, averaging 600 pages to the vol.
Publishers' price............$2.50
Our price. $1.00
Postage extra 30c

**52216.** Hugo's Works, complete in 7 Vols. Library edition printed on calendered paper from new plates made from long primer type, averaging 650 pages to the vol. bound in extra cloth, stamped in gold, gilt top, containing 14 full page inserted illustrations, printed on plate paper.
Publishers' price..$8.75 Our price......$4.25

**52218.** George Eliot's Works. Printed from clear type on fine quality paper, illustrated, durably bound in heavy cloth, complete 8 vols.
Publishers' price.....................$6.00
Our price. $3.25
**Cheaper edition**, in 6 vols, 12 mo., size uniform.
Publishers' price..$4.50 Our price.....$2.65

**52220.** Opie Read's Works. Substantially and neatly bound in extra cloth, gilt top, printed on fine paper from clear type, 5 vols.
Per set. $3.20
Separately per vol. .75c
Postage each extra 12c
My Young Master.
The Jucklins.
The Kentucky Colonel.
The Tennesee Judge.
On The Swanee River.

**52222.** Emerson's Essays. Two volumes, complete, substantially and attractively bound in binder's silk cloth, 12mo. size in neat box.
Publisher's price......$0.75
Our price................40
Postage extra, 24c.

**52224.** Samuel Smile's Works. Attractively bound in English silk cloth, gilt top, printed from clear type on fine paper, 12mo. uniform, 4 volumes.
Duty. Thrift. Character. Self-Help.
Publisher's price...$1.75 Our price. .....$1.10
Postage extra, 45c.
Separately, per volume............30
Postage each, extra 12c.

**52230.** Victor Hugo's Works. Les Miserables, library edition complete and unabridged, printed on calendered paper from new plates, made from large type, 650 pages to the volume, 10 inserted illustrations printed on plate paper, durably bound in extra silk finish cloth, stamped in gold, (neatly boxed).
Publisher's price..........................$2.50
Our price.....................................95
Postage extra, 30c.

**52232.** Alexander Dumas' Works. Complete in eight volumes. Printed on finest quality paper from large clear type, averaging 560 pages to the volume beautifully bound in extra silk finish cloth, stamped in gold, gilt top, containing 16 full page inserted illustrations. Contents of volumes as follows:
Edmund Dantes.        The Count of Monte Cristo.
Twenty Years After.   The Man in the Iron Mask.
Louise De La Valliere. Vicomte De Bragellone.
The Son of Porthos.   The Three Guardsmen.
Publisher's price.......................$10.00
Our price. 5.75

**52234.** J. Fennimore Cooper's Works. Leather Stocking Tales, Illustrated. Large, clear type edition, printed on fine paper from clear type, each volume containing from 400 to 450 pages. The volumes are very durably bound in binder's silk finish cloth. Contents of the five volumes as follows:
The Deerslayer.
The Pathfinder.
The Prairie.
The Pioneers.
The Last of the Mohicans.
Publisher's price.........................$3.75
Our price. 1.00
Postage, extra, 58c.

**52236.** Cooper's Sea Tales. Durably bound in binder's silk finish cloth, printed on extra quality paper from new clear type, containing the following:
Water Witch.        The Pilot.
Red Rover.          Wing and Wing.
The Two Admirals.
Publishers' price..$3.75   Our price.... $1.00
Postage extra, 58c.

## DIALOGUES AND RECITATIONS

**52242. The Tuxedo Reciter.** This new book contains only such original and selected recitations as have been approved and in many cases tested and received the sanction of the most prominent elocutionists in this country and Europe. Apart from the orignial pieces in the work, there are many rare and curious selections which cannot be found in any other publication. The popular recitations, "Lasca," "The Chariot Race" from "Ben Hur," "A Tuxedo Romance," "The Face Upon The Floor," "Kissing Cup's Race," and many other new and famous pieces are incorporated in this elegant work. "The Tuxedo" is the most complete and attractive book ever published. 317 pages, extra cloth, top gilt. Price............$0.60
Postage, 12 cents.

**52244.** Quotations. By Agnes H. Morton, B. O. This is a clever compilation of pithy quotations selected from a great variety of sources and alphabetically arranged according to the sentiment. An important division of the book is the characteristic lines from well-known authors. In it are hundreds of familiar sayings of widely varying application, accredited to their original sources. It contains all the popular quotations in present use, together with many rare bits of prose and verse not generally found in similar collections. Cloth, price....$0.40

**52246 Hand-Book of Pronunciation.** By John H. Bechtel. This work contains over five thousand carefully selected words of difficult pronunciation alphabetically arranged. Two forms of pronunciation are given. The first employs as few diacritical marks as possible and is designed for those to whom such marks are a stumbling block instead of a help. The second is a close phonetic analysis of the word, in which every vowel is marked, every necessary sign employed, every silent letter omitted and every accent, primary and secondary, carefully noted. Cloth, price............................$0.40

**By mail, 8 cents extra.**

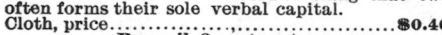

**52248 Practical Synonyms.** By John H. Bechtel. This volume avoids the tedious prolixity of the more scholarly works on the one hand and the fatal mistake of an insufficiency of related words on the other. It will be found to meet the wants of the busy merchant or lawyer, the thoughtful clergyman or teacher, and the wide-awake school boy or girl who is ambitious to express the thoughts of the mind in more fitting phrase than the crude slang that two often forms their sole verbal capital.

Cloth, price............................$0.40
**By mail, 8 cents extra.**

**52250 Parlor Games.** For the Wise and Otherwise. This complete and attractive volume contains a splendid collection of games for all kinds of amusement, entertaiment and instruction, thus answering most happily that puzzling question, "What shall we do?" so frequently propounded on rainy days and long winter evenings. The games are not adapted to young people alone, but to older persons as well, for the most staid and sedate adult will find many of them both profitable and entertaining. Cloth, price............................$0.40

**By mail, 8 cents extra.**

**52252 Etiquette.** By Agnes H. Morton. B. O. Some manuals of etiquette treat almost exclusively of "state occasions," while others are made up of sundry rules, often illiterate in style and of doubtful authority. Both of these classes of manuals are obviously inadequate to the needs of the great mass "who dwell within the broad zone of the average." For this large class a book that gives information as to the essential points of correct behavior in social life,—points equally applicable to the rich and to the poor,—is the ideal manual. And such a book is this volume.

Cloth, price............................$0.40
**By mail, 8 cents extra.**

**52256 Choice Humor.** For Reading and Recitation. By Charles C. Shoemaker. As its name implies, the selections are chosen with the greatest care, avoiding the coarse and vulgar on the one hand, and the flat and insipid on the other. The repertoires of many of the best amateur and professional readers have been examined, and the choicest bits of humor have been carefully culled and bound up in this rich golden sheaf and are here offered to the public for the first time in book form. Paper bound. Price............................$0.25

**By mail, 3 cents extra.**

**52258 Humorous Dialogues and Dramas.** By Charles C. Shoemaker. After the severe labors of the day every one enjoys that which will afford relaxation and relieve the mind of its nervous tension. The dialogues are humorous without being coarse, and funny without being vulgar. Many of them are selected from standard authors, but a number of others have been specially written for the book by experienced writers. Paper binding. Price............................$0.25

**Postage, 4 cents extra.**
Cloth, price, (Postage, 8 cents extra)........$0.40

**52260 North's Book of Love-Letters.** With directions how to write and when to use them. By Ingoldsby North. This is a branch of correspondence for the various phases incident to Love, Courtship and Marriage. Few persons are able to express in words the promptings of the first dawn of love, and how to follow up a correspondence with the dearest one in the world, and how to smooth the way with those who need to be consulted in the matter. The hundred and forty letters and answers in this book, aided in many instances by the author's sensible comments on the specimen letters, and his valuable hints under adverse contingencies. Cloth, price............................$0.60
Bound in boards, price, (By mail, 8c extra). 0.40

**52262 How to Conduct a Debate.** A Series of Complete Debates, Outlines of Debates, and Questions for Discussion. By Frederick Rowton. In the complete debates, the questions for discussion are defined, an array of arguments adduced on either side, and the debate closed according to parliamentary usages. The second part consists of questions for debate, with heads of arguments, for and against, given in a condensed form. In addition to these are a large Collection of Debatable Questions.

Bound in boards, price. $0.60 Paper covers..$0.40
**By mail, 6c extra.**

**52264 Ogden's Skeleton Essays; or Authorship in Outline.** Consisting of Condensed Treatises on popular subjects, and directions how to enlarge them into essays, or expand them into lectures. By Christol Ogden. In this work is a thorough analysis of some seventy prominent and popular subjects, some of which are discussed and ably argued on both sides of the question, thus presenting also well digested matter for debate, essays, etc.
Bound in boards....$0.60 Paper covers......$0.40
**By mail, 6c extra.**

**52266 McBride's Choice Dialogues.** A collection of fifteen Exhibition Dialogues for young persons from twelve to sixteen years. By H. Elliott McBride. They are dramatic in their construction, and excellent exercises in stage action, mimicry and characteristic dialects.
Bound in boards....$0.40 Paper covers......$0.25
**By mail, 6c extra.**

**52268 McBride's New Dialogues.** Specially designed for young people of ten to sixteen years of age, for representation at juvenile entertainments. By H. Elliott McBride. This new and entirely original series contains twenty-five very amusing dialogues, some of them introducing different dialect characters.
Bound in boards....$0.40 Paper covers......$0.25
**By mail, 6c extra.**

**52270 Diverting Dialogues.** Consisting of twenty Comedies and Farces by various authors, written expressly for this book, and specially suitable for parlor performance by young ladies and youths. Seven of the plays are illustrations of well-known proverbs. It includes also elaborate directions for exhibiting Living Pictures and Tableaux, with a complete programme of beautiful Tableaux for a complete entertainment.

Bound in boards............$0.40
Paper covers............ 0.25
**By mail, 6c extra.**

**52272 Dick's Stump Speeches and Minstrel Jokes.** Contains all the materials necessary for Minstrel Shows, providing Jokes, Gags, Conundrums and Funny Sayings for the end men, stilted remarks for the middle man, with Burlesque Sermons and Stump Speeches, choice Farces, Interludes and Negro Acts, in sufficient variety for a number of minstrel entertainments, warranted to "bring down the house" every time.
Bound in boards............$0.40
Paper covers............ 0.25
**By mail, 6c extra.**

**52274 McBride's Comic Dialogues.** Designed expressly for school exhibitions and literary entertainments; containing "From Punkin Ridge" and eighteen other original dialogues. By H. Elliott McBride. They afford ample scope for the display of dramatic talent in young persons of twelve years and upwards, introducing Irish, Yankee and other characteristic eccentricities.

Bound in boards............$0.40
Paper covers............ 0.25
**By mail, 6c extra.**

**52276. Sut Lovingood.** Yarns spun by "A Nat'ral Born Durn'd Fool." Warped and wove for Public Wear by George W. Harris. Illustrated with seven full page engravings. from designs by Howard. The Preface and Dedication are models of sly simplicity, and the 24 Sketches which follow are among the best specimens of broad burlesque for which the Southwest is so distinguished.

Cloth binding............$1.15
**By mail 12c extra.**

**52278. Dick's Commercial Letter Writer.** A book of General Commercial Correspondence and Correct Business Forms. It contains about two hundred original letters and replies, in business style and correct phraseology, suitable for those about to commence, or already engaged in mercantile pursuits, with models of applications for clerkships, etc., and of acceptance or rejection. A special feature of this book consists of different series of letters between the several parties involved in a business transaction, requiring in some instances from fourteen to seventeen letters in continuous correspondence. This work has been widely adopted as a text-book by leading business colleges.
Bound in boards............$0.40
**By mail 6c extra.**

**52280. Dick's Original Album Verses and Acrostics.** A very handy book for selecting an appropriate verse for insertion in a lady's album, or for a suitable sentiment of congratulation on all the Wedding Anniversaries, on birthdays, and other occasions; also for accompanying Philopena forfeits or Bouquets, and for Valentines of every kind; besides acrostic verses, which spell out two hundred and eighteen different ladies' names with the derivation and meaning of each.
Cloth binding............$0.60
Paper covers............ .40
**By mail 6c extra.**

**52282. Martine's Sensible Letter-Writer.** A complete Guide to Correct Correspondence, giving instructions on Style, Arrangement of Ideas, Grammar and Spelling, the use of Capitals and Punctuation Marks, and contains about three hundred letters and notes with appropriate replies, covering all contingencies of business, social, family and domestic life, Love, Courtship and Proposal.
Cloth binding............$0.60
Bound in boards............ .40
**By mail 8c extra.**

**52284. Young Folks' Recitations.** By Mrs. J. W. Shoemaker. For young people of fifteen years, Containing Readings, Recitations, Dialogues, and Tableaux, suited to the Home Circle, Juvenile Concerts, School Exhibitions, Sunday-School Gatherings, etc., etc. While some of the old favorites have been retained, this book is largely made up of fresh, crisp, and wholesome selections, many of them appearing for the first time in permanent form.
Bound in boards............$0.20
Paper covers............ .12
**By mail 4c extra.**

**52286. Child's Own Speaker.** By E. C. and L. J. Rook. For children of six years. A collection of Recitations, Motion Songs, Concert Pieces, Dialogues, and Tableaux, in all 100 pieces, many of which are entirely new as well as novel in arrangement, and have been specially written for this book. While the tender age of the little ones for whom this collection is intended has been kept in mind, mere baby-talk has been excluded and only such pieces as contain some thought worth memorizing have been inserted.
Paper binding............$0.12
**By mail 4c extra.**

**52288. Shoemaker's Best Selections.** For Readings and Recitations. Teachers, Readers, Students, and all persons who have occasion to use books of this kind, concede this to be the best series of speakers published. The different numbers are compiled by leading elocutionists of the country, who have exceptional facilities for securing selections, and whose judgment as to their merits is invaluable.

Cloth............$0.40
Paper bindings............ .25
**By mail 6c extra.**

**52290. Young Folk's Entertainments.** By E. C. and L. J. Rook. Absolutely new and original. School Entertainments of the present time generally present a much more varied performance than of old, and the call for variety has been met in this book by the careful preparation of Motion Songs, Charades, Tableaux, Dialogues, Concert Recitations, Motion Pieces, Drills, etc.
Paper bindings............$0.20
**By mail 4c extra.**

**52292. The Peerless Reciter, or Popular Program.** Containing the choicest selections, recitations and readings from the best authors, for schools, public entertainments, social gatherings, sunday schools etc., including recitals in prose and verse, dialogues and dramas, selections in dialect, together with rules, and instructions for gesture, expression and cultivation of the voice; vast collection comprising eloquence and sentiment, pathos and humor, dramatic and descriptive selections, juvenile readings, readings with lesson talks, dialogues and tableaux, etc., one large volume of over 500 pages, embellished with phototype engravings in rich colors. Bound in extra fine cloth, marbled edges.
Publishers' price............$1.75
Our price............ 0.95
Bound in full morocco, gilt edges, publishers' price............ 2.50
Our price............ 1.40
**Postage each extra 30c.**

**52294. Choice Series of Comical Recitations and Readings.** Attractively bound in paper covers, each 20 cents, by mail extra 3 cts.

Wilson's Modern Dances, 128 pp.
DeVere's Negro Sketches.
Cushing's Manual, 200 pages.
March's Dialogues and Speeches.
German at a Glance, 96 pages.
Burdett's Dutch Dialect Recitations.
French at a Glance, 96 pages.
DeVere's Laughable Recitations
Spanish at a Glance, 96 pages.
Casey's Recitations and Comic Songs.
Josh Hayseed's Trip to New York.
Italian at a Glance, 96 pages.
Bro. Gardner's Stump Speeches.
Mason's Fancy Drills and Marches.
Wilford's Dialogues for Young Folks.
Payne's Rules of Order.
Burdett's Negro Dialect Recitations.
Drummer's Yarns.

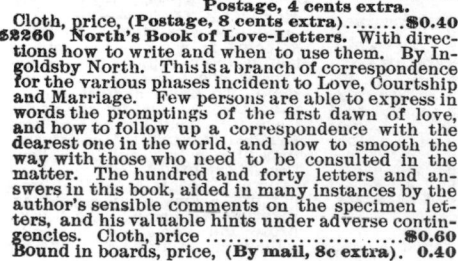

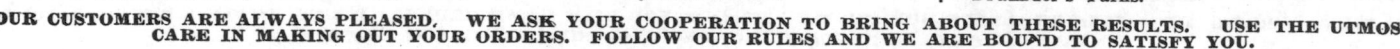

**52294. The Speakers' Favorite, or Best things for Entertainments, Home, Church and Schools.** Consisting of Recitations, Dialogues and Dramas, Pathetic, Tragic, Humorous, Narrative, Oratorical, Didactic and impersonative. Explanatory Head Notes, instructions on speaking, entertainments etc. Very attractively bound in red cloth, illustrated covers, contains 234 pages and many illustrations. Price......**$1.00**
**By mail 18c. extra.**

**52298 Ventriloquism Self-Taught.** A thoroughly reliable guide to the **art of voice throwing and vocal mimicry**, by an entirely novel system of graduated exercises, tested and proved successful by the author during years of tuition. By Prof. Robert Ganthony. Illustrated; including vocal imitation of musical instruments, the construction and management of puppets, and hints on entertaining........(**By mail 4 cents extra.**)........ **20c**

**52300 Hoyle's Games.** By "Trumps." A complete Manual of the games of skill and chance as played in America, and an acknowledged arbiter on all disputed points; thoroughly revised and corrected in accordance with the latest and best authorities. It contains the modern laws and complete instructions for the games of chess, draughts, dominoes, dice, backgammon and billiards, as well as all the games with cards at present in vogue, including: baccarat, duplicate, whist, Cayenne whist, Hearts, grabouche, newmarket, solo whist, cinch or high five, etc. Profusely illustrated. **By mail 10c extra** Bound in boards, **60c.**; Paper covers............**40c.**

**52302 Richardson's Monitor of Freemasonry.** A comprehensive book containing the work, lectures and ceremonies of initiation of the three blue lodge degrees, and of the chapter, council and commandery degrees of the Ancient York Rite. Also the Lodges of Perfection, the Chapters of the Red Cross, and the councils and consistories of all the ineffable and historical degrees of the Scottish Rite, including the Degree of the Heroine of Jericho.
Bound in leather pocket-book style......... **$1.75**
Paper covers .......................... **.60**
**By mail 6 cents extra.**

**52304 Lander's Revised Work of Odd-Fellowship.** Prepared in conformity with the important amendments and alterations adopted by the **Sovereign Grand Lodge.** By Edwin F. Lander. This gives the regulations for opening, conducting and closing the lodge, with the complete work, and lectures in initation, and in the three Lodge Degrees of Friendship, Brotherly Love and Truth; in the Patriarchal, Golden Rule and Royal Purple Degrees of the Encampment, and in the Rebekah, or Ladies' Degree.......................... **20c**
**By mail 4 cents extra.**

**52306 Morgan's Freemasonry Exposed and Explained.** Showing the **origin, history** and **nature** of Masonry and containing a key to all the Degrees of Freemasonry. Giving a clear and correct synopsis of the manner of conferring the different degrees. Paper bound............... **20c**
**By mail 4 cents extra.**

**52308 Locomotive Catechism.** By Robert Grimshaw. A most practical and useful work on the catechism of the steam engine, boiler, etc., with questions and answers. 200 illustrations and 7 folding plates; 12mo.
Publisher's price ................ **$3.00**
Our price.......................... **1.75**
**By mail 14 cents extra.**

**52310 Haswell's Engineers' Pocket-book.** Mechanics' and engineers' pocket-book of tables, rules and formulas pertaining to mechanics, mathematics and physics. By C. H. Haswell. Fifty-sixth edition. 12mo. leather pocket-book form. Publisher's price .................. **$5.00**
Our price.......................................... **2.90**
**By mail 12 cents extra.**

**52312 Roper's Young Engineer's Own Book.** Containing an explanation of the principal theories of the steam engine. For the use of educational institutions where students are intended to engage in mechanical pursuits, and for the private instruction of youths who show an inclination for steam engineering. By Stephen Roper; with 106 illustrations; 363 pages; 18mo. tuck; gilt edge. Publisher's price................. **$3.00**
Our price........................................ **2.10**
**By mail 10 cents extra.**

**52314 Steel Square, Part 1st.** Its uses. etc. By Fred Hodgson; 12mo.; cloth........................ **75c**
**Postage extra 6 cents.**

**52316 Steel Square, Part 2d.** A continuation to part first, giving new problems. By Fred Hodgson; 12mo. cloth......(**Postage extra 6 cents.**)........ **75c**

**52318 Camp Life in the Woods and the Tricks of Trapping and Trap Making.** Containing comprehensive hints on camp shelter, log huts, boat and canoe building, and valuable suggestions on trapping, etc.; also all the tricks and valuable bait receipts of the profession. Full directions for use of steel traps, all kinds, etc. Very attractively bound in cloth; 16mo.; with hundreds of illustrations. Price....(**Postage 10c extra**)...... **70c**

# Popular Fiction

## IN SPECIAL BINDING.

**The Most Readable Works of the Best Authors, all bound handsomely and worth double our price. 3 per cent discount where cash in full accompanies orders.**

**52320, Edward Bulwer Lytton's Works. Library Edition with Frontispiece.**
Last Days of Barons, 12mo.................. **$0.67**
Last Days of Pompeii, 12mo.................. .25
Rienzi, 12mo.................. .25
Ernest Maltravers, 12mo.................. .67
Eugene Aram, 12mo.................. .67
Paul Clifford, 12mo.................. .67
The Coming Race, 12mo.................. .25
My Novel, 2 vols., 12mo.................. .67
Night and Morning, 12mo.................. .67
The Pilgrims of the Rhine, 12mo.................. .67
Alice, 12mo.................. .35
The Caxtons, 12mo.................. .67
Kenelm Chillingly, 12mo.................. .25
The Disowned, 12mo.................. .67
Calderon, 12mo.................. .67
**Postage each, extra 12c.**

**52322. J. Fennimore Cooper's Works.** Durably bound in binder's silk cloth, uniform, 12mo. size.
Precaution..........**67c** Afloat and Ashore.**67c**
The Prairie..........**20c** The Red Rover....**67c**
Homeward Bound...**67c** The Deerslayer....**20c**
The Chainbearer....**67c** The Headsman....**67c**
The Two Admirals..**67c** Wing and Wing...**67c**
Mercedes of Castile..**67c** The Sky..........**67c**
The Bravo..........**67c** The Pathfinder....**20c**
Home as Found......**67c** The Pilot..........**20c**
Last of the Mohicans**20c** Oak Openings......**67c**
Wept of the Wish-ton-wish................**67c**
**Postage each, extra 12c.**

**52324. R. D. Blackmore's Works.** Handsomely bound in silk cloth, 12mo.
Kit and Kitty, 12mo.................. **$0.88**
**By mail 12c. extra.**
Lorna Doone, illustrated, 12mo.............. .70
**By mail 10c. extra.**
Springhaven, illustrated, 12mo.............. 1.05
**By mail 13c. extra.**
Perlycross Post 8vo.............. 1.23
**By mail 15c. extra.**

**52326. Marie Corelli's Works. Cloth bound,** 12mo.
Ardath............**25c** Wormwood..........**25c**
Thelma............**25c** Vendetta..........**25c**
Barrabas..........**70c** The Sorrows of Satan**80c**
Romance of Two Worlds..................**25c**
**Postage each extra 12c.**

**52328. Alexander Dumas' Works.** Substantially bound in silk cloth,
Monte Cristo .................. **$0.70**
Twenty Years After.................. .25
Marguerite DeValois.................. .70
Forty-five Guardsmen.................. .70
The Regent's Daughter.................. .70
The Queen's Necklace.................. .70
The Three Musketeers.................. .20
The Countess DeCharney.................. .70
Viscomte DeBragelonne.................. .25
Chicot the Jester.................. .70
The Conspirators.................. .70
Memoirs of a Physician.................. .70
Taking the Bastile.................. .70
The Chevalier.................. .70
DeMaison Rouge.................. .70
**Postage each, etxra 12c.**

**52330. George DuMaurier's Works.**
Trilby, a Novel.................. **$1.15**
**Postage extra 14c.**

**52332. George Eber's Romances.**
An Egyptian Princess.................. **$0.20**
The Bride of the Nile, 2 volumes.................. .53
The Emperor, 2 volumes.................. .53
Cleopatra.................. .20
Uarda.................. .20
Homo Sum, 2 volumes.................. .53
**Postage extra 12c.**

**52334. Edward Eggleston's Works, cloth bound, uniform, 12mo.**
The Circuit Rider.................. **$1.05**
The Hoosier Schoolmaster.................. .88
The Hoosier Schoolboy.................. .88
**Postage extra 12c.**

**52336. Augusta J. Evans' Novels, cloth bound, uniform, 12mo.**
Beulah...........**$1.17** St. Elmo........**$1.34**
Macaria..........**$1.17** Vashti..........**$1.34**
Inez..............**$1.17** Infelice ........**A1.34**
At the Mercy of Tiberius..................**$1.34**
**Postage extra 14c.**

**52338. Thomas Hardy's Works, cloth bound uniform, 12mo.**
Jude, the Obscure.................. **$1.05**
Tess, of the D'arberville.................. 1.05
**Postage extra 15c.**

**52340. Mary J. Holmes' Novels, cloth bound, uniform, 12mo.**
Tempest and Sunshine........**53c**
Marion Grey..................**95c**
Dr. Hathern's Daughters......**95c**
Lena Rivers..................**95c**
Darkness and Daylight.........**95c**
**Postage extra 15c.**

**52342. Washington Irving's Works, cloth bound, uniform, 12mo.**
Alhambra..................**20c**
Sketch Book..................**20c**
Granada...........**25c** Knickerbocker....**25c**
Wolfert's Roost.....(**Postage extra 12c.**).....**50c**

**52344. Captain Charles King's Works, cloth bound, uniform, 12mo.**
Under Fire......**88c** A War Time Wooing.**70c**
Marion's Faith..**88c** Fort Frayne..........**88c**
Laramie; or the Queen of Bedlam...........**70c**
**Postage extra 12c.**

**52346. Edna Lyall's Works, cloth bound, uniform, 12mo.**
Donovan..........**25c** In the Golden Days.**22c**
We Two...........**25c** A Hardy Norseman.**25c**
Knight Errant...**22c** Won by Waiting....**22c**
**Postage extra 12c.**

**52348. Ian Maclaren's Works, cloth bound, uniform, 12mo.**
Beside the Bonnie Briar Bush.................. **88c**
The Days of Auld Lang Syne.................. **88c**
**Postage extra 12c.**

**52350. Works of E. P. Roe.** Attractively bound in silk cloth, uniform, 12mo.
Each ........................**$0.90**
**By Mail each 11c extra.**
Miss Lou.
His Somber Rivals.
A Face Illumined.
The Home Acre.
Nature's Serial Story.
Near to Nature's Heart.
Barriers Burned Away.
Without a Home.
He Fell in Love with His Wife.
What Can She Do?
Driven Back to Eden.
A Day of Fate.
Opening of a Chestnut Burr.
A Knight of the XIX. Century.
From Jest to Earnest.

**52352. The Following of E. P. Roe's Works** bound in 16mo. size, each.................. **$0.30**
**By Mail each 8c extra.**
An Original Belle.
Opening of a Chestnut Burr.
A Young Girl's Wooing.
Barriers Burned Away.

**52354. Sir Walter Scott's Works.** Cloth bound, uniform, 12mo.
Bob Roy..........**$0.25** The Pirate.......**$0.22**
Waverly ..........**.25** The Talisman.... **.50**
Ivanhoe..........**.22** **Postage, 12c extra.**

**52356. Robert Louis Stephenson's Works.** Cloth bound, uniform, 12mo.
Kidnapped .................. **$0.55**
**Postage 12c extra.**
Treasure Island..**$0.20** Kidnapped.......**$0.20**
Prince Otto.......**.20** Master of Ballantre **.20**
**Postage 8c extra.**

**52358. Gen. Lew Wallace's Works.** Cloth bound, uniform, 12mo.
Ben Hur, A Tale of the Christ ..................**$0.95**
**Postage 13c extra.**
The Fair God, or The Last of The Tzins..........**$0.95**
**Postage 13c extra.**
The Prince of India, 2 vols..................**$1.75**
**Postage 22c extra.**

**52360. Stanley J. Weyman's Works.** Cloth bound, 12mo.
A Gentleman of France **$0.88**
My Lady Rotha .......... **.88**
The Man in Black........ **20**
**Postage 12c extra.**

**52362. Ten Nights in a Bar-Room, and What I Saw There.** By T. S. Arthur, illustrated, 12mo., Price..........(**By Mail 12c extra.**)............**$0.45**

**52378. Shams; or, Uncle Ben's Experience with Hypocrites.** A delightfully humorous and entertaining book by **"Uncle Ben Morgan."** It tells the story in a pleasant manner of simple country life, and gives a clear picture of every day life and incidents in the rural districts, that every one who has ever crossed a farm or halted in front of a country school house will readily recognize. Also of Uncle Ben's trip to the City of Chicago and to California, and his amusing experience with the shams and sharpers of the metropolitan world. **Full of good sense, funny incidents, interesting narrative and keen satire,** thoroughly readable and yet full of moral lessons for young and old. Illustrated with over 100 original illustrations by True Williams. A large, quarto book, bound in cloth.
Publishers' price.................. **$1.00**
Our price.................. **.40**
**My mail 14c extra.**

## Every Household Necessity...

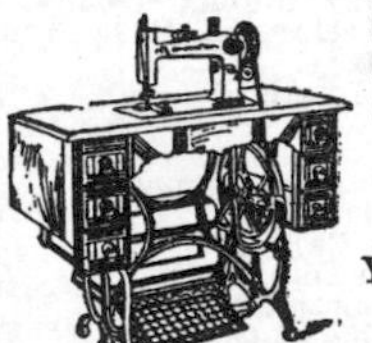

**SINKS INTO INSIGNIFICENT WHEN COMPARED WITH THE VALUE OF A FINE ......**

**SEWING ...MACHINE**

You used to be asked **$75.00** for a good one. Most agent's now **Ask $40.00 to $60.00.**

**WE SELL THE MACHINES under our own name at from $18.00 to $21.00.**

☞ See our Sewing Machine Department or send for Free Catalogue.

**WE WILL SEND GOODS ON OUR LIBERAL C. O. D. TERMS, AND YOU HAVE FULL PRIVILEGE OF EXAMINATION. MOST CUSTOMERS SEND CASH IN FULL AND GET THREE (3) PER CENT DISCOUNT, ON OUR GUARANTEE THAT GOODS SHALL BE AS REPRESENTED.**

## IDEAL LIBRARY

**52364** Comprising 150 titles of standard works, representing authors of established merits; printed from large clear type on extra quality of paper and bound in attractive paper covers in such a way that they open easily and flexibly, thus making their perusal of pleasure and comfort.

**Eight cents per Volume; 7 books for 50 cents.**
**By mail Extra 2 cents each.**

Clarabel's Love Story, Bertha M. Clay.
The Old Mam'selle's Secret. E. Marlitt.
Her Desperate Victory, Mrs. Rayne.
The Son of Clemenceau, Alexander Dumas.
Conquest of Spain. Washington Irving
Vivian the Beauty. Mrs. Annie Edwards.
Vicar of Wakefield, Oliver Goldsmith.
Only One Sin, Bertha M. Clay.
Dodo, F. F. Benson.
John Halifax. Miss Mulock.
The Last of the Mohicans, J. Fennimore Cooper.
Sketch Book, Washington Irving.
Ships that Pass in the Night, Beatrice Harradan,
Deerslayer, J. Fennimore Cooper.
Oliver Twist, Dickens.
The Evil Genius, Wilkie Collins.
Marvel, The Duchess.
Pathfinder, J. Fennimore Cooper.
Pioneers, J. Fennimore Cooper.
Love Letters of a Worldly Woman, Mrs. W. K. Clifford.
Vendetta, Marie Corelli.
Tour of the World in 80 days, Jules Verne.
Gulliver's Travels, Swift.
Thorns and Orange Blossoms, Bertha M. Clay.
Tales of a Traveler, Irving.
Cleopatra, H. Rider Haggard.
Lord Lynn's Choice, Bertha M. Clay.
Ivanhoe, Walter Scott.
Jane Eyre, Charlotte Bronte.

East Lynne, Mrs. Henry Wood.
Thelma, Marie Corelli.
King Solomon's Mines. H. Rider Haggard.
Miawa's Revenge, H. Rider Haggard.
Mildred Trevanion, The Duchess.
A Romance of Two Worlds, Marie Corelli.
Last Days of Pompeii, Lord Lytton.
Adam Bede, George Elliot.
The Legacy of Cain, Wilke Collins.
Romola, George Elliot.
The Mysterious Island, Jules Verne.
20,000 Leagues Under the Sea, Jules Verne.
A Crooked Path, Mrs. Alexander.
The Mill on the Floss, George Eliot.
Called Back, Hugh Conway.
A Pair of Blue Eyes, Bertha M. Clay.
Dark Days, Hugh Conway.
The Lamplighter, Maria Cummins.
Madcap Violet, William Black.
Camille, Alex. Dumas.

Vanity Fair, W. M. Thackeray.
The Wide, Wide World, E. Wetherell.
Willy Rielly, Will Carleton.
Bound by a Spell, Hugh Conway.
Woman Against Woman, Mrs. M. E. Holmes.
Black Beauty, Anna Sewell.
On Her Wedding Morn, Bertha M. Clay.
Sunshine and Roses, Bertha M. Clay.
Hunted Down, Max Hilary.
Natural Law in the Spiritual World, Drummond.
The Duke's Secret, Bertha M. Clay.
Dora Thorne, Bertha M. Clay.
Beyond Pardon, Bertha M. Clay.
Handy Andy, Samuel Lover.
A Golden Heart, Bertha M. Clay.
Children of the Abbey, Regina Maria Roche.
A Mad Love, Bertha M. Clay.
The Frozen Pirate, W. Clark Russell.
Wife in Name Only, Bertha M. Clay.
The Dream of Love, Zola.
Kenilworth, Sir Walter Scott.
Dark Marriage Morn, Bertha M. Clay.
Saddle and Saber, Hawley Smart.
A Young Girl's Love, Bertha M. Clay.
A Woman's Error, Bertha M. Clay
Won by Waiting, Edna Lyall.
Forging the Fetters, Mrs. Alexander.
Lucile, Owen Meredith.
Viscount DeBragelonne, Alex. Dumas.
Woman's War, Bertha M. Clay.
Wooed and Married, Rosa Nouchette Carey.
A Hardy Norseman, Edna Lyall.
We Too, Edna Lyall.
Donovan, Edna Lyall.
Louise de la Valliere, Alexander Dumas.
Knight Errant, Edna Lyall.
Wee Wifie, Rosa Nouchette Carey.
Edmund Dantes, Alexander Dumas.
Her Sister's Bethrothed, Bertha M. Clay.
Love's Chain Broken, Bertha M. Clay.
Foiled by Loving, Bertha M. Clay.
Twenty Years After, Alexander Dumas.
The Son of Porthos, Alexander Dumas.
Lover or Friend, Rosa Nouchette Carey.
The First Violin, Jessie Fothergill.

The Count of Monte Cristo. Alexander Dumas.
Three Guardsmen, Alexander Dumas.
To Be or Not to Be, Mrs. Alexander.
The Light of Love, Bertha M. Clay.
An Egyptian Princess, Geo. Ebers.
From Out the Gloom, Bertha M. Clay.
Her Only Sin, Bertha M. Clay.
Dick's Sweetheart, The Duchess.
The Pirate, Sir Walter Scott.
Rob Roy, Sir Walter Scott.
The Wife's Sacrifice, A. D. Ennery.
House of Seven Gables, Nathaniel Hawthorne.
Story of an African Farm, Olive Schreiner
Dreams, Olive Schreiner.
Reveries of a Bachelor, Ik Marvel.
Dream Life, Ik Marvel.
Worth Winning, Mrs. H. Lovett.
Ardath, Marie Corelli.
Wormwood, Marie Corelli.
Ideala, Sara Grand.
Micah Clark, A. Conan Doyle.
A Study in Scarlet, A. Conan Doyle.
A Bird of Passage, Beatrice Harradan.
Beyond the City, A. Conan Doyle.
The Sign of the Four, A. Conan Doyle.
The Idle Thoughts of an Idle Fellow, Jerome K. Jerome.
The Bondsman, Hall Caine.
The Deemster, Hall Caine.
Treasure Island, Robert Louis Stevenson.
Beside the Bonnie Brier Bush, Ian Maclaren.
Robinson Crusoe, Daniel De Foe.
The Scarlet Letter, Nathaniel Hawthorne.
Life in London, Edwin Hodder.
The Abbe Constantin. Ludovic Halevy.
The Coming Race, Lord Lytton.
Mosses from an Old Manse, Nathaniel Hawthorne.
Drummond's Addresses, Prof. Drummond.
The Confessions of an English Opium Eater, Thomas De Quincy.
Winsome but Wicked, Meredith.
Fantine, Victor Hugo.
Cosette, Victor Hugo.
Marius, Victor Hugo.
Saint Denis, Victor Hugo.
Jean Valjean, Victor Hugo.
Rienzi, Lord Lytton.
Ernest Maltravers, Lord Lytton.
Alice, Lord Lytton.
A Case of Identity, A. Conan Doyle.
Child's History of England, Charles Dickens.
The Two Orphans, R. D'Ennery.
Widow in Thrums, J. M. Barrie.
When a Man's Single, J. M. Barrie.
Gold Elsie, E. Marlitt.
Was it a Crime?

## THE PARKSIDE SERIES

**52366.** A Choice Selection of Writings by Well-Known Authors, very attractively bound in heavy paper. Price each 5c; 23 for $1.00.
Postage each, extra 2 cents.

Fairy Gold.
A Man of Mark.
The Evil Genius.
Mona's Choice.
The Sign of the Four.
Barbara.
Dark Days.
Blind Love.
Lady Hutton's Ward.
The Light that Failed
The Duchess.
Valerie.
Cleopatra.
Tracking the Truth.
A Marriage at Sea.
The Danver's Jewels.
Kidnapped.

A Matter of Skill.
Chiffon's Marriage.
Living or Dead.
A Crooked Path.
A Change of Air.
The House of the Wolf.
Love's Martyr.
A Fight for a Fortune.
Jack and the Three Jills.
The Great Keinplatz Experiment.
The Master of Ballantrae.
Treasure Island.
Vere.
A Little Rebel.
A Study in Scarlet.
The Heir of Linn.
The Big Bow Mystery.

**52368. Abraham Lincoln.** His early History and Political career; together with his Speeches, Messages, Proclamations and other Officials, Documents illustrative of his eventful administration, containing 478 pages substantially bound in cloth. 12mo.
Publishers price........$0.70
Our price............... 0.30
By Mail 12 cents extra.

**52370. P. T. Barnum.** His early life and struggles, bold ventures and brilliant successes, wonderful career in which he made and lost fortunes. His genius, wit, eloquence and life as a citizen.
Printed from clear new type on good quality paper. Contains over 500 pages, beautifully illustrated, bound in fine cloth, marbled edges.
Publishers price, $1.50; Our price.............75c.
By mail 24 cents extra.

**52372. James G. Blaine.** Containing a full account of his early life; his career as a teacher; services as secretary of state, his illness and death. The whole forming a complete and graphic account of America's most distinguished statesman. Printed from clear new type on calendered paper, embellished with beautiful engravings. One large octavo volume of 600 pages.
Publishers price, $1.50; Our price.............75c.
By mail 28 cents extra.

**52376. The Farmer's Encyclopedia. The Encyclopedia of Practical Information and Universal Knowledge.** A very large 780 page volume of universal knowledge. A book of ready reference for every occupation, trade and profession. **Eight volumes in one.** It contains the following departments: Medical, Trades, Agricultural, Household, Business, Mineral, Educational and Miscellaneous. It is a book that should be in every library in every household. There is hardly anything of general knowledge and information that cannot be found in this volume. The book is size 10x8x3 and weighs about four pounds.
Publishers' price, $2.00; Our price.............98c.
By mail 45c extra.

**52380. The Columbian Gallery.** A collection of reproductions of photographs from the World's Fair, including the chief palaces, interiors, statuary, architectural and scenic groups, characters, typical exhibits, and marvels of the Midway Plaisance. The pictures in the "Gallery" embrace views of all the Main, State and Foreign buildings, the Court of Honor, the Ferris Wheel, the Wooded Island and Lagoons, the most striking interiors and exhibits, and the features of the **Midway Plaisance.** Size 13x11 inches. 210 full page plates. Brown cloth binding.
Publishers' price, $2.50; Our price.............65c.
Postage 30c extra.

**52382. Indian Horrors; or, Massacres by the Rod Men.** Being a thrilling narrative of bloody wars with the merciless savages; startling descriptions of fantastic Ghost dances; desperate Indian braves; scalping of helpless settlers, etc. The whole comprising a **fascinating history of the Indians** from the discovery of America; their manners, customs, modes of warfare, etc. Printed from clear new type and comprised in one octavo volume of 600 pages. It is illustrated with fine engravings. **Printed in colors,** bound in fine cloth, marbled edges. Postage extra 28c.
Publishers' price, $1.50; Our price............. 95c.

**52384. The Sands of Time.** A book of Birthday Gems, by Thos. W. Handford. 32mo cloth. This handsome book is superbly illustrated with 13 full page engravings, is bound in extra gold embossed silk cloth, with full gilt edges. It contains a text, a sentiment and a proverb for every day in the year, taken from the works of 150 different authors, besides a blank space for the autographs of friends. This is an unique and acceptable gift book.
Publishers' price............$1.50
Our price..................55
By mail 14c extra.

**52388. Earth, Sea and Sky, or Marvels of the Universe.** Being a full and Graphic Description of all that is Marvelous and Wonderful in every Continent of the Globe, containing **Thrilling Adventures on Land and Sea,** and Renowned Discoveries of the World's Greatest Explorers in all Ages. Embracing the Peculiar Characteristics of the Human Race, of Animals, Birds, Insects, etc., including a **Vivid description of the Monsters of the Deep, Beautiful Sea-Shells and Plants, Singular Fishes and Dwellers in the World of Waters,** Remarkable Ocean Currents, etc., etc. Together with the Amazing Phenomena of the Solar and Starry Systems. The work is printed from large, clear new type, on fine calendered paper, and comprised in one large octavo volume of 864 pages. It is embellished with 329 fine and appropriate engravings. Bound in cloth. Silk Finish, Marbled Edges. By mail 28c extra.
Publisher's price.........................$2.75
Our price in Cloth...........................95
Our price in Full Morocco.................. 1.40

**52390 Conquering the Wilderness;** Or Heroes and Heroines of Pioneer Life an Adventure. By Col. Frank Triplett. An interesting account of the romantic deeds, lofty achievements and marvelous adventures of **Daniel Boone, Davy Crockett, Sam Houston, Kit Carson, Buffalo Bill, General Freemont, General Kearney,** and scores of other noted Indian fighters and celebrated pioneers. Conquering the Wilderness depicts **border life past and present,** of **gold diggings, Indian raids, Judge Lynch, hunting, trapping and ranching.** The book contains 200 portraits and many original and striking engravings from special sketches by Nast and Darbey. Bound in heavy cloth.
Publisher's price .......................... $2.00
Our price ................................. .85

**By Mail 35c extra.**

**52392 Explorations and Adventures of Henry M. Stanley.** Being a graphic account of thrilling adventures, marvellous discoveries and strange phenomena in all parts of the globe. Containing **Wonders of the Tropics,** Wild Sports of the Jungle and Plain, Curious Customs of Savage Races, with vivid descriptions of **Ferocious Animals; Death Dealing Reptiles, Superb Scenery,** etc; Renowned Explorations of Modern Heroes of Discovery, with their startling and fascinating adventures. The most interesting and instructive of all modern works on travel and adventure. Contains 816 large octavo pages and 314 fine appropriate engravings, substantially bound in heavy cloth.
Publisher's price ........................... $.250
Our price ................................ 1.00

**By mail 25c extra.**

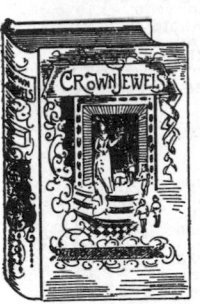

**52396 Crown Jewels or Gems of Literature, Art and Music.** Being choice collections from the writings of the most celebrated authors from the earliest times to the present day, comprising **Narratives, Ballads, Songs, Poems of Heroism, Romance, Adventure and Patriotism.** Choice selections from Religious Literature. Masterpieces of Dramatic Literature, Romance, Wit, Humour, etc. A vast treasure of gems for every taste, sentiment or condition of life. This work covers the whole field of literature. Every page is resplendent in its array of noble and inspiring thought. **Its jewels should sparkle in every home throughout the land.** Bound in one large octavo volume of 632 pages, in extra fine cloth, marble edges. The beautiful steel plate engravings with which it is embellished are alone worth the whole cost of the book.
Publisher's price .......................... $2.50
Our price ................................ 1.25

**Postage extra 28c.**

**52398 From Pole to Pole.** Includes renowned explorations and voyages in the torrid and frigid zones; **thrilling sketches of the great heroes of modern discovery,** with their startling adventures and fascinating narratives. The work is printed from clear, new type, on fine calendered paper, and comprised in one large octavo volume of 816 pages. It is embellished with 324 fine and appropriate engravings. Bound in silk finished cloth, marbeled edges.
Publisher's price.......................... $2.75
Our price ............................... 1.25

**By mail, 28c. extra.**

**52400 A Trip Around the World.** Contains a rare and elaborate collection of **Photographic Views** of the entire world of Nature and Art. Presenting and describing choicest treasures of Europe, Asia, Africa, Australia, North and South America. Printed on fine calendered paper. Size 12x13 inches.
Publisher's price... .......................... $3.00
Our price ................................ .75

**By mail 30c. extra.**

**52402 Alta Edition, comprises 154 titles of standard works,** embracing fiction, essays, poetry, history, travels, etc., selected from the world's best literature, written by authors of world wide reputation, printed from large clear type on good paper. Each book is bound in a handsome manner with a beautiful black and gold back stamp, ornamented sides and silk ribbon marker. This edition is composed of books of sterling quality, and are well adapted for school and other libraries. In point of manufacture they are superior to any other line.
Publishers' price, each vol...50c
Our price ................. 25c
Five or more at one time ....23c
**Postage each extra 12c.**

1 Robinson Crusoe, by Daniel De Foe.
2 Arabian Nights Entertainments.
3 Swiss Family Robinson.
4 Thaddeus of Warsaw, by Jane Porter.
5 Children of the Abbey, by Regina Marie Roche.
6 Don Quixote, by Cervantes.
7 Vicar of Wakefield, by Goldsmith.
8 Bunyan's Pilgrim's Progress.
9 Gulliver's Travels, by Swift.
10 Child's History of England, by Charles Dickens.
11 Æsop's Fables, 50 illustrations.
12 Baron Munchausen.
13 Ivanhoe, by Sir Walter Scott.
14 Guy Mannering, by Sir Walter Scott.
15 Stories from French History, by Sir Walter Scott.
16 Tom Brown's School Days at Rugby, Thomas Hughes.
17 Dog Crusoe, by R. M. Ballantyne.
18 Gorilla Hunters, by R. M. Ballantyne.
19 Wild Man of the West, by R. M. Ballantyne.
20 Gascoyne, by R. M. Ballantyne.
21 Freaks on the Fells, by R. M. Ballantyne.
22 Shifting Winds, by R. M. Ballantyne.
23 Floating Light, by R. M. Ballantyne.
24 Bear Hunters, by Anne Bowman.
25 Kangaroo Hunters, by Anne Bowman.
26 American Family Robinson, by D. W. Belisle.
27 Adventures in Canada, by John G. Geikie.
28 Under the Holly, by Mrs. Margaret Hosmer.
29 A Million too Much, A Temperance Tale, by Julia McNair Wright.
30 Gavroche, by Victor Hugo.
31 Grimm's Popular Tales.
32 Grimm's Household Stories.
33 French Fairy Tales, by De Segur.
34 Standard Fairy Tales.
35 Lady Green Satin, by Deschesnez.
36 Pickwick Papers, by Charles Dickens.
37 Martin Chuzzlewit, by Charles Dickens.
39 Oliver Twist, Italy and American Notes, by Charles Dickens.
40 David Copperfield, by Dickens.
41 The Vicissitudes of Bessie Fairfax, by Holme Lee.
42 Katerfelto, A Story of Exmoor, by G. J. Whyte Melville.
43 Valentine, the Countess, by Carl Detlef.
44 Chaste as Ice, Pure as Snow, by Mar M. C. Despard.
45 Complete Letter Writer.
46 Prehistoric World, by Berthet.
47 Stories From History, by Agnes Strickland.
48 English History, Tales from, by Agnes Strickland.
49 Ancient History, True Stories from, by Agnes Strickland.
50 Pique, A Tale of English Aristocracy.
51 Orange Blossoms, by T. S. Arthur.
52 Bar Rooms at Brantly, by T. S. Arthur.
53 Cook's Voyages around the World.
54 Camp-Fires of Napoleon, by Henry C. Watson.
55 Romance of the Revolution, by Oliver B. Bunce.
56 Remarkable Events in the World's History, by L. H. Young.
57 Evening Amusements, by Planche.
58 Modern Classics, by E. E. Hale, Bayard Taylor and others.
59 Travels in Africa, by Charles Williams.
60 In the Arctic Seas, by Captain McClintock.
61 Children's Bible Stories.
62 Memorable Scenes in French History, by Samuel M. Schmucker.
63 Frontier Life, Tales of the Southwestern Border, by F. Hardman.
64 Celebrated Female Sovereigns, by Mrs. Jameson
65 Pioneer Women of the West, by Mrs. Ellet.
66 Thrilling Adventures on Land and Sea, by J. O. Brayman.
67 Modern Story Teller, Selections from the best authors.
68 Christmas Stories, Selections from the best writers.
69 Sea and Shore, by Hector Malot.
70 King of Conjurers, by Houdin.
71 Speeches of Daniel Webster, by B. F. Teft.
72 Daniel Webster, Life of, by B. F. Teft.

73 David Crockett, Life of, by Edw. S. Ellis.
74 Andrew Jackson, Life of, by John S. Jenkins.
75 Zachary Taylor, Life of, by H. Montgomery.
76 Duchess of Orleans, Life of.
77 Joan of Arc, by David W. Bartlett.
78 Patrick Henry, Life of.
79 Old Curiosity Shop, and reprinted pieces by Charles Dickens.
80 Barnaby Budge, and Hard Times, by Charles Dickens.
81 Bleak House, by Charles Dickens.
82 Little Dorrit, by Charles Dickens.
83 Dombey & Son, by Charles Dickens.
84 In the Days of My Youth, by Amelia B. Edwards.
85 Gentianella, by Mrs. Randolph.
86 Underground City.
87 Tour of the World in Eighty Days, by Jules Verne.
88 At the North Pole, by Jules Verne.
89 Desert of Ice, by Jules Verne.
90 Twenty Thousand Leagues under the Sea, by Jules Verne.
91 Wreck of the Chancellor, by Jules Verne.
92 Whimsicalities, Whims and Oddities, by Thos. Hood.
93 Miscellanies and Hood's Own, by Thomas Hood.
94 Up the Rhine, by Thomas Hood.
95 Christmas Books, Uncommercial Traveler, by Charles Dickens.
96 Tale of the Two Cities and Great Expectations, by Charles Dickens.
97 Edwin Drood, Sketches, Master Humphrey's Clock, etc., by Charles Dickens.
98 Three in Norway.
99 Emma, by Jane Austen.
100 Mansfield Park, by Jane Austen.
101 Sense and Sensibility, and Persuasion, **by Jane Austen.**
102 Helen Ford, by Horatio Alger Jr.
103 Jane Eyre, by Charlotte Bronte.
104 Lucile, by Owen Meredith.
105 Andersen's Fairy Tales.
106 Macaulay's England, Vol. I.
107 Macaulay's England, Vol. II.
108 Macaulay's England, Vol. III.
109 Macaulay's England, Vol. IV.
110 Macaulay's England, Vol. V.
111 Charles O'Malley, by Lever.
112 Handy Andy, by Samuel Lover.
113 Three Guardsmen, by Dumas
114 Tom Brown at Oxford, by Thos. Hughes.
115 East Lynne, by Mrs. Henry Wood.
116 John Halifax, Gentleman, by Miss Mulock.
117 The Last of the Mohicans, by James Fenimore Cooper.
118 Adam Bede, by George Eliot.
119 Hold the Fort, by D. L. Moody.
120 Evenings with Moody and Sankey.

121 Child's History of Rome, Seven Kings of Seven Hills, by C. H. B. Laing.
122 Child's History of Rome, Conquest of the Seven Hills, by C. H. B, Laing.
123 Mary and Florence, by Ann Fraser Tytler.
124 Mary and Florence at Sixteen, by Ann Fraser Tytler.
125 Plain Thoughts on the Art of Living by Washington Gladden.
126 Uncle Grandesir's Matches, by E. Martineau Deschesnez.
127 Daniel Deronda, Vol. I, by George Eliot.
128 Daniel Deronda, Vol. II, by George Eliot.
129 The Deerslayer, by J. Fenimore Cooper.
130 Felix Holt, by George Eliot.
131 Mill on the Floss, by George Eliot.
132 Old Mamselle's Secret, by E. Marlitt.
133 The Pathfinder, by J. F. Cooper.
134 Romola, by George Eliot.
135 The Heart of Midlothian, by Sir Walter Scott.
136 The Monastery, by Sir Walter Scott.
137 The Abbott, by Sir Walter Scott.
138 Kenilworth, by Sir Walter Scott.
139 The Pirate, by Sir Walter Scott.
140 The Betrothed, by Sir Walter Scott.
141 Woodstock, by Sir Walter Scott.
142 The Fair Maid of Perth, by Sir Walter Scott.
143 Anne of Geierstein, by Sir Walter Scott.
144 Count Robert of Paris, by Sir Walter Scott.
145 Chronicles of the Cannongate, by Sir Walter Scott
146 The Antiquary, by Sir Walter Scott.
147 Rob Roy, by Sir Walter Scott.
148 The Fortunes of the Nigel, by Sir Walter Scott.
149 Peveril of the Peak, by Sir Walter Scott.
150 Quentin Durward, by Sir Walter Scott.
151 St. Ronan's Well, by Sir Walter Scott.
152 Red Gauntlet, by Sir Walter Scott.
153 The Talisman and Castle Dangerous, by Sir Walter Scott.
154 Washington and his Generals
155 Pilgrim's Progress.

## POSTAGE MUST BE INCLUDED

When you send for goods to go by mail. If you send too much we will send back the balance.

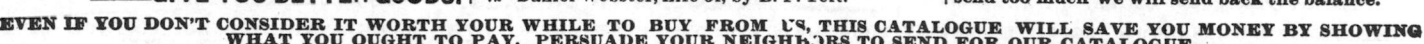

## Alpine Edition.

**52406 Fill your library for $20.44.** We are offering at 28 cents per volume, the choicest works of the world's greatest authors. Books that were published to sell at 70 cents. This edition comprises 73 titles, and for $20.44 you get as nice an assortment of finely bound books as you can find at double our price. These books are bound in the finest silk cloth and are very handsome in appearance, and most suitable for the finest library. These books have gilt top, and are printed in handsome, large type, on a superior quality of paper. 3% discount if cash in full accompanies order. If you buy the full list of the Alpine series, the net cash price will be only $19.83, and you will have the choicest selection of standard works at a price less than half the price your local dealer will charge. Publisher's price, per volume........ 70c
Our price, per volume (Postage 12c extra).. 28c

Abbe Constantin. Ludovic Halevy.
Adam Bede. George Eliot.
Thaddeus of Warsaw.
Aesop's Fables.
Alhambra. Washington Irving.
Anderson's Fairy Tales.
Arabian Night's Entertainment.
Ardath. Marie Corelli.
Astoria. Washington Irving.
Autocrat of the Breakfast Table. Oliver Wendell Homes.
Bacon's Essays. Francis Bacon.
Black Beauty. Anna Sewell.
Bondsman, The. Hall Caine.
Bracebridge Hall. Washington Irving.
Character. Samuel Smiles.
Children of the Abbey. Regina Marie Roche.
Child's History of England. Charles Dickens.
Count of Monte Cristo, The. Alexander Dumas.
Confessions of an English Opium Eater. Thos. DeQuincey.
Crayon Papers, The. Washington Irving.
Daniel Deronda. George Eliot.
Deemster, The. Hall Caine.
Donovan. Edna Lyall.
Don Quixote, by Cervantes.
Dream Life. Donald G. Mitchell (Ik. Marvel.)
Drummond's Addresses.
Duty. Samuel Smiles.
East Lynne. Mrs. Henry Wood.
Edmund Dantes. Alemander Dumas.
Egyptian Princess, An. George Ebers.
Felix Holt. George Eliot.
First Violin, The. Jessie Fothergill.
Grimm's Fairy Tales. Brothers Grimm.
Gulliver's Travels. Dean Swift.
Handy Andy. Samuel Lover.
Hardy Norseman, A. Edna Lyall.
House of Seven Gables, The. Nathanel Hawthorne.
Hypatia. Charles Kingsley.
Imitation of Christ. Thomas A'Kempis.
Ivanhoe. Sir Walter Scott.
Jane Eyre. Charlotte Bronte.
John Halifax. Miss Mulock.
Kenilworth. Sir Walter Scott.
Knickerbocker History of New York. Washington Irving.
Lamplighter, The. Maria Cummings.
Last Days of Pompeii. Lord Lytton.
Last of the Mohicans, The. J. Fenimore Cooper.
Lorna Doone. R. D. Blackmore.
Lucile. Owen Meredith.
Middlemarch. George Eliot.
Mill on the Floss, The. George Eliot.
Misjudged. W Heimburg.
Mosses from an old Manse. Nathaniel Hawthorne.
Mysterious Island, The. Jules Verne.
Natural Law in the Spiritual World. Drummond.
Old Mam'selle's Secret. E. Marlitt.
Oliver Twist. Charles Dickens.
Our Mutual Friend. Charles Dickens.
Pathfinder, The. J. Fenimore Cooper.
Pilgrim's Progress, The. John Bunyan.
Reveries of a Bachelor. D. G. Mitchell (Ik.Marvel)
Robinson Crusoe. Daniel DeFoe.
Romance of Two Worlds, A. Marie Corelli.
Romola. George Eliot.
Scarlet Letter, The. Nathaniel Hawthorne.
Scottish Chiefs. Jane Porter.
Self Help. Samuel Smiles.
Sesame and Lilies. John Ruskin.
Sign of the Four, The. A. Conan Doyle.
Silas Marner. George Eliot.
Sketch Book. Washington Irving.
Story of an African Farm. Olive Schreiner.
Uncle Tom's Cabin. Harriet Beecher Stowe.

## Cook Books and Household Medical Works.

**52407. White House Cook Book.** Size 8x10x12 inches. 570 pages, illustrated. Cream whited enameled cloth bindings; large type; wide margins; complete indexes. By Hugo Ziemann, chef of White House under President Harrison. Without a doubt the soundest and most practical cook book before the public. It contains over 1,600 tested cooking recipes, besides numerous hints and helps for the toilette and household. Too well known for further comment except the price which is positively the lowest yet offered. Publisher's Price...............$1.75
Our Price (Postage 30c Extra)..............90

---

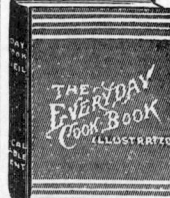

**52408 Every Day Cook Book and Cyclopedia of Practical Recipes,** by Miss E. Niel. Economical, Reliable and Excellent. Neatly bound in oilcloth; 12mo.
Publisher's Price........$1.00
Our Price...............30
**Postage 15c extra.**

**52409 The Housekeeper's Cook Book.** A work of unparalled excellency; 2500 recipes; ten modes of preparing each dish; complete, practical, simple. Bound in oilcloth, size 6¼ x 9 inches.
Publisher's Price.....$1.00
Our Price..............50
**Postage 12c Extra.**

**52410 The Buckeye Cook Book,** an entirely new edition with hints on practical housekeeping. Revised and enlarged; 8 vo; attractively bound in oilcloth.
Publisher's Price.....$2.00
Our Price..............1.15
**Postage 14c Extra.**

**52411 Ladies' and Gentlemen's Etiquette,** by E. B. Duffy. A complete manual of the manners and dress of American Society, containing forms of letters, invitations, acceptances, and regrets. Very attractively bound in silk cloth 12mo.
Publisher's Price..........$1.50
Our Price..............1.00
**By mail 15c Extra.**

**52412 Favorite Cook Book.** The most complete culinary encyclopedia published. New, original, practical, perfect, approved. Contains over 1600 recipes, each one guaranteed perfect. Printed in large clear type. Bound in white oilcloth. If it becomes soiled, can easily be cleaned by an ordinary cloth. Size 8x12 inches, 528 pages.
Publisher's Price...........................$3.00
Our Price................................1.50
**By mail 30c extra.**

**52413. Science of Life or Creative and Sexual Science** by Prof. O. S. Fowler. Including manhood, womanhood, and their mutual and interrelations. Love, its laws, powers, etc. A work pure and elevated in tone, and eloquent in its denunciation of vice. Illustrated with numerous engravings. 8vo.
Publisher's price..$3.00
Our price...........1.35
**Postage, 28c extra.**

**52414 The Ladies' New Medical Guide,** by Dr. S. Pancoast. An Instructor, Counselor and Friend in all the delicate and wonderful matters peculiar to women. Fully explaining the nature and mystery of the reproductive organs in both sexes; love, courtship, marriage, pregnancy, labor, and childbirth, with the causes, treatment and symptoms of all their own special diseases and diseases of children. Illustrated with about 125 engravings and diagrams explanatory of the human system. Octavo. Cloth.
Publisher's price.. .................$2.50
Our price..............................1.35
**Postage, 20c extra.**

**52415. Robb's Family Physician.** Being a concise and comprehensive treatise on diseases as they occur in every day life. The Causes, the Symptoms and Treatment, and demonstrating the cure of the various ills humanity is subject to. By J. V. Bean, M. D., R. L. Robb, M. D., and Sarah L. Robb, M. D. Illustrated with numerous engravings. Large octavo. Cloth.
Publisher's price......................$3.00
Our price................................1.10
**Postage, 25c extra.**

**52416. Medical Companion and Household Physician,** by J. W. Bate. M. D. No family can afford to be without this valuable book. It contains many valuable recipes and advise concerning the preservation of health and the prevention of diseases. Durably bound in full cloth. 319 pages.
Publisher's price.....$1.50
Our price..............35
**Postage, 14c extra.**

---

## Poetry.

**OUR BEST EFFORTS** have been given to compile a series of poetical works that will meet the demands of all tastes. We are conscious of having succeeded in securing the choicest works of all favorite poets at greatly reduced prices and take pleasure in inviting your attention to the list quoted below. You will be bound to admit that nothing desirable has been left out, and when the quality of binding, elegance of print and paper are considered, none can compete with us in price.

**52417. Red Line Edition of the Poets.** Printed on toned paper, bound in extra English cloth, stamped in black and gold. 12mo.
Gold edges, each......$0.45
Ten or more at one time, each.............0.42
**By Mail 11c each, extra.**

Beauties of Shakespeare.
British Female Poets.
Browning, Mrs.
Browning, Robert.
Bryant (Early Poems).
Burns. Byron.
Campbell. Dante.
Eliot, George.
Milton. Moore.
Emerson, Ralph Waldo (Early Poems).
Faust. Mulock, Miss.
Favorite Poems. One Thousand and One
Goethe. Gems.
Goldsmith. Pilgrim's Progress.
Hemans, Mrs. Poe, Edgar Allan.
Holmes, Oliver Wendell Poets of America.
(Early Poems). Pope.
Homer's Iliad. Procter.
Homer's Odyssey. Religious Poems.
Household Poems. Schiller.
Hugo, Victor. Scott.
Imitation of Christ. Scottish Cavaliers.
Ingelow, Jean. Shakespeare.
Keats. Shelley.
Kingsely, Charles. Songs for the Household.
Language and Poetry of Tennyson.
Flowers. Thompson.
Longfellow (Early Poems). Virgil.
Lowell (Early Poems). Willis.
Lucile. Whittier (Early Poems).
Macaulay. Wordsworth.
Meredith.

## Household Edition of the Poets.

**52418.** Each volume is complete, printed from good type and tastefully bound; suitable for private, public and school libraries. Most of them contain Portraits. 12mo.
Cloth, each...............$1.15
**By Mail, 15 cents each extra.**

Aldrich's Poems. Bret Hart's Poems.
Bryant's Poems. Cary's Poems.
Emerson's Parnassus. Emerson's Poems.
Holmes' Poems. Humorous Poetry.
Larcom's Poems. Longfellow's Christus.
Longfellow's Poems. Lowell's Poems.
Owen Meredith's Pomes. Parton's Humorous Poetry.
Saxe's Poems. Songs of Three Centuries
Stedman's Poems. Taylor's Dramas.
Taylor's Poems. Tennyson's Poems.
Whittier's Poems.

## Woodbine Edition of the Poets.

**52419.** Padded leather covers, handsomely embossed. Gilt edges. A neat gift edition. Each volume boxed. 12mo. Per volume..............$0.90
**By Mail 13 cents per vol. extra.**

Browning, Mrs.
Browning, Robert.
Bryant, (Early Poems).
Burns.
Byron.
Dante.
Don Juan.
Emerson, Ralph Waldo Lowell, Early Poems.
(Early Poems). Lucile.
Faust. Milton.
Favorite Poems. Moore.
Goethe. One Thousand and One
Golden Leaves from the Gems.
American Poets. Pilgrim's Progress.
Golden Leaves from the Poe, Edgar Allan.
British Poets. Proctor.
Golden Leaves from the Schiller.
Dramatic Poets. Scott.
Golden Leaves from the Shakespeare.
English Poets. Tennyson.
Goldsmith. Whittier, (Early Poems).
Hemans, Mrs. Wordsworth.
Holmes, Oliver Wendell (Early Poems).
Ingelow, Jean.
Longfellow, Early Poems.

**52420. The Fireside Encyclopedia of Poetry.** Thoroughly revised, collected and arranged, by Henry T. Coates. Imperial 8vo, handsomely bound in silk cloth, gilt sides and edges.
Publishers price...........$4.00
Our price.................2.45
**By Mail 35 cents extra.**

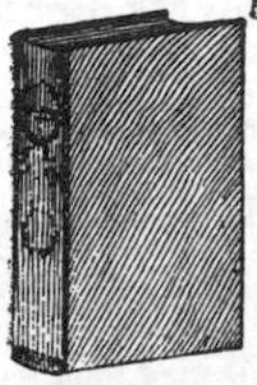

**52421 Hurst's Plain Edition of Poets** Neatly bound in binders' silk cloth, and printed on good paper from clear new type. 12mo. Publishers price each.......... **$0.70**
Our price each, **0.30**
**By Mail, 11 cents each extra.**

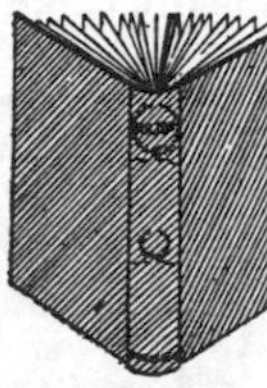

| | |
|---|---|
| Arnold, Edwin. | Homer's Odyssey. |
| Browning, Mrs. | Hugo, Victor. |
| Browning, Robert. | Ingelow, Jean. |
| Bryant. | Keats. |
| Burns. | Language and Poetry of Flowers. |
| Byron. | Longfellow. |
| Campbell. | Lowell. |
| Dante. | Lucile. |
| Eliot. | Milton. |
| Emerson, Ralph Waldo. | Moore. |
| Faust. | One Thousand and One Gems. |
| Goethe. | Poe, Edgar Allan. |
| Golden Leaves from the American Poets. | Pope. |
| Golden Leaves from the Dramatic Poets. | Scott. |
| Goldsmith. | Shakespeare. |
| Holmes, Oliver Wendell. | Tennyson. |
| Homer's Iliad, | Whittie r. |

**52422 Shakespeare Art Edition.** With the story of each drama classified as **Comedies, Tragedies and Histories,** including also a list of familiar Shakespearean quotations; by Charles and Mary Lamb and Mary Seymour, **760 royal quarto pages and over 175 full page and other illustrations,** printed from large, clear type, on a superior quality of paper, bound in full embossed Russia leather, full gilt edges and stamped in gold from an unique design. The most elaborate and handsome art edition of Shakespeare ever published.

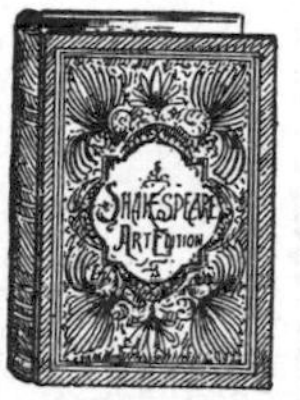

Publisher's price ........................................ **$6.00**
Our price.......................................................... **1.98**
**By mail 30c extra.**

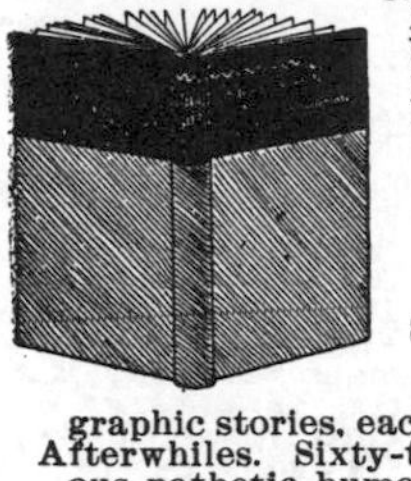

**52423 James Whitcomb Riley's Works.** Tastefully bound in English silk cloth, uniform, 16mo. size.
Neighborly Poems. Thirty-six poems in Hoosier dialect, including "The Old Swimmin' Hole and 'Leven More Poems." By Benjamin F. Johnson. With eight halftone illustrations.
Sketches in Prose. Originally published as "The Boss Girl and other Stories." Twelve graphic stories, each prefaced by a poem.
Afterwhiles. Sixty-two poems and sonnets, serious, pathetic, humorous and dialect, with frontispiece.
Pipes o' Pan. Five sketches and 50 poems. The sketches are separated by four books of 12 poems each, with frontispiece.
Rhymes of Childhood. One hundred and two dialect and serious poems. Not for children only, but of childhood days, with frontispiece.
The Flying Islands of the Night. A weird and grotesque drama in verse.
Green Fields and Running Brooks. One hundred and two poems and sonnets, dialects, humorous and serious.
Old Fashioned Roses. Sixty-one selected poems, published in England.
Armazindy, Hoosier Airs and Others.
Publisher's price ........................................ **$1.25**
Our price, each.................................... **.88**
**By mail 8c each extra.**

**52424 William Shakespeare's Complete Works, Windsor Edition,** dramatic and poetical, with the "Epistle Dedicatorie," and the address prefixed to the first edition of 1623. History of the early drama and the stage in the time of Shakespeare, a full and comprehensive life; by J. Payne Collier, A. M.; Shakespeare's will; critical and historical introductions to each play and glossarial and other notes and references. Edited by George Long Duyckinck. 8 vols. 16mo. With steel illustrations. Handsomely bound in cloth.
Publisher's price ........................................ **$9.00**
Our price ........................................................ **4.40**
**By mail 60c extra.**

**PAY NO MONEY**
**If you are not entirely pleased with our goods.**
**READ OUR LIBERAL**
**... C. O. D. TERMS ...**
**IN FRONT OF BOOK.**

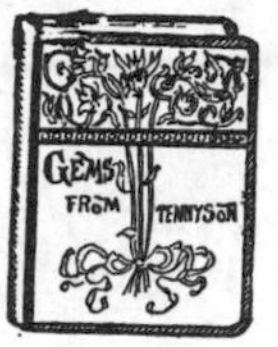

**52425 Bell's Series.** Each volume elegantly illustrated with engravings from original designs, printed on finest plate paper, bound in ivorone with side stamped in ornamental design, gilt edges. Small quarto, Boxed.
Each........................................ **$0.60**
**By mail 8 cents extra, each.**
The Cotter's Saturday Night. By Robert Burns.
The Deserted Village. By Oliver Goldsmith.
From Greenland's Icy Mountains. By Reginald Heber.
The Night Before Christmas. By Clement C. Moore.
Bingen on the Rhine. By Caroline E. Norton.
The Bells. By Edgar Allen Poe.
Lady Clare. By Alfred Tennyson.
Gems from Tennyson. By Alfred Tennyson,
Beauties of Tennyson. By Alfred Tennyson.

**52426 The Yale Series of Poets.** Very attractively and durably bound in English silk finish cloth, printedon extra quality of paper from clear new type, uniform, 12mo. size.
Price each.................................................. **$0.75**
**Postage each 12 cents extra.**

| | |
|---|---|
| Browning, [Robert.] | Lights of Asia. |
| Bryant. | Longfellow. |
| Burns. | Milton. |
| Byron. | Moore. |
| Chaucer. | Odyssey. |
| Coleridge. | Pope. |
| Dante. | Rossetti. |
| Faust. | Shakespeare. |
| Hood. | Shelley, |
| Iliad. | Swinburn, |
| Ingoldsby Legends. | Tennyson. |
| Keats. | Whittier. |

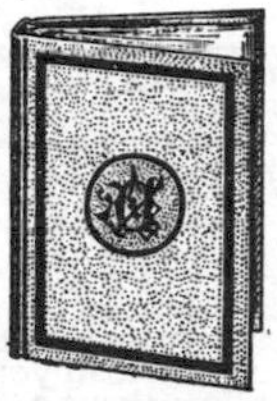

**52428 Art Edition of Tennyson.** The most elaborate, complete, artistic and attractive edition ever published. The illustrations are appropriate to the texts and are drawn by the **foremost artists,** printed from entirely new plates on a superior quality of paper, containing 843 royal octavo pages and over **300 full page and other illustrations;** bound in silk finish cloth, stamped in gold and ink from original designs. Cloth.
Publisher's Price......... **$3.00**
Our Price................ **1.50**
Embossed Russia leather, full gilt edges and stamped in gold on the front and back.
Publisher's Price.................................... **$5.00**
Our Price............................................ **2.30**
**Postage 35c extra.**

**52430 Shakespeare complete in one large volume,** clear type edition, size 6½x9 inches, contains 1227 pages. A magnificent edition, issued in the most convenient form possible. Bound in **Best English Cloth,** embellished with numerous full page illustrations,
Publisher's Price........................................ **$4.00**
Our Price................................................... **1.95**
**Postage, 30c extra.**
Three volumes, [as above,]................. **2.50**

**52432 Bryon's Complete Works.** Reprinted from the original editions, with copious explanatory notes, references, introductions, etc. The work is **conveniently and substantially bound** in one and two volume size 6½ by 9 inches; printed from large clear type on fine paper, with numerous full page illustrations,
One volume bound in English cloth...... **$1.90**
Two " " " " ...... **$2.30**
**Postage, 28c extra.**

## Religious.

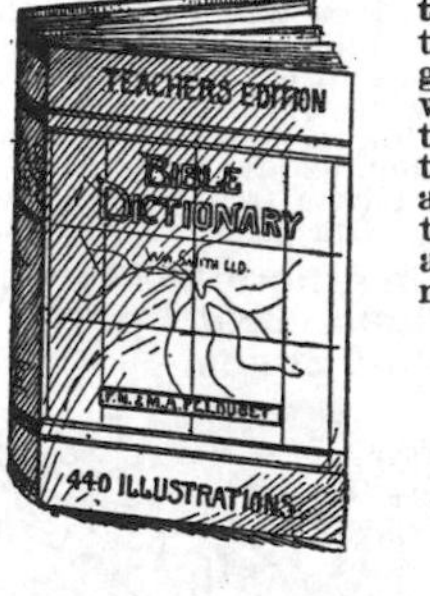

**52436. Smith's Bible Dictionary.** Comprising Antiquities, Biography Geography, Natural History, with numerous illustrations and maps, also contains complete concordance, together with four thousand questions and answers on the old and new testaments. Cloth.
Publishers' price, **$3.00**
Our price........... **1.40**
Sheep, marbled edges, publishers' price........ **5.00**
Our price........... **2.20**
**By mail 25c. extra.**

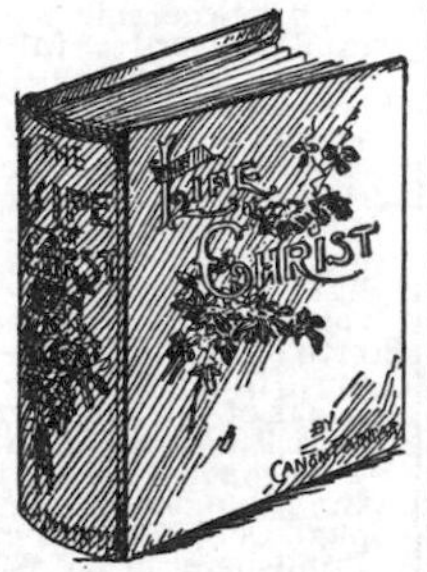

**52438. The Life of Christ.** By Canon Farrar. This Life of Christ meets the wants of the time more fully than any other work. It comprises the birth, infancy and early Life of Jesus, His work, ministry, etc. 600 pages, bound in extra English silk cloth.
Publishers' price..**$3.00**
Our price.......... **1.25**
**By mail 32c. extra.**

**52432 The Pictorial History of the Bible from the Creation of the World to the close of the Apostolic Era.** A full and complete account of the events narrated in the Sacred Scriptures; **History of the Jews** after the dispersion, from the taking of Jerusalem by Titus down to the present time.
The work is printed from plain, new type, on fine calendered paper, made expressly for this work, comprised in one large octavo volume of 1104 pages, splendidly embellished and illustrated with 250 beautiful engravings and maps, by the best artists of England and America. Bound in fine cloth, full gilt back, marbled edges.
Publishers' price............................................ **$2.75**
Our price.................................................... **1.50**
**Postage extra 35c.**

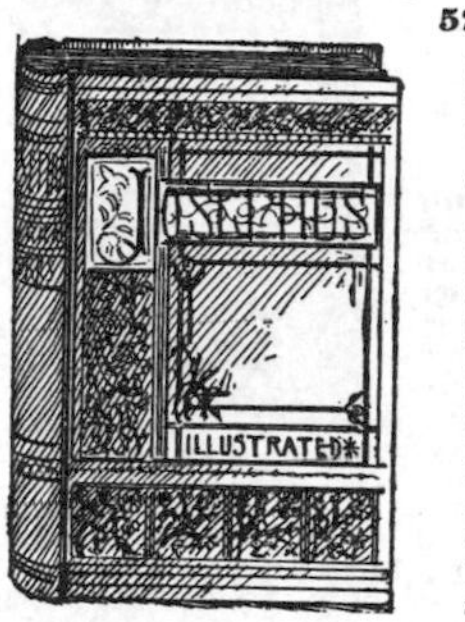

**52444. Flaviu Josephus complete works.** Comprising the History and Antiquities of the Jews with the destruction of Jerusalem by the Romans, and dissertations concerning Jesus Christ, John the Baptist, James the Just, and the sacrifice of Isaac, together with discourse on Hades, or Hell—with the autobiography of Josephus, translated by William Whiston, A. M., to which is added an analytical index to the entire work. Embellished with **16 full page illustrations and maps.** Writers and critics have borne unanimous testimony to the high character of the writings of Josephus. They are a great aid to the study of the history, geography and archæology of scripture. 790 quarto pages. Cloth.
Publishers' price............................................ **$2.25**
Our price.................................................... **1.15**
Sheep, marbled edges, publishers' price.. **3.00**
Our price.................................................... **1.60**
**By mail 35c. extra.**

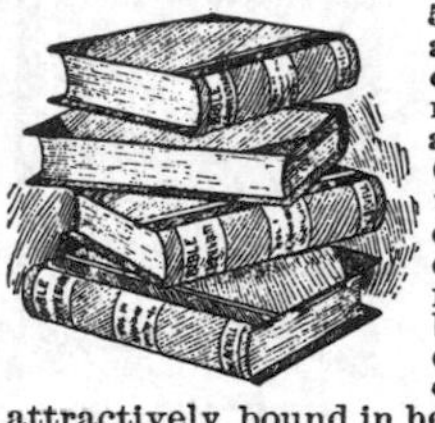

**52446. Jamiesone, Fausset and Brown's Commentary on the Old and New Testament. Critical, Practical and Explanatory.** This Commentary has been **tried, tested and proven,** during one of the most active periods ever known in Biblical research. That it has not been found wanting is evident in the **still unabated demand.** The volumes are attractively bound in heavy cloth, printed on a fine quality paper, from clear type.
Cloth, publishers' price.................. **$ 8.50**
Our price.......................................... **4.80**
Half morocco, publishers' price.......... **11.00**
Our price.......................................... **6.00**
**By mail 75c. extra.**

**52448 The Home Beyond, or Views of Heaven,** by Samuel Fallows. Taken from the works of over **four hundred promiuent thinkers and writers.** Complete treatise on the following: Man, Life, Death, the Dying, Immortality, Resurrection, Heaven, etc. Contains 512 royal pages, 80 full page engravings, 8vo.
Publisher's price............................................ **$2.00**
Our price.................................................... **.85**
**By mail 22c. extra.**

**52450 The Christian's Secret of a Happy Life.** By Hannah Whitall Smith, standard edition, 12mo.
Cloth.............................................................. **60c**
Cloth, gilt edges............................................ **70c**
Half white cloth, boxed.................................. **88c**
**Postage, 12 cents.**

**52452 Side Talk with Girls.** By Ruth Ashmore. 12mo. The dominant note in these confidential talks with girls of all ages is a loving and sympathetic sympathy, with the point of view of the average girl in her attitude toward the world. The talks cover a wide range of subjects—social, literary, religious, domestic manners, courtship, marriage, etc., and will be found as entertaining as they are helpful.
Price.................................................................. **70c**
**Postage, 10 cents.**

**52454 Bridal Etiquette.** A sensible guide to the etiquette and observances of the marriage ceremony. By Mme. de Chatelain. Containing complete instructions for bridal receptions, for bridesmaids, groomsmen, sending cards, etc........................... **10c**
**By mail, 2 cents extra.**

**52456 Before He is Twenty.** Five perplexing phases of the boy question considered. By Robert J. Burdette, Francis Hodgson Burnett, Edward W. Bok, Mrs. Burton Harrison and Mrs. Lyman Abbott. With portraits of the authors; 16mo, cloth, gilt top.................................................. **65c**
**Postage 8 cents.**

**52458 Nineteen Beautiful Years,** Or Sketches of a Girl s Life. By Francis E. Willard. With preface by John G. Whittier. New and revised edition. 12mo. 'A very sweet and tender record of an exceptionally beautiful life."—John G. Whittier.
Price.................................................................. **60c**
**Postage 8 cents.**

**52460 Her Christmas and Her Easter.** Rev. E. A. Rand. 12mo, 187 pages. A story of life in a New England seaport, full of incident and helpful to our young people who are in earnest for that which is good.
Price.................................................................. **60c**
**By mail 10 cents extra.**

**IN ORDERING BOOKS OR ANY KIND OF MERCHANDISE, YOU WILL CONFER A FAVOR ON US AND FACILTATE THE FILLING OF YOUR ORDER BY ALWAYS GIVING NAME OF ARTICLE WANTED, AS WELL AS ARTICLE NUMBER AND PRICE.**

## Self Pronouncing S. S. Teachers' Bible.

**New Large Type Edition.**

Our Sunday School Teachers' Bible is by far the most instructive and exhaustive compendium of every kind of information essential to Biblical study, and will be found an invaluable companion for every minister, teacher and student. The text conforms exactly to that of the Oxford Bible.

**52466**

**Helps to the study of the Bible.** Prepared by the most eminent Biblical scholars; a **Complete Series of New Maps**, illustrating the geography of Palestine and the surrounding countries, embodying the most recent discoveries; a very full concordance, containing over 40,000 references, history and summary of the books of the Bible, historical, chronological and geographical tables, new subject index to the Bible, a dictionary of scripture proper names with their pronunciation and meaning, tables of miracles, parables, etc.

**4,000 Questions and Answers for the aid of Sunday**

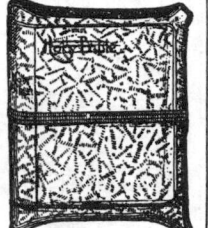

**52462**

**School Teachers and other students of the Bible.** Critical and exhaustive descriptions of the botany, zoology and geology of bible lands, glossary of antiquities, customs, etc.

**64 pages of Engravings** Reproducing in fac-simile authentic documents, monuments, pictures and portraits illustrating the history of the Bible.

**52464**

| | Pub. price | Our price |
|---|---|---|
| **52462** French Seal, limp, round corners, gilt edges | $5.50 | $2.60 |
| **52464** Imperial Seal, tuck edges, known as the "Divinity Circuit," linen lined, round corners, gilt edges | 6.00 | 2.90 |
| **52466** Tampico Morocco. Divinity Circuit, leather lined, round corners, red under gold edges | 7.50 | 3.50 |
| **52468** Persian Seal, Divinity Circuit, leather lined, silk sewed, round corners, red under gold edges | 9.00 | 4.50 |
| **52470** Palestine Levant, Divinity Circuit, leather lined, silk sewed, round corners, red under gold edges | 10.00 | 4.95 |
| **52472** Self-pronouncing Combination Bible, Palestine Levant, Divinity Circuit, leather lined, silk sewed, round corners, red under gold edges | 10.00 | 5.30 |

Postage each extra 28c.

**52476 The Self-Pronouncing S. S. Teachers' Reference Bible.** Conforms exactly to the Oxford Teacher's Edition. Containing all the Celebrated Oxford Teachers' Helps to the study of the Bible, together with a complete concordance with context; over 40,000 references indexed to persons, places and subjects; a complete series of new maps illustrating the geography of Palestine and the surrounding countries from the earliest times, and embodying the most recent discoveries, also exhaustive articles on Bible History, Geography, Natural History. Etymology, Botany, etc., and a **complete history of the Gospels**; all proper names are divided into syllables, and every vowel is marked and the syllable inflected showing the sounds and accents as they are given in a dictionary, thus enabling the reader to properly pronounce every word. Printed from large, clear new type on the finest quality of paper; imperial seal binding, tucked edges, linen lined, round corners, full gilt edges.

Publisher's price, with Denison's index.... $5.50
Our price ........................................ 1.95
Without index ................................. 1.65

"Its compactness, durability and beauty of finish, all commend it to the general use."
By mail 20c extra.

## REFER TO INDEX FOR ANY ARTICLE YOU CAN'T FIND.

---

**42478 Oxford Edition Teachers' Bibles, from Photographic Plates;** minion 8vo., size 5x7¾x½ inches, complete edition with references, maps, concordance, helps, etc.

| | Pub. price. | Our price. |
|---|---|---|
| **52478½** French seal, divinity circuit, round corners gilt edge | $2.25 | $1.10 |
| **52478¾** Same bible, with Silvera patent index cut on the edges | $3.25 | $1.55 |
| **52479** Russia seal, silk sewed, flexible gilt edges, leather lined | 4.00 | 1.40 |
| **52479½** Same bible, with Silvera patent index cut on the edges | 4.75 | 1.75 |

By mail 23c extra.

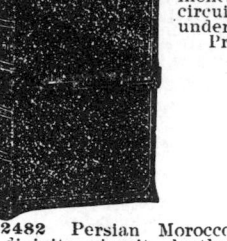

**52480 Oxford New Testaments,** Ruby 32mo., size 4x2¾ inches. French seal, divinity circuit, round corners, red under gold edges.
Price .................... $0.35
By mail 6c extra.

**52482 Persian Morocco,** divinity circuit, leather lined, silk sewed, round corners, red under gold edges. Price ....... $0.90
By mail 14c extra.

**52484** French Morocco, square corners gilt edges.
Price ........... $0.25
By mail 6c extra.

**52486** Maroon cloth, gilt edges, flexible, round corners, gold side title, with brass clasp.
Price ........ (By mail 6c extra.) ........... $0.18

## FAMILY BIBLES.

Bible agent's make immense profits and when you buy from agent's or book dealers, the extra profits come out of your pockets. Bible publishers usually allow agent's 40 to 50% commission on such books. Our prices are less than half retail prices; less than what agents and storekeepers pay. We save you the difference and make it well worth your while to buy or use. These Bibles are published by one of the leading book publishers in the country and have a great reputation for the excellent paper, clear print and splendid binding. It will be better to have such heavy books sent by express or by freight with other goods. 3% discount if full cash accompanies order.

### Family Bible bound in American Morocco Padded Sides, Handsome Design.

**52488—**

gold side and back titles, gilt edges. Containing two phototypes and sixteen full-page Dore engravings; self-pronouncing edition of Smith's Bible Dictionary, illustrated; self-pronouncing dictionary of proper names in the Bible; a complete concordance of the holy scriptures; maps of the holy land and numerous biblical illustrations; Psalms of David in metre; chronological index to the Holy Bible, giving years when remarkable events occurred and passages wherein they are recorded; a History of the Holy Bible; a summary of its contents and many valuable aids and helps to Bible students; marriage certificate, family record, etc. Publishers' price. $6.25; Our price ........ $3.60

### Family Bible Bound in American Morocco Raised, Panel Sides, Gold Centre Stamps, Gold Edges.

**52490** Containing both versions of the pronouncing Old and New Testaments in parallel columns; History of the Bible; marriage certificate; family record; 28 full page illustrations; 1,600 pages; forty scriptural tables; colored maps of Palestine; Ancient and Modern Jerusalem; History of Religious Denominations of the World; Smith's Bible Dictionary. History of the books of the Bible, embellished with forty-six full-page illustrations; a description of the Israelitish Tabernacle in the Wilderness; natural history of the Bible; the Proverbs of Solomon and many full-page Dore engravings. One photograph card. Publishers' price. $10.00; Our price ........ $4.95

---

### Family Bible Bound in American Morocco Paneled, Comb Edges.

**52492** Containing pronouncing parallel Old and New Testaments, marriage certificate, family record, temperance pledge, full page engravings, etc.; printed on fine quality of paper from new electrotype plates made from large modern clear type; 12½ in. long, 10½ in. wide. This is the cheapest parallel self-pronouncing Bible ever sold.

Publishers' price .......................... $4.50
Our price ..................................... 2.15

### Family Bible Bound in American Morocco New Crushed Panel Sides, Gold Back Stamp and side Title, Comb Edges.

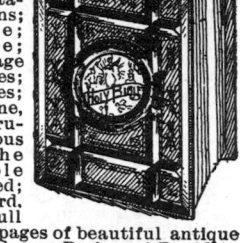

**52494** Containing both versions of the pronouncing Old and New Testament, in parallel columns; history of the bible; marriage certificate; family record; 28 full page illustrations; 1600 pages; forty scriptural tables; colored maps of Palestine, Ancient and Modern Jerusalem; history of religious denominations of the world; Smith's bible dictionary, illustrated; the parables of our Lord, illustrated with ten full page engravings and 32 pages of beautiful antique text; a complete concordance; Psalms of David in metre; full page illuminated plates; temperance pledge and many other valuable aids and helps to bible students.

Publisher's price .......................... $6.00
Our price ..................................... 2.95

### Approved Holy Catholic Bibles.

**50496** Containing Bible Dictionary, History of the Holy Catholic Bible, Life of the Blessed Virgin, Dr. Horstmann's Tabular Matter, Parables of our Lord (plain plates), Great Events in Catholic History and History of the Holy Catholic Church. In all nearly 300 pages of extra explanatory matter, and seventy full page illustrations. American Morocco; calf finish; paneled; full gold sides and back; gold edges.

Retail price .................................. $11.00
Our price ..................................... 5.25
**52498 American Morocco;** calf finish; paneled; gold cross on back; combed edges.
Retail price .................................. $8.00
Our price ..................................... 4.00
**52500 Quarto Bible.** Bound in American morocco; raised panels; full gold sides and edges; emblematic designs; embossed in gold.
Retail price .................................. $13.00
Our price ..................................... 6.50

"The above Bibles contain about 1600 pages, and are printed from large, clear type. The paper is of the finest quality. The bindings are of the most durable and attractive character, from new and elegant designs made expressly for them."

---

**ALL ORDERS WHETHER LARGE OR SMALL RECEIVE OUR MOST CAREFUL ATTENTION. WE ONLY URGE LARGE ORDERS FOR YOUR OWN BENEFIT. THEY CAN BE SHIPPED BY FREIGHT AT MUCH LESS EXPENSE.**

## ALBUMS.

Money doesn't buy better Photograph Albums than those shown below. Agents and dealers are accustomed to charge 100 per cent profit on such goods, and these profits are saved when purchasing from us.

Our stock is entirely free from ancient styles, such as are found in retail stores, and in making your selection from our goods, you have the satisfaction of getting not only better goods, but far better prices than you can get elsewhere.

Our terms are liberal. Either C. O. D. on our regular terms, or a discount of 3 per cent is allowed when cash in full accompanies order.

**52520 Detachable Swivel Easel Album.** Bound in fine motled silk plush, a beautiful pattern; interior imitation mahogany, with openings for 75 pictures; heavily padded front lid; round corners; handsome and appropriate ornaments with heart-shaped German plate mirror in centre.
Retail Price..................$6.50
Our Price.....................3.10

**52522 Marine Album. Oblong Celluloid Front.** Bound in handsome silk plush, celluloid front and appropriate ornaments, with imitation mahogany interior and openings for 75 pictures.

The Beautiful Design lithographed upon the celluloid front of this album is a copy of a famous painting, showing a harbor scene at night, freight upon the wharf, lights gleaming through the windows of the lookouts, boats lying quietly at anchor, and the full moon beaming through the rifts in the flying clouds, lighting up the water with a weird sheen of changable silver, makes the picture delightful to study.
Retail price.....................$6.50
Our price.......................3.25

**52524 Flat Oblong Album,** bound in superfine morocco hinge pattern. The interiors are imitation mahogany with openings for sixty cabinets and eighteen card photographs; nickel plated, patent extension clasp, gilt edges.
Retail Price......................$5.50
Our Price........................2.50

**52526 Quarto size 9x11 inches.** Bound in superfine silk plush, garnet embossed cat-talis and word "Album," elegant interior, gold bevel openings.
Retail price....$3.00
Our price......1.80

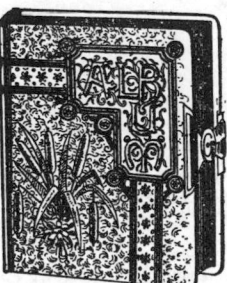

**52528 Crescent Mirror Album.** Bound in mottled silk plush, imitation mahogany interior, handsome ornaments and crescent-shaped

mirror on side. Openings for 75 pictures. At the base of the album on ornamental drawer is built to receive extra photographs.
Retail Price....$6.50
Our Price.....3.50

**52530 Fine Morocco Bound Album.** Embossed in gold, oval centre, fancy corners; handsome interior, gold bevel openings.
Retail price....$5.50
Our price......2.15

**We Sell Cameras for 90c.**

---

### TABLETS.

**Our Line Includes an Assortment of Everything, from the Cheapest to the Best.**

Everything from a 400 page tablet of fair paper for 4 cents, to one of fine cream laid paper. They are a convenient form in which to get your writing paper, and you should include one with every order.

**ORDER BY NUMBER**

**53000 "The Captain" Pencil Tablets.** Handsome design in natural colors; 400 pages, ruled; size 6x9.
Each 4c; per doz.......$0.40
Per 100..................3.50

**53002 "Echo" Pencil Tablet.** Cover lithographed in many bright colors and gold. 300 pages highly finished pencil paper; size 6x9 ruled.
Each 4c; per doz. 43c; per 100..................$4.00

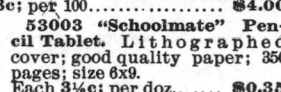

**53003 "Schoolmate" Pencil Tablet.** Lithographed cover; good quality paper; 350 pages; size 6x9.
Each 3½c; per doz. .....$0.35
Per 100.................3.80

**53005 Good Luck Ink Tablet.** Cover lithographed; 160 pages fine paper; blotter attached; size 5x8.

Each 3½c; per doz.........$0.35
Per 100.....................3.80

**53007 "Polar Waltz" Pencil Tablet.** Lithographed cover; 300 pages, fine quality pencil paper; size 6x9.
Each 4c; per doz 40c; per 100. $3.90

**53009 "Saxony Linen" Ink Tablet.** Cover lithographed in gold. Extra quality paper ruled; blotter attached.

| | Size | pages | each | doz. |
|---|---|---|---|---|
| Com'l note... | 5x8 | 110 | $0.06 | $0.65 |
| Packet note | 5½x9 | 96 | .06 | .65 |
| Letter...... | 8 x10 | 07 | .07 | .67 |

**53010 "Daisy" Writing Tablet.** Tinted cardboard cover; fine quality paper, blotter attached. 114 pages; size 5x8.
Each 6c; per doz...........$0.65

**53012 "Old Glory" Writing Tablet.** Designs in natural colors; blotter attacted; fine white wove paper.

| | Size | Pages | Each | Doz. |
|---|---|---|---|---|
| Com'l note... | 5x8 | 100 | $0.07 | $0.67 |
| Packet note | 5½x8 | 96 | .07 | .67 |
| Letter........ | 8x10 | 80 | .06 | .65 |

---

**53013 "Scorcher" Pencil Tablet.** Lithographed cover; 400 pages, white paper; size 6x9; weight, packed, 18 ounces.
Each 6c; per doz.............$0.65
Per 100....................5.00

**53014 "Floral Beauties" Pencil Tablet.** Floral design on cover, handsomely lithographed in colors. 300 pages, fine white paper.
Each 4c; per doz. 40c; per 100 $3.20

**53016 "Strange Lands" Ink Tablet.** Tinted cardboard cover, hansomely lithographed in gold. 130 pages fine quality paper, ruled. Com'l size, 5½x8. Each 8c; per doz $0.75

**53017 "Seal" Ink Tablet.** Fine quality, highly finished cream wove paper; cover lithographed in gold and colors; 90 pages. Sizes, 5½x8 in. Each 6c; per doz.... $0.65

**WE CAN SAVE YOU ENOUGH MONEY ON A POUND OF TEA TO PAY FOR A YEAR'S SUPPLY OF WRITING MATERIAL.**

**53020 Soo,** finest quality cream wedding plate finished paper, ruled, cover lithographed in gold and blue; blotter attached. Commercial note, 200 pages. Each. $0.11
Per doz.....................1.00
Packet note, 150 pages. Each. 0.11
Per doz.....................1.00

**53022 Prince of India.** Beautiful lithographed cover, fine quality, high plate finished cream paper; blotter attached, ruled. Commercial note size 5x8, 140 pages. Each......$0.12
Per doz....................1.30
Packet note 5½x8. pages 120.
Each, 16c; per doz..$1.78
Letter 8x10, 140 pages. Each, 25c; per doz......$2.50

**53024 Knickerbocker,** writing tablet, cover beautifully lithographed in high colors, cream laid paper, blotter attached. Size 5x8, 170 pages. Each......$0.13
Per doz..............1.40
Packet note 5½x8; 200 pages. Each, 18c; per doz..$1.90
Letter 8x10; 150 pages. Each, 27c; per doz..$2.85

**53026 Book-keeping Blanks,** for practice in schools and colleges, excellent quality white paper, blank book finish, colored press board covers, 38 pages to book. Size 8½ x 14 inches, weight each 8 ounces, ruled as follows: Day Books, Record, Journal, Cash Book, D. E. Ledger, S. E. Ledger and Trial Balance. "Always mention kind of rulingwanted." Each..........$0.08
Per doz....................0.70

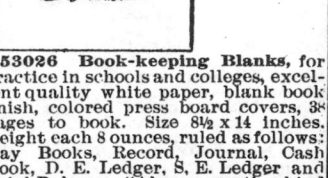

---

**POSTAGE must always be included when goods are to go by mail.**

**Refer to the Index in back of book if you don't see what you want.**

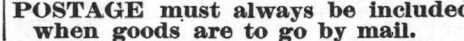

## Ream Paper.

**Ruled and folded. Excellent quality, fine paper for personal and commercial correspondence.**

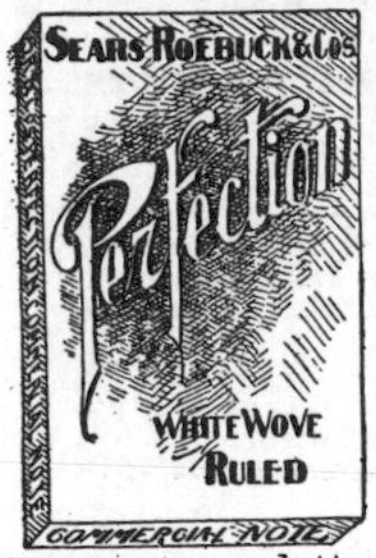


| | ¼ R'm. | Rm. |
|---|---|---|
| **53029** Sears, Roebuck & Co.'s "Perfection" superfine white wove commercial note, size 5x8 in., 4 lbs to ream | 16c | $0.55 |
| **53030** S., R. & Co.'s 5 lb commercial note, superfine white wove, size 5x8 in. | 20c | .75 |
| **53032** S., R. & Co.'s 6 lb commercial note, superfine white wove, size 5x8 in. | 25c | .90 |
| **53034** S., R. & Co.'s "Perfection" white wove congress letter, size 8x10 in., 12 lbs to ream | 40c | 1.50 |
| **53036** S., R. & Co.'s "Perfection" white wove foolscap, size 8x12½ in., 14 lbs to ream | 50c | 1.85 |
| **53038** S., R. & Co.'s "Perfection" superfine white wove legal cap, size 8x12½ in., 14 lbs to ream | 50c | 1.85 |

## Electric Mills.

**Fine quality paper for general correspondence.**

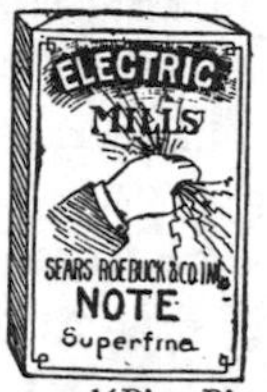


| | ½ R'm. | R'm. |
|---|---|---|
| **53040** Electric commercial note, size 5x8 in., 3 lbs. to ream | 20c | $ .35 |
| | ¼ Rm. | R'm. |
| **53042** Electric commercial note, size 5x8 in., 5 lbs. to ream | 16c | .55 |
| **53044** Electric commercial note, size 5x8 in., 6 lbs. to ream | 22c | .80 |
| | ¼ R'm. | R'm. |
| **53046** Electric congress letter, size 8x10 in., 12 lbs. to ream | 35c | $1.80 |
| **53048** Electric foolscap, size 8x12 in., 14 lbs, to ream | 45c | 1.70 |
| **53050** Electric legal cap. size 8x12 in., 14 lbs. to ream | 45c | 1.70 |

## Envelopes.

**Highest grade, best quality of paper.**

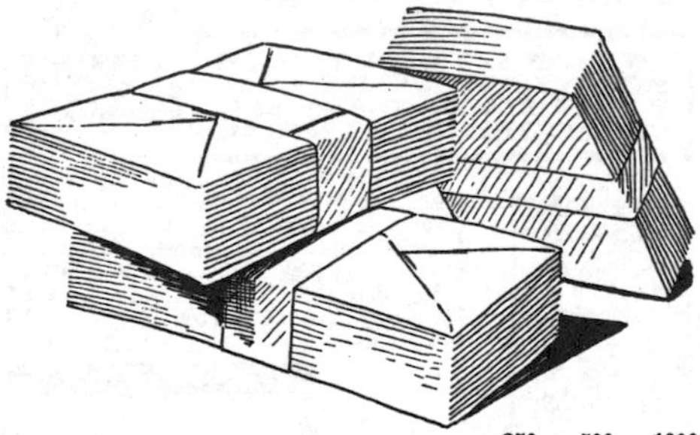

| | 250 | 500 | 1000 |
|---|---|---|---|
| **53055.** Manilla envelopes, No. 5, XXX stock, 3x5½ in., weight ber box of 500 52 ounces | $0.32 | $0.48 | $0.70 |
| **53057.** Manilla envelopes No. 6¼, 4x6½ in., XXX, weight per box of 500 50 ounces | .34 | .50 | .75 |
| **53059.** Manilla envelopes No. 6¾, No. 1 XXX stock, 4x6½ in., weight per box of 500 63 ounces | .35 | .55 | .80 |
| **53061.** Duplex envelopes, white outside blue inside, No. 5, high cut, XX stock, weight per box of 500 65 ounces | .35 | .55 | .95 |
| **53063.** Duplex envelopes, high cut, superior quality, No. 6¼, XX stock, weight per box of 500 67 ounces | .38 | .65 | 1.10 |
| **53065.** Duplex envelopes, best quality. high cut, No. 6¾, XX stock, weight per box of 500 80 ounces | .43 | .75 | 1.18 |
| **53066.** Special white cream wove high cut envelopes, weight per box of 500 78 ounces | .35 | .67 | 1.10 |
| **53067.** Envelopes, white, cream wove, high cut, No. 5, 3⅝x6 in., No. 218X stock, weight per box of 500 83 ounces | .45 | .75 | 1.30 |
| **53070.** Envelopes, white cream wove, commercial high cut, No. 6¾, 218 XX stock, weight per box of 500 95 ounces | .50 | .90 | 1.40 |
| **53072.** No. 152 XX stock, white cream wove envelopes, high cut, extra quality, No. 5, weight per box of 500 5 lbs. | .48 | .74 | 1.28 |
| **53073** No. 152, 6¼ XX cream wove commercial high cut, superior quality, weight per box of 500 96 ounces | .60 | 1.08 | 1.75 |
| **53076.** Envelopes, high cut, cream wove, No. 162, 6¼ XXX, superior quality, weight per box of 500 8½ lbs. | .60 | 1.07 | 1.75 |
| **53078.** Envelopes, cream wove, high cut, No. 162. 6¾ XXX, superior quality, weight per box of 500 8½ lbs. | .61 | 1.28 | 1.90 |
| **53080.** Photograph envelopes, cabinet size, 4⅜x7⅜ in., white | | | 1.35 |
| **53082.** Photo. envelopes, imperial white, size, 5⅝x7½ in. | | | 1.06 |

## Papeteries.

**Fine Writing Paper in Boxes, Envelodes to Match.**

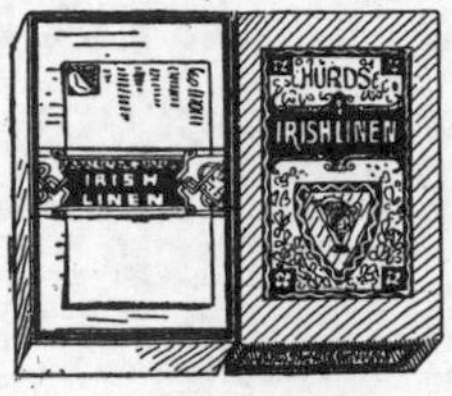


**53090 Hurd's Irish Linen,** cream wove, finest grade paper made. Pure linen, rough surface commercial note. 5 quires or 120 sheets in tinted box. Weight. packed, 21 oz.
Per box ........... **$0.45**

**53091 Square Envelopes to Match.** (125)
Per box .......... **$0.45**

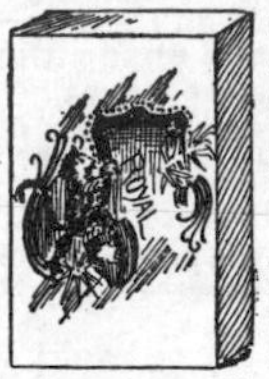

**53093 "Royal."** Superfine, cream wove, ruled octavo note paper, with square envelopes to match. In tinted box. Weight, packed, 12 oz.
Per box, **15c**; per doz. boxes. **$1.50**

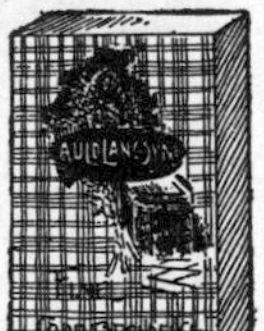


**53095 "Auld Lang Syne."** Fine correspondence, tinted, antique wove, ruled octavo note paper. Square envelopes to match, in tinted box. Weight, packed, 12 oz.
Per box, **17c**; per doz. boxes **$1.35**

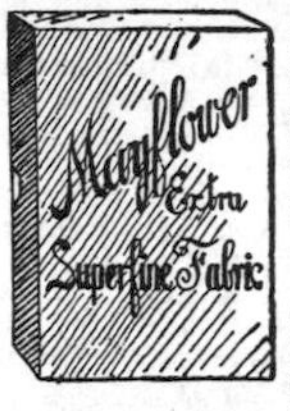


**53097 Mayflower.** Extra superfine fabric for fine correspondence. Ruled octavo notepaper and square envelopes **to match. In** tinted box. Weight packed, **11 oz.**
Per box **13c**; per doz. boxes. **$1.40**

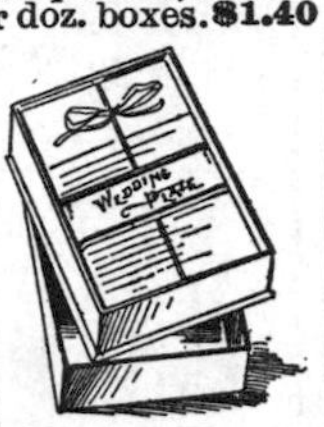


**53099 Wedding Plate.** Cream Wove superfine ruled note paper and square envelopes to match. Suitable for men's or ladies' correspondence. In white box. Wt, 12 oz.
Per box, **15c**; per doz. boxes **$1.70**

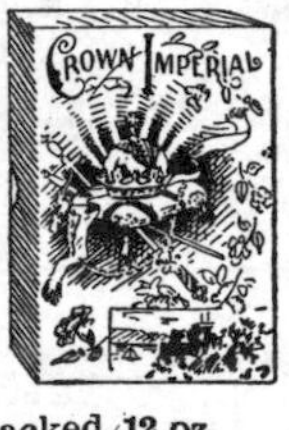


**53100 Crown Imperial.** Extra superfine cream finish, octavo note paper. Square envelopes to match. Weight, packed, 13 oz.
Per box, **20c**; per doz. boxes **$2.00**

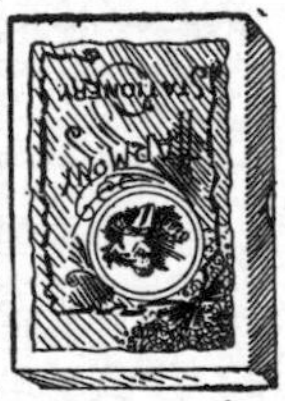

**53102 Harmony Stationery.** Cream wove, ruled octavo note paper; square envelopes in neat box. Weight, packed, 12 oz.
Per box, **16c**; per doz. boxes... **$1.80**

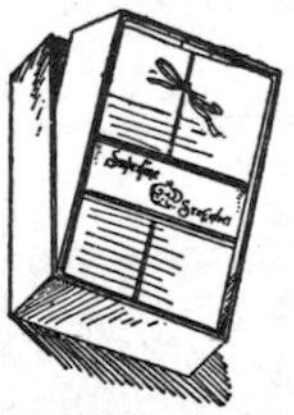

**53104 Superfine Stationery.** Cream wove, smooth finish, ruled octavo, in tinted box.
Per box **10c**; per doz. boxes.. **$1.05**

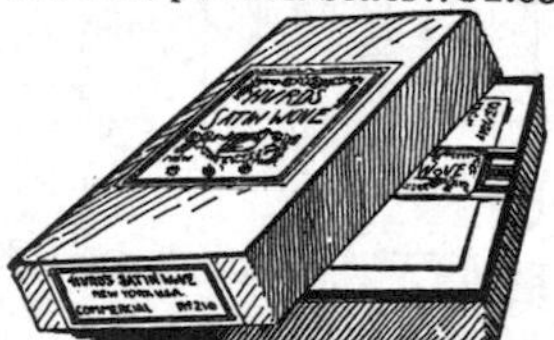


**53106 Hurd's Satin Wove.** Cream finish; perfectly smooth surface for fine correspondence. Commercial note. 5 quires or 120 sheets in tinted box. Weight packed, 27 oz.
Per box .......... **$0.45**

**53108 Square Envelopes to match,** 125 iu box.
Per box .......... **$0.45**

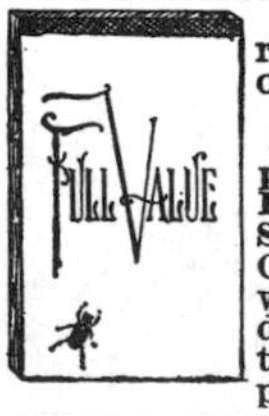


**53110 "Full Value,"** smooth finish, ruled note paper, with square envelopes to match. Weight, packed, 8 oz.
Per box **5½c**; per doz. boxes... **$0.60**

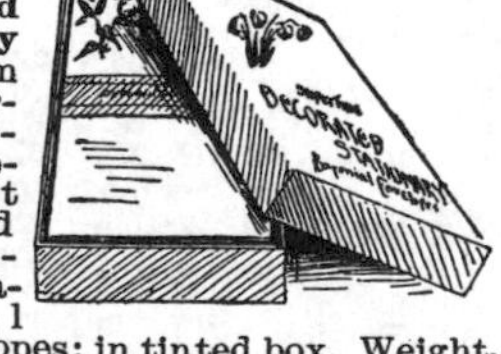


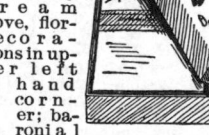

**53112 Superfine Decorated Stationery** Cream wove, flordecorations in upper left hand corner; baronial envelopes; in tinted box. Weight, packed, 10½ oz.
Perbox, **16c**; per doc. boxes **$1.85**

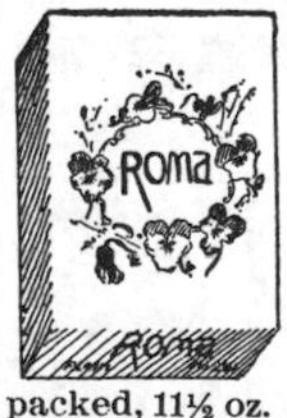


**53113 Roma.** Cream wove ruled octavo note paper, for general correspondence. Square envelopes to match. In tintde box. Weight. packed, 11½ oz.
Per box, **15c**; per doz. boxes **$1.65**

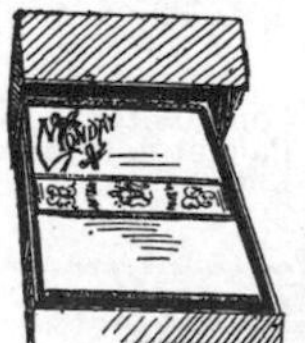

**53115 Society.** Extra cream wove octavo note paper; smooth surface; with days of week printed in upper left hand corner of sheet; square envelopes to match. Weight packed, 10 oz.
Per Box .......... **$0.13**
Per dozen boxes .......... **1.45**

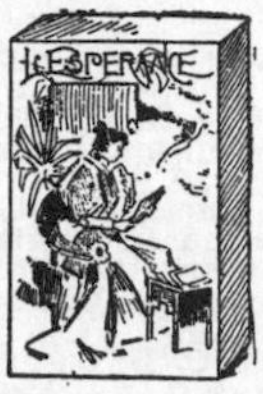


**53117 L'Esperance Papeterie,** for ladies fine correspondence, cream wave note paper in tinted box; envelopes to match; weight packed, 11 oz. Per box ..... **$0.17**
Per dozen boxes .......... **1.80**

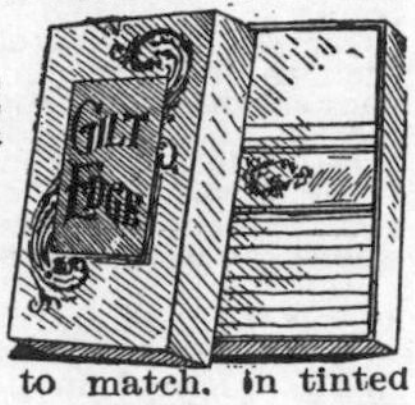


**53118 Gold Edge Papeterie,** super fine wove, tinted ruled octave note paper with fine gold edges, round corners; baronial envelopes to match, in tinted box. Weight packed, 12 oz.
Per box .......... **$0.20**
Per dozen boxes .......... **2.00**

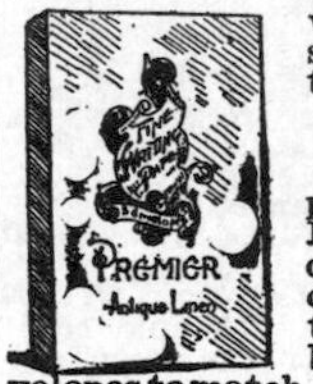


**53119 "Premier,"** fine grade writing paper, antique linen, square envelopes to match, in tinted box, weight packed 11 oz.
Per box .......... **$0.15**
Per dozen boxes .......... **1.70**

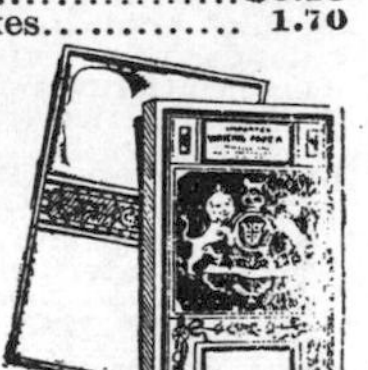

**53120 Imperial Writing Paper,** finest quality, ruled cream laid antique, in tinted box, square envelopes to match, wt., p'k'd, 17 oz.
Per Box .......... **$0.30**
**Per dozen boxes .......... 3.00**

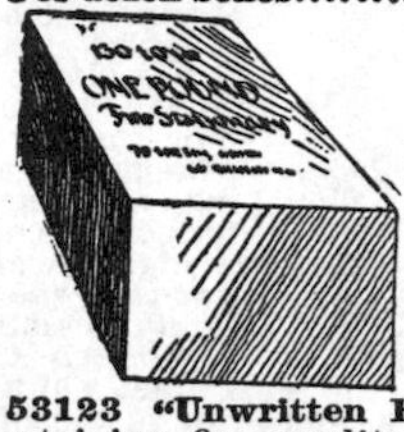


**53121 "One Pound Papeterie,"** containing 60 sheets cream wove, smooth finish fine quality octavo note paper, ruled, baronial envelopes to match, in tinted box; weight packed, 21 oz. Per box ..... **$0.18**
Per dozen boxes .......... **2.00**

**53123 "Unwritten History," Book Shape Box,** containing fine quality cream wove ruled octavo note paper and baronial envelopes to match; weight packed, 15 oz. Per box .......... **$0.14**
Per dozen boxes .......... **1.55**

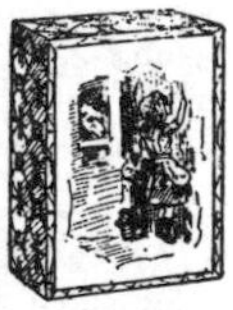

**53125 Juvenile Papeterie,** Paper and envelopes especially for children's correspondence. cream wove, ruled note paper and envelopes to match. Size 3⅜x4⅞ inches in chromo top box; weight packed 5½ oz. Per box... **$0.07**
Per dozen boxes .......... **0.70**

**53127 Mourning Paper,** fine quality, octavo cream wove, ruled baronial envelopes to match; weight per box, 12 ounces. Per box .......... **$0.20**
Per dozen boxes .......... **2.00**

**53129 Mourning Paper,** extra quality, cream wove finish medium border, square envelopes to match, ruled; weight per box, 12 ounces.
Per box, **25c.**; Per dozen boxes .......... **$2.45**

## Papeteries in Fancy Bazes.

**Nothing more appropriate for birthday or wedding present. Useful, ornamental and necessary. Postage, 1 cent per ounce.**

## Misses' Silk Plush Work Box.

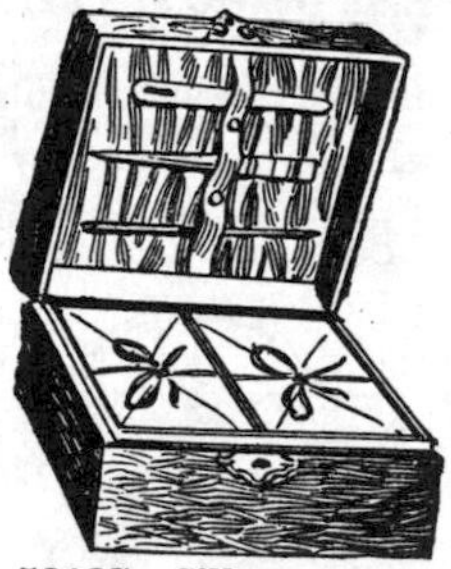

**5135. Misses Silk Plush Work Box,** containing fine quality, cream wove, juvenile note paper and envelopes to match, also bone tape needle, bodkin, crochet hook, size 5x4x 2¾ inches. weight packed 13 ounces.
Price .......... **35c**

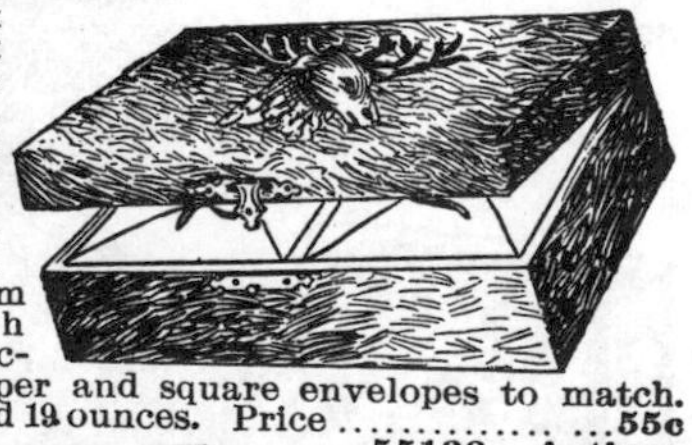

**53137. Silk Plush Work Box,** size 8x5½ x2⅝ inches, with silvered catch, ornamented cover, lined with puffed satin, contains cream wove. smooth finish ruled octavo note paper and square envelopes to match. Weight packed 19 ounces. Price .......... **55c**

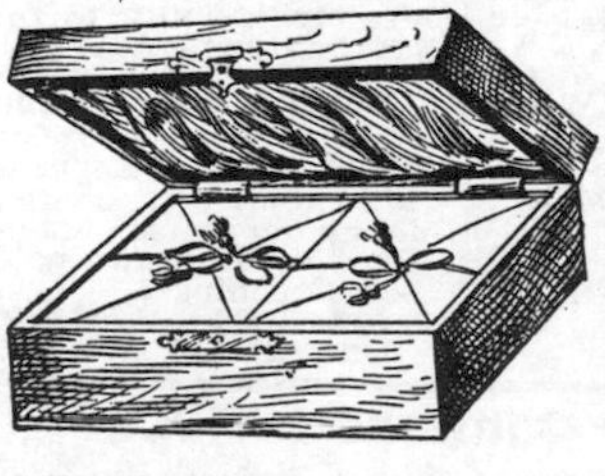

**55138. Antique Oak Box,** handsomely polished with nickled catch and hinges, lined with puffed satin, contains fine quality of ruled octavo note paper and square envelopes to match, Size 8¾ x3¼ ins. Weight packed 20 ounces.
Price .......... **37c**

**WE HAVE HAD GREAT PLEASURE IN SEEING HUNDREDS OF OUR OLD CUSTOMERS IN OUR STORE. IF YOU EVER GET TO CHICAGO, COME AND SEE US.**

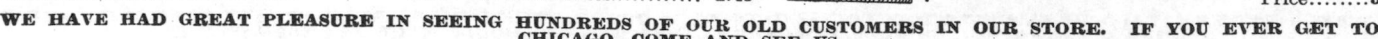

## Handkerchief Box.

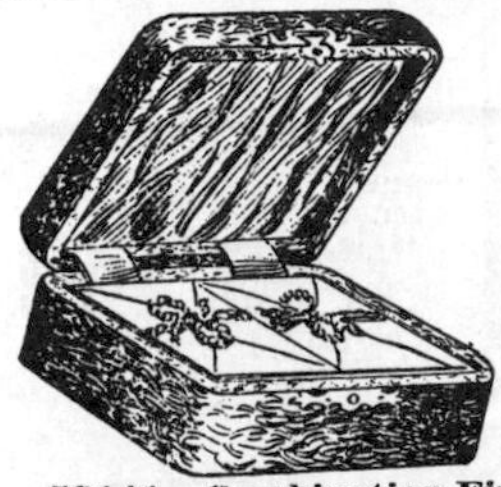

**53140. Handkerchief Box,** silk tiger plush, lined with satin, contains cream wove smooth finish note paper and baronial envelopes to match. Size 7¾x5½x3 inches. Weight packed 23 ounces.

Price ..............80c

**53141. Combination Fine Silk Plush and Celluloid Work Box.** Can be used as a handkerchief case. Extension base, silvered catch, hinges, ball feet, cover lined with satin and fitted with plate glass

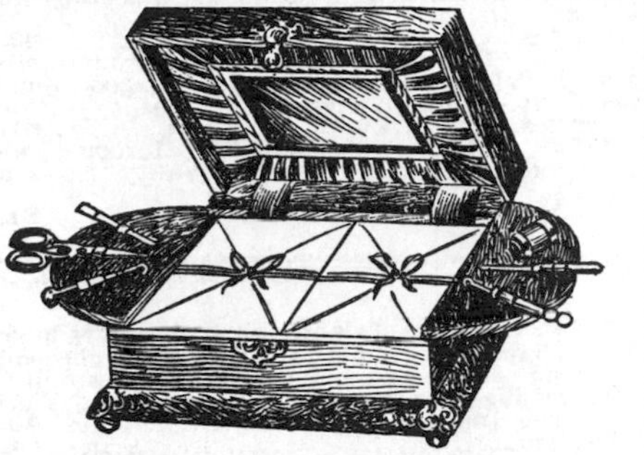

mirror; contains bodkin, crochet hook, scissors, glove hook, tape needle and thimble; also superfine smooth finish cream note paper and square envelopes to match. Weight packed 40 ounces.
Price ..............................................$1.85

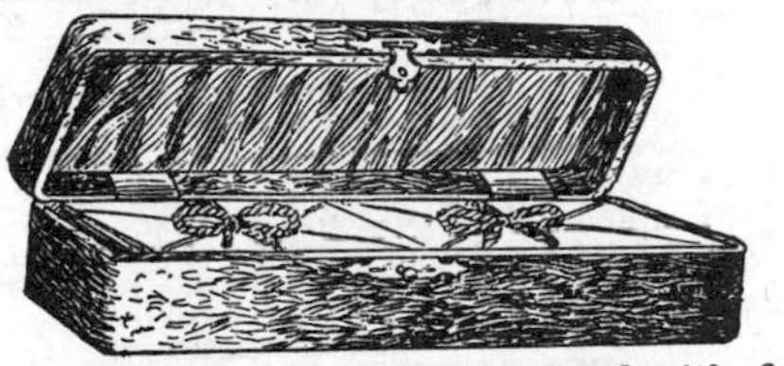

**53142 Silk Plush Glove Box,** lined with fine puffed satin, silvered catch and hinges; contains extra fine cream corresponding cards and envelopes to match. Size, 11¾x4x3 inches. Weight, packed, 24 ounces. Price..........................................$0.80

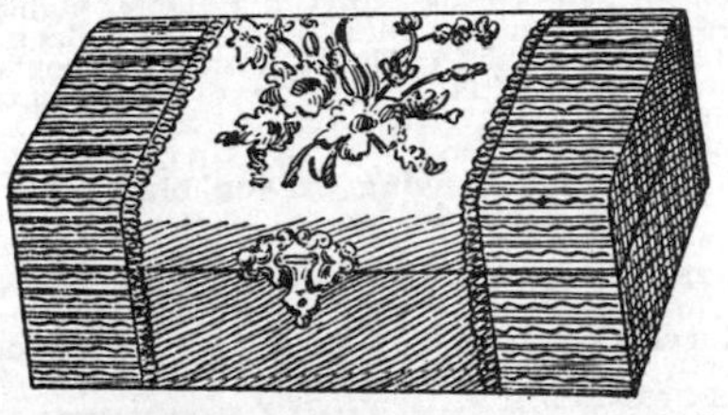

**53143 Ivory Finish Celluloid Combined Jewel and Handerchief Box,** satin lined, silvered catch and hinges; contains fine cream wove, smooth finish, note paper and envelopes to match; lined compartments for jewelry, handkerchiefs, etc. Weight, packed, 40 ounces. Price.............................$1.85

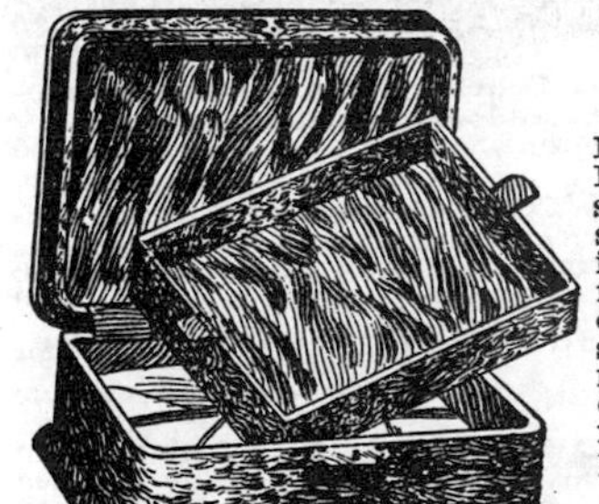

**53145 Red Plush Jewel Box,** satin lined, silvered catch; size, 8¼x6x3¼ inches; contains fine quality cream wove, smooth finish note paper and envelopes to match. Weight, packed, 28 ozs. Price....$0.80

**53147 Silk Plush Work Box,** with celluloid cover, satin lined; contains bodkin, glove hook, crochet hook, scissors and tape needles, finest cream wove ruled octavo note paper and square envelopes to match. Weight, packed, 24 ounces.
Price .... $0.95

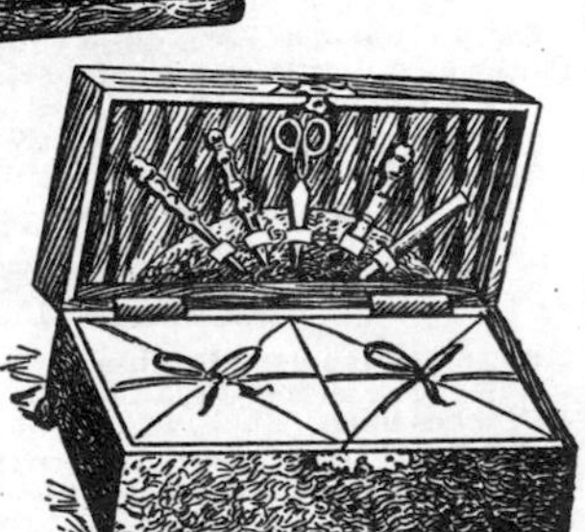

## Inks.

### Diamond Chemical Writing Fluid.

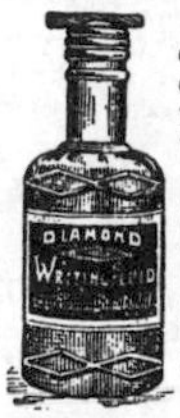


Writes a beautiful blue color which changes to a coal black. This is the ink for book-keeping and fine writing.

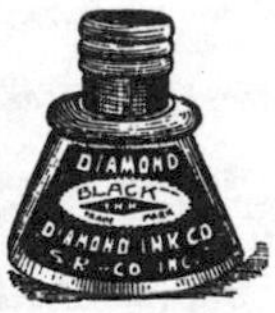


**53150** 4 oz. desk stands, enameled top, 3 dozen in box. Per doz........$0.65
Per bottle ........ 0.06
**53151** One half pint bottles with spouts, 1 doz. in box. Per doz.....$1.65
Per bottle.......... 0.15
**35152** One pint bottles with spouts, 1 dozen in box. Per doz..........$2.55
Per bottle........................................... 0.24
**53153** One quart bottles with spouts, 1 dozen in box. Per doz.......$4.50. Per bottle ...........$0.42

### Diamond Cardinal Red Ink.

**53154** 2 oz. square stands, enameled tops, 1 dozen in box. Per doz....$1.20 Per bottle..............$0.11

### Diamond Magic Black Ink.

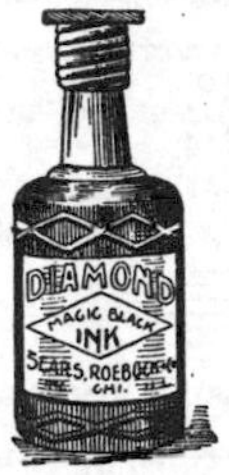


**53155** One-half pint bottles, with spouts, 1 dozen in box. Per doz.$1.50
Per bottle...................... 0.14
**53156** One pint bottles, with spouts, 1 dozen in box. Per doz.$2.40
Per bottle...................... 0.22
**53157** One quart bottles with spouts, 1 dozen in box. Per doz.$4.20
Per bottle...................... 0.42

### Diamond Black Ink.

**53158** 2 oz. paper bottles, 3 dozen in box. Per gro.$2.50 Per doz.$0.28
Per bottle ..................... 0.03

### Diamond Violet Ink.

| | Per gro. | Per doz. | Per bot. |
|---|---|---|---|
| **53159** 1½ oz. round stands, wood tops, 3 doz. in box.......... | $3.65 | $0.35 | $0.04 |

### Diamond Violet Writing and Copying Ink.

| | Per doz. | Per bot. |
|---|---|---|
| **53160** ½ pint bottles, with spouts, 1 doz. in box.............. | $2.10 | $0.19 |
| **53161** 1 pint bottles, with spout, 1 doz. in box.............. | 3.60 | 0.33 |
| **53162** 1 quart bottles, with spouts, 1 doz. in box.............. | 6.00 | 0.55 |

### Diamond Green Ink.

| | Per gro. | Per doz. | Per bot. |
|---|---|---|---|
| **53163** 2 oz. square stands, enameled tops, 3 doz. in box..... | $5.65 | $0.50 | $0.05 |

### Diamond Combined Writing and Coqying Fluid.

| | Per doz. | Per bot. |
|---|---|---|
| **53164** ½ pint bottles, with spouts, 1 doz. in box.............. | $2.40 | $0.22 |

### Ink Powders.

| | Per gro. | Per doz | Per bot. |
|---|---|---|---|
| **53165** Put up in glass vials, each vial contains enough powder to make pint of good ink. Green. Violet, Red and Black. In ordering be sure and give the color.............. | $13.50 | $1.25 | $0.12 |

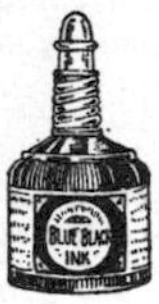


**53166 Sanford's Fountain Filler Blue Black Ink,** for use in stylographic and fountain pens; writes blue and changes to black; 4 oz. flint glass bottle with filler; a cap screws into sleeve on neck of bottle, which holds bulb and filler in place and seals bottle; weight, packed. 15 oz.
Per bottle...............................$0.17

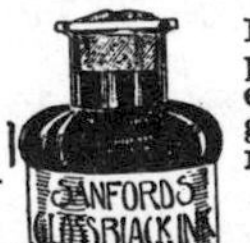


**53167 Sanford's Gloss Black Ink** for ornamental penmanship, card writing, engrossing, etc.: dries jet black with a snooth, glossy surface like varnish: in 1½ oz. round bottle; weight, packed, 10 oz.
Per bottle....................... $0.07
Per dozen bottles.................... .70

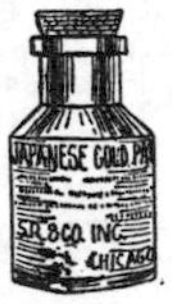


**53168 Japanese Gold Ink,** for corresponding, designing, decorating, etc.; a brilliant gold ink which writes fluently with a common steel pen; in half oz. bottle; weight (packed for mailing). 7 oz.
Per bottle..............................9c

### Indelible Ink.

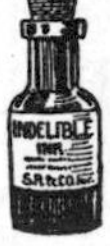


**53169 Payson's Indelible Ink,** for marking linen, silk and cotton with a common pen; no preparation is required. It becomes deep black when dry. Weight, per bottle. 2 oz. Per bottle 19c

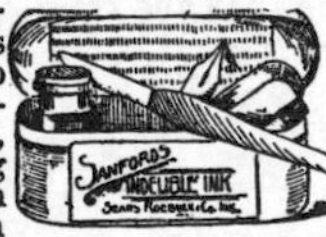


**53170 Sanford's Indelible Ink,** writes dark, changes to deep black and is permanent; put up in practical bottle, with stretcher for holding fabric while marking, and pen and penholder in decorated tin box. Weight, packed, 4 oz....... ...................19c

**IF YOU NEVER BOUGHT OF US** YOU ARE MANY DOLLARS WORSE OFF THAN YOU MIGHT BE.

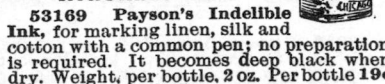

## Mucilage.

### Diamond Liquid Glue.

**Mends Anything Strong as a Rock.**

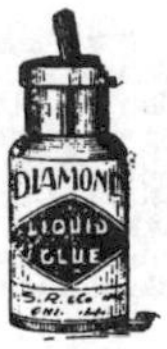


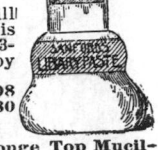

| | Doz. | Each. |
|---|---|---|
| **53171** 1½-oz. bottles Glue, 1 doz. in box.......... | $0.70 | $0.07 |
| **53172** 2-oz. patent tin cans Glue, 1 doz. in box..... | 1.28 | 0.12 |
| **53173** 4-oz. patent tin cans, Glue, 1 doz. in box.... | 2.00 | 0.18 |
| **53174** ½-pt. tin cans Glue, 1 doz. in box........... | 2.40 | 0.22 |
| **53175** Pint tin cans Glue, 1 doz. in box......... | 3.95 | 0.35 |
| **53176** Quart tin cans Glue, 1 doz. in box.......... | $6.75 | $0.54 |
| **53177** ½-gal. tin cans Glue, ½ doz. in box.......... | 10.70 | 0.66 |
| **53178** 1-gal. tin cans Glue, ½ doz. in box..... | 19.15 | 1.70 |

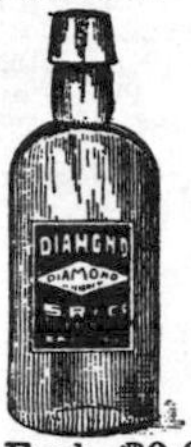


**53180 Diamond Gum Mucilage,** quart bottles, 1 doz. in box.
Each, $0.44; per doz.....................$4.80

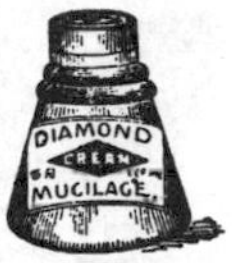


**53181 Diamond Cream Mucilage,** the quickest sticker there is, 3-oz. bottles, 1 doz. in box.
Each.................$0.07
Per doz............... 0.75

**53182 Diamond Magic Invisible Cement,** for mending china, glassware, crockery, ornaments, etc.; small bottles, 1 doz. in box.
Each, $0.08; per doz.....................................$0.80

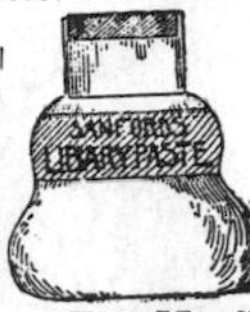


**53183 White Library Paste;** will not discolor materials on which it is used; sticks and dries quickly; in 3-oz. glass bottles; cannot be sent by mail.
Per bottle.............................$0.08
Per dozen bottles..................... 0.80

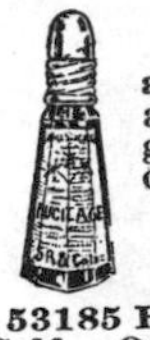

**53184 "Imperial" Sponge Top Mucilage Bottle,** filled with a strong, clear mucilage; has a direct feed and will not clog; good value at the price; weight, packed, 12 ounces.
Per bottle...................................$0.13
Per dozen bottles............................ 1.20

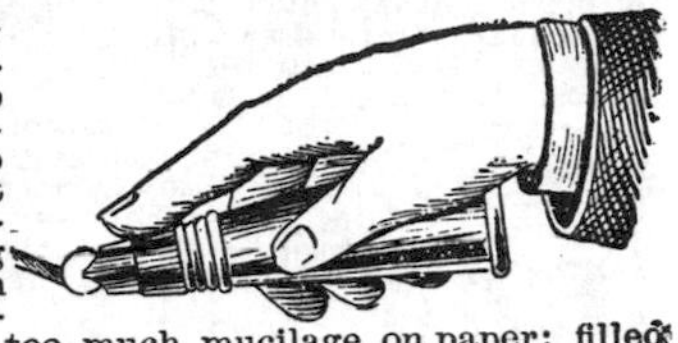

**53185 Handy Self - Operating Mucilage Bottle;** requires no brush; does not get out of order; revolving wheel at mouth of bottle prevents getting too much mucilage on paper; filled with a strong, clear mucilage. Very handy for scrap albums, Weight, packed, 13 ounces.
Each, $0.23; per dozen.......................$2.40

## Inkstands.

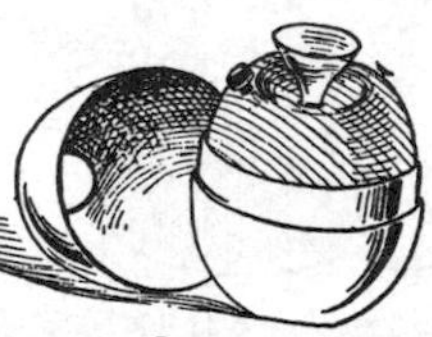

Open.

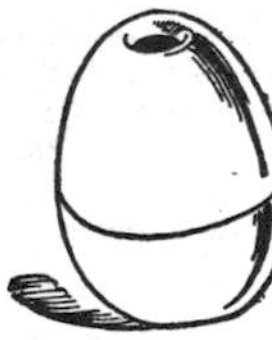

Ready for use.

**53165½. "The Columbus Egg."** Made of pure Aluminum; is indistructable, and will not tarnish; may be turned over and thrown about without spilling contents, and will right itself of its own accord. Inside the aluminum shell is the ink receptacle, which is made of pure India rubber, and will last a lifetime. No ink spots on desk or table cover. No annoyance, always bright and clean as new silver.
Price.......................................$0.50
Postage, 5 cents extra.

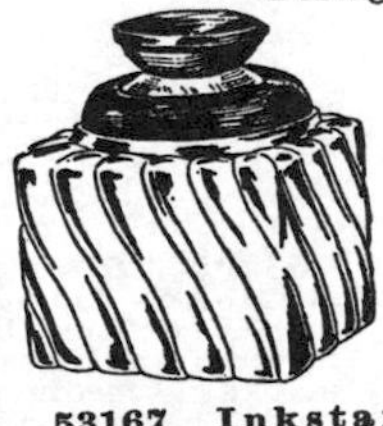

**53166. "Bankers" Inkwell.** Easy acting; will not spill; keeps ink fresh; rubbered funnel and rubber top 2 inches square.
Price......................$0.25

**53167 Inkstand, Single Bottle,** enamel finish. High horse shoe shaped rack, with ornamental head on top. 6½ inches high; base 3¾ by 2½ inches. Each.....35c

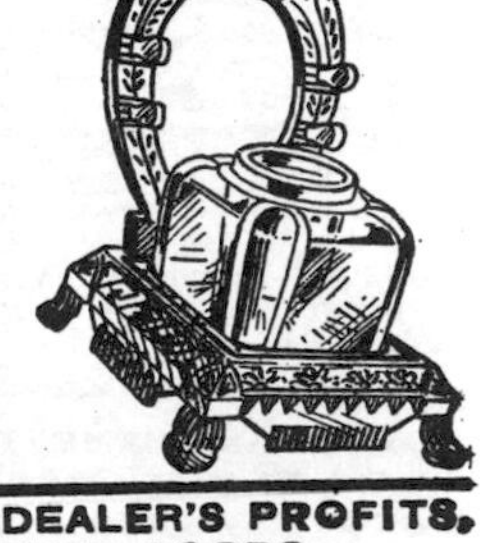



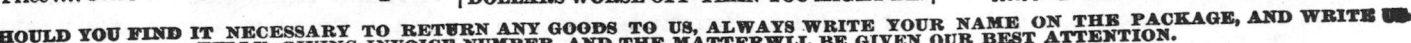

SHOULD YOU FIND IT NECESSARY TO RETURN ANY GOODS TO US, ALWAYS WRITE YOUR NAME ON THE PACKAGE, AND WRITE US FULLY, GIVING INVOICF NUMBER, AND THE MATTERWLL BE GIVEN OUR BEST ATTENTION.

**53168** Ink-stand, enamel finish, iron base with postal card and pen rack, crystal glass ink bottle with cap. 5 inch. high; base. 5¾ by 5¾ inches. Each........45c

**53169** Inkstand, double enamel finish, iron base and pen rack; two heavy flint glass bottles; 4½ inches high; base, 5½x8½ inches. Each........$0.40

**52170** Revolving Inkstand, enameled, iron frame with pen rack, heavy flint glass bottle; 4½ inches high; base, 2½x 4½ inches. Each.............$0.20

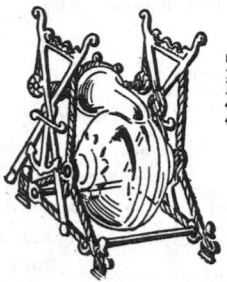

**53171** Inkstand, finished in bronze, iron cover and base; heavy flint glass; bottle 3 inches high; base, 3½x3½ inches. Each.........$0.19

**53172.** **Common Sense Ink Stand** for commercial and general use. No evaporation, no spilling of ink. The most practical and useful ink stand made. Each, 11c; per dozen.......$1.20

**53173.** **Pocket Inkstand for Travelers.** Leather covered, double spring covers, silvered finish; 1¾ inch in diameter; will fit any ordinary vest pocket. Weight, packed, 3 ounces. Each...............$0.30 Per dozen............ 3.00

## Pencils.

**53199.** Faber's "Hexagon Gilt," extra fine rosewood, polish gold stamp, grades 1, 2, 3, 4, 5 and 6. smooth, tough leads. No. 1 soft, No. 6 hard. Per doz....$0.49

**53200.** **Dixon's American Graphite Pencils.** Round, plain cedar, 7 inches long, extra quality. Weight per dozen.. 6 oz. Per doz. $0.03 Per gross..... .30

**53202.** **Dixon's Artisan.** Round polished cedar with inserted rubber eraser. medium lead, "best pencil made for the money." Weight per doz., 4 oz. Per doz....$0.07 Per gross... .75

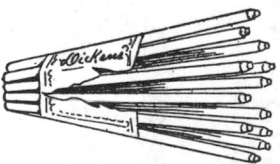

**53204.** Round, black or red polished. with inserted rubber eraser. Per dozen.......$0.08 Per gross...............85

---

**53206. Tip Top.** Maroon finish, gilt stamp, short nickel tip and rubber eraser. No. 2 lead. "Best pencil made for the money." Weight per doz., 4 oz. Per doz.........$0.14 Per gross..................... 1.40

**53208. Dixon's "Rover."** Round maroon finish, gilt stamp.. Ladies' size. No. 2 lead. short nickel tip and rubber eraser. Weight. per doz., 4 oz. Per dozen..........$0.14 Per gross...........$1.40

**53210. Dixon "Cabinet."** Highest grade lead, gold stamp, round satin finish, nickeled tip, rubber eraser, of superior quality. No. 2 and 3 lead. Weight, per doz. 5 oz. Per doz...$0.30 Per gross., 3.00

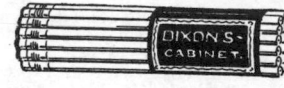

**53212.** Faber's "Commercial" Hexagan No. 2. Nickel tip, rubber inserted. Rosewood, black or natural finish. Best pencil made for school and commercial use. Weight, per dozen, 6 oz. Per dozen.......$0.30 Per gross........3.00

**53214.** Faber's "Commercial." Round, as above. Per dozen.....0.25 Per gross.......$2.80

**53216.** Dixon "Secretary." Round tablet size, Nos. 2 and 3 lead. Nickeled tip with rubber eraser. Weight, per doz., 5 oz. Per doz......30c Per gross....$3.25

**53218. Dixon "Traveler."** Round, maroon finish, gilt stamp. Nos. 2 and 3 lead of high grade; nickeled tip and rubber eraser. Weight, per doz., 4 oz. Per doz...........$0.20 Per gross........$2.00

**53220. Faber's "Editor,"** Round, natural polish, grade 1 and 2, large soft lead, especially valuable to newspaper men. Weight, per doz., 6 oz. Per doz..........$0.35 Per gross...........$3.90

**53221.** Faber's "Black Monarch." Yellow polish, gold stamp, hexogon shape; 6 B grade, very soft thick lead "a very good pencil for drawing." Weight per doz., 7 oz. Per doz...$0.40 Per gross..... 4.15

**53222** Dixon's "Cosmos," round, rosewood polish, circular rubber eraser. The tip on this pencil is a point protector. and the rubber can be turned as it wears. thereby bringing a sharp edge always into service. Weight per doz. 6 oz. Per doz. ...........$0.27 Per gross............. 3.00

**53224** American "Eclectic," round, polished, medium lead, nickel tip with rubber eraser. Weight per doz. 5 oz. Per doz...........$0.18 Per gross........... 1.85

**53226** "Helmet," round, rosewood polish, nickeled tip, rubber inserted with helmet shield. The helmet is so arranged that it covers the rubber tip and keeps it clean. Weight, packed, 6 oz. Per doz......................$0.30 Per gross........... 3.25

**53228** Dixon's "Triangle," extra fine, assorted polished. gold stamp. The triangular shape makes it exceedingly popular, as it fits the fingers, does not tire the hand from continuous use. or roll when laid on slanting desk. Nickeled tip with rubber eraser. Weight, packed, 6 oz. Per doz......$0.40 Per gross........... 4.25

**53230** Faber's "Memo," round. red finish, tablet size. grade 2 and 3, a very desirable pencil for tablet use. Weight, packed, 4 oz. Per doz......................$0.25 Per gross..................... 2.80

---

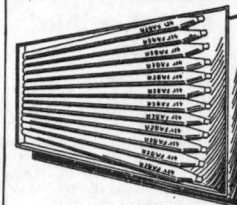

**53232** Faber's "Bank," conic shape, highest grade, No. 2 and 3 lead, highly polished. Weight. packed, 7 oz. Per doz........$0.20 Per gross...... 4.10

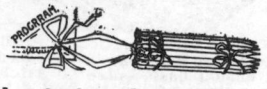

**53234** "Programme" pencils round, enameled in colors with gilt tip and ring, very handy for memorandum books and especially suitable for balls, dances, etc. No. 3 lead. Per dozen.......$0.20 Per gross.......$2.00

**53236** "Imperial" Maroon polish, round, silver stamp, nickel tip with rubber eraser, good quality lead. No. 2 and 3. Weight packed 5 oz. Per dozen.......$0.15 Per gross...........$1.60

**53238** Faber's "Housatonic" Maroon polish, Hexagon silver stamp. good quality, No. 2 and 3 leads. Weight per doz. 5 oz. Per doz.......$0.12 Per gross...........$1.30

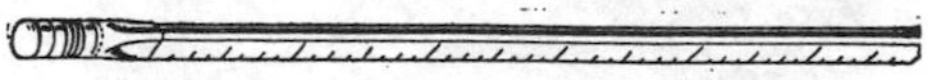

**53240** Faber's Triangular highest grade lead. This shape prevents the fingers from becoming cramped while writing and also the possibility of their rolling from the desk. Highly polished. Weight per dozen, 6 ounces. Per dozen..................$0.38 Per gross..................... 4.40

**53242** Carpenters' Pencils, oval polished cedar, 9 inches long, best quality lead, weight per doz., 7 ounces. Per dozen ....................$0.20 Per gross ..................... 2.00

**53244** Carpenters' Pencils, oval polished cedar, 7 inches long, weight per doz. 5 ounces. Per dozen....................$0.18 Per gross..................... 1.75

**53244** Carpenters' Pencils, plain cedar, 7 inches long, good quality lead, weight per dozen, 5 ounces. Per dozen....................$0.16 Per gross..................... 1.65

**53246** Fine Grade Copying Pencils, highly polished. gold stamp; violet, blue, red, or black leads. Letters written with this grade can be copied the same as copying ink. Weight per dozen, 5 ounces. Per dozen....................$0.30 Per gross ..................... 3.00

**53448** "Sun" Copying Crayon, blue, red, or purple. Each, 4c; per dozen..................$0.35 Per gross..................... 3.25

**53250** Red and Blue Lead Pencils, Hexagon, 9 inches long, red in one end, blue in the other; very useful for checking purposes. Weight per dozen, 6 ounces Each, 3c; per dozen..........................$0.30 Per gross..................... 3.00

**53252** Crayon Pencils, Blue Lead Round Polished Cedar, 7 inches long. Weight per dozen. 5 ounces. Each, 3c, per dozen..........................$0.30 Per gross..................... 3.00

**53254** Crayon Pencils, Red Lead, Round Polished Cedar, 7 inches long. Weight per doz., 4 oz. Each, 3c, per dozen..........................$0.30 Per gross..................... 3.00

**53256** Crayon Pencils, Green Lead, Round Polished Cedar, 7 inches long. Weight per doz., 5 oz. Each 3c, per dozen..........................$0.30 Per gross..................... 3.00

## Acme Indellible Marking Pencils.

**53258** Acme Indelible Marking Pencils, one doz. in box; length, 4 inches; in black, red, blue, or assorted colors; will not rub or wash off. Each 3c, per doz....$0.30

**53260** Excelsior Marking Crayons; clean, strong material; takes the place of marking pot and brush; will not rub off; black or blue; 2 sizes. Large size, each, $0.03; per doz..............$0.30 Small size, each. $0.02; per doz.............$0.20

## Lumber Pencils.

**53262** Dixon's "Regular" Black Lumber Pencil, hexagon shape, ½ inch in diameter, 4¾ inches long. Each, 4c; per dozen..........$0.42 Per gross..................... 4.85

**53264** Dixon's Red Lumber Pencil, hexagon shape, paper covered. Japan finish, ½ inch in diameter, 4¾ inches long. Each, 7c; per doz.......$0.75 Per gross..................... 8.50

---

## Automatic Pencils and Leads.

**53266 Eagle Automatic Pencil (Stop Gauge)**, with copying ink lead, which writes black and copies green; length, 5 inches. Each, 8c; per doz.....**$0.85**

**53268 Copying Ink Leads** for the above pencil; 3 leads in metallic box. Per box, 8c; per doz.....**$0.85**

**53269 Eagle Automatic Pencils**, with violet ink lead, 4¾ inches long. Each, 4c; per doz.....**$0.40**

**53270 Copying Ink Leads** (violet) for the above; 3 leads in box. Each, 4c; per dozen boxes.....**$0.40**

**53271 Automatic Pencils**, with purple copying lead (stop gauge); 5 inches long. Each.....**$0.18**
Per dozen.....**2.00**
**53272 Purple Copying Ink Leads** for above; 3 leads in flat box. Per box.....**$0.15**
Per dozen boxes.....**1.65**

## Propel and Repel Pencils.

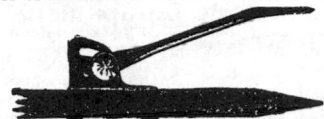

**53274 "Wire Screw" Business Propel and Repel Pencil**; screw pattern, metal case, nickel plated, black lead. Each, 13c; per doz.....**£1.40**

**53275 Cross's Business Pencil.** Cut nail pattern, metal case, 4 inches long, nickel plated, black lead. Each, 8c; per dozen.....**$0.85**

**53278 Black Leads** for above pencils, 6 leads in box, Per box.....**$0.08**

**53279 "Eagle" Combination Pocket Pencil.** compass, pencil point protector, pencil holder, envelope opener and rubber eraser; will draw circle 9 inches in diameter; a handy compass for school use. Each, 8c; per dozen.....**$0.85**

**53279½ "Eagle" Compass and Divider**, reliable in its work and useful for school children, mechanics, artists, draughtsmen and architects; a child can readily and freely use it; nicely nickel plated, regulated by screw and spring adjustment, each in neat box, with nickel box containing 6 extra leads. Weight, packed, 3 ounces. Each, 20c; per dozen.....**$2.10**

**53280 "Eagle" Magic Knife and Reversible Automatic Pencil combined**, nickeled, spiral handles, length, opened, 6½ inches, black lead in pencil. Each.....**$0.12**
Per doz.....**1.25**

**53281 "Eagle" Magic Knife**, with nickeled spiral handle and blade, which moves in or out when pressure is applied to the cap, length, open, 5 inches. Each.....**$0.08**
Per dozen.....**0.85**

**53283 Steel Ink Erasers**, cocoa wood handles, with spear point, length 5 inches. Each.....**$0.25**

**53285 Polished Ebony handles, Steel Ink Eraser and Pencil Sharpener**, length 6 inches.
Each.....**$0.36**

**53288 Steel Brush Ink Eraser**, consists of a number of very fine steel wires in the shape of a brush with bone tip for smoothing paper after erasing. Price.....**$0.18**
Per dozen.....**2.00**

**53289 Cocoa handle Steel Ink Eraser**, double edge curved blade, length, 5½ inches. Each..**$0.25**

**53291 Bone handle Steel Tip Ink Eraser**, with brush, can be used as pencil sharpener and ink eraser, the brush removes particles of dust after erasing. Price.....**$0.45**

---

**53292 Steel Eraser and Letter Opener**, aluminum handles, very useful article. Price.....**$0.75**

**53293 Steel Knife Eraser and Letter Opener**, a very handsome article, and is especially useful around ladies' desk; it serves as a paper folder, cutter and pencil sharpener. Price.....**$2.00**

## Slate Pencils.

**53295 Slate Pencils**, encased in cedar wood, like lead pencils, 7 inches long. Weight per dozen 4½ ounces. Each.....**$0.01**
Per dozen.....**0.09**
**53297 German Slate Pencils**, union pointed in sliding pasteboard box, containing 12 pencils, a very convenient box for scholars. Each.....**$0.03**
Per dozen.....**0.28**
**53300 Best American Soapstone Slate Pencils**, union pointed, 5½ inches long, 100 in box. Weight, packed, 28 oz. Per box of 100.....**$0.10**
Per 1000.....**.80**
**53302 American Soapstone Slate Pencils**, pointed, each wrapped in flag paper, 5½ inches long. Weight, packed, per box, 22 oz.
Per box.....**$0.12**
Per 1000.....**1.05**

## Pencil Holders.

**53304 Sears, Roebuck & Co.'s "Safety" Pocket Pencil and Penholder**, with three compartments, imitation black Russia leather.
Each.....**$0.10**
Per doz.....**1.00**

**53305 Nicol's Leather Pocket Holder**, very convenient for vest pocket, holds three pencils.
Each.....**$0.09**
Per doz.....**.90**

**53306 "Dove" Nickel Pencil Holder**, made to fit any pocket.
Each.....**$0.07**
Per doz.....**.75**

**53307 "Handy" Pencil Holder**, leatherette, plush lined, with metal spring, will hold 4 pencils.
Each.....**$0.08**
Per doz.....**.85**
**53309 "Eureka" Leather Pocket Holder**, with nickel spring, will hold 3 pencils.
Each.....**$0.08**
Per doz.....**.85**

Nor 53307.   No. 53309.

**53310 Specialty Pencil Holder**, a handy device for using up short pencils, black polished handle, 4½ inches long. Each.....**$0.05**
Per doz.....**.50**

**53312 Magic Pencil Holder**, self adjusting, will not work off. Each.....**$0.04**
Per doz.....**.40**

## Pencil Sharpeners.

**53313 Faber's Improved Long Bevel Lead Pencil Sharpener.**
Each.....**$0.05**
Per doz.....**.55**

**53315 "Columbus" Lead Pencil Sharpener.** Aluminum blade. Can be removed and sharpened. Requires no adjusting, always ready for use.
Each.....**$0.18**
**53317 3 Extra Blades** for Columbus pencil sharpener in nickel box.....**$0.15**
**53318 "Ever Ready" Self-Adjusting Pencil Sharpener.** Cannot get out of order.
Each, 10c; per dozen.....**$1.00**

## Colored Crayon Pencils.

**53319 Colored Crayon Pencils**, in size for map drawing. 4 inches long one each light blue, brown, green, yellow, dark blue, red, in chromo box.
Per box, 7c; per dozen boxes.....**$0.75**

---

**53321 Franklin's Colored School Crayons.** For teaching colors, combinations of colors and general color work in kindergarten and primary grades. 7 colors in box.
Per box, 4c; per dozen boxes.....**$0.40**
**53322 Educational Drawing Crayons.** For teaching colors, combination of same and general color work. 12 bright clear colors in box.
Per box, 8c; per dozen boxes.....**$0.85**
**53324 Colored Crayons for General Use.** Assorted round polish wood. Gold stamp, full length. One each of brown, blue, yellow, black, violet, red, green, in slide box.
Each, 25c; per dozen.....**$2.75**
**53326 "Artists'" Crayon Pencils**, in sets. Finest quality crayon for artists and teachers. Full length, polished, round, gold stamp. 7 vivid colors, in slide box.
Per box.....**$0.40**
Per dozen boxes.....**4.00**

## Pen Holders.

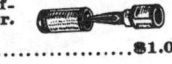

**53329 Straight Handled Pen Holder**, accommodation tips, for school use. Per doz.....**$0.03**
Per gross.....**0.30**

**53330 Swell Pen Holder**, polished cedar handle, with blue steel tip, medium size. Each, 2c; per doz. 15c; per gross.....**$1.40**

**53331 Japanned Swell Pen Holder**, cedar handle, nickel tip, in three colors, black, red or natural; medium. Each, 3c; per doz., 25c; per gross...**$2.40**

**53332 Or-tho-dac-tye-ic**, polished cedar holder, with finger rests, which assist the hand to assume the proper position in writing. The only pen holder recommended by instructors in penmanship. Each, 4c; per doz., 40c; per gross.....**$3.55**

**53334 Oblique Pen Holder**, large size, polished cedar handle. A favorite with expert pen and card writers. Each, 4c; per doz., 40c; per gro..**$4.00**

**53335 The "Bank" Pen Holder**, taper, natural finish, with cork lip. The cork tip is very agreeable and easy to the touch; does not tire the fingers. Each, 6c; per doz.....**$0.65**

**53336 Aluminum Pen Holder**, black taper handle, steel pen in each holder. Each, 8c; per doz.....**$0.85**

**53338 Medium Size Taper Pen Holder**, with hard rubber tip; "guaranteed to last." Each, 8c; per doz.....**$0.90**

**53339 Taper Handle Medium Size Pen Holder**, natural finish, fluted soft rubber tip; very agreeable to the touch. Each, 7c; per doz.....**$0.75**

**53340 Rubber Tip Pen Holder**, long taper handle; a favorite with expert penmen. Each, 8c; per doz.....**$0.85**

**53341. Sears, Roebuck & Co.'s Natural Finished Penholder**, with red rubber sleeve which prevents the ink from staining fingers. Each.....**6c.** Per dozen.....**65c.**

**53343. Pen-Ejecting Holder**, long taper swell polished cedar handle, with a corrugated hard rubber tip. By sliding the rubber tip back it readily ejects the pen without soiling the fingers. Each.....**4c.** Per dozen.....**43c.**

**53345. Hard Rubber Penholder**, long black or mottled. Each.....10c. Per dozen.....**$1.00**

## Penholders—Continued.

53346. **Rubber Pedholder,** reversible, medium size, black or mottled.
Each.................17c. Per dozen........$1.95

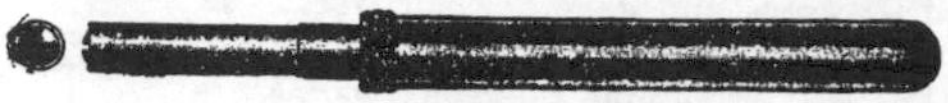

53347. **Rubber Penholder.** pocket reversible, large size; for Nos. 5, 6 or 7 gold pen.
Each...............22c. Per dozen..........$2.40

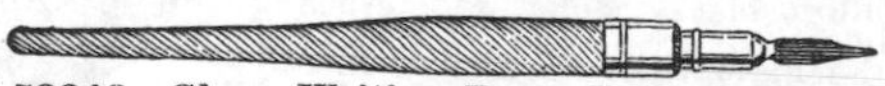

53348. **Glass Writing Pen.** Twisted glass for point in nickeled barrel. Black enameled holder.
Each.................9c. Per dozen.. .........90c.

53349. **Steel Point Stylus,** for writing on manifold paper, nickel mounted, black japanned, taper handle. Each............8c. Per dozen........85c.
53351. **Porcelain Point Stylus,** for writing on manifold paper, nickel mounted, black japanned handle. Each.....................9c.; per doz. $0.90

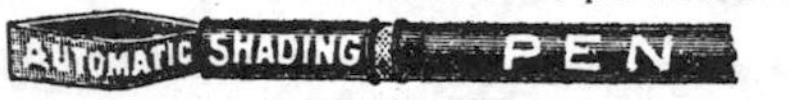


53353. **Automatic Shading Pens,** for engrossing, fancy lettering, card writing, etc.

| Nos. | 0 | 1 | 2 | 3 | 4 | 5 |
|---|---|---|---|---|---|---|
| Width | 1-16 in. | ⅛ in. | 3-16 in. | ¼ in. | ⅜ in. | ½ in. |

Each.......................$0.15 Per dozen.........$1.65
53354. No. 6, ⅝ inch wide. Each..............$0.20
53355. No. 8, ⅞ inch wide. Each............. 0.20

## Ink for Automatic Shading Pens.

53356. **Shading Pen Ink,** prepared especially for use with automatic shading pens; in wide mouth, round, flint glass 1½ oz. bottles. Colors: red, violet, blue, green, black.
Per bottle......$0.10. Per dozen bottles....$1.10
Postage, 11 cents per bottle.

53357. **Spencerian Ruling or Bow Pen,** glass finish wood handle, imitating mottled rubber; nickel plated double blade with flat spring at joint to keep points together; slight pressure on finger-plate causes blades to spread so that filler or spoon-shaped blade may be inserted in ink-stand and enough ink taken and retained when closed upon smaller blade to rule 36 lines six inches long, with one dip in ink. The best pen made for bookkeepers' use and general purposes; weight, packed, 2 ounces.
Each............. $0.20. Per dozen...............$2.00

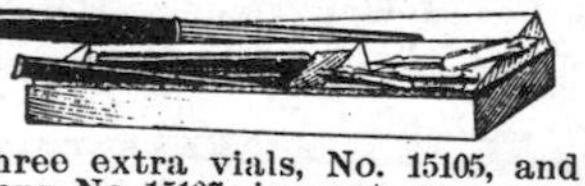

53358. **Eagle Fountain Pen;** assortment contains one fountain pen No. 15103, three extra vials, No. 15105, and one dozen extra pens, No. 15107, in neat compartment box. A complete, popular and useful outfit; weight, packed, 5 oz. Per box........$0.20. Per doz. boxes...$2.00
53359. **Fountain Pen Filler,** for fountain pen use; strait glass with seamless rubber bulb.
Each .. ..................................................4c.

## Initial Seals.

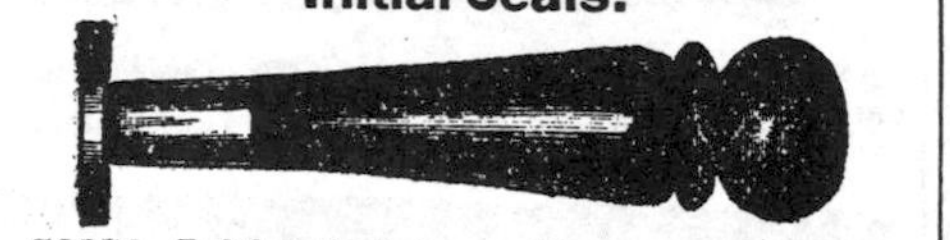

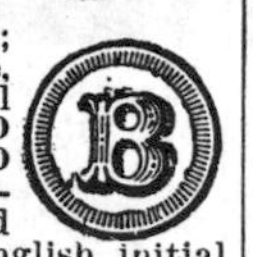

53370 **Initial Seal** for sealing wax; length, 2⅛ inch, black enameled handle, nickel metal die with rustic initial letter. Our special price, each... $0.10
Per doz................................ 1.00
53371 **Initial Seal** for use with sealing wax; length 3 inch, black enameled handle, nickeled metal die with Old English initial letter. Our price, each...........................$0.10
Per doz............................................ 1.00

## Sealing Wax.

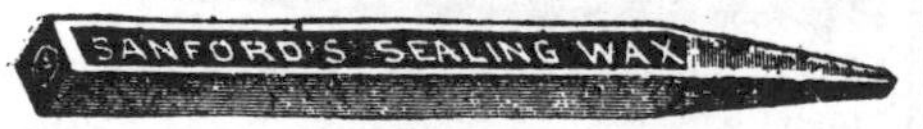


53372 **Sanford's No. 2 Red Express Sealing Wax;** 4 four-ounce sticks to pound or 8 two-ounce sticks to pound. Per 4 oz. stick.............. $0.12
Per 2 oz. stick 6c; per pound (either size)........ .30
53374 **Sanford's Green Express Sealing Wax;** 4 or 8 sticks to the pound box. Per 4 oz. stick.. $0.12
Per 2 oz. stick 6c; per pound (either size)...... .24
53376 **Superfine London Black Letter Sealing Wax.** Per 1 oz. stick 5c; per 2 oz. stick....... $0.10
Per pound (either size)............................. .60
53378 **Perfumed Sealing Wax** for use in fine correspondence; 5 sticks, assorted colors in box; weight, per box. 4 ounces. Per box............$0.22

**OUR LIBERAL DISCOUNT** of Three (3) per cent. for full cash with order should be taken advantage of. Our goods as represented or they may be returned.

## Steel Pens.

The cut shows exact size of pens. We quote a varied line and warrant every one to be the best that can be found. Not less than a dozen of any kind sold.

## Easterbrook Steel Pens.

53380 **"Bank"** (No 14) bronze finish, medium point, an excellent and popular pen for business use. Per doz 7c; per gross....... $0.48

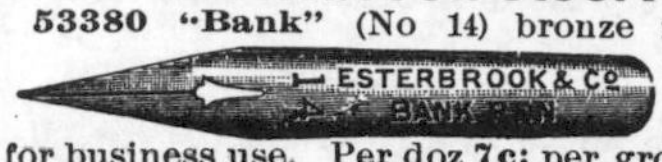


53381 **"Falcon"** (No. 048), bronze finish, medium point. The most popular pen in use for general business purposes.
Per doz 6c; per gross.................................... $0.48

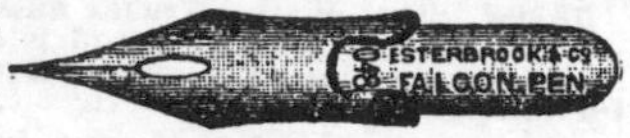


53382 **"Extra Fine Elastic"** (No. 128), gray finish. The favorite pen for college and professional penmen.
Per doz. 6c; per gross...................................... $0.52

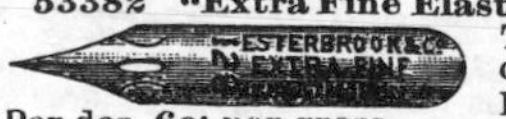

53383 **"Short Nib Engrossing,"** or Stub (No. 161 F) bronze finish, medium fine stub. Very popular.
Per doz 8c; per gross $0.60

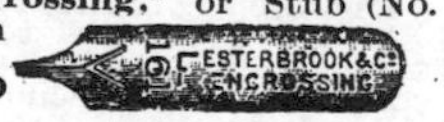


53384 **"Ladies' Falcon"** (No. 182), bronze finish, fine and easy action.
Per doz........... $0.06
Per gross ......... .44

53385 **"Judges' Quill"** (No. 312) gray finish, fine point stub; a large engrossing pen, very popular.
Per doz....... $0.07
Per gross........................................... $0.60

53386 **"School"** (444) bronze finish, medium fine; largely used in the public schools.
Per doz........... $0.06
Per gross......... .40

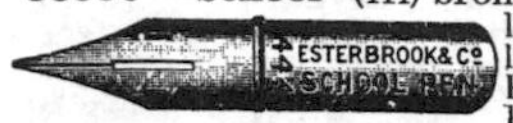


## Spencerian Steel Pens.

53387 **"College"** (No. 1), point fine, elastic, and action perfect, largely used by the best penmen in the country.
Per gross......... $0.80
Per ¼ gross............................................ $0.25

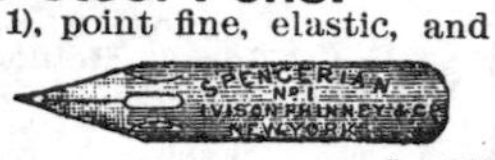

53388 **"School"** (No. 5), point fine, medium inflexibility.
Per gross........ $0.80
Per ¼ gross....... .25

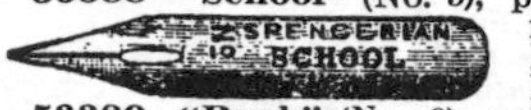

53389 **"Bank"** (No. 9), point long and flexible; great favorite with accountants, tellers, etc. Per gross $0.80
Per ¼ gross............................................. $0.25

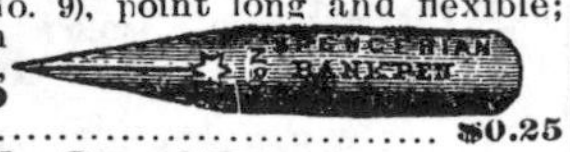

## Gillott's Steel Pens.

53390 **"Principality Pen"** (No. 1) extra fine point, and will make heavy down stroke, excellent in flourishing and ornamental pen work. Per doz 10c; per gross.......................... $0.90

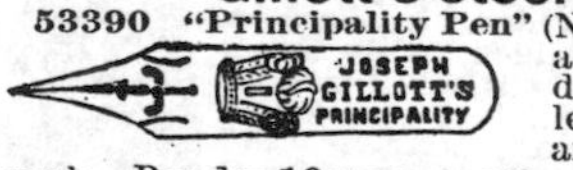


53391 **"Ladies' Pen"** (No. 170), extra fine point, designed especially for ladies' use. Per doz. 8c; per gross.................. $0.65

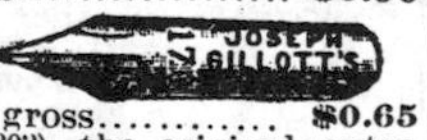

53392 **"Victoria"** (No. 303), the original extra fine pen and most widely used.
Per doz........... $0.10
Per gross........ .90

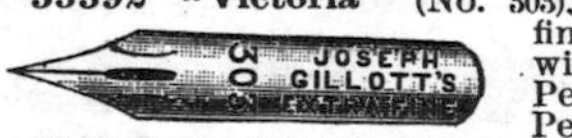

53393 **"Public Pen"** (No. 404), with bead, fine point. Very popular for fine writing and school use,
Per doz....... $0.06
Per gross........................................... $0.49

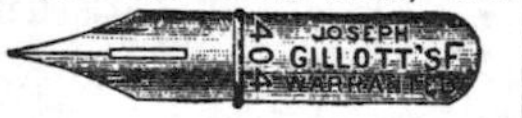

53394 **"Magnum Quill"** (No. 601 E, F.), extra fine point, for fine and ordinary writing, very popular for general use.
Per gross.............................................. $0.83
Per ¼ gross............................................. .25

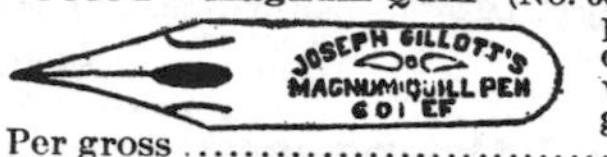


53395 **"Double Elastic"** (No. 604 E, F.), extra fine point. The original double elastic pen, a favorite with professors of penmanship and teachers in business colleges.
Per gross 60c; Per ¼ gross.............................. $0.20

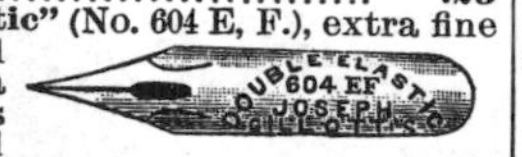

53397 **"Double Line Ruling"** (No. 344 C), gray finish. This pen makes two lines with one stroke and is very useful for the work of architects, engineers, draughtsmen and bookkeepers; one dozen pens on card with holder to suit Weight packed 3 oz. Per card.................. $0.22

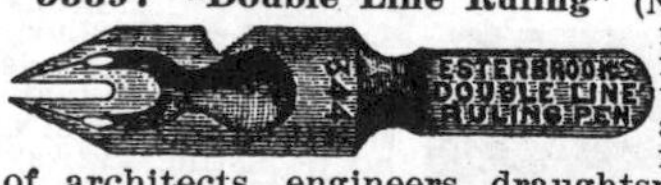


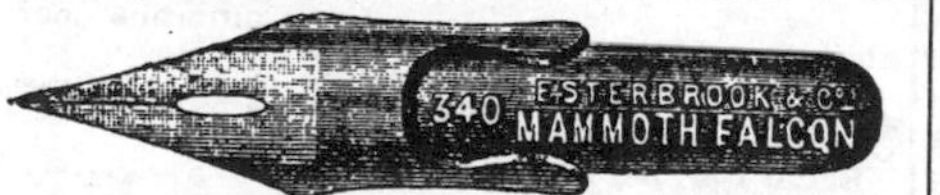


53398 **"Mammoth Falcon"** (No. 340 B). bronze finish, easy action. For general correspondence and for bank, shipping and entry clerks' use; 12 pens and a holder to suit on card. Per card........ $0.24
Postage 3 cents.

**A Superior Line of Fountain Pens in Jewelry Department. See page 433.**

**Easterbrook's Celebrated Steel Pens** in metalic boxes, containing one dozen pens each.
Postage 1 cent per box; 8 cents per doz.

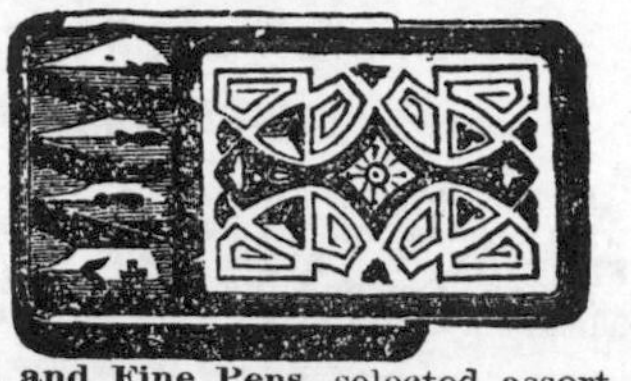

53402 **School and Fine Pens,** selected assortment of styles. Per box 6c; per doz boxes.... $0.60
53403 **Superior Business Pens,** selected assortment of styles. Per box 6c; per doz boxes.... $0.60
53404 **Assorted Stub or Engrossing Pens,** specially selected for use by lawyers and professional men. Per box 6c; Per doz. boxes............ $0.60

## Pen Racks.

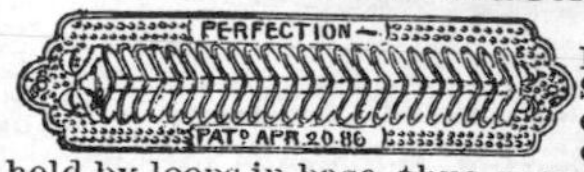


53406 **Keep's Patent Perfection Spiral Pen Rack,** each coil permanently but loosely held by loops in base, thus preventing springs from being weakened or displaced by use. Size, 6¼x1¼x1½ inches. Weight, packed, 3 oz. Each........ $0.08
Per dozen ................................................ 0.80

## Wooden Rulers.

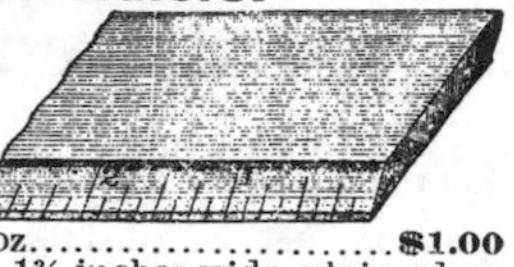

53407 **Maple Ruler,** with inlaid brass edges. Paper cutter. 12 inches long. Each... $0.08
Per doz...... 0.85
53409 15 inches long. Each, 10c; per doz.......................... $1.00
53410 **Maple Ruler,** 1⅜ inches wide, plain edge; suitable for school and office use. 12 inches long. Each, 5c; per doz.................................... $0.60
53411 15 inches long. Each, 7c; per doz... $0.75

## Scholar's Companions.

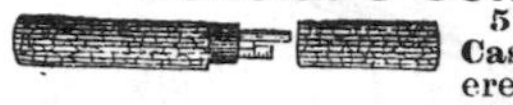

53413 **Turned Wood Case,** fancy paper covered, furnished with slate and lead pencil, pen holder and ruler. Each, 3c; per doz.............$0.30
53415 **Unique Scholar's Companion,** varnished maple box, with sliding cover, 9-inch ruler attachment with scale, fitted with lead pencil, slate pencil and pen holder. Size, 9x2x1⅛ inches. Each, 8c; per doz............................. $0.85

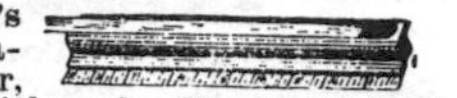

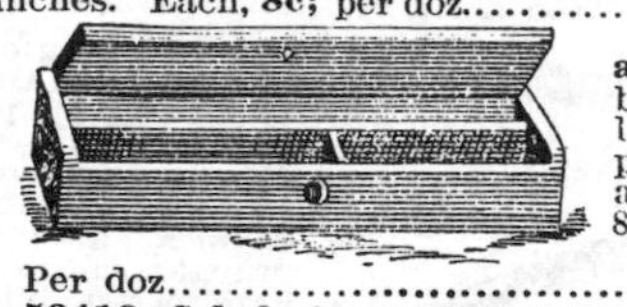

53417 **Scholar's Companion,** bass wood, shellac finish, 3 compartments each and key. Size, 8¼x2½ inches.
Each...... $0.07
Per doz.................................................... 0.75

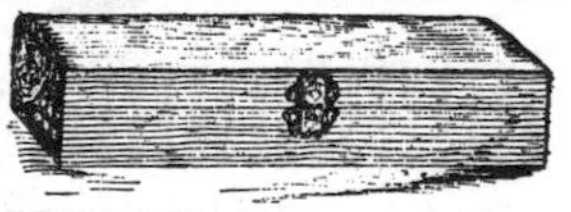

53419 **Scholar's Companion,** varnished bass wood, 3 compartments, fancy spring catch. Size, 7½x2¼.
Each....... $0.06
Per doz.................................................... $0.65

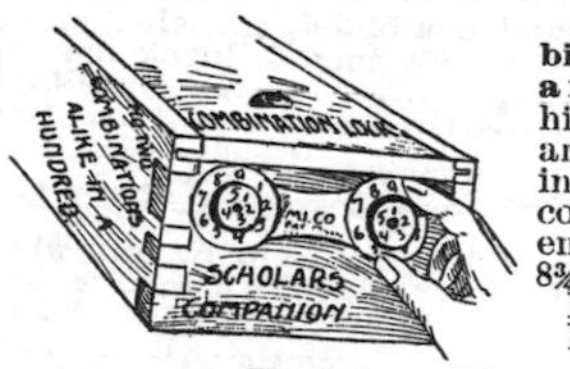


53421 **Magic Combination Lock, Scholar's Companion,** highly finished ash and cherry wood sliding cover, fastened by combination lock on end of cover. Size, 8¾x2½ inches.
Each ............ $0.08
Per doz....... 0.70

## Rubber Erasers.

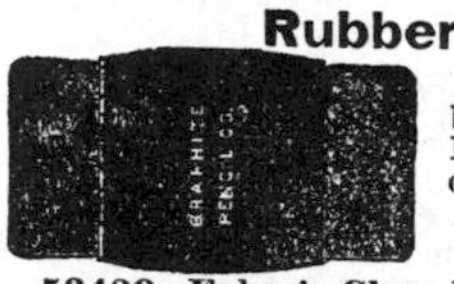

53425. **Faber's Combined Ink and Pencil Eraser,** wood center, best quality erasive rubber.
Each.............. $0.07
Per dozen............. .75
53429 **Faber's Clasp Eraser.** Especially handy for typewriters, the thin strip of erasive rubber, within the metal clasp, presents a sharp, stiff edge to the paper. To adjust, loosen by means of sliding band. Each........................................... 9c
Per doz........................................... 95c
53430 **Faber's Comet Eraser.** Same composition as the circular eraser, with the addition of a brush that will effectually clean the paper after erasure.
Each........................................................ 9c
Per dozen.................................................. 95c

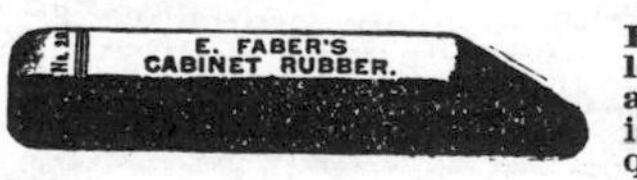


53431 **Cabinet Bevel Point Oblong Rubber Eraser.** Velvet finish, superior quality, small size. Weight, per dozen, 4 oz. Each........................................ 1c
Per dozen.................................................. 9c
Per pound, 100 pieces..................................... 80c
53432 **Cabinet Eraser,** medium size. Weight, per dozen, 6 oz. Each...,................................ 3c
Per dozen.................................................. 30c
Per pound, 40 pieces..................................... 80c
53433 **Cabinet Eraser,** large size. Weight, per dozen, 12 oz. Each........................................ 5c
Per dozen.................................................. 50c
Per pound, 20 pieces..................................... 80c

**WE GIVE THE VARIOUS WEIGHTS OF OUR STATIONERY, AND WITH POSTAGE AT 1 CENT PER OUNCE, YOU CAN CALCULATE THE AMOUNT OF STAMPS TO ENCLOSE TO PREPAY WHEN SENT BY MAIL.**

## Rubber Erasers Continued.

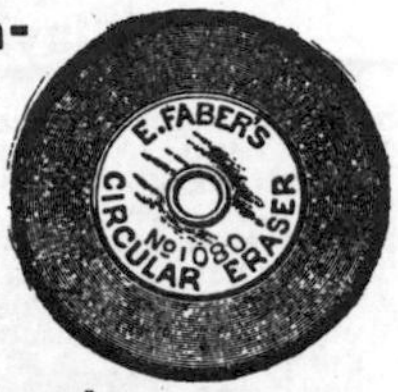


**53434, Faber's Circular Eraser,** for Typewriter ink or pencil. The circular shape is very convenient, giving a sharp continuous edge for use until worn out.
Each....................4c.
Per dozen...............40c.

## Rubber Bands.

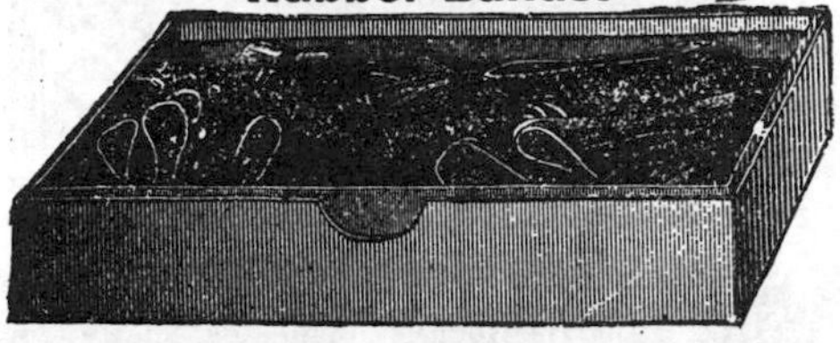

**53435. Faber's Assortment of Rubber Bands,** for office or home use. Weight packed 6 ounces.
Per box....................30c

## Thread Bands.

**53436. Thread Bands.** One gross in a box. We do dot sell less than a box.

| Nos. | 8 | 10 | 12 | 14 |
|---|---|---|---|---|
| Length | ⅜ in. | 1¼ in. | 1⅝ in. | 2 in. |
| Per box | 8c. | 10c. | 12c. | 14c. |
| Per dozen boxes | 85c. | $1.00 | $1.20 | $1,40 |
| Wgt per doz boxes | 11 oz. | 11 oz. | 14 oz. | 14 oz. |

**53437. Rubber Bands,** one-quarter inch wide.

| Number. | Length. | Per doz. | Per gross. |
|---|---|---|---|
| 000¼ | 3 in. | $0.07 | $0.70 |
| 0000¼ | 3½ in. | .09 | .80 |

**53439. Rubber Bands,** one-half inch wide.

| Number. | Length. | Per doz. | Per gross. |
|---|---|---|---|
| 00½ | 2½ in. | $0.11 | $1.05 |
| 000½ | 3 in. | .12 | 1.15 |
| 0000½ | 3½ in. | .14 | 1.25 |

**53441. Rubber Bands,** three-quarter inch wide.

| Number. | Length. | Per doz. | Per gross. |
|---|---|---|---|
| 000¾ | 3 in. | $0.15 | $1.50 |
| 0000¾ | 3½ in. | .18 | 1.75 |

We do not sell less than one dozen of a size.

**53443. Heavy Rubber Bands,** five-eighth inch wide.

| Number. | Length. | Each. | Per doz. |
|---|---|---|---|
| 105 | 5 in. | $0.05 | $0.45 |
| 107 | 7 in. | .06 | .60 |
| 109 | 9 in. | .07 | .75 |

## Dean's Universal Bill File.

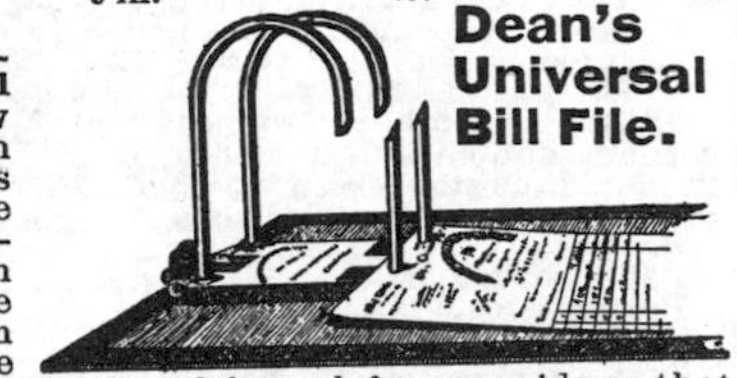

**55461 Dean's Universal Bill File**—A new double arch file. It does not require a perforator. When the bills are placed on the needle pointed post the tips of the arch form a guide, so that the bills are punctured the same distance from the top. The file is securely fastened with copper rivets to book binders, heavy tar board, covered with marbled paper, bound with heavy cloth. This is the strongest and most efficient file made.
Note size—7 x 12—Each....................$0.53
Letter size—9 x 14½—Each....................60
Cap size—9 x 17—Each....................70

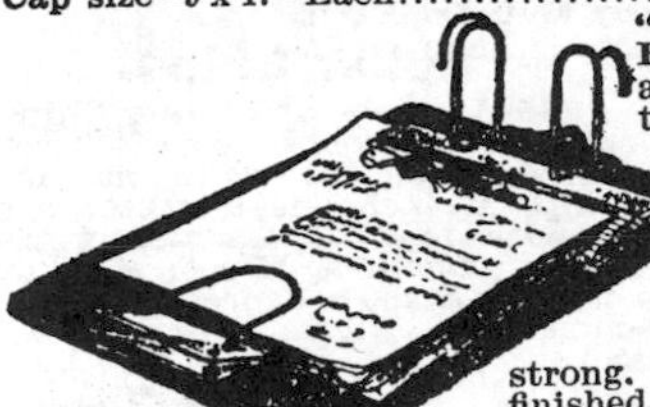

**"Globe" Union File,** a double arch file in which the arches swing outward, opening and closing together—either arch operating both; strong, durable, well-finished, and the best double arch file made. Quotations are for the file and board only; indexes and perforators not included.

| | | Each. |
|---|---|---|
| 54463. | Note, 7x12, file and board only...... | $0.66 |
| 53464. | Letter, 9x14¼, file and board only.... | .73 |
| 53465. | Cap, 9x17, file and board only........ | .82 |
| 53456. | Perforator for Globe Union File, each | .24 |
| 53457. | Alphabetical Index for Globe Union File, each .... .05 Per dozen .......... | .50 |

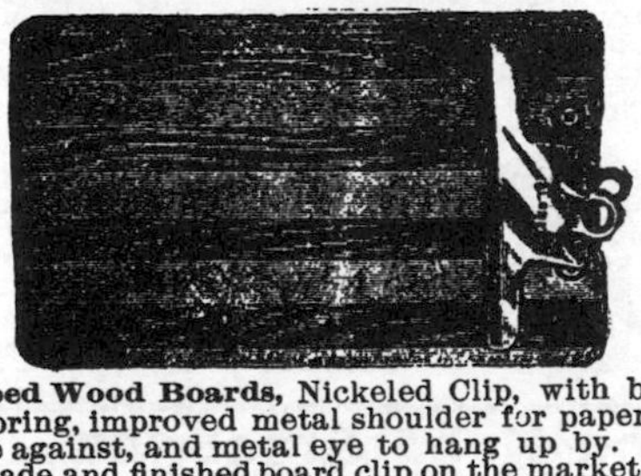

**Striped Wood Boards,** Nickeled Clip, with brass wire spring, improved metal shoulder for papers to square against, and metal eye to hang up by. The best made and finished board clip on the market.

| | | Each. | | Per doz. |
|---|---|---|---|---|
| 53468. | Note size. | $0.27 | Per doz.. | $3.05 |
| 53569. | Letter size. | .30 | Per doz.. | 3.35 |
| 53470. | Cap size, | .33 | Per doz.. | 3.65 |

## Paper Clips.

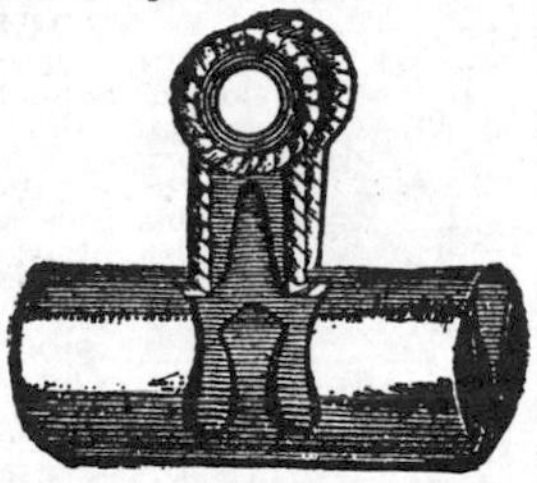

**"Ever Handy" Paper Clips,** for holding together notes, receipts, invoices, letters and memoranda of every description, made from best spring steel and brass double length.

**53473. "Ever-Handy" Paper Clip,** small size, with jaws 1¼ inches wide,
Each ..........$0.04
Per dozen...... 0.40

**53474. "Ever-Handy" Paper Clip,** medium size, with jaws 2½ inches wide. Each..$0.06 Per doz..........$0.60

## "Spencerian" Ever-Handy Paper Clip.

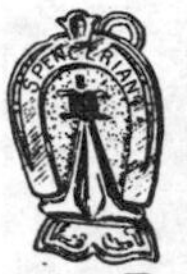


**53475. "Spencerian" Paper Clip,** Horseshoe shape; brass, size 1¾ x 2¾ inches.
Each ....................$0.04
Per dozen....................0.43

## Paper Files.

**53476 Hanging Paper File,** tinned wire back and hook with protected point; weight, packed, 9 ounces. Each.........$0.04
Per dozen..............0.40

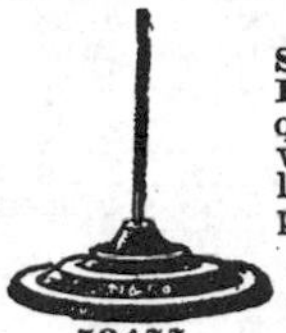
53477.

**53477 Jumbo Standing Paper File,** 4-inch lacquered iron base, wire 8 inches long; weight, packed, 9 ounces.
Each,.......$0.07
per dozen 0.75

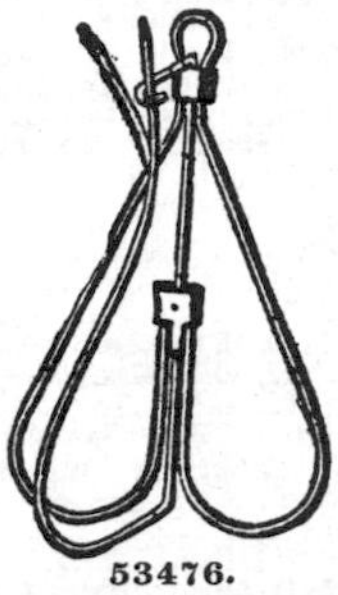
53476.

## Paper Fasteners.

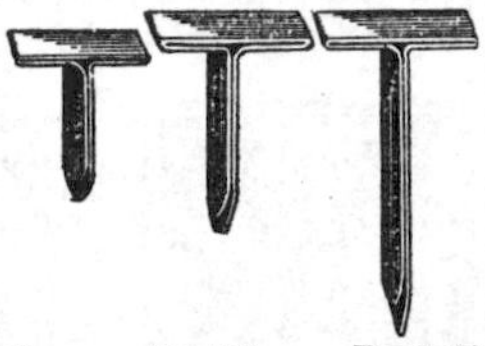

**53478. Commercial Paper Fasteners,** made from best quality brass, for binding manuscript, pamphlets, records and papers for references, etc. 100 in brass box.

| No. | Length. | Per 100. | Per 1000 |
|---|---|---|---|
| 1 | ¼ inch. | 10c. | $0.80 |
| 2 | ½ inch. | 12c. | 1.00 |
| 3 | ¾ inch. | 14c. | 1.20 |
| 4 | 1 inch. | 17c. | 1.40 |

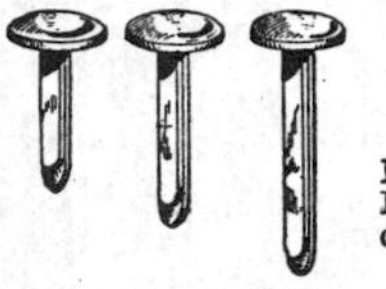

## "Never Break" Round Head Brass Paper Fasteners.

**52479. "Never Break" Round Head, Brass Paper Fasteners,** made from first quality brass.
100 in brass box.

| No. | Length. | Per 100. | Per 1000. |
|---|---|---|---|
| 1 | ¼ inch | $0.12 | $1.00 |
| 2 | ½ inch | $0.14 | $1.20 |
| 3 | ¾ inch | $0.14 | $1.60 |
| 4 | 1 inch | $0.23 | $2.00 |

## Eureka Staple Driver.

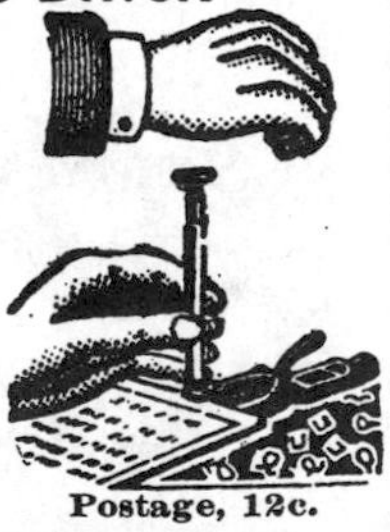

**53480 Eureka Staple Driver.** for binding books, papers, pamphlets, etc., putting down cloth or matting, putting up curtains, shades on rollers, and driving small steel staples for a hundred purposes. Requires no skill to use it; staple is placed in holder, driven to place, and driver returns to place, ready for use. Packed in neat card board box containing driver, clincher and 400 assorted staples.
Each, 38c.; per doz., $4.25
Postage, 12c.

## Desk Blotting Pads.

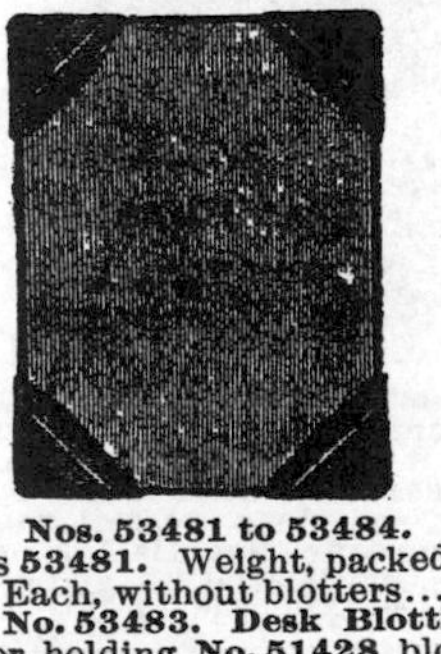
Nos. 53481 to 53484.

### Without Blotting Paper.

**No. 53481. Desk Blotting Pad,** 10x12¼ inches, for use on ladies' desks, made of heavy binder's board, covered with blue paper, red roan leather corners, morocco paper back, for holding 51424 blotters. Weight, packed, 11 oz. Each, without blotters..........$0.19

**No. 53482. Desk Blotting Pad,** 12¼x19¼ inches, for holding No. 51426 blotters, otherwise same as 53481. Weight, packed, 18 oz.
Each, without blotters....................$0.20

**No. 53483. Desk Blotting Pad,** 19¼x24¼ inches, for holding No. 51428 blotters, otherwise same as 51431. Weight, packed, 32 oz.
Each, without blotters....................$0.30

**53484 Star Blotting Paper,** put up in 12 in package, assorted colors in package. Per package, 4c; per dozen packages....................$0.40

**53485 Climax Heavy Blotting Paper,** blue, buff, cherry, 9¼x12 inches, for use in No. 53481 desk pad. Per sheet, 3c; per dozen sheets..............$0.30

**53486 "Climax,"** 12x19 inches, for use in No. 53482 desk pad. Per sheet, 4c; per dozen sheets.....$0.40

**53487 "Climax,"** 19x24 inches, for use in No. 53483 desk pad. Per sheet, 5c; per dozen sheets....$0.50

## Postage Stamp Boxes.

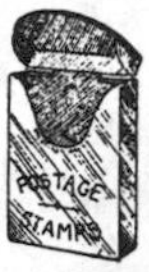

53488

**53488 "Harvard" Postage Stamp Box,** polished nickel hinged cover,
Each, 8c; per dozen... $0.85

**53489 "Handy" Postage Stamp Box,** nickel and silver finish ball catch, assorted, with fancy design on front. Size, 1⅜x1⅛ in.
Each....................$0.10
Per doz....................1.00

**Always Order by Number.**

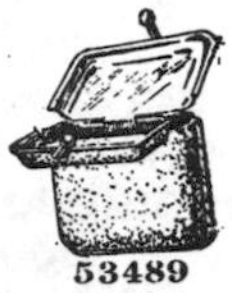
53489

## School Bags.

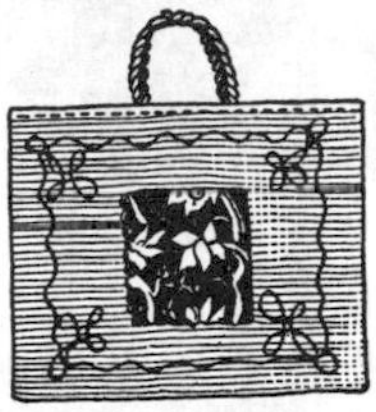

**53490. School Bag.** Fancy Hemp, embroidered front, with pocket; size 11½ x 14 inches; weight packed 5 oz.
Each....................$.08
Per doz....................80

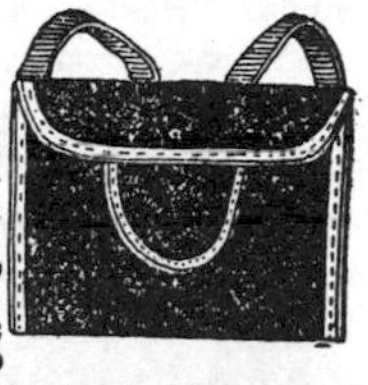

**53491. Waterproof School Bag,** with outside pocket, shoulder strap and flap, bound edges. Weight packed 5 oz.
Each, 14 in....................$.10
Per doz....................95
Each, 16 inch....................12
Per doz....................1.20

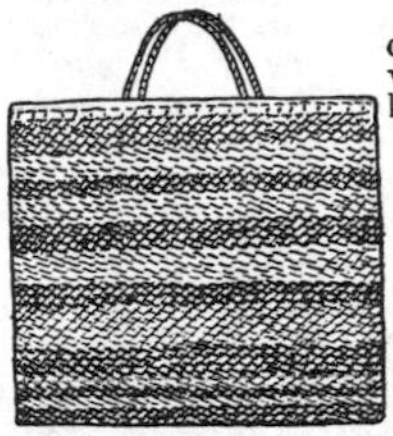

**53492. School Bag,** hard cotton cord, closely woven in variegated colored stripes. lined, cord handles, 14 inches.
Each....................$0.15
Per doz....................1.07

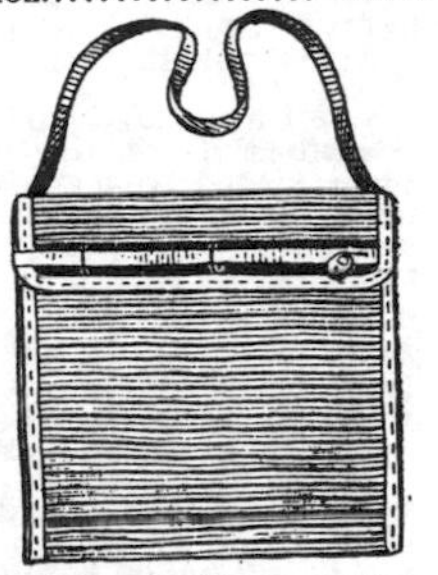

**53493. School Bag,** Brown Duck, flap fastens with strap and lock, leather shoulder strap. Size 9½x14. Very durable.
Each..............$0.18
Per doz............. 1.90

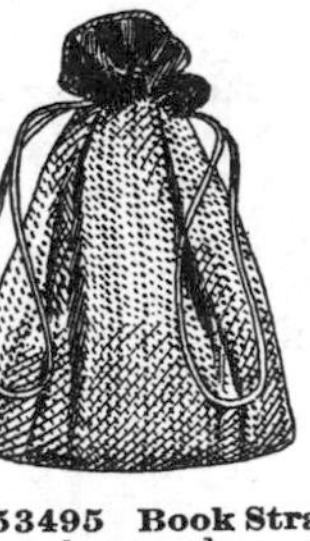

**53494 School Bags,** cotton cord in variegated colored stripes. lined with colored cambric, with drawing strings, size when open 14x17½ inches.
Each....................$0.20
Per dozen....................2.00

**53495 Book Straps,** flexible leather, handle with cross-bars and name plate, 36 inch strap.
Each....................$0.10
Per doz....................1.00

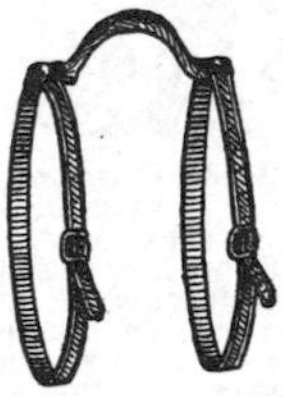

**53496 Heavy Leather Handle,** stitched edges, covered cross-bars, grain leather straps, 42 inches long and ⅝ inch wide. Each......$0.20
Per dozen....................2.00

**53497 Book Strap,** solid metal handle, nickeled with 36 inch russet grained straps, ½ inch wide.
Each....................$0.15
Per dozen....................1.45

## Chalk Crayons.

**53500 White Chalk Crayons;** round; one gross in box. Weight, 2½ lbs.
Per box, 7c; per doz. boxes....................$0.70

**53501 Colored Chalk Crayons;** round: one gross, assorted colors in box. Weight, 2⅛ lbs.
Per box (one gross), 30c; per doz. boxes......$3.25

**53504 "National Dustless Crayon,"** for schools and seminaries; makes a white, distinct mark, smoothly, softly and silently, and is easily erased; contains no grease, soap nor gummy substance; cheaper than common chalk, because it lasts five times as long; medium grade for artificial surfaces, hard grade for real slate blackboards. One gross in box; weight, packed, 4 lbs.
Per gross, 35c; per case (25 gross)..................$8.25

## Blackboard Erasers.

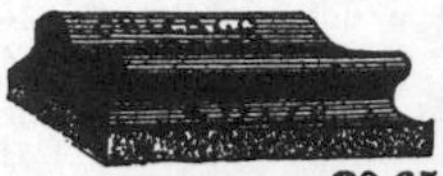

**53508 Chicago Dustless Eraser**, wool felt, cleans the board thoroughly, very durably made. Weight, packed, 4 ounces. Each 6c.

Per doz ........ $0.65
Per gross ........ 6.95

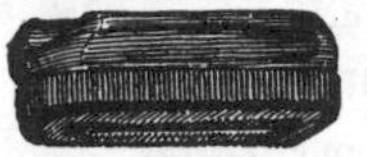

**53510 The Matchless Dustless Eraser**, made of thin fancy colored felt, firmly secured, forming a substantial and perfect eraser.

Each........ $0.05
Per doz........ .55
Per gross........ 5.45

## Youth's Companion and Reversible Blackboard.

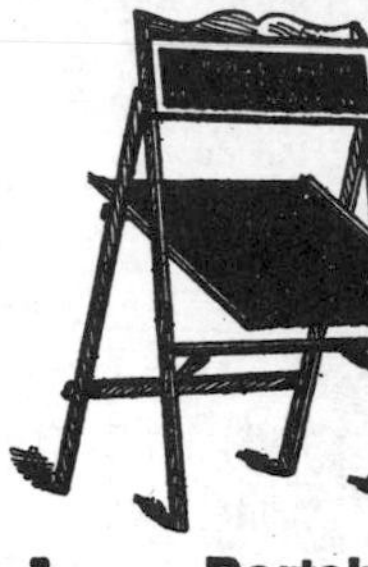

**53512 Combination Writing and Drawing Desk.** Suitable for home, Sunday and private schools. Both sides slated, hard wood frame. 3 feet 11 inches high, 2 feet wide. The most complete, perfect and reliable black board made. Price..... $3.00

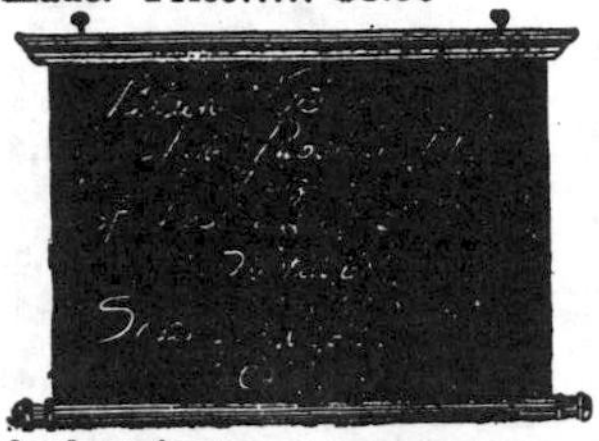

## Portable Black-Boards.

**53514 Portable Blackboard** of cloth with best black liquid slating surface on both sides, mounted on rollers with hook and rings complete for hanging.

| Size. | Each. | Size. | Each. | Size. | Each. |
|---|---|---|---|---|---|
| 2x2 ft. | $0 54 | 3x5 ft. | $1 90 | 4x5 ft. | $2 30 |
| 3x4 ft. | 1 14 | 3x6 ft. | 2 30 | 4x6 ft. | 2 85 |
| 3x4 ft. | 1 50 | 4x4 ft. | 1 90 | 4x7 ft. | 3 30 |

With music lines, $1.25 each, additional.

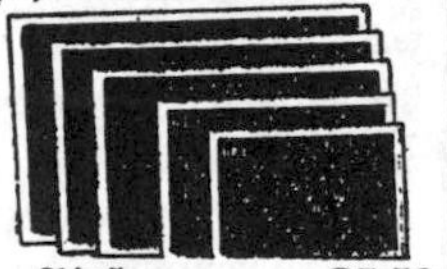

**53516 Portable Blackboard of Hyloplate**, slated both sides; with ash frame; for use on wall, easel or table.

| | | | |
|---|---|---|---|
| 2x3 ft. | $2.60 | 3½x5 | $5.50 |
| 3x2 ft. | 3.60 | 4 x6 | 7.15 |
| 3x4½ ft. | 4.55 | | |

With music lines, $1.25 each additional.

Reversible portable blackboards, same as No. 51516, mounted on hardwood standards, for private schools, Sunday schools, lecture rooms, etc. Prices will be quoted on application.

## Slated Paper and Cloth.

**53518 For Blackboard; excellent for any flat Surface.** Per yard.

Paper, 3 ft. wide, slated one side, black...... $0.47
Paper, 4 ft. wide, slated one side, black...... .60

53520
Cloth, 3 ft. wide, slated one side, black....... .54
Cloth, 4 ft. wide, slated one side, black....... .67
Cloth, 3 ft. wide, slated two sides, black...... .67
Cloth, 4 ft. wide, slated two sides, black...... .80

## Liquid Slating for Blackboands.

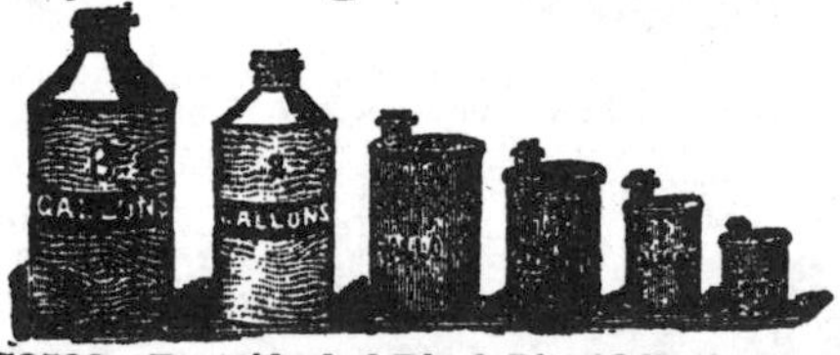


**53522. Best Alcohol Black Liquid Slating**; may be applied to hard finish plaster, paper, boards, or to old blackboards of any kind; does not become greasy, is not easily scratched, does not crack, blister or glaze when applied to suitable surface according to directions which accompany each can, dries in a few minutes, hardens in a day. A gallon will cover about 250 square feet, three coats. Put up in tin cans. Cannot be sent by mail.

Per pint........ $0.45
Per quart........ .75
Per half-gallons........ 1.45
Per gallon........ 2.85

**53524 Flat Brush for Applying Liquid Slating**, 3 inches wide. Each........ $0.75

**Don't be afraid** that you live too far away to order goods from us.

**Dealers take advantage from large Centers of Trade and you have to Pay for it**

**Some of our biggest customers are in Texas, Arizona, Colorado, California, Washington and Oregon.**

## School Slates With Wood Frames.

**53526 "Hyatt" Patent Wire Bound School Slates** combine strength, lightness, durability, and uniformity of finish of surface; being wire bound, they cannot come apart, and machine smoothed they present an absolutely even writing surface, free from ridges.

| Size. | Each. | Per doz. | Wt., Ea. |
|---|---|---|---|
| 6x 9 | $0.04 | $0.42 | 18 oz. |
| 7x11 | 0.05 | 0.48 | 22 oz. |
| 8x12 | 0.06 | 0.60 | 25 oz. |

6x 9, 12 doz. in case, per case........ $4.75
7x11, 10 doz. in case, per case........ 4.50
8x12, 8 doz. in case, per case........ 4.50

## "Hyatt Noiseless Slates.

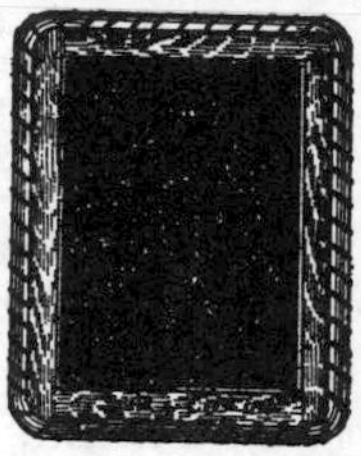

**53528 Strength, lightness and durability combined.** Best quality slate with perfectly finished, even writing surface, free from ridges. Frame is wire bound (cannot come apart) and covered with fine bright red (fast color) wool felt, securely fastened.

**"Hyatt" Noiseless Slate**, single.

| Size. | Each. | Per doz. | Wt., Ea. |
|---|---|---|---|
| 6x 9 | $0.08 | $0.80 | 18 oz. |
| 7x11 | 0.10 | 1.00 | 23 oz. |
| 8x12 | 0.12 | 1.20 | 26 oz. |

6x 9, 12 doz. in case, per case........ $9.00
7x11, 10 doz. in case, per case........ 9.00
8x12, 8 doz. in case, per case........ 8.40

**53529 "Hyatt" Noiseless Slate**, double, hinged with strong webbing, firmly riveted to frames.

| Size. | Each. | Per doz. | Wt., Ea. |
|---|---|---|---|
| 7x11 | $0.20 | $2.00 | 40 oz. |
| 8x12 | 0.24 | 2.40 | 46 oz. |

7x11, 5 doz. in case, per case........ $9.00
8x12, 4 doz. in case........ 8.40

## Victor Slates.

**53530 Best Quality Slates**, with perfectly smooth surface; frame covered with bright red wool felt and securely fastened.

| Size. | Each. | Per doz. |
|---|---|---|
| 5x7 | $0.08 | $0.80 |
| 6x9 | .09 | .95 |
| 7x11 | .10 | 1.05 |
| 8x12 | .12 | 1.25 |

## Silicate Book Slates.

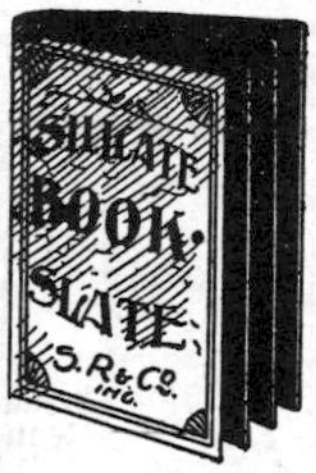


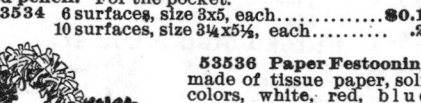

**Superior quality, strongly made**, bound in fine black cloth covers. Superior slate surface for the slate pencil. For school or office use.

| | | Size. | Each. |
|---|---|---|---|
| 53532 | 6 surfaces | 5x8½ | $0.25 |
| | 6 surfaces | 6x9 | .35 |

Silicate Book Slates, neatly and strongly bound in fine cloth, with superior **ivorine surface, for the lead pencil.** For the pocket.

53534 6 surfaces, size 3x5, each........ $0.15
10 surfaces, size 3¼x5½, each........ .25

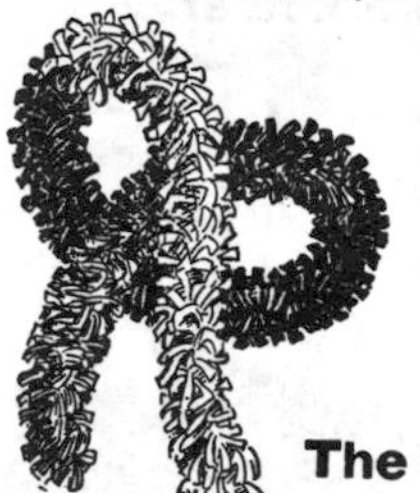

**53536 Paper Festooning**, made of tissue paper, solid colors, white, red, blue, green, yellow, pink and lilac, also red, white and blue combined for decorating halls, stores, arches, stands etc. 10 yards in roll, weight per roll 8 ounces. "Sold by the roll only."

Per roll (10 yds.)........ $0.20
Per doz. rolls (120 yds) 1.95

## The Hafew Check Protector.

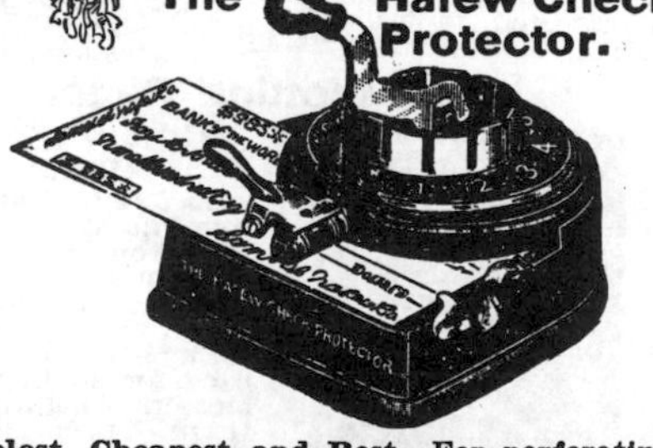

**53538**

**Simplest, Cheapest and Best.** For perforating the original amounts in checks, drafts, bonds, stock certificates, etc., **so that it cannot be raised.** For cimplicity and excellence of construction, ease of operation, durability and clean, perfect work, not only has this punch no equal, but it is the only machine which in all respects fills the bill, and cannot get out of order. Size 6x4½ in., 3 in. high. Price, each........ $7.20

**Mammoth Vehicle Catalogue Free on Application.**

## Playing Cards.

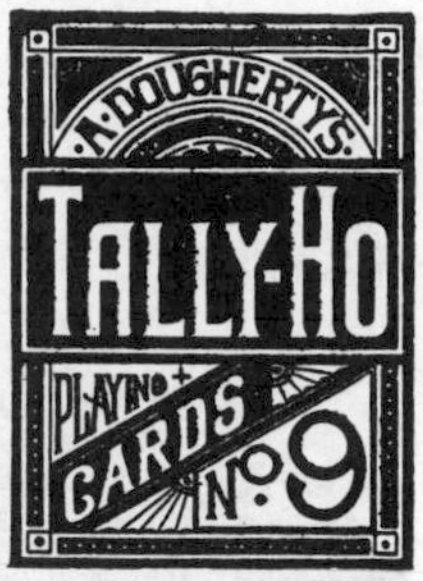


**53539 "Tally-ho" No. 9**, half linen, round cornered, double index, extra enameled; large variety of handsomely designed backs in different tints and colors; the best enameled card at price in the market. Weight, packed 4 ounces.

Per pack........ $ 0.17
Per dozen........ 1.84
Per gross........ 19.80

**By mail 5c extra.**

**53540 "Outing," No. 17**, fine enameled, double indexed, assorted backs. Weight, packed, 4 ounces.

Per Pack........ $ 0.13
Per dozen packs........ 1.30
Per gross packs........ $14.60

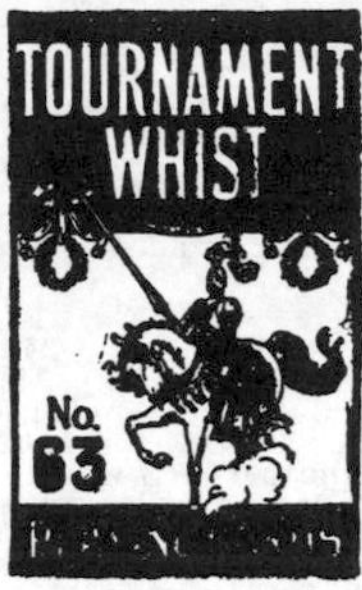


**53541 "Tournament Whist," No. 2**, size 2½x3½ inches, made especially for regular and duplicate whist, enameled, round corners, double indexed, assortment of fancy backs and colors. Weight packed, 4 ounces.

Per pack........ $ 0.19
Per dozen packs........ 2.00
Per gross packs........ 21.60

**By mail 5c extra.**

**53542 "Bicycle," No. 808**, superior ivory enameled finish; numerous popular and appropriate backs. Largely used by card players throughout the world. Weight packed, 4 ounces. Per pack..... $ 0.17

Per dozen........ 1.85
Per gross........ 19.80

**By Mail 5c. Extra.**

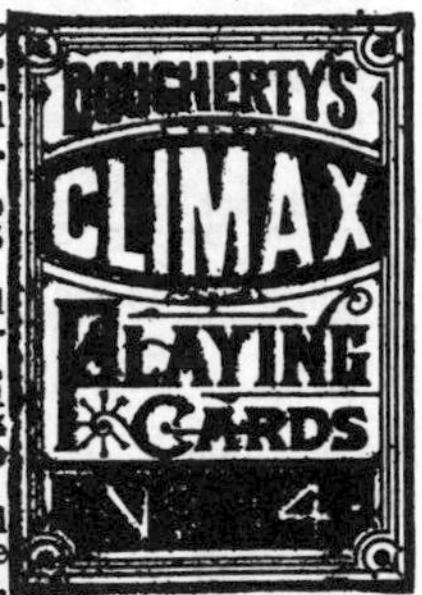


**53543 "Climax" No. 14**, enameled, round cornered, "linen cards," double indexed, beautifully designed backs in tints and colors. Weight packed, 4 ounces.

Per pack........ $0.30
Per doz........ 3.35

**By Mail 5c. extra.**

**53544 "Cruiser,"** round corners, double indexed, assorted backs. Weight packed, 4 ounces. Per pack... $ 0.11

Perdoz........ 1.15
Pergross packs........ 13.00

**By Mail 5c. Extra.**

**53546 "Steamboat,"** round corners, double index, made in plaid blue star, green star, Spanish wave and calico backs. Weight packed, 4 oz.

Per pack........ $0.08
Per dozen packs........ .85
Per gross packs........ 9.00

**By Mail 5c. Extra.**

**53547 "Barcelona" No. 49, "Spanish Monte Cards,"** 48 cards in pack, assortment of black and colors. Weight packed, 3 ounces. Per pack... $0.30

Per dozen packs........ 3.35

**By Mail 5c. Extra.**

**53549 "Empire," No. 97**, round corners, double indexed, assorted backs. Weight per package, 4 oz.

Per pack........ $0.15
Per dozen packs........ 1.45

**By Mail 5c. Extra.**

## Poker Chips.

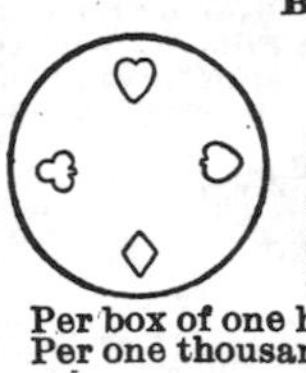

**53561 Embossed Poker Chips**, depressed colored spots, 4 "ace" embossed on red, white and blue chips, 1¼ inches in diameter, one hundred in a box, assorted as follows: 50 white, 25 red, 25 blue, weight packed 30 ounces.

Per box of one hundred........ $1.10
Per one thousand........ 9.00

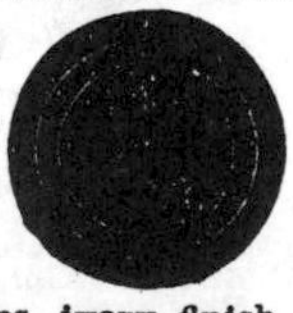

**53563 Composition Ivory**, 1¼ inches in diameter, superior quality and finish, one hundred in box, assorted as follows: 25 red, 25 blue, 50 white, weight, packed, 27 ounces.

Per box of one hundred.. $ 1.20
Per one thousand........ 10.00

**53565 Composition Poker Chips**, ivory finish, warranted not to chip or warp, 1¼ inches in diameter, one hundred in a box, assorted as follows: 50 white, 25 red, 25 blue; weight, packed, 25 ounces.

Per box of oue hundred........ $0.30
Per one thousand........ 2.75

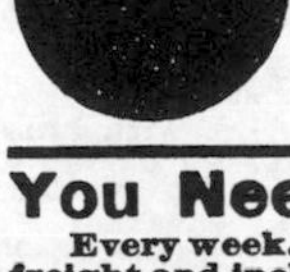

**53567 Plain Poker Chips**, composition, ivory finish, warranted not to chip or warp, one hundred in box, assorted as follows: 50 white, 25 red, 25 blue; weight, packed, 30 ounces.

Per one hundred........ $0.65
Per one thousand........ 5.20

**You Need Groceries . . .**

**Every week. Order a month's supply, ship by freight and include the stationery and other small articles at NO ADDITIONAL EXPENSE.**

**IF YOU NEED SOME STATIONERY, A NEIGHBOR, A SET OF HARNESS; ANOTHER, A PLOW; AND ANOTHER SOME GROCERIES. GET TOGETHER AND SEND IN A CLUB ORDER, SHIPPING ALL BY FREIGHT.**

# MATHEMATICAL AND DRAWING INSTRUMENTS and MATERIALS.

Customers desiring this line of goods may be assured that any selection they may make will be entirely satisfactory. We buy from leading manufacturers, both abroad and in this country, and handle only such instruments as are perfectly accurate, reliable and durable. We guarantee every item as represented, or it may be returned to us. 3 % off when cash in full accompanies order.

**53600** Pencil Compass, for general and school use, easily adjusted, makes circle from ½ to 8 inches in diameter, good quality nickel tip lead pencil. Price, 15c; per doz....**$1.50**

**By mail 2c. each extra.**

**53602** Bow Compass, brass, 3½ inch, with handle, fixed needle point. Pin and pencil points. Price, 35c; per doz.........**$4.00**

**By mail 2c. each extra.**

**53604** Bow Compass, made from best German silver, 3½ inches, with handle, fixed needle points. Pen and pencil points. Price.....................**$0.55**

**By mail 3c. extra.**

**53607** Improved Polygraph. More than 10,000 mathematical figures can be produced; gives correct curves and degrees; nickel plated. Full directions accompany each. Put up in neat box,
Price each............**$0.25**
Per doz............**$2.50**
Postage 5c. extra.

## Nickel Plated Instruments in Sets.

The most complete for school and general use.

**53609** "Amateur" Pencil Compass, 5 inches long, with pencil point adjustments; nickel divider. Fitted in velvet, card board case. Weight, 2½ oz. Price......**$0.22**

**53611** Drawing Set, in wood case, with sliding cover; 5 inches long, velvet fittings, containing 4½ inch divider, ruling pen, and lengthening bar. Weight, 4½ ounces. Price.................**$0.27**

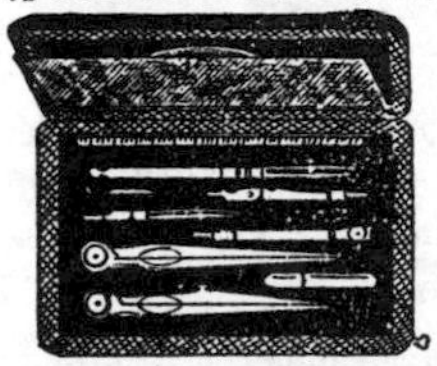

**53613** Drawing Set containing 4¾ inch divider, lengthening bar, ruling pen, metal protractor, pen 3 inches, needle point and ink cups in a beautiful leatherette case lined with velvet. Weight, 6¼ ounces. Price per set **$0.80**

**53614** Scholar's Companion, fitted with nickel plated instruments, in leatherette case, lined with black velvet; containing 4¾ inch dividers, with pen, pencil point, plain divider, ruling pen, metal protractors, ink cups. Weight, 7½ ounces. Price per set.......**$1.25**

**53616** Fitted in Leatherette Case with 4¼ inch dividers; pen and pencil point, plain dividers, ruling pen, metal protractor, rule and ink cups; velvet lined, weight 8½ ounces. Price.................**$1.25**

**53617** Containing 4¾ inch Divider, fixed needle point, pen and pencil points, lengthening bar, plain divider 2½ inch divider, ruling pen, metal protractor, rule and ink cups. fitted in leatherette case, lined with black velvet. Weight, 9 oz. Price....**$1.65**

**53619** "Our Leader" Drawing set in a beautiful leatherette case, velvet lined, fitted with 4¾ inch divider, pen and pencil points, plain divider, lengthening bar, spring bow pen, metal protractor, rule and ink cup. The best set made for school use. Weight 11 oz. Price......**$1.70**

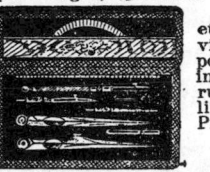

## Kern's Swiss Drawing Instruments.

Made of the best German Silver and English Steel.

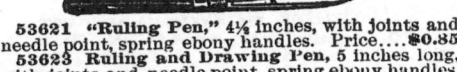

**53621** "Ruling Pen," 4½ inches, with joints and needle point, spring ebony handles. Price....**$0.85**

**53623** Ruling and Drawing Pen, 5 inches long, with joints and needle point, spring ebony handles. Price.........................**$0.90**

**53625** Ruling and Drawing Pen, with spring joints and needle point, 5½ inches long, ebony handle. Price.........................**$1.05**

**53627** Ruling and Drawing Pen, with spring joints and needle point, 4¾ inches long, ivory handle. Price.........................**$1.25**

**53628** Drawing and Ruling Pen, with joints and needle point, 5¼ inches long, ivory handle. Price.........................**$1.50**

**53629** Drawing and Ruling Pen, 6¼ inches long, with joints and needle point, ivory handle. Price.........................**$1.75**

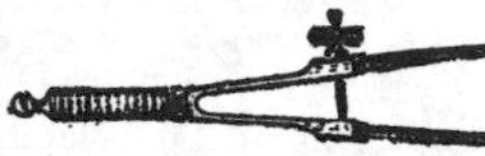

**53631** Steel Spring Bow Dividers, screw on a right and left thread, holds the points firmly in any position, 3¼ inches long, metal handle. Price.........................**$1.90**

**53632** Steel Spring Bow Pen, 3½ inches long, screw on a right and left thread, holds the points firmly in any position, ivory handle. Price...**$1.95**

**53634** Steel Spring Bow Pen, 3½ inches long, metal handle, otherwise same as No. 53632. Price.........................**$2.15**

## Superior Swiss Instruments.

Made of selected German silver and best English steel, are of a very graceful form, light in weight.

**53636** Plain Divider, 3½ inches long, with handle joint. Pivot joint. Price....**$1.70**

**53638** Hair Spring Divider, Silver plated, 3½ inches long. Price.........................**$2.30**

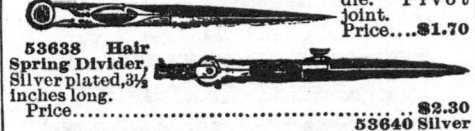

**53640** Silver Plated Dividers, first quality, 5½ inches, with fixed needle point, pen, pencil point and lengthening bar. Price..**$6.00**

**53642** Silver Plated Dividers, with fixed needle point, and pencil point, pen and lengthening bar, 3½ inches long. Price.........................**$3.80**

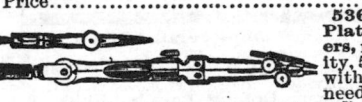

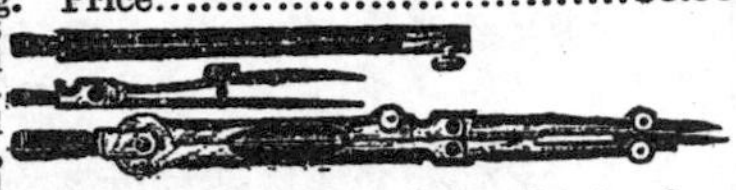

**53643** Hand Made, Silver Plated Divider, with fixed needle point, pen, pencil point and lengthening bar. 5½ inches long. Price.........................**$5.90**

## Extra Fine German Silver and Steel Instruments.

**53645** Drawing Pen, Best quality steel, 4¾ inches long; ebony handle. Cheap but very durable. Price.........................**$0.55**

**53647** Drawing Pen 5¼ inches long. Otherwise same as No. 53645. Price...........**$0.60**

**53649** Drawing Pen with improved bent spring. Ebony handle 4½ inches long. Price...**$0.65**

**53651** Drawing Pen, 5¼ inches long, with improved bent spring. Ebony handle. Price.**$0.75**

**53653** Ivory Handle, needle point drawing pen, with German silver blades for colored inks; very fine point. Price.........................**$0.75**

**53655** Dotting Wheel, made of the very best German steel; white bone handle. Price....**$0.95**

**53657** Improved Drawing Pen. The pen is connected with bar which runs through the center of holder and is operated by loosening screw at the end of handle. It will readily follow any curve without blotting the edge of curved ruler. Superior quality German silver. Price......**$1.40**

**53659** Improved Drawing Pen, a perfect pen for line work. Opens and closes by turning thumbscrew at upper end of handle, and is so made that it cannot get out of order. Superior quality English steel. Price...................**$1.35**

**53661** Improved Railroad Pen, 5½ inches long, both blades face the same way. Ivory handle. Price.........................**$2.20**

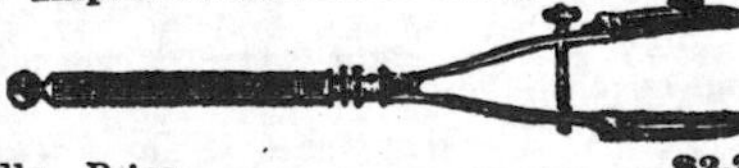

**53662** Improved Railroad Pen, 5½ inches long. Ivory handle. Price.........................**$2.15**

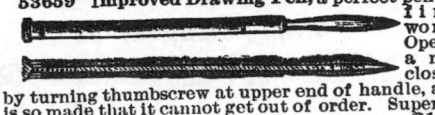

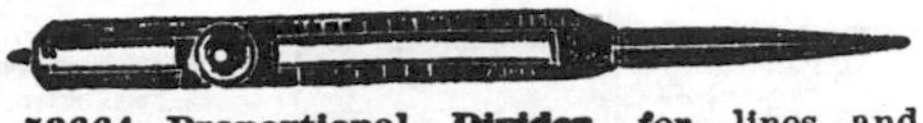

**53664** Proportional Divider, for lines and circles, 6¼ inches, made of best quality English steel. Price.........................**$2.00**

**53666** Proportional Divider, with rack motion, 8½ inches for lines and circles; made of superior quality German silver. Price.........**$9.00**

**53668** Proportional Divider, for lines, circles, planes and solids, with micrometer adjustments. 9 inch, made of first quality German silver; in beautiful leatherette case. Price ........**$12.00**

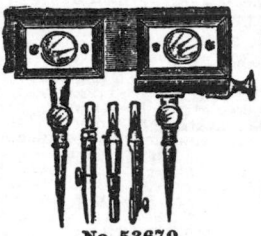

**53670** Beam Compass, improved pattern, to fasten to a straight-edge or bar, with tangent attachments, pencil, pen, needle and two round points, also wheel attachment in case. Price..........**$10.00**

**53672** Beam Compass, to fit on any straight-edge, with two plain points, one needle point. Pen and pencil fitted in neat leather case. Price.........................**$4.60**

**No. 53670.**

**53674** Beam Compass, 20 inches long, 2 bars, with pen and pencil and 2 straight points. Price.........................**$7.50**

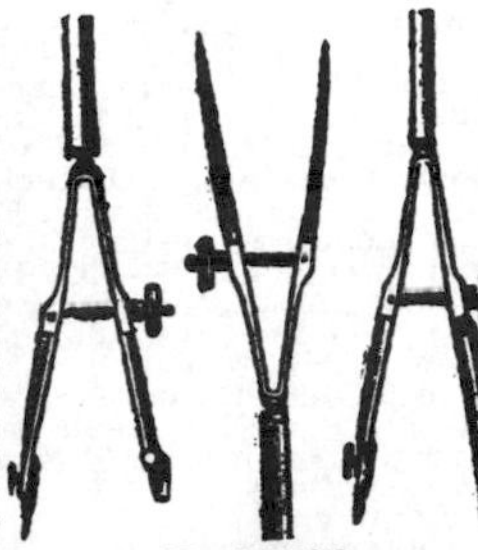

**53676** Steel Spring Bow Divider, 3 inches, round point, ivory handle. extra German make and shaped like the Swiss bows. Price............**$1.30**

**53678** Steel Spring Bow Pencil, extra fine German make, needle point, ivory handle, shaped like the Swiss bows. Price........**$1.60**

**53680** Steel Spring Bow Pen, extra fine German make, needle point, shaped like the Swiss bows ivory handle. Price.........**$1.60**

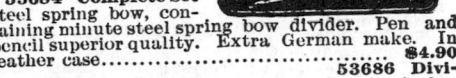

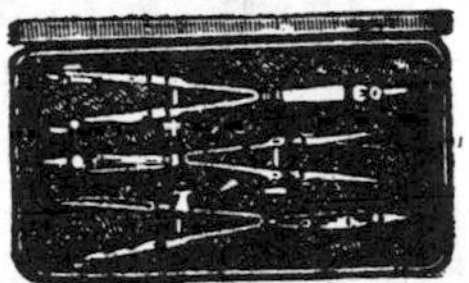

**No. 53676.**

**53682** Set Containing steel spring bow pen, pencil and divider. Extra German make and shaped like Swiss bows. Price..........**$3.95**

**53684** Complete Set steel spring bow, containing minute steel spring bow divider. Pen and pencil superior quality. Extra German make. In leather case.........................**$4.90**

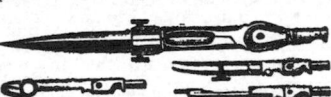

**53686** Divider 3½ inches long with fixed needle. Pen and pencil point superior quality. Price....**$4.25**

**53688** Plain Divider 3½ inches long, Price **$1.00**

**53690** Plain Divider 6 inches long. Price, **$1.50**

**53691** Extra Finish compass 3½ inches, with fixed needle point. Pen and pencil point, price...........**$3.00**

**53693** Compass, made of selected German silver; 3½ inch, with fixed needle and pen point; light weight, hand made. Price.**$2.60**

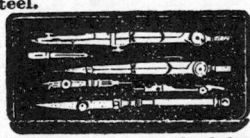

**53695** Compass Set, best German silver; 4½ inch divider, with fixed needle point, pen, pencil point and lengthening bar. Price......**$5.30**

## Extra Fine German Instruments.

Made of First Grade German Silver and English Steel.

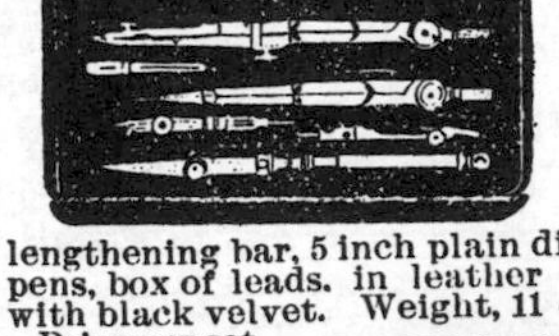

**53697** Fine German Silver Set, for use in school, containing 5½ inch steel jointed dividers with fixed needle point, pen and pencil points, lengthening bar, 5 inch plain divider, 5 inch ruling pens, box of leads. in leather covered case. lined with black velvet. Weight, 11 ounces. Price per set.........................**$2.35**

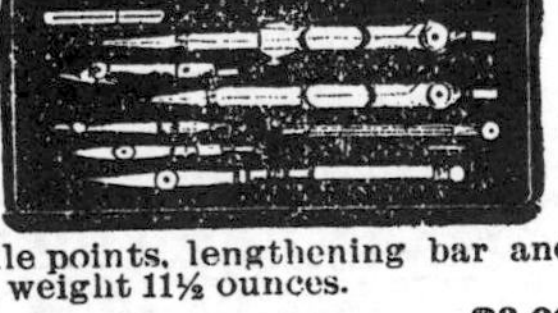

**53698** Best Quality German Silver Set, in leather covered case lined with velvet containing ivory handled 5½ inch dividers, 5 inch ruling pen, pen, pencil and needle points, lengthening bar and 5 inch plain divider, weight 11½ ounces. Price, per set.........................**$3.00**

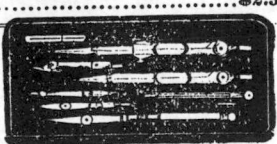

IT IS VERY NECESSARY THAT YOU GIVE THE CATALOGUE NUMBER OF EACH ARTICLE YOU ORDER, TO AVOID CONFUSION. IF YOU ORDER FROM A SPECIAL CATALOGUE OR CIRCULAR, ALWAYS MENTION IT IN YOUR ORDER.

**53699** Containing finest quality German silver instruments 5½ inch steel jointed divider with fixed needle point, steel spring bow pen, drawing pen, lengthening bar, pen and pencil points 5½ inch plain divider, steel jointed drawing pen, ivory handles in a beautiful leather case velvet lined, weight 12 ounces.
Price ....................$3.50

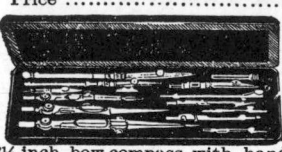

**53700** German Silver Set in morocco case containing 5½ in. compass with pen, pencil needle points and lengthening bar, 5½ inch divider, 3½ inch bow compass with handle, pen, pencil and needle points, key and 5½ inch ruling pen with hinge, 4 inch ruling pen, hinge, ivory handle. Weight, 12½ ounces. Price ....................$4.95

**53702** Extra Fine German Drawing Instruments, in polished walnut case, with tray, lock and key, containing 5½ inch compasses with pen, pencil, needle points and lengthening bar, 5 inch dividers, 3½ inch bow compass with pen, pencil and needle points, 3 inch steel spring bow pen, 5½ inch ruling pen with hinge and pin, 4 inch ruling pen, lead case, key, 6 inch scale, rubber triangle, metal protractor. The retail price of this set is $30.00.
Our special price .....................**$15.00**

**No 53705** Superior German Drawing Instruments, made of best quality German silver in polished walnut case, lined with finest velvet. Tray lock and key. Containing: 6½-inch proportional dividers, 5½-inch Compasses, with Pen, Pencil, Needle Points and Lengthening Bar, 5-inch Hair Spring Dividers, 5-inch Dividers, 3½-inch Bow Compasses, with Pen, Pencil and Needle Points, 3½-inch Dividers, with handle, 3-inch Steel Spring Bow Pen, 3-inch Spring Bow Pencil, 3-inch Spring Bow Dividers, Railroad Pen, 5½-inch Ruling Pen, with hinge and pin, 4-inch Ruling Pen, Key, Lead Case, 1 dozen Tacks, 6-inch Ivory Scale, Rubber Triangle, Metal Protractor and Wooden Curve.
Retail price ......................$40.00
Our special price ..................26.00

## Protractors.

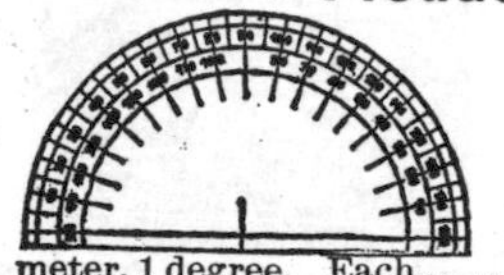

**53707** Half Circle Brass Protractor, 3½ inches in diameter, 1 degree. Each,....$0.10
Per doz .......... 1.00

**53709** Brass Protractor, first quality, half circle, 6⅜ inches in diameter. Each...$0.40
**53710** Half Circle Protractor. German silver, 5½ inches in diameter. ½ degree. Each......$0.60
**53712** Best quality German silver Half Circle Protractor, ½ degrees, 8½ inches in diameter. Each.............................$1.25
**53714** Full Circle Horn Protractor, 5½ inches in diameter. ½ degrees. Each....$0.90
**53716** Metal Horn Protractor, 7 inches in diameter. ½ degrees. Each, $0.23, Per...$2.00
**53718** Half Circle Vernier Protractor, with horn center, 10 inches in diameter, ¼ degrees. Vernier reading to one minute, arm extending over outer edge of Protractor, 6½ inches in diameter. Price..........................$15.30
**53720** Swiss Half-Circle Protractor, best German silver, center on outer edge, 6 inches in diameter, ¼ degrees. Each .....................$3.05
**53721** Swiss Half-Circle Protractor, best German silver, center or inner edge, 5 inches in diameter, ½ degrees. Each ...................$2.45
**53722** Ivory Protractor, 6 inches long, 2½ inches wide, divided into ½ degrees, ⅛, ¼, ⅜, ½, ⅝, ¾, ⅞, 1, 1⅛, 1¼, 1⅜, 1½, 1¾, 2 inch scale. Scale of chords, 10, 20, 30, 40, 50, 60, 70, 80, 90, parts to inch, diagonal scale, Scale 40 on lower edge. Each..........$4.00
**53724** Ivory Protractor, 6 inches long, 2 inches wide, divided, whole degrees, ⅛, ¼, ⅜, ½, ⅝, ¾, ⅞, 1 inch scales. Scale of chords, 10, 20, 30, 40, 50, 60, 70, 80, 90 parts to inch and diagonal scale. Price....$1.75

## Platting Scales.

**53724** Boxwood Platting Scale, 6 inches. Each.......................$0.10
**53725** Ivory Platting Scale, 6 inches. Each.......................$0.60
**53727** Gunter Scale, boxwood, 24 inches. Each.......................$0.75
**53728** Boxwood Gunter Scale, 12 inches, Each.......................$0.55

## Machine Divided Drawing Scales.

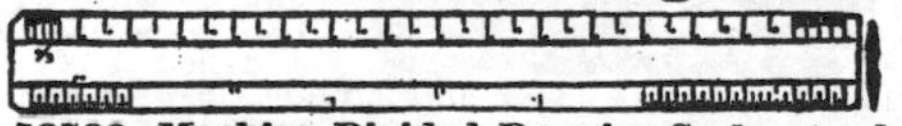

**53730** Machine Divided Drawing Scale, standard best quality flat boxwood, bevelled and divided on both sides. 24 inches long.........$2.50
18 inches long....................2.20
12 inches long....................1.10
6 inches long.....................50
**53732** Ivory, best quality, 12 inches long...3.40
**53734** Ivory, best quality, 6 inches long....1.80
**53735** Boxwood, ivorine edge, 6 inches long.......................$0.80

---

**53736** Flat Boxwood, universal scale, 12 inches long, divided on one side ⅛, ¼, ½, 1, 1-5-16, ⅝, ⅜, 1¼, divided on other side ⅜, ¾, 1½, 3, 1¾, 2, 2¼, 2½ inch to foot. Each........................$0.80
**53737** Ivory, same as No. 53736............2.60

### Triangular Boxwood Scales.

**53738** Triangular Boxwood, 24 inch, divided ⅛, ¼, ¼, ¾, 1, 1½, 2, 3, 4 inch to foot and 1-16. Price............................$3.85
**53739** Triangular Boxwood, 12 inch, divided 3-32, 3-16, ⅛, ¼, ⅜, ½, ¾, 1, 1½, 3 inch to foot and 1-16 inch. Price............................$1.50
**53740** Triangular Boxwood, 6 inch, divided 3-32, 3-16, ⅛, ¼, ⅜, ½, ¾, 1, 1½, 3 inch to foot and 1-16 inch. Price............................$0.70

### Engineers' Triangular Scales.

**53742** Triangular Boxwood, 6 inch, divided 10, 20, 30, 40, 50, 60 parts to inch. Price......$0.70
**53743** Triangular Boxwood, 12 inch, divided same as No. 53742. Price...............$1.35
**53744** Triangular Boxwood, 18 inch, divided same as No. 53742. Price...............$2.30
**53745** Triangular Boxwood, 24 inch, divided same as No. 53742. Price...............$3.90

**53747** Triangular Scale Guard, a very convenient article made of plated metal; can be attached to any part of scale. Price......$0.23

### Parallel Rulers.

**53748** Parallel Rulers, made of pure ivory, German silver bars, 6 inch. Price..........$1.35
**53749** Parallel Rulers, ebony, brass bars.

| Length | 6 in. | 9 in. | 12 in. | 18 in. | 24 in. |
|---|---|---|---|---|---|
| Price | 18c | 30c | 40c | 60c | $1.45 |

**53751** Ebony Rolling Parallel Ruler, with ivory divided edges, 9 inches. Price...........$3.30
**53752** Extra Fine Finish Ebony Parallel Ruler, with ivory divided edges. Price...........$4.10
**53754** Ebony Rolling Parallel Ruler, 9 inch........................$2.00
**53755** Ebony Rolling Parallel Ruler, extra finish, 15 inch.....................$3.00

### Skeleton Pocket Rules.

**53757** Skeleton Rule, self-acting springs; thin and light; will not shrink; 2 feet, 4 fold, 1-16 inch, on both sides..........................$0.30
**53759** Accurate, Self-Acting, Spring Skeleton Rule; thin and light; will not shrink; 4 feet, 8 fold, 1-16 inch, on both sides. Price...........$0.55
**53761** Thin, Light-Skeleton Rule, self-acting springs, accurate, 5 feet, 10 fold. Price....$0.80
**53763** Skeleton Rule, 2 feet, 4 fold, 1-16 inch, on both sides. Price.........................$0.20
**53765** Skeleton Rule, 2 feet, 4 fold, 1-6 inch on one side, meter on other. Price..........$0.20
**53767** Flexible Skeleton Rule, 4 feet, 8 fold, 1-16 inch on one side, meter on other. Price...$0.50

### Triangles.

**53770** Cherry Triagles, framed, mortised joints, 30°x60°.

| Size, inches, | 7 | 9 | 12 | 14 |
|---|---|---|---|---|
| Each, | $0.18 | .20 | .25 | .35 |

**53771** Cherry Triangles, framed, mortised joints, 45°.

| Size, inches | 5 | 7 | 9 | 12 |
|---|---|---|---|---|
| Each, | $0.18 | .20 | .25 | .35 |

**53772** Transparent, "Ambro" Triangles, open center, 30°x60°.

| Size, inches, | 6 | 8 | 10 | 12 | 14 | 16 |
|---|---|---|---|---|---|---|
| Each | $0.35 | .50 | .70 | 1.00 | 1.50 | 2.00 |

**53773** Transparent "Ambro" Triangles, open center, 45°.

| Size, inches, | 6 | 8 | 10 | 2 | 114 | 16 |
|---|---|---|---|---|---|---|
| Each, | $0.50 | .70 | 1.00 | 1.00 | 2.25 | 3.00 |

*(Note in margin: "All triangles measured this way." with "30°x60° 450." and "30°x60° 450.")*

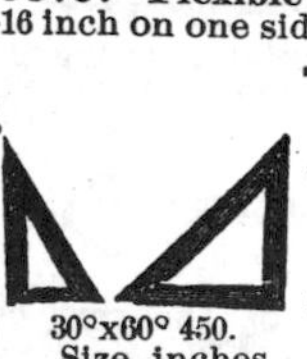

### Straight Edges.

**53775** Cherry, one edge beveled.

| Size, inches, | 18 | 24 | 30 | 36 | 42 |
|---|---|---|---|---|---|
| Each, | $0.20 | .25 | .30 | .40 | .50 |

**53776** Mahogany, ebony lined.

| Size, inches, | 24 | 30 | 36 | 42 | 48 |
|---|---|---|---|---|---|
| One edge beveled, each, | $0.50 | .60 | .75 | 1.00 | 1.25 |

**53777** Steel Straight Edges, nickel plated, one edge beveled, the other square.

| Size, inches, | 15 | 18 | 24 | 30 | 36 |
|---|---|---|---|---|---|
| Each, | $1.75 | 2.00 | 3.00 | 4.00 | 5.00 |

**53779**

| Size, inches, | 42 | 48 | 60 | 72 |
|---|---|---|---|---|
| Each, | $6.50 | 8.00 | 11.00 | 15.00 |

---

## T Squares.

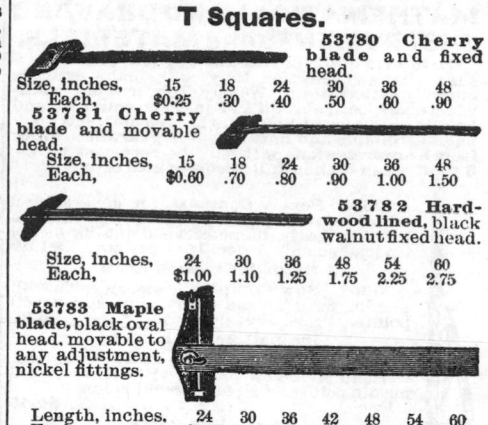

**53780** Cherry blade and fixed head.

| Size, inches, | 15 | 18 | 24 | 30 | 36 | 48 |
|---|---|---|---|---|---|---|
| Each, | $0.25 | .30 | .40 | .50 | .60 | .90 |

**53781** Cherry blade and movable head.

| Size, inches, | 15 | 18 | 24 | 30 | 36 | 48 |
|---|---|---|---|---|---|---|
| Each, | $0.60 | .70 | .80 | .90 | 1.00 | 1.50 |

**53782** Hardwood lined, black walnut fixed head.

| Size, inches, | 24 | 30 | 36 | 48 | 54 | 60 |
|---|---|---|---|---|---|---|
| Each, | $1.00 | 1.10 | 1.25 | 1.75 | 2.25 | 2.75 |

**53783** Maple blade, black oval head, movable to any adjustment, nickel fittings.

| Length, inches, | 24 | 30 | 36 | 42 | 48 | 54 | 60 |
|---|---|---|---|---|---|---|---|
| Each | $1.75 | 1.90 | 2.10 | 2.25 | 2.40 | 2.55 | 2.70 |

## Drawing Boards.

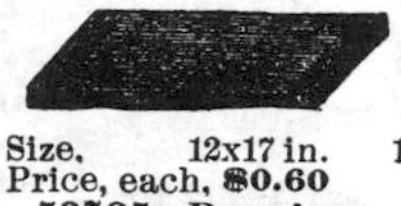

**53784** Light Drawing Board for school use. Polished pinewood with two drawing surfaces.

| Size, | 12x17 in. | 15x21 in. | 18x24 in. | 20x25 in. |
|---|---|---|---|---|
| Price, each, | $0.60 | .85 | 1.00 | 1.30 |

**53785** Drawing Board, extra finish pinewood with hardwood ledges. Dovetailed to allow contraction or expansion.

| Size, | 20x25 in. | 23x31 in. | 27x36 in. | 31x42 in. |
|---|---|---|---|---|
| Price, each, | $1.50 | 2.20 | 3.10 | 3.40 |

## Folding Stands.

**53787** Folding Stand, made of polished hardwood, nicely finished, with adjustable leather straps to set to convenient height, and hinged top board to set the drawing board standing. Price..$6.75

**53789** Folding Drawing Table, hardwood base and pine top, for use either as a drawing or reference table, well braced and substantially made, can be carried without inconvenience.
Size, 24x34 in., 29 in. high. Price, each,....$3.40
Size, 32x42 in., 38 in. high. Price, each,......5.10

## Fastening Pins or Thumb Tacks.

**53790** German Silver, best quality, points screwed in and riveted, covered with blue paper.
Round Head 7-16 inch in diameter. Per doz....$0.40
Round Head ⅝ inch in diameter. Per doz......50
Round Head ⅝ inch in diameter. Per doz......75
**53792** "Bayonet" Tacks, made of one piece of steel, a portion of the head forming the point.
5-16 in. in diam., per box of 100, 60c; per doz...$0.06
⅝ " " " 100, 75c; " ...08
7-16 " " " 100, 90c; " ...12

## German Silver and Brass Tacks.

**53794** Swedged Head, point cannot push through head, and less liable to be pulled out of head.
Round Head, German silver ⅝ in. in diameter. Per dozen.................$0.18
Round Head, German silver, 7-16 in. in diameter. Per dozen.................$0.18
Round Head, German silver, ½ in. in diameter. Per dozen.................$0.23
**53795**
Round Head, brass, ⅝ in. in diameter, Per doz.$0.12
" " 7-16 " " " " .15
" " ½ " " " " .20

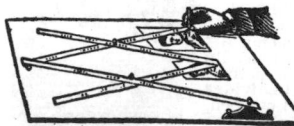

**53796** Improved Pantograph, made of hard wood. A simple mechanical apparatus, which without any instruction enables one to enlarge portraits using ordinary cabinet sized pictures. Maps, ornamental designs, music, monograms and patterns can be enlarged to any size by the use of this instrument.
Price, each.......................$0.20
**53798** Higher Grade Improved Pantograph, brass mounted, movable point and elbow joint pencil handle. Otherwise same as No. 53796.
Price, each.......................$0.80

## Carbon Paper.

**53800 Black Transfer Carbon Impression Paper,** for drawing or painting, for outlining work of every description on any surface desired. Nos. 53800 to 53802 papers are prepared on one side only, and are not intended for manifold use. Size, 10x15, Per sheet ........ **$0.05**
Per dozen ........ **$0.50** Per quire ........ **$1.00**
**53801** Size, 20x30. Per sheet ........ **$0.15**
Per dozen ........ **$1.20** Per quire ........ **$2.30**
**53802 Transfer Carbon Impression Papers,** in colors, red, blue, green, yellow, brown and white. Size, 11x18. Per sheet ........ **$0.09**
Per dozen ........ **$0.85** Per quire ........ **$1.60**
**53803 Transfer Carbon Impression Paper,** prepared on **both** sides for manifold use. Made in **black** only. Size, 17x28. Per sheet ........ **$0.20**
Per dozen ........ **$2.00** Per quire ........ **$3.50**

## Drawing Paper in Sheets.

**Whatman's Hand-made.**

The Whatman paper differs in surface as follows, viz.:

C. P. signifies "cold pressed," and has a slightly grained surface; used for general drawings and finely finished water color drawings.

H. P. signifies "hot pressed," and has a smooth surface; mostly used for very fine drawings and pen-and-ink sketches.

R. signifies "rough," and has a coarsely grained surface; used for very bold drawing and water color work (Torchon paper).

In ordering please specify which surface is desired, C. P., H. P. or R.

We furnish all sizes of Whatman's papers, but we list only the following ones, because they are most profitable to buy, as they are made of heavier paper, and cost no more in proportion to size than the smaller sheets. We cut the sheets up if desired, thus furnishing small sheets of heavier paper.

**53805 Whatman's with H. P. or C.P. surface,** select quality, imperial, 22x30 inches, per quire, **$2.75**
Double elephant, 27x40 inches. Per quire ........ **$5.00**
**53806 Whatman's with R. surface,** selected best quality (Torchon paper). Imperial, 22x30 inches, per quire, **$3.15.** Double elephant, 27x40 inches. Per quire ........ **$5.40**
**53807 Whatman's extra heavy,** with surface as below, selected quality. Imperial, 22x30, H. P., C. P. or R., per quire, **$7.25.** Per sheet ........ **$0.35**
Double elephant, 27x50, C. P. or R., per quire. **$10.75**
Per sheet ........ **$0.50**
**53808 German Drawing Paper,** especially adapted for colleges and schools:

| | | Per quire. |
|---|---|---|
| Cap, | 14x17 inches, | $0.25 |
| Demy, | 15x20 inches, | .40 |
| Medium, | 17x22 inches, | .55 |
| Royal, | 19x24 inches, | .75 |
| Imperial, | 22x30 inches, | 1.00 |
| Double Elephant, | 27x40 inches, | 2.00 |

**53810 "Cream" Drawing Paper.** For description see No. 53815. Double elephant, 27x40 inches; per quire ........ **$2.00**
**53811 Patent Office Bristol Board,** plain, 10x15 inches. Per dozen ........ **$0.50**
**53812 "Ivory White" Bristol Board,** for pen and ink drawings. Per sheet, 20x30 inches ........ **$0.25**
30x40 inches ........ **.40**

## Drawing Paper in Rolls.

**53813 Detail Paper,** cold pressed, is expressly made for drafting purposes, of selected stock, with slightly grained surface. It stands erasing to fair extent, and will take India Ink and pencil well.

| | Per roll of 100 yds. Medium. | Thick. | Per roll of 10 yds. Medium. | Thick. |
|---|---|---|---|---|
| 36 inches wide, | $4.00 | $4.50 | $0.50 | $0.60 |
| 42 inches wide, | 4.50 | 5.50 | .60 | .70 |
| 48 inches wide, | 5.25 | 6.75 | .70 | .80 |
| 54 inches wide, | 6.00 | 8.00 | .80 | 1.00 |

**33814 Cream Drawing Paper** is the finest paper in the market for preliminary and general drawing and sketching. It will stand erasing perfectly, and will take ink, pencil, and water color well. Unlike other papers of similar kind, it will not break in folding. Its cream tint is agreeable to the eye, and will admit of much handling without soiling.

| | Per 100 yds. | Per 50 yds. | Per 25 yds. | Per yd. |
|---|---|---|---|---|
| 21 inches wide, | $ 6.00 | $3.25 | $1.75 | $0.08 |
| 27 inches wide, | 8.00 | 4.25 | 2.25 | .10 |
| 36 inches wide, | 10.50 | 5.50 | 3.00 | .15 |
| 42 inches wide, | 14.25 | 7.50 | 4.00 | .20 |
| 56 inches wide, | 17.50 | 9.25 | 5.00 | .25 |

**53815 "German" Drawing Paper** is a strong white paper, excellent erasing properties, with slightly grained surface, suitable for work in ink, pencil and color.

| | Per 50 yds. | Per 25 yds. | Per yd. |
|---|---|---|---|
| 27 inches wide, | $ 5.60 | $3.00 | $0.15 |
| 36 inches wide, | 7.20 | 4.00 | .20 |
| 42 inches wide, | 8.75 | 4.75 | .24 |
| 62 inches wide, | 14.25 | 7.40 | .35 |

**53817 Eggshell Drawing Paper.** It is made of the best paper stock. Owing to its peculiar surface, drawings made upon it show up most effectively; unsurpassed for perspective drawing and water color work.

| | Per 25 yds. | Per 10 yds. | Per yd. |
|---|---|---|---|
| 36 inches wide, | $6.75 | $2.85 | $0.33 |
| 42 inches wide, | 7.50 | 3.25 | .36 |
| 58 inches wide, | 9.75 | 4.20 | .47 |

**63818 Eggshell Smooth Drawing Paper** is made of the same stock as the preceding and differs from it only in the surface, which is cold pressed or medium smooth.

| | Per 25 yds. | Per 10 yds. | Per yd. |
|---|---|---|---|
| 36 inches wide, | $6.75 | $2.85 | $0.32 |
| 42 inches wide, | 7.50 | 3.25 | .36 |
| 58 inches wide, | 9.75 | 4.20 | .47 |

## Mounted Roll Drawing Papers.

**For maps and other valuable drawings made to last, that should not tear or break by much handling or folding, the following papers mounted on muslin will be best adapted:**

**53820 German Mounted,** the same paper as described under No. 53815.

| | Per 10 yds. | Per yd. |
|---|---|---|
| 36 inches wide ........ | $ 6.50 | $0.80 |
| 42 inches wide ........ | 7.30 | .90 |
| 56 inches wide ........ | 10.25 | 1.20 |

**53821 Egg-shell Mounted,** the same paper as described under No, 53817.

| | Per 10 yds. | Per yd, |
|---|---|---|
| 36 inches wide ........ | $ 7.85 | $1.00 |
| 42 inches wide ........ | 8.85 | 1.10 |
| 58 inches wide ........ | 11.75 | 1.40 |

**53824 Eggshell Smooth Mounted,** the same paper as described under No. 53818.

| | Per 10 yds, | Per yd. |
|---|---|---|
| 36 inches wide ........ | $ 7.85 | $1.00 |
| 42 inches wide ........ | 8.85 | 1.10 |
| 58 inches wide ........ | 11.75 | 1.40 |

## Tracing Cloth and Tracing Paper.

**53826 "Imperial," or Universal Tracing Cloth,** one side glazed, the other dull.

| | Per roll of 24 yds. | Per yd. |
|---|---|---|
| 30 inches wide ........ | $ 6.90 | $0.35 |
| 36 inches wide ........ | 7.60 | .40 |
| 42 inches wied ........ | 10.50 | .50 |

**53827 Tracing Parchment,** a strong transparent "German" paper for pencil or ink. Size, 20x30; per sheet, **5c**; per quire, **85c.** Size 30x40, per sheet, **10c;** per quire ........ **$1.80**
**53828 Detail Tracing Paper for Pencil,** 40 in. wide. Per roll 100 yards, 40 in, wide, **$2.50;** 48 in. wide ........ **$3.25**
**53829 Bond Drawing and Tracing Paper,** 42 in. wide. Per roll 50 yards, **$4.95;** per yard ........ **$0.15**
**53830 "Natural" Tracing Paper,** unglazed; the best for detail or full size tracings; 54 in. wide. Per roll of 44 yards, **$5;** per roll of 22 yards ........ **$2.50**
Per yard ........ **0.18**
**53831 "Natural" Tracing and Sketching Paper,** 62 in. wide. Per roll of 50 yards ........ **$3.50**
**53832 "Parchment" Tracing Paper,** very fine, medium thick, 37 inches wide. Per roll 20 yds. **$3.25**

## Higgins' Liquid Drawing Inks.

**53834 Higgins' Waterproof Ink,** black. Each ........ **$0.20**
**53836 Higgins' General Ink, black.** Each ........ **$0.20**

## Turck's Diamond Drafting Inks.

**53840 Indelible Black,** mammoth size, 8-ounce bottles. Each ........ **$3.00**
**53841 Indelible Black,** or not Indelible, "8 B" Black for Tracing Cloth and for general use. Extra large, 4-ounce bottles. Each ........ **$1.70**
**53842 Indelible Carmine, Indelible Blue,** extra large size, 4-ounce bottles. Each ........ **$1.50**
**53843 Indelible Green, Indelible Yellow, Indelible Orange, Not Indelible Burnt Sienna.** extra large size, 4-ounce bottles ........ **$1.50**
**53844 Indelible Black, Indelible Carmine, Indelible Blue, Indelible Green, Indelible Yellow, Indelible Orange.** Not Indelible Burnt Sienna for Coloring. Not Indelible "8 B" Black for tracing cloth and for general use. Meidum size, 1-ounce bottles. Each ........ **$0.40**
**53845 Indelible Black. Indelible Carmine, Indelible Blue, Indelible Green, Indelible Yellow, Indelible Orange,** not Indelible Burnt Sienna for coloring, not Indelible "8 B" Black for tracing cloth and for general use. Small size, ½-ounce bottles. Each ........ **$0.20**

## Borman's Celebrated German Indelible Drawing Inks.

**Borman's Indelible Inks are specially adapted for mechanical drawing.** The lines drawn with these colors are indelible and will not blur or be defaced by frequently applied brush tints, nor by exposure in outdoor work.

**53850 Liquid Indelible Drawing Ink,** black, brown, blue, green, scarlet, carmine. or yellow. Each ........ **$0.25**

## Chinese or India Ink.

**53852 Black,** oval, polished, 2½ inch. Price ........ **$0.10**
**53853 Lion Head,** black, oval, polished, 3 inch. Price ........ **$0.25**
**53854 Square,** black, super, 2⅜ inch. Price ........ **$0.40**
**53855 Square,** black, super, 3⅝ inch. Price ........ **$0.90**
**53856 Square, blue, Chinese Inks,** about 2¾ inch. Price ........ **$0.50**
**53857 Square, red, Chinese Inks,** about 2¾ inch. Price ........ **$0.50**
**53858 Square, yellow, Chinese Inks,** about 2¾ inch. Price ........ **$0.50**

## Don't Fail to Preserve this Catalogue

IT WILL BE OF SERVICE TO YOU LATER, IF YOU ARE NOT READY TO BUY NOW.

REMEMBER—OUR CATALOGUES ARE ISSUED REGULARLY IN MARCH AND SEPTEMBER.

## Ink and Color Slabs.

**53860 Slate Inkstone,** 5 in. with heavy glass cover. Price ........ **$0.45**
**53861 Slate Inkstone, 3½ in.** with heavy glass cover. Price ........ **$0.30**
With these stones the ink can be quickly and uniformly ground, the slate surface is smooth, but not polished. The deep well in the center gathers the ink, and makes it more convenient for filling the pen.
**53863 Patent Ink Slab,** with cover 2⅛x5⅛ inches. Price ........ **$0.50**
**53865 Patent Ink Slab,** with cover 1¾x4½ inches. Price ........ **$0.35**

**53867 Faber's Drawing Pencils.** Siberian. Nos. 1 to 6. Each ........ **$0.13**
Per doz. ........ **$1.20**

**53869 Faber's Siberian Artists' Pencils,** with movable lead, Nos. 6H, 3H, 2H, HF, B and BB. Each ........ **$0.30**
**53871 Faber's Siberian Artists' Pencil,** with single point. Each ........ **$0.20**

**53873 Faber's Siberian Artists' Leads** for artists' pencil. 6 leads in box. Per box ........ **$0.55**

## L. & C. Hardtmuth's Lead Pencils.

L. & C. Hardtmuth are the oldest and largest pencil manufacturers in the world.

**53874 "Koh-i-Noor,"** Nos. B, HB, F, H, 2H, 3B, 4H, 5H, 6H. Every dozen done up separately in a box. Per doz ........ **$1.25**

By a new process of manufacture the graphite assumes a highly compressed form, which secures for it remarkable lasting qualities, the pencil point remaining sharp for a surprisingly long time. For the draftsman and others, where the preservation of a fine point is of importance, the Koh-i-noor pencils and leads will be found invaluable.

**53875 Hardtmuth's red hexagon,** Nos. B, HB, F, H, 2H, 3H, 4H. Per doz ........ **$0.75**
**53876 Artists' Pencil,** with Koh-i-Noor lead, double pointed. Each ........ **$0.35**
**53877 Artists' Pencil,** with Koh-i-Noor lead, single pointed. Each ........ **$0.25**
**53878 Koh-i-Noor leads,** 6 in box, Nos. HB, 4H, 6H. Per box ........ **$0.65**
**53879 L. & C. Hardtmuth's red and blue combination pencils.** Per doz ........ **$0.75**

## Erasers.

**53880 A perfect rubber eraser,** Tower's Multiplex, specially prepared for draftsmen and the accountant.

| Size. | | Per lb. | Each. |
|---|---|---|---|
| 2¾x¾x¾ | Oblong, 12 to lb. | $2.50 | $0.25 |
| 2½x⅝x⅝ | Oblong, 20 to lb. | 2.50 | .15 |
| 2x9-16x½ | Oblong, 30 to lb. | 2.50 | .10 |
| 1½x½x7-16 | Oblong, 60 to lb. | 2.50 | .05 |

## Steel Pens for Drawing.

**53882 Gillott's Crow Quills,** on cards with Holder.
**Per card of one doz. $0.60**

**53884 Gillott's mapping pens,** on cards, with holder. Per card of one doz., **$0.60**
**53886 Gillott's lithographic pens,** on cards, with holder. Per card of one doz ........ **$0.60**

SPORTING GOODS DEPARTMENT SHOWS CONPLETE ASSORTMENT OF GUNS AND HUNTING SUPPLIES, FISH RODS AND SUNDRIES, BASE BALL GOODS AND EVERY CONCEIVABLE KIND ON SUPPLIES FOR OUT-OF-DOOR SPORT.

## The Sketchette.

An Instrument based on thoroughly scientific **principles** that will enable anyone to **draw or paint a picture.** It is in use by many of the leading artists in the United States and Canada. Has been adopted by the German army for sketching fortifications and is invaluable to the amateur. With the **Sketchette** anyone can successfully sketch, in any size, draw in pencil, crayon, or paint in colors anything visible in nature or still life, in exact reproduction of figure, form or color.

**Objects, Pictures, Views from Nature,** or anything that can be seen, can be reflected on any kind of working material and focused any size desired. The reflection will be absolutely perfect. All that that is required of the operator is to fill in the outlines and go over the colors (simply fixing the reflection on the working material), thereby obtaining a faithful reproduction of the subject, true perspectives in line and color and perfect in every detail. A result which would be impossible to accomplish by any other means.

**CHINA AND TAPESTRY PAINTING.**—For Oils, Water-colors, Crayons, Pastels, China and Tapestry Painting, anyone can make their own enlargements or reductions and use anything as a subject, as reproductions, books, flowers, animals, clippings from a magazine or a scene from nature. Color as well as form will appear on the working material.

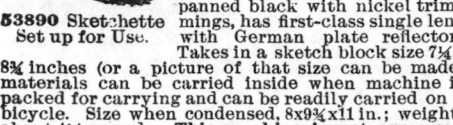

**53890 Sketchette.** In designing this machine our object was to produce a first-class sketching device of neat appearance, that would pack compact, be perfectly light proof, weigh little, of almost indestructible nature. All these qualities are combined in this machine. The body is constructed of well seasoned wood, with dove-tailed or glued corners and securely nailed where needed, is covered with best quality of English book cloth imitation black grained levant morocco leather, has solid leather sliding strap handles, metal parts are japanned black with nickel trimmings, has first-class single lens with German plate reflector.

**53890 Sketchette** Set up for Use.

Takes in a sketch block size 7¼x 8¾ inches (or a picture of that size can be made) materials can be carried inside when machine is packed for carrying and can be readily carried on a bicycle. Size when condensed, 8x9¾x11 in.; weight, about 4¼ pounds. **This machine is not arranged for making enlargements.** Is best suited for outdoor sketching. Our special price............**$1.75**

**53893 Sketchette.** This instrument is binocular and intended for making larger pictures than No. 1, and for making enlargements and reductions, has a rack and pinion focusing arrangement that adds value to its convenience in adjusting (hand wheel is inside the box). The head can be set at right angles to the position occupied to that while in ordinary sketching, for the purpose of making enlargements, has a first-class single lens secured in position by a rubber washer that forms a rest for pasteboard diaphrams for cutting out the light (to make image appear sharp to the edges), has German plate reflector, body is iron japanned black with nickel trimmings, supporting rod is malleable iron, and nickel-plated; the box it packs in forms the table while in use is made of basswood and polished in the natural wood; size when closed 4x10x17 inches, forms a table size 14x17 inches; for making sketches size 12x14 inches or under and enlargements up to same size; has solid leather sliding strap carrying handle; the curtain is made of black gossamer rubber cloth and is fastened to the head by means of an elastic drawstring, forming a convenient and almost light-proof covering. The hand of the operator is inserted under the cover while sketching; he looks at his work through the hooded aperture in the body. Weight, 7½ lbs. Price............................**$3.00**

**53894 Sketchette.** This instrument has same head, curtain supporting rod, focusing arrangement and handle that No. 53893 has, is very carefully fitted and finished. The carrying case or table is longer and constructed of heavier lumber, is stained imitation walnut, has hard oil finish, rubbed and polished. The table is supported with Dean's improved folding knee tripod (unexcelled for its rigidity) constructed of hard maple and varnished, has japanned iron head with nickel-plated thumbscrew. Makes sketches and enlargements the same as No. 53893. With each instrument is included one of Dean's

improved three-leg folding camp stools, legs are white birch, round, with brass ferrules to prevent splitting, has heaviest quality striped Amoskeag ticking seat with wire cable hemmed in edge and is sufficiently strong to support the heaviest person. The above makes the most complete field for outdoor

sketching ever produced. Camp stool and tripod pack inside of case with ample room for other materials. Weight 9¼ pounds. Price............**$6.00**

**Note**—We do not recommend Nos. 53893–53894 for professional portrait artists as only single lens is used in the instruments.

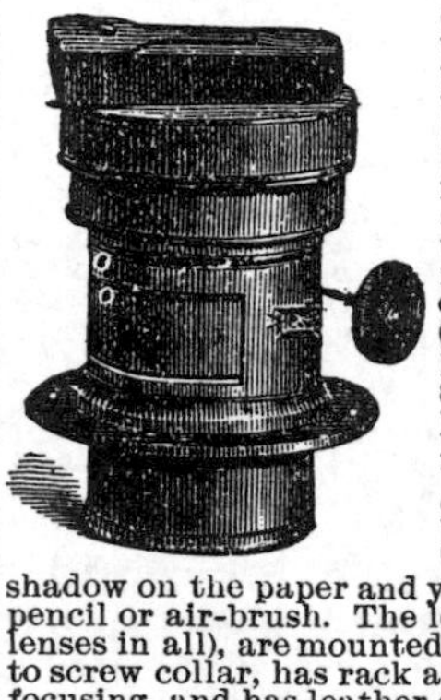

**53896 Lens for Sketchette.** For professional use, is the same in every particular as No. 53894 with the exception of an extra head, lens and window board or box for excluding light from room, while at the same time admitting it to the object to be reflected for the purpose of making enlargements (so necessary in crayon portrait work). This instrument dispenses with the necessity of having to have a "shadow" or a "bromide" made to work over, as is commonly done by crayon portrait artists. The instrument puts the shadow on the paper and you can "fix" it with either pencil or air-brush. The lenses are achromatic (four lenses in all), are mounted in a brass tube, and fitted to screw collar, has rack and pinion adjustment for focusing, and has leather cap (no diaphrams go with lens). Is imported from France and one of the strongest projecting lenses known, the manufacturer claims that under favorable circumstances it will project an image from diameter of lens to ten feet in diameter. To get good results, the room operated in must be absolutely without light when the lens is capped, all light entering room must come through the lens. The copy to be reflected must be lit up with a strong sunlight. The window board or box is made adjustable so it will fit any ordinary window and by drawing down the roller shade (commonly on windows) to edge of board, the room can be darkened, if not sufficient, hang some light proof substance over the curtain to get the desired result. If the object to be reflected is six inches long and the screen to receive it is two feet behind the lens it will be enlarged to twice the size, or at that ratio as the screen is run back from lens.

Price ..................................... **$15.00**

## Enamels.

**53900 Ready Mixed Liquid Enamels** in gold, silver and illuminum for all kinds of artistic and decorative painting and gilding, especially deirable for fancy glassware, photograph frames and artistic work. Can be washed with soap, will not rub off or tarnish, dries perfectly hard in one hour forming a smooth ivory like surface, put up in two ounce cans.

Each 13c; per doz......................**$1.35**
By mail 5 cents extra.

**53901 Wythe's Brilliant Enamel Gloss,** ready for instant use, can be used for painting vases, chairs, table furniture, baskets, etc.; dries perfectly hard in one hour, forming an ivory like surface. New beautiful and delicate shades put up in 4 oz. cans: white, black, green, blue, maroon, orange. indian red, scarlet and yellow. In ordering always specify color wanted.

Price per can 25c; per doz......................**$2.10**

**53902 Japanese Gold Ink,** for corresponding, decorating, etc.; a beautiful gold ink which writes fluently with common steel pen, put up in ½ ounce bottles. Per bottle 9c; per doz..........**95c**

## Artists' Material.

**53905 Finely Prepared Colors for Artists.** "Our tube paints are prepared from carefully selected pigments. The system employed in their manufacture is such that it secures that firm consistency and fineness of texture required by artists. Put up in collapsible tubes, price each....................**5c**
Per dozen ...................................**53c**
In ordering always specify colors wanted.

| | |
|---|---|
| American Vermillion, | Lamp Black, |
| Antwerp Blue, | Light Red, |
| Asphaltum, | Light Raw Sienna, |
| Bistre, | Magenta, |
| Bitumen, | Meglip, |
| Black Leaf, | Mummy, |
| Blue Black, | Naples Yellow, 00-E P, |
| Bone Brown, | Naples Yellow, 0-P. |
| Brilliant Yellow, | Naples Yellow, No. 1, |
| Brown Ochre, | light, |
| Brown Pink, | Naples Yellow, No, 2, |
| Buant Umber, | medium, |
| Burnt Roman Ochre, | Naples Yellow, No.3, deep, |
| Burnt Sienna, | Neutral·Tint, |
| Burnt Terre Verte, | New Blue, |
| Caledonian Brown, | Olive Lake, |
| Cappah Brown, | Olive Tint, |
| Cassel Earth, | Orpiment, |
| Cork Black, | Oxford Ochre, |
| Copal Meglip, | Paris Blue, |
| Chrome Green No. 0-9. | Paris Green, |
| Chrome Green No. 1, light, | Payne's Grey, |
| Chrome Green No. 2, | Permanent Blue, |
| medium, | Permanent Yellow, |
| Chrome Green No. 3, deep, | Permanent White, |
| Chrome Yellow, No. 1, | Permanent Green, light, |
| light, | Permanent Green, medi'm, |
| Chrome Yellow, No. 2, | Permanent Green, deep, |
| medium, | Persian Red, |
| Chrome Yellow, No. 3 | Prussian Blue, |
| deep, | Prussian Brown, |
| Chrome Orange, | Purple Lake, |
| Chrome Red, | Raw Sienna, |
| Cologne Earth, | Raw Umber, |
| China White, | Red Brown, |
| Chinese Blue, | Roman Ochre, |
| Cremnitz White, | Rome's Yellow, |
| Crimson Lake, | Scarlet Lake, |
| Emerald Green, | Silver White, |
| Flake white. | Sugar of Lead, |
| French Green, | Transparent Gold Ochre. |
| French Naples Yellow, | Terra Rosa. |
| Flesh Ochre, | Terre Verte, |
| Geranium Lake, | Vandyke Brown, |
| Gamboge, | Venetian Red, |
| Gold Ochre, | Ferdigris, |
| Greenish Naples Yellow, | Verona Brown, |
| Indian Lake, | Veronese Green, |
| Indian Red, | Yellow Lake, |
| Indigo, | Yellow Ochre, |
| Italian Pink, | Zinc White, |
| Ivory Black, | Zinnober Green, light. |
| Kings Yellow, | |

### Special Colors.

**53907.**

| | |
|---|---|
| Blue Verditer, | English Vermilion, |
| Brown Madder, | French Vermilion, |
| Burnt Lake, | Gaude Lake, |
| Cornation Lake, | Green Lake, |
| Cerulean Blue, | Imperial Orange, |
| Chinese Green, | Perfect Yellow, |
| Chinese Vermilion, | Ruben's Madder, |
| Citron Yellow, | Sepia. |

Per tube............12c; Per dozen..............**$1.20**

### American Vermilion.

**53909**      **Double size Tubes.**

| | |
|---|---|
| Antwerp Blue, | Light Red, |
| Asphaltum, thick, | Magenta, |
| Bitumen, | Mauve, |
| Black Lead, | Mauve No. 2, |
| Bone Brown, | Medium Imp. Meglip, |
| Brilliant Yellow, | Meglip, |
| Brown Ochre, | Mummy, |
| Brown Pink, | Naples Yellow, French |
| Burnt Roman Ochre, | Naples Yellow, |
| Burnt Sienna, | Neutral Tint, |
| Caledonian Brown, | New Blue, |
| Cappah Brown, | Nottingham White, |
| Cassel Earth, | Olive Lake. |
| Chinese Blue, | Orpiment, |
| Chrome Yellow, No. 1, | Oxford Ochre, |
| Chrome Yellow, No. 2, | Papne's Gray, |
| Chrome Yellow, No. 3, | Permanent Blue, |
| Chrome Yellow, | Permanent White. |
| Chrome, deep, | Permanent Yellow, |
| Chrome, Lemon, | Prussian Blue, |
| Chrome, Orange, | Prussian Brown, |
| Chrome, Red, | Purple Lake, |
| Cinnebar, Green-light, | Pyne's Meglip, |
| Cinnebar, Green-medium, | Raw Sienna, |
| Cinnebar, Green-deep, | Raw Unber. |
| Cologne Earth, | Roman Ocher, |
| Cool Roman Ochre, | Sap Green. |
| Copal Meglip, | Scarlet Lake, |
| Cork Black, | Silver White, |
| Cremnitz White, | Sugar of Lead, |
| Crimson Lake, | Terra Rosa, |

| | |
|---|---|
| Emerald Green, | Terra Verta, |
| Flake White, | Transparent Gold Ochre, |
| Gamboge, | Vandyke Brown, |
| Indian Red, | Venetian Red, |
| Indigo, | Verdigris, |
| Italian Pink, | Verona Brown, |
| Ivory Black, | Yellow Lake, |
| King's Yellow, | Yellow Ochre, |
| Lamp Black, | Zinc White. |

Per tube..........15c, Per dozen..........**$1.20**

## Special Colors.

**53910** **Single Tube, No. B.**

| | |
|---|---|
| Brown Madder, | Geranium Lake, |
| Burnt Lake, | Indian Lake, |
| Cerulean Blue, | Rembrandt's Madder, |
| Chinese Vermilion, | Ruben's Madder, |
| Chinese Green, | Sepia |
| French Vermilion, | Vermillion. |

Per tube..........20c; Per dozen..........**$1.90**

**53912** **Single Tubes, No. C.**

| | |
|---|---|
| Brilliant Ultramarine, | Mars Red, |
| Carmine No. 2, | Mars Violet, |
| Citron Yellow, | Mars Yellow, |
| Cobalt Blue, | Mineral Gray, |
| Extra Malachite Green, | Orange-Vermilion, |
| Extract of Vermilion, | Oxide of Chromium, |
| French Ultramarine, | Oxide of Chromium, trans. |
| French Veronese Green, | Pink Madder. |
| Indian Yellow, | Purple Madder, |
| Lemon Yellow, Pale, | Rose Madder, |
| Lemon Yellow, | Scarlet Vermilion, |
| Madder Lake, | Strontian Yellow, |
| Malachite Green, | Scarlet Madder, |
| Mars Brown, | Viridian. |
| Mars Orange, | |

Per tube..........30c; Per dozen..........**$3.00**

## Winsor & Newton's Water Colors in Cakes.

**53913** **Half Cakes.**

| | |
|---|---|
| Antwerp Blue, | Orange Chrome, |
| Bistre, | Payne's Grey, |
| Blue Black, | Prussian Blue, |
| British Ink, | Prussian Green, |
| Brown Ochre, | Raw Sienna, |
| Brown Pink, | Raw Umber, |
| Bronze, | Red Lead, |
| Burnt Sienna, | Roman Ochre, |
| Burnt Umber, | Sap Green. |
| Chinese White, | Terre Verte, |
| Chrome Yellow, | Vandyke Brown, |
| Cologne Earth, | Venetian Red, |
| Chrome, Deep, | Vermilion, |
| Dragon's Blood, | Yellow Lake, |
| Emerald Green. | Yellow Ochre. |

Half cakes, per dozen..........**$1.45**

**Whole Cakes.**

| | |
|---|---|
| Flake White, | Gamboge, |
| Hooker's Green No. 1, | Hooker's Green No. 2, |
| Indigo, | Italian Pink, |
| Indian Red, | King's Yellow, |
| Ivory Black, | Light Red, |
| Lamp Black, | Neutral Tint, |
| Naples Yellow, | New Blue, |
| Olive Green. | |

Whole cakes, per dozen..........**$2.30**

## French Water Colors on Card Board Palettes.

**53914** Oval, 12 colors with brush..........**10c**
**53915** Oval metalic surface, 6 colors..........**15c**
**53916** Square imitation light porcelain, 12 large olors..........**45c**

## French Water Colors in Boxes.

**53917** White wood, sliding cover, containing 12 whole cakes and 4 plain cups. Price, each.....**$0.23**
Per dozen..........**2.40**

**53918** Containing 12 whole cakes, 2 gilt cups and color crayons in imitation satin wood polished box, hinge lid. Price..........**40c**

**53919** Mahogany polished box with tray, lock, hinged lid, containing 18 half cakes, 4 gilt cups, colors, crayons and sundries. Price..........**$1.40**

**53920** Inlaid in plush mahogany case with hinged lid, tray, lock, containing 18 half cakes, one whole cake each Sepia, Carmine and India Ink, 4 gilt cups, color crayons and sundries. Price..........**$2.00**

**53921** Handsome finished wood, brass inlaid, name plate with hinged lid, tray lock, 2 hexigon whole cakes Indian ink, 4 jars moist colors, gold and silver, cups, water glass, cabinet nest with saucers, crayons, charcoal stumps and sundries. Price..........**$8.00**

## Acme Transparent Water Colors.

**53924 For Coloring and Painting Photographs, portraits**, on all kinds of paper, views, lantern, slides, transparencies, engravings, artotypes and prints of all kinds, also tapestry, Paris tinting, and all kinds of dye or fabric painting, in large tin boxes with palettes, containing Chinese White, Brown, Madder, Carmine, Dark Green, New Rose, Flesh, New Violet, Dark Brown, Pink Madder, Blue Black, Blue Grey, Deep Yellow, Scarlet, Gold and Deep Blue. Price each..........**$2.50**

**53925 Containing Deep Blue, Flesh, Deep Yellow, Dark Brown, Scarlet and Chinese White.** Instructions with each box.
Small boxes, price each..........**$1.00**

## Water Color Box.

**53926 A Perfect Box and Outfit for Moist Colors, Japanned tin, 7½ inch x 10½ inch x 1⅛ inch deep tray, holds 24 whole or 48½ pans moist colors with space beneath for a further supply of colors or other articles, partition for sundries, brush washer, water bottle, brushes, brush holders for protecting the points, space in lid for a 7 inch x 10 inch sketch book. This is the most perfect and complete outfit made and is intended for either out door sketching or studio use.** Price..........**$10.75**

## Tin Palette Cups.

**53927 Japanned**, single without cover, 5c; Japanned, double without cover..........**10c**
**53928 Japanned**, with brass screw, 15c; Japanned, with tin hinged cover..........**15c**

## Palette Knives.

**53929 Artists' Palette Knife with Fine Ebony Handle**, 3 inches long..........**20c**
Artists' Palette Knife with fine ebony handle 3½ inches long..........**20c**
Artists' Palette Knife with fine ebony handle 4 inches long..........**25c**
**53930 Artists' Pocket Palette Knife with Pearl Handle**..........**$1.10**
Artists' Pocket Palette Knife with Ivory handle..........**75c**

## French Varnishes Preparations, etc

**53931 Soehnees' Retouching Varnish No. 2**, for water colors. Per bottle..........**18c**
**53932 Soehnees' Retouching Varnish**, for oil painting. Per bot..........**18c**

## Devoe's Artist Oils, Varnishes, Etc.

**53933 Linseed Oil**, purified, 2 oz bot. Each.**10c**
**53934 Siccatif De Harlem**, 2 oz. bot. Each..**25c**
**53935 Pale Drying Oil**, 2 oz. bot. Each......**13c**
**53936 Siccatif De Cambrai**, 2 oz bot. Each..**15c**
**53937 Spirits of Turp.**, rectified, 2 oz. bot. Each..........**10c**
**53938 Fixatif**, 2 oz bot. Each..........**18c**
**53939 Ebony Beach**, 2 oz. bot. Each..........**18c**
**53940 Picture Mastic Varnish**, 2 oz. bot. Each**25c**
**53941 White Damar Varnish**, 2 oz. bot. Each**18c**
**53942 French Varnish**, 2 oz. bot. Each.....**18c**
**53943 Retouching Varnish**, 2 oz. bot. Each.**18c**
**53944 Japan Solid Size**, 2 oz. bot. Each.....**18c**
**63945 Nut Oil**, 2 oz. bot. Each..........**18c**
**53946 Poppy Oil**, 2 oz. bot. Each..........**15c**

**53951 Devoe's Prepared Sketching Canvas. Best English Linen.**

| Size. | Each. | Size. | Each. |
|---|---|---|---|
| 8x10, smooth...... | **$0.30** | 18x30, smooth...... | **$0.90** |
| 9x15, smooth...... | **.40** | 22x36, smooth...... | **1.15** |
| 12x24, smooth...... | **.50** | 40x54, smooth...... | **3.00** |
| 16x28, smooth...... | **.60** | | |

**53952 Devoe's Prepared Sketching Canvas, in rolls of 6 yards.**
Size, 28 inches wide, smooth, per roll..........**$2.35**
Size, 31 inches wide, smooth, per roll..........**2.70**
Size, 42 inches wide, smooth, per roll..........**3.15**

**53953 Pastel Canvas, six yards in roll.**
31 inches wide, per roll of 6 yards..........**$ 6.00**
37 inches wide, per roll of 6 yards..........**7.90**
42 inches wide, per roll of 6 yards..........**10.50**

## Drawing Copy Books.

**53954 Vere Foster's Water Colored Copy Books**—On landscape painting for beginners, teaching the use of one color, outlining, and how to sketch properly, with full instructions in the use of the brush, etc. Price..........**70c**
**Postage extra, 10c.**

**53955 Extra soft Pastel Crayons**, 1 dozen assorted shades. Packed in a wooden box.

| | | |
|---|---|---|
| **GREYS.** | | |
| Deep Grey.......... | Nos. 1, 2, or 3..........box, | $0.50 |
| Light Grey.......... | 1, 2, 3, 4, 5 or 6...... | .50 |
| Yellow Grey.......... | 1, 2, 3, 4, or 5.......... | .50 |
| **BROWNS.** | | |
| Burnt Umber.......... | Nos. 1, .. 3, 4, 5, 6 or 7....box, | $0.50 |
| Burnt Sienna.......... | 1, 2, 3, 4, 5, 6, 7 or 8.. | .50 |
| Italian Earth.......... | 1, 2, 3 or 4.......... | .50 |
| Purple Brown.......... | 1, 2, 3. 4, 5 or 6.......... | .50 |
| Raw Umber.......... | 1, 2, 3. 4. 5, 6 or 7.... | .50 |
| Red Brown.......... | 1, 2, 3. 4, 5 or 6.......... | .50 |
| Vandyke Brown.......... | 1, 2. 3 or 4.......... | .50 |
| **BLUES.** | | |
| Indigo.......... | Nos. 1, 2, 3, 4, 5, 6 or 7....box, | $0.50 |
| Prussian Blue.......... | 1, 2, 3, 4, 5, 6 or 7.... | .50 |
| Ultramarine.......... | 1, 2, 3, 4, 5 or 6...... | .50 |
| Cobalt.......... | 1.......... | 2.00 |
| **GREENS.** | | |
| Deep Chrome.......... | Nos. 1, 2, 3, 4, 5 or 6.....box, | $0.50 |
| Deep Blue Green.... | 1, 2, 3 or 4.......... | .50 |
| Emerald Green.......... | 1, 2, 3, 4, 5 or 6....... | .50 |
| Emeraude Green..... | 1, 2, 3, 4 or 5.......... | .50 |
| Light Chrome Green. | 1, 2, 3, 4, 5 or 6....... | .50 |
| Olive Green.......... | 1, 2, 3, 4, 5, 6 or 7.... | .50 |
| Terre Verte.......... | 1. 2. 2, 4, 5, 6 or 7.... | .50 |
| Viridian.......... | 1, 2, 3, 4, 5 or 6....... | .50 |
| Yellow Green.......... | 1, 2, 3, 4, 5, 6 or 7.... | .50 |

## French Stomps, for Crayon Shading.

**53957**

| **YELLOW LEATHER.** | | **GREY PAPER.** | |
|---|---|---|---|
| No. 1..........each, | $0.07 | No. 1..........each, | $0.02 |
| 2.......... | .08 | 2.......... | .03 |
| 3.......... | .09 | 3.......... | .05 |
| 4.......... | .10 | 4.......... | .05 |
| 5.......... | .12 | 5.......... | .06 |
| 6.......... | .14 | 6.......... | .07 |
| 7.......... | .16 | 7.......... | .08 |
| 8.......... | .18 | 8.......... | .09 |

Tortillon Stomps, White..........per doz., $0.10
" " Grey.......... " .08

## SEND YOUR ORDERS TO US

**FOR ANYTHING IN THE LINE OF PERSONAL OR HOUSEHOULD SUPPLIES. IF WE DON'T PLEASE YOU, WILL REFUND MONEY. WE GUARANTEE SATISFACTION.**

**53959 Artist's Prussia Sable Brushes** for oil painting, polished handles, nickel-plated ferrules; round and flat.

| | | | |
|---|---|---|---|
| No. 1. | Price, each.....5c | No. 7. | Price, each.....7c |
| No. 2. | Price, each.....5c | No. 8. | Price, each.....7c |
| No. 3. | Price, each.....6c | No. 9. | Price, each.....8c |
| No. 4. | Price, each.....7c | No. 10. | Price, each.....8c |
| No. 5. | Price, each.....7c | No. 11. | Price, each.....9c |
| No. 6. | Price, each.....7c | No. 12. | Price, each.....10c |

## Bristle Brushes.

**53960 Artist's "English" Bristle Brushes**, for oil painting. Red polished handles, tin ferrules, round and flat.

| | | | |
|---|---|---|---|
| No. 1. | Price, each.....4c | No. 7. | Price, each.....6c |
| No. 2. | Price, each.....4c | No. 8. | Price, each.....7c |
| No. 3. | Price, each.....5c | No. 9. | Price, each.....7c |
| No. 4. | Price, each.....5c | No. 10. | Price, each.....7c |
| No. 5. | Price, each.....5c | No. 11. | Price, each.....8c |
| No. 6. | Price, each.....5c | No. 12. | Price, each.....9c |

**53962 DeVoe's Special Artists' Superfine Bristle Brushes for Oil Painting.**
**STYLE B**, double pointed, affording a peculiar touch when pressed laterally on the canvas. Price..........**20c**
**STYLE C**, in 3 parts, to prevent the color from accumulating and clogging the bottom of the brush. Price..........**20c**
**STYLE D**, with a long feathery edge, affording a sweeping touch. Price..........**20c**
**STYLE E**, short wedged shape. Price..........**20c**
**STYLE G**, long and perfectly straight hair, having a good spring, enabling square touches to be placed with accuracy. Price..........**20c**
**STYLE K**, chiseled edge. Price..........**20c**
**STYLE L**, long, elastic and thin edge, with soft flag, suitable for foliage. Price..........**20c**

**53963 Camel Hair Lacquering Brushes**, round polished handles, tin ferrules.
No. 1 each **05c** No. 3 each **07c** No. 5 each **10c**
No. 2 each **06c** No. 4 each **08c** No. 6 each **12c**

**53965 Extra Fine Sable Brushes**, for water color painting, polished handles, round and flat; albata ferrules.
No. 0 each **30c** No. 2 each **33c** No. 5 each **40c**
No. 1 each **30c** No. 4 each **33c** No. 6 each **50c**

**53967 Extra Fine Sable Brushes** for oil painting, firm square touching, and general landscape work, polished handles, nickel plated ferrules.

| | | | |
|---|---|---|---|
| No. 1, each.......... | **$0.08** | No. 6, each.......... | **$0.15** |
| No. 2, each.......... | **.09** | No. 7, each.......... | **.19** |
| No. 3, each.......... | **.10** | No. 8, each.......... | **.25** |
| No. 4, each.......... | **.12** | No. 9, each.......... | **.35** |
| No. 5, each.......... | **.14** | | |

**53968 Leather Board Plaques.** For oil painting.
5 inches in diameter. Each..........**12c**
6 inches in diameter. Each..........**17c**
7 inches in diameter. Each..........**25c**
8 inches in diameter. Each..........**27c**
9 inches in diameter. Each..........**33c**
10 inches in diameter. Each..........**40c**
12 inches in diameter. Each..........**45c**
14 inches in diameter. Each..........**57c**
16 inches in diameter. Each..........**65c**

**23969 Frosted Porcelain Plaques, Opal, White.**
5 inches in diameter, each..........**$0.22**
6 inches in diameter, each..........**.34**
7 inches in diameter, each..........**.37**
8 inches in diameter, each..........**.43**
9 inches in diameter, each..........**.53**
10 inches in diameter, each..........**.65**
11 inches in diameter, each..........**.75**
12 inches in diameter, each..........**.85**
13 inches in diameter, each..........**1.15**
14 inches in diameter, each..........**1.35**

**53970 Celluloid.** Each size, 20x50 inches.
White, No. 44 AG, polished one side. Per sheet, **$1.30**
White, No. 44 AS, polished two sides. Per sheet, **1.50**

**53971 Celluloid**, pink, No. 405, polished one side. Per sheet..........**$1.30**

**53972 Celluloid**, cream, yellow, green, blue, red, tortoise, mottled, each polished on one side. Per sheet..........**$1.35**

**53973 Celluloid**, silk finish, pink, blue, or yellow. Per sheet..........**$1.90**

**53974 Celluloid**, transparent, silk finish. Red or blue. Per sheet..........**$2.10**

## Tracing Papers.

**53975 French Vegetable, Extra Fine.**
Size 13x17 inches, per sheet..........**$0.04**
Size 14x19 inches, per sheet..........**.05**
Size 15x20 inches, per sheet..........**.06**
Size 18x22 inches, per sheet..........**.07**
Size 19x24 inches, per sheet..........**.08**
Size 22x28 inches, per sheet..........**.10**
Size 24x34 inches, per sheet..........**.15**
Size 26x40 inches, per sheet..........**.25**

## Transfer Papers.

**53976 In Blue, Black, Green, Red, Yellow, Purple, and White.** Each size 11x18 inches. Per sheet, **5c**

**53977 Peerless Tracing.** Paper in rolls 40 inches wide, 22 yards long; tough and transparent. Per roll, 2.50; Per yard..........**20c**

**53978 Parchment Tracing Paper**, 38 inches wide, 22 yards long. Per roll, **$3.75**; per yard..........**23c**

## Utility Easels

The following Utility Easel will accommodate various sizes of stretched canvass. It has an auxiliary frame to hold the canvass which can be adjusted in any angle, either to the rear, upright or inclined to the front, so that the most desirable position can be obtained, according to the character of the work. This is a very useful easel in tapestry painting.

**53979** Utility, pine wood, 6 feet 3 inches high. Price..........**$ 6.25**

**WHEN YOU SEND YOUR ORDERS DON'T FORGET THAT WE MUST HAVE SUCH INFORMATION AS WILL BE NECESSARY TO DETERMINE JUST WHAT YOU WANT.**

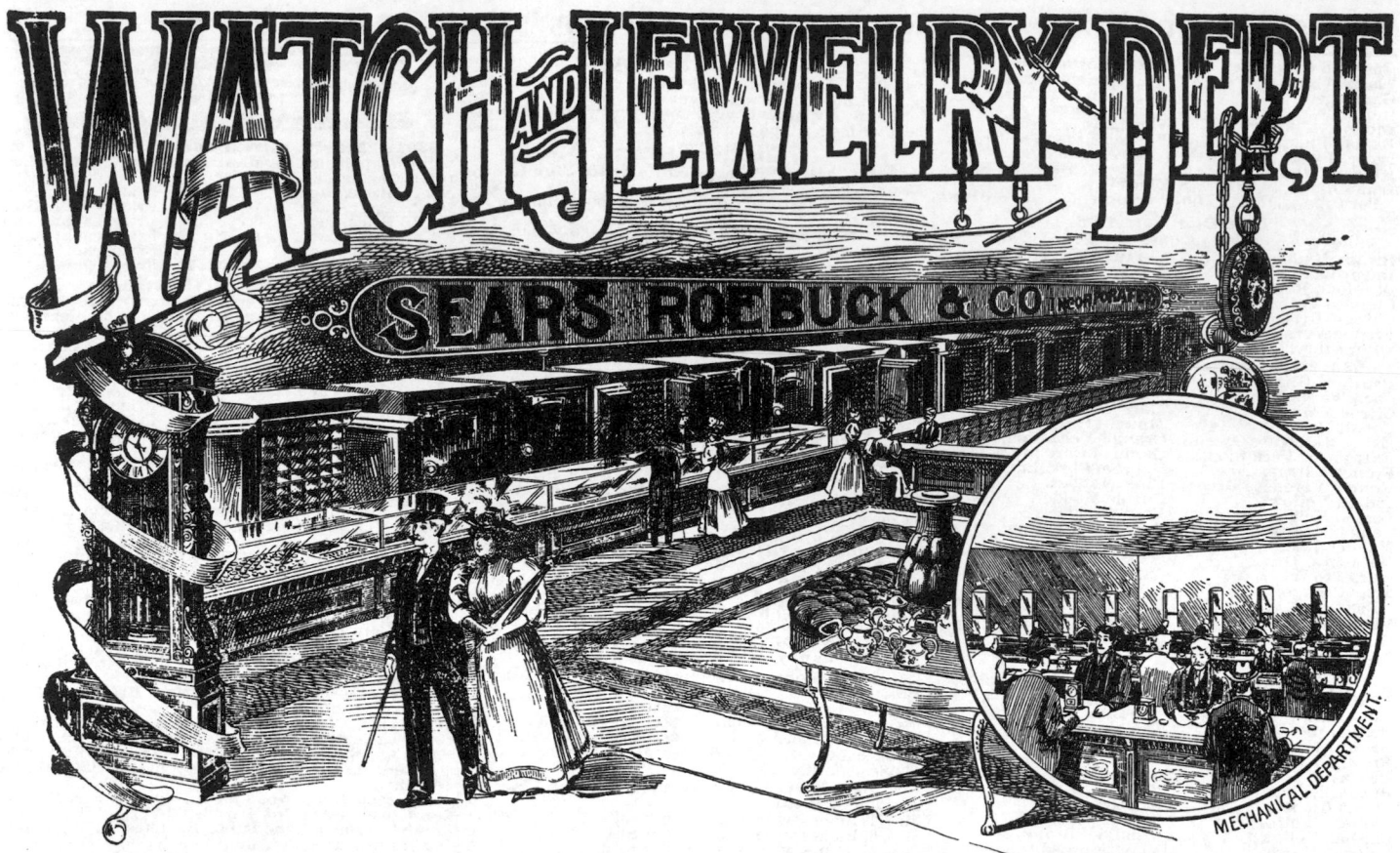

MECHANICAL DEPARTMENT.

# WATCH AND JEWELRY DEPARTMENT.

**The Watch and Jewelry Department wishes to thank our many customers** for their very liberal patronage during the past year. We are glad to note the increase in the orders for very high grade watches, also a very large increase in the diamond trade, which indicates the appreciation of the higher class of watches and jewelry. Our shipments from the Watch Department throughout the year have averaged several hundred per day. Any one day's shipment would make a very large stock for the average retail jeweler. We think that our customers should be able to understand from this that a very small profit on each article sold will satisfy a concern whose aim it is to give the most value they possibly can for the money. We have undertaken to describe every article in the catalogue exactly as it is and to fill every order exactly according to description. By so doing our customers are always satisfied; in fact, it is the only way to retain their good will and constantly increase our trade. **We have devoted three pages** in the beginning of this department to a careful description of the different movements listed, how gold filled cases are made, etc., it being our aim to place our customers in position to decide intelligently what they should have, and know what they will get for their money before they order.

**OUR GUARANTEE.** With every gold filled, silver or solid gold watch, we give a certificate of guaranty. With gold filled watches the certificate guarantees the case to wear and keep its color for fifteen or twenty years, and the movement to be an accurate timekeeper for five years. This guaranty is given in addition to the guaranty which is fitted in the back of the watch case. As to the value of our guaranty, we will refer you to the first page of this book under the head of **OUR RELIABILITY.**

**OUR PRICES.** In watches and jewelry we buy nearly everything direct from the manufacturers in large quantities for spot cash, and as we sell for cash, having no bad debts, we are satisfied to sell at prices which the retailer pays, and on a large per cent of goods for much less money.

**YOU CAN MAKE MONEY** Selling watches, jewelry, silverware, etc., for when you can buy them for the same, or less money, than the retail dealer who sells on from 30 to 100% profit and has large expenses in the way of rent, clerk hire, fuel, light, etc., you can readily see that you could undersell him and still make a handsome profit for yourself.

**DISCOUNTS** For cash with order we allow a discount of 3 per cent. on orders amounting to $50.00 or under. Over $50.00 and under $100.00 4 per cent., on $100.00 and upwards 5 per cent. Do not ask for further discounts on quantities, as the margin of profit is based on the sale of large quantities, whether they be shipped to one or more persons. Our profits are so small that they will not admit of our making any further reduction.

**OUR VERY LIBERAL TERMS** We desire to make our terms of shipment as liberal as possible, consistent with safety and good business principles. Watches, jewelry, diamonds, silverware, clocks and optical goods will be shipped C. O. D. by express when desired, when a deposit of sufficient amount to pay the express charges both ways is sent with the order, the balance to be paid when goods have been received. Goods cannot be sent by mail C. O. D. When to be sent by mail the full amount of cash must accompany the order, also enough to pay postage. Be sure to enclose enough to pay postage, and if any amount remains it will returned to you. When goods are to be shipped C. O. D. we will require deposits as follows:

**AMOUNT OF DEPOSIT REQUIRED** For watches and jewelry 50 cents must accompany the order; for diamonds, optical goods, silverware, clocks and other heavy goods we require $1.00 with the order. Orders for surveyors' instruments must be accompanied by at least $5.00. We never consign goods to be sold on commission, nor do we sell goods on time. Our terms are strictly cash in full with order or C. O. D.

**MAIL SHIPMENTS** We recommend sending jewelry, watches, etc., by mail, as it is perfectly safe and far the cheapest. Postage is 1 cent per ounce. A watch packed for shipment weighs from 6 to 8 ounces; chains, rings and other small articles of jewelry about 2 ounces. Packages amounting to $1.00 or over should be registered, which costs 8 cts. extra. We guarantee the safe delivery of all registered mail packages. Be sure to send enough for postage, and if any balance remains we will return it to you.

**ENGRAVING** We charge for engraving in script on jewelry, watches, etc, 2½ cents per letter; in old English, small, 5 cents per letter; small script monograms on jewelry, etc., from 25c to 75c. Engraving on flat ware such as spoons, forks, etc., in quantities of 6 or more pieces 1½ cents per letter. Jewelry and watches to be engraved cannot be sent C. O. D.; the full amount of cash must accompany the order.

**WATCH REPAIRING** We have a thoroughly equipped Mechanical Department, which is fitted with all of the latest tools and appliances for the repairing of all kinds of watches. We have a large force of thoroughly skilled watch makers under the supervision of a very competent foreman, and any watch sent to us for repairs will command very careful and prompt attention. We do not solicit for watch repair work, but are willing to accommodate our customers who wish to have work done in a thoroughly first class manner. Our charges are about half what is usually charged by the retail dealers, but the work will be done in a very superior manner. We cannot give an accurate estimate of the cost of repairs without a thorough examination. Our charges are merely enough to cover cost of manufacture and labor. None but a thoroughly competent watch maker should ever take a watch to pieces for the chances are that he will ruin it.

# PLAIN TALK FOR YOUR BENEFIT
## WE BEG OF YOU TO READ IT ALL, IT WILL OPEN YOUR EYES.

Throughout this department we have referred in many places to the difference between **our** prices for goods and the prices charged by retailers. We feel that in order to make ourselves thoroughly understood, and to place the matter before our customers in such a manner that they will understand both sides of the question, it is necessary for us to thoroughly canvass the situation and give them a few pointers that will place them in a position to judge for themselves as to the merits of our argument. It is our intention not to make any statement in this catalogue that we cannot fulfill or prove to the entire satisfaction of anyone.

A few years ago such a thing as sending away for goods was almost unknown, but now the custom is becoming so popular that it bids fair to soon be the medium for purchasing the larger portion of goods the consumer uses. Some people, as we are aware, are afraid to send away for goods for fear of being swindled. It is true there are some individuals who advertise in a flashy manner goods which have but little value, using a firm name, and place on their advertising matter a picture of some large building, allowing the customer to draw the conclusion that they occupy the whole of it when probably the truth is they occupy only one or two small rooms. These concerns, however, are little known, and if the customer patronizes only those houses of well-known reputation there is no danger of being deceived.

Retail dealers, however, undertake to convince their customers that all advertising houses will swindle them. We shall take the position of fighting them with their own weapons. We will cut our argument short, but still undertake to give you the points and you can draw your own conclusions.

**The retailer's hobby** is to make himself socially as popular as possible, and if his town supports any secret or other societies he endeavors to make himself an influential member, using at all times the social garb to attract and bring him trade. He wins the confidence of his customers through personal acquaintance, and while he endeavors to sell goods that will give satisfactory results, it does not alter the fact that his customers pay from one-half more to twice what the goods are worth. There is probably no merchant who sells so few articles during the year and makes such large profits as the local jeweler. Step into his store at almost any time and you will find him gossiping with a neighbor merchant, reading the newspaper or both he and his clerks are cleaning up and polishing some of the old shop-worn goods that have been in the house for years, trying to make them look like new.

**A large per cent** of his sales are made **on time,** by reason of which he naturally loses a great deal, as every credit business does by selling on time, and in order to carry as large a stock as possible he is compelled to buy on time, and is almost always in debt to some wholesale house which places him in such a position that he cannot take advantage of a bargain if the market was flooded with them. Neither is his output for goods such as would put him in a position to buy in any quantity.

**In addition** to the losses which the retail dealer is compelled to stand by reason of bad debts, the wholesale houses who sell him have a great deal of the same experience, for every time a merchant fails from one to several wholesale houses lose a considerable amount, and in addition to these losses the wholesale houses have expensive traveling salesmen's salaries and expenses to pay (and many traveling salesmen's salaries and expenses amount to from $5,000.00 to $10,000.00 per year).

As the manufacturer sells to the wholesaler on time, and often wholesale houses fail, he too is subject to loss from that direction. The goods in each case must be sold sufficiently high to meet these losses, as there is a certain number of failures calculated on every year, and this is a strong reason why cash customers can always buy much cheaper than those who buy on time.

His store, in order that he may be successful, must be located on the best part of the best street in the town where the rent is very high; his fuel and lighting expenses are very large, besides clerk hire, care of the store, interest on the investment, profits, his own living (and he usually lives well), all of which must be included. Take into consideration all these expenses, then consider the small number of sales he makes during the year, and you can understand how he must have from 33⅓ to 100 per cent gross profit on every article he sells. If it is not fraud to sell goods for twice what they are worth, it is certainly the next thing to it.

**The proprietor** of such a store in small places usually **poses as a watchmaker,** when the fact probably is he has learned his trade by a service of six months to one year in a jewelry store, running errands and repairing jewelry and clocks. Where the trade is thoroughly learned it is customary to spend one year on jewelry and clocks, and then from two to three years on watches, and even then the person must have natural mechanical ability, and the circumstances must be most favorable in the way of having plenty of watch repair work to do. As only about one watch out of ten needs anything more than a thorough cleaning there is no opportunity for learning the watchmaker's trade in the average retail store short of ten years. Oftentimes you find some one with no previous experience at all collects some tools and starts to work. Do not be deceived even though he may have succeeded in starting someone's watch on which some watchmaker has worked; the chances are that he may not know himself how he did it.

**The watchmaker's trade** cannot be learned in that way. For example, there is a firm in London who will not employ a man as an apprentice until he has had three years of previous experience, and then they require an apprenticeship of five years additional. People who claim to have worked in watch factories, nine times out of ten are not practical workmen, because they know how to make but one part, and that is made by machinery. The kind of watchmakers above referred to usually **ruin every watch they undertake to repair.** We have had expensive high-grade movements returned to us a few months after they were purchased which had been in the hands of such a workman, and we found that the temper had been drawn from the pinions, the leaves of which were full of rust from contact with acids or careless cleaning, the wheels blackened and the temper drawn from the brass, and in fact, the movement in an utterly worthless condition. **Is this not fraud?**

The retailers are constantly **writing to the trade journals** urging upon them the necessity of taking some concerted and combined action in order to prevent the manufacturers from selling goods to us, claiming that it is ruining their business, and that when we are constantly sending advertising matter into their locality, offering goods at the prices they have to pay, and often less, that their trade is being killed. The American Watch Jobbers' Association has even gone so far on several occasions as to order special meetings, and send out orders to the different manufacturers not to sell us. Can you wonder that the dealer is compelled to misrepresent his goods in order to sell them under such circumstances.

In the matter of **taking your watch in exchange** the dealer usually turns a clever trick. He will offer you more for your old watch than it is worth, and you would naturally suppose that he would sell the watch to some one else for the same money, or even more than he allowed you for it. It is a very easy matter for him to allow you a good price for the old watch, for the profit that he has added to the new one is usually so large that after the exchange is made he owns your watch and a good cash profit on the transaction besides. If you are a clever trader you can catch him on this scheme. Ask him what he will allow in cash for your old watch, and if you insist you will find that he is not willing to allow you any more than the metal in the cases is worth, providing you give him no encouragement that you will purchase from him. It is a very exceptional occasion that the old watch taken in exchange is sold again for anything but old metal, and the movement is usually put in the scraps, for which it is of little value. Old gold is worth 56c. per pennyweight for 14 karat, and 40c. per pennyweight for 10 karat. Old silver is worth 56c. per ounce. These are the highest market values, and no one will pay you any more for it unless he is sure of making a sale to you in order to make it back.

## NOW FOR OUR SIDE: 
Our method of getting trade is to give the best goods at lower prices than they can be had elsewhere, and from one-third to one-half less than retail prices. We waste no time waiting for a customer to make a selection, for they do that at home by their own fireside, and when the order comes in the selections are all made, and all that is required for us to do is to take the goods from our stock, see that they are in good condition, make the necessary record, and ship them. Our clerks are as busy as bees from morning till night filling orders in this manner, and the work is so divided as to accomplish the best results. Our goods are not scattered about over valuable space for show, but are kept in regular wholesale style, requiring but little storage room to accommodate immense stocks of goods. Our sales are so large that our stocks are constantly changing from day to day, and even though our 110x170 feet, six stories and basement building is crowded with stock, on an average our entire stock changes often during the year. We buy for cash direct from the manufacturer, and sell for cash; hence, our customers pay for nobody's bad debts. We give the customer the advantage of being able to select from a line which represents everything made that is worthy of notice. Our sales are so large that there are no bankrupt stocks or forced sales that we are not in a position to take advantage of. With nearly 1,000 shipments daily going out from our jewelry department alone, we think you can understand that it takes but a small percentage of profit to satisfy us.

**As to monopolies and trusts** we do not propose to be dictated to by them. We consider it wrong to uphold any action that will cause the consumer to pay more for his goods than they are worth. **Our course is honorable,** and we propose to pursue it to a finish. So long as we are equipped with cash we will have no trouble in buying all the goods we want, and our customers will get them at a very small percentage in advance of what we pay for them.

**We will buy any old gold or silver** that you may wish to dispose of, and will pay you the highest market price either in cash or trade. As to our mechanical department, would say that we have a large force of watchmakers who are every one skilled workmen, and each one is the possessor of a fine set of modern watchmaker's tools. Any work done by any of our workmen is done in such a perfect manner that as a rule even a mechanic cannot detect that the watch has ever been broken, and that is the only way repair work should be done on watches.

We do not cater for repair work, but when our customers want their watches cleaned or repaired we are always glad to accommodate them and do the work in the most thorough manner, and at the lowest wholesale prices, which cover only the cost of material and labor.

**We have given you facts,** and we feel sure that with what we have laid before you you will be in a position to pass a just decision for yourself. Yours for honorable dealing and strict business principles,

# DESCRIPTION OF THE MOVEMENTS WE LIST.

To save space by avoiding repetition we have adopted the following as the best method of describing movements, because we are able to give a more complete and intelligent description than if inserted in a condensed form on each page.

On the following page will be found an explanation of the different terms used.

## WE GUARANTEE FOR FIVE YEARS, ALL THE MOVEMENTS SOLD BY US.

This does not refer to the life of the movement, but that we will for five years from date of purchase, correct free of charge any fault which may occur from defective material or workmanship. Any well made movement will run a life-time if properly cared for.

### DESCRIPTION OF 18 SIZE MOVEMENTS.

**THE "TRENTON"** Movement is made at Trenton, New Jersey, and will be furnished in full plate or ¾ plate, seven jeweled, nickel damaskeened, has compensation balance and patent pinion.

**THE SETH THOMAS** Movements are three-quarter plate, nickel damaskeened, and are quoted in the 7 jeweled grade only. They have safety pinion, compensation balance and are a good reliable movement. They are made by the old reliable Seth Thomas Clock Co., whose reputation for fine clocks is a sufficient guarantee for the quality of the watch movements they make.

**THE SEVEN JEWELED** Waltham, Elgin and Hampden Movements have compensation balance, patent pinions, and are finished in gilt only.

**ELEVEN JEWELED** Elgin and Waltham movements have recently been discontinued by the factories, hence we will be unable to furnish them hereafter. The Hampden Movement is still made in the eleven jeweled grade and can be furnished in nickel only. They have patent pinion, compensation balance, and are damaskeened. The train jewels in this grade are set in the plate instead of settings.

**FIFTEEN JEWELED** Elgin, Waltham and Hampden Movements have compensation balance, patent pinions, patent regulators, and plate jewels in settings. The Waltham and Elgin will be furnished in both gilt and nickel, but list only the nickel grade.

**THE G. M. WHEELER** Elgin Movement is now made with 17 jewels. Until this year it was made only with fifteen jewels. It has safety pinion, train jewels in settings; compensation balance, adjusted, patent Breguet hair spring, patent micrometer regulator and is furnished in either gilt finish or nickel damaskeened. Is stamped on the plate "17 jewels adj."

**THE P. S. BARTLETT** Waltham Movement is now made with 17 jewels; until this year made with fifteen jewels only. The train or plate jewels are in composition settings. It has compensation balance, adjusted patent pinion, patent regulator, and patent Breguet hair spring, hardened and tempered in form, double sunk dial, bright flat screws, and will be furnished in either gilt finish or nickel damaskeened.

**THE APPLETON, TRACY & CO.** Movement is a well known grade of the Waltham which is now made with 17 ruby jewels in gold settings, compensation balance, adjusted to temperature, isochronism and position, with patent regulator, patent Breguet hair spring, hardened and tempered in form, patent pinion and double sunk dial. It is furnished in either gilt finish, or solid nickel beautifully damaskeened.

**THE B. W. RAYMOND** Movement is a grade of the Elgin Watch Co.'s now made with 17 ruby jewels, in fine composition settings. It has compensation balance, adjusted, safety pinion, patent micrometer regulator, patent Breguet hair spring, double sunk dial and is furnished in gilt finish or solid nickel, beautifully damaskeened.

**THE ANCHOR** grade of the Hampden Watch Co., is made with 17 extra fine ruby jewels in solid gold settings, patent micrometer regulator, patent center pinion double sunk dial, compensation balance accurately adjusted, Breguet hair spring, Crescent hands and the Hampden back action main spring. This movement is furnished in solid nickel, beautifully damaskeened.

**THE NEW RAILWAY HAMPDEN** Movement has 17 extra fine ruby jewels in solid gold settings, 14 karat gold patent regulator, compensation balance accurately adjusted to temperature, isochronism and five positions, has Breguet hair spring, patent center pinion, double sunk dial, gilt screws, is solid nickel elegantly engraved and damaskeened, Fleur de Lis hands and the Hampden back action main spring.

**THE NO. 150 ELGIN** is made with 21 fine ruby jewels, compensation balance adjusted to temperature, isochronism and position, escapement cap jeweled, gold settings, patent regulator, Breguet hair spring, safety pinion, glass enameled double sunk dial, solid nickel with gilt letters and ornaments. The above is the latest production of the Elgin Watch Factory in 18 size movements, and has been on the market but about a year. It is a movement built especially to meet the demands of railroad men and others who require a very close time-keeper.

**THE "VANGUARD" WALTHAM** Movement is made with 21 extra fine ruby jewels in raised gold settings, double roller on balance staff, exposed pallets, embossed gold patent micrometer regulator, compensation balance adjusted to temperature, isochronism and position, patent safety barrel, exposed winding wheels, patent Breguet hair spring, hardened and tempered in form, elaborately finished nickel plates with gold letters, plate and jewel screws gilded, steel parts chamfered, double sunk dial. The balance wheel of this movement sets in a recess in the plate so as to make a thinner and better proportioned movement as well as adding very much to the appearance. This is the finest 18 size movement made by the Waltham Watch Company, and is intended to meet the requirements of those who want a very accurate timepiece.

**NON-MAGNETIC WALTHAM** Movements will be furnished in 18 size only at the following additional prices: For the 7 jeweled grade, non-magnetic, add $2.50 to the regular price. For the Crescent Street add $5.00. For the Vanguard add $5.00. A special grade 15 jeweled nickel, adjusted to temperature, isochronism and position, will be furnished for $7.00 more than the Bartlett.

**THE HAMPDEN SPECIAL RAILWAY** Movement is nickel, has 17 extra fine ruby jewels in solid gold settings, jeweled center, magnificently damaskeened and finished; bevel head screws, 14 karat gold; patent regulator, perfectly compensated and accurately timed to all positions and isochronism; double sunk glass, enameled dial, with red marginal minute figures; patent Breguet hair spring, steel work highly polished; patent center pinion, elegantly engraved and damaskeened; fine escapement; fleur de lis hands, and the Hampden back action main spring. This is the finest 18 size movement made by the Hampden Watch Company, and is especially adapted to the requirements of railroad men and others who need a very fine timepiece.

**THE WALTHAM 16 SIZE MOVEMENTS** are all made in ¾ plate. We quote them in five grades as follows;

**THE "NO. 20" WALTHAM** has 7 jewels, compensation balance, with Breguet hair spring, hardened and tempered in form, exposed winding wheels, and is finished in gilt.

**THE "NO. 28" WALTHAM** has 15 jewels in settings, patent regulator, compensation balance, safety pinion, patent Breguet hair spring, hardened and tempered in form, exposed winding wheels, and is made in solid nickel.

**THE "ROYAL" WALTHAM** has 17 jewels in settings, center setting raised, exposed pallets, patent regulator, compensation balance, adjusted, patent Breguet hair spring, hardened and tempered in form, exposed winding wheels, and is solid nickel damaskeened.

**THE "RIVERSIDE" WALTHAM** has 17 ruby jewels in gold settings, exposed pallets, patent regulator, compensation balance, adjusted to temperature, and position, patent Breguet hair spring, hardened and tempered in form, safety pinion, exposed winding wheels, solid nickel plates, finished in gilt and damaskeened.

**THE "AMERICAN WATCH CO." WALTHAM** has 17 fine ruby jewels in gold settings, exposed pallets, patent regulator, compensation balance adjusted to temperature, isochronism and position, patent Breguet hair spring, hardened and tempered in form, safety pinion, exposed winding wheels and fine solid nickel damaskeened plates. The above is a very fine movement, designed to meet the requirements of those who want a very accurate time piece, such as railroad men, etc.

**THE ELGIN 16 SIZE MOVEMENTS** are now made only in the new (1895) models, which are very thin and are fitted in a much neater and more symmetrical case than the old model. They are all made with exposed winding wheels, which adds very much to their appearance. As none of these movements are named, we quote them under the manufacturers numbers, which do not appear on the movements, but are used by the manufacturers and dealers to indicate the grade.

**THE "NO. 151" ELGIN** is ¾ plate, has 7 jewels, Breguet hair spring, compensation balance, safety pinion and dust band, and is finished in gilt only.

**THE "NO. 152" ELGIN** is ¾ plate, has 15 jewels in settings, patent micrometer regulator, compensation balance, safety pinion, Breguet hair spring and dust band, and solid nickel damaskeened plates.

**THE "NO. 154" ELGIN** is ¾ plate, has compensation balance, adjusted to temperature, 17 jewels in settings, patent micrometer regulator, Breguet hair spring, moon hands, dust band, thoroughly well finished, and is made with solid nickel damaskeened plates.

**THE "NO. 155" ELGIN** is ¾ plate, has compensation balance, adjusted to temperature and position, 17 ruby jewels with gold settings, micrometer regulator, patent Breguet hair spring, double sunk dial, dust band, first quality moon hands, finely finished throughout and has solid nickel damaskeened plates.

## DESCRIPTION OF SIX SIZE MOVEMENTS.

**THE TRENTON and SETH THOMAS** movements are ¾ plate, nickel damaskeened, and will be furnished in the 7 jeweled grade. They have patent pinion and compensation balance.

**THE SEVEN JEWELED** grade of Elgin, Waltham and Hampden has compensation balance, patent center pinion, and is furnished in gilt finish only.

**THE FIFTEEN JEWELED** grade of Elgin and Hampden, has compensation balance, patent center pinion, jewels in settings, and is solid nickel, damaskeened. This grade is not now made by the Waltham factory.

**THE "NO. 168" ELGIN** has 16 ruby jewels, raised settings, compensation balance, Breguet hair spring, fine oval finished patent micrometer regulator with gold index, safety pinion and solid nickel damaskeened plates.

**THE "ROYAL" WALTHAM** has 17 fine ruby jewels in raised settings, exposed pallets, patent regulator, dust band, compensation balance, adjusted, patent Berguet hair spring, hardened and tempered in form, patent center pinion, and is solid nickel, beautifully damaskeened.

**THE "RIVERSIDE" WALTHAM** has 17 fine ruby jewels, raised gold settings, exposed pallets, patent center pinion, patent regulator, compensation balance, adjusted, patent Breguet hair spring, hardened and tempered in form, and is solid nickel, beautifully damaskeened.

**THE HAMPDEN** 17 jeweled grade is solid nickel and has 17 fine ruby jewels, raised gold settings, patent center pinion, highly polished center and escape wheels, is beautifully damaskeened in gilt and nickel, Hampden back action mainspring, finest grade hair spring, gilt bevel screws, fine gilt hands, adjusted to five positions and very accurately timed.

**THE DESCRIPTION OF O SIZE MOVEMENTS** is the same as for six size. The Hampden and Trenton are not made in 0 size.

---

**CAUTION:—During the past year several grades of movements that formerly were made with 15 jewels are now made with 17 jewels, and in most cases the prices have remained the same or been reduced. Retail stocks are made up of the old 15 jewel movements and we warn intending purchasers against paying more money for an old style movement than we ask for clean fresh goods with all the latest improvements.**

**We can furnish any movement or case made. Our catalogue is very complete, but if you do not find what you want, write us.**

# Explanation of the Terms Used in the Description of Watch Movements.

**To assist our customers in making an intelligent selection of a movement best suited to their requirements, and that they may know exactly what they are buying, we give below an explanation of the terms used on the opposite page.**

**Remember** That the "numbers" which are always engraved on watch movement have nothing to do with our catalogue number, or the manufacturer's number, which indicates the grade. Every movement is numbered consecutively, and you will find no two movements made by the same factory that have the same number.

**Jewels** Are not used to add to the intrinsic value of a movement, as is supposed by many, but for the purpose of equalizing and reducing friction, which will reduce the variation, and cause the pivots and bearings to wear much longer, and thus retain the good qualities of the movement for an indefinite length of time. They are made of garnet or ruby. The ruby, being harder and more expensive, is used only in the higher grade movements. A great deal depends on the quality and perfect finish of the jewels.

In movements of lower grade than fifteen jewels, the jewels are used in places where there is the most friction.

With the seven-jeweled grade, the pivots of the balance wheel each run in a jewel and, in addition to this, is used what is called "cap" jewels, which serves as a bearings for the ends of the balance pivots, which are made with conical instead of square shoulders, and the ends of the pivots rest on the cap jewels, instead of the shoulders resting on the hole jewels. By this method the friction can be equalized, and the watch will keep the same rate, whether on its edge, face or back. Two jewels are used in the pallet, which operates on the 'scape wheel, and one, called the "roller" jewel, is set in the roller table, which is under the balance wheel on the balance staff.

In the eleven-jeweled grade, seven are used in the escapement as above indicated, and in addition to this the four top pivots, viz.: The third wheel, the fourth wheel, the 'scape wheel and pallet are jeweled.

In the fifteen-jeweled grade, seven jewels are used in the escapement and eight plate jewels are used, four of which are set the same as in the eleven-jeweled movement, and the other four on the opposite pivots in the lower plate.

In the seventeen-jeweled grades, the jewels are distributed as in the fifteen, with the addition of one for each pivot of the center wheel.

In the twenty-one-jeweled grades, the jewels are distributed as in the seven-jeweled grade, with the addition of two cap jewels each for the pallet and 'scape wheel.

**The Compensation Balance** Is made of a combination of hammer hardened brass and steel, in such proportions as to compensate for the variations in temperature. The brass is used on the outside and steel on the inside. The brass being softer than steel is more sensitive to changes of temperature, and as the rim of the balance wheel is cut in two places, and the balance wheel has but two arms, it leaves each half of the rim attached at one end and leaves the other ends of the rim free to be influenced by the expansion or contraction of the brass on the outside of the rim. A small balance wheel used with the same hair spring would run much faster than a large balance wheel. At a high temperature the entire balance wheel would naturally expand in bulk and consequently run slower. But, with the compensation balance, while the entire bulk of the balance wheel expands, the expansion of the brass on the outside of the rim is greater than the steel on the inside, consequently it throws the loose end of the rim of the balance wheel in toward the center of the wheel, thus making the circumference enough smaller to compensate for the increased volume.

By the results of experience it is possible to make these wheels by machinery, so nearly correct, that the rate is sufficiently close for all ordinary purposes. For closer rate the balance wheel must be adjusted to temperature.

**Adjustment.** There are three kinds of adjustment which affect the rate of a watch. These are used in the finer timepieces, such as those for railroad men, sailors and others, who require a timepiece which can be depended on for a very close rate. The adjustment of a movement requires the most skill at the hands of a workman of any of the departments of watchmaking. Adjustments are perfected only by experiment and a great deal of careful hand labor on each individual movement. The first adjustment is that of heat and cold. Every compensation balance is provided with screws in the rim of the balance wheel, by the use of which the adjustment to heat and cold may be changed by the workman. The movement is tested in an ice box and in an oven, and if it does not keep the same rate in both extremes of temperature, as well as the average temperature, the screws in the balance wheel are shifted to or from the loose end of the balance rim, so as to bring about the desired results.

The second adjustment is that of position. The watch must keep the same rate when lying on its face, on its back, or on the edge with pendant up, pendant down, three up and nine up. This adjustment is accomplished by having the jewels in which the balance pivots rest, of the proper thickness in proportion to the diameter of the pivot, and at the same time it must equal the surface on the end of the pivot, which rests on the "cap" jewel; also the balance wheel, as well as pallet and 'scape wheel must be perfectly poised. A wheel is perfectly poised when the pivots can be supported on two flat surfaces, perfectly smooth and polished, and the wheel placed in any position, when it will remain exactly as it is placed. If it is not perfectly poised, the heaviest part of the wheel will always turn to the point immediately under the lines of support.

The third adjustment is that of isochronism. This is the result of careful calculation and experiments in the way of selecting a hair spring of the exact proportions as to length, strength, etc., which will cause the balance wheel to give the same length of arc of rotation, when the main spring is wound full up, as it does when nearly run down. The natural tendency is for the watch to run slower when nearly run down than it does when wound full up. This is why your watchmaker will sometimes tell you to always wind your watch at the same time every day. This adjustment overcomes that serious difficulty. While the variations from that cause is not sufficient to be of any consequence in a watch for ordinary use, it is very important with very fine timepieces.

**The Patent Regulator** Is a device which is used on all gents' watches of high grade, for the purpose of assisting in the finer manipulation of the regulator. It is so arranged that the regulator can be moved the shortest possible distance, without fear of moving it too far. They always have a fine graduated index attached, which makes it possible to see just how much the regulator has been moved.

**The Hair Spring** In general use on the ordinary and medium grade watches is known as the flat hair spring. A great deal depends on the form and temper of any style hair spring, in order that it may retain its elasticity and give the best results. The Breguet hair spring is an improvement over the flat hair spring and is used on high grade watches. The inside coil of any hair spring is attached to what is called a "collet" on the balance staff, and the end of the outside coil of the hair spring is attached to a stud, which is held firmly by a screw in the balance wheel bridge. Two small pins, with the end of each fastened to a projection in the regulator, clasp the outer end of the hair spring a short distance from where it is fastened in the stud. If the regulator is moved toward "S," these pins, called guard pins, are moved toward the stud, which lengthens the hair spring and allows the balance wheel to make a longer arc of rotation, which causes the watch to run slower, because it requires a longer time for the wheel to perform the longer arcs. When the regulator is moved toward "F," these pins are moved from the stud, which shortens the hair spring and makes shorter the arcs of the balance wheel, thus causing the movement to run fast. It sometimes happens that the next coil to the outside one, from a heavy jar, will catch between these guard pins, which will shorten the length of the hair spring just one round, causing a gaining rate of about one hour per day. When such does occur, the hair spring can be easily released, and it will resume its former rate. Under such conditions your local jeweler is very apt to tell you that the watch needs a new hair spring, which is not true.

**The Breguet Hair Spring** Is a recent improvement, which accomplishes two objects. It prevents the liability of the hair spring catching on the guard pins, and at the same time there is no lateral or side motion given to the balance wheel, as the expansion is equal all around, owing to the fact that the outside coil of the spring is bent up and turned around, so as to pass near the center and across to the opposite side and is attached to the stud above the level of the body of the spring.

**The Patent or Safety Pinion** Is now used in most of the American watches, and was invented for the purpose of protecting the train from reaction, caused by breakage of the main spring, which is liable to happen in any grade of watch at any time, without apparent cause; sometimes from over-winding. It is the pinion of the center staff with which the barrel (the hollow wheel which contains the main spring) engages. In case the mainspring breaks, the recoil and backward action given to the main wheel disengages the pinion from the center staff and allows it to turn freely on the staff.

When solid pinions are used, balance staffs, jewels, teeth of wheels and other serious damage has resulted from the breaking of the main spring. The patent pinion prevents all such accidents.

**Full Plate** Movements are those on which usually the **balance wheel** only is exposed to view; with some the flat steel winding wheeler are also on top of the upper plate.

**Three-Quarter Plate** Movements are those which have a portion of the upper plate cut away, so as to expose a portion of the train wheels, pallet, etc. Three-quarter plate is used mostly on 16, 6 and 0 size movements. The Seth Thomas movements quoted by us are made in three-quarter plate.

**Non-Magnetic Movements** Have the balance wheel, hair spring, roller table and pallet made of non-magnetic metal, which is a composition of iridium, paladium and other metals. (Both of the above named metals are four times as valuable as gold). The balance wheel and escapement (except in the non-magnetic watches) is made largely of hardened steel. If hardened steel comes in contact with a strong electric current, it is liable to become magnetized, a portion of which will be retained, and will be very detrimental to the time-keeping qualities of the watch. The non-magnetic metal will not in any way be influenced or attracted by electricity or magnetism. It is a comparatively recent discovery, and is especially valuable to those who work about electric cars, electric light plants, etc.

In non-magnetic movements we list only those made by the Waltham Watch Company; the Elgin Watch Company do not make them.

**We Guarantee for Five Years** All the movements sold by us. This does not refer to the life of the movement, but that we will for five years from date of purchase, correct free of charge any fault which may occur from defective material or workmanship. Any well made movement will run a lifetime if properly cared for.

**Remember** That your watch should not run longer than one and one-half years without having the old oil cleaned off and fresh oil applied. This must be done at the expense of the purchaser.

The balance wheel of all modern watches makes 18,000 beats or revolutions per hour; 432,000 per day, or 157,788,000 per year. An engine or sewing machine will be oiled several times per day, but we have known people to carry a watch for ten years without having it cleaned or fresh oil applied. Usually, a movement thus treated is of no value, being entirely worn out. Take good care of your watch if you wish it to perform its duty properly, for it is a very delicate machine. Our charge for cleaning and oiling is 75 cents. The regular retail price is $1.50.

We can furnish any movement or case made. If you do not find in our catalogue what you want, write us.

# HOW GOLD FILLED CASES ARE MADE.

**A**S GOLD FILLED CASES have become so popular in the past thirty years, and there is so little known by the general public of the relative proportions of the different materials that enter into their construction and the methods employed in making them, we feel that it will be interesting to our customers and their friends to know more about such an important industry. With every line that we handle and list in our catalogue, we make ourselves thoroughly familiar as to the manner in which the goods are made, and the quality and proportion of each kind of material which enters into their construction. It is very necessary for us to do this in order to protect the interests of our customers, for their interests are our own. We employ men in each department who are thoroughly familiar with the construction of the goods they handle, know where to look for weak and strong points, and are thoroughly competent to judge and to protect the interests of both our customers and ourselves from being imposed upon by fraudulent concerns whose only object is to make up cheap, showy goods and market them to the unsuspecting public in competition with goods of real merit, which, if bought right, can be owned for the same or even less than the shoddy goods. We can say without fear of contradiction that the average merchant does not employ competent people and even himself is not a practical man. Let us repeat that we leave nothing undone to thoroughly understand and know the merits of everything we sell.

There are at the present time eleven watch case factories in the United States, with a daily average of about 4,500 filled cases, or 1,498,500 per year. Most of the watch case factories in operation at the present time are reputable makers who have been established a great many years, and have proven by the experience of over a quarter of a century that gold filled cases, when properly made, are not only theoretically, but practically, a success, and have given their owners entire satisfaction. We might say that it has been our good fortune and pleasure to have had the privilege of examining a great many gold filled watch cases which have been in constant use from 20 to 30 years, and, without exception, we found all of those which were made by reputable concerns to be in good condition, and to all appearances equal to a solid gold case. (Of course, the joints were somewhat loose from wear, which is a natural consequence with any watch case.) Even though the first filled cases were satisfactory as to wear and appearance, improved machinery and years of experience have made it possible to turn out cases at a very low price, which for style and appearance are far superior to a solid gold case and for wear are all that could be wished for. The following article, together with accompanying illustrations, will give the reader a good general idea of how gold filled cases are made.

The first operation is to prepare a sheet of material which is composed of two plates of gold with a plate of hard composition metal between. Instead of rolling all three plates out to the required thickness before soldering them together, which would be a very difficult operation and attended with unsatisfactory results, such as uneven thickness of the plates, not being soldered well together, etc., the material is made ready, as shown in Figure 1, by taking one piece of gold about 4 inches long by 2 inches wide, and another of the same width and length but thinner for the inside of the case, as there is no wear on the inside. Now, a hard piece of composition metal of the same width and length is placed between the two pieces of gold, and after placing a few bits of hard gold solder between the plates the three are put into a furnace kept at a very high heat by a charcoal fire and a hot air blast. The solder soon melts, and all three of the original pieces of metal are in one solid piece as seen in Figure 1.

This piece is passed between adjustable hard steel rollers, which are brought closer together by a set screw after each time the plate has been passed through until it is reduced to a thin sheet a little less than 1-16 of an inch in thickness. Figure 2 represents a plate after having been passed through several times. By this method all three of the original sheets are reduced proportionately equal so that neither the gold nor the composition metal will be thicker in one place than another.

The next operation is to cut the plate into strips of such width as to accommodate the different parts of the case, which are to be stamped out by large automatic rotary presses. The back, front and cap of the cases are stamped out in a circular plate as shown in Fig. 3, and the piece of the strip that is left is represented by Fig. 4. Cuts are about one-third size.

By a single operation these round plates are forced into a steel die in a large rotary press which turns up the edges all round so as to give it a bowl shaped appearance, as shown in Fig. 5. In another operation the edges are turned down as shown in Fig. 6, which is called the snap.

The next step is to place the piece thus shaped into a sectional hard steel concave die. On the inside is operated with very heavy pressure a small hard steel polished roller (see Fig. 8) which forces the metal into the die in all parts, which shapes the piece to conform to the style of case which is being made. If the case is to have corrugated edges, or Star vermicilli work, or heavy engraving, it is formed in this die. This operation also shapes the inside edges of the piece so as to form the snap as seen in Fig. 7.

The piece thus shaped is put on edge turned out a little with a sharp fectly on the center of the case. propelled at a high speed is run the joint (hinge). Two pieces of in length (joint wire is made in with a small hole running the entire of the required length with a saw), is placed in the seat cut by the tool and bound in place with fine wire. Some bits of fine hard gold solder are then laid over the crevice and the pieces are held in a gas jet which is stimulated by an air blast. The solder is melted and secures the joints, after which the binding wire is taken off. A piece of solid gold is soldered on in the same way on the edge of the back of case to form the thumb piece.

**This Cut Shows a Section of Joint Wire Enlarged.**

the head of a lathe and the inside tool to make it snap and fit perfectly. After this is done a rotary cutter across one edge to cut the seat for gold joint wire about ⅜ of an inch sticks about 4 inches in length length, and is cut into pieces

The center of the case is made by taking a strip of stock (prepared in the same way as described in the first part of this article) about ¾ of an inch wide by about 7 inches long (see Fig. 9), which is bent in a circle and the ends soldered so as to form a band or ring a little over two inches in diameter. This piece is placed in a sectional die (see Fig. 10), which is held securely in a very heavy frame. A small hard polished roller is rolled on the inside of the ring with very heavy pressure until the metal comes in contact with every part of the die. The inside of the die is made in the exact shape of the outside of center of case so that when the metal has been well pressed in, it is shaped complete as seen in Fig. 12. The rough edges on the inside are now turned out (on the lathe) to the standard size to fit the movement.

The seats for the joints are milled out and joints soldered on as described above, except that one piece of joint wire instead of two are put on. The pendant (see Fig. 13) is made by forcing a small piece of stock into a die. A small concave seat is cut in the center (Fig. 12) to receive it, and it is bound in place and soldered on with gold solder.

The pendant bow (usually called the ring) is made of solid gold. The bezel (crystal ring) is made in much the same way as the center. All the joints (hinges) are now filed and broached so as to fit perfectly, the case springs are secured in their places and the different parts of the case are fitted together.

The next operation is to engrave the case, which is done by hand with a small tool about five inches in length (see Fig. 14), which is held as seen in Fig. 15. Engraving is very fine work and requires years of practice as well as natural ability to master the art. After the engraving is done the case is polished inside and out on cotton buff wheels from one to five inches in diameter, which run at the rate of about 3,000 revolutions per minute and are saturated with alcohol and red rouge (very fine powdered oxide of iron). The case is now washed carefully, put in a soft cotton bag and is ready for the market.

See description under Nos. 4018 to 4023, which explains how electro gold plated cases are made.

**GRADES OF GOLD.** For the benefit for those of our customers who are not familiar with what is meant by 10, 14 or 18 karat gold, we make the following explanation: 24 is taken as a basis. For 14 karat gold, fourteen twenty-fourths of the composition is pure gold and ten twenty-fourths is alloy. For 10 karat, ten twenty-fourths is pure gold while fourteen twenty-fourths is alloy.

Fig. 1.

Fig. 2.

Fig. 3.

Fig. 4.

Fig. 5.

Fig. 6.

Fig. 7.

Fig. 8.

Fig. 9.

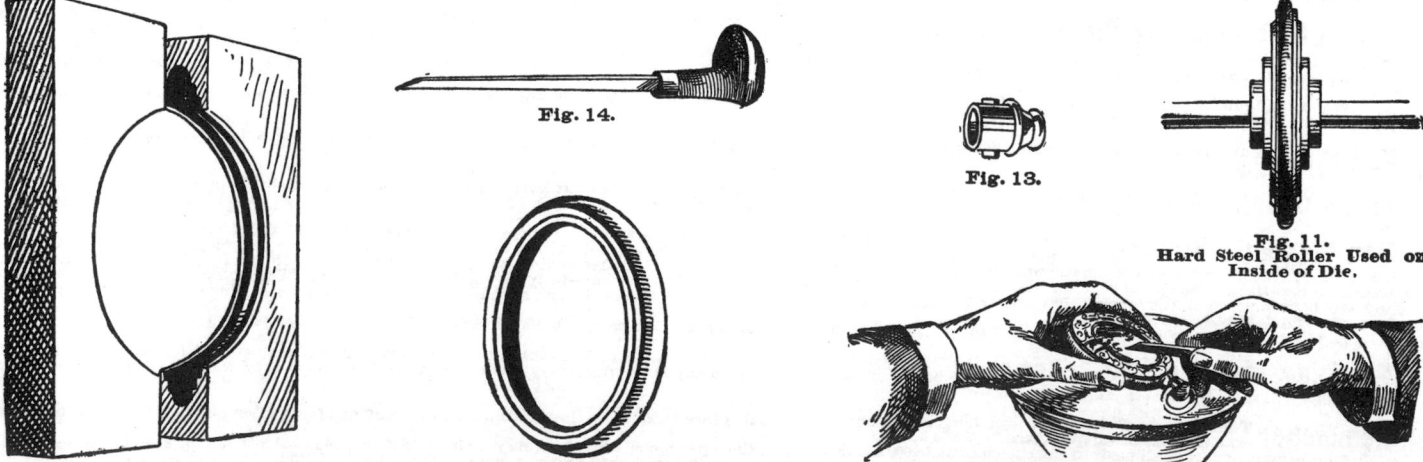

Fig. 10.     Fig. 14.     Fig. 13.     Fig. 11. Hard Steel Roller Used on Inside of Die.     Fig. 12.     Fig. 15.

**RAISED COLORED GOLD ORNAMENTATION** is mentioned in different parts of our Watch and Jewelry department. Gold can be made in many different colors by using different kinds of metal for alloy. Pure Gold is Bright Yellow; Gold of a Reddish color is made by using Copper for alloy; very Light Colored Gold is made by using Silver for alloy; Green Gold is made with light alloys and colored by a chemical treatment. A white metal is also used in raised colored decorations which is Platinum, and when pure it will not tarnish or corrode.

# WATCHES ALMOST GIVEN AWAY.

Don't go without a watch and continue to ask your neighbor the time of day when you can have one of your own for a little money. The Boys, the Girls, the Rich and the Poor can all carry watches at the prices we ask. By our one-small-profit plan, from manufacturer to consumer, you can own a watch at a very few cents advance on cost to manufacture, and by the use of improved and automatic machinery, watches can now be made and sold for $2.00 or $3.00 which are a credit to those sold fifty years ago for $25.00 to $40.00.

Those illustrated and quoted on this page are all complete in every detail, and are warranted to be as represented. Our terms are most liberal. We want you to see for yourself. Any of these watches will be sent to any address C. O. D., by express. subject to examination, on receipt of 50 cents, in stamps or cash, as a guarantee of good faith. The watch can be examined thoroughly at the express office, and if not found to be as represented, or even more, you can refuse to accept it and we will refund the amount you have deposited.

We advise you to send cash in full with your orders and save the 3 per cent. cash discount. It is perfectly safe, and, if you are not in every way satisfied with the watch when it arrives, you can return it and your money will be refunded. Most of our customers send cash in full. It saves return charges on the collection, and the goods go by registered mail if 14 cents extra is sent to pay postage.

**WE LEAD ON LOW PRICES. OUR TERMS ARE MOST LIBERAL.**

**SEND US A TRIAL ORDER IF YOU HAVE NOT ALREADY DEALT WITH US AND BE CONVINCED.**

No. 65001.     No. 65002.     No. 65003.

No. 6001. Nickel-plated metal case, of regular 18-size heavy glass, stem wind and stem set, patent lever movement, and runs 30 to 36 hours with one winding, is American made, and is a very good timekeeper. It is only by contracting for several thousand of these watches on a spot cash basis that we are enabled to sell them at such an extremely low figure. The movement of this watch is of very strong construction, and will stand much more rough usage than the average watch. There is nothing that you could buy as a present to a boy which would give him so much real pleasure for the money as a watch.
Price........$0.98

No. 6002. Another wonderful bargain nickel-plated metal case, very strong, with heavy glass, stem wind and stem set with good cylinder escapement, jeweled movement, enameled dial, and is a good watch that retails at $3.00

**IF YOU WANT TO MAKE MONEY,** there is no better way to do it than to save it on your purchases. Remember the old adage "A dollar saved is a dollar earned." We can save you many of them.

**FOR 50 CENTS** you can see and examine any of these watches at your express office. If not satisfactory we will refund the deposit.

to $5.00. These watches are made by the poor peasants in the mountains of Switzerland, where entire families work during the winter months at watchmaking, for which they average about 15 cents each per day.
Our Price........$1.68

No. 6003. Genuine Dueber Silverine, 3½-ounce case, with heavy, flat bevel-edge glass. The Dueber silverine cases are made of the same solid silverine metal through and through, and will wear and retain their beautiful silver color a lifetime. They will be furnished with good jeweled imported movements, hard white enamel dial, key or stem-wind and are good timekeepers.
Price for key-wind movement and case complete........$2.25
Price for stem-wind movement and case complete........2.95

**A DISCOUNT** of 3 per cent will be given for cash in full with your orders; 4 per cent will be allowed on orders over $50.00 and 5 per cent on orders over $100.00.

No. 65004.     No. 65005.     No. 65006.     No. 65007.

No. 6004. Our Boys' Watch, warranted solid nickel case, with heavy bevel-edged crystal. The case is solid nickel through and through and warranted not to tarnish. It is fitted with a jeweled imported well-made stem-wind and stem-set movement and is a good timekeeper. The watch is a trifle larger than the illustration and fills a long felt want for a boys' watch, a little smaller than the regular gents' size, and at the price we offer them no boy need be without one.
Price........$1.75

No. 6005. A genuine all-American solid nickel watch. This case is made of solid nickel through and through, beautifully polished, and is fitted with heavy bevel-edged glass and guaranteed not to tarnish. The movement is made by the New York Standard Watch Co., is nickel damaskeened, stem wind and stem set, patent lever, seven jewels, train bearings in metal settings, safety pinion, compensation balance, and are fully warranted by both the manufacturers and ourselves. The New York Standard Watch Co.'s movements are well known, and we recommend them as being most excellent value for the money. This watch will retail in first-class stores at from $5.00 to $7.00.
Our Price........$2.75

All of the above watches are open face. We cannot furnish them in hunting case.

No. 6006. A genuine coin-silver, engraved, open-face watch. Never before has a genuine coin-silver watch been offered at so little money. The case is solid coin silver, well made and beautifully engraved, as seen in above cut, and is fitted with heavy bevel-edged glass. The movement is made by the New York Standard Watch Co., is nickel damaskeened, stem wind and stem set, patent lever, seven jewels, train bearings in metal settings, safety pinion, compensation balance, and is fully warranted by the manufacturers and ourselves.
Our Price........$4.75

No. 6007. A genuine all-American, gold-filled, open-face watch. Something new. This is the first time that we have been able to offer a genuine gold-filled watch at anywhere near the price we ask for this. The case is made of two plates of gold over an inner plate of composition metal, is beautifully engraved and guaranteed by the manufacturers to wear for five years; a certificate of guarantee accompanies each watch.

The movement is made by the New York Standard Watch Co., is nickel damaskeened, stem wind and stem set, patent lever, seven jewels, train bearings in metal settings, safety pinion, compensation balance, and is fully guaranteed by both the manufacturers and ourselves.
Our special price for the complete watch is........$5.50

WITH SALES OF SEVER-
AL HUNDRED WATCHES
PER DAY A FEW CENTS
PROFIT ON EACH IS SUF-
FICIENT.

WE HAVE NO EXPEN-
SIVE TRAVELING MEN
OR AGENTS SALARIES TO
PAY. OUR CATALOGUE
DOES IT ALL.

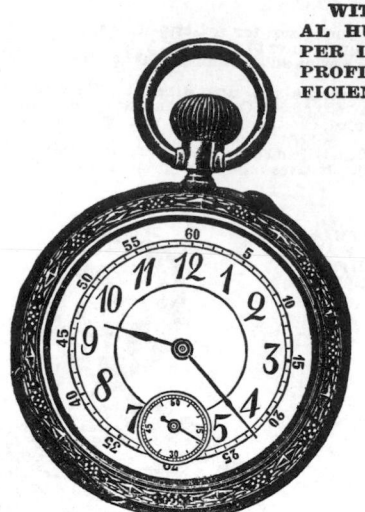

### No. 65008.
### OUR BOYS' SOLID COIN SILVER WATCH.

The **Case is** made of Solid Coin Silver, well **finished**, beautifully engraved and is fitted with heavy **beveled** edge glass.

The **movement** is an imported, jeweled, cylin-**der** escapement, stem wind and stem set, and has **hard** enameled dial.

It is well finished and regulated, and is warranted **a good** timekeeper.
Price..................................$3.85

### No. 65009.
### A SOLID COIN SILVER ALL AMERICAN OPEN FACE WATCH.

The **case** is Solid Coin Silver, and is fitted with heavy beveled edge glass. It is made in a most thor-ough manner by one of the best and largest case manufacturers in America.

The **movement** is made by the **Trenton Watch Co.,** Trenton, N. J., and is guaranteed by both the manufacturers and ourselves. Is seven jeweled, nickel, damaskeened, with safety pinion, and compen-sation balance; patent lever escapement, stem wind and stem set, and is carefully regulated, and war-ranted an accurate timekeeper.
Price, with engine turned case..................$5.45
Price, with fancy engraved case................ 5.75

### No. 65010.
### SOLID COIN SILVER HUNTING GENUINE ALL AMERICAN WATCH.

The case is Solid Coin Silver, hunting style, well made and engine turned or engraved. It is made by one of the most reputable case manufacturers in the United States, and is fully warranted.

The **movement** is made by the **Trenton Watch Co.,** Trenton, N. J., and is nickel, damaskeened, stem wind and stem set, seven jeweled, compensation bal-ance, patent center pinion, and is carefully regulated and guaranteed an accurate timekeeper.

**Compare** our prices with those of your local jeweler, and you will find that we can sell an all American Solid Silver Watch for much less than he can sell you a cheap trashy low grade imported watch, which cannot be depended upon.

This watch would retail at from $10.00 to $13.00.
Our Price, with engine turned case..............$5.75
Our Price, with fancy engraved case............ 6.00

WE ARE HEADQUAR-
TERS FOR WATCHES JEW-
ELRY SILVERWARE, ETC.,
NO MATTER WHAT YOU
WANT WE CAN FURNISH
IT.

WITH OUR ONE SMALL
PROFIT PLAN FROM MAN-
UFACTURER TO CON-
SUMER YOU GET FULL
VALUE FOR YOUR MONEY.

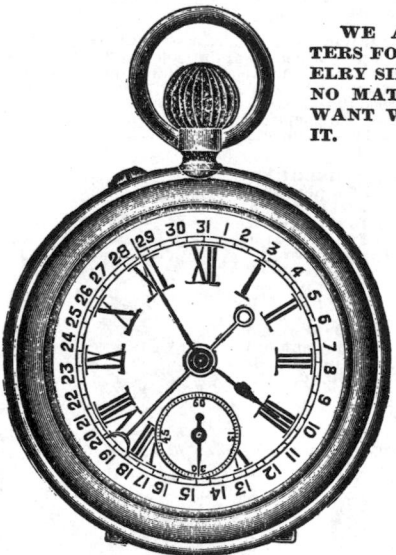

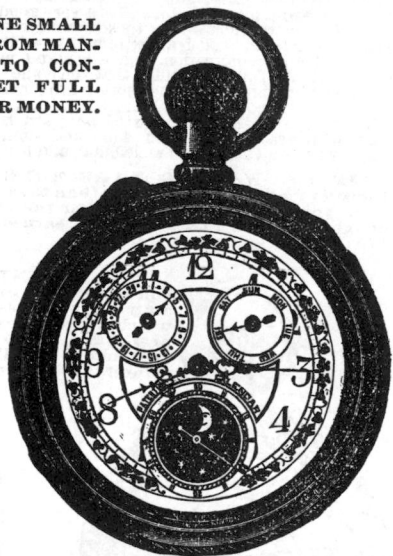

### No. 65011.
### CALENDAR WATCH.

If you own one of these watches you will not find **it** necessary to consult an almanac or ask some one to tell you the day of the month.

The case is nickel plated, and fitted with a heavy beveled edge glass.

The **movement** is imported, stem wind and stem set, jeweled, cylinder escapement, hard enam-eled dial, and in addition to being complete in every **respect** as a timekeeper, it has a complete calendar, **which** works automatically, always indicating cor-**rectly** the day of the month.
Price..................................$4.45

### No. 65012.
### SOLID SILVER MOON CALENDAR WATCH.

**This watch is a mechanical wonder,** but at the same time is offered at a price which is within the reach of all.

The case is **Solid Silver,** beautifully engraved, **and** fitted with a heavy beveled edge glass.

The **movement** is stem wind and stem set, patent lever escapement, jeweled bearings, and in addition to being a complete timepiece, it is also a complete calendar, indicating the day of the week, day of the month, month of the year, and the changes of the moon. At the same time it is so simple that it is not more liable to get out of order than an ordinary watch. It is fully guaranteed by both the manu-facturers and ourselves.

We can furnish it in open face only.
Price..................................$9.50

### No. 65013.
### GOLD FILLED OPEN FACE MOON CAL-ENDAR WATCH.

The case is Genuine Gold Filled, made of **Two Plates of Solid Gold** over a fine hard composition metal, and warranted by certificate to wear and re-tain its color for twenty years.

The **movement** is stem wind and stem set, patent lever, jeweled escapement, compensation bal-ance, and warranted a good timekeeper.

In addition to being a regular timepiece, with hour, minute and second hand, it is a complete calen-dar, correctly indicating the day of the week, day of the month, and changes of the moon.

It is in every respect a thorough and practical watch, is reliable and simple in construction, and warranted an accurate timekeeper. A certificate of guarantee accompanies each watch covering both case and movement.
Our Price..................................$18.45

**Our competitors, the manufacturers, and our customers all wonder** how it is possible to build up such an enormous trade **in every corner of the United States** as well as nearly all foreign countries. It is very easy to explain. Our customers are always so well satisfied with their purchases, by reason of our sending them the **best** goods on the market for from one-third to one-half less than they can be purchased at home, that one sale makes another, and one customer makes another customer. **We** try to treat our customers as we would like to be treated were we in their places. This is the only way. Send us a **trial order** and be convinced.

# THE CELEBRATED DUEBER SILVERINE WATCHES.

**Down! Down!! Down!!!** Down with prices, and every reduction that we succeed in getting from the manufacturers, with the assistance of cash, experience and a reputation as the largest buyers of watches in the world, our customers always get the benefit. You ask, why do we not keep on selling at the same high prices and make more money? We answer, we have built up a reputation as the Cheapest Supply House on Earth, and we must sustain it by continuing with the same methods as those which have built up our business. Even though we have the reputation for the best goods at the lowest prices, it would be very easy for us to lose it were we to adopt any other policy. We think we need offer no other argument than the fact that we are selling on an average of over 5,000 of this one kind of watch per month to convince you that we are in a position to place them in your hands at a very small per cent above cost of manufacture.

The John C. Dueber Silverine Cases have a world-wide reputation, and are known to be the only genuine and reliable silverine case. It is solid through and through, weighs about 3½ ozs., is a very dense and tough metal, takes a beautiful polish, holds a color almost as white as coin silver, and is warranted not to tarnish. A certificate of guarantee, a fac simile of which we give below, accompanies each case.

Fahay's Screw Back and Bezel or Crescent Screw Bezel, dust proof cases if desired, 25 cents extra.

All American movements are now made in stem wind and stem set only.

Our Catalogue numbers have nothing to do with the consecutive numbers which are always engraved on both case and movement.

**No. 65014.**
A picture of the Open Face. The back is plain polished.

**No. 65015.**
A picture of back of Hunting Case. Stag or Bird engraving. For price add 75c. to list below.

**No. 65016.**
A picture of front of Hunting Case. Back plain polished. For price add 75c. to list below.

## WE FIT THESE CASES WITH THE FOLLOWING 18 SIZE MOVEMENTS:

| | GILT. | NICKEL. | | GILT. | NICKEL. |
|---|---|---|---|---|---|
| 7 jeweled, Trenton | | $3 00 | Full 17 jeweled, "Appleton, Tracy & Co.," Waltham; "B. W. Raymond," Elgin; or "Anchor," Hampden, adjusted | | $18.45 |
| 7 jeweled, Seth Thomas, ¾ plate | | 3 50 | Full 17 jeweled, "Crescent Street," Waltham, adjusted | | 18.85 |
| 7 jeweled, Waltham, Elgin or Hampden | $4.25 | | Full 21 jeweled, "No. 150," Grade Elgin, fully adjusted | | 25.60 |
| Full 15 jeweled, Waltham, Elgin or Hampden | | 8.00 | Full 21 jeweled, "Vanguard," Waltham, fully adjusted | | 33.85 |
| Full 17 jeweled, "G. M. Wheeler," Elgin; "P. S. Bartlett," Waltham; or "Hampden," adjusted | | 10.75 | Full 17 jeweled, "New Railway," Hampden, fully adjusted | | 25.75 |
| | | | Full 17 jeweled, "Special Railway," Hampden, fully adjusted | | 35.75 |

We guarantee all of the above movements for five years. For full description of the same see introductory pages.

# GOLD ONLAID DUEBER SILVERINE CASES.

Below we illustrate two very pretty designs of gold onlaid work on silverine cases. The Stag and Locomotive, as well as some other parts of the picture, on the back of the case, is in solid gold plate. The contrast between the gold and the silverine metal creates a very beautiful effect. The cases are the same as described above, with the exception of the gold inlaying, which is very heavy, and will wear an indefinite length of time.

All of the Dueber open face cases are fitted with extra heavy beveled edge glasses, and being made extra heavy and strong throughout, they make an excellent watch for anyone who is engaged in any kind of heavy work. Many people prefer a fine movement and a cheap case. This case fills all the requirements. We cannot recommend them too highly. For prices on the gold inlaid cases add 75c. to the prices listed above.

A DISCOUNT of 3 per cent will be given for cash in full with your order; 4 per cent will be allowed on orders over $50.00 and 5 per cent on orders over $100.00.

16 cents will carry a gents' watch to any point in the United States by registered mail; 25 cents to almost any point by express.

DUEBER CASES are not made with Screw Back and Bezel, but Fahy's Screw Back and Bezel, or the Crescent Screw Bezel DUST PROOF Cases can be furnished when desired for 25 cents more than prices quoted for the Dueber.

**No. 65017.**
A picture of the Gold Inlaid Dueber Silverine Case. Add 75c. to prices listed above. Open face only.

**DUEBER'S GUARANTEE.**
A picture of the Manufacturer's Own Guarantee which goes with every Silverine Case.

**No. 65018.**
A picture of the Gold Inlaid Dueber Silverine Case. Add 75c. to prices listed above. Open face only.

**SOMETHING NEW.** A CASE WITH GLASS ON BOTH SIDES.

SEE PAGE No. 380.

YOU CAN MAKE MONEY selling our watches and jewelry. Why not, when you can buy as low and lower than your retail dealer? You would be satisfied with smaller profits because what you make is clear gain. He has heavy expenses, such as store rent, fuel, clerk hire, etc.

# GOLD PLATED WATCHES.

**Do not be deceived by this class of goods.** We sell them for what they are. They are handled largely by Newspaper Advertising concerns as Premium Offers with newspapers; by Jewelry Auction Houses, Peddlers, and by unprincipled Retail Dealers, and sold under various descriptions, such as Gold Filled, Solid Gold Plated, Heavy Gold Plated on composition metal, etc. To make our line complete, and to satisfy the wants of those who wish to buy them, we must list them. But to protect our customers against fraudulent representation, and that they may know the difference between these and reliable goods, we have resorted to this method of caution.

In the introductory pages of this department we have given you a brief article on "How Gold Filled Cases are Made." That you may be able to understand the difference between Gold Plated and Gold Filled Cases we will explain **How Electro Gold Plated Cases are Made:** The material of which these cases are made is Sheet Brass. The different parts are stamped out and shaped in dies similar to those in which gold filled cases are made, with the exception that they are made with less care, and as the joints and different parts do not fit properly they do not even protect the movement thoroughly from the intrusion of dust and dirt. They are made largely by small boys and girls. After the case is finished and put together it is then hung on a wire hook and suspended in a gold plating solution, through which a current of electricity passes and causes a portion of the gold in the solution to adhere to the case. There are several methods of saturating the solution with gold. One is to dissolve chloride of gold (gold in very fine powdered form) in a solution of cyanide of potassium. Another is to hang in the battery a piece of solid gold, by which the action of the battery eats off a portion of the same, carries it over to the article being plated and deposits it thereon. The film of gold deposited is very thin, the thickness of which depends on the length of time it is allowed to remain in the battery and the strength of the electric current. In any event, however, but a very light plating can be put on by this method.

The plating on all cases offered on this page will wear from thirty to ninety days. It is not possible to put on a plating by the electro-plating process that can be depended upon to wear more than three years, and is much more expensive than filled work in proportion to the cost. To those wanting goods that will wear longer than those offered on this page we recommend the five-year filled cases. The movements in these cases are all cylinder escapement, imported, either key or stem wind. They will keep very good time, but we do not warrant them. We do, however, guarantee that they will reach the purchaser in good condition.

**BUY WATCHES AND JEWELRY OF A RELIABLE CONCERN.**

No. 65019.

No. 6019. Gents' 18 size, Hunting Case, Key Wind, Price.................................$2.80
No. 6019. Gents' 18 size, Hunting Case, Stem Wind. Price.................................. 3.65

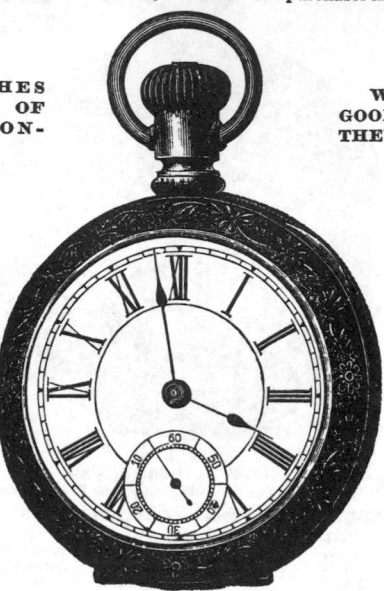

**WE REPRESENT GOODS FOR WHAT THEY ARE.**

No. 65020.

No. 6020. Gents' 18 size, Open Face, Key Wind. Price.................................$2.75
No. 6020. Gents' 18 size, Open Face, Stem Wind. Price................................. 3.55

No. 65021.

No. 6021. Gents' 18 size, Hunting, Key Wind. Price.................................$2.80
No. 6021. Gents' 18 size, Hunting, Stem Wind. Price................................. 3.65

**YOU RUN NO RISK** when dealing with a reliable concern. We refer to the National Banks of Illinois and Republic, among the largest in the city. See their letters in this book.

No. 65022.

No. 6022. Ladies' Hunting, Key Wind. Price..$2.80
No. 6022. " " Stem " .. 3.95

No. 65023.

No. 6023. Ladies' Hunting, Key Wind. Price..$2.80
No. 6023. " " Stem " .. 3.95

These watches are bought largely by traders who wish to drive a good bargain regardless of the value they give.

No. 65024.

No. 6024. Gents' 18 size, Hunting, Louis XIV, Box Joint, Stem Wind. Price.................$3.90

**Cash in full must accompany all orders for these watches.** They will not be sent C. O. D. We can furnish Nos. 4019 and 4021 with a gold plating, which will wear for about six months and fitted with Trenton movement when desired, for $2.00 extra on above prices. The above watches make a good appearance, and by an inexperienced person they cannot be told from a high-grade watch except by comparison. **We cannot send these watches C. O. D.**

16 cents will carry a gents' watch to any point in the United States by registered mail; 25 cents to almost any point by express.

**YOU CAN MAKE MONEY** selling our watches and jewelry. Why not, when you can buy as low and lower than your retail dealer. You would be satisfied with smaller profits because what you make is clear gain. He has heavy expenses, such as store rent, fuel, clerk hire, etc.

**SEE HOW GOLD FILLED CASES** are made, on introductory pages of this department.

# TIMERS AND CHRONOGRAPHS.

Do not entertain the idea that these watches are intended only for timing horses, etc. While they are indispensable for timing horses, bicycle races, foot races, etc., there is no watch that is more interesting and useful as a regular pocket timepiece than a Chronograph. Thousands of people carry them who have no desire to time race horses. There is no watch so handy and useful to a doctor for counting the pulse as a Chronograph. The sweep second hand which goes once around the dial every minute, and can be started, stopped at any point on the dial, or made to fly back to the figure 12 by simply pushing the crown, makes it an easy matter to count, and at the same time makes the watch very attractive and interesting. In addition to the sweep second hand they all have the regular small second hand. The sweep second hand can be allowed to run all the time or stopped without interfering with the timekeeping qualities of the watch. They are good timekeepers, are comparatively simple in construction, and not liable to get out of order. But a few years ago the prices on Chronograph Watches were such that but few people could afford to own one. Now we have succeeded in placing a very fine line at the disposal of our customers, at prices within the reach of everyone.

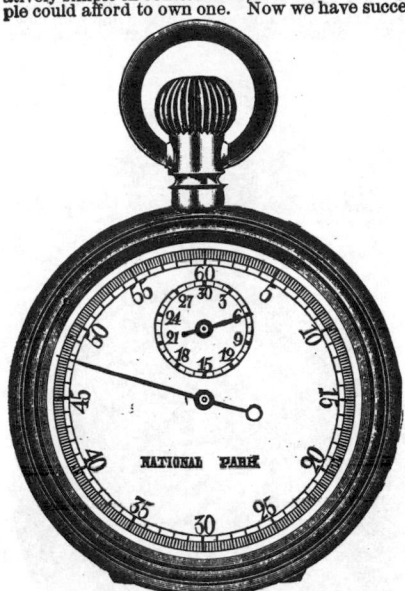

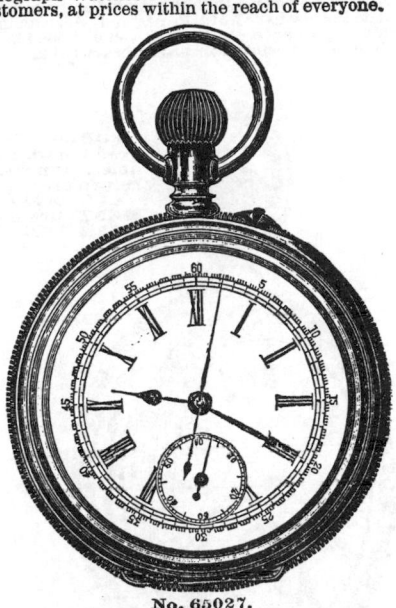

### No. 65025.
### HORSE TIMER ONLY,

and is not a regular watch. It has start, stop and fly-back arrangement, operated from the crown. It is also provided with minute register. It has a metal case, heavily Nickel Plated, plain polished, and fitted with cylinder escapement imported movement. Just the thing for those who do not wish to invest much money in a timer for races of any kind.
Our special price.....................$4.75

### No. 65026.
### SPLIT SECOND HORSE TIMER,

with minute register, start, stop and fly-back attachment, operated from the crown. This is the best cheap Split Second Horse Timer made. The two sweep second hands operate independently of each other, and are used for timing two participants in the same race at the same time. The case is made of metal, heavy Nickel plated, and fitted with a good reliable movement.
Our special price............................$12.95

### CHRONOGRAPH WATCH.

This is a regular watch with a timing attachment. It has a fine gilt movement, expansion balance, patent lever escapement, quick train, is well finished in every respect, is a perfect timekeeper and a perfect horse timer combined. Start, stop and fly-back is operated from the crown. Beats fifth seconds.
Our special price in Solid Nickel Case...$10.95
Solid Coin Silver Case, price.............13.95
10-karat Gold Filled Case, warranted to wear for 20 years, price............ 17.90

### Read our Plain Talk on third introductory Page of this department.

**YOU RUN NO RISK** when dealing with a reliable concern. We refer to the National Banks of Illinois and Republic, which are among the largest in the city. See their letters in this book.

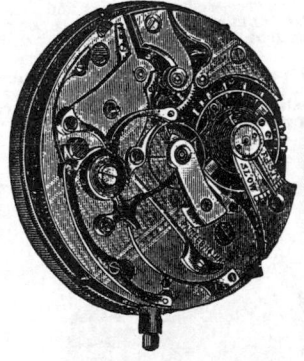

Picture of Dial and Movement, engraved from a photograph.

### No. 65028.
### CHRONOGRAPH WATCH.

Is a perfect watch with **Horse Timer and Minute Register** combined. The movement is thoroughly well made in every respect, is Full Jeweled, Quick Train, Patent Lever Escapement, Expansion Balance, beats fifth seconds, and warranted an accurate timepiece. The start, stop and fly-back are operated from the winding crown.
Our special price for Solid Nickel Case.....................$15.50
For Solid Coin Silver Case, price.............. 21.40
For 10-karat Solid Gold Case, price.............. 36.40
For 14-karat Solid Gold Case, price ...................... 47.50

If you return watches or jewelry for exchange or repairs, be sure to follow our instructions. See front page of this book.

A **DISCOUNT** of 3 per cent. will be given for cash in full with your order. Four per cent. will be allowed on orders over $50.00, and 5 per cent. on orders over $100.00.

### No. 65029.
### A GENUINE AMERICAN WATCH AND CHRONOGRAPH COMBINED.

This is the first time that a genuine all American Chronograph watch and case have ever been offered at a price within the reach of the average individual. **American Chronograph Watches** have sold at from $50.00 upwards. This, too, is the first interchangeable Chronograph Watch ever made. We can fit it in any open face 18 size American case. The movement is made by the **Trenton Watch Company,** of Trenton, N. J., has Patent Pinion, Expansion Compensation Balance, beats fifth seconds, and is warranted an accurate timekeeper. The timing attachment is constructed on the most common sense simple plan of any chronograph on the market. The mechanism is very simple, and is not liable to get out of order.
Our special price for this watch, in Silverine, Open Face, plain polished case.........................................................$12.50
In 20-year Gold Filled Case ............................................. 16.75

The cut represents the back of gold filled case. Chronograph Watches will be furnished in open face only. We can fit this movement in any open face case you desire. Prices will be furnished on application. 50 cents, as guarantee of good faith, must accompany all orders for Chronograph watches. When desired, they will be sent C. O. D. by express for the balance.

# AMERICAN COIN SILVER WATCHES.

**Do not be lured into paying** your retail jeweler one-third to one-half more than our prices for a watch because he poses as a personal friend of yours. **Business is business,** and if you do not look after your own interests, we assure you that other people will not look after them for you. Do not have so little confidence **in your own judgment,** that you are afraid to buy of anyone but your local merchant. Any person of ordinary intelligence can, with a little inquiry and attention, post **themselves** sufficiently that there is no reason for being deceived. Keep in mind the old adage, "a dollar saved is a dollar earned." We propose to save you many dollars. **Our silver watches** are made by the very best, oldest and largest manufacturers of silver watch cases in the world. They are all perfectly fitted, are dust proof, and **warranted solid coin silver.** In open face we can furnish you either jointed cases with gold joints, or screw bezel, patent crescent, dust-proof cases, as shown in the open **engraving below.** Both the jointed and screw open face cases listed below are fitted with **heavy, thick, flat, bevel-edge glasses, and weigh 3 ounces.** The hunting cases **listed below** have gold joints and weigh 3 ounces. Jointed or screw open face cases can be furnished in 4 ounce when desired for $1.10 additional on prices quoted below; **hunting 4 ounce, $1.60 extra.** Jointed open face in 5 ounce, $3.00 extra; hunting, $3.50 extra. Jointed open face in 6 ounce, $5.00 extra; hunting, $5.50 extra. Screw open **face cases** cannot be furnished heavier than 4 ounce.

**FOR 50 CENTS** you can see and examine watches at your express office. If not satisfactory we will return the deposit. **ALL AMERICAN MOVE-MENTS** are now made in STEM WIND AND STEM SET only.

**MOST OF OUR CUSTOMERS** send cash in full with their orders and save the discount and return charges on the collection. **YOU RUN NO RISK.** We will refund all your money if you are not satisfied with your purchase.

**No. 65030.**
Front view of jointed case.

Back view of screw case.
**No. 65030½.**

**No. 65031.**
For plain hunting 3 oz. cases add 50c. to list below.
For fancy engraved hunting case add $100 to list below.

## WE FIT THESE CASES WITH THE FOLLOWING 18 SIZE MOVEMENTS:

| | GILT. | NICKEL. |
|---|---|---|
| 7 jeweled, Trenton | | $ 7.95 |
| 7 jeweled, Seth Thomas, ¾ plate | | 8.45 |
| 7 jeweled, Waltham, Elgin or Hampden | $8.95 | .... |
| Full 15 jeweled, Waltham, Elgin or Hampden | | 12.72 |
| Full 17 jeweled, "G. M. Wheeler" Elgin, "P. S. Bartlett" Waltham, or Hampden, adjusted | | 15.45 |

| | NICKEL. |
|---|---|
| Full 17 jeweled, "Appleton, Tracy & Co." Waltham, "B. W. Raymond" Elgin, or "Anchor" Hampden, adjusted | $22.26 |
| Full 17 jeweled, "Crescent Street" Waltham, adjusted | 22.46 |
| Full 21 jeweled, "No. 150" Grade Elgin, fully adjusted | 29.40 |
| Full 21 jeweled, "Vanguard" Waltham, fully adjusted | 37.67 |
| Full 17 jeweled, "New Railway" Hampden, fully adjusted | 29.66 |
| Full 17 jeweled, "Special Railway" Hampden, fully adjusted | 39.67 |

We guarantee all of the above movements for five years.    For full description of the same, see introductory pages.

# GOLD INLAID SOLID COIN SILVER CASES.

The contrast between the solid gold and the coin silver creates a **most beautiful effect.** The **Stag and Locomotive,** as well as a portion of the scenery on cases Nos. **4032** and **4033** are made of a plate of solid gold laid in a recess cut in the silver and soldered with fine silver solder. They are then finished and engraved by hand, and are fully **warranted.** They will be furnished only in open face at above prices. For prices on gold inlaid, open face, dust proof, screw bezel watches, add $1.10 to prices **above.** Hunting gold inlaid cases can be furnished to order for $3.00 on prices listed above. Cash in full must accompany orders for hunting inlaid cases.

**The best protection** to a movement is a screw dust and damp proof case, with a tight case the oil will be preserved much longer.

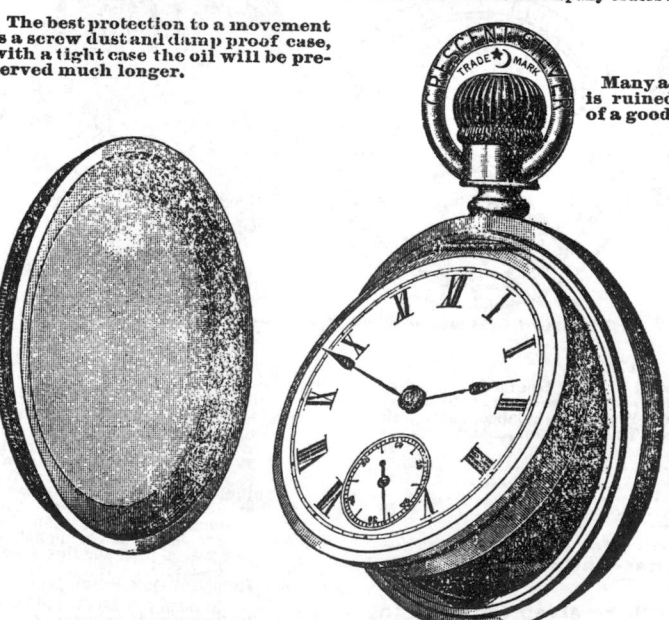

**Many a movement** is ruined for want of a good case.

**No. 65032.**
For prices on gold inlaid engraving, add $1.10 to prices listed above.

This picture shows open-face screw case open.
**65030½**

**No. 65033.**
For prices on gold inlaid engraving add $1.10 to prices listed above.

# A TWENTY-YEAR, GOLD-FILLED, SCREW BACK AND BEZEL, DUST-PROOF WATCH FOR $6.60.

Let competitors undertake to meet our prices. It will be of no use. They cannot do it. The reasons why they cannot do it are many. Never before was a gold filled, screw back and bezel, dust-proof case offered at anywhere near such prices. We have for several years consumed the entire product of the factory that makes this line of cases; not one is sold to anyone else. The manufacturers are under contract not to sell any of these cases to anyone else. The fact of the matter is, it keeps them busy to supply us. In making arrangements with them we figured the cost of material, the cost of making, etc., added only a reasonable percentage for manufacturers profit, and these figures established the prices we pay for the goods. We realize that this is a snap, and that if we desired we could just as well make more money, only for the fact that we must sustain our reputation as the cheapest supply house on earth, and on just such deals as this it affords us an excellent opportunity to sell far below any competitors. Of this one kind of watch we sell several thousand per month, all of which have given the most excellent satisfaction. These cases are made of two plates of solid gold over an inner plate of fine composition metal, and are warranted by special certificate to wear and retain their color for twenty years. We show in the accompanying illustration a fac simile of the guarantee. These cases are made in the best possible manner; the designs are the very latest, the material is heavy, but still they are made in the new thin model, and are beautifully engraved and finished in the most perfect manner. There is no case made which affords better protection to the movement from the intrusion of dust, dirt or dampness than this one. We invite you to most carefully investigate this watch. Look where you may and get prices on twenty-year gold filled, screw back and bezel and dust-proof watches. Your own judgment in the matter is all we ask. You will find that you will be compelled to pay from 50 per cent. to 100 per cent. more than the prices we ask. You run no risk whatever, for if you are not thoroughly satisfied upon receipt of the watch you can return it to us at our expense and we will refund all your money. We will be glad to send these watches on our regular terms C. O. D. by express, subject to examination, when desired. Watches can be sent to almost any point in the United States by express for 25 cents; by registered mail to any point, 14 cents. We allow for cash in full with order a discount of 3 per cent.; on amounts over $50.00, 4 per cent.; amounts over $100.00, 5 per cent. Most all our customers send cash with their orders.

This cut shows case open with front and back unscrewed, showing just how the case is made and put together.

**Warranted Dust Proof.**

No. 65036.

**Warranted Best Gold Filled.**

This is a picture of our Special Guarantee which goes with every watch.

FRONT OF CASE.

BACK OF CASE.

| We fit these cases with the following 18 size movements: | GILT. | NICKEL. |
|---|---|---|
| 7 jeweled, Trenton | ..... | $6.60 |
| 7 jeweled, Seth Thomas, ¾ plate | ..... | 7.10 |
| 7 jeweled, Waltham, Elgin or Hampden | $8.30 | 11.40 |
| Full 15 jeweled, Waltham, Elgin or Hampden | ..... | |
| Full 17 jeweled, "G. M. Wheeler" Elgin, "P. S. Bartlett" Waltham, or Hampden, adjusted | ..... | 14.10 |

We guarantee all of the above movements for five years.

| | GILT. | NICKEL. |
|---|---|---|
| Full 17 jeweled, "Appleton, Tracy & Co." Waltham, "B. W. Raymond" Elgin, or "Anchor" Hampden, adjusted | ..... | $20.90 |
| Full 17 jeweled, "Crescent Street" Waltham, adjusted | ..... | 21.30 |
| Full 21 jeweled, "No. 150" Grade Elgin, fully adjusted | ..... | 28.05 |
| Full 21 jeweled, "Vanguard" Waltham, fully adjusted | ..... | 36.30 |
| Full 17 jeweled, "New Railway" Hampden, fully adjusted | ..... | 28.30 |
| Full 17 jeweled, "Special Railway" Hampden, fully adjusted | ..... | 38.30 |

For full description of the same, see introductory pages.

# A GENUINE GOLD FILLED 18 SIZE WATCH FOR $6.60.

A Watch for $6.60, equal in appearance and finish to a $20.00 Watch. If you want to post yourself on the newest and best goods on the market, and want to own them at the lowest prices, always consult our catalogue. It is an Encyclopaedia of Bargains.

How is this for a hot drive at our competitors? They cannot keep pace with us, there is no use of their trying. They are not in our class. A genuine gold filled watch, made of two plates of solid gold over an inner plate of fine composition metal, beautifully finished and engraved, made and warranted by the Illinois Watch Case Company, of Elgin, Illinois. The finish and workmanship on these cases is equal to the best, and are made in the latest and most stylish patterns; warranted by certificate to wear and retain their color for five years. This does not imply that they will wear only for five years, but that they are warranted for that length of time. They may wear for ten years or longer.

**BUY WATCHES AND JEWELRY DIRECT AND SAVE 30 TO 50 PER CENT.**

**RETAIL JEWELERS MUST HAVE LARGE PROFITS, AND THEY PAY TOO MUCH FOR THEIR GOODS.**

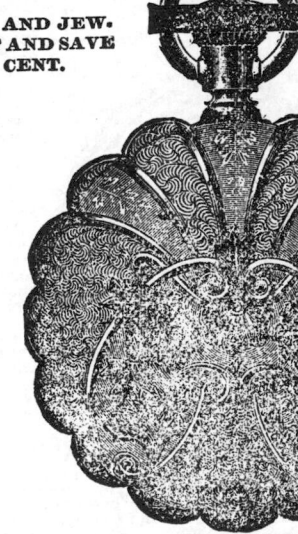

No. 65037.

No. 65038

No. 65039.

| We fit these cases with the following 18 size movements: | GILT. | NICKEL. |
|---|---|---|
| 7 jeweled, Trenton | ..... | $6.60 |
| 7 jeweled, Seth Thomas, ¾ plate | ..... | 7.10 |
| 7 jeweled, Waltham, Elgin or Hampden | $8.30 | 11.40 |
| Full 15 jeweled, Waltham, Elgin or Hampden | ..... | |
| Full 17 jeweled, "G. M. Wheeler" Elgin, "P. S. Bartlett" Waltham, or Hampden, adjusted | ..... | 14.10 |

We guarantee all of the above movements for five years.

| | GILT. | NICKEL. |
|---|---|---|
| Full 17 jeweled, "Appleton, Tracy & Co." Waltham, "B. W. Raymond" Elgin or "Anchor" Hampden, adjusted | ..... | $20.90 |
| Full 17 jeweled, "Crescent Street" Waltham, adjusted | ..... | 21.30 |
| Full 21 jeweled, "No. 150" Grade Elgin, fully adjusted | ..... | 28.05 |
| Full 21 jeweled, "Vanguard" Waltham, fully adjusted | ..... | 36.30 |
| Full 17 jeweled, "New Railway" Hampden, fully adjusted | ..... | 28.30 |
| Full 17 jeweled "Special Railway" Hampden, fully adjusted | ..... | 38.30 |

For full description of the same, see introductory pages.

# A 14 Karat, Gold Filled, 18 Size Watch for $11.95.

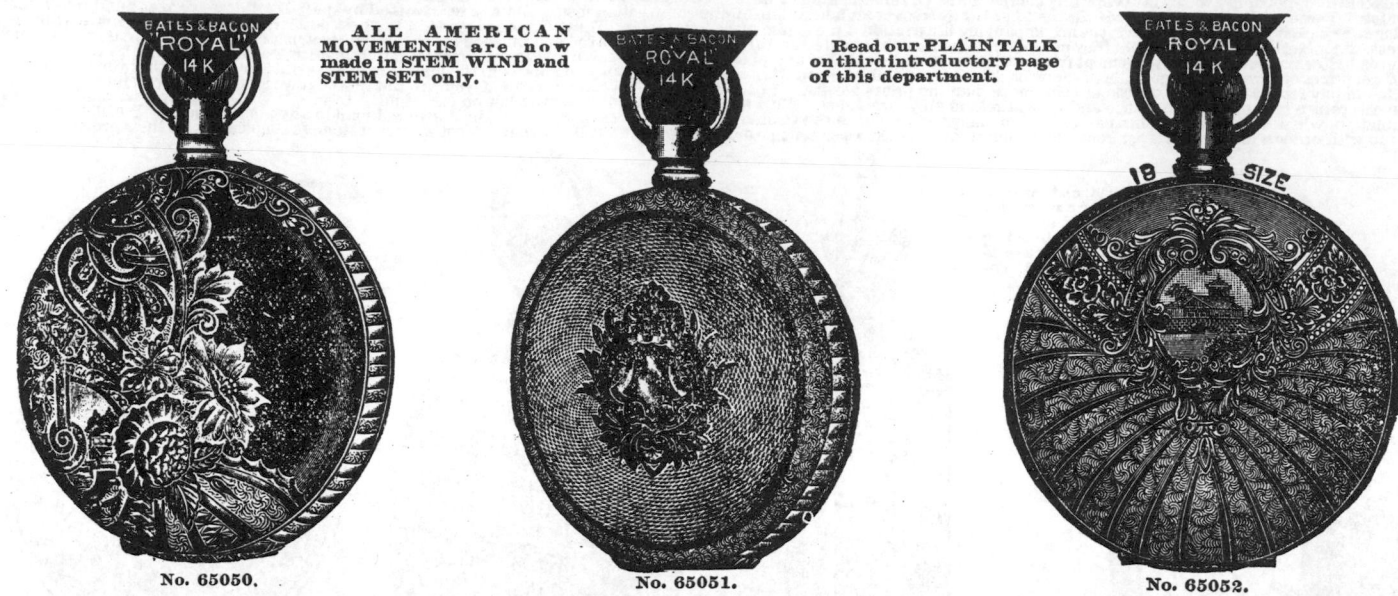

**ALL AMERICAN MOVEMENTS are now made in STEM WIND and STEM SET only.**

**Read our PLAIN TALK** on third introductory page of this department.

No. 65050.       No. 65051.       No. 65052.

**Nothing like it ever advertised before. Something entirely new.** Our stock is always fresh with new and up-to-date goods. We allow no shop-worn or old goods to accumulate on our hands. Step inside a retail store and you will find goods that have been in the house for ten years, if the store has been in existence that long. In our establishment you will seldom find a piece of goods that is six months old, and the majority of our stock changes every few weeks. No concern can carry a full line and always have fresh and new goods at the lowest prices except that they have an immense trade that will keep their stock moving all the time. Let us say here that our **trade is simply enormous.** You could have no idea unless you could call on us and see for yourself. When you come to the city you must not fail to **give us a call.** It will be the strongest argument we can present to convince you that we are in a position to do as we say.

These cases are made of solid 14 karat gold over fine composition metal; are beautifully finished, elaborately engraved, and are made and warranted by the celebrated **Bates & Bacon Watch Case Company** to wear and retain their color for fifteen years.

### WE FIT THESE CASES WITH THE FOLLOWING 18 SIZE MOVEMENTS.

| | Gilt. | Nickel. | | Gilt. | Nickel. |
|---|---|---|---|---|---|
| 7 jeweled, Trenton | | $11 95 | Full 17 jeweled, "Appleton, Tracy & Co." Waltham, "B. W. | | |
| 7 jeweled, Seth Thomas, ¾ plate | | 12 45 | Raymond" Elgin, or "Anchor" Hampden, adjusted | | $26 35 |
| 7 jeweled, Waltham, Elgin or Hampden | $12 95 | | Full 17 jeweled, "Crescent Street" Waltham, adjusted | | 26 75 |
| Full 15 jeweled, Waltham, Elgin or Hampden | | 16 35 | Full 21 jeweled, "No. 150" grade Elgin, fully adjusted | | 33 75 |
| Full 17 jeweled, "G. M. Wheeler," Elgin, "P. S. Bartlett," Waltham, or "Hampden, adjusted | | 19 20 | Full 21 jeweled, "Vanguard" Waltham, fully adjusted | | 43 35 |
| | | | Full 17 jeweled, New Railway" Hampden, fully adjusted | | 34 15 |
| | | | Full 17 jeweled, "Special Railway" Hampden, fully adjusted | | 44 15 |

We guarantee all of the above movements for five years. For full description of the same see introductory pages.

## 16 SIZE, 14 KARAT, GOLD FILLED.

Manufactured by the same concern as the 18 size cases listed above, and are the same quality. These cases are made in the **new thin model** for **Elgin** or **Waltham** 16 size movements. They can be furnished in a variety of the very latest and most desirable shapes.

We fit these cases with the following 16 size movements:

7 jeweled, Trenton or Standard, nickel............$13 10
7 jeweled, Elgin or Waltham, gilt.................. 14 15
Full 15 jeweled, Elgin or Waltham, nickel......... 16 75

Full 17 jeweled, "No. 153" grade Elgin or "Royal" Waltham, adjusted nickel..........$23 55
Full 17 jeweled, "Riverside" Waltham, adjusted, nickel.......... $32 45
Full 17 jeweled, "No. 155" grade Elgin, fully adjusted.....$34 10
Full 17 jeweled, "American Watch Company" Waltham fully adjusted, .............$45 10

The thin model, 16 size cases, are rapidly growing in favor by reason of their thinness, and being smaller than the 18 size. When you order be sure to state the style and engraving you want, and grade of movement.

No. 65053½.

**Watches will be sent C. O. D.** on receipt of 50 cents (cash or stamps), with order as a guarantee of good faith on your part. The 50 cents will be refunded if goods are not satisfactory.

## SOMETHING NEW. Glass On Both Sides.

**You can see the movement in your watch at any time without opening the case.** Nothing about a watch is more fascinating or interesting than to see the movement, with its different parts, such as train wheels, the pallet, hair spring and the balance wheel which makes 18,000 beats per hour, 432,000 per day or 157,788,000 per year. As the ordinary cases are constructed, you cannot see the movement except that you open the cases, which exposes the movement to dampness in the atmosphere and to the intrusion of dust and dirt.

**With the case we offer here it is different.** The body of the case is made of **solid silverine metal by the Dueber Watch Case Co.,** whose reputation for the manufacture of fine watch cases is too well known to need any further comment. **The metal very closely resembles solid silver** and is warranted to retain its color. They have a very heavy bevel edged crystal glass fitted on both sides.

**Don't be afraid** that they are not strong enough for we believe that if they were placed on the floor, they would support the weight of an ordinary man without breaking.

We have sold a large quantity of these watches which have, without one exception, given entire satisfaction. **We can furnish them only with Trenton, Seth Thomas or Hampden Movements. The Seth Thomas Movement** will be found to be the most satisfactory, as it has ¾ plate which exposes to view the most of the wheels. **The Seth Thomas** movements are very carefully made, are well finished and are good timekeepers. We guarantee all movements for 5 years. You run no risk in ordering one of these watches, for if you are not satisfied with it it can be returned (if not too much worn) and exchanged for anything you may select from our catalogue or money refunded as you desire. Prices for complete watch as follows: With 7 jeweled Trenton nickel movement, $3.00; with 7 jeweled Seth Thomas nickel movement, $3.50; with 7 jeweled Hampden movement, $4.25.

**All of these movements are stem wind and stem set and are warranted for 5 years**

No. 65054½.

# A 20-Year, Hunting Case, Gold Filled, 18 Size Watch for $7.95

We are always at war with high prices. We care not for any kind of opposition. Dealers are constantly writing the trade journals to make some effort to stop us from ruining their business. They say they cannot sell goods when we are constantly sending advertising matter into their vicinity and offering watches and jewelry at wholesale prices and less. Monopolies and Watch Trusts have undertaken many times to stop us from getting certain lines of goods. This has been done in the interest of the retailer; but still we go on pounding down prices. Our course is honorable and we propose to pursue it to a finish. We consider that it is wrong to uphold any monopoly or trust that will cause the consumer to pay more for goods than they are worth. We believe in putting goods on the market at a very small per cent of advance on cost of manufacture; this we are doing. On this Watch, as well as our screw No. 4036, dust-proof cases and ladies' special 6 size cases, Nos. 4194 to 4199, we are controling the production of one of the largest factories in this country. To do this means to sell several thousand of their cases every month.

We have handled these goods for many years, and it is not only from a thorough knowledge of the quality and proportion of material that goes into their construction, but also from practical experience that we can speak of their merits. The cases are made of two plates of fine solid gold, over fine hard composition metal, are well finished, beautifully engraved in a variety of styles, as illustrated on this page, and are warranted by special certificate to wear and retain their color for twenty years. They are very beautiful watches, are thoroughly up to date, and one that any man can justly be proud of. In addition to the certificate on the inside of the case a large certificate of guarantee for both case and movement is furnished by us.

Any of these watches will be sent on our regular terms to any express office, subject to examination, provided 50 cents accompanies the order, as guarantee of good faith. Most of our customers send cash in full with their order and take advantage of the 3 per cent discount. If goods are to be sent by mail, send extra money for postage and registering, and state how much you enclose for that purpose.

**THE LATEST STYLES.**

**THE FINEST ENGRAVINGS.**

No. 65055.  No. 65056.  No. 65057.

## WE FIT THESE CASES WITH THE FOLLOWING 18-SIZE MOVEMENTS:

| | GILT. | NICKEL. |
|---|---|---|
| 7 jeweled, Trenton | | $7.95 |
| 7 jeweled, Seth Thomas, ¾ plate | | 8.50 |
| 7 jeweled, Waltham, Elgin or Hampden | $9.65 | .... |
| Full 15 jeweled, Waltham, Elgin or Hampden | | 12.75 |
| Full 17 jeweled, "G. M. Wheeler," Elgin; "P. S. Bartlett," Waltham; or Hampden, adjusted | | 15.45 |

| | NICKEL. |
|---|---|
| Full 17 jeweled, "Appleton, Tracy & Co.," Waltham; "B. W. Raymond," Elgin; or "Anchor," Hampden, adjusted | $22.25 |
| Full 17 jeweled, "Crescent Street," Waltham, adjusted | 22.45 |
| Full 21 jeweled, "No. 150," Grade Elgin, fully adjusted | 29.45 |
| Full 21 jeweled, "Vanguard," Waltham, fully adjusted | 37.95 |
| Full 17 jeweled, "New Railway," Hampden, fully adjusted | 29.85 |
| Full 17 jeweled, "Special Railway," Hampden, fully adjusted | 39.85 |

We GUARANTEE all of the above movements for five years. For full description of the same, see introductory pages.

**THE BEST GOODS.**

**THE LOWEST PRICES.**

No. 65058.  No. 65059.  No. 65061.

**ANY STYLE IN OPEN FACE, 50 CENTS LESS.**

A CERTIFICATE OF GUARANTEE for both case and movement accompanies every watch we sell.

SEE HOW GOLD-FILLED CASES ARE MADE, on introductory pages of this department.

Read our plain talk on third introductory page of this department.

Sixteen cents will carry a gent's watch to any point in the United States by registered mail; 25 cents to almost any point by express.

# GOLD FILLED, 10-KARAT, 18 SIZE WATCHES

Made by the **Joseph Fahys Watch Case Company** (makers of the Montauk case), of Brooklyn, N. Y.; the **Deuber Watch Case Company**, of Canton, Ohio; the **Crescent Watch Case Company**, of Newark, N. J.; **Bates & Bacon Watch Case Company** (manufacturers of the Peer case), Attleboro, Mass.; **Wadsworth Watch Case Company**, Newport, Ky., and the **Keystone Watch Case Company** (makers of the James Boss case), of Philadelphia, Pa.   The above are the oldest and most reliable makers in the case business.

The cases listed on this and the opposite page are all made of **Two Plates of solid 10-karat gold** over fine hard composition metal, and are guaranteed by certificates from the manufacturers.

The Deuber 10-karat cases are warranted to wear for 20 years, while all of the others are warranted for 15 years.

We wish to call special attention to the **most excellent finish, quality and style** of goods made by the **Deuber, Wadsworth, Fahys** and the **Illinois Watch Case Companies.**

Our limited space will not permit us to illustrate all of the styles made by these three companies, but we can furnish them in any **style** listed on these two pages.   We can also furnish styles not listed here when desired.

We are the originators of the LIBERAL POLICY of sending goods C. O. D. on small deposit for examination.

We will furnish anything. If you don't find what you want in our catalogue, write us.

No. 65070.            No. 65071.            No. 65072.

### WE FIT THESE CASES WITH THE FOLLOWING 18 SIZE MOVEMENTS:

| | GILT. | NICKEL. |
|---|---|---|
| 7 jeweled, Trenton | | $10.95 |
| 7 jeweled, Seth Thomas, ¾ plate | | 11.45 |
| 7 jeweled, Waltham, Elgin or Hampden | $11.95 | |
| Full 15 jeweled, Waltham, Elgin or Hampden | | 15.35 |
| Full 17 jeweled, "G. M. Wheeler" Elgin, "P. S. Bartlett" Waltham or "Hampden" adjusted | | 18.20 |
| Full 17 jeweled, "Appleton, Tracy & Co." Waltham, "B. W. Raymond" Elgin or "Anchor" Hampden, adjusted | | 25.80 |
| Full 17 jeweled, "Crescent Street" Waltham, adjusted | | 26.25 |
| Full 21 jeweled, "No. 150" Grade Elgin, fully adjusted | | 32.75 |
| Full 21 jeweled, "Vanguard" Waltham, fully adjusted | | 42.35 |
| Full 17 jeweled, "New Railway" Hampden, fully adjusted | | 33.15 |
| Full 17 jeweled, "Special Railway" Hampden, fully adjusted | | 43.15 |

We **GUARANTEE** all of the above movements for five years.   For full description of the same, see introductory pages.

OUR POLICY is to TREAT OUR CUSTOMERS AS WE WOULD LIKE TO BE TREATED WERE WE IN THEIR PLACES. Its the only road to success.

If you will follow our instructions in the front of this book when making up your orders, there will be little chance for mistakes.

No. 65073.            No. 65074.            No. 65075.

OPEN FACE jointed cases $1.00 less. For open face, screw, dust-proof cases see Nos. 6036 and 6123 to 6128.

A DISCOUNT of 3 per cent will be given for cash in full with your order.  Four per cent will be allowed on orders over $50.00, and 5 per cent on orders over $100.00.

BE SURE TO STATE both the number and name of case and grade of movement wanted when you order.

# GOLD FILLED 10 KARAT WATCHES—Continued.

### FOR PRICES, SEE PREVIOUS PAGE.

No. 65076.

No. 65077.

No. 65078.

If you return watches or jewelry for exchange or repairs, be sure to follow our instructions. See front page of this book.

If we should make a mistake in your order, let us know immediately. Any house is liable to make a mistake.

No. 65079.

No. 65080.

No. 65081.

Our clerks are all instructed to treat our customers as they would like to be treated were they in the customer's place.

Our customers interests are our own. Without their good will we would soon loose our trade.

No. 65082.

No. 65083.

No. 65084.

For smaller gents' or boys' gold filled watches, see 12 size, Nos. 4342 and 4343.

FOR 50 CENTS you can see and examine watches before paying for the same at your express office. If not satisfactory we will refund the deposit.

SEE HOW GOLD FILLED CASES are made, on introductory pages of this department.

24

# 14 Karat, Gold Filled, 18 Size Watches.

Made by the **Joseph Fahy's Watch Case Company** (makers of the Monarch case), of Brooklyn, New York; the **Dueber Watch Case Company**, of Canton, Ohio; the **Crescent Watch Case Company**, of Newark, New Jersey; the **Illinois Watch Case Company** (makers of the Elgin Commander case), of Elgin, Illinois; the **Bates & Bacon Watch Case Company** (makers of the Puritan case), of Attleboro, Mass.; the **Wadsworth Watch Case Company**, of Newport, Ky., and the **Keystone Watch Case Company** (makers of the James Boss cases), of Philadelphia, Pa.

The above named concerns are all the oldest and most reliable makers in the case business. The cases represented on these two pages are made of **two plates of solid 14 karat gold** over fine composition metal, and are warranted by certificate from the manufacturers to wear and retain their color for twenty years.

Your special attention is requested in favor of the **Dueber, Fahy's** and **Illinois Watch Case Company's** goods, on account of the **most excellent finish,** quality and style of the same. Limited space will not permit us to illustrate all the shapes, styles and different engravings of the three last named concerns; but we can furnish goods made by them in any style listed on these two pages.

For Engraving on watch cases: Script, 2⅗ cents per letter; Old English, 5⅗ cents.

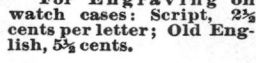

A certificate of guarantee from us for both case and movement will accompany every watch we sell.

No. 65085.                     No. 65086.                     No. 65087.

## WE FIT THESE CASES WITH THE FOLLOWING 18-SIZE MOVEMENTS:

|  | GILT. | NICKEL. |  | GILT. | NICKEL. |
|---|---|---|---|---|---|
| 7 jeweled, Trenton.......... | ...... | $14.95 | Full 17 jeweled, "Crescent Street" Waltham, adjusted............. | ...... | $30.10 |
| 7 jeweled, Seth Thomas, ¾ plate............ | ...... | 15.45 | Full 21 jeweled, "No. 150" Grade Elgin, fully adjusted............. | ...... | 36.57 |
| 7 jeweled, Waltham, Elgin or Hampden.................... | $15.95 | ...... | Full 21 jeweled, "Vanguard" Waltham, fully adjusted............. | ...... | 45.10 |
| Full 15 jeweled, Waltham, Elgin or Hampden........ | ...... | 19.25 | Full 17 jeweled, "New Railway" Hampden, fully adjusted......... | ...... | 37.00 |
| Full 17 jeweled, "G. M. Wheeler" Elgin, "P. S. Bartlett" Waltham, or Hampden, adjusted...... | ...... | 22.00 | Full 17 jeweled, "Special Railway" Hampden, fully adjusted...... | ...... | 47.00 |
| Full 17 jeweled, "Appleton, Tracy & Co." Waltham, "B. W. Raymond" Elgin, or "Anchor" Hampden, adjusted........... | ...... | 29.70 |  |  |  |

We **GUARANTEE** all of the above movements for five years. For full description of the same, see introductory pages.

A guarantee from the manufacturer will be found in the back of every filled case we sell.

If you ever get any goods from us that are not satisfactory, return them to us immediately for exchange.

No. 65088.                     No. 65089.                     No. 65090.

Open face, jointed cases, $1.00 less. For open face, screw, dust-proof cases see Nos. 4036, and 4123 to 4128.

**YOU CAN MAKE MONEY** selling our watches and jewelry. Why not, when you can buy as low and lower than your retail dealer. You would be satisfied with smaller profits, because what you make is clear gain. He has heavy expenses, such as store rent, fuel, clerk hire, etc.

**SEE HOW GOLD FILLED CASES** are made, on introductory pages of this department.

# 14 KARAT GOLD FILLED 18 SIZE CASES.—Continued.

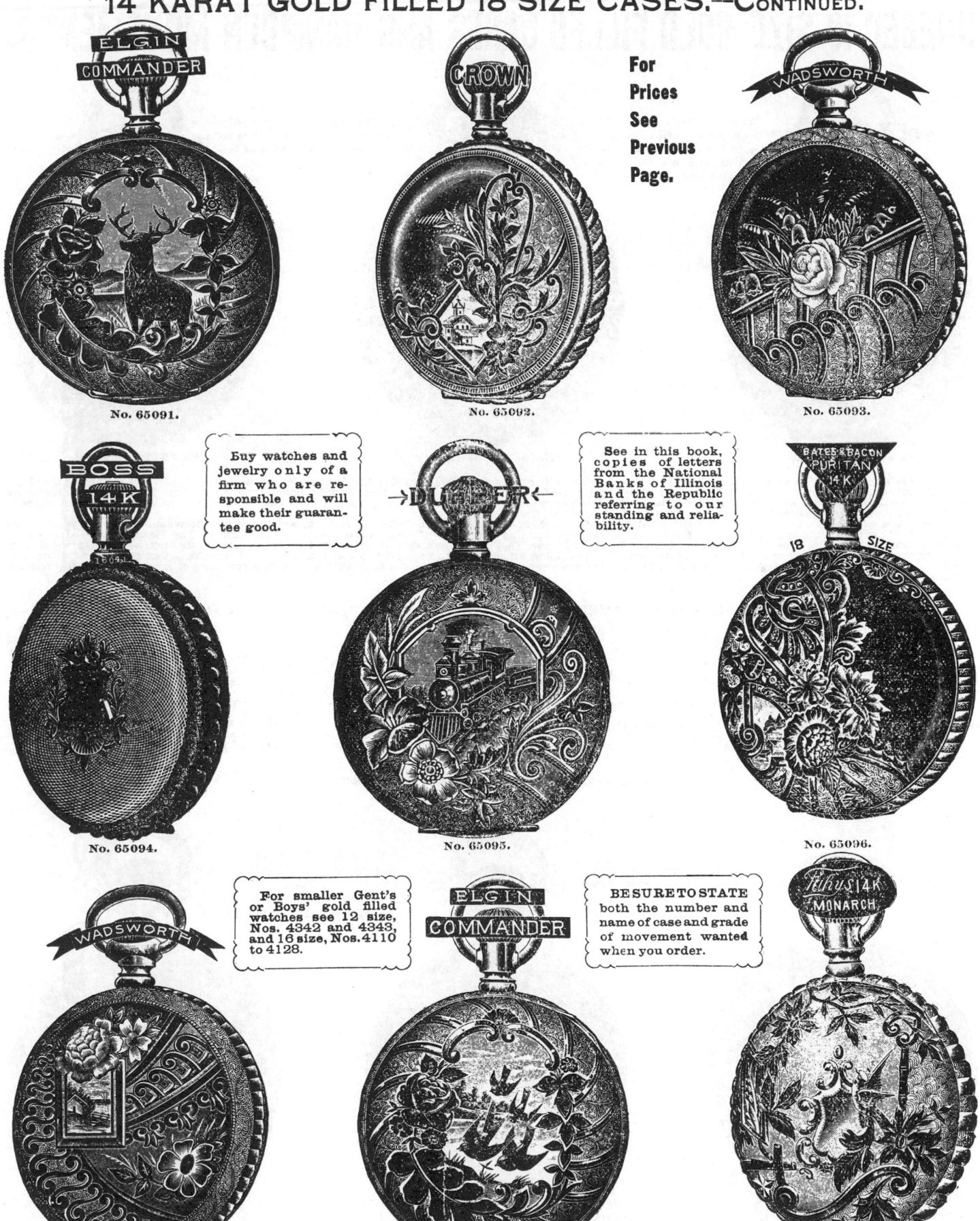

For
Prices
See
Previous
Page.

No. 65091.

No. 65092.

No. 65093.

Buy watches and jewelry only of a firm who are responsible and will make their guarantee good.

See in this book, copies of letters from the National Banks of Illinois and the Republic referring to our standing and reliability.

No. 65094.

No. 65095.

No. 65096.

For smaller Gent's or Boys' gold filled watches see 12 size, Nos. 4342 and 4343, and 16 size, Nos. 4110 to 4128.

BE SURE TO STATE both the number and name of case and grade of movement wanted when you order.

No. 65097.

No. 65098.

No. 65099.

OUR LIBERAL TERMS allow you to examine the goods before paying for the same.   No other concern offers such fair treatment.

# DUEBER 16 SIZE, GOLD FILLED CASES AND HAMPDEN MOVEMENTS.

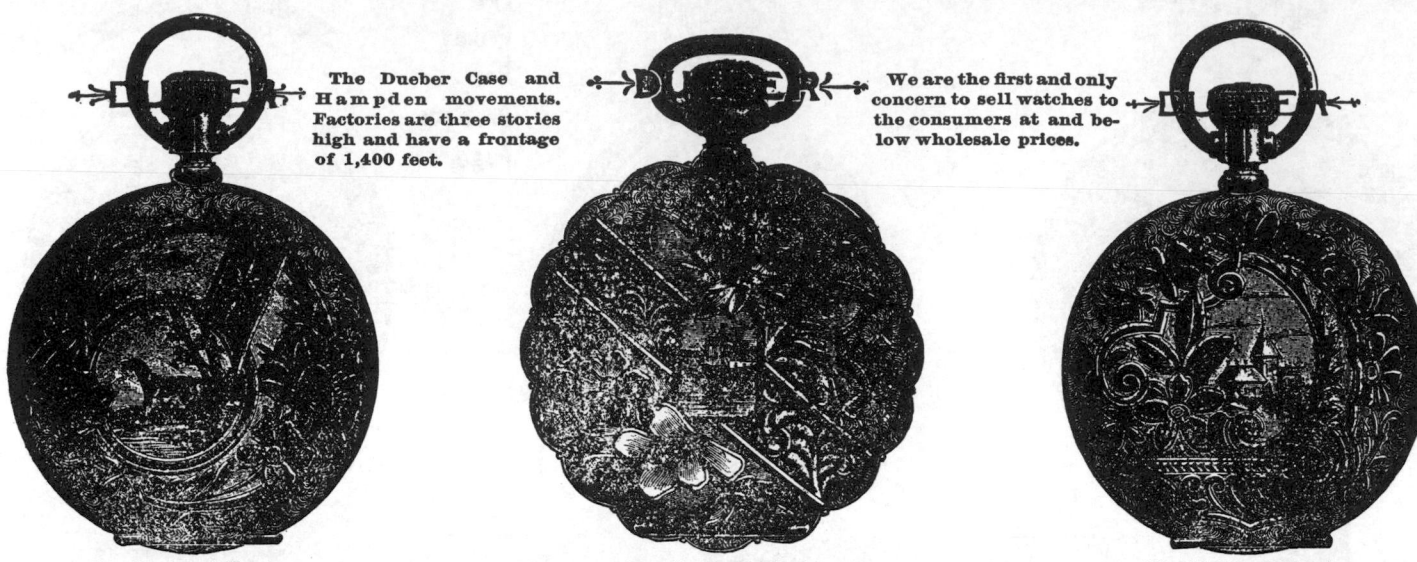

The Dueber Case and Hampden movements. Factories are three stories high and have a frontage of 1,400 feet.

We are the first and only concern to sell watches to the consumers at and below wholesale prices.

No. 65110. 10 Karat.          No. 65111. 10 Karat.          No. 65112. 10 Karat.

The Dueber cases and Hampden movements have a reputation for quality, finish and durability that is **excelled by none**. Both factories are among the **oldest** and their goods are known the world over. We list on this page 16 size cases and movements complete. This size is becoming more popular year by year as being the **most desirable gentleman's size**, where their work does not make it necessary for them to have a very heavy case. These cases, however, are made very strong and there is not much difference, so far as strength is concerned, between these and the 18 size.

These cases are made of two plates of solid gold over hard composition metal, and both the 10 and 14 karat are warranted to wear for twenty years. The Dueber Watch Case Company has a reputation for the finest engravings, and they finish all their cases in the most thorough manner. The Hampden 16 size movements are made to fit Dueber cases only, and cannot be furnished in any other. They have several special features in their mechanical construction which has assisted them in building up such an enviable reputation as fine timekeepers. They are all well made, and are warranted by both the factory and ourselves. The two highest grades are especially adapted to the requirements of railroad men, where a fine timekeeper is essential, and where it is necessary to have a certificate of inspection from the railroad company.

## WE FIT IN THESE CASES HAMPDEN MOVEMENTS ONLY, AS FOLLOWS:

|  | With 10 Karat Case. | With 14 Karat Case. |
|---|---|---|
| 7 Jeweled, Hampden, gilt | $11.90 | $13.90 |
| 11 Jeweled, Hampden, gilt | 12.90 | 14.90 |
| 13 Jeweled, Hampden, nickel | 14.40 | 16.40 |
| 17 Jeweled, Hampden, nickel, patent regulator | 17.90 | 19.90 |
| 17 Jeweled, Hampden, nickel, patent regulator, adjusted, with Breguet hairspring | 19.90 | 21.90 |
| 17 Jeweled, Hampden, nickle, patent regulator, adjusted, double sunk dial, and Breguet hairspring. A fine movement for railroad use | 22.90 | 24.90 |

|  | With 10 Karat Case. | With 14 Karat Case. |
|---|---|---|
| 17 Extra fine ruby Jewels, in gold settings, gold bevel head screws, patent Breguet hairspring, double sunk dial, patent micrometer regulator, compensation balance, accurately timed and adjusted to temperature, position and isochronism. Especially adapted to railroad use | $42.90 | $44.90 |

The above is the highest grade 16 size movement made by the Hampden Watch Co. The Dueber Watch Case Co. and the Hampden Watch Co. are both located at Canton, Ohio. The factories are three stories high and occupy a frontage of 1,400 feet.

All of the above movements are warranted for five years.

We speak for your trade and offer you every possible inducement to get it.

Our only salesman is our catalogue. If this one is not yours, send 15 cents to partly pay postage and you shall have one.

No. 65113. 14 Karat.          No. 65114. 14 Karat.          No. 65115. 14 Karat.

Open face jointed cases $1.00 less. For open face screw dust-proof cases see Nos. 6036 and 6123 to 6128.

A DISCOUNT of 3 per cent. will be given for cash in full with your order; 4 per cent. will be allowed on orders over $50.00 and 5 per cent. on orders over $100.00.

If you return watches or jewelry for exchange or repairs, be sure to follow our instructions. See front page of this book.

# Wadsworth, Boss and Elgin 16 Size, Gold Filled Watches.

Our line of 16 size filled cases is very complete, and represents all of the best manufacturers. For want of space we illustrate but three each of the 10 and 14 karat, but will furnish any style or make desired. Those illustrated are the latest and most popular patterns. They are made in the new thin model for the latest **Elgin** and **Waltham** 16 size movements. Thin watches are growing in favor very rapidly, as they do not disfigure the clothing like a heavy thick watch. While we only illustrate one each of the **Wadsworth** cases, we can furnish them in any design and pattern of engraving listed on this page. The engravings on these watches are of the very finest done by hand, and the cases are finished in the highest style of the art. They are made by the **Wadsworth Watch Case Company** of **Newport, Ky.,** and the **Keystone Watch Case Company** (makers of the **Boss** case), of **Philadelphia, Pa.** They are constructed of two plates of solid gold, over fine hard composition metal. The 10 karat cases are warranted to wear for fifteen years, and the 14 karat cases for twenty years.

No. 4121. Case is satin finished, and is especially adapted when desired for the engraving of a large monogram.

The prettiest, best and latest, and latest style goods on the market are always listed by us.

When you have learned to buy your goods by mail you will often wonder why you did not do so before.

No. 65116. 10 karat, 16 size.

No. 65117. 10 karat, 16 size.

No. 65118. 10 karat, 16 size.

No. 65119. 14 karat, 16 size.

## WE FIT THESE CASES WITH THE FOLLOWING 16 SIZE MOVEMENTS:

|  | For 10 karat case. | For 14 karat case. |
|---|---|---|
| 7 jeweled, Elgin or Waltham, gilt | $12.75 | $16.50 |
| Full 15 jeweled, Elgin or Waltham, nickel | 15.85 | 19.60 |
| Full 17 jeweled, "No. 153" Grade Elgin or "Royal" Waltham, adjusted, nickel | 22.10 | 25.85 |
| Full 17 jeweled, "Riverside" Waltham, adjusted, nickel | 28.70 | 32.45 |
| Full 17 jeweled, "No. 154" Grade Elgin, adjusted, nickel | 24.85 | 28.60 |
| Full 17 jeweled, "No. 155" Grade Elgin, fully adjusted, nickel | 30.45 | 34.20 |
| Full 17 jeweled, "American Watch Co." Waltham, fully adjusted, nickel | 41.35 | 45.10 |

We GUARANTEE all the above movements for five years. For full description of the same, see introductory pages.

**SEE HOW GOLD FILLED CASES are made, on introductory pages of this Department.**

**Open face jointed cases $1.00 less. For open face screw dust-proof cases, see Nos. 6036 and 6123 to 6128.**

**BE SURE TO STATE both the number and name of the case and grade of movement wanted when you order.**

**For smaller gents' or boys' gold filled watches see 12 size, Nos. 6342 and 6343.**

If the BEST GOODS at the LOWEST PRICES and PROMPT ATTENTION will secure your patronage, IT IS OURS.

You can sit down by your own fireside and with our catalogue you have all the advantages of a metropolitan store.

No. 65120. 14 karat, 16 size.

No. 65121½. 14 karat, 16 size.

No. 65122. 14 karat, 16 size.

# GOLD FILLED, SCREW BACK AND BEZEL, DUST-PROOF, 18 SIZE CASES.

Prices lower than ever before. Anybody can own a gold filled watch at our prices. Screw dust-proof cases have become very popular, and are being so much appreciated by all who desire an open faced watch that the sales have grown to an enormous number. They are symmetrical in design, have no joints to wear out the pockets, and they afford the movement the most perfect protection from intrusion of dust or dampness, and retain the oil in a fluid form for a greater period of time. They are especially adapted to the requirements of millers and others exposed to dust. For street car men, they preserve the movement from exposure to dampness.

The cases illustrated on this page are manufactured by the celebrated **Joseph Fahy's Watch Case Company** of Brooklyn, N. Y. They are made of **two plates of solid gold** over fine hard composition metal, are very strong, beautifully engraved, thoroughly finished in every respect, and warranted by certificates from both the manufacturers and ourselves. The 10 karat cases are guaranteed to wear for fifteen years, and the 14 karat cases for twenty-one years. They can also be furnished in engine-turned engraving, and with antique or plain pendants, as desired. They are all fitted with **heavy bevel edge glasses.**

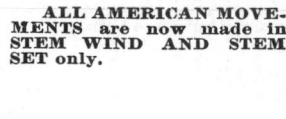

**ALL AMERICAN MOVEMENTS** are now made in **STEM WIND AND STEM SET** only.

**SEE HOW GOLD FILLED CASES** are made, on introductory pages of this department.

No. 65123.                No. 65124.                No. 65125.

## WE FIT THESE CASES WITH THE FOLLOWING 18 SIZE MOVEMENTS:

| | For 10 karat case. | For 14 karat case. | | For 10 karat case. | For 14 karat case. |
|---|---|---|---|---|---|
| 7 jeweled, Trenton, nickel | $7.10 | $9.95 | Full 17 jeweled, "Crescent Street" Waltham, adjusted, nickel | $22.95 | $26.80 |
| 7 jeweled, Seth Thomas, ¾ plate, nickel | 7.60 | 10.45 | Full 21 jeweled, "No. 150" Grade Elgin, fully adjusted, nickel | 29.45 | 33.30 |
| 7 jeweled, Waltham, Elgin or Hampden, gilt | 8.20 | 12.05 | Full 21 jeweled, "Vanguard" Waltham, fully adjusted, nickel | 37.95 | 41.80 |
| Full 15 jeweled, Waltham, Elgin or Hampden, nickel | 12.05 | 15.90 | Full 17 jeweled, "New Railway" Hampden. fully adjusted, nickel | 29.85 | 33.70 |
| Full 17 jeweled, "G. M. Wheeler" Elgin, "P. S. Bartlett" Waltham, or Hampden, adjusted, nickel | 14.90 | 18.70 | Full 17 jeweled, "Special Railway" Hampden, fully adjusted, nickel | 39.85 | 43.70 |
| Full 17 jeweled, "Appleton, Tracy & Co." Waltham, "B. W. Raymond" Elgin or "Anchor" Hampden, adjusted, nickel | 22.50 | 26.35 | | | |

We guarantee all of the above movements for five years. For full description of the same, see introductory pages.

# FAHY'S GOLD FILLED, SCREW BACK AND BEZEL, DUST-PROOF, 16 SIZE CASES.

The same general description applies to these cases as to the 18 size listed above, except that they are smaller. **These 16 size cases we believe to be the most beautiful and symmetrical open face cases on the market.** For style, finish and neatness they are beyond description. If you want an open face watch, do not fail to give these the attention they deserve. Like the above, they have **heavy bevel edge glasses**, are very strong and thoroughly well made.

**YOU RUN NO RISK** when dealing with a reliable concern. We refer to the National Banks of Illinois and Republic, among the largest in the city. See their letters in this book.

**OUR LIBERAL TERMS** allow you to examine the goods before paying for the same. No other concern offers such fair treatment.

No. 65126.                No, 65127.                No. 65128.

## WE FIT THESE CASES WITH THE FOLLOWING 16 SIZE MOVEMENTS:

| | For 10 karat case. | For 14 karat case. | | For 10 karat case. | For 14 karat case. |
|---|---|---|---|---|---|
| 7 jeweled, Elgin or Waltham, gilt | $9.20 | $13.05 | Full 17 jeweled, "No. 154" Grade Elgin, adjusted, nickel | $22.55 | $25.85 |
| Full 15 jeweled, Elgin or Waltham, nickel | 11.60 | 15.35 | Full 17 jeweled, "No. 155" Grade Elgin, fully adjusted, nickel | 28.05 | 31.35 |
| Full 17 jeweled, "No. 153" Grade Elgin or "Royal" Waltham, adjusted, nickel | 19.80 | 23.10 | Full 17 jeweled, "American Watch Co." Waltham, fully adjusted, nickel | 39.05 | 42.35 |
| Full 17 jeweled, "Riverside" Waltham, adjusted, nickel | 26.40 | 29.70 | | | |

We guarantee all of the above movements for five years. For full description of the same, see introductory pages.

## No. 65129—A GOLD FILLED, BOX JOINT, 18 SIZE WATCH FOR $9.90.

This Case is made in **Louis XIV.** style, **box joint**, is made of **two plates of solid gold** over fine hard composition metal, is beautifully engraved and well finished in every respect, and is warranted by certificate to **wear for twenty years.** The price quoted above is for **Elgin, Waltham** or **Hampden,** 7 jeweled, compensation balance, patent pinion, stem wind and stem set, gilt movement, price $9.90. For prices with other movements add $1.70 to prices listed for No. 4125.

## No. 65130—A Gold Filled, Open Face, Plain Polished, Screw Dust-Proof, 18 Size Watch for $8.20.

This Case will be furnished in either 10 or 14 karat gold filled, warranted for fifteen and twenty years. It is made by the **Muhr Watch Case Co.,** of Philadelphia, Pa., is plain polished or engine turned, Basine pattern, fitted with **heavy bevel edge glass,** has screw back and bezel, is dust proof, and will be fitted with a 7 jeweled expansion balance, patent pinion, stem wind and stem set, **Waltham, Elgin** or **Hampden gilt movement.** The price quoted above is for 10 karat; for 14 karat with same movement, $12.05. For prices with other movements, same prices as Nos. 4123 to 4128.

## No. 65131—DUEBER, 14 KARAT, BOX JOINT, FULL ENGRAVED, 18 SIZE CASES.

These cases are of the **Louis XIV.** box joint pattern, made of two plates of solid gold over composition metal and warranted to wear and retain their color for twenty years. They are made by the celebrated **Dueber Watch Case Company,** of Canton, Ohio, whose reputation for fine watch cases is **known the world over.** They are thoroughly finished in every respect and elaborately engraved by hand. Price for 10 karat case, fitted with **Waltham, Elgin** or **Hampden,** 7 jeweled, expansion balance, patent pinion, stem wind and stem set movement, $18.15. This case can be furnished in 16 size when desired. For 18 karat case, with same movement, $18.15. For other grades of movements in 14 karat cases, add $1.60 to No. 4085.

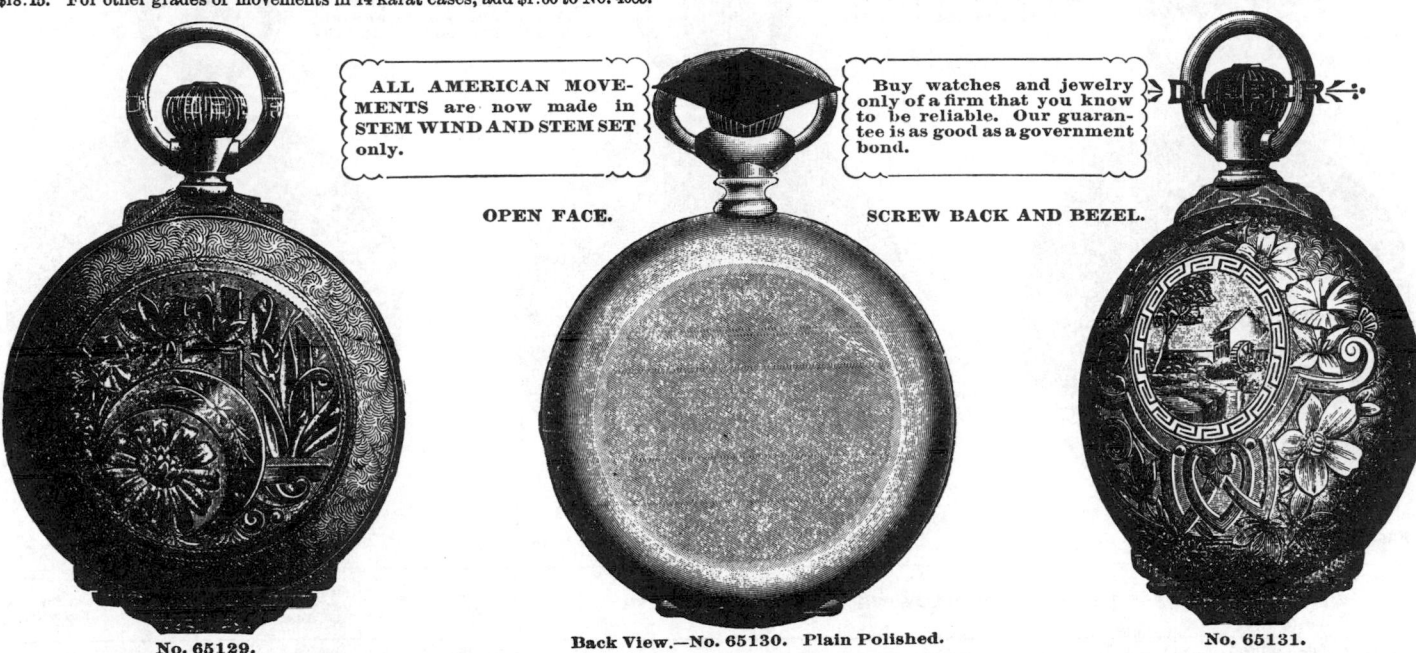

ALL AMERICAN MOVE-MENTS are now made in STEM WIND AND STEM SET only.

Buy watches and jewelry only of a firm that you know to be reliable. Our guarantee is as good as a government bond.

OPEN FACE.        SCREW BACK AND BEZEL.

No. 65129.     Back View.—No. 65130. Plain Polished.     No. 65131.

# SOLID GOLD, 14 KARAT, NEW THIN MODEL, 16 SIZE CASES.

In **Solid Gold Cases** we handle nothing but **the very best solid gold through and through,** and made only by the oldest and most reputable case makers. You will not find cases of such high grade and finish as we offer you in the average retail store. They are only to be found in the largest and finest retail stores in the large cities, such as Chicago and New York. We give you the advantage of having the largest and most complete stock to select from, and at the same time **save you from 33⅓ to 50 per cent** on your purchase. Our line is very complete, and if you do not find here what you want, write us, giving an idea of what you wish and we will be pleased to quote you. We illustrate here three of the latest and prettiest designs, which are all very popular. No. 4150 can be furnished in satin finish instead of engine turned, if desired. Furnished in that style it is especially adapted for monogram work. (Large monograms engraved on watch cases can be furnished at from $2.00 to $6.00, depending on style, quality, etc.) We carry in stock and can furnish **raised colored gold and diamond set solid gold cases,** in either 16 or 18 size when desired. Prices furnished on application. **Open Face Cases, $1.00 less.**

Watches will be sent C. O. D. on receipt of 50 cents (cash or stamps) with the order as a guarantee of good faith on your part. The 50 cents will be refunded if goods are not satisfactory.

Other styles of 16 size solid gold cases will be furnished if desired, also colored, ornamented, and diamond set.

16 cents will carry a gents' watch to any point in the United States by registered mail. 25 cents to almost any point by express.
Read our plain talk on third introductory page of this department.

If you write for prices on any SPECIAL STYLE, please state as near as possible what you want.

No. 65150.        No. 65151.        No. 65152.

Solid 14 karat Gold, 16 size, Plain Polished, Engine Turned or Satin Finished; weight, 31 dwt.    Solid 14 karat Gold, 16 size, Fancy Engraved; weight, 32 dwt.    Solid 14 karat Gold, 16 size; weight, 48 dwt. Fancy Engine Turned or Satin Finished.

### WE FIT THESE CASES WITH THE FOLLOWING 16 SIZE MOVEMENTS:

| | No. 65150. | No. 65151. | No. 65152. | | No. 65150. | No. 65151. | No. 65152. |
|---|---|---|---|---|---|---|---|
| 7 jeweled, Elgin or Waltham ............Gilt, | $27.40 | $29.40 | $43.40 | Full 17 jeweled, "No. 154" Grade Elgin, adjusted..Nickel, | $39.50 | $41.50 | $55.50 |
| Full 15 jeweled, Elgin or Waltham ................Nickel, | 30.15 | 32.15 | 45.15 | Full 17 jeweled, "No. 155" Grade Elgin, fully adjusted ...............................Nickel, | 45.00 | 47.00 | 61.00 |
| Full 17 jeweled, "No. 153" Grade Elgin, or "Royal" Waltham, adjusted ...............Nickel, | 36.75 | 38.75 | 52.75 | Full 17 jeweled, "American Watch Co." Waltham, fully adjusted...............................Nickel, | 56.00 | 58.00 | 72.00 |
| Full 17 jeweled, "Riverside" Waltham, adjusted " | 43.35 | 45.35 | 59.35 | | | | |

We GUARANTEE all of the above movements for five years. For full description of the same, see introductory pages.

# SOLID 14 KARAT GOLD, 18 SIZE CASES.

If you want the best that money will buy, get a solid gold case, but don't pay the retail prices for it. Your jeweler will say you cannot buy a good solid gold case at our prices, or your friends who have been accustomed to buying at retail may say the same. But do not be deceived. We will give you a pointer. If you have any doubts ask your dealer what he will pay you in cash per pennyweight for old 14-karat gold. Do not accept a trade proposition, but talk on the basis of cash, and not with the promise that you will buy a watch from him. The market value of 14 karat gold is 56 cents per pennyweight. After it is refined it is worth about 10 cents more. The average gent's solid gold case weighs from 30 to 45 pennyweights. To the cost of gold we add cost of making and engraving, and our small per cent. of profit for handling, and there you have it. Figure for yourself. You need take the statement of no one for it. It has always been our disposition to place everything before our customers in a plain and concise manner, then they can understand what they are buying, and are easier to satisfy.

Our solid gold cases are the best to be had, are solid 14 karat gold through and through, and made by the best makers in the watch case business, concerns who furnish the largest and finest stores in New York City, Chicago, and other large cities. They are all stamped inside, "14 karat solid gold," warranted United States Mint Assay. We do not handle anything below 14 karat in solid gold cases, as the difference in the cost of gold is but a few cents per pennyweight and would not justify the purchaser in making a sacrifice on the quality. We furnish with each gold watch a certificate of guarantee, warranting the case for a lifetime and the movement for five years.

Engraving on watch cases, script 2½ cents per letter, old English 5½ cents per letter.

When watches are to be engraved the full amount of cash for both goods and engraving must accompany the order.

**No. 65153.**
Fancy engraved, solid gold, weight 40 dwt.

**No. 65154.**
Engine-turned engraving, solid gold, weight 38 dwt.

**No. 65155.**
Fancy engraved, solid gold, weight 40 dwt.

| WE FIT THESE CASES WITH THE FOLLOWING 18 SIZE MOVEMENTS: | Prices for Case No. 65154. | Prices for Cases Nos. 65153, 65155, 65158. | Prices for Case No. 65157. | Prices for Case No. 65156. |
|---|---|---|---|---|
| 7 jeweled, Trenton..................................................nickel, | $27.80 | $32.80 | $35.80 | $40.10 |
| 7 jeweled, Seth Thomas, ¾ plate.............................nickel, | 28.40 | 33.40 | 36.40 | 40.70 |
| 7 jeweled, Waltham, Elgin or Hampden.......................gilt, | 28.90 | 33.90 | 36.90 | 41.20 |
| Full 15 jeweled, Waltham, Elgin or Hampden...............nickel, | 32.75 | 37.75 | 40.75 | 45.05 |
| Full 17 jeweled, "G. M. Wheeler" Elgin, "P. S. Bartlett" Waltham or Hampden, adjusted...........nickel, | 35.60 | 40.60 | 43.60 | 47.90 |
| Full 17 jeweled, "Appleton,Tracy&Co." Waltham, "B.W.Raymond" Elgin, or "Anchor" Hampden, ajsd..nickel, | 43.20 | 48.20 | 51.20 | 55.50 |
| Full 17 jeweled, "Crescent Street" Waltham, adjusted........nickel, | 43.65 | 48.65 | 51.65 | 55.95 |
| Full 21 jeweled, "No. 150" grade Elgin, fully adjusted......nickel, | 50.40 | 55.40 | 58.40 | 62.70 |
| Full 21 jeweled, "Vanguard" Waltham, fully adjusted........nickel, | 58.65 | 63.65 | 66.65 | 70.95 |
| Full 17 jeweled, "New Railway" Hampden, fully adjusted....nickel, | 51.50 | 56.50 | 59.50 | 62.85 |
| Full 17 jeweled, "Special Railway" Hampden, fully adjusted..nickel, | 61.50 | 66.50 | 69.50 | 72.85 |

We GUARANTEE all of the above movements for five years. For full description of the same, see introductory pages.

**Open Face Cases, $1.00 less.**

Every gold case we sell is stamped: "Warranted 14 karat" U.S. Mint Assay.

We can furnish 10 karat solid gold cases when desired, but we do not catalogue them. If you want them write for prices.

**No. 65156.**
Fancy engraved, escalloped center, solid gold, weight 45 dwt.

**No. 65157.**
Fancy engraved, solid gold, weight 42 dwt.

**No. 65158.**
Fancy engraved, solid gold, weight 40 dwt.

WE WILL FURNISH CASES similar to the above, or any style you may desire, set with diamonds, at from $8.00 up, according to size of diamond. For $8.00 extra we will set a ¼-K. diamond; for $14.00 a ¼-K. diamond. Fancy settings and colored gold work extra, according to the amount of work. In writing for prices please specify as near as possible what you want.

YOU RUN NO RISK when dealing with a reliable concern. We refer to the National Banks of Illinois and Republic, among the largest in the city. See their letters in this book.

# Ladies' Imported and American Chatelaine Watches, Nickel and Silver.

**No. 65182.**

Ladies' nickel open face chatelaine watch. Case is plain polished, and same size as illustrated; is stem wind and stem set, has an imported cylinder escapement movement, and is a good timekeeper.
Price............................$2.25

**No. 65183.**

Ladies' open face silver chatelaine watch, same size as illustration, with solid silver engraved case; has imported stem wind cylinder escapement movement, and is a good timekeeper.
Price............................$3.15

**No. 65184.**

Ladies' solid silver, engraved, open face chatelaine watch; is stem wind and stem set, has good quality imported cylinder escapement movement with second hand, and is a good timekeeper. This watch is finished better and has heavier case than No. 4183, and has second hand.
Price............................$3.45

**No. 65185.**

Ladies' solid silver hunting chatelaine watch. Is stem wind and stem set and fitted with an imported cylinder escapement movement. Case is full engraved. Watch is a good timekeeper.
Price............................$3.95

**FOR OPEN FACE** sky light gold filled watches see No. 4344.

**SEE HOW GOLD FILLED CASES** are made, on introductory pages of this department.

**No. 65186.**

All American, solid nickel ladies chatelaine watch. This is an American made solid nickel case; will be fitted with your choice of Waltham or Elgin, 0 size, stem wind and pendant stem set, 7 jeweled movement.
Price............................$6.25

**YOU CAN MAKE MONEY** selling our watches and jewelry. Why not, when you can buy as low and lower than your retail dealer. You would be satisfied with smaller profits because what you make is clear gain. He has heavy expenses such as store rent, fuel, clerk hire, etc.

See other open face watches Nos. 4344 to 4347.

**No. 65187.**

All American, solid silver, open face ladies' chatelaine watch. The case is solid coin silver, satin finish or engraved. Waltham or Elgin, 0 size, stem wind and pendant stem set, 7 jeweled movement.
Price............................$6.95

**12 cents** will carry a ladies' chatelaine watch to any point in the United States by registered mail. **25 cents** to almost any point by express.

**No. 65188.**

All American, solid silver, open face chatelaine watch. Case is made of solid silver, either satin finish with gold inlaid stars or ornamented with gold inlaid bunch of flowers. Will be fitted with your choice of Waltham or Elgin, stem wind and pendant stem set, 7 jeweled movement.
Price............................$7.50

**No. 65189.**

Ladies' all American, solid silver, hunting case watch. The case is made of solid coin silver, beautifully engraved, with extended, scalloped or plain center, in either 0 or 6 size; will be fitted with your choice of Waltham or Elgin, stem wind and pendant stem set, 7 jeweled movement.
Price in 6 size....................$7.75
Price in 0 size....................  8.50

---

## GENUINE GOLD FILLED, 6 SIZE, LADIES' WATCHES.

Never before were genuine gold filled watches offered at such prices. We are bound to be at the head of the procession in establishing low prices, and we do not forget that the ladies appreciate a bargain as well as the gentlemen. The prices at which we are selling these genuine gold filled watches makes it possible for ladies to wear a beautiful watch which cannot be told from solid gold, who have been compelled to do without one or wear something that they were not proud of.

These watches are genuine gold filled; made of two plates of solid gold over composition metal, and warranted by certificates from the manufacturers to wear for five years. Do not think because they are cheap that everybody would know that you were wearing a cheap watch, for it is not true. We will defy anyone who is not thoroughly familiar with the different grades and makes of watch cases to detect the difference between one of these watches and any of the high priced watches, so far as outward appearance is concerned. They are perfectly fitted and finished, elaborately engraved, and for beauty are not surpassed by anything on the market.

Any of these watches will be sent on our regular terms, C.O.D. to any express office for examination. If you send cash in full with your order you are entitled to a discount of 3%; on orders over $50, 4%; on orders over $100, 5%. 25c will carry a watch to almost any point in the United States by express; 13c will carry a ladies' watch to any point in the United States by mail. If you send cash with your order, be sure to enclose extra money for postage.

**No. 65190.**

**No. 65191.**

**No. 65192.**

**No. 65193.**

**WE FIT THESE CASES WITH THE FOLLOWING 6 SIZE MOVEMENTS:**

| | |
|---|---|
| 7 jeweled, Trenton, nickel............................$ 6.75 | Full 16 jeweled, Elgin, Waltham or Hampden, nickel............$13.00 |
| 7 jeweled, Seth Thomas, nickel............................ 7.25 | Full 16 jeweled, "Royal," Waltham or Hampden, nickel....... 16.70 |
| 7 jeweled, Elgin, Waltham or Hampden, gilt............ 7.85 | Full 17 jeweled, "Riverside" Waltham or Hampden, adjusted, nickel... 23.50 |
| Full 15 jeweled, Elgin, Waltham, or Hampden, nickel............ 10.10 | For full description of above movements, see introductory pages. |

**We GUARANTEE** all of the above movements for five years.

# 20-YEAR GOLD-FILLED WATCHES, LADIES' 6 SIZE FOR $7.75.

Your retail dealer will not sell you one of these watches because he cannot get them except of us, and if he did sell them would want two prices. On these, as well as two special gents' watches, we control the entire production of one of the largest Watch Case factories in the world. They are made under contract for us according to our own specifications and designs. We have figured the cost of material, the cost of making and engraving, and allow the manufacturers a small per cent of advance for their profit. This enables us to place the goods in your hands at a small per cent of advance on cost to manufacture, instead of your having to buy the goods in the regular way after a large profit has been added by the manufacturer and a profit for the general selling agent, still another for the jobber or wholesale dealer, and then a large profit for the retail dealer, after which you would have to pay twice the price for a watch of the same quality as the one we offer you. Your jeweler will naturally make every effort possible to induce you to buy at home, and if persuasion will not do he usually resorts to trickery by trying to intimidate you by saying that if you send away for goods you will make a mistake; but he can produce no argument to substantiate it. We have given you all the argument we think necessary to the contrary. You run no risk whatever, for you can see the goods before you pay for them, if you desire. Besides this, you have a certificate of guarantee from us and an agreement that if the watch is not satisfactory and does not fulfill the requirements of our guarantee that we will refund your money. This is all that is necessary when you are dealing with a thoroughly reliable concern.

These cases are made of two plates of solid gold over fine hard composition metal, are thoroughly well made in every respect and beautifully engraved. They are warranted by certificate to wear and retain their color for twenty years. So far as finish, quality and design is concerned there is nothing made that will surpass them. You must not get the impression that on account of the low price at which they are sold that they would have an appearance of cheapness, for it is not true. We can lay them side by side with any of the other best grade of cases on the market and you cannot tell the difference.

12 cents will carry a ladies' watch to any point in the U.S. by registered mail; 25 cents to almost any point by express.

Buy watches and jewelry of a firm that has a good financial standing.

When watches or jewelry are to be engraved the full amount of cash for goods and engraving must accompany the order.

No. 65194.      No. 65195.      No. 65196.      No. 65197.

## WE FIT THESE CASES WITH THE FOLLOWING 6 SIZE MOVEMENTS:

| | GILT. | NICKEL. | | NICKEL. |
|---|---|---|---|---|
| 7 jeweled, Trenton | | $7.75 | Full 16 jeweled, Elgin, Waltham or Hampden | $14.90 |
| 7 jeweled, Seth Thomas | | 8.25 | Full 16 jeweled, "Royal" Waltham or Hampden, adjusted | 17.70 |
| 7 jeweled, Elgin, Waltham or Hampden | $8.85 | | Full 17 jeweled, "Riverside" Waltham, or Hampden, adjusted | 24.30 |
| Full 15 jeweled, Elgin, Waltham or Hampden, | | 11.60 | | |

WE GUARANTEE all of the above movements for five years. For a full description of the same see introductory pages.

We are thoroughly responsible. Our guarantee is as good as a bond.

See how gold filled cases are made on introductory pages of this department.

Read our Plain Talk on third introductory page of this department.

No. 65198.      No. 65199.      No. 65200.      No. 65201.

**LEARN PHOTOGRAPHY.** It's a most delightful and instructive pastime for both young and old. Can be learned in a few hours by following our instructions. Our prices are far below manufacturers. See photo goods department.

**WATCHES** will be sent C. O. D. on receipt of 50 cents, (cash or stamps) with order as a guarantee of good faith on your part. The 50 cents will be refunded if goods are not satisfactory.

**A DISCOUNT** of 3 per cent. will be given for cash in full with your order; 4 per cent. will be allowed on orders over $50, and 5 per cent. on orders over $100.

# GOLD FILLED, 10 KARAT 0 SIZE LADIES' WATCHES.

Made by the **Wadsworth Watch Case Company**, of Newport, Ky.; the **Dueber Watch Case Company**, of Canton, Ohio; the **Muhr Watch Case Company** (makers of the Crown Case), of Philadelphia, Pa.; the **Keystone Watch Case Company** (makers of the Boss Case), of Philadelphia, Pa., and the **Fahy's Watch Case Company** (makers of the Montauk Case), of Brooklyn, New York.

The above concerns are all the oldest and most reliable makers in the watch case business. These cases are all made of **two plates of 10 karat solid gold** over fine hard composition metal, and are warranted by certificates from the manufacturers. The **Dueber** 10 karat cases are **warranted to wear for twenty years**, while all the rest are warranted for fifteen years.

**We wish to direct your attention** especially to the **Wadsworth, Dueber** and **Crown** Cases, on account of the **most excellent finish, quality** and **style.** For want of space we cannot illustrate all of the styles of each manufacturer, but we can furnish the **Crown, Fahy's** and **Wadsworth** Cases in any style listed on this page. **The 0 Size Watches are becoming very popular,** as has been demonstrated by their increased sale. They are a little smaller than the 6 size, but the reduction in size does not in any way interfere with their timekeeping qualities.

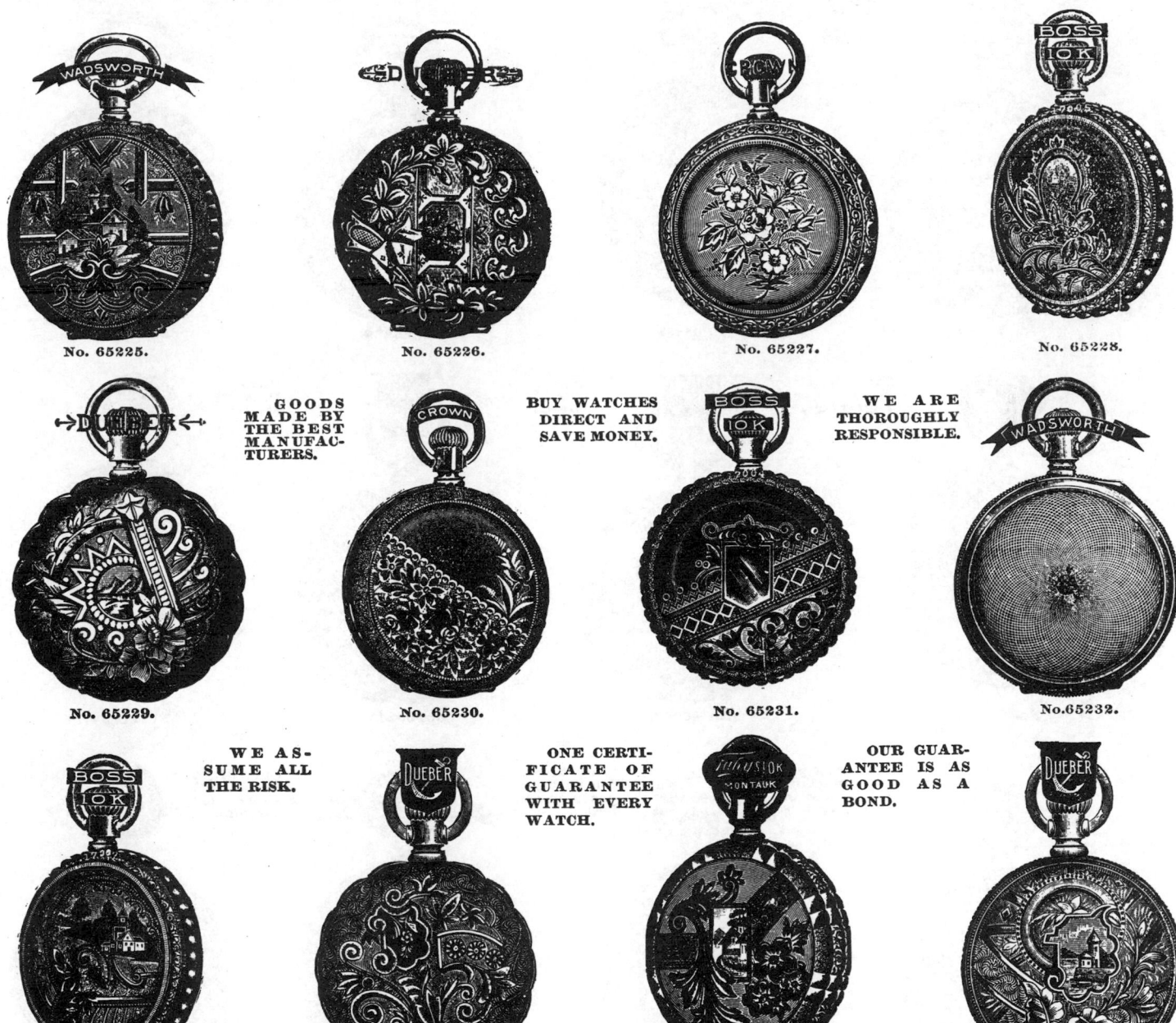

No. 65225.  No. 65226.  No. 65227.  No. 65228.

**GOODS MADE BY THE BEST MANUFAC-TURERS.**  **BUY WATCHES DIRECT AND SAVE MONEY.**  **WE ARE THOROUGHLY RESPONSIBLE.**

No. 65229.  No. 65230.  No. 65231.  No. 65232.

**WE AS-SUME ALL THE RISK.**  **ONE CERTI-FICATE OF GUARANTEE WITH EVERY WATCH.**  **OUR GUAR-ANTEE IS AS GOOD AS A BOND.**

No. 65233.  No. 65234.  No. 65235.  No. 65236.

## WE FIT THESE CASES WITH THE FOLLOWING 0 SIZE MOVEMENTS.

| | | Nos. 65226, 65227, 65230, 65232, 65236. | Nos. 65225, 65228, 65229, 65231, 65233, 65234, 65235. |
|---|---|---|---|
| 7 jeweled, Elgin or Waltham | Gilt, | $12.20 | $12.75 |
| Full 15 jeweled, Elgin or Waltham | Nickel, | 14.70 | 15.25 |
| Full 16 jeweled, Elgin or Waltham | Nickel, | 18.80 | 19.35 |
| Full 16 jeweled, "Royal" Waltham, adjusted | Nickel, | 21.55 | 22.10 |
| Full 17 jeweled, "Riverside" Waltham, adjusted | Nickel, | 27.05 | 27.60 |

We GUARANTEE all of the above movements for five years. For full description of same, see introductory pages.

---

**BE SURE TO STATE** both the number and name of case and grade of movement wanted when you order.

**OUR LIBERAL TERMS** allow you to examine the goods before paying for the same. No other con-cernoffers such fair treatment.

**FOR OPEN FACE** sky light gold filled watches see No. 6344.

**SEE HOW GOLD FILLED** CASES are made on introduc-tory pages of this department.

# Gold Filled, 14 Karat, 0 Size, Ladies' Watches.

Made by the Dueber Watch Case Company, of Canton, Ohio; the Keystone Watch Case Company (makers of the Boss case), of Philadelphia, Pa.; the Muhr Watch Case Company (makers of the Crown case), of Philadelphia, Pa.; the Wadsworth Watch Case Company, of Newport, Ky.; the Crescent Watch Case Company, of Newark, N. J., and the Fahy's Watch Case Company (makers of the Monarch case), of Brooklyn, New York.

The above named concerns are all the oldest and most reliable makers in the case business. The cases listed on this page are made of two plates of solid 14 karat gold over fine, hard composition metal, and are warranted by certificate from the manufacturers to wear and retain their color for twenty years. The Crown, Fahy's and Wadsworth Cases can be furnished in any style listed on this page. We recommend them for their most excellent finish and beauty of style and engraving. For want of space we cannot illustrate a full line of engravings and styles of each maker. The engravings listed on this page are a selection from the prettiest and latest designs now on the market.

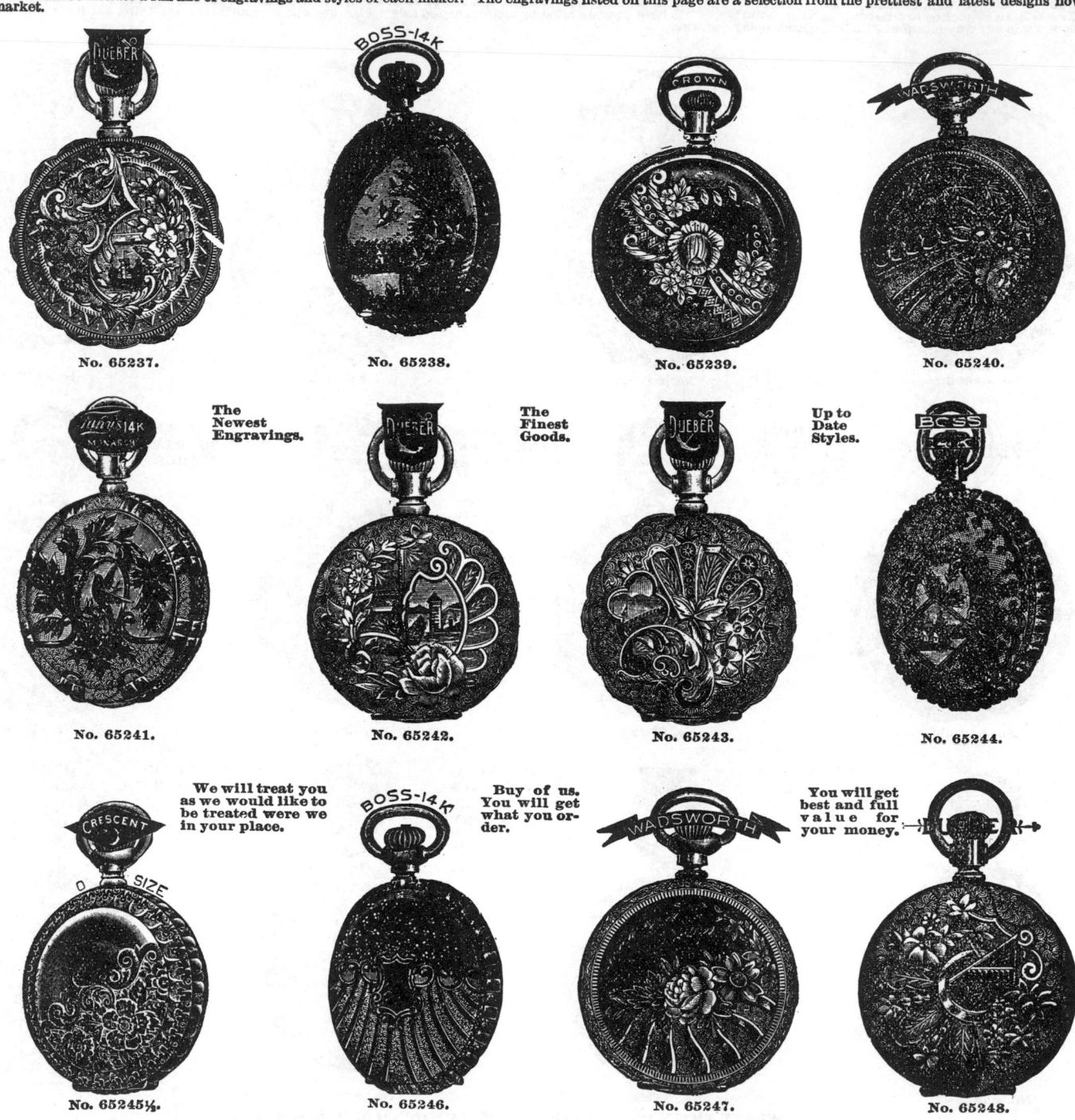

No. 65237.    No. 65238.    No. 65239.    No. 65240.

The Newest Engravings.    The Finest Goods.    Up to Date Styles.

No. 65241.    No. 65242.    No. 65243.    No. 65244.

We will treat you as we would like to be treated were we in your place.    Buy of us. You will get what you order.    You will get best and full value for your money.

No. 65245½.    No. 65246.    No. 65247.    No. 65248.

### WE FIT THESE CASES WITH THE FOLLOWING 0 SIZE MOVEMENTS:

| | Nos. 65239, 65242, 65245, 65247, 65248. | Nos. 65237, 65238, 65240, C5241, 65243, 65244, 65246. |
|---|---|---|
| 7 jeweled, Elgin or Waltham | Gilt........ $13.20 | $13.75 |
| Full 15 jeweled, Elgin or Waltham | Nickel........ 15.70 | 16 25 |
| Full 16 jeweled, Elgin or Waltham | " ........ 19.80 | 20.35 |
| Full 16 jeweled, "Royal" Waltham, adjusted | " ........ 22.55 | 23.10 |
| Full 17 jeweled, "Riverside" Waltham, adjusted | " ........ 28.05 | 28.60 |

We GUARANTEE all of the above movements for five years. For full description of the same see introductory pages.

A DISCOUNT of 3 per cent will be given for cash in full with your order. 4 per cent will be allowed on orders over $50.00, and 5 per cent on orders over $100.00.

FOR 50 CENTS YOU CAN SEE AND examine watches at your express office. If not satisfactory we will refund the deposit.

BE SURE TO STATE both the number and name of case and grade of movement wanted when you order.

FOR OPEN FACE skylight gold filled watches see No. 4344.

# GOLD FILLED, 10 KARAT, 6 SIZE, LADIES' WATCHES.

Made by **The Illinois Watch Case Company** (makers of the Elgin Giant), of Elgin, Illinois; **The Wadsworth Watch Case Company**, of Newport, Ky.; **The Dueber Watch Case Company**, of Canton, Ohio; **The Keystone Watch Case Company** (makers of the Boss Case), of Philadelphia, Pa., and **The Fahy's Watch Case Co.** (makers of Montauk Cases), of Brooklyn, New York.

The concerns mentioned are all among the oldest and most reliable makers in the watch case business. All of the cases illustrated on this page are made of **two plates of solid 10 karat gold** over fine, hard composition metal, and are warranted by certificate from the manufacturers. The Dueber Cases are warranted to wear for **twenty years**, while the rest are warranted for fifteen years. Our limited space in this catalogue will not allow us to illustrate all the different styles from the different makers. We have illustrated a variety which covers all of the latest and prettiest patterns of engravings and designs of cases on the market. We recommend the Wadsworth, Fahy's and Illinois Watch Case Company's goods for their excellent finish and quality of material, and can furnish them in any style listed on this page.

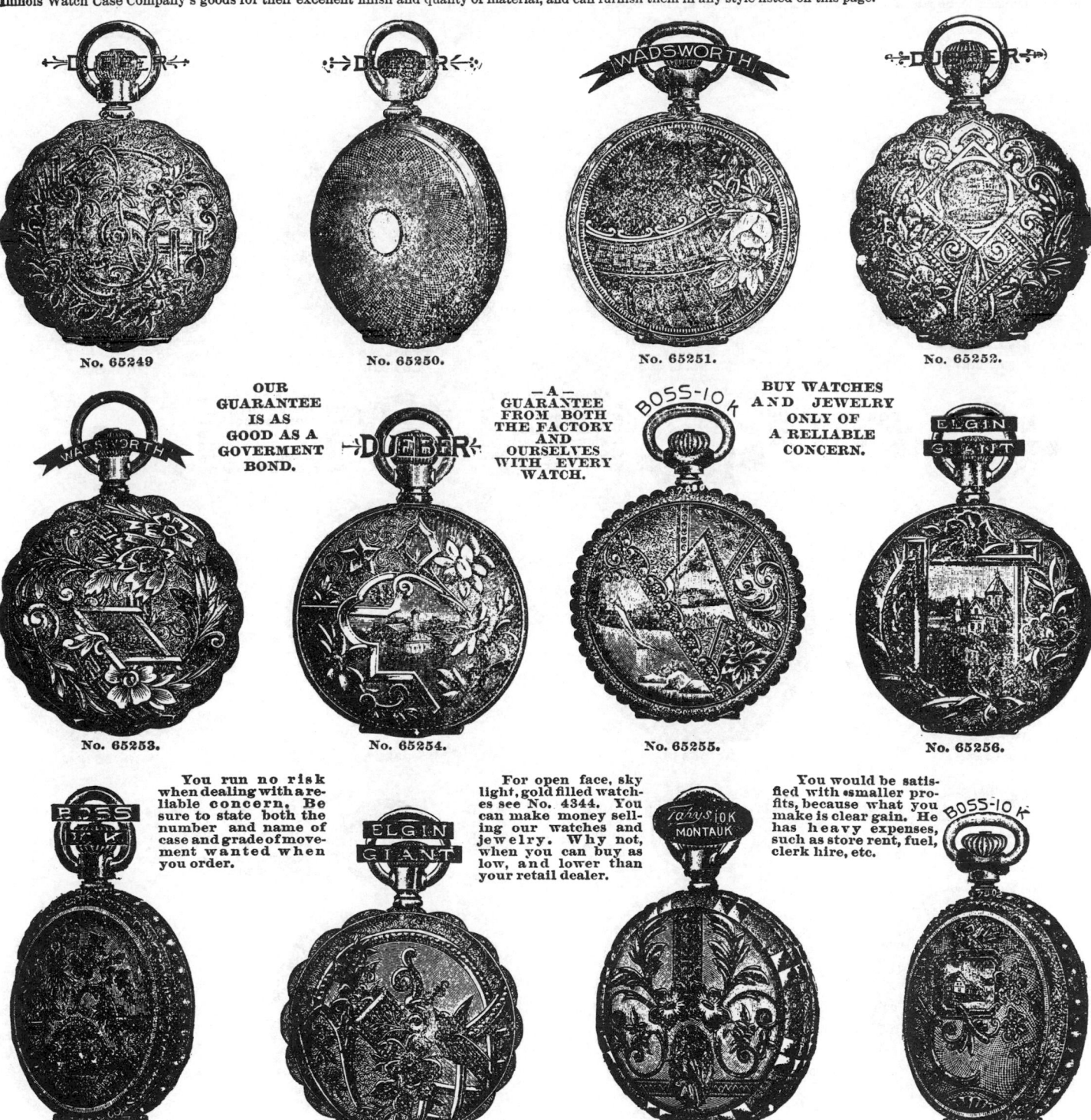

No. 65249.  No. 65250.  No. 65251.  No. 65252.

OUR GUARANTEE IS AS GOOD AS A GOVERMENT BOND.

—A— GUARANTEE FROM BOTH THE FACTORY AND OURSELVES WITH EVERY WATCH.

BUY WATCHES AND JEWELRY ONLY OF A RELIABLE CONCERN.

No. 65253.  No. 65254.  No. 65255.  No. 65256.

You run no risk when dealing with a reliable concern. Be sure to state both the number and name of case and grade of movement wanted when you order.

For open face, sky light, gold filled watches see No. 4344. You can make money selling our watches and jewelry. Why not, when you can buy as low, and lower than your retail dealer.

You would be satisfied with smaller profits, because what you make is clear gain. He has heavy expenses, such as store rent, fuel, clerk hire, etc.

No. 55257.  No. 65258.  No. 65259.  No. 65260.

## WE FIT THESE CASES WITH THE FOLLOWING 6 SIZE MOVEMENTS:

|  | | Nos. 65250, 65251, 65254, 65256. | Nos. 65249, 65252, 56253, 65255, 65257, 65258, 65259, 65260. |
|---|---|---|---|
| 7 jeweled, Trenton | nickel, | $10.55 | $11.65 |
| 7 jeweled, Seth Thomas | nickel, | 11.05 | 12.15 |
| 7 jeweled, Elgin, Waltham or Hampden | gilt, | 11.65 | 12.75 |
| Full 15 jeweled. Elgin, Waltham or Hampden | nickel, | 13.85 | 14.95 |
| Full 16 jeweled, Elgin, Waltham or Hampden | nickel, | 17.70 | 18.80 |
| Full 16 jeweled, "Royal" Waltham or Hampden, adjusted | nickel, | 20.45 | 21.55 |
| Full 17 jeweled, "Riverside" Waltham or Hampden, adjusted | nickel, | 27.05 | 28.15 |

We guarantee all of the above movements for five years. For full description of the same, see introductory pages.

# GOLD FILLED, 14 KARAT, 6 SIZE, LADIES' WATCHES.

Made by the Illinois Watch Case Company (makers of the Elgin Commander) of Elgin, Ill.; the Wadsworth Watch Case Company, of Newport, Ky.; the Keystone Watch Case Company (makers of the Boss Cases), of Philadelphia, Pa.; the Dueber Watch Case Company, of Canton, Ohio, and the Fahy's Watch Case Company (makers of the Monarch Cases), of Brooklyn, New York.

The above-mentioned concerns are all among the oldest and most reliable makers in the watch case business. The goods listed on this page are all made with two plates of solid 14 karat gold over fine composition metal, and are warranted by certificate from the manufacturers to wear for twenty years. For want of space we are unable to illustrate a full line of each of the different manufacturers, but we wish to call your attention especially to the Elgin Commander, Fahy's, Dueber and Wadsworth Cases, which can be furnished in any design and style of engraving on this page. The quality and finish of their goods, together with the handsome designs and finest engravings, have won for them a most excellent reputation. A certificate of guarantee from the manufacturers accompanies each case. In addition to this we furnish a certificate of guarantee covering both case and movement.

No. 65261.

No. 65262.

No. 65263.

No. 65264.

FOR OPEN FACE skylight gold filled watches see No. 6344.

No. 65265

12 cents will carry a ladies' watch to any point in the United States by registered mail; 25 cents to almost any point by express.

No. 65266.

Our catalogue numbers have no relation to the consecutive numbers which are always engraved on the case and movement.

No. 65267.

No. 65268.

BE SURE TO STATE both the number and name of case and grade of movement wanted when you order.

No. 65269.

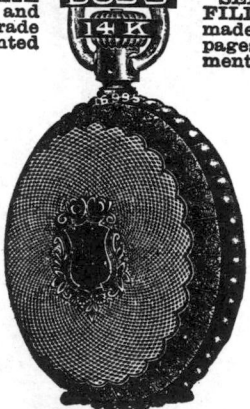

SEE HOW GOLD-FILLED CASES are made, on introductory pages of this department.

No. 65270.

If you return watches or jewelry for exchange or repairs, be sure to follow our instructions. See front page of this book.

No. 65271.

No. 65272.

## WE FIT THESE CASES WITH THE FOLLOWING 6 SIZE MOVEMENTS:

| | | Nos. 65263, 65266, 65270. | Nos. 65261, 65262, 65264, 65265, 65267, 65268, 65269, 65271, 65272. |
|---|---|---|---|
| 7 jeweled, Trenton | Nickel, | $11.55 | $12.65 |
| 7 jeweled, Seth Thomas | Nickel, | 12.05 | 13.15 |
| 7 jeweled, Elgin, Waltham or Hampden | Gilt, | 12.65 | 13.75 |
| Full 15 jeweled, Elgin, Waltham or Hampden | Nickel, | 14.85 | 15.95 |
| Full 16 jeweled, Elgin, Waltham or Hampden | Nickel, | 18.70 | 19.80 |
| Full 16 jeweled, "Royal" Waltham, or Hampden, adjusted | Nickel, | 21.45 | 22.55 |
| Full 17 jeweled, "Riverside" Waltham or Hampden, adjusted | Nickel, | 28.05 | 29.15 |

We GUARANTEE all of the above movements for five years. For full description of the same see introductory pages.

# A LADIES' GOLD FILLED, 14 KARAT, 6 SIZE WATCH FOR $9.90.

**Would sell at retail for $15.00 to $40.00.** For beauty and finish they are surpassed by none. Just out, and are made in the very latest and most fashionable shapes and patterns. They are made of **two plates of solid 14 karat gold** over fine composition metal, are ornamented with the latest and most beautiful hand engravings, and are guaranteed by the manufacturers to wear and retain their color for fifteen years. These cases are made by the old reliable **Bates & Bacon Watch Case Company,** of Attleboro, Mass., who have a **world-wide reputation** for the manufacture of fine watch cases. A certificate of guarantee, signed by the manufacturers, accompanies each case.

No. 65273.

No. 65274.

No. 65275.

No. 65276.

### WE FIT THESE CASES WITH THE FOLLOWING 6 SIZE MOVEMENTS:

| | | |
|---|---|---|
| 7 jeweled, Trenton | nickel, | $ 9.90 |
| 7 jeweled, Seth Thomas | nickel, | 10.50 |
| 7 jeweled, Elgin, Waltham or Hampden | gilt, | 11.00 |
| Full 15 jeweled, Elgin, Waltham or Hampden | nickel, | 13.20 |
| Full 16 jeweled, Elgin, Waltham or Hampden | nickel, | $17.05 |
| Full 16 jeweled, "Royal" Waltham or Hampden, adjusted | nickel, | 19.80 |
| Full 17 jeweled, "Riverside" Waltham or Hampden, adjusted | nickel, | 26.40 |

# 14 KARAT SOLID GOLD O SIZE LADIES' WATCHES.

**The finest goods made at the lowest prices.** We have absolutely no competition on solid gold cases. No concern is willing to meet our prices. They say they will have a good profit or they will not sell them. Our solid gold cases are the very best made. They are made of solid 14 karat gold through and through, and are manufactured by the best makers, who supply the largest retail stores in the large cities and whose reputation is a sufficient guarantee for their goods. We carry a full line of the latest and prettiest patterns of engraved, satin finished, engine turned, escalloped and beaded centers, raised colored gold ornamented and diamond set cases. We will put your monogram or name in plain or fancy engraving, raised colored gold ornamentation or in diamonds or semi-precious stones when desired. If you do not find here what you want, please advise us, stating what you desire, and we will be pleased to quote you prices. Our stock is very large, but for want of space we illustrate here only the latest and most popular designs. We claim that we can save you from 33⅓ per cent to 50 per cent on prices charged by retail dealers for solid gold watches, and in addition to this we always furnish strictly up-to-date goods. See what we have to say about gold watches on gents' 18 size page. A certificate of guarantee accompanies each solid gold case, warranting it for a lifetime.

No. 65300.

No. 65301.

**Read our plain talk on third introductory page of this department.**

No. 65302.

No. 65303.

**12 cents will carry a ladies' watch to any point in the United States by registered mail; 25 cents to almost any point by express.**

**YOU CAN MAKE MONEY** selling our watches and jewelry. Why not, when you can buy as low and lower than your retail dealer.

**OUR MOTTO,** good goods far below all competition. Make one article sell another and treat our customers as we would like to be treated were we in their places.

No. 65304.
Raised colored gold, ornamented.

No. 65305.
Raised colored gold, ornamented and set with 1 large and 3 small diamonds.

No. 65306.
Raised colored gold, ornaments and set with large diamond.

No. 65307.
Satin finished, and set with 1 diamond and 3 emeralds or rubies.

### WE FIT THESE CASES WITH THE FOLLOWING O SIZE MOVEMENTS:

| | | Nos. 65300, 65303. | Nos. 65302 | Nos. 65304, 65307. | No. 65305. | No. 65306. |
|---|---|---|---|---|---|---|
| 7 jeweled, Elgin or Waltham | gilt, | $15.95 | $19.90 | $23.90 | $25.80 | $28.40 |
| Full 15 jeweled, Elgin or Waltham | nickel, | 18.37 | 22.26 | 26.26 | 28.16 | 30.76 |
| Full 16 jeweled, Elgin or Waltham | nickel, | 23.10 | 27.15 | 31.15 | 31.00 | 35.65 |
| Full 16 jeweled, "Royal" Waltham, adjusted | nickel, | 25.85 | 28.90 | 32.90 | 32.90 | 38.20 |
| Full 17 jeweled, "Riverside" Waltham, adjusted | nickel, | 31.35 | 35.40 | 39.40 | 39.40 | 44.80 |

We guarantee all of the above movements for five years. For full description of same see introductory pages.

# SOLID 14 KARAT GOLD, 6 SIZE, LADIES' WATCHES.

If you are hard to please and want the best that money will buy, get a solid gold watch, but do not let your retail dealer fool you on an exchange. He is most always willing to take your old watch in exchange, and apparently allow you a good price on it. He may allow you more than the market value IN TRADE. We think you are broadminded enough to see how he could do that if he has the price for his goods set high enough. Then he will sell your case for metal and put the movement in the scrap (which is worth very little). See what we have to say about this in "Plain Talk" on third introductory page of this department.

All of our solid gold cases are 14 karat, solid gold through and through, and warranted for a lifetime. In fixing the price on gold watches we figure the value of the gold, add the cost of making and engraving, a small per cent for the manufacturers' profit, and offer the cases to you at only a slight advance on cost to manufacture. We do not ask you to take our statement. You can figure it for yourself. Refined 14 karat gold is worth about 66 cents per dwt., the average 6-size case weighs from 16 to 20 dwt.; but let us say here that you will often find cases in retail stores that, with the springs taken out, there would hardly be sufficient material in the case to resist the least pressure, and will not afford the movement the protection it needs. All of our cases are made very heavy, from 17 to 20 dwt. We list here only a few of the most popular and stylish designs, but we can furnish anything that is made. We handle a very fine line of raised, colored, gold, ornamented, and diamond-set cases. We wish to direct your attention especially to No. 4318, which can be furnished with any name to order, but it will require about ten days after the order is received to make shipment of this watch. Watches with names or engravings on cannot be sent C. O. D., but they must be accompanied by the full amount of cash.

Our lifetime guarantee accompanies each solid gold case.

Every case stamped on the inside "warranted 14 karat" U. S. mint assay.

No. 65308.   No. 65309.   No. 65310.   No. 65311.

The finest material, the best finish.

The latest styles, the prettiest engravings.

The lowest prices, and the most liberal terms.

No. 65312.   No. 65313.   No. 65314.   No. 65315.

A DISCOUNT of 3 per cent will be given for cash in full with order; 4 per cent will be allowed on orders over $50, and 5 per cent on orders over $100.

Watches will be sent C. O. D., on receipt of 50 cents (cash or stamps) with the order as a guarantee of good faith on your part. The 50 cents will be refunded if goods are not satisfactory.

IF YOU WANT TO MAKE MONEY there is no better way to do it than to save it on your purchases. "A dollar saved is a dollar earned." We can save you many of them.

No. 65316.   No. 65317.   No. 65318.   No. 65319.

No. 65316. Fancy engraved, set with one large diamond. For price of this case and movement complete, add $4.50 to prices quoted for No. 6311.

No. 65317. Plain polished case, with raised colored gold decorations, one large diamond and twenty-four fine pearls. A very rich and beautiful case. For price of this watch with movement complete, add $11.45 to prices quoted for No. 6311.

No. 65318. Plain, satin finished case, six diamonds set in star and crescent; plain, but very rich in appearance. For price of this watch with movement complete, add $12.45 to prices of No. 6311.

No. 65319. Case satin finished. Any name to order. Set with two diamonds and three rubies; requires about ten days to fill an order for this watch, and cash in full must accompany your order. For price on this watch with movement complete, add $4.25 to prices quoted for No. 65311.

## WE FIT THESE CASES WITH THE FOLLOWING 6 SIZE MOVEMENTS.

|  | | No. 65310. | Nos. 65312, 65313. | Nos. 65308, 65309. | Nos. 65311, 65315. 36514 |
|---|---|---|---|---|---|
| 7 jeweled, Trenton | nickel, | $15.85 | $16.85 | $18.35 | $23.35 |
| 7 jeweled, Seth Thomas | nickel, | 16.45 | 17.45 | 18.95 | 23.95 |
| 7 jeweled, Elgin, Waltham or Hampden | gilt, | 16.95 | 17.95 | 19.45 | 24.45 |
| Full 15 jeweled, Elgin, Waltham or Hampden | nickel, | 19.25 | 20.20 | 21.75 | 25.70 |
| Full 16 jeweled, Elgin, Waltham or Hampden | nickel, | 23.00 | 24.00 | 25.50 | 30.50 |
| Full 16 jeweled, "Royal" Waltham or Hampden adjusted | nickel, | 25.75 | 26.75 | 28.25 | 33.25 |
| Full 17 jeweled, "Riverside" Waltham, or Hampden, adjusted | nickel, | 32.35 | 33.35 | 34.85 | 39.85 |

We GUARANTEE all the above movements for five years. For full description of the same, see introductory pages.

# HIGHEST GRADE GOLD FILLED CASES MADE.

### RAISED COLORED GOLD ORNAMENTATION AND GENUINE DIAMOND SETTINGS.

The first four cases following represent the highest art in watch case making, and will certainly satisfy the desires of those who wish to obtain the best filled case that money will purchase, Nos. 65340, 65350 and 65351 are made by the Wadsworth Watch Case Company of Newport, Kentucky; and No. 65352 is made by the Crescent Watch Case Company, formerly a part of the Waltham Watch Company; both concerns are among the oldest watch case makers, and are noted for the manufacturing of the finest goods, and as they are old in the business their reliability is established beyond a doubt.     They are all made of two plates of solid 14 karat gold over fine hard composition metal and are warranted by certificates from the manufacturers to wear and retain their color for 20 years. In addition to this certificate we add our certificate of guarantee, which warrants the case to wear for 20 years and the movement an accurate time keeper for 25 years.     They are all decorated with raised colored gold ornamentation in the most beautiful and handsome floral designs.     For the benefit of those who do not understand how the raised ornamentation is made, we will say that the ornaments are all composed of solid gold laid on to the case after it has been finished, firmly secured and then engraved.     Deep yellow flowers and ornaments are composed of pure gold, 24 karat fine, while the light yellow colored ornaments are composed of gold alloyed with silver.     Reddish colored ornaments are alloyed with copper, the same as rings, watch cases, etc.     The white ornaments are alloyed with platinum and silver, while the green gold is alloyed with silver and colored with chemicals.     The prices for either 0 or 6 size are the same.  Cases Nos. 65340, 65350 and 65352 are 6 size, while 65351, as illustrated, is 0 size.  Please state when you order which size is wanted.

For 50 cents you can see and examine watches at your express office. If not satisfactory we will refund the deposit.

12 cts will carry a ladies' watch to any point in the United States by registered mail; 25 cents to almost any point by express.

ALL AMERICAN MOVEMENTS ARE now made in STEM WIND and STEM SET only.

**No. 65350.**
65350 raised colored gold ornamentation, 6 size.

**No. 65340.**
65340 raised colored gold ornamentation set with a fine diamond 6 size.

**No. 65351.**
65351 raised colored gold ornamentation, any initial desired, 6 size.

**No. 65352.**
65352 raised colored gold ornamentation, 6 size.

Six size cases will be fitted with any of the movements listed below, but the Naught size cases cannot be fitted with Trenton or Seth Thomas movement.

| | | 65350 | 65340 | 65351 | 65352 | | | 65350 | 65340 | 65351 | 65352 |
|---|---|---|---|---|---|---|---|---|---|---|---|
| 7 jeweled, Trenton | Nickel, | $14.85 | $19.25 | $16.50 | $15.40 | Full 15 jeweled, Elgin or Waltham | Nickel, | 18.10 | 22.50 | 19.75 | 18.65 |
| 7 jeweled, Seth Thomas | Nickel, | 15.35 | 19.75 | 17.00 | 15.90 | Full 16 jeweled, Elgin or Waltham | Nickel, | 21.00 | 26.40 | 23.65 | 22.55 |
| 7 jeweled, Elgin or Waltham | Gilt, | 15.95 | 20.35 | 17.60 | 16.50 | Full 16 jeweled, Royal Waltham, adjusted | Nickel, | 24.75 | 29.15 | 26.40 | 25.30 |
| Full 17 jeweled, Riverside, Waltham or Hampden adjusted | | | | | | | Nickel, | 31.35 | 35.75 | 33.00 | 31.90 |

The prices for the 6 and 0 size watches are the same, for while the cases in six size cost a little more the movements for the 0 size cost the most, which evens up the cost for the complete watches. Above movements are all guaranteed for 5 years.  For full description see the introductory pages.

**No. 65344.  Gold-filled, 14 karat, open face, skylight chatelaine.** Is made of two plates of 14 karat gold over composition metal and warranted by certificate from the Wadsworth Watch Case Company, of Newport, Ky., to wear and retain its color for twenty years.  This is a very beautiful little watch, elaborately engraved, and will be fitted with either **Waltham** or **Elgin** O size movement.  Price $11.00.  For 50 cents extra will furnish fancy gilt enamel dial.  This watch is strictly in style and is very neat and handy.

**No. 65345.  Solid nickel, 6 size, open face watch.** The case is made of solid nickel, is well finished and plain polished. The movement is nickel, thin model, damaskeened, 7 jewels, train bearings in metal settings, compensated balance, and warranted by the **New York Standard Watch Company.**   Price $3.75.

**No. 65346.  Solid coin silver, 6 size, open face watch.**  Case is made of solid silver, is fancy engraved, well finished, and is made in thin model; movement is nickel, damaskeened, 7 jewels, train bearings in metal settings, compensated balance, and made and warranted by **New York Standard Watch Company.**  Price $5.20.

**No. 65347.  Gold-filled, 6 size, open face (thin model) watch.**  Case is made of two plates of solid gold over fine composition metal, and is warranted by the **New York Standard Watch Company** to wear and retain its color for five years.  The movement is nickel, damaskeened, 7 jewels, train bearings in metal settings, compensated balance, and warranted.   Price $6.00.

MOST OF OUR CUSTOMERS send cash in full with their orders and save the discount and return charges on the collection.

YOU RUN NO RISK when dealing with a reliable concern. We refer to the National Banks of Illinois and Republic, among the largest in the city. See their letters in this book.

If you return watches or jewelry for exchange or repairs, be sure to follow our instructions. See front page of this book.

**No. 65344.**

**No. 65345.**

**No. 65346.**

**No. 65347.**

# PHOTOGRAPHS ON WATCH CASES AND DIALS.

An ever-present reminder of your relatives or friends, in the form of a photograph on the dial or back cap of your watch, at a trifling expense.   The work is done by the Photographic Enamel Process, and is as perfect in detail and finish as the best cabinet photographs, and with ordinary care will last forever.   It is an excellent place to carry a picture of the baby, your wife or husband, or your sweetheart.   No extra charge for group if the pictures are all on same photo. When group picture is wanted and pictures are on separate photographs, add $1.50 for each extra figure.   Send us your watch by mail or express, carefully packed in a small strong box, well wrapped in some very soft material (cotton batting or similar substance is best), together with a photo to copy from (size makes no difference.   As soon as the work is done we will return the watch and picture uninjured.   It usually requires about a week after we get the watch and picture to complete the work.

We are doing a great deal of this work, which has in every case given most excellent satisfaction.   We have received many letters of testimonials speaking in the highest terms, and that the work was far nicer than they could have expected, and that they could not find words to express their appreciation and thanks. The work can be done on any kind or size of watch.   Gold or gold-filled are the best for cap work, but it makes no difference for dial work.   Be sure to state whether you want the picture on the dial or on the cap.

**No. 65348.**
The above is a sample of dial work.  Price $1.75

**No. 65349.**
The above is a sample of work on the cap in back of watch. Price $2.25.

# WATCHMAKERS' TOOLS AND MATERIALS.

The numerous inquiries we have received from time to time have induced us to list a line of watchmakers' and jewelers' tools. For want of space we can illustrate only the most useful and desirable, and have been compelled to reduce the cuts in order to illustrate what we do. The goods, however, are all of standard make and size, and of the best quality. If there is anything that you want that you do not find illustrated, send us your order, enclosing market price for same, and give an accurate description. If you do not know what the cost is, be sure to enclose enough, and we will return what is left.

We guarantee our prices to be as low as any, and you will find that we always furnish goods at lowest wholesale prices. We will be glad, however, to quote you if you desire prices before ordering.

When ordering material for repairs, always send a sample if possible. If not, fully describe the size and make of watch or clock for which parts are intended. When ordering materials you will save both time and trouble by making a remittance of sufficient funds to cover all possible charges for cost of goods and mailing. We will always refund any balance left after paying cost of goods and mailing.

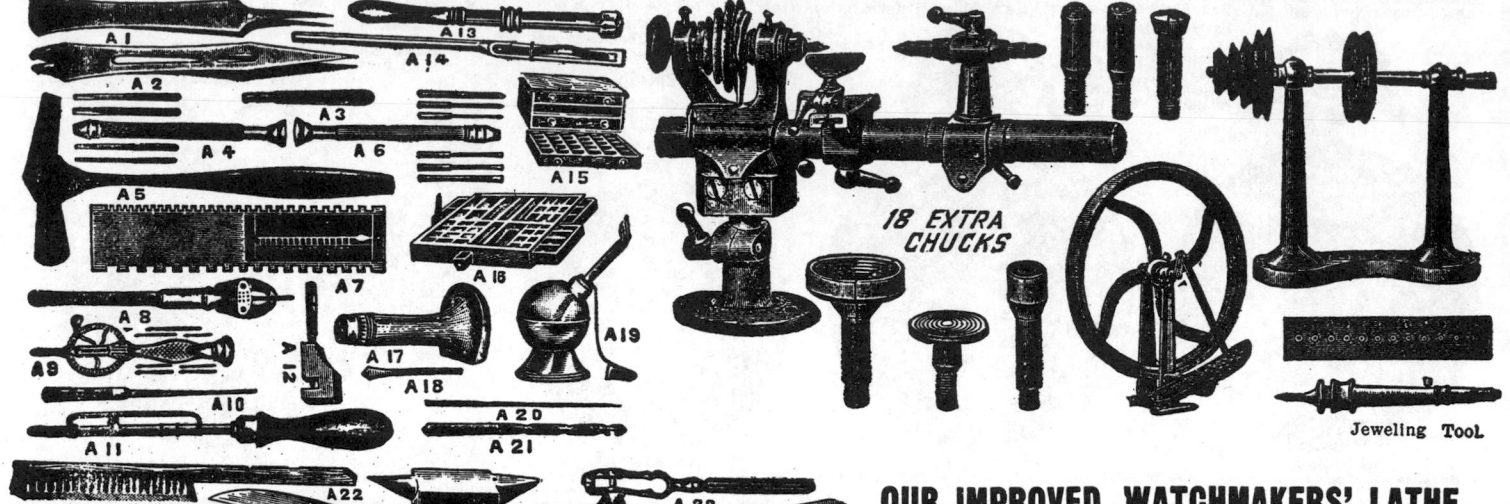

Jeweling Tool

## OUR IMPROVED WATCHMAKERS' LATHE,
### WITH INDEX POINTER AND LATCH.

Length of bed, 10 inches; bed to centers, 1½ inches; will swing a wheel or plate up to 3 inches in diameter.

This is the best watchmakers' lathe in the market for the money. The bed is made of turned steel, slightly flattened on one side. It is very rigid, is well finished, and perfectly true. The spindles and bearings are hardened, and carefully ground to insure them running true. Cone pulley is made of steel, with three steps for different speeds; with index pointer and latch at cone, as shown in cut, with rubber knob on end of draw-in spindle. The tail stock is provided with taper center, hardened and ground. The bed can be raised to suit the operator, or can be removed from the pedestal entirely by simply loosening the small lever on same.

The lathe is beautifully nickle plated and has 18 extra chucks, including a complete assortment of split chucks, wheel chucks, and one cement chuck, with brasses.

Price of lathe complete with 18 extra chucks..................$22.00
Counter-shaft (as shown in cut), extra.......................... 3.00
Foot wheel (as shown in cut), extra............................ 8.50

### A WORD OF CAUTION.

In ordering mainsprings all that is necessary is to enclose a piece off the outer end about one inch in length, and state what kind of watch it is for.

Watch glasses cannot be fitted from any measurement that you can give or statement of the kind of watch it is for, as the sizes vary so much, as also do the kinds. It requires a very large stock of glasses for a proper assortment and even then sometimes they have to be ground to fit. We cannot fit glasses except that we have the case.

In sending for any kind of materials always be sure to state kind of watch it is wanted for and enclose the piece as a sample.

Watch or clock materials cannot be exchanged. We will do any kind of watch work at jobbing price, which is about one-half the price charged by retail dealers.

When goods are to go by mail be sure to enclose money enough to cover postage. Any balance will be returned to you.

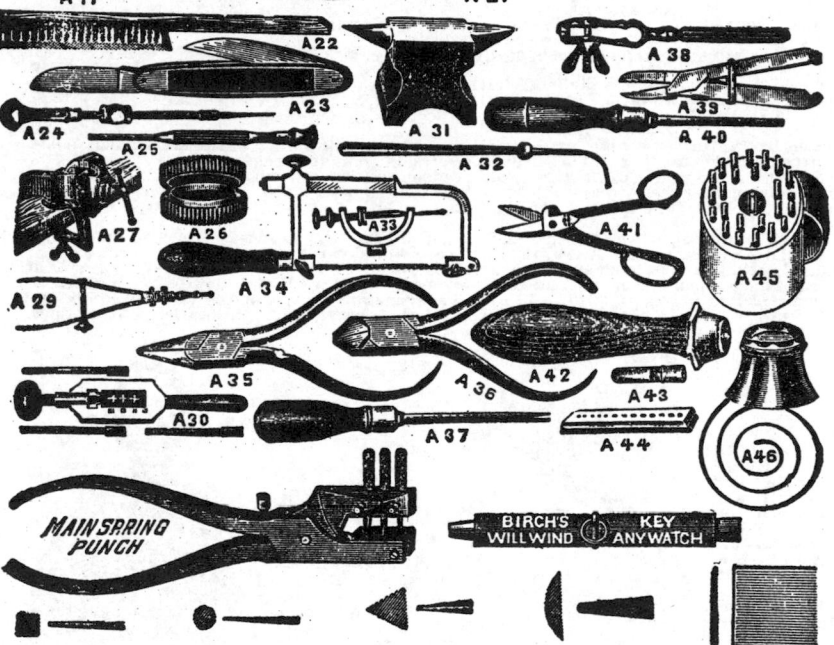

MAINSPRING PUNCH

BIRCH'S KEY WILL WIND ANY WATCH

No. A 71 S | No. A 71 R | No. A 71 M | No. A 75 O | No. A 73 F

Cuts R, O, M, F and S, show width and shape of files. The average length is about 6 inches.

| No. | | | No. | | | No. | | |
|---|---|---|---|---|---|---|---|---|
| A 50 | Alcohol Cups...................each | $0.35 | A 77 | Files, screw head.................each | $0.25 | A117 | Punch, Mainspring, Swiss (3 punches)..each | $1.25 |
| A 31 | Anvil (jewelers')................each | .75 | A 7 | Gauge, Mainspring................each | 1.00 | A 45 | Punches, set of 24, with hollow stake, in hard- | |
| A 53 | Plow Pipes, common brass.......each | .25 | A 79 | Gauge, Degree, nickle plated, with rule..each | 1.00 | | wood box, per set.......................... | 1.25 |
| A 32 | Plow Pipes, nickle plated, with ball...each | .50 | A 5 | Hammers, according to size........each 40 to | .75 | A 35 | Plyers, round, square or snipe bill......each | .65 |
| A 23 | Bench Knife (jewelers'), with case opener, | | A 81 | Hammer Handles, ebony ..............each | .25 | A 36 | Plyers, Stub's best side cutting.......each | 1.00 |
| | each | .50 | A 83 | Hands, Watch, per pair, 10c.; per dozen pair | .50 | A119 | Plyers, cutting, regular Swiss.........each | .65 |
| A 55 | Buffs, Chamois or Felt, round or flat.....each | | A 84 | Hands, Second, each, 5c..............per dozen | .30 | A 41 | Shears and Wire Cutters.............each | 1.25 |
| A 22 | Brushes, best bristle, watch or clock......each | .30 | A 85 | Hands, Clock, per pair, 5c.; per dozen pair | .42 | A 11 | Screw Holder and Driver combined....each | .75 |
| A 59 | Burnishers, jewel and other........each, 25 to | .75 | A 17 | Handles, adjustable, for graver or small files, | | A 25 | Screwdriver, Watch.................each | .25 |
| A 10 | Broaches, Stub's best quality, assorted sizes | | | each | .15 | A 4 | Screwdriver, Watch, adjustable, 4 sizes, per | |
| | from No. 75 to 40.............per dozen | 1.00 | A 42 | Handles, adjustable, for medium files...each | .25 | | set............................... | .60 |
| A 3 | Broach Handle...................each | .10 | A 87 | Jeweling Tools, Swiss, in box.........each | 1.50 | A 14 | Second Hand Holder, nickle plated....each | .40 |
| A 29 | Broaches, Swiss joint.............per dozen | .25 | A 89 | Jewelers' Cement, per bottle..........each | .25 | A 44 | Stake, Riveting, hard steel...........each | .25 |
| A 16 | Cabinet, for small material..........each | 1.50 | A 91 | Jewel Pin Setter....................each | .88 | A 34 | Saw Frame, Swiss, extra quality, nickle | |
| A 15 | Cabinet, for large material..........each | 4.50 | A 43 | Jewel Bottle.......................each | .08 | | plated............................ | 1.10 |
| A 20 | Calipers, Pinion, plain.............each | .25 | A175 | Jeweling Tool, complete (see cut)....... | 1.50 | A121 | Saws for above....................per dozen | .15 |
| A 61 | Calipers, regular brass.............each | .30 | A 93 | Keys, Watch, common..............per dozen | .25 | A123 | Saw Frame, Stub's.................each | 1.75 |
| A 63 | Calipers, nickle plated, with bar and screw, each | .65 | A 95 | Keys, Watch, wind any watch, (see cut) each | .20 | A125 | Saw Blades, Stub's.................each | .25 |
| A 49 | Clock Screwdriver.................each | .28 | A 97 | Keys, Watch, for bench use..........each | .50 | A127 | Soldering, copper..................each | .20 |
| A 57 | Clock wire bender.................each | .20 | A 99 | Keys, Clock, iron or brass...........each | .10 | A129 | Soldering fluid, per bottle...........each | .25 |
| A 65 | Counter Sinks, per set of three............. | 1.00 | A 19 | Lamps, Alcohol, patented, large.......each | 1.75 | A131 | Solder, Silver.....................per package | .25 |
| A 67 | Counter Sinks, per set of six............. | 2.00 | A101 | Lamps, Alcohol, faceted glass........each | .88 | | Solder, Gold......................per package | 1.00 |
| A 6 | Counter Sinks, adjustable handle, per set...... | .75 | A103 | Mainsprings, Watch, each 25c.......per dozen | 1.75 | A 30 | Screw Stock and Dies, per set........ | 2.00 |
| A 26 | Cups, Oil, for watch or clock..........each | .25 | A105 | Mainsprings, Clock, 1 day...........each | .15 | A 1 | Tweezers, fine, medium or heavy.......each | .35 |
| A 18 | Drills, common...................per dozen | .36 | A107 | Mainsprings, Clock, 8 day...........each | .45 | A 2 | Tweezers and hand raiser.............each | .45 |
| A 21 | Drills, Morse, Twist, assorted....per dozen | 1.25 | A160 | Mainspring Punch, improved..........each | 1.25 | A 89 | Tongs, 2 hole, hand................each | .40 |
| A 33 | Drills, Stock, common..............each | .50 | A100 | Oil, Watch or Clock, per bottle.......each | .20 | A 27 | Vise, jewelers', 1½ inch jaw..........each | 1.75 |
| A 9 | Drill Bow, to use with above.........each | .20 | A111 | Oiler, Watch......................each | .15 | A133 | Vise, amateur.....................each | .40 |
| A 24 | Drill Stock, patent spiral...........each | .65 | A113 | Oil Stone, best Arkansas, in box......each | 1.00 | A137 | Watch Glasses, hunting style, each, fitted.... | .10 |
| A 9 | Drill Stock, patent guard...........each | 1.00 | A 13 | Pin Slide, common medium...........each | .35 | A139 | Watch Glasses, per ½ dozen of one No..... | .15 |
| A 46 | Eyeglass, Watchmakers', common......each | .30 | A 38 | Pin Vise, hollow handle.............each | .75 | A141 | Watch Glasses, assorted, per gross..... | 2.50 |
| A 46 | Eyeglass, Watchmakers', with coil spring, each | .50 | A 13 | Pin Vise, nickle plated, patented......each | 1.25 | A143 | Watch Glasses, thick, open face, fitted...each | .20 |
| A 71 | Files, 3 cornered, round and square, small, each | .12 | A146 | Plating Solution, silver, per bottle...... | 1.00 | A155 | Watch Glasses, thick open face, per doz... | .40 |
| A 73 | Files, flat, regular................each | .35 | A147 | Plating Solution, gold, per bottle...... | 2.50 | A 95 | Watch Keys, Birch's................each | .20 |
| A 75 | Files, rounding and entering........each | .35 | A 12 | Punch, Mainspring, English...........each | .75 | | | |

The above is the only list of tools and materials that we issue, but we will fill orders for anything wanted at the lowest market prices.

# Genuine Diamonds and Solid 14 Karat Gold Mountings.

On diamonds **we have absolutely no competition.** No concern has ever offered diamonds at anywhere near our prices. Our diamonds are **pure white, clean and well cut.** The value **of a diamond** depends largely on the cutting, for if it is not well cut the stone will not be brilliant. We import our diamonds direct from Europe in large quantities and pay spot cash, thus securing them at the lowest possible figure. Our Buyer is an expert in his line and buys nothing but perfect goods. We buy our mountings in large quantities and do our own setting. Every stone is carefully weighed on fine diamond scales before it is set, and you will be charged only for the actual weight of the stone and value of the mounting. The stone we send you will sometimes vary a small fraction from the one ordered but the price will be changed accordingly. Diamonds are as good as gold. They never wear out and if bought of us you can realize very near, if not more than you paid for them.

We send with each diamond a **Guarantee and Refund Certificate** in which we guarantee the stone to be a **genuine perfect diamond** and we agree to take it back at any time within one year from date of purchase and refund the purchase price less 10 per cent. Where is there another concern that will do this? Don't buy diamonds at retail and pay two prices for them.

**Diamonds will be sent C. O. D.** for examination at your express office, providing $1.00 accompanies your order as a guarantee of good faith. If goods are not found to be as represented the deposit will be refunded to you

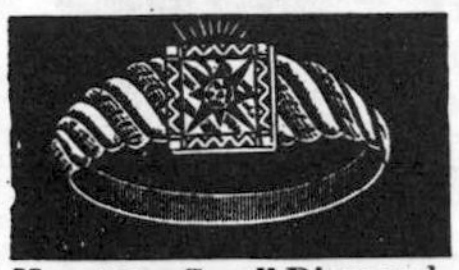
No. 6400. Small Diamond. Price, $4.60

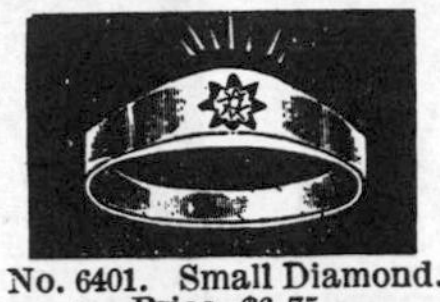
No. 6401. Small Diamond. Price, $6.75

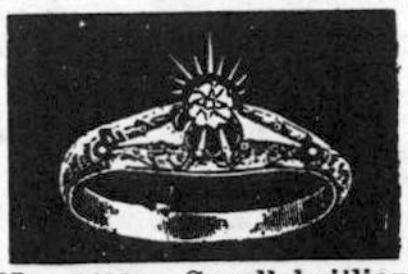
No. 6402. Small brilliant cut Diamond. Price, $8.15

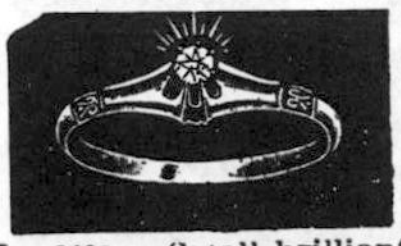
No. 6403. Small brilliant cut Diamond. Price, $8.50

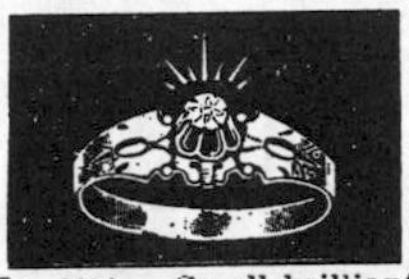
No. 6404. Small brilliant cut Diamond. Price, $8.90

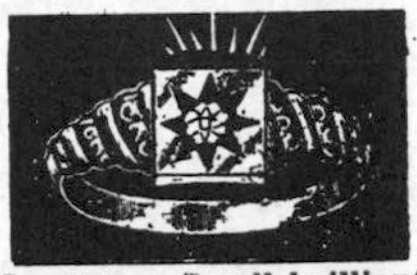
No. 6405. Small brilliant cut Diamond. Price, $9.05

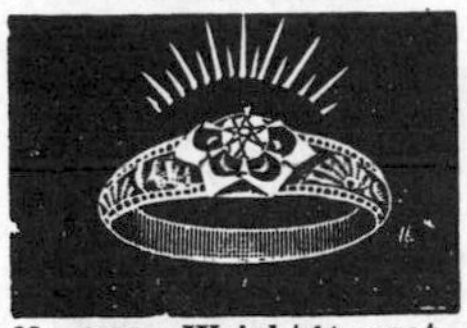
No. 6406. Weight ⅛ carat. Price, $9.50

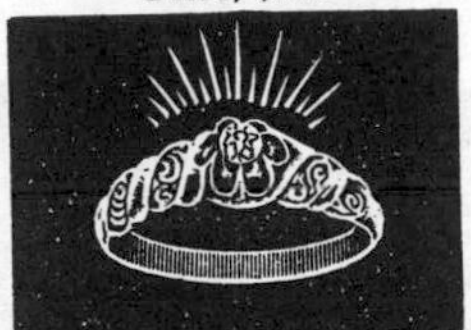
No. 6407. Weight ⅛ carat. Price, $9.50

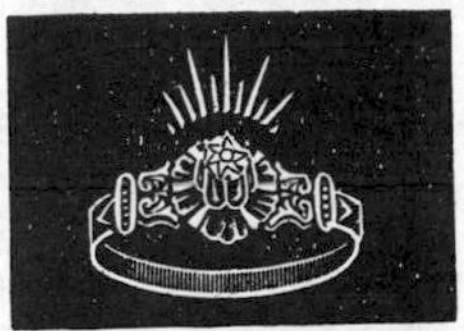
No. 6408. Weight ⅛ carat. Price, $9.50

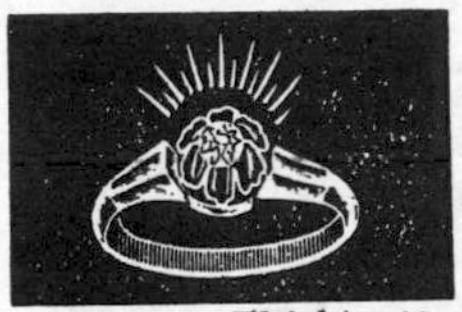
No. 6409. Weight 3-16 carat. Price, $12.50

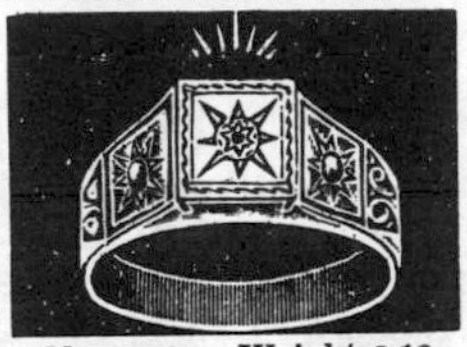
No. 6410. Weight 3-16 carat. Price, $12.50

No. 6411. Weight 3-16 carat. Price, $12-50

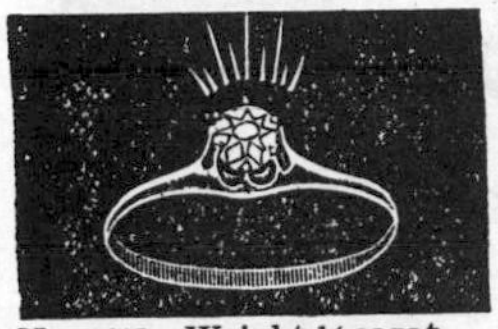
No. 6412. Weight ¼ carat. Price, $15.95

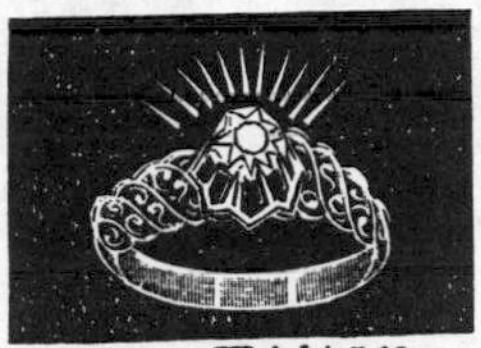
No. 6413. Weight 5-16 carat. Price, $19.25

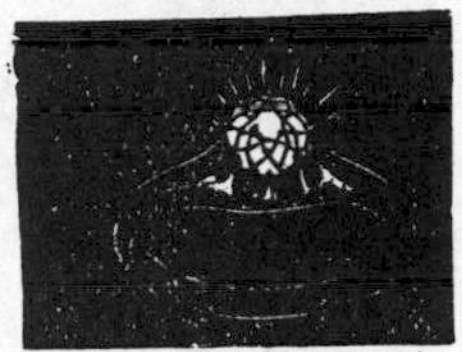
No. 6414. Weight ⅜ carat. Price, $22.50

No. 6415. Weight ½ carat. Price, $29.75

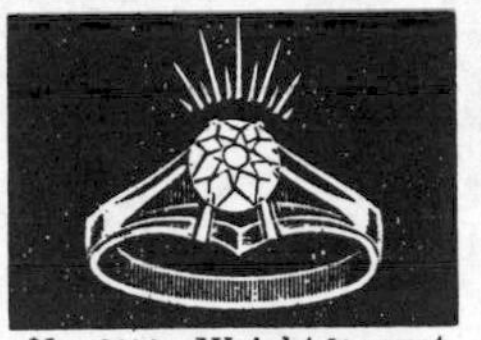
No. 6416. Weight ⅝ carat. Price, $38.95

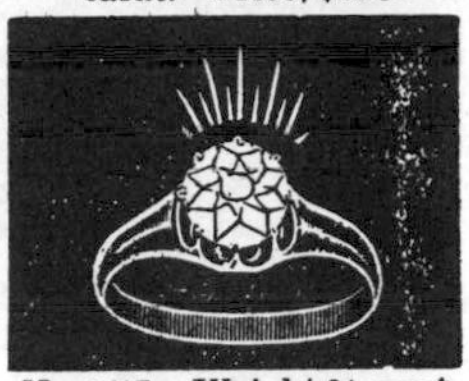
No. 6417. Weight ¾ carat. Price, $51.10

No. 6418. Weight 1 carat. Price, $74.00

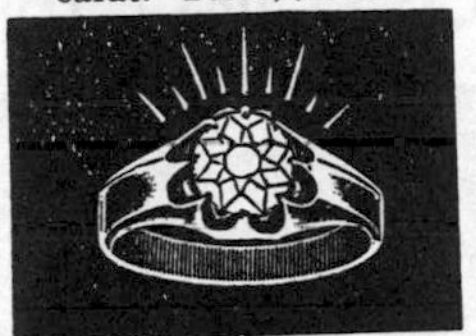
No. 6419. Weight 1¼ carat. Price, $92.00

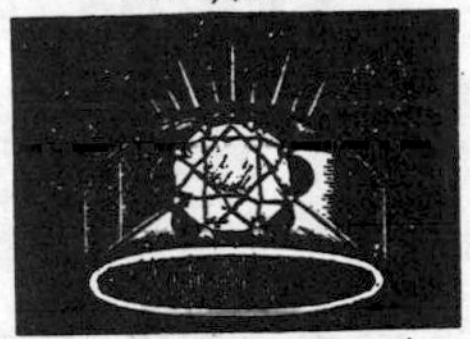
No. 6420. Weight 1½ carat. Price, $111.00

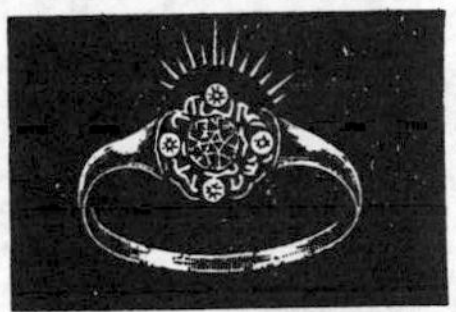
No. 6421. 4 Diamonds, 1 Emerald, Ruby or Sapphire. Price, $5.95

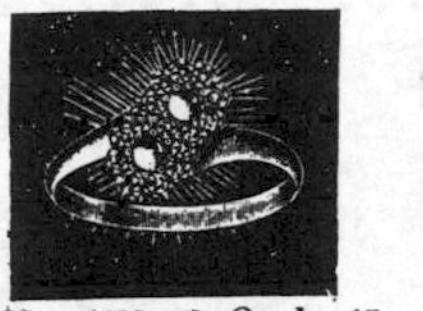
No. 6422. 2 Opals, 15 Diamonds. Price, $8.50

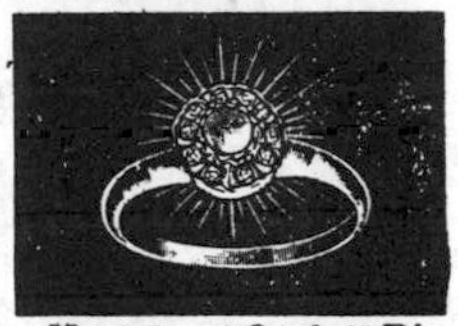
No. 6423. 1 Opal, 10 Diamonds. Price, $10.25

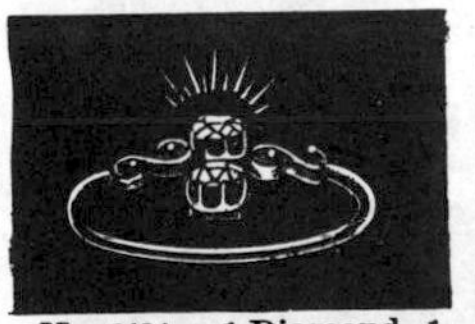
No. 6424. 1 Diamond, 1 1 Ruby, Sapphire or Emerald. Price, $11.95

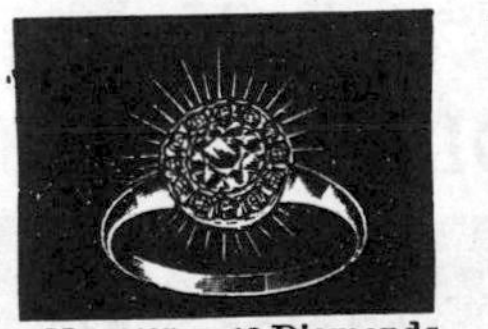
No. 6425. 12 Diamonds, 1 Ruby, Emerald, or Sapphire. Price, $13.40

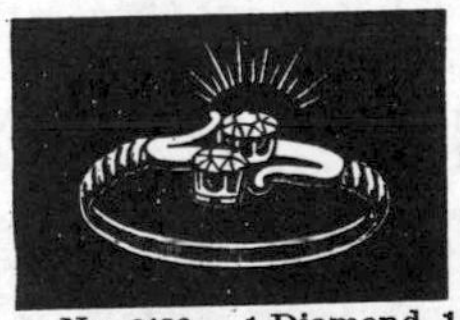
No. 6426. 1 Diamond, 1 Ruby, Sapphire or Emerald. Price, $14.60

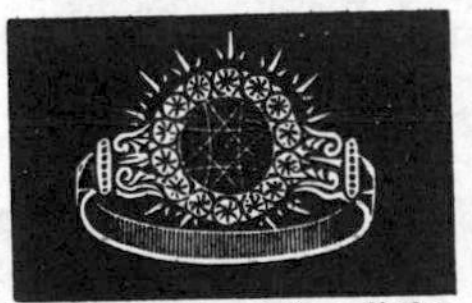
No. 6427. 1 fine Ruby, 14 Diamonds. Price, $15.20

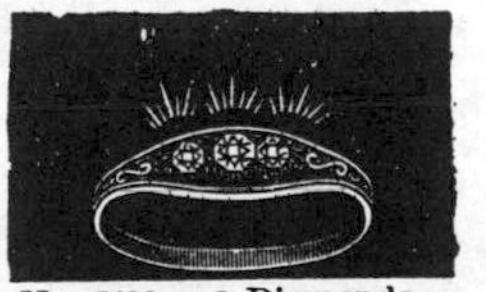
No. 6428. 3 Diamonds. Price, $15.90

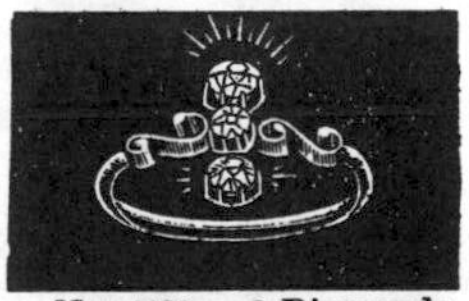
No. 6429. 2 Diamonds, 1 Emerald, Sapphire or Ruby. Price, $15.90

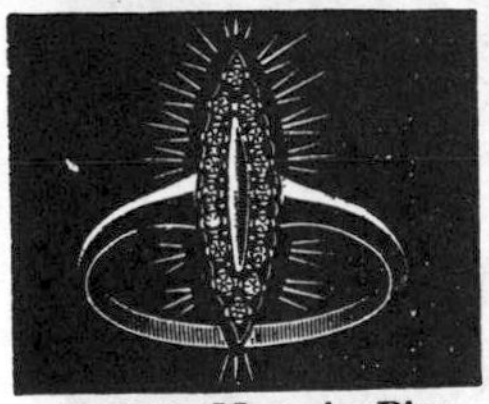
No. 6430, Marquise Ring, 16 Diamonds, 1 Turquoise in center. Price, $17.50

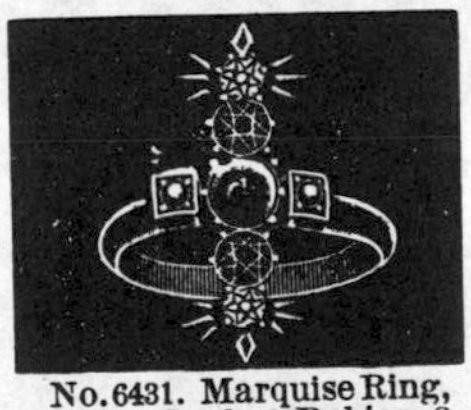
No. 6431. Marquise Ring, 1 large Opal, 2 Rubies, 2 fine Diamonds and 2 Pearls. Price, $21.25

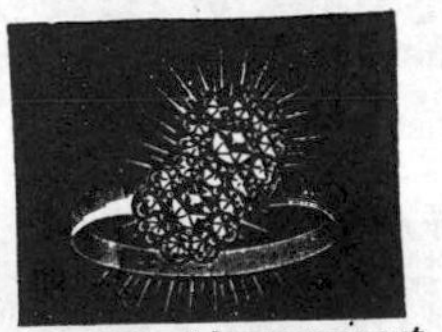
No. 6432. 2 large rose cut Diamonds. 17 small Diamonds. Price, $16.75

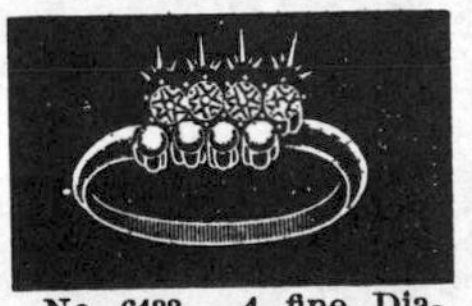
No. 6433. 4 fine Diamonds, 4 Pearls. Price, $23.75

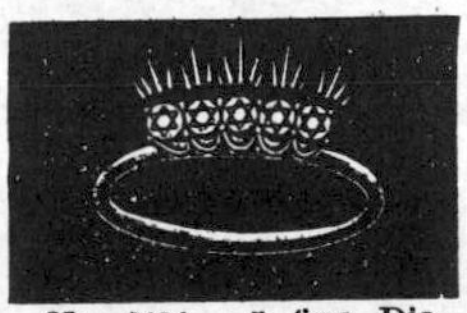
No. 6434. 5 fine Diamonds. Price. $24.95

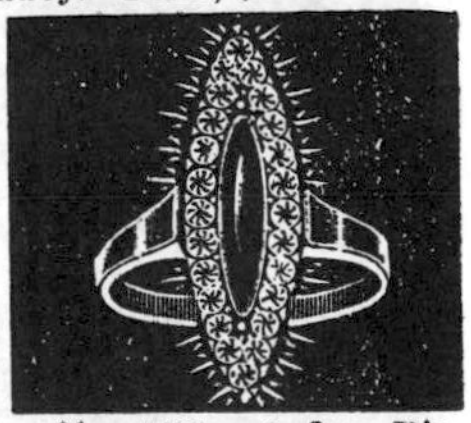
No. 6435. 8 fine Diamonds, 1 Ruby, Emerald or Sapphire. Price, $36.75

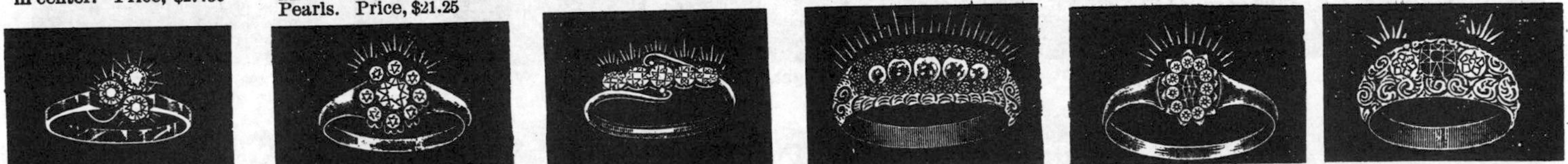
No. 6436. 3 fine Diamonds. Price, $26.25

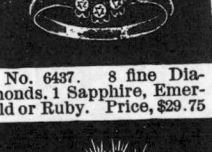

No. 6437. 8 fine Diamonds. 1 Sapphire, Emerald or Ruby. Price, $29.75

No. 6438. 5 fine Diamonds. Price, $29.75

No. 6439. 26 Diamonds, 5 Opals or Rubies. Price, $30.45

No. 6440. 10 Diamonds, 1 Opal. Price, $35.00

No. 6441. 2 Fine Diamonds, 1 Ruby. Price, $35.50

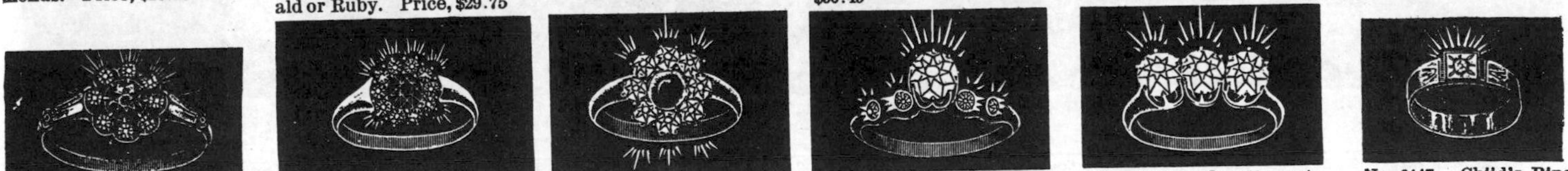
No. 6442. 8 Diamonds, 1 Ruby, Sapphire or Emerald. Price, $17.50

No. 6443. 24 fine Diamonds, 1 Turquoise. Price, $59.25

No. 6444. 8 fine Diamonds, 1 fine Opal. Price, $63.75

No. 6445. One ⅝ carat fine Diamonds. 4 small Diamonds. Price, $72.00

No. 6446. 3 fine ⅝ carat Diamonds. Price, $120.00

No. 6447. Child's Ring, small Diamond. Price, $1.35

# SOLID GOLD DIAMOND SET SCARF OR STICK PINS.

We sell diamonds to some of the largest jewelry manufacturers in Chicago. They sell to the wholesale houses, who sells the retailer, and the retailer sells the consumer. Each one must make a good profit. You can save one-half by buying direct.

 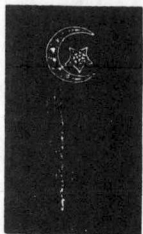 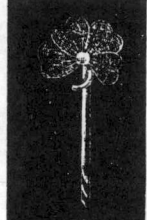    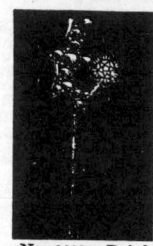 

No. 6460. Roman-finished Crescent, 1 diamond. Price, $1.75.

No. 6461. Bright cut Crescent, 7 pearls, 1 diamond. Price, $2.25.

No. 6462. Green Gold, chased leaves, 1 diamond. Price, $2.60.

No. 6463. Engraved, 4 pearls, 1 diamond Price, $2.90.

No. 6464. Enameled leaves, 2 pearls, 1 diamond. Price, $4.35.

No. 6465. Green and brown gold leaves, engraved, 1 diamond. Price, $4.50.

No. 6466. Bright cut, 11 pearls, 1 diamond. Price, $5.25.

No. 6467. Bright cut, engraved, 6 pearls, 2 diamonds. Price, $5.50.

No. 6468. Bright cut, engraved, 11 pearls, 1 diamond. Price, $5.75.

No. 6469. Bright cut, engraved, 12 pearls, 2 rubies, 1 diamond. Price, $6.50.

No. 6470. One amethyst, 4 diamonds. Price, $5.95.

No. 6471. Brig cut, Masonic emblem, 5 pearls, 6 turquoise, 3 diamonds. Price, $6.50.

No. 6472. Bright cut, butterfly, 3 rubies, 4 diamonds. Price, $6.85.

No. 6473. Bright cut, 18 pearls, 1 fine diamond. Price, $8.75.

No. 6474. Masonic, bright cut. enameled cross, 10 diamonds. Price, $9.70.

No. 6475. One fine opal, 12 fine diamonds. Price, $25.00.

# DIAMOND SHIRT STUDS, WITH SOLID GOLD MOUNTINGS.

   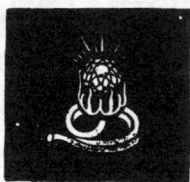   

No. 6476. Weight, 1-16-carat. Price. $5.95.

No. 6477. Weight, ⅛-carat. Price, $9.00.

No. 6478. Weight, ¼-carat. Price, $15.75.

No. 6479. Weight, ⅜-carat. Price, $22.00.

No. 6480. Weight, ½-carat. Price, $29.50.

No. 6481. Weight, ¾-carat. Price, $51.00.

No. 6482. Weight, 1 carat. Price, $73.00.

# DIAMOND EAR DROPS, WITH SOLID GOLD MOUNTINGS.

  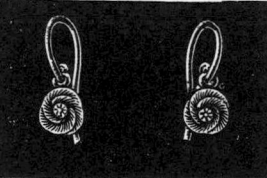 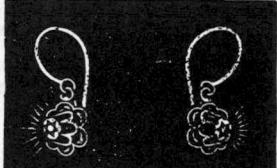 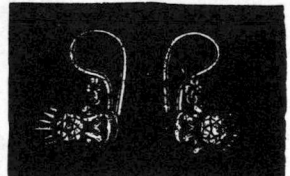

No. 6490. Fancy Roman-finished, each set with 1 small diamond. Per pair, $7.90.

No. 6491. Roman-finished, engraved, each set with diamond. Per pair, $8.60.

No. 6492. Fancy Roman knot, each set with diamond. Per pair, $9.75.

No. 6493. Weight, ⅛-carat. Per pair, $10.35.

No. 6494. Weight, ¼-carat. Per pair, $17.00.

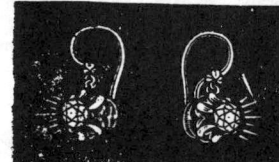 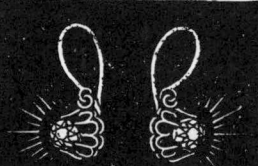  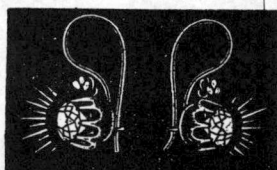 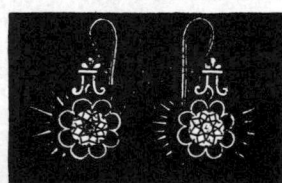

No. 6495. Weight, ⅜-carat. Per pair, $23.50.

No. 6496. Weight, ½-carat. Per pair, $31.00.

No. 6497. Weight, ¾-carat. Per pair, $42.50.

No. 6498. Weight, ⅞-carat. Per pair, $56.30.

No. 6499. Weight, 1 carat. Per pair, $65.60.

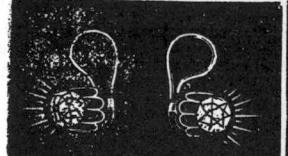 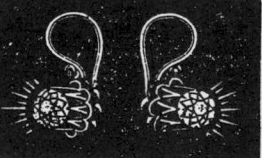 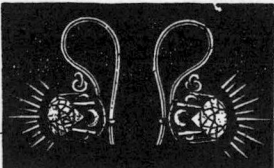 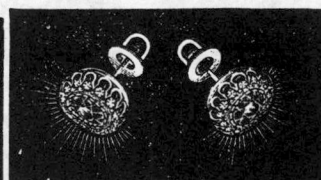 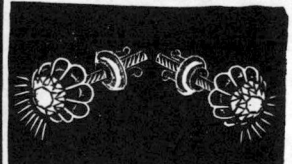

No. 6500. Weight, 1⅛-carat. Per pair, $69.75.

No. 6501. Weight, 1½-carat. Per pair, $99.50.

No. 6502. Weight, 2 carats. Per pair, $152.00.

No. 6503. Screw Ear Sets, fine rubies, encircled with small diamonds. Per pair, $24.50.

No. 6504. Screw Ear Sets. Weight, 1 1-16 carat. Per pair, $69.50.

The weights given above are the total weight for the two stones. We can furnish for any size stone, from ⅛ to 2 carats, any style of setting, from Nos. 6493 to 6502, without extra charge.

There is a vast difference in the value of diamonds depending on the color, cutting, and whether they are clean or not. Our diamonds are pure white, clean and perfectly cut.

# Fine Diamond Jewelry, with Solid 14-Karat Gold Mountings.

| ⅛ | ¼ | ⅜ | ½ | ⅝ | ¾ | ⅞ | 1-C. | 1⅛-C. | 1¼-C. | 1⅜-C. | 1½-C. |

For the benefit of those who are not familiar with the sizes of diamonds, we illustrate above the approximate sizes of stones from ⅛ to 1½-carats. Stones of the same weight vary a trifle in width, depending on the thickness. The illustrations are as near correct as is possible to make them.

Send us your diamond orders and we will give you such value for your money that you will buy no more jewelry at retail. All we ask is that you carefully compare side by side our goods with goods bought of any other concern.

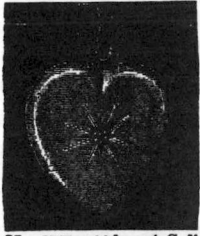

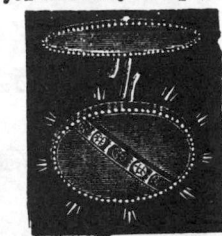

**No. 6515.** 14-karat Solid Gold Locket, for two pictures, Roman finished, 1 diamond. Price, $8.65.

**No. 6516.** Solid 14-karat Gold Locket, for two pictures, satin finished, 1 fine diamond. Price, $7.90.

**No. 6517.** Solid 14-karat Gold Locket, for two pictures, satin finished, 1 fine diamond. Price, $7.45.

**No. 6518.** Solid 14-karat Gold Locket, for two pictures, satin finished, with 3 diamonds. Price, $11.90.

**No. 6519.** Solid Gold Cuff Links, raised, ornamented border, Roman finished; each set with a diamond. Per pair, $9.55.

**No 6520.** Solid Gold Cuff Links, fancy edges, satin finished, each set with 8 emeralds and 2 diamonds. Per pair, $14.80.

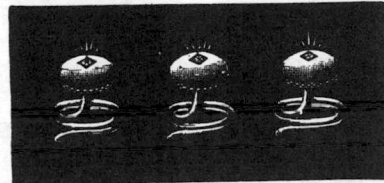

**No. 6521.** Fine Solid Gold Brooch Pin, enameled leaves, bright cut engraved, 25 real pearls, 1 fine diamond. Price, $11.50.

**No. 6522.** Fine Solid Gold Brooch Pin, bright cut engraved, 55 real pearls, 1 fine diamond. Price, $13.75.

**No. 6523.** Solid Gold Roman finished Dress Shirt Stud, each set with diamond.
Price, each ........................ $ 3.50
"   set of three.............. 10.25

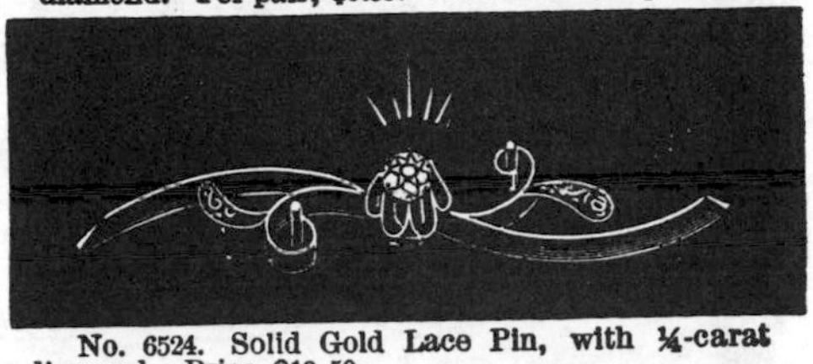

**No. 6524.** Solid Gold Lace Pin, with ¼-carat diamond. Price, $19.50.

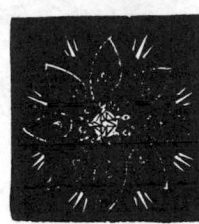

**No. 6525.** Fancy Solid Gold Brooch Pin, Roman-finished leaves, diamond in center. Price, $8.75.

**No. 6526.** Fancy Solid Gold Brooch Pin, Roman-finished leaves, fine diamond in center. Price, $9.50.

**No. 6527.** Solid Gold Wreath, 4 leaves, enameled; 4 leaves set with 12 diamonds; an be worn as a brooch or pendant. Price, $14.85.

**No. 6528.** Fancy Solid Gold Brooch or Pendant, fine diamond in center. Price, $12.45.

**No. 6529** Fancy Solid Gold Brooch and Pendant combined, 1 fine diamond in center. Price, $10.65.

**No. 6530.** Solid Gold Brooch and Pendant combined; can be worn as either; fancy Roman finished leaves, fine diamond in center. Price, $9.95.

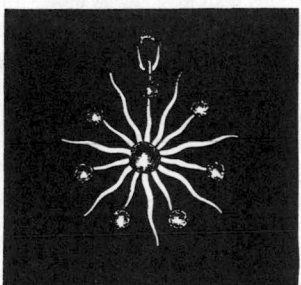

**No. 6531.** Fine Solid Gold Pendant and Brooch; can be worn as either; fine ½-carat diamond in center. Price, $35.00.

**No. 6532.** Fine Solid Gold Pendant and Brooch; can be worn as either; 1 fine diamond in center and 27 real pearls. Price, $24.90.

**No. 6533.** Solid Gold Pendant and Brooch, 8 fine diamonds. Price, $57.50.
Same, with 1 diamond and 7 pearls. Price, $22.50.

**No. 6534.** Solid Gold Pendant and Brooch combined; can be worn as either; 11 fine diamonds and 40 real pearls. Price, $114.50.

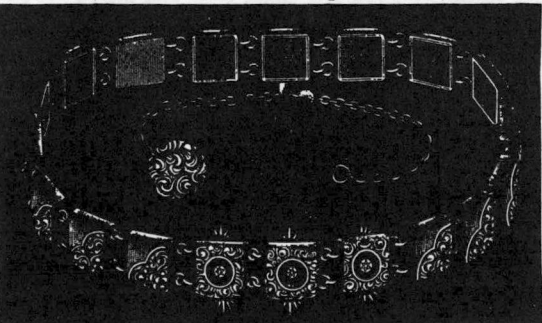

**No. 6535.** Fine Solid Gold Brooch and Pendant combined; can be worn as either; set with 61 diamonds. Price, $225.00.

**No. 6536.** Solid 14-karat Gold Bracelet, Roman finished, square box links, fancy raised ornamentation, solid gold Safety Chain with Bangle, set with 3 diamonds. Price, $18.50.

**No. 6537.** Solid 14-karat Gold Bracelet, Roman finished, hand engraved and fancy ornamented, with solid gold Safety Chain and Bangle, set with fine large diamond. Price, $29.75.

The above Pendants, 6531, 6533, 6534 and 6535, will be made to order only and must be accompanied by at least $10.00 as a guarantee of good faith. If the goods are not found to be as represented, they can be refused and the $10.00 will be promptly refunded. If you want any special design in diamond jewelry write us, stating as near as possible what you want, and we will be glad to furnish estimates.

# Finest Quality Rolled Gold Plated Gents' Vest Chains.

Chains known to the trade as "Fire Gilt" and "Electro Gold Plated" are handled largely by retail dealers and some advertising concerns. We wish to warn our customers against such goods, as they will not hold their color but a short time, and are usually sold for more than the prices we ask for genuine Rolled Gold Plated goods. All of the Chains listed on this page are the best quality Rolled Gold Plated and warranted to wear and retain their color for five years.

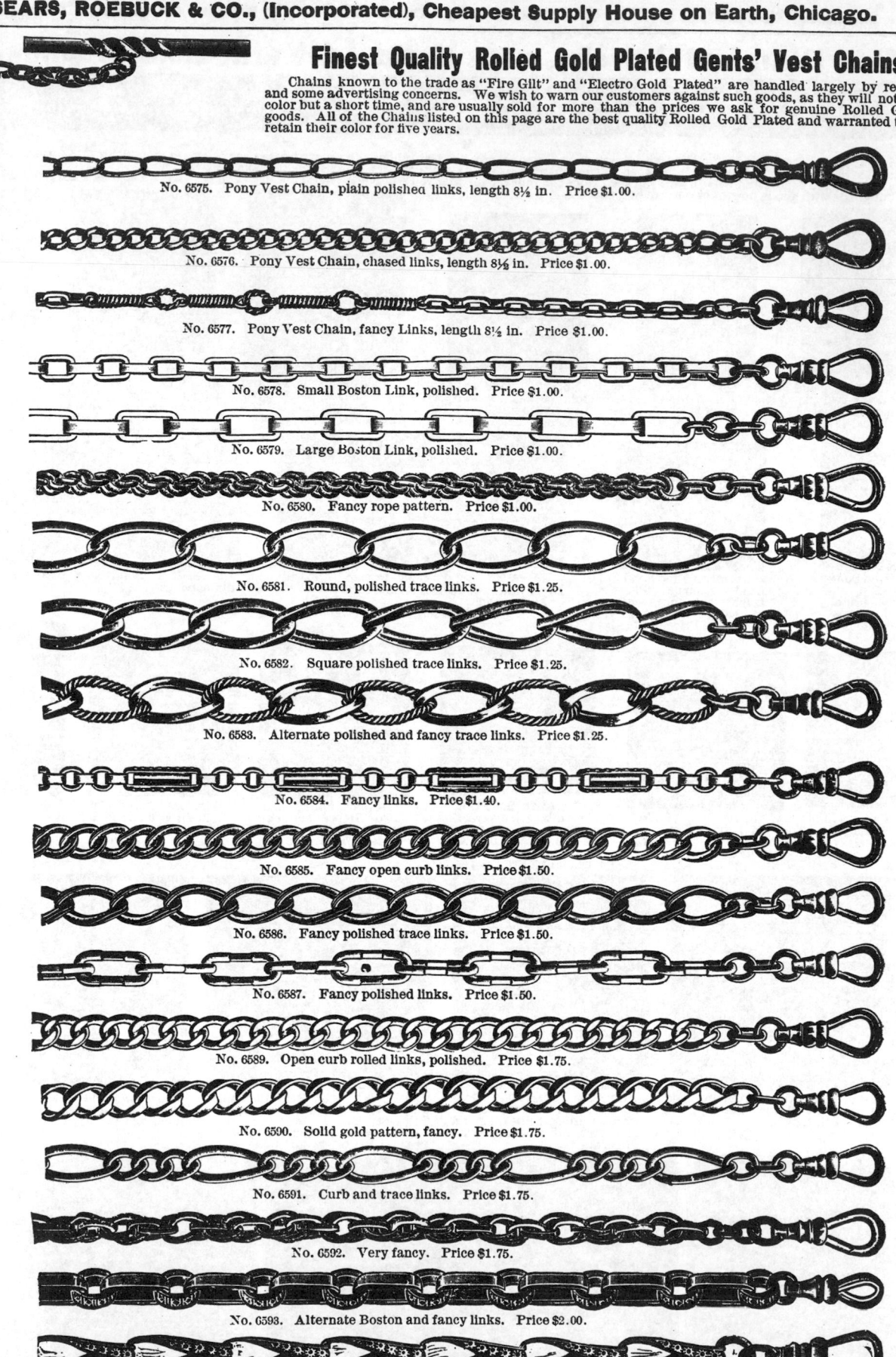

No. 6575. Pony Vest Chain, plain polished links, length 8½ in. Price $1.00.

No. 6576. Pony Vest Chain, chased links, length 8½ in. Price $1.00.

No. 6577. Pony Vest Chain, fancy Links, length 8¼ in. Price $1.00.

No. 6578. Small Boston Link, polished. Price $1.00.

No. 6579. Large Boston Link, polished. Price $1.00.

No. 6580. Fancy rope pattern. Price $1.00.

No. 6581. Round, polished trace links. Price $1.25.

No. 6582. Square polished trace links. Price $1.25.

No. 6583. Alternate polished and fancy trace links. Price $1.25.

No. 6584. Fancy links. Price $1.40.

No. 6585. Fancy open curb links. Price $1.50.

No. 6586. Fancy polished trace links. Price $1.50.

No. 6587. Fancy polished links. Price $1.50.

No. 6589. Open curb rolled links, polished. Price $1.75.

No. 6590. Solid gold pattern, fancy. Price $1.75.

No. 6591. Curb and trace links. Price $1.75.

No. 6592. Very fancy. Price $1.75.

No. 6593. Alternate Boston and fancy links. Price $2.00.

No. 6594. Fancy flat trace links. Price $2.00.

No. 6595. Knurled trace and curb links. Price $2.00.

*(left margin)* No. 6588. Plain polished open curb links. Price $1.75.

All of the above Chains, except the three first, are full length, 12 inches long, with bar and drop attachment for Charm. Postage on Gents' Chains, 3 cents. State how much extra is enclosed for postage, registry, or insurance.

# Gents' Finest Quality Gold Filled Vest Chains.

All of the chains listed on this page are the finest quality gold filled, made of solid gold over composition metal and warranted to wear for twenty years. Our line includes all of the latest and strictly up-to-date patterns, and at prices below all competition.

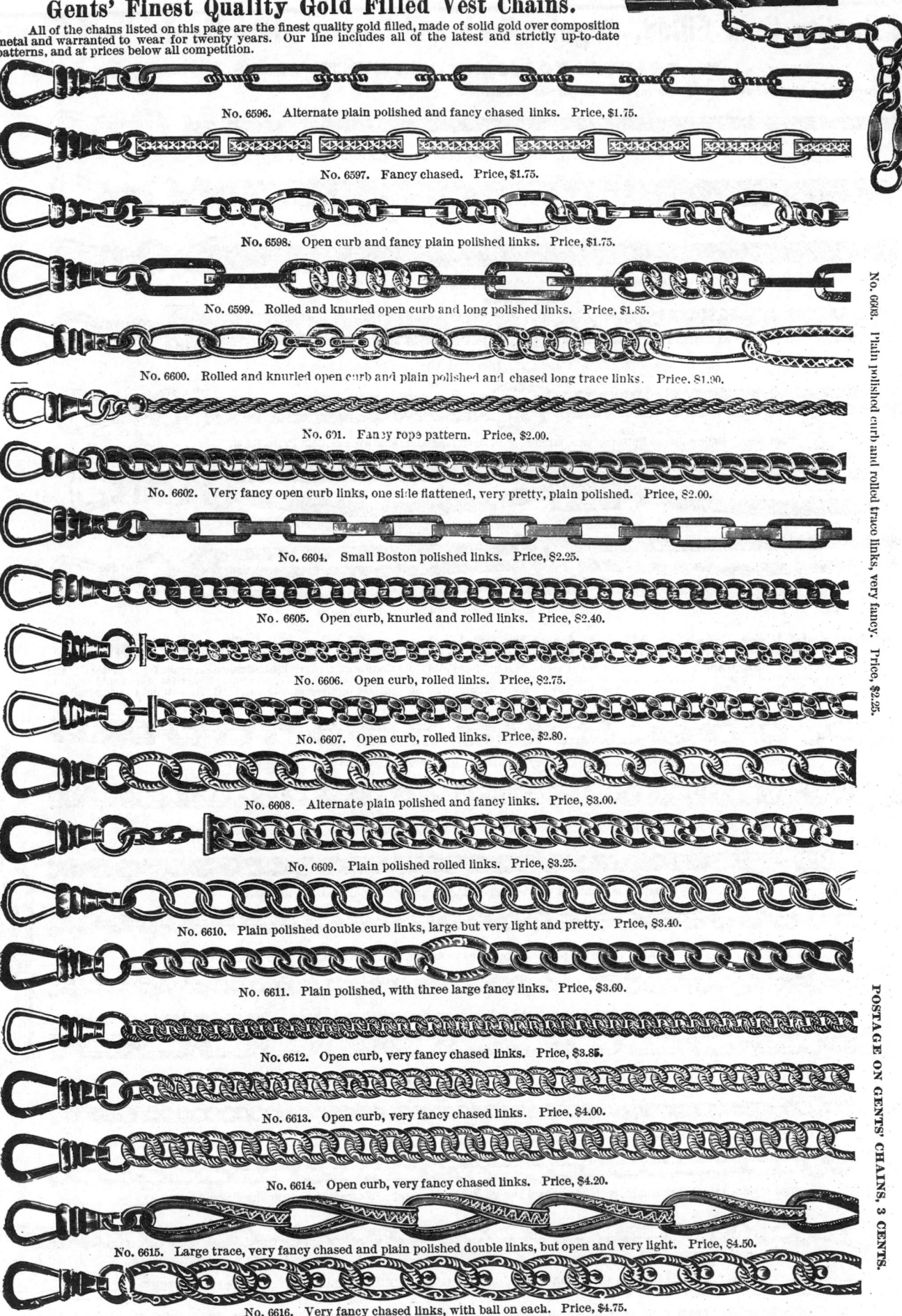

No. 6596. Alternate plain polished and fancy chased links. Price, $1.75.

No. 6597. Fancy chased. Price, $1.75.

No. 6598. Open curb and fancy plain polished links. Price, $1.75.

No. 6599. Rolled and knurled open curb and long polished links. Price, $1.85.

No. 6600. Rolled and knurled open curb and plain polished and chased long trace links. Price, $1.90.

No. 601. Fancy rope pattern. Price, $2.00.

No. 6602. Very fancy open curb links, one side flattened, very pretty, plain polished. Price, $2.00.

No. 6604. Small Boston polished links. Price, $2.25.

No. 6605. Open curb, knurled and rolled links. Price, $2.40.

No. 6606. Open curb, rolled links. Price, $2.75.

No. 6607. Open curb, rolled links. Price, $2.80.

No. 6608. Alternate plain polished and fancy links. Price, $3.00.

No. 6609. Plain polished rolled links. Price, $3.25.

No. 6610. Plain polished double curb links, large but very light and pretty. Price, $3.40.

No. 6611. Plain polished, with three large fancy links. Price, $3.60.

No. 6612. Open curb, very fancy chased links. Price, $3.85.

No. 6613. Open curb, very fancy chased links. Price, $4.00.

No. 6614. Open curb, very fancy chased links. Price, $4.20.

No. 6615. Large trace, very fancy chased and plain polished double links, but open and very light. Price, $4.50.

No. 6616. Very fancy chased links, with ball on each. Price, $4.75.

All of the above chains are 12 inches in length, and have regular bar and drop attachment for charm.

No. 6603. Plain polished curb and rolled trace links, very fancy. Price, $2.25.

POSTAGE ON GENTS' CHAINS, 3 CENTS.

**We will send jewelry, when desired, amounting to over $2.00 C. O. D. by express on receipt of 50 cents as a guarantee of good faith**

# Finest Quality Gold Filled, Regular Curb and Rope Pattern Gents' Vest Chains,

## WARRANTED TO WEAR FOR TWENTY YEARS.

Regular Curb Chains always have been and always will be popular and stylish.

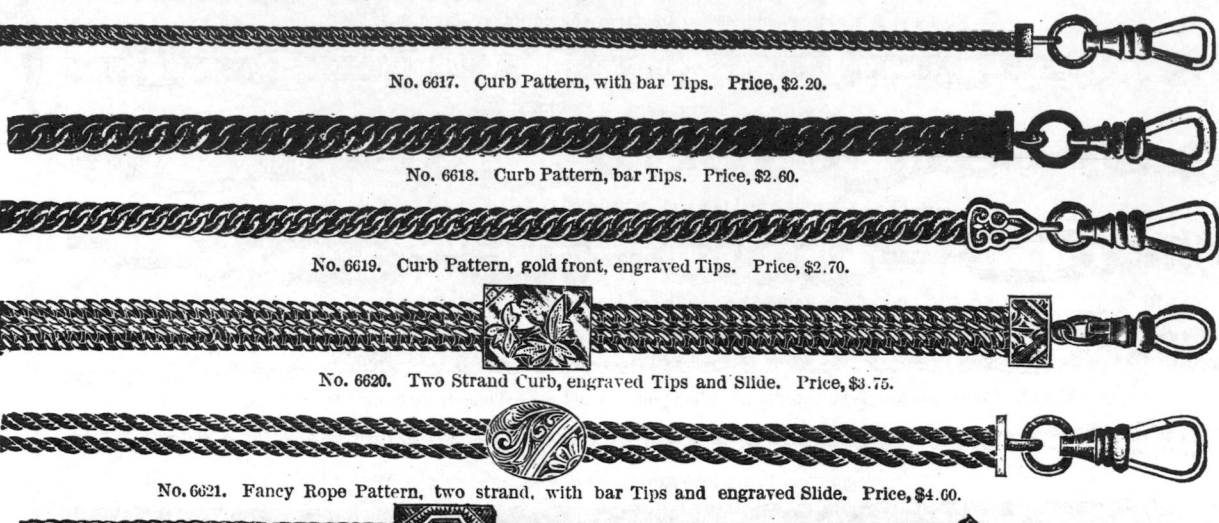

No. 6617.  Curb Pattern, with bar Tips.  **Price, $2.20.**

No. 6618.  Curb Pattern, bar Tips.  **Price, $2.60.**

No. 6619.  Curb Pattern, gold front, engraved Tips.  **Price, $2.70.**

No. 6620.  Two Strand Curb, engraved Tips and Slide.  **Price, $3.75.**

No. 6621.  Fancy Rope Pattern, two strand, with bar Tips and engraved Slide.  **Price, $4.60.**

No. 6622.  Two Strand Curb, with engraved Tips and Slide.  **Price, $3.95.**

No. 6623.  Three Strand, curb engraved Tips and Slide.  **Price, $4.95.**

# Gents' Solid Gold Vest Chains, All Full Length, 12 Inches, with Bar and Charm Attachment.

These Chains are solid Gold through and through, and are warranted.  We sell our Solid Gold Chains at a very slight advance on cost of the material and making.  When you own a solid gold chain you have the satisfaction of knowing that it is the best that money will buy, and at any time that you should wish to dispose of it you can realize on it at a large per cent of the cost.  Any of these chains will be sent on our regular terms, C. O. D., subject to examination, providing 50 cents, as a guarantee of good faith, accompanies your order.

No. 6650.  Plain Polished Boston Link, a very popular chain.  Warranted solid gold.  Price, $12.95

No. 6651.  Heavy, Strong, Curb Link Chain, plain polished; no more durable chain made.  Warranted solid gold.  Price, 13.90.

No. 6652.  Fancy Rope Chain; a very strong chain.  Warranted solid gold.  Price, $9.95.

No. 6653.  Very Fancy Link Chain, fancy engraved and plain polished links alternate.  Warranted solid gold.  Price, $6.95.

No. 6654.  Very Fancy Trace Link Chain, each link flattened and polished; no more stylish chain made.  Warranted solid gold.  Price, $5.90.

No. 6655.  Beautiful Square Boston Link Chain.  Warranted solid gold.  Price, $6.50.

No. 6656.  Beautiful Fancy Open Curb Link Chain, links flattened and polished; very neat and stylish chain.  Warranted solid gold.  Price, $5.95.

No. 6657.  Beautiful Round Trace Link Chain, with bar, swivel and charm attachment.  Warranted solid gold.  Price, $4.95.

No. 6658.  Beautiful Square Flattened Trace Link Chain.  Warranted solid gold.  Price, $6.95.

All our chains are full length, 13 inches, with fancy bar, swivel and charm attachments.

Postage on Gents' Chains 3 cents.  When goods are to go by mail be sure to inclose enough money to pay postage and registry or insurance.  If any balance remains it will be promptly refunded.

When cash in full accompanies your order we allow a discount of 4 per cent, and you save on the express charges.

# FINEST QUALITY GOLD FILLED WELLINGTON AND PONY VEST CHAINS.

These are the latest thing out, and are becoming very popular. They are all the finest quality gold filled, and warranted to wear for twenty years.

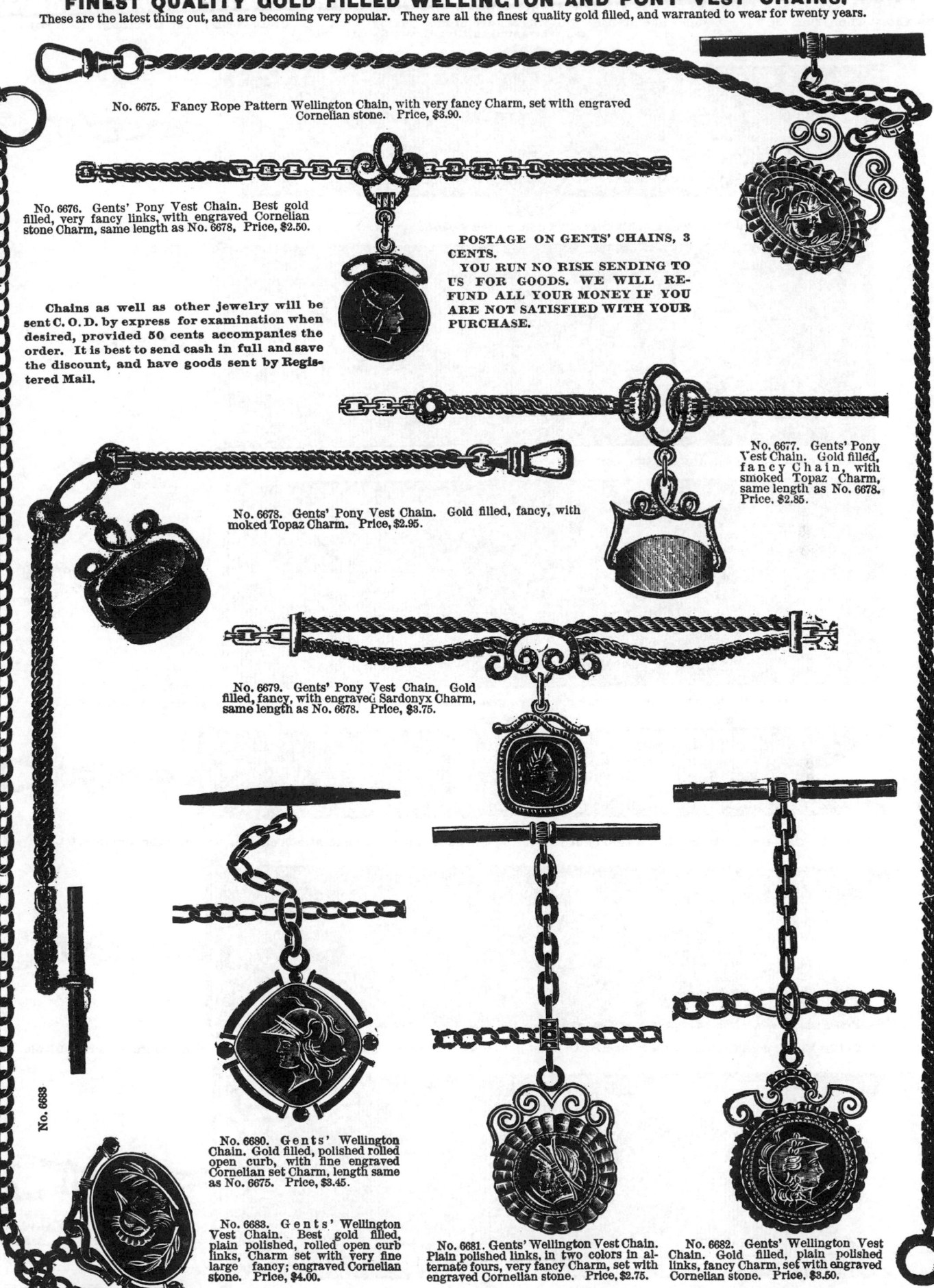

No. 6675. Fancy Rope Pattern Wellington Chain, with very fancy Charm, set with engraved Cornelian stone. Price, $3.90.

No. 6676. Gents' Pony Vest Chain. Best gold filled, very fancy links, with engraved Cornelian stone Charm, same length as No. 6678, Price, $2.50.

**POSTAGE ON GENTS' CHAINS, 3 CENTS.**

**YOU RUN NO RISK SENDING TO US FOR GOODS. WE WILL REFUND ALL YOUR MONEY IF YOU ARE NOT SATISFIED WITH YOUR PURCHASE.**

**Chains as well as other jewelry will be sent C. O. D. by express for examination when desired, provided 50 cents accompanies the order. It is best to send cash in full and save the discount, and have goods sent by Registered Mail.**

No. 6677. Gents' Pony Vest Chain. Gold filled, fancy Chain, with smoked Topaz Charm, same length as No. 6678. Price, $2.85.

No. 6678. Gents' Pony Vest Chain. Gold filled, fancy, with moked Topaz Charm. Price, $2.95.

No. 6679. Gents' Pony Vest Chain. Gold filled, fancy, with engraved Sardonyx Charm, same length as No. 6678. Price, $3.75.

No. 6680. Gents' Wellington Chain. Gold filled, polished rolled open curb, with fine engraved Cornelian set Charm, length same as No. 6675. Price, $3.45.

No. 6683. Gents' Wellington Vest Chain. Best gold filled, plain polished, rolled open curb Charm set with very fine large fancy; engraved Cornelian stone. Price, $4.00.

No. 6681. Gents' Wellington Vest Chain. Plain polished links, in two colors in alternate fours, very fancy Charm, set with engraved Cornelian stone. Price, $2.75.

No. 6682. Gents' Wellington Vest Chain. Gold filled, plain polished links, fancy Charm, set with engraved Cornelian stone. Price, $3.50.

No. 6683

# Best Quality Silk Watch Fobs with Rolled Gold Plated and Gold Filled Mountings.

**The** Latest Thing Out. Is Very Poplular and Stylish. The Ribbons are of Fine Quality Black Gros Grained Silk. The Mountings are of Extra Quality and Warranted to Give Entire Satisfaction.

No. 6707.—Gros Grained Black Silk, with fine rolled gold plated mounting, with ring to attach charm. Price without charm, 60 cents.

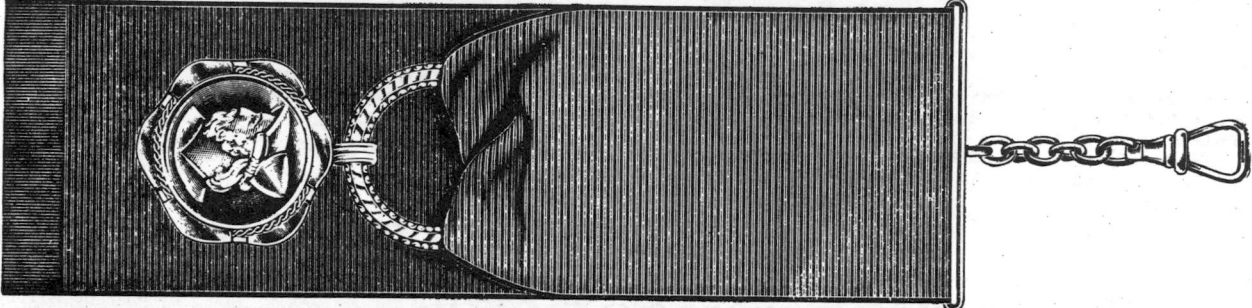

No. 6708.—Gros Grained Black Silk, with fine rolled gold plated mounting and charm with entaglio setting. Price, 85 cents.

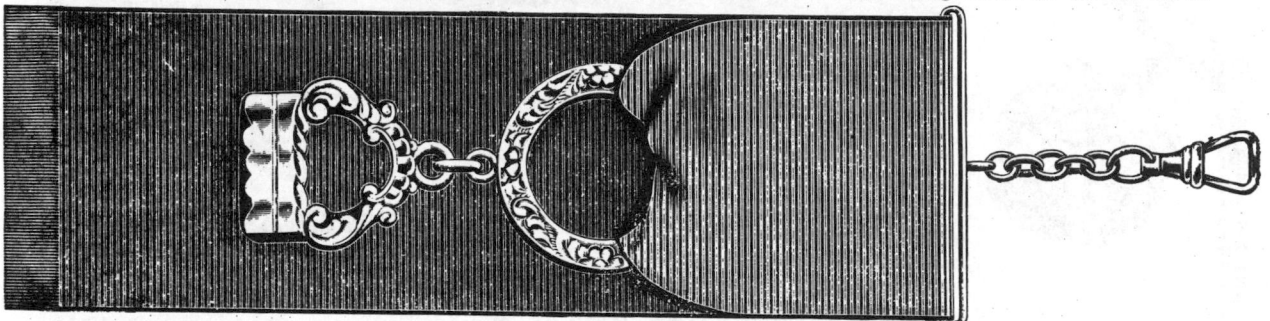

No. 6709.—Gros Grained Black Silk, with fine rolled gold plated mountings and charm, fancy stone setting. Price, $1.25.

No. 6710.—Gros Grain Black Silk, with gold filled mounting and buckle, spring ring to attach charm. Price, without charm, $1.35.

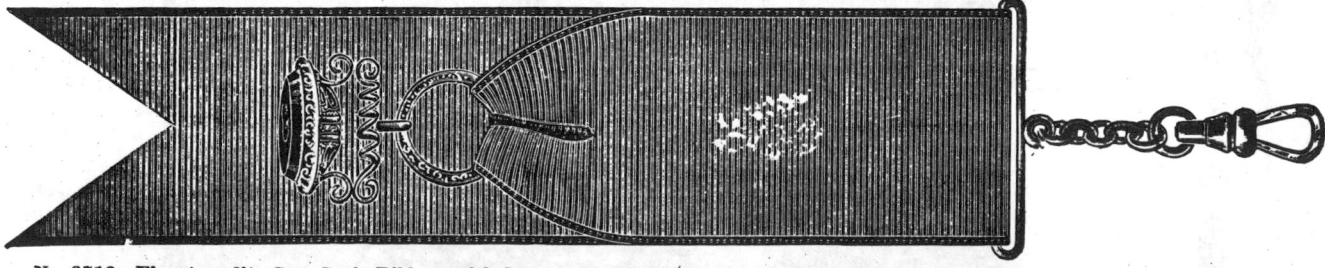

No. 6712.—Finest quality Gros Grain Ribbon, with finest gold filled mountings, and fancy charm set with engraved stone. Price, $3.00.

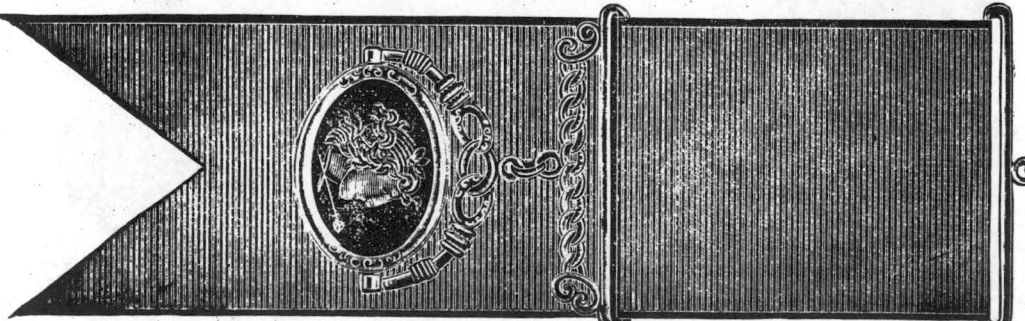

THE THREE LAST LISTED AS GOLD FILLED ARE WARRANTED TO WEAR FOR 20 YEARS.

No. 6713.—Finest quality Gros Grain Black Silk Ribbon, with fine quality gold filled mounting and charm. Charm set with fine engraved cornelian stone. Price, $4.00.

# Gents' Fine Quality Rolled Gold-Plated Curb Vest Chains, all Full Length, 12 inches, with Bar and Charm Attachment.

No. 6715. Two-strand Rolled Gold Plated Curb, with engraved tips and slide. Price, $1.70.

No. 6716. Two-strand Rolled Gold Plated Curb. with engraved tips and slide. Price, $2.25.

No. 6717. Three-strand Rolled Gold Plated Curb, engraved tips and slide. Price, $2.95.

## BEST QUALITY SILK AND HAIR VEST GUARDS, WITH GOLD-FILLED MOUNTINGS.

- No. 6718. Best quality two strand Flat Silk Vest Guard, with gold-filled engraved mountngs. Price. 65 cents.

No. 6719. Best quality two-strand Flat Silk Vest Guard, gold-filled and ornamented mountings. Price, 75 cents.

No. 6720. Best quality two-strand Braided Silk Vest Guard, with fancy gold-filled and ornamented mountings. Price, 90 cents.

No. 6721. Best quality two-strand Braided Silk Vest Guard, with fancy ornamented gold-filled mountings. Price, $1.10.

No. 6722. Best quality two-strand Braided Silk Vest Guard, with fine ornamented gold-filled mountings. Price, $1.25.

All of the above have regular bar and toggle and are 10½ inches in length.

No. 6723.      Fancy Woven Hair Vest Guard, 8½ in. long, with very fancy gold-filled mountings. Price, $1.75.   We are not in position to quote prices on this Guard made to order.

## SOLID STERLING SILVER AND WHITE METAL VEST CHAINS.

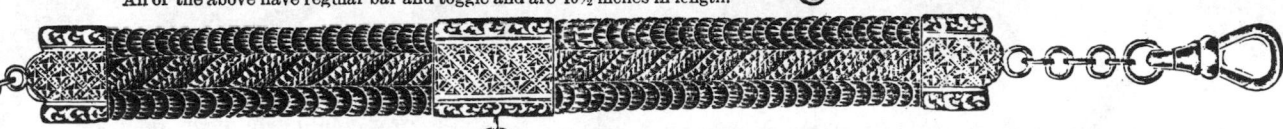

No. 6724. Alternate polished and fancy trace links. Price, in silver, $1.65; solid white metal. 30 cents.

No. 6725. Curb Chain, with tips. Price, in solid sterling silver, $1.70; solid white metal, 20 cents.

No. 6727 Two-strand Curb, with tips and slide. Price, in solid sterling silver, $2.50; in solid white metal, 45 cents.

No. 6726. Fancy rope pattern, solid sterling silver. Price, $2.50; in solid white metal, 35 cents.

All of the above Chains are full 12 inches long, with bar and toggle.

# LONG SILK WATCH GUARDS.
## LENGTH 48 INCHES, OR 24 INCHES WHEN DOUBLED.

No. 6728. Fine Silk Guard, with gold-filled Trilby heart, slide and gold-filled swivel. Price, 50 cents.

No. 6729. Fine Silk Guard, with gold-filled buckle, slide and swivel. Price, 55 cents.

No. 6730. Fine Silk Guard, with solid silver slide and swivel, and enameled emblem for Epworth League or Christian Endeavor. Price, 85 cents.

Postage on Gents' Chains, 3 cents; Silk and Hair Guards, 2 cents. We will send jewelry amounting to over $2.00 anywhere by express C. O. D., for examination, when a deposit of 50 cents accompanies your order.

# BEST QUALITY LADIES' ROLLED GOLD PLATED AND GOLD FILLED VICTORIA CHAINS.

In Chains we handle nothing of lower grade than the best quality of Rolled Gold plate. Anything that could be furnished for less money would be of no practical value to the owner. We guarantee all of our Rolled Gold plated Chains to be exactly as represented, and to wear and retain their color for five years.

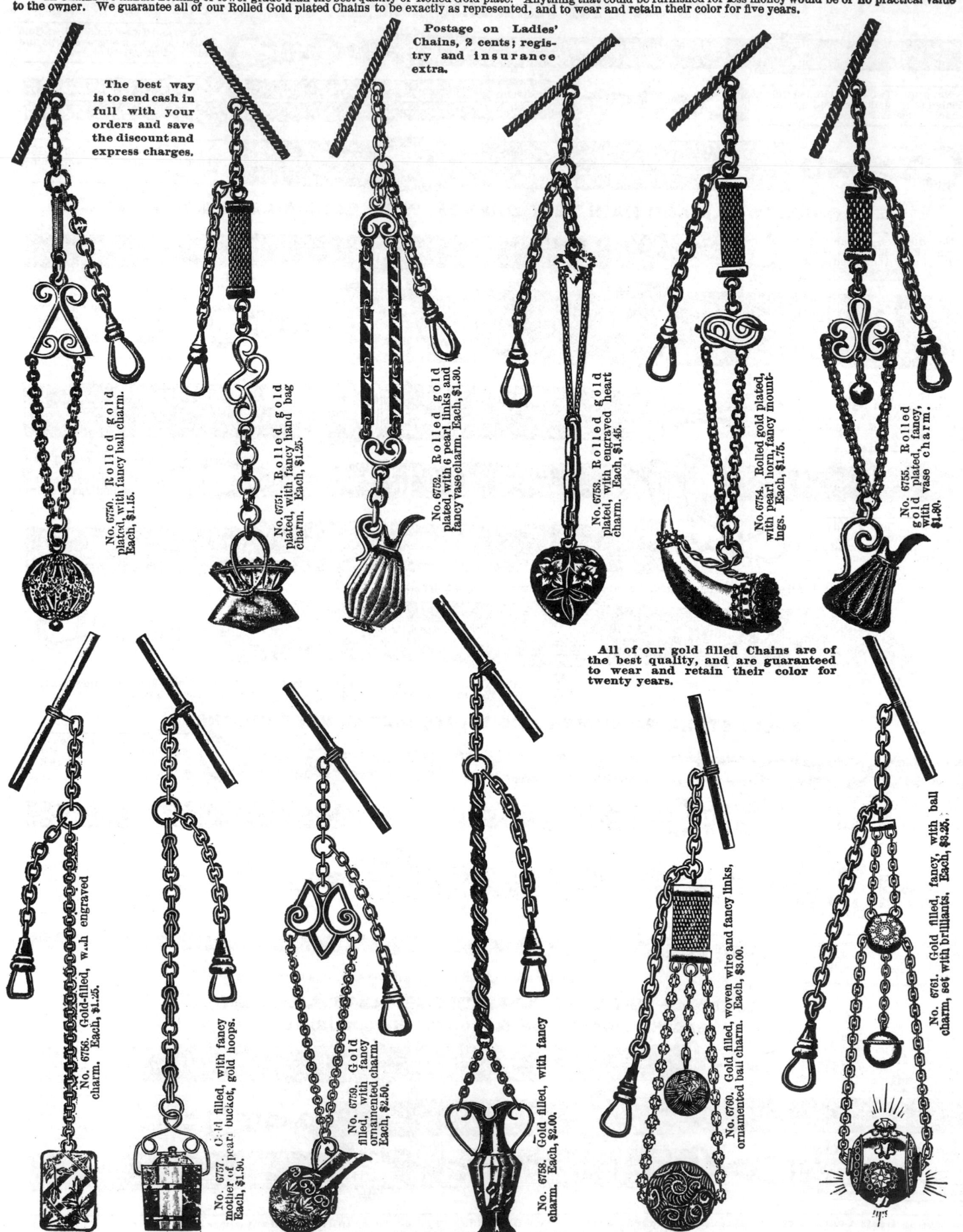

The best way is to send cash in full with your orders and save the discount and express charges.

Postage on Ladies' Chains, 2 cents; registry and insurance extra.

No. 6750. Rolled gold plated, with fancy ball charm. Each, $1.15.

No. 6751. Rolled gold plated, with fancy hand bag charm. Each, $1.25.

No. 6752. Rolled gold plated, with 6 pearl links and fancy vase charm. Each, $1.30.

No. 6753. Rolled gold plated, with engraved heart charm. Each, $1.45.

No. 6754. Rolled gold plated, with pearl horn, fancy mountings. Each, $1.75.

No. 6755. Rolled gold plated., fancy, with vase charm. $1.80.

All of our gold filled Chains are of the best quality, and are guaranteed to wear and retain their color for twenty years.

No. 6756. Gold-filled, with engraved charm. Each, $1.25.

No. 6757. Gold filled, with fancy mother of pearl bucket, gold hoops. Each, $1.90.

No. 6759. Gold filled, with fancy ornamented charm. Each, $2.50.

No. 6758. Gold filled, with fancy charm. Each, $2.00.

No. 6760. Gold filled, woven wire and fancy links, ornamented ball charm. Each, $3.00.

No. 6761. Gold filled, fancy, with ball charm, set with brilliants. Each, $3.25.

# Finest Quality Ladies' Gold Filled Victoria Chains, with Attach Pins.

## WARRANTED TO WEAR FOR 20 YEARS.

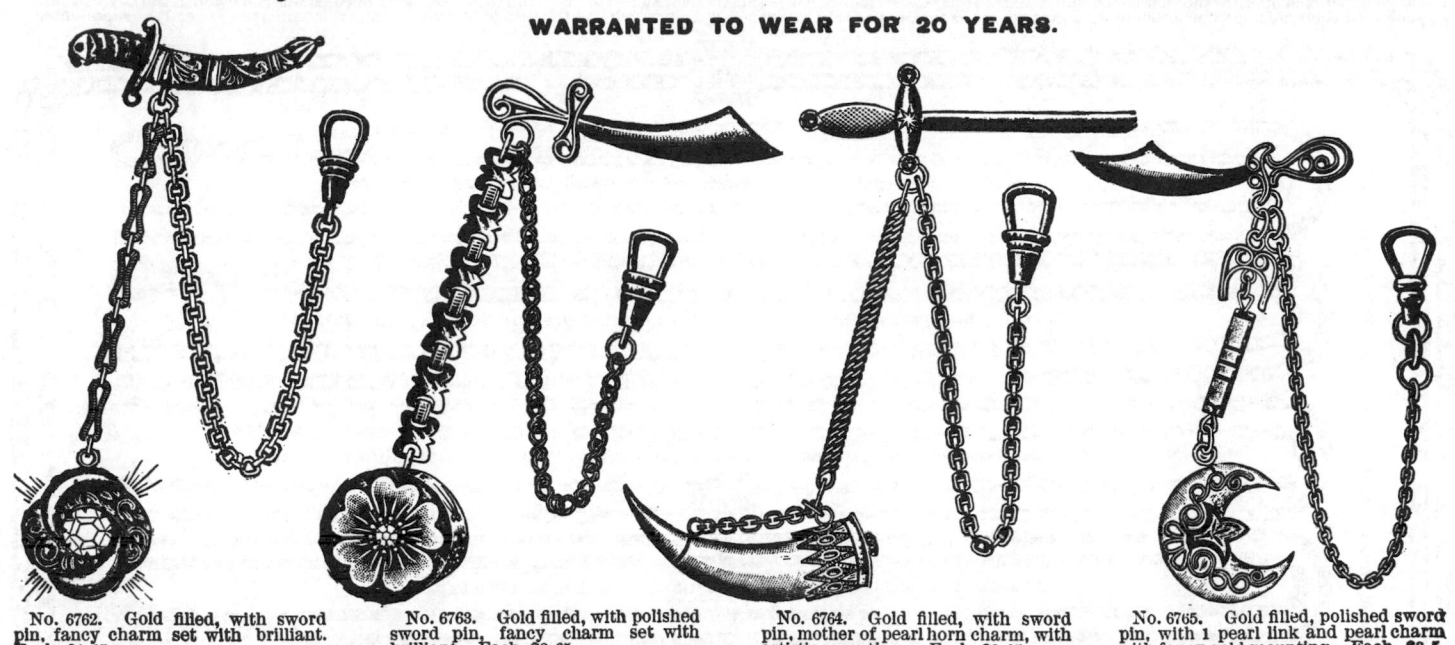

No. 6762. Gold filled, with sword pin, fancy charm set with brilliant. Each, $1.95.

No. 6763. Gold filled, with polished sword pin, fancy charm set with brilliant. Each, $2.65.

No. 6764. Gold filled, with sword pin, mother of pearl horn charm, with artistic mountings. Each, $2.95.

No. 6765. Gold filled, polished sword pin, with 1 pearl link and pearl charm with fancy gold mounting. Each, $3.5.

# Ladies' Finest Quality Gold Filled, Slide, Adjustable and Regular Vest Chains.

## ALL WARRANTED TO WEAR FOR 20 YEARS.

The three first chains can be made longer or shorter as desired. They are very popular, and have always been good sellers.

No. 6766. Ladies' gold filled adjustable vest chain, with solid gold front slide, hand engraved, with spring ring for charm. Each, $1.75.

No. 6767. Ladies' gold filled adjustable vest chain, solid gold front slide, hand engraved, with fancy stone set in charm. Each, $1.95.

No. 6768. Ladies' gold filled adjustable vest chain, solid gold front slide, hand engraved, with fancy stone set in charm. Each, $2.50.

No. 6769. Ladies' gold filled vest chain, very strong, with square polished links, solid gold front slide, set with 3 stones. Each, $2.95.

No. 6770. Ladies' gold filled vest chain, fancy woven wire, polished and engraved slide, set with 3 stones. Each, $3.20.

The cut of No. 6769 is ⅝ inch, and 6770 1⅛ inch, shorter than the chains they represent.

Postage on ladies' chains, 2 cents; insurance or registry extra. See front of book for instructions.

Jewelry orders over $2.00 will be sent C. O. D. when desired, if 50 cents accompanies the order.

No risk, we will refund deposit if goods are not satisfactory.

# FINEST QUALITY LADIES' ROLLED GOLD PLATED, GOLD FILLED AND SOLID GOLD LORGNETTE CHAINS.

The lorgnette style of chains are now the most popular of any for ladies' wear. Our line is very complete, and represents all of the desirable patterns on the market. Our rolled gold plated chains are the very best quality, and are guaranteed to give entire satisfaction, and wear for five years. Our gold filled chains are made in the same manner as gold filled rings, and are warranted to wear for twenty years. Our solid chains are solid gold through and through of fine quality, and warranted to be exactly as represented.

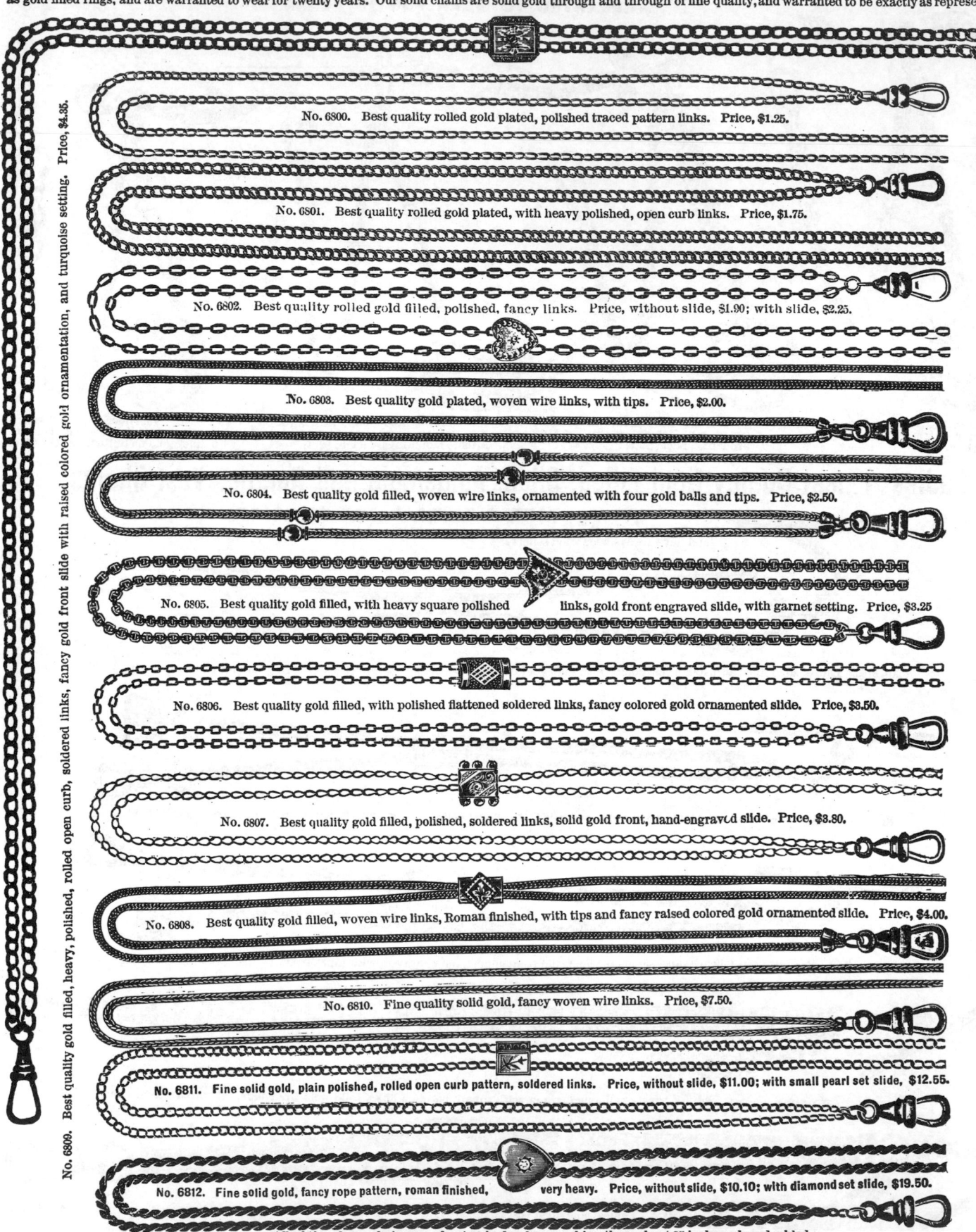

No. 6809. Best quality gold filled, heavy, polished, rolled open curb, soldered links, fancy gold front slide with raised colored gold ornamentation, and turquoise setting. Price, $4.35.

No. 6800. Best quality rolled gold plated, polished traced pattern links. Price, $1.25.

No. 6801. Best quality rolled gold plated, with heavy polished, open curb links. Price, $1.75.

No. 6802. Best quality rolled gold filled, polished, fancy links. Price, without slide, $1.90; with slide, $2.25.

No. 6803. Best quality gold plated, woven wire links, with tips. Price, $2.00.

No. 6804. Best quality gold filled, woven wire links, ornamented with four gold balls and tips. Price, $2.50.

No. 6805. Best quality gold filled, with heavy square polished links, gold front engraved slide, with garnet setting. Price, $3.25.

No. 6806. Best quality gold filled, with polished flattened soldered links, fancy colored gold ornamented slide. Price, $3.50.

No. 6807. Best quality gold filled, polished, soldered links, solid gold front, hand-engraved slide. Price, $3.80.

No. 6808. Best quality gold filled, woven wire links, Roman finished, with tips and fancy raised colored gold ornamented slide. Price, $4.00.

No. 6810. Fine quality solid gold, fancy woven wire links. Price, $7.50.

No. 6811. Fine solid gold, plain polished, rolled open curb pattern, soldered links. Price, without slide, $11.00; with small pearl set slide, $12.55.

No. 6812. Fine solid gold, fancy rope pattern, roman finished, very heavy. Price, without slide, $10.10; with diamond set slide, $19.50.

All of the above chains are about 50 inches long, making them about 25 inches when doubled.

# LADIES' SOLID GOLD VICTORIA CHAINS.

These chains are all of the finest quality solid gold through and through, and are fully warranted. We only ask you to compare our prices on solid gold chains with those of your retail dealer to be convinced that we can furnish you the latest patterns in solid gold goods on the market, at about one-half the price he asks for old style and inferior quality of goods.

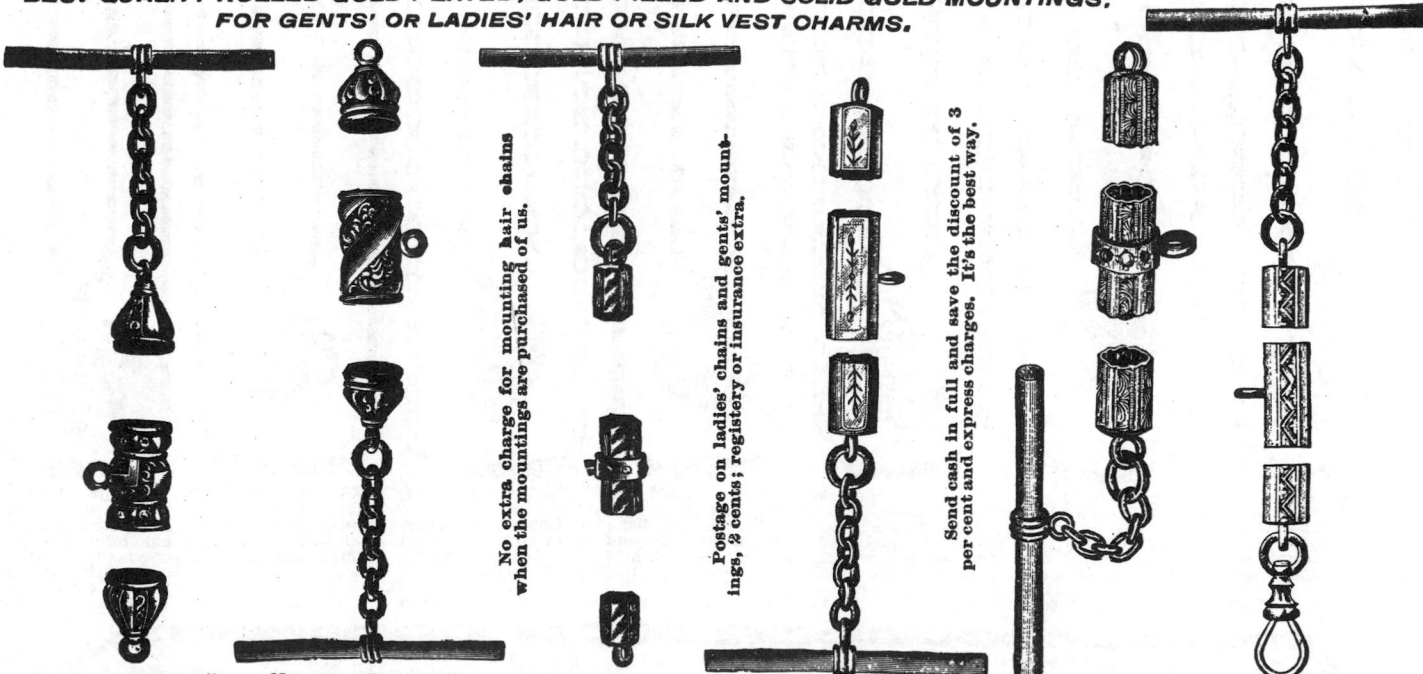

No. 6825. Solid gold, polished links and heart locket. Each, $3.95.

No. 6826. Solid gold, square polished, trace pattern links, fancy hand engraved and enameled charm, set with real pearl. Each, $4.90.

No. 6827. Solid gold, very fancy chain, with raised, ornamented Roman finished ball charm, set with 4 real pearls in raised stars. Each, $6.75.

No. 6828. Solid gold, very fancy soldered links, hand-engraved charm, set with 6 real pearls. Each, $7.60.

No. 6829. Solid gold, heavy, with very fancy links, Roman finished and fancy raised, ornamented pitcher charm, set with 8 real pearls and 1 turquoise. Each, $9.45.

No. 6830. Solid gold, Roman finished, fancy rope pattern, with raised ornamented, bright cut hand-engraved and enameled charm. Each, $6.45.

### BEST QUALITY ROLLED GOLD PLATED, GOLD FILLED AND SOLID GOLD MOUNTINGS, FOR GENTS' OR LADIES' HAIR OR SILK VEST CHARMS.

No extra charge for mounting hair chains when the mountings are purchased of us.

Postage on ladies' chains and gents' mountings, 2 cents; registery or insurance extra.

Send cash in full and save the discount of 3 per cent and express charges. It's the best way.

No. 6852. Best quality rolled gold plated, hard soldered. Per set, including swivel, 75c.

No. 6853. Best quality gold filled, fancy chased and ornamented. Each, including swivel, 90c.

No. 6854. Best quality gold filled, engraved, octagon shape, set with pearl and 2 garnets. Each, including swivel, $1.15

No. 6855. Best quality gold filled, fluted pattern, engraved. Each, including swivel, $2.25.

No. 6856. Finest quality gold filled, fancy fluted pattern, chased and polished, set with pearl and 2 garnets. Each, including swivel, $2.70.

No. 6857. Fine solid gold, fluted pattern, engraved. Each, including swivel, $7.00.

No. 6859. Hair chain, braided to order, in two pieces like above. Price, $1.00.

No. 6860. Hair chain, made to order, two pieces, like above. Price, $1.50.

# Best Quality Gold Filled and Solid Gold Neck Chains with Pendants.

Our gold filled neck chains all have soldered links, thus making them very strong, and are all warranted to wear and retain their color for twenty years. Our gold chains are solid gold through and through, and are warranted to be as represented. Our line represents the latest, prettiest and most stylish patterns, and are all sold at astonishingly low prices. We can save you on the same grade of goods from 33⅓ to 50 per cent over prices charged by retail dealers.

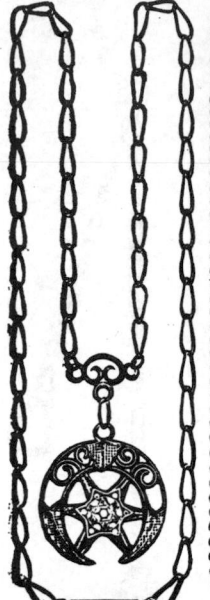

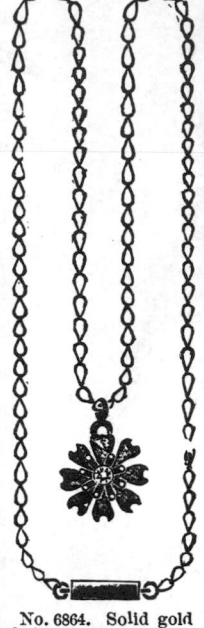
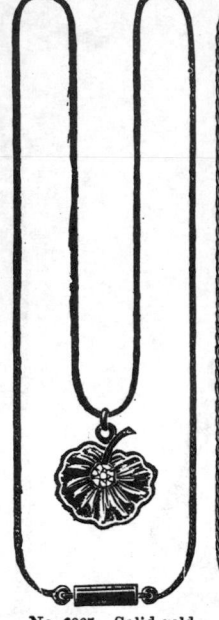

**No. 6861.** Gold-filled chain, fancy crescent and star pendant, set with large white brilliant. Price............$1.45

**No. 6862.** Gold-filled chain, with colored gold ornamented charm, set with stone. Price............$1.85

**No. 6863.** Solid gold chain, Roman finished, fancy links, solid gold, satin finished, heart pendant. Price............$2.00

**No. 6864.** Solid gold chain, trace pattern links, solid gold flower, fancy pendant, set with real diamond. Price............$3.85

**No. 6865.** Solid gold, woven wire chain, solid gold leaf pendant, set with real diamond. Price............$4.75

**No. 6866.** Solid gold, woven wire chain, with solid gold, Roman finished gold heart, set with 12 pearls and 1 real diamond. Price............$5.40

**No. 6867.** Solid gold chain, heavy trace pattern links, with solid gold bird and twig pendant, colored gold leaves, 7 turquoise and diamond eye. Price............$5.90

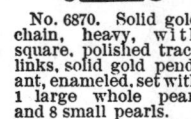

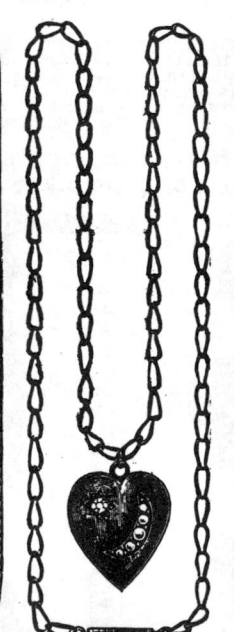
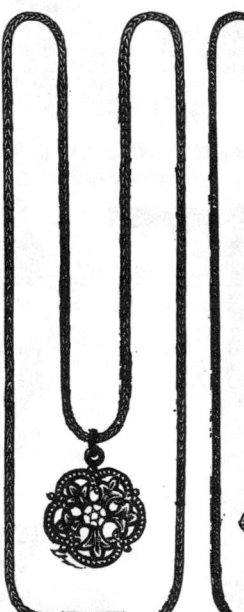

**No. 6868.** Solid gold, heavy chain, square, polished links, trace pattern. Solid gold crescent pendant, set with ruby and 7 real pearls. Price............$5.00

**No. 6869.** Solid gold chain, Roman finish, fancy trace links, Roman finished solid gold heart, set with 1 diamond and 14 real pearls. Price............$6.50

**No. 6870.** Solid gold chain, heavy, with square, polished trace links, solid gold pendant, enameled, set with 1 large whole pearl and 8 small pearls. Price............$6.75

**No. 6871.** Solid gold fancy link chain, solid gold, bright cut, hand engraved, crescent pendant, set with 9 real pearls and 1 real diamond. Price............$7.50

**No. 6872.** Solid gold, very heavy, square polished trace links, satin finished, solid gold heart, set with 5 pearls and 1 fine brilliant cut diamond. Price............$7.75

**No. 6873.** Solid gold woven wire links, fancy pendant, with colored gold leaves, set with brilliant cut diamond. Price............$7 80

**No. 6874.** Solid gold woven wire chain, heavy solid gold pendant, bright cut, hand engraved, set with 16 real pearls and 1 fine brilliant cut diamond. Price............$8.00

**No. 6875.** Gold filled neck chain, warranted to wear twenty years. Set with 10 fine imitation diamonds. Price................................$3.25.

All of the above neck chains are 13 inches long.

**POSTAGE ON NECK CHAINS, 2 CENTS. JEWELRY ORDERS OVER $2.00 WILL BE SENT BY EXPRESS C. O. D. WHEN DESIRED IF 50 CENTS ACCOMPANIES YOUR ORDER AS A GUARANTEE OF GOOD FAITH.**

# GOLD-FILLED AND SOLID STERLING SILVER BRACELETS.

No. 6910. Misses' Gold-Filled Bracelet, plain polished links, with raised, ornamented an polished lock, length 5 inches. Price, $1.15.
No. 4910½. Solid Sterling Silver, with satin-finished links, raised, ornamented and satin-finished lock, length 5 inches. Price, 95 cents.

In Gold-Filled and Silver Bracelets we handle nothing but the finest quality, and our line embraces all of the desirable patterns on the market. Chain Bracelets are now the most stylish. They are all full length and are adjustable. Our Gold-Filled Bracelets are all warranted to wear and retain their color for twenty years.

No. 6911. Gold-Filled Bracelet, best quality, bright polished trace pattern links, polished lock. Price, $1.75.

No. 6912. Gold-Filled Bracelet, best quality, fancy chased links, raised, ornamented and polished lock. Price, $2.00.

No. 6913. Gold-Filled Bracelet, best quality, with fancy chased links, raised, ornamented and polished lock. Price, $2.45.
No. 6913½ Solid Sterling Silver, chased satined links, raised, ornamented and satin finished lock. Price, $1.75

No. 6914. Gold-Filled Bracelet, best quality, plain polished links and lock. Price, $2.25.

No. 6915. Gold-Filled Bracelet, best quality, flattened links, fancy chased, raised, ornamented and polished lock. Price, $2.90.
No. 6915½. Solid Sterling Silver Bracelet, flattened chased links, raised, ornamented and satin lock. Price, $2.55.

No. 6920. Gold Filled Bracelet, best quality flattened links, small at the ends and graduated to large in the middle, roman finished and fancy chased links and lock, spring lock with key. Is very pretty and stylish. Price, $2.45.

No. 6922. Gold Filled Bracelet, best quality, large hollow links, giving it a massive and rich appearance, but at the same time it is light. Links and lock are both satin finished, has spring lock with key and is exceptional value. Price, $2.80.

No. 6918. Gold-Filled, best quality, very fancy, with flattened rolled links, fancy chased, set with five garnets and five sapphires in center, fancy lock. Price, $3.75.

No. 6919. Gold-Filled, best quality, very large hollow Links, fancy chased, with raised, ornamented and polished lock. Price, $4.50.
No. 6913½. Solid Sterling Silver, satin and very fancy chased large hollow Links, satined and raised, ornamented lock. Price, $2.25.

All of the above Bracelets, except Nos. 6910 and 6910½ are 7 inches long.    FOR SOLID GOLD BRACELETS SEE DIAMOND PAGES.

Postage on Bracelets, 3 cents, registry or insurance extra. We advise you to send cash in full and save the discount of 3 per cent and express charges. We assume all the risk, for if you are not satisfied we will refund your money.

# GOLD=FILLED RINGS.

## How Gold-Filled Rings Are Made.

We have given in the front part of this department an article explaining the manner in which gold-filled cases are made, and as we offer you here a page of gold-filled rings, we believe it would be interesting to you and much more satisfactory before making a purchase of a gold-filled ring to know just how they are made. It would seem to the average person and even a mechanic that it would be a difficult problem to completely envelop a piece of hard composition metal with solid gold, and at the same time turn out and place the goods on the market at such a low price. The operation, however, is very easy when it is understood. To start with, a piece of solid gold tube from 1½ to 2 inches in diameter is taken and the hole on the inside made perfectly smooth, after which a piece of hard, fine composition metal is placed on the inside of the tube so as to fit the opening perfectly. Some fine gold solder is now placed in the crevice and the whole is inserted in the furnace. As soon as the two pieces are heated sufficiently the solder flows into the crevice, after which it is removed from the furnace, and after it is cold the two original pieces are one. You will see a section of such a piece illustrated in Fig. 1.

One end of this piece is then hammered and drawn out, so as to make it a little smaller, after which it is inserted in what is called the draw plate, which is a long steel plate with a number of holes in it of such shape as the pieces which it is desired to make. These holes are graduated in size, at one end being very large and at the other end small. The piece of material to be worked on is inserted in the large hole first and with a pair of tongs it is drawn through; this reduces the piece, when it is again hammered at the end to make it small enough to be inserted in the next smaller hole and in turn drawn through this. (All kinds of wire for whatever purpose it may be intended is drawn in the same manner. Sometimes a wire will be drawn in this manner to a mile or more in length). The edges of the holes are all polished so as not to scrape, but to press the metal. This drawing hardens the metal to such an extent that after drawing it through several times it would break easily. It is then annealed by inserting it in the fire and allowing it to cool gradually. After the piece has been drawn out to the required shape and size, one end is bent around a steel mandrill until it has formed a circle of the size the ring is to be made. It is then cut off at the proper place and both ends are carefully surfaced in order to bring them together and make a perfect joint, and on this joint is placed some fine gold solder and the ring inserted in a furnace sufficiently heated to cause the solder to flow into the joint. The ring is then polished carefully on a cotton buff wheel with tripoli and rouge, after which it is ready for the market. Solid gold rings are made in the same manner with the exception of the composition metal on the inside.

The market is flooded with cheap brass rings which are electro-gold plated, and are called rolled plate or rolled gold plate, and which are utterly worthless. In gold-filled rings we handle nothing but the very best. The gold used is 14-karat, will wear an indefinite length of time, and is guaranteed to give entire satisfaction.

## SEE OUR PRICES ON ——— BEST QUALITY 14-KARAT GOLD-FILLED RINGS ——— WILL BE FURNISHED IN SIZES 5 TO 11.

**No. 6964.** Plain oval band. Price, 60 cents.
**No. 6965.** Plain oval band. Price, 95 cents.
**No. 6966.** Plain oval band. Price, $1.30.
**No. 6967.** Plain oval band. Price, $1.65.
**No. 6968.** Plain flat band. Price, $1.30.
**No. 6969.** Plain flat band. Price, $1.70.
**No. 6970.** Flat band chased. Price, 80c.

**No. 6971.** Flat band, fancy engraved and embossed. Price, $1.00
**No. 6972.** Flat band, fancy engraved and embossed. Price, $1.30.
**No. 6973.** Flat band, engraved and embossed. Price, $1.40.
**No. 6974.** Flat band, fancy engraved and embossed. Price, $1.55.
**No. 6975.** Flat band, fancy engraved and embossed. Price, $1.70.
**No. 6962.** Solid gold. Fancy engraved, with polished hearts. Price, $1.25.
**No. 6963.** Solid gold. Tiffany Belcher setting with fine imitation diamond. Price, $1.50.

## LADIES' AND GENTS' SOLID STERLING SILVER RINGS.

**No. 6980.** With Christian Endeavor bangle. Price, 30 cents.
**No. 6981.** With Epworth League bangle. Price, 30 cents.
**No. 6982.** Engraved, set with garnet. Price, 35 cents.
**No. 6983.** Engraved, set with garnet. Price, 50 cents.
**No. 6984.** Engraved, set with 3 garnets. Price, 75 cents.
**No. 6985.** Engraved, set with 3 fine garnets. Price, $1.00.
**No. 6986.** Snake pattern, set with fine garnet, emerald eyes. Price, $1.25.

## CHILDREN'S AND MISSES' SOLID GOLD RINGS, SIZES 0 TO 5.

**No. 6987.** One Garnet. Price, 75 cents.
**No. 6988.** One pearl, 2 garnets. Price, 85 cents.
**No. 6989.** Three pearls, 3 garnets. Price, $1.00.
**No. 6990.** Two pearls, 4 garnets. Price, $1.10.
**No. 6991.** Fancy, 1 garnet. Price, $1.20.
**No. 6992.** Fancy setting, 1 small diamond. Price, $1.30.
**No. 6993.** Set with 1 garnet, sizes, 5 to 8. Price, $1.35.

## RULES FOR MEASUREMENT—SCALE SHOWING SIZES OF RINGS.

BE SURE TO FOLLOW THESE INSTRUCTIONS in ordering rings, whether Gold-Filled or Solid Gold; we must know the size from this scale. Take a narrow slip of paper and measure around the finger, making sure that when both ends meet it will fit exactly as ring should. To get number of size measure slip on gauge by placing one end of the slip even with the left end of the gauge here illustrated. The figure which the other end meets will indicate the size required. When ordering always write number of size, as slip is sometimes lost and order delayed until another is received.

Use a slip of paper about the width of the above gauge.

---

**BEFORE YOU SEND YOUR ORDER, PLEASE REFER TO OUR INSTRUCTIONS ON THE FIRST PAGE OF THIS DEPARTMENT.**

# SOLID GOLD ENGRAVED BAND RINGS. EVERY ONE IS SOLID GOLD THROUGH AND THROUGH.

These rings will be furnished in sizes as follows: Nos. 61000 to 61003, sizes 0 to 3. Nos. 61004 to 61006, sizes 3 to 5. Nos. 61007 to 61010, sizes 5 to 8. Nos. 61011 to 61048 sizes 5½ to 11½. Larger sizes than 11½ must be made to order and will be charged for extra. Cash in full must accompany all orders for special rings. The prices on gold rings are based according to the weight and engraving. No. 61007 is a guard ring to prevent rings that are too large from coming off.

 No. 61000, 25c.
 No. 61001, 40c.
 No. 61002, 50c.
 No. 61003, 55c.
No. 61004, 58c.
No. 61005, 65c.
No. 61006, 70c.

 No. 61007, 60c.
 No. 61008, 65c.
No. 61009, 75c.
 No. 61010, $1.10.
 No. 61011, $1.25.
No. 61012, $1.50.
 No. 61013, $1.75.

 No. 61014, $1.80.
No. 61015, $1.80.
No. 61016, $1.85.
No. 61017, $1.85.
No. 61018, $1.85.
No. 61019, $1.85.
 No. 61020, $1.90.

No. 61021, $1.90.
No. 61022, $1.90.
 No. 61023, $1.90.
No. 61024, $1.90.
No. 61025, $1.95.
No. 61026, $1.90.
No. 61027, $2.00.

 No. 61028, $2.00.
No. 61029, $2.10.
 No. 61030, $2.10.
No. 61031, $2.15.
No. 61032, $2.15.
 No. 61033, $2.20
No. 61034, $2.20.

 No. 61035, $2.35.
 No. 61036, $2.70.
No. 61037, $3.00.
 No. 61038, $3.00.
No. 61039, $3.20.
 No. 61040, $3.20.
No 61041, $3.30.

 No. 61042, $3.30.
No. 61043, $3.55.
No. 61044, $3.70.
 No. 61045, $3.80.
No. 61046, $3.80.
 No. 61047, $3.85.
No. 61048, $3.90.

## FINEST QUALITY, 10, 14 AND 18 KARAT SOLID GOLD PLAIN BAND RINGS.

These rings are all finished in the best possible manner and are warranted to be exactly as represented. Wedding rings should be made of 18 karat gold.

**OVAL BAND.**          **SOLID GOLD.**          **FLAT BAND.**

| | No. 61100 2 pwt. | No. 61101 3 pwt. | No. 61102. 5 pwt. | No. 61103. 6 pwt. | No. 61104. 2 pwt. | No. 61105. 4 pwt. | No. 61106. 6 pwt. |
|---|---|---|---|---|---|---|---|
| 10-karat | $1.20 | $1.80 | $3.60 | $3.60 | $1.20 | $2.40 | $3.60 |
| 14-karat | 1.60 | 2.40 | 4.00 | 4.80 | 1.60 | 3.20 | 4.80 |
| 18-karat | 2.00 | 3.00 | 5.00 | 6.00 | 2.00 | 4.00 | 6.00 |

## FINE SOLID GOLD, INTERCHANGEABLE INITIAL AND EMBLEM RINGS.

The price of the different mountings vary according to the weight and amount of work on same. No. 61107 is a medium weight ring, while 61110 is very heavy. These rings are very stylish for gentlemen's wear, and are all of the very latest designs. Both the initials and emblems are mounted on black onyx. The initial is of solid gold, nicely engraved. The society emblems are of solid gold, and all but the Masonic, Odd Fellows, and Masonic and Odd Fellows combined are beautifully enameled. We have quoted each mounting, excepting 61111 and 61112, with gold initial, set with six diamonds and with all emblems. When desired we can furnish ring at a small additional cost with both emblem and initial, which can be interchanged at any time the owner may desire.

 No. 1.
 No. 2.
 No. 3.
 No. 4.
 No. 5.
 No. 6.
No. 7.
No. 8.
No. 9.
 No. 10.

No. 61107.
Gold initial, $3.00.
Gold initial, 6 diamonds, $6.45.
Emblem, $3.50.

No. 61108.
Gold initial, $5.10.
Gold initial, 6 diamonds, $8.15.
Emblem, $5.60.

No. 61109.
Gold initial, $7.05.
Gold initial, 6 diamonds, $9.75.
Emblem, $7.55.

No. 61110.
Gold initial, $7.25.
Gold initial, 6 diamonds, $9.90.
Emblem, $7.75.

No. 61111. Heavy solid gold mounting, onyx setting with gold initial set with 6 diamonds. Price, $7.80.

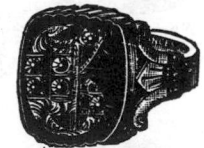
No. 61112. Very heavy gold mounting, fancy design, black onyx setting, with beautiful raised gold initial, set with 6 fine diamonds. Price, $11.50.

**rings Nos. 61108, 61109 and 61110 Show the Shanks only, but the Prices are Quoted for the Complete Ring.**

# LADIES', GENTS', AND MISSES' FINE SOLID GOLD SEMI-PRECIOUS STONE AND DIAMOND SET RINGS.

Our Solid Gold Stone Set Rings are all of the very latest design, finished in the best possible manner, made by the best manufacturers, and every one are guaranteed to be exactly as represented. The first row will be furnished in sizes from 5 to 8 only. All the rest will be furnished in sizes from 5½ to 11. There will be an extra charge for sizes larger than 11, and cash in full must accompany orders for extra sizes.

No. 61124. Fancy Mounting, 1 opal. Price, $1.25.

No. 61125. Plain mounting, 1 garnet. Price, $1.35.

No. 61126. Plain mounting, 2 garnets and 1 emerald. $1.50.

No. 61127. Fancy mounting, 1 small diamond. Price, $1.50

No. 61128. Plain mounting, 3 garnets. Price, $1.75.

No. 61129. Fancy mounting, 1 large moon stone. $1.80.

No. 61130. Engraved mounting, 1 large amethyst. Price, $1.90.

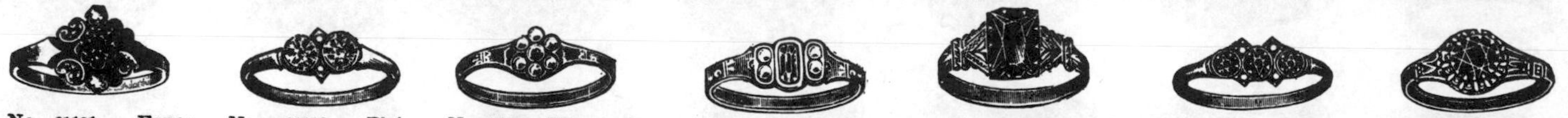

No. 61131. Fancy mounting, 1 garnet and 2 brilliants. $1.90.

No. 61132. Plain mounting, 2 brilliants. Price, $1.95.

No. 61133. Engraved mounting, 1 turquoise, 6 real pearls. $2.00.

No. 61134. Engraved mounting, 1 emerald, 4 real pearls. $2.15.

No. 61135. Engraved mounting, 1 large ruby. Price, $2.25.

No. 61136. Plain mounting, 3 rubies, 4 real pearls. $2.50.

No. 61137. Engraved, fancy mounting, 1 large ruby. $3.25.

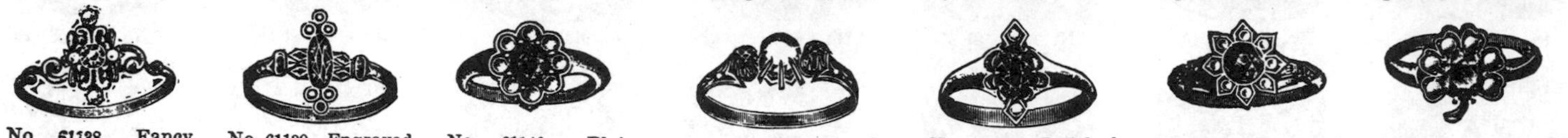

No. 61138. Fancy mounting, 1 ruby, 4 real pearls. $3.00.

No. 61139. Engraved mounting, 1 ruby, 6 real pearls. $3.00.

No. 61140. Plain mounting, 1 ruby, 8 real pearls. $3.10.

No. 61141. Engraved mounting, 2 rubies, 1 moon stone. $3.35.

No. 61142. Polished mounting, 1 garnet, 2 pearls. Price, $3.35.

No. 61143. Engraved mounting, 1 ruby, 8 pearls. Price, $3.35.

No. 61144. Polished mounting, 1 ruby, 6 pearls. Price, $3.50.

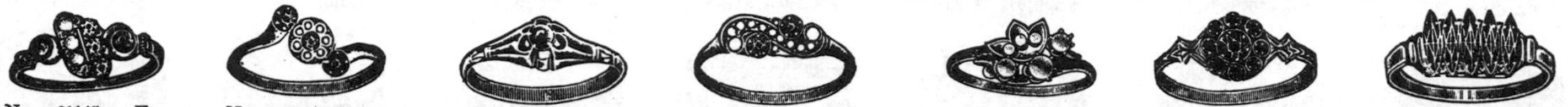

No. 61145. Fancy mounting, 3 rubies, 3 moon stone. $3.50.

No. 61146. Polished mounting, 3 rubies, 6 real pearls. $3.70.

No. 61147. Polished claw mounting, 1 moon stone. Price, $3.70.

No. 61148. Polished mounting, 2 rubies, 9 real pearls. $3.85.

No. 61149. Polished fancy mounting, 3 opals, 3 pearls. $4.15.

No. 61150. Fancy mounting, 9 rubies. Price, $4.25.

No. 61151. Polished mounting, 5 fine rubies. Price. $4.30.

No. 61159. Polished mounting, fancy, 10 rubies, 5 real pearls. Price, $4.45.

No. 61160. Polished mounting, 6 pearls, 1 ruby. Price, $4.50.

No. 61161. Polished mounting, 3 rubies, 10 pearls. Price, $4.60.

No. 61162. Polished mounting, 5 rubies, 24 pearls. Price, $5.00.

No. 61163. Polished mounting, 3 emeralds, 8 whole pearls. Price, $5.25.

No. 61164. Round and fancy mounting, 1 large opal. Price, $5.75.

No. 61165. Polished mounting, 1 opal, 12 real pearls. Price, $6.90.

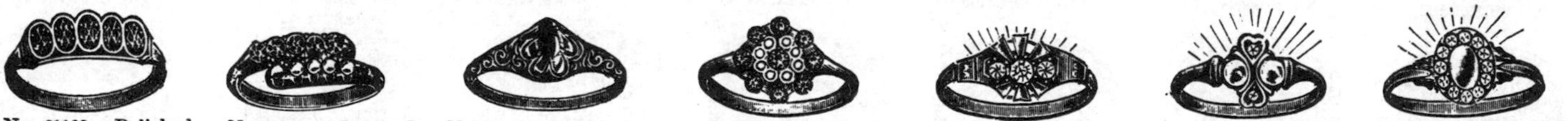

No. 61166. Polished mounting, 5 rubies. $4.50.

No. 61167. Polished mounting, 5 rubies, 5 large whole pearls. Price, $7.00.

No. 61168. Fancy engraved mounting, 1 large opal. Price, $7.25.

No. 61169. Polished mounting, 9 rubies, 8 real pearls. Price, $6.00.

No. 61170. Fancy mounting, 3 real diamonds. Price, $7.75.

No. 61171. Polished mounting, 2 opals, 2 real diamonds. Price, $8.50.

No. 61172. Polished mounting, fine large opal, 12 real diamonds. Price, $12.50.

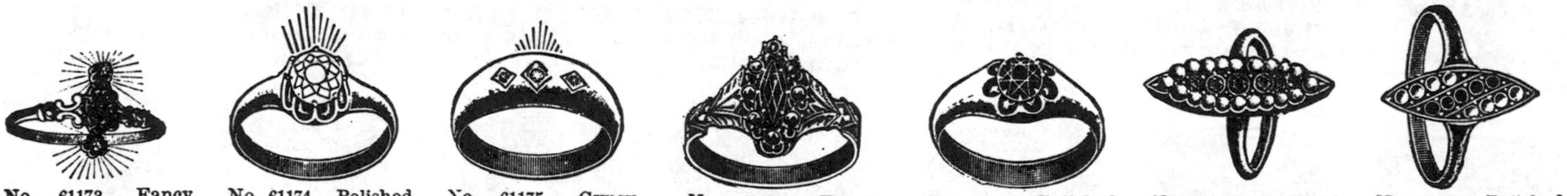

No. 61173. Fancy mounting, 1 ruby, 2 small diamonds. Price, $2.70.

No. 61174. Polished mounting, 1 large imitation diamond. Price, $3.25.

No. 61175. Gypsy style mounting, 1 emerald, 1 ruby, 1 small diamond. Price, $3.75.

No. 61176. Fancy engraved mounting, 8 moon stones, 1 ruby. Price, $3.80.

No. 61177. Polished mounting, 1 ruby. Price, $4.75.

No. 61178. Polished mounting, marquise pattern, 5 rubies or emeralds, 22 pearls. Price, $5.75.

No. 61179. Polished mounting, marquise pattern, 5 rubies, 8 pearls. Price, $6.90.

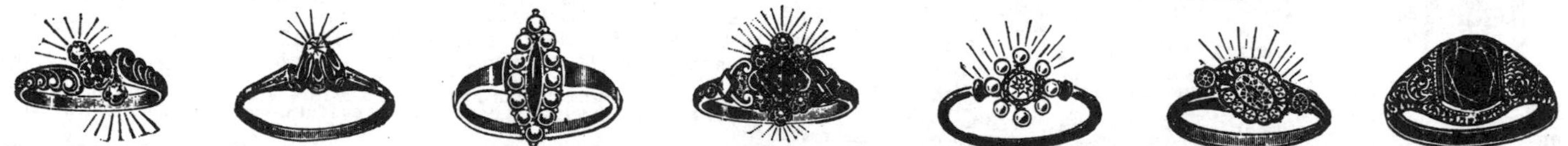

No. 61180. Fancy mounting, 1 ruby, 2 small diamonds. $2.75

No. 61181. Fancy mounting, 1 real diamond. Price, $4.25.

No. 61182. Polished mounting, marquise pattern, turquoise or ruby center, 12 pearls. Price, $4.60.

No. 61183. Fancy mounting, ruby center, 6 real diamonds. Price, $6.75.

No. 61184. Polished round mounting, 1 real diamond, brilliant cut, 8 whole pearls. Price, $9.25.

No. 61185. Polished mounting, 3 rubies, 10 real diamonds. Price, $9.85.

No. 61186. Fancy engraved mounting, 1 fine ruby. Price, $5.40.

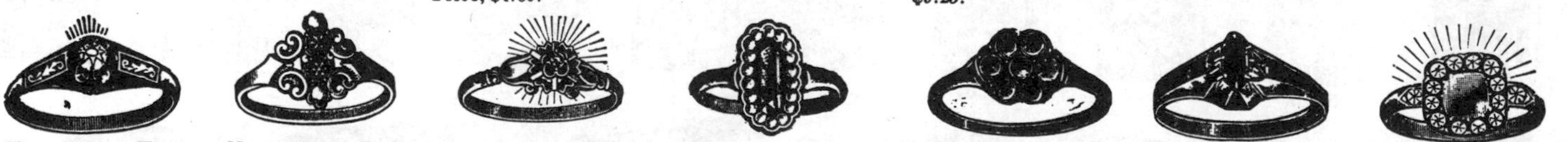

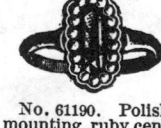

No. 61187. Fancy mounting. 1 opal or ruby. Price, $3.75.

No. 61188. Fancy mounting, 2 rubies and 2 whole pearls. Price, $4.10.

No. 61189. Fancy mounting, 1 real diamond. Price, $4.25.

No. 61190. Polished mounting, ruby center, 18 pearls. Price, $5.10.

No. 61191. Polished mounting, 1 large pearl, 6 beautiful opals. Price, $7.25.

No. 61192. Polished mounting, 1 carbunkle. Price, $6.25.

No. 61193. Polished mounting, 1 large opal, 14 real diamonds. Price, $18.40.

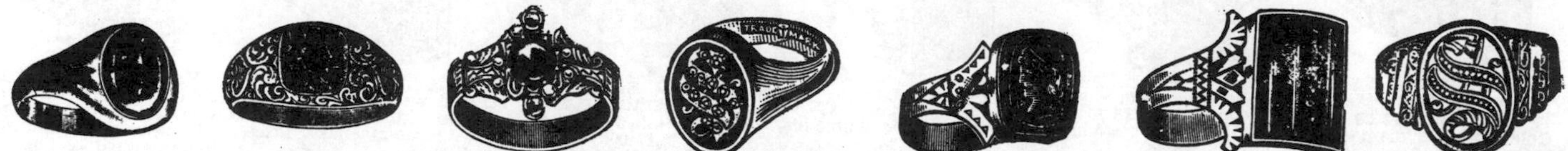

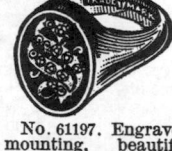

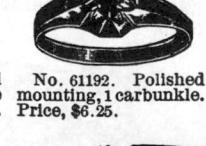

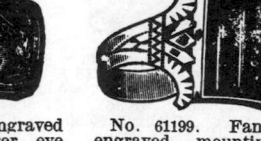

No. 61194. Solid gold polished mounting, 1 carbunkle. Price, $2.75.

No. 61195. Fancy engraved mounting, 1 fine ruby. Price, $4.25.

No. 61196. Engraved mounting, carbunkle center, 2 brilliants, 2 turquoise. Price, $3.70.

No. 61197. Engraved mounting, beautiful colored initial, incrusted in black onyx.

No. 61198. Engraved mounting, tiger eye stone, beautifully cut. Price, $1.95.

No. 61199. Fancy engraved mounting, plain polished black onyx setting. Price,

No. 61200. Plain polished mounting, gold initial incrusted in black onyx, 5 dia-

# FINE QUALITY GOLD FILLED WATCH CHARMS.

No. 61250. Compass. Each, 25c.

No. 61251. Fancy painted, tiger eye back. Each, 25c.

No. 61252. Stone settings, one side engraved. Each, 25c.

No. 61253. Fancy stone setting. Each, 25c.

No. 61254. Engraved stone setting. Each, 25c.

No. 61256. Painted dog's head, cornelian stone back. Each, 25c.

No. 61255. Compass. Each, 35c.

No. 61257. Lantern Charm, ruby glass. Each, 50c.

No. 61258. Cornelian stone. Each, 30c.

No. 61259. Bicycle Charm. Each, 50c.

No. 61260. Compass. Each, 30c.

No. 61261. Anchor. Each, 50c.

No. 61262. Engraved stone, fancy mounting. Each, 45c.

No. 61263. Engraved stone. Each, 45c.

No. 61264. Fancy mounting, painted setting. Each, 30c.

No. 61265. Genuine crystal. Each, 35c.

No. 61266. Watch, engraved, brilliant setting. Each, 40c.

No. 61267. Large topaz. Each, 60c.

No. 61268. Genuine crystal, engraved. Each, 90c.

No. 61269. Padlock, brilliant setting. Each, 75c.

No. 61270. Fancy engraved, stone setting. Each, 95c.

No. 61271. Engraved stone setting. Each, 35c.

No. 61272. Chased horse, ruby eyes. Each, 75c.

No. 61273. Engraved, brilliant setting. Each, 60c.

No. 61274. Engraved, with brilliant setting. Each, 40c.

No. 61275. Fancy Odd Fellows' Charm. Each, 32c.

No. 61276. Raised colored gold ornamentation. Each, 80c.

No. 61277. L. A. W. Bicycle Charm. Each, 80c.

No. 61278. Eight brilliants, incrusted in fancy stone. Each, 32c.

No. 61279. Large topaz. Each, 40c.

No. 61280. Topaz. Fancy mounting. Each, 55c.

No. 61281. Pearl and cornelian, brilliant center. Each, 35c.

No. 61282. Pearl and black onyx, brilliant center. Each, 45c.

No. 61283. Raised horseshoe, brilliant in center. Each, 65c.

No. 61284. Fancy compass. Each, 40c.

No. 61285. Painted horse and tiger eye, in watch. Each, 85c.

No. 61286. Real crystal. Each, 33c.

No. 61287. Fancy engraved, with three stones. Each, 55c.

No. 61288. Fancy pearl logs, with rope mounting. Each, 95c.

No. 61289. Pearl ring, with openwork Masonic emblem. Each, $1.00.

No. 61290. Fancy mounting, Knights of Pythias emblem on both sides, enameled in four colors. Each, $1.25.

No. 61291. Pearl, with chased mounting, emblem enameled in two colors. Each, $1.35.

## FINEST QUALITY GOLD FILLED AND STERLING SILVER WATCH CHARMS.

No. 61292. Printer's Stick. Each, 95c.

No. 61293. Raised gold Dogs. Each, $1.10.

No. 61294. Team of Horses, well finished. Each, 70c.

No. 61295. Compass Charm, is reliable. Each, $1.50.

No. 61296. Aluminum Horse, heavy gold plated, with ruby eyes, is very light. Each, $1.85.

No. 61297. Engraved stone. Each, 95c.

No. 61298. Plasterer's Trowel, tiger eye handle. Each, 90c.

No. 61299. Fine Compass Charm, very accurately poised needle, with onyx back, thoroughly reliable. Each, $1.75.

No. 61300. Fancy mounting, engraved cornelian setting. Each, 75c.

No. 61301. Fancy Horse Shoe and Horse. Each, $1.25.

No. 61302. Fancy Compass, perfectly accurate. Each, $1.25.

No. 61303. Base Ball. Each, $1.30.

No. 61304. Leather Knife, tiger eye handle. Each, $1.25.

No. 61305. Mail Pouch. Each, 40c.

No. 61306. Butcher's Charm. Each, 75c.

No. 61307. Barber's Charm and Cigar Cutter. Each, 90c.

No. 61308. Butcher's Cleaver, tiger eye handle. Each, 95c.

No. 61309. Sterling silver jointed Fish, garnet eyes. Each, 75c.

No. 61310. Steel blade Cigar Cutter, sterling silver handle. Each, $1.25.

No. 61311. Mason's Trowel, tiger eye hndl. Each, 95c.

No. 61312. Carpenter's Charm. Each, 75c.

No. 61313. Farmer's Charm. Each, $1.25.

No. 61314. Locket, engrav'd. Each, 60c.

No. 61315. Locket, engraved, brilliant setting. Each, 75c.

No. 61316. Locket, solid gold front, sapphire, ruby and brilliants, hnd. engvd. Each, $1.90.

No. 61317. Locket, raised, ornamented, brilliant setting. Each, 90c.

No. 61318. Locket, raised, ornamented, brilliant setting. Each, 95c.

No. 61319. Locket, raised colored gold, ornamented and engraved. Each, $1.05.

No. 61320. Locket, engraved, with two brilliants in wheels. Each, $2.25.

No. 61321. Locket, raised ornamentation and brilliant setting. Each, $1.90.

No. 61322. Locket, raised colored gold ornamentation. Each, $1.05.

No. 61323. Locket, raised, ornamented and Roman finished, brilliant setting. Each, $1.10.

No. 61324. Locket, engraved stone setting. Each, $1.75.

No. 61325. Locket, solid gold front, sapphire, ruby and brilliants, hand engraved. Each, $1.85.

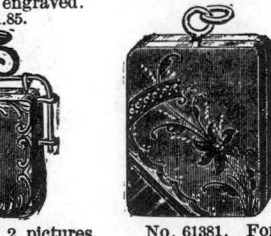
No. 61326. Locket, engraved Horse Shoe, brilliant setting. Each, 75c.

## SOLID 14 KARAT GOLD LOCKETS.

No. 61375. For 2 pictures, satin finished, hand engraved.

No. 61376. For 2 pictures, satin finished, bright cut

No. 61377. Satin finished, engraved. Each, $2.25.

No. 61378. Satin finished, bright cut edges, engraved, for 2 pictures. Each $4.10.

No. 61379. For 2 pictures, satin finished, engraved. Each, $3.95.

No. 61380. For 2 pictures, bright polished, raised ornamented border, fancy mounting. Each, $4.75.

No. 61381. For 2 pictures, satin finished, hand engraved. Each,

# BEST QUALITY GOLD FILLED AND ENAMELED EMBLEM CHARMS.

These Charms are all well finished in every respect, beautifully enameled and cannot be told in appearance from Solid Gold goods.

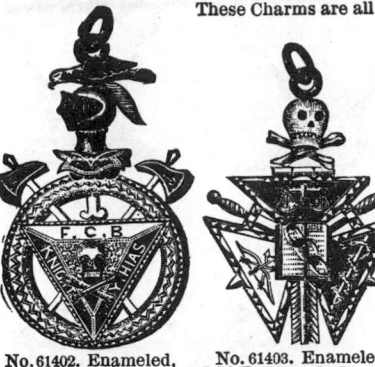     

No. 61402. Enameled, K. of P. very fancy. Each, $3.25.

No. 61403. Enameled, Odd Fellows. $1.75.

No. 61404. Enameled, Ancient Order of Forresters. Each, $1.20.

No. 61405. Enameled, A. O. U. W. Each, $0.95.

No. 61406. Enameled, Masonic, Keystone, Each, $1.35.

No. 61407. Enameled, Sr. O. U. A. M. $0.85.

No. 61408. Enameled, Masonic. Each, $2.50.

No. 61409. Enameled, Odd Fellows. $2.00.

No. 61410. Enameled, K. of P. Each, $2.75.

No. 61411. Enameled, Modern Woodmen. Each, $1.75.

No. 61412. Enameled, Christian Endeavor. Each, $0.95.

No. 61413. Masonic and Odd Fellows combined fancy engraved. Each, $1.20.

No. 61414. Enameled, K. of P. Each, $1.60.

No. 61415. Enameled, G. A. R. Each, $1.95.

No. 61416. Pearl Center with gold filled and enameled emblem and mounting. Each, $1.45.

No. 61417. Enameled, O. R. T. Each, $1.45.

No. 61418. Pearl Center, gold filled and enameled, emblem and mounting. Each, $1.35.

No. 61419. Enameled, Sons of Veterans. Each, $1.20.

No. 61420. Enameled, Masonic. Each, $1.20.

No. 61421. Enameled, Masonic. Each, $1.20.

No. 61422. Enameled, Odd Fellows, $1.20.

# FINE SOLID GOLD ENAMELED EMBLEM CHARMS.

In Solid Gold Emblem goods we handle nothing but the best quality and those made by the largest and most reputable manufacturers. We guarantee every one to be exactly as represented

No. 61423. Masonic, movable visor, enameled 3 colors. $12.50.

No. 61424. Masonic, Black Onyx setting, Solid Gold mounting and emblem. $6.50.

No. 61425. Odd Fellows, enameled. Each, $9.00.

No. 61426. Masonic, heavy keystone. Each, $5.50.

No. 61427. Masonic and Odd Fellows, combined fancy engraved. Each, $4.00.

No. 61428. K. of P., movable visor, enameled, $7.00.

N. 61429. Masonic, movable visor, onyx settings, enameled, set with rubies and 5 diamonds. Each, $22.50.

No. 61430. Masonic, enameled emblem, fancy raised edge. Each, $4.75. Odd Fellows same price.

No. 61431. Masonic. Each, $3.75.

No. 61432. Masonic, enameled. Each, $3.25.

No. 61433. Odd Fellows, enameled 3 colors. Each, $5.75.

No. 61434. K. of P., enameled 3 colors. Each, $2.00.

No. 61435. Masonic, fancy engraved. Each, $2.25.

No. 61436. Masonic, enameled figures. Each, $3.50.

No. 61437. A. O. U. W. enameled three colors, $3.75.

# FINEST QUALITY GOLD FILLED EMBLEM PINS.

These Pins are well made, are enameled and are equal in appearance to the Solid Gold goods.

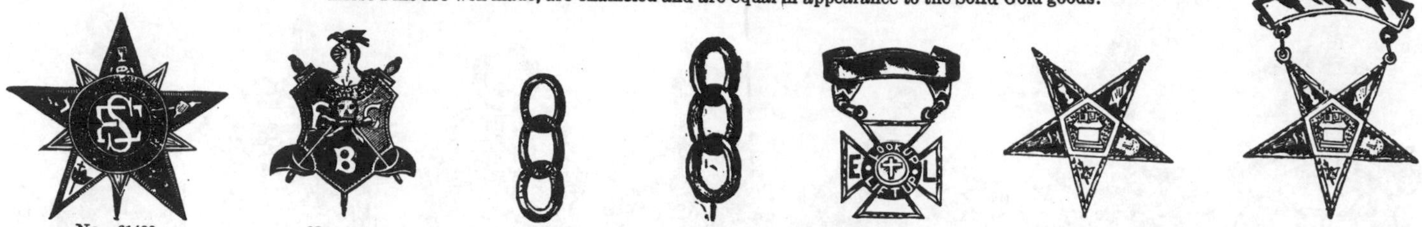

No. 61480. Eastern Star, enameled. 70c.

No. 61481. K. of P., enameled. 60c.

No. 66482. Odd Fellows, enameled, 50c.

No. 61483. Odd Fellows, 60c.

No. 61484. Epworth League, enameled, 70c.

No. 61485. Eastern Star, enameled, 65c.

No. 61486. Eastern Star, enameled, 85c.

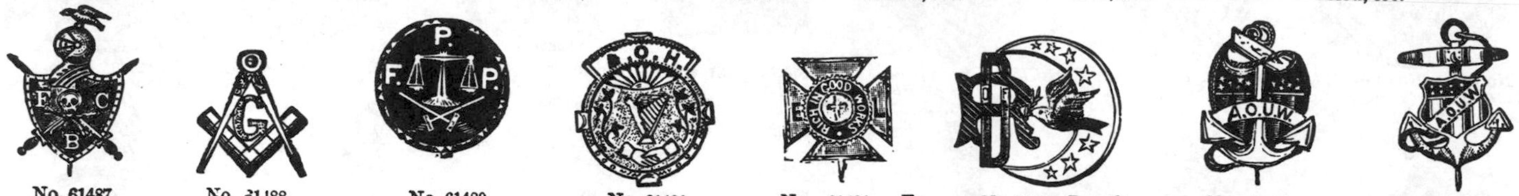

No. 61487. K. of P., enameled 55c.

No. 61488. Masonic, engraved, 20c.

No. 61489. A. P. A., enameled, 45c.

No. 61490. A. O. H., enameled, 45c.

No. 61491. Epworth League, enameled, 40c.

No. 61492. Daughters of Rebecca. enameled, 60c.

No. 61493. A. O. U. W., enameled, 55c.

No. 61494. A. O. U. W., enameled, 40c.

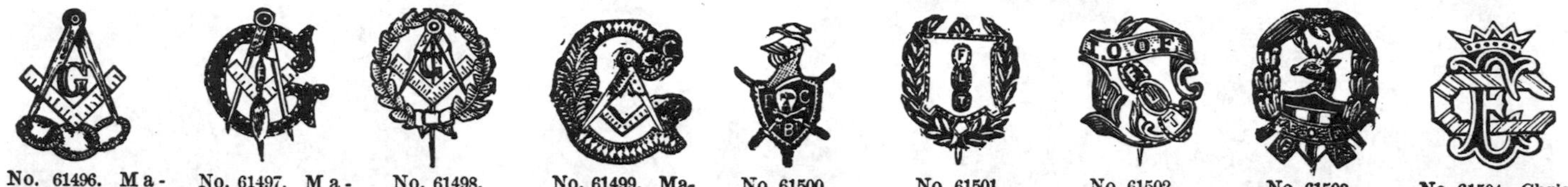

No. 61496. Masonic and Odd Fellows, engraved, 35c.

No. 61497. Masonic, engraved and enameled, 45c.

No. 61498. Masonic, enameled, 55c.

No. 61499. Masonic, fancy engraved, 45c.

No. 61500. K. of P., enameled, 35c.

No. 61501. Odd Fellows., enameled, 40c.

No. 61502. Odd Fellows, enameled, 50c.

No. 61503. A. O. F., enameled, 60c.

No. 61504. Christian Endeavor, enameled, 45c.

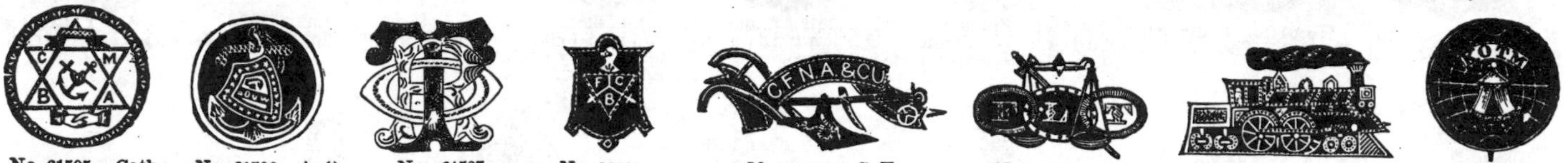

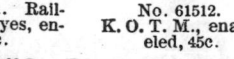

No. 61505. Catholic M. B. Association, enameled, 45c.

No. 61506. A. O. U. W., enameled, 45c.

No. 61507. O. R. T., enameled, 65c.

No. 61508. K. of P., enameled, 30c.

No. 61509. C. E. N. A. and C. U., enameled, 50c.

No. 61510. Odd Fellows, enameled, 40c.

No. 61511. Railway employes, enameled, 45c.

No. 61512. K. O. T. M., enameled, 45c.

## FINEST QUALITY GOLD FILLED AND ENAMELED LAPEL BUTTONS, WITH SCREW BACKS. EACH, 38C.

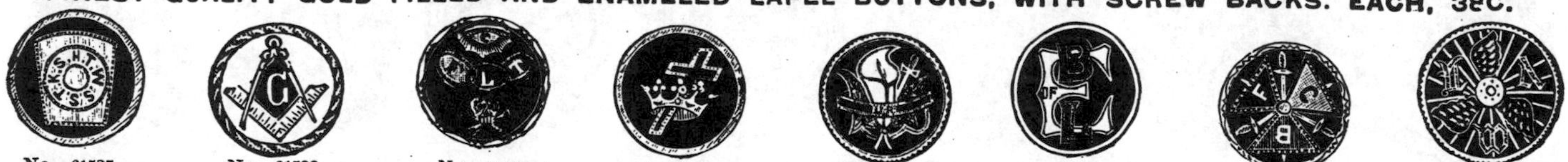

No, 61525. Masonic.

No. 61526. Masonic.

No. 61527. Odd Fellows.

No. 61528. Masonic.

No. 61529. K. of P.

No. 61530. B. of L. E.

No, 61531. K. of P.

No. 61532. L. A. W.

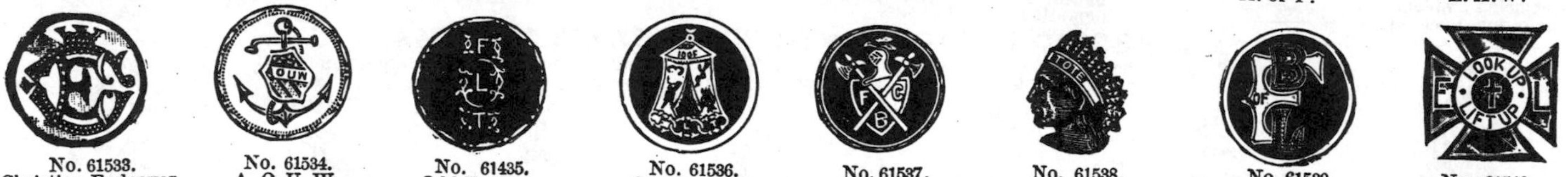

No. 61533. Christian Endeavor.

No. 61534. A. O. U. W.

No. 61435. Odd Fellows.

No. 61536. Odd Fellows.

No. 61537. K. of P.

No. 61538. Red Men.

No. 61539. B. of L. F.

No. 61540. Epworth League.

## MEDALS AND BADGES IN SOLID GOLD AND SILVER, FOR COMPETITION PRESENTATIONS ETC.

We list them only in Solid Silver and Solid Gold, but they can be furnished when desired in Solid Silver, with heavy gold plate and bright cut engraving, at $1.75 additional on silver prices.

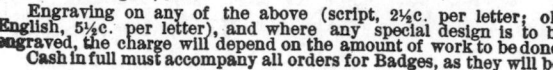

No. 61550. Marksman's Badge, for gun club competitions. Price, in solid silver, $3.00; in solid gold, $6.50.

No. 61551. Bicycle Badge, beautifully engraved. Price, in sterling silver, $5.00; in solid gold, $10.00.

No. 61552. Blank Badge, can be engraved in design suitable for any kind of presentation; border is beautifully engraved by hand. Price, in solid silver, $3.00; in solid gold, $6.00.

No. 61553. Blank Badge, suitable for class or any kind of presentation; can be engraved with design to suit requirements. Price, in solid silver, $4.00; in solid gold, $9.00.

No. 61554. Blank Badge, very fancy, hand engraved and ornamented, suitable for class or other presentation; can be engraved with design to suit requirements. Price, in solid silver, $5.00; in solid gold, $10.00.

Engraving on any of the above (script, 2½c. per letter; old English, 5½c. per letter), and where any special design is to be engraved, the charge will depend on the amount of work to be done.

Cash in full must accompany all orders for Badges, as they will be made to order only.

# FINEST QUALITY SOLID GOLD EMBLEM PINS.

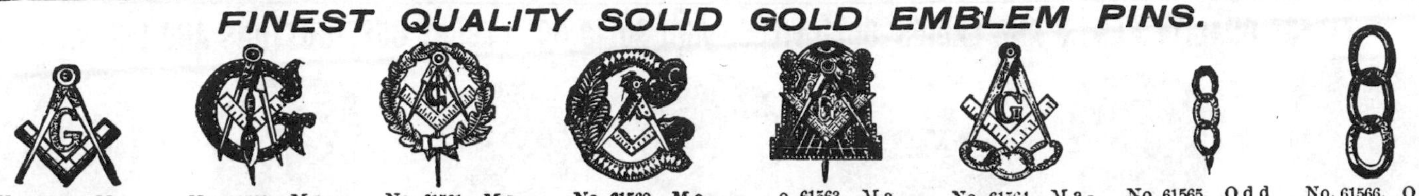

No. 61559. Masonic, engraved. Each, 50c.

No. 61560. Masonic, engraved, enameled. Each, 85c.

No. 61561. Masonic, engraved. Each, 78c.

No. 61562. Masonic, fancy engraved. Each, 82c.

o. 61563. Masonic, engraved and enameled. Each, $1.25.

No. 61564. Masonic and Odd Fellows. Each, 52c.

No. 61565. Odd Fellows. Each, 40c.

No. 61566. Odd Fellows. Each, 90c.

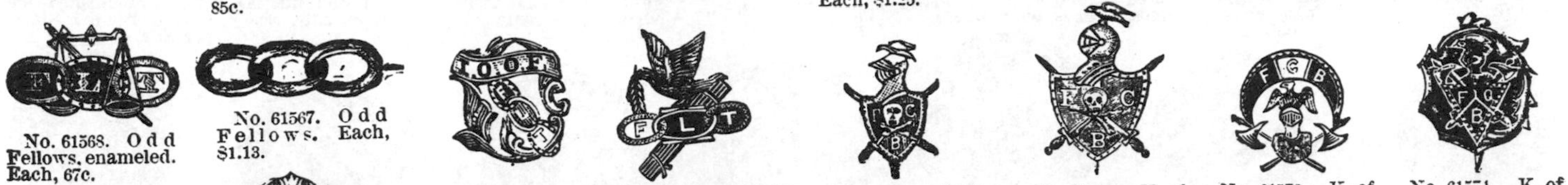

No. 61568. Odd Fellows, enameled. Each, 67c.

No. 61567. Odd Fellows. Each, $1.13.

No. 61569. Odd Fellows, enameled. Each, 70c.

No. 61570. Odd Fellows, enameled and engraved. Each, 95c.

No. 61571. K. of P., enameled. Each, 65c.

No. 61572. K. of P., enameled. Each, 95c.

No. 61573. K. of P., enameled. Each, 85c.

No. 61574. K. of P., enameled. Each, $1.20.

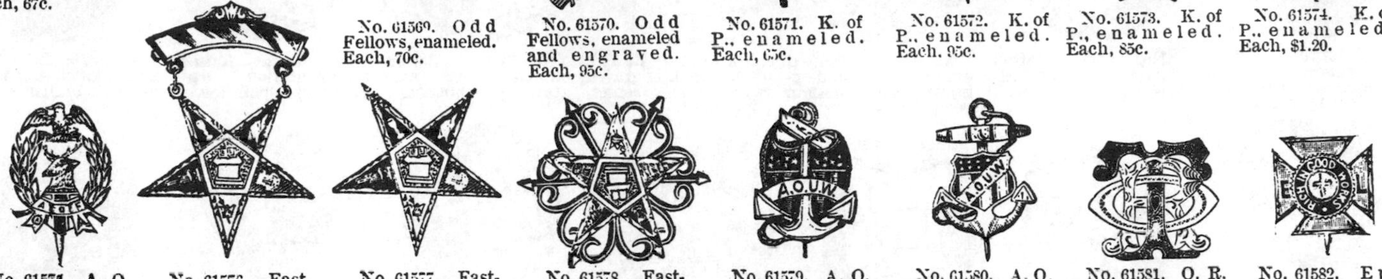

No. 61575. A. O. F., enameled. Each, $1.40.

No. 61576. Eastern Star, enameled. Each, $1.95.

No. 61577. Eastern Star, enameled. Each, $1.24.

No. 61578. Eastern Star, fancy enameled, $3.75.

No. 61579. A. O. U. W., enameled. Each, $1.10.

No. 61580. A. O. U. W., enameled. Each, 65c.

No. 61581. O. R. T., enameled and engraved, $1.25.

No. 61582. Epworth League, enameled, 70c.

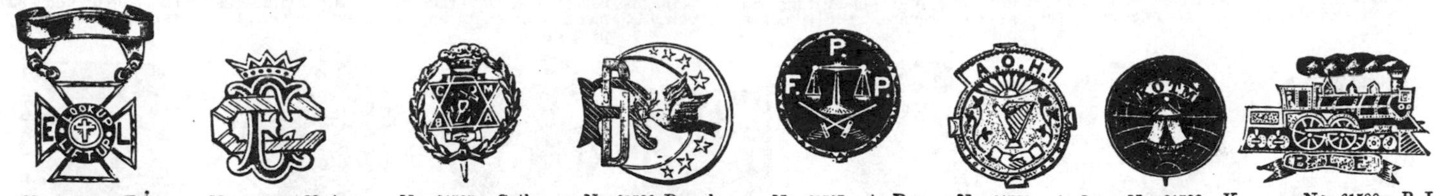

No. 61583. Epworth League, enameled. Each, $1.40.

No. 61584. Christian Endeavor, engraved and enameled. Each, $1.25.

No. 61585. Catholic M. B. Association, enameled. Each, 95c.

No. 61586. Daughters of Rebecca, enameled. Each, $1.14.

No. 61587. A. P. A., enameled. Each, 90c.

No. 61588. A. O. H., enameled. Each, 95c.

No. 61589. K. O. T. M. Each, 85c.

No. 61590. B. L. E., or B. L. F. enameled. Each. $1.30.

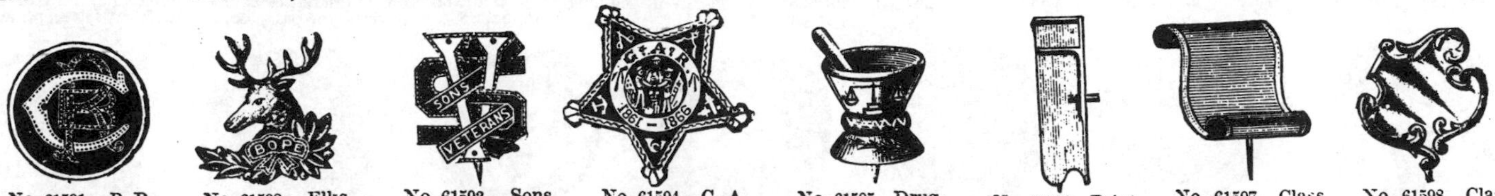

No. 61591. B. R. C., enameled. Each, 95c.

No. 61592. Elks, enameled. Each, $1.25.

No. 61593. Sons of Veterans, enameled. Each, $1.10.

No. 61594. G. A. R., enameled. Each, $1.25.

No. 61595. Druggists, enameled. Each, 95c.

No. 61596. Printers Stick. Each, $1.20.

No. 61597. Class Pin, or can be engraved for any order. Each, $1.06.

No. 61598. Class Pin, or can be engraved for any order. Each, 95c.

## FANCY SKELETON SOLID GOLD LAPEL BUTTONS, WITH SCREW BACKS.

These Buttons are all made in open work, which adds very much to their appearance. They are the latest and neatest thing on the market.

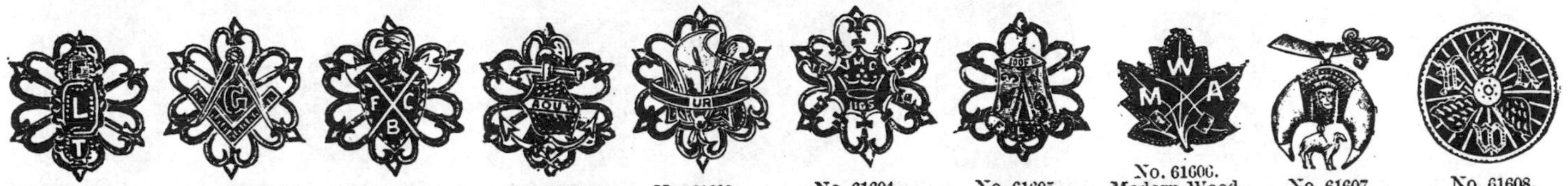

No. 61599. Odd Fellows, enameled. Each, $1.20.

No. 61600. Masonic, enameled. Each, $1.20.

No. 61601. K. of P., enameled. Each, $1.20.

No. 61602. A. O. U. W., enameled. Each, $1.20.

No. 61603. K. of P., enameled. Each, $1.20.

No. 61604. Royal Arcanum, enameled. Each, $1.20.

No. 61605. Odd Fellows, enameled. Each, $1.20.

No. 61606. Modern Woodmen, green enameled, not open. $1.15.

No. 61607. Masonic, enameled. Each, $1.90.

No. 61608. L. A. W., enameled, not open. Each, 95c.

## SOLID GOLD ENAMELED LAPEL BUTTONS, WITH SCREW BACKS. PRICE EACH, 87 CENTS.

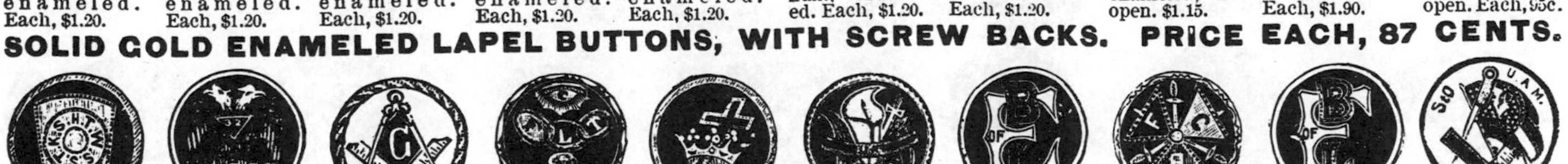

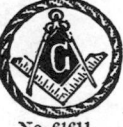

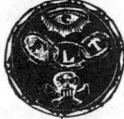

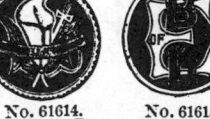

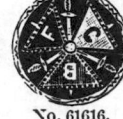

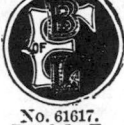

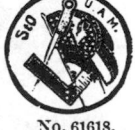

No. 61609. Masonic.

No. 61610. Masonic.

No. 61611. Masonic.

No. 61612. Odd Fellows.

No. 61613. Masonic.

No. 61614. K. of P

No. 61615. B. of L. E.

No. 61616. K. of P.

No. 61617. B. of L. F.

No. 61618. Sr. O. U. A. M.

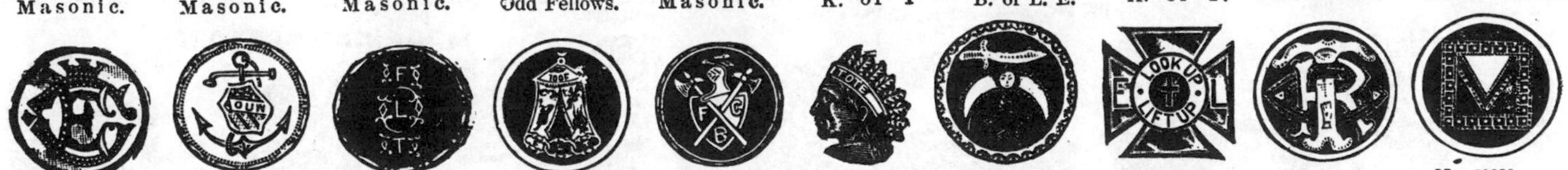

No. 61619. Christian Endeavor.

No. 61620. A. O. U. W.

No. 61621. Odd Fellows.

No. 61622. Odd Fellows.

No. 61623. K. of P.

No. 61624. Red Men.

No. 61625. Masonic.

No. 61626. Epworth League.

No. 61627. O. R. T.

No. 61628. Royal League.

In addition to the above list of Emblem Goods we can furnish anything that is made, at lowest wholesale prices. We will allow discount of 10 per cent. net from the above prices on orders for a dozen or more articles of one kind. This is our best quantity price, and will not be allowed on orders for less than one dozen of a kind.

# FINEST QUALITY GENTS' AND LADIES' GOLD FILLED AND SOLID GOLD FRONT CUFF BUTTONS AND LINKS.

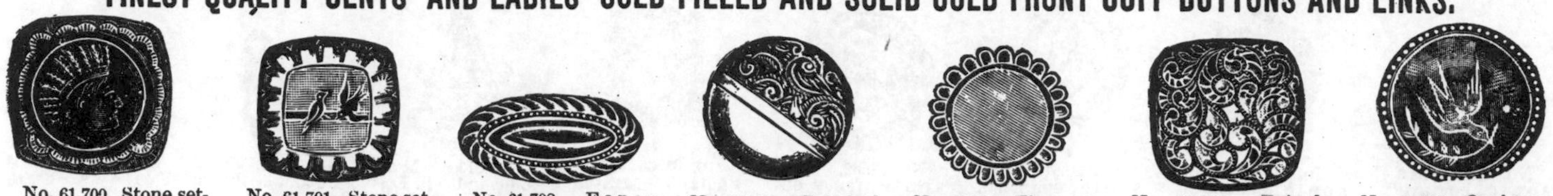

No. 61,700. Stone settings, chased edges, per pair, 25c.

No. 61,701. Stone settings, hand painted birds, chased edges, per pair, 25c.

No. 61,702. Fancy stone settings, chased edges, per pair, 30c.

No. 61,703. Polished and engraved, per pair, 32c.

No. 61,704. Tiger eye settings, escalloped edges, per pair, 35c.

No. 61,705. Raised ornamentation and engraved, per pair, 40c.

No. 61,706. Oval center, satin finished, engraved, beaded edges, per pair, 42c.

No. 61,707. Raised and colored ornamentation, set with brilliants, per pair, 44c.

No. 61,708. Raised ornamentation and engraved, per pair, 45c.

No. 61,709. Raised ornamentation and engraved, shell design, per pair, 45c.

No. 61,710. Raised, ornamented, engraved edges, satined center, per pair, 48c.

No. 61,711. Raised ornamentation, engraved, per pair, 50c.

No. 61,712. Raised ornamentation, engraved, per pair, 55c.

No. 61,713. Raised ornamentation, engraved set with brilliants, per pair, 59c.

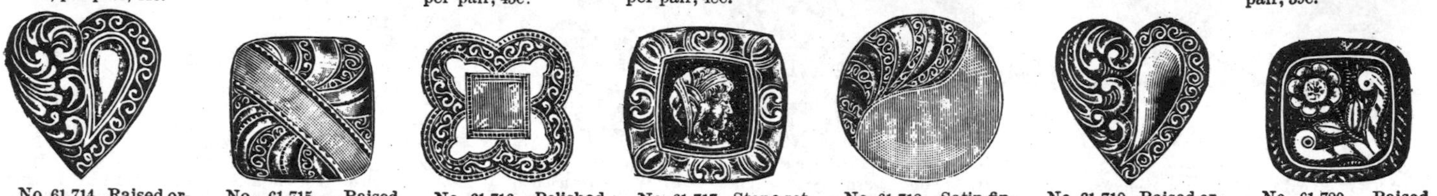

No. 61,714. Raised ornamentation, engraved set with pearls, per pair, 58c.

No. 61,715. Raised and colored ornamentation, engraved, per pair, 60c.

No. 61,716. Polished and engraved, open around square, per pair, 60c

No. 61,717. Stone settings, raised ornamented edges, per pair, 65c.

No. 61,718. Satin finished and raised ornamentation, engraved, per pair, 70c.

No. 61,719. Raised ornamentation with satined shield, per pair, 70c.

No. 61,720. Raised, ornamented and engraved, per pair, 75c.

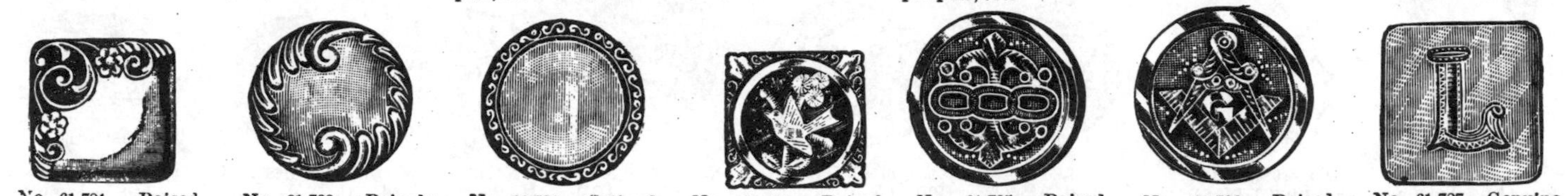

No. 61,721. Raised, ornamented and engraved, per pair, 75c.

No. 61,722. Raised, ornamented, satined center, per pair, 80c.

No. 61,723. Satined centers, raised ornamented edges, per pair, 85c.

No. 61,724. Raised and colored gold, ornamented and engraved, per pair, 95c.

No. 61,725. Raised colored gold ornamented, engraved, Odd Fellow's button, pair, 95c.

No. 61,726. Raised colored gold, ornamented, engraved, Masonic button, per pair, 95c.

No. 61,727. Genuine pearl buttons with gold filled and engraved initial, any letter, pr, 98c.

No. 61,728. Open work, plain, polished and engraved, per pair, 98c.

No. 61,729. Fancy stone setting, escalloped edges, per pair, 98c.

No. 61,730. Satined center, raised ornamented edges and engraved, warranted 20 years, per pair, $1.25.

No. 61,731. Raised, ornamented and engraved, warranted 20 years, per pair, $1.50.

No. 61,732. Raised, ornamented, satin finished and engraved, warranted 20 years, per pair, $1.50.

No. 61,733. Raised gold ornamentation, satin finished and engraved, warranted 20 years, per pair, $1.75.

No. 61,734. Raised gold ornamentation, satin finished and engraved, warranted 20 years, per pair, $1.85.

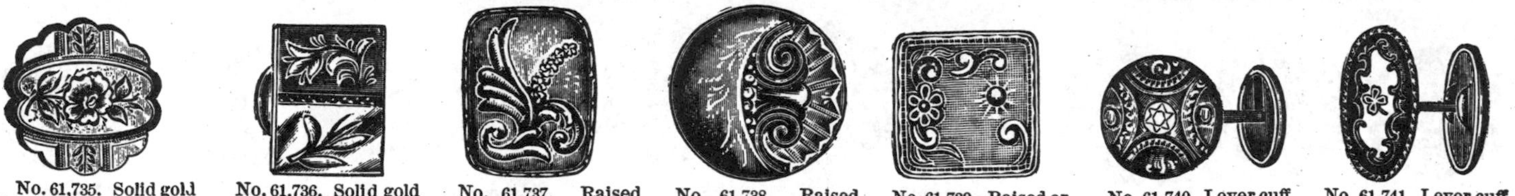

No. 61,735. Solid gold front, satin finished, hand engraved, per pair, $1.85.

No. 61,736. Solid gold front, satin finished and plain polished, hand engraved, pair, $1.90.

No. 61,737. Raised gold, ornamented, satin finished, very fine, warranted 20 years, per pair, $1.95.

No. 61,738. Raised gold ornamentation, satin finished, hand engraved, warranted 20 years, per pair, $2.00.

No. 61,739. Raised ornamentation, each set with real pearl, per pair, $2.00.

No. 61,740. Lever cuff links, raised, ornamented, set with brilliants, per pair, 45c.

No. 61,741. Lever cuff links, enameled in colors, per pair, 60c.

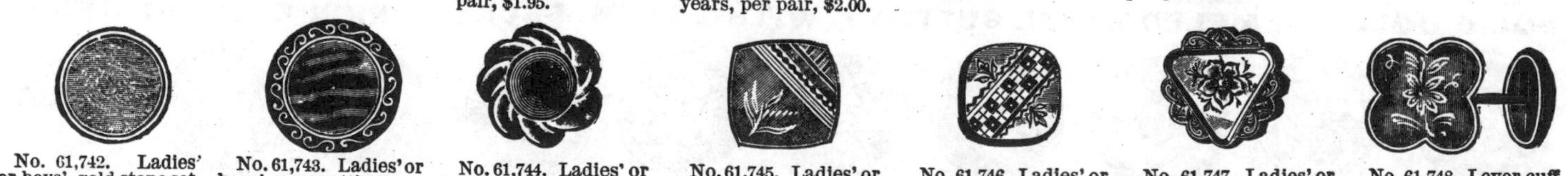

No. 61,742. Ladies' or boys', gold stone setting, per pair, 23c.

No. 61,743. Ladies' or boys', onyx settings, ornamented edges, per pair, 25c.

No. 61,744. Ladies' or boys', moonstone settings, escalloped edges, per pair, 35c.

No. 61,745. Ladies' or boys', solid gold fronts, hand engraved, per pair, 85c.

No. 61,746. Ladies' or boys', solid gold fronts, hand engraved, per pair, 90c.

No. 61,747. Ladies' or boys', solid gold fronts, hand engraved, per pair, $1.00.

No. 61,748. Lever cuff links, polished and engraved, per pair, $1.10.

## MOURNING BUTTONS.

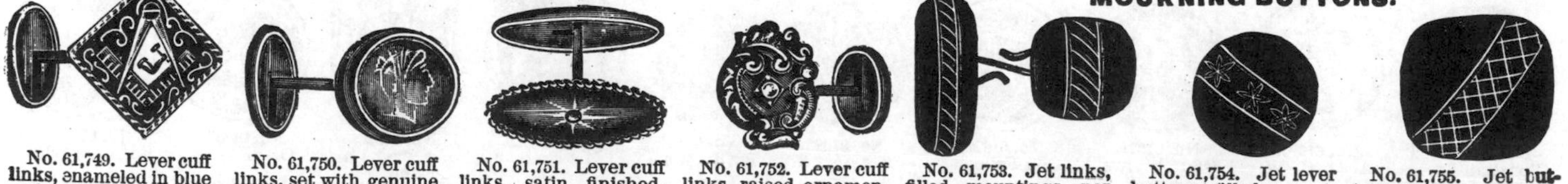

No. 61,749. Lever cuff links, enameled in blue and white, Masonic emblem, per pair, $1.10.

No. 61,750. Lever cuff links, set with genuine cornelian stone, engraved, per pair, $1.50.

No. 61,751. Lever cuff links, satin finished, raised ornamented edges, set with turquoise, per pair, $1.50.

No. 61,752. Lever cuff links, raised ornamentation and engraved, set with real pearls, per pair, $1.75.

No. 61,753. Jet links, filled mountings, per pair, 90c.

No. 61,754. Jet lever buttons, filled mountings, per pair, 35c.

No. 61,755. Jet buttons, lever, per pair, 45c.

All of the cuff buttons listed on this page have patent lever backs.

# Fine Solid Gold Cuff Buttons, Links, Collar Buttons and Studs.

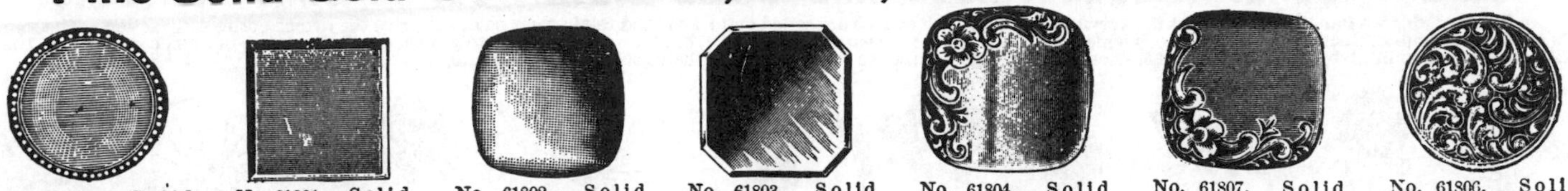

No. 61800. Solid gold, satin finished, beaded edge. Per pair, $2.50.

No. 61801. Solid gold, satin finished, polished edge. Per pair, $3.00.

No. 61802. Solid gold, plain polished. Per pair, $3.40.

No. 61803. Solid gold, satin finished, polished bevel edges. Per pair, $3.45.

No. 61804. Solid gold, plain polished and raised ornamentation. Per pair, $3.50.

No. 61807. Solid gold, satin finished, raised ornamentation. Per pair, $4.50.

No. 61806. Solid gold, very fancy, raised ornamentation, hand engraved. Per pair, $4.00.

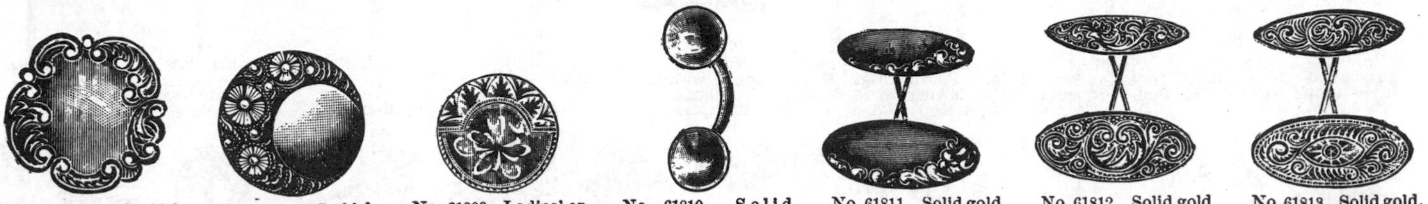

No. 61805. Solid gold, polished center, raised ornamented edges, fancy. Per pair, $3.85.

No. 61808. Solid gold, plain polished, fancy raised ornamentation. Per pair, $4.75.

No. 61809. Ladies' or boys, fine solid gold, hand engraved. Per pair, $2.75.

No. 61810. Solid gold Dumb Bell Links, Per pair, $2.90.

No. 61811. Solid gold Cuff Links, plain polished and raised ornamentation. Per pair, $2.85.

No. 61812. Solid gold Cuff Links, very fancy, raised ornamentation, Roman finish. Per pair, $3.50.

No. 61813. Solid gold, very fancy, raised ornamentation, set with 2 diamonds. Per pair, $5.50.

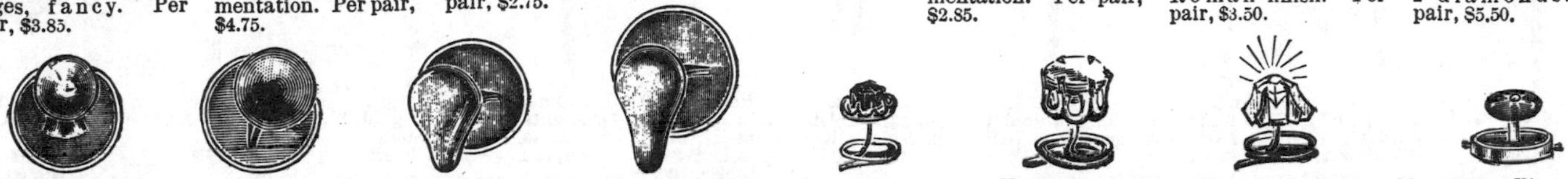

No. 61830. Solid gold Collar Button, solid top. Each, $1.00.

No. 61831. Solid gold Collar Button, lever top. Each, $1.00.

No. 61832. Solid gold Collar Button, lever top. Each, $1.00.

No. 61833. Solid gold Collar Button, lever top. Each, $1.25.

No. 61834. Solid gold Stud, 1 ruby. Each, 75c.

No. 61835. Solid gold Stud, 1 opal. Each, 90 cents.

No. 61836. Solid gold Stud, fine white brilliant. Each, $1.00.

No. 61837. Fine solid gold, dress shirt Studs with real Pearls, separable. Each, $1.50. Per set of 3, $4.25.

## STERLING SILVER AND PLATED LINKS AND SETS.

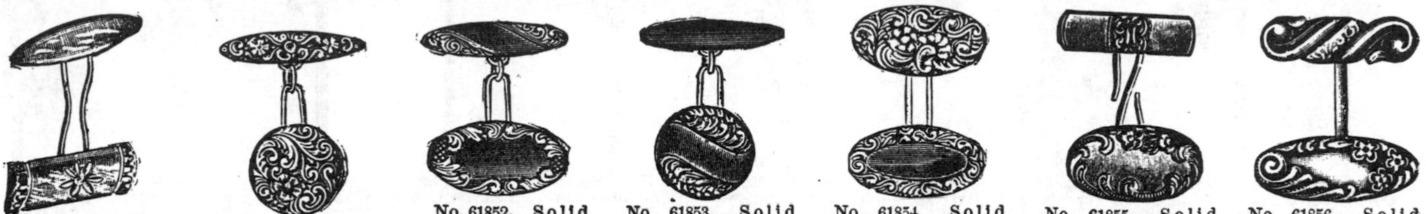

No. 61850. Pearl, beautifully engraved, with strong attachments. Per pair, 20c.

No. 61851. Solid sterling silver, heavy, fancy raised ornamentation. Per pair, 65c.

No. 61852. Solid sterling silver, fancy engraved. Per pair, 60c.

No. 61853. Solid sterling silver, fancy engraved. Per pair, 55c.

No. 61854. Solid sterling silver, large and heavy, raised ornamentation and engraved. Per pair, 75c.

No. 61855. Solid sterling silver, beautifully enameled, with raised ornamentation. Per pair, 75c.

No. 61856. Solid sterling silver, enameled, fancy raised ornamentation. Per pair, 90c.

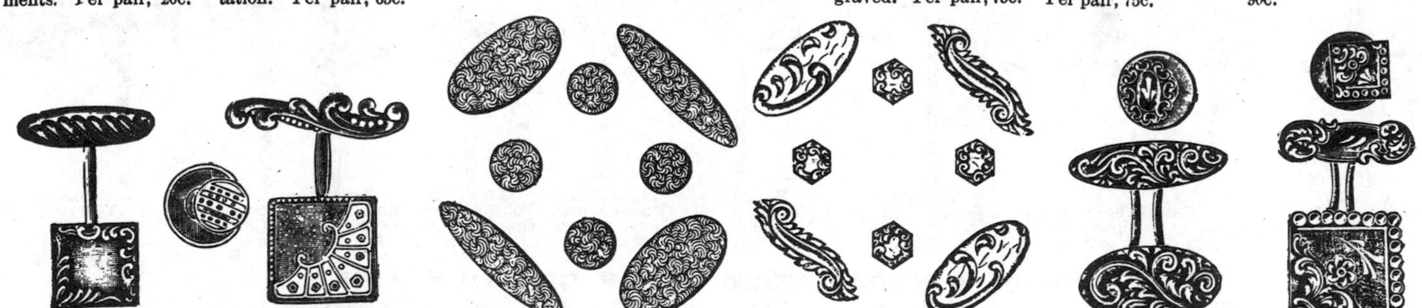

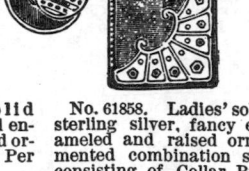

No. 61857. Solid sterling silver and enameled, with raised ornamentation. Per pair, $1.10.

No. 61858. Ladies' solid sterling silver, fancy enameled and raised ornamented combination set, consisting of Collar Button, 3 Dress Buttons and 1 pair of Cuff Buttons. Per set, $1.50.

No. 61859. Ladies' solid sterling silver, raised ornamented combination set, consisting of Collar Button, 3 Dress Buttons and 1 pair Cuff Links. Per set, $1 05.

Same style in white metal, silver plated. Per set, 35c.

No. 61860. Ladies' solid sterling silver, fancy enameled and raised ornamented, combination set consisting of 1 Collar Button, 3 Dress Buttons and 1 pair of Cuff Links. Per set, $1.25.

No. 61861. Per set, 35c.

No. 61862. Per set, 50c.

Nos. 61861 and 61862. Ladies' Combination Set, gold plated on white metal, bright cut and hand engraving, which shows the white metal through the gold, making a pretty contrast; consists of 1 Collar Button, 3 Dress Buttons, 1 pair Cuff Links.

## FINE QUALITY GOLD FILLED COLLAR BUTTONS AND STUDS.

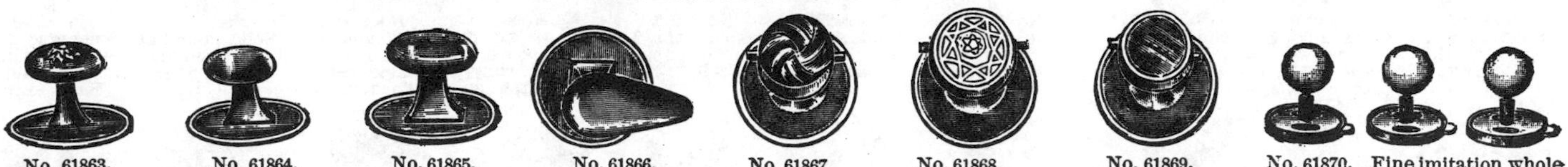

No. 61863. Stationary top, brilliant setting, celluloid back. Each, 20c.

No. 61864. Patent shank, lever top. Each, 10c.

No. 61865. Patent shank, lever top. Each, 25c.

No. 61866. Patent shank, lever top, Each, 20c.

No. 61867. Separable, celluloid back. Each, 10c.

No. 61868. Pearl top, with brilliant, celluloid back, separable. Each, 15c.

No. 61869. Tiger eye top, celluloid back, separable. Each, 15c.

No. 61870. Fine imitation whole pearls, separable backs. Set of 3, 30c.

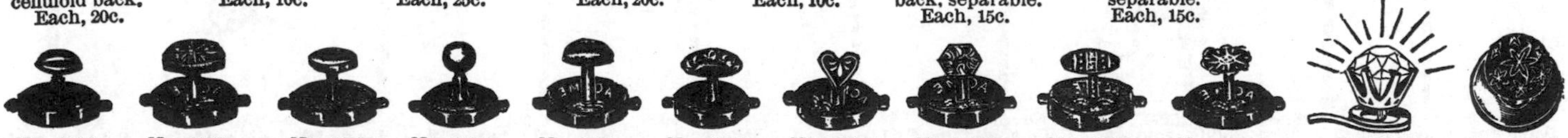

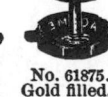

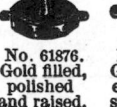

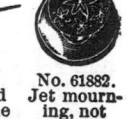

No. 61871. Mother of pearl, separable. Set of 3, 20c.

No. 61872. Mother of pearl, separable. Set of 3, 25c.

No. 61873. Gold filled, polished, separable. Set of 3, 30c.

No. 61874. Gold filled, polished, separable. Set of 3, 35c.

No. 61875. Gold filled, satined, separable. Set of 3, 40c.

No. 61876. Gold filled, polished and raised, ornamented, separable. Set of 3, 45c.

No. 61877. Gold filled, engraved, separable. Set of 3, 50c.

No. 61878. Gold filled, fancy engraved. Set of 3, 60c.

No. 61879. Sterling silver, white and blue enameled, separable. Set of 3, 65c.

No. 61880. Satin and engraved, separable. Set of 3, 75c.

No. 61881. 14 karat solid gold, with fine imitation diamond. Each, $1.25.

No. 61882. Jet mourning, not separable, Set of 3, 38c.

# FINEST QUALITY GOLD FILLED AND SOLID SILVER SCARF OR STICK PINS.

In Scarf Pins we handle nothing but the very best goods, which can be depended on to wear and retain their color and give the owner entire satisfaction. The market is flooded with cheap electro gold plated goods which make a very nice appearance when new, but for wear are absolutely worthless. Our trade in every corner of the United States has been built up by furnishing our customers with good goods and we expect to retain their good will by continuing in the same manner.

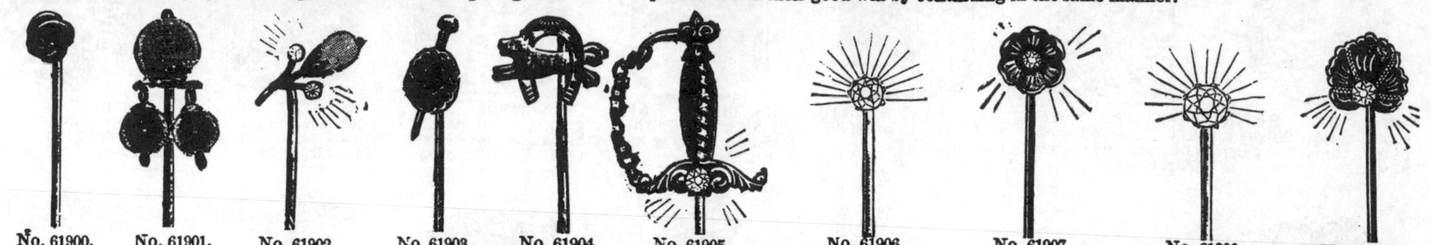

No. 61900. Bright Polished Knot. Each, 23c.

No. 61901. 3 Spar Balls. Each, 23c.

No. 61902. Imitation Pearl Bud, 2 brilliants. Each, 25c.

No. 61903. Bright Polished, with Amethyst, 30c.

No. 61904. Bright Horse Shoe, Chased Dog, 33c.

No. 61905. Sword. with 1 brilliant. Each, 34c.

No. 61906. Imitation Diamond. Each, 35c.

No. 61907. Gold plate on solid silver, 1 brilliant, 35c.

No. 61908. Fine Imitation Diamond. Each, 36c.

No. 61909. Gold plate on solid silver, 1 brilliant, 36c.

No. 61910. Gold plate on solid silver, 1 brilliant, 36c.

No. 61911. Bright polish, 2 garnets, 1 brilliant, 36c.

No. 61912. Bright and Roman Turquoise Set, 36c.

No. 61913. Colored gold, 3 garnets, 1 brilliant, 38c.

No. 61914. Roman finish, polished silver Axe, 38c.

No. 61915. Gold plated on solid silver, 1 pearl, 1 turquoise, 39c.

No. 61916. 7 brilliants, 1 turquoise. Each, 39c.

No. 61917. Colored gold, 3 brilliants. Each, 43c.

No. 61918. Horse Shoe, 10 pearls. Each, 43c.

No. 61919. Sword, Roman finish, 5 brilliants, 1 sapphire, 50c.

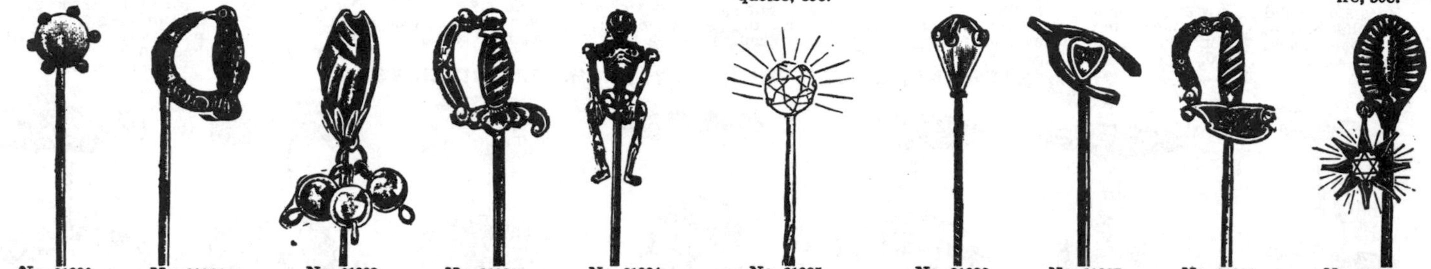

No. 61920. Opal Setting. Each, 45c.

No. 61921. Polished and chased Crescent, ruby eye, 48c.

No. 61922. 3 spar balls, 1 real sea shell. Each, 48c.

No. 61923. Sword, gold plate on solid silver, 48c.

No. 61924. Roman finished skeleton, loose joints, garnet eyes, 50c.

No. 61925. Fine imitation Diamond. Each, 53c.

No. 61926. Pearl, with turquoise on top. Each, 53c.

No. 61927. Wishbone Stone Sets. Each, 53c.

No. 61928. Sword, gold plate on solid silver, 55c.

No. 61929. Real shell, 1 brilliant. Each, 55c.

No. 61930. Gold plate on solid silver. Each, 60c.

No. 61931. Bright Polished, 1 brilliant. Each, 62c.

No. 61932. Solid silver, satined garnet eyes, 62c.

No. 61933. Whip, bright polish, 3 brilliants, 75c.

No. 61934. Cornet, bright polish. Each, 75c.

No. 61935. Chased Arrow, Horse Shoe, 9 brilliants, 85c.

No. 61936. Polished mounting, large garnet, 90c.

No. 61937. Bug, 1 emerald, 1 ruby, 2 pearls. Each, $1.25.

No. 61938. Solid silver Christian Endeavor bangle. Each, 35c.

No. 61939. Solid silver Epworth League bangle. Each, 35c.

## SOLID 14 KARAT GOLD SCARF OR STICK PINS.

No. 61975. Solid gold, 1 pink pearl. Each, 65c.

No. 61976. Solid gold, 1 ruby. Each, 65c.

No. 61977. Solid gold Bug, 1 ruby, 3 pearls, 75c.

No. 61978. Solid gold fancy, large opal. Each, 90c.

No. 61979. Solid gold, 1 ruby, 1 whole pearl, 95c.

No. 61980. Solid gold, 2 rubies, 1 opal. Each, $1.20.

No. 61981. Solid gold Wishbone, 1 emerald, 1 ruby, 1 brilliant, $1.35.

No. 61982. Solid gold colored, 1 ruby, 1 whole pearl. Each, $1.75.

No. 61983. Solid gold, fine imitation diamond, $1.85.

No. 61984. Solid gold, fancy, 6 brilliants, 1 emerald. Each, $1.90.

No. 61985. Solid gold fine imitation diamond. Each, $1.90.

No. 61986. Solid gold double crescent, chased, 1 sapphire, $2.20.

No. 61987. Solid gold, 3 rubies, colored wings, $2.50.

No. 61988. Solid gold, fancy, 1 opal. Each, $2.20.

No. 61989. Solid gold, bright cut engraving, 5 brilliants, 1 emerald, $2.25.

No. 61990. Solid gold, enameled leaves, 3 pearls, bright cut, $2.10.

No. 61991. Solid gold, fancy, large opal. Each, $2.90.

No. 61992. Solid gold horse shoe and clover leaf, 1 sapphire. Each, $2.95.

No. 61993. Solid gold, fancy enameled leaf, large pearl. Each, $3.25.

No. 61994. Solid gold horse shoe, 11 real diamonds. Each, $11.40.

# Best Quality Gold Filled and Solid Gold Front, Engraved Lace Pins.

### ALL OF OUR PINS HAVE A PATENT SAFETY CATCH.

No. 62050. Solid gold front (engraved name, when desired, 15c. extra.) Each, 30c.

No. 62051. Gold filled, 1 garnet. Each, 35c.

No. 62052. Gold filled, fancy. Each, 35c.

No. 62053. Gold filled, knife pattern, engraved handle. Each, 35c.

No. 62054. Gold filled, fancy, 2 garnets, 1 pearl. Each, 40c.

No. 62055. Gold filled, fancy, 1 garnet. Each, 43c.

No. 62056. Gold filled, fancy, 1 garnet. Each, 45c.

No. 62057. Gold filled, with fancy ends, satin finished, plain polished center, 1 garnet. Each, 50c.

No. 62058. Gold filled, fancy, 1 garnet. Each, 60c.

No. 62059. Gold filled, fancy, 1 garnet. Each, 60c.

No. 62060. Gold filled, fancy, 2 garnets. Each, 66c.

No. 62061. Gold filled key, engraved. Each, 75c.

No. 62062. Gold filled, fancy, 2 garnets. Each, 60c.

No. 62063. Gold filled, fancy, 1 garnet. Each, 65c.

No. 62064. Gold filled, fancy, 1 garnet. Each, 50c.

No. 62065. Solid gold front, engraved. Each, $1.30.

No. 62066. Solid gold front, engraved. Each, 65c.

No. 62067. Solid gold front, engraved. Each, 75c.

No. 62068. Solid gold front, engraved. Each, 65c.

No. 62069. Solid gold front, fancy, engraved. Each, 70c.

No. 62070. Solid gold front, fancy, engraved. Each, $1.75.

No. 62071. Solid gold front, satin finished and fancy engraved, 1 garnet, 1 turquoise, 1 pearl. Each, $1.35.

No. 62072. Solid gold front, engraved, 2 garnets, 1 pearl. Each, 55c.

No. 62073. Fine gold filled spoon, engraved handle. Each, 70c

No. 62074. Fine gold filled fork, engraved handle. Each, 70c.

No. 62075. Solid gold front, engraved, 1 garnet. Each, 45c.

No. 62076. Solid gold front, fancy engraved. Each, 90c.

No. 62077. Fancy gold filled slipper, with engraved toe, satin finished lining, very fine. Each, 95c.

No. 62078. Solid gold front, engraved. Each, 75c.

No. 62079. Solid gold front, fancy engraved. Each, 65c.

No. 62080. Gold front, engraved, 1 sapphire, 1 brilliant, 1 garnet. Each, 95c.

No. 62081. Solid gold front, engraved, raised gold, ornamented and polished, 2 garnets. Each, $1.50.

No. 62082. Solid gold front, fancy engraved. Each, $1.10.

Name engraved on Nos. 42067-68-76-78, when desired, 20 cents extra. Postage on pins, 2 cents; insurance or registry extra. Always state how much is enclosed for postage, also how much on each article.

Jewelry will be sent C. O. D. by express for examination when desired, providing the order amounts to $2.00 or over, and 50 cents as a deposit accompanies the same.

# BEST QUALITY GOLD FILLED, SOLID GOLD FRONT, AND STERLING SILVER BROOCH PINS.

No. 62083. Gold filled crescent, with raised colored pansy; 1 brilliant. Each, 45c.

No. 62084. Gold filled; 2 emeralds, 1 pearl. Each, 40c.

No. 62085. Gold filled, fancy finish; 2 emeralds, 1 brilliant. Each, 40c.

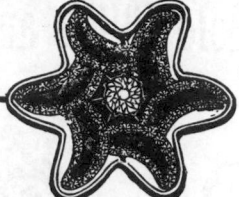
No. 62086. Gold filled, fancy center; 1 brilliant. Each, 35c.

No. 62087. Gold filled crescent; 3 brilliants. Each, 35c.

No. 62088. Gold filled, raised, ornamented, satin finished; 1 brilliant. Each, 90c.

No. 62089. Gold filled; 1 turquoise. Each, 30c.

No. 62090. Gold filled; 1 brilliant. Each, 35c.

No. 62091. Trilby hearts; 1 engraved, 1 plain polished. Each, 60c.

No. 62092. Gold filled; 1 emerald, 2 brilliants. Each, 42c.

No. 62093. Gold filled; 2 garnets, 1 brilliant. Each, 48c.

No. 62094. Gold filled; 4 garnets, 1 brilliant. Each, 60c.

No. 62095. Gold filled, ornamented with colored gold leaves; 1 brilliant. Each, 55c.

No. 62096. Gold filled, raised, ornamented, satin finished. Each, 70c.

No. 62097. Gold filled; 1 large brilliant. Each, 50c.

No. 62098. Gold filled pansy leaves, fancy Roman finished; 2 fine brilliants. Each, $1.50.

No. 62099. Gold filled, fancy Roman finished leaves; 1 pearl. Each, 95c.

No. 62100. Gold filled, raised, ornamented, satin finished; Each, 95c.

No. 62101. Gold filled, raised, ornamented, satin finished; 1 fine brilliant. Each, $1.05.

No. 62102. Gold filled, Roman finished leaves; 1 fine brilliant. Each, $1.15.

No. 62103. Gold filled, Roman finished leaves; 1 fine brilliant. Each, $1.20.

No. 62104. Gold filled violin, with tail piece, bridge, strings, finger board, sound holes and keys, a perfect imitation, beautifully finished. Each, $1.30.

No. 62105. Fancy gold filled, raised, ornamented; large beautiful genuine amethyst. Each, $1.40.

No. 62106. Solid gold front, fancy engraved and satin finished; 1 fine garnet. Each $1.45.

No. 62107. Solid gold front, fancy engraved, plain polished. Each, $1.45.

No. 62108. Solid gold front crescent, fancy engraved, satin finished; 3 garnets. Each, $1.50.

No. 62109. Pearl crescent, gold filled mounting; 3 white brilliants, and ornamented with colored gold. Each, 93c.

No. 62110. Gold filled, fancy Roman finished, with garnet eyes. Each, $1.55.

No. 62111. Gold filled, fancy Roman finished and engraved leaves; fine, large brilliant. Each, $1.85.

No. 62112. Gold filled, fancy Roman finished, engraved; 1 large garnet, 4 brilliants. Each, $1.80.

## SOLID STERLING SILVER BROOCH PINS.

No. 62113. Solid silver, raised, ornamented and engraved. Each, 60c.

No. 62114. Solid silver, raised, ornamented edges and engraved. Each, 50c.

No. 62115. Solid silver, raised ornamented edges and engraved. Each, 55c.

No. 62116. Solid silver bicycle badge; 1 small garnet. Each, 95c.

No. 62117. Solid silver, fancy filigree work, bright cut, engraved; large, genuine amethyst. Each, $2.50.

**POSTAGE ON BROOCH PINS, 2c; INSURANCE OR REGISTRY EXTRA. SEE FRONT PAGE FOR INSTRUCTIONS.**

# Finest Quality Solid Gold, Solid Gold Front and Gold Filled Brooch, Lace and Baby Pins.

No. 62149. Solid Gold Brooch Pin with colored gold (variegated) leaves, set with real pearls. A very beautiful piece of jewelry. Each, $4.25.

No. 62151. Fine solid gold, with enameled wreath leaves, beautifully finished. Each, $5.25.

No. 62152. Fine solid gold, fancy design, fine large whole pearl in center and 16 small pearls. Each, $7.60.

No. 62153. Fine solid gold, fancy design, 4 beautiful enameled leaves, 1 fine opal, 4 pearls. Each, $6.50.

No. 62154. Fine solid gold, fancy design, ornamented with colored gold leaves, 1 fine opal, 4 fine large whole pearls, 20 small pearls. Each, $12.25.

No. 62175. Solid gold front, fancy engraved, polished. Each, 85c.

No. 62176. Solid gold front, fancy engraved, polished. Each, 95c.

No. 62177. Solid gold front, fancy engraved, satin finished. Each, $1.05.

No. 62178. Solid gold front, fancy engraved, satin finished. Each, $1.25.

No. 62179. Fine gold filled Pin Set, fancy raised ornamentation, Each, 90c.

No. 62180. Fine gold filled Pin Set, raised ornamentation. Each, 65c.

No. 62181. Solid gold Pin Set, fancy raised ornamentation. Each, $3.50.

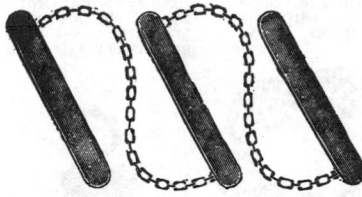

No. 62182. Solid gold front Pin Set, satin finished. Each, $1.50.

No. 62183. Solid gold front Pin Set, fancy pattern, engraved, satin finished. Each, $1.65.

No. 62184. Solid gold front engraved Pin Set, 1 garnet, 1 pearl, 1 sapphire. Each, $1.60.

# CHILDS' BIB PINS.

No. 62185. Gold filled, 2 brilliants, 1 garnet. Each, 20c.

No. 62186. Solid gold front, engraved. Per pair, 40c.

No. 62187. Fine gold filled, raised ornamentation. Per pair, 45c.

No. 62188. Fine gold filled, raised ornamentation. Per pair, 45c.

No. 62189. Gold front, raised ornamented ends. Per pair, 55c.

No. 62190. Fine gold filled, raised ornamentation. Per pair, 58c.

No. 62191. Solid gold front, engraved. Per pair, 70c.

No. 62192. Solid gold front, engraved. Per pair, 70c.

No. 62193. Solid gold front, engraved. Per pair, 70c.

No. 62194. Solid gold front, engraved. Per pair, 70c.

No. 62195. Solid gold front, engraved. Per pair, 65c.

No. 62196. Solid gold front, engraved, 1 garnet, 1 pearl, 1 sapphire. Per pair, 85c.

No. 62197. Solid gold front, fancy engraved, 1 garnet. Per pair, 90c.

No. 62198. Solid gold front, engraved, 1 garnet, 1 pearl, 1 turquoise. Per pair, $1.00.

No. 62199. Solid gold front, engraved, satin finished, 2 garnets, 2 pearls, 1 turquoise. Per pair, $1.00.

No. 62200. Solid sterling silver, embossed ends, satin finished center. Per pair, 48c.

No. 62201. Fine solid gold, polished center, beaded edges. Per pair, $2.00.

No. 62202. Fine solid gold, polished, raised ornamentation. Per pair, $2.25.

No. 62203. Silver plated, raised ornamented Belt Pin. Each, 12c.

No. 62204. Silver plated and enameled Belt Pin. Each, 10c.

No. 62205. Fine gold filled Belt Pin, plain polished, beaded edge, patent safety catch. Each, 35c.

No. 62206. Fine gold filled, engraved. Each, 35c.

No. 62207. Fine solid sterling silver. Each, 60c.

No. 62208. Solid gold front, fancy engraved, satin finished. Each, 85c.

No. 62209. Fine solid gold, fancy engraved, satin finished. Each, $2.50.

It is perfectly safe and much better to send cash in full with your orders. You save the discount and express charges, and we guarantee safe delivery.

Postage on above goods 2 cents; registry or insurance extra.

# FINE SOLID GOLD BOHEMIAN GARNET AND AMBER JEWELRY.

The jewelry listed under this heading if manufactured in this country could not be sold for twice the prices at which we offer them. These goods are made in the forest regions of Germany by poor peasant families who realize from 15 to 25 cents per day for their work. If you will stop and think that every one of the stones must be cut, ground and polished, besides the cost of material and the work of mounting you can get some idea of the amount of labor required to make these goods.

No. 62210. Brooch Pin, Solid Gold Mounting, set with garnets. Price, $1.25.

No. 62211. Brooch Pin, Solid Gold Mounting, set with garnets. Price, $1.75.

No. 62212. Brooch Pin, Solid Gold Mounting, set with garnets. Price, $2.25.

No. 62213. Brooch Pin, Solid Gold Mounting, set with garnets. Price, $2.13.

No. 62214. Hair Ornament. Solid Gold Mounting, set with garnets. Price, $2.50.

No. 62215. Brooch Pin, Solid Gold Mounting, set with first quality fine cut garnets. Price, $5.75.

No. 62216. Brooch Pin, Solid Gold Mounting, set with first quality fine cut garnets. Price, $5.85.

No. 62217. Brooch Pin, Solid Gold Mounting, set with first quality fine cut garnets. Price, $5.85

No. 62218. Brooch Pin, Solid Gold Mounting, set with first quality fine cut garnets. Price, $5.75.

No. 62219. Ear Drops, Solid Gold Mountings and wires, set with garnets. Per pair, $0.85.

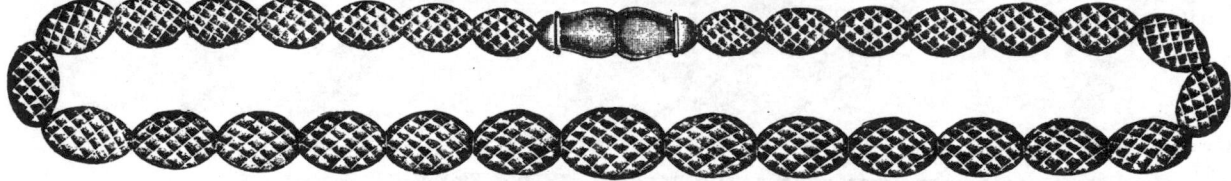 

No. 62221. Genuine Amber Bead Necklace. This is a genuine amber bead necklace of fine quality, strung on linen cord. The beads are beautifully cut and very transparent. It is thought by many that Amber when worn as a necklace acts as a preventative against colds, sore throat and the contagious diseases to which children are subject. They are very light and make a beautiful and inexpensive necklace. Price, $1.00.

62220. Ear Drops, Solid Gold Mountings and wires, set with garnets. Per pair, 85c.

## FINE JET MOURNING JEWELRY.

No. 62222. Ear Drops, Jet balls, Solid Gold wires. Per pair. 50c.

No. 62223. Ear Drops, Jet flowers, Solid Gold wires. Per pair, 65c.

No. 62224. Ear Drops, Jet flowers, Solid Gold wires. Per pair, 80c.

No. 62225. Ear Drops, Jet leaves, polished ball center, Solid Gold wires. Per pair, 95c.

No. 62326. Ear Drops, Jet balls and flowers, polished center, Solid Gold wires. Per pair, $1.20.

No. 62227. Ear Drops, Jet Flowers, real pearl centers, Solid Gold wires. Per pair, $1.25.

No. 62228. Jet Lace Pin, polished and engraved. Price, 20c.

No. 62229. Jet Lace Pin, polished and fancy engraved. Price, 30c.

No. 62230. Polished Jet Lace Pin, with small gold ornament set with real pearl. Price, 75c.

No. 62231. Jet Lace Pin, polished ball in flower. Price, 75c.

No. 62232. Jet Lace Pin. Engraved, small gold ornament set with real pearl. Price, 90c.

No. 62233. Jet Lace Pin, set with real pearl. Price, 90c.

No. 62234. Jet Brooch Pin. Jet flowers, Gold Filled Mounting. Price, $1.50.

No. 62235. Brooch Pin. Jet Flower, ball center, Gold Filled Mounting. Price, 85c.

No. 62236. Brooch Pin. Jet Flower, small gold ornament in center, set with real pearl, Gold Filled Mounting. Price, 90c.

No. 62237. Brooch Pin. Fine Jet Flowers. Fancy Gold Filled Mounting, set with one real pearl. Price, $1.75.

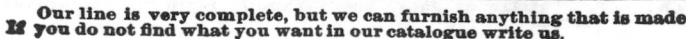

Our line is very complete, but we can furnish anything that is made. If you do not find what you want in our catalogue write us.

Postage on above goods 2 cents. Registry and insurance extra. State how much is inclosed for postage, also how much for each article.

# Finest Quality Gold Filled and Solid Gold Front Ear-Rings and Drops.

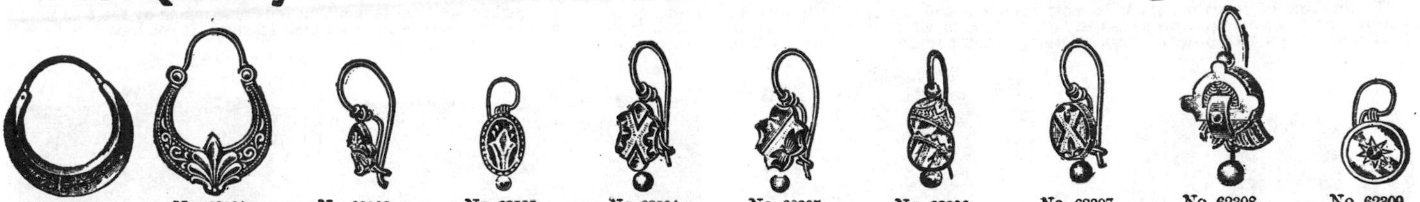

No. 62300. Gold filled hoop Rings, engraved, solid gold wires. Per pair, 35c.

No. 62301. Gold filled hoop Rings, engraved, solid gold wires. Per pair, 45c.

No. 62302. Solid gold fronts, engraved. Per pair, 45c.

No. 62303. Solid gold fronts, engraved, ball pendants. Per pair, 50c.

No. 62304. Solid gold fronts, engraved, ball pendants. Per pair, 54c.

No. 62305. Solid gold fronts, engraved, ball pendants. Per pair, 55c.

No. 62306. Solid gold fronts, engraved, ball pendants. Per pair, 58c.

No. 62307. Solid gold fronts, engraved, ball pendants. Per pair, 60c.

No. 62308. Gold filled, fancy, set with garnets. Per pair, 65c.

No. 62309. Solid gold fronts, engraved, set with garnets. Per pair, 65c.

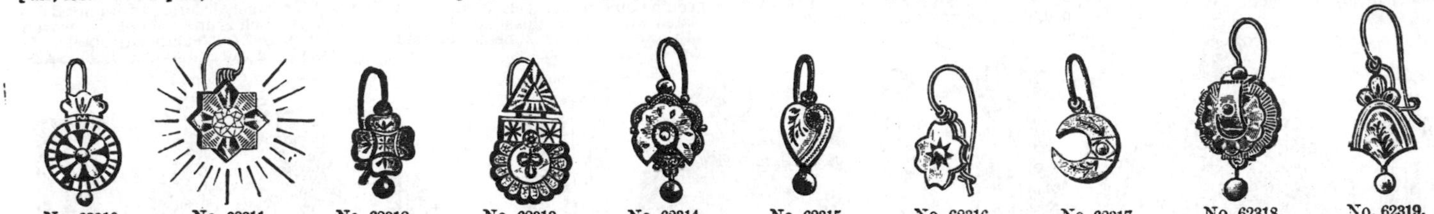

No. 62310. Gold filled, enameled, ball pendants, solid gold wires. Per pair, 75c.

No. 62311. Solid gold fronts, with imitation diamonds. solid gold wires. Per pair, $1.15.

No. 62312. Solid gold fronts, engraved. Ball pendants. Per pair, 85c.

No. 62313. Gold filled, raised colored ornamentation, set with garnets. 85c.

No. 62314. Solid gold fronts, set with garnets, ball pendants. Per pair, $1.50.

No. 62315. Solid gold fronts, engraved, ball pendants. Per pair, 92c.

No. 62316. Solid gold fronts, engraved, with garnets. Per pair, 98c.

No. 62317. Solid gold fronts, engraved, with garnets. Per pair, $1.00.

No. 62318. Fancy gold filled, with garnets, ball pendants. Per pair, $1.00.

No. 62319. Solid gold fronts, engraved, ball pendants. Per pair, $1.10.

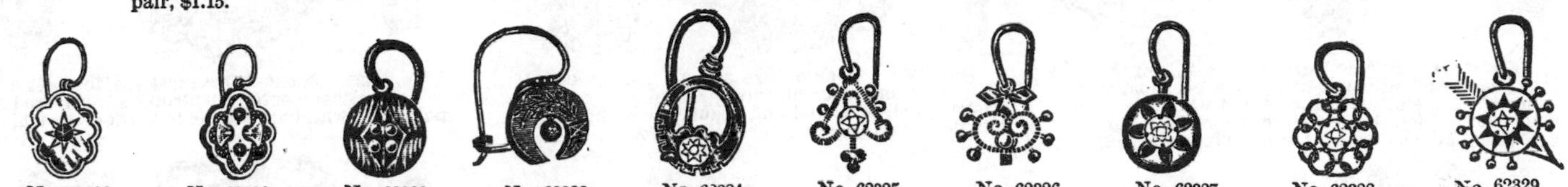

No. 62320. Solid gold fronts, escalloped, set with garnets. Per pair, 75c.

No. 62321. Solid gold fronts, raised ornamentation, solid gold wires. Per pair, $1.25.

No. 62322. Gold filled balls, solid gold wires, gold front ornamentation. Per pair, $1.45.

No. 62323. Solid gold fronts, engraved, ball pendants. Per pair, 90c.

No. 62324. Solid gold fronts, with garnets. Per pair, $1.55.

No. 62325. Solid gold fronts, fancy Roman, with moonstones. Per pair, $1.65.

No. 62326. Solid gold fronts, with turquoise, fancy. Per pair, $1.70.

No. 62327. Solid gold fronts. Per pair, $1.75.

No. 62328. Gold filled, fancy, Roman finish, set with moonstones. Per pair, $1.90.

No. 62329. Gold filled, with imitation diamonds, incrusted in blue stone. Per pair, $1.95.

## 14-KARAT SOLID GOLD EAR-RINGS, DROPS AND SETS.

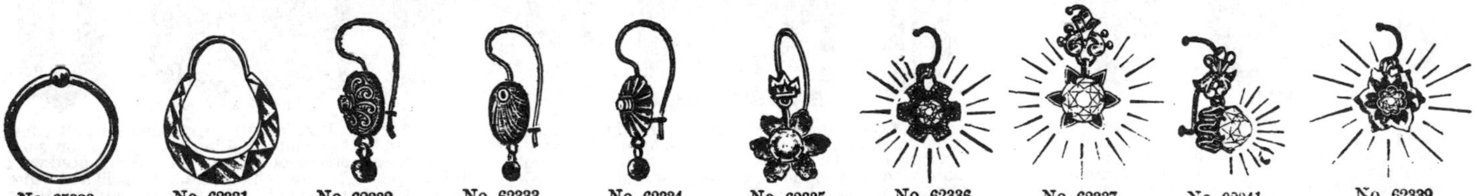

No. 65330. Solid gold Rings. Per pair, 65c.

No. 62331. Solid gold hoop Rings, facited and polished. Per pair, 98c.

No. 62332. Solid gold, with real pearls, ball pendants. Per pair, $1.10.

No. 62333. Solid gold, with garnets. ball pendants. Per pair, $1.20.

No. 62334. Solid gold, with garnets, ball pendants. Per pair, $1.25.

No. 62335. Solid gold, with large imitation pearls. Per pair, $2.00.

No. 62336. Solid gold, with imitation diamonds. Per pair, $1.95.

No. 62337. Solid gold, with fine imitation diamonds. Per pair, $2.25.

No. 62341. Solid gold, with imitation diamonds. Per pair, $1.59.

No. 62339. Solid gold, with imitation diamonds. Per pair, $1.85.

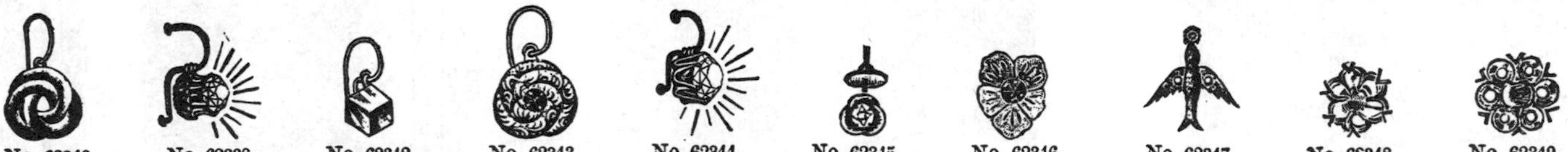

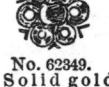

No. 62340. Solid gold knots, Roman finish, heavy. Per pair, $1.85.

No. 62338. Solid gold, with imitation diamonds. Per pair, $1.50.

No. 62342. Solid gold, polished cube. Per pair. $1.00.

No. 62343. Solid gold knot, fancy, Roman finish, ruby settings. Per pair, $2.25.

No. 62344. Solid gold, with imitation diamonds. Per pair, $1.65.

No. 62345. Solid gold screw Ear Sets, with whole pearls. Per pair, $1.60.

No. 62346. Solid gold screw Ear Sets, ruby settings, Roman finish, fancy engraved. Per pair, $1.85.

No. 62347. Solid gold Ear Sets, 1 ruby. 2 pearls in each. Per pair, $2.25.

No. 62348. Solid gold Ear Sets, very fancy, with opals. Per pair, $3.75.

No. 62349. Solid gold Ear Sets, very fancy, with opals. Per pair, $4.30.

## 14-KARAT SOLID GOLD STICK PINS, Etc.

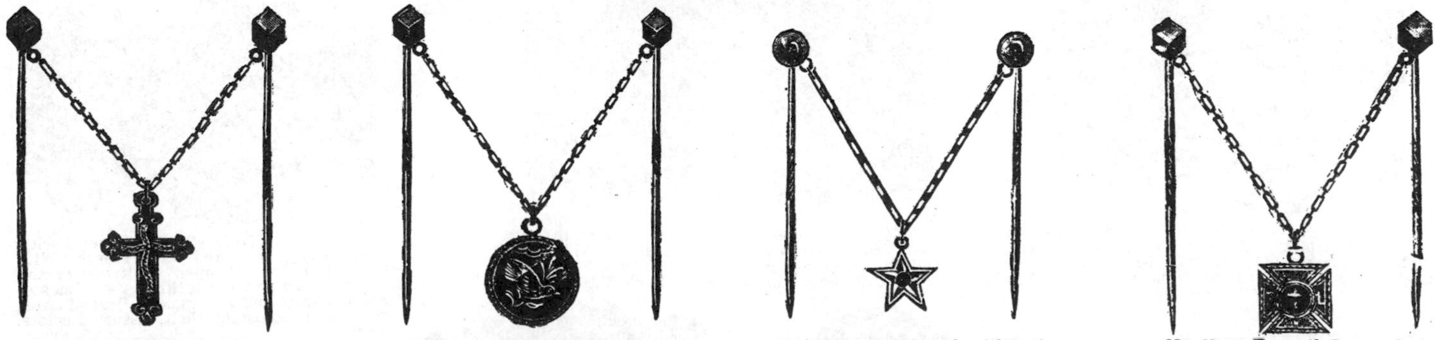

No. 62350. Solid gold, with engraved cross. Price, $1.30.

No. 62351. Solid gold, with fancy engraved bangle. Price, $1.45.

No. 62352. Solid gold, with real pearl in star. Price, $1.60.

No. 62353. Epworth League bangle, enameled in two colors. $1.85.

**Postage on above goods 2 cents; registry or insurance extra. State how much you inclose for postage, also how much for each article.**

# SOLID STERLING SILVER AND PLATED BUCKLES AND BELTS.

**In this line of goods our stock is most complete and always fresh with the latest styles. As to quality, we handle none but the finest, made by the best manufacturers, and by so doing we always satisfy our customers, which is the only way to hold their trade and make new customers among their friends. If you have not already bought of us, send a trial order at once. Nothing is more appropriate than a belt as a present to a lady.**

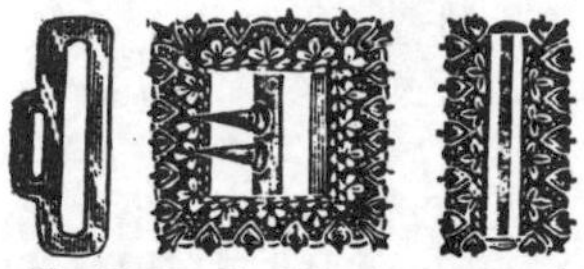

No. 62400. Buckle (size 1⅜x1⅛ in. for belt ¾ in. wide) with attachments. Gold plated and ornamented with enameled border. Each, 40 cents.

No. 62401. Buckle (size 1⅞x1⅜ in. for belt 1⅛ in. wide) and attachments. Quadruple silver plated over solid white metal and ornamented with bright cut engravings. Each, 40c.

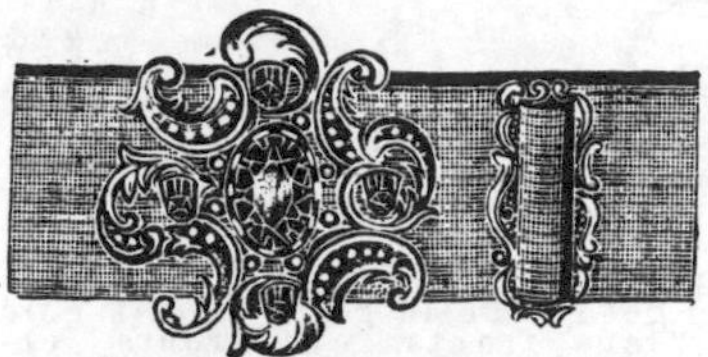

No. 62402. Buckle and Belt (width of belt 1⅛ in.) with attachments. Buckle is gold plated and set with 5 genuine amethysts; belt is fine gold plated woven wire tinsel, full length, adjustable. Is very beautiful and stylish. Each, $2.40.

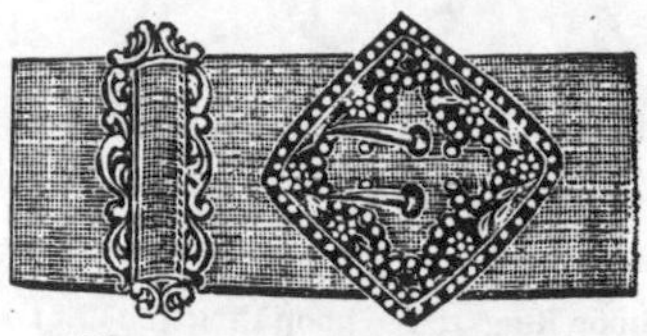

No. 62403. Buckle and Belt (width of belt 1⅛ in.) and attachments. Buckle is gold plated and ornamented with enamel, decorated with floral designs. Belt is fine gold plated, woven wire tinsel, full length, adjustable. Is very beautiful and stylish. Each, $2.25.

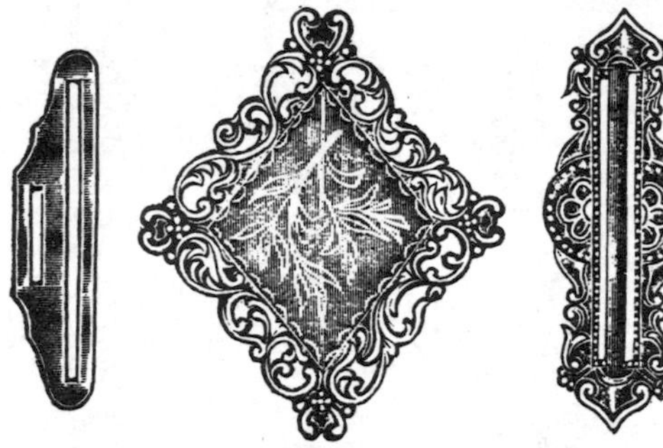

No. 62404. Buckle (size 3¼x2¾ in. for belt 2 ins. wide) and attachments. Fine gold plated on solid white metal and ornamented with bright cut engraving, which shows the white metal through the gold and produces a very beautiful effect. Each, $1.50.

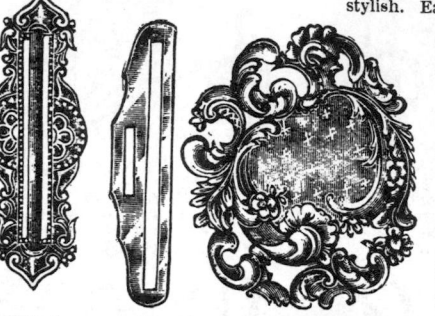

No. 62405. Buckle (size 3½x2½ ins. for belt 2 ins. wide) and attachments. Embossed pattern, quadruple silver plated and beautifully ornamented with decorated enamel center. Each, 75c.

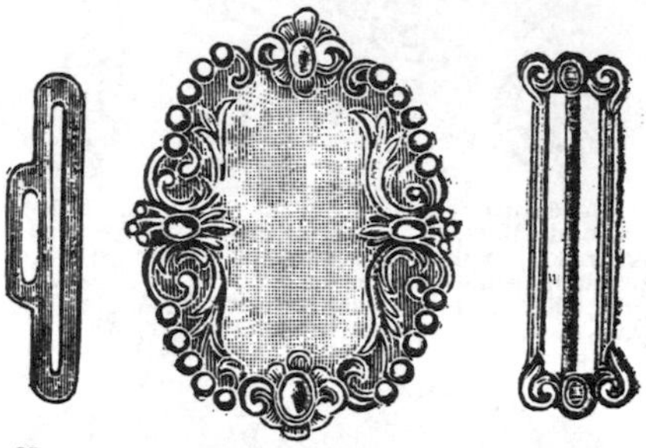

No. 62405. Buckle (size 3x2¼ ins. for belt 2 ins. wide) and attachments. Quadruple silver plated and ornamented with blue enamel in border. Each, 35c.

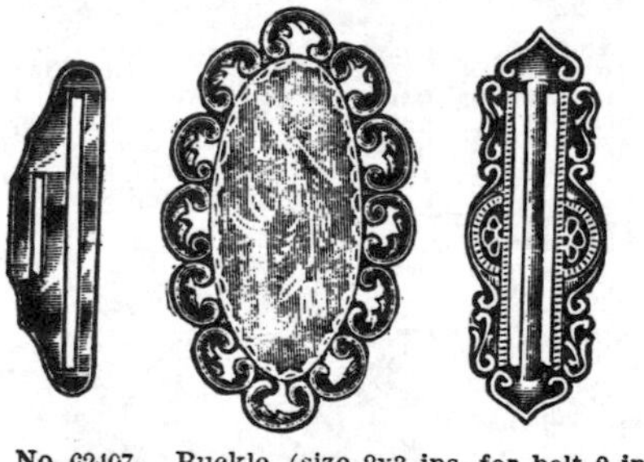

No. 62407. Buckle (size 2x3 ins. for belt 2 ins. wide) and attachments. Fine gold plated on solid white metal, and ornamented with beautiful, bright cut engraving, which shows the polished white metal through the gold plate. This is a very beautiful buckle to [illegible] the cut does not do justice. Each, $1.75.

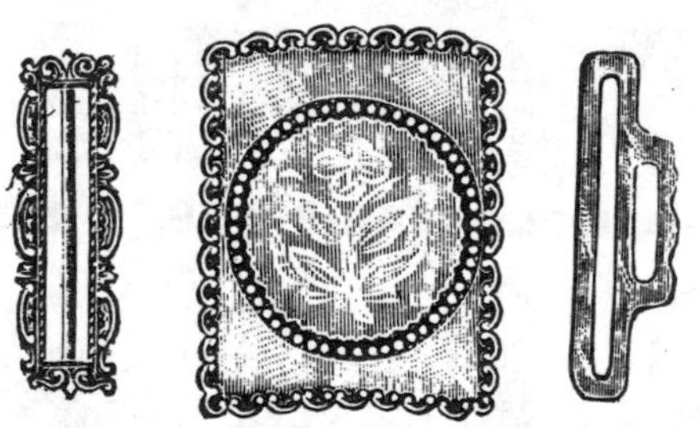

No. 62408. Buckle (size 2¾x2½ ins. for belt 2 ins. wide) and attachments. Quadruple silver plated, embossed border and [illegible] with bright cut engraving and enamel, in floral design, is modest and very pretty. Each, 60c.

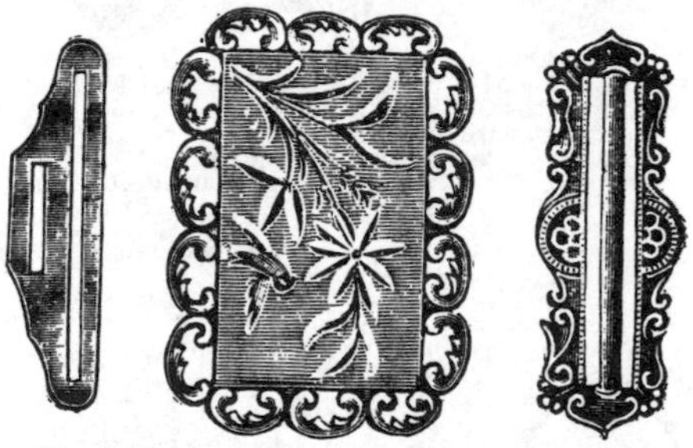

No. 62409. Buckle (size 2¾x2¼ ins. for belt 2 ins. wide) and attachments. Fine gold plated on solid white metal, embossed border and ornamented with bright cut engraving, which shows the polished white metal through the gold plate. The contrast produces a very beautiful effect. Price, $1.05.

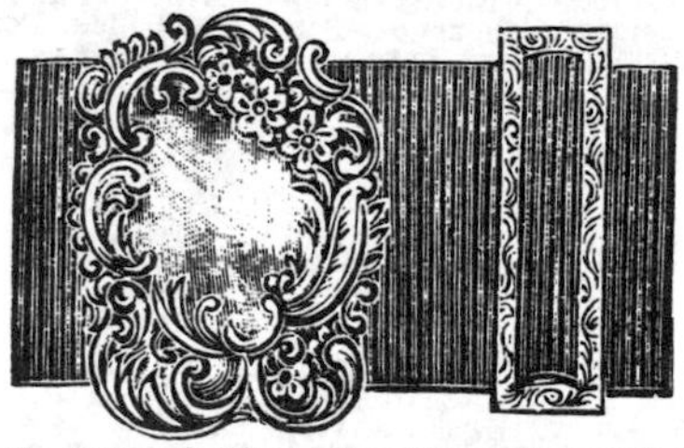

No. 62410. Solid Sterling Silver Embossed Buckle (size 2½x1⅞ ins.) and attachments. With best Silk Webb Adjustable Full Length Belt, assorted colors. Each, $1.50.

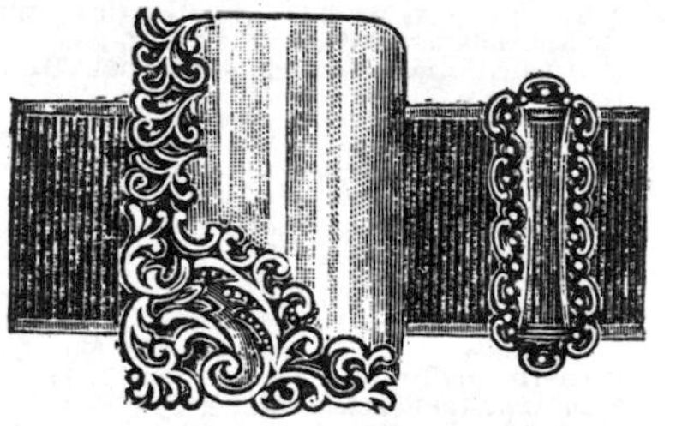

No. 62411. Solid sterling silver buckle (Size 2⅝x1¾ ins.) and attachments. Best silk web, adjustable full length belt, assorted colors. Each, $2.25.

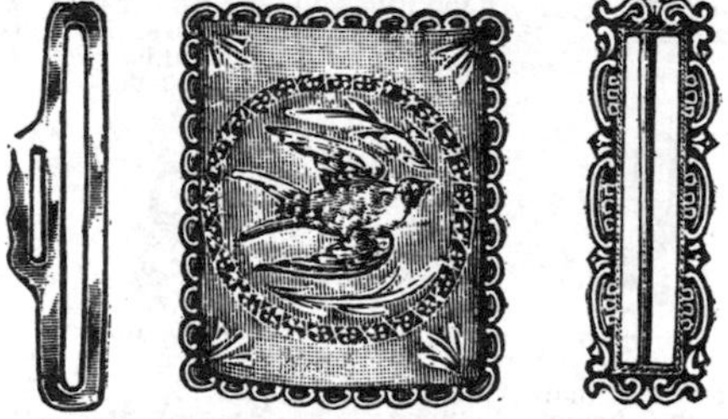

No. 62,412. Buckle (size 2¾x2⅛ ins.) and attachments. Quadruple silver plated on solid white metal, embossed border, bright cut engraving and ornamented with raised bird in center. Each. 75c.

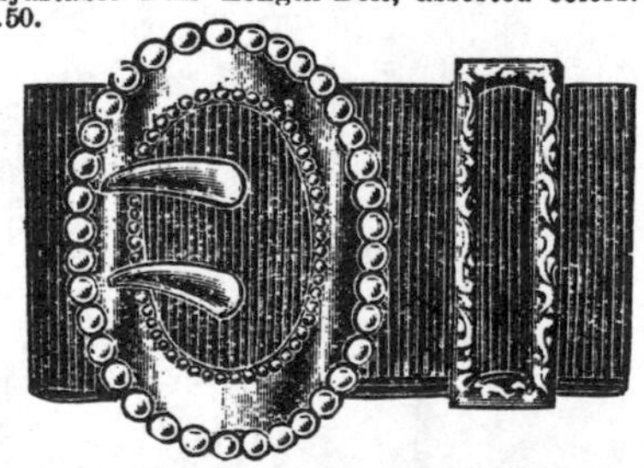

No. 62413. Solid sterling silver buckle (size 2⅞x2¼ ins.) and attachments. Very strong with embossed border, all bright polished, with best silk web, full length adjustable belt, assorted colors. Each, $2.75.

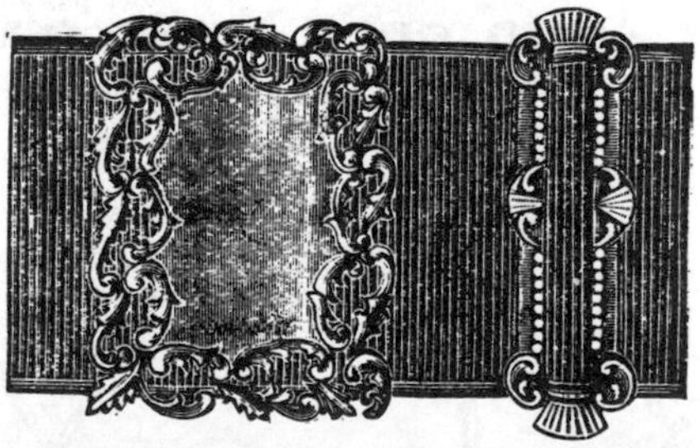

No. 62414. Solid sterling silver buckle (size 2¾x2 ins.) and attachments. Beautiful embossed border, satin finished center with best silk web, full length adjustable belt, assorted colors. Each, $3.00.

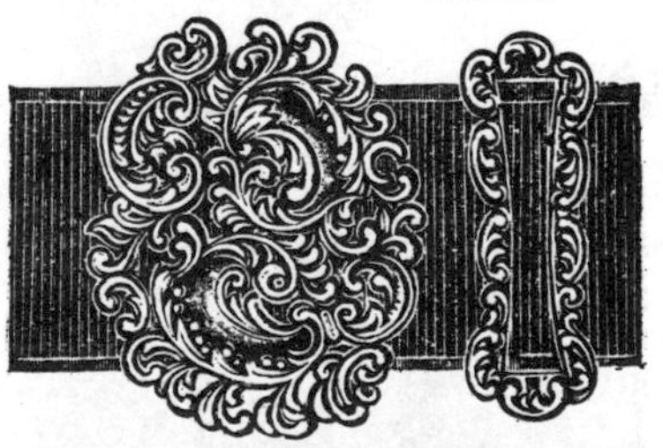

No. 62415. Solid sterling silver buckle (size 2⅝x1¾ ins.) and attachments. With beautiful embossed, open work border and center (showing the belt through the buckle) and two satin finished shields. Best silk web, full length adjustable belt, assorted colors. Each, $2.50.

No. 62416. Buckle (size 2 ins. for belt 1⅛ in. wide) and attachments. Quadruple silver plated on solid white metal embossed border and ornamented with bright cut engraving on satin finished center. Each, 45c.

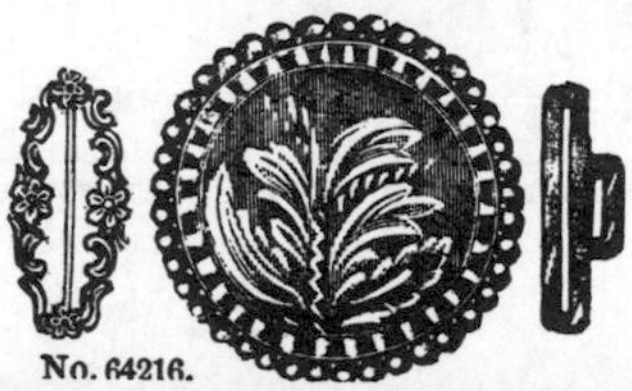

No. 64216.

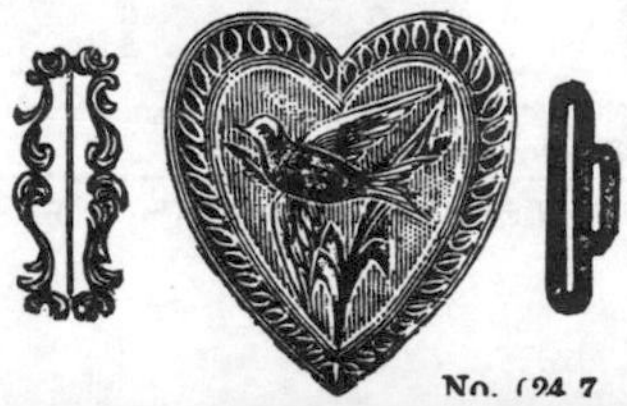

No. (24 7

No. 62417. Buckle (size 2⅛x1⅞ ins., for belt 1⅛ ins. wide) and attachments. Quadruple silver plated on solid white metal, embossed border with bright cut engraving, center satin finished with bright cut engraving and raised bird. Each, 45c.

# FOUNTAIN PENS.

Before listing a line of Fountain Pens we have taken every possible precaution and spared no pains to place at the disposal of our customers the best Pens made. There is probably nothing more annoying than a Fountain Pen of poor quality. We wish to direct your attention especially to the very simple manner of construction, and at the same time they have all the latest improvements. Every one of our Fountain Holders are fitted with a solid gold 16-karat Pen, (except the Globe, No. 62451, which has a solid gold 14-karat Pen.) They all have genuine iridium points (called diamond points), which will last with proper care for a lifetime. They have the latest improved feeds, both over and under, which insures a good flow of ink. The Holders are made of the very best quality of rubber, in a variety of styles, as shown in illustration, and are finished in the best possible manner. We have carefully investigated and thoroughly tested every line of Fountain Pens on the market, and we now feel that in offering you this line of Pens we can give you more value for the money than would be possible for us to do with any other line. Every one is thoroughly warranted by both the manufacturers and ourselves, and we will make good at any time any Pen which is found to be in bad order from defective material or workmanship. Of course, we cannot be responsible for accidents.

The market has been flooded with Pens of poor quality, and still sold at higher prices than we ask for the best goods. The Pens are of low grade, and will turn black or of a brownish color after being in use for a short time. They have poor points, which will soon wear out, and the material is so thin and poorly tempered that they have not the necessary elasticity. The holders are poorly constructed, the feeds fitted hurriedly and not of proper shape, which has been the means of many a person becoming disgusted with a Fountain Pen.

No. 62460. Gold filled, fancy chased Magic Pencil. Price, 95c. When closed the Pencil is about one-half the length as seen above.

No. 62461. Gold filled screw Pencil. Price, 80c. When not in use the point is drawn inside the case by simply turning the top. Toothpick of the same style can be furnished at the same price.

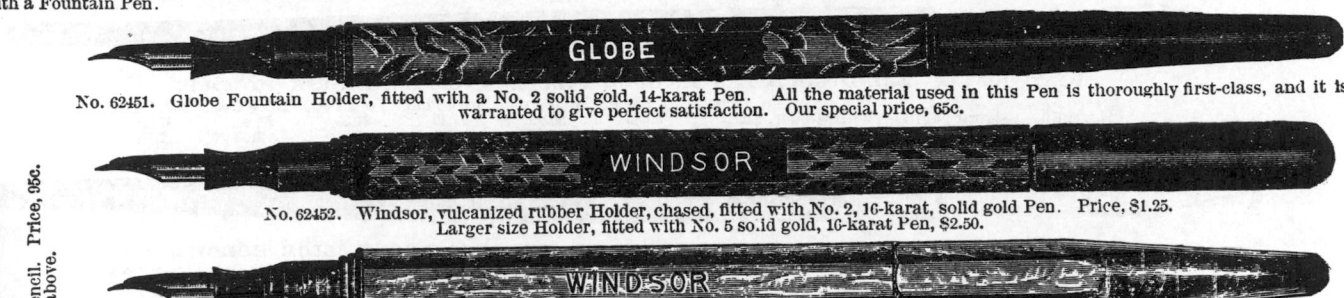

No. 62451. Globe Fountain Holder, fitted with a No. 2 solid gold, 14-karat Pen. All the material used in this Pen is thoroughly first-class, and it is warranted to give perfect satisfaction. Our special price, 65c.

No. 62452. Windsor, vulcanized rubber Holder, chased, fitted with No. 2, 16-karat, solid gold Pen. Price, $1.25.
Larger size Holder, fitted with No. 5 solid gold, 16-karat Pen, $2.50.

No. 62453. Windsor, black vulcanized rubber Holder, hexagonal shape, tapered cap, vented, fitted with No. 2 solid gold, 16-karat Pen. Price, $1.50.
Larger Holder, fitted with No. 5 solid gold, 16-karat Pen. Price, $2.75.

No. 62454. Windsor, black vulcanized rubber Holder, spiral finished, with tapered cap, vented, fitted with No. 2 solid gold, 16 karat Pen. Price, $2.35.
Can be furnished with black and brown variagated Holder at 25c extra, when desired

No. 62455. Ladies' Windsor, black vulcanized rubber Holder, chased finish, mounted with two gold-filled bands, taper cap, vented, fitted with No. 2 solid gold, 16-karat Pen. Price, $2.50. This Pen is made especially for ladies' use, and has met with enormous sales.

No. 62456. Columbian, vulcanized rubber Holder, chased finish, mounted with fine gold-filled bands and taper cap, vented, fitted with No. 2 solid gold, 16-karat Pen. Price, $2.75.
Larger holder, fitted with No. 5 solid gold, 16-karat Pen. Price, $3.25.

All of the above Fountain Pens are guaranteed to give satisfaction. Any that fail to do so can be returned to us for exchange, or money will be refunded, as desired. Do not question the quality of these goods because the prices are low. We guarantee them, without any exception, to be unsurpassed by any goods on the market.

## SOLID GOLD, GOLD FILLED AND STERLING SILVER PENS, PENCILS, HOLDERS AND PICKS.

Please read what we have to say regarding our gold Pens and Pencils on next page.

No. 62457. Solid sterling silver Holder, beautifully chased and tapered, very pretty and stylish. Price, $1.25.

No. 62458. Gold filled and ebony telescopic Holder, with best quality iridium pointed pens.

| | No. 3 Pen. | No. 4 Pen. | No. 5 Pen. | No. 6 Pen. | No. 7 Pen. |
|---|---|---|---|---|---|
| 10-karat Pen with Holder, | $1.10 | $1.20 | $1.55 | $1.95 | $2.30 |
| 16-karat Pen with Holder, | 1.35 | 1.60 | 1.95 | 2.30 | 2.75 |

No. 62459. Gold filled, improved telescopic Pen Holder and combined screw Pencil. When it is desired to use the Pencil the Pen can be slid back into the holder by means of a band on the outside, and the Pencil can be brought into position.

| | No. 3 Pen. | No. 4 Pen. | No. 5 Pen. | No. 6 Pen. |
|---|---|---|---|---|
| 16-karat Pen with Holder, | $1.95 | $2.50 | $2.75 | $3.45 |

No. 62462. Fine solid gold, fancy chased Toothpick and Ear Spoon. Price, $1.55.

Nos. 62462 and 62463 are made of fine solid gold throughout, and are exceptional value for the money. The Picks and Ear Spoon can be drawn inside of the case when not in use.

No. 62463. Fine solid gold, fancy chased, cut stone head Toothpick. Price, $1.50.

**GOLD PENS REPOINTED.**

## Finest Quality Solid Gold Pens.

Long Nib with Fine or Medium Points.

| No. 62464— | 10-karat. | 16-karat. |
|---|---|---|
| No. 1, | $0.42 | $0.54 |
| No. 2, | .45 | .63 |
| No. 3, | .50 | .76 |
| No. 4, | .60 | .89 |
| No. 5, | .80 | 1.05 |
| No. 6, | .90 | 1.27 |
| No. 7, | 1.10 | 1.40 |
| No. 8, | 1.53 | 1.73 |
| **STUB.** | | |
| No. 4, | .60 | .89 |
| No. 5, | .80 | 1.05 |
| No. 6, | .90 | 1.27 |
| No. 7, | 1.10 | 1.40 |

**LONG NIBS.**  **STUB.**

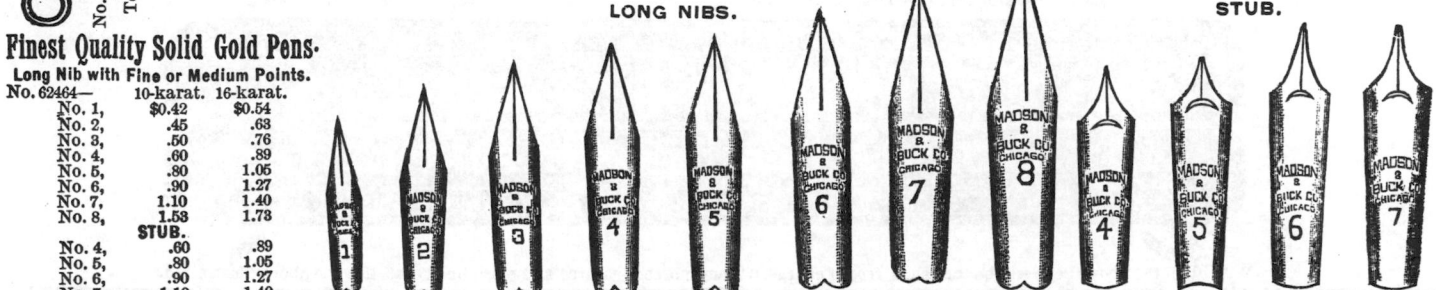

Postage on Fountain Pens, Holders and Picks, 3 cents. Registry or insurance extra.

If Jewelry is returned for exchange, or any other reason, be sure to follow instructions in front part of this book.

# FINEST QUALITY GOLD PENS AND HOLDERS.

Our Pens are all mounted with the best quality of gold filled stock, and are warranted not to tarnish. The pearl used is all of first quality, and is beautifully finished. Our gold Pens are all of the finest quality, solid gold through and through, heavy and well tempered, with genuine iridium points (called diamond points), perfectly finished, and with ordinary care will last a lifetime. The market has been filled with cheap, trashy gold Pens of low grade, which will soon turn brown, are not properly tempered and have not sufficient material to hold their elasticity; by reason of which they are of no value to write with, and certainly are not an ornament. The Holders are cheap plated goods, which will soon tarnish, and the pearl of third or fourth grade, which has no lustre; and even though they are sold for as much as we ask for first-class goods, they are of little value.

We take particular pride in offering you a line of solid gold Pens and gold filled mounted Holders, which is not surpassed by any on the market. These goods are largely sold for presentations, and as there is nothing more embarrassing than to make your friend a present of a worthless article, we advise you to buy none but the best.

These goods are made by one of the best and most reputable manufacturers of this line of goods, and are fully warranted to us. We guarantee them to our customers, and will gladly make good any Pen or Holder that is not fully equal to our description, or money will be refunded if you desire it.

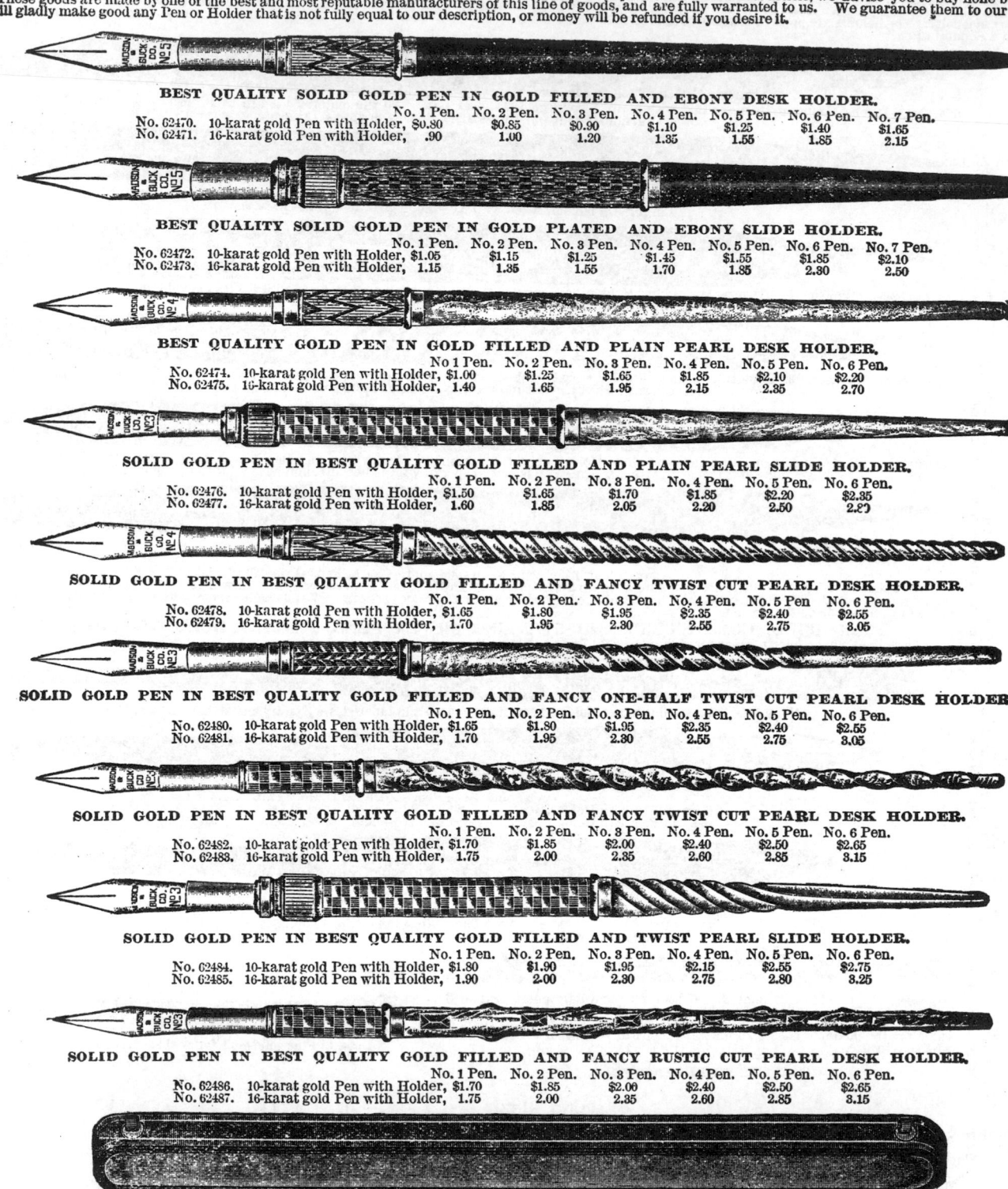

## BEST QUALITY SOLID GOLD PEN IN GOLD FILLED AND EBONY DESK HOLDER.

|  | No. 1 Pen. | No. 2 Pen. | No. 3 Pen. | No. 4 Pen. | No. 5 Pen. | No. 6 Pen. | No. 7 Pen. |
|---|---|---|---|---|---|---|---|
| No. 62470.  10-karat gold Pen with Holder, | $0.80 | $0.85 | $0.90 | $1.10 | $1.25 | $1.40 | $1.65 |
| No. 62471.  16-karat gold Pen with Holder, | .90 | 1.00 | 1.20 | 1.35 | 1.55 | 1.85 | 2.15 |

## BEST QUALITY SOLID GOLD PEN IN GOLD PLATED AND EBONY SLIDE HOLDER.

|  | No. 1 Pen. | No. 2 Pen. | No. 3 Pen. | No. 4 Pen. | No. 5 Pen. | No. 6 Pen. | No. 7 Pen. |
|---|---|---|---|---|---|---|---|
| No. 62472.  10-karat gold Pen with Holder, | $1.05 | $1.15 | $1.25 | $1.45 | $1.55 | $1.85 | $2.10 |
| No. 62473.  16-karat gold Pen with Holder, | 1.15 | 1.35 | 1.55 | 1.70 | 1.85 | 2.30 | 2.50 |

## BEST QUALITY GOLD PEN IN GOLD FILLED AND PLAIN PEARL DESK HOLDER.

|  | No 1 Pen. | No. 2 Pen. | No. 3 Pen. | No. 4 Pen. | No. 5 Pen. | No. 6 Pen. |
|---|---|---|---|---|---|---|
| No. 62474.  10-karat gold Pen with Holder, | $1.00 | $1.25 | $1.65 | $1.85 | $2.10 | $2.20 |
| No. 62475.  16-karat gold Pen with Holder, | 1.40 | 1.65 | 1.95 | 2.15 | 2.35 | 2.70 |

## SOLID GOLD PEN IN BEST QUALITY GOLD FILLED AND PLAIN PEARL SLIDE HOLDER.

|  | No. 1 Pen. | No. 2 Pen. | No. 3 Pen. | No. 4 Pen. | No. 5 Pen. | No. 6 Pen. |
|---|---|---|---|---|---|---|
| No. 62476.  10-karat gold Pen with Holder, | $1.50 | $1.65 | $1.70 | $1.85 | $2.20 | $2.35 |
| No. 62477.  16-karat gold Pen with Holder, | 1.60 | 1.85 | 2.05 | 2.20 | 2.50 | 2.80 |

## SOLID GOLD PEN IN BEST QUALITY GOLD FILLED AND FANCY TWIST CUT PEARL DESK HOLDER.

|  | No. 1 Pen. | No. 2 Pen. | No. 3 Pen. | No. 4 Pen. | No. 5 Pen | No. 6 Pen. |
|---|---|---|---|---|---|---|
| No. 62478.  10-karat gold Pen with Holder, | $1.65 | $1.80 | $1.95 | $2.35 | $2.40 | $2.55 |
| No. 62479.  16-karat gold Pen with Holder, | 1.70 | 1.95 | 2.30 | 2.55 | 2.75 | 3.05 |

## SOLID GOLD PEN IN BEST QUALITY GOLD FILLED AND FANCY ONE-HALF TWIST CUT PEARL DESK HOLDER.

|  | No. 1 Pen. | No. 2 Pen. | No. 3 Pen. | No. 4 Pen. | No. 5 Pen. | No. 6 Pen. |
|---|---|---|---|---|---|---|
| No. 62480.  10-karat gold Pen with Holder, | $1.65 | $1.80 | $1.95 | $2.35 | $2.40 | $2.55 |
| No. 62481.  16-karat gold Pen with Holder, | 1.70 | 1.95 | 2.30 | 2.55 | 2.75 | 3.05 |

## SOLID GOLD PEN IN BEST QUALITY GOLD FILLED AND FANCY TWIST CUT PEARL DESK HOLDER.

|  | No. 1 Pen. | No. 2 Pen. | No. 3 Pen. | No. 4 Pen. | No. 5 Pen. | No. 6 Pen. |
|---|---|---|---|---|---|---|
| No. 62482.  10-karat gold Pen with Holder, | $1.70 | $1.85 | $2.00 | $2.40 | $2.50 | $2.65 |
| No. 62483.  16-karat gold Pen with Holder, | 1.75 | 2.00 | 2.35 | 2.60 | 2.85 | 3.15 |

## SOLID GOLD PEN IN BEST QUALITY GOLD FILLED AND TWIST PEARL SLIDE HOLDER.

|  | No. 1 Pen. | No. 2 Pen. | No. 3 Pen. | No. 4 Pen. | No. 5 Pen. | No. 6 Pen. |
|---|---|---|---|---|---|---|
| No. 62484.  10-karat gold Pen with Holder, | $1.80 | $1.90 | $1.95 | $2.15 | $2.55 | $2.75 |
| No. 62485.  16-karat gold Pen with Holder, | 1.90 | 2.00 | 2.30 | 2.75 | 2.80 | 3.25 |

## SOLID GOLD PEN IN BEST QUALITY GOLD FILLED AND FANCY RUSTIC CUT PEARL DESK HOLDER.

|  | No. 1 Pen. | No. 2 Pen. | No. 3 Pen. | No. 4 Pen. | No. 5 Pen. | No. 6 Pen. |
|---|---|---|---|---|---|---|
| No. 62486.  10-karat gold Pen with Holder, | $1.70 | $1.85 | $2.00 | $2.40 | $2.50 | $2.65 |
| No. 62487.  16-karat gold Pen with Holder, | 1.75 | 2.00 | 2.35 | 2.60 | 2.85 | 3.15 |

With all of the above Pens will be furnished, free of charge, a fancy morocco-covered and plush-lined case, like the above illustration.

We guarantee safe delivery. You run no risk whatever. We also guarantee all goods sold by us to give entire satisfaction.

Postage on above goods, 3c; registry or insurance extra. Be sure to state how much is inclosed for postage, and follow instructions in front of book.

# FANCY HAIR ORNAMENTS AND HAT PINS.

**No. 62500.** Gold Filled Hat Pin, raised ornamentation, set with Emerald, 5½ inches long. Price, $1.25. Postage, 3 cents.

**No. 62501.** Gold Filled sword Hat or Hair Pin, very fancy Roman handle, set with eight Pearls and one Amethyst, bright polished Silver Blade 6½ inches long. Cut as ¾ size. Price, $2.15. Postage, 3 cents.

**No. 62502.** Gold Filled Hair Pin, fancy, engraved and ornamented, imitation Tortoise Shell prong, 5½ inches long. Cut as ½ size. Price, $1.15. Postage, 3 cents.

**No. 62503.** Heavy Gold plated and Solid Silver, with bright cut engraving to show Silver, very beautiful effect. Cut is about ½ size, top is 3½ inches wide, and Pin 6 inches long. Imitation of Tortoise Shell prong. Price, $3.95. Postage, 4 cents.

**No. 62504.** Gold Filled Hair Pin, very fancy, hand-engraved and ornamented. Cut as ¾ size' 6 inches long, imitation Tortoise Shell prongs. Price, $3.59. Postage, 4 cents.

## Silver, Gold Filled and Solid Gold Thimbles. Postage, 2 Cents.

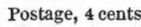

**No. 62506.** Solid Silver. Price, $0.20.

**No. 62607.** Solid Silver. Price, $0.30.

**No. 62508.** Solid Silver, beautifully engraved. Price, $0.45.

**No. 62509.** Solid Silver, hand-engraved. Price, $0.55.

**No. 62510.** Gold Filled, warranted. Price, $0.75.

**No. 62511.** Gold Filled, engraved, warranted. Price, $1.15.

**No. 62512.** Solid 10-karat Gold. Price, $1.90.

**No. 62512½.** Solid 14-karat Gold. Price, $3.75.

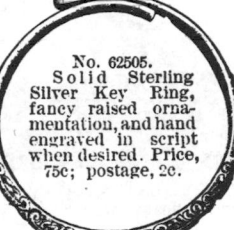

**No. 62505.** Solid Sterling Silver Key Ring, fancy raised ornamentation, and hand engraved in script when desired. Price, 75c; postage, 2c.

## SOLID STERLING SILVER MOUNTED GOODS.

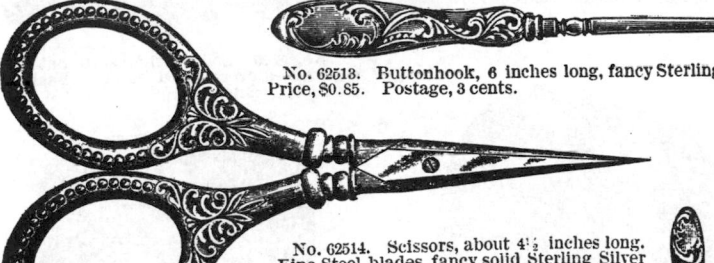

**No. 62513.** Buttonhook, 6 inches long, fancy Sterling Silver handle. Price, $0.85. Postage, 3 cents.

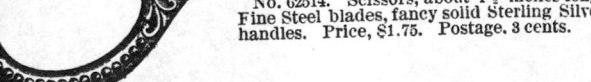

**No. 62514.** Scissors, about 4½ inches long. Fine Steel blades, fancy solid Sterling Silver handles. Price, $1.75. Postage, 3 cents.

**No. 62515.** Scissors, 4⅗ inches long. Fine Steel blades, very fancy, Solid Sterling Silver handles. Price, $2.00. Postage, 3 cents.

**No. 62517.** Hair Curler. Fancy Solid Sterling Silver handle, length 6¾ inches. Price, $0.90. Postage, 4 cents.

**No. 62516.** Scissors, 4 inches long. Fine Steel blades, very fancy Solid Sterling Silver handles. Price, $1.50. Postage, 3 cents.

**No. 62519.** Manicure and Buttonhook set, fancy, Solid Sterling Silver handles, length, 3½ inches. Per set, $0.95. Postage, 4 cents.

**No. 62518.** Nail Cleaner and File, fancy, Solid Sterling Silver handle, length 5½ inches. Price, $0.85. Postage, 3 cents.

**No. 62520.** Silk Satin Garter. Solid Sterling Silver Mountings, very fancy, raised ornamentation. Price, $1.90. Postage, 4 cents.

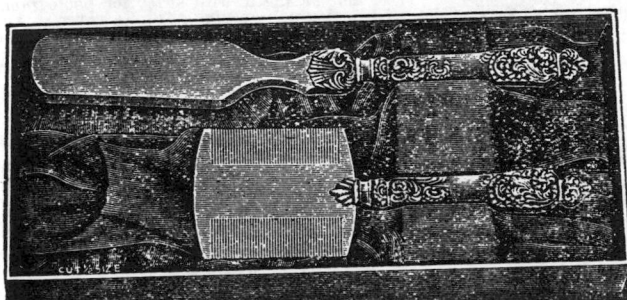

**No. 62521.** Child's Toilet Set, consisting of Comb and Brush; fancy Solid Sterling Silver handles, in fancy satin lined case. Price, $1.85. Postage, 6 cents.

**No. 62522.** Chamois Nail Polisher, fancy Solid Sterling Silver mountings. Price, $1.90. Postage, 4 cents.

# GOLD HEADED CANES.

Guaranteed best quality gold headed canes, mounted on fine polished genuine ebony sticks.

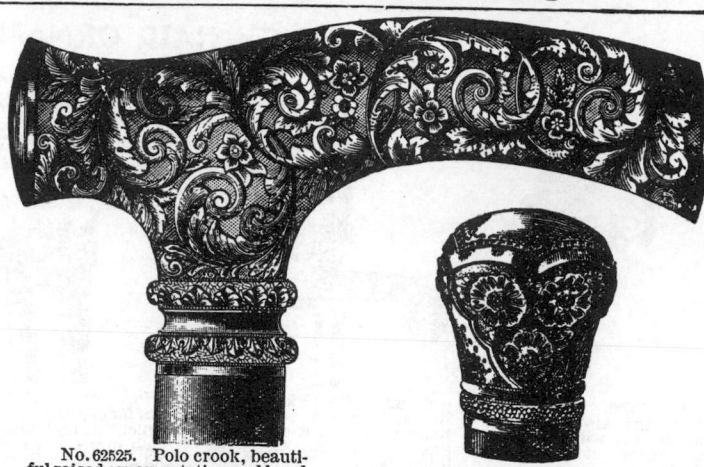

No. 62523. Round head, raised ornamentation and hand engraved, plain polished top, ⅝-in. stick, 10 karat gold. Each, $4.45.

No. 62524. Round head, fancy, raised ornamentation and hand engraved, plain polished top, ⅝-in. stick, 14 karat gold. Each, $6.95.

No. 62525. Polo crook, beautiful raised ornamentation and hand engraved, polished ends, ⅝-in. stick, 10 karat. Each, $9.95.
Same in 14 karat. Each, $14.90.

No. 62526. Round head, raised ornamentation and hand engraved, plain polished top, stick ⅝-in., 10 karat gold. Each, $3.50.

Any of the above mountings can be engraved with any name or inscription in script at 2½ cents per letter, or old English 5½ cents per letter. We will send any of these canes to any address C. O. D., subject to examination, on receipt of 50 cents with order, as guarantee of good faith. If you wish us to engrave canes, or other goods, cash in full must accompany the order, as they could not be sold to anyone else if for any reason they were not accepted. Canes cannot go by mail.

## Fine Sterling Silver and Gold Filled Novelties.

All of our sterling silver goods are solid sterling silver, $\frac{925}{1000}$ fine through and through, and are fully warranted.

No. 62527. Solid sterling silver coat hanger, heavy and strong. Each, 75c. Postage, 2 cents.

No. 62528. Knife, solid sterling silver handle, beaded border, with two fine quality steel blades. Each, 95c. Postage, 2 cents.

No. 62529. Solid sterling silver hat mark, with raised ornamented border. Each, 20c. Postage, 2 cents.

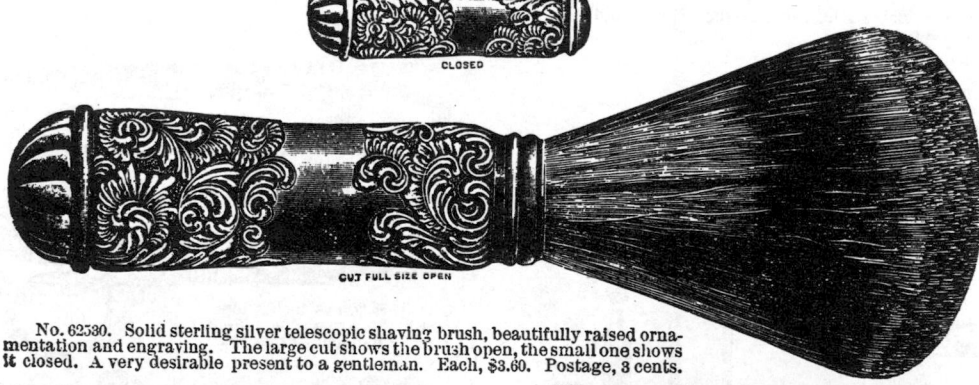

CLOSED

CUT FULL SIZE OPEN

No. 62530. Solid sterling silver telescopic shaving brush, beautifully raised ornamentation and engraving. The large cut shows the brush open, the small one shows it closed. A very desirable present to a gentleman. Each, $3.60. Postage, 3 cents.

No. 62536. Match Safe, solid sterling silver, embossed ornamentation and engraving with spring top. Price, $1.35.

No. 62537. Match Safe, satin finished with very fancy raised and embossed ornamentation with spring top. Price, $1.65.

No. 62532. Solid sterling silver match safe, with beautiful raised ornamentation, and arranged with space for photograph; photograph opening has mica cover. Any photo of the proper size can be fitted in and changed when desired. Each, $2.85.
Same in white metal, silver plated. Each, 95c. Postage, 3 cents.

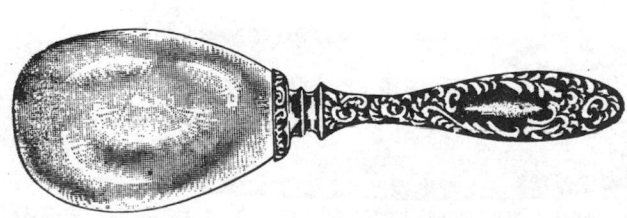

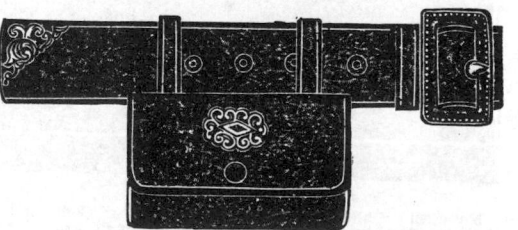

No. 62533. Solid sterling silver mounted hose darner. The ball is made of enameled wood, while the handle is made of solid sterling silver, with raised ornamentation. The handle is detachable, and has a receptacle on the inside for needles. A very desirable present for an elderly lady or anyone who has such work to do. Each, $1.75. Postage, 5 cents.

No. 62534. Solid sterling silver garter buckle, and garter complete. Buckle is heavy, has raised ornamentation and bright cut hand engraved. Each complete, $2.25.
No. 62534½. Buckle only. Each, $1.75. Postage, 2 cents.

No. 62535. Ladies' bicycle belt and buckle, made of real seal. Belt 1¾ in. wide, full length, adjustable, with black buckle and solid silver ornaments. The purse is made of seal skin with solid silver name plate, embossed and engraved. A very useful article for a lady who rides a bicycle. Price complete, $2.25.

# SOLID STERLING SILVER AND SILVER-MOUNTED NOVELTIES.

These goods are the finest on the market and very desirable for presentations.

No. 62538. Hair Brush, solid black celluloid handle, beautifully grained, with solid sterling silver, raised, ornamental mountings, has aluminum bristle supports, heavy stiff bristles, and is so arranged as to be very easily cleaned. It is impossible for us to describe or give by illustration any idea of the beauty of this brush; length, 9¼ inches. Price, $2.25. Postage, 6 cents.

No. 62541. Baby Rattle, heavy solid **pearl** ring, with two solid sterling silver bells. **Price, 98** cents. Postage, 2 cents.

No. 62539. Imitation Tortoise Shell Comb, solid sterling silver, raised, ornamented mounting; length, 6⅞ inches. Postage, 3 cents. Price, 98 cents.

No. 62539½. Larger and heavier Comb, with very heavy, full sterling silver back, raised, ornamented. Price, $1.95. Postage, 4 cents.

No. 62542. Imitation Tortoise Shell Side Combs, solid sterling silver, raised, ornamental mountings. Per pair, $1.30. Postage, 2 cents.

No. 62540. Solid Sterling Silver Handkerchief Holder, raised, ornamented and bright cut, hand engraved, center satin finished; has pin on back to attach to dress. Price, 85 cents. Postage, 2 cents.

No. 62543. Fine, solid sterling silver-mounted Hair Brush. Price, $1.90. Postage, 6 cents. (Cut is about one-fourth size).

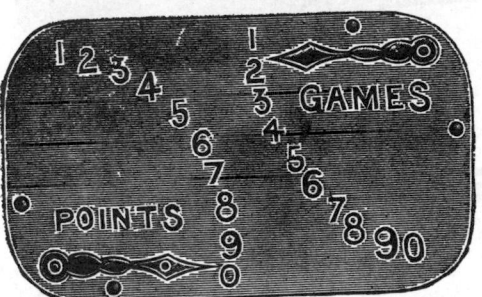

No. 62544. Game Counter, made of solid mother of pearl, with solid sterling silver pointers and stops; figures and letters are of black enamel. Price, 93 cents. Postage, 2 cents.

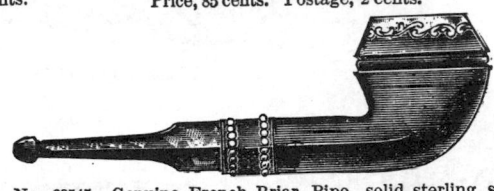

No. 62545. Genuine French Briar Pipe, solid sterling silver, raised, ornamental mountings, genuine Amber mouthpiece. Price, $1.60. Postage, 4 cents.

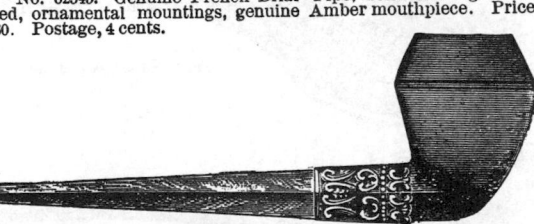

No. 62546. Genuine French Briar Pipe, with solid sterling silver, raised, ornamented mounting, long genuine amber mouthpiece. Price, $2.50. Postage, 4 cents.

No. 62547. Satchel Tag, heavy **solid** sterling silver, with raised ornamentation; satin space for name. Price, 75 cents. Postage, 2 cents.
(We can furnish solid silver **tags for** about one-half the above price, but **they** are so light that we could not recommend them.)

No. 62548. Match Safe, genuine seal leather, solid sterling silver, raised, ornamented mounting. Price, 50 cents. Postage, 2 cents.
(Cut is full size. Are sometimes used to attach to one end of a Dickens or Wellington Chain.)

No. 62549. Fine black grained leather Cigar Case, solid sterling silver, raised, ornamented mounting, satin finished center. Size, 3¼x4¾. Price, $1.60. Postage, 3 cents.

No. 62550. Memorandum Book and Case, made of genuine seal; book is interchangeable, has solid sterling silver, raised, ornamented mounting and pencil with rubber. Size, 2⅜x4¼. Price, 95 cents. Postage, 2 cents.

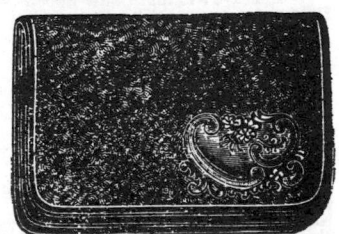

No. 62551. Ladies' genuine Seal Purse, beautifully finished, with solid sterling silver, raised, ornamented mounting and satin space for name. Size, 2½x3¼. Price, $1.25. Postage, 3 cents.

## ALASKA SILVERWARE.—A New Discovery.

**The cheapest and best flat ware made.** The Alaska Silverware is not plated, but is the same solid metal through and through, and will hold the same color as long as there is any portion of the goods left. Do not be deceived by any dealer who undertakes to sell you any of the numerous imitations of this ware that are sold on the market for more money than we ask for the genuine. The genuine Alaska Silverware can be had only of us.

Before taking hold of this new discovery we left nothing undone to thoroughly investigate the properties of this metal, and to test the same in every conceivable manner to satisfy ourselves that it was all that it was represented to be. After having made all sorts of experiments, and it stood all tests, we made a contract with the factory to handle the goods. It has now been about two years since we began to handle this line, and it has not only proved from experiment to be as represented, but with two years of actual service in the hands of many thousands of our customers, who send us the most flattering recommendations in praise of these goods, and with the rapidly increasing sales, we feel that we cannot recommend it too highly.

The metal is very dense and tough, is almost as white as genuine silver, takes a beautiful polish and requires no care as does silver plated ware. You can scrape kettles or pots, or subject it to any kind of service without fear of damage.

We have this year added a beautiful engraved pattern, which is equal in appearance and artistic finish to any of the best silver plated or solid silver goods on the market. The engravings are as fine as can be made, the handles of an oval shape, and will be furnished at only a slight advance over the prices of the plain pattern. The immense quantities of these goods we handle, and the condition of our contract direct with the factory, puts us in position to furnish this genuine Alaska Silverware at a slight advance over cost to manufacture.

### Hereafter all these Goods except the Knives will be Stamped "Sears, Roebuck & Co.'s Alaska Silverware."

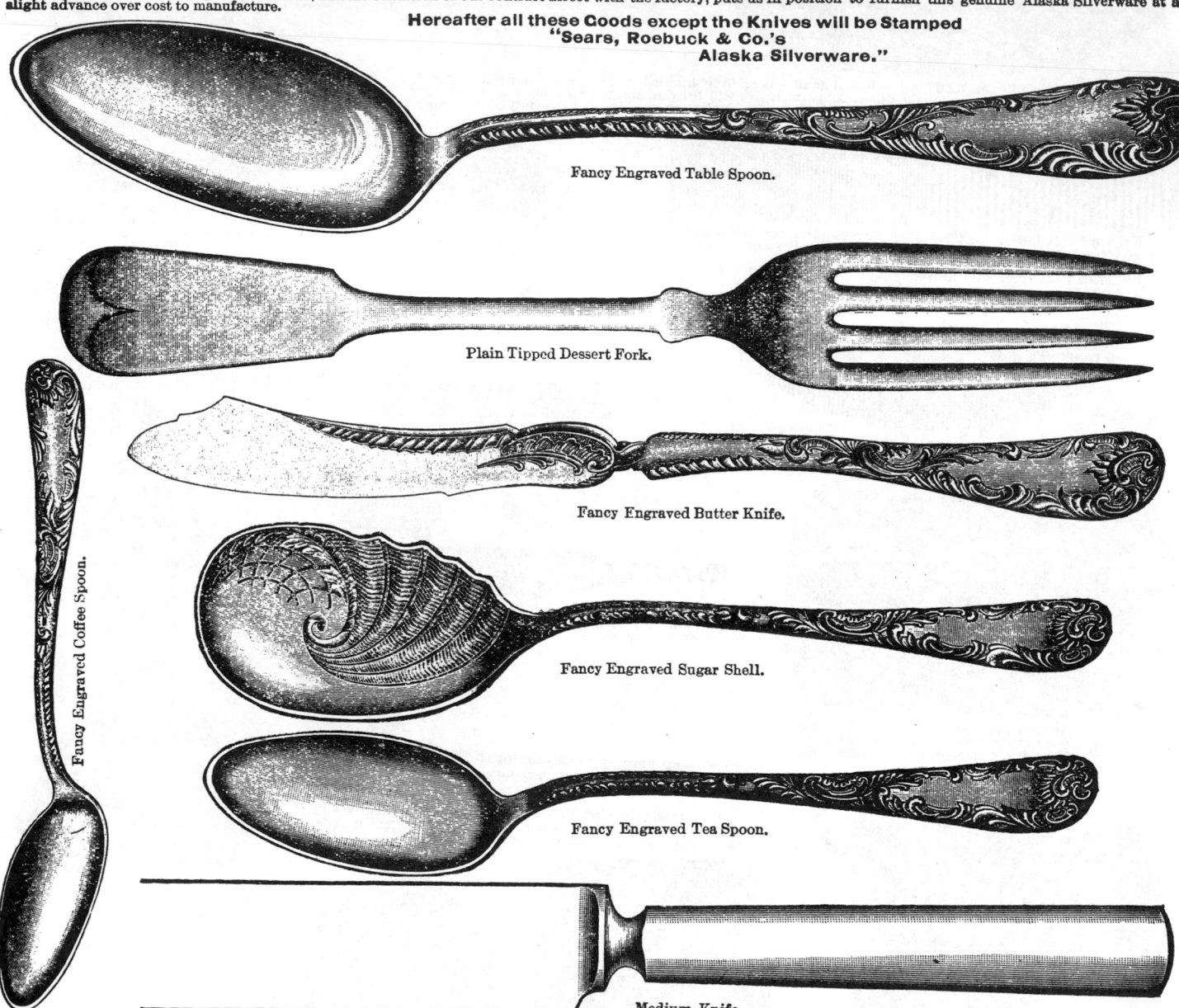

Fancy Engraved Table Spoon.

Plain Tipped Dessert Fork.

Fancy Engraved Butter Knife.

Fancy Engraved Coffee Spoon.

Fancy Engraved Sugar Shell.

Fancy Engraved Tea Spoon.

Medium Knife.

**Relative lengths:** Coffee Spoons, 4¾ inches; Teas, 5¾ inches; Dessert Spoons, 7¼ inches; Table Spoons, 8¼ inches; Dessert Forks, 7 inches; Medium Forks, 7½ inches; Dessert Knives, 8 inches; Medium Knives, 9 inches; Sugar Shells, 5¾ inches; Butter Knives, 7 inches.

### OUR SPECIAL PRICES.

Any of these goods can be sent by mail on receipt of price and additional amount named to pay postage.

Plain tipped pattern (like fork above).

|  |  | | | |  |
|---|---|---|---|---|---|
| No. 62600. | Coffee Spoons | | set of ½ doz., | | $0.51 |
| No. 62601. | Tea " | " | " | " | .51 |
| No. 62602. | Dessert " | " | " | " | .85 |
| No. 62603. | Table " | " | " | " | 1.02 |
| No. 62604. | Medium Forks (regular size) | " | " | " | 1.02 |
| No. 62605. | Dessert " | " | " | " | .85 |
| No. 62606. | Plain handle Dessert Knives | " | " | " | 1.10 |
| No. 62607. | " medium " | " | " | " | 1.25 |
| No. 62608. | Sugar Shells | | | each, | .15 |
| No. 62609. | Butter Knives | | | " | .15 |

Fancy Engraved like all but the Fork above.

|  |  | | | |  |
|---|---|---|---|---|---|
| No. 62610. | Coffee Spoons | | set of ½ doz., | | $0.56 |
| No. 62611. | Tea " | " | " | " | .56 |
| No. 62612. | Dessert " | " | " | " | .90 |
| No. 62613. | Table " | " | " | " | 1.07 |
| No. 62614. | Medium Forks (regular size) | " | " | " | 1.07 |
| No. 62615. | Dessert " | " | " | " | .90 |
| No. 62616. | Sugar Shells | | | each, | .16 |
| No. 62617. | Butter Knives | | | | 16 |

Postage on the above goods, if to go by mail, will be extra per ½ dozen as follows: On coffee spoons, 5 cents; tea spoons, 6 cents; dessert spoons or forks, 12 cents; table spoons or medium forks, 15 cents; sugar shells (or butter knives, 2 cents; and dessert or medium knives, 18 cents. It is cheaper to send them by express, if you have an express office near by.

**The standard of quality and finish** of the above goods **are guaranteed** by the manufacturer to us, and we guarantee them to our customers. You run no risk whatever in purchasing this ware, for if you do not find them to be exactly as represented, they can be returned to us and your money will be refunded. Be sure to state catalogue number and pattern wanted when you order.

We will send any of the above goods by express, C. O. D., subject to examination, providing a deposit of $1 as a guarantee of good faith is sent with order.

The best way is to send cash in full and save the discount of 3 per cent and charges on the collection.

# FINE SILVER PLATED WARE.

**On Silverware of all kinds we take the lead. Others follow.** They are either unable or unwilling to sell goods at the prices we do. We are satisfied with small profits, and buy at prices that put us in position to furnish you goods as cheap as your retail dealer can buy them. On goods illustrated on this page we can save you at least 50 per cent.

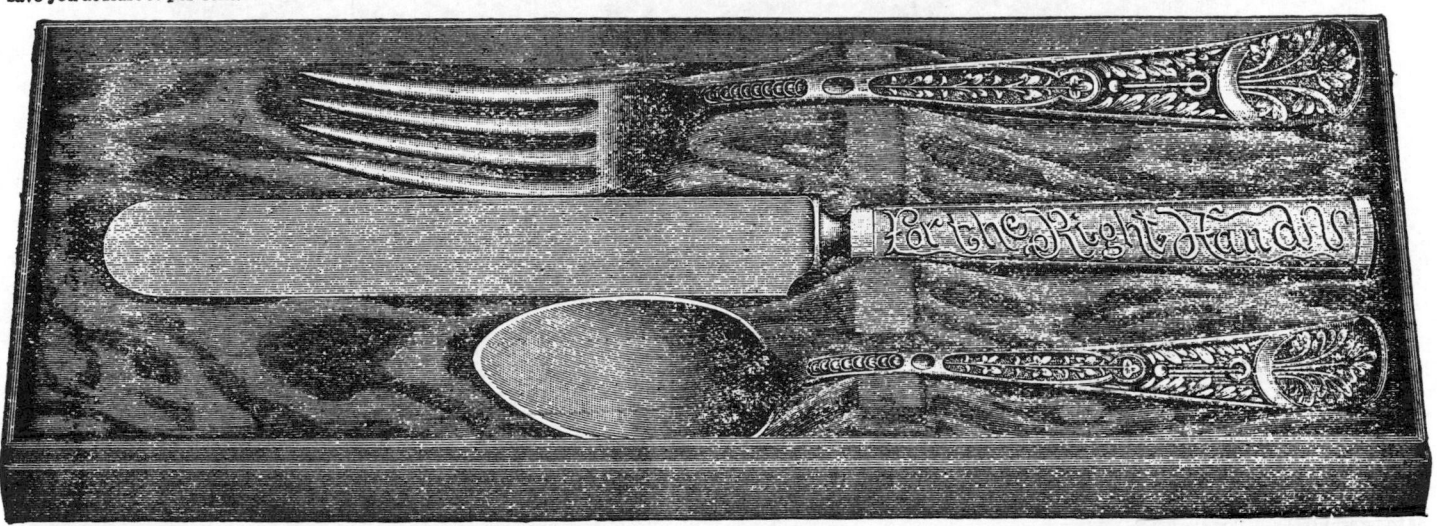

No. 62619. **Kindergarten Child's Set** of three fine silver plated pieces, consisting of knife, fork and spoon in satin lined box with cover. Price, 70c. If to go by mail, postage extra, 7c.

No. 62620. **Silver plated Pepper or Salt.** Is plated on fine nickel silver metal. Price, each, 18c. If to go by mail, postage extra, 4c.

Do not compare these goods with the cheap Britannia ware, which is poorly finished and plated with tin instead of silver.

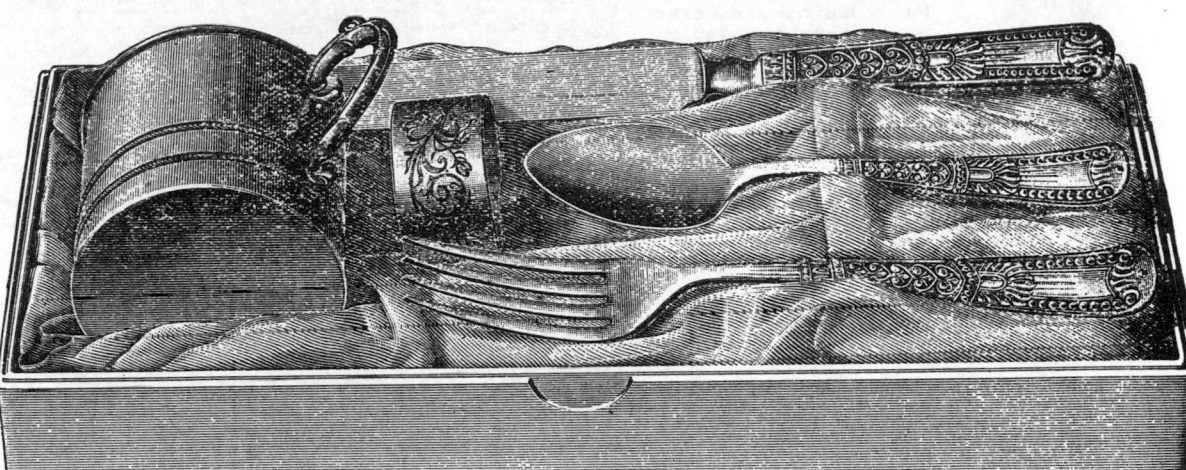

No. 62621. **Five Piece Child's Set,** consisting of knife, fork, spoon, cup and napkin ring. Cut is two-thirds size. The cup and napkin ring are made of solid nickel silver; the knife, spoon and fork of fine hard metal. All are plated with coin silver, and make a very beautiful and serviceable set, in satin lined box with cover. Price, complete, $1. If to go by mail, postage extra, 14c.

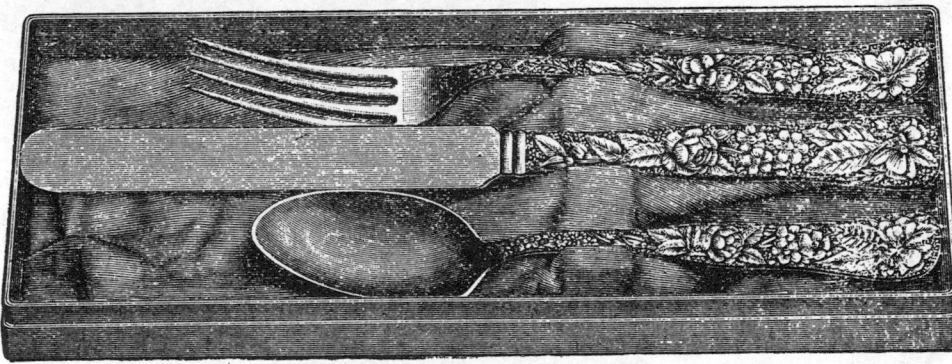

No. 62623. **Three Piece Child's Set,** made of fine steel heavily plated with coin silver, in satin lined box; is beautifully engraved and well finished in every respect. Our sales on this set are very large, and by making a special contract we are in position to give exceptional value. Our special price for the complete set, 45c. If to be sent by mail, extra, 7c.

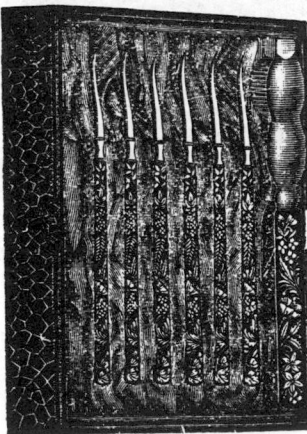

No. 62622. **Nut Crack Set,** in satin lined box. The set consists of six picks and one nut crack, all made of fine steel, beautifully finished and engraved, and triple plated with coin silver. Per set, $1.60. If to be sent by mail, extra, 15c.

(The above cut is reduced size. Goods are regular size.)

No. 62624. **Fruit Knives,** set of six in a box. These knives are made of solid cast steel, well finished, and are plated with coin silver. Our special price per set of six, 95c. If by mail, extra, 15c.

We give a discount of 3 per cent. for cash in full with your orders; 4 per cent. on orders over $50; 5 per cent. on orders over $100.

**You run no risk. We will refund all your money if you are not satisfied with your purchase.**

## FINE SILVER PLATED TABLE WARE.

All goods listed below, with the exception of the Knives and Knife Handled Forks, are made of fine composition metal in beautifully engraved and embossed designs, and are plated with genuine coin silver. The Knives and Knife Handled Forks are made of solid cast steel, and are plated with pure coin silver. All these goods are most excellent values for the money and are guaranteed to be as represented.

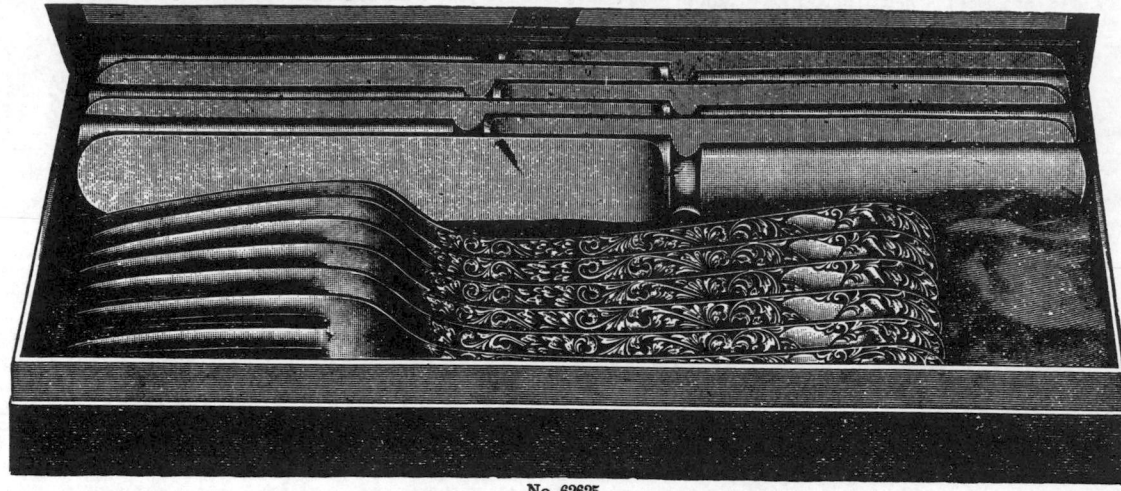

No. 62625.

No. 62625. Set of six each **Medium Table Knives and Victoria Pattern Forks** in satin lined box. The Knives have plain handles, but the Forks are engraved like the Victoria Pattern Spoon below. They are heavily silver plated, the Forks on fine composition metal and the Knives on solid cast steel. Per set, $2.00. If to be sent by mail, postage extra, 35c.

Nevada Pattern.

No. 62626. Set of six each, **Fancy Knives and Forks with engraved handles.** Both the Knives and Forks are made of solid cast steel with a heavy plate of coin silver, and are finished in a very thorough manner. Cut is reduced but the goods are full regular size, all put up in a neat satin lined box. Per set, $2.60. If to be sent by mail, postage extra, 35c.

No. 62627. **Nevada Pattern Sugar Shell and Butter Knife,** made of fine composition metal, plated with pure coin silver, beautifully finished and engraved; the two pieces in satin lined box. Price, 35c. If to go by mail, postage extra, 5c.

### NEVADA PATTERN SILVER PLATED WARE.

The Nevada ware is made of fine composition metal, heavily plated with pure coin silver, is beautifully ornamented and engraved and warranted to give entire satisfaction. This ware is put up in lots of ½ dozen each, without boxes, and will not be sold in smaller quantity than three pieces of any one kind.

No. 62634. Coffee Spoons, per ½ dozen, 60c.
No. 62635. Tea Spoons, per ½ dozen, 60c.
No. 62636. Table Spoons, per ½ dozen, $1.15.
No. 62637. Medium Forks, per ½ dozen, $1.15.
No. 62638. Sugar Shell, each, 16c.
No. 62639. Butter Knife, each, 23c.

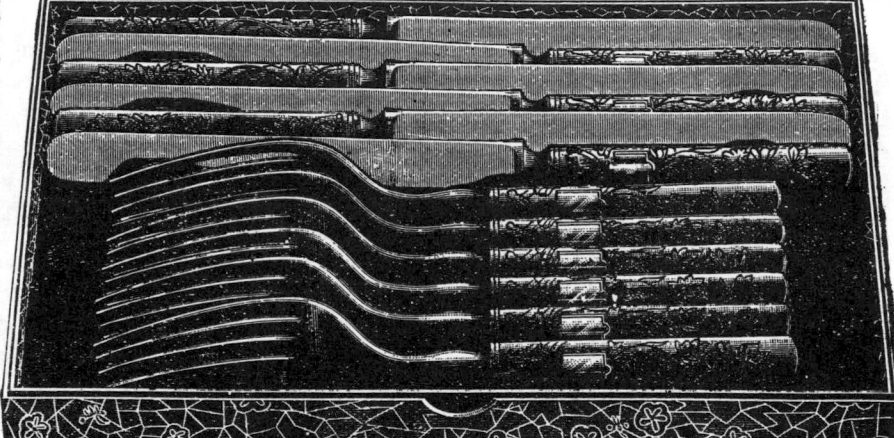

No. 62626.

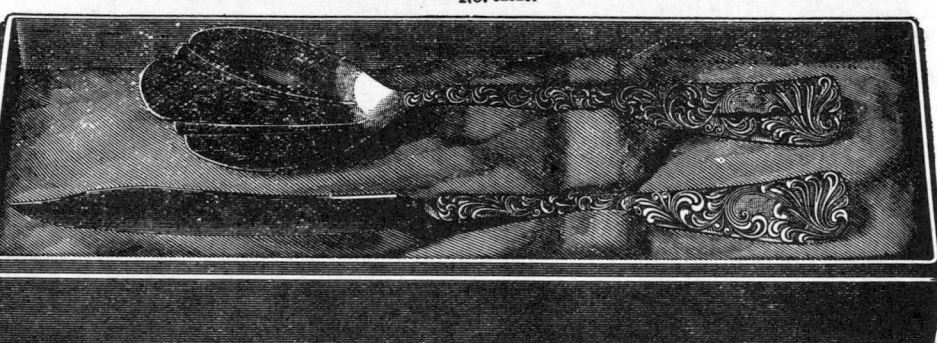

No. 62627.

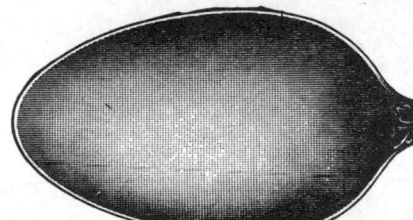

Victoria Pattern.

### FINE VICTORIA PATTERN PLATED WARE.

This ware is made of fine composition metal, heavily plated with pure coin silver, is beautifully engraved, well finished and guaranteed to be as represented. We quote this ware in lots of ½ dozen each, without boxes, and will not sell a smaller quantity than three pieces of any one kind.

| | | |
|---|---|---|
| No. 62628. Coffee Spoons, per set of six, 40c. | No. 62630. Table Spoons, per set of six, 80c. | No. 62632. Sugar Shell, each, 12c. |
| No. 62629. Tea Spoons, per set of six, 40c. | No. 62631. Medium Forks, per set of six, 80c. | No. 62633. Butter Knife, each, 16c. |

If to go by mail the postage on the Victoria and Nevada unboxed goods will be extra as follows: Coffee Spoons, 5c; Tea Spoons, 6c; Table Spoons, 15c; Medium Forks, 15c; Sugar Shells, 2c; Butter Knife, 2c.

The illustrations of boxed goods above are all reduced, but the goods are full regular size.

**Buy jewelry and silverware of a reliable concern.** We guarantee everything we sell, and what's more we always make our guarantee good. Flat silverware will be sent C. O. D., when desired, on receipt of $1 with order. Balance payable after goods have been examined.

# WILLIAM ROGERS' AND C. ROGERS' FINE SILVER PLATED GOODS IN PLUSH LINED BOXES.

These goods are all of fine quality, made of solid white metal and heavily plated with pure coin silver. Both of the above manufacturers have been prominent in the silverware business for years, are well known and make nothing but the best goods.

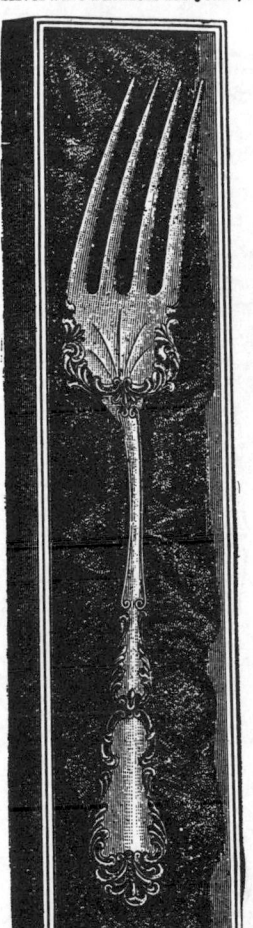

No. 62634.

No. 62635.

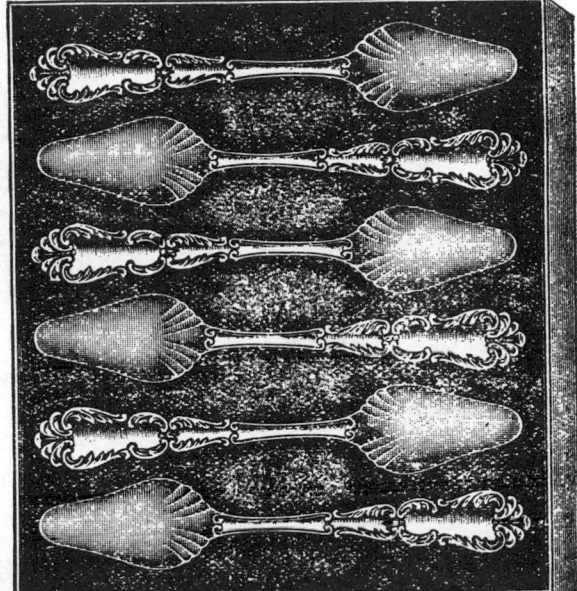

No. 62636.

No. 62635. **Sugar Shell and Butter Knife, Regent pattern**, very fancy, made by **C. Rogers & Bros.**, in fine plush lined box. Price, per set, 95c.

No. 62635¼. **Sugar Shell only**, in plush lined box. Price, 45c.

No. 62635½. **Butter Knife only**, in plush lined box. Price, 50c.

Gold plated bowl on Sugar Shell 20c extra.

Gold plated blade on Butter Knife, 30c extra.

No. 62636. **Regent pattern, Orange Spoons**, in fine plush lined box, fancy pattern, and are made by **C. Rogers & Bros.** Price per set of 6, $1.65.

Same as above, with gold plated bowls, extra, $1.

No. 62634. **Regent pattern, Cold Meat Fork**, made by **C. Rogers & Bros.**, fancy pattern, in fine plush lined box. Price, $1.

No. 62637. **Yale pattern, Berry Spoon**, in plush lined box, is made by the Wm. Rogers Mfg. Co., is very fancy, a real work of art. Price each, $1.25.

Note—Same as above with gold plated bowl, extra, 35c.

No. 62638. **Regent pattern, Berry set**, in fine plush lined box, is made by **C. Rogers & Bros.**, is finished in the best possible manner, and is a most beautiful set. Price, per set of one spoon and six forks, $2.90.

For set with bowl of spoon gold plated, 40c extra.

All of the above cuts are considerably reduced, but the goods are full regular size. All goods on this page are fully guaranteed by both the manufacturers and ourselves.

**We want your trade, and we are in position to serve you as no other concern can. Best goods, largest variety, lowest prices and quick service.**

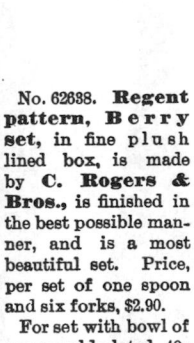
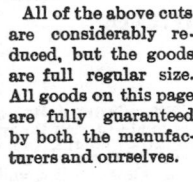

No. 62637.

No. 62638.

# C. ROGERS & BROS.' FINE SILVER PLATED WARE.

## THESE GOODS ARE MANUFACTURED BY C. ROGERS & BROS., OF MERIDEN, CONN.

They are made of solid white metal, heavily plated with coin silver, are well known and guaranteed by both the manufacturers and ourselves to give entire satisfaction. They are made in a variety of fancy and very pretty patterns, as illustrated below. We have made special arrangements with the manufacturers of these goods, and are in position to furnish them to our customers at a very slight advance on cost to manufacture.

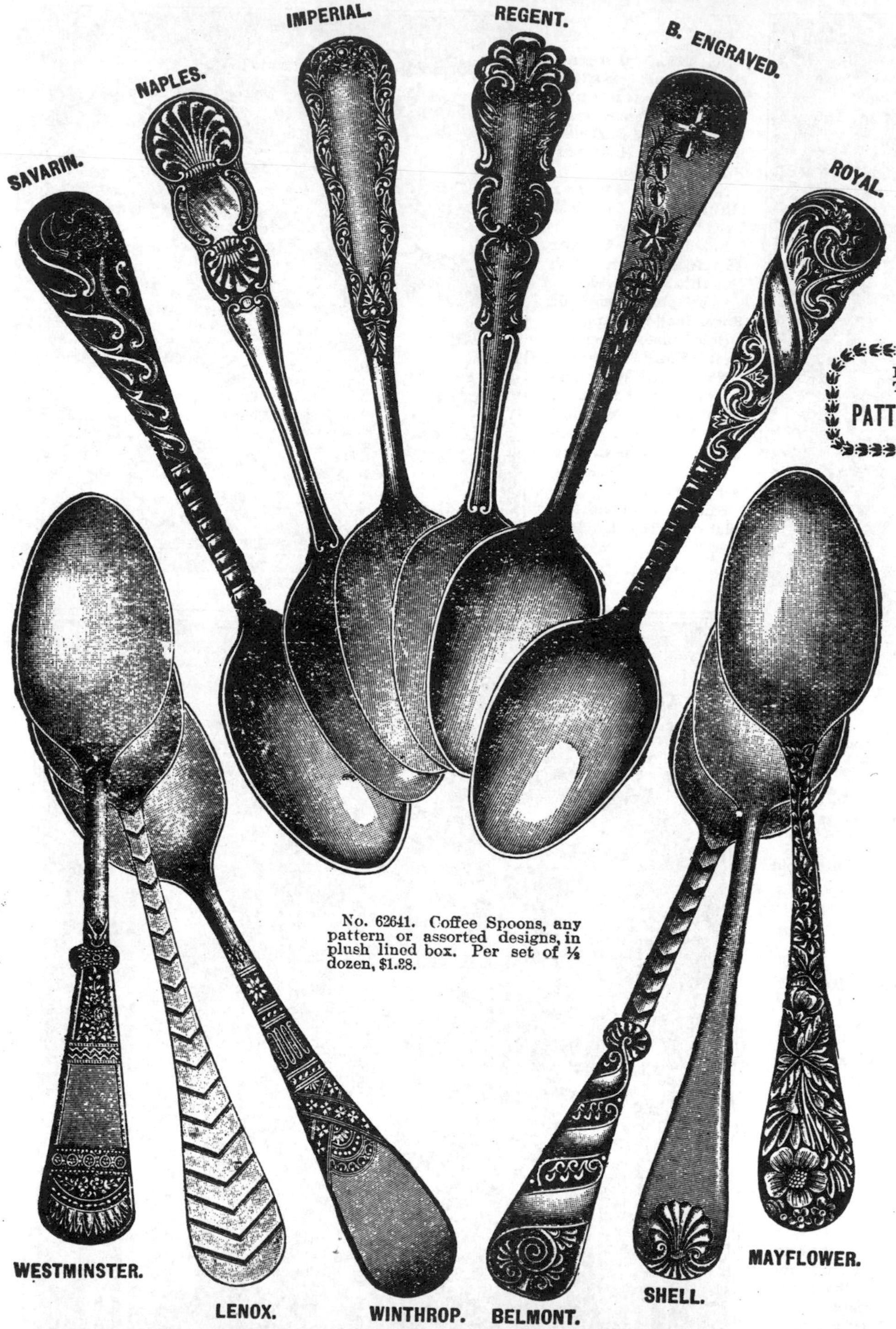

SAVARIN.    NAPLES.    IMPERIAL.    REGENT.    B. ENGRAVED.    ROYAL.

BE SURE TO STATE **PATTERN WANTED.**

No. 62641. Coffee Spoons, any pattern or assorted designs, in plush lined box. Per set of ½ dozen, $1.28.

WESTMINSTER.    LENOX.    WINTHROP.    BELMONT.    SHELL.    MAYFLOWER.

No. 62639. **Berry Spoon, Regent pattern,** in fine plush lined case, is made in very fancy embossed pattern, and is beautifully finished and engraved; length, 8½ inches. Price, each, $1.20.

**There will be an extra charge** for the B engraved Spoons, as per note below the list, and the Naples and Savarin patterns are made only in Coffee Spoons.

No. 62642. Tea Spoons, as above. Price per ½ dozen, $1.26.
No. 62643. Dessert Spoons as above. Price per ½ dozen, $2.22.
No. 62644. Dessert Forks as above. Price per ½ dozen, $2.22.
No. 62645. Table Spoons as above. Price per ½ dozen, $2.47.
No. 62646. Medium Forks as above. Price per ½ dozen, $2.47.
No. 62647. **Pie Knife, Yale pattern,** made by the **Wm. Rogers Manufacturing Co.,** fine silver plated and beautifully embossed and ornamented, in plush lined box. Price, $1.80. With gold plated blade, 50c extra. Cut is made reduced, but the goods are full regular size.

**Any flat Silverware will be sent by express C. O. D.,** subject to examination, when desired, providing the order is accompanied with a deposit of $1.
**If you send cash in full,** we will allow you a discount of 3 per cent. We assume all the risk.

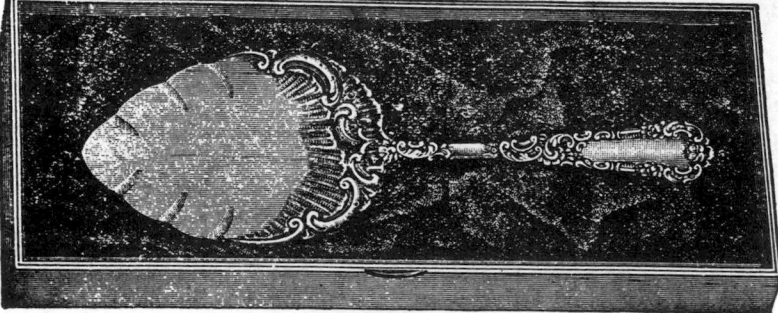

No. 62647.

# "ROGERS BROS. 1847," SILVER PLATED WARE.

### THE "ROGERS BROS. 1847" GOODS ARE AND ALWAYS HAVE BEEN THE BEST SILVER TABLE WARE MADE.

Do not be deceived by allowing any dealer to sell you any other Rogers' goods, claiming that they are the same or as good. These goods are all stamped "**Rogers Bros. 1847**," and no goods without that stamp are genuine. They are made by the **Meriden Britannia Company**, of **Meriden, Conn.**, who are one of the oldest and most reliable manufacturers in the silverware business. The goods are all made of fine **solid white metal** and **heavily plated with coin silver**. The **Knives** and **Knife Handled Forks** are **made of fine solid case steel**, first plated with Copper then with **coin silver**. We have this year placed a very heavy contract direct with the manufacturers on a spot cash basis, which enables us to sell the goods to the consumer for the same or less money than the retail dealer pays for them. You may wonder how this can be, but it is plain enough when you understand it. In the regular way the manufacturer sells the general agent, the general agent sells the jobber or wholesale dealer, and the wholesale dealer sells to the retail dealer. Each one of these concerns employs expensive traveling salesmen, and has other very heavy expenses, in addition to a liberal allowance which must be made for losses by failures, etc., all of which must be added to the price the retail dealer pays for his goods.

We handle a very complete line of the **Rogers Bros. 1847 goods**, but our limited space will not permit us to list but a portion of the same. We, however, have represented one of each of nearly all the styles in which these goods are made, which includes all of the very latest and best patterns. We list these goods in two grades, namely, what is known as the **extra plate** and the **triple plate**, the latter of which is the best and highest grade of silverware ever made.

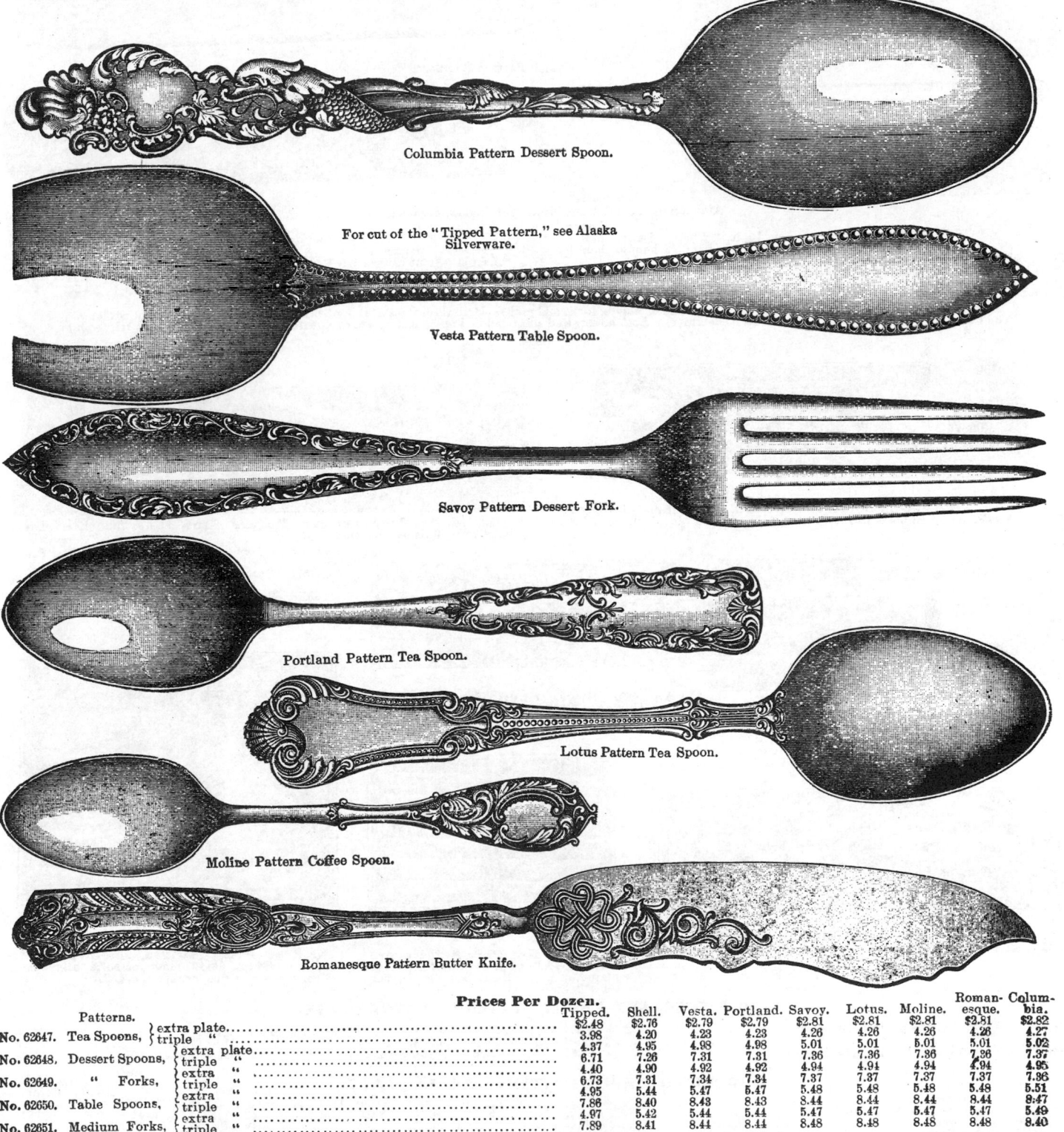

Columbia Pattern Dessert Spoon.

For cut of the "Tipped Pattern," see Alaska Silverware.

Vesta Pattern Table Spoon.

Savoy Pattern Dessert Fork.

Portland Pattern Tea Spoon.

Lotus Pattern Tea Spoon.

Moline Pattern Coffee Spoon.

Romanesque Pattern Butter Knife.

### Prices Per Dozen.

| Patterns. | | | Tipped. | Shell. | Vesta. | Portland. | Savoy. | Lotus. | Moline. | Romanesque. | Columbia. |
|---|---|---|---|---|---|---|---|---|---|---|---|
| No. 62647. | Tea Spoons, | extra plate | $2.48 | $2.76 | $2.79 | $2.79 | $2.81 | $2.81 | $2.81 | $2.81 | $2.82 |
| | | triple " | 3.98 | 4.20 | 4.23 | 4.23 | 4.26 | 4.26 | 4.26 | 4.26 | 4.27 |
| No. 62648. | Dessert Spoons, | extra plate | 4.37 | 4.95 | 4.98 | 4.98 | 5.01 | 5.01 | 5.01 | 5.01 | 5.02 |
| | | triple " | 6.71 | 7.26 | 7.31 | 7.31 | 7.36 | 7.36 | 7.36 | 7.36 | 7.37 |
| No. 62649. | " Forks, | extra " | 4.40 | 4.90 | 4.92 | 4.92 | 4.94 | 4.94 | 4.94 | 4.94 | 4.95 |
| | | triple " | 6.73 | 7.31 | 7.34 | 7.34 | 7.37 | 7.37 | 7.37 | 7.37 | 7.36 |
| No. 62650. | Table Spoons, | extra " | 4.95 | 5.44 | 5.47 | 5.47 | 5.48 | 5.48 | 5.48 | 5.48 | 5.51 |
| | | triple " | 7.86 | 8.40 | 8.43 | 8.43 | 8.44 | 8.44 | 8.44 | 8.44 | 9.47 |
| No. 62651. | Medium Forks, | extra " | 4.97 | 5.42 | 5.44 | 5.44 | 5.47 | 5.47 | 5.47 | 5.47 | 5.49 |
| | | triple " | 7.89 | 8.41 | 8.44 | 8.44 | 8.48 | 8.48 | 8.48 | 8.48 | 8.40 |

We can not fill orders for less than ¼ dozen of any one kind. All the forks in the above list have spoon pattern handles.

**For engraving on flat ware, spoons, forks, etc., 1½c per letter for script engraving on lots of 6 or more pieces. On all other kinds of work the charge is 2½c per letter for script, and 5c for old English.**

# "ROGERS BROS. 1847" SILVER PLATED WARE.

Plain Handle.

Shell Pattern Handle.

Arabesque Fancy Handle, bright cut finished ornamentation.

| Patterns. | Plain handle. | Shell handle. | Fancy handle. | Fancy hollow handle. |
|---|---|---|---|---|
| No. 62652. Dessert Knives, per doz | $3.20 | ..... | $4.15 | ..... |
| No. 62653.   "   Forks,  "  " | 3.20 | ..... | 4.15 | ..... |
| No. 62654. Medium Knives,  "  " | 3.30 | $8.40 | 4.25 | $6.00 |
| No. 62655.   "   Forks,  "  " | 3.30 | 3.40 | 4.25 | 6.00 |

| Patterns. | Plain handle. | Shell handle. | Fancy handle. | Fancy hollow handle. |
|---|---|---|---|---|
| No. 62656. Fruit Knives, per ½ doz | $1.50 | $1.65 | $1.75 | ..... |
| No. 62657. Nut Picks,  "   ½ doz | 1.35 | 1.40 | 1.50 | ..... |
| No. 62658. Three Piece Carving Sets, per set | 3.50 | ..... | 4.50 | $6.00 |

We can not fill orders for less than ¼ dozen of a kind of knives, forks and picks. Medium Knives are 9 inches long. Dessert Knives 7½ inches long. The Forks in this list have handles to match the knives. Both hollow and solid handled fancy Knives are bright finished and quoted only in triple plate.

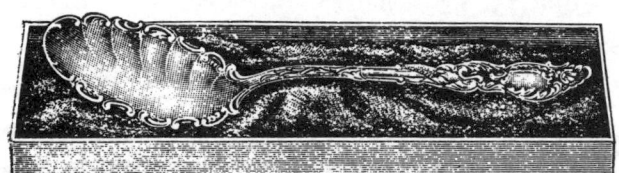

No. 62673. **Berry Spoon, Columbia pattern,** fine silver plated, **Rogers Bros. 1847,** fancy embossed, very beautifully finished, in plush lined box. **Price, $1.25.**

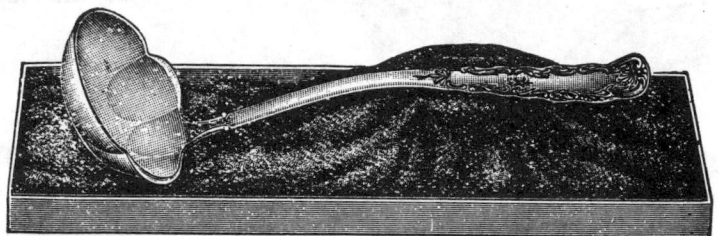

**Ladle, Portland pattern, Rogers Bros. 1847,** fine silver plated, beautifully finished and embossed.

No. 62676. Gravy Ladle, in plush lined box. Price, $1.25.
No. 62677. Oyster Ladle, in plush lined box. Price, $1.25.
No. 62678. Soup Ladle, in plush lined box. Price, 2.50.

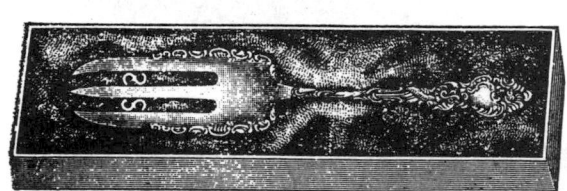

No. 62679. **Sugar Shell** and **Twish Butter Knife, Portland pattern, Rogers Bros. 1847,** silver plated, in plush lined box. Price, $1.10.

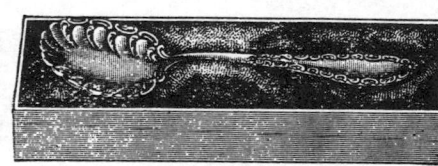

No. 62680. **Sugar Shell, Savoy pattern, Rogers Bros. 1847,** silver plated, fancy finished and embossed, in plush lined box. Price, 65c.

No. 62681. **Cake Fork, Columbia pattern, Rogers Bros. 1847,** silver plated, very fancy, in plush lined box. Price, $1.15.

No. 62682. **Nut Pick Set, Rogers Bros. 1847,** made of solid steel, silver plated, in plush lined box. Price, per set of 6, $1.35.

No. 62683. **Fruit Knives, Shell pattern, Rogers Bros. 1847,** made of solid cast steel, silver plated. Price, per set of 6, $1.75.

## ODD PIECES, ANY FANCY PATTERNS, EXTRA PLATE.

| | | |
|---|---|---|
| No. 62659. Pie Knife, any pattern, price each | $2.08 | |
| No. 62660. Cake  "   "   "   " | 2.05 | |
| No. 62661. Cream Ladle, any pattern, price each | .85 | |
| No. 62662. Sugar Tongs, any pattern, price each | $1.00 | |
| No. 62663. Salt Spoon,  "   "   "   " | .21 | |
| No. 62664. Oyster Forks,  "   "   "   per ½ doz | 2.05 | |

## ODD PIECES, FANCY PATTERNS, EXTRA PLATE.

| Patterns. | Tipped. | Shell. | Vesta. | Portland. | Savoy. | Lotus. | Moline. | Roman-esque. | Colum-bia. |
|---|---|---|---|---|---|---|---|---|---|
| No. 62665. Butter Knives, price each | $0.48 | $0.50 | $0.50 | $0.51 | $0.53 | $0.52 | $0.52 | $0.52 | $0.52 |
| No. 62666. Sugar Shells,  "   " | .40 | .44 | .45 | .45 | .49 | .47 | .47 | .47 | .47 |
| No. 62667. Pickle Forks,  "   " | .32 | ..... | ..... | .46 | ..... | ..... | .46 | .46 | ..... |
| No. 62669. Coffee Spoons, price per doz | ..... | 3.75 | 3.77 | 3.77 | 3.80 | 3.78 | 3.79 | 3.79 | 3.79 |
| No. 62670. Mustard Spoons,  "   each | .22 | .33 | .35 | .35 | .38 | .37 | .36 | .36 | .36 |

**Postage extra, as follows, when goods are to go by mail:** Coffee Spoons, 5c; Teas, 6c; Dessert Spoons or Forks, 12c; Table Spoons or Medium Forks, 15c; Dessert or Medium Knives, 18c; Sugar Shells in box, 3c; Butter Knife in box, 3c. Will be sent C. O. D. when desired on receipt of $1 with order.

# SOLID STERLING SILVER FLAT WARE.

**In Solid Silver Flat Ware we recognize no competitors, nor do we care for combinations or trusts.** Recently there has been formed a combination by the manufacturers of solid silverware in order to keep up the prices. They have pledged themselves not to sell any concern who will cut the prices and interfere with the dealer, who must have larger profits, and by reason of the many hands through which the goods pass before he gets them, he pays as much for them as the consumer should pay. We repeat, we do not care for such combinations. We have fought them for years, and we will always find some way to get the goods at the right prices, and will not be dictated to as to the prices at which we sell them.

We illustrate and handle a complete line, with the prettiest and latest patterns on the market, and at prices from one-third to one-half less than you will have to pay your retail dealer. Our solid silver goods are all guaranteed to be solid sterling silver through and through, 925-1000 fine. We guarantee that there is nothing better on the market, and never before has such a complete and beautiful line been offered to the consumer direct. We illustrate one or more pieces of each pattern and list them below, in all the patterns.

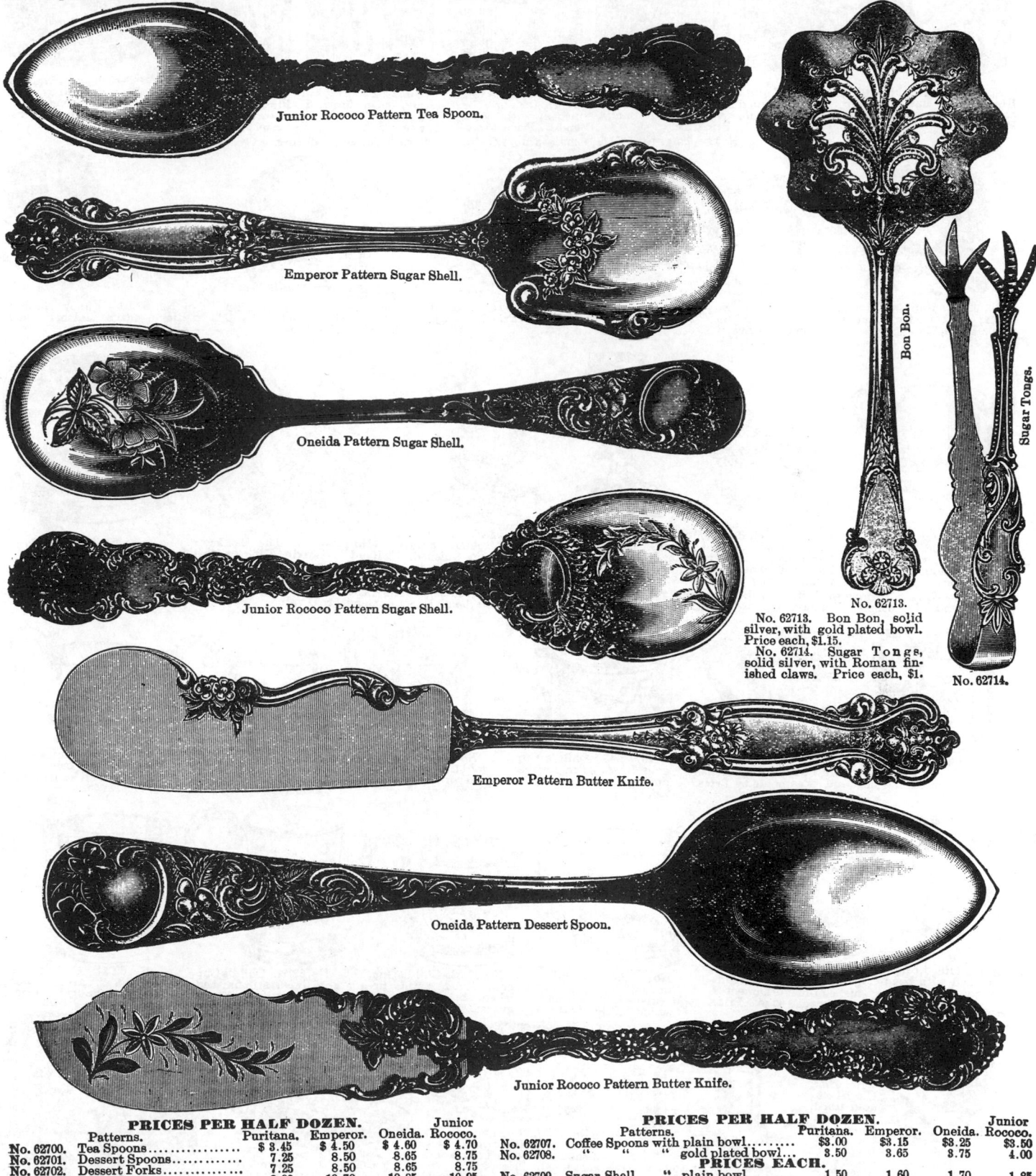

Junior Rococo Pattern Tea Spoon.

Emperor Pattern Sugar Shell.

Oneida Pattern Sugar Shell.

Junior Rococo Pattern Sugar Shell.

Emperor Pattern Butter Knife.

Oneida Pattern Dessert Spoon.

Junior Rococo Pattern Butter Knife.

Bon Bon.

Sugar Tongs.

No. 62713.

No. 62713. Bon Bon, solid silver, with gold plated bowl. Price each, $1.15.
No. 62714. Sugar Tongs, solid silver, with Roman finished claws. Price each, $1.

No. 62714.

## PRICES PER HALF DOZEN.

| Patterns. | | Puritana. | Emperor. | Oneida. | Junior Rococo. |
|---|---|---|---|---|---|
| No. 62700. | Tea Spoons................ | $ 3.45 | $ 4.50 | $ 4.60 | $ 4.70 |
| No. 62701. | Dessert Spoons........... | 7.25 | 8.50 | 8.65 | 8.75 |
| No. 62702. | Dessert Forks............. | 7.25 | 8.50 | 8.65 | 8.75 |
| No. 62703. | Table Spoons............. | 8.90 | 10.70 | 10.85 | 10.95 |
| No. 62704. | Medium Forks............. | 8.90 | 10.75 | 10.85 | 10.95 |
| No. 62705. | Dessert Knives........... | ..... | ..... | ..... | 15.50 |
| No. 62706. | Medium Knives........... | ..... | ..... | ..... | 17.00 |

## PRICES PER HALF DOZEN.

| Patterns. | | | Puritana. | Emperor. | Oneida. | Junior Rococo. |
|---|---|---|---|---|---|---|
| No. 62707. | Coffee Spoons with plain bowl......... | | $3.00 | $3.15 | $3.25 | $3.50 |
| No. 62708. | " " gold plated bowl... | | 3.50 | 3.65 | 3.75 | 4.00 |

### PRICES EACH.

| | | | Puritana. | Emperor. | Oneida. | Junior Rococo. |
|---|---|---|---|---|---|---|
| No. 62709. | Sugar Shell | plain bowl......... | 1.50 | 1.60 | 1.70 | 1.85 |
| No. 62710. | " | gold plated bowl... | 2.05 | 2.15 | 2.25 | 2.40 |
| No. 62711. | Butter Knife | plain blade........ | 2.50 | 2.60 | 2.70 | 2.90 |
| No. 62712. | " | gold plated blade.. | 3.30 | 3.40 | 3.50 | 3.75 |

**Sterling Silverware** will be sent C. O. D., providing $1.00 accompanies the order. If to be sent by mail, postage will be about the same as on Alaska Silverware.

# BEST QUALITY QUADRUPLE PLATED SILVERWARE.

## IS PLATED WITH PURE SILVER ON FINE SOLID WHITE METAL, AND IS WARRANTED.

We buy all of our silverware direct from the best manufacturers and save you all middlemen's profits. We guarantee every article of silverware we sell to be **exactly** as represented or money will be refunded.

 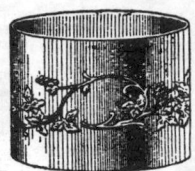 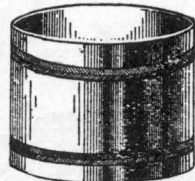 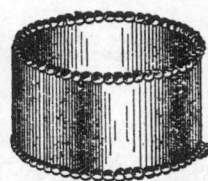   

No. 62725. Napkin Ring, satin finished and ornamented. Price, 15c.

No. 62726. Napkin Ring, satin finished and ornamented. Price, 18c.

No. 62727. Napkin Ring, satin finished, with chased bands. Price, 20c.

No. 62728. Napkin Ring, bright burnished, with beaded edges. Price, 45c.

No. 62729. Napkin Ring, satin finished, engraved "Mother." Price, 50c.

No. 62730. Napkin Ring, satin finished, engraved "Father." Price, 50c.

No. 62731. Napkin Ring, very fancy, with raised ornamentation and open work. Price, 60c.

NOTE—Rings Nos. 62729–30 make a most desirable present to father or mother.

No. 62732. Napkin Ring, fancy, with raised ornamentation. Price, 75c.

No. 62733. Napkin Ring, with bird on wish-bone, fancy. Price, 90c.

No. 62734. Napkin Ring on lily, satin finished, fancy. Price, $1.05.

No. 62735. Fancy Napkin Ring, satin finished and chased. Price, $1.30.

No. 62736. Fancy Napkin Ring, satin finished and chased. Price, $1.30.

No. 62737. Tooth Pick or Match Holder, gold lined, bright burnished, with fancy raised ornamentation. Price, 60c.

No. 62738. Tooth Pick or Match Holder, gold lined, bright burnished, with very fancy raised ornamentation. Price, $1.05.

No. 62739. Tooth Pick Holder, gold lined, satin finished, with fancy ornamentation. Price, $1.35.

No. 62740. Tooth Pick Holder, gold lined, satin finished, with fancy ornamentation. Price, $1.35.

No. 62741. "The Monkey Band" Napkin Ring, with very fancy raised ornamentation and chased. Price, 75c.

No. 62742. Napkin Ring, satin finished, fancy. Price, 90c.

NOTE—We can furnish the "Monkey Band" Napkin Ring in the following pieces, namely: The Leader, First Violin, Base Viol, Clarionet, Bassoon, Triangle, **Cymbals,** and a few others. We have bought the entire lot of these Rings and are selling them at about one-half real value.

No. 62743. Child's Cup, gold lined, satin finished and ornamented. Price, 65c.

No. 62744. Child's Cup, gold lined, satin finished and ornamented. Price, 75c.

No. 62745. Child's Cup, gold lined, satin finished and ornamented. Price, 55c.

No. 62746. Child's Cup, gold lined, satin finished and ornamented, fancy. Price, 90c.

No. 62747. Child's Cup, gold lined, bright burnished and ornamented. Price, $1.05.

No. 62748. Child's Cup, gold lined, bright burnished and engraved. Price, $1.55.

No. 62749. Child's Cup, gold lined, bright burnished with beaded edge. Price, 50c.

No. 62750. Child's Cup, gold lined, bright burnished, fancy ornamented, with beaded edge. Price, $1.35.

No. 62751. Child's Cup, gold lined, bright burnished, fancy ornamented. Price, $1.50.

No. 62752. Child's Cup, gold lined, satin finished, bright cut engraved. Price, 80c.

No. 62753. Child's Cup, gold lined, satin finished, bright cut engraved. Price, 95c.

No. 62754. Child's Cup, gold lined, satin finished, fancy engraved. Price, 75c.

No. 62755. Goblet, gold lined, satin finished and fancy, bright cut engraved. Price, $1.25.

No. 62756. Cup and Saucer, bright burnished, fancy pattern. Price, $2.40.

No. 62757. Cup and Saucer, fancy pattern, bright burnished with beaded edges and gold lined. Price, $2.70.
No. 62757½. Bright burnished, engraved and gold lined. Price, $3.15.

No. 62758. Cup and Saucer, gold lined, satin finished, bright cut engraved, fancy. Price, $2.95.

No. 62759. Child's Cup, satin finished and ornamented, in satin lined box. Price, 50c.

Plain band napkin rings weigh boxed ready for shipment, about 4 ounces; fancy rings, pick holders and cups about 8 ounces; cups and saucers about 12 ounces.

**Silverware takes first-class express and freight rates. See front of book for further instructions.**

# BEST QUALITY QUADRUPLE PLATED SILVERWARE.
## IS PLATED WITH PURE SILVER ON FINE SOLID WHITE METAL, AND IS WARRANTED.
Best goods, latest patterns, lowest prices, prompt shipment and courteous treatment.

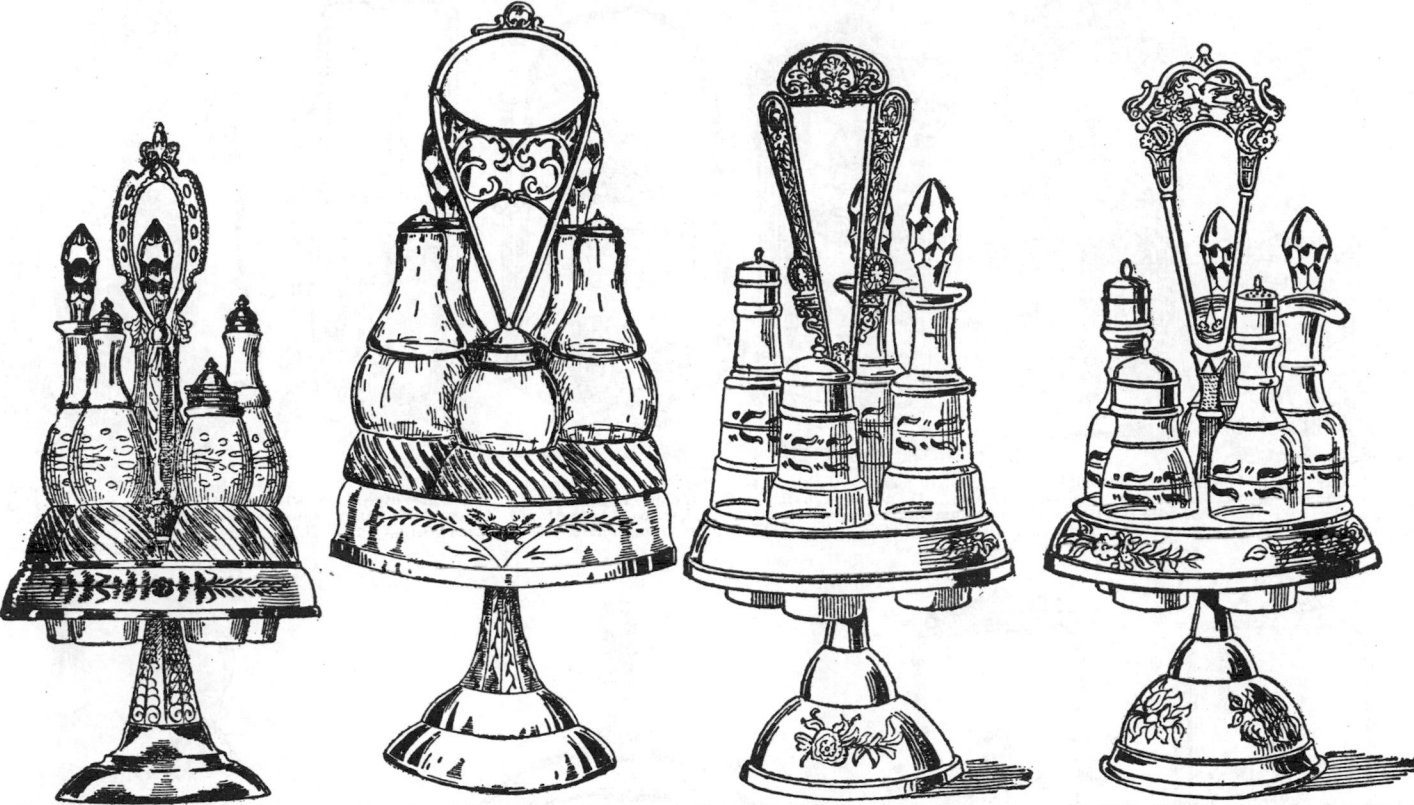

No. 62760. Dinner Castor, with five ornamented bottles, satin finished and engraved. Price, 90c.

No. 62761. Dinner Castor, with five bottles, satin finished and engraved. Price, $1.15.

No. 62762. Dinner Castor, five ornamented bottles, fancy handle and extra engraving. Price, $1.80.

No. 62763. Dinner Castor, five ornamented bottles, fancy handle, and extra bright cut engraving. Price, $2.

No. 62764. Castor, 8½ inches high, with vinegar, pepper and mustard, fancy bottles. Price, $1.20.

## SPECIAL DRIVE IN QUADRUPLE SILVER PLATED CASTORS.

As Castors are the best selling pieces in hollow silverware, we have made special preparations for this year's trade by contracting for an immense quantity of these goods direct with the manufacturers on a spot cash basis. These goods are made by the best silverware manufacturers, whose reputation is a sufficient guarantee for their goods. They are all made of a fine grade of solid white metal, are quadruple plated with pure silver, beautifully engraved, and are warranted in every respect. The bottles are all made of fine quality of flint glass, the stoppers ground in so as to insure their fitting perfectly, and nothing is left undone to make them the best goods on the market. They are guaranteed by the manufacturers to us, and we in turn guarantee them to our customers. We are prepared to furnish you with these goods at from one-third to one-half the prices you would have to pay for them at retail. We ask you to investigate, compare prices and see for yourself. We want your orders, and if low prices and good goods will secure them, they are ours. If you have not dealt with us before, and are in need of anything of this kind, lose no time in sending us a trial order, and be convinced that we are indeed the Cheapest Supply House on Earth.

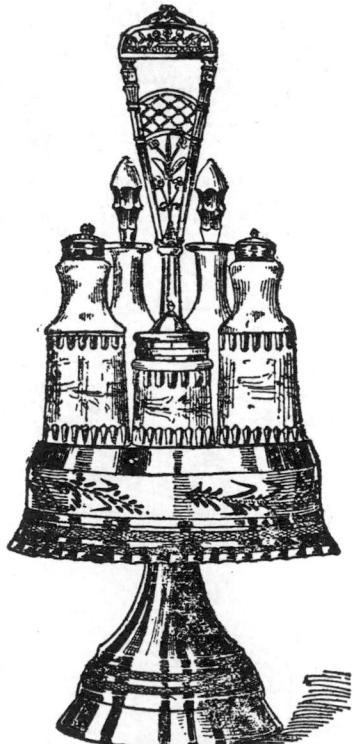

No. 62765. Castor, 8 inches high, with very fancy imitation cut-glass bottles for pepper, mustard and vinegar. Price, $2.70.

No. 62766. Castor, length 6 inches, height 4½ inches, very fancy, with genuine cut-glass bottles for pepper, salt and mustard. Price, $1.50.

No. 62767. Castor, 4½ inches high, with two fancy genuine cut-glass bottles for pepper and salt. Price, $1.05.

No. 62768. Dinner Castor, with five fancy bottles, fancy handle and extra engraving, a very fine castor. Price, $2.20.

Weight of lunch castors boxed, about 2 lbs. Weight of 5 bottle castors, about 5 lbs.; boxed, ready for shipment, about 11 lbs.

# BEST QUALITY QUADRUPLE PLATED SILVERWARE.
## IS PLATED WITH PURE SILVER ON FINE SOLID WHITE METAL, AND IS WARRANTED.

Silverware was never offered at such prices before.   We mean just what we say, and only ask that you investigate and judge for yourself.

 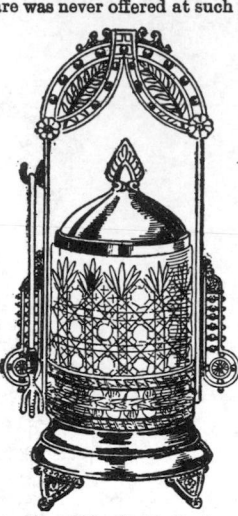    

No. 62769.   Pickle Cas-ter, height 11 inches, with tongs and fancy glass bottle.  Price, 90c.

No. 62770.   Pickle Caster, height 11½ inches, fancy handle and stand, with tongs and imitation cut glass bottle.  Price, $1.10.

No. 62771.   Pickle Cas-ter, 11 inches high, fancy handle, with fancy bottle.  Price, $1.20.

No. 62772.   Pickle Caster, 9½ inches high, fancy stand, with tongs and fancy colored glass bottle.  Price, $1.30.

No. 62773.   Pickle Caster, 11½ inches high, fancy, with tongs and fancy square glass bottle.  Price, $1.50.

No. 62774.   Pickle Caster, 10½ inches high, with very fancy stand and tongs, fine colored glass bottle, with raised decorations.  Price, $2.90.

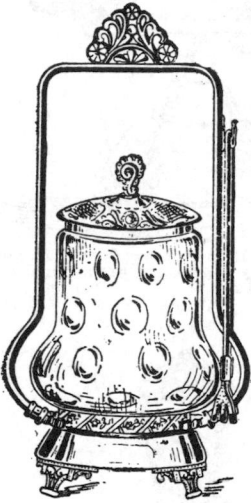   

No. 62775.   Pickle Caster, 10½ inches high, with fancy stand, tongs and fine colored glass bottle.  Price, $2.50.

No. 62776.   Pickle Caster, 10½ inches high, with fancy stand, tongs and fine colored glass bot-tle.  Price, $3.

No. 62777.   Crumb Set.  9 inches wide, satin finished, with fancy handles and beaded border.  Price, $2.90.

No. 62778.   Crumb Set, 9 inches wide, with very fancy handles, satin finished, with raised orna-mented border and bright cut engraved.  Price, $3.50.

No. 62779.   Butter Dish, satin fin-ished and engraved, with handles and knife-rests.  Price, 95c.

No. 62780.   Butter Dish, satin finished and fancy bright cut engraved, with knife-rests.  Price, $1.30.

No. 62783.   Butter Dish, satin fin-ished and engraved.  Price, 90c.

No. 62784.   Butter Dish, satin finished, with fancy bright cut engraving, handles and knife-rests.  Price, $1.35.

No. 62781.   Butter Dish, satin finished and fancy bright cut engraved.  Price, $1.05.

No. 62782.   Butter Dish, satin finished and fancy bright cut engraved, with handles and knife-rests.  Price, $1.55.

NOTE—The Butter Dishes listed above all have drainers, and are from 5¼ to 6 inches in width.

You run no risk by sending cash in full with your orders.  We guarantee safe delivery, give a discount of 3 per cent. for cash, and refund your money if goods are not satisfactory.  Weight of Pickle Caster, about 2 lbs.; boxed, about 4 lbs. Butter dish, boxed, about 2 lbs.

Silverware takes first-class express and freight rate.  See front of book for further instructions.

We buy all of our silverware direct from the best manufacturers, saving you all middlemen's profits.  We guarantee every article of silverware we sell to be exactly as represented or money will be refunded.

# BEST QUALITY QUADRUPLE PLATED SILVERWARE.

## IS PLATED WITH PURE SILVER ON FINE SOLID WHITE METAL, AND IS WARRANTED.

In the past, only those possessed of considerable means could afford to dress the table with a nice outfit of silverware. At our prices almost anyone can afford it

No. 62786. Berry or Fruit Dish, fancy and burnished stand, with handles and crystal glass dish. Price, $1.10

No. 62787. Berry or Fruit Dish, with burnished and fancy stand, fancy handles, with imitation cut crystal glass dish. Price, $1.30.

No. 62788. Berry or Fruit Dish, with very fancy handle fancy raised ornamented base, with beautiful escaloped china dish, white on the outside, pink on the inside and beautifully ornamented in raised gold work. Price, $5.80.
NOTE—It is impossible for us by description or illustration to give any idea of the beauty of this dish.

No. 62789. Berry or Fruit Dish, fancy ornamented handle and base, with imitation cut-glass crystal dish. Price, $1.25.

No. 62790. Berry or Fruit Dish, with very fancy ornamented and open work handle, fancy stand, with heavy imitation cut-glass crystal dish. Price, $2.75.

No. 62791. Berry or Fruit Dish, large fancy base, with fancy ornamented handle, heavy imitation cut-glass crystal dish. Price, $1.35.

No. 62792. Card Receiver, 6 inches high, satin finished and fancy engraved. Price, $1.40.

No. 62793. Celery Holder, 10½ inches high, with satin finished stand and fancy glass cup. Price, $1.10.

No. 62794. Syrup with plate, height 7 inches, satin finished, bright cut engraved and raised ornamentation; very pretty. Price, $1.45.

No. 62795. Card Receiver, 5½ inches high, satin finished and engraved. Price, $1.30.

No. 62796. Syrup with plate, height 6 inches, satin finished and engraved. Price, $1.10.

No. 62797. Syrup with plate, height 6 inches, satin finished and fancy bright cut engraved. Price, $1.60.

No. 62798. Syrup with plate, 3¾ inches high, plate has raised ornamented border; syrup is genuine cut-glass with fancy plated mountings. Price, $1.90.

No. 62799. Bouquet Holder and Card Receiver, 8⅝ inches high, very fancy, with ornamented crystal glass vase, satin finished and raised ornamented receiver. Price, $2.10.

Berry Dishes weigh, net, about 3½ lbs.; boxed, about 9 lbs.; syrups, etc., boxed, about 2 lbs. We give weights to assist you in calculating the shipping charges if you desire.

# BEST QUALITY QUADRUPLE PLATED SILVERWARE.

### IS PLATED WITH PURE SILVER ON FINE SOLID WHITE METAL, AND IS WARRANTED.

Our most pleasant hours are spent at the table, why not have it "well dressed" when it can be done for so little money.

No. 62810. Cake Dish, 10½ inches high, satin finished, with raised ornamentation. Price, $1.25.

No. 62811. Cake Dish, satin finished and bright cut engraved, fancy border and handle. Price, $2.75.

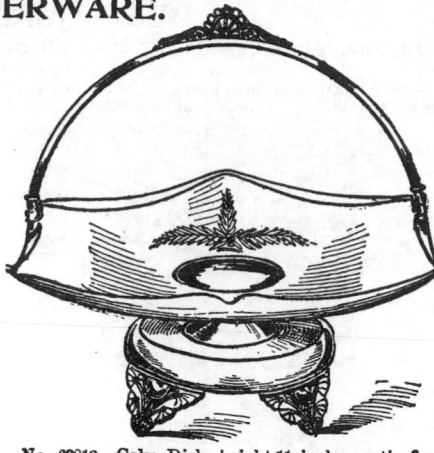

No. 62812. Cake Dish, height 11 inches, satin finished and bright cut engraved. Price, $1.10.

No. 62813. Cake Stand, regular size, diameter 8¼ inches, satin finished top, bright cut engraving, burnished stand. Price, $1.45.

No. 62814. Cake Dish, diameter about 8½ inches, fancy embossed edge and engraving, satin finished. Price, $1.70.

No. 62815. Cake Dish, 10½ inches high, very fancy pattern, ornamented border, satin finished, with bright cut engraving. Price, $3.20.

No. 62816. Bon Bon, gold lined, width 5½ inches, satin finished and fancy ornamented. Price, $1.90.

No. 62817. Cake Dish, diameter 8½ inches, satin finished, with bright cut engraving. Price, $1.

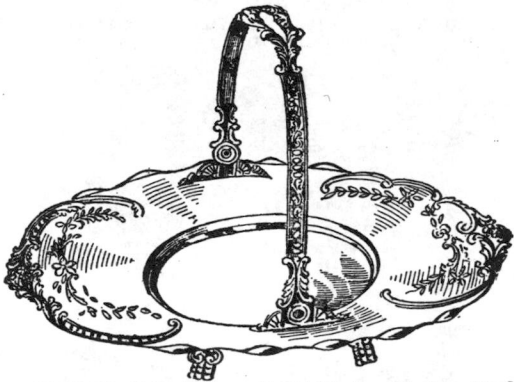

No. 62818. Cake Dish, satin finished, with burnished center, fancy bright cut engraving and ornamentations, very fancy handle. Price, $2.80.

No. 62819. Bon Bon, gold lined, diameter 4½ inches, bright burnished, with fancy ornamented border and handle. Price, $1.20.

No. 62820. Nut or Fruit Bowl, diameter 6¼ inches, height 5¼ inches, octagon shaped, bright burnished, with fancy ornamentations, gold lined. Price, $3.25.

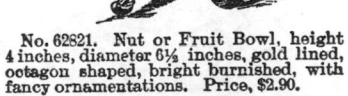

No. 62821. Nut or Fruit Bowl, height 4 inches, diameter 6½ inches, gold lined, octagon shaped, bright burnished, with fancy ornamentations. Price, $2.90.

Weight of Cake Stands net, about 1½ lbs.; boxed, about 4 lbs.; Nut Bowls and Bon Bons a little less.

**Silverware takes first-class express and freight rates. See front of book for further instructions.**

No. 62822. Bon Bon, diameter 5½ inches, satin finished, with fancy ornamentations and beaded border, gold lined. Price, $1.55.

## BEST QUALITY QUADRUPLE PLATED SILVERWARE.
### IS PLATED WITH PURE SILVER ON FINE SOLID WHITE METAL, AND IS WARRANTED.
The retail jeweler has always depended to a large extent on Silverware for good profits, hence the high prices at which it is sold by them.

No. 62840. Four piece Tea Set, consisting of Tea, Sugar, Cream and Spoon Holder, satin finished and fancy bright cut engraved, very fancy pattern, Cream and Spoon Holder gold lined. Price for complete set, $5.90.

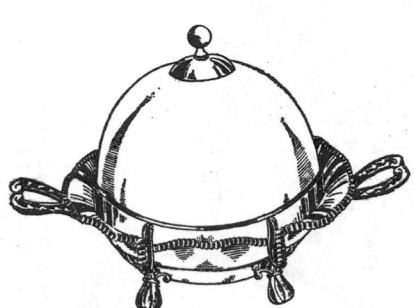

No. 62841. Butter Dish, bright burnished, with fancy ornamentations, handles and knife-rests. Price, $2.95.

NOTE—The above Butter Dish matches Tea Set No. 62842.

No. 62842. Tea Set, consisting of Tea 7 inches high, Sugar 5 inches high, Cream and Spoon Holder each 4 inches high. Set is bright burnished, with fancy border and fancy ornamented handle, Cream and Spoon Holder gold lined; is a very beautiful and high grade Tea Set. Price complete for four pieces, $9.50.

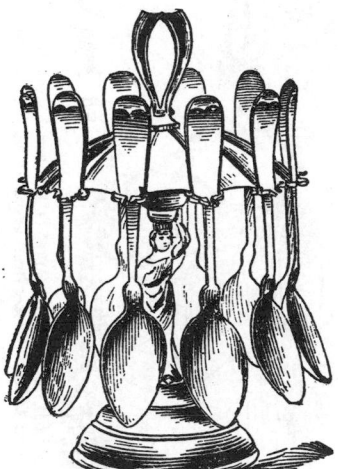

No. 62483. Spoon Holder for twelve spoons, is bright burnished. Price without spoons, $1.20.

No. 62844. Fancy Sugar, bright burnished, with fancy handles, and spoon holders for 12 spoons, raised ornamentation. Price, $1.00.

No. 62845. Sugar, fancy and burnished mounting with holders for 12 spoons, fancy glass bowl. Price, $1.60.

No. 62846. Sugar, with fancy mounting, imitation cut glass bowl, with hook to support cover when off the bowl. Price, $3.85.

No. 62847. Syrup with plate, height, 6 inches, satin finished and fancy ornamented. Price, $1.40.

No. 62848. Bake Dish, diameter 9 inches, satin finished and bright cut engraved. Price, $2.90.

No. 62849. Bake Dish, diameter 9 inches, satin finished and bright cut engraved. Price, $2.25.

NOTE—All of the above Bake Dishes are provided with a porcelain dish, in which puddings, etc., can be baked, and when ready for serving, the Bake Dish with contents can be set inside the plated dish with cover.

Tea Sets weigh net about 5 lbs., boxed about 11 lbs.; Bake Dishes about 9 lbs., boxed. Silverware will be sent C. O. D. on receipt of $2 with order.

**Silverware takes first-class freight and express rates. See front of book for further instructions.**

# BEST QUALITY QUADRUPLE PLATED SILVERWARE.
## IS PLATED WITH PURE SILVER ON FINE SOLID WHITE METAL, AND IS WARRANTED.

What is nicer than a table dressed with beautiful silverware? Why not have it when it costs so little money?

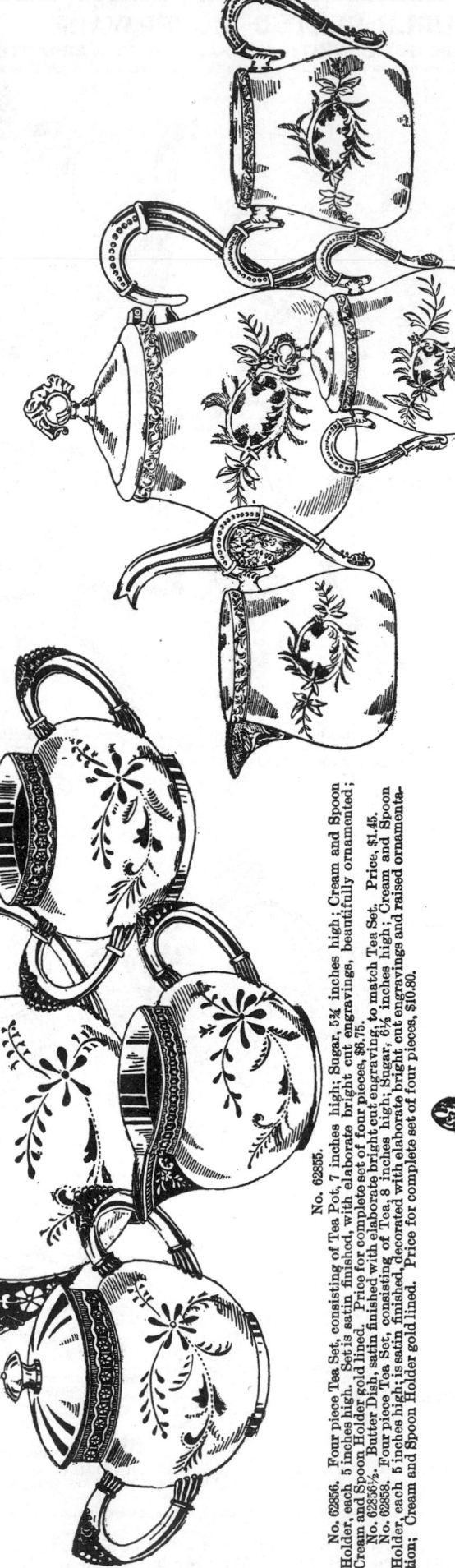

No. 62854. Tea Set, consisting of Tea Pot, 6½ inches high; Sugar, 4½ inches high; Spoon Holder and Cream, each 3½ inches high. The set is satin finished, beautifully ornamented with bright cut engravings and bright burnished shield; Cream and Spoon Holder gold lined. Price for complete set of four pieces, $4.50.

No. 62855. Tea Set, consisting of Tea Pot, Sugar, Cream and Spoon Holder. Set is satin finished, is beautifully ornamented and decorated with a very pretty pattern of bright cut engraving; Cream and Spoon Holder gold lined. Price for complete set of four pieces, $4.90.

No. 62854.

No. 62855.

No. 62856. Four piece Tea Set, consisting of Tea Pot, 7 inches high; Sugar, 5¾ inches high; Cream and Spoon Holder, each 5 inches high. Set is satin finished, with elaborate bright cut engravings, beautifully ornamented; Cream and Spoon Holder gold lined. Price for complete set of four pieces, $6.75.

No. 62856½. Butter Dish, satin finished with elaborate bright cut engraving, to match Tea Set. Price, $1.45.

No. 62858. Four piece Tea Set, consisting of Tea, Sugar. 6½ inches high; Cream and Spoon Holder, each 5 inches high; is satin finished, decorated with elaborate bright cut engravings and raised ornamentation; Cream and Spoon Holder gold lined. Price for complete set of four pieces, $10.80.

No. 62856.

No. 62858.

Tea Sets weigh, net, about 5 lbs.; boxed, about 11 lbs. Will be sent C. O. D. when desired, but the best way is to send cash with your order. If goods are not satisfactory, you will lose nothing. Silverware takes first-class freight and express rates. See front of book for further instructions,

# FINEST QUALITY QUADRUPLE PLATED SILVERWARE.

## IS PLATED WITH PURE SILVER ON FINE SOLID WHITE METAL, AND IS WARRANTED.

We don't handle anything but the best goods. If we should do otherwise, we could not expect to retain the good will of our customers, and without that we would soon have no patronage.

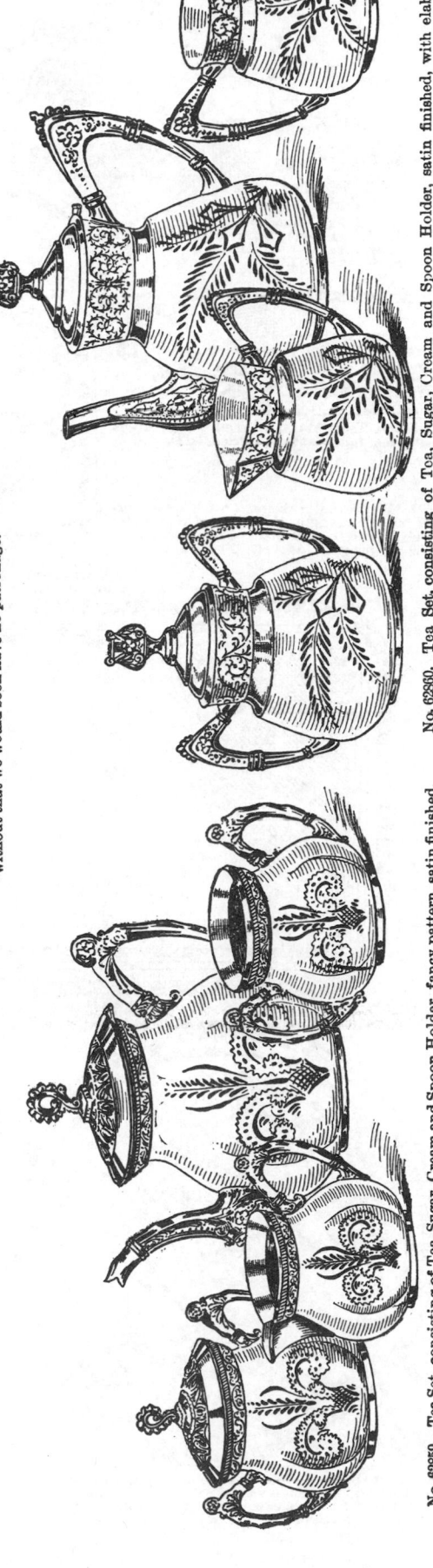

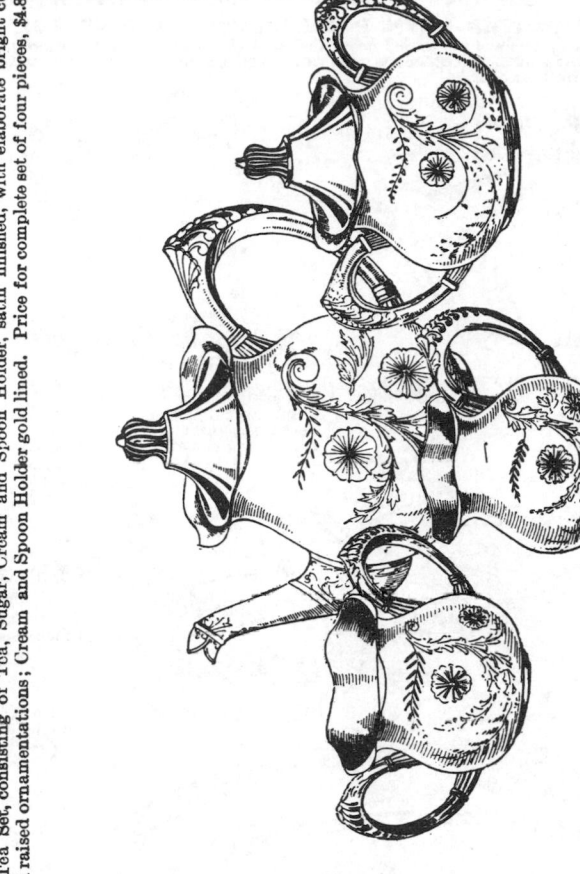

No. 62859. Tea Set, consisting of Tea, Sugar, Cream and Spoon Holder, satin finished, with elaborate bright cut decorated with elaborate bright cut engraving and raised ornamentations; Cream and Spoon Holder gold lined. Price for complete set of four pieces, $4.85. gold lined. Price for complete set of four pieces, $7.85.

No. 62860. Tea Set, consisting of Tea, Sugar, Cream and Spoon Holder, fancy pattern, satin finished, engravings and raised ornamentations; Cream and Spoon Holder gold lined. Price for complete set of four pieces, $7.85.

No. 62861. Tea Set, very fancy, consisting of Coffee, 8½ inches high; Tea, 7½ inches high; Sugar, 6½ inches high; Cream, Spoon Holder and Butter Dish, each 6 inches high; Cream and Spoon Holder gold lined. All are satin finished and decorated with elaborate bright cut engravings. Coffee, $4.20; Tea, $4; Sugar, $2.75; Cream, $2.20; Spoon Holder, $2.20; Butter, $2.87. Price for complete set of four pieces, consisting of Tea, Sugar, Cream and Spoon Holder, $11.

No. 62862. Tea Set, consisting of Tea, 7 inches high; Sugar, 6 inches high; Cream and Spoon Holder, 5 inches high. It is a very fancy pattern, satin finished, elaborately decorated with fancy bright cut engraving and raised ornamentation; Cream and Spoon Holder gold lined. Price for complete set of four pieces, $5.95.

Tea sets weigh, net, about 5 lbs.; boxed, about 11 lbs. We will send tea sets or other silverware any place in the United States C. O. D., providing a deposit of $2 accompanies the order. Balance can be paid at the express office, after examination, if goods are in every way satisfactory; if not, they can be refused and we will refund the deposit. Could we make an offer more fair than this?

**Silverware takes first-class freight and express rate. See front of book for further instructions.**

# BEST QUALITY QUADRUPLE PLATED SILVERWARE.

## IS PLATED WITH PURE SILVER ON FINE SOLID WHITE METAL, AND WARRANTED.

We sell everything on a basis of the lowest possible cost of the goods. Retail dealers don't fix their prices that way. They sometimes sell what they call a very staple article as low as they can. Then on goods with which the public is not familiar with values they make long profits. That is deception. Another bad feature is that he pays too much for his goods.

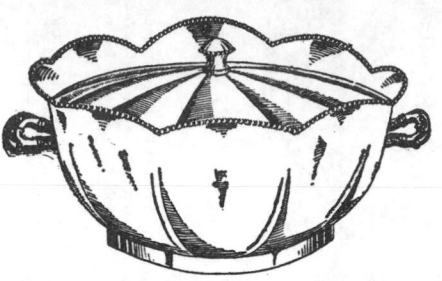

No. 62863. Soup Tureen, holds two quarts, is bright burnished, fancy pattern, with beaded edge. Price, $5.90.

No. 62864. Syrup with plate, 6½ inches high, matches Tea Set No. 62858, is satin finished, decorated with very fancy bright cut engraving and raised ornamentation. Price, $3.20.

No. 62865. Bon Bon, diameter 4½ inches, is burnished, fancy ornamented and gold lined. Price, $1.70.

No. 62866. Nut Bowl or Fruit Dish, diameter 9 inches, is bright burnished, with fancy raised ornamented border and gold lined. Price, $3.10.

No. 62868. Bread Tray, satin finished, with bright cut fancy engraving, fancy border. Price, $1.20.

No. 62870. Waiter, satin finished, with raised ornamented border. Length, 13 inches. Price, $3.30.
No. 62870¼. Length, 15 inches. Price, $4.50.
No. 62870½. Length, 17 inches. Price, $5.90.

No. 62869. Biscuit Jar, height 6½ inches, satin finished, with bright cut engraving. Price, $2.40.

No. 62867. Dessert Set of four pieces, consisting of Sugar, 5 inches high; Cream and Spoon Holder, each 3 inches high; Tray, 10¾ inches diameter; is satin finished, bright cut engraved, with raised ornamentations; Cream and Spoon Holder gold lined; very fancy. Price, $4.60.

**Silverware takes first-class freight and express rate. See front of book for further instructions.**

No. 62870.

No. 62871. Waiter, diameter 14 inches, round, satin finished, with raised ornamentation and bright cut engravings. Price, $2.15.
Single pieces and sets, except the large Trays, on this page, weigh, boxed, from 2 to 7 lbs.; Round Tray, boxed, about 7 lbs.; Square Tray, boxed, about 8 to 10 lbs.

No. 62872. After Dinner Coffee Set of four pieces, consisting of Sugar, height 3 inches; Cream and Spoon Holder, height each 2 inches; and Tray, diameter 7¾ inches. All are satin finished, decorated with bright cut engraving, raised ornamentation. Cream and Spoon Holder gold lined. Price, for complete set, $3.40.

# BEST QUALITY QUADRUPLE PLATED SILVERWARE.
## IS PLATED WITH PURE SILVER ON FINE SOLID WHITE METAL, AND WARRANTED.

The goods listed on this page will not be found in the average retail store. Where you do find them see what prices you will have to pay: $20 to $30 for a Tilting Water Set, and other things in proportion.

**No. 62873.** Tilting Water Set, height 19 inches, satin finished, with bright cut engraving. Price, $4.25.

**No. 62874.** Tilting Water Set, 21 inches high, with Cup and Slop, Cup gold lined; satin finished, with bright cut engraving and fancy raised ornamentation. Price, $8.60.

**No. 62875.** Tilting Water Set, 19 inches high, with Slop and fancy ornamented and gold lined Goblet, satin finished, with bright cut engraving and very fancy raised ornamentation. Price, $8.90.

No. 62873.    No. 62874.    No. 62875.

**No. 62876.** Water Pitcher, satin finished, with bright cut engraving. Price, $1.75.

**No. 62877.** Water Pitcher, satin finished, with elaborate bright cut engraving and raised ornamentation, very fancy. Price, $4.50.

**No. 62878.** Water Pitcher, height 8 inches, satin finished, with embossed border and ornamentation. Price, $3.

No. 62878.

No. 62876.    No. 62877.

No. 62881¼.

No. 62881.

No. 62881½.    No. 62881¾

## CHURCH SERVICE OR COMMUNION SET.

**No. 62881.** Flagon, 3 pint, burnished. Price, $5.40.
**No. 62881¼.** Baptismal Bowl, burnished. Price, $2.35. Same, gold lined. Price, $2.86.
**No. 62881½.** Plates, burnished. Price, each, $2.15.
**No. 62881¾.** Goblets, burnished. Price, $1.75. Same, gold lined. Price, $2.10.
The above set is guaranteed to be the best quality made.

No. 62879.

No. 62882.

No. 62880.

**No. 62879.** Water Pitcher, height 7¾ inches, capacity about 2 qts., is satin finished, with elaborate bright cut engraving, and beautiful raised ornamentation. Price, $3.50.
**No. 62880.** Three piece Water Set, consisting of Pitcher 8 inches high, gold lined Cup, and Tray 9 inches long. All are bright burnished, with raised ornamented border, and gold lined. Price for complete set, $7.45.

**No. 62882.** Gravy Boat, with plate, 4 inches high, 9 inches long, fancy legs, and fancy raised ornamented border to boat and plate, all satin finished, boat gold lined. Price, $3.90.
**No. 62883.** Card or Spoon Holder, 4 inches high, satin finished, with very fancy ornamented handle and raised ornamented edge, gold lined. Price, $2.40.

No. 62883.

Tilting Water Set weighs, boxed, about 16 lbs.; Water Set including Tray, Pitcher and Cup weighs, boxed, about 11 lbs.
**Any silverware will be sent C. O. D. on receipt of a deposit of $2.**

# BEST QUALITY QUADRUPLE PLATED SILVERWARE.
## IS PLATED WITH PURE SILVER ON FINE SOLID WHITE METAL, AND IS WARRANTED.
### Once a customer always a customer.  If you have not dealt with us before, send an order immediately and be convinced.

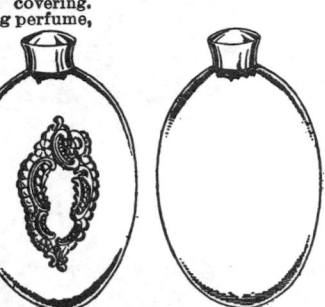

No. 62886. Puff Box, satin finished, bright cut engraving and gold lined, with puff. Price, $1.50.

No. 62887. Hair Pin Box, satin finished, and bright cut engraved, with fancy raised ornamentation, size 2x4½ inches. Price, $1.15.

No. 62887.

No. 62886.

No. 62884. Perfume, the celebrated Lundborg's, 2 oz. bottle, height 4¾ inches, with very fancy open work silver plated covering. Price, including perfume, $2.25.

No. 62885. Perfume, the celebrated Lundborg's, 1 oz. bottle, satin finished, with very fancy bright cut engraving and open work silver plated covering. Price, including perfume, $1.45.

No. 62888. Hair Curling Set, with alconol lamp, is bright burnished and engraved, with raised ornamentation. Price, including fine plated curling iron, $2.90.

No. 62889. Vaseline Box, satin finished, with raised ornamentation, just the size to admit a vaseline bottle. Price, 90c.

No. 62891. Drinking Flask, capacity ¾ pint, satin finished, with screw top. Price, $2.

No. 62892. Drinking Flask, capacity ½ pint, satin finished and raised ornamented, with screw top. Price, $2.20.

No. 62892½. Same as above, with capacity ¾ pint. Price, $2.50.

No. 62891.

No. 62892.

No. 62893. Drinking Flask, capacity ¾ pint, satin finished and raised ornamentation, with screw top. Price, $2.60.

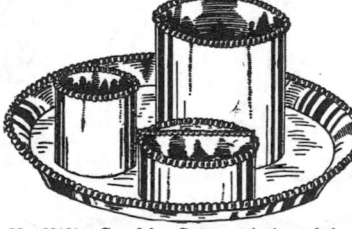

No. 62894. Puff Box with cover, height 4½ inches, satin finished, with elaborate bright cut engravings, gold lined. Price, including puff, $2.25.

No. 62895. Smoking Set, for cigars or pipe and tobacco, height 4 inches, length 7 inches, satin finished, with very fancy raised ornamentation. Price, $2.40.

No. 62890. Cologne, Lundborg's Rhenish, 4 oz. bottle, 9½ inches high, with very fancy open work silver plated covering. Price, including cologne, $1.80.

No. 62897. Shaving Mug, is bright burnished and gold lined, beaded edge. Price, $2.70.

No. 62897½. Brush to match above, of genuine badger hair, plated mounting. Price, $1.20.

No. 62896. Shaving Mug, height 3 inches, diameter 4 inches, satin finished and gold lined, with compartment for soap. Price, $2.90.

No. 62898. Smoking Set, consisting of cigar holder 3½ inches high; match holder and ash cup, all gold lined, with tray 7 inches in diameter, all bright burnished, with beaded edges. Price, for complete set, $4.90.

No. 62899. Fern Dish, 7 inches in diameter, satin finished, with fancy raised ornamentation and removable silver plated pan. Price, $2.85.

No. 62900. Shaving Mug, gold lined, satin finished, with bright cut engraving and raised ornamentation. Price, $2.60.

No. 62900½. Brush to match above, genuine badger hair, with plated mounting. Price, $1.50.

No. 62903. Ink Set, size 6x2¼ inches, 2 inches high, bright burnished, with embossed ornamentation, two ink wells, stamp and pen compartments. Price, $2.75.

No. 62901. Ink Set, height 3½ inches, with fancy raised ornamented mounting and cut-glass bottle. Price, $1.45.

No. 62902. Fern Dish, diameter 7 inches, very fancy, with bright cut engraving, raised ornamentation and removable silver plated pan. Price, $7.30.

No. 62902½. Base for fern tray, or other fancy table ornament, 11½ inches diameter, with beautiful beveled escaloped edge mirror, diameter 10 inches, fancy raised ornamentation. Price, $5.70.

NOTE—The cuts can give you no idea of the beauty and elegance of the above two pieces.

**We can furnish anything that is made in the silverware line. If you don't find what you want in our catalogue write us with a description of what you want and we will be glad to quote you prices.**

# OUR CLOCK DEPARTMENT.

In clocks we represent all of the oldest and most reliable makers, those who' have built up a reputation for their goods by making only such clocks as they could guarantee.

We list clocks made by the following concerns, viz.: The Waterbury Clock Company, of Waterbury, Conn.; New Haven Clock Company, of New Haven, Conn.; Ansonia Clock Company, of Ansonia, Conn. and the Seth Thomas Clock Company, of Thomaston, Conn.

(We wish to state that the Waterbury Clock Company has no connection whatever with the Waterbury Watch Company, but is a much older concern.)

Every clock we sell is warranted to us by the manufacturers, and we warrant them to our customers. Any clock bought of us that is not in every way satisfactory can be returned, and it will be exchanged or money will be refunded. We sell clocks at astonishingly low prices, but do not get the idea that the grade is correspondingly low, for we cover almost the entire line of each of the best makers. Do not think that the shipping charges would advance our prices to anywhere near the prices you would have to pay your retail dealer, because he would have to pay the same freight or express rate as you, and therefore you would be on an equal footing with him, and at our prices you are in position to buy as low and even lower than he. We wish you to investigate for yourself, and be convinced that we can save you from 30 to 50 per cent on clocks.

We give at the bottom of each page the approximate weight of the clocks represented on that page, boxed ready for shipment, from which you can estimate the cost of the shipping charges if you desire.

It is not necessary for you to pay the shipping charges in advance. The best way is to pay them when you get the goods.

**Clocks will be sent to any address by express C. O. D.** when desired, providing a deposit of $2.00 is sent with order. The balance can be paid at the express office after examination. If the goods are not satisfactory the goods can be refused and the money advanced will be refunded.

**When cash in full** is sent with order you are entitled to a discount of 3 per cent.; on orders over $50, 4 per cent.; over $100, 5 per cent.

**You run no risk** by sending cash in full, for if the goods are not satisfactory they can be returned at our expense and your money will be refunded.

Clocks take first-class freight and express rates. For further instructions on rates, etc., see front of this book.

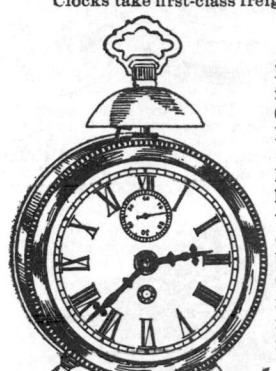

**Imported.** No. 62909. Nickel Alarm Clock, 4 inch dial, similar to No. 62910, a very good timekeeper. Price, 57c.

**Beacon.** No. 62910. Nickel Alarm Clock; height, 6½ inches; width, 4¼ inches; 4 inch dial; made by the celebrated New Haven Clock Company; lever movement, best grade nickel clock made, warranted. Price, 78c.

**Beacon Luminous.** No. 62911. Nickel Alarm Clock, with luminous dial; height, 6½ inches; width, 4¼ inches; 4 inch dial, and is manufactured by the New Haven Clock Company of New Haven, Conn.; best grade lever movement. Price, 97c.

NOTE—The dial on above clock is luminous, and will show distinctly the time in the dark. The darker it is the brighter it glows.

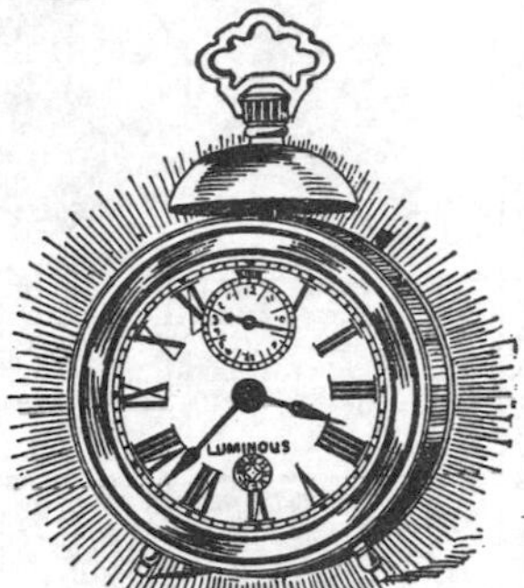

**"Must Get Up."** No. 62912. Nickel Alarm Clock; height, 5⅞ inches; dial, 4½ inches; made by the Waterbury Clock Company. This clock has very large bell on the back of the clock; the alarm runs five minutes with one winding; can be made to run a short, medium, long, or extra long time, and can be stopped at pleasure. The movement is best grade lever escapement and warranted. Price, $1.40.

**Spinning Wheel.** No. 62913. Fancy Clock, in silver plate or gilt bronze finish; dial, 2 inches; beveled-edged glass; height, 3¾ inches; made by the Waterbury Clock Company; good lever movement; has no alarm. Price, $1.40.

**Patrol.** No. 62914. Fancy Nickel Alarm Clock; height, 6 inches; dial, 2½ inches; has glass sides to show the movement; gilt front and handle; fine lever escapement movement; bell underneath; made by the Waterbury Clock Company. Price, $1.85.

**Guide.** No. 62915. Fancy Nickel Alarm Clock (similar to 62914); height, 7 inches; dial, 2½ inches; glass sides to show movement; gilt front and handle; bell underneath; made by the Waterbury Clock Company. Price, $2.

No. 62915½. Same as above, but strikes hours and halves, and has alarm. Price, $2.40.

Nos. 62914, 62915, 62915½.

**Basket.** No. 62916. Fancy Basket Clock, in gilt bronze or silver plate; height, 4⅞ inches; dial, 2 inches, beveled glass, fine lever movement, made by the Waterbury Clock Company. Price, $1.65.

No. 62916.

**Capitol.** No. 62917. Fancy Clock, finished in gilt or silver plate; height, 5⅜ inches; dial, 2 inches, beveled glass, good lever movement, made by the Waterbury Clock Company. Price, $2.10.

No. 62917½. Same as above, with alarm. Price, $2.62.

Nos. 62917 and 62917½.

**Liberty.** No. 62918. Beautiful Bronze Case, representing Liberty and the Liberty Bell, with trumpet and flag; height, 12½ inches; width, 9½ inches; diameter of dial, 3 inches; has good lever escapement movement, is well finished, and is a very beautiful little clock for the money. Price, $1.85.

No. 62918.

## PORCELAIN CLOCKS.

Porcelain Clocks have of late become very popular and are having a wonderful sale. The cases are made of one solid piece of porcelain, in irregular and fancy shapes, beautifully ornamented with raised work and colored gold decorations. The porcelain case is especially desirable in addition to its beauty for the reason that it will never become soiled. The finish is indestructible, and can be cleaned without any fear of damage. They have always been sold at very high prices, but we have made special arrangements by which we are able to sell them at a price which brings them within the reach of anyone. In fact, everything considered, they are the cheapest clock made. The cuts do not do these clocks justice. They must be seen to be appreciated.

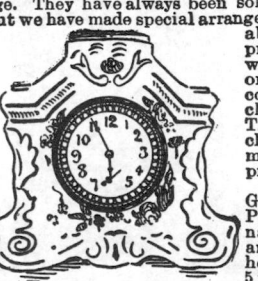

**Cilicia.** No. 62919. Genuine imported white Porcelain Case, fancy ornamented with colors, and hand painted; height, 5 inches; width, 5 inches; dial, 2 inches. Movement is made by the New Haven Clock Company; a good timekeeper. Price, $1.50.

**Boudoir No. 19.** No. 62920. Genuine imported white Porcelain Case, with gilt and colored hand painted decorations; height, 4⅞ inches; diameter, 4⅝ inches; dial, 2 inches; with beveled glass; fine lever movement made by the Waterbury Company. Price, $1.65.

**Boudoir No. 20.** No. 62921. Same as No. 62920, except the height, which is 6¼ inches; diameter, 5⅞ inches; dial, 3½ inches; with alarm. Price, $2.15.

Nos. 62920 and 62921.

**Boudoir No. 10.** No. 62922. Genuine Porcelain Case, ornamented with gilt and colored, hand painted decorations; height, 7½ inches; length, 5⅝ inches; beveled glass, 2 inch silver dial; has fine lever movement made by the Waterbury Clock Company. Price, $2.50.

**Ardmore.** No. 62923. Fancy genuine imported Porcelain Case, with gilt and colored hand painted decorations; height, 9½ inches; width 5 inches; dial 2 inches, very fancy; made by the New Haven Clock Company. Price, $3.00.

**Boudoir No. 13.** No. 62924. Genuine Porcelain Case, with gilt and colored hand painted decorations; height, 8⅞ inches; length, 7¼ inches; dial 3½ inches; has fine lever movement made by the celebrated Waterbury Clock Company; with alarm. Price, $3.45.

**Parlor.** No. 62925. Genuine imported white Porcelain Case, with gilt and colored hand painted decorations; height, 8⅞ inches; length, 7¼ inches; ivory dial, 3½ inches; fancy gilt center, cast gilt sash and bezel 8 day; strikes hours and half hours on cup bell; has fine lever movement; made by the celebrated Waterbury Clock Company. Price, $5.75.

Nos. 62924 and 62925.

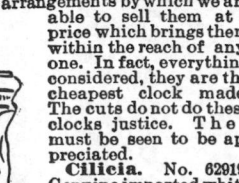

### Clock Department—Continued.

**Bonaparte.** No. 62926. Genuine imported Porcelain Case, with very fancy gilt and colored hand painted cupid decorations; height, 10½ inches; width, 9¾ inches; 3 inch dial; fine 8 day movement; made by New Haven Clock Company; strikes hours and half-hours; is an elegant clock. Price, $6.40.

**Porcelain L.** No. 62927. Fine genuine imported Porcelain Case, with fancy colored hand painted decorations; height, 12 inches; width, 10½ inches; French rococo sash and porcelain dial; fine 8 day movement; made by the Ansonia Clock Company; strikes hours and half-hours on fine Cathedral gong bell. Price, $8.25.

**Dorda.** No. 62928. Polished, ebonized Wood Case, with gilt ornaments and gilt engraving; very fancy, in imitation of black onyx; height, 12 inches; length, 11 inches; dial, 4½ inches, with fine 8 day movement; made by the Waterbury Clock Company; strikes hours and half hours on cathedral gong bell. Your choice of American white dial with Roman figures, or American gilt dial with Arabic figures like cut. Price, $4.50.

**Aragon.** No. 62929. Very fancy and enameled Iron Case; a most excellent imitation of Tennessee marble, with very fancy colored and gilt ornamentation; height, 11 inches; width 10 inches; 6 inch white or gilt dial; fine 8 day movement made by the New Haven Clock Company; strikes hours and half hours on cathedral gong bell. Price, $7.50.

**Savoy.** No. 62930. Fancy enameled Iron Clock, with colored and gilt bronze ornamentations; height, 9¾ inches; width, 9 inches; fine 8 day movement made by the Ansonia Clock Company; strikes hours and half hours on cathedral gong bell; fancy dial and very fancy sash. Price, $5.90.

**Leona.** No. 62931. Very fancy enameled Iron Case, showing variegated blue finish, in imitation of marble, with fancy colored and gilt ornamentations; height, 12 in.; width, 9¼ in.; 6 inch white or gilt dial; fine 8 day movement made by the New Haven Clock Company; strikes hours and half hours on cathedral gong bell. Price, $5.95.

**Castanet.** No. 62932. Very fancy enameled Iron Case, showing oak-wood finish, with fancy colored and gilt ornamentations; height, 12⅝ inches; width, 8½ inches; 6 inch white or gilt dial, with fine 8 day movement made by the New Haven Clock Company; strikes hours and halves on cathedral gong bell. Price, $6.25.

**Batavia.** No. 62933. Fine polished Wood Case in imitation of black onyx, with gilt engraving; fancy bronze side ornaments and feet; fancy dial and sash; height, 10½ in.; length, 11¾ inches; dial 5½ inches, with fine 8 day movement, made by the Waterbury Clock Company; strikes hours and halves on cathedral gong bell; with American gilt or white dial. Price, $4.40.

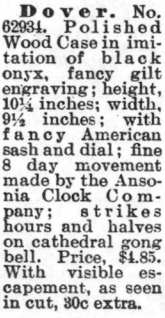

**Dover.** No. 62934. Polished Wood Case in imitation of black onyx, fancy gilt engraving; height, 10¼ inches; width, 9¼ inches; with fancy American sash and dial; fine 8 day movement made by the Ansonia Clock Company; strikes hours and halves on cathedral gong bell. Price, $4.85. With visible escapement, as seen in cut, 30c extra.

**New Monaco.** No. 62935. Very fancy enameled Iron Case smoked finish; a most excellent imitation of marble, with fancy colored and gilt decoration; height, 11½ inches; width, 12 inches; 6 inch white or gilt dial; fine 8 day movement made by the New Haven Clock Company; strikes hours and halves on cathedral gong bell. Price, $7.80.

**Amiens.** No. 62936. Enameled Iron Case, with very fancy colored and gilt ornamentations and feet; height, 10¼ inches; width, 13½ inches; fancy gilt dial and sash; fine 8 day movement made by the Ansonia Clock Company; strikes hours and halves on cathedral gong bell. Price, $7.90.

**Fresno.** No. 62937. Very fine polished Wood Case, in imitation of black onyx, fancy gilt engraving, marbleized columns, with gilt bronze bases and caps, fancy sash; height, 10⅝ inches; length, 16 inches; dial, 5½ inches; fine 8 day movement; made by the Waterbury Clock Company, strikes hours and halves on cathedral gong bell, American white dial, Roman figures, or American gilt dial with Arabic figures. Price, $5.40.

**Chester.** No. 62938. Fine polished Wood Case, in imitation of black onyx, with gilt engraving, gilt bronze side ornaments and feet, very fancy sash; height, 10½ inches; width, 16 inches; fine 8 day movement, made by the Ansonia Clock Company, strikes hours and halves on cathedral gong bell, fine American gilt dial with Arabic figures. Price, $6.60.

**Porcelain Clocks on this page weigh, boxed, about 20 lbs.; Enameled Iron Clocks, 22 to 37 lbs.; Marbleized Wood, 15 to 19 lbs.**

**Clock Department—Continued.**

**Java.** No. 62939. Polished Wood Case in imitation of black onyx, fancy gilt engraving, 6 marbleized columns with artistic bronze caps and bases, large fancy bronze side ornaments and feet; height, 11¼ inches; length, 18¼ inches; dial, 5½ inches; fine 8 day movement made by the Waterbury Clock Company, strikes hours and half hours on cathedral gong bell, American white dial with Roman figures, or fancy gilt dial with Arabic figures. Price, $6.30.

**Sicily.** No. 62940. Very fancy polished Wood Case, in imitation of black onyx, with elaborate gilt engravings; large fancy bronze handles, feet and moulding; height, 11 inches; length, 17 inches; very fine 8 day movement, made by the Ansonia Clock Company, strikes hours and half hours on cathedral gong bell, fine American sash and dial, with fine visible escapement. Price, $6.90.

**Marble.** No. 62942. Very fancy polished Wood Case, in imitation of brown Italian or verde antique (green) marble top base and columns, with imitation black onyx body; fancy gilt engraving, with fancy gilt bronze ornaments and tops and bases to columns; also heavy bronze side ornaments and feet; length, 17 inches; height, 11¼ inches. The top of the clock is ornamented by beautiful gilt bronze figure of lady and harp; height, 8½ inches; is fitted with fine 8 day movement, made by the Waterbury Clock Company; strikes hours and halves on cathedral gong bell; very fancy gilt dial with Arabic figures in black enamel; has a patent regulator by which the clock can be regulated without touching the pendulum. Price, $6.45.

The above clock is a work of art, and must be seen to be appreciated. It has the appearance of a clock that would sell at from $50 to $60. It is a most beautiful clock, to which we cannot do justice by any description or engravings we could possibly give you.

**Pointer.** No. 62943. Fine bronze ornament for mantle or top of mantel clock; height, 4 inches; length, 7⅜ inches. Price, 95c.

62943.

**Onyx.** No. 62945. Wood Case, with new process indestructible finish, which is a most excellent imitation of Mexican onyx, and except that it is examined very closely no one would believe that it was not a real onyx clock. It holds a beautiful polish, and with proper care would last a lifetime. If case gets soiled or dirty it can be wiped off with a damp cloth without any fear of injury; has fancy bronze feet, made in artistic scroll designs; fine Corinthian style bronze tops and bases to columns; bronze lions' heads, with rings in mouth, as side ornaments; fancy gilt dial and sash, with black enameled figures; length, 17 inches; height, 11½ inches; has fine 8 day movement, made by the old reliable Seth Thomas Clock Company of Thomaston, Conn., and is fully warranted by them; strikes hours and halves on cathedral gong bell; has patent regulator by which the clock can be regulated without touching the pendulum. If you are in need of a clock, now is your opportunity to have one of the finest in town. If your old clock needs repairs, it will pay you better to discard it and add a little to what the repairs would cost and have a new one. Price, $5.90.

NOTE.—This clock is being sold by retail jewelers and installment houses for $12 and $14.

62946.

**Ormonde.** No. 62946. Beautiful bronze figure of horse, for mantel ornament or top of mantel clock; height, 7½ inches; length, 8 inches. Price, $1.75.

**Knight.** No. 62941. Elaborate gilt bronze case, with very fancy engravings and scroll decorations, ornamented with a fine statue of a bugler; very fancy sash, with fine visible escapement; height, 15 inches; width, 15 inches; has fine 8 day movement; made by the Ansonia Clock Company; strikes hours and halves on beautiful cathedral gong bell. Price, $14.85.

NOTE—Such a clock as this cannot be found in the average retail store, but is a real work of art, one that you will not find in any other than the finest stores in the large cities. It is a clock that will retail at $25 and upwards. Price, $3.25.

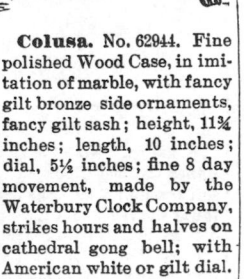

**Colusa.** No. 62944. Fine polished Wood Case, in imitation of marble, with fancy gilt bronze side ornaments, fancy gilt sash; height, 11¾ inches; length, 10 inches; dial, 5½ inches; fine 8 day movement, made by the Waterbury Clock Company, strikes hours and halves on cathedral gong bell; with American white or gilt dial. Price, $4.50.

**No charge for boxing or cartage. The prices we quote are for the goods carefully packed and delivered on board the cars in Chicago.**

62947.

**Ceres.** No. 62947. Fine bronze statue of lady with bundle of wheat and sickle. Makes a beautiful ornament for mantel or top of mantel clock; height, 7 inches; length, 7⅞ inches. Price, $1.90.

**Tick Tack.** No. 62948. Height, 11 inches; dial, 5 inches, with mahogany finish, one day time only. Price, 70c.

No. 62948½. Same as above, with alarm. Price, 95c.

62948.

**Don't overlook our Grocery Department, and make up an order of 100 pounds or more, and thus secure the very lowest tariff rate possible.**

**Marbleized Wood Clocks on this page weigh, boxed, from 15 to 19 lbs.; Bronze Clock, about 40 lbs.; Bronze Mantel Ornaments, about 15 lbs.**

## Clock Department—Continued.

62949.

**Duxbury.** No. 62949. Cabinet Clock, in solid oak or walnut, 22½ in. high; carved 6 in. dial; 8 day movement; made by the New Haven Clock Company. Strikes hours and halves on wire bell. Price, $2.

**Beaver.** No. 62953. Very fancy Cabinet Clock, in black walnut only; fancy carved and ornamented; height, 22½ inches; dial, 6 inches; fine 8 day movement; made by the Ansonia Clock Company; strikes hours and halves on wire bell. Price, $2.90; cathedral gong bell when desired, 30c extra.

62953.

**Saranac.** No. 62957. Fancy Cabinet Wall Clock, in solid oak or walnut; very fancy carved and turned ornamentations; height, 29 inches; dial, 6 inches; has accurate barometer and thermometer; fine 8 day movement; made by the Waterbury Clock company; strikes hours and halves on cathedral gong bell. Price, $3.90; alarm additional, when desired, 30c. This Clock has an Ornamental Base and is intended to be hung on the wall and not be set on a shelf.

**Flint.** No. 62950. Cabinet Clock, solid oak or walnut, fancy carved; height, 22 inches; dial, 6 in.; movement made by the Waterbury Clock Company, one day strike. Price, $2.25.
No. 62950¼. Eight day, strikes hours and halves on wire bell. Price, $2.50.
No. 62950½. Eight day, strikes hours and halves on cathedral gong bell. Price, $2.75.

62950.

No. 62950¾. Same as above, 8 day; strikes hours and half hours on gong bell, and has calender. Price, $3. The Calender Clock cannot be fitted with alarm. Alarm on Nos. 62950 and 62950½, 30c extra.

**Clarence.** No. 62954. Fancy Cabinet Clock, 22½ inches high; dial, 6 inches; made in oak only; beautifully carved and ornamented; fine 8 day movement; made by the Ansonia Clock Company; strikes hours and halves on wire bell. Price, $2.75; gong bell when desired, 30c extra.

62954.

**Buffalo.** No. 62958. Fancy Cabinet Clock in solid black walnut only; very fancy ornamented and carved case; height 26⅞ inches; dial, 8 inches; fitted with fine 8 day movement; made by the Waterbury Clock Company; strikes hours and halves on wire bell with calendar. Price, $3.70.
No. 62958½. Same as above but with cathedral gong bell. Price, $4.

**Niantic.** No. 62951. Cabinet Clock, in solid oak or walnut beautifully carved; height, 22½ inches; dial, 6 inches; fine 8 day movement; made by the New Haven Clock Company; strikes hours and halves on wire bell. Price, $2.40; cathedral gong bell on above when desired, 30c extra.

62951.

**Richland.** No. 62955. Fancy Cabinet Clock, in solid oak or walnut; very fancy carved and ornamented; height, 22 inches; dial, 6 inches, with fine 8 day movement; made by the Waterbury Clock Company; strikes hours and half hours on wire bell. Price, $3.40. Cathedral gong bell when desired, 30c extra; alarm extra, when desired, 30c.

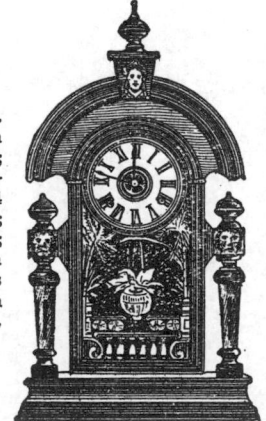

**Triumph.** No. 62959. Very fancy Cabinet Clock in black walnut only; fine carved and turned ornamentations; height, 24½ inches; dial, 6 inches; with fancy bronze ornaments, plate glass mirrors in each side; silver cupid statues; fine 8 day movement; made by the Ansonia Clock Company; strikes hours and halves on cathedral gong bell. Price, $5.55.

**Recorder.** No. 62952. Cabinet Clock, in solid oak or walnut, fancy carved and ornamented case; height, 23 inches; dial, 6 inch; fine 8 day movement; made by the New Haven Clock Company; strikes hours and half hours on wire bell. Price, $2.75.
No. 62952½. Same as above, with cathedral gong bell. Price, $3; alarm extra when desired, 30c.

62952.

**King.** No. 62956. Fancy Cabinet Clock, in solid walnut or oak; fancy carved and ornamented; height, 24 inches; dial, 6 inches; fine 8 day movement; made by the Ansonia Clock Company. Strikes hours and halves on cathedral gong bell. Price, $3.90.

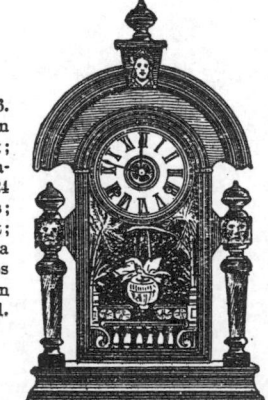

**Monarch.** No. 62960. Very fancy Cabinet Clock, in black walnut only; fancy carved, with bronze ornaments and fancy French sash. Height, 24½ inches; dial, 6 inches; with fine 8 day movement; made by the Ansonia Clock Company; strikes hours and halves, with fancy pendulum. Price, $6.15; cathedral gong bell, 30c extra.

**The Mantel Clocks on this page weigh, boxed, from 22 to 30 lbs.** Compare our prices with those you would have to pay in your own town at your retail jeweler's, if you wish to know how much you can save by buying of us.

## Clock Department—Continued.

**Viol.** No. 62961. Fancy Mantel Clock, in solid oak or mahogany, fancy carved and ornamented; height, 16 inches; dial, 5½ inches; fine 8 day movement; strikes hours and halves on cathedral gong bell; American gilt dial with Arabic figures. Price, $3.25.

**Watson.** No. 62962. Fancy oak or walnut Mantel Clock, beautifully engraved and carved cases. Height, 16 inch; dial, 5½ inch; 8 day movement; made by the Waterbury Clock Company; strikes hours and halves on cathedral gong bell; American gilt dial with Arabic figures. Price, $3.75.

**Tivoli.** No. 62963. Fancy Mantel Clock, with black walnut, case; height, 15 inches; width, 11½ inches; fancy carved, extra finish case; fine 8 day movement; made by the Ansonia Clock Company; strikes hours and halves on cathedral gong bell; very fancy sash, and dial 5¾ inches. Price, $3.25.

**Perpetual Calendar.** No. 62964. Fine solid walnut or oak case, elegantly carved, height, 24 inches; dial, 6 inches. This clock is made by the Waterbury Clock Company; has fine 8 day, hour and half hour strike movements, with cathedral gong bell and calendar. The calendar is perpetual, showing the day of the week, the month and day of the month; is guaranteed to be thoroughly reliable and accurate. Price, $5.25.

This clock can be furnished with alarm, when desired, for 25c extra.

**Seth Thomas.** No. 62965. This is the genuine old reliable Seth Thomas Weight Clock, made by the Seth Thomas Clock Company, of Thomaston, Conn. The case has rosewood or walnut finish, with one day weight strike movement; height, 25½ inches. Price, $5.20.

No. 62965½. With 8 day weight strike movement; height, 29½ inches. Price, $7.45.

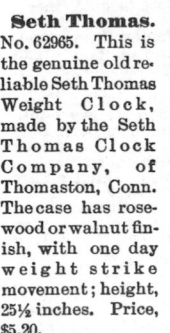

**Octagon Lever.** No. 62966. Has oak, walnut or cherry veneered octagon case or round nickel case; movement is patent lever, is made by the Waterbury Clock Company, and is a good reliable timepiece. This clock is especially desirable for offices, schools, churches, etc.; one day, with 4 inch dial, time only. Price, $1.45.

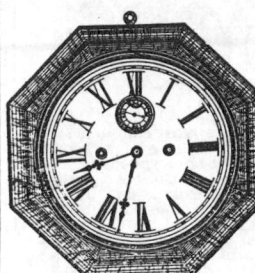

62966 to 62972.

No. 62967. One day, 6 inch dial, time only. Price, $2.10.
No. 62968. One day, 8 inch dial, time only. Price, $2.35.
No. 62969. One day, 10 inch dial, time only. Price, $2.95.
No. 62970. 8 day, 10 inch dial, time only. Price, $3.45.
No. 62971. 8 day, 10 inch dial; strikes. Price, $4.50.
No. 62972. 8 day, 12 inch dial; strikes. Price, $4.90.

**Saxon.** No. 62973. Rosewood veneered case, well finished; height, 22 inches; dial, 10 inches; is made by the New Haven Clock Company, and is especially designed for offices, schools, churches, etc.; 8 day; time only. Price, $3.40.

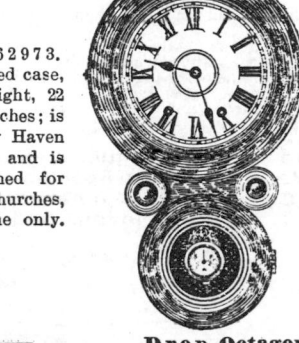

**Drop Octagon.** Has solid oak or fine veneered case; movement is made by the Waterbury Clock Company and is thoroughly reliable. Is designed for offices, schools or churches.

No. 62974. 8 day, 10 inch dial; time only. Price, $3.45.
No. 62975. 8 day, 10 inch dial; time only, with calendar. Price, $3.75.
No. 62976. 8 day, 10 inch dial; strikes hours and halves, with calendar. Price, $4.30.
No. 62977. 8 day, 12 inch dial, time only. Price, $3.70.
No. 62978. 8 day, 12 inch dial; strikes hours and halves. Price, $4.40.

62974 to 62979.

No. 62979. 8 day, 12 inch dial, time only, with calendar. Price, $3.95.
NOTE—The height of the clocks with 10 inch dial is 21 inches; 12 inch dial, 23½ inches.

**Bruce.** No. 62980. Oak, walnut or cherry case, beautifully carved and turned ornaments. Height, 38¼ inches; width, 14¾ inches; dial 8 inches; has fine 8-day movement with wood pendulum rod, which is not affected by changes of temperature; made by the Waterbury Clock Company, and is a very fine timepiece. Price, $6.70.

The above makes a very beautiful clock for office, school or church.

**Regulator.** No. 62931. Has solid oak or handsome veneered and very fine finished case. Height, 32 inches, with 12 inch dial; has very fine 8 day movement, with calendar; made by the Waterbury Clock Company; has wood pendulum rod, which is not affected by changes of temperature, and is a very fine timepiece; makes a very fine office clock or regulator. Price, $5.85.

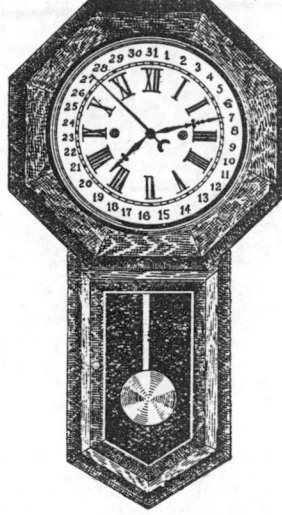

**No. 62982. Cuckoo Clock.** These Clocks are largely in use in Europe and have of late years become very popular in this country. The clock is quite a novelty, but is thoroughly practical and is certainly a very interesting and pretty ornament in any home. The little door above the dial opens every half hour; a bird appears, flaps its wings and calls Cuckoo, once for half hours and as many times as it is necessary to denote the time on the hours. Before the cuckoo has called the hours the clock strikes the hours in the regular way. The clock is fitted with a solid brass movement, cut steel pinions and has two copper finished fancy iron weights. The height of the case is 19 inches, width 13 inches, made of fancy carved German walnut ebonized ornaments, has white bone hands and figures. Price............$5.50

**No. 62983. Calendar Eight Day Clock with Thermometer and Barometer.** A most wonderful and complete clock for a little money. This clock has been one of the greatest bargains that we have ever been able to offer to our customers, and the best evidence that they have appreciated the same has been demonstrated by the very large sales. It has been one of the best selling clocks we have ever offered. We buy them in immense quantities for spot cash, and the price at which we offer them will save you, we believe, fully 50 per cent. over the prices asked by retail dealers. The clock will be furnished with solid black walnut or antique oak case, as desired, beautifully carved, ornamented and decorated. The picture really does not do it justice, for it is a work of art. The height is 24 inches with dial 6 inches. The movement is one of the best made, and is warranted to be an accurate time keeper; has a complete calendar attachment which works automatically and always indicates correctly the day of the month. It has a perfect thermometer on one side and on the other side a barometer. The barometer always indicates the condition of the atmosphere and always correctly foretells the probabilities of the weather; both are artistically set and add very much to the appearance and beauty of the clock. It is eight day and strikes the hours and halves on a beautiful gong bell. We cannot furnish it with alarm; in fact, an alarm should not be used on a cabinet clock. This clock will last a life time if properly cared for and we will guarantee satisfaction in every respect. Weight of clock, boxed ready for shipment is 17 lbs. Price............$3.65

# OPTICAL GOODS

**In this Department** we carry a most complete line of all kinds of optical goods. While we are compelled to carry some cheap goods to supply the demand for such, our specialty is the best quality of goods. You will find every article described exactly as it is and any goods which are not satisfactory to the purchaser can be returned to us for exchange, or if desired the money will be cheerfully refunded. Optical goods as well as watches and jewelry are sold by retail dealers and local merchants at enormous profits, while we are satisfied with our usual small per cent in advance of net cost to us. Opticians make a practice of imposing on their customers by charging from $3.00 to $12.00 for spectacles and eye glasses and give as an excuse for the prices charged, "that the lenses were ground to order." Grinding to order is necessary only in cases where one or both eyes are affected by what is called astigmatism, which is of very rare occurrence. Do not get the idea that it is necessary for you to have a personal interview with an optician, and that instruments called optimeters are necessary to fit you with glasses.

We have during the past year fitted many thousand people to their entire satisfaction. Many people think that the longer they put off wearing glasses the better, but this is not true for often irreparable injury is done by such neglect. The wearing of glasses is made necessary by a defect in the shape of the eyes and not until the strain on the muscles (in their vain effort to adjust the defective vision) is relieved, will the injury cease.

If you will carefully follow our instructions, we will have no trouble in selecting glasses which will fit you perfectly.

State your age; state whether glasses have been worn or not; if so, state whether for reading or distant objects or both. State whether glasses are wanted for reading or distant objects or both.

State the distance from the center of one eye to the center of the other. You can take the measure with a rule or tape across the nose. State whether the bridge of the nose is prominent or flat.

The proper reading distance is from 12 to 14 inches from the eyes, and when it is necessary to hold the book nearer, spectacles for near sight are required. When farther away spectacles for far sight.

## TO TEST THE EYES FOR ASTIGMATISM.

If some of the arms of the above figure appear more distinct than others, it is evident that your eyes are affected with astigmatism. This difficulty can be corrected only by having cylindrical lenses carefully ground to order from an oculist's prescription, or by personal fitting. The presence of astigmatism is, however, very rare.

### TEST FOR NEAR SIGHT.

State the greatest distance from the eyes at which paragraph 24 in the test type below can be distinctly seen. The number of inches between the eyes and this page will indicate the number of concave lenses required.

### TEST FOR OLD OR FAR SIGHT.

Hold this page in a good light at 12 to 14 inches from the eyes and state the finest print that can possibly be read at that distance. The number of the paragraph will indicate the number of convex glasses required for reading, sewing, etc.

No. 48.

The smallest size letters on this card should be read easily at fifteen inches from the eye. If you cannot do so you should wear spectacles. It does not pay to buy cheap spectacles.

No. 36.

They disturb the rays of light, disturb the angles of vision, cause pain and discomfort and injure the

No. 30.

eyesight. When it is necessary to hold work or reading matter farther than fifteen

No. 26.

inches from the eyes in order to see distinctly, it is a sure sign of failing vision

No. 24.

and much annoyance, discomfort and pain will be prevented by

No. 18.

having a pair of glasses fitted.

No. 16.

## Buy no other kind.

No. 14.

## Crystalline are

No. 10.

the best

**The Following Illustrations Show The Various Styles of Spectacles and Style Glasses. See Adjoining Column for Full Descriptions and Prices.**

Style A. Spectacles, straight temples, steel, alumnico, gold or gold filled frames.

Style B. Spectacles, straight temples, gold or gold filled frames.

Style C. Spectacles, riding bow temples, steel, alumnico, gold or gold filled frames.

Style D. Spectacles, with cable riding bow temples and gold or gold filled frames.

Style E. Spectacles, frameless, riding bow temples, gold or gold filled mountings.

Style F. Spectacles, flat eye, straight or riding temples, steel or solid gold frames.

Style A H. Spectacles, showing straight bi-focal lenses.

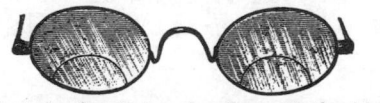

Style A J. Spectacles, showing perfection bi-focal

## STEEL SPECTACLES WITH STRAIGHT TEMPLES. FOR CUTS SHOWING STYLES SEE ADJOINING COLUMN.

**No. 69500. Steel** frames, common, straight temples, similar to style A, plano convex lenses (not recommended), all numbers. Price......................10c

**No. 69501. Style A**, steel frames, better quality, straight temples, screws in joints with plano convex lenses (not recommended) all numbers. Price....25c

**No. 69502. Style A**, steel frames, straight temples, good finish, nickel plated, periscopic lenses. Price................................................50c

**No. 69503. Style A**, steel frames, tempered, fine quality, wide, flat, nose bridge, nickel plated with finest periscopic lenses. Price.....................75c

**No. 69504. Style A**, steel frames, tempered, best quality, straight temples, wide, flat, nose bridge, extra finish and nickel plated with finest quality periscopic Brazillian lenses. Price.......................$1 75

## STEEL SPECTACLES WITH RIDING BOWS. FOR CUTS SHOWING STYLES SEE ADJOINING COLUMN.

**No. 69510. Style C**, steel temples, fine quality, riding bow temples, with broad nose piece, nickel plated with fine quality periscopic lenses. Price.........75c

**No. 69511. Style C**, steel frames, extra fine, broad nose piece, riding bow temples, nickel plated with finest quality periscopic lenses. Price..........$1.25

**No. 69513. Style F**, steel frames, good quality, phantoscopic or flat eye spectacles, with straight temples, nickel plated periscopic convex lenses. Price.....75c

This style of spectacle frame is very convenient for reading spectacles, as the wearer can look over them when he wishes to see a distance. They can also be furnished in solid gold if desired.

**No. 69514. Style F**, steel frames, fine quality, straight temples, nickel plated with finest periscopic lenses. Price..................................$1.00

When desired Nos. 69513 and 69514 can be furnished with riding bow temples for 15 cents extra.

## ALUMNICO SPECTACLES.

Alumnico is a new alloy which is as white as silver and will not tarnish or rust. It is fast becoming very popular for spectacle frames and we highly recommend it.

### For Cuts Showing Styles See Adjoining Column.

**No. 69518. Style A**, alumnico frames with straight temples, fine periscopic lenses. Price..........$1.00

**No. 69519. Style C**, alumnico frames with riding bow temples, broad nose piece, fine periscopic lenses. Price.................................................$1.25

## GOLD FILLED SPECTACLES.

Gold filled spectacles are becoming very popular for the reason that they are equal in appearance to solid gold and cost much less. The frames for gold filled spectacles are made in the same manner as gold filled watch cases. They are warranted to give entire satisfaction.

### For Cuts Showing Styles See Adjoining Column.

**No. 69525. Style B**, gold filled frames, fine quality flat eye wire and straight temples, broad nose piece, fine periscopic lenses. Price.....................$1.25

**No. 69526. Style A**, gold filled frames, finest quality, round eye wire, straight temples, broad nose piece, with finest periscopic lenses. Price............$1.75

**No. 69530. Style C**, fine gold filled frames, riding bow temples, broad nose piece, fine periscopic lenses. Price.................................................$1.25

**No. 69531. Style C**, gold filled frames, finest quality, warranted for 10 years, riding bow temples, broad nose piece, with finest quality periscopic lenses. Price.................................................$1.50

**No. 69532. Style C**, gold filled frames, finest quality, warranted for 10 years, with extra showy cable temples, broad nose piece, fitted with finest periscopic lenses. Price...........................$2.20

Cable temples are larger but much more flexible than the regular riding bow temples, which makes them much more comfortable to the wearer.

**No. 69535. Style E**, gold filled mountings, finest quality, frameless, riding bow temples, broad nose piece, with fine periscopic lenses. Price........$1.70

## SOLID GOLD SPECTACLES.

In solid gold spectacles we list both 14 and 10 karat, but nothing lower. The 10 karat grade we will guarantee to give entire satisfaction and it will not tarnish. There is nothing better made than the 14 karat grade. Both the workmanship and the grade are fully guaranteed.

### For Cuts Showing Styles See Adjoining Column.

**No. 69540. Style A**, solid gold frame, round eye wire, straight temples, with finest quality periscopic lenses. Price in 10 karat......................$4.00

Price in 14 karat.................................. 4.90

**No. 69543. Style B**, solid gold frame, flat eye wire, straight temples, broad nose piece, with finest quality periscopic lenses. Price in 10 karat.........$4.15

Price in 14 karat.................................. 5.20

**No. 69545. Style C**, solid gold frame, medium weight, riding bow temples, broad nose piece, with finest quality periscopic lenses. Price in 10 karat..$3.75

### Gold Spectacles—Continued.

No. 69546. **Style C, solid gold frames**, heavy weight with riding bow temples, broad nose piece, finest quality periscopic lenses. Price in 10 karat.......... **$4.20**
Price in 14 karat.......................... **4.90**

No. 69548. **Style D, solid gold frames**, heavy weight, broad nose piece with cable temples, finest quality periscopic lenses. Price in 10 karat.............. **$4.60**
Price in 14 karat.......................... **5.50**

No. 69550. **Style E, solid gold mountings** frameless, medium weight temples, broad nose piece, with finest quality periscopic lenses. Price in 10 karat.......................... **$3.75**
Price in 14 karat.......................... **4.55**

### BI-FOCAL SPECTACLES.

Bi-Focal spectacles are a very great convenience for the reason that the upper lenses are double convex, can be furnished in any number, focused for distance, while the lower lense is focused for reading. They can be furnished in frames, styles A, B, C and D, with steel, alumnico, gold filled or solid gold frames in any grade listed at 25 cents or over; for style H bi-focal lenses add 25 cents, for style J bi-focal lenses add 50 cents.
For cuts showing styles see adjoining column.

### EYE-GLASSES.

With all Eye-Glasses costing 50 cents or over (except those with offset guards) we give a case and silk cord free.

### RUBBER FRAMES.

For cuts showing styles see adjoining column.

No. 69560. **Style K, rubber frame**, convex lenses only (not recommended). Price.......................... **15c**

No. 69562. **Style R, rubber frames**, cork guards, double convex lenses, fair quality. Price.......... **28c**

No. 69563. **Style M, shell zylonite frames**, adjustable cork guards, bronzed steel spring, finest quality periscopic lenses. Price.......................... **90c**

### STEEL EYE-GLASSES.

For cuts showing styles see adjoining column.

No. 69564. Style similar to M, not adjustable, good steel frames, blue or bronze with cork guards and periscopic lenses. Price.......................... **55c**

No. 69565. **Style R, steel frames**, extra fine, light, nickel plated with cork guards and finest quality periscopic lenses. Price.......................... **85c**

No. 69568. **Style L, steel frames**, extra fine, light, nickel plated, adjustable cork guards with finest quality periscopic lenses. Price.......................... **90c**

No. 69570. **Style N, steel frames**, extra fine, light, nickel plated, offset cork guards, with finest quality periscopic lenses. Price.......................... **75c**

### ALUMNICO EYE-GLASSES.

For cuts showing styles see adjoining column.

No. 69575. **Style L, alumnico frames**, adjustable cork guards, periscopic convex lenses. Price... **$1.10**

### GOLD FILLED EYE-GLASSES.

For cuts showing styles see adjoining column.

Gold Filled Eye-Glasses are very popular and are equal in appearance to solid Gold and are fully warranted by us.

No. 69577. **Style N, gold filled frames**, fine quality seamless wire, offset cork guards, with fine periscopic lenses. Price.......................... **$1.20**

No. 69578. **Style N, gold filled frames**, extra quality, warranted for 10 years, offset cork guards, with fine periscopic lenses. Price.......................... **$1.75**

No. 69580. **Style M, gold filled frames**, fine quality, seamless wire, adjustable cork guards, finest periscopic lenses. Price.......................... **$1.20**

No. 69582. **Style P, gold filled**, skeleton mountings, fine quality, offset cork guards, frameless, fine quality periscopic lenses. Price.......................... **$1.50**

### SOLID GOLD EYE-GLASSES.

For cuts showing styles see adjoining column.

In solid gold eye-glasses we list both 10 and 14 karat, but nothing lower. The 10 karat grade we guarantee to give entire satisfaction and not to tarnish. The workmanship and quality are fully warranted.

No. 69590. **Solid gold frames**, (similar to style O.) medium weight, cork nose pieces, with finest quality periscopic lenses. Price in 10 karat.............. **$3.50**
Price in 14 karat.......................... **4.50**

No. 69592. **Style L, solid gold frames**, medium weight, patent adjustable cork nose piece, with finest quality periscopic lenses. Price in 10 karat..... **$3.90**
Price in 14 karat.......................... **5.25**

No. 69594. **Style P, solid gold mountings**, skeleton, offset cork guards, finest quality periscopic lenses.
Price in 10 karat.......................... **$3.25**
Price in 14 karat.......................... **3.90**

No. 69596. **Style O, solid gold mountings**, skeleton, handle and catch, cork guards, with finest quality periscopic lenses. Price in 10 karat.............. **$3.75**
Price in 14 karat.......................... **4.45**

### COLORED LENS EYE-GLASSES.
### For Weak Eyes.

Colored lens eye-glasses and spectacles are not made with focus to assist the sight, but are intended only to protect the eyes from strong light. They are a very great comfort to those whose eyes are weak and do much to preserve the sight. They can be furnished in either coquille or flat lenses. The coquille are convex, concave or oval shape, as indicated under style W. When ordering please state which are wanted.
For cuts showing styles see adjoining column.

No. 69605. **Style K, rubber frames**, coquille or flat lenses, smoke or blue (not recommended). Price..**15c**

No. 69606. **Style R, rubber frames**, with fine coquille or flat lenses, smoke or blue. Price.............. **15c**

No. 69608. **Style R, steel frames**, fine quality, cork guards, fine quality coquille or flat lenses, smoke or blue. Price.......................... **50c**

No. 69609. **Style R, steel frames**, fine quality, cork guards, finest quality ground, flat or coquille lenses. Price.......................... **90c**

The following illustrations show the various styles of spectacles and eye glasses. See adjoining columns for full descriptions and prices.

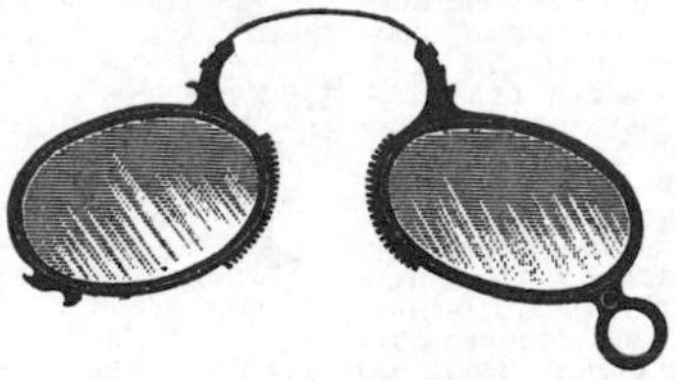

Style K. Eye Glasses, hard rubber frames

Style L. Eye Glasses, adjustable rubber nose pieces, steel or nickel frames.

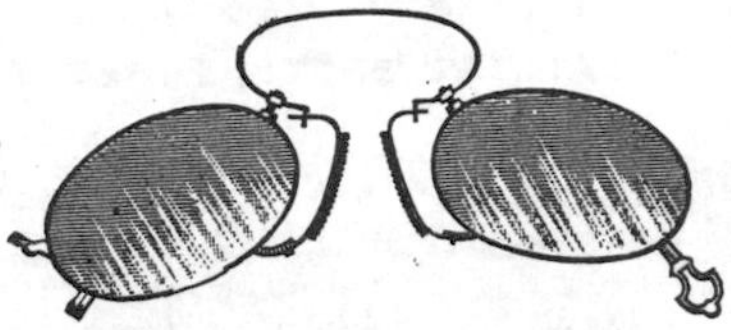

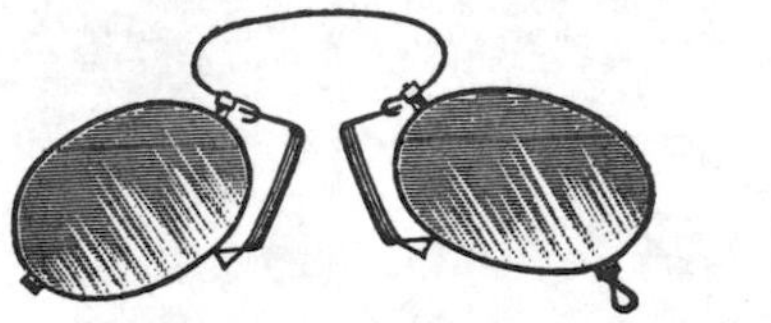

Style M. Eye Glasses, adjustable cork nose pieces, gold or gold filled frames.

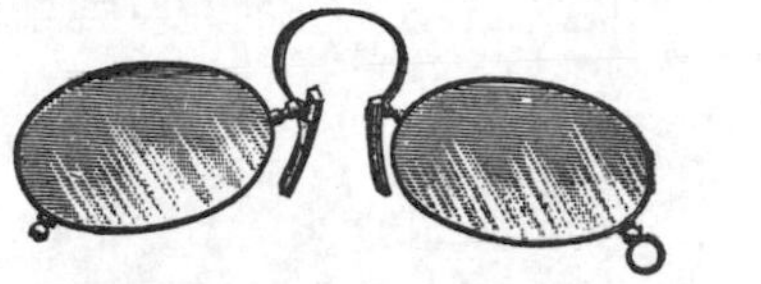

Style N. Eye Glasses, offset cork nose pieces, steel gold or gold filled frames.

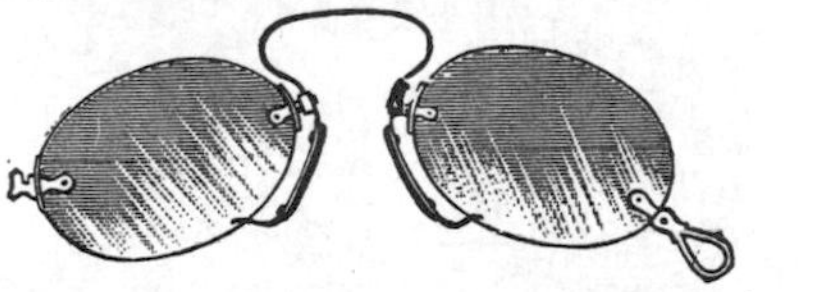

Style O. Eye Glasses, skeleton, cork nose pieces, gold or gold filled mountings.

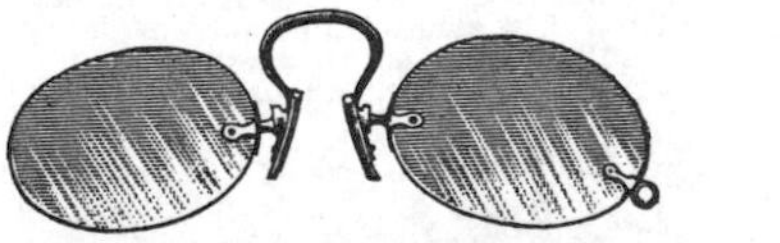

Style P. Eye Glasses, skeleton, offset cork nose pieces, gold or gold filled mountings.

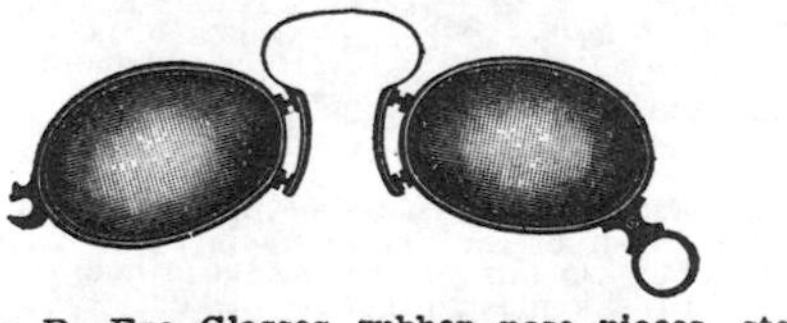

Style R. Eye Glasses, rubber nose pieces, steel frames, smoked or colored lenses.

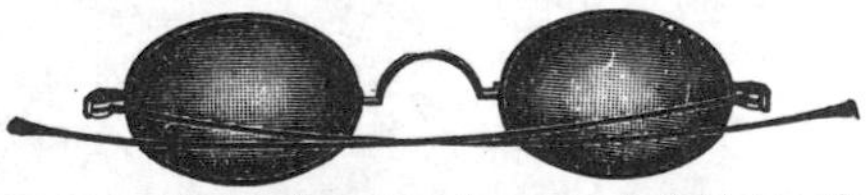

Style T. Spectacles, steel frames, straight temples, smoked or colored lenses.

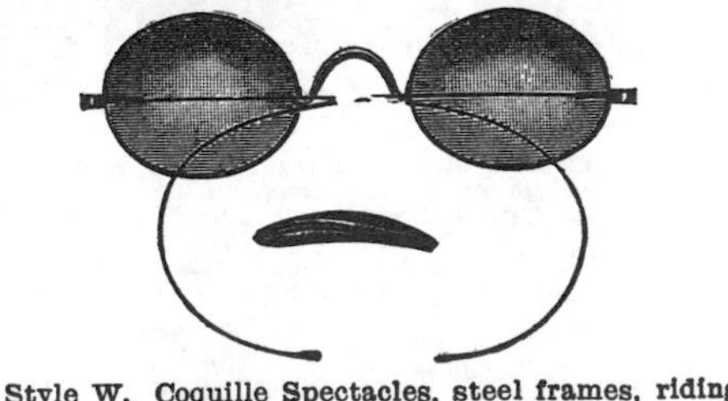

Style W. Coquille Spectacles, steel frames, riding bow temples, smoked or colored lenses.

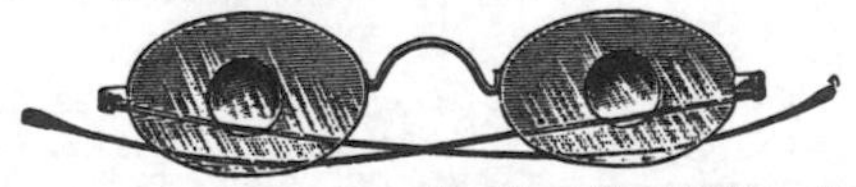

Style X. Scenery or Shooting Spectacles, steel frames, straight temples.

### COLORED LENS SPECTACLES,
### For Weak Eyes.

No. 69612. **Style T, steel frame**, straight temples, untempered, with coquille lenses for weak eyes, smoke or blue, common quality (not recommended).
See previous column for cuts showing styles.
Price.......................... **20c**

No. 69613. **Style T, steel frames**, straight temples, better quality and finish, coquille or flat lenses, smoke or blue. Price.......................... **35c**

No. 69614. **Style T, steel frames**, tempered, fine quality, straight temples, with first quality coquille or flat lenses, smoke or blue. Price.................. **85c**

No. 69618. **Style W, steel frames**, ordinary riding bow temples, coquille lenses, smoke or blue. Price, **25c**

No. 69619. **Style W, steel frames**, fine quality, riding bow temples, fine quality coquille lenses, smoke or blue. Price.......................... **50c**

No. 69620. **Style W, steel frames**, fine quality, riding bow temples, nickel plated, extra finish, with finest quality coquille flat lenses, smoke or blue. Price..**90c**

### SCENERY OR SHOOTING SPECTACLES.

While these spectacles are commonly known as shooting spectacles they are very largely used by tourists for looking at scenery, as it very much improves the view, and as they are amber tinted they are soothing to the eyes when in a bright light. The lenses are sanded so as to exclude the view except the small circle in the middle of each.
See previous column for cuts showing styles.

No. 69625. **Style X, steel frames**, tempered, good quality, nickel plated, straight, temples, amber tinted diaphragm lenses, Price.......................... **25c**

No. 69626. **Style X-C steel frames**, fine quality, riding bow temples, nickel plated, fine quality, amber tinted diaphragm lenses. Price.......................... **50c**

### GOGGLES.

When ordering goggles be sure to state the color of lenses you desire.

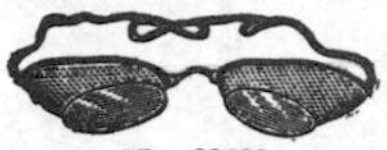

No. 69628.

No. 69628. **Goggles**, wire gauze, ordinary quality, with smoke, blue, white or green lenses, in a tin box with hinge cover.
Price.......................... **9c.**

No. 69629. **Goggles**, wire gauze, fine quality, velvet bound edges with smoke, blue or white glasses, in morocco cases. Price.............. **35c.**

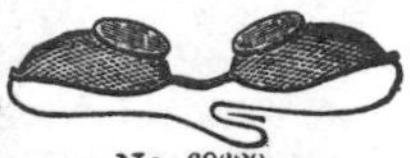

No. 69629.

### RAILROAD OR DRIVING SPECTACLES.

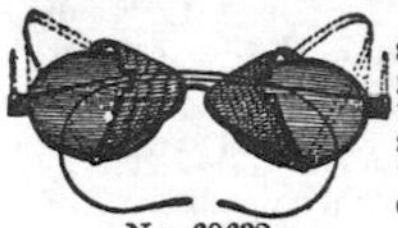

No. 69632.

No. 69631. **Steel frames**, straight temples, with wire gauze side protectors closing with the temples (making them as compact as an ordinary spectacle) with smoke or white coquille lenses. Price.... **85c.**

No. 69632. **Steel frames**, same as above, but with riding bow temples. Price.......................... **$1.15**

### STONE CUTTERS SPECTACLES.

No. 69633. Steel frames, strong plain white lenses, large eyes and turn pin temples, for protecting the eyes from injury. Each.......................... **20c.**
Postage 5 cents.

### MICA EYE PROTECTORS.

No. 69634. This is a very neat and light patent arrangement which will thoroughly protect the eyes from the intrusion of dust. Is also very desirable for bicyclists and others riding at night, to protect their eyes from bugs and flies. Each section of the rim holds a selected sheet of mica, around which is securely fastened a perforated strip of corrugated felt with an elastic cord to encircle the head of the wearer. Furnished in either smoke, blue or white; each one in a neat pocket case.
Price.......................... **45c**

### SPECTACLE CASES.

With all spectacles costing 50 cents or over, we furnish a case free. When spectacle and eye-glass cases are to be sent by mail be sure to allow 2 cents extra for postage.

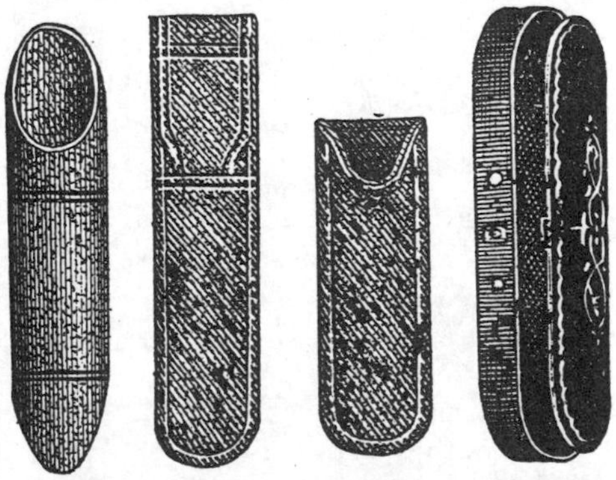

Style 1. Style 2. Style 3. Style 4.

No. 69635. Style 1. **Leather**, medium quality case for straight temple spectacles, open end. Each... **5c**

No. 69636. Style 1. **Leather**, fine quality case for straight temple spectacles, open end. Each...... **10c**

No. 69637. Style 2. **Leather**, medium quality case for straight temple spectacles with closed ends. Each..**5c**

**Our Prices on Spectacles and Eye Glasses are from one-half to one-fourth the prices charged by oculists and opticians for the same quality of goods. We do not recommend Spectacles or Eye Glasses listed at less than 50 cents.**

## Spectacle Cases—Continued.

No. 69638. Style 2. **Leather,** fine quality case for straight temple spectacles, closed end. Each......**10c**
No. 69640. Style 3. **Leather,** fine quality case for riding bow spectacles, open end. Each............**8c**
No 69641. Style 3. **Leather,** fine quality case for riding bow spectacles with closed end. Each......**10c**
The two last numbers can be furnished for coquille spectacles when desired, but it will be necessary to mention the same when you order.
No. 69642. Style 1. **Papier mache,** very strong case for straight temple spectacles, open end. Each...**20c**
No. 69643. Style 4. **Papier mache** case with inlaid design on cover, nickel jointed with catch, made 6¾ inches for straight temple, or 4¾ inches for riding bow spectacles; a very strong case. Each..............**25c**
NOTE.—The case for riding bow opens at the end instead of at the side.

## EYE-GLASS CASES.

With all eye-glasses costing 50c or over (except those with offset guards) we give a case and silk cord free. Postage on eye-glass cases 2c.

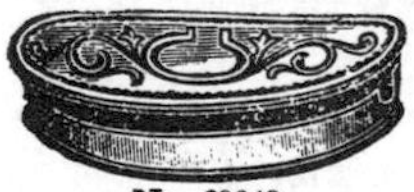
No. 69648.

No. 69648. Style 10. **Nickel** eye-glass case, velvet lined, cover engraved. Each....**20c**

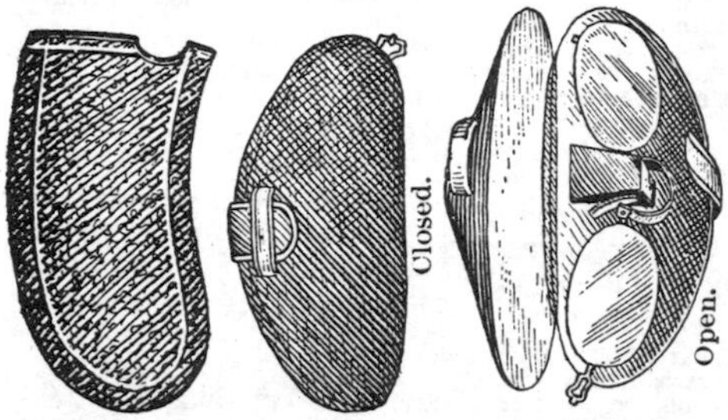

No. 69649. No. 69651. No. 69651.

No. 69649. Leather eye-glass case, fine quality. Each..........**5c**
No. 69650. **Eye-Glass Case** similar to the above, except that it is about one-half the length for folding eye-glasses. Fine quality leather. Each............**5c**
No. 69651. **Leather** case, fine quality, for offset eye-glasses with strap. Each..........................**20c**

## EYE-GLASS CORDS AND CHAINS.

Length about 19 inches when doubled.

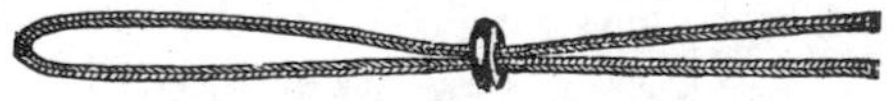
No. 69655.

No. 69655 **Eye-Glass Cord,** pure silk, light weight with bead slide. Each..............................**5c**

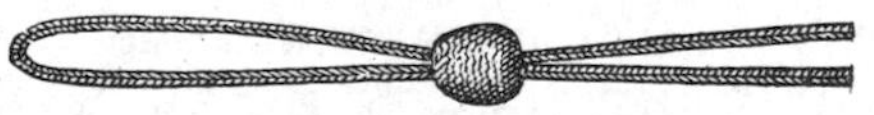
No. 69656.

No. 69656. **Eye-Glass Cord,** pure silk, fast dye, medium weight with silk covered slide. Each.....**10c**

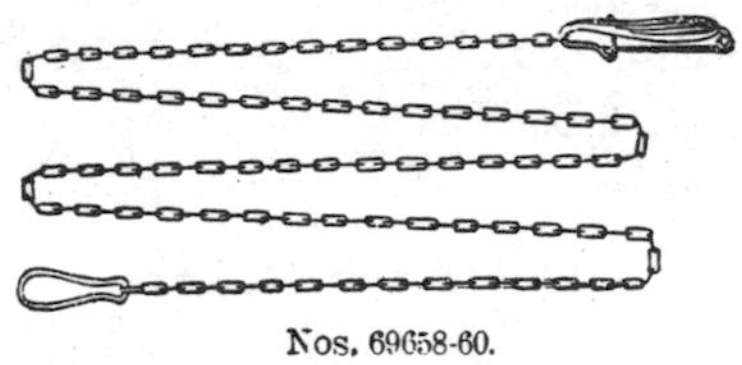
Nos. 69658-60.

No. 69658. **Eye-Glass Chain,** rolled gold plated with hook. Each..............................**70c**
No. 69659. **Eye-Glass Chain,** fine quality gold filled, with hook. Each ..........................**$1.00**

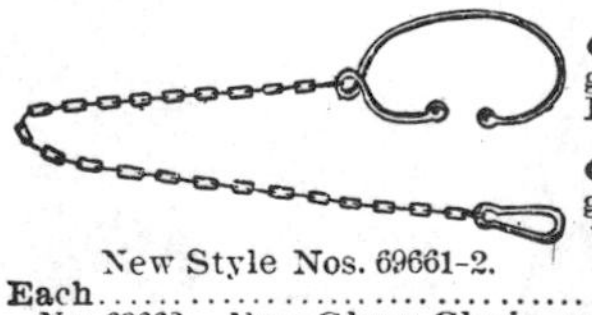
New Style Nos. 69661-2.

No. 69660. **Eye-Glass Chain,** solid gold with gold hook. Each..........**$2.00**
No. 69661. **Eye-Glass Chain,** best gold filled new style, with loop to go around the ear. Each..............................**90c**
No. 69662. **Eye-Glass Chain,** solid gold, new style with loop to go around the ear. Each..........**$1.80**
The above chains we consider the most desirable eye-glass chains made. The chain is short, is not liable to catch and the hook is almost invisible when around the ear.

No. 69665. **Eye-Glass Hook,** gold filled. Each................... **30c**
No. 69666. **Eye-Glass Hook,** solid gold. Each ......................................**90c**

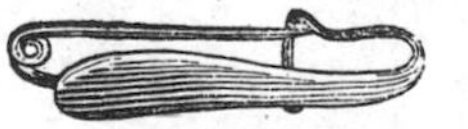
Nos. 69665-6.

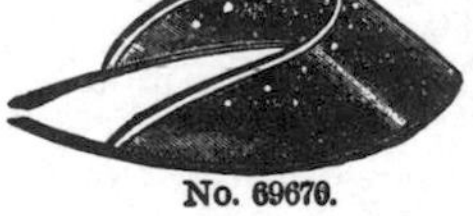
No. 69670.

## EYE SHADES.

No. 69670. **Eye-Glass Shade** with metal rim, leather bound edge and ventilated. Each..................**12c**

## DUST PROTECTOR.

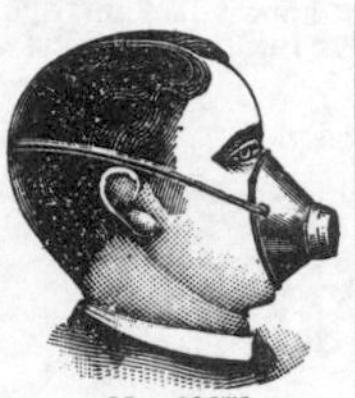
No. 69672.

No. 69672. The **Patent Dust Protector** protects the nose and mouth from the intrusion of dust which is so injurious to the head and lungs. They are of great value in mills, elevators, around threshing machines and in other places where dust is so troublesome. They have been used for years with the most satisfactory results. They afford perfect protection with liberal ventilation Are made of metal, smooth polished and nickel plated; are light and comfortable. Price, each.......................................**90c**

## EAR TRUMPETS, TUBES, ETC.

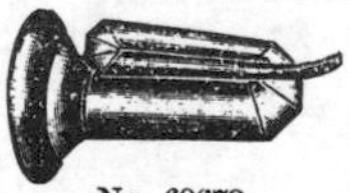
No. 69673.

No. 69673. **Ear Trumpet,** bugle shape, made of japanned metal in three sizes, small, medium or large. Each.......**$1.90**
No. 69674. **London Hearing Horn,** nickel plated, size 2¼ to 4 inches in length. They are for the use of those who are moderately deaf and are easily concealed in the hand when in use. Each......**$2.25**

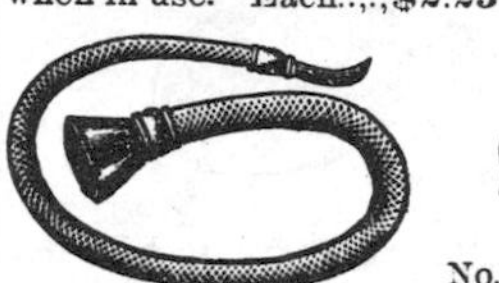
No. 69675.

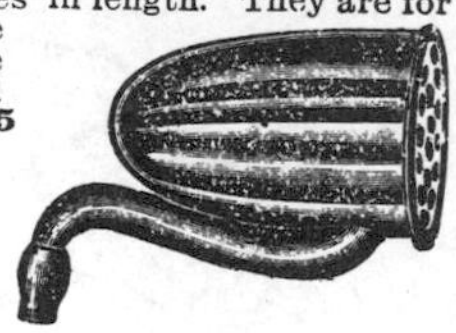
No. 69674.

No. 69675. **Conversation Tube** of flexible mohair, 3 feet in length with rubber ends. This tube is suited to the most obstinate cases of deafness. Each.........**$2.75**

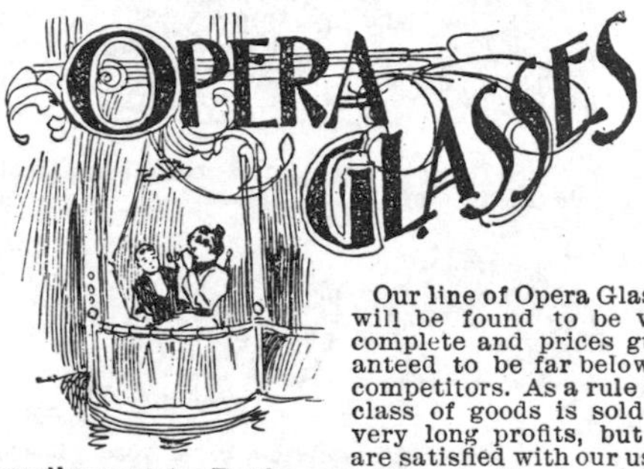


Our line of Opera Glasses will be found to be very complete and prices guaranteed to be far below all competitors. As a rule this class of goods is sold on very long profits, but we are satisfied with our usual small per cent. By the use of lines in the description of opera and field glasses is meant the diameter of the largest lens. The system of measurement is of French origin. 13 lines are equal to about 1 5-32 inch and 15 lines 1⅝ inch, there being about 11 lines to the inch.

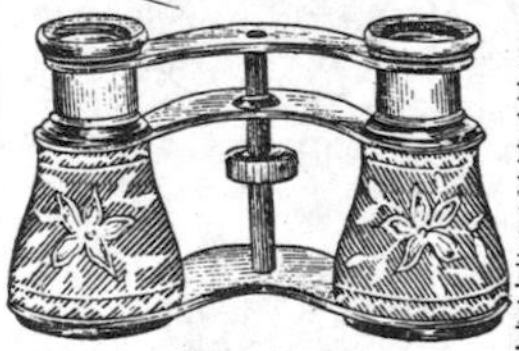
Nos. 69685-6.

No. 69685. **Opera Glass** 15-line, bodies of white metal enameled in blue with bright cut engraving nickel plated frame with gilt draws, tops and trimmings. Lenses of good quality. Price, including silk plush bag. Each ..............**$1.65**

No. 69686. **Opera Glass** 15 line, bodies of white metal blued, bright cut engraving, gilt trimmings, nickel frame and draws, lenses of good quality, Price including silk plush bag with nickel clasps and cord attached. Each..................................**$1.75**

No. 69687. **Opera Glass** 15 line, black leather covered, with enameled frame and draws, morocco case. Each..............**$2.00**
No. 69688. **Opera Glass** 15-line, black leather covered, with enameled frame and draws, achromatic lenses, morocco case. Each ............**$3.40**
No. 69689. **Opera Glass** 17-line, black leather covered, enameled frame and draws, achromatic lenses, morocco case. Each..............**$3.75**

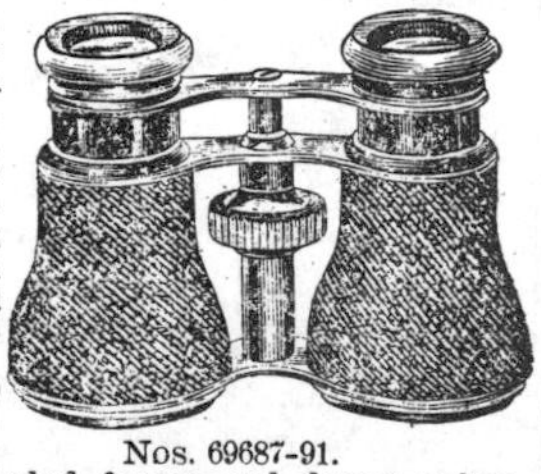
Nos. 69687-91.

No. 69690. **Opera Glass** 15-line, black morocco cover, with nickel frame and draws, first quality achromatic lenses. This is the best quality plain opera glass made, in neat leather case. Each...................**$5.50**

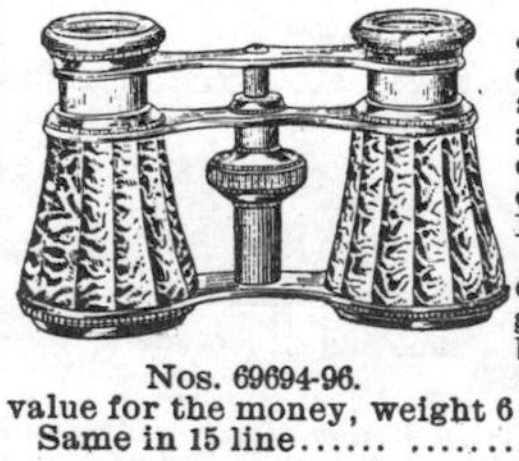
Nos. 69694-96.

No. 69694. **Opera Glasses** 17 line, black morocco cover, enameled frame and draws, first quality achromatic lenses, same quality as one above but one size larger. Each................**$6.25**
No. 69694. Fancy pearl opera glasses 13-line with gilt draws, nickel cross bars and tops, achromatic lenses and is exceptional value for the money, weight 6 ounces, each......**$4.50**
Same in 15 line...... **5.50**

No. 69695. **Pearl Opera Glasses, white or Oriental,** with pearl tops, gilt cross bars and slides 15-line, very fine achromatic lenses, in morocco case. Each ..**$6.90**
Same in 15-line.................................**$7.85**
No. 69696. **Pearl Opera Glasses, white or Oriental** (light or dark), gilt cross bars, pearl slides and tops, 13-line, finest achromatic lenses, each............**$8.60**
Same in 15-line ..................................**$9.75**
No. 69697. **Aluminum Opera Glasses,** bodies embossed in beautiful scroll and floral designs, all parts made of aluminum, bright polished, pearl inlaid tops 15-line, finest achromatic lenses, thoroughly first class in every respect, weight but 5 ounces, in fine morocco case, each ........................................**$11.75**

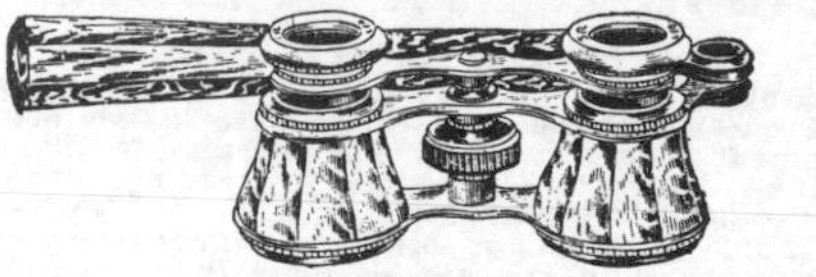
No. 69698.

No. 69698. **Pearl Opera Glasses, Oriental,** with extension pearl mounted handle, has gilt cross bars, slides and trimmings, 13-line, finest achromatic lenses, is one of the latest designs and is rapidly becoming very popular. The handle can be drawn out to nearly double the length which appears in the engraving as closed. Weight 9 ounces in long plush bag. Ea., **$12.75**

## UNIVERSAL EXTENSION OPERA GLASS HANDLES.

These handles are easily adapted to any opera glass, can be attached or detached instantly, are telescopic, folding within themselves to about one-half length. They are very desirable inasmuch as they prevent the arm from becoming tired.

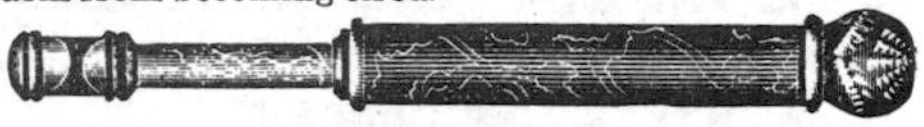
Nos. 69700-2.

No. 69700. **Solid silverine** mountings. black celluloid handle, each .....................................**$2.60**
No. 69701 **Gold filled** mountings, black celluloid handle, each..........................................**$3.15**
No. 69702. **Solid sterling silver** mountings, black celluloid handle, each...................................**$3.15**

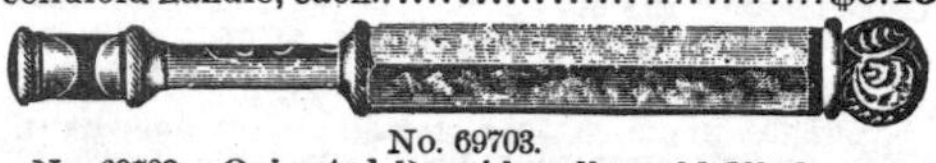
No. 69703.

No. 69703. **Oriental Pearl** handle, gold filled mountings, each .......................................**$6.75**

## OPERA GLASS BAGS.

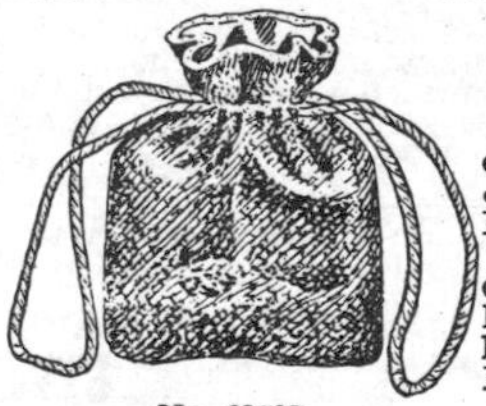
No. 69703.

No. 69703. Bags for opera glasses made of chamois, assorted colors, Each.............................**95c**
No. 69704 Bags for opera glasses, chamoise-long, with pocket for handle, assorted colors. Each...............**$1.55**

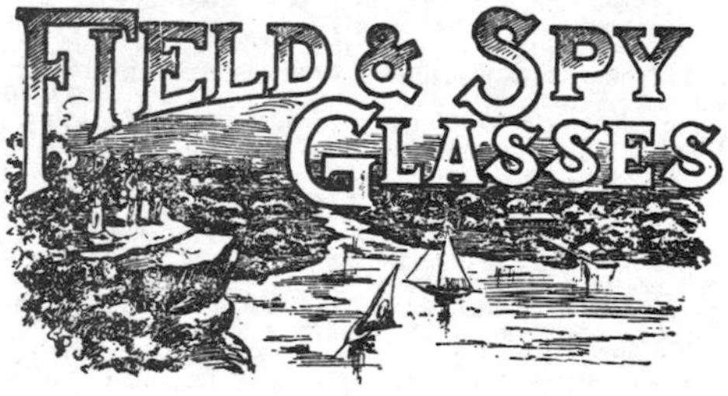


We carry in stock a very large assortment of field glasses at prices on which we defy competition. Our cheap field glasses are fitted with good lenses and are most excellent value for the money. Unlike other concerns we sell our better finished and higher grade glasses on the same small margin of profit. Our field glasses are all guaranteed to give entire satisfaction. The size of field glasses is indicated by the diameter of the largest or the front lens, which is measured by the French ligne system, one inch being equal to about eleven lignes. A lens measuring thirteen lignes is equal to about 1 5-32 inches and fifteen lignes 1⅝ inches.

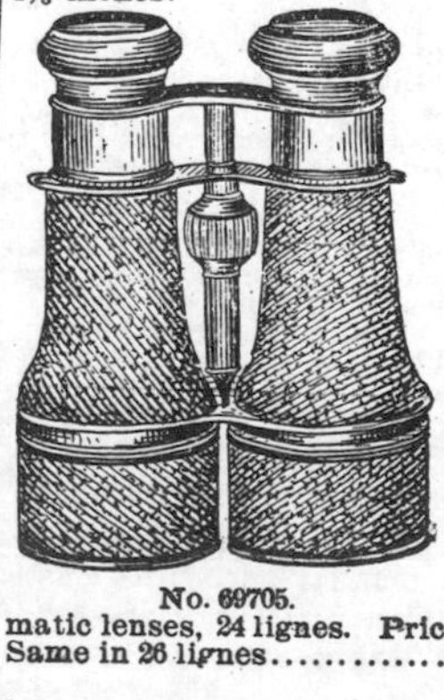
No. 69705.

No. 69705. **Field or Marine Glasses,** leather covered body with black finished bars, slides and trimmings, large lenses, 24 lignes, with case and shoulder strap, weight 2¼ lbs. Price.... **$4.00**
Same style, but with extension hood, black oxidized trimmings and achromatic lenses.....**$5.25**
No. 69706. **Field or Marine Glasses,** leather covered body with extension hood, black oxidized bars, draws and trimmings, more powerful and better definition than the one preceding, with neat case and shoulder strap, weight 2¾ lbs achromatic lenses, 24 lignes. Price....................**$8.50**
Same in 26 lignes................................**8.90**

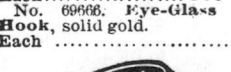

## Field and Marine Glasses—Continued.

**No. 69707. Field or Marine Glasses** with extension hood, black oxidized bars, draws and trimmings, leather covered body, fine finish, extra quality high power achromatic lenses, with neat case and shoulder straps, weight 2½ lbs.
Price in 24 ligne.......................................$12.50
Price in 26 ligne..........................................14.50

**No. 69708. Field and Marine Glasses,** black morocco body with extension hood, black oxidized cross bars, draws and trimmings, has 12 finest achromatic lenses and highest known power for day or night; has been used by the United States Signal Service, length when closed 6 inches, extended 7⅜ inches, 26 lignes, weight 2½ lbs. with fine leather case and shoulder strap. Price.......................................$21.00

**No. 69709. Tourist's Field Glasses** with short body, morocco covered and long draw tubes, finest achromatic lenses, length when closed about 4 inches, when extended about 5½ inches, 19 ligne, achromatic lenses, weight 1 lb. and 4 oz.
Price with neat case and strap.....................$8.75

**No. 69710. Cavalry Field Glasses** with rapid adjustment for ranchmen, tourists, etc. are constructed with short bodies and long draw tubes, so that while capable of being extended to give necessary power they occupy when closed comparatively small compass. They are fitted with a patent adjustment, by means of which they can always be kept at the proper focus for the owner's eyes; having once been adjusted by the screw, as in the ordinary field glass, they can then be closed by simply pushing them together, and when needed they can be instantly pulled out and are ready for immediate use, the adjustment to the eyes having remained undisturbed. They have fine enameled frames, draw tubes and trimmings, morocco covered with finest achromatic lenses, 21 lignes, length when closed 5 in., when extended 7 in.; very powerful.
Each.............................................$19.50

**No. 69711. Field Glass** with rapid adjustment, same as above, but with 24 ligne lenses; length when closed 5¼ in., extended 7 in.; highest known power.
Each..................$23.00
The cut represents the case and strap furnished with field glasses.

## NON-ACHROMATIC SPY GLASSES.

These glasses have two single lenses each, which are non-achromatic, but have considerable magnifying power. They are excellent value for the money, but are not to be compared with the superior finished achromatic glasses described further on.

**No. 69712. Non-achromatic,** red japanned body, 3 inches long when closed with objective glass ⅞ inches in diameter. Each with one draw...................25c
Each with three draws........................50c
**No. 69713. Non-achromatic** imitation rosewood, japanned body, 5 inches long when closed, objective glass 1⅛ inch in diameter.
Each with one draw.........................$0.95
Each with two draws............................1.15
Each with three draws..........................1.30
Postage on above 5 to 8 cents.

## ACHROMATIC SPY GLASSES AND TELESCOPES.

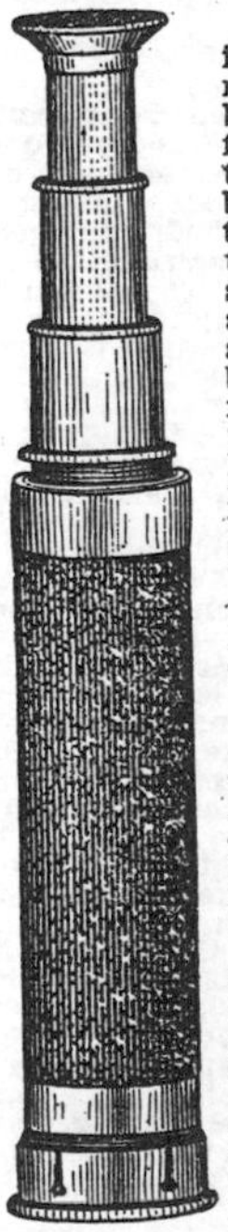

The instruments we list here are all intended for practical purposes, are made with fine achromatic lenses, bodies well finished and accurately fitted and should not be compared with the cheap, light, trashy toys advertised by "Cheap John" houses and sold by toy dealers. If on receipt of any of these instruments they are not entirely satisfactory they can be returned to us and your money refunded. Spy glasses are very convenient and are used largely by travelers, hunters, farmers, stock men and others. We give the measurements of the front or objective lens. Eleven lignes are equal to about 1 inch. All of our spy glasses are provided with a slide cover for the small lens and a cap for the front lens.

**No.69714. Spy Glass,** leather covered with 10 ligne, achromatic objective lenses, 4 sections, magnifying power 10 diameters, length when closed 5 inches, when open 13¼ inches. Each... $1.85
Postage, 10 cents.

**No. 69715. Spy Glass,** leather covered with 14 line achromatic objective lenses, magnifying power 15 diameters, 4 sections, length when closed 6¼ inches, when open 16 inches.
Each.......................$2.75
Postage, 10 cents.

**No. 69716. Spy Glass,** leather covered with 4 sections, fine achromatic lenses, 16 lines, magnifying power 20 diameters, length when closed 8 inches, when open 22 inches. Each............$4.00

**No. 69717. Spy Glass,** leather covered, 4 sections with extension hood, fine achromatic lenses, 19 lignes, magnifying power 30 diameters, length when closed 10 inches, when open 30 inches, range about ten miles, weight 35 oz.
Nos. 69714-8. Each............$5.60

**No. 69718. Spy Glass,** black morocco covered body, 5 sections, with sun shade, finest achromatic lenses, 22 lignes, very high power and a superior finished instrument, length when closed 10½ inches, when open 36 inches, range 14 miles, weight 3 lbs. Each....$8.35

**No. 69719. Spy Glass,** black morocco covered body, 5 sections, burnished draw tubes with sun shade to extend over objective lenses, loops for shoulder strap, finest achromatic lenses, 25 lignes, magnifying power 45 diameters (range about 18 miles), length when closed about 12 inches, when open 38 inches, weight 4 lbs. Each............................................$13.50

**No. 69720. Spy Glass,** 5 sections, polished mahogany covered body, burnished brass draws, sun glass to eye piece, a superior finished instrument. It affords excellent views of the moon, sun, etc., in addition to terrestrial powers; finest achromatic lenses, 22 lines, magnifying power 45 diameters, excellent definition, range 18 miles, length when closed 11½ inches, when open 36¼ inches, weight 2¾ lbs. Each..$14.25

**No. 69721. Spy Glass,** polished mahogany covered body, 5 sections, burnished brass draws with sun glass to the eye piece, superior finished achromatic lenses, 25 lignes, magnifying power 50 diameters, range 22 miles, length when closed about 12 inches, when open 42 inches. Each.........................$17.75

**No. 69722. Celestial Eye Piece** in long draw tube for spy glass 69721, increasing the magnifying power to 135 diameters. Each....................$5.20
NOTE.—Both numbers 69720 and 69721 are very superior glasses for terrestrial observations and also afford excellent views of the sun, moon, satellites of Jupiter, etc. To produce the best results they should be used on a striped stand or with clamp rests.

Nos. 69723-4.

**No. 69723. Tourists' Spy Glass.** morocco covered, 5 sections, oxidized, with sun shade, leather caps and carrying straps, length when closed 7¾ inches, when open 29 inches, fine achromatic lenses, 19 lignes, weight 1¾ lbs., a very fine glass. Each.......$15.00
**No. 69724. Spy Glass,** morocco covered body, 5 sections, burnished draws with sun shade, leather caps and carrying strap, length when closed 11 inches, when extended 36 inches, fine achromatic lenses, 22 lignes, magnifying power 33 diameters, with very fine definition, especially adapted to rifle range work, as it will show in a clear atmosphere, a bullet mark at 1,000 yards; weight 3 lbs., best glass made for size.
Each..........................................$21.00

ASTRONOMICAL AND LANDSCAPE TELESCOPES

No. 69725.

**No. 69725. Astronomical Telescope,** brass body, 40 inches long, fine achromatic object glass, 3 inches in diameter, one terrestrial eye piece with power of 500 diameters, one celestial eye piece with sun glass with power of 125 diameters, with rack and pinion for adjustment of focus; has vertical and horizontal movements, mounted upon a cast iron folding tripod for table use, packed in a strong wood case.
Price, complete, each............................$47.00
**No. 69726. Astronomical Telescope,** same as 69721, but with the addition of a long, strong, hardwood tripod, a part of which is shown in the cut, all packed in a strong wood case. Price, each.............$59.00

## TRIPODS FOR TELESCOPES.

**No. 69727. Tripod** of hard wood with vertical and horizontal motion, with clasps for securing the telescope upon which to place the telescope or spy glass; has sufficient steadiness for all ordinary purposes.
Price, each.........................................$4.75
**No. 69728. Tripod** of hard wood, stronger and more steady than the above, has vertical and horizontal motion, also an arrangement for raising and lowering the telescope, with clamps for same.
Price, each..........................................$6.90

## CLAMP RESTS FOR TELESCOPES OR SPY GLASSES.

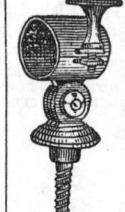

**No. 69729. Clamp Rest** as shown in cut has a brass collar for clamping the telescope with a steel gimlet screw for fastening to a tree, post, window frame or other support, which avoids fatiguing the arms during long observations and gives a much more steady and satisfactory view.

No. 69729.

Each...14....16....19....22....25 lignes.
.$1.20  1.65  2.35  2.60  3.00
Be sure to state the size wanted when you order.

## POCKET SPY GLASSES.

**No. 69630. Pocket Spy Glass** with black morocco covered body, highly burnished brass draw tubes, round polished nickel caps for both ends, finest achromatic lenses, 10 lignes, length when closed, 5½ in., length when open 14¾ in., magnifying power 10 diameters, four sections. Each.........................$3.25
Postage 10 cents.

No. 69734.

**No. 69734. Pocket Spy Glass,** same as above, except the length, when closed 6 in., when open 16 in., diameter in lenses 12 lignes, magnifying power 15 diameters. Each....................$3.75
Postage 12 cents.
**No. 69735. Pocket Spy Glass,** same as 69730, except the length, when closed 6¾ in., when open 17 in., magnifying power 20 diameters, diameter of objective lenses 14 lignes. Each..........................$4.50

MICROSCOPES.

IN Microscopes and Magnifying Glasses we carry a most complete line to fill the requirements for professional use as well as for ordinary purposes. We use a great deal of care in the selection of optical goods in this line and we guarantee every instrument to give entire satisfaction.

**No. 69740. Tripod microscope,** adapted to a variety of uses where a short focus and high magnifying power is desirable. The focus is adjustable by means of a screw, has a strong compact frame 1⅝ inches in diameter, standing on three legs, with very strong double lenses. Each......38c
Postage 5 cents.

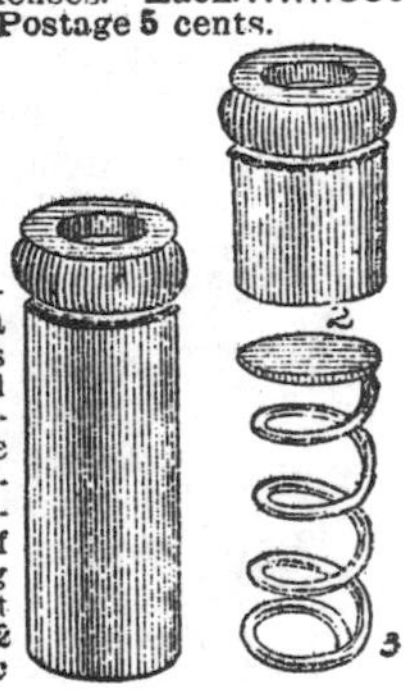

**No. 69741. Cupid Microscope.** This instrument has a high magnifying power, and is arranged to confine very small objects for inspection. The object is placed on the glass at the top of the spring and is inserted in the tube for examination. By placing a drop of water on the glass and holding toward a good light the result will astonish you; length 2 inches. Each...........15c
Postage 4 cents.

**No. 69742. Cage or Seed Microscope,** 1¼ inches high by 1½ inches in diameter, has strong lenses, nickel plated mounting with glass body, is used for the examination of seeds, grain, live bugs or insects, etc. Each.......................25c
Postage 5 cents.

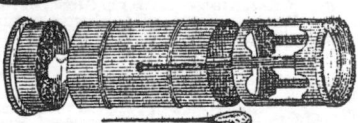

**No. 69743. Combination Microscope** with lacquered brass case, 2 inches in length, has two lenses, one of very high power, the other of medium power; is especially adapted for the pocket. Price, including one insect holder, each...................35c
Postage 5 cents.

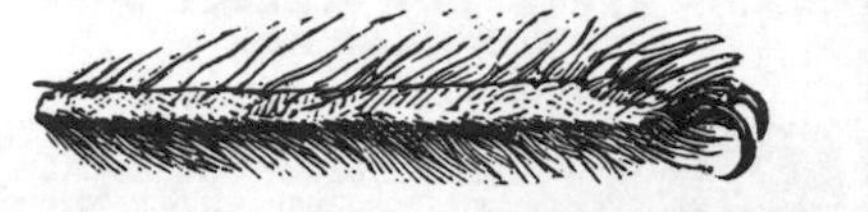

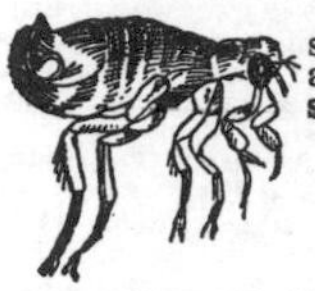

The two cuts above represent a small insect about the size of a flea and a spider's foot under a microscope.

## MAGNIFYING GLASSES.

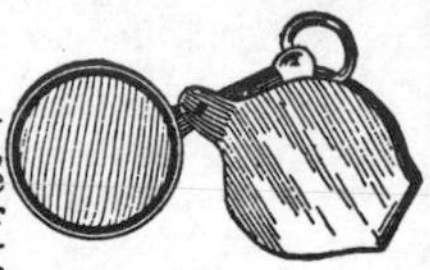

No. 69745. **Folding Magnifying Glass**, nickel plated, with folding handle. The handle of this glass folds over the lens, affording it protection, thus adapting it for pocket use, has a strong lens ¾ inch, Each........30c
Postage 3 cents.

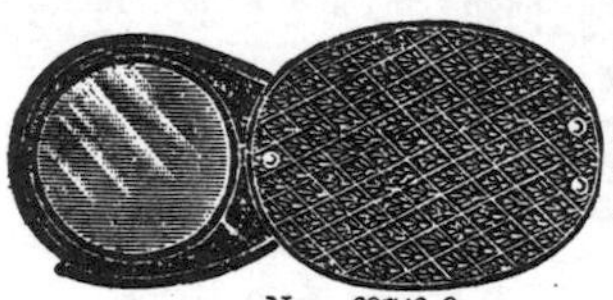

Nos. 69746-9.

No. 69746. **Folding Magnifying Glass** with well finished hard rubber case, strong lens ¾ in. in diameter. Each.....25c
Postage 3 cents.

No. 69747. **Folding Magnifying Glass** with well finished hard rubber case, single lens 1¼ inches in diameter. Each.......................60c
Postage 4 cents.

No. 69748. **Folding Magnifying Glass**, well finished hard rubber case, single lens 2 inches in diameter, also makes a good sun glass for lighting pipes, cigars. etc. Each.................................$1.00
Postage 5 cents.

No. 69749. **Magnifying Glass**, oxidized metal case, designed for rough service. single lens 1 3-16 inches in diameter. Same style as No. 69746. Each.........50c
Postage 2 cents.

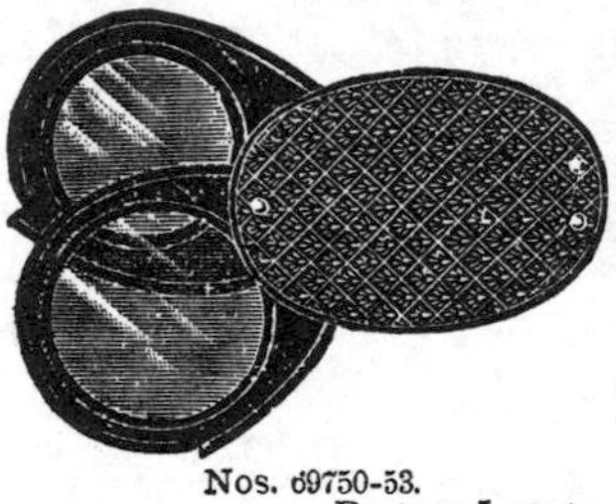

Nos. 69750-53.

No. 69750. **Folding Magnifying Glass** well finished with hard rubber case, two lenses ⅝ inch and ¾ inch in diameter. Each ....55c
Postage 3 cents.

No. 69751. **Folding Magnifying Glass**, well finished hard rubber case, two lenses ¾ inch and 1 inch in diam. Each.90c
Postage 5 cents.

No. 69752. **Folding Magnifying Glass**, well finished, hard rubber case two lenses 1 inch and 1¼ inches diameter. Each...................................$1.10
Postage 5 cents.

No. 69753. **Folding Magnifying Glass**, well finished, hard rubber case, two lenses 1½ inches and 1¾ inches diameter, a very strong magnifier and a fine sun glass. Each...............................$1.25
Postage 5 cents.

No. 69754. **Folding Magnifying Glass**, well finished, hard rubber case, two lenses 1 inch and 1⅞ inches diameter, of high magnifying power, especially adapted to the use of mineral prospectors; also for sun glass. Each, $2.00
Postage 5 cents.

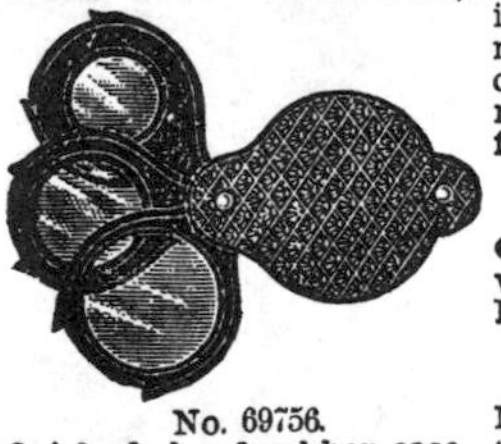

No. 69756.

No. 69755. **Magnifying Glass**, same as above, but with two lenses same size. Each...................70c
Postage 5 cents.

No. 69756. **Folding Magnifying Glass**, well finished, hard rubber case, three lenses ⅝, ¾ and ⅞ inch diameter, very powerful. Each....................90c
Postage 5 cents.

No. 69757. **Watchmakers' Eye-Glass**, with hard rubber mounting, 2-inch to 4-inch focus, same as used by all watchmakers. Each.........................30c
Postage 5 cents.

No. 69758. **Watchmakers' Eye-Glass, with hard** rubber mounting and spring to go around the head for holding the glass to the eye, 2 to 4-in. focus. **Each, 50c**
Postage 5 cents.

No. 69759. **Watchmakers' Eye-Glass**, hard rubber mounting, with two lenses, giving two strengths and two lengths of focus, very powerful. Each...............60c
Postage 5 cents.

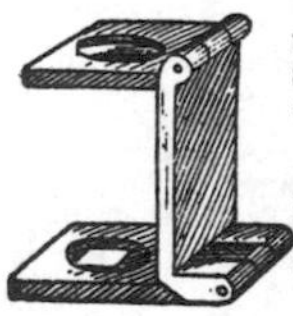

No. 69760. **Folding Pocket Magnifier**, with brass frame, folds into space ¼x⅝x1 inch, but has very strong magnifying power. Each..25c
Postage 3 cents.

No. 69761. **Folding Pocket Magnifier**, same as above, but better finished, with achromatic lenses, frame nickel plated. Each.............60c
Postage 3 cents.

## CODDINGTON MAGNIFIERS.

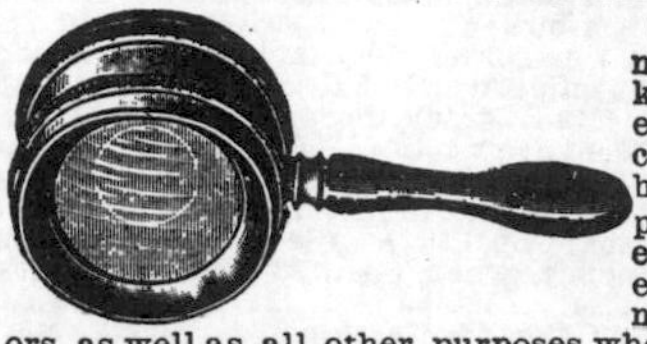

Coddington Magnifiers are well known for their excellent finish, compactness and high magnifying power. They are especially adapted to the use of mineral prospectors, as well as all other purposes where a strong magnifying glass is required.

No. 69762. **Coddington Magnifier**, or miner's glass, double achromatic lenses, ⅝ inch in diameter, lacquered brass frame and handle. Each..................$1.00
Postage 4 cents.

No. 69763. **Coddington Magnifier**, same as above, but with lenses 1 inch in diameter. Each........$1.25
Postage 6 cents.

No. 69764. **Coddington Magnifier**, same as above, but with lenses ⅞ inch in diameter. Each......$1.50
Postage 6 cents.

## With Nickel Plated Folding Metal Cases.

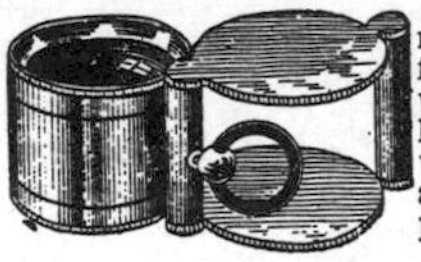

No. 69765. Coddington Magnifier, with folding metal frame, nickel plated, with ring, very fine double achromatic lenses ¾ inch in diameter, very high power, especially adapted for carrying in the pocket. Each.........$1.25
Postage 4 cents.

No. 69766. Coddington Magnifier, same as the above, but with lenses 1 inch in diameter. Each........$1.50
Postage 5 cents.

No. 69767. Coddington Magnifier, same as No. 69765, but with lenses 1¼ inch in diameter. Each......$1.75
Postage 6 cents.

No. 69768. Coddington Magnifier, same as No. 69765, but with lenses 1⅜ inch in diameter. Each......$2.10
Postage 7 cents.

## READING GLASSES

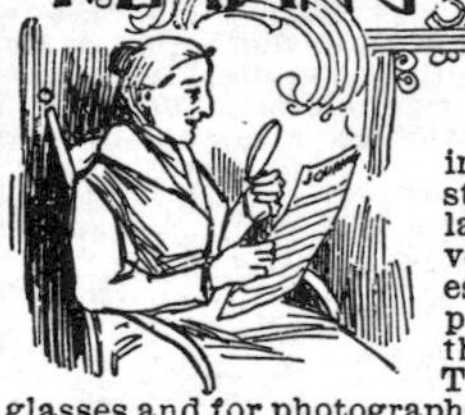

Are very desirable for reading fine print and as they are strong magnifiers and give a large range of vision they are very restful to the eyes and especially desirable for old people, enabling them to read the finest print with ease. They are also used for sun glasses and for photographs, as they bring out the details and add a great deal to the beauty of the picture. The principle is the same as the graphoscope. The lenses are well finished, the frames of metal nickel plated and the handles of wood enameled in black.

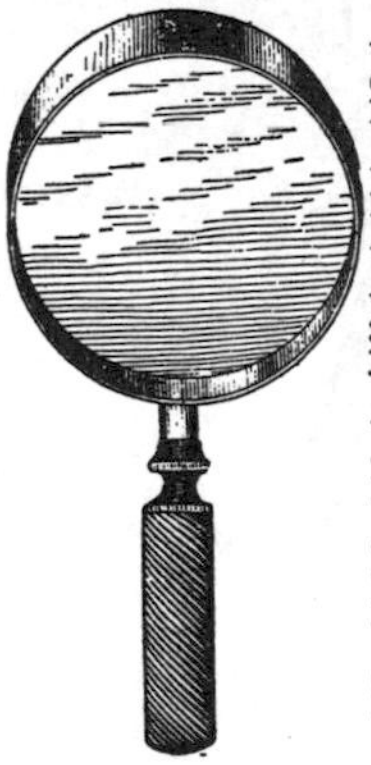

No. 69780. **Reading Glass**, wood handle, nickel frame, diameter of lens, 2¼ in., weight 4 oz. Each..............................55c

No. 69781. **Reading Glass**, wood handle and nickel frame, lens 2¾ in. diameter, weight 6 oz. Each..............................70c

No. 69782. **Reading Glass**, wood handle, nickel frame, lens 3½ in. in diameter, weight 8 oz. Each..............................90c

No. 69783. **Reading Glass**, wood handle, nickel frame, lens 4 in. in diameter, weight 10 oz. Each..........................$1.25

No. 69784. **Reading Glass**, wood handle, nickel frame, lens 7 in. in diameter, weight 1 lb. Each..........................$1.90

Reading Glasses are also used extensively for sun glasses, to light a pipe, cigar, etc.

## MICROSCOPES FOR STUDENTS, HOME EDUCATION, AMUSEMENT AND PROFESSIONAL USE.

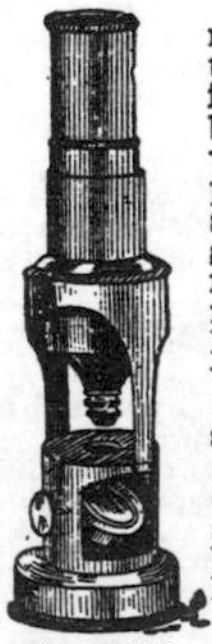

No. 69790.

No. 69790. Gem Microscope. This is a neatly finished instrument, designed for the use of those who wish to pursue their investigation beyond the powers yielded by a simple microscope. The low price at which it is sold, its simplicity and compact form has made it a very popular instrument. The lenses are accurately ground and are of such power as to render minute objects, animal, vegetable and mineral distinctly visible. The Gem Microscope is substantially made with a vertical brass body 6 inches high. It has one eye piece and one objective giving a power of 40 diameters or 1,600 areas; has a mirror beneath the stage for the illumination of transparent objects, two glass slips, one prepared object and one pair of brass tweezers, all packed in a nice French polished case. Each.......$2.25
Postage, 25 cents.

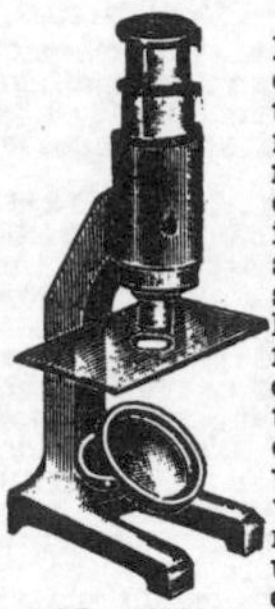

No. 69791.

No. 69791. **Household Microscope.** Many years of experience in the sale of microscopes has demonstrated that the public appreciate a microscope of not too complicated construction of moderate price, but still well made, easily managed, capable of affording instruction and to supply this demand a Household Microscope has been designed. It is a compound Microscope having all the essential parts of a first-class instrument. It is a model of the most approved and modern pattern with a range of magnifying powers affording an opportunity for investigating the minutia of animal and vegetable life by which we are surrounded and which are to so many an unknown world. The animalcules, commonly present in stagnant water, the pollen of flowers, etc., can be well observed and studied with it. It is 7 inches high, as shown in the engraving. The base is of bronzed iron, has hinged joint allowing the instrument to be used at any convenient angle. The body is brass, finely finished, stage large and steady with brass springs for holding the object; has a mirror beneath the stage for the illumination of transparent objects; two crown glass objectives affording magnifying powers of every range from 30 to 75 diameters (500 to 7,500) areas); one glass slip, plain, one glass slip with concave cell for holding liquid or insects, one prepared object, all packed in a neat box, weight 1½ lbs. Price.................................................$4.50

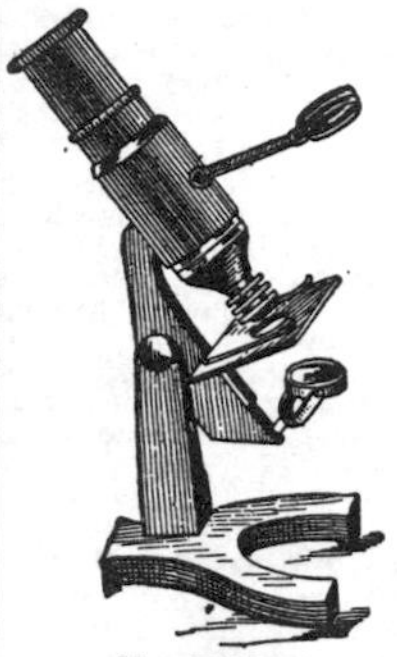

No. 69792.

No. 69792. **Household Microscope**, same as 69791 but has three objectives which are separable, giving three powers from 30 to 125 diameters, or 500 to 10,000 areas, and has condensing lens for the illumination of opaque objects, weight 1¾ lbs. Each.......................$6.00

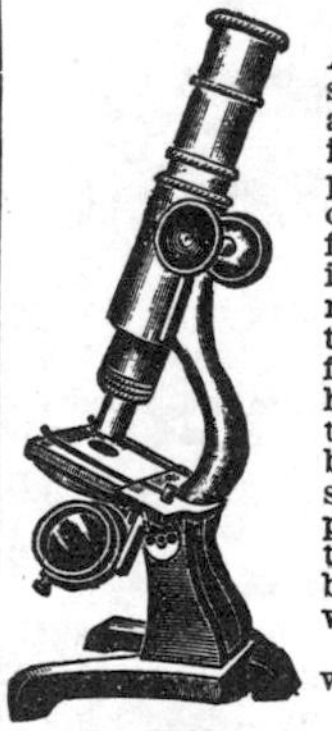

No. 69793.

No. 69793. **Students' Microscope.** American model mounted on substantial, well japanned, iron base and has inclination joint for adjusting to any angle, has a fine rack and pinion movement, one eye piece and one dividing objective giving power from 80 to 350 diameters, has revolving diaphragm with adjustable mirror under stage for illuminating transparent objects with two rings for holding steady in position. It has a society screw which permits the use of other objectives that can be purchased when needed. The instrument is very attractive in appearance, substantial in construction, powerful but low priced, which brings it within the reach of all, weight 5 lbs.

Price complete packed in neat wood case, each..............$15.00

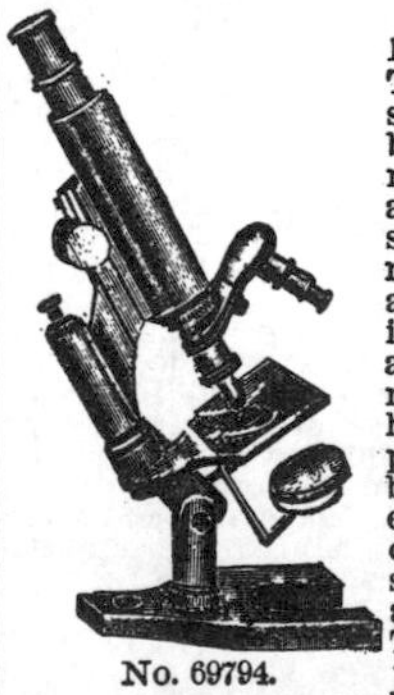

No. 69794.

No. 69794. **The Continental Professional Microscope.** This microscope is of new construction, the coarse adjustment being accomplished by diagonal rack and pinion, while the fine adjustment is by micrometer screw giving very delicate movement. The draw tube is adjustable for the tube length. This instrument is particularly adapted to American requirements and is very complete, of high grade workmanship, simple and is offered at a price far below other instruments of equal grade. The base is made of japanned iron of the horse shoe form with rounded corners and of ample size for stability. The pillar is of lacquered brass with joint for inclination of the body. The stage is of brass oxidized and with removable spring clips. The mirror bar switches to an obliquity below the stage and is provided with both plain and concave mirrors. This instrument is especially recommended for high school laboratories, as it fully meets all the requirements for the scientific work prescribed, and on account of its moderate cost it is brought within the reach of all. The height is 12 inches, weight about 12 lbs, has strong and well finished case with handle, lock and key, furnished with one eye piece and ⅚ in. and 1-6 in. objectives with power of from 75 to 540 diameters and can be fitted to 2950 diameters. Price complete.......$34.50

No. 69795. **Continental Microscope**, same as above but with double nose piece (as shown in cut) to which both objectives are attached and which enables either one to be instantly shifted into use.
Price complete...........................................$39.00

# COMPASSES

**No. 69800.** Pocket Compass, open face, paper dial, heavy beveled edge glass, brass case with ring.
Diameter 1 in. each.........15c
Diameter 1¼ in. each......20c
Diameter 2 in. each.........25c
Postage 4 cents.

· No. 69800.

**No. 69801.** Pocket Compass, open face with brass case and ring, silvered metal dial, heavy beveled edge glass.
Diameter 1¾ in. each........40c
Postage 5 cents.

**No. 69802.** Pocket Compass, open face with brass case and ring, silvered metal dial and stop, heavy beveled edge glass.
Diameter 1¾ in. each........60c
Postage 5 cents.

**No. 69803.** Pocket Compass, brass case with ring, hinged cover silvered metal dial with full circle division, jeweled cap to needle, slide stop. Diameter 1¾ in. each.
Diameter 2 in. each.

Nos. 69800–3.
..................$1.40
...... 1.50
Postage 6 cents.

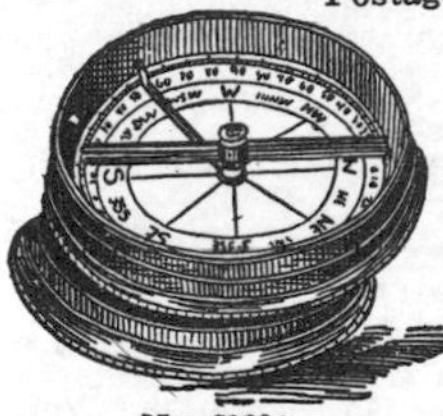

**No. 69804.** Pocket Compass with brass case, cap cover, no ring, paper dial.
Diameter 1½ in. each...25c
Diameter 1¾ in. each...30c
Postage 6 cents.

**No. 69805.** Pocket Compass, brass case with heavy milled edge, cap cover, silvered metal dial with full divisions, jeweled cap to needle, sliding stop.
Diameter 1¾ in. each....90c
Diameter 2 in. each..$1.10

No. 69804.
Diameter 2¼ in. each............ 1.25
Postage 8 cents.

**No. 69806.** Pocket Compass, nickel plated, silvered metal dial, full circle division with slip cover, jeweled English bar needle with automatic stop. (By automatic stop is meant the pressure of the cover raises the stop.)
Diameter 2½ in. each............$2.50
Diameter 3 in. each.......... 3.00
Postage 10 cents.

**No. 69807.** Pocket Compass with strong brass case, slip cover and case, English jeweled bar needle, silvered metal dial marked with double degrees and raised circle division to level of needle, extra heavy edge glass, automatic stop.
Diameter 3¼ in. each............$3.75
Postage 15 cents.

**No. 69808.** Compass with wood case and cover hinged, diameter 2¾ in., metal dial, automatic stop, jeweled cap to needle, each..75c
Postage 10 cents.

**No. 69809.** Compass with wood case square and cover hinged, silvered metal dial with full circle division, English bar needle, jeweled, automatic stop each, $1.75
Postage 10 cents.

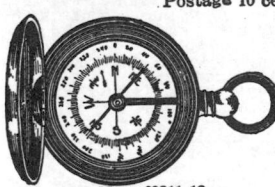

Nos. 69808–10.
**No. 69810.** Compass with wood case square, and cover hinged, silvered metal dial with raised circle division to level of needle, jeweled English bar needle with automatic stop. Diameter 2¾ in. each.....$2.00
Postage 10 cents.

**No. 69811.** Pocket Compass, watch shape, dust proof with ring cover, silvered metal dial with full divisions, 2 inches in diameter, English bar needle with automatic stop, heavy convex beveled edge glass, a very fine compact little instrument.
...........$3.50

Nos. 69811–12.
Each.......
**No. 69812.** The Woodmans' Compass, double thick oxidized case with hinged cover made for rough service, jeweled English bar needle, with automatic stop, silvered metal dial with full divisions, degree marked from 0 to 160, heavy beveled edge glass, weight 9½ oz. Each.........$4.90

**No. 69815.** Pocket Compass with sun dial, jeweled needle with full circle divisions, nickel plated case with hinged cover, slide stop, 2 in. in diameter, will indicate the time fairly close when the sun is shining.
Price each.. ...........$4.00

No. 69815.

# BOAT COMPASSES

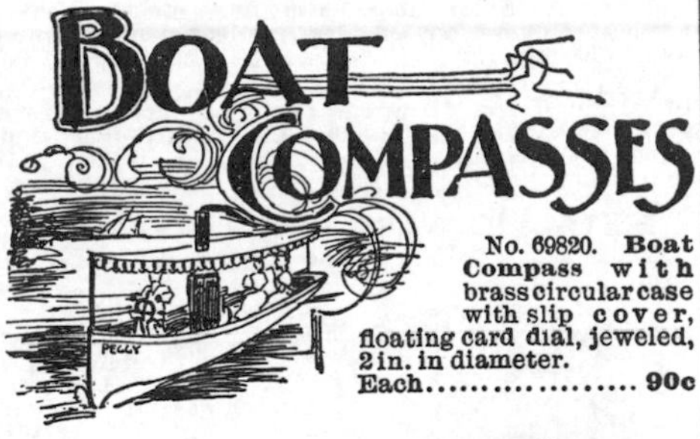

**No. 69820.** Boat Compass with brass circular case with slip cover, floating card dial, jeweled, 2 in. in diameter.
Each.................. 90c

**No. 69821.** Boat Compass, skeleton with brass gimbal mounting, with screw holes in base to secure it in position, floating card dial 1¾ in. in diameter, jeweled cap, a very handsome little instrument.
Each...................$3.50

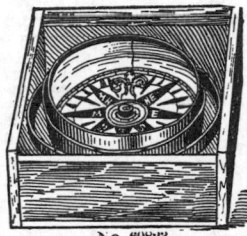

No. 69822.

**No. 69822.** Boat Compass, skeleton with brass gimbal mounting with screw holes in base to secure it in position, floating card dial 1¾ in. in diameter, jeweled cap, a very handsome little instrument.
Each...................$3.50
Postage 8 cents.

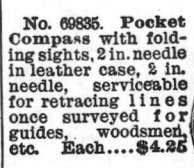

**No. 69823.** Boat Compass with brass bowl and gimbal rings, mounted in a strong oak box with sliding cover, jeweled and mounted on a hardened pivot, bowl heavily weighted to insure steadiness.

No. 69823.
With 6 in. box and 3¼ in. floating card dial, price $4.50
With 8 in. box and 5 in. card dial, price.......... 6.00
With 10 in. box and 7 in. card dial, price.......... 8.00
**No. 69824.** Boat Compass with floating card dial, jeweled, a well finished instrument in square wood box 5¾ x 5¾ in. with hinged cover. Each......$4.00

## COMPASSES FOR GUIDES, WOODS-MEN, ARCHITECTS, BUILDERS, SURVEYORS, ETC.

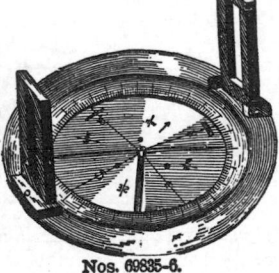

**No. 69835.** Pocket Compass with folding sights, 2 in. needle in leather case, 2 in. needle, serviceable for retracing lines once surveyed for guides, woodsmen, etc. Each....$4.25

Nos. 69835–6.
**No. 69836.** Pocket Compass with folding sights, same as above but with 2½ in. needle, leather case. Each....................$6.00
**No. 69837.** Pocket Compass with bar needle, hinged cover, nickel plated, with folding sights, 2 in. in diameter, suitable for same purpose as preceding numbers. Each................$4.30

**No. 69838.** Pocket Compass, same as above, but 2¾ in. in diam. Each..$5.00
**No. 69839.** Pocket Compass with cover and folding sights, same as 69837, but 2¾ inches in diameter. Each....$6.20

Nos. 69837–9.

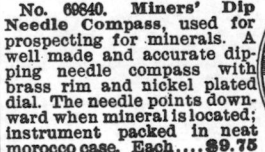

**No. 69840.** Miners' Dip Needle Compass, used for prospecting for minerals. A well made and accurate dipping needle compass with brass rim and nickel plated dial. The needle points downward when mineral is located; instrument packed in neat morocco case. Each....$9.75

No. 69840.

# SURVEYORS INSTRUMENTS AND COMPASSES

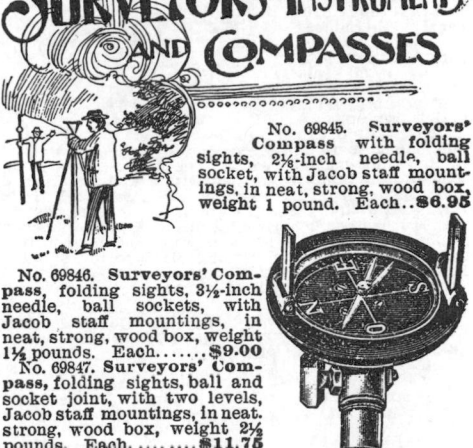

**No. 69845.** Surveyors' Compass with folding sights, 2½-inch needle, ball socket, with Jacob staff mountings, in neat, strong, wood box, weight 1 pound. Each..$6.95

**No. 69846.** Surveyors' Compass, folding sights, 3½-inch needle, ball sockets, with Jacob staff mountings, in neat, strong, wood box, weight 1½ pounds. Each.......$9.00
**No. 69847.** Surveyors' Compass, folding sights, ball and socket joint, with two levels, Jacob staff mountings, in neat, strong, wood box, weight 2½ pounds. Each.........$11.75
**No. 69848.** Surveyors' Compass, folding sights, 4½-inch needle, ball and socket joint, with two levels, Jacob staff mountings, in neat, strong, wood box, weight 2¾ pounds. Each...........$13.25

Nos. 69845-8.

**No. 69849.** Tripod with Jacob staff top for the above compasses, metal shoes. Each.........$2.40
**No. 69850.** Jacob staff with metal shoe to stick in the ground, for use of the above compasses instead of tripod, weight 2¼ lbs. Each.....90c

**No. 69851.** Vernier Compass for surveyors, folding sights, two levels, 3½-inch needle, in neat strong wood box, weight complete with tripod 7 pounds, weight without tripod 2½ pounds. Price complete...............$19.00
Price without tripod... 15.00
**No. 69852.** Vernier Compass with folding sights, two levels, 4½-inch needle, in neat strong wood box, weight complete 7¼ pounds, weight without tripod, 3 pounds. Price complete........$21.00
Price without tripod......... 17.00

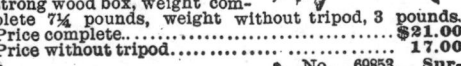

No. 69851.

**No. 69853.** Surveyors' Vernier Compass, high grade, two straight levels, 5-inch needle, Jacob staff mountings, with ball and socket joint, brass cover, outkeeper, vernier under the glass for adding or substracting the magnetic variations of the needle, sights graduated for taking angles of elevations and depressions, sights detachable but very firm; is a strictly high grade instrument, all packed complete without tripod in a substantial mahogany box with lock and strap for carrying. Price..............$35.00
Price with regular tripod.......... 40.00

No. 69853.

NOTE—For the benefit of those who do not understand the Jacob staff mountings will say that they include a metal shoe for the bottom of the staff, and the mounting of the compass has a socket to receive the other end of the staff. Anyone can make the staff in a few minutes which is to be used by inserting one end in the ground. The ball socket joint allows the compass to be turned at any angle to level the same.

**No. 69854.** Builders' or Farmers' Drainage Level, combining simplicity and compactness with efficiency at the least possible cost; is especially adapted to the uses of builders and drainage contractors; has 11 in. telescope made especially for this instrument with achromatic objective lens 1 in. in diameter, necessary eye piece, having ½ mile range, cross hairs, rack and pinion adjusted to the eye piece, vernier with clamp reading to one degree, wooden tripod and metal base for use on walls of buildings in course of erection, with strong carrying case complete. Each..........................$35.00

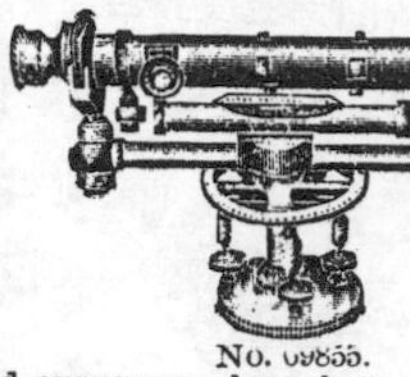

No. 69855.

No. 69855. **Architects' Level.** This admirable instrument, although recently introduced in its improved form, has met with a very large sale among architects, builders, millrights and those engaged in construction, also among engineers and surveyors, by whom it is used in city and contract work. The telescope is 12 in. long, of the finest optical qualities and is arranged and adjusted as in the regular engineers' level. It is furnished with a carefully ground long level, instrument turns upon a horizontal circle 3 in. in diameter, graduated from 0 to 90 each way, and is read to 5 minutes by a vernier, which is fixed to the spindle. Price complete, including a strong hard wood tripod and substantial box with strap, each..........**$44.00**

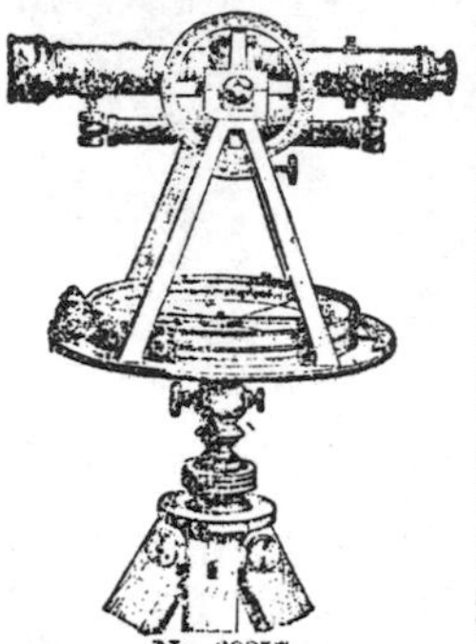

No. 69857.

No. 69856. **Vernier Transit Compass,** has the same general properties as the Vernier Compass, but is furnished with a telescope in place of ordinary sights. The telescope is from 10 to 12 in. long and is sufficiently powerful to see and set a flag at a distance of two miles on a clear day. The vernier or complete circle is within the box under the glass. The needle lifting screw is also underneath the plate, but is not shown in the cut with 5 in. needle, telescope and tripod complete. Each.....**$74.00**

No. 69857. **Vernier Transit Compass,** same as above, except that it has a 3½ in. vertical circle, level and telescope with clamp and tangent movement to axis of telescope, including tripod.
Complete..........................................**$100.00**

NOTE.—We can furnish anything wanted in the line of compasses transits, etc. We have quoted here a complete line of medium and low priced instruments, but if you are interested in anything more complete write us; we will be glad to furnish quotations on same.

## SURVEYORS' CHAINS, TAPES, ETC.

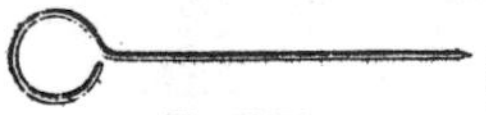

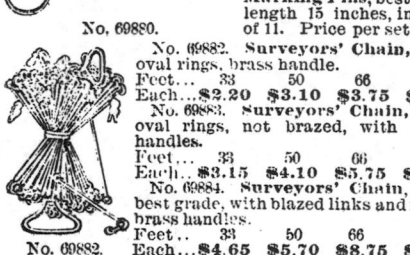

No. 69880.

No. 69880. **Arrows or Marking Pins,** best steel, length 15 inches, in sets of 11. Price per set..**90c**

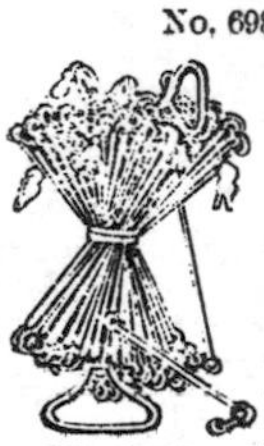

No. 69882.

No. 69882. **Surveyors' Chain,** iron, oval rings, brass handle.

| Feet... | 33 | 50 | 66 | 100 |
|---|---|---|---|---|
| Each... | $2.20 | $3.10 | $3.75 | $4.80 |

No. 69883. **Surveyors' Chain,** steel, oval rings, not brazed, with brass handles.

| Feet... | 33 | 50 | 66 | 100 |
|---|---|---|---|---|
| Each.. | $3.15 | $4.10 | $5.75 | $6.90 |

No. 69884. **Surveyors' Chain,** steel, best grade, with blazed links and rings, brass handles.

| Feet.. | 33 | 50 | 66 | 100 |
|---|---|---|---|---|
| Each... | $4.65 | $5.70 | $8.75 | $9.80 |

## STEEL TAPE MEASURES.

The general favor with which these tapes are received show that in the future they will take the place of the heavy chains with their hundreds of wearing places and inconvenience on account of bulk and weight. These tapes are intended for use wherever the chain can be used, and can be used in many places where the chain cannot. They are not intended to take the place of the light fine graded ones, but are especially designed for convenience and durability, and to take the place of the chain in all land surveying, railroad and canal work and town platting. They are made of the best tempered spring steel ⅜ inch wide. Each consecutive foot is graduated by a brass rivet and each 5 or 10 feet have plates with figures stamped thereon. For country and field work these tapes have given excellent satisfaction, and if they are nickel plated (with dull finish) they are much less liable to rust and do not require oiling or cleaning after use. The tape is not easily broken by fair usage, but should an accident of that kind occur it is easily mended by brightening the surface near the ends, then clamping them with a sleeve of thin brass or tin and letting a little solder flow in, being careful, of course, to keep the ends butted together and keep it straight while cooling. The handles are made to detach, that when drawing the tape through the brush it is not liable to catch anywhere.

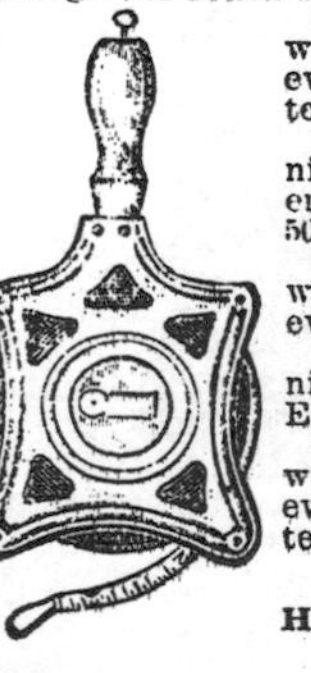

No. 69885. **Steel Tape Measure,** without nickel plate, graduated every foot, end feet graduated in tenths, 50 feet long. Each.....**$3.60**

No. 69886. **Steel Tape Measure,** nickel plated, graduated every foot, end feet graduated in tenths, length 50 feet. Each..................**$4.50**

No. 69887. **Steel Tape Measure,** without nickel plating, graduated every link, length 66 ft. Each, **$4.50**

No. 69888. **Steel Tape Measure,** nickel plated, graduated every link. Each ..........................**$5.40**

No. 69889. **Steel Tape Measure,** without nickel plating, graduated every foot, end feet graduated into tenths, 100 feet long. Each ...**$4.50**

No. 69890. **Steel Tape Measure,** nickel plated, graduated every foot, end feet graduated into tenths, length 100 feet. Each..............................**$5.85**

The above tape measure can be furnished in lengths of 200 and 300 feet if desired. The prices includes brass reel with handle, also detachable handles for each end of the tape measure.

## METALLIC WARP LINEN MEASURE TAPES.

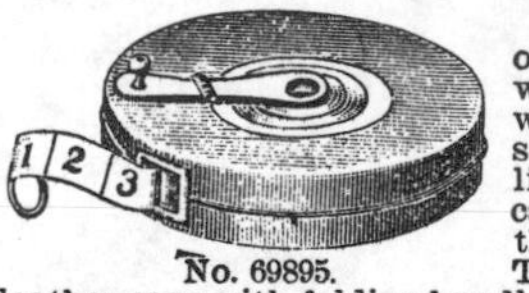

No. 69895.

These tapes are made of linen thread interwoven with fine brass wire, not so liable to stretch as the usual linen tape and better calculated to withstand the effects of moisture. They have a substantial leather case with folding handle.

No. 69895. **Metallic Linen Tape,** leather case, folding handle divided into feet and twelfths with links on the back.

| Feet......... | 25 | 33 | 50 | 66 | 75 | 100 |
|---|---|---|---|---|---|---|
| Price....... | $1.75 | $2.00 | $2.50 | $2.75 | $3.00 | $4.00 |

No. 69896. **Metallic Linen Tapes,** same as above, but divided into 1-10 foot for engineers' use.

| Feet......... | 25 | 33 | 50 | 66 | 75 | 100 |
|---|---|---|---|---|---|---|
| Price...... | $1.75 | $2.00 | $2.50 | $2.75 | $3.00 | $4.00 |

No. 69897. **Steel Tape** with folding flush handle, leather case, nickel trimmings, marked for feet and inches, links on the back.

| Feet ........ | 25 | 33 | 50 | 66 | 75 | 100. |
|---|---|---|---|---|---|---|
| Price..... | $3.75 | $4.50 | $6.00 | $7.75 | $9.00 | $11.00 |

No. 69898. **Steel Tape** with folding flush handle, in leather case, nickel trimmings, divided into feet and tenths of feet instead of inches, for engineers' use.

| Feet.......... | 25 | 33 | 50 | 66 | 75 | 100 |
|---|---|---|---|---|---|---|
| Price..... | $3.75 | $4.50 | $6.00 | $7.75 | $9.00 | $11.00 |

No. 69905. **Steel Pocket Tape** ⅜ in. wide, folding flush handle, nickel plated, brass case, marked on one side only, in feet, inches and eighths. This tape measure is intended principally for the use of carpenters, contractors, builders and others who do not feel inclined to invest in a higher priced measure. While the prices are very low none of the good features have been sacrificed. With care one will last an indefinite length of time and its accuracy can always be depended upon. The tape is easily detached from the case and an extra handle is furnished for the inside end.

| Feet........................... | 25 | 50 | 75 | 100 |
|---|---|---|---|---|
| Price..................... | $3.00 | $3.75 | $5.00 | $6.50 |

The 25 foot length weighs but 6 oz.

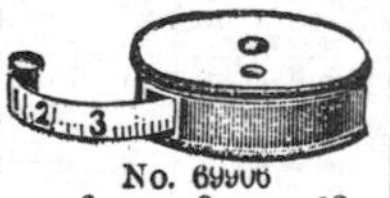

No. 69906

No. 69906. **Steel Pocket Tape,** in German silver case, with a spring which winds up the tape automatically; also a spring stop, divided into feet, inches and eighths.

| Feet............................ | 3 | 6 | 9 | 12 |
|---|---|---|---|---|
| Price........................ | $0.95 | $1.25 | $1.75 | $2.25 |

No. 69907. **Steel Pocket Tape,** same as above, divided into eighths and meters.

| Feet.......................... | 3 | 6 | 9 | 12 |
|---|---|---|---|---|
| Price..................... | $1.35 | $2.10 | $2.70 | $3.40 |

## STEREOSCOPES.

Stereoscopes and Views never were more popular than at the present time. With the large assortment of views which we list, there is an endless amount of entertainment to be obtained from an outfit of this kind, at a very small expense. We do not list the cheapest line of stereoscopes made, for we cannot conscientiously recommend them to our customers. The prices on what we list are so low that there would be no advantage whatever for us to offer anything of poorer quality. We offer a good quality of stereoscope for less money than others ask for the cheapest goods made.

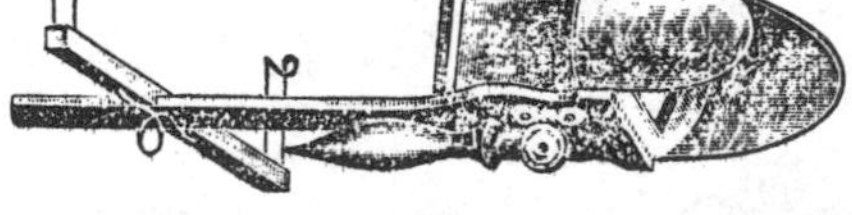

Nos. 69908-11.

No. 69908. **Stereoscope, Cherry frame,** medium sized lenses, patent folding handle with varnished hood. Each..................................................**25c**

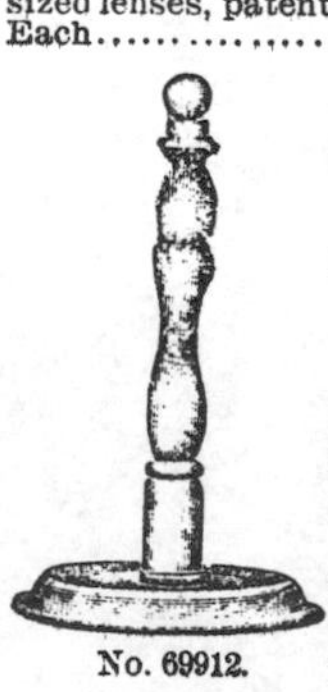

No. 69912.

No. 69909. **Stereoscope, Walnut frame,** medium sized lenses, patent folding handle with varnished walnut hood. Each............**40c**

No. 69910. **Stereoscope, Cherry frame,** large lens, patent folding handle, cherry hood, nicely varnished. Each...................**45c**

No. 69911. **Stereoscope, Walnut frame,** extra large lenses of fine quality, patent folding handle, polished tulip wood hood, first quality throughout. Each...............**90c**

No. 69912. **Stand for Stereoscopes,** walnut frame or cherry with round wood base, can be attached to any folding handle stereoscope, polished. Each.................**35c**

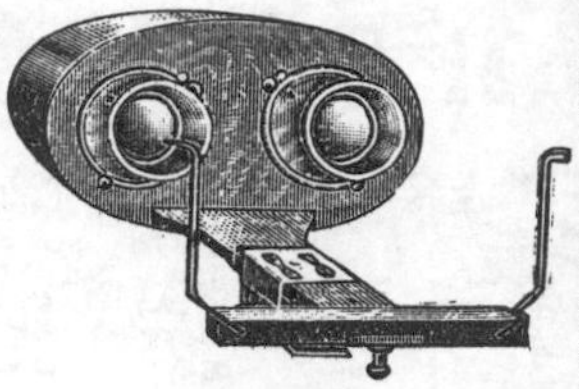

No. 69914.

No. 69913. **Stand for Stereoscopes,** polished rosewood with nickel legs; can be attached to any folding handle stereoscope. Each, **$1.00**

No. 69914. **Stereo-Graphoscope.** This is a combination of a perfect stereoscope and graphoscope for magnifying either single or stereoscopic pictures; as a graphoscope the lenses are reversed by a very simple mechanical arrangement; made of oiled cherry with polished cherry hood; instructions accompany each instrument.
Each, Small, 50c; Medium, 65c; Large.........85c

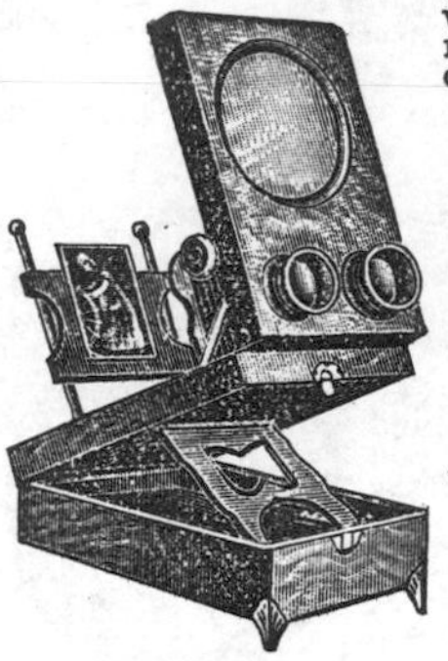

Nos. 69915-16.

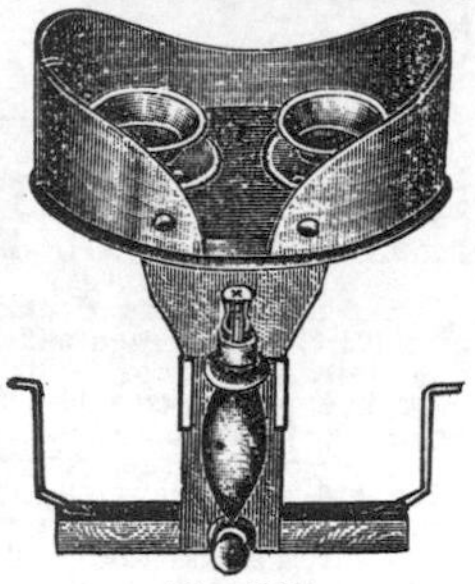

No. 69914.

No. 69915. **Stereo-Graphoscope,** folding box style with ebonized finish, with 4 inch lens of fine quality for graphoscopic views, and two fine stereoscopic view lenses. Each......................................**$4.25**

No. 69916. Stereo-Graphoscope, folding box style, made of olive wood with 5 inch graphoscopic lenses of fine quality for viewing single pictures and two fine stereoscopic lenses, a very fine instrument.
Each..............................................**$8.40**

## STEREOSCOPIC VIEWS.

In Stereoscopic Views we do not list the cheap, trashy printed views, but only those which are printed on the regular photographic paper from a negative. When seen through the stereoscope the value of these views will readily be appreciated on account of their superior quality. We have made arrangements with a first-class stereoscopic view artist who does only the best class of work. We list under each number several different subjects, and if you do not state your selection from that number we will send them assorted.

Postage on stereoscopic views size 3½ x 7 in. 6 cents per dozen; sizes 4 x 7 in. 9 cents per dozen.

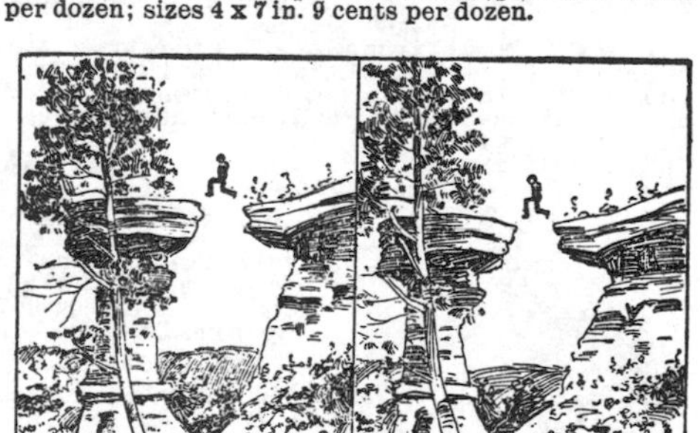

The above view was taken among the Dells of the Wisconsin, showing a man in the act of leaping across a chasm 9 feet in width and 60 feet deep. This is given only as a sample.

We cannot furnish any special pictures. You must take them as they come of our own assortment (except as to subjects.) The profit on these goods will not permit of any extra expense in making special selections.

There are several subjects listed under most numbers. Please state which are wanted.

No. 69917. **Stereoscopic Views,** size 3½x7 in.
Illustrating picturesque points of America, (100 subjects.)
The principal cities of America, (50 subjects.)
Picturesque points of Europe and Africa, (50 subjects.)
The principal cities of Europe, Yellowstone Park, America's wonderland (50 subjects).
Any of the above subjects or assorted.
Each..................................**5c; per dozen, 40c**

No. 69918. **Stereoscopic Views,** size 3½x7 inches, of the World's Fair, Chicago's Famous White City (50 subjects). Scandinavian cities and scenery of Norway and Sweden (50 subjects). Antiquities illustrating the ruins of ancient times (50 subjects). Sporting scenes of hunting, fishing, and woods life (50 subjects). Comic views, a large and varied collection of funny pictures, children, adults, etc., in funny predicaments; very amusing (150 subjects).
Any of the above subjects or assorted.
Each.................................**7c; per dozen, 70c**

No. 69919. **Stereoscopic Views,** 3½x7 inches, comic scenes in different colors, funny pictures in child and adult life (150 subjects).
Each.......................................**7c; per dozen, 70c**

SUCCESSFUL ANTELOPE ON SADDLE

**No. 69920. Stereoscopic Views**, highest grade made, size 4x7 inches, on heavy mounts, all taken from original negatives. Sporting series, hunting, fishing, canoeing, camping scenes and life in the woods (200 subjects). Yellowstone National Park, with hot springs, geysers, falls, canons, etc. (200 subjects). Alaska, the Land of the Midnight Sun, the glaciers, mountains, Indian life, Totempoles, etc. (50 subjects). Florida, tropical scenes, southern life, etc. (50 subjects). Niagara Falls in summer and winter (50 subjects). Dells of Wisconsin with stereoscopic views of river, rocks, glens, etc. (50 subjects). World's Fair, with realistic views of the fair grounds, buildings, Midway, etc. (200 subjects).

Any of the above subjects or assorted.

Each..........10c; per dozen, **$1.00**

**No. 69921. Stereoscopic Views**, religious subjects, size 3½x7 inches. The Crucifixion, representing the nativity, early life, trial, crucifixion, and resurrection of Christ, and the Life of Christ representing the story of Christ's life before and after the crucifixion. These views are from photos of the Passion Play presented at Oberamergau; a description of each view is printed on the back of all the Crucifixion Series. The Crucifixion Series contains 12 views; the Life of Christ, 12 views. For uncolored views, either series.

Each..........7c; per dozen, 70c

**No. 69922. Stereoscopic Views**, size 3½x7, Crucifixion or Life of Christ series, same as above, but colored.

Each..........9c; per dozen, 90c

The two series of views above are especially adapted to the use of Sunday schools, churches, and church societies.

**No. 69923. Graphoscope Views of Chicago.** New and interesting photographs of Chicago's public buildings, street scenes, parks, boulevards, stock yards, works of art and statuary from the Art Institute, size 6x8 inches (75 subjects), all first class work, large size. Each..........9c; per dozen, 90c

## CABINET PHOTOGRAPHS.

All photographs are our own selection; that is, they must be taken as they come. We cannot fill orders for specific subjects.

**No. 69924. Photographs**, cabinet size, of actresses, good finish, assorted. Each..........5c
Per dozen..........50c

**No. 69925. Photographs**, cabinet size, comic subjects, very amusing. Each..........6c
Per dozen..........60c

**No. 69926. Photographs**, cabinet size, taken from life, representing prominent actresses of the vaudeville stage in full costume, finished and mounted on heavy cards. Each..........10c
Per dozen..........$1.00
Postage on cabinet photographs 7 cents per dozen.

# THERMOMETERS

Our lines of thermometers embraces a complete variety for home as well as scientific purposes and are manufactured by the representative and most reputable concerns in this country and abroad. We handle nothing except such goods as we can fully guarantee to give entire satisfaction. Thermometers should not be sent by mail as they are liable to be broken.

**No. 69940. Japanned Tin Case Thermometer**, silvered scale with black enameled figures reading from 40 to 60 below to 120 and 170 above. The 12 in. can be furnished with a spirit tube and scale reading from 30 to 50 below if desired. The tubes are of standard size and are reliable for ordinary use; mercury tubes will be sent unless otherwise ordered Length 8 inches, mercury only. Each..........25c

**No. 69941.** Length 10 inches, mercury only. Each..........35c

**No. 69942.** Length 12 inches, spirit or mercury. Each..........45c

**No. 69943.** Same description as above but with seasoned tubes, carefully tested for accuracy, case, scale and tubes, all extra heavy, length, 8 inches mercury only. Each..........60c

**No. 69944.** Length 10 inches, same as No. 69943, mercury only. Each..........80c

**No. 69945.** Length 12 inches, same as No. 69943. Each..........$1.00

**No. 69946. Enameled Metal Case Thermometer**, light color, top and bottom rolled on, 8 in. fluted with scale for distant reading. Each..........20c

Nos. 69946-7. No. 69948. Nos. 69949-50. Nos. 69951-2.

**No. 69947. Enameled metal case**, 8 in. light color, black figures on white scale, strongly made. Each, 25c

**No. 69948. Enameled metal case**, 10x3 in., with larger figures and scale for distant reading. Each 35c

**No. 69949. Black ebonized wood Thermometer**, graduated on the face with white figures, sunken tube, nickeled trimmings, 8 inches. Each..........22c

**No. 69950. Boxwood Thermometer**, finished with oval top, high grade with magnifying mercury, sunken tube, graduation plain in double degrees; a very pretty thermometer. Each..........44c

**No. 69951. Cabinet or House Thermometer** with magnifying tube, white figures and polished black japanned index plate, mounted upon polished beveled wood backs, bold figures and scale for distant reading; 8 in. Each..........60c

**No. 69952.** Same, 10 inches long. Each..........75c

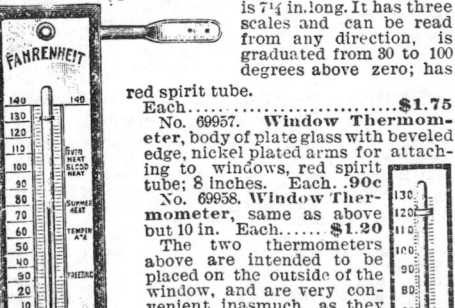

No. 69953.  Nos. 69954-5.  No. 69956.

**No. 69953. Cabinet or House Thermometer**, 9 in. scale magnifying tube, aluminum figures on polished black japanned plate with large scale and figures for distant reading, mounted on fancy polished oak frame with beaded edge; a very pretty thermometer.
Each..........70c

**No. 69954. Cabinet or House Thermometer** with wood back, porcelain scale, reading 40 to 40 degrees below zero; a very rich and artistic instrument, 8 in.
Each..........95c

**No. 69955. Cabinet or House Thermometer**, same as above but 10 in. Each..........$1.40

**No. 69956. Radial Scale Thermometer** with chain and snap for attaching to chandelier or other support, is finished in polished brass, has decorated ends and is 7¼ in. long. It has three scales and can be read from any direction, is graduated from 30 to 100 degrees above zero; has red spirit tube.
Each..........$1.75

**No. 69957. Window Thermometer**, body of plate glass with beveled edge, nickel plated arms for attaching to windows, red spirit tube; 8 inches. Each..90c

**No. 69958. Window Thermometer**, same as above but 10 in. Each..........$1.20

The two thermometers above are intended to be placed on the outside of the window, and are very convenient inasmuch as they can be read from the inside of the room.

**No. 69959.** Thermometer for decorative art, nickel plated, metal plate, from 2 to 6 in. in length. All lengths. Each..........14c

No. 69957.  No. 69959.

## SELF REGISTERING THERMOMETER.

Self Registering Thermometers are a very great convenience, inasmuch as the highest and lowest temperature will be registered and it is not necessary to watch the thermometer from time to time to know the highest or lowest point which has been reached. The tube in the Minimum Thermometer is filled with red spirit. It also contains a small float which follows the spirit to the lowest point but remains when the spirit advances with rise of temperature until it is again set. The Maximum Thermometer is for registering heat. The tube is filled with mercury which has a cut-off near the bulb. The mercury rises to the highest point, but when the temperature begins to decrease the mercury separates, thus leaving the column in the tube standing at the highest point reached until it is set for use again.

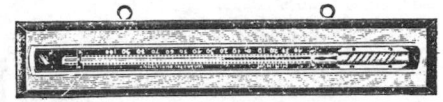

No. 69960.

**No. 69960½ Minimum Thermometer**, boxwood, self registering, for cold from 40 degrees below to 120 above, 10 in., with red spirit. Each..........80c

**No. 69961½ Minimum Thermometer**, boxwood, same as above, but registers to 50 degrees below zero; very accurate. Each..........$1.60

**No. 69962½ Maximum Thermometer**, boxwood, 10 in., mercury tube self registering for heat. Each..........$1.20

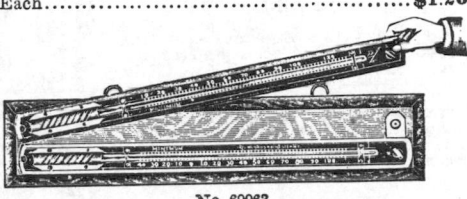

No. 69963.

**No. 69963½ Maximum and Minimum Thermometer**, boxwood, 10 in., for registering both heat and cold, same as two described above. Each..........$1.75

No. 69964.

**No. 69964. Standard Maximum Thermometer**, self registering, 12 in. long with brass insulated strap to fasten in position, graduated on metal plate.
Each..........$2.50

**No. 69965. Standard Signal Service Minimum Thermometer**, self registering with brass insulated strap to fasten in position, graduated metal plate.
Each..........$3.50

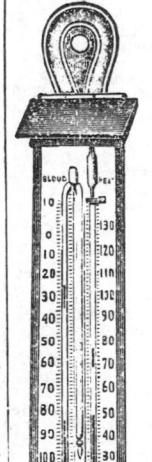

No. 69966.

**No. 69966. Maximum and Minimum Thermometer combined** (Six's patent) for registering both heat and cold, boxwood, with a long continuous tube filled with mercury, creosote and compressed air; each side of the tube contains a small steel index which remains at the highest point reached until it is drawn to place by a magnet which accompanies each instrument; scales read from 50 below to 150 above zero; 8 in. Each..........$2.85
10 in. Each..........3.75

## STORM GLASS AND THERMOMETER.

**No. 69967. Storm Glass and Thermometer combined.** The barometer will foretell the weather with a fair degree of accuracy for 24 hours in advance; polished wood case (like cut) 3x9 in.; a very popular instrument. Each..........20c

**No. 69968.** Antique oak barometer and storm glass combined, size 3½x8½ in with fancy beaded edge, silvered metal scale to thermometer with brass mountings, large barometer tube; a very fine instrument.
Each..........90c

**No. 69969. Weather House.** This is a simple and interesting little instrument, which indicates the changes of the weather by two small figures. The man comes out before the approach of stormy weather and a lady appears when the indications promise fair weather. The case is made of tin, handsomely decorated in different colors and has thermometer attached. Each..........$1.35

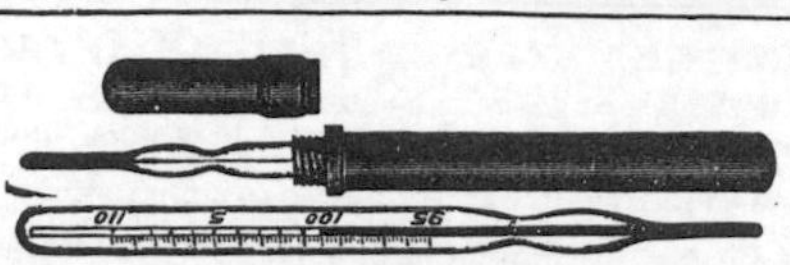

No. 69970.

No. 69970. **Clinical Thermometer,** for physicians' and nurses' use, self registering, 4 in. long in a neat hard rubber case, straight pattern with bulb very accurate. (The two cuts represent the thermometer in and out of the case.) Each....................**$1.00**

No. 69971. **Clinical Thermometer,** for physicians' and nurses' use, self registering, 4 in. long, in plain enameled case with gilt band, safety chain and clasp to prevent it being lost from the pocket; a certificate of accuracy is furnished with each one of these thermometers. Each.......**$2.00**

No. 69972. **Chemical Thermometer,** all glass, with graduations etched on tube with scale up to 300 or 600 degrees Each..............................**$1.75**

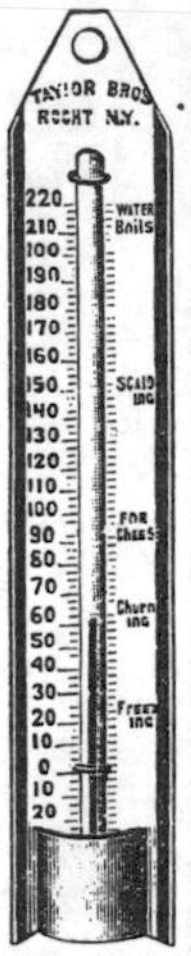


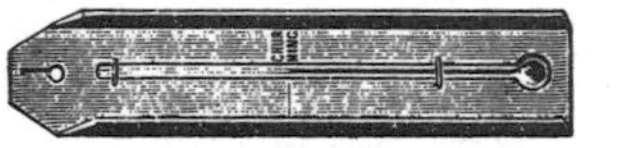

No. 69973.

No. 69973. **Churn Thermometer** with flange scale, tested at 62 degrees for churning. Each.....................**15c**

No. 69974. **Dairy Thermometer** with flange like cut for general dairy use.
Each 8 in..............................**15c**
Each 10 in.............................**25c**

No. 69974.

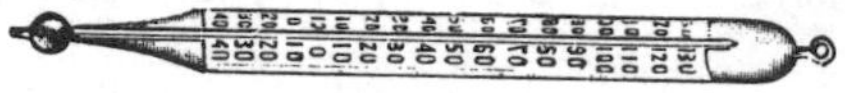

No. 69975.

No. 69975. **Dairy or Bath Thermometer,** all glass; a very desirable instrument and easy to keep clean. Each.................................................**20c**

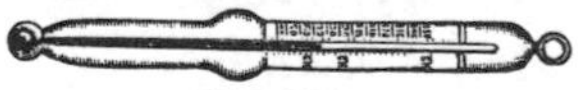

No. 69976.

No. 69976. **Dairy Thermometer,** all glass, standard floating; a new and superior instrument, 9 in. long with swell tube, floats upright.
Each, Small, 30c.; Large..............................**50c**

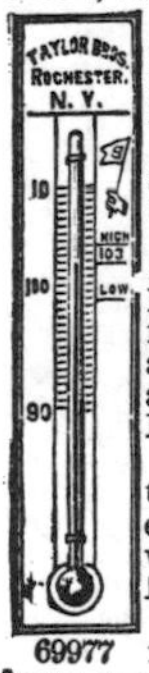


69977

No. 69977. **Incubating Thermometer,** each 4½ or 6 in., long with graduated metal scale, very sensitive and accurate Each......................................**50c**

No. 69978. **Bath Thermometer.** 8 in. glass tube, with scale, white wood frame, with round handle. Each....**40c**

No. 69979. **Hot Bed Thermometer,** round 15 in., hard wood frame with handle and sharp pointed hollow brass ferule to penetrate the soil, red spirit and boxwood scale; is an indispensable article to gardeners or florists. Each......................................**$1.80**

No. 69980. **Evaporating Thermometer,** for drying fruit, ovens, dry kilns, etc., reading to 300 degrees and over, with flanged scale, extra heavy. Each......................................**$1.65**

No. 69981. **Confectioner's Thermometer,** heavy copper case, 12 in. long, scale reading up to 350 or 400 degrees, very accurate. Each..........................**$1.75**

No. 69982. **Lactometer,** for testing the quality of milk, shows the effects produced by changes in the animals diet, as different articles of food produce milk of different density; also shows the amount of water contained in milk; complete instructions accompany each instrument. Each..........................................**35c**

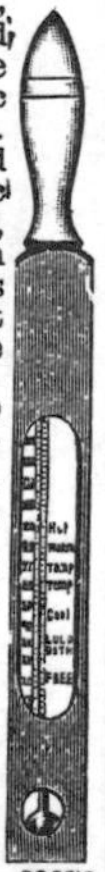

69978

No. 69983. **Urinometers,** used for determining the condition of the system by the specific gravity and the quality of the urine; a circular accompanies each instrument, giving full instructions as to how it should be used, complete with jar enclosed in a round wood box. Each.......................................**35c**

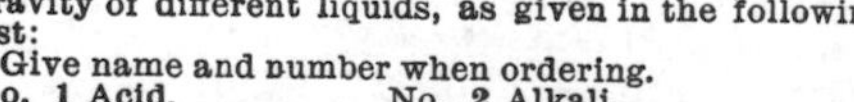

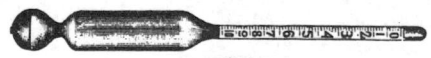

No. 69984.

No. 69984. **Hydrometers,** for testing the specific gravity of different liquids, as given in the following list:

Give name and number when ordering.

| | |
|---|---|
| No. 1 Acid. | No. 2 Alkali. |
| No. 3 Sugar and Syrup. | No. 4 Vinegar. |
| No. 5 Salt, 0 to 50. | No. 6 Salamander, 0 to 100. |
| No. 7 Cider. | No. 8 Shellac. |
| No. 9 Spirit, plain. | No. 10 Bark (for tanners.) |
| No. 11 Liquids heavier than water. | |
| No. 12 Liquids lighter than water. | |
| No. 13 Sachrometers. | No. 14 Ammonia. |
| No. 15 Coal Oil. | |

Price of any of the above. Each.................**50c**

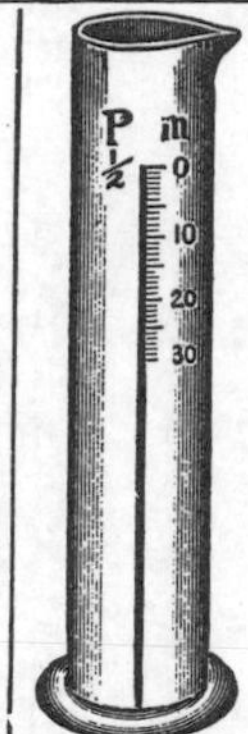

No. 69986.

No. 69985. **Hydrometer Jars,** with foot and pouring spout, but without degrees, weight 6 to 8 oz., height 10 in., diameter 1½ in. Each............**30c**
Height 12 in., diameter 2 in. Each...**40c**
Height 15 in., diameter 2 in. Each...**50c**

No. 69986. **Hydrometer Jars,** with foot and pouring spout, degrees engraved from 0 to 30, weight 6 to 8 oz. Height 10 in., diameter 1½ in.
Each..........................................**50c**
Height 10 in., diameter 1½ in. 0 to 90 degrees.
Each..........................................**60c**

No. 69987. **Rain Gauge,** 3 in. in diameter, copper funnel with galvanized overflow and measuring stick used by the Signal Service. Each........**$2.25**

No. 69988. **Hygrometer or Moisture Gauge,** mounted on wood base for the use of florists, gardeners, incubators, etc. Each..........**$1.25**
Postage 10 cents.

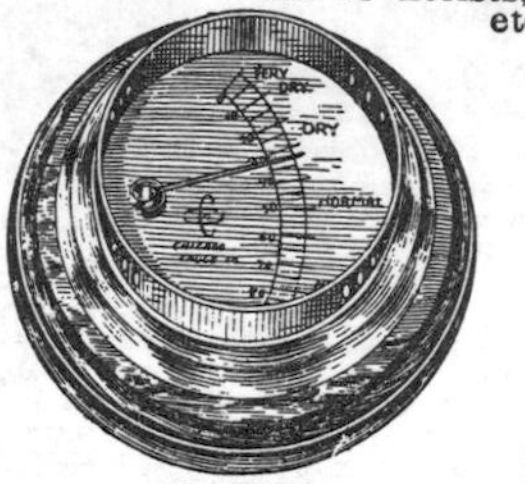

No. 69988.

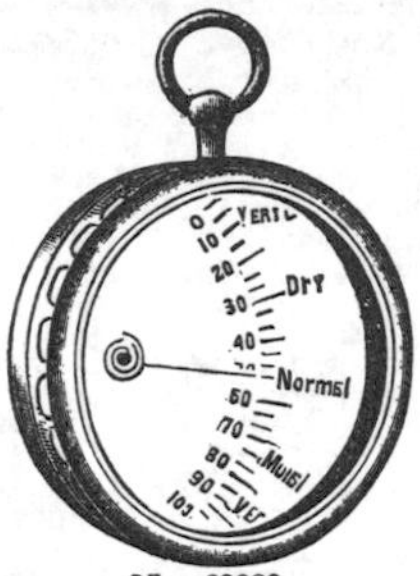


No. 69989.

No. 69989. **Hygrometer or Moisture Gauge, German,** with brass case, card dial, 2¼ inches in diameter; weight, 4 ounces, for general purposes. Each.......................**$1.75**

## BAROMETERS.

For the benefit of those who do not know, we will explain that barometers are scientific and practical instruments, used to fortell the indications of the weather by the varying pressure of the atmosphere. They are of inestimable value to farmers, gardeners, mariners, etc They are also used by tourists in the mountain regions to determine the altitude or distance abovethe sea level. Full instructions accompany each instrument.

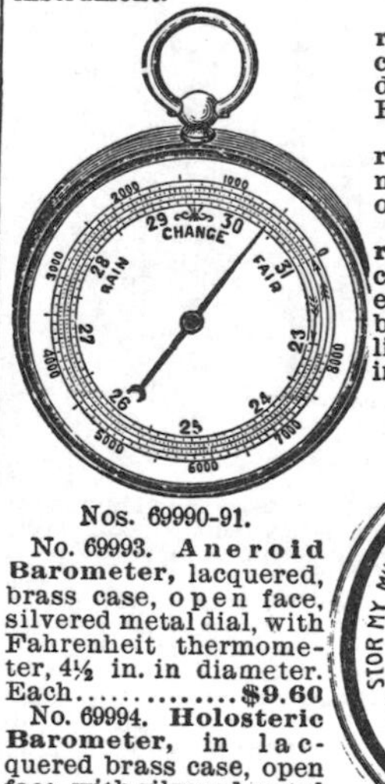


Nos. 69990-91.

No. 69990. **Aneroid Barometer,** in nickel plated case, open face, with card dial, 2½ inches in diameter. Each ............................**$2.00**

No. 69991. **Aneroid Barometer,** brass case, with metal dial, 4 in. in diameter, open face. Each,....**$3.50**

No. 69992. **Aneroid Barometer,** lacquered, brass case, entire open face dial etched on plate glass front, beveled edge; a very fine little instrument, 4 inches in diameter. Each..**$5.50**

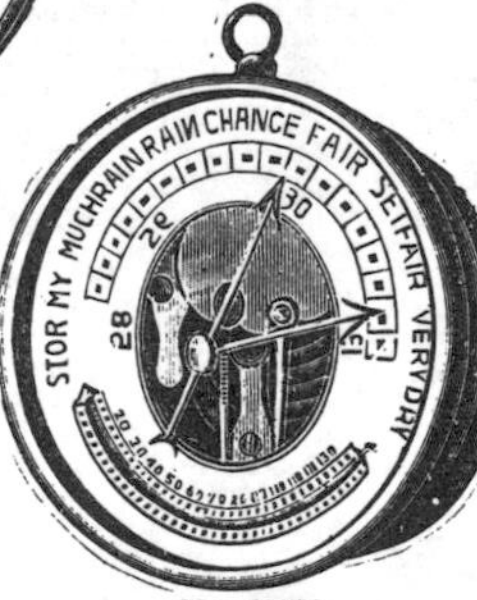


No. 69993.

No. 69993. **Aneroid Barometer,** lacquered, brass case, open face, silvered metal dial, with Fahrenheit thermometer, 4½ in. in diameter. Each..............**$9.60**

No. 69994. **Holosteric Barometer,** in lacquered brass case, open face, with silvered metal dial, 6 inches in diameter, with two thermometers representing the Fahrenheit, Centigrade and Reaumur scales. This instrument is a standard of very fine quality. Each, **$15.50**

## MOUNTAIN POCKET BAROMETERS.
### For Measuring Heights.

These instruments are now made nearly as portable as an ordinary watch, and yet are fully as accurate as the larger sizes. They are of great service to engineers and tourists, as well as to scientific observers, especially in mountain districts, as they indicate correctly the distance above the sea level.

No. 69995. **Pocket Aneroid Barometer,** watch size, 1⅞ inches in diameter, nickel case, metal dial, open face, without thermometer, reading to 10,000 feet. Each..............................................**$7.65**

No. 69996. **Pocket Aneroid Barometer,** watch size, 2 inches in diameter, nickel case, open face, metal dial, with revolving ring, reading to 15,000 feet, compensated for temperature, thermometer and compass on the reverse side; a very complete and accurate instrument. Each..........................................**$10.35**

## MERCURIAL BAROMETERS.

No. 69997. **Mercurial Barometer,** 39 in. long, with porcelain scales, light and dark frame. Each...**$5.00**

No. 69998. **Standard Mercurial Barometer,** same principle as those used by the weather bureau, 36 inches long, ivory scales, oak frame; a very complete and practical instrument. Each ......................**$10.85**

## TELEGRAPH INSTRUMENTS AND APPARATUS.

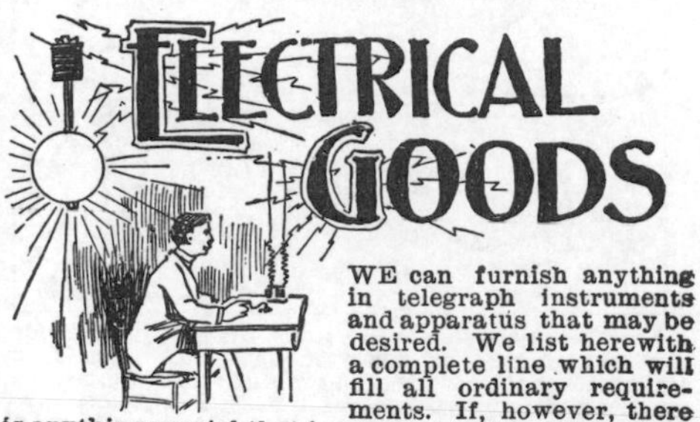


WE can furnish anything in telegraph instruments and apparatus that may be desired. We list herewith a complete line which will fill all ordinary requirements. If, however, there is anything special that is wanted kindly advise us and we shall be glad to make quotations. Our prices will be found to be far lower than the manufacturers, and we believe that a trial order placed with us for anything that may be needed in this line will convince the purchaser that we can save him much money and that we shall be able to merit his future patronage. In addition to our Learner's Instrument, we wish to call special attention to the fact that we list the high grade Standard Western Union instruments, which need no further recommendation.

## TERMS OF SHIPMENT.

**Electrical goods will be sent by express C. O. D.** when desired, providing $1.00 accompanies the order as a guarantee of good faith. The balance can be paid at the express office after examination.

**It is best to send cash in full** with your order and save the discount of 3 per cent. also return express charges on money.

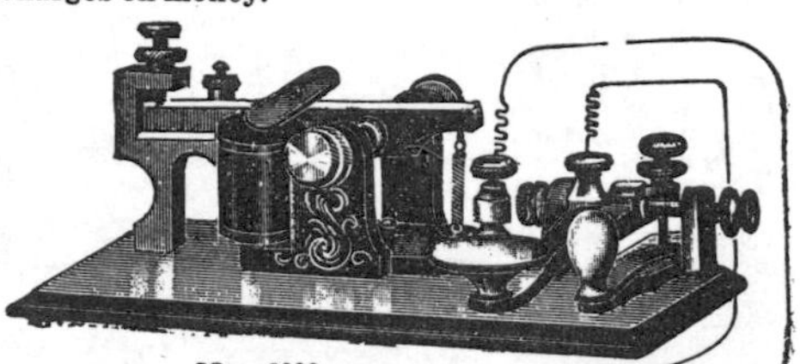

No. 6000.

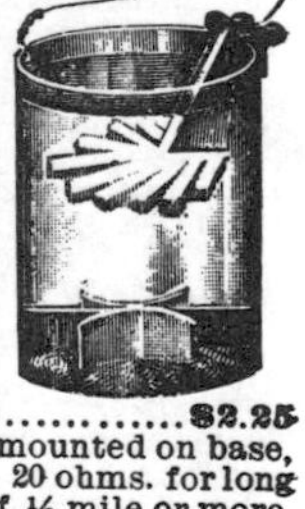

No. 6000. **Learner's Outfit,** complete, for telegraphy, consisting of full size sounder and key, mounted on polished cherry base; has full sized battery, with wire, chemicals and complete book of instructions, with everything necessary for operating for private practice, complete weight about 10¼ lbs. Price..........................**$3.00**

No. 6001. **Learner's Instrument,** same as above, without battery, weight about 2 pounds. Each....................**$2.25**

No. 6002. **Learner's Instrument,** mounted on base, as above, but has sounder wound to 20 ohms. for long distance and should be used on line of ½ mile or more, as it will give better results, weight 2 pounds. Each.....................................................**$2.90**

No. 6006. **Private Line Instrument,** the highest grade, made with steel lever, key and tubular sounder, same style as Western Union, but one size smaller, on polished cherry wood base, with polished rubber covered coils, wound to 20 ohms resistance. Each..**$3.90**

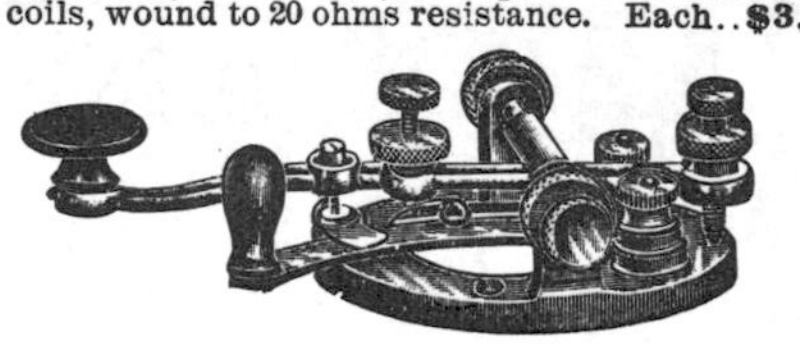

No. 6009.

No. 6008. **Steel Lever Key. Standard Western Union,** with legs to go through the table. These keys are of the latest and most improved type, the lever and trunions being made of solid steel, nickel plated, instead of brass, as in the old type of instrument. The same strength is secured with much lighter weight and the liability of loose trunions completely avoided. This is without doubt one of the most handsome and best working keys on the market. Its adoption by the Western Union Company is certainly a sufficient recommendation for it. Price, each.................**$1.50**
Postage 10 cents.

No. 6009. **Steel Lever Key, Standard Western Union,** legless, with two binding posts to receive the wires. This key is the same as the one described above, with the exception of not having the legs. It is more desirable for screwing on the top of a table. Price, each .....................................**$2.00**
Postage 10 cents.

# POSTAGE

**must always be included when goods are to be sent by mail.**

**DON'T FORGET.**

**The Graphophone—the wonder of the Centure and heretofore only bought by the wealthy is now within the reach of limited means. Special Catalogue free.**

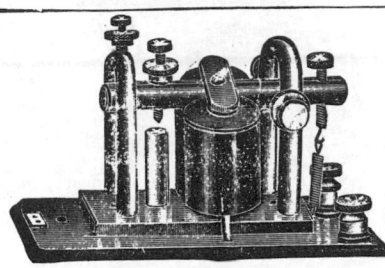

No. 6012.

No. 6012. **Pony Sounder Tubular**, same style as Western Union, but a little smaller; a very fine instrument for short lines or local practice; has polished cherry base with heavy metal sub-base; fine polished rubber covered magnets and a very loud and clear sounder wound to 4 ohms resistance. Each............$2.25
Postage 17 cents.

No. 6013. **Pony Sounder, Tubular**, same as above but wound to 20 ohms resistance for lines up to 15 miles in length. Each............................$2.50
Postage 17 cents.

No. 6014. **Giant Sounder, Tubular.** Standard Western Union size, otherwise same description as above, very loud and clear sound, wound to 4 ohms resistance. Each............................$2.40
Postage 20 cents.

No. 6015. **Giant Sounder, Tubular**, Standard Western Union size, same as above but wound to 20 ohms resistance, for main line use. Each.......$2.80

No. 6024.

No. 6024. **Pony Relay**, made of bronze metal, hand finished, mounted on solid mahogany base with metallic sub base; a thoroughly reliable and practical instrument. Price, with magnets wound to 20 ohms resistance.............................$3.40
No. 6025. **Pony Relay**, same as above, but wound to 50 ohms resistance. Each.............$3.90
No. 6026 **Relay**, Standard Western Union, tubular mountings, mounted on solid mahogany base, wound to 150 ohms resistance, with rubber covered coils, adjustable magnets and finished in a most thorough manner. Price.........................$4.85

No. 6027.

No. 6027. **Box Sounding Relay**, Western Union pattern, both box and base made of polished mahogany; all metal parts nickel plated, with complete adjustments for increasing or decreasing the sound at will, wound to 50 ohms resistance.
Price, without key.........................$5.90
For the benefit of those who do not know we wish to say that for local practice, or for short lines up to ¼ or ½ mile in length, and where only two instruments are used on lines, a sounder of 4 ohms resistance will give very good results, especially if a complete metallic circuit be used, which is recommended for very short lines. For lines longer than ½ mile, or where more than two instruments are to be used, unless the line be very short, the magnets should be wound to 20 ohms resistance.

No. 6035.

No. 6035. **Pocket Galvanometer**, for testing the strength of electric currents; a well finished instrument. Each.............................$5.75
No. 6035½. **Pocket size**, little different in construction, hard rubber case. Each.................$4.60

---

## ESTIMATE FOR A HALF MILE PRIVATE LINE.

No 6036. Two instruments the same as 6002 wound with fine wire to 20 ohms resistance.
Each.........................$2.90.........$5.80
½ mile of No. 14 BB galvanized iron wire about 50 lbs.
at.........................$0.06½.........$3.25
14 pony glass insulators at.....  .04.........  .56
15 oak brackets at ..............  .03.........  .45
5 cells of gravity battery at.....  .50.........  2.50
2 pounds of office wire at......  .32.........  .64
10 pounds of blue vitrol at......  .06.........  .60
Complete,.........................13.80
The above estimate is for a complete and practical working line.

We shall be glad to furnish information to any who are anticipating the building of a private line. It is a very popular practice where there are several students in telegraphy within a reasonable distance of each other, to build a line connecting each of their homes. In this way they have practical experience in telegraphy and the distance makes the study very pleasant as well as more valuable. Complete instructions for building private lines, together with diagrams accompany each set of instruments free of charge.

## GRAVITY BATTERY.

The Gravity Battery is a closed circuit battery which is used for telegraph work, or can be used for operating electric bells, but is not so desirable for bell work on account of evaporation and the necessity of renewing the battery more often.

FOR CUT OF SAME SEE LEARNER'S OUTFIT, No. 6000, SEE PAGE 470.

No. 6037. **Gravity Battery**, cell complete, size 5x7, weight about 5 pounds. Each.....................50c
No. 6088. **Gravity Battery**, cell complete, size 6x8, weight about 7 pounds. Each.....................60c
No. 6089. **Battery Jar**, glass, 5x7. Each ........25c
No. 6040. **Battery Jar**, glass, 6x8. Each ........30c
No. 6041. **Zinc**, for 5x7 battery. Each..........20c
No. 6042. **Zinc**, for 6x8 battery. Each..........40c
No. 6043. **Copper**, for 5x7, or 6x8 battery. Each.15c
No. 6044. **Blue Vitrol**, per pound.................6c

## OPEN CIRCUIT BATTERIES.

For electric bells, burglar alarms, telephone work, etc.

No. 6048.

These batteries are intended for use where the circuit is closed only a small portion of the time. If placed on a continuous closed circuit they will soon be exhausted, but for open circuit work such as bells, telephone work, etc., they will last from 12 to 18 months without renewal.
No. 6048. **La Clede Battery**, per cell, complete............50c
No. 6049. **Le Clanche Battery**, complete, per cell....60c

**Extra Parts for the Above Batteries.**

No. 6050. A Porus Cup. Each...................40c
No. 6051. Glass Jar. Each.....................10c
No. 6052. Zinc. Each.........................5c
No. 6053. Sal-ammoniac. Per lb................15c

## DRY BATTERIES.

**Dry Batteries** when first introduced were not very successful, but now they are largely displacing the wet batteries of La Clede and Le Clanche type for nearly all kinds of work. The principle is the same as the Le Clanche. They are clean in every respect and will last from 4 to 18 months, depending largely on the amount they are used. They require no attention to keep them in order. When they have run out they are not to be recharged, but must be replaced by a new one. These batteries are largely used for electro medical work also.
No. 6055. Dry Battery, the Western or Mesco Cell. Each..........................70c

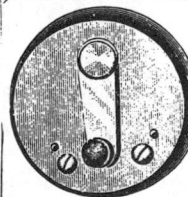

No. 6055.

## EDISON LA LANDE BATTERY.
For motor work.

These batteries have been designed especially for motor work, lighting and other work where a very strong and continuous current is required.

No. 6058. **Edison La Lande Battery**, type J, cell capacity 50 ampere hours. Each.............$1.25

### RENEWAL PARTS.

No. 6059. Copper oxide plate (one charge).......12c
No. 6060. Zinc Plate (one charge)...............8c
No. 6061. Caustic Potash, two sticks (one charge.)
Each.........................................12c
No. 6062. Paraffine Oil (one charge)............5c
No. 6063. **Edison La Lande Battery**, Type Q Cell, capacity 150 ampere hours, cell complete.
Each.......................................$1.90

### RENEWAL PARTS.

No. 6064. Copper oxide plate, one charge........24c
No. 6065. Two Zinc Plates, one charge.........25c
No. 6066. Caustic Potash, two sticks, one charge.
Each.......................................17c
No. 6067. Paraffine Oil, one charge............5c

---

## IRON BOX BELLS.

Used for Door Calls, Alarm Work, Etc.

No. 6090 With 3 in. gong Each ...........50c
No. 6091. With 4 in. gong. Each..........60c

## BUZZERS, WITH METAL BOX.

Buzzers are sometimes used in place of bells, as they make a low buzzing sound No. 6091. which can be heard but a short distance.
No. 6095. **Buzzer**, with nickel or wood box. Each...........60c

## PUSH BUTTONS.

Push Buttons are arranged to make electrical connections and are used for door bells and other work.

No. 6099. **Push Buttons**, oak. Each....................15c
No. 6100. **Push Buttons**, fancy or polished bronze. Each....................40c
No. 6101. **Floor Push** for servants' call, etc. Each....................75c

No. 6099.

## ELECTRIC BELL OUTFITS.

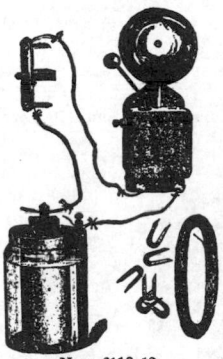

Consisting of bell, battery, push button, wire and full instructions for putting up the same.
No. 6110. **Door Bell Outfit**, complete with battery, wood push button.
Each....................$2.00
No. 6111. **Door Bell Outfit**, complete with battery and bronzed push button.
Each....................$2.50
No. 6112. **Burglar Alarm Outfits**, with bell, battery and door or window spring, complete.
Each....................$2.75

Nos. 6110-12.

## CALL ANNUNCIATORS.

Call Annunciators are arranged with bell, complete. and have a hand which points to the number indicating the portion of the house or other place from which the call originated; also used for burglar alarm purposes.
No. 6120. **Annunciator** with four numbers.
Each.............................$5.00
No. 6121. **Annunciator** with six numbers.
Each.............................$7.00
No. 6122. **Annunciator** with eight numbers.
Each.............................$8.50

## BURGLAR ALARM SPRING.

Used for making window or door connections which close the circuit and sound the alarm when a window or door is opened.
No. 6130. **Door Spring**. Each...................25c
No. 6131. **Window Spring**. Each...............25c

## MATTING.

No. 6032. **Electric Matting**, to be placed under the carpet or mat, and when connected with bell or battery, pressure on the mat will close the circuit and cause the bell to ring. Per square foot, each......50c

## SWITCHES.

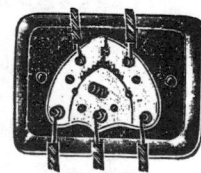

Switches with wood base for making electric connections; metal parts nickel plated.
No. 6140. **Switch with one point.** Each............30c
No. 6141. **Switch with two points.** Each............35c
No. 6142. **Switch with three points.** Each.............40c

No. 6140.

No. 6150. **Lightning Arrester** and ground wire switch for short line telegraph work. Each............80c
No. 6151. **Lightning Arrester** and ground wire switch, adjustable.
Each.............$1.20

No. 6150.

## WIRE.

No. 6175. **Annunciator Wire**, double cotton covered and paraffined for electric bells, telegraph and telegraph work or other inside wiring, per lb., (about 150 feet)............30c
No. 6175.  No. 6178. **Galvanized iron** telegraph or telephone wire, No. 14, about 100 lbs. to the mile, in ½ mile coils, per lb...............6½c

## INSULATORS.

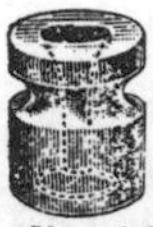

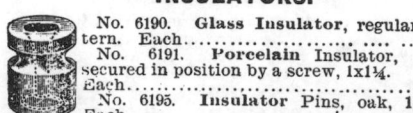

No. 6190. **Glass Insulator**, regular pattern. Each .................... 4c

No. 6191. **Porcelain Insulator**, to be secured in position by a screw, 1x1¼. Each .................... 2c

No. 6195. **Insulator Pins**, oak, 1¼ in. Each .................... 2c

No. 6198. **Insulator Brackets**, wood, No. 9191. patent. Each .................... 3c

No. 6200. **Staples**, ½ in. for securing wires on inside work, per lb .................... 15c

## MAGNETS.

No. 6201. Horse Shoe Magnets, superior quality.

| Length, inches, | 2 | 3 | 4 | 6 |
|---|---|---|---|---|
| Price, each, | $0.06 | .15 | .25 | .44 |
| Length, inches | 8 | 10 | | 12 |
| Price, each, | $0.85 | 1.35 | | 1.80 |

No. 6202. Bar Magnets.

| Length, inches, | 4 | 6 |
|---|---|---|
| Price, each, | $0.18 | .25 |

No. 6203. Loadstone or Natural Magnet, sold in pieces as follows:

| | Small size. | Med. size. | Large size. |
|---|---|---|---|
| Price, per piece, | $0.20 | .45 | .70 |

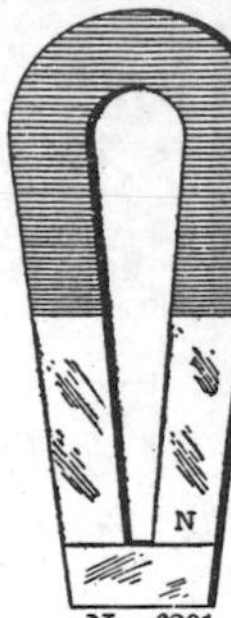


No. 6201.

## ELECTRIC MOTORS.

We list the Porter electric motors which are so well known that we believe a lengthy description is unnecessary. They are arranged to be run with batteries. Almost any cell or battery will suffice where the work to be done is not too heavy, but where the motor is to perform heavy and continuous work they should be operated by the Edison La Lande Battery.

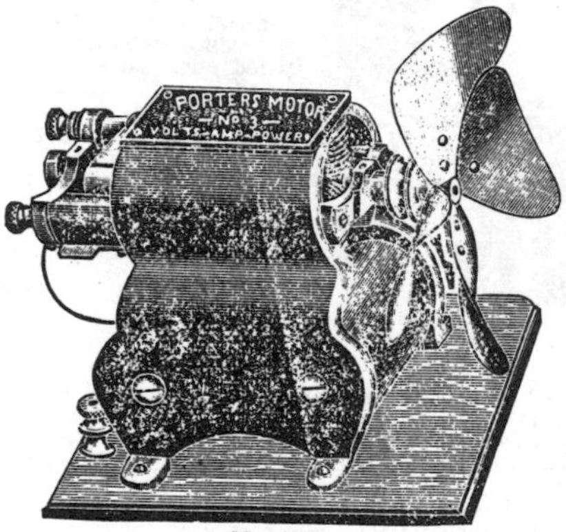


No. 6235.

No. 6235. **Porter Motor** No. 1 size, small but develops a considerable amount of power, can be operated with one cell of battery and will furnish power for mechanical toys, revolving window show, etc.; weight about 1¾ lbs.
Price, each, without battery .................... $2.90

No. 6236. **Porter Motor** No. 2 size, same construction as above but larger, weighing about 3 lbs and has a capacity of about 1-20 horse power. Price, each, without battery .................... $4.75

No. 6237. **Porter Motor** No. 3 size, 5½ in. long by 4½ in. high by 4½ in. wide. This motor will run a small ventilating fan, a dentist's buffer, a grinding machine or other light work. The normal speed is about 2,200 revolutions per minute, and when using 4 cells of battery it will generate about 1-15 horse power, weight about 6 lbs. Each, .................... $9 00

No. 6238. **Porter Motor** No. 4 size, built same style as No. 3 but is a much larger and stronger motor. It is wound for from 2 to 10 volts, and with 8 volts and 10 amperes will develop about 1-6 horse power. It is mounted on a ¾ in. cherry base, has brass binding posts and a two point switch for regulating the speed by changing the number of batteries in the circuit; weight with base about 12 lbs., clears an 8 in. fan.
Price, complete, .................... $13.50

No. 6239. **Iron Base**, artistically made and japanned, for elevating the height of motors Nos. 3 or 4 to permit the use of larger fans. Each, .................... $1.00

## FANS FOR PORTER MOTORS.

No. 6240.

| Inches | 4 | 5 | 6 | 8 | 10 |
|---|---|---|---|---|---|
| Blades | 3 | 3 | 4 | 4 | 6 |
| Each | $0.25 | .35 | .40 | .75 | 1 25 |

**YOU CAN EASILY LOSE $20.00**

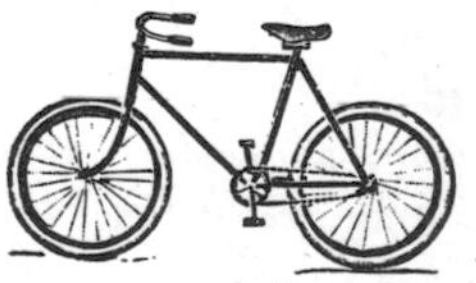

By buying your
... BICYCLE ...
From a Local Agent.

**Our "Uno" at $35.00**

Is the rarest of Bargains. See page 612.

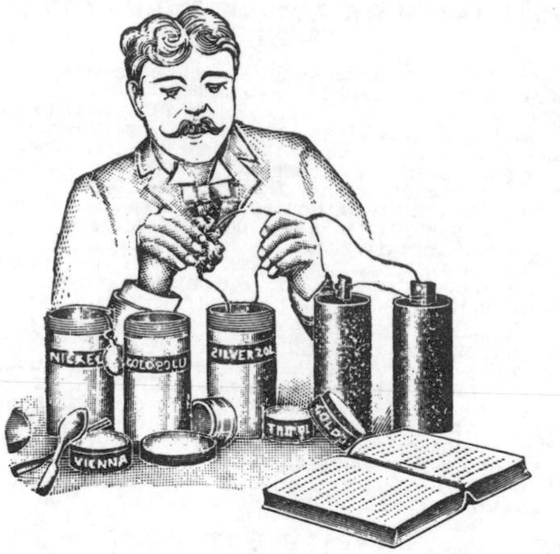


No. 6250.

## GOLD AND SILVER PLATING OUTFITS.

No. 6250. These are intended for plating small bright articles of jewelry, such as watches, rings, chains, tea spoons, etc. As they are used with dry batteries to generate the electric current the use of acids being dispensed with, thereby rendering them more desirable and popular for home amusements, and instruction in the beautiful art of electro-metalurgy. This outfit plates well with gold, silver, nickel or copper. It consists of two dry batteries, two glass tanks, the necessary solutions, salts, etc., making a complete outfit. It is packed in a strong box with cover and weighs, complete, about 9½ lbs. Price, each .................... $10.00

## BOOKS ON ELECTRICITY.

No. 6275. **Electric Bell Hangers'** Hand Book (by Badt). Each .................... $1.00

No. 6276. **Electric Bells** and All About Them (by Bottone). Each .................... 50c

No. 6277. **The Telephone** (by Dolbear). Each .................... 50c

No. 6278. **Electro Metalurgy**, a complete treaties on electro-plating .................... $1.00

## TELEPHONES.

The demand for telephones has so largely increased of late that we have been induced to give the matter special attention with a view to selecting a 'phone which is strictly up-to-date, and at the same time one which can be furnished at a moderate cost. Until within the past year the telephone patents have been so closely guarded that a strictly first-class and up-to-date instrument could not be furnished for the use of private individuals or telephone exchanges except the Bell and a few others. Many of the most valuable patents have now expired and others have been introduced to take the places of those which have not as yet expired. We are now prepared to offer telephones which are not only suitable for private use, but are being furnished for the use of corporations for city exchanges. The telephone as now made is very much simplified, and while it is a delicate instrument we have taken particular care to select one which we can guarantee to give entire satisfaction. We caution buyers of telephones against purchasing instruments of concerns who have not an established reputation, as there are many 'phones on the market which cannot be depended upon and are practically worthless.

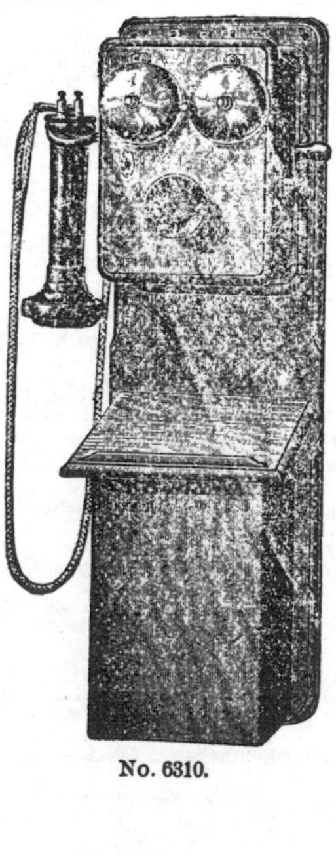

No. 6310.

No. 6310. **The Improved long distance battery telephone** of the regular Bell telephone style with solid oak or walnut case, magneto call with 10,000 ohm generator, double bells, compound pole receiver with end nickel plated to prevent rust; a very sensitive granulated chemically treated carbon transmitter, and box on case for two batteries. The chemical treatment of the granulated carbon prevents it from packing, which has been a very fatal objection with granulated carbon transmitters.

Price complete including 2 cells of dry battery.
Each .................... $13.50

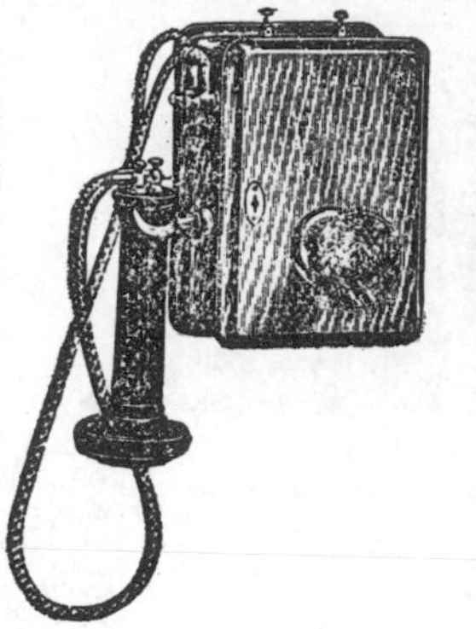

No. 6311.

No. 6311. **Improved long distance telephone**, with transmitter and receiver, same as above but with a battery call instead of the magneto call, the connection is to be made with a push button, and is a thoroughly reliable instrument.

Price with case complete as shown in cut, made of oak or black walnut.
Each .................... $7.00

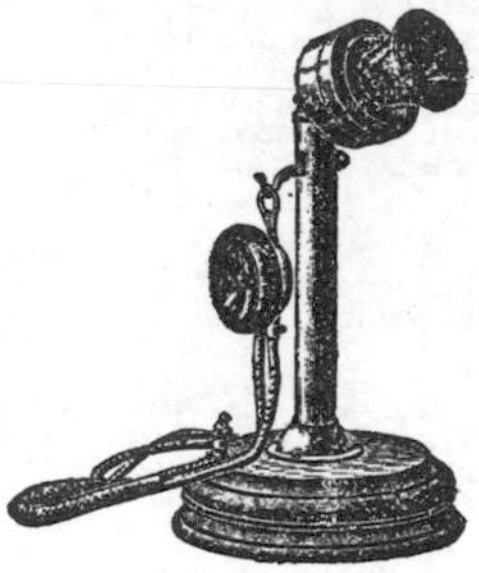

No. 6312. **Desk 'phone**, one of the neatest and most artistic desk 'phones made; has neat pedestal with nickel plated standard. Our regular type of long distance transmitter with the small new style receiver.
Each .................... $11.50

No. 6313. **Desk 'phone**, same style as above, but with magneto call bells included. Each .................... $16.50

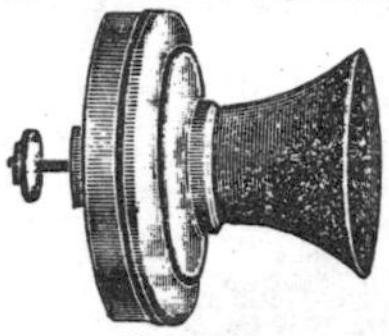

No. 6314.

No. 6314. **Transmitter**, long distance with granulated carbon; can be attached to telephones of any make on which the transmitter is not satisfactory or has given out, same as used on our improved long distance telephones, but made to screw on the front of the box; is very easily attached.
Price .................... $2.00

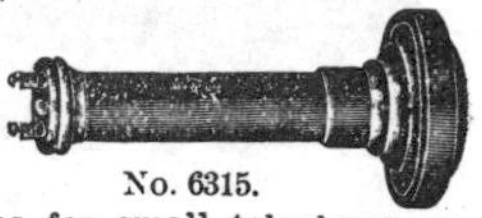

No. 6315.

No. 6315. **Receiver**, same as used on our regular 'phones with compound bar magnets, hard rubber case.
Each .................... $1.50

No. 6320. **Plug Switches** for small telephone exchanges, five connections or over.
Each connection .................... 20c

## ELECTRO MEDICAL BATTERIES

### For Home or Physicians' Use.

The Electro Medical Battery as a curative agent is becoming more appreciated from day to day. In cases of nervous trouble and partial paralysis it has brought about phenomenal results. The best physicians prescribe its use even when all else fails, and even under such adverse circumstances it often cures. For rheumatism, neuralgia, paralysis and all nervous disorders it seems to be nature's own cure. There need be no fear from the use of these machines, as there can be no bad results derived. An invalid may use them with perfect safety. There are a great variety of electrical machines and batteries on the market, from which we have selected of each kind those in which we can furnish our customers with the best value for the amount of money expended.

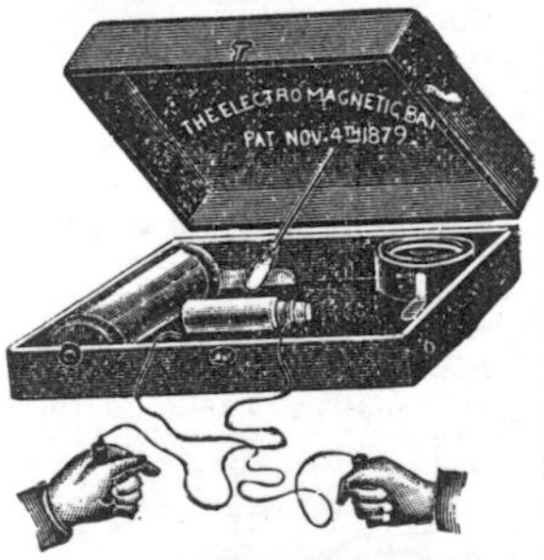


No. 6350.

No. 6350. **The Little Wonder.** A complete and perfect working little battery, neat, portable, and powerful, and produces an electric current from a small cell of zinc and carbon. This is a small machine that embodies all of the features of the larger ones and produces an electric current of great tensity and long duration with a very small charge of chemicals. There are no dangerous acids to handle, and it is so simple that any child can operate it; full instructions accompany each battery.
Each .................... $1.35

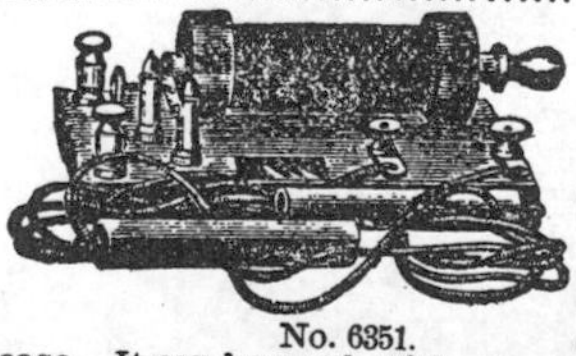

No. 6351.

No. 6351. **Induction Coil** without battery. This instrument is very strong and is practically the same as the next following, except that it has not the battery included, and consequently a smaller case. It can be used with any acid battery, or with one or two cells of dry battery which are listed further on in this department. This instrument is especially desirable for the use of travelers, inasmuch as it is very small and portable; size of base 5¾x2¾, but still it has all the power of the larger instruments. Price of instrument complete, including pair of hand electrodes, cords and sponge holder of the best quality.
Each .................... $3.50

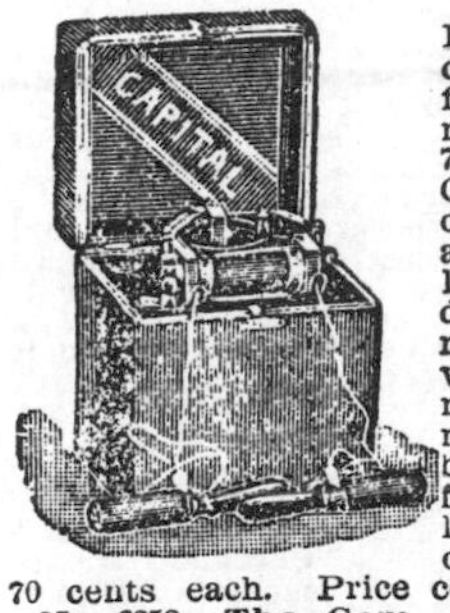


**No. 6352. The "Capital" Battery**, imitation mahogany case made of cherry and well finished with rounded corners, handle and catch, height 7¼ inches, width 6½x5¾. One of the principal features of this battery is that it uses a Mesco dry cell, which will last from four to nine months, depending largely on how much it is used. It develops a very strong current, is well made throughout, with parts nickel plated and is one of the best batteries on the market for the price; weighs a little less than 5 pounds. New cells of battery can be furnished at 70 cents each. Price complete.................**$4.50**

**No 6353. The Gem Electro Medical Battery.** This battery, like the one preceding, uses a dry cell, but the entire apparatus is made in a much more compact form and has a very fine polished oak case which is better proportioned than the one represented by the cut and has a nice carrying handle. The size is

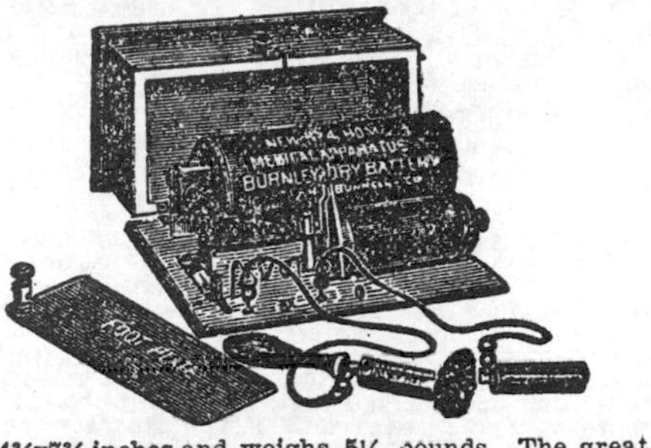


4½x4¾x7¾ inches and weighs 5½ pounds. The great advantage to be derived from these batteries is a strong and even current combined with the entire absence of acids of any kind, which are liable to be spilled and injure clothing, furniture, etc. This instrument is furnished complete with cords and handles, one foot plate and two sponge electrodes with wood handles. Price complete..................**$5.75**
Extra battery, per cell..........................**70**

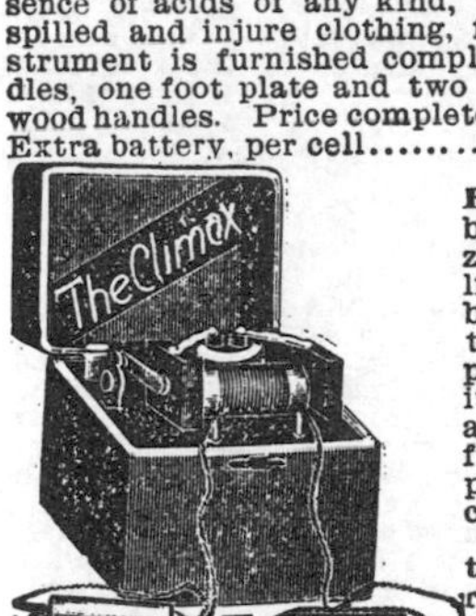


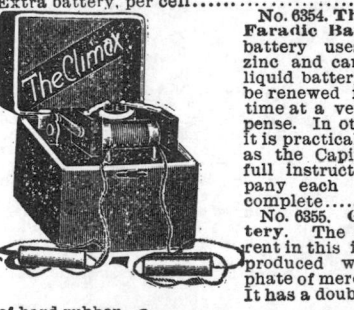

**No. 6354. The "Climax" Faradic Battery.** This battery uses a regular zinc and carbon cell of liquid battery, which can be renewed from time to time at a very small expense. In other respects it is practically the same as the Capital battery; full instructions accompany each one. Price, complete..............**$4.00**

**No. 6355. Gaiffe's Battery.** The electric current in this instrument is produced with a bisulphate of mercury battery. It has a double cell made of hard rubber, each cell having a carbon and zinc plate. The double battery cell can easily be removed from the case for cleansing or recharging. The

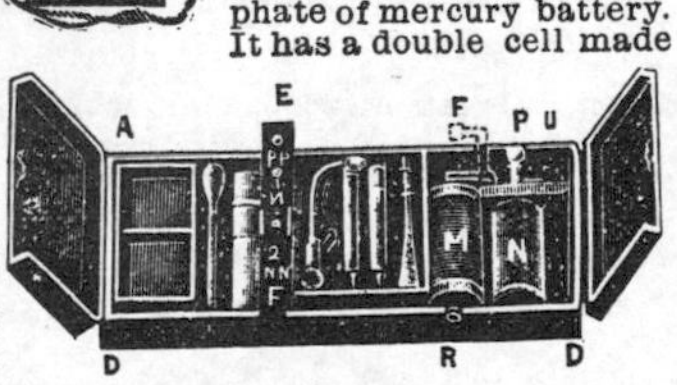


currents produced by these batteries are as follows:

1. Primary current.
2. Secondary current.
3. The current of the first two combined in tensity.
4. Shocks slow or fast according to the use of the contact breaker or lever.

This is the celebrated Gaiffe system for physicians and family use. It is very compact, is all enclosed in a polished mahogany case 4x1¾x7½ inches, and weighs 1¾ lbs. Complete with full instructions. Each..**$6.50**

**No. 6356. Gaiffe's Battery** with same sized coil as in the preceding, but produces two currents only instead of three, is mounted in single cover, polished mahogany case, size 4x1½x6½ inches, with two insulated handles and one vial bisulphate of mercury for charging the battery. Each..................**$5.40**

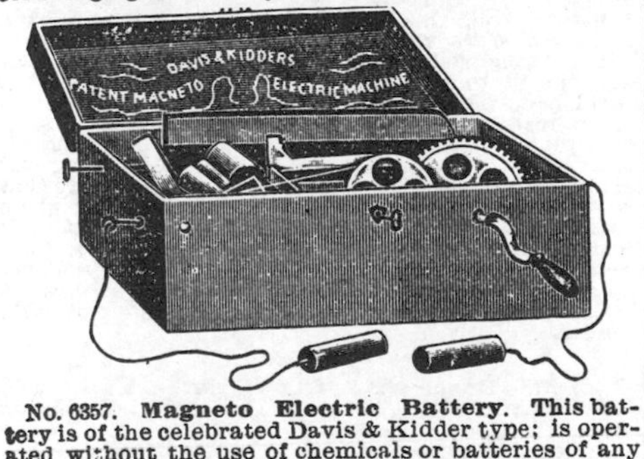


**No. 6357. Magneto Electric Battery.** This battery is of the celebrated Davis & Kidder type; is operated without the use of chemicals or batteries of any kind. The electric current is produced by the revolving of fixed electro magnets by turning a handle from the outside of the case. This machine produces a very powerful current and will last a lifetime if properly cared for. Size of case 4x4½x8¼; weight about 5¾ lbs.

No. 6358. **Magneto Electric Battery**, same as above, but larger and stronger; size of case, 4½ x 5 x 10 inches. Each..........................................**$6.75**

## BECKWITH THERMO OZONE BATTERY
### A New Discovery.

No. 6359. **The "Beckwith" Battery** constitutes an entirely new discovery in the use of electricity, as a remedial agent. It only generates a current of thermo-galvanism when there exists a difference of temperature between the battery and its poles. In the treatment of disease, the battery must be placed in

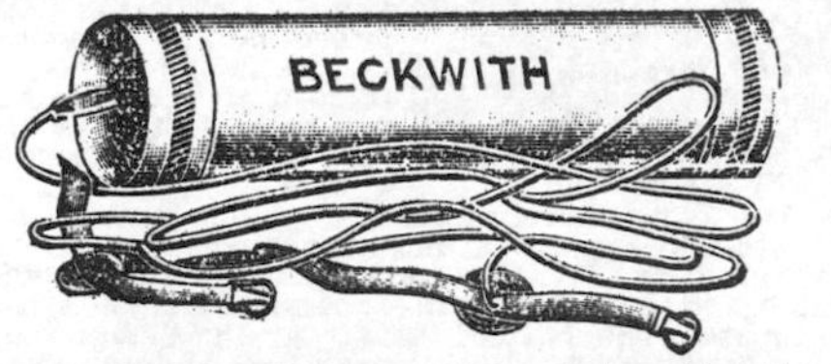


water not less than 30 degrees Fahrenheit, colder than the poles when applied to the body. It sets free from water and air in contact with the positive poles, oxygen and ozone, and the force of the current sends these neutral curative agents into the blood circulation between the poles. The same force by the use of wired wood pulp tablets, having medicine put on their surfaces in contact with the body and under the positive pole, conveys the medicine into any organ of the body. The battery is constant—will last for years and has no switches or corroding points to get out of order. Its force is regulated by the degree of cold surrounding the battery, and can be regulated by the person using it to meet the needs in every case. It is intended for family use, as well as physicians. Many hundreds of families have used it in home treatment, and state that they have been able to cure many diseases at their beginning, thereby avoiding danger, suffering and expense. It is put up in compact form, with book giving complete directions and explanations. Price complete, each.................................................**$9.00**

## BATTERY PARTS, ETC.

No. 6360. **Sponge Holder**, electrode, for any of the above batteries. Each..................................**50c**
No. 6261. **Handles** for any of the above batteries. Per pair...............................................**75c**
No. 6262. **Battery Cords** for above batteries, about 4 feet in length. Per pair..........................**50c**
No. 6363. **Battery**, dry cell. Each..............**50c**
No. 6364. **Zinc** for the Climax battery. Each...**20c**
No. 6365. **Carbon** for Climax Battery. Each....**25c**
No. 6366. **Glass Jar** for Climax battery. Each, **25c**
No. 6367. **Bisulphate of Mercury** for charging batteries. Per oz., **10c**; per ½ lb. **75c**; per lb., **$1.25**
No. 6368. **Metallic Hair Brush**, with electric attachments for use with any of the above batteries. Each..................................................**$1.25**

## ELECTRIC RING FOR RHEUMATISM.

No. 6370. These are the first rings introduced into the United States, all others being imitations. Their popularity has caused many rings to be placed on sale that are without any curative properties. Gray metal polished.
Price, each...........................................**75c**
No. 6371. Same as above, but gold plated. Price, each..................................................**$1.00**

## PHOTOGRAPHIC GOODS.

Photography is one of the most fascinating and fast becoming one of the most popular of pleasures. It is something in which everybody can indulge, and is not a fleeting pleasure which lasts but a few minutes, but is instructive and entertaining as well. It enables one to collect mementos from time to time, at home, while traveling, etc., which will become treasures in after years. We list a large variety of cameras as well as photographic sundries. Our line of hand cameras, folding hand cameras and view cameras are listed complete in this book, but those who are interested in studio outfits will be furnished with a special catalogue with quotations on same. We have carefully examined the cameras and accessories made by all the reputable manufacturers and have, after careful consideration, selected a line which is complete with the latest improvements and in which we can furnish our patrons a thoroughly first-class article; in fact, the best on the market for the least money. We wish to say briefly that the art of photography is much more simple than is generally believed. If it was generally known that it could be so easily mastered there would be thousands of people enjoying the art who now feel afraid to undertake it. Complete instructions for the manipulation of the camera, taking pictures, developing, printing and finishing the same, accompanies each camera. The instructions are made so simple that even a child with very little experience can do very good work. We are at all times glad to answer any inquiries concerning photographic goods, and also to assist our patrons should they experience any difficulty in finishing the pictures.

## HAND CAMERAS.

The Hand Camera is the simplest form of photographic camera and one which appeals strongest to those who have not had previous experience. Some are constructed for the use of films only, others for both films and dry plates and a few for dry plates only. The film cameras are most convenient for the traveler, for all that he has to do after having loaded his camera is to make exposures one after the other until the roll of film has been consumed, after which it is replaced by a new one. A roll of film weighs but a few ounces and takes up but very little space. The film cameras are also most desirable for those who wish to make the exposures only and have the pictures developed and finished by a professional photographer. The majority of amateurs, however, derive fully as much pleasure from the developing and finishing of their pictures as they do from making the exposures, and we believe that if it was more generally known that the art is so easily mastered there would be but a small amount of work taken to the photograph gal-

## TERMS OF SHIPMENT.

**Photographic goods** when ordered to the amount of $2.00 or more **will be sent C. O. D.** if desired, providing $1.00 accompanies the order as a guarantee of good faith. Orders to the amount of $20.00 and over must be accompanied by $2.00. These are the most liberal terms ever offered on this class of goods and we trust that our patrons will appreciate the same.

**Liquids and Glass can be sent by mail** at the rate of 4 cents per oz. Liquids (not more than 4 oz.) may be bottled and packed in wooden boxes as provided by the U. S. postal laws. Allow 5 cents for liquid cases in addition to the postage. Small dry plates can also be sent in the same way.

**Photographic goods cannot be returned** for exchange after they have been used, for even though they may have been used but a little they become second-handed, and we have no means of selling second-handed goods.

The above rule, however, does not refer to any goods which might be defective. We guarantee all goods to give entire satisfaction.

**We advise sending cash in full**, as you save the discount of 3 per cent., also return charges on the money.

## THE ZAR POCKET CAMERA.

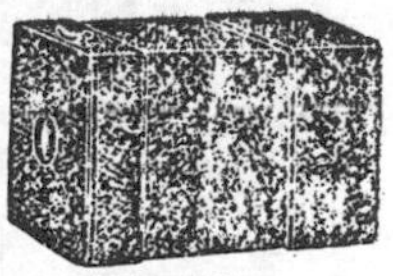
No. 6500.

No. 6500. The cheapest camera ever sold. Even though this little instrument is offered for less than $1.00 it is a complete and practical working camera. The case is covered with black leatherette, which is a most excellent imitation of morocco. It has a good single lens and a very simple but practical shutter, which works equally well for instantaneous or time exposures. The instrument is extremely simple with nothing about it to get out of order. It takes a picture 2x2 inches on regular dry plates. The camera holds but one plate, but can be re-loaded either with a loading sleeve, a dark closet or any place from which the light is excluded. With each camera is included a half dozen regular dry plates and complete instructions for making, developing, printing and toning pictures. The camera measures 2¼x2¼x3¾.
Price, complete............................................**85c**
Postage, 15 cents.

## THE GEM CAMERA.

No. 6503. This camera has been well named, inasmuch as it fills a much felt want, for a camera which will take a good sized picture, but at a price which will come within the reach of all. It is the most exceptional bargain that we have ever been able to offer, and at the same time is thoroughly reliable in every respect. It is so simple that it is almost out of the question to get it out of order. It uses glass plates only, size 3¼x4¼, which is sufficiently large to fill the requirements of the average amateur. It has a space on the inside for three holders, and the case on the outside measures but 4½x6x7 inches and weighs but one pound. It is fitted with a first-class achromatic lense with the Rochester safety shutter and one regular double plate holder with rubber slides which hold two plates. It is only necessary to purchase two other plate holders to have a capacity for six pictures which is quite sufficient for any ordinary outing. The exposed plates can be exchanged for fresh ones in any dark room or closet. The shutter is a very simple and convenient arrangement, which adapts it for both instantaneous and time exposures. It has two brilliant view finders, one for horizontal and the other for upright pictures, and the case is covered with a good quality of black grained leather.

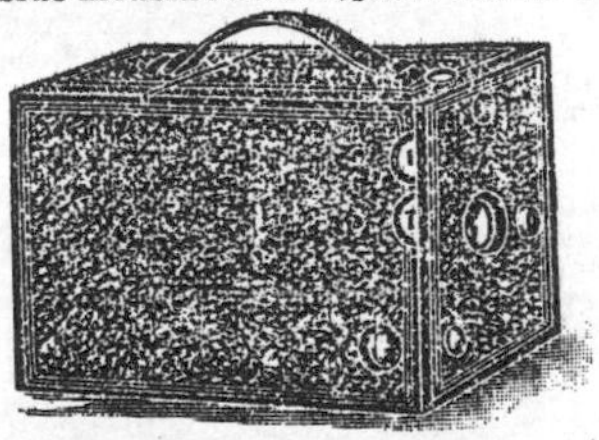

Price of Gem Camera with one plate holder.....**$4.25**
Extra double plate holders. Each...............**.35**

Gem developing and printing outfit, consisting of one metal ruby lamp, three fibre trays, one 8 oz. little developing solution, one 8 oz. bottle of toning solution, one graduate, one printing frame, one pound of hypo, one dozen sensitized paper. Price complete.......**$1.75**

The above camera and accessories we can conscientiously recommend to anyone desiring a good low-priced outfit. A complete instruction book accompanies each outfit.

## THE BABY HAWKEYE CAMERA.

No. 6506. This camera is arranged for the use of films only. It takes a picture 2 x 2½ and has a capacity for 12 exposures. The outside dimensions are 2½ x 3½ x 4 inches. The entire weight is only 7 ounces. It will be readily understood that this makes the camera very convenient for carrying about. It has a brilliant view finder, which enables the operator to correctly center the camera upon any object of which he wishes to take a picture. A great deal of difficulty has been experienced with most of the so called daylight cameras on account of the light reaching the sensitive surface of the films while placing it in position, or removing it from the camera. This camera is supplied with a very late device which entirely overcomes this trouble and enables us to offer a small camera which can be safely loaded in broad daylight without any extr

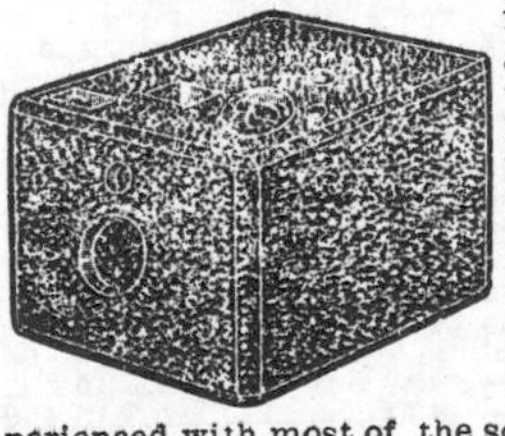

structed that the length of an exposure can be varied as to time which is the means of good results even when the light is very weak. It has an automatic tally which shows correctly at all times the number of exposures that have been made. The lens is a single achromatic always in focus and of the best quality obtainable. The covering is of the best selected morocco grain cow hide, and the finish throughout is equal to that of any of the larger cameras. Making photographs with this camera is so simple that it is hardly necessary to consult the guide book which is furnished. The Baby Hawkeye complete with one film for 12 exposures. Price.......................................$5.40
Extra rolls of sunlight film for 12 exposures, each. .35
Developing outfit, complete.......................1.00

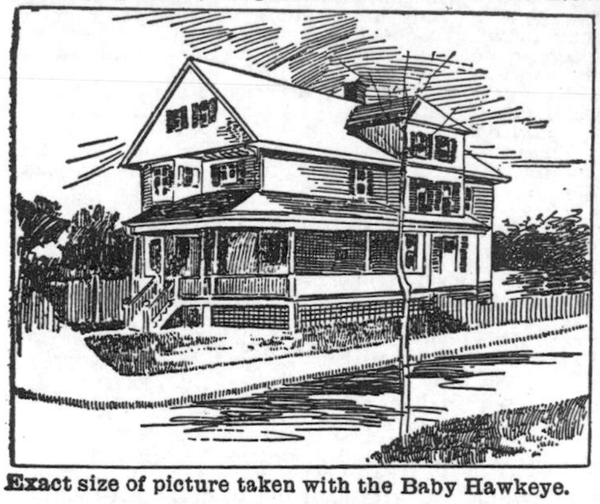

Exact size of picture taken with the Baby Hawkeye.

## THE HAWKEYE JUNIOR CAMERA.

No. 6507. Many people appreciate a camera which can be used for either roll films or glass plates, as it enables them to use either, depending upon the circumstances. If only a few pictures are to be made and developed, glass plates can be used to the best advantage, but if going off on a trip where a large number of pictures are to be taken, the films to the average individual are considered most desirable. The Hawkeye Junior camera takes a picture 3½x3¼ inches. The outside dimensions of the case are 4¼x4½x6 inches and weighs but 20 ounces. The case is well made, is covered throughout with best grain leather and is supplied with neat carrying handle. The lens is the single achromatic offset focus, very rapid and capable of doing good work indoors as well as in the open air. The shutter is supplied with a late improvement which allows time exposures to be made without danger of jarring the camera, which is the difficulty experienced when undertaking to make such exposures with the majority of small cameras. The speed can be regulated for snap shots, which will properly time the negative even in a weak light, and is provided with an improved indicator for counting the number of exposures which never fails. The automatic tally always shows at a glance the number of pictures which have been taken. A brilliant square view finder centers the view accurately upon the surface of the film.

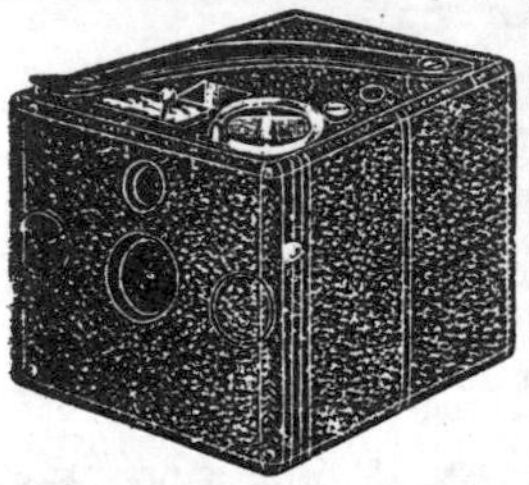

Price of the Hawkeye Junior covered with black grain leather, without roll of film, or plate holder. Each.......................................$7.20
Double Dry Plate Holder for dry plates. Each.. .90
Sunlight Film for twelve exposures. Per roll... .55

## THE HAWKEYE JUNIOR CAMERA.
### For, 4x5 Pictures.

No. 6508. This camera is similar in design to the smaller "Hawkeye Junior," although different in some respects. It has a good single achromatic lens, and is provided with a focusing lever and scale by which the camera can be quickly focused for near or distant objects. It has both vertical and horizontal view finders, interior ground glass screen for testing the focus, automatic registering tally, showing number of exposures made, and a tripod plate for time work is provided. This camera like the smaller size, uses either the sunlight film or regular dry plates. With the film it can be loaded and unloaded in bright daylight without the least danger of destroying the material. The advantages of using either film or glass plates is of great importance, as often one wishes to make but one or two exposures, which are required for immediate development, and by the use of the holder with plates much annoyance is saved. The size of the case is 5¾x6¾x9 inches; takes a picture 4x5 inches, and weighs but 2 pounds and 14 ounces, with a capacity for 18 exposures. Price of the 4x5 "Hawkeye Junior," covered with black grained leather, without roll of film or plate holder....$14.40
Double dry plate holder for dry plates, each.... .90
Sunlight film for 12 exposures, per roll........ .80

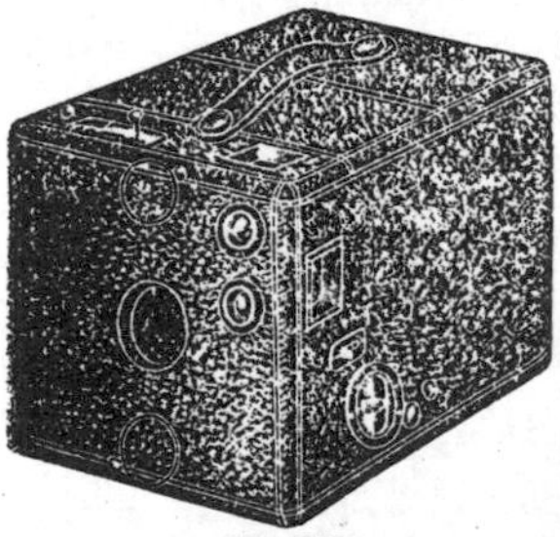

No. 6508.

## THE COMET CAMERA.

No. 6512. The "Comet" is arranged for the use of glass dry plates or cut films only. The cut films being used in holders of the same type as the plate holders. This camera is sold at a very low price, but is thoroughly well made in every respect; in fact the company which makes this camera turns out no other kind of goods. It contains some of the adjustments heretofore found only in the higher priced outfits, is light in weight, simple and compact. It has a single achromatic lens with great depth of focus, flatness of field and wonderful definition, and will be found entirely satisfactory for general work. No other lens can be furnished for the "Comet" camera. It is fitted with the safety pattern shutter which can be set without any danger of accidentally exposing the plate. The shutter is set by turning a small milled head on the front of the camera. The time exposures are made with the time lever at the side, while the speed for snap shots is adjusted by a brass lever. It is provided with both an upright and horizontal view finder and has two plates for attaching the tripod. The "Comet" is provided with a full sized ground glass screen, permitting it to be used as a regular view camera by dropping the hinged panel in the back. The Perfection Junior plate holder is used being the same as furnished for the Premo cameras. The "Comet" is exceedingly compact, measuring only 5⅝x7x9¼ inches including space for three double plate holders, or a capacity of six pictures without re-filling the holders. It is made only in size 4x5 and cannot be used with roll film.

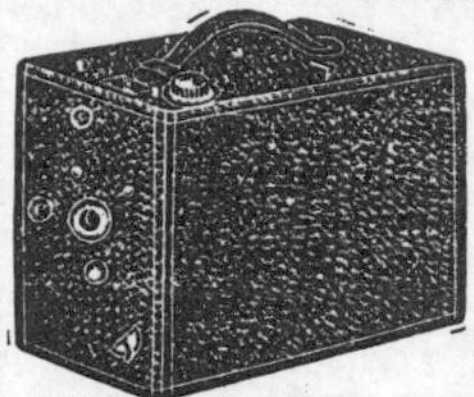

### PRICE.

Camera including one 4x5 Perfection Jr. plate holder. Each.......................................$8.00
Extra double plate holders for two plates. Each..1.05
Cut film holders for two cut films Each.........1.15

## THE PREMIER CAMERA.

No. 6514. This camera is one of the best and most complete hand cameras on the market at anywhere near the price and possesses many advantages over all others. It can be used for either dry plates, cut films or rolled films and is equally adapted for home use or the tourist. The construction of the shutter is such that it works without jar or noise, which is a very desirable feature, and the speed may be regulated at the will of the operator from a slow movement to one of great rapidity, which is governed by the tension of the spring lever at the side of the camera. Time exposures are made by simply extending the time stop, located above the spring lever. To open the shutter a button is pressed and it is closed by pressing the time stop. The front of the camera can be removed if desired and exposure made with a lens cap. The Premier camera is provided with two view finders, one for horizontal and the other for vertical pictures; also two tripod plates. It also has a ground glass screen full size of plate on which the pictures can be focused by dropping the hinged panel at the back. It has a focusing scale at the side which is accurately marked with white figures on a black dial. Either the single view lens or rapid rectilinear lens will be furnished, both of which are provided with rotating diaphragms for regulating the light. It is arranged so that other lenses may be substituted if desired. The "Premier" is made to hold either four or six plate holders; the difference in length being 1⅛ inches. The price is the same for either size, but it will be necessary to state which is wanted when ordering. The camera for four holders measures only 6½x7¼x11¼ inches and weighs but 4 pounds. It is covered with black morocco leather throughout; has a leather handle for carrying and presents a very handsome appearance, made only in size 4x5.

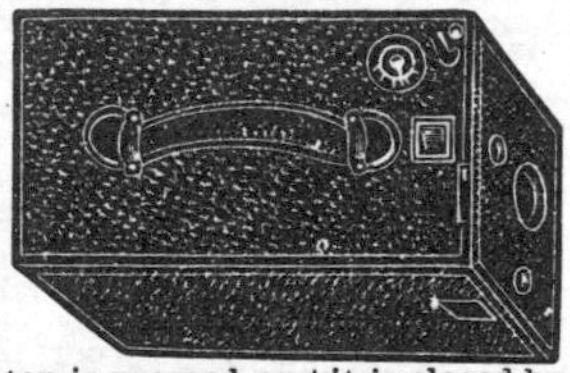

### PRICE.

With single lens including one double dry plate holder.......................................$12.75
With rapid rectilinear lens and one double dry plate holder.......................................$17.85
Extra double dry plate holders. Each........ .85
Facile film holder for holding cut films. Each. 1.05
Roll holder, empty, for using roll films........ 7.20
Roll of films for 24 exposures.................. 1.43
Roll of films for 48 exposures.................. 2.85
Canvas covered cases for the Premo with shoulder strap.......................................$2.25
Leather covered case with shoulder strap.... 2.70

We can furnish the Premo camera as described above with either single or double achromatic lens, provided with a swing back and rising and falling front. The swing back and rising and falling front are used to advantage principally when photographing tall buildings, etc. In order to take the picture the full size of the plate have it perfectly upright without too much foreground.

For prices of these extras add $2.50 to prices quoted above.

## FOLDING HAND CAMERA.

The Folding Hand Camera is fast becoming the most popular among amateurs. It is very simple, is easy of manipulation and one of the strongest advantages is its portability. A camera taking a large size picture will fold into an extremely small space, and they are so nicely arranged that the time required for ascertaining and adjusting the camera preparatory to taking a picture consumes but a few seconds. They are equally well adapted to snap shot or tripod work. They all have plates both on the bottom and on the end for attaching the tripod. They have a square view finder by which they can be accurately focused for snap shot work. Or for tripod work they can be focused from the glass screen. For all time exposures a tripod should be used. Our line of folding cameras we believe to be the best on the market, and are listed by us considerably below the manufacturers' prices. If you are at a loss to know what kind of camera you should have, if you will write us stating what kind of work you wish to do, we shall be glad to give you the benefit of our experience.

## THE PREMO "D" CAMERA.

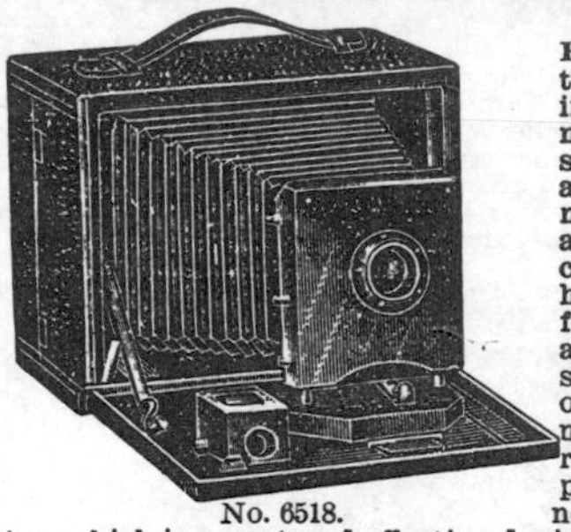

No. 6518.

No. 6518. The Premo "D" is the cheapest folding camera on the market, but at the same time it is a thoroughly well made instrument and will do excellent work. It has sliding front for adjusting sky and foreground, single achromatic or rapid rectilinear lens with rotating diaphragm, and the new safety shutter, which is a neat and effective device for both time and instantaneous work. The shutter is set by a lever at the side, the leaves remaining stationary. The camera is furnished with a reversible view finder attached in a convenient position on the bed. When closed the 4x5 size measures only 5¼x5¼x6¾ inches, and has space on the inside for three plate holders, or roll holder and weighs but a trifle over 2 lbs. It is a thoroughly practical camera using glass plates, cut or rolled films, and will fully meet the demands of a large class of amateurs.

### PRICE.

| | 4x5 | 5x7 |
|---|---|---|
| Camera complete, including one plate holder single achromatic lens...... | $ 8.50 | $15.30 |
| With rapid rectilinear lens .... ...... | 12.75 | 22.10 |
| Extra Premo plate holder ...... | 1.05 | 1.28 |

Other extras same price as on Premo Sr.

## THE PREMO "C" CAMERA.

Fo. 6519. The Premo "C" Camera is similar to the Premo "D" with the exception that it is provided with swing back and sliding front, and the ground glass screen is spring actuated, and recedes to allow the insertion of the plate holder. A hinged panel at the back permits the full sized image to be seen while focusing. The back swings from the center. It has two tripod plates with view finder attached in convenient position on the bed, and is reversible for both upright and horizontal pictures. The Premo "C" Camera in size 4x5 measures only 4⅝x5⅝x5⅝ inches, which include space on the inside for three plate holders, or roll holders, and weighs but a little over 2 lbs. Glass plates, cut or roll films can be used.

Prices includes camera, lens, shutter and one plate holder.

| PRICE. | 4x5 | 5x7 |
|---|---|---|
| Premo "C" camera with single achromatic lens.......................... | $10.20 | $17.00 |
| Premo "C" camera with rectilinear lens.......................... | 14.45 | 23.80 |
| Extra Premo plate holders.......... | 1.05 | 1.28 |

Other extras at same prices as for the Premo Sr

## THE PREMO "B" CAMERA.

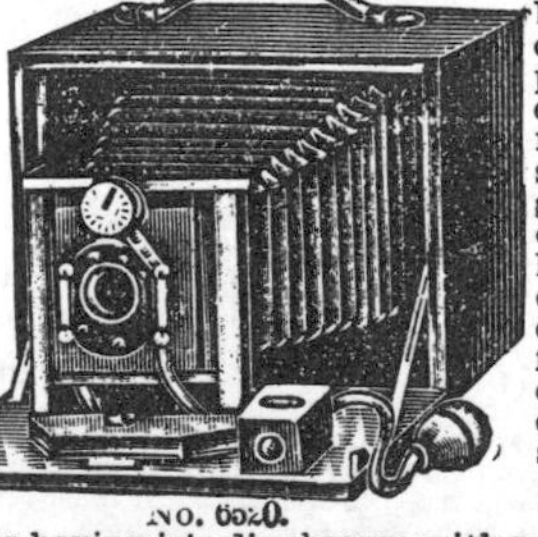

No. 6520.

No. 6520. The Premo "B" is one of the most popular hand cameras on the market. It is strictly high grade throughout, great care having been exercised in its construction, and for a high grade camera at a moderate price it stands second to none. It is fitted with the Victor shutter having iris diaphragm with pneumatic release, and can also be released by the lever; has the new center swing back with rising and falling front thus adapting it to either snap shot or tripod work. It is furnished with either a single achromatic or Victor rapid rectilinear lens, as may be preferred. A reversible view finder is fitted to the bed for both vertical and horizontal pictures; has spring actuated ground glass screen and two tripod plates. It has room inside for three double plate holders, weighs a little over 2 lbs., and the 4x5 measures only 4⅝x5⅝x5⅝ inches when closed. It is covered with fine grained black leather; has handle for carrying. It will use glass plates, cut or rolled films, as may be desired. Price includes camera, lens, shutter and one plate holder.

### PRICE.

| | 4x5 | 5x7 |
|---|---|---|
| Price the Premo "B" with single achromatic lens.......................... | $13.60 | $19.55 |
| Price the Premo "B" with Victor rapid rectilinear lens.......................... | 17.85 | 25.50 |
| Extra Premo plate holder............ | 1.05 | 1.28 |

Other extras same as quoted for Premo Sr.

## THE PONY PREMO CAMERA.

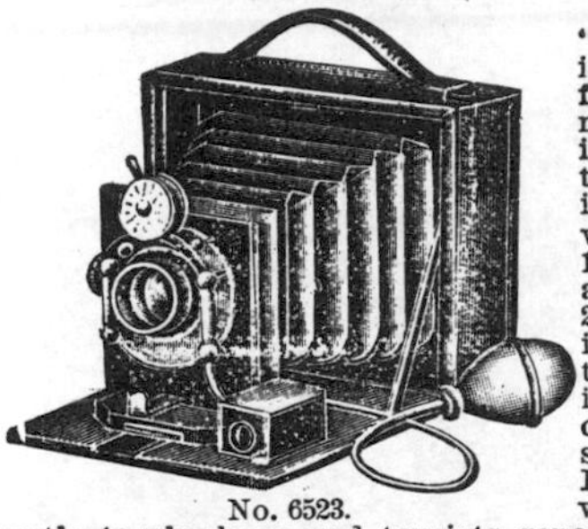

No. 6523.

No. 6523. The "Pony Premo" is the smallest folding camera made, and while it takes a picture 4x5 inches, it measures when closed but 1⅞x5x6 inches, and weighs but 26 ounces. Owing to its extreme portability and lightness of weight, this style of the Premo camera will appeal directly to wheelmen and tourists generally, yet it is a favorite among a large class of amateurs who desire a thoroughly practical outfit to occupy the smallest possible space. Although it is extremely compact, every part is perfectly adjustable and works so perfectly that its manipulation is a pleasure. It is made of thoroughly seasoned mahogany; is handsomely covered with fine black leather, which, in contrast with the polished interior and lacquered brass trimmings and rich red leather bellows, presents an elegant appearance. The back is spring actuated and recedes to allow the insertion of the plate holder. The panel covering the ground glass will open upward to allow the image to be focused, and act as a shield for focusing. When it is desired to use a roll holder, the back is removed by simply pressing a small brass lever, the roll holder is then attached to the supports at top and bottom, which change can be made in a few seconds. The "Pony Premo" is furnished with the Victor rapid rectilinear lens and shutter, which is well adapted to all classes of work. The shutter is fitted with iris diaphragm and pneumatic release, same as the Premo Sr. It has reversible view finder and two tripod plates. The "Pony Premo" is furnished with a neat leather case, as shown in illustration, which holds the camera, lens, shutter and three plate holders, or roll holder, and may be carried by the shoulder strap or attached to the frame of a bicycle in the same manner as a tool bag. The roll holder is the latest pattern, fitted with automatic indicator for registering the number of exposures made. The roll holder is fitted with a shield, which permits its being attached or detached in full daylight. The price includes the camera, lens, shutter, one double dry plate holder, leather case and strap.

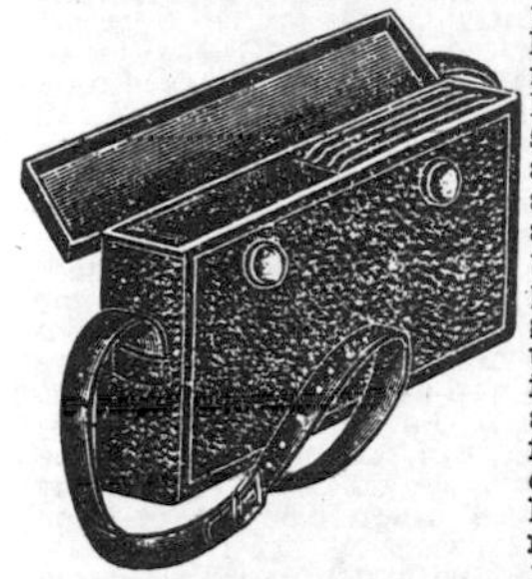

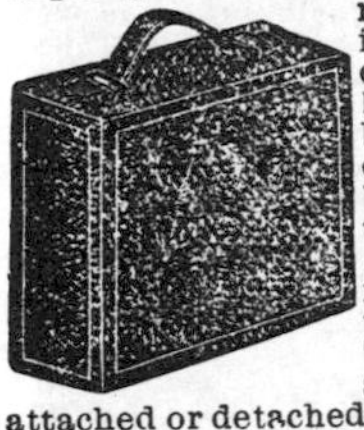

PRICE.

| | |
|---|---|
| Pony Premo, with rapid rectilinear lens | $20.40 |
| Extra double plate holders | 1.05 |
| Roll holder, empty | 9.00 |
| Roll of films for 48 exposures | 2.85 |

## THE PREMO SR. CAMERA.

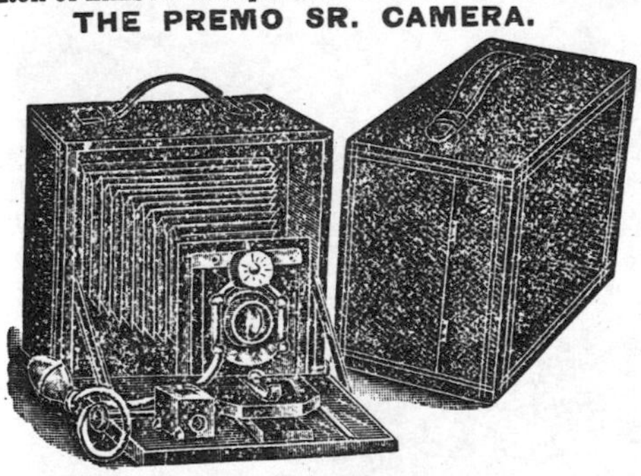

No. 6526.

No. 6526. The "Premo Sr." in our estimation represents the very highest type of the folding hand camera. It is thoroughly equipped with the latest improvements, making it highly prized by the advanced worker and at the same time equally well adapted to the use of the novice in the art. This instrument has been constantly gaining favor until we now believe it is one of the best known hand cameras made. The "Premo Sr." is made of selected mahogany throughout and is covered with fine black leather. The finely polished bed and inside work, with lacquered metal trimmings, makes such a perfect contrast with the black leather covering that it gives the camera an extremely handsome appearance when open. It is fitted with all the essential features necessary for either hand or tripod work, snap shots or time exposures and at the same time is very simple and easily manipulated. It is fitted with a double swing back and double sliding front, which enables the operator to take full sized pictures of tall buildings, or of objects in confined locations. It has rack and pinion movement for focusing, the working parts of which are entirely within the case. When the camera is closed it is merely a neat leather-covered box, presenting no appearance of what is within. It has both the horizontal and vertical swings, which are at the center of the plate and may be quickly adjusted by means of a spring lever, working in a series of notches in a brass plate at the side. A spring lever secures the "swing back" in any position it may be placed. The double sliding front is of equal importance with the swing back for working in confined situations. The "Premo Sr." is fitted with two tripod plates, has a panel at the back for focusing, and a reversible view finder on the bed, which can be used for either horizontal or upright pictures. The view finder is used for snap shot work. The lens used in the "Premo Sr." is the Victor rapid rectilinear, which possesses great power and is constructed especially for hand camera work. It may be removed from the shutter and a wide angle lens substituted when desired, as the cells of both lenses are interchangeable. The wide angle lens is principally of use for taking pictures indoors, in order to expose as much of a room as possible, also buildings, architectural or other subjects in confined places. It is fitted with iris diaphragm for regulating the amount of light and the new Victor shutter, both being practically first class in every respect. Both diaphragm and shutter works between the lenses, the shutter working without noise or jar, may be adjusted for time exposures as well as for rapid instantaneous work. The speed for snap shots may be varied from one second to one hundredth of a second, working automatically. It is set by revolving the metal disc at the top to the right or left until the pointer indicates the speed desired. Glass plates, cut or roll films may be used. The Perfection Jr. holder, with rubber sides, is furnished for use of glass plates. The roll holder is the latest pattern, fitted with automatic device for measuring the film, an indicator for registering the number of exposures made. The change from glass plates to films is but the work of a moment and can be made in full daylight. The size of the "Premo Sr." when closed is only 4⅝x5⅝x7 inches, with space inside for three double plate holders or roll holder; weight is 2½ lbs. The price includes camera, lens, shutter and one plate holder.

| | 3¼x4¼ | 4x5 | 5x7 | 6½x8½ |
|---|---|---|---|---|
| Premo Sr. and 1 plate holder | $25.50 | $25.50 | $34.00 | $42.50 |
| Extra for wide angle lens | ........ | 9.00 | 10.80 | 13.50 |
| Cut film holders | 1.15 | 1.15 | 1.35 | 1.58 |
| Dry plate holders | 1.05 | 1.05 | 1.27 | 1.40 |
| Roll holder, empty | 9.00 | 9.00 | 11.25 | 14.40 |
| Leather covered carrying case | 2.25 | 2.25 | 2.70 | 3.00 |

| | 5x7 | 6½x8½ | 3¼x4¼ | 4x5 |
|---|---|---|---|---|
| | 32 exp. | 24 exp. | 60 exp. | 48 exp. |
| Roll of films | $3.80 | $3.80 | $2.50 | $3.00 |
| | 54 exp. | 48 exp. | | |
| Roll of films | $5.70 | $7.60 | | |

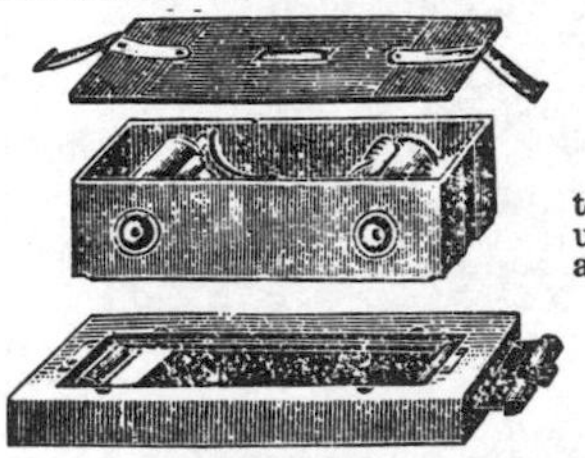

This cut represents the "Roll Holder" used in the Premo and hand cameras.

## THE LONG FOCUS PREMO CAMERA.

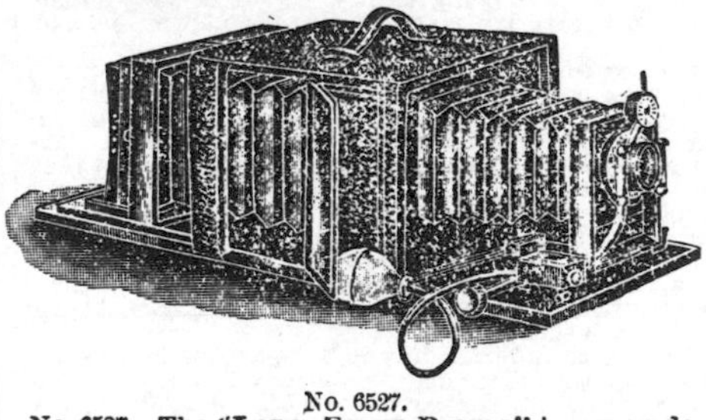

No. 6527.

No. 6527. The **"Long Focus Premo"** is a new departure in hand cameras. It is a most complete instrument, and will be very highly appreciated by many. It combines all the features of advantage in the Premo Sr. camera; is similar in appearance and may be used in the same manner for either hand or tripod work. While when closed it is no larger than the Premo Sr. it has double the focal capacity, adapting it to use for copying and many other purposes, requiring an extended length of bellows. It uses the Victor lens, which is symetrical and allows the front combination to be removed and the camera used with the rear lens alone when desired, which approximately doubles the length of focus. For different views this is very desirable, as objects in the view are about twice the size that they would be with the regular lenses. There are many views which can be brought out to better effect at a long distance with this camera than could possibly be done by taking them at a short distance. As the lens board is removable, any other lens can be readily attached if desired. It is also interchangeable with the wide angle lens. It is made throughout of mahogany, handsomely polished, and is covered with fine black leather; in fact, in every other respect is like the Premo Sr.

Focal capacity or length of bellows:

| 4x5 | 5x7 | 6½x8½ | 8x10 |
|---|---|---|---|
| 15 inches. | 19 inches. | 22 inches. | 28 inches. |

Price includes the camera, lens, shutter and one plate holder.

PRICE.

| | 4x5 | 5x7 | 6½x8½ | 8x10 |
|---|---|---|---|---|
| Long focus Premo | $29.75 | $38.25 | $46.75 | $55.25 |

Extras same prices as for Premo Sr.

## THE STEREOSCOPIC PREMO CAMERA.

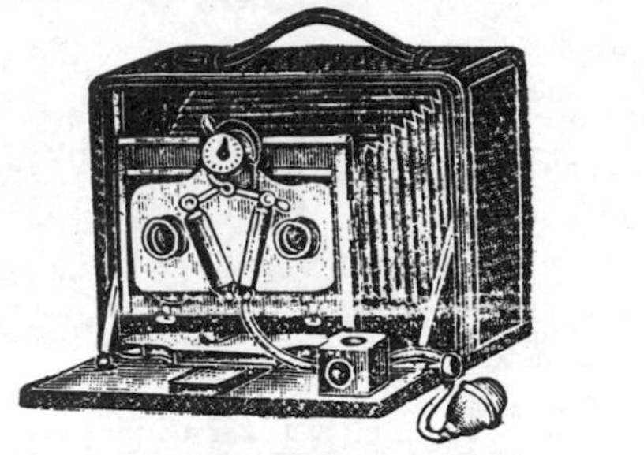

No. 6528.

No. 6528. As Stereoscopic Photography has become such a fascinating and interesting branch of the art and as the hand camera is especially adapted to this class of work, this camera has been designed to fill a popular demand. It is in construction the same as the Premo Sr., except that it is furnished only in sizes 5x7 and in 6½x8½, and the lens board is made wider than for the regular "Premo." A matched pair of 4x5 Victor rapid rectilinear lenses are used, fitted with Bausch & Lomb stereo shutter, which works on the principal of the diaphragm shutter. The shutter may be regulated automatically, so as to give a speed of from three seconds to the hundredth part of one second, and by turning the time lever exposures of any length can be made. Both finger and pneumatic release are used, same as on the Premo Sr. The price includes a Victor rapid rectilinear lens and shutter for full sized views and also a pair of stereo lenses and shutter, together with a division in the camera and one plate holder. Glass plates, cut or roll films may all be used. The roll holder is of very late design. Wide angle lenses may also be used, same as in the Premo Sr.

Stereo Premo Sr., with One Plate Holder.

5x7..................$63.75 | 6½x8½..................$72.25

Stereo Premo, Same as Above but Without Rack Pinion Adjustment.

5x7..................$59.50 | 6½x8½..................$68.00

Extra for Wide Angle Lenses.

5x7..................$10.20 | 6½x8½..................$12.75

Extra Plate Holders.

5x7..................$1.27 | 6½x8½..................$1.50

| | 5x7 | 6½x8½ |
|---|---|---|
| Cut film holder | $1.37 | 1.58 |
| Roll holder, empty | 11.25 | 14.40 |
| Roll of films for 32 exposures | 3.80 | ...... |
| 24 exposures | ...... | 3.80 |
| Leather covered carrying case | 2.70 | 3.10 |

## VIEW CAMERAS.

View Cameras are intended principally for taking landscapes, architectural, buildings and other outside views, also interiors and portrait work, but cannot be used for tintype work. Tintype work requires a special camera and lenses. We have outfits suitable for both tintype and portrait work combined, prices of which will be furnished on application. All of our View Cameras are made to fold, thus making them very compact and portable. The prices quoted for View Cameras, with a few exceptions, do not include lenses or tripods. A lens must be selected, and if desired we will fit the same to the front board of the camera before shipping it. If at a loss to know what kind of an outfit should be purchased, we will give our patrons the benefit of our experience if they will advise us what class of work is to be done.

## THE NEW MODEL CAMERA.

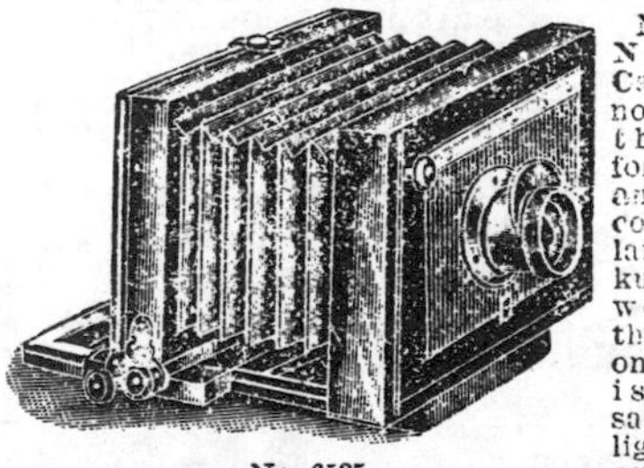

No. 6535.

No. 6535. The **New Model Camera** has now been on the market for 12 years, and has become so popular and well known that we consider that comment on its merits is unnecessary. It is very light, compact and makes a very desirable outfit for the amateur who wishes to invest but a small amount of money. It is made of selected cherry, well finished and has nickel trimmings. It is provided with sliding front, folding bed and is easily reversed for upright pictures by the use of a new adjustable reverse clamp which places the strain entirely on the bed where it belongs. The folding part of the bed is held rigid and firm by a new clamp hook, which is the quickest, easiest and most effective device that can be used for the purpose. The price includes a good single-view lens, standing folding tripod, a carrying case with handle and one Perfection plate holder (except the 8x10 size, with which neither lens or tripod are included.) The carrying case will hold two extra plate holders.

| Size of View. | Weight. | With Single Swing. |
|---|---|---|
| 3¼x 4¼ | 1⅜ lbs. | $ 8.50 |
| 4 x 5 | 1⅝ " | 8.50 |
| 4½x 6½ | 2 " | 9.35 |
| 5 x 7 | 2¼ " | 10.20 |
| 5 x 8 | 2½ " | 10.20 |
| 6½x 8½ | 2¾ " | 12.75 |
| 8 x10 | 5 " | 11.90 |

The 8x10 does not include lens or tripod.

**If you have any reason to complain of any article sent, write us just as soon as you get the goods, and you may be sure of a prompt adjustment of your claims.**

## THE NEW MODEL IMPROVED VIEW CAMERA.

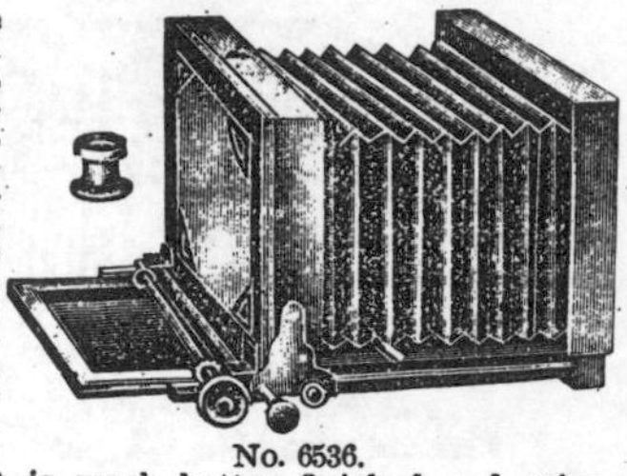

No. 6536.

No. 6536. The **New Model Improved** is a strictly first-class camera with all necessary improvements, but is sold at a price which brings it within the reach of the ordinary amateur. It is made after the same general style as the New Model, but is much better finished and enjoys the reputation of being the most popular amateur camera on the market. The New Model Improved is made of the best Honduras mahogany, highly polished with nickel trimmings, has sliding front, folding bed and is reversible by means of a new adjustable reversing clamp. It is very light, compact and an excellent instrument for a small amount of money. It has rack and pinion for focusing and folding bed held rigid by a new clamp hook. The price includes a fine single view lens with Carlton sliding tripod, carrying case and one Perfection plate holder (except the 8x10, which has neither lens nor tripod.) The carrying case will hold two extra plate holders.

| Size of View. | Weight of Camera. | Single Swing. | Double Swing. |
|---|---|---|---|
| 3¼x4¼ | 1⅝ lbs. | $11.05 | $12.75 |
| 4x5 | 1¾ " | 11.90 | 13.60 |
| 4¼x6½ | 2⅛ " | 13.60 | 15.00 |
| 5x7 | 2⅜ " | 15.30 | 17.00 |
| 5x8 | 2¾ " | 15.30 | 17.00 |
| 6½x8½ | 3¼ " | 18.70 | 20.40 |
| 8x10 | 5½ " | 12.75 | 14.40 |

The 8x10 quoted above has neither lens nor tripod.

## THE NEW MODEL STEREOSCOPIC CAMERA.

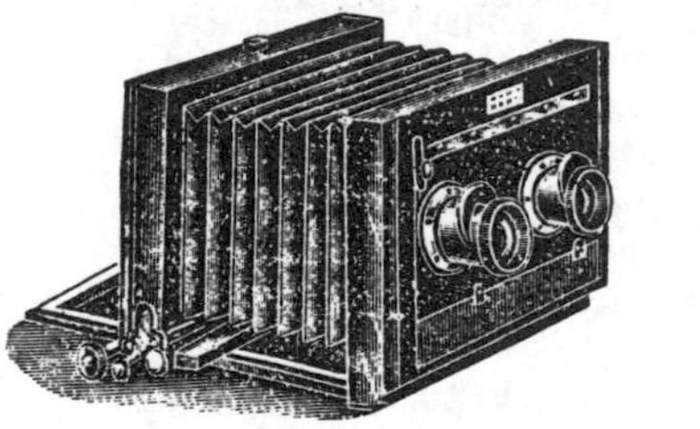

No. 6537.

No. 6537. The **"New Model Stereoscopic" Camera** has an enviable reputation, which has been well earned. It has found favor with all who are interested in this most fascinating branch of photography. It is patterned closely after the New Model Improved Camera, and is the lightest, most compact and simplest instrument yet placed on the market, combining the many features needed for stereoscopic work. It is made of the best Honduras mahogany, highly polished and has nickel trimmings. It has rack and pinion for focusing, sliding front, folding bed and is reversible by means of the new adjustable reversing clamp. The folding bed is held rigid and firm by a clamp hook, which is considered the quickest, easiest and best device for the purpose. The partition and front board can be removed so that the camera may be used if desired with a lens of sufficient focus to cover the full plate. Each camera is furnished with a neat canvas case with room for two extra plate holders. It will be furnished only in size 5x8 with a matched pair of achromatic lenses, improved sliding tripod and one Perfection double plate holder complete .......... **$18.70**

Camera and tripod, complete, without lenses. **13.60**

Camera without lenses or tripod.............. **11.90**

We are always glad to furnish information to parties who are undecided as to what accessories they should have with a camera, or what camera they should have to do the kind of work required.

## THE EMPIRE STATE CAMERA WITH REVERSIBLE BACK.

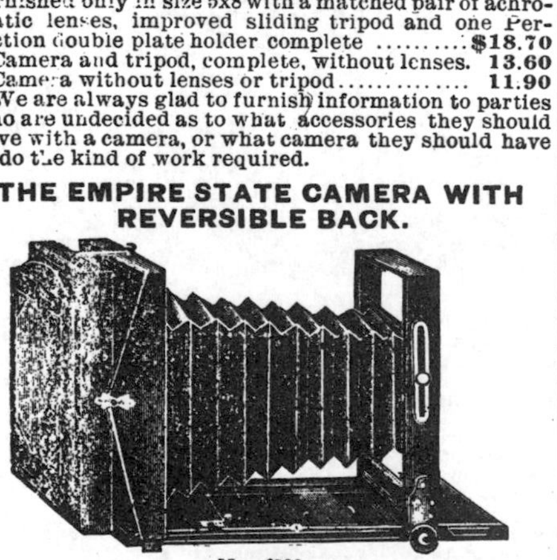

No. 6539.

No. 6539. The **Empire State Camera** has all of the adjustments necessary for general work, and while sold at a moderate price it fully meets the requirements of the professional as well as the amateur, and is constantly gaining favor. This camera is constructed with an idea of satisfying all the movements necessary in a camera for both indoor and outdoor photography rather than beauty and fine finish. It is, however, made from selected mahogany, well finished with trimmings of polished brass. It has a front rack and pinion movement for focusing, which is held firmly after being set, by turning a milled head placed inside of the one used for focusing. The bed is hinged with two joints and folds completely under the camera, thus allowing lenses of extremely short focus to be used. The front board is made wide enough for stereoscopic lenses and there is ample rise and fall which is a desirable feature for work in confined situations. It has both single and double swing, both swinging from the center, a feature which is rare in modern priced cameras, but which will be appreciated by the professional. The horizontal swing is attached in a very simple manner, occupying no additional room, consequently the double swing takes up no more room than would the single swing. The back of the Empire State Camera has a spring actuated, ground glass frame, which allows the plate holder to be inserted between the ground glass and the camera back. The slide may be drawn from the top, bottom or either side. We feel that we can thoroughly recommend the Empire State Camera as being a practical instrument, which will in every way meet with the approval of the professional as well as the amateur, and we believe that those not familiar with the instrument would be agreeably surprised after examining the same. The 14x17 and larger are made in back focus, focusing with a handle instead of rack pinion. With sizes above 11x14 the English book plate holder will be furnished. The carrying case will hold two extra plate holders.

| Size of View. | Weight of Camera. | Single Swing. | Double Swing. |
|---|---|---|---|
| 5x7 | 5 lbs. | $14.45 | $16.25 |
| 5x8 | 5½ " | 16.30 | 17.00 |
| 6½x8½ | 5¾ " | 17.00 | 18.70 |
| 8x10 | 7¾ " | 18.70 | 20.40 |
| 10x12 | 8¾ " | 23.80 | 25.50 |
| 11x14 | 11½ " | 27.20 | 30.60 |
| 14x17 | 23¾ " | 36.00 | 38.25 |
| 17x20 | 30 " | 40.80 | 45.90 |
| 20x24 | 46 " | 66.30 | 73.95 |

The above prices include canvas carrying case with one Perfection holder but no lens or tripod.

## THE IDEAL CAMERA.

Reversible Back

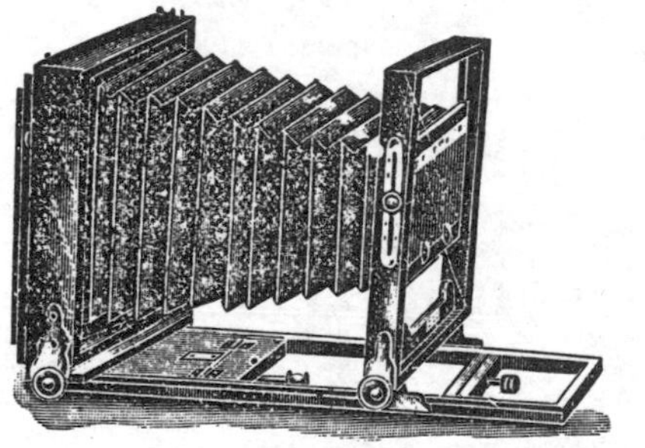

No. 6540.

No. 6540. The **"Ideal" Camera** is one of the best view cameras ever placed on the market. It is made of selected mahogany, is finished in the best possible style, every part being as nearly perfect as possible. All metal parts are made of brass, polished and lacquered.

The perfection of this camera is the result of much study and many experiments and is a favorite for both professional and amateur photography. It has reversible back with spring actuating ground glass frame, by which the plate holder is inserted between the ground glass and camera back. The bellows are cone shape but the 5 x 7 and all sizes above are made with fronts wide enough for stereoscopic lenses. By using a very simple method of attaching the horizontal swing it takes up no more room than does the single swing. The bed has two joints which admit of the use of lenses of short focus.

Sizes up to and including 6½ x 8½ are made the same as the above engraving; but sizes 8 x 10 to 11 x 14 inclusive are made similar to the "Empire State." The 14 x 17 and larger are made with back focus and with focusing handle instead of rack and pinion.

The price includes one perfection plate holder and canvas carrying case (which will hold three plate holders in addition to the camera) but has no lens or tripod. With sizes above 11 x 14 the English book plate-holder is furnished instead of the regular type of plate-holder.

| Size of view. | Weight of camera. | Single swing. | Double swing. |
|---|---|---|---|
| 3¼ x 4¼ | 2 lbs. | $14.45 | $16.15 |
| 4 x 5 | 2½ " | 15.30 | 17.00 |
| 4¼ x 6½ | 3 " | 17.00 | 18.70 |
| 5 x 7 | 4½ " | 18.70 | 20.40 |
| 5 x 8 | 4¾ " | 20.40 | 22.10 |
| 6½ x 8½ | 5¼ " | 22.10 | 23.80 |
| 8 x 10 | 8 " | 25.50 | 28.05 |
| 10 x 12 | 9 " | 28.05 | 30.50 |
| 11 x 14 | 12 " | 32.30 | 35.70 |
| 14 x 17 | 23¾ " | 42.50 | 46.75 |
| 17 x 20 | 30 " | 51.50 | 57.80 |
| 18 x 22 | 38 " | 61.20 | 68.00 |
| 20 x 24 | 46 " | 76.50 | 85.00 |

# THE INDEX

**is the guide to this Catalogue. Refer to it often and don't lose track of the rare bargains we offer.**

## THE MONITOR CAMERA.

Reversible Back.

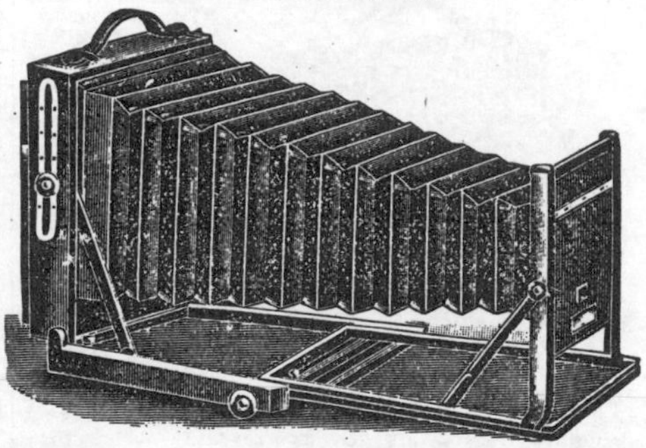

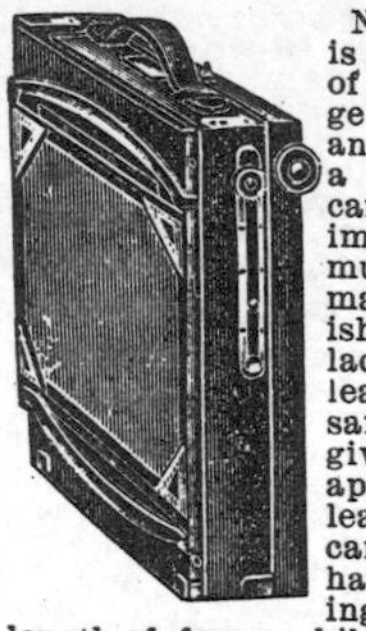

No. 6542. The **"Monitor" Camera** is a new form of the compact style of view camera and while similar in general appearance to the Carlton and designed with a view of making a strictly high grade compact camera possessing all the latest improvements, it is furnished for a much lower price. It is made of mahogany throughout, highly polished with brass work polished and lacquered, bellows of the finest leather and is finished with the same care as the Carlton, which gives it an exceedingly handsome appearance. It is provided with a leather handle by which it can be carried without case if desired. It has extra long draw; thus allowing the use of the lenses of extreme length of focus while the back will slide forward by loosening two milled heads which is necessary when using extreme wide angle lenses.

The Monitor is provided with double swing back, rising and falling fronts and rack and pinion movement for adjustment. The rising and falling front is controlled by a spring working in a rachet which does away with milled heads. The back is easily reversed for either vertical or horizontal pictures. The ground-glass is spring actuated and recedes for the insertion of the plate holder, which slides between the ground-glass frame and the back of the camera.

The Monitor Camera up to and including 8 x 10 are supplied with either short or long canvas case. The short case carries the camera with three holders, while the long one carries six holders and combination tripod and in sizes up to 6½ x 8½ inclusive, there is space for lenses. In ordering be sure to state which size case is wanted. This camera is furnished only in double swing.

| Size of View. | Focal Capacity. | Weight of Camera. | Double Swing. |
|---|---|---|---|
| 4x5 | 13 inches. | 2 lbs. | $20.40 |
| 5x7 | 17 " | 3½ " | 23.00 |
| 5x8 | 19 " | 4¼ " | 25.50 |
| 6½x8½ | 20¼ " | 4⅝ " | 28.00 |
| 8x10 | 24 " | 6¾ " | 30.60 |
| 10x12 | 26½ " | 9½ " | 36.00 |
| 11x14 | 30¾ " | 12 " | 38.25 |

## THE CARLTON CAMERA.

Reversible Back.

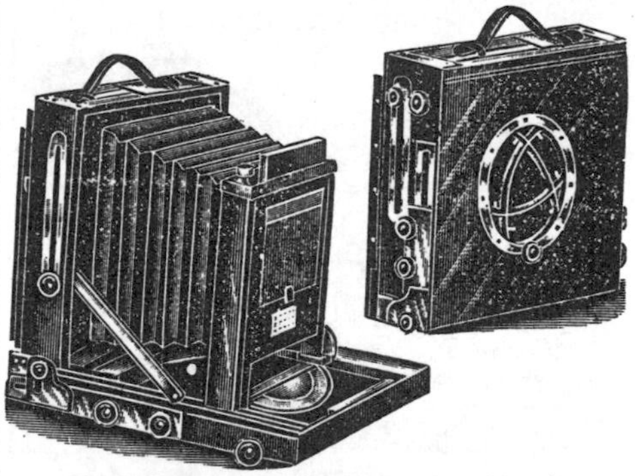

Partly Open. No. 6544. Closed.

No. 6544. The **"Carlton" Camera** without question represents the highest perfection attained in professional view cameras. This camera has achieved great popularity throughout the United States and Canada, which it fully deserves as it is complete in every respect, with all modern improvements. Ideas suggested by practical experience have been carefully watched and all those which were deserving of merit have been as near as possible combined in this camera.

It satisfies the ideas of the enthusiastic amateur as well as the most fastidious professional, who is not satisfied without having the best of everything.

The Carlton Camera is made from selected mahogany throughout; is finished in the best possible style and has all the latest improvements. No pains have been spared to make every part as near perfect as possible.

The camera box is square and has a reversible back by which pictures can be taken with the plate either horizontal or vertical, the change being made in five seconds. The ground glass frame is held to the front by two springs which allow it to recede for inserting the plate holder between the glass and the camera

back. This method prevents the necessity of removing the glass screen, which prevents the liability of breaking. While very compact the camera is very simple of manipulation and has no loose screws or parts. It has a fine rack and pinion movement for adjusting the focus and all metal work is of brass, polished and lacquered.

The camera back has a forward movement for adjustment when extreme wide angle lenses are to be used. The movement is quickly made by the use of two milled heads, which loose permit the back to be placed above the bed, in which position it can be moved forward.

A very great improvement in the Carlton Camera is that it carries its own tripod top, which is adapted to the combination tripod. The top is made of metal; is neatly fitted in the bed and revolves easily and with great smoothness, permitting the operator to adjust the camera in any position. A small milled head secures it firmly when set. It has double swing back and is furnished with one mahogany perfection double plate holder, with rubber sides, mahogany combination tripod and canvas case, but no lens. Sizes to 8x10, inclusive, are furnished with either a long or short canvas case. The short case carries the camera with three plate holders only. The latter will hold the camera, six holders, combination tripod, and in sizes 6½x8½, inclusive, there is a compartment for lenses.

In ordering be sure to state which size of case is desired.

| Size of View. | Focal Capacity. | Weight of Camera. | Double Swing. |
|---|---|---|---|
| 4x5 | 13 inches. | 2⅞ lbs. | $29.75 |
| 4½6½ | 15½ " | 4 " | 30.60 |
| 5x7 | 17 " | 4¾ " | 34.00 |
| 5x8 | 19 " | 5¾ " | 35.70 |
| 6½x8½ | 20½ " | 7 " | 38.25 |
| 8x10 | 24 " | 9¼ " | 42.50 |
| 10x12 | 26¾ " | 12¾ " | 46.75 |
| 11x14 | 30¾ " | 15¼ " | 52.70 |

## HORSEMANS' ECLIPSE PHOTOGRAPH OUTFITS FOR AMATEURS.

These Cameras are made of polished cherry and the outfit is furnished with tripod and all necessary chemicals.

No. 6545. The "Eclipse Outfit No. 2" fills a popular demand for an instrument and accessories for little money. It consists of a polished cherry camera with leatherette bellows, brass mounted lens, ground glass frame hinged to camera, one double dry plate holder for plate size 3¼x4¼ inches with tripod and carrying case. A complete chemical outfit for developing and printing is furnished including ruby lamp, ½ dozen dry plates, two japanned iron trays, two bottles developer, one box hypo-soda, 12 sheets sensitized paper, one printing frame, one bottle toning solution and one dozen card mounts. The camera alone weighs two pounds, the complete outfit about 10 lbs.
Price complete..........................................$4.50
No. 6546. The "Eclipse Outfit No. 3" is similar to No. 2 except that it makes a full cabinet size picture or photograph 4½x6½ and has polished cherry camera with folding bed, double plate-holders, brass mounted lens with set of stocks, folding tripod, carrying case, printing frame and complete chemical outfit, weighs about 15 pounds. Price complete................$9.00

## SUNDRIES FOR HORSEMANS' ECLIPSE OUTFITS.

No. 6547.
Plate holders for No. 2 Cameras, size 3¼x4½, each...................................................45c
Plate holders for No. 3 camera, size 4½x6½. Each.......................................................90c
Eclipse Developer "A," per bottle...............10c
Eclipse Developer "B," per bottle...............10c
Both "A" and "B" developer are to be used in combination.
Eclipse Toning Solution..........................10c
For Dry Plates for the above Cameras, see our regular list further on. We do not duplicate the same brand as furnished with the Cameras.

## VIEW FINDERS.

No. 6565. A View Finder is made on the same principle as a small camera, having a lens and ground glass; is about 1¼ inch square and assists the operator in locating the view. They are attached to the camera by means of a spring clamp. They are principally of advantage when snap shots are to be taken. As the plate is in the camera for exposures the operator is unable to obtain the exact location of the picture in any other way. They can be attached to any camera. Price.................................................$1.35

## PLATE HOLDERS.

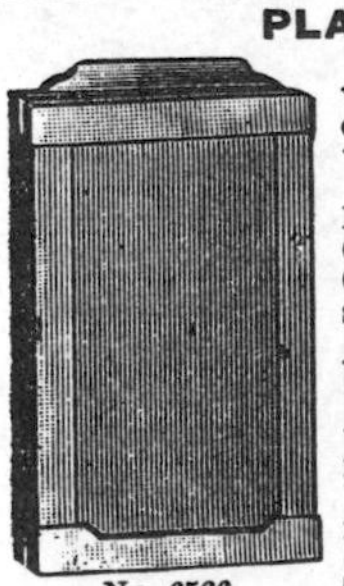

No. 6566.

When ordering Plate Holders it will be necessary to state the name of the camera for which they are wanted.
No. 6566. The Perfection Plate Holders are to be used in the View Camera listed under Nos. 6535 and 6544 inclusive. This is one of the simplest plate holders on the market, the plate being held in place by a spring bar at the lower end. By simply pressing the spring bar with the thumb the plate will fall in or out of place. As the plate is held in place by the ends only the full width is exposed and but 1-16 of an inch is cut off from each end. The Perfection Plate Holders are also made of mahogany, polished and with rubber slides, as a few customers who buy the higher priced cameras prefer them. It is, however, only a matter of satisfaction, as they are not any better than the regular board slides. The regular holders have pressed board slides.

| | | | |
|---|---|---|---|
| 3¼x4¼.....$0.85 | 5 x7 ....$1.06 | 8x10....$1.57 |
| 4 x5 ...... .85 | 5 x8 .... 1.15 | 10x12.... 2.55 |
| 4½x6½.... 1.06 | 6½x8½.... 1.37 | 11x14.... 3.40 |

Prices on Mahogany Holders Furnished on Application.

## THE PERFECTION JR. HOLDER.

No. 6567. The Perfection Jr. Holders are made on the same principle as the Perfection, but are more compact and has rubber slides. They are to be used with the hand cameras only.

| | | |
|---|---|---|
| 3¼x4¼.....$1.05 | 5 x8 .......$1.35 | 10x12....$3.40 |
| 4 x5 ...... 1.05 | 6½x8½.... 1.50 | 11x14.... 4.25 |
| 5 x7 ...... 1.32 | 8 x10 .... 1.90 | |

## THE FACILE FILM HOLDER.
### For Cut Films.

No. 6568. The "Facile" Film Holder is made interchangeable with the dry plate holders, so that either may be used on the same camera. It is very simple to load and unload, and is considered to be one of the best film holders on the market.

| | | |
|---|---|---|
| 3¼ x 4¼........$1.05 | 5 x 8 .......$1.35 |
| 4 x 5 ........ 1.05 | 6½ x 8½.... 1.57 |
| 4¼ x 6½........ 1.22 | 8 x 10 ...... 1.85 |
| 5 x 7 ........ 1.32 | |

## INSIDE KITS.

No. 6570. A "Kit" is a thin woolen frame about the thickness of glass made

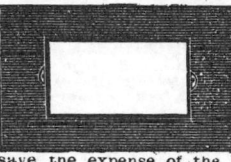

to fit in the dry plate holder, with an opening for holding smaller plates, which are secured by small buttons. They are to be used when it is desired to take smaller pictures than the regular size of the camera, and thus save the expense of the larger plates.

| | | | |
|---|---|---|---|
| 4 x 5 | to hold 3¼x4¼ plates. Each...............20c |
| 4¼x 6½ | " 3¼x4¼ " "...............20c |
| 5 x 7 | " 3¼x4¼ or 4x 5 plates. Each...............25c |
| 5 x 8 | " 3¼x4¼, 4x5 or 4¼x6½ plates. Each...25c |
| 6½x 8½ | " 4 x5, 4¼x6½, 5x7 or 5x8 plates. " 30c |
| 8 x10 | " 4¼x 6½, 5x7, 5x8 or 6½x 8½ plates. Each...........35c |
| 10x12 | to hold 5x 7, 5x 8, 6½x8½ or 8x10 plates. Each, 40c |
| 11x14 | " 8x10 or 10x12 plates. Each...50c |
| 14x17 | " 8x10, 10x12 or 11x14 plates. Each....65c |
| 17x20 | " 11x14 or 14x17 plates. Each........85c |
| 18x22 | " 14x17 or 17x20 " "..........$1.30 |

## TRIPODS.

No. 6572. The "Gem Folding" Tripods for cameras 5x7 or smaller; has folding ash legs riveted to the head with brass trimmings, and screw for attaching to camera is included with each. Length extended 52 inches, when folded 28½. This is we believe far the best cheap tripod on the market. Each......$1.25

No. 6574. "Sliding" Tripod. The legs are made in three pieces which render the tripod firm when set up, and it has a special advantage over the folding tripod, as it is easier to level the camera in rough places by adjusting the length of the tripod legs. It can be set up or taken down very quickly. The tripod is of wood and has cloth covered top, brass clamps and is in every way a thoroughly well made tripod.

No. 6572. No. 6575.

| | |
|---|---|
| No. 1—For cameras up to 5x7... | $1.95 |
| No. 2—For cameras 5x8 and 6½x8½. | 2.10 |
| No. 3—For cameras 8x10 and 10x12.. | 2.55 |
| No. 4—For cameras 11x14 and 14x17. | 3.40 |
| No. 5—For cameras 17x20 to 20x24.. | 4.25 |

No. 6575. "Combination" Tripod, with combined sliding and folding legs. This is one of the most convenient forms of tripod on the market. It is quickly set up for use and readily adjusted to any height. It has two joints, the lower section of which slides into the second, while the upper section folds back upon the first. They are made of the best seasoned ash with fine brass trimmings, are perfectly rigid and durable; length when extended 59 inches, when closed 23¼ inches. The head is detachable from the legs.

| | |
|---|---|
| No. 1—For cameras up to 5x7. | $2.55 |
| No. 2—For 5x8 and 6½x8½... | 2.75 |
| No. 3—For 8x10 and 10x12..... | 2.95 |
| No. 4—For 11x14 and 14x17.... | 3.80 |
| No. 5—For 17x20 to 20x24.... | 5.10 |

No. 6578. The "Premo" Tripod, is designed especially for use with hand cameras. It is the lightest and most compact form ever made, yet it is rigid and perfectly durable in all its parts. It is made with three joints. The lower section slides into the second, these two into the third, while the upper section folds back upon the third. By this means extreme compactness and portability are secured. It measures when closed but 16 inches and weighs but 14 ounces. Including the aluminum top. Length when extended is 55 inches. It is quickly set up for use and readily adjusted. It is made from seasoned spruce and has handsome brass trimmings.
For 4x5 and 5x7 cameras, each.................$4.50

## LENSES.

No. 6581. The "Excelsior" Rapid Rectilinear Lens, will meet the wants of the amateur who desires a better lens than the single view lens, and yet at a moderate cost. They are perfectly rectilinear, have great depth of focus and flatness of field, giving brilliant definition. They will be found excellent for landscapes, architectural subjects, as well as groups and portraits. They will be fitted with Water House stops or with iris diaphragms. We confidently believe this lens to be the best value of any lens on the market, and equal to many lenses sold at a much higher price.

No. 6581.

## Excelsior Lenses—Continued.

| Size of Camera. | PRICE. Water House Stops. | Iris Diaphragms |
|---|---|---|
| 4x5 | $ 9.50 | $14.25 |
| 5x8 | 11.40 | 16.60 |
| 6½x8½ | 14.25 | 19.45 |
| 8x10 | 19.00 | 25.20 |
| 10x12 | 29.50 | 36.10 |
| 12x15 | 42.75 | 51.30 |

Our aim is to list a line of lenses which will meet with the requirements of the amateur as well as the professional. The selection of the lens is very important, inasmuch as the quality of the work depends largely on the quality of the lens used. A single view lens will do work which will satisfy the average amateur when the conditions are favorable, but for fine work a rapid rectilinear lens should be used.

No. 6580. The Single View Lens although designed for landscape work, will make very good groups and even good portraits. It must be remembered that our descriptions of these lenses are from a professional standpoint, and that a single view lense will give results which will more than please those who have not had a considerable amount of experience.

No. 6580.

| Size of Camera. | Price. |
|---|---|
| 4x5 | $2.70 |
| 4½x6½ | 3.15 |
| 5x8 | 3.60 |
| 6½x8½ | 4.50 |
| 8x10 | 6.30 |

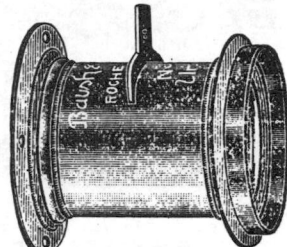

No. 6582.

No. 6582. Bosh & Lomb Rapid Universal Lenses are among the best known on the American market and have gained a popularity which we believe is beyond any of their class. They are of the rectilinear compound type, especially adapted to studio work as well as all kinds of outdoor photography. They are in no manner an imitation of any form, but have a construction peculiarly their own, which is the result of years of experiment and practical observation. The glass used in the lens is of unusual hardness and brilliancy with the practical advantage that the lenses are not liable to become scratched or undergo chemical changes. The mountings are of neat design, well finished and carefully centered. Every lens is supplied with morocco cap case and eight stops. Unless otherwise mentioned brass stops will be furnished, but they can be furnished with hard rubber stops, if desired. The hard rubber being very light and especially adapted for the purpose, it is preferred by many.

| Large Stop Covers Plate. | Diameter of Lenses. In. | Equivalent Focus. In. | Price. |
|---|---|---|---|
| 3¼ x 4¼ | ⅞ | 5¼ | $16.00 |
| 4 x 5 | 1 1-16 | 6¼ | 20.00 |
| 5 x 8 | 1⅜ | 8½ | 24.00 |
| 16½ x 8½ | 1⅝ | 11¼ | 32.00 |
| 18 x 10 | 1⅞ | 13 | 44.00 |
| 10 x 12 | 2⅛ | 16 | 56.00 |
| 12 x 15 | 2⅜ | 19½ | 70.00 |
| 16 x 18 | 3½ | 23¾ | 90.00 |
| 20 x 22 | 4⅛ | 30 | 120.00 |

## THE ZEISS ANASTIGMAT LENSES.
### Series III A. f:9.

**For Instantaneous Out-Door Work, Also for Groups and Large Portraits.**

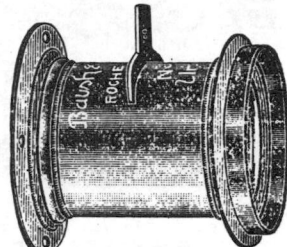

No. 6588. Among the many advantages claimed for these lenses are extreme flatness of field, absolute uniformity of illumination, unusual depth of focus and freedom from astigmatism. They are all fitted with iris diaphragms. The lenses of the series III-A have an aperture of 90 degrees.

No. 6588.

| Size of Plate Covered with Stop f 12-5. In. | Free Diameter of Largest Lens. | Equivalent Focus. In. | Price. |
|---|---|---|---|
| 4 x 5 | ⅝ | 4¾ | $21.00 |
| 4¼ x 6½ | ¾ | 5¾ | 25.00 |
| 5 x 7 | ⅞ | 6¾ | 30.00 |
| 5 x 8 | 1 | 7 11-16 | 33.00 |
| 6½ x 8½ | 1¼ | 9 1-16 | 43.00 |
| 7 x 9 | 1 7-16 | 10¾ | 52.00 |
| 8 x 10 | 1⅝ | 12½ | 65.00 |

## THE EXCELSIOR WIDE ANGLE LENS.

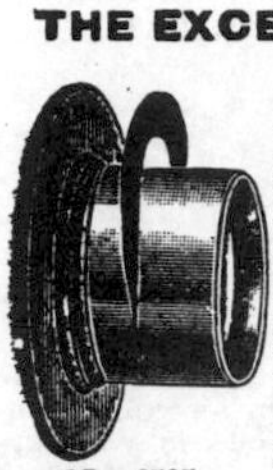
No. 6595.

No. 6595. The "Excelsior" Wide Angle Lens will be found as valuable for the character of work for which they are designed as the well known and popular rapid rectilinear series. They are adapted for interiors of buildings, landscapes and all work in confined situations where lenses of longer focus cannot well be used. All Wide Angle Excelsior Lenses have rotating diaphragms. They embrace an angle of 90 to 100 degrees and admit of being much nearer to the object photographed, but are not so quick working as those of ordinary angles.

| Length Focus. | Size View. | Price. |
|---|---|---|
| 3½ inches. | 4 x 5 | $ 9.50 |
| 5 " | 5 x 8 | 14.25 |
| 6¼ " | 6½ x 8½ | 17.80 |
| 8 " | 8 x 10 | 20.90 |

## THE UNIVERSAL DROP SHUTTER.

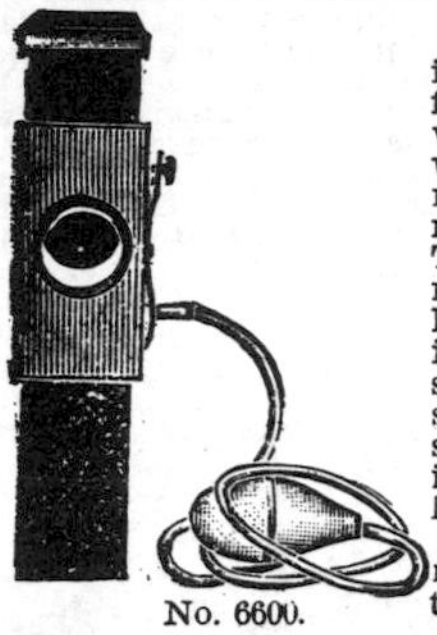
No. 6600.

No. 6600. The "Universal" is a very simple yet effective form of shutter. The slide when released falls of its own weight, and by the use of a rubber band any degree of rapidity may be obtained. The body of the shutter is made of mahogany and is very heavy. A thin strip of rubber is placed on the top of the shutter to lessen the concussion caused by the falling slide. Maximum opening 3 inches. Price with spring release .......................85c
Price with buttons, pneumatic release bulb and tube.......................$1.15

## UNIVERSAL SHUTTER FOR STEREOSCOPIC LENSES.

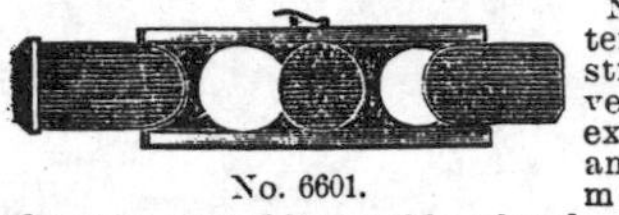
No. 6601.

No. 6601. This shutter is similar in construction to the universal drop shutter, except for two lenses, and as the slides move horizontally they are moved by a rubber band. Price, each. $1.35

## THE WELLER WING SHUTTER.

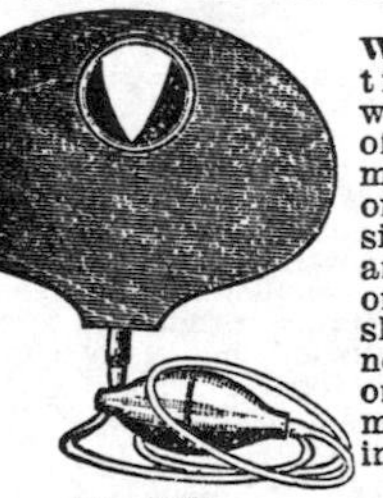
No. 6502.

No. 6502. The "Weller Wing" Shutter is for both time and instantaneous work. We consider it one of the best shutters on the market for either amateurs or professionals. It is very simple in its construction and cannot well get out of order. It works with only a slight jar and is nearly noiseless. It is made to fit on the end of the lens. The maximum opening is 2¼ inches, Each.........$3.30

## THE LOW "KAZOO" SHUTTER No. 1.

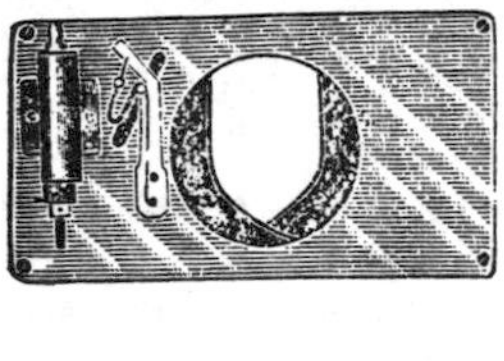
No. 6603.

No. 6603. The Low "Kazoo" Shutter No. 1 is made of metal handsomely finished and nickel plated. It is provided with a spring back that will fit any size of lens tube, and is intended to be used on the front end of the lens. It can be instantly changed from time to instantaneous exposures by simply moving the small lever to one side. It gives the correct exposures and requires no setting after either time or instantaneous movement, as it sets itself after every exposure without opening the wings. It is one of the most desirable shutters on the market.

| | | | |
|---|---|---|---|
| 1½ inch opening | 4 inches long | by 2¾ wide | $5.40 |
| 1¾ " " | 4⅜ " " | " 2⅞ " | 5.85 |
| 2 " " | 4⅞ " " | " 3⅛ " | 6.30 |
| 2¼ " " | 5⅝ " " | " 3⅞ " | 6.75 |
| 2½ " " | 6 " " | " 4½ " | 7.20 |

## THE LOW "KAZOO" SHUTTER NO. 2.

No. 6604. The Low "Kazoo" Shutter No. 2 is designed to be placed on the inside of the camera and attached to the front board. It can be operated entirely from the outside of the camera and at any distance away. It can be changed from time to instantaneous exposures by simply pushing in or pulling out a small brass pin which is passed through the front board and into the shutter. It will balance open for any length of time for focusing. It gives the correct exposures, lighting the drapery or foreground most.

| | | | |
|---|---|---|---|
| 1½ inch opening, 4 | inches by | 2¾ outside | $5.40 |
| 1¾ " " | 4⅜ " | " 2⅞ " | 5.85 |
| 2 " " | 4⅞ " | " 3½ " | 6.30 |
| 2¼ " " | 5⅝ " | " 3⅞ " | 6.75 |
| 2½ " " | 6 " | " 4½ " | 7.20 |

Can furnish other shutters at a discount from Manufacturers lists. Prices quoted on application.

## PRINTING FRAMES.

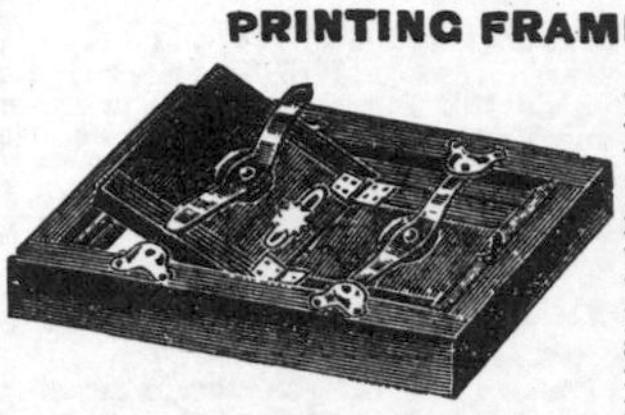
No. 6607.

No. 6607. Our printing frames will be found to be lighter than the ordinary frames, a feature which will be very much appreciated. They are very carefully made and well finished and equally as serviceable as the heavier frames. When printing with film negatives a plain glass should be used on top of the film. The heavier frames can be furnished when desired at a slight advance.

| Size. | Each. | Size. | Each. |
|---|---|---|---|
| 3¼x4¼ | $0.30 | 10x12 | $0.75 |
| 4x5 | .30 | 11x14 | 1.30 |
| 4¼x6½ | .34 | 14x17 | 1.70 |
| 5x7 | .38 | 16x20 | 2.10 |
| 5x8 | .41 | 17x20 | 2.25 |
| 6½x8½ | .45 | 18x22 | 3.00 |
| 8x10 | .65 | 20x24 | 3.75 |

## DEVOE'S PRINTING EASEL.

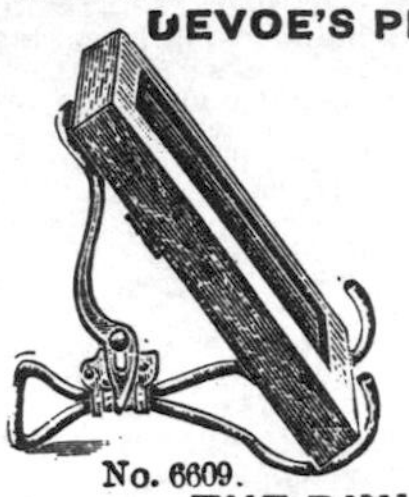
No. 6609.

No. 6609. The Devoe Printing Easel holds the frame at any desired angle. It economizes space, keeps your negative square to the sun and makes more symetrical vignettes. It also prevents the printing frames from slipping down and breaking the negatives. Size suitable for frames up to 10x12 inches.
Each.....................30c

## THE DIXIE VIGNETTER.

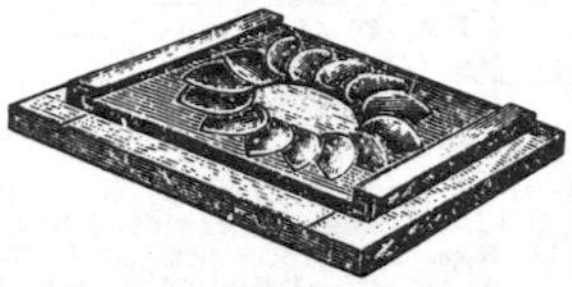
No. 6610.

No. 6610. The Dixie we consider the most perfect instrument on the market for the purposes. It is always ready for use and can be adjusted to any shape in a few seconds. It has adjustable leaves for not only gauging the size of the opening but to alter the shape of the same; made of white wood and neatly finished.

| Size. | Each. | Size. | Each. |
|---|---|---|---|
| 3¼x4¼ | 25c | 5x8 | 25c |
| 4x5 | 25c | 6½x8½ | 35c |
| 4¼x6½ | 25c | 8x10 | 50c |
| 5x7 | 25c | 10x12 | 60c |

## DEVELOPING AND TONING TRAYS

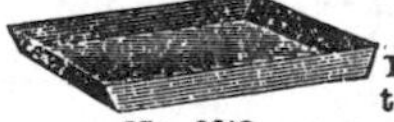
No. 6612.

No. 6612. Japanned Tin Trays for developing and toning.

| Size. | Each | Size. | Each |
|---|---|---|---|
| 4x5 | 20c | 5x8 | 25c |
| 6½x8½ | 30c | 8x10 | 40c |
| 10x12 | 50c | | |

## COMPRESSED FIBRE DEVELOPING AND TONING TRAYS.

No. 6613. Compressed Fiber is one of the latest discoveries in trays. They are black, smooth, well finished, strong and have the appearance of hard rubber trays, but cost much less. They are guaranteed to be both acid and alkali proof, and they are furnished both in deep and shallow. The deep trays all have a lip.

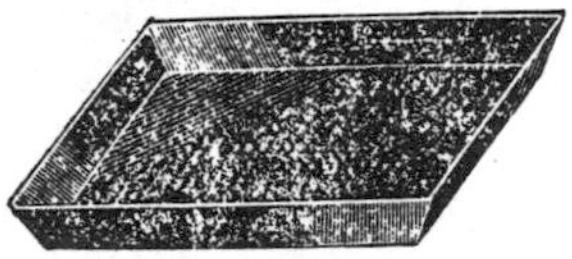
No. 6613.

The above cut represents the shallow style.

| | Shallow. | Deep. |
|---|---|---|
| 3¼x4¼ | $0.15 | ....... |
| 4¼x5½ | .20 | $0.40 |
| 5½x8½ | .40 | .50 |
| 7x9 | .55 | .60 |
| 8½x10½ | .80 | 1.10 |
| 10½x12½ | | 1.30 |
| 12x16 | | 1.80 |

## RUBBER TRAYS.

No. 6614. "Rubber" Trays vulcanized, either deep or shallow. The depth of the shallow trays in size 4x5 on the inside is a trifle over ¾ inch, the larger sizes being deeper. The depth of the 8x10 deep tray is 1⅝ inch; others in proportion.

| For plates. | Shallow. | Deep. |
|---|---|---|
| 4 x 5 | $0.25 each | $0.50 |
| 5 x 8 | 55 " | 70 |
| 7 x 9 | 70 " | 85 |
| 8 x 10 | 1.00 " | 1.15 |
| 10 x 12 | | 1.75 |
| 12 x 16 | | 2.40 |
| 18 x 22 | | 5.00 |
| 19 x 24 | | 5.75 |

## AMBER GLASS TRAYS.

No. 6615. "Amber Glass" Trays are preferred by some for developing. They are heavy and shallow.

| Size. | Each. |
|---|---|
| 4 x 5 | 25c |
| 5 x 8 | 35c |
| 8 x 10 | 75c |

## FIXING BATHS.

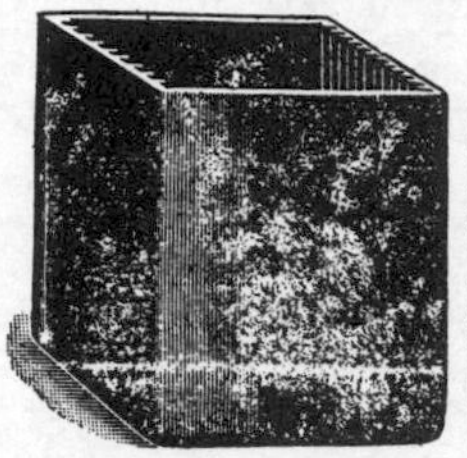

No. 6616. Hard Rubber "Fixing Baths" are a very great convenience for fixing negatives. The plates less liable to accident and a large number can be handled safely at one time. After the plate has been developed it is only being necessary to drop it into the fixing bath. Each box holds one dozen plates.

| | | | |
|---|---|---|---|
| 3¼ x 4¼ | $1.60 | | |
| 4 x 5 plates | $1.80 | 5 x 8 plates | 2.25 |
| 4¼ x 6½ plates | 1.95 | 6½ x 8½ | 2.70 |
| 5 x 7 plates | 2.00 | 8 x 10 | 3.15 |

## GRADUATED GLASSES.

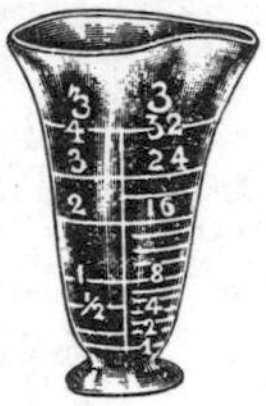

No. 6618. Graduated Glasses for measuring liquids. Each has a graduated scale, with ounces and drams marked.

| | | | |
|---|---|---|---|
| 1 ounce | 15c | 8 ounces | 40c |
| 2 " | 15c | 12 " | 50c |
| 4 " | 25c | 16 " | 65c |
| 6 " | 30c | 24 " | 90c |

## GLASS MORTARS AND PESTLES.

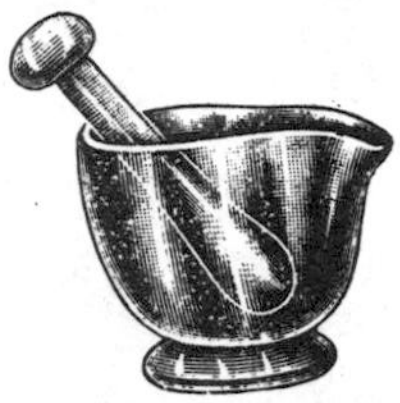

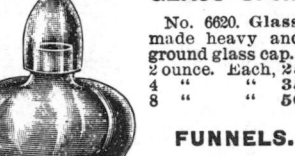

No. 6619. Glass Mortars and Pestles used for mixing chemicals.

| | | |
|---|---|---|
| 1 ounce, | 2½x2¼. | Each...15c |
| 2 " | 3 x2¾. | " ...20c |
| 4 " | 4 x3. | " ...25c |
| 8 " | 4¼x3½. | " ...35c |

## GLASS SPIRIT LAMPS.

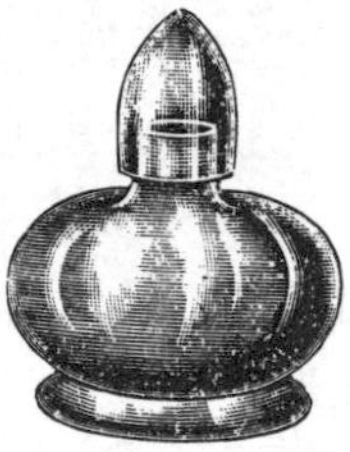

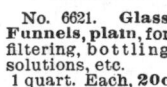

No. 6620. Glass Spirit Lamps, made heavy and strong, with ground glass cap.
2 ounce. Each, 25c
4 " " 35c
8 " " 50c

## FUNNELS.

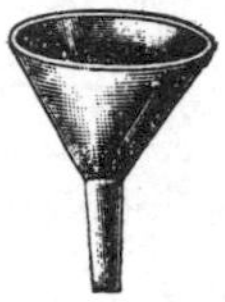

No. 6621. Glass Funnels, plain, for filtering, bottling solutions, etc.
½ pint. Each, 10c    1 quart. Each, 20c
1 " " 15c    2 quarts. " 25c

## FLUTED GLASS FUNNELS.

No. 6622. Glass Funnels, fluted, for filtering.
½ pint. Each.......15c    1 quart. Each.......30c
1 " " .......20c    2 " " .......40c

## HARD RUBBER FUNNELS.

No. 6623. Rubber Funnels are very durable, as they are not easily broken.
¼ pint. Each........40c    1 pint. Each.........55c
½ " " ........50c    1 quart. " .........60c

## SCALES AND WEIGHTS.

No. 6624. Hand Scales, small, with 5-inch beam; pans, 2⅛ in. In box, with weights. Price....50c
Postage 10 cents.

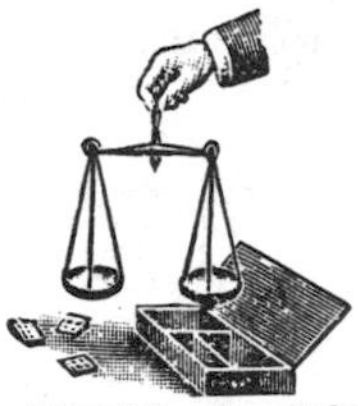

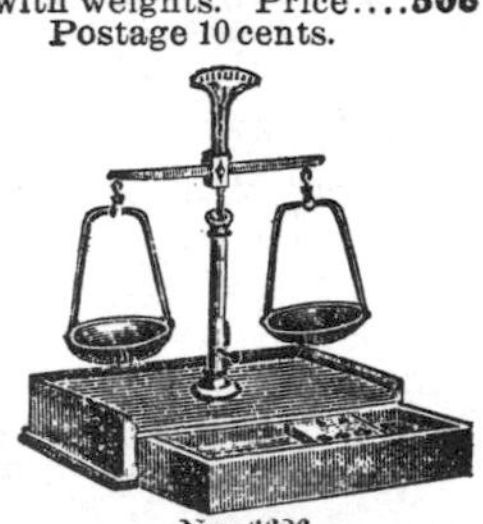
No. 6626.

No. 6626. Prescription Scales. A polished cherry or walnut box, with drawer; has pillar and 6-in. beam, 2 ½-inch pans and full set of weights; weight, 1½ lbs. Price.......$2.25

No. 6627. Prescription Scales with pillar and 8 inch beam, on polished walnut box with drawer, nickel plated, pans 2¾ in diameter, brass work lacquered; has full set of weights. Price..........................$3.75
Scale No. 6627 can be taken apart and packed in drawer of the stand.

## FLASH LAMP.

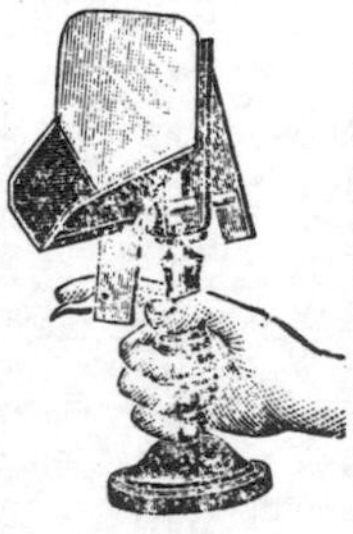

No. 6630. The "James" Flash Lamp is the simplest yet most practical device ever invented for burning flash light powders of all kinds. It dispenses entirely with the use of alcohols gasoline, etc. The powder is ignited with a common parlor match by simply pulling the trigger with the finger when you are ready. The action lights the match which is forced by a spring into the powder in the flash pan exploding it. The charge of powder can be governed to suit the requirements.
Price..............................$1.60

We aim to bring you in way of price at the very door of the manufacturer, and on our liberal terms of shipment and guarantee of quality secure your patronage and influence.

No. 6631. The "Perfection" Magazine Flash Lamp is one of the best yet produced for pure magnezium. The magazine when loaded to its full capacity contains powder sufficient for 20 flashes. An instantaneous flash or a continuous flame of light may be produced, thus making the length of exposures to suit the will of the operator. A piece of circular wick saturated with alcohol produces a large flame, which entirely consumes the charge of powder. A mouthpiece and rubber tubing is supplied with each lamp, but a bulb can be attached if preferred. The Perfection lamp is easy of manipulation, extremely simple and the results produced will commend it to all. Price ........................ $1.80

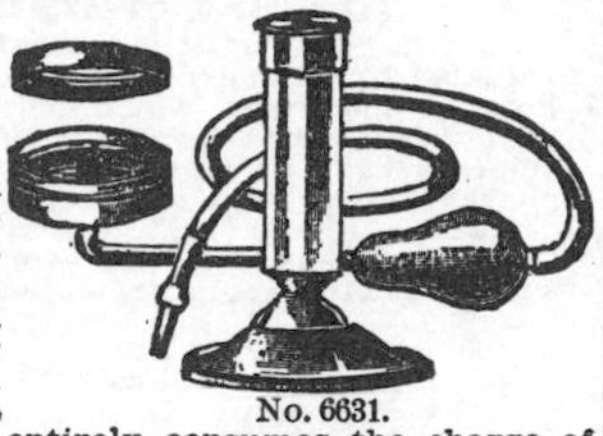
No. 6631.

## RUBY LANTERNS.

For Use in the Dark Room.

No 6635. **Ruby Lamp**, very compact, size 6x2⅝x1½ with ruby glass front; burns oil. Price ........... 50c

No. 6636. **Ruby Lamps**, similar to the above, but made of polished brass with rounded top, size 7x2½x1¾ inches; a first class lamp. Each ................ 85c

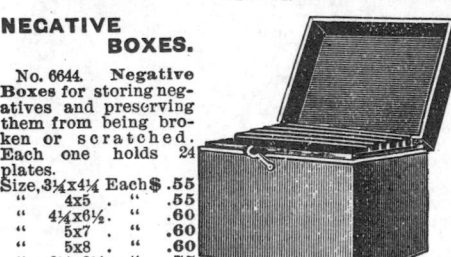

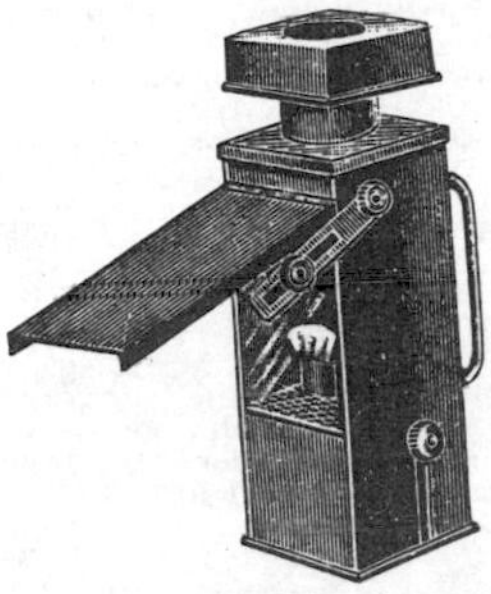
No. 6635.

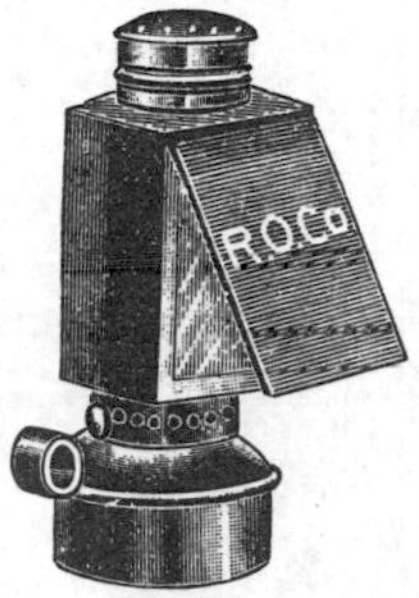

No. 6636.

No. 6637. The **"Universal" Lamp**; a very desirable and practical lamp; height 9 inches with illuminating surface fitted with Ruby glass 2½x4 inches; burns oil. Each ................ 75c

No. 6638. **Universal Ruby Lamp**, size larger than the above ................ 90c

The above lamps are the most popular on the market.

## FOLDING NEGATIVE RACK.

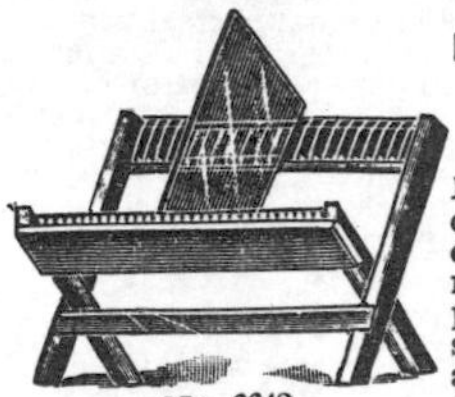
No. 6642.

No. 6642. The **Folding Negative Rack** is a very convenient and necessary accessary for the support of negatives while drying and prevents them from being scratched: will hold 24 negatives. For plates up to 6½ x 8½, each ........... 25c

## NEGATIVE BOXES.

No. 6644. **Negative Boxes** for storing negatives and preserving them from being broken or scratched. Each one holds 24 plates.

| Size | Each |
|---|---|
| 3¼x4¼ | $ .55 |
| 4x5 | .55 |
| 4¼x6½ | .60 |
| 5x7 | .60 |
| 5x8 | .60 |
| 6½x8½ | .75 |
| 8x10 | .90 |
| 10x12 | 1.50 |

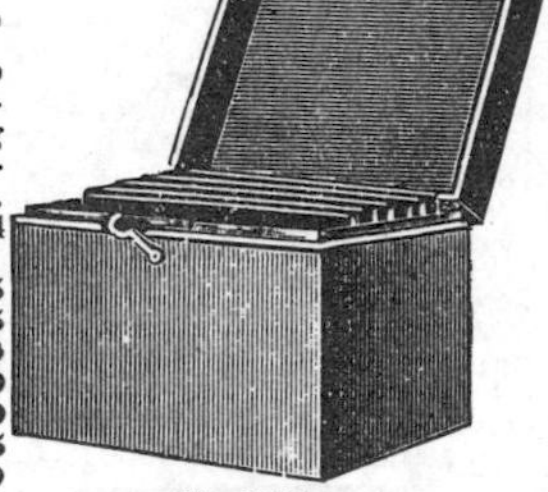
No. 6644.

## PRINT ROLLERS.

Are for rolling down the prints after mounting. A large per cent of amateurs do not use a roll burnisher at all and depend entirely on the print roller for finishing their work.

No. 6646. **Print Roller** with wood center, rubber covered, malleable iron frame with wooden handle.

| | |
|---|---|
| 6 inch | $0.60 |
| 8 inch | .75 |
| 10 inch | 1.00 |

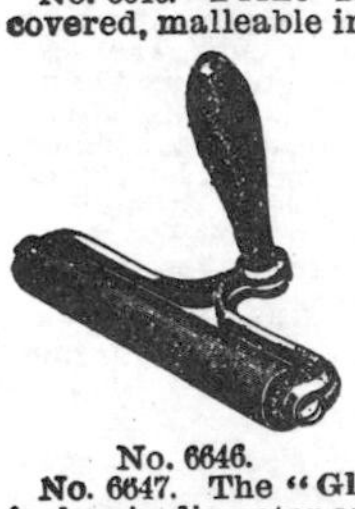
No. 6646.

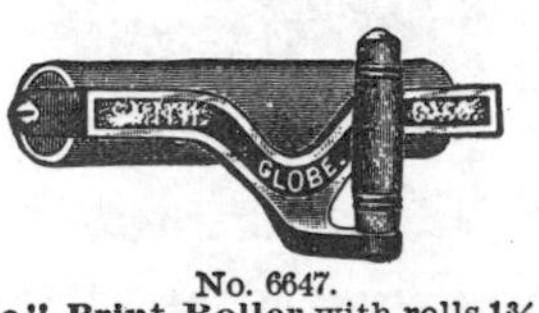

No. 6647.

No. 6647. The **"Globe" Print Roller** with rolls 1¾ inches in diameter and handle placed in position which enables the operator to produce the strongest pressure with the least exertion. The frame is of iron nickel plated, the roller of iron covered with soft rubber.

| | |
|---|---|
| With 6 inch roller | $1.35 |
| " 8 " " | 1.60 |
| " 10 " " | 1.80 |

## BURNISHERS.

We list but three styles of burnishers, but have made a careful selection which will fill the requirements of both the professional and the amateur. They are three of the best burnishers on the market for the money, and we take pleasure in recommending them to our customers. We can furnish the old style drag burnishers if desired, but do not recommend them. We can also furnish other styles of burnishers.

## THE MODEL DUPLEX BURNISHER.

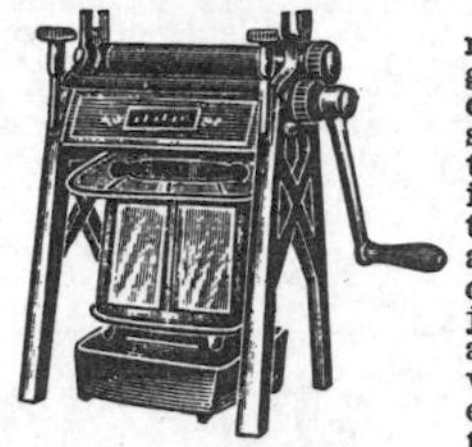

No. 6655. This is a new machine built to meet the growing demand for a good double roll burnisher in small sizes at lower prices than heretofore offered. It is well made in every detail. The top roll is hinged and the pressure can be quickly and perfectly adjusted, and does its work in a first-class manner. It will be furnished with either oil or gas heater at the same price. Be sure to state which is wanted when you order.

| | |
|---|---|
| Price 6 in. with oil or gas heater | $7.25 |
| Price, 8 in. with oil or gas heater | 9.00 |
| Price, 10 in. with oil or gas heater | 11.25 |
| Price 12 in. with oil or gas heater | 14.00 |

The cut shows burnisher with oil heater.

The same burnisher as above, but with one roller and drag at **$7.20** and **$8.90** (not recommended.)

The above in 8 and 10 inch only.

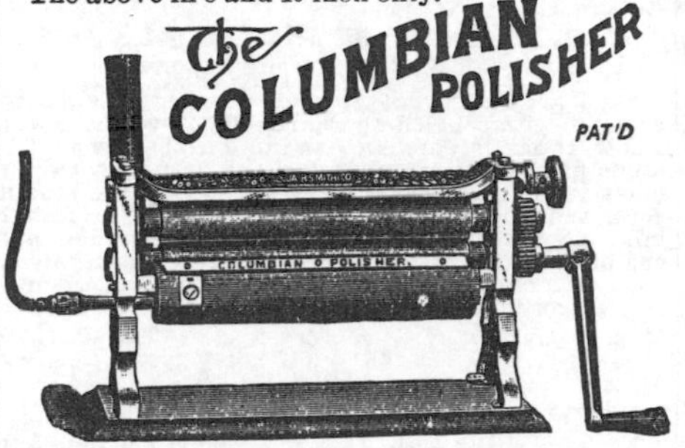


No. 6657. **The Columbian** is the best solid double roll two-cog burnisher ever produced. The rolls do not sweat and the heat is so confined that it does not inconvenience the operator. The fire box for heating the lower roll is a new device with closed bottom and chimney attachment at the opposite end from the crank for conducting the surplus heat. These are the most important improvements for solid two roll machines ever introduced, and does away almost entirely with sweating. It will be furnished with either gasoline or gas heater, which will heat in about half the time required by the oil heater; are more powerful, cleaner, smokeless and in every way more satisfactory than oil. They have automatic spring above the bearings which makes the pressure always uniform and quickly adjusted with one hand wheel. This machine fills all requirements for the professional as well as the amateur.

| | Each. |
|---|---|
| 8 in. with gas or gasoline heater | $13.50 |
| 10 " " " " " | 21.75 |
| 15 " " " " " | 27.00 |
| 20 " " " " " | 36.00 |

## GLOBE ENAMELER.

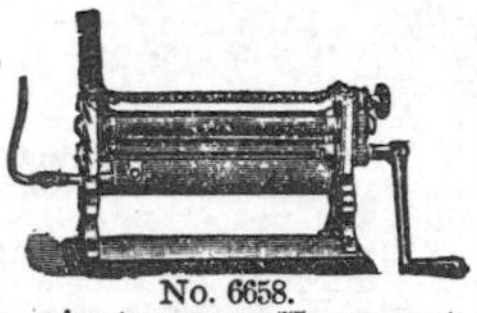
No. 6658.

No. 6658. The **Globe Enameler** with quadruplex system of gearing rolls; has Humphrey's patent hollow roll, the advantages of which are as follows:

They heat in three to five minutes, save 75 per cent. of gas, no smoke; either gas or gasoline can be used, gives the finest gloss, does not scratch, rolls never sweat a particle, pictures not liable to stick to the roll or pull off the cards, oil from the journals does not get on the rolls and soil them, the polishing roll does not attract the dust and moisture from the atmosphere and become soiled, as in solid rolls; has a chimney for conducting the heat and creates a circulation of air through the roll, which secures perfect combustion of gas.

| | |
|---|---|
| 10 in | $27.00 |
| 15 " | 36.00 |
| 20 " | 45.00 |
| 25 " | 54.00 |

In ordering do not forget to specify whether gas or gasoline attachment is wanted in any of above machines.

## BRUSHES.

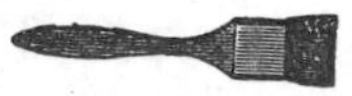
No. 6660.

No. 6660. **Bristle Brushes** for mounting photographs, also good for dusting out plate holders, etc.

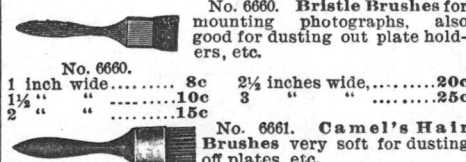

| | | | |
|---|---|---|---|
| 1 inch wide | 8c | 2½ inches wide | 20c |
| 1½ " " | 10c | 3 " " | 25c |
| 2 " " | 15c | | |

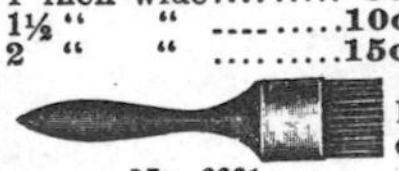
No. 6661.

No. 6661. **Camel's Hair Brushes** very soft for dusting off plates, etc.

| | | | |
|---|---|---|---|
| 1 inch wide | 20c | 2½ inches wide | 40c |
| 1½ " " | 25c | 3 " " | 50c |
| 2 " " | 30c | | |

No. 6665. **Blotting Paper**, used for rolling down prints, size 9x12 in., per dozen sheets ............ 25c

No. 6666. **Absorbant Cotton**, used for filtering, etc. 2 oz. package, each ............ 20c
4 " " " ............ 30c

No. 6667. **Filtering Paper**, best gray, 13 in. in diameter, round, per package of 10 sheets ............ 10c
Per package " 100 " ............ 75c

No. 6668. **Litmus Paper**, best, in red or blue, 100 sheets in bottle. Per bottle ............ 14c

No. 6669. **Yellow Paper** for illuminating the dark room. Per sheet, 3c; per dozen ............ 30c

No. 6670. **Ruby Paper**, Carbutt's, size 20x25. Per sheet ............ 20c

No. 6671. **Envelopes** for preserving negatives, made of strong manilla, the proper size for negatives, open at the end and have notched cut for admitting thumb and finger in removing; printed on the face with lines for number, description, etc.; put up in packages of 50 each.

| Size. | Per pkg. | Size. | Per pkg. |
|---|---|---|---|
| 3¼x3¼ | 15c | 5x8 | 30c |
| 4¼ or 4½x5½ | 20c | 6½x8½ | 32c |
| 4x6½ | 25c | 8x10 | 40c |
| 5x7 | 28c | 10x12 | 70c |

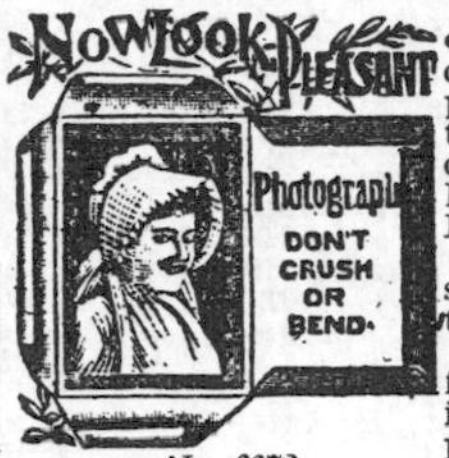

No. 6672.

No. 6672. **Mailing Envelopes** for photographs. You can mail your letter and photograph well protected in the same sealed envelope if desired. In cabinet sizes only. Price per package of 25 **$0.35**
Per box of 125 ............ 1.25

The above envelopes are stiffened for the protection of the photograph.

No. 6673. **Ground Glass** for replacing broken screens in cameras, making transparencies, etc.

| | Each. | | Each. |
|---|---|---|---|
| 3¼ x 4¼ | 10c | 8 x 10 | $0.25 |
| 4 x 5 | 10c | 10 x 12 | 35 |
| 4¼ x 6½ | 10c | 11 x 14 | 50 |
| 5 x 7 | 15c | 14 x 17 double thick. | 1.00 |
| 5 x 8 | 15c | 18 x 22 " " | 1.25 |
| 6½ x 8½ | 20c | | |

No. 6674. **Ruby or Orange Glass** for dark rooms where it is desired to have the lenses on the outside, replacing broken lantern glass, etc.

| Size. | Per Light. | Size. | Per Light. |
|---|---|---|---|
| 6½ x 8½ | 20c | 11 x 14 | 45c |
| 8 x 10 | 25c | 12 x 20 | 75c |
| 10 x 12 | 35c | | |

Be sure to state which color is wanted.

No. 6675. **Ferrotype Plates** with polished surface, used for drying prints when it is desired to have a glossy finish without burnishing. These cannot be sent by mail. Size 10 x 14 inches, each ............ 10c

No. 6676. **Retouching Pencils**, artist's style with Siberian lead single point. Each ............ 25c
Siberian leads, 6 in a box, Nos. 2-B to 6-H. Per box ............ 65c

No. 6677. **Smith's Metallic Points** for retouching. Each ............ 15c

No. 6678. **Plate Lifters** to prevent soiling the fingers. Each ............ 10c

No. 6679. **Rubber Finger Tips "The Alpha"** in sets of three. Per set ............ 15c

No. 6680. **Focusing Cloth**, best quality gossamer. Each ............ 50c

No. 6681. **Glass Forms** for trimming photograph prints to shape, before mounting.

| | Each. |
|---|---|
| Stereoscopic, arched top | 35c |
| 3¼ x 4¼, square corners | 25c |
| 4 x 5 | 35c |
| 4¼ x 6½ | 50c |
| 5 x 8 | 50c |
| 6½ x 8½ | 75c |

No. 6682. **Trimmer's "Robinson's"** Straight for trimming photos. Each ............ 20c

No. 6683. **Trimmers, "Robinson's,"** with revolving cutter for trimming photos. Each ............ 25c

No. 6684. **Clipps, "Lockwood's,"** photo. Each ............ 25c

No. 6685. **Hydrometers** for photographers' solutions, single degree. Each ............ 50c

No. 6686. **Note Book** for photographers, simple and compact for recording exposures and other notes, neatly bound, size 8x4½ in., including pencil. Each ............ 20c

## The Amateur ...Photographer

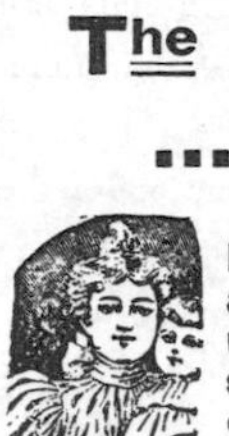

**A Complete and Simple Instruction Book. Tells all about how to take pictures and finish them. Is so plain a child can understand it.**

**Price, Postage Paid ....... 20c**

## If You Don't Know

**What kind of an outfit you should have write us stating how much you can invest and state what class of work you are most interested in whether portrait or landscape, for traveling or home use, for pleasure or business and we will give you our advice in the matter.**

**The Camera is as popular as the Bicycle. We sell both and can save you from 25 to 40 per cent. We solicit a trial order and can convince you.**

## "OUR SPECIAL" ARISTOTYPE ALBUMA PRINTING PAPER.

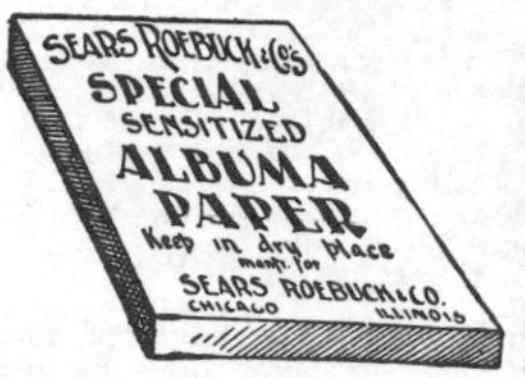

No. 6700.

No. 6700. This paper is the simplest working paper on the market and has many points of superiority over other papers. The film is insoluable, will not soften in warm water, tones in either combined or separate bath, and in any good alkaline bath requires no hardener in the mixing bath or at any other time during manipulation. It prints quickly and tones to any tint with clear whites. The superiority of this paper and the low price commends it to all. The smallest size we list is 3½x3½, but if smaller sizes are desired, you can purchase the most convenient larger size which can be divided to the size you desire.

| Size. | Dozen. | Gross. |
|---|---|---|
| 3½x3½ | $ .10 | $ .70 |
| 3¼x4¼ | .10 | .75 |
| 4x5 | .12 | 1.00 |
| 3⅞x5½ Cabinets | .12 | 1.00 |
| 4x6 | .15 | 1.20 |
| 4¼x6½ | .15 | 1.40 |
| 5x7 | .20 | 1.75 |
| 5x8 | .25 | 2.00 |
| 5½x7¾, Paris Panel | .30 | 2.50 |
| 6x8 | .30 | 2.75 |
| 6½x8½ | .35 | 3.00 |
| 7x9 | .35 | 3.50 |
| 7½x9½ | .40 | 3.75 |
| 8x10 | .45 | 4.00 |
| 9x11 | .55 | 5.00 |
| 10x12 | .65 | 6.00 |
| 11x14 | .75 | 7.50 |
| 14x17 | 1.15 | 12.00 |
| 16x20 | 1.50 | 16.00 |
| 18x22 | 2.00 | 20.00 |
| 20x24 | 2.00 | 22.00 |
| 10 foot roll, 25 inches wide | | 1.10 |

SECONDS.—A limited quantity of Cabinet Seconds at **75c.** per gross. Proofs 4x5, and Cabinets **50c.** per gross.

"Our Special" paper is sold in dozen and gross packages only. We will not break dozen packages. Seconds and proofs are discarded from the selected paper only by reason of very small imperfections.

Postage on cabinet size paper amounts to about 15 cents per gross.

## KIRKLAND'S LITHIUM PAPER.

No. 6701. If you have never tried **Kirkland's Lithium Paper** it will pay you to lose no time in doing so. It is a gelatine paper which requires no ice in the summer and no thermometer to test your solutions. It is especially adapted for coloring on account of its being capable of producing the purest high lights and richest shadows of any paper on the market. It takes water colors readily.

PRICE.

| | Glossy. Doz. | Gross. |
|---|---|---|
| 2¼x3¼, Carte devisite | $ .15 | $ .75 |
| 3x4 Mantello | .15 | 1.00 |
| 3¼x3¼, "Quad" | .18 | 1.15 |
| 3½x3½, "Bull's Eye" | .20 | 1.20 |
| 3¼x4¼ | .20 | 1.20 |
| 3¾x3¾, "Cyko" | .20 | 1.25 |
| 3⅞x5½, Cabinet | .25 | 1.50 |
| 4x6 | .25 | 1.50 |
| 5x7 | .35 | 2.65 |
| 5x8 | .40 | 3.00 |
| 5½x7¾, Paris Panel | .45 | 3.40 |
| 6x8 | .50 | 3.75 |
| 6½x8½ | .55 | 4.10 |
| 7x9 | .65 | 5.25 |
| 7½x9½ | .70 | 5.75 |
| 8x10 | .75 | 6.00 |
| 10x12 | 1.10 | 9.00 |
| 11x14 | 1.25 | 11.20 |
| 14x17 | 1.85 | 18.00 |
| 16x20 | 2.50 | 24.50 |
| 18x22 Half doz., 1.75 | 3.00 | 30.00 |
| 20x24 " " 2.00 | 3.00 | 33.00 |

NOTE—Cabinets by mail, 15 cents extra per gross.

We can furnish a limited quantity of cabinet size seconds, per gross ........ **$1.00**

4x5 seconds, trimmed, per hundred ........ **.75**

The above paper can be furnished in rolls of 10 feet long and 25 inches wide, per roll ........ **$1.50**

Orders for less than one gross will be charged at dozen rates.

## BROMIDE PAPER.

Fo. 6702. Is used for enlarging and contact printing. The "Standard" grade should be used for ordinary negatives or daylight. The "Quick" grade for heavy negatives, or printing in artificial light. Be sure to state which kind is wanted when ordering.

| Size. In. | Per doz. | Size. In. | Per doz. |
|---|---|---|---|
| 3¼ x 4¼ | $0 15 | 11 x 14 | $2.15 |
| 4 x 5 | 25 | 12 x 15 | 2.40 |
| 4¼ x 5½ | 30 | 14 x 17 | 3.60 |
| 4 x 6½ | 35 | 16 x 20 | 4.80 |
| 4¾ x 6½ | 40 | 17 x 20 | 5.25 |
| 5 x 7 | 50 | 18 x 22 | 6.00 |
| 5 x 7¼ | 55 | 20 x 24 | 7.25 |
| 5 x 8 | 60 | 22 x 27 | 8.50 |
| 6½ x 8½ | 90 | 24 x 30 | 10.00 |
| 8 x 10 | 1.20 | 25 x 30 | 10.50 |
| 10 x 12 | 1.80 | 24 x 36 | 13.00 |
| 10 x 14 | 2.00 | 30 x 40 | 18.00 |

If ordered in packages of less than one dozen **25c** extra will be charged for packing.

The exposure on bromide paper varies with the density of the negative and the quality and density of the light.

## CELERITE PAPER.

No. 6703. **A new process Matt Surface Paper;** nothing like it or even similar to it in the market; no gelatine, no colodion; uses no gold and no hypo. The results are somewhat similar to those obtained on platinum paper, but are much more preferable. It is almost as simple as making a blue print. It prints in about half the time required for other papers, hence, a great saving of time; makes strong prints from weak negatives, or soft prints from strong ones. Can be toned to suit any taste from sepia to coal black. The prints never curl; always lie flat and can therefore be bound in book form without mounting. The finished prints cost less than any other, except blue prints, and but little more than the latter. No prints produced by the action of light are more permanent, and if you do not continue to use it, you will be a rare exception. Not sold in less quantities than ¼ gross. If smaller sizes than those listed are wanted, get the most convenient size which can be cut in two. The papers will keep in good condition three or four months, or even longer. Prints have been made on paper over six months old that could not be distinguished from those on fresh paper.

PRICES.

| | | | |
|---|---|---|---|
| 4 x 5, per ¼ gross | $0.40 | Per gross | $1.50 |
| Cab, per ¼ gross | 40 | " | 1.50 |
| 5 x 7 per ¼ gross | 70 | " | 2.60 |
| 6 x 8 per ¼ gross | 80 | " | 3.00 |
| 6½ x 8½ per ¼ gross | 1.10 | " | 4.00 |
| 8 x 10 per ¼ gross | 1.60 | " | 6.00 |
| 10 x 12 per dozen | 80 | | |
| 11 x 14 " | 1.00 | | |
| 20 x 24 " | 3.00 | | |

A complete set of chemicals sufficient for about 300 4-5 prints will be supplied for **40c.** (See list of chemicals.

## C. S. BINDERS OR PHOTO ALBUMS.

For Binding Celerite Paper.

No. 6704. The covers are made of substantial boards covered with pebbled cloth and embossed. The word Photographs is embossed in ink on the cover. The stubs of the cover are perforated with two pairs of holes with nickel eyelets through which the binding cords and ribbons are passed, and then tied securely to hold the picture firmly in place. Any desired number can be bound in this way. Full instructions furnished with each binder. Covers should be ordered about ½ inch larger than the prints to be mounted.

| | | | |
|---|---|---|---|
| 5¾ x 7¾ | 25c | 9 x 12 | 50c |
| 7 x 10 | 35c | 10¾ x 13¾ | 60c |
| 7 x 11 | 40c | | |

## FERRO-PRUSSIATE OR BLUE PAPER.

No. 6705. **Blue Paper** is very easy to manipulate, as it requires no toning. Prints can be made from it very rapidly and no chemicals are necessary. It is merely printed for about 10 minutes in the sunlight and then washed thoroughly in clean water. It will retain its sensitiveness longer than any other paper, and full instructions for working accompanies each package. It is a good paper for beginners for printing landscapes, etc. The prints are in blue on white, put up in light proof packages of 24 sheets.

| Size. | Per Package. | Size. | Per Package. |
|---|---|---|---|
| 3¼ x 4¼ | 16c | 5 x 8 | 40c |
| 4 x 5 | 20c | 6½ x 8½ | 50c |
| 4¼ x 6½ | 30c | 8 x 10 | 65c |
| 5 x 7 | 36c | | |

## DRY PLATES.
## The "Stanley" and "Wuestner New Eagle."

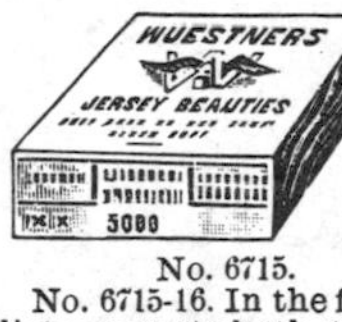

No. 6715.

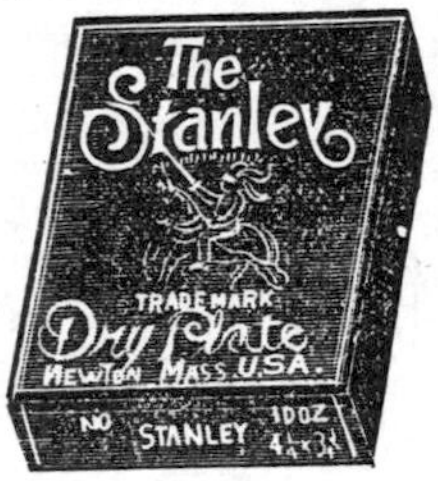

No. 6716.

No. 6715-16. In the following list we quote both the Stanley and the Wuestner New Eagle. The Stanley plates are made in sensitometers, both No. 35 and No. 50, of which the 35 is medium and 50 is rapid. The Stanley plates have an enviable reputation among the leading photographers, who consider them among the best plates for portrait work, flash-light and out-door photography, and amateurs find them to give most excellent results for snap shots and short exposures. If used according to instructions they are guaranteed to give the best results. We carry a very large stock of the Stanley plates, and it will be seldom that we will not be able to fill orders the same day they are received. The Wuestner New Eagle plates are made in sensitometers, "Jersey Beauties XX," medium for landscape and general viewing and "Cyclones XXX" for snap shots, quick studio work or flashlight. If you do not state which we should send we will use our best judgment. Please state in your order whether we may substitute or not, provided we happen to be out of the particular brand you order.

| Size. | Price. Per doz. | Size. | Price. Per doz. |
|---|---|---|---|
| 2 x 2 (Stanley) | 15c | 4¼ x 6½ | 54c |
| 2¼ x 2¼ | 15c | 5 x 7 | $0.66 |
| 2½ x 4 | 18c | 5 x 8 | 75 |
| 3¼ x 3¼ | 25c | 6½ x 8½ | 1.00 |
| *3½ x 3½ (for Quad Camera) | 25c | 7 x 10 | 1.32 |
| | | 8 x 10 | 1.44 |
| 3¼ x 4¼ | 35c | 10 x 12 | 2.28 |
| *4 x 4 (For Cyko Camera) | 40c | 11 x 14 | 3.00 |
| | | 14 x 17 | 5.40 |
| *4¼ x 4¼ (For Vive Camera) | 40c | 16 x 20 | 7.50 |
| | | 17 x 20 | 7.80 |
| 4 x 5 | 40c | 18 x 22 | 9.30 |
| 4 ¼x 5½ | 46c | 20 x 24 | 11.00 |

Those marked with a star will be furnished in Stanley only.

## WUESTNER NEW EAGLE "ORTHO-CHROMATIC" AND "IMPERIAL NON-HALATION" PLATES.

No. 6716. The **Orthochromatic** plates are especially valuable by reason of their being sensitive to yellow, red and green, which makes them particularly adapted to the photographing of oil paintings, water colors and general landscape photography. They are guaranteed to keep for years. The **Imperial Non-Halation** are patented and are of value for all interior work, and especially wherever halation is present, such as photographing machinery, silverware, signs, etc.

| Sizes. | Price per doz. Orthochromatic. | Non-Halation. | Sizes. | Price per doz. Orthochromatic. | Non-Halation, |
|---|---|---|---|---|---|
| 3¼x4¼ | $0.37 | $0.47 | 8x10 | $ 1.90 | $ 2.55 |
| 4 x5 | .53 | .68 | 10x12 | 3.00 | 4.00 |
| 4¼x5½ | .60 | .77 | 10x14 | 4.00 | 5.31 |
| 4¼x6½ | .70 | .94 | 14x17 | 7.20 | 9.57 |
| 4¾x6½ | .80 | 1.02 | 16x20 | 10.00 | 13.38 |
| 5 x7 | .90 | 1.18 | 17x20 | 10.40 | 13.81 |
| 5 x8 | 1.00 | 1.32 | 18x22 | 12.40 | 16.36 |
| 6½x8½ | 1.30 | 1.79 | 20x24 | 14.80 | 18.98 |
| 7 x10 | 1.75 | 2.29 | | | |

## SEED'S DRY PLATES (Sens. No. 27.)

No. 6717. These plates are well and favorably known by those interested in photography. Directions for using accompanies each package. The No. 27 is very rapid.

| Size. | Price, Per Doz. | Size. | Price, Per Doz. |
|---|---|---|---|
| 3¼x 4¼ | $0.40 | 10x12 | $ 3.40 |
| 4 x 5 | 0.60 | 11x14 | 4.50 |
| 4¼x 6½ | 0.80 | 14x17 | 8.10 |
| 5 x 7 | 1.00 | 16x20 | 1.25 |
| 5 x 8 | 1.13 | 18x22 | 13.95 |
| 6½x 8½ | 1.50 | 20x24 | 16.65 |
| 8 x10 | 2.15 | | |

## CELLULOID FILMS.

No. 6718. **Celluloid Films** are of advantage to tourists and travelers by reason of their lightness. They are used in the same manner as dry plates, except that they require a special holder. Ten dozen films weigh about the same as one dozen dry plates

| Sizes. | Price, Per Doz. | Sizes. | Price, Per Doz. |
|---|---|---|---|
| 3¼x4¼ | $0.50 | 5x8 | $1.40 |
| 4x5 | 72 | 6½x8½ | 1.90 |
| 4¼x6½ | 1.00 | 8x10 | 2.70 |
| 5x7 | 1.25 | | |

## PHOTOGRAPHIC CHEMICALS, SOLUTIONS, ETC.

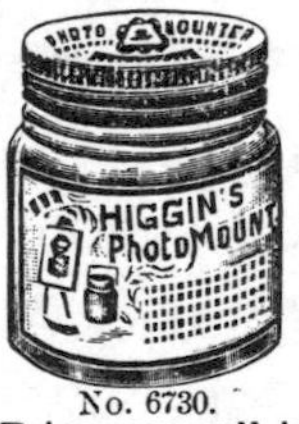

No. 6730.

No. 6730. **"Higgin's" Photo Mounter** is a most perfect paste for mounting photos. It always adheres, will not spill, spatter or drop off the brush; does not cockle, harden, separate, become gritty or strike through or change the tone; does not mould, sour or deteriorate in any way.

Price per small jar ........ **23c**

" " pound " ........ **45c**

No. 6731. **AntiTache** is an article which will be appreciated by all. It prevents the fingers and nails from becoming stained, and the hands from becoming rough and chapped. It is perfectly harmless, antiseptic and condensed. The emulsion is of a rose tint, and forms an absolute protection to the hands against the action of any developer, toner or acid solution. It renders the hands impervious to all, whether hypo, metol, silver, iron or acid stains. Its action on the skin is softening, healing and cleansing and it will not contaminate with the most delicate solution.

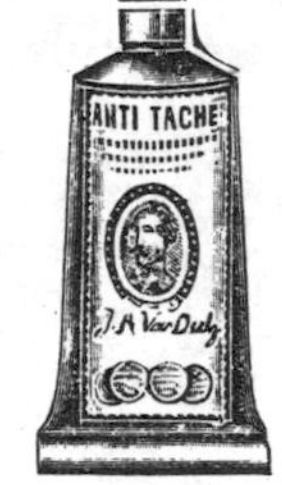

No. 6731.

¼ oz. in collapsible tube ........ **25c**

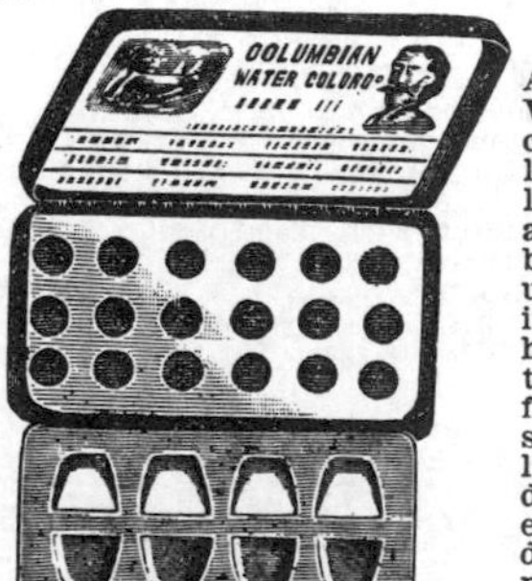

No. 6732.

No. 6732. **"New Acme" Transparent Water Colors** for coloring portraits, landscape views and lantern slides. They are not liquid colors, but are moist and put up in cups, the set being contained in a handsome tin case. As they are in condensed form they have greater strength than the liquid colors, are more durable to light and easy to apply. No difficulty in burnishing prints after coloring.

Price for complete outfit, amateur size ........ **$0.95**

" " " professional size ........ **2.25**

No. 6733. **"Photinto," Liquid Colors** for tinting photos, magazine pictures, etc. Full instructions how to use it accompany each box and it can be learned in 10 minutes.

Price per box of 6 bottles, assorted colors, including directions ........ **50c**

Cannot be sent by mail.

**You will be 3 per cent. the gainer by taking advantage of our liberal discount of 3 per cent. for full cash with order. Besides, you can save the express charges on return of cash when you buy that way.**

No. 6734. **Negative Varnish** (Flint's) for preserving negatives.
6 oz. bottle .......... 40c

No. 6735. **Diamond Varnish** for positives on tintypes. For 6 oz. bottle .......... 32c

No. 6736. **Retouching Varnish**, 6 oz. bottle .... 45c

No. 6737. **Liquid Opaque**, for making any portion of negative opaque. Per bottle .......... 36c

No. 6738. **Glace Polish**, for applying to photographs before burnishing. Ready for use.
Per box .......... 20c

No. 6739. **Flashlight Powder "Blitz Pulver,"** a well-known flashlight powder. Per oz .......... 60c

No. 6740. Flash Cartridges; a desirable size for home use, small interiors, ordinary portrait work, etc.
Per box of 6 catridges .......... 25c

## OUR OWN CHEMICALS.

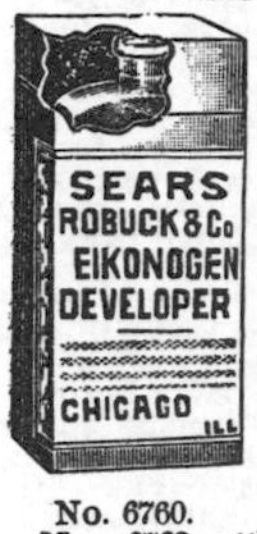


In justice to our customers we have decided to put up a line of our own photo chemicals, such as developers, toning solutions, etc. They are put up under the supervision of a thoroughly competent and experienced chemist, which enables us to guarantee the quality, this being a very important question in the matter of ready prepared solutions.

No. 6760. **"Eikonogen" Developer**, ready mixed, concentrated with directions. Per 8 oz. bottle .......... 30c

No. 6761. **"Hydro Chinon,"** a good concentrated developer, with instructions. Per oz. bottle .......... 30c

No. 6760.

No. 6762. **"Eiko-Hydro" Developer** and concentrated solution of eikonogen and hydrochonin, with directions. Per 8 oz. bottle .......... 30c

No. 6763. **"Hydro-Metol" Developer**, a concentrated solution of hydrochinon and metol, an excellent developer, with instructions.
Per 8 oz. bottle .......... 40c

No. 6764. **"Ferrous Oxalate" Developer** concentrated in two solutions, is especially desirable for lantern slides, bromide paper, etc., with instructions.
Per package of two bottles .......... 45c

No. 6765. **"Pyrogallic Acid" Developer** put up in two concentrated solutions, with instructions.
Per package of two 8 oz. bottles .......... 50c

No. 6776. **Intensifier**, for strengthening weak negatives. Per 4 oz. bottle .......... 25c

No. 6777. **Reducer**, for the reduction of dense negatives, bromide prints, transparencies, etc.
Per 8 oz. bottle .......... 25c

No. 6778. **Soaking Solution**, for the emersion of roll films after development to prevent curling.
Per 8 oz. bottle .......... 30c

No. 6779. **"Toning and Fixing" Solution** combined, is ready for use and suitable for all aristotype papers. Per 8 oz. bottle .......... 30c
Per 16 oz. bottle .......... 50c

No. 6780. **"Toning" Solution**, concentrated for aristotype and albuma papers. It has only to be diluted and it is ready for use.
Per 4 oz. bottle .......... $ .35
Per 8 oz. bottle .......... .60
Per 12 oz. bottle .......... .85
Per 16 oz. bottle .......... 1.10

No. 6781. **Print Hardener** for hardening albuma or aristotype prints. Per 8 oz. bottle .......... 30c

No. 6782. **Eikonogen Developing Powders.** This is a very convenient means for preparing the liquid Eikonogen developer; avoids the risk of breakage in transportation and always insures a fresh and stronger developer. Each package contains six sets of powders, which is sufficient to prepare from 1¼ to 2 pints of concentrated developer. Price, per package .......... 25c
Postage, 4 cents.

No. 6783. **Pyro Developing Powders.** These powders are highly esteemed by all who use but small quantities of this developer at a time. It is well known that all liquid Pyro developers soon discolor and become worthless, but with these powders it is only necessary to mix the developer just when it is needed, by which arrangement the solution is always fresh and strong. Each package contains six sets of powders, which is sufficient to prepare from 1½ to 2 pints of strong developer. Price, per package .......... 25c
Postage, 4 cents.

No. 6784. **Toning Powders, "Hale's."** A good toner put up in dry form and especially desirable for mailing. Per ¼ lb. box .......... 25c
Per ½ lb. box .......... 40c
Per 1 lb. box .......... 65c

No. 6785. **Chemicals for "Celerite Paper,"** sufficient for about 300 4x5 prints with instructions.
Per set .......... 40c

No. 6787. **Toning Powders, "Our Special."** This is a most excellent toning powder and works well on all kinds of Albuma Aristotype papers. It is especially desirable for tourists, and also for shipment, as there are no bottles to be broken. It is put up in neat pasteboard boxes, with full and complete instructions.
Per ¼ pound box .......... 25c
Per ½ pound box .......... 40c
Per 1 pound box .......... 65c
Postage on developing powders, 10c, 18c and 25c.

NOTE.—Dry developing powders do not include the gold. Chloride of gold should be ordered for use with same.

## PHOTOGRAPHIC CHEMICALS.

No. 6800. Chemicals are bought and sold by avoirdupois weight, but mixed by apothecary's weight. In the avoirdupois weight there are 16 oz. to the lb. and 437½ grains to the oz., while in apothecary's weight their are 12 oz. to the lb. and 480 grains to the oz. Please remember that if you get but 437½ grains of any chemical for an oz. it is not short weight, as all chemicals are bought and sold that way.

| | |
|---|---|
| Acid, acetic, No. 8, 1 lb. bottle | $0.16 |
| Acid, citric, 1 oz. bottle | 10 |
| Acid, muriatic, 2 oz. bottle; | 18 |
| Acid, nitric, 1 oz. bottle | 15 |
| Acid, nitric, ¼ oz. bottle | $0.10 |
| Acid, oxalic, 2 oz. bottle | 15 |
| Acid, pyrogallic (H. & F.) 1 oz. can | 35 |
| Acid, pyrogallic (Anthony's) 1 oz. bottle | 35 |
| Acid, pyrogallic (Schering's) 1 ox. can | 35 |
| Acid, pyrogallic (Mailinkrodt's) 1 oz. can | 43 |
| Acid, Salicylic, 1 oz. package | 25 |
| Acid, salicylic, ½ oz. package | 15 |
| Acid, sulphuric C. P., 1 oz. bottle | 12 |
| Alcohol, ½ pint bottles, 98 per cent. deodorized | 25 |
| Alum, pulverized, 1 lb. package | 18 |
| Alum, chrome, ½ lb. bottles | 20 |
| Ammonia, liquid conc., U. S. P., 1 lb. bottle | 26 |
| Ammonia, bromide, 1 oz. bottle | 12 |
| Ammonia, bichromate, bottle included, per lb. | 1.25 |
| Ammonia, carbonate, bottle included, per lb. | 40 |
| Ammonia, chloride, 1 oz. bottle | 10 |
| Ammonia, sulpho cyanide, 1 oz. bottle | 14 |
| Chloroform, 1 oz. bottle | 15 |
| Ether, sulphuric concentrated, 1 lb. bottle | 85 |
| Eikonogen, crystals, 1 oz. bottle | 35 |
| Eikonogen, crystals, per ¼ lb. | 1.20 |
| Glycerine, 2 oz. bottle | 15 |
| Glycerine, 1 oz. bottle | 8 |
| Gold, chloride and sodium, 15 gr. bottle | 35 |
| Gold chloride (dry), pure, 15 gr. bottle | 50 |
| Hydrochinon, in tins, per ounce | 35 |
| Iodine, resub., 1 oz. bottle | 38 |
| Iodine, tincture 1 oz. bottle | 20 |
| Iron, protosulphate, 1 lb. package | 8 |
| Iron, protosulphate, 1 lb. bottle | 20 |
| Lead, nitrate, 1 oz. bottle | 15 |
| Lead, acetate, 1 oz. bottle | 25 |
| Lime, chloride, ¼ oz. bottle | 12 |
| Lime, chloride, in bottles, per lb. | 25 |
| Metol, Hauff, per 1 oz. bottle | 70 |
| Metol, Hauff, per ¼ lb. bottle | 2.60 |
| Mercury, bi-chloride, 1 oz. bottle | 15 |
| Mercury, bi-sulphate, per oz. | 15 |
| Mercury, bi-sulphate, ½ bottle | 75 |
| Mercury, bi-sulphate, 1 lb. bottle | 1.25 |
| Magnesium, pure, per oz. | 49 |
| Potasssium, meta-bi-sulphite, per oz. | 15 |
| Potassium, meta-bi-sulphite, ¼ lb. bottle | 25 |
| Potassium, meta-bi-sulphite, ½ lb. bottle | 50 |
| Potassium, meta-bi- sulphite, 1 lb. bottle | 1.00 |
| Potassium, bromide, 1 oz. bottle | 10 |
| Potassium, bromide, 2 oz. bottle | 15 |
| Potassium, carbonate, ½ lb. bottle | 20 |
| Potassium. carbonate, 1 lb. bottle | 27 |
| Potassium, cyanide, 2 oz. bottle | 14 |
| Potassium, cyanide, ¼ lb. bottle | 25 |
| Potassium, cyanide, 1 lb. bottle | 65 |
| Potassium, ferri-cyanide (red prussiate) per oz. | 20 |
| Potassium, ferri-cyanide (red prussiate) per lb. | 80 |
| Potassium, ferri-cyanide (yellow prussiate), per oz. | 12 |
| Potassium, ferri-cyanide (yellow prussiate), per lb. | 60 |
| Potassium, iodide, 1 oz. bottle | 35 |
| Potassium, neutral oxalate, 1 lb. pack | 30 |
| Platinum chloride, per 15 gr, bottle | 70 |
| Platinum chloride, per oz. | 7.00 |
| Silver, nitrate, 1 oz. bottle, per doz | 65 |
| Silver, nitrate, 8 oz. bottle, per bottle | 4.00 |
| Silver, bath, solution, 40 grains strong, 1 pint bottle | 1.75 |
| Silver, bath solution, 40 grains strong, 1 quart bottle | 3.25 |
| Soda, acetate, 2 oz. bottle | 15 |
| Soda, bi-carbonate, 1 lb. package | 12 |
| Soda, carbonate (Sal,), 1 lb. package, granular | 10 |
| Soda, carb. (Sal.), crystals, 1 lb. bottle | 20 |
| Soda, citrate, 1 oz. bottle | 18 |
| Soda, hyposulphate, per lb. | 5 |
| Soda, phosphate, ½ lb. bottle | 30 |
| Soda, sulphite, granular, ½ lb. bottle | 30 |
| Soda, sulphite, crystals, 1 lb. bottle | 25 |
| Soda, tungstate, 1 oz. bottle | 15 |

## MOREHOUSE PHOTOGRAPH ALBUMS.

For Mounted or Unmounted Photographs.

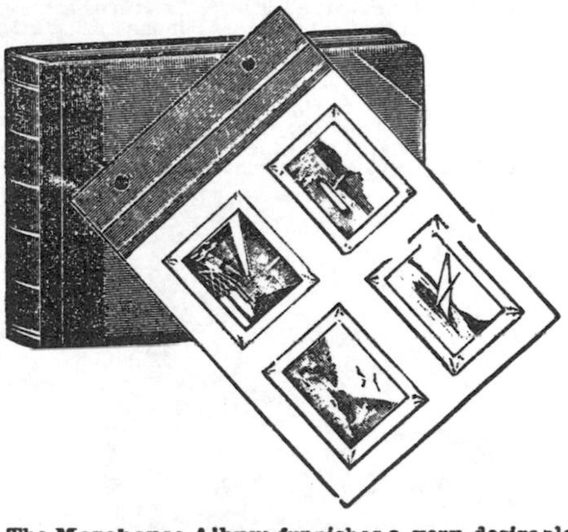

The **Morehouse Album** furnishes a very desirable means of preserving pictures and has several advantages over other albums.

The first number is for unmounted photos. The leaves are full size and prints can be mounted on the leaves instead of on cards. It is desirable with medium sized prints to select a size which is large enough to mount two on a page. It affords a precaution against those who are inclined to take photographs from a collection, which is often very annoying. Leaves can be taken out or put in when desired, as the extensions are adjustable. As many as 50 or 60 leaves may be put in without injuring the appearance of the book.

No. 6870. **Album for Mounted Photographs.** These books are furnished with 25 gummed stubs to which the already mounted photographs can be attached. The stubs being gummed, all that is necessary to be done is to moisten them and attach to the mounts to form a perfect leaf which will fit neatly in the album.

| Size. | Style "A," full cloth. | Style "B," seal back and corners. | Extra gummed stubs or hinges. Per pkg. of 25 |
|---|---|---|---|
| 6x 7 | $0.95 | $1.65 | $0.35 |
| 7x10 | 1.18 | 1.90 | .45 |
| 10x12 | 1.42 | 2.13 | .55 |
| 11x14 | 1.66 | 2.37 | .65 |

No. 6871. **Album for Unmounted Photographs.** Each book furnished with 25 No. 1 mounts with perforated stubs attached. It is only necessary to mount prints on the leaves same as any other mount, then place the leaf in the album.

| Size. | Style "E," bound in half leather and half cloth embossed. | Style "F," seal grain back and corners embossed and rolled in gold leaf. | Extra perforated leaves Per. doz. |
|---|---|---|---|
| 6x 7 | $1.38 | $1.88 | $0.35 |
| 8x10 | 1.85 | 2.38 | .50 |
| 10x12 | 2.40 | 3.08 | .75 |
| 11x14 | 2.85 | 3.75 | 1.00 |
| 14x17 | 3.80 | 4.75 | 1.50 |

## CARD MOUNTS.

**Card Mounts** are the cards on which the print is pasted after having been toned and finished. A photo is very much improved in appearance by a neat and pretty card mount. Card mounts are put up by the manufacturers in packages of 25 each, and we cannot

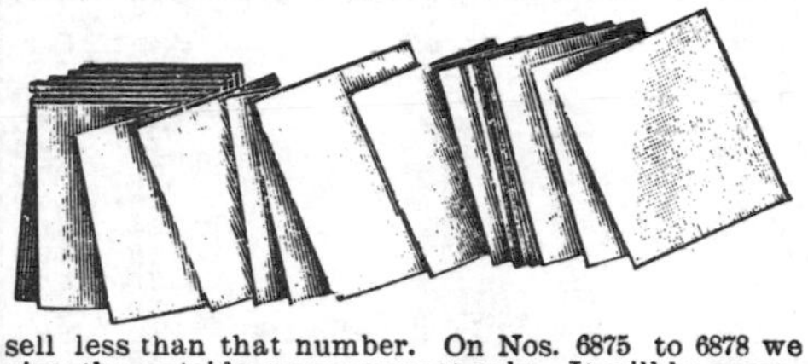

sell less than that number. On Nos. 6875 to 6878 we give the outside measurement only. It will be necessary to order the cards a little larger than the prints you wish to mount. Photographers should use their own judgment as to the amount of margin, but it will be found that a liberal margin always looks best. Professionals are now leaving much larger margins than formerly.

No. 6875 **White Card Board Mounts**, heavy, with square corners.

| Size | Per pkg. | Per 100 | Size | Per Pkg. | Per 100 |
|---|---|---|---|---|---|
| 3½x3½ | $0.10 | $0.35 | 7x 9 | $0.45 | $1.70 |
| 4 x5 | .15 | .40 | 8x10 | .55 | 2.00 |
| 5 x8 | .30 | .95 | 10x12 | .85 | 3.00 |
| 6½x8½ | .40 | 1.50 | 11x14 | 1.00 | 3.75 |

No. 6876. **Round Corners**, plain edges, good quality, white or gray.

| Size | Per pkg. | Per 100 |
|---|---|---|
| 2½x 4¼ (Carte de Visite) | $0.10 | $0.30 |
| 3½x 4½ | .10 | .35 |
| 4¼x 5¼ | .15 | .45 |
| 4¼x 6½ (Cabinet) | .15 | .45 |
| 5 x 7 | .20 | .65 |
| 5 x 8 | .22 | .80 |
| 5¼x 8½ | .22 | .80 |
| 6½x 8½ | .30 | 1.00 |
| 6⅞x 9⅞ | .38 | 1.40 |
| 6 x10 | .40 | 1.55 |

No. 6877. **Beveled Edge**, round corners, heavy weight, white or gray.

| Size | Per pkg. | Per 100 |
|---|---|---|
| 4¼x 5¼ (Cabinet) | $0.25 | $0.75 |
| 4¼x 6½ | .30 | 1.05 |
| 5 x 7 | .35 | 1.20 |
| 5 x 8 | .45 | 1.45 |
| 6½x 8½ | .55 | 1.70 |
| 8 x10 | .70 | 2.45 |
| 10 x12 | 1.00 | 3.45 |

No. 6878. **Gold Beveled Edge**, heavy weight, gray or white; a very stylish mount.

| Size | Per pkg. | Per100 |
|---|---|---|
| 2½x 2½ (white only) | $0.15 | $0.50 |
| 2½x 4¼ " " | .15 | .50 |
| 3½x 4½ | .30 | .90 |
| 4¼x 5¼ | .35 | 1.10 |
| 5 x 7 | .55 | 1.90 |
| 6½x 8½ | .70 | 2.65 |
| 8 x10 | 1.00 | 3.90 |

No. 6879. **Gold Beveled Edge**, dark maroon, fine quality; makes a very pretty and stylish mount.

| Size. | Per Pkg. | Per 100 |
|---|---|---|
| 2½x4¼ (Carte de Visite) | $0.25 | $0.85 |
| 4¼x6½ (Cabinet) | .45 | 1.75 |

## ..PHOTOGRAPHY..

**Is one of the most interesting, delightful and instructive of pleasures**

**IT'S EASY ...TO MAKE** GOOD PICTURES

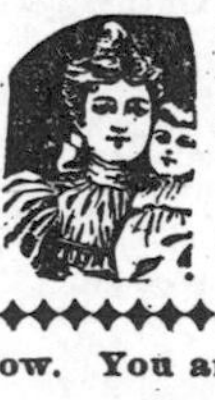

**If you will but follow carefully the printed instructions which accompanies each outfit.**

**IF INTERESTED IN**

**PROFESSIONAL STUDIO OUTFITS**

Send for Special Catalogue of STUDIO CAMERAS, ETC.

**We sell only the best goods that the market affords. Don't be afraid if our prices seem unusually low. You are at liberty to return any article not satisfactory.**

## MANTELLO CARD MOUNTS.

**No. 6880.** Mantello Card Mounts are the latest and most stylish mount on the market. We furnish them in both gray and white. They have raised center with an embossed or matted border, are heavy and of fine quality and improve very largely the appearance

of the pictures. This style card mount is now being almost exclusively used by the leading professional photographers. We recommend the gray as being most desirable, as it is not easily soiled and the tint seems to harmonize with the picture much better than the white. Try the gray and we believe you will be well pleased.

| Size of card. | Size of picture. | Per pkg. | Per 100 |
|---|---|---|---|
| 2⅝x3½ | 1½x2 | $0.10 | $0.40 |
| 2 x3 | 1⅜x2¼ | .12 | .45 |
| 3½x3½ | 2 x2 | .15 | .55 |
| 2⅝x4½ (white only) | 1⅝x2⅞ | .20 | .70 |
| 3¼x3¾ | 2 x2½ | .20 | .70 |
| 3¾x3¾ | 2⅞x2⅞ | .24 | .85 |
| 3⅞x5½ | 2½x3⅞ | .28 | .90 |
| 5 x5 | 3½x3½ | .30 | 1.05 |
| 4¼x6 | 3¼x4¼ | .30 | 1.05 |
| 5¼x6¼ | 3¼x4¼ (horizontal) | .32 | 1.20 |
| 5½x5½ | 4 x4 | .35 | 1.50 |
| 5⅝x6¼ | 4 x5 | .35 | 1.25 |
| 5⅝x7¾ | 4⅛x5⅝ | .45 | 1.40 |
| 7 x9 (very heavy) | 4 x5¼ | .60 | 2.20 |
| 8 x10 " | 4 x6 | .70 | 2.65 |
| 8 x10 " | 5 x7 | .70 | 2.65 |

## STEREOSCOPIC MOUNTS, TINTYPE HOLDERS, ETC.

**No. 6885.** Stereoscopic Mounts, 3½x7 inch, dark buff. Per pkg. 15c Per hundred 45c.

**No. 6886.** Stereoscopic Mounts, fine quality, enameled, pink or buff, 4x7 inch, Per pkg 16c Per hundred 60c.

**No. 6887.** Ferrotype Cases (Caterson's) card size, in assorted tints, with red borders, oval opening. Per pkg. 10c Per hundred 35c.

**No. 6888.** Ferrotype Cases, (Caterson's) cabinet size, with arched opening, in assorted tints. Per pkg. 30c Per hundred 90c.

## DEVELOPING OUTFITS.

For the benefit of those who are not familiar with photography, and who are at a loss to know what they should have, will say that a complete outfit for finish-

ing photographs in addition to the camera consists of the following items:

A ruby lamp for the dark room.
Trays for developing and toning (three).
Glass graduate for measuring liquids.
Printing frame.
Developing solution.
Toning solution.
Hypo sulphite.
One dozen sensitized paper for making prints.
One copy of the "Amateur Photographer" which gives complete instructions for developing, printing, toning, etc.

**No. 6895.** Developing and Printing Outfit, consisting of the articles mentioned above for 3¼x4¼ and smaller sizes, complete..........................$1.75

**No. 6896.** Developing and Printing Outfit, consisting of articles named above for 4x5 and smaller sizes, complete...........................$2.35

## MAGIC LANTERNS.

The magic lantern is an optical instrument by which transparent views made on small plates of glass are illuminated by means of condensed light, and are projected on the surface of the wall or screen, and thus made visible as enlarged images, and may be viewed by large crowds of spectators. The origin of the magic lantern, like that of many other useful inventions is unknown. It has been claimed that the priests of ancient Egypt used such instruments to further mystify their religion. The first authentic account of them dates back about 300 years, and even though they must

at that time have been a very rude and primitive affair, the revelations appeared so marvelous to the uneducated people of that period that the instrument was named "Magic Lantern." For centuries afterwards it was regarded as a toy for the amusement of children; but eventually its value as an educational adjunct and a source of intelligent entertainment was recognized, which has resulted in the perfecting of the apparatus, until now the magic lantern has been elevated to the position of a scientific and popular instrument of vast and varied utility.

### TERMS OF SHIPMENT.

Magic Lantern Slides, etc., will be sent C. O. D. when desired. Orders amounting to $15.00 or less will be sent on receipt of $1.00 with order as guarantee of good faith. With orders amounting to over $15.00 will require $2.00 with the order. Magic Lanterns cannot be returned for exchange after they have been used, for even though they have been used but little they are second-hand and we have no means of disposing of second-hand goods. This rule, however, does not refer to any goods which might be defective. We guarantee all of our goods to give entire satisfaction.

We recommend that you send cash in full with your order and save both the return charges on the money and the cash discount of 3 per cent.

Juvenile Magic Lanterns and Outfit.

We believe that money cannot be spent to better advantage for the amusement of children than for a magic lantern and outfit. They derive a great deal of pleasure from giving magic lantern exhibitions, posting circulars, and all of the detail connected with an amateur entertainment.

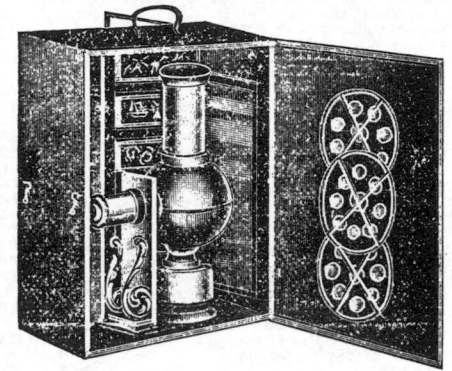

No. 61000.

**No. 61000.** The "Home" Magic Lantern for parlor entertainments: has metal body, handsomely japanned, with gilt decorations, and has kerosene lamp with six colored slides, with views 1⅛ inches wide, magnifying picture to about one foot. Each...................75c

**No. 61001.** The "Home" Magic Lantern, same as above, but has one dozen views, 1⅜ inches in diameter, magnifying picture to about 1½ foot. Each....$1.00

**No. 61002.** The "Home" Magic Lantern, same as above, but has three finely ground lenses in each lantern, twelve colored slides, 1½ inches wide, with three to four pictures on each slide, magnifying the picture to about two feet in diameter. Each...........$1.75

**No. 61003.** The "Home" Magic Lantern, same as No. 61002, with slides 1¾ inches wide; magnifying picture to about 2½ feet diameter. Each...........$2.25

**No. 61004.** The "Home" Magic Lantern, same as No. 61002, except that it has slides 2⅜ inches wide, magnifying pictures to about 3 feet in diameter. Each...........$3.00

**No. 61005.** The "Home" Magic Lantern, same as No. 61002, except that it has slides 3½ inches wide, magnifying the pictures to about 3½ feet in diameter. Each...........$4.00

**No. 61006.** The "Home" Magic Lantern, same as No. 61002, except that it has slides 4 inches wide, magnifying picture to about 4 feet in diameter. Each..$5.60

One dozen fancy colored slides are furnished with each of the above lanterns; for extra slides see list of juvenile slides. Extra glass chimneys for above lanterns, 25c, 30c, and 35c each, depending on the size. We furnish free of charge with the above lanterns a quantity of admission tickets and show bills.

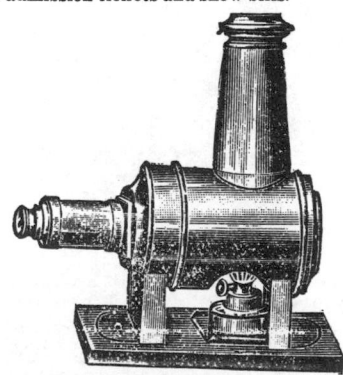

No. 61010.

**No. 61010.** The "Brilliant" Magic Lantern. It is highly finished entirely in brass, mounted on polished wood stand, with staff head, six long glass slides 1⅜ inches wide, four views on each slide and three glass discs with six views on each disc. The picture

is magnified to about two feet in diameter. Packed in a neat box, with handle and hooks, as shown in cut. Each...........................$1.75

**No. 61011.** The "Brilliant" Magic Lantern, same as above, but has six long glass slides, 1¾ inches in diameter, four views on each, with three glass discs, six views on each, magnifying pictures to about three feet in diameter, complete in box. Each........$3.50

**No. 61012.** The "Brilliant" Magic Lantern, same as 61010, but has six long glass slides two inches wide, with four views on each and three glass discs, six views on each, magnifying the pictures to about four feet, complete in box. Each..................$4.50

For extra slides see list of juvenile slides further on. With the above lantern we furnish admission ticket and show bills free of charge.

No. 61025.

**No. 61025.** The New "Gem" Magic Lantern. This lantern is especially adapted for amateur parlor exhibitions; is handsomely japanned, has nickel-plated lens tube, brass trimmings, and 2-wick kerosene lamp, high illuminating power. With each lantern we furnish show bills, admission tickets, one fire work chromatrope, one colored comic slip slide, two movable sceneries, in which the figures are made to interchange and move about; 12 handsomely colored slides, with four views on each slide, slides 2 inches wide, magnifying the figures to about four feet in diameter. Each...................................$5.00

**No. 61026.** The New "Gem" Magic Lantern, same as the one described above, except that the views are 2¾ inches wide, magnifying the views to about five feet in diameter. Each......$6.75

**No. 61027.** The New "Gem" Magic Lantern, same as No. 61025, except that the views are 2¾ inches wide, magnifying pictures to about six feet in diameter. Each...................................$8.00

## MAGIC LANTERN SLIDES FOR JUVENILE LANTERNS.

These slides come from the manufacturers put up in boxes holding one dozen each. There are from three to five different series of views only. In ordering extra sets of slides, to prevent the possibility of your getting the same as you received before, you should state what subjects you have. We cannot fill orders for special subjects. All slides for juvenile lanterns are highly colored and are made up in combinations of very funny pictures, such as the Mother Goose Melodies, Nursery Tales, American and foreign scenery, etc

### PLAIN COLORED SLIDES.
Width 1⅛ inch, weight about 7 ozs.

No. 61035.

| | | | | | | |
|---|---|---|---|---|---|---|
| Per doz........................................ | | | | | | $0.35 |
| Width 1⅜ inch., weight about 7 ozs. Per doz... | | | | | | .45 |
| Width 1½ " | " | " | 10 " | " | " | .50 |
| Width 1¾ " | " | " | 15 " | " | " | .60 |
| Width 2 " | " | " | 1¼ lbs. | " | " | .90 |
| Width 2⅜ " | " | " | 1¼ " | " | " | 1.00 |
| Width 2¾ " | " | " | 2½ " | " | " | 1.50 |
| Width 3⅛ " | " | " | 3 " | " | " | 1.75 |

### MOVABLE SLIDES WITH COLORED COMIC PICTURES.

No. 61036.

| | | |
|---|---|---|
| Width 1½ inches...........Each, 10c; per doz., | | $1.00 |
| Weight 1¼ lbs. per doz. | | |
| Width 1¾ inches...........Each, 14c; per doz., | | $1.50 |
| Weight 1¾ lbs. per doz. | | |
| Width 2⅜ inches...........Each, 20c; per doz., | | $1.75 |
| Weight 2 lbs. per doz. | | |
| Width 3½ inches...........Each, 25c; per doz., | | $2.50 |
| Weight 3¾ lbs. per doz. | | |
| Width 4 inches...........Each, 35c; per doz., | | $4.00 |
| Weight 4½ lbs. per doz. | | |

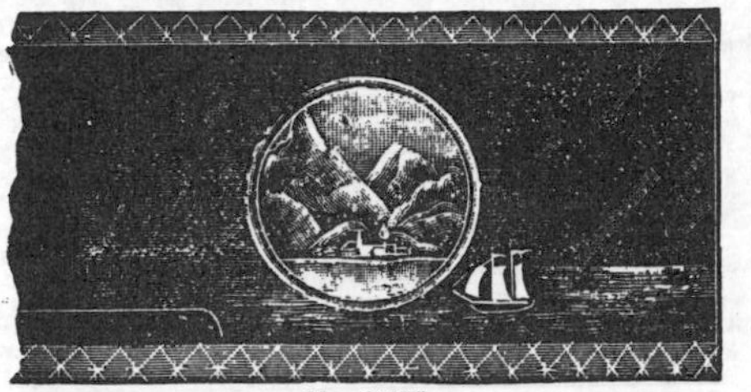

No. 61037.

## MOVABLE SLIDES WITH COLORED LANDSCAPES.

No. 61037. Such as a train moving across a bridge, boats sailing across a river or lake, etc. The object which moves passes along the entire distance of the landscape and disappears.

Width 1¾ inches............Each, 20c; per doz., $1.80
Weight 1 lb. per doz.

Width 2⅜ inches............Each, 25c; per doz., $2.80
Weight 1½ lbs. per doz.

Width 3⅛ inches............Each, 50c; per doz., $5.50
Weight 2 lbs. per doz.

Width 4 inches.............Each, 75c; per doz., $7.20
Weight 4½ lbs per doz.

The 3⅛ and 4-inch views can be used in the professional lanterns also.

Lantern slides cannot be sent by mail, they should be sent by express.

## "BRILLIANT" MAGIC LANTERN SLIDES.

No. 61041. The cheapest outfit of slides for amateurs' lanterns on the market. These are transparencies printed on mica, giving a class of pictures never before offered in anything but high priced slides; they are two inches wide and are substantially bound with metal, and so perfectly transparent that low priced lanterns will show them up with a great brilliancy. They can be used in any lanterns that will take slides two inches in diameter or larger, but when used with larger lanterns they must be used with a carrier, which can easily be made of pasteboard or light wood, so as to center them before the lenses. Each series consists of 12 slides, with three pictures on each slide, making 36 views in all.

Series A—Noted places around the World, 36 views, per set.............................................50c

Series M—American and Foreign Scenery, 36 views, per set.............................................50c

Series H—Bible Views, spirited drawings from the Old and New Testaments, 36 views, per set........50c

Series B—Miscellaneous views, 36 views, per set. 50c
(These are mostly very comic views.)

Series "I"—Comic, each one good for a smile, per set.............................................50c

## GEOMETRICAL CHROMATROPE SLIDES.

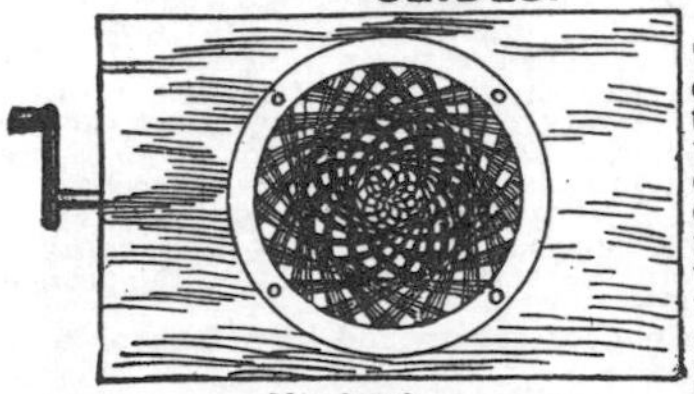

No. 61042.

No. 61042. These slides consist of two transparent wheels painted with geometrical radiations and revolved by means of a small crank in opposite directions, which produces a highly illuminated and very brilliant effect.

| | | | | |
|---|---|---|---|---|
| Width, | 1½ inch. | 2⅜ inch. | 3⅛ inch. | 4 inch. |
| Price, | 35c. | 50c. | 75c. | $1.00 |

The postage on the 4-inch slide, 7c., on the others, 5c. each.

## THE POLYOPTICON.

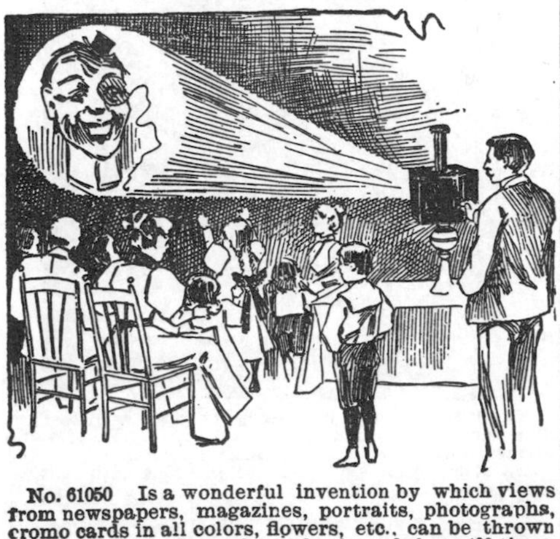

No. 61050 Is a wonderful invention by which views from newspapers, magazines, portraits, photographs, cromo cards in all colors, flowers, etc., can be thrown upon a screen in the parlor and enlarged about 400 times One is always finding cuts in magazines or pictures on cards that would make a pretty parlor exhibition if they could only be thrown upon a sheet by some means that would not be too complicated or costly. In the invention of the polyopticon this problem has been solved. It throws pictures upon a screen or wall four to five feet in diameter.

The instrument consists mainly of two wooden boxes, with highly polished nickel plated brass reflector, lamp and burner, large lens, and a door so swung that the exhibition of pictures, when properly cut and mounted, is very convenient and speedy. The wooden boxes are preferable to metal for this reason that they do not become too hot to handle; there are special means for ventilating and cooling not possessed by any other magic lantern apparatus.

Polyopticon parties are becoming very popular in both city and country. Each guest will bring with him a few of the ordinary advertising cards and a photograph, or natural flowers, whereby an entire change of views can be seen every evening.

Over 100 plain pictures are furnished with each Polyopticon, thus affording a number of diversified subjects for immediate use, including, Around the World in 80 sights; Bible pictures (Old and New Testaments), Ancient and Modern Statues, Portraits of Prominent Persons, Illustrations from Robinson Crusoe, Illustrations of a Temperance Lecture, Comical German figures in Procession, Silhouettes, Animals, Insects, Fishes, Birds, Comic Scenes, Balloons, Transformations, etc.

Price of the Polyopticon and 100 pictures, complete, each $4.40. Weight, complete, about, 3½ lbs.

Extra pictures (series No. 2 or 3), colored, over 100 different subjects, each series.............................50c

## PROFESSIONAL MAGIC LANTERNS.

Magic Lanterns are now being used for the purpose of illustrating lectures, showing up foreign and domestic scenery, by Sunday schools, for illustrating Bible scenes, by secret societies for illustrating the different signs of the order together with the history of the same, by colleges for illustrating scientic views, miscoscopic pictures, by both the amateur and professional theatrical companies and in fact its use is almost unlimited. There is in every locality an opening for someone to do a good business in giving exhibitions in the way of public entertainments to Sunday-schools, churches, families, etc. They are usually given on the shares for the use of the hall, church or Sunday school room. There is practically no expense connected with the business and it is very remunerative.

As a means of raising funds for Churches, Sunday schools, etc., we know of no better method than by giving magic lantern exhibitions, and the nature of the views used can be strictly in accordance with the ideas of the congregation.

We are at all times ready to give suggestions or information to those about to engage in the business, and all questions will be cheerfully answered by a thoroughly competent person.

All professional lanterns are quoted without slides. Slides must be purchased extra, and will be found listed after the magic lanterns.

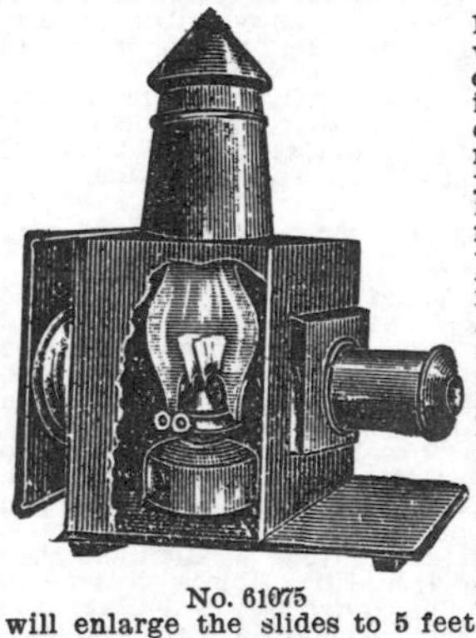

No. 61075

No. 61075. **The Duplex Lantern**, while low in price, combines good quality and simplicity in construction. It is made of metal, with japanned body 6x8 inches square and is mounted on a neat walnut base 7x14 inches. It is provided with an improved duplex lamp using kerosene oil, and one first quality 3½-inch plano-convex condensing lens. One first quality double object glass which will admit any of the standard size professional slides listed further on and will enlarge the slides to 5 feet in diameter. Price complete without slides..............................$9.50

No. 61076. A pair of No. 61075 lanterns arranged together on one large base for dissolving views. Price complete.............................................$19.50

A dissolving view apparatus consists of two magic lanterns similar in construction, magnifying power, etc., and so placed that the views projected from both will cover exactly the same disc on the screen. By a simple device which is furnished with the lantern and called a dissolver the views proceeding from one lantern is gradually blended or dissolved into that proceeding from the other lantern; one view fades away and the other replaces it, the screen never being vacant and no handling of the views being perceived by the audience.

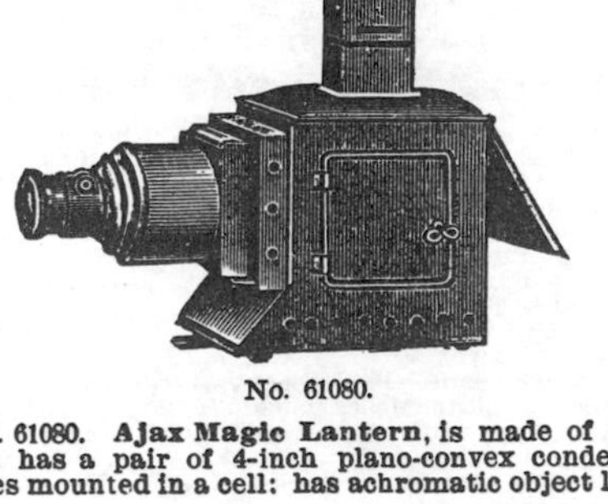

No. 61080.

No. 61080. **Ajax Magic Lantern**, is made of sheet iron; has a pair of 4-inch plano-convex condensing lenses mounted in a cell; has achromatic object lenses with rack and pinion for adjustment of focus, first quality three-wick lamp, sheet iron carrying case; is good quality throughout and will give excellent satisfaction. Price complete without views.........$15.00

No. 61085. **The Imperial Sciopticon** (similar to the Ajax) is made of Russian sheet iron, has extension fronts with brass hood, which shuts off all reflected and diffused light, spring clip for holding carrier with slide, patent Tri-unial lamp, the light of which is intensely white, the flame is regulated by an opening in the rear of the lantern through a tinted glass, which avoids confusing the sight, giving a picture about 10 feet in diameter. Has fine achromatic objective lenses, with rack and pinion for adjustment of focus; a pair of 4-inch plano-convex condensing lenses mounted in brass, adjusted to heat and cold (contraction and expansion). Packed in a neat Russian sheet iron case, which can be used as a stand for the lantern. Price complete without views..............................$20.00

NOTE--The above lantern can be furnished in matched pairs for dissolving views if desired. Prices quoted on application.

No. 61090. **The Peerless Sciopticon with Peerless Tri-Unial Lamp.** A most excellent lamp for public entertainment, army posts, societies, Sunday schools, etc. The Peerless is made of Russian sheet iron, has double body—the outer one being perforated to avoid heating. Extention front, with nickel plated hood which shuts off all diffused light, spring clip for holding carrier for slide; has patent tri-unial lamp—the light of which is intensely white. The flame is regulated by an opening in the rear of the lantern—

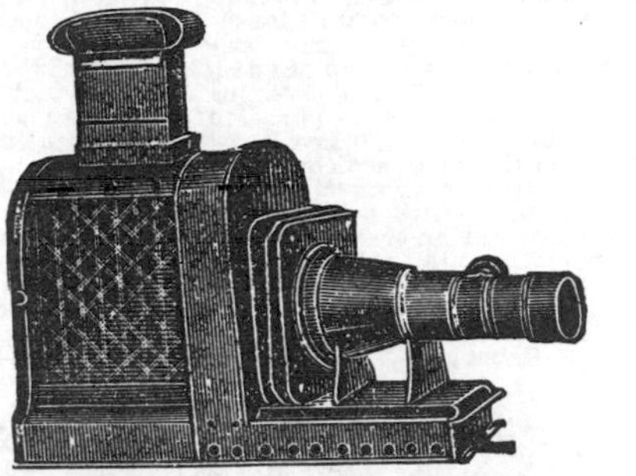

through a tinted glass which avoids confusing the eyesight, and gives a uniform 10-foot sharp cut picture at a distance of about 18 feet from the screen. Has fine Achromatic Objective Lenses, with rack and pinion and adjustment for focus; a pair of 4-inch plano-convex condensing lenses for condensing the light upon the view, mounted in brass. The mounting for the condensing lenses is adjusted to heat and cold (expansion and contraction) which is a safeguard against possible breakage of lenses. The lantern is packed in a neat Russian sheet iron case, with rack which can be used as a stand for the lantern. Price, complete, without views, each........................................$27.50

NOTE.—The above lantern, with opaque attachment No. 61092, is very extensively used by photographers for enlarging crayon portraits.

No. 61091. A pair of Peerless Sciopticons, with tri-unial

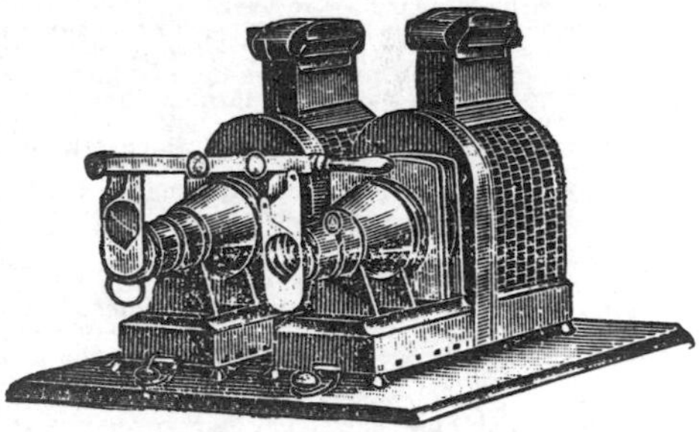

lamps mounted on wooden platform, with dissolving apparatus for dissolving views. Price, complete $60.00

For explanation of dissolving view apparatus, see note following No. 61076.

## OPAQUE ATTACHMENT.

No. 61092. A newly constructed apparatus which makes a very excellent accessory to lantern No. 61090, for parlor entertainments and class instructions; also for artist's use for enlarging photographs to life size, for crayon and portrait drawing, also for architects, draughtsmen and civil engineers. For obtaining working drawings of increased size, engravings, illustrations, watch movements, coins, medals, flowers, etc., can be shown affording an inexhaustible source of enjoyment. This is done by reflected light from the object, but does not however, equal in brilliancy that of the transparent glass magic lantern views. Price, each..............................................$4.75

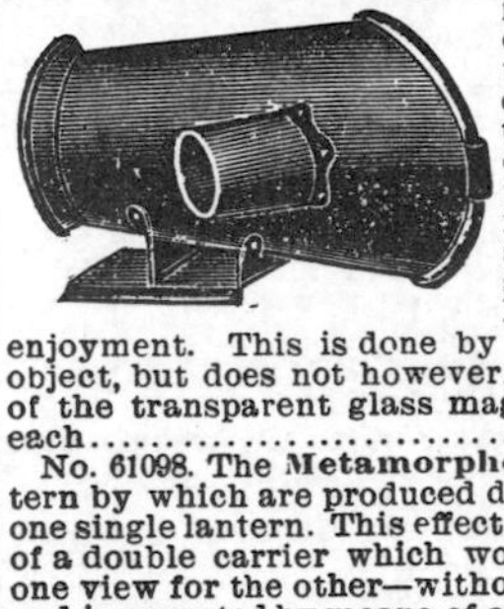

No. 61098. The **Metamorphoser**, a new patented lantern by which are produced dissolving effects from the one single lantern. This effect is accomplished by means of a double carrier which works vertically—changing one view for the other—without any interval between, and is operated by means of a lever. This enables one view after another to be shown, thus dispensing with the unsightly disc of light seen on the screen while changing the slides in an ordinary lantern.

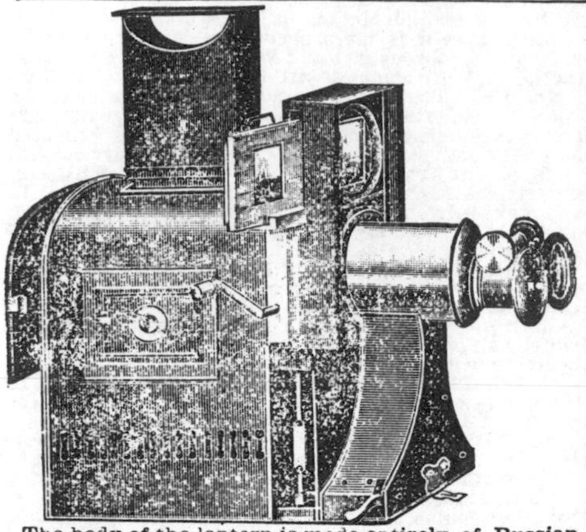

The body of the lantern is made entirely of Russian iron and riveted throughout with copper rivets, and the front tube and sliding O. G. tube for the lenses of solid brass beautifully finished and lacquered. The lantern is fitted with a 4-inch compound condensing lens mounted in a brass cell (two plano-convex lenses) and a one-fourth plate portrait lense front with specially large sized lenses in the back combination (thus giving greater light) and has double pinion to the rack attachment. It has also a high-grade 4-wick lamp with wicks 2 inches wide (placed to form two wedges like the letter "W" (M) inverted, thus preventing the flicker of the wicks seen on the screen when they are parallel to one another) and the tall jointed Russian iron chimney with a large oil can and filler; the oil can when not in use fits into the chimney, and the chimney then slides into the lantern body underneath the lamp, thus making the box into which the lantern is packed as small as possible. (Size 6x11½x15 inches.) Price for this most excellent lantern complete without views. Each....................$45.00

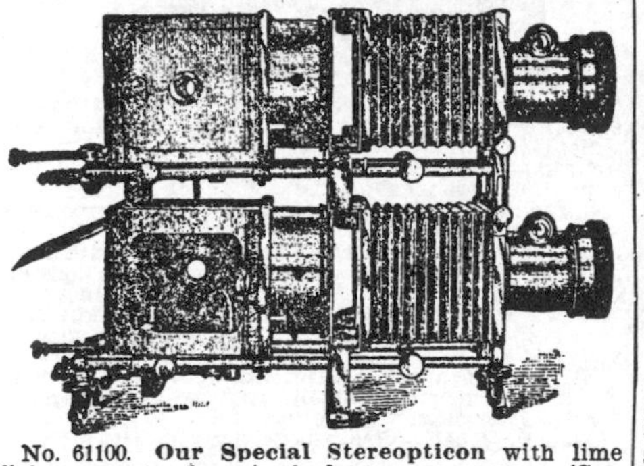

No. 61100. **Our Special Stereopticon** with lime light apparatus for using hydro-oxygen gasses. (Can also be used with lamps.) In response to the general demand for a cheaper instrument for use with hydro-oxygen gasses we have been induced to make special arrangements whereby we could furnish our patrons with an apparatus not only for less money than they have heretofore been sold, but one which we could guarantee in every respect.

In our Special Stereopticon we have included all of the good features of the higher-priced instruments and are in a position to offer an outfit which we can guarantee to give entire satisfaction. One of the special features of this lantern is the leather bellows with the sliding telescope frame arrangement which enables the lantern to be packed in a very small space. It has 4¾ inch condensing lenses of the best grade. The objective or front lenses are made by Darlot, of Paris. The jets are of brass with stop cocks and mechanical lime movement for revolving the limes. Price complete, including medium pressure dissolving key for using gasses from bags......$98.00

NOTE.—In the above lantern the dissolving effect is accomplished with the dissolving key which gradually extinguishes the light from one lantern while the light in the other lantern at the same time develops until one has been so far extinguished that only a blue flame remains, which gives no light and the other is turned out in full.

## GAS MAKING OUTFIT.

No. 61101. For a complete gas-making apparatus including bags for holding the gasses, the generating outfit, etc., ready for use, add to the above price $67.50. The production of gas for these outfits is very simple and costs but a few cents for the light of an evening's entertainment. The light from a gas outfit is intensely white and approaches nearest in intensity to an electric arc light.

Lime light is used almost exclusively in the fancy stage effects in the theatres. For further details on limelight outfits, professional views, etc., see our Special Magic Lantern Catalogue.

## CONDENSING LENSES FOR MAGIC LANTERNS.

Condensing lenses are those which are used between the light and the view for condensing the light for the purpose of increasing the intensity.

No. 61120. **Plano-convex lens,** diameter 3½ inches. Each....................$2.40

No. 61121. **Plano-convex lens,** diameter 4 inches. Each....................$2.85

No. 61122. **Plano-convex lens,** diameter 4½ inches. Each....................$3.75

No. 61123. **Plano-convex lens,** diameter 5 inches. Each....................$5.70

All of the above are single lenses.

## CONDENSING LENSES IN PAIRS MOUNTED IN TIN.

The pairs are very much stronger than the single lenses and are used in the higher priced lanterns.

No. 61125. **Plano-convex lenses,** diameter 3½ inches. Each....................$5.25

No. 61126. **Plano-convex lenses,** diameter 4 inches, Price....................$6.15

No. 61127. **Plano-convex lenses,** diameter 4½ inches. Price....................$7.95

No. 61128. **Plano-convex lenses,** diameter 5 inches. Price....................$11.90

## CONVEX CONDENSING LENSES IN PAIRS MOUNTED IN BRASS.

No. 61130. **Plano-convex lenses,** diameter 3½ inches. Price....................$6.65

No. 61131. **Plano-convex lenses,** diameter 4 inches. Price....................$7.65

No. 61132. **Plano-convex lenses,** diameter 4½ inches. Price....................$9.60

No. 61133. **Plano-convex lenses,** diameter 5 inches. Price....................$12.75

## SCREENS.

Our screens are made of the best white material with loops sewed on the four sides so that the frames may be dispensed with and the muslin hung up and drawn tightly by ropes attached to wall, window frames or other convenient support.

No. 61150. **Muslin screen,** 8 feet square, each..$2.75

No. 61151. **Muslin screen,** 10 " " " .. 4.00

No. 61152. **Muslin screen,** 12 " " " .. 6.50

Quotations furnished on larger sized screens if desired.

## LECTURER'S LAMP.

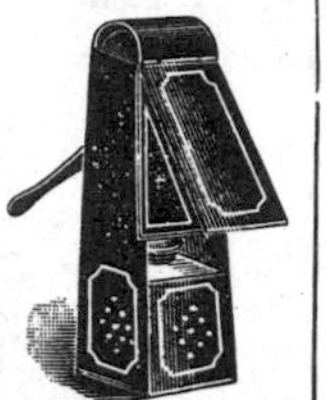

This lamp throws a sufficient amount of light for reading the lectures accompanying the views, and is so arranged that it will not illuminate the hall so as to interfere with the brilliancy of the views on the screen. Price complete..$2.25

## BOOK OF THE LANTERN.

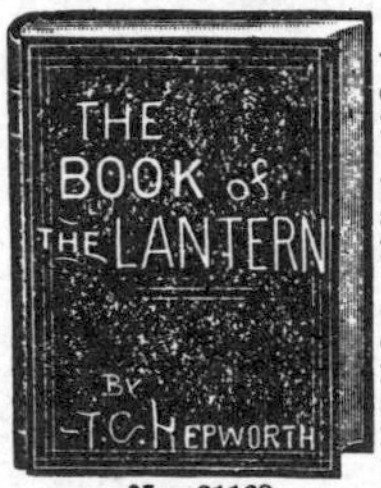


No. 61168.

No. 61168. This book is a very valuable assistant to anyone expecting to engage in the business or giving magic lantern entertainments. It gives full and precise directions for making and coloring lantern slides and manipulating the magic lantern, the size, appearance and value of the different lenses both condensing and objective in a business like way without being superficial. The book is written in such a way as to interest those who have a slight knowledge of the subject and without being too technical it gives a practical explanation of the minute details of construction and operation. Price each....................$1.80

## SLIDES OR VIEWS FOR MAGIC LANTERN AND STEREOPTICONS.

The regular size of slides for use in the Standard Magic Lantern is 3¼x4 inches, one view on each slide; but we have recently made arrangements whereby we are able to offer a very desirable collection of slides, known as the Gem Slides which have three views on each slide and we can sell the slides at 45 cents each. This reduces the price of each view to 15 cents, while the regular slides cost 45 cents for each view. The Gem slides are 2½ inches wide by 8 inches long and each slide has three views each 2 inches in diameter. The quality of the views is beyond question and they will make a picture on a screen two-thirds as large as the regular 3¼x4 inch slides and they are suitable for use in any lantern having a slide stage not less than the width of the slide which is 2½ inches.

The list of Gem Slides comprises illustrations from Natural Scenery, History, Comic, Statuary, Temperance, the Bible, Anatomy, Astronomy, etc., topics of educational and special interest. They appeal particularly to lantern exhibitors who do not aspire to exhibiting on a large scale, to Schools, Sunday schools, amateurs and the home circle. We cannot guarantee the price to remain at 45 cents; it is liable to advance at any time.

We quote herewith a list with abridged descriptions of the Gem Slides. For detailed list, see our Special Catalogue on Magic Lanterns.

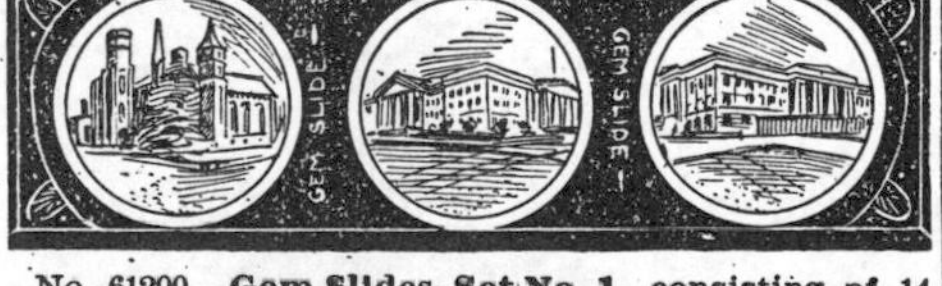


No. 61200. **Gem Slides, Set No. 1,** consisting of 14 slides, 42 pictures, including landscape views, buildings, etc., from 1, America; 2, England; 3, Venice; 4, Ireland; 5, Switzerland; 6, Constantinople; 7, Egypt; 8, Jerusalem; 9, Germany; 10, Russia; 11, Scotland; 12, Rome; 13, Rome; 13, Paris.

Price of each slide....................45c

Price per set of 14 slides....................$6.30

No. 61201. **Gem Slides, Set No. 2.** Scripture, 6 slides, 18 pictures.

15, Joseph Sold. 16, Rebecca at the well. 17, The Annunciation, 18, Moses Saved. 19, Baptism of Christ. 20, Last Supper. Price each slide....................45c

Price per set....................$2.70

No. 61203. **Gem Slides, Set No. 4.** The Bottle, 3 slides, with nine pictures.

25, The bottle for the First Time. 26, Unable to obtain employment. 27, The Husband kills His Wife

Price each slide....................45c

Price per set....................$1.35

No. 61204. **Gem Slides, Set No. 5.** Ten Nights In a Bar Room, 4 slides with 12 pictures. 28, Arrival at the "Sickle and Sheaf;" 29, Joe Morgan with Delirium Tremens; 30, Willie Hammond Induced to Gamble; 31, Frank Slade Kills His Father. Price each slide...45c

Price per set....................$1.80

No. 61205. **Gem Slides, Set No. 6.** Statuary Roger's groups, etc., 9 slides with 27 pictures. 32, Rip Van Winkle at Home; 33, Thorwaldsen's Gems; 34, Thorwaldsen's Gems; 35, Parting Promise; 36, Mail Day; 37, The Bushwacker; 38, We Boys; 39, Eve before the Fall; 40, Serenade. Price each slide....................45c

Price per set....................$4.10

No. 61206. **Gem Slides, Set No. 7,** miscellaneous. 9 slides with 27 pictures. 41, The Ill Fated Ship; 42, Fate of the Steamship; 43, Fort Sumter in Peace; 44, Bay of Naples and Mt. Vesuvius; 45, Courtship of the Second Wife: 46, The First Meeting; 47, Frigid Zone; 48, Steamboat Race on the Mississippi; 49, Sick Monkey. Price each slide, plain....................45c

Price per set, plain....................$4.10

No. 61207. **Gem Slides, Set No. 8,** comic, 6 slides, 18 pictures. 60, Romance; 61, Bulldozing; 62, Dey Say I Can't—But I'se Gone Done It; 63, Nip and Tuck; 64, Come Into the Garden, Maud; 65, 'Twere Vain to Tell Thee All I Feel. Price per slide, plain....................45c

Price per set, plain....................$2.70

No. 61208. **Gem Slides, Set No. 9,** United States History, etc., 5 slides, 15 pictures, 66, Landing of Columbus; 67, Penn's Treaty with the Indians; 68, Declaration of Independence; 69, Capture of Major Andre, 1770; 70, "Old Abe After the Battle." Price per slide, plain..45c

Price per set, plain....................$2.25

No. 61210. **Gem Slides, Set No. 12,** comic, 3 slides, 9 pictures. 89, Another Negro Rising; 90, Poor Donkey; 91, The Three Graces. Price per slide........45c

Price per set....................$1.35

No. 61213. **Gem Slides, Set No. 15.** Rip Van Winkle, 2 slides, 6 pictures.

100. Rip Van Winkle with the Children, 101. Rip Van Winkle on the Mountains. Price per slide...45c

Price per set....................90c

No. 61215. **Gem Slides, Set No. 17,** Uncle Tom's Cabin, 4 slides, 12 pictures.

104. George Harris takes leave of his wife, 105. Uncle Tom sold and leaving his family. 106. George Harris resists the slave hunters. Each 45c; Set $1.80

107. Eva's dying farewell.

No. 61216. **Gem Slides, Set No. 19,** 6 slides, 18 pictures.

112, Creation of Light. 113, Saul and the witch of Endor. 114, Flight into Egypt. 115, Christ and the Samaritan Woman. 116, Christ preaching on the sea, 117. Saul on the way to Damascus.

Price per slide....................$0.45

Price per set....................2.70

## LECTURE SETS.

Our lecture sets consist of choice photographs used in carriers, each set accompanied by an interesting descriptive lecture. To render an exhibition thoroughly enjoyable a proper description of the views presented to the audience is an absolute necessity, and to obtain the exact information requires access to extensive libraries, books of travel, etc., beyond the reach of many. The following sets of views have therefore been arranged with an interesting lecture for each set covering the points of historical or other information necessary for the proper information of each view used, thus enabling a lecturer to go before an audience and fully describe the various scenes intelligently. Each view is on a slide 3¼x4 with a protecting or covered glass both sealed together and can be used in any of the carriers for any of the professional lanterns.

Lecture does not accompany slides when not ordered in sets.

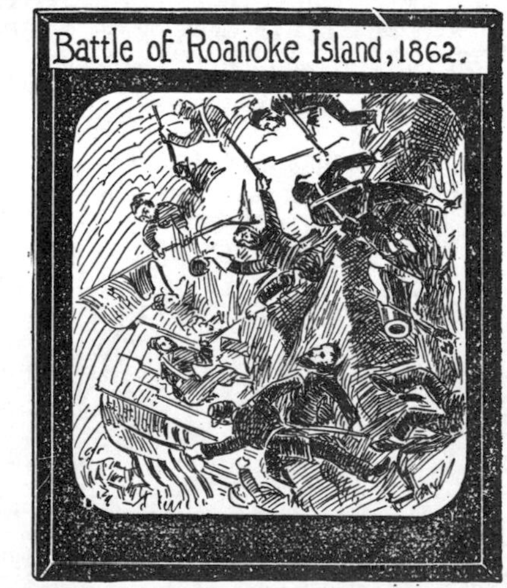


No. 61225. **Views of Venice.** 12 slides with lecture, Price complete....................$4.50

Price each....................42

No. 61226. **Views of London,** 12 slides with lecture. Price for complete set....................$4.50

Price each....................42

No. 61227. **Views of Paris,** 12 slides with lecture. Price for complete set....................$4.50

Price each....................42

No. 61228. **Views of Rome,** 12 slides with lecture. Price, per set complete....................$4.50

Price, each....................42

No. 61229. **Views of Germany and the Rhine.** 12 slides with lecture. Price, per set....................$4.50

Price, each....................42

## Lantern Slides—Continued.

No. 61230. **Views of Switzerland and Italy**. 12 slides with lecture. Price, per set ........ $4.50
Price, each ........ 42

No. 61231. **Views Here and There in the United States.** 12 slides with lecture.
Price, complete set ........ $4.50
Price, each ........ 42

No. 61232. **Views of Yellowstone Park,** 12 slides with lecture. Price, complete set ........ $4.50
Price, each ........ 42

No. 61233. **A Walk or Ramble About New York,** 12 slides with lecture. Price, complete ........ $4.50
Price, each ........ 42

No. 61234. **Views of Philadelphia,** 12 slides with lecture. Price per complete set ........ $4.50
Price, each ........ 42

No. 61235. **Views of Washington,** 12 slides with lecture. Price, per set ........ $4.50
Price, each ........ 42

No. 61236. **Views of Boston,** 12 slides with lecture, Price, per set ........ $4.50
Price, each ........ 42

No. 61237. **Views of Chicago,** 12 slides with lecture. Price, per set ........ $4.50
Price, each ........ 42

No. 61238. **Views of Richmond, Va.,** 12 slides with lecture. Price per set ........ $4.50
Price each ........ 42c

No. 61239. **Life of Christ,** plain, per set .... 6.00
Price per set colored ........ 11.50
Price, each ........ 1.00

No. 61240. **Mary Queen of Scotts,** plain per set ........ 4.00
Price colored, per set ........ 7.50
Price, each ........ 1.00

No. 61241. **Jack and the Beanstalk,**, size 3½ x 4 inches. Price per set, plain ........ 2.24
Price, each, plain ........ 35
Price, per set, colored ........ 4.25
Price, each, colored ........ 70

## SECRET SOCIETY VIEWS.

**Fine Colored Photographs.** Price, each, **$1.42** (Three inches in diameter, each view mounted in a slider 4 x 7 inches.)

## MASONIC.

No. 61242. **Entered Apprentice's Degree,** 14 views.
No. 61243. **Fellowcraft's Degree,** 7 views.
No. 61244. **Master Mason's Degree,** 16 views.
No. 61245. **Royal Arch Chapter,** 1 view.
No. 61246. **Commandery,** 4 views.
No. 61247. **Prelate,** 14 views.
No. 61248. **Grand Army of the Republic,** 20 views.

NOTE. The above views in plain square photographs not framed, price each ........ 1.42
Price per hundred ........ $40.00

## ODD FELLOWS.

**Fine Colored Photographs.** Price **$1.42** each. (Three inches diameter, each view mounted in a slide 4 x 7 inches.

No. 61249. Initiatory Degree, 4 views.
No. 61250. First degree, 2 views.
No. 61251. Second Degree. 5 views.
No. 61252. Third Degree, 4 views.
No. 61253. Encampment Emblems, 6 views.
No. 61254. **The Buildings of the Columbian Exposition,** 89 views. Price uncolored ........ $1.42
Price, colored, unframed, each ........

## CHICAGO.

Views consisting of prominent business houses, Masonic Temple, Parks, Boulevards, Residences. Theatres, Hotels, etc. Price, uncolored, each ... $ .42
Price, colored, unframed, each ........ 1.15

## CHOICE COLORED SLIDES WITH MOTION.

No. 61256. **Rat Catcher,** man sleeping, awakes and swallows one rat after another in quick succession, very laughable. Each ........ $3.25

No. 61257. **Mount Vesuvius Eruption;** throws out fire and smoke; good for one lantern. Each ..... $3.00

No. 21258. **Moving Waters,** represents the waters moving in the moonlight, a very beautiful and natural effect. Each ........ $2.25

No. 21259. **Good Night in Wreath.** A wreath of flowers in which appears a sleepy child in her night-gown holding a candle, she disappears and is succeeded by the words "Good Night." Each ........ $2.25

No 21260. **The Earth's Rotundity.** Proved by a ship sailing around the globe and a line drawn from the eye of an observer placed on an eminance.
Each ........ $3.00

No. 21261. **The Dancing Skeleton,** a new and striking effect. Each ........ $4.00

No. 21262. **Curtain Slide.** Represents the rolling up of a curtain, each ........ $3.00

No. 21263. **Swiss Water Wheel.** Wheel revolves, each ........ 3.00

No. 21264. **The Aquarium,** in which fish move about, each ........ 3.50

No. 21265, **The Bee-Hive,** surrounded by flying bees, each ........ 3.50

## CHROMATROPES OR ARTIFICIAL FIRE-WORKS.

These slides are singularly curious, the effect being very similar to that of the kaleidoscope. The pictures are produced by brilliant designs painted upon two circular glasses, and the glasses made to rotate in different directions. An endless variety of changes in the patterns are caused by turning the wheel—sometimes slowly, then quickly—backward and forward. Size, 4 inches wide.

No. 21266. **"The Geometrical"** Chromatrope, each ........ 1.50

No. 21267. **"The Geometrical"** Chromatrope, superior quality, each ........ 3.00

No. 21268. **"The Washington"** Chromatrope, each ........ 3.75

No. 21269. **"The Lincoln"** chromatrope, each ... 3.75

No. 21270. **"The Good Night"** Chromatrope, each ........ 3.75

No. 21271. **"The Garfield"** Chromatrope, each ... 3.75

## COMIC CRAYON CARICATURES.

Plain photographs, size 3¼x4 inches. Can be used in carriers we list. Price per hundred ........ $40.00

No. 61272. Comic crayon caricatures, 30 views. Each ........ 42

## MOVABLE COMIC VIEWS.

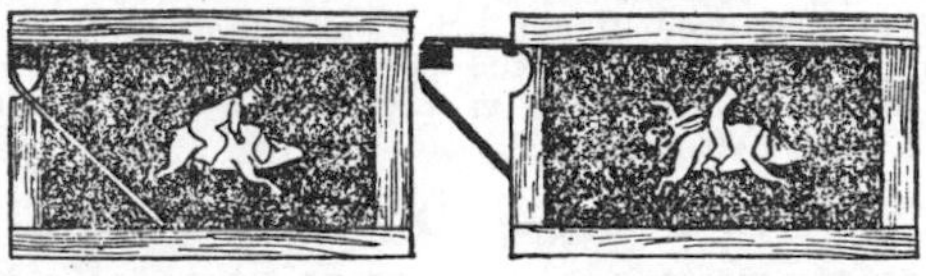

On slides 4x7 inches. Highly colored with fantastic life-like and unexpected motions to the figure. The movement is produced by a portion of the figure being painted on a glass plate which is quickly drawn to one side, giving the above effect.

No. 61273. **Movable Comic Views,** 50 different subjects. Price each ........ $0.55
Price per dozen ........ 6.25

For an itimized list of any of the preceding series, also a large additional list of views, see our Special Magic Lantern Catalogue.

## GRAPHOPHONES OR TALKING MACHINES.

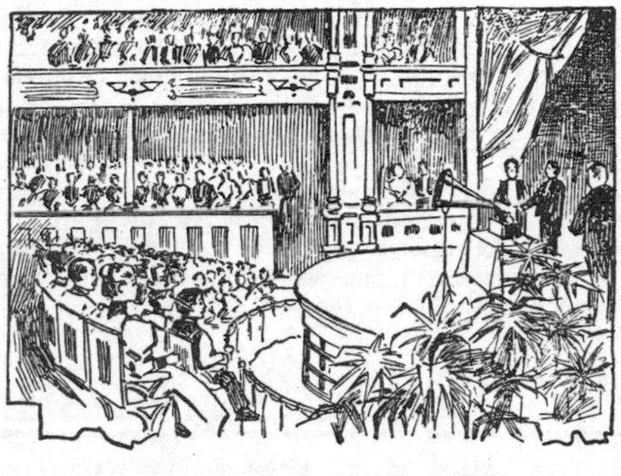

**A Graphophone Exhibition.**

You can hear in your own home all of the latest songs, instrumental music, speeches, etc., from the best artists in the metropolitan cities. The Graphophone or Talking Machine is a most wonderful invention, but until recently the prices were so high that their use has not become very general. All this is now changed and they are becoming so popular that thousands of private families are purchasing them for home entertainment. They also afford a most excellent means for money making by traveling from place to place and giving public exhibitions. By using the horn they can be distinctly heard in every part of a large hall. An outfit with records complete for an evenings entertainment can be purchased for a small amount of money. We list here but one style of machine, but the coin-in-the-slot machines as well as a large variety of records, etc., will be found listed in our special phonograph catalogue, which will be sent on application.

**Graphophones, records, etc., will be sent C. O. D.** when desired, on receipt of $2.00 with order as a guarantee of good faith. The balance can be paid at the express office after having examined the goods, but we advise sending the full amount of cash and save the 3 per cent. discount, also the return charges on the money.

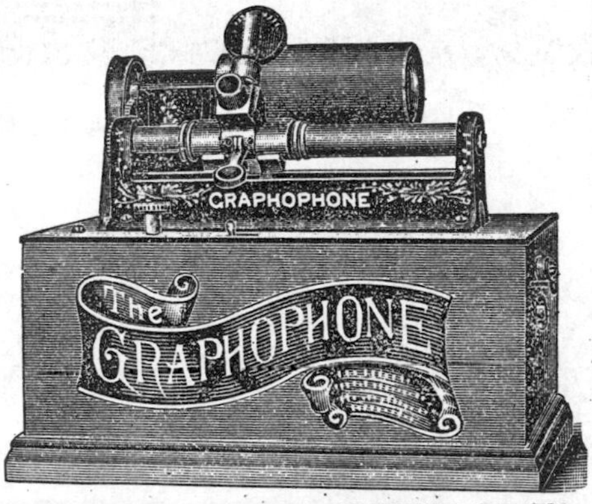


## OUR HOME ENTERTAINMENT OR EXHIBITION OUTFIT.

No. 6400. Our **Home Entertainment or Exhibition Outfit** consists of the following pieces:

One graphophone talking machine and oak carrying case, one recording diaphragm, one automatic extra loud reproducing diaphragm, one speaking tube, one bottle of oil and one screw driver, complete .... $25.00
12 Musical and Talking Records, your own selection ........ 6.00
1 Hearing Tube for three persons ........ 3.00
1 Small Horn for concert work ........ 1.00

Price of outfit complete ........ $35.00

On the complete outfit we will allow a special discount of three per cent. for cash in full with order. The above machine is so much simplified that anyone can operate it. The motor is a very simple arrangement which is wound up by a detachable crank in a similar manner to a musical box. The cover is fastened by safety hooks, and when attached makes a complete carrying case with handle. An instruction book accompanies each outfit, and they are guaranteed to give entire satisfaction. The recording diaphragm can be used to make any records desired, which can be made on blanks furnished for the purpose. Any of the records can be shaved off many times and others put on.

## CARRYING CASE.

No. 6445. **Canvas Carrying Case,** for holding 36 records. Each ........ $5.00

No. 6447. Blank Cylinder, made of wax, for the phonograph or graphophone. Each ........ 20c

No. 6448. Same as above, but prepared for recording music. Each ........ 25c

No. 6449. **The Bijou.** A new shaving device for shaving off old records to prepare them for new. Each ........ $5.00

## MUSICAL AND OTHER RECORDS READY PREPARED.

We have a large list of records, including the latest songs, instrumental music, dances, speeches, etc., but for want of space will list but a few of them.

Those who are interested should send for our special phonograph catalogue if a larger selection is wanted than the list following.

The list of records we quote here includes the latest and best pieces, and we would advise that you either make your first selection from the same or leave it to us and we will select for you.

**Price 50 cents each.** A special discount of 5 per cent. will be allowed when ordered in lots of one dozen or more. This is in addition to the 3 per cent. discount for cash with order.

**Opera Selections.**

From Issler's Orchestra.

List No.

Anvil Chorus (from Il Trovatore) ........ 21
Flower Song (Blumenthal) ........ 19
Intermezzo from Cavaleria Rusticana ........ 1
Selection from Bohemian Girl ........ 12
Selection from Erminie ........ 6

**John Philip Sousa's Marches.**

El Capitan March (the march from the final of the second act) ........ 23
Directorate (Sousa) ........ 159
Honeymoon March (hit of the season) ........ 150
King Cotton (Sousa's greatest) ........ 195
Liberty Bell ........ 166
Manhattan Beach ........ 167
Marching Through Georgia ........ 178
'Rastus on Parade (great) ........ 188
Washington Post ........ 176

**U. S. Marine Band.**

**Marches.**

High School Cadets ........ 826
Manhattan Beach ........ 834
The Directorate ........ 833
Washington Post ........ 825

**Waltzes.**

Beautiful Blue Danube ........ 102
Gasperone ........ 107
Gypsy Baron (by Strauss) ........ 61
Lion du Bal ........ 87
Nanon Waltz ........ 83
The Sirens ........ 62

**Lancers and Quadrilles.**

Furtuna Lancers (with calls) ........ 752
Gems of Ireland (Quadrille with calls) ........ 753
Gaiety Girl Lancers ........ 750

**Lancers, with Calls.**

Apollo (one of the best) ........ 258
Little Trooper (Della Fox) ........ 256
Merry Monarch ........ 267
Trip to Chinatown ........ 263
Wang ........ 259

**Quadrilles, with Calls.**

Æolian ........ 302
Right In It ........ 303

**Polkas.**

Laughing Polka (this is great) ........ 333

**Gavotte.**

Little Beauty ........ 354

**Schottisches.**

Little Irish Queen (with Cornet Solo, Dana) ........ 426
Trilby (the craze) ........ 425

**Songs and Dances with Clog Effects.**

Alabama Coon ........ 460
Darky Shuffle ........ 461

**Plantation Melodies, with Clog, Shouts, Etc.**

Cocoanut Dance (with imitations) ........ 483
Kentucky Jubilee Singers ........ 481
Virginia Skedaddle ........ 478

**Miscellaneous.**

And Her Golden Hair was Hanging Down Her Back . 510
Dixie ........ 507
Midway Dance du Ventre ........ 506
She May Have Seen Better Days ........ 539
Sidewalks of New York ........ 524
There is Only One Girl in the World for Me (latest hit) ........ 500
Rock-a-Bye Baby ........ 894
Cotton Pickers (with clog) ........ 776

**Cornet Solo by D. B. Dana.**

Home, Sweet Home ........ 1756

**Cornet Solos by W. S. Mygrant.**

Emmett's Lullaby ........ 1809
Old Black Joe (with variations) ........ 1814

**Cornet Solo by W. P. Chambers.**

Nearer My God to Thee ........ 1851

**Clarionet Solo by Wm. Tuson.**

Old Kentucky Home ........ 1901

**Banjo Duet, Mays and Hunter.**

Memories of Dixie ........ 2262

# OUR ORGAN AND PIANO DEPARTMENT.

Our aim is to put high grade Organs and Pianos on the market at less money than they can be sold to any other concern. **To furnish our customers strictly high grade instruments at less money than the retail dealer can buy, and for far less money than other catalogue houses quote them.** In order to do this we have contracted with two of the largest makers in the country for their entire output of high grade organs and pianos. Our organs and pianos should not be classed with the cheap, poorly constructed instruments which are being so extensively advertised, but we do invite a close comparison of our instruments with any of the high class standard makes in the market. We build them on honor, send them out on trial, send a most binding ten years' guarantee, and for quality, beauty, style and price, **WE DEFY COMPETITION.**

## ——OUR SPECIAL TERMS AND CONDITIONS OF SHIPMENT——

We have so much confidence in the excellency of our instruments, and we are so anxious you should compare them with any instrument you can buy elsewhere, **WE MAKE THIS MOST EXTRAORDINARY OFFER. Send us $10.00 with your order** as a guarantee of good faith, and we will send any organ or piano to you by freight; you can examine the instrument at the depot, and if found perfectly satisfactory and exactly as represented pay the agent our price and freight charges, less the $10.00 sent with order. If not satisfactory, **return it at our expense,** and we will refund your $10.00. After 30 days' trial, if you become dissatisfied with the instrument, return it at our expense and we will refund your money. **STILL ANOTHER OFFER.** Deposit with your banker the price of instrument wanted, take his receipt which should read as follows:

Received from Mr. ........................................................., ..................................................................,............Dollars in payment for one of Sears, Roebuck & Co.'s................................. I agree to hold this money until instrument has been received by Mr.................................... and he has had fifteen days' trial, when I shall forward the amount to Sears, Roebuck & Co., unless in the meantime Mr.................................... returns the instrument to Sears, Roebuck & Co., and presents railroad company's bill of lading for same to me, when I shall return all money to Mr.........................

--------------------------------------------------

Banker Signs Name Here.

**Send this receipt to us.** We will then ship the instrument direct to you, your banker will hold the money deposited fifteen days after arrival of instrument, during which time you can give it a thorough trial and if you are not in every way satisfied you can return the instrument to us, present the railroad company's receipt to your banker and he will refund all your money. **THREE PER CENT. CASH DISCOUNT.** We allow a discount of three per cent. if cash in full accompanies your order. If you send the full amount of cash with your order you may deduct three per cent. from our prices. The best way is to send cash in full with your order, for you not only save the three per cent. discount, but you save all trouble of making arrangements at your bank, and you save return charges on money to us if sent C. O. D. Nearly all our customers send cash in full, and take advantage of the three per cent. cash discount. Yet take no risk, for we will immediately refund your money if you are not perfectly satisfied.

**OUR BINDING TEN YEARS' GUARANTEE.** The longest, strongest and most binding guarantee given with any instrument, is sent with every instrument we sell. During the ten years if any piece or part gives out by reason of defect of material or workmanship, we will replace it free of charge.

**ABOUT THE FREIGHT.** In the introductory pages of this catalogue we quote a schedule of rates per hundred pounds by freight to various points in every state and territory. As the shipping weights are given with each instrument, you can readily estimate just what the freight will be. You will find that the transportation charges are a very small item and not worth considering when you think of the 30, 40 or 50 per cent. we save you in the price of the instrument. Pianos and organs are accepted by the railroad companies as first-class freight.

## THE SEARS, ROEBUCK & CO.'S PIANOS

Are instruments of great solidity, every part being thoroughly and honestly made. **The tone** is powerful, yet full, rich and sonorous. **Our cases** are double veneered and of very finest select hardwood, thoroughly kiln dried and seasoned. **Our pianos** contain full iron frame, covering the wrist plank, with the exception of the space occupied by the tuning pins. **Our wrist plank** is made of rock maple composed of a number of layers, with the grain running diagonally, which insures the piano keeping in tune. **The back** is of hardwood, containing six posts four inches square, each post being made of two pieces so glued together that the grains run different ways, which insures strength and solidity. **The action** is finely constructed, containing the best felts and materials to be had. It is double repeating, and regulated with a view of giving the piano a light, easy touch, so much desired by artistic players. **Only the most skilled labor** is employed, and the material used is the very best money can buy. There is no piano more honestly made, and wherever one of our pianos go people will have no other.

## OUR $125.00 S., R. & CO., SPECIAL PIANO. ‖ YOU CAN'T DUPLICATE IT FOR LESS THAN $300.00.

We send the piano to any address on receipt of $10.00, balance to be paid after piano is received. **We will ship piano to any address on fifteen days' trial, if $125.00 is deposited in your bank.** (See terms and special offer above.) **Three per cent. discount or $121.25 pays for the piano if cash in full accompanies your order.** We refund your money if you are not perfectly satisfied. Our binding ten years' guarantee goes with every piano. This piano is very large and showy. Height, 4 feet 8½ inches; width, 2 feet 3½ inches; length, 5 feet 3 inches; **weight, 800 pounds.** See the rate per 100 pounds for 1st class freight to points in your state. Multiply the rate per 100 pounds by 8 and you have the amount of freight on this piano to your place.

NO. 71.

....DESCRIPTION OF....

## OUR $125.00 PIANO.

### A REGULAR $300.00 INSTRUMENT.

**$125.00 IS THE PRICE IF SENT C. O. D., SUBJECT TO EXAMINATION. $121.25 IS THE PRICE IF CASH IN FULL ACCOMPANIES YOUR ORDER. YOUR CHOICE OF FINISH. FANCY IMPORTED ITALIAN BURLED WALNUT OR MAHOGANY AS DESIRED.**

**No. 71 PIANO** Seven and one-third octaves. Overstrung scale. Double roll fall board. Full swing music desk. Ivory or celluloid keys as desired. Polished ebony sharps. Fine hardwood case throughout. Beautifully carved panels. Fancy carved trusses. Tone excellent, full and round. Good action and hammers. Light, easy touch. You will be more than pleased with this beautiful, large upright piano. Think of the price, $125.00 C. O. D., or $121.25 cash with order. If you doubt our reliability, you are at liberty to send your order and money to the National Bank of Illinois, with instructions not to turn it over to us unless they know us to be perfectly reliable.

**DON'T YOU KNOW US? THEN ASK YOUR NEIGHBOR. NEARLY EVERY ONE KNOWS US AS THE CHEAPEST SUPPLY HOUSE ON EARTH. IT PAYS AS WELL TO KNOW WHERE YOU CAN BUY ON THE BEST TERMS, AS TO KNOW HOW TO BUY.**

NO. 72—ORDER BY NUMBER.

## No. 73. Our $169.00 Piano.

A piano that retails at $350.00 to $400.00. At $169.00 we send the piano C. O. D., subject to examination, on receipt of $10.00, balance, $159.00, and freight, to be paid after piano is received. Or we will send it to any address if you will deposit $169.00 in your bank to be held until piano has been received and you have given the instrument fifteen days' trial. **If you send cash in full** with your order, you may deduct 3 per cent. from our prices, when **$163.93 pays for the instrument.** You take no risk, for we will immediately refund your money if you are not perfectly satisfied.

A ten years' binding guarantee goes with every piano.

This is a picture of our Style C Piano at $169.00. The cut is engraved from a photograph, but no illustration we can show will begin to do the instrument justice. Size—Length, 5 feet 3½ inches; height, 4 feet 8½ inches width, 2 feet 4½ inches. Weight, when boxed, 850 pounds.

### Description of our $169.00 No. 73 Piano.

Seven and one-third octaves, Cabinet Grand, double veneered case, exquisitely finished, double roll fall board, full swing music desk. Beautifully carved panels of unique design, moulded ends, Queen Anne trusses, over-strung scale, ivory keys, polished ebony sharps, double repeating action, continuous nickel plated hinge on fall board, two pedals—in all a most beautiful instrument. Case is ebony finish and makes one of the finest appearing pianos on the market. **When you can buy a strictly high grade, extra large piano for $169.00,** and on such liberal terms, **there is no reason** in paying local dealers $300.00 to $400.00 for a piano of the same grade. Our system of selling direct from manufacturer to consumer on a one small profit plan, makes it possible for you to **own a high grade piano at less price than any dealer can buy.**

## OUR $159.00 S., R. & CO. PIANO.

Can't be had at retail for less than $350.00. At $159.00 we send the piano to any address, C. O. D., subject to examination. $154.23 buys the piano if cash in full accompanies your order. Nearly all our customers send cash in full and save the 3 per cent. cash discount. This is a very large, showy instrument. Height, 4 feet 6½ inches; width, 2 feet 4 inches; length, 5 feet 3¼ inches. $159.00 Piano is in fancy ebony case. We also furnish the piano finished in either Rosewood, Mahogany, Italian Walnut, Circassian Walnut or Quarter-Sawed Oak at $169.00, less 3 per cent. discount if cash in full accompanies your order.

### Description of our Special No. 72 $159.00 Piano.

See terms and conditions of shipment fully explained. You can have fifteen days' trial by depositing the price of piano with your banker, who will hold the money until you have received the piano and given it fifteen days' trial in your home. If it is not satisfactory return it to us and the banker will refund your money.

This Elegant Piano has seven and one-third octaves, double veneered case of artistic design, beautifully finished, handsomely carved panels, swinging music desk, fancy trusses, full iron frames and continuous hinge on fall board, ivory keys, polished ebony sharps, double repeating action, nickel plated rail, brackets and pressure bar, three pedals. Our $159.00 grade is finished in highly polished Ebony. At $10.00 extra we furnish this piano in Rosewood, Mahogany, Italian Walnut, Circassian Walnut or Quarter-Sawed Antique Oak.

If you order our Style B Piano at $159.00 you will not only be thoroughly satisfied, but every one who sees the instrument and learns the price of it will want one. Our motto is to make one instrument sell another.

NO. 73—ORDER BY NUMBER.

## Our Special, No. 74.

### Our $179.00 Upright Cabinet Grand Piano.

Money can't buy a better piano. Everyone who buys a Sears, Roebuck & Co. Piano speaks in the highest of praise of it. Our D Grade is the very finest we make and a magnificent instrument. This, our highest grade piano, is 5 feet 3½ inches long; 4 feet 8½ inches high, 2 feet 4½ inches wide. Weight, boxed, 800 pounds. You can tell what the freight will be by referring to introductory pages of this catalogue, where rate per 100 pounds is quoted to the different States.

### Description of our Finest Upright Grand Piano.

This piano is built without regard to necessary expense, a thoroughly honest and elegant instrument, very large, and makes a grand appearance.

Seven and one-third octaves, Full Cabinet Grand, double veneered case, exquisitely finished, double roll fall board, full swing music desk.

Beautifully carved panels of unique design, Queen Anne trusses, over-strung scale, ivory keys, polished ebony sharps, double repeating action, continuous nickel plated hinge on fall board, Sostenuto pedal. In all a most beautiful instrument.

At $179.00 we furnish this piano in fine ebony case.

For $189.00 we furnish the instrument in Rosewood, Mahogany, Italian Walnut, Circassian Walnut or Quartered Oak as desired.

If you send cash in full with your order you may deduct 3 per cent. from our advertised prices.

NO. 74—ORDER BY NUMBER.

ALL WE ASK IS A TRIAL ORDER TO SATISFY YOU THAT OUR GOODS ARE ALL THAT WE REPRESENT, AND THAT WE CAN SAVE YOU A LARGE PERCENTAGE ON EVERY PURCHASE. 5 PER CENT DISCOUNT ON ALL CASH ORDERS OVER $100.00.

No. 75.

# $38.95 Buys a $100.00 Parlor Organ.

We ship organs on the same terms and conditions as pianos, viz: **C. O. D.,** subject to examination, on receipt of $10.00, balance and freight payable after organ is received, or deposit $38.95 with your banker and send the receipt to us and we will send the organ on 15 days' trial. 3 per cent. discount allowed if cash in full accompanies your order. Our organs are built of the finest material and by the highest skilled mechanics, which materializes an organ with the softest touch, richest tone, and necessitates the least effort to operate. A binding ten years' guarantee goes with every organ.

No. 75. Order by number. Solid Quartered Antique Oak or Black Walnut, as desired. Height, 77 inches; length, 42 inches; depth, 23 inches. Weight, boxed, 400 pounds. Stool and instruction book free.

## Description of our No. 75, $38.95 Organ.

In putting this design on the market we do so to fill the demands of people who cannot afford to pay for our more elaborately designed organs, and yet insist on an organ with our superior action at a low price. The style of this case is entirely constructed with a view towards making a very presentable appearance, yet being inexpensive in the cost of the construction. To do this we are compelled to employ the latest, greatest labor-saving machinery, in the possession of which we lead all other factories. The case is made of Solid Oak or Walnut Lumber, thoroughly seasoned, handsomely carved, and finished with three coats of varnish and hand-rubbed in oil. The action is the same as in our most costly cases, made up of the best wires, leather, felts, etc.

Bellows are made of the best rubber cloth, and of three-ply bellow stock, and the finest sheep-skin leather in the valves.

Among the fittings of this organ you will find Bevel Face Celluloid Stop Knobs, Nickel Plated Pedal Frames, with best Brussels Carpets, Casters, Extension Lamp Shelf and Handles.

No. 75. Action 580, 5 Octaves. Contains 4 sets of Reeds, two of three Octaves, two of two Octaves each. Eleven (11) Stops, as follows: Diapason, Principal, Dulciana, Melodia, Celeste Cremona, Bass Coupler, Treble Coupler, Diapason Forte, Principal Forte, Vox Humana; 122 Reeds.

# $41.50 BUYS A $100.00 PARLOR ORGAN.

This organ retails at $100.00 to $125.00. For elegance of design, finish and durability you will find no organ equal to our S., R. & Co. instruments. A 10-years' guarantee with every organ. Your choice, Solid Antique Oak, Quartered, or Black Walnut.

Dimensions: Height, 77 inches; length, 42 inches; depth, 23 inches. Weight, boxed for shipping, 400 pounds.

Our special price, $41.50. Stool and instruction book free.

## Description of our No. 76, $41.50 Organ.

In putting this design on the market we do so to fill the demands of people who cannot afford to pay for our more elaborately designed organs, and yet insist on an organ with our superior action at a low price. The style of this case is entirely constructed with a view towards making a very presentable appearance, yet being inexpensive in the cost of the construction. To do this we are compelled to employ the latest, greatest labor-saving machinery, in the possession of which we lead all other factories. The case is made of Solid Oak or Walnut Lumber, thoroughly seasoned, handsomely carved, and finished with three coats of varnish and hand-rubbed in oil. The action is the same as in our most costly cases, made up of the best wires, leather, felts, etc.

Among the fittings of this organ you will find an elegant 10 x 16 inch Beveled French Plate Mirror, Bevel Face Celluloid Stop Knobs, Nickel Plated Pedal Frames, with best Brussels Carpets, Casters, Extension Lamp Shelf, and Handles.

No. 76. Action 580½, 5 Octaves. Contains 4 sets of Reeds, two of three Octaves, two of two Octaves each. Eleven (11) Stops, as follows: Diapason, Principal, Dulciana, Melodia, Celeste, Cremona, Bass Coupler, Treble Coupler, Diapason Forte, Principal Forte, Vox Humana; 122 Reeds. Stool and instruction book free. We make no charge for boxing or cartage.

No. 76.

**THE FREIGHT ON AN ORGAN SINKS INTO INSIGNIFICANCE WHEN YOU CONSIDER WHAT YOU SAVE. YOU HAVE TO PAY THE FREIGHT FOR THE RETAILER AND A BG PROFIT BESIDE WHEN YOU BUY THAT WAY. BETTER PAY $2.00 FREIGHT OUTRIGHT AND SAVE FROM $30.00 TO $60.00.**

## $44.00 Buys a $125.00 Organ.

Your dealer would ask from $100.00 to $125.00 for such an instrument. **Our price is $44.00**, and we send it to any address, C. O. D., subject to examination. A ten years' guarantee goes with every organ. Your choice, **Solid Antique Quartered Oak** or **Black Walnut**, as desired.

**DIMENSIONS:** Height, 77 inches; length, 42 inches; depth, 23 inches; weight boxed, 400 pounds. **Stool and Instruction Book free.** We make no charge for boxing or cartage.

### Description of our No. 77 Organ at $44.00.

This is a full sized, new designed, handsome Organ, with canopy top. It is profusely carved and ornamented. The turnings and scroll frets are of the latest and most popular design. The case is made of solid oak or walnut lumber, thoroughly seasoned, and finished with three coats of fine piano varnish and hand rubbed in oil. The action, as in all our organs, consists of the best grade of Reeds, Felts, Leathers, etc., obtainable, and are made only by highly experienced men, who produce the most accurate workmanship which is responsible for the best results alone. Bellows are made of the best rubber cloth and of three-ply bellows stock, and the finest sheepskin leather in the valves. Among the fittings of this organ you will find Bevel Face Celluloid Stop Knobs, Nickel Plated Pedal Frames, with best Brussels Carpet, Extension Lamp Shelf and Handles.

No. 77. Action, five octaves. Contains four sets of Reeds, two of three Octaves, two of two Octaves each. Eleven (11) stops, as follows: Diapason, Principal, Dulciana, Melodia, Celeste, Cremona, Bass Coupler, Treble Coupler, Diapason Forte, Principal Forte, Vox Humana; 122 Reeds. Price, **$44.00**.

**Stool and Instruction Book free.** We make no charge for boxing or drayage.

**NO. 77.**

## $51.00 Buys a $140.00 Parlor Organ.

**One of the Finest Organs on the market.** Our prices are at least 33 per cent. below all competition, and our instruments are the very finest it is possible to produce. Every Organ guaranteed for 10 years. Any Organ sent on Trial before paying. Your choice, Solid Antique Quartered Oak or Black Walnut DIMENSION: Height, 81 inches; length, 48 inches; depth, 24 inches. Weight boxed, 450 pounds.
Our Special Price with No. 78 Action......$51.00 } 3 per cent. discount if cash in
Our Special Price with No. 79 Action...... 54.00 } full accompanies your order.
  (Six Octave Organ $6.00 extra.) Stool and Instruction Book Free. We make no charge for boxing or cartage.

### Description of Our No. 78, $51.00 Parlor Organ.

In putting this design on the market the manufacturers realize that their conception of the ornamentation is entirely novel, and different from what has ever been produced in an organ before, and yet at the time of this writing, wherever it has been shown, it produced the greatest enthusiasm and approval. Nothing has ever been received with such favor. Description—The case is made in such a manner that its construction will be approved and admired by the most critical cabinet maker. The ends are paneled like those of the most costly piano, and the entire front or every large surface is paneled, which makes it impossible for any part to crack or warp, and gives it besides the most imposing appearance. The scroll work and carving is of the latest aesthetic design. The top for solidity is built on the same principle as the base, the beautiful canopy—which is a work of art and an ornamentation anywhere—is securely fastened to the paneled back and held by heavy pillars which are firmly secured on a very heavy base. The shelf which surrounds the French Plate Mirror is such that it harmonizes with the design throughout. The panels in the top are deeply carved, in fact all our ornamentation is cut into the wood. We have no "pressed" figures as are commonly used in organs because they are cheaper. This, as in the materials and construction of the interior, is of the highest grade obtainable. No cheapening will be considered. Our policy is to improve. The action is the feature to which we always point with pride. Through our especial facilities we are enabled to make it in such a way that it never varies in perfection. No two organs of the same grade have ever been found to vary in tone and effect. The felts, leather and wires we use are unequaled. The bellows are made of the best rubber cloth and three-ply built up stock, and are made after our improved system, which necessitates the least possible physical energy to operate the organ. The tone which these improved features develop is of the richest order. With the Dulciana and Cremona stops only in use you have a tone so soft, yet clear and distinct, so sweet that it suggests ethereal voices. Then add the various more powerful stops and you eventually reach the climax of a volume of music which in its power, beauty and grandeur have never been equaled. No. 78 Action. 5 Octaves. Contains 4 sets of Reeds, two of three Octaves, two of two Octaves each. Eleven (11) Stops, as follows: Diapason, Principal, Dulciana, Melodia, Celeste, Cremona, Bass Coupler, Treble Coupler, Diapason Forte, Principal Forte, Vox Humana; 122 Reeds. Price, $51.00. No. 79 Action. 5 Octaves. Contains 5 sets of Reeds, three of three Octaves, two of two Octaves. Thirteen Stops: Diapason, Principal, Dulciana, Melodia, Celeste, Cremona, Flute, Viola, Bass Coupler, Treble Coupler, Diapason Forte, Principal Forte, Vox Humana. Grand Organ and Knee Swell; 159 Reeds.
No. 79. This Organ with Action No. 79 ........................ $54.00
  (We furnish this Organ in 6 Octaves at $6.00 extra.)

**NO. 79.**

WHEREVER OUR GOODS ARE ONCE INTRODUCED WE HAVE NO TROUBLE IN SELLING TO OTHERS. WE UNDERTAKE TO HAVE OUR GOODS ADVERTISE US, AND THEY DO. ONE ORDER ALWAYS BRINGS ANOTHER.

## $56.00 BUYS A $200.00 PARLOR ORGAN.

**This is our Finest Organ.** No picture, no illustration, no description can do it justice. Money can't buy better. **Our Binding 10-Years' Guarantee** goes with every instrument. When you see this organ, you will wonder how it is possible to produce such an instrument at anything like the price. For a strictly High Grade Organ, an organ possessing the good features of all organs, with the defects of none, we recommend our No. 80 at $56.00. There is nothing finer.

To see and examine it, it is only necessary to send us $10.00, when we will send it to you by freight. You can examine it at the freight depot, and if found perfectly satisfactory, exactly as represented, and one of the most magnificent Organs you ever saw, pay the agent the balance, $46.00 and freight, and the instrument is yours. You have your choice, Solid Quartered Antique Oak or Black Walnut, as desired. Don't forget all our instruments are guaranteed for ten years. Other concerns give five year guarantees.

This Organ is 81 inches high, 48 in. long and 24 in. deep; weighs, boxed, 450 lbs.

No. 80. Our price, with No. 730 Action, is .................................. $56.00
No. 81. " " " 731 " " .................................. 60.00
No. 82. " " " 732 " " .................................. 66.00

Six octaves $6.00 extra. **Stool and Instruction Book Free.** No charge for boxing or cartage.

### DESCRIPTION OF OUR NO. 80 HIGHEST GRADE ORGAN.

The illustration of this style proves it to be a Case of the richest design, having an appearance of massiveness and solidity, yet being in accordance with good taste in its entirety. The raised carving and turning is of the heaviest order, the scroll work in the frets is of that peculiar pattern that harmonizes so well with the style of carving that we employ. It will be easily noticeable that every line of architecture of this Case has something in common with the others. The greatest feature of our Cases is their finish, on which is used three coats of the best piano varnish and hand rubbed in oil, giving it that superior finish found on pianos. The action, as in all our Organs, consists of the best grade of Reeds, Felts, Leathers, etc., obtainable, and are made only by highly experienced men, who produce the most accurate workmanship, for which the best results alone are responsible. The bellows are made of the best rubber cloth and three-ply built-up stock, and are made after our improved system, which necessitates the least possible energy to operate the Organ. These organs are fitted with a 10x16 inch Bevel French Plate Mirror and Bevel Faced Celluloid Stop Knobs, Nickel Plated Pedal Frames, Best Brussels Carpet and Extension Lamp Shelf.

**No. 80, Action No. 730.** Contains four sets of Reeds, two of three Octaves, two of two Octaves each. Eleven (11) Stops, as follows: Diapason, Principal, Dulciana, Melodia, Celeste, Cremona, Bass Coupler, Treble Coupler, Diapason Forte, Principal Forte, Vox Humana, Grand Organ and Knee Swell; 122 Reeds.

**No. 81, Action No. 731.** Contains five sets of Reeds, three of three Octaves, two of two Octaves each. Thirteen (13) Stops; Diapason, Principal, Dulciana, Melodia, Celeste, Cremona, Flute, Viola, Bass Coupler, Treble Coupler, Diapason Forte, Principal Forte, Vox Humana. Grand Organ and Knee Swell; 159 Reeds.

**No. 82, Action No. 732.** Contains eight sets of Reeds, four of four Octaves, four of two Octaves each. Fifteen (15) Stops; Diapason, Principal, Dulciana, Melodia, Bourdon, Clarionet, Cornet, Cornet Echo, Cremona, Flute, Bass Coupler, Treble Coupler, Diapason Forte, Principal Forte, Vox Humana, Grand Organ and Knee Swell; 244 Reeds.

No. 81.

# OUR $36.90 CHAPEL ORGAN.

These Organs are especially adapted for Churches, Lodges and Halls. Made in solid oak or walnut as desired. Every Organ covered by a most **Binding 10 Years' Guarantee.**

The back is perfectly finished with handsome panels and fancy open fret work and presents a rich appearance. Height, 4 feet 2 inches; length, 3 feet 8 inches; depth, 2 feet. Weight, 300 pounds.

### DESCRIPTION.—OUR NEW $36.90 ORGAN.

In this Chapel Organ we present a style that being simple in design, should lack neither in dignity nor in a presentable appearance for any surrounding for which a Church Organ would be appropriate, and our assurance that we have succeeded, is attested to by the increasing demand for this particular style. Though its popularity is attributable in part to its outward appearance, yet most is due to the superior construction and finish of the action, which possesses properties that make a tone of the greatest delicacy, power and expression, and an almost perfect imitation of the small pipe organ, for which it has often been found a most satisfactory substitute. The case is made of solid Oak or Walnut lumber, thoroughly seasoned, handsomely carved, and finished on all sides with three coats of varnish and hand-rubbed in oil. The action is made of the best Wire, Leather, Felt, etc. Bellows are made of the best Rubber Cloth and three-ply built-up stock, and are made after our improved system, which necessitates the least possible physical energy to operate the organ. Among the fittings will be found Bevel faced Celluloid Stop Knobs, Nickel Plated Pedal Frames, with best Brussels Carpet, Extension Lamp Shelf and Handles.

**No. 83, Action 211. 5 Octaves.** Contains four sets of Reeds, two of three Octaves, two of two Octaves each. Eleven (11) Stops, as follows: Diapason, Principal, Dulciana, Melodia, Celeste, Cremona, Bass Coupler, Treble Coupler, Diapason Forte, Principal Forte, Vox Humana; 122 Reeds.

No. 83. Front view of our $36.90 Chapel Organ.

**ALL OUR ORGANS AND PIANOS ARE SPECIALLY FINISHED AT THE FACTORY BEFORE SHIPPING. IT REQUIRES FROM THREE TO SIX DAYS AFTER THE ORDER IS RECEIVED BEFORE SHIPMENT CAN BE MADE, EXCEPT IN CASE OF URGENT HASTE.**

# Musical Goods Department.

**No Department** in our **vast establishment** has grown more rapidly in popular favor than that of musical instruments. Under the **supervision of a competent and experienced manager,** our trade in this line has been cared for with the **greatest satisfaction** to ourselves and **our customers.** No better evidence of this fact exists than the second, third and constant orders from the same customer and orders from entirely new customers who have seen our goods in the hands of friends and neighbors. We have included in this department an assortment of musical instruments that positively has no equal for quality, cheapness and variety. We are better prepared than any other house in existence to serve you, not only by furnishing the best goods at the lowest prices, but we offer an assortment from which all tastes may be satisfied. Our terms are the most liberal of any. We are ready and willing and anxious that prospective purchasers may be sure of getting just the instruments they want. By our fair and easy C. O. D., subject to examination plan you may be sure of securing just the article that will suit you. Except when otherwise specified we will ship any instrument to any one, any where, C. O. D., subject to examination and approval, on receipt of $1 with order as a gurantee of good faith. You can examine the instrument at the express office, and if it is to your entire liking you can pay the agent the balance due, with charges, and the instrument is yours. Otherwise it can be returned to us and money will be refunded less express charges. Furthermore, in order that there may be the most entire satisfaction we shall allow you to return any instrument to us prepaid after five days' careful trial if you find that it does not meet your requirements.

Bear in mind three facts: Fact 1—All the instruments and sundries are imported by us directly from European manufacturers or purchased by us direct from the most reliable American manufacturers, and purchasers may rest assured that they are getting only the very finest goods it is possible to produce. Fact 2—Our prices are based on our one small profit plan, direct from manufacturer to consumer, and you own the goods at about what the retailer pays. Fact 3—Our terms are most liberal. We give you the same chance that the retailer does to see and examine the goods before paying for them. These three facts make it very plain that nowhere else can you get invariably select goods, nowhere else can you secure such low prices and nowhere else can you avail yourself of such fair and liberal terms.

☞ Remember, we allow a discount of 3 per cent. where cash in full accompanies order. It is better to send full cash, as you save the 3 per cent., besides the express company's charge for returning money to us. Our guarantee on the goods is just the same, and any article not satisfactory may be returned and money refunded.

☞ The line of musical merchandise is so enormous that even with the space allotted for same in this catalogue we cannot list everything. If you do not find just what you want quoted herein write us. We shall be pleased to give you net wholesale prices.

## Violins.

We can sell a violin for 44 cents, but we would not accept an order for the inferior instrument at that price. Those quoted below are up to the standard of quality demanded by critical buyers and are our own importations from largest and most reputable European manufacturers. Our entire confidence in these superior instruments prompts us to make the most liberal terms of sale. We will send any violin to any express office C. O. D., subject to examination, asking only a deposit of $1.00 with the order as a guarantee of good faith. If the instrument is not found satisfactory or not as represented, it can be returned to us and money refunded. We further agree that where full cash accompanies order, customer will have the privilege of returning the instrument to us, if, after **five days' trial,** it proves unsatisfactory. We appreciate the desire to secure a violin that will give the most pleasing results, and take this method of enabling customers to test the instrument just as fully as though examined in a retail store.

As to our prices, they speak for themselves. No one who has ever examined our Violins has failed to express the greatest surprise at the invariable high quality, at prices beyond all competition. For instruments of fine

model and finish, as well as for full, round, resonant and beautiful tone, our violins will stand in competition with any others in the world.

We include a valuable instruction book free with each instrument, and pack it in a pasteboard case. We list in this catalogue a very complete line of violin furnishings, at one-half to one-third retail prices. All sorts of violin furnishings quoted farther on in this book. Violins boxed weigh about 10 lbs.

**No. 725.** Genuine Salzard Model Violin; dark red color, polished, inlaid edges, full strung.
Price, each,_____$2.85

**No. 726.** Genuine Hopf Model Violin; brown color, swelled top and back, ebony fingerboard and tailpiece. Very excellent quality, full set of strings.
Price, each,_____$3.70

**No. 728.** Genuine Stainer Model Violin; reddish brown color, very highly polished and finished, ebony fingerboard and tailpiece. An instrument of remarkable tone and quality at a very low price. Full set of strings. Price, complete_____$5.25

**No. 730.** Genuine Stradivarius model Violin, light red or old amber color, shaded, highly polished, ebony fingerboard and tailpiece. Excellent neck, superior tone, full set of strings. Weight, boxed, 10 lbs.
Our special price_____$5.95

**No. 731.** German Violin, Italian School, Guarnerius Model; reddish brown color, very fine finish. A superior model violin that possesses a full, round bell tone of remarkable purity. Full set of superfine strings.
Our price, complete_____$6.25

**No. 733.** Genuine Stradivarius Model Violin; excellent imitation of old instrument, mottled reddish brown color, finished neck, ebony fingerboard and tailpiece. A very excellent instrument with an admirable tone. Full set of strings; weight, boxed, 10 lbs.
Our special price_____$7.95

**No. 736.** Grand Concert Violin; genuine Stradivarius model, and a fine imitation of an old instrument, so sought after by connoisseurs and artists. Reddish brown color, oil varnished, ebony fingerboard and tailpiece. A most desirable model; producing a remarkably pure, sweet tone. Full set of superfine strings. Weight, boxed, 10 lbs. Our special price_____$9.30

**No. 738.** Genuine Maggini Model Violin; a model much sought after by professionals. Medium red color, double row of inlaying around edges. Very highly polished, ebony fingerboard and tailpiece; finely finished neck, superfine strings. We recommend this instrument to be equal to violins retailing at from $15.00 to $20.00. The tone is of exquisite purity and sweetness and will captivate any intending purchaser who may examine it. Weight, boxed, 10 lbs.
Our special price_____$8.00

☞ **Bear in mind that we send any violin C. O. D., subject to examination, on deposit of $1.00, Three per cent. discount when full cash comes with order. Remember that you may return any violin not found satisfactory after five days' trial.**

**No. 741.** "Vuillaume" Violin. This special professional violin possesses a decidedly pleasing tone, being full, round and resonant, bell-like in quality and at the same time rich and mellow. The model is a decidedly pleasing one, with an amber varnish finish in light red color, highly polished. The swelled back is made of one piece of selected maple; white edges, full ebony trimmed. The fine scroll neck is made of curly maple. Superfine strings. Weight, boxed, 10 lbs.
Our special price_____$12.20

**No. 742.** Genuine Stradivarius Model Violin; very fine imitation of old instrument, reddish brown color, finely finished and full ebony trimmed, Superfine strings, perfect finished neck. Very fine selected materials used throughout. An instrument that will prove most satisfactory to any purchaser, amateur or professional. Weight, boxed, 10 lbs.
Our special price_____$16.70

**No. 743.** Artist Violin is made by the most celebrated Berlin manufacturer, Henry Eichheimer. The model is very similar to the Stradivarius and is exceptionally handsome. It is a very handsome red color, richly oil varnished and polished. This violin has a fine scroll neck of small size and polished ebony trimmings throughout. The superior grade of material and expert workmanship render this instrument much sought after by artists and professionals, as well as by amateurs, by reason of its supurb quality of tone, which is ordinarily found only in violins retailing at from $50.00 to $75.00. Full set of superfine strings. Weight, boxed, 10 lbs.
Our special price_____$20.95

**No. 745.** The Celebrated Lowendall Conservatory Violin. This instrument has a justly earned reputation which has been built up by the genuine and unusual good quality. This quality is not intermittent, but every instrument is exceptionally fine. We import these direct from Europe, and although we have full and entire confidence in the rigid inspection before they leave the factory, we use the most extreme care in examination ourselves, that every instrument shall be perfection itself. The tone is superb. The finish is unexcelled. Comes in dark red color, very tastily finished, with full ebony trimmings. Sent C. O. D., subject to examination, on receipt of $1.00. Guaranteed positively as to quality and tone. Weight, boxed, 10 lbs. Our special price,_____$17.65

See our list of violin furnishings for selection of bows, cases and full line of extras at one-third dealers' prices.

**No. 747.** Lowendall's Imperial Violin. The most celebrated make. Superb model, amber oil varnish, beautifully finished, full ebony trimmings. This elegant instrument is the pride of many professional players, who place it ahead of any other make. It is an elegant violin for orchestra leaders. The tone is perfect in quality, being pure and bell-like, full, round, and resonant. We can recommend this violin to the most exacting and critical buyer, being assured that

our recommendation will be appreciated after the instrument has been put to a test. Full set of superfine strings. Weight, boxed, 10 lbs.
Our special price_____$36.55

☞ **We send any violin C. O. D., subject to examination.**

**No. 749.** Lowendall's Artist Violin; a violin intended especially for the soloist. It is beyond anything ever carried in any retail store outside of a few largest cities. It is a violin so far superior to the cheaper instruments sold elsewhere, that it is impossible to give more than a faint idea of its supurb quality. So far as the tone is concerned the intending purchaser can only realize its wonderful purity by a thorough test. In model and finish it has no superiors. Amber oil varnish, beautifully polished and full ebony trimmed. Light red color, full set of superfine strings. We ask you to remit $1.00 with your order and we will send this elegant instrument C. O. D., subject to approval. Weight, boxed, 10 lbs. Our special price_____$46.95

### Ladies' Violin.

**No. 751.** To enhance the popularity of the violin as a musical instrument for the ladies' use, we have had manufactured especially for our trade, by one of the leading European manufacturers, this elegant instrument, four-fifths the regular size. This size will especially commend itself to the ladies—for whom it is designed, being lighter, more easily handled and less cumbersome than the ordinary violin. It is reddish brown in color, beautifully shaded, oil varnished, ebony fingerboard and tailpiece. The tone is a feature of this elegant instrument that will commend itself to critical players. We send it C. O. D., subject to examination. Weight, boxed, 10 lbs.
Our special price_____$7.95

### Boys' or Small Size Violins.
#### Half or three-quarter size.

State which size is wanted. No difference in price. Instruction book included free.

**No. 753.** Half or Three-quarter size Violin; good model, red shaded, excellent finish, imitation ebony fingerboard. Weight, boxed, 7 lbs.
Our special price,_____$1.95

**No. 755.** Small Size Violin, either half or three-quarter size. German make, after Italian school. Dark brown color, good model and finish; plain trimmings. This violin has an admirable tone and will please the purchaser in both quality and price. Weight, boxed, 7 lbs. Our special price_____$2.75

**No. 756.** Half or Three-quarter Size Violin; red color, good model and excellent finish, solid ebony fingerboard and tailpiece. Very nice tone. Weight, boxed, 7 lbs. Our special price_____$4.60

**No. 758.** Half or Three-quarter Size Violin; genuine Stradivarius model, medium red color, beautifully shaded and highly polished, solid ebony fingerboard and tailpiece. The tone is full, round and extremely pleasing in quality. Weight, boxed, 7 lbs.
Our special price_____$7.15

### Violas or Tenor Violins.

All violas are full strung with superfine strings, and complete instruction book is furnished free. Weight, boxed, about 10 lbs.

**No. 760.** Viola; light reddish brown in color, inlaid edges, good model and finish. The tone is that of a viola for which you would pay $10.00 or $12.00. We send the instrument C. O. D., subject to examination on our liberal terms. Our special price_____$4.35

**No. 762.** Viola; medium brown color, beautifully finished and decorated with fancy inlaid edges. Fancy tailpiece and fancy pegs. The tone is surprising in quality. The finish is equal to that of violas at double the price named. Our special price_____$6.55

**No. 763.** Viola; genuine Stradivarius model, reddish brown color, very finely polished and finished to perfection. The model is an especially desirable one, one that is much sought after by professionals. Solid ebony fingerboard and tailpiece. The tone of this instrument will please the most exacting critic.
Our special price_____$8.55

**WE PREFER ALL ORDERS TO BE MADE OUT ON OUR REGULAR ORDER BLANK. WE FURNISH THESE FREE ON APPLICATION. IF YOU HAVE NONE AT HAND, USE CARE TO GIVE EXACT DESCRIPTION, CATALOGUE NUMBER AND PRICE OF ARTICLES WANTED.**

# An Unexampled Sale of Violin Outfits.

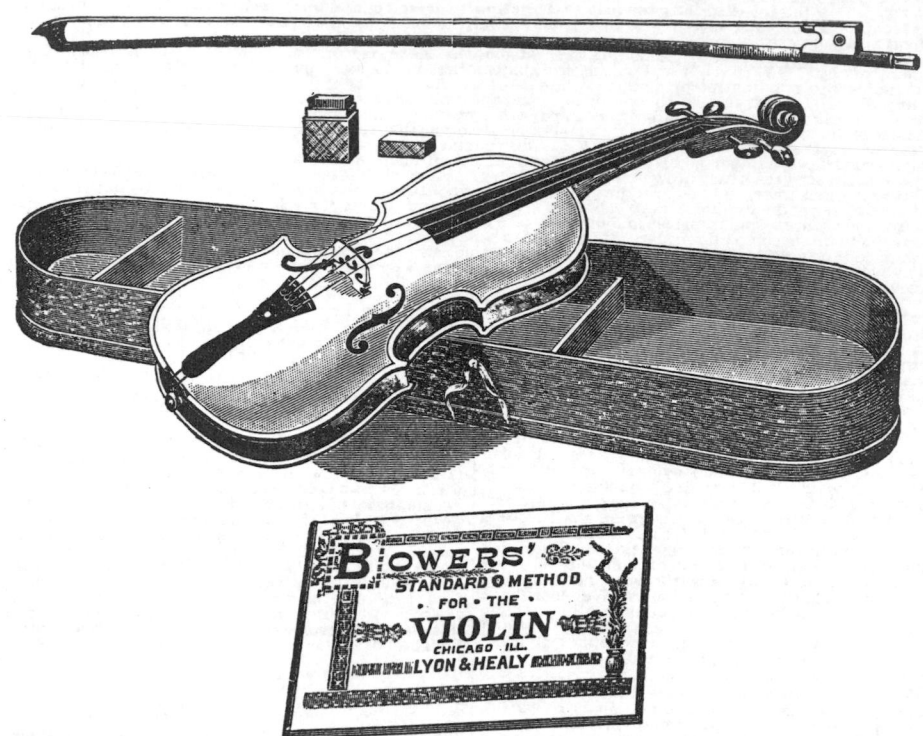

**FOR CASH** we have imported direct from the largest European manufacturers one of the largest consignments of violins ever shipped into the United States. The makers of these violins have a world-wide reputation. Only the most expert and experienced workmen are employed. Only the finest selected material is used in the making. The result is that every violin is the acme of perfection from a mechanical standpoint.

**The Cheapest Instrument** we quote, possesses a beautiful tone and finish. We could buy cheaper ones, but it is our settled policy to handle none but such as will give the most perfect satisfaction. What the instruments cost to make, with the small import duty added, is but a small proportion of the price of a violin when it passes through all the numerous middlemen's hands finally to the consumer. We bridge over the wide chasm between maker and user, and by our perfect economic factory-to-consumer system lay the goods down at your door at even less than the retailer himself pays. In fact, many retail dealers endeavor to buy all their stock from us, knowing the fact that we are direct importers and can undersell the wholesale house. Buying these superb violins through us on our one small profit plan you are practically securing them direct from Europe. In most cases we offer violins of a grade not found in the retail stores at all or only in the largest cities. The cheap grades we refuse to sell are the instruments most frequently found in local dealers' shops. Our desire to get our trade in musical instruments thoroughly established in every community leads us to make an offer unsurpassed in liberality, an offer that no competitive concern cares to make. Such is our implicit confidence in the violin outfits, fully illustrated and described below, that we make the following liberal offer. Select any violin outfit and inclose $1.00 with your order as a guarantee of good faith. We will ship the outfit selected to you, C. O. D., subject to examination and approval. All that we ask is that you give the outfit a careful examination, see that every piece and part is exactly as we say; judge for yourself the quality and model of the violin. If you do not find it the most complete and the handsomest violin and furnishing you ever saw or heard of at the price, the privilege is yours to send it back at our expense and get your money. We will have no dissatisfaction on the part of our customers. We realize fully that our continued trade, our reputation, in fact, depends on the class and quality of goods we send you, we realize, also, that quality only is remembered, long after the price is forgotten. Hence we supplement this remarkable offer by holding out to every purchaser of these violin outfits the privilege of returning any instrument after 5 days' trial. If it does not prove satisfactory or does not meet requirements, it can be returned to us prepaid, and we will either refund money in full or exchange for any other instrument.

In opening up to you an avenue for escape from the exorbitant prices of retail dealers and in the development of this new factory-to-consumer method of merchandising, we ask as a special favor that each customer who receives one of these outfits and finds it even far better than expected, shall do us the great kindness of speaking a favorable word for us to their friends and neighbors. You will not only oblige us greatly, but you will at the same time be rendering your acquaintances a service by pointing out to them a sure, safe and sensible way of economizing.

A liberal discount of 3 per cent. is allowed where full cash is sent with order. This is the wisest method of ordering, as you save not only our cash discount, but also the return charges of money to us. In all cases our guarantee assures you that anything unsatisfactory may be returned to us, and full cash refunded.

**No. 770—Violin Outfit for $2.00.** No. 770 is a special offer of **more value for a little money than has ever before been heard of.** We include in this outfit a violin of excellent model, and possessing a tone of surprising quality, purity and volume. **The bow is** made of selected maple, imitation snakewood with black frog, bone button and inlaid dot. Full set of fine **strings.** Cake of bow **rosin.** Marbilized pasteboard **case.** This special bargain outfit is complete with a fine **Instruction book** for the violin, the best instruction book published; weight, boxed, 10 pounds. Our special price, complete, $2.00.

**No. 772—Our $2.65 Complete Violin Outfit.** This complete outfit includes a **special violin,** imported particularly to meet the demand for an excellent model, possessing a full, powerful and rich tone, and one that can be sold by us at less than half the regular retail price. Red in color, with a nice finish. Inlaid edges. Best seasoned top. Accurate finger-board. Full set German transparent strings. The **bow** is made of maple, painted and polished; ebony frog and inlaid dot. The bow rosin is superior quality medium sized cake. The case is fancy marbleized pasteboard, with compartments for extras. We also include one of the best **violin instruction books** published, a splendid book for beginners; with it the expensive services of a teacher may be dispensed with. Our special price for this complete outfit is only $2.65. We send it C. O. D., subject to examination, on receipt of $1.00 with order. If it is found entirely satisfactory and exactly as represented, pay the balance, $1.65, with express charges, to the agent and the outfit is yours; 3 per cent. discount if full cash comes with order, and the outfit costs only $2.57, and the violin alone is worth $5.00.

**No. 775—Our Famous $3.25 Outfit.** This violin possesses a full, round, bell tone—sweet, yet powerful; a tone seldom found in violins at even **five** times our price for the complete outfit. Model, reddish-brown color, varnish finish; edges inlaid with purfling; beautiful curly maple back and sides. Top, best seasoned pine, selected especially for violins. True finger-board, hardwood pegs, maple bridge, three scrolls. **Full** set German transparent and polished **strings.** The **Bow**—Selected maple, painted mahogany red, polished and varnished; ebony frog, inlaid dot, bone slide and button. Violin **Case**—Fancy marbleized pasteboard, fancy ribbon fastenings, special compartments for violin, bow, rosin, etc. **Rosin**—Good quality, German importation; medium-sized cakes. **Instruction Book**—Bowers' Violin Instructor, one of the very best instruction books for beginners, so arranged that a good idea of tuning, fingering, etc., can be obtained in a short time without the aid of a teacher; also a nice selection of easy pieces, embracing waltzes, etc., sent complete in above instruction book. $3.15, cash with order, or $3.25 C. O. D. You never will have such an opportunity again. **Worth three times our price,** but offered to our customers this one time only as a special leader and to complete our grand combination of bargains.

**No. 777—Violin Outfit for $4.48.** This most complete outfit consists of one **genuine Salzard model violin,** a model that is much sought after by experts and artists. The color is dark red, and it is elegantly polished and further decorated with handsome inlaid edges. This is an instrument that will please the most exacting. The regular retail price is $5.00. The **violin bow,** furnished free, is a special grade of maple, black finished, has bone slide and button, bone frog and inlaid eye; a bow that is fully up to the high standard of the violin itself. Regular retail price, 50c. The **violin case,** as shown in the picture, is a genuine solid wood case. Not one of the cheap pasteboard cases, but a case that will stand wear and tear and keep your instrument from damage. It is black varnished and half lined with flannel, has handsome handle and hooks. No lock. We sustain our reputation on the outfit by giving you a case that is made on honor. Regular retail price, $1.95. We also include a full set of fine transparent Gut E, A and D strings and wound G string. E string is four lengths, A 2½ lengths, D 2½ lengths and G 1 length. Regular retail price per set, 60c. We give free, also, a cake of superior bow rosin, in neat pasteboard case. Retail price, 5c. As a final inducement, we give free in this remarkable outfit a **violin instructor,** the finest of its kind. By its use the novice can take up the study of the violin without the expense of a teacher. Regular retail price, 50c. Figure all these up and you will find that you would have to pay **$9.10** for the items of this No. 777 outfit, which we offer you for $4.48.

**No. 779—Our $6.15 Complete Violin Outfit.** The violin is a genuine Stradivarius model, medium red varnish, light shaded, ebony finger-board and tail piece. Fine violin bow, redwood, natural color, solid ebony frog, inlaid dot, bone button and pearl slide. Fine American made wood case, black varnished, half lined with flannel, complete with handle and hooks; complete set of superfine quality strings, full cake of bow rosin, in pasteboard case. We also include the most superior violin instruction book published; weight, boxed, 10 pounds. Our price complete, $6.15. The surprising quality we are able to offer in these violin outfits make them the most wonderful bargains in musical merchandise. The violin we include in this outfit possesses a tone that will delight the most critical judge. We send the outfit C. O. D., subject to examination, on receipt of $1.00. Remember our 3 per cent. cash discount for full cash with order. You can examine the outfit at the express office, and if found exactly as represented, pay the agent the balance and express charges, and it is yours. Our special C. O. D. price, $6.15, our special cash price, $5.97.

**OUR MUSICAL GOODS DEPARTMENT IS RECEIVING A LARGE SHARE OF OUR CUSTOMERS' ATTENTION. OUR PRICES AND TERMS MAKE OUR SALES ENORMOUS, AND THE QUALITY OF THE GOODS IS SUCH THAT CUSTOMERS ARE ALWAYS PLEASED.**

**No. 781—Our Special $8.65 Violin Outfit.** We include in this outfit a **genuine Stainer model violin**, which alone retails at more than our price for the complete outfit. It is reddish-brown in color, shaded and handsomely polished, and has ebony fingerboard and tail piece. The **violin bow** is of special quality, made of Brazil wood, with ebony frog, pearl slide and full German silver trimmed. The **violin case** is of selected wood, black varnished, full lined with flannel and complete with nickel plated lock, handle and hook hasps. Strings are of superfine quality. The instruction book, sent free, is the most complete published. Good-sized cake of bow rosin also included; weight, boxed, 10 pounds. Our special price, complete, $8.65. The above is an outfit of remarkable superiority. Many a violin alone has been retailed at double our complete outfit price and was not equal in tone, quality or finish to the one we furnish. Keep in mind our liberal C. O. D. terms.

## Our Genuine Gaspar Da Salo Model Violin and Complete Outfit for $16.50.

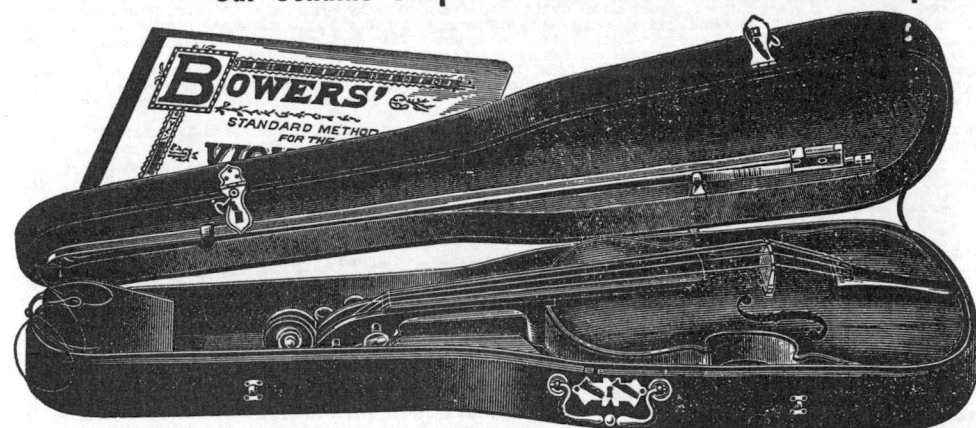

No. 783. A most amazing offer. **The violin** is a beautiful model, with name carved in scroll, and very fancy inlaying in back. The instrument is one that will attract the interest of professionals, on account of its beautiful full, round tones, as well as the richness of the finish and desirability of model. Full ebony trimmed. Reddish-brown color. We include a **violin bow** of decided excellence, it being made of Brazil wood. Round stick, with rounded ebony frog, German silver lined, fancy German silver button, pearl eye and pearl slide. The **fine wood violin case** is exposition shape, black varnished, full lined with flannel, with handle, lock and clasps. The **full set of strings** is of the most select superfine quality. The very best "**Reform Rosin**," on metal spools, in pasteboard box. **Instruction book** given is the best and most complete ever published. This complete outfit would retail at $30.00 or more. The violin alone is one that sells at $25.00 in the few retail stores that handle goods of such high grade; weight, boxed, about 12 pounds. Our special price, $16.50.

## DOUBLE BASS VIOLS.

We quote below a complete line of double bass viols, one-quarter, one-half and three-quarter size. Prices include complete instruction book and bow of superior quality. Weight, boxed, averages about 125 pounds.

### ONE-QUARTER SIZE.

**No. 784—Double Bass Viol.** One-quarter size, 4 strings, dark red shaded, finely polished, special quality, patent head. Our special price, $19.95.

### ONE-HALF SIZES.

**No. 785—Double Bass Viol.** One-half size, 3 strings, dark red shaded, handsomely polished, very excellent quality, patent head. Our special price, $18.35.

**No. 786—Double Bass Viol.** Same as No. 785, above, with 4 strings. Our special price, $19.40.

**No. 787—Double Bass Viol.** 3 strings, dark red shaded, highly polished, finely decorated, inlaid edges, very fine quality, patent head. Our special price, $29.90.

**No. 788—Double Bass Viol.** Dark red shaded, very finely polished, inlaid edges, swelled back, very superior quality. This instrument possesses a tone of remarkable purity and power. A bass viol far superior to anything found in an ordinary retail store. Patent head, 4 strings. Our special price, $44.95.

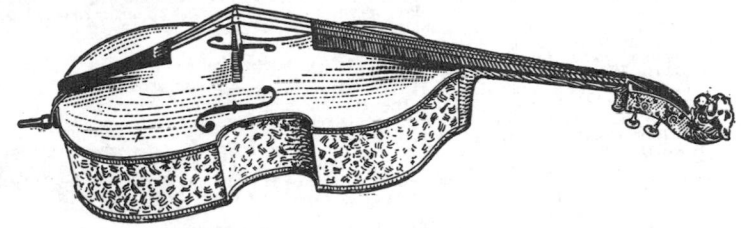

### THREE-QUARTER SIZES.

**No. 789—Double Bass Viol.** Three-quarter size, dark red, shaded, polished, very excellent quality, and possesses a tone of decided quality. Patent head. Our spceial price, $22.50.

**No. 790—Double Bass Viol.** Same, with 4 strings, $24.00.

**No. 791—Double Bass Viol.** 4 strings, dark red, shaded, finely polished, inlaid edges, superior quality in make and finish, patent head, rich and mellow tone. Our special price, $34.95.

**No. 792—Double Bass Viol.** 4 strings, patent head, dark red color, shaded, beautifully polished, inlaid edges, swelled back. The tone of this instrument is exceptionally fine and the finish is superb. Our special price, $45.00.

## VIOLONCELLOS.

The following violoncellos are with peg head. We also quote a line with patent head. Instruction book included, free. Customers will find a very complete list of violoncello bows and other furnishings further along in the catalogue quoted at from one-half to one-third dealers' prices. Sent C. O. D., subject to examination. Weight of violoncellos, boxed, about 45 pounds.

**No. 793.** Reddish-brown color, very good quality, peg head. Our special price, $7.65.

**No. 794.** Reddish-brown color, superior quality, rich tone and fine finish, peg head. Our special price, $8.35.

**No. 795.** Light red color, very good quality, inlaid edges, excellent finish and superior tone, peg head. Our special price, $10.95.

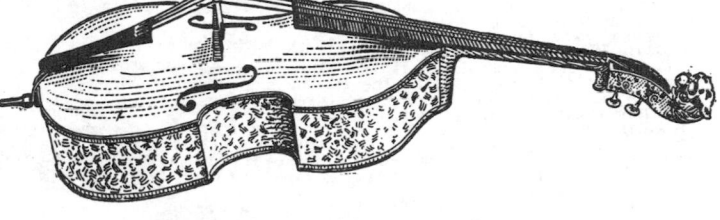

## Violoncellos with Patent Head.

**No. 796.** Reddish brown color, very excellent finish and good quality, patent head. Our special price, $7.90.

**No. 797.** Medium brown color, finely polished and finished, quality is excellent and tone is especially good for a low priced instrument, patent head. Our special price, $9.35.

**No. 798.** Reddish-brown color, inlaid edges, brass plates. This instrument is especially excellent both in tone and quality. Made by the same factory that manufactures all our fine instruments. This one fact is sufficient guarantee of genuine high grade of material and workmanship. Weight, boxed, 43 pounds. Our special price, $11.55.

**No. 799.** Dark brown color, superior model, decorated with fancy inlaid edges, brass plates, patent head. The tone is rich and resonant. Our special price $15.20.

☞ We send any violoncello C. O. D., subject to examination, on receipt of $2 with order as guarantee of good faith.

**IF ANY MUSICAL INSTRUMENT DOES NOT MEET YOUR APPROVAL AFTER 5 DAYS' FAIR AND HONEST TRIAL, IT CAN BE RETURNED TO US PREPAID, AND ENTIRE AMOUNT REFUNDED.**

# 12 FROM 1000.

Much time and money have been spent by our experienced buyer in examining over a **thousand samples of guitars** and from all the vast array of instruments, good, bad and indifferent, he has selected twelve of the choicest, made by the acknowledged leading manufacturer of the world. **No sharper contrast exists** between the heaped-up-profit prices of the retailer and our Factory-to-Consumer prices, than on Guitars. Our cash purchases of guitars to meet the season's demands exceed the combined yearly purchase of hundreds of retailers. Furthermore, buying direct from the factory, and not from the wholesaler as in the retailer's case, we have a further immense advantage. Buying for spot cash, the manufacturer is absolutely safe from bad accounts. These three important facts secure to us, prices that no retailer can even approach, and enable us to place these elegant guitars in your hands at the actual cost to make, with only one small margin of profit added. Aside from the matter of price, the quality is beyond criticism. In fact, few retail dealers outside of very large cities, carry in stock such elegant instruments as are herein illustrated and described. The manufacturer has a reputation for superior goods, that is second to none. The fact is that the name of the maker is so widely known and the products of the factory have become so justly famous, that the mere name is sufficient guarantee of the superb quality.

Every scrap of wood that enters into the construction of these guitars has been seasoned in the drying rooms of the factory from one to two years, thus insuring the instrument against cracking or checking in any climate. The most expert workmen only are employed. The skilled artisans in our factory are amongst the highest salaried workmen in the world. Material and workmanship are absolutely guaranteed, and we warrant each instrument for one year. No other house can compete with us on price and no other concern can meet **our liberal terms.**

On receipt of $1.00 we send any guitar C. O. D., subject to examination. You have the privilege of making a rigid examination of the instrument, and if you find it just as represented and satisfactory in every respect, pay the express agent the balance with express charges and the guitar is yours.

**THIS LIBERAL OFFER** is intended for the benefit of those who are not acquainted with our house and our business integrity. Old customers almost invariably send full cash in advance, thus taking advantage of our 3 per cent. cash discount, which we allow on all orders accompanied with full amount.

## SPECIAL GUITARS.

Anybody can learn to play without a teacher. We include a complete instruction book free. Full set of strings with each guitar. Every instrument comes ready to play. On account of the general inferiority of imported Guitars and the constant tendency of some **to check and crack**, we have entirely ceased carrying them in stock. We hence **quote below only the American made instrument, the finest in the world.**

**Bear in mind** that even after the acceptance of any guitar, you are extended **the privilege of returning the instrument prepaid, after 5 days' fair and** honest trial, if it does not meet your requirements. We shall refund your money in full in such a case, or will send another instrument as you may wish. We desire in all cases that **you shall be entirely pleased with each and every purchase.**

**No. 7100.**

**No. 7100. Our Spanish Guitar,** American make. The best low priced guitar on the American Market. Not only well constructed and handsome in appearance, but made to withstand all climates. So far as quality of tone is concerned, it will far exceed the expectations of the most critical buyer. We can safely say that this instrument is far superior to other makes, retailed at double our price. Has select birch back and sides, finished in imitation mahogany, with imitation cedar neck, accurately fretted, inlaid sound hole, and patent head. Weight packed, 15 lbs. Our price, each.........$3.95

**No. 7101. Our Columbian Standard American Guitar.** Regular size, solid birch back and sides, fine rosewood finish, colored wood inlaying around sound hole, ebonized finger board, position dots. We caution intending purchasers against imitations of this instrument. While it is true that imitation is the sincerest flattery, it is also true that the imitation is always inferior to the original. Weight, boxed, 15 lbs. Our Special price.................................$5.20

**No. 7102. Our "Euterpe" Guitar,** made in selected quartered oak, a most desirable and resonant wood when selected and properly prepared. The finish is extremely handsome; the scale is perfect; the neck delicately proportioned; the patent head is of American make and the best in the world. The strings furnished are of the very best quality. Our old customers who have purchased this guitar have been delighted with it and pronounce it far superior to any instrument ever seen at anything near our price. As stated, it has solid quartered oak back and sides, antique finish, inlaid around sound hole, ebonized fingerboard, position dots, orange top, patent head, standard size. Weight, boxed, 15 lbs. Our price........$5.75

**No. 7103.** We have the same instrument as Guitar No. 7102 above described, but in special concert size. The concert size is a much larger instrument than the regular size and possesses a much more powerful tone. A size especially in favor with professionals. Weight, boxed, 18 lbs. Our Special price.....................................$10.65

Bear in mind our liberal C. O. D. terms. We ship any guitar C. O. D., subject to examination. Note terms at head of the page. You will find a full line of guitar cases and all other furnishings farther on.

**No. 7104. Our "Collegian" Guitar.** A guaranteed guitar that is the most thoroughly satisfactory low priced instrument ever put on the market. As with all our guitars, this instrument is warranted for one year. Instruction book with each guitar. This beautifully modeled guitar is made of quartered sycamore, the stock being selected from handsomely figured wood. The instrument is most attractive in appearance. It is finished in imitation rosewood and mahogany, and is neatly inlaid around sound hole. The neck is imitation cherry, nicely finished, ebonized finger board, position dots, with patent machine head of American make. We present the "Collegian" as the best guitar for anything like the price that has ever been offered. The tone is remarkably good for such a low priced instrument, and the general appearance is such as to command for it immediate recognition. Weight, boxed, about 15 lbs. Our Special price...........................$6.45

**No. 7106.**

**No. 7105. Our "Famous" Guitar.** This instrument is made by a celebrated manufacturer whose guitars have a world wide reputation. Absolutely guaranteed to stand all climates. Is made of the finest selected bird's-eye maple sides and back, with beautiful cedar front. Dark rosewood oval fingerboard. Inlaid sound hole and position dots. Patent machine head. One of the most beautiful guitars made. You would pay $20.00 or $25.00 for a guitar at retail, and not secure an instrument so fine in construction or perfect in tone. Weight, boxed, 15 lbs. Our Special price.................$9.65

See another page for guitar strings and other furnishings.

**No. 7106. The "Troubadour"** was the first mahogany guitar to score a success. Previous to its appearance, the few instruments that had been offered in this wood had proven failures; but the "Troubadour" with its splendid tone, neat and substantial appearance, fine finish and absolutely correct scale, leaped at once into public favor and is now one of the standard guitars of the country. The result was that many cheap dealers began to copy it, and now these imitations are legion. The best of them is not for a moment to be compared with the original and reliable "Troubadour." Be sure to see and try this guitar, you will buy no other. "Troubadour," solid mahogany back and sides, Brazilian cedar neck, ebonized convex fingerboard and bridge, pearl position dots, patent machine head, colored wood inlayings around sound hole, finished with orange colored top, handsomely hand polished.....................$8.65

**No. 7107.** Same as No. 7106, with white celluloid inlaid edges....................... 8.95

We offer Nos. 7106 and 7107 guitars as products of the finest factory in the land. As such, they are warranted positively flawless in construction and possessing a beautiful tone found only in the very highest grade of instruments. See another page for guitar furnishings and strings. Do not forget that we ship any guitar C. O. D., subject to examination.

**No. 7108. Our improved "American Artist" guitar.** A beautifully modeled instrument that is pleasing alike to amateur and artist. Every piece and part that enters into its construction is the most select and perfect. Finely finished solid rosewood back and sides. Handsome French polished, beautiful orange colored front, patent American made machine head, cedar neck. Absolutely correct in scale, as all guitars offered by us are guaranteed to be. Colored wood inlaying around sound hole, white inlaid stripe down the back, plain edges, ebonized finger-board, position dots. Weight boxed, 15 lbs. Our Special price.................$11.95

**No. 7109. "American Artist"** guitar precisely the same as No. 7108 above described, but extra large concert size. Weight packed, 18 lbs. Our Special price, 13.95

**No. 7110. The Celebrated Washburn Guitar.** Standard size. A guitar perhaps better known than any other make. It is as perfect in all the details of construction as the most expert and experienced workmen can make it. Not an ounce of inferior material enters into its make-up, but on the contrary, the markets of the world provide no better than that used in making the Washburn guitar. Made of beautiful rosewood, with plain finished edges. Colored wood inlayings around sound hole, and handsome inlaid stripe down the back. Oval finger-board, with pearl position dots. Weight packed, 15 lbs. Sent C. O. D. anywhere on receipt of $1.00. Our Special price.................................$22.00

**No. 7111.** We have the Washburn guitar exactly same as No. 7110 above described, but in large Concert size. Weight boxed, 18 lbs. This special concert guitar is particularly designed to meet the demands of expert players who are only satisfied with the choicest in the market. Our Special price.........................$27.00

**NOTE.**—On our American guitars gut and silk wound strings are recommended under all circumstances. The efforts of the manufacturers are directed toward the production of a rich mellow tone, and in order to accomplish this result they use a sensitively constructed sounding board, which is not made to withstand the strain of wire strings. By using great care some of them will stand this heavy strain without serious detriment, but we wish it understood that we will not be responsible for the failure of a guitar where steel strings are used. See another page for guitar strings and all kinds of guitar furnishings.

# BEST BARGAINS IN BANJOS.

The banjo is a popular instrument. It deserves to be. The main reason for its comparatively little use lies in the fact that retail prices have been so outrageously high, that most people have been kept from buying. It gives us pleasure to announce **AN ENORMOUS DEAL**, putting us in possession of our season's supply of banjos at a price far below any other price ever named to wholesale buyers. Our season's contracts cover only the finest output of the factory. Our expert buyer made a personal selection to meet the demands of the most critical player, and we are now putting in the hands of the user a line of banjos never seen in retail stores outside of large cities. Or, if found at all the prices asked were at least double what we name. Our aim is to supply our trade with banjos that have intrinsic musical value. The perfect Scale, artistically Shaped Neck, first quality Head, as well as the accurately made and fitted metal parts, are features that distinguish our banjos from all others sold. These distinguishing features apply to our cheapest instruments as well as to our best. The manufacturers with whom we have contracted for our entire stock have unlimited facilities and the finest machinery known, as well as the most skillful workmen, enabling them to turn out the most exquisite productions of modern musical instruments at the lowest cost of production. The prices we name for these highest grade banjos are the lowest ever known. Our economic, factory-to-consumer plan revolutionizes trade relations, cuts off the constantly increasing expenses and profits of middlemen and enables the user of the article to procure it at the very door of the factory that makes it. By the time-worn system—manufacturing, wholesaling and retailing—it costs twice as much to sell an article as it originally cost to make it. Every customer who purchases on our method of merchandising has learned the lesson of economy as we teach it. Aside from the matter of price, our terms are so liberal that the most skeptical can readily be convinced that we have harnessed price and quality together, and that our goods are as superior **On Receipt of $1.00** we send any **C. O. D., Subject to Examination.** You inspect the banjo as our prices are low. banjo at your express office, and see that it is just as represented and entirely satisfactory, and pay the express agent the balance and charges and the banjo is yours at half the retail price. If it is not as represented, you return the banjo and we refund your money. This is the most liberal offer ever made. You can't say you buy a "pig in a poke." We combine quality, price and fair and easy terms to such a degree that we deserve the liberal patronage of every reader of this catalogue. With every banjo we include free an excellent Instruction Book. Each instrument is full strung with fine strings and ready to play.

**No. 7120.** Banjo, maple shell with nickel band, imitation cherry neck, 10-inch calfskin head, 6 screw brackets, full strung, accurately fretted. Weight, boxed, 18 lbs. **Our Special Price**............................................**$2.10**

**No. 7122.** Banjo with nickel shell, wood lined, stained imitation cherry neck, with 7 nickel plated hexagon brackets, 10-inch calfskin head, accurately fretted, full strung. Weight, boxed, 18 lbs. **Our Special Price** ........................**$2.75**

**No. 7124.** Banjo with nickel shell, 13 nickel plated hexagon brackets, wood lined shell, 11-inch calfskin head, birch neck, raised frets, superior quality tailpiece. This banjo possesses qualities of tone and finish found only in the case of high grade instruments. Weight, boxed, 18 lbs. **Our Special Price**.............**$3.70**

**No. 7126.** Nickel shell, wood lined, birch neck, raised frets, 25 brass hexagon brackets, 11-inch calfskin head. A superior instrument at a very low price. Weight, boxed, 18 lbs. **Our Special Price** ....................................**$4.35**

**No. 7127.** Banjo with extra heavy nickel shell, wood lined, wire edge, French polished birch neck, scroll head, imitation ebony fingerboard, raised frets, inlaid position dots. Best quality 11-inch calfskin head. A splendid banjo. See illustration above; 31 nickel plated hexagon brackets. Weight, boxed, 18 lbs. **Our Special Price**...........................................................**$6.35**

**No. 7129.** Professional Banjo. 11-inch heavy nickel shell, wood lined, wired edges, heavy strainer hoop rabbeted, 25 brackets and patent tailpiece. Finely decorated head, finely polished mahogany neck, solid ebony fingerboard, decorated with fancy inlayings of pearl and metal, raised frets. This banjo is made with extra care, is handsomely ornamented, carefully adjusted and is intended to supply the want for a thoroughly desirable professional instrument at a medium price. Weight, boxed, 18 lbs. **Our Special Price**...........................................**$9.80**

**No. 7130.** Professional Banjo, suitable alike to amateurs and experts, although designed especially for the use of the latter. Metal parts are all of extra weight. Extra heavy German silver shell, fully nickel plated. Both edges wired, heavy maple hoops (inside), ebonized and polished. Finely polished birch neck, raised frets, extra heavy rabbetted strainer hoops, brass bracket screws, with hexagon heads and washers nickel plated. Extra heavy ebony fingerboard, neck handsomely ornamented with pearl, 7-inch head and 13 elbow brackets. Weight, boxed, 18 lbs. **Our Special Price**........................................................**$10.95**

**No. 7132.** Same as No. 7130 with 9-inch head and 15 brackets. **Our Special Price, $14.10**

**No. 7134.** Same as No. 7130 with 10-inch head and 17 brackets. **Our Special Price, $15.95**

**No. 7135.** Same as No. 7130 with 11-inch head and 21 brackets. **Our Special Price, $17.80**

**No. 7136.** Same as No. 7130 with 12-inch head and 29 brackets. **Our Special Price, $19.35**

No. 7127.

**No. 7137.** Same as No. 7130 with 13-inch head and 31 brackets. **Our Special Price** ........................................................................**$21.00**

**No. 7139.** Semi-Professional Banjo, with 12-inch extra quality calfskin head. A special instrument designed for fine trade at a very reasonable price. Retails at $25.00. Has fine heavy German silver shell, wood lined, rosewood veneered inside. Both edges wired, rabbeted strainer hoops, French polished birch neck, with metal stay pieces, rosewood fingerboard, pearl position ornaments, raised frets, celluloid imitation ivory pegs, 19-inch neck, 31 nickel globe brackets, with safety nuts. Weight, boxed, 18 lbs. **Our Special Price** ....................................................**$16.10**

# BANJORINE.

This instrument is intended for use with one or more Banjos as a leading instrument; the tone being of a penetrating quality is consequently prominent in duets, quartettes, etc. The neck is made short, being less in length than the diameter of the shell, the Fingerboard extending over the head similar to a guitar. It is very easy of execution, the frets, of course, being nearer together than on the ordinary banjo neck. The instrument is tuned differently from the regular banjo—being a fourth higher. For instance: When the banjorine is played in Key of E, the regular banjo should be tuned to A.

## 12-Inch German Silver Shell.

**No. 7140.** Wood lined, finished in black inside, both edges wired, plain strainer hoop, birch neck, ebony finger board, with pearl position dots and raised frets, black pegs, 25 nickel plated hexagon brackets...........**$13.35**

## 12 1-2 Inch German Silver Shell.

**No. 7142.** Wood lined, rosewood, veneered inside, both edges wired, rabbeted strainer hoop, French polished birch neck and metal stay piece, heavy ebony finger board,

Banjorine.
position ornaments and raised frets, imitation ivory pegs, 31 nickel globe brackets with safety nuts. **Our special price**........................................**$18.65**

It is past the comprehension of our competitors how it is possible for us to offer such liberal terms of shipment of goods. The explanation is simple. We do not try to make all the profit on one order. The smallest possible margin is all we ask on each order, and customers come again.

# A SPECIAL DRIVE IN MANDOLINS
## MADE POSSIBLE BY A TREMEDOUS DEAL ON A SPOT CASH BASIS.

In contemplation of a large purchase, our expert buyer spent much time in visiting the largest American factories. We have discarded all imported mandolins on account of their worthlessness as a musical instrument. Hence only American made instruments were considered. The result of our investigation was the weeding out of all but strictly the best, and we finally settled on a line which presents a sharp and welcome contrast to the cheap instruments found in retail stores, a line of mandolins made by the largest manufacturer in America, whose reputation for high grade goods is second to none.

### THESE ELEGANT MANDOLINS Combine to an unexampled degree, the four essential points, Tone, Finish, Model and Durability.

The Tone is accomplished by a delicate and proper construction of the instrument. The mandolins herein quoted are made in the most thorough manner by experts, who have had years of experience and a knowledge gained by time and many costly experiments. The Finish has made these mandolins justly celebrated. The work is done by men who are simply perfect in the art. It is the finish that appeals to the eye. These goods are not equaled in the world for handsome finish, beautiful shadings and perfect lustre.

These mandolins are genuine Neapolitan models, considered by artists the most desirable model made.

The question of durability comes in especial importance, and, in selecting our line, our buyer required that the manufacturer should positively guarantee these mandolins for one year. The guarantee might just as well be for ten years. Not a scrap of wood enters into the construction of these instruments but what is seasoned in the dry rooms of the factory for twelve months, and in fact some of the more important parts are seasoned for twice that length of time. There are no weak spots in any of these instruments.

In closing our contract for our season's stock of mandolins, the persuasive power of spot cash secured for us prices far below any prices ever before quoted even to the largest wholesale buyers. On our one small profit plan we offer these elegant mandolins at the actual cost to produce, with only a narrow margin of brokerage added. You are brought to the door of the factory, as it were, and, through us, you secure your goods from the hands of the manufacturer who makes them. Our economic system is revolutionizing trade and bringing about an entire change in business methods. According to the old way it cost far more to deliver an article to the actual user, by the doubled and tripled expenses and profits of several middlemen, than it cost to make it. By our economic system we point the way to economy on a large scale. Heaping advantage on advantage, we not only give the consumer the tremenduous benefit of unheard of low prices, but we enable him to actually see and examine his goods before paying for them. This is, of course, a desirable privilege to those who have never dealt with us and who are unacquainted with our integrity and business methods.

To those who are not familiar with our house we make this liberal

## SPECIAL OFFER:

Remit $1.00 with your order for any of the special mandolins quoted herein, and we will ship it at once to you. You can examine the instrument at the express office to see that it is exactly as represented and perfectly satisfactory in every way. If (and there is no doubt) you are entirely satisfied that the mandolin is just as we say, you pay the agent the balance, and you are the possessor of the instrument. Otherwise you return it at our expense and we will cheerfully refund your deposit.

Furthermore, should you accept the mandolin and after five days' honest test, find it unsatisfactory or not suited to your wants, you can return it to us prepaid, and we will refund the entire amount paid.

In relation to our liberal and unheard of terms, let us say in explanation that we are prompted to make them so fair, from the fact, that many so-called mail order houses have imposed on the confidence of the people. Our regular customers are acquainted with us and our honorable dealings, but there are many who have never dealt with us. In order that they may not class us with the numerous swindlers, we make it possible for new customers to see and examine their goods before paying for them.

To our old customers, or in fact to all who prefer to send full cash with order, we allow a discouut of 3 per cent., when amount in full accompanies the order. By remitting entire cash with order you thus have the benefit of the 3 per cent. discount and also save the return express charges on the C. O. D.

We invite your special attention to the following mandolins at the best prices the world has ever seen.

No. 7145. Mandolin. Every purchaser who desires a thoroughly first-class instrument with the investment of a small sum will find this mandolin fully up to every possible requirement. In buying it he has the assurance of guaranteed quality, the makers being the most reputable as well as the largest musical instrument manufacturers in America. The materials and workmanship are remarkably superior. The instrument is made of maple, with five ribs, inlaid between each rib with a black strip. Orange colored top, ebonized fingerboard, patent head, accurately fretted, celluloid guard plate, position dots, inlaid around sound hole, celluloid inlaid edges, nickel plated tailpiece and sleeve protector, satinwood finish, hand polished. Complete, with pick and instructor. Weight, packed, 8 pounds. Our special price........................................................................................................................$3.45

No. 7147. This mandolin is made of select maple, with seven ribs, having black inlaid strip between. Beautiful rosewood finish, hand polish. Orange colored top, ebonized fingerboard and guard plate, position dots, black and white celluloid edges, nickel covered tail piece, American patent head. This mandolin is made after the Neopolitan model and is particularly handsome in appearance. The purity of tone distinguishes it from the cheap instruments found in retail stores. Is full strung and has a perfect scale. Mandolin pick and instruction book free. Weight, boxed, 8 pounds. Our special price...............................................$5.25

All our Mandolins are absolutely warranted for one year not to split or crack.

No. 7149. Mandolin. Made of beautifully finished birch and maple, seven ribs, with black inlaying between and finely hand polished. Orange colored top, ebonized fingerboard and guard plate. Perfectly arranged frets, pearl position dots, black and white celluloid edges, nickel covered tail piece, patent machine head. Full strung and ready to play. Guaranteed in finish, quality and tone. The design is the beautiful Neopolitan model. Intending purchasers will be delighted with this instrument on examination. Complete, with pick and instruction book. Weight, boxed, 8 pounds. Our special price........................................................$6.95

We guarantee every mandolin for one year. We send any mandolin C. O. D., subject to examination.

No. 7150. Mandolin. One of the most pleasing instruments on the market. Beautiful Neopolitan model. Made of walnut and maple, nine ribs, alternating walnut and maple, with black inlaying between. Brazilian cedar neck, hand polished throughout and elegantly finished. Orange colored top, ebonized fingerboard, celluloid guard plate, pearl inlaid position dots, black and white celluloid edges, nickel plated tail piece, patent machine head. This mandolin is perfect musically and the combination of different colored woods is very pleasing. An ideal instrument at a moderate price that is commended alike to professionals and amateurs. Complete, with pick and instruction book. Weight, boxed, 8 pounds. Price.........................................................$9.90

No. 7151. Mandolin. Is precisely the same as No. 7150 described fully above, but the nine ribs are alternating mahogany and oak. Our special price....$11.20

No. 7153. Mandolin. Only needs a trial to delight an intending purchaser. Eleven ribs of select mahogany and redwood, with red colored wood inlaying between, beautifully polished, orange colored top, ebonized finger board, celluloid guard plate, pearl position dots, inlaying around sound hole and edges, celluloid inlaid edge, nickel-plated tailpiece, patent head, perfectly fretted scale, full strung with eight strings. This instrument is the famous Neopolitan model and is without a rival at anything like the price. Complete with pick and instruction book. Weight, boxed, 8 pounds. Our special price...............................................$14.10

☞ We send any instrument anywhere, to anyone, C. O. D., subject to examination, and guarantee every one for one year.

No. 7154. Mandolin is just the same in every point of description as No. 7153, as described above, but has 15 alternate mahogany and ebony ribs and richly inlaid around sound hole. Our special price.................................................................$16.10

No. 7156. Mandolin. All lovers of the mandolin pronounce this the most perfect instrument ever produced. It is alike famous for its magnificent tone and beautiful design. It commands the admiration of professional and amateur. Has 11 alternate rosewood and curly maple ribs, with inlaid stripes between, handsomely polished, orange colored top, neat inlay around oblong sound hole, celluloid inlaid edge, ebonized fingerboard and guard plate, with perfectly regulated scale, Spanish cedar neck, pearl position dots, rosewood veneered headpiece, nickel-plated covered patent machine head, nickel-plated tailpiece, full strung with 8 strings and ready to play, Complete with pick and instruction book. Weight, 8 pounds, packed. Fully guaranteed. Our special price.................................................$19.85

SUCH AN ASSORTMENT OF SUITABLE SUITS AT SATISFACTORY PRICES WAS NEVER SEEN IN ANY CATALOGUE OR STORE, AS IS INCLUDED IN THE PAGES OF THIS BOOK. WE SHIP C. O. D., SUBJECT TO EXAMINATION.

# THE APOLLO HARP.

The most simple and attractive Musical Instrument the mind of man could conceive of. With absolutely no knowledge of music whatever, the merest novice can soon learn to play this remarkable instrument, and that, too, **positively without the aid of a teacher** No use paying hundreds of dollars learning to play the organ or piano, when with the Apollo Harp you can have the finest music in the world.

**The Action** is somewhat that of **a Piano.** Each string is vibrated by means of a small felt hammer, which strikes the string when pressed by the finger. **The picture shows the cross bars with the hammers between.** By running your finger over one row of hammers a complete chord is sounded.

You can readily see that the playing of chords is simplicity itself. **The execution of more complicated music is** rendered easy by reason of the simple and comprehensive instructions we send with each instrument.

**Anyone can play** the Apollo Harp with skill in a very short time, and produce **high-class music.** There is absolutely nothing in the range of musical ability that cannot be beautifully and **expressively played** on it. **The Apollo Harp is be**yond the shadow of a doubt without a rival in the **production of sweet, pure music** of every variety known, with so little effort on the part of the performer.

Buy one of these elegant Harps, and delight the whole family. **If there is no musical ability** in your family, that need make no difference, as anyone can play it whether he has any knowledge or not. **The price is not "boosted up"** because it is a new thing, and there is a patent on it. **We are on the inside** when it comes to the price.

Our Economic Factory-to-Consumer-Plan cuts off the host of middlemen's profits and expenses, placing the consumer on the same footing as the largest dealer when it comes to buying. We ship C. O. D., subject to examination, on most **liberal terms.** You are under no obligation to **keep unsatisfactory goods.**

No. 7230 Apollo Harp as illustrated, fitted with a fixed 3 bar keyed bridge, set in key of C. This Harp has 19 strings and produces 3 principal chords. An ordinary range of select music can be played on this instrument. Weight, boxed, 7 lbs.

### OUR PRICE, - $3.00.

No. 7235. Apollo Harp is chromatically strung with 33 strings. It is fitted with 3 bar keyed sliding bridge. This Bridge can be adjusted to play in any of the following keys, viz.: C, C sharp, D, E flat, E or F, and produces 3 chords in each or **18** chords in all. The range of the instrument is unusual for one so low priced. Weight, packed, 10 lbs.

### OUR PRICE, EACH, - - $4.00.

No. 7237. Apollo Harp is made of handsome imitation Rosewood and is chromatically strung with 33 strings. Has a sliding 4 bar keyed bridge, as illustrated, which can be adjusted to play 4 chords, viz.: Tonic, Dominant 7th, Sub-Dominant and Minor in keys of C, C sharp, D, E flat, E, F, F sharp and G, or 32 chords in all. This instrument permits a wide range of music, simple or classical, sacred or gay. Weight, packed, 12 lbs.

### OUR SPECIAL PRICE, - $8.85.

No. 7239. Apollo Harp is 12½ x 21 in. in size and handsomely made in imitation of Rosewood. It has 34 strings chromatically strung, and is fitted not only with a 5 bar sliding keyed bridge which produces 5 chords in every key, but has an additional attachment of great merit. This is known as the Symphonic attachment, like shown in the illustration of No. 7244 below, except that it has only 5 bars. This Symphonic attachment is made similar to the sliding keyed bar, but is covered with felt on the underside, with openings to correspond exactly with the keys in the keyed bar. The latter is removed and the Harp played with Symphonic attachment instead. With the keyed bridge, the most beautiful and wonderfully perfect Dulcimer effects are obtained, and all kinds of music, even the most rapid and repeating notes are played. Yet with the Symphonic attachment, "ear hath never before heard" such exquisite tone, nor has any known musical instrument ever approached in distant degree, such delightful and sympathetic harmony as can be brought forth on the Apollo Harp with the Symphonic attachment. Complete with both Keyed Bar and Symphonic and Instruction Book. Weight, packed, about 15 lbs.

### OUR SPECIAL PRICE, $16.75.

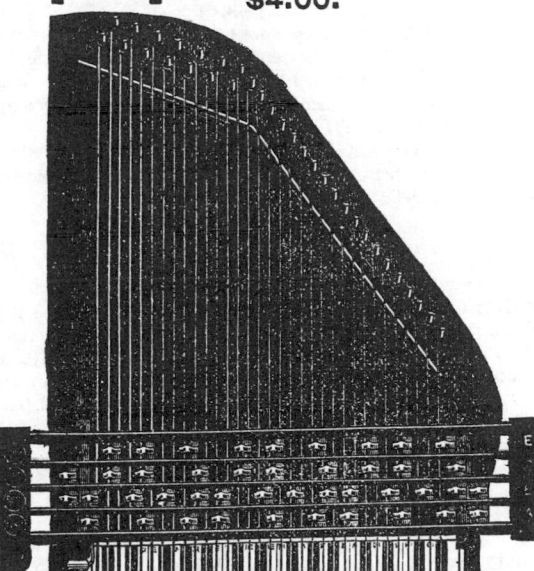

**No. 7237.**

No. 7241. Apollo Harp, is finely finished and handsome in design; exactly the same as No. 7244 illustrated but plain in finish. Has 36 strings, strung in chromatic scale and fitted with 6 bar sliding keyed bridge, which can be adjusted at the will of the performer to produce any and every chord in any key. The Symphonic attachment fully described with No. 7239 Harp, and illustrated with No. 7244 is included free. This instrument has every requirement for producing the most difficult and classical music in any key, and gives opportunity for modulating from any key to another, equal to the Piano or Organ. Thus a grand result is obtained in this elegant instrument that can be found in no other. Weight, packed, about 15 lbs.

#### OUR SPECIAL PRICE, $20.00.

No. 7244. Apollo Harp is exactly as illustrated. It has 6 bar sliding keyed bridge, as well as Symphonic attachment, producing all chords in all keys. In capacity and capability it is just the same as No. 7241 above. But upon No. 7244 have been exhausted the skill of the designer, the carver and the finisher. The result is the most beautiful instrument of its kind. In it are preserved all the delightful tone qualities and capabilities, and added to them is an especially elegant appearance. A harp that will grace any parlor or music room. Weight, packed, about 15 lbs.

#### OUR SPECIAL PRICE, $29.30.

**No. 7230.**

**No. 7244.**

The Apollo Harp is constructed on an entirely new principle. The novel feature of extending the strings from the pin block down and around the end of the Harp and back to the other side of the same block, is of great importance: the compressing of the sounding board renders a clearer, sweeter, and very much better tone or singing quality than in any box, or other form of Harp. The liability of twisting or bending is entirely obviated, so that when the strings are once stretched they will stay in tune indefinitely, while in all other Harps even after the strings are stretched the possibility of twisting, curving, and bending always exists and usually happens, thereby upsetting the most careful tuning. All the material in our Harps and slides, both Keyed and Symphonic, is the most carefully selected and of the very best quality to be found, and the workmanship and finish of the highest grade.

**LOOK IN THE INDEX, AND YOU WILL FIND HUNDREDS OF NECESSARY ARTICLES ARE ADVERTISED WHICH YOU MIGHT OVERLOOK. THE INDEX IS A COMPLETE GUIDE TO WEALTH. THE CATALOGUE IS A STORE FROM WHICH YOU CAN BUY EVERYTHING YOU EAT, OR WEAR, OR USE, FOR PROFIT, BUSINESS OR PLEASURE.**

# THE AUTOHARP.

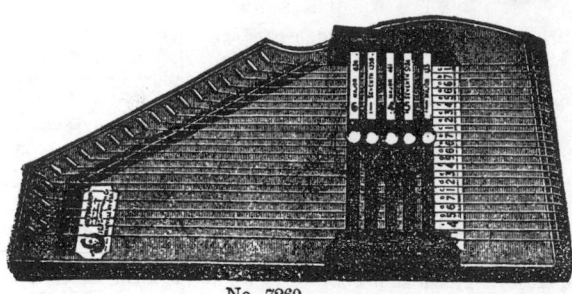

The Autoharp has become one of the most popular musical instruments. There are two of the very best reasons for this popularity. It requires but little practice or musical ability to master the instrument and play it in a manner enjoyable alike to audience and player. At the same time its simplicity does not preclude the playing of difficult and classical music, and while the amateur musician will find it remarkably easy to play, the autoharp is in decided high favor with the finest professional musicians. A second reason for its popularity is the remarkable sweetness and purity of tone, rendering the music delightful to amateur and artist alike. The Autoharp has a handsome case, full strung, and with three or more bars. These bars have felt dampers at proper intervals on the under side, and when any bar is pressed on the strings a complete and perfect chord is played by drawing the pick across the strings. Otherwise it is played similar to the zither.

No. 7260.          No. 7259. Autoharp No. 1 has 21 strings, 3 bars and produces 3 chords. Complete, with instruction book, music and ring for playing. Our special price, each, **$2.75.**

No. 7260. Autoharp No. 2¾ has 23 strings and 5 bars, producing 5 chords. Instruction book, music and ring for playing. See illustration above. Our special price, each, **$3.60.**

No. 7261. Autoharp No. 2⅞ is an entirely new style just on the market. It has 28 strings and 7 bars, producing 7 chords. Every nickel paid for this elegant instrument represents more music than can possibly be secured from other sources for twice the money. Weight, boxed, about 8 pounds. Our special price, **$6.00.**

No. 7262. Autoharp No. 3 has 28 strings and 4 bars with shifters, producing 9 chords. Complete, with instruction book, music and ring for playing. Our special price, each, **$8.60.**

No. 7263. Autoharp No. 4 has 28 strings, 5 bars with shifters, producing 11 chords. This elegant instrument is made of imitation rosewood, with inlaid edges, sides and bottom. Complete, with music, instruction book and ring for playing. Each, **$10.65.**

No. 7264. Autoharp No. 5 has 28 strings, 5 bars with shifters and produces 13 chords. Made of beautiful rosewood, veneered, with inlaid edges, tops and sides. A charming instrument for solos, accompaniment or for concerts. Complete with music, instruction book and ring for playing. Our special price, each, **$13.50.**

No. 7265. Autoharp No. 6 is a special instrument designed for the highest class of music. It has 32 strings, 6 bars and produces 16 chords. Is made of handsome imitation rosewood, with inlaid edges, sides and bottom. Complete with music, ring for playing and instruction book. Our special price, each, **$18.50.**

# ZITHERS.

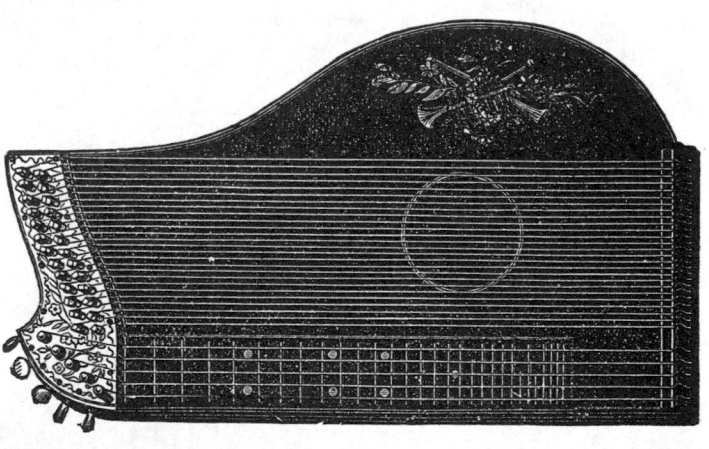

Our line of Zithers is selected with care from the stock of the most widely and favorably known manufacturer of these popular instruments. We hence assure customers the best satisfaction. We send any zither, C. O. D., subject to examination, on receipt of $1.00 with order. Weight, boxed, about 12 pounds.

No. 7270. Imitation rosewood, inlaid sound hole and edges, full strung, plain head, excellent grade and finish. In pasteboard case. Each, **$3.70.**

No. 7272. Zither, imitation rosewood, inlaid sound hole and edges, patent head, full strung, very excellent quality and model, fine finish. In pasteboard case. Price, each, **$5.35.**

No. 7273. Solid Rosewood Zither, finely polished and finished, pearl inlaid around sound hole, inlaid edges, patent head. In lined wood case, with lock handles and catches. Each, **$10.25.**

### CONCERT ZITHER.

No. 7275. Solid rosewood, highly polished, inlaid sound hole and edges, full strung, patent head. A very fine instrument. In excellen pasteboard case. Each, **$11.90**

# DULCIMERS

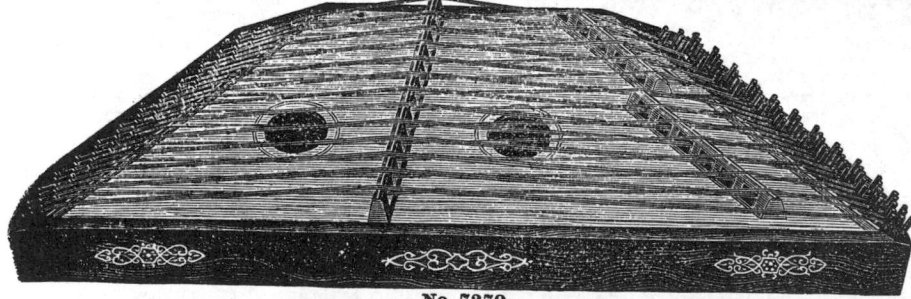

No. 7279.

No. 7279. The Dulcimer illustrated is selected for our trade, having in view the fact that the best is none too good. We are aware that there are Dulcimers on the market that are cheaper in price. They do not compare with the one we illustrate, either in appearance, tone or durability, and purchasers are invariably disappointed because of their general inferiority. This Dulcimer is finely finished, in imitation rosewood, and with neatly decorated body, chromatically strung. Can be perfectly tuned in any and all keys. Positively the most complete and most carefully made instrument of the kind. Weight, packed, 15 lbs. **Price, each, $22.90.**

# THE COLUMBIA ZITHER.

No. 7285 is a Musical Instrument in every sense of the word. It requires but little practice or musical ability to master and play in a manner enjoyable alike to audience and performer.

The 17 plain or melody strings at the right are played with the right hand, while the bass and accompaniment strings are played with the left hand, and the combination of sounds thus evoked is of a most agreeable nature.

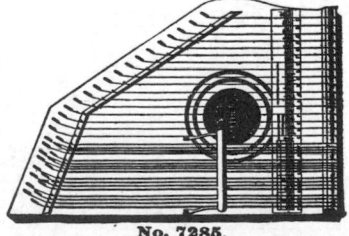

No. 7285.

34 Strings, Imitation Rosewood, Fine Finish, Complete in Pasteboard Case, with Picks, Tuning Key, and Instruction Book, containing also many pieces of Figure Music. Each, **$4.50.**

**FARTHER ALONG IN THIS DEPARTMENT WE SHOW A COMPLETE ASSORTMENT OF STRINGS AND MUSICAL INSTRUMENT FURNISHINGS. IF YOU DON'T SEE WHAT YOU WANT, LOOK IN THE INDEX. IF YOU DON'T FIND IT THERE, WRITE US ABOUT IT AND WE'LL QUOTE YOU THE BEST PRICES YOU EVER HEARD OF.**

# THE REGINA.

**The Queen of Automatic Musical Instruments.** The first of the kind ever manufactured in America, and it surpasses anything of similar nature manufactured by anyone anywhere. The mechanism of these music boxes is entirely different from any other. Interchangeable music sheets are used instead of the round cylinder in the old style music box. In the case of the latter, only one to a dozen tunes could be played without the great expense of an extra cylinder. With the Regina however, the expense of extra tune sheets is only about that of ordinary piano and organ music and they can be obtained in any quantity. The latest airs on the market can be secured almost simultaneously with their publication in paper form. This one fact is sufficient to render the Regina the most popular instrument of the kind on the market. The motive force in the Regina consists of an extremely solid, and yet in its unique combination, an extremely simple clockwork. One valuable feature of this clockwork lies in the fact that all the parts are interchangeable and we are able to supply duplicates of any part that may be broken by accident or otherwise.

The Regina is therefore an instrument of the highest standard, and one that with reasonable care will last a lifetime. Of an equally high degree of perfection, are the musical appointments. A clear melodious tone combined with a most remarkable sounding capacity has made the Regina the favorite of the music loving public.

The various features of the Regina are protected by many patents, some particulars of which we will mention:

In the larger sizes, the tune sheets are actuated from the outside by a sprocket wheel, engaging in holes near the edge of the disc, a very ingenious device, securing steady and easy motion. All instruments are provided with a speed-regulating device, by means of which an even tempo is obtained from beginning to end. Independent steel dampers are used, and their construction is the most perfect in existence. A silent winding arrangement is a special feature of the "Regina," and does away with the disagreeable noise occasioned in winding other music boxes. A safety winder is introduced, to prevent the over-winding or breaking of the main spring.

**No. 7300.**

The Regina is the only music box having duplex combs. The two combs face each other; the steel tongues are tuned and actuated in pairs, by corresponding star-wheels. An extraordinary volume and sweetness of tone is the result, and makes it possible to have as many as 156 keys in a small space, a range far exceeding that of the piano. All cases are made of solid American wood, such as mahogany, oak, walnut, etc., and are of elegant design and finish. The list of tunes increases every day, and is already large and varied enough to meet the taste of every purchaser. The metallic tune sheets are easily interchanged, thus making it possible for each individual box to play an unlimited variety of airs. The sale of these tune-sheets at very reasonable prices will continue for years after the boxes are sold. A guide for operating, oiling and repairing the Regina music box goes free with each instrument.

No. 7300. Regina music box as illustrated is one of the smaller ones, but is just as perfect in its working parts as the most expensive. The case is made of solid oak or solid mahogany and is highly polished. Dimensions are 9¾ inches long, 8¾ inches wide and 7 inches high, tune sheets are 8½ inches in diameter. Has 41 steel tongues. Spring movement. Plays classical music, sacred and popular airs, in fact every kind that can be produced on any instrument. Weight packed, about 20 lbs. Our Special price, complete with one tune sheet......................$14.95 Extra tune sheets, 30 cents each. List of nearly 200 airs for this instrument sent on application.

No. 7301. Regina is precisely the same as No. 7300 described above, but instead of having a spring movement and running automatically, it is played by turning a crank. It is just the same size, has same tune sheets and same mechanism with the exception of motive power. Extra tune sheets 30 cents each. Our Special price........................................$8.70

No. 7302. Regina music box shown in the illustration is made with handsome oak and mahogany case highly polished. This case is 13 inches long, 12 inches wide and 8¾ inches high. The mechanism contains 56 steel tongues. Tune sheets are 11 inches in diameter. Weight, boxed, about 25 lbs. Our Special price, complete with one tune sheet.................................$29.75

Extra tune sheets, 55 cents each. List of music for this instrument sent free on application.

No. 7305. Regina music box. Case is made either of mahogany, 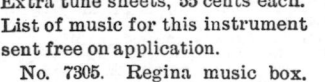 maple or oak beautifully polished. Size is 21 inches long, 18½ inches wide by 9½ inches high. Working part contains 156 steel tongues, while the tune sheets are 15½ inches in diameter, rendering possible the rendition of the most difficult and classical music with perfect precision and charming execution. With this magnificent instrument, you can have rendered in your home, such music as the most brilliant pianist is capable of and that without the slightest musical talent or the expenditure of the hundreds of dollars necessary to secure musical education. The extra music costs little more that would the same were it in paper form. Weight boxed, about 40 lbs. Our Special price, complete with all attachments and one tune sheet...........$78.95 Extra tune sheets 76 cents each. List of over 300 musical selections free on application.

**We ship these Magnificent Instruments** C. O. D., subject to examination, on receipt of $5.00 with order, balance to be paid to express agent when you find everything to your satisfaction.

**We are more than anxious** to introduce a Regina into every neighborhood. It is so novel in action, so wonderful in perfect and accurate mechanism and so exquisite in its music producing qualities, that one sale in a locality will mean a certain sale of many more. All the power and purity of piano music is duplicated on this most unique and elegant instrument of the age. Years of study at an expense of hundreds of dollars would not enable a musician to execute more accurately or produce more pleasing music than the Regina renders automatically. An instrument for the wealth-

**No. 7302.**

**No. 7305**

iest homes and just as popular and desirable for those who are less able to invest in luxuries.

**The Price of the finest Regina** is much less than would have to be paid at retail for an inferior Parlor Organ which requires a musician to render it of any value. **We guarantee every Regina** absolutely perfect in mechanism and will replace any defective part free of all charge.

## Music Boxes.

We import our entire line of Music Boxes from the most reputable manufacturers of Switzerland. We can thus insure our customers that our line is the most select ever introduced into the American market. Importing direct, we are in a position to name the very lowest prices obtainable, and a careful inspection of this department will reveal bargain prices to be secured nowhere else, quality being considered. Our terms are most liberal. On receipt of $5.00 with order, we will send any Music Box C.O.D., subject to examination, allowing customer the privilege of **returning the instrument if found unsatisfactory. Money will be cheerfully refunded.**

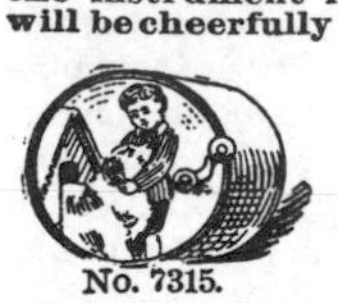

No. 7315.

No. 7315. Small Music Box, has 12 teeth, plays one tune by turning crank at top. Well adjusted and accurate in construction. Round nickel case, with fancy chromo top. Weight, 10 oz. Our special price ........ $0.48

No. 7316. Music Box, same style as above, but has 36 teeth and plays two airs. Large, round, nickel case, fancy chromo top. Our special price ........ $1.05

No. 7317. Music Box, oblong wood case, 4x3½ inches in size. Fancy chromo top. Has 18 teeth and plays two airs by turning small crank in top. A music box that will please old as well as young and last a long time. Made substantially by one of the best European manufacturers.

Our special price, each $0.78

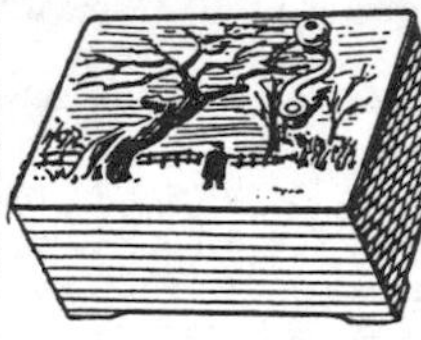

No. 7317

No. 7318. Music Box like No. 7317 illustrated and described above, but larger in size. Has 18 teeth and plays three popular airs.

Our special price, each ........ $1.24

No. 7319. Music Box is also an oblong wood box case with chromo top and larger size. Has 60 teeth and plays two airs. Remarkable for beautiful tone.

Our special price, each ........ $1.85

## Music Boxes with Spring Movements and Key.

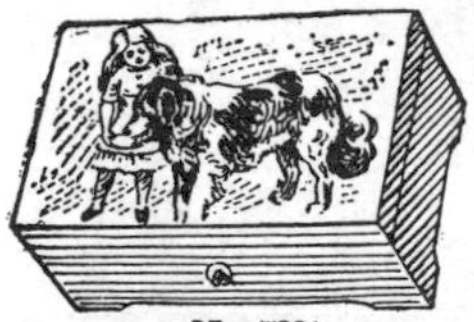

No. 7321.

No. 7321. Music Box, as shown in the illustration, is 4¾x2½ inches in size, winds up with key and runs automatically by spring movement. Has 1¼ inch cylinder, plays two airs, and is self-changing. The handsome wood case has chromo top. Lid opens, exposing cylinder. Weight, 16 oz. Our special price, each ... $2.35

No. 7322. Music Box. Is like No. 7321, shown and described above, but is much larger, having a 3 inch cylinder and playing three airs automatically. Is wound with key and is self-changing. Handsome wood case, with chromo top on hinged lid. Weight, 19 oz. Our special price ........ $4.95

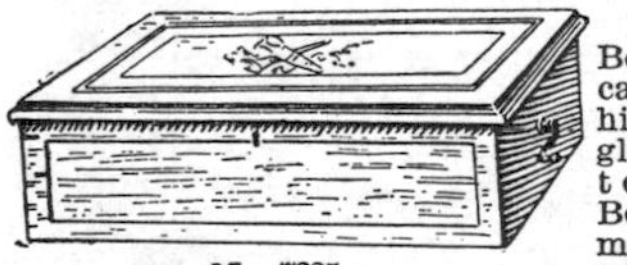

No. 7325.

No. 7325. Music Box. Fancy wood case with decorated hinged lid. Interior glass cover to protect mechanism. Best spring lever movement with winding key on outside as shown in picture, or with inside rachet lever as desired. Plays all the tunes without rewinding; 3⅜ inch cylinders. Plays four popular airs. Self changing. A music box is an entertaining instrument, and especially so in cases where no member of the family is a musician. Weight, 15 pounds, boxed.

Our special price ........ $7.95

No. 7326. Music Box is precisely like No. 7325 shown and described above, but plays six airs. And has outside winding attachment only. Our special price .. $8.35

No. 7327. Music Box is also like No. 7325 above, but is very much larger and more complete. Has large 6 inch cylinder and plays ten of the latest and most popular airs. Has either outside or inside winding arrangement. Weight, packed, about 25 pounds.

Our special price ........ $15.35

No. 7330. This music box is one of the most desirable instruments manufactured. The charming music so much admired is due partly to the wonderful precision rendered possible by the perfect construction of cylinder and teeth. An extraordinary volume and sweetness of tone is a feature of this elegant music box. The cylinder is 6 inches long and plays six tunes. The case is a beautiful one, made with rosewood top, decorated with variegated wood inlaying. Interior glass cover to protect mechanism; fancy nickel plated spring lever movement, furnished with either inside ratchet or outside crank winding; can be stopped at end of any tune by a lever; it can be made to repeat any air or can be made self-changing so that all the airs will be played in succession. Weight, boxed, about 30 lbs. Size, 16½ long, 7½ wide, 5½ high. Complete, as described, with time dial. Our special price ........ $16.95

No. 7331. Music box. Follows the same general description of No. 7330 above, but is larger and has a greater capacity. Size of case is 20 inches long by 7½ inches wide, 8 inch cylinder, playing ten airs. Case, attachments, etc., just as No. 7330.

Our special price ........ $22.45

We quote zither attachments with either of last two music boxes at $1.40 extra. This attachment consists of a small roll of thin paper attached to the underside of an ornamental nickel bar, and when pressed against the teeth of the comb produces the effect of a zither. It can be detached at will, allowing the box to play in its natural tone.

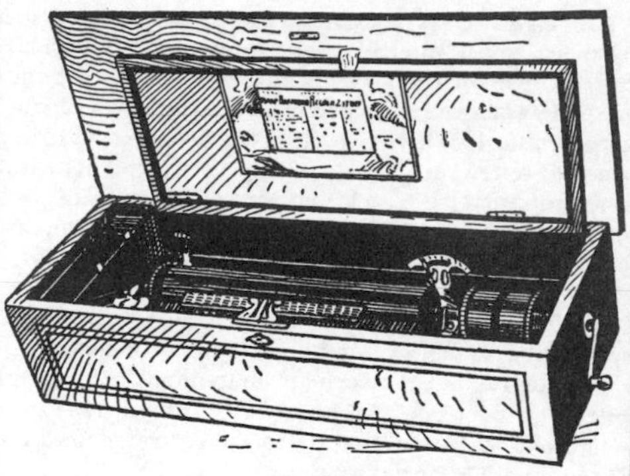

No. 7334.

o. 7334. Musical Box. Is a superb instrument, producing music most pleasing to all lovers of harmony. The case is decidedly beautiful, with solid rosewood top, variegated wood inlaying, interior glass cover, spring lever, nickel plated movement, time dial, safety check, tune skipper and speed regulator. Extra large 13 inch cylinder, playing twelve airs. An additional feature is the Zither attachment, as described with No. 7331 Music Box. The sublime harmony of this elegant instrument is unexcelled for beauty, and no purchaser will ever regret the investment.

The Box is furnished with either a ratchet lever inside, or outside crank winding attachment, as desired. We guarantee this instrument to be as represented or money refunded. If desired we will ship C. O. D. subject to examination and approval on receipt of $5 with order; balance, with express charges, to be paid to express agent when found satisfactory. Three per cent. off on all full cash orders. Weight, boxed, about 40 lbs.

Our Special Price ........ $32.45

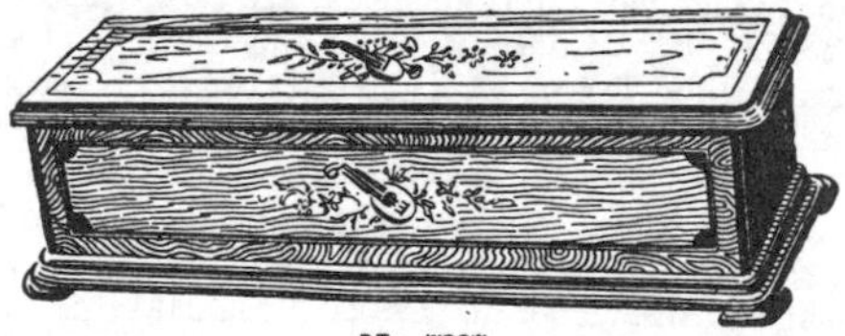

No. 7337.

No. 7337. Music Box, shown in the accompanying illustration, has an especially rich and imposing appearance, that is, fully in accord with its superb quality. The case is of rich rosewood, with beautiful variegated inlayings. The interior has glass covers to protect working parts. Case has handsome moulded base. Spring movement is wound by inside nickel plated ratchet or nickeled outside crank, as ordered. The special cylinder is 11 inches long, and plays eight airs, with guitar-mandolin effect. The pleasing qualities of the music are still further enhanced by the extra attachment for producing zither effect when desired. The combination possible on this music box is productive of especially delightful effects in music of rapid movement, as every note is brought out clear and distinct.

Additional features of this elegant instrument are the tune dial, showing the tune being played; safety check, tune skipper, enabling anyone to change the instrument to play any tune; speed regulator, causing it to play fast or slow; lever to repeat same tune, or play all airs in rotation. Size, 20 in. long by 7½ in. wide. Weight, packed, 40 lbs.

Our special price ........ $43.35

## Not A Toy.

No. 7340. Our Favorite Roller Organ for $4.95 is made to please the artistic ear of the most accomplished musician. At the same time, it is so simple that a little child can play it. One of the most perfect musical instruments ever produced. Thousands would not think of being without a musical instrument of some kind in the house, if it had not been for the expense of the instrument itself, and the time and money it would take to learn to play it.

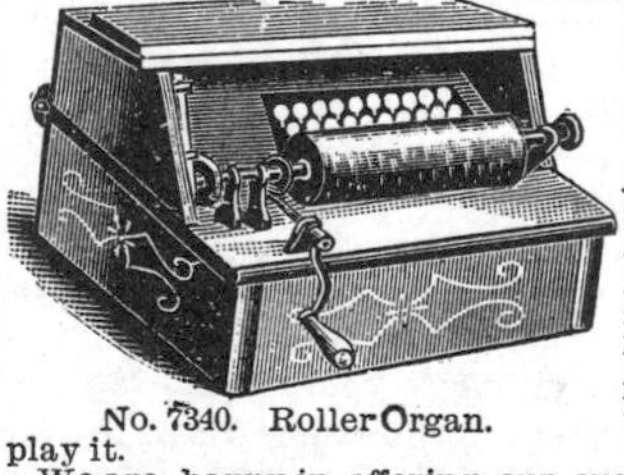

No. 7340. Roller Organ.

We are happy in offering our customers as sweet-toned an instrument as heart could desire. We are especially pleased that we can make the price at a point within the reach of everybody. Furthermore, the Gem Roller Organ requires only the simple turning of the handle, and the music is yours.

As you will note in the picture, the music is obtained from the roller, which has teeth or pins like those on the roller of a music box. These pins operate on the valve keys, and the roller is turned by gearing, which also works the bellows. The mechanism is after the same plan of the parlor organ. You can get rollers of anykind of music you want—Sacred, Spanish or German music, popular airs, waltzes, or any kind of dance music. These rollers cost only the same or less than ordinary sheet music. This is an especially durable instrument. The reeds are of full organ size, and the volume of tone is equal to that of a fine parlor organ. The case is an elegant one of Imitation Black Walnut, and is 16 inches long, 14 inches wide, and 9 inches high. Weight boxed, 15 pounds. No. 7340 our special price with three rollers of music free ........ $4.95

Send for complete list of extra music rollers.

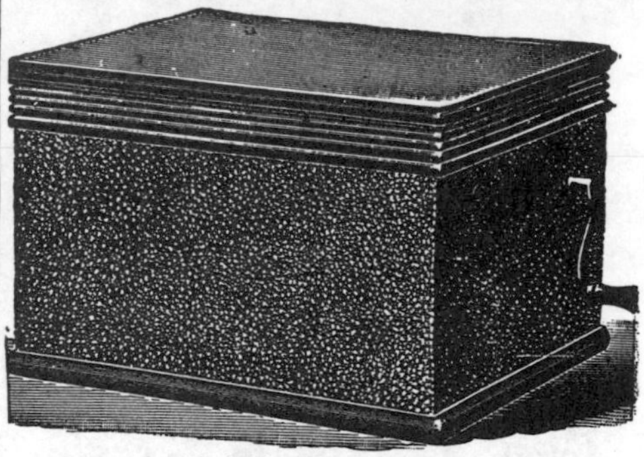

No. 7341. The Angelica.

No. 7341. You might spend hundreds of dollars in music lessons and not be able to produce sweeter music than this most wonderful musical instrument of the age. No knowledge of music necessary, Just turn the handle and any popular or religious air can be played. If you couldn't see the Angelica when it was being played, you would think there was a grand parlor organ in the house, played by an artistic musician.

The Angelica is the greatest and latest improvement over the old style Organette. It contains fourteen reeds, and the case is made of black walnut moulding and cover, with real leatherette sides. The entire case is beautifully finished, and makes a pleasing and elegant ornament for any house, be it ever so rich or ever so humble.

The size of this beautiful musical instrument is 12½ inches long, 10 inches high, and 9¼ inches wide.

The music is produced by means of perforated paper, which is rolled on spools. We have all the latest tunes in stock, as well as the old time melodies. Extra music costs you less than the sheet music for organ or piano. We furnish one roll of music free with the Angelica. We have printed lists of music, and will send list on application. These lists include Sacred, German, Norwegian, Swedish and Spanish music, popular airs and dance music. If you want to dan e, the Angelica will give you the music. If you want to sing, the Angelica is just the thing for an accompaniment. For church service, for lodge, for the home, the Angelica is an inexpensive instrument that will delight everyone. The price cuts no figure, it is so small. We want to introduce one of these Angelicas into your neighborhood. We know that you will be delighted, and everybody else will be crazy for one. Just to get you started to buying your musical instruments through us, we make you a special price. No. 7341, packed in a neat light box, complete with one roll of music, $6.50.

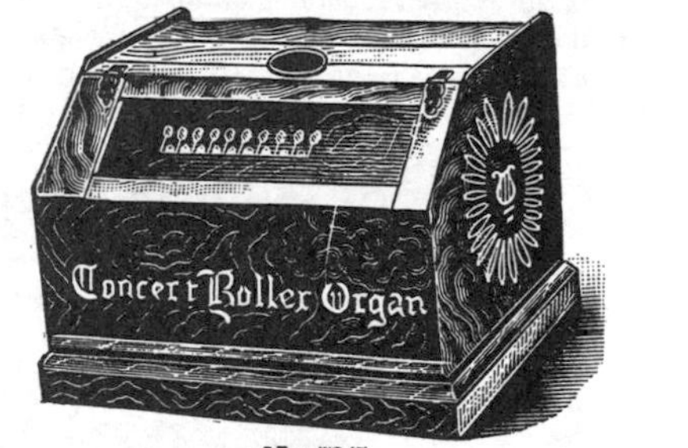


No. 7345.

No. 7345. The Concert Roller Organ is a delightful instrument for the household. It is of quite good size, and hence capable of producing a greater volume of tone than most roller organs. The case is of handsome black walnut, with glass top and finely finished. It is 19 inches long, 16 inches wide and 14 inches high. Has extra strong bellows and fine reeds. Weight, boxed, about 30 lbs.

Price, complete, with five music rollers ........ $9.00

We can furnish extra rollers playing one tune each at 23 cts.; postage, 7 cts. each, extra. Music lists free on application.

## Accordeons.

We import our accordeons direct from European manufacturers, selecting them with a view to securing instruments superior for quality, tone, beauty and durability. We claim for the line quoted below that it includes the very choicest accordeons made and sold anywhere. We ship on the most liberal C. O. D. terms and allow you to examine each instrument if you so desire before paying in full. All orders should be accompanied with $1.00 as a guarantee of good faith. We allow a discount of 3 per cent. on all full cash orders.

(See next page.)

BY REFERRING TO THE INDEX, YOU CAN LOOK UP THE CROCKERY DEPARTMENT, WHICH CONTAINS A NEW LINE JUST IMPORTED FROM EUROPE AND PRICED AT EUROPEAN PRICES.

### Our $4 Accordeon for $1.85.

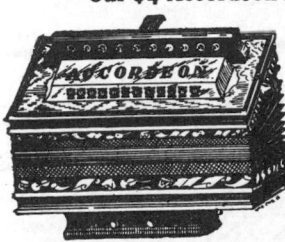

No. 7365. Requires little musical ability and less money. An accordeon with the merit of a high priced musical instrument. Has fancy decorated moulded frame, enameled cloth trimmed bellows and nickel key cover. 10 keys, 1 stop, and 2 full sets of reeds. Packed in a light box, weighs about 7 pounds. We send it

No. 7365.

C. O. D. subject to examination on receipt of $1 Pay 85 cts. balance to agent when found as we say.

### Accordeon. Our Price, $2.05.

No. 7367. Sent C. O. D. subject to examination. A special accordeon at a special price. Worth double what we ask. Fancy ebonized moulding. with nickel edges; open key-board. The ten nickel keys are ornamented with gilt stars. The panels, corners and clasps are handsomely bronzed. This accordeon has two stops, two sets of reeds and double bellows. Send $1.00 deposit with order and we send accordeon by express subject to examination. Pay agent $1.05 balance when you see it's all right.

No. 7367.

### Accordeon.

**Special quality. Our special price...........$2.25**

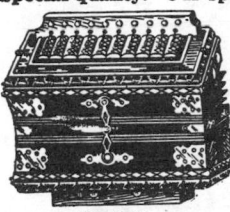

No. 7369. Nothing of equal value to be had at retail for $6.00. Made in imitation solid oak, with hand carved moulding and keys. Special broad reeds. Corners and clasps heavily nickel plated. Double bellows. Flannel-lined leather straps. This accordeon has ten fancy keys, two stops and two sets of reeds. Sent C.O.D.,

No. 7369. subject to examination, on $1.00 deposit. Three per cent. off for full cash with order, and $2.18 is the price.

### Our $2.45 Accordeon.

No. 7370. Made by the best known Berlin manufacturer. Quality unsurpassed. Rich full tones equal to parlor organ. Beautiful moulded frame with open keyboard and ten nickel plated keys. Corners and clasps are also extra nickel plated. Double bellows, two stops and two sets of reeds. We send this accordeon C. O. D., subject to examination on receipt of $1.

No. 7370.

### Accordeon. Our special Price, $2.65.

No. 7373. A musical instrument of powerful tone and general superiority. One of the most popular styles made by a celebrated Berlin manufacturer. Made in imitation of solid oak with fancy moulding and panels. Open keyboard, corners and clasps nickel plated; double bellows; ten keys, two stops and two sets of reeds. Sent C.O.D.,subject to

No. 7373. Balance, $1.65, paid at express office. Weight, packed, 7 lbs. approval on receipt of $1.00.

No. 7374. Miniature Accordeon. A hand painted accordeon for $4.25. A beautiful instrument, capable of producing music that will captivate the most artistic musician. The panels and moulding are handsomely ebonized, and have tasty hand painted ornaments; ten patent nickel plated keys, clasps and corners likewise nickel plated, double bellows, two stops, two sets of reeds. Weight, packed, about 8 lbs.

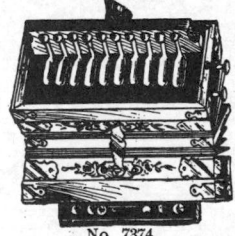

No. 7374.

C.O.D., subject to examination, on receipt of $1.00.

---

No. 7376. Kalbe's Imperial Accordeon with twelve fancy keys for $3.85. Usually retailed for $8. Weight, packed, about 8 pounds. Broad ebonized mouldings, with beautifully decorated and hand painted bellows frame, open key board, nickel plated corners and clasps. Double leather bound bellows, two stops, two sets of reeds. The two basses and twelve keys, including two half tones, render possible the play-

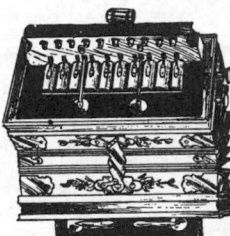

No 7376.

ing of more difficult music, thus making the instrument desirable for professionals. Sent C. O. D., subject to examination upon receipt of $1. Weight, packed, about 8 pounds.

No. 7379. Accordeon for $3.95, sent C. O. D. subject to examination.

Has more music to the cubic inch than any other Accordeon made. Requires little musical ability. Is one of the simplest instruments made. Has ten nickel plated keys, nickel plated corners and clasps. The fancy moulded frame has nickel ornamented panels. Sixteen fancy trumpets in moulding and ten trumpets in key cover. Triple bellows, two stops and two sets of reeds. Send $1 with order and we send this beautiful accordeon C. O. D. subject to examination. Weight, packed, about 8 lbs.

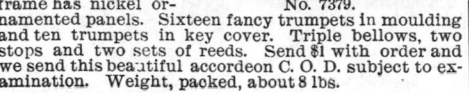

No. 7379.

No. 7380. The "Tuxedo" Accordeon, with "Vox Humana" or Tremola attachment. Kalbe's Imperial. Our special price, $4.65. Sold only in large cities by retailers at double our price. A musical instrument whose powerful and full round tones are a delight to amateur and expert alike. Made with handsome ebonized mouldings and panels.

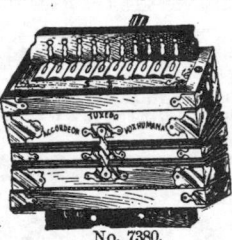

No. 7380.

Open key board with ten nickel plated keys and two basses. The hand painted ornaments on panels and the nickel plated corners and clasps make the instrument one which will delight the eye, as well as the ear. The double bellows are leather bound. Two stops and two sets of reeds with Vox Humana attachment. C.O.D., subject to examination, on receipt of $1.00. Weight, packed, about 9 lbs.

No. 7381. A Genuine Kalbe Imperial Accordeon, New Model, for $4.75. Sent C.O.D., subject to examination on receipt of $1.00. Guaranteed to be as described or money refunded. An instrument that will give as much of a musical treat as a hundred dollar organ or a three hundred dollar piano. Broad ebonized mouldings, sunken panels. Bellows are double and leather bound, bellows frame handsomely decorated, nickel plated clasps and corners, ten round nickel plated keys, two stops, two sets extra quality reeds. Weight, packed, about 9 lbs.

No. 7381.

No. 7382. Medium Size Kalbe's Imperial Accordeon. Warranted Genuine German Make. Our Special Price, $4.95.

We include a very complete instruction book with this special accordeon. With this book anyone can soon be an expert player. Accordeon has ebonized mouldings and panels. The bellows frame is silver stamped. The corners and clasps are nickel plated and the extra strong bel-

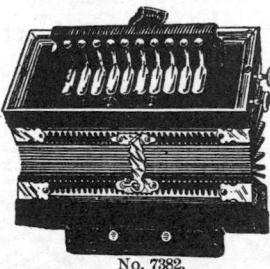

No. 7382.

lows are nickel protected, ten keys and two basses heavily plated, two stops, two sets broad reeds. Sent C. O. D., on receipt of $1. If not as represented it can be returned to us at our expense and money refunded. Weight, packed, about 9 pounds. Our special price, $4.95.

---

No. 7384. Special High Grade Accordeon. A $10 Instrument for $5.45. We import direct from Germany and can sell at what they cost the retailer. We give a complete instruction book free with each instrument. This special accordeon is made with broad ebonized mouldings and fancy gilt stamped panels. Ten patent nickel plated keys and two bases. Extra strong leather bound bellows, with nickel protectors.

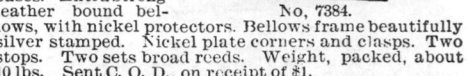

No. 7384.

Bellows frame beautifully silver stamped. Nickel plate corners and clasps. Two stops. Two sets broad reeds. Weight, packed, about 10 lbs. Sent C. O. D., on receipt of $1.

No. 7386. Accordeon. Our Special Introduction Price, $5.85. A decided hit in the accordeon line; a novelty that meets the popular demand for an instrument that will produce just as fine music as would one costing as many dollars as this does nickels. The moulded frames are fancy decorated, while the panels have handsome nickel ornamentation, mirrored nickel round rings, etc.; nickel plated corners and clasps; double leather bound bellows; seventeen keys, two stops, four sets extra quality broad reeds. C. O. D., for $1.00. Examine at express office and pay agent balance of $4.85. Weight, packed, about 10 lbs.

No. 7388. The Climax Accordeon. Our special price, $5.90. A special instruction book free with each accordeon. This superior instrument has broad ebonized mouldings, sunken keyboard, copper and silver br'nz'd panels, ten nickeled keys, sixteen

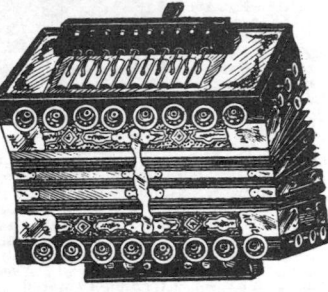

decorated trumpets, fancy plated corners and clasps, extra triple bellows, leather bound, fancy gilt ornaments throughout, six stops and tremolo, three sets of reeds. Weight, packed, about 11 lbs. Sent C. O. D., subject to examination on receipt of $1.00.

### A $12 Accordeon for $6.15.

No. 7390. No use paying the retail price when you need pay only our special importers price. We throw in a complate instruction book and it saves you all the expense of a teacher. This decidedly superior instrument is faultless in construction, appearance, and musical possibilities. Has ebonized mouldings and panels, nickle bordered. Open key board. Gold

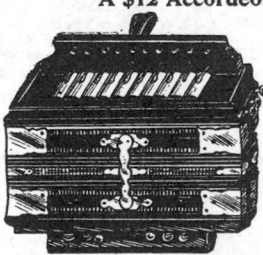

No. 7390.

stamped leatherette double bellows. Ten nickel keys, nickel plated corners and clasps, three stops, three sets reeds. Weight, packed, about 11 pounds. Sent C.O.D., on receipt of $1 and you can examine it at the express office.

No. 7391. New Style Accordeon. Special Price, $6.95. The "Empress" professional instrument. Broad mahogany mold'd frames, mahogany panels and keys. The frame and panels are ornamented with handsome gilt and nickel ornaments. Clasps and corners fully nickel plated. Sunken open key board, double ribbed bellows, ten keys, eight stops, four sets of reeds, tuned in chords. Complete instruction book free. Weight, packed, about 18 lbs. Sent C. O. D., subject to examination on receipt of $1.

---

**OUR SPORTING GOODS DEPARTMENT INCLUDES EVERYTHING FOR OUTDOOR SPORTS. THE BICYCLE RIDER, THE FOOT BALL PLAYER, THE BASE BALL PLAYER, THE TENNIS PLAYER, EVERY SPORTSMAN WILL FIND COMPLETE OUTFITS AT WHOLESALE PRICES.**

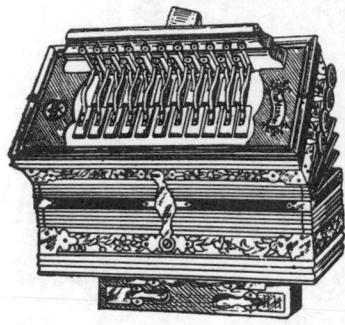

**No. 7393.** Genuine Pitzschier Accordeon. Retails for $18.00. Our special price, $9.45. A special importation direct from Berlin Germany. Most remarkably superior in richness and purity of tone, ease of action, as well as in details of construction. Fine fluted mouldings in imitation mahogany; panels, genuine mahogany; all wood work finely polished and finished; sunken open-action keyboard; 19 nickel keys; heavy double bellows, with nickel protectors; nickel plated corners and clasps; four stops; four fine sets of reeds. A complete instruction book free. Weight, packed, about 20 lbs. We send it C.O.D., anywhere on receipt of $1.00. Pay balance, $8.45, to express agent when you see the instrument is all right.

**No. 7394.** Accordeon is just the same in every way as No. 7393, described above, but has twenty-one nickel plated keys, as shown in the illustration. Weight, packed, about 20 lbs. Sent C.O.D. on receipt of $1.00. Our special price.....................$10.60

**No. 7395.** Accordeon shown in the illustration is the Accordeon we sell at $11.80. Retailers sell it at $20.00. This beautiful instrument is one of the most elegant on the market, and will delight the most exacting professional. It is, however, designed to meet the demands of the amateur as well as of

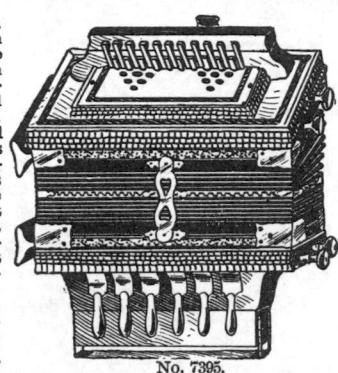

No. 7395.

the expert. The frame is made with carved mahogany mouldings and walnut panels with marquetry inlayings; case and bellows are morocco covered and gilt stamped. Additional features are the knee pieces, as shown in the illustration. The thumb guide is moveable; twenty-one long ivory keys, with sound holes; six upright bass keys, with leather hand rest; corners and clasps heavily nickel plated; double bellows, leather bound; four stops, four sets finest reeds made. Instruction book, sent free, will enable anyone to learn the instrument thoroughly in a short time. Weight, packed, about 23 lbs. This elegant musical instrument is sent C.O.D., subject to examination, on receipt of $1.00. You examine it at the express office and if found as we represent it, pay the agent the balance and the Accordeon is yours.

**No. 7396.** Accordeon is precisely the same style as above, same keys, bellows, knee rests, etc., but a plainer finish. Our special price....................$11.25

### Concertinas.

**No. 7400.** Our Price $2.15. Retails at $4.

**CONCERTINA.**

Description: Mahogany, full size, 20 keys, bone buttons, nickel sound rings, good tone. Weight boxed 7 pounds. C.O.D. to any one on receipt of $1, balance $1.15 to be paid at express office.

No. 7400.

**No. 7401.** Concertina at one-half the regular retail price. Our Special Price, $2.55. Beautifully toned and pleasing in general appearance. Has twenty full-sized keys and is made with mahogany tops, decorated with German silver edges and inlaying. Fancy sound rings. Well protected double bellows. Send $1 and we send this concertina C.O.D. subject to examination. Weight, boxed, about 7 lbs.

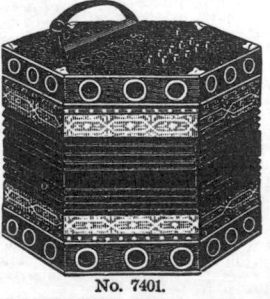

No. 7401.

**No. 7404.** Concertina. Our special price, $2.85. A most popular instrument and one capable of producing music of remarkable sweetness and variety. The one shown in the illustration has twenty keys. Mahogany tops decorated with nickel ornaments. Nickeled sound rings. Extra quality large bellows. Weight packed about 7 pounds. Sent C.O.D., subject to examination on receipt of $1.

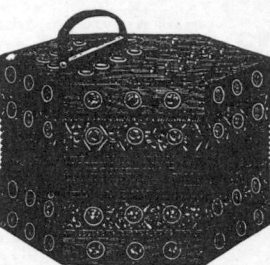

No. 7404.

**No. 7406.** Concertina shown in the illustration is of special quality and sold by us at a price far below retail value. The real rosewood tops are handsomely decorated with neat figured mouldings. Twenty bone keys; extra quality large bellows. Only the most select reeds are used in this concertina, so as to insure the most satisfactory results to the player. Weight, packed, 7 lbs.

No. 7406.

Our special price.....................$3.85
Sent C.O.D., for examination on receipt of $1.00.

**No. 7408.** Our Price $5.60. Retails at $10.

**CONCERTINA.**

Description: Mahogany case, German silver inlayings, leather bound bellows, twenty keys, broad reeds, heavy tone, finely finished. Weight boxed 8 pounds.
C.O.D., on receipt of $1.

No. 7408.

**No. 7410.** Our Price $9.35. Retails at $20.

**English Concertina.**

Description: Anglo-German pattern, made of mahogany, twenty keys, leather bound bellows, five folds. In wood case. Weight boxed 6 pounds.
This is one of the finest instruments made and our price is about one-half the regular retail price.

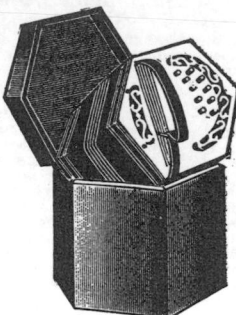

No. 7410.

## HARMONICAS.

Our assortment is the best ever offered. We import in large quantities from European manufacturers and quote at the lowest possible prices, based on our economic factory-to-consumer system. Weight, from 3 to 7 oz.

**No. 7425. Brass Band Harmonica. The King of all Harmonicas.** The best in quality, the strongest toned, the most durable instrument of the kind. Has the best bell metal reeds. The tone is remarkably rich and powerful, as well as delightfully smooth, a characteristic which makes the instrument especially desirable to professionals. Has solid brass reed plates, solid metal covers (hence the reeds are perfectly protected), extension ends, ten single holes, twenty bell metal reeds. Tuned accurately to concert pitch and can be had in any key. Postage, 4 cts. Our Special Price.................$0.22     Per dozen......................2.40

THE BRASS BAND HARMONICA
Extra Full Tone
BELL     METAL     REEDS

**No. 7426. The finest Instrument of the kind in the World.** Made by a most celebrated manufacturer, it has just been put on the market, and met already with an enormous sale. We import these elegant instruments direct from Europe in large quantities, securing the lowest net manufacturer's price. For purity and volume of tone this Harmonica has no equal. The reeds are made of the finest bell metal, and are extremely sensitive, producing a remarkably smooth tone. The covers are flaring at the back, and are made of solid brass, heavily nickel plated, and are consequently of unusual strength, thus protecting the reeds perfectly. Accurately tuned to concert pitch. The Brass Band Harmonica, illustrated, has ten double holes, forty bell metal reeds, brass reed plates and extension ends. It is in high favor with professional and amateur alike. Retails for $1 and is worth every cent of it. On our one small profit plan direct from the factory we sell at less than half retail price. We include a handsome lined case, as shown in the illustration. Postage......................$0.08
Our Special Price, as described......................$0.50     Per dozen......................5.40

(See full assortment of harmonicas on next page).

**THE TERMS ON WHICH WE SHIP ARE SO LIBERAL THAT NO ONE NEED FEAR DISSATISFACTION. WE SEND ALMOST ALL GOODS C. O. D., SUBJECT TO EXAMINATION, ON A SMALL DEPOSIT. IF THE GOODS ARE NOT ALL RIGHT, YOU DON'T TAKE THEM AND YOU GET YOUR DEPOSIT BACK.**

**(Harmonicas Continued.)**

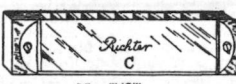

No. 7427. Genuine Richter Harmonica, ten single holes, brass reed plates, nickel covers.

Special price, each.............$0.05
Per doz..............................0.50

No. 7428. Genuine Richter Harmonica, is same as above, but is double, having ten single holes at each side, twenty single holes in all.
Our special price, each...............$0.10
Per doz.........................................1.05

No. 7429. "The New Troubadour" Harmonica. Perfectly tuned and of excellent tone; ten single holes; white reed plates, nickel plated covers.
Price, each............$0.08
Per doz...................0.90

No. 7429.

No. 7430. The harmonica shown is a genuine Gebruder Ludwig-Richter pattern, and the best cheap instrument made.
No. 7430.
Ten single holes; brass reed plates; nickel covers.
Price, each............$ .12
Per doz...................1.28

No. 7432. Genuine Gebruder Ludwig harmonica, Richter pattern; superior reeds, affording a rich resonant tone. Ten single holes on each side; twenty holes in all; brass reed plates; nickel plated covers.
Price each............$ .23
Per doz...................2.55

No. 7432.

No. 7433. Professional Concert Harmonica. The celebrated Gebruder Ludwig make, ten double holes, forty superior reeds. Brass reed plates. Engraved German silver covers. An instrument of exceptional quality and one that is especially admired by professional players. Our special price, each..................$0.36
Per dozen............................................4.25

No. 7435. The Improved Emmet Harmonica. A neat little instrument very pleasing to all admirers of music. Has ten single holes. Brass reed plates and nickel plated covers.
Our special price, each.....$0.12
Per dozen........................1.38

No. 7435.

No. 7436. Harmonica. Ten single holes; best steel bronze reeds; nickel plated reed plates and covers. A universal favorite. Our special price, each............$ .15
No. 7436.
Per doz...................1.70

No. 7437. The Silver Tongued Richter. Rightly named. A harmonica of special quality. Ten double holes; brass reed plates; nickel covers.
Our special price, each............$ .17
Per doz...................2.00

No. 7437.

No. 7439. The Columbia Exhibition Harmonica. An instrument that has met with great favor, and fully deserves it. Has ten single holes, nickel reed plates and covers, full set superior German silver reeds, bronzed wood. Extra quality throughout.
Our special price, each............$0.20
Per doz...................2.30

No. 7439.

No. 7441. The M. Hohner Harmonica, one of the best known and best liked Harmonicas made; ten single holes, best reeds and brass reed plates. Nickel covers. Price, each.
No. 7441.
Per dozen............2.25

No. 7442.

No. 7442. A special Hohner Harmonica with ten double holes, forty excellent reeds, brass reed plates and nickel covers. Price, each.............$0.45
Per dozen.......................................5.15

No. 7444.

One of the finest Hohner Harmonicas, sixteen double holes; thirty-two superfine reeds, perfectly tuned in chords. Brass reed plates. Nickel covers.
Our special price, each.............$0.55
Per dozen.............................5.85

No. 7446.

No. 7446. Hohner Harmonica. A double instrument of powerful and pleasing tone. Has ten double holes on each edge, twenty double holes in all; eighty very fine reeds, brass reed plates, nickel covers.
Our special price, each.............$0.85
Per doz..............................9.60

No. 7447. Carl Essbach's Richter harmonica, good quality, 10 single holes, 20 reeds, brass reed plates, nickel cover. Each, $0.10
Per dozen..............$1.00

No. 7447.

Weight, 3 oz.

No. 7448. Carl Essbach's new French harp extra fine quality, pure tone, perfectly tuned; 10 single holes, 20 German silver reeds, brass reed plates nickel covers, extension ends. Each.............$0.13
Per dozen....................................1.40

No. 7448.

Weight, 3 oz.

No. 7449.

No. 7449. Essbach's Miniature concert harmonica. 10 double holes, 40 reeds, brass reed plate, nickel covers. This harmonica fills a long felt want, it being a full concert, but of small size, therefore the tones are easily produced, besides, it can be covered with the hands, same as the Richters. Each.............$0.32
Per dozen.............................................$3.45

Weight, 4 oz.

No. 7450.

No. 7450. Harmonica, with celluloid shell. A novelty that is in universal demand. The celluloid shell adds resonance to the tone and makes playing easier. Ten single holes; twenty fine reeds; brass reed plates. Our special price, each.............$ .25
Per doz.............................2.70

No. 7452. Harmonica with celluloid shell. The celebrated Doerfel's International concert system. Justly famous for the general excellence of its make and the remarkable purity and harmony of tone. Has ten double holes; forty best reeds; brass reed plates and an especially desirable feature, the celluloid case, which adds not only to the tone but also to the ease of playing. Price, each.............$ .45
Per doz.............................4.75

No. 7452.

No. 7455.

No. 7455. Harmonica. Our special Ph. Brunnbauer instrument for $1.15. Worth $2.00. One of the most powerful toned harmonicas made. Beautiful gilt and fancy enameled covers decorated with flowers, etc. Best brass reed plates, finest reeds, thirty-two double holes. Will produce the most exquisite music in the hands of an expert player. Our special price, each, $1.15

No. 7456. Harmonica is the same genuine Ph. Brunnbauer make as above described, but has forty double holes. Our special price each.............$1.30

No. 7459. Genuine Richter Bell Harmonica, with bell. The best quality of reeds is used in this instrument; 10 single holes, brass reed plates, German silver covers, extended ends, one bell.
No. 7459.
Our price, each.............$0.25
Per doz.............................2.95
No. 7459½. Same, with two bells. Each.............0.39
Per doz.............................4.60

No. 7460.

No. 7460. Our Special Concert Harmonica, with bells. Best quality; ten double holes with forty reeds, brass reed plates, fancy engraved German silver covers. Two bells. Our special price, each.............$0.65
Per doz.............................7.65

No. 7462. Harmonica Set. Genuine Wilhelm Thie-Richter patterns: special quality reeds, beautifully toned reeds. Ten single holes; brass reed plates; nickel covers; set consists of four harmonicas in assorted keys.
Our special price, per set.....$ .55

No. 7462.

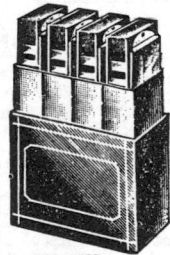

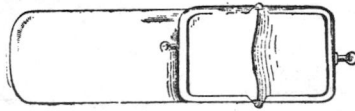

No. 7465.

No. 7465. Harmonica Pouches or Pocket Cases, made of best calf leather with nickel plated frame with clasp. To hold ten hole Richter model.
Our special price, each.............$0.10
No. 7466. Same to hold ten hole Concert Harmonica.
Our special price, each.............$0.15

No. 7467. Harmonica Holder. Made of metal, painted or varnished. Made to hold either Richter or Concert pattern. Tube has opening at one end to produce either mute or tremulo effects. No artistic player should be without one of these holders. Weight, 6 oz.
No. 7467.
Price, each.............$0.10
Per dozen.............................1.00

**THE QUESTION OF CAUSE AND EFFECT: LOW PRICES THE CAUSE, ECONOMY THE EFFECT. GOOD QUALITY THE CAUSE, SATISFACTION THE EFFECT. PLEASED CUSTOMERS THE CAUSE, ENORMOUS BUSINESS THE EFFECT.**

## Harmonica Holders.

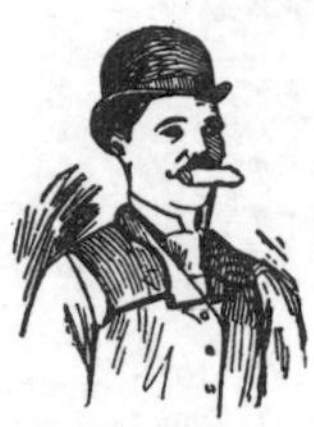

No. 7468.

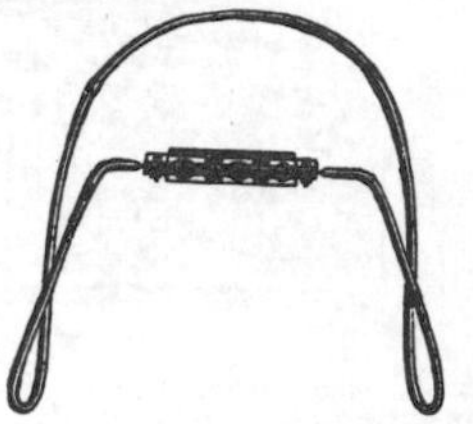

No. 7470.

No. 7468. Harmonica Holder, an especially advantageous attachment for the player as the harmonica is held firmly in position, leaving the hands free for playing another instrument. The only harmonica holder on the market that answers all demands for perfect adjustment. Made of the best nickel plated wire, and fastens at the arm holes and around the neck. Holds any size harmonica and can be folded up into small compass. Weight, 8 oz.
Our special price, each .......... $0.34

No. 7470. Harmonica Holder, made of copper plated wire, to go around the neck; holds any size harmonica. Best cheap holder made. Our special price, each .. $0.09

## Flute Harmonicas.

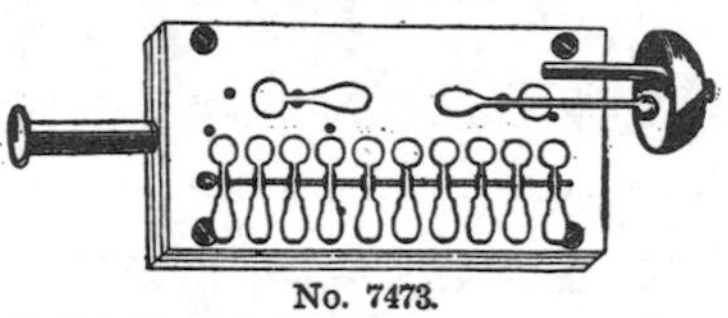

No. 7473.

No. 7473. Finest flute harmonica made; powerful tone; nickel plated frame with ten long keys; two basses and bell. A simple musical instrument pleasing to both professional and amateur. Weight, 22 oz.
Our special price .......... $0.85

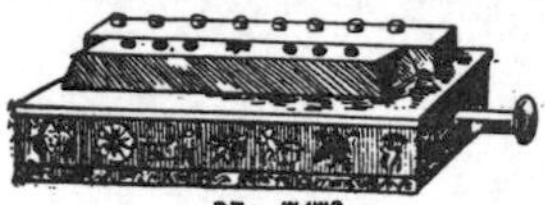

No. 7476.

No. 7476. Flute Harmonica, a musical instrument, easy to play and pleasing in tone. Wooden case, with nickel top and fancy paper covered; eight round keys. Weight, about 18 oz.
Special price, each .......... $0.29

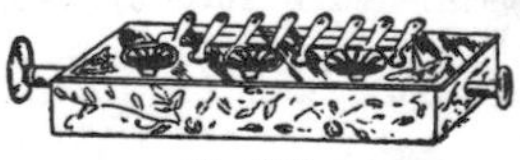

No. 7478.

No. 7478. Flute Harmonica. Fancy decorated case, eight long keys, fancy gilt trumpets, mouthpiece and trumpet, excellent quality reeds. Weight, 19 oz.
Our special price .......... $0.39

## The Clariophone.

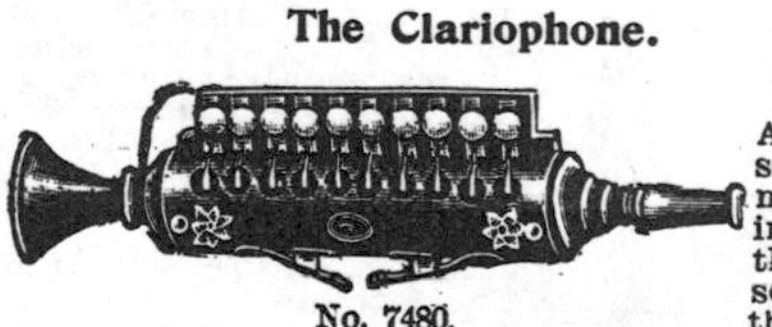

No. 7480.

No. 7480. A handsome little musical instrume't that possesses all the necessary qualities for pleasing the ear with melodious sounds. Wood body, with fancy metal ornaments and cord. Ten keys, two bases and excellent reeds. Weight, about 28 oz.
Our Special Price .......... $1.10

## Flute Accordeons.

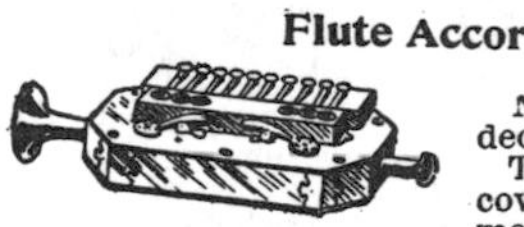

No. 7482.

No. 7482. Flute Accordeon. Our special price, 82c. Ten bone keys; nickel covered case; projecting metal bell. An instrument that is capable of producing a fine class of music. Note the low price we make. Weight, about 26 oz.

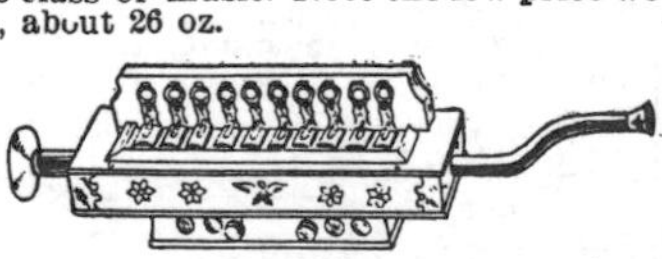

No. 7483.

No. 7483. Is one of our finest flute accordeons and is better made than the ordinary instruments found in retail stores; has ten patent nickel keys; two basses, ebonized sides and keyboard with gilt ornaments; nickel plated corners; trumpet and mouthpiece. Weight, about 30 oz.
Our special price .......... $1.35

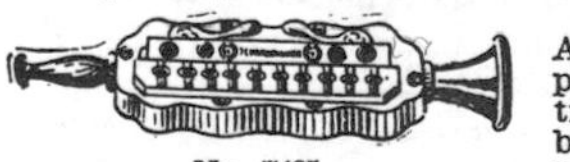

No. 7485.

No. 7485. Flute Accordeon. Special price, $0.78. Substantially made with ten bone keys, two basses and excellent reeds. Wood case, with projecting bell. Weight, 20 oz.

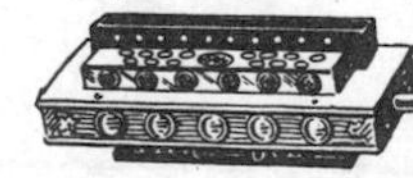

No. 7487. Flute Accordeon. Wooden case, nickel trimmed, ten keys and two basses. Excellent quality of tone. Weight, 21 oz.
Our special price ..... $0.71

## Fifes.

Key of B Flat and C only. Instruction Book 12 cts.

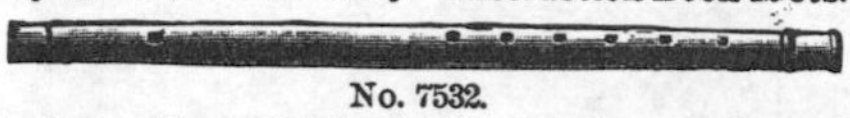

No. 7532.

No. 7530. Key of B Flat or C. Maple; natural color; brass tipped. Each .......... $0.20
No. 7531. Imitation ebony; B Flat or C; nickel plated ferrules. Each .......... $0.25
No. 7532. Key of B Flat or C; solid rosewood, brass ferrules. (See cut.) Each .......... $0.32
No. 7533. Key of B Flat or C. Cocoa wood; brass ferrules. (See cut.) Each .......... $0.40
No. 7534. Key of B Flat or C. Cocoa wood; nickel plated ferrules. (See cut.) Each .......... $0.50
No. 7535. Key of B Flat or C. Solid ebony; nickel plated ferrules. Each .......... $0.55
No. 7536. Key of B Flat or C. Solid ebony; long metal ferrules; Crosby model; extra fine quality. Each .......... $0.80

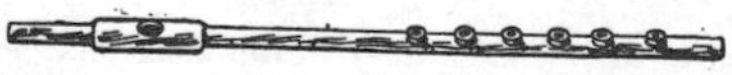

No. 7537. Key of B Flat or C. Nickel plated, with raised finger holes. (See illustration.) Each .... $0.80
No. 7538. Same as No. 7537, with gutta percha embouchure. Each .......... $0.85

## Flageolets.

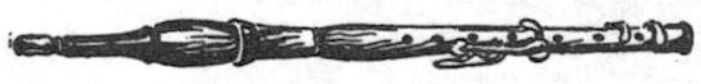

In Pasteboard Boxes.

No. 7539. Key of D. Boxwood; black; 1 key. Each .......... $1.30
No. 7540. Key of D. Grenadilla; German silver trimmed; 1 key. Each .......... $1.60
No. 7541. Key of B♭. Grenadilla; German silver trimmed; 1 key. Each .......... $2.00
No. 7542. Key of D. Grenadilla; German silver trimmed; 4 keys. Each .......... $2.25
No. 7543. Key of D. Grenadilla; German silver trimmed; 6 keys. Each .......... $2.60

## Piccolo-Flageolets.

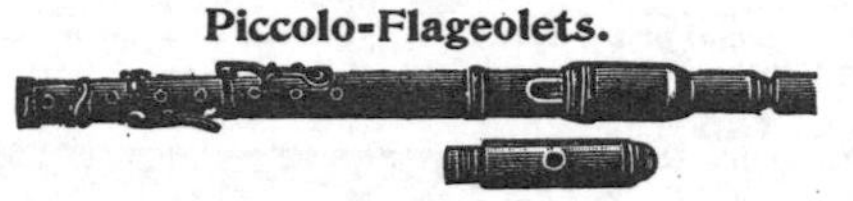

With extra mouthpiece; can be played either as a piccolo or as a flageolet. In pasteboard boxes.

No. 7546. Key of D. Boxwood, German silver trimmed, 1 key. Each .......... $1.85
No. 7547. Key of D. Grenadilla, German silver trimmed, five keys. Each .......... $2.55
No. 7548. Key of D. Grenadilla; German silver trimmed; six keys. Each .......... $2.75

## Nightingale Flageolets.

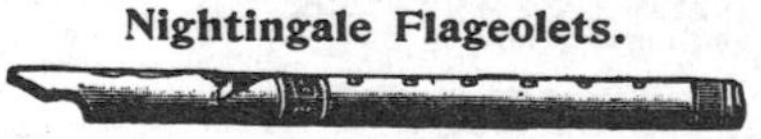

No. 7552. Nightingale Flageolets, as shown above, made of brass, nickel plated. A reliable and well made instrument that must not be compared with cheap imitations. A sheet of instructions with each instrument. Furnished in any of the following keys: B, C, D, E, F, G. Each .......... $. 25

## Clark's London Flageolets.

No. 7555. Clark's London Flageolet, a very popular low-priced instrument, simple to play and producing good tone. Similar in shape to the Nightingale Flageolet, shown above; tin, key of D.
Our special price, each .......... $0.09
No. 7557. Same, brass. Each .......... 0.14
No. 7558. Same, finely nickel plated. Each .... 0.18

## Piccolos.

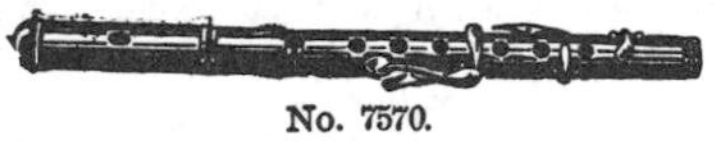

No. 7570.

No. 7565. Key of D or E♭. Made of cocoa wood, 1 key, German silver trimmed, in pasteboard box. Weight, 6 oz. Price, each .......... $0.55
No. 7566. Key of D or E♭. Made of cocoa wood, with 1 key, and tuning slide, German silver trimmed, in pasteboard box. Each .......... $0.80
No. 7567. Key of D or E flat, Grenadilla wood, with tuning slide and four keys, German silver trimmed, in pasteboard box. Each .......... $1.65
No. 7570. Key of D or E Flat, Grenadilla wood, with tuning slide, six keys, German silver trimmed, (See cut above), in pasteboard box. Price, each .. $2.15

## Meyer Patterns.

In Fine Cases. (See Illustration.)

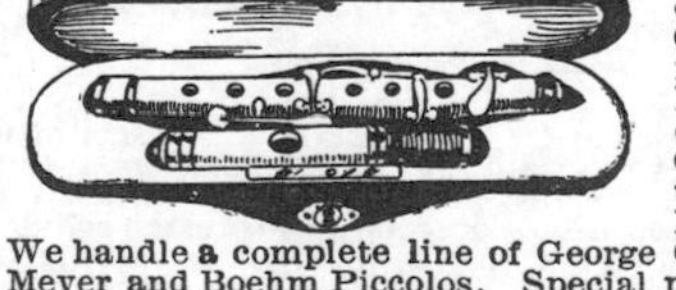

No. 7573. Key of D or E Flat, Grenadilla, ivory head, six keys, with slide cork joints, German silver trimmed.
Each .......... $4.65

We handle a complete line of George Cloos, Genuine Meyer and Boehm Piccolos. Special prices on application.

## Flutes.

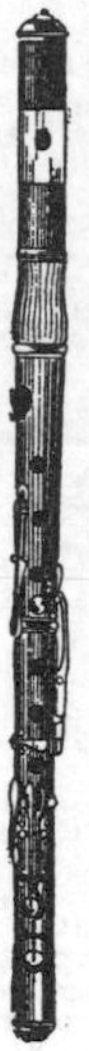

No. 7574. Genuine cocoa, German silver trimmed with tuning slide and one key, in pasteboard box. Each .......... $1.60
No. 7576. Boxwood, imitation ebony, German silver trimmed, with tuning slide, four keys, in pasteboard box. Each .......... $2.00
No. 7578. Cocoa, German silver trimmed, with tuning slide, with four keys, in pasteboard box. Each .......... $2.60
No. 7579. Boxwood, imitation ebony, with tuning slide, German silver trimmed, with six keys, in pasteboard box. Each .......... $2.75
No. 7581. Cocoa, with tuning slide, German silver trimmed, six keys, in pasteboard box. Each .......... $2.85
No. 7583. Cocoa, with tuning slide, cork joints, German silver caps and trimmings, six keys, in pasteboard box. Each .......... $2.95
No. 7585. Grenadilla, with tuning slide, cork joints, German silver caps and trimmings. Each .......... $3.75
No. 7586. Grenadilla, with tuning slide, cork joints, German silver caps and trimmings and embouchure, as illustrated. Each .......... $4.50
No. 7587. Grenadilla, with tuning slide, cork joints, German silver head joint. Each .. $6.90
No. 7589. Fine imitation of Meyer Flute, D, eight keys, grenadilla wood, with tuning slide, cork joints, in fine morocco case, as shown, velvet lined, with joint caps, grease box, swab pads and screw driver. Weight, 26 oz.
Our special price .......... $6.25
No. 7590. Fine Imitation of Meyer Flute, key of D, ten keys, grenadilla wood, with tuning slide and cork joints. In fine morocco case velvet lined, as shown, complete with joint caps, grease box, swab, pad and screw driver. Weight, 26 oz. Our special price .......... $9.85

No. 7586.

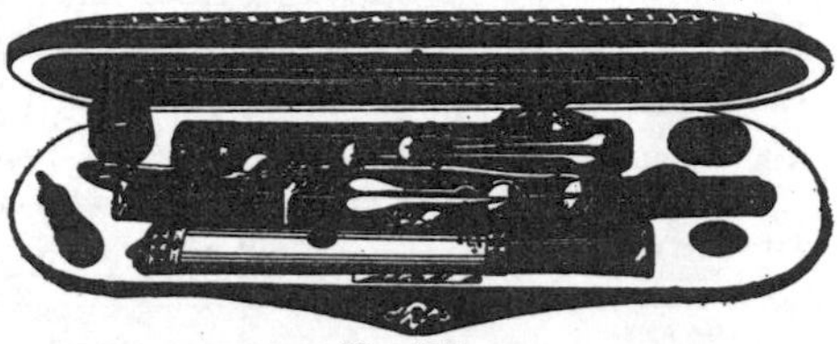

No. 7591.

No. 7591. Fine Imitation of Meyer Flute, key of D, exactly same as No. 7590 above, but with genuine ivory head, as illustrated above. In fine velvet lined morocco case, with joint caps, grease box, swab, pads and screw driver. Weight, 26 oz.
Special price .......... $15.10

## Clarionets.

Genuine French manufacture and superior in tone and quality. American Pitch. Come in any of the following keys: A, B♭, C, D and E♭. Be sure to state what key is desired. We include a valuable instruction book free with each instrument.

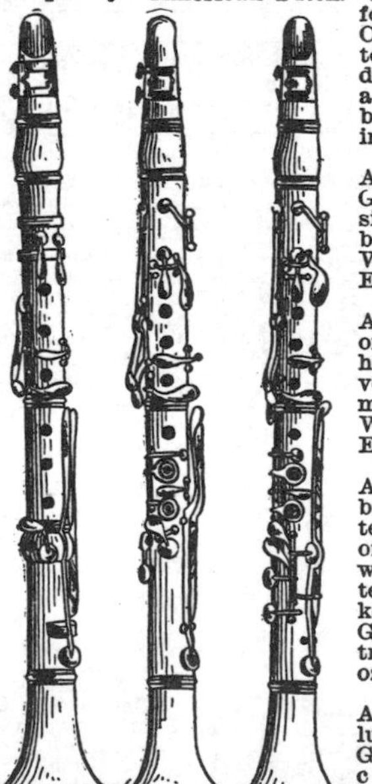

No. 7599. No. 7600. No. 7601.

No. 7598 Clarionet. Any key, made of Grenadilla wood, has six brass keys and is brass trimmed. Weight, 16 oz, Each .......... $4.35
No. 7599. Clarionet. As illustrated, made of Grenadilla wood, has ten German silver keys and is German silver trimmed. Weight, 18 oz. Each .......... $6.55
No. 7600. Clarionet. As illustrated celebrated Albert system, any key. Made of Grenadilla wood, with cork joints, thirteen German silver keys, two rings and German silver trimmed. Weight, 20 oz. Each .......... $12.45
No. 7601. Clarionet. Albert system, as illustrated. Made of Grenadilla wood, with cork joints. fifteen German silver keys, (except B♭ and C sharp) two rings, German silver trimmed. Weight, 23 oz. Price, each .......... $14.85

## Important.

Proper care must be taken of clarionets, flutes, piccolos and similar wooden instruments. They are liable to crack or check at any time through carelessness on the part of the owner or user. They are susceptible to changes of atmosphere and especially so when damp from usage or otherwise. Always after using they should be wiped dry, inside and outside, and rubbed with sweet oil. No music dealer will be responsible for checking or cracking. We examine each instrument with scrupulous care and we warrant every one to leave our house in perfect condition.

# We are Outfitters for Drum Corps.

We will quote special prices on application for complete Fife and Drum Corps outfits. The line of Snare or Tenor Drums, as well as of Bass Drums, is made by a well known manufacturer, who makes a specialty of this particular kind of instrument. The shell, hoops, heads and trimmings are all of special quality, warranted extra select, and put together by skilled workmen, whose expertness is the result of years of experience. We consequently offer prospective purchasers a line of drums that must not be compared with the cheap, dingy instruments found in ordinary music stores, or by competitive houses. In fact, few retailers outside of large cities carry a stock of Drums. The retailer has to send away to some wholesale house. The advantage is very apparent for you to get such goods direct from the factory.

Anticipating the unusual demand for Drums during the presidential campaign, we have contracted for a very large supply. To prevent carrying over any stock, we cut right into the bottom price at once and name prices on the best drums made that cannot be duplicated by any concern.

We scarcely think it possible to duplicate these prices again. But, while our contracts hold good with the manufacturer, we shall stand by the prices we make below. We ship any drum C. O. D., subject to examination, on receipt of $5.00 as a guarantee of good faith.

As stated above, we shall be glad to name a special price on quantities to clubs. In writing, always state the exact style and number of instruments you want. If you do not find described herein just what you need, write us.

Additional supplies for drum corps, in the shape of fifes, piccolos, drum majors' batons, etc., will be found in this catalogue farther on.

☞ **Many imitations of these special pattern drums are now on the market. Bear in mind that price alone does not make a bargain. Quality must have just as great consideration.**

Through our factory-to-consumer plan we combine quality and price in a degree of economic perfection never seen before. We claim the best goods at the least money, and only ask a fair chance to back up every assertion.

## SNARE DRUMS.

We are headquarters for Snare Drums. We are especially well prepared to furnish complete outfits for Fife and Drum corps. We invite correspondence where it is desired to purchase the drums and fifes for an entire corps. The quotations in this catalogue are based on our economic factory-to-consumer methods, and we invite comparison of our prices with those of anyone, anywhere, quoting the same high grade of goods. We ship goods C. O. D., subject to examination. We guarantee all instruments to be as represented. Shipping weight of snare drums is about 16 pounds.

No. 7615. Snare Drum, Prussian pattern; maple hoops with ebonized or imitation rosewood finish, white metal plated trimmings, 14-inch maple shell, 6 inches high, 7 rods, 6 snares, 2 calfskin head. Our special price, complete with 2 rosewood sticks $4.85.

No. 7617. Snare Drum, Prussian pattern: maple hoops, ebonized or imitation rosewood finish: white metal plated trimmings, 16-inch maple shell, 6 inches high, 8 rods, 8 rawhide snares, 2 calfskin heads, 2 rosewood sticks. Our special price, each, $5.00.

No. 7619. Same as No. 7617, above, but with brass shell. Our special price, $5.00.

No. 7620. Snare Drum, Prussian pattern; maple hoops with fancy Decalcomaine ornamentation, white metal plated trimmings, 16-inch rosewood or brass shell, 6 inches high, 8 rods, 8 rawhide snares, 2 calfskin heads. Each, $6.25.

No. 7622. Same as No. 7620, above, but brass shell. Each, $6.25.

**PRUSSIAN PATTERN.**

No. 7626. Snare Drum, regulation pattern, bird's-eye maple shell, maple hoops, ebonized or imitation rosewood finish, 14-inch shell, 8 inches high, varnish finish, cord hooks, 7 braces, 6 snares, new pattern snare strainer, 2 calfskin heads, two rosewood sticks. Weight, each, packed, 14 pounds. Our special price, each, $4.60.

No. 7628. Snare Drum, regulation pattern, bird's-eye maple shell, maple hoops, ebonized or imitation rosewood finish, 16-inch shell, 9½ inches high, fine varnish finish, cord hooks, 8 braces, 8 snares, new pattern snare strainer, 2 calfskin heads, two rosewood sticks. Weight, packed, about 14 pounds. Our special price, each, $4.90.

No. 7630. Same as No. 7628 above, but with rosewood shell. Each, $4.90.

**REGULATION PATTERN.**

Descriptions below are for Regulation Pattern Bass Drums as illustrated. We can furnish same sizes in Prussian pattern at same prices. Prussian pattern Bass Drums are all 9½ inches high.

## BASS DRUMS.

No. 7640. 24-inch shell Regulation Pattern Bass Drum, bird's-eye maple or imitation mahogany shell, maple hoops, ebonized or imitation rosewood finish, Italian hemp cord, improved pattern cord hooks, 10 inches high, with 11 braces, 1 calfskin and 1 sheepskin head. Weight, packed, 50 pounds. Buckskin head stick included. Our Special price, $9.95.

No. 7641. Same as above, with 2 calfskin heads, $10.65.

No. 7643. Bass Drum, regulation pattern, 26-inch shell, either bird's-eye maple or imitation mahogany, 11 inches high, 12 braces, 2 calfskin heads, maple hoops, ebonized or imitation rosewood finish, Italian hemp cord, improved pattern cord hooks. Weight, boxed, about 55 pounds. Buckskin head stick included. Our special price, $11.15.

No. 7645. 28-inch Regulation Bass Drum, 12 inches high, 13 braces, otherwise just the same description as No. 7643 above. Weight, 60 pounds. Our special price, $12.35.

No. 7647. 30-inch Regulation Pattern Bass Drum, 12 inches high, 14 braces, otherwise just like No. 7643, described above. Weight, 65 pounds. Price, each, $13.50.

**REGULATION PATTERN.**

No. 7649. 32-inch Regulation Pattern Bass Drum, 15 braces, otherwise just the same as No. 7643 above. Weight, 70 pounds. Our special price, $15.65.

No. 7650. 34-inch Regulation Pattern Bass Drum, 16 braces, otherwise just the same as No. 7643, described above. Weight, packed, 80 lbs. Our special price, $17.15.

☞ We can furnish same size, shells of same description as above in Prussian pattern at same prices.

## YOUTHS' SNARE DRUMS, STICKS AND SLINGS INCLUDED.

No. 7652.

No. 7652. 12-inch fancy stamped imitation brass shell, **Regulation Pattern**, fancy cord, sheepskin heads. Complete with sticks and slings. Price, each, $1.35.

No. 7653. 10-inch fancy wood shell, nickel inlaid hoops, 5 rods, snare strainer, 1 calfskin and 1 sheepskin head. Complete with sticks and slings. Prussian pattern. Price, each, $2.05.

No. 7654. Same as No. 7653, with 12-inch shell and 6 rods. Price, each, $2.75.

No. 7655. Same as No. 7653, with 14-inch shell and 8 rods. Price, each, $3.10.

No. 7656. Regulation pattern, 14-inch nickel shell, nickel inlaid hoops, snare strainer, 1 calfskin and 1 sheepskin head. Complete with sticks and sling. Each, $3.60.

## CYMBALS.

No. 7670. Turkish Cymbals, 8-inch, composition metal, with leather handles. Weight, 35 ounces. Per pair, $4.50.

No. 7671. Turkish Cymbals, 9-inch, made of composition metal, with leather handles. Weight, 43 ounces. Per pair, $5.25.

No. 7672. Turkish Cymbals, 10-inch, made of composition metal, with leather handles. Weight, 50 ounces. Per pair, $6.25.

No. 7673. Turkish Cymbals, 11-inch, made of composition metal, with leather handles. Weight, 60 ounces. Per pair, $7.25.

No. 7674. Turkish Cymbals, 12-inch, composition metal, with leather handles. Weight, 6 pounds. Price, per pair, $8.75.

No. 7675. Turkish Cymbals, 13-inch, composition metal, with leather handles. Weight, 7½ pounds. Our price, per pair, $9.45.

No. 7676. Turkish Cymbals, 14-inch, composition metal, with leather handles. Weight, 9 pounds. Our special price, per pair, $10.20.

No. 7680. 10-inch Brass Cymbals, with leather handles. Weight, 35 ounces. Per pair, $1.85. No. 7681. 11-inch Brass Cymbals, with leather handles. Weight, 40 ounces. Per pair, $2.10. No. 7682. 12-inch Brass Cymbals, with leather handles. Weight, 45 ounces. Per pair, $2.30. No. 7683. 13-inch Brass Cymbals, with leather handles. Weight, 50 ounces. Per pair, $2.50.

**TURKISH.**

**THE LINE OF BAND INSTRUMENTS QUOTED FARTHER ON IS MOST COMPLETE. THESE INSTRUMENTS ARE THE BEST THE MARKETS OF THE WORLD AFFORD. WE INVITE CORRESPONDENCE FROM BANDS AND DRUM CORPS. OUR TERMS ARE MOST LIBERAL.**

## Band Instruments.

There is perhaps no line of musical instruments on which a larger profit is made than on band instruments. Few dealers carry anything like an adequate stock and what few sales they do make are subjected to an enormous profit. The actual first cost of the cornet, bass, or trombone is completely buried beneath a mass of middlemen's expenses and profits

Dealing, as we do, on the economical factory to consumer plan, we practically hand you the instruments from the manufacturer's door, with only our one small margin of brokerage added. One can well imagine what a saving we effect.

As regards the superb quality of these instruments, we need only say that they are made by a manufacturer whose reputation for superior workmanship is such that his very name is sufficient guarantee to professionals, of unexcelled quality and purity of tone.

Added to the quality of the instruments themselves, and the factory prices we name, are **the exceedingly liberal terms on which we ship.**

Send $1.00 with your order as a guarantee of good faith and we will ship you any band instrument listed, no difference how expensive, subject to examination. You have the privilege of seeing and examining the instrument at the express office. If you find it perfectly satisfactory and just as represented, pay the express agent the balance, with express charges and the instrument is yours. Otherwise, return it to us and we will refund your money, less the express charges.

We make the above offer wide open to every one. We allow 3 per cent. cash discount where full cash accompanies order. Customers who have dealt with us once almost invariably send full cash in advance, thereby taking advantage of our cash discount and saving the express charges on return of C. O. D.

We are especially well prepared to fill orders for complete band or orchestra outfits, We handle any instrument, from the least expensive up to a double Bb bass listing at $230.00, or a saxaphone for $135.00. If you do not find all the instruments wanted quoted herein on account of limited space, write us with specifications and we shall be glad to send pictures and quotations.

**On our exceedingly favorable terms you can buy any instrument made, with just as satisfactory a personal examination, and at from 33 1-3 to 50 per cent. lower price than at any retail store.**

We allow a further privilege to every purchaser, of returning any instrument to us prepaid after 5 days' fair trial, if it is not satisfactory or not up to requirements. We make this additional liberal offer in order that every prospective purchaser may be assured of entire satisfaction.

We give below a variety of combinations for bands, indicating the proper assortment of instruments.

| BAND OF 6. | BAND OF 7. | BAND OF 8. |
|---|---|---|
| 1 Eb Cornet.<br>2 Bb Cornets.<br>1 Eb Alto.<br>1 Bb Tenor.<br>1 Eb Bass. | 1 Eb Cornet.<br>2 Bb Cornets.<br>1 Eb Alto.<br>1 Bb Tenor.<br>1 Bb Baritone.<br>1 Eb Bass | 1 Eb Cornet.<br>2 Eb Cornets.<br>2 Eb Altos.<br>1 Bb Tenor.<br>1 Eb Baritone.<br>1 Eb Bass. |

| BAND OF 9. | BAND OF 10. | BAND OF 11. |
|---|---|---|
| 2 Eb *Cornets.*<br>2 Bb Cornets.<br>2 Eb Altos.<br>1 Bb Tenor.<br>1 Bb Baritone.<br>1 Eb Bass. | 2 Eb Cornets.<br>2 Bb Cornets.<br>2 Eb Altos.<br>2 *Eb Tenors.*<br>1 Bb Baritone.<br>1 Eb Bass. | 2 Eb Cornets.<br>2 Bb Cornets.<br>2 Eb Altos.<br>2 Bb Tenors.<br>1 Bb Baritone.<br>1 *Bb Bass.*<br>1 Eb Bass. |

| BAND OF 12. | BAND OF 13. | BAND OF 14. |
|---|---|---|
| 2 Eb Cornets.<br>2 Bb Cornets.<br>3 Eb *Altos.*<br>2 Bb Tenors.<br>1 Bb Baritone.<br>1 Bb Bass.<br>1 Eb Bass. | 2 Eb Cornets.<br>2 Bb Cornets.<br>3 Eb Altos.<br>2 Bb Tenors.<br>1 Bb Baritone.<br>1 Bb Bass.<br>2 *Eb Basses.* | 2 *Eb Cornets.*<br>3 Bb Cornets.<br>3 Eb Altos.<br>2 Bb Tenors.<br>1 Eb Baritone.<br>1 Bb Bass.<br>2 Eb Basses. |

| BAND OF 15. | BAND OF 15. | BAND OF 17. |
|---|---|---|
| 3 Eb Cornets.<br>3 Bb Cornets.<br>3 Eb Altos.<br>2 Bb Tenors.<br>1 Bb Baritone.<br>1 Bb Bass.<br>2 *Eb* Basses. | 3 Eb Cornets.<br>4 Bb Cornets.<br>3 Eb Altos.<br>2 Bb Tenors.<br>1 Bb Baritone.<br>1 Bb Bass.<br>2 *Eb Basses.* | 3 Eb Cornets.<br>4 *Bb Cornets.*<br>4 Eb Altos.<br>2 Bb Tenors.<br>1 Bb Baritone<br>1 Bb Bass.<br>2 Eb Basses. |



## Our $4.95 Eb Cornet.

**Retails anywhere for $10.00.**

No. 7690. This very fine brass instrument is beautiful in tone and finish. It is of especially fine model and susceptible to the most artistic playing. Has music rack, water keys, German silver mouthpiece and German piston valves. Our special price ............ $4.95

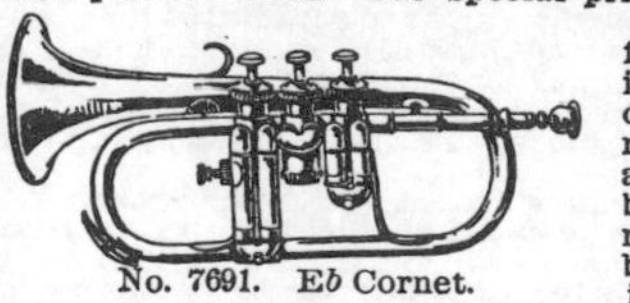
No. 7691. Eb Cornet.

No. 7691. Very fine Eb cornet, as illustrated, is one of the best instruments of the kind and is made of brass, all finely nickel plated and beautifully finished. Has German piston valves, German silver mouthpiece and water keys. Our special price ............ $5.95

## Our $5.65 Bb Cornet.

**Retails at $12.00.**

No. 7693. Our Special Bb Cornet is an instrument of remarkable beauty of model and purity of tone. Superior to many instruments retailed as high as $12.00 or more. Made of brass and has music rack, German piston valves, water keys and German silver mouthpiece. Our special price ............ $5.65

No. 7694. Bb Cornet is just the same as 7693 above, but is very finely nickel plated throughout and handsomely finished. We send any instrument C. O. D., subject to examination. Our special price ............ $6.60

## Our Eb Alto for $7.10.

**Retails for $14.00.**

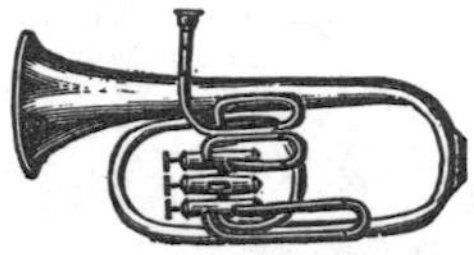
No. 7696.

No. 7696. The Eb Alto, as illustrated with Bell up, is an especially desirable instrument. The well known reputation of the manufacturer assures the purchaser of the best that experience and unequaled facilities will produce. Made of brass, finely finished and complete with music rack, German silver mouthpiece, water key and German piston valves. Weight, boxed, 8 lbs. Our special price ............ $7.10

No. 7697. Eb Alto is precisely the same as No. 7696, illustrated and described, but is beautifully nickel plated throughout. Our special price ............ $8.95

No. 7698. **Bb Tenor,** Bell up, is precisely the same model as No. 7696 Eb alto, illustrated above. Is made by the same well-known manufacturer, and possesses all the requisite features of an high grade instrument. Is made of brass, with a superior finish, and fitted with music rack, German piston valves, German silver mouthpiece and water key. Weight, boxed, 9 lbs. Our special price ............ $8.95

No. 7699. **Bb Tenor.** Bell up, is the same as No. 7698 above, but is made additionally desirable by reason of special finish of fine nickel-plating throughout. Weight, boxed, 9 lbs. Our special price ............ $11.65

No. 7700. **Bb Baritone,** Bell up, is just the same model as No. 7696 Eb alto, illustrated above, and has the same superior principles of construction which render these instruments so easily distinguishable from the cheap articles on the market. Made of brass with a special finish, and fitted with music rack, German silver mouthpiece, German piston valves and water key. Weight, boxed, 10 lbs. Our special price ... $10.65

No. 7701. **Bb Baritone,** Bell up, only differs from No. 7700 described above in the fact that it is elegantly nickel plated throughout and presents a very handsome appearance in addition to its superb quality of tone. Weight, boxed, 10 lbs. Our special price .. $13.45

## Our Special Eb Alto Trombone for $6.95.

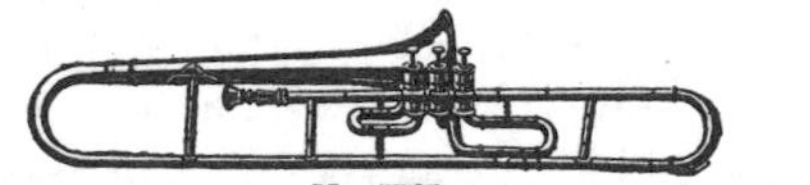
No. 7705.

No. 7702. The Eb Alto Valve Trombone illustrated is of a quality seldom found in a retail store. We have special facilities for furnishing unusual value in band instruments, and we only ask the privilege of sending you this splendid trombone to try. It is made of brass, finely finished and furnished with German silver mouthpiece, German piston valves, water key and music rack. Our special price ............ $6.95



No. 7703. Eb Valve Trombone is just the same as No. 7702, but is extra heavily nickel plated and is espceially beautiful in model and finish. Our special price ............ $8.95

## Our $15 Bb Tenor Trombone for $9.15.

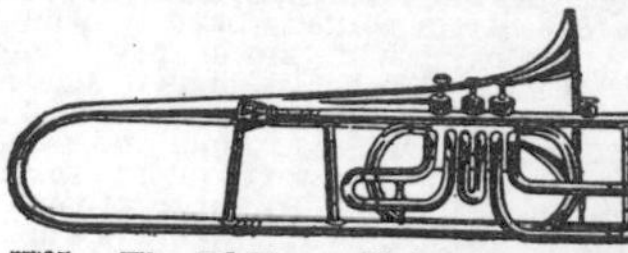

No. 7705. The Bb Tenor Valve Trombone, illustrated above is a special quality instrument that is made unusually desirable by reason of the most exacting care used in its construction. We take great pleasure in assuring intending purchasers that in sending for it they may expect nothing less than the best that expert workmen of long experience can produce. Is made of brass and fitted with music rack, German silver mouthpiece, German piston valves and water key. Weight, boxed, 9 lbs. Our special price ............ $9.15

No. 7706. Bb Tenor Valve Trombone is just like No. 7705, above, in every respect, except that it is beautifully nickel plated throughout. Our special price. $11.65

## Our Special $7.95 Eb Alto Slide Trombone.

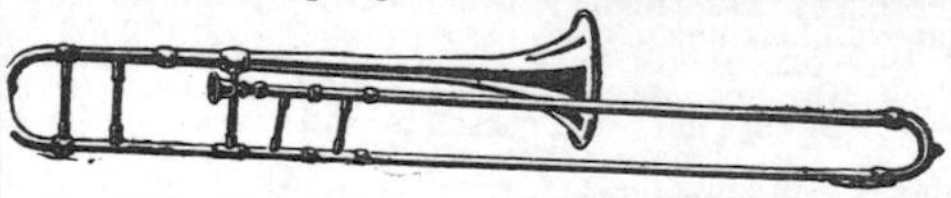

No. 7707. This Eb Alto or Bb Tenor Slide Trombone is made expressly for our best trade by the leading French manufacturer. It is one of the best made and will give the purchaser entire satisfaction in tone, quality and finish. It is made of brass, complete with water key, German silver mouthpiece and music rack. Weight, boxed, 8 lbs. Our special price ............ $7.95

No. 7708. Eb Alto or Bb Tenor Slide Trombone is precisely the same instrument as No. 7709 illustrated and described above, but is finely nickel plated. Weight, boxed, 8 lbs. Our special price ............ $10.45

## Bb Bass.

No. 7709. Bb Bass, Bell up is the same model as No. 7696, Eb Alto illustrated above. It is of course much larger and weighs, boxed, 15 lbs. This instrument is one that will please the most critical judge, and we shall be only too glad to send it C. O. D. subject to examination on our liberal terms, to any intending purchaser. It is fitted with music rack, German silver mouthpiece, German piston valves and water key. Our special price ............ $11.45

No. 7710. Bb Bass, Bell up, has all the features of No. 7709 above, but is handsomely nickel plated throughout. Weight, boxed, 15 lbs. Our special price ............ $14.45

## Our $16.25 Eb Bass.

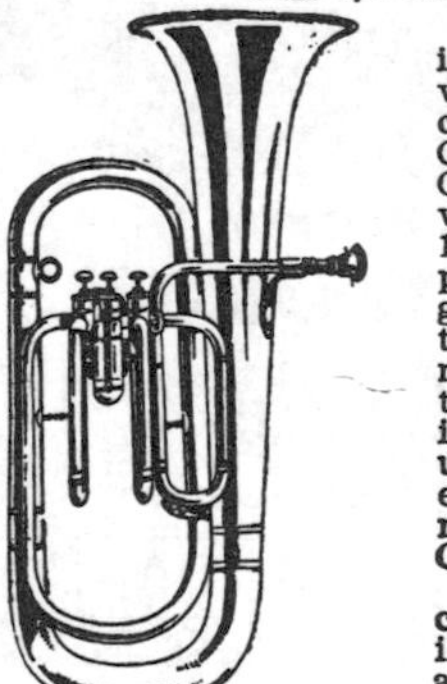
No. 7711.

No. 7711. The **Eb Bass** illustrated is made of brass, with a very fine finish. It is complete with music rack, German silver mouthpiece, German piston valves and water key. Weight, boxed, 18 lbs. We shall take pleasure in sending this elegant instrument to any intending purchaser for examination on our liberal C.O.D. terms. Every customer is invariably surprised at the unusual value, finding it equal to any $25.00 instrument in the retail market. Our special price ...... $16.25

No. 7712. **Eb Bass** is precisely the same instrument illustrated and described above, but has added value, by reason of the full nickel plating throughout. Weight, boxed, 18 lbs. Our special price .... $20.25

No. 7713. **Eb Contra Bass** Is a superb instrument with a rich, round, powerful tone of remarkable purity. Every purchaser has expressed great delight with the unusual value they have received. This instrument is made of brass, with a fine finish, and fitted with music rack, German piston valves, German silver mouthpiece and water key. Weight, boxed, 22 lbs. Our Special Price ............ $18.75

No. 7714. **Eb Contra Bass.** Only differs from No. 7713 described above in the fact that it is fully nickel plated throughout. Weight, boxed, 22 lbs. Our Special Price ............ $22.75

## Our Celebrated French Light Action Silver Piston Band Instruments.

## Our $6.40 Eb Cornet.

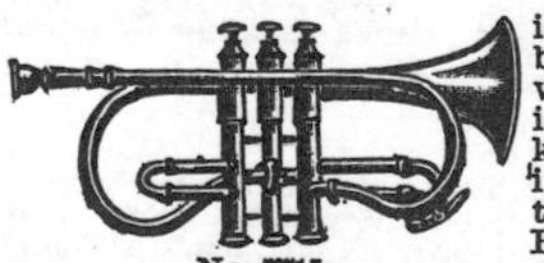
No. 7715.

No. 7715. Eb Cornet is fitted with the celebrated Light action silver piston valves, and is an instrument of acknowledged superiority over the many imitations on the market. Finely made of brass with a handsome finish. We furnish free an excellent music rack. This instrument has German silver mouthpiece and water key. Weight, boxed, 6 pounds. Our special price ...... $6.35

No. 7716. Eb Cornet is in every way the same as No. 7715 illustrated and described above, but is finely nickel plated throughout. Weight, boxed, 6 pounds. Our special price ............ $7.30

## Our Celebrated $6.55 Bb Cornet.

**Retails at $12.**

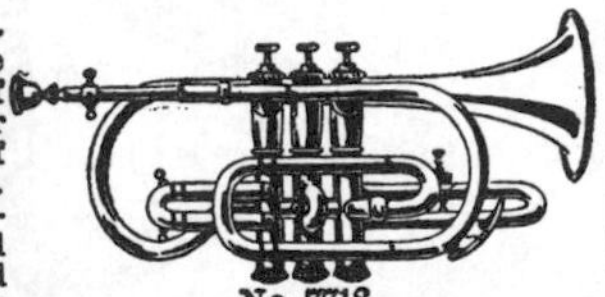
No. 7718.

No. 7718. Bb Cornet is one of the best productions of a factory noted for the excellence of their instruments. It is made of beautifully finished brass, and is fitted with the popular Light Action silver piston valve. The mouthpiece is of German silver, and the cornet is complete with water key and music rack. Weight, boxed, 7 pounds. Our Special Price ....$6.55

No. 7719. Bb Cornet is the same as No. 7718 above illustrated and described, but is handsomely nickel plated. Weight, boxed, 7 pounds. Our special price, $7.55

## Our $10.45 Solo Eb Alto.

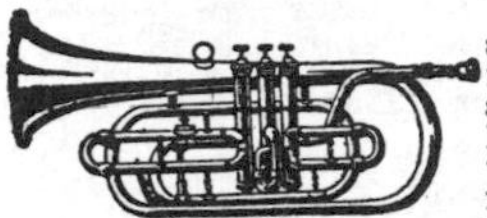
No. 7721.

No. 7721. Solo Eb Alto, as illustrated, is seldom retailed at less than $18, and more usually at $20. By our economic system we are able to cut off all middlemen's profits and make a price no retail dealer can even approach. This elegant instrument is made of brass and has the Light Action silver piston valves, of peculiarly advantageous construction. We fit it also with German silver mouthpiece, water key and music rack. Weight, boxed, 6 lbs. Our Special Price ....$10.45

No. 7722. Solo Eb Alto. Is very finely nickel plated, but otherwise the same exactly as No. 7721, illustrated and described above. Weight, boxed, 6 lbs. Our Special Price ....$12.45

## Our $10.55 Eb Alto Trombone.

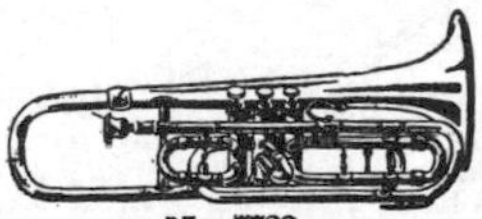
No. 7723.

No. 7723. Eb Alto Valve Trombone, as shown in the illustration, is a special instrument designed to meet the demands of professionals, as well as of amateurs. It is very finely made of brass, with a handsome finish. The valves are the French Light Action silver piston valves. We fit the instrument with water key and German silver mouthpiece. We also furnish free a fine music rack. Weight, boxed, 9 lbs. Our special price ....$10.55

No. 7724 Eb Alto Valve Trombone is exactly the same as No. 7723, described above, but is finished and extra nickel plated throughout. Weight, boxed, 9 lbs. Our special price ....$12.55

## Our Bb Tenor Valve Trombone for $12.60.

No. 7725. Bb Tenor Trombone is precisely the same model as our Eb Alto Trombone illustrated above and is a beautiful as well as splendidly toned instrument. It is made by high class workmen who thoroughly understand the scientific construction of musical instruments. It is of brass, finely finished and is fitted with water key and German silver mouthpiece. An additional desirable feature with this trombone is the celebrated Light Action silver piston valves. We furnish with each instrument a fine music rack. Weight boxed 10 pounds. Our special price ....$12.55

No. 7726. Bb Tenor Trombone is the same as No. 7725 illustrated above, but is finely nickel plated throughout. Weight, boxed, about 10 pounds. Our special price ....$14.95

No. 7727. **Bb Baritone Valve Trombone** is the same style and model as No. 7723 Eb Alto, illustrated. It is made of brass and has the very desirable Light Action silver piston valves, and is fitted with water key and German silver mouthpiece. We also furnish music rack free with each instrument. Any intending purchaser can examine this improved French Piston Trombone before paying for it. We ship on the most liberal terms and give every opportunity to be satisfied that the instrument is just as we represent it and satisfactory in every way. Weight, boxed, 11 lbs. Our special price ....$12.55

No. 7728. Bb Baritone Valve Trombone is very finely nickel plated, but otherwise the same in every respect as No. 7727, described above. Weight, boxed, 11 lbs. Our special price ....$16.55

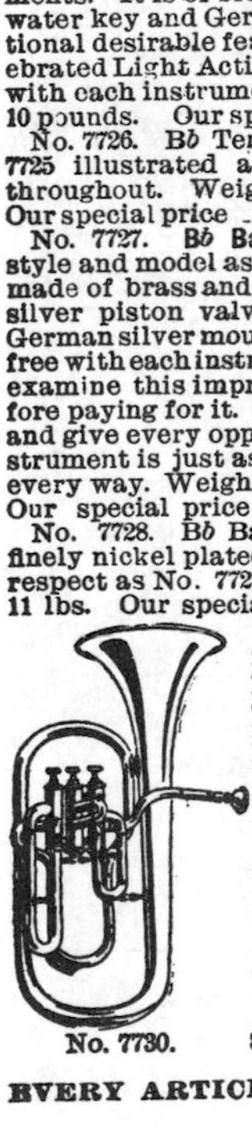
No. 7730.

No. 7730. **Eb Alto, bell up.** This is a special instrument designed particularly for experts, and made of brass with the utmost care. It is made by one of the most celebrated French manufacturers, and is the improved model. The Light Action silver pistons are a very valuable feature. The instrument is fitted with water key, German silver mouthpiece, and music rack. Weight boxed, 8 lbs. Our Special Price ....$10.50

No. 7731. Eb Alto, bell up, is precisely like No. 7730, illustrated and described, but is beautifully nickel plated throughout. Weight, boxed, 8 lbs. Our Special Price ....$12.50

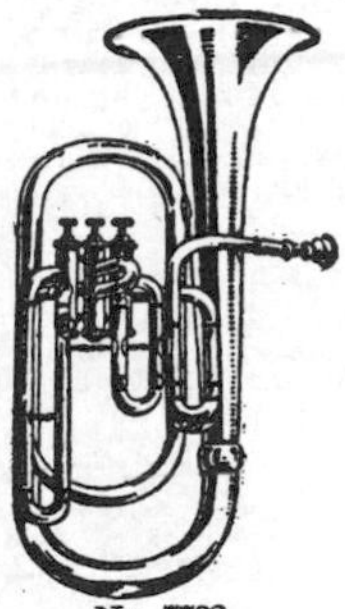
No. 7732.

No. 7732. **Bb Tenor,** with bell up, has had the utmost care bestowed upon it to produce an instrument as near perfect as the hand of man can make it. The tone is unexcelled in purity and power. The instrument is made of finely finished brass and has the celebrated Light Action silver pistons. The model is the improved style of French design and manufacture. Fitted with German silver mouthpiece, water key and music rack. Weight, boxed, 10 lbs. Our special price ....$12.50

No. 7733. Bb Tenor, with bell up, is just like No. 7732, illustrated and described above, but is made additionally attractive and valuable by being nickel plated throughout. Our special price ....$14.95

No. 7734. **Bb Baritone,** bell up, is just the same style and model as No. 7732 Bb Tenor illustrated and described above. Made of brass beautifully finished, the improved model with Light Action of French design and manufacture. This action has silver pistons, and is especially sought after by professionals. We fit the instrument with German silver mouthpiece, water key and fine music rack; weight boxed 11 pounds. Our special price ....$12.75

No. 7735. Bb Baritone, bell up, is just the same as No. 7734 above described, but is very finely nickel plated; weight boxed 11 pounds. Our special price $16.70

No. 7737. **Bb Bass.** Improved Model, light action with silver pistons, is just the same style and model as No. 7732 Bb Tenor, illustrated above. It is made of brass, finely finished and fitted with German silver mouthpiece, water key and music rack. This elegant instrument is the best French manufacture and made especially for best trade. We ship this instrument on our liberal terms. C.O.D., subject to examination. A personal examination will assure the most critical judge that we effect a remarkable saving in the line of band instruments of higest grade. Weight, boxed, 16 lbs. Our special price ....$16.10

No. 7738. Bb Bass is the same instrument as No. 7737, above described, but is an unusual quality and finely nickel plated throughout. Price ....$19.10

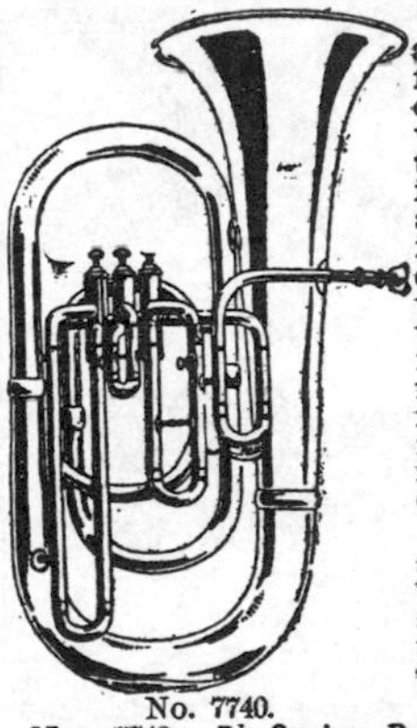
No. 7740.

No. 7740. **Eb Bass** is such an instrument as cannot be found in any retail store outside of large cities, and where it can be found it retails at from $40 to $45. We import it direct from France and are in a position to offer it at less than the retailer can buy. It has light action, with silver pistons, and is the improved model. We fit it with German silver mouthpiece and music rack, made of brass. Handsomely finished. Weight, boxed, 25 lbs. Our Special Price ....$22.95

No. 7741. Eb Bass, is the same instrument as No. 7740, illustrated and described above, but is finely nickel plated. Our Special Price ....$26.95

No. 7742. **Eb Contra Bass** is precisely the same model and style as No. 7740, Eb Bass, illustrated and described above. It has the celebrated light action, with silver pistons, and is the improved model so popular with professionals. The finest factory in France makes up these instruments for us, and each one is thoroughly examined and tested before shipping. We fit it with German silver mouthpiece and water key, and also furnish free a fine music rack. This instrument is made of brass, elegantly finished. Weight, boxed, 30 lbs. We send any instrument C.O.D., subject to examination or allow 3 per cent. discount when cash accompanies order. Our special price ....$34.25

No. 7743. Eb Contra bass, only differs in description from No. 7742, above, in the fact that it is elegantly nickel plated, and hence a much more valuable instrument. Our special price ....$39.95

## Solo Bb Cornets.

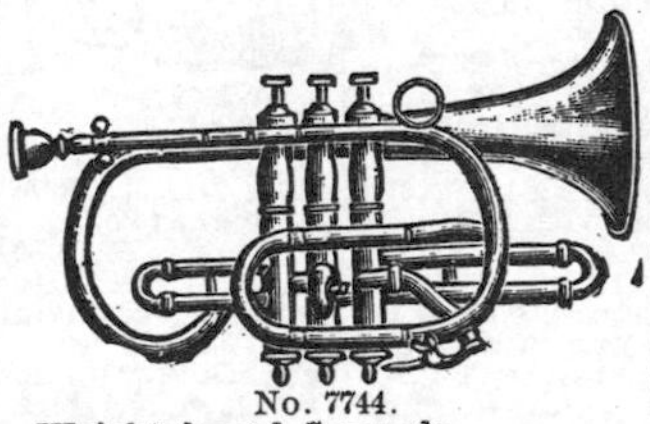
No. 7744.

No. 7744. Bb Cornet, brass long model, German silver, light action, French piston valves, water key, German silver mouthpiece, "A" set piece. A superb instrument. Price ....$8.50
Weight, boxed, 7 pounds.

No. 7745. Bb Cornet. Same as above. Nickel plated ....$10.25

No. 7746. Bb Cornet, light action, improved model, French manufacture, extra quality, richly mounted with figured metal. German silver pistons and mouthpiece, with double water keys and "A" set piece. Brass ....$18.00
Weight, boxed, 8 pounds.

No. 7747. Bb Cornet, same style as No. 7746. Nickel plated. Each ....$20.00

## Solo "C" Cornets.

No. 7748. "C" Cornets, brass, improved model, French manufacture, light action, German silver piston valves, with water key, extra Bb crook. Each ....$8.50

No. 7749. "C" Cornet, same style as No. 7748. Nickel plated. Each ....$10.25

NOTE.—We guarantee our band instruments to be in perfect condition, as each one is thoroughly examined by an experienced workman before being shipped.

## Bugles.

No. 7750. The Officers Bugle, made of brass and finely finished, key of C; weight boxed 5 pounds. Our special price ....$1.50

No. 7751. Same, finely nickel plated. Our special price ....$2.15

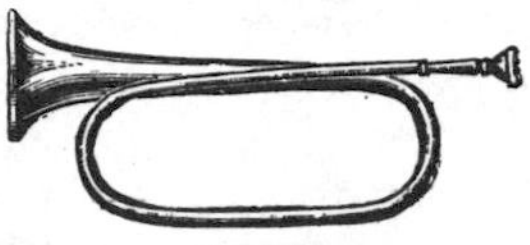
No. 7752.

No. 7752. Cavalry Bugle, brass, key of F; weight boxed 6 pounds. Our special price. $2.00

No. 7753. Same, nickel plated ....$2.65

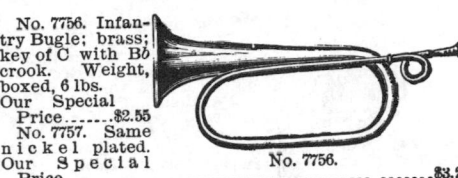

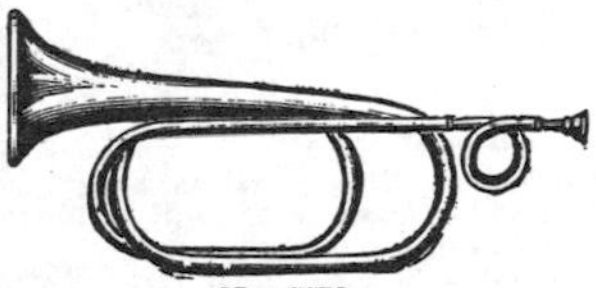
No. 7752.

No 7754. Artillery Bugle, brass, key of G; weight boxed 6 pounds. Our special price ....$2.65

No. 7755. Same, finely nickel plated. Our special price ....$3.20

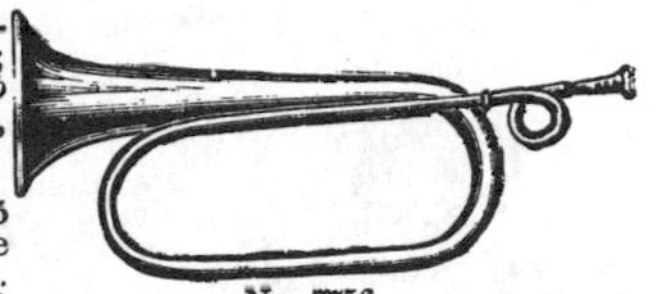
No. 7756.

No. 7756. Infantry Bugle; brass; key of C with Bb crook. Weight, boxed, 6 lbs. Our Special Price ....$2.55

No. 7757. Same nickel plated. Our Special Price ....$3.25

## Bicycle Bugles.

No. 7758. Bicycle Bugles: brass, with chain. Weight boxed, 5 lbs. Our Special Price ....$1.55

No. 7759. Same, nickel plated. Our Special Price ....$2.15

## Hunting Horns.

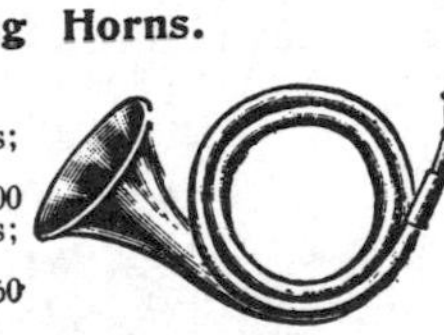
No. 7761.

No. 7761. Hunting Horns; brass. One turn. Each ....$1.00

No. 7762. Hunting Horns; brass; three turns. Each ....$1.50

## MISCELLANEOUS MUSICAL INSTRUMENTS.

## Jews' Harps.

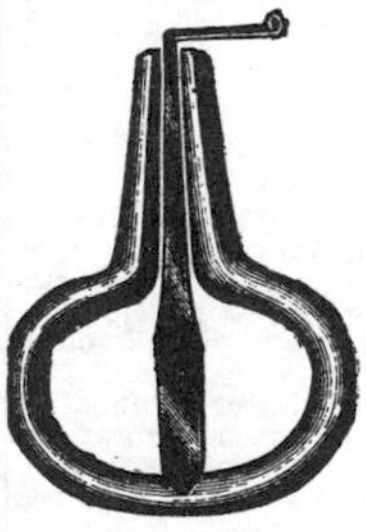
No. 7765.

No. 7765. Jews' Harp. Common old style pattern, as illustrated; good quality. Weight, 2 to 3 oz. Each ....$0.05

No. 7766. Jews' Harp. White metal frames, fancy file finished. Medium size ....$0.10
Large size .... 0.12
Extra Large size .... 0.20

7768. Smith's Iron Frame Jews' Harp, plated, brass tipped tongues. 2½ inch frame. Each ....$0.15

No. 7769. Same, 3 inch frame Each ....$0.18

No. 7771. Smith's "Jumbo" Jews' Harp, 3¾ inch iron frame. Each ....$0.40

**Whether you buy a Jews' Harp or a Piano, your order will receive the same attention.**

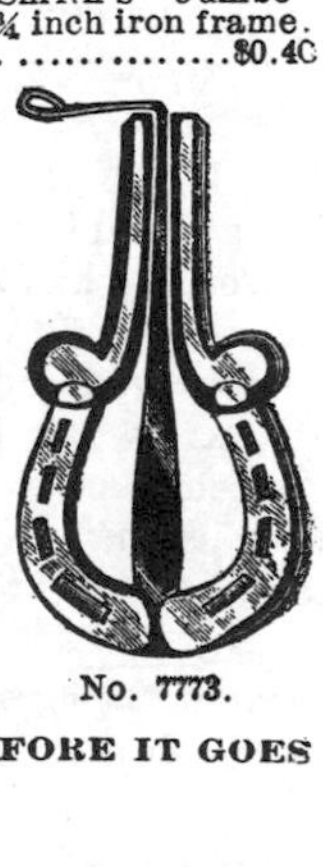
No. 7773.

No. 7773. Jews' Harp. Horseshoe pattern, as illustrated, 2½ inch plated iron frame, steel tongue. Weight, 2 oz. Each ....$0.10

No. 7775. English fancy pattern, with 2¾ inch frame. Weight, 2 oz. Each ....$0.10

**The list of Music Folios and Instruction Books is very complete. You will find them several pages farther along.**

**EVERY ARTICLE WE SHIP IS CAREFULLY INSPECTED, AND PASSES THROUGH THE HANDS OF THREE CHECKERS BEFORE IT GOES OUT. WE GUARD AGAINST ERRORS WITH THE UTMOST CARE.**

## The "Midway Musette."

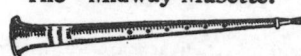

No. 7777.

No. 7777. The music of "Midway Musette" is an exact reproduction of the wierd oriental music, so familiar to those who visited the Midway Plaisance at the World's Fair. Anyone can play it. Nickel plated, with reed, each................$0.75

## Kazoos.

No. 7778. The Kazoo is the simplest musical 'nstrument made. No trouble to learn. Insert

No. 7778.

some noise at the one end, the pleasing music is emitted from the other. Made of maple with metal ring.
Each ..................$0.08
Per dozen .................0.85

No. 7780.

No. 7780. The Kazoo Cornet, illustrated, is made of brass and is attached to the Kazoo as shown. Gives the voice an exact imitation of the cornet.
Price, each, without Kazoo..................$0.60
Per dozen.................7.00

## Fanfares.

No 7781.

No. 7781. The Faufare is a simple instrument with reed valves. Made of brass. Price, with six reed valves, superior quality, each.........$0.50
No. 7782. Same, with eight reed valves. Each... 0.65
No. 7783. Same, with ten reed valves. Each.... 0.75

No. 7784. Toy Piano, for the little people. The keys are real keys and the piano will play a real tune. Strongly made and neat; fifteen keys, with steel bars. Weight, about 4 lbs. Each .............$1.25

No. 7784.

## Parlor Bells.

No. 7785.

No. 7785. Parlor Bells. A popular instrument for accompanying piano, organ or guitar. Made with twelve lettered blued steel bars on a handsome frame. Perfectly tuned. Music is produced by beaters, which are furnished as shown. Key of A, Ab or C, as desired. Weight about 4½ lbs. Price, complete.............$1.35

## Orchestra Bells.

No. 7786.

No. 7786. Orchestra Bells. Made with especial care, and intended particularly for professional use. Either for solo or orchestra purposes. Twenty-five finished steel bars, chromatic

scale, tuned perfectly to concert pitch. Mounted in fine polished walnut case. There are inferior instruments in the market similar to this, that are gotten up to sell cheap, and no attention is paid to musical effect. We recommend this as the best made. Weight, packed, about 20 lbs. Twenty-five notes, two beaters. Price, each..................$8.40

## Xylophones.

A musical novelty of great popularity. Made of maple, on a frame. Each bar producing a different tone, when struck with the beater.

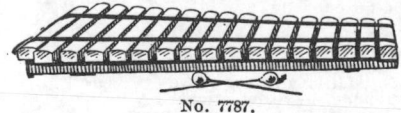

No. 7787.

No. 7787. Fifteen maple bars, as illustrated, letter C to C; fifteen notes, key of C; on frame; excellent quality and tone.....................$0.95
No. 7788. Twenty-five maple bars, ten extra bars for chromatic scale, letter F to F, key of F; on frame. Fine quality. Each..................$3.75

## Bones and Clappers.

No. 7789. Bones, hardwood, 5½ inches. Weight, 5 oz. Per set of four ............$0.12
No. 7790. Bones, rosewood, 5½ inches. Weight, 5 oz. Per set of four ............$0.15
No. 7791. Bones, rosewood, 7 inches, large. Weight, 6 oz.

No. 7789.

Per set of four.......................$0.20
No. 7792. Bones, solid ebony, 5½ inches. Weight, 6 oz. Per set of four.......................$0.25
No. 7793. Bones, solid ebony, 7 inches large. Weight, 7 oz. Per set of four.......................$0.35

No. 7794. Clappers. Made of walnut, with patent steel spring and lead clappers. Per set of two.... $0.10

No. 7794

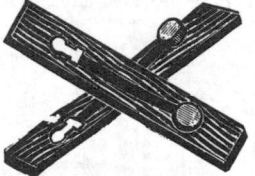

No. 7795.

No. 7795. Cymbalet. Made of two pieces of bent wood, fastened together with two loose brass jingles at each end. Produces same effect as tambourine, and is easier to handle. Each.......................$0.05
Per doz .......................0.50

## Castanets.

No. 7796.

No. 7796. Castanet. Made of solid ebony, with cord to fasten on wrist. Price, per pair, large.$0.50
Price, per pair, small 0.40

## Tambourines.

No. 7797. Seven inch maple rim, with tacked sheepskin head and three sets of jingles; weight 10 oz.

No. 7797.

Price, each...................$0.25
Per dozen .................2.75
No. 7798. Same, with 8 inch head; weight 12 oz.
Each .......................$0.33
Per dozen .................3.75
No. 7799. Same, with 10 inch head; weight 14 oz.
Each .......................$0.36
Per dozen .................4.05
No. 7800. Maple painted rim, 8 inch tacked calfskin head, nine sets of jingles; weight 16 oz. Each... $0.65
No. 7801. Maple painted rim, 10 inch tacked calfskin head, twelve sets jingles; weight 19 oz. Each......$0.88
No. 7802. Maple rim fancy painted and ornamented, 10 inch calfskin head, fastened with metal band, without tacks, three sets jingles; weight 16 oz. Each..$0.80

## Salvation Army Tambourines.

No. 7803. 11 inch Maple Hoop, calfskin head, nineteen sets brass jingles, metal band fastening. Each$1.75
No. 7804. 11 inch Nickel Hoop, wood lined, calfskin head, nineteen sets nickel plated jingles, invisible metal band fastening. Each.......................$2.50

## Triangles.

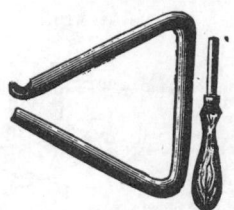

No. 7805.

No. 7805. 4 inch, nickeled steel, with hammer. Weight, 7 oz. Each.......................$ .25
No. 7806. 6 inch, nickeled steel, with hammer. Weight, 9 oz. Each.......................$ .30
No. 7807. 7 inch, nickeled steel, with hammer. Weight, 12 oz. Each.......................$ .45
No. 7808. 8 inch, nickeled steel, with hammer. Weight, 15 oz. Each.......................$ .60
No. 7809. 10 inch, nickeled steel, with hammer. Extra heavy. Weight, 20 oz. Each.......................$ .95
No. 7810. 12 inch, nickeled steel, with hammer. Extra Heavy. Weight, 25 oz. Each.......................$1.35

## Musical Sleigh Bells.

No. 7811. Musical Sleigh Bells. A musical novelty that consists of an oak frame about 30 inches long by 24 inches high, with eight straps, each having six bells attached. Each set of six bells representing different notes. The sets are tuned as follows: B flat, C, D, E flat, F, G, A and B flat, or one full octave in key

No. 7811.

of B flat. Very simple to play and decidedly pleasing to the ear, as well as novel. They come packed compactly in a pasteboard box, and are easily put together. Weight about 4 lbs. Price per set.......................$10.65

## Ocarinas.

A very popular instrument easy to learn and simple to play. Instruction sheet with each instrument.

## Fiehn's Vienna Make.

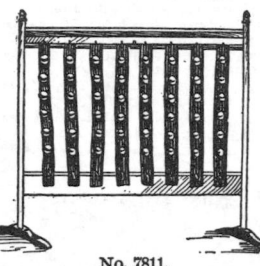

| No. | | | Each. |
|---|---|---|---|
| 7812. | Key of C, | Soprano | $0.18 |
| 7813. | " | Bb, " | 0.18 |
| 7814. | " | A, " | 0.22 |
| 7815. | " | G, " | 0.24 |
| 7816. | " | F, " | 0.25 |
| 7817. | " | E, " | 0.27 |
| 7818. | " | Eb, " | 0.28 |
| 7819. | " | D, Alto | 0.30 |
| 7820. | " | C, " | 0.32 |
| 7821. | " | Bb, " | 0.35 |
| 7822. | " | A, " | 0.39 |
| 7823. | " | Ab, " | 0.49 |
| 7824. | " | G, " | 0.52 |
| 7825. | " | F, " | 0.60 |
| 7826. | " | E, " | 0.87 |
| 7827. | " | Eb, " | 0.87 |
| 7828. | " | D, Bass | 0.98 |
| 7829. | " | C, " | 1.26 |
| 7830. | " | Bb, " | 1.54 |
| 7831. | " | A, " | 1.75 |
| 7832. | " | Ab, " | 1.96 |
| 7833. | " | G, " | 2.31 |
| 7834. | " | F, " | 2.45 |
| 7835. | " | Eb, Contra Bass | 2.60 |
| 7836. | " | D, " " | 3.15 |
| 7837. | " | C, " " | 3.50 |

7837½. Quartettes, 1st and 2nd Tenor, 1st and 2nd Bass.......................Per Set, 3.65
7838. Sextettes, Soprano, 1st and 2nd Tenor, 1st and 2nd Bass, and Contra Basses.....Per Set, 9.75
Sopranos, weight 4 oz.; Altos, 14 oz; Bass, 26 oz.; Contra Bass, 40 oz.
When ordering for a quartette or sextette be sure to have all in the same key. A sheet of instructions with each instrument showing exactly how it is played.

Not an ounce of inferior stock can be found in any of our Harness.

## Strings.

We import direct from European manufacturers and handle none but the best strings made. Not an inferior string sold by us at any price. We guarantee every one to be perfectly made of the best quality material. We do not guarantee them against breaking, but they will stand anything that can be expected of the best strings made. We solicit your orders on this particular line, knowing that we can please you to an eminent degree and save you from 50 to 60 per cent. on every purchase.

We wish to caution our trade in buying strings against being misled by "fancy" names and high prices quoted by other dealers. We buy all our gut strings (steel and wound strings are made in this country) direct from the best European manufacturers, select only first quality, and are selling them at "rock bottom" prices. A trial order will convince you that this statement is correct. Violin and banjo strings, weight 2 oz. per set; guitar and violoncello strings, 4 oz. per set.

### Violin Strings.

| | | Each. | Pr dz. |
|---|---|---|---|
| No. 7839. | E, superior Italian, 4 lengths, polished | $0.12 | $1.25 |
| No. 7840. | E, superior quality, rough finish | 0.12 | 1.25 |
| No. 7841. | A, superior Italian, 2½ lengths | 0.12 | 1.25 |
| No. 7842. | D, superior Italian, 2½ lengths | 0.15 | 1.60 |
| No. 7843. | G, superior Italian, 1 length | 0.08 | 0.85 |
| No. 7844. | Per set of four, 40 cts. | | |

### Extra Fine Quality Violin Strings.

| | | Each. |
|---|---|---|
| No. 7845. | E, best quality, 4 lengths | $0.15 |
| No. 7846. | A, best quality, 2½ lengths | 0.15 |
| No. 7847. | D, best quality, 2½ lengths | 0.18 |
| No. 7848. | G, best quality, 1 length | 0.10 |
| No. 7849. | Full set of above, 50 cts. | |

### Steel Violin Strings.

| | Silver Plated. | Each. | Per doz. |
|---|---|---|---|
| No. 7850. | E, 1 length, best quality | $0.02 | $0.20 |
| No. 7851. | A, 1 length, best quality | 0.02 | 0.20 |
| No. 7852. | D, 1 length, best quality, covered, silver plated | 0.06 | 0.65 |
| No. 7853. | G, 1 length, best quality, covered, silver plated | 0.06 | 0.65 |
| No. 7854. | Full set, 10 cts. | | |
| No. 7855. | Silk violin strings, E, 4 lengths, very fine quality, French | 0.12 | 1.25 |

### Banjo Strings.

| | | Each. | Per doz. |
|---|---|---|---|
| No. 7856. | B or 1st, and E or 5th | $0.08 | $0.85 |
| No. 7857. | G or 2nd | 0 10 | 1 00 |
| No. 7858. | E or 3d | 0 10 | 1.00 |
| No. 7859. | A or 4th bass | 0.08 | 0.85 |
| No. 7860. | Full set of five, fine quality, 35 cts. | | |

### Extra Fine Quality Banjo Strings.

| | | Each. |
|---|---|---|
| No. 7861. | B or 1st, and E or 5th | $0.10 |
| No. 7862. | G or 2nd | 0.14 |
| No. 7863. | E or 3d | 0.14 |
| No. 7864. | A or 4th | 0.10 |
| No. 7865. | Full set of five, 45 cts. | |

### Steel Banjo Strings.

| | | Each. | Per doz. |
|---|---|---|---|
| No. 7866. | B or 1st E or 5th | $0.02 | $0.20 |
| No. 7867. | G or 2d | 0.02 | 0.20 |
| No. 7868. | E or 3d | 0.02 | 0.20 |
| No. 7869. | A or 4th | 0.07 | 0.65 |
| No. 7870. | Full set of 5, per set, 12c. | | |

### Guitar Strings.

| | | Each. | Per doz. |
|---|---|---|---|
| No. 7871. | E or 1st, superior quality gut. | $0.12 | $1.25 |
| No. 7872. | B or 2nd, superior quality gut. | 0.12 | 1.25 |
| No. 7873. | G or 3rd, superior quality gut. | 0.15 | 1.60 |
| No. 7874. | D or 4th, silvered wire on silk | 0.10 | 1.00 |
| No. 7875. | A or 5th, silvered wire on silk | 0.10 | 1.00 |
| No. 7876. | E or 6th, silvered wire on silk. | 0.10 | 1.00 |
| No. 7877. | Full set of 6, 60c. | | |

### Extra Quality Guitar Gut Strings.

| | | Each |
|---|---|---|
| No. 7878. | E or 1st | $0.15 |
| No. 7879. | B or 2nd | 0.15 |
| No. 7880. | G or 3rd | 0.18 |

### Steel Guitar Strings.

| | | Each. | Per doz. |
|---|---|---|---|
| No. 7881. | E or 1st, silvered steel, best quality | $0.02 | $0.20 |
| No. 7882. | B or 2nd, silvered steel, best quality | 0.02 | 0.20 |
| No. 7883. | G or 3rd, silvered wire wound on steel | 0.10 | 1.00 |
| No. 7884. | D or 4th, silvered wire wound on steel | 0.10 | 1.00 |
| No. 7885. | A or 5th, silvered wire wound on steel | 0.10 | 1.00 |
| No. 7886. | E or 6th, silvered wire wound on steel | 0.10 | 1.00 |
| No. 7887. | Full set of 6, steel, 38c. | | |

### Mandolin Strings.

| | | Each. |
|---|---|---|
| No. 7888. | First string, steel wire, silver plated | $0.04 |
| No. 7889. | Second string, steel wire, silver plated | 0.04 |
| No. 7890. | Third string, steel, wound with silver wire | 0.08 |
| No. 7891. | Fourth string, steel bound with silver wire | 0.08 |
| No. 7892. | Full set of 8, 40c. | |

### Violoncello Strings.

| | | Each. |
|---|---|---|
| No. 7893. | A, best Italian | $0.15 |
| No. 7894. | D, best Italian | 0.20 |
| No. 7895. | G, best wired gut | 0.15 |
| No. 7896. | C, best wired gut | 0.20 |
| No. 7897. | Full set of four strings. Per set | 0.65 |

### Double Bass Strings.

| | | Each. |
|---|---|---|
| No. 7898. | G or 1st, genuine Italian, fine quality | $0.60 |
| No. 7899. | D or 2d, genuine Italian, fine quality | 0.75 |
| No. 7900. | A or 3d, genuine Italian, fine quality | 0.90 |
| No. 7901. | A or 3d, wound silvered wire on gut | 1.00 |
| No. 7902. | E or 4th, wound silvered wire on gut | 1.10 |
| No. 7903. | Per set of three | 2.00 |
| No. 7904. | Per set of four | 3.00 |

NOTE.—When ordering sets of double bass strings state whether you want "A" string plain or wound.

### Autoharp Strings.

We do not sell less than full set.

| | | |
|---|---|---|
| No. 7905. | Full set for No. 1 | $0.40 |
| No. 7906. | Full set for No. 2¾ | 0.45 |
| No. 7907. | Full set for No. 2⅞ or 3 | 0 50 |
| No. 7908. | Full set for No. 4 or 5 | 0.60 |
| No. 7909. | Full set for No. 6 | 0.65 |

### Zither Strings.

No. 7910. Steel and brass for finger board. Each $0 05

No. 7911. Accompaniment and bass wound on steel wire. Each 0.07

No. 7912. Full set wound on steel wire. Weight, per set, 6 oz. $1.75.

NOTE.—When ordering strings for zither be sure and give number and letter of string wanted.

### Violin Furnishings.

VIOLIN CASES.

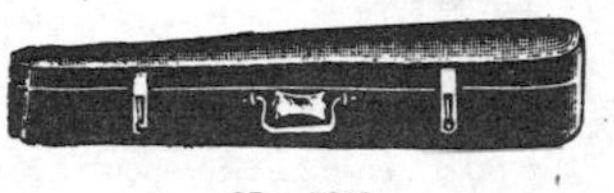

No. 7913.

From the best factories. Unless otherwise ordered we always send full size, where cases are made in full sizes, ¾ and ½ sizes.

No. 7913. Violin case, made solidly of wood, finely varnished black, exposition shape, full lined throughout with flannel; complete with nickeled lock, handle and spring clasps. Full, ¾ or ½ size. Our special price. Each $2.65

No. 7914. Violin case, common shape, made of select wood, American, black varnished, full lined with flannel, complete with nickel plated lock, handles and hook clasps. Our special price $2.30

No. 7915. Violin case, common shape, well made of wood, and half lined with flannel, complete with handle hooks and lock. Our special price $1.30

No. 7916. Same as No. 7915, above, but without lock. Our special price $1.10

No. 7917. Violin Case, similar shape to No. 7916, illustrated above, full leather covered and full lined with velvet, leather handles, nickel plated lock and hook hasps. Comes either in black or russet color. Especially good value. Our price. Each $5 15

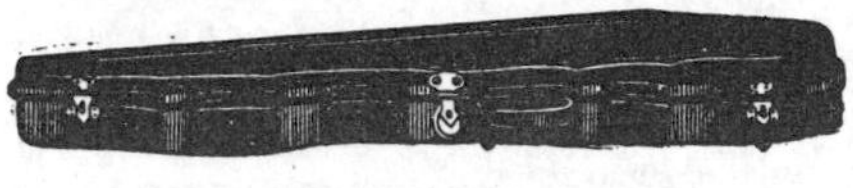

No. 7918.

No. 7918. Violin Case shown in the illustration is made of fine papiermache, fancy French shape, full lined with baize, nickeled lock, handle and hasps, very light and durable. Our special price $2.85

VIOLIN BOWS.

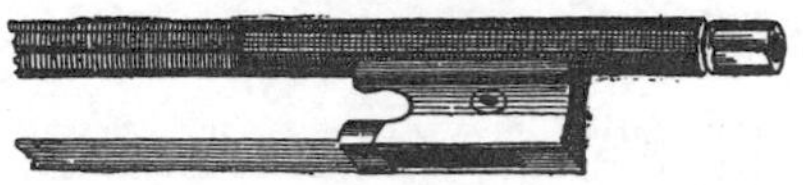

No. 7919.

No. 7919. Violin Bow, octagon shaped stick, made of select maple, finished black, bone frog, inlaid eye, bone slide and button. A good bow that will give excellent satisfaction. Our special price $0.32

No. 7920. Violin Bow, made of maple, imitation snakewood, ebony frog, inlaid dot, pearl slide, German silver button. Our special price $0.41

No. 7921. Violin Bow, genuine "L. Weizel," Brazil wood, ebony frog, pearl slide, pearl eye, German silver lined, German silver button, superior quality bow hair. Our special price. Each $0.59

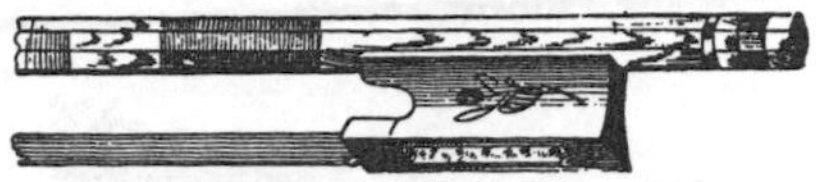

No. 7922.

No. 7922. Violin Bow, made of select Brazil wood, imitation snakewood, ebony frog, inlaid pearl dot, pearl slide, German silver button, octagon stick. An excellent fancy bow that is pleasing alike to amateur and professional. Price, Each $0.93

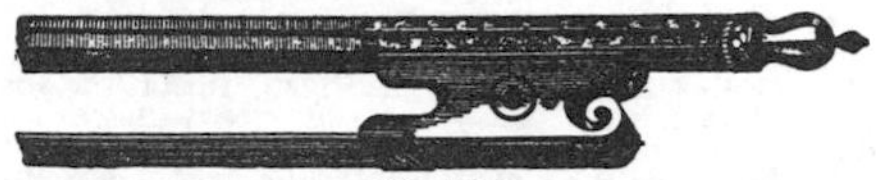

No. 7923.

No. 7923. The illustration describes a very fine genuine snakewood bow. Has ivory frog, double pearl eye, German silver lined and ivory button. Only the finest quality of bow hair with this bow. Our special price, each $2.80

No. 7924. Violin Bow is just the same as the illustration of No. 7923, but is made of select Brazil wood, imitation of snakewood. Has ivory frog, ivory button, double pearl eye, and is German silver lined. Best bow hair. Our special price, each $1.55

### Violin Bow Frogs.

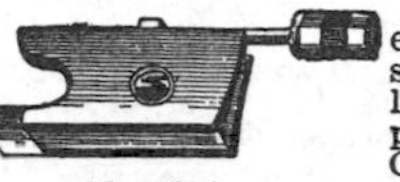

No. 7925.

No. 7925. Violin Bow Frog, ebony, with pearl inlaid in sides. Full German silver lined, German silver button, pearl slide. Our price, each $0.38

No. 7926. Violin Bow Frog, ebony, German silver dot inlaid in sides, German silver button, pearl slide. Our price, each $0.22

### Violin Bow Screws.

No. 7927. Bow Screw, with bone button, octagon shape, inlaying in end. Price, each $0.06

No. 7928. Bow Screw with ebony and German silver button, octagon shape, inlaying in end. Price, each $0.12

### Violin Patent Heads.

No. 7930. Violin Patent Head, made of solid brass, with handsome engraving on sides, bone buttons. Weight, 4 oz. Our price, complete, per set $0.35

No. 7931. Violin Patent head, handsomely nickel plated, fancy engraved sides, bone buttons. Weight, 4 oz. Our price, per set $0.50

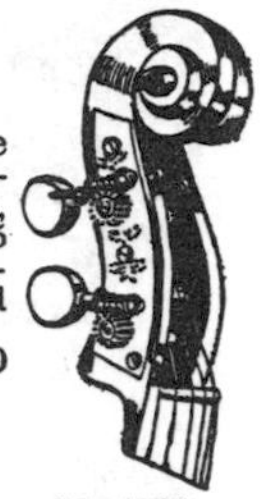

No. 7930.

### Violin Pegs.

No. 7933. Maple Violin Peg, black stained, hollow shape, pearl dot in head. Our price, each $0.02
Per set of four .07

No. 7935. Maple Violin Peg, imitation ebony finish, hollow shape, pearl dot in head. Our price, each $ .04
Per set of four .14

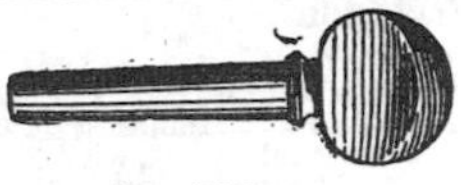

No. 7937.

No. 7937. Solid Ebony Violin Peg, hollow shape pearl dot in head.
Price, each $ .05
Per set of four .18

No. 7938. Violin Peg, made of celluloid in imitation of amber, with hollow shape head.
Our price, each $ .09
Per set of four .32

No. 7940. Celluloid Violin Peg, imitation amber, with Greek cross head. (See cut).
Our price, each $ .14
Set of four .52

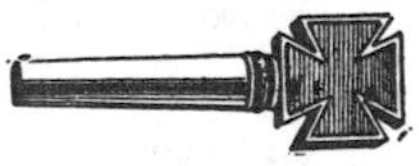

No. 7940

No. 7942. Genuine Ivory Violin Pegs, highly polished, finest quality, Greek cross head.
Our special price, each $ .66
Set of four 2.40

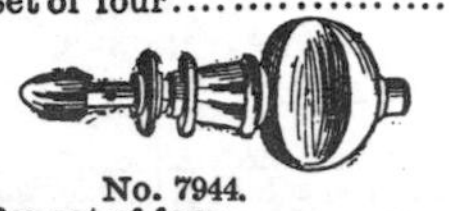

No. 7944.

No 7944. Genuine Celluloid Violin Peg. The best patent violin peg made, imitation ebony, or all white, nickel mounted.
Per set of four $0.80



NINE-TENTHS OF THE ERRORS THAT ARE MADE IN FILLING ORDERS ARE THE RESULT OF CARELESSNESS ON THE PART OF THE CUSTOMER IN MAKING OUT HIS ORDER. ALWAYS READ YOUR ORDER OVER A SECOND TIME BEFORE SENDING IT TO BE SURE YOU MAKE NO MISTAKES.

## Violin Tail Pieces.

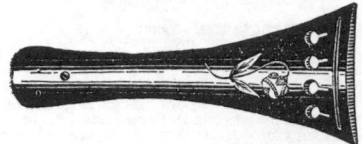

No. 7952.

No. 7946. Maple Violin Tail piece, black stained, with plain pearl inlaying. Our price, each........$0.05
No. 7948. Maple Violin Tail Piece, imitation ebony finish, inlaid with fancy colored pearl flowers and leaves. Our price, each......................$0.09
No. 7950. Solid Ebony Violin Tail Piece. Excellent model and finish. Price, each...............$0.10
No. 7952. Solid Ebony Tail Piece, inlaid with colored pearl flower and two leaves (see cut).
Our price, each.............................$0.22

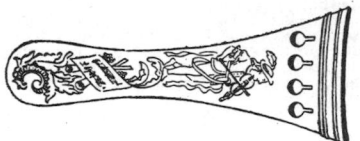

No. 7953.

No. 7953. Celluloid Violin Tailpiece, imitation of amber, tortoise or ivory, with violin player, music, etc., in relief, as shown in illustration. Good model.
Our special price...........................$0.48

## Violin Chin Rests.

No. 7954. Violin Chin Rest, solid ebony, with nickel-plated double screw fastenings. Each........$0.25
No. 7955. Violin Chin Rests, velvet covered, with German silver double screw fastening. 6 oz.
Our Special Price, each.....................$0.45

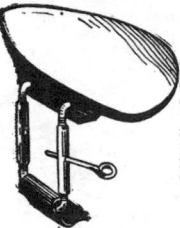

No. 7956. Violin Chin Rest. Becker's celebrated patent. Ebonite and nickel, as shown in cut. Our Special Price......$0.58
No. 7957. Same as above, with shoulder rest combined The most perfect and complete violin rest made. Weight 6 oz.
Our Special Price........ --$1.10

No. 7956.

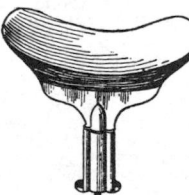

No. 7958. Violin Chin Rest, made of gutta percha, with nickel-plated mountings. This chin rest is adjustable to any size instrument. Weight, 4 oz.
Our special price........$1.35

No. 7958.

## Violin Bridges.

No. 7960. Violin Bridge, made of maple, "Panpi" model, three scrolls, good quality. Each..$0.03
No. 7962. Violin Bridge, three scrolls, same as above. extra fine quality, "Panpi." Each....$0.05
No. 7963. Violin Bridge, Vuillaume model, made of extra select maple, three scrolls, very fine quality. Each ................$0.09

No. 7960.

No. 7964. Violin Bridge, made of maple, superfine quality, three scrolls, made for artists' use. Our price ..............$0.18

No. 7964.

## Violin Mutes.

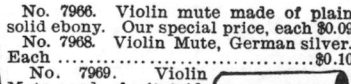

No. 7966. Violin mute made of plain solid ebony. Our special price, each $0.09
No. 7968. Violin Mute, German silver. Each............................$0.10
No. 7969. Violin Mute, made of celluloid, in imitation of amber, tortoise shell, or ivory.
Each........$0.19
No. 7966.
No. 7971. Violin Mute, as illustrated, is made of German silver and has tuning pipe A and string gauge.
Our price, each ..................$0.25    No. 7971

## Violin Fingerboards.

No. 7973.

No. 7973. Violin Fingerboard, made of maple, imitation ebony finish, excellent model.
Our price, each..........................$0.16
No. 7974. Solid Ebony Fingerboard, fine model, highly finished.
Our special price, each....................$0.25

**Our new building covers nearly half a block, and we are still crowded for space.**

## Violin End Pins.

No. 7976.

Each.
No. 7976. Maple, imitation ebony finish, pearl dot inlaid in head......................$0.02
No. 7977. Ebony, best model, pearl dot inlaid in head .04
No. 7978. Cocoa, with movable pin in center, allowing view of sound post .10
No. 7979. Ebony, with "A" tuning pipe in center .12

## Bow Hair.

Per Bunch.
No. 7980. Siberian, good quality, for full length bows .09
No. 7981. French, finest quality, but slightly bleached .15
No. 7982. Russian, extra quality .20

## Violin Bow Rosin.

No. 7984. Bow Rosin, small-sized cakes in oblong pastboard box. Price, each.......... $0.03
No. 7985. Bow Rosin, large sized cakes in oblong pasteboard box. Price, each........$0.05
No. 7986. Large-sized Cakes Bow Rosin, in neat wood case, to be used without removing from case. Price, each....$0.07

No. 7984

## Violin Necks.

No. 7987. Violin Necks, maple, unfinished, carved scroll. Each...........................$0.20
No. 7988. Violin Necks, maple, unfinished, fine quality, finely carved scroll. Each.................$0.70
No. 7989. Violin Necks, curly maple, unfinished, best quality, finely carved scroll. Weight, 8 oz, Each..$1.15

## Viola Furnishings.

### VIOLA CASES.

No. 7990. Wood, American, black varnished, half lined, hooks and lock. Price, each...............$1.65

### BRIDGES.

Each
No. 7992. Maple, three scrolls, good quality .... $0.05
No. 7993. Maple, three scrolls, fine quality, Vuillaume model .15
No. 7994. Maple, three scrolls, superfine quality, selected old wood .40

### BOW HAIR.

No. 7995. Siberian, finest quality, each filling tied up separately .20

### BOW FROGS.

No. 7996. Ebony, pearl eye, full German silver lined, German silver button, pearl slide........ .75

### FINGER BOARDS.

No. 7998. Ebony, plain, fine model and finish .... .32
No. 7999. Ebony, superior model and finish...... .48

### MUTES.

No. 71001. Ebony, plain, good model and finish.. .14
No. 71002. Ebony, beveled top, new model....... .20

### NECKS.

No. 71004. Maple, finely carved scroll........... .80
No. 71005. Curly maple, finely carved scroll, extra quality 1.30

### PEGS.

No. 71006. Boxwood, hollow shape, imitation ebony finish, pearl dot inlaid in head .......... .07
No. 71007. Ebony, hollow shape, highly polished .09
No. 71008. Ebony, hollow shape, highly polished, extra quality .12

### TAIL-PIECES.

No. 71009. Ebony, plain, good model and finish.. .19
No. 71010. Ebony, plain, best model and finish, extra quality .28

## Double Bass Viol Furnishings.

### DOUBLE BASS BOWS.

No. 71012. Made of maple, red painted, light wood frog, excellent quality, common model. Each.... $1.25
No. 71014. Redwood, natural color, ebony frog, good quality, common model. Price, each ..............$2.25

No. 71015.

No. 71015. Pernambuco wood, natural color, ebony frog, German silver lined, pearl inlaid eye, professional model, like cut. Price, each ..............$4.45

### DOUBLE BASS BOW FROGS.

No. 71018. Made of solid ebony, plain, good model and finish.
Each....................$1.20

No. 71018.

### DOUBLE BASS BOW HAIR.

No. 71019. Siberian black, fine quality.
Price, each filling...........................$0.22
No. 71020. Siberian, white, finest quality.
Price, each filling...........................$0.27

### DOUBLE BASS BRIDGES.

No. 71022. Maple, plain scroll, fine quality. for ½ size or ¾ size double bass. Price, each..........$0.40
No. 71024. Maple, superfine quality selected old wood, for ½ or ¾ size double bass. Price, each...$1.20

### DOUBLE BASS MUTES.

No. 71025. Solid ebony, best model and finish.
Each .......................................$0.95

### DOUBLE BASS FINGERBOARDS.

No. 71026. Maple, imitation ebony finish, fine quality. Each .................................$1.05
No. 71027. Solid ebony, fine quality and finish.
Each .......................................$3.45

### DOUBLE BASS TAILPIECES.

No. 71029. Maple, imitation ebony finish, pearl dot inlaid, for three or four string bass. Each .......$0.60
No. 71030. Solid ebony, fine finish, for three or four string bass. Each.............................$1.95

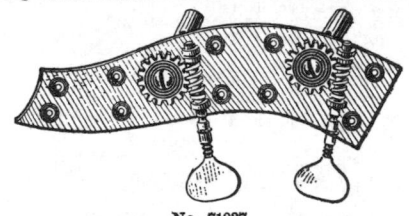

No. 71037.

### DOUBLE BASS PATENT HEADS.

No. 71033. Iron plates and screws, good quality, for three string bass. Per set of three ...........$1.70
No. 71034. Same for four stringed bass.
Per set of four.................................$2.10
No. 71035. Brass plates and iron screws, fine quality for three string bass. Per set of three..........$2.40
No. 71036. Same for four string bass.
Per set of four.................................$3.10
No. 71037. Full brass, with engraved side plates, same as illustrated. Per full set.................$6.60

### DOUBLE BASS BOW RESIN.

No. 71039. Good quality, in oblong pasteboard box.
Each.......................................$0.09
No. 71041. Wood boxes, to be used without removing from box. Each.............................$0.11

## Violoncello Furnishings.

### VIOLONCELLO CASES.

No. 71045. Wood, black varnished, lined with flannel, with lock, handle and spring clasps. Each ......$13.05

### VIOLONCELLO BAGS.

No. 71046. Excellent quality green cloth, with buttons. Each...............................$3.05
No. 71047. Superior grade canvas, fleece lined, patent fasteners. Price, each...................$3.30

### VIOLONCELLO BOWS.

No. 71048. Redwood, plain ebony frog, bone button, good quality, weight, 8 oz. Each ..............$0.65
No. 71049. Redwood, ebony frog, pearl eye, German silver button. Weight, 10 oz. Each..........$1.00
No. 71050. Brazil wood, ebony frog, double pearl eye, full German silver lined. pearl slide, German silver button. Weight, 10 oz. Each................$1.55

No. 71051.

No. 71051. Pernambuco wood, ebony frog, double pearl eye, full German silver lined, German silver button. Weight, 10 oz. Each..................$2.35

**YOU WILL FIND ALL MUSICAL INSTRUMENT FURNISHINGS ARRANGED CONSECUTIVELY IN THE SAME ORDER AS THE INSTRUMENTS THEMSELVES. BE SURE TO LOOK IN THE INDEX IF YOU DON'T FIND WHAT YOU WANT.**

## Violoncello Furnishings.—Continued.

**VIOLONCELLO BOW FROGS, WITH SCREW.**

No. 71052. Ebony, pearl dot inlaid in side, pearl slide, bone button. Our price, each........$0.25
No. 71053. Solid ebony, with pearl dot in side, German silver lined, pearl slide, German silver button. Price, each..........$0.45

**VIOLONCELLO BOW HAIR.**

No. 71054. Fine quality Siberian bow hair, each filling tied separately. Our special price, each......$0.20

**VIOLONCELLO BRIDGES.**

No. 71055. Maple, good quality, with two scrolls. Weight, 3 oz. Each..........$0.18
No. 71056. Maple, fine quality, with three scrolls. Weight, 3 oz. Each..........$0.27

**VIOLONCELLO TAIL PIECES.**

No. 71057. Maple, imitation ebony finish, pearl dot inlaid on top. Weight, 4 oz. Each..........$0.28
No. 71058. Ebony. plain, best model and finish. Weight, 4 oz. Each..........$0.70

### Violoncello Nuts.

No. 71059. Ebony for upper end of fingerboard. Each..........$0.40
No. 71060. Ebony to support tail-piece string. Each..........40

### Violoncello Fingerboards.

No. 71061. Ebony, plain, good model and finish. Each..........$1.20
No. 71062. Plain solid ebony, extra quality finish and special model. Each..........$2.75

### Violoncello Mutes.

No. 71064. Ebony, plain, good model and finish. Each..........$0.16
No. 71065. Ebony, beveled top, new model. Each. 0.55

### Violoncello Patent Heads.

No. 71068. Brass plates and iron screws, maple pegs, with pearl dot inlaid in head. Per set..........$0.19
No. 71069. Full brass, with engraved side plates. Price, per set..........$0.40

### Violoncello Tailpieces.

No. 71071. Maple, imitation ebony finish, pearl dot inlaid in top. Our Special Price. each..........0.28
No. 71072. Plain solid ebony. Good model and finish. Each..........$0.65

### Violoncello Pegs.

No. 71075. Solid ebony, hollow shape, highly polished, pearl dot inlaid in head. Each..........$0.28
Per set of 4..........1.05
No. 74077. Solid ebony, plain oval shape, highly polished. French model. Each..........$0.24
Per set of 4..........0.90

### Violoncello Bow Rosin.

No. 71079. Medium size round boxes, good quality, "Ole Bull." Each..........$0.08
No. 71081. Reform Rosin, on metal spools. Fine quality, in pasteboard boxes. Each..........$0.10

## GUITAR FURNISHINGS.

### Guitar Cases.

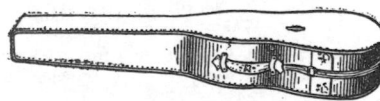

No. 71087.

No. 71086. Wood, superior quality, American made, half lined, with lock, handle and hooks; for standard size guitar. Each..........$2.00
No. 71087. Brown canvas, as illustrated, leather bound edges, open on end, complete with strap, buckle and handle. Standard or regular size. Each..........$1.50
No. 71088. Same, for concert size. Each..........$1.90
No. 71089. Hand sewed leather, embossed, black or russet, very superior quality, for standard size guitar. Each..........$5.25
No. 71090. Same, for concert size. Each..........$5.75

### Guitar Bags.

No. 71092. Fine green cloth with buttons for ordinary concert or grand concert guitar. Each........$0.95
No. 71094. Canvas, fleece lined, patent fasteners, fine quality, for ordinary concert or grand concert size guitar. Each..........$1.15

### Guitar Patent Heads.

No. 71098.

No. 71096. Brass, good engraving on sides, bone buttons, fine quality. Per set..........$.70
No. 71097. Nickel plated, good engraving on sides, bone buttons, fine quality. Per set..........$.85
No. 71098. Brass, polished and lacquered, white celluloid buttons, (see cut). Per set..........$1.50

## Guitar Tailpieces.

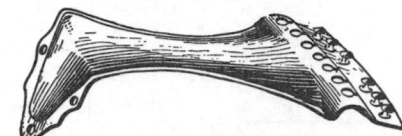

No. 71102.

No. 71101. Celluloid, imitation ivory or amber, for ordinary size guitar. Each..........$.50
No. 71102. Brass, nickel plated, for any size guitar. Each..........$.75

## Guitar Fingerboards.

No. 71107.

No. 71106. Ebony, plain, without frets, Each...$.60
No. 71107. Ebony, with frets, (see cut). Each.. 1.00

## Guitar Capo D'Astros.

Used to clamp on fingerboard to facilitate playing in flat keys.

No. 71110.

No. 71110. Brass, nickel plated, rubber covered clamps, vest pocket model. Our price, each......$0.20

No. 71111. Capo D'-Astro, nickel plated, spring action, felt covered clamps. (See cut). Price, each..........$0.30
No. 71112. Same as above made of aluminum, polished. Each..........$0.50

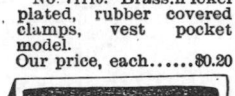

No. 71111.

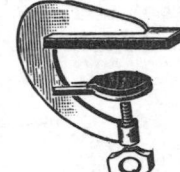

No. 71115.

No. 71115. Capo D'Astro, made of brass, polished and lacquered, cork lined clamps, improved model, extra weight and strength. Each..........$0.25
No. 71116. Same, Brass, finely nickel plated. Each..........$0.35

## Guitar Furnishings.

**GUITAR BRIDGES.**

No. 71121.

No. 71119. Ebony, plain, best model and finish. Each..........$0.20
No. 71120. Ebony, neat pearl inlaying at each end. Each..........$0.60
No. 71121. Ebony, engraved and pearl inlaying at each end. Each..........$1.05
No. 71122. Celluloid, imitation amber or ivory. Each..........$0.45

**GUITAR BRIDGE PINS.**

No. 71125.

No. 71124. Maple, black stained, polished head. Each..........$0.02
Per set of six..........10
No. 71125. Ebony, polished pearl inlaying in head (see cut). Each..........$0.03
Per set of six..........12
No. 71126. Ivory, polished pearl inlaying in head. Each..........$0.06
Per set of six..........30
No. 71127. Celluloid, imitation amber, tortoise shell or ivory. Each..........$0.06
Per set of six..........30

**GUITAR END PINS.**

No. 71130.

No. 71129. Ebony, plain, polished heads. Each..........$0.03
No. 71130. Ebony, plain, polished heads, with pearl dot inlaid. Each..........$0.04

**GUITAR FRETS.**

No. 71133.

No. 71133. Brass, in sets of eighteen. Per set..$0.17
No. 71134. German silver in sets of eighteen. Per set..........$0.30
No. 71135. German silver, in coils. Per pound.. 3.75

## Banjo Furnishings.

**BANJO CASES.**

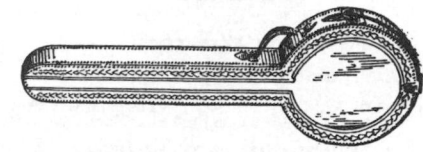

No. 71140.

No. 71136. Wood, black varnished, flannel lined, complete with lock, handle and hooks, for 11 inch banjo. Each..........$2.00
No. 71138. Brown Canvas Case, superior quality, edges bound with leather, flannel lined, with handle, for any size banjo from 7 to 13 inch. Each........$1.75
No. 71140. Extra fine black or russet leather case, embossed, flannel lined, open on end, complete as illustrated, with strap, buckle and handle, for 10 or 11 inch banjo..........$4.50
No. 71141. Same, for 12 or 13 inch banjo. Each..$5.10

**BANJO BAGS.**

No. 71142. Fine Green Cloth, with buttons, for 10 to 13 inch banjo. Each..........$0.75
No. 71144. Canvas, fleece lined, patent fastners, for 10 to 13 inch banjo. Each..........$0.90

**BANJO BRIDGES.**

No. 71146. Maple or rosewood; professional model; special make. Each..........$0.05
No. 71148. Solid ebony, regular model. Each...$0.05

No. 71149. Celluloid; special professional model, see cut. Imitation of amber, tortoise shell or ivory. Each......$0.10

No. 71149.

**BANJO TAILPIECES.**

No. 71151. Plain solid ebony. Each..........$0.05
No. 71153. Celluloid; imitation of amber, tortoise shell or ivory. Solid heel piece. Price, each....$0.22

No. 71155. Brass, heavily nickel plated. Special make. See cut. Price, each..........$0.35

No. 71155.

No. 71157. Genuine walrus ivory, highly polished and nicely engraved. Artist model. See cut. Price, each..........$0.58

No. 71157.

### Banjo Pegs.

No. 71160. Imitation ebony, hollow shape, pearl dot on handle, regular. Each..........$0.03
No. 71161. Same, side pegs. Each..........$0.03
No. 71163. Solid ebony, hollow shape, pearl dot in each end, regular. Each..........

No. 71160.

No. 71164. Same, side peg. Each..........$0.06
No. 71166. Celluloid, imitation of amber, Greek cross pattern, polished, regular. Each..........$0.12
No. 71168. Side pegs to match. Each..........$0.12

No. 71166.

Full set of 5..........55
No. 71170. Celluloid, imitation ebony, nickel mounted, the celebrated "Champion" patent. Per set of 5..........$1.00
No. 71172. Same, white, nickel mounted. Per set of 5..........$1.00

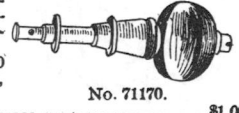

No. 71170.

### Banjo Brackets.

No. 71174. Leaf Pattern. (See cut) New style, solid brass, cast with bolt and nut. Per doz..........$0.70
No. 71176. Same, nickel plated. Per doz..........$1.00
No. 71177. Hexagon pattern, new style, solid brass, turned and polished, with bolt and nut. Per doz........$0.78
No. 71180. Same, nickel plated. Per doz..........$1.25
No. 71182. Globe pattern, solid brass, turned and polished, with bolt and new pattern safety nut. Per doz..........$1.05
No. 71184. Same, nickel plated. Per doz..........$1.25

No. 71174.

### Banjo Patent Heads.

No. 71186. Patent head, nickel plated, engraved sides, bone buttons, good quality. Per full set..........$0.58

### Banjo Thimbles.

No. 71188. German silver, imported pattern. Each ........ $0.05

### Banjo Wrenches.

No. 71190. Brass, key shape, nickel plated. Each ........ $0.12
No. 71192. Solid cast brass, fancy shape, finely ground and lacquered, for ¼ or 5-16 inch nut. Each ........ $0.24

## MANDOLIN FURNISHINGS.

### Mandolin Cases.

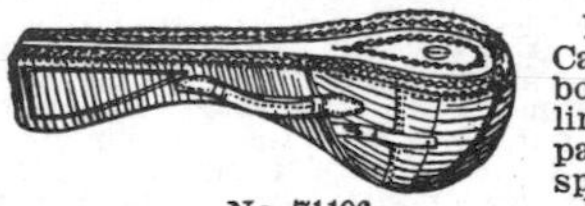

No. 71196.

No. 71194. Brown Canvas, leather bound edges, flannel lined, handle and patent fastenings. Our special price, each $1.50
No. 71196. Mandolin Case made of russet or black leather, extra quality, hand sewed, flannel lined, same as illustration. Special price, each ........ $5.25

### Mandolin Bags.

No. 71198. Mandolin Bag, made of green cloth with buttons, good quality. Each ........ $0.70
No. 71200. Mandolin Bag, made of best canvass, full fleece lined, patent fasteners, superior quality. Each ........ $0.85

MANDOLIN PICKS.

No. 71202. Genuine tortoise shell, oval shape (like cut), polished or unpolished. Price, each ........ $0.05
No. 71204. Same, extra large, extra quality. Price, each ........ $0.08
No. 71206. Genuine tortoise shell, triangular shape. Each ........ $0.05
No. 71208. Gutta percha, fine quality, oval shape. Each ........ $0.08

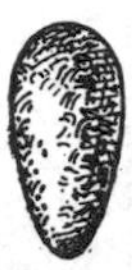

No. 71202.

MANDOLIN PATENT HEADS.

No. 71210. Brass, nickel plated, white celluloid buttons, extra fine quality. Price, per set ........ $1.95
No. 71212. German silver, full plate style, fancy engraved, very fine quality. Per set ........ $3.05

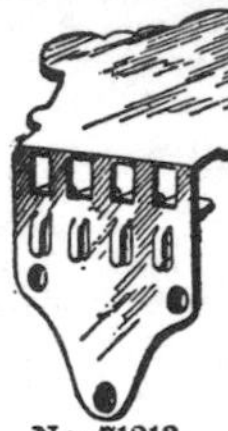

No. 71213.

MANDOLIN TAIL PIECES.

No. 71213. Tail piece, brass, nickel plated, fine model (see cut). Each ........ $0.31

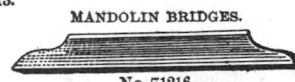

MANDOLIN BRIDGES.

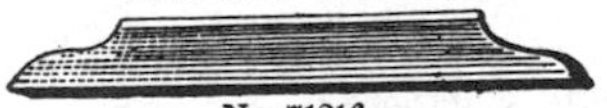

No. 71216.

No. 71214. Bridges, ebony, plain finish. Each ... $0.25
No. 71216. Bridges, ebony, ivory inlaid. Each ... $0.35

### Autoharp Cases.

No. 71220. Wood, black varnished, half lined with flannel, complete with hooks, handle and lock, to fit Nos. 1 to 5 autoharps. Each ........ $1.30
No. 71224. Same, to fit No. 6 autoharp. Each ... $1.75
No. 71225. Autoharp case made of brown canvas, bound all around the edges with leather, flannel lined, superior model and quality, complete with handle, strap and name plate, to fit Nos. 1 to 5 Autoharps. Our Special price ........ $2.70
No. 71227. Same as No. 71225, to fit No. 6 autoharp. Our Special price ........ $2.95

### Autoharp Furnishings.

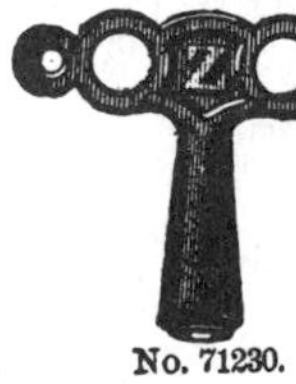

No. 71230.

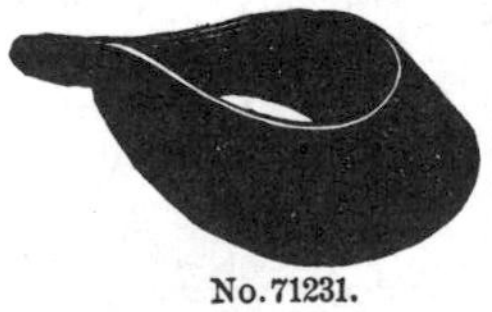

No. 71231.

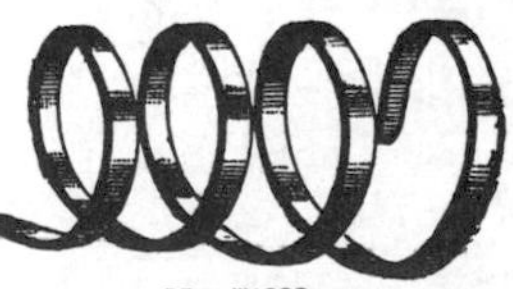

No. 71233.

| | | Each |
|---|---|---|
| No. 71230. | Tuning Hammers, malleable iron | $0.10 |
| No. 71231. | Picks, celluloid | .06 |
| No. 71232. | Picks, horn | .10 |
| No. 71233. | Picks, brass, spiral | .05 |

### Zither Cases.

No. 71233½. Zither Case. Made of select wood, black varnish, lined with flannel, with lock, handle and hooks to fit. Prim zither. Each ........ $1.95

### Zither Furnishings.

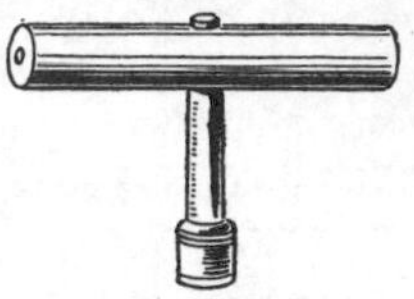

No. 71234.

No. 71234. Zither Tuning Hammer, black handle. Each ........ $0.20
No. 71235. Zither Tuning Hammer, ivory handle. Each ........ $0.75

ZITHER BRUSHES.

No. 71236. Zither Brush, bone handle. Each ... $0.65
No. 71237. Zither Duster, bone handle. Each ... $0.75

ZITHER RINGS.

No. 71238. Zither Ring, made of German silver. Each ........ $0.03
No. 71239. Zither Ring, made of horn. Each ... $0.05
No. 71240. Zither Ring, German silver improved pattern (see cut). Each ... $0.10

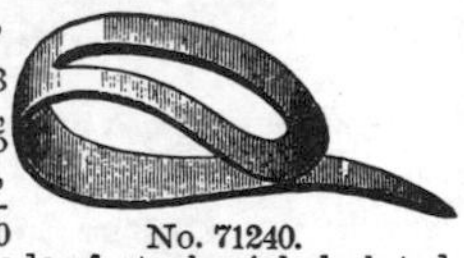

No. 71240.

No. 71241. Zither Ring, made of steel, nickel plated, new model, sizes 1 to 6. Price, each ........ $0.12

ZITHER PATENT HEADS.

No. 71243. Zither Patent Head, nickel plated, engraved, fine quality. Each ........ $2.05

### Dulcimer Furnishings.

TUNING HAMMERS.

No. 71245. Maple handle, square hole. Each ... $0.48
No. 71246. Maple handle, oblong hole. Each ... $0.48

DULCIMER BEATERS.

No. 71247. Flexible handles, felt covered heads. Per pair ........ $0.48

DULCIMER TUNING PINS.

No. 71248. Blued steel, square head. Per doz ... $0.12
No. 71249. Blued steel, oblong head. Per doz ... $0.12

### Fife and Piccolo Mouthpieces.

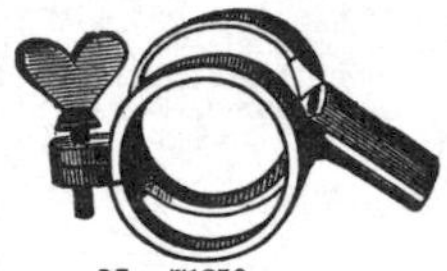

No. 71250.

No. 71250. Composition metal, adjustable with screw, for fife or piccolo. Each ........ $0.12

### Flute and Flageolet Mouthpieces.

No. 71251. Flute Mouthpiece, composition metal, adjustable with screw. Each ........ $0.20
No. 71252. Flageolet Mouthpiece, made of bone. Each ........ $0.14

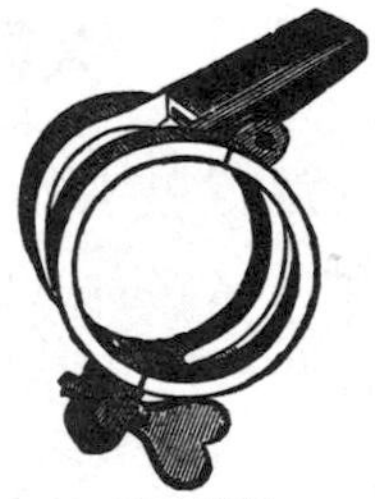

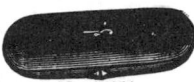

No. 71251.

### Flute and Piccolo Cases.

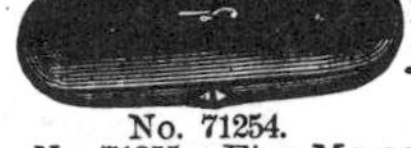

No. 71254.

No. 71253. Morocco covered case for 4, 6 or 8 keyed D flute, very fine, velvet lined. Price, each ........ $1.85
No. 71254. Same for 10, 11 or 13 keyed D flute. Each ... $2.30
No. 71255. Fine Morocco covered, velvet lined case, for D or E flat piccolos. Each ........ $1.20

### Clarionet Furnishings.

CLARIONET REED HOLDERS AND PROTECTORS.

No. 71256. German silver, with adjusting screws, for A, B♭, C, D or E♭. Each ........ $0.25
No. 71257. German silver combination reed holder and protector, for A, B♭, C, D or E♭. Each ........ $0.50

CLARIONET MOUTHPIECE CAPS.

No. 71258. Grendilla, polished, for A, B♭, C, D or E♭ mouth-pieces. Each ........ $0.28
No. 71259. Nickel plated, for A, B♭, C, D or E♭ mouthpieces. Each ........ $0.25

CLARIONET REEDS.

No. 71260. Martin, for A, B♭, C, D or E♭ clarionet. Each ........ $0.05
Per doz. ........ .50
No. 71261. Cottereau, fine quality, for A, B♭, C, D or E♭ clarionet. Each ........ $0.06
Per doz. ........ .65
No. 71262. Barbu, superfine, for A, B♭, C, D or E♭ clarionet. Each ........ $0.08
Per doz. ........ .85

Our Clarionet Reeds are made expressly for us by a reedmaker of great celebrity.

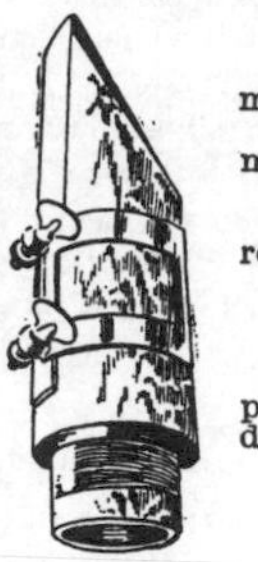

CLARIONET MOUTH-PIECE CASES.

No 71263. Leather covered, for single mouthpiece. Each ........ $0.72
No. 71264. Leather covered, for two mouthpieces. Each ........ $0.85

CLARIONET REED CASES.

No. 71265. Leather pocket case, for six reeds. Each ........ $0.50

CLARIONET REED TRIMMERS.

No. 71266. Brass, nickel plated, Flach's patent, with circular cutter and file underneath for finishing. Each ........ $1.75

CLARIONET MOUTHPIECES.

Give Key of Clarionet.

No. 71268. No. 71268. Solid ebony with German silver reed holder, for A, B♭, C, D or E♭. Each ... $0.65
No. 71269. Same, any key, without reed holder. Each ........ $0.42
No. 71270. Grenadilla, with German silver reed plate, but without reed holder, any key. Each ... $1.95

### Clarionet Cases.

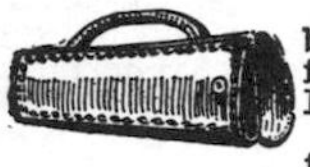

No. 71276.

No. 71276. Clarionet Case. Leather bag, lined, with handle and catch, for clarionet of any key. Each ........ $1.60
No. 71277. Clarionet Case. Satchel form, leather covered, flannel lined, with handle, hooks and lock. Made to carry three clarionets. Our Special Price ........ $3.50

### Cornet Cases.

No. 71280. Wood, select quality, black varnished, lined; with lock, handle and hooks. Each ........ $1.05

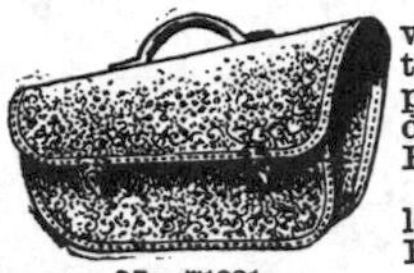

No. 71281.

No. 71281. Russet leather, very fine, satchel form, as illustrated; flannel lined, nickel plated trimmings, with shoulder strap. Each ........ $1.80
No. 71282. Same, Pebbled leather. Each ........ $1.85

### Drum Furnishings.

BASS DRUM STICKS.

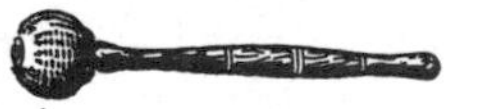

No. 71284.

No. 71284. Rosewood handle, with felt head screwed on handle. Each ........ $1.60
No. 71286. Hickory handle with chamois skin head. Each ........ $0.40

SNARE DRUM STICKS.

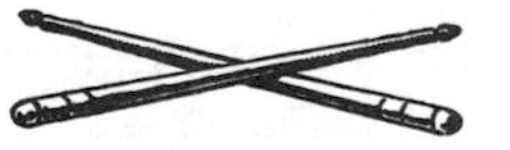

No. 71288.
Weight, 6 to 9 oz.

No. 71288. Rosewood, 17 inch, fine model, French polished. Per pair ........ $0.25
No. 71289. Ebony, 17 inch, fine model, French polished. Per pair ........ $0.50
No. 71290. Ebony, 17 inch, with nickel plated ferrules, French polished. Per pair ........ $1.00
No. 71291. Snakewood, 17 inch French polished. Per pair ........ $1.20
No. 71292. Snakewood, 17 inch, with nickel plated ferrules, French polished ........ $2.00

KEYS OR WRENCHES FOR SNARE DRUMS.

No. 71294. Square hole, for ordinary rods. Each. $0.10
No. 71295. Wrench, for patent rods ........ $0.10

SNARE DRUM SLINGS.

No. 71299. Colored webbing, narrow for boys' drums. Each ........ $0.15
No. 71301. Striped webbing, improved pattern, best quality, with snap for snare drums. Each ........ $0.25
No. 71303. Striped or white webbing, with button, allowing webbing to be taken out for washing. For snare drums. Each ........ $0.50

BASS DRUM SLINGS.

No. 71305. White or striped webbing, improved pattern, best quality, with snap. Price, each ........ $0.45
No. 71306. Fine quality leather, extra well made, with snap. Our price, each ........ $0.70

Since our prices for high grade goods that you do want are lower than the prices on the out of date shopworn goods that you don't want, it is quite natural that our trade keeps on increasing at the most rapid rate ever known in the commercial world.

THE GREATEST GOOD TO THE GREATEST NUMBER. OUR FACTORY TO CONSUMER SYSTEM MAY BE HARD ON THE MIDDLEMEN, BUT IT'S EASY ON THE CONSUMER. WHICH CLASS DESERVES THE MOST CONSIDERATION?

## Drum Furnishings.—Continued.

### CALFSKIN HEADS.

**For Drums, Banjos and Tambourines.**

| No. | | | | Each. |
|---|---|---|---|---|
| 71310. | 12 in., for 10 in. | Drum, Tambourine or Banjo | | $0.22 |
| 71311. | 13 " | 11 " | " | .30 |
| 71312. | 14 " | 11½ " | " | .35 |
| 71314. | 15 " | 12 " | " | .40 |
| 71315. | 16 " | 13 " | " | .50 |
| 71316. | 17 " | 14 " | | .60 |
| 71317. | 18 " | 15 " | | .70 |
| 71318. | 19 " | 16 " | | .80 |
| 71319. | 20 " | 17 " | | .90 |
| 71320. | 22 " | 19 " | | 1.00 |
| 71321. | 28 " | 24 " | Bass Drum | 1.50 |
| 71322. | 30 " | 26 " | | 1.80 |
| 71323. | 32 " | 28 " | | 2.00 |
| 71324. | 34 " | 30 " | | 2.25 |
| 71325. | 36 " | 32 " | | 2.75 |
| 71326. | 38 " | 34 " | | 3.00 |
| 71327. | 40 " | 36 " | | 3.50 |
| 71328. | 42 " | 38 " | | 4.00 |

### EXTRA QUALITY SPECIAL BANJO HEADS.

| No. | White's Opaque. | Each. |
|---|---|---|
| 71330. | 13 inch, White, for 11 inch Banjo | $0.55 |
| 71332. | 14 " " 11½ " | 0.75 |
| 71333. | 16 " " 13 " | 0.00 |

## Drum Major's Batons and Furnishings.

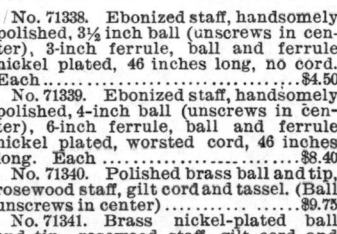

No. 71338. Ebonized staff, handsomely polished, 3½ inch ball (unscrews in center), 3-inch ferrule, ball and ferrule nickel plated, 46 inches long, no cord. Each............$4.50

No. 71339. Ebonized staff, handsomely polished, 4-inch ball (unscrews in center), 6-inch ferrule, ball and ferrule nickel plated, worsted cord, 46 inches long. Each............$8.40

No. 71340. Polished brass ball and tip, rosewood staff, gilt cord and tassel. (Ball unscrews in center)............$9.75

No. 71341. Brass nickel-plated ball and tip, rosewood staff, gilt cord and tassel. (Ball unscrews in center.) Each............$11.00

No. 71342. Brass silver-plated ball and tip, rosewood staff, gilt cord and tassel. (Ball unscrews in center.) Each............$14.40

No. 71343. Same as No. 71342, but gold plated. Each............$18.00

No. 71344. 4-inch brass ball and ferrule, without stick or cord. Each. $4.50

No. 71345. Brass staff, tapered, 4-inch ball (unscrews in center). All finely nickel plated, 45 inches long, no cord. Each............$12.00

### BATONS.

No. 71350. Rosewood, plain polished, tapering, Each............$0.48

Rosewood, nickel plated top on each end, French polished, tapering. Each............$0.82

No. 71352. Solid ebony, tapering, with genuine fancy ivory handle, German Silver mounted, very fine. Each............$5.55

## Band Instrument Mouthpieces.

Professional models, all silver plated and burnished. In ordering, send an impression of tube where mouth piece is to enter, and attach same to order.

The **Higham Models** have a medium cup, rather a wide surface for lips, and medium bore.

The **Austin Models** have a small cup, a small surface for lips, well rounded, and a large bore, especially recommended for playing with ease in the upper register. See cut.

The **Hutchins Models** have a large surface for lips, with a rather sharp inner edge, a good sized cup, and a medium bore; is a very easy model on the lip, and can be played upon a long time without tiring the performer.

No. 71354. No. 71354. Mouthpiece for E♭ or B♭ cornet, either Austin model like cut, or Higham or Hutchins model as above described. Each............$0.80

### AUSTIN OR HIGHAM MODEL MOUTHPIECES.

| No. | | Each. |
|---|---|---|
| 71357. | E♭ Alto | $1.05 |
| 71358. | B♭ Tenor | 1.25 |
| 71359. | B♭ Baritone | 1.25 |
| 71360. | B♭ Bass | 1.65 |
| 71361. | E♭ Bass | 2.00 |
| 71362. | E♭ Contra Bass | 2.25 |

The following are all German silver, French model band instrument mouthpieces:

| No. | | Each. |
|---|---|---|
| 71366. | E♭ Cornet | $0.40 |
| 71367. | B♭ Cornet | .40 |
| 71368. | E♭ Alto | .65 |
| 71369. | B♭ Tenor | .70 |
| 71370. | B♭ Baritone | .75 |
| 71371. | B♭ Bass | .85 |
| 71372. | E♭ Bass | .95 |
| 71373. | E♭ Contra Bass | .95 |
| 71374. | BB♭ Helicon Bass | 1.05 |
| 71375. | B♭ Flugelhorn | .75 |
| 71376. | French Horn | .90 |
| 71377. | Bugle | .90 |

### TROMBONE MOUTHPIECES.

No. 71380. Trombone mouthpiece, Brann's model, very fine. Each............$2.50

## Band Instrument Mutes.

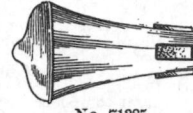

No. 71385.

No. 71385. Improved Model Cornet Mute, made of brass, plain. Price, each............$1.10

No. 71387. Same, brass, finely nickel plated. Each............$1.25

## Organ and Piano Stools.

No. 71389.

No. 71389. Organ or Piano Stool, 13½x13½ inch seat, covered with durable haircloth covering, dark rosewood finish, fancy covered legs, adjustable seat. Weight, 25 lb, packed. Our special price............$1.25

No. 71301. Same as above, mohair plush, plain or embossed, in maroon or crimson color. Our special price............$2.15

No. 71391. Piano or Organ Stool, 12x15 inch framed seat, upholstered in plain mohair plush, maroon or crimson, blue or old gold, 3 fancy heavy legs, adjustable seat, mottled walnut or oak. Each............$3.25

No. 71395. Same in embossed mohair plush, maroon or crimson. Each............$3.25

No. 71396. Same in silk plush, any standard color. Each............$3.25

No. 71398. An elegant and very attractive solid wood Piano Stool. Entire stool, including seat, made of select hardwood, finished in rosewood, mahogany, plain or mottled, ebony or oak. Fancy turned legs, with braces, and mounted on bronze metal claw feet with round ball bases. Seat is adjustable to any height desired. Weight, packed, about 30 lbs. Our special price............$2.35

No. 71400. Piano stool, as illustrated, with 13x 16½ Ottoman seat. An elegant design upholstered in plain mohair. Plush in either maroon, crimson, blue, olive or old gold. Three fancy decorated legs. Seat is adjustable in height. Wood is selected stock and finished regularly in ebony or antique oak. Rosewood, mahogany or mottled walnut finished to order at no extra charge. A remarkably handsome stool. Weight, boxed, 35 lbs. Our Special Price....$4.80

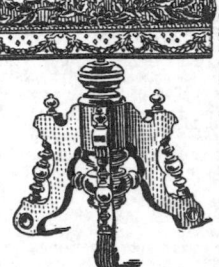

No. 71400.

No. 71401. Same in embossed mohair plush, in maroon or crimson. Our Special Price............$4.80

No. 71402. Same in silk plush, any standard color. Each............$4.80

## Upright Piano Scarfs.

No. 71406. Piano Scarf, made of finest quality of felt, 6-inch drop; fine quality, plush front, fine embroidery almost entire length, with cord and tassels. Our Special Price............$2.85

No. 71408.

No. 71408. All silk plush, as illustrated above. Good quality, full length, 6-inch drop, tastily embroidered front. Our Special Price, each............$3.95

No. 71410. Finest lustre English plush; rich and artistic hand-embroidered 9-inch front, with silk cord and tassels. Our Special Price, each............$5.95

There is not a shadow of a difference between the promise and the fulfillment of our statements. You don't have to take them with a grain of salt.

## Music Racks for Band Instruments, etc.

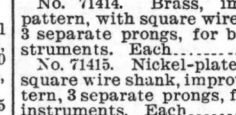

No. 71414. Brass, improved pattern, with square wire shank, 3 separate prongs, for band instruments. Each............$0.45

No. 71415. Nickel-plated, with square wire shank, improved pattern, 3 separate prongs, for band instruments. Each............$0.66

No. 71416. Brass, improved pattern, 3 separate prongs, with plate for bass drums. Each, $0.66

No. 71417. Nickel plated, improved pattern, 3 separate prongs, with plate for bass drums. Each............$0.84

No. 71418. Brass, improved pattern, 3 separate prongs, with plate for snare drums. Each, $0.66

No. 71419. Nickel plated, improved pattern, 3 separate prongs, with plate for snare drums. Each... 0.84

No. 71420. Clamp for holding music rack on any bass or snare drum............0.45

No. 71421.' Nickel plated rack, with adjustable ring, for clarionets (see note) 3 separate prongs. Each 0.74

No. 71422. Brass, improved pattern, 3 separate prongs, with strap to buckle on arm for fifes, piccolos, etc. Each............$1.00

No. 71423. Brass, improved pattern, 3 separate prongs, with long shank for slide trombones. $1.05

No. 71424. Nickel plated, improved pattern, 3 separate prongs, with long shank for slide trombones. Each............$1.20

No. 71414.

NOTE.—Always give key of clarionet for which music rack is wanted.

## Music Stands.

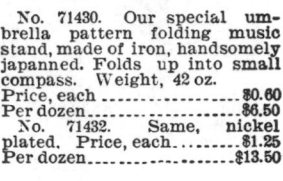

No. 63430.

No. 71430. Our special umbrella pattern folding music stand, made of iron, handsomely japanned. Folds up into small compass. Weight, 42 oz.
Price, each............$0.60
Per dozen............$6.50
No. 71432. Same, nickel plated. Price, each............$1.25
Per dozen............$13.50

## Music Folios.

No. 71438.

No. 71436. Music Folio, cloth back, black morocco paper sides, "Music" in gilt on side. Each............$0.57

No. 71438. Music Folio, as illustrated, bound in full cloth back and sides, assorted colors, "Music" and flowers in gilt and black. Each, $1.05

No. 71440. Music Folio, bound in seal leather back and sides, "Music in elaborate raised oxydized letters. Each............$2.65

## Music Wrappers.

No. 71442. Music Folio, glazed cloth, lined, with leather strap and buckle, etc. Each............$0.45

No. 71444. Music Folio, English saddle leather, embossed, russet, orange, black or maroon color, with strap and handle. Each............$0.75

No. 71446

No. 71446. Music Wrapper, as illustrated, made of select embossed leather, russet, black or maroon color, lined strap and leather covered buckle. Each...$1.00

## Tuning Forks.

**NEW STANDARD OR LOW PITCH.**

No. 71500. Steel, A or C, philharmonic. Each............$0.09

No. 71502. Nickel plated steel, A or C, superior quality. Each............$0.20

No. 71504. Blued steel, A or C, superior quality. Each............$0.30

## Tuning Pipes.

**NEW STANDARD OR HIGH PITCH.**

No. 71506. German silver, keys of A or C combined, extra fine quality in white metal boxes. Each............$0.12

No. 71508. Same, keys of C and G combined. Each............$0.12

AMERICAN, OR HIGH PITCH.

No. 71510. E, A, D and G combined, for tuning violin or mandolin, (like cut). Weight, 3 oz. Per set...$0.30

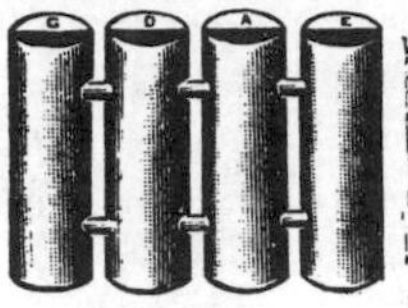

No. 71510.

No. 71512. Set of 5, B, G sharp, E, A and E, combined, for tuning banjo. Weight, 3 oz. Per set...$0.40

No. 71514. Set of 6, E, B, G, D, A and E, combined, for tuning guitar. Weight, 2 oz. Per set...$0.50

NOTE—Beginners on violin, mandolin, banjo, or guitar, will find above sets very convenient for tuning instruments. They are made of German silver and tuned to a standard concert pitch.

PIANO TUNING HAMMER.

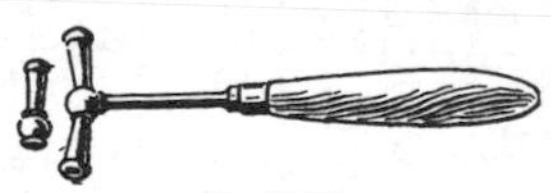

No. 71516.

No. 71516. Long Rosewood handle, double head with oblong holes, and single head with star hole. Extra quality warranted. Each...$1.60

## Metronomes.

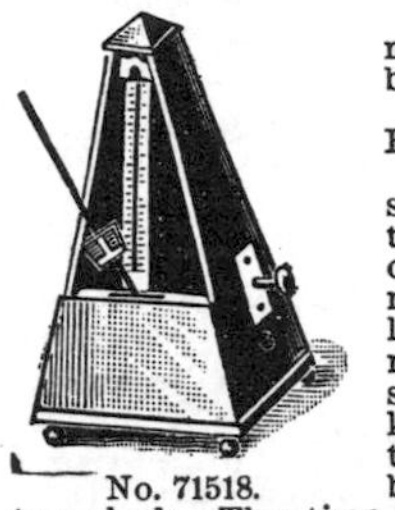

No. 71518.

No. 71518. Metronome, solid mahogany, fixed key, without bell, Maelzel system. Each, $2.45

No. 71520. Same, with bell. Each...$3.50

The metronome is used by students of music, especially of the piano, to indicate the tempo or time. The upright rod moves backward and forward like an inverted pendulum, the movement being actuated by a spring which is wound up with a key. The time is indicated both to eye and ear, the movement being in sight and ticking similar to a clock. The time is regulated fast or slow by the sliding weight on the "pendulum," while the latter has a graduated scale. This is an invaluable instrument for pupils of the piano or organ especially.

## Music Paper.

No. 71526. Super Royal Music Paper, size 10¼x13¼ in. Ruled 10, 12, 14, 16, or 24 staves. Octavo or oblong, for vocal or piano. Any ruling or style at same price. Customers must be specific in ordering. Weight, per quire, about 21 oz. Price, per quire...$0.31
Per ream...$5.25

No. 71527. French Gummed Paper, for mending sheet music. Per sheet...$0.14

## Ruling Pens.

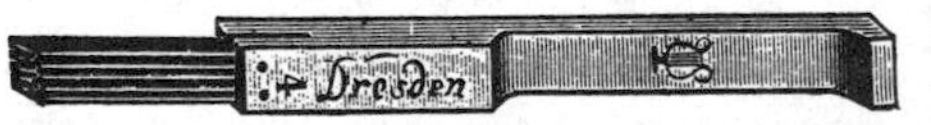


No. 71528.

No. 71528. Ruling Pens, with five lines for drawing staff. Each...$0.10

No. 71530. Steel Pens, with three points, for writing music, special make, with L. & H. brand. Per dozen...$0.18

**VOCAL AND INSTRUMENTAL MUSIC.**

**The assortment of Music Books, Folios and Instruction Books includes the latest productions of the best authors. We invite special attention to this selection, on the part of music lovers, as the assortment is made up by an expert musician and every Book and Folio may be depended on as a CHOICE GEM OF MUSIC.**

## Vocal Music Folios.

(Words and Music).

No. 71600. Musical Chatterbox, No. 2, contains both vocal and instrumental music, every piece a popular favorite, choice, easy and medium piano pieces; beautiful songs for the young folks: just the collection for home; it contains, besides the music, eight beautiful illustrations. Price...$0.40
Extra, by mail, 8 cts.

No. 71601. The Song Bouquet. A companion to the Parlor Bouquet, a beautiful collection of the latest popular songs, everything new, complete and unabridged. Size, 10x12½ inches, 224 pages. Nothing like it ever before published. Price...$0.40
Extra, by mail, 8 cts.

No. 71602. The "Maywood" Folio, a new collection of popular songs and instrumental music by George Schleifforth, 111 pages, every piece new and good. Price...$0.40
Postage, 10 cts.

No. 71603. Whitney's Golden Folio for the cabinet organ, containing a choice variety of music, both vocal and instrumental, by well known authors. Price, each...$0.40
Postage, extra, 10 cts.

No. 71604. Whitney's Silver Folio, a companion to the Golden Folio, arranged on the same order. Every piece a gem. Price...$0.40
Postage, 10 cts.

No. 71605. Superb Songs, a new book which contains over 200 pages of choice music and words arranged for piano or organ accompaniment. This is a companion to the celebrated "Song Folio," the most popular book of the class ever issued. It has illuminated paper covers and contains 15 elegant lithograph portraits of the celebrated singers of the day, both male and female. Our price...$0.40
Extra, by mail, 11 cts.

No. 71606. Selected Songs, by eminent composers. A new collection of the latest and best vocal music. Full sheet music size, paper covers. Price, each...$0.40
Extra, by mail, 8 cts.

No. 71607. Excelsior Song Folio. A beautiful collection of the latest and most popular songs and ballads by American and European composers; 192 pages. Retail price, 50 cents. Our special price...$0.40
Postage, 10 cents.

No. 71608. Superior Song Collection. A large variety of the latest and choicest songs and ballads; 192 pages. Our special price...$0.40
Postage, 11 cents.

No. 71609. Sweet Old Songs We Like to Sing. Hitchcock's collection of songs that reach the heart, comprising many popular favorites, good for all times to come; 192 pages. Our special price...$0.40
Postage, 11 cents.

No. 71610. Songs That Always Live. A superb collection of songs pleasing to all tastes: 192 pages. Our special price...$0.40
Postage, 10 cents.

No. 71615. Smith's Musical Album. A very complete book of popular select music, containing 208 pages, the selection including a wide variety of vocal and instrumental music, suiting all tastes. Our special price...$0.40
Postage, 12 cents.

No. 71617. The International Piano and Song Folio. A choice collection of music gathered from the great composers of all nations, containing 200 pages. Our special price...$0.40
Postage, 17 cents.

No. 71618. The National Waltz Song Folio. Containing 160 pages; devoted entirely to very popular waltz songs. Our special price...$0.40
Postage, 10 cents.

No. 71620. Old Homestead Songs. This folio is devoted entirely to the popular airs that never grow old, and contains 175 pages. Our special price...$0.40
Postage, 9 cents.

No. 71621. Songs We Never Forget. A beautiful collection of standard songs, containing 168 pages, devoted to gems of music that are popular to all tastes. Our special price...$0.40
Postage, 8 cents.

No. 71623. The National Classical Song Folio of select and classical songs; 160 pages. Our special price...$0.40
Postage, 9 cents.

No. 71624. Treasures of the Musical World. A collection of standard and popular favorites in vocal and instrumental music by the world's greatest composers; contains 320 pages. Our special price...$0.40
Postage, 15 cents.

No. 71626. The International Song Folio. A choice collection of popular songs, together with the old compositions of all nations. Contains 154 pages. Our special price...$0.40
Postage, 11 cents.

No. 71628. Peerless Collection of Vocal Music. Containing a large variety of the choicest songs and ballads by eminent American and European composers. 190 pages. Our special price...$0.40
Postage, 12 cents.

No. 71630. Choice Baritone and Bass Songs. A collection of twenty-six of the latest and best songs for male voices with piano or organ accompaniment, published by T. B. Harms, full sheet music size. Price each...$0.40
Extra, by mail, 8 cents.

## Vocal Duets.

No. 71634. Vocal Duet Folio. A rare collection of late and popular vocal duets for similar and mixed voices. 96 pages, full sheet music size. Price...$0.40
Postage, extra, 10 cents.

## G. A. R. Songs.

No. 71638. Grand Army Songs. A valuable collection of war and camp songs, to which is added a selection of memorial songs and hymns for Decoration Day, etc.; choruses all arranged for male voices, organ or piano accompaniment; 100 pages; heavy paper covers. Price...$0.45
Extra, by mail, 5c.

## College Song

No. 71642. College Songs. A collection of eighty new and popular songs (with music) sung in American colleges. This new and already widely used collection contains not only the college songs proper, but the light comic songs one hears everywhere. It is brimful of fun, and can hardly be spared from any social party, where they are all musical. Price, paper covers...$0.45
Extra, by mail, 8c.

## Juvenile Vocal Music.

No. 71643. Our Children's Favorite Songs. Beautiful collection of vocal music, especially adapted for the entertainment of the little ones; 144 pages. Our special price...$0.40
Postage, 8 cents.

No. 71646. The Evening Party. Containing a selection of the very best and most popular compositions. American copyright. Songs, ballads and piano-forte selections, 128 pages. Our special price...$0.40
Postage, 9 cents.

## Quartette Books.

No. 71649. Emerson's New Male Quartette. A specially choice selection of bright, sparkling quartettes for male voices, 129 pages. Our special price...$0.50
Postage, 4 cents.

## Minstrel, Comic and Topical Songs.

No. 71654. Jubilee and Plantation Songs as sung by Hampton Students, Jubilee Singers, Fisk University Students and other concert singers. This book also contains a number of pleasing selections. Our special price...$0.50
Postage, 4 cents.

No. 71656. J. W. Pepper's American Minstrel Songster. New and enlarged edition, 50 songs, words and music. Our special price...$0.10
Postage, 4 cents.

No. 71658. 100 Popular Songs, including all the favorite minstrel and home gems, words and music both. 100 pages. Our special price...$0.10
Postage, 4 cents.

No. 71660. Harvest of Minstrel Songs. A specially desirable collection of minstrel songs, one that will prove exceedingly popular, and has had an unusually large sale; 207 pages. Our special price...$0.40
Postage, 11 cents.

No. 71662. Minstrel Songs, old and new, book of 214 pages, board covers, containing a collection of over 100 of the famous minstrel and plantation songs, including the most popular of the celebrated Foster melodies, arranged with piano and organ accompaniment...$1.25

No. 71663. The Celebrated Dockstader Songster, containing 50 minstrel and variety songs, with words and music. Price...$0.08
Postage, 2 cents.

No. 71665. The Jolly Songster. A fine collection of 200 pieces, including comic and patriotic songs, popular ballads and favorite Negro melodies. Price, paper covers...$0.20
Postage, 5 cents.

No. 71666. Famous Comic Songs, the best collection of comic songs ever published. Contains 35 of the very latest, including "A Job Lot," "What a Difference in the Morning," "Irish Spree," "I've Worked Eight Hours To-day," "Mary and John," "Near It," "Sweet Katie Connor," "When You Wink the Other Eye," etc., etc. Words and music complete with piano and organ accompaniment. Price, each...$0.45
Extra, by mail, 8 cents.

No. 71670. Humorous Coster Songs, as sung by Albert Chevalier. Printed on fine paper and containing 68 pages. Our special price...$0.40
Postage, 5 cents.

No. 71672. Old and New Popular Comic Songs, for the people who sing and be happy; 136 pages. Our special price...$0.40
Postage, 8 cents.

No. 71673. "They're After Me" Folio of Funny Songs for the Whole World. A new collection of the very latest comic songs by the most popular song writers of every nation; very funny; 128 pages. Our special price...$0.40
Postage, 8 cents.

No. 71674. Recent Gems of Songs, containing many of the most popular songs of the day; 120 pages. Our special price...$0.10
Postage, 4 cents.

No. 71678. Hitchcock's Collection of Songs of Ireland. 50 Moore's Irish melodies, 120 pages. Composed by eminent composers. Our special price...$0.40
Postage, 9 cents.

No. 71679. J. W. Pepper's Gems of Ireland Songster. 50 songs, words and music, postage 4 cents. Our special price...$0.10
Postage, 2 cents.

No. 71680. Songs of Scotland, full sheet music size, containing 100 of the most popular Scotch Songs, with piano or organ accompaniment. Paper covers...$0.40
Extra, by mail, 7 cents

## Gospel Hymns.

No. 71685. Consolidated, Nos. 1, 2, 3, 4. Large type words and music; 400 pages.
Each...$0.75
Per dozen...7.72
Postage, 10 cents.

No. 71686. Same as 71685. Bound in half-leather, red edges, words and music.
Each...$1.50
Per dozen...15.40
Postage, each, 10 cents.

No. 71687. Words only, Nos. 1, 2, 3, 4.
Each...$0.20
Per dozen...2.15
Postage, 4 cents.

No. 71688. Gospel Hymns, No. 5, with words and music; board covers.
Each...$0.30
Per dozen...3.10
Postage, each, 6 cents.

No. 71689. Same as No. 71688. Bound in limp cloth, very handsome.
Each...$0.50
Per dozen...5.40
Postage, each, 6 cents.

No. 71690. Gospel Hymns, No. 6, bound in boards.
Each...$0.30
Per dozen...3.10
Postage, each, 6 cents.

No. 71691. Same as No. 71690. Bound in limp cloth, very handsome.
Each...$0.50
Per dozen...5.40

No. 71692. Just out. Nos. 5 and 6, combined. Words and music.
Each...$0.70
Per dozen...7.00
Postage, each, 8 cents.

**WE SHIP PIANOS AND ORGANS SUBJECT TO 20 DAYS' TRIAL. YOU CAN HAVE A REPUTABLE MUSIC TEACHER COME IN AND GIVE YOU A PROFESSIONAL OPINION AS TO WHETHER THE INSTRUMENT IS ALL THAT WE REPRESENT.**

**Gospel Hymns.—Continued.**

No. 71693. Same as 71692. Words only.
Each ............ $0.22
Per dozen ............ 2.30
Postage, each, 4 cents.

No. 71694. Gospel Choir, by Ira D. Sankey and James McGranahan; 128 pages, board covers.
Each ............ $0.40
Per dozen ............ 4.00
Postage, each, 10 cents.

## Gospel Hymns, Arranged for the Cornet.

No. 71695. Melodies of the Gospel Hymns, Nos. 1, 2, 3, 4, consolidated. Arranged for the cornet by Hayslip, for use in Sabbath schools, gospel meetings, etc. A piano or organ played from the regular edition will agree perfectly with the cornet played from this.
Price, paper covers ............ $1.00
Extra by mail, 8 cents.

No. 71697. Gospel Hymns, No. 5, arranged for the cornet, containing the melodies and altos of all the members.
Price, paper covers ............ $0.80
Postage, 5 cents extra.

## Instrumental Music Folios.

**For Piano.**

No. 71700. Excelsior Dance Folio. A superb collection of latest dances, arranged for the piano; 192 pages. Our special price ............ $0.40
Postage, 10 cents.

No. 71702. Strauss Dance Collection. A selection of the best and latest compositions of Johann, Eduard and Josef Strauss, from the repertoire of the Strauss Imperial Court Orchestra; 160 pages of the very choicest selections. Our special price ............ $0.40
Postage, 10 cents.

No. 71704. Superior Dance Collection. Containing the latest and most popular dances arranged for the piano; composed by celebrated American and European authors; includes gallops, marches, waltzes and miscellaneous dance music; 192 pages.
Our special price ............ $0.40
Postage, 12 cents.

No. 71706. Peerless Collection of Dance Music. Containing the latest popular waltzes, polkas and other dances by American and European composers; 192 pages. Our special price ............ $0.40
Postage, 12 cents.

No. 71708. Excelsior Piano Folio, No. 1. A choice collection of instrumental compositions for the pianoforte; 192 pages. Our special price ............ $0.40
Postage, 12 cents.

No. 71710. Excelsior Piano Folio, Vol. 2. A superb selection of popular and classical compositions for the pianoforte, containing no duplicates of those in Vol. 1, above; 192 pages. Our special price ............ $0.40
Postage, 12 cents.

No. 71711. Golden Hours. A fine collection of popular piano music, consisting of a large variety of marches and miscellaneous dance music, four-hand pieces, etc., forming a select library of elegant music. 224 pages. Our special price ............ $0.40
Postage, 12 cents.

No. 71712. Peerless Collection of Piano Music, containing a collection of beautiful compositions by some of the foremost composers of America and Europe. This handsome folio contains 192 pages, neatly bound. One of the best music books to be found. Our special price ............ $0.40
Postage, 12 cents.

No. 71713. Dance Treasury. A collection of the popular dances of the day, arranged for the piano. A collection of dance music suitable for all tastes and occasions. 144 pages Our special price ............ $0.40
Postage, 11 cents.

No. 71715. The International Piano Folio. A choice collection of music gathered from the great composers of all nations. 192 pages. Our special price ............ $0.40
Postage, 8 cents.

No. 71716. Young People's Folio, containing an admirable collection of music for the piano and especially adapted for beginners. 160 pages. Our special price ............ $0.40
Postage, 10 cents.

No. 71717. Queen of Waltzes, a splendid collection of beautiful waltzes, everyone a gem, nearly 100 pages, sheet music size. (Brainard's Dollar Library.)
Price ............ $0.40
Extra by mail, 11 cents.

No. 71718. The Parlor Bouquet, companion to the "Song Bouquet," a fine collection of instrumental music, comprising new and sparkling gems and standard favorites. Every piece complete. Sheet music size, 224 pages. The Parlor Bouquet should adorn every piano in the land, and the low price brings it within the reach of all. Each ............ $0.40
Extra by mail, 10 cents.

No. 71719. Whitney's "Folio Gems," a choice collection of recent compositions, including marches, waltzes, polkas, schottisches, etc., by popular composers. 150 pages, sheet music size. Price, each ............ $0.40
Extra, by mail, 10 cents.

No. 71720. Whitney's "Folio Leaves," a companion to Folio Gems, containing same style of music (no duplicates), 250 pages. Price each ............ $0.40
Extra, by mail, 10 cents.

## Four-Hand Folios for Two Pianos.

No. 71725. Excelsior Four-Hand Folios, a superior collection of instrumental duets for pianoforte. 192 pages. Our special price ............ $0.40
Postage, 12 cents.

No. 71726. Royal Collection Four-Hand. A specially fine collection of instrumental music for two pianos, arranged with great care and selected from the best authors. 160 pages. Our special price ............ $0.40
Postage, 9 cents.

No. 71728. The Prize Four-Hand Pianoforte Collection. A selection of specially choice instrumental music for two pianos. 160 pages. Our special price ............ $0.40
Postage, 9 cents.

## Instrumental Folios for Piano or Cabinet Organ.

No. 71740. The 'Monarch' Waltz Collection; 16 of the very latest and best waltzes, arranged for organ or piano; published by T. B. Harms; every one a favorite. Price, each ............ $0.40
Extra, by mail, 8 cents.

No. 71741. Whitney's Folio of Pearls. Containing brilliant pieces for the piano, also pieces especially arranged for cabinet organ; 150 pages full sheet music size. Each ............ $0.40
Extra, by mail, 10 cents.

No. 71743. Kinkel's Folio, Vol. 1. A rare collection of bright instrumental gems for young players, arranged for piano and organ. No better books for pupils can be obtained, and we especially recommend them to teachers. Price ............ $0.40
Extra, by mail, 10 cents.

No. 71744. Kinkel's Folio, Vol. 2 Containing pieces of an advanced order. Price ............ $0.40
Extra, by mail, 10 cents.

No. 71746. Famous Dance Music. A new collection of the very latest and most popular waltzes, polkas, marches, etc., by Waldteufel, Roeder and others, arranged for piano or organ; full sheet size. Price ............ $0.40
Extra, by mail, 10 cents.

No. 71748. Parlor Dance Folio. Contains choice collection of the latest dances; also the German, with quadrille calls, etc., arranged for piano or organ; full sheet music size; paper covers; just the book for parlor dancing. Price ............ $0.40
Extra, by mail, 10 cents.

No. 71750. Superb Solos. A magnificent collection for the piano or cabinet organ; contains simple and classical airs, popular and sacred music, and is suitable to a large variety of tastes; 208 pages.
Our special price ............ $0.40
Postage, 11 cents.

No. 71752. Excelsior Juvenile Collection. A book of easy and beautiful pieces for the piano or cabinet organ; specially adapted for teaching purposes and for the home circle; 192 pages. Our special price ............ $0.40
Postage, 12 cents.

No. 71754. Musical Sketch Book, No. 1, for the piano or organ. A magnificent collection of solos, waltzes, marches, etc., by favorite authors, arranged for the piano or organ and compiled by S. W. Frederic; 142 pages. Our special price ............ $0.40
Postage, 9 cents.

No. 71755. Musical Sketch Book, No. 2. A superior collection of solos, waltzes, marches, etc., by favorite authors, arranged for piano or organ; compiled by S. W. Frederic; 142 pages; no duplicates of numbers in No. 1. Our special price ............ $0.40

No. 71757. Marches. Selected from the works of celebrated composers for pianoforte or organ, regular sheet music size. A large folio of the very best selections. 160 pages. Our Special price ............ $0.40
Postage, 9 cents.

No. 71759. Everyday melodies for Cabinet Organ or Piano. A collection of popular melodies within the compass of five octaves, suitable either for cabinet organ or piano. 144 pages. Our Special price ............ $0.40
Postage, 11 cents.

No. 71760. Elite. Collection of dance music for piano or cabinet organ. Each piece is complete and unabridged. A collection made up from the most popular authors. 144 pages. Our special price ............ $0.40
Postage, 8 cents.

No. 71762. Folio Gems for Piano or Cabinet Organ. A specially fine selection of instrumental music, including popular airs of dance music and operatic airs. 162 pages. Our Special price ............ $0.40
Postage, 12 cents.

## Instrumental Music for Cabinet Organ.

No. 71775. Reed Organ Folio, a new collection of the best and most popular music of the day, arranged especially for the five octave organ. Over 60 pieces, full sheet music size, paper covers. Each ............ $0.40
Extra, by mail, 10 cents.

No. 71776. Reed Organ at Home. A collection of reed organ music, containing favorite melodies and a variety of dance music, operatic music, etc. 128 pages. Our Special price ............ $0.40
Postage, 8 cents.

## Instrumental Music for Violin.

No. 71778. The Young Violinist's Favorite. A collection of popular music for the violin, including overtures, quadrilles, and a wide selection of dance music; 50 pages. Our special price ............ $0.40
Postage, 4 cents.

No. 71779. The Young Violinist's Favorite No. 2. An entirely different edition from Folio No. 1 above, containing no duplicates. Contains 50 pages.
Our special price ............ $0.40
Postage, 4 cents.

No. 71781. Musician's Omnibus. A book containing 1500 pieces, arranged for violin, consisting of waltzes, polkas, schottisches, galops, quadrilles, jig and clog dances, etc. Publisher's price, $2.00. Our price... $1.50

No. 71782. Ryan's 1050 Reels and Jigs, a very popular collection of lively music arranged for violin.
Price, each ............ $1.50
Extra, by mail, 12 cents.

## Instrumental Music for Violin and Piano.

No. 71790. Popular Duets for Violin and Piano No. 1. This is a new collection of the very latest music, including "Loves' Dreamland" Waltzes, Mendelsshon's "Wedding March," "Hornpipe Polka," etc., 84 pieces, 122 pages. Full sheet music size paper covers, every piece a gem. Price, each ............ $0.40
Postage, 10 cents.

No. 71791. Popular Duets for Violin and Piano No. 2, contains a collection of still later music. Full sheet music size, 120 pages. These are the best collections ever put on the market in book form. Price, each, $0.40
Postage, 10 cents.

No. 71793. Violin Solos. A new and popular edition containing duets for violin and piano. Contains 42 pages of very choice selections. Our special price, $0.40
Postage, 4 cents.

No. 71794. Violin Solos, No. 2. A second edition of this particularly popular folio containing choice duets for violin and piano. No duplicates. Contains 42 pages. Our special price ............ $0.40
Postage, 4 cents.

No. 71795. Musical Evenings. A folio devoted entirely to a collection of new and popular music by favorite authors, music for violin and piano. 92 pages.
Our special price ............ $0.40
Postage, 7 cents.

No. 71796. Society Dance Journal. A collection of original and select compositions for violin and piano by Chas Escher, Jr. 70 pages. Our special price, $0.40
Postage, 5 cents.

No. 71797. Excelsior Piano and Violin Folio. A grand collection of new, popular and classical pieces for the violin and piano by celebrated composers. 128 pages. Our special price ............ $0.40
Postage, 8 cents.

No. 71798. Popular Duets, No. 1. A new and popular edition of duets arranged especially for the violin and piano. 122 pages. Our special price ............ $0.40

No. 71799. Popular Duets No. 2. A second edition of above number, but containing no duplicates. Contains a very fine selection of duets arranged for violin and piano. 142 pages. Our special price ............ $0.40

## Guitar Music, Vocal and Instrumental.

No. 71800. Royal Collection of Vocal Guitar Music. A fine selection of vocal music arranged specially for the guitar; 80 pages. Our special price ............ $0.40
Postage, 5 cents.

No. 71802. Brainard's Vocal Guitar Folio. One of the most popular collections of vocal music for the guitar ever published; 96 pages. Our special price $0.40
Postage, 7 cents.

No. 71804. Guitar Jewels, a magnificent collection of vocal and instrumental selections for the guitar, together with a number of duets and trios. This folio contains 112 pages of popular and classical music.
Our special price ............ $0.40
Postage, 8 cents.

No. 71805. Royal Collection of Instrumental Guitar Music. This folio contains some of the choicest selections of guitar music, including both popular and classical airs with an excellent proportion of dance music.
Our special price ............ $0.40
Postage, 5 cents.

No. 71806. Brainard's Instrumental Guitar Folio. A most popular edition of instrumental music for guitar only: 96 pages. Our special price ............ $0.40
Postage, 6 cents.

## Banjo Music, Vocal and Instrumental.

No. 71815. The Banjo Companion. A new collection of select vocal music for the banjo; nothing like it ever put into book or sheet form.
Our special price ............ $0.40
Postage, 6 cents.

No. 71817. Banjo Songs. A choice collection of the most popular songs of the day, carefully arranged with banjo accompaniment; 72 pages.
Our special price ............ $0.40
Postage, 6 cents.

No. 71818. Hamilton's Banjo Folio. A collection of late and popular arrangements for one or two banjos, with piano accompaniment and banjo solos; 92 pages. Our special price ............ $0.40
Postage, 7 cents.

No. 71820. Banjo Companion—Book Two. Instrumental. A new collection of select instrumental music for banjo; one of the best ever put into book form; arranged with great care; 72 pages.
Our special price ............ $0.40
Postage, 7 cents.

No. 71822. Hamilton's Banjo Folio. A splendid collection of beautiful banjo music, suitable for amateur or artist. Contains collections for solos and duet. Full sheet, music size ............ $0.40
Postage, 10 cents.

No. 71823. "Banjoists' Budget." A grand collection of 50 jigs, hornpipes, reels, clog dances, walk-arounds, etc., etc., arranged and correctly fingered for the banjo by A. Bauer; best collection of banjo music published; paper covers. Price ............ $0.45
Extra, by mail, 5 cents.

## Mandolin and Piano Music.

No. 71825. Society Dance Journal. A collection of original and select compositions for mandolin and piano; 70 pages. Our special price ............ $0.40
Postage, 5 cents.

**YOU CAN MAKE UP AN ORDER OF GROCERIES EACH MONTH AND INCLUDE SUCH OTHER ARTICLES AS MAY BE NEEDED. IN SHIPPING ALL YOUR GOODS BY FREIGHT, THE CHARGES ARE VERY SMALL.**

## Mandolin Music.

**Arranged for Mandolin and Guitar.**

No. 71826. Benjamin's Amateur Mandolin and Guitar Collections. No. 1 contains thirteen easy and popular pieces, arranged for mandolin or violin, with guitar accompaniment; also the piano accompaniment. Our special price.....$0.30
Postage, 4 cents.

No. 71828. Excelsior Mandolin and Guitar Folio. This book has become immensely popular and has a great and increasing sale; contains 72 pages of the very choicest music for the mandolin and guitar. Our special price.....$0.40
Postage, 5 cents.

No. 71829. Champion Mandolin and Guitar Folio. Containing the latest arrangements and compositions for these popular instruments; printed on fine supercalendered paper; 96 pages. Our special price.....$0.40
Postage, 8 cents.

No. 71831. Ideal Mandolin and Guitar Folio. A very superior collection of instrumental music arranged for the mandolin and guitar duets; 2 parts, 40 pages each. Our special price.....$0.40
Postage, 3 cents.

No. 71833. Superior Mandolin and Guitar Folio. A choice collection of music by eminent composers, arranged for mandolin and guitar; printed on fine supercalendered paper, and containing 92 pages. Our special price.....$0.40
Postage, 7 cents.

## Cornet Solos.

No. 71835. Cornet Solos. Ferazzi's new and popular edition, No. 1, of select duets for cornet and piano, 42 pages. Our Special price.....$0.40
Postage, 4 cents.

## Cornet and Piano Duets.

No. 71837. Popular Duets. This is a new and popular edition of select duets for cornet and piano, edition No. 1. 122 pages. Our Special price.....$0.40
Postage, 11 cents.

## Orchestra Music.

No. 71850. Favorite Dance Album, first series, arranged for orchestra of nine instruments, viz.: 1st and 2nd violin, cornet, clarionet, flute, viola, trombone, bass and piano; contains 11 pieces of assorted dance music, each piece new and good. Price, each book (except piano).....$0.25
Piano book.....0.35
Extra, by mail, 3 cents.

No. 71851. Favorite Dance Album. second series, arranged for same instruments as No. 71850, contains 11 pieces choice dance music. Price, each book (except piano).....$0.25
Piano book.....0.35
Extra, by mail, 3 cents.

No. 71853. Beginners' Orchestra Journal, No. 1, by A. S. Bowman. Contains 25 easy and popular pieces of dance music arranged for orchestra of 8 instruments, viz: 1st and 2nd violin, cornet, clarionet, flute, trombone (either clef), bass and piano, each part separate. Price, each book (except piano).....$0.25
Piano book.....0.50
Extra, by mail, 3 cents.

No. 71855. Beginners' Orchestra Journal, No. 2, by A. S. Bowman; 25 pieces dance music arranged for orchestra, same as No. 1, but contains a more difficult grade of music. Price, each book (except piano).....$0.25
Piano book.....0.50
Extra, by mail, 3 cents.

No. 71856. Gems of the ball room, No. 1, by McCosh and others. A collection of 33 pieces of choice dance music, all kinds, arranged for orchestra of eight instruments, viz: 1st and 2nd violin, cornet, clarionet, flute, trombone, (double clefs), bass and piano, each part separate. Price, each book (except piano).....$0.50
Price, each book, in lots of 5 or more (excepting piano).....$0.45
Prices piano book each.....1.00

No. 71857. Gems of the Ball Rooms, No. 2. A collection of the latest dance music, arranged for orchestra of eight instruments, same as Gems No. 1. Contains 33 pieces, including the new military schottische "Berlin," "York," etc. Price, each book, (excepting piano).....$0.50
Price, each book, in lots of 5 or more (excepting piano).....$0.45
Price, piano book, each.....1.00

No. 71859. Gems of the Ball Room, No. 3, arranged for same instruments as Nos. 1 and 2, and contains 33 pieces of new dance music, also some of the old "Contra" dances. Price, each book (except piano).....$0.50
Price, each book, in lots of five.....0.45
Price, piano books, each.....1.00

No. 71861. Gems of the Ball Room, No. 4, arranged for same instruments as the other numbers; contains 32 pieces of the latest and best dance music.
Price, each book (excepting piano).....$0.50
Price, each book (excepting piano), in lots of five. 0.45
Price, piano book.....1.00

No. 71863. Gems of the Ball Room, No. 5. This is the latest edition of these very popular orchestral collections, and contains thirty-two pieces of the best new dance music; arranged for same instruments as Nos. 1 and 2. Price, each book (excepting piano).....$0.50
Price, each book (excepting piano), in lots of five. 0.45
Price, piano book.....1.00
Extra, by mail, each 2 cents.

There are no duplicates in Gems of the Ball Room and every orchestra leader should have the complete set.

No. 71865. Echoes from the Ball Room. This collection contains everything in music essential to dancing. It includes the latest dances, also the old standards; 31 pieces, arranged for 1st and 2d violin, cornet, clarionet, bass, flute, viola, trombone and piano.
Price, each book (excepting piano).....$0.50
Price, each book, in lots of five.....45
Price, piano book.....1.00

No. 71867. Beauties of the Ball Room, No. 1. Choice selection of dance music, arranged for either first or second violin or any orchestral instrument.
Price per part for orchestral instrument.....$0.50
Price of piano book.....90
Postage, 2 cents.

No. 71869. Beauties of the Ball Room, No. 2. This is a second volume of the book described above, but containing no duplicates.
Price of book for any orchestral instrument.....$0.50
Price of piano book.....90

No. 71870. Parlor and Ball Room Album. A new collection of best music by Prof. Francis Goetz, a composer for string bands, and who is one of the most popular writers of the day. In this collection he has even surpassed himself. Our price, each book.....$0.50
Postage, 2 cents.

No. 71872. The Beginners Concert Orchestra Journal, by A. S. Bowman, the composer of the popular ball room quadrille journals and other favorite dance music.
Price per single part for either first or second violin, bass viol, flute, clarionet or other instruments.....$0.25
Our price with piano accompaniment.....35
Postage, 2 cents.

## Brass Band Music.

71880. The Combination Band Book, arranged by McCosh, just published, and is already becoming very popular, as it contains sixteen pieces of choice music for every occasion. Marches, quicksteps, waltzes, polkas, overtures, etc., etc. Just the book for young bands. Arranged for full band of twenty pieces. Price, single book, each.....$0.25
Set of six or more, each.....20

No. 71883. National Band Journal No. 1. Contains eight pieces of music, including our national airs, together with the best of our grand old war songs, arranged for full band. Price, all parts complete, $0.90
Postage, 4 cents.

No. 71884. The Ever Ready Band Books. A new collection of choice quicksteps, marches, watltzes, etc., by McCosh, Fox, Ruby and other composers, arranged for full brass band. Price, single books, each.....$0.25
Set of six or more, each.....20
Postage, 4 cents.

No. 71885. Sacred Band Journal, contains ten familiar hymns, arranged for full band. This journal is invaluable for Sunday playing, Sunday school picnics, concerts, etc. Price, all parts complete.....$0.90

No. 71887. The Golden Crown Band Book, by Prof. Francis Goetz. This book has attained a greater popularity than perhaps any other selection of compositions. Thousands of bands already own it and everyone of them are delignted with it. Our special price.....$0.45
Lots of ten or more, each.....40
Postage, 2 cents.

No. 71888. Band Book No. 1. A collection of specially desirable music for bands, arranged for various instruments. Our special price, each book.....$0.25
Ten or more, each.....$0.22
Postage, 2 cents.

No. 71890. George Southwell's Band and Orchestral Book. A collection of sixteen easy, yet very showy, pieces for the ball room. This set of books is so arranged that they can be played with almost any combination of orchestra instruments. Price per book for any orchestral instrument.....$0.45

No. 71892. Beginner's Band Book Instrumentation. Arranged for solo B flat cornet. A superb collection for this instrument. Our special price.....$0.25
Postage, 2 cents.

## Instruction Books—Piano.

No. 71894. Lebert & Stark Piano School, Parts 1, 2 and 3; board covers; retail price per volume.....$2.00
Our price, per volume.....1.25
Postage, 14 cents.

We have elegant plate editions of this celebrated school, carefully edited and corrected. This work is endorsed by the greatest musicians, and is fast coming into popular favor.

No. 71895. Karl Merz Piano Method, complete. Publisher's price $3.00; our price.....$2.00
Postage, 24 cents.

No. 71896. Richardson's New Method for Piano. Publisher's price, $3.00; our price.....$2.10
Postage, 28 cents.

No 71897. Root's New Musical Curriculum, complete and revised. Publisher's price, $3 00; our price.....$2.10
Postage, 28 cents.

No. 71899. The Ideal Method for the Piano. Containing simple and clear instructions and a large number of operatic and other popular airs, carefully selected from the latest publications and arranged with special reference to the piano. Our special price, $0.60
Postage, 3 cents.

No. 71900. First Instruction Book for the Pianoforte. A thorough course for teachers and pupils by Edward Wagner. Is translated from the German and edited by J. H. Cornell. This is one of the most valuable instruction books ever issued. The first part is devoted to the rudiments of music.
Our special price.....$1.05
Postage, 9 cents.

No. 71902. First Instruction Book for Pianoforte, Part 2. This part takes up the instruction of the pupil on the pianoforte where part 1 leaves off. Bound in boards. Our special price.....$1.05
Postage, 9 cents.

No. 71904. Bellak's Analytical Method for the Pianoforte. A very popular method of instruction and remarkably complete, containing besides the elements of music and general instructions, a dictionary of musical terms and a number of easy waltzes and airs for the piano. Bound in boards, our special price, $0.65
Bound in paper, our price.....0.55

No. 71906. Wilson's Complete Method for the Piano. A complete method for the pianoforte, containing elements of music, also musical dictionary and terms used in music. Complete series of instructions and exercises as well as a number of easy and popular airs for the piano. Bound in paper cover, our special price.....$0.45
Postage, 6 cents.
Bound in boards, our special price.....$0.65
Postage, 8 cents.

No. 71910. Winner's Eureka method for the piano. An instruction book that is in very great demand and is deservedly popular, contains besides instruction a number of selections and melodies; bound in paper. Our special price.....$0.55
Postage, 6 cents.

## Cabinet or Parlor Organ.

No. 71914. Winner's Eureka Method for the organ. The latest and best of all instruction books; bound in paper, 80 pages. Our special price.....$0.55
Postage, 6 cents.

No. 71915. Bentley's Method for the Parlor Organ. This work has met with a very large sale and has been very kindly received by teachers and students of music throughout the country. This is the new Columbian edition and attention is called to the excellence of the elementary department. This book is recommended as one of the very best published; bound in boards.
Our special price.....$0.65
Postage, 11 cents.

No. 71917. Eclectic Teacher of the Parlor Organ. An analytical and synthetical method for students desiring to become familiar with the cabinet or reed organ together with music associated therewith. A thorough text book and guide in the principles of organ playing. Containing a large number of studies, etc., also songs. Bound in boards.
Our special price.....$0.95
Postage, 14 cents.

No. 71919. Lyon's Eclectic Organist for the Cabinet Organ. This instruction book for the organ will be found a marked improvement on all other works; bound in boards. Our special price.....$1.25
Postage, 13 cents.

No. 71921. White's Method of Reed Organ. Publisher's price, $2.50. Our price.....$0.80
Extra, by mail, 15 cents.

No. 71922. Karl Merz's Modern Method for Reed Organ. Publisher's price, $2.50. Our price.....$1.25
Extra, by mail, 18 cents.

No. 71923. Getze's Method for Reed Organ. Publisher's price, $2.00. Our price.....$1.00
Extra, by mail, 16 cents.

No. 71925. Whitney's Improved Easy Methods for the Parlor Organ. New and enlarged edition. This is a new and attractive system, by which the pupil may rapidly learn to play the organ. Besides a thorough course in music, this book contains a choice collection of vocal and instrumental pieces, progressively arranged, so that a careful study of each in their order will enable the student to correctly perform all the different styles of music. Publisher's price, $1.50.
Our price.....$0.60
Postage, 13 cents.

No. 71926. Improved Easy Method for the Parlor Organ. A new and attractive system by which pupils may rapidly learn to play. A choice selection of vocal and instrumental music, including dance music, operatic music, ballads, etc.; bound in boards. Retail price, $1.50. Our special price.....$0.95
Postage, 12 cents.

No. 71928. Winner's Instruction Books for Organ. Retail price, 25 cents. Our price.....$0.12

## Violin Instruction Books.

No. 71932. Violin Without a Master. Containing new and complete rules and exercises, with full directions in bowing and all necessary instructions to perfect the learner in the art of playing the violin: to which is added a large selection of popular airs and dance music, as well as operatic airs. with several pieces arranged as duets. Our special price.....$0.30
Postage, 3 cents.

No. 71934. Self Instructor for the Violin. Containing the elements of music, complete instructions, and a large collection of violin music, consisting of popular airs, dance music, etc.; compiled by Elias Howe.
Our price.....$0.50
Postage, 2 cents.

No. 71936. Bower's Standard Method for the Violin. One of the most complete standard instruction books for this instrument; contains besides instructions a large number of instrumental pieces, both popular and classical. Our special price.....$0.25
Postage, 4 cents.

No. 71937. Winner's Eureka Method for the Violin. Instruction book that meets the demand of all students; thoroughly complete and very popular.
Our special price.....$0.55
Postage, 6 cents.

No. 71937½. Winner's Instruction Book for Violin. Retail price, 25 cents. Our price.....$0.12

No. 71938. L. A. Benjamin's Violin School. Comprises elementary and more advanced studies for the violin. Conveys a comprehensive and valuable knowlege of the instrument. Our special price.....$0.70
Postage, 5 cents.

No. 71940. Maza's Complete Violin School. Publisher's price, $2.00. Our price.....$0.75
Extra, by mail, 7 cents.

**IT IS VERY NECESSARY THAT CUSTOMERS EXERCISE CARE IN ORDERING. ALWAYS GIVE CATALOGUE PAGE AND CATALOGUE NUMBER OF THE ARTICLE, AS WELL AS NAME AND PRICE. WHERE SIZES, COLORS, ETC., ARE NECESSARY, DO NOT FAIL TO GIVE ALL INFORMATION.**

## Violin Instruction Books.—Continued.

**No. 71941.** Benjamin's Illustrated Violin Method. This is the latest publication in the way of a violin instructor, and is the best work for the beginner ever put on the market. It contains the complete elementary course, is profusely illustrated; also contains a collection of popular music; 79 pages, sheet music size. Each _____$0.50

Extra, by mail, 5 cents.

**No. 71942.** Wichtl's Young Violinist. Publisher's price, $2.25. Our price_____$0.80

Extra, by mail, 10 cents.

**No. 71944.** Howe's Original Violin School, new and enlarged edition. Contains complete rules and exercises, together with a collection of over 450 pieces of every variety. Hundreds of old familiar airs never before published for violin. Extra large type and fine paper. Each _____$0.40

Extra, by mail, 4 cents.

**No. 71946.** Howe's "Diamond" School for the Violin, contains complete instruction, full directions for bowing, and 558 pieces of dance music. Each_____$0.45

Extra, by mail, 4 cents.

## Guitar Instruction Books.

**No. 71948.** Winner's Eureka Method for the Guitar. An instruction book for this instrument that meets all requirements and is very widely recommended by the most noted music teachers. Our special price_____$0.55

Postage, 6 cents.

**No. 71949.** The Common Sense Guitar Instructor. A new and concise method in which the instructions are so simply treated that anybody may become a performer on this favorite instrument. This book also contains the elements of music and a complete collection of the newest songs and pieces arranged for this work to be found nowhere else. Our special price_____$0.50

**No. 71951.** Bower's Standard Method for the Guitar. Positively the most popular instruction book for the guitar ever published, bound in paper. Our special price_____$0.25

Postage, 4 cents.

**No. 71952.** Elite Guitar Instructor, arranged by Arling Shaeffer, particularly with reference to a thorough and complete understanding of the instrument itself and proper knowledge of its methods for learning it thoroughly. The purpose of this book is to furnish a course of instruction for the guitar, which if clearly observed and diligently practiced will enable those who are lovers of this most beautiful stringed instrument to become accomplished and artistic performers; bound in boards. Our special price_____$1.85

Postage, 12 cents.

**No. 71953.** Carcassi's Guitar Method. Complete.$1.00

Extra, by mail, 12 cents.

**No. 71954.** Winner's Instruction Book for Guitar; retail price 25 cts. Our price_____$0.12

**No. 71955.** Instruction Book of Chords for the Guitar. A new system of learning to play the chords of the guitar without notes or teacher. Each_____$0.25

Extra, by mail, 1 cent.

## Banjo Instruction Books.

**No. 71956.** Dobson's New System for the Banjo. Containing a course of complete instructions, together with practical exercises, selections and arrangements; bound in boards. Our special price_____$0.75

Postage, 10 cents.

**No. 71957.** Bowers' Standard Method for the Banjo. This publication is one of the most complete books of its kind ever offered to lovers of the banjo. Our special price_____$0.25

Postage, 3 cents.

**No. 71959.** Instruction Book of Chords for Banjo; publisher's price 50 cts. Our price_____$0.25

Extra, by mail, 1 cent.

**No. 71960.** Winner's Instruction Books for Banjo; retail price, 25 cts. Our price_____$0.12

## Mandolin Instruction Books.

**No. 71962.** Bowers' Standard Method for the Mandolin. Very popular and sought after by students of this desirable instrument; bound in paper. Our special price _____$0.25

Postage, 4 cents.

**No. 71964.** Winner's Eureka Method for the Mandolin. One of the latest and best instruction books for this popular instrument; bound in paper and printed on very fine super-calender stock. Our special price _____$0.55

Postage, 6 cents.

**No. 71966.** Elite Mandolin Instructor. Containing Arling Schaeffer's new system for the mandolin, complete and graduate system of exercises, together with a number of popular airs and dance music, arranged particularly for the mandolin. Sixth edition, bound in boards. Our special price_____$0.95

Postage, 12 cents.

**No. 71968.** Benjamin's Illustrated Method for the Mandolin, containing complete course in the rudiments of music, is fully illustrated and contains a choice collection of music. Price_____$0.50

Extra, by mail, 5 cents.

**No. 71970.** Ryan's True Mandolin Instructor. Publisher's price 75 cts. Our price_____$0.25

## Miscellaneous Instruction Books.

**No. 71978.** Howe's Army and Navy Fife Instructor, containing complete course of instructions, also calls, signals, and the complete camp and garrison duties as practiced in the United States army and navy, besides the National Airs and a large collection of marches, quicksteps, waltzes, etc., etc. Price each, paper cover_____$0.40

Extra, by mail, 4 cents.

**No. 71979.** Winner's Instruction Book for Flute; retail price, 25c. Our price_____$0.12

**71980.** Winner's Instruction Books for Fife; retail price, 25c. Our price_____$0.12

**No. 71981.** Winner's Instruction Book for Cornet; retail price, 25c. Our price_____$0.12

**No. 71982.** Winner's Primary School for Accordeon, Organ, Violin, Guitar, Banjo, Flute, Fife, Violoncello, Clarionet and Cornet. Not condensed; unabridged. (Specify for which instrument book is wanted.) Price, per volume_____$0.18

Extra, by mail, 3 cents.

**No. 71983.** Pepper's New Self Instructor for the Piccolo. Contains complete instructions for this popular instrument. Each_____$0.45

Extra, by mail, 4 cents.

**No. 71984.** Winner's Instruction Book for Accordeon; retail price, 25c. Our price_____$0.12

**No. 71985.** Ryan's True Zither Instructor. Publisher's price, 70c. Our price_____$0.25

Extra, by mail, 3 cents.

**No. 71986.** Ryan's True Double Bass Instructor; publisher's price, 72c. Our price_____$0.25

Extra, by mail, 3 cents.

**No. 71988.** Ryan's True Ocarina Instructor; publisher's price, 75c. Our price_____$0.25

Extra, by mail, 3 cents.

**No. 71989.** Ryan's True Harmonica Instructor; publisher's price, 75c. Our price_____$0.25

Extra, by mail, 3 cents.

**No. 71991.** Arban's World Renowned Cornet Method, in cloth binding, gilt letters. Each_____$1.60

Extra, by mail. 16 cents.

## Miscellaneous.

**No. 71998.** Organ Voicing and Tuning. A thoroughly practical work on organ tuning, voicing and repairing. This book is illustrated, and a careful study of it will obviate the necessity of sending for a tuner every time your organ gets out of order. Our price_____$0.25

Postage, 3 cents.

**No. 71999.** Rudiments of Music. A concise and thoroughly practical course of instruction on the art of singing by note; prepared by J. R. Murray. Teachers' classes and individuals will find in the above inexpensive work everything that is necessary to a complete understanding of the art of reading and singing by note. Our price_____$0.10

Postage, 2 cents.

**No. 72002.** Construction, Tuning and Repairing of the Piano. A book that tuners, repairers, teachers and owners of pianos and organs ought to possess. Bound in board cover. Our special price_____$0.60

Postage, 4 cents.

**No. 72003.** Burrow's Pianoforte Primer. Containing the rudiments of music; calculated either for class or private teaching. Our special price_____$0.20

Postage, 4 cents.

**No. 72004.** Pronouncing Pocket Dictionary of over 500 musical terms. A book of great convenience to students and teachers. Our special price_____$0.12

Postage, 1 cent.

**No. 72005.** Jones's Musical Catechism. A book of special desirability to students and teachers alike. Contains a revised dictionary of musical terms: bound in paper. Our special price_____$0.16

Postage, 2 cents.

## Ball Room Guides and Call Books.

**No. 72006.** Prof. Clendenen's Fashionable Quadrille Book and Guide to Etiquette. This book contains all the necessary instructions, both with reference to etiquette on the ball room floor, as well as description of figures and calling; 64 pages. Our special price_____$0.25

Postage, 2 cents.

**No. 72008.** Howe's New American Dancing Master. Containing 400 dances and including 100 figures of the German; all the latest and most fashionable dances are included, with full explanation of the latest and most approved figures and calls for the different changes, as well as rules on deportment and toilet, and etiquette of dancing; 140 pages. Our special price.$0.50

Postage, 4 cents.

**No. 72009.** Pepper's Universal Dancing Master, Prompter's Call Book and Violinists' Guide. This work is intended as a complete instructor in the art of dancing and prompting. It contains an elaborate description of the steps and figures used in the round, square and fancy dances, including the very latest, such as the "York," "Berlin," "Lœmo," "German," etc., etc.; also an appropriate collection of music, easily arranged for the violin and plainly marked for prompter's calls; over 200 pages; board covers. Every violinist should have one of these books. Our price_____$0.80

Postage, 14 cents.

**No. 72012.** Revised Edition of Dick's Quadrille Call Book and Ball Room Prompter. This edition is thoroughly revised and illustrated by diagram directions how to call off figures of every dance; also 100 figures of the German, as well as sensible guide to deportment; 200 pages. Our special price_____$0.50

Postage, 4 cents.

## TO GIVE YOU AN IDEA

of what our customers think of our Watch and Jewelry Department, we take the liberty of printing a few of the thousands of letters we constantly receive.

**EVERY ITEM SHIPPED OUT IS CAREFULLY INSPECTED THREE TIMES BEFORE SHIPPING, TO SEE THAT IT IS AS ORDERED AND IN PERFECT CONDITION.**

# Sears Roebuck & Co. INCORPORATED
## SPORTING GOODS DEPARTMENT

**WE ARE HEADQUARTER FOR EVERYTHING** In Guns, Revolvers, Ammunition, Gun Implements, Hunters' Clothing, Fishing Tackle, Tents, Base Ball, Tennis and other athletic goods and Lake and River Seines.

**WE CAN SAVE YOU MONEY** on everything in this line, no matter how little or how much you wish to buy we will be just as thankful for your order and will save you 33⅓ per cent.

**GUN CLUB MEMBERS** Are especially invited to compare our prices with those of other houses. **WE ARE SUPPLYING GUN CLUBS** everywhere. If your club does not buy from us, they are paying too much for goods, and we would thank you for calling their attention to our prices herein.

**WE HAVE NO COMPETITORS** In this line, so far as price is concerned. **NO ONE MEETS OUR PRICES.**

**WE MAKE THE PRICES BELOW ALL OTHERS** By contracting each season with different manufacturers for a seasons supply, always a very large amount, and **ALWAYS FOR CASH. SMALL EXPENSE OF HANDLING** is another advantage in our favor. We believe we have the most economically managed **Sporting Goods Department** in America. It is but **one of many departments** in our house; therefore we are not compelled to look to this department alone to defray all our expenses, and to satisfy our entire earnings. On the contrary, we can add the **smallest kind of a profit** to the actual **NET COST** on **seasons cash contract purchase basis**, allowing nothing for bad debts, for we have none, and that is our prices to you. ☞ **COMPARE THESE PRICES**—Take Guns. We sell the Parker Gun as low as $36.45 Hammerless Parker, $41.70; Colt Hammerless, $51.30; L. C. Smith Hammerless, $31.75, and everything in the line in proportion. Does another firm meet these prices?

**..TERMS..**

We will ship **Guns, Revolvers, Sporting Goods** by express, C.O.D., subject to examination on the following conditions: **REVOLVERS**—We will send any revolver to any address by express, C.O.D., subject to examination, on receipt of **One Dollar** as a guarantee of good faith. You can examine it at your express office, and if found perfectly satisfactory and exactly as represented. pay the express agent the balance and express charges. **GUNS**—We will send any gun to any address by express C. O. D., subject to examination, on receipt of **three dollars** as a guarantee of good faith. You can examine the gun at your nearest express office, and if found perfectly satisfactory and exactly as represented. pay the express agent the balance and express charges. **GUN IMPLEMENTS, AMMUNITION** and other **SPORTING GOODS** we will send to any address by **express or freight**, C.O.D., subject to examination, on receipt of a sufficient **cash deposit to pay** freight or express both ways, balance to be paid when received.

**DISCOUNT FOR CASH.** We allow a discount of **Three Per Cent** if cash in full accompanies your order. If you send the full amount of cash with your order you may deduct **three per cent from our prices. NEARLY ALL OUR CUSTOMERS** send cash in full. Always consider our 3 per cent cash discount when comparing our prices with other houses. As a rule the 3 per cent will nearly and in many cases more than pay the freight or express charges.

**OUR BINDING GUARANTEE.** We guarantee every article we show in this department to be **exactly as represented** and of the **very highest grade, and** if not found so we will return your money. **IF YOU HAVE ANY DOUBT AS TO OUR RELIABILITY** you are at liberty to send your order and money to any Express Co. in the city, to the **Metropolitan National Bank** or **National Bank of Commerce** with instructions not to turn it over to us unless they know us to be thoroughly reliable. **GIVE US ONE ORDER** for ammunition or other goods, and if we don't save you 20 per cent or more send the goods back and **we will refund your money and pay freight both ways.**

---

### THE WELL-KNOWN PARKER HAMMER GUN FOR $36.45.

**If you will compare the price** of $36.45 with any price you have seen quoted on any Parker gun, you can then appreciate what it means by placing your orders in our hands, what our economic one small profit plan saves the consumer on the merchandise bought. See that your Parker guns are stamped "Parker Bros." All others are only imitations and cheap grade common guns.

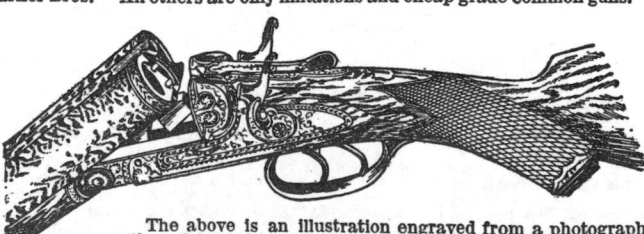

The above is an illustration engraved from a photograph of the celebrated breech loading double gun, top lever, made by Parker Bros., of Meriden, Conn. All grades of these guns as quoted below are breech loading, all have the top lever action, double bolt and improved check hook and pin, fore-end lock, solid head plunger, extension rib, rebounding locks and low hammers. In ordering guns give first and second choice on weights and dimensions. We shall always do our best to give the first choice, and generally will be able to do so. All Parker guns are choke bored for close shooting and are accompanied by a target made at the factory. 12 gauge weigh 7½ to 9½ lbs.; 10 gauge, 9½ to 10½ lbs. Length of barrels, 30 or 32 inches as desired. Our guns are the very best made in these grades, every gun warranted, all bored for long range, and the cheapest will shoot as well as the most expensive.

| | 12 gauge. | 10 gauge. |
|---|---|---|
| **No. 81.** Parker twist barrel, American stock, engraved and checkered pistol grip | $36.45 | $39.50 |
| **No. 82.** Parker fine Damascus steel barrels, fine figured American or imported stock, engraved rubber butt plate, checkered pistol grip | 51.30 | 54.25 |

### THE CELEBRATED PARKER HAMMERLESS GUN.

No better shooting gun made. The Parker gun is so well known that little comment need be made by us.

The above illustration engraved from a photograph gives you some idea of the appearance of the Parker Hammerless gun. Cut shows style of engraving on the $150.00 grade. Our special price..................$98.75

All these guns have top lever, choke bore and are made by Parker Bros., of Meriden, Conn., and so plainly stamped, fine Damascus steel barrels, fine figured American or imported walnut stock, pistol grip, checkered, handsomely engraved hard rubber butt plates, beautifully finished throughout, every gun warranted highest quality to the grade, matted ribs.

| | | List price. | Our price. |
|---|---|---|---|
| **No. 83.** | E. H. grade, 10 gauge | $85.00 | $54.52 |
| **No. 83½.** | G. H. grade, 12 or 16 gauge, 28, 30 and 32-inch barrel | 80.00 | 51.30 |
| **No. 84.** | D. H. grade, 10, 12 and 16 gauge | 100.00 | 64.25 |
| **No. 85.** | Fine twist barrels, 12 and 16 gauge | 65.00 | 41.70 |

Weight, 12 gauge, 7½ lbs. to 9 lbs.; 10 gauge, 8½ to 10 lbs. Length of barrel 28 to 32 inches. Drop of stock, 2½ to 3¼ inches. Stocks (measured from center of first trigger to center of butt plate) 14 to 14¼ inches. We can make shorter or longer barrels and different stocks to special order at prices according to extra amount of labor. Higher priced guns made to order.

Understand, any of these guns will be sent to any address C. O. D., subject to examination, on receipt of $3.00, balance and express charges payable at express office.

**BEFORE RETURNING ANY GOODS FOR ANY REASON READ FULL INSTRUCTIONS CONCERNING RETURNED GOODS IN FRONT OF THIS BOOK.**

## THE CELEBRATED COLT'S NEW HAMMERLESS BREECH LOADING GUN FOR $51.30.

We guarantee our prices on these guns to be below any competition, and if upon comparison you do not find this to be the fact we will not ask you to favor us with your orders for anything in the merchandise line.

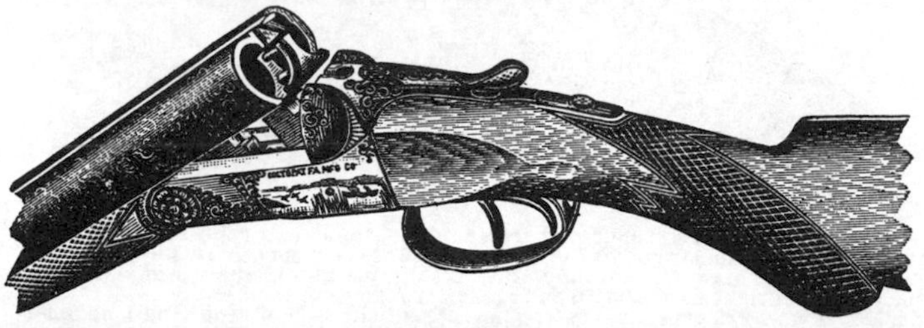

The above is an illustration of the new Colt's Hammerless Breech loader engraved from a photograph, made by the Colt's Patent Fire Arms Mfg. Co. at Hartford, Conn., and every genuine gun bears their name. The 10 bore is a long range duck gun, a gun that generally retails at $75.00 to $90.00, and at our price we consider it one of the best guns on the market for the money; the finest material, best workmanship, beautiful finish, and no better shooting gun at any price. Safer than a hammer gun, simple and few parts, no better gun made for durability and shooting qualities; all have pistol grip, all are choke bored, all have extension rib, all are warranted as represented or can be returned at our expense; long range, hard shooters, all warranted highest quality to the grade.

No. 86. Fine Damascus steel barrels, neatly engraved, fancy imported walnut stock, pistol grip, fancy rubber butt plate, checkered grip and fore end, case hardened lock plates and actions and finely finished, 12 gauge, 30 and 32-inch barrels, 7½ to 9 lbs., our special price....$51.30

No. 87. 10 gauge, 30 and 32-inch barrels, 8½ to 10 lbs., our special price....51.30

No. 88. Regular $125.00 grade, finest Damascus barrels, beautifully finished and engraved, 10 or 12 gauge, our special price....$84.95

Higher priced guns made to order. All have automatic safety and every one a beauty at the trap or in the field.

## NOTE OUR SPECIAL BARGAINS IN THE FAMOUS L. C. SMITH HAMMERLESS GUNS.

We carry everything in the line of L. C. Smith guns, and at prices 25 per cent lower than your local dealer can buy in quantities, in fact, there is no dealer in America who pretends to meet our competition in the way of prices on the famous L. C. Smith hammerless shot guns. We only ask you to compare our prices with those of any other concern in existence, and if you do not freely admit that we have no competitors then we will not ask for your patronage; but if after a close comparison of our prices with those of others you find you can save money by placing your orders in our hands we would ask that you favor us with your orders for such goods in the sporting goods line as you require, and if you will use your kind influence in our behalf with your friends who are in need of sporting goods we will feel amply repaid for the effort we have made in pounding down prices.

## $31.75 BUYS A $50.00 L. C. SMITH HAMMERLESS GUN.

We ask you have you ever seen an L. C. Smith Hammerless gun offered at any such price? Understand any gun will be sent to any address by express C. O. D. subject to examination on receipt of $3.00, balance and express charges payable at express office.

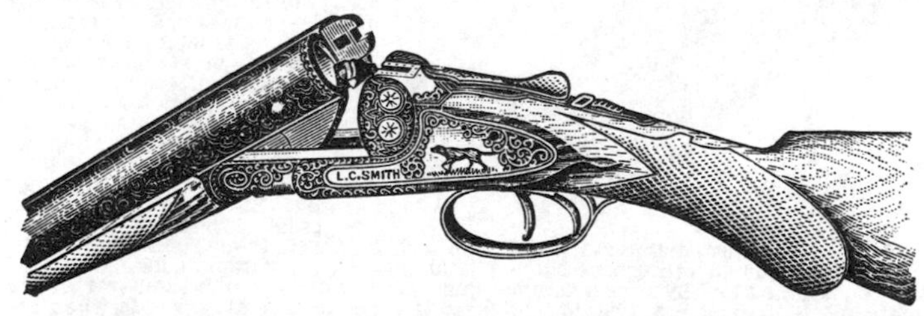

The above illustration is engraved from a photograph and will give you an idea of the appearance of this grade Smith gun. It is improved for the season of 1896 and made by The Hunter Arms Co., at Fulton, N. Y. All have top lever, all have choke bore, all have pistol grip, and all are warranted, bored for nitro and black powders and warranted never to get loose or shaky with any nitro powder. Wide, heavy breech, narrow muzzles, greatly improved for this season, no better shooting gun at any price.

No. 809. Fine twist barrels, imported walnut stock, pistol grip, rubber butt, case hardened lock plates and action, plain finished but a good gun, every one warranted: 10 or 12 gauge, 30 or 32-inch barrel, our special price....$31.75

No. 810. No. 1 quality, fine laminated steel barrels, imported walnut stock, pistol grip and fore end, rubber butt plate, hardened lock plates and action. No fancy engraving, but well made and desirable and just as good a shooter as a higher priced gun. 10, 12 or 16 gauge as desired and 30 or 32-inch barrel. Our special price....$37.22

Sixteen gauge guns, 28 or 30-inch barrels, 6¾ to 7¼ lbs.; 12 gauge, 28, 30 or 32-inch barrels, weigh 7¼ to 9 lbs.; 10 gauge guns have 30 or 32-inch barrels and weigh 8¾ to 9¾ lbs.

## THE L. C. SMITH HAMMERLESS GUN, GRADE No. 2.

The regular price of this gun is $80.00; our special offer price is $49.63.

The above illustration is engraved from a photograph, and will give you an idea of the appearance of the gun. Every gun is warranted up to grade and all stamped with the name of the maker.

No. 811. No. 2 quality, good Damascus steel barrels, imported walnut stock, pistol grip, checkered and engraved, finely finished, 10, 12 or 16 gauge, 28, 30 and 32-inch barrels, our special offer price....$49.63

## L. C. SMITH HAMMERLESS GUN, No. 3 GRADE, AT $61.20 AND $89.75.

These guns are offered at retail at about double the price.

No. 812. Very fine Damascus or Crown steel barrels to order. Very fine English walnut stock, beautifully checkered, very finely engraved, 10, 12 or 16 gauge. Our special price....$61.20

## THE L. C. SMITH PIGEON GUN.

No. 813. The L. C. Smith Pigeon Gun, finest Crown steel barrel, blued finish; straight grip, highly finished and engraved; bore for nitro powder and made especially for trap shooting, beautifully balanced and made in the highest style of the art of gun making; 12 gauge, 30-inch barrels, 7¼ to 8 lbs. Our special offer price....$89.75

This gun can be furnished with pistol grip stock at same price.

## THE CELEBRATED L. C. SMITH AUTOMATIC EJECTOR HAMMERLESS GUNS AT $49.75 AND UPWARDS.

We offer these guns at about one-half the regular retail price, and we believe you will appreciate this fact when you have compared our prices with those of other Houses.

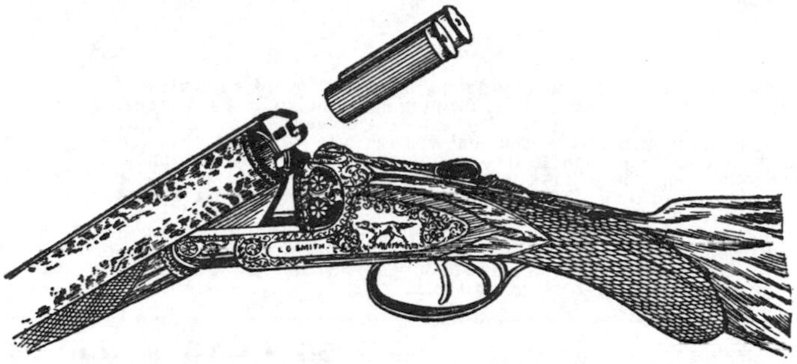

No. 814. No. 1 ejector, pistol grip, laminated steel barrel, line engraving, neatly finished, well made and durable, warranted full choke bore unless otherwise ordered, 12 gauge, 30 or 32-inch barrels, 7½ to 8½ lbs....$49.75

No. 815. No. 2 ejector, Damascus barrels, neatly engraved, pistol grip, English walnut stock warranted, 12 gauge, 30 or 32-inch barrel, 7¼ to 8¾ lbs. Our special price....$68.90

No. 816. No. 3 ejector, fine Damascus barrels, pistol grip, handsomely engraved, beautifully finished, 12 gauge, 30 or 32-inch barrel, 7¼ to 8½ lbs., our special price....$78.90

No. 817. Quality A1 ejector, very fine Damascus steel barrel, very fine imported English walnut stock, fine checkering and engraving, choke bored on the multiplied system and warranted close hard shooters, 12 gauge, 28, 30 and 32-inch barrel, 7¼ to 8½ lbs., our special price....$99.50.

The Smith ejectors are perfect and positive in their working parts and never fail to eject the empty shell. They are not liable to get out of order.

## WE OFFER THE CELEBRATED CHARLES DALY HAMMERLESS EJECTOR GUN AT $129.00,

And we are willing to guarantee the price and also guarantee the Charles Daly Hammerless Ejector was never before offered at any such money.

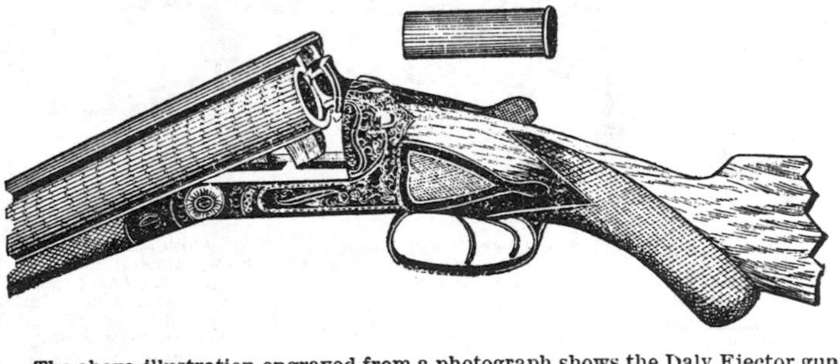

The above illustration engraved from a photograph shows the Daly Ejector gun of the latest improved 1894 model, all bored for nitro or black powder, with all the latest improvements; improved quality, reduced price, quality the best.

No. 818. No. 250 diamond quality automatic ejector, highest grade Damascus barrels, automatic lock, trigger safety, pistol grip, beautifully engraved Turkish walnut stock. There is no gun in the world superior to it; it will bear comparison with the finest Purdy, the highest priced gun made. 12 and 16 gauge, our special price....$189.50

No. 819. No. 150, Damascus barrels, automatic ejector, fine plain engraving, selected stock, matted rib, 12 and 16 gauge, a perfect ejector. Our special offer price, $129.00. 12 gauge guns weigh 7¼ to 7¾ lbs., 28 or 30-inch barrels.

The Daly ejectors are the handsomest, strongest and most perfect ejectors made at any price. They are perfect in every respect. No gun in the world surpasses them in shooting or wearing qualities. Can be returned if not as represented.

## THE CELEBRATED CHARLES DALY HAMMERLESS GUN FOR $95.75.

No. 820. This fine Daly Hammerless (not automatic ejecting), high grade Damascus barrel, beautifully finished, neatly engraved, all the latest improvements, greatly improved for this year, shooting qualities guaranteed, best material, finest workmanship, the best gun for the money on the market, all choke bored, good for nitro or black powder, 12 or 16 gauge, our special price....$95.75

Weight, 12 gauge, 7¼ to 7¾ lbs. Length of barrel 28 and 30 inches.

No. 821. The No. 120, 12 gauge feather weights 26-inch barrel, weight 5¾ lbs. Our price....$102.64

**DON'T FORGET US ON LOADED SHOT SHELLS.**

Order in time to be ready when shooting season opens. **We can save you so much** in price you can't afford to buy at retail. **Order in lots of 500** or more and let us ship by freight at lowest freight rate. **It will pay you.**

**The advantages of buying your gun of us are you get a lower price than you can get elsewhere. You get the highest grade No. 1 standard tested guns. Every gun is carefully tested and targeted before it leaves our hands, and is fully guaranteed.**

## THE WORLD RENOWNED W. W. GREENER EJECTOR GUN FOR $187.50.

This gun is one that sells everywhere at $250.00. You have never seen it listed at any less price.

The above illustration engraved from a photograph shows the W. W. Greener high grade ejector gun, made at Birmingham, England. The Greener gun is made as a fine gun, in fact, is the highest development of the sporting gun in every particular. Workmanship and material are the very best. The ejector gun only throws out the shell that is fired or both shells when both are fired. Breech action is self-fastening, the lock is self-locking and the extractor is self-ejecting. Beautiful in design and finish. The Greener gun is so well known that it is not necessary to mention all its superior qualities.

No. 822. No. 3 quality Greener ejector, hammerless, finely engraved, fine Damascus barrels, treble wedge, fastening self-acting ejector, has all the improvements of the higher cost guns but made plainly finished, still a high grade gun; 12 gauge, 30 inch barrel, 7¼ to 8 lbs., our special price..........................$187.50

## THE FACILE PRINCEPS GREENER FOR $93.75,

A gun that wholesales at $125.00.

The above illustration engraved from a photograph shows the Facile Princeps grade, the most popular gun of the Greeners. More of them are used by noted trap shooters and sportsmen than any other high grade gun in the world. They are made for downright hard service and are long range close shooters.

No. 823. Facile Princeps, quality Greener, cross bolt, treble wedge, best hammerless gun made, best material, neatly finished, well balanced, light and strong, fine Damascus barrels, matted ribs and a good one. Made especially to order for trap shooting; no better shooting gun at any price. 12 gauge, 30 inch barrel, 7¼ to 8¼ lbs., our special price..........................$93.75

### FORESTER GRADE GREENER FOR $69.95.

No. 824. No. 6 Greener Forester Hammerless gun, Anson & Deely action, treble wedge fast, cross bolted. Matted ribs, laminated barrels, finely finished, well-balanced, choke bored, made for service and a good shooter. The value of these guns is in the barrels and lock work which are made specially for us. They shoot just as well as the higher priced ones and wear just as long. 12 gauge, 30 inch barrels, 7½ to 8 lbs., our special price..........................$69.95

## $27.50 BUYS A $50.00 HAMMERLESS SHOT GUN.

We offer you at $27.50 a hammerless shot gun which can not be duplicated in any market for less than $50.00. This gun is made expressly for us by the Crescent Fire Arms Co. under patents controlled by Charles Lancaster. We guarantee this gun equal to any gun on the market, regardless of price. There is no better shooting gun made at any price. Our sale of these guns has been enormous, and from everywhere we are receiving the most flattering testimonials. We are able to offer the special price of $27.50 by reason of having contracted with the manufacturers for the entire product, and on the basis of the actual cost to produce the gun with only the manufacturer's profit added, and the result is we can offer you a strictly high grade hammerless gun for less money than your retail dealer can buy in quantities. These guns are made by a concern whose reputation for the manufacture of high grade guns ought to be a sufficient guarantee for their quality. Every gun is warranted in every respect, and if not found perfectly satisfactory it may be returned to us, and your money will be cheerfully refunded. Our terms are very liberal. Send us $3.00 as a guarantee of good faith, and we will send you the gun by express C. O. D., subject to examination. You can examine the gun at the express office, and if found perfectly satisfactory pay the express agent the balance, $24.50, and express charges, and the gun is yours. A discount of 3 per cent. will be allowed if cash in full accompanies your order, in which case $26.65 pays for the gun, and you will also save 25 cents to 50 cents express charges on return of money to us. You take no risk for if the gun does not suit you in every way you can return it at our expense, and we will cheerfully refund your money.

### No. 825. ORDER BY NUMBER.

The above is a picture of our special $27.50 gun, engraved from a photograph, and will give you some idea of its general appearance. There is no better gun made. This gun is known as the genuine Triumph hammerless double barrel shot gun, manufactured by the Crescent Fire Arms Co., under patents owned by Charles Lancaster. Everything up to date, the latest and best full choke bored, no stronger shooter made, treble bolt, strongest made, long strong extension rib, matted rib, 12 gauge only, 12 gauge with 28, 30 or 32-inch barrels as desired, weight 7 to 8 lbs. Be sure to state weight and length of barrel wanted. Barrels very finest quality twist, latest and strongest

top snap break, very fine checkered and imported Italian walnut stock, patent fore end, line engravings, diamond matted rib, full choke bored, fancy rubber butt plate. This gun is simple in construction and superior in workmanship. It has rebounding locks and the barrels can be taken off and put on again without cocking the gun. These two features will commend the gun. The tipping of the barrels and cocking of the gun is done as easily as on a hammer gun, which is a great point in favor of the Triumph. Most hammerless guns are hard to open and put together. The automatic safety bolt is so constructed behind the lever that the gun is always safe when the word "safe" is exposed, and by pushing the safety bolt forward it is ready to shoot. The lugs are steel and swing on a circle, which makes the gun open and close easily. The extension rib is L shaped, which grips the frame firmly and makes a strong lock. The frame is forged, which is far superior to case or malleable iron frames. The Triumph is a strictly high grade American gun, manufactured in this country under valuable patents owned by Charles Lancaster, who stands at the head of English gun makers. It is bored and guaranteed to shoot hard and close. Every gun is tested as to its shooting qualities before leaving the factory, and the target of each gun is on the tag attached to the gun when you get it.

While we have figured the price of every gun as low as possible, figured on the basis of a very small percentage of profit added to the actual cost in large quantities under season contract with the manufacturers, we believe there is no gun offered of so great a value for $27.50 as our Triumph, and we are extremely anxious to receive your order because we know it will lead to many more orders from your neighborhood.

## THE CELEBRATED ITHACA HAMMERLESS GUN FOR $26.00.

For the first time we are able to offer the Ithaca hammerless gun at $27.50, a gun which has retailed at $50.00 and upwards and wholesaled at $35.00 to $40.00. Understand our terms are alike on all guns. On receipt of $3.00 we will send any gun by express C. O. D. subject to examination. You can examine it at the express office,

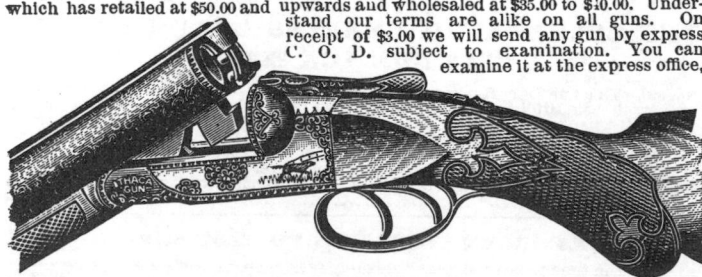

and if found perfectly satisfactory and exactly as represented, pay the express agent the balance and charges, and the gun is yours.

The illustration is engraved from a photograph and will give you some idea of the general appearance of the Ithaca Hammerless gun. This gun is too well known to require comment from us. It is bored for nitro and black powders. Barrels can be put on and taken off same as hammer gun whether gun is cocked or not. Locks are rebounding, automatic safety, can be changed to independent by a touch of the thumb for rapid firing. All have pistol grip, all have extension rib, all choke bored, all finely finished and greatly improved for the season of 1896. All have matted ribs. The stub twist barrels used on these guns are better than laminated or cheap Damascus barrels. 30 inch barrels, 12 gauge, weigh 7½ to 8½ pounds. 32 inch weighs 7¾ to 9½ lbs.

No. 826. Fine English stub twist barrels, American walnut stock, pistol grip checkered, line engraving, 10, 12, or 16 gauge, our price..............$26.00

No. 827. A better finished gun, nicely engraved, decorated, imported walnut stock, 10, 12 or 16 gauge, our special price.........................$32.45

No. 828. Fine Damascus steel barrels, English walnut stock, pistol grip, checkered, neat engravings, 10, 12 or 16 gauge, our price.....................$36.82

**Look at our No. 850 gun at $6.68.** No. 851 at $8.69. No. 854 at $10.75. No. 855 at $12.95. Our T. Barker at $11.85 and $16.35. Our Greener action No. 859 at $17.90. No such bargains were ever offered us. In addition consider our liberal $3.00 in advance, C. O. D. terms of shipment and our 3% discount for cash in full.

**Our stock is immense, but we may sometimes be out of the exact weight or length of barrel. If you will give us the privilege of sending the next in length or weight it will insure the prompt filling of your order.**

# THE NEW ITHACA EJECTOR HAMMERLESS GUN.

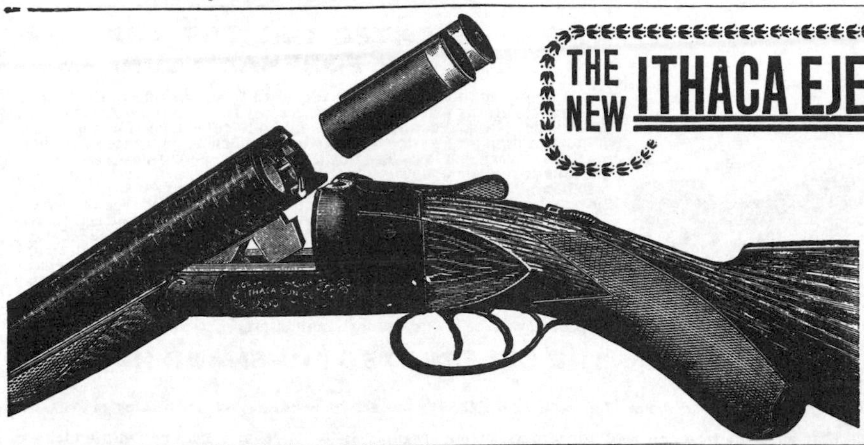

THE ABOVE ILLUSTRATION is engraved from a photograph of "THE NEW ITHACA EJECTOR HAMMERLESS GUN" and will give you an idea of the appearance of this gun. The Ithaca Gun is so well known that it is unnecessary for us to make a full description of every detail. "The New Ejector" in addition to having all of the advantages of the Ithaca Hammerless Gun, has the "New Automatic Ejector" made expressly for this gun and is more simple than any other ejector on the market. That it works direct on the Extractor and is all contained in the lug, makes it less complicated, and therefore less likely to get out of order. It is all made of tool steel, and is not only more durable, but is stronger and more positive than the other ejectors, which are made more complicated.

**No. 828½.** With fine English stub twist barrels, with checkered walnut pistol grip stock, 10 or 12 gauge, 30 or 32 in. barrels. Our special price........................................**$36.00**

## THE NEW ITHACA HAMMER GUN FOR $19.95.

This is the late improved model for 1896, manufactured by the Ithaca Gun Co., of Ithaca, New York.

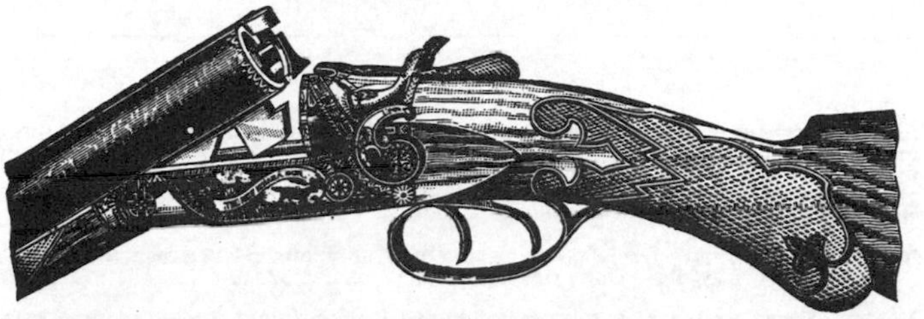

The above illustration is engraved from a photograph, and will give you some idea of the appearance of this gun. Made of the best materials, simplest and best locks, low hammers, top lever swinging over them when cocked; self compensating, taking up wear at every point, never gets loose and shaky, matted rib and all have walnut pistol grip, stock checkered, case hardened lock plates and blued mountings. All guns are choke bored to shoot the closest pattern. No extra charge for 10 gauge over 12 gauge, or a heavy weight over a light weight. Only the best English twist and Damascus steel barrels used. All have rubber butt plate, top lever, extension rib, all are choke bored, every gun warranted, and all have matted rib.

No. 829. Fine English stub twist barrels, American Walnut stock, pistol grip, checkered, 10, 12 or 16 gauge, neatly engraved, our price........................$19.95

No. 830. Fine Damascus steel barrels, selected American walnut stock, pistol grip, checkered, 10, 12 or 16 gauge, engraved, our price........................$30.47

10 gauge, length of barrel, 30 and 32 inches.
12 gauge, length of barrel, 30 and 32 inches.
12 gauge, weighs 7¼ to 9 lbs.
10 gauge, weighs 8½ to 11 lbs.
16 gauge, weighs 6½ to 7 lbs.

No better shooting gun at any price. The best buck gun. Heavy 10 gauge guns are bored for buck shot when you state in your order for buck shot. For long range shooting and big game a 10 gauge Ithaca gun has no superior,

## THE CELEBRATED REMINGTON NEW BREECH LOADING DOUBLE BARREL SHOT GUN FOR 22.50.

For the first time we are able to offer you the latest model Remington shot gun at this price. It will be sent to any address by express, C. O. D., subject to examination, on receipt of $3, as a guarantee of good faith. 3 per cent. discount allowed if cash in full accompanies your order. We hope you will compare our prices with those of other concerns, and thus be convinced of the wonderful saving by placing your orders in our hands.

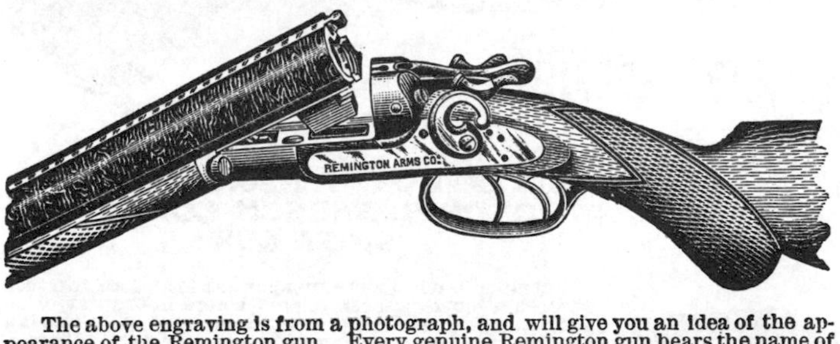


The above engraving is from a photograph, and will give you an idea of the appearance of the Remington gun. Every genuine Remington gun bears the name of the maker. They are manufactured by the Remington Arms Co., of Ilion, N. Y. Every gun is covered by a most binding guarantee, and if any piece or part gives out by reason of defective material or workmanship it will be replaced free of charge. The 10 gauge Remington is known as a long range duck and trap gun, and there is no better shooting gun made at any price. We offer you the very latest improved model, top lever, extension rib, with rebounding bar locks, large head strikers, patent fore-end. All have pistol grip and all are choke bored. Every gun is carefully and rigidly tested before leaving the factory, and satisfaction guaranteed. Lengths, 12 gauge, 30 and 32 inches. Weights, 10 gauge, 8½ to 10 lbs. Lengths, 10 gauge 30 and 32 inches. Weight, 12 gauge, 7¾ to 9 lbs. The barrels of the Remington guns are choke bored on the best principles and the parts are interchangeable. Only the best material and workmanship are used in the construction of these guns. All have matted ribs and circular hammers.

No. 831. Fine decarbonized steel barrels, walnut stock, 10 or 12 gauge, pistol grip, just as good a shooter as the Damascus, list price........................$19.56

No. 832. Twist barrels, selected walnut stock, 10 or 12 gauge, pistol grip, list price........................$22.00

No. 833. Damascus pattern, steel barrels, selected walnut stock, pistol grip, 10, or 12 gauge, list price........................$23.75

**We Carry a Full Line of Reloading Implements and Hunter's Supplies.**

## THE CELEBRATED REMINGTON HAMMERLESS EJECTOR DOUBLE BARREL SHOT GUN.

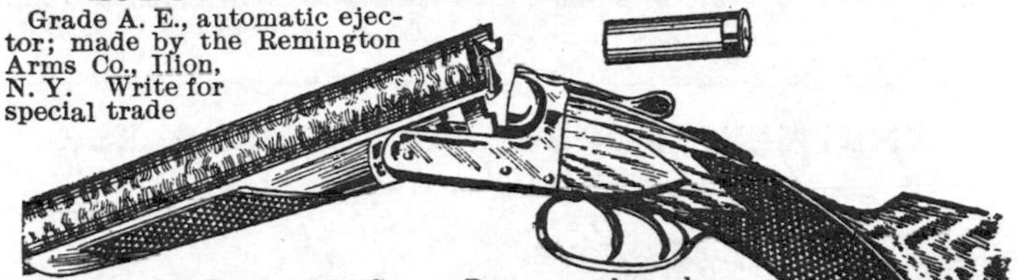

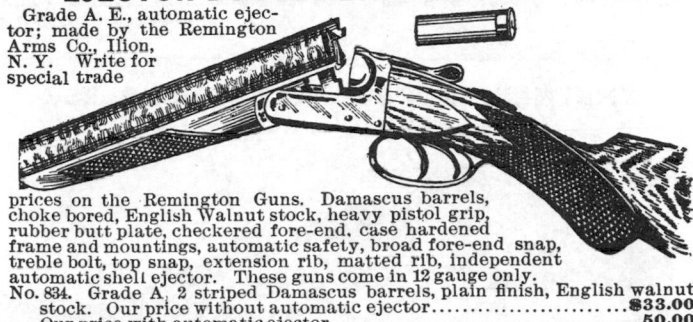

Grade A. E., automatic ejector; made by the Remington Arms Co., Ilion, N. Y. Write for special trade prices on the Remington Guns. Damascus barrels, choke bored, English Walnut stock, heavy pistol grip, rubber butt plate, checkered fore-end, case hardened frame and mountings, automatic safety, broad fore-end snap, treble bolt, top snap, extension rib, matted rib, independent automatic shell ejector. These guns come in 12 gauge only.

No. 834. Grade A, 2 striped Damascus barrels, plain finish, English walnut stock. Our price without automatic ejector........................**$33.00**
Our price with automatic ejector........................**50.00**

No. 835. Grade B, fine 3 stripe Damascus barrels, line engraving, fine English walnut stock. Our price without automatic ejector........................**$50.00**
Our price with automatic ejector........................**70.00**
These guns come in 28, 30 and 32 inch barrels, and weigh 6¾ to 8¾ lbs. Drop 2¼ to 3⅛ inches.

## THE IMPROVED NEW BAKER DOUBLE BARREL BREECH LOADING SHOT GUN FOR $19.85.

We guarantee our prices below all others.

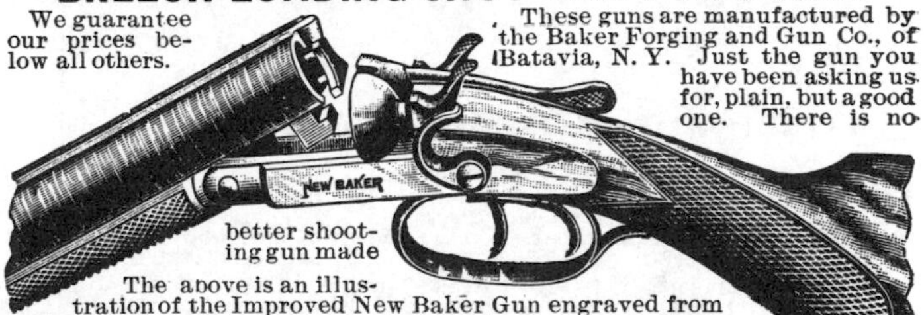


These guns are manufactured by the Baker Forging and Gun Co., of Batavia, N. Y. Just the gun you have been asking us for, plain, but a good one. There is no better shooting gun made

The above is an illustration of the Improved New Baker Gun engraved from a photograph. The makers claim for this gun even pattern, powerful shooter, and equal to any gun in the market for durability and simplicity. It has English steel twist barrels, extension rib, checkered pistol grip, fancy English walnut stock, rubber butt plate, low circular hammers, solid strikers, rebounding locks, top snap action, interchangeable parts, choke bored unless otherwise ordered. No better shooting gun made at any price. A plain, well balanced, neatly finished gun, made of the best material, compensating fore-end, cannot get loose and shaky in hinge joint, in fact, just the gun for business and at a moderate price. Every gun is fully warranted. All have matted ribs.

No. 836. Regular $30.00 grade, 12 gauge, 30 and 32 inch barrel, 7¼ to 8½ lbs. Our special price........................**$18.65**
Ten gauge, 30 and 32 inch barrel, 8½ to 10½ lbs. Our price........................**18.65**

## THE CELEBRATED BAKER HAMMERLESS GUN

With positive automatic block to firing pin, cross bolted, no better shooting gun made at any price, every gun fully warranted. Bored for nitro or black powder.

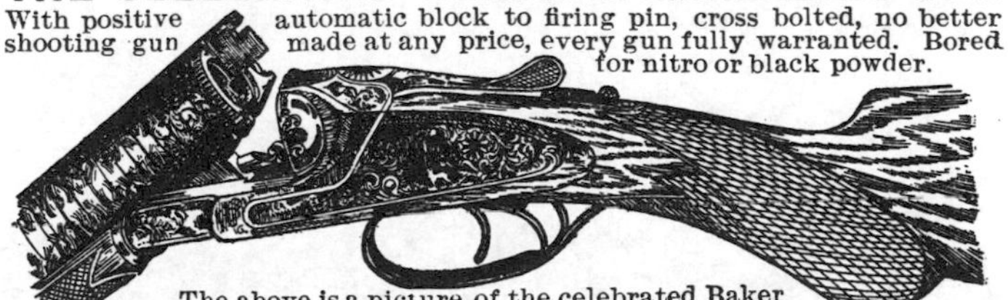

The above is a picture of the celebrated Baker Hammerless Gun engraved from a photograph, and will give you some idea of its general appearance. An accidental discharge of either barrel or simultaneous firing of both is rendered impossible. There is no condition, position or situation by which this can be discharged other than by a pull of the trigger. Gun is locked by solidly cross bolting extension ribs. There is no retracting bolt, in consequence of which the frame is not cut away but is left intact, solid and strong. Beautiful in design and finish, wide breech, made for downright hard service. Not liable to get out of order. One of the best American guns on the market and stands the racket of nitro powder every time. 10 gauge same price as 12 gauge.

No. 837. Fine Damascus barrels, beautifully engraved, finely finished, equal to many $150.00 grade guns. 12 gauge, 28, 30 or 32 inch barrels, weight 7¼ to 9½ lbs. 16 gauge, 30 and 32 inch barrels, 8¾ to 10½ lbs........................**$57.95**

No. 828. Grade "A." Fine four blade Damascus barrels, beautifully engraved, choke bored for best possible shooting, every gun warranted, handsome, well made and durable, 12 gauge, 28, 30, or 32 inch barrels, 7¼ to 9 lbs. 10 gauge, 8 to 10 lbs. Our price........................**$36.25**

No. 839. Finest twist barrels, neatly engraved, choke bored for best possible shooting, every gun warranted perfect and a good shooter, 12 gauge, 30 or 32 inch barrels, 7¼ to 8½ lbs. 10 gauge, 30 and 32 inch barrels, 8 to 10 lbs. Our special price........................**$31.75**

No. 840.

## THE CELEBRATED EJECTOR AND NON-EJECTOR FOREHAND GUN.

We call your attention to the Forehand gun as one of the best in the market at any price. Manufactured by the Forehand Arms Co., at Worcester, Mass., a concern whose enviable reputation for the manufacture of high grade guns ought to be a sufficient guarantee for their quality. Every gun is covered by a most binding guarantee, and if any piece or part give out by reason of defective material or workmanship it will be replaced free of charge. We offer you this gun at $33.00. It will be sent by express C. O. D., subject to examination upon receipt of $3.00. You can examine it at the express office, and if found perfectly satisfactory and exactly as represented, pay the express agent the balance, $30.00, and express charges, and the gun is yours. 3 per cent discount allowed if cash in full accompanies your order. Do not forget our cash discount. In figuring the price of anything in this book where there is a discount allowed it should be taken into consideration, and when so considered you can be sure that no dealer, let him be wholesaler or importer, will meet our net cash manufacturer to consumer prices.

## THE CELEBRATED FOREHAND HAMMER GUN.

**$22.90 Buys a $40.00 Gun** and remember our terms are liberal, 3 per cent discount for cash or **C. O. D.** subject to examination on receipt of **$3.00.** Balance and express charges payable at express office.

The above illustration engraved from a photograph shows you as near as a picture can the appearance of our regular $40.00 Forehand hammer gun which we are selling at $22.90. This gun is made by the old and reliable Forehand Arms Co., at Worcester, Mass., which is a guarantee for its quality. **No better shooting gun made at any price.** Imported Italian Stock, Extension rib of double strength, straight and matted, 12 or 16 gauge as desired, 30 or 32 inch barrel, 7½ to 8½ lbs.

No. 840.   Our special offer price with finest Twist Barrels......................$21.00 | No. 841 with finest Damascus Barrels...........................................$24.00

No other house offers such a bargain. Order by number.

## THE NEW FOREHAND HAMMERLESS DOUBLE GUN.

The above illustration engraved from a photograph will give you an idea of the appearance of the Forehand gun. This gun has rebounding locks and the barrels can be taken off and put

on again without cocking the gun, and when cocked the hammers may be let down gradually and without the full force of the blow. It is simple in construction, having very many less parts than any other hammerless gun. No better shooting gun at any price. Easily tipped and cocked, bored for the best possible shooting, small bore for nitro or black powder.

No. 842.   Finest twist barrels, no engraving but finely finished, 12 gauge, 30 or 32 inch barrels, 7½ to 8½ lbs.   Our price.............................................$33.00

No. 843.   Fine Damascus barrels, dark finished Italian walnut stock, full pistol grip, checkered grip and fore end, engraved action mounting, handsome, well made and durable. Every gun warranted a good shooter.  12 gauge, 30 inch barrels, 7½ to 8½ lbs.   Our price................................................$37.50

**If you want to buy anything you do not see in this catalogue, first refer to the complete index in the back of the book, and if you don't find it mentioned there, write us for prices, before you buy elsewhere.**

## FOREHAND AUTOMATIC EJECTOR GUNS.

No. 844.   Finest twist barrels, our price...........................$50.00
No. 845.   Fine Damascus barrels, our price..........................55.00
No. 846.   Extra fine Damascus barrels, extra fine finish, beautifully engraved, our price.............................................$75.00

Made in 12 gauge only, 30 inch barrels, 7 to 8 lbs. The Forehand gun is made for downright hard service and is a first-class gun in every particular.

**If we don't get your trade on Bicycles, it is because you have no trade to give. Our terms match the grade of the wheels and the prices, in that they are the best ever offered.**

# ...DAVIS HAMMER GUN...

No. 849.

## $17.90 BUYS A $30.00 DOUBLE BARREL BREECH LOADING SHOT GUN.

A genuine Davis American-made gun for $17.90. No such a bargain has ever been offered before in the way of an American double barrel breech-loading shot gun. This is a genuine Davis gun, warranted in every respect. There is no better shooting gun made, no stronger gun made.

The above illustration is engraved from a photograph and will give you some idea of the appearance of this gun. It comes in 12 gauge only, 30 or 32 inch barrels, finest grade twist, weight, 7½ to 8½ lbs. Bar rebounding locks, strongest and most simple lock made, double bolt, so constructed and and so strong that the gun can never wear loose re-enforced breech, patent applied only on the Davis gun. The barrels are double thickness over shell chamber, fine selected imported walnut stock, fancy checkered full pistol grip, fancy rubber butt plates, latest style low circular hammers, best and latest top snap break, strong, long extension rib, large firing pin, best automatic shell extractor,

case hardened and engraved mountings, choke bored. Every gun is tested to target before leaving the factory, and for a perfect target and penetration gun there is no better gun made. At our special price of $17.90 there is no American gun made that will compare with it. We will allow you a discount of 3 per cent. if cash in full accompanies your order, or the gun will be sent C. O. D. subject to examination on receipt of $3.00 as a guarantee of good faith, balance and express charges payable at express office.

**WHEN YOU ARE IN CHICAGO, YOU WILL FIND NO MORE HEARTY WELCOME ANYWHERE THAN IN OUR HOUSE. YOU CAN CHECK YOUR BUNDLES HERE, GET INFORMATION ABOUT THE CITY, AND MAKE YOURSELF AT HOME.**

## THE DAVIS HAMMERLESS GUN.

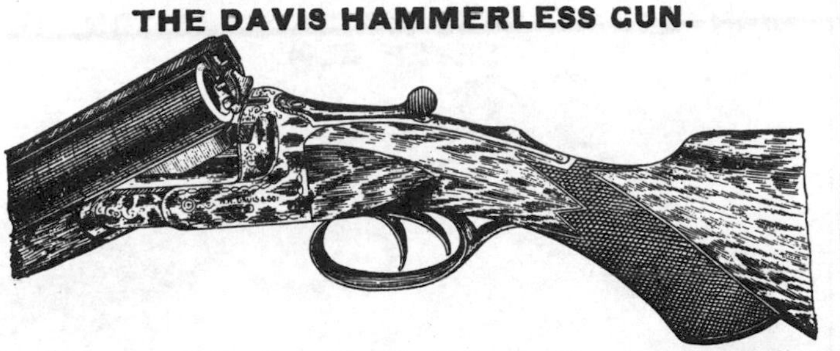

No. 847½. Best quality Twist Barrels, Choke Bored, extended matted rib, double bolt, one on Lug of Barrel and square Cross Bolt through extended rib, patent fore end. Full pistol grip stock, stock and tip checked. All parts nicely engraved. Cocks by the opening of barrels, and by the action of closing them the Sears and Triggers are both blocked by a positive motion, thus avoiding all danger from jarring off or premature pulling off, by trigger or otherwise, and is absolutely safe. Safety can be used as automatic or independent, a very desireable feature for rapid firing. Gun can be put together or taken apart with hammers in any position, and without any extra operation. Hammers may also be let down without snapping, which is always preferable.

Price, with fine twist barrels, American walnut stock, 12 guage, 28 to 32 inches long, 7 to 8½ lbs....... $23.95

## THE HOLLENBECK OR SYRACUSE HAMMER-LESS GUN.

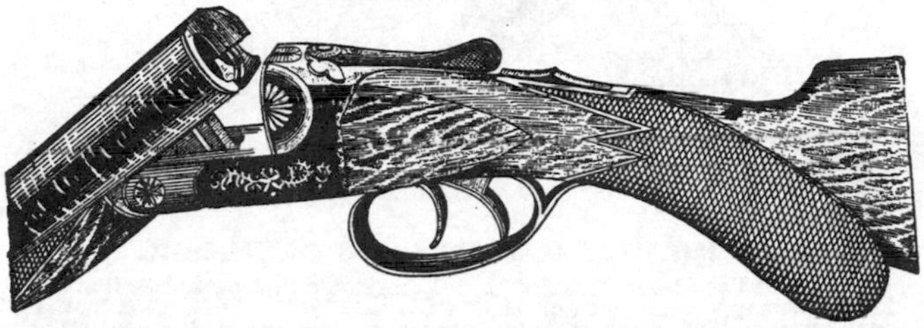

No. 848¾. The hollenbeck Hammerless Gun made by the Syracuse Arms Co. is cross bolted, top lever, matted extended ribs, pistol grip, patent fore-end automatic safety catch, bored for nitro or black powder, choke bored, well made and durable, good shooter.

Fine Twist Barrel, 12 gauge, 6¾ to 8½ lbs. Each....... $27.00

No. 848½. Three Blade Damascus Barrels....... 35.80

## THE NEW S. R. & CO. HAMMERLESS DOUBLE BARREL SHOT GUN.

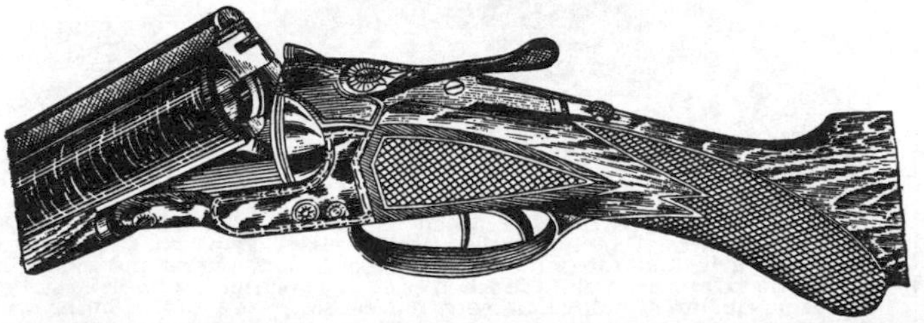

We offer at $35.00 a gun that sells regularly at $65.00. We offer at $29.00 a gun that sells regularly at $50.00. We guarantee it equal to any gun in the market, and there is no better gun made at any price.

The above illustration engraved from a photograph shows the general appearance of the **Sears, Roebuck & Co.** high grade hammerless shot gun with all the latest and best features of the high priced guns, and the latest model for the season of 1897. Made of best material, handsome in design and finish, well balanced, easy booking—the weight of the barrel doing the work; for beauty of outline it has no superior at any price. Top lever, cross bolted, pistol grip, English walnut, patent compensating snap fore-end, case hardened lock plates and action, finely matted tapering rib, wide heavy breech, narrow at muzzle, neatly engraved, bored for nitro or black powders, will shoot either kind, good at trap or in the field, in fact a first-class all around gun for a small amount of money, no better shooting gun at any price. Come in two grades only below mentioned, the same in design and finish, the only difference being in the grade of barrel stock and finish. The twist barrels are just as good as the Damascus. All choke bored unless otherwise ordered. Every gun tested, and target accompanies each gun.

No. 847. Fine Damascus steel barrels, 12 gauge, 30 inch barrels, 7 to 8½ lbs., our price....... $35.00

No. 848. Finest laminated twist steel barrels, 12 gauge, 30 inch barrels, 7 to 8½ lbs., our price....... $29.00

## LEFAUCHEAUX ACTION BREECH LOADER,

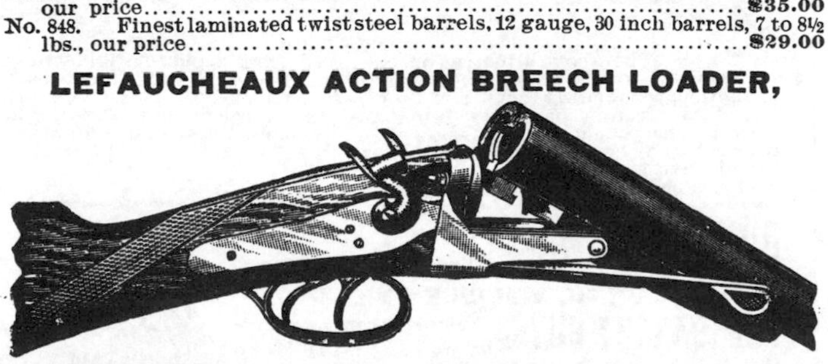

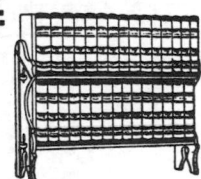

No. 850½. The Lefaucheaux Action Double Breech Loading Shot Gun, decarbonized blued steel barrel, back action locks, checkered grip, bottom lever and shell ejector.

12 gauge, 30 and 32 inch barrels, 7½ to 8¼ lbs....... $5.65

10 gauge, 30 and 32 inch barrels, 8½ to 9¼ lbs....... 5.90

## OUR LINE OF IMPORTED DOUBLE BARREL SHOT GUNS.

Our line of imported guns is very extensive and embraces the products of some of the best European makers. We recognize no competition in this line, and a comparison of our prices with those of other houses will convince you that we have none. We aim to handle only thoroughly first-class goods, guns that will stand service and give the best satisfaction, and every gun we offer is warranted in every respect.

In our line of imported guns we would call your attention to our $6.68 Double Barrel Breech loader, our T. Barker at $11.95 our special Greener action guns, and our high grade machine guns. We are in a position to make you prices on this class of goods at least 50 per cent. below any competition, and if you will favor us with your order we know you will be so well pleased that you will not only give us your future orders but recommend our house to your friends.

## A $10.00 GUN FOR $6.68.

We offer you the celebrated Lefaucheaux action double barrel shot gun at $6.68, a better grade than is generally sold in this make, and yet the price is lower than the price made by others.

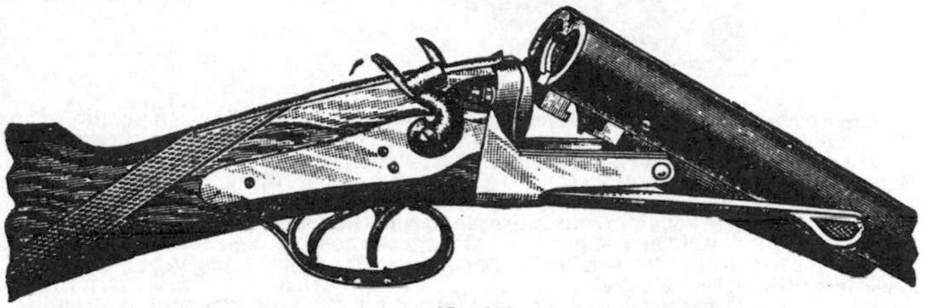

No. 850.

No. 850. The celebrated Lafaucheaux action, no stronger action made, guaranteed the best gun of this make in the market, double barrels, blued decarbonized steel barrels, back action lock, checkered grip, bottom lever, automatic shell ejector. 30 or 32 inch barrels, 12 gauge, weight, 7½ to 8¾ lbs. Our special steel barrels, back action lock with case hardened mountings, checkered grip, bottom lever, automatic shell ejector, 30 or 32 inch barrels, 12 gauge weight 7½ to 8¾ lbs. Our special price....... $6.68

10 gauge, weight 8½ to 9½ lbs., our special price....... $6.95

16 gauge, 30 and 32 inch barrels, our special price....... $7.45

Our 16 gauge is full checked Pistol Grip Stock and **Laminated Steel** barrels

## $8.69 BUYS A $15.00 GUN.

We offer you a high grade, imported, double-barrel shot gun at $8.69, which can not be duplicated elsewhere for less than $15.00. We import these guns direct. Every gun is a direct blow at monopoly. The result is you buy a gun for less than one-half the retail price, 40 per cent cheaper than other houses advertise, and far below the price your retail dealer pays. We guarantee every gun, and if you are not perfectly satisfied we will refund your money on return of the gun to us.

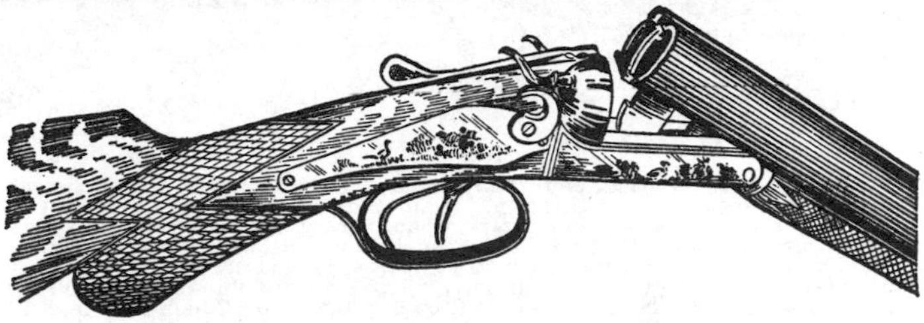

No. 851.

The above illustration, engraved from a photograph, will give you an idea of the appearance of this gun. Double barrel breech loader, top lever snap action, rebounding back action locks, walnut stock, case hardened lock plates and mountings, automatic shell ejector, twist barrels and fancy butt plate.

No. 851. 10 or 12 gauge as desired, 30 or 32 inch barrel, 7½ to 9 lbs., our special price....... $8.69

## THE CELEBRATED BELGIAN BACK ACTION GUN.

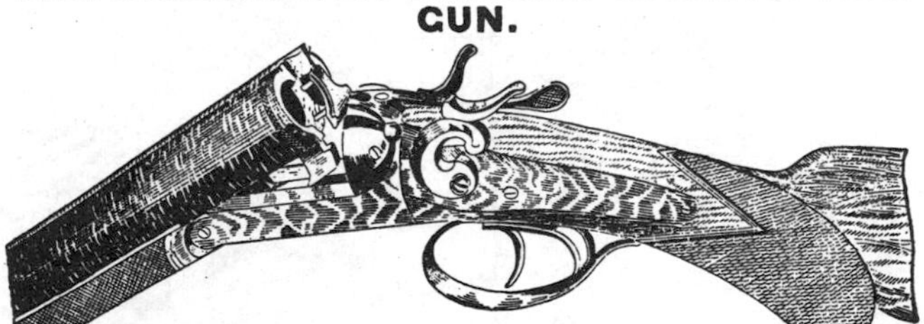

No. 851½. The Celebrated 'Belgian Back Action" Gun with top lever extension rib, **laminated finish** barrels, low circular hammers, patent snap fore-end, case hardened locks, checkered pistol grip, stock and fore-end with checked iron butt plate.

12 gauge, 30 and 32 inch barrels, 7½ to 8 lbs, our special price....... $7.95

10 gauge, 30 and 32 inch barrels, 9 to 10 lbs, our special price....... 8.25



See Pages 336 to 349.

**IN ORDERING GUNS, YOU MUST ALWAYS GIVE EXPLICIT INSTRUCTIONS. STATE GAUGE, LENGTH OF BARRELS AND WEIGHT WANTED. ALWAYS NOTING WHETHER OR NOT OUR DESCRIPTION STATES THAT THE GUN IS MADE AS YOU WANT IT.**

## THE CELEBRATED PIEPER COMBINED SHOT GUN AND RIFLE FOR $23.45.

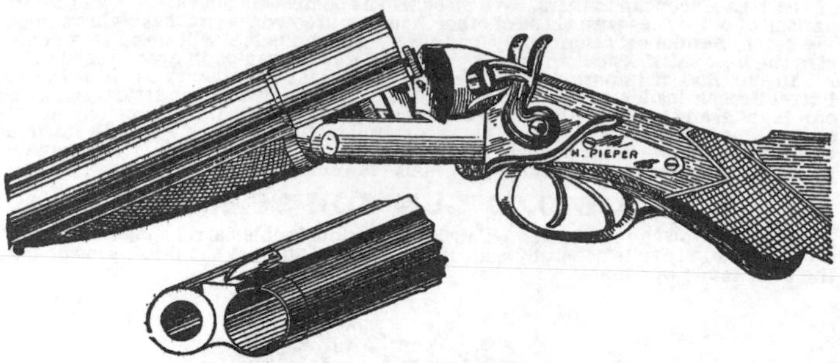


The above illustration, engraved from a photograph, will give you an idea of the appearance of the celebrated Pieper gun. The rifling is the best, in accuracy and range as good as the best rifle in the market. The boss gun to have around a farm. Pieper's patent re-inforced breech-loading shot gun and rifle combined, barrels side by side, having blued steel barrels and steel butt plate, sporting rear sight, sliding to right or left, white metal front knife sight, shot gun stock, checkered pistol grip. This is without doubt the handsomest, strongest shooting, and most accurate combined arm ever offered for sale in this or any other market. 12 gauge and 44 W. C. F. caliber, 30 inch barrels, weight about 8½ lbs. Our price........................$23.45

No. 852. Pieper's patent combined shot gun and rifle, 12 gauge and 38 caliber, 55 grains powder, 255 grains lead, barrels 30 inches. 8½ lbs., side lever, our price........................$23.45

No. 853. Pieper's combined shot gun and rifle, side snap lever, blued barrel, good on game up to 300 yds., accurate and reliable. 12 gauge, 32 W. F. C. caliber, 30-inch barrel, 8½ lbs., price........................$23.45

Understand these guns will be sent C. O. D., subject to examination, on receipt of $3.00, balance to be paid at the express office, and 3 per cent discount is allowed if cash in full accompanies your order.

## $10.75 BUYS A $20.00 GUN.

We offer at $10.75 a gun which cannot be duplicated elsewhere for less than $20.00.

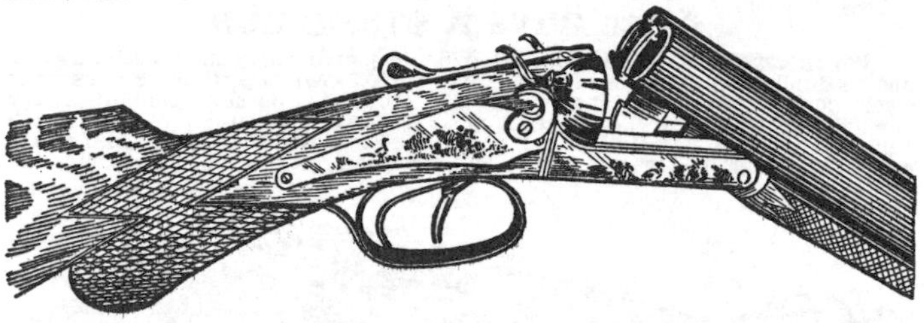

No. 854.

The above illustration, engraved from a photograph, will give you some idea of the appearance of this gun. It is made in Belgium by one of the largest and most reliable makers, is a thoroughly first-class arm in every respect, has fine laminated steel twist finished barrels, back action rebounding locks, low circular hammers, below line of sight, pistol grip, fancy rubber butt plate, patent fore end, beautifully checkered and finished, large firing pins, top snap break, comes in either 10 or 12 gauge, 30 or 32 inch barrels, and 7¼ to 9½ lbs. in weight.

Our special price........................$10.75

## $12.95 BUYS A REGULAR $25.00 GUN.

This gun is equal to guns that retail in many stores at $25.00. It is a strictly first-class imported Belgium gun and warranted in every respect. It is well made and a good shooter, and for penetration and pattern equal to many guns that sell at four and five times our price.

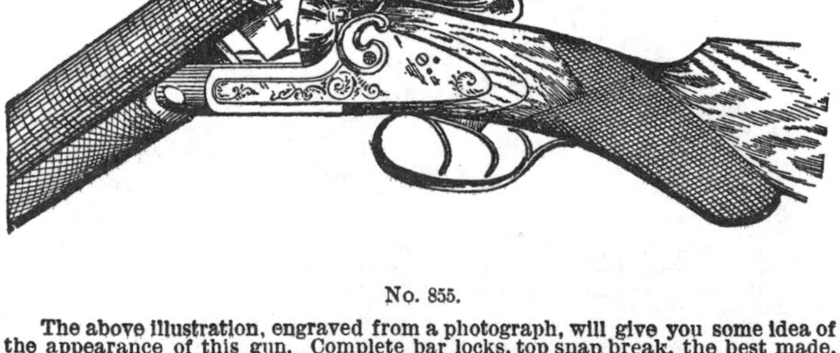

No. 855.

The above illustration, engraved from a photograph, will give you some idea of the appearance of this gun. Complete bar locks, top snap break, the best made, finest twist finished steel barrels, rebounding hammer, strong extension rib, pistol grip, selected walnut stock, finely checkered fore end, large strong firing pins, fancy rubber butt plate. 10 or 12 gauge as desired, 30 or 32 inch barrel as desired, weight 7¼ to 9½ lbs. The gun will be sent to any address on receipt of $3.00 as a guarantee of good faith; 3 per cent discount allowed if cash in full accompanies your order. Price........................$12.95

**THIS IS A BIG CATALOGUE**

**IF YOU WANT TO FIND YOUR WAY ABOUT IN IT, GET A GUIDE**

**THAT'S THE INDEX.**

## HIGH-GRADE, BELGIUM BACK ACTION, TOP LEVER GUN.

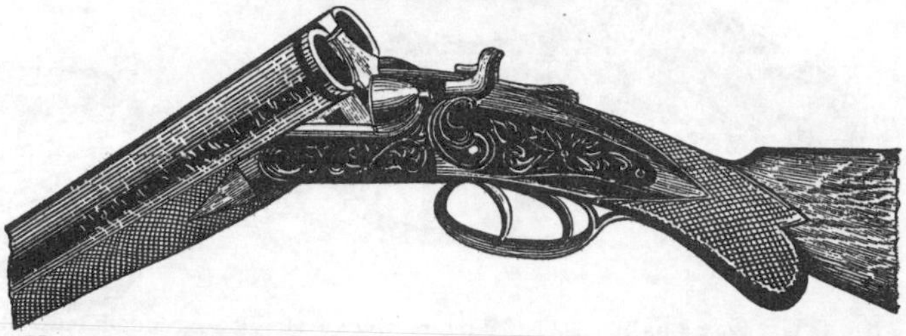

No. 854½. High Grade Belgium Back Action Double Barrel Breech Loader. Genuine laminated steel barrels, extra engraved lock plates and action, top lever, rebounding back action locks, pistol grip, walnut stock, checkered grip and fore end, extension matted rib, low circular hammers, out of line of sight, patent snap fore end, gun easily taken apart and put together again, barrels polished bright and smooth inside, well made and durable, a good shooter, safe and reliable; one of our "big sellers;" left barrel full choke bored, right barrel modified choke. Factory price, $20.00.

12 gauge, 30 or 32 inch, 7¼ to 8¾ pounds........................$11.85
10 gauge, 30 or 32 inch, 8¾ to 9¾ pounds........................12.25

## THE ENGRAVED BAR LOCK GUN.

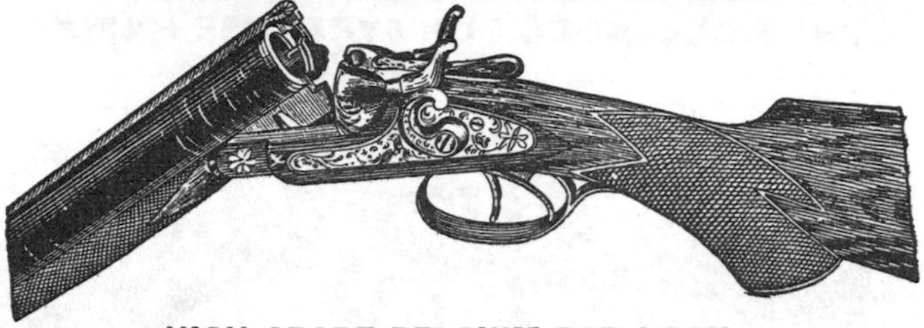

### HIGH-GRADE BELGIUM BAR LOCK.

No. 855¼. The above illustration taken from a photograph will give you an idea of the appearance of our **HIGH-GRADE BELGIUM BAR LOCK GUN**, with engraved locks, low circular hammers below line of sight, full checkered pistol grip stock and fore end, matted extension rib, fine twist barrels, Scott's patent top lever break and checked butt plate.

12 gauge, 30 or 32 inch barrels, price........................$13.70
10 gauge, 30 or 32 inch barrels, price........................13.95

## OUR PLAIN BAR LOCK GUN.

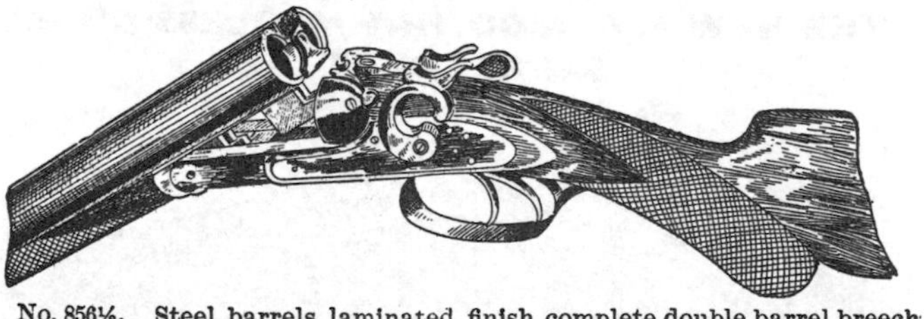

No. 856¼. Steel barrels laminated finish complete double barrel breech loader, top lever, rebounding bar locks, pistol grip, oil walnut stock, checkered grip and fore end, case-hardened lock plates and mountings, automatic extractor; a plain finished gun but a good one; solid head strikers, extension rib, low circular hammers, patent snap fore end. The browning will wear as long as on a genuine twist barrel, and they are just as good shooters, and sold by many as genuine laminated steel. Barrels polished bright and smooth inside. For a gun for ordinary use this gun will fill the bill every time.

12 gauge, 30 or 32 inch barrels, 7½ to 8¾ lbs., price........................$9.75
10 gauge, 30 or 32 inch barrels, 8¾ to 9¾ lbs., price........................9.95

## THE CELEBRATED THOMAS BARKER DOUBLE BARREL BREECH LOADING SHOT GUN FOR $12.95.

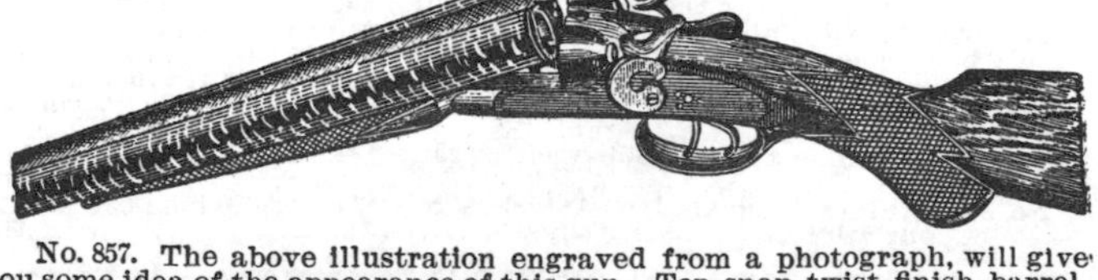

No. 857. The above illustration engraved from a photograph, will give you some idea of the appearance of this gun. Top snap twist finish barrel, bar action, rebounding locks, matted rib, full checkered, (P. G. stock) pistol grip stock, circular hammers, patent fore end, large firing pins, fancy butt plate, left barrel choked, extension rib, double bolt, a first-class gun in every respect. They come in 10, 12 and 16 gauge, (the price is the same). 30 or 32 inch barrels, and from 7¼ to 9¾ lbs.

Price each........................$11.95

**DON'T BUY WAISTS**

**...UNTIL YOU SEE OUR PRICES.**

**YOU CANNOT BUY** to better advantage anywhere in the world than from our catalogue. SEE THE ELEGANT LINE we show in our DRY GOODS DEPARTMENT.

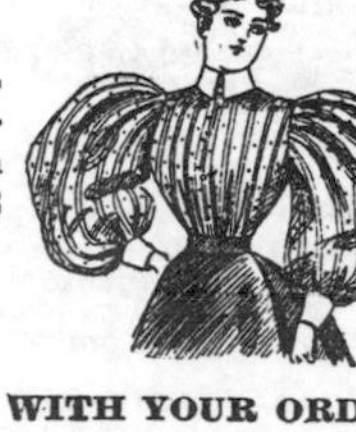

**THE MOST STYLISH GOODS.**

**THE LOWEST PRICES.**

YOUR GUN WILL DO YOU NO GOOD WITHOUT CARTRIDGES. ALWAYS INCLUDE WHAT AMMUNITION YOU WANT WITH YOUR ORDER. RELOADING TOOLS WILL BE NEEDED. WE HAVE EVERYTHING AT LOWEST PRICES.

### Damascus Finish Barrels, Top Snap, Bar Action, Matted Extension Rib. Circular Hammers, Highly Engraved, 10, 12 and 16 Gauges.

No. 858. We offer you at $16.35 a gun which cannot be duplicated in any retail store at even 50 per cent above our price. Remember there is 3% discount if cash in full accompanies your order, and any gun will be sent C. O. D. subject to examination on receipt of $3.00.

The above illustration engraved from a photograph will give you but a little idea of the beautiful appearance of this gun. It has Royal Damascus finished barrels, with top lever action, matted extension rib, automatic ejector, beautifully engraved bar locks, inlaid with silver plated hunting dog which adds greatly to its appearance. Has low circular rebounding hammers below line of sight, full checkered pistol grip stock

**No. 858.**

and Deeley & Edge patent fore-end and rubber butt plate. This line is elaborately decorated, engraved and finished by hand. We furnish in either 10, 12, or 16 gauge; 10 and 12 gauge come in 30 and 32 inch barrels as desired, 16 gauge in 28 or 30 inch; 10 gauge weighs 8¼ to 9½ lbs., 12 gauge weighs 7¼ to 8½ lbs.. and 16 gauge weighs 6¾ to 7¾ lbs. Our special price in any size.... ...................................................$16.35

## THIS CELEBRATED GREENER ACTION BREECH LOADING SHOT GUN FOR $17.90.

This gun is one we have imported from Europe at a price which enables us for the first time to place it on the market at $17.90, less than half the price charged by retail dealers for guns of this quality. You will find this gun equal to anything on the market at any price. There is no better shooting gun made.

No. 858. This gun has top snap break, the best break made, very beautiful Damascus finished barrel, bar action rebounding locks, fancy pistol grip, Deely & Edge fore end, treble bolt cross bolt, extension rib, the celebrated Greener cross bolt with engraved locks and mountings, nicely checkered stock and fore end, left barrel modified choke. right barrel cylinder bored, double bolt and lock, fancy cap on pistol grip, rubber butt plate. Gun comes in 10 or 12 gauge, 30 or 32 inch barrels. Ten gauge weighs 8½ to 9¾ lbs., 12 gauge weighs 7¼ to 8½ lbs.

**No. 859.**

We cannot recommend this gun too highly, and we are extremely anxious to receive your order for one of them, for we know it will mean the sale of many more. There is nothing in the market at anything like the price. Under our system of one small profit direct from the manufacturer to the consumer, you will own this gun at less money than your local dealer can buy in quantities.

### OUR $19.90 BARGAIN.

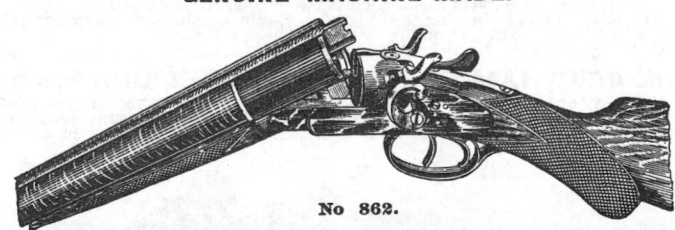

**No. 861**

The above illustration is engraved from a photograph, and shows one of the finest guns made in Belgium and a gun that is sold in this market at two and three times our special offer price. Under the old system of handling guns it costs about as much to sell them as it does to make them, but we change this and you pay the actual cost to produce with only one small profit added. We guarantee every gun to be exactly as we represent it, and if you find it is not at any time you may return it to us and we will refund your money.

This beautiful machine-made gun has fine laminated steel barrels, top snap break, rebounding bar locks, solid plungers, low circular hammers, tapered and extended matted rib, double bolt, snap fore end, English walnut pistol grip, stock checkered and engraved, rubber butt plate, left barrel full choked, right barrel modified choked, comes in 10 or 12 gauge as desired, and 30 or 32 inch barrel as desired. 12 gauge weigh 8 to 9 lbs., 10 gauge weigh 9 to 10 lbs. Price...........$19.90

## PIEPER'S PATENT, MODIFIED DIANA PATTERN.
### GENUINE MACHINE MADE.

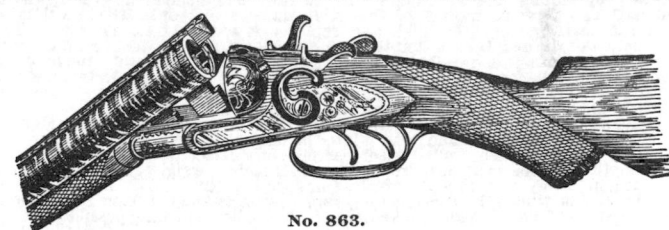

**No 862.**

The barrels are screwed in the breach; they remain perfectly round and straight, and are not pinched together, as is the case in the old way of manufacture. The lumps and the steel breach are in one solid piece thus avoiding, lumps becoming loose.

The barrels being independent of each other, the expansion is even, and the penetration and shooting qualities in general is thereby increased. Barrels are choked after the most approved system and are flat at the breech.

This gun has the Scott patent lever top snap, genuine laminated barrels, matted extension rib, improved patent snap fore end, rebounding bar locks, low circular hammers below line of sight, full checkered pistol grip stock, rubber butt plate, left barrel full choke bored, right barrel modified. The peculiar construction of this gun positively prevents it from getting loose and shaky and makes it especially adapted to nitro or smokeless powders. We furnish them in either 10, 12, 16 or 20 gauge as follows:

| | |
|---|---|
| 10 gauge, 30 or 32-inch barrels, weight 8½ to 10 lbs., price............. | $17.90 |
| 12 gauge, 30 or 32-inch barrels, weight 7¼ to 8¾ lbs., price.............. | 17.30 |
| 16 gauge, 28 or 30-inch barrels, weight 6¼ to 7 lbs., price............. | 17.65 |
| 20 gauge, 28 or 30-inch barrels, weight 6 to 6½ lbs., price............. | 17.80 |

NOTE—There are cheap imitations of this gun on the market with breech ends of barrels painted instead of being made separate and barrels screwed into the blued breech—LOOK OUT FOR THEM! OURS ARE THE GENUINE.

NOTE—We can furnish any of these guns in Damascus barrels at $5.00 extra.

## OUR GENUINE ENGLISH MACHINE MADE GUN.

**No. 863.**

After much hard study and careful investigation, we have succeeded in obtaining a gun for all purposes, which combines the fine material and workmanship together with the beauty and finish of the high-grade American guns as well as the strength and durability required to withstand the heavy charges of nitro or smokeless powder.

The above illustration, taken from a photograph of **Our Genuine English Machine Gun**, will give you an idea of the appearance of this gun, which is high grade and strictly first class in every sense of the word. This gun has genuine fine twist barrels with fine matted extension rib, double bolt. **Case hardened locks and mountings finely engraved.** Low circular hammers below line of sight, top lever brake, full checkered pisto grip stock and checked patent fore end, fancy engraved rubber cap on grip and checked rubber butt plate; the left barrel full choke bored, right barrel modified. While this gun has all the advantages of a $50.00 American gun we furnish it to you in either 10 or 12 gauge, 30 or 32 inch barrels; 12 gauge, 7½ to 8½ lbs., 10 gauge, 8½ to 10 lbs.

Our special price.................................................................$22.75

## OUR HIGH GRADE $13.65 BELGIUM GUN.

Many imitate us, but none furnish the same gun at the same money. They can not do it. This gun, like all foreign made guns, we import direct from Europe. We buy them in Belgium from the best makers at the lowest prices for cash, pay the import duty, and sell them at the smallest profit possible consistent with the class of goods we handle. We make our terms very liberal. We send these goods C. O. D., subject to examination, on receipt of a small deposit, balance and express charges to be paid at the express office, or 3 per cent discount is allowed if cash in full accompanies your order.

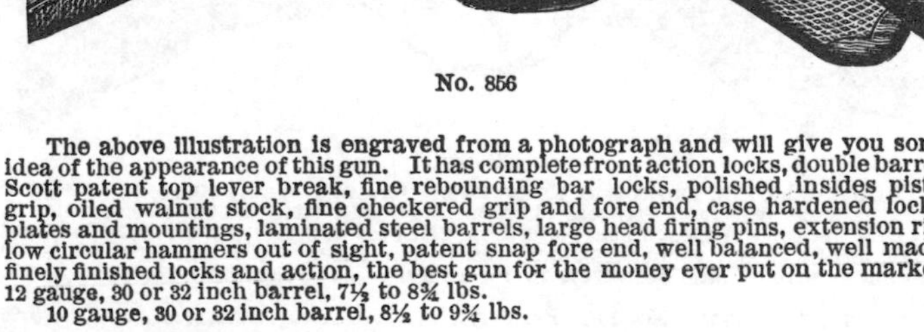

**No. 856**

The above illustration is engraved from a photograph and will give you some idea of the appearance of this gun. It has complete front action locks, double barrel, Scott patent top lever break, fine rebounding bar locks, polished insides pistol grip, oiled walnut stock, fine checkered grip and fore end, case hardened locks, plates and mountings, laminated steel barrels, large head firing pins, extension rib, low circular hammers out of sight, patent snap fore end, well balanced, well made, finely finished locks and action, the best gun for the money ever put on the market. 12 gauge, 30 or 32 inch barrel, 7½ to 8¾ lbs.

10 gauge, 30 or 32 inch barrel, 8½ to 9¾ lbs.

Our special price..................................................$13.65

**WE SHIP GUNS C. O. D. SUBJECT TO EXAMINATION, AND WE GUARANTEE YOU WILL BE PLEASED OR YOU NEED NOT ACCEPT THE GOODS. 3 PER CENT DISCOUNT FOR CASH WITH ORDER.**

## WINCHESTER REPEATING SHOT GUNS.

Six shooter. Retails at $25.00. Our price, $16.88. Our terms, the same on all shot guns, C. O. D. to any one on receipt of $3.00, balance payable at express office. Order by number. No. 864. Price.......................................$16.88

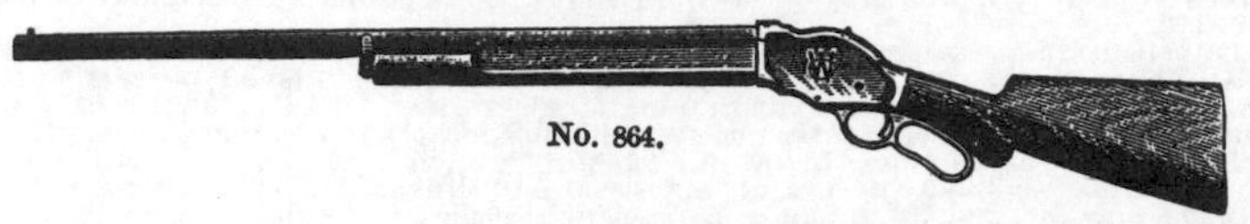

No. 864.

Description.—No better shooting gun made. The barrel can be examined and cleaned from the breech. The magazine and carriers hold five cartridges, which with the one in the chamber, makes six at the command of the shooter. The forward and backward motion of the finger lever, which can be executed while gun is at shoulder, throw out empty shells, raises a new cartridge from magazine, and puts into the barrel. The gun is then ready to be fired. Finest quality rolled steel barrels, case hardened frame and pistol grip, walnut stock. All guns are full choked, and no gun will be sent out that will not make a perfect target. The standard gun will have a stock 12¾ inches in length and 2⅝ inches drop, any variation from standard length or drop will be charged for extra.

12 gauge, 30 or 32 inch barrel, weight 7¾ lbs., our special price...................$16.88
10 gauge, 30 or 32 inch barrel, weight 9 lbs., our special price...................16.88

The best gun made for ducks, chickens, partridges, etc., as you can fire much more rapidly than with any double barreled gun, besides, the penetration of these guns is simply wonderful.

## LATEST REPEATING SHOT GUN MADE.

Just put on the market. Model of 1893. Winchester repeating shot gun. Shoots 6 times. Retails at $25.00. Our special price, $16.88. Order by number. No. 865. Price.......................................$16.88

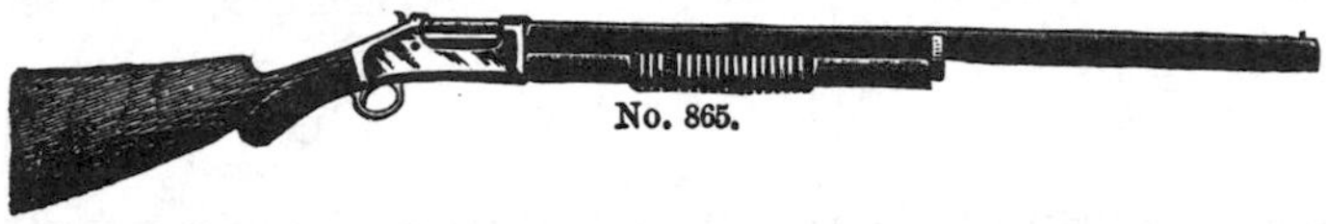

No. 865.

We will ship C. O. D. to any one anywhere on receipt of $3.00 as a guarantee of good faith, examine the gun at express office, and if found satisfactory, pay the express agent the balance, $13.88, and express charges, otherwise pay nothing and the agent will return it to us and we will refund your $3.00 less express charges.

Description.—Best gun made for ducks, chickens or partridges, no stronger shooting gun made, has wonderful penetration and makes a perfect pattern. Operated by sliding fore arm below the barrel. When the hammer is down the backward and forward motion of this slide unlocks and opens the breech lock, ejects the cartridge or fired shell and replaces it with a fresh cartridge. The construction of the arm is such that the hammer cannot fall, or the firing pin strike the cartridge until the breech lock is in place and locked fast, while the hammer stands at the full cock notch, the gun is locked against opening. In this position the firing pin must be pushed forward to open the gun; when the hammer stands at half-cock, the gun is locked both against opening and pulling the trigger.

To load the magazine turn the gun with the guard upward, lay the cartridge on the underside of the carrier and push it into the magazine.

Finest quality, patent rolled steel barrels, fine selected walnut stock, pistol grip, length of stock 13 inches, drop of stock 2¾ inches, weight 7¾ lbs., shoots six times, 12 gauge only, 30 or 32 inch barrel. Our special price....................$16.88

This gun is simple in construction, very few parts and not liable to get out of order, most rapid action made, choke bored to do the best shooting possible.

## NEW MODEL SPENCER REPEATING SHOT GUN.

Our special price $27.65. Retails at $40.00. Six shooter, single barrel, latest model. Can be taken apart to pack. Order by number. No. 866. Price......$26.95

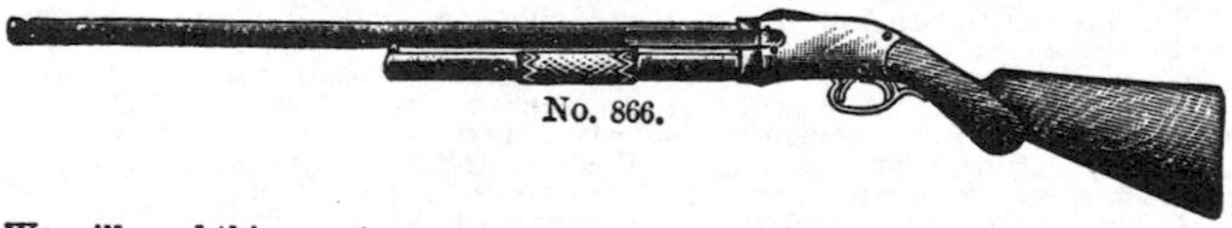

No. 866.

We will send this gun to any one C. O. D. subject to examination on receipt of $3.00, balance, $24.65, and express charges, to be paid at express office.

Description.—The magazine is located under the barrel and will hold five cartridges. Fine genuine Damascus barrels, fine selected Italian walnut stock, pistol grip, handsomely checkered, beautifully finished throughout and is far superior to any double barrel shot gun in precision and penetration. Has few parts and is solid and substantial, can be used as a single loader and cartridges in magazine held in reserve. 30 and 32 inch barrels, 7¾ to 8¼ pounds, 12 gauge.

Compare our prices with those of other houses. Consider our **terms.** **We** can save you money. Can we have your trade?

No. 866½. The Spencer Gun, same as No. 866, except has **"Twist Barrel"** and Wood Slide (and not checkered grip); in 12 gauge, 30 inch barrel, 7¾ to 8½ pounds. Length of stock, 13½ to 14 inches. Drop of stock, 3 inches. Our special price.......................................$17.85

## SINGLE BARREL BREECH LOADING SHOT GUN FOR $5.95.

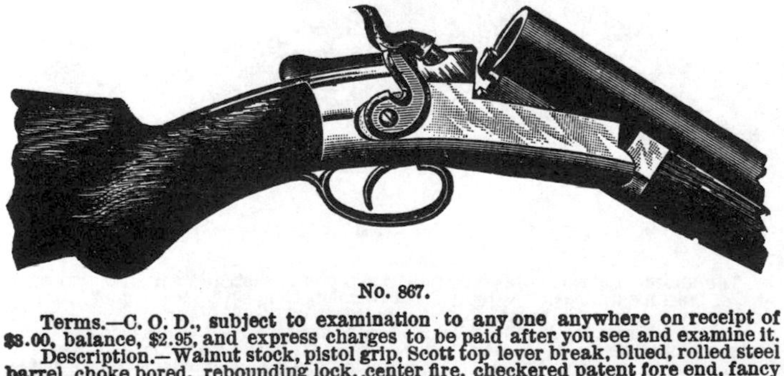

No. 867.

Terms.—C. O. D., subject to examination to any one anywhere on receipt of $3.00, balance, $2.95, and express charges to be paid after you see and examine it.

Description.—Walnut stock, pistol grip, Scott top lever break, blued, rolled steel barrel, choke bored, rebounding lock, center fire, checkered patent fore end, fancy butt plate, 30 or 32 inch barrel, 6½ to 7½ pounds. 12 gauge, each, $5.95; 16 gauge, each, $5.95.

Order by number. No. 867. Price.......................................$5.95

## OUR NEW "TAKE DOWN" SINGLE BARREL SHOT GUN.

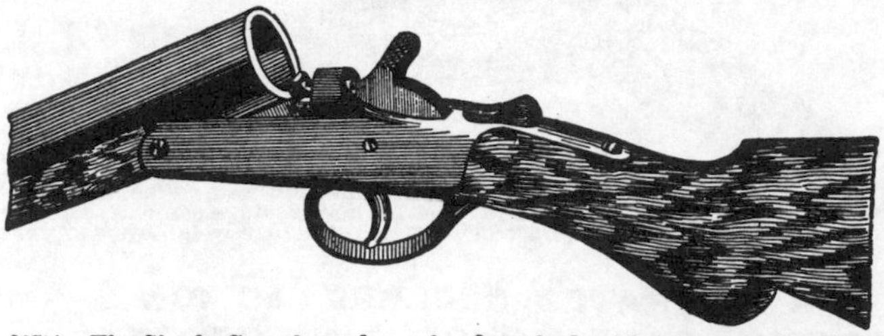

No. 867½. The Single Gun; barrel can be detached without removing the fore end, top snap blued frame, rebounding lock with direct firing pin, oiled walnut stock, fine blued steel barrels bored from solid metal, choke bored, positive extractor, long bolted lug; all working parts made of best drop forged steel, machine fitted. Waarranted in every way. 12 gauge, 30 inch, 6½ lbs. Each.......................................$5.56

## FOREHAND & WADSWORTH SINGLE BARREL BREECH LOADING SAOT GUN FOR $6.90.

Made by the Forehand Arms Co. at Worcester, Mass., and guaranteee one of the best single guns made. Retails for $12.00; we sell it at $6.90.

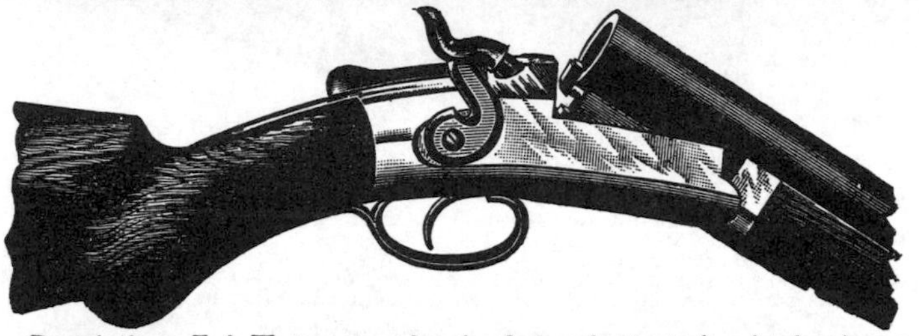

Description.—F. & W. top snap break; fine walnut stock, pistol grip, rebounding locks, snap fore end, nicely checkered, solid block strikers, choke bored, finest blued steel barrels, 12 gauge, 30 or 32 inch barrel, 7 pounds.

Order by number. No. 868. Price.......................................$6.90

## REMINGTON SEMI-HAMMERLESS SINGLE BARREL BREECH LOADING SHOT GUN.

Handsome and well made. Can you match it for $6.95. Our special price is $5.95. It retails for $12.

You can examine it at your nearest express office by sending $3.00 as a guarontee of good faith; the balance, $3.95, and express charges to be paid atter you get the gun. You will get free a complete set of re-loading tools if you send cash in full with your order, and we will refund your money if you are not perfectly satisfied.

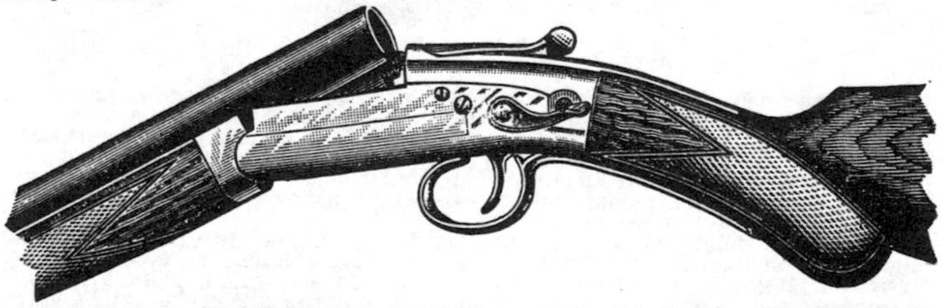

Description.—The Remington Semi-Hammerless Single Barrel Breech Loading Shot Gun, top lever break, the best break made, blue steel barrels, choke bored, side cocking lever, case hardened frame and butt plate, pistol grip stock, rebounding lock. The material, finish and shooting qualities are the some high standard as the Remington double barrel gun. Every gun is warranted perfect and a strong shooter. They are all put to a test before leaving the factory and none are allowed to go out until a perfect pattern hat been shown.

You take no risk in buying the old and reliable Remington. 12 gauge only; 30 or 32 inch barrel; 6 to 6½ pounds.

Order by number. No. 869. Special Price.......................................$6.95

## THE BEST HAMMER SINGLE BARREL GUN MADE.

Madc by the Crescent Fire Arms Co, Retails at $15. Our special price $6.75. Compare our prices with those of other houses. You will find our prices below all others. Consider our terms: C. O. D. to any one on receipt of $3, balance to be paid at express office.

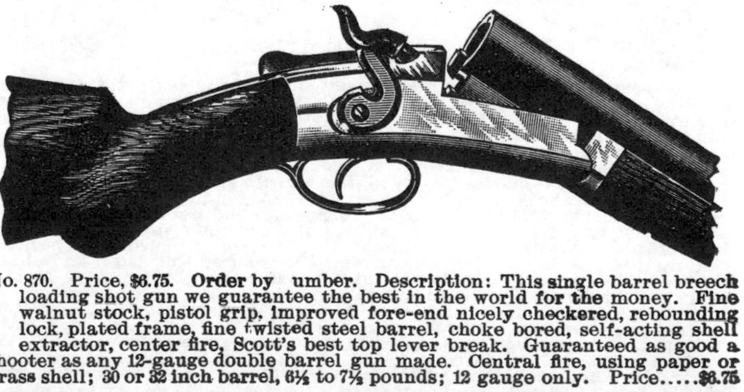

No. 870. Price, $6.75. **Order by umber.** Description: This single barrel breech loading shot gun we guarantee the best in the world for the money. Fine walnut stock, pistol grip, improved fore-end nicely checkered, rebounding lock, plated frame, fine twisted steel barrel, choke bored, self-acting shell extractor, center fire, Scott's best top lever break. Guaranteed as good a shooter as any 12-gauge double barrel gun made. Central fire, using paper or brass shell; 30 or 32 inch barrel, 6½ to 7½ pounds; 12 gauge only. Price.....$6.75

**GREAT SALE OF MACKINTOSHES.** **See Index.**

**YOU WOULD CONSIDER A MAN FOOLISH WHO WOULD SELL HIS WHEAT AT 20 CENTS A BUSHEL LESS THAN MARKET PRICE. HE'S NOT MORE SO THAN THE MAN WHO PAYS 20 TO 50 PER CENT MORE THAN ACTUAL WORTH OF GOODS HE BUYS.**

## $6.75 for the New York Arms Company's Latest Patent Automatic Ejector, Single Barrel Breechloading Shot Gun.

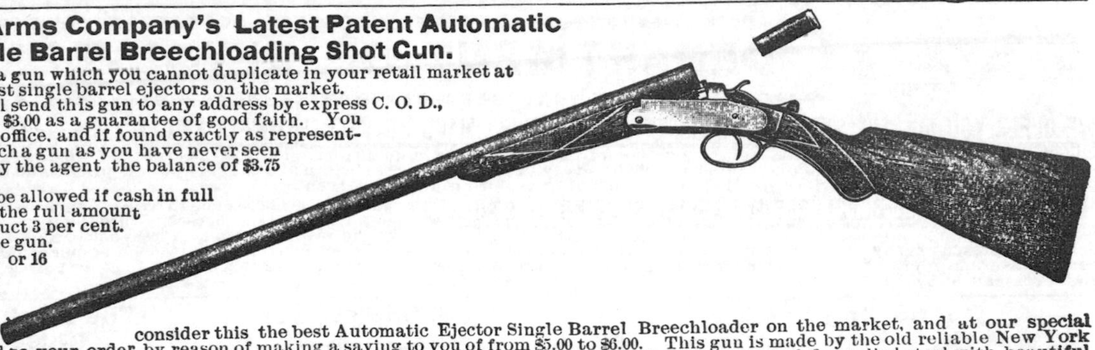

**No. 869¼** For $6.75 we offer you a gun which you cannot duplicate in your retail market at less than $12.00. This is one of the best single barrel ejectors on the market.

At our special price of $6.75 we will send this gun to any address by express C. O. D., subject to examination, on receipt of $3.00 as a guarantee of good faith. You can examine the gun at your express office, and if found exactly as represented and perfectly satisfactory, and such a gun as you have never seen before at anything like the price, pay the agent the balance of $3.75 and express charges.

**Three per cent. discount** will be allowed if cash in full accompanies your order. If you send the full amount of cash with your order you may deduct 3 per cent. from our price, when $6.55 pays for the gun.

We furnish this gun in either 12 or 16 gauge, 30 or 32 inch barrel, as desired. In ordering be sure to state gauge and length of barrel wanted.

No such gun was ever before offered at anything like the price. We consider this the best Automatic Ejector Single Barrel Breechloader on the market, and at our special price of $6.75 we think we are entitled to your order by reason of making a saving to you of from $5.00 to $6.00. This gun is made by the old reliable New York Arms Company, which is a guarantee in every respect. It is made from the very best material throughout. The barrels are of fine rolled steel with beautiful blued finish. They are full choke bore, which makes them shoot very hard and close. For a perfect pattern and penetration this gun is equal to breechloaders that sell at ten times the price. You will get the same service, the same execution, the same convenience from this automatic ejecting single barrel gun that you would from a $200.00 ejector. The hammer is hung in the center so as to strike the cartridge square. The automatic ejector device is very strong and simple and cannot get out of order. The barrel is detachable, making it convenient to carry with ejector apart in a Victoria style gun case. The stock is made of selected walnut, pistol grip, fancy butt, rebounding lock, top snap break. The frame and trigger guard are case hardened and beautifully finished.

At $6.75 shipped C. O. D., or $6.55 cash in full with order, we feel confident of a very large trade on these guns; so confident, in fact, that we have accepted a proposition from the manufacturer for a quantity by reason of which we are able to make this price. We would advise you when looking for a single barrel shot gun to consider this before all others. When you stop to consider that for only $6.55 you get a thoroughly first-class, high grade New York Company's breechloading shot gun, and with the latest patent self-acting automatic shell ejector, we believe we are entitled to your order.

**Do not forget the price,** $6.75 when shipped C. O. D., $6.55 if cash in full accompanies your order.

## The Celebrated Davenport Ejector For $6.45.

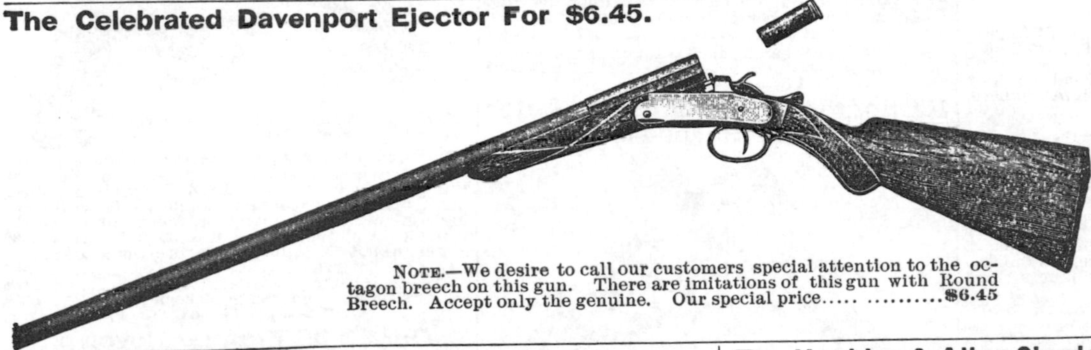

NOTE.—We desire to call our customers special attention to the octagon breech on this gun. There are imitations of this gun with Round Breech. Accept only the genuine. Our special price..... ..........**$6.45**

**No. 869½.**

**A Regular $15.00 Gun.** Consider our liberal $3.00 deposit, C.O.D. terms, our 3 per cent. discount, and compare, our prices with those of any other concern.

The above illustration shows the celebrated Davenport automatic ejector, model of 1895 gun. **The best single barrel breech loader made.** Top snap, octagon breech, rebounding lock, automatic ejector, finely checkered pistol grip stock and fore end, fancy rubber butt plate, 30 inch barrel; **12, 16 or 20 gauge,** as desired. Weight, 5¾ to 6¼ pounds.

**On the basis of lower prices than** any one else can possible give, we earnestly speak for your trade.

## Hammerless Single Barrel Breech Loader.

Made by the Forehand Arms Co. The finest, the best single breech loading shot gun made. Retails everywhere at $20 and upwards. Our special drive price, **$12.35.** Terms: C. O. D. to any one on receipt of $3, balance $9.35 and express charges to be paid after you have received and examined the gun.

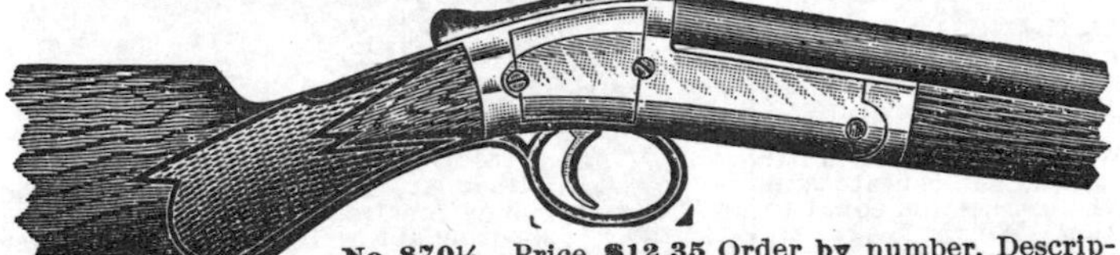

**No. 870½.** Price, **$12.35** Order by number. Description: Best, safest, most durable single barrel shot gun made. Top snap, break, pistol grip nicely checkered and finished, patent snap fore-end, automatic action, with an absolute safety-catch to lock the trigger to prevent accidental discharge, simple in construction, perfectly safe and made of the very best material, choke bored, finest twist steel barrel, using brass or paper shells, center fire, 12 gauge, 30 inch barrel; weighs 7 pounds. We guarantee the shooting qualities of this gun fully equal to any 12 gauge gun made.

## The Hopkins & Allen Single Barrel Shot Gun, "Take Down" Style, $6.00.

The "Take Down" Hopkins & Allen Shot Gun, a perfectly safe and good shooting gun, that can be taken apart without tool and put into very small compass. It has a rebounding lock and a vertical sliding breech block operated by the guard as a leaver, which, when thrown down, ejects the empty

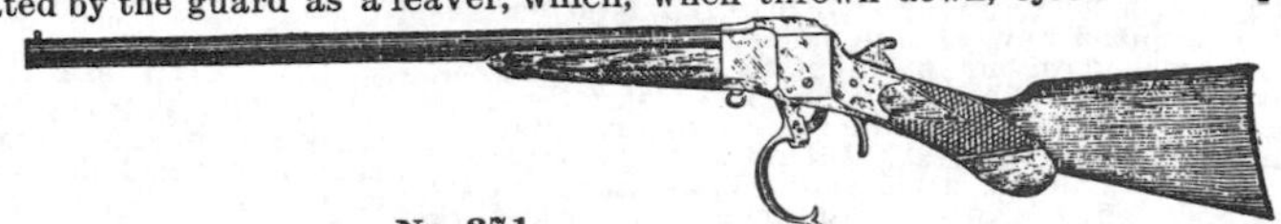

**No. 871.**

shell from the chamber, and with sufficient force to carry it 6 to 8 feet from the shooter. The barrel is fastened to the frame by a tapering screw key, easily removed by the hand, which passes through the frame and section of the barrel laterally, keeping the barrel always in its proper position. Finest blued steel barrel, case-hardened mountings, choke bored. The barrels are bored out of solid metal; oiled walnut pistol grip stock, double bolt. One of the strongest and best made guns in the market. **12 gauge only, 30 inch barrels, 6½ to 7 pounds.** Each..... .................................**$6.00**

NOTE.—The H. & A. "Take Down" gun never gets loose and shaky in the hinge joints like the "tip up" barrel guns, as it has no joints, and barrel does not "tip up" but is firmly fastened to the breech action.

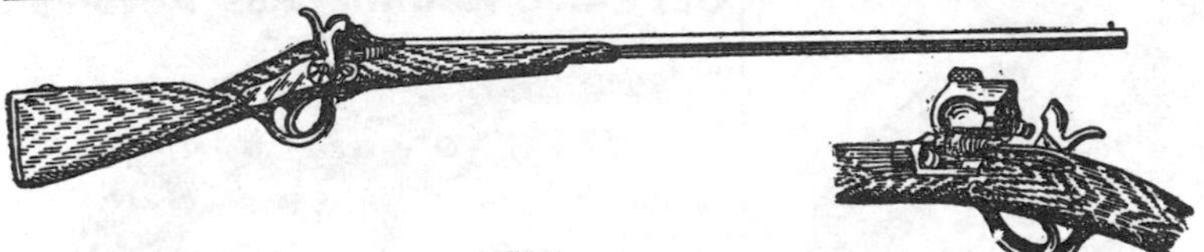

**871½.**

## "The Zulu" Breech Loading Shot Gun $3.40.

Our Genuine "Zulu" Breech Loading Shot Gun. A safe, strong and close shooter to load. The hammer must be raised to half cock, the breech block brought over by the thumb from left to right. The extractor is attached to the breech block; by pulling the block backward the shell is extracted. There is a spiral spring that carries block back to position. This is a very strong and durable gun for general purposes; 12 gauge only.

Our special price.........................................**$3.40**

## DOUBLE BARREL MUZZLE LOADER. $5.35 to $9.60.

**Our Terms:** C. O. D., subject to examination to anyone anywhere on receipt of $3.00, balance to be paid at express office. If not satisfactory, return the gun at our expense, and we will refund your $3.00 less express charges.

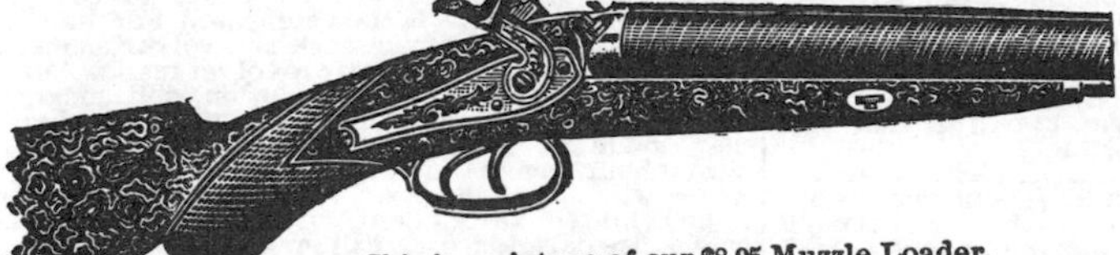

This is a picture of our $8.95 Muzzle Loader.

**No. 872. Imitation Twist Barrels,** back action locks, plain breech, gauge 11, 12, 13, 14. Our price.......................................**$5.35**

**No. 873. Genuine Twist Barrels,** oiled walnut stock, patent breech, back action locks, checkered grip, 12 to 14 bore, 7 to 8½ lbs.. 30 to 34 inch barrel. A good, safe and reliable gun. Our price..................................**$7.95**

**No 874. Laminated Steel Barrels,** back action lock, oiled walnut stock, patent breech and break off, checkered pistol grip. Our price...........**$8.95**

**No. 875. Genuine Twist Barrels,** bar lock, walnut stock, checkered pistol grip, gauge 11, 12, 13 and 14; length of barrels, 30 te 34 inches; weight, 7½ to 8¾ pounds. Our price.........................................**$9.60**

## BOYS' MUZZLE LOADERS—SINGLE BARREL.

**Our special price, $2.65.** Retails at $7.00. A great bargain. Cash in full must accompany your order for tnis gun. If you don't find it satisfactory, return it at our expense, and we will immediately refund your money.

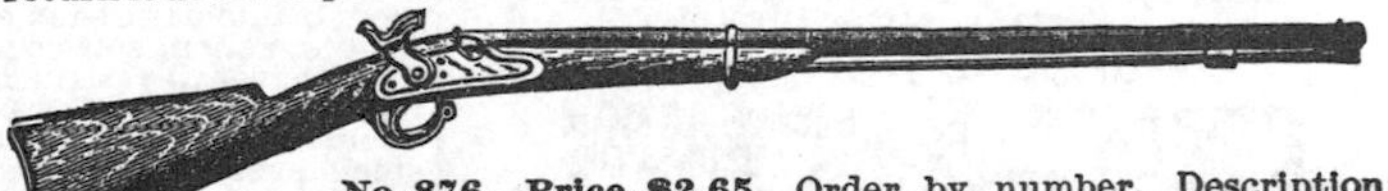

**No. 876. Price, $2.65.** Order by number. Description: Boys' muzzle loader, single barrel, wood ramrod, blued barrel; a good, safe gun, small nipple for GD or EB caps, 31 inch barrel, 4½ pounds, 16 gauge.

## A CUT-DOWN MUSKET FOR $1.95.

Never before sold at less than $3.00. We have bought 2,000, which we can close out at $1.95, and when these are gone there will be no more at any price.

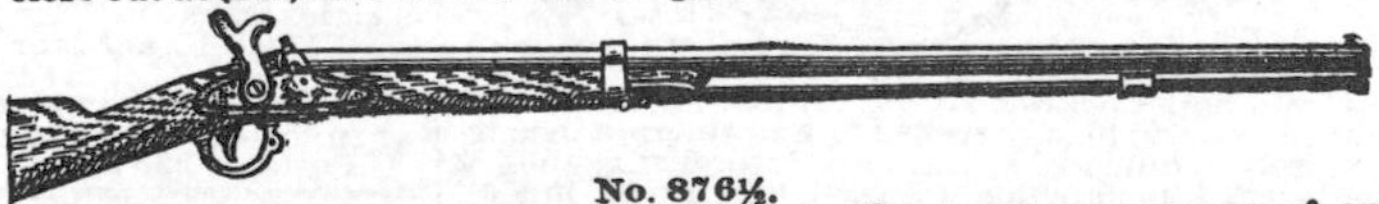

**No. 876½.**

**No. 876½.** The above illustration shows the exact appearance of our **Special $1.95 Cut-down Musket. U. S. Springfield Model 1893.** Altered to shot gun, front action lock, case hardened mountings and locks, blued barrel, steel rod. **For quality of material, shooting qualities and durability** these goeds are too well known to require any comment from us.

**Such a bargain was never before offered.**

# DEPARTMENT OF REVOLVERS.

**WE OFFER YOU ALL THE STANDARD MAKES OF REVOLVERS AT MANUFACTURERS' LOWEST PRICES.** When you get our price you are getting the manufacturers' price with only our one small profit added, and owning the revolver for less money than any dealer can buy in quantities. For the season of 1897 we have many special bargains to offer, as our contracts with the different manufacturers have been so very large that we are able to make the very closest prices, and a comparison of our prices with those of any other concern will convince you there is a saving of from 25 per cent. to 75 per cent.

**IN ORDERING SINGLE REVOLVERS WE ADVISE SENDING BY MAIL.** This can be done where enough extra is enclosed to cover postage. The postage is one cent per oz., or fraction thereof. We will ship revolvers by express C. O. D., subject to examination. on receipt of $1.00 as a guarantee of good faith. You can examine the revolver at the express office, and if found perfectly satisfactory and exactly as represented, pay the express agent the balance and express charges and the revolver is yours. Three per cent. discount is allowed if cash is full accompanies your order. We advise sending cash in full, deducting 3 per cent. for cash, and adding enough to cover postage, insurance or registry fee, and have the revolver sent by mail.

## Our 68c Revolver.

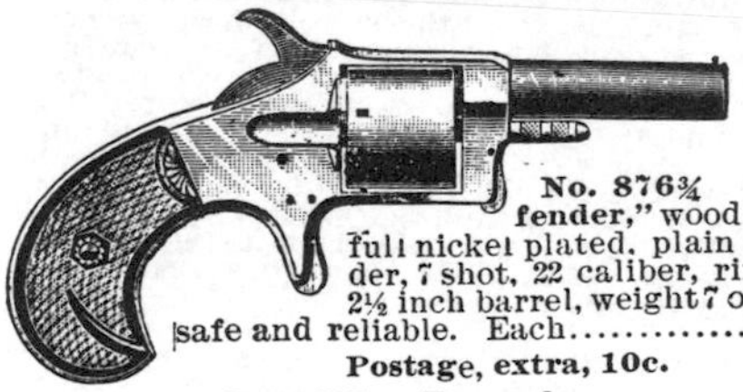

**No. 876¾** "Defender," wood stock, full nickel plated, plain cylinder, 7 shot, 22 caliber, rim fire, 2½ inch barrel, weight 7 ounces. safe and reliable. Each............**$0.68**

**Postage, extra, 10c.**

## Our 85c Revolver.

**No. 877** Rosewood handle, 7 shot, full nickel plated, 22 caliber, long or short, rim fire, weight, 7 oz., 2½ inch barrel, safe and reliable. Price....**$0.85**

**No. 877½** Rubber Handle, 7 shot, 22 caliber, long or short, rim fire, full nickel plated, weight 7 ounces, rifled barrel. Our special price................**$0.95**

## Defender, 32 Caliber.

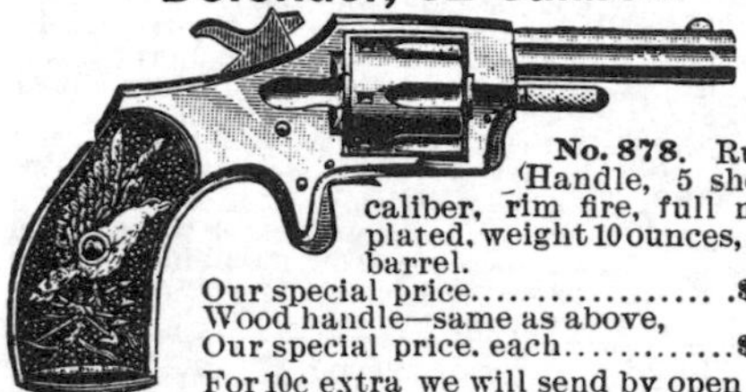

**No. 878.** Rubber Handle, 5 shot. 32 caliber, rim fire, full nickel plated, weight 10 ounces, rifled barrel.

Our special price.................. .**$1.20**

Wood handle—same as above,

Our special price. each............**$0.85**

For 10c extra we will send by open mail. For 18c extra we will send by registered mail.

## Bull Dog Revolvers.

American Bull Dogs all double action, self-cocking; all have rubber stocks, all beautifully nickel plated; all have plated cylinders, all have octagon barrels, all warranted new and in perfect order. Regular retail price $3.00; our special price..............**$1.35**

**Description:** These revolvers are strictly first-class in every respect. The quality of material and workmanship is the best. All have rifled barrels and are good shooters; all 5 shot. These are not toys, but good guns. No one can meet our prices on these goods.

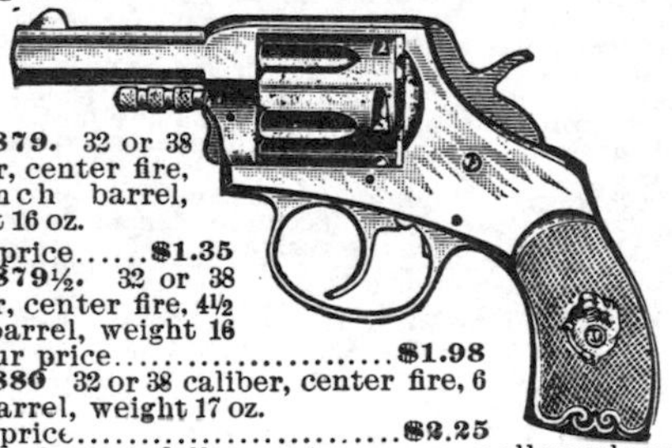

**No. 879.** 32 or 38 caliber, center fire, 2½ inch barrel, weight 16 oz.

Our price......**$1.35**

**No. 879½.** 32 or 38 caliber, center fire, 4½ inch barrel, weight 16 oz. Our price......................**$1.98**

**No. 880** 32 or 38 caliber, center fire, 6 inch barrel, weight 17 oz.

Our price..........................**$2.25**

Remember one dollar must accompany all revolver orders to be sent C. O. D., balance to be paid at express office. 3 per cent. discount if cash in full accompanies your order.

For 20c extra we will send by open mail. postpaid. For 28c extra we will send by registered mail, postpaid.

**No. 880½** Rubber handle, 7 shot, 22 caliber, long or short. rim fire, full nickel plated, weight 7 oz., rifled barrel, price................. ..........**$1.35**

**Postage, extra, 10c.**

## Our $1.45 Revolver.

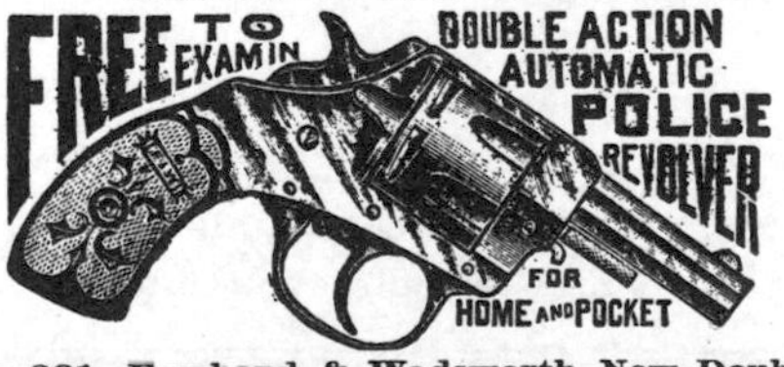


**No. 881 Forehand & Wadsworth New Double Action. Self-Cocking Revolver,** full nickel plated, rubber stock, rifled barrel, safe and reliable. accurate, rebounding locks, parts are interchangeable, 32 caliber, 2½ inch octagon barrel, weight 12 ounces. Our price.........................................**$1.45**

**No. 882** 38 caliber, 2½ inch octagon barrel, 5 shot, weight about 15 oz. Our price..................**$1.45**

**Postage, extra, 17c.**

## Our $1.55 Revolver.

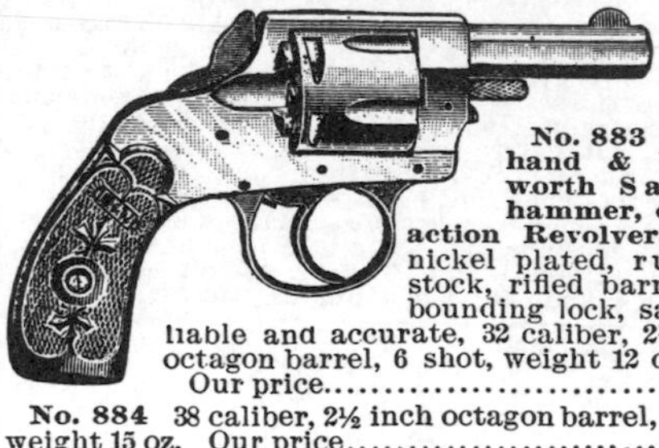

**No. 883 Forehand & Wadsworth Safety hammer, double action Revolver,** full nickel plated, rubber stock, rifled barrel, rebounding lock, safe. reliable and accurate, 32 caliber, 2½ inch octagon barrel, 6 shot, weight 12 ounces. Our price.........................**$1.55**

**No. 884** 38 caliber, 2½ inch octagon barrel, 5 shot, weight 15 oz. Our price..............................**$1.55**

**Postage, extra, 17c.**

## Harrington & Richardson Automatic Revolvers.

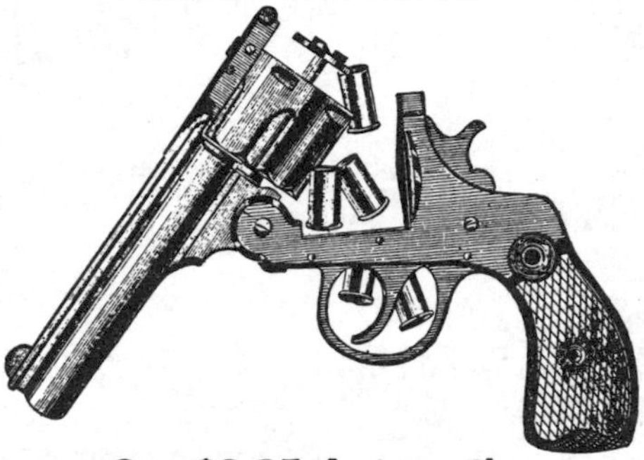

## Our $2.85 Automatic.

**No. 885.** This revolver would retail in any first-class gun store at from $5 to $6. It is the celebrated Harrington & Richardson improved automatic, self extracting, double action, self-cocking revolver, modeled on the Smith & Wesson pattern, beautifully nickel plated, rubber stock, as accurate and durable as any revolver on the market and equal to the Smith & Wesson in shooting. Weight 18½ oz., 3¼ inch barrel. 6 shot, 32 caliber. center fire.

Our price.............................................**$2.85**

**No. 886.** 5 shot. 38 caliber, central fire.

Our price.............................................**$2.85**

**Postage, extra, 22c.**

## Our $2.70 Revolver.

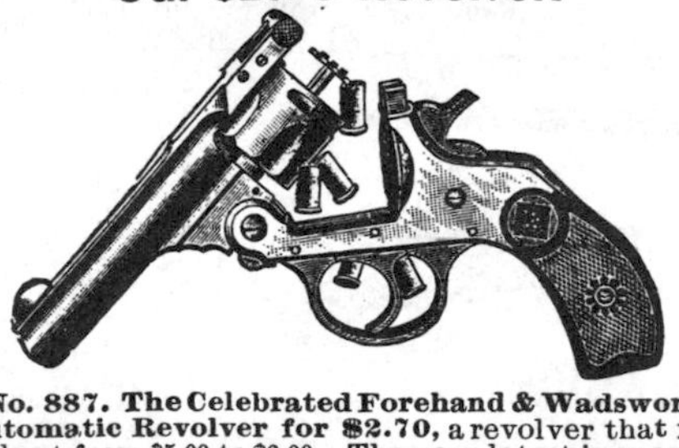

**No. 887. The Celebrated Forehand & Wadsworth Automatic Revolver for $2.70,** a revolver that retails at from $5.00 to $6.00. The very latest improved model, automatic shell extractor, rebounding locks, double action, self-cocking, simple and accurate, interchangeable parts made from drop steel forgings. The frame is cast steel, no malleable iron about it, nickel plated throughout, fancy rubber stock, every revolver is fully warranted, length of barrels 3¼ inches, weight 17 oz., entire length 7¾ inches. The fact that we sold over 10,000 of these revolvers during the last year is evidence of the general satisfaction they give. 32 caliber, Smith & Wesson center fire cartridges, 6 shot.

Our price...........................................**$2.70**

**No. 888.** 38 caliber, Smith & Wesson center fire cartridges, 6 shot. Our price......................**$2.70**

**No. 889.** Either 32 or 38 caliber with 5 inch barrel. Our price..............................................**$3.45**

We can furnish these revolvers in blued finish when so desired at 50c. extra.

**Postage, 25c extra; 5 inch barrels, 35c extra.**

**NOTICE: Owing to the heavy advance at the factory, in the price of Revolvers, our present prices apply to STOCK ON HAND, and are subject to change without notice. Take advantage of our low prices and order at once.**

## The Celebrated Harrington & Richardson Automatic Police Revolver for $2.95.

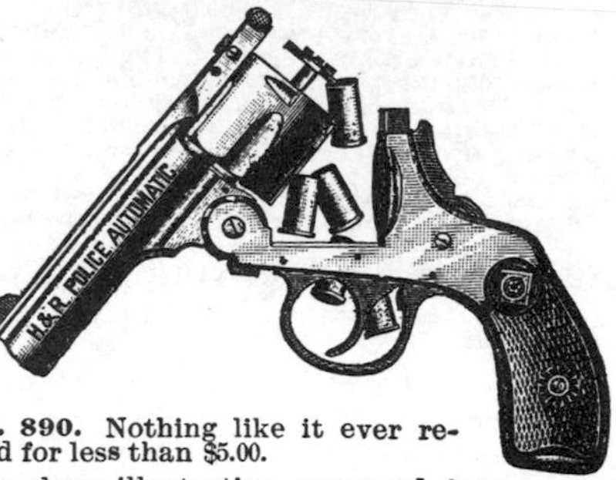


**No. 890.** Nothing like it ever retailed for less than $5.00.

The above illustration, engraved from a photograph, will give you some idea of the appearance of this gun. It is the celebrated Harrington police, automatic, safety hammer, double action, self-cocking, automatic shell extractor, fancy rubber stock, full nickel plated, center fire, 32 or 38 caliber; 32 caliber 6 shot; 38 caliber 5 shot; weighs 18 to 22 oz.

Our special price.......................................**$2.95**

Five-inch barrel.......................................**3.95**

Extra for pearl handle in place of rubber....**1.75**

**Postage, 24c. extra.**

## Our $3.80 Frontier Revolver.

Remember the 3 per cent. discount for cash is allowed when comparing our prices with those of other houses.

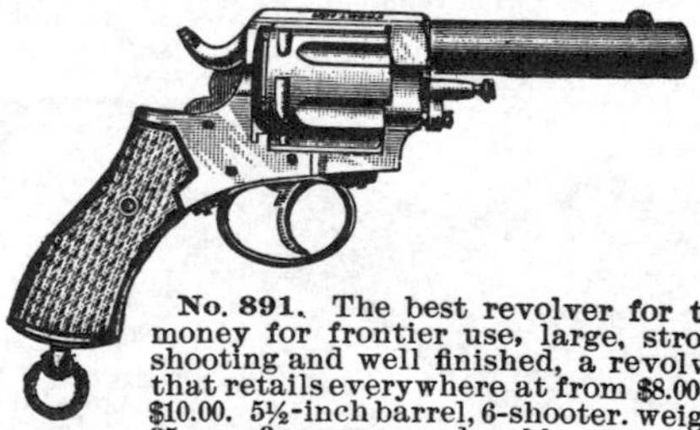

**No. 891.** The best revolver for the money for frontier use, large, strong shooting and well finished, a revolver that retails everywhere at from $8.00 to $10.00. 5½-inch barrel, 6-shooter. weighs 35 oz., fine engraved rubber stock. 44 caliber, central fire, full nickel plated. This revolver is adapted to 44 caliber Winchester cartridges so that a person having a rifle need not change ammunition but can use the same cartriges in both. Price, **$3.80**

**Postage, extra, 35c.**

## Our $4.70 Hammerless Revolver.

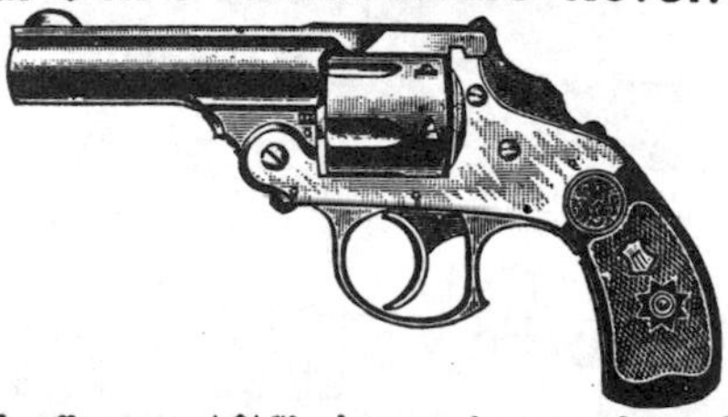

We offer you at $4.70 a hammerless revolver which has never been retailed at less than $8.00 to $10.00. No other house will meet our price. Make a comparison and decide for yourself, always considering that we allow a discount of 3 per cent. for cash in full with order. This is the celebrated Forehand & Wadsworth new style hammerless revolver made by Forehand Arms Co., no better revolver made. Automatic shell extractor, double action, self-cocking, rebounding lock, absolutely safe catch to lock hammer, made of best material, beautifully finished throughout, accurate and reliable. No revolver made will shoot better. All central fire, nicely nickel plated throughout, uses Smith & Wesson center fire cartridges, 32 caliber 6 shot, 28 caliber 5 shot.

**No. 891½** 32 caliber, our price ..... ........**$4.70**

**No. 891¾** 38 caliber. our price .............. **4.70**

We can furnish the revolver with 5 inch barrel when so desired at $5.35.

**Postage, 25c extra.**

Always consider our 3 per cent. cash discount when comparing our prices with those of other houses.

**IT WILL PAY YOU TO GET YOUR NEIGHBORS INTERESTED IN OUR CATALOGUE. IF YOU COULD GET SEVERAL OF THEM TO JOIN YOU IN CLUB ORDERS, IT WILL BE AN EXTRA SAVING TO YOU ON FREIGHT.**

## $2.75 BUYS AN $8.00 HAMMERLESS REVOLVER.

We say an $8.00 hammerless revolver for the reason we believe this revolver is equal to many that retail as high as $8.00. We are able to offer the price of $2.75 by reason of a very large quantity we have purchased and at a forced sale.

No. 892. The above illustration engraved from a photograph will give you some idea of the appearance of this revolver, and at our price of $2.75 it will surely prove a death blow to competition. It is a genuine American hammerless revolver. Dealers may say it is impossible. Some may say we do not furnish it but we do. We propose to demonstrate to the consumers of the world that our trade, reaching into every State in the Union and then into every country on the globe, places us in a position to go to the manufacturers with such large orders for cash that we can buy and offer our leaders at prices that will strike terror to dealers and competitors. We use the word "competitors" but we have none, and a comparison of our prices with those of other houses will convince you of this fact. Our policy is 10,000 revolvers at a profit of 10c. each which amounts to $1000.00 rather than 100 revolvers at $2.00 each and amount to only $200.00. It pays to sell cheap. We make more money by selling a revolver at 10c. profit than at $2.00 profit. Every one who buys from us talks for us. We treat them right, we give them unheard of values for their money, and in consequence they will talk—talk words of praise. You can't stop them. Dealers try to, so do certain would-be competitors try to stop them, but they can't. Our customers sound our praise, and as a result our bargain list grows bigger and bigger as each leader succeeds the other.

This new hammerless revolver is made by the New York Arms Co., and is known as the Bull's Eye Hammerless. Solid frame, full nickel plated, fancy ornamented rubber handle, patent safety lock so arranged that accidental discharge is impossible, uses Smith & Wesson central fire cartridges, 22, 32 and 38 caliber as desired. 22 caliber is adapted to rim fire cartridges. 22 caliber has 2½ inch barrel and weighs 9 oz. 32 and 38 calibers have 3¼ inch barrels and weigh 14 and 17 oz. respectively. If you buy one you will buy more.

You can sell them at $5.00 each.

Our terms are C. O. D. to any one on receipt of $1.00 as a guarantee of good faith. Examine the revolver at the express office, and if satisfactory pay the express agent the balance, $1.75, and express charges. The best way is to send cash in full. You can then deduct 3 per cent. cash discount, and for 23c. extra we will send the revolver by mail, postage prepaid.

## A $10.00 HAMMERLESS REVOLVER FOR $3.95.

We offer for $3.95 a hammerless revolver that is the equal of anything sold by retail dealers at $10.00. If you will allow us to send it to you by express C. O. D. subject to examination and you do not find it as represented and equal to revolvers that retail at $10.00 and more, you can return it at our expense.

No. 893. The above illustration engraved from a photograph will give you an idea of the appearance of this revolver. It is one of the best known perfect safety hammerless revolvers in the market. It is known as the Perfect Safety Hammerless and is adapted to Smith & Wesson central fire cartridges, is made by one of the largest and most reliable manufacturers in America, a concern whose reputation for the manufacture of this kind of work is a guarantee for the quality of the arm; is full nickel-plated, has automatic shell extractor and patent safety catch, making accidental discharge impossible. It works automatically in every respect; all parts are steel and interchangeable; the barrel and all working parts are made of drop steel forgings; cylinder is locked when hammer is either up or down; is the strongest, simplest made; the safety catch is hung behind the lock. This revolver comes in 38 caliber only, 3¼ inch barrel, and weighs 16 oz. Will be sent to any address C. O. D. subject to examination on receipt of $1.00 as a guarantee of good faith, balance and express charges payable at express office; 3 per cent. discount allowed if cash in full accompanies your order. For 23c. extra we will send it by mail, postage prepaid.

## IVER JOHNSON SMALL FRAME AUTOMATIC REVOLVER.

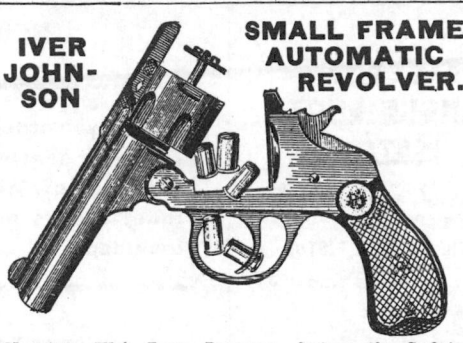

No. 894. The Iver Johnson Automatic Safety Hammer Revolver, double action, self-cocking, 5-shot, 11 oz. weight, 3 inch barrel, finely nickel plated, neatly finished. Every one warranted. 32 caliber, center fire, Smith & Wesson cartridges. Each.........................................$2.85
No. 895. 38 caliber, 3¼ inch barrel, Weight 16 ounces. Each.........................................$2.85
4 inch, either caliber...........................3.25
5 inch, either caliber...........................3.50

## IVER JOHNSON HAMMERLESS AUTOMATIC REVOLVER.

No. 896. The above illustrated revolver is the celebrated Iver Johnson automatic hammerless double action; high grade finish, fine adjustments. Its trigger locking device makes it one of the safest revolvers to carry in the pocket. Automatic self-ejector, rebounding lock, safety trigger locking device, chambered cylinder, rifled barrel, nickel plated, 32 caliber, Smith & Wesson small frame, 5 shot, weight 13 oz., length of barrel 3 inches; a revolver that retails at from $7.00 to $10.00.
Our special price.........................$4.35
Or 38 caliber, 3¼ inch.......................4.35

## HOPKINS & ALLEN AUTOMATIC HAMMERLESS DOUBLE ACTION REVOLVER FOR $4.85.

Consider our price and our cash discount of 3 per cent. also our liberal terms, C. O. D. offer, and the fact that this revolver will be sent by mail on receipt of 22c. extra to pay postage, and you will then have the advantages to be gained by placing your order in our hands.

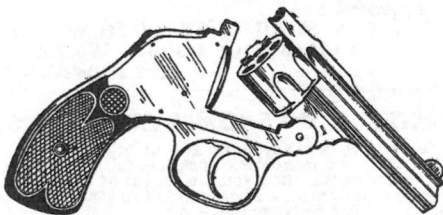

No. 897. The above illustrated revolver is the celebrated Hopkins & Allen automatic hammerless double action; high grade finish, fine adjustments. Its trigger locking device makes it one of the safest revolvers to carry in the pocket. Automatic self-ejector, rebounding lock, safety trigger locking device, chambered cylinder, rifled barrel, nickel plated, 32 caliber, Smith & Wesson small frame, 5 shot, weight 13 oz., length of barrel 3 inches, a revolver that retails at from $7.00 to $10.00, our special price.........................$4.85
No. 898. 38 caliber Smith & Wesson large frame, weight 18 oz., length of barrel 3½ inches, our price.......4.85
We furnish either of the above revolvers when so desired in blued finish at the same price. Pearl handles.........................$2.20 extra.

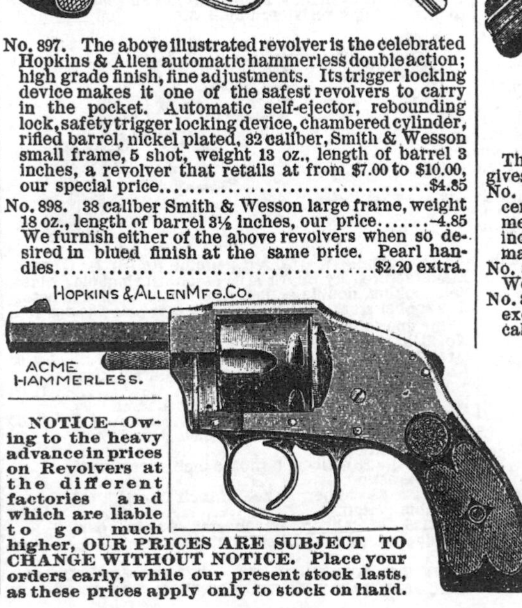

HOPKINS & ALLEN MFG. CO.

ACME HAMMERLESS.

NOTICE—Owing to the heavy advance in prices on Revolvers at the different factories and which are liable to go much higher, OUR PRICES ARE SUBJECT TO CHANGE WITHOUT NOTICE. Place your orders early, while our present stock lasts, as these prices apply only to stock on hand.

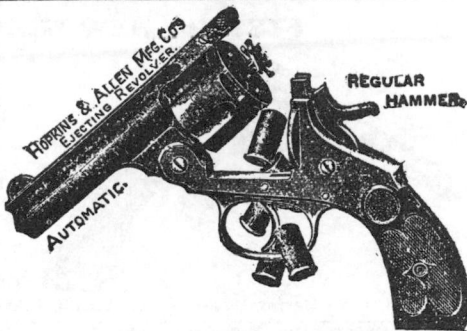

The above illustration shows you the Hopkins & Allen shell ejecting double action self-cocking revolver. Very finest forged steel barrels and cylinders, in all respects the best material and finish, guaranteed accurate, safe and reliable, nickel plated rubber stock, a high grade revolver at a heretofore unheard of price.
No. 8100. 32 caliber, 5 shot, 12 oz., 3 inch barrel, our price.........................$3.65
No. 8101. 38 caliber, 5 shot, 17 oz., 3¼ inch barrel, our price.........................$3.65
No. 8102. 22 caliber, rim fire, 7 shot, 12 oz., 3 inch barrel, our price.........................$3.65
We can furnish these revolvers in blued finish when so desired at 30c extra.

## HOPKINS & ALLEN DOUBLE ACTION REVOLVER FOR $1.70

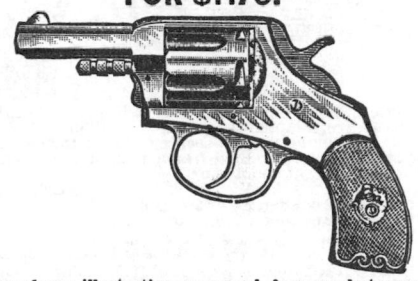

The above illustration engraved from a photograph shows you the double action, self-cocking revolver, nickel plated rubber stock, finely finished, accurate and reliable, rifled barrels, weight 16 oz., a thoroughly first-class arm.
No. 8106. 32 caliber, 3 inch barrel, our price........$1.70
No. 8107. 38 caliber, 3 inch barrel, our price........1.70

## THE HOPKINS & ALLEN AUTOMATIC SHELL EJECTING FOLDING HAMMER REVOLVER FOR $3.95.

The above illustration engraved from a photograph gives you an idea of the appearance of this revolver.
No. 8103. Hopkins & Allen automatic shell ejecting center fire, double action, self-cocking, folding hammer revolver, 32 caliber, 3 inch barrel or 38 caliber, 3¼ inch barrel, nickel plated, fancy rubber stock, finely made and accurate, 5 shot, 17 oz., our price.......$3.95
No. 8104. Same revolver as above only 32 or 38 Smith & Wesson caliber, blued finish.......................$4.10
No. 8105. Hopkins & Allen revolver, same as above, except 5¼ inch barrel, nickel plated rubber stock, 38 caliber, weight 19 oz.............................$4.90

## HOPKINS & ALLEN ACME HAMMERLESS DOUBLE ACTION SELF-COCKING REVOLVER FOR $2.60.

The above illustration shows you the Hopkins & Allen double action self-cocking rebounding lock, safety trigger locking device, chambered cylinder; safe, reliable and accurate, a regular $5.00 revolver.
No. 899. 32 caliber, 5 shot, weighs 11 oz., 2¾ inch octagon barrel. Our price.......$2.60
Postage extra, 19c.

## STEVENS' NEW MODEL

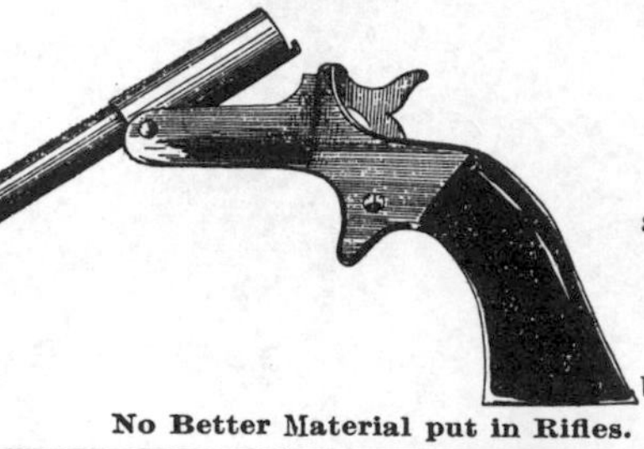

### STEVENS' SINGLE SHOT PISTOL

8108 Tip-up barrel, plated finish, 3½ inch barrel, 22 caliber only, rim fire.

A FINE TARGET PISTOL.

Price ....................$2.25

No Better Material put in Rifles. Weight 8 oz.

## REMINGTON DERRINGERS.

When you order revolvers sent by mail, postage must always be included.

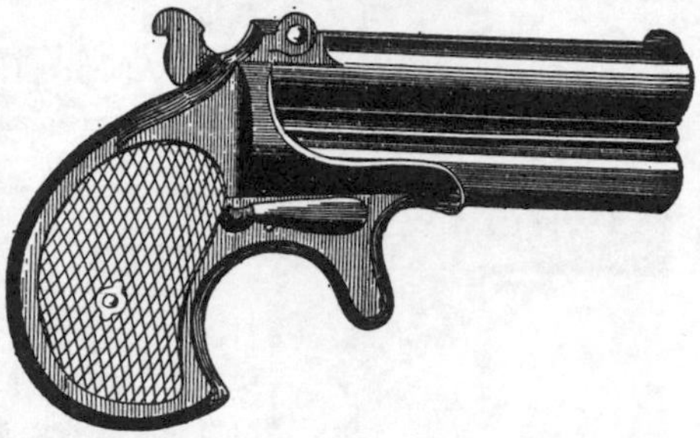

8109 Remington Double Derringer, 41 caliber, rim fire, nickel plated or blued, checkered rubber stock, length of barrels 3 inches, length over all 5 inches. Weight 12 oz. Price........................................$5.15

## COLT'S REVOLVERS.

The same terms on Colt's revolvers, C. O. D., to any-one anywhere, subject to examination on receipt of $1.00. Examine them at the express office, and if found satisfactory, pay our price and express charges, less the $1.00 sent with your order, otherwise pay nothing. If cash in full accompanies your order, we will allow you a discount of 3 per cent. Besides, we will ship any Colt's revolver, by registered mail, postage paid, on receipt of 25c. extra to pay postage.

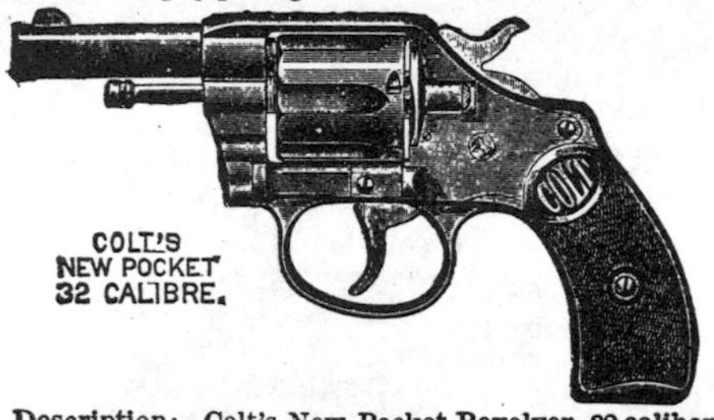
COLT'S
NEW POCKET
32 CALIBRE.

Description: Colt's New Pocket Revolver, 32 caliber, central fire, adapted to long and short Colt's C. F. Cartridges, double action, self-cocking, blued or nickel plated, as desired, jointless solid frame with simultaneous extractor. Weight about 14 oz.

| | | Our Special Prices. |
|---|---|---|
| No. 8112. | 32 caliber, 2½ or 3½ inch barrel | $10.00 |
| No. 8113. | 32 caliber, 6 inch barrel........ | 11.00 |

## COLT'S ARMY DOUBLE ACTION REVOLVER.

Sent to anyone C. O. D., subject to examination on receipt of $1.00, balance payable at express office. If cash in full accompanies your order, we allow a discount of 3 per cent.

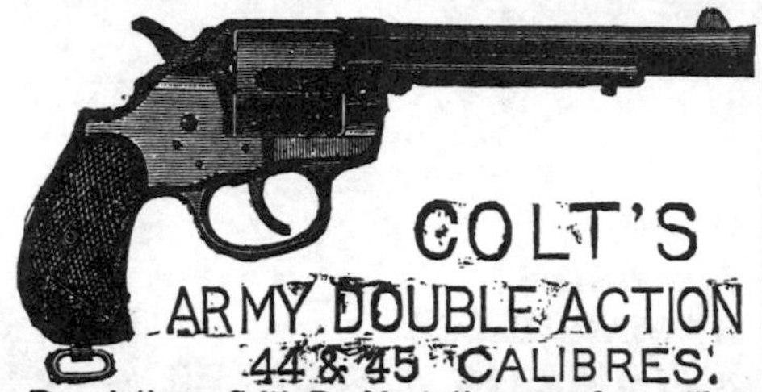
COLT'S
ARMY DOUBLE ACTION
44 & 45 CALIBRES.

Description: Colt's Double Action. 44 and 45 caliber. Every one warranted. Made by the Colt's patent Fire Arms Co., Hartford, Conn. Colt's Revolver, army size, double action, self-cocking, 44 and 45 caliber, Winchester center fire, case hardened, nickel plated or blued, as desired. Rubber stock with sliding spring ejector barrels, 4¾, 5½ or 7½ inches long, as desired; 6 shooter.
No. 8115. Price.......................................$13.75

## COLT'S DOUBLE ACTION REVOLVER.

C. O. D. to anyone, $1.00 in advance, balance payable at express office. For cash in full with order 3 per cent discount allowed.

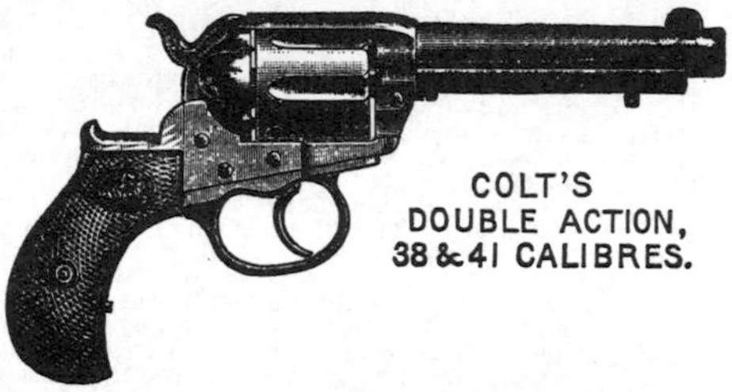
COLT'S
DOUBLE ACTION,
38 & 41 CALIBRES.

Description: Colt's Double Action, sliding ejector. Every one warranted. 38 or 41 caliber, 6 shooter, center fire, nickel plated or blued, as desired, 4½, 5 or 6 inch barrel, as desired.
No. 8116. Our special price.................................$12.00
Remember, you get a 3 per cent discount if cash in full accompanies your order.

## COLT'S ARMY MODEL, 1892.

C. O. D. to anyone on receipt of $1.00, balance payable at express office. Discount of 3 per cent for cash in full.

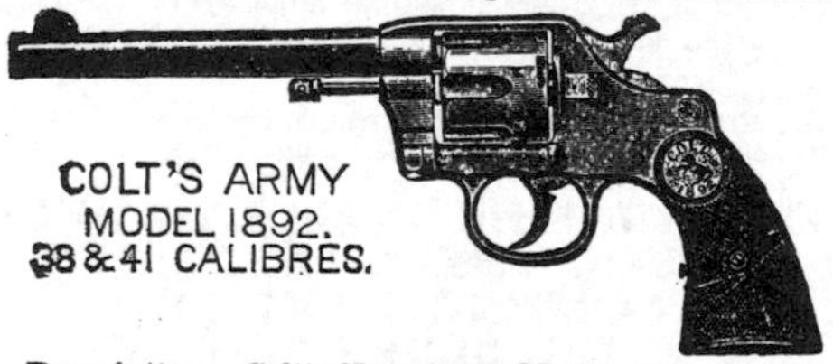
COLT'S ARMY
MODEL 1892.
38 & 41 CALIBRES.

Description: Colt's New Army Model, 1892. Double action, self-cocking, jointless solid frame with simultaneous ejector. Blued or nickel plated, as desired. Weight 2 lbs., 6 shooter, 38 or 41 caliber, length of barrel 3, 4½ or 6 inches as desired.
No. 8114. Our special price................................$12.00
By registered mail, 48c extra to pay postage.

## COLT'S SINGLE ACTION ARMY, FRONTIER AND TARGET REVOLVERS.

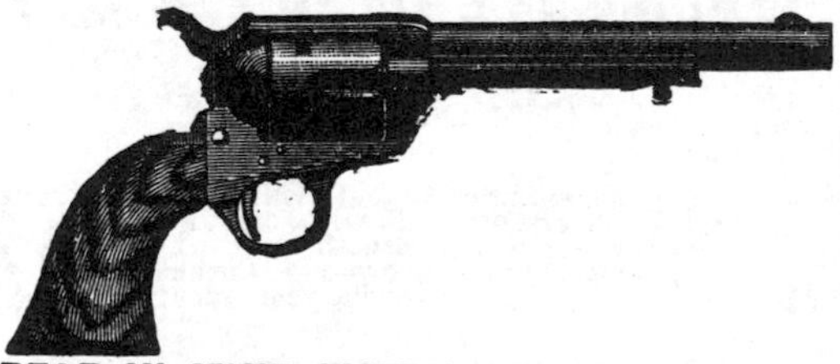

Barrels 7½ inches, weight 2 lbs. and 5 ozs. C. O. D. to anyone, $1.00 in advance, balance payable at express office. 3 per cent discount for cash.

Description: Single action, six shooter, rubber stock, solid frame, the best quality and finish, warranted perfect and accurate in every detail. Nickel plated or blued, as desired. Barrel 7½ inches; length 12½ inches; 32, 38, 44, 41 or 45 caliber, as desired.
No. 8117. Our special price.......................$12.95

**BEAR IN MIND EVERY GUN WE SELL is thoroughly tested and targeted before it leaves our house. We handle only the HIGHEST GRADE goods, and ALWAYS AT LOWEST PRICES.**

## COLT'S NEW NAVY, MADE BY THE COLT'S PATENT FIRE ARMS COMPANY, HARTFORD, CONN.

This revolver has been adopted by the U. S. navy, and every one has to pass a rigid inspection.

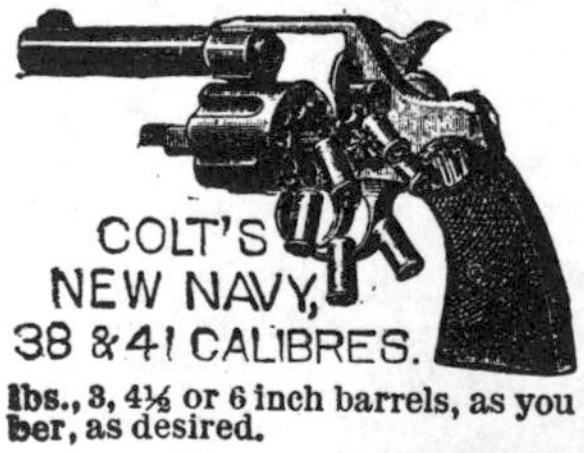
COLT'S
NEW NAVY,
38 & 41 CALIBRES.

Description: Colt's New Navy double action, self-cocking, automatic shell ejecting revolver, nickel plated or blued, as desired, rubber stock, beautifully finished, finest material, length about 12½ inches, 6 shooter, weight 2 lbs., 3, 4½ or 6 inch barrels, as you desire, 38 or 41 caliber, as desired.

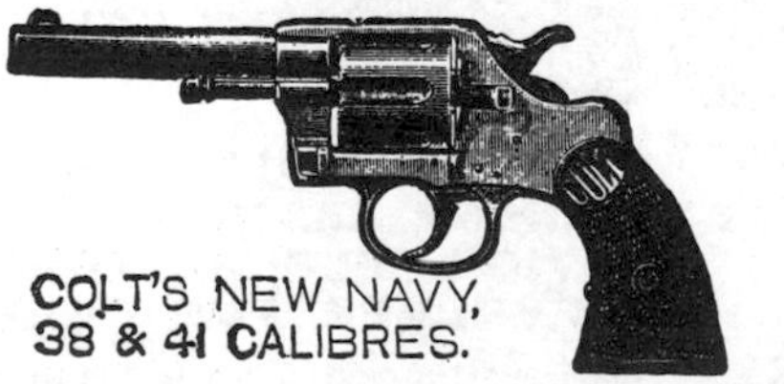
COLT'S NEW NAVY,
38 & 41 CALIBRES.

No. 8117½. Price.......................................$12.00
Our special price, $12. C. O. D. to anyone, $1.00 in advance, balance payable at express office. A 3 per cent, discount allowed if cash in full accompanies your order.

## SMITH & WESSON REVOLVERS.

Terms C. O. D. to anyone on receipt of $1.00, balance to be paid at express office. If cash in full accompanies your order we will allow you a discount of 3 per cent. If to be sent by mail, send cash in full and 25 cents extra to pay postage; registered mail, 33c.

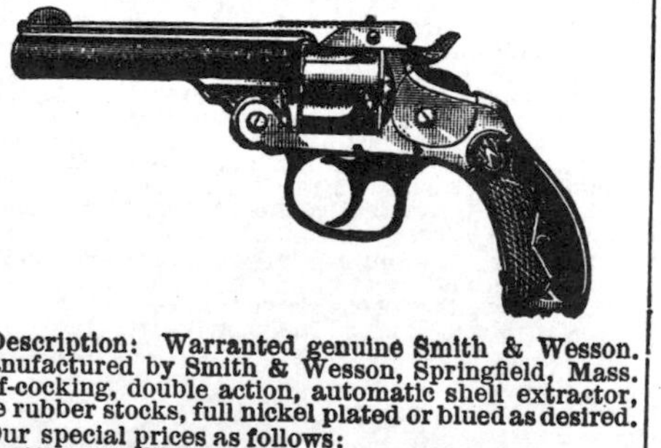

Description: Warranted genuine Smith & Wesson. Manufactured by Smith & Wesson, Springfield, Mass. Self-cocking, double action, automatic shell extractor, fine rubber stocks, full nickel plated or blued as desired.

Our special prices as follows:

| | | |
|---|---|---|
| No. 8118. | 32 caliber, 5-shot, 3 and 3½ inch barrel, best double action.......... | $9.95 |
| No. 8119. | 32 caliber, 5-shot, 6 inch barrel, best double action.......... | 11.00 |
| No. 8120. | 38 caliber, 5-shot, 3¼ inch barrel, best double action.......... | 11.00 |
| No. 8121. | 38 caliber, 5-shot, 4 inch barrel, best double action.......... | 11.25 |
| No. 8121½. | 38 caliber, 5-shot, 5 inch barrel, best double action.......... | 11.50 |
| No. 8122. | 38 caliber, 5-shot, 6 inch barrel, best double action.......... | 12.00 |
| No. 8123. | 44 caliber, Winchester, 5-shot, cartridge, 4 inch barrel, best double action.......... | 13.00 |

No. 8124 S. & W. 44 caliber, 5 shot, 6 or 6½ in. barrel, chambered for either 44 Winchester center fire, or 44 S. & W. Russian model cartridges. Price...$13.75

| | |
|---|---|
| Extra for ivory stock, 32 or 38 caliber.......... | 1.25 |
| Extra for ivory stock, 44 caliber.......... | 2.00 |
| Extra for pearl stock, 32 or 38 caliber.......... | 2.00 |
| Extra for pearl stock, 44 caliber.......... | 4.00 |

## SMITH & WESSON HAMMERLESS REVOLVERS.

Terms: C. O. D. to anyone on receipt of $1.00, balance to be paid at express office. If cash in full accompanies your order we will allow 3 per cent. discount. If to be sent by mail, send cash in full and 25c. extra to pay postage; registered mail, 33c.

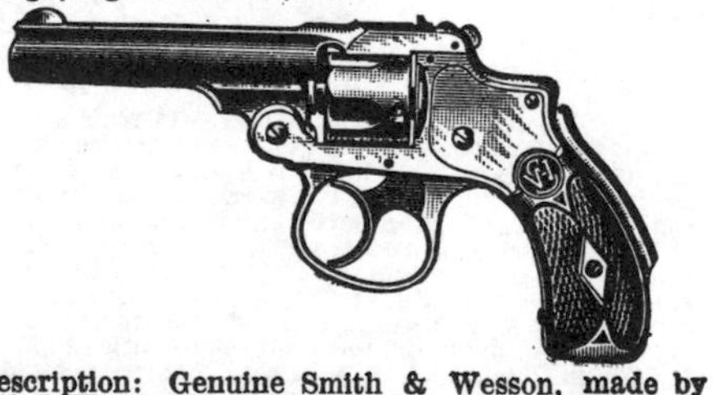

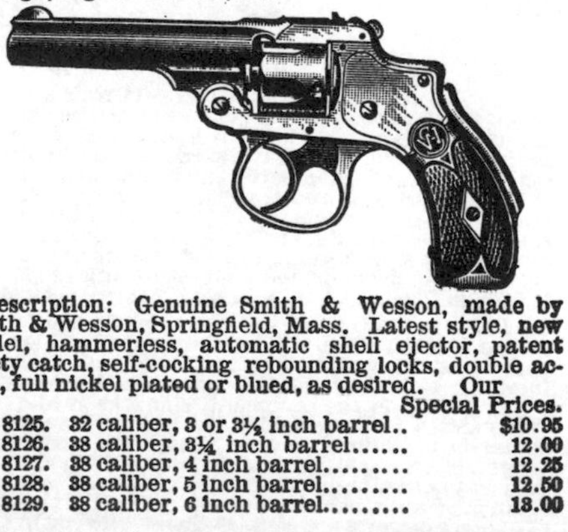

Description: Genuine Smith & Wesson, made by Smith & Wesson, Springfield, Mass. Latest style, new model, hammerless, automatic shell ejector, patent safety catch, self-cocking rebounding locks, double action, full nickel plated or blued, as desired.

| | | Our Special Prices. |
|---|---|---|
| No. 8125. | 32 caliber, 3 or 3½ inch barrel.. | $10.95 |
| No. 8126. | 38 caliber, 3¼ inch barrel...... | 12.00 |
| No. 8127. | 38 caliber, 4 inch barrel...... | 12.25 |
| No. 8128. | 38 caliber, 5 inch barrel...... | 12.50 |
| No. 8129. | 38 caliber, 6 inch barrel...... | 13.00 |

IF WE MAKE A MISTAKE, WE ASK A CHANCE TO CORRECT IT. WITH 600 EMPLOYEES FILLING THOUSANDS OF ORDERS, AN OCCASIONAL ERROR CANNOT BE AVOIDED.

# AIR RIFLES AND BELONGINGS—THE CHICAGO AIR RIFLE.

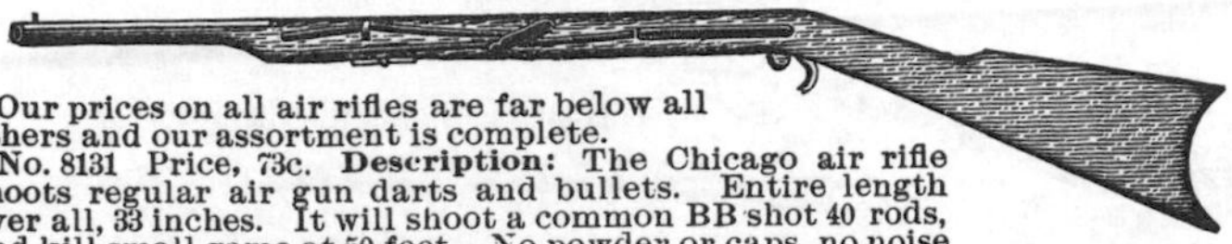

Our prices on all air rifles are far below all others and our assortment is complete.
No. 8131 Price, 73c. Description: The Chicago air rifle shoots regular air gun darts and bullets. Entire length over all, 33 inches. It will shoot a common BB shot 40 rods, and kill small game at 50 feet. No powder or caps, no noise not dangerous to handle. By its use a person can become a perfect shot. It costs but one cent to shoot 100 times. The barrel, air chamber and all working parts are made of brass and steel. The stock is maple, nicely stained and varnished, representing rosewood. The air chamber and barrel are of mandrel drawn brass, accurately bored and polished. The barrel has a perfect device for holding the ball tight to place. The plunger and piston is of the very best of steel and made specially for this purpose. All parts are made to stand continued usage and not get out of order.
**Postage Extra, 35 cents.**

## THE KING AIR RIFLE SINGLE SHOT.

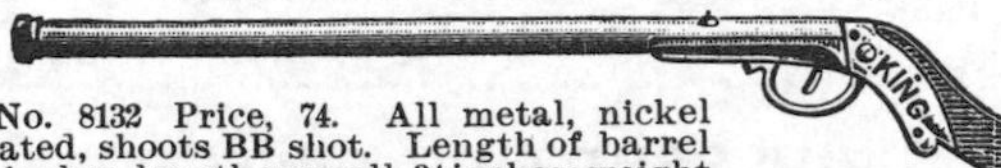

No. 8132 Price, 74. All metal, nickel plated, shoots BB shot. Length of barrel 19 inches, length over all, 34 inches; weight 2 lbs. The King air rifle shoots common BB shot accurately and with sufficient force to go through ¼-inch soft pine. The barrel and all working parts can be easily removed by simply unscrewing the metal cap on front part of gun, a feature when seen that must be appreciated. as it makes the removal of shot that are sure to become lodged in all muzzle-loading air guns a very simple and easy matter. Each gun is sighted with movable sights and packed in paper box, with sample package of shot and directions.
No. 8132½ New King Repeater, shoots 150 times, made by the same concern that makes King single shot and the appearance of the rifle is almost the same. Best repeater made. Onr special price, $1.15.
**Postage, 35 cents.**

## THE DAISY AIR RIFLE.

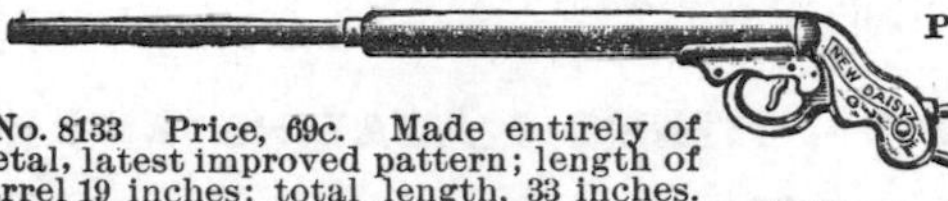

**Postage, 35 cents.**

No. 8133 Price, 69c. Made entirely of metal, latest improved pattern; length of barrel 19 inches; total length, 33 inches. Weight, 2½ lbs. Is now fitted with globe sights, each rifle carefully tested before leaving factory.

## THE DANDY REPEATING AIR RIFLE.

No. 8134 Price, $1.75. Shoots 45 times without reloading. Full length, 29 inches. Nickel plated barrel, 16 inches long. One movement in loading. Nice, light colored hardwood stock, shoots BB shot; cocking lever works similar to those on the Winchester repeating rifle.

## MATCHLESS REPEATING AIR RIFLE.

No. 8135 Price, $1.75 Shoots 65 times without reloading. Length of gun. 36 inches; weight 3 lbs. 4 oz., weight packed ready for shipment, 5 lbs. The Matchless for BB shot. The accompanying cut gives a good idea of the shape of the "Matchless" rifle. The stock is made of black walnut, nicely finished. The barrel is made of heavy brass tubing, nickel plated with block nickel.
No. 8135¼ Same as No. 8133, except has wood stock and is more finely finished. **Our special price each, 85 cents.**
No. 8135½ BB shot especially for the above rifles.
Per 1 lb. package, 10c. Per 5 lb. bag, 40c.
No. 8135¾ Main springs for Chicago, King or Daisy, 10c. each. Matchless, 15c.

## QUACKENBUSH IMPROVED NICKEL PLATED AIR GUN.

No. 8136 Price. $5.95. No. 1—$2-100 caliber full length, 36 inches; weight, 4½ lbs. Shoots darts and slugs. Each gun is neatly boxed, with 6 patent darts, 6 paper targets. 100 slugs, together with a combined claw and wrench. The gun can be instantly taken apart for the convenience of carrying in trunk or valise.

## DARTS, SLUGS, ETC.

| | |
|---|---|
| 17-100 Darts for Quackenbush rifle, per doz | $0 50 |
| 21-100 " " " " " | 0 50 |
| 17-100 Felted slugs for Quackenbush rifle, per 100 | 0 15 |
| 21-100 " " " " | 0 15 |
| BB shot, 5 lb. bag | 0 50 |
| BB shot, 25 lb. bag | 2 00 |

## FLOBERT RIFLES—$1.65 BUYS A $3.00 RIFLE.

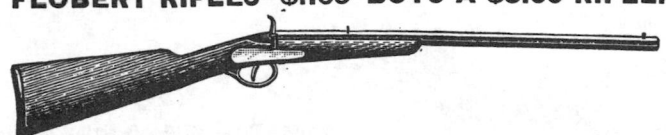

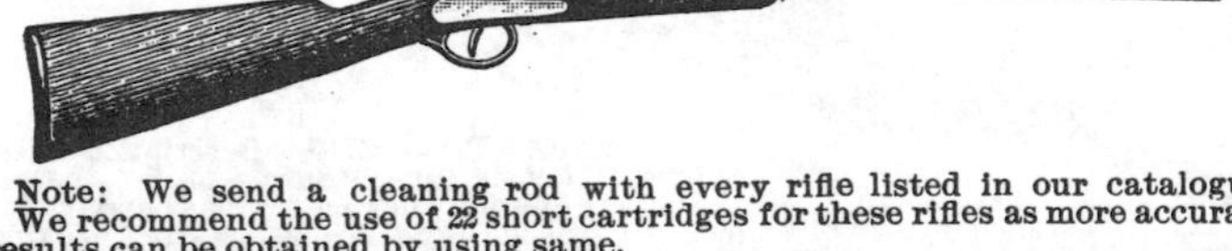

Note: We send a cleaning rod with every rifle listed in our catalogue. We recommend the use of 22 short cartridges for these rifles as more accurate results can be obtained by using same.
No. 8137 Price, $1.65. Cash in full must accompany your order for these rifles. We sell them at a few cents profit and can't afford to ship C. O. D. If gun does not prove satisfactory you can return it at our expense and we will refund your money. **Description:** This rifle is made for BB caps, has side extractor, bright mountings, varnished stock, 32 inch barrel, weighs about 4½ lbs. **Our special price, $1.65.**

## REMINGTON SYSTEM FLOBERT RIFLE.

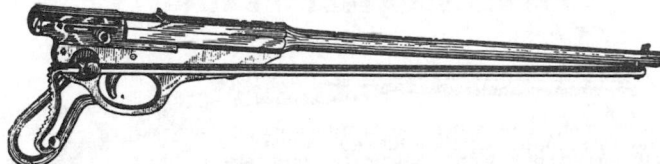

No. 8138 Price, $2.85. Description: Remington system, for 22 caliber (rim fire) cartridges, polished barrel, Remington action, scroll guard, light barrel, rifled, oiled stock, dark mountings, fine checkered pistol grip, 22 inch barrel, weighs about 4½ lbs. Our special price, $2.85.

## WARNANT SYSTEM FLOBERT RIFLE.

No. 8139 Price, $3.00. Description: Warnant, or Springfield action, polished heavy barrel, rifled pistol grip, fancy butt, scroll guard, carved stock, dark mountings, 24 inch barrel, weight about 6 lbs. Uses 22 caliber rim fire cartridges. Our special price, $3.00.

No. 8139¼ Same as above, lighter for boys use, well made and accurate. The safest rifle for boys. Our special price, $2.50.
No. 8139½ New model Warnant action, oiled walnut stocks, checkered pistol grip, 24 inch barrel, 32 caliber, short rim fire, shell extractor, barrel very finely rifled, weight 6½. Our special price, $2.90.

## BICYCLE RIFLE.

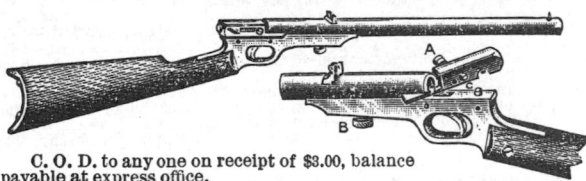

No. 8139¾ Perfectly accurate. all steel, beautifully finished and can be used either as a rifle or a pistol.
Breech system same as that used on the Quackenbush Safety Rifle. The skeleton stock can be moved in and out quickly and is held firmly when in place. The form of stock and pistol grip are such that the rifle comes to the shoulder, hand and eye, as conveniently as any rifle. Each rifle is tested before leaving the works.
Shoots 22 short, 22 long, 22 long rifle, or 22 short cartridges, or BB caps.

| 22 caliber, whole length 27 inches, closed 16 inches, 12 inch barrel, weight 31 oz. | each, $4 20 |
|---|---|
| Canvas Holster for same, to attach to bicycle | each, 0 35 |
| Leather Holster for same, to attach to bicycle | each, 0 70 |

Postage on rifle if mailed, 40c. On canvas Holster, 5c. Leather Hotster, 8c. If sent by registered mail add 8c. for same.

## THE QUACKENBUSH JUNIOR SAFETY RIFLE— $4.00 BUYS AN $8.00 RIFLE.

No. 8140. Price, $4.25. Description.—The Quackenbush Junior Safety rifle has a fine steel nickel plated skeleton stock, which can be easily detached for carrying in small space. Nickel plated barrels, finely rifled. Whole length, 33 inches. Weight 4 pounds, 22 inch caliber, rim fire only. Safe, accurate and reliable, and fully warranted by the manufacturers. Our special price .................... $4.00

## QUACKENBUSH'S SAFETY CARTRIDGE RIFLE— $4.65 BUYS A $10.00 RIFLE.

C. O. D. to any one on receipt of $3.00, balance payable at express office.
No. 8141. Price. $4.70 Description—Fine steel barrel, automatic cartridge extractor. Stock is black walnut, handsomely finished, and so fastened to the barrel that the two may be easily and quickly separated, making the arm handy to carry in a trunk, valise or package. The barrel and parts are well and durably nickeled, except the breech block, which is case hardened in color. Whole length 33 inches, 18 inch barrel, weight about 4½ lbs., 22 caliber for regular rim fire. "BB" or long and short cartridges. Plain open sights, as shown in cut. Our price with 18 inch barrel...$4.65
Our price with 22 inch barrel .................... 4.85

## REMINGTON RIFLE. NEW MODEL No. 4, SINGLE SHOT.

Description : Remington Rifle No. 4, oiled walnut stock, case hardened frames and mountings, open front and rear sights. As finely rifled as any rifle in the market, and made of the very best rifle material. Perfectly accurate, and every one warranted. No better or longer range rifles made of these calibers. Warranted as represented.
No. 8142. Our special price, 22 caliber, rim fire, 22½ inch octagon barrel, weight 4½ lbs., rifle butt. A fine little rifle and an accurate shooter................$5.00
No. 8143. Our special price, 32 caliber, rim fire, 24 inch octagon barrel, weight 4½ lbs., rifle butt.................... $5.00

**SEE OUR WONDERFUL BARGAIN $17.90 DAVIS HAMMER GUN ON PAGE 566 WE SHIP ALL GUNS C. O. D. SUBJECT TO EXAMINATION ON A SMALL DEPOSIT.**

## STEVENS' FAVORITE RIFLE—DETACHABLE BARREL.

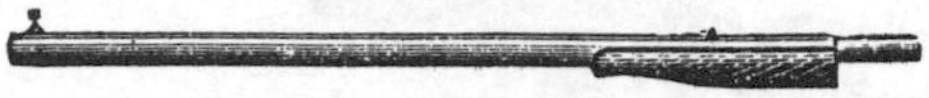

This picture shows barrel and stock detached.

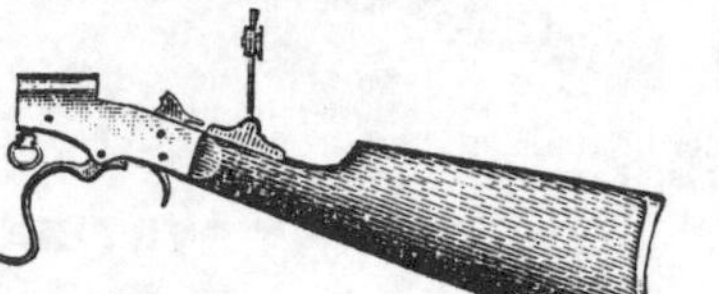

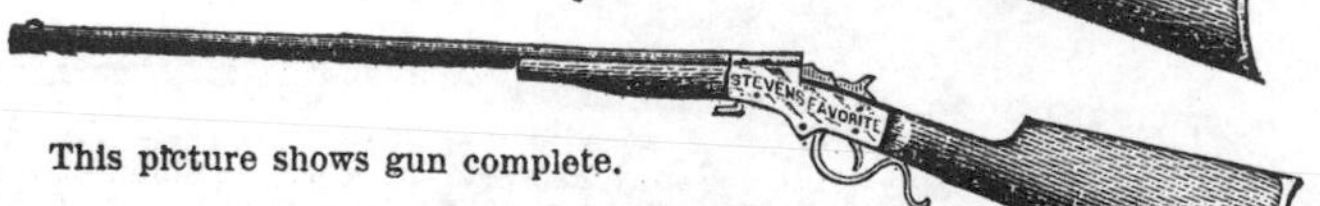

This picture shows gun complete.

No. 8167. Price, $6.00. Description: Guaranteed as well finished and rifled a barrel as found in the most costly rifles. Entirely new model. The barrel is held to stock by a set screw, and easily separated or put together. Rifling and quality of barrel same as the higher cost rifle. Case hardened frame, walnut stock, finely finished, warranted accurate, rim fire, 22 caliber, using long or short cartridges, 22 inch barrel, weight, 4½ lbs. Our special price..............................$6.00

## STEVENS' LATEST IDEAL RIFLE.

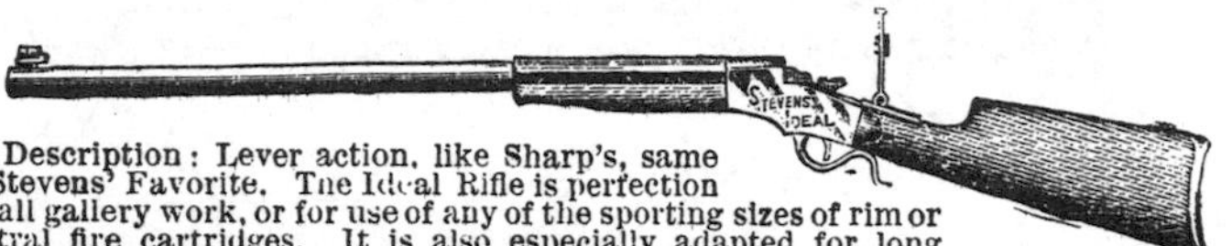

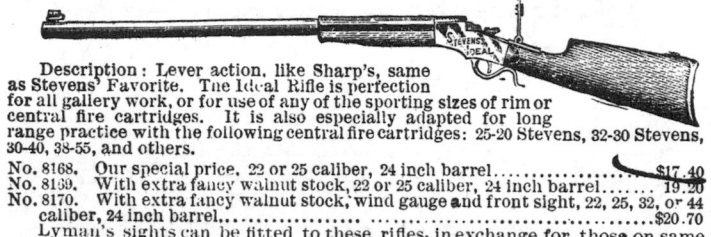

Description: Lever action, like Sharp's, same as Stevens' Favorite. The Ideal Rifle is perfection for all gallery work, or for use of any of the sporting sizes of rim or central fire cartridges. It is also especially adapted for long range practice with the following central fire cartridges: 25-20 Stevens, 32-30 Stevens, 30-40, 38-55, and others.

No. 8168. Our special price, 22 or 25 caliber, 24 inch barrel..............$17.40
No. 8169. With extra fancy walnut stock, 22 or 25 caliber, 24 inch barrel........ 19.20
No. 8170. With extra fancy walnut stock, wind gauge and front sight, 22, 25, 32, or 44 caliber, 24 inch barrel..............................$20.70

Lyman's sights can be fitted to these rifles, in exchange for those on same at our regular prices for sights.

Extra for each 2 inches in length of barrel over 24 inches.................. 1.20

## REMINGTON FINE TARGET RIFLE.

No. 8144. Rim fire, 22 caliber, using "B. B." cap, or 22 long or short cartridge, 24 inch octagon barrel, weight 5¼ to 6 lbs. Our special price..................$8.72
No. 8145. Rim fire, 32 caliber, using long or short rim fire cartridges, 28 inch octagon barrel, weight, 5¾ to 6 lbs. Price..............................$8.75

## REMINGTON NO. 3, LONG RANGE TARGET RIFLE.

Their best rifle. Over 1,000,000 sold. No other single shot rifle has such a wonderful sale. Latest model guaranteed. Every rifle warranted by the manufacturers. This rifle is especially designed for long range hunting and target purposes. It has a solid breech block, with direct rear support, rebounding hammer, so that it always stands with the trigger in the safety notch, rendering premature discharge impossible. This rifle makes a flatter trajectory than other rifles, and is unequaled for target and sporting use. No better or more accurate rifle in the market. All have side lever, oiled walnut stock, pistol grip checkered, rebounding hammer, case hardened frame and mountings, open front and rear sights, full octagon barrels. Set trigger $2.75 extra.

No. 8146. 32-30 caliber, 30 inch, 8½ to 9 lbs. Price..............................$14.75
No. 8147. 32-40 caliber, 30 inch octagon barrel, 8½ to 9 lbs. Sure at 200 yards. 14.75
No. 8148. 38-55 caliber, 30 inch octagon barrel, 8½ to 9½ lbs. Sure at 100 to 500 yards..............................$14.75
No. 8149. 40-65 caliber, 30 inch octagon barrel, 4¾ to 10 lbs. weight. Sure at 150 to 600 yards..............................$14.75
No. 8150. 40-90 caliber, 32 inch octagon barrel 10 to 11 lbs. weight. Long range, 16.75
No. 8151. 45-70 caliber, 30 inch octagon barrel, 10 lbs. Sure at 20 to 1000 yards. 14.75

Our Remington rifles are the best, and every rifle is fully warranted.

You know our terms:—C. O. D. to any one on receipt of $3.00, balance to be paid at express office. If you send cash in full with your order, a nice present will be sent you. You take no risk for we will cheerfully refund your money if you are not perfectly satisfied.

## MERWIN, HULBURT & CO.'S RIFLE AND SHOT GUN COMBINED. PRICE $13.50.

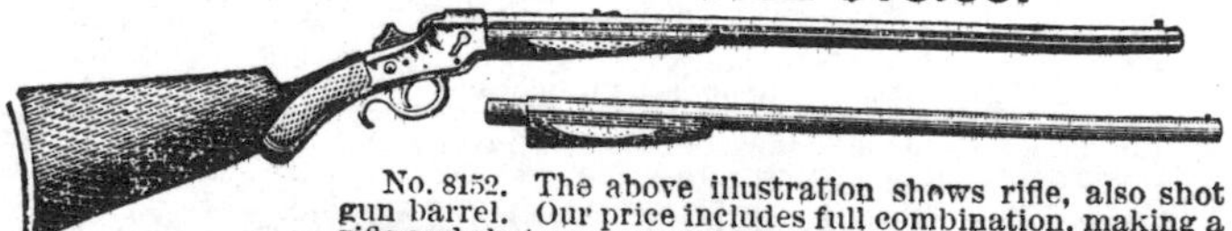

No. 8152. The above illustration shows rifle, also shot gun barrel. Our price includes full combination, making a rifle and shot gun complete in one arm.

The barrels are interchangeable, and can be easily taken apart by withdrawing a thumb screw, which, being tapered, takes up all wear that any gun is subject to, and makes it the most solid single barrel breech loader.

This combination shot gun and rifle is provided with rebounding locks and automatic shell ejector.

Our special price for 22 or 32 caliber (as desired), rim fire, 26 inch rifle barrel, and 16 gauge, 30 inch shot gun barrel, $13.50.

Our terms always the same—C. O. D. to any one on receipt of $3.00, balance to be paid at express office.



## MERWIN, HULBERT & CO.'S RIFLES.

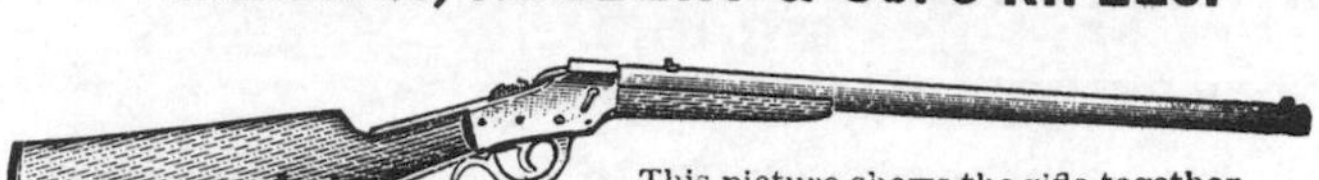

This picture shows the rifle together.

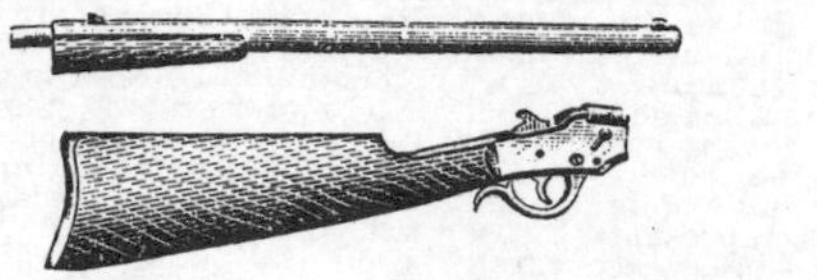

No. 8153. Price $4.95. Description.—Merwin, Hulbert & Co.'s Junior Rifle, single-shot, barrel easily removed from stock for packing or cleaning, blued barrel, case hardened lock plates, 22 inch round barrel, weighs 4½ lbs., perfectly reliable and accurate, barrel as well rifled as the best rifles, 22 caliber, rim fire, using BB caps and 22 long and short cartridges, ejects the empty shell from the gun when lever is thrown down. Our special price..............................$4.95

For 32 caliber, 22 inch round barrel, rim fire, long and short cartridge, ivory bead and sporting rear sights..............................$6.75

## MERWIN, HULBERT & CO.'S RIFLE.

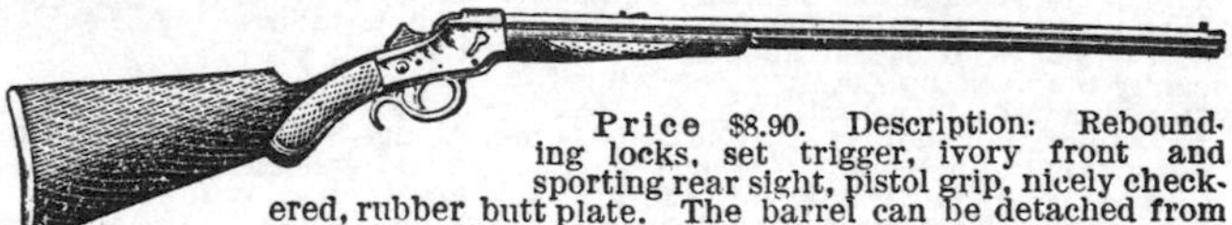

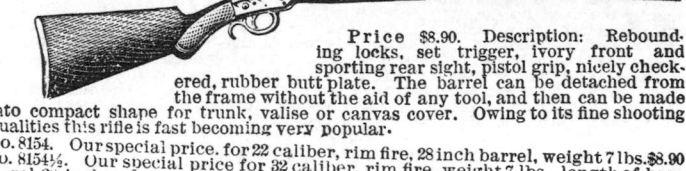

Price $8.90. Description: Rebounding locks, set trigger, ivory front and sporting rear sight, pistol grip, nicely checkered, rubber butt plate. The barrel can be detached from the frame without the aid of any tool, and then can be made into compact shape for trunk, valise or canvas cover. Owing to its fine shooting qualities this rifle is fast becoming very popular.

No. 8154. Our special price. for 22 caliber, rim fire, 28 inch barrel, weight 7 lbs.$8.90
No. 8154½. Our special price for 32 caliber, rim fire, weight 7 lbs., length of barrel 28 inches..............................$8.90
No. 8154¾. Our price, 32 caliber, W. C. F., 26 inch octogon barrel..........$8.75

## COLT'S NEW LIGHTNING MAGAZINE RIFLES.

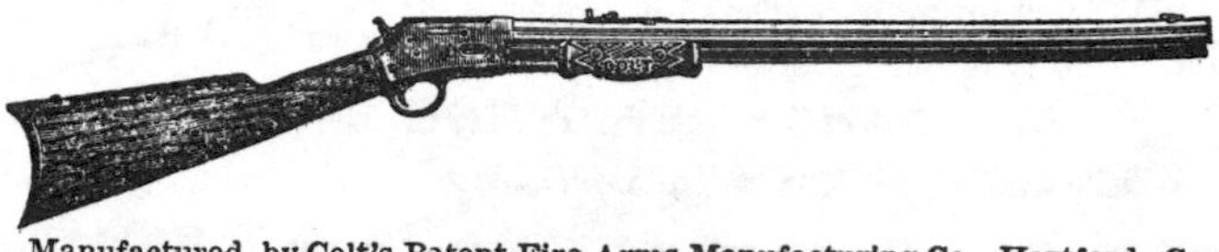

Manufactured by Colt's Patent Fire Arms Manufacturing Co., Hartford, Conn. Constructed upon entirely new principles. The workmanship is of the same high standard as that of other arms manufactured by this company. Old shell ejected and new cartridge inserted by sliding motion of the forearm, and as it can be done with the left hand, it is at once convenient and rapid. Every rifle warranted. 22 caliber is rim fire; all others are center fire, using same cartridges as Winchester rifles of same caliber, or U. M. C. special make.

| | | | | | | | | |
|---|---|---|---|---|---|---|---|---|
| No. 8155—22 | Caliber, 15 shot, | weight | 6¾ lbs., | 24 inch | octagon | barrel | .......... | $ 9.72 |
| No. 8156—32 | " 15 " | " | 6¾ " | 26 " | round | " | .......... | 10.94 |
| No. 8157—32 | " 15 " | " | 7¼ " | 26 " | octagon | " | .......... | 11.86 |
| No. 8158—38 | " 15 " | " | 6¾ " | 26 " | round | " | .......... | 10.94 |
| No. 8159—38 | " 15 " | " | 7¼ " | 26 " | octagon | " | .......... | 11.86 |
| No. 8160—44 | " 15 " | " | 6¾ " | 26 " | round | " | .......... | 10.94 |
| No. 8161—44 | " 15 " | " | 7½ " | 26 " | octagon | " | .......... | 11.86 |

## STEVENS' NEW MODEL POCKET RIFLE.

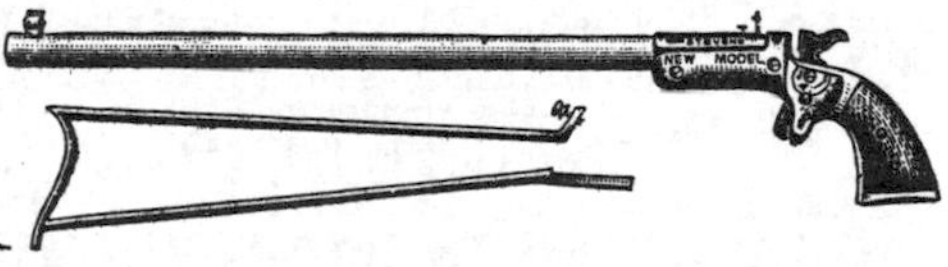

Description.—A fine target or squirrel rifle. Good for 100 yards. Latest model, 22 caliber, rim fire, shoots short cartridge or BB caps.

No. 8163. 12 inch barrel, weight 2¼ lbs. Our special price..............................$ 8.95
No. 8164. 15 inch barrel, weight 2½ lbs. Our special price.................. 10.13

## STEVENS' HUNTER'S PET RIFLE.

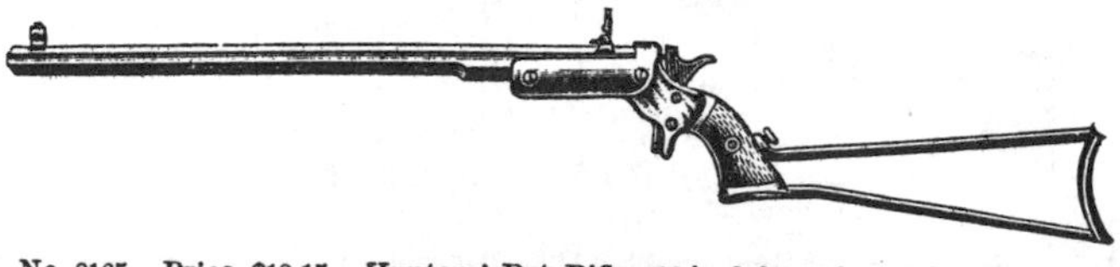

No. 8165. Price, $12.15. Hunters' Pet Rifle, 18 inch barrel, weight, 5¼ lbs., and good 40 rods, 22 or 32 caliber, rim fire cartridge. Our price, $12.15. Extra for 20 inch barrel, 85 cents.

## STEVENS' RIFLES.

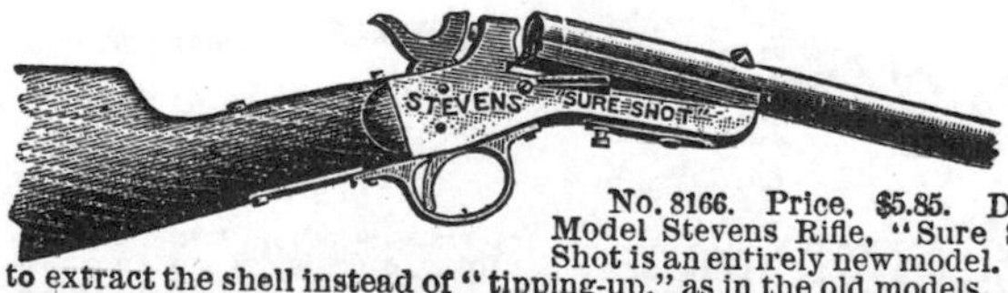


No. 8166. Price, $5.85. Description: New Model Stevens Rifle, "Sure Shot." The Sure Shot is an entirely new model. The barrel swings to extract the shell instead of "tipping-up," as in the old models. Barrels are rifled same as in the higher grades, and is a wonderful shooter. Frame nickel plated, walnut stock, rebounding lock, German silver front sight, finely finished throughout. Stock and barrels easily separated to clean or pack. Barrel 20 inches long. Entire length 34 inches, weight 3¼ lbs., 22 caliber, rim fire short, long or long rifle cartridge. Every rifle warranted as long range and as accurate as any 22 caliber rifle in the market. Our special price..............................$5.85

## MARLIN REPEATING RIFLES.

All arms of this make have solid top frames and eject to the side. The solid top keeps out rain, snow, twigs, pine needles, alkali dush, sand, etc., and protects the head of the shooter from any accident. The side ejection is much more convenient than the old-fashioned systems that throw the shell into your face, fill your nostrils and eyes with smoke and gas and generally interfere with a quick second or third shot. All barrels are exactly the same as **Ballard Target Barrels** made by the Marlin Company and so long recognized as the standard of accuracy throughout the world.

**Our Terms Always the Same.** Send us $3.00 as a guarantee of good faith and we will send any gun by express C. O. D., subject to examination, you can examine it at the express office and if found perfectly satisfactory pay the express agent the balance and express charges. **3 per cent discount if cash in full** accompanies gun order.

### MARLIN REPEATING RIFLES. MODEL 1892.

Rifles of this model have blued frames. Cut shows rifle with round barrel. In one and the same rifle, without adjusting, may be used any or all of the following rim fire cartridges; 22 short, 22 long, 22 long rifle and 22 short. This is the only repeater that will do this. Other systems require two or three rifles to do the same work. 22 short cartridges are accurate up to 100 ft. 22 long up to 150 ft. 22 long rifle up to 600 ft. The **Marlin** is the only repeater using the long rifle cartridge. These are guaranteed to shoot any of these cartridges as accurately as any arms made. This model takes entirely to pieces without tools, allowing of perfect cleaning.

No. 8171. Octagon barrel, 22 caliber, 24 inch, 6 lbs., 25 short, 20 long or short or 18 long rifle cartridge.................................. $11.85
No. 8172. Round barrel, same as above, 6¼ lbs.............................. 10.90
Pistol grips and all extra except take downs, set locks and short magazines.

### MARLIN REPEATING RIFLES. MODEL 1891.

Rifles of this model have blued frames. All rifles sent out with two firing pins. This rifle is so made that in the same rifle may be used 32 short rim fire, 32 long rim cartridges and by changing the firing pin 32 short center fire and 32 long fire. This ammunition is cheap, and as compared to repeaters using the 32-20 cartridge will save the entir cost of rifle on first 2,000 cartridges. The ammunition is what costs. Get the only repeter made for these cheap cartridges.

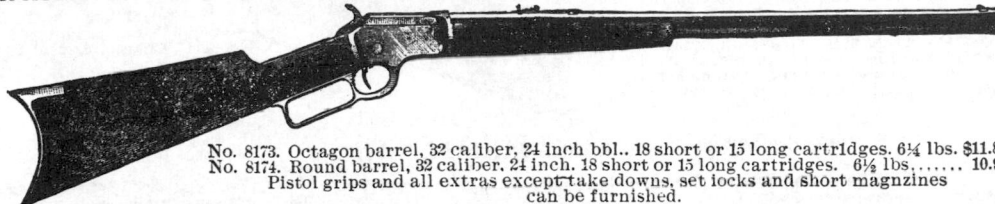

No. 8173. Octagon barrel, 32 caliber, 24 inch bbl.. 18 short or 15 long cartridges. 6¼ lbs. $11.85
No. 8174. Round barrel, 32 caliber, 24 inch. 18 short or 15 long cartridges. 6½ lbs....... 10.94
Pistol grips and all extras except take downs, set locks and short magazines can be furnished.

### MARLIN REPEATING RIFLES. MODEL 1894.

Rifles of this model have case hardened frames.

**Special Discount of 3 per cent When Cash in full accompanies order.**

No. 8175. Octagon barrel, 25-20 Marlin caliber, 24 inch barrel, 14 shots, 6⅞ lbs.................... $11.85
No. 8176. Round barrel. 25-20 Marlin caliber, 24 inch barrel, 14 shots, 7¼ lbs.................... 10.94
No. 8177. Octagon barrel, 32-20 caliber, 24 inch barrel, 14 shorts, 6⅞ lbs.................... 11.85
No. 8178. Round barrel, 32-20 caliber, 24 inch barrel, 14 shots, 7¼ lbs.................... 19.94
No. 8179. Octagon barrel, 38-40 caliber, 24 inch barrel, 14 shots, 6⅞ lbs.................... 11.85
No. 8180. Round barrel, 38-40 caliber, 24 inch barrel, 14 shots, 7¼ lbs.................... 10.94
No. 8181. Octagon barrel, 44-40 caliber, 24 inch barrel, 14 shots, 6⅞ lbs.................... 11.85
No. 8182. Round barrel, 44-40 caliber, 24 inch barrel, 14 shots, 7¼ lbs.................... 10.94

Extras of all kinds such as pistol grip, take down, etc., can be furnished on this model except set lock.

### MARLIN REPEATING CARBINE. MODEL 1894.

**ANY RIFLE SENT C. O. D. SUBJECT TO EXAMINATION ON RECEIPT OF $3.00 WITH ORDER**

Carbines have blued frames.
No. 8183. Can be furnished in 25-20 Marlin, 32-20, 38-40 or 44-40 calibers, 20 inch barrel, 12 shots, 6 lbs........ $10.64

### MARLIN "TAKE DOWN" ON MODELS 1892, 1893, 1894 AND 1895.

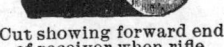

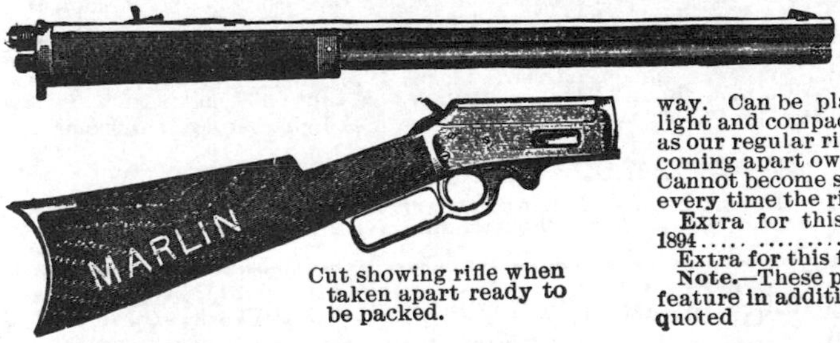

In this system the barrel is screwed into the frame exactly as in a solid rifle. No part of the thread is cut away, nor is this union weakened in anyway. Can be placed in a "Victoria" case. As light and compact to carry as a shot gun. Strong as our regular rifle; no looseness; no danger of coming apart owing to accident or carelessness. Cannot become shaky, as all wear is taken up every time the rifle is put together.

Extra for this feature models 1892, 1893 and 1894...........$3.07
Extra for this feature models 1885......... 3.37
**Note.**—These prices are for the "Take down" feature in addition to prices of rifles, as above quoted

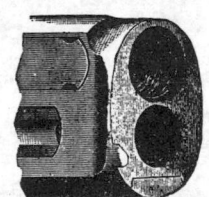

Cut showing rifle when taken apart ready to be packed.

Cut showing forward end of receiver when rifle is apart.

Cut showing breach end of barrel and magazine when rifle is apart.

### MARLIN PISTOL GRIP.

**Any of these special features can be had with any Marlin Rifle herein quoted, when the extra price is added.**

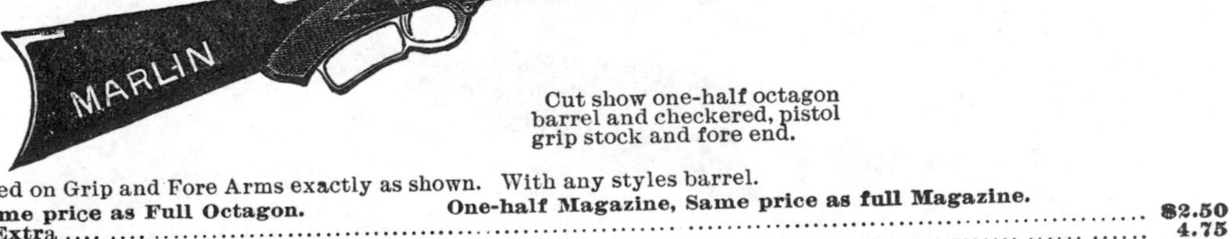

Cut show one-half octagon barrel and checkered, pistol grip stock and fore end.

Checked on Grip and Fore Arms exactly as shown. With any styles barrel.
One-half Octagon barrel, Same price as Full Octagon. One-half Magazine, Same price as full Magazine.
Plain Pistol Grip Stock without Checkering Extra .................................................... $2.50
Plain Walnut Checkered Pistol Grip Stock and Fore End Extra.................................... 4.75
Extra Select English Walnut Pistol Grip Stock, Full Checkered and Checkered Fore End........... 11.00
High grade work is the specialty of the Marlin Company. If you want anything fine write us for complete Marlin catalogue and our special prices. It take ordinarily two week to make a special rifle, depending, of course, on amount of extra work to be done.
Engraving costs from $5.00 up owing to Style of Engraving and amount of Labor required.

**ALL ABOVE FEATURES ARE EXTRAS, AND WHEN YOU WANT A MARLIN RIFLE WITH ANY OF THESE SPECIAL FEATURES, THE**

## MARLIN REPEATING RIFLES, MODEL 1893.

**Rifles have Cast Hardened Frames.**

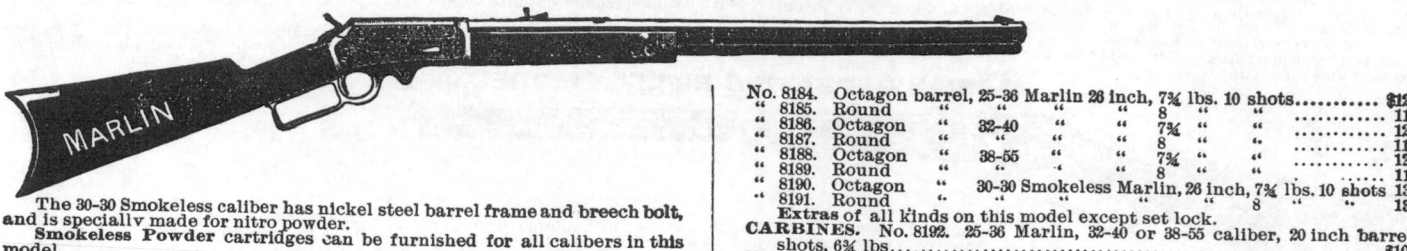

The 30-30 Smokeless caliber has nickel steel barrel frame and breech bolt, and is specially made for nitro powder.

Smokeless Powder cartridges can be furnished for all calibers in this model.

| | | | | | | | | |
|---|---|---|---|---|---|---|---|---|
| No. 8184. | Octagon barrel, | 25-36 Marlin | 26 inch, | 7¾ lbs. | 10 shots | $12.11 |
| " 8185. | Round | " | 8 | " | " | 11.26 |
| " 8186. | Octagon | " 32-40 | " | 7¾ | " | 12.11 |
| " 8187. | Round | " | 8 | " | " | 11.26 |
| " 8188. | Octagon | " 38-55 | " | 7¾ | " | 12.11 |
| " 8189. | Round | " | 8 | " | " | 11.26 |
| " 8190. | Octagon | " 30-30 Smokeless Marlin, | 26 inch, | 7¾ lbs. | 10 shots | 13.21 |
| " 8191. | Round | " | 8 | " | " | 13.21 |

Extras of all kinds on this model except set lock.

CARBINES. No. 8192. 25-36 Marlin, 32-40 or 38-55 caliber, 20 inch barrel, 7 shots, 6¾ lbs.........................$10.96

No. 8193. 30-30 Smokeless (nickel steel) 20 inch, 7 shots, 6¾ lbs............12.75

## MARLIN REPEATING RIFLES, MODEL 1895.

**Rifles of this Model have Case Hardened Receivers.**

The barrels in rifles of this model are made of nickel steel and guaranteed to fill government tests. The increasing use of nitro-powders makes this feature important. The barrels are also slighly tapered, giving extra strength around the chamber and making the balance of the rifle much better.

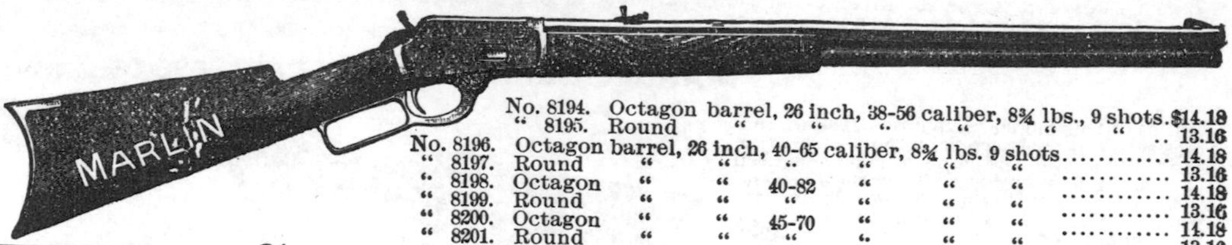

With shot gun rubber butt plate and half magazine a rifle will weigh about one-half pound less.

Ths 38-56 criliber Marlin uses the 38-56-255 cartridge. Smokeless cartridges in this size will be ready soon.

The 40-65 caliber Marlin uses the 40-65-260 or the 40-60-260 Marlin cartridge in the same rifle. Smokeless cartridges ready soon.

The 40-82 Marlin uses the 40-82-260 cartridge. Smokeless cartridges with metal patched bullets can be furnished.

The 45-70 Marlin uses the 45-70-405 Marlin, the 45-70-405 Government, the 45-70-500 Government, the 45-70-330 Gould's Express, the 45-70-350 or the 45-85-

| | | | | | | | |
|---|---|---|---|---|---|---|---|
| No. 8194. | Octagon barrel, 26 inch, | 38-56 caliber, | 8¾ lbs., | 9 shots. | $14.18 |
| " 8195. | Round | " | " | " | " | 13.16 |
| No. 8196. | Octagon barrel, 26 inch, | 40-65 caliber, | 8¾ lbs. | 9 shots | 14.18 |
| " 8197. | Round | " | " | " | " | 13.16 |
| " 8198. | Octagon | " 40-82 | " | " | " | 14.18 |
| " 8199. | Round | " | " | " | " | 13.16 |
| " 8200. | Octagon | " 45-70 | " | " | " | 14.18 |
| " 8201. | Round | " | " | " | " | 13.16 |
| " 8202. | Octagon | " 45-90 | " | " | " | 14.18 |
| " 8203. | Round | " 45-90 | " | " | " | 13.16 |

Marlin cartridges in the same rifle. Smokeless cartridges with metal patched bullets can also be furnished.

The 45-90 Marlin uses the 45-90-300, the 45-85-350, the 45-82-405, or the 45-85-300 Express cartridges in the same rifle. Smokeless cartridges with metal patched or mushroom bullets can be furnished.

All rifles of this model can be furnished with pistol grip, with take down and all other extras except set locks.

No. 8204. **Carbines** in this model 38-56, 40-65, 40-82, 45-70 or 45-90 caliber, 20 inch barrel, 6 shots, 7¾ lbs............$12.82

## WINCHESTER RIFLES. MODEL OF 1873.

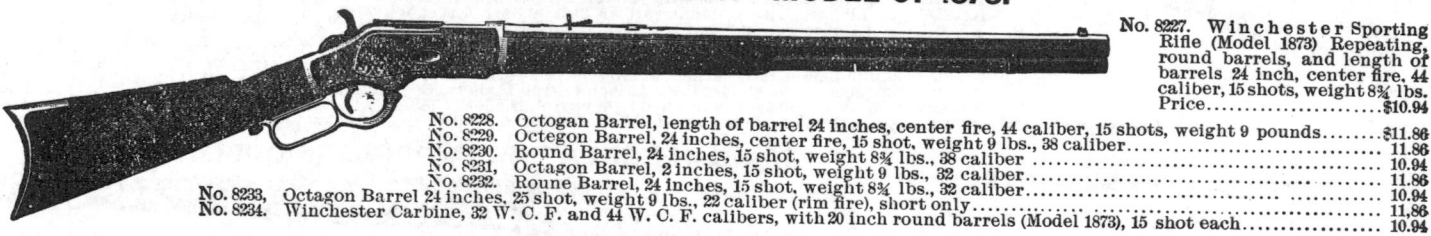

No. 8227. Winchester Sporting Rifle (Model 1873) Repeating, round barrels, and length of barrels 24 inch, center fire, 44 caliber, 15 shots, weight 8¾ lbs. Price..................$10.94

| | | |
|---|---|---|
| No. 8228. | Octogan Barrel, length of barrel 24 inches, center fire, 44 caliber, 15 shots, weight 9 pounds | $11.86 |
| No. 8229. | Octegon Barrel, 24 inches, center fire, 15 shot, weight 9 lbs., 38 caliber | 11.86 |
| No. 8230. | Round Barrel, 24 inches, 15 shot, weight 8¾ lbs., 38 caliber | 10.94 |
| No. 8231. | Octagon Barrel, 2 inches, 15 shot, weight 9 lbs., 32 caliber | 11.86 |
| No. 8232. | Roune Barrel, 24 inches, 15 shot, weight 8¾ lbs., 32 caliber | 10.94 |
| No. 8233. | Octagon Barrel 24 inches, 25 shot, weight 9 lbs., 22 caliber (rim fire), short only | 11.86 |
| No. 8234. | Winchester Carbine, 32 W. C. F. and 44 W. C. F. calibers, with 20 inch round barrels (Model 1873), 15 shot each | 10.94 |

## WINCHESTER MODEL 1892 REPEATER.

The system is the same as the Model of 1886, now so well known. Manipulated by a finger lever, the firing pin is first withdrawn; the gun unlocked and opened; the shell or cartridge ejected, and a new cartridge presented and forced ints the chamber, the firing pin held back until the gun is rgain locked. The locking bolts are always in sight, and when the gun is closed, support the breech-bolt symmetrically against the force of the explosion. The same cartridges are used as in the Model of 1873-.44, .38 and .32 Winchester center fire, their widely extended sale having proved their value for general use, and in addition the W. C. F. cartridge. The gun is light, strong, handsome and simple in construction.

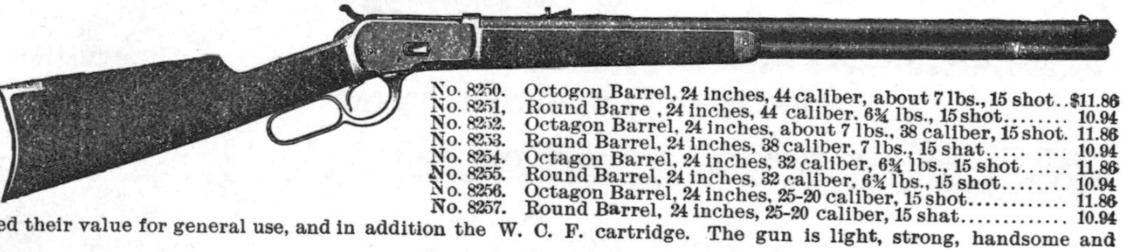

| | | |
|---|---|---|
| No. 8250. | Octogon Barrel, 24 inches, 44 caliber, about 7 lbs., 15 shot | $11.86 |
| No. 8251. | Round Barre , 24 inches, 44 caliber. 6¾ lbs., 15 shot | 10.94 |
| No. 8252. | Octagon Barrel, 24 inches, about 7 lbs., 38 caliber, 15 shot. | 11.86 |
| No. 8253. | Round Barrel, 24 inches, 38 caliber, 7 lbs., 15 shot. | 10.94 |
| No. 8254. | Octagon Barrel, 24 inches, 32 caliber, 6¾ lbs., 15 shot. | 11.86 |
| No. 8255. | Round Barrel, 24 inches, 32 caliber, 6¾ lbs., 15 shot. | 10.94 |
| No. 8256. | Octagon Barrel, 24 inches, 25-20 caliber, 15 shot. | 11.86 |
| No. 8257. | Round Barrel, 24 inches, 25-20 caliber, 15 shat. | 10.94 |

### MODEL 1892—"TAKE DOWN."

No. 8258. Octagon barrel, 24 inches. 32, 38, 44 and 25-20 calibers, each.............$15.00

No. 8259. Model 1892 carbine, with 20 in. round barrel, full magazine in 32, 38 or 44 calibers, 6¼ lbs. Each.............$10.40

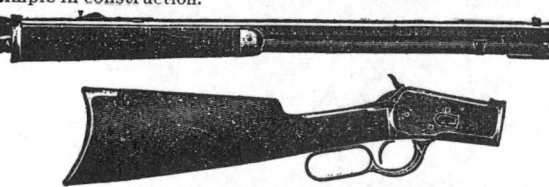

**RIFLE TAKEN APART.**

## WINCHESTER RIFLE. MODEL 1894. NEW 30 CALIBER AND 25-35 CALIBERS.

**WE BOX ALL GUNS CAREFULLY FOR SHIPPING AND GUARANTEE SATISFACTION.**

| | | |
|---|---|---|
| No. 8260. | Octagon barrel, 26 inches, 10 shot, 7½ lbs., 32-40 caliber | $11.86 |
| No. 8261. | Octagon barrel, 26 inches, 10 shot, 7½ lbs., 38-55 caliber | 11.86 |
| No. 8262. | Round barrel, 26 inch, 10 shot, 7¼ lbs., 32-40 caliber | 10.94 |
| No. 8263. | Round barrel, 26 inch, 10 shot, 7¼ lbs., 38-55 caliber | 10.94 |
| No. 8264. | Round barrel, 26 inch, 10 shot, 7¾ lbs., 30 caliber Winchester smokeless cartridges, each | $13.98 |
| No. 8265. | Round barrel, 26 inch, 10 shot, 7¾ lbs., 25-35 Winchester smokeless cartridges, each | $13.98 |

For "Take Down" Rifle Model, 1894, add $3 to above prices in any Caliber.

**IN ORDERING GUNS, DO NOT FAIL TO SPECIFY JUST WHAT MODEL, LENGTH OF BARREL, WEIGHT, ETC., YOU WANT. ALWAYS GIVE NAME, CATALOGUE NUMBER AND PRICE.**

## WINCHESTER RIFLES.

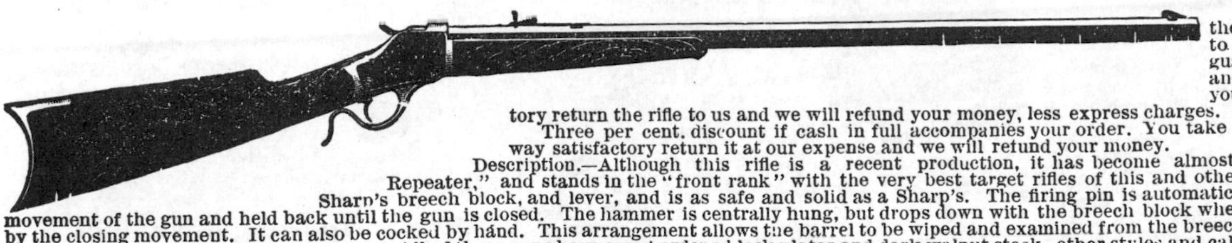

On rifles, our terms are exactly the same as on all other guns; C. O. D. to any one on receipt of $3.00 as a guarantee of good faith, the balance and express charges to be paid after you receive the rifle. If not satisfactory return the rifle to us and we will refund your money, less express charges.

Three per cent. discount if cash in full accompanies your order. You take no risk. If the rifle is not in every way satisfactory return it at our expense and we will refund your money.

Description.—Although this rifle is a recent production, it has become almost as famous as the "Winchester Repeater," and stands in the "front rank" with the very best target rifles of this and other countries. This gun has the old Sharp's breech block, and lever, and is as safe and solid as a Sharp's. The firing pin is automatically withdrawn at the first opening movement of the gun and held back until the gun is closed. The hammer is centrally hung, but drops down with the breech block when the gun is opened, and is cocked by the closing movement. It can also be cocked by hand. This arrangement allows the barrel to be wiped and examined from the breech. In our line everything has been done to make the gun pleasing to the eye. All of these guns have case hardened lock plates and dark walnut stock, other styles and caliber made to order.

Every rifle warranted perfect and accurate. These rifles are not made with double trigger. The set locks are adjustable by a little screw in rear of trigger, and can be set to pull as desired or not used at all. Pushing the trigger forward places it in the "hair pull" notch, same as working a double trigger. All rifles have sporting rear sights.

## OUR SPECIAL PRICES.

| | Price. |
|---|---|
| No. 8205. 22 caliber (rim fire), BB caps, short or long cartridge, 24 inch octagon barrel, weight 7 lbs. (plain trigger) | $10.13 |
| No. 8206. 22 caliber (rim fire), BB caps, short or long cartridge, 26 inch octagon barrel, weight 7 lbs. (plain trigger) | 11.00 |
| No. 8207. 32 caliber (rim fire), extra short, short or long cartridges, 26 inch octagon barrel, weight 7 lbs. (plain trigger) | 10.13 |
| No. 8208. 22 caliber (center fire), 26 inch octagon barrel, weight 7 lbs. (plain trigger) | 10.75 |
| No. 8209. 25 caliber (center fire), 28 inch octagon barrel, weight 7 lbs. (plain trigger) | 10.13 |
| No. 8210. 32 caliber (center fire), 28 inch octagon barrel, weight 8½ lbs. (plain trigger) | 10.40 |
| No. 8211. 32-40 caliber (center fire) 30 inch octagon barrel, weight 9 lbs. (plain trigger) | 10.13 |
| No. 8212. 32-40 caliber (center fire), 30 inch octagon barrel, weight 9 to 9¼ lbs. (set trigger) | 12.13 |
| No. 8213. 38 caliber (center fire), 28 inch octagon barrel, weight 8½ lbs. (plain trigger) | 11.00 |
| No. 8214. 38-55 caliber (center fire), 30 inch octagon barrel, weight 9 lbs. (plain trigger) | 10.13 |
| No. 8215. 38-55 caliber (center fire), 30 inch octagon barrel, weight 9 lbs. (set trigger) | $12.75 |
| No. 8216. 40-60 caliber (center fire), 30 inch octagon barrel, weight 9¼ lbs. (set trigger) | 12.75 |
| No. 8217. 40-82 caliber (center fire), 30 inch octagon barrel, weight 9½ lbs. (plain trigger), long range | 10.13 |
| No. 8218. 40-90 caliber (center fire), 32 inch octagon barrel, weight 9½ to 11 lbs. (set trigger) | 14.75 |
| No. 8219. 45-70 caliber (center fire), 30 inch octagon barrel, weight 9¼ lbs. (plain trigger), long range | 11.00 |
| No. 8220. 40-65 caliber (center fire), 30 inch octagon barrel, weight 9½ lbs., a good target rifle | 11.00 |
| No. 8221. 45-90 caliber (center fire), 30 inch octagon barrel, weight 9½ lbs., long range | 11.00 |
| No. 8222. 40-70 caliber (center fire), 30 inch octagon barrel, weight 9½ lbs. (plain trigger), each | 10.13 |
| No. 8223. 30 U. S. caliber, 30 inch special round barrel | 23.00 |

This rifle uses the 30 U. S. army (smokeless powder) cartridge. Only one style barrel furnished.

## EXTRAS ON RIFLES.

All deviations from standard styles and sizes involve a large proportional outlay for hand labor and when ordered will be subject to the following charges:
For additional length of barrel and magazine add to price 75 cents per inch; on model 1886, $1.00.
For set triggers on model 1873, $2.00.
Extra for plain walnut pistol grip, stock not checkered, $4.75.
Extra for fancy walnut pistol grip, stock checkered, $11.00.
Sling straps and swivels, $1.50 per set. Extra for plain pistol grip, stock not checkered. $2.50

## WINCHESTER 22 CALIBER REPEATING RIFLE—MODEL '90—"TAKE DOWN."

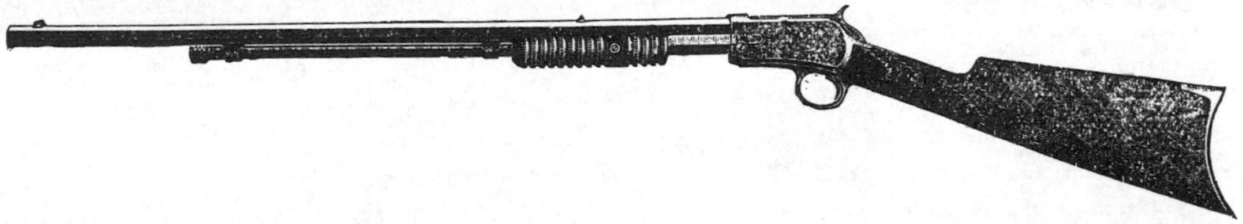

Winchester Model, 1890, Repeating Rifle. Loads and ejects the shell by the sliding motion of the forearm. All 24 inch Octagon barrels, and 5¾ pounds weight. New model stock and barrel, can be separated by removing a screw.

| | |
|---|---|
| No. 8224. For 22 caliber, rim fire short, only 15 shot. Our special price | $9.72 |
| No. 8225. For 22 caliber, rim fire long, only 12 shot. Our special price | 9.72 |
| No. 8226. For 22 caliber, rim fire, special Winchester cartridges, 10 shot. Our special price | $9.72 |

NOTE.—Only the cartridge mentioned can be used in the above rifles as they are only chambered for one size cartridge and are warranted to be accurate and reliable.

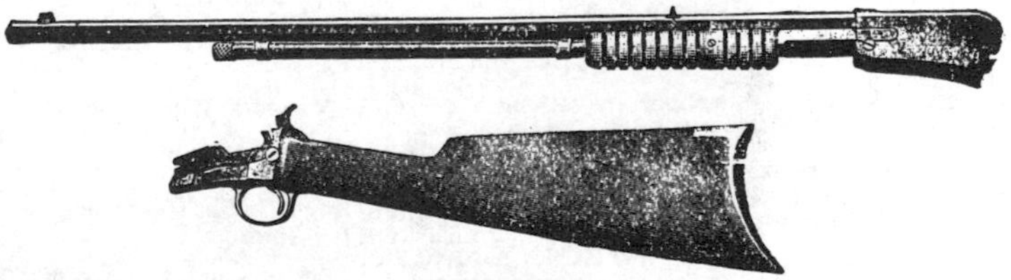

Taken apart.

## WINCHESTER RIFLES. MODEL 1886.

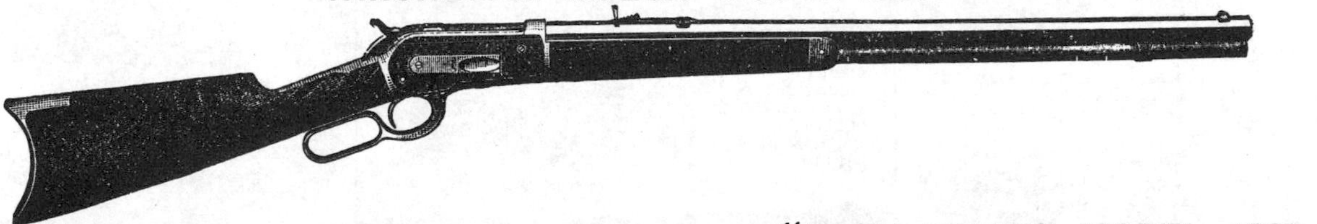

| | |
|---|---|
| No. 8235. Octagon Barrel, 26 inches or under, 9½ lbs., 40-82 caliber, 260 grain bullet, 8 shot | $14.18 |
| No. 8236. Round Barrel, 40-82 caliber | 13.16 |
| No. 8237. Octagon Barrel, 26 inches or under, 9¼ lbs., 45-70 caliber, 405 grain bullet, using a regular (government cartridge,) 9 shot | $14.18 |
| No. 8238. Round Barrel, 26 inches or under, 9 lbs., 45-70 caliber | 13.16 |
| No. 8239. Octagon Barrel, 26 inches or under, 9¼ lbs., 45-90 caliber, 300 grain bullet, 8 shot | $14.18 |
| No. 8240. Round Barrel, 26 inches or under, 9 lbs., 45-90 caliber | 13.16 |
| No. 8241. Octagon Barrel, 26 inches, 9¼ lbs., 38-56 caliber, 8 shot | 14 18 |
| No. 8242. Round Barrel, 26 inches, 9¼ lbs., 38-56 caliber | 13.16 |
| No. 8243. Octagon Barrel, 26 inches, 9¼ lbs., 40-65 caliber | 14.18 |
| No. 8244. Round Barrel, 26 inches, 40-65 caliber | 13.16 |
| No. 8245. Octagon Barrel, 26 inches, 50-110 caliber, Express | 14.18 |
| No. 8246. Octagon Barrel, 26 inches, 9¼ lbs., 38-70-255 caliber | 14.18 |
| No. 8247. Octagon Barrel, 26 inches, 9¼ lbs., 40-70-330 caliber | 14.18 |
| No. 8248. Model, 1886, Carbine can be furnished 22 inches, round barrel, in any of the above calibers at | $12.83 |

The standard length of barrel will be 26 inches. Guns taking the 45-70 cartridge will have the Sporting Leaf Sight, and all other the Sporting Rear Sight. Each gun will be accompanied by a cleaning rod FREE. Set Triggers, $2.25 extra.

## "TAKE DOWN" MODEL 1886.

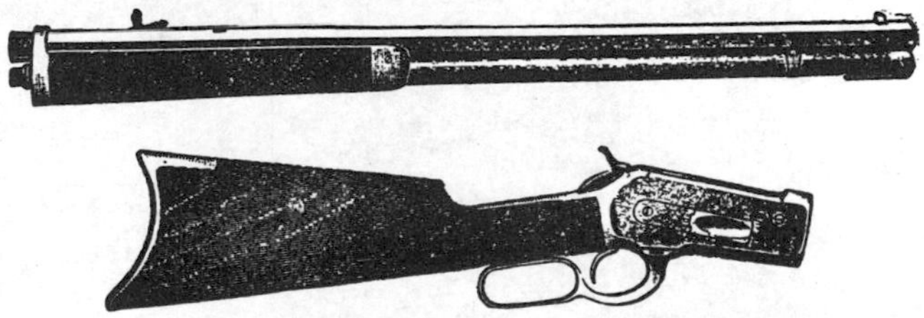

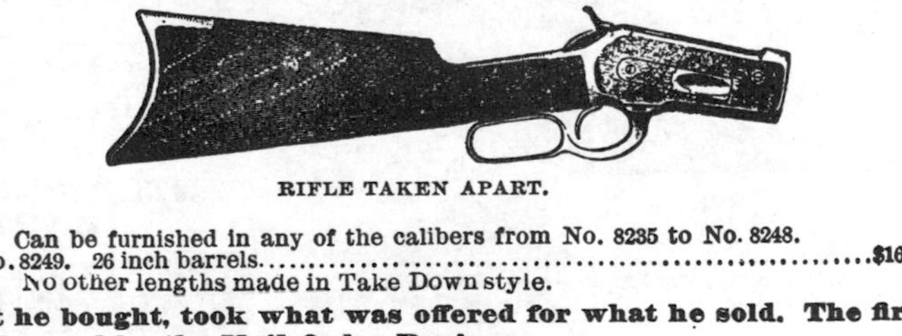

RIFLE TAKEN APART.

Can be furnished in any of the calibers from No. 8235 to No. 8248.

No. 8249. 26 inch barrels. .......... $16.88

No other lengths made in Take Down style.

**There was a time when the consumer paid what was asked for what he bought, took what was offered for what he sold. The first condition, at least, is radically changed,—changed by the Mail Order Business.**

## SPORTING AND MILITARY RIFLE SIGHTS.

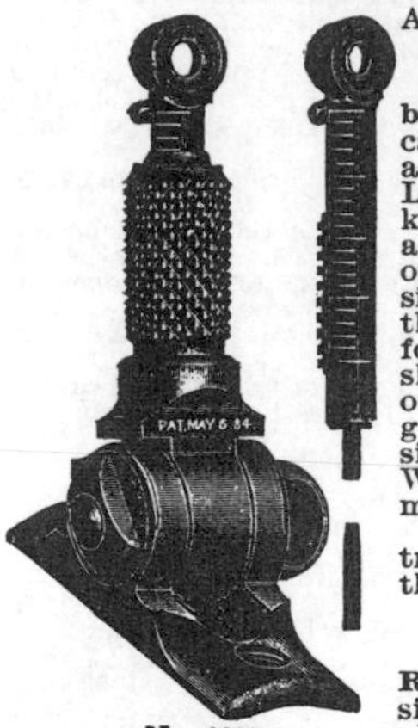


No. 8266

Always state model of rifle sights are wanted for.

**Lyman's Patent Combination Sight.** Any one can attach these sights to a rifle in a few minutes. Lyman's sights of all kinds can be furnished for almost every kind of rifle on the market. These sights more than double the value of a rifle, either for hunting or target shooting, for instantaneous aim can be taken with great accuracy. The sights are made in all sizes. When ordering give the make and gauge of rifle.

The sight stem is illustrated separately to show the point blank stop pin. Price of sight .......$2.40

**Lyman's Patent Ivory Read Front Sight.** This sight gives the sportsman a clear white bead which can be seen distinctly against any object in the woods or in the bright sunlight. Price....................$0.75

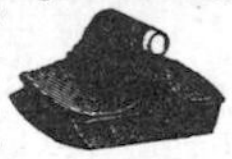

No. 8268

No. 8277 **Lyman's Patent Improved Ivory Front Hunting Sight.** This sight is better than the bead sight for a hunting rifle. The Ivory is so well protected by the surrounding metal that there is no danger of its being injured. Price...............$0.40

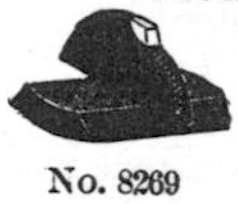

No. 8269

**Lyman's Patent Ivory Shot Gun Sight with reamer.**
No. 8273 Price..........$0.55

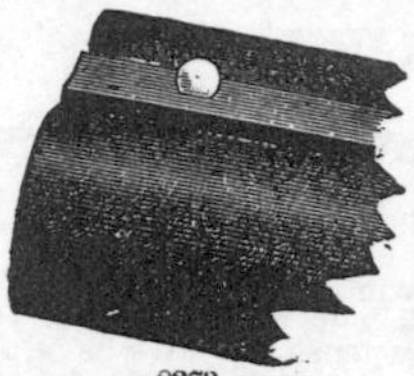

8273

**Lyman's Patent Combination Ivory Front Sight.** One cut shows the sight with the Ivory open part in use and the other with the globe turned up. No. 8274. Price........$0.75

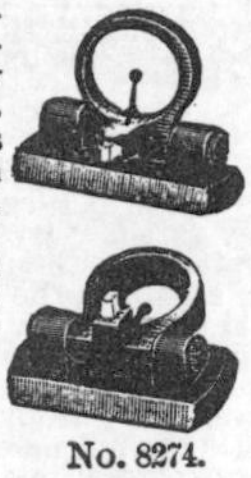

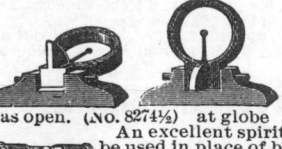

No. 8274.

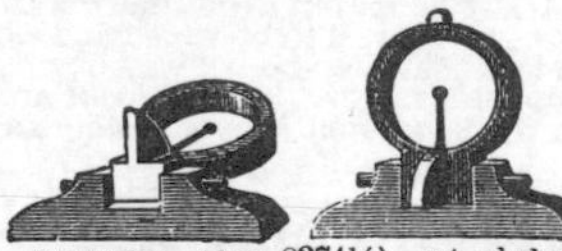

as open. (No. 8274½) at globe

**Beach Combination Sight.** No. 8274½
Price.........$0.75

An excellent spirit level, which can be used in place of blank piece. No. 8275 Price...........$0.75

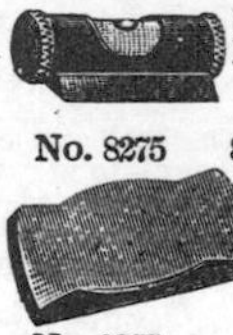

No. 8275

**RockyMountain Front Sight.** No. 8275½. Price..$0.44

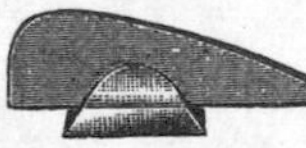

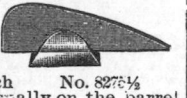

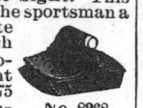

No. 8275½

Black piece to replace the crotch sight, which is usually on the barrel when the rifle is purchased; this should always be removed when peep sights are used.
No. 8277. Price...................$0.20

No. 8277

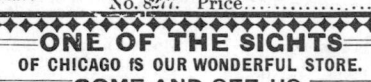

**ONE OF THE SIGHTS**
**OF CHICAGO IS OUR WONDERFUL STORE.**
**COME AND SEE US.**

## Winchester Graduated Peep Sight.

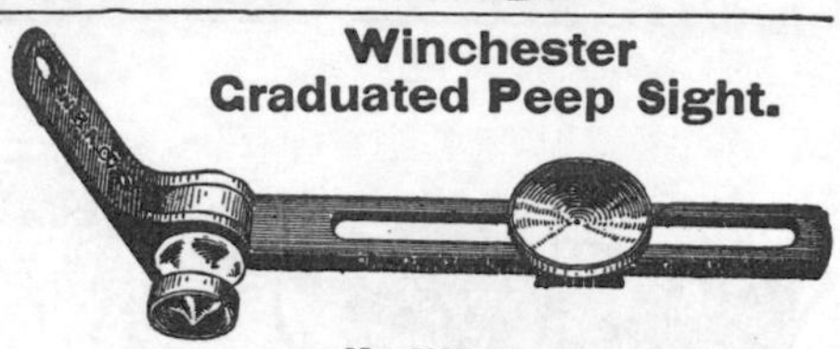

No. 8272

Graduated peep sight, complete, with screws to fasten to stock of rifle. Price.....................$2.25

## Sporting Rear Sight.

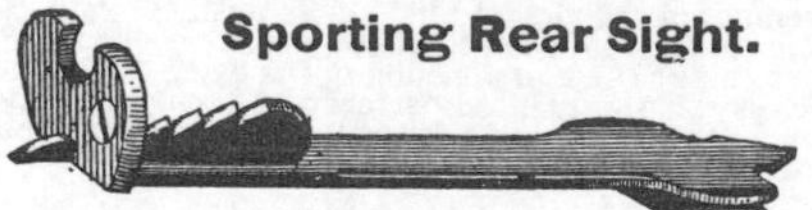

No. 8270

Sporting Rear Sight. Graduated from 50 to 300 yards. Price.........................................$0.60

## Lyman's Rear Leaf Sight.

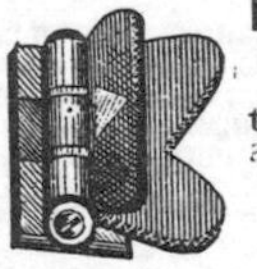

8270½ One leaf is a bar with a triangular Ivory center, the other is a wide open V crotch.
Price......... .. ............... ..$0.75

8270¾ **Sporting Front Sight.** Price.$0.30

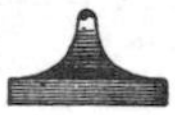

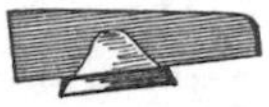

**8271 Knife Blade Front Sight.**
German Silver or Ivory Price $0.48

## LOADED METALLIC CARTRIDGES.

We do not send Cartridges C. O. D. when ordered alone. We can furnish all kinds of cartridges not on this list at lowest market price.

Cartridges can be shipped with other goods by express or freight. Cartridges cannot be sent by mail.

Prices subject to change without notice. U. M. C., U. S., Lowell and Winchester makes, all the same price and kept in stock.

## RIM FIRE CARTRIDGES.

No. 8276. Cartridge, 22 caliber, BB cap, 100 in box, per box, 14c; per 1000, $1.25; weight, ¼ lb. per box.

No. 8276¼. Conical Ball Cap Cartridge, 22 caliber, rim fire, box of 100, 22c; per 1000, $2.00; weight, ¼ lb. per box.

No. 8277. Cartridges, 22 caliber, short, rim fire, U. M. C. make "U," 50 in box, 12c; per 1000, $2.25.

No. 8278. Cartridges, 22 caliber, short, rim fire, Winchester make "H," 50 in box, 12c; per 1000, $2.25.

No. 8279. Cartridges, 22 caliber, short, rim fire, U. S. make, 50 in box, 12c; per 1000, $2.25.

No. 8280. Cartridges, 22 caliber, short, rim fire, 50 in box, 12c; per 1000, $2.25.

No. 8281. Cartridges, 22 caliber, long, rim fire, 50 in box, 15c; per 1000, $2.85; weight, ¾ lb. per box.

No. 8282. Cartridges, 22 caliber, long rifle, rim fire, 50 in box, 15c; per 1000, $2.85.

No. 8283. Cartridges, 22 caliber, extra long, rim fire, 100 in box, 46c; per 1000, $4.30; weight, 1¼ lb. per box.

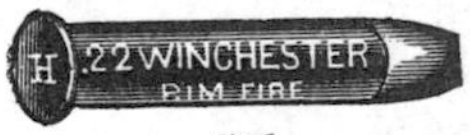


8284

No. 8284. Cartridges, special 22 caliber, for Winchester model '90, repeating rifle, 7 grains powder, 45 grains lead; per 50, 24c; per 1000, $4.57

No. 8285. Cartridges, 25 caliber, for Stevens, Maynard and Winchester single shot rifles, 11 grains powder, 65 grain ball, rim fire, 50 in box, 40c; per 100, 70c.

No. 8286. Cartridges, 30 caliber, short, rim fire, 50 in box, 23c; per 100, 44c; weight, ¾ lb.

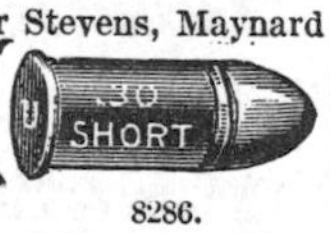


8286.

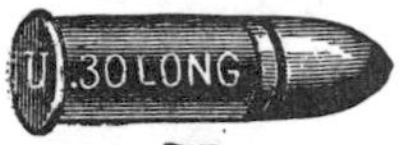


8287.

No. 8287. Cartridges, 30 caliber, long, rim fire, 50 in box, 28c; per 100, 51c; per weight. ¾ lb.

No. 8288. Cartridges, 32 caliber, extra short, rim fire, 50 in box, 25c; per 100, 46c; weight, ½ lb. per box.

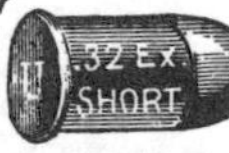


8288.

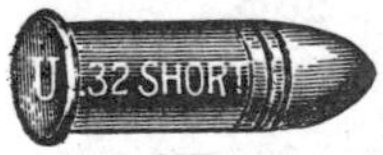


8289.

No. 8289. Cartridges, 32 caliber, short, rim fire, 50 in box, 26c; per 100, 48c; weight, ¾ lb.

No. 8290. Cartridges, 32 caliber, long, rim fire, 50 in box, 30c; per 100, 56c; weight, 1 lb.

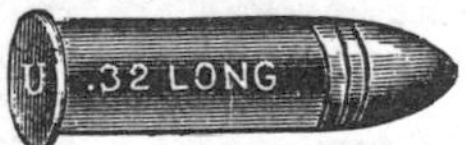


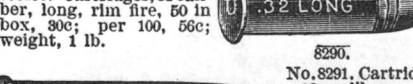

8290.

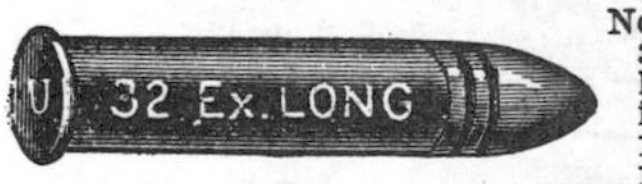


8291.

No. 8291. Cartridges, 32 caliber, extra long, rim fire, 50 in box, 48c; per 100, 80c; weight, 1¼ lb. per box.

No. 8292. Cartridges, 38 caliber, short, rim fire, 50 in box, 42c; per 100, 79c; weight, 1¼ lb.

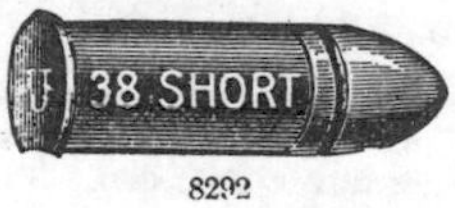


8292

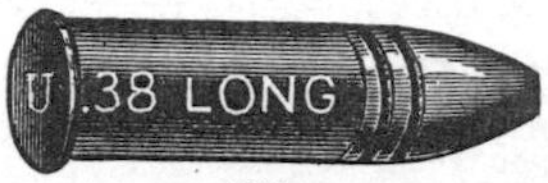


8293.

No. 8293. Cartridges, 38 caliber, long, rim fire, 50 in a box, 47c; per 100, 87c; weight, 1½ lbs.

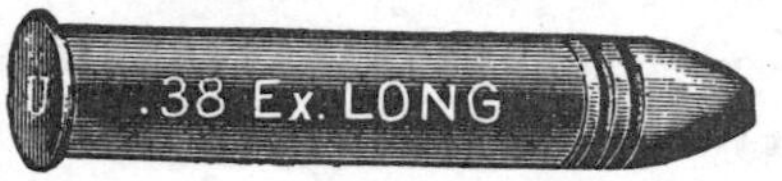


8294.

No. 8294. Cartridges, 38 caliber, extra long, rim fire, 50 in box, 65c; per 100, $1.20; weight, 1¾ lbs.

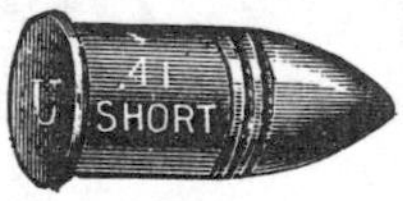


8295.

No. 8295. Cartridges, 41 caliber, rim fire, for Remington Derringer pistol, per box of 50, 40c; per 100, 72c; weight, 1¼ lbs.

No. 8296. Cartridges, 41 caliber, long, rim fire, 50 in box, 45c; per 100, 85c.

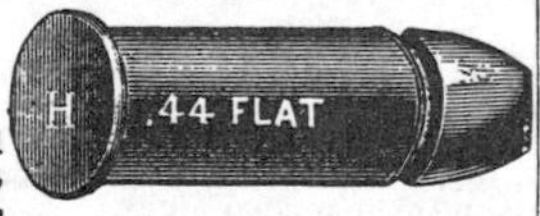


8297.

No. 8297. Winchester, model '66, rim fire, 28 grains powder, 200 grain ball, 50 in box, 62c; per 100, $1.17; weight, 1¾ lbs. per box.

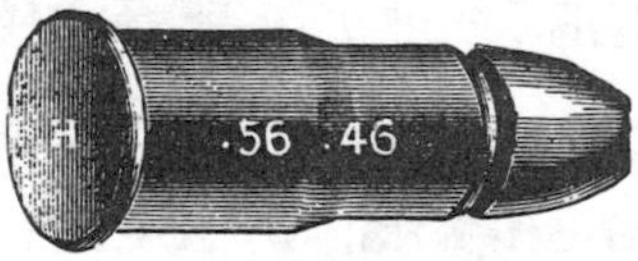


8298.

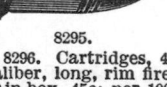

No. 8298. Cartridges, 56-46, Spencer carbine, rim fire, 25 in box, 52c; per 100, $1.94; weight, 2 lbs.

No. 8299. Cartridges, 56-50 Spencer carbine, rim fire, 25 in box, 52c; per 100, $1.94; weight, 2¼ lbs. per box.

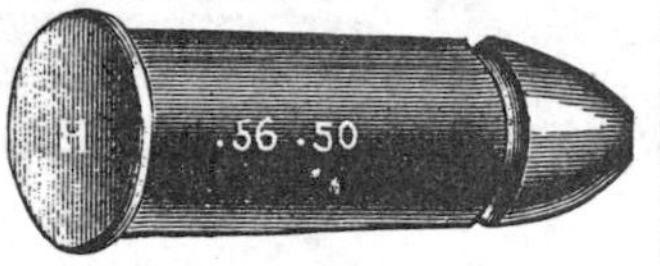


8299.

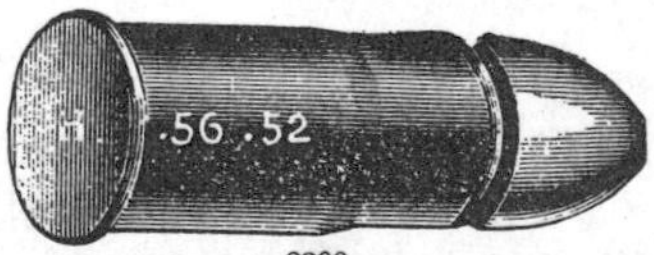


8300.

No. 8300. Cartridges, 56-52, Spencer rifle, rim fire, 25 in box, 52c; per 100, $1.94.

No. 8301. Cartridges, 56-56, Spencer carbine, rim fire, 25 in box, 52c; per 100, $1.94.

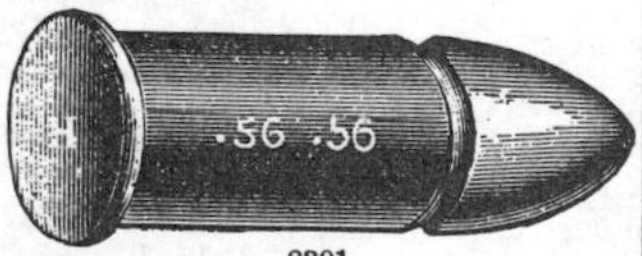


8301.

## CENTER FIRE PISTOL AND RIFLE CARTRIDGES.

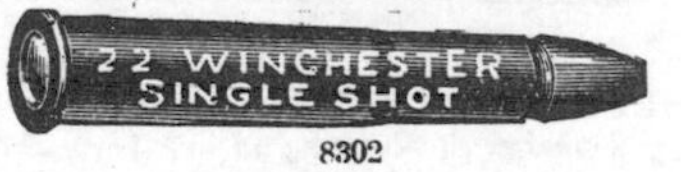


8302

No. 8302. Cartridges, 22 caliber, center fire, 15 grs. powder, 45 gr; bullet for Winchester single shot rifle, box of 50, 58c. per 100.; $1.10, weight 1 lb, per box.

No. 8303 Cartridges, 25-20 caliber, 19 grains powder, 86 grain ball, for Stevens', Maynard and Winchester single shot rifles, box of 50, 75c.; per 100, $1,35; weight 1¼ lbs.

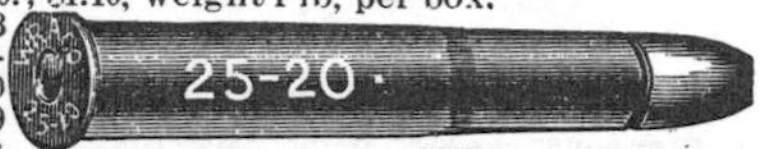


8303

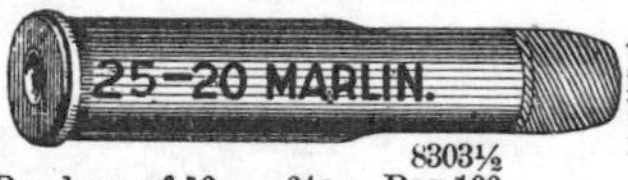


8303½

No. 8303½ Center fire, 25-22 caliber, 86 grains ball, for Marlin repeating rifle.
Per box of 50 ....64c.; Per 100 .......................$1.10

No. 8304 Cartridges, 32 caliber. Smith & Wesson, center fire, 50 in box, 44c.; per 100 80c.; weight, 1¼ lbs. Using No. 1 primers if made by W. R. A. Co., using No. 0 primer if made by U. M. C. Co.

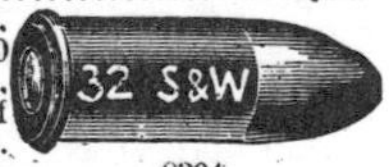


8304

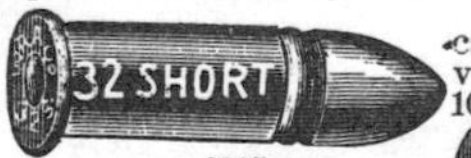


8305

No. 8305 Center fire, 32 caliber, short, for Colt's revolver, 50 in box, 44c.; per 100, 80c.; weight 1¼ lbs.

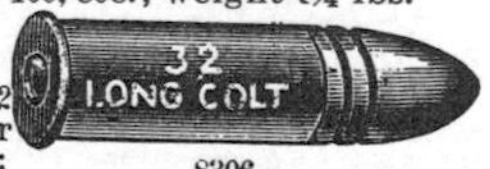


8306

No. 8306 Center fire, 32 caliber, long, Colt's or Ballard, 50 in box, 48c.; per 100, 88c.; weight 1½ lbs.

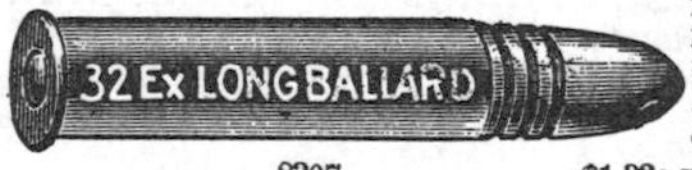


8307

No. 8307 Cartridges, 32 caliber, extra long, center fire, 50 in box. 72c.; per 100 $1.32; weight 1¾ lbs.

No. 8308 Cartridges, center fire. 32 caliber, for Colt's lightning repeating rifle, 20 grains powder, 100 grains lead, box of 50, 64c.; per 100, $1.16; weight 1¾ lbs.

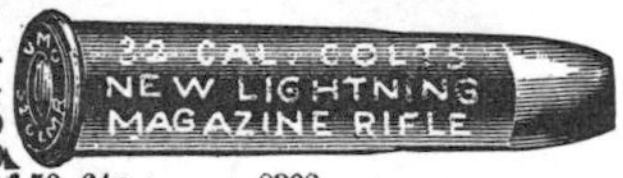


8308

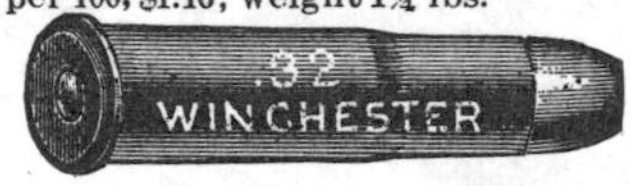


8309

No. 8309 Cartridges, for Winchester rifle. 32 caliber, center fire, 20 grains powder, 115 grs. lead, weight, 1¾ lbs., per box of 50, using No. 1 primer, 64c.; per 110 $1.16

No. 8310 Cartridges, 38 caliber. center fire, Smith & Wesson, 50 in box, 54c., per 100, 98c.; weight 2 lbs. per box.

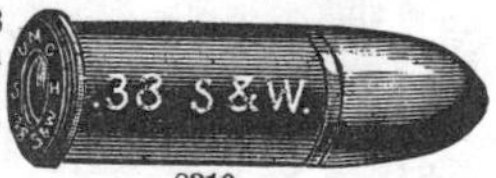


8310

No. 8311 32 Ideal Cartridge, 1¾ inch straight shell, 25 grains powder, 150 grains lead, per box of 50, 75c.; per 100, $1.40.

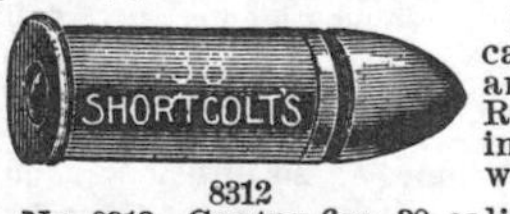


8312

No. 8312 Center fire, 38 caliber, short, for Ballard rifles, Colt's and Remington revolvers, 50 in box, 54c.; per 100, 98c.; weight 2 lbs.

No. 8313 Center fire, 38 caliber, long, for Ballard rifles and Colt's revolvers, 50 in box, 58c.; per 100, $1.06; weight 2¼ lbs. per box.

.....A GREAT LINE OF.....
....MEN'S OUTING SHIRTS AND SWEATERS....
....On Pages 211 to 214....

ALWAYS GIVE CATALOGUE NUMBER AND DESCRIPTION, AS WELL AS SIZES ETC. OF ARTICLES WANTED.

Center Fire Pistol and Rifle Cartridges.—Continued.

8314

No. 8314. Center fire, 38 caliber, extra long, 38 grains powder, 148 grains lead, for Ballard rifle No. 2, 50 in box, 92c; per 100, $1.67; weight 2½ lbs.

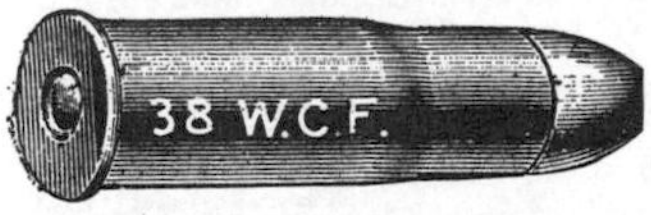

8315

No. 8315. Winchester (model '73), center fire, 38 caliber, 40 grains powder, 180 grains lead, 50 in box, using No. 1 primer. Per box, 69c; per 100, $1.38; weight 2¾ lbs. per box.

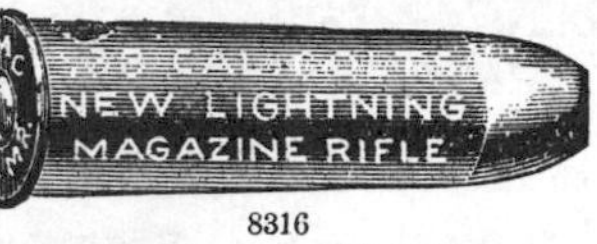

8316

No. 8316. Cartridges, center fire, 38 caliber for Colt's Lightning Repeating Rifle, 40 grains powder, 180 grains lead. Per box of 50, 70c; per 100, $1.37; weight 2¾ lbs. per box.

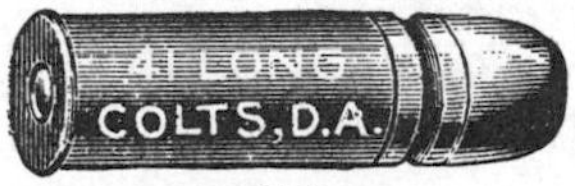

8317

No. 8317. Colt's revolver, caliber 41, center fire (long D A), 50 in a box. Per box, 70c; per 100, $1.28; weight 1½ lbs. per box.

No. 8318. Cartridges, Colt's revolver, 41 caliber, center fire (short DA), 50 in a box. Per box, 60c; per 100, $1.15; weight 1½ lbs. per box.

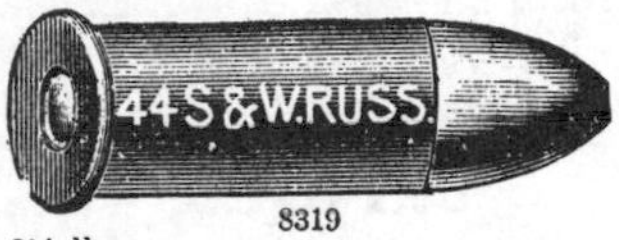

8319

No. 8319. Cartriges, 44 caliber Smith & Wesson, center fire, No. 3 Russian, 50 in a box. Per box, 80c; per 100, $1.42; weight 2½ lbs.

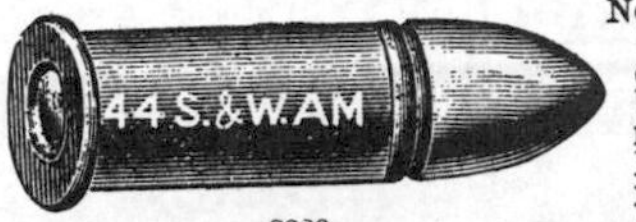

8320

No. 8320. Smith & Wesson, American model, caliber 44, center fire, 50 in a box. Per box, 76c; per 100, $1.38; weight, 2½ lbs.

No. 8321. Cartridges for Colt's pistol, 44 caliber, center fire, 50 in a box. Per box, 80c; per 100, $1.45; weight 2½ lbs. per box.

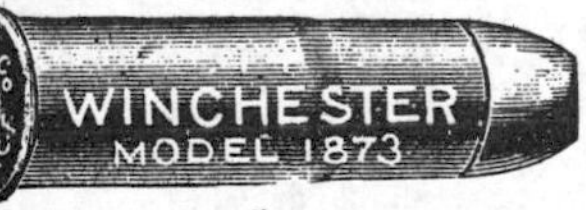

8322

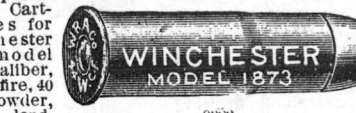

No. 8322. Cartridges for Winchester rifle, model '73, 44 caliber, center fire, 40 grs. powder, 200 grs. lead, 50 in a box, using No. 1 primer. Per box, 70c; per 100, $1.38; weight 1¾ lbs.

No. 8323. Cartridges, 44 caliber, long, center fire, for old Ballard rifles, 50 in a box. Per box, 88c; per 100, $1.60; weight 2½ lbs.

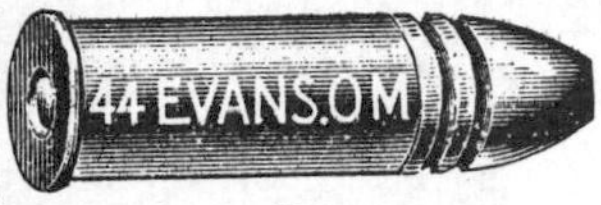

8324

No. 8324. Cartridges, Evans' old model repeating rifle (34 shot), shell 1 inch long, 33 grs. powder, 220 gr. bullet, 50 in a box. Per box, 88c; per 100, $1.60; weight 2¼ lbs. per box.

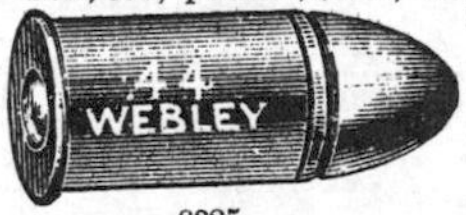

8325

No. 8325. Cartridges, caliber 44, Webley center fire, for bull dog revolver, 50 in a box. Per box, 68c; per 100, $1.20; weight 2½ lbs. per box.

## LOADED METALLIC CARTRIDGES.

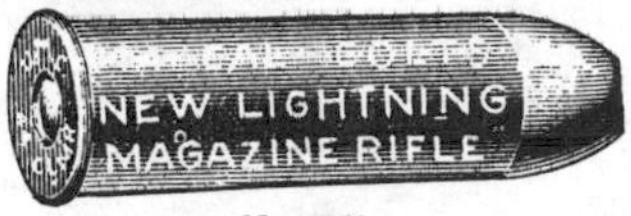

No. 8326.

No. 8326. Cartridges, center fire, caliber 44, for Colt's Lightning Repeating rifle, 40 grains powder, 217 grains lead. Per box of 50, 70c; per 100, $1.37; weight, 2¾ lbs.

### Central Fire Cartridges for Target and Sporting Rifles.

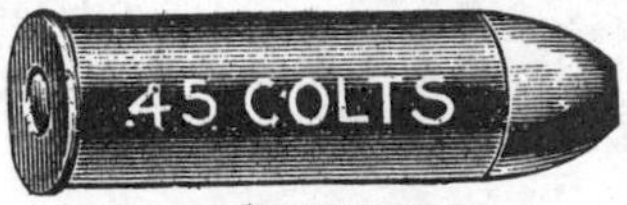

No. 8327.

No. 8327. Colt's Army and D A revolvers, 45 caliber, center fire. Per box of 50, 84c; per 100, $1.57; wt. 3¼ lbs. per box.

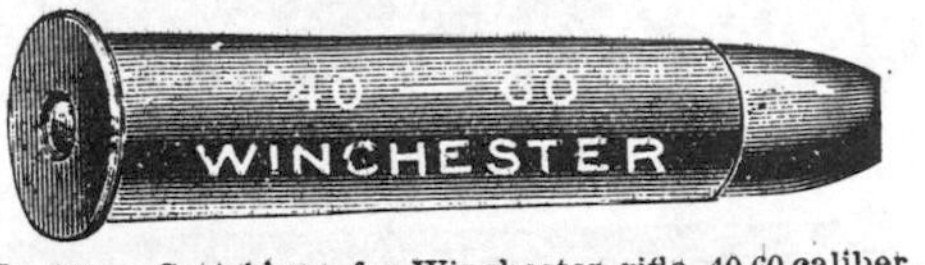


No. 8334. Cartridges, for Winchester rifle, 40-60 caliber, 60 grains powder, 210 grains lead, weight 1 5-16 lbs. Per box of 20, 54c; trade price of 100, $2.62.

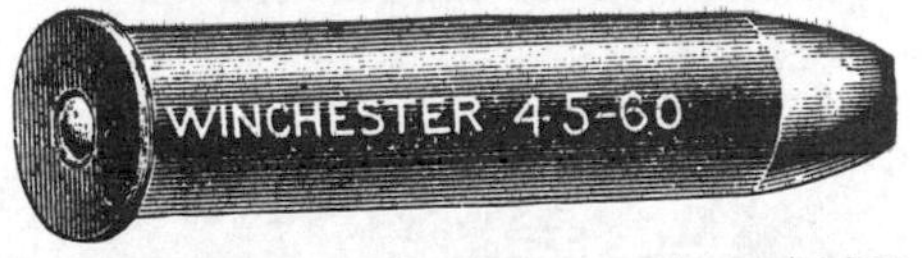


No. 8338. Cartridges, for Winchester rifle, model 1876, 45 caliber, center fire, straight shell, 60 grains powder, 300 grains lead. Per box of 20, 60c; per 100, $2.72; weight per box, 1⅝ lbs.

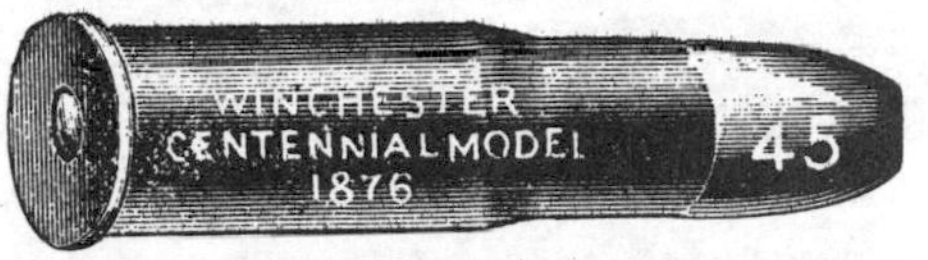


No. 8339. Cartridges, for Winchester rifle, model 1876, 45 caliber, center fire, 75 grains powder, 350 grains lead. Per box of 20, 63c; per 100, $3.00; weight, 1⅛ pounds.

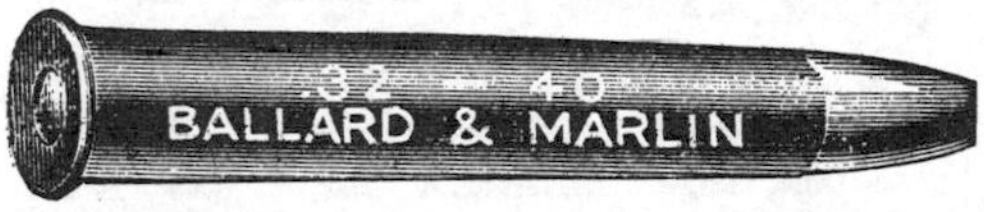


No. 8328. Cartridges, for Ballard, Marlin and Winchester single shot rifles, center fire, 32 caliber, 40 grains of powder, 165 grains lead, weight 1¼ lbs. Per box of 20, 47c.; per 100 ........ $2.29.

No. 8329. Cartridges, for Ballard, Marlin and Winchester single shot, short range, 32-40 caliber, 13 grains of powder, 98 grains lead, weight 1¼ lbs. Per box of 20, 48c.; per 100 ........ $2.33

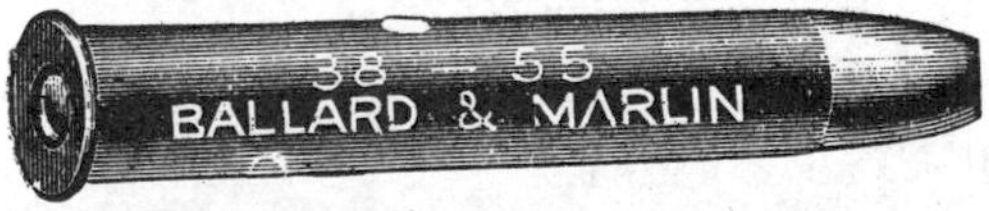


No. 8330. Center fire, 38-55 caliber, 55 grains powder, 255 grains lead, for Ballard, Marlin and Winchester single shot rifles of this caliber, 20 in a box, weight, 1½ lbs., 60c.; per 100 $2.72.

No. 8331. Cartridges, for Ballard, Marlin and Winchester single shot, 38-55 caliber, short range, 20 grains of powder, 155 grains lead, same length shell as No. 8330. Per box of 20, 60c.; per 100 ........ $2.72

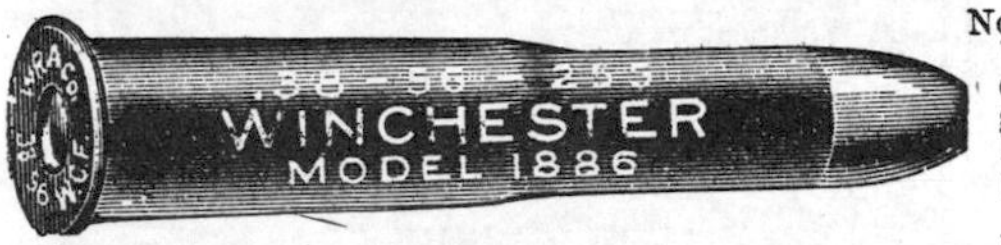


No. 8332. Cartridges, for Winchester rifles, models 1886, 38-56 caliber, 255 grains, weight 1⅝ lbs. Per box of 20, 60c.; trade price per 100 ........ $2.70

No. 8333. Cartridges, center fire, for Colt's lightning rifle, 40 caliber, 60 grains powder, 260 grains lead, weight 1¾ lbs. Per box of 20, 55c.; trade price per 100 ........ $2.62

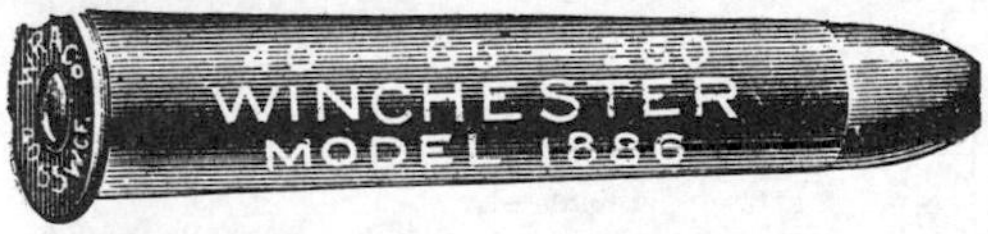


No. 8335. Cartridges; for Winchester repeating rifle, model 1886, 40-65, 260 caliber, center fire, weight 1½ lbs. Per box of 20, 59c.; trade price per 100 ........ $2.70

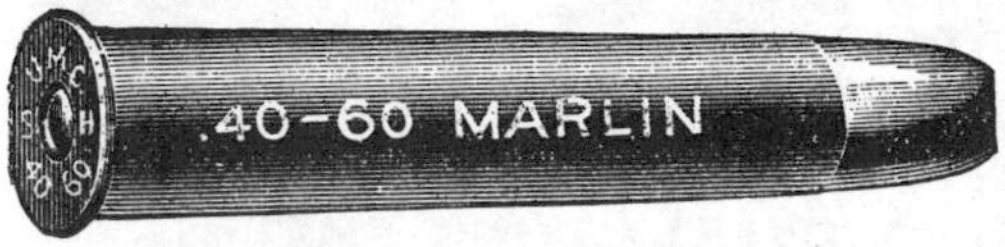


No. 8336. Cartridges, for Marlin rifle, 40-60 caliber, center fire, 60 grains powder, 260 grains lead, weight, 1⅛ lbs. Per box of 20, 59c.; trade price per 100 ........ $2.70

No. 8336½. Cartridges for Winchester rifle, model '86, 40-70-330, 20 in box.
Per box ........ $0.65
Per 100 ........ 3.00

No. 8337. Cartridges, 40-70-330, straight shell, grooved ball, weight 1¾ lbs. Per box of 20, 70c.; trade price per 100 ........ $3.30

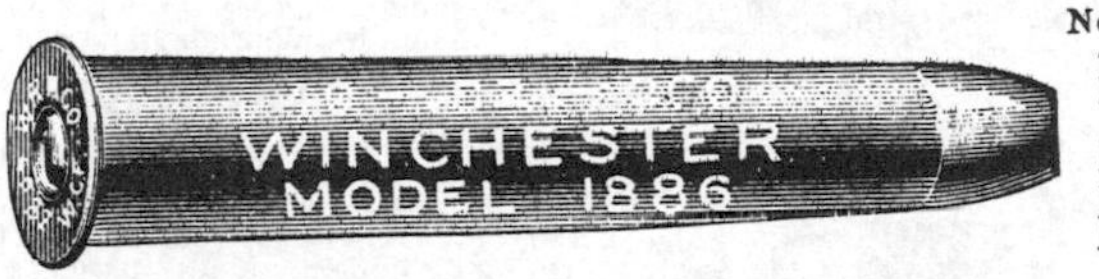


No. 8340. Cartridges, 40 caliber, 82 grains powder, 260 grain bullet, center fire, for Winchester rifle, model 1886.
Per box of 20 ........ $0.64
Per 100 ........ 2.97

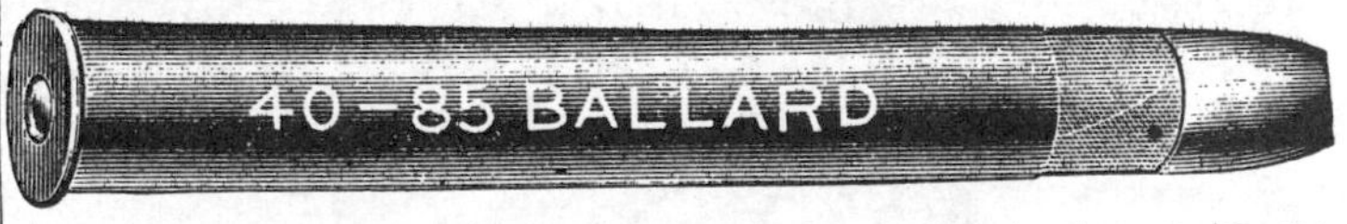


No. 8341. Cartridges, 40-85 caliber, center fire, straight shell, for Ballard rifle, this caliber, 85 grains powder, 370 grains lead. Per box of 10, 45c; per 100 ........ $4.12

No. 8342. Cartridges, for Sharp's rifle, 40-90, Sharp's Remington and Winchester single shot rifles, center fire, 3¼ inches, straight shell, 90 grains powder, 370 grains lead. For shape of shell see 40-85 Ballard. Per box of 10, 45c; per 100 ........ $4.12

No. 8343. Cartridges, 40-110, express, 3¼ inch shell, 110 grains powder, 260 grains lead. Per box of 10, 72c; per 100 ........ $6.80

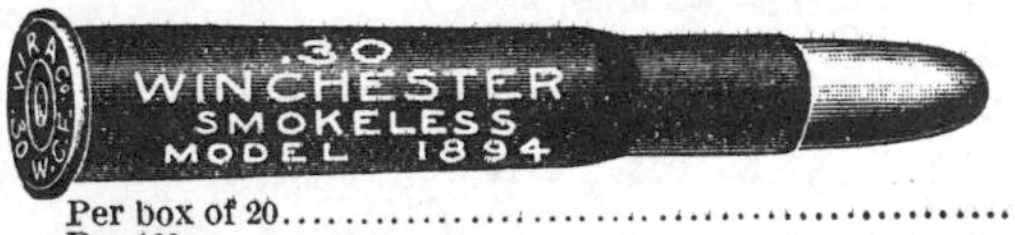


No. 8347. Cartridge, 30 caliber, Winchester smokeless powd'r, 30 grains powder, 160 grain metal patch bullet.
Per box of 20 ........ $0.75
Per 100 ........ 3.20

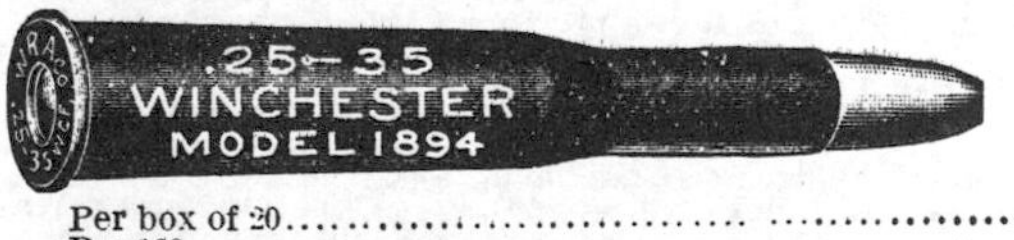


No. 8348. Cartridge, 25-35 Winchester smokeless powder, 26 grains smokeless powder, 117 grain soft nose metal patched bullet.
Per box of 20 ........ $0.70
Per 100 ........ 3.00

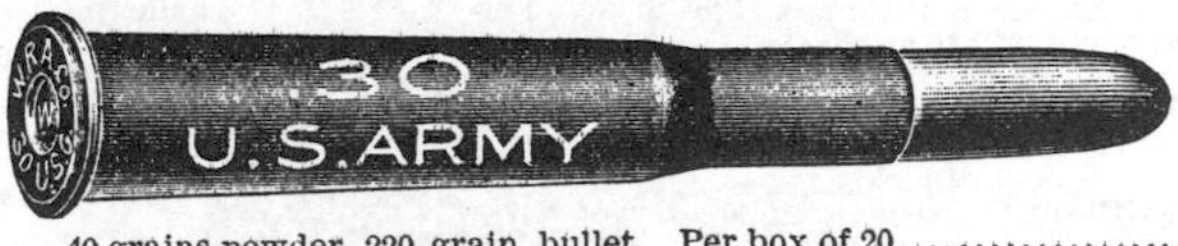


No. 8349. U. S. Army Cartridge. Smokeless powder, steel jack'd bullet. 40 grains powder, 220 grain bullet. Per box of 20 ........ $0.90
For Winchester single shot rifle, per 100 ........ 4.25

No. 8350. Cartridge for model 1886 Winchester rifle 38-70-255, 20 in a box.
Per box ........ $0.60
Per 100 ........ 2.85

## CARTRIDGES, SMOKELESS POWDER LOADED.

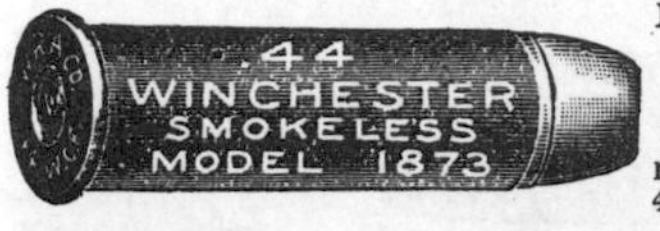


No. 8352. 44 caliber 17 grains smokeless powder, 200 grains metal patched bullet.
Per 100..............................$2.35
Per box of 50..............................1.30
Adapted to Winchester repeating rifles, models of 1873 and 1892, and single shot rifles, 44 caliber.

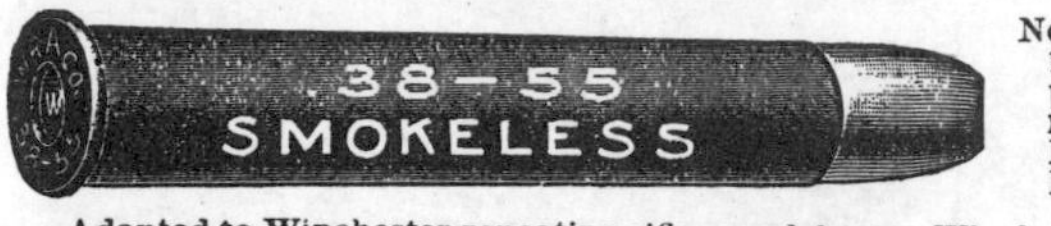


No. 8353. 38-55 caliber, 19 grains smokeless powder, 255 grains metal patched bullet.
Per 100..............$3.40
Per box of 20.... 0.75

Adapted to Winchester repeating rifles, model 1894. Winchester single shot rifles and Marlin rifles. 38-52 caliber.

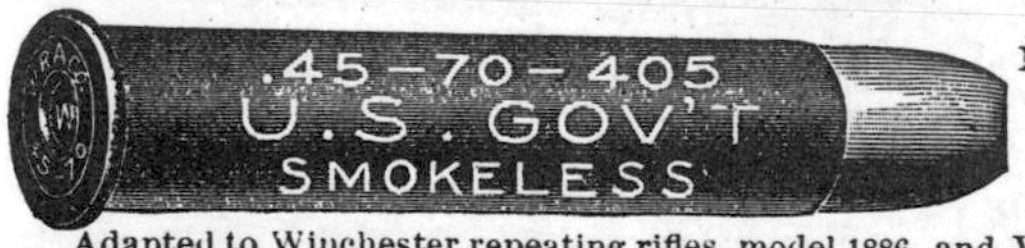


No. 8354. 45-70 caliber, 31 grains smokeless powder, 405 grains metal patched bullet.
Per box of 20...$0.80
Per 100......... 3.80

Adapted to Winchester repeating rifles, model 1886, and Winchester single shot rifle, 45-70 caliber.

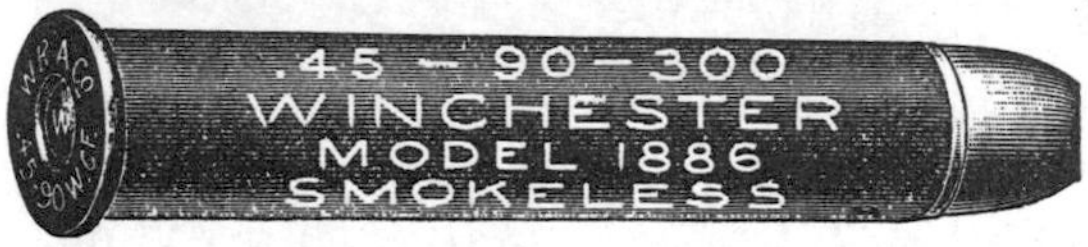


No. 8355. 45-90 caliber, 37 grains smokeless powder, 300 grains metal patched bullet. Per box of 20........$0.85
Per 100 45-90 caliber........$3.80

## LOADED METALLIC CARTRIDGES.

No. 8356. Cartridges, 45 caliber, center fire, for Winchester rifle, model 1886, 70 grains powder, 405 grains lead, weight 36 oz. Per box of 20, 67c; per 100, $2.98.

No. 8357. Cartridges, for Marlin rifle and Winchester model '86 rifle, 45 caliber, center fire, 70 grs. powder, 405 grains lead. Per box of 20, 67c; per 100, $2.98; weight 36 oz.

No. 8358. Cartridges, for single shot rifles, 45-70 caliber, for armory practice, 5 grains powder, 140 grains lead, round ball. Per box of 20, 67c; per 100, $2.98; weight 20 oz.

No. 8359. Cartridges, for Marlin rifle or any other 45-70 caliber rifle, 45 caliber, 45-85 grains powder, 285 grain bullet. Per box of 20, 67c; per 100, $2.98; weight per box 30 oz.

No. 8360. Cartridges, for Winchester repeating rifle, model 1886, 45 caliber, 90 grains powder, 300 grains bullet, box of 20, 70c; 100, $3.17; weight per box, 28 oz.

No. 8361. Sharp's, only 2¼ inch necked shell, 44-77-405. Box of 20, 80c; 100, $3.62; weight per box, 30 oz.

No. 8362. Cartridges, U. S. government, 45 caliber, 70 grains powder, 21-10 inch shell, 500 grain ball, special long range target, for Winchester and other 45-70 caliber rifles. Box of 20, 72c; 100, $3.23; weight per box, 36 oz.

No. 8363. Cartridges, 50 caliber, U. S. government, center fire, 70 grains powder, 1¾ inch shell, weight 44 oz. Per box of 20, 80c; per 100, $3.62.

No. 8364. Cartridges, regular and Remington, 44-77-470, necked 2¼ inch shell, weight 44 oz. Per box of 20, 80c; per 100, $3.62.

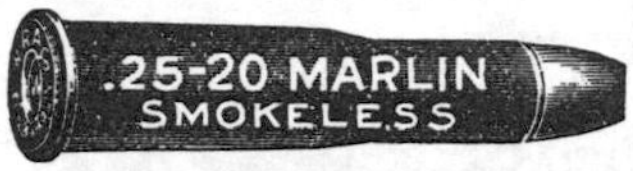


No. 8344. Special cartridge, 25 and 20 caliber, 86 grain ball, for Marlin repeating rifle.
Per box of 50, center fire..............................$0.75
Per 100.............................................. 1.39

No. 8345. Cartridge Marlin rifle, model 1893. 25-36 caliber, 36 grains powder, 106 grain metal patch bullet.

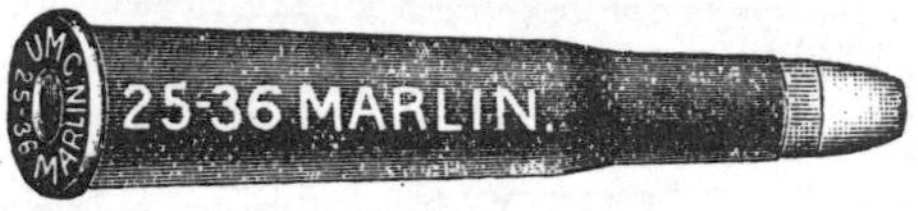


Per box of 20..............................................$0.55
Per 100.............................................. 2.00

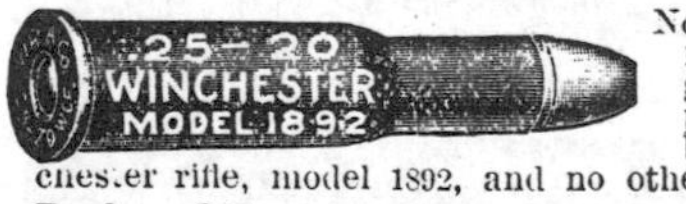


No. 8346. Cartridge, 25-20, 17 grains black powder, 86 gr. ball for Winchester rifle, model 1892, and no other rifle.
Per box of 50..............................................$0.70
Per 100.............................................. 1.35

No. 8365. Sharp's straight 2 7-8 inch shell, 45-105-550. Box of 20, $1.08; weight, 55 oz.

No. 8366. Cartridges, 50-95 Winchester Express rifle, 95 grains powder, 300 grains bullet. Per box of 20, 76c; per 100, $3.35.

No. 8367. Cartridges, 50-110-300, Winchester Express Per box of 20, 87c; per 100, $3.92.

## CARTRIDGES FOR REMINGTON RIFLE.

No. 8368. 32 caliber, center fire, 30 grains powder, 125 grains lead, weight, 36 oz. Per box of 50, 90c; per 100, $1.70.

No. 8369. 38 caliber, center fire, 1¾ inch, 40 grains powder, 245 grains lead, straight shell. Box of 20, 60c; 100, $2.65.

No. 8370. 38 caliber, center fire, 2¼ inch straight shell, 50 grains powder, 245 grains lead. Box of 20, 63c; 100, $2.88.

No. 8371. 40 caliber, center fire, 45 grains powder, 265 grains lead, 1⅞ inch straight shell, weight 24 oz. Per box of 20, 62c; per 100, $2.88.

No. 8372. 40 caliber, center fire, 65 grains powder, 330 grains lead, 2⅜ inch straight shell, weight 38 oz. Per box of 20, 71c; per 100, $3.30.

No. 8373. 32-44 caliber, center fire, S. & W. target cartridge, grooved ball, 19 grains powder, 83 grain bullet. Per box of 50, 71c.

No. 8374. 32-44 S. & W. gallery cartridges, center fire, round ball, 6 grains powder, 50 grain bullet. Per box of 50, 68c.

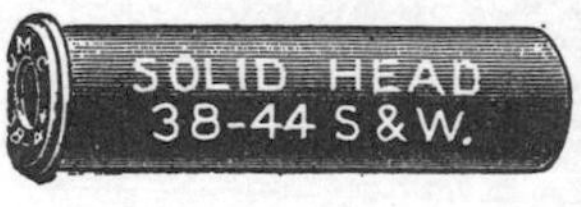


No. 8375. 38-44 caliber, center fire, S. & W. target cartridge, grooved ball, 23 grains powder, 140 grain ball. Per box of 50, 87c.

No. 8376. 38-44 caliber, center fire, S. & W. gallery, round ball, 6 grains powder, 70 grain ball. Per box of 50, 70c.

## PATENT METAL PATCH BULLET CARTRIDGES.

These cartridges are made up with the regular shell, and vary only in charge of powder and weight and kind of bullet. The patent metal patched bullet gives increased accuracy, penetration and cleanliness. The bullet has a covering of copper instead of paper patch, and is smooth instead of being grooved.

No. 8377. Metal patch cartridge, 38-56-255, for Winchester model 1886 rifle, per box of 20, 65c; per 100, $3.00.

No. 8378. Metal patch cartridge, 40-65-245, for Winchester rifle, model 1886, per box of 20, 65c; per 100, $3.00.

No. 8379. Metal patch cartridge, 40-82-245, for Winchester rifle, model 1886, per box of 20, 68c; per 100, $3.20.

No. 8380. Metal patch cartridge, 45-90-295, for Winchester rifles, per box of 20, 75c; per 100, $3.30.

## BLANK CARTRIDGES.

**Order No. 8381.**

Primed and regular powder charge, but without ball. Weight per box of 50, ¾ to 1¼ lbs.

| | |
|---|---|
| 22 caliber, rim fire, per box of 100.................. | $0.15 |
| 32 caliber, rim fire, per box of 50.................. | .14 |
| 45-70 caliber, per box of 20.................. | .60 |
| 50-70 caliber, per box of 20.................. | .72 |
| 32 S. & W. blanks, per 100.................. | .55 |
| 38 " " per 100.................. | .70 |

## EMPTY RIFLE AND PISTOL SHELLS.

**Order No. 8382.**

Sold in any quantity from one shell to a thousand. All center fire. Shells cannot be sent by mail.

| | Weight. | Per 100. |
|---|---|---|
| 25-20 Marlin.............................. | 1 lb. | $0.80 |
| 22 caliber, Winchester.............................. | 1 lb. | 0.77 |
| 25-20 caliber Winchester.............................. | 1 " | 1.02 |
| 32 caliber, for Smith & Wesson.............................. | 1⅛ " | .55 |
| 32 caliber, for Winchester, 1873 model... | 1⅜ " | .75 |
| 32-44 S. & W. gallery.............................. | ¾ " | .90 |
| 32-44 S. W., target.............................. | ¾ " | .91 |
| 32 caliber, for Colt's rifle.............................. | 1⅜ " | .78 |
| 38 caliber, for Smith & Wesson.............................. | 1⅛ " | .64 |
| 38 caliber, for Colt's pistol.............................. | " | .63 |
| 38 caliber, for Winchester, model 1873... | 1¾ " | .85 |
| 38-44 S. & W., gallery.............................. | 1⅛ " | 1.08 |
| 38-44 S. & W., target.............................. | 1⅛ " | 1.08 |
| 41 caliber, for Colt's long D A pistol..... | 2 " | .63 |
| 44 caliber, for Smith & Wesson, Russian. | 2 " | .85 |
| 44 caliber, for Winchester, model 1873... | 1¾ " | .85 |
| 44 caliber, for Colt's Lightning rifle...... | 1¾ " | .86 |
| 44 caliber, for Evan's rifle, new model... | 1 5-16 | 1.00 |
| 44 caliber, Webley.............................. | ⅞ " | .68 |
| 45 caliber, for Colt's revolvers.............. | 1 5-16 | .90 |
| 32-40 caliber, Ballard & Marlin.............. | 2 " | 1.30 |
| 38-55 caliber, Ballard & Marlin.............. | 2½ " | 1.50 |
| 40-60 caliber, Winchester, mod. '76, 210 gr. | 2¾ " | 1.68 |
| 40-85 caliber, Ballard.............................. | 2¾ " | 2.20 |
| 40-65 caliber, Winchester, model 1886.... | 2¾ " | 1.55 |
| 45-60 caliber, Winchester, model for 1876. | 2½ " | 1.68 |
| 40-82 caliber, Winchester, model for 1886. | 2¾ " | 2.00 |
| 45-70 caliber, U. S. government.............. | 2¾ " | 1.90 |
| 45-75 caliber, Winchester, model of 1876. | 2¼ " | 1.75 |
| 44-77 caliber, Sharp's only, necked...... | 2¼ " | 2.00 |
| 40-90 Ballard.............................. | 2¾ " | 2.20 |

| | Weight. | Per 100 |
|---|---|---|
| 45-90 Winchester.............................. | 2⅞ " | $ 2.00 |
| 50-70 Government.............................. | 2¾ " | 1.80 |
| 40-70 Remington, straight.............................. | 2½ " | 1.85 |
| 40-90 Sharp's, straight.............................. | 3¼ " | 2.26 |
| 38-56 Winchester.............................. | 2⅞ " | 1.60 |
| 40-90 Sharp's necked.............................. | 2⅝ " | 2.26 |

Prices of cartridges, shot and ammunition in general are subject to market changes without notice.

## GROOVED BULLETS.

**Order No. 8383.**

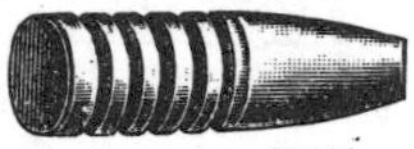

Weight per 100, 1¾ lbs. to 4 lbs., according to size.

32-165

| Sizes. | Description. | Weight Grains. | Price per 100. | Weight per 100. |
|---|---|---|---|---|
| 22 | Winchester.................. | 45 | $0.21 | 1 lb. |
| 32-40 | Short range.................. | 98 | .45 | 2 " |
| 38-55 | Short range.................. | 155 | .63 | 2¼ " |
| 25-20 | Stevens'.................. | 86 | .35 | 1¾ " |
| 32 | Smith & Wesson.................. | 85 | .25 | 1¾ " |
| 32-73 | Winchester.................. | 115 | .35 | 2 " |
| 32-40 | Ballard & Marlin.................. | 165 | .60 | 2½ " |
| 32-40 | Ballard & Marlin.................. | 185 | .61 | 4 " |
| 32-44 | S. & W.................. | 83 | .47 | 1 " |
| 32-44 | S. & W., round ball.................. | 146 | .36 | 1½ " |
| 38-44 | S. & W.................. | 140 | .48 | 1¼ " |
| 38-44 | S. & W., round.................. | 70 | .37 | 1 " |
| 38 | Smith & Wesson.................. | 145 | .38 | 3 " |
| 38-73 | Winchester.................. | 180 | .42 | 4 " |
| 38-55 | Ballard & Marlin.................. | 255 | .78 | 4 " |
| 40-60 | Winchester.................. | 210 | .66 | 3½ " |
| 40-60 | Marlin.................. | 260 | .75 | 4½ " |
| 45 | .................. | 285 | .95 | 4½ " |
| 44-73 | Winchester.................. | 200 | .50 | 3¼ lbs. |
| 44 | Smith & Wesson, Russian... | 256 | .54 | 4 " |
| 45 | Colt, D. A.................. | 260 | .58 | 4¼ " |
| 45-60 | Winchester.................. | 300 | .75 | 4½ " |
| 45-75 | Winchester.................. | 350 | .79 | 5¼ " |
| 45-70 | Government.................. | 405 | 1.00 | 6 " |
| 45-70 | Government.................. | 500 | 1.25 | 7¼ " |
| 50-70 | Government.................. | 450 | 1.15 | 6¾ " |
| 50-95 | Hollow Ball, Express........ | 300 | .90 | 5¼ " |
| 50-95 | Solid Ball, Express.......... | 312 | .76 | |

## PATCHED BULLETS.

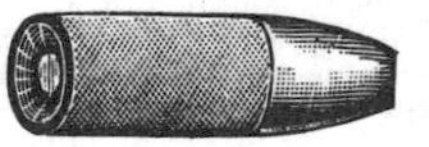

**Order No. 8384.**

| Sizes. | Description. | Weight Grains. | Weight per 100. | Price per 100. |
|---|---|---|---|---|
| 32-40 | Ballard.................. | 165 | 3¼ lbs. | $0.90 |
| 32-40 | Ballard.................. | 185 | 3¼ " | .95 |
| 38-55 | Ballard.................. | 255 | 4¼ " | .95 |
| 40-85 | Ballard.................. | 370 | 5¾ " | 1.05 |
| 40-90 | Sharp & Winchester, straight.................. | 370 | 4¾ " | 1.05 |
| 44-77 | Remington.................. | 470 | 7 " | 1.35 |
| 44-90 | Remington.................. | 550 | 8 " | 1.40 |
| 45-70 | Sharp's.................. | 420 | 6¼ " | 1.25 |
| 45-105 | Sharp's.................. | 550 | 10¼ " | 1.89 |
| 45 | .................. | 500 | 7½ " | 1.48 |
| 40 | .................. | 330 | 5 " | .96 |

## EVERLASTING SHELLS.

**Order No. 8385.**

| No. | Size. | Description. | Each. |
|---|---|---|---|
| 239 | 45-70 | Ballard Everlasting Shells.......... | $0.08 |
| 240 | 45-100 | Ballard Everlasting Shells.......... | .07 |

By mail, 1 cent extra.

## SHOT CARTRIDGES.

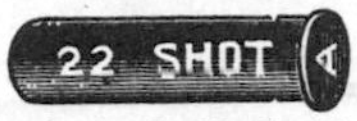


Loaded with shot instead of ball. For use in rifles and revolvers.

| No. | | Weight. | Per box. |
|---|---|---|---|
| 8386. | 22 caliber, rim fire, 50 in box, per 100.................... | ¾ lbs. | $0.50 |
| 8387. | 32 caliber, long rim fire, 25 in box. per 100................ | 2 " | 1.10 |
| 8388. | 32 caliber, S. & W., center fire, 50 in box, per 100......... | 2 " | 1.17 |
| 8389. | 38 caliber, S. & W., center fire, 50 in box, per 100......... | 4 lbs. | 1.30 |
| 8390. | 44 caliber, Winchester, model 1873, center fire, 50 in box, per 100.................... | 5 " | 1.64 |
| 8391. | 32 caliber, center fire, Winchester, model 1873, 50 in box, per 100............... | 2⅛ " | 1.86 |
| 8392. | 38 caliber, center fire, Winchester, model 1873, 50 in box, per 100............... | 4½ " | 1.65 |
| 8393. | 56-52 caliber, Spencer, rim fire, per 100.................... | | 2.50 |
| 8394. | 56-56 caliber, Spencer, rim fire, per 100, 25 in box......... | | 2.50 |

## PIN FIRE PISTOL CARTRIDGES.

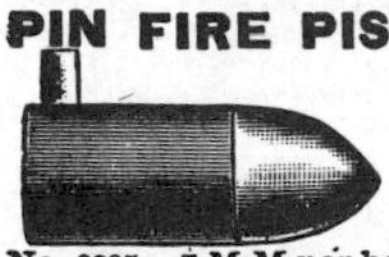

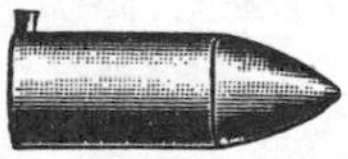

No. 8395. 7 M-M per box of 50, weight 18 oz.........$0.40
No. 8396. 9 M-M per box of 50, weight 24 oz......... .50

In sizes 7 M-M is 32 caliber, 9 M-M is 38 caliber, 12 M-M is 44 caliber.

No. 8397. 12 M-M per box of 50, weight, 24 oz.........$0.65

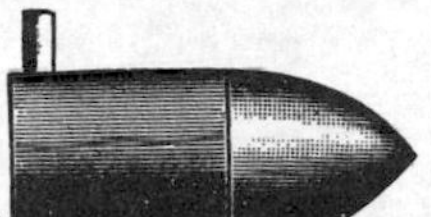

## MACHINE LOADED PAPER SHOT SHELLS

**Every Shell warranted.**

**Loaded Shells can go by freight, or express, alone or with other goods.**

The shells used are the celebrated WATERPROOF RIVAL and Club, U. M. C. and Winchester make. (Waterproof paper shells.) Put up in boxes of 25 shells, 20 boxes or 500 shells to the case. These shells are loaded with two thick black edge wads, and one CARDBOARD wad over the powder, and one thin cardboard wad over the shot.

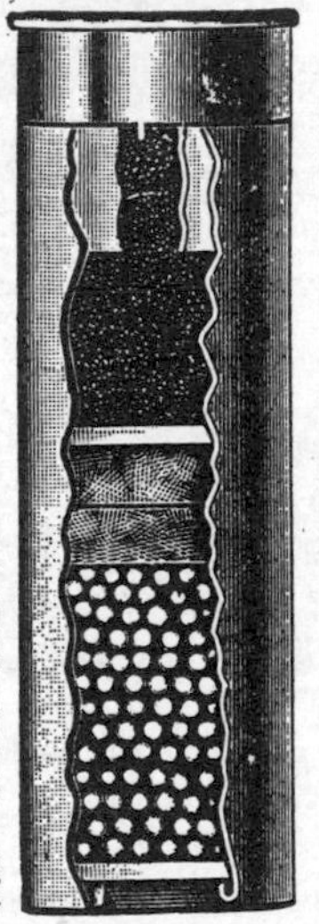

**NO BETTER MADE.**

The uniformity of the material used and the regularity of the machine work, insure level seating of wads and even pressure of powder, the compression being such as to secure the *highest explosive force*, thereby giving absolute perfection of loading, and becoming at once the most salable form of fixed ammunition. We can usually furnish these goods, loaded with Dupont, Laflin & Rand, or Hazard dead shot powders.

**Prices subject to change without notice.** Weight per case, 12 gauge, 65 lbs.; 10 gauge, 77 lbs., 500 shells in a case.

**N. B. 5 per cent. discount for cash on 500 lots or over. 10 per cent. discount for cash on 1,000 or over in case lots.**

### Order No. 8398. 12 Gauge.
BLACK POWDER.

| Load No. | Am't of Powd'r | Am't of shot | Size shot | Adapted to Shooting | Price per 25 | Price per 100 |
|---|---|---|---|---|---|---|
| 701 | 3 dr. | 1 oz. | 10 | Woodcock .......... | $0.30 | $1.29 |
| 707 | 3¼ dr. | 1⅛ oz. | 8 | Quail & Prairie C's | 31 | 1.36 |
| 709 | 3½ dr. | 1⅛ oz. | 8 | Prairie chicken.... | 33 | 1.39 |
| 713 | 3¼ dr. | 1¼ oz. | 8 | Inanimate Targets | 33 | 1.41 |
| 717 | 3¼ dr. | 1¼ oz. | 7 | Clay pigeons....... | 33 | 1.41 |
| 719 | 3¼ dr. | 1⅛ oz. | 7 | Ruffed Grouse..... | 35 | 1.36 |
| 721 | 3½ dr. | 1⅛ oz. | 7 | Teal................ | 34 | 1.39 |
| 725 | 3¼ dr. | 1⅛ oz. | 6 | Bluebill............ | 32 | 1.36 |
| 727 | 3½ dr. | 1⅛ oz. | 6 | Pintail............. | 33 | 1.39 |
| 729 | 3½ dr. | 1⅛ oz. | 5 | Mallard............ | 35 | 1.39 |
| 733 | 3¾ dr. | 1⅛ oz. | 3 | Canvas-back........ | 34 | 1.41 |
| 739 | 4 dr. | 1⅛ oz. | BB | Goose ... ... ...... | 38 | 1.45 |
| 741 | 3 dr. | 1 oz. | 9 | .................... | 33 | 1.29 |
| 743 | 3 dr. | 1 oz. | 8 | .................... | 33 | 1.29 |
| 747 | 3 dr. | 1 oz. | 7 | .................... | 32 | 1.29 |
| 749 | 3 dr. | 1 oz. | 6 | .................... | 32 | 1.29 |
| 751 | 3¼ dr. | 1⅛ oz. | 5 | .................... | 35 | 1.36 |
| 755 | 3 dr. | 1 oz. | 5 | .................... | 31 | 1.29 |
| 757 | 3 dr. | 1 oz. | 4 | .................... | 32 | 1.29 |
| 759 | 3¼ dr. | 1⅛ oz. | 4 | .................... | 31 | 1.36 |
| 761 | 3½ dr. | 1⅛ oz. | 4 | .................... | 33 | 1.39 |
| 763 | 3¾ dr. | 1⅛ oz. | 2 | .................... | 34 | 1.41 |
| 765 | 3¾ dr. | 1⅛ oz. | B | .................... | 35 | 1.41 |
| 767 | 3¾ dr. | 1⅛ oz. | BB | .................... | 37 | 1.45 |
| 769 | 4 dr. | 1⅛ oz. | 4 | .................... | 34 | 1.45 |
| 771 | 4 dr. | 1⅛ oz. | 5 | .................... | 38 | 1.45 |
| 773 | 4 dr. | 1⅛ oz. | 5B'k | .................... | 40 | 1.54 |

### Order No. 8398½. 10 Gauge.
MACHINE LOADS. BLACK POWDER.

| Load No. | Am't of powd'r | Am't of shot. | Size shot | Adapted to shooting | Price per 25 | Price per 100 |
|---|---|---|---|---|---|---|
| 700 | 3½ dr. | 1⅛ oz. | 10 | Woodcock.......... | $0.38 | $1.45 |
| 702 | 3½ [illegible] | 1⅛ oz. | 9 | Snipe.............. | 38 | 1.45 |
| 704 | 3¾ dr. | 1⅛ oz. | 8 | Quail............... | 36 | 1.47 |
| 706 | 4¼ dr. | 1⅛ oz. | 8 | Quail & Prairie C's | 38 | 1.52 |
| 710 | 4 dr. | 1¼ oz. | 8 | Inanimate Targets | 39 | 1.57 |
| 714 | 4½ dr. | 1¼ oz. | 8 | Live Pigeons....... | 40 | 1.60 |
| 718 | 4¼ dr. | 1⅛ oz. | 7 | Ruffed Grouse...... | 38 | 1.52 |
| 720 | 4½ dr. | 1⅛ oz. | 7 | Teal................ | 39 | 1.54 |
| 726 | 4½ dr. | 1⅛ oz. | 6 | Pintail... ......... | 39 | 1.54 |
| 728 | 4½ dr. | 1⅛ oz. | 5 | Mallard............ | 39 | 1.54 |
| 730 | 4½ dr. | 1⅛ oz. | 4 | Red-head.......... | 39 | 1.54 |
| 732 | 4½ dr. | 1⅛ oz. | 3 | Canvas-Back....... | 40 | 1.56 |
| 738 | 5 dr. | 1⅛ oz. | BB | Goose.............. | 43 | 1.71 |
| 746 | 4 dr. | 1⅛ oz. | 6 | .................... | 38 | 1.50 |
| 748 | 4 dr. | 1¼ oz. | 7 | .................... | 38 | 1.50 |
| 750 | 4½ dr. | 1¼ oz. | 5 | .................... | 38 | 1.60 |
| 752 | 4½ dr. | 1¼ oz. | 2 | .................... | 37 | 1.61 |
| 754 | 4½ dr. | 1¼ oz. | 1 | .................... | 36 | 1.61 |
| 756 | 5 dr, | 1¼ oz. | 4B'k | .................... | 50 | 1.93 |

### Order No. 8399. 16 Gauge.
MACHINE BLACK POWDER.

| Load No. | Am't of powd'r | Am't of shot | Size shot | Adapted to Shooting | Price per 25 | Price per 100 |
|---|---|---|---|---|---|---|
| 808 | 2¾ dr. | 1 oz. | 8 | .................... | $0.35 | $1.34 |
| 810 | 2¾ dr. | 1 oz. | 7 | .................... | 35 | 1.34 |
| 812 | 2¾ dr. | 1 oz. | 6 | .................... | 35 | 1.34 |
| 815 | 2½ dr. | 1 oz. | 8 | .................... | 35 | 1.32 |
| 816 | 2½ dr. | 1 oz. | 7 | .................... | 35 | 1.32 |
| 818 | 2¾ dr. | 1 oz. | 5 | .................... | 35 | 1.34 |

## Smokeless Powder, Machine Loaded Paper Shells.

Smokeless Loaded Paper Shells. Loaded 25 shells in a box. Sold in boxes of 25 at the 100 shell rates if desired; ten per cent discount in 1000 lots cash with the order.

### 12 Gauge—Order 8399 1-2.

| No. | Am't of powd'r | Am't of shot | Size shot | Smokeless Powder Machine Loaded. | Per 100. |
|---|---|---|---|---|---|
| 19 | 2¾ dr. | 1⅛ oz. | No. 9 | .................... | $2.20 |
| 18 | 2¾ dr. | 1⅛ oz. | No. 8 | .................... | 2.22 |
| 38 | 3 dr. | 1⅛ oz. | No. 8 | .................... | 2.23 |
| 58 | 3 dr. | 1¼ oz. | No. 8 | .................... | 2.29 |
| 17 | 2¾ dr. | 1⅛ oz. | No. 7 | .................... | 2.22 |
| 37 | 3 dr. | 1⅛ oz. | No. 7 | .................... | 2.23 |
| 57 | 3 dr. | 1¼ oz. | No. 7 | .................... | 2.29 |
| 17 | 2¾ dr. | 1⅛ oz. | No. 6 | .................... | 2.22 |
| 36 | 3 dr. | 1⅛ oz. | No. 6 | .................... | 2.23 |
| 35 | 3 dr. | 1⅛ oz. | No. 5 | .................... | 2.23 |
| 34 | 3 dr. | 1⅛ oz, | No. 4 | .................... | 2.23 |
| 57½ | 3 dr. | 1⅛ oz. | No. 7½ | .................... | 2.35 |

### 10 Gauge—Order 8400.

| No. | Am't of powd'r | Am't of shot | Size shot | Smokeless Powder Machine Loaded. | Per 100. |
|---|---|---|---|---|---|
| 29 | 3½ dr. | 1¼ oz. | No. 9 | .................... | $2.60 |
| 28 | 3½ dr. | 1¼ oz. | No. 8 | .................... | 2.60 |
| 27 | 3¼ dr. | 1⅛ oz. | No. 7 | .................... | 2.60 |
| 127 | 3½ dr. | 1¼ oz. | No. 7 | .................... | 2.73 |
| 26 | 3½ dr, | 1¼ oz. | No. 6 | .................... | 2.73 |
| 25 | 3½ dr. | 1¼ oz. | No. 5 | .................... | 2.73 |
| 44 | 3¾ dr. | 1¼ oz. | No. 4 | .................... | 2.70 |

### 16 Gauge—Order 8400 1-2.

| No. | Am't of powd'r | Am't of shot | Size shot | Smokeless Powder Machine Loaded. | Per 100. |
|---|---|---|---|---|---|
| 328 | 2½ dr. | ⅞ oz. | No. 8 | .................... | $2.09 |
| 327 | 2½ dr. | ⅞ oz. | No. 7 | .................... | 2.09 |
| 336 | 2½ dr. | 1 oz. | No. 6 | .................... | 2.09 |
| 335 | 2½ dr. | 1 oz. | No. 5 | .................... | 2.09 |

## SHOT SPREADERS.

**PATENTED.**

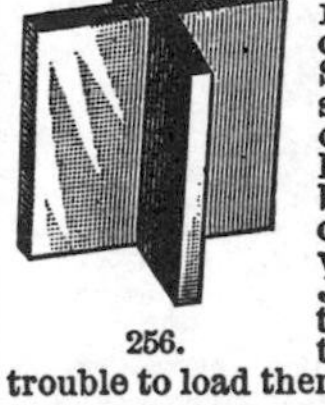

256.

8401. Full chokes made to spread MORE than cylinders. SHOT SPREADERS do it. A FULL CHOKE makes a circle of about 12 inches at 15 yards. Shot spreaders make the same gun scatter from 24 to 30 inches. No use of carrying two sets of barrels on a hunting trip. They are made of pasteboard, and pass loosely through the choke. Very successful in the bushes where shooting is done at short range. Just right for quail, woodcock, partridge and rabbits. Do not mangle the game at close quarters. No trouble to load them.

12 gauge and 10 gauge. To load: In a 2⅝ inch shell use 2¾ drs. powder; 1 B. edge and 1 card wad on powder. Drop the spreader down onto the powder wads and then pour in 1⅛ ounces shot. 1⅛ ounce fills the spreader and a little over. Lay on an ordinary card wad and turn over the shell. If your shell is more than 2⅝ inches long use any load of powder and wads you have room for. Price, per 100, 50c. Box of 50, 25c.

All 12 gauge will work in 10 gauge, also.

## EMPTY PAPER SHOT GUN SHELLS.

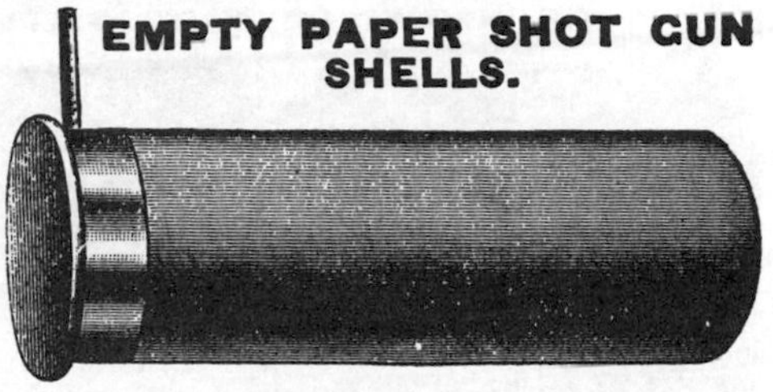

Pin Fire.

No. 8402. Pin-fire Paper Shells, 20 gauge; per box of 100, weight, 2 lbs...............................$0.65
No. 8403. Pin-fire Paper Shells, 14 gauge; per box of 100, weight, 2 lbs...............................$0.65
No. 8404. Pin-fire Paper Shells, 16 gauge; per box of 100, weight, 2 lbs...............................$0.65
No. 8405. 12 gauge; per box of 100, pin-fire, weight, 4¼ lbs...............................$0.90
No. 8406. 10 gauge, pin-fire paper shells, per box of 100...............................$1.20

## U. M. C. SMOKELESS EMPTY PAPER SHELLS.

Salmon.

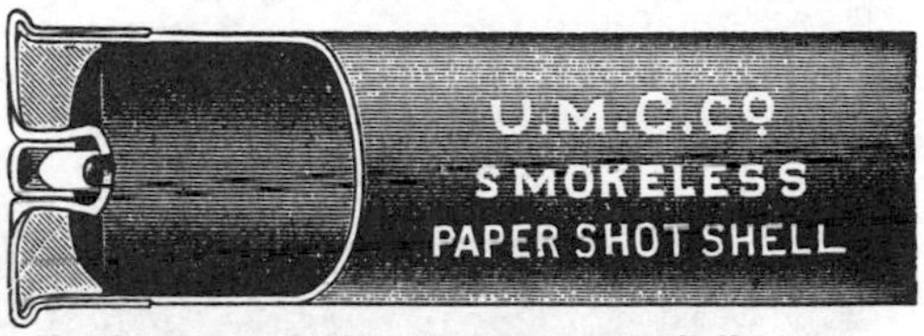


The Smokeless Shell is the boss paper shell.

No. 8407. The New U. M. C. Smokeless, Red or Salmon Colored Empty Paper Shell, made expressly for (SS) smokeless powder, and the best low pricsd shell for E. C. Schultze and Wood powders, using the LONG STRONG No 3 primer, made by the U. M. C. Company only. With "Nitro" powder of any kind this is much the QUICKEST and strongest shell now upon the market for the price. See that your shells take the LONG No. 3 PRIMER, for they are MUCH the BEST. (The long No. 3 primer is twice as long as other primers.)

| | Per box of 100. | Per 1,000. |
|---|---|---|
| 12 gauge, 2⅝ in., weight, 2¼ lbs....... | $0.83 | $7.75 |
| 12 " 2¾ in., " 2½ lbs...... | .88 | 8.40 |
| 10 " 2⅞ in., " 2¾ lbs....... | .89 | 8.40 |
| 16 " 29-16 in., " ...... | .87 | 8.50 |

NOTE.—These shells are not loaded.

## GREEN TRAP U. M. C. EMPTY PAPER SHELL.

Prices subject to change without notice.
(Empty shells, not loaded.) All center fire.
Weight, per box, 12 gauge, 2½ lbs., 10 gauge, 3¼ lbs.; 8 gauge, 4¼ lbs.

The Trap Shell is the best and strongest paper shell made, and is used by all experts in live-bird "matches," and where heavy charges are required, and are warranted gas tight.

No. 8408. Paper U. M. C. Trap Shell, metal reinforced, green colored paper, gas tight, especially adapted to E. C. Schultze, Wood and all nitro powders; crimp same as any paper shell; reloadable, using No. 3 long, quick, strong primer.

| | Per 100 | Per 1,000 |
|---|---|---|
| 10 gauge, 2⅞ in.......................... | $1.32 | $12.57 |
| 12 gauge, 2⅝ in.......................... | 1.25 | 12.00 |
| 12 gauge, 2¾ in.......................... | 1.32 | 12.55 |
| 12 gauge, 2⅞ or 3 in...................... | 1.32 | 12.57 |

## U. M. C. "MAROON" EMPTY PAPER SHELL.

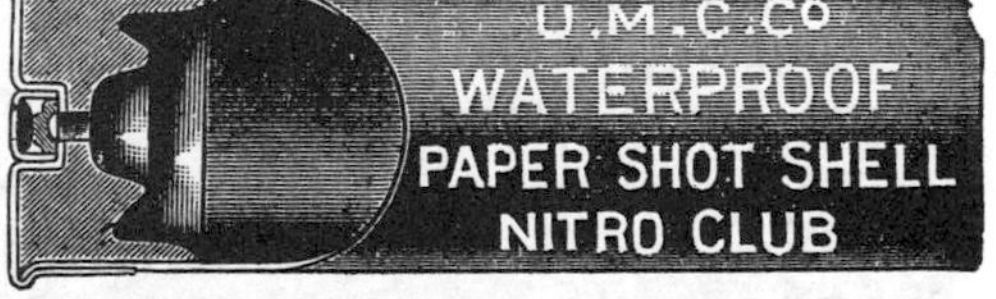


No. 8409. U. M. C. Maroon Paper Shell for black and nitro powder, using No. 5 primer. Can be reloaded.

| | Per 100 | Per 1,000 |
|---|---|---|
| 12 gauge, 2⅝ in.......................... | $0.49 | $4.65 |
| 12 gauge, 2¾ in.......................... | .55 | 5.40 |
| 10 gauge, 2⅞ in.......................... | .55 | 5.39 |
| 16 gauge, 2⅜ in.......................... | .56 | 5.39 |
| 20 gauge, 2½ in.......................... | .56 | 5.40 |

## BLACK CLUB PAPER SHELL.

No. 8410. The New Club Nitro or Black Powder Shell, with special strong primer. Strong and quick. No. 2. Can be reloaded.

| | Per 100 | Per 1,000 |
|---|---|---|
| 12 gauge, 2⅝ in.......................... | $0.49 | $4.65 |
| 12 gauge, 2¾ in.......................... | .55 | 5.30 |
| 10 gauge, 2⅞ in.......................... | .55 | 5.30 |

**GROCERIES MAKE GOOD FREIGHT SHIPMENTS.**

**Make up a freight order and ship your shells with it. . . . . . . . .**

**PRICES ON CERTAIN LINES OF GOODS ARE CONSTANTLY CHANGING. WE ARE QUICK TO ALLOW REDUCTION WHERE THE PRICE DROPS. AND WHEN IT RISES, WE ARE OF COURSE COMPELLED TO MEET THE ADVANCE WITH A RISE.**

## WINCHESTER GREEN TRAP EMPTY SHELL.

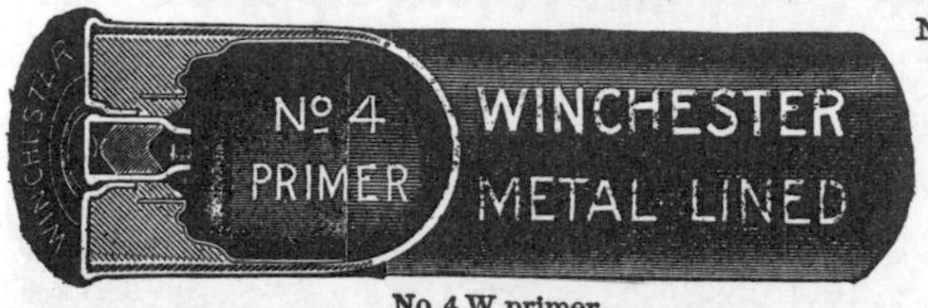


No. 8411. The new trap paper shell made by the W. R. A. Co., reinforced inside and outside with brass, as shown in the cut, for nitro or black powder—new, strong.

No. 4 W primer.

| | | Per 1000. |
|---|---|---|
| 12 gauge, 2⅝ in., per box of 100 | $1.25 | $11.50 |
| 12 gauge, 2¾ in., per box of 100 | 1.33 | 12.60 |
| 10 gauge, 2⅞ in., per box of 100 | 1.33 | 12.60 |

## WINCHESTER "LEADER" EMPTY PAPER SHELL.

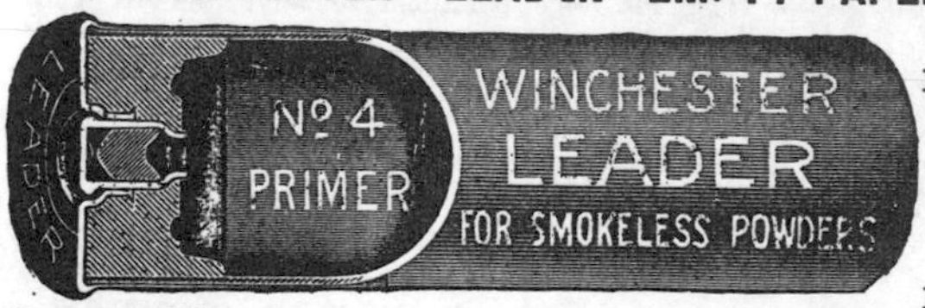


No. 8412. Winchester Leader, smokeless paper shells; can be reloaded; for nitro or black powders; using No. 4 W nitro primer.

| | Per 100. | Per 1,000. |
|---|---|---|
| 12 gauge, 2⅝ in | $0.83 | $7.75 |
| 12 gauge, 2¾ in | .89 | 8.40 |
| 12 gauge, 3 in | 1.00 | 9.50 |
| 10 gauge, 2⅞ in | .89 | 8.50 |
| 10 gauge, 3 in | 1.00 | 9.65 |
| 16 gauge | .85 | 8.25 |

## WINCHESTER "BLUE" RIVAL EMPTY PAPER SHELLS.

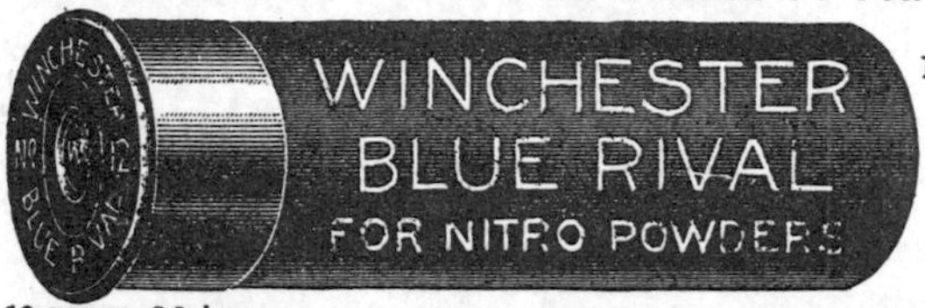


No. 8413. Winchester Blue Rival paper shells, waterproof, quick and reliable, using No. 3 W primer; can be reloaded; for black or nitro powders.

| | Per 100. | Per 1.000. |
|---|---|---|
| 16 gauge, 2 9/16 in | $0.56 | $5.39 |
| 12 gauge, 2⅝ in | .49 | 4.65 |
| 12 gauge, 2¾ in | .54 | 5.30 |
| 12 gauge, 3 in | .65 | 5.90 |
| 10 gauge, 2⅞ in | .54 | 5.30 |

## RIVAL EMPTY PAPER SHELLS.

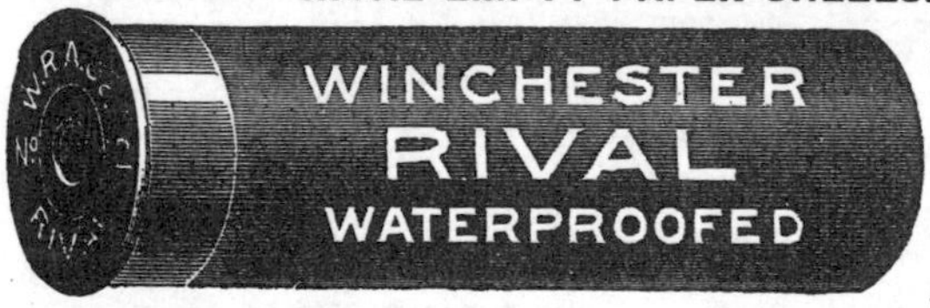


No. 8414. Winchester "Rival" paper shells, warranted perfect; a good shell, waterproof, U. M. C. or Winchester No. 2 primer; can be reloaded.

| | Per box. | Per 1,000. |
|---|---|---|
| 12 gauge, 2⅝ in., weight 2¼ lbs | $0.49 | $4.65 |
| 12 gauge, 2¾ in | .54 | 5.30 |
| 10 gauge, 2⅞ in | .54 | 5.30 |
| 14 gauge, 2 9/16 in | .56 | 5.40 |
| 16 gauge, 2 9/16 in | .56 | 5.40 |
| 20 gauge, 2½ in | .56 | 5.40 |

## WINCHESTER REPEATER EMPTY PAPER SHELL.

Yellow.

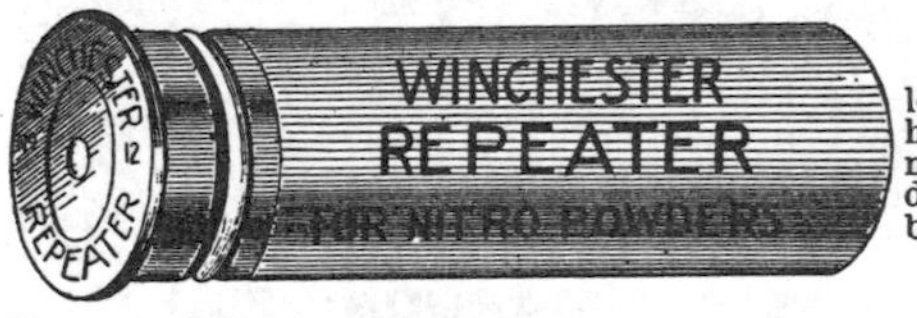


Repeater Paper Shell (yellow), long corrugated brass head, especially adapted to medium loads of nitro powder; new No. 6 primer; can be reloaded.

| | Per 100 | Per 1,000 |
|---|---|---|
| 12 gauge, 2⅝ in. long (empty) | $.49 | $4.65 |
| 12 gauge, 2¾ in. long (empty) | .54 | 5.35 |
| 12 gauge, 3 in. long (empty) | .60 | 5.45 |
| 10 gauge, 2⅞ in. long (empty) | .56 | 5.30 |

## EMPTY BRASS SHELLS.

Give gauge and length when ordering shells,

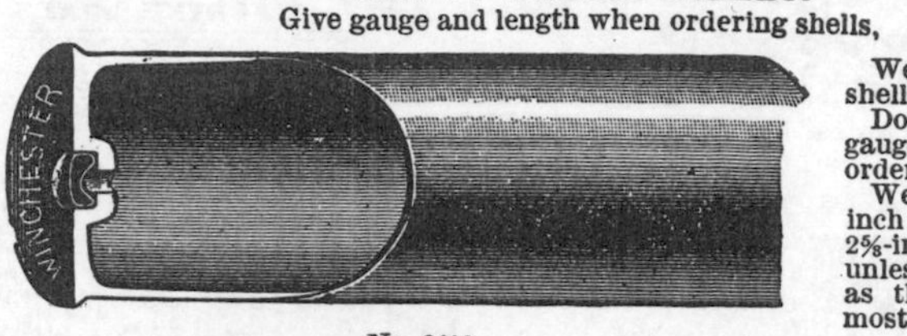

No. 8416.

Weight per box of 25 shells, about [illegible] lbs.

Don't forget to give gauge wanted when ordering shells.

We always send 2⅝-inch in 12 gauge and 2⅝-inch in 10 gauge unless length is given, as this is the size most used.

## WINCHESTER "RIVAL" BRASS SHELLS.

No. 8416. Brass shells, "Rival," using any No. 2 primer. A good, strong shell, but lighter than the first quality, 12 gauge, 2½ and 2⅝ inches long, each....... 4½c
Per box of 25........ 80c

No. 8417. Brass shells, "Rival," 10 gauge, 2⅝ or 2⅞ inches long, each....... 4½c
Per box of 25........ 80c

N. B.—The Rival shells are sold by many dealers as "The very best quality." Don't be fooled. Send to us for samples at box rates.

## WINCHESTER "BEST" BRASS SHELLS.

Order No. 8418.

Winchester brass shells, first quality, using Winchester No. 2. primer.

| | |
|---|---|
| 20 gauge, 2¼ inches long, per box of 25 | $1.15 |
| 16 gauge, 2½ inches long, each 5c., per box of 25 | 1.16 |
| 14 gauge, 2⅜ inches long, each 5c., per box of 25 | 1.17 |
| 12 gauge, 2½ and 2⅝ inches long, each 5c., per box of 25 | 1.18 |
| 12 gauge, 2¾ and 2⅞ inches long, each 5c., per box of 25 | 1.19 |
| 10 gauge, 2⅝ inches long, each 5c., per box of 25 | 1.20 |
| 10 gauge, 2⅞ and 3 inches long, each 5½c., per box of 25, weight 1¾ lbs | 1.21 |
| 8 gauge, 3 inches long, each 9c., per box of 25, weight 3¼ lbs | 2.10 |

In ordering shells be careful to give gauge of gun for which you wish the shells.

## U. M. C. BRASS SHELLS.

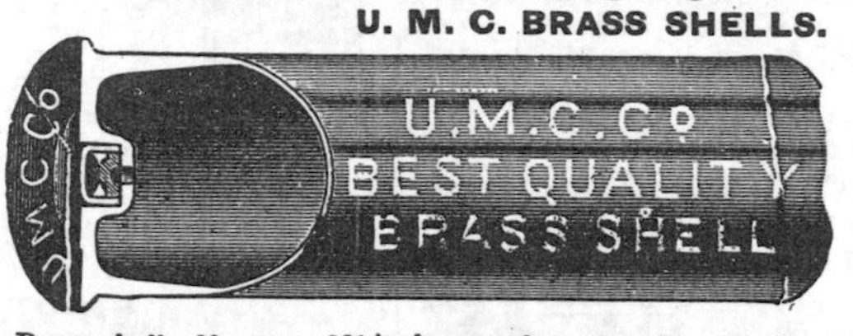


**Order No. 8419.**

Give gauge and length when ordering shells.

**Using U. M. C. No. 2 Primer.**

| | |
|---|---|
| Brass shells, 20 gauge, 2⅝ inches, each 5c., per box of 25 | $1.15 |
| Brass shells, 16 gauge, 2½ inches, each 5c., per box of 25 | 1.16 |
| Brass shells, 14 gauge, 2⅜ inches, each 5c., per box of 25 | 1.17 |
| Brass shells, 12 gauge, 2½ or 2⅝ inches long, per box of 25 | 1.18 |
| Brass shells, 10 gauge, 2¾ or 2⅞ inches long, per box of 25 | 1.18 |
| Brass shells, 10 gauge, 2⅝ or 2¾ inches long, per box of 25 | 1.20 |
| Brass shells, 10 gauge, 2⅞ inches long, per box of 25 | 1.25 |
| Brass shells, 10 gauge, 3 inches long, per box of 25, weight 1¾ lbs | 1.25 |
| Brass shells, 8 gauge, 3 inches long, per box of 25, weight 2¼ lbs. | 2.10 |

## U. S. CLIMAX. EMPTY.

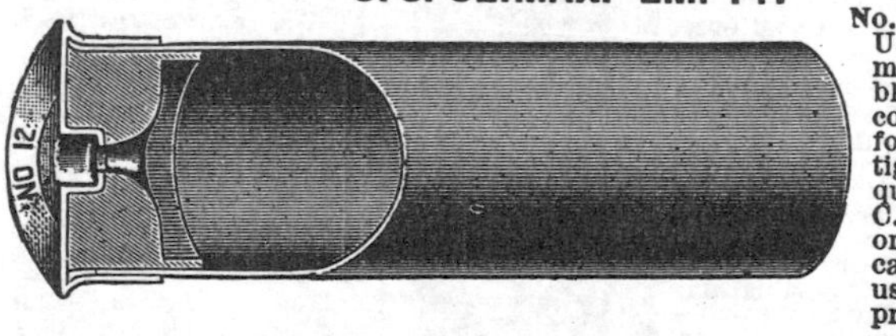


No. 8415. The new U. S. Lowell "Climax" paper shell, black waterproof, conical base, re-enforced base, gas-tight, extra strong, quick primer, for E C. Wood, Schultze or black powders; can be reloaded, using any No. 2 primer.

| U. S. Climax Shells. Continued. | | Per 100. | Per 1,000. |
|---|---|---|---|
| 12 gauge, 2⅝ in. | Weight, 2¼ lbs | $0.49 | $4.65 |
| 12 gauge, 2¾ in. | " 2 5/16 " | .54 | 5.30 |
| 12 gauge, 2⅞ in. | " 2⅜ " | .54 | 5.30 |
| 10 gauge, 2⅞ in. | " 2⅞ " | .54 | 5.30 |
| 14 gauge | | .56 | 5.30 |
| 16 gauge | | .56 | 5.40 |
| 20 gauge | | .56 | 5.30 |

OUR HOUSE IS...
THE BARGAIN CENTER

## GUN CAPS AND PRIMERS.

Showing size of Showing size of Primers.

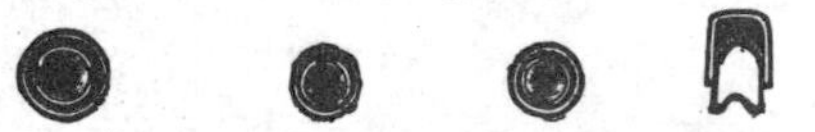

No. 2 and 2½. No. 1. No. 1½. No. 3.

Cannot go by mail.

| | |
|---|---|
| No. 8420. Primer for pin-fire paper shell, per box of 250, 60c.; per M | $2.00 |
| No. 8421. Primer for pin-fire pistol cartridges, per box of 250, 50c.; per M | 1.80 |
| No. 8422. The W. R. A. Waterproof gun caps for muzzle loaders, per box, 6c.; per M | .45 |
| No. 8423. U. S. musket caps, 10 boxes (1,000 caps), per box, 5c.; per M | .65 |
| No. 8424. Gun caps, G. D. percussion, per box, 4c.; per M | .40 |
| No. 8425. Gun caps (Ely E. B.), single waterproof, 10 boxes (1,000), per box, 7c.; per M | .65 |
| No. 8426. Primers, centre fire, for shot gun shells and cartridges, U. M. C., No. 2½, 2, 1, 1½, 0, per box of 250, 35c.; per M | 1.20 |
| No. 8427. Primers for Winchester cartridges and shot gun shells, Nos. 1, 1½, 2, 2½ per box of 250, 35c.; per M | 1.20 |
| No. 8428. Primers No. 3 for U. M. C. Trap and "Smokeless" grade paper shells. These primers are twice as long as the regular primers, and are the only No. 3 primer known to the trade. They are much stronger and quicker than any other primer. Per box of 250, 35c.; per M | 1.20 |
| No. 8429. Winchester No. 3 W primer for Rival paper shells, when nitro powder is used, per box, 35c.; per M | 1.20 |
| No. 8429½. Primers No. 5, per box, 35c.; per M | 1.20 |
| No. 8429¾. Winchester No. 4 Primers, for "Leader" and "Green Trap" Winchester paper shells, per box of 250, 35c.; per M | 1.20 |
| Winchester No. 6 Primer, for "New Repeater" paper shells, per box of 250, 35c.; per M | 1.20 |

**DON'T FORGET POSTAGE WHEN GOODS ARE ORDERED BY MAIL.**

When ordering **Primers** be sure to give **manufacturer's** name of shell or **our** catalogue number. **Primers cannot go by mail.**

## WADS.

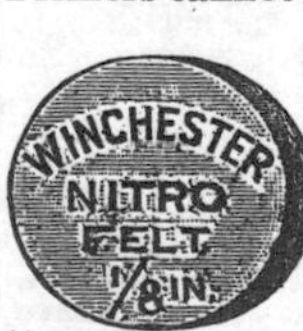


No. 8430, **Winchester "Nitro"** powder wad, made of elastic felt soft and pliable, unlubricated, perfectly dry and free from all greasy matter, covered both sides with thin, soft blue paper. 125 in a box.

| | ⅛ Per box. | ⅛ Per 1,000. | ¼ Per box. | ¼ Per 1,000. | ⅜ Per box. | ⅜ Per 1,000. |
|---|---|---|---|---|---|---|
| 11 or 12 gauge | $0.07 | $0.48 | $0.13 | $0.88 | $0.27 | $1.92 |
| 9 or 10 " | .10 | .66 | .15 | 1.00 | .30 | 2.16 |

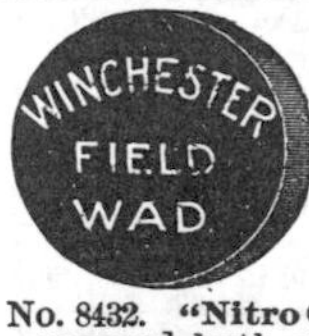


No. 8431. **Winchester Field Wad,** elastic white felt, covered with black waterproof material on one side and blue paper on the other, unlubricated, for use over powder.

| | Per box. | Per 1.000. |
|---|---|---|
| 10 gauge, 250 in box | $0.26 | $1.00 |
| 12 " " | .24 | .80 |

No. 8432. **"Nitro Card" Wad,** extra thick card-board, covered both sides with this paper, for use over powder. The claim for this wad is improved pattern and preventing balling of shot, when used in combination with the Winchester "Nitro" and field wad.

| | Per box. | Per 1,000. |
|---|---|---|
| 9 or 11 gauge, 250 in a box | $0.07 | $0.20 |
| 11 or 12 " " " | .05 | .15 |

No. 8433. **The New Thin Top Shot Wad.** For trap shooting, made of specially prepared paper, less than one-fourth as thick as regular card wads. Advantages of this wad: Evener distribution of shot; closer pattern, more space for powder wads and shot, blows to pieces when "fired" and offers less resistance to the shot, and yet stiff enough to hold shot in place when crimped, and does not "bulge" in crimping.

| | Per box. | per 1,000. |
|---|---|---|
| 10 gauge, per box of 500 | $0.20 | $0.35 |
| 12 " " " | .10 | .20 |

Weight per box about 4 oz.

No. 8434. Engraved **"Thin" Top Shot Wads.** The best yet. Try them once and be convinced. Size of shot engraved on both sides. Sizes of shot Nos. 5, 6, 7, 8 and 9.

| | Per box. | Per 1,000. |
|---|---|---|
| 12 gauge, per box of 500 (weight 6 oz. per 1,000) | $0.15 | $0.25 |
| 10 gauge, per box of 500 (weight 7 oz. per 1,000 | .18 | .30 |

**IF ANY CUSTOMER EVER HAS CAUSE TO COMPLAIN, LET US HEAR FROM HIM BY ALL MEANS. WITH 600 EMPLOYEES, SOME OF THEM MAY GET CARELESS. WE WANT TO FIND IT OUT, AND RECTIFY ANY FAULT, IF SUCH SHOULD OCCUR.**

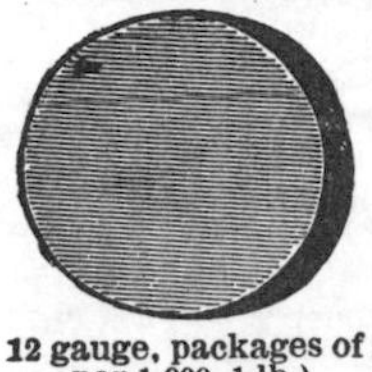

No. 8435. **Salmon Felt Wads, "soft,"** for use over nitro powder. Gives the best satisfaction of any wad in the market for "top powder" use. Has soft hair on one side, thin salmon colored paper glued on the other side.

| | Per box. | Per 1,000. |
|---|---|---|
| 12 gauge, packages of 250 (weight per 1,000, 1 lb.) | $0.18 | $0.60 |
| 10 gauge, packages of 250 (weight 1¼ lbs. per 1,000) | .20 | .70 |

### WADS—U. M. C. AND WINCHESTER MAKE.

No. 8436. **Pink Edge Wads,** ¼ inch thick, 250 in a box.

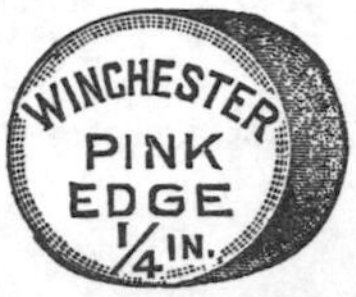
WINCHESTER
PINK
EDGE
1/4 IN.

| | Per box. | Per 1,000. |
|---|---|---|
| 11 or 12 gauge | $0.33 | $1 20 |
| 9 or 10 " | .38 | 1.40 |

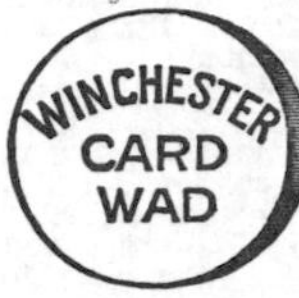
WINCHESTER
CARD
WAD

No. 8437. **Card-board Wads** for use over shot. Weight per 1,000 1¼ lbs.

| | | Per 1,000. |
|---|---|---|
| 7 gauge, per box of 250 | $0.07 | $0.21 |
| 8 " " " | .07 | .20 |
| 9 or 10 gauge " " | .06 | .18 |
| 11 to 20 " " | .05 | .15 |

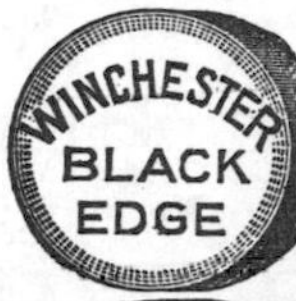
WINCHESTER
BLACK
EDGE

No. 8438. **Black Edge Wads,** for use over powder. Weight per 1,000 2 to 3½ lbs., according to size.

| | | Per 1,000. |
|---|---|---|
| 6 gauge, per box of 250 | $0.28 | $1.08 |
| 7 " " " | .19 | .65 |
| 8 " " " | .19 | .64 |
| 9 or 10 gauge " " | .17 | .56 |
| 11 to 20 " " | .13 | .48 |

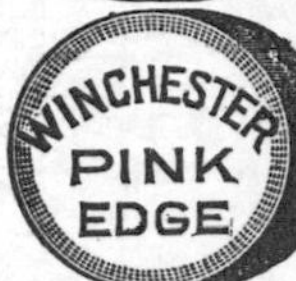
WINCHESTER
PINK
EDGE

No. 8439. **Pink Edge Wads,** for use over powder. Weight per 1,000, 2 to 3½ lbs.

| | | Per 1,000. |
|---|---|---|
| 6 gauge, pink edge, per box of 250 | $0.40 | $1.40 |
| 7 " " " " " | .34 | 1.21 |
| 8 " " " " " | .33 | 1.20 |
| 9 to 10 gauge " " " " | .30 | 1.00 |
| 10 to 20 " " " " | .23 | .80 |

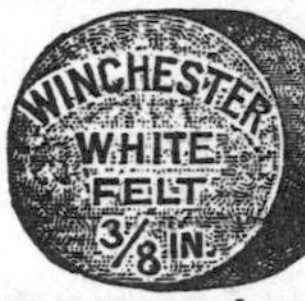
WINCHESTER
WHITE
FELT
3/8 IN.

No. 8440. **White Felt Wads,** ⅜ inch thick, for use over powder. Weight per 1,000 5 to 6 lbs.

| | | Per 1,000. |
|---|---|---|
| 7 gauge, per box of 125 | $0.47 | $3.60 |
| 8 " " " | .41 | 3.20 |
| 9 or 10 gauge, per box of 125 | .33 | 2.37 |
| 11, 12, 14, 20 gauge, per box of 125 | .29 | 2.18 |

No. 8441. The new **"Trap" Wool Felt Wad,** one side black waterproof, reverse side salmon color paper; sometimes called express or field wads; about the same thickness as a pink edge, for over powder, not as hard "finish" as most wads of this kind, and consequently better than any other wad of this kind on the market; weight, 1½ to 1¾ lbs. per 1,000.

| | | |
|---|---|---|
| 10, gauge, per box of 250 | $0.25 | $1.00 |
| 11 and 12 gauge, per box of 150 | .24 | .80 |

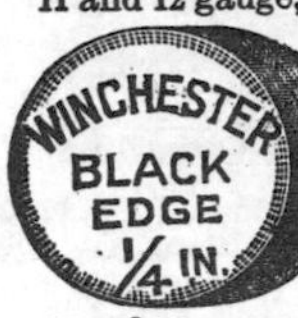
WINCHESTER
BLACK
EDGE
1/4 IN.

No. 8442. **Black Edge, ¼ Inch Wads;** weight, per 1,000, 2¼ to 3 lbs. 9 or 10 gauge, per box of 250 ........ $0.24 ........ $0.85
11 and 12 gauge, per box of 250 ........ .20 ........ .72

No. 8443. **Black Edge Wads,** ⅜ inch thick, 125 in a box, 9 and 10 gauge ........ $0.29 ........ $2.16
11 and 12 gauge; weight per 1,000, 3¼ to 4¼ lbs. ........ .26 ........ 1.92

N. B.—In 12 gauge brass shells, use 10 gauge wads; in 10 gauge brass shells use 8 gauge wads. In paper shells use wads the same size as shell. Always put the wad down to place flat and evenly, otherwise the shooting quality of your gun will be greatly impaired.

### WAD CUTTERS.

Postage 5c extra. Be sure and give gauge wanted.

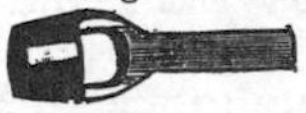

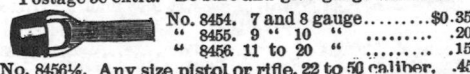

| | | |
|---|---|---|
| No. 8454. | 7 and 8 gauge | $0.35 |
| " 8455. | 9 " 10 " | .20 |
| " 8456. | 11 to 20 " | .15 |
| No. 8456½. | Any size pistol or rifle, 22 to 50 caliber | .45 |



### Dupont Smokeless or Nitro Powder.

**The Dupont Smokeless Nitro Powder** is a fine grain, hard powder, safe and reliable. It may be loaded the same as black powder, except the quantity should be less; use paper shells only; load measured in reguler powder measure; 16 ga. 2 to 2½ drams; 12 ga. 2¼ to 3 drams; 10 ga. 2¾ to 3½ drams. One of the most satisfactory nitro powders.

| | |
|---|---|
| 12½ pound cans, equal in bulk to 25 pounds black powder | $13.20 |
| 6¼ pound cans equal in bulk to 12½ pounds black powder | $6.75 |
| 3⅛ pound cans equal in bulk to 6¼ pounds black powder | $3.45 |
| ½ pound cans equal in bulk to 1 pound black powder | $0.60 |

See directions on package for loading.

N. B.—All nitro or smokeless powders can be shipped by express or freight, either alone or with other goods.

### Schultze Powder.

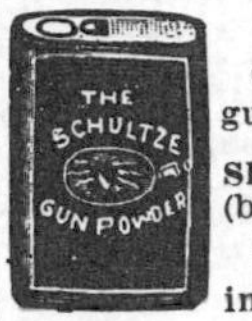
THE
SCHULTZE
GUN POWDER

These powders are made for first-class guns.

No. 8458. **Schultze Powders for Shot-guns,** very little smoke.

| | |
|---|---|
| 1 pound (bulk) cans | $0.50 |
| 10 pound (bulk) drums | $4.80 |

Follow the directions on can for loading.

### E. C. Powder.

No. 8444. **E. C. Shot-gun Powder,** little or no smoke. It is becoming more popular every year.

| | |
|---|---|
| 1 pound (bulk) cans, per can | $0.55 |
| 10 " " " " | 5.35 |

Great care must be taken in loading these powders to obtain the best results. Directions for use on each can.

The great advantage of Dupont's Smokeless, Schultze S. S. and E. C. Powders over common powders is the fact that there is much less recoil and no smoke to prevent seeing game or target for second shot.

### THE NEW GRADE (S.S.) SMOKELESS POWDER.

**THE BEST SMOKELESS OR NITRO POWDER YET PRODUCRD.**

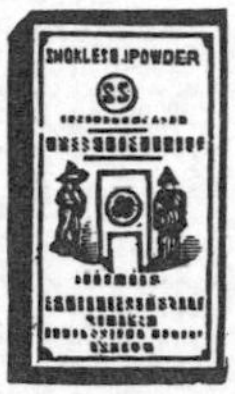
SMOKELESS POWDER
SS

**No. 8445. The New Smokeless (S. S.) Shot-Gun Powder;** does not weigh as much, bulk for bulk, as black powder.

| | |
|---|---|
| 1 pound can (bulk) price | $0.50 |
| 10 " " " " | 4.25 |

The superiority of the S. S. powder consists in its high velocity, long range, reduced recoil, reduced smoke, reduced fouling and more regular patterns. (S. S.) is the highest development in "nitro" compounds. In consequence of the absence of "jar" and the reduced recoil it is the most agreeable of powders to shoot.

### DUPONT RIFLE AND SHOT GUN BLACK POWDER.

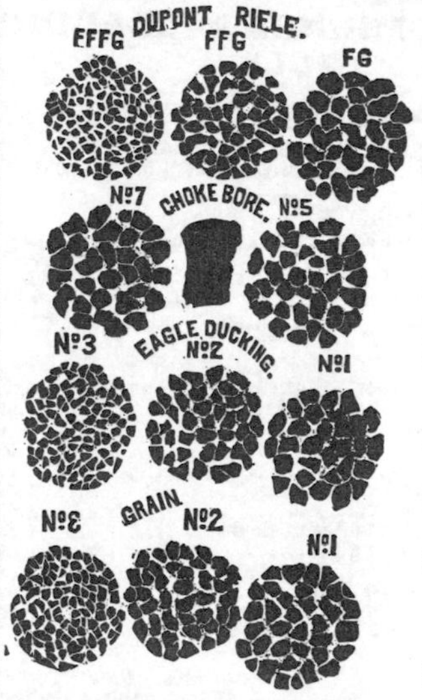
DUPONT RIFLE.
FFFG
FFG
FG
Nº7
CHOKE BORE.
Nº5
Nº3
EAGLE DUCKING.
Nº2
Nº1
Nº3
GRAIN
Nº2
Nº1

Showing size of grains of different powders. Hazard Powder same price as Dupont.

The Messrs. Dupont & Co., are the oldest powder makers and have the most extensive works in the country. We consider their powder the best. Every pound warranted good and clean. In air tight metallic kegs; Fg. coarse; FFg, medium; FFFg, fine.

No. 8446. Kegs, Fg, FFg, FFFg, 25 lbs. ....$4.00
No. 8447. ½ kegs, Fg, FFg, FFFg, 12½ lbs. ....$2.25
No. 8448. ¼ kegs, Fg, FFg, FFFg, 6¼ lbs. ....$1.25
No. 8449. 1 pound cans, Fg, FFg, FFFg, per can, ....$0.25

**Choke Bore.**

No. 8450. Kegs, Nos. 5 and 7, 25 lbs. ....$5.00
No. 8451. ½ kegs, Nos. 5 and 7, 12½ lbs. ....$2.75

| | | |
|---|---|---|
| No. 8452. | Kegs, Nos. 5 and 7, 6¼ lbs. | $1.50 |
| No. 8453. | 1 lb. cans, Nos. 5 and 7 | $0.40 |

**Note:** Some firms claim to ship powder by express. **We do not.** We wish to not only comply with the Inter-state laws, but also to insure our customers from any risk or inconvenience which would arise if an attempt to ship by express were found out. We ship all powder by freight. Include some with your order if going by freight.

### DUPONT EAGLE DUCK.

| | | |
|---|---|---|
| No. 8459. | Kegs, Nos. 1, 2, 25 lbs. | $8.00 |
| No. 8460. | ½ kegs, Nos. 1, 2, 12½ lbs. | 4.25 |
| No. 8461. | ¼ kegs, Nos. 1, 2, 3, 6¼ lbs. | 2.25 |
| No. 8462. | 1 lb. cans, Nos. 1, 2, 3 | .45 |

Powder cannot be shipped by express, but must be sent in separate kegs or cases and marked "gun powder," and sent by freight. Freight charges are double first-class rates on powder.

### DUPONT'S "V. G. P,"

No. 8463. The new Trap Powder—black, moist, quick, clean and strong (not a nitro); 12½ lb. kegs....$2.25
6¼ lb. kegs .... 1.25

**Prices quoted on any make of powder in the market.**

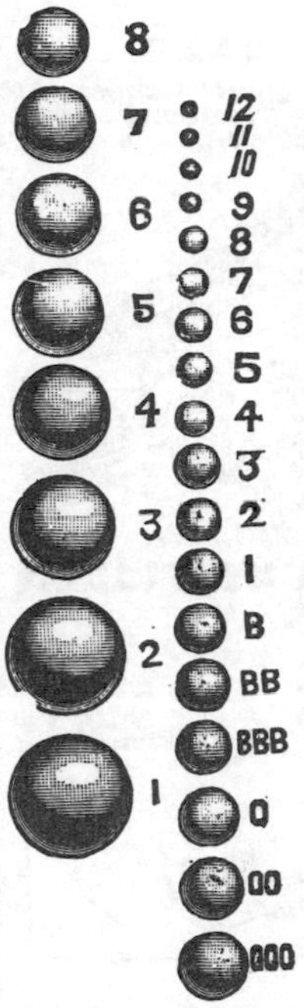
8
7
6
5
4
3
2
1
12
11
10
9
8
7
6
5
4
3
2
1
B
BB
BBB
O
OO
OOO

### SHOT AND BAR LEAD.

Subject to market changes without notice.

Chilled and dropped shot in sacks of 5 pounds and 25 pounds at lowest market rates. We do not sell less than a sack. The price of shot fluctuates so much that we cannot quote permanent price.

| | |
|---|---|
| No. 8464. Drop shot, all sizes, 1 to 12, per 25 lb. sack | $1.30 |
| No. 8465. Drop shot, all sizes, 1 to 12, per 5 lb. sack | .35 |
| No. 8466. Chilled shot, all sizes, 2 to 10, per 25 lb. sack | $1.60 |
| No. 8467. Chilled shot, all sizes, 2 to 10, per 5 lb. sack | .45 |
| Buck shot, B to No. 8, 25 lb. sack | $1.60 |
| Buck shot, B to No. 8, 5 lb. sack | .45 |

In case of fluctuation chilled shot is always 25 cents higher in 25 lb. sacks, and 10 cents higher in 5 lb. sacks than drop shot. We will always bill shot at the lowest market rates.

No. 8468. Bar lead for running bullets at market price; average price about 6¼ cents per pound.

**We always bill at lowest market prices.**

We guarantee lowest market price on cartridges, shells, primers, powder, shot, etc.

Prices subject to change without notice.

We cannot sell 5 lb. sacks at 25 lb. sack rates.

### GALLERY TARGETS.

**BIRD AND STAR TARGET.**

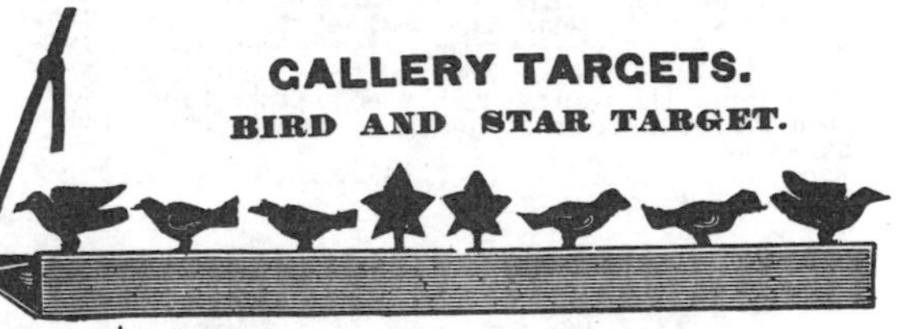

The birds and stars fall back out of sight when hit, and are reset by rope from shooting stand. It is one of the most satisfactory targets in the market, and is made to last. Heavy wrought iron face plate.

No. 8469. (ex) Target of 6 extra heavy birds and stars, weight, 14 to 18 lbs., each....$2.30

No. 8470. (o) Target of 8 extra heavy birds and stars, weight, 18 to 22 lbs., each....$2.75

### EMPIRE TRAP AND TARGETS.

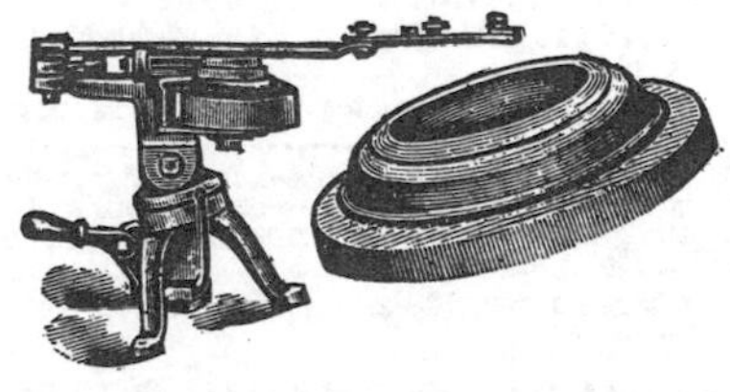

No. 8471. The New Empire Composition Target can be thrown for any trap except the "Old Peoria."

| | |
|---|---|
| Per barrel of 500 targets | $2.50 |
| Per 1,000 targets | 5.00 |

Weight, per barrel, about 135 pounds.

No. 8472. The Empire Amateur Trap can be changed instantly to throw any angle.

Each ....$4.50

Weight, 12 pounds.

**DID YOU EVER GET SHOT AT SUCH PRICES AS WE NAME? CAN YOU BUY ANYTHING FOR THE PRICES WE SELL AT?**

**THREE TIMES IN TWO YEARS HAVE OUR CUSTOMERS COMPELLED US TO MOVE, EACH TIME INTO A BUILDING WITH TWICE THE ROOM AS THE PRECEDING ONE. WE GET INCREASED BUSINESS BY PLEASING OUR TRADE.**

## BLUE ROCK EXTENSION TRAP.

No. 8479. Blue Rock Extension Trap. Each........$4.50 Empire Targets work just as well in Blue Rock Traps as other targets. We furnish Score Cards free.

## BLUE ROCK TRAP.

No. 8480. The new Blue Rock "Expert" traps, ea..$6.00
No. 8481. Paul North's Electric Trap Pulls, complete with wire and battery. Weight 35 lbs.

For one trap..........$10.00
For three traps........ 25.00
For five traps.......... 30.00

Shooting clubs are being formed all over the country, even among the farmers. They find it pays in the increased amount of "work" the boys and "hired" men perform.

## RUDOLPH'S GROUND PIGEON TRAP.

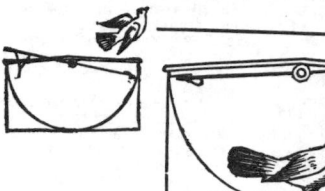

8482.

No. 8482. Rudolph's Ground Pigeon Trap, for live pigeon match shooting. The most satisfactory trap for the purpose, and used by many of the State associations for eight years. Made of heavy galvanized sheet iron. This trap has filled a long-felt want for a good trap at a reasonable price. Every club should have a set.
Each ...............................................$2.15
Weight 6½ lbs. each.

## ROUND IRON TARGETS.

Bell rings when bull's eye is hit, and self-setting round iron, no figure.
No. 8473. (C) 12 inches diameter, for Flobert ball caps; weight, 12½ lbs.....................$1.00
No. 8474. (A) 12 inches diameter, heavy, for 22 cartridges....$1.45

## ROUND IRON FIGURE TARGETS.

Figure springs up and rings bell when bull's eye is hit; reset with rope from shooting stand.
No. 8475. (B) 12 inch diameter, for Flobert ball caps; weight, 15 lbs.....................$1.95
No. 8476. (R) 12 inch diameter, heavy, for 22 cartridges; weight, 15 to 18 lbs..................$2.20
No. 8477. 12 inch diameter, steel faced, ¼ inch thick. Bird is thrown up and bell rings when bull's eye is hit. For air guns or cartridges not larger than 22 long; weight, 12½ pounds, each.......................$2.90
Paper targets for rifle and pistol practice furnished. Write for prices.

## WINCHESTER MAKE RELOADING TOOLS, INCLUDING BULLET MOLDS, COMPLETE SET.

8483

A set of implements comprises the reloading tool, a bullet mold and charge cup. The re-

loading tool removes the exploded primer and fastens ball in the shell, at the same time swaging the entire cartridge to the exact form and with absolute safety. Wood handles on bullet molds. Blued finished and polished. Perfect in every respect.
No. 8483. Extra by mail 42 and 45 cts. Per set.

| | | | | | | Per set. |
|---|---|---|---|---|---|---|
| 22 caliber, center fire, Winchester | | | | | | $1.70 |
| 25-20 | " | " | " | " | | 1.71 |
| 32 | " | " | " | " | model '73 | 1.76 |
| 38 | " | " | " | " | " | 1.77 |
| 44 | " | " | " | " | " | 1.78 |
| 32 | " | " | " | " | S. & W. | 1.68 |
| 38 | " | " | " | " | | 1.69 |
| 38-90 Winchester Express | | | | | | 2.75 |
| 44 caliber, center fire, Webley cartridge | | | | | | 1.80 |
| 40-90 caliber, Sharp's patched straight | | | | | | 2.80 |
| 40-70 Ballard patch ball | | | | | | 2.81 |
| 40-110 caliber, Winchester Express | | | | | | 2.40 |
| 40-60 caliber | | | | | | 2.15 |
| 44 S. & W., Russian | | | | | | 1.80 |
| 44 S. & W., American | | | | | | 1.80 |
| 45-75 caliber, Winchester | | | | | | 2.26 |
| 50-95 | " | " | Express | | | 2.70 |
| 50-70 | " | U. S. Government | | | | 2.50 |
| 45-60 | " | " | Winchester | | | 2.22 |
| 50-110 Express | | | | | | 2.40 |

No. 8484. Reloaders, only 22 to 44 caliber...... 1.45
No. 8484½. Reloaders, only from 40-90 to 45-60 caliber, each............................................. 1.85
No. 8485. Bullet Molds, any caliber, each.......... .85
No. 8486. Brass charge cups......................... .10
Mention caliber when ordering tools.

## NEW MODEL WINCHESTER TOOL, INCLUDING BULLET MOLD, AND COMPLETE SET. RELOADS AND RESIZES THE SHELL.

Winchester New Model Tool, including bullet mold with wood handles. A complete set. Reloads and resizes the shell. Weight 3¼ lbs. Polished blued finish. Perfect in every respect.
Order by number.

No. 8488.

| | | | Per set. |
|---|---|---|---|
| 32-40 caliber, Winchester | | | $2.10 |
| 38-55 | " | " | 2.10 |
| 38-56 | " | " | 2.10 |
| 38-70 | " | " | 2.10 |
| 40-60 | " | " | 2.10 |
| 45-60 | " | " | 2.10 |
| 40-65 | " | " | 2.10 |
| 45-75 | " | " | 2.18 |
| 40-70 | " | " | 2.16 |
| 40-82 | " | " | 2.16 |
| 45-70 | " | Government 405 | 2.18 |
| 45-70 | " | Government 500 | 2.17 |
| 45-90 | " | Winchester | 2.10 |
| 50-110 Winchester Express | | | 2.22 |
| 45-70-330 Hollow Ball (Gould bullet) | | | 2.50 |
| 50-70 Government | | | 2.50 |
| 45-70-350 Solid Bullet | | | 2.52 |
| 50-100-450 Winchester | | | 2.50 |

## IDEAL COMBINED RELOADING TOOLS.

### IDEAL RELOADING TOOLS.

These tools will reload shells using patched balls, but to run smooth balls you require an extra bullet mold.

A set of reloading tools includes bullet mold, recapper, decapper, ball seater, all in one tool. Powder measure with each set.

8489.

No. 8489. Any caliber. State caliber wanted. Per set.

| | | | Per set. |
|---|---|---|---|
| 22 caliber, center fire, U. M. C | | | $1.59 |
| 32 | " | short | 1.59 |
| 32 | " | long | 1.59 |
| 32 | " | S. & W. | 1.59 |
| 32 | " | extra long | 1.59 |
| 38 | " | short | 1.59 |
| 38 | " | long, outside lubricator | 1.59 |
| 38 | " | extra long | 1.59 |
| 38 | " | S. & W. | 1.59 |
| 41 | " | Colt's D. A. pistol | 1.59 |
| 41 | " | long, Colt's D. A. pistol | 1.59 |

Postage on above tools about 30 cents extra.

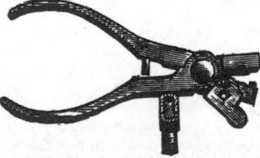

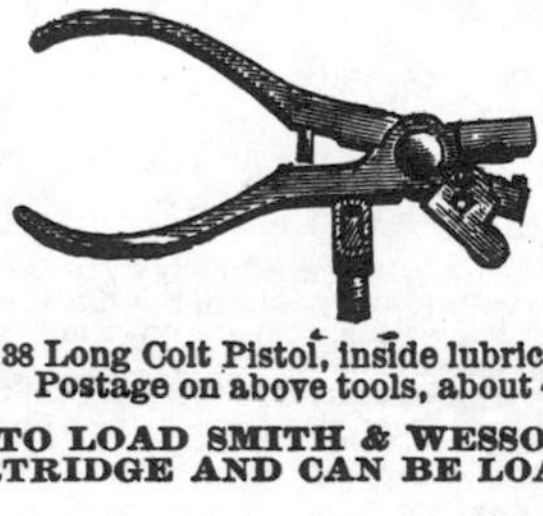

No. 8490. Ideal Tools. State caliber when ordering.
32-44 S. & W. grooved Ball. Per set....$3.50
32-44 S. & W. gallery, round ball. Set..$3.50
38-44 S. & W. target grooved.............$3.50
38-44 S. & W. gallery round .............$3.50
38 Long Colt Pistol, inside lubricator, per set........ 8.00
Postage on above tools, about 40c extra.

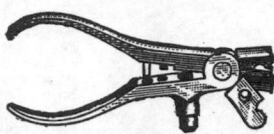

No. 8491. Ideal Tools. 25-20 caliber, Winchester.
Per set. .......$1.70
32 caliber, Colt's Lightning Rifle.
Per set......$1.71

| | | | |
|---|---|---|---|
| 32 caliber, Winchester Rifle, Model '92 and '73..$1.72 | | | |
| 32-20 | " | Marlin | 1.73 |
| 32-30 | " | Remington | 1.75 |
| 38-40 | " | Winchester Model '73 and '92 | 1.74 |
| 38-40 | " | Colt's Rifle | 1.75 |
| 38-40 | " | Marlin Rifle | 1.76 |
| 44-40 | " | Colt's Rifle | 1.77 |
| 44-40 | " | Winchester Model '73 and '92 | 1.78 |
| 44-40 | " | Marlin | 1.79 |
| 44 | " | S. & W. Russian Model | 1.80 |
| 44 | " | S. & W. American Model | 1.80 |
| 45 | " | Colt's Pistol | 1.70 |

Postage on above tools about 30c extra.

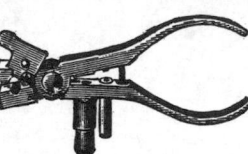

No. 8492. Ideal Reloading Tools. State caliber wanted.
25-36 caliber, Marlin,.......................$2.13
25-35 Winchester. 2.12
30-30 caliber, Marlin, or Winchester...$2.15
32-40 Ballard and Marlin. Per set..$2.10

| | | | |
|---|---|---|---|
| 32-40 caliber, Remington | | " | 2.11 |
| 38-40 caliber, Remington | | " | 2.12 |
| 38-50 caliber, Remington | | " | 2.13 |
| 38-55 Marlin | | " | 2.14 |
| 38-56 Winchester & Colt | | " | 2.15 |
| 40-60 Winchester | | " | 2.16 |
| 40-60 Colt & Marlin | | " | 2.17 |
| 40-65 Winchester | | " | 2.18 |
| 40-70 Sharp's straight groove | | " | 2.70 |
| 40-82 Winchester | | " | 2.19 |
| 44 Evans' new model | | " | 2.30 |
| 45-60 Winchester | | " | 2.20 |
| 45-70 405 Government | | " | 2.12 |
| 45-70 500 Government | | " | 2.24 |
| 45-70 Marlin | | " | 2.14 |
| 45-85 285 | | " | 2.25 |
| 45-90 Winchester | | " | 2.22 |
| 50-70 Government | | " | 2.24 |
| 40-90 Sharp's straight 3¼ inch shell | | " | 3.00 |

Postage on above tools about 45c extra.
Can furnish any other caliber in the Ideal Tools that are made, including those for Winchester rifles, etc.

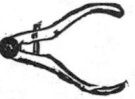

No. 8493. Shell Reducer and Resizer for any size from 32-40 and larger.
Each.............$1.75
Order size wanted.
Every good rifle shooter needs these tools. 
Postage extra, 15c.

No. 8494. Ideal Bullet Sizer for making bullets to exact size, and one standard die.
Each.........................$1.50
Extra dies.................. .50
You require a die for each style of bullet. Postage extra, 18c.

No. 8495. Ideal Re- and De-capper for pistol cartridges. One tool will only re- and de-cap the one size shell. Each,$1.00 Postage extra 8c.
No. 8496. Ideal Loading Flask No. 1 for rifle. 38 to 50 caliber, $2.25.

No. 2 for Rifles and Pistols, 38 to 22 caliber........$2.20
Extra shell receiver from 22 to shot gun size...... .50
Postage extra, 20c.

## BULLET MOLDS ONLY.

Be sure and give size wanted.
For all sporting and military sizes of cartridges.
Extra by mail........16c

No. 8497. To make Grooved Balls.............each, $0.85
No. 8498. " Express Balls............. " 1.25
No. 8499. " Round Balls............. " 1.15
No. 8500. " Smooth Balls for cartridges made only with patched bullet,..................$1.00

No. 8501. Bullet Molds for making round bullets, from 12 to 120 bullets to the pound. One mold will only make one size of bullet. Extra by mail, 2c to 6c. Each......25c
No. 8502. Patch Paper for cartridges, using patched ball.
Per quire................................................55c
Per sheet................................................7c

DON'T ORDER A SHORT OR A "LONG" TOOL TO LOAD SMITH & WESSON CARTRIDGES, FOR THEY WILL NOT DO THE WORK, AS THE S. & W. IS A SPECIAL CARTRIDGE AND CAN BE LOADED ONLY WITH TOOLS MARKED "S. & W."

Reloading Tools.—Continued.

No. 8503. Ideal Dipper for running bullets. Each............40c Postage extra, 10c.

## IDEAL MELTING POT.

No. 8504. Ideal Melting Pot for melting lead, 38c Postage extra, 15c. No. 8505. Adjustable Cover to fit any stove for Ideal Melting Pot, 38c Extra for postage, 24c.

Melting Pot, Cut ⅓ size.

Cover.

## MELTING LADLES.

Weight 1 to 3 lbs.

No. 8506. Melting ladles, for melting lead, etc. Each.
3-inch diameter bowl....................$0.22
4-inch diameter bowl.................... 25
5-inch diameter bowl.................... 40
6-inch diameter bowl.................... 45

## LOADERS, 10 AND 12 GAUGE.

Extra by mail, 4c.

No. 8507. Cocobolo Loader, complete, 10 & 12 guage. Each................12c
No. 8508. Common Loader, complete. Each......8c
No. 8509. Loader without tube, 10 and 12 gauge, each, 6c

All with extracting pin. Be sure and give gauge wanted.

No. 8510. Barclay Loader with inside spring wad starter, 10 and 12 gauge, each, 40c; 8 gauge, 75c.
No. 8511. Nitro Powder Loader, cocobolo rammer and base, nickel tube, spring equal to 10 lb. pressure in rammer, 10 or 12 gauge only. Each.......... .35c

## RELOADING TOOLS.

For 14, 16 and 20 gauge only. These are the only styles and prices we have in these gauges. In ordering state size wanted.
No. 8512. Cocobolo Loader with nickel tube and extracting pin, 14, 16 or 20 gauge only, 18c. extra; by mail 3c.
No. 8513. Recapper, bronzed iron, for 14, 16 or 20 gauge only, 15c; extra by mail 3c.
No. 8514. Shell Crimper, best quality, for 14, 16 or 20 gauge only, 70c; extra by mail 10c.
No. 8515. Ring Shell Extractor, for 14, 16 or 20 gauge only, 10c; extra by mail 1c. (State gauge wanted.)

## 8 GAUGE RELOADING TOOLS.

These tools are of the very best quality and are the only style made for this gauge.
No. 8516. Cocobolo Loader with tube and extracting pin, weight 4 ounces, 8 gauge only................ .50
No. 8517. Shell Crimper, best quality, 8 gauge only, weight 24 ounces.......................$1.50
No. 8518. Recapper, red japanned, polished joints, 8 gauge only, weight 5 ounces....................$0.84
No. 371. Ring Shell Extractor, 8 gauge only........ 0.20

## RE-CAPPER AND DE-CAPPER.

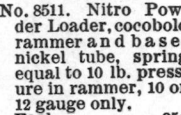

## SHELL EXTRACTOR AND RAMMER.

No. 8519. The Ideal shell Loader, including funnel and base, bronze finish, compact and handy to carry in the pocket, re- and de-caps and seat wads, weight 4 ounces.
Each, 16 gauge........................42c
" 12 " .......................40c
" 10 " .......................40c

---

8520. The Ideal Hand Shell Closer for paper shells; handy to carry in pocket; always ready for use; weight 5 ounces.
Each, 16 gauge.....................28c
" 12 " .....................29c
" 10 " .....................30c

"IDEAL" HAND CLOSER.

No. 8521. Ideal Powder and Shot Measure combined. Nickel plated cap, wood handle. Each, 9c; postage, extra, 2c.

## 10 AND 12 GAUGE RELOADING TOOLS.

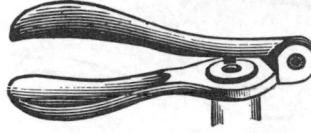

No. 8522. Red Japanned Recapper, neat and handy, 12 gauge, weight 2 oz., each 8c; 16 or 20 gauge 12c.

No. 8523. Recapper, with flat automatic spring handle, 10 and 12 gauge, weight 3 oz., each..................10c

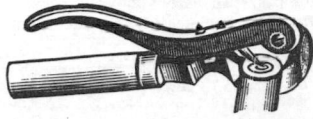

No. 8524. Remington De- and Re-capper, 10 and 12 gauge, each 50c. Be sure and give gauge wanted when ordering de- and re-cappers or implement sets. Postage 11c extra.

**If You Haven't Got Mann's De-and Re-capper, Don't Find Fault if Your Gun Missfires.**

No. 8525. Mann's De- and Re-capper is first-class in every respect, nickel plated shell post, cocobolo handle. A simple, convenient and effective implement, de-capping and re-capping the cartridge shell without removing from the shell post or reversing the lever, doing its work easily, rapidly and perfectly. Missfires will be avoided by its use. Weight 8 oz. 12 gauge 90c; 10 gauge 95c.

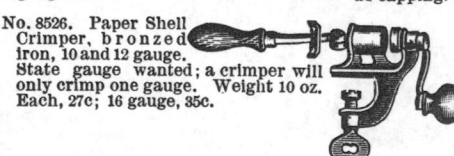
When de-capping.

No. 8526. Paper Shell Crimper, bronzed iron, 10 and 12 gauge. State gauge wanted; a crimper will only crimp one gauge. Weight 10 oz. Each, 27c; 16 gauge, 35c.

No. 8527. Paper Shell Crimper, bronzed and brass, with expelling pin, 10 and 12. State gauge wanted. Weight, 12 ounces. Price each, 10 or 12 gauge 35c; 16 or 20 gauge, 45c.

No. 8528. The B. G. I. Paper Shell Closer, red japanned, brass and ebony trimmings, expelling pin; a good, strong closer. Gauge 10 or 12, each, 54c.; gauge, 16 or 20, each, 64c; weight 13 ounces.

No. 8529. The New Improved Spangler Square Crimper. New straight feed lever, with steel grip. The only tool that will crimp every shell alike, no matter what the variations of load may be. The only tool having an automatic plunger, that prevents the end of the shell from spreading over the wad. All wearing parts are of steel. The best crimper ever made; 10 or 12 and 16 gauge only. Weight 30 oz. Each..................$1.60

Showing style of crimp.

---

No. 8530. The New No. 3 B. G. I. Crimper, with reversible crimp, making either the oval or the square crimp with the same tool; a good, strong, and durable article, 10 or 12 gauge, $1.28. Postage extra, 32c. Order by gauge or shell you wish to crimp. A 10 gauge will not crimp a 12 gauge.

No. 8531. Cleaning Rods, hardwood, patent brass joints, and three implements, swab, scratch brush and wiper, 10, 12, 16 gauge. Weight, 7 oz.; per set, 25c.
No. 8532. Cleaning Rod, 3 joints, lancewood, nickel trimmings, four implements, swab, scratch brush, wormer and wiper; 10, 12 and 16 gauge. Weight, 7 oz.; each.......................50c
No. 8533. Cleaning Rod, three joints, ebony wood, nickel trimmings, four implements, swab, scratch brush, wormer and wiper; a fine rod; 10, 12 and 16 gauge. Weight, 7 oz.; each.......................70c
No. 8534. Snakewood Cleaning Rod, nickel trimmings and implements; 10 or 12 gauge....................90c

No. 8535. Brass Wire Brush for removing lead caking and rust spots; can be attached to any joint rod; 10, 12, 16 and 20 gauge. Order by gauge, as one brush will fit but one gauge. Each, 45c; postage extra, 2c.

8535.

No. 8536. Field Cleaner, large bristle brush, slotted wiper, string and oil bottle, weight, fine leather pouch, with clasp; 8, 10 and 12 gauge. Weight, 3 ounces. Each..........88c

8536.

No. 8537. Expansion Felt Swab, to fit jointed rod, 10 or 12 gauge; weight 2 oz.; each.......................35c

8537.

No. 8538. Three row Wire Brush to fit jointed rods; 10 and 12 gauge, each, 30c; weight, 3 oz. 16 and 20 gauge, each.......................45c

8538.

8539.          8540.          8541.

No. 8539. Wool Swab to fit jointed rods; 10 and 12 gauge. Weight, 2 oz. Each.......................8c
No. 8540. Flannel Wiper to fit jointed rods; 10 and 12 gauge. Weight, 1 oz. Each.......................6c
No. 8541. Wire Scratch Brush to fit jointed rods; 10 and 12 gauge. Weight, 1 oz. Each.......................6c

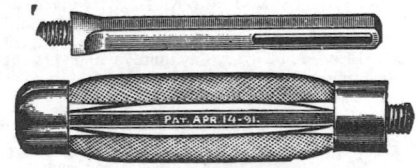
By mail 3c. extra.

8542.

No. 8542. Budd's Improved Petmecky Gun Cleaner; 10 or 12 gauge; screws on to all jointed rods; the best cleaner in the market.......................50c

8543.

No. 8543. The Tomlinson Gun Cleaner, for shot gun; wire gauze cleaner; fits any standard jointed cleaning rod. Each, 80c; postage extra, 4c.

## SHELL EXTRACTOR.

No. 8544. The Universal Shell Extractor will extract any shell from 8 to 22 caliber, 15c. By mail, 1c. extra.

8544.

---

**YOU OUGHT TO GET INTO THE HABIT OF SENDING IN A REGULAR ORDER OF GROCERIES, AND SHOULD YOU NEED ONLY A FEW OTHER SMALL ARTICLES, THEY CAN BE INCLUDED WITH NO INCREASED FREIGHT.**

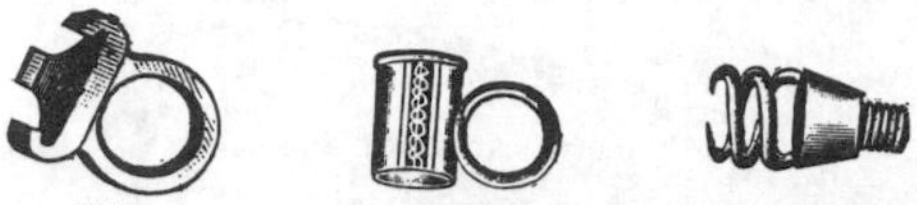

8546. 8547. 8545.

No. 8545. Wormers to fit jointed rods; 10 and 12 gauge. Weight, 1 oz. Each....6c

No. 8546. Ring Shell Extractor, polished: 10 and 12 gauge; nickel finish. Weight, 1 oz. Each....8c

No. 8547. Powder and Shot Measure combined, ring handle, polished nickel finish. Weight, 1 ounce. Each....15c

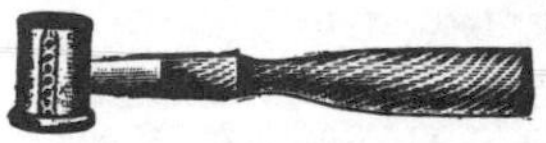

8548.

No. 8548. Powder and Shot Measure combined; cocobolo handle, polished nickel finish. Weight, 2 oz. Each....10c

No. 8549. B. G. I. Standard Nitro Powder Measures, 3¼ drams, 45 grains; or 3½ drams, 49 grains; will only measure one size charge. Each....20c

## RIFLE CLEANING RODS.

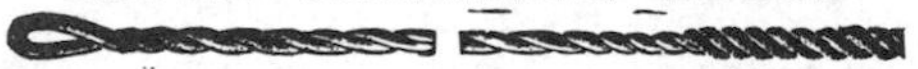

No. 8550. Twisted wire, bristle brush on end, 22 caliber. Weight, 2 oz....4c

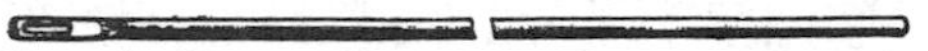

No. 8551. Plain brass wire, slotted for 22 caliber. Weight, 4 oz....12c

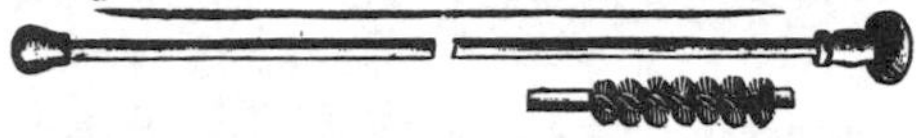

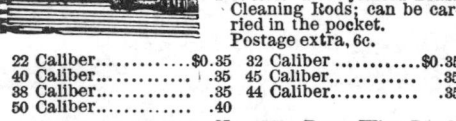

No. 8552. French Iron Wire Rod, with screw off and bristle and wire scratch brushes; 22 caliber....19c
32 caliber, weight 4 oz....18c

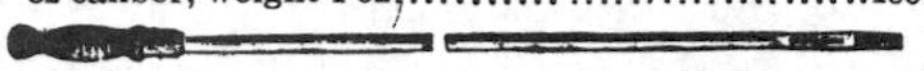

No. 8553. Cocobola handle, brass wire, jagged, slotted, and knob for 32 and 22 caliber. Weight, 4 ounces. Each....35c

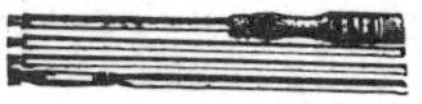

No. 8554. Four-jointed Brass Cleaning Rods; can be carried in the pocket. Postage extra, 6c.

| | | | |
|---|---|---|---|
| 22 Caliber | $0.35 | 32 Caliber | $0.35 |
| 40 Caliber | .35 | 45 Caliber | .35 |
| 38 Caliber | .35 | 44 Caliber | .35 |
| 50 Caliber | .40 | | |

No. 8555. Brass Wire Brush to fit 8554. Rods 12, 32, 38, 40, 44, 45 and 50 Calibers.
Postage extra, 2c. Each....$0.20

## GUN IMPLEMENT SET.

State gauge wanted.

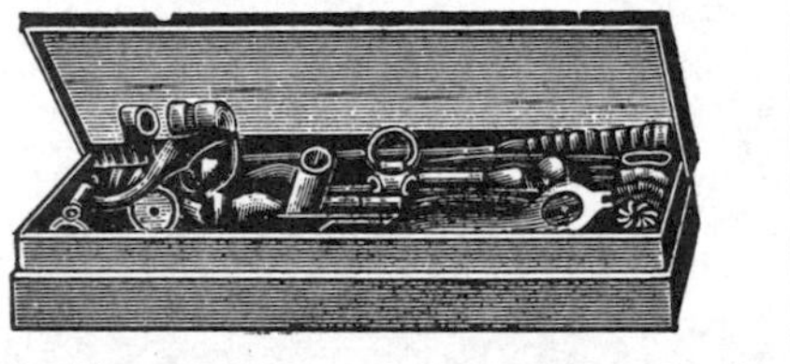

No. 8557. The complete gun implement set, embracing loader, paper shell crimper, re- and de-capper, shell extractor, powder and shot measure, and cleaning rod with implements. This set comes in a strong pasteboard box, neatly divided into compartments for each article, and each implement is made of *good material*, and recommends itself to every owner of a breech-loading shot gun. **The best ever offered for the money.** Size of box, 5x13 inches. Price per set, best quality, 10 or 12 guage, with 20 hole loading block; weight 3 lbs....$1.60

No. 8558. Price per set, medium quality, 10, 12, 16 and 20 gauge, without loading block....$0.95

No. 8559. Price, good every day quality, 10 or 12 gauge; weight 2 lbs....$0.70

(State gauge wanted.)

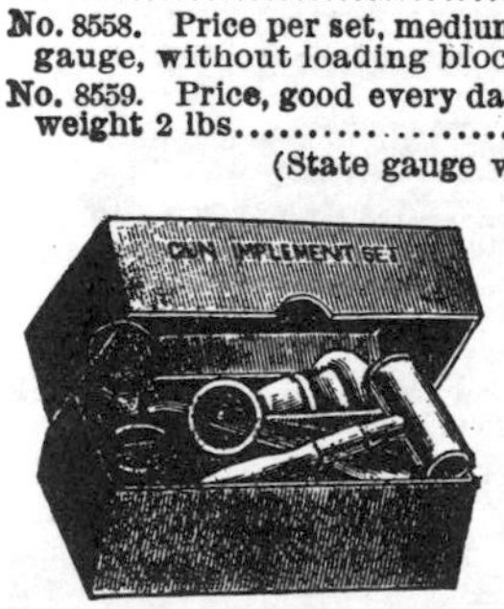


No. 8560.

No. 8560. Reloading set consisting of rammer and de-capper, with base block, nickel loading tube and re-capper, ring extractor, and patent paper shell crimper, graduated powder and shot measure, all inclosed in a strong paper box, making a neat and convenient set of tools. Per set, 16 or 20 gauge, weight 1 lb....$0.49

No. 8561. Per set, 10 or 12 gauge....45

No. 8562. Per set, for brass shells only, no crimper.
10 or 12 gauge only, weight 12 oz....$0.15
16 or 20 gauge, " "....20

## SHELL-LOADING BLOCK.

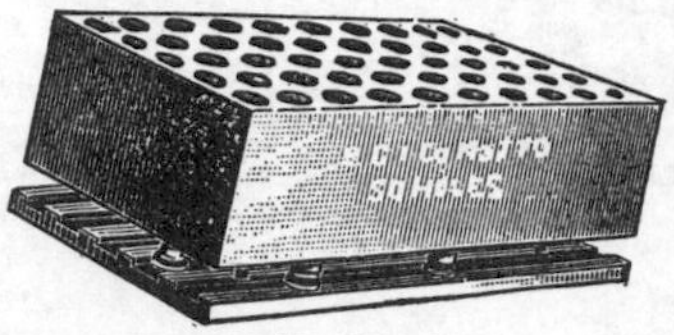

No. 8563.

New model, made of white wood, holes bored with shoulder to fit entire length of shell; top of hole reamed out in place of wad-starter; shell does not come within ¼ inch of top of block; shells cannot "bulge or break down." Just the thing to load shells for the Smith or Parker guns, or where wads larger than shell are required; weight 3 lbs.

No. 8563. Holding 50 12 gauge shells....$0.85
No. 8563. " 50 10 " " ....85
No. 8564. Metal-lined block, same as above. Weight, 6¾ lbs. Each....$5.55

## SHOT POUCHES.

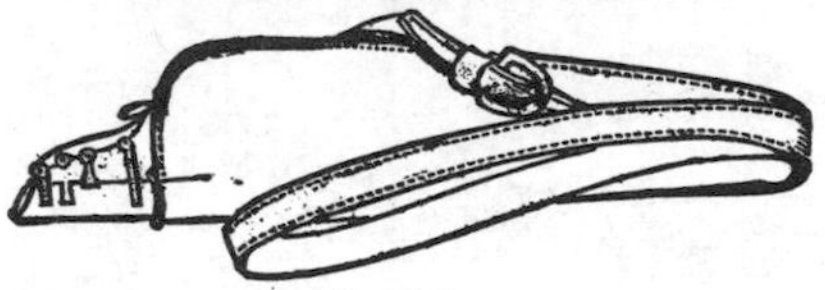

No. 8565.

By mail, 3 to 5c extra.

No. 8565. Single Belts, with Irish charger....$0.35
No. 8566. Single Belts, with lever charger.... .70
No. 8567. Double Belts, with patent charger.... 1.00

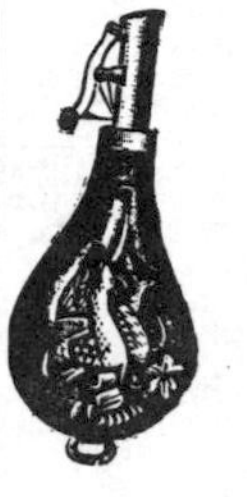

Pouch.

No. 8568. Pouches, 2½ lbs., with common Irish charger, not illustrated. Each....$0.30

No. 8569. Pouch 2½ lbs., with lever charger. Extra by mail, 3 to 5c. Each....$0.60

## POWDER FLASKS.

No. 8570. 8 oz., with cord, common top, 29c.

No. 8571. 12 oz., with cord, common top, 48c.

No. 8572. 16 oz., with cord, common top, 50c.

Postage, extra, 6c.

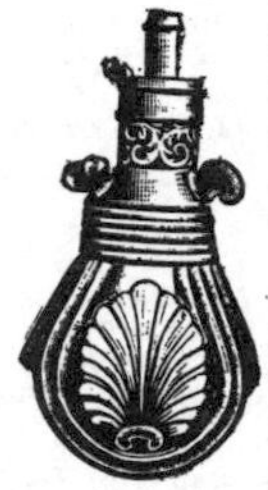

## SHELL BAGS.

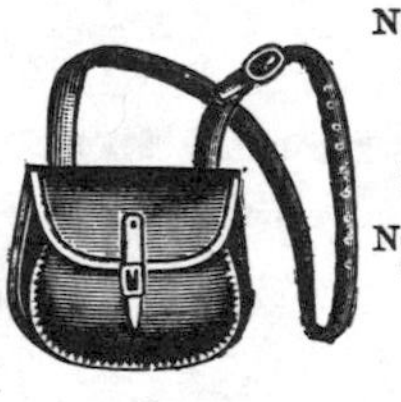

No. 8573. Brown Canvas Bags' leather bound, with pocket' weight 12 oz.
50 shells....$0.30
75 shells.... .35
100 shells.... .37
Weight 15 oz.

No. 8574. Leather bags, extra finished; weight 10 to 20 oz.
100 shells....$1.18
75 shells.... 1.06
50 shells.... .93

No. 8575. Heavy drab colored canvas shell bag, bound with red leather, 2 pockets, extra shoulder piece, handsome and durable. Each.
50 shells....$0.60
75 shells.... .70
100 shells.... .85
Weight 9 to 14 oz.

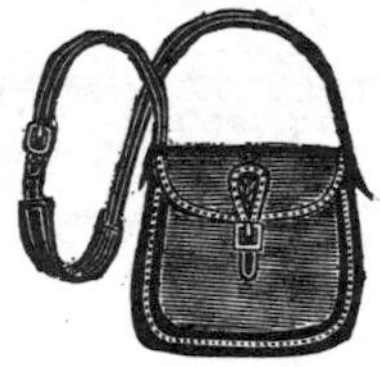

## BEDELLS' PATENT GAME SKIRT.

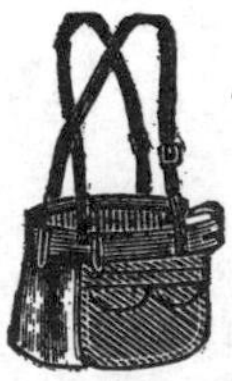

No. 8579. Bedells' patent game and cartridge holder, heavy russet leather belt with game hooks, double leather shoulder straps, heavy brown canvas skirt with pocket to carry 100 shells. The best game and cartridge holder for field shooting in the market. Each, $2.00. Postage, extra, 26 cents.

By mail, 15 to 20 cents extra.)

**THE ONLY DIFFERENCE BETWEEN A POOR SADDLE AND A**

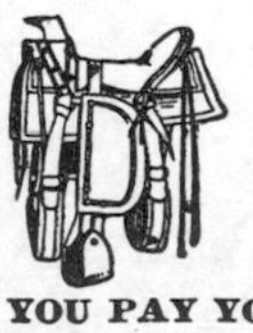

**GOOD SADDLE**

**IS THE NUMBER OF MILES YOU ARE FROM CHICAGO.**

**IN OTHER WORDS, WE SELL A GOOD SADDLE AT THE PRICE YOU PAY YOUR DEALER FOR A POOR ONE.**

——SEE PAGES 750 TO 757.——

## GUN COVERS AND CASES.

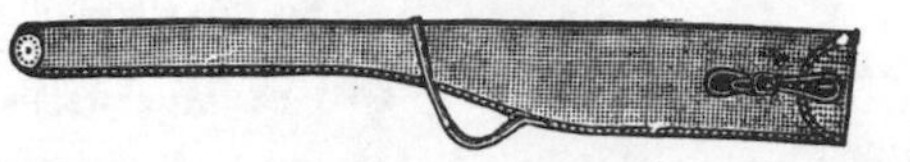

Gun Covers, Nos. 8580 to 8582.

No. 8580. Brown Canvas, leather bound, leather handle and muzzle protector, cotton flannel lining, 30 to 40 inch barrel. Each 50c. Per doz....$5.50

No. 8581. Brown canvas, same style as 434 but lighter material, for single barrel shot guns and small rifles 24 inch to 34 inch. Each....38c

No. 8582. Best Quality Brown Canvas, leather bound, with leather lock and muzzle protector and handle, cotton flannel lined. Each 70c. Per doz....$7.50

Rifle Covers—waterproof.

No. 8583. Rifle Cover, best brown canvas, leather bound, leather sling, cotton flannel lined, best quality, 24 to 32 inch barrel. Each....58c

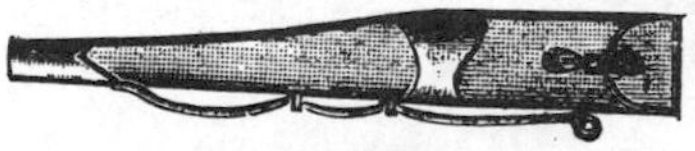

No. 8584. Rifle Cover, same as 8583, with heavy leather lock and muzzle protector. Each, 75c. Per doz..$8.40

No. 8585. Rifle Cover, with sling straps, all heavy bag leather, russet color, made same style as the canvas covers. Waterproof and a good one....$1.50
Extra, by mail, 24c.

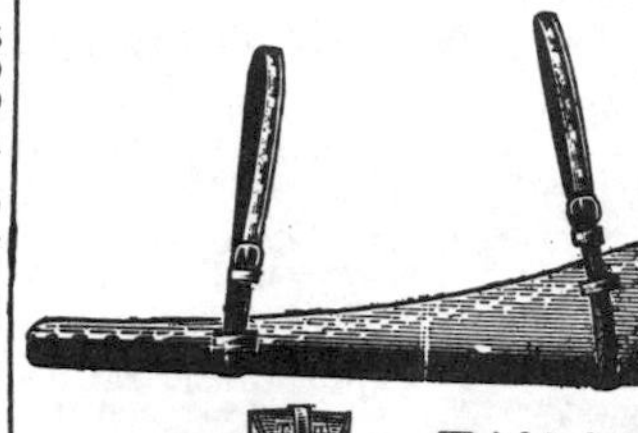

No. 8586. Rifle and Carbine Sheath or "Saddle Holster."....$1.15

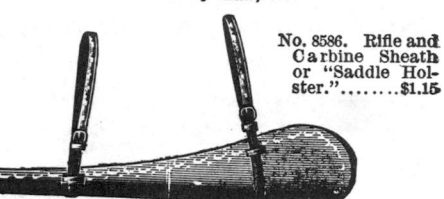

Weight for carbines, 13 oz.; model '73, 16 oz., mod. '76 and '86, 26 oz.

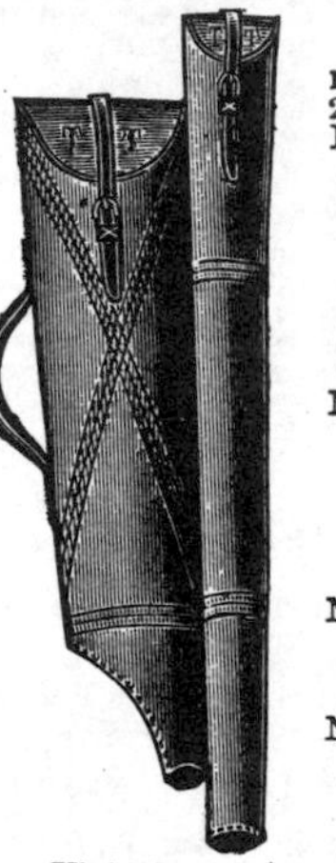

Victoria.

No. 8587. Rifle and Carbine Sheath, best russet leather, for Winchester carbines and models 1873, 1876 and 1886 rifles. These sheaths are not full length covers, but are for carrying rifle on saddle, leaving the stock of rifles exposed to be easily grasped. Each....$1.15

No. 8588. Victoria Gun Case, best brown canvas, leather bound, with leather handle, lock and muzzle protector, with heavy leather and with tool pocket on outside; weight 32 oz. Each $1.00. Per doz....$11.00

No. 8589. Victoria Gun Case, same as 8588, but without lock and muzzle protector; weight 25 oz. Each 65c. Per doz....$7.20

No. 8590. Victoria Gun Case, brown canvas, leather bound, with leather handle, cotton flannel lined, no tool pocket, a good cover; weight 20 oz. Each 44c. Per doz....$4.80

No. 8591. Victoria Gun Case, extra heavy russet leather, good, strong and durable, 30 and 32 inch barrels, with tool pocket outside....$2.40

No. 8592. Victoria Gun Case, heavy russet sole leather, cotton flannel lined, tool pocket outside, 30 and 32 inch barrels. Weight 36 oz. Each....$3.00

No. 8593. Victoria Gun Case, extra heavy leather, good, strong and durable, no outside pocket, 30 and 32 inch barrels. Each....$2.00

No. 8594. Victoria Gun Case, extra heavy russet colored sole leather, highly finished, with tool pocket, flannel lined, 30 and 32 inch barrels; weight 44 oz. Each....$3.25

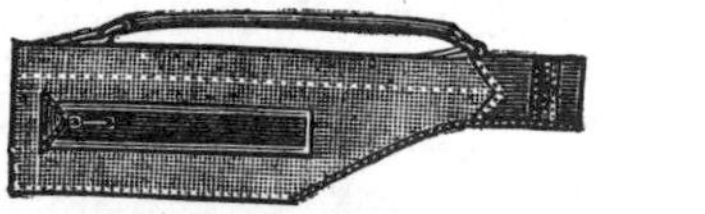

No. 8595. California style gun case. Heavy brown canvas, leather muzzle protector, tool pocket and sling strap. Well made, strong and durable. Each $0.75. Postage, extra, 25c.

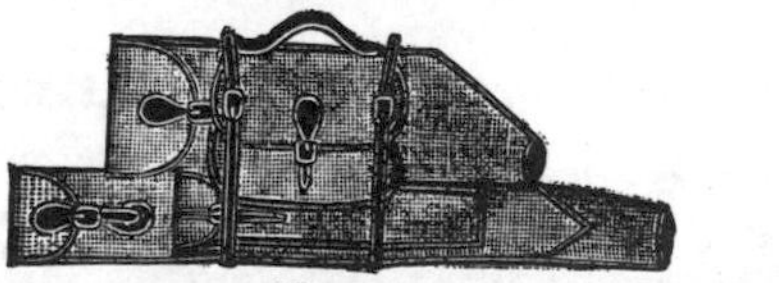

No. 8596.

No. 8596. Victoria Gun Case, heavy waterproof canvas reinforced on stock and barrel, with pocket for cleaning rod, also shell bag to hold 50 shells. The most complete cover offered to sportsmen and trap shooters. Each....$1.27
Postage, extra, 35c.

**REFER TO THE VOLUMINOUS INDEX IN THE BACK PART OF CATALOGUE FOR ANYTHING YOU DON'T SEE IN THE BOOK. ABOUT EVERYTHING YOU WANT IS QUOTED.**

## ENGLISH VICTORIA GUN CASE.

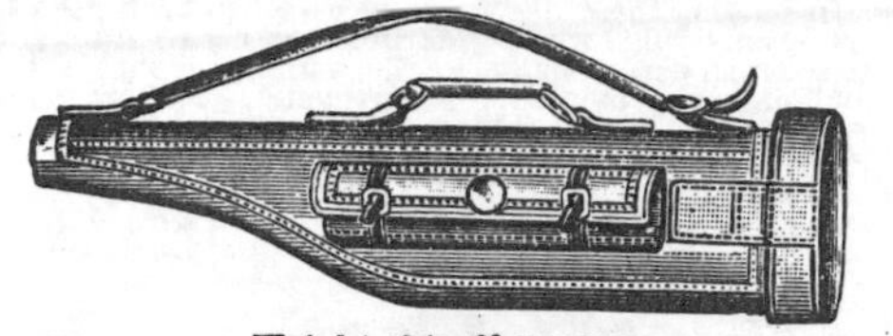

Weight 40 to 60 ounces.

**No. 8587.** English Victoria Gun Case, extra heavy **orange** leather, plain finish, nickel plated trimmings, patent fastening, staple for lock. A fine case, well made and very durable, 30 and 32 inch barrels. Each....................$3.75

## ENGLISH VICTORIA.

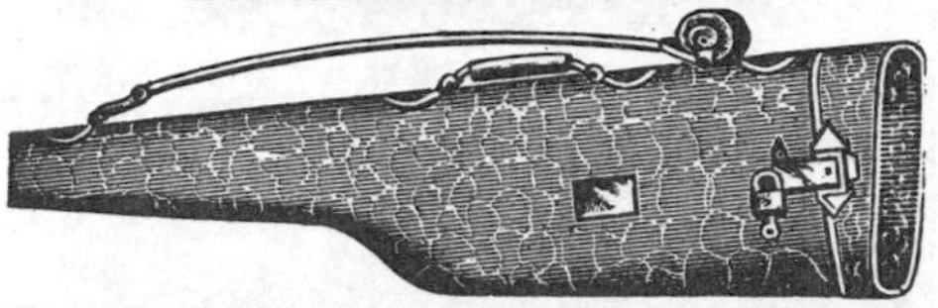

No. 8598. English Victoria, oak tanned russet colored leather, brass trimmings with lock buckle, a beauty, 28, 30 or 32 inch barrels. Flannel lined, each....................$3.75

**No. 8599.** Same as 8598 with tool pocket on outside. Each....................$4.75

## ENGLISH VICTORIA.

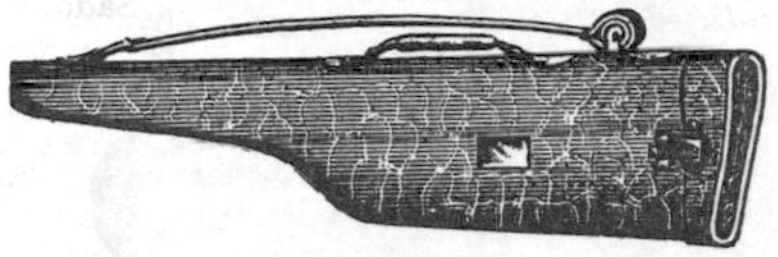

No. 8600.

**No. 8600.** English Victoria, imitation alligator, chestnut colored leather, heavy and strong, a fine case. Each....................$4.40

Any of above cases lined with lambskin with the wool left on for $1.50 extra, to order chamois lined $1.50 extra.

No. 8601. English Victoria Gun Case, made of the very best orange color finish sole leather, burnt ished brass trimmings, made up in the very best style; no tool pocket; elegant in design and finish. Each....................$5.50

No. 8602. Victoria Case, same as 8601, with tool pocket on the outside. Each....................$6.25

All leather Victoria Cases are the best and handsomest covers for guns. The leather being thick and heavy protects the guns from being injured or getting rusty. These cases are called sole leather and are almost as heavy as sole leather. (Mention length of gun barrels.

## LEATHER RIFLE CASE.

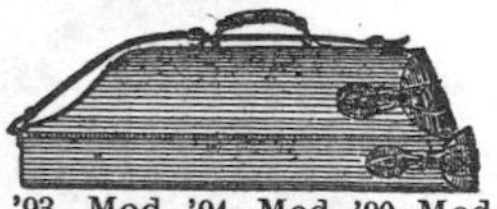

No. 8603. Heavy Russet Grained Leather Rifle Case, flannel lined, well made. This case is made for the Take Down Rifles only, namely, Mod. '92, Mod. '93, Mod. '94, Mod. '90, Mod '86. Each....................$2.25

## SHELL BOXES.

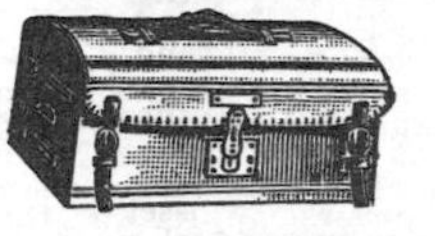

Weight, 5 lbs.

No. 8606. Sole Leather Shell Boxes, tin lined, with compartments, nickel plated trimmings. Dimensions, 12½ in. long, 6 in. wide, 7½ in. high; holding 200 shells. Each....................$3.00

No. 8607. Sole Leather Shell Boxes, same as 8606. Dimension: 13¾ inches long, 8½ inches wide, 8 inches high; holding 300 shells. Each....................$3.50

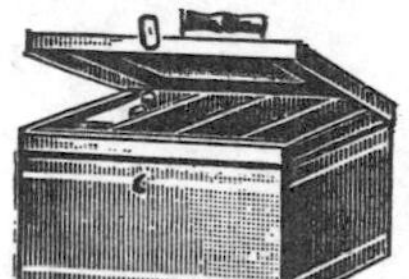

No. 8608. Metallic Shell Box; length 11 in., width 6½ in., depth 5 in., capacity 100 No. 12. Each....................$1.75 Weight 3 lbs.

No. 8609. Length 13 in., width 8½ in., depth 7½ in.; capacity, 400 No. 12. Each....................$2.75

The material of this box is very heavy, so it could be used for a seat or stool to sit upon without damage. All are nicely painted and ornamented; weight about 4 lbs.

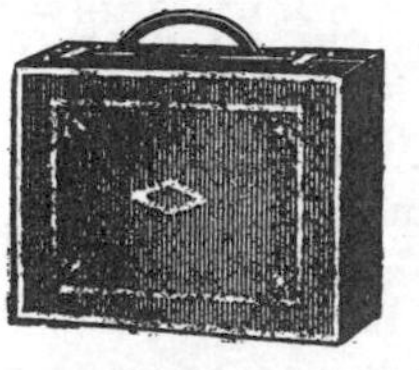

No. 8610. Trap Shooter's Leather Ammunition Cases; heavy russet sole leather, tin lined, partitioned for 25 shells in each space; tray for cleaning rod and three partitions for sundries; holds 150 shells. Each....................$4.96 Weight 5 lbs.

## PISTOL HOLSTERS.

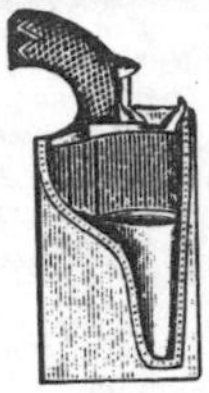

No. 8611. Russet Leather Pocket Holster (as adopted by police officers), heavy russet leather, for 3¼ inch barrel, 32 and 38 caliber. Made to wear in the hip pocket; sweat proof; each 30c. Per doz....................$3.25

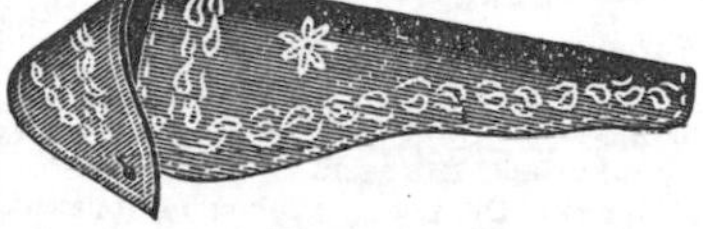

No. 8611½–8612.

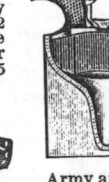

Army and Navy Holsters, by mail 5c. extra.

No. 8611½. Pistol Holster with loop similar to cut, heavy russet leather, 32 caliber. Each....................25c

No. 8612. Pistol Holster with loop similar to cut, russet leather, 38, 44 and 45 caliber. Each....................38c

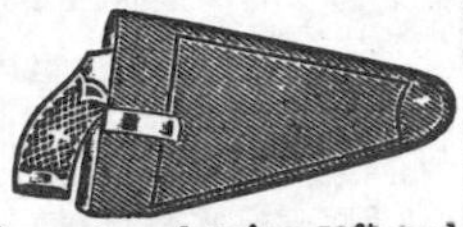

No. 8613. Rubber Pocket Holster with steel hook.
32 caliber ....................29c
38 " ....................35c
44 " ....................40c
Postage, 4 cents extra.

The rubber Holster is rust proof, and being soft and pliable, it is the best and most convenient holster ever made to carry a revolver in the pocket. Will hold revolvers with 3¼ inch barrel, or shorter.

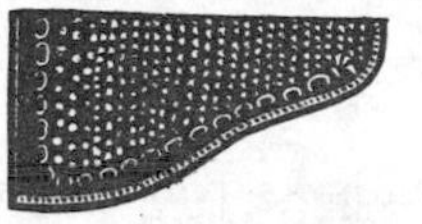

No. 8614. Pocket Pistol Holster, soft russet leather (no loop for belt) for pocket use only; 22, 32 and 38 calibers. Each, 15c. Per dozen..$1.65 Postage, 3 cents.

## PISTOL HOLSTERS.

(By mail, 5 cents extra.)

No. 8615. Pistol Holster with loop for belt; heavy russet leather, 22 and 32 caliber; each........20c

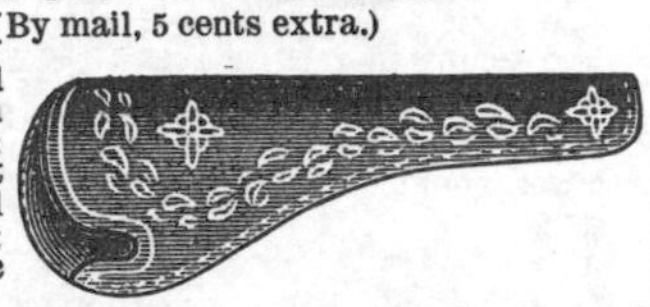

No. 8616. Pistol Holster with loop for belt; best russet leather, 38 caliber; each....................25c

No. 8617. Pistol Holster with loop for belt; best russet leather, 44 caliber; each....................35c

No. 8617½. Pistol Holster with loop for belt; best russet leather, 45 caliber; each....................40c

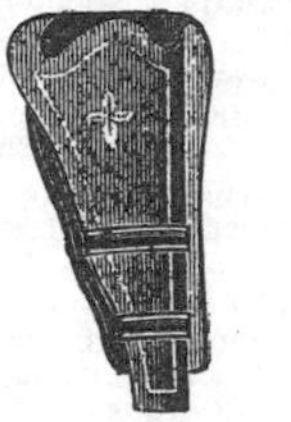

No. 8618. Mexican Holster, best russet leather, heavy and durable, 32 and 38 caliber; each....................45c
44 caliber; each....................50c
45 " " ....................55c
By mail, 6 cents extra.

## LEATHER BELTS.

**Our Leather Goods are the Best in the Market.**

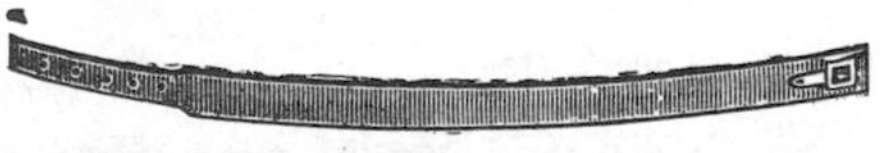

No. 8619. Belts only, russet leather, without loops for cartridges. By mail, 5 cents extra. Each..........15c

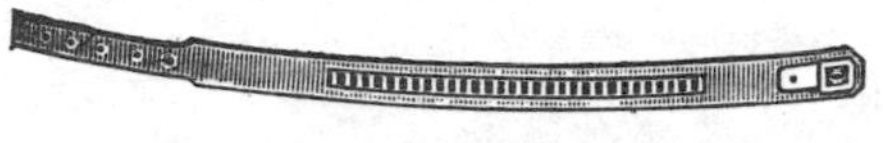

No. 8620. Belts only, russet leather, with loops for cartridges; 32 and 38 caliber, 1½ inches. Wide plain roller buckle. By mail, 5 cents extra. Each.......30c

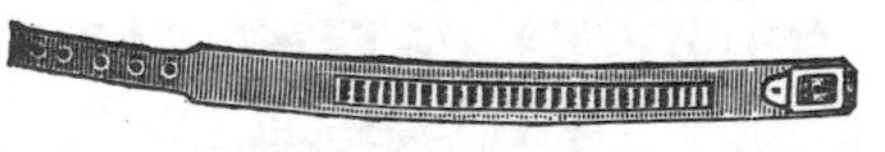

No. 8621. Belts only, fine russet leather, with loops for cartridges; 32, 38, 44 and 45 caliber, 2⅛ inches wide, large nickel plated buckle. By mail, 10 cents extra. Each....................45c

## RIFLE CARTRIDGE BELTS.

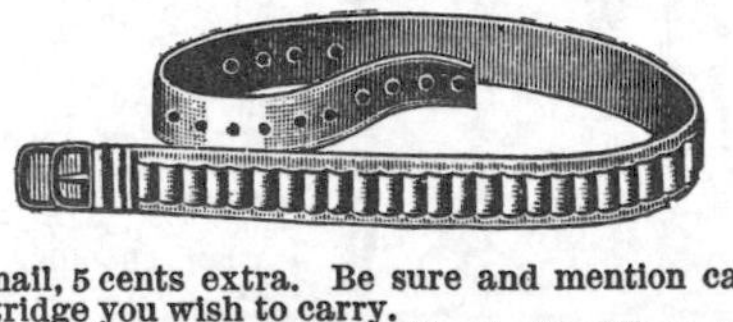

By mail, 5 cents extra. Be sure and mention caliber of cartridge you wish to carry.

No. 8622. Webb rifle belt, 32, 38, 44, 45 caliber, heavy and strong....................35c

No. 8623. Leather rifle belt, 32, 38, 44, 45 caliber, 2⅛ inches wide, best quality, heavy....................50c

## CARTRIDGE AND SHOT BELTS.

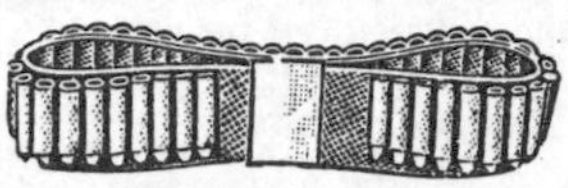

No. 8624. The woven cartridge belt, invented by Col. Anson Mills, U. S. A. The main body of the belt, as well as the loops which hold the cartridge, is woven in one solid piece. The belt is soft and pliable, particularly adapted to rifle cartridges. In ordering be sure to give caliber and name of cartridges you wish to carry. 32 to 50 caliber. By mail, 20 cents extra. Each....................$1.40

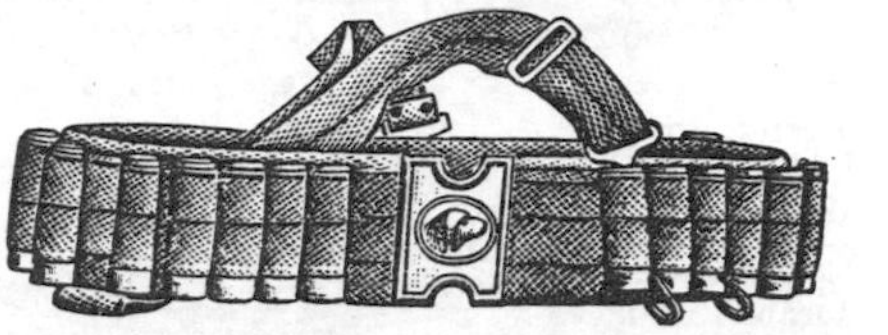

No. 8625. The Anson Mills woven shot shell belts, 10 gauge and 12 and 16 gauge, with shoulder strap and game hooks. By mail, 22 cents extra. Each.....$1.40

## SHELL BELTS.

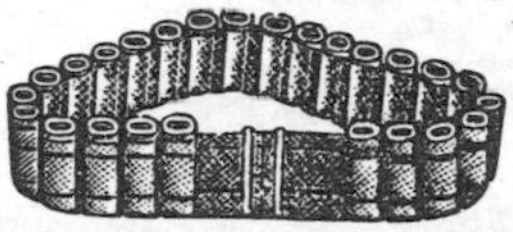

No. 8626. Anson Mills hunters' belt. The loops are woven, closed at the bottom, protecting the crimped end of shell; no sewing on the belt whatever; weight, 5 ounces: 10 or 12 gauge. Each....................$1.10

No. 8627. Light Webb shell belts; no shoulder straps or welt on bottom; weight, 4 ounces. Each..........18c

No. 8628. Canvas shell belts, 10, 12, 16 and 20 gauge, with shoulder strap; weight, 15 ounces. Each..........40c

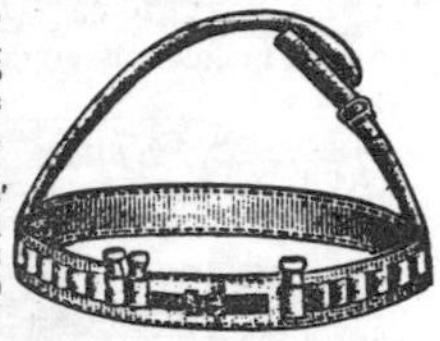

No. 8629. Russet leather shell belt, with shoulder strap, 10, 12, 16 and 20 gauge. Each 46c

No. 8630. Russet leather shell belt, with shoulder strap; 8 gauge only. Each .....$1.00
By mail, 16 cents extra.

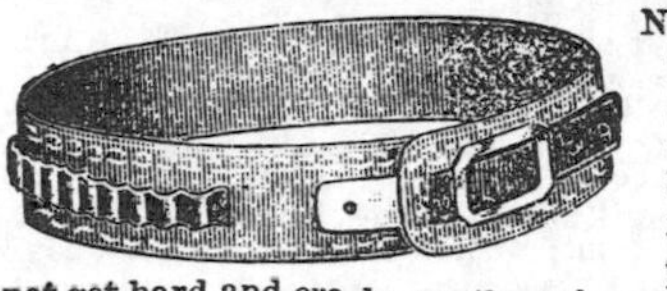

No. 8631. Mexican combined Cartridge and Money Belt, made of the very best russet leather; Belt 3 inches wide, soft and pliable and will not get hard and crack; neatly embossed; 32 and 38 caliber, 80c. 44 caliber, 90c. 45 caliber, 90c. By mail, 13 cents extra. Don't forget to state caliber wanted.

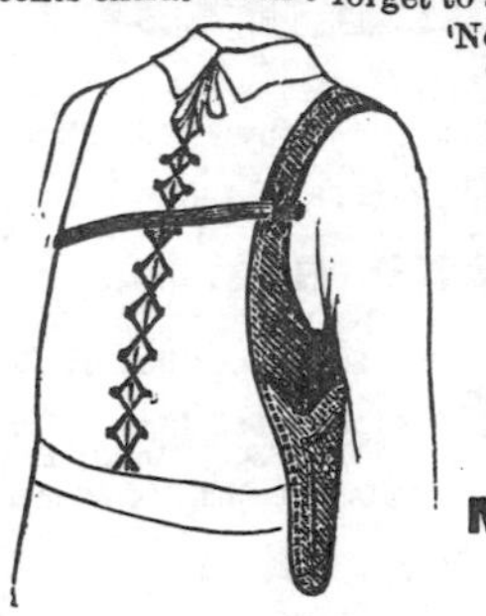

No. 8632. "The Pop" shoulder holster, with breast and shoulder strap to wear under coat, on the left side, as shown in cut. Made of fine soft russet leather, any caliber or length of barrel. Each, 60c **Always state caliber and length of barrel, if** you are in a hurry for your goods, and then it will not be necessary to write you for size.

## MONEY BELTS.

By mail, 3 cents extra.

No. 8633. Money belts, chamois skin, with three compartments; width, 3 inches; to be worn around waist under clothing. Each, 40c. Per dozen..........$5.00

No. 8634. Money belts, soft pliable leather, 3 compartments, sweat proof, never get hard or stiff, the best thing in the world. Each, 75c. Per dozen..........$7.70

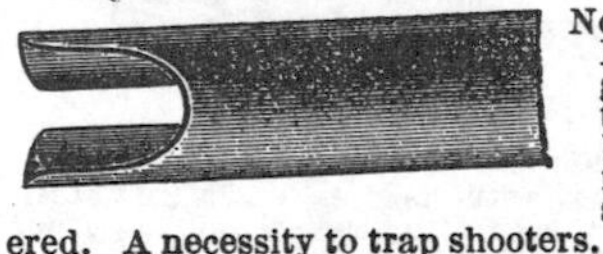

No. 8635. Heik's Hand Protector, for shot gun barrels; a protection from cold barrels or hot barrels, made of spring steel, leather covered. A necessity to trap shooters. Each..........69c.
By mail, 3 cents extra.

## RECOIL PADS.

By mail, 5 cents extra.

No. 8636. Rudolph's Popular Recoil Pad, leather, with lacing; will not become loose. Each.......60c. Postage extra, 10c.

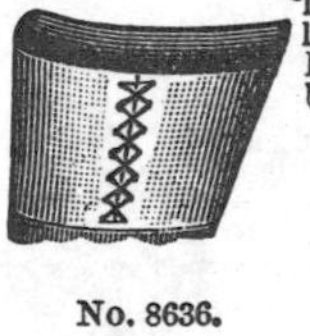

No. 8636.

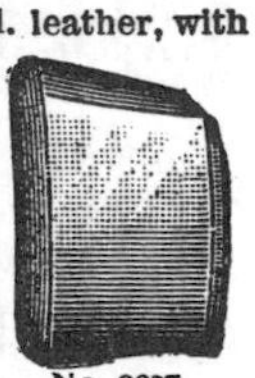

No. 8637.

No. 8637. The Rubber Recoil Pad, made entirely of rubber, well padded, and will fit any gun, its elasticity keeping it in position, and preventing the shock of the recoil doing injury to the shoulder. Price, each 35c. Per dozen..........$3.95

**We do as much for your pocketbook as would the man who would offer you 75 cents for your wheat, when the market price is only 50 cents.**

## Recoil Pads—Continued.

No. 8638. Pure Red Rubber Recoil Pad, the best pad in the market. Two sizes. Nos. 3 and 4. No. 3 smallest. Give length of heel plate on gun for which you want the pad. Each, 75c. Postage, extra, 7c.

No. 8639. The "Cow Boy" Holster, made of heavy red, oiled leather, raised embossed work; made to match in color and style our Cow Boy Saddles. The best holster on the market.
38 caliber................$1.40
44 "................1.50
45 "................1.60
Postage, extra, 11c.

No. 8640. the "Cow Boy" Combined Cartridge and Money Belt, made of heavy red, oiled leather, strong and durable, designed to match our Cow Boy Saddles. 38, 44 and 45 caliber. Each, $2.25. Postage, extra, 8c.

## HUNTING KNIVES.

All these knives are of the very best quality steel.

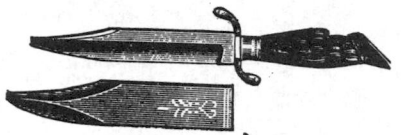

No. 8641. Deer Foot.

No. 8641. Hunting Knife, deer's foot handle, 7 inch clip blade, best steel, leather sheaths, with loops to attach to belt, nickel bolstered, (see cut)................$1.50

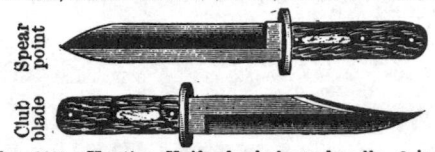

Spear point

Club blade

No. 8642. Hunting Knife, buck horn handle, 6 inch steel clip blade, leather sheath, with loop to attach to belt; entire length 11 inches; by mail, 8c extra....75c.
No. 8643. Hunting Knife, same description as No. 8642, 6 inches, spear point; by mail, 8c extra............95c.
No. 8644. Hunting Knife, same description as No. 8642, 6 inches, spear point; weight, 13 oz................$1.65

(By mail, 8c extra.)

No. 8645. Hunting Knives, scored ebony handle, bolstered with guard, best steel blade, 6 inch blades. Each, 50c. 6¼ inch blades, each, 60c. 7 inch blades, each................70c.

## SHEATHS AND BELTS.

(By mail, 8c. extra.)

No. 8646. Leather Knife Sheaths.
6 in.....10c. 7 in.....12c.
8 in.....15c. 9 in.....18c.
No. 8647. Leather Belts for knife sheaths, 1¼ inches wide, 15c.

## HUNTER'S AX.

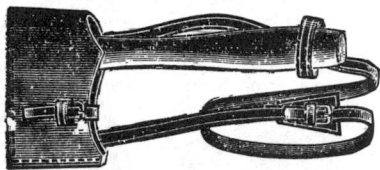

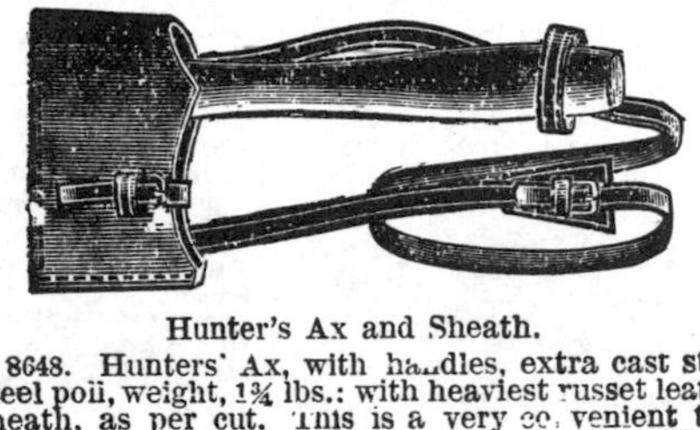

Hunter's Ax and Sheath.

No. 8648. Hunters' Ax, with handles, extra cast steel, steel poll, weight, 1¾ lbs.; with heaviest russet leather sheath, as per cut. This is a very convenient tool, It makes a light ax or a heavy hatchet. Price, each................$1.40

## POCKET OILERS.

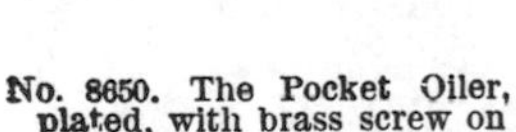

No. 8649. The C. & D. Perfection Gun Oiler, the best and handiest gun and revolver oiler in the market. Each........20c.

No. 8650. The Pocket Oiler, flat, nickel plated, with brass screw on top, entirely preventing the escape of oil; can be carried in the vest pocket; about the size of a watch. Each................10c.
Extra, by mail, 2c.

No. 8650.

REFER TO INDEX FOR GOODS YOU WANT.

## GUN OIL, Etc.

Winchester Gun Grease, put up by the Winchester Repeating Arms Company.

No. 8651. The Winchester Gun Grease is the best rust preventer manufactured. It has been in use in this factory for years. For any steel or polished iron surface, and for inside or outside of gun or rifle barrels, it has no equal. Put up in neat metallic tubes. Per tube, 11c. Per box of 10 tubes................$1.15
Postage, 12c. extra.
No. 8652. Paraffine Gun Oil, put up exclusively for guns, gun locks, and fine machinery and furniture; removes rust and will not gum. 2 oz. bottles. Price per dozen, 50c., 3 bottles for 15c. Postage 18c. per bottle.
No. 8653. Popular Lubricating Oil; best oil in the market for guns, locks, sewing machines, bicycles, and any small machines; will not freeze, gum, rust, or corrode or become rancid. Per bottle, 8c. Per dozen, 80c. Unmailable.
No. 8654. RUST REMOVER, coarse, for removing rust from iron, steel, brass or any metal where cutting properties are desired. Per bottle................20c.
No. 8655. Rust Remover, medium................18c.
No. 8656. Rust Remover, fine, 19c. Postage, 5c. extra.
No. 8657. WOOD POLISH. Nothing like it for bright, clean and lustrous polish on furniture, desks, gun stocks and all walnut, oiled or varnished furniture. Per bottle, 20c. Unmailable.

## BIRD CALLS.

By mail, 2 to 3 cents each.

No. 8658. Grubb's Improved Illinois River Duck Call. The most natural toned call made; easy to blow; not easy to get out of repair, having a fine tempered reed; makes it so you can call teal, wood-duck and bluebill, as well as mallard. This is the only call you can do this with. Each........50c
No. 8659. The Perfection duck call, made of red cedar, silver mounted, with silver reed which gives it a perfect tone. This is the finest duck call made, perfect, similar in style to the Grubb's call, and are warranted. Each........$1.00

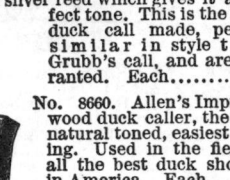

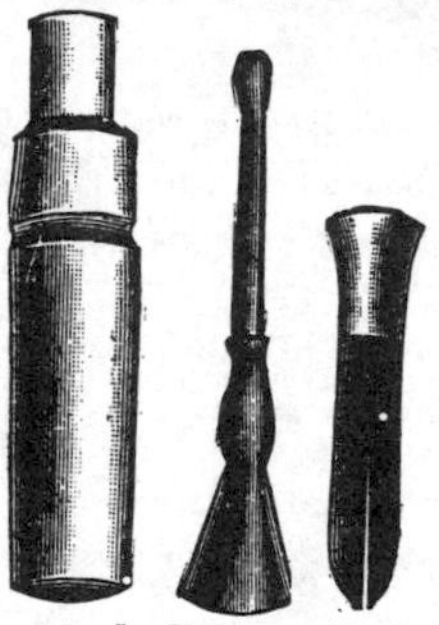

No. 8660. Allen's Improved wood duck caller, the most natural toned, easiest blowing. Used in the field by all the best duck shooters in America. Each....40c.
No. 8661. Duck calls, B. G. L. with rosewood mouthpiece, each................25c.
No. 8662. Turkey calls, horn, with rosewood mouthpiece, each................27c.
Extra, by mail, 3c.
No. 8663. Snipe calls, (no cut), each............18c.
Postage, extra, 2c.

Allen's Turkey Call.    Duck Call.

No. 8664. Fuller's Metallic wild goose caller, each............80c.
Extra, by mail, 5c.

No. 8664½. The Cartridge Whistle or Dog Call is one of the most popular calls now in use. This Whistle is the exact shape and about the size of a 45 caliber Colt's cartridge. With polished brass shell and silver plated bullet. With ring in end to fasten to watch chain. Makes a shrill whistle call. Our price 23c. each.

## BARNUM'S PATENT GAME CARRIER.

By mail, 3 cents extra.

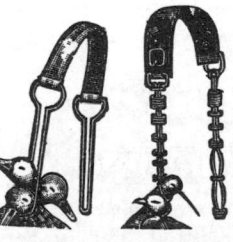

Barnum's.    Rudolph's.

No. 8665. Worth its weight in gold; a blessing to feathered game shooters; weight, 2½ ounces; folded, 8½ inches long, ½-inch thick; can be carried in the pencil pocket, yet holds securely 18 ducks, balanced on the shoulders, on the belt, gun barrel, or in the hand. Price, each. $0.14
Per dozen................1.40
No. 8666. Rudolph's Compact game carrier, with leather shoulder strap, each................$0.30
Per dozen................3.00
By mail, extra, 3c.

SPECIAL LINE OF BICYCLE SUITS IN OUR CLOTHING DEPARTMENT.

## DECOYS.

In making these decoys great care has been used to select only sound white Cedar for their construction and to secure a perfect balance. They are light, substantial and naturally painted. Assortments: Mallard, canvas back, red head, blue bill, teal, pin or sprig tails. Weight, per dozen, 35 to 40 pounds.

No. 8667. No. 1 best decoy ducks, per doz........$3.25
No. 8668. No. 2 good decoy ducks, per doz........2.90
No. 8669. Cords and anchors for decoys, per doz..  .50

No. 8671. Folding canvas decoys. The best imitation of the natural duck in the market. Made of best canvas, beautifully painted in natural colors, waterproofed. Weight, 4 oz. each. Packed 1 dozen in a neat wooden box 2¾x9 inches. We sell any quantity. Mallards, red heads, canvas back and blue bills. Per dozen................$5.95

No. 8672. Danz's folding decoy geese. Collapsable canvas, with the latest improved legs and neck. Packed 1 dozen in a case. Will sell any quantity at dozen rates.
No. 1 is goose without wings, or wings painted on body. Price, per dozen..$7.50
No. 2. The best goose on the market, with wings and perfect in every respect. Price, per dozen........$11.00

## GRASS SUITS.

No. 8673. For wild goose, duck and all kinds of shore bird shooting; made of long tough marsh grass into cape coat with hood. Weigh less than four pounds, are convenient to wear and shoot from. Make good waterproofs in rainy weather, are easily packed and carried. Hunters appreciate the value of these suits, as no blind or bough house is necessary when shooting on marshes. Single suits, each................$1.75

FREIGHT IS THE CHEAPEST METHOD OF TRANSPORTATION. IT WON'T PAY YOU TO SHIP A GAME CARRIER ALONE BY FREIGHT, BUT YOU NEED GROCERIES ALL THE TIME, AND IT WILL PAY YOU TO MAKE UP A FREIGHT ORDER OF SUGAR, COFFEE, TEA, FISH, MEATS, ETC., AND INCLUDE THE SMALL ARTICLES WITH IT.

## HUNTER'S CLOTHING.

**Also good for Farmers, Teamsters and Mechanies. Finest quality and the best made goods in the market. All double stitchad and never rip. Extra by mail 40 to 50 cents on canvas coats.**

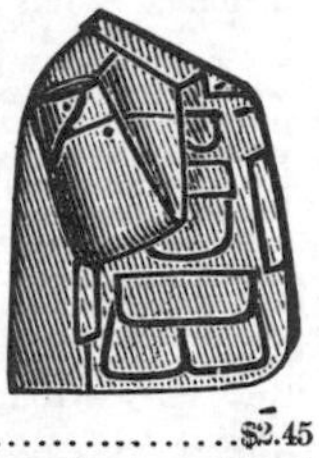

No. 8674. Hunting Coat, full length, double filled, 10 oz. duck. Full pattern, full drill lined. Corduroy collar and cuffs, adjustable seven outside shell and whistle cut-in-pockets with flaps. Three game pockets with entrance from outside edges and outside back seams, shoulders reinforced double stitched, three buttons and full leather bound. Our special price.. $2.95

No. 8675. Same coat as aboue, but not leather bound. Our special price ........ $2.45

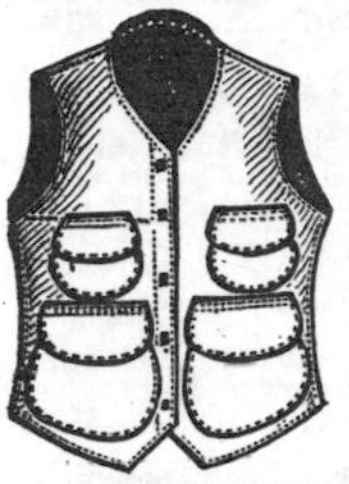

8676.

No. 8676. Hunting Vest, made of the best 8 ounce duck. Waterproof to match coat with four patch pockets which will carry forty shells or more. Size, 32 to 42. Our special price.... $0.70

No. 8677. Hunting Coat, made of heavy 10 ounce army duck, lined throughout with 8 oz. duck, dead grass color oil tanned leather bound. Corduroy collar and cuffs, adjustable, otherwise same description as number 8674. The best hunting Coat on the market. Our special price ............ $3.40

No. 8678 Hunting Coat, fine 8 oz. duck, full pattern, drill lined, corduroy collar and cuffs adjustable, six outside shell and whistle patch pockets with flaps, three game pockets with entrance from edges and outside back seams, shoulders reinforced, double stiched. three buttons, full oil tanned leather bound to prevent wearing out of edges. Price ............. $2.35

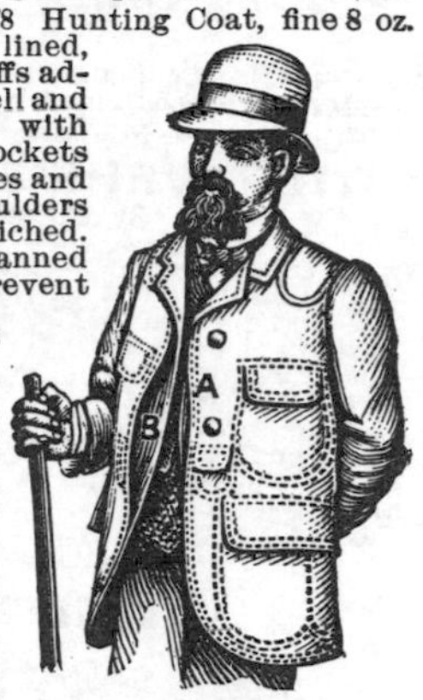


No. 8677.

No. 8679. Same Coat as No. 8678. Without leather binding. Price..... $2.10

No. 8680. Coat, lighter duck, six pockets outside, full game pocket inside, corduroy collar; sizes 36 to 46, a good coat. Each......... $1.30

No. 8681. Coat, same as 8680, except leather bound all around. Each ............. $1.48

No. 8682. Hunting Coat, dead grass color, duck, 6 outside pockets, one large game pocket, full size of coat inside, with outside entradce on each side. Each .......... 85c
**Extra by mail ........... 25c**

No. 8683. Hunting suit, greenish drab color, 8 oz. duck for hunting or fishing, before the foliage is dead, or in the south, six outside pockets, full inside game pocket, entrance on the outside, shoulders reinforced. Made in first-class manner; a good suit, coat, pants and vest ........... $4.50
Coat only ........... 2.40
Vest only ........... .95
Pants only ........... 1.27

Caps and hats, any hunting style, same prices as the dead grass colored.

N. B.—We can furnish the above coats heavy flannel lined, $1.50 extra. No other coat is needed where No. 1 coat is lined.

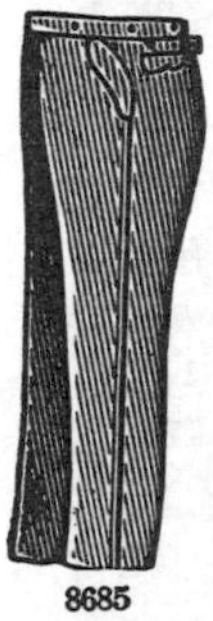

8685

No. 8684. Vest same as 8676, but with shell bands instead of pockets; sizes, 36 to 44. Price, each ........... $1.00
Extra by mail 15c.
Give chest measure for coat and vest.

No. 8685. Hunting Pants, made of heavy, 8 oz. waterproof duck to match coat and vest, with two long pockets in front, one hip pocket, full length, regular make, double stitched, never rip until worn out. Each...... $1.30
Extra by mail 25c.

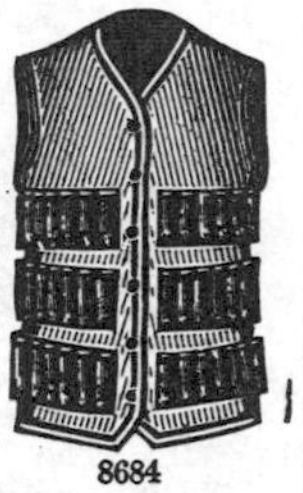

8684

No. 8686. Canvas Vest, dead grass color, with sleeves; sizes, 36 to 44. Each ........... $1.15
Extra by mail 16c.

No. 8687. Skeleton coat canvas, dead grass color with game pockets. Sizes breast measure 36 to 44. Each ........... $0.90
Extra by mail 16c.

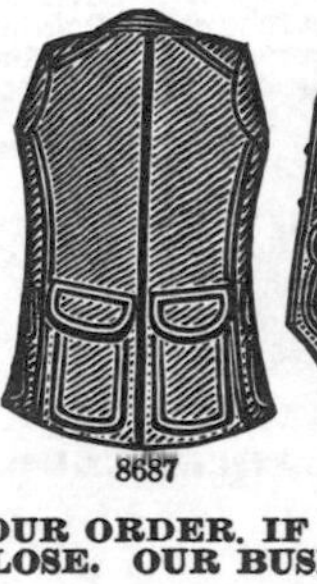

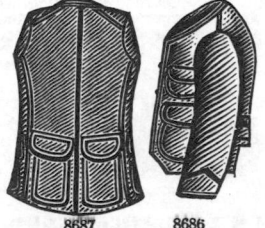

8687

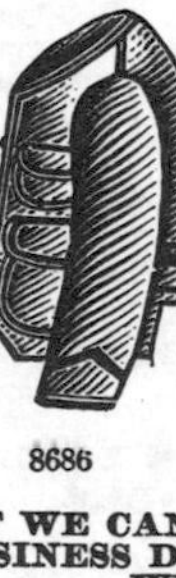

8686

## BEST IMPORTED CORDUROY SUITS.

Weights—coat 42 oz; Pants, 33; Vest, 16 to 20 oz.

No. 8 88. Corduroy coat; size 36 to 44 ........... $5.75
No. 8689. Corduroy vest; size 36 to 44 ........... 2.50
No. 8690. Corduroy pants; give waist and inside seam measure; full length, regular make ........... 4.10
No. 8691. Corduroy Hunting Coat, dark drab color not as heavy as 8688, but well made and durable. (Many prefer them to the heavier goods.) Each, 3.85
No. 8692. Corduroy pants, same ........... 3.15
No. 8693. Corduroy vest, same ........... 1.80

Our Corduroy clothing is made of **Imported goods**, and is free from any "objectionable odor," such as is found in some "so called" imported corduroys. They are well made and nice fitting goods, and all warranted as represented. Coats are all sack style, similar to our hunting coats in design and finish.

## OIL TANNED HORSEHIDE SUITS.

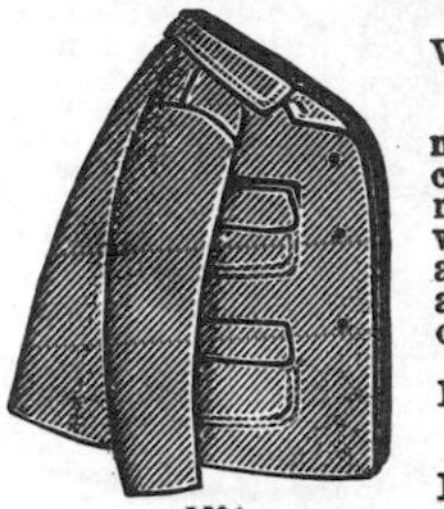

8694

Weight—Coats, 56 to 60 oz.

Positively the best garment made in this or any other country for those exposed to rough weather. They are water and wind-proof, pliable and soft as kid, and will always remain so. Made with outside pockets.

No. 8694. Horsehide coat, reversible with corduroy; sizes, 36 to 44 .......... $10.90
No. 8695. Horsehide coat, heavy cassimere lined $8.95
No. 8696. Vest, Cassimere lined horsehide .......... $3.90
No. 8697. Vests, reversible, with corduroy .......... $5.60
No. 8698. Pants, horsehide, cassimere lined, weight about 3 lbs. Full length regular make ............ $6.95
No. 8699. Horsehide Pants reversible, with corduroy ........... $8.50

Our horsehide clothing is genuine horsehide, and not "goatskin" or "sheepskin" or "dogskin" (which is another name for "sheepskin" in most cases), and will never peel off or get rough, no matter how sharp the thorns or how thick the brush and trees are, and can be oiled like a boot or harness, grows softer and more pliable the longer it is worn.

No. 8700. "Shooting Sweater." Dead grass color. heavily reinforced at shoulder with shell pockets in front. Sizes, from 26 to 44 in. These sweaters make a close fitting, wind proof garment and being elastic are desirable for trap shooting as well as hunting. Our special price ........... $3.25

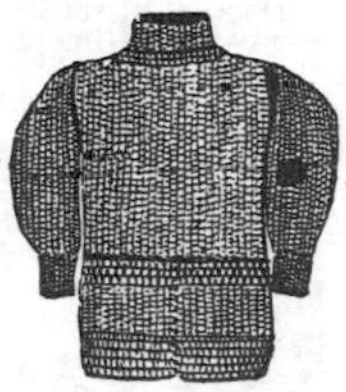

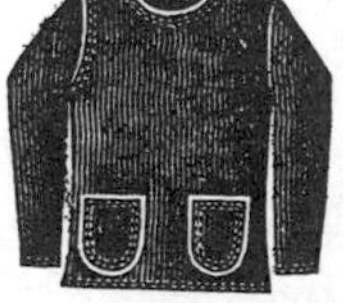

## SHOOTING BLOUSE.

No. 8701. Thurman's Shooting Blouse. For trap shooters; made of the very best knit jersey. Colors: brown or navy blue, each ........... $1.80
Postage, 10c. extra.

## CHAMOIS SHIRT.

No. 8702. This shirt is made of fine Swiss Chamois and lined with a light cassimere—has the extra protector on chest. It is pronounced by our leading trap shooters to be the most comfortable garment on the market. It is proof against the wind. Soft and light. Does not interfere with the proper handling of the gun. For measure, send size of collar worn, breast measure and length of sleeve, price net...... $6.00
Weight, 35 to 40 oz.

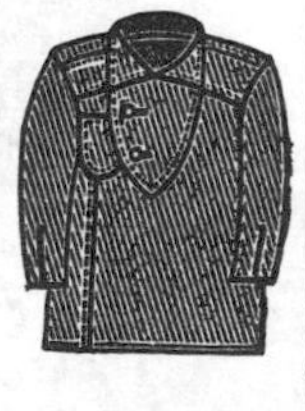

## HUNTING HATS AND CAPS.

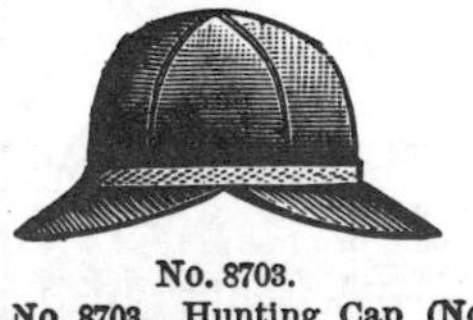

No. 8703.

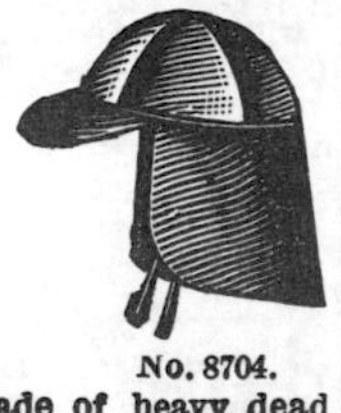

No. 8704.

No. 8703. Hunting Cap (No. 1) made of heavy dead grass colored duck, with double visor. Give size of hat worn. Weight, 5 oz., each ........... $0.38
No. 8704. Hunting Cap, same as above, one visor, has havelock cape to protect the neck from storm or sun. Taped seams, light flannel lined. Weight 12 oz., each ........... $0.48

**Our Canvas goods are the best in the market. We do not handle the cheap stuff.**

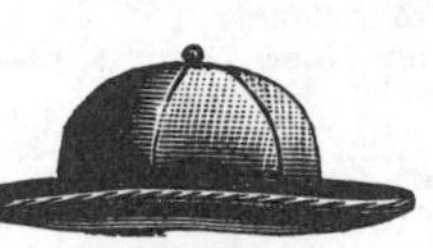

No. 8705.

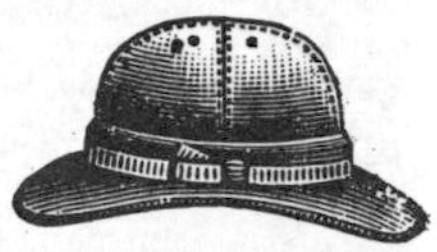

No. 8706.

No. 8705. Hunting Hat, dead grass colored duck, all around rim taped seams, weight 10 oz., each.... $0.38
No. 8706. Solar Hunting Hat, dead grass color, with ventilated sweat band inside ........... $0.60
No. 8707. Corduroy Hats, round top, light drab color, taped seams ........... $0.85
No. 8708. Corduroy Hat, square top, light drab color, taped seams ........... $0.85
No. 8709. Corduroy Cap, double visor, light drab color, taped seams ........... $0.60
No. 8710. Corduroy Cap, with short cape, light color taped seams ........... $0 75
Postage extra, 12c.

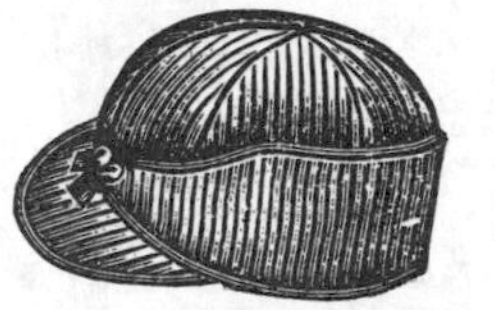

No. 8711. Corduroy Cap, each ........... $0.75
Postage, extra, 12c.
For lined duck clothing, see "Clothing Department."

## CLOTHES BAGS.

No. 8712. Made of heavy white duck, with drawing strings fastened on the top, with round bottom; weight, 2 lbs ........... $0.50
Postage extra, 35c.

## LEGGINGS.

For Hunting Boots and Shoes see Index.

**When ordering leggings, be sure and give size of calf of leg outside of pants.**

No. 8713. Reynold's Army Style Legging, made of heavy 10 oz. brown water-proof canvas, with eyelets and hooks to lace all the way; 12 inches long. In ordering send size around calf of leg. Per pair, 70c; per doz ........... $8.00
No. 8713½. Men's Knee Leggings to buckel, brown canvas. Per pair, 48c; per doz ........... $5.40
Postage extra, 4 cents.

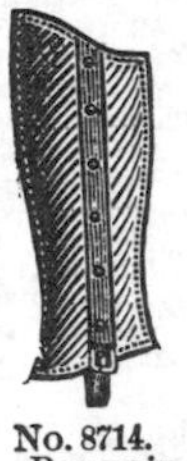

No. 8714.

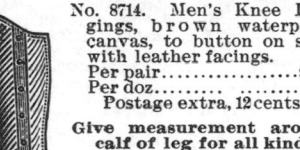

No. 8714. Men's Knee Leggings, brown waterproof canvas, to button on side. with leather facings.
Per pair ........... $0.45
Per doz ........... 4.75
Postage extra, 12 cents.

**Give measurement around calf of leg for all kinds of leggings.**

No. 8716. Men's Knee Leggings, brown canvas, waterproof, leather bound top and bottom to buckle, like cut.

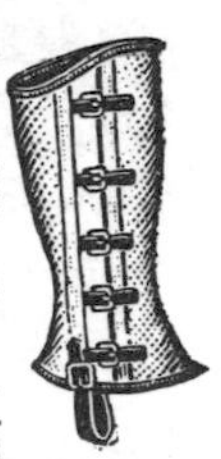

No. 8716.

Per pair, 55c; per doz ........... $6.00
No. 8716½. Same as No. 8716, to lace instead of buckle. Price ........... $0.60
Postage extra, 21 cents.

No. 8717. Men's Leggings, same as 8716. except has steel spring fastenings on side instead of buckels or buttons. Each, 85c; per doz ........... $9.85
Postage extra, 25 cents.

No. 8718. Men's Thigh Leggings, brown canvas waterproof, leather bound top and bottom, buckle at knee, lace to thigh, extra long, weight, 28 oz. Per pair, 95; per doz ........... $10.00
Postage extra, 30 cents.

No. 8718½. Same as No. 8718, with side spring steel fastener to knee, lace to thigh. Price ........... $1.00

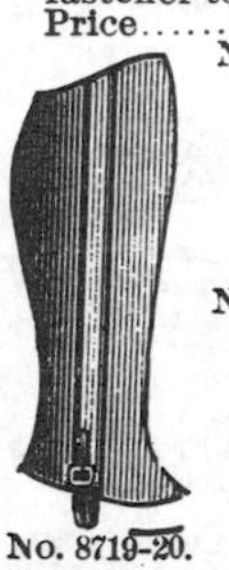

No. 8719-20.

No. 8719. Men's Leggings, black grain leather, with steel spring stiffener on side, the new and convenient fastening, like cut. Weight, 44 ounces.
Per pair ........... $ 1.85
Per doz ........... 19.85

No. 8720. Men's Leggings, russet grain leather, with steel spring stiffener on side, the new and convenient fastening, like cut; 18 inches, weight 40 oz.
Per pair ........... $ 1.85
Per doz. ........... 19.85
Postage extra, 45.

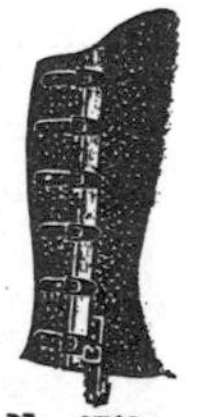

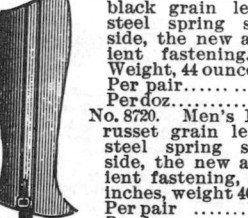

No. 8719.

No. 8721. (OAP) Men's Knee Leggings, black grain leather to buckle all the way up, weight, 32 oz.
Per pair ........... $ 1.70
Per doz ........... 18.70
Postage extra, 35 cents.

No. 8722. Men's Leggings, russet grain leather, like cut 8720, to buckle all the way up, 18 inches long, weight 32 ounces.
Per pair ........... $ 1.70
Per doz ........... 18.70

**WONDERFUL BARGAINS .....IN..... HARNESS AND SADDLES.**

See Pages 736 to 757.

**WE DON'T WANT YOUR ORDER. IF WE CAN'T SAVE YOU MONEY. WE DON'T WANT YOU TO FEEL THAT IT IS A CASE OF LUCK IF YOU WIN OR LOSE. OUR BUSINESS DEPENDS ON SATISFYING YOU, AND TO DO SO WE MUST GIVE YOU GOOD SERVICE. WE HAVE EVERY FACILITY FOR SAVING YOU MONEY.**

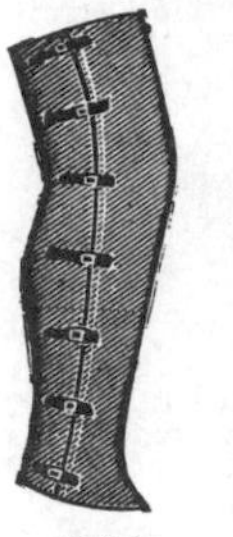

Thigh.

Horsehide Leggings, either "Knee" or "Thigh" lengths. To lace all the way. Same price as to buckle.

No. 8723. Men's Knee Leggings, russet tanned horsehide, to lace, weight 28 oz.
Per pair........................$ 2.39
Per dozen........................ 25.00

No. 8724. Men's Thigh Leggings, russet tanned horsehide, to buckle and lace; weight, 36 oz.
Per pair........................$ 3.20
Per dozen pair................... 33.75

Showing shape of thigh legging, all buckle.

N. B.—The horsehide leggings are the handsomest and best in the market; are always soft and pliable.

Horsehide leggings to lace all the way; same price as buckle.

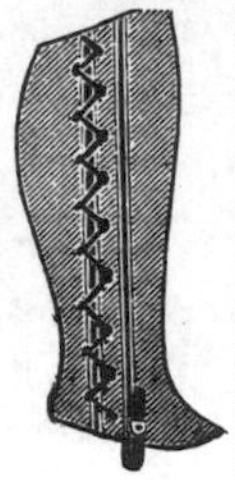

No. 8725. Men's Knee Leggings, imported corduroy, to buckle.
Each............................$ 1.35
Per doz.......................... 15.00
Weight, 23 oz. To lace.
Per pair......................... 1.40
Per doz.......................... 16.00

Always send measurement around calf of leg for leggings, or we will be obliged to hold the order and write you for size.

## DOG COLLARS.

### BIG BARGAINS.

By mail, 5 to 14c extra.

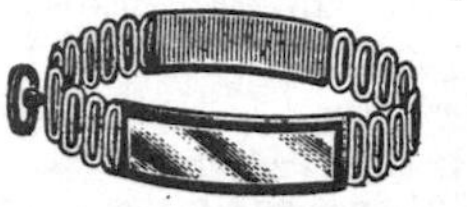

No. 8726. Dog collar, nickel, wide, flat links, nickel name plate, with staple for padlock. The most popular and a big seller. Very attractive; 14, 16, 17 and 18 in. width, 1 inch.
Each..................$0 20

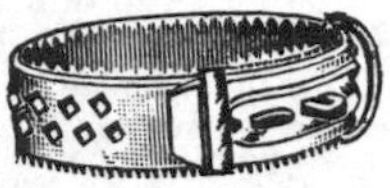

No. 8727. Dog Collar, fine orange leather, chamois lined large nickel plated studs, nickel name plate and trimmings, to lock; length 17, 19 and 21 in.; 1 in. wide.
Each......................$0.60

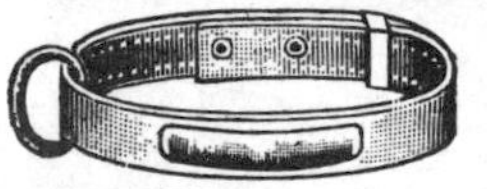

No. 8728. Dog collar, double harness leather, black stitched edges, nickel trimming, ring name plate and staple to lock; length, 17 to 21 inches; width 1 inch.........................$0.49

No. 8729. Length, 19 to 23 in ; width, 1¼ in., each.. .55
No. 8730. " 21 " 25 " " 1½ " " .. .60
No. 8731. Dog collar, same as 8728, except to buckle; length, 17 to 21 in.; width, 1 in.; each..........$0.45
No. 8732. Length, 19 to 23 in.; width, 1⅛ in.; each.. .50
Length, 21 to 25 in.; width, ½ in.; each.. .55

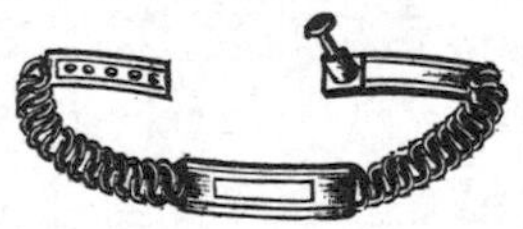

No. 8733. Dog collar, polished steel name plate, chain and padlock in one; strong and durable; will last a lifetime; single chain 14 and 16 in., ea., $0.35

No. 8734. Same style, double chain, 14, 15, 17, 18 and 20 in.; each..............................$0.65

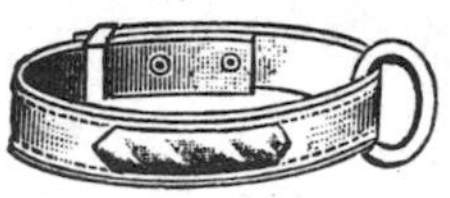

No. 8735. Dog collar, fancy leather, assorted colors, nickel trimmings and name plate; length, 8, 9, 10, 12 and 13 in.; width, ⅝ inch.
Each....................$0.15
Per doz.................. 1.60

No. 8736. Length, 13, 14, 15, or 16 in.; width, ⅞ in.
Each..............................$0.27
Per dozen.......................... 2.75

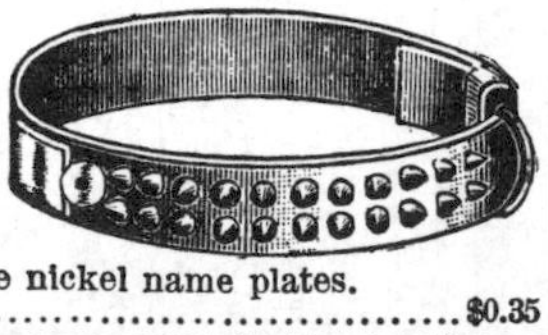

No. 8737. (ABOt) Dog collar, best English single russet harness leather, studded, nickel name plate and ring to buckle, length, 14, 15, 16, 17, 18 and 20 in.; width, 1 in. All collars have nickel name plates.
Each..............................$0.35

No. 8738. Dog collar, same as 8737; double row, heavy plated studs, is 1¼ to 1½ inches wide; to buckle, 21 in., 22 in. long. Each..........$0.44

No. 8739. Dog collar, same as 8737; fine nickel plated studs, is 1½ in. wide, to buckle 15, 16, 17, 18 and 20 in. long. Each..........$0.59

No. 8740. Dog collar, same as 8737, except to lock, 1¼ in. wide, 2 rows, heavy nickel plated studs, fine russet leather, 16, 17, 18, 19, 20, 21 in. long. Each..........$0 65

No. 8741. Dog collar, extra quality, single harness leather, studded to lock, (locks not included in price named) 1 in. wide, 17, 19 and 21 in.; each..........$0.55

No. 8742. Three rows studs, with staple to attach lock; 1¼ to 1½ inches wide; 14, 15, 17, 19, 21 and 23 in.
Each..............................$ .70

No. 8743. Dog collar, same as No. 8740, with staple to attach lock, 2¼ inches wide, four rows nickel plated studs, 15, 16, 17, 18, 19, 20, 21, 22 and 24 inches long.
Each..............................$0.95

Postage extra 12c.

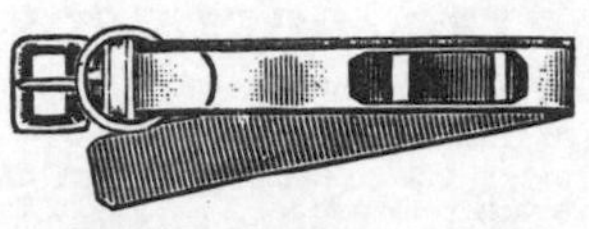

No. 8744. (AOCt) Dog collar, russet leather, nickel name plate and ring to buckle; length, 14 to 18 in.; width, 1 in.
Each..............................$0.22
Per dozen.......................... 2.15
Length, 9 to 12 in., 1½ in. wide. Each.......... .20

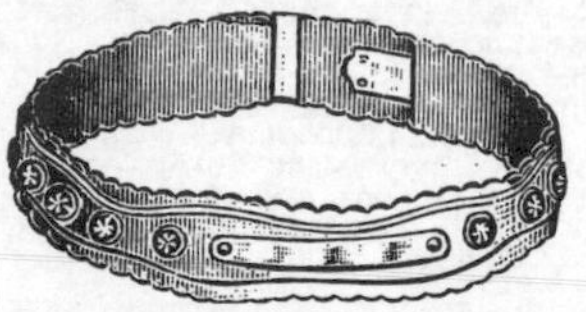

No. 8745. (CTP) Scalloped russet leath'r, to lock, chamois lined, new style ornaments. Width ¾ in; length, 13, 15 or 17 inches.
Each.........$0.35
Per doz.........3.60

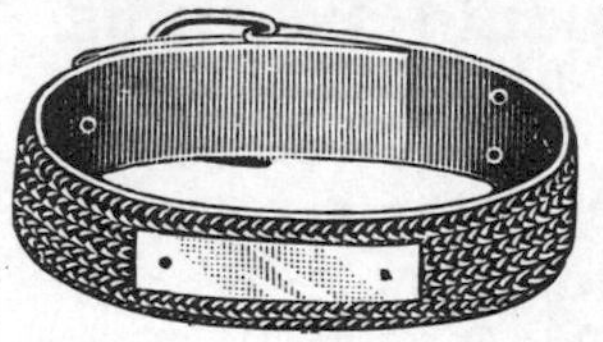

No. 8746. (ctHc(Cl). Nickel plated, woven steel wire chain, leather and chamois lined, handsome and stylish, 1 in. wide, staple to lock. Lengths, 17, 19, 21 in. Each.....$0.60
Per doz....... 6.48

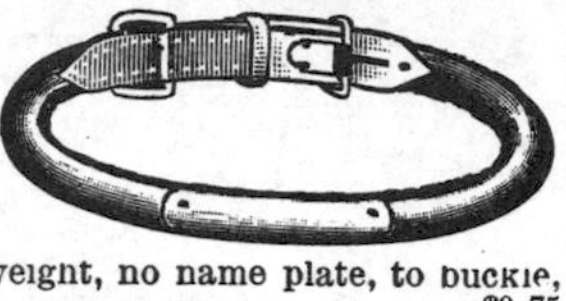

No. 8747. Round Dog Collar, to buckle. Fine heavy block leather, with name plate, 16, 18, 20 in.
Each..........$0.75

No. 8748. Round Dog Collar, orange leather, very light weight, no name plate, to buckle, 14, 16, 18 in. Each.........$0.75

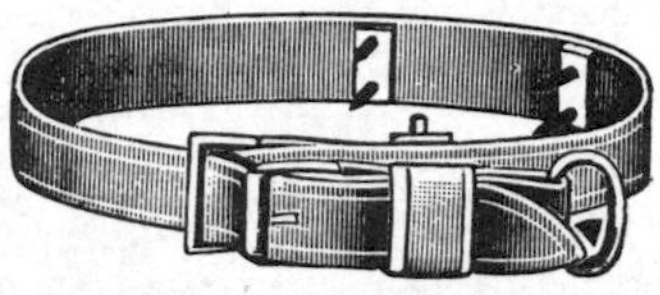

No. 8749. D. Watter's Spike Collar, pronounced by all dog trainers the best collar ever made for training purposes. Simple and durable, and cannot twist. Hence the points are always towards the dog's neck. It works freely and will not mutilate any dog. Punishment can be applied or ended instantly in forcing a dog to retrieve. Every owner of a dog should have one. Made of *good* black leather. Each..............................$1.50

Extra by mail, 10c.

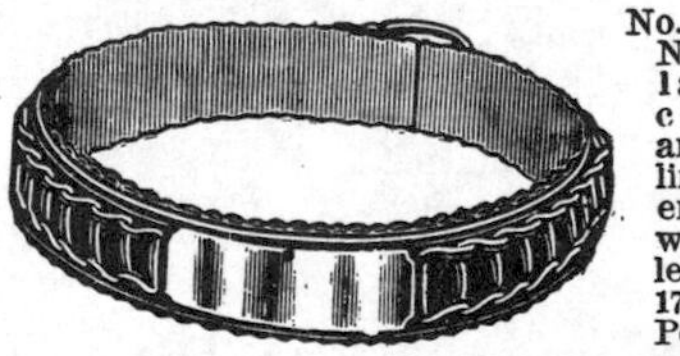

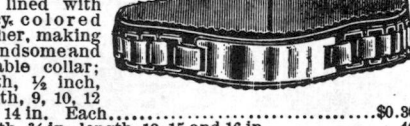

No. 8750. (CTARcl) Nickel plated ladder link chain, leather and chamois lined; a big seller (to lock); width, ¾ inch, length, 13, 15 and 17 in. Each.$0.40
Per doz..... 4.00

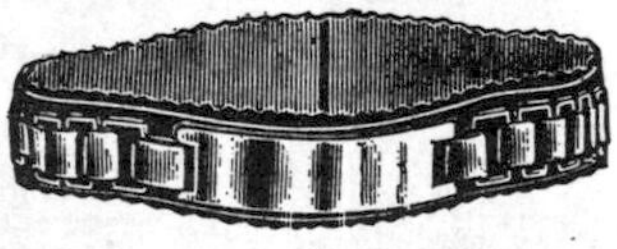

No. 8751. Dog Collar, lined with fancy colored leather, making a handsome and durable collar; width, ½ inch, length, 9, 10, 12 and 14 in. Each..............................$0.30
Width, ¾ in., length, 13, 15 and 16 in.......... .40
Width, 1 in., length, 14, 15, 16, 17, 18 and 20 in., each .50

## DOG COMBS.

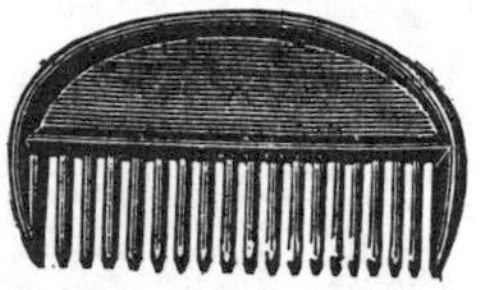

No. 8752. Rubber Dog Combs, best quality.
Each..............$0.25

## DOG COLLAR PADLOCKS.

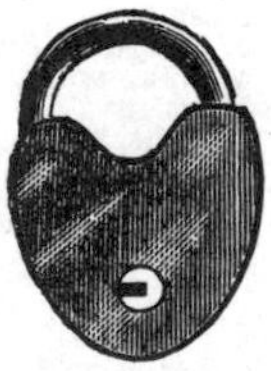

No. 8753. Padlock, 1x¾ in., all nickel plated, with key. Each........$0.20
Per doz..................... 2.20

No. 8754. Padlock, 1x¾ in., brass, with key. Each..............$0.20
Per doz..................... 2.20

Extra by mail, 1c.

No. 8755. Scandinavian Padlock for dog collar.
Small..............$0.20
Large.............. .25
Postage extra, 2c.

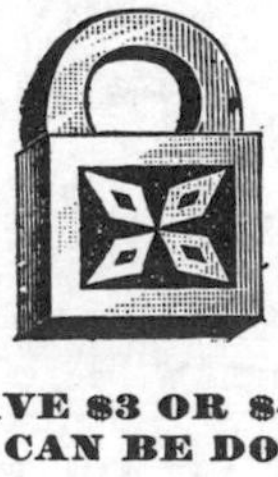

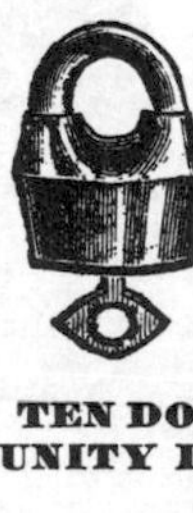

No. 8756. Dog Collar Padlock, made of aluminum, almost as light as a feather, ¾ in. by 1⅜ in. (CTC.)
Each..............$0.20
Per doz........... 2.25

## DOG LEADS.

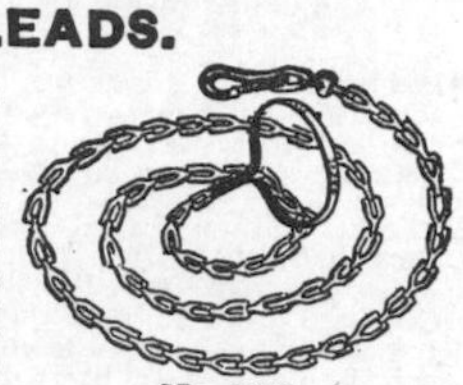

No. 8757.

No. 8757. Dog Lead, bright safety link chain, swivel snap, with hand grasp as shown in cut. Length, 48 inches. Each .....$0.25

No. 8758. Dog Lead, same style as No. 8757, except with ring hold, heavy nickel plated, very strong and durable, large link, 4½ feet long.
Price, each..........$0.30

No. 8758½. Same style as above, medium link, 4½ feet long..............................$0.27

No. 8759. Same style as above, small link. Length, 4½ feet, a little beauty..............................$0.24

No. 8760. Heavy Dog Lead, polished iron, flat safety link, very strong and durable. Length, 4½ feet.
Each..............................$0.18

No. 8761. Dog Leads, hand braided leather, round, with loop and snap, 40 inches. Each..........$0.39

## KENNEL DOG CHAINS.

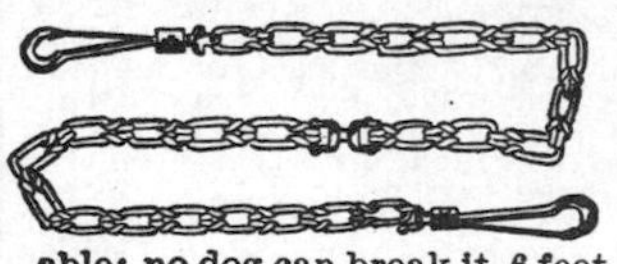

No. 8763. Kennel Dog Chains, polished steel, round wire, new style safety links, 3 swivels, 2 hooks, well made and durable; no dog can break it, 6 feet, weight 16 oz.
Each..............................$0.65

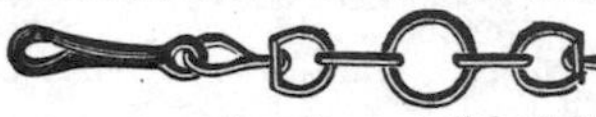

No. 8764. Dog Couplings, polished steel, large ring in center, snap hook on each end, two swivels; weight, 5 oz. Each..............................$0.40

## THE SURPRISE WHISTLE.

By mail, 1c. extra.

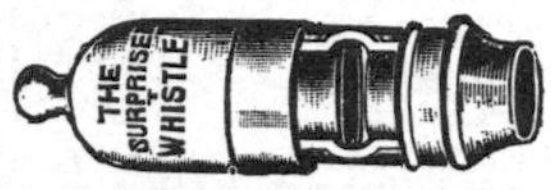


No. 8765. The Surprise Whistle, the loudest and best dog call in the market. By squeezing in the bulb at the end you can regulate the sound and produce any effect, from purling or muffled notes up to a great swelling, booming, two mile piercing note. A good snipe or plover call also. Each..............................$0.20
Per doz.............................. 2 00

Postage extra, 2c.

## WHISTLES.

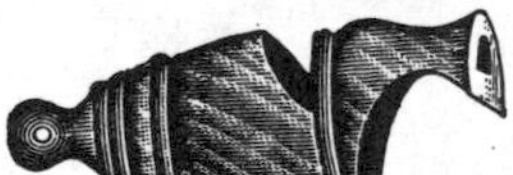

No. 8766. Celluloid Dog Call or Whistle. A loud one.
Small, each.......$0.20
Large, each....... .25
Postage extra, 2c.

## DOG WHIPS.

By mail, 8 cents extra.

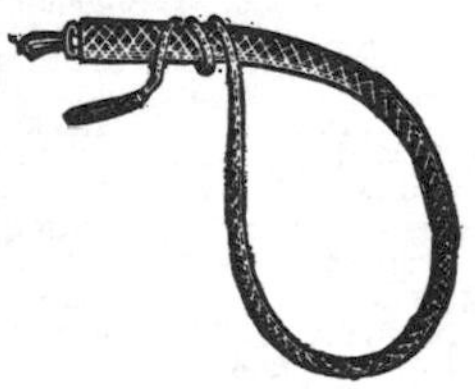

No. 8767. Whips, hand braided russet leather, whistle on handle, heavy and durable. Each..73c

No. 8768. The Never Break Whip, same as 8767, with snap on end instead of whistle, making a good lead as well as whip; can be folded into small compass and carried in pocket. Each .......50c

No. 8769. The Never Break Whip, 12 plait braided leather, with leather loop on end, loaded butt, strong and durable. Each.......80c

## DOG MUZZLES.

By mail, 4 to 6 cents extra.

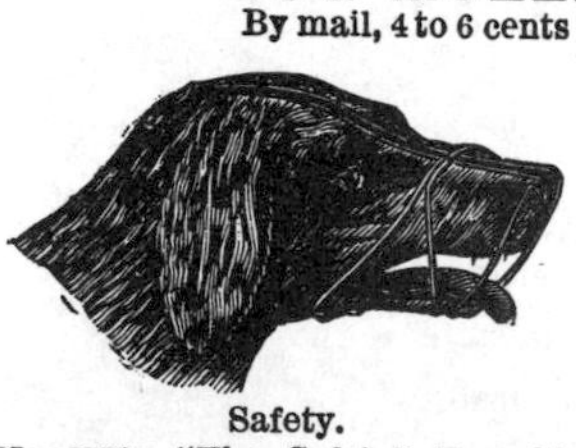

No. 8770. Dog Muzzles, common iron wire, with strap to buckle around the neck. Basket style to cover nose and mouth. Each..25c

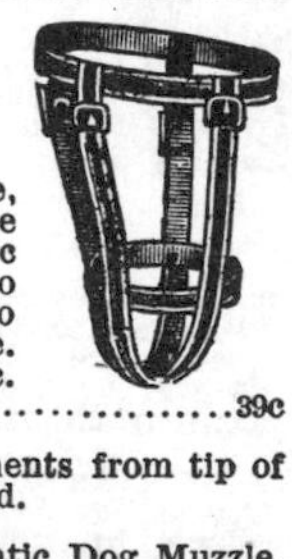

Safety.

No. 8771. "The Safety" Dog Muzzle, made of iron wire with strap to buckle around neck. Each..............25c

No. 8772. Leather strap Dog Muzzle, to buckle around neck and buckle to take up around head if too large. Small size, 15c. Medium size, 30c.
Large size..............................39c

Give measurements from tip of nose to top of head.

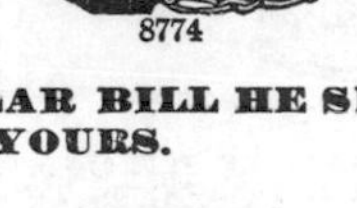

8774

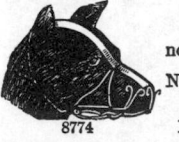

No. 8773. Automatic Dog Muzzle, wire and leather. Permits dog to open mouth to drink or eat.
Each..............................70c

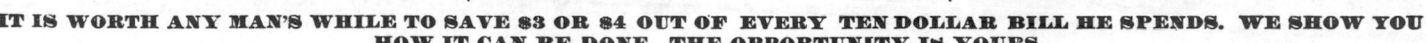

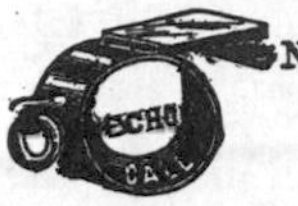
ECHO
CALL

No. 8774. The Echo Call, the loudest yet, beautifully nickel plated. Can be carried in the vest pocket. Each........15c

## DRINKING CUPS.

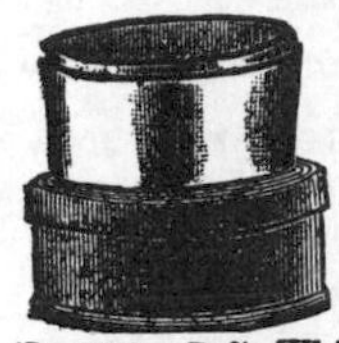

No. 8775. Drinking Cups. Britannia collapsing telescope height, full length 3¼ inches, width across top 2⅜ in., flaring bottom, comes in round japanned box; size 2½x1⅜ in. One of the handiest and most convenient articles ever invented for hunters, tourists and teamsters; can be carried in pocket easily. Price only 20 cents; per doz. $2.00. By mail 4c extra.

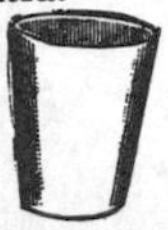

No. 8776. Soft, White Rubber Drinking Cup, tumbler shape, will hold about as much as a common table tumbler, flexible and can be folded and put in pocket. Each.....18c By mail, 3 cents extra.

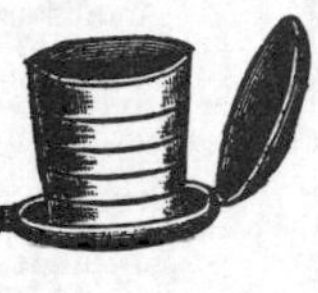

No. 8777. Patent Collapsing Pocket Cup, in nickeled tin watch case. Cup stands about 2 inches high when open. Case exact size of a watch. One of the best novelties ever invented. Price, each 25c. By mail 4c extra.

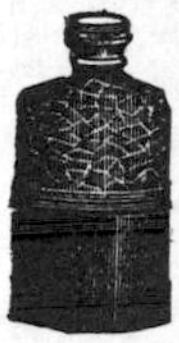

No. 8778. Olry Pocket Flasks, leather covered, with metal drinking cup on bottom, and white metal screw-off top or stopper. Almost a household necessity.

| | |
|---|---|
| ¼ Pint | $0 75 |
| ½ Pint | 87 |
| ¾ Pint | 1 10 |
| 1 Pint | 1 25 |
| 1 Quart | 2 10 |

## DOG REMEDIES.

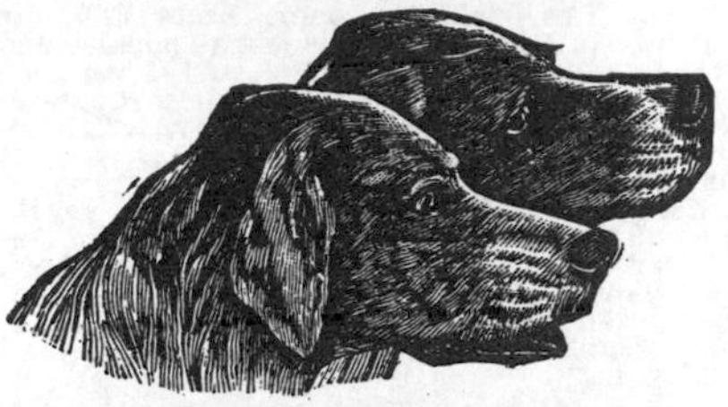

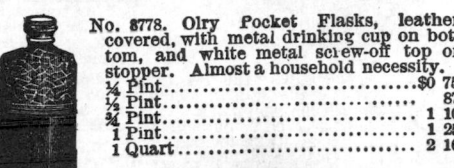

No. 8779. "Spratts Patent" Tonic Condition Pills for debility arising from disease, and of great value in preparing dogs for work requiring endurance. Unequaled in preparing dogs for bench shows. Price per box, 35c. Postage........4c

No. 8780. "Spratts Patent" Mange Cure, which rarely fails to speedily cure mange in every form, and the destruction of fleas, lice, ticks, etc., in the Dog, Horse Ox, Pig and other animals, is non-poisonous; full directions wrapped around each bottle. Price, 40c. Postage........10c

No. 8781. "Spratts Patent" Worm Cure. A speedy and sure destroyer of these troublesome parasites, which are the source of so many forms of canine diseases. Price per box, 35c. Postage........4c

No. 8782. "Spratts Patent" Distemper Cure, the new antiseptic remedy, an effective cure for the scourge of the kennel; each packet contains very minute directions for the treatment of dogs suffering under distemper. Price per box, 40c. Postage........4c

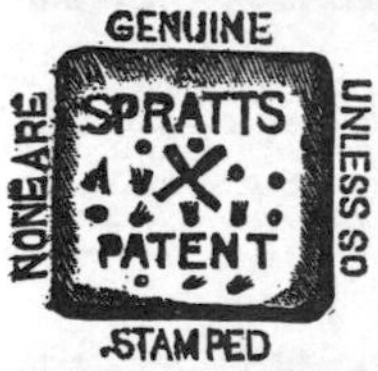
GENUINE
SPRATTS
PATENT
NONE ARE
UNLESS SO
STAMPED

No. 8783. "Spratts Patent" Fibrine Dog Cakes (with Beetroot), these celebrated biscuits are supplied to all the leading kennels and are used at the principal dog shows in America and England, and have been before the public for more than a quarter of a century. Price per 50 lb. bag, $3.25. 25 lb. boxes, per box, $1.70. 5 lb. boxes, per box........40c

No. 8784. "Spratts Patent" Dog Soap; this is of the greatest value to dog owners as it is entirely free from poison and at the same time most effective in the destruction of lice, fleas and ticks; it is the only soap that should be used in preparing dogs for exhibition, as it leaves the coat smooth and glossy. Printed directions for using the soap on each wrapper. Price per cake, 20c. Extra by mail........7c

## SLUNG SHOTS AND BILLIES.

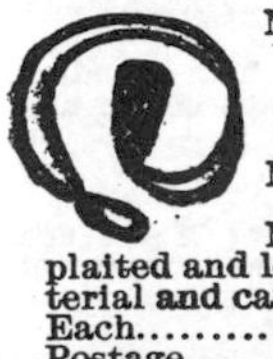

No. 8786. Braided Leather Slung Shot, made of the best material, cannot be broken.
Each........$0.40
Postage, extra........05

No. 8785. Plaited Billy, Leather. Each........30

No. 8785½. Braided Leather Billy, plaited and loaded with shot, made of the best material and cannot be broken; 9½ inches; weight 6 oz. Each........$0.90
Postage........06

No. 8786½. Knucks, heavy nickel plated and polished. $0.30 per pair. Postage........$0.03

**Complete Hardware Department** commences on page 38. Look over the 100 or more pages for what you need.

## LAWN TENNIS GOODS, ETC.

No. 8789. Best Jointed Poles, polished, with brass ferrules, ornamented. Per pair........$1.50
No. 8790. Ordinary Jointed Poles. Per pair........70
No. 8791. Lawn Tennis guy ropes find pins; complete; 2 ropes, 4 guys and 4 pins; per set, 25c, 50c, 75c, according to quality.
No. 8792. Tennis M3rkinfl or Boundary Tapes, for marking out the court with pins or staples. Per set, single court, $3.35; per set, double court, $3.75.
No. 8793. Dry Powder Court Marker, cylinders and handle complete........$1.70
No. 8794. Tennis Fork to hold net up in center, made of smooth iron. Each........$0.75 Weight, 2¼ lbs.
No. 8795. Tennis Marking Plates for marking angles of court. Made of iron; per set of 10 plates........$0.90

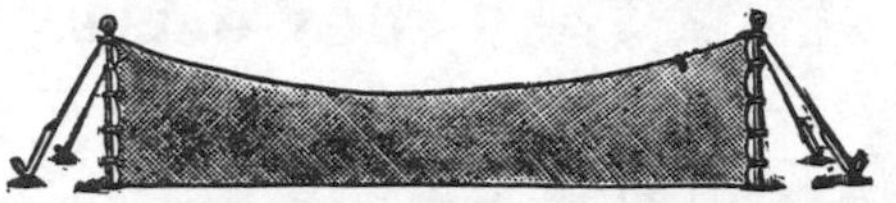

No. 8796. Tennis nets, 27 x 3 feet, 12 threads, weight 27 oz. Each........$0.90
No. 8797. Tennis net, 36 x 3 feet, 15 thread, weight 32 oz. Each........$1.40
No. 8798. Tennis nets, 42 x 3, 15 thread, weight 32 oz. Each........$1.50
No. 8799. Stop nets, 50 x 7 feet, No. 12 thread. Each........$2.90

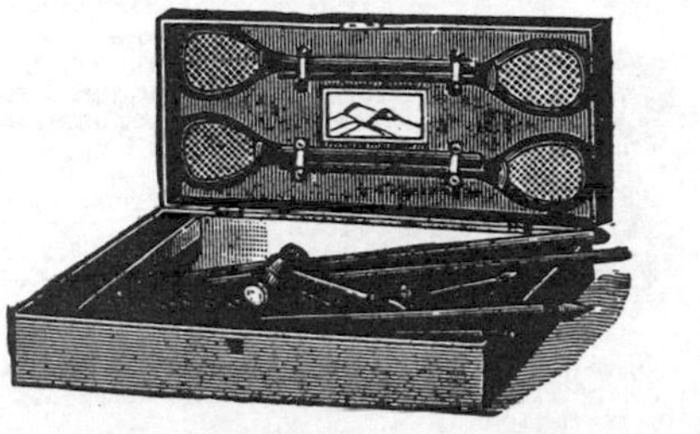

No. 8800. Popular Lawn Tennis set, contains 4 strung gut bats, 4 balls, portable poles, net 3 x 27 feet, lines and runners, mallet and book complete in box, a good plain set, small bats........$8.40
No. 8801. Popular lawn tennis set, contains 4 regulation bats, 4 balls, good net, 3 x 33 feet, portable poles, lines and runner, mallet and book of instructions, complete in box........$10.00
No. 8802. Picnic lawn tennis set, contains 4 regulation racquets, regulation net, 4 regulation balls, pointed poles, jointed guys, ropes, pe⸱⸱ and mallet, with book of instructions, complete in case........$12.00
Better sets, complete $18.00, $20.00, $25.00, $30.00.

## LAWN TENNIS BALLS.

No. 8803. Plain rubber for wet weather use........$0.18
No. 8804. Regulation covered........28
No. 8805. Tournament, regulation covered........35
No. 8806. Champion Tennis Balls. Wright and Ditsons'........40

## LAWN TENNIS BATS. "RACQUETS."

Our Tennis Bats this year are the latest improved.

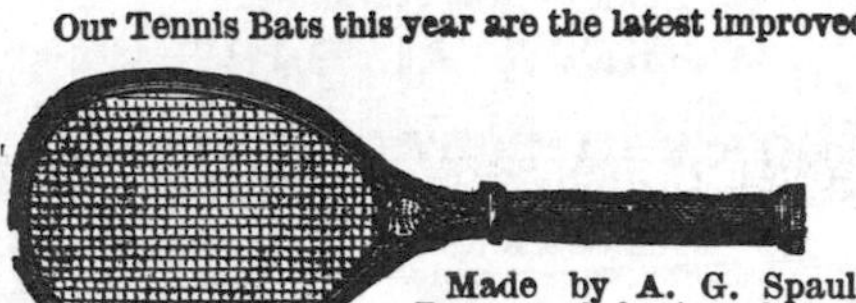

Made by A. G. Spaulding Bros., and best makers, and warranted A 1 quality. If not satisfactory for price, can be returned at our expense after examination. These prices are from 30 to 50 per cent. less than regular retail prices.

No. 8807. Practice bat, ash frame, gut strong....$0.75
No. 8808. Boys' and Girls' Favorite, made of good ash, cedar handle, gut strong........$1.00
No. 8809. "Geneva," made of good ash, cedar handle, gut strong, a good bat for beginners, 10 to 11½ ounces........$1.65
No. 8810. "Greenwood" bat, made of gcod ash, cedar handle, domestic gut, length 26½ inches, bow 7¼x10½........$2.00
No. 8811. "Lakeside" bat, made of good white ash, cedar handle, fair quality of domestic gut; a well finished bat, 11 to 15 oz........$2.40
No. 8812½. "Slocum Jr." bat, made of fine white ash, cedar handle, good quality all white gut, a strong bat, 11 to 15 oz., checkered handles, cherry throat piece........$3.00
No. 8814½. "Slocum" frame bat, made of the finest white ash, cedar handle, strung with finest red and white gut, 12 to 15 oz., fine finish........$3.75
No. 8815½. Bat, same as 8814½, cork handle......$4.25
No. 8816½. "Slocum" Tournament Racquet, extra fine Oriental gut, polished mahogany handle, Slocum pattern........$5.49
No. 1817½. "Slocum Oval" Racquet, oval handle, finest white gut, handsomely polished and finished in antique oak, scored sides........$5.75
No. 8818. Tennis Bat Covers, made of green felt. Each........$0.45
No. 8819. Tennis Bat Covers, made of canvas. Each........$0.90
No. 8820. Rubber Handle Covers for Tennis Bats. Each........$0.20

## CROQUET SETS.

Weight 16 to 28 Pounds.

No. 8821. Four-ball Croquet Set, plain mallets, oiled balls and stakes varnished, ten arches, with book, in neat box with hinged cover........$0.65
No. 8822. Same as No. 8821, with 8 balls in dovetailed box with hinged cover........$1.10
No. 8823. Eight-ball Croquet Set, mallets of neat design, painted and striped, also balls, 2 large fancy stakes, heavy coppered arches. An excellent set at a low price (6)........$1.75
No. 8824. Eight-ball Croquet Set, handsome maple, with fancy striped mallets, handles and balls, 2 elegant beaded stakes, heavy pointed arches painted, superior workmanship and materials in every part (7)........$2.20
No. 8825. Eight-ball Croquet Set, shellac finish, 8 fancy striped 6 inch ebonized and bronzed mallets, handles and balls beautifully finished, painted and striped, 2 elegantly beaded stakes, heavy arches with sockets, an elegant set........$3.40

## OUR SPECIAL LEADER MEN'S BOXING GLOVES.

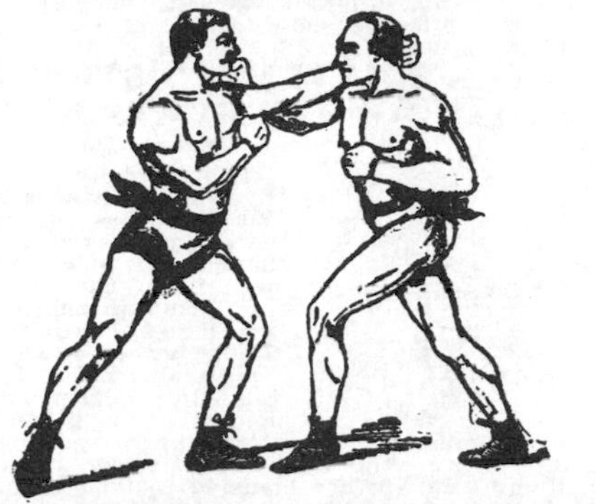

No. 8826. This glove is made of the best select French kid, and is of a chocolate brown color, extra strongly stitched and welted, separate finger parts, stuffed toe and heel pads, laced and elastic wrist band as shown in the picture. Ventilated palms, full leather lined. This is a special glove, made to order for us, and stuffed with the best superfine curled hair. Weight, 8 ounces each. Sold only in complete sets of four gloves. Retail price, $6 per set; our special price, packed one set in a box, per set........$2.95

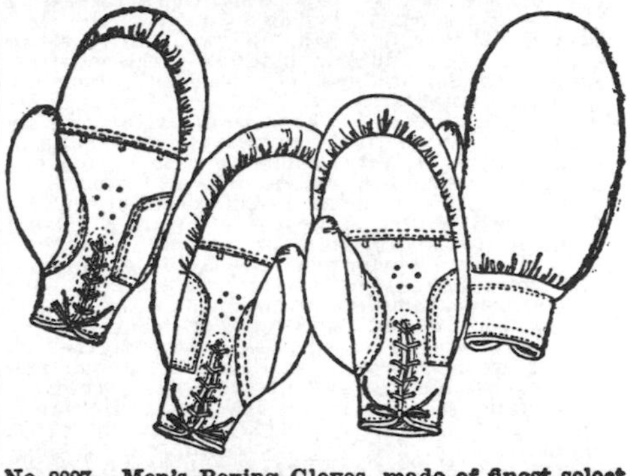

No. 8827. Men's Boxing Gloves, made of finest select California "Napa" tan kid, and stuffed with superfine curled hair. Stuffed toe and heel pads, ventilated palms, double stitched and welted all round, stitched fingers, full leather lined, laced and elastic wristbands. Weight, 8 ounces each. This is a glove that is endorsed by amateurs and professionals alike. Equal to anything on the market that retails at $6 or $7 per set; our special price, per set of four........$3.25
Instruction Book Free with each set.

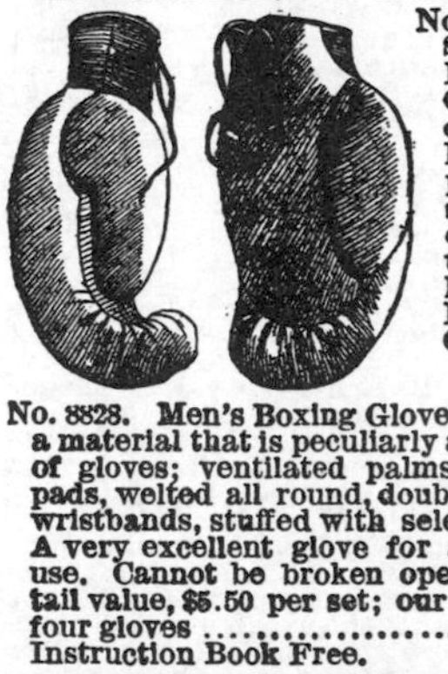

No. 8827½. S. R. & Co.'s Special. The new style Boxing Glove. Genuine Corbett pattern. Padded on ends of fingers; ventilated palms and side heel pads; seal brown color; stuffed with the finest curled hair, and lined throughout with fine kid. Weight, each 8 oz. Regular price, $7.50. Our special price, per set of four........$5.25

No. 8828. Men's Boxing Gloves, made of best white kid, a material that is peculiarly adapted to this high class of gloves; ventilated palms, full leather lined, heel pads, welted all round, double stitched fingers, elastic wristbands, stuffed with select superfine curled hair. A very excellent glove for amateurs or gymnasium use. Cannot be broken open by legitimate use. Retail value, $5.50 per set; our special price, per set of four gloves........$2.85
Instruction Book Free.

**Timers and Chronographs . . .**
**Stop Watches at $4.95, $10.95, $12.95 up to $47.50. Page 377.**

No. 8829. Men's Boxing Gloves, made of all white kid. These gloves are stuffed with fine curled hair, and have ventilated palms; are full leather lined and have elastic wristband; double stitched all round and double stitched fingers; extra strong, and will give superior service. Our price is special. You may not get such a chance again. Our price gets as good, if not better, gloves than you can buy at retail for $5. Special price, per set of four ........................$2.40
Instruction Book Free with each set.

No. 8830. Men's Boxing Gloves, made of extra quality sheepskin and stuffed with fine curled hair; double stitched fingers, ventilated palms, elastic wristbands. Best glove in the world for the money—a glove that will stand hard usage and very soft for practice. Our special price, per set of four ........................$1.75
Instruction Book Free with each set.

No. 8831. Boys' Boxing Gloves, made extra strong, of superior sheepskin. A durable and excellent shaped glove, with ventilated palms and stuffed with fine curled hair; very soft and a favorite with the boys; elastic wristbands. Retails at $3 per set; our special price, per set of four ........................$1.35
Instruction Book Free with each set.

No. 8832. Boys' Boxing Gloves, made of all white kid and stuffed with a good quality of curled hair; ventilated palms, elastic wristbands; good shape; a well made glove that is durable and soft. Retails at $2.50; our special price, per set of four gloves..........$1.25
Instruction Book Free with each set.

## FRAZER'S PATENTED STRIKING BAG PLATFORM.

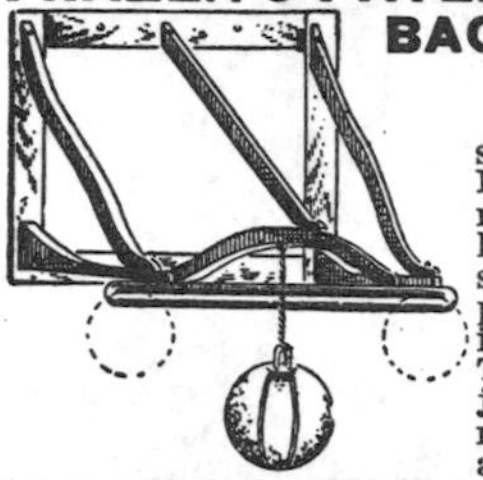

**Description.**

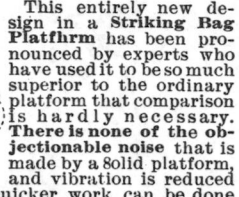

This entirely new design in a **Striking Bag Platfhrm** has been pronounced by experts who have used it to be so much superior to the ordinary platform that comparison is hardly necessary. **There is none of the objectionable noise** that is made by a Solid platform, and vibration is reduced to a minimum. Much quicker work can be done on it, owing to the fact that the bag strikes a small and solid surface, causing a lively rebound. The bag striking in the same position on the rim causes it to swing true from all sides. **All parts are made of highly polished hardwood.** This platform, although designed for gymnasium purposes, is particularly well adapted for home use, its neat appearance makes it possible to put it up where it may be accessible to every member of the family. Price, complete, ready to attach to wall, without bag..$9.75

## SINGLE END STRIKING BAGS.

No. 8833. **Single End Striking Bag**, 33 inches in circumferance, used by suspending from a low ceiling by the top rope. This bag is made of the **Best Selected Heavy Calfskin**, and will outwear two ordinary bags. Rubber bladder furnished free. Retails for $5; our special price, each, complete with attachments ........................$2.60

No. 8834. **Single End Striking Bag**, extra strongly made, of heavy calfskin, extra well sewed, and of great werring quality; complete with upper rope and rubber bladder. When inflated for use it is 33 inches in circumferance. Color, seal brown. **No Better Bag Made.** A most popular and desirable addition for gymnasium or private use. More muscular development can be had from this appliance than from any other indoor exercise. Our special price, complete, each........................$2.45

No. 8835. **Single End Striking Bag**, made of very excellent vuality of sheepskin, strongly sewed, and of superior wearing quality. Comes complete, with rubber bladder and attachments. When inflated for use the bag is 33 inches in circumference. Sold at retail up to $4. Our special price, each........................$1.85

(Special).—S., R. & Co's Canvas Striking Bags. Light and durable; single end; leather top loop. Complete, with rope and bladder. Our special price........................$1.25

## DOUBLE END STRIKING BAGS.

No. 8833½. Double End Striking Bag, with leather loop at top and bottom. Complete, with rope for ceiling, and rubber floor connection. Screw hook and bladder. Bag made of the **Best Select Calfskin**, 33 inches in circumference. One of the best made bags on the market. Regular price $6. Our special price...$3.65

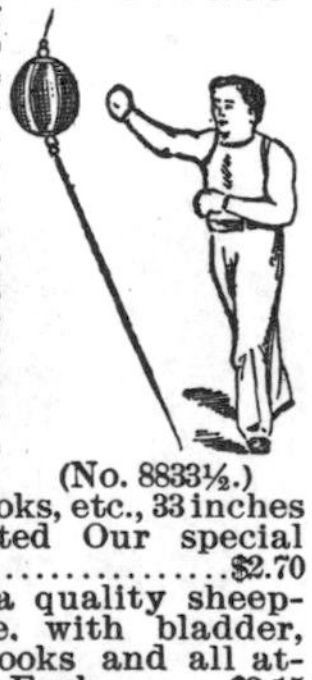

(No. 8833½.)

No. 8834½. Double End Striking Bag, made of fine calfskin, color seal brown, with strong leather loop at top and bottom. Complete, with rubber bladder, rope for attaching to ceiling, and rubber floor connection and screw hooks, etc., 33 inches in circumference when inflated Our special price........................$2.70

No. 8835½. Double End Bag, extra quality sheepskin, strongly made. Complete, with bladder, rope, rubber floor connection, hooks and all attachments. Each........$2.15

## INDIAN CLUBS.

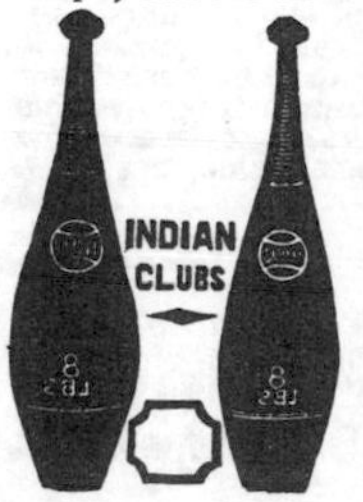


No. 8836. Sold in pairs only, and made of the best rock maple, and finely polished. Weight given is the weight on each club. If you order one pair 1 lb. clubs, you get two 1 lb. clubs, etc.

| | Per Pair. |
|---|---|
| 1 pound | $0.25 |
| 1½ pounds | .30 |
| 2 " | .35 |
| 3 " | .4s |
| 4 " | .55 |
| 5 " | .60 |

## DUMB BELLS.

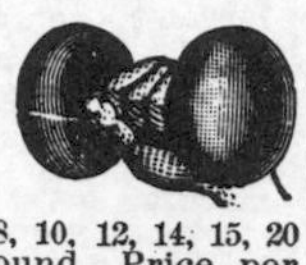

Our Iron Dumb Bells are Cast from pure gray iron, and are very much stronger and more durable than those ordinarily sold, which are usually made from scrap iron, tin, etc., and are very brittle and break easily. We make them with weights as follows: 1, 2, 3, 4, 5, 6, 8, 10, 12, 14, 15, 20 and 25 pounds each. Sold by the Pound. Price, per lb., 3c.; 50 lbs. 5c.; 75 lbs. 6c.; 100 lbs. 7c. per pound.

No. 8837. Wood Dumb Bells, made of polished maple.

| Weight | 1 lb. | 2 lb. | 3 lb. | 4 lb. |
|---|---|---|---|---|
| Per pair | 25c. | 30c. | 40c. | 50c. |

## FOOT BALLS.

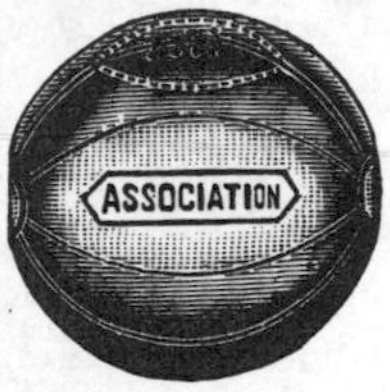


No. 8838. The Association Foot Ball, genuine, made of best Indian rubber bladder, with fine leather outside case, hand sewed, laced, round. Postage, about 20c. extra.

| | Each. |
|---|---|
| 22-inch circumference | $1.35 |
| 24-inch " | 1.55 |
| 27-inch " | 1.85 |
| 30-inch " | 1.95 |
| 33-inch " | 2.20 |

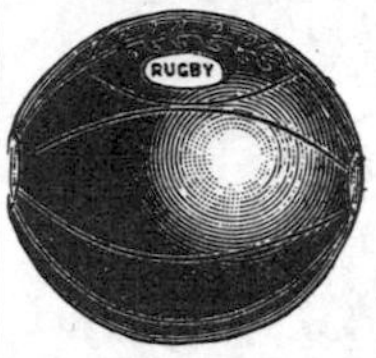


No. 8338. Rugby Foot Ball, oval shape, made of the best India rubber bladder, with outside leather case, hand sewed, laced. Best quality.

| | Each. |
|---|---|
| 22-inch circumference | $1.35 |
| 24-inch " | 1.45 |
| 27-inch " | 1.60 |
| 30-inch " | 1.80 |
| 33-inch " | 1.15 |

No. 8840. Extra Foot Bladders for either Rugby or Association Foot Balls. In ordering, state what kind is wanted.

| | Each. |
|---|---|
| For 22-inch ball, weight 8 oz | $0.45 |
| For 24-inch ball | .50 |
| For 27-inch ball | .59 |
| For 30-inch ball | .65 |
| For 33-inch ball | .70 |

## RUBBER FOOT BALLS.

No. 8841. American Rouod Rubber Foot Ball. By mail, 7c. to 12c. extra.

| | |
|---|---|
| No. 1, 6-inch diameter | $0.35 |
| No. 2, 7-inch " | .40 |
| No. 3, 8-inch " | .47 |
| No. 4, 9-inch " | .54 |
| No. 5, 10-inch " | .62 |
| No. 6, 11-inch " | .69 |

No. 8842. Extra keys for foot ball, etc., 5c.

## FOOT BALL INFLATERS.

No. 8843. Pocket Foot Ball Inflaters, nickeled tubes for filling up bladders, 35c.

Rubber Foot Balls, Rugby shape, made of heavy rubber, one size only, regulation, No. 5, each $1.90.

No. 8844. Foot Ball Inflaters, large club size, solid brass metal, new design and the best, polished brass, length 13½ in. Each 75c. By mail 6c. extra.

Prices on Foot Ball Clothing will be furnished on application. Lowest prices guaranteed.

## HORIZONTAL BARS.

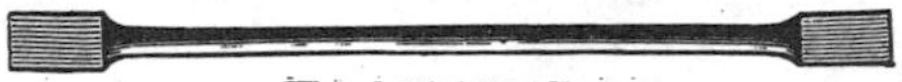

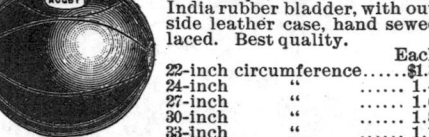

Weight 4½ to 6 lbs.

No. 8845. Made of the best quality second growth straight hickory, square ends.

| | |
|---|---|
| 4 ft. long | $0.50 |
| 4½ ft. long | .60 |
| 5 ft. long | .70 |
| 5½ ft. long | .95 |
| 6 ft. long | 1.20 |

## TRAPEZE BARS.

Weight, 2 to 3½ pounds.

No. 8246. Made of the best second growth hickory, Without ropes.

| | Each. |
|---|---|
| 2 ft. Bar, without ropes | $0.45 |
| 2½ ft. Bar, " | .48 |
| 3 ft. Bar, " | .55 |
| 3½ ft. Bar, " | .60 |
| 4 ft. Bar, " | .70 |

We make any length of rope to order, 8c. per foot.

## BASE BALL GOODS.

The largest and best manufacturers in the world contribute to this department. We show the most select line of Base Ball supplies ever put on the market. Our past and steadily increasing trade warrants our making an unusually large contract, and by so doing we have secured prices far lower than any retail dealer dreams of getting. We hence offer the best goods at prices against which none can compete. We have one favor to ask in connection with this department. Do not compare our goods with the cheap, trashy Base Ball supplies usually carried in stores. The greater part of such goods sold at retail are not worth carrying away. As stated above, our goods are made by the best factories, are good goods and stay good.

## OUR LIBERAL TERMS.

**On all orders amounting to more than $4.00** we ship C. O. D. by express, subject to examination, when one-fourth cash accompanies order, balance, with express charges, to be paid to express agent when goods are examined and found exactly as represented and perfectly satisfactory. You can easily dispose of a dozen balls and can sell at double the price you pay and **then undersell all local dealers.** make some pin money for yourself and let us supply you with goods that are of the very best that can be had in the country. We are anxious to push our Base Ball supplies this season, as it is going to be one of the greatest base ball years ever known. We can supply Base Ball Clubs at prices never equaled.

**SPECIAL RATES TO CLUBS BUYING $20 OR MORE SUPPLIES.**

Write for prices.

## BASE BALLS.

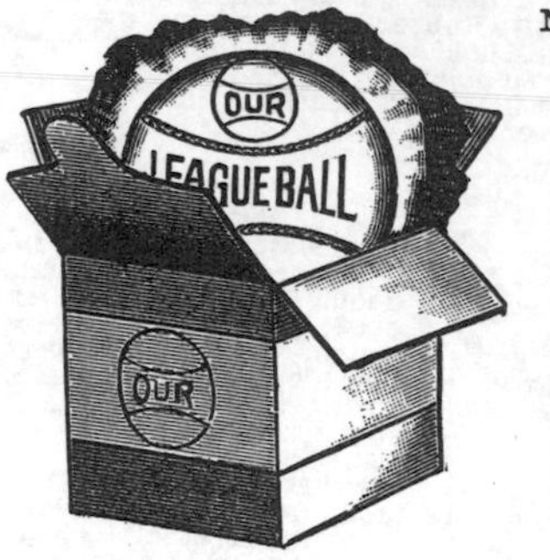


No. 8880. The Genuine Spalding League Ball, the Official Base Ball adopted by the League and American Association of Professional Base Ball Clubs. Warranted to last a full game without ripping or losing its elasticity or shape. Positively the finest Base Ball made. Each ball in a separate box. Our special price.... ...$1.25
Postage 8c.

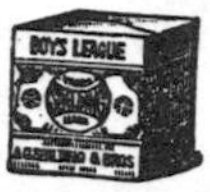


No. 8881. The Spalding Official Boys' League Ball, for junior Clubs. The best of the kind made. The only satisfactory ball used by boys' clubs. Each ball in a separate sealed box.
Our special price........................$ .72
Special dozen price........................ 8.25
Extra by mail 8c.

No. 8882. The Spalding Double Seam Ball, double stitched. A Base Ball that is just as popular and desirable as the Official League Ball, and of just the same quality and durability. Each ball in a separate box and sealed. Our special price........................$ 1.10
Per dozen........................ 12 95
Postage 8c.

No. 8883. Wright & Ditson's League Ball, regulation size and weight, warranted to last a full game. In fact this ball will give the same service as any other ball. Each ball in a separate box and sealed.
Our special price........................$ .85
Per dozen........................ 9.95
Postage 8c.

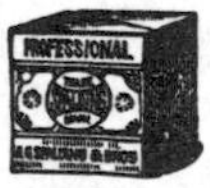


No. 8884. "Professional" Ball, regulation size and weight. A ball that will give best of service and one that is bought very largely by semi-professional clubs. Each ball in a separate sealed box.
Our special price each.............$ .73
Per dozen........................ 8.00
Postage 8c.

No. 8885. Boys' "Professional" Base Ball, same as No. 8884 above, but of smaller size. A ball of wonderful wearing quality and one that retails at twice our price. Each ball in a separate sealed box.
Our price each........................$ .36
Per dozen........................ 4.00
Postage 8c.

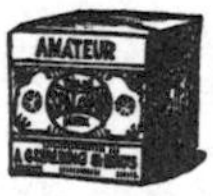


No. 8886. Amateur Ball. A Base Ball that has had a very large sale with us. Has fine horsehide cover and is regulation size. Each ball in a separate sealed box.
Our special price each.............$ .58
Our special dozen price............ 6.30
Postage 8c.

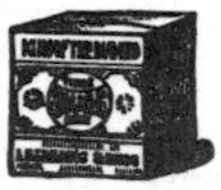

No. 8887. "King of the Diamond," regulation size and well made. The best cheap Base Ball ever sold. Each ball in a separate sealed box. Our special price each........................$ .35
Per dozen........................ 3.75
Postage 8c.

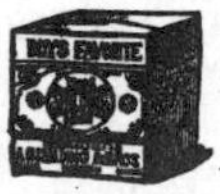

No. 8888. "Boys Favorite," regulation size Base Ball with strong horsehide cover. A ball that will stand a great deal of usage. Retails at 30c. Each ball in a separate sealed box. Each....$ .22
Per dozen........................ 2.20
Postage 8c.

No. 8889. League Junior Base Ball. Well made with fine horsehide cover, strongly sewed. Slightly under regulation size. Each........................$ .20
Per dozen........................ 2.20
Postage 8c.

No. 8890. "Bouncer." A very lively and high bounding Base Ball, unusually well made of select center and cover. Each........................$ .18
Per dozen........................ 2.00
Postage 7c.

No. 8891. "Victor" Ball. Regulation size. A good one for the money, one that will outlast two or three of the cheap ones sold at a higher price elsewhere. Each, 14c; per dozen, $1.50; postage, 7c.

No. 8892. Boys' "Amateur" Ball, a little under regulation size, but a splendid ball for the money. Sold ordinarily for 20 to 25 cents. Our special price, 13c; per dozen, $1.20; postage, 8c.

No. 8893. Eureka Base Ball, nearly regulation size, and will give best of satisfaction. Each, 8c; per dozen, 85c; postage, 5c.

No. 8894. "Boys' Lively" Ball, a high bounder; well made and durable. Our special price, each 8c: per dozen, 80c; postage, 5c.

No. 8895. "Rocket" Ball, the best anywhere at twice the price. Each, 5c; per doz., 55c; postage, 5c.

No. 8896. "Dandy" Ball, made with a strong two-piece cover. Each, 4c; per doz., 45c; postage, 5c.

No. 8897. "Boss" Ball, a good one to knock around and is worth three times our price. Each, 3c; per dozen, 35c; postage, 5c.

## BASE BALL BATS.

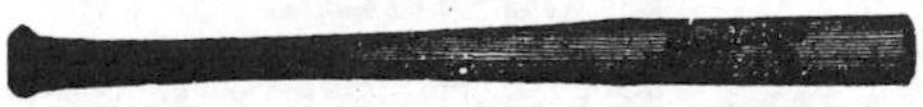

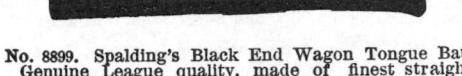

No. 8898. Genuine Spalding League Model Bats, made of finest selected and season timber, oil finish. This is the finest and best balanced bat made and will stand harder usage than any other bat on the market. Each bat in a separate bag. Lengths, 33, 34, 35 and 36 inches. Each ........................ $0.75

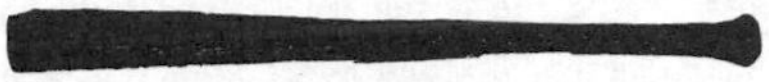

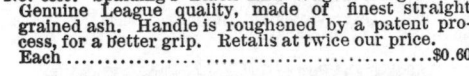

No. 8899. Spalding's Black End Wagon Tongue Bat. Genuine League quality, made of finest straight grained ash. Handle is roughened by a patent process, for a better grip. Retails at twice our price. Each ........................ $0.60

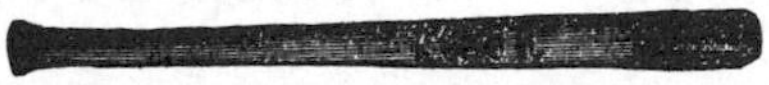

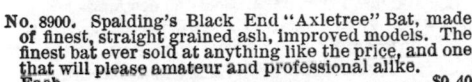

No. 8900. Spalding's Black End "Axletree" Bat, made of finest, straight grained ash, improved models. The finest bat ever sold at anything like the price, and one that will please amateur and professional alike. Each ........................ $0.40

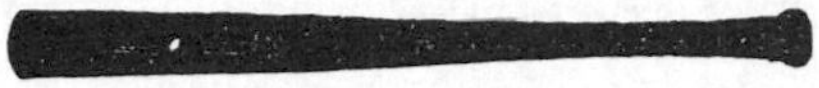

No. 8906. Spalding's Black End "Antique" Finish Bat, made of extra quality ash. Very strong and well made. Each ........................ $0.20

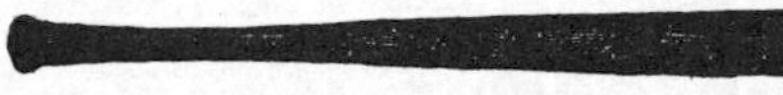

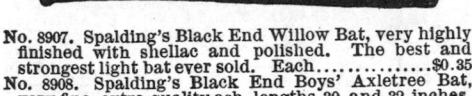

No. 8907. Spalding's Black End Willow Bat, very highly finished with shellac and polished. The best and strongest light bat ever sold. Each ............ $0.35

No. 8908. Spalding's Black End Boys' Axletree Bat, very fine, extra quality ash, lengths 30 and 32 inches. A special grade that will give best satisfaction. Each ........................ $0.20

No. 8909. Spalding's Black End Youth's Maple Bat, stained and polished, and decorated with gilt stripes. Extra value and worth double the money. Each .. $0.10

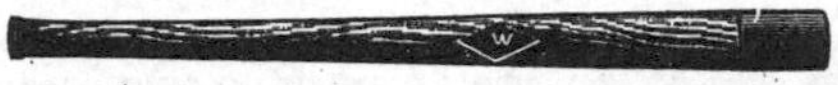

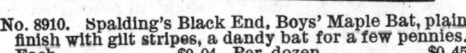

No. 8910. Spalding's Black End, Boys' Maple Bat, plain finish with gilt stripes, a dandy bat for a few pennies. Each ............ $0.04 Per dozen ............ $0.45

## BASE BALL MITTS.

Our stock includes all kinds, Catchers, Basemen's, Infielders' Mitts, as well as Infielders' Gloves, all of the very best that can be made. Special inducements to clubs purchasing $20.00 or more at one time. Our terms on all orders of $5.00 or more are very liberal. C. O. D., subject to examination on receipt of one-fourth of order.

## SPALDING'S CATCHERS' MITTS.

All of our Mitts are furnished for either the right or left hand. The Left Hand Mitt always sent unless otherwise ordered. **No Throwing Glove** furnished with any of our Mitts this season.

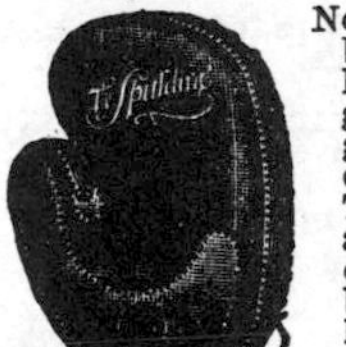


No. 8912.

No. 8912. Basemen's Mitt. This Mitt bearing the trade mark of our highest quality goods, is sufficient guarantee that it is the most perfect glove in all its details that our past experience enables us to produce. The leather is of the finest quality adapted for that purpose, the padding and workmanship of the very best, and the additional feature of lace back make it—as we intend it shall be—the "PERFECTION" of Catchers' Mitts. Made in rights and lefts. Regular price ..... $7.50
Our price, each ........................ $5.50

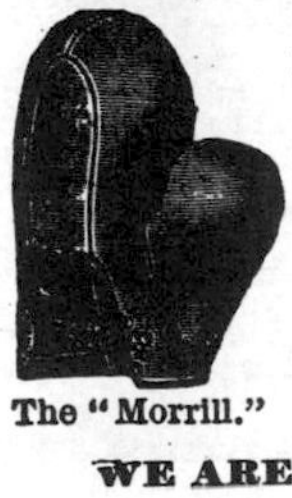

The "Morrill."

No. 8913. The "Morrill" Mitt is after the design of the well-known ball player, John Morrill, and has become very popular. It is made throughout of finest quality drab buckskin, is very heavily padded with the softest felt, and thumb laced to palm to prevent ripping. An extremely easy fitting mitt. Made in rights and lefts. Not laced back. Each ............ $4.50

Base Ball Mitts.—Continued.

No. 8914. League Mitt. Is made throughout of specially tanned and selected hogskin, making a strong and durable mitt, the same time being very soft and pliable. It has our patent lace back and heavily padded. Made in rights and lefts. Each ............ $3.75

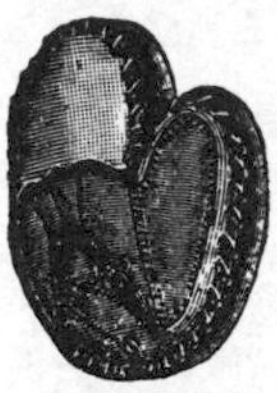

No. 8916.

No. 8915. The Spalding Mitt, face, sides and finger-pieces are made of velvet tanned deerskin, and the back of fine hogskin, making an exceedingly easy-fitting and durable mitt. It has our patent lace back and well padded. Made in rights and lefts. Each ............ $2.15

No. 8916. Spalding's "Decker Patent" Mitt is made exactly the same as our No. 8915 Mitt, with the addition of a heavy piece of sole leather on back for extra protection to the hand and fingers, as shown in cut. It has as well the patent lace back, and is extremely well padded. Made in rights and lefts. Each ........................ $2.50

No. 8917. Spalding's Amateur Mitt is made of extra quality asbestos buck, perspiration proof and extremely tough and durable. It has our patent lace back, reinforced at thumb and well made and padded. Made in rights and lefts. Each .............. $1.65

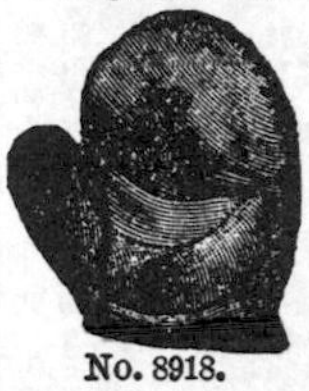

No. 8918.

No. 8918. The Spalding Practice Mitt. The face and finger-piece of our Practice Mitt are made of light brown tanned suede leather, the edge strip and back of ecru tanned suede. It has our patent lace back, reinforced at thumb and substantially padded. Made in rights and lefts.
Each ........................ 75c

## SPALDING'S BOYS' CATCHERS' MITTS.

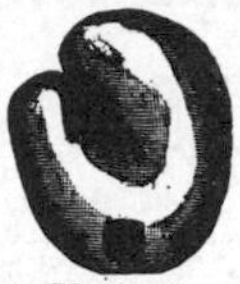

No. 8920.

No. 8919. Spalding's "Decker Patent" Boys' League Mitt; face, edge strip and finger-piece made of velvet tanned deerskin, the back of fine hogskin, very soft and perspiration proof. The heavy piece of sole leather on back affords extra protection to hand and fingers. It has the patent lace back and is extra well padded. Made in rights and lefts. Each ........ $1.80

No. 8920. Spalding's Boys' Mitt; face and finger-piece of mitt made of dark tanned leather, the back and edge strip of light tanned asbestos buck. It has our patent lace back, well padded and finished and reinforced at thumb. Made in rights and lefts, and little larger in size than our regular Boys' Mitts. Each ......... $1.25

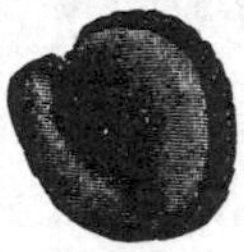

No. 8921.

No. 8921. Spalding's Boys' Mitts; front and finger-piece of this mitt are made of light brown tanned suede leather, the back and edge strip ecru tanned. It is extremely well padded and nicely finished throughout, and has our patent lace back. Made in rights and lefts. Each ........................ 39c

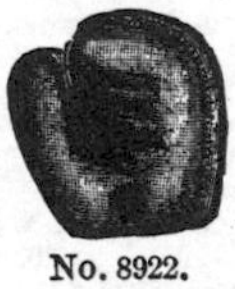

No. 8922.

No. 8922. Spalding's Boys' Mitt; front and back made of ecru tanned leather, the edge strip of lighter tanned leather. Well made throughout, heavily padded and superior to any boys' mitt ever offered at the price. Each ........................ 20c

## SPALDING'S BASEMEN'S MITT.

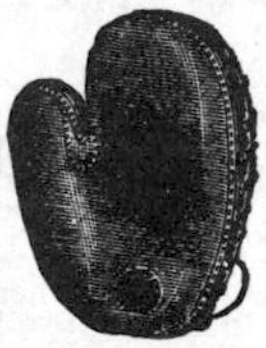

No. 8923.

No. 8923. Basemen's Mitt, made of fine selected and specially tanned calfskin, extremely well made throughout and padded to meet the special requirements of a baseman's mitt. It adapts itself nicely to the conformation of the hand without undue straining, and the addition of our patent lace back and "Highest Quality" trade mark is a sufficient guarantee of its quality and merits. Made in rights and lefts. Each ........ $3.60

## SPALDING'S BASEMEN'S AND INFIELDERS' MITTS.

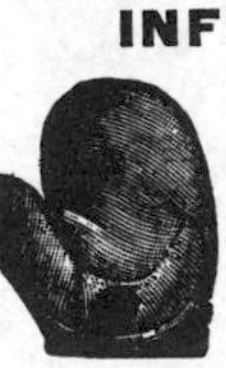

No. 8924.

No. 8924. Mitt, made of the very best and softest light tanned buckskin; the thumb and at wrist are extra well padded with the highest quality felt, making it a very safe and easy fitting mitt combined with strength and durability. The mitt throughout is of the best workmanship, as indicated by our "Highest Quality" trade mark. Made in rights and lefts. Each ............ $2.55

Base Ball Mitts.—Continued.

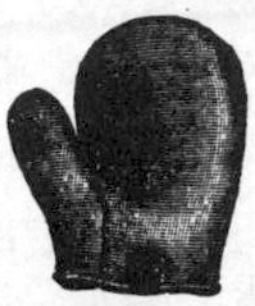

No. 8925.

No. 8925. Spalding's Basemen's and Infielders' Mitt is constructed throughout of velvet tanned deerskin and edges morocco bound. It is well padded with fine felt and carefully sewed and finished. Made in rights and lefts. Each ............ $1.80

No. 8926. Spalding's Basemen's and Infielders' Mitt, made of good quality suede leather, nicely padded, and constructed throughout in a most substantial manner, making an exceedingly good mitt at a popular price. Made in rights and lefts. Each ...... 85c

### BOYS' BASEMEN'S AND INFIELDERS' MITT.

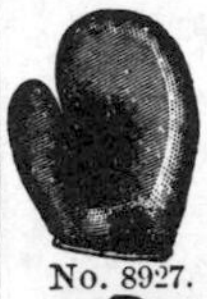

No. 8927.

No. 8927. Spalding's Boys' Basemen's Mitt is made throughout of a good quality leather. It is well padded and makes a good and substantial mitt for boys. Made in rights and lefts. Each ...... 40c

## INFIELDERS' GLOVE.

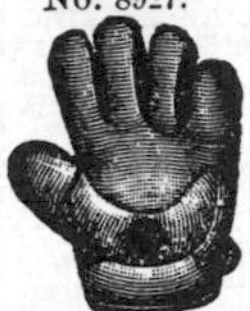

No. 8928.

No. 8928. Infielders' Glove is made throughout of selected velvet tanned buckskin, lined and correctly padded with finest felt. It fits the hand perfectly and our trade mark "Highest Quality" is a guarantee that the glove is perfect in all its details. Made in rights and lefts.
Each ........................ $2.25

### INFIELDERS' GLOVES.

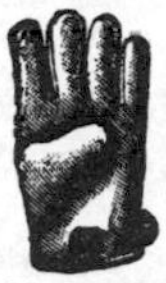

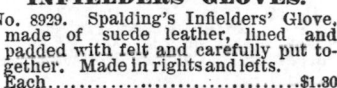

No. 8929.

No. 8929. Spalding's Infielders' Glove, made of suede leather, lined and padded with felt and carefully put together. Made in rights and lefts.
Each ........................ $1.30

No. 8930. Spalding's Men's Infielders' Glove, all leather; a substantial glove at a popular price. Each ............ $0.95

### BOYS' INFIELDERS' GLOVES.

No. 8931. Spalding's Boys' Infielders' Glove, quality and style as our No. 8929 in boys' sizes. Each ............ $0.95

## PITCHER'S TOE PLATES.

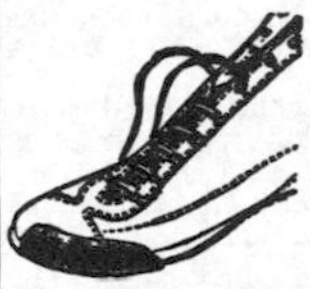

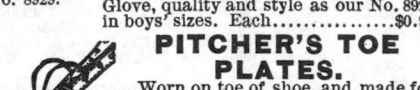

Worn on toe of shoe, and made for left or right foot. A valuable assistant in pitching.

No. 8932. Aluminum toe plate, Each, ........................ $0.35

No. 8933. Brass toe plate. Each .18

### SPALDING'S MASKS.

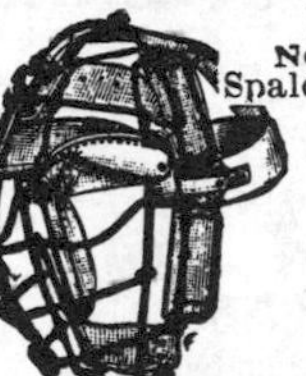

No. 8935.

Black Enameled Sun Protecting No. 8935. Mask—Patented. Spalding's League. This is not only the "Highest Quality" mask made, but has also patent sunshade, which is formed by a piece of molded leather securely fastened to top, forming a perfect shade to the eye without obstructing the view or materially increasing the weight of the mask. Made of best soft annealed steel wire, extra heavy and black enameled, thus further preventing the reflection of light. The mask throughout is constructed of the very best material and has been highly endorsed by the leading catchers. Each ........................ $4.00

### SPALDING'S BLACK ENAMELED MASKS.

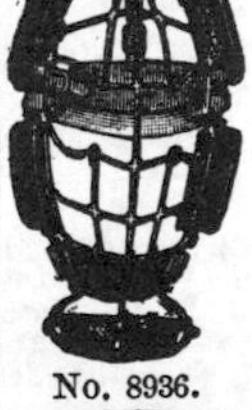

No. 8936.

No. 8936. Patent Neck Protecting Mask has an extension at bottom giving absolute protection to the neck, without interfering in the least with the movements of the head. The wire is of best annealed steel, is extra heavy and covered with black enamel to prevent the reflection of light. The padding is filled with goat hair and faced with finest imported dogskin, which, being impervious to perspiration, always remains soft and pleasant to the face. Each ........ $2.50

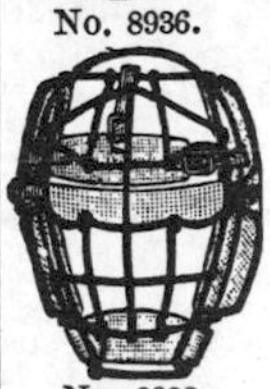

No. 8938.

No. 8937. Special League Mask, made of extra heavy and best soft annealed steel wire, black enameled, the padding filled with goat hair and covered with finest imported dogskin. Each ........................ $1.95

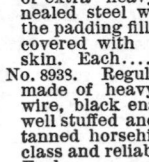

No. 8938. Regulation League Mask, made of heavy soft annealed steel wire, black enameled, the padding well stuffed and faced with specially tanned horsehide. Warranted first-class and reliable in every particular. Each ........................ $1.85

## REGULATION LEAGUE MASKS.

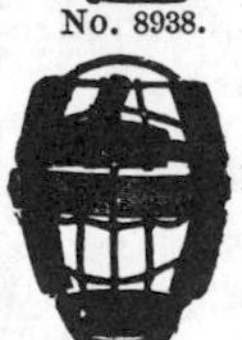

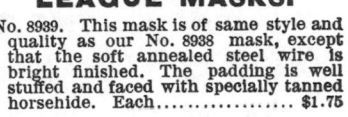

No. 8939.

No. 8939. This mask is of same style and quality as our No. 8938 mask, except that the soft annealed steel wire is bright finished. The padding is well stuffed and faced with specially tanned horsehide. Each ........................ $1.75

WE ARE SELLING AGENTS FOR THE CELEBRATED WINCHESTER REPEATING SHOT GUNS AND RIFLES, AND MARLIN REPEATING RIFLES.

## SPALDING'S AMATEUR MASKS

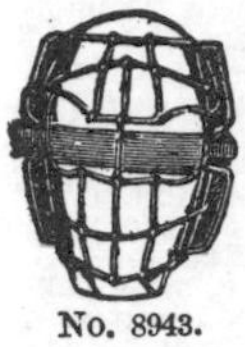

No. 8943.

No. 8940. Spalding's Amateur Mask, made in same size and general style as our League masks, but of lighter soft annealed steel wire, well padded, strongly constructed and warranted perfectly safe. Each............ $1.10

No. 8941. Spalding's Amateur Boys' mask, made in same style and quality as No. A mask, only smaller in size, for boys. Each ............................ $0.85

No. 8942. Spalding's Youth's Masks, heavy wire and well padded, without head or chin piece. Each............................ $0.55

No. 8943. Spalding's Youths' Masks, light wire padded, without head or chin piece. Each......... $0.40

No. 8944. Spalding's Boys' Masks, light wire and padded, without head or chin piece. Each........... $0.20

## SPALDING'S INFLATED BODY PROTECTOR.

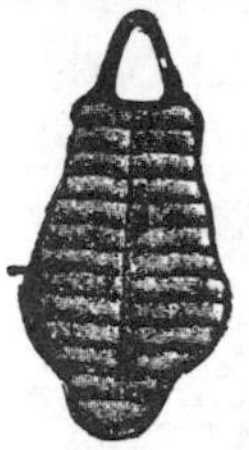

No. 8948.

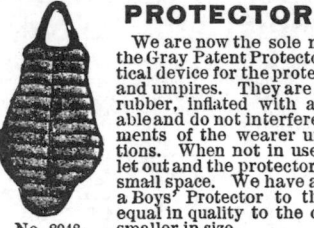

We are now the sole manufacturers of the Gray Patent Protectors, the only practical device for the protection of catchers and umpires. They are made of the best rubber, inflated with air, light and pliable and do not interfere with the movements of the wearer under any conditions. When not in use the air may be let out and the protector rolled in a very small space. We have added this season a Boys' Protector to the line, which is equal in quality to the other styles, only smaller in size.

No. 8948. League Catchers' Protector............. $7.50
No. 8949. Amateur Catchers' Protector.......... 4.25
No. 8950. Boys' Catchers' Protector.............. 4.15

## SPALDING'S SPECIAL LEAGUE SHOE PLATES. (Patented.)

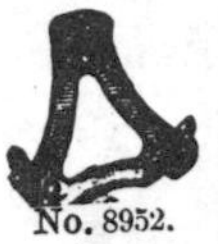

No. 8952.

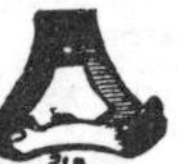

No. 8953.

Our Special League Plates are made of the finest tempered steel and the strength increased almost fourfold without increasing weight by our patent reinforced brace, which is formed as shown in cut by splitting the metal at each corner and depressing the center, thus forming a brace at each side.

No. 8952. Spalding's Special Hand Forged Steel Toe Plates........pair $0.35
No. 8953. Spalding's Special Hand Forged Steel Heel Plates.......pair .35
Per dozen pairs............................ 4.00

## PROFESSIONAL SHOE PLATES.

No. 8954.

No. 8954. Spalding's Professional Toe Plates, best quality steel........pair $0.20
No. 8955. Spalding's Professional Heel Plates, best quality steel.......pair .20
Per dozen pairs............................ 2.25

## AMATEUR SHOE PLATES.

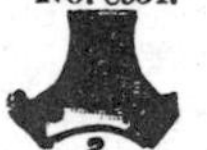

No. 8956.

No. 8956. Spalding's Amateur Shoe Plates, fine steel..............pair $0.08
Per dozen pairs........................... .09

## SPALDING'S UMPIRE INDICATOR.

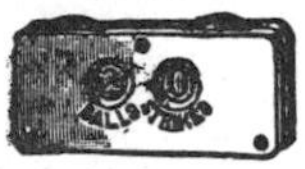

No. 8958.

No. 8958. Made of celluloid, exact size 3 x 1½ inches. It is intended for keeping tally of balls and strikes. Endorsed and used by all League umpires............... $0.39

## SPALDING'S SCORING TABLET.

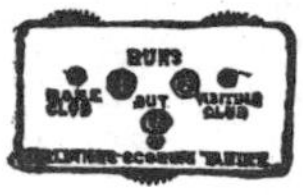

No. 8959.

No. 8959. A simple, convenient and accurate device for the record of runs and outs. It is made of celluloid and can easily be carried in any vest pocket......$0 .29

## SPALDING'S BASES.

Three Bases to a set.

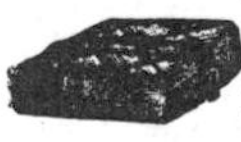

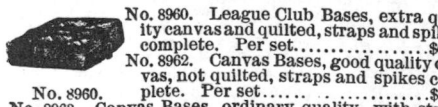

No. 8960.

No. 8960. League Club Bases, extra quality canvas and quilted, straps and spikes, complete. Per set................$6.55

No. 8962. Canvas Bases, good quality canvas, not quilted, straps and spikes complete. Per set......................$4.75

No. 8963. Canvas Bases, ordinary quality, with straps and spikes, complete. Per set..................$3 40

Home plates not included in above sets.

## SPALDING'S HOME PLATES.

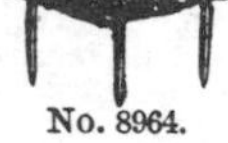

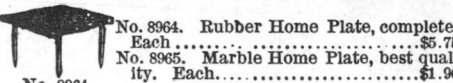

No. 8964.

No. 8964. Rubber Home Plate, complete, Each ........................................$5.75

No. 8965. Marble Home Plate, best quality. Each....................................$1.90

## SPALDING'S PITCHER'S BOX PLATES.

No. 8966.

Made in accordance with National League regulations and of extra quality white rubber. Complete with pins.

No. 8966. Spalding's Pitcher's Box Plates. Each.......................$4.50

## SPALDING'S CLUB BAGS.

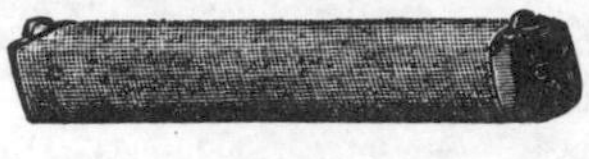

No. 8970.

No. 8968. League Club Bag, sole leather, for 18 bats. Each...........................................$15.00
No. 8969. Canvas Club Bag, leather ends, for 24 bats. Each.............................................$ 4.35
No. 8970. Canvas Club Bag, leather ends, for 12 bats. Each..............................................$ 3.40

## INDIVIDUAL BAGS.

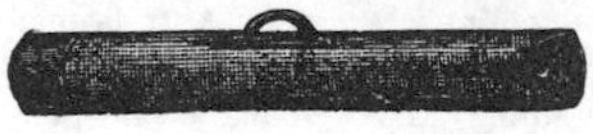

No. 8972.

No. 8971. Sole Leather Bag, for two bats. Each...$3.60
No. 8972. Heavy Canvas Bag, Leather reinforce at both ends. Each..........................................$1.45
No. 8973. Canvas Bag, Leather reinforce at one end. Each..............................................$ .90

## SCORE BOOKS.

CLUB SIZES.

No. 8975. Board Cover, 30 games. Each...........$0.75
No. 8976. Cloth Cover, 60 games. Each............ 1.30
No. 8977. Cloth Cover, 90 games. Each............ 1.90
No. 8978. Cloth Cover, 102 games. Each........... 2.25

POCKET SIZES.

No. 8979. Paper Cover, 7 games. Each..............8c
No. 8980. Board Cover, 22 games. Each.............19c
No. 8981. Board Cover, 46 games. Each.............38c
Score Cards, per dozen, 19c.

## BASE BALL CAPS.

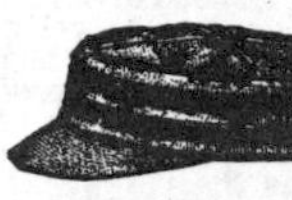

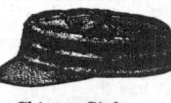

Chicago Style.

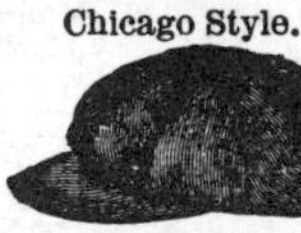

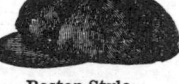

Boston Style.

Chicago or Boston styles.

No. 8983. Quality, best flannel. Each..............................90c
No. 8984. Quality, lighter flannel. Each.........................73c
No. 8985. Quality, good flannel. Each..............................60c
No. 8986. Quality, ordinary flannel. Each........................45c
No. 8987. Quality, light flannel. Each..............................32c

## BASE BALL BELTS.

**Worsted Web Belts.**

In all colors.

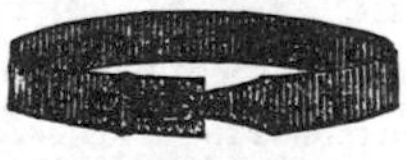

No. 8988.

No. 8988. Special League Belt, worsted web, 2½ inches wide, leather lined, large nickel plated buckle. Each ........................72c

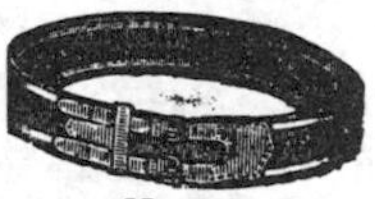

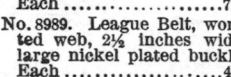

No. 8990.

No. 8989. League Belt, worsted web, 2½ inches wide, large nickel plated buckle. Each ........................45c

No. 8990. Worsted Web Belt, 2½ inches wide, double strap, leather covered buckles. Each...............36c

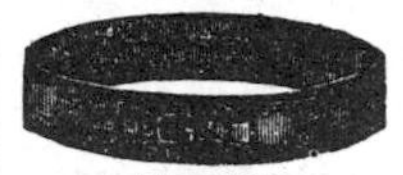

No. 8991.

No. 8991. Worsted Web Belt, 2½ inches wide, single strap, leather covered buckle. Each.......................36c

**Cotton Web Belts.**

Colors: Red, Navy, White, Maroon and Stripes.

No. 8992. Cotton Web Belt, 2½ inches wide, double strap, nickel buckles. Each.................................21c
No. 8993. Cotton Web Belt, 2½ inches, leather mounted, single strap and buckle. Each...............................14c

**ATHLETE'S UNIFORM BAG.**

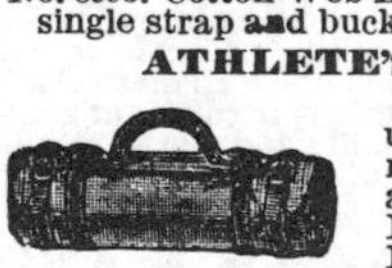

For carrying base ball and other uniforms. Made to roll, and will not wrinkle or soil same. Separate compartments for shoes.

No. 8994. Canvas. Each....$1.95
No. 8995. Fine bag leather. Each ..................................$4.00

## SPALDING'S BASE BALL SHOES.

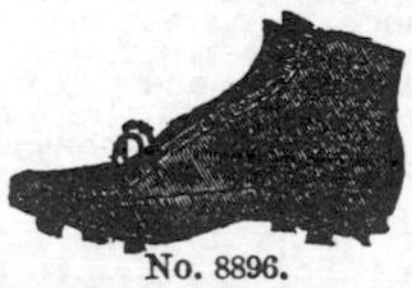

No. 8896.

No. 8996. Selected kangaroo, hand made throughout, and special steel plate riveted to heel and toe. Per pair...$6.50

No. 8997. Spalding's "University" base-ball shoe, kangaroo calf, hand-sewed and hand-forged steel plates riveted to heel and sole. Per pair..$5.75

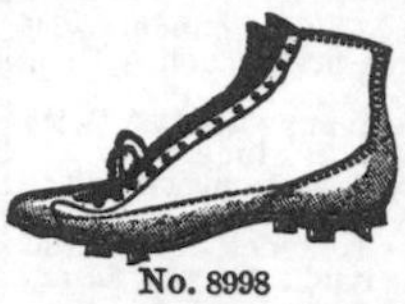

No. 8998

No. 8998. Spalding's "Club Special" shoe, satin calf-skin, steel plates riveted to heel and sole. Per pair........$4 25

No. 8999. Spalding's "Amateur Special" Shoe, good quality calfskin, plates riveted to heel and sole. Per pair ......$2.95

## SPALDING'S BASE BALL STOCKINGS.

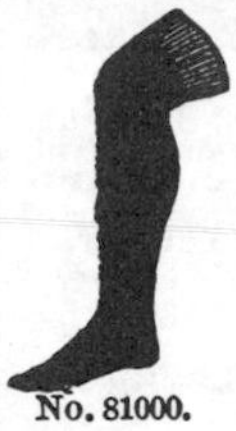

No. 81000.

No. 81000. Stocking, heavy ribbed, full fashioned and special weave. Colors: Black, Maroon, Navy, Gray, and other colors to order. Per pair ........$1.30
Per half dozen ........................................ 7.50

No. 81000½. Same stocking in any combination of colors. Per pair........$1.45
Per half dozen...................................... 8.25

**REGULAR STOCKINGS.**

Made in full lengths and furnished in following stock colors: Black, Navy, Maroon, Red and Royal Blue.

| | | Per pair. | Per half doz. |
|---|---|---|---|
| No. 81001. | Heavy all wool stocking | $0.90 | $5.00 |
| No. 81002. | Medium weight, all wool | .66 | 3.60 |
| No. 81003. | Ordinary weight stocking | .42 | 2.40 |
| No. 81004. | Cotton stocking | .25 | 1.40 |

## SPALDING'S LINEN SOLE STOCKINGS.

Soles knit of finest linen. Cool and comfortable.

No. 81005. Heavy weight, ribbed. Pair............$1.15
Half dozen pairs.......................................... 6.50

**STOCKING SUPPORTERS.**

The most comfortable hose supporter made.

No. 81006. Supporters, shoulder, per pair..........$0.40
No. 81007. Supporters, waist ......................... .28

## SPALDING'S BASE BALL SHIRTS.

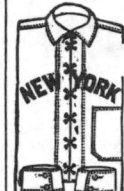

In lace or button front.

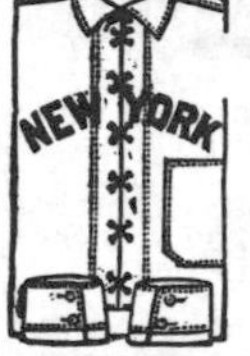


Each.

No. 81010. Shirt, any style..........$5.25
No. 81011. The "University" shirt, any style...........................$4.15
No. 81012. "Interscholastic" shirt, any style..........................$3.75
No. 81013. "Club Special" shirt, any style...........................$2.50
No. 81014. "Amateur Special" shirt, any style...........................$1.85

Price includes lettering on shirts.

## SPALDING'S BASE BALL PANTS.

Our Pants are all heavily padded and quilted.

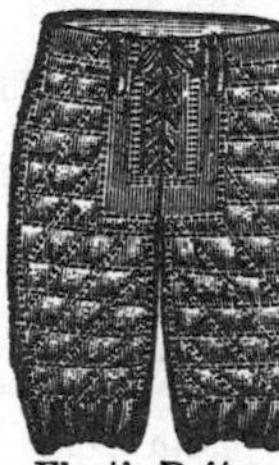

Elastic Bottom.

In tape or elastic bottom. All padded.

Pair.

No. 81015. Pants..............$5.80
No. 81016. "University" pants 4.40
No. 81017. "Interscholastic" pants ........................$3.40
No. 81018. "Club Special" pants ........................$2.40
No. 81019. "Amateur Special" pants ......................$1.75

## SPALDING'S BASE BALL UNIFORMS.

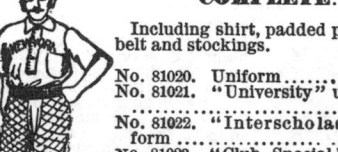

**COMPLETE.**

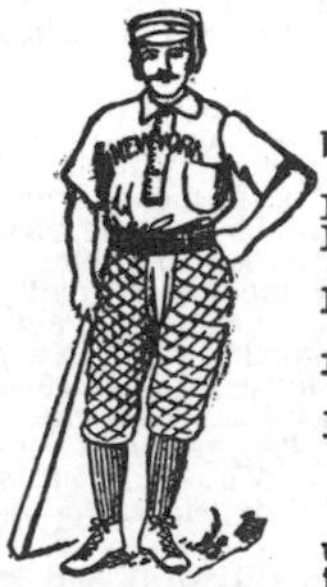

Including shirt, padded pants, cap, belt and stockings.

No. 81020. Uniform ...........$13.50
No. 81021. "University" uniform... ..................................$10.65
No. 81022. "Interscholastic" uniform ............................$8.70
No. 81023. "Club Special" uniform ..................................$6.25
No. 81024. "Amateur Special" uniform ...........................$4.30

Our line of flannels for base ball uniforms consists of the best qualities in their respective grades, and the most desirable colors for base ball uniforms. Each grade is kept up to the highest point of excellence and quality improved wherever possible every season. Owing to the heavy weight flannels used in our Nos 81020 and 81021 uniforms, we have found it desirable, after many years of experience, to use a little lighter weight material for the shirts; this makes them more comfortable, much cooler, and wear just as well as the heavier weight. If, however, you prefer the heavier goods for the shirts, they will be supplied at same price, but only when *specially ordered.*

**OUT-OF-DOOR SPORTSMEN WANT SWEATERS AND SUITS AND ALL THE ETCETERAS NECESSARY FOR SPORT. WE ARE HEADQUARTERS FOR CLOSE BUYERS.**

## SPALDING'S ELASTIC BANDAGES.

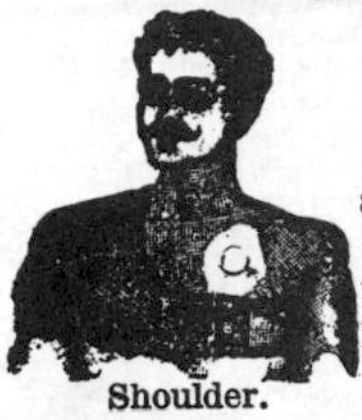
Shoulder.

### SHOULDER CAP BANDAGE.

In ordering, give circumference around arm and chest separately.

Each.
No. 81030. Cotton thread......$3.25
No. 81031. Silk thread......... 4.40

### ELBOW BANDAGE.

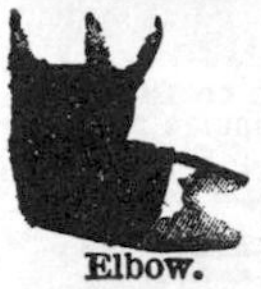
Elbow.

In ordering, give circumference above and below elbow, and state whether intended for light or strong pressure.

Each.
No. 81032. Cotton thread..........$1.45
No. 81033. Silk thread.............. 1.85

### FORE ARM BANDAGE.

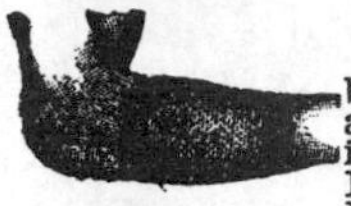
Fore Arm.

In ordering, give circumference below elbow and just above wrist, and state if light or strong pressure is desired. Each.
No. 81034. Cotton thread.......$1.45
No. 81035. Silk thread.......... 1.85

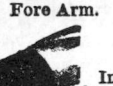

### KNEE CAP BANDAGE.

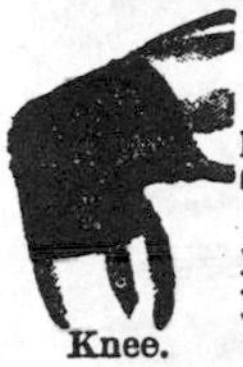
Knee.

In ordering, give circumference below knee, at knee, and just above knee, and state if light or strong pressure is desired.

Each.
No. 81036. Cotton thread............ $1.45
No. 81037. Silk thread................ 1.85

### ANKLE BANDAGE.

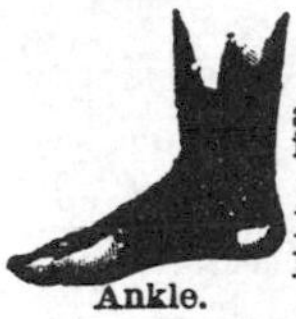
Ankle.

In ordering, give circumference around ankle and over instep, and state if light or strong pressure is desired.

Each.
No. 81038. Cotton thread..........$1.45
No. 81039. Silk thread............... 1.85

### WRIST BANDAGE.

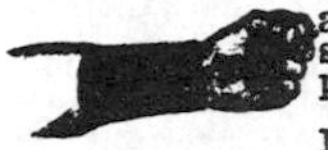
Wrist.

In ordering, give circumference around smallest part of wrist, and state whether for light or strong pressure.

Each.
No. 81040. Cotton thread.........$0.62
No. 81041. Silk thread............ .85

## SUPPORTERS AND BANDAGES.

### IMPROVED MORTON SUPPORTERS.

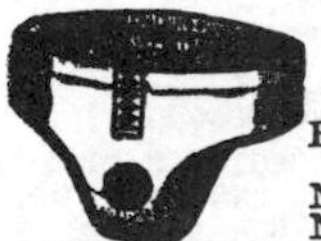
Morton Supporter.

Made of Canton flannel, lace front. Each supporter in separate box.

Each.
No. 81042. Improved Morton.....$0.25
No. 81043. Elastic on sides and back.......................... .45

### ELASTIC BANDAGES

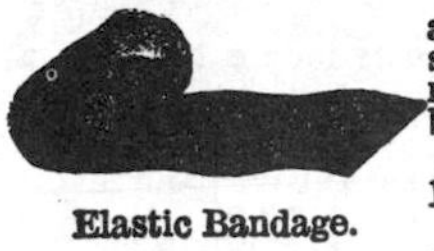
Elastic Bandage.

This bandage is light, porous and easily applied. The pressure can be applied wherever necessary and quickly secured by inserting end under last fold.

Each.
No. 81044. Width 2¼ inches 5 yards long (stretched) $0.50
No. 81045. Width 3 inches, 5 yards long (stretched) .75

### LEATHER WRIST SUPPORTER.

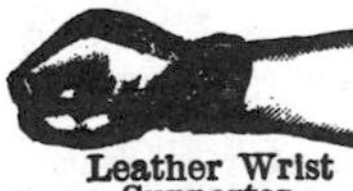
Leather Wrist Supporter

A perfect support and protection to the wrist. Invaluable to base ball, tennis and cricket players, or in any game where the strain is on the wrist.

Each.
No. 81046. In Domestic Grain Leather — Tan Orange or black..........$0.21
No 81047. In Imported Grain.................... .37

### THE HACKEY ANKLE SUPPORTER.

Patented May 24, 1887.

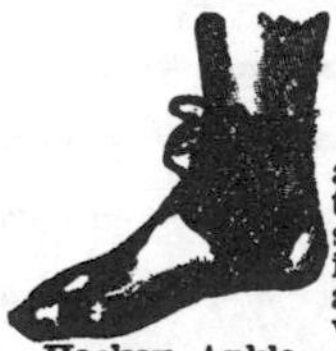
Hackey Ankle Supporter.

Relieves pain immediately, cures a sprain in a short time, and prevents turning of the ankle. Made of fine, soft leather, and is worn over stocking, lacing very tight in center, loose at top and bottom. The shoe usually worn can be used.

Pair.
No. 81048. Hackey Supporter...$1.00

### THE SPALDING SUSPENSORIES.

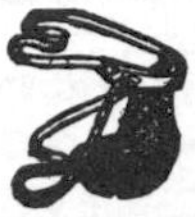

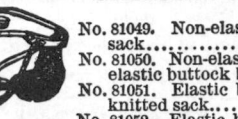

Each.
No. 81049. Non-elastic bands, knitted sack......................................$0.19
No. 81050. Non-elastic waist bands, full elastic buttock band, knitted sack. .38
No. 81051. Elastic bands, fine English knitted sack........................... .56
No. 81052. Elastic bands, all silk sack, warranted not to chafe............ .75
No. 81053. Elastic bands, fine Swiss bolting silk sack, satin top piece.......... .95
No. 81054. Silk elastic bands, finest Swiss bolting silk sack, satin trimmings...................... 1.50

### OLD POINT COMFORT SUSPENSORIES.

Each.
No. 81055. Elastic bands, adjusting buckles, lisle thread sack ..................................$0.75
No. 81056. Elastic bands, adjusting buckles, satin trimmings, fine knitted silk sack.......... 1.10
No. 81057. Silk elastic bands, adjusting buckles, trimmings, fine knitted silk sack............. 1.50

## GOODYEAR'S ROUND RUBBER HEALTH PULL.

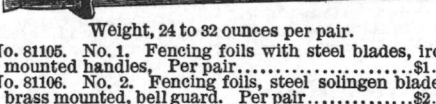

No. 81100. No. 5, for ladies and children, 14 years and upwards. Each...................................$1.25
No 81101. No. 6, for men of moderate strength, Each................................................ 1.45
No. 81102. No. 7, used by ladies, children or men; is fitted with screw eye to attach to wall or floor, Each.................................................$1.90
No. 81103. No. 8, for men of extra strength, made like No. 7. Each...........................................$2.40

## FENCING FOILS, MASKS AND GLOVES.

All goods standard make and quality.

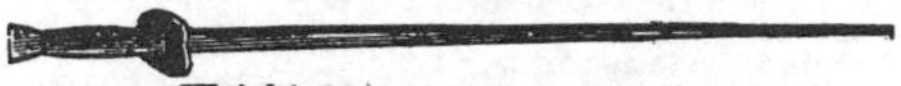

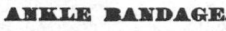

Weight, 24 to 32 ounces per pair.

No. 81105. No. 1. Fencing foils with steel blades, iron mounted handles, Per pair.......................$1.35
No. 81106. No. 2. Fencing foils, steel solingen blades, brass mounted, bell guard. Per pair.............$2.25
No. 81107. No. 3. Fencing foils, best steel, Solingen blades, brass mounted, wound handles. Pair...$2.75

## FENCING MASKS.

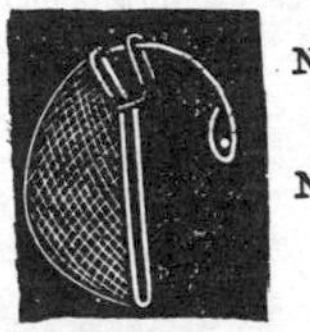

Weight, 24 to 28 oz.
No. 81108. No 10. French pattern, standard quality, per pair........$2.25
No. 81109. No. 11, French pattern, standard quality, with ears. Per pair........$2.65

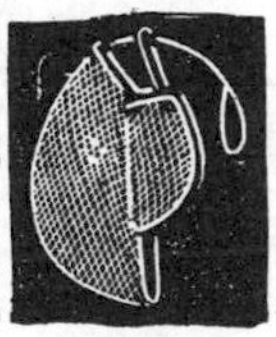

## FENCING GLOVES, BUCKSKIN.

Weight, 10 to 15 ounces.

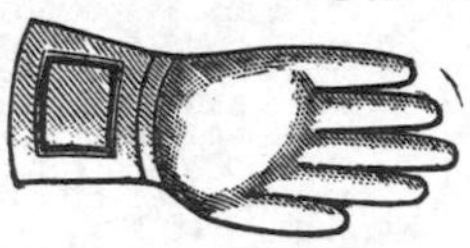

No. 81110. No. 14. Fencing gloves, without gauntlet. Per set of 2 gloves...$1.75
No. 81111. No. 15. Fencing gloves, with gauntlet. Per set of 2 gloves, ......................$2.70

## FENCING STICKS.

No. 81112. Fencing sticks, with cane willow basket hilt, Per pair.......$0.75

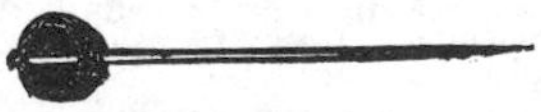

## FULL SLEEVE SHIRTS.

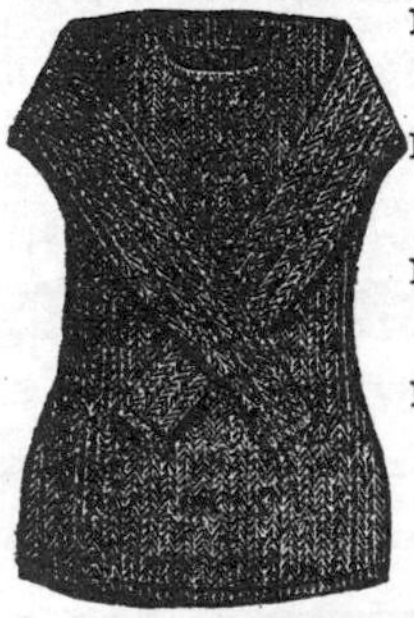

No, 81117. Long Sleeve Shirts, made of the very best worsted, perfect fitting, any color and any size, price $2.95
No. 81118. Long sleve, fine worsted; colors, navy, black or maroon, any size. Price ..........................$2.25
No. 81119. Long sleeve, fine cotton; colors, white, black or flesh color, any size. Price...................................$1.25
No. 81120. Long Sleeve, cotton, white or black, any size. Price..........................$1.10

## SLEEVELESS SHIRTS.

30, 32, 34 and 36 Chest.

No. 81122. Worsted, any color, plain, sleeveless. $2.50
No. 81123. Cotton, white, navy or black.......... 75
By mail, extra, 10c.

## QUARTER SLEEVE SHIRTS.

26, 28, 30, 32 and 36 Chest Measure.

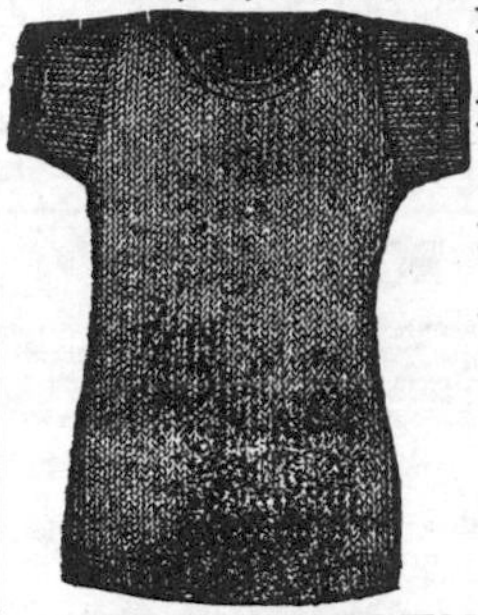

No. 81124. Shirts, best worsted, plain, any color, seamless. each...$2.70
No. 81125. Shirts, worsted ½ sleeve, black or navy blue or maroon, medium weight. Each.......$1.35
No. 81126. Shirt, cotton, ¼ sleeve, white or black, good weight. Each..$.50
No. 81127. Shirt, cotton, ¼ sleeve, white or black, fast colors, light weight, but firm and good wearing quality. Each..$0.40

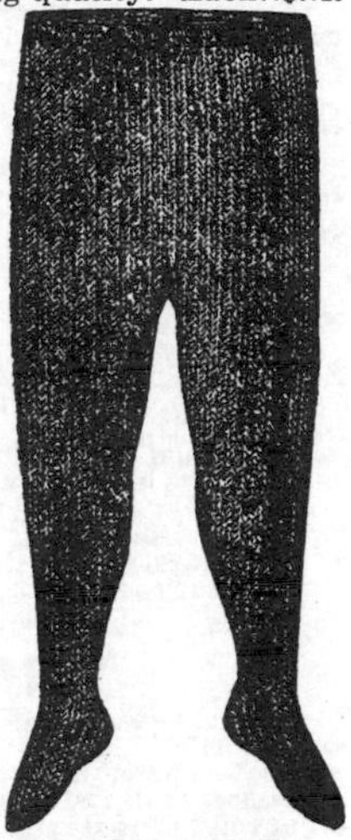

## FULL LENGTH TIGHTS.

No. 81128. Full length cotton tights, white or black. Per pair..............................$1.00
No. 81129. Full length tights, best worsted, any color. Per pair.................$3.25
Postage 15c.
No. 81130. Full length tights, worsted, medium weight, black, navy blue or maroon. Per pair.......... ......$2.10

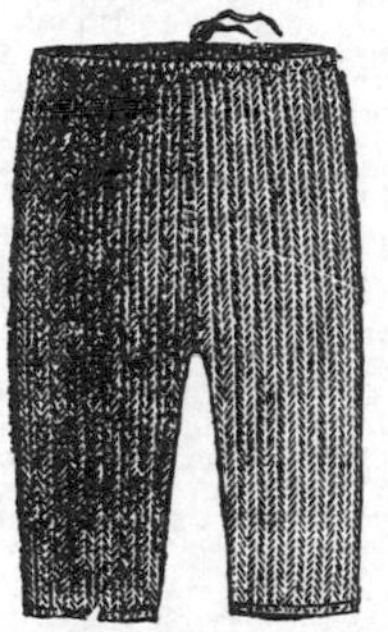

## KNEE TIGHTS.

No. 81131. Knee tights, cut Jersey goods, plain black, navy blue or maroon. Per pair .......................$1.30
No. 81132. Worsted plain black. Per pair........$2.00
No. 81133. Best worsted, any color. Per pair....$2.25
No. 81134. Cotton, white, navy and black, also make good bathing trunks. Per pair........ ..........$0.45
By mail, extra 10c.
No. 81135. Trunks, worsted black, navy, maroon. Per pair...............................................$1.45
No. 81136. Bathing trunks, fancy colored cotton in stripes, assorted sizes. Per pair.................$0.20
No. 81137. Bathing trunks, heavy, fancp colored cotton in stripes, assorted sizes. Each............$0.30
By mail, extra 5c.
No. 81138. Cotton trunks, white or black. Pair. $0.50
No. 81139. Puffed velvet trunks, block, red, navy or maroon. Pair.......................................$1.00

## WHITELEY EXERCISERS.

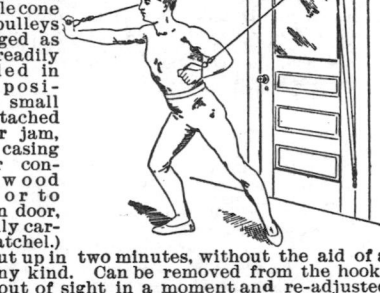

The Whitely Exerciser consists of a pure gum cable, of many strands, covered to protect it from the weather, with adjustable handles and swiveled attachments, running over three absolutely noiseless and adjustable cone bearing pulleys so arranged as to be readily suspended in various positions on small hooks attached to door jam, window casing or other convenient wood work, or to hinges on door, (Can easily carry in satchel.) Can be put up in two minutes, without the aid of a tool of any kind. Can be removed from the hooks and put out of sight in a moment and re-adjusted for use just as quickly. The hooks are of steel wire, strong though small, The workings of Exercise are absolutely noiseless. No straps to buckle. No weights to change. Resistance self-adjusting. No. jerks. No dead weights. Exercises all the muscles of the body. All parts warranted. For home use this exerciser is far superior to the chest weights and other cumbrous machines which cost much more money. Order No. 81140½.

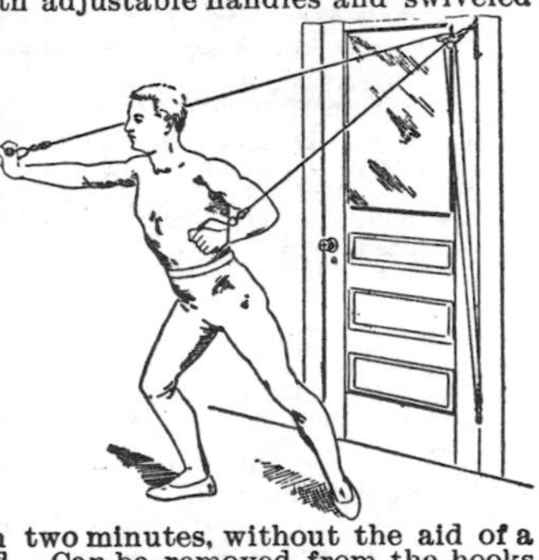

No. 1 quality complete with cone-bearing pulleys, etc. Price,..............................................$2.95
No. 0 quality, same style but not so well finished. Price...................................................$1.85

## COMMON SENSE EXERCISERS.

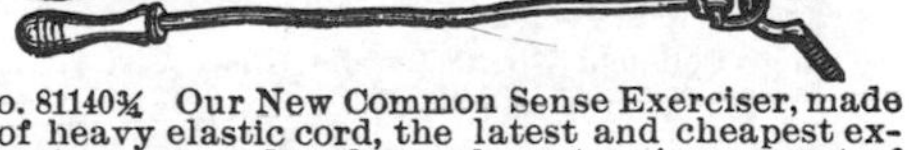

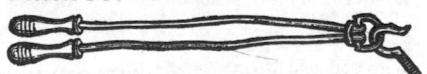

No. 81140¾ Our New Common Sense Exerciser, made of heavy elastic cord, the latest and cheapest exerciser yet produced, can be put up in any part of the room. Our price, complete.................$0.75

WE ARE ANXIOUS FOR A TRIAL ORDER, NO DIFFERENCE HOW SMALL. A SMALL ORDER WILL NOT SHOW YOU SO WELL WHAT SAVING CAN BE EFFECTED AS A LARGE ONE. HOWEVER, SEND IN YOUR ORDER AND WE WILL PLEASE YOU.

# FISHING RODS.

In selecting the goods in this department we have endeavored to put only those goods that we could rely on as standard goods. We have looked over a great many lines of fishing rods and have endeavored to procure only those that are made of the best quality woods and finished in the best manner.

You will notice our line is very complete, ranging in prices that will suit almost any one. Our cheap rods are selected with just as much care as the high grade rods. As we sell a great many more of these rods than the higher grade ones, we endeavor to make a good advertisement for ourselves by sending out the best goods for the money.

Any rod not found exactly as described can be returned at our expense and money refunded, if returned as soon as examined and not used.

## WOOD RODS.

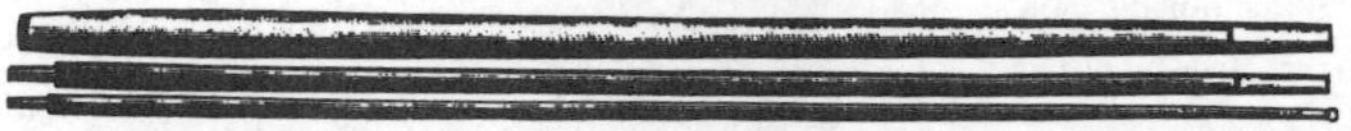

Our prices are lowest jobbing prices on fishing tackle, that is why the prices made seem low for good goods.

No. 81200. Three-jointed fishing rod, made of maple with single ferrules, brass mounted. A good rod for light fishing, 10½ ft. Put up in neat paper bag. Price each....9c

No. 81201. Maple rod, three joints, brass mounted, single ferrules, ringed for lines, 10½ ft. Put up in neat paper bag. Price, each....14c

No. 81202. Maple rod, four joints, brass mounted, single ferrules, ringed and stained. A very neat rod. Length, 12 ft. Price, each....18c

No. 81203. Three joints, brass mounted, double ferrules, stained, ringed reel bands and butt caps. A rod that is giving satisfaction all over the country. Length, 10½ ft. Price, each....30c

No. 81204. Three joints, same as No. 81203, except nickel mountings and in much finer finish. One of the neatest rods in our catalogue. 10½ ft. Price, each.50c

No. 81205. Four joints, brass mounted, double ferrules, ringed, stained reel bands and butt cap, with lancewood tip. 12 ft. Price, each....65c

No. 81206. This rod is our leader in wood rods, one that is made specially for our trade, and one on which we anticipate a very large trade this season. This rod is one we have had a great call for and are sure it will satisfy customers. Three piece bait rod, the butt and second joint being of maple, and the tip of lancewood. Handsomely varnished and filled with oil. Nickel mounted, silk wound tie guides, solid reel seat, new enameled grip, metal plugs. This rod is finished in rosewood and is one of the best bass rods we can secure for this season. Length, 10 ft. Put up in cloth bag. Price, each....$1.00

## BRISTOL STEEL RODS.

We take pleasure in presenting this line of Bristol rods, which is very complete and includes the new rods that have been lately added. No fisherman's outfit is complete without a supply of Bristol's steel fishing rods, in the latest pattern. The demand for this rod is constantly growing, and notwithstanding the competition of other rods, is used largely throughout the country.

These rods are all guaranteed from breakage, flaws or defects in the manufacture. They have been subjected to much abuse, such as being bent double and all manner of unnecessary tests. Against such tests we cannot undertake to guarantee our rods, but we will guarantee them from all breakage when in actual use, by reason of flaws in material or workmanship and within a reasonable time of their purchase.

## STEEL RODS—BRISTOL STEEL FISHING RODS.

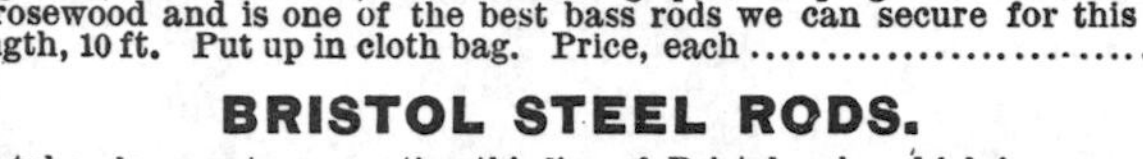


No. 81220. (1) Bass rod, 9 ft. 6 inches in length, full nickel mounted, with solid reel seat above the hand. Line runs through the center of the rod. When telescoped, the rod is 32 inches in length, all enclosed within the butt length. With celluloid wound handle. Weight 11¾ oz. Price, each....$3.95

## BRISTOL STEEL FISHING ROD.

No. 81222. (5) Fly Rod, 9 ft. 6 in. in length, full nickel mounted, with solid reel seat below the hand; line runs through the center of the rod. When telescoped the rod is 32 inches in length, all inclosed within the butt length.
With Celluloid Wound Handle, price....$3.90
Weight, 11¾ ounces.

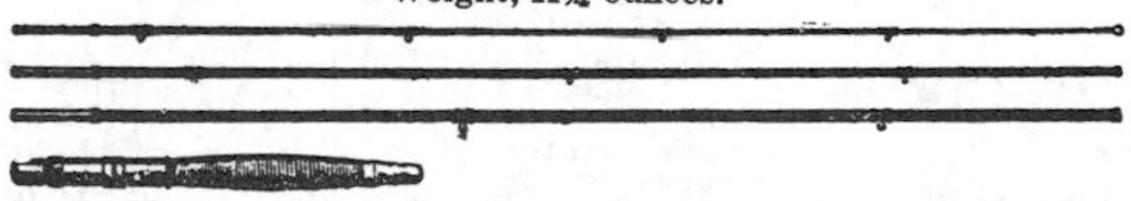

No. 81224. (8) Fly Rod, 10 ft. in length, full nickel mounted, with solid reel seat below the hand. This rod is jointed, fitted with two ring German silver tie guide and one ring German silver fly tip. Is made with three joints and handle; the joints are 38 inches long. Does not telescope.
With Celluloid Wound Handle, price....$4.65
With Cork Grip Handle, price....4.80
Weight, 9½ ounces.

No. 81226 (11) The "Henshall's" Pattern Bass Rod, 8 ft. 6 in. in length, nickel mounted, with solid reel seat above the hand. This rod is jointed, fitted with two ring German silver tie guides and German silver three ring tip. Is made with three joints and handle; the joints are 32 inches long. Does not telescope. This rod is the best bass or pickerel rod made.
With Celluloid Wound Handle, price....$4.75
With Cork Grip Handle, price....5.00
Weight, 10 ounces,

No. 81228. (13) The "St. Lawrence" Bass Rod, 7 ft. 6 in. long, full nickel mounted, with solid reel seat above the hand. This rod is jointed, fitted with two ring German silver tie guides and German silver three ring tip. Is made with three joints and handle; the joints are 28 inches long. We have good reason for believing this is the best bait casting or boat rod on the market.
With Celluloid Wound Handle, price....$4.50
With Cork Grip Handle, price....4.75
Weight, 9 ounces.

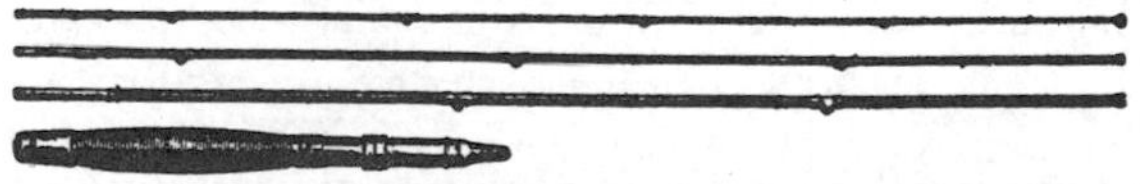

No. 81230. (15) The "Expert" Bait Casting Rod, 6 ft. 6 in. in length, full nickel mounted, with solid reel seat above the hand. This rod is jointed, fitted with two ring German silver tie guides and German silver three ring tip. Is made with three joints and handle; the joints are 24 inches long. This is a fine rod for long casts and for heavy work.
With Celluloid Wound Handle, price....$4.65
With Cork Grip Handle, price....4.85
Weight, 8¼ ounces.

No. 81232. (17) The "Favorite" Bait Casting Rod. 7 ft. in length, full nickel mounted, with solid reel seat above the hand. This rod is jointed, has German silver Trumpet guides and solid silver double-hole tip; the strongest and freeest running tip made, excepting the Agate. Is made with three joints and handle; the joints are 26 inches long. For bait casting and general heavy work this rod has no equal.
With Cork Grip Handle, weight 8¾ ounces, price....$6.00
With Cane Wound Handle, weight 8¾ ounces, price....6.25

## JOINTED BAMBOO FISHING RODS.

The Bamboo rods quoted below are light, handy and strong. Can be used with or without reels. The best trolling rods in the market. The most popular rods on the market are the Japanese and Calcutta bamboo. They can be handled as a high grade one cannot be, and will stand a great deal of abuse and are very durable.

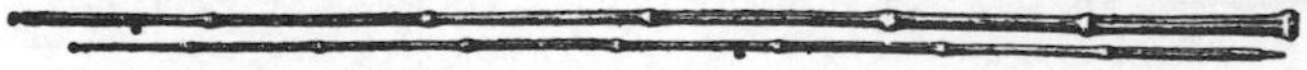

No. 81240. Two piece, plain straw color, double ferrules, ringed for line, 8 to 9 ft. Price, each....12c.

No. 81242. Three piece, plain double ferrules, straw color, ringed 13 to 15 ft. Price, each....30c.

No. 81243. Three piece, plain straw color, double ferrules, ringed and reel bands. Price, each....45c.

No. 81244. Four piece, plain double ferrules, ringed, 14 to 17 ft. Price, each....40c.

No. 81245. Four piece, plain double ferrules, ringed, reel bands, 14 to 17 ft. Price, each....55c.

## CALCUTTA BAMBOO RODS.

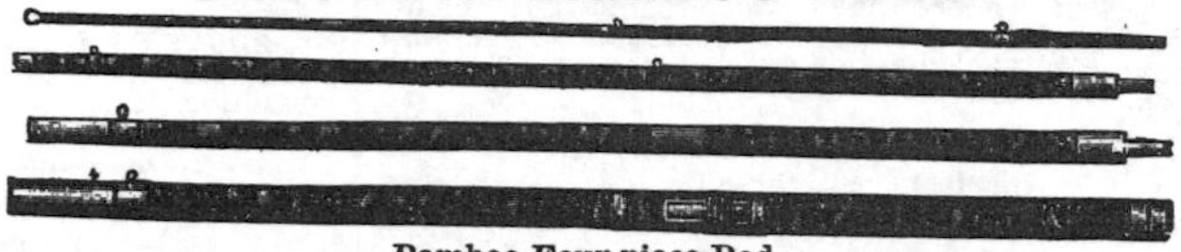

Bamboo Four-piece Rod.

No. 81250. Three joints, double ferrules, plain, 9 to 12 feet. Price, each....$0.25

No. 81252. Three joints, double ferrules, butt cap, ringed reel bands, 8½ to 10 ft. Price, each....$0.45

No. 81254. Four joints, double ferrules, butt cap, ringed reel bands, 12 to 15 feet. Price, each....$0.80

No. 81256. Club House Rod, three joints, celluloid wound handle, reel bands and butt cap, silk wound guides, nickel mounted, silk whippings between guides. Made very heavy for boat or light sea fishing. 9 to 10 feet. A very popular rod. Price, each....$0.95

No. 81258. Western Bass Rod, three joints, silk wound tie guides, full mounted solid reel seat, white and black celluloid grip, with extra lance tips, nickel mountings, 10½ feet. Price, each....$1.00

No. 81260. Three joints, celluloid wound grip, Calcutta bamboo 1st and 2d joints and lancewood tips, nickel mounted guide and reel bands, 9 to 10 ft. Ea. $0.75

No. 81262. Two joints, enameled scored grasp, reel bands, butt cap, silk wound guides, nickel mountings, silk whippings between guides, solid reel seat, 7 to 8 feet. Price, each....$1.00

## LANCEWOOD RODS.

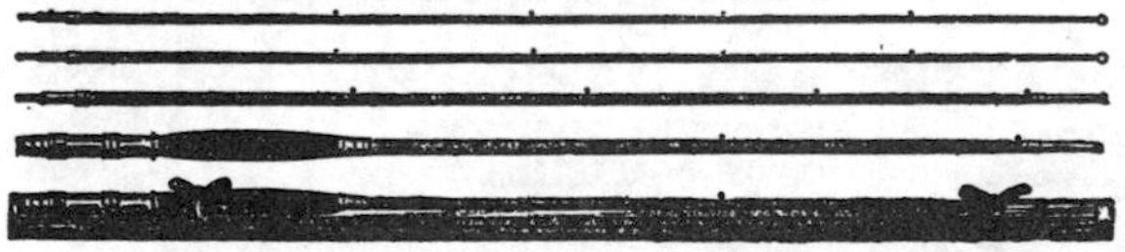

No. 81264. Bass Rod, three joints, lancewood throughout, with extra tip, nickel mountings, silk wound tie guides, solid reel seat above hand, corrugated grip, metal plugs, length 10 feet, All in cloth bag and wood form. Price, each....$1.15

No. 81266. Fly Rod, same description as above rod, except reel seat is below hand and is made especially for light trout fishing. Price, each....$1.25

No. 81268. Bass Rod, three joints, solid lancewood, carefully selected, extra tip, nickel mountings, welted ferrules, close wrappings of red silk, solid reel seat above hand, enameled grips, metal plugs, length 10 feet. Put up in neat cloth bag in wooden form. Price, each....$1.65

No. 81270. Fly Rod, same as above, except is fly rod and made for light fishing, a very fine one for the money. Price, each....$1.60

No. 81272. Bass Rod, three joints, solid lancewood throughout, carefully selected natural collar with extra tips, nickel mountings, welted ferrules, close wrappings of red silk, edged with black, scored grips, solid reel seat above hand metal plugs, in wood form and cloth back, length 10 feet. Price, each....$2.35

No. 81274. Fly Rod, same as above and one of the best obtainable for fishermen who are looking for a light fly rod, strongly made, cork grip, length 9½ feet. Price, each....$2.30

## GREENHEART RODS.

Greenheart Fly and Bass Rods, nickel mountings, solid reel seat, cork grip, close alternate wrappings of red and green silk, welted ferrules, metal plugs, in wooden form and cloth bag.

No. 81276. Bass Rod, 10 feet, with extra tip. Price, each....$2.75

No. 81278. Fly Rod, 8½ feet, with extra tip. Price, each....$2.65

## TRUNK RODS.

These rods are very popular with all those who do much traveling. A rod is a very unhandy thing to carry, unless it is short enough to be carried in a trunk or large size grip. From this the rod gets its name of "Trunk Rod."

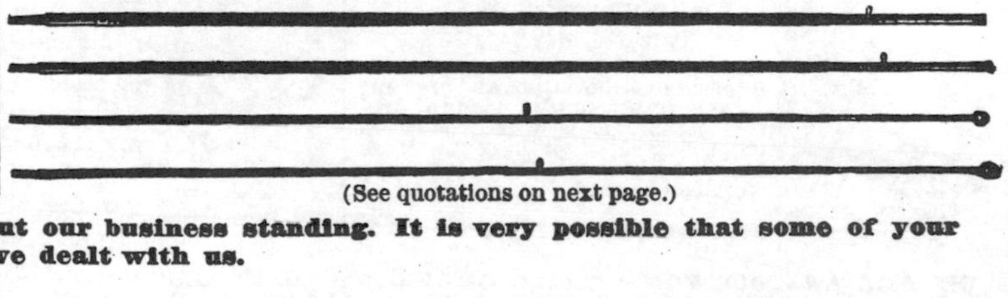

(See quotations on next page.)

**If you have never dealt with us, you can very easily find out our business standing. It is very possible that some of your neighbors have dealt with us.**

## TRUNK RODS.

(See cut on previous page.)

**No. 81280.** Five joints. Ash—dark stained, ring guides and reel band with lancewood tip. 9 feet. Price, each ........................ $0.85

**No. 81282.** Six joints, special quality, with extra lancewood tips, corrugated grasp, solid reel seat, welted ferrules, metal plugs, silk wound raised tie guides, nickel mountings, 12 feet ........................ $1.45

**No. 81284.** First quality lancewood trunk Bass Rod, tapered zylonite grip, balance of rod lancewood, nickel mountings, welted ferrules, covered dowels, silk wound tie guides, solid reel seat, 10 feet 5 inches, joints and extra tip. Price, each ........................ $2.25

## SPLIT BAMBOO RODS.

Our rods may vary in length from 6 in. to 1 ft. We endeavor to fill orders as ordered.

Our split bamboo rods we wish particularly to call attention to, as they have been selected from the very best we have been able to secure all over the country. Do not judge the quality of the rods by the exceedingly low prices we have them catalogued at, as we are able to obtain these prices by the large quantities we buy and we know that all the rods we send out in this line will be a lasting advertisement for us. Our "Split Bamboo" prices are 50 to 100 per cent. lower than the regular retail prices, and any rods not found just as represented can be returned at our expense, provided you do so immediately.

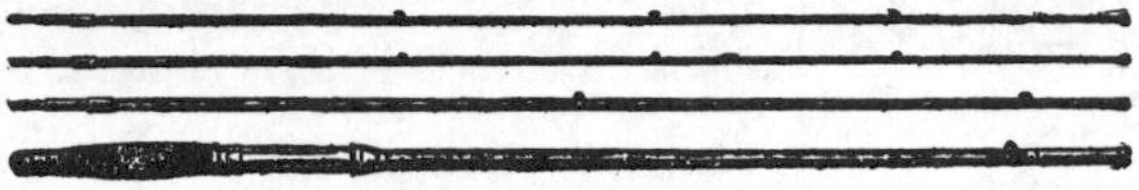

**No. 81290.** Split and glued bamboo fly rod. Silk-wound rings, with alternate silk wrappings of red and green silk. This rod is one of the best rods we know of in the country for the money. Price, each ........................ $1.05

**No. 81292.** This rod is one that we are making a run on at an exceedingly low price and are positive the rod cannot be duplicated for twice the amount, anywhere in the country. Split and glued bamboo bass rods. Silk-wound wire guides, with alternate silk wrappings of red and green silk, enameled grasp, solid reel seat, metal plugs, nickeled mountings. In wooden form and cloth bag. With extra tip. 9½ ft. Price, each ........................ $1.00

**No. 81294.** Same style as 81290, made with cork handles, 9 and 9½ ft. Price, each 1.25

**No. 81296.** Same style as 81292, only made with cork handles, 8 and 9½ ft. " 1.35

**No. 81298.** Split and glued bamboo fly rod, swelled butt, silk-wound rings with very close wrappings of red silk, cork grasp, solid reel seat, welted ferrules, metal plugs, nickel mountings. In covered form and cloth bag with extra tip. 9½ ft. Price, each ........................ $2.00

**No. 81300.** Split and glued bamboo bass rods, same as 81294, but heavier and reel seat above hand. With extra tip. 10 ft. Price, each ........................ $1.95

NOTE.—Split rods Nos. 81298 and 81300 are made of bright clear cane and in every respect are the best split bamboo rods on the market.

## SPECIAL GRADES SPLIT AND GLUED BAMBOO RODS.

**No. 81302.** Split and glued bamboo fly rod, special selected cane, swell butt, silk wound rings, with very close silk wrappings of yellow silk, edged with black, cork grasp, solid reel seat, welted ferrules, metal plugs, nickeled mountings. In covered form, 8½ and 10½ ft. Price, each ........................ $2.75

**No. 81304.** Split and glued bamboo bass rod, "specially selected cane" silk-wound raised tie guides, with very close wrappings of yellow silk edged with black, solid reel seat, welted ferrules, cork grasp, metal plugs, nickeled mountings. In cloth covered form and bag. 9½ ft. Price, each ........................ $2.70

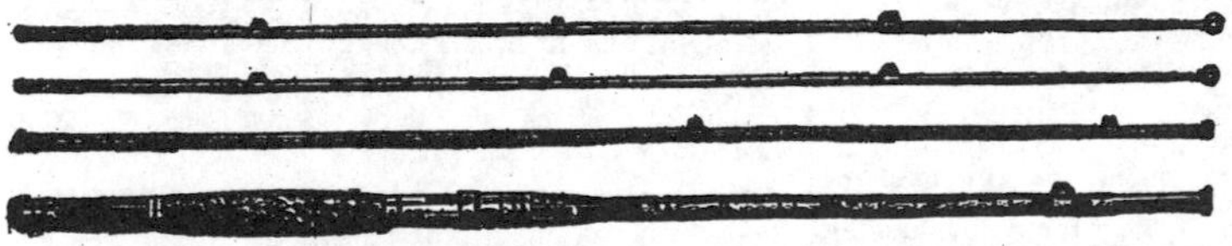

**No. 81306.** Bass rods, finest quality, three piece hexagonal selected split bamboo bass rod, hand-made throughout; weight, 9 oz.; length, 8 ft. 3 in. Fine nick milled mountings, improved waterproof rimmed shoulder ferrules, anti friction, rimmed silk-wound guides, nickel reel-seat, full swell, inlaid with cedar and bamboo cork grip, alternate silk windings at short intervals, extra full length tip, in covered form and cloth bag. A bargain. Price each ........................ $4.50

**No. 81308.** Fly Rods, same as above, with reel seat below hand. Price, each ...... 4.75

**No. 81310.** Split Bamboo Fly Rod, swell butt, specially selected cane, silk-wound rings, with very close wrappings of red silk, special German silver mountings, heavy welted ferrules, cork grasp, solid reel seat, metal plugs. In cloth covered form and bag, 8½, 9, 9½, 10 and 10½ ft. Price, each ........................ $5.00

**No. 81312.** Split Bamboo Bass Rod, same as 81310, but heavier, and reel seat above hand, 9½ to 10½ ft. Price, each ........................ $4.95

## SPECIAL FLY ROD.

**No. 81314.** We particularly call the attention of anglers to this special fly rod. This rod is made of absolutely perfect cane, the ferrules fit perfectly, being all taper ground to bear their entire length. The ritting and gluing of the sections are done by the most perfect process, the same as the highest grade rods made. The wrappings of silk are red and green and are extremely close to still further strengthen the sections. They are varnished most thoroughly with the best spar varnish. These rods have solid drawn ferrules and reel seat, and for a high grade of fly rod, we would recommend this one.

**DESCRIPTION.**

Cane-wound grasp, solid reel seat. Welted and milled ferrules. Metal plugs German silver mountings. In cloth cover, form and cloth bag.
Price, each ........................ $5.00

**WE HOPE TO FILL YOUR ORDERS WITH SUCH RESULTING SATISFACTION TO YOU THAT YOU MAY FEEL FREE TO RECOMMEND US AND OUR METHODS TO YOUR FRIENDS. THIS IS THE BEST ADVERTISING WE COULD ASK . . . . . . . . . .**

**Better Gun Than He Expected.**

SARVERSVILLE, Pa.

SEARS, ROEBUCK & CO..
*Dear Sirs:* I received the gun to-day and am well pleased. It is better than I expected.
Yours truly, CHAS. SAUTERS.

QUITMAN, Miss., May 27, 1895.

SEARS, ROEBUCK & CO.
*Dear Sirs:* I received the revolver; was well pleased with it. I will say it was all that you claimed for it; you can use my name in any way you choose. I expect to continue to patronize your house. Yours truly, W. W. PURVIS.

**Very Nice Gun For The Money.**

CAMERON, Ga., Nov. 16, 1895.

SEARS, ROEBUCK & CO.
*Gentlemen:* The gun sent G. B. Evans, C. O. D., has been delivered O.K., and money returned. He is very well pleased with it so far. I think it a very nice gun for the money. Respectfully, J. A. EVANS, Ex. Agt.

**Will Give Us More Orders.**

SEARS, ROEBUCK & CO.
*Dear Sirs:* I received goods all O.K. I have tried the gun and it proved satisfactory. The reason why I did not write sooner was because I was away. We expect to favor you with another order soon.
Yours truly, EDWARD MOORE.

**May Expect More Orders.**

BUTLER, Freestone Co., Tex.

MESSRS. SEARS, ROEBUCK, & CO., Chicago, Ill.
*Dear Sirs:* Am glad to say I received my gun all OK, and after careful examination, was very much pleased with it. I have tried it on shooting, and it has proved a success; you may expect more orders from my friends and self in short time. Please find inclosed 15 cts. in postage, for which you will please send me one of your big catalogues. I am your customer, A. B. BROWN.

## ROD CASES.

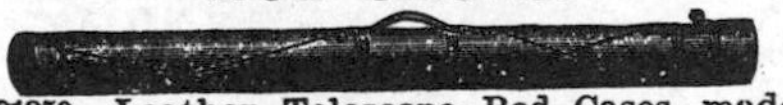

**No. 81350.** Leather Telescope Rod Cases, made of heavy russet leather, with handle. This is a new style of rod case which can be adjusted to fit any size rod, and is suitable to carry any kind of a pointed rod in. Price, each ........................ $0.95

Cheaper quality leather, neatly finished, 40 to 50 in. long, 2 in. diameter, each ........................ 1.75

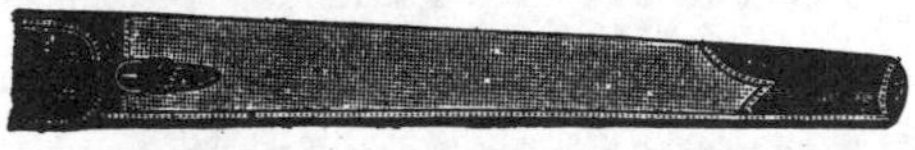

**No. 81352.** Canvas Rod Cases, leather top and bottom, a dandy for the money; weight, 6 to 8 oz.; 40 to 50 in. long; each ........................ 60c

**No. 81353.** Canvas Rod Case; plain, heavy canvas; each ........................ 40c

**No. 81354.** The "Handy" fish rod holder; can be carried in the vest pocket; screws on gunwale of boat; is covered with rubber. Ordinary size, each ........ 13c
Large size, each ........ 15c

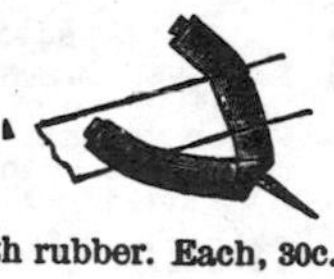

**No. 81356.** Fish Rod Holder; a good one for the money; screws on any part of the boat; forks covered with rubber. Each, 30c.

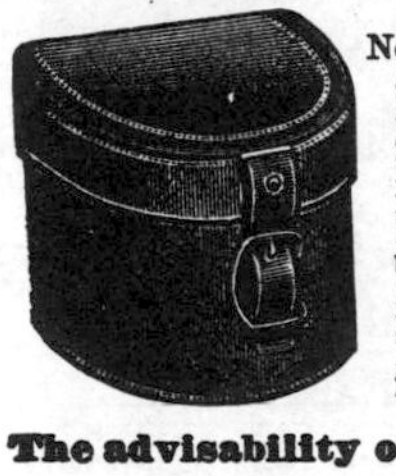

**No. 81358.** Leather Reel Cases; are made of bleached oak finest leather, felt lined, with leather-covered buckles.
No. 11, to hold small single-action reel ........ 55c
No. 12, to hold large single-action reel ........ 65c
No. 13, to hold small multiplying reel ........ 70c
No. 14, to hold large multiplying reel ........ 90c

## UNIVERSAL FISH ROD HOLDER.

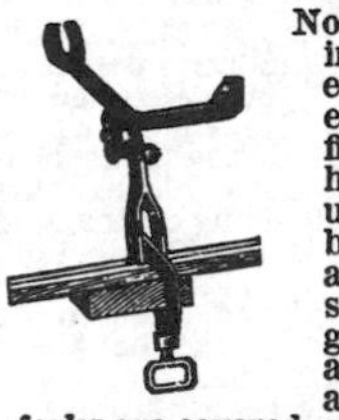

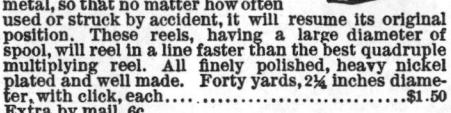

**No. 81360.** For trolling and still fishing in a boat. It can be fastened either to the gunwale or seat. It enables a person, if he desires, to go fishing without a guide to row for him, or to have two or three rods in use without their being all over the bottom of the boat, to be stepped on and broken. By means of a thumbscrew it can be adjusted to any angle or any direction, as it works on a ball-and-socket joint. It is neatly and strongly made, is tinned, and forks are covered with rubber. It will take any rod, from ¾ to 2 inches diameter at butt. Weight, 26 oz. Each ........................ $1.00

## FISHING REELS.

(Reels by mail, 10 to 15 cents extra.)

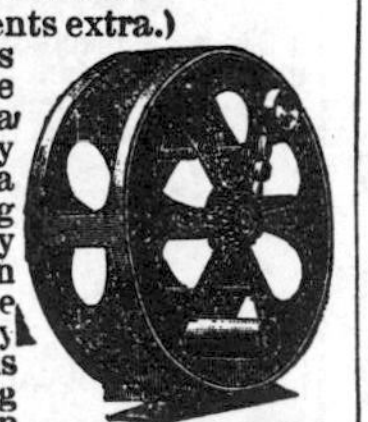

**No. 81362.** The Expert Reel. This reel has an entirely new device for use in casting or "playing" a fish, whereby the angler may vary the reel from a free-running to a delicate drag, heavy drag, or bring it to a complete stop, simply by the pressure of the thumb upon the guard. By this device the line may be stopped instantly at any desired point when casting. This guard is made of extra-hard spring metal, so that no matter how often used or struck by accident, it will resume its original position. These reels, having a large diameter of spool, will reel in a line faster than the best quadruple multiplying reel. All finely polished, heavy nickel plated and well made. Forty yards, 2¼ inches diameter, with click, each ........................ $1.50
Extra by mail, 6c.
Seventy yards, 3 inches diameter, with click, each ........................ 1.65
Extra by mail, 7c.

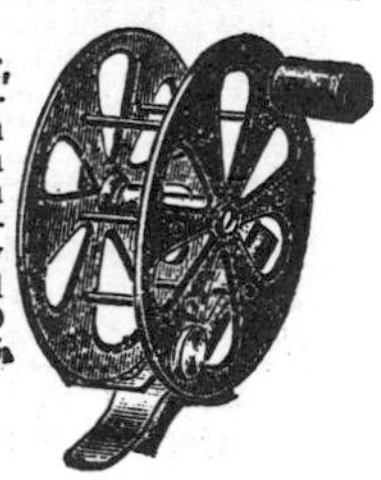

**No. 81364.** The famous amateur, drag reel, fine nickel plate, allowing line to dry quickly; can be changed to a free runner in an instant by simply pressing down on spring; beats the best multiplier in reeling in the line. Very light weight, and fits any reel band. Small ........ $0.90
Medium ........ 1.15
Extra by mail, 5c.

## FISHING REELS.

Our fishing Reels are carefully selected from our past experience in the fishing tackle business, and we have adopted reels that are popular all over the country.

## THE "FEATHERLIGHT" REELS

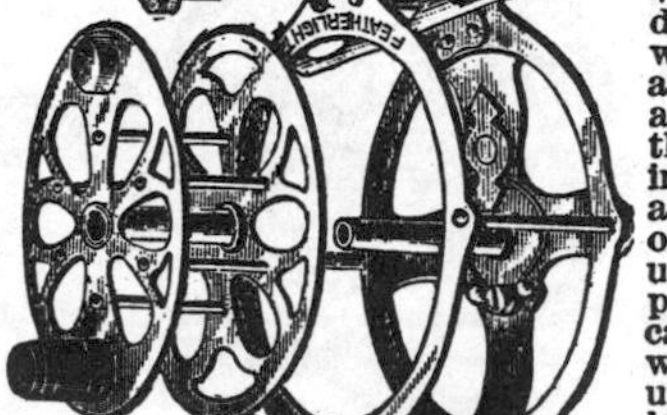


Something new. We always endeavor to keep up with the times, and when a new article comes out that is going to be in demand, we are notified at once by the manufacturers and put same in our catalogue; hence, we have a strictly up to date catalogue all the time. This reel has movable spool as shown in the cut, which makes it very handy for cleaning same. It can also be used as a line dryer. Has back sliding steel click and steel spindle. Fine nickel finish. Best workmanship. Lightest reel made.

**No. 81370.** 80 yards, size spool, 2¼x3¼ in. Price each, ........................ $1.35
Postage extra, 10c.

**The advisability of Freight Shipments is very obvious, as the charges are so small. If you happen to need only a few small items you can include enough Groceries to make up at least 100 lbs.**

## THE "ALLRIGHT" REELS.

Closed back to keep out dirt. Removable spool. Back sliding steel click and steel spindle. Fine nickel finish. Best workmanship. This reel is an excellent casting reel and one of the most durable reels made.
No. 81372. 80 yds., size spool, 2¼x1 in. Made especially for bass casting.
Price, each.....................$1.55

## THE COMPETITOR.

No. 81373. Single action, raised pillar, riveted brass reel, no click or drag. 25 yds...................9c

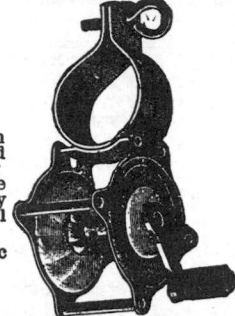

No. 81374. Single action raised pillar, riveted brass reels, with ring clamp, made to fit the plain bamboo rod. A very popular and useful reel for light fishing.
25 yds., each........ .. 20c
Extra by mail, 3c.

No. 81376. Single action, screwed hard rubber reels, with bushed bearings, click, brass spools and polished. A very good and strong string reel for light trout fishing.
25 yds...................... 40c
40 yds...................... 45c
60 yds...................... 50c
Extra by mail, 5c.

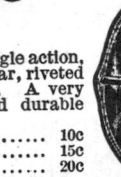

No.81378. Single action, raised pillar, riveted brass reel. A very strong and durable reel.
25 yds.......... 10c
40 yds.......... 15c
60 yds.......... 20c
Extra by mail, 4c.

No. 81380. Same as above reel except has click.
25 yds...................15c   40 yds................... 20c
60 yds...................25c   Extra by mail 4c.

No. 81382. Double multiplying raised pillar, balance handle, screwed brass reel, with patent adjustable slide drag and back sliding click, polished.
40 yds.............. .. 40c
60 yds............... 45c
80 yds............... 50c
Extra by mail, 7c.

No. 81384. This reel is one of which we have sold a great many and are positive it will give satisfaction wherever sent. Same as above, nickel plated.
40 yds...................50c   60 yds............... 60c
80 yds...................70c   Extra by mail, 7c.

No. 81386. Rubber cap, double multiplying raised pillar, balance handle, screwed nickle plated reels, with patent adjustable slide drag and back sliding click.
40 yds...$0.90
60 yds... 1.00
80 yds... 1.10
Extra by mail 7c.

## THE MATTER OF PRICE CONCERNS
## THE SHREWD BUYER.

That there is nothing the matter with our prices is very evident from the trade they induce. Our prices not only sell the Goods, but the Goods stay sold. They are just as we represent; and, in fact, many of our customers write and say "they are even better than you said." . . . .

No. 81388. Double multiplying, round disc, balance handle, screwed brass reels, with brass pivots, patent adjustable slide drag, back sliding click, and nickle plated.
40 yds.............$0.85
60 yds............. .90
80 yds............. 1.00
100 yds............ 1.15
Extra by mail, 7c.

No. 81390. Quadruple, round disc, balance handle, screwed brass reel, with fine steel pivots in bronzed bushed bearings, patent adjustable slide drag, back-sliding click, and nickel plated.
40 yards.............$1.45
60 " ............. 1.65
Extra by mail, 10c.

No. 81392. Single-action, extra fine quality screwed hard rubber reels, with flush balance handle, bushed bearings and backsliding click, nickel plated.
25 yards.............$1.00
40 " ............. 1.10
60 " ............. 1.20
Extra by mail, 7c.

## PENELL REEL.

No. 81394. Extra quality nickeled quadruple multiplying Reel, with sliding click and drag, steel pivots, bridge over cogs; one of our leaders for this season. It is a high-grade reel, and one that we are offering at

a very much reduced price; high grade, and made of the best material possible. Constructed for all of those fishermen who are looking for a fine-looking reel at a low figure. Extra by mail, 12c.
40 yards.............$2.25
60 " ............. 2.50
80 " ............. 2.75
100 " ............. 3.00

No. 81396. Abbey & Imbrie's patent compensating quadruple, finest quality throughout, beautifully nickel plated, backsliding click and sliding drag. The steel pivots are so made that any wear may be adjusted in a few moments, so that the reel is practically everlasting, and a beauty besides. Easily oiled and readjusted.
40 yards.............$7.00   60 yards.............$7.55
80 yards............. 8.00   Extra by mail, 8c.

## VOM HOFE'S REELS.

There is probably no reel on the market that is so popular as the Vom Hofe Reel. We have put the prices within the reach of all desiring a high-grade reel, and recommend the following reels to be guaranteed and strictly high-grade in every respect:
No. 81398. Vom Hofe's patent rubber and nickel plated multiplying steel pivot reels. Backsliding click (steel spring and ratchet), with patent adjusting pivot cap.
60 yards ............$3.50
80 " ............. 3.75
Extra by mail, 8c.

No. 81400. Vom Hofe's patent rubber and nickel plated quadruple multiplying steel pivot reels. Backsliding click (steel spring and ratchet), with patent adjusting pivot cap.
60 yards ............$4.95   80 yards.............$5.25
Extra by mail, 8c.

## FISH LINES.

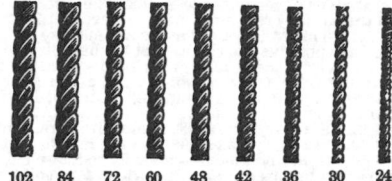

9 8 7 6 5 4 3 2 1

No. 81450. Eureka fish lines, colored sea island cotton, put up in 15 foot lengths, connected. Price per doz. pieces of 15 foot each.

| No. | Per doz. | Per 12 doz. | No. | Per doz. | Per 12 doz. |
|---|---|---|---|---|---|
| 1 | $0.05 | $0.45 | 6 | $0.11 | $0.85 |
| 2 | .06 | .50 | 7 | .12 | 1.10 |
| 3 | .07 | .60 | 8 | .13 | 1.20 |
| 4 | .08 | .70 | 9 | .15 | 1.30 |
| 5 | .10 | .80 | | | |

### LINEN LINES IN HANKS, DRAB COLOR.

No. 81452. Linen fish lines, each line 15 ft. long, 180 ft. to the dozen. (Numbers to correspond to Eureka fish lines.)

| Nos. | 1 | 2 | 3 | 4 |
|---|---|---|---|---|
| Per doz. | $0.10 | $0.11 | $0.13 | $0.15 |
| Per gross, pieces | 1.00 | 1.15 | 1.35 | 1.42 |

No. 81454. Linen lines, 25 feet or 300 feet to the dozen.

| No. | 5 | 6 | 7 | 8 |
|---|---|---|---|---|
| Per doz. | $0.20 | $0.25 | $0.30 | $0.35 |
| Per gross, pieces | 2.19 | 2.50 | 3.10 | 3.47 |

### WHITE COTTON LINES

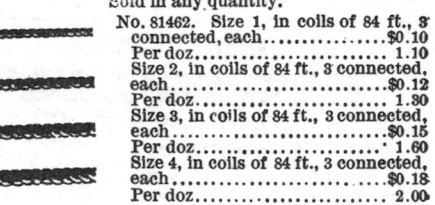

102 84 72 60 48 42 36 30 24

No. 81456. White cotton lines, put up in 20 feet lengths, 12 connected. Illustrations show larger than actual size, but as near as can possibly be shown on paper. Price per dozen pieces of 20 feet each.

| Nos. | 24 | 30 | 36 | 42 | 48 | 60 | 72 | 84 | 102 |
|---|---|---|---|---|---|---|---|---|---|
| Doz. | $0.10 | $0.12 | $0.13 | $0.15 | $0.16 | $0.20 | $0.22 | $0.27 | $0.30 |
| 12 doz. | 1.10 | 1.36 | 1.44 | 1.70 | 1.95 | 2.19 | 2.30 | 2.50 | 2.79 |

### BROOK TROUT LINEN LINES.

In coils of 25 feet, 12 connected. A fine line, best quality. Smallest reel line made.
No. 81458. Size 140, trout linen in coils of 25 feet, 12 connected, each.......................................$0.04
Per dozen coils, 12 connected......................... .35

### SEA ISLAND COTTON FISH LINES.

No. 81460. Extra fine quality 25 foot coils, 12 coils connected; sold in any quantity; a beautifully finished line and good reel, trolling or bass line. Made of the longest staple Sea Island cotton, and perfectly smooth, straight, and of even strength. (Nos. correspond to Nos. 1, 2, 3,4 and 5 of "Eureka" fish lines.)

| Nos. | 9 | 12 | 15 | 18 | 21 |
|---|---|---|---|---|---|
| Each | $0.03 | $0.04 | $0.05 | $0.06 | $0.07 |
| Per dozen | .25 | .29 | .35 | .40 | .45 |

### BROWN LINEN TROLLING LINES.

Sold in any quantity.
No. 81462. Size 1, in coils of 84 ft., 3 connected, each.............$0.10
Per doz. 1.10
Size 2, in coils of 84 ft., 3 connected, each.............$0.12
Per doz. 1.30
Size 3, in coils of 84 ft., 3 connected, each.............$0.15
Per doz. 1.60
Size 4, in coils of 84 ft., 3 connected, each.............$0.18
Per doz. 2.00

### BROWN LINEN CABLE OR HAWSER LAID TROLLING LINES.

No. 81464. Made of the very best linen, extra strength. The No. 4 will hold the largest fish. In coils of 84 feet, 4 connected if desired. Same size as above.

| | Each. | Per doz. |
|---|---|---|
| Size 1, cable laid coils of 84 feet | $0.16 | $1.79 |
| Size 2, cable laid coils of 84 feet | .17 | 1.84 |
| Size 3, cable laid coils of 84 feet | .18 | 1.95 |
| Size 4, cable laid coils of 84 feet | .23 | 2.20 |

### BRAIDED COTTON LINES.

No. 81466. Braided cotton lines in coils; strong and durable; made of best Sea Island cotton, guaranteed even strength. No. 1 the largest. Nos. 2, 3, 4, 5 running smaller; in coils of 84 feet. Nos. 5, 4, 3, each, 9c; per doz., 75c; Nos. 2, 1, 12c; per doz., 85c.

### HARD BRAIDED LINEN LINES.

Much stronger than twisted or laid lines. Sizes 1, 2, 3, 4, 5, 6. No. 1 is the largest. (4 lines connected if desired.)
No. 81468. Hard braided linen lines, in coils of 25 yds. See illustrations of braided cotton lines for sizes. Each, 15c; per 100 yds.............................55c

All sorts of canned goods for Fishing and

Picnic Parties will be found in

our Grocery Department.

If there is any particular style of Reel or Rod you want, and you don't find it priced herein, write us the name and description, and we shall name you a price far below the Retail Value.

## BRAIDED LINEN LINES.

On 25 yd. blocks. For bass, pike and other large fish. A good trolling line (4 lines connected if desired.)
No. 81470. Braided linen lines on blocks. Sizes 1, 2, 3, 4, 5. No. 1 is the largest on blocks of 25 yds. See illustrations of braided cotton lines for sizes. Each, 10c; per 100 yds....................................38c

## BEST BRAIDED LISLE THREAD LINES.

No. 81472. A special grade line, finely made, strong and even. Comes on blocks of 25 yds. each, 4 connected.

| Size No. | 1 | 2 | 3 | 4 | 5 |
|---|---|---|---|---|---|
| Per 25 yds. | 10c | 10c | 10c | 10c | 10c |
| Per 100 yds. | 35c | 35c | 35c | 35c | 35c |

## FINE TWISTED SILK LINES

In hanks, for trout and other small fishing.
No. 81473. Assorted colors, 15 ft. in each hank.

| Size | 2 | 4 |
|---|---|---|
| Each | 5c | 9c |
| Per dozen | 50c | 95c |

Our silk lines are all silk and fine quality.
In silk lines, No. 4 is for small bass, No. 1 for large fish.

## BRAIDED SILK LINES.

The illustrations of lines appear a little larger than the line, but they are the exact diameter of the lines they represent. This applies to all the illustrations of fish and seine lines.
No. 81474. Braided dressed lines on 25 yard block. Four connected.
Nos. 1 2 3 4 5
Price 40c, 35c, 30c, 25c, 20c. per 25 yds.
No. 81476. Fine quality braided oil silk lines, in coils of 25 yards each; 4 connected. A big seller and a good one.
Nos. 1 2 3 4 5
Prices 48c, 35c, 30c, 25c, 20c.per 25 yds.
No. 81478. High grade raw braided silk lines, on blocks of 25 yds. each; 4 connected.
Nos. 1 2 3 4 5
Prices 35c, 30c, 25c, 20c, 15c per 25 yds.

## It Is a Very EXCELLENT PLAN for You

To make up a Club Order of such Fishing Tackle and Sporting Goods in general as you and your acquaintances may want. By having all shipped together, your part will cost you very little for transportation. Refer to introductory pages for

## ...Special Discounts on Club Orders...

## COHANTIC SPECIAL BRAIDED SILK LINES.

No. 81480. We call special attention to this line as the very best Braided Silk line made. The silk used is made especially for this line and combines great strength and smooth finish to a greater degree than any other similar line made. Put up in 25 yard lengths, 4 connected on cards.
No. 1½ is smallest and is the one mostly used by bait casters; will hold the largest bass.

| | Per 25 yards. | Per 100 yards. |
|---|---|---|
| No. 1½ " " | $0.30 | $1.00 |
| No. 3 " " | 40 | 1.35 |
| No. 5 " " | 50 | 1.75 |
| No. 5½ " " | 60 | 2.25 |

NOTE—No. 1½, 3, 5, are black and white mottled. No. 5½ is drab color.

## SPECIAL SILK TROUT LINES, ENAMEL FINISH.

No. 81482. These lines are in special demand, being of small diameter, and possessing great strength. This result is obtained not only by using the highest grade of silk, but by braiding more strands into each line and plaiting very close. One line in a box, 25 yard length; per 25 yard line, each.......................35c

## FINEST QUALITY MARTIN'S BRAIDED SILK LINES.

No. 81484. This line meets the demand for one of great strength, and smoothly braided. They are made of a greater quantity of stock and of a higher quality silk than other lines on the market, and have double the breaking strength of any other similar line sold. Come in 25 yard blocks; 4 connected.

| Size No. | 1 | 2 | 3 | 4 | 5 |
|---|---|---|---|---|---|
| Per 25 yd. line | 60 | 50 | 40 | 30 | 25 |
| Per 100 yds | $2.00 | $1.60 | $1.20 | 80c | 60c |

## SUPERIOR WATERPROOF BRAIDED SILK LINES.

No. 81486. Enameled braided silk lines, hard enameled and run free on the reel. In 25 yard coils, 4 connected; can order 25, 50, 75 or 100 yards in

| Nos. | 3 | 4 | 5 | 6 |
|---|---|---|---|---|
| Per 25-yard coil | $1.25 | $1.00 | $0.76 | $.75 |

No. 81490. Highest quality waterproof braided silk, luster finish, fly lines. The best highly polished line made. No. 6 or G is the smallest, 25 yard coils, 4 connected; can order 25, 50, 75 or 100 yards in a line.

| Nos. | 26 or G | 5 or F | 4 or E | 3 or D |
|---|---|---|---|---|
| Price, per 25 yards | $0.95 | $1.15 | $1.40 | $1.60 |

## CUTTY HUNK LINEN LINE.

No. 81492. Best and strongest line made. Cutty hunk linen lines, best quality. The best linen reel line in the market, runs smooth and even and does not kink. 150 feet blocks. 9 threads, each, 25c; 12 thread, each, 30c; 15 thread, each, 35c; 18 thread, each, 40c; 21 thread, each, 50c.
No. 81494. In 300 feet lengths, 9 thread, each, 50c; 12 thread, each, 60c; 15 thread, each, 75c; 18 thread, each, 80c; 21 thread, each, $1.00.

## LINEN REEL LINES.

In Coils.
No. 81496. Made of best improved gilling thread. (No. 35), in 50-feet coils, connected. (See Cutty Hunk lines for sizes.

| Nos. | 6 | 9 | 12 | 15 | 18 |
|---|---|---|---|---|---|
| Each coil | 9c | 10c | 11c | 13c | 14c |

## SEA GRASS LINES.

In 8 ounce catties.
No. 81498. Six lines in bunch, 10 to 15 feet in a line. One of the best and strongest lines made, fine as silk. No. 1, for trout, per bunch of 6, 45c; No. 2, for bass, per bunch of 6, 50c; No. 3, for pike, etc., per bunch of 6, 55c.

## FISH LINES RIGGED.

No. 81500. Fishing lines, rigged with hook and float; a good line, each, 3c; per doz., 25c; Medium laid line, each, 4c; per doz., 35c. Silk line, each, 15c; per doz...............................$1.75

## FISH HOOKS.—DOUBLE REFINED CAST STEEL.

All best English manufacture. There are cheaper hooks in the market, but we do not carry them in stock, as they are no good for catching fish.

These illustrations show the different sizes of Limerick, Kirby, Carlisle and all other kinds of hooks as nearly as possible.
The cuts illustrate full size of hooks.

SOLD ONLY IN BOXES OF 100.

State Kind Wanted.
(See prices elsewhere.)

### FISH HOOKS.

Weight per box of 100, No. 12 to 2-0, 3 oz.; 4-0 to 5-0, 6 oz.; 6-0, 8 oz.; 7-0, 10 oz.; 8-0, 14 oz.; 9-0, 18 oz.; 10-0, 20 ounces.

### LIMERICK HOOKS.

No. 81502. Limerick Fish Hooks, superfine ringed; put up in boxes of 100 hooks. Nos. 12, 11, 10, 9, 8, 7, 6, 5, 4, 3, 1, per box, 5c; 1-0, 7c; 2-0, 8c; 3-0, 9c; 4-0, 10c; 5-0, 12c; 6-0, 15c; 7-0, 18c; 8-0, 25c; 10-0, 35c.
Per 1000, No. 12 to No. 1...............$0.50

### KIRBY HOOKS

No. 81504. Kirby bent fish hooks, superfine ringed. Put up in boxes of 100 each. Nos. 12, 11, 10, 9, 8, 7, 6, 5, 4, 3, 1, per box, 5c; 1-0, 7c; 2-0, 8c; 3-0, 9c; 4-0, 10c; 5-0, 12c; 6-0, 14c; 7-0, 16c; 8-0, 20c; 9-0, 35c; 10-0, 40c.
We do not break boxes at these prices. If you purchase more than you require for yourself you can easily sell enough to pay for your whole purchase, so that for your own use would cost you nothing.

### CARLISLE HOOKS.

No. 81506. Fine quality English "O. V. B." blue spring steel Kirby bend, hollow point Carlisle hook, ringed. Put up in boxes of 100 each, only one size in a box; 100 hooks in a box.
No. of size.........

| | 1 to 8 | 1-0 | 2-0 | 3-0 | 4-0 | 5-0 | 6-0 | 7-0 |
|---|---|---|---|---|---|---|---|---|
| Per box | 25c | 28c | 30c | 35c | 40c | 50c | 60c | 65c |

We ask no man to buy of us who has the least doubt of our willingness to fulfill all that we advertise. We shall consider it a favor if you will investigate our standing first.

Carlisle Hooks.—Continued.

**No. 81507.** Carlisle Hooks, good quality, blued, not so good as No. 81506, just as strong, but not so nicely blued. Put up 100 in a box, only one size in a box.

| Nos.... | 8 | 7 | 6 | 5 | 4 | 3 | 2 | 1 |
|---|---|---|---|---|---|---|---|---|
| Per box | 10c. | 10c. | 10c. | 10c. | 10c. | 10c. | 10c. | 10c. |
| Nos.... | 1-0 | 2-0 | 3-0 | 4-0 | 5-0 | 6-0 | 7-0 | 8-0 |
| Per box | 13c. | 15c. | 17c. | 20c. | 23c. | 25c. | 30c. | 35c. |

## ABERDEEN HOOKS.

**No. 81508.** Superfine English blued spring steel round bend Aberdeen hooks, ringed. Put up in boxes of 100 each; only one size in a box.
100 hooks in a box.

| Size | 6 to 1 | 1-0 | 2-0 | 3-0 | 4-0 | 5-0 | 6-0 | 7-0 |
|---|---|---|---|---|---|---|---|---|
| Per box | 25c | 30c | 32c | 35c | 40c | 58c | 60c | 69c |

## SPROAT HOOKS.

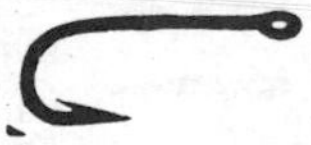

Superfine English blued spring steel sproat hooks, ringed. Put up in boxes of 100 each, only one size in a box.

**No. 81510.** 100 hooks in a box.

| Size | 8 to 1 | 1-0 | 2-0 | 3-0 | 4-0 | 5-0 | 6-0 | 7-0 |
|---|---|---|---|---|---|---|---|---|
| Per box | 20c | 30c | 40c | 45c | 50c | 55c | 70c | 75c |

## SOMETHING NEW.

**No. 81512.** Warren's Never Strip Snelled hooks, put up in wrapper envelopes; the hooks are all in view the moment the package is opened, and can be taken out singly or in any quantity desired without tangling the balance. We carry in stock Carlisle, Sproat and Aberdeen, tied in a good and serviceable manner, at prices and in sizes quoted below. In ordering be sure and state KIND wanted. If no kind is mentioned we will send Carlisle. One dozen of a size in a package. Price for single snelled, per package: 3-0, 30c; 2-0, 25c; 1-0, 22c; 1 to 10, 20c.

## SNELLED HOOKS.

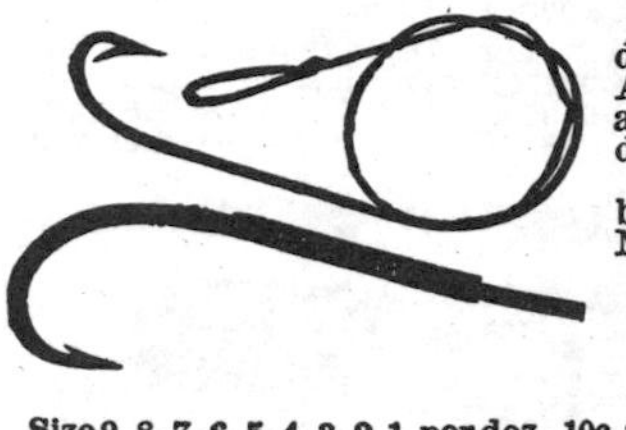

Sold in one-half dozen lots or over. Always give size and price when ordering.

Full length gut; best tied.

**No. 81514.** Superior Limerick hooks to single gut, and superior Kirby bent hook to single gut. Size 9, 8, 7, 6, 5, 4, 3, 2, 1, per doz., 10c.; 1-0, 11c.; 2-0, 14c.; 3-0, 18c.; 4-0, 25.

**No. 81516.** Superfine quality Limerick hooks to double gut; best quality full length double gut. Sizes 6 to 1, per doz., 22c.; 1-0, 25c.; 2-0, 30c.; 3-0, 35c.; 4-0, 40c.; 5-0, 45c.; 6-0, 55c.

**No. 81520.** Sproat hooks to 9-inch best quality double gut. Sizes 2 or 1, per doz., 35c.; 1-0, 40c.; 2-0, 42c.; 3-0, 45c.; 4-0, 50c.; 5-0, 55c.; 6-0, 65c.

Snelled hooks or hooks to gut sold in any quantity at above prices.

**No. 81522.** Aberdeen Hooks, tied to best quality full-lenght double gut. (Sold in half-dozen lots or over.)

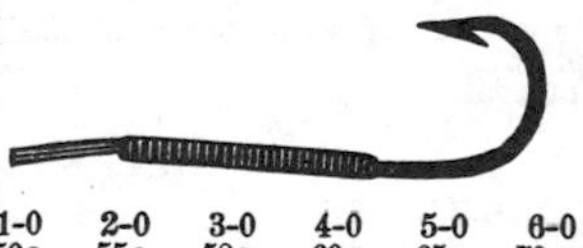

| Size | 4 to 1 | 1-0 | 2-0 | 3-0 | 4-0 | 5-0 | 6-0 |
|---|---|---|---|---|---|---|---|
| Per doz.. | 40c. | 50c. | 55c. | 58c. | 60c. | 65c. | 70c. |

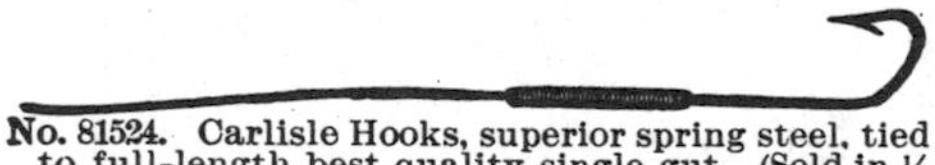

**No. 81524.** Carlisle Hooks, superior spring steel, tied to full-length best quality single gut. (Sold in ½ dozen lots or over.)

| Sizes | 8 to 1 | 1-0 | 2-0 | 3-0 |
|---|---|---|---|---|
| Per doz | 15c. | 20c. | 22c. | 25c. |

**No. 81526.** Carlisle Hooks, superior spring steel, tied to full-length best quality double gut.

| Size | 4 to 1 | 1-0 | 2-0 | 3-0 | 4-0 | 5-0 | 6-0 |
|---|---|---|---|---|---|---|---|
| Per doz.. | 20c. | 25c. | 28c. | 30c. | 33c. | 35c. | 40c. |

**No. 81528.** Sneck Kendall Hooks, spring steel, tied to full-length best quality single gut.

| Sizes | 1 | 2 | 3 | 4 | 5 | 6 |
|---|---|---|---|---|---|---|
| Per doz | 25c. | 25c. | 25c. | 25c. | 25c. | 25c. |

(State size wanted.)

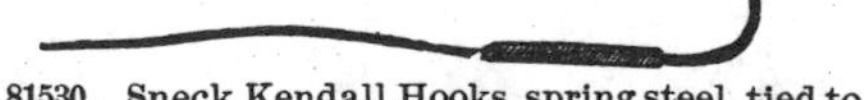

**No. 81530.** Sneck Kendall Hooks, spring steel, tied to full-length best quality double gut.

| Size | 1 to 4 | 1-0 | 2-0 | 3-0 | 4-0 | 5-0 |
|---|---|---|---|---|---|---|
| Per doz | 40c. | 50c. | 52c. | 55c. | 58c. | 68c. |

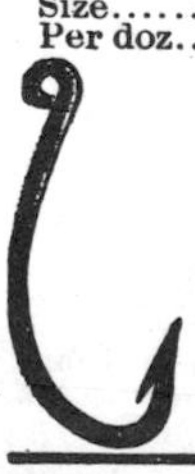

## CENTRAL DRAFT HOOK.

No. 81534. Central draft hooks, ringed.

| | | Per doz. | Gross. |
|---|---|---|---|
| No. 9—4⅜ in. long | | $0.20 | $2.15 |
| No. 10—4½ | " | 18 | 1.95 |
| No. 11—3⅞ | " | 15 | 1.60 |
| No. 12—3¾ | " | 10 | 1.10 |
| No. 13—2⅞ | " | 08 | 85 |
| No. 14—2½ | " | 06 | 60 |

WHEN YOU GO FISHING TAKE ALONG SOME OF OUR CANNED MEATS.
SEE PAGE 14.

## PLAIN TREBLE HOOKS.

(Ringed.)

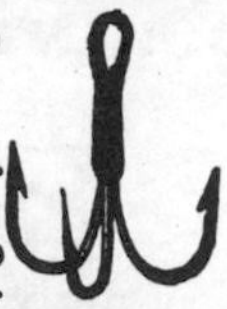

**No. 81536.** Treble hooks, plain ringed. Sizes 8, 7, 6, 5, 4, 3, 2, 1, per doz., 15c.

| Size | 1-0 | 2-0 | 3-0 | 4-0 | 5-0 | 6-0 | 7-0 |
|---|---|---|---|---|---|---|---|
| Per doz.. | 17c | 18c. | 21c. | 28c. | 30c. | 35c. | 40c. |

## TAPERED TREBLE HOOKS.

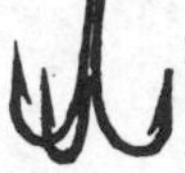

**No. 81538.** Tapered Treble Hooks. Sizes 10, 9, 8, 7, 6, 5, 4, 3, 2 or 1, each 4c.; per doz. 15c.

| Size... | 1-0 | 2-0 | 3-0 | 4-0 | 5-0 | 6-0 | 7-0 | 8-0 |
|---|---|---|---|---|---|---|---|---|
| Doz... | 17c. | 18c. | 21c. | 25c. | 28c. | 35c. | 40c. | 45c. |

## FEATHERED TREBLE HOOKS.

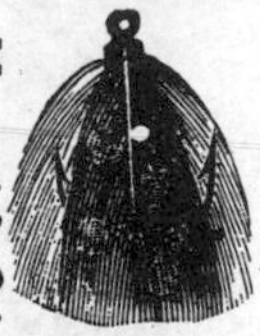

**No. 81540.** Feathered Treble Hooks. Sizes 10, 9, 8, 7, 6, 5, 4, 3, 2, 1, per dozen, 50c.

| Size, | 1-0 | 2-0 | 3-0 | 4-0 | 5-0 | 6-0 | 7-0 | 8-0 |
|---|---|---|---|---|---|---|---|---|
| Doz. | 50c. | 55c. | 60c. | 65c. | 70c. | 75c. | 80c. | 85c. |

## THE ST. LAWRENCE GANG.

Patented in England and the United States.

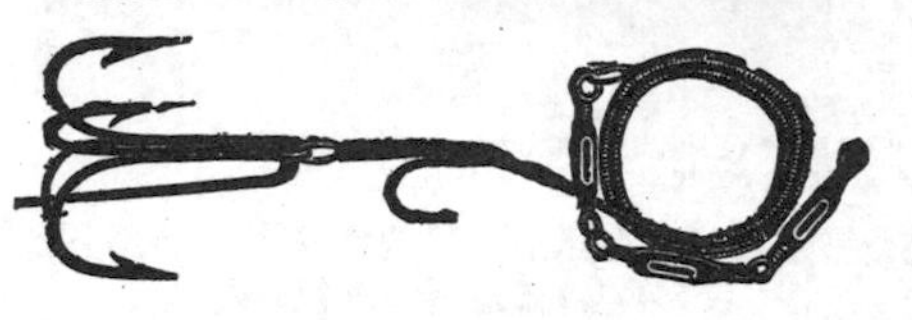

**No. 81542.** Nos. 1, 2 and 3, each, 20c.; per doz., $2.25. Nos. 1-0 and 2-0, each, 25c.; per doz., $2.90. No. 3-0, each, 35c.; per doz. ........ $4.15.

All have patent hooks, with baiting needle, adjustable lip hook and treble swivel, best silk metal-wound gimp on hook to attach line to.

This is the most ingenious invention and radical improvement in trolling tackle yet made. Its manifest superiority over all gangs now in use is evident to every expert angler. A few of the peculiar excellences are: It is the only gang on which a bait can live. It is the only gang which can be adjusted to any sized minnow instantly and perfectly. It is not only the simplest, but also the strongest gang made. It does not scare away the big and wary fish by a long array of treble hooks. The treble swivel insures perfect revolution of bait and reduces to the lowest possible point the liability of kinking the line.

## FIRST QUALITY OF EXCELSIOR FLOATS.

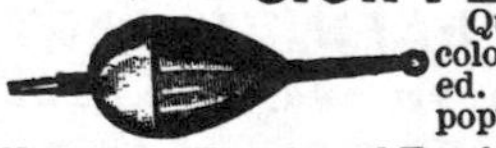

Quill top; painted in two colors and varnished; assorted. This is one of the most popular lines of floats.

**No. 81544.** Egg-shaped Excelsior.

| | 1½ in. | 1¾ in. | 2 in. | 2¼ in. | 2½ in. |
|---|---|---|---|---|---|
| Each | 2c. | 3c. | 4c. | 5c. | 6c. |
| Per doz | 22c. | 27c. | 30c. | 37c. | 47c. |

## CORK FLOATS.

**No. 81546.** Unbound, egg-shape, quill top. Painted in two colors.

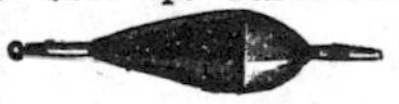

| | 1¼ in. | 1¾ in. | 2⅛ in. | 2½ in. |
|---|---|---|---|---|
| Each, | 4c. | 5c. | 6c. | 8c. |
| Doz., | 35c. | 51c. | 75c. | 87c. |

**No. 81548.** Barrel shape, best bound quill top. Painted in two colors.

| | 2 in. | 3 in. | 4 in. |
|---|---|---|---|
| Each | 5c. | 8c. | 18c. |
| Per doz | 46c. | 78c. | $1.75 |

## BRASS BOX SWIVELS.

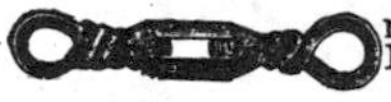

Sold in any quantity at dozen rates.

**No. 81550.** Brass Box Swivels. No. 8, smallest, ½ inch long. 3-0, largest, 1¾ inches long.

| Sizes | 1 to 8 | 1-0 | 2-0 | 3-0 |
|---|---|---|---|---|
| Per doz | 12c. | 22c. | 30c. | 40c. |

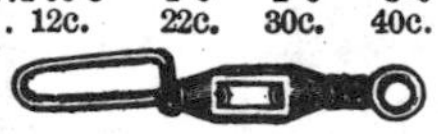

**No. 81552.** Brass Hook Swivels. Sizes, 1-0, 2, 4, 6, 8. No. 1-0, largest, about 2¼ inches long; 8, smallest, 1 in. long. 1-0, per doz., 65c.; Nos. 2, 4, 6, 8, per doz., 50c.

## SINKERS.

**No. 81554.** Patent adjustable sinkers. These can be attached or detached by a single turn of the line. No. 1, smallest, ⅞ inch long; No. 7, largest, 2 inches long.

| Size | 1 | 2 | 3 | 4 | 5 | 6 | 7 |
|---|---|---|---|---|---|---|---|
| Per dozen.. | $0.09 | $0.12 | $0.16 | $0.17 | $0.19 | $0.22 | $0.24 |

Sold in any quantity at dozen rates.

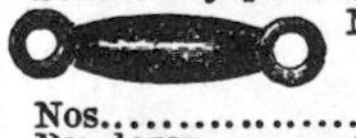

**No. 81556.** Ringed sinkers. Smallest Nos. 1, 2, 3 and 4, per doz....... 8c.

| Nos. | 5 | 6 | 7 | 8 | 9 | 10 |
|---|---|---|---|---|---|---|
| Per dozen | $0.09 | $0.10 | $0.15 | $0.18 | $0.20 | $025 |

No. 1 smallest ¾ inch long; No. 10 largest, 3 inches long, weight 2¼ oz.

## SPLIT SHOT.

For light sinkers and fly casting when it is windy. By mail, 1c extra for box.

**No. 81558.** Split shot for sinkers, ¼ gross in wood box per box ........ $ .03
Per dozen boxes ........ .20

BUY OUR $35.00 BICYCLE.

## GUT LEADERS.

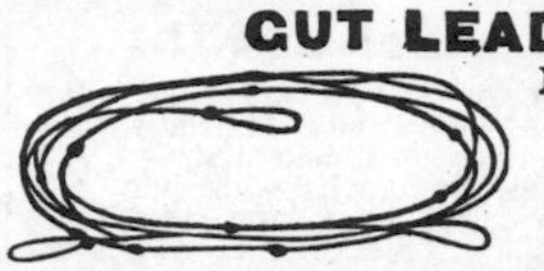

**No. 81559.** Spanish silk worm gut. Leaders, 3 ft. single, each 3c; per dozen, 20c. Leaders 3 ft. double, each 5c; per dozen, 35c.

**No. 81560.** Leaders, good heavy, 3 ft., single, each, 4c, per dozen, 30c; 6 ft. single, each, 5c, per dozen, 50c; 9 ft. single, each, 10c, per dozen, $1.00.

**No. 81562.** Leaders, good extra heavy, 3 ft. single, each, 6c, per dozen, 65c; 6 ft., single, each, 10c, per dozen, $1.00; 9 ft. single, each, 16c, per doz., $1.70.

**No. 81564.** Leader, heavy bass and salmon, 3 ft. single, each, 15c, per dozen, $1.50; 6 ft. single, each, 30c, per dozen, $3.00; 9 ft. single, each, 45c, per dozen, $4.50.

**No. 81566.** Leaders, regular quality, 3 ft. double, each, 8c, per dozen, 86c; 6 ft. double, each, 14c, per dozen, $1.65; 9 ft. double, each, 25c, per dozen, $2.70.

**No. 81568.** Leaders, best heavy, double. 3 ft. double, each, 20c, per dozen, $2.25; 6 ft. double, each, 37c, per dozen, $4.00; 9 ft. double, each, 60c, per dozen, $6.50.

**No. 81570.** Leaders, spliced knots twisted. 3 ft. long, each, 20c, per dozen, $2.00; 6 ft. long, each, 40c, per dozen, $3.60; 9 ft. long, each, 75c, per dozen, $5.00.

## SILKWORM GUT.

No. 81572. Put up 100 in a bunch.

| | | |
|---|---|---|
| E, | 11 inches long, fine, per bunch | $ .35 |
| N, | " " heavy, " | .70 |
| Q, | " " " " | .95 |
| S, | " " " " | 1.45 |

## TROUT FLIES AND HACKLE.

Our stock of trout flies is made up of the best known and most popular varieties and patterns, and adapted to all water, and seasons. We selected the most popular and best killing varieties made, and carry them in stock in three grades, viz: A, B and C, grade C being the best fly made; the B grade, the standard fly (sold by many dealers as the *best*), and the grade A being the same fly with less hackle and wing, and cheaper quality of tying. All of our flies are tied on Harrison spring steel needle pointed sproat hook and guaranteed as such. We list and describe the following most popular styles.

Sizes of hooks, 6, 8 and 10. These are the sizes used by expert fly fisherman. All flies tied on best single gut.

Always mention name and grade wanted when ordering flies. *We guarantee our flies to be a better quality grade for grade than any other dealer can furnish at these prices. A comparison is all we ask.*

## SOMETHING HANDSOME.

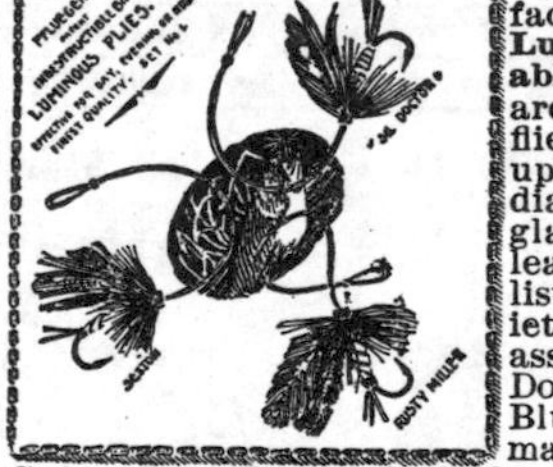

The engraving is a fac-simile of **"Pflueger's Luminous Indestructable Body Flies."** These are the most beautiful flies on the market; put up assorted (3) on a card, diamond shaped, white glazed, printed in gold leaf. The following is a list of the different varieties contained in this assortment: Sexton, Sil Doctor, Rusty Miller—Blue Jay, Royal Coachman, Ibis—Ethel May, Guinea, Coachman—Seth Green, Gow Dung, Lake George—Prince Albert, Evening Bell, Great Scott—Professor. Gueen of Water. White Miller—Raven, Pembria, Sargant—Governor, Montreal, Yellow Beauty—Golden Doctor, Oliver. Princes—Peacock, Snake Doctor. Grizzly King—Blue Bottle, Black Ant, Yellow May—Arcade. Parnell. Blue Prince—Partridge, Rocky River. Jaguar—Aldan, May Flower, Red Wood, Mallard, May Queen. Fire Fly—Romo, Pyramid, Countess—Queen, Sylph, Imperial, Tipperlinn, Duke, Amazon—Alden Cock, Bishop, Monarh—Gipsy, Dwarf, Emerald Gnat, Chippy, Yellow Robbin, Yellow Governor—Wild Roosser, Indian Crow, Cock Robin—Lake Huron, Toronta, Oregon—Snow Flake, Golden Duke, Soldier—Deer Fly, Orange Dun, Golden Black—Silver Black, Turkey, Portlaad—Polka, Alexandria, Beaverkill—Oriole, Abbey, Ferguson—Red Ant, Royal Coachman, Rueb Wood—Dark Spinner, Apolla, White Miller. These flies are strictly "high grade" and usually sell at 15c to 20c per single fly. We offer them by card only, containing (3) assorted flies of the acove variety.

**No. 81575.** Trout Flies to single gut leader, on No. 4, 6 or 8 hooks only. Per card of (3) flies ........ $0.25
Per dozen cards (or 3 dozen flies) ........ 2.85

**No. 81576.** Bass Flies to double gut leaders, with spoon hooks. Same assortment on No. 1-0, 1 or 2 hooks. Per card of (3) flies ........ $0.30
Per dozen cards (or 3 dozen flies) ........ 3.25

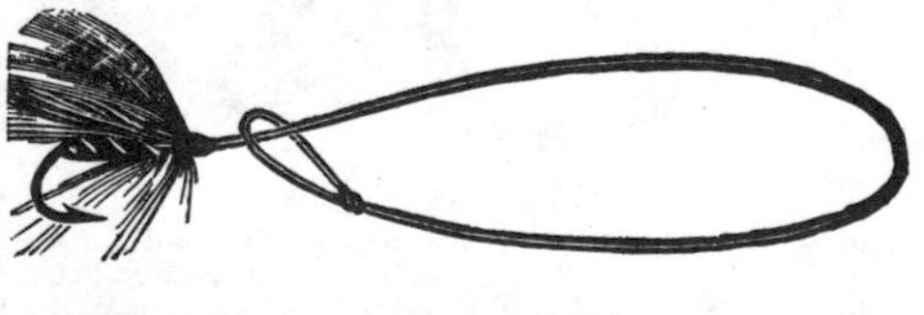

*Always mention size of hook, name and grade wanted.* Prices are per dozen, sizes 6, 8 and 10 hooks. We do not break dozens of A Grade flies. Not less than one dozen of this grade will be sold. We will sell ½ dozen of either B or C Grade, but not less.

**No. 81580.** **Professor**, yellow body, gold bound and tipped scarlet tongue, ginger hackle, black and white mottled wings. A, 20c. B, 35c. C, 50c.

**No. 81582.** **Governor Alvord**, peacock body, cinnamon hackle, dark gray or mouse colored wing. B, 35c. C, 50c.

Trout Flies and Hackle.—Continued.

No. 81616. **Evening Dun**, silk wound scarlet body, gold tipped, dark hackle, light dove colored wing. B, 35c. C, 50c.
No. 81618. **Silver Doctor**, silver bound body, yellow hackle, variegated colored wing. B, 35c. C, 50c.
No. 81620. **Seth Green**, green body, bound with gold, fawn colored hackle, brown dappled wing. B, 35c. C, 50c.
No. 81622. **Capt. Scott**, turkey bronze body, tipped with red, black hackle, light gray and white dappled wing. B, 35c. C, 50c.
No. 81624. **Cow Dung**, dark brown body, light brown hackle, dove colored wing, tied on best single gut. A, 20c. B, 35c. C, 50c.
No. 81626. **Queen of Waters**, large body silver bound, dark ginger hackle, light mottled black and white wing. B. 35c. C, 50c.
No. 81628. **June**, body in rings of two colors (white and red) black hackle, brown and black hackled wing, B, 35c. C, 50c.
No. 81630. **Grizzly King**, green body, bound with silver, red tongue, gray and black hackle, light gray and dark brown mottled wing. A, 20c. B, 35c. C, 50c.
No. 81632. **Dark Coachman**, wings, lead color; body, peacock; herl legs, brown hackle. A, 20c. B, 35c. C, 50c.
No. 81634. **Brown Palmer**, wing, red; body, red silk, wound with a brown hackle. A, 20c. B, 35c. C, 50c.
No. 81636. **Brown Palmer**, green body; body green silk, wound with brown hackle. A, 20c. B, 35c. C, 50c.
No. 81638. **Brown Stone**, wings, brown mallard; body, brown mohair; tail, brown mallard legs, dark brown hackle. B, 35c. C, 50c.
No. 81640. We can furnish any of the above named flies on 3, 4, or 5 hooks in grade "C" only.
Price per dozen....50c.
No. 81642. **Midges**, or small trout flies. Superior midget flies tied on sproat hooks; Nos. 12 and 14, of which the following is a list: Golden Spinner, Royal Coachman, Abbey, March Brown, Black Hackle, Beaverhill, Coachman, Hare's Ear, Professor, White Miller, Great Dunn, Brown Hackle, Dark Coachman, Yellow May, Gray Hackle, Red Spinner, Brown Ant, Governor, Grizzly King, Black Knat, Dark Cowdung. The above selection are "Killers." Per dozen.....50c.

## TROUT HACKLE FLIES.

Tied on same quality and size hooks and gut as regular flies.
No. 81644. Black hackle, brown hackle, gray hackle, grizzly hackle, golden or yellow hackle, ginger hackle, peacock black hackle, peacock brown hackle, peacock gray hackle, red hackle, white hackle. Price....$0.35

## HIGHEST GRADE TROUT FLIES.

No. 81646. High grade trout flies, reversed wing. Tied on best spring steel hooks and the best gut in the best possible manner. Names: Black Palmer, Brown Palmer, Grey Palmer, Black Knat, Beaver Kill, Bee, Captain, Coachman, Royal Coachman, Cow Dung, Grizzly King, Golden Spinner, Gov. Alvord, Hare's Ear, Scarlet, March Brown, Dark Montreal, Parmachenee Bell, Professor, Queen of Waters, Silver Doctor, Shoemaker, White Miller, 3, 4, 6, 8, 10 and 12 hooks.
Each....$0.10
Per dozen....1.00
In ordering, give catalogue number and name of fly and size of hook.

## BASS FLIES.

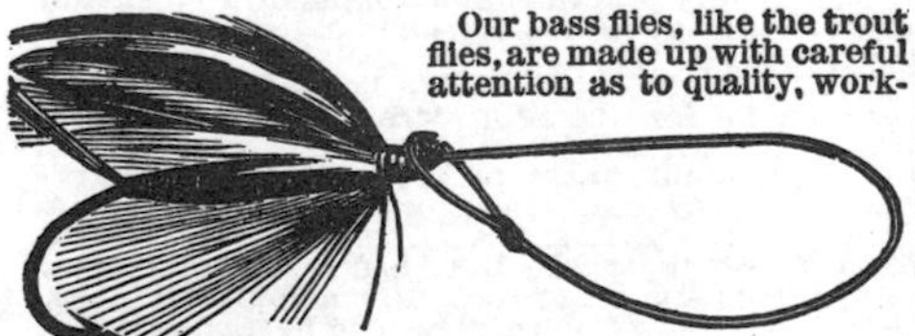

Our bass flies, like the trout flies, are made up with careful attention as to quality, workmanship and combination of natural colors. They are tied on best spring steel needle pointed limerick and sproat hooks. Sizes 1 and 2, 1-0, 2-0, 3-0 hooks, nicely mounted in cardboard. By mail, 2 to 4 cts. per dozen extra. Sold in any quantity at dozen prices.
No. 81648. Bass flies consisting of the following styles: Windsor, Sweep, Oak, Olive, Montreal, Professor, Cock Robin, Captain, Governor, Soldier, Snowflake, Polka, Golden Ibis, Lake Huron, White Miller, March Brown, Lake Erie and Scarlet Ibis. Each....$0.10
Per dozen....1.00

## EXTRA FINE SPECIAL BASS FLIES.

No. 81649. **Seth Green**, tied to finest double gut, on best steel spring sproat hooks, made of the very best material, gold plush body, green necked, silver tipped, mottled tongue, heavy brown hackle, wing of female mallard, brown mottled feather. Sizes, 4-2-1, 1-0, 2-0 and 3-0. Prices, each....$0.15
Per dozen....1.00
No. 81650. **Royal Coachman**. Sizes 1-0, 2-0 and 3-0. Price, each....$0.15
Per dozen....1.40
No. 81652. **Professor**. Sizes, 1-0, 2-0 and 3-0. Price, each....$0.15
Per dozen....1.40
No. 81654. **Black June**, Peacock breast body, gold tipped, hair tongue, black hackle, raven wing. Sizes, 1-0, 2-0 and 3-0. Price each....$0.15
Per dozen....1.40

## ARTIFICIAL BAITS.

We have selected the best and most used baits, all of which we can recommend. Any bait not satisfactory at the price can be returned as soon as examined.

### SKINNER'S SPOON BAIT.

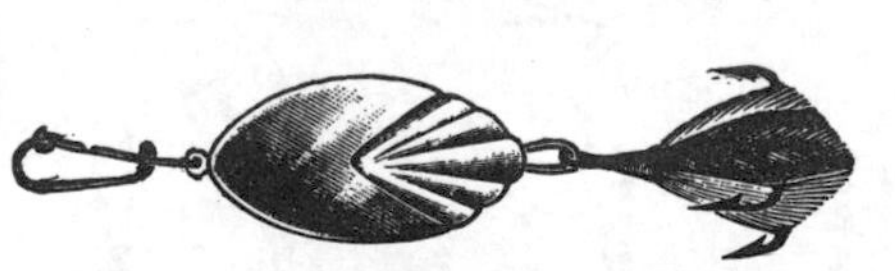

**Skinner's Spoons, Nickel Plated.**

No. 81670. Suitable for black bass, trout, etc. Nos. 1, 2, 3, 4, 4½, 4¾, each....$0.18
Per dozen....2.20
No. 12909. Suitable for pickerel, lake trout, pike and muskallonge, medium. Nos. 5 and 6, each....$0.24
Per dozen....2.50
Nos. 7 and 8, each....30
Per dozen....3.20

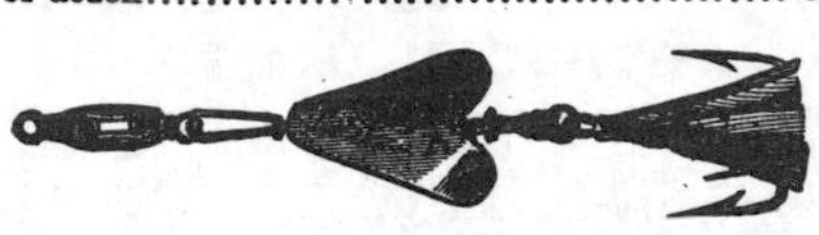

No. 81672. Black bass spinners, finely plated, with swivel, revolving spoon, feathered hooks. Sizes, 1, 2, 3, 4, 5 and 6. No. 1 is smallest. Each....$0.10
Per dozen, assorted....1.10

### KIDNEY SPOON BAITS.

All good baits.

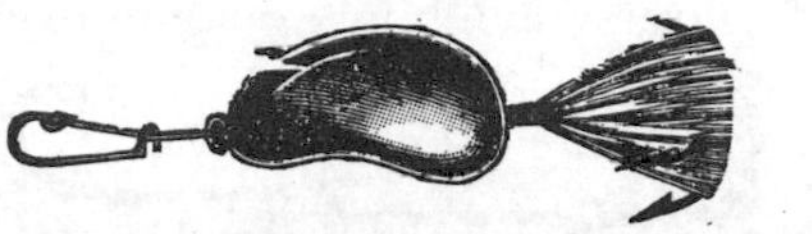

No. 81674. Kidney nickel plated spoon bait, nickel plated spoons, fine feathered treble hooks. Sizes 1, 2, 3, 4, 5 and 6. No. 1 spoon is about 1 in. long, No. 2 is 1¼ in., No. 3 is 1⅜ in., No. 4 is 1⅝ in., No. 5 is 1⅞ in., No. 6 is 2¼ in. Each....$0.10
Per dozen....1.00
No. 81676. Pickerel bait, same shape and sizes of No. 81674, is tinned with feathered treble hook; box swivel attached; a good one. Each....$0.05
Per dozen....55
No. 81678. Bass, pickerel or pike bait, kidney shape with swivel. Same shape and sizes as No. 81674. Each....$0.10
Per dozen....1.00

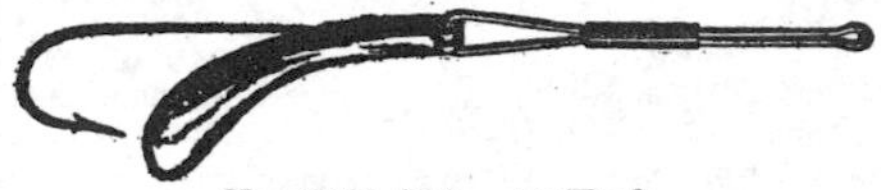

No. 81680 (901). 4-0 Hook.

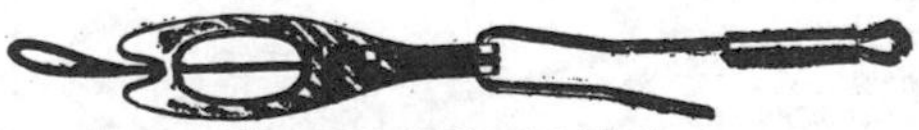

No. 81681 (4 R). 4-0 Hook.

In addition to the great merits of this device as a weed guard, it is a sinker in the right place and helps out the bait-caster. It also lands the frog belly down and trolls the minnow in a natural manner. For casting a pork rind bait it is simply *perfection*. When using Nos. 900 to 902, hook the frog or minnow from the top down, the point of the hook pointing downward, as shown in the illustration. The guard will hang downward, leaving the point of the hook well exposed; when obstructions are reached, the guard instantly closes over the point of the hook. Nos. 2R to 7R are reversible and can be used in either way, making an absolute weed guard with the hook pointing downward and a three-quarter weed guard when pointing upward.

| | | Each. |
|---|---|---|
| No. 900. | 2-0, Best Carlisle hooks.... | $0.25 |
| No. 901. | 4-0, " " " .... | .25 |
| No. 902. | 7-0, " " " .... | .25 |
| No. 2R. | New reversible, 2-0, best Carlisle hooks... | .25 |
| No. 4R. | " " 4-0, " " " ... | .25 |
| No. 7R. | " " 7-0, " " " ... | .25 |

Two hooks accompany each guard. Sent by mail postpaid.

## THE "SUCCESS" LUMINOUS BAIT.

No. 81684. The "Success" minnow head, fluted spoon, a "great killer" and one of the best trolling baits ever placed on the market, with patent reversible hinge leg, with gimp leader, and swivel.

| | No. 2, smallest. | No. 4. | No. 6. | No. 8. |
|---|---|---|---|---|
| Price, each..... | $0.20 | $0.23 | $0.27 | $0.35 |

Don't fail to order a sample of this bait.

## FLUTED SPOON BAIT.

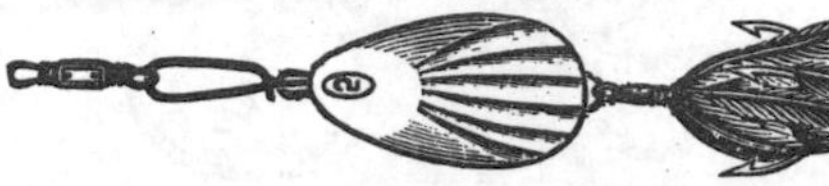

No. 81690. Fluted trolling spoon, full nickel plate, same shape spoon as Skinner's and same size hook, treble hook and fly; a first-class spoon. No. 1, smallest, 1¼-inch spoon. Nos. 1, 2, 3, 4, 4½, 4¾, each, 7c; Nos. 5 and 6, each, 10c; Nos. 7 and 8, each....$0.10

## AMERICAN SPINNER.

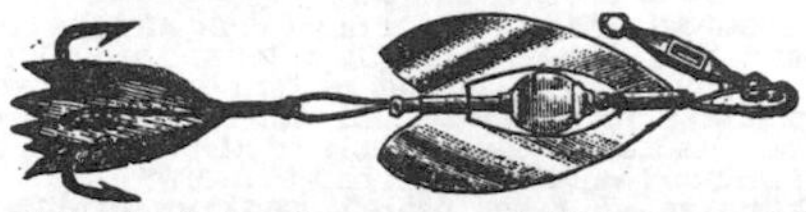

No. 81692. Best plated spoon, one-half hammered, best material and a rapid spinner, for bass, pickerel, etc. Nos. 2, 3, 4, 5 and 6, smallest, each, 20c per dozen.$2.25

## SPOON MINNOWS.

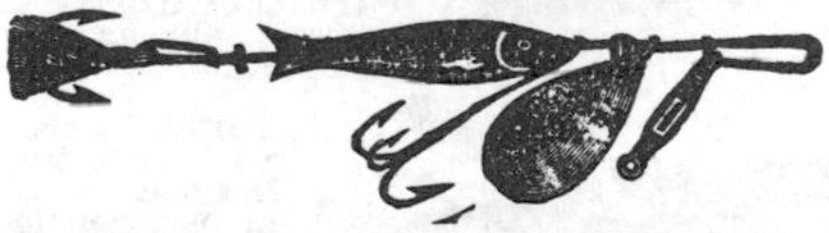

No. 81694. Fine nickel plated spoon, rubber minnows, best material, treble hook; a good bait for large fish. Nos. 4, 5, 3½ each, 65c; per dozen....$6.70

## HAMMERED SPOON BAITS.

In ordering state kind of fishing wanted for

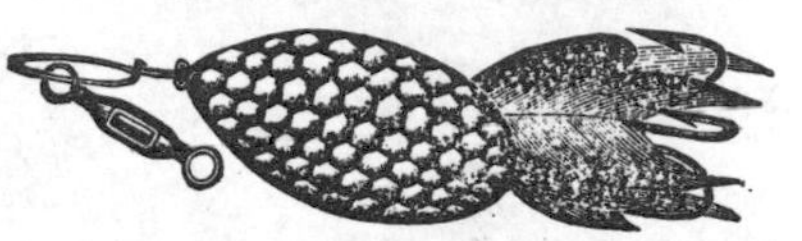

No. 81696. Best nickel plated spoon, feathered treble hook. One of the most successful baits in the market. No. 1, smallest, 1 inch; No. 7, largest, 2½ inch. Nos. 1, 2, 3, 4, 5, 6, 7, each, 10c; per dozen....$1.09

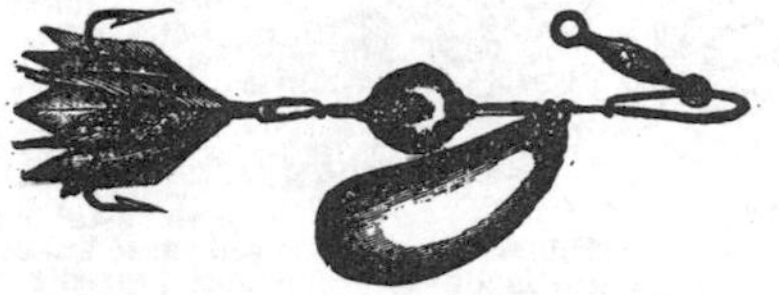

No. 81698. Ball bait, good nickel plate spoons, feathered treble hook. No. 1, smallest for small bass; larger ones for pickerel, pike and muskallonge. Nos. 1, 3½, 3, 3½, 4, 5, 6 and 7. No. 7, largest, about 2¾ inches, each, 15c; per dozen....$1.75

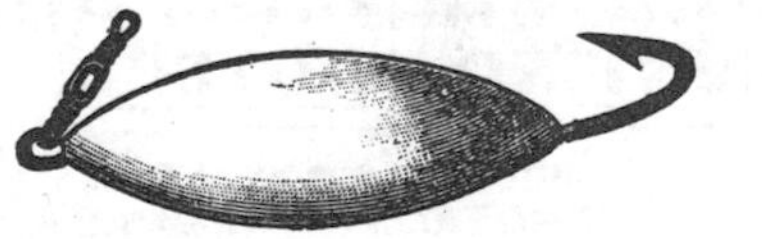

No. 81699. Salmon trout bait, plated spoon, one hook. No. 1, smallest, 2¼ inches long, 4 inches long and 3¼ inches long, each, 20c; per dozen....$2.40

## THE MUSKALLONGE OR TARPON BAITS.

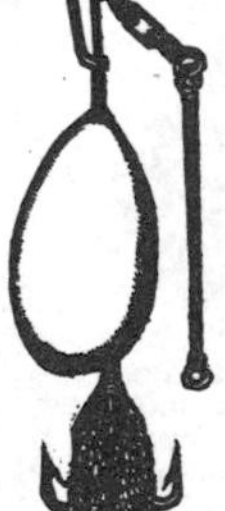

The herculean strength of this bait will tell its own story to the fisherman in the pursuit of large game. For the St. Lawrence, the western lakes and rivers and the coast of Florida they will fill the bill to perfection.
No. 81700. Fine nickel plated spoon, treble hook, feathered, very best material, 2¾ inch spoon for 10 to 25 lb. fish.
Each....$0.25
Per dozen....2.70
3½-inch spoon, for 20 to 100 lb. fish.
Each....$0.30
Per dozen....3.00

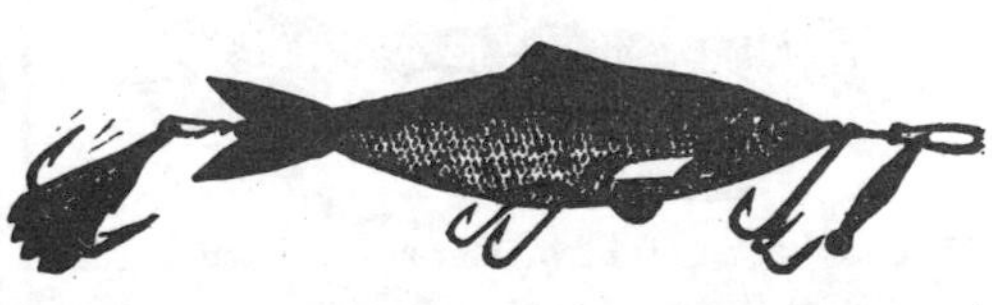

No. 81702. Muskallonge trolling minnow, solid rubber, accurately decorated to represent the live minnow; the finest bait in the world to capture "Muskey." Entire length of minnow 6½ inches. Price, each.$1.20

NEVER CUT A PICTURE OR DESCRIPTION FROM YOUR CATALOGUE. GIVE THE CATALOGUE NUMBER AND NAME OF ARTICLE, WITH SIZES, COLORS, ETC., WANTED, AND WE CAN DETERMINE WHAT YOU DESIRE.

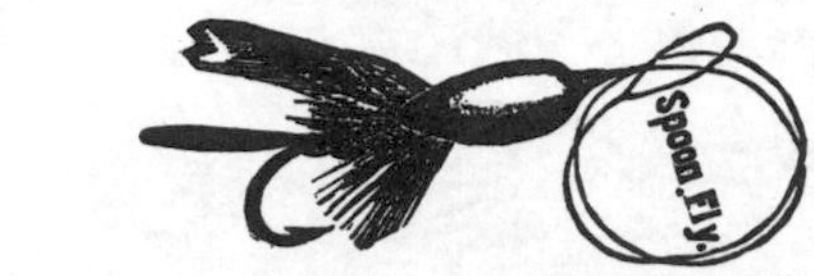


No. 81704. Adirondack spinner spoon fly, smallest nickel spoon, feathered hook for small trout, etc. Small, about ¾-inch spoon; medium, 1 inch; large, 1¼ inch, each, 15c; per dozen....................$2.25

## THE PATENT LUMINOUS FISH BAIT.

The most attractive lure for day fishing and the only successful bait in deep and rolly water and after dark. Every suitable size, style and pattern made for bass, pike, pickerel, muskallonge and other game fish of America. As game fish do most of their feeding by night, luminous bait is the best bait to fish with.

DIRECTIONS.—For day fishing, use same as ordinary baits. For night fishing, expose baits to light during the day.

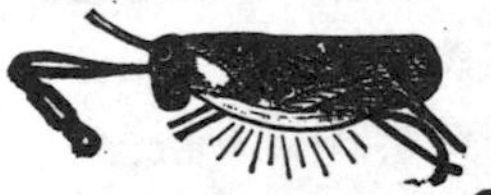

No. 81705. Luminous soft rubber grasshopper. The most natural and most durable article on the market, each...$0.30

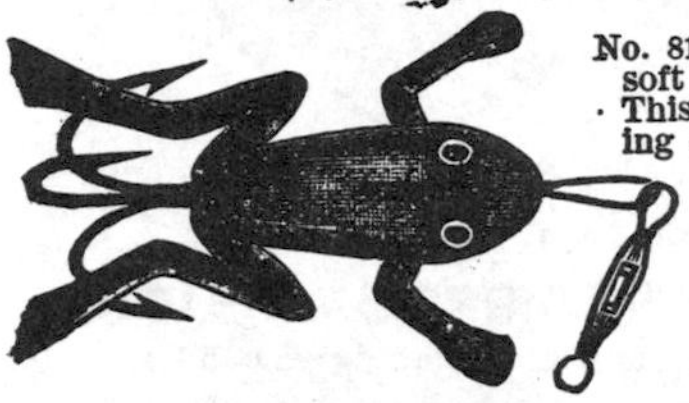

No. 81706. Luminous soft rubber frogs. This bait is a lasting one, combined with luminous qualities. It is a decided improvement over live frogs. Each......30c

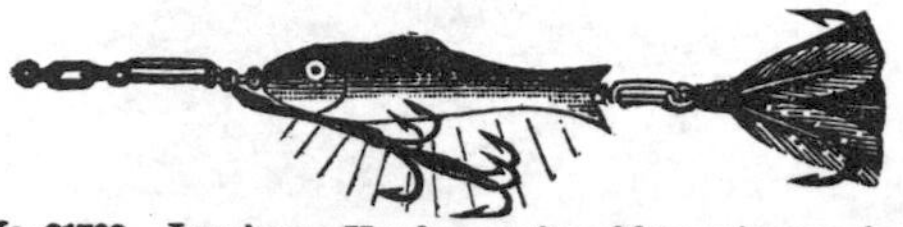

No. 81708. Luminous Hard or soft rubber minnow, indestructible. The best imitation of a minnow, finely colored. The "cut" is poor, but the bait is the best in the market. Nos. 7, 8 and 9. Price each, all sizes.40c

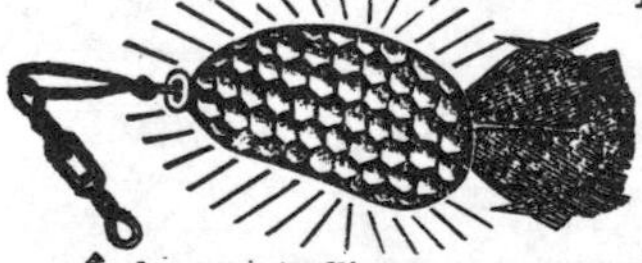

No. 81712. Pflueger's luminous baits are too well known to require any extended description. Their killing qualities are well established and wherever trolling spoons are used these baits are found. They are made with the best brazed treble hooks, well feathered, and the spoons are heavily nickel plated. 3 smallest and 8 largest.

Nos. 3 and 4, each....................27c
Nos. 5 and 6, each....................30c
Nos. 7 and 8, each....................35c

## HUNTING BOOTS.

SEE OUR BOOT AND SHOE DEPARTMENT.

LOWEST PRICES. BEST QUALITY.

## PHANTOM MINNOWS.

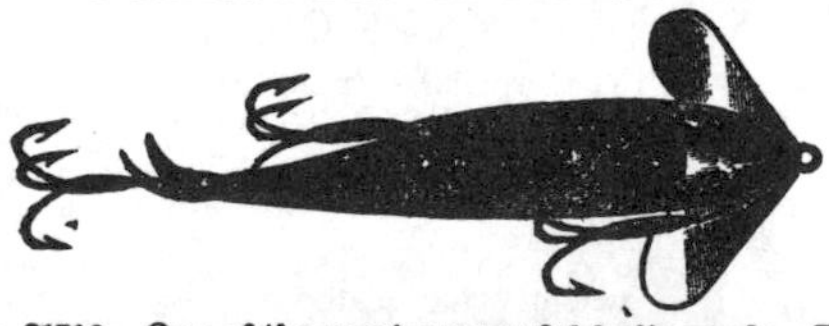

No. 81716. One of the most successful baits made. The body is made of silk waterproofed, nicely mounted, assorted colors and shades. Nos. 2, 3, 4, 5, 45c; No. 6, 49c; No. 7, 55c; No. 8....................60c

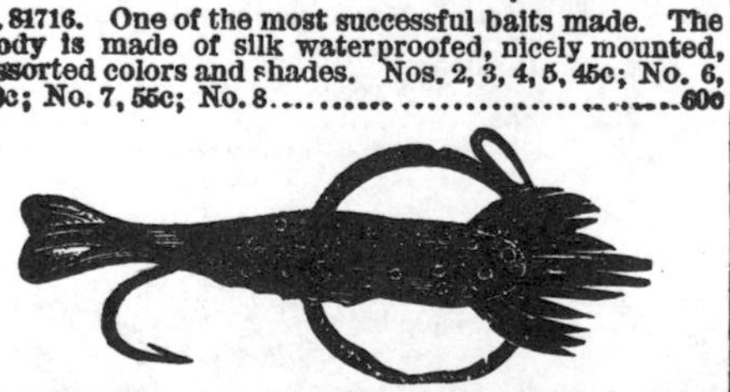

No. 81720. Large crawfish, soft rubber. Each......25c.

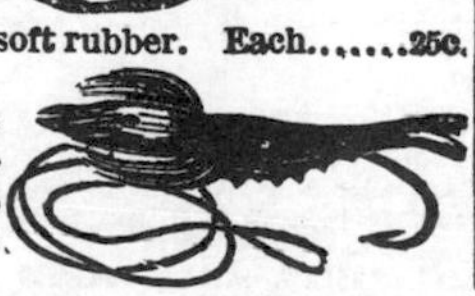

No. 81722. Shrimps, small, Each....................20c.
No. 81724. Shrimps, large, Each....................27c.

## HELGAMITES.

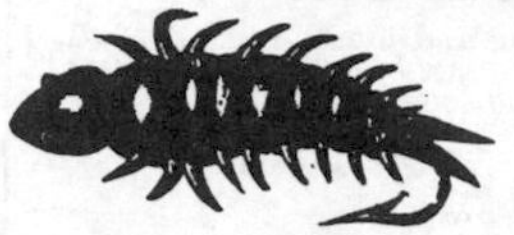

No. 81726. Helgamite or Dobson soft rubber, with swivel. Each, 25c.

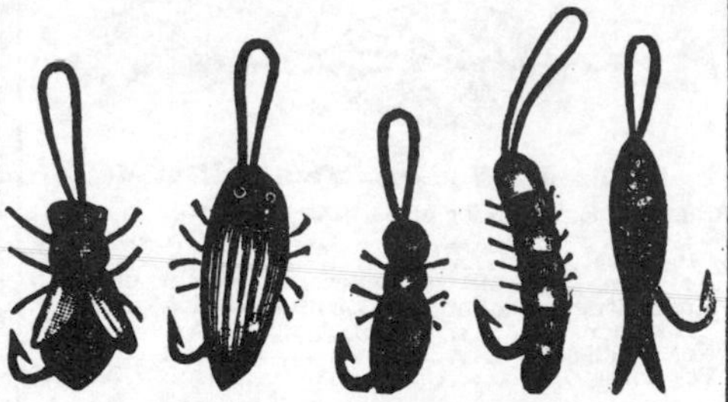

## ARTIFICIAL BAITS.

No. 81728. Bumble bee, cockchafer, beetle, caterpillar, fly-minnow, wasps, blue bottle, lady bird, spider, cricket and house fly; assorted colors. Each......15c.
Grasshopper, small, each....................15c.
Grasshopper, large, each....................25c.
No. 81730. Frogs, small; soft rubber. Each..........20c.
No. 81732. Frogs, large; soft rubber. Each..........25c.

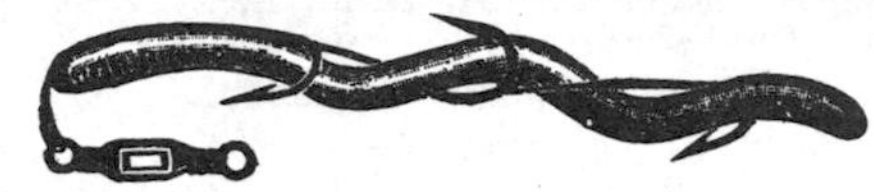

No. 81734. Angle worms; a perfect imitation. Each....................20c.

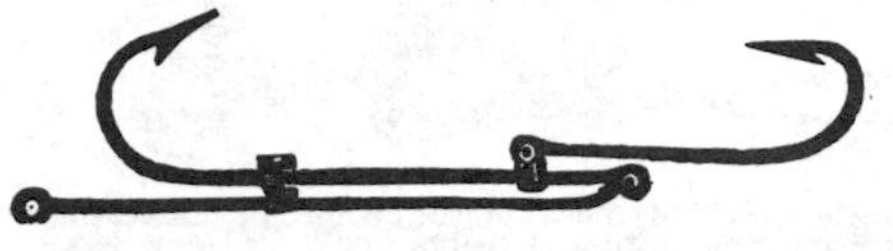

No. 81736. Greer's patent lever fish hook; no more fish lost and baits to reset; no coming home without your largest fish; a dead sure thing on getting your fish if it bites; it is easily adjusted to all kinds of fishing, by sliding the little clamp on the rod; made on 3-0 Carlisle hooks. Each.......10c. Per Doz..........$1.00

## SPRING HOOKS.

No. 81738. The Sockdologer spring fish hook.

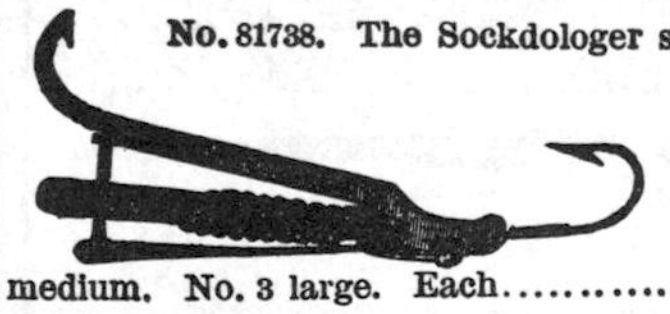

Easy to set and sure to catch any fish that takes it. For large fish. No. 1 small. No. 2 medium. No. 3 large. Each....................23c.

No. 81740. The snap and catch 'em spring fish hook. Easily set. Fish cannot get away once he is hooked.

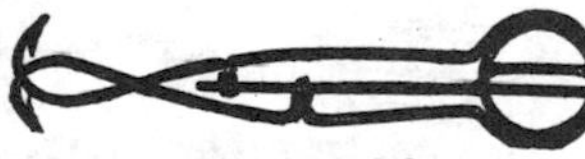

For small fish.

No. 20 small, No. 19 medium, No. 18 large. Each....................10c.

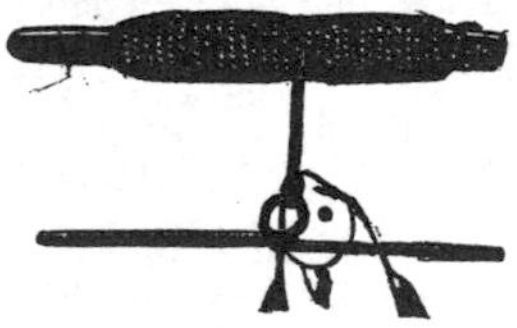

## FISH STRINGERS.

No. 81742. Fish stringer, No. 1 XC plate complete with line. By mail, 2c extra.
Each.................. 5c.
Per Dozen.........45c.

## CHAIN FISH STRINGER.

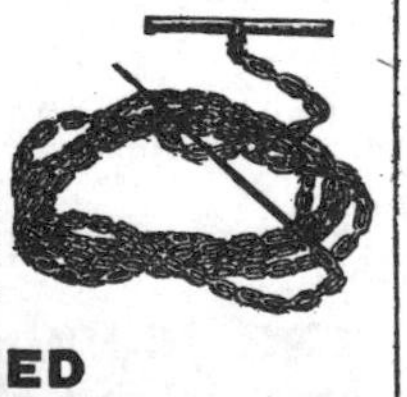

No. 81744. Chain fish stringers, brass links, heavily nickel plated, strong and durable, will hold 100 pounds of fish and not break. Each..............25c.

## COMBINED FISH HOOK EXTRACTOR AND FISH STRINGER.

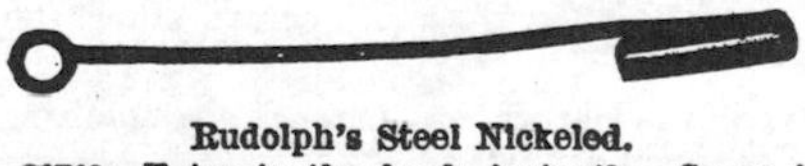

Rudolph's Steel Nickeled.

No. 81746. Extracts the hook instantly. Saves time, line, hook and fish. Each....................$ .15
Per Dozen....................1.55

UNCLE SAM MAKES IT EASY FOR YOU TO BUY BY MAIL.

## CLEARING RINGS.

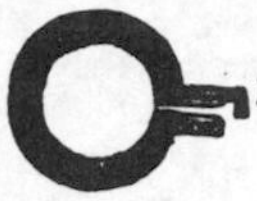

No. 81748. Clearing rings to free the hook when it gets caught under the water. Each....................54c.

## FROG SPEAR.

No. 81750. Frog spear, 3 tines, with socket to put pole in. Each.........15c.

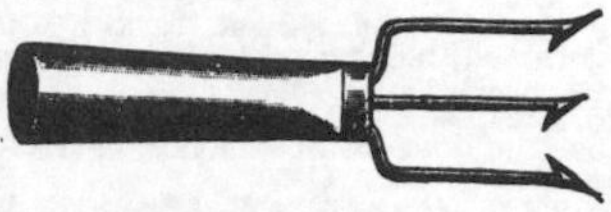

## FISH SPEARS.

Lengths given the entire length of prongs; weight, 8 to 12 ounces each.

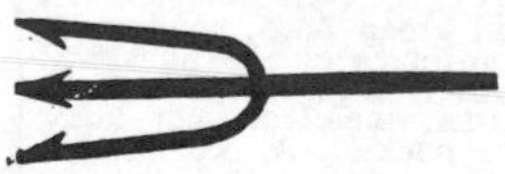

No. 81752. 3 prongs, 2¼ in. long, tanged. Each....................20c.
No. 81754. 5 prongs, 4 in. long, tanged. Each....................25

No. 81756. 5 prongs, 4½ inches, with sockets. Each..........50c.
No. 81758. Five prongs, 5 in. with socket. Each.....65c.
Lengths given are length of prong.

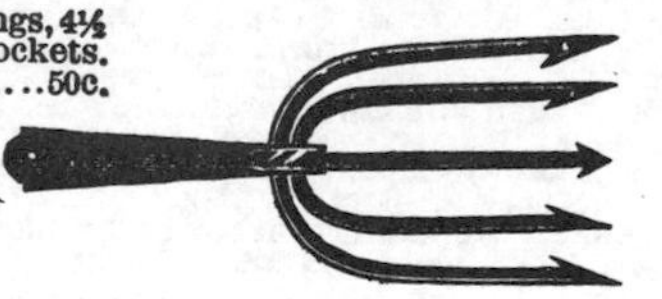

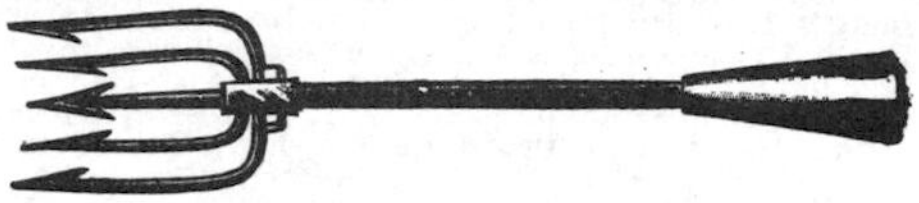

The best spear on the market.

No. 81760. Hand made fish spear, all best steel, except socket and wedge; beards of each tine made on solid shank, screws into socket and makes its own thread in wood (of handle); the outside tines can be removed if smaller spear is wanted at any time by putting in larger wedge; width about 4¼ to 4½ in.; entire length of tines, about 6½ in.; entire length 22 in. Weight about 1¾ lbs. Each....................$ 2.25
Per Dozen....................24.00

## LANDIS TACKLE BOXES.

The very best in the market.

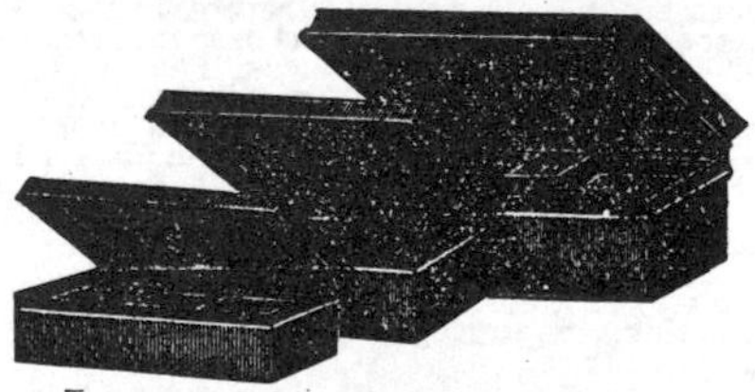

Showing comparative sizes of 81762-6.

This is a very practical and ornamental box made of heavy tin, double seamed and soldered, and will stand hard service.

No. 81762. Single outfit tackle box, has four compartments for tackle; size, 8x4¾x2¼ inches. Price....................$0.75
No. 81764. Double outfit tackle box, has 4 compartments, 1 tray and space for reel. Size, 8x4¾x3¼. Price....................$1.00
No. 81766. Stock tackle Box, has 4 compartments, tray, space for large reel, any amount of lines, hooks, etc. They must be seen to be appreciated. All are made black finish, gilt stripe and ornamentation. Size, 16⅜x5½x4. Price..............$1.25
No. 81768. Wilson's pocket tackle box, 7x4x1½ inches. Has center leaf which projects slightly beyond the two halves of the box, so that when the box is opened this leaf is caught and raised with the half uppermost, thus retaining in their places the tackle in that half. Has corks for books. Space for gang hooks attached to the trolling spoons. Each....................$0.95

## BORCHERDT'S FISHING TACKLE BOX.

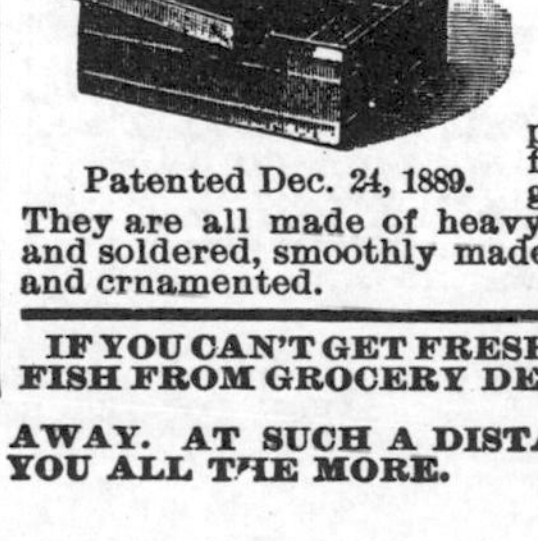

Patented Dec. 24, 1889.

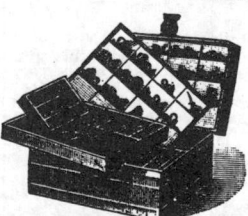

No. 81770. Size, 9½x7x3, has 1 tray, space for 2 reels, and any amount of lines, hooks, etc., with pockets in cover for flies, as shown in cut. Each..........$2.85
No. 81772. 10¾x9½x3¾, 1 tray, space for two reels, trolling line, etc., and pockets in cover. Each......$3.00
These boxes were planned by a practical fisherman, and have given satisfaction to all. They are all made of heavy stock, double seamed and soldered, smoothly made and elegantly painted and ornamented.

IF YOU CAN'T GET FRESH FISH, BUY CANNED FISH FROM GROCERY DEP'T ON PAGE 14.

IF YOU ARE 1500 MILES FROM CHICAGO, DON'T FEAR THAT YOU ARE TOO FAR AWAY. AT SUCH A DISTANCE FROM TRADE CENTERS, DEALERS' PRICES ARE ENORMOUS, AND WE CAN SAVE YOU ALL THE MORE.

## POCKET TACKLE BOOKS.

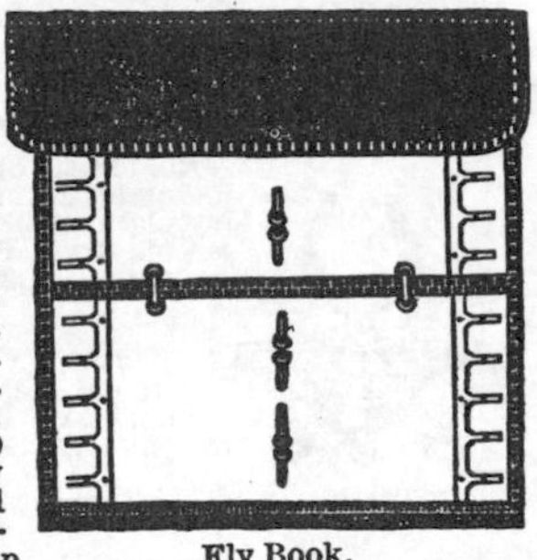

Fly Book.

No. 81774. Solid leather tackle books, bound and stitched edges, strap fastening, six compartments. Six in. long........$1.65
7 in. long..... 2.13

No. 81776. Pocket fly book, patent celluloid leaves, clip fly holders, morocco leather covered, snap fastening; a good book. 7 in long...., .$1.50

No. 81778. Pocket fly book, made of good strong morocco colored leather, snap fastening; made of best materials throughout, not a cheap article, but made for service, patent clips; a fine book. 8 leaves, 64 clips, 7 in. Each..............................$1.83

No. 81780. Pocket fly book, leather covered, patent fastenings, well made, patent clips, parchment leaves, 7 in. Each..............................$0.70

No. 81782. Pocket fly book, leather covered, patent clips, snap fastening, good shape, parchment leaves, but not made of fine material, 6 in. long. Each..............................$0.40

No. 81784. "Best South Side," solid leather, fine quality, celluloid leaves, two compartment pockets, two leather pockets, clips to hold 5 dozen flies, felt pads for keeping flies moist; size of book, 7x4. An elegant book for the money. Price, each..............................$3.00

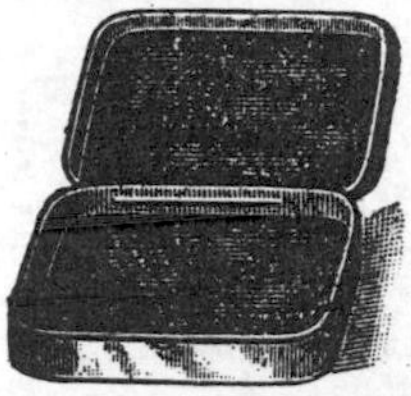

No. 81785. Leader boxes, heavy nickel plated leader boxes; size, 4½ to 3¼; has felt pad to keep leaders moist; no more whipping off of leaders or wasting of time trying to get them in shape after you are at your fishing grounds. Each..............................$0.50

## BAIT BOXES.

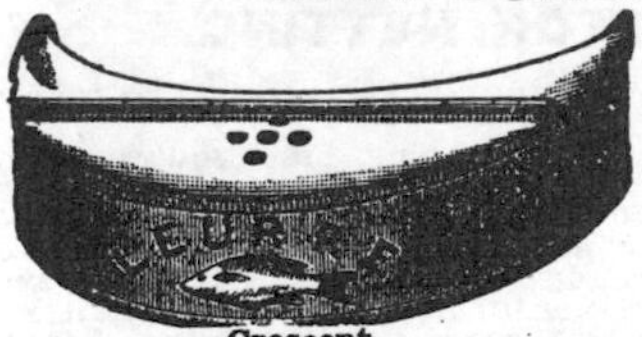

Crescent.

No. 81786. Oval pattern. Each, ..........$0.09

No. 81788. Padlock pattern, ea. ..........$0.09

No. 81790. Ketchem pattern, ea., ..........$0.09

No. 81792. Crescent, each, $0.15

No. 81794. Bait box straps, leather, ¾ inch wide, 36 in. long, each..............................$0.18

## THE HARVARD ICE TOP MINNOW PAIL.

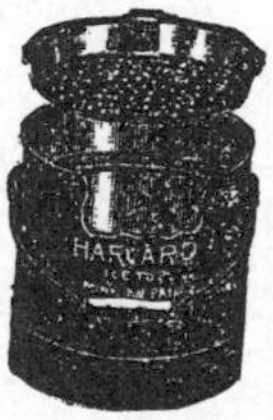


No. 81796. Made of tin, neatly Japanned. It has a perforated ice top cover to enable one to carry a lump of ice to keep the water cool and the minnows fresh.

| | 6 qt. | 8 qt. | 10 qt. |
|---|---|---|---|
| Each.......... | 50c | 65c | 80c |

## RUDOLPH'S CELEBRATED FLOATING MINNOW BUCKETS

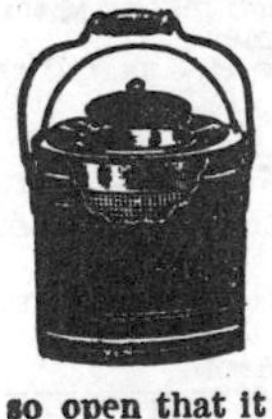

No. 81798. Handiest, lightest, noiseless and most complete minnow bucket ever put on the market. Will not sink, free circulation of air and water, attracts the fish to it, thereby making good fishing around the bucket. No loss of bucket or bait should you drop it overboard. Ice top to carry ice if desired, to keep the minnows fresh while in transit. When you arrive at the lake drop inside bucket into the water, where it will remain on the surface, the waterproof wire making it so open that it affords full flow of fresh water all the time, bringing to your minnows the insect food upon which they exist, as well as attracting other fish to it. Weight 3½ to 5½ pounds.

| Quart.......... | 6 | 8 | 10 | 12 |
|---|---|---|---|---|
| Each.......... | $1.15 | $1.35 | $1.55 | $1.65 |

## FLOATING MINNOW POCKET.

(Rudolph's Patent.)

When several ladies and gentlemen go fishing together, they may provide themselves with floating minnow pocket each so that when they arrive at the fishing ground each may have their own minnows, avoiding the necessity of more than one minnow bucket in the party. When not in use, are so small that they will go in an ordinary coat pocket and no thicker than your hand.

No. 81799. Floating minnow pocket, each ...... ..............................$0.90

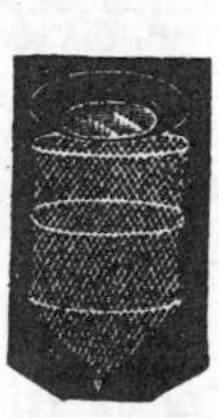

When in use.

## LIVE NETS.

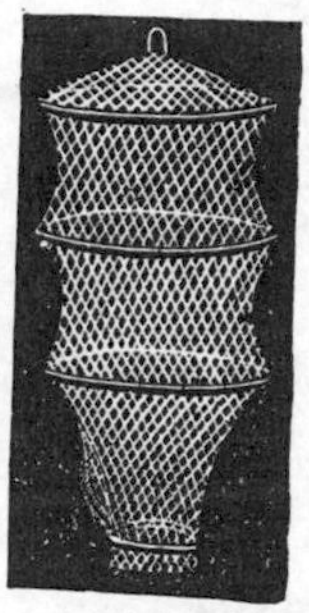

81800.

No. 81800. These nets are to put fish in when caught, keeping them alive. Price, each, 10-inch, 45c; 12-inch, 50c; 14-inch, 55c.

## MINNOW DIP NETS.

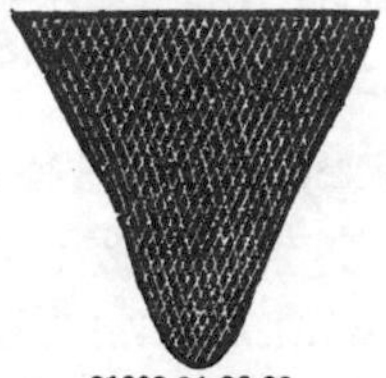

81802-84-86-88.

No. 81802. Linen minnow dip nets.

| Inches deep.......... | 16 | 18 | 20 | 24 | 30 | 36 |
|---|---|---|---|---|---|---|
| Each.......... | 35c | 40c | 45c | 50c | 73c | $1.00 |

## LINEN LANDING NETS.

No. 81804. 20-inch, 25c; 24-inch, 30c; 30-inch, 40c.

## BRAIDED WATERPROOF LANDING NETS.

(Cotton.)

No. 81806. 24 inches deep, each, 60c; 30 inches, 78c.

No. 81808. Crab nets, made of 12-thread cotton seine twine, regulation meshes. 16 inches deep, each 12c; 20-inch, 15c; 24-inch..............................20c

## LANDING NET RINGS.

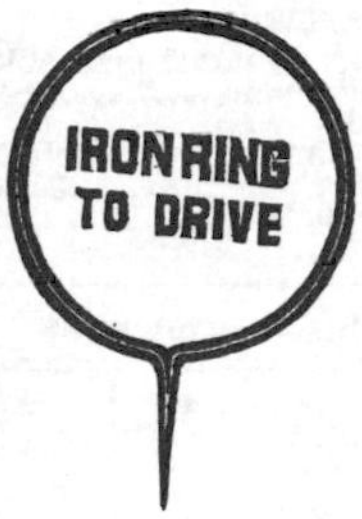


No. 81810. Iron net rings for landing and crab nets. 12 in. diameter, 15c; 14 in. 20c; 16 in. 25c; 18 in..........30c.

No. 81812. Plain 6 foot ash handles for crab and landing nets. Each..... ..........18c

## THE "HARRIMAC" STEEL NET RING.

As good as anybody wants.

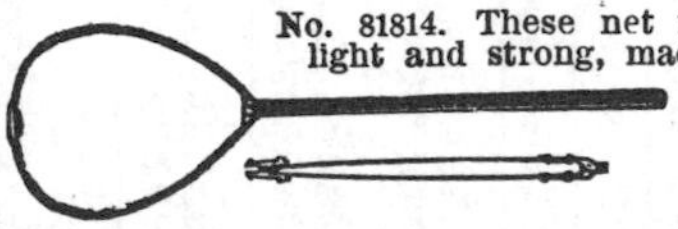

No. 81814. These net rings are very light and strong, made of the best tempered steel. The screw on ring is made in one piece. No parts to get lost. Net is left on ring when not in use. Put up in partitioned bag. No. 9, with 12 inch wood handle, each, $1.25; No. 10, with 4 foot jointed bamboo handle, each..............................$1.68

## CREELS.

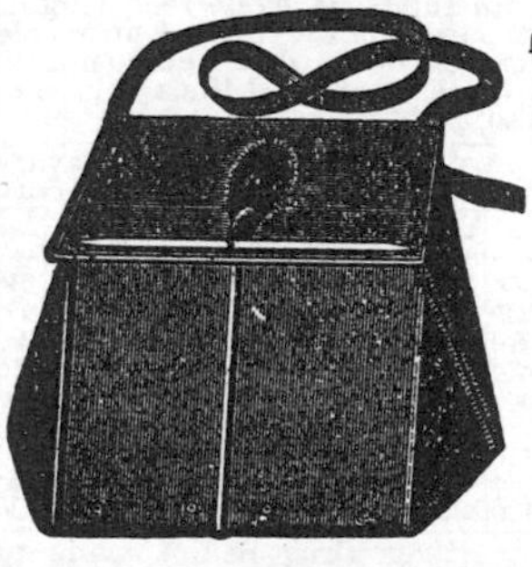

No. 81816. Patent folding canvas creels or trout baskets, with shoulder strap made of heavy brown canvas. Can be folded and carried in large pocket.
(A) capacity, 12 lbs..........$0.95
(B) capacity, 20 lbs..........$1.00
(C) capacity, 25 lbs..........$1.15

## TROUT BASKETS.

Weight, 1 to 1¾ lbs.

No. 81818. 7¼x10¾ inches on back, 70c; capacity 6 lbs.

No. 81820. 7½x12 inches on back, 80c; capacity 9 lbs.

No. 81822. 9x13 inches on back, 98c; capacity 12 lbs.

No. 81824. 9½x14½ inches on back $1.25; capacity 20 lbs.

No. 81826. 16x16 inches on back, $1.45; capacity 25 lbs.

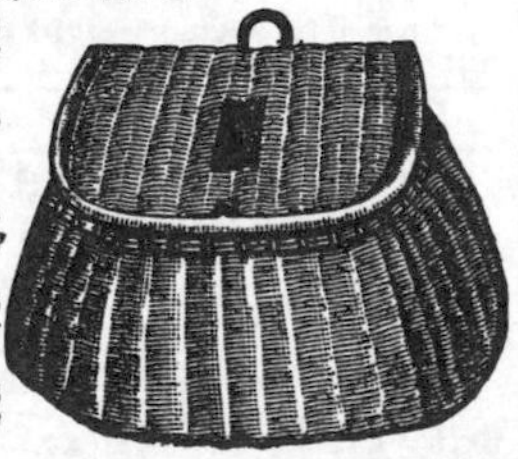

## TROUT BASKET STRAPS.

No. 81828. Leather basket straps, each..............................15c

No. 81830. Webbing basket straps, each..............................25c

No. 81832. Patent sliding straps, leather and web combined, each..............................30c

## MOSQUITO HEAD NETS.

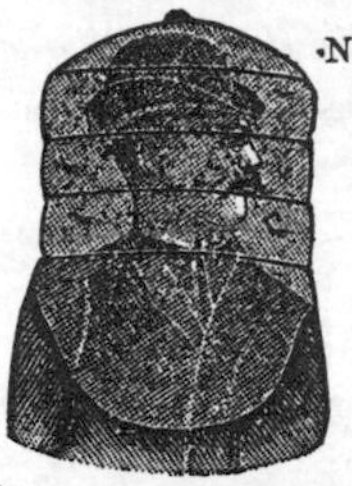

No. 81834. To be worn over the hat or cap. Made of white tarletan. Fitted with five light steel springs. Can be folded up and put in ordinary coat pocket. Weight, 5 oz. Each, 60c; per doz..........$7.1[illegible]

## LANDING NETS.

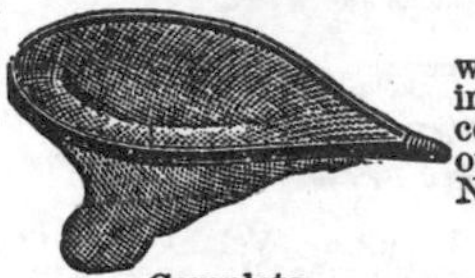

Complete.

This is a fac-simile of our wooden frame landing net, 12 inch screw-off handle; a very complete and necessary part of a fishing outfit.

No. 81836. Wooden frame landing net with 12 inch handle. Weight, about 3 lbs. Each..............................85c

No. 81838. Wood frame landing net, with 3 foot screw-off handle, complete with net. Weight, about ¾ lb. Each..............................95c

No. 81840. Landing net, cane bow, wound handle, 6 inch handle, bow 9 inch diameter, complete with net. Each..............................55c

## GAFF HOOKS.

No. 81842. Gaff hooks, japanned with 3 foot wood handle. Each..............................50c

No. 81844. Plain japanned steel. Each..............................20c

## FISH ROD MOUNTINGS.

No. 81846. Rod ring guides and keepers, all sizes. Per doz..............................15c

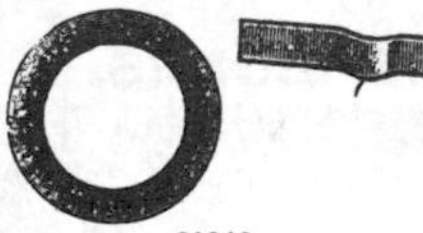

81846

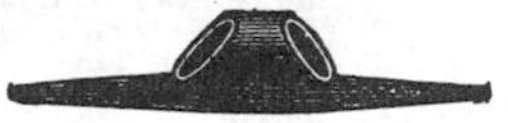

81848

No. 81848. Rod tie guides, brass, all sizes. Per doz..25c

No. 81850. Rod standing guide, brass, 6-32 to 1¼ inch. Per doz..............................50c

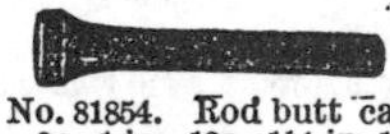

No. 81852. Rod tips funnel, brass, sizes 6 to 12. No. 6 smallest. Each..............................10c

No. 81854. Rod butt caps, solid brass, ¾ in. ⅞ in. each, 8c; 1 in., 12c; 1¼ in. 1½ in..............................17c

No. 81856. Rod screw butt caps, brass. ⅞ in. each, 15c; 1 in., 18c; 1¼ in..............................20c

## ROD FERRULE—BRASS.

Measurements are for diameter of outside ferrule No. 81858.

DESCRIPTION.

| No. | Diam. inches. | Plain per pair. | No. | Diam. inches. | Plain per pair. |
|---|---|---|---|---|---|
| 00 | 5-32 | $0.05 | 11 | 11-16 | $0.13 |
| 0 | 6-32 | .05 | 12 | 23-32 | .14 |
| 2-0 | 7-32 | .05 | 13 | ¾ | .14 |
| 1 | ¼ | .05 | 14 | 25-32 | .15 |
| 1½ | 9-32 | .05 | 15 | 13-16 | .17 |
| 2 | 10-32 | .05 | 16 | ⅞ | .17 |
| 3 | 11-32 | .05 | 17 | 15-16 | .18 |
| 4 | ⅜ | .06 | 18 | 31-32 | .19 |
| 5 | 13-32 | .07 | 19 | 1 | .19 |
| 6 | 7-16 | .07 | 20 | 1 1-16 | .19 |
| 7 | ½ | .08 | 21 | 1⅛ | .20 |
| 8 | 9-16 | .09 | 22 | 1 5-32 | .20 |
| 9 | 19-32 | .10 | 23 | 1 3-16 | .20 |
| 10 | 10-16 | .11 | 24 | 1¼ | .20 |

## BRASS DOWELS.

For size, see Ferrule.

No. 81860. Nos. 0, 1, 2 and 3, price, per doz., 25c; Nos. 4, 5, 6, 7 and 8, per doz., 30c. Nos. 0, 10, 11, 12, 13 and 14, per doz.............................. 35c

## BRASS REEL BANDS.

No. 818[illegible].

| Size.......... | ¾ in. | ⅞ in. | 1 in. | 1⅛ in. | 1¼ in. |
|---|---|---|---|---|---|
| Price per set of three, | 12c | 12c | 15c | 15c | 20c |
| Price per set of three, nickeled and polished | 18c | 18c | 20c | 20c | 25c |

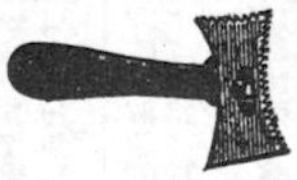

No. 81863. Fish scale scraper. Steel plate, iron handle, one end is sharpened to cut off the heads. The best thing out for the purpose. Each, 35c; extra by mail..........10c

## FISH ROD MOUNTINGS.

No. 81864. Lancewood tips, nickel mounted. For fly rods, each ..........$0.50
For bait rods, each .......... .75
No. 81866. Lancewood tips, unmounted. For fly rods .35
For bait rods .......... .50
No. 81868. Split bamboo tips, silk wound, nickel mounted. For fly rods ..........$1.25
For bait rods .......... 1.00
No. 81869. Split bamboo tips, unwound. For fly rods .75
For bait rods .......... .50
In ordering mounted tips you must give size of ferrule.

## FISH ROD CEMENT.

No. 81870. Ferrule cement for fish rods, in 4-inch stick, water proof. Per stick ..........15c

## FISH ROD VARNISH.

No. 81872. Fish rod varnish, put up in about 2 oz. bottles, best quality, camel's hair brush with each bottle.
Per bottle ..........$ .25
Per dozen .......... 2.40

## WEIGH YOUR FISH.

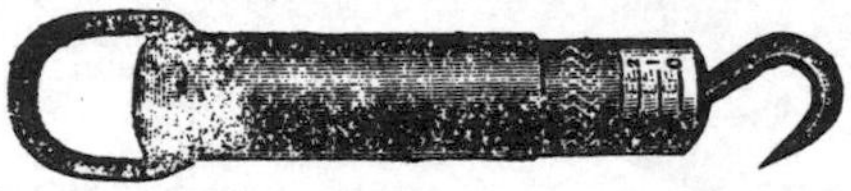

No. 81874. Novelty spring balance. Weighs from 1 to 15 lbs. by ¼s. A good scale with tare allowance. Every pair warranted perfect. Each ..........30c.
Extra by mail 5c.

## ROD WINDING SILK.

No. 81876. Special winding silk, 100 yards on spool size "A" in black, yellow, green or scarlet. Price per spool ..........20c.

**You can have our elaborate Bicycle Catalogue for the asking . . . . . .**

**Our Electric Bicycle for $39.90 is the most popular of the year 1896 . . . .**

## WHITE ASH OARS.

Weight of oars, 8½ to 15 lbs. per pair.

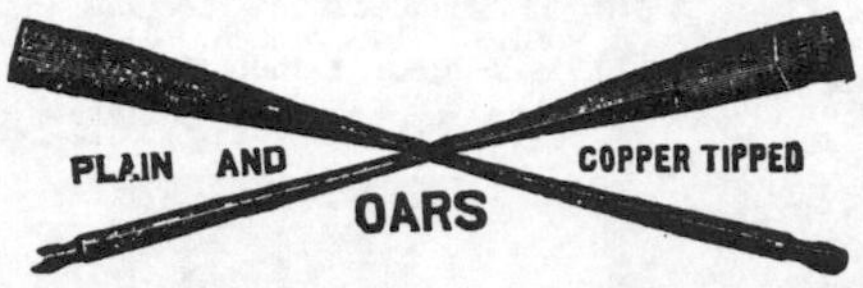


## COPPER TIPPED ASH OARS.

| No. 81878. Length | 6 ft. | 6½ ft. | 7 ft. | 7½ ft. | 8 ft. |
|---|---|---|---|---|---|
| Per pair | $0.88 | $0.94 | $1.00 | $1.12 | $1.20 |
| Length | 8½ ft. | 9 ft. | 9½ ft. | 10 ft. | |
| Per pair | $1.25 | $1.32 | $1.39 | $1.46 | |

## PLAIN ASH OARS.

| No. 81880. Length | 6 ft. | 6½ ft. | 7 ft. | 7½ ft. | 8 ft. |
|---|---|---|---|---|---|
| Per pair | $0.78 | $0.82 | $0.88 | $0.95 | $1.04 |
| Length | 8½ ft. | 9 ft. | 9½ ft. | 10 ft. | |
| Per pair | $1.10 | $1.16 | $1.19 | $1.25 | |

## OAR LOCKS.

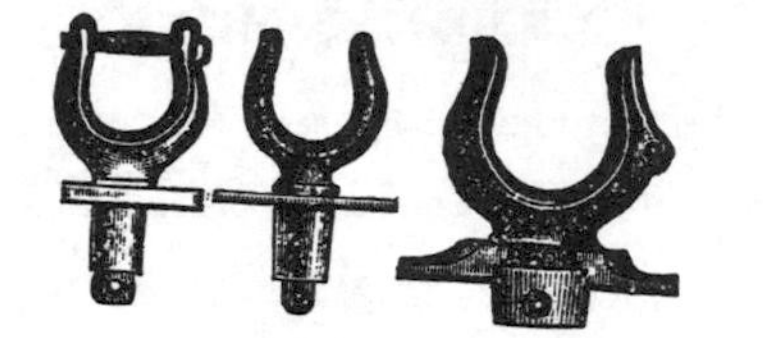

81890. 81892. 81894.

No. 81890. North River oar lock, galvanized malleable iron, 2 inches between horns. Per pair ..........25c.
Weight per pair, about 2 pounds.
No. 81892. Socket oar lock, galvanized iron; weight 24 to 50 oz., width 1½ inches. Per pair ..........$0.16
Width 2 inches between horns, per pair .......... .49
Width 2¼ inches, per pair .......... .25

No. 81894. Patent swivel oar locks, galvanized iron, weight, 48 to 60 oz., per pair; width 1¾ inches .... .60
Width 2 inches .......... .65
Width 2¼ inches .......... .79
Width 2½ inches .......... .85

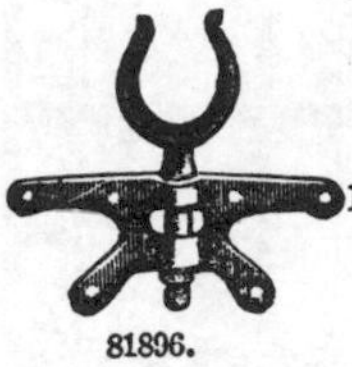

81896.

No. 81896. Side plate oar lock, plain malleable iron. Per pair ......35c.

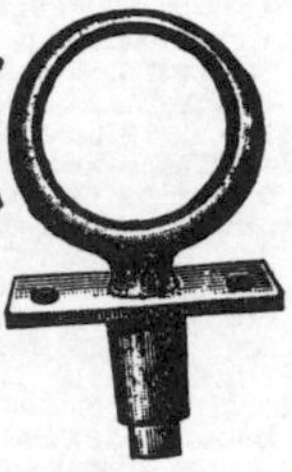

No. 81898. Round socket oar locks. Per pair ......40c.

## BOAT ANCHORS.

No. 81900. Boat anchors, black wrought-iron, regular shape.

| | Per lb. |
|---|---|
| 6 to 15 lbs .......... | $ .15 |
| 15 to 30 lbs .......... | .13 |
| 30 to 50 lbs .......... | .12 |
| 50 to 100 lbs .......... | .11 |
| 100 lbs. or over .......... | 10 |

## LIFE PRESERVERS.

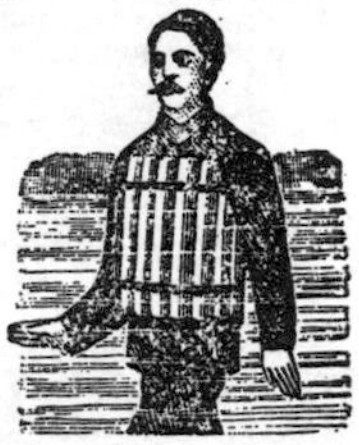

No. 81902. "Never Sink," corl jackets, adopted as standard and the government inspector's stamp on each one, and easily put on, durable and has great buoyancy. Weight, 9 pounds; each ..........$ 1.25
Per dozen .......... 13.50
No. 81903. Life belts, in squares, similar to the "Never Sink" and buckles on the same way. One of the best in the market; safe and durable. Weight, 9 pounds; each ..........$ 1.10
Per dozen .......... 10.20

## LAKE AND RIVER SEINES.

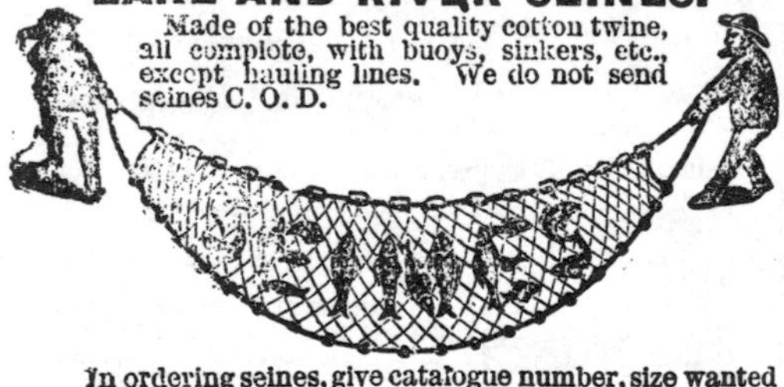


Made of the best quality cotton twine, all complete, with buoys, sinkers, etc., except hauling lines. We do not send seines C. O. D.

In ordering seines, give catalogue number, size wanted and price.

Special prices are given upon request, for large lake seines and other lengths and depths not in this list.

These seines all have top line ¼ inch manilla rope, tarred, and bottom lines ¼ inch manilla rope tarred, doubled, with reversed twist to prevent rolling. We use new improved cast lead sinkers on all our seines. Twine, Woodbury's best.

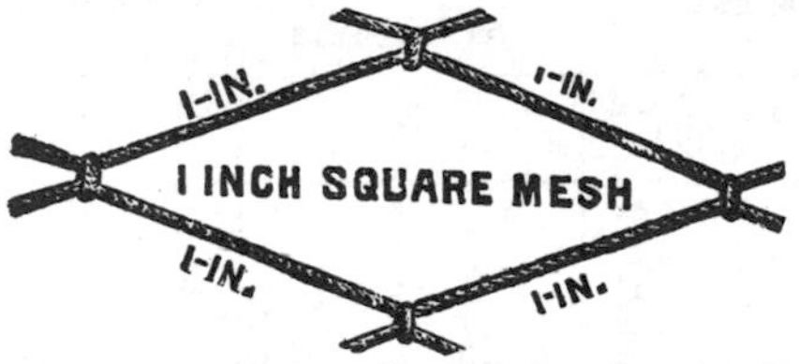


N. B.—A seine mesh is diamond shaped, and a 1 inch square mesh measures 1 inch on each of the four sides. A 1¼ measures 1¼ on each of the four sides, etc., etc. One inch square mesh is 2 inches stretched mesh; 1½ inch square mesh is 3 inch stretched mesh.

**12 Thread Cotton Seine Twine—Square Mesh.**

| No. | Length. Ft. | Depth Center. Ft. | Depth at ends. Ft. | 1 inch Mesh. Price. | 1¼ inch Mesh. Price. | 1½ inch Mesh. Price. | 2 inch Mesh. Price. |
|---|---|---|---|---|---|---|---|
| 82000 ...... | 20 | 4 | 3 | $ 0.94 | $ 0.82 | $ 0.74 | $ 0.68 |
| 82001 ...... | 30 | 4 | 3 | 1.38 | 1.21 | 1.11 | .99 |
| 82002 ...... | 40 | 5 | 4 | 2.07 | 1.82 | 1.63 | 1.43 |
| 82003 ...... | 50 | 5 | 4 | 2.63 | 2.27 | 2.06 | 1.79 |
| 82004 ...... | 60 | 6 | 5 | 3.46 | 3.00 | 2.70 | 2.27 |
| 82005 ...... | 72 | 7 | 6 | 4.76 | 4.00 | 3.56 | 3.04 |
| 82006 ...... | 90 | 7 | 7 | 6.60 | 5.53 | 4.84 | 4.09 |
| 82007 ...... | 100 | 8 | 7 | 7.33 | 6.13 | 5.37 | 4.52 |
| 82008 ...... | 120 | 10 | 8 | 10.40 | 8.68 | 7.62 | 6.36 |
| 82009 ...... | 150 | 12 | 10 | 14.75 | 12.18 | 10.50 | 8.60 |
| 82010 ...... | 180 | 12 | 10 | 18.14 | 14.32 | 12.87 | 10.61 |
| 82011 ...... | 200 | 14 | 10 | 19.97 | 16.53 | 14.27 | 10.77 |
| 82012 ...... | 250 | 14 | 10 | 26.65 | 21.98 | 17.02 | 13.12 |
| 82013 ...... | 300 | 14 | 10 | 38.75 | 26.33 | 22.71 | 18.61 |

**Wading Pants on Page 196.**

**16 Tread Cotton Seine Twine—Square Mesh.**

| No. | Length. Ft. | Depth Center. Ft. | Depth at ends. Ft. | 1 inch Mesh. Price. | 1¼ inch Mesh. Price. | 1½ inch Mesh. Price. | 2 inch Mesh. Price. |
|---|---|---|---|---|---|---|---|
| 82014 ...... | 20 | 4 | 3 | $ 1.02 | $ 0.94 | $ 0.85 | $ 0.70 |
| 82015 ...... | 30 | 4 | 3 | 1.53 | 1.43 | 1.23 | 1:09 |
| 82016 ...... | 40 | 5 | 4 | 2.27 | 2.15 | 1.84 | 1.51 |
| 82017 ...... | 50 | 5 | 4 | 3.04 | 2.67 | 2.35 | 2.07 |
| 82018 ...... | 60 | 6 | 5 | 3.84 | 3.49 | 3.07 | 2.55 |
| 82019 ...... | 72 | 7 | 5 | 5.29 | 4.91 | 4.13 | 3.40 |
| 82020 ...... | 90 | 8 | 7 | 7.34 | 6.78 | 5.70 | 4.72 |
| 82021 ...... | 100 | 8 | 7 | 10.57 | 7.55 | 6.75 | 5.10 |
| 82022 ...... | 120 | 10 | 8 | 11.58 | 10.68 | 8.95 | 6.55 |
| 82023 ...... | 150 | 12 | 10 | 16.53 | 14.50 | 12.64 | 9.88 |
| 82024 ...... | 180 | 12 | 10 | 20.17 | 18.52 | 15.36 | 12.14 |
| 82025 ...... | 200 | 14 | 10 | 22.40 | 20.61 | 17.05 | 13.44 |
| 82026 ...... | 250 | 14 | 10 | 26.37 | 24.30 | 20.22 | 16.28 |
| 82027 ...... | 300 | 14 | 10 | 35.94 | 32.70 | 27.22 | 21.50 |

Above seines are hung with leads, floats and lines ready for use, except hauling lines.

## STRAIGHT SEINES.

No. 82030. Seines. In thirty yards (90 feet) lenghts or over. No lengths less than 30 yards. The depths given are straight from end to end, and do not taper. Hung with leads, floats and lines. Made of Woodbury's best soft laid twine.

| | Prices per running yard 12 Thread—Soft. | | | | | Prices per running yard 16 Thread—Soft. | | | | |
|---|---|---|---|---|---|---|---|---|---|---|
| Mesh, inches ..... | 1 | 1¼ | 1½ | 1¾ | 2&3 | 1 | 1¼ | 1½ | 1¾ | 2&3 |
| 6 ft. deep | 19c | 17c | 15c | 13c | 12c | 21c | 19c | 17c | 15c | 13c |
| 8 ft. deep | 23c | 19c | 17c | 15c | 13c | 25c | 23c | 20c | 18c | 16c |
| 10 ft. deep | 27c | 23c | 21c | 19c | 16c | 31c | 28c | 24c | 20c | 19c |
| 12 ft. deep | 33c | 27c | 23c | 21c | 19c | 36c | 34c | 28c | 25c | 21c |
| 14 ft. deep | 36c | 31c | 25c | 23c | 20c | 41c | 38c | 31c | 28c | 24c |
| 15 ft. deep | 38c | 32c | 27c | 25c | 21c | 45c | 40c | 33c | 30c | 25c |
| 16 ft. deep | 41c | 35c | 29c | 36c | 23c | 46c | 42c | 35c | 31c | 26c |
| 18 ft. deep | 45c | 37c | 33c | 28c | 25c | 51c | 46c | 38c | 35c | 29c |
| 20 ft. deep | 48c | 39c | 34c | 29c | 27c | 56c | 47c | 41c | 37c | 32c |

No. 82031. Lake or River Drag Seines made of Woodbury's best white cotton, soft laid, seine twine. No better seine made at any price. Hung with leads, floats and line ready for use. Square mesh.

These seines are straight from end to end, and do not taper; all complete; ready for use.

| | | No. 9 Thread. | | | No. 12 Thread. | | | |
|---|---|---|---|---|---|---|---|---|
| Length. | Depth. | 1 inch Mesh. Price | 1¼ inch Mesh. Price | 1½ inch Mesh. Price | 1 inch Mesh. Price | 1¼ inch Mesh. Price | 1½ inch Mesh. Price | 2 to 3 inch Mesh. Price |
| 20 ft. | 4 ft. | $0.90 | $0.81 | $0.73 | $0.99 | $0.85 | $0.79 | $0.62 |
| 30 ft. | 5 ft. | 1.51 | 1.36 | 1.08 | 1.69 | 1.46 | 1.30 | 1.19 |
| 40 ft. | 6 ft. | 2.17 | 1.74 | 1.67 | 2.49 | 2.13 | 1.89 | 1.60 |
| 50 ft. | 7 ft. | 3.05 | 2.70 | 2.30 | 3.49 | 2.90 | 2.59 | 2.17 |
| 60 ft. | 8 ft. | 3 95 | 3.50 | 2.90 | 4.56 | 3.84 | 3.32 | 2.82 |
| 75 ft. | 8 ft. | 4.93 | 4.40 | 3.64 | 5.70 | 4.76 | 4.19 | 5.43 |

## COTTON NETTING.

**White Only. Just the Netting. No Floats, Leads or Lines.**

No. 82032. 12-thread, soft twine, 1 inch square mesh, or larger, per lb ..........48c
No. 82033. 16 or 20 thread, soft twine, 1 inch square mesh, or larger, per lb ..........45c
No. 82034. 12-thread, medium twine, 1 inch, square mesh, ar larger, per lb ..........50c
No. 82035. 15 or 18 thread, medium twine, 1 inch square mesh, or larger, per lb ..........47c
Can furnish any depth required.

When ordering seines or netting give full description of what is wanted, and state if length ordered is just the length wanted or you want it to hang a net that length. Don't fail to give depth wanted.

## CREEK SEINES.

**Square Mesh, Half-Inch Mesh Center, One-Inch Mesh Ends.**

| No. | Depth. | 4 Ft. Price. | 5 Ft. Price. | 6 Ft. Price. | 7 Ft. Price. |
|---|---|---|---|---|---|
| 82036 | 10 ft long | $0.94 | $1.08 | $1 47 | $1.95 |
| 82037 | 15 ft long | 1.33 | 1.58 | 2.14 | 2.42 |
| 82038 | 20 ft long | 1.72 | 2.10 | 2.52 | 3.15 |
| 82039 | 25 ft long | 2.10 | 2.52 | 3.15 | 3.92 |

Each end of a creek seine is of 1-inch mesh; ¼ the length oi a seine in center is ½-inch mesh.

When ordering seines give size and price as well as catalogue number.

## MINNOW SEINES.

**Hung with Leads and Floats, Three-Eighths Inch Square Mesh.**

Minnow Seines are the same width from end tc end. Runs from 3½ to 5½ feet to the pound.

**Minnow Seines, ⅜-Inch Mesh,**

| No. | Depth. | 3 Ft. | 4 Ft. | 5 Ft. | 6 Ft. |
|---|---|---|---|---|---|
| 82040 | 10 ft long | $1.23 | $1.63 | $1.96 | $2.31 |
| 82041 | 12 ft long | 1.54 | 1.96 | 2.37 | 2.79 |
| 82042 | 15 ft long | 2.02 | 2.42 | 2.83 | 3.36 |
| 82043 | 20 ft long | 2.52 | 3.28 | 3.85 | 4.58 |
| 82044 | 25 ft long | 3.15 | 3.99 | 4.87 | 5.66 |

Rigged ready for use except hauling line.

When ordering seines give size and price as well as catalogue numbec.

Minnow Seines, hung with floats and leads, ready for use except hauling lines, ¼ inch square mesh. Runs 3¼ to 2½ feet to the pound.

**Minnow Seines, ¼-Inch Mesh.**

| No. | Depth. | 3 Ft. | 3 Ft. | 5 Ft. | 6 Ft. |
|---|---|---|---|---|---|
| 82045 | 10 ft long | $2.00 | $2.58 | $3.10 | $3.68 |
| 82046 | 12 ft long | 2.38 | 3.08 | 3.75 | 4.42 |
| 82047 | 15 ft long | 2.93 | 3.85 | 4.68 | 5.54 |
| 82048 | 20 ft long | 3.96 | ·5.15 | 6.95 | 7.30 |
| 82049 | 25 ft long | 4.94 | 6.38 | 7.78 | 9.24 |

**HIGH GRADE BICYCLES. LOWEST PRICES CATALOGUE FREE.**

## MINNOW NETTING.

No. 82050. Minnow Netting, made of cotton twine, just the netting only; no sinkers, floats or lines. Price is by the running yard, stretched measure.

| | 3 ft. deep. per yd. | 4 ft. deep. per yd. | 5 ft. deep. per yd. |
|---|---|---|---|
| ¾ in. square mesh | 16c. | 17c. | 21c. |
| ½ in. square mesh | 21c. | 28c. | 35c. |
| ⅜ in. square mesh | 25c. | 32c. | 42c. |
| ¼ in. square mesh | 42c. | 56c. | 70c. |

Price is per running yard, stretched. The mesh is described on the square.

## THE COMMON SENSE MINNOW SEINE.

No. 82051. Minnow Seines; ⅛ inch mesh, made of a light woven netting. Not as strong or as lasting as the regular goods as quoted above, yet a good article for the money. Hung with leads, floats and lines.

| Size | 4x10 ft. | 4x12 ft. | 4x15 ft. | 4x20 ft. | 4x25 ft. |
|---|---|---|---|---|---|
| Each | 77c. | 92c. | $1.16 | $1.44 | $1.72 |

## THE PEERLESS FYKE OR HOOP NET.

### With Wings.

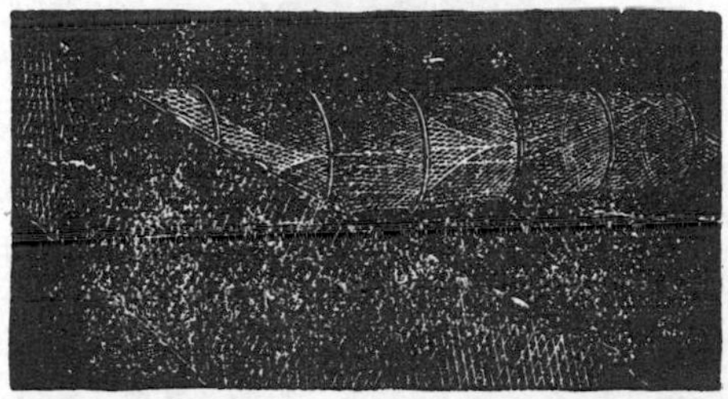

Wts. 2 ft. 10 lbs.
Wts. 2½ ft. 12 lbs.
Wts. 3 ft. 20 lbs.
Wts. 4 ft. 25 lbs.
Wts. 5 ft. 35 lbs,
Wts. 6 ft. 45 lbs

| No. | | Height Mouth. | Number Hoops. | Length Net. | Full Length Wings. | No. Twine. | Size of mesh, Inches Square. Front. | Middle. | Tail. | White Twine. Price Each. |
|---|---|---|---|---|---|---|---|---|---|---|
| | | | | ft | ft | | | | | |
| 82052. | Single throat. | 2 ft | 4 | 6 | 12 | 9 | ¾ | ¾ | ¾ | $2.35 |
| 82054. | Single throat. | 3 ft | 6 | 10 | 18 | 24 | 1¼ | 1¼ | 1¼ | 4.25 |
| 82055. | Single throat. | 4½ ft | 8 | 18 | 30 | 24 | 1½ | 1½ | 1½ | 6.75 |
| 82056. | Double throat. | 2½ ft | 6 | 8 | 12 | 16 | 1 | 1 | 1 | 3.65 |
| 82057. | Double throat. | 3 ft | 6 | 10 | 18 | 24 | 1¼ | 1¼ | 1¼ | 4.45 |
| 82058. | Double throat. | 4 ft | 7 | 16 | 24 | 24 | 2 | 1¾ | 1½ | 5.65 |
| 82059. | Double throat. | 4½ ft | 8 | 18 | 30 | 24 | 2½ | 2 | 1½ | 6.95 |
| 82060. | Double throat. | 5 ft | 8 | 18 | 30 | 28 | 2½ | 2 | 1½ | 7.67 |
| 82061. | Double throat. | 6 ft | 8 | 18 | 40 | 28 | 2½ | 2 | 1½ | 9.67 |

For Fyke nets made of preservative tarred twines, add ⅓ to above prices. Lengths on wings are for both wings from end to end.

Our Peerless has the hoops on the outside of netting, thus greatly saving the netting.

Made of best quality cotton twine. Hung ready for use. Netting can be furnished without hoops if desired.

## FUNNEL NETS. WITHOUT WINGS.

Same style as the Peerless, but has no wings. With hoops complete.

| Description. | | Weight. | Height Mouth. | No. Hoops. | Length. | Square Mesh. Front. | Tail. | Each. |
|---|---|---|---|---|---|---|---|---|
| | | lbs. | ft. | | ft | in. | in. | |
| 82062. | Single throat | 7 | 2 | 4 | 6 | ¾ | ¾ | $1.40 |
| 82064. | Single throat | 10 | 3 | 6 | 10 | 1¼ | 1¼ | 2.59 |
| 82065. | Single throat | 20 | 4½ | 8 | 18 | 1½ | 1½ | 3.78 |
| 82066. | Double throat | 9 | 2½ | 6 | 8 | 1 | 1 | 2.25 |
| 82067. | Double throat | 15 | 3 | 6 | 10 | 1¼ | 1¼ | 2.91 |
| 82068. | Double throat | 20 | 4 | 7 | 16 | 2 | 1½ | 3.15 |
| 82069. | Double throat | 25 | 4½ | 8 | 18 | 2½ | 1½ | 3.85 |
| 82070. | Double throat | 30 | 5 | 8 | 18 | 2½ | 1½ | 4.13 |
| 82071. | Double throat | 35 | 6 | 8 | 18 | 2½ | 1½ | 4.90 |

Made of the best quality cotton twine.

When ordering seines give size, price and catalogue number, to avoid error.

N. B.—We make all kinds of fish nets to order, if you will fully describe what you want and send diagram of shape. Money must accompany the order, as they cannot be sent C. O. D. or returned when made to order.

## QUAIL OR PARTRIDGE NETS.

Weight, 3½ pounds.

No. 82072. No. 1, 25 feet long, 20 feet wing each side, with funnel, each ........ $4.20
No. 82073. No. 2, 20 feet long, 20 feet wing each side, with funnel, each ........ 3.78
No. 82074. No. 3, 20 feet long, 20 feet wing each side, without funnel, each ........ 3.40
No. 82075. No. 4, 15 feet long, 20 feet wing each side, without funnel, each ........ 2.95
No. 82076. No. 5, 12 feet long, 15 feet wing each side, with funnel, each ........ 2.52

Front hoops of our quail nets are of wood. Netting 1¼ inches, square mesh, 12 thread cotton.

## GILL NETTING.

No. 82077. Linen netting for gill nets or inside of trammel nets made of best silver gray 3 cord linen twine. Any depth required. This netting is for "gill" or "set" net, and not for "drag" seines, the twine being too small for such use.

| No. Order. | Square Mesh. | Price per pound. No. 18 twine | No. 20 twine | No. 25 twine | No. 30 twine | No. 35 twine | No. 40 twine |
|---|---|---|---|---|---|---|---|
| 82077 | ¾ in. | $1.84 | $1.95 | $2.18 | $2.35 | $2.60 | $2.81 |
| | 1 in. | 1.57 | 1.73 | 1.90 | 2.19 | 2.56 | 2.79 |
| | 1¼ in. | 1.50 | 1.63 | 1.82 | 2.08 | 2.46 | 2.65 |
| | 1½ in. | 1.47 | 1.58 | 1.79 | 2.06 | 2.44 | 2.63 |
| | 1¾ in. | 1.42 | 1.53 | 1.74 | 2.00 | 2.39 | 2.60 |
| | 2 in. | 1.36 | 1.47 | 1.70 | 1.96 | 2.34 | 2.55 |

No. 82079. Cotton netting for outside of trammel nets from 6 to 8 inch square mesh. Per pound, 45c.

## IMPROVED PERFECTION TRAMMEL NET.

It has three nets hung upon a single top and a single bottom line. Of the three nets two have large meshes of cotton seine twine. The inside net is made of best linen gilling twine, which is hung slack, forming a bag in which fish coming from either side are caught, unable to escape. These nets are not "drag seines," but are to be "set" in the water, the same as a gill net.

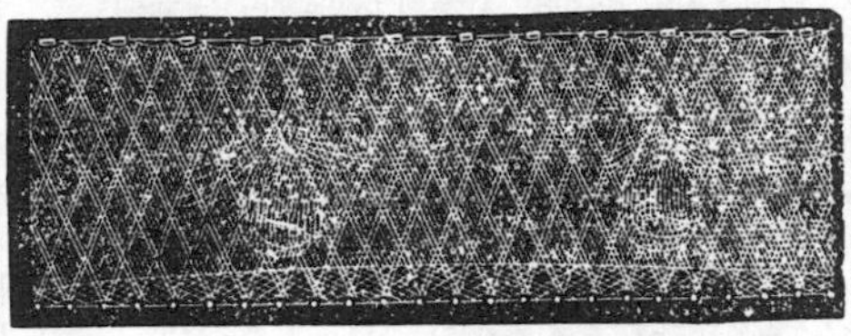

Price is per running yard in length, hung measure, the three nets combined, complete with leads and floats. Square mesh. Weight per yard, about one-half pound.

| No. | Depth. | Outside Mesh. | Inside Mesh. | Inside Linen Twine. | Outside Cotton Twine. | Price per Yard. |
|---|---|---|---|---|---|---|
| | Feet. | Inches. | Inches. | No. | No. | |
| 82080 | 3½ | 6 | ¾ | 25 | All No. 16, Soft Laid. | $0.23 |
| 82081 | 3½ | 6 | 1 | 25 | | 21 |
| 82082 | 3½ | 6 | 1¼ | 25 | | 17 |
| 82083 | 4 | 6 | 1 | 25 | | 22 |
| 82084 | 4 | 6 | 1¼ | 25 | | 18 |
| 82085 | 4½ | 7 | 1¼ | 20 | | 20 |
| 82086 | 4½ | 7 | 1¼ | 25 | | 19 |
| 82087 | 4½ | 7 | 1½ | 18 | | 19 |
| 82088 | 4½ | 7 | 1¾ | 18 | | 18 |
| 82089 | 4½ | 7 | 2 | 18 | | 16 |
| 82090 | 5 | 8 | 1 | 25 | | 27 |
| 82091 | 5 | 8 | 1½ | 18 | | 19 |
| 82092 | 5 | 8 | 2½ | 18 | | 16 |
| 82093 | 5 | 8 | 3 | 18 | | 15 |
| 82094 | 6 | 8 | 1 | 25 | | 32 |
| 82095 | 6 | 8 | 1½ | 18 | | 24 |
| 82096 | 6 | 8 | 2 | 18 | | 18 |
| 82097 | 6 | 8 | 2½ | 18 | | 16 |
| 82098 | 6 | 8 | 3 | 18 | | 15 |
| 82099 | 7 | 8 | 1½ | 18 | | 25 |
| 82100 | 7 | 8 | 2 | 18 | | 21 |
| 82101 | 7 | 8 | 2½ | 18 | | 18 |
| 82102 | 7 | 8 | 3 | 18 | | 17 |
| 82103 | 8 | 8 | 1½ | 18 | | 28 |
| 82104 | 8 | 8 | 1¾ | 18 | | 24 |
| 82105 | 8 | 8 | 2 | 18 | | 22 |
| 82106 | 8 | 8 | 2½ | 18 | | 21 |
| 82107 | 8 | 8 | 3 | 18 | | 19 |

Other styles made to order. Meshes as given above are diamond square. Hung complete for use except hauling lines. When ordering nets give size, price, and catalogue number.

N. B.—Trammel Nets are made to order only, and if order is filled correctly we cannot take the goods back, as we seldom have any two orders "just alike" in every particular, consequently if the net was returned it would be a "dead loss" to us.

## GILL OR SET NET.

A gill net is a single net, hung with floats and leads complete, without hauling lines. Made of best imported linen twine. These nets cannot be used for "drag" seines, the twine being too fine. They are set in the water and allowed to remain from 5 to 24 hours. Commencing at one end, "lift" gently when taking up net. The fish are caught by the gills, hence the name "gill" or "set" net.

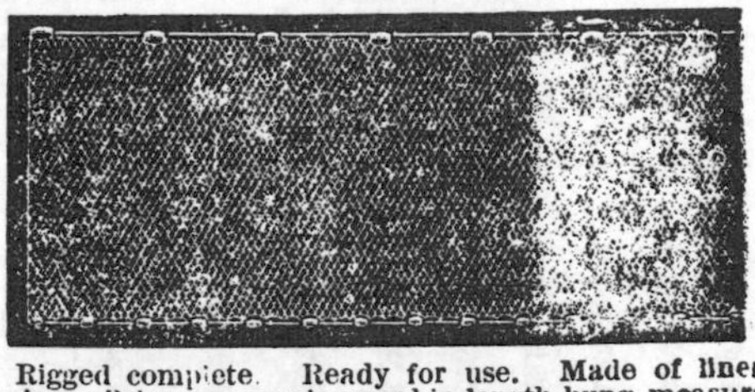

Rigged complete. Ready for use. Made of linen twine. Price per running yard in length hung measure. Weight per yard, about ¼ pound.

| No. | Depth. | No. Twine, Linen. | Size of Mesh. Square. | Price per Yard |
|---|---|---|---|---|
| | Feet. | | | |
| 82108 | 3½ | 40 | 2 | $0.09 |
| 82109 | 4 | 40 | 1 | 15 |
| 82110 | 4 | 40 | 1¼ | 13 |
| 82111 | 4 | 35 | 1½ | 12 |
| 82112 | 4 | 35 | 1¾ | 11 |
| 82113 | 4 | 40 | 2 | 11 |
| 82114 | 5 | 40 | 1 | 17 |
| 82115 | 5 | 40 | 1¼ | 14 |
| 82116 | 5 | 35 | 1½ | 14 |
| 82117 | 5 | 25 | 1¾ | 13 |
| 82118 | 5 | 40 | 2 | 12 |
| 82119 | 5 | 40 | 2¼ | 11 |
| 82120 | 5 | 40 | 2½ | 10 |
| 82121 | 6 | 40 | 1 | 22 |
| 82122 | 6 | 40 | 1¼ | 17 |
| 82123 | 6 | 35 | 1½ | 15 |
| 82124 | 6 | 35 | 1¾ | 14 |
| 82125 | 6 | 35 | 2 | 15 |
| 82126 | 6 | 40 | 2¼ | 13 |
| 82127 | 6 | 40 | 2½ | 12 |
| 82128 | 7 | 25 | 1½ | 17 |
| 82129 | 7 | 20 | 1¾ | 16 |
| 82130 | 7 | 20 | 2 | 15 |
| 82131 | 8 | 25 | 1½ | [illegible] |
| 82132 | 8 | 20 | 1¾ | [illegible] |
| 82133 | 8 | 20 | 2 | 16 |

Other styles made to order. Our gill nets are made of Knox best Scotch linen twine.

## COTTON TROT LINE.

No. 82134. Cotton Trot Lines in 50-feet coils, 6 connected, best quality, sold in any quantity at dozen rates.

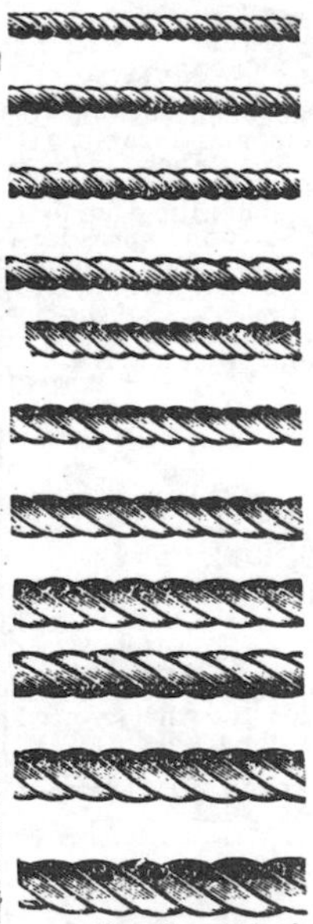

| No. | Per doz. coils. | Wt. per doz. |
|---|---|---|
| 1 | $0.38 | 15 oz. |
| 2 | .47 | 16 oz. |
| 3 | .57 | 19 oz. |
| 4 | .63 | 20 oz. |
| 5 | .79 | 23 oz. |
| 6 | .88 | 24 oz. |
| 7 | .99 | 32 oz. |
| 8 | 1.08 | 36 oz. |
| 9 | 1.24 | 44 oz. |
| 10 | 1.37 | 52 oz. |
| 11 | 1.64 | 56 oz. |
| No. 12. 3-16 inch diam | 1.71 | 96 oz. |

**Your local dealer doesn't like to lose your trade. He says: "you'll get bit," and does all he can to prevent you from being satisfied with your dealings with us. If we can't please you, we will not complain if you go back to your dealer.**

**If you ever find it necessary to make a complaint, always write us at once upon receipt of goods, and state the Invoice number of your order. See instructions in front of book.**

## GILLING TWINE.
### The Best Quality Imported.

Gilling twine is a small, all-linen twine used for gill or set nets, and cannot be used to make a drag, lake or river net.
No. 82135.

Linen Gilling Twine, No. 12, 3 cord, per lb........$0.78
"　　"　　"　　No. 14, 3 "　　"　　.............82
"　　"　　"　　No. 16, 3 "　　"　　.............95
"　　"　　"　　No. 20, 3 "　　"　　.............98
"　　"　　"　　No. 25, 3 "　　"　　.............1.10
"　　"　　"　　No. 30, 3 "　　"　　.............1.15
"　　"　　"　　No. 35, 3 "　　"　　.............1.30
"　　"　　"　　No. 40, 3 "　　"　　.............1.50
"　　"　　"　　No. 50, 3 "　　"　　.............1.85

Gilling twine comes in ½-lb. balls.

### SEINE TWINE.

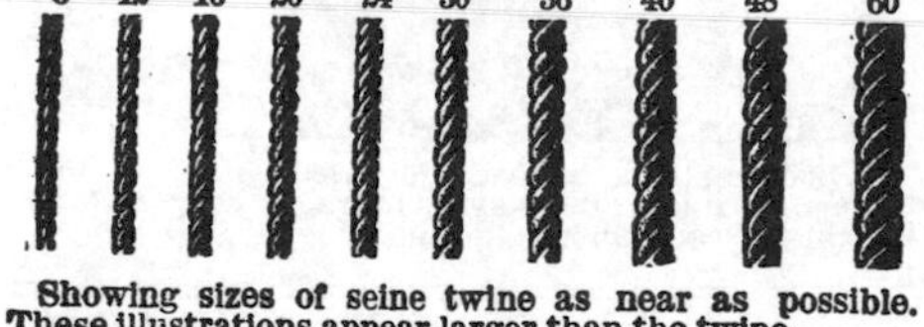

6　12　16　20　24　30　36　40　48　60

Showing sizes of seine twine as near as possible. These illustrations appear larger than the twine.

Our seine twine is the best in the market, laid smooth and even, and uniform in size. We do not handle the loosely laid, bunchy, cheap goods.

No. 82136. White seine twine, soft laid, in skeins of of about 1 to 1¾ lb. each. Nos. 6, 9, 12, 16, 20, 24, 28, 32, 36, 40, 44, 48, 60. No. 6 smallest, No. 60 largest. 32 to 48 is the proper size for fly nets; 16 to 24 is the hammock size. Per lb., in less than 5-lb. lots, 20c.; per lb., in 5-lb. lots and over.................................19c.

No. 82137. White seine twine, medium laid, for seines and hammocks, in skeins. Nos. 9, 12, 15, 18, 21, 24, 27, 30, 33, 36, 42, 48, 54, 60. No. 9 smallest. Per lb., in 5-lb. lots and over, 21c.; per lb...........................24c.

No. 82138. White seine twine, hard laid, in skeines Nos. 9 to 60, same size as in medium laid. Per lb., in 5-lb. lots or over, 23c.; per lb..........................24c.

N. B.—In the small size the hanks weigh about 1 lb.; in the larger sizes they run about 1½-lb. to the skein. We do not break skeins.

## COLORED TWINE FOR HAM-MOCKS AND FLY NETS.

No. 82139. Colored seine twine, for hammocks and fly nets. Colors: Blue, red, brown and orange. Nos. 24 and 32 only; No. 24 for hammocks and No. 32 for fly nets. Per lb...........................................30c.

Price on rope and seine rigging quoted on application. We can furnish nearly everything in this line at low prices.

### SEINE NEEDLES.

No. 82140. Seine knitting needles, made of white wood.
Size........... ½ in.　¾ in.　1 in.　1¼ in.　1½ in.
Each........ 10c.　12c.　15c.　16c.　17c.

For quotations on sailors' palms, needles and twine, see index.

### HAMMOCKS.

No. 82146.

No. 82146. Hammocks for children, open mesh, cotton cord, mixed bright colors, strong and durable, 6 ft. 6 in. bed by 4 ft. wide; weight, 8 oz. Each......$0.35
No. 82146½. Child,s hammock, double cord open mesh, bright colors, curved spreaders on each end, entire length from end to end 8 ft. 6 in., spreaders, 2 ft. 6 in, long, strong, well made and durable; weight, 1½ lbs., each ..................$0.50
No. 82147. Hammocks, full size, made of heavy double seinetwine, full width, entire length, end to to end, 14 ft., fancy bright colors; weight 2 lbs. Each..................................................$0.90

No. 82148.

No. 82148. Hammocks, Mexican woven, white sisal, entire length, 12 ft. 6 in., bed, 6 ft., with knotted edge, clinch thimbles, strong and durable. Each.............................................$0.70
No. 82149. Hammocks, Mexican woven sisal, assorted colors, same size and style as No. 82148. Price each..................................................$0.80

No. 82150.

No. 82150. Hammocks, Mexican woven, made of sisal sea grass, yellowish white bed, fancy colored valon each side, bright colored end strings, clinch thimble on each end, entire length 14 ft., length of bed 6 ft. 6 in., full width; weight, 4 lbs. Each......$1.59

---

No. 82151.

No. 82151. Hammocks, close woven body, fancy colors, with pillow and one spreader, size of bed 38x78 incees. Price, each...............................$1.35
No. 82152. Hammocks, close woven body, full fancy, bright colors, with two curved spreaders concealed, and pillow, size of bed 42x80 inches. Price, each..................................................$1.60

No. 82153.

No. 82153. Hammocks, close excelsior woven, with fancy fringe valance, full fancy bright colors, 2 curved wooden spreaders, with pillow, size of bed 42x80 inches. Price, each...........................$1.85
No. 82153½. Hammocks. close excelsior woven, with deep woven valance, fluted full fancy bright colors, with 2 curved wooden spreaders and pillow. Size of bed 42x80 inches. Price, each...........$2.15

No. 82163.

No. 82163. Hammocks, close woven fancy weave in full fancy bright colors, 5 ply weave, with extra deep fancy finted valance, with one straight heavy spring steel spreader concealed, and pillow, size of bed 42x84 inches; a beau,t Our special price, $2.65.
No. 82164. Hammock. fancy close Grecian wove, full fancy bright colors throughout, extra deep fluted valance, two straight heavy spring steel spreaders. with heavy steel triangular spreader rings, very strong and durable, size of bed 48x90 inches. Price...........................................$3.40
No. 82165. Hammock, same description as No. 82164, with two pillows, bed 54x96 inches; this hammock is suitable for two persons, strong and durable. Price...........................................$4.25

No. 82155.

No. 82155. Hammocks, close woven body, cotton weave, in bright fancy colors, mostly red mixed with other bright colors, wide balance on each side, with pillow, 42x84 inch, heavy and strong. Weight, about 6 lbs. Each.........$3.75

### PEERLESS HAMMOCK SPREADER.

No. 82166. Is made of a solid hard piece of hardwood, bent bow shape, with hooks on its lower edge. It is designed to sustain a heavy weight, and is so simple in its construction and application that all will understand how to use it. Each, 8c; per dozen, 75c. Weight, 1 lb. each.

## HAMMOCK ROPES AND HOOKS.

No. 82167. Hammock ropes, 7 feet long, with galvanized iron anchor fastening that remains where you place it; no knots to tie after attached to hammock, no slipping while in hammock. Hammock can be raised and lowered in an instant. Each, 8c; two for 15c.

No. 82172. Screw hammock hooks, tinned. 7-16 inch diameter, to screw in. Each, 6c; per dozen. 65c.

No. 82173. Plate hammock hooks, tinned, 7-16 inch in diameter, to screw on. Each, 9c; per dozen, $1.00.

---

## TENTS.
### How to Pitch a Tent.

Having unrolled the tent in the exact position you want it to be when up, place the ridge pole, rounded side up, inside the tent, and on a line with the large eyelet holes, which are in the center of the roof; then insert the uprights in the holes bored in the ridge pole, and let the pikes in the upright pole come through the top of the tent. If a fly is used let the pikes also go through that, in precisely the same way as the tent; then take hold of the uprights and raise tent and fly together; secure the corner guys first and then the others between them. Do not drive the stakes straight, but angling; they hold very much better in this way. The tent being now up and guys all adjusted so that they bear equal strain, then proceed to dig a V-shaped trench all around the tent, about three inches deep; this will insure you a dry floor at all times. Do not take the tent down when wet or even damp. Heat and dampness is the cause of mildew, which destroys more tents than all other causes combined.

SPECIAL NOTE.—If you are interested in other styles of tents not listed in this catalogue, we invite your correspondence. Quotations given on applications, and at bottom prices. We can meet your expectation.

### "A" OR WEDGE TENTS.

Weight without poles, 18 to 40 lbs.; weight of poles, 14 ounces to the foot in length.

| Order No. | Length and Breadth. Feet. | Height. Feet. | Price 8 oz. Duck. | Price 10 oz. Duck. | Price 12 oz. Duck. |
|---|---|---|---|---|---|
| 82198 | 7 x 7 ft. | 7 ft. | $3.65 | $4.25 | $5.65 |
|  | 7 x 9 ft. | 7 ft. | 4.40 | 5.15 | 6.80 |
|  | 9 x 9 ft. | 7 ft. | 4.85 | 5.75 | 7.60 |
|  | 9½x12 ft. | 7½ft. | 5.95 | 7.00 | 9.40 |
|  | 12 x14 ft. | 9 ft. | 8.65 | 10.00 | 13.50 |

### MINERS' TENTS.

Weights without poles 14 to 30 pounds; poles 13 ounces per foot in length.

| 82198 | | Price, Complete. | | |
|---|---|---|---|---|
| Size of Base. | Height | 8 oz. Single Filling Duck. | 10 oz. Single Filling Duck. | 12 oz. Double Filling Duck. |
| 7 ft. x 7 ft. | 7 ft. | $2.30 | $2.90 | $4.10 |
| 9 ft. x 9 ft. | 8 ft. | 3.80 | 4.40 | 6.15 |
| 12 ft. x 12 ft. | 9 ft. | 5.80 | 6.70 | 9.80 |

### REFRESHMENT TENTS.

(Plain White Duck.)

Oblong or Refreshment tent, made of PLAIN WHITE DUCK, not striped, as shown in cut. Price includes poles, pins, guys, etc., complete, ready to set up. The cut shows front open, it can be closed, or stretched out in front for an awning or taken off altogether, as it is put on with hooks for these changes.
No. 82199.

| Size. | Wall. | Center. | 8 oz. White Duck. | 10 oz. White Duck. | 10 oz. Double Filling Duck. |
|---|---|---|---|---|---|
| 9x14 | 6 ft. | 10 ft. | $13.20 | $14.90 | $15.60 |
| 9x16½ | 6 ft. | 10 ft. | 14.65 | 16.65 | 17.70 |
| 9x19 | 6 ft. | 10 ft. | 15.96 | 18.50 | 19.70 |
| 12x19 | 6 ft. | 11 ft. | 17.95 | 20.40 | 22.25 |
| 12x21½ | 6 ft. | 11 ft. | 21.48 | 24.60 | 26.80 |
| 14x21½ | 6 ft. | 11 ft. | 22.00 | 25.15 | 27.85 |
| 14x23½ | 6 ft. | 11 ft. | 27.10 | 31.10 | 34.85 |

NOTE.—Where 8 oz. stripe, blue or brown, is wanted, the price will be the same as 10 oz. "double filling" white duck.

TAKE ECONOMY PILLS FOR THAT... POVERTY FEELING.

---

## REFRESHMENT TENT TOPS.

No. 82206. (Without wall)

| Size. | Center. | 8 oz. White Duck. | 10 oz. White Duck. | 10 oz. Double Filling Duck. |
|---|---|---|---|---|
| 9x14 | 10 ft. | $ 7.55 | $ 8.25 | $10.10 |
| 9x16½ | 10 ft. | 8.58 | 9.35 | 11.65 |
| 9x19 | 10 ft. | 9.65 | 10.56 | 13.10 |
| 12x19 | 11 ft. | 10.75 | 11.90 | 15.20 |
| 12x21½ | 11 ft. | 12.40 | 14.65 | 18.75 |
| 14x21½ | 11 ft. | 13.80 | 15.90 | 19.70 |
| 14x23½ | 11 ft. | 17.30 | 19.20 | 25.15 |

The above prices include everything complete ready for putting up. Where 8 oz. stripe is wanted the prices will be the same as 10 oz. double filling.

## WALL TENTS.

We can furnish tents in large or small quantities on short notice generally. Our tents are the best quality; they are *all full size*, and all have a *good "pitch"* to roof, to turn rain, and all made in a durable and substantial manner. Prices in lots of 5 or more furnished on application. Tents will not be sent C. O. D., as they have to be made to order. We warrant them to be exactly as represented. In ordering give catalogue number, length and breadth and price.

We can make to order all kinds of tents canopies, etc.

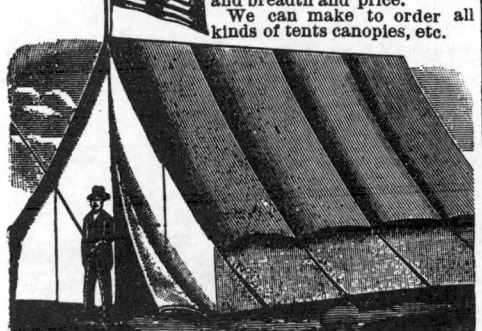

Wall Tent No. 82213.

Weights without poles, 7x7, 30 lbs.; 9½x12, 40 to 50 lbs.; 14x16, 66 to 76 lbs.; 16x24, 120 to 130 lbs.; 18x32, 147 to 160 lbs. Ridge poles weigh 22 ounces to the foot. Upright poles, 14 oz. to the foot. Pins weigh ¼ to ¾ pounds each. All of our 12 ounce duck tents are double filling, best quality, 29 inch duck.

| No. | Length and Breadth Feet. | Height Wall. Feet. | Height Pole. Feet. | 8 oz. Duck. | 10 oz. Duck. | 12. oz. Duck. |
|---|---|---|---|---|---|---|
| Order 82213 | 7 x 7 | 3 | 7 | $4.75 | $5.45 | $7.40 |
| | 7 x 9 | 3 | 7 | 5.50 | 6.50 | 8.50 |
| | 9 x 9 | 3 | 7½ | 6.40 | 7.50 | 9.55 |
| | 9½ x 12 | 3 | 7½ | 7.60 | 8.75 | 11.70 |
| | 9½ x 14 | 3 | 7½ | 8.60 | 9.95 | 13.20 |
| | 12 x 12 | 3½ | 8 | 8.95 | 10.50 | 13.90 |
| | 12 x 14 | 3½ | 8 | 10.10 | 11.85 | 15.60 |
| | 12 x 16 | 3½ | 8 | 11.25 | 13.20 | 17.50 |
| | 12 x 18 | 3½ | 8 | 12.45 | 14.60 | 19.15 |
| | 14 x 14 | 4 | 9 | 12.00 | 14.10 | 18.80 |
| | 14 x 16 | 4 | 9 | 13.30 | 15.60 | 20.70 |
| | 14 x 18 | 4 | 9 | 14.80 | 17.30 | 23.10 |
| | 14 x 20 | 4 | 9 | 16.35 | 19.15 | 25.10 |
| | 14 x 24 | 4 | 9 | 18.60 | 21.60 | 28.10 |
| | 16 x 16 | 5 | 11 | 16.90 | 19.48 | 25.75 |
| | 16 x 18 | 5 | 11 | 18.10 | 21.20 | 28.80 |
| | 16 x 20 | 5 | 11 | 19.35 | 23.40 | 30.50 |
| | 16 x 24 | 5 | 11 | 22.70 | 26.40 | 34.60 |
| | 16 x 30 | 5 | 11 | 27.50 | 32.05 | 41.88 |
| | 16 x 35 | 5 | 11 | 30.75 | 35.95 | 46.90 |
| | 18 x 18 | 5 | 11 | 20.75 | 24.70 | 32.80 |
| | 18 x 20 | 5 | 11 | 22.85 | 26.60 | 34.90 |
| | 18 x 24 | 5 | 11 | 25.50 | 29.75 | 38.95 |
| | 18 x 30 | 5 | 11 | 30.55 | 35.65 | 46.75 |
| | 18 x 35 | 5 | 11 | 34.25 | 39.70 | 52.85 |

Where higher wall is wanted add 5 per cent. for each 6 inches in extra height of wall.

Poles and pins included in above prices. Prices on any size of wall tent not mentioned above, given on application. Can furnish any style of tent wanted.

A tent fly makes an extra movable or double roof to a tent, and affords a greater protection from sun and rain, and can be made to serve as an awning, either in front or rear of tent. They are not really necessary, and are not included in prices of tents, but we can furnish them, if ordered, at one-half the price of tents of corresponding size and quality.

**This Catalogue is intended to be to you a correct guide for economic buying. It is plain to the most skeptical that we are in a position to quote far lower prices direct from factory to consumer than can your local dealer. That we do quote lower prices is easily proven. You have the privilege of examining anything you may order.**

## PHOTOGRAPHERS' TENTS.

No. 82238. Weight, without poles, 66 to 176 pounds. Ridge poles, 22 to 25 oz. per foot in length.

| Size. | Pole. | Wall. | 8 oz. single fill'g duck. | 10 oz. single filling, duck. | 10 oz. double filling duck. |
|---|---|---|---|---|---|
| | | | Price, complete, without dark room. | | |
| 12x16 ft...... | 11 ft. | 6 ft. | $17 23 | $19.40 | $23.15 |
| 12x21 ft...... | 11 ft. | 6 ft. | 21.05 | 24.30 | 28.65 |
| 12x24 ft...... | 11 ft. | 6 ft. | 23.40 | 26.95 | 31.60 |
| 14x16 ft...... | 12 ft. | 6 ft. | 19.35 | 22.85 | 27.50 |
| 14x21 ft...... | 12 ft. | 6 ft. | 23.40 | 26.90 | 32.50 |
| 14x24 ft...... | 12 ft. | 6 ft. | 25.45 | 29.60 | 35.10 |
| 14x28 ft...... | 12 ft. | 6 ft. | 28.90 | 33.65 | 39.80 |
| 16x18 ft...... | 13 ft. | 6 ft. | 22.85 | 26.65 | 31.85 |
| 16x24 ft...... | 13 ft. | 6 ft. | 28.15 | 32.75 | 38.90 |
| 16x28 ft...... | 13 ft. | 6 ft. | 31.90 | 37.15 | 44.20 |
| 16x30 ft...... | 13 ft. | 6 ft. | 34.20 | 39.80 | 47.40 |

Prices on tents include poles, pins, guys, etc. Tent complete, ready to set up.

Dark rooms extra, 6x6 feet, $7.80; 4½x4½ feet, $6.50. Our dark rooms are made of same material, same weight and color as the tent—all white. We make the room only, the artist can darken it to suit his own taste. Some use black silesia, some yellow, etc.

The above prices include poles, pins, guys, etc., ready to set up tent. Quotations on other sizes on application and at bottom prices.

Prices on stable tents, stable tops, Sibley tents, canopy tops without wall, photographers' tents, square hip-roof tents, or any other style, given on application and at bottom prices.

## PALMETTO OR LAWN TENTS.

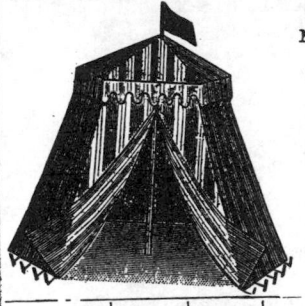

No. 82249. These tents have but one pole, and that is in the center. Top is supported by a light iron frame sewed into tent around eaves. They are made of 8 ounce awning material. Color, blue and white, brown and white, blue and old gold, etc., in alternate shades.

| Size of Base. | Size of Top. | Height in Center. | Height at Side. | Price without Awning. | Price with Awning. |
|---|---|---|---|---|---|
| 7x 7........ | 2 ft. 4 in. | 7 ft. 6 in. | 6 ft. | $5.00 | $6.95 |
| 8x 8........ | 2 ft. 4 in. | 8 ft. | 6 ft. | 5.80 | 7.65 |
| 9x 9........ | 3 ft. 6 in. | 8 ft. 6 in. | 7 ft. | 7 80 | 9.25 |
| 10x10........ | 3 ft. 6 in. | 9 ft. | 7 ft. 6 in. | 8.20 | 10.60 |

## BLACK OILED WAGON COVER.

These covers, although black and called tarpaulins, have no tar in their composition. Our waterproof dressing is an oil preparation and is entirely free from anything calculated to rot or burn the canvas, but adds to the durability of the cover, being impervious to water and very soft and pliable. It will neither rot nor mildew from damp, nor break from being too hard. They are invaluable to all persons who are shipping and receiving goods which are liable to damages from wet weather. In ordering give catalogue number, size and price.

Weight, 9 to 28 lbs. 6x12, 12 lbs.; 6x9, 9 lbs.; 7x12, 16 lbs.; 7x14, 19 lbs.

| No. | Size. | Price. | Size. | Price. | Size. | Price. |
|---|---|---|---|---|---|---|
| 82254 | 6x 8 ft. | $2.70 | 7x 9 ft. | $3.55 | 8x10 ft. | $4.50 |
| | 6x 9 ft. | 3.05 | 7x10 ft. | 3.90 | 8x12 ft. | 5.42 |
| | 6x10 ft. | 3.35 | 7x12 ft. | 4.70 | 8x14 ft. | 6.35 |
| | 6x12 ft. | 3.95 | 7x14 ft. | 5.50 | 8x16 ft. | 7.20 |
| | 6x14 ft. | 4.75 | 7x16 ft. | 6.30 | 9x14 ft. | 7.09 |

## WAGON COVERS.

No. 82258. Wagon covers, white duck (see cut). Always give size when ordering. Weight, 7 to 50 lbs.; 10 x 10, 8 oz., 7 lbs.; 10 x 12 10 oz., 16 lbs., 12 x 22, 40 to 50 lbs.

| Size—Feet. | 8 oz. Duck. | 10 oz. Duck. | 12 oz. Duck. |
|---|---|---|---|
| 10x10 | $1.65 | $2.00 | $3 10 |
| 10x12 | 1.95 | 2.45 | 3 65 |
| 10x14 | 2.25 | 2.85 | 4 30 |
| 10x15 | 2.40 | 3.15 | 4 60 |
| 10x16 | 2.50 | 3.25 | 4 90 |
| 11x15 | 2.30 | 2.90 | 4 50 |
| 11x15 | 2.70 | 3.40 | 5 15 |
| 11x18 | 3.25 | 4.10 | 6 25 |
| 12x15 | 3.00 | 3.80 | 5 75 |
| 12x16 | 3.30 | 4.00 | 6 15 |
| 12x20 | 4.19 | 5.00 | 7 75 |

## STACK, MACHINE AND MERCHANDISE COVERS, CALLED PAULINS.

Weight from 15 to 100 lbs.; 16x14, 10 to 26 lbs.; 14x20, 25 to 30 lbs.; 20x20, 38 to 45 lbs.

No. 82259. White Duck. Always state size wanted when ordering. Prices quoted on application on sizes not mentioned here. Our 12 ounce duck is best double filling. These goods are not tents, but "stack covers" or paulins.

| Size.—Feet. | 8 oz. Duck. | 10 oz. Duck. | 12 oz. Duck. |
|---|---|---|---|
| 10x16 | $ 2.32 | $ 2.85 | $ 4.25 |
| 10x18 | 2.60 | 3.20 | 4.73 |
| 12x14 | 2.52 | 3.12 | 4.56 |
| 12x16 | 2.98 | 3.56 | 5.24 |
| 12x18 | 3.27 | 4.00 | 5.89 |
| 12x20 | 3.66 | 4.45 | 6.56 |
| 14x16 | 4.09 | 4.72 | 6 30 |
| 14x18 | 4.34 | 5.32 | 7.09 |
| 14x20 | 4.85 | 5.92 | 7.88 |
| 14x24 | 5.80 | 7.10 | 9.45 |
| 16x16 | 4.43 | 5.40 | 7.20 |
| 16x18 | 4.97 | 6.10 | 8.10 |
| 16x20 | 5.55 | 6.75 | 9.00 |
| 16x24 | 6.62 | 8.12 | 10.80 |
| 18x20 | 6.24 | 7.60 | 10.12 |
| 18x24 | 7.47 | 9.12 | 12.15 |
| 18x28 | 8.70 | 10.50 | 14.18 |
| 18x30 | 9.30 | 11.40 | 15.19 |
| 20x24 | 8.30 | 10.12 | 13.50 |
| 20x36 | 12.35 | 15.15 | 20.20 |
| 24x30 | 12.41 | 15.20 | 20.25 |
| 24x40 | 15.30 | 18.75 | 26.40 |
| 24x50 | 19.15 | 23.45 | 33.00 |

Stack covers have short ropes, but no poles; machine and merchandise covers have eyelets around side. Any other size furnished on short notice. Prices on application.

## BINDER COVERS.

No. 82264. Weight, 6½ to 7¼ lbs. Fitted to cover the binder and not the whole macine. Will fit any binder. Made of white duck.

| | 8 oz. | 10 oz. |
|---|---|---|
| Price, each........................... | $1.85 | $2.15 |

## STOCKMEN'S BED SHEETS.

Weights, 10 to 22 lb. Fitted with snap rings or eyelets as may be ordered.

Made of very best heavy white duck.

| Order No. | Feet. | 13 oz. | 15 oz. | 18 oz. |
|---|---|---|---|---|
| 82265 | 6x12 | $2.58 | $3.15 | $3.35 |
| | 6x14 | 2.92 | 3.60 | 3.85 |
| | 6x15 | 3.20 | 3.85 | 4.18 |
| | 6x18 | 3.90 | 4.60 | 4.90 |
| | 7x12 | 3.00 | 3.57 | 3.90 |
| | 7x14 | 3 40 | 4.12 | 4.60 |
| | 7x15 | 3.70 | 4.45 | 4.90 |
| | 7x18 | 4.35 | 5.25 | 5.80 |
| | 8x12 | 3.75 | 4.50 | 4.85 |
| | 8x14 | 4.30 | 5.20 | 5.67 |
| | 8x18 | 5.50 | 6.65 | 7.25 |

**We list a fine line of Cameras in our Optical Goods Department. You can get a vast deal of pleasure from reviewing past scenes of outing trips where you have taken your camera along.**

## ARCTIC SLEEPING BAGS.

No. 82268. The Improved. Made of heavy waterproof tan-colored duck, lined with sheepskin with the wool left on; inside of sheepskin lining is a heavy drill lining that can be taken out and cleaned at any time. Large enough to cover any man entirely. Can cover up "head and ears," and still have plenty of air. Loops on sides, so that it can be hung up with ropes if desired. With these bags all beds and bedding can be dispensed with. It rolls up into small package, so that it can be fastened to a saddle or "packed on back." The best bed ever invented for out door sleeping or tent camping. Weight, about 20 lbs. Each................................$13.00

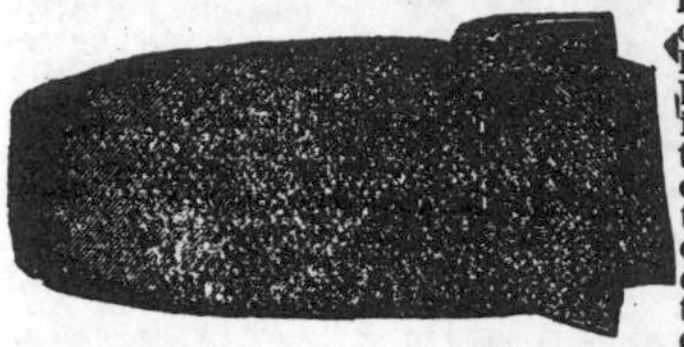

## CAMPERS' CLOTHES BAG.

No. 82269. These bags are made of heavy white duck, round bottom, drawing string top fastening; handy for extra clothing, shells, boots and other "truck." Regular sailor's bag. Doesn't cost much; always useful. Every family needs them. Each..............60c

## CAMPERS' "CARRYALL" BAG

(Try one on your next outing trip.)

No. 82270. This bag is made of heavy waterproof, tan-colored duck, with leather lap over mouth, leather lock-strap, fastening mailbag style. Durable and strong, large size. The BEST and most USEFUL bag a "cowboy," hunter or camper could suggest. No camper's outfit complete without one; about 20x30 inches. Each.........$3.50

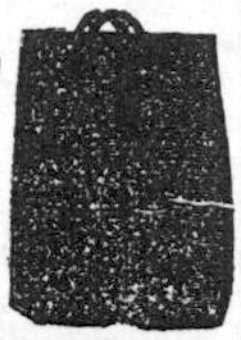

## KIT BAG.

No. 82271. Made of 10-ounce brown canvas, fastened with straps and buckles. Neat, handy and durable. Length, 27 inches; width, 20 inches. Each...$1.20

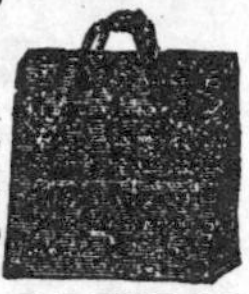

## THE ACME FOLDING CANVAS BOAT.

No. 82285. (2) The Acme folding canvas boat. Painted dark green. Length, 12 feet: beam, 45 inches; depth at stem and stern, 22 inches; depth amidships, 14 inches; weight, light form, 35 lbs.; weight, complete, 46 lbs.; capacity, two and three passengers. Complete with one pair 6½-foot oars, pair adjustable oar-locks, 2 folding seats, 1 adjustable back and shipping case. Price, complete................................$35.00

This is our most popular boat. It is a good general purpose boat. It can be made up in a light form, weighing but 35 pounds, by leaving out some of the parts which are necessary only when the boat is loaded to its full capacity. It can be made up into two bundles of equal size and weight. For from one to three passengers, we would recommend it above any of the other sizes.

## THE EUREKA CANVAS FOLDING BOAT.

No. 82286. (No. 1.) Length, 10 feet; beam, 36 inches; depth at ends, 20 inches; depth at center, 12 inches; weight 35 lbs.; capacity, one to three passengers. Price, with one pair 6-foot ash oars, malleable row-locks and two folding seats, Grade A............$24.00

The No. 1 has a full model, the full beam being carried well up to the ends. It has great carrying capacity for a boat of its length and weight, and is very steady on the water. It is a boat capable of carrying safely two or three persons, and yet light enough and compact enough to be easily carried long distances by hand.

The Eureka does not fold as compactly as the Acme, and, of course, is not as well made, but yet is strong and durable.

## THE KOSHKONONG HUNTING SKIFF.

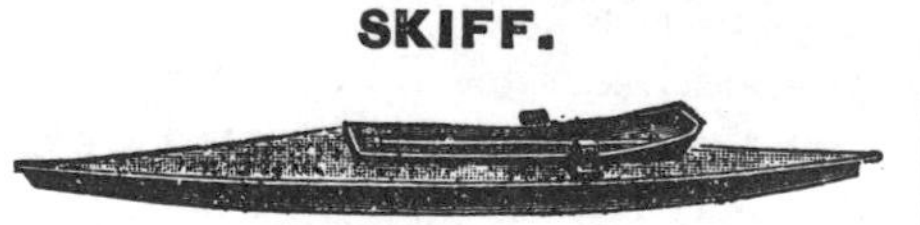

"Sets on the water like a duck."

No. 82288. The celebrated Koshkonong Hunting Boat is without doubt the best in the world, all things considered. Fifteen feet long, three feet beam, cockpit five feet long, two feet wide, pointed at both ends, deck boarded and canvas covered—can walk all over deck. Folding canvas wing around cockpit. Overlocks not fitted, can put on any kind of locks desired. Water and air tight chamber in each end., good in open rough, as well as shallow water. Can not be tipped over, easy rowing, foot rack in bottom, made especially for running easily over grass and weeds, sets low on the water. Capacity, 1,200 to 1,500 pounds. Just what every hunter and fisherman has been looking for; "easy as a rocking chair." Weight about 90 pounds. Boat only................................$22.00

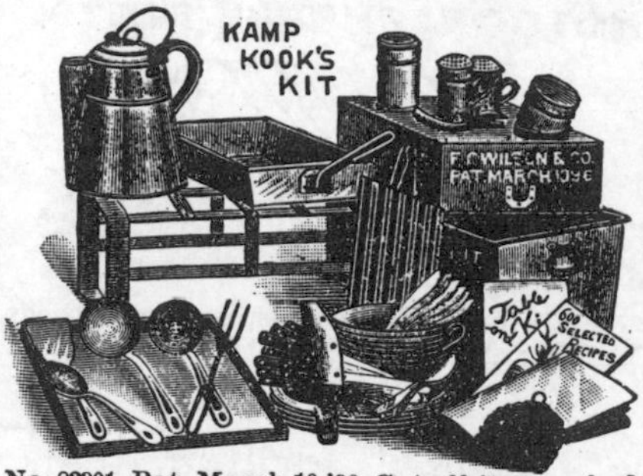


No. 82301. Pat. March 10,'96. Cut of kit unpacked

## CAMPING OUTFITS.

No. 82301. Wilson's Kamp Kook's Kit. Just the thing for camping out. 53 pieces. Fire jack, 2 boilers suitable for using as an oven, fry pan, coffee pot and all utensils and tableware for a party of six. Everything first-class. Boilers are made of 26 gauge smooth steel. The entire kit nests in small space, and when packed ready for shipment makes a package 24½x10½x8 inches, all nested together and can be firmly locked up by an ordinary pad lock. Weight, complete 80 pounds. Price complete..........................$9.00

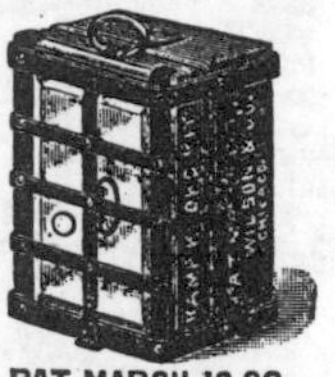

PAT. MARCH 10,96. No. 82301. Cut of kit packed for shipment.

No. 82302. 20 piece set, containing the stove and complete apparatus, without the table ware. Price....$7.00

No. 82303. Wilson's Kamp Komfort Tent Heater. The largest and best tent heater on the market. Size, 15½x12x15 inches, with 9 joints of pipe which telescope and packed inside of the stove for shipping. This stove burns anything, is air-tight with down draught. Holds fire all night. Has spark arrester which insures perfect safety. The pipe nests so closely in this stove, it leaves plenty of room for our "Kamp Kooks Kit." Complete with fire jack. Body made of No. 22 sheet steel. No. 16 lid with hasp for pad lock, making a secure shipping case with handles ready to check as baggage. One size only. Price...$6.50

No. 82303. Pat. pending.

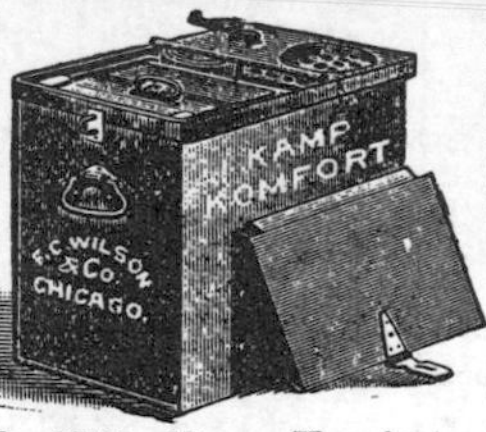


No. 82303. Kamp Komfort Tent Heater.

## THE "U. S." FOLDING COT.

No. 82305. The "U. S." Folding Cot. Just the thing for camping purposes Covered with either white or brown 10 oz. duck. This is the lightest, strongest and most compact folding cot made. It has the only practical pillow ever put on a cot. It is easier opened and closed and folds into less space than any other cot. The duck will wear longer and legs stand more strain.and will stand on more uneven ground because not being stretched with a stretcher. Length, 6 feet 3 inches. Width, 29 inches. Dimensions when folded and ready for shipment, 6 ft. 3 in.x5in.x2 in. Weight, 15 lbs. Price complete with pillow, each..$1.75. Price complete without pillow, each..$1.50.

82305.

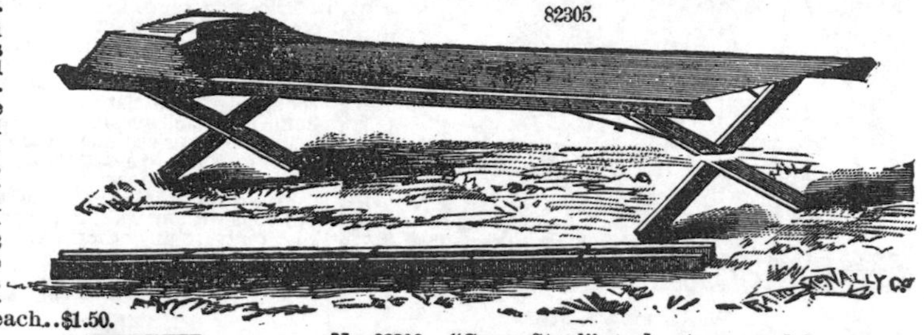

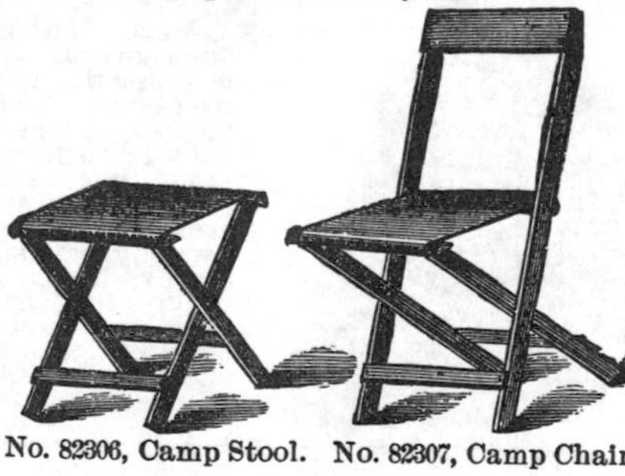

No. 82306, Camp Stool. No. 82307, Camp Chair.

No. 82306. "Camp Stool" made strong and durable to fold flat and easily packed. Price with heavy duck top each............50c. With carpet top, each.............75c

No. 82307. "Camp Chair," same style as No. 82306 except has back, like cut.

Price with heavy canvass top, each....................55c

No. 82308. "The Repose Folding Chair." A most luxuriant chair for camp or garden, covered with strong canvas; has a high comfortable back. Made with easy recline and is arranged so as to give perfect rest. The most portable and efficient chair yet invented; can be folded into very small package and carried in the hand without inconvenience.

Price, each..........................................$1.95

**NOTE—No camp is complete without our "Kamp Kook's Kit," "Tent Heater," "U. S." Cot and Chairs or Stools.**

## Outdoor Lamps. For Lighting Tents, Etc.

No. 82310. The New "Chicago" Outdoor Lamp. For lighting tents, lawns, or outdoor meetings of any kind there is nothing to equal them. They are perfectly safe, give a very clear, steady light, make no smoke or smell and will stand any wind. Can be hung up anywhere and make an excellent headlight for boating. To insure best results, with brilliant light and no smoke, use gasoline of 74 degrees gravity.

Price with 1 gallon tank, each...................$2.25 Price with 2 gallon tank, each...................$3.75

## FERGUSON'S (PATENT) UNIVERSAL REFLECTING LAMP.

### WITH SILVER PLATED LOCOMOTIVE REFLECTOR.

No. 1.

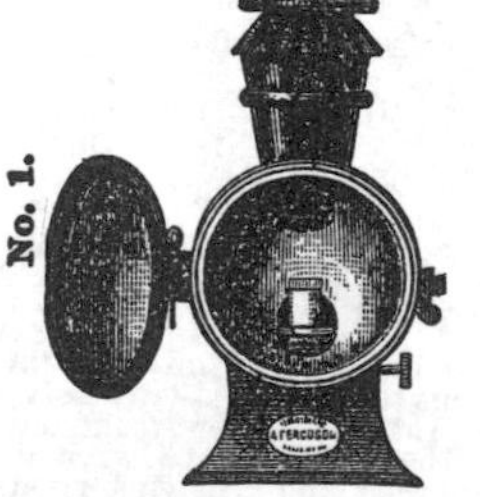

No. 2.

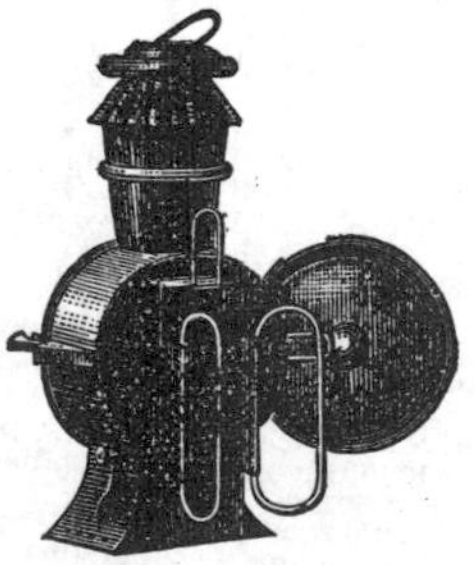

No. 3.

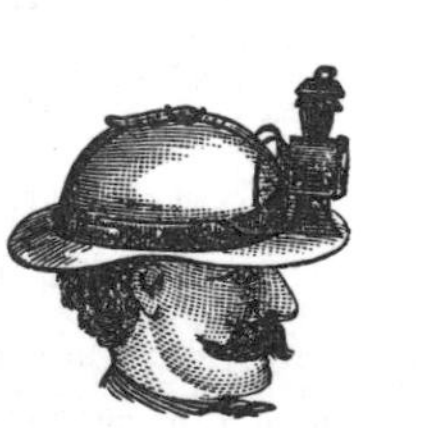

No. 82312. The Celebrated Ferguson Hunting and Fishing Lamps. This is the most practical lamp ever invented for hunting, fishing, boating, traveling or driving at night, lighting log cabins, tents or shanties. It will burn the oil from eight to nine hours without refilling and gives a powerful light, by which an object from 40 to 60 yards distant can be readily seen. It will "shine" an animals eyes at 100 yards distance. It has folding handles at the back, also a catch by which it may be hung in any desired position. It can a be secured to the waist by passing a strap or cord through an aperture at the back made for this purpose. It may also be worn on the head by using the head attachment, without any inconvenience and on any kind of a hat. This lamp burns any ordinary lantern oil. Best results obtained from "signal oil," or "lard oil mixed with kerosene."

Figure 1. Represents front view of the lamp.

Figure 2. A back view showing the outside wick regulator, the folding handles, the catch for suspending the lamp and the cap or door held open by the side catch.

Figure 3. Showing the lamp adjusted to the front of the head by means of the head attachment.

The door or cap may be closed when desired, making a dark lantern without extinguishing the light. Black japanned lamp, height, 8½ inches; depth, 2¾ inches; face, 3¾ inches; weight 17 ounces.

Price without head attachment................$5.00 Price complete with head attachment..........$6.50

# BICYCLE DEPARTMENT.

For the season of 1897 we offer a line of **STRICTLY HIGH GRADE BICYCLES, which for price, beauty of design, quality of material used, workmanship, and, in fact, general perfection, is not excelled, if, in fact, equalled by any line of Bicycles made. We have made our arrangements with a view to selling at least 10,000** Bicycles this season, and to do this it is necessary to put our prices below all kinds of competition. We have not only done this, but by a careful comparison you will observe that our prices are far lower than any other concern, and yet by the terms of our guarantee you can see that we have not cut the prices at the expense of quality. On the contrary, we make and stand ready to defend ourselves on this bold statement: **Every one of our Bicycles, excepting the $24.95 Wheel, is STRICTLY HIGH GRADE;** every one is covered by the same binding guarantee; no matter what you pay, you cannot buy a poor bicycle from us.

**Do not buy your Bicyles at retail and pay $75.00 to $100,00,** when you can buy a strictly first class, two year guaranteed **Electric Wheel from us at $29.90,** or a cheap wheel, such as is sold by others at $40.00 to $50.00, for **$24.95,** and our **Strictly High Grade Uno Bicycle for $35.00.**

**You can see and examine the Wheels** at your own express office before paying for same. You will not be expected to take the Bicycle unless it is found exactly as represented, perfectly satisfactory, and much cheaper than you could possibly buy elsewhere.

**OUR BINDING GUARANTEE.** While our Bicycles will with care last a lifetime, to confirm our statements regarding quality, we send with every Wheel **a Special Certificate of Guaranty for Two Years,** during which time we agree to make all repairs and keep the wheel in perfect order against trouble occasioned by **defect in material or workmanship.** This guaranty is practically as good as if it was for ten years, for if a wheel will stand two years without showing the slightest defect, it is a mechanical acknowledgement that it will stand ten years. **This guaranty does not cover our Special Electric $24.95 Bicycle,** which is offered with **no guaranty,** simply to compete with cheap wheels on the market, but every wheel except our special $24.95 Electric **is guaranteed for two years, and a written binding guaranty accompanies the wheel. Please understand by this guaranty that we do not hold ourselves responsible for damages occasioned by carelessness or accident.** Repairs of this kind sent us will be charged for at the actual cost of the labor and material. **Pneumatic tires are all guaranteed by the manufacturers,** and they earnestly request that all tires for repairs be sent direct to them and not to us. **In making claims for new parts to replace those which are broken or defective,** the old ones must in every case be sent to us prepaid, accompanied by a written statement from the sender, giving the name and number of the wheel and when purchased. If you fail to state the name and number of the wheel and when it was purchased it is liable to lead to serious delay. Please do not overlook this.

**TERMS AND CONDITIONS OF SHIPMENT.** **To make it easy to see and examine our Bicycles, we make this most extraordinary offer: On receipt of $1.00 we will ship any Bicycle by express C. O. D., subject to examination,** to the following States: Illinois, Indiana, Wisconsin, Michigan and Ohio. **To all other States east of the Rocky Mountains we will ship Bicycles on receipt of $5.00,** balance and express charges to be paid at the express office after you have seen and examined the wheel. Understand, if you live in any of the five States mentioned, you can see and examine any bicycle by sending us $1.00; from the other States east of the Rocky Mountains, $5,00. Orders for Bicycles from States and Territories west of the Rocky Mountains must be accompanied by cash in full.

**DISCOUNT FOR CASH.** **WE ALLOW A DISCOUNT OF 3 PER CENT. IF CASH IN FULL ACCOMPANIES YOUR ORDER.** If you send the full amount of cash with your order, you can deduct 3 per cent. from the prices quoted. **You take no risk in sending cash in full, for** we will immediately refund your money if you are not perfectly satisfied. You have this advantage, you save the 3 per cent., save the express charges on **return** of money to us, and besides you insure prompt delivery, as C. O. D. goods are sometimes delayed a trifle to complete shipping records.

# OUR SPECIAL $24.95 1897 MODEL GENTS' BICYCLE.

## Our Special Electric Wheel for $24.95.

**To meet a class of competition which is offering poor wheels at $30.00 to $40.00** we have arranged to supply this **Special Electric for $24.95.** We offer the wheel in competition with all other low grade wheels, but do not feel safe in guaranteeing it. In fact, it is like all cheap wheels on the market, made to sell and not for service. **If you want a cheap wheel we** can furnish you this for **$24.95** with full assurance that it is as good a wheel as you can buy elsewhere at from $30.00 to $40.00.

**It should be distinctly understood** that we are under no obligations whatever, and for any defect in material or workmanship, for any breakage or accident that may accur from any cause, we are not to be held responsible.

### DESCRIPTION.

**FRAME** is made of 1⅛ inch tubing; ¾ inch rear forks and stays.
**HANDLE BARS** are made of ⅞ inch tubing.
**WHEELS** are 28 inch; 32 and 36 spokes.
**TIRES** are single tube, pneumatic.
**RIMS** are wood of good quality.
**HUBS** are of the late tubular pattern.
**SPOKES** are nickeled and a fair grade.
**PEDALS** are rat trap.
**CHAIN**, ¼ inch, hardened cutters and cranks 6½ inch.
**BEARINGS**, fair grade, case hardened.
**TREAD**, 5 inches.
**SPROCKETS**, nickeled.
**GEAR**, 64, 68 or 72, as desired.
**SADDLE**, good fair quality, 1897 model.
**WEIGHT**, 26 lbs.

Each wheel furnished with tool bag complete. Furnished in black only. **$24.95 is our net cash with order price for this Special Electric wheel, and we will not send it C. O. D. subject to examination.** In fact, we are not anxious to receive orders for this wheel, but feel compelled to offer it in order to meet competition which is offering the exact same wheels at various prices and under very lengthy guaranties. **Do not ask us to send this wheel C. O. D.,** but if wanted enclose **$24.95** with your order and the wheel will be shipped to you by express at once.

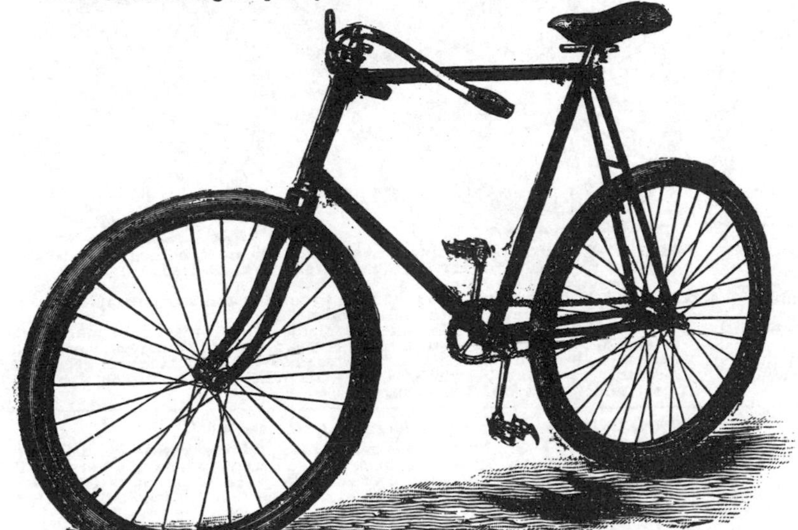

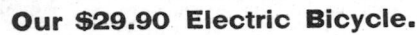

## Our $29.90 Electric Bicycle.

**No. 83000 Is made of good material,** but is not so highly finished as our higher priced wheels.
**FRAME**—Is made of 1⅛ inch tubing in the main, and ¾ inch in the rear forks and stays. This makes a very handsome frame. It is 24 inches deep, as this size has been found most desirable.
**CONNECTIONS**—Are all sheet stampings and crucible steel.
**FORK CROWN**—Is a standard pattern, very strong and handsome.
**HANDLE BARS**—Are made of ⅞ inch tubing, very gracefully curved, either up or down, as desired.
**WHEELS**—28 inch, 32 and 36 spokes.
**TIRES**—Are single tube, guaranteed, or Morgan & Wright (Quick Repair).
**RIMS**—Wood, very good quality.
**HUBS**—Tubular, the latest pattern.
**SPOKES**—Nickeled, and are very good ones.
**PEDALS**—A light rat-trap pedal, very neat.
**CHAIN**—¼ hardened Cutters.
**CRANKS**—6½ inch, round and threaded.
**BEARINGS**—All case hardened.
**TREAD**—5 inches.
**SPROCKETS**—Nickeled, very handsome.
**GEAR**—64, 68, 72.
**SADDLE**—A high-grade road saddle.
**WEIGHT**—24 lbs., wheel base 44 inches.

Each wheel furnished with a tool bag complete. Furnished in colors of blue and black only.

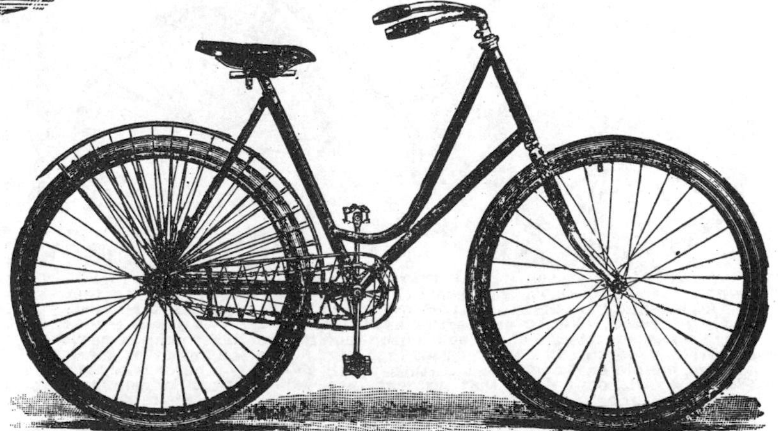

## Our Ladies' $29.90 Electric Bicycle.

**No. 83001 Made of the same material as the Gents' No. 83000.** It is a very neat and graceful wheel.
**FRAME**—Is 22 inches deep, made 1⅛ inch tubing in main and ¾ inch in rear forks and stays.
**FORK CROWN**—Is the same as on the gents'.
**HANDLE BARS**—Are made of ⅞ inch tubing, very gracefully up curved.
**WHEELS**—Are 28 inches in diameter, 32 spokes in front and 36 in rear.
**RIMS**—Are wood.
**TIRES**—Used on this wheel are single tube, guaranteed.
**HUBS**—Are the tubular pattern, very handsome.
**SPOKES**—Are nickled.
**PEDALS**—Are light and neat; rubber or rat trap.
**CHAIN**—Is ¼ inch; hardened centers.
**CRANKS**—Are 6½ inches; round and threaded.
**BEARINGS**—Are all case hardened.
**TREAD**—5 inches.
**SPROCKETS**—Are both nickel plated; ¼ inch; geared to 64 or 68.

Fitted with a good saddle suitable for ladies. Entire weight, 24 lbs. Furnished with a tool bag complete. Furnished in colors of blue and black only.

## Our Uno Bicycle at $35.00.

**TOO MUCH CANNOT BE SAID IN FAVOR OF OUR UNO BICYCLE AT $35.00.** As is illustrated and described below, we have them in both ladies' and gents'. The price is the same, **$35.00,** and this bicycle will compare favorably with any bicycle you can buy in your local market at $75.00. **IT IS STRICTLY HIGH GRADE IN EVERY RESPECT.** Nothing has been spared or left undone to make this a wheel that will give the very best service. **IT IS A WHEEL THAT WE CAN GUARANTEE** in every respect and we issue with each **a binding guarantee for two years.** As will be seen by the description it is the very latest 1897 model, thoroughly complete in every respect. **WE FEEL PERFECTLY SAFE IN ASSURING** you, that if favored with your order, you will receive such a bicycle as has never been seen in your section at anything like the price.

**DO NOT OVERLOOK OUR LIBERAL TERMS.** We send these wheels C.O.D., subject to examination, on receipt of from **$1.00** to **$5.00,** according to distance, the bicycle to be examined at the express office, and if found perfectly satisfactory and exactly as represented, pay the agent our price and express charges, less the amount sent with order and the bicycle is yours.

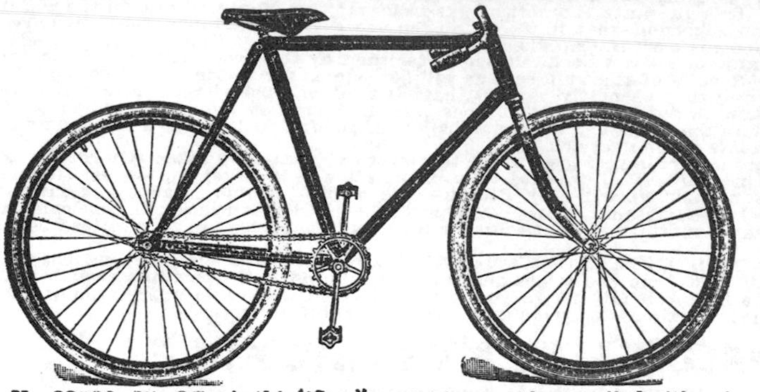

**No. 83002 We Offer in this Wheel** one tnat cannot be equalled either in quality or price, by any other firm in existence. **We ask you to read the specifications of this wheel carefully,** and compare them with the specifications of other high grade wheels, and be convinced of what a rare bargain we offer.

**SPECIFICATIONS.**

**FRAME**—Is a true diamond, 24 inches deep, made of 1⅛ inch tubing in the main frame, and ¾ inch in the rear forks and stays, and 1¼ inch in the head. This combines to make the strongest frame on the market, and the depth, 24 inches, is just what everybody wants.

**FORK AND CROWN**—Are two features to which we wish to call your special attention. The crown is the beautiful arched crown; it is the strongest made, and is used on nearly all high grade wheels. The fork, crowns and ends are nickeled, giving it a beautiful appearance. A strong fork is one of the most essential features of a bicycle, and we know from tests that have been made, that this fork is one of the strongest made.

**HANDLE BARS**—Are made of ⅞ inch tubing, very gracefully curved, up or down, or ram's horn as desired. Our ram's horn bar is the neatest and most comfortable made.

**WHEELS**—Are made of the best material. They are 28 inches in diameter; front wheel containing 32 spokes, rear wheel 36.

**SPOKES**—Are Washburn & Moen's extra select, 14-16 swaged; these spokes cannot be excelled, and tests have proved that 14-16 is the best size.

**HUBS**—Are tubular, with an improved oiling process. They are turned from solid bar steel and are very handsome.

**RIMS**—Are the best non-warpable wood, highly polished, and will not split or crack. They are fastened with a dovetail joint the strongest made.

**WHEELS**—Are fitted with the following guanteed tires: Morgan & Wright double tube, Akron India Tire Co's arrow tread single tube or the new Brunswick Tire Co's "Messenger." Basket Tread Single Tube. Always specify what tire you wish. The above tires are the best made, and we work on the plan throughout that the best is none too good for our patrons.

**PEDAL**—We use a very handsome rat trap pedal on this wheel, but the combination will be supplied if desired.

**CRANKS**—Nothing but the finest forgings are used in the cranks on this wheel, which are 6½ inches long, round and threaded and heavily nickeled on copper.

**CONNECTIONS**—All connections in this wheel are extra select drop forged and selected steel.

**BEARINGS**—Are the finest tool steel and are properly hardened Balls are accurate and true to gauge, thereby making an easy running wheel. Large size 5-1? inch in hanger. The tread is 4⅞ inches—the most desirable, and neatest width.

**SPROCKETS**—Are both select forgings, heavily nickeled; rear sprocket is detachable. We use the large sprockets, which does away with a great deal of friction, and makes a wheel look much neater.

**CHAIN**—Is as good as the best, ¼ of an inch with hardened centers, and one that will last a lifetime. Any gear from 64 to 76 will be furnished. As the gear of 70 is the most desirable, our wheels will be shipped with this gear unless otherwise specified.

**SADDLE**—Is another point that demands attention, and our wheels are fitted with either a B. & W. Hygeinic, or a Garford Road Saddle, as desired. These are just as good saddles as there are made.

We use a very handsome T seat post on this wheel. Each wheel is furnished with a handsome tool bag, and complete set of tools, pump, repair kit, wrench, and oiler. The entire weight of this wheel is 23lb. They are enameled with 4 coats of enamel, handsomely striped and transfers and varnished over all, which prevents scratching off, and always retains its beautiful lustre. Your choice of blue, black or green as desired.

**DO NOT FORGET THAT THIS WHEEL IS GUARANTEED FOR TWO YEARS TIME. THIS IS AN UNQUESTIONED PROOF OF ITS QUALITY**

**No. 83003 This is the Companion to our Gent's "Uno" Wheel,** and the same high-grade material and fine workmanship is maintained it in its make up.

**SPECIFICATIONS.**

**FRAME**—In this wheel is a very handsome one, as the cut shows, made of 1⅛ inch tubing in main, 1¼ inch in head, and ¾ inch in rear forks and braces. This is without doubt one of the strongest drop frames made.

**CONNECTIONS**—Are selected steel and drop forgings.

**FORK CROWN**—The arched fork crown on this wheel makes it a very beautiful one, and is certainly a thing of beauty and joyforever. A ladies' wheel is **hard to keep out of the repair shops.** We have built this one so it will **stay out,** and we know that our customers will find it so. **The fork ends and crown** are nickel plated. **HANDLE BARS**—Are made from selected ⅞ inch tubing, very gracefully up-curved.

**WHEELS**—Contain the best material obtainable. They are 28 inches in diameter, 32 spokes in front, and 36 in rear.

**SPOKES**—Are Washburn & Moen's extra select 14-16 swaged.

**HUBS**—Are turned from solid bar steel, tubular in shape and have improved oiling process. The cups and cones in this wheel, throughout, are case hardened, and will always give satisfaction.

**RIMS**—Are the best non-warpable wood, highly polished.

**TIRES**—The wheel will be fitted with either Morgan & Wright tire, or the Akron India Tire Co.'s single tube tire, as desired; both are guaranteed.

**PEDALS**—We use a very light and beautiful rubber pedal that can be changed to a rat-trap if so desired.

**CRANKS**—Are 6½ inches, round and threaded, and heavily nickeled, nothing but the best forgings are used in making these cranks.

**BALLS**—Are large size throughout. **TREAD**—Is 4⅞ inches.

**SPROCKETS**—Both are handsomely nickeled, the rear being detachable. The large sprockets are used and do away with a great deal of friction, and also make handsome wheels. **CHAIN**—Same chain is used on this wheel as the one on the Gent's "Uno." **No better made.**

**GEAR**—Furnished in 64, 68 or 72 as desired. **GUARDS**—We have paid especial attention to the mud and chain guards, and we have as pretty and strong guards as there are made. They are very handsomely laced.

## Our Special Ladies' "Uno" Bicycle.

**$35.00.**

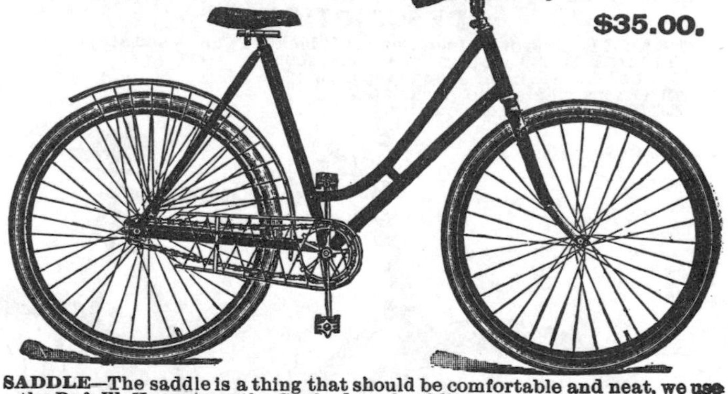

**SADDLE**—The saddle is a thing that should be comfortable and neat, we use the B. & W. Hygenic or the Garford road saddle as desired.

**T POSTS**—Are put on every wheel.

**TOOL BAG**—Each wheel supplied with a tool bag and tools, complete, consisting of pump, repair outfit, oiler, and wrench.

**ENTIRE WEIGHT**—Of this wheel is 23 lbs. It is finished in four coats of enamel, handsomely striped and ornamented with transfers; varnished over all to prevent scratching off. Your choice of blue, black, or green, as desired. Unless otherwise specified, this wheel will be shipped in blue, 68 gear, and Morgan & Wright tires.

## Our Gent's Utah.

## Price, $43.00

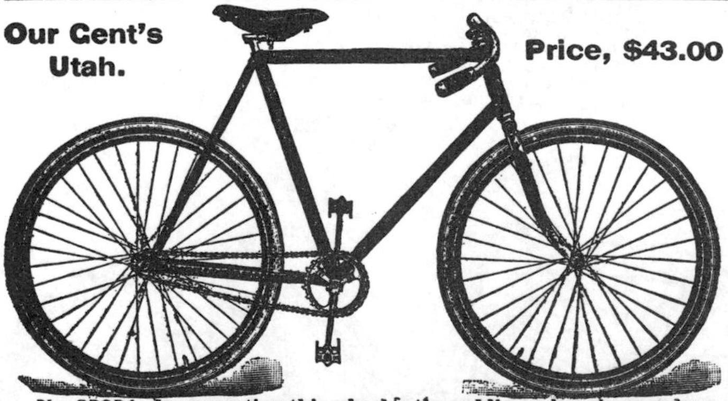

**No. 83004 In presenting this wheel to the public,** we havehave endeavored to combine strength, beauty and price, to meet with the approval of all. Special attention is called to the **fork crown,** which is a patented feature, and is protected. We alse call particular attention to the **two piece crank** which we use on this wheel, which is unequalled for simplicity and beauty, as well as strength. It will be noticed that we give you the option of gear, saddles, handle bars and tires, a feature which should not be overlooked. We can say without a doubt that our gents' and ladies' "Utah" wheels are the market for anywhere near our price. The gents' Utah is made in the following manner:

**SPECIFICATIONS.**

**FRAME.**—24 inches deep, best seamless tubing, 1⅛ inch in main frame, 1¼ inch head and ¾ inch rear forks and braces.

**CONNECTIONS.**—Are all drop forged and selected steel.

**FORK CROWN.**—On this wheel is one of the special features. It is first a rough forging, but after it goes through the factory, comes out a very beautiful and one of the strongest crowns made. The cut shows its exact appearance. **FORK.**—Is tapering and is one-fourth nickeled, making a very handsome fork.

**HANDLE BARS.**—Made from select steel, ⅞ inch; either drop, up curve or ram's horn, as desired. Wood bars will be furnished if preferred.

**WHEELS.**—28 inches in diameter, 32 spokes in front, 36 in rear.

**SPOKES.**—Washburn & Moen's best 14-16, heavily nickeled. **HUBS.**—Turned from solid bar steel, tubular in shape, with improved oiling process.

**CUPS AND CONES.**—All turned from tool steel and hardened in bone, a process which makes them as near perfect as it is possible. **RIMS.**—The best made. We use nothing but the finest rims obtainable, on this wheel.

**TIRES.**—Your choice of Morgan & Wright double tube tires, or Vim, and Volt basket tread single tube tires. These tires are as good as any that can be obtained, and are found at the head of the list.

**PEDALS.**—Can be furnished either rat trap or rubber, as desired.

**CRANKS.**—6½ inches, made of the best forgings. The two piece crank which we use on this wheel is another feature found only on high grade wheels.

**BALLS.**—Finest made, large size throughout.

**TREAD.**—4⅞ inch, which is considered just right by all riders.

**SPROCKETS.**—Both drop forged, heavily nickeled, and detachable. The large sprockets are used on this wheel also. **GEAR.**—Any gear from 64 to 76 will be furnished. Unless otherwise specified we will ship in 70 gear.

**SADDLE.**—For a saddle we use the famous Messenger, which is unequalled for comfort. For those who desire a road or racing saddle, we recommend the American, which is made on the pattern of the famous "Brooks." T seat post. **TOOL BAG.**—A tool bag and outfit complete accompanies each wheel. **WEIGHT.**—22 pounds.

**FINISH.**—Finished in a manner which is the envy of all other manufacturers. It never loses its handsome appearance or lustre. It is handsomely striped in gold and ornamented with transfers.

**COLOR.**—Unless otherwise specified, will be shipped in blue. Other colors, black, maroon, coach green and yellow.

**No. 83005 The Companion to No. 83004,** is one of the Finest Wheels made. The handsome hollow crown adds greatly to the appearance of this wheel, and the two piece crank makes the mechanism so simple, that any lady can take apart and assemble the wheel with ease. The chain and mud guards are of the finest material and are closely laced. The saddle is the most important point of a ladies' wheel, and, with this fact in view, we have fitted our "Utah" with a Messenger saddle. This saddle is unequalled for comfort and that is what a lady desires in a wheel, as much as anything else.

### SPECIFICATIONS.

**FRAME**—In this wheel is the drop style like cut, 22 inches high, made of the best grade seamless tubing, 1⅛ inch in main frame, 1¼ inch in head, and ¾ in rear forks and braces.

**CONNECTIONS**—Are all selected steel and drop forgings.

**FORK CROWN**—On this wheel the same as on gents' "Utah" and fork is tapered and ¾ nickeled in a like manner.

**HANDLE BARS**—Are curved upward, made of the best ⅞ inch tubing. We use nothing but the best material in the construction of the wheels; they are 28 inches in diameter; front wheel has 32 spokes, rear wheel 36.

**SPOKES**—Are Washburn & Moen's extra select, heavily nickeled. The wood rims are of a very superior quality, and will not break or split. The method of dove tailing joints is used on these rims, and they are consequently almost impossible to get apart at the joint.

**HUBS**—Are the same high grade as the ones on the gents' wheel, and are very handsome. The question of tires is settled at your option; you have your choice of Morgan & Wright, Vim, or the Messenger basket tread. The latter tires are single tube, and are unequalled for their easy riding qualities. Where a great deal of road riding is done, we recommend the Vim or the Messenger.

**CRANKS**—Are of the same two piece pattern as those on gent's wheel, and are very simple, and strong, as they are made of the best forgings.

**SPROCKETS**—Are ¼ inch, both detachable and both heavily nickeled. The large sprockets are used on this wheel also, as we have found that they reduce friction to a great extent. A very handsome ¼ inch chain is used, and which is subjected to a very severe strain before being allowed to pass. Any gear from 64 to 72; unless otherwise specified 68 gear will be sent, as it is the most desirable.

## Our Ladies' "Utah." For $43.00.

**PEDALS**—Are rubber combination, which can be changed to rat trap. They are very light and handsome.

**T POST**—On each wheel, and each one fitted regularly with a Messenger saddle. Garford will be sent if preferred.

**TOOL BAG**—Set of tools, consisting of pump, wrench, oiler and repair kit is furnished with each wheel.

**ENTIRE WEIGHT**—Is 22 pounds.

**FINISHED**—In the colors of blue, black, coach green, maroon or yellow. Each wheel is hand striped, transfers and varnished over all. This manner of finish cannot be equalled by any other concern making wheels.

**Our special price.** .................................................$43.00

## Our Special "Yukon" Gents' Bicycle. For $56.50.

**No. 83006 Our Yukon Bicycle** is without doubt the finest production of mechanical skill, fine material and beauty, that will be put on the market for 1897. The cut, we are very sorry to say, does the bicycle an injustice, as it is not one-third as handsome as wheel really is. The special features, such as the Fauber Hanger, Internal Expanders, and the drop in hanger, are never found anywhere but on $100 wheels, and we challenge the world on Our Special $56.50 Wheel. The rims are laminated, making the strongest one made. The hubs and hanger have ball retainers, and while we do not claim the hubs to be absolutely dust proof, they are as near it as the best mechanical skill can make them. The arch fork crown is another feature worthy of particular attention, as it is the handsomest and strongest crown made. The finish of these wheels is unequalled, and is the admiration and envy of the whole cycling world. They are enameled in four coats of enamel, then hand striped and the transfers put on, and over all this is put a coat of transparent varnish which protects the enamel and gives it a lustre that never dulls. The D tubing also adds greatly to the appearance of this wheel, and it is another feature that is found only on $100 wheels. Why pay $100 for a wheel that is no better than Our "Yukon" for $56.50? Bear in mind that this wheel is

guaranteed for two years time, while all others are guaranteed from six months to a year. There is not one piece of material used in the construction of this wheel that is not of the highest order, and we are therefore able to say that our wheel is as good as the best, and it certainly stands second to none. We ask you to read carefully the specifications printed below, and when you have finished you cannot fail to see what a bargain this wheel is at $56.50.

### SPECIFICATIONS.

**FRAME**—22, 24 or 26 inch, made of 1⅛-inch seamless tubing in main frame, 1¼-inch in head, and ¾-inch D shape in rear stays.

**CONNECTIONS**—All drop-forged and selected steel.

**FORK-CROWN**—The handsome and strong arch crown; nickel plated.

**FORK**—Large size, tapering; ¾ nickeled.

**HANDLE BARS**—⅞-inch, 7-inch bar as shown in cut, or regular up-curve, or drop bar; wood or steel as desired. The expander used here does away with the objectionable handle bar clamp, and makes it look much neater.

**WHEELS**—28-inch; 32 spokes in front wheel, 36 in rear.

**RIMS**—Best rock elm, laminated. Conceded to be the best on the market.

**TIRES**—Morgan & Wright, or Vim, 1½-inch tires furnished if desired. 1⅝-inch will be regularly sent.

**SPOKES**—Selected, 14-16 swaged.

**RUBS**—Tubular, turned from solid bar steel, with improved oiling device by which the oil is carried direct to the balls where it should be, fitted with improved ball retainers.

**PEDALS**—The Record '97 model; rat trap or rubber.

**CHAIN**—¼-inch; the handsomest chain made; "B" links.

**CRANKS**—6½-inch round, and threaded for ½ by 20 pedal; made of select drop-forgings.

**CUPS AND CONES**—Turned from tool steel the best that can be made.

**HANGER**—The celebrated "Fauber," one piece crank and hanger with a drop of 2 to 2½ inches, is used on this wheel.

**BALLS**—Large size throughout; 5-16-inch in hanger.

**TREAD**—4⅞-inches.

**SPROCKETS**—Drop-forged, detachable front, 19 to 25-tooth; detachable rear, 7, 8 or 9 tooth. Heavily nickeled.

**GEAR**—64, 68, 70, 72, 76, 80, as desired.

**SADDLE**—Your choice of a Hygienic or Racing saddle. The Messenger Hygienic, or the Plew or American racing saddle.

**SEAT POST**—The Forward L pattern, with internal expander, which does away with the aggravating seat post bolt.

**FURNISHED**—With a handsome tool bag and tools complete.

**ENTIRE WEIGHT**—22 pounds.

**COLOR**—Your choice of the following: Vermilion, royal blue, coach green, yellow, black and ivory white. It will be sent in vermilion unless otherwise specified.

**Our special price.**...........................................$56.50

### SPECIFICATIONS.

**No. 83007 FRAME**—20 or 22 inch, made of 1⅛ inch seamless tubing in main frame, 1¼ inch in head, and ¾ inch D shaped in rear stays.

**CONNECTIONS**—All drop forged and selected steel.

**FORK CROWN**—The handsome and strong arch crown; nickel plated.

**FORK**—Large size, tapering; ¾ nickeled.

**HANDLE BARS**—⅞ inch; 7 inch bar as shown in cut, or regular up-curve; wood or steel as desired. The expander used here does away with the objectionable handle bar clamp, and makes it look much neater.

**WHEELS**—28 inch; 32 spokes in front wheel, 36 in rear.

**CHAIN AND MUD GUARDS**—Alluminum chain and wood mud guard.

**RIMS**—Best rock elm, laminated. Conceded to be the best on the market.

**TIRES**—Morgan & Wright or Vim, 1½ inch tires furnished if desired. 1⅝ in. will be regularly sent.

**SPOKES**—Selected 14-16 swaged.

**HUBS**—Tubular, turned from solid bar steel, with improved oiling device by which the oil is carried direct to the balls where it should be; and improved ball retainers.

**PEDALS**—The Record '97 model; rat trap or rubber.

**CHAIN**—¼ inch, the handsomest chain made. "B" links.

**CRANKS**—6½ inch, round, and threaded for ½x20 pedal. Made of select drop forgings.

**CUPS AND CONES**—Turned from tool steel, the best that can be made.

**HANGER**—The celebrated Fauber. One piece crank and hanger is used on this wheel—another conclusive proof of its quality—with a drop of 2½ inches.

**BALLS**—Large size, throughout; 5-16 inch in hanger.

**TREAD**—4⅞ inch.

**SPROCKETS**—Drop forged, detachable front 19 to 25 tooth; detachable rear, 7, 8 or 9 tooth. Heavily nickeled.

**GEAR**—64, 68, 70, 72, 74 or 80 as desired.

**SADDLE**—Messenger Hygienic.

**SEAT POST**—The forward L pattern, with external expander, which does away with the obnoxious seat post bolt.

## Our "Yukon" Ladies' Wheel. For $56.00.

**FURNISHED**—With a handsome tool bag and tools complete.

**ENTIRE WEIGHT**—22 pounds.

**COLOR**—Your choice of the following: Vermilion, royal blue, coach green, yellow, black, and ivory white. It will be sent in vermilion unless otherwise specified.

**Price.**.............................................$56.50

**IT IS VERY NECESSARY THAT CUSTOMERS EXERCISE CARE IN ORDERING. ALWAYS GIVE CATALOGUE PAGE AND CATALOGUE NUMBER OF THE ARTICLE, AS WELL AS NAME AND PRICE. WHERE SIZES, COLORS, ETC., ARE NECESSARY, DO NOT FAIL TO GIVE ALL INFORMATION.**

# JUVENILE BICYCLES.

**OUR LINE OF JUVENILES** FOR 1897 IS THE MOST COMPLETE, as well as the best line that has been put before the public. They are built of the SAME HIGH GRADE MATERIAL THAT IS USED IN OUR REGULAR BICYCLES, as our experience has taught us that the juvenile wheel must be built just the same as the regular size wheel, except of course it must be smaller to suit the respective sizes. THE JUVENILE WHEEL receives rougher usage, and is more apt to be broken than the regular size wheels, as a child can not take the care that an older person would. WE HAVE ENDEAVORED TO BUILD A WHEEL which will contain the following points, viz: STRENGTH FIRST, BEAUTY NEXT, and last but not least, a wheel that will give excellent service and one that will stay out of the repair shops. The same material is used throughout our entire line of Juveniles. For instance, Our Child's 20 Inch Wheel Has Just as Good Material in it as Our 26 Inch Wheel. The difference in price is caused by the difference of expenses in making the different sizes. To make juvenile wheels, a factory must have special tools which necessitates a greater outlay of expense, and for this reason there are so Few Juvenile Wheels on the Market, Which Can Absolutely Be Called HIGH GRADE.

**ANOTHER IMPORTANT ITEM,** OUR JUVENILES ARE GUARANTEED. The majority of juveniles are not. AS REGARDS OUR PRICES, we wish to say that in some unaccountable manner, people have an erroneous idea that a small wheel can be built much cheaper than a regular size. As a matter of fact, there is NO manufacturer who would not rather build a 28 inch wheel and sell it for $35.00 than to build a juvenile and sell it for the same price. THEREFORE WHEN YOU ARE COMPARING OUR PRICES ON JUVENILES with those of the cheap and entirely out of date wheels, we wish you to also COMPARE THE DIFFERENCE IN MATERIAL AND CONSTRUCTION.

We have found that it is poor policy to give a child a cheap wheel, for in the end, after you have paid for numerous repairs, to say nothing of the dissatisfaction of the child and yourself, you will readily see that it would have Been Much Cheaper to Purchase a Wheel of Good Quality and to Have Paid More For It. You would be dissatisfied with a wheel that was ever out of order, so will the child.

Make the little one doubly happy by purchasing a HIGH GRADE JUVENILE from us.

## Our Boy's 26 Inch Wheel for $33.00.

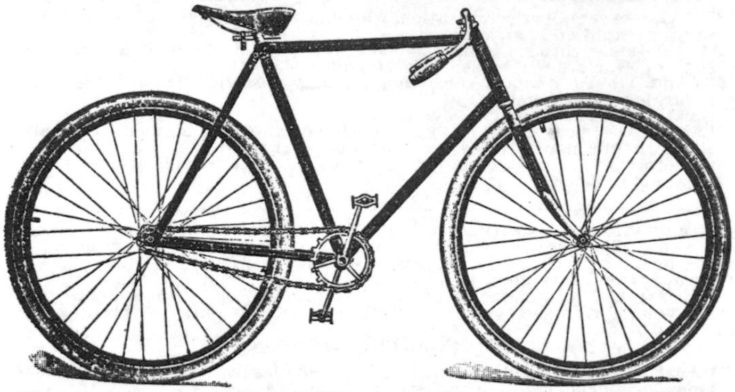

**No. 83008 Our Boys' 26 inch Wheel,** is made of exactly the same material as our Special "Uno" bicycle, except it is fitted with 26 inch wheels instead of 28 inch. This wheel is very suitable for small men, and it will safely bear up any weight that can be put on it.

SPECIFICATIONS.

FRAME—Which is made of 1⅛ tubing in main, 1¼ in head and ¾ in rear forks and braces, is the strongest frame ever used on a Juvenile wheel.
FORK CROWN—Is one that cannot be excelled for strength and beauty.
WHEELS—Are 26 inch—14-16 spokes highly nickeled. The same hub is used as is used in No. 83000. RIMS—Are as good as any rim made.
CUPS AND CONES—Are all turned from tool steel and properly hardened.
BALLS—Are perfect gauge, and therefore make the wheel easy running.
SPROCKETS—Are both nickeled, made of the finest steel forgings. Any gear will be furnished from 60 to 70. We recommend 68 as it is the most desirable.
CRANKS—Are 6½ inches long, round and threaded.
CHAIN—Is ¼ inch, the strongest made.
HANDLE BARS—Will be furnished either up curve or drop, as desired. T seat post, Garford saddle, and Morgan & Wright tires. Single tube tires furnished if desired.

Entire weight of wheel is 22 lbs. Finished in royal blue, black or green as desired. Our Special Price.............................................. $33.00

## Our Special 26 Inch Girl's Wheel for $33.00.

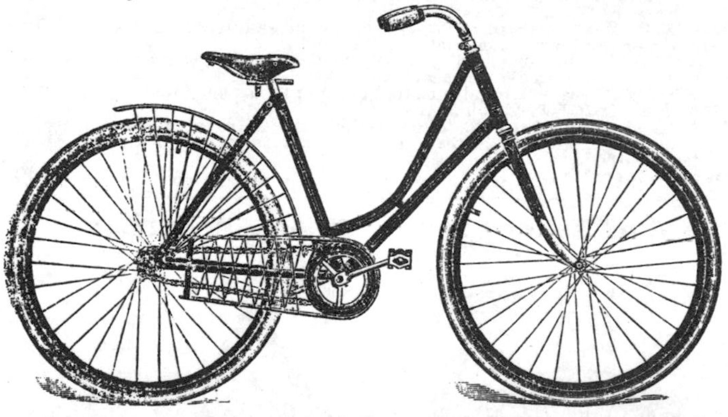

**No. 83009 It is seldom, indeed, that manufacturers take much pains with juvenile wheels,** and we do not hesitate to say that more care is taken with our line of Juveniles, than any other on the market. The **same careful workmanship and high grade material** that is put in our regular stock is put on this wheel. It must be remembered that in order to be able to guarantee our wheels for two years' time, we must put in good material, and careful workmanship. Read carefully the specifications of our Special 26 Inch Girls' Wheel. Suitable for girls from the age of 12 to 16, and for small ladies. For ladies who do not wish to ride a 28 inch wheel, we recommend this one as just the thing.

SPECIFICATIONS.

FRAME—Drop, 22 inches deep, 1⅛ inch tubing in main frame, ¾ inch in rear stays. FORK—Double plate crown, handsomely nickeled.
WHEELS—26 inch; spokes 14-16, highly nickeled. HUBS—Tublar design—the strongest and handsomest made. CUPS AND CONES—Turned from tool steel. BALLS—The finest steel obtainable. RIMS—Non-warpable wood, highly polished.
SPROCKETS—Both nickeled and made of the best forgings. GEAR—56, 60 and 64. CRANKS—6½ inch, finely nickeled. CHAIN—¼ inch, hardened links.
HANDLE BARS—Up curve, or drop; ⅞ inch tubing. SADDLE—Garford.
SEAT POST—"T" nickeled.
WEIGHT—Entire weight of wheel equipped, 22 lbs. Each wheel supplied with tools and bag complete. Furnished in royal blue or black, and fitted regularly with Morgan & Wright tires. Our special price............ $33.00

## Our Boy's 24 Inch Wheels. For Children from age of 8 to 12 Years for $31.00.

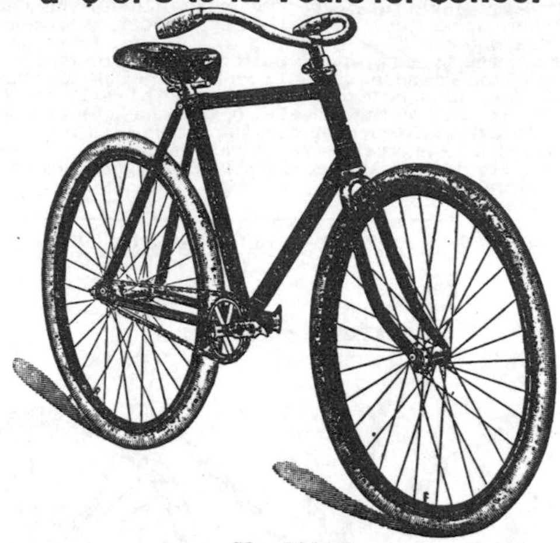

No. 83010

SPECIFICATIONS.

FRAME—Diamond, made of 1⅛ inch tubing in the main frame, ⅝ inch tubing in rear stays; height of frame 17½ inches.
FORK—A standard pattern crown, nickel plated.
WHEELS—26 inch with wood rims.
HUBS—Tubular, finest quality.
SPOKES—Nickeled.
CUPS AND CONES—Turned from tool steel.
SPROCKETS—Both nickeled and made of forgings.
CRANKS—Made of forgings and heavily nickeled.
SADDLE—A high grade Juvenile saddle on each wheel.
HANDLE BARS—Up-curve, or drop, ⅞ inch handsomely nickeled.
GEAR—52 and 54. Ball bearing throughout. Each wheel equipped with tool bag and tools complete. Entire weight about 23 pounds. Finished handsomely in 4 coats of black enamel and varnished over all for protection. Fitted with the same high grade single tube tires as our other Juveniles.

Our Special Price.............................................. $31.00

## Our Girl's 24-Inch Wheel for $31.00.

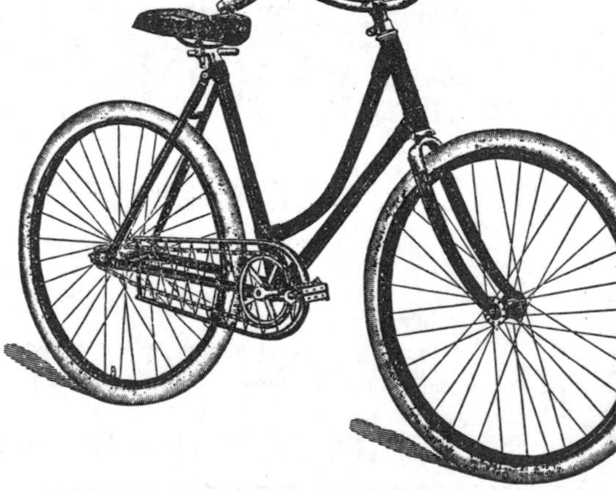

**No. 83011 For Girls from the Age of 8 to 12 Years.**

SPECIFICATIONS.

FRAME—Drop made of 1⅛ inch tubing in the main frame, ⅝ inch tubing in rear stays; height of frame 17½ inches.
FORK—A standard pattern, crown nickel plated.
WHEELS—26 inch, with wood rims.
HUBS—Tubular, finest quality.
SPOKES—Nickeled.
CUPS AND CONES—Turned from tool steel.
SPROCKETS—Both nickeled and made of forgings.
CRANKS—Made of forgings and heavily nickeled.
SADDLE—A high-grade Juvenile saddle on each wheel.
HANDLE BARS—Up-curve, ⅞ inch, handsomely nickeled.

Geared to 52 and 54. Ball bearing throughout. Each wheel equipped with tool bag and tools, complete. Entire weight about 23 pounds. Finished handsomely in four coats of black enamel, and varnished over all for protection. Fitted with the same high-grade single tube tires as our other Juveniles. Our special price.............................................. $31.00

## Our 20 Inch Wheel For $29.00.

### For Boys from the Age of 5 to 8 Years.

**No. 83012 FRAME** is made of best steel tubing, 1⅛ inch in main frame, and ⅝ inch in rear stays, making a very strong and handsome frame. Height of frame 14 inches.

**FORK**—Is made of the strongest material obtainable, handsomely nickel plated.

**WHEELS**—20 inch, made from the finest material; wood rims.

**HUBS**—Are tubular same as in our regular wheels only smaller. Ball bearings throughout.

**SPOKES**—Are the standard nickel plated.

**CUPS AND CONES**—Turned from tool steel.

**GEAR**—About 42 or 43.

**PEDALS**—A very neat and light rubber pedal will be used.

**HANDLE BARS**—Upturned, or drop, handsomely nickeled.

**SADDLE**—A high grade comfortable child's saddle. The entire weight of this wheel is about 20 lbs.

Will be finished in black enamel with 4 coats, varnish over all to protect it. A tool bag will be sent with each wheel, together with complete set of tools. We shall fit them regularly with a high grade single tube tire, guaranteed. as it is found troublesome to repair the small double tube tires.

Each wheel is guaranteed.

Our Special price, each........................................ $29.00

### Girls' Wheel, 20-inch. For $29.00

#### No. 83013.
#### SPECIFICATIONS.

**FRAME**—Is made of the best steel tubing 1⅛ inch in main frame, and ⅝ inch in rear stays, making a very strong and handsome frame. Height of frame 14 inches.

**FORK**—Is made of the strongest material obtainable, handsomely nickel plated.

**WHEELS**—20-inch, made from the finest material, wood rims.

**HUBS**—Are tubular, same as in our regular wheels, only smaller.

**SPOKES**—Are the standard, nickel plated.

**BALL BEARING** throughout.

**CUPS AND CONES**—Turned from tool steel.

**GEAR**—About 42 or 43.

**PEDALS**—A very neat and light rubber pedal will be used.

**HANDLE BARS**—Up-turned, or drop, handsomely nickeled.

**SADDLE**—A high grade comfortable child's saddle.

The entire weight of this wheel is about 20 pounds. Will be finished in black enamel with 4 coats, varnish over all to protect it. A tool bag will be sent with each wheel, together with complete set of tools. We shall fit them regularly with a high grade, single tube tire, guaranteed, as it is found troublesome to repair the small double tube tires. Each wheel is guaranteed.

Our special price, each.................. ...............................$29.00

## ....WHAT THE PEOPLE SAY....

### Could not fit me better if you took the measure yourself.

SMARTSVILLE, CAL., Jan. 4th, 1897.

SEARS, ROEBUCK & CO.

DEAR SIRS: The suit of clothes received and am very much pleased with them; they could not fit better if you had taken the measure yourself. I hope you received the money all right. I will send for your catalogue in a short time. Please send me some samples of plaid and other dress goods, and oblige, Yours Respectfully,

MRS. W. H. COLLING.

### Unequaled for Beauty and Fit.

Torrington, Conn.

SEARS, ROEBUCK & CO.

Gentlemen—I am very much pleased with the suit I bought of you, and I think that I could not have done better anywhere. Everyone remarks on the beauty of the suit, and the fit could not be better if your tailor had measured me. I will gladly recommend to any desiring to purchase of you. Yours respectfully, E. W. JERVISS.

### Our Goods Sell Themselves on Sight.

DENISON, TEXAS, Jan. 10, 1897.

SEARS, ROEBUCK & CO., Chicago, Ill.

GENTLEMEN: Many thanks for the prompt manner in which you filled my order for a mackintosh, the coat received all O. K., it is much better than I had expected; I think it will be the means of selling others; I will do all I can to sell more, it would not be any trouble to sell if it were not for the scarcity of money. With best wishes I remain,

W. S. WHITE.

## Tricycles and Velocipedes.

**Notwithstanding the immense popularity of the bicycle, the tricycle and velocipede still remain in favor.** Many parents prefer them for their children by reason of their safety, convenience and the ease with which they can be run by the little girl or boy. The tricycle, which we illustrate, is made for girls or boys from two to fifteen years. They are constructed with especial care and will stand the abuse they very frequently receive. They are very easy running and handsomely finished. The improved spring seat takes all vibration, and being upholstered in plush and furnished with back, makes riding easy and comfortable. Frame is enameled black. Quoted with iron tire wheels or C plate rubber tire wheels. The illustration shows the tricycle with fenders. We quote without fenders. The following are our special prices with iron tire wheels:

| | | |
|---|---|---|
| No. 85018 | Rear wheels 18 inch, for girls 2 to 4 years............... | $3.35 |
| No. 85019 | Rear wheels 20 inch, for girls 3 to 5 years............... | 4.45 |
| No. 85020 | Rear wheels 22 inch, for girls 4 to 7 years............... | 5.30 |
| No. 85021 | Rear wheels 26 inch, for girls 7 to 10 years............... | 6.35 |
| No. 85022 | Rear wheels 30 inch, for girls 10 to 15 years............... | 7.35 |

### Prices with Rubber Tire Wheels. No Fenders.

| | | |
|---|---|---|
| No. 85023 | Rear wheels 18 inch, for girls 2 to 4 years........... | $ 5.70 |
| No. 85024 | Rear wheels 20 inch, for girls 3 to 5 years........... | 6.35 |
| No. 85025 | Rear wheels 22 inch, for girls 4 to 7 years........... | 8.25 |
| No. 85026 | Rear wheels 26 inch, for girls 7 to 10 years........ | 9.95 |
| No. 85027 | Rear wheels 30 inch, for girls 10 to 15 years........... | 11.65 |

### Boys' All Steel Velocipede.

Give the boy all the fun he wants at an expense of a few pennies.

We show an all steel velocipede that will stand a "heap of racket" on the part of the restless youth. There are no nuts or bolts in the head connections to rattle or come loose. is adjustable and can be taken apart in shipping. The coil spring in seat does not sag or get out of repair. We use the best drive wheel made, in this velocipede. The manner in which the fork and backbone are secured to head and axle is a new method, far superior to any other, and makes them doubly strong.

The handle is of one piece and stationery. The frames are made of malleable iron. Made both with steel tires or rubber tires. Prices as follows:

| STEEL TIRES. | | | RUBBER TIRES. | | |
|---|---|---|---|---|---|
| 85028 | Front wheel, 16 inch........ | $1 35 | 85033 | Front wheel, 16 inch........ | $2 95 |
| 85029 | Front wheel, 20 inch........ | 1 75 | 85034 | Front wheel, 20 inch........ | 3 45 |
| 85030 | Front wheel, 24 inch........ | 2 15 | 85035 | Front wheel, 24 inch........ | 3 95 |
| 85031 | Front wheel, 26 inch........ | 2 55 | 85036 | Front wheel, 26 inch........ | 4 45 |
| 85032 | Front wheel, 28 inch........ | 2 95 | 85037 | Front wheel, 28 inch........ | 4 95 |

## These Are Not Bicycle Shoes.

BUT WE SHOW A COMPLETE LINE IN OUR SHOE DEPARTMENT.

SEE FARGO'S FAMOUS BALL BEARING BICYCLE SHOE.

**DON'T FORGET THE LIBERAL C. O. D. SUBJECT TO EXAMINATION TERMS ON WHICH WE SHIP OUR GOODS. WE SHOW OUR CONFIDENCE IN THE GOODS WE SELL.**

## Saddles.

**No. 83020 Our Special Hygienic Padded Saddle.** This saddle has undergone innumerable critical tests during the last year by every class of riders. It has also been submitted to the most eminent physicians in the country, and has earned unlimited approval and praise from all who have used it. We have placed it on the market at a price within reach of all, and for those who saddle desire a padded but do not care to pay a high price, this is the saddle. It is made from the finest selected black leather, the cantle and springs are of the finest steel, and the workmanship cannot be excelled. It will never lose its shape. Our special price........$1.55

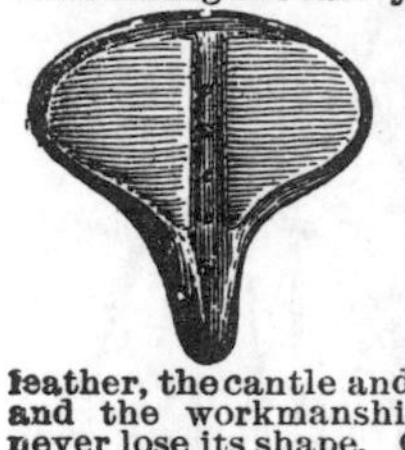

**N. B.—Every Saddle Positively Guaranteed.**

**No. 83021 Our Special Road Saddle,** made of the best quality black leather. The same material is used in this saddle as that in 83020, except this one is not padded. Has a very unique device by which it is made to keep its shape. For general riding this saddle can not be excelled. Our special price.$1.20

**No. 83022 The American.** For track or road riding cannot be excelled. It is the most durable and comfortable saddle on the market at present. The leather is a special English tannage, soft and pliable, and reinforced. It is made on the same pattern as the famous Brooks Saddle, which was so popular in 1896. We can honestly recommend this saddle to all of our customers. Our special price..............................$1.65

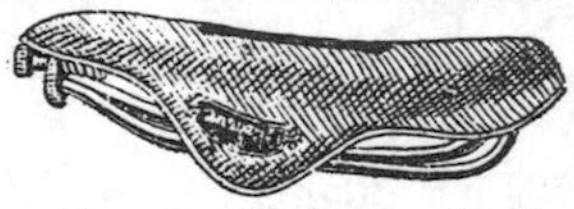

## The Plew. Its Nose Is Soft.

**No. 82023 The Plew** is so constructed as to fill the wants of the many riders who prefer a firm saddle without the objectionable hard pommel. The part upon which the body rests is shapely and firm, with a nose not too long, narrow and perfectly soft, thereby creating that which is rarely found in saddles—security and absolute comfort.

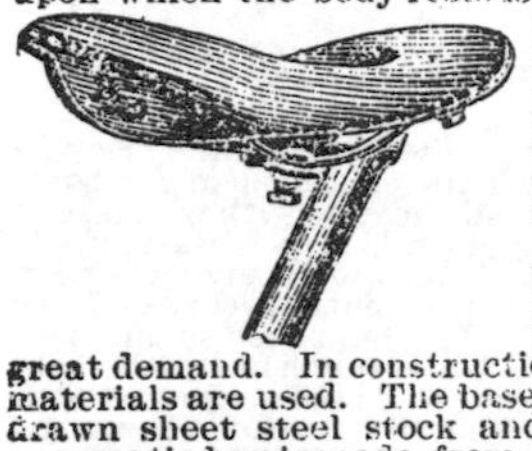

**The Plew** is the only padded saddle on the market with a pneumatic nose, and is in great demand. In construction only the very finest materials are used. The base is stamped out of cold drawn sheet steel stock and will not break. The pneumatic bag is made from the best pure rubber tubing, vulcanized at each end and provided with valve of standard make. Being held in place by lacing it is easily accessible. The spring is bent out of best quality wire spring steel and guaranteed not to break. Clamps are of a pattern which allows saddle to set low on seat post. **Finished in a superb manner, in two styles.**

**The Plew Model B.**

| | | | |
|---|---|---|---|
| Model B. | Ladies' Black | each, | $2.70 |
| " | " Tan | " | 2.70 |
| " | " Russet | " | 2.70 |

**The Plew Model C.**

| | | | |
|---|---|---|---|
| Model C. | Gents' Black | each, | $2.70 |
| " | " Tan | " | 2.70 |
| " | " Russet | " | 2.70 |

## No Hard Projection in Front.

**No. 83024 The Duplex Saddle** has no metal or rigid projection in front, on to which a rider can be thrown and injured, the pommel carries no weight—you cannot sit on it, it is simply an extention between the legs of the rider so that he cannot slip sideways. The saddle has been greatly improved by the addition of soft pads, covered with soft, durable leather, making the easiest seat ever designed either for the new and experienced rider of either sex, yet permitting the springs to act with the body as heretofore. Price..........................................$2.75

**No. 83025 Messenger Saddle** is something new and a saddle that will be very popular with all riders who are looking for an easy-riding and strong saddle. Construction: Woven rattan base, first to make the seat firm but elastic. This is then covered with felt to soften, and this in turn is covered with leather to add durability and comfort. V shaped aperture is cut through both felt and leather to relieve all injurious pressure. The most popular, the best saddle in the world. Costs more, but is worth more. Men's and boys', Prich each. $3.00

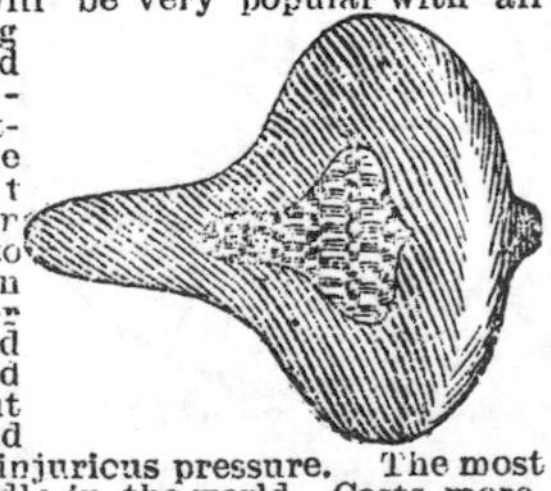

**No. 83026** Same, women's and girls'. Price. 3.00

**N. B.—See our Special Bicycle Catalogue for a more complete line of fine saddles.**

## Tool Bags.

Our tool bags are the best the market can afford. We have a line to suit the tastes of all persons.

**No. 83030 This bag is made of handsome seal leather;** black, strongly riveted, buckles heavily nickeled; never loses its shape, and will keep its handsome appearance forever. A model bag.

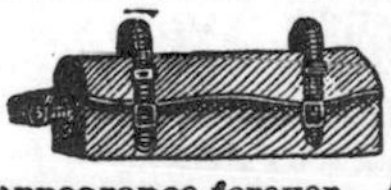

Our special price, each..............................$0.20
Per dozen...................................................2.25

**No. 83031 Made of fine grain leather;** square shape; riveted ends, and fastens with clasps instead of buckles; always easy to open; no straps or buckles to fumble over; handsomely finished, and an attractive attachment for any bicycle.
Odr special price, each.....$0.30
Per dozen.......................3.40

**No. 83032 Made of polished grain leather;** extra quality; triangular shape; fastened with clasp; very strongly riveted, and handsomely embossed; furnished in black or russet. This is one of the handsomest bags made, and is the prevailing style. Our special price, each.$0.45

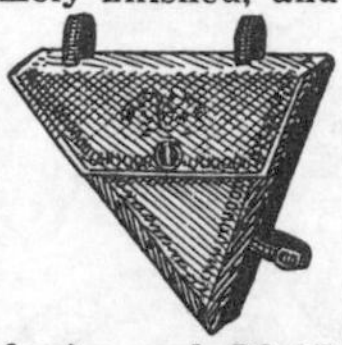

**No. 83033 Made of extra select polished grain leather,** fastened by clasp shaped to fit frame of gent's wheel under saddle, and the popular bag for ladies wheels made in the same manner as the rest of our tool bags, strong, durable and handsome finished in black or russet.
Our special price, each..............................$0.40

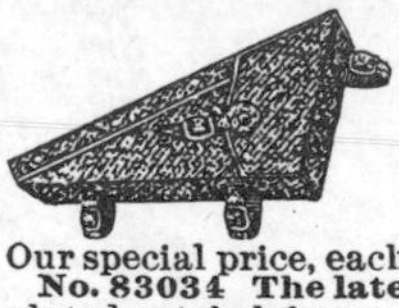

**No. 83034 The latest thing in a tool bag.** Nickel plated satchel frame, opening entire length of bag like a satchel or purse. Made of extra quality black seal leather, and owing to the "Satchel Opening" which it has, it is a most convenient article to carry not only tools but any small article you may desire to take with you. Have one of these and you will be up-to-date. Our special price.................$0.50

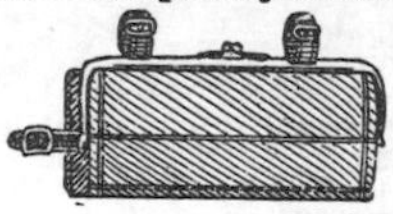

**No. 83035** Furnished in very fine oak tanned russet leather, each..............................$0.75

**N. B.—The above bags are never sold elsewhere for less than 75c and $1.00.**

## Lunch Boxes.

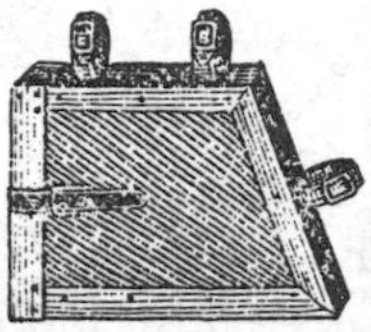

**No. 83037 Well made of** compressed fibre board and fitted with straps and buckles. Shaped to fit the wheel. Size, 3½x6¾x9⅝. Price each..$0.55

**No. 83038 Similar to 83037.** Made of waterproof oil cloth, zinc lined; keeps food in prime condition; don't miss this. Our special price.........$0.75

## Bicycle Tourists' Cases.

These cases are light, capacious and durable. They are easily, quickly and securely attached to the bicycle frame and are no hindrance or inconvenience to the rider. Every bicyclist needs one.

**No. 83039 Triangular Shape** (formed after shape of frame work of bicycle), made of strong canvas, cloth lined, securely riveted, fitted with straps and buckles. Dimensions, 18¾ inches long, 3½ inches thick, 16⅝ inches greatest width and 5½ inches narrowest width. Price each....$0.90

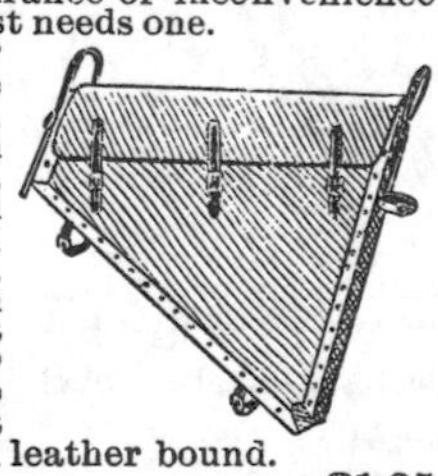

**No. 83040 Same Style and size as No. 83039,** but of extra quality canvas and leather bound. Price each..............................$1.25

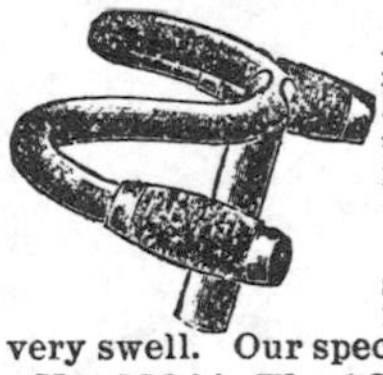

**No. 83042 Our Ram's Horn Handle Bar** is the handsomest bar on the market. With a Ram's Horn Bar you always have complete control of your wheel. Bent forward 5 inches. It is impossible to have a cut of this bar to do it justice. Once seen, it will immediately be admired. Makes your wheel look very swell. Our special price..................$2.25

**No. 83044 The "Chicago" Adjustable Steel Handle Bar.** In this handle bar all the good features of an adjustable bar are embodied. It can be adjusted to any desired position, from the "jolly scorchers" favorite to the position which the elderly person desires, that is, an up curve bar, so he may sit perfectly erect. The dotted lines show the position when up curve is desired.

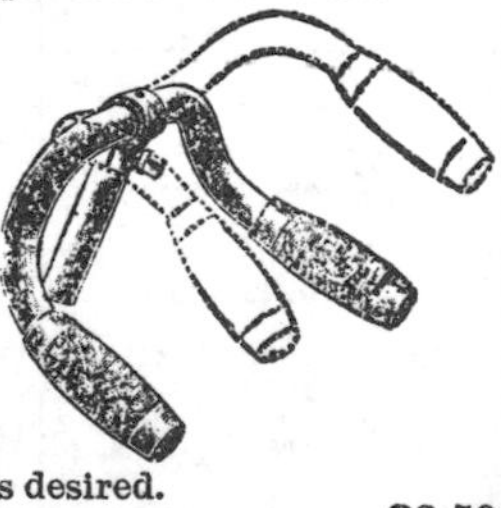

Our special price..............................$2.50

**N. B.—See our Special Bicycle Catalogue for a complete list of Handle Bars.**

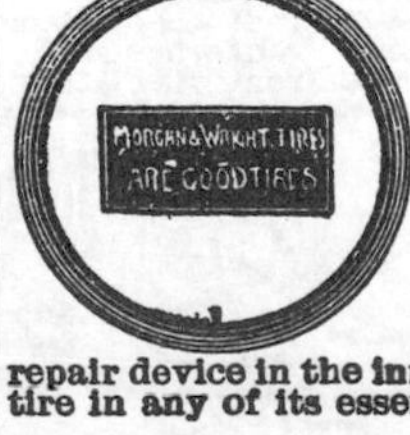


**No. 83046 The Morgan & Wright Quick Repair Tire** was the most popular double tube tire on the market in 1896, and will be just as popular in 1897. By aid of the quick repair outfit, this tire can be easily and permanently repaired in almost all cases, without removing the tire from the wheel. This is a great advantage in itself. The quick repair device in the inner tube does not change the tire in any of its essential features, as it is merely an addition of a thin web or film of rubber, which goes inside the inner tube. It has no effect on the resistancy of the tire and it is simplicity in the plainest form. The merits of this tire are too well known for us to go into details, and we therefore leave it to our customers to decide which tire they want to ride for 1897. Our special price, per pair of 24, 26 or 28x1⅝ tires, including pump and quick repair box..............................$8.40
For one tire only..............................4.25

**No. 83047 Inner Tubes,** each..............................$1.60

**No. 83048 Outer Casings,** each..............................$2.60

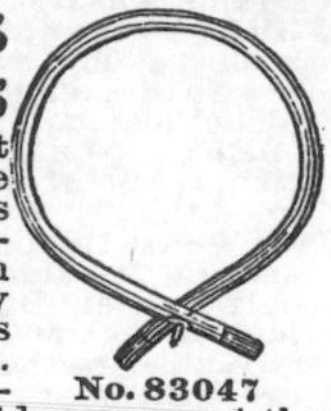

No. 83047

**No. 83049 Owing to the great demand for a "Clincher" tire,** we have decided to list the famous Gormully & Jeffrey tire of this pattern. This tire is too well known to go into details, but we will say that it has won hosts of friends throughout the entire country. Where a tire of this pattern is desired, we should recommend the G. & J. above all others, and as the price heretofore has been quite high, we beg to call our customers' attention to the reduction which we have made.
For one pair of 26 or 28x1⅝ tire, include rims and pump, $12.00
For ½ pair of above, no pump included.........6.00

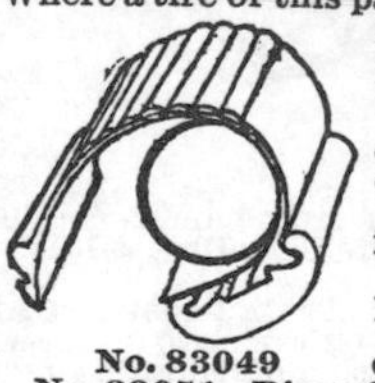

No. 83049

**No. 83050 Inner Tubes,** each.................... 1.00
**No. 83051 Rims Only,** per pair............. 1.50
**No. 83052 Outer Casings,** each............ 3.50

**Tandem and Special Tires Quoted on Application.**

**No. 83053 As we have had a great demand for a single tube tire,** we list the Vim Pebble Tread for those who desire a "bang up" single tube tire. The Pebble tread has made this tire famous on the track as well as in a number of road races. It also gives the tire a very handsome appearance. Vim tires do not puncture easily, but if they should, they are easily repaired with "Vinoid," the very useful tool which accompanies every pair of tires sent out. This is a great advantage over the '96 tire, as plugs were used to repair punctures, and many riders were disgusted with a single tube on that account. A pump accompanies every pair of tires. We furnish them in green, or the natural color, which is the same color as other tires. Our special price per pair of 26 or 28 in. by 1⅝.....$10.00

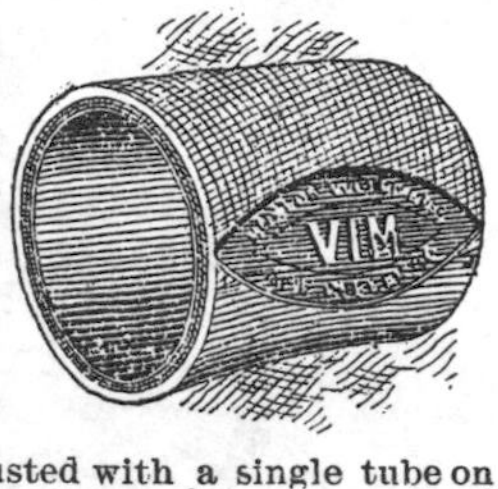


**No. 83054 The Vim Tandem Tire.** Same as above, only heavier and stronger. Per pair..$15.00

## League Tires.

**No. 83056 The League Tire** is made by the New York Belting and Packing Co., and is one of the most famous single tube tires on the market. The League tires "Get There and Get Back." It is very hard to puncture, is easily repaired when punctured, and it is a strong, durable and fast tire. The entire weight of a pair of these tires is 4½ pounds. Furnished in the embossed or smooth tread as desired. Guaranteed the same as all other high grade tires. A pump and repair accompanies every pair. Our Special Price per pair of 26 or 28x1½ or 1⅝..............................$8.25

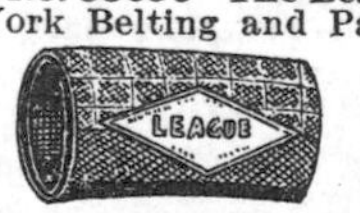


**No. 83058** For those who desire a **Single Tube Tire of superior quality,** and handsome appearance, and who do not care to pay so much for a tire, we recommend the Akron "Arrow Tread." This is destined to be a most popular tire for 1897, and our patrons will appreciate the fact that we are putting within the reach of all a good single tube tire. Our special price per pair of 28 inch x1⅝, including pump and repair kit..............................$7.00

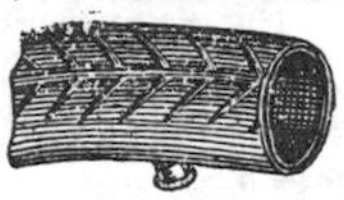

**The "Arrow Tread" on this tire prevents slipping.**

### Manufacturers' Guaranty on Tires for 1897.

We agree to make good by repair or replacement, when delivered to us, transportation prepaid, any imperfections or defects in material or manufacture of tires, not caused by misuse or neglect, Provided such tire is accompanied by a signed statement from the owner, together with the name and number of the wheel on which it was used, and that all imperfect or defective tires shall be referred to us, before any claim for repairs or replacement shall be allowed.

We agree to repair, free of charge, any tire that can be repaired, Providing such tire is delivered to us, transportation prepaid.

This agreement does not apply to tires into which any of the so-called anti-leak preparation has been introduced.

MORGAN & WRIGHT,
GORMULLY & JEFFRY,
BOSTON WOVEN HOSE & RUBBER CO.
NEW YORK BELTING AND PACKING CO.
AKRON INDIA TIRE CO. (All Chicago.)

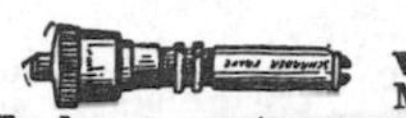

**No. 83060 The Schroeder Valve** is the same style as the Morgan & Wright, only larger. Used on a great many of the leading tires.
Our special price for valve and stem complete.. $0.17
Our special price for valve and stem complete, per dozen........ 1.94
**No. 83062** Morgan & Wright valve and stem complete........ .14
Morgan & Wright valve and stem complete, per dozen........ 1.64

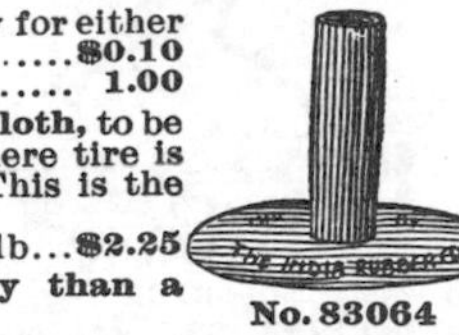
No. 83064

**No. 83064 Stems** only for either of the above. Each.........$0.10
Per dozen........ 1.00
**No. 83066 Friction Cloth**, to be put over inner tubes, where tire is laced, for protection. This is the best cloth made.
Our special price, per lb...$2.25
**Sold in less quantity than a pound at same price.**

## Bicycle Pumps.

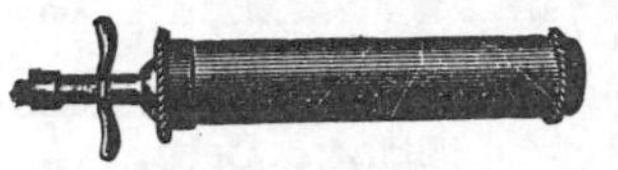

**No. 83068 The Morgan & Wright Hand Pump** for 1897 will not be nickel plated. Don't be fooled and buy a cheap nickeled pump, for you will regret it. The M. & W. hand pump for '97 can be identified by its handsome black finish. The best on the market. Our special price, each...$0.20
Per dozen........ 2.30

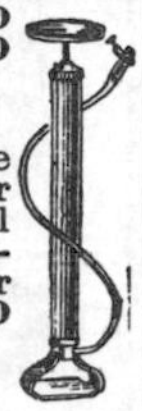

**No. 83069 Our Special Foot Pump** the best on the market for anywhere near our price. Has a good strong pressure and will fit any valve. Very handsomely nickel plated, a beautiful and serviceable pump. Our special price, each........ $0.80

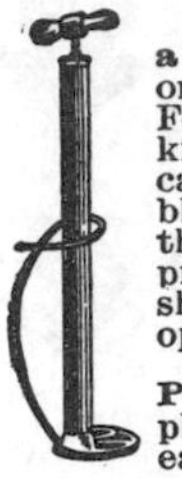

**No. 83070 There is a great demand for a Pump which will do quick work**, and one which will be serviceable in every way. For persons desiring a cheap pump of this kind, we recommend our Floor Pump which can be securely fastened to the floor or a block. You can pump your tire up with this while thinking about it. Very strong pressure. A handsome pump for a repair shop or dealer. Don't miss this splendid opportunity. Our special price.......$1.80
**No. 85071 The Universal Coupling for Pumps**, which fits all valves. A very simple and strong one. Our special price, each........ $0.15

## Pedals.

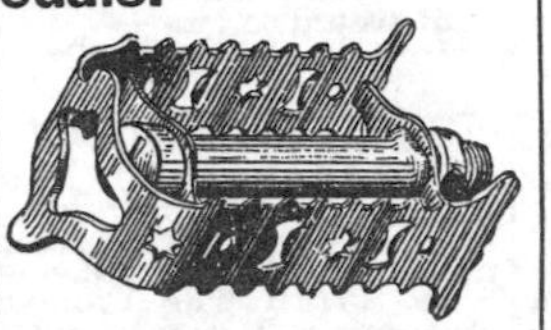

**No. 83073 Star Pedal for gent's wheels.** Rat trap pattern, thoroughly dust proof and will withstand all hard usage to which pedals are subjected. This is a very handsome pedal. Our special price per pair....$2.00

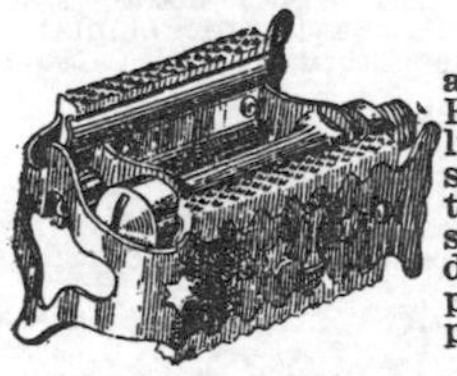

**No. 83074 Star Combination Pedal with Rubbers.** For the ladies' wheels, a very light, neat, and best of all, serviceable pedal. Made the same as the Star Rap, slightly smaller. These pedals can't be beat at the price. Our special price, per pair........ $2.25

**No. 83075 The W. & E. Pedal, for Slotted Crank.** This is a very handsome, serviceable and well made pedal; for use on wheels which have the slotted crank; furnished in Rat Trap or Combination.
Our Special Price for Rat trap per pair,........$2.00
Our Special Price for Combination, per pair.. 2.10

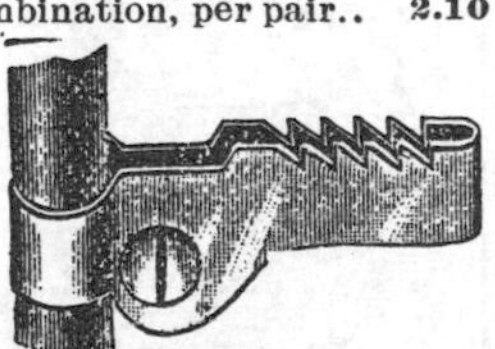

**No. 83076 Adjustable Foot Rests or Coasters** very light but strong and neat in design.
Per pair...........$0.25



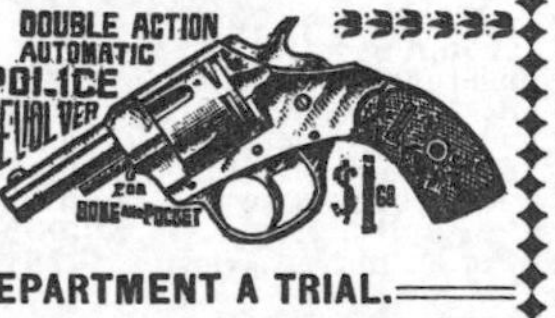




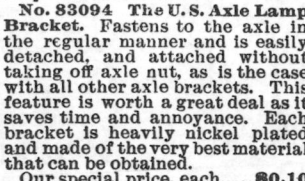

## Lamps.

**No. 83080 No More Greasy Lamps. The Light of 1897.** The never out lamp for bicycles and carriages, is in our opinion the handsomest and best lamp on the market. It is honestly built on scientific principles, made of best drawn brass throughout, riveted. No solder to melt. The insulated kerosene reservoir renders it impossible to get oil on the hands or clothing, and is an absolute preventative against explosions. It has an automatic wick lock device, which renders the wick jar proof. An intense, steady, and piercing light is obtained by means of a properly focused double convex photo lens, backed by a most powerful reflector. The rear danger signal, together with the handsome appearance of this lamp, makes it a beautiful ornament for any wheel or carriage. The reversible rigid bracket permits the lamp to be used on either side of the fork or dashboard. (No other bracket required). All up to date improvements such as red and green lights; cotton packed reservoir, etc. Burns kerosene 16 hours at one filling. This lamp costs more than the average lamp, but as our patrons will discover by experience with cheap lamps, it is worth it. Our special price each........ $4.00

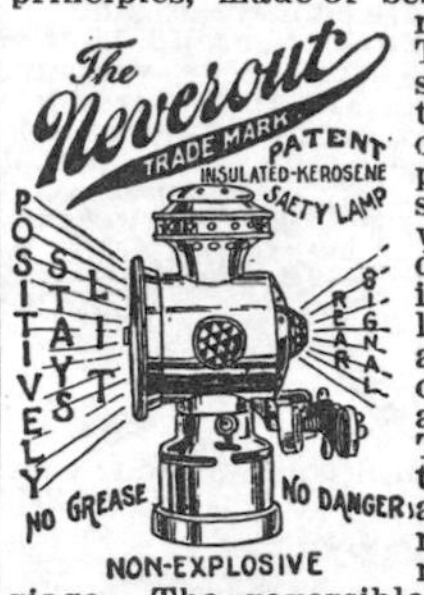


**N. B.—Every Lamp Positively Guaranteed.**
**No. 83081 The "Search Light."** A high grade lamp, burning kerosene oil. Will burn ten hours without trimming. Made entirely of brass. Perfect in mechanical construction, always cool. Wick is held firmly in position by means of a jam nut and will not work down from jarring of wheel. Can be easily taken apart and cleaned. Filled and lighted from the outside. Locked to wheel with removable key, finished in nickel only. This lamp has been adopted by the U. S. Government. Price, each........ $3.75

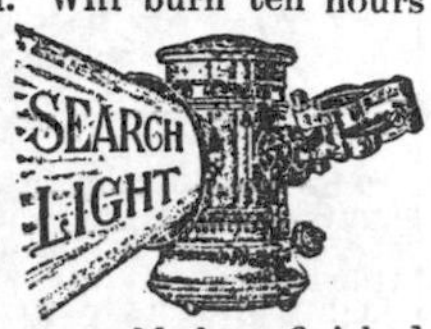


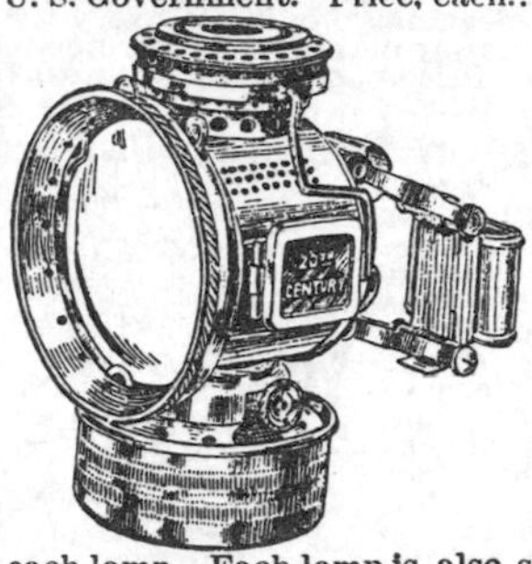


**The 20th Century Lamp for '97** is made on the same standard of excellence as was the '96 pattern; stays lit; as a driving lamp with the detachable carriage attachment, it can be placed on the dash board or side irons, at any angle. By raising bail handle it makes a very superior hand lantern. An extra red lens accompanies each lamp. Each lamp is also supplied with a fine gossamer hood to protect it when not lighted. Entire weight, nickel 9 oz.; aluminum 7 oz.

Our Special Price:

| | | |
|---|---|---|
| No. 83082 | Nickeled. each........ | $3.00 |
| No. 83084 | Aluminum, each........ | 3.25 |
| No. 83085 | Japanned, each........ | 3.00 |
| | TANDEM SIZE. | |
| No. 83086 | Nickel........ | $4.00 |
| No. 83087 | Japanned........ | 4.00 |
| No. 83088 | Aluminum........ | 4.25 |

**No. 83089 The Demon Lamp.** We sell large numbers of Demon Lamps. They are good lamps and cheap—two very essential qualities. This lamp has 2¼ inch beveled plate glass in front, with ruby side lights. Front is hinged. Large wick, detachable reflector. Has spring check and rubber-cushined socket. Can be attached to any bicycle. Height 4½ inches. Weight 12 oz. Price, each........$0.60

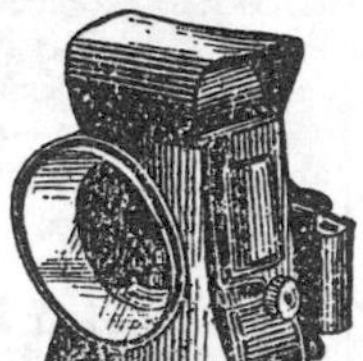

**No. 83090 The Comet.** Made of the same high grade material as the Demon. It is a smaller lamp, but it has a powerful lens and reflector, and will burn kerosene or lard oil. The lard oil or any good cycle lamp oil gives better results. Our special price, each. $0.50
**The Sunbeam** is a lamp that is all that its name implies. It has a bevel plate glass lens, front opening and colored side lights. A strong, well made and durable lamp at a moderate price. Weighs 9 ounces. Furnished in japanned or nickel.
**No. 83091** Our special price, japanned. Each........ $0.90
**No. 83092** Our special price, nickel. Each. 1.00

## Lamp Brackets.

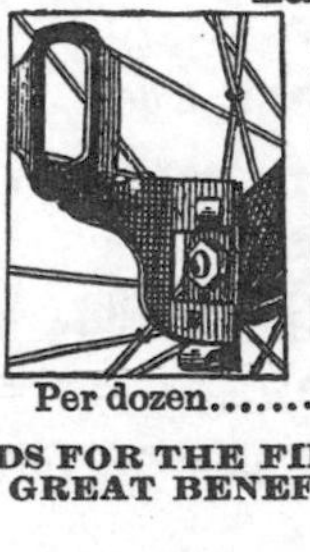

**No. 83094 The U. S. Axle Lamp Bracket.** Fastens to the axle in the regular manner and is easily detached, and attached without taking off axle nut, as is the case with all other axle brackets. This feature is worth a great deal as it saves time and annoyance. Each bracket is heavily nickel plated and made of the very best material that can be obtained.
Our special price, each.....$0.10
Per dozen........ 1.00

**No. 83095 The special feature of this lamp bracket**, is the spring grip fingers which fit the lamp socket tightly, holding the lamp fast and firm, thus preventing the annoying rattle, or the lantern falling off the wheel. It is made of specially rolled steel, heavily nickel plated; fits any wheel.
Our special price. Each........ $0.15
Our special price. Per dozen........ $1.60

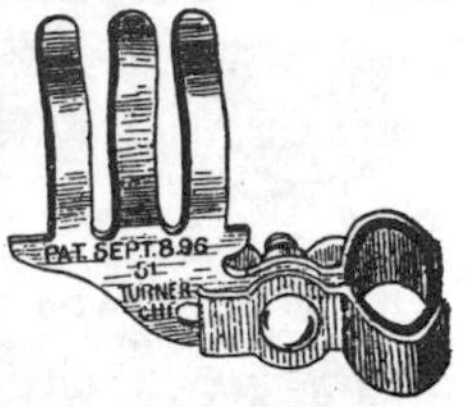


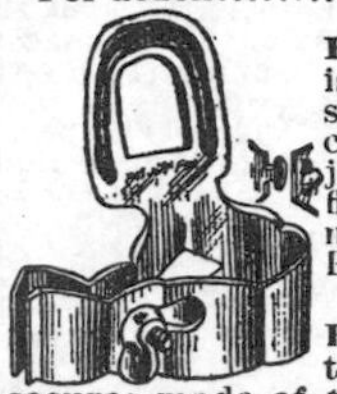

**No. 83096 Combination Lamp Bracket** for head or frame or fork is an "up-to-date" original accessory; unique in design, simple in construction, hence easily adjusted, light, durable, made and finished in the best possible manner. Weight 1½ oz. Nickeled steel. Price each........ $0.20

**No. 83097 The Axle Bracket**, fastens on axle, the nut making it secure; made of the best material; handsomely finished; as it is small and light, and always out of the way; it is a very desirable bracket.
Our Special Price. each........ $0.05
Our Special Price. per doz........ .50

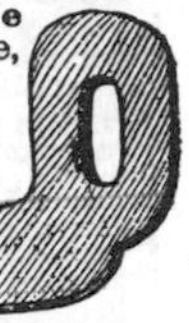

## Cyclometers.

**No. 83098 The Atom Cyclometer.** This little cyclometer is the best cheap one on the market. It is made of the very best material, very finely nickel plated. The lens, instead of being made of glass, which so often breaks, is made of very fine transparent celluloid, and blows and falls will not injure it. There are no springs used in its construction, therefore it does not get out of order. It registers 1,000 miles and repeats. Figures are very plain and easily read from the saddle. Weighs but one ounce. So small it is never in the way. Full directions in each box. Every one backed by a binding guarantee. If it gets broken, send it in and get a new one. Mileage absolutely correct. Every one can own a cyclometer at our special price of........ $0.55
**N. B.—For 28 inch wheels only.**

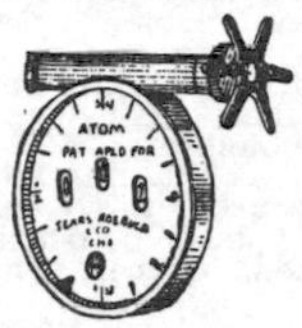


## The U. S. Cyclometers.

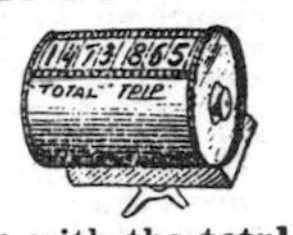

**No. 83099 The U. S. Cyclometer Model 1** is sure to be one of the leading cyclometers for 1897. This model has a total register of 10,000 miles, also an independent recorder of 100 miles. By turning the end of case the trip can be set to "0" at will without interfering with the total record. The trip record shows daily trips or local distances, while the total keeps a perfect record of the season's mileage. Perfect mechanism and largest figures. Made for 26 or 28 inch wheels.
Our special price, each........ $1.50

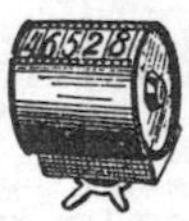

**No. 83100 The U. S. Model 2** registers 10,000 miles from tenths up, and repeats. It is easily set. Weighs but 1 ounce. Smallest and lightest thing out and is less liable to injury.
Our special price, each........ $1.00

## Bells.

Our line of bells for the se[illegible] 1897 is very complete and as they are made [illegible]ecially for our bicycle trade, we can warrant them to be second to none. A wheel is not complete without one, as it prevents accidents not only to others but to yourself. Packed, one in a neat pasteboard box.

**No. 83101 This Bell is Stamped from Sheet Steel.** Finely nickel plated; rings clear and loud; won't wake the dead, but comes as near it as any of them; 2½ in. Price each........$0.10

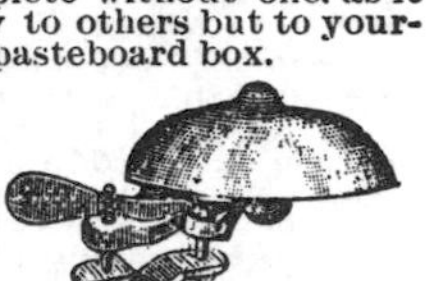
No. 83101.

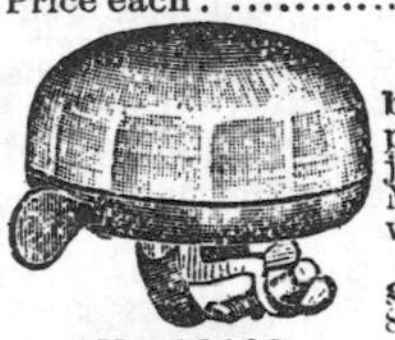
No. 83102.

**No. 83102 This is Our Double-Stroke Bell.** 1¾ in., nickel plated. There may be be some just as good, but none better. Made from pure bell metal; weight 3 oz. Price, each..$0.30
**No. 83103 This is Our Single-Stroke Bell**, similar to No. 83102. Finely nickel plated; made from pure bell metal; don't be without one. When people see a bicycle, they want to "hear dem bells." 2⅛ in.; weight 4¼ oz. Price each........ $0.25
**No. 83104 Made from Pure Bell Metal**, similar shape to No. 83102; 2⅛ in., nickel plated; weight 4¼ oz.; with the famous electric stroke. A very popular one. You might just as well get a good bell while you are about it. Get this one. Price ..$0.55

## The Siren Whistle.

**No. 83105 The Siren Whistle** will produce any kind of a sound, from a groan to an unearthy shriek, at the will of the operator. It is a strong, well made whistle, of a very convenient size, and each one is handsomely nickel plated. Never sold for less than 10c. Our special price $0.06
Postage on the above when ordered by mail........ .02
Per dozen........ $0.65

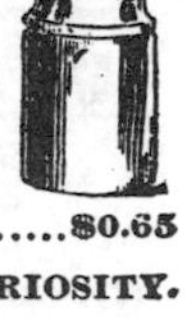

**IF THIS CATALOGUE COMES INTO YOUR HANDS FOR THE FIRST TIME, WE HOPE YOU HAVE NOT GOTTEN IT MERELY OUT OF CURIOSITY. WE CAN BE OF GREAT BENEFIT TO YOU IF YOU WILL GIVE US A CHANCE.**

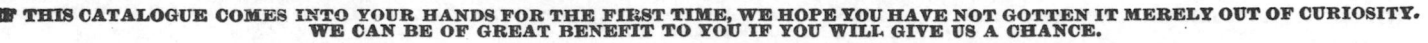

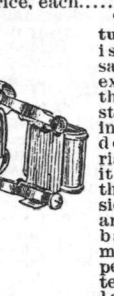

## Bicycle Whistles.

No. 83106.

83107.

**No. 83106. The Duplex Whistle;** gives two clear and distinct notes; made of brass, heavily nickel plated, complete with chain and hook. Price. $0.25

**83107 The Gem Whistle;** gives a soft, loud alarm; a favorite whistle. Price, with chain .......... $0.15

**No. 83108 Single Tube Whistle,** the strongest and shrillest whistle in use. The slightest effort is all that is required to use it. Price .......... $0.18

## Bicycle Horns.

**No. 83109** Fastened to the handle bars and very handy and light. You know how to work this horn. Press the rubber bulb and you hear a so... like unto no other ... hly sound.

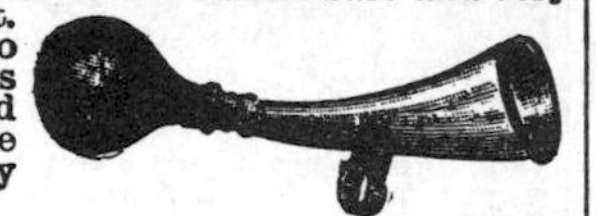

No. 1, small, Price, each .......... $0.85
No. 2, large. Price each .......... 1.00

## Bicycle Locks.

**No. 83110 Pure Aluminum Bicycle Lock.** All are finished with raised parts, higly polished, and depressed parts, luster polished. They are spring, self-locking, with spring shackles and fitted with 16-inch strong and shapely chain. Each ...... $0.30
Per dozen .......... 3.50

**No. 83111 Same as above,** except is made of best bronze, highly polished. Cannot be broken.
Our special price, each .......... $0.20
Our special price, per dozen .......... 2.30

**No. 83112 The Emperor Sprocket Lock** is one of the best on the market. All parts are accurately machine fitted; spring self locking; spring opening. Has rolled bronze metal rod bolts, formed and milled. Nickel plated steel key. The proper place to lock a wheel is on the sprocket, and you want a strong lock, for a poor lock is worse than none. Our special price, each ..... $0.25
Our special price, per dozen .......... $3.00

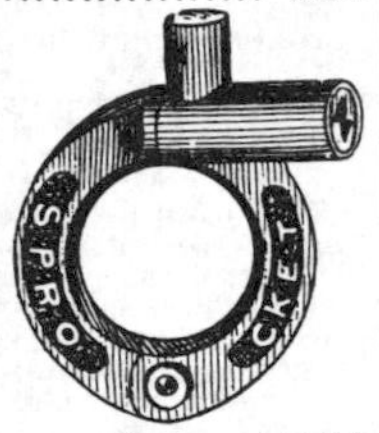


## Bundle Carriers.

**No. 83115 The Lamson Bundle Carrier** can be attached to the bicycle in a moment, and when not attached can be used as a shawl strap; it weighs a mere trifle, and can be easily carried in the pocket when not in use. Price ....... $0.80

**No. 83116** Similar to 83115, but is made still lighter, of small but stiff steel wire, nickeled and has narrower straps, made for small parcels like a coat, bathing suit, etc. Price, each .......... $0.75

**No. 83117 Made on same principles** as No. 83115, resting on handle bars and fastened around the head. Made for large packages and of one continuous piece of spring steel wire. Price, each .......... $0.95

**No. 83118 Made with double straps;** will carry a small camera and tripod, or anything else, and is an excellent carrier to take on a short tour. Its carrying capacity is remarkable; is made larger than No. 83117 and attached in same manner. Price, $1.50

## Kalamazoo Folding Parcel Carrier.

The net is made of black linen twine, manufactured especially for this purpose,

Set in front of the Handle Bar.

Folded, as carried when not in use.

**No. 83120 The illustrations show the celebrated Kalamazoo Package Carrier,** both open and folded. It attaches in front or behind the handle bar, as the rider may wish. Weighs but 16 oz., and will carry 15 lbs. Has black linen twine net and nickel plated frame. A very necessary addition to a cyclist's accessories. Our special price, each .......... $1.50

TAKE A CAMERA WITH YOU . . .

SOLD AT FROM 90 CENTS UP IN OUR SPECIAL PHOTOGRAPHIC CATALOGUE.

## Brownie Child's Seat.

Can be attached securely to the bicycle in five seconds without the aid of clamps, bolts or straps. Cannot injure the tubing or enamel. It is adapted to carry little babies or children until they are eight years old.

**No. 83122 Frame 5-16 steel spring wire.** Seat, veneered board. Fits all modern bicycles except drop frames.
Weight, 28 ozs. Price .......... $2.00

**No. 83124. The Kalamazoo Baby Carrier** has a reversible clamp, enabling the carrier to be used in position shown by cut, or in front of the handle bar. This is a very desirable feature, especially on a ladies' machine. It is very strong and will support a child three or four years of age. Price .......... $2.75

## Mud Guards.

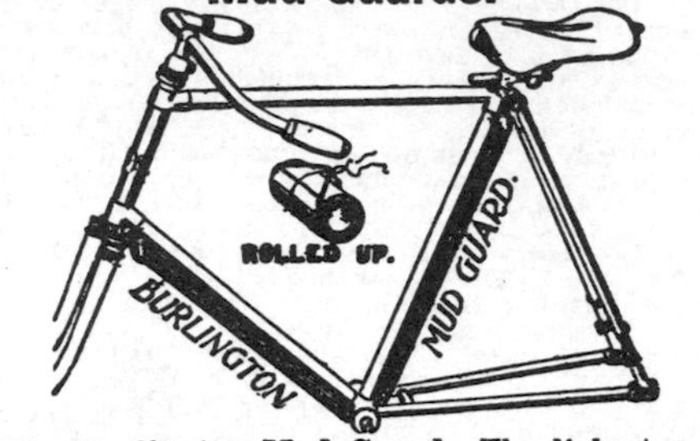


**The Burlington Mud Guard.** The lighest mud guard made. There is no metal used in the construction of this guard, being made entirely of pure thin rubber. It is a very effective article, and thoroughly protects frame. When not in use, it rolls up, in a small coil which can be easily carried. Don't spoil that new coat of enamel that you have just had put on your wheel. Use this little guard and save the annoyance of cleaning your frame every time you wish to go out, to say nothing of the protection it gives the enamel. Price, each .......... $0.25
Per dozen .......... 2.75

## The Burlington Cyclists' Cape.

**No. 83127 This illustration** will give a general idea of the Burlington Cyclists' Cape. It is put up in a neat leather case with straps so it can be attached to any part of the wheel without any inconvenience to the rider, and carried at all times same as the tool bag. Any rider limiting himself with a few tools can put them in this case if he so desires, and the annoying rattle incident will be overcome.

You no doubt have debated in your mind, whether or not you had better take your coat, when out for a ride; this cape fills the place exactly. It is thoroughly waterproof, when worn it forms an umbrella like shape and protects the rider from the rain.
Our special price, each .......... $1.50

## Oilers.

**No. 83128 Perfect Pocket Oiler.** The cleanest and handsomest pocket oiler in the world.
Price .......... $0.20

**No. 83129 Bicycle Oiler** Can be carried in the pocket. Price, each, tinned .......... $0.08
Nickeled .......... .12

**See our Special Bicycle Catalogue for more complete line of sundries.**

THE RAIN

FALLS ALIKE ON THE

JUST AND UNJUST.

All should be supplied with

MACKINTOSHES

SEE THE BEST LINE OF

Wet Weather Protectors

EVER SOLD

...ON PAGES 177 TO 179...

SAMPLES FREE.

## Toe Clips.

A few reasons why bicycle riders should use Thiem's Toe Clips: First. They are the lightest and strongest. Second. They can be easily adjusted to fit any shoe. Third. The foot cannot slip off the pedal sideways or forward. Fourth. By their use a rider can travel faster. Fifth. In going up or down a steep grade, the rider can push or hold back all the way around.

No. 83131

No. 83132

**No. 83131 Thiem's Toe Clips** are made of crucible wire. The foot cannot slip from the pedal with this clip, and nothing but a severe accident will put it out of shape. Use only screw driver to apply to pedal. Price, per pair .......... $0.35

**No. 83132 The Standard Toe Clip** is made of tempered steel and is a very popular clip. Fits any pedal. No fast riding without one. Price, per pair ... $0.20

## Spoke Grip.

**No. 83134 The Chicago Grip** is made for both straight and tangent spokes and has a differential screw which gives far greater power than any hitherto placed on the market, and can be screwed up with the thumb and fingers enough to hold any spoke made.
Price each .......... $0.50

**No. 83136 The Perfect Nipple Grip,** the best on the market. Everybody knows what the Perfect grip is.
Our Special Price .......... $0.60

## Spoke and Nipple Grip.

**No. 83138 Our Universal Spoke and Nipple Grip** we claim is the neatest, lightest and strongest on the market. Can be carried in the pocket on account of its small size. Made of hardened steel and is nickel plated. Price each ........ $0.25

## Wrenches.

Our wrenches are selected from a large line, and guaranteed to be durable and combine strength and lightness.

**No. 83140 In Presenting this Wrench** we have endeavored to put a wrench in our customers' hands that would be durable and compare with any wrench on the market for twice the price. Made specially for us in large quantities, we are able to guarantee them to be all that we represent them to be. Heavily nickel plated on forged steel. Price, each ..... $0.30

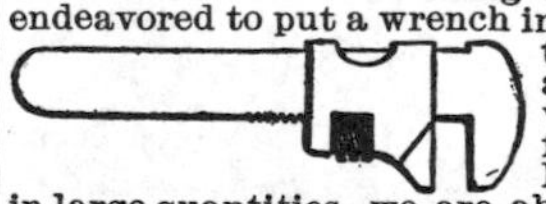

**No. 83142 The Famous Barnes Wrench,** the strongest and most beautiful wrench made. Made of the finest forging, and heavily nickel plated. Weighs 5½ ounces. Our special price, each .... $0.40

## Cork and Corkaline Grips.

**No. 83144 We can furnish Cork Grips** in either square or round ends. Made of best material, with nickel plated ferrules on each end.

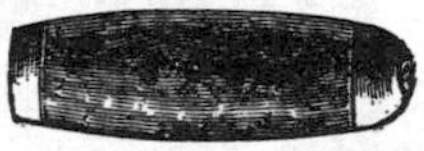

Square ends, per pair .......... $0.25
Round ends, per pair .......... 0.20

**No. 83146 The Corkaline Grip** is the strongest made and with black combination tips makes a very attractive handle. Price per pair .......... $0.25

## Repair Kits.

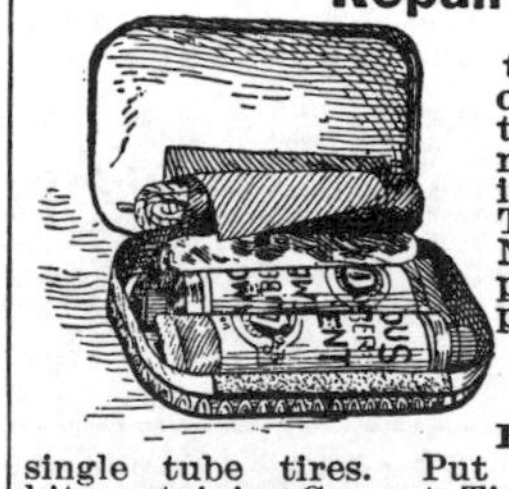

**No. 83148** Do not fail to get one of our repair outfits for double tube tires, consisting of Cement, Cement cloth, Patching Rubber, Tire Tube, Tire Lacing and Needle. No cyclist equipment complete without one. Our price is below competition.
Price, each ........ $0.12
Price, per doz ........ 1.38

**No. 83149 Single Tube Repair Kits,** for mending single tube tires. Put up in a neat leather kit, containing Cement, Tire Tape, Plugs, etc.
Our special price, each .......... $0.35
Our special price, per doz .......... 3.80

## Tire Tape.

**No. 83152 No Cyclist** should be without this very useful part of a repair outfit. We have put the price where it is as low as it is possible to put it. Put up in neat rolls, 16 to the pound.
Per Roll .......... $0.05
Per Pound .......... 0.70

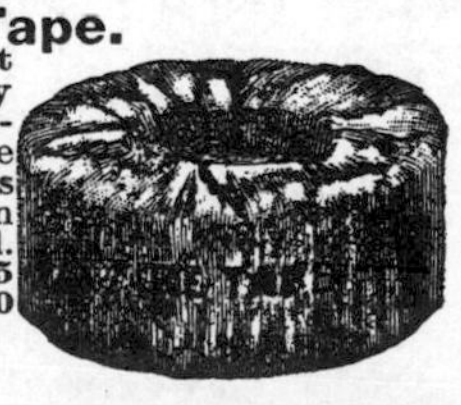

## Patching Rubber.

**No. 83154 Don't Try to Patch or Mend a Tire With Poor Rubber.** It does not pay. Our patching rubber is made from the purest Para Rubber. Put up 12 sheets in a package. Per package........$0.15
Per dozen packages.............................. 1.70

## Patching Plugs.

**No. 83156 Patching Plugs** for mending single tube tires, made of the finest quality rubber. Put up one dozen assorted in a package.
Per package.............................................$0.12
Per dozen packages.................................... 1.38

## Illuminating Oil for Bicycle Lamps.

**This Illuminating Oil** is made by a concern that has had years of experience in this line, and has profited by same. We therefore can honestly claim that our illuminating oils rank with the finest, and furthermore we guarantee it, as we do all the rest of our goods. Your lamp will not burn well with cheap oil. Use nothing but good oil and your lamp will certainly be a jewel. Too many good lamps are ruined by using poor oil. Do not be among the class that cannot keep a lamp lighted, but buy a can of our illuminating oil and your lamp will never be found wanting.

83157 Per ½ pint can....... $0.15
83158 Per 1 pint can.................................$0.25

## Bicycle Lubricating Oil.

**Too much care cannot be exercised as regards oiling a bicycle.** A great many people have trouble with their wheels because they use an inferior grade of oil. Our Lubricating Oil stands second to none, and while there may be cheap oils on the market, yet we caution our customers against their use. We think the best is none too good for our trade, and we know that there is none better. We put our goods in cans, in order that our customers may order by mail or express without fear of breakage.

No. 83160. No. 83162.

**83160 Lubricating Oil** in 4 oz can with spout. Each..........................................................$0.10
**83163 Lubricating Oil** in ½ pint can with spout. Each..........................................................$0.18
4 oz cans per doz..................................... 1.00
½ pint cans per doz.................................. 2.10

**No. 83164 When you are out riding,** a long ways from home, and your chain begins to creak, and your wheel to run hard, then you wish that you had used some of our lubricant on your chain before you started. Wise riders are never without a stick of our lubricant, as they know that we use the best only. It is composed of the very finest graphite, and it will stay on the chain and do good. Put up in a neat lithographed tube 4x1 with bottom which pushes up as graphite is used.
Per tube, (color black,) each........$0.10
**No. 83165 Same as above in wood box.** Each.................................................$0.10
Can be used without soiling the hands in any way at all. Does not injure clothing.

## Rubber Cement.

**Pure Rubber Cement** for mending tires, rubber boots, etc. Guaranteed absolutely pure. Put up in 1 x 6 inch tubes.
**No. 83167** Per tube.............$0.10
Per dozen tubes....................... 1.00
**No. 83169 Rubber Cement,** same as above. Put up in ¾ x 4 inch tubes.
Per tube.......................................$0.06
Per dozen tubes.................................. .60
**No. 83170 Same as above in 4 oz cans.**
Per can.......................................$0.12
Per doz. cans.................................$1.38
**No. 83170 Rubber Cement.**
Per pint.......................................$0.35
**No. 83171 Rubber Cement.**
Per ⅛ pint.....................................$0.20
N. B.—Full directions for applying accompanies all cement.

No. 83167

## Wood Rim Liquid Cement.

**Our Wood Rim Cement** is absolutely the best made. Do not waste your money and time by purchasing the cheap, sloppy stuff with which the market is flooded. We guarantee our cements.
**No. 83173 Wood Rim Cement,** in 1x6 inch tubes. Per tube, 10c.; Per dozen tubes.................$1.00
**No. 83174 Wood Rim Cement,** in 4 oz. cans. Per can, 12c.; Per dozen cans.......................$1.38
**No. 83175 Wood Rim Cement,** in ½ pint cans. Each.............................................................$0.20
**No. 83176 Wood Rim Cement,** in pint cans. Each.............................................................$0.35

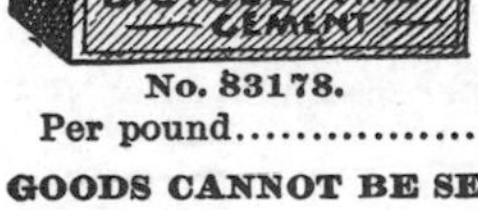


No. 83178.

**No. 83178 Wood or Steel Rim Cement,** in 3 ounce cakes, the best on the market.
Per cake.........$0.07
**No. 83180 Wood or Steel Rim Cement,** in 1 pound cakes.
Per pound..............................................$0.30

## Enamel.

**83182 Notwithstanding** that there has been a number of so called air drying enamels on the market, we still stick to the old reliable, "Gerstendorfers," because we know that it will always give the best satisfaction. Put up in 4 oz. cans; enough in a can to enamel one wheel; drys with an exceedingly fine luster. In colors, green, black, maroon, blue, yellow, pink, ivory white and others. The colors mentioned are the most popular.
Per 4 oz. can 15c; per doz. cans...........................$1.70
**No. 83183 Varnish to use over Enamel.** Gives it an elegant finish, and insures against scratching enamel off so easily. Easy to apply.
Per 4 oz. can, 15c; per doz. cans.......................$1.70
**No. 83184 Finest Camel's Hair Brush,** for applying above enamel and varnish. Made especially for this purpose. In order to do a good job of enameling it is essential to use a good brush.
Price, each, 5c; per dozen................................$0.50

## Hose Supporters.

**No. 83185 Hose Supporters.** Consists of a belt to go around the waist, with elastic straps, with patent fastenings to attach to the hose to hold them smoothly in their place. They are adjustable to waist and length of limb. State size of waist when ordering. Per pair....................$0.25
**No. 83186 Shoulder Stocking Supporter.** An article that meets the popular demand of wheelmen. These supporters do away with elastic bands which bind upon the limbs, causing numbness or swollen veins. Adjustable for any size person. Price, per pair.............................................$0.25

No. 83187

**No. 83187 Morton's Supporters.** Made of best quality Canton flannel. Cool and pleasant to wear. The best fitting and most effective supporter made. Be sure and give waist measurement.
Price, per pair..............................$0.25
**No. 83188 Ostergren's Patent Trouser Guard,** a neat and handy device for saving the pants from dirt and grease; can be carried in the vest pocket or worn around the legs under the pants when not in use.
Price, per pair........$0.05

**No. 83190 The Perfection Trouser Guard,** made of finest spring steel, to wear around ankle, same as Ostergren's.
Our special price, per pair...........................$0.03
Per dozen................................................. .35

## Chains.

**The phenomenal and unprecedented success of these Chains, is due** to the fact that they are accurate, and are made strictly on their merits. **These Chains are all guaranteed,** and you will always be safe if you have one of our chains on your wheel.

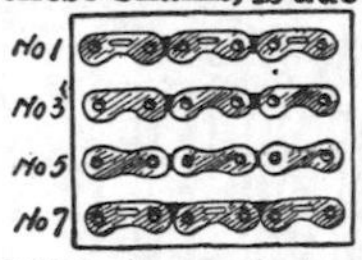


**No. 83200 Style 1, M. and M. W.** B links for ¼ inch 3-16 inch sprockets. Our special price, each...$2.00
**No. 83201 Style 3, Indiana Pattern,** B links ¼ or 3-16 inch. Our special price, each...........$1.50
**No. 83202 Style 5, Indiana Pattern,** Figure 8 links, ¼ or 3-16 inch. Our special price each ..$1.50
**No. 83203 Style 7, M. and M. W.,** Special B links, ¼ or 3-16 inch. Our special price, each.........$2.00
**N. B.—Unless otherwise specified, ¼ inch Chains will be sent.**

## Chain Parts.

No. 83205 **Blocks** for 3-16 or ¼ chain. Per dozen.................................................................$0.30
No. 83207 **Sides** for chain, blued. Per doz. 0.20
No. 83209 **Rivets** for chains 3-16 or ¼. Per dozen.................................................................$0.08
No. 83210 **Chain Bolt and Nut,** complete. each, ..........................................................................$0.08
N. B.—When ordering blocks or rivets for chains, specify whether ¼ or 3-16 is desired.

## Chain Adjusters.

**No. 83312 Don't wait until you break** your chain adjuster before ordering new ones. Order now, and when your adjuster breaks, as the best of them will do, you will not be occasioned any unnecessary delay. Our adjusters are made from select material, and are the strongest kind made.
Our special price per pair, each pair heavily nickeled.................................................................$0.15

**A CHOICE ASSORTMENT OF SWEATERS ON PAGES 213 AND 214.**

**THE BEST LINE OF BICYCLE CLOTHING ON PAGE 167.**

**No. 83214 This Hub is made upon an entirely new plan** which secures greatest strength with lightest material. The stock from which these Hubs are made is of the toughest fiber and of highest flanging quality, thus the danger of loops and eyelets stripping is entirely done away with. The workmanship is beyond question, absolutely the finest. All cups and cones are turned. Bearings are of three-point contact order. The sprockets are fastened with unusual security and furnished in 7, 8 or 9 tooth, for either 3-16 or ¼ inch chain, and so adjusted as to distribute strain equally upon cones at both ends. This Hub is furnished for 5 or 5¼ inch tread and with or without ball retaining devices. When ordering Hubs, be sure to state whether for 3-16 or ¼ chains, and what tread is desired. When not otherwise specified, 5 in. tread and ¼ sprocket will be sent. Our special price.
Per pair, without ball retaining device.... ..$3.20
Per pair, with ball retaining device.......... 3.50

## Wood Rims.

**Our Wood Rims** are all extra selected ones, and our customers may feel that they will get the best when ordering from us. Our special prices:
**83216** Extra select rims for 1½ inch tire, for 26 or 28 inch wheel, per pair. ...................... $1.00
**83218** Extra select rims for 1⅝ inch tire, for 26 or 28 inch wheel, per pair.................. 1.00
**83220** Extra select rims for 1¾ inch tire, for 26 or 28 inch wheel, per pair.................. 1.00
Our rims are all drilled ready for use when shipped to you. We charge nothing extra for drilling them. Unless otherwise specified they will be shipped for 28 inch wheels, drilled, 32 holes in one and 36 in the other. When ordering rims always state diameter, and for what size tires. Also how many holes you wish drilled. They will be shipped undrilled if desired.

## Wheels Built Up and Trued Ready for Use.

**WITHOUT TIRES.**

This cut represents our wheel built up and trued ready to put in the frame. The material together with the workmanship put in on these goods is unexcelled. The hubs are the celebrated W. & E. tubular, '97 pattern. The spokes are extra select Excelsior Needle Co.'s stock; rims of the finest non-warpable wood; cups and cones turned from solid bar steel. A wheel built of the above material cannot be excelled. They are furnished in the following sizes: 28x 1½ to 28x1¾ inclusive.
Per Pair.....................................................$10.00
**No. 83224** 26x1½ to 26x1¾ inclusive,
Per pair.....................................................$10.00
**Every Wheel Guaranteed.**

## Tandem Wheels.

Built of same material as the above, only heavier for tandems.
**No. 83226** 28x1½ to 28x1¾ inclusive; single or double sprocket. Our Special price, per pair $12.00

## Spokes and Nipples.

**Headed, Bent and Threaded.**

**Excelsior Needle Co.'s Cold Swaged Spokes** furnished in sizes of 14-16 and 15-17 only.
**No. 82228** 15-17 headed, bent, threaded and nickel plated. Per 100.................................................$1.60
**No. 83230** 14-16 headed, bent, threaded and nickel plated. Per 100...............................................$1.60
**No. 83231 Nipples** will be furnished with spokes for 40c extra per 100.
**No. 83234 When sold by the dozen** the spokes will be fitted with nipples.
Price per dozen complete.............................$0.30
**No. 83236 Washers** for wood rims.
Per 100, 15c; per 1,000.................................$1.00
**Steel Balls, highest grade, guaranteed true to gauge.** Made of the finest case hardened tool steel. Beware of cheap balls, made of poor material. They are worse than worthless for they ruin your wheel. Our special price:

| | Per doz. | Per 100 |
|---|---|---|
| No. 83238½, 5-32, 3-16 | $0.10 | $0.75 |
| No. 83239¼ | .18 | 1.35 |
| No. 83240 5-16, ⅜ | .25 | 1.50 |
| No. 83241, 7-16 | .40 | 3.00 |

**No. 83244 Fluxine is universally used as a Brazing Compound** because it is the cheapest and best; cause the spelter to flow deep into the joints with positively no air chambers. Requires little heat, therefore causing no brittleness of steel and forms no scale. Flows smooth, uniform and quick. Brazes four times as much as borax will, and requires only one half as much spelter.
Our special price, 1 lb. box, per lb...........$0.35
5 lb. box, per lb...$0.30 10 lb. box, per lb....27½c

**GOODS CANNOT BE SENT BY MAIL UNLESS POSTAGE IS PREPAID. WE REQUIRE FOR MAIL SHIPMENT, THAT ENTIRE CASH SHALL ACCOMPANY ORDER, AND EXTRA POSTAGE MUST BE ADDED.**

# SEARS ROEBUCK & CO INCORPORATED FURNITURE DEPARTMENT

**OUR FURNITURE DEPARTMENT** includes almost every modern thing in Furniture. If you don't find just what you want in this book you will surely find it in **Our Special Furniture Catalogue** which you should send for.

**OUR SPECIAL FURNITURE CATALOGUE** is the largest and most complete furniture catalogue, and like in this book you will find the prices based on the actual cost to manufacture with only our one small percentage of profit added, which means you can buy furniture from us cheaper than from any other house, in fact for less money than local dealers can buy in car lots.

**OUR SPECIAL TERMS.** We will send Furniture to any address by freight C. O. D. subject to examination on receipt of sufficient deposit to cover freight charges both ways, balance to be paid when received.

**DISCOUNT FOR CASH.** We will allow a **DISCOUNT OF THREE PER CENT.** if cash in full accompanies your order. Nearly all our customers send cash in full.

**OUR GUARANTEE.** We guarantee every piece of Furniture we advertise to be exactly as represented. Made from selected material in a first-class mechanical manner, and if not found so you can return it to us and **We will Refund Your Money.**

## SPECIAL LEADERS

~ IN ~

## KITCHEN AND DINING ROOM CHAIRS.

### Our 34 Cent Chair.

**No. 91** We offer this Wood Seat Kitchen or Dining Chair at the lowest price ever known for a really first-class chair. It has three spindles and bow back, hard wood finished plain, in antique or dark, as may be desired.
Our Special Price,
Each ............... $0.34
Per Set of six ...... 2.00

No. 91.

### Our 38 Cent Chair.

**No. 92** The Wood Seat Chair shown in the illustration is especially well constructed and is fancier than the chair preceding. This is a kitchen chair that can seldom be obtained at retail at 50c. Our special price is made with a view of proving our ability to render better value than any other house in existence. This chair is made with four spindles, bow back, **fancy ornamental stripes.** It is made of hardwood and finished in antique.
Our Special price, each ... ............ $0.38
Per set of six................ 2.20

No. 92.

No. 93.

### A Wonderful Bargain for 75 cts.

**No. 95** A $1.25 Chair for 75 cents, a special bargain in bedroom chairs. Made of best kiln dried elm, finished antique, and has fancy embossed carvings on back panel, and strong spindles in back.
Our special price.... $0.75
Per set of six...... 4.30

No. 95.

No. 97.

### A $1.25 Chair for 75 Cents.

**No. 97** This is a special new pattern for 1897, and is one of the handsomest cheap dining chairs ever put on the market. It has cane seat, high back, strong, fancy turned spindles, and in general is thoroughly well made of the best kiln-dried elm, finished in antique oak.
Our special price,
each...................... $0.75
Per set of six.......... 4.30

### A Dollar Chair for 60 Cents.

**No. 93** A very strong, durable, and well made Dining Chair, high back, wood seat, made of hardwood and finished in antique. It is substantially made with bent arms securely bolted to the seat, legs and spindles are well constructed, and the chair is very strong throughout.
Our special price.... $0.60
Per set of six....... 3.48

### 90c. Pays for a $1.50 Dining Chair.

**No. 98** This is a strictly new and desirable pattern, just put on the market, and the newest thing out for 1897 trade. You will not find any such chairs in your retail store at anything like our price; in fact, the chances are you will not find them in any local dealer's stock whatever. It has a beautifully embossed high back, with 7 spindles, bent arm braces securely fastened to back and seat, woven cane seat, strongly built legs and spindles. The chair is a decided bargain and is offered by us at about half of what you will ordinarily pay, for a chair of equal value at retail. **Made of solid oak.** While the best kiln-dried elm makes a very excellent chair, there is nothing superior to **fine selected oak**, and when you can buy a solid oak, cane seat, dining-room chair at 90c you are securing an unheard-of bargain.
Our special price................................. $0.90
Per set of six.................. .................... 5.10

No. 98.

### Our Great Bargain for 85 Cents.

**No. 910** We have this Dining Chair as illustrated and described with solid arm braces securely fastened to seat and back, making a firm and most durable chair. Our Special Price, each ............ $0.85
Per set of six.......... 4.90

**No. 911** We have also the same design as the Diner illustrated and described above in a very handsome ladies' rocker, with bent arm and seat braces, woven cane seat, and same pattern of carving as shown in illustration above. This ladies' rocker is very desirable and unusually cheap.
Our Special Price..... $1.48

A SET OF SIX CHAIRS BY FREIGHT WILL COST BUT LITTLE FOR TRANSPORTATION. ORDER YOUR GROCERIES AND CLOTHING AT THE SAME TIME AND SHIP ALL TOGETHER.

# OUR GRAND PAGE OF BARGAINS IN DINING CHAIRS.

**Our Former Prices were Low.  THESE ARE LOWEST . .**
**Our Former Chairs were high-grade.  THESE are the BEST.**

### A $2.00 DINING CHAIR FOR $1.10.

**No. 915.** A most wonderful bargain in solid oak dining chair, made of the best selected oak, handsomely finished and very stylish in appearance. High back, beautifully carved, **fancy turned spindles**, woven cane seat, bent arm braces, giving great additional strength. Made by one of the best manufacturers in the country. A rare bargain.

Our special price, each....$1.10    Per set of 6..........$6.30

### ELEGANT CARVED SOLID OAK CHAIR.

**No. 917.** We take pride in offering such an elegant selection of dining room chairs to our customers, knowing that they demand the very choicest the market affords. In this connection we have no hesitation in saying that the chair shown in illustration is as **handsome as anything** that can be found at wholesale or at retail. We offer this chair as one of the highest productions of the cabinet maker's art. It has **high back with beautiful hand carving**, elegantly turned spindles, woven cane seat, extra well braced in every respect. This chair is made of **solid oak**, very handsomely finished and is beautiful in design and workmanship.

Our special price, each....$1.20    Per set of 6..........$7.00

No. 913.        No. 915.

No. 917.        No. 920.

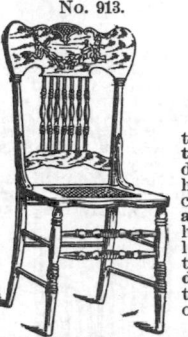

### A LEADER AT $1.00.

**No. 913.** We are constantly in the market for the newest designs and the most desirable goods in the furniture line, and we offer the dining room chair shown in illustration, believing it to be one of the choicest productions of the best manufacturer in the country. **We buy these chairs in large quantities** and shipping direct from the factory as to offer them at about half the ordinary retail price. This particular chair is made with high back, **beautifully carved and embossed panel**, elegantly turned spindles, has a fine hand woven cane seat, fancy turned legs, bent braced arm pieces securely fastened to back and seat. It is made of the **choicest kiln dried rock elm**, is warranted to be perfectly put together and substantially finished in antique oak. Our special bargain price, each........$1.00
Per set of 6............    5.75

No. 918.

### A $2.00 CHAIR FOR $1.25.

**No. 918.** The manufacturers of dining room furniture have put forth every effort to place on the market a line of furniture for the season of 1897 which is far superior to anything ever previously offered. We show in illustration **one of their handsomest designs**, something that you will not find in retail stores. This dining chair has high back with fancy carved top of beautiful pattern, seven fancy turned spindles, stong hand woven cane seat, turned legs and braces, bent arm braces strongly attached to back and seat. Throughout it is a chair which is not only beautiful but exremely serviceable, finished in antique oak, and sold by us at an unheard of price.

Our special price, each........$1.25
Per set of 6 ..................    7.20

### A $2.00 CHAIR FOR $1.35.

No. 924.

**No. 924.** The demand for the Vienna dining chairs has been growing very largely, and there is excellent reason for it in the fact that they are thoroughly well constructed, very comfortable and unusually cheap. The one which we show in illustration **has bent arm pieces**, securely fastened to back and seat, woven cane seat, bent legs securely braced with heavy spindles. We furnish this chair finished either imitation mahogany or antique, as may be desired. Our special price, each................$1.35
Per set of 6............................    7.80

No. 923.

### THE NEWEST DINER OUT.

**No. 923.** Knowing the great demand for as fine a grade of goods as can be manufactured, we show in illustration one of the choicest patterns that has been put on the market for 1897. It has what is known as a **box seat with beautifully carved panels**, elegantly shaped solid back with fancy hand carving. Fancy bent legs, well braced, with fancy turned spindles. It is made of the **very finest solid oak**, elegantly hand polished, finished in antique oak. This is an entirely new design, and in buying this chair you will be sure of having something that cannot be compared with anything else in your neighborhood; in fact, the chances are, that it is as fine a chair as your neighbors may have to pay $6.00 or $7.00 each for.

Our special price, each.....$3.95
Per set of 6..................    23.50

### A $3.00 CHAIR FOR $1.75.

**No. 920.** You will seldom if ever see the cheapest kind of a solid oak dining chair with box cane seat in any **retail** store at less than $3.00 each. That shown in the accompanying illustration is decidedly new with a **very tasty carved top**, very strong posts, fancy turned spindles, **box cane seat**, hand woven, new shaped legs well braced with fancy turned spindles. A remarkable bargain at the very low price offered below.

Our special price, each....................$1.75
Per set of 6............................    10.20

### THE LATEST DESIGN FOR 1897.

**No. 922.** There is quite a demand for a solid back dining chair, plain in finish but very rich in appearance. The dining chair shown in the accompanying illustration is as handsome a chair as we have ever handled. It is something entirely new, just on the market for 1897 trade. Beautifully shaped **high solid back**, very strong seat posts, fancy turned legs, well braced with turned spindles, hand woven cane seat. Made of the very choicest **quarter sawed oak**, beautifully hand polished. This chair is equal to anything on the market that retails at $3.00 or even more.

Our special price, each........$1.95
Per set of 6....................    11.50

No. 923.        No. 922.

### OUR $1.75 VIENNA DINER.

**No. 925.** We offer the Vienna dining chair as shown in the illustration at the unheard of price, of $1.75. It is thoroughly well made of the most select rock elm with harp back. It is the most desirable bent wood chair made. **The seat and back are reenforced** in strength by bent arm pieces which are securely fastened, while the bent legs are given additional means of a circular piece of wood as illustration. **Cane seat is well woven**, chair you will have great comfort, ity. Finished in either **imitation mahogany or antique oak.**

Our special price.............................$1.75
Per set of 6............................    10.20

No. 925.

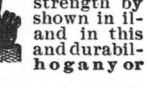

strength by shown in illustration and in this and durability, hogany or antique oak.

---

# OUR WONDERFUL COMBINATION OFFER!

**TO INDUCE** a wider range of combination orders and to outbid all possible competition, we will allow a SPECIAL CASH DISCOUNT OF 5%, when cash in full accompanies order for the DINING TABLE below in any size, together with 6 DINING CHAIRS, any one style on this page.

### A $6.00 DINING TABLE FOR $3.30.

When we name the above price on such a table as we illustrate in the picture and such a table as we describe, customers will more than likely think that it is certainly poorly constructed or something is the matter with it. We would say in this connection, however, that the main reason why this doubt will arise in our customers' minds is the fact that they have been accustomed to pay the exorbitant retail prices charged by local dealers. They have not yet learned, perhaps, that there is a more economical method of distributing goods. They forget the fact, perhaps, that before the goods reach them through the retail dealers, they have passed through several middlemen's hands, and the profits and expenses have been accumulating, until the price which they pay is two, or three, or four times the actual cost to produce the particular article. We have developed an entirely new system for the distribution of merchandise, and ship from the door of the factory to your door every article that you need for household or personal use. You can readily see that by cutting off all the middlemen's profits, how it is possible for us to furnish you this elegant and substantial dining table at the remarkable low price of $3.30. about 100 lbs.

This table when closed has a 42x42 inch top and is made of the very finest selected and kiln dried ash, both top, rims and legs. The rim of this table, as shown in the illustration is plain. We have persuaded the manufacturer, however, to make a special feature of this table for our customers, in the way of decoration, and the purchaser will find it very much more handsome than the one shown in the illustration, from the fact that the one which we shall ship will have fancy ornamentation and moulding on the rim. The legs are of extra strength and are fancy turned and carved, while the center panel and cross pieces are also decorated and carved. This table, as shown in the illustration has six legs, with a complete set of fine patent castors. We pack all our tables carefully, so that there will be no danger of rubbing or scratching, and the customer may be sure of receiving the goods in the best of condition. The finish is beautiful, being our best gloss finish, equal to the polish finish of other factories. We make this table in four lengths, viz.: 6 ft., 8 ft., 10 ft. and 12 ft., and the prices which we name are less than one-half the ordinary price charged by retailers for the same or inferior goods. The weight of this table ready for shipment is

No. 926. 6 ft., price......$3.30    No. 927. 8 ft., price......$4.45    No. 928. 10 ft., price......$5.60    No. 929. 12 ft., price......$6.75

**THIS SPECIAL DEVIATION** from our regular cast iron terms of 3% for cash is only made possible by special large spot cash contracts with leading manufacturers, and from our desire to induce you to place all your furniture order with us. The table is a great bargain at $3.30, $4.45, $5.60, $6.75.

No such table can be found in retail stores at 50% more than our prices. THE DINING CHAIRS are the latest designs for 1897, and for price and quality are marvels.

**REMEMBER** our special cash offer of 5% off is only when cash in full accompanies order for table and set of six chairs. **FOR EXAMPLE**, you order table No. 927, 8 ft., price $4.45, and set of 6 chairs, No. 917, price $7.00; total, $11.45 less special offer cash discount of 5%, and the combination costs you but $10.88. The chairs alone would cost you that much at retail. **REMEMBER**, if chairs alone or table alone is bought, our regular discount of 3% only will be allowed.

# RARE BARGAINS IN LADIES' ROCKERS, ARM CHAIRS AND LARGE ROCKERS.

No. 927    No. 926

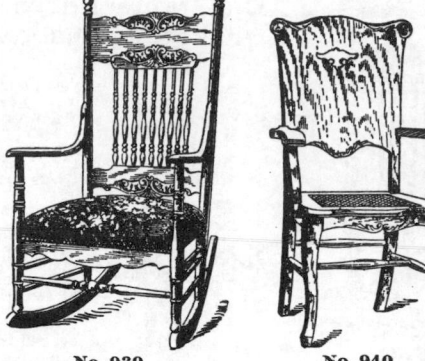

No. 939      No. 940

### A $1.50 Rocker for 85 Cents.

**No. 926**   The Bargain which we offer in this rocker is something which will not be overlooked by the economical buyer. We are able to make the price we do by reason of **our immense trade which secures spot cash prices** the retailer cannot get. From this reason as well as from the fact that we sell on the closest possible margin we are able to furnish you goods at prices which your retailer himself could not obtain. This Ladies' Wood Rocker is made of best selected rock elm, and is well made throughout. **Solid Wood Seat,** strongly braced legs securely fastened to rockers. Finished in antique oak.
Our special price, each.......................$0.85

### A $3.00 Rocker for $1.68.

**No. 927**   From out of thousands of designs, we illustrate here the the best selections we have been able to secure from the **leading manufacturers of the country.** This rocker is one of the best bargains we have secured. We offer it with the assurance it will give the greatest satisfaction to our trade. It is made of the **very finest rock elm,** handsomely finished in antique oak, **fancy carved back,** handsome turned spindles, well braced back and seat with bent arm braces securely bolted, and in general it is extra strong throughout.
Our special price, each..... .........$1.68

**No. 928**   We can furnish the same rocker if desired in the best selected solid oak, handsomely finished, and unusually good value.
Our special price, each.................... .... ......$1.80

### A $4.00 Rocker for $2.80.

**No. 930**   This is a decidedly new pattern in the line of ladies' rockers and will immediately catch your attention from the general appearance of comfort and durability. It is made of the **very finest selected quarter sawed oak,** which is kiln dried before it is made up into chairs, hence you are sure of an article of furniture that will be exceedingly durable. The full panel back is very comfortable and is fancy shaped and handsomely finished. **The bent brace arms,** which are securely bolted to the back and seat, give great additional strength. Fine hand **woven cane seat,** bent legs securely fastened to rockers. We finish this rocker in birch with imitation mahogany polish finish.
Our special price, each...........................$2.70

No. 930.

**No. 931**   We have a Dining Room Chair made exactly the same as the rocker above illustrated and described, but is higher and of course has no rockers. In every other way it is precisely the same chair.
Our special price, each, $2.05; Per set of 6........12.00

**No. 932**   We have in the same design and pattern a very handsome gent's arm chair, with large comfortable arms securely attached to seat and back. This chair is a german than the diner, and is a very comfortable addition to any library. Finished in oak or mahogany.
Our special price, each........................$2.90

### A Large Well-Made Rocker for $2.15.

**No. 933**   We offer this Comfortable Rocker at the unusually low price mentioned, having secured it from the manufacturer on a special deal which enables us to give our customers the benefit of the great bargain. It is very securely constructed of the **very best rock elm,** has comfortable bent arms securely bolted to back and seat, **woven cane seat,** solid legs and rockers, finely finished in antique oak.
A decided bargain at our special price, each.$2.15

No. 933

### A Leader for $2.85.

**No. 935**   The Rocker which we show in the illustration is one of the **old fashioned comfortable rockers,** for which there is such a large demand not only on account of their beauty but by reason of their durability and comfort. This rocker is something entirely new, in fact, we are securing from the factory the first consignment that they have turned out. You will not find anything like this in your retail store. It is made of the very choicest rock elm, **beautifully finished in antique oak.** As shown in illustration, it is handsomely carved, and you will be even more pleased with it on its receipt than you think you will from seeing it in illustration. It is put up in the **most substantial manner,** the arms being securely bolted to the seat; easy woven cane seat, strong legs with rockers securely fastened. One advantage in the rocker is that it is built on scientific principles and hangs very comfortably. Most cheap rockers on the market swing too far forward or too far back, and are not built on proper lines.
Our special price, each.. .......................$2.85

### Finest Solid Oak for $3.48.

**No. 937**   We have the same rocker as above illustrated and described, but instead of being rock elm it is made of the very **finest solid oak,** beautifully finished in antique.
Our special price, each.....$3.48

### A $3.25 Rocker for $2.15.

**No. 938**   We show in the illustration a Rocker which is in great favor. It is a new design for 1897 and is built on the lines of comfort and durability. It is made either in solid oak or in birch, with imitation mahogany finish. Fancy carved top. Arms are given additional strength by means of bent arm braces underneath, which are securely attached to back and arms; hand woven cane seat. In general, this chair is unusually strong and will last a lifetime with ordinary usage. A chair that will retail everywhere at $3.25.
Our special price, each..........................$2.15

No. 938

### $4.00 Rocker for $2.55.

**No. 939**   We have been handling this rocker during the past season with great success and the demand has been so large for it that we have decided to continue it so long as our present stock lasts. We have secured the last of the manufacturer's stock, and are offering the rocker at a reduced price from that at which we sold it last year. **Easy spring seat** is upholstered in **silk plush or brocoline.** You can have in the plush any desirable colors, such as blue, olive or red. The high back has fancy carving on the panels, while the back posts are elegantly turned. Rocker has fancy shaped front, very strong, well braced legs, with rockers securely attached. You will find this rocker **a special bargain,** and we recommend it to you with the assurance that you will find nothing that will please you better at anything like our factory to consumer price.
Our special price, each........................$2.55

### Great Bargain for $5.25.

**No. 940**   For the library there is nothing more desirable than a handsome arm chair that is not only **beautiful but comfortable.** The one shown in the illustration answers all requirements for elegance, durability and comfort. It is elegantly made of the **very finest quarter sawed oak,** it has beautifully carved full panel back, **woven cane seat, box pattern,** bent legs well braced. It is such a chair as ordinary retail dealers will ask from **$8.00 to $10.00** for, and at our special price below is an unusual bargain. We offer it with the assurance that customers who receive it will be delighted with it, and will consider it **one of the finest bargains** they have ever seen in the furniture line.
Our special price, each........................$5.25

**No. 941**   We have also a dining chair to match the above illustrated arm chair exactly in every way except that it is somewhat smaller and has no arms. It has the same **beautifully carved panel back, box cane seat,** and matches the arm chair exactly. Many customers desiring a set of 6 dining room chairs will purchase 5 of the diners and one arm chair for a complete set.
Our special pric for Diner, each, $2.90; Per set of 6...............$17.10

No. 943

### Our $1.40 Library Chair.

**No. 943**   The Library or Arm Chair which we show in the accompanying illustration is very reasonable in price and very comfortable. It is constructed of the finest rock elm, **finished in antique oak,** has high back, fine bent arms bolted to back and seat. Back posts are also securely bolted to seat. **Extra strong legs and spindles,** wood seat. Finished in antique oak, and is as its appearance implies, a "Solid Comfort" chair.
Our special price, each........................$1.40

**No. 944**   We have the same chair with cane seat instead of wood seat.
Our special price, each...... ......... .......$1.70

### A $4.00 Rocker For $2.00.

**No. 947**   You can scarcely believe it possible for you to secure such a rocker as shown in the illustration as low even as $4.00 from the fact that it is well made of the **finest selected oak,** has beautiful carved top, handsome turned spindles, **solid leather cobbler seat,** large comfortable arms, strong elegantly turned and well braced legs, all finished in antique. This is one of the choicest patterns for the season of 1897 and is offered at a price against which no one can possible compete. We trust that you will favor us with your order for one of these rockers for the entire satisfaction it will give you, and we feel sure that the chair will be a great advertisement for us and will enable us to build up a large trade in your neighborhood.
Our special price, each.......... .......................$2.00

No. 947

### An Elegant Saddle Seat Rocker.

**No. 949**   This is a rocker that is elegant enough for the richest home, and at the same time the price brings it within the reach of the most limited pocket book. We have a tremendous leverage on prices by reason of the tremendous trade which we carry on with the leading manufacturers. We consequently **are able to offer you this rocker at an extremely low price,** in fact, as low a price as your dealer can ordinarily buy it. The rocker is made of handsome quarter sawed oak. The top of back has **handsome carving** as well as the lower panel. The arms are wide and comfortable and the wood seat is known as the saddle seat. We solicit your trade in the furniture line knowing that we can please you very highly, and in no instance can we give you better value than that which we offer in this particular rocker.
Our special price, each.......... ...........$2.55

**No. 950**   We also furnish the same rocker in curly birch with imitation mahogany finish. This makes a very handsome rocker. In other respects it is just the same as No. 949.
Our special price, each....................................$2.25

## $3.50 Rocker for $2.00.

**No. 951** Our buyers have been devoting a great deal of time to securing late designs and most desirable patterns for this season's trade, and we show in the illustration a rocker which illustrates the success of their efforts to get the best the market affords. This rocker is what is known as the cobbler seat rocker with an embossed leather sunken seat, very comfortable, handsome, and in great demand. The back is fancy carved, spindles elegantly turned, and the rocker is put up strongly and sub-stantially, We furnish this rocker in antique oak or imitation mahogany, as may be desired.
Our special price......
Each.............$2.00

## Easy Upholstered Rocker for $5.15

**No. 952** We are offering a special bargain in the rocker shown in illustration. In construction it is **particularly well made**, in appearance it is beyond comparison with goods sold at twice our price by most local dealers, while in comfort it has no superior. This rocker has high back and is made with a **solid oak frame upholstered in silk plush** in a variety of popular colors, such as olive, blue, red, etc. The sea has spring bottom and the back is padded and ornamented with fancy tassels, handsome carving on top of back, and the rocker as a whole is one of the most tasty low priced rockers we have for sale.
Our Special Price, each......................$5.15

## A $10.00 Rocker for $6.48.

**No. 956** When it is possible to secure all the comfort that can possibly be afforded by a rocker at the extremely low factory price which we are making, it is certainly an object to you to take ad-vantage of the bargains which we are offering in this catalogue. The magnificent piece of furniture which we show in illustration is as good an example as we can show of the opportunities you can take advantage of through our factory to consumer method of doing business. This rocker is one that will seldom be bought at retail at $10.00 In fact, retailers will frequently ask $12.00 to $14.00 for one no better. It is made of the very finest selected material, finished in antique oak. It is upholstered in silk plush. The cushion on back is loose and can be removed if desired. It is kept in position by fancy tasseled cords as shown in the illustration. The bottom of cushion is also upholstered in very fine silk plush and is removable. The upholstering can be had in any of the popular colors. This large comfortable rocker is a picture of ease and at our special bargain price you can not afford to be without at least one handsome rocker in the house.
Our Special Price, each .......................$6.48

## $2.78 Invalid's Chair.

**No. 957** We show in the accompanying illustration a chair which is a very great convenience in the sick room, and which is thoroughly well constructed of the best rock elm, finished in antique oak. Has high back, fancy painted panel and top, strong bent arms securely bolted to seat, fancy turned legs and spindles.
Our special price....$2.78

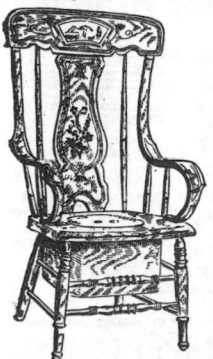

## A $2.00 Chair for $1.05.

**No. 958** It has never been in our power to secure such bargains in the line of furniture as we have at the present time. We are offering in this catalogue un-heard of bargains and this is one of them. This youth's high chair is made of very fine selected rock elm, hand-somely finished, with elegant carved back and turned back posts. Additional strength is given by means of the bent arm braces, which are attached to the back. The legs are fancily turned, and thoroughly well braced. The seat is wood. This chair is as neat and durable as one could desire. The price leaves no question of doubt of its desirability as a great bargain. Our special price, each....$1.05

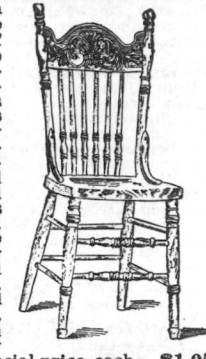

## $1.15 Youth's High Chair.

**No. 959** The Youth's High Chair shown in this cut, is a pat-tern that the leading manufacturer considers one of the best. It has **handsomely carved back**, bent arm braces securely fastened to back and seat. Back post is one continuous piece, being a continu-ation of the legs, hence adding ad-ditional strength to the chair. Cane seat. A very substantial Youth's or Misses' High Chair at about one-half what retailers will ordinarily charge for it. Finished in antique oak.
Our special price............$1.15

## Misses' Rocker for $1.20.

**No. 961** The Misses' Rocker shown in illustration is an en-tirely new pattern, never on the market before, a style that will prove unusually pleasing and satisfactory. The back has a beautiful design and carving, the back posts are handsomely turned, and bent arms are se-curely fastened to the seat posts. Legs are fancy turned and well braced with turned spindles. Rockers securely attached. This rocker is made of the very best rock elm, handsomely finished in antique oak.
Our special price, each...$1.20

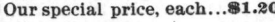

## $1.10 Child's Rocker.

**No. 966** One of the best made little Rockers we have ever handled, and turned out by a manufacturer who makes a specialty of children's chairs. It has handsome carved back with turned spindles, woven cane seat, comfortable arms well braced and securely at-tached to back and seat. This is a thoroughly well construct-ed little rocker and will stand a great deal of battering. Made of best rock elm, handsomely finished in antique oak.
Our special price, each..$1.10

## Our 90 Cent Child's Rocker.

**No. 967** We take pleasure in offering this Rocker as one of the most substantial little pieces of children's furniture we have ever catalogued. It is made of kiln dried and thoroughly sea-soned rock elm, handsomely fin-ished in antique oak, has beau-tifully carved top, bent arms securely bolted to back and seat, wood seat, strong legs well braced and with rockers thoroughly well attached. A good honest rocker at a good honest price.
Our special price, each...$0.90

## Bargain for $1.45.

**No. 968** The Child's Rocker which we show in cut is an entirely new pattern. There is nothing on the market like it. When you buy a rocker for the little one, you might as well have as nice a one as there is to be gotten, providing the price is right. Offering this as we do at $1.45, you will get something you would pay your retail dealer $2.50 for, and an article that will please your child. The comfortable back is beautifully carved and has an elegant appearance. The arms are securely attached to back and seat. Seat is woven cane, legs are strong and well braced, the rockers are securely attached to them. We make this rocker of the very best kiln dried elm and finish it in antique oak.
Our special price, each................ ... ...$1.45

## 48 Cent Child's Rocker

**No. 969** We show a handsome little Rocker that will delight the the children. It is well made and thoroughly substantial. Strongly braced arms, bent back, with four turned spindles, wood seat. Fin-ished in antique oak.
Our special price, each........48c

## Our 80 Cent High Chair.

**No. 970** This bargain gives you another taste of our facil-ities for hammering down prices. You will readily see from the illustration that it is strongly built and very handy. It is made of the best rock elm, **kiln dried and thoroughly seasoned**, bow back, adjustable table which swings over child's head so that the child can be placed in the chair before ad-justing the table. It is seldom that such a chair will be offered at retail for less than double our factory to consumer price. The chair is finished either in red or antique, as may be de-sired. In purchasing this chair you will secure a bargain you have **never seen or heard of before**.
Our special price.......................80c

## Child's High Chair for $1.00.

**No. 971** This Child's High Chair is made of selected ma-terial, thoroughly well con-structed; in fact, this is an ab-solute necessity in a child's high chair, otherwise it will last but a comparatively short time. We are fortunate in dealing with manufacturers who have a reputation to sus-tain in all their work and turn out nothing but the best qual-ity of goods. This chair is made of the very finest selected kiln dried elm, and is put up to last as well as for the sake of appearance. The swing table is made to swing over the child when seated in the chair. The position when the table is swung back is the same as shown in the cut of the chair following. This chair is fin-ished in antique oak, has wood seat, and is very de-sirable in every respect.
Our special price, each.......................$1.00

## $2.00 Chair for $1.35.

**No. 972** It is scarcely neces-sary for us to dwell on the handsome appearance of this chair, as the illustration speaks for itself. However, the cut does not do it justice, as the handsome design cannot be brought out by our artist. The back is **fancy carved**, and it is in all a very attractive piece of furniture. The swing table can be thrown forward into pos-ition while the child is sitting in the chair. The legs are strong and well braced, in fact, the chair is put together very sub-stantially, made for wear as well as for appearance.
Our special price in antique oak finish...................$1.35

## 85 Cent Nursery Chair.

**No. 974** This chair is really a household necessity, and no fami-ly with children should be without one. It is made up handsomely of the best rock elm, handsomely dec-orated, has full back with three spindles and table in front. It is strongly constructed, handsomely finished either in regular or an-tique oak.
Our special price, each.....$0.85

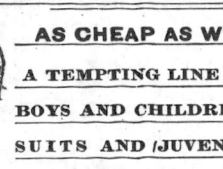
**IF YOU** NEED A CHAIR OR ROCKER..
ORDER ENOUGH GROCERIES TO MAKE UP 100 LBS. AND SHIP ALL BY FREIGHT, AND THE CHARGES WILL BE LITTLE IF ANY MORE THAN ON THE CHAIR ALONE.

SHOULD YOU HAVE ANY MISUNDERSTANDING ABOUT AN ORDER, KEEP IN MIND THE FACT THAT IT IS TO YOUR INTEREST TO PRE-VENT MISTAKES, AND IT IS BETTER TO DELAY YOUR ORDER FOR INSTRUCTIONS THAN TO RUN THE CHANCE OF FILLING IT WRONG.

## $5.10 Office Chair.

**No. 975 The Office Chair** which we show in illustration is a very handsome and desirable piece of furniture. Solid back panel, heavy back posts with comfortable arms, and iron rod running from arm to seat, giving additional strength. Solid embossed leather cobbler's seat. This office chair **has screw and spring** so that the tension of the spring can be adjusted if desired. Can also be adjusted in height by means of screw in the legs. This elegant effice chair is made of **the finest quarter sawed oak,** handsomely finished, very strong and durable.
Our Special Bargain Price.................. **$5.10**

## Great Bargain for $3.75.

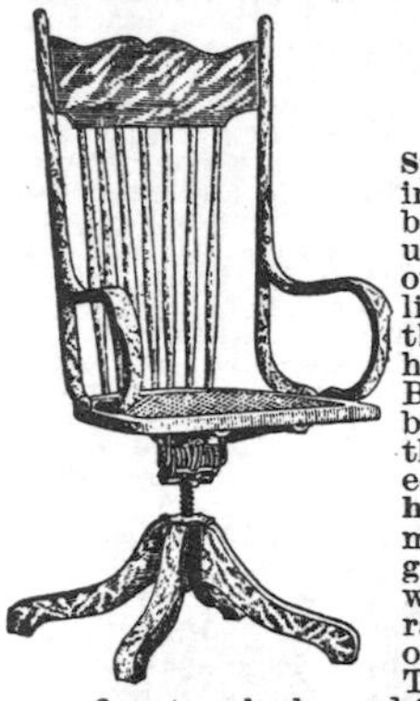

**No. 977 The Screw and Spring Office Chair** shown in the cut is very well made by one of the leading manufacturers whose greatest output of chairs is in this line. It is very comfortable, thoroughly well made and handsome in appearance. Bent arms are securely bolted to back and seat and the back posts are also bolted to seat. **Cane seat is hand woven,** and the spring may be adjusted to any degree of tension desired, while the chair may be raised or lowered by means of the screw in steel plate. This chair is made of the very finest rock elm and **finished in antique oak.**
Our special price, each........................... **$3.75**
**No. 978 We have the same chair** as above illustrated and described but with wood seat instead of cane seat. Our special price .................... **$3.48**

## Our $4.60 Office Chair.

**No. 980 The Office Chair shown in this illustration** is one of the latest designs for 1897. We have arranged our **dealings with one of the largest manufacturers of office chairs, and offer this as one of the choicest designs in their stock. It is made with screw and spring** so that the tension may **be regulated, has fancy carved back,** comfortable arms, fancy **solid** leather cobbler seat.
Our special price, each..**$4.60**

## Office Chair for $4.50.

**No. 982** We take **pleasure in offering for the attention of our customers** the elegant office chair shown in the illustration. It is a very desirable pattern, large, roomy and comfortable, with handsomely carved back panel, **bent arms securely bolted to back and seat,** and given additional strength by fancy turned spindles. The front panel of seat is also handsomely carved. The seat has full cane bottom. **The spring in chair** can be adjusted to any degree of tension by means of screw. The height can be regulated by screwing the chair up or down. This is a thoroughly well constructed chair, made of the very finest rock elm, kiln dried **before manufactured. It is handsomely finished** and presents an elegant appearance.
Our special price, each........................... **$4.50**

**No. 983 We have this chair also in solid oak,** finished antique. Same style **carving,** same cane seat, **and** in every other way just **the** same as illustrated **above.** Our special price, Each ................**$5.00**

## Our $2.24 Bargain

**No. 984 We also have the same pattern** as above illustrated office chair in **Gent's Large Arm Chair.** This **arm** chair is constructed of **best** rock elm, has some **fancy** carving on back and top of arms as shown in illustration above; solid wood seat, heavy legs firmly braced with fancy turned spindles. This is a decided bargain at our special price.........**$2.24**

## Our $1.85 University Chair.

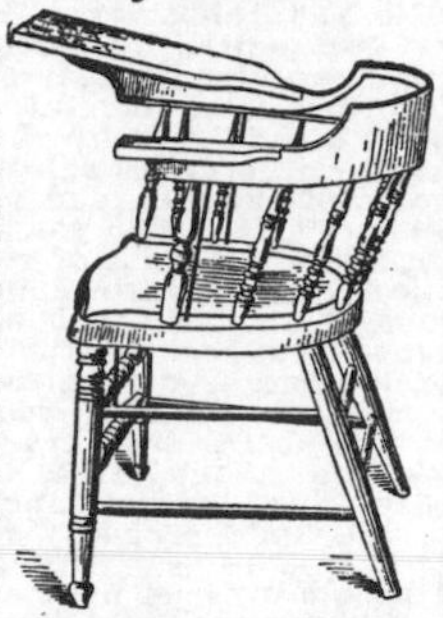

**No. 986 One of the most convenient chairs manufactured is the University** Chair, with side table or book rest as shown in illustration. This chair is **thoroughly well made** from very fine rock elm. The back and arms are extra well braced by means of iron rods passing through seat. The chair is decidedly comfortable, and after being once used is considered an absolute necessity. Wood seat, nicely finished in **antique oak or dark finish, as** desired.
Our special price, each.... ..........................**$1.85**

## Wood Seat Stool for 38 cents.

**No. 987 The low stool which we show in the accompanying illustration** comes handy in a great many instances. It is thoroughly well constructed of the finest elm, **finished in antique oak.** Stands 18 inches high and is thoroughly well made and substantial. Wood seat.
Our special price....**$0.38**
Six for................ **2.10**

## 47c Counter Stool.

**No. 989 The Counter Stool which we show in the cut** is especially desirable for stores, but is bought for a variety of purposes. It is sold by us at a lower price than even the cheapest kind of stools sell elsewhere. **Made of best rock elm,** 24 inches high, finished in antique oak.
Our special price........**$0.47**
6 for ............................ **2.50**
**No. 990 We have the same stool** with cane seat instead of wood seats.
Our special price, each, 75c; 6 for............**$4.00**

## Our 68 cent High Desk Stool.

**No. 991 The High Desk Stool which** we illustrate is substantially made, strongly braced, handsomely finished and has an excellent appearance. It is made of very fine rock elm, kiln dried, has a wood seat, and is **finished in antique oak.** The legs are handsomely turned, strongly braced. It is an excellent stool for the money and can not be secured for less than **50 per cent above our price.**
Our special price, each**$0.78**
Six for .............. **3.18**
**No. 993 We have the same stool** with cane seat, instead of wood seat, constructed in the same manner, after the same style, thoroughly well made.
Our special price, each,.................... **$0.93**
Six for........................................... **5.40**

## A Fine Lawn Chair for $2.90.

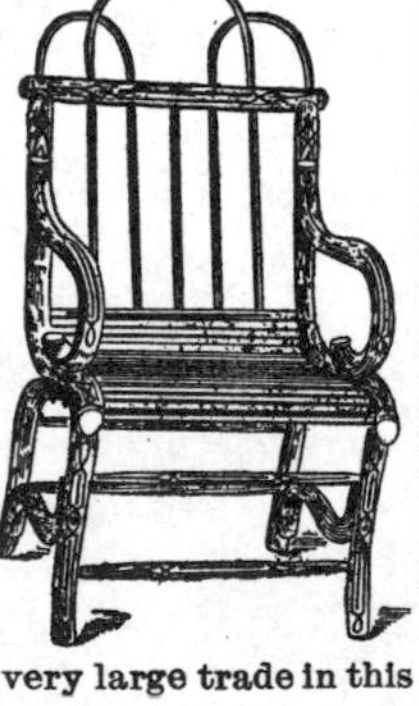

**No. 995 The desirability of these lawn or porch chairs** and seats leads us to add to our line the comfortable lawn or porch chair which we show in the cut. This chair is made by one of the leading manufacturers in bend wood furniture, and a manufacturer who has no rival in the quality of the goods which he turns out, and hence we offer this chair as one of **unusual strength and durability,** one that will not become rickety or fall to pieces after comparatively short usage. It is thoroughly well constructed of the best kiln dried wood, securely put together in the most workmanlike manner, handsomely **finished in red, green or antique oak.** It is a very desirable piece of furniture to have for summer use, and we anticipate a very large trade in this particular chai.
Our special price, each................................**$2.90**
**No. 996 We can furnish the same design as the above chair** illustrated and described, **in large arm rocker.** The rocker will be constructed in the same manner, in fact, will be the same chair exactly with the addition of rockers.
Our special price, each.................................**$3.40**

...MAMMOTH...
FURNITURE CATALOGUE FREE.

## A Fine Lawn Rocker for $2.25.

**No. 997 The illustration will give you some idea of the appearance,** comfort and durability of our **Veranda Rocker** with **reed seat and back.** This rocker is just as strong and just as comfortable as the all reed or rattan rockers which are sold by retail dealers at from $6.00, to $8.00 or $9.00. It is thoroughly well constructed, the frame being of fine kiln dried wood and the entire chair being **finished in shellac or cherry.** A very necessary article of furniture for the summer months, and a rocker that will be found just as comfortable and just as desirable for house use.
Our special price, each............................**$2.25**
**No. 998 We also have the same rocker** finished in red instead of shallac or cherry.
Our special price, each.................................**$2.50**

## A Leader at $3.10.

**No. 9100 We take great pleasure in being able to offer such a decided bargain** in the way of the beautiful lawn or porch settee illustrated. This settee **has solid seat and back,** with very fancy carved panels, extra strong bent arms securely bolted to seat and back. The settee is thoroughly well constructed with the best selected material, and we **finish it in either red or antique oak. It is very ornamental in appearance** and handsomely finished. It will be found ornamental as well as extremely useful and unusually desirable for porch or lawn uses. This settee is 43 inches long, very roomy, and a decided bargain at the price named below.
Our special price, each.........................**$3.10**
**No. 9101 We have the same settee with rocker attached** which gives additional comfort. This rocker settee is of the same design as shown above and is constructed on the same general principles of strength and durability.
Our special price, each.............................**$3.75**

## Our $3.00 Lawn Settee.

**No. 9103 Desiring to meet all the demands of our trade, we** add to our already large list of furniture this handsome and comfortable **Lawn Settee.** It is very desirable for use on **Lawns or Porches,** and is just the thing for summer when the greatest comfort is to be secured in sitting out of doors. With one of these settees on your lawn or yard you will wonder how you had previously done without it. **It is made of select kiln dried wood** and is finished in either **regular, green or antique oak.** We can furnish this settee in 4 styles. Prices as follows:
4 feet long, price each.......................... **$3.00**
5 feet long, price each.......................... **3.25**
6 feet long, price each.......................... **3.50**
8 feet long, price each.......................... **4.50**

## A Wonderful Bargain for $1.25.

**No. 9105 We show two illustrations of this special settee,** one showing it opened and the other when folded. This is a moderate priced settee that meets all the requirements **for lawns, piazzas, or for public halls and exhibitions.** It is thoroughly well constructed of the best **selected** hard wood, handsomely finished in vermillion, while the seats are finished in light color, and all nicely varnished. **It is put together with screws and rivets,** and is a light, strong, durable and at the same time comfortable settee. When folded it **occupies but a very small space.** Length 3 feet 6 inches.
Our special price................................**$1.25**

## GREAT SALE OF CARPETS...

CHOICE PATTERNS OF INGRAINS, TAPESTRY AND BODY BRUSSELS, MOQUETTES AND VELVETS.
REFER TO INDEX AND SEE FULL PLATE PAGES.
OUR PRICES ARE THE RIGHT PRICES.

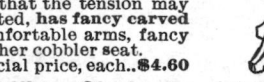

**DON'T LET ANY CONCERN MAKE YOU BELIEVE THEY ARE THE GREAT AND ONLY. IF YOU CAN MAKE A BETTER DEAL WITH ANY OTHER HOUSE THAN WITH US, MAKE IT. EVERY TUB STANDS ON ITS OWN BOTTOM.**

# ...RATTAN CHAIRS...

## A $3.25 Rocker for $2.05.

**No home is complete** without one or more of these handsome reed rockers. They are desirable for summer and out of door use, or for parlor or library at all seasons of the year. Odd pieces of furniture are sought after more largely than ever, and nothing is more fashionable than these elegant reed goods. The one which we show in illustration is cheap in price but thoroughly well made by the leading manufacturer in the country. The arms and back posts are cane wound, **woven cane roll at top,** woven cane seat, fancy turned legs, well braced, rockers well attached. Only the best selected reed is used in its manufacture. You cannot do better than include one of these rockers in your next order.

9114 Our special price, each, natural finish................................................$2.05
9116 Our special price, each, shellac finish................................. 2.50

No. 9125.

## Large Comfort Rocker for $4.00.

A Comfort Rocker in order to be all that the name implies must be **built on lines of beauty, comfort and durability.** The peculiar points of excellence about this rocker are in the superior quality of the reed from which it is made, the perfect shape and expert workmanship which is employed to turn it out. **The full woven reed scroll** around back extends entirely down the front to rockers. Easy full woven reed seat, fancy woven reed back with **ornamental turned balls,** cane wound legs amply strengthened by cross braces. No better reed can be found than that which

No. 9114.

we use in this particular rocker, and the purchaser will find it to be a **piece of furniture of which he will be proud,** and which will give more service and durability than anything which could be secured from a retail store at 50% more than our price.

9125 Our special price, each, natural finish....$4.00
9126 Our special price, each, shellac finish.... 4.75

## Ladies' Comfort Rocker for $3.90.

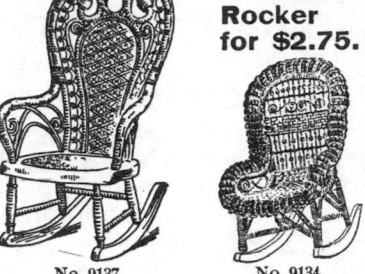

**One of the best bargains ever offered** in a genuine Comfort Rocker. More satisfaction can be gotten out of one of these chairs than anything else in the furniture line. The best present you can give your wife. A chair that is made for service and durability as well as for comfort. **The manufacturer who makes these** reed goods **has no rival in the market,** and we take particular pleasure in offering this line, knowing the excellent service it will give. This rocker is made of the best selected reed with fancy open back, **fancy woven rim around back and seat,** woven reed seat, cane wound legs and braces, in fact, throughout it is as substantial a rocker as you could obtain at retail stores at double our price. This is positively the lowest priced first class Comfort Rocker ever put on the market.

No. 9117.

9117 Our special price, each, natural finish....$3.90
9118 Our special price, each, shellac finish.... 4.65

**Your choice of either shellac or natural finish. Always state in your order which finish you desire.**

## A $6.00 Rocker for $3.90.

**This line of goods represents the newest designs for the season of 1897,** in fact, they are stylish and desirable patterns not to be found in retail stores. We contract for these in large quantities with the manufacturer, and hence are able to offer them at about the prices that retailers pay for the same quality of goods. Nothing more handsome or more comfortable made. **Their durability is beyond question** for they are made of the choicest select reed, which is very pliable and consequently will not crack like that from which the cheap rockers are made. **We guarantee that you will be pleased** with this rocker and if it is not just what we represent it to be, it may be returned and we will gladly refund your money. Full roll woven reed, back and arms are peculiarly adapted to comfort and strength. Fancy woven reed back **ornamented with turned balls.** Close woven cane seat. Very strong fancy turned legs and spindles. Rockers securely attached to legs.

No. 9121.

9121 Our special price, each, natural finish....$3.90
9122 Our special price, each, shellac finish.... 4.65

## Our $8.00 Rocker for $5.85.

**We are offering** so many handsome and stylish **ladies' rockers** that it is difficult to suggest which one is really the nicest. The one shown in the accompanying illustration is an entirely new pattern just brought out, and, in fact, as the catalogue goes to press has only been manufactured in comparatively small quantities. Fancy star pattern woven reed back surrounded by **very ornamental hand woven reed.** All scrolls on our reed rockers such as the scrolls shown in this rocker are tied to posts and frame instead of being tacked on as is the case with the cheap rockers on the market. This gives them additional strength and durability, a point which you must not overlook when comparing these goods with others which you will see advertised. **Fancy cane wound arms,** close woven cane seat with fancy ornamentations in front and sides. The legs are cane wound, well braced with cane wound braces. Legs are securely attached to rockers. We furnish this rocker **either in natural finish or shellac finish,** as desired.

9127 Our special price, each, natural finish..$5.85
9128 Our special price, each, shellac finish... 6.85

No. 9127.

## Our Finest Reed Rocker for $6.50

We take great pride in directing the attention of our customer to the very beautiful **Ladies' Reed Rocker** as shown in the accompanying illustration. The best efforts of the most expert designers have been used towards bringing out this elegant pattern. This rocker, like our other reed goods, is made by the **leading manufacturer in this line,** a manufacturer who has no real competitors, and whose goods have a reputation that has been sustained for many years. This rocker is made of the choicest reed, **fancy scroll arms, fancy woven back,** very close woven center, back posts decorated with reed ornamentations. The seat is of close woven cane with fancy reed panel in front. Cane wound legs, well braced and securely attached to rockers. This **is** one of the finest pieces in furniture we have ever had the pleasure of cataloguing, and we assure any one who wishes something particularly fine that this rocker will give them far more pleasure than they can even expect from our description or the illustration.

No. 9129.

9129 Our special price, each, natural finish.. $6.50
9130 Our special price, each, shellac finish.... 7.50

**ANY FURNITURE C. O. D. SUBJECT TO EXAMINATION ON RECEIPT OF REGULAR DEPOSIT. 3 PER CENT OFF FULL CASH.**

## A Choice Rocker for $2.75.

No. 9137.          No. 9134.

**The wants of the little ones** must not be overlooked in laying in your supply of furniture. Nothing more handsome, durable or comfortable can be purchased than the beautiful Comfort Rocking Chair for children which is illustrated in accompanying cut. It has **full woven reed roll** around arm and back, fancy ornamented back, **cane wound legs** given additional strength by means of cross braces.

9134 Our special price, each, in natural finish.........................$2.75
9135 Our special price, each, finished in shellac.................... 3.25

## A Very Handsome Rocker for $2.85.

**Nothing will please the little one better** than the rocker which we show in the illustration. Our price is so much lower than you could get anything of similar value for from your local dealer that you cannot afford to buy elsewhere. We wish to emphasize the fact that the quality of these reed goods is unsurpassed, that no other manufacturer in the world makes anything to equal them, hence it is with every confidence that we solicit your trade in this line, knowing that the goods will prove satisfactory to you, not only upon their immediate receipt but after years of usage. This is something that must be taken into consideration in buying goods. This Child's Rocker is made of the usual high grade selected reed found in all our reed goods. Close woven cane seat, fancy star pattern reed back with ornamental scrolls, cane wound arms, fancy turned legs amply well braced and securely attached to rockers.

9137 Our special price, each, natural finish...............................$2.85    9138 Our special price, each, shellac finish...........................$3.50

## A Very Handsome Window Chair for $5.90.

The best efforts of the most expert designers have been put forth in bringing out decidedly new and attractive patterns for 1897. Nothing will exhibit the success of their efforts better than the beautiful Reception or Window Chair as shown in illustration. It is made of the very finest select reed, finely hand woven. **The back is an ornamental scroll,** in fancy design, and the strength is reinforced by braces which are continuations of the rear legs. The seat is close woven reed with fancy woven reed rim. Handsome turned and cane bound legs re-enforced by cross braces. Nothing more handsome can be added to your furniture. It will serve not only as an ornament to any room, but will be found a most desirable and comfortable piece of furniture.

9139 Our special price, each, natural finish............$5.60
9140 Our special price, each, shellac finish.............$6.90

## One of the Newest Designs for 1897.

A peculiarly handsome and decidedly striking pattern that will show off to wonderfully good effect in any home, whether rich or poor. It is, however, not made for ornament alone but for comfort and durability. It is decidedly well constructed of the very finest selected reed, close woven seat, embellished with handsome ornamentations in the way of reed scrolls, balls, etc. The extra strong legs are cane wound and given great additional strength by means of cane wound cross pieces and braces.

9147 Our special price, each, in natural finish........$6.50
9148 Our special price, each, in shellac finish.......$7.50

## A Most Stylish Chair for $6.00.

The illustration will give you some little idea at least of the graceful outline and elegant appearance of this beautiful Reception Chair. It is made like all our reed goods of the best selected reed that can be procured. This Reception Chair has fine close woven cane seat, woven reed back and arm rest. The top of back has very fancy ornamental scroll work of reed, all scrolls being tied to the frame. The front of chair is handsomely ornamented in the way of reed scrolls. The legs are cane wound, well braced. In this chair you will have one of the handsomest pieces of furniture you could place in your parlor. We offer it at 50 per cent. less than the ordinary retail price for the same class of goods.

9149 Our special price, each, natural finish.$6.00
9150 Our special price, each, shellac finish.$7.00

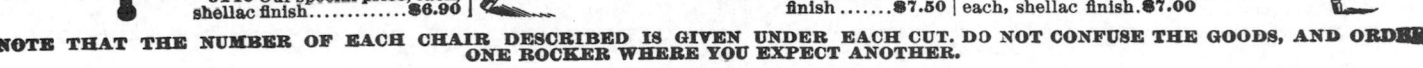

**NOTE THAT THE NUMBER OF EACH CHAIR DESCRIBED IS GIVEN UNDER EACH CUT. DO NOT CONFUSE THE GOODS, AND ORDER ONE ROCKER WHERE YOU EXPECT ANOTHER.**

### Latest 1897 Style Reception Chair.

**No. 9151** We show in the illustration something entirely new in the way of Fancy Ornamental Chairs. The frame is made of the very finest selected material, fancy turned, hand ornamented. The back has fancy turned spindles. The seat is of close woven cane, very comfortable and durable. The legs are well braced with **fancy spindles.** The most ornamental part of this chair can not be brought out in illustration, and that is the finish. We furnish these chairs in **all white enamel or all gold leaf,** as may be desired, and in either finish it is more elegant than we can express in this description or show in an illustration. We only ask you to see this chair that you may be satisfied it is all we claim for it in **elegance and durability.** We guarantee if it is not as represented it may be returned to us and we will cheerfully refund your money.

Our Special Price, each...................$3.60

In ordering be sure to state whether you wish it finished in White Enamel or Gold Leaf.

**No. 9151.**

### Reception Chair in White Enamel or Gold Leaf.

**No. 9152** We show in illustration another **Fancy Reception Chair** which is all the rage at the present time, and one of the most fashionable and desirable chairs on the market. The frame is of the very finest selected, thoroughly seasoned wood and is far more desirable than can be made to appear in illustration. **The back, legs and spindles** throughout are **fancily turned,** giving the chair an elegant appearance without detracting in any way from its strength. Fancy hand carving on back pieces. Hand woven cane seat. The fancy arm braces give additional strength to the back. This is **one of the most artistic chairs** ever put on the market, and we finish it either in White Enamel or Gold Leaf, adding very greatly to its already handsome appearance. In ordering be sure to state whether you want it in White Enamel or Gold Leaf. Remember or special terms. When cash in full accompanies order, 3% may be deducted for cash. Our Special Price, each...................$5.50

**No. 9152.**

### Our Special $2.75 Work Basket.

To those who wish something large, strong and desirable in every respect. We offer the work basket as illustrated herewith. The work basket has large upper and lower compartments. The upper basket is 15x15 in. in size. The lower one is slightly smaller. Both baskets are very roomy and the handle makes it very convenient to move around from place to place. This basket is made of the very best reed that can be procured, handsomely hand woven. The four legs are cane wound and extra well braced.

9153 Our special price, each, in Natural Finish............$2.75
9154 Our special price, each, in Shellac Finish............$3.25

### Child's Cabinet Chair.

9155 A household necessity where there are children. Made of selected reed, with supported table in front. Reed covered seat. This cabinet chair **must not be compared** with cheap willow goods at low prices. Our special price.....$1.75

---

## ✳ THREE HANDY CHAIRS AT CAR-LOAD PRICES. ✳

### Our 52 Cent Folding Chair.

**No. 9157** A convenient, light and handy folding chair is something very much to be desired for camping or outing parties or for lawn use. The chair is made with **a hard maple wood seat,** is constructed of the best seasoned material, thoroughly well put together by the best workmen. When folded it makes a **very compact bundle,** as can be seen by the illustrations accompany-ing.

Our special price, each...................$0.52
Price per dozen.......  6.00

### A 50 Cent Camp Stool for 30 Cents.

**No. 9158** This is the lightest, strongest and most lasting camp stool on the market at anything like our prices. We have very large quantities of these on hand direct from the manufacturer, and are offering them as one of the most convenient articles of the kind that can be produced. This camp stool is made of **best selected frame with duck seat,** wedged and nailed. It folds into a small compass and is very light and convenient to handle. Our special price, each....$0.30
Price per dozen....................  3.40

**No. 9110** We have the same camp stool as above described but without the back. In all other respects it is the same as No. 9109 above.
Our special price, each..$0.20; Per dozen..$2.20

### Our $1.18 Folding Step Ladder.

**No. 9162** The illustration shows our step ladder chair opened for use as a step ladder. The back and rear legs have very strong braces, so that as a step ladder alone it is thoroughly substantial and very rigid. When closed **as a chair** it makes a very desirabe article and **excellent for kitchen use.** It is made of very best hardwood handsomely finished in antique oak and with nicely carved back. It is a step ladder chair that will last for a lifetime and stand rough usage when necessary.
Our special price. each....$1.18

---

## DINING-ROOM AND KITCHEN TABLES. 🌱

### Any Table C. O. D., Subject to Examination, on a Deposit of $5.00. 3 per cent. Discount when Cash in Full Accompanies Order.

### Our $1.35 Kitchen Table.

**No. 9164** The Kitchen Table which we show in the accompanying illustration is made of **bass wood with hard wood legs** and large roomy drawer.

It is strongly constructed and has bolt leg fastenings. It can be taken apart for shipping, thus saving very largely on freight. This table is a household necessity and no kitchen is complete without it. It is made in three sizes, nicely finished. Weighs about 40 lbs. Prices as follows:

| Size of Top. | Price. |
| --- | --- |
| 28x42 inches | $1.35 |
| 30x54 inches | 1.70 |
| 30x60 inches | 2.00 |

**No. 9164½** We have the same table as above illustrated and described, but without drawer. In every other respect it is just the same as above. Made also in three sizes, well finished. Prices as follows:

| | |
| --- | --- |
| Size of top, 28x42 inches, price | $1.25 |
| Size of top, 30x54 inches, price | 1.45 |
| Size of top, 30x60 inches, price | 1.75 |

### Our $5.50 Handy Kitchen Table.

**No. 9165** Among the inventions for assisting the **housekeeper** we know of nothing that is more convenient or satisfactory for household uses than the kitchen table we illustrate above. You can gain but very little idea from the illustration of the genuine value of this special table. It saves the tired housewife many a weary step, and keeps all the articles which can be contained therein sweet and clean. It contains, as shown in illustration, **two flour bins,** one with two compartments and the othe: with one, all of them large and roomy.

Besides, it has two drawers with compartments for cutlery, etc., and **two convenient slides.** This kitchen table is made of the best hard wood with bass wood top and the size of top is 30 x 48 inches. The table is strongly constructed and will last a lifetime. It is well finished and presents a good appearance. It weighs about 60 lbs., and goes as second-class freight. Our special price...................$5.50

### Our $2.10 Breakfast Table.

**No. 9166** This is one of the most desirable and necessary articles of furniture and one that is convenient for breakfast use or for general kitchen use. This is not an extension table, but the leaves at either side may be dropped so that the table will take up little space when not in use. It is made of selected kiln dried ash with handsome antique finish, and we furnish it in either oval top as illustrated or square top as may be desired. The size of top in either case is 42 inches wide by 52 inches long. The table can be taken apart and shipped knocked down, thus saving freight charges.
Our Special Price Each...................$2.10

### Our $3.40 Extension Table.

The **Old Fashioned Round drop Leaf Table** which we show in the illustration is an old time favorite and never goes out of date, nor does it lose any of its desirable features. This table is especially well constructed by one of the best manufacturers in this line of goods. **It is made of fine oak** with an oval top, the size of which is 42x52 inches. Can be taken apart and shipped knocked down, thus saving very largely in the freight rate.

It comes in three lengths at the following prices:

| | | |
| --- | --- | --- |
| No. 9167 | 6 feet | $3.40 |
| No. 9168 | 8 feet | 4.50 |
| No. 9169 | 10 feet | 5.60 |

**A SPLENDID ASSORTMENT OF TABLE LINEN IN OUR DRY GOODS DEPARTMENT. SHIP YOUR TABLE CLOTH AND NAPKINS WITH THE TABLE AND SAVE EXTRA CHARGES. REFER TO INDEX.**

# SIX SPECIAL LEADERS IN DINING TABLES.

### .....A RECORD BREAKING SALE OF HIGH ART FURNITURE.....

## A $5.00 Table for $2.64.

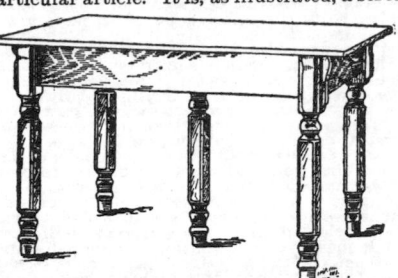

**Never before has such a price been named on a dining table that** possesses any of the qualifications of service and durability found in this particular article. It is, as illustrated, **a strong, substantial table,** not remarkable for beauty, but **excellent for service and entirely presentable in appearance.** It has a very nicely finished solid ash top with hard wood rims and very fancy carved hard wood legs of **extra strength.** This table is made to meet the demands of those who desire an excellent and substantial piece of furniture for the dining room, without the necessity of expending a large amount of money. It is, so far as cabinet work is concerned, thoroughly well constructed, of a material, while not of the highest grade of wood, **very superior in quality and excellently selected.** It possesses an additional feature in the fact that the legs are fastened by bolts to the top of the table, and in shipping they can be taken off, **thus reducing the transportation charges to a minimum.** Weight, packed, about 70 lbs. We make this table in four lengths, 6 ft., 8 ft., 10 and 12 ft. Our special prices are as follows, carefully packed and delivered on board cars at Chicago.

| | | | |
|---|---|---|---|
| No. 9170 | 6 ft. | Price | $2.64 |
| No. 9171 | 8 ft. | Price | 3.52 |
| No. 9172 | 10 ft. | Price | 4.40 |
| No. 9173 | 12 ft. | Price | 5.28 |

## Our $12.75 Extension Table.

**No. 9176 The illustration will give you some idea** of the appearance of one of the **Finest Extension Tables** we have ever handled. Nothing but the finest material enters into its construction. The grain of the quarter sawed oak is unusually handsome, while **the polished finish** given to it by expert workmen is **equal to that of a fine piano.** The top is 46 inches in size, with a solid beaded and ornamented rim. The legs are fancy turned and beaded, while the cross pieces are handsomely decorated and have fancy brackets. The table rests on the most expensive nickle-plated ball-bearing castors, and in every respect it is an article of furniture to be proud of. We pack these tables with the utmost care, and can assure you that they will reach you in the most perfect condition. **Remember that we allow 3 per cent cash discount** if full amount accompanies order. Our guarantee extends to every article we sell whether paid for in advance or not—that it may be returned to us if not as represented.
We make this table in three sizes at the following prices:

| | |
|---|---|
| 8 feet long when extended | $12.75 |
| 10 feet long when extended | 15.50 |
| 12 feet long when extended | 17.50 |

## A Great Bargain for $11.75.

**9177 The Table** which we show in this illustration is one of the latest designs just put on the market. This is a pattern which has just been designed by one of the most expert designers in cabinetwork. The table is made by a **manufacturer whose reputation is second** to none, and the value of the furniture rests not only on its elegant appearance but the quality of the material which enters into its construction and the expert workmanship employed thereon. In fact, the **finest cabinet makers** are employed in the factory from which we get these tables, hence you can be assured you are getting something that is equal to the finest in the land. This table is made of the choicest solid oak with a beautiful hand polished finish. **The top is 46 inches wide. The massive** legs are handsomely beaded and ornamented, extra well braced by fancy cross pieces and upright brackets. The top is surrounded by a solid rim beautifully ornamented, while the castors are the very best nickel plated **ball bearing castors.** We ship these tables securely packed so that there may be no danger of their reaching customers in other than first class condition. We make this table in three sizes when extended, prices as follows:

| | |
|---|---|
| Length 6 feet, our special price | $11.75 |
| Length 10 feet, our special price | 14.00 |
| Length 12 feet, our special price | 16.00 |

## A $15.00 Table for $10.00.

**No. 9179 To get an idea** of the value of the furniture which we offer, it is necessary for you to see and examine it. We would be only too glad to ship one of these tables into your neighborhood, knowing the tremendous benefit it would be to us as an advertisement, and the resulting trade which we would secure from your locality. **It is impossible in a cut to show the handsome grain of the quarter sawed oak** from which this table is made. The top is beautifully hand polished and is 46 inches wide with a solid beaded rim. The legs are handsomely carved, well braced with cross braces, fancily decorated. Nickel plated ball bearing castors of the very best quality, making the table very easy to move about from place to place. We make the table in three lengths at the following prices:

| | |
|---|---|
| Length 8 feet when extended, Our Special Price | $10.00 |
| Length 10 feet when extended, Our Special Price | 14.00 |
| Length 12 feet when extended, Our Special Price | 16.00 |

## A Special Leader at $10.50.

**No. 9180** This Specially handsome extension table is made of the finest of quarter sawed oak. It is a table which will give delight to every purchaser, and we can not recommend it too highly. **We guarantee that if you are not pleased with anything in this line you can return it to us and we shall be pleased to refund your money.** The top is 46 inches wide, has massive carved and beaded legs 6 inches in diameter. The table rests on the **best ball bearing nickel plated castors,** and is a piece of furniture that will retail at 50 per cent. more than our factory to consumer price. We can not speak too highly of the specially fine workmanship that is displayed in this article. The material is the best that the market affords and the manufacturer is the best in his line. Hence, in this piece of furniture you will have **something unusually fine** at a price which you would pay for inferior goods from your local dealer. Made in three lengths at the following prices:

| | |
|---|---|
| Length 8 feet when extended | $10.50 |
| Length 10 feet when extended | 14.25 |
| Length 12 feet when extended | 16.25 |

## An $18.00 Table for $12.00.

**No. 9181.** The illustration is scarcely sufficient to enable you to determine the excellent value of this elegant Pillar Extension Table. It is, however, made of the very finest selected solid oak with a beautiful hand polished finish equal to that of the finest piano. In appearance it is decidedly handsome and is unusually massive, the legs being 6 inches in diameter and are fitted with the very finest nickel plated **ball bearing castors.** The castors which we furnish with this table are unusually desirable from the fact that there is no danger of wrinkling or tearing the carpet when moving the table in any direction. The size of the top when table is closed is 46 inches wide. It has a **solid rim, handsomely ornamented.** This is beyond doubt one of the best bargains we have ever been able to offer in the way of extension tables, not only by reason of the unusually handsome appearance, but by reason of the construction. the table being made by one of the leading manufacturers, who takes especial **pride in the quality of the goods** he turns out. Remember that we allow a discount of 3 per cent. when full cash accompanies order. Our guarantee on every article we sell is that it shall be as represented, or it can be returned to us and **money will be refunded.** This table comes in three lengths. Prices as follows:

| | |
|---|---|
| 8 feet long when extended | $12.00 |
| 10 feet long when extended | 14.50 |
| 12 feet long when extended | 16.50 |

**WE PACK OUR GOODS WITH GREAT CARE. WE MAKE NO CHARGE FOR BURLAP, PACKING OR BOXING. GOODS ARE SURE TO REACH YOU IN FIRST CLASS ORDER.**

# WONDERFUL BARGAINS IN SIDEBOARDS, BUFFETS AND CHINA CLOSETS.

## A $12.50 Sideboard for $8.50.

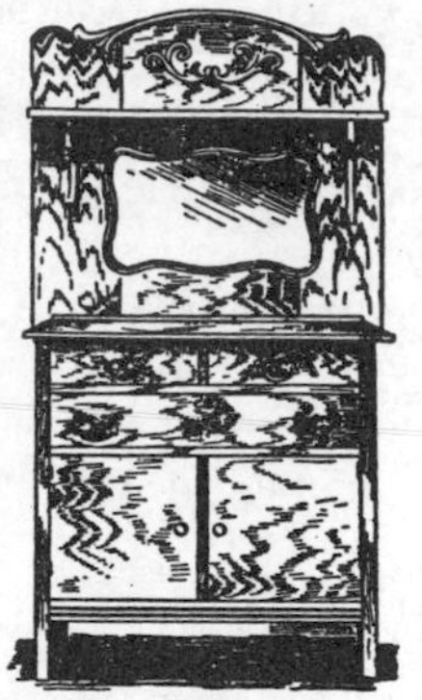

**No. 9189 The Solid Oak Sideboard which we illustrate** is the product of one of the best manufacturers in the country. The designs which we show in sideboards are entirely new for the season of 1897, and while this sideboard is **unusually cheap** for the quality, the style of decoration and general appearance are that of a much more expensive one. **The top is ornamented with hand carving** and is fitted with a convenient shelf supported by brackets. The fancy pattern mirror is 14x24 inches in size, and is made of the best imported plate glass. The top of the base is 20x38 inches in size. The base is **fitted with one large and two small drawers**, one of the small drawers being **lined with plush** for silverware. The drawers are fitted with cast brass handles and locks and keys. Below are large compartments with doors. The height of the sideboard is six feet and the sides are paneled and perfectly finished. Weighs when packed for shipment about 75 lbs.
Our special price.... ........................**$8.50**

## Wonderful Bargain $14.00 Sideboard.

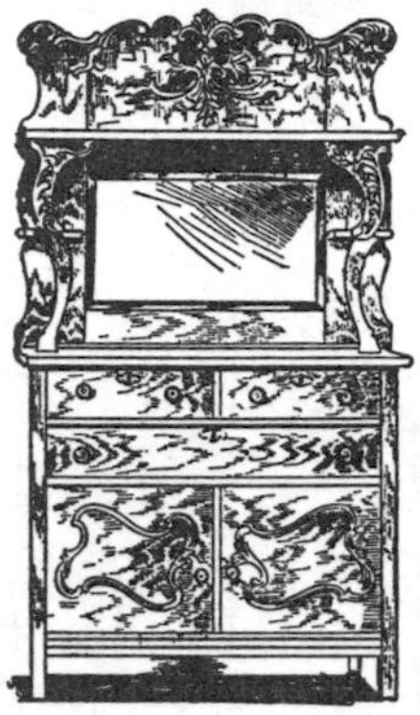

**No.9190 You can only appreciate the unheard-of value** we are offering in this sideboard by seeing the article itself. We would take pleasure in receiving your order, either with cash in full when we will allow a discount of 3 per cent., or with a deposit as required. when we will ship the sideboard C. O. D, subject to examination. **We know that you would be so well pleased** with it and with the value that we give you for your money that you could not help recommending us to your friends and neighbors, and we would thus be sure of an increased trade in your locality. This sideboard is made of the **very finest solid oak**, beautifully quarter-sawed and elegantly finished. **The top is fancy shaped** and decorated with a beautiful moulding and hand-carving. The top shelf is supported by very **fancy brackets.** There are also two small shelves on either side of the mirror. These are very convenient for china, vases, etc. **The mirror is square**, 16x28 inches in size, and made of the **finest imported German bevel plate** glass. The top of the base is fancy curved pattern shaped, entirely different from the old style usually found in small retail stores. The top is 20x42 inches in size. It is fitted with large and small drawers and **roomy compartments.** The drawers have cast brass knobs while the doors below are decorated with very fine pattern rococo moulding. The base board is beaded and the sides are paneled and finished. One of the small drawers is lined with plush for silverware. The height of the dresser is 6 feet and it weighs when packed for shipment about 200 pounds, Our special price, each.................................. **$14.00**

## A $30.00 Sideboard for $20.00.

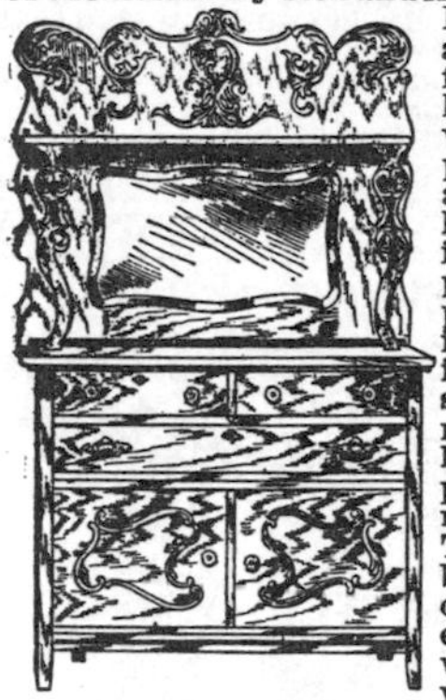

**No. 9191 It is impossible for you to gain from the illustration** any idea of the decidedly rich and imposing appearance of this magnificent sideboard. It is made of the very choicest quarter sawed oak and thoroughly well finished throughout with a finish equal to that of the finest piano. The top has the **finest hand carving** imaginable after a **very graceful design,** while the shelf is fancy pattern shaped and the supports are decorated with hand carving. The mirror is handsome pattern shape and is 17 x 30 inches in size, made of the best **imported German plate-glass.** The top of the base is also fancy pattern shape, the ends and sides being curved instead of square. The top is 23 inches by 46 inches in size. The base is fitted with **large and small drawers** as well as large, roomy compartments. The drawers are fitted with cast **brass handles and knobs,** while the doors to the compartments are decorated with **beautiful rococo molding,** and are fitted with cast brass knobs. The sides are handsomely paneled and finished, base board is beaded. The height of the sideboard complete is 6 feet 4 inches. One of the small drawers is lined with plush for silverware. Weight, when packed for shipment, about 200 lbs. We would take pleasure in shipping this sideboard to your locality, knowing the excellent satisfaction it would give and the increased trade is would direct to us. If you desire to take advantage of **our liberal C. O. D. terms,** we shall be glad to send the sideboard subject to examination, balance to be paid upon receipt of goods. **If cash in full** accompanies order we will allow a discount of 3 per cent. **We guarantee satisfaction** on all our furniture. Our special price, each............**$20.00**

## A $30.00 China Closet for $20.00.

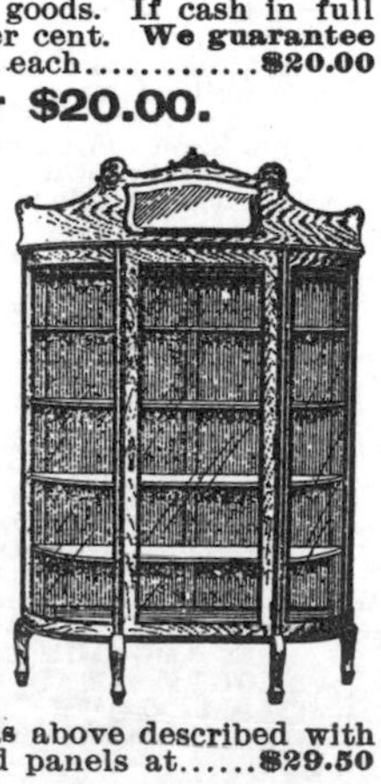

**No. 9196. The only way in which you can form any idea of the elegance** of this beautiful china closet is to see the article itself. The illustration can not do it half justice, you can form no idea of of its elegant appearance. It is made of the **finest quarter sawed oak with swell sides and swell front.** The wood work is all highly polished by hand, the finish being equal to that of the finest piano. The height of the case is 73 inches and the width 48 inches. The **shelves are adjustable.** The case weighs about 175 lbs. Nothing can be more attractive for a dining room than this beautiful china closet, and those who have handsome china to display will find it one of the most desirable articles they could purchase. **We guarantee it to be wonderful value,** and if any customer who purchases it does not find it exactly as represented we shall certainly be glad to have them return it to us and we will promptly refund money. We have this much confidence in the goods we sell.

We make the special price on this buffet as described above................ ..............**$20.00**

**No. 9197. We can also furnish the same buffet** as above described with **fancy mirror back** in rear of shelves instead of wood panels at......**$29.50**

## A $32.00 Sideboard for $21.00.

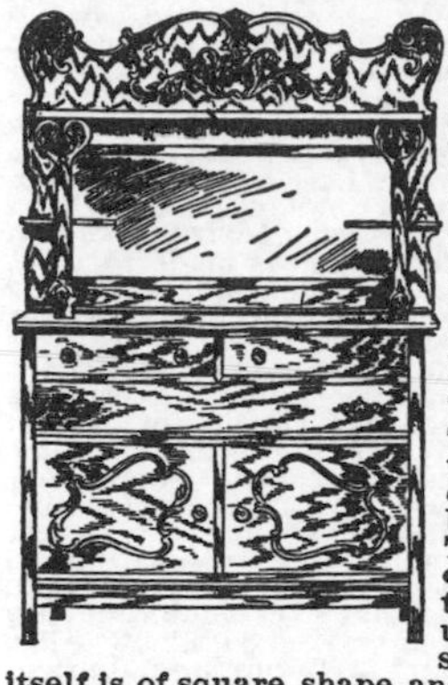

**No. 9192. We save you one-third of what the retailer would charge** you for these elegant goods. It is only possible for us to supply our customers with these stylish and high grade goods by furnishing them direct from the factory on the smallest possible percentage of profit. The prices are furthermore greatly reduced from the fact that our buying facilities are such that we are able to make special cash offers for large quantities, thus securing prices which no retail dealer can ever expect to receive. **We share all these benefits** with our customers, and believe that we can give you more value for your money than any other concern in existence. **If** you want to see a more complete line of sideboards send for our **special Furniture Catalogue. The Sideboard** which we will show in illustration is massive in appearance, unusually well constructed of the very **finest quarter sawed oak,** beautifully polished and finished throughout. The illustration can not do half justice to the **elegant hand carving** or fancy pattern shape of the top. **The large top shelf** is supported by unique design supports while there are two small shelves at each side of the mirror. The mirror itself is of square shape and unusually large in size. **It is massive in appearance,** being 18x40 in. in size, and is made of the best imported German bevel plate glass. The top of the base is fancy curved pattern instead of the old style square shape. The base has a large roomy drawer for linens and two small drawers for silverware, one of them being **lined with plush.** The smaller compartments below have large doors with **cast brass knobs** and are decorated with fancy rococo molding. The base board is beaded and the sides are paneled and finished. Height of sideboard complete is 6 feet 4 in. and it weighs when packed for shipment about 250 lbs. We pack and crate these sideboards with the utmost care, and they are sure to reach you in the best possible condition. Our special price.............................. **$21.00**

## Our Finest Sideboard for $25.00.

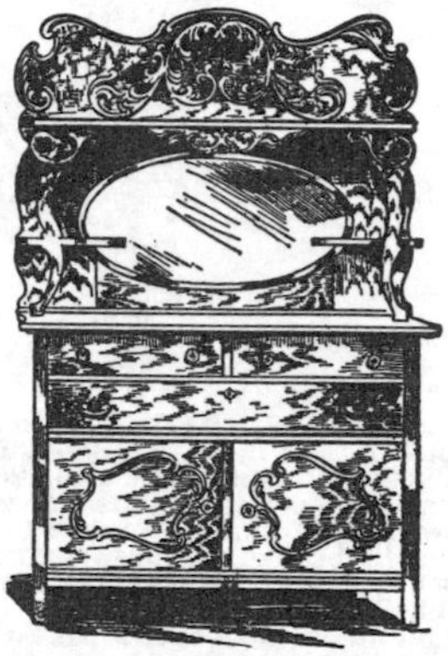

**No. 9193 You cannot expect to find such a Sideboard** as we show in illustration in any retail store at **less than $40.00,** and, in fact it is **difficult** to presume that you would find such a quality of goods in any of the smaller local dealers' stocks. These goods are the very latest and most fashionable designs for 1897, goods that are just being made for the first time by the leading manufacturer, and goods that we offer at an unheard of price from the fact that we are able to contract for them in large quantities. It is scarcely possible to describe this sideboard and do it half justice. We know that the illustration will not give you an idea of **its superb and massive appearance.** The style of the **carving on the top,** the **fancy pattern shaped mirror,** the elegantly **ornamented front,** are things whose value you can only perceive by seeing the sideboard itself. The large shelf at top has fancy hand carved front and is supported by unique supports decorated with hand carving. The two additional shelves at each side of the mirror are very convenient for vases, etc. The mirror itself is made of the very best **French bevel plate,** is oval in shape and 18x36 inches in size. The top of base is fancy carved pattern and is 23x53 inches in size. The height of the sideboard is 6 feet 4 inches, so you can see it is not only very attractive in appearance but very large and massive. The drawers and doors in base are fitted with cast brass knobs. The doors are decorated with fancy molding, and one small drawer is **lined with plush for silverware.** The base board is beaded and sides are handsomely paneled. This sideboard is made of choicest oak, beautifully quarter-sawed, showing the grain of the wood perfectly and so finely polished that it presents an elegant appearance. Weighs complete when packed for shipment, about 250 pounds. Our special price, each..................................**$25.00**

## Our $24.50 Buffet.

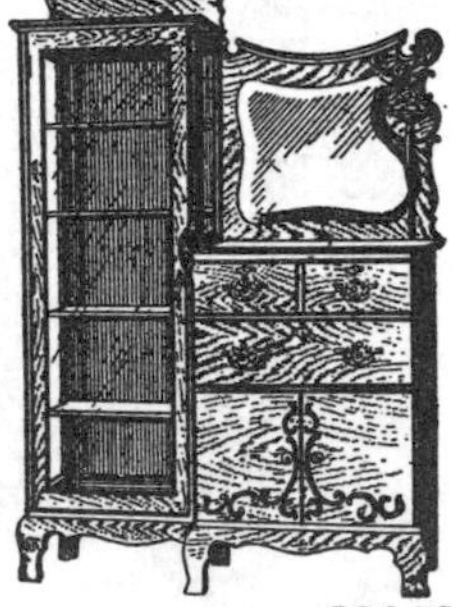

**No. 9194. We have had a growing demand for handsome dining room furniture** in the way of well made and attractive buffets. We have been fortunate in making contracts with one of the leading manufacturers in this line of goods, and are offering the beautiful buffet in **quarter sawed oak,** as shown in illustration, at an unusually low price. This buffet stands 75 in. high and is 50 inches wide. It is, as stated above, made from choicest quarter sawed oak, decorated with beautiful hand carving. The extra **heavy bevel plate mirror** is fancy pattern shape and 18x22 inches in size. The door of cabinet is fitted with **double thick glass,** and has lock and key and fancy handle. The drawers are large and roomy, one drawer being lined with plush for silverware. Large cupboard at bottom with doors. Fancy pattern base. The buffet weighs about 175 lbs. when packed for shipment. Our Special Price............ ............**$24.50**

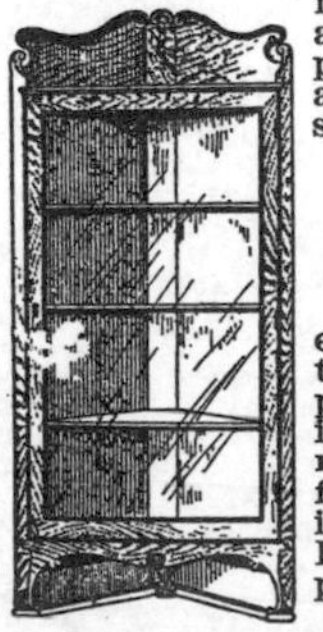

## Our $10.00 Corner China Cabinet.

**No. 9196 The Corner China Cabinet** is one of the most economical and desirable pieces of furniture one can add to his home. It takes up very little space as it can be placed in a corner of the dining room, and at the same time it is attractive in outline and beautiful in finish. It is **made of the finest quarter sawed oak** with fine polished finish. The large glass in the door is of double strength and is the best clear glass made. The shelves are portable. Height of the case is 70 inches; width 31 inches; weight packed for shipment about 75 lbs.
Our special price....................................**$10.00**

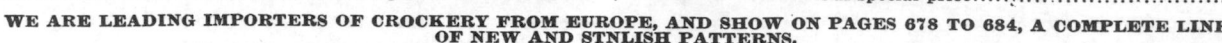

WE ARE LEADING IMPORTERS OF CROCKERY FROM EUROPE, AND SHOW ON PAGES 678 TO 684, A COMPLETE LINE OF NEW AND STNLISH PATTERNS.

# Challenge Sale of Parlor Tables.

**Prices that Defy Competition. Shipped on Liberal Terms, C. O. D., Subject to Examination, or 3 per cent. for full cash with order.**

## PARLOR TABLES.

**OUR 95c BARGAIN.**

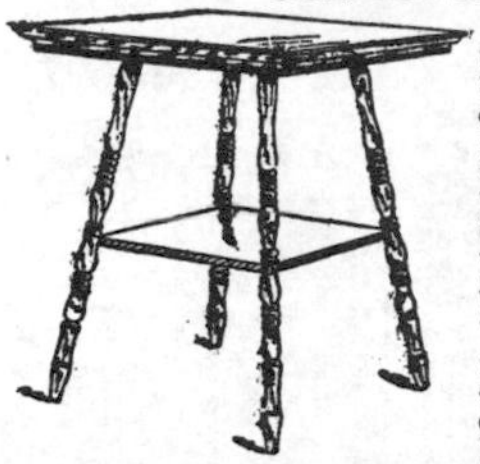

**No. 9200 It does not seem possible that any manufacturer can turn** out an elegant, large parlor table, thoroughly well made, at anything like the price we offer. This table is made by the leading manufacturer in this line, a manufacturer whose reputation is second to none in the quality of the goods that he turns out. We contracted for a large supply of these tables, and our only fear is that we may not be able to supply the immense demand which will naturally result from putting on the market a fine, high-grade table at the low price we name. **This table is made of the choicest selected and well seasoned ash,** finished in antique oak. Size of the top is 24 x 24 inches. Fancy turned legs, large shelf, which is convenient for books, magazines, etc. This center table can be taken apart and shipped knocked down, thus saving very largely on the freight. It is very easily set up, extra strong, and just as handsome as you could wish. Weighs about 25 pounds. Last year we could not secure a table of this quality to sell for less than $1.20.

Our special price now, each....................**$0.95**

## Fine Parlor Table for $1.30.

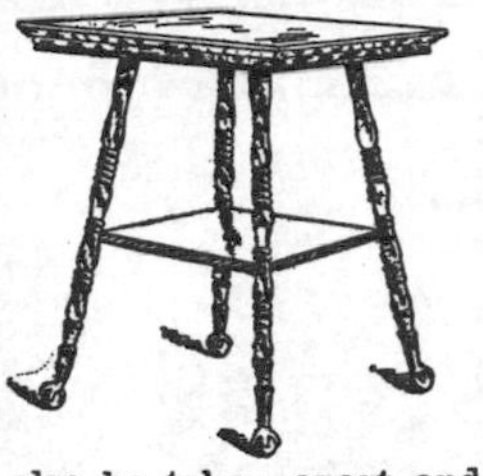

**No. 9202. This table** is very similar to No. 9200, illustrated and described above. It is the same size and is made of the very best kiln dried ash, **finished in antique oak.** The extra feature about this table is the **solid brass claw feet,** which add very greatly to its appearance and save the carpet from the wear occasioned by other tables. This table can also be taken apart and shipped knocked down, weighing about 25 lbs.

Our Special Price, each....................**$1.30**

## A Large Solid Oak Parlor Table for $1.35.

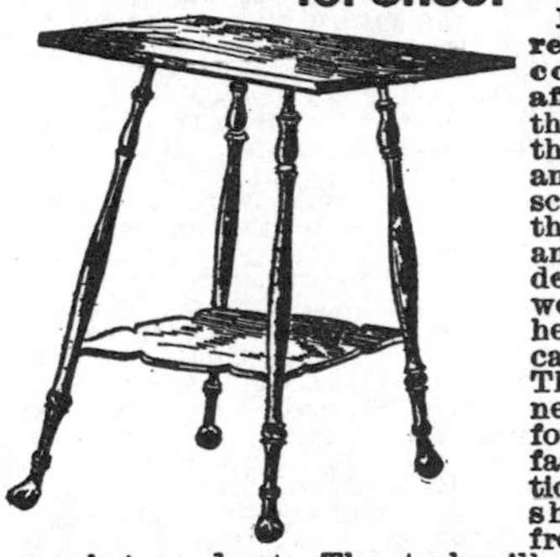

**No. 9204 No retail dealer could possibly afford** to sell you this table for less than $2.25 to $2.50, and, in fact, it is scarcely possible that you will find any of the new designs such as we are showing herein in your local dealer's store. This is one of the newest patterns for 1897, and, in fact, the illustration which we show is made from the first sample turned out. The stock will scarcely be on the market until this catalogue reaches your hands, and hence you will not be able to find such goods in your town. We are making the price exceedingly low for we want your trade. As stated above, this table is made of the **very finest solid oak,** top is 20x20 inches in size, with a **very fancy pattern** below. Legs are fancy turned with brass feet. Weight about 35 lbs. Our special price, each..........**$1.35**

## A $3.25 Table for $2.05.

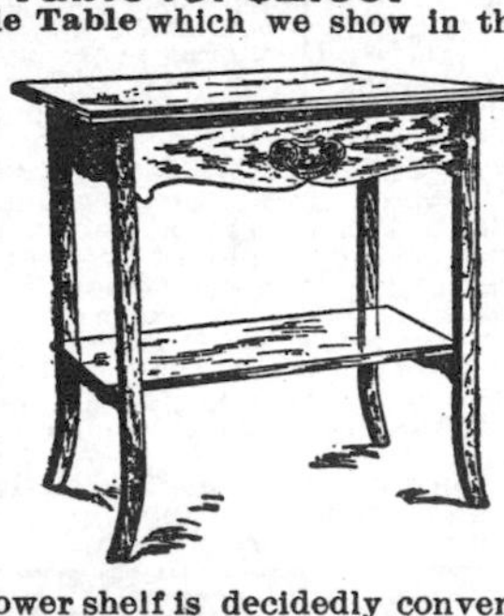

**No. 9206 The Side Table** which we show in the cut is a very desirable piece of furniture, and at our factory to consumer price is within the reach of the most limited means. This table is made of the very finest kiln dried ash with an **elegant antique oak finish.** The size of top is 20 inches wide by 28 inches long. It has one **drawer with cast brass handle.** This table is thoroughly well made, and the lower shelf is decidedly convenient. Weight packed for shipment, about 40 pounds. Our special price, each....................**$2.05**

## A Solid Oak Table for $1.48.

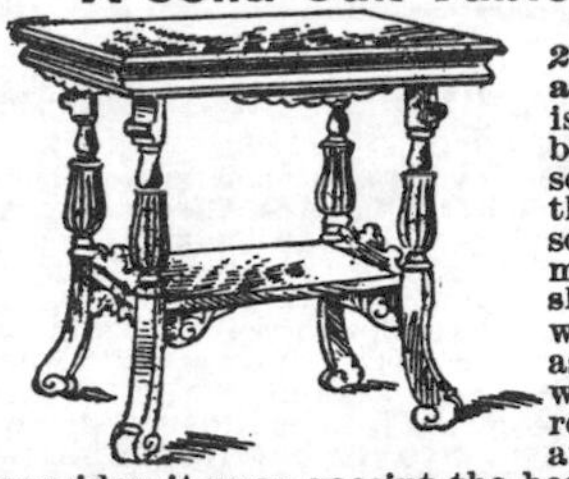

**No. 9207 The top is 22 x 28 inch. in size, and the table entire** is made of the very best solid oak, handsomely finished throughout. Top has solid rim, fancy ornaments. **The lower shelf is ornamented** with similar design as top. This table weighs about 35 lbs., ready for shipment, and if you do not consider it upon receipt the best bargain you ever saw for the money you are at liberty to return it to us and we will cheerfully refund you the amount paid. We want you to be pleased, and are prepared to do everything in our power to satisfy you.

Our special price, each....................**$1.48**

## A $3.00 Table for $2.00.

**No. 9209. We illustrate in this table** another very great reduction in price which our buying facilities have secured. In fact, we are offering this table now at 20 per cent. less than last year's price. Size of top is 22x30 inches, **with solid rim** all around and fancy lower shelf handsomely decorated. The legs are very strong and elegant in appearance. We offer this table as one of the best bargains that we have ever secured, and guarantee that every customer receiving it will be **delighted with the value** which he gets. Nothing can be secured from retail dealers of the same value for **less than 50 per cent.** more than our price. Remember our 3 per cent. discount when **cash** in full accompanies order.

Our Special Price for this table....................**$2.00**

## A $4.50 Table for $2.90.

**No. 9211 The Table which we show in this illustration** is also made of the very finest selected solid oak, beautifully polished, legs turned and carved, **fancy shelf with ornamental braces.** The top of this table is 22 inches wide and 30 inches long with solid rim. The illustration does not do the table half justice, and we can only assure our customers that they will not be disappointed in its unusually high quality; in fact, it is impossible to give you more than half an idea of the appearance of any of these goods from the illustrations herein. If you will take our word for it that **no such bargains exist elsewhere** as we are able to catalogue; we will guarantee you entire satisfaction, and assure you that if goods are not entirely up to our representations they may be returned and we will promptly refund your money. We want your trade and are determined that if we once secure it we shall keep it by giving you such goods as you could not secure elsewhere for the price.

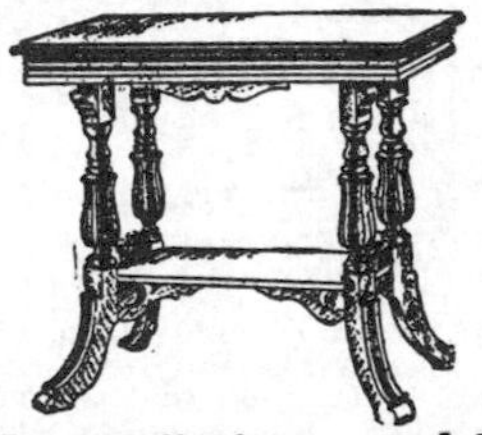

Our special price....................**$2.90**

## Our Wonderful $1.38 Offer.

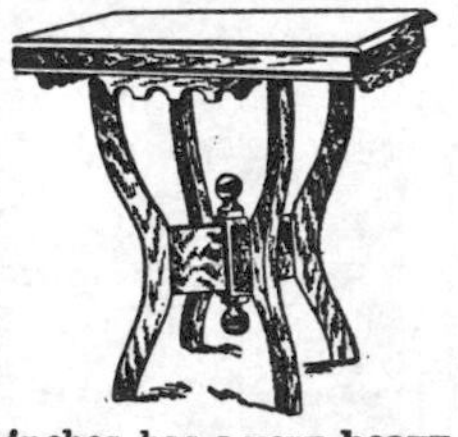

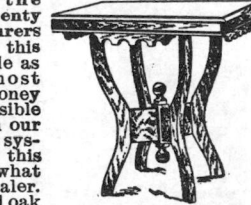

**No. 9212 From the Samples of Over Twenty Different Manufacturers** we have selected this beautiful parlor table as representing the most value for the least money of anything it is possible for us to secure. On our factory to consumer system we offer to you this table at about half what you pay your retail dealer. It is made of fine solid oak with a top 22 inches by 28 inches, has a very **heavy solid ornamental rim,** is well finished and well made. The fancy shaped legs are well braced by cross pieces, decorated in the center with turn balls. We would like nothing better than to introduce one of these tables into your neighborhood for we know if your neighbors would know you had paid but $1.38 for this table they would be anxious to become our customers for similar goods. **We depend upon our old customers** for new trade, and take extra pains to serve them and save them money on every article they purchase. Our special price, each........**$.138**

## Our $2.98 Parlor Table.

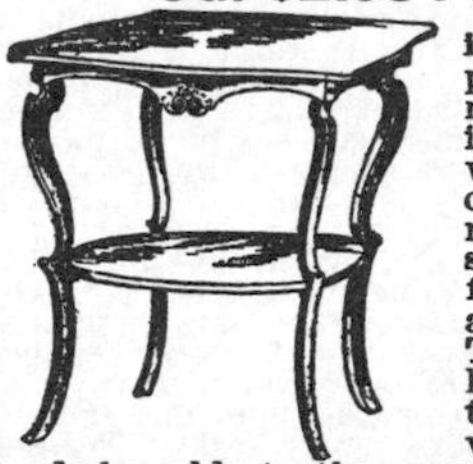

**No. 9214 We are giving wonderful values in** parlor tables, and this is not better illustrated than in the case of the table which we show in the accompanying cut. It is made of the **very finest solid oak, with a beautiful polished top,** having an elegantly carved rim. **The fancy shaped legs are** handsomely carved, while the oval lower shelf is a very great convenience and also adds to the appearance of the table itself. This table weighs about 50 lbs., packed for shipment, and the freight will be very little compared with what we can save you in price. In fact, we can lay this table down at your freight depot and when you have paid the freight on it you will find that **you have secured it at 50 per cent less** than your local dealer would charge you for goods put up by inferior manufacturers and goods that will not stand the usage this table can receive.

Our special price, each....................**$2.98**

## A $6.00 Table for $3.50.

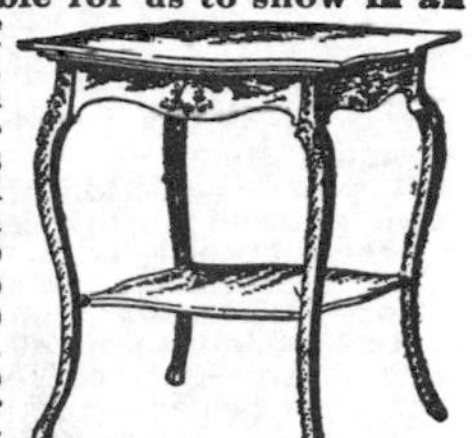

**No. 9216 It is impossible for us to show in an Illustration** but a few of of the points of beauty, strength and finish which are contained in this elegant parlor table. It is of unique and **graceful design, handsome enough for the parlor of the richest home** and cheap enough to be within the means of the poorest. This table is made of the choicest selected **quarter sawed oak,** very finely polished and finished, in fact, has a finish equal to that of the finest **piano.** Very fancy pattern shaped rim with elegant **hand** carving. The top of legs are also **handsomely decorated** while the pattern-shaped lower shelf is **very** convenient and adds greatly to the appearance **and** strength of the table. Packed for shipment **it** weighs about 40 lbs. Our Special Price, each..**$3.50**

## A $6.50 Table for $4.10.

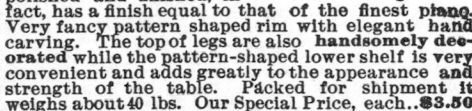

**No. 9218 The chances are that you will never see such an elegant piece of furniture in a local dealer's store, or if it is found** the price will be so exorbitant that you will not feel able to afford it. **By placing large contracts with the leading manufacturers** in the line of parlor tables we are able to secure such prices as will put you on the same footing as your local dealer in the matter of prices. We take pride in calling your attention to the table illustrated above, from the fact that it is one of the best productions of the leading manufacturer in the country. **This table is made of the choicest birch,** with an imitation mahogany finish, **making the prettiest table** it is possible to produce. The top is 26x26 inches in size, with solid rim, while the **fancy turned legs** have polished **brass** claw feet. The fancy pattern lower shelf is attached to the legs and supported by polished brass brackets, a unique design adding very greatly to the appearance and strength of the table. The weight of the table when packed for shipment is about 50 lbs.

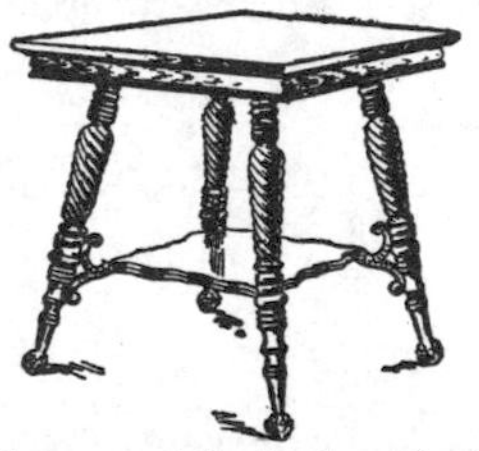

A wonderful bargain at our special price of..**$4.10**

**No. 9218½ We can also furnish the same table in** solid quarter sawed oak, elegantly finished and polished. Our special price, each............**$4.60**

## A Wonderful Bargain at $8.95.

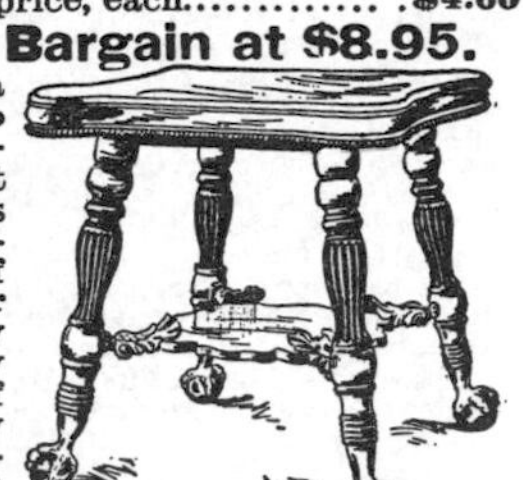

**No. 9219 This is a table that has only to be seen to be fully appreciated.** We cannot show in a cut any of its best points of excelence. It is made of the very finest **quarter sawed oak or curly birch with mahogany finish.** Either style of wood is sufficiently handsome for the richest parlor. It is a large table, the top being 28x 28 inches, with a fine **polish finish like that of the finest piano.** The feet are made of highly polished brass, claw shaped with glass balls. The fancy pattern shelf is supported by and attached to the legs by means of brass brackets. In fact, in every way this is a table to be proud of, will give the longest service and will never lose its beauty. Weight packed for shipment, 65 pounds.

Our special price, each....................**$8.95**

**No. 9220 We also have the same table in solid mahogany,** decidedly rich in appearance and magnificent in design. Our special price, each....**$12.25**

**THE MOST STYLISH LINE OF LACE CURTAINS EVER IMPORTED FROM EUROPE IS QUOTED ON FULL PLATE PAGES OF DRY GOODS DEPARTMENT.—— SEE INDEX.**

**OUR MAMMOTH SPECIAL FURNITURE CATALOGUE IS FREE.** IT QUOTES EVERYTHING KNOWN IN THE FURNITURE TRADE. We won't quarrel on Prices.

**WE QUOTE A FULL LINE OF TABLE SCARFS, ETC., IN OUR DRY GOODS DEPARTMENT. BUY SUCH ARTICLES AS YOU NEED AT THE SAME TIME YOU GET YOUR FURNITURE AND SAVE EXTRA FREIGHT.**

# LIBRARY AND OFFICE FURNITURE.

**The Choicest Bargains Selected from the Leading Products of Foremost Manufacturers. Shipped on Liberal C. O. D. Terms, or 3 Per Cent. off for Full Cash.**

### A $3.00 Table for $1.98.

No. 9221 **We doubt if you will find anything in your local market** to equal this table in style or appearance at anything like the retail price named above. This table is made of fine quarter sawed oak or curly birch with mahogany finish. Either wood is very desirable and in either case the table will be as handsome as one could desire. It is handy as well as ornamental. It is light and can easily be moved from place to place. **The fancy pattern top** is 24x24 inches in size with the very best finish. The pattern shelf below is very convenient as a **receptacle for books, magazines,** and at the same time adds strength. We offer this as one of the best results of the cabinet maker's art, and assure our customers that if it is not **just as represented in every respect** it can be returned to us and we will cheerfully and promptly refund your money. Remember our 3 per cent discount for cash in full with order. Weight of this table about 35 lbs. Our special price......**$1.98**

### A $8.50 Library Table for $5.65.

No. 9222 **The Library Table which we show** in the illustration is an entirely new pattern and is made by the acknowledged leaders in the manufacture of Library and Parlor Tables. We have selected this table from over 100 different designs submitted to us for selection, and consider it the best bargain we could possibly secure for our trade. **On our one small profit plan** we are offering this table at 50 per cent less than retailers would ever care to sell it for. It is made of the **finest quarter-sawed oak with an elegant polish finish** equal to that of a fine piano. The large roomy drawer has fancy cast brass handle, which adds greatly to the appearance of the table itself. **Fancy French bent legs** are decorated with carving, while the shelf is supported by and attached to the legs by fancy brass brackets. Size of the top is 22 inches wide by 32 inches long. In this table you have a large and convenient piece of furniture, which is thoroughly well constructed, **beautiful in outline** and most desirable in price. Weight, packed for shipment, about 65 lbs. Our special price..**$5.65**

### A Special Bargain for $11.50.

No. 9223 **The Library Table** which we show in illustration is made of the **choicest quarter sawed oak** of a very high polish finish, equal to that of the finest piano. The size of top is 28 inches wide by 42 inches long. You can judge therefore that the table is a large one, very roomy as well as handsome in appearance. The top has drawer with fancy cast brass handle. **The Elegant Turned Legs have Polished Brass Claw Feet** with round glass balls. The fancy pattern shelf is supported by and attached to the legs by **Polished Brass Brackets.** The weight of this table is about 85 lbs. when packed for shipment. It is a table that would ordinarily retail at not less than $15.00 to $18.00.

Our Special Price, each.................. **$11.50**

### $8.75 Pays for a $12.00 Toilet Table.

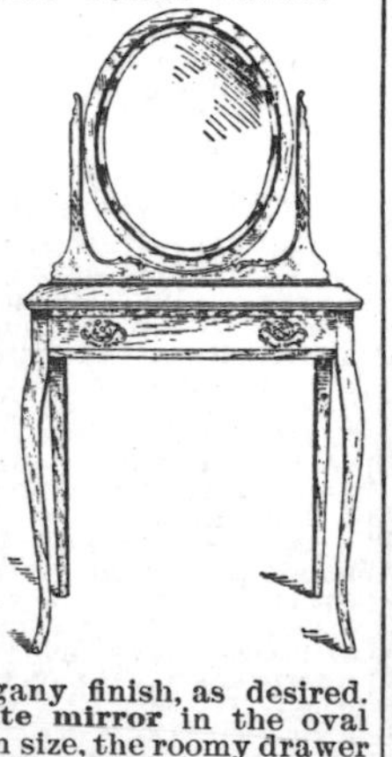

No. 9224 **We have secured for the benefit** of our customers a remarkable bargain in the way of **a Toilet Table,** and our artist has endeavored to give you some idea of its appearance in the illustration. However, you can only form half an idea of its beautiful appearance and **elegant design,** and we can only ask you to depend on it that it is the best bargain in the way of a toilet table that has ever been offered. **We guarantee that you will be pleased** with it, and if you do not find it unusually high value and just as represented it may be returned to us and we will promptly return your money. This toilet table is made of **selected quarter sawed oak** or **fine birch** with imitation mahogany finish, as desired. The fine **French bevel plate mirror** in the oval swing frame is 18x28 inches in size, the roomy drawer has fancy handles and the French bent legs are after the latest patterns. Our special price....**$8.75**

**No. 9224½ We have this Toilet Table** also in very choice select bird's-eye maple, a wood that is peculiarly handsome and always desirable.

Our special price............................**$10.00**

### A $15.00 Combination Book Case for $9.50.

**It seems impossible for a manufacturer to turn out such an elegant Library Case and Secretary** as we show in the accompanying cut for the price we mention. In order to appreciate the unusual value which we give in this line of goods it is necessary to see and examine the article itself. The illustration can give you but a small idea of the general excellence and the **high class workmanship** employed in the manufacture of these goods. This book case is made of the best and most select solid oak, very handsomely finished throughout. The top is decorated with **hand carving,** the drop leaf secretary has also handsome ornamentation. The door to the book case is fitted with **double thick glass,** while the shelves are adjustable and can be placed at any height desired. The secretary is **fitted with pigeon holes and drawer,** and below is a compartment very handy for magazines, etc., fitted with lock and key. The case rests on castors and is very convenient to move about. Height, 5 feet 8 inches, width, 3 feet 4 inches. Weight, packed for shipment, about 140 lbs. **No. 9238.** Our special price.....**$9.50**

### Our $18.00 Case for $11.00.

No. 9240 **The Demand for the Combination Book Case** which we illustrate has been so unusually large during the past season that we have made arrangements with the manufacturer to make us up a large quantity for 1897 trade. By reason of placing a large contract we are able to reduce the price somewhat, and are now selling for $11.00, a case that could not ordinarily be purchased in a retail store for less than $18.00, and the chances are that you would find no such elegant case in any local dealer's stock. This case is made of **Beautiful Quarter Sawed Oak,** handsomely carved by hand, and has an elegant French beveled plateglass mirror in back, fancy shaped. The **Drop Leaf Writing Table** is handsomely decorated and the interior is supplied with pigeon holes and drawers. The door to the book case is fitted with double thick glass 14 inches wide by 44 inches high. There is a large compartment below with door fitted with lock and key. The height of case is 66 inches and the width is 33 inches. It is handsomely finished throughout. Weighs packed for shipment, about 135 lbs.

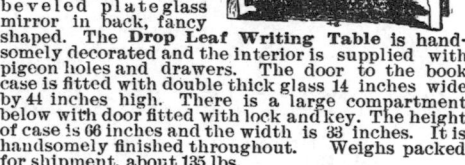

Our Special Price.................................. **$11.00**

**We can furnish the same case in Imitation Mahogany for $11.50.**

### Our $11.50 Bargain.

No. 9241 **The Combination Book Case** which we show in the illustration, is one of the choicest designs for the season of 1897. It is made either in **oak or birch** at prices given below. This book case has glass door with extra thick heavy glass and the shelves in the book case proper are removable and can be adjusted to any height desired. The very **handsome hand carvings** on this case add very greatly to its appearance, while the beautiful French plate mirror at the top is 10 by 14 inches in size and adds much to its attractiveness. The height of the case is 64 inches and the width 39 inches. **The case has drop leaf secretary** with pigeon holes and compartments within. The weight of the case complete is 125 lbs. As stated above, we make it in oak or birch at the following prices: Oak.............................................**$11.50**
Birch............................................ **12.00**

### An $18.00 Book Case for $11.75.

No. 9242 **Only by contracting for very large quantities** of the book cases shown in illustration are we able to hammer the prices down to the lowest ever known. This case is not only made of the best selected oak but the fine quarter-sawing adds **great elegance to its general appearance.** The decorations in the way of fancy pattern top and handsome hand carving add very greatly to the attractiveness of the case. **This case is 69 in. high and 40 in. wide.** The door to the book case is fitted with double-thick glass of extra strength, while the shelves are adjustable. The drop-leaf writing table is decorated with hand carving while the inside of the secretary is fitted with **pigeon holes and drawers.** Fancy pattern shaped mirror, size 10 x 14 inches. Large roomy compartment below. Fancy pattern base. Best castors. Weight, packed for shipment, about 155 lbs. Our special price........................**$11.75**

### A $35.00 Cylinder Book Case for $23.00.

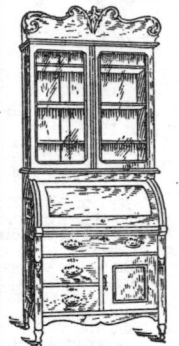

No. 9243 **Nothing can possibly be more desirable** for a library than the **handsome Cylinder Book Case** which we have undertaken to illustrate in the accompanying cut. We regret that we can give you so little idea of its elegant appearance. However, we can say that it is made of the choicest quarter sawed oak, with a beautiful polished finish, and is made by a manufacturer who has no rivals in this particular line. We have taken unusual pains this season to handle nothing but the best goods on the market, and in offering this book case can assure our customers that we are giving them the benefit of the lowest price and the best goods that have ever been secured. This book case has **large roomy shelves,** the shelves being adjustable to any height. The top is beautifully decorated with **hand carving,** while the doors of the book case are fitted with double thick glass. **The secretary has cylinder cover,** which can be pushed back into the case, leaving the writing desk exposed, with **drawers, cabinets and pigeon holes.** Below the writing desk is one large roomy drawer and two small ones, also handy compartment with door. The drawers have fancy cast brass handles, while compartment has lock and key. The sides of the book case are **handsomely paneled and elegantly finished.** The case rests on excellent castors. The height of the case is 7 feet 6 inches and width 38 inches, depth 24 inches. Case, packed for shipment, weighs about 175 lbs.

Our special price....................................**$23.00**

### Solid Oak Book Case for $4.35.

No. 9244 **There may be Book Cases on the Market** that are sold at lower prices, but there is nothing **within 50 per cent more** than our price which will equal the above case in quality and appearance. Most cheap book cases are made of second growth ash or elm, and being very poorly constructed are liable to fall to pieces after short usage. We list in our catalogue only such goods as we can guarantee to give entire satisfaction, not only upon immediate receipt but after **years of usage.** We hence recommend this case as a very desirable bargain. It is made of select solid oak and is very handsomely finished throughout. The height of this book case is 4 feet 11 inches, width is 32 inches, and it weighs about 60 lbs. when packed for shipment. **Shelves are adjustable.** The top of the case is fitted with rod and rings for hanging a curtain to cover the books, keeping out dust and dirt. The top is fancy pattern shaped.

Our Special Price, each..... ................ **$4.35**

....SEE WHAT THE.....
**METROPOLITAN NATIONAL BANK SAYS ABOUT US.**
PAGE 7.

## $10.75 Buys an $18.00 Combination Book Case and Medicine Cabinet.

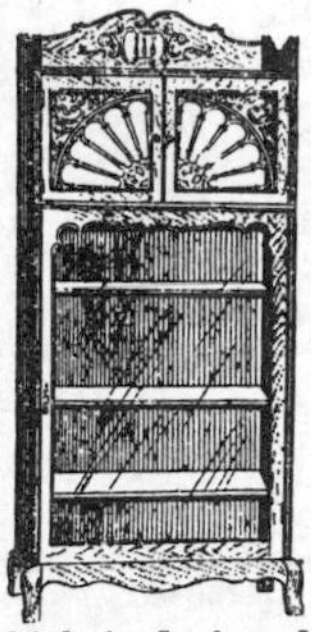

**No. 9247 One of the most unique and desirable pieces of** furniture which has been put on the market for the season of 1897 is the **Combination Library Case and Medicine Cabinet** which we undertake to show you in the illustration. This is a decidedly convenient piece of furniture and is made attractive enough for the handsomest library. By reason of our tremendous purchases in the line of furniture we are able to make the price within the most limited means. This case is made either of **oak or birch** as may be desired at the prices named below. When furnished in birch we finish **it in imitation mahogany**, a most elegant and desirable finish. Height of case 68 inches, width 31 inches. The upper part of case, which is designed for a medicine cabinet, is fitted with two doors with lock and key and decorated with **ornamental chip glass** back of the **carved veneer work**, giving the case a most elegant appearance, such as will only be found in the most expensive cases sold at retail at from $25.00 to $30.00. The top of the case is further decorated with fancy spindles and pattern shelf. The door of the book shelves is fitted with fancy pattern shaped double thick glass and has lock and key. The shelves are adjustable. The weight of the case when packed for shipment is about 75 lbs.

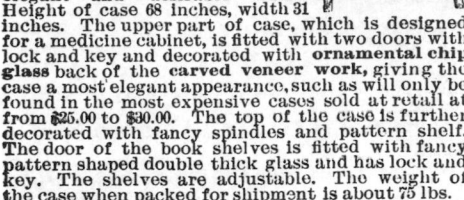

Our special price each, in oak.............................. **$10.75**
Our special price each, in birch.............................. **11.45**

## A Most Stylish Cabinet for $18.00.

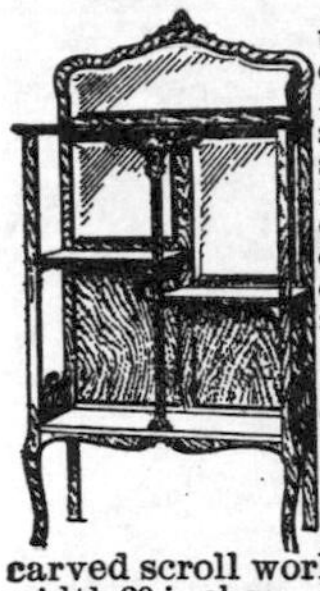

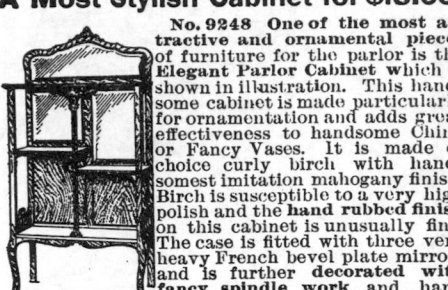

**No. 9248 One of the most attractive and ornamental pieces** of furniture for the parlor is the **Elegant Parlor Cabinet** which is shown in illustration. This handsome cabinet is made particularly for ornamentation and adds great effectiveness to handsome China or Fancy Vases. It is made of choice curly birch with handsomest imitation mahogany finish. Birch is susceptible to a very high polish and the **hand rubbed finish** on this cabinet is unusually fine. The case is fitted with three very heavy French bevel plate mirrors and is further **decorated with fancy spindle work** and hand carved scroll work. The height is 56 inches and the width 29 inches. It weighs packed for shipment 75 lbs. This is a case that would ordinarily retail at not less than $25.00 or $30.00.

Our special price, each.............................. **$18.00**

**No. 9249 We have this case also in solid mahogany if desired.** We furnish it in mahogany in just the same design as the one in illustration and with beautiful hand polished finish.

Our special price.............................. **$20.00**

## A $25.00 Book Case for $16.75.

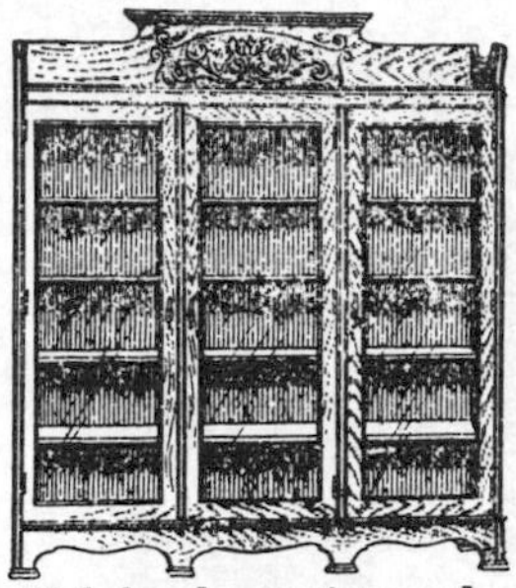

**No. 9250. The Library Book Case** which we show in illustration is one which would ordinarily retail in any furniture store for $25.00. At our special factory to consumer price you are securing something unusually handsome, and in fact, **a quality of goods not ordinarily found in retail stores anywhere** outside of large cities. This book case is made of the most select quarter-sawed oak with beautiful hand carving and a variety of ornamentation. It has a high hand polished finish and in every respect is one of the most attractive pieces of furniture we have to sell. This book case **has three glass doors**, the glass being extra thick and strong. The shelves are all portable and can be changed in height if desired. **The case is 72 inches high and 51 inches wide**, being as you will note unusually large and roomy. We pack these cases with the greatest care so that they may be delivered to customer without damage. Weight, complete, 150 lbs.

Our special price, each.............................. **$16.75**

## A $12.00 Desk for $8.95.

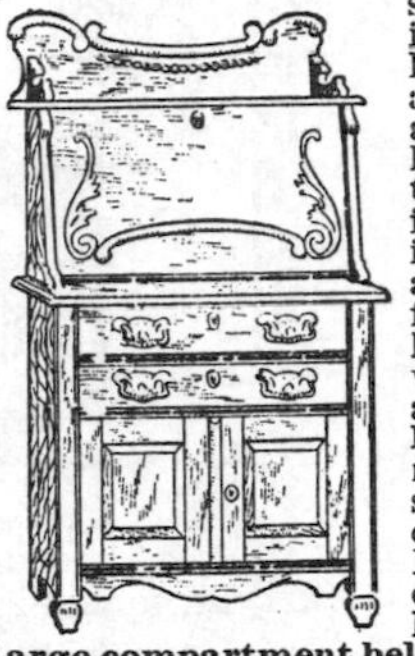

**No. 9251 This is one of the most convenient pieces of furniture,** especially where ladies are personally concerned. While it is designed specially for ladies' use, it will be found a very convenient desk for all purposes. Is decidedly handsome as well as **extremely useful.** This desk is 4 feet 8 inches high, 31 inches wide and weighs about 65 lbs. when packed for shipment. It is very handsomely ornamented with fancy hand carving and pattern top. **The drop leaf writing table** is very neatly ornamented, and the secretary is fitted with compartments and drawers. Below are two roomy drawers with cast brass handles and lock and key. **Large compartment below** with two doors. Sides are handsomely paneled and the desk being made of the choicest solid oak is thoroughly substantial and will last a lifetime.

Our special price.............................. **$8.95**

**FINE WRITING PAPER**
**AND EVERY VARIETY OF CHOICE STATIONERY IN OUR STATIONERY DEPARTMENT. Pages 349 to 356.**

## A $7.50 Desk for $4.75.

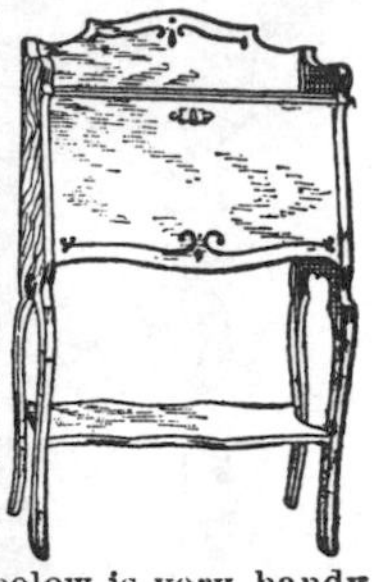

**No. 9253 We have been very fortunate** in securing some of the choicest goods from the stock of a leading manufacturer in this line of goods, and by placing large contracts are able to secure these goods at unusually close prices. We are giving our customers the benefit of these prices, and are hence able to offer this **Beautiful Ladies Desk** at 40 per cent less than retailers are able to offer. This desk is made of very handsome oak, finely finished and thoroughly well constructed. The drop leaf writing table is **fancy pattern shaped,** handsomely ornamented with roomy shelf below. Inside is fitted with pigeon holes, and is very convenient for **Writing Materials, Letters,** etc. The shelf below is very handy for books, magazines, etc. Weight packed for shipment about 35 lbs. Our Special Price.......... **$4.75**

## Our $7.50 Music Cabinet.

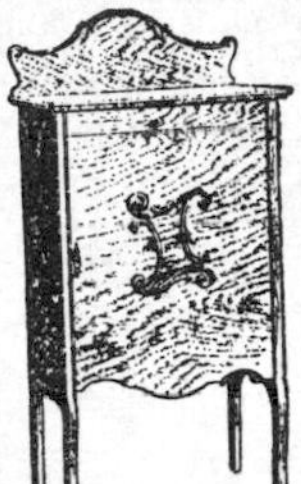

**No. 9254 The Music Cabinet as shown in the illustration is** made of the finest curly birch, finished in **imitation mahogany.** This is one of the handsomest finishes in which furniture is now made, in fact, it is preferred by many to solid mahogany, as the grain of the wood, except in the most expensive mahogany, is **very much handsomer.** The **beautiful polished finish** given to this article of furniture is equal to that of the finest piano. This music cabinet is fitted with a door handsomely decorated with rococo molding and has lock and key. The interior is fitted with roomy shelves and the cabinet is especially made for music, although it can be used for magazines and papers when so desired. The height of the case is 45 inches, and the width 23 inches. The weight of the cabinet, when packed for shipment, is about 35 lbs. Our special price.................. **$7.50**

## Great Bargain for $8.00

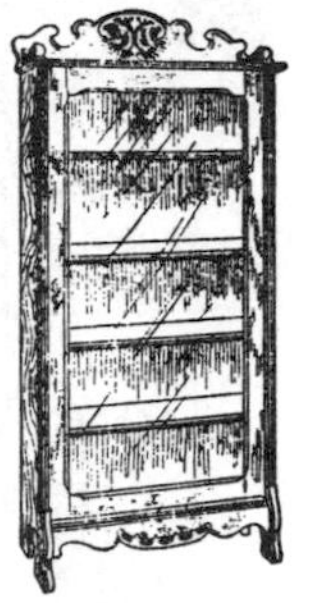

**No. 9255 The Book Case shown in illustration** is a particularly desirable piece of furniture at a price within the means of the limited pocketbook. It is not only thoroughly well constructed of the best **selected solid oak**, but it is very ornamental in design, handsomely decorated with hand carving, pattern panels, etc. The large door is fitted with **double thick glass** of extra strength and furnished with lock and key. The base board is fancy pattern shaped. **Shelves are adjustable.** The height of the case is 6 feet and the width 2 feet 6 inches. Weight, packed for shipment, about 85 lbs.

Our special price, each..... **$8.00**

# OFFICE DESKS.

**Any Desk shipped C. O. D. on receipt of $5.00, balance to be paid after examination. 3 per cent off for full cash with order.**

## Our $14.50 Curtain Top Desk.

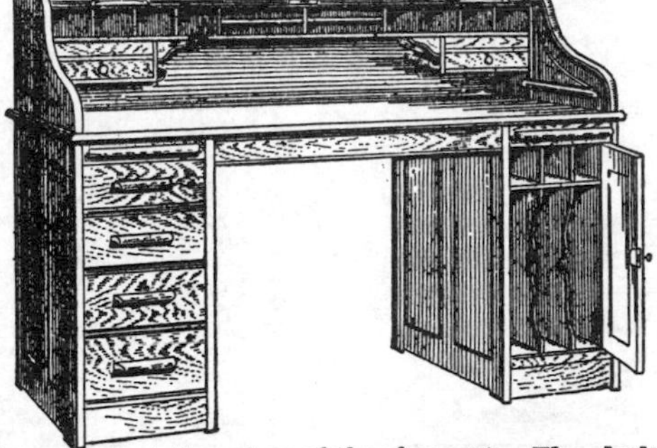

**No. 9260 We have used the utmost care in selecting** our line of office furniture. We are perfectly well aware of the fact that the market is flooded with a large variety of cheaply constructed office desks. **A curtain desk in order to be serviceable** must necessarily be made of the most select material and put together by expert mechanics in such a way that it will stand usage. The difficulty with the cheap desks on the market is that material is inferior and poorly seasoned, and hence after short usage the desk will warp and crack and the joints come apart, and your desk is practically worthless. **We guarantee the goods which we illustrate and describe** to be the best the market affords, and we are able to sell you these goods at the prices of the cheapest. **The desk illustrated is made of solid oak,** perfectly kiln dried and thoroughly seasoned. Nicely finished throughout. It has convenient roll top, which moves up and down very easily. This curtain top is fitted with spring lock. The interior is fitted with 4 pigeon holes, 6 open drawers and 2 closed drawers, also with pen and pencil racks, etc., etc. On the left are 4 large roomy drawers, and the right is fitted with compartments for books and small pigeon holes for papers. Ends and inside are handsomely paneled and thoroughly well finished throughout. Further convenience arises from the fact that arm rests are fitted on both sides. Weight, packed for shipment, about 235 lbs. All drawers lock automatically when curtain top is pulled down. We furnish this desk in three sizes, but in all cases the desk will be 2 feet 6 inches deep, and 3 feet 9½ inches high. Prices as follows:

**Desk as above described,** 5 feet long .............................. **$20.00**
4 feet 6 inches long.............................. **17.50**
4 feet long.............................. **14.50**

## Our $7.50 Office Desk.

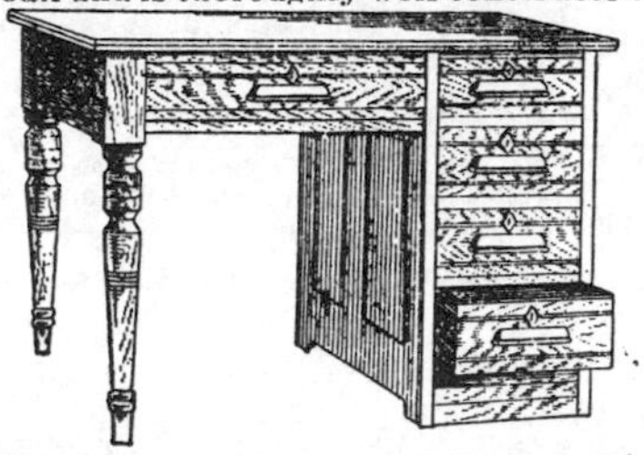

**No. 9263 The demand for a cheap, convenient and well constructed flat top desk** has been so large that we have made specially desirable contracts on the one which we illustrate. **This desk is** made of selected solid oak and is thoroughly well constructed by a leading manufacturer who employs only the best cabinet makers in furniture of this kind. This insures our customers securing **furniture that will not only look well** but will be of such **quality as will endure the service of a lifetime.** The top of desk is 3 feet long by 27 inches wide, fitted with four large roomy drawers on side and one in top, all drawers being fitted with locks and keys. **The sides are paneled** and handsomely finished. The desk is strong in every respect and is guaranteed to be exactly as represented or it may be returned to us and money will be refunded. Remember our 3 per cent. discount when cash in full accompanies order. Weight of desk, packed for shipment, is about 80 lbs. Our special price **$7.50**

## A $16.00 Desk for $10.75.

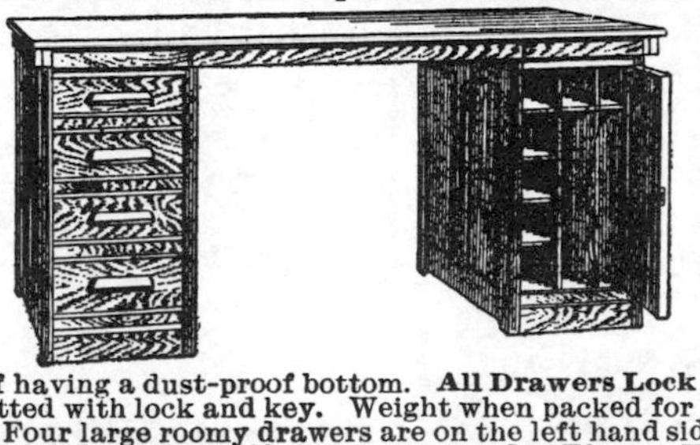

**No. 9266 The Flat Top Desk Illustrated** in the cut is selected from the choicest leaders of a number of manufacturers. We have selected this desk by reason of its unusual superiority in workmanship, material and appearance, and at the same time on account of the exceedingly low price at which we are able to offer it. It is made of **Very Choice Solid Oak** with **Beautiful Polished Top.** This desk has the advantage of having a dust-proof bottom. **All Drawers Lock Automatically** and are fitted with lock and key. Weight when packed for shipment about 125 lbs. Four large roomy drawers are on the left hand side and the right is fitted with a door, the inside being composed of **Pigeon Holes and Compartment** for books. The desk is also fitted with arm slides at both sides. This desk is made in three different sizes, the desk being in all cases two feet 7 inches wide. Desk as above described, 5 feet long, our price.............................. **14.00**

Same, 4 feet 6 inches long,.... **12.75** Same, 4 feet long, ........ **10.75**

**WE MAKE IT A POINT TO SHIP AS PROMPTLY AS POSSIBLE, IN FACT MOST SHIPMENTS ARE MADE THE NEXT DAY AFTER ORDER IS RECEIVED. SOMETIMES A DELAY IS UNAVOIDABLE, GOODS BEING TEMPORARILY OUT OF STOCK, OR ALTERATIONS HAVE TO BE MADE. WE NEVER DELAY IF WE CAN HELP IT.**

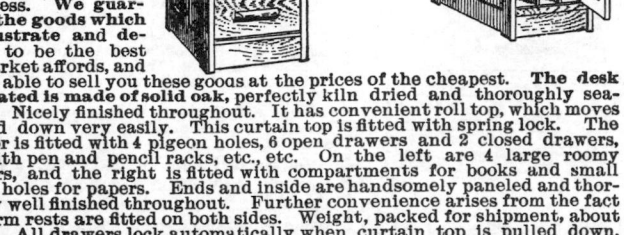

## A $15.00 Office Table for $9.25.

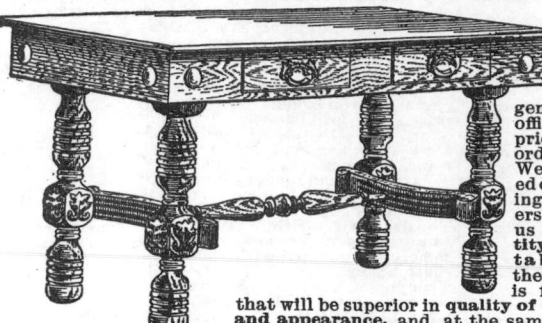

No. 9275 It has hitherto been exceedingly difficult to secure a genuine first class office table at a price within the ordinary means. We have persuaded one of the leading manufacturers to make up for us a large quantity of these office tables, knowing the demand there is for something that will be superior in quality of workmanship and appearance, and, at the same time, low in price. It is seldom you will ever see anything to equal this table at less than $15.00. It is made of the very finest solid oak with hand rubbed polish on top, giving it a beautiful finish. Size of top 30 inches wide by 54 inches long. Fitted with two drawers having fancy cast brass handles. Legs are heavy and massive in appearance and of unusual strength, being well braced. This table, packed for shipment, weighs about 100 lbs., and is one of the most decided bargains ever put on the market.
Our special price.......................$9.25

## Our $8.00 Standing Desk.

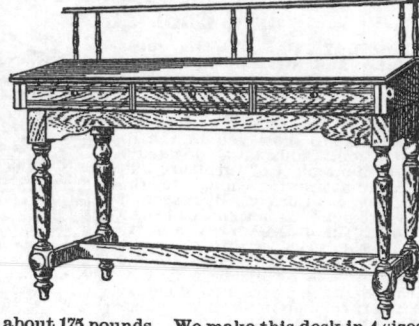

No. 9268 One of the most convenient pieces of office furniture which can be secured is the standing office desk which we show in illustration. This desk is made of solid oak and is fitted with three large roomy drawers having locks and keys. Book rack at back of top. Fancy turned legs of unusual strength and thoroughly well braced. This desk can be taken apart in shipping and shipped knocked down, thus saving very largely on the freight. It can very readily be put together and is one of the most substantial desks of the kind we have ever had.
Weight packed for shipment about 175 pounds. We make this desk in 4 sizes, the desk in all cases being 2 feet 11 inches wide. Prices as follows:

| | |
|---|---|
| Standing Desk, 4 feet long, price | $ 8.00 |
| Standing Desk, 5 feet long, price | 11.50 |
| Standing Desk, 6 feet long, price | 13.50 |
| Standing Desk, 8 feet long, price | 17.85 |

## A $16.00 Bed Room Suit for $10.00.

No. 9300.

No. 0304.

No. 9300. In this Suit we offer more value for the money than was ever before offered in the line of bed room furniture. We illustrate the bed and dresser only, but the suit consists of three pieces, including a very handsome wash stand. The bed is 6 feet high and has 4 foot 6 inch slats. The head of the bed is handsomely decorated with heavy molding; bed sides are thoroughly substantial, and the construction of the bed is such that you can expect great service. The square dresser is very handsome and has beautifully carved top, with a large square German plate mirror 20x24 inches in size. Fitted with three very large roomy drawers having cast brass handles. The suit throughout is finished very handsomely in antique oak. The commode or wash stand has three drawers and door, with splasher back. Weight of suit complete is about 300 pounds.
No. 9300. Price for the above suit, consisting of three pieces, Bed, Square Dresser and Commode.........................$10.50
No. 9303. We can furnish dresser with very fine German bevel plate. The price of the suit will then be.......................$11.00

## Onr Special $12.50 Bed Room Suit.

This Chamber Suit has the same bed and commode as No. 9300 illustrated above, but instead of the square dresser shown above we furnish the suit with an elegant and stylish cheval dresser, as shown in the accompanying illustration. This dresser has a very large German plate mirror 17x30 inches in size in swing frame. Base is fitted with two large roomy drawers, having cast brass handles and locks and keys. Weight, complete, about 220 pounds.
No. 9304. Our special price for above suit, consisting of Bed, Cheval Dresser and Commode.......................$12.50

These Bed Room Suits will compare most favorably with furniture sold in retail stores at from 50 to 75 per cent more than our prices.

Any suit C.O.D. subject to examination on receipt of $5 with order.

## Our $16.00 Elegant Solid Oak Bed Room Suit.

No. 9305.

No. 9305

No. 9305. This Bed Room suit is made of the very finest solid oak and is finished by the best workmen in this line. The bed is six feet high, the corner posts at the head being decorated with tasty hand carving, the panels at both head and footboard are handsomely finished and fitted, while the top panel has the tastiest ornament in the way of fancy hand carving. The bed has 4 foot 6 inch slats and is very solidly constructed by the most expert cabinet makers.
The Dresser No. 9305 is what is known as the Chevalle Dresser, and has a very heavy mirror 18x30 inches, made of the very best imported bevel plate. The dresser is decorated with very fancy hand carving, which matches the ornamentation of the bed exactly. It has very convenient hat cabinet and two small drawers. The top of dresser base is the fancy late style curved pattern with round corners, and is 21x42 inches in size. The two drawers in the dresser base are large and roomy and fitted with cast brass ornamented handles. The height of Dresser is 6 feet 6 inches. The Commode shown in the illustration matches the suit in every particular and is about 5 feet to top of splasher and has 17x33 inch top. The weight of this suit complete is about 225 lbs. Complete suit, 3 pieces.
Our special price.......................$16.00

No. 9306.

## Our $15.00 Bed Room Suit.

No. 9306 We also have this suit consisting of the same Bed and Commode as above described but including the square dresser No. 9306, which is also illustrated. The ornamentation in the way of hand carving, etc., is precisely the same and matches the bed exactly. The drawers all have fancy cast brass handles, while the dresser top is fancy curved pattern, 21x42 inches in size. Heavy bevel plate mirror, 24 x 30 inches in size. All of these suits are furnished with best of patent castors. The weight of this suit is about 225 lbs.
No. 9306. Bedroom Suit consisting of bed, commode and including No. 9306 square dresser. Our special price.......................$15.00

Our Special Furniture Catalogue, mailed free on application, contains a most elaborate display of strictly new furniture, and a class of goods not to be had elsewhere at anything like our prices

## Our Special $7.85 Bed Room Suit

No. 9306½. We show in the illustration a Chamber Suit of two pieces, suitable for hotels or for bed rooms that are too small for the larger size three piece suits. Made of the best selected and most carefully seasoned elm, and is thoroughly well put together by expert workmen. Finished in antique oak. The bed is 6 feet high and has 4 foot 6 inch slats. The top of the head board is fancy pattern shaped and decorated with heavy molding, giving it a very neat appearance. The combination wash stand and dresser is of a style which matches the bed perfectly. The top is handsomely carved. The dresser is fitted with two large roomy drawers and large compartment below the doors. The mirror is of excellent imported German plate glass and is 14x24 inches in size. Weight of suit complete about 200 lbs. Our special price, complete, two-piece suit.......................$7.85

## A $35.00 Bed Room Suit for $22.75.

No. 9316     No. 9316.

No. 9317.

**No. 9316** Our artist has endeavored to give you some idea of the appearance of this elegant suit by drawing it direct from a photograph, but we regret that many of the details have been left out, and you can not form an accurate idea of its value. We should desire nothing better than to have one of these suits shipped **into your neighborhood,** knowing the value it would be to us **as an advertisement.** We are exceedingly anxious to get you started buying your furniture from us, as we know that we can give you better value than you could secure elsewhere, and that after having made one purchase in this line you will find it to your interest to make all your purchases from us where you can secure the best value to be had anywhere.

**This Bed Room Suit is one of the best examples** of our facilities for buying at lowest spot cash prices. This suit is made of the **choicest quarter-sawed oak,** a quality of wood that is susceptible of a very high finish and which presents in quarter-sawed effect a beautiful appearance. **The bed** is 6 feet 1 inch high with 4 feet 6 inch slat. The top of bed is fancy pattern shaped with handsome hand carving. The foot is also decorated with carving to match the head board. All panels are handsomely finished and do not present the crude appearance which you will find in the cheap suits held at high prices by retail dealers. **The dresser top is 20x41 inches in size, fancy pattern shaped. The dresser** is fitted with large roomy drawers, having cast brass handles, each drawer having lock and key. Sides are handsomely paneled and finished. **The wash stand** is not shown in the cut, but is of a quality and style to match the other pieces of the suit. The top is 18x22 inches in size and is fitted with towel rack, drawers and compartment. The suit is furnished **complete** with casters and weighs, packed for shipment, about 250 pounds. Our special price for complete suit, concisting of No. 9316 Bed, No. 9316 Dresser and Wash Stand to match............$22.75

### Special $24.00 Suit.

**No. 9317** We can also furnish the same suit as above described with Bed No. 9316 and the Wash Stand described with suit above, but with **Cheval Dresser No. 9317** as illustrated above. **This dresser** is a very popular design. The top is 20x41 inches in size and stands about 6 feet high. It is decorated in the same style of ornamentation as the bed, and is beautifully finished. The fine bevel plate mirror is 18x40 inches in size and is the best imported German bevel plate to be secured. At the side of the mirror is a handsome drawer and large compartment for ladies' hat, gloves, etc. The weight of this suit, complete, packed for shipment, is about 275 pounds.
Our special price, each...........................$24.50
Complete suit consists of Bed No. 9316, Chevalle Dresser No. 9317 and handsome commode to match.
Our Special offer. Send deposit of $5.00 and we will send by freight C. O. D. subject to examination. You examine it at the depot, and if as represented, pay the agent the balance with freight.

## A $30.00 Bed Room Suit for $20.50.

NC. 9318     No. 9318.

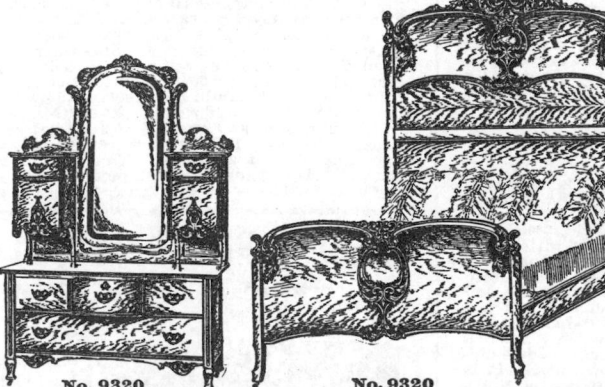

No. 9319

**No. 9318** We have just contracted with the leading manufacturer in the west for a large number of **the bed room sets** which we show in the illustration. This is an **entirely new design** just put on the market, a style that is handsome, attractive and very rich in appearance. This suit is made of the very finest quarter-sawed oak, the grain of the wood being very beautiful, and being brought out especially handsome by reason of the superior finish given to it. **The bed** is 6 feet 4 inches and has 4 foot 6 inch slats. The top of the head board is handsomely ornamented with rich and **imposing hand carving.** The foot board is a handsome large piece of quarter-sawed oak with the grain of the wood shown very handsomely and decorated with fancy hand carving. **The bed** sides are thoroughly substantial and the panels are all handsomely finished. **The square dresser** which we show in the illustration has beautiful hand carving on the top, matching the decoration of the bed exactly. The large square mirror is 24x30 inches in size and is made of the **best imported French bevel plate.** This dresser has the new style swell front. The top of the base is **fancy pattern shaped,** being curved on front and sides. The drawers are also curved in front instead of straight, thus giving it a beautiful appearance. **The two large and two small drawers** are fitted with cast brass handles and have locks and keys. The sides are handsomely paneled. **The comode,** which we do not show in the illustration, completes the suit, anb is also made of the best selected quarter-sawed oak, matching perfectly the balance of the suit. It has 18x31 inch top, splasher back and fitted with drawers and large compartment. We furnish free the very finest plate casters. The weight of this suit, when packed for shipment, is about 290 pounds. It is one which will delight you by reason of its substantial makeup, **excellent** quality of its material and **handsome appearance.**
Our special price, each,..............$20.50

### Our Special $23.00 Bed Room Suit.

**No. 9319** The bed is just the same as bed No. 9318 illustrated. The complete suit consists of cheval dresser shown, bed No. 9318, with handsome comode to match. **The cheval dresser No. 9319** is 6 feet 4 inches high, decorated at the top with fancy hand carving, has a large French bevel plate mirror, 18x40 inches in size, in fancy swing frame. At the side are a **large compartment** and two handy drawers. It is fitted with one large and two small roomy drawers. Weight, complete, about 300 pounds. Our special price for 3-piece suit, consisting of bed No. 9318, cheval dresser No. 9319 and **commode**............................$23.00

---

# THE MOST STYLISH SUIT EVER SOLD.

**WE OFFER...**

The Bed Room Suit illustrated in the accompanying cut to those who are desirous of purchasing

**THE FINEST THAT THE MARKET AFFORDS,**

and at the same time do not wish to pay an exorbitant price, such as retail dealers charge who are able to carry such expensive goods. We can furnish this suit either with No. 9320 dresser or No. 9321 dresser, as may be desired. In both cases the Bed and Wash Stand will be the same.

**THE BED**

is one of the latest designs for 1897 trade, and is a pattern made and designed by one of the most expert artists in the furniture line.

No. 9320     No. 9320     No. 9321

**THIS BED**

Stands 6 feet and 4 inches high, with 4 feet 6 inch slat. The superb and massive hand carving on head board and foot board cannot be fully appreciated from the illustration. We can say that there is nothing on the market which is superior to it in elegance. The panels of the head board are beautifully finished and the suit being made of choicest quarter-sawed oak, the grain stands out prominently and adds very greatly to the elegance of the general appearance. The foot board is one solid piece. The side boards are of extra strength and fancily decorated. The posts are fancy shaped and suit is fitted with best quality casters.

Dresser No. 9320 has fancy pattern shaped mirror, 30x36 inches in size. This mirror is made of the choicest extra heavy French bevel plate in a handsome swing frame. The ornamentations are exceedingly rich and match in outline those of the bed. The dresser top is 22x48 inches in size. This dresser has a fancy pattern swell front, preserving the same outline as the top; 2 extra large roomy compartments below. All drawers are fitted with fancy cast brass handles. The dresser has handsome pattern shaped base board. Sides are finished with handsome panels. The wash stand, which is not shown in the cut, is the same high grade of workmanship and material as the bed and dresser. The wash stand top is 19x36 inches in size, and has towel rack, drawers and compartments below. The weight of this suit when packed for shipment is about 350 pounds. Our special price...........$65.00

**No. 9321.** As stated above, we also furnish this suit complete with dresser No. 9320 as illustrated. This dresser has square heavy German bevel plate mirror, set in fancy swing frame with ornamentation to match the decorations of bed. The dresser top is 20x48 inches in size. This dresser has two small and two large roomy drawers, all drawers having fancy cast brass handles. Sides of dresser are handsomely paneled. The suit is fitted throughout with a very heavy set of plate casters. Suit weighs, complete, 325 pounds when carefully packed for shipment.
Our special price............................$59.00
Both our Cash and C. O. D. terms are very liberal. Any bedroom suit sent C. O. D. subject to approval on a deposit of $5.00. Three per cent. off when full cash accompanies order.

**FOR OTHER STYLISH AND DESIRABLE FURNITURE SEND FOR OUR SPECIAL FREE FURNITURE CATALOGUE MAILED FREE.**

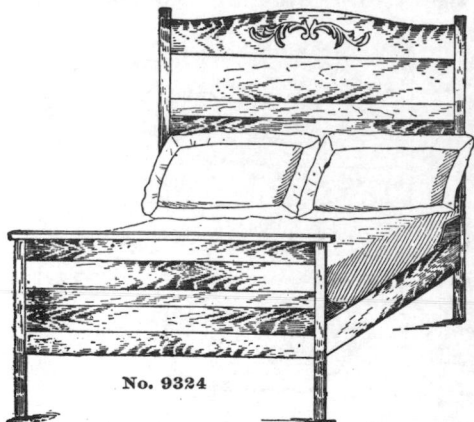

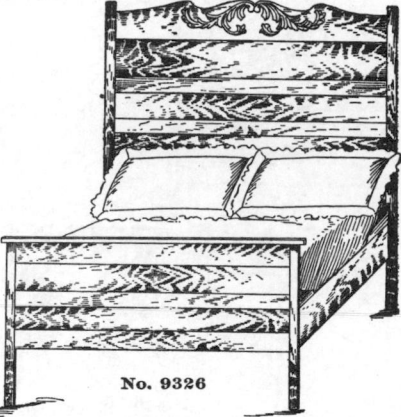

## A $2.50 Bed for $1.65.

**No. 9324** The bed which we illustrate is offered to meet the demand for something very low priced and at the same time a bed that will stand usage and is thoroughly well constructed of excellent material. This bedstead is made of the best kiln dried rock elm, is well finished in **antique oak**, is put together substantially and carefully by the best workmen and will give ample service. It is 5 feet high at the head and has 4 feet 2 inch slats. We can also furnish it in 3 foot 6 inch width if so desired, the price being the same. Our special price, either size..........**$1.65**

## Our Special Bargain $2.10 Bed.

**No. 9326** We buy the bed shown in the cut from a manufacturer who has a reputation for the high grade of his goods, and we offer this article as one that is very substantial. At our factory to consumer price it is at least **40 per cent below what retailers** would charge for an article no better and perhaps not so good. It is made of fine selected rock elm, thoroughly seasoned, and is very handsomely finished in antique oak. The decoration on the headboard is a **fancy style of molding** while the panels are handsome and well finished. The bed sides are substantial and strong, and throughout it is well put together and unusually cheap. The height is 5 feet 6 inches, the slat is either 4 feet 2 inches or 3 feet 6 inches as desired. Our special price, each.............................**$2.10**

No. 9324

No. 9326

**No. 9327** We have the same bed as No. 9326 above described and illustrated, but **in solid oak** instead of solid elm, otherwise being just the same having the ornamental carving, etc. Our special price, each.........................................................................**$2.58**

## FOLDING BEDS.

### Our $6.75 Folding Bed.

**No. 9330** The Mantel Folding Bed is a great convenience in that **it** will take up very little room when closed and furthermore that it can be used in many rooms which are not usually intended for bedrooms. The bed which we show in illustration is much more handsome in appearance than you would judge from illustration which does not do it half justice. It is **remarkably well made** when you consider the extremely low price at which we are able to furnish it. It is made of selected kiln dried elm, thoroughly well put together by the best workmen, and will stand the usage of an ordinary lifetime. It is made **for curtain front**, so that when the bed is closed it can be concealed by drapery. The head and foot-board are alike, giving choice of ends for the head. The legs close up when the bed is closed. The bed is handsomely finished and will please any one. **We furnish free with the bed a woven wire mattress.** Size of bed when closed 53 inches high, 81 inches long and 14 inches deep. When opened inside measurements are 48 inches wide and 72 inches long. Weight, packed for shipment, about 100 lbs. Our special price..........**$6.75**

### An $18.00 Bed for $11.50.

**No. 9331** A Folding Bed in order to be desirable in every respect must be **thoroughly well constructed** on the best scientific principles, so that it can be handled with ease, and also that it may be thoroughly substantial in every respect and stand the usage of many years. While the **folding bed shown in illustration** is remarkably cheap in price, it is very finely made of the best selected rock elm with very handsome built-up **veneered oak panels** and is finished in **antique oak**, a very handsome and desirable finish. The size of this bed when closed is 54 inches high, 55 inches wide and 20 inches deep. When opened, the size, outside is 55x75 inches, and inside 48x72 inches. A **mattress to fit this bed should be 3 feet 10 inches wide by 6 feet long** and should be made of such material as will fold easily, such as wool, moss, cotton, hair, etc. **This folding bed** is best known as the mantel style, and when opened the footboard, which is the top of the bed when closed, is drawn out, stretching the **wire mattress, furnished free** with the bed, tightly and making the bed full size. This bed is **easy to open and close**, a very convenient and attractive piece of furniture, especially desirable where bed rooms are of comparatively small size. Weight, packed for shipment is about 200 pounds. Our special price.....................**$11.50**

### Our $14.50 Bargain.

**No. 9334** This bed is made to supply the demand for a kind of furniture which is convenient, well made and low priced. The material is the best kiln dried and seasoned elm with **built-up veneered oak panels**, and finished in **antique oak**. The legs drop down when the bed is opened, while the end or foot board pulls and tightens the woven wire mattress with which the bed is fitted. The ornamentation of the bed is **decidedly handsome**, and adds much to its already neat appearance. It is fitted with a **handsome bevel plate mirror**, 14 inches high by 24 inches wide. The size of the bed when closed is 57 inches high, 55 inches wide and 20 inches deep. Size when opened, outside, 55x75 inches; inside, 48x72 inches. As stated above, **woven wire mattress is free.** Filled mattress should be 3 feet 10 inches wide by 6 feet long, and made of such material as wool, moss, etc., which will fold easily. Weight, packed for shipment about 250 pounds. Our special price...............**$14.50**

## A $28.00 Folding Bed for $18.50.

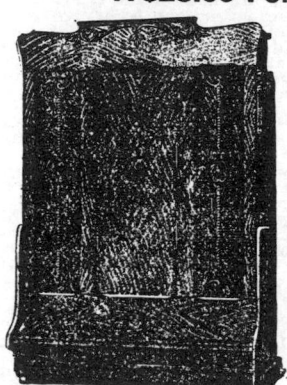

**No. 9335** We offer the folding bed which we show in the illustration as one of the best and most substantial as well as attractive beds ever offered at anything like our factory to consumer price. It is made of the **best kiln dried rock elm** with **built-up veneered oak panels**, and is as handsome as most beds sold by retail dealers at 50 per cent. more than our price. It is finished in antique oak, hand rubbed and given an elegant polish such as is found on fine pianos. **It has self-adjusting and self-locking metal legs** which swing automatically when the bed is lowered. This bed is made on the best scientific principles, and is so perfectly adjusted that there is no danger of the back tipping over. The size of the bed when closed is 78 inches high, 57 inches wide and 24 inches deep. Size opened, outside, 57 inches high and 80 inches long; inside. 50 x 72 inches. We furnish a substantially woven wire mattress free with each bed. Filled mattress for it should be 4 feet wide by 6 feet long and should be made of such material as will fold easily. Weight packed for shipment about 400 pounds. Our special price.........................**$18.50**

## A $35.00 Folding Bed for $21.25.

**No. 9338** We have found the folding bed which **we illustrate** herewith to have given such **unusual satisfaction** to our customers during the past season that we have made new contracts with the manufacturers so that they will supply us for the coming season for the same bed, gotten up in their usual high class style and with the best workmanship. This bed is made of the best selected elm that can be secured with **built-up veneered oak panels**. It is finished in antique oak and **very highly polished**, giving it an elegant appearance. Everything about this bed is in accordance with **late patents and improvements.** It has self-adjusting metal swing legs which swing down and lock themselves automatically when the bed is opened. The bed is so perfectly adjusted that in no possible way can the back tip over. The very handsome **hand carvings** and ornamentations throughout give the bed a beautiful appearance, and it will be an ornament to any bed room. The **elegant bevel plate mirror** is 18 x 40 inches in size. We give a fine woven wire mattress free with each bed. Size when opened 57 x 80 inches outside, or 50 inches x 72 inches inside. Size when closed, 78 inches high. 57 inches wide and 24 inches deep. A filled mattress to fit with the bed should be 4 feet wide by 6 feet long, and should be made of material that will fold easily. Everything about this bed is of the same class of workmanship and quality of material as will be found in the most expensive kept only in high class stores. It is very easily handled—a child can open and close it with ease. The bedding is perfectly ventilated from the back. Weight packed for shipment about 400 pounds. **Woven wire mattress free with every bed.** Our special price...........................**$21.25**

**FREIGHT CUTS NO FIGURE IN THE SAVING WE CAN EFFECT FOR YOU. WHEN YOU BUY AT RETAIL YOU PAY THE FREIGHT JUST THE SAME, AND WITH A PROFIT ADDED.**

# A GREAT LEADER IN FOLDING BEDS.

**We Ship on Liberal C. O. D. Terms when $5.00 Accompanies Order, 3 per cent. off for Full Cash with Order and this Elegant Bed Costs You but $23.30 in Elm or $25.65 in Solid Oak.**

## The Best Folding Bed Made.

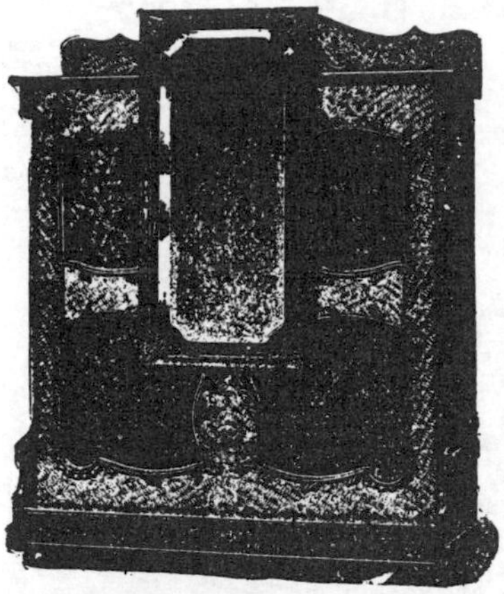

No. 9341, with glass turned and elevated for use as cheval or pier glass.

**The New Departure Mantel Folding Beds. Recent patents** have been given, covering certain **improvements on folding beds** which are of such unusual desirability that we have made arrangements with the manufacturers to act as selling agents to our customers. These arrangements have been completed on the most satisfactory terms, and we are now in a position to offer folding beds such as you will only find in the very largest stores in cities, and when found the prices are of such magnitude that only the wealthy are enabled to purchase. **By our factory to consumer system** we place our customers on the same footing as the largest trade. We enable them to take advantage of the newest and best goods on the market at prices which retailers would charge for inferior furniture. **These beds, which we attempt to illustrate** in the accompanying cuts, are provided with an **adjustable mirror.** This mirror is so mounted as to be entirely concealed by the back when the bed is opened. This is a very desirable feature for many purchasers of folding beds find difficulty in preventing the glass from being broken from underneath when the bed is opened. **Another decided advantage** in this adjustment can be seen from the two illustrations which we show. This advantage is that the glass may be retained in the ordinary **horizontal position** when the bed is closed, or it may be turned to an **upright position** and elevated so as to be at a very convenient height for use as a pier mirror. The size of this beautiful and **massive French mirror** is 18 inches wide by 40 inches long. The bed itself is made in either elm or oak at the prices named below. In either case the wood is hand rubbed and beautifully polished, while the panels are surrounded and decorated with **beautiful molding and carved work,** adding greatly to the already attractive appearance. The top of the bed is handsome pattern shaped, also decorated with carved molding. The size when closed is 55 inches wide and 58 inches high by 20 inches deep. Size when opened completely, outside, 55x75 inches; inside measurement, 48x72 inches when opened. We furnish a **woven wire mattress with each bed.** Filled mattress for the bed should be 3 feet 10 inches wide by 6 feet long, and should be made of wool, moss, cotton, hair, etc., or such material as will fold easily. We offer this New Departure Bed with the assurance that **every customer will be highly delighted** with it. It is strictly **up-to-date** with all the latest patents, and it has the exclusively desirable feature in the way of pivoted mirror. The weight when packed for shipment is about 300 lbs. We pack and crate all of our folding beds with extreme care, so that they may be sure to reach our customers in the very best condition. We solicit your order on any of these folding beds, and can assure you if you do not find it to be exactly as represented and entirely satisfactory it may be returned to us and we shall refund your money.

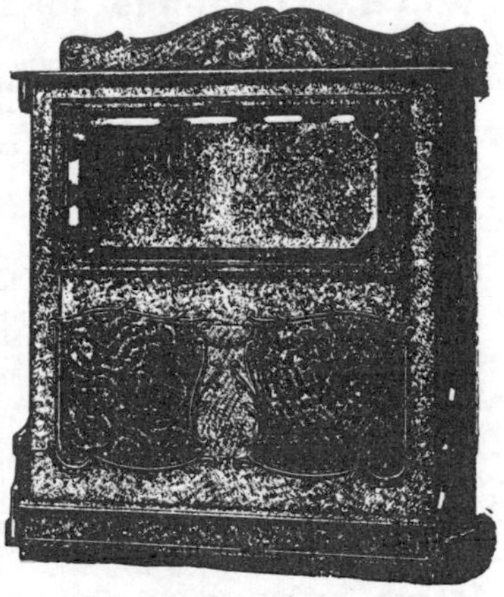

No. 9341, with glass in ordinary position,

**No. 9341** Our Special Price for **New Departure Bed** in Elm............ **$23.00**
**No. 9343** Our Special Price **in solid oak, beautifully hand polished**............ **$26.45**

# GREAT ANTI-TRUST SALE OF DRESSERS.

**The Choicest Leaders from Five Different Factories. The Finest Made Furniture in the World. Shipped to Anyone Anywhere C. O. D., Subject to Examination on Deposit of $5.00. 3 per cent. off for Full Cash with Order.**

## Our Special Bargain $6.75 Dresser.

**No. 9350 The Dresser which we show** in the illustration is made of a very fine quality selected rock elm, kiln dried and thoroughly seasoned. It is handsomely **finished in antique oak,** and presents an elegant appearance. The fancy oval mirror is fitted in a decorated swing frame held by odd design uprights, and the dresser complete presents a very attractive appearance. **The mirror** is 20x24 inches in size and is made of the best imported plain **German plate glass. The base** is fitted with three large roomy drawers having cast brass handles, and the sides are paneled and finished handsomely. Weight complete when packed for shipment about 100 lbs. Our special price, each.... **$6.75**

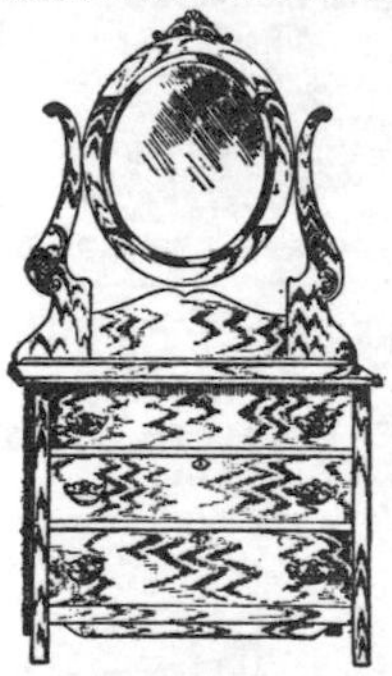

## An $18.00 Dresser for $12.50.

**No. 9351 The dresser which we show in the illustration** is very rich in design and is the product of one of the leading manufacturers in this line, a manufacturer who takes particular pride in making goods that will stand all the service that is needful, a dresser that will give satisfaction not only upon its receipt but after years of usage. This dresser is made of solid **quarter sawed oak,** the quarter sawing giving a **beautiful appearance** and taking an especially fine polish. The mirror is the best heavy **German bevel plate** and is 24x30 inches in size. The mirror is in handsome swing frame decorated with beautiful hand carving. The top of the dresser is **fancy swell front,** and is 20x41 inches in size. The dresser is fitted with three large roomy drawers having **cast brass handles** and lock and key. Fancy pattern base board. Paneled ends. Weight of dresser complete packed for shipment about 100 lbs, Set of castors furnished free. Our special price............ **$12.50**

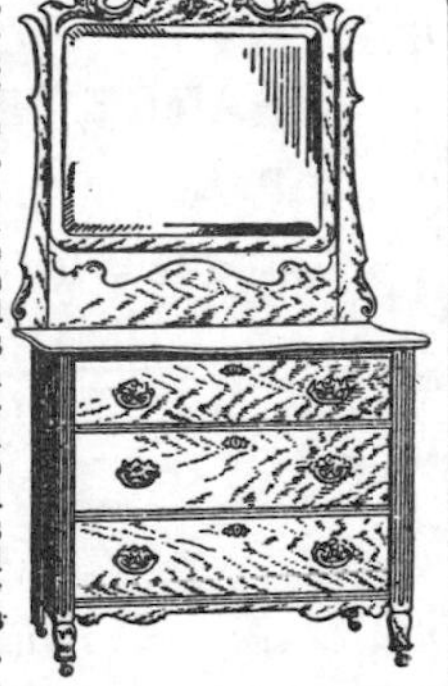

## Our Great Bargain.

**No. 9352 The dresser which we show in illustration** is after the same style and design as No. 9351 above, but is **cheval style,** having long mirror, 18x40 inches in size, instead of square. This dresser is made of quarter sawed oak with a **very fine hand polished finish.** At side of mirror is a handy drawer and compartment for gloves, etc. The top of base is 20x41 inches in size with swell front and two large roomy drawers. Handsomely finished and polished, fancy pattern base board. **Castors free.** Weight packed for shipment about 110 lbs. Our special price.... **$14.95**

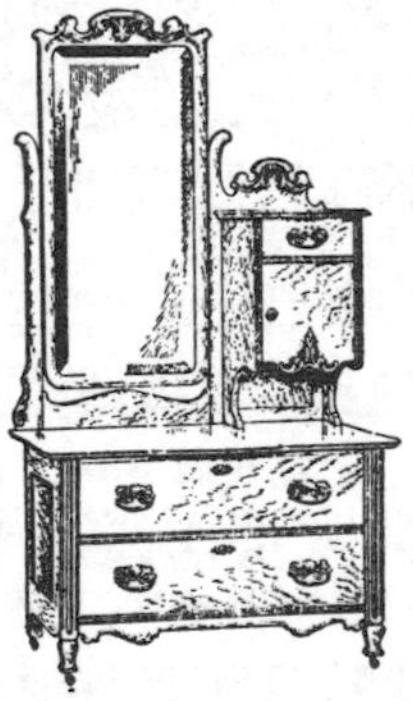

## Our $13.75 Solid Oak Dresser.

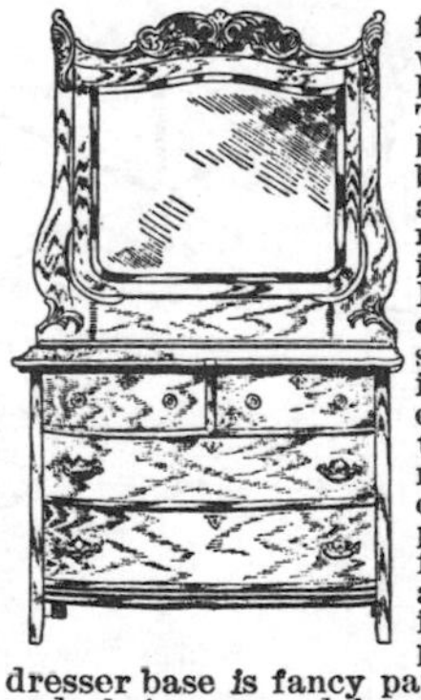

**No. 9354. The Beautiful Solid Oak Dresser** which we illustrate is one of the latest designs for 1897 trade. The most expert artists have used their skill in bringing out patterns which are extremely **tasty and rich in appearance.** This is one of the most desirable. It is made of **choice solid oak,** beautifully quarter sawed, handsomely finished in finest polish and elegant throughout. The top is handsomely ornamented with choice hand carving, while the **fancy pattern mirror** in swing frame is 24x30 inches in size and is made of the very best imported **German bevel plate glass.** The top of the dresser base is fancy pattern shaped, the sides and ends being curved handsomely instead of square. The dresser base has also **curved front,** or swell front, as it is sometimes known, a feature of the dresser which we can not bring out in illustration. The base is fitted with two small and two large, roomy drawers fitted with **cast brass knobs** and handles and having locks and keys. These drawers are all perfect fitting and move in and out readily, a feature not to be found in the **cheap dressers for sale in retail stores.** The sides are handsomely paneled and perfectly finished. The dresser is furnished complete with a fine set of castors; weighs when packed for shipment about 350 lbs. This will be a **very popular dresser** to be used in connection with one of our fancy iron beds; in fact, the demand for iron beds and odd dressers is much greater than formerly, a great many people preferring a suit of that style to the complete wood suit.
Our special price............ **$13.75**

## Our Finest $22.00 Dresser.

**No. 9355 The illustration can not do half justice** to this elegant piece of furniture, **a dresser that** would be an **ornament to any chamber,** and, at our factory to consumer price, is placed within the limit of moderate means. It is **decidely rich and imposing** in appearance, being decorated throughout with the finest of ornamentation. The very large and massive mirror is fancy **pattern shaped** and fitted in a **swing frame of ornamental design,** being decorated with beautiful hand carving. The sides or supports of the mirror are also ornamented in a manner which harmonizes perfectly with the balance of the dresser. The dresser base is a beautiful curved pattern shape. The top is the handsome late style swell front, and has large and small roomy drawers fitted with cast brass knobs **and** handles and locks and keys. The dresser base has handsome paneled sides, and in its completeness the dresser is beyond a rival at anything like **the** price, being made of the **best quarter sawed solid oak,** finished with a handsome polish equal to **that** of the finest piano. At our factory to consumer price you have a dresser equal to those which retail at $40.00 or more. We furnish it complete with **best plate castors** and pack it very carefully for shipment. It weighs complete when packed about 175 lbs.
Our special price............ **$22.00**

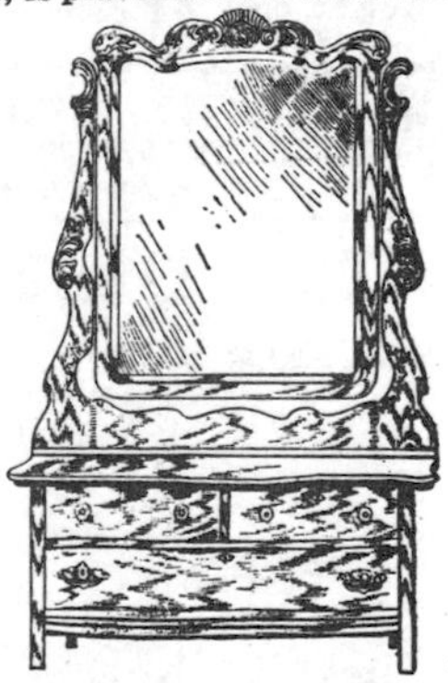

## A $22.00 Dresser for $15.00.

**No. 9357 This Dresser is manufactured especially** for those who wish to purchase an iron bed and desire an odd dresser to complete the suit. **This** desirable and fancy shaped dresser is made of **the best quarter sawed oak** with a fine polished finish. The oval mirror is made of the best imported bevel plate, and set in fancy swing frame, decorated with fancy carving, The mirror is 24x30 inches in size. Top of dresser is 19x41 inches in size. Three large roomy drawers, fitted with cast brass handles. Paneled ends, perfectly finished. **The Dresser is fitted with castors** complete. This is an **especially good bargain** and we take the greatest care in packing **it** for shipment that it may reach customers in perfect condition. Weight, packed, about 110 lbs.
Our special price............ **$15.00**

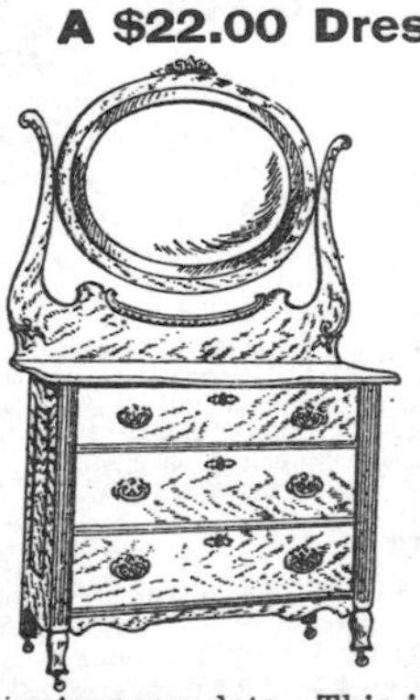

## A ROYAL UPRIGHT PIANO FOR $125.00.

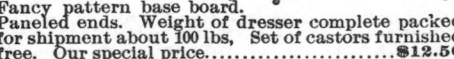

**C. O. D. ON LIBERAL SUBJECT TO EXAMINATION TERMS.**

**Twenty days trial allowed.**

**ORGANS AT LESS THAN $25.00.**

**SPECIAL GRAND PIANO AND ORGAN CATALOGUE FREE.**

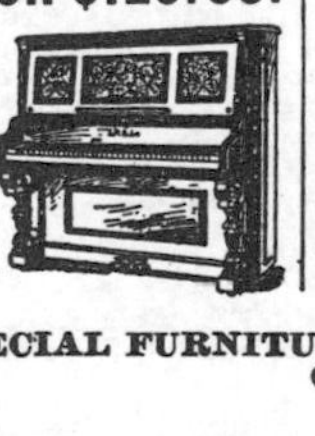

**SEND FOR OUR MAMMOTH SPECIAL FURNITURE CATALOGUE. WE FURNISH YOUR HOUSE FROM CELLAR TO GARRET. SPLENDID LINE OF CARPETS IN OUR CARPET DEPARTMENT.**

# SPECIAL BARGAIN SALE OF CHIFFONIERS AND BUREAUS.

### SEND FOR OUR SPECIAL FURNITURE CATALOGUE FOR MORE COMPLETE LINE TO SELECT FROM.

## An $8.00 Chiffonier for $5.25.

**No. 9359** No dressing room is complete without **a chiffonier**. It is a convenient receptacle for all dressing accessories. At our unusually low price no one need be without an article of this kind. We have taken particular pains to secure nothing but what is well made, and that of the very best material, and we take pleasure therefore in offering to your attention the chiffonier shown in illustration as an example of what can be done in the matter of price. Thisc hiffonier is made of very fine **solid oak**, has four large roomy drawers, is excellently finished, and presents a handsome appearance. It is 4 feet 2 inches in height, and the top is 18x31 inches in size. Handsomely decorated top and paneled sides. **Pattern base board.** Weight packed for shipment about 85 lbs. Our special price..........................$5.25

## A $12.00 Chiffonier for $7.25.

**No. 9361** This Chiffonier **is** made of the choicest kiln dried solid oak, thoroughly seasoned and guaranteed to be perfectly free from warping or checking. The height of the Chiffonier is 5 feet 6 inches. The size of the top is 18 by 31 inches. Fancy German bevel plate mirror set in swing frame decorated with hand carving. The drawers are fitted with fancy cast brass handles and are perfectly made, so that they may be moved in or out without difficulty, a feature which will commend itself to those who have been bothered with cheap furniture. Sides paneled and perfectly finished, Weight, packed for shipment, about 100 lbs. Our special price..........................$7.25

**WE PACK ALL FURNITURE** WITH THE UTMOST CARE AND **DELIVER WITHOUT EXTRA CHARGE ON BOARD CARS AT CHICAGO.** . . . .

## Our Special $8.00 Bureau.

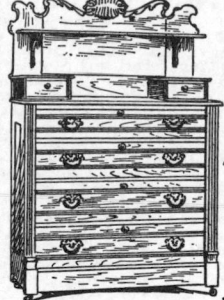

**No. 9362** To meet the demand for these desirable articles of furniture, we have completed our contracts with leading manufacturers in this line of goods, and take pleasure in presenting to your attention the bureau shown in the illustration. This bureau is made of the best **solid oak, handsomely finished.** It is fitted with **four very large roomy drawers in base and two small drawers at top**. It has further convenience in the way of shelf at top, suppo ted by fancy brackets. The top of bureau is handsomely decorated with beautiful and **massive carving.** S des are perfectly finished and paneled. Castors free. Weight, packed for shipment, about 70 lbs. Our special price..$8.00

**No. 9363** We can also furnish the Bureau same as No. 9362, illustrated and described above, with a **fancy imported bevel plate mirror**, 12x28 inches in size, instead of wood panel back, if desired. Weight, packed for shipment, 85 lbs. Our special price.**$10.00**

## $12.75 is the Price.

**No. 9368** The Bureau which we show in the illustration is one of the new patterns for 1897. Its desirability is unquestioned, for even from the faint idea you can get from the cut you can judge of its elegant appearance. **The most expert artists** have designed this pattern, and the bureau is superior to anything that is on the market. This bureau is made of **fine solid oak; beautiful hand carved ornaments on front and on mirror frame. The mirror in swing frame is made of the best heavy bevel plate glass, and is 20x24 inches in size. Four large, roomy drawers with cast brass handles in base and two small convenient drawers in top. The sides are handsomely finished and paneled. Fancy pattern base board; castors free.** Weight of bureau when packed for shipment, about 85 lbs. Our special price........................$12.75

## Latest Design for 1897.

**No. 9367** We wish it were possible for you to see this bureau which we illustrate in the cut. We know that if you could see it, at the price which we name you would not hesitate a minute before deciding to own it yourself. **It is so thoroughly well made** of the best quarter sawed oak and finely finished, it is so handsomely decorated with massive hand carving in front and top, and the outline and richness of design are **so attractive** that you could not help but acknowledge it the best bargain you had ever seen or heard off at anything like our price. Four very large roomy drawers with **massive hand carving** and fitted with fancy cast brass handless. Two small decorated and convenient drawers at top. Fancy c a r v e d and beaded pillars in front. Sides are perfectly finished and paneled. **Fancy pattern** base board fitted with best quality castors free. Weight of this bureau is about 90 lbs. We pack these goods very c a r e f u l l y and guarantee them to be exactly as represented or money will be refunded. Remember our 3 per cent. cash discount when full amount accompanies order. We ship on the most liberal C. O. D. terms, and want you to be perfectly satisfied that the goods are what we represent them to be. Our special price.. ..................................$12.00

# OUR WONDERFUL COMBINATION BED-ROOM SUIT.

**THE SALE OF THIS SUIT HAS REACHED THE HIGHEST POINT EVER KNOWN IN THE FURNITURE TRADE. WE BUY BY CARLOADS, AND ARE THUS ABLE TO MAKE A PRICE AGAINST WHICA NONE CAN COMPETE. SEND $5.00 AND WE WILL SEND COMPLETE SUIT C. O. D. SUBJECT TO EXAMINATION. SEE OUR ELEGANT IRON BEDS ON NEXT PAGE. SEND FOR OUR GREAT SPECIAL FURNITURE CATALOGUE.**

## A MODERN $30.00 SUIT FOR $15.00.

**IF PRICES ARE ANY OBJECT TO YOU**

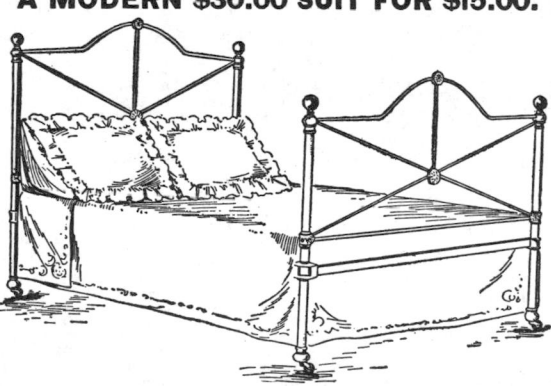

**THIS IS THE CHANCE OF A LIFETIME.**

Price for this Dresser only, $7.95

**No. 9374**
Price for Iron Bed only........$3.50
Price for complete Suit......$15.00

Price of Commode..:...$3.68

For $15.00 we offer a suit your local dealer would ask $30.00 for. **OUR TERMS ARE EASY.** We will send the suit to any address by freight, C. O. D., subject to examination on receipt of $5.00. You can examine the suit at your local station and if found satisfactory pay the freight agent the balance, $10.00, and freight charges and the suit is yours. 3 per cent. discount allowed if cash in full accompanies your order, when $14.55 pays for the suit.

You can order any one of pieces or the complete suit at prices above named.

**Description of Iron Bed.** We offer this iron bed at about one-half the regular retail price. It is a strong heavy made bed, the very latest style, a new pattern just out. Height, 4 feet 2 inches. Your choice of following sizes: 3 feet, 3 feet 6 inches, 4 feet 6 inches, the price is the same. Be sure to state width wanted. All beds are 6 feet 6 inches long, have 1 inch pillars and filling of ⅜ inch, ornamented with brass knobs, beautifully finished in white enamel throughout. No better bed ever offered. Iron Beds are the proper thing, there are ten iron beds sold to one wooden bed. They are cleaner, neater, healthier and more stylish. Remember our price, **$3.50.**

**Description of Dresser.** This is a beautiful hardwood, white enameled dresser, such as would retail at double our price. The very latest and most stylish thing in a dresser, made to match the white enameled iron bed. Size of top 20x38 inches, with a very fine beveled plate imported mirror, size 20x24, has 3 large roomy drawers, which are trimmed with heavy fancy brass handles, top of mirror frame is finely carved, the base is made with fancy panel and fitted with patent socket castors.

Our special price for dresser only ........$7.95

**Description of Commode.** This beautiful Commode is made of hardwood, finished in white enamel to match white enamel iron bed and dresser. Size of top 17x30 inches, splasher back and made with panel base, has 2 drawers and 2 doors, fitted with patent socket castors.

Our special price for Commode........$3.68

**No. 9374** Price for Complete Suit of 3 pieces, Iron Bed, Dresser and Commode ........$15.00

**YOU CAN ORDER A BED-ROOM SUIT OR DRESSER AND HAVE CLOTHING, DRY GOODS, SHOES AND ALL SMALL ARTICLES PACKED IN THE DRAWERS. FREIGHT WILL THEN BE PRACTICALLY NO MORE THAN ON THE FURNITURE ALONE.**

# THE BEST IRON BEDS AND THE CHEAPEST. Typical of Strength Cleanliness and Beauty.

**Nowhere else are such Values. Nowhere else such Liberal C. O. D. Terms. 3 per cent off for full cash with orders, or C. O. D. subject to examination on $5.00 deposit.**

## Very Desirable and Only 90 Cents.

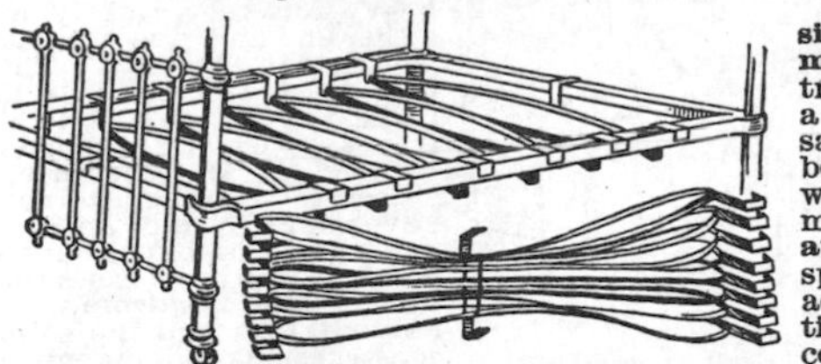

**9386 Where it is desirable to use a coil spring mattress,** or a wire mattress which is not made on a wooden frame, a necessary addition to an iron bed is a slat of some kind which will sustain the mattress. **We call special attention** to the patent spring slats shown in the accompanying illustration. They are ingeniously constructed and composed of strips of untempered steel, set on edge and riveted together. This forms **a complete bed bottom,** and it is the strongest for the purpose that could possibly be built. It is very compact for shipment and far stronger than wood slats. **It is perfectly adjusted** to slight variations in length or width of bedsteads, and by means of the adjustable hangers can be so adjusted as to drop the spring bed down to suit any taste as regards the height of the bed. Our special price.......................................................**$0.90**

## A $7.00 Iron Bed at Half Price.

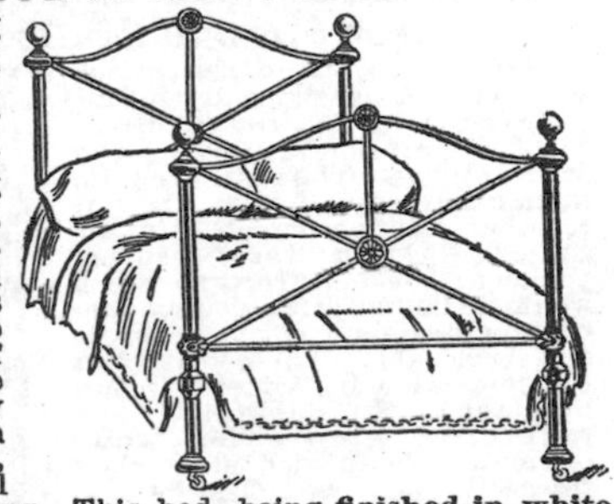

**9388 We have had an unusual demand during the past season** for iron beds with odd dressers, and the trade has been very rapidly increasing. In order to meet the demand for **an extremely cheap bed** which will be handsome in appearance as well as strong and substantial, we offer the one which we show in the accompanying illustration as the most desirable low priced bed it has been possible to secure. **This iron bed,** is made with 1⅛ inch iron pillars, while the cross rod and fillings are made of 5-16th and ⅜th inch material. The posts are surmounted by **very fancy brass mounts** and vases. We furnish this bed either in 3 feet, 3 feet 6 inch, 4 feet, or 4 feet 6 inch width. In all cases the bed is 6 feet, 4 inches long. This bed, being **finished in white enamel,** presents a very elegant appearance and is very substantial in every respect, being made by one of the leading manufacturers in this line in this country. The weight, when packed for shipment, is about 65 lbs.
Our special price.......................................................**$3.50**

## Our Latest Iron Bed for $4.85.

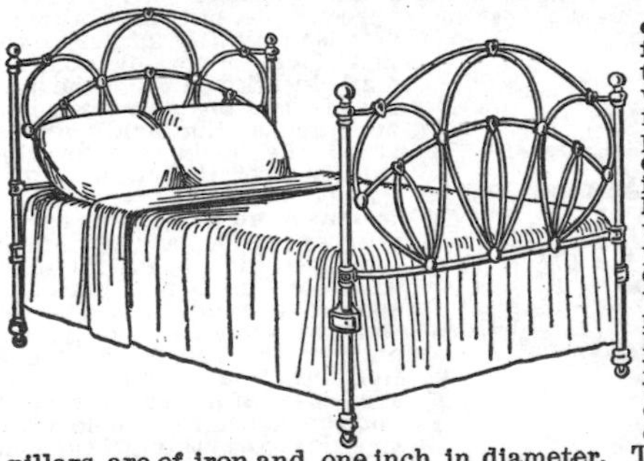

**9390 An entirely new departure in the way of fancy designs** has been taken by the manufacturer with whom our contracts for iron beds have been placed this season. The design which we show in illustration is one of the **latest for 1897 trade,** and we feel certain that any purchaser who is fortunate enough to secure this bed will be delighted with it, not only by reason of its handsome appearance, but furthermore by reason of the unusual strength and **durability of the material** of which it is made. The pillars are of iron and one inch in diameter. The filling is 5-16ths inch in diameter. The rods are **surmounted by fancy brass vases,** adding elegance to an already handsome bed. The height of the head is 51 inches and the height of the foot is 46 inches. We furnish this bed in three sizes, 3 feet 6 inches, 4 feet or 4 feet 6 inch wide, as may be desired. In all cases the bed is 6 foot 4 inches long. It is finished with **a very desirable grade of white enamel** in several coats. With any of the separate dressers which we show in this catalogue, together with wash-stand, you have a bedroom suit which is out of the usual order of things, and will give you a great deal of satisfaction. Weight, packed for shipment, about 100 lbs.
Our special price.......................................................**$4.85**

## An $8.00 Bed for $5.60.

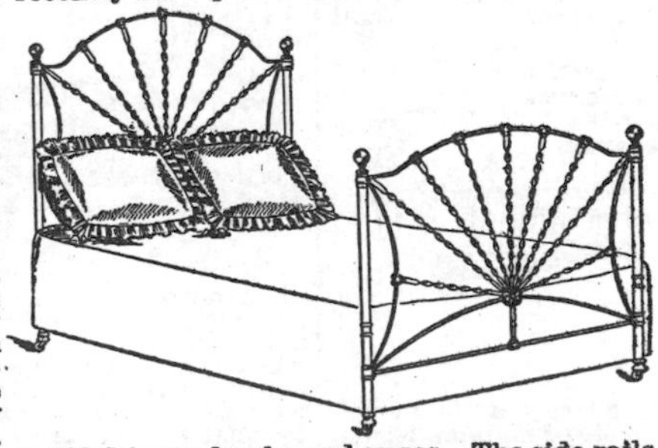

**9392 From the variety of handsome and desirable patterns** in the way of iron beds which have recently been put on the market, we have selected the one shown in illustration as one of the most desirable and attractive designs that can be secured. **This bed is made by a manufacturer** whose reputation is well known for the unusually high quality of the goods he makes, and we offer this bed as a substantial and durable piece of furniture, which is as durable as it is cheap and as cheap as it is thoroughly well made. **The solid iron pillars** are 1 inch in diameter and the cross rods are 5-16 inch in diameter. **Fancy iron work** at head and foot. Pillars are surmounted by **beautiful brass knobs and vases.** The side rails are of unusual strength and are fitted accurately and closely in the joints, giving the bed a rigidity which can not be found in cheap articles of furniture on the market. This bed is made 4 feet wide, or 4 feet 6 inches wide. The bed is **finished in very handsome white enamel** of the best quality, and presents a very beautiful appearance. Weight, when packed for shipment, is about 100 pounds. We pack and crate these beds very securely, so that they may be certain to reach you in proper condition.
Our Special Price.......................................................**$5.60**

## A $12.00 Iron Bed for $7.25.

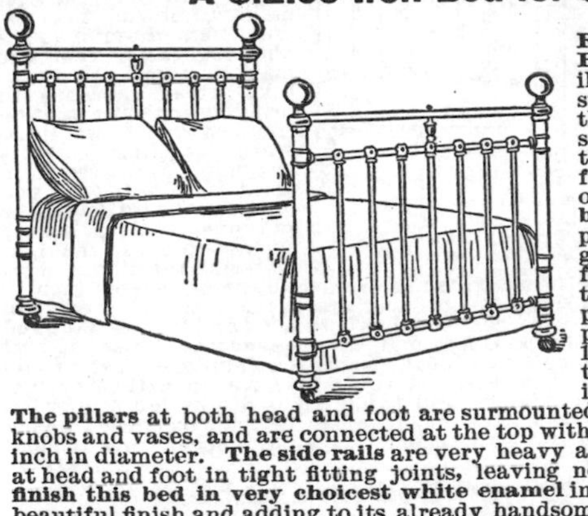

**9394 The Massive and Rich Appearing Iron Bed** which we show in the illustration is unusually strongly constructed from the very best and most selected materials by the the same leading manufacturer who makes all of our iron beds. **The very best workmen** are employed in making these goods, and we are therefore assured that our customers will be very highly pleased with them. The pillars are made of iron 1⅛ inch in diameter, while the rodding throughout is is ⅜ inch in diameter. **The pillars** at both head and foot are surmounted by very handsome brass knobs and vases, and are connected at the top with a solid brass top rail ⅝ inch in diameter. **The side rails** are very heavy and strong, and are fitted at head and foot in tight fitting joints, leaving no room for vermin. **We finish this bed in very choicest white enamel** in several coats, giving it a beautiful finish and adding to its already handsome appearance. We make this bed in three sizes, either 3 feet 6 inches wide, 4 feet wide or 4 feet 6 inches wide, the beds in all cases being 6 feet 2 inches long. Bed is fitted **with casters free of charge.** In ordering coil spring mattress for this bed you should also order extra slats, which are quoted on another page. The steel slats are necessary for mattresses of the kind mentioned. If a woven wire mattress is used you will not need steel slats as we make them with extended rails especially for iron beds. This bed, when carefully packed and crated for shipment, weighs about 100 lbs.
Our Special Price.......................................................**$7.25**

## A $12.50 Iron Bed for $7.95.

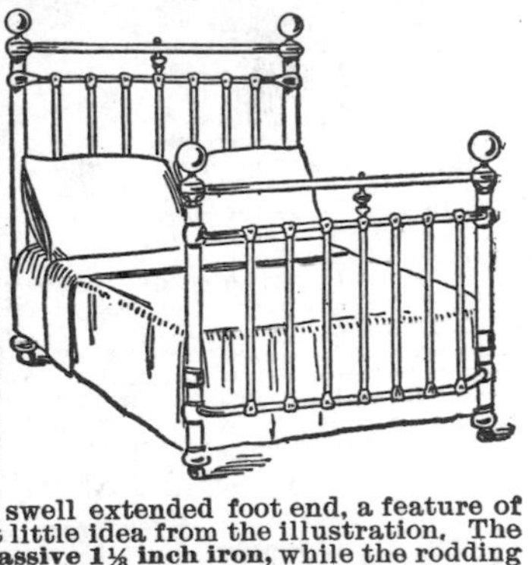

**9396 It is impossible for you to gain any idea of the handsome appearance** of this iron bed from the illustration. The artist is not able to do it justice, although he has drawn it from a photograph. However, we can assure you that this is **one of the most desirable bargains** in the way of iron beds ever offered, and we should be pleased to send it to you C. O. D. subject to examination on our liberal C. O. D. terms. If you do not find it exactly as represented and entirely satisfactory it can be returned to us and **we will cheerfully refund your money.** If you wish to send cash in full with order, remember that we **allow a discount of 3 per cent.** and in all cases if goods are not up to our representation they may be returned to us and money will be refunded. This handsome iron bed is made with swell extended foot end, a feature of whose attractiveness you can gain but little idea from the illustration. The corner posts are made of **heavy and massive 1⅛ inch iron,** while the rodding and filling throughout are made of ⅜ inch iron. The posts are surmounted by **handsome brass knobs and vases** connected with a **solid brass top rod** at both head and foot, this top rod being ⅝ of an inch in diameter. **The finish** of this bed is of the same high order as all our best beds, viz: in several coats of beautiful white enamel, very durable and handsome. The bed is fitted with the **best casters** free of charge. We make this bed in three sizes, viz: 3 feet 6 inches, 4 feet, or 4 feet 6 inches wide, in all cases the beds being 6 feet 2 inches long. Weight, when very carefully packed and crated for shipment, 100 pounds. Bedding, of course, is not included.
Our special price.......................................................**$7.95**

## Our $8.50 Brass Trimmed Iron Bed.

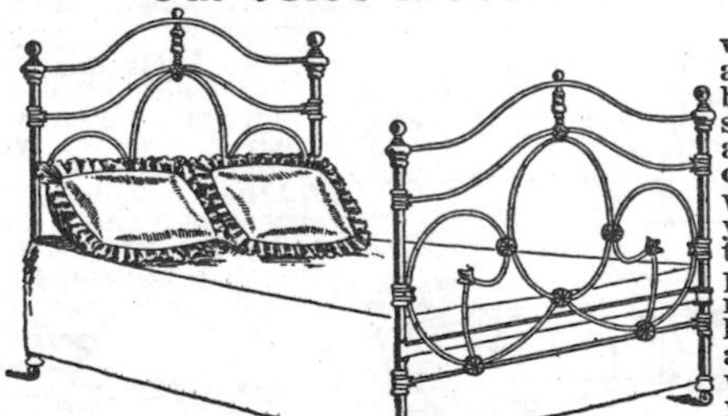

**9398 To appreciate the wonderful values** which we are giving in the line of iron beds, it is absolutely necessary that you see one of the articles themselves. **On our liberal C. O. D. terms,** we should be glad to have you take the opportunity to examine one of the beds, providing you desire to make such a purchase. We know that you can not help admitting that the **bargains we are offering** are such as you have never seen or heard of, and that we are giving you better value than could possibly be secured through any other source. **This beautiful and substantial iron bed** is made of the best selected material with one inch iron pillars and 5-16ths inch filling. **The ornamental iron work** is of the highest degree of art, and the pillars are such as you will find only in the most expensive furniture. We make this bed in two sizes, either 4 feet or 4 feet 6 inches wide by 6 feet 2 inches long. We furnish casters free of charge. Weight when packed for shipment about 100 lbs.
Our special price.......................................................**$8.50**

## IF YOU HAVE NEVER DEALT WITH US

**YOU CAN ASK YOUR BANKER TO LOOK UP OUR FINANCIAL STANDING. HE WILL TELL YOU THAT WE ARE**

**Thoroughly Responsible.**

**WRITE TO THE METROPOLITAN NATIONAL BANK**

**OF CHICAGO, ENCLOSING STAMP IF YOU WANT TO KNOW MORE.**

**WE QUOTE A VERY DESIRABLE AND REMARKABLY CHEAP LINE OF STYLISH PARLOR, BANQUET AND TABLE LAMPS IN LAMP DEPARTMENT. MAKE NO MISTAKE BY BUYING ELSEWHERE.**

## A $16.00 Bed for $10.00.

**9400** Such value as we are offering in the bed shown in illustration is unusual, in fact, were you to see the article itself you could hardly believe that it was possible to make it at the price which we name. We have placed our contracts for the year of 1897 with the best manufacturer in the

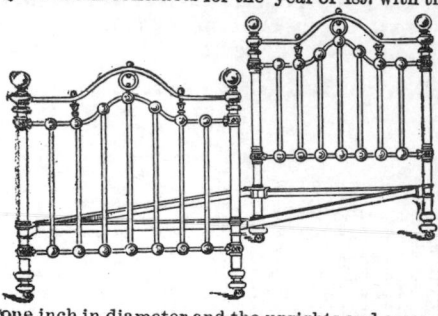

country, a manufacturer whose **line of iron beds is superior** to anything else turned out. We make it a point to contract for such goods with only the best makers, knowing that our customers deserve t h e choicest goods that the markets afford. We hence take great pleasure in bringing to your attention the bed which we illustrate, knowing that its purchase would result in great credit to us and **entire satisfaction to the purchaser.** It is solidly constructed of the best material, the pillars being one inch in diameter and the uprights and cross rods being 5-16ths inch in diameter. The pillars at both head and foot are surmounted by **beautiful two inch brass knobs or vases,** connected at both head and foot with **top rod of solid brass,** beautifully polished, and very **handsome brass ring at center.** The side rails and all parts of the bed throughout are substantially made, thoroughly well put together, and you will have an article of furniture which possesses the strength and durability to last a lifetime of wear. We make this bed in two sizes, 4 feet or 4 feet 6 inches wide by 6 feet 2 inches long, and finish it in beautiful white enamel. Weight, packed for shipment, 125 lbs. Our special price.................................................$10.00

## A $15.00 Iron Bed for $10.50.

**9402** It is impossible for us in a short description and a small illustration to give you a complete idea of the value and durability as well as **elegant appearance** of

this **remarkably cheap iron bed.** We show this bed in a larger illustration in our Special Furniture Catalogue, and would recommend that you send for that catalogue if you contemplate placing a furniture order. This bed is made of the best selected iron, **all rods and cross pieces, pillars,** etc., being of the **very best material.** The pillars are one inch in diameter, the spindles, cross rods, ornamental iron work being 5-16 inch in diameter. The pillars are surmounted by handsome brass knobs. **The Design** is new and ornamental while the extended foot rail adds to its already handsome appearance. **The pattern** is one which you will not find in local stores, as the bed is only sold by the finest retail dealers in large cities. We furnish this bed in two sizes, either 4 feet or 4 feet 6 inches wide by 6 feet 2 inches long, and finish it in handsome white enamel of the very best quality. Weight packed for shipment, 125 lbs. We **crate these** beds with the utmost care that they may reach you in the most perfect condition. Remember our 3 per cent. discount when cash in full accompanies order. Our Special price.................................$10.50

## A $6.50 Child's Bed for $4.50.

**9306** The **Great Advantage** in iron beds is their cleanliness, in fact that is one of their great points of superiority over the old fashioned wood bed which always gives so much chance for dirt and vermin. **These Beds** are substantially constructed of the very best material with ½ inch posts and **strong iron filling.** We finish these beds in handsome white enamel, the same beautiful finish as is found in all our best work. Size, 2 feet 6 inches wide by 4 feet 6 inches long. Weight when packed for shipment about 65 lbs.
Our special price.................$4.60

## Our $42.50 Solid Brass Bed.

**9404** The **Illustration of Our Very Finest Solid Brass Bed** will give you some idea of its elegant appearance. It is made with swell foot end,

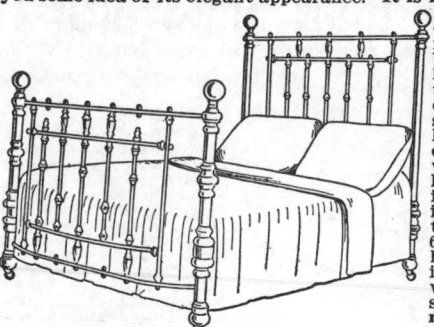

has 2 inch solid pillars decorated with handsome ornaments and surmounted by 3½ inch **solid brass knobs.** The cross rods and upright rods are ⅝ inch in diameter. The end rails are solidly constructed, very heavy, fit very tightly at either end and give the bed **very great strength.** The height of the head is 58 inches; height of foot is 37 inches. We make this up in three sizes, all beds being 6 feet 4 inches long. You have your choice of 3 foot 6 inch, 4 foot or 4 foot 6 inch width. Price in all cases the same. **The handsome ornamentation** and the solid construction render it one of the most desirable beds on the market. **The rods throughout, all posts, uprights, knobs, ornamentations and decorations are solid brass.** We fit the beds with the **very finest casters** and it is easily handled and most substantial in every respect. It is a bed that would ordinarily retail in high class retail stores, in which it would only be found, at from **$75.00 to $85.00.** To those who are in the market for a most substantial and desirable piece of furniture which can be handed down to future generations we recommend this as the best purchase they could possibly make.
Our special price.....................................$47.50

## Our Special $5.95 Child's Iron Bed.

**9408** We show in illustration a very choice pattern of Child's Iron Bedstead. It is very substantially made of the most select material and will stand long and rough usage. The bed is all iron with **fancy iron scroll fillings.** The posts are ½ in. in diameter, and all parts are put

together with the utmost care by skilled workmen, thus insuring you an article of furniture which would be not only **handsome and ornamental** but most desirable and serviceable. The bed is 2 feet 4 inches wide by 4 feet 6 inches long, and all the iron work is carefully coated with the finest white enamel. We furnish steel slats free with each bed. Casters also free. Weight, packed for shipment, about 75 pounds. Our special price ..... .........................$5.95

## A $12.00 Iron Bed for $8.75.

**9410** These Child's Beds are made by a manufacturer who has a world-wide reputation for the unusual high quality of his goods. Not only is the material (which is iron) the most select procurable, but the workmanship is unusually fine, since the manufacturer employs none but skilled workmen, men who have been in the business for years, and hence thoroughly understand the business of making furniture of this style, which will be **extremely durable as well as handsome.** The corner posts of this bed are ½ inch in diameter, with beautiful brass knobs or vases, and brass top rods. The handsome iron scroll work adds much to the appearance of the bed. We furnish iron slats free. The side rails are heavy, of unusual strength, and the bed on the whole is far superior to anything of the kind made by other manufacturers. Size, 2 feet 6 inches wide by 4 feet 6 inches long. Sides are made to let down for convenience. The weight packed for shipment is about 80 lbs. Our special price...................$8.75
We furnish a superior woven wire mattress with above bed at $1.10 extra.

## Our $1.95 Child's Crib.

It is difficult to imagine how it is possible for manufacturers to turn out a crib which possesses so many points of general excellence as the one which we show in illustration at the unheard-of price

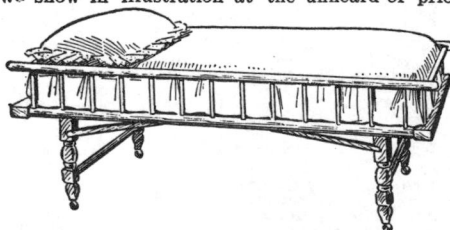

which we name below. **This folding crib** is made of choicest maple, either **natural finish or imitation mahogany,** either finish being extremely desirable. It has **adjustable brace,** and is held extremely rigid when open. The legs are made to fold close to bottom of bed so that it occupies but little space when not in use. **The side rails** are well constructed and securely fastened, giving unusual strength. **The wire mattress** furnished free is of excellent material. We furnish the crib in two sizes, and it weighs, packed for shipment, about 50 lbs.
No. 9412 **Child's Folding Crib,** size, 30x34 inches.
Price.................................................$1.95
No. 9414 **Child's Folding Crib,** size, 36x60 inches.
Price....................................................$2.25

## Our $2.30 Folding Crib.

The **Folding Crib** which we show in illustration is practically the same as No. 9412 above, but is fitted **with folding top** which adds considerable to the height when opened, and by means of the **patent folding attachment** does not occupy any more space than the ordinary crib when closed. This crib is fitted with **new adjustable brace** which makes the **legs extremely rigid** when raised. We mount

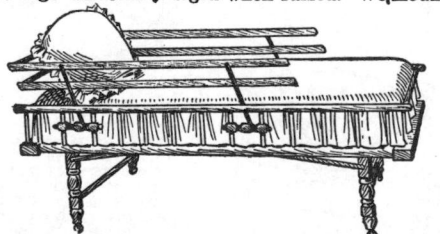

this crib on casters, and it is hence readily moved about. The castings are all made of malleable iron, and the crib throughout is substantially constructed, making it the neatest crib of the kind on the market. **The extra high sides** secured by the folding attachment are the most practical folding sides on the market and add greatly to the desirability of this article. Weighs, when packed for shipment, about 65 lbs. We furnish the crib in natural maple or imitation mahogany, as desired. It is made in the following sizes:
No. 9416 **Child's Folding Crib,** size 30 x 54 inches.
Price..................................................$2.30
No. 9417 **Child's Folding Crib,** size 36 x 60 inches.
Price..................................................$2.65

## Child's Folding Bed for $4.30.

**9419** The **Child's Folding Bed** which we **Show** in the Illustration is one of the most economical pieces of furniture that can be purchased. This

folding bed contains all the latest improvements in the way of folding devices, etc., is very light and **put together with an idea of strength and neatness.** The castings are all malleable iron and thoroughly well made. **The material** is the best selected maple handsomely finished. At the end of the bed there is a **drapery rod** so that when the bed is closed the front can be covered with drapery, and when opened the drapery can be thrown over the end of the bed as shown in illustration. The drapery and bedding are not furnished. We guarantee that **customers will be delighted** with the bed, not only from the fact that it is unusually cheap but that it is desirable in every respect by reason of the superior quality of material and excellent workmanship. It weighs when packed for shipment about 75 pounds. It is consequently light and easy to handle. We finish the wood in either natural maple or imitation mohogany. Size of bed is 30 inches wide by 60 inches long.
Our Special price...........................$4.30
No. 9420 **We have the Same Folding Bed** as above illustrated and described, 40 inches wide and 60 inches long.
Our Special price...........................$5.00

## A $2.50 Cradle for $1.40.

**9423 You would not think after seeing this cradle** that it was possible to make it for the price, but the manufacturers are long on cradles and short on cash, and we are hence able to name our own figures. We give our customers **the advantage of every squeeze in the market.** We recommend this article as most desirable in every respect and quoted at an unheard of price. **This cradle** is made of the best selected hard wood with bent wood work and finished in antique or dark finish, as desired. The size is 24 inches by 44 inches, and is shipped knocked down when taken apart, thus saving very largely on freight. It is very easily set up and put together with screws.

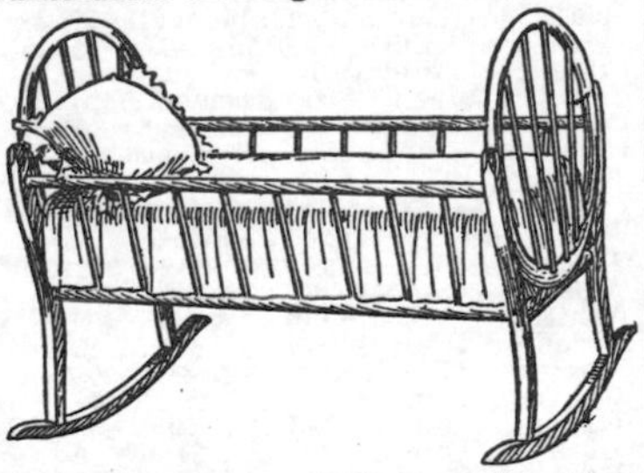

Our special price........................................ **$1.40**

## A Bargain for $2.00.

**This is one of the most unique and desirable Cradles ever put on the market.** The base is very strongly constructed and extremely rigid. **The cradle swings very easily,** the body being hung on patented hangers, making it one of the most easily operated cradles on the market. It is thoroughly

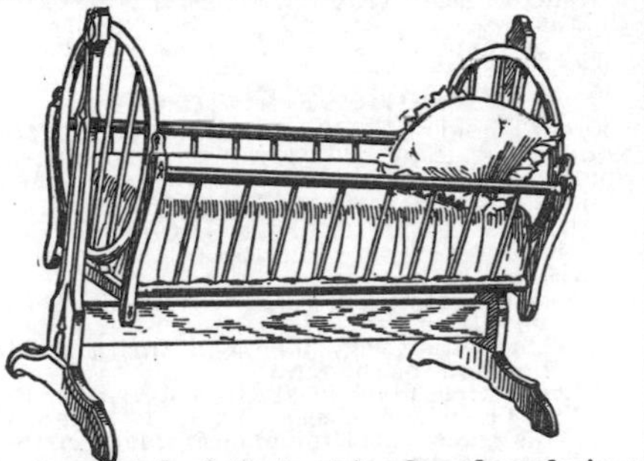

well constructed of the best hardwood, made in a fancy shape and finished either in **antique oak or dark finish,** as may be desired. It presents an elegant appearance, and your neighbor will not believe you when you mention the price which you paid for it. Comes in size 24 x 44 inches, and is taken apart for shipping, thus saving very largely on the freight. Our special price.................................. **$2.00**

## Our $1.05 Wire Cot.

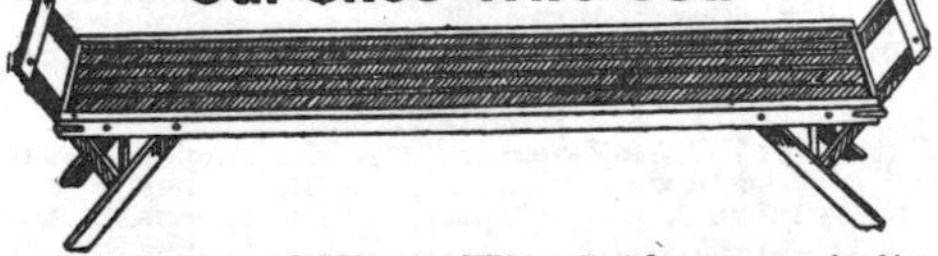

**The Universal Woven Wire Cot** has many imitations on the market, which is the best proof in the world of its general excellence. This cot is the most desirable low priced article of furniture on the market, and is so constructed that the head and foot are raised by opening the legs. **It is very substantial,** the frame being made of selected hard wood and fitted with a woven wire mattress. No house is complete without a c cot of this kind. When not in use **it takes up very small space,** and being unusually light is easily moved from one part of the house to another when convenience demands it. We make this cot in two sizes, prices as follows:

**No. 9426** 2 feet 6 inches wide by 6 feet long. Our special price........................................ **$1.05**

**No. 9427** 3 feet wide by 6 feet long. Our special price........................................ **$1.20**

## $1.75 Cot for $1.10.

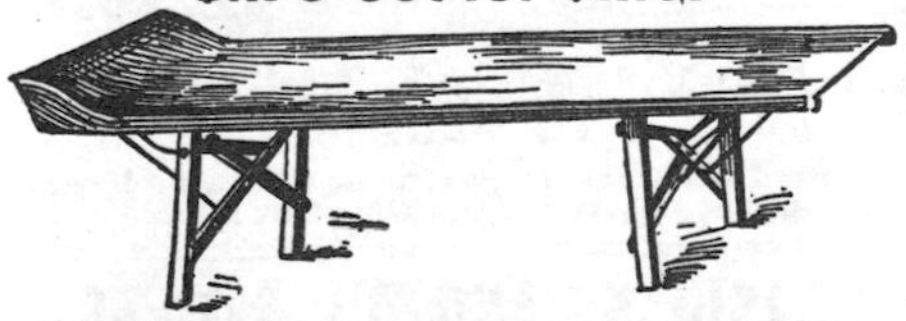

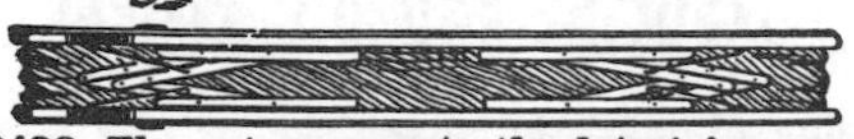

**9428 The cut represents the latest improved Folding Cot** on the market. We offer it to our customers as an article of comfort, neatness, strength and simplicity. It is constructed with the latest **improved head rest or pillow,** which is in itself a most valuable feature, forming as it does a perfect rest or pillow for the head. The lower illustration shows how compactly the cot can be packed together, and for camping parties, hotels or private use the **Eclipse Cot is without a rival.** The frame is made of the best selected hard wood, and is constructed throughout with a view to durability as well as compactness and neatness. In size it is 29 inches wide. Our special price........................ **$1,10**

## Our 95 Cent Wire Mattress.

**No. 9429 This is the Regular Standard Mattress for the Million.** The frame is made of thoroughly hard seasoned maple and with thick batten. It has **perfectly tight joints** between end rail and batten, while the batten crowning as shown gives great

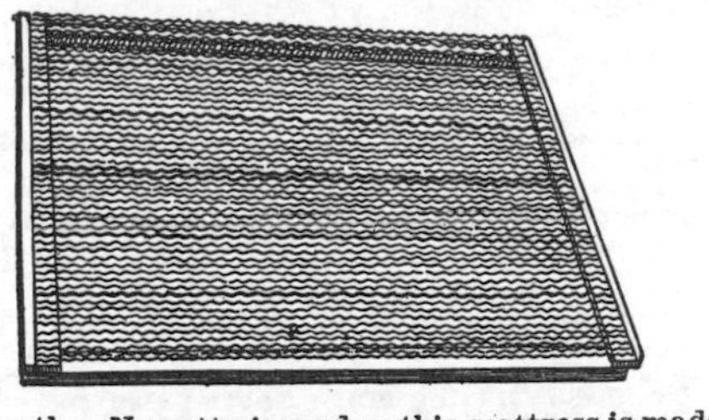

strength. No putty is used as this mattress is made by a leading manufacturer in his line and who puts out goods which will invariably add to his reputation. This is the **best low priced mattress made.** It has patent end fasteners for the fabric, making it impossible for any of the wires to become loosened by such strain as will be put upon them. This is a feature which no other wire mattress in the market posesses. Our special price, each.............. **$0.95**

**No. 9438 Woven Wire Mattress.** This mattress possesses the same good qualities as No. 9429 above with medium weave wire composed of the very **best drawn steel** very heavily corded. The frame is manufactured with especial care from the very best selected kiln dried stock. **This Mattress has a Special Advantage** not posessed by No. 9429 above, viz: **a Special Screw Extension.** This extension is shown in the cut of No. 9431 below. The advantage posessed by this attachment lies in the fact that the best woven wire fabric will after long usage stretch somewhat and lose part of its tension. By use of the screw attachment the mattress can be drawn taunt again, giving it the **same tension as it originally possessed.** Our special price.................. **$1.60**

## A $2.00 Mattress for $1.20.

**No. 9431 The Mattress which we show in the illustration** is made on the very best selected hardwood frame and carefully put together by the best mechanics that can be employed, hence having per-

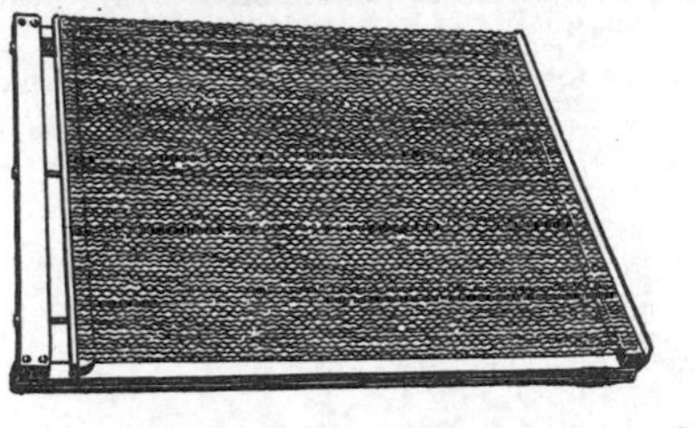

fectly tight joints, in which case no putty is needed as is the case with the cheap mattresses on the market. By means of the double end bar and side screw extension, of which the illustration gives you some little idea, **the fabric can be stretched to any desired tension** when after long usage it becomes slightly loose. This is the only positive and practical extension made. Having this double end bar and the fabric being made of a high grade of steel wire, this mattress will last a lifetime.

Our special price.................................. **$1.20**

**No. 9432 This Woven Wire Mattress differs from No. 9531 above** in that it has an extra heavily corded spring and is made of finer material throughout than the one above. **It is made on the same general principles as the one illustrated** with the latest practical set screw extension, and is very durable in every respect. Always state size of bed when ordering mattress.

Our special price in regular sizes ............ **$1.75**

## $1.45 Buys a $2.50 Mattress.

**9434 The illustration will give you some idea** of the unusually desirable features of this bed. It is made of the **finest corded woven wire fabric,** on a thoroughly seasoned and unusually well built frame of selected and thoroughly seasoned hard wood. The illustration shows the bottom of the

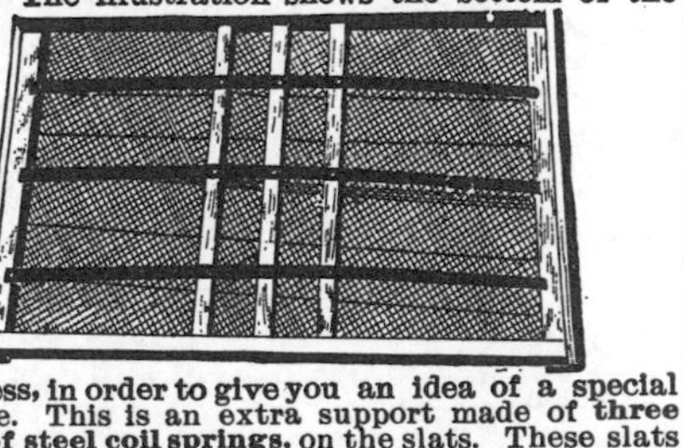

mattress, in order to give you an idea of a special feature. This is an extra support made of **three rows of steel coil springs,** on the slats. These slats are supported by three substantial iron straps running from the head to the foot of the spring. The slats are free at the end and the support is very rigid and substantial. It is impossible for us to express the general excellence of the spring better than to say that it is positively the most comfortable and durable mattress of the kind ever put on the market. It is made in regular sizes. Always mention size of bed when ordering.

Our special price for any regular size....... **$1.45**

## Our Special $1.40 Mattress.

**9436 We acknowledge no competition on this class of goods.** We invite you to compare this mattress with those you will see in any other catalogue. You will be compelled to admit that we set the pace for low prices. Not only do we believe our prices are lower than anyone else can make, but we have confidence in the unusual superiority of the goods which we sell. **This mattress is**

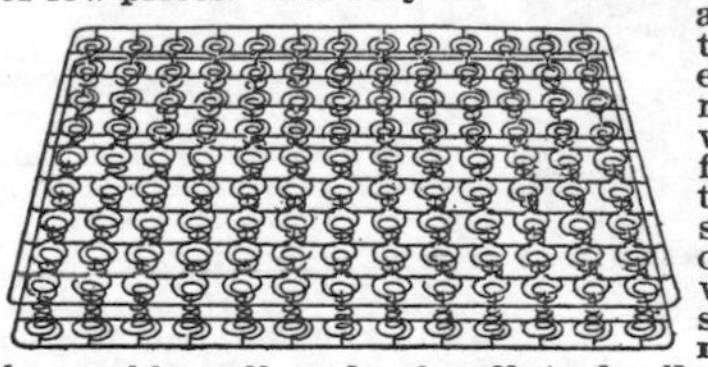

thoroughly well made, the **all steel coils** being handsomely japanned. The top and bottom surfaces are alike, the cone springs being double and connected by broad steel clasps of great strength. This bed is **elastic and yielding** in all its parts, conforming perfectly to the form and weight of the person lying on it. It is **unusually simple in construction,** which adds to its durability from the fact that there is scarcely anything to get out of order. Full size mattress has 117 double coil springs.

Our special price for regular size............ **$1.40**

## A $4.00 Bed Spring for $2.25.

**No. 9439 This is a Famous Spring** and is in every way worthy of the reputation which it has established for itself. We only ask that you give this mattress a trial to be assured that you will be thoroughly satisfied with it. The manufacture of goods of this nature is a practical science, and

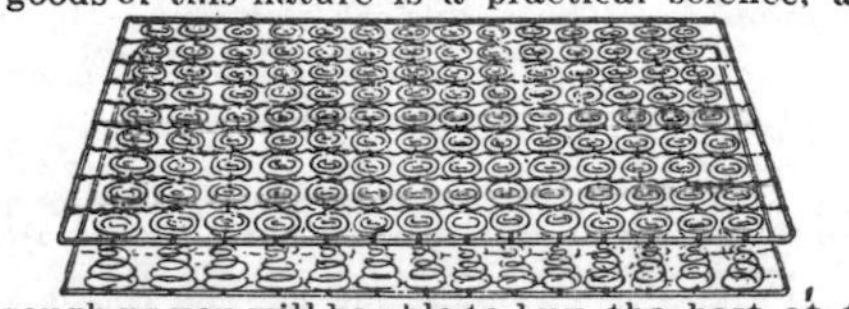

through us you will be able to buy the best at the price of the cheapest. The **scientific construction** of a satisfactory bed spring is only carried out in detail by the best manufacturers. The spring is made of the finest No. 12 steel wire and has **117 springs, tempered perfectly** and finely japanned. Each spring is made of a **double reverse coil,** made on a neat and perfect principle. Always state size of bed when ordering.

Our special price for regular size............ **$2.25**

**No. 9440 We have the same spring** as No. 9439 illustrated and described above, but **made to fold in the center** so that when moving from one bed to another it can be folded together and handled more readily, or if not in use will occupy much less space. Our special price .................... **$2.50**

## Special Steel Frame Bed Spring.

**No. 9442 The Woven Wire Mattress which we illustrate** is the most desirable from the fact that it is made on a **metal frame composed of solid angle steel.** Sides are composed of iron pipe. **The woven wire fabric is stretched tightly** and is the very best on the market, being composed, as it is, of the steel tempered wire. This wire mattress is so ar-

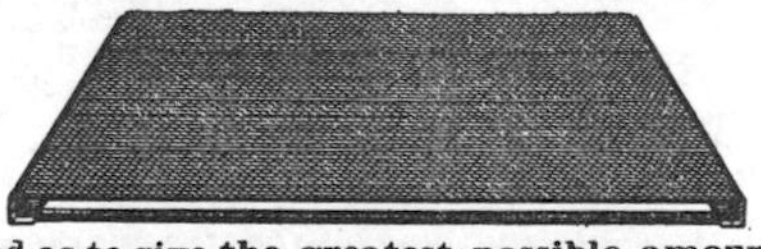

ranged as to give **the greatest possible amount of strength** for its weight, and is beyond a doubt the peer of any mattress on the market, while on the other hand it is superior to the majority of cheaply constructed mattresses which you will very frequently find in local retail stores. It is especially **desirable for metallic bedsteads,** but can, of course, be used for any bed, whether wood or iron. We furnish this mattress in four sizes, all being 6 feet long. The widths are 3 feet, 3 feet 6 inches, 4 feet or 4 feet 6 inches. In ordering be sure to state the width wanted. Our special price .................... **$3.38**

## A $7.00 Wire Mattress for $4.25.

**No. 9444 The Mattress which we show in** the illustration is precisely the same as No. 9442 illustrated above, but in the illustration we show the bottom of the mattress which has an additional feature not possessed by No. 9442 above, viz: **a steel supporter** attached to the frame with **six extra strong springs.** This supports **four rows of coil springs,** giving not only additional strength to the mattress itself but also adding **great elasticity,** both

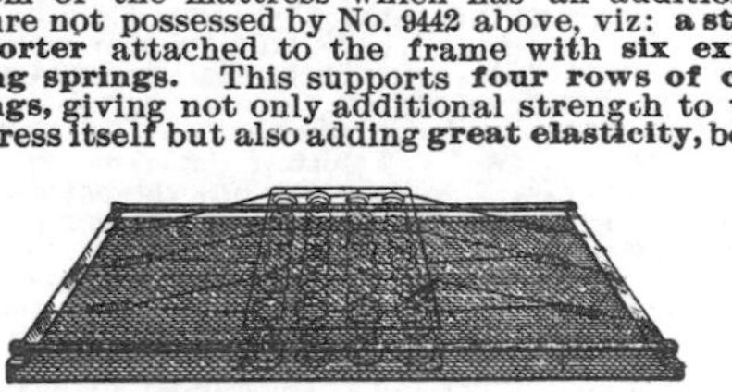

of which features commend themselves to the careful buyer. While No. 9442 above is unusually desirable you can readily perceive that these additional features render the mattress much more valuable, and we can assure any purchaser that they will find it the most satisfactory article of the kind ever purchased. We make this mattress in the following widths: 3 feet, 3 feet 6 inches, 4 feet, and 4 feet 6 inches, all mattresses being 6 feet long. Always mention size wanted when ordering.

Our special price.. ................................ **$4.25**

**IF YOU EVER HAVE CAUSE FOR ANY COMPLAINT WHATSOEVER, DO NOT HESITATE TO WRITE US FULLY, GIVING INVOICE NUMBER AND DATE OF SHIPMENT. WE ARE ANXIOUS TO PLEASE YOU.**

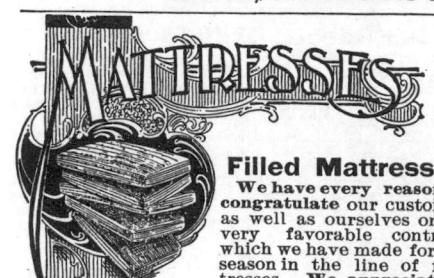

# MATTRESSES

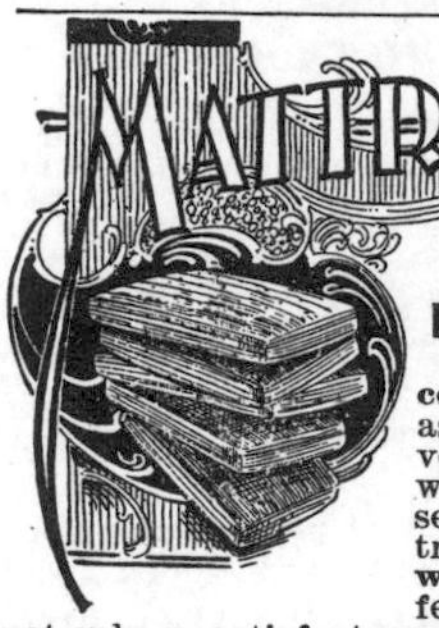

## Filled Mattresses.

**We have every reason to congratulate** our customers as well as ourselves on the very favorable contracts which we have made for this season in the line of mattresses. **We appreciate as well as** any one can that inferior goods of this class are not only unsatisfactory but entirely undesirable. We have consequently taken particular pains to **contract for our stock from a leading manufacturer,** one whose reputation has been made on a **high grade of goods,** and who turns out a quality equal to or better than anything else in the market. We quote a superior line of **excelsior, wool, cotton, moss and hair mattresses** that are guaranteed to give thorough satisfaction, are just as represented in every respect, and if not found to be up to our representation we will cheerfully refund money upon their return to us. Always state size of bed for which mattress is intended when ordering.

**No. 9446 This is an all excelsior mattress** made with plain ticking filled with excellent, pure and clean excelsior; easy and comfortable.
Our Special Price, each........................ **$1.70**

**No. 9448 A superior excelsior mattress made with wool top.** The excelsior which we use in this mattress is of the very best and cleanest quality, and the wool top adds greatly to its comfort. The ticks are bound and ticking used is of a superior quality, far better than you would ordinarily find and what retailers would consider cheap for $3.00.
Our Special Price, regular size.............. **$2.05**

**No. 9450 An all excelsior mattress with cotton top.** Like all our excelsior mattresses the quality of material is very nice and clean. The cotton top makes the mattress all the more desirable, giving it ease and comfort. The ticks are bound and the ticking is of superior quality. Our special price for regular size........................................ **$2.15**

**No. 9453 All Excelsior Mattress with Cotton Top and Bottom.** The mattress is consequently reversible, and when side becomes hard or packed, can be turned over and your mattress is just as soft and comfortable as when new. The material is clean and pure, while the ticking is of the very nicest quality. Ticks are bound. Special price, each.. **$2.75**

**No. 9454 Plain Husk Mattress.** The husks which we use in these mattresses are thoroughly well cleaned and are free from sticks or other foreign matter which loses for the mattress a certain extent of its comfort. The mattress is thoroughly well made of a superior quality of ticking.
Our special price for regular size............ **$2.70**

**No. 9455 Mixed Husk Mattresses with Wool or Cotton Top.** For a cheap mattress there is nothing better made. The husk is elastic and is not liable to crack like other filling, while the wool or cotton top gives added comfort. Ticks are bound and the ticking is of superior quality.
Our special price for regular size............ **$2.85**

**No. 9456 Extra No. 2 Wool Mattress.** Full weight, superior quality wool, thoroughly first class ticking, bound ticks—a very durable, soft and comfortable mattress. Our special price, each ... **$3.00**

**No. 9457 Palm Leaf Mattress.** Palm leaf is a quality of filling used in some of the most desirable mattresses made, in fact, many people prefer a palm leaf mattress to anything else on the market. We make this mattress with wool or cotton top, thus giving you an elastic mattress, as well as one that is soft and comfortable. Ticks are bound and have two rows of tufting on edges. Special quality of ticking used. Our special price for regular size, **$4.25**

**No. 9459 Sanitary Sea Moss Mattress with Cotton Top.** This mattress possesses many sanitary qualities which are gained from the moss. **Many physicians consider a mattress of sanitary sea moss** to be of great benefit to invalids. This mattress is made with cotton top and is extremely comfortable. The ticks are bound with two rows of tufts on edges. Ticking of superior quality.
Our special price for regular size............ **$4.35**

**No. 9460 Extra No. 1 All Wool Mattress.** A wool mattress is very desirable, especially when made of perfectly clean and pure wool such as the manufacturer uses in these goods. The mattress is full weight and covered with the **latest and most desirable pattern of ticking.** Ticks are bound with two rows of red tufts on edge.
Our special price for regular size ............ **$4.65**

**No. 9461 Extra No. 2 Cotton Mattress.** Many of our customers will buy nothing but the cotton mattresses, considering them, as they have good reason to do, the best medium priced mattresses that are made. The one which we quote here is **extra choice, guaranteed full weight** and strictly first-class in every respect. **The workmanship is No. 1 throughout.** The most desirable pattern and best grade of ticking is used. The ticks are bound and have two rows of tufts on edges. Our special price...... **$5.75**

**No. 9463 Extra No. 2 Doubled Ginned Moss Mattress.** In the opinion of many the moss mattress is equal in every respect to a hair mattress, **possessing all the elasticity and other features for which the hair mattress is considered especially desirable.** This moss mattress is filled with best selected moss, and we guarantee it to be satisfactory or money will be refunded. The ticking is very desirable and of superior strength. Ticks are bound and have two rows of tufts on edge.
Our special price for regular sizes ........... **$5.75**

## Hair Mattresses.

**Particular attention** is called to the fact that the hair we use in these mattresses is **thoroughly cured and perfectly clean** in all cases, whether the mattress is cheap or high priced. We have the hair mattresses **made specially to order** after the order is received. This is a very desirable feature. The ticking used is either plain or fancy, and in all cases the **most desirable patterns** and thoroughly excellent quality. We guarantee these mattresses to be full weight.

**No. 9465 No. 1 Black or Grey Mixed Hair Mattress.** A very good quality of **clean pure hair** is used in this mattress, and you will receive one which will not only be comfortable but will give you a lifetime's service. Our special price............... **$7.25**

**No. 9466 Very Fine Black Hair Mattress** filled with an excellent quality of curled hair, **very springy and comfortable.** Covered with fine ticking, and thoroughly well made and superior in every respect. Our special price....................... **$8.95**

**No. 9468 Having Made Special Contracts** with a leading manufacturer in this line, we are able to offer this **all black hair mattress,** full size, 35 lbs. in weight, excellent grade of hair and ticking, at an unusually low price. This is a mattress which would ordinarily retail at from $11.00 to $12.00.
Our special price, full size.... .............. **$7.25**

**No. 9470 Black Hair Mattress.** This mattress is filled with **long curled black hair,** absolutely clean, **thoroughly cured,** and covered with a superior quality fancy or plain ticking, as may be desired. This is a substantial, **comfortable and serviceable mattress** at an unusually low figure.
Our special price, full size.... ............ **$12.50**

**No. 9471 Black Hair Mattress.** A 35 lb. black hair mattress of the very best quality, the hair being thoroughly cured and perfectly cleaned. **This mattress we recommend** to our customers as a desirable and **thoroughly well made article,** which can be relied upon for comfort as well as durability. We use on this mattress the most durable and substantial ticking of the finest quality, and the pattern is the newest and most desirable. This mattress is made in full size. Our special price.......... **$14.90**

**No. 9473 White Hair Hattress.** This mattress is filled with long curled hair, thoroughly cured, perfectly cleaned, superior in every respect, and will **last for a lifetime or more.** Very elastic and covered with the best and newest design of ticking.
Our special price................................ **$16.50**

**No. 9475 A Pure White Mattress,** filled with the choicest quality of long curled hair. It is covered with a **superior grade of ticking** and is very springy and comfortable. A hair mattress of this quality is the **purchase of a lifetime,** and we are saving you from 25 to 40 per cent. on the purchase. Weight, 25 lbs. A splendid bargain. Our special price.. **$19.75**

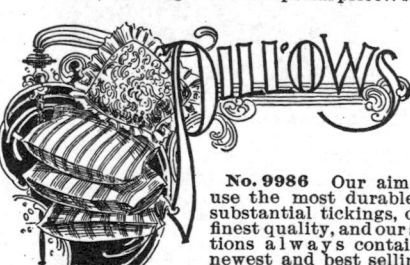

# PILLOWS

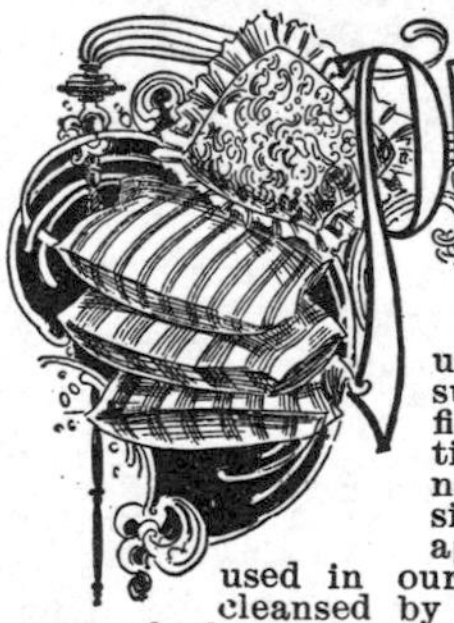

**No. 9986** Our aim is to use the most durable and substantial tickings, of the finest quality, and our selections always contain the newest and best selling designs. Samples sent upon application. All feathers used in our pillows are thoroughly cleansed by our latest improved processes, which, at the same time, gives the feather an unexcelled filling capacity. Prices given are per pair in sizes most generally acceptable. We, however, make pillows of any desired weight or size at same price per pound.

| Grades: | | 4lb. pr. | 5lb. pr. | 6lb. pr. | 7lb. pr. | 8lb. pr. |
|---|---|---|---|---|---|---|
| AAA........ | Size | 20x27 | 21x28 | 23x29 | 24x30 | |
| | Price | $3.50 | $4.40 | $5.26 | $6.10 | |
| AAAA....... | Size | 20x28 | 21x29 | 24x29 | 24x30 | |
| | Price | $4.40 | $5.10 | $6.00 | $7.10 | |
| AA.......... | Size, | 20x26 | 22x27 | 23x28 | 25x29 | 26x30 |
| | Price, | $2.75 | $3.48 | $4.45 | $4.85 | $5.50 |
| A.......... | Size, | 20x26 | 22x27 | 23x28 | 24x29 | 25x30 |
| | Price, | 2.60 | 3.25 | 3.95 | 4.45 | 5.25 |
| GP .......... | Size, | 19x26 | 21x27 | 22x28 | 23x29 | 24x30 |
| | Price, | 2.30 | 2.90 | 3.50 | 4.10 | 4.75 |
| B.......... | Size, | 19x26 | 21x27 | 22x28 | 23x29 | 24x30 |
| | Price, | 2.50 | 3.15 | 3,75 | 4.40 | 5.00 |
| C.......... | Size, | 18x26 | 20x27 | 21x28 | 22x29 | 24x29 |
| | Price, | 2.30 | 2.90 | 3.50 | 4.10 | 4.75 |
| CD .......... | Size, | 18x26 | 20x27 | 21x28 | 22x29 | 23x29 |
| | Price, | 2.10 | 2.60 | 3.15 | 3.68 | 4.18 |
| D.......... | Size, | 17x26 | 19x26 | 20x26 | 21x27 | 22x28 |
| | Price, | 1.80 | 2.30 | 2.75 | 3.20 | 3.68 |
| Special ..... | Size, | | 19x25 | 20x26 | 21x27 | 22x27 |
| | Price, | | 1.95 | 2.30 | 2.75 | 3.20 |
| Acme ..... | Size, | | 18x26 | 19x26 | 20x26 | 21x28 |
| | Price, | | 1.60 | 1.95 | 2.30 | 2.60 |
| Nonpareil .. | Size. | | | 18x25 | 19x26 | 20x27 |
| | Price, | | | 1.50 | 1.60 | 1.80 |
| Champion .. | Size, | | | 18x25 | 19x26 | 20x27 |
| | Price, | | | 1.18 | 1.35 | 1.45 |
| Standard ... | Size, | | | 18x25 | 19x26 | 20x27 |
| | Price, | | | 0.95 | 1.20 | 1.35 |
| Leader ..... | Size, | | | 17x25 | 19x26 | 20x26 |
| | Price, | | | 0.80 | 0.95 | 1.20 |

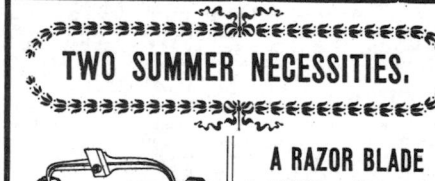

**BED QUILTS, COMFORTERS AND BLANKETS** In endless variety and at tempting Prices in Dry Goods Department, WHICH SEE.

## Down Sofa Cushions.

**IN FANCY FIGURED SATEEN CREPE OR TINSEL.**

**No. 9482** Grade, King.

| Size.................... | 16x16 | 18x18 | 20x20 | 22x22 | 24x24 |
|---|---|---|---|---|---|
| Price, each, plain.... | $0.75 | $0.82 | $1.15 | $1.45 | $1.75 |
| Price, each, flounced | .87 | 1.05 | 1.38 | 1.70 | 2.00 |
| Grade, Queen. Sizes same as King. | | | | | |
| Price, each, plain.... | $0.68 | $0.80 | $1.13 | $1.20 | $1.40 |
| Price, each, flounces | .86 | 1.00 | 1.25 | 1.45 | 1.72 |

## Down Sofa Cushions.

**No. 9480 In White Cambric.**

| Grade: | Size, | 16x16 | 18x18 | 20x20 | 22x22 | 24x24 |
|---|---|---|---|---|---|---|
| Popular | Ounces | 6 | 8 | 12 | 16 | 20 |
| White. | Each, | $0.40 | $0.55 | $0.82 | $1.10 | $1.35 |
| Nevada | Ounces, | 6½ | 8 | 12 | 16 | 20 |
| Grey. | Each, | $0.42 | $0.48 | $0.75 | $1.00 | $1.20 |
| Eclipse | Ounces, | 10 | 14 | 19 | 23 | 30 |
| Grey. | Each, | $0.45 | $0.50 | $0.70 | $0.88 | $1.14 |
| Oriol | Ounces, | 8 | 12 | 16 | 20 | 26 |
| Grey. | Each, | $0.42 | $0.48 | $0.65 | $0.75 | $0.98 |

## Down Pillows.

**IN FANCY FIGURED SATEEN OR CREPE.**

**No. 9478** Grade 1.

| Grades. | 4lb. pr. | 4½ lb. pr. | 5lb. pr. |
|---|---|---|---|
| Size.............................. | 22x28 | 24x30 | 25x30 |
| Weight .............................. | 4 lbs. | 4½ lbs. | 5 lbs. |
| Price, per pair.................. | $6.98 | $7.85 | $8.79 |
| Grade 1½. Size.............. | 22x28 | 24x30 | 25x30 |
| Weight.............................. | 4 lbs. | 4½ lbs. | 5 lbs. |
| Price. per pair.................. | $5.55 | $6.25 | $6.95 |
| Grade 2. Size ............... | 20x26 | 21x26 | 21x27 |
| Weight.............................. | 4 lbs. | 4½ lbs. | 5 lbs. |
| Price, per pair.................. | $3.65 | $4.10 | $4.50 |
| Grade 3. Size.............. | 20x26 | 21x26 | 21x27 |
| Weight... ......................... | 4 lbs. | 4½ lbs. | 5 lbs. |
| Price, per pair.................. | $2.80 | $3.10 | $3.50 |

## Odorless Feathers.

Every pound of feathers which we sell is treated by our latest improved process and, upon examination, they will be found to bear witness to the fact, that for the price their quality leads.

**FEATHERS IN SACKS.**
**Any Quantities.**

**No. 9488**

AA Selected prime live geese..............per lb $0 70
A Prime live geese..........................per lb 65
(This grade is very good, and almost as nice in appearance as the AA.)
GP Grey Prime Live Geese................per lb $0 55
B Fair Prime Live Geese.................per lb 60
(This grade will be found desirable when the best is not required.)
C Mixed Geese and Duck. ..............per lb $0 55
CD Good Mixed Grade.......................per lb 45
(Above two grades are very satisfactory for filling purposes.)
D Well Mixed Grades........................per lb $0 43
(Especially good for pillows, fully as clean as best grades.)
**Lower grades also, from 15 to 35 cents per lb.**
AAA Extra Selected Prime, with a reasonable proportion of Down.......... .........per lb $0 73
AAAA Small Selected Feathers, with a good proportion of Down..................per lb $0 82

**DOWN.**

Extra No. 1 White Down ....................per lb $2 00
No. 1 Geese Down .............................per lb 1 75
No. 1½ Down. ...................................per lb 1 40
No. 1¾ Down......................................per lb 95
No. 2 Down.........................................per lb 75



**OUR DISCOUNT OF 3 PER CENT. FOR FULL CASH WITH ORDER IS WELL WORTH CONSIDERING. IN FACT MOST OF OUR CUSTOMERS TAKE ADVANTAGE OF IT TO HELP PAY THE FREIGHT.**

# PRINCELY PARLOR FURNITURE.

WE ARE anxious for a trial order from each neighborhood in this particular line of furniture. It will be the best advertisement we could have in your locality. One of our Parlor Suits or Parlor Chairs is bound to sell others. When people once see our goods and learn our prices, our trade with them is assured. This Elegant Furniture is made by the three foremost factories in the United States. This is sufficient guarantee of its elegant quality and general style. Our line comprises the latest designs for 1896. Our prices speak for themselves. We ship anywhere to anyone, C. O. D., subject to examination, on receipt of $5.00 deposit as a guarantee of good faith. If as represented, you pay the balance and goods are yours. Otherwise, send them back and get money remitted. We pack our upholstered furniture with especial care. A parlor suit weighs about 130 to 290 pounds. Our Upholstered Furniture is built on honor and for wear, the material and workmanship is of the highest standard, and wherever we make one sale we have no trouble in making many more in the same neighborhood. We carry the furniture in tobacco, maroon, crimson, olive, blue, gold, steel, coral, nile, copper and pomegranate. Leather we have in maroon, dark olive and brown. The prevailing style in furniture is to have the various odd pieces upholstered in harmonizing colors of different shades.

WE SEND SAMPLES FREE ON APPLICATION. Always state which quality you desire. Please state just what sample is wanted, and thus save us the expense of sending samples which will be of no use to you.

Be particular to state what kind of finish is desired, whether mahogany or antique oak; also state grade and color of upholstering, and price any number. We would recommend that you leave it to our designer, as he is an artist in combining colors on Parlor Furniture, so as to harmonize with the colors in any parlor.

The grades of upholstery are as follows:

Grade A.—Good Cotton Tapestry.
Grade B.—No. 2 Corduroy or Kizer Plush.
Grade C.—High Grade Corduroy or Normandy Plush.
Grade D.—Brocaline Crushed Plush.
Grade E.—Silk Tapestry.
Grade F.—Wilton Rug.
Grade G.—Silk Brocatelle.
Grade H.—Satin Damask.
Grade I.—Silk Damask.

## A $16.00 PARLOR SUIT FOR $11.35.

GRADE A UPHOLSTERING $11.35

GRADE D UPHOLSTERING $14.50

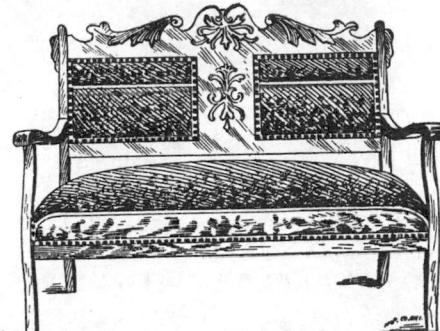
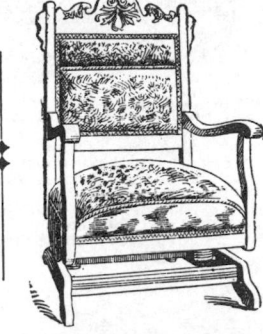

No. 9500. When we call this a $16.00 Parlor Suit, we are really very much underestimating its retail value. It is seldom that you can find any kind of a 5-piece parlor suit in a retail store at less than $20.00, and when you do it is of such inferior material and so poorly upholstered that there is no satisfaction to be gained from it. You get very little idea of the handsome appearance of the suit from the illustration. We can say, however, that it is well made on a solid oak frame, with a very handsome carved top, and the suit presents a handsome appearance and will be an ornament to any parlor. The suit consists of a Large Sofa, Large Easy Rocker, one Large Easy Arm Chair and two Parlor Chairs. Each piece has an easy spring seat with hard edge, the fronts being of plush handsomely corded. We furnish casters free, and the suit complete weighs about 195 pounds. It is difficult to imagine how it is possible for a manufacturer to turn out such goods at the price we name, but it is the fact nevertheless, and we will be glad to ship one of these suits to you C. O. D., subject to examination, as we know you will admit it the best value you have ever seen at anything like the price. We pack these suits very carefully and wrap each piece in burlap, so that it will reach you in the best possible condition. This 5-piece suit is upholstered in either grade A or D. Grade A upholstering is a handsome quality cotton tapestry. Grade D is a handsome brocoline crushed plush. In all cases the patterns will be very neat and artistic and the colorings will harmonize handsomely.

Our Special Price for the above Suit in Grade A Upholstering.........................$11.35
Our Special Price for the above Suit in Grade D Upholstering.............................14.50

## ...OUR SPECIAL...
## $18.50 PARLOR SUIT.
### SIX PIECES.

No. 9501. We show herewith an illustration of a very handsome Divan, which is included with the above 5-piece suit No. 9500, and goes to make up an elegant 6-piece suit. In fact, this suit is just the same in appearance as No. 9500 above, but has the addition of the very handsome divan as shown in the accompanying cut. It differs very materially, however, from No. 9500, from the fact it is better made of better material, the seats having spring edges instead of hard edges, and in every other way it is much superior as well as being a larger suit. The bands on the back of each piece are composed of very handsome silk plush. The

fronts are also of choice silk plush. This suit is upholstered in grades A, D, E or F upholstering. Grade A is a nice cotton tapestry; grade D, a handsome brocoline crush plush; grade E, a fine grade of silk tapestry, and grade F is the always popular Wilton rug. In all cases the patterns will be artistic, and the colorings will harmonize perfectly. We recommend that you leave the combinations of colors to our designer, who will combine them to blend with perfect harmony. The weight of this suit when packed complete for shipment is about 225 pounds.

Our Special Price for Suit described above, Upholstered in Grade A.............................$18.60
Our Special Price for same Suit Upholstered in Grades D or E.................................21.50
Our Special Price for same Suit Upholstered in Grade F.........................................25.75
Be sure to state the grade of upholstering wanted, and if you have any choice of color mention that also in order.

## OUR SPECIAL $15.00 OVERSTUFFED PARLOR SUIT.
In ordering, be sure to state the grade of upholstering wanted and colors desired, if you have any choice.

No. 9502. We endeavor to show you in the illustration the handsome design of this Parlor Suit which we are able to offer at such an unheard of price. While the price is exceedingly low, we wish to say that the suit is made by a manufacturer whose reputation is of the highest order for the quality of goods which he makes, and who will not allow it to suffer by inferior workmanship in any respect. The most capable and expert upholsterers are employed by this manufacturer, and we offer this suit as the best that can be secured for anything like the price. This suit is in a variety of designs and colorings, and if you will leave it to our designer we will furnish you with an assortment of colors in the suit which will harmonize beautifully and present an artistic appearance. The back panel of sofa is upholstered in the same material as the seat with handsome tufted sides. All the pieces are ornamented with fringe and tassel valance around bottom

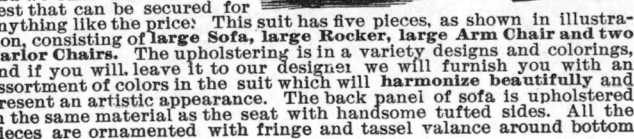
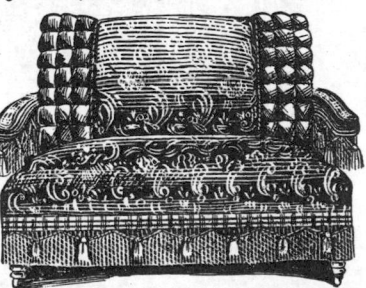

and around arms. You will note on another page a complete description of our styles of upholstering, and this suit is quoted at different prices depending on the grade of the upholstering. The frame of the suit is of the very best selected kiln dried material, and you can depend upon it that it is strong and substantial as well as durable. It weighs, when packed for shipment, 250 pounds. We will send this suit C. O. D., subject to examination, on receipt of $5.00, balance to be paid upon receipt of the goods and upon finding them entire satisfactory and just as represented. We allow 3 per cent. discount for cash. When cash in full accompanies an order you may deduct 3 per cent. from the prices named below. We pack these suits very carefully, covering them with burlap.

This suit has five pieces, as shown in illustration, consisting of large Sofa, large Rocker, large Arm Chair and two Parlor Chairs.

Our Special Price for 5-piece Parlor Suit as above described in cotton tapestry.......................................$15.00
Same Suit, Our Special Price upholstered in crushed plush.........20.50
Same Suit, Our Special Price upholstered in silk tapestry.........24.00

# $23.00 BUYS A $45.00 PARLOR SUIT

**OUR SPECIAL OFFER:** SEND US $5.00 as a guarantee of good faith and we will send you the suit by freight. C. O. D., subject to examination; you can examine it at your freight depot, and if found perfectly satisfactory pay the freight agent the balance, $18.00 and freight. Three per cent. discount allowed if cash in full accompanies your order, when $22.31 pays for the suit.

**No. 9503** This elegant Turkish parlor suit consists of 1 Tete-a-Tete, 1 Rocker, 1 Gents' Easy Chair, 1 Parlor or Reception Chair. All these pieces are made in extra large size, high backs and large comfortable seats, and are very latest design. The upholstering or cover of this suit is in the latest design and pattern of imported goods; each piece is covered in a different color. We will be pleased to mail you samples of six different colors to select from, or if left to us to make selection in colors our upholsterer will in all cases give you colors on this suit that will please you in every respect. The suit is finely upholstered, with plush band and rolls on top and sides of back and trimmed with a heavy worsted fringe. This suit is made with good steel spring seats and spring edges and every piece is made with spring backs. This is without a doubt one of the best parlor suits ever put on the market at the price we ask for it and will be an ornament in any home. We can furnish this same parlor suit upholstered in good grade of crushed plush, assorted colors, and other styles of covering.

| | |
|---|---|
| 4 piece Parlor Suit, price in cotton tapestry | $23.00 |
| 4 piece Parlor Suit, price in crushed plush | 25.50 |
| 4 piece Parlor Suit, price in silk brocatelle | 29.50 |
| 4 piece Parlor Suit, price in silk damask | 34.00 |

## A $35.00 PARLOR SUIT FOR $24.00.

In offering this Parlor Suit of six pieces for $24.00 we fully believe that no such suit can be secured at less than $35, and if bought at retail at that price you would consider it a great bargain.

Made with a solid oak or a solid birch frame If furnished in solid birch it is finished in imitation mahogany, a most desirable and attractive finish.

**No. 9504** The backs of this suit are upholstered in the same quality of material as the seat, and the decorations in the way of hand carving are decidedly unique and attractive. Easy spring seat and edges corded with handsome cord with silk plush banded front. The suit is furnished complete with a full set of casters, and weights, when packed for shipment, about 250 lbs. We show in illustrations only pictures of the large sofa, large rocker and large parlor chair. The six piece parlor suit complete consists in addition to the three shown of a divan, same as the sofa only smaller; an extra Parlor Chair and a large Arm Chair of same size as rocker shown. Bear in mind that our C. O. D. terms of shipment are very liberal, also that we allow a discount of 3 per cent when full cash accompanies order. Most of our customers send full cash with order, knowing the goods are guaranteed and may be returned if not satisfactory and money refunded.

Upholstered as follows:

| | |
|---|---|
| Our special price for 6 piece suit in an excellent grade of cotton tapestry | $24.00 |
| Our special price for same upholstered in a very excellent quality of imported corduroy | 26.50 |
| Our special price for same upholstered in a fine grade of brocaline crushed plush or silk tapestry | 30.00 |
| Our special price for same upholstered in very fine brocatelle or choice silk damask | 33.00 |

Be sure to advise us when ordering, what special combinations of colors are desired. We can furnish you with a suit which for harmony of colors as well as durability and elegance will delight you more than you could possibly expect.

## A $50.00 PARLOR SUIT FOR $33.00.

**No. 9505** It is difficult to imagine a more beautiful and artistic suit than the one which we show in the illustration. Our artist has endeavored to draw the different pieces so that you can get an idea of the handsome design. It is one of the richest and most stylish appearing parlor suits made for the season of 1897. It is after a design executed by expert artists in this line, and the manufacturers are taking particular pains that the suit shall be not only perfect in detail and handsome in outline, but thoroughly substantial and durable in every respect. it is a suit that will last a lifetime and a suit that you will never become tired of. It is made with a solid oak frame or a frame made of curly birch with imitation mahogany finish. Either wood is decidedly handsome and thoroughly substantial. The frames are beautifully carved after the most stylish pattern, and the suit as a whole has the appearance of one which would retail frequently at from $75.00 to $80.00. It consists of 6 pieces, a large sofa, a large divan, large easy rocker, large arm chair and two parlor chairs. We upholster this suit in five different styles of upholstering. D. E. F. G and H. D is a very fine blocaline crush plush; E is an elegant silk tapestry; F a superb Wilton rug; G a choice grade of silk brocatell and H a very handsome and durable satin damask. You have your choice of upholstering. In all grades the patterns are the very latest designs, and in coloring you will have your choice of all the popular shades. We recommend, however, that you leave the matter of coloring in general to our designer, as we make these parlor suits specially to order and will upholster the various pieces in the latest popular shades, all harmonizing perfectly. The weight of the suit when packed very carefully for shipment is 300 lbs. We pack each of these pieces with the utmost care, covering all parts with burlap so that they will reach you in perfect condition. Casters free.

| | |
|---|---|
| Our special price for above 6 piece Parlor Suit, upholstered in grade D or E | $33.00 |
| Same Suit, upholstered in grade F, our special price | 37.00 |
| Same Suit, upholstered in grade G or H, our special price | 38.00 |

# OUR GREATEST BARGAIN PARLOR SUIT. ...A $75.00 PARLOR SUIT FOR... $47.00.

A Wonderful Offer in Parlor Furniture.

Divan, Large Arm Chair and Extra Parlor Chair INCLUDED.

**No. 9506** We show in the accompanying cuts illustrations of three pieces of this most elegant and stylish parlor suit. The suit complete consists of large sofa, as illustrated, a very handsome divan of same shape and design as sofa but smaller in size, two parlor chairs like the one in illustration, one large easy rocker, as illustrated, and one large arm chair same as the large arm rocker but with legs instead of rockers. This elegant parlor suit is made of the very choicest **quarter sawed oak or solid birch** as may be desired. When furnished in birch it is finished in handsome imitation mahogany, an elegant finish which gives the suit even a nicer appearance than **solid mahogany** itself. The backs of all the pieces are elegantly carved by hand and are **exceedingly rich in design.** They are furthermore decorated with upholstered centers, the upholstering in all cases being the same as the seat. This parlor suit is made by one of the leading manufacturers, a manufacturer who takes particular pride in the quality of his goods, and we offer the suit as **equal to anything that can be found anywhere at** $75.00 or more. The seats are very easy and comfortable, being fitted with the best Bessemer steel springs. They have spring seats and the edges are corded with silk gimp cord. Fronts are banded with the same material as the general upholstering. A full set of casters are furnished free with each suit. We shall be glad to send this parlor suit to any address C. O. D., subject to examination on our liberal C. O. D. terms, and we know that you will be so well pleased with it that you would not sell it for **50 per cent more than you paid for it** if you knew you could not get another. Weight when packed for shipment about 350 lbs. We pack these parlor suits with the utmost care so that they may be sure to reach you in the very best possible condition. Upholstered as follows:

Our special price in fine brocaline crushed plush or silk tapestry, **$47.00**
Our special price for 6-piece suit upholstered in very handsome and expensive brocatell........................**$53.00**
Our special price in very choicest satin damask....................**$55.00**

**In ordering** be sure to state style of upholstering desired, as well as combination of colors which you prefer.

# A $12.00 ROCKER FOR $8.95.

## Our Wonderful $6.75 Rocker.

**No. 9507** It is difficult to imagine a rocker which would present a handsomer appearance than the one which we show in the illustration. It is an entirely new design, something that you will not find in your retail stores, a pattern that will be very pleasing in effect and will add greatly to the appearance of any room. It is made of **choice curly birch,** a very popular wood, which we finish either in **natural color or imitation mahogany,** as desired. It is very finely hand polished and is elegantly finished throughout. The very easy spring seat is upholstered in the best grades of material, and taken as a whole considering the superiority of the material, **the handsome carving** and elegant upholstering, you will have a chair at a medium price that is superior to anything you would ordinarily secure from a retail store at less than $10.00. See description of rocker 9509 for materials used in upholstering.

Our special price upholstered in grade E.........**$6.75**
Our special price upholstered in grade G or H....... 7.35
Our special price upholstered in grade I......... 8.70
Our special price upholstered in grade L......... 9.65

## $12.00 Rocker for $7.50.

**No. 9508** It will be difficult for you to find anything in the stocks of your local dealers that will equal in appearance or quality the elegant large arm rocker which we show in illustration. This rocker is made of the very finest birch with an elegant mahogany finish, **and very finely polished.** It has mahogany veneer back with marquetrie, the new style decoration. The illustration does not do it half justice. We can only say that if you will order this rocker and are not satisfied that it is the finest bargain you have ever seen, you are at liberty to return it to us and we will cheerfully refund your money. We have no fears, however, but what you will be even more delighted with it than you would expect from the illustration. The seat is made extra easy with best **Bessemer Steel Springs,** and is upholstered in satin damask in the very choicest shades. This rocker is one that will last a lifetime and is put up in a way that

will warrant it to do so with ordinary use.
Our special price, each....................**$7.50**

**No. 9509** The Purchaser of the rocker which we show in illustration will have something that he will be proud of, a rocker that cannot be matched by those purchased by his neighbors for less than $12.00. In fact, it is seldom that such a rocker is **carried in any ordinary retail store.** The prices which retail dealers are compelled to charge for such goods are invariably so high that they generally do not find it worth while to carry them in stock. **The appearance of this rocker cannot** be exaggerated. The illustration does not do it half justice. **The arms are handsomely ornamented with beautiful carving,** while the back panels are also decorated with very fine workmanship. **The rocker** is constructed of the **finest curly birch,** and is either finished in natural color or in imitation mahogany with a very fine hand polish. Curly birch is a wood which is very popular for chairs of this nature, and is very stylish. **The easy spring seat** is upholstered in the best grades of material, either grade E, fine silk tapestry, grade G, which is a silk brocatell, grade H, a satin damask, grade I, a silk damask, or grade L, in genuine leather. In ordering, always state style of covering wanted. Prices are as follows:

Our special price in grade E..... **$8.95**
Our special price in grade G or H..... 9.65
Our special price in grade I..... 10.50
Our special price in grade L..... 11.40

## Our $12.75 Easy Chair.

**No. 9570** The **Large Gent's Easy Chair** which we illustrate is a strictly new design, one which has just been put on the market, and by reason of its **wonderfully comfortable shape,** its splendid construction of high grade material, will undoubtedly meet with a very large sale. It is impossible for us to describe here in a few words the desirability of this easy chair. It is roomy and comfortable, has a **very soft easy spring seat and edge,** and is made with the **finest solid oak or birch** frame, as desired. It is handsomely decorated in front with hand carving and is fitted with casters. We upholster this easy chair in grade E, which is a fine quality of silk tapestry, or in grade L, genuine leather. We pack the chair very carefully, and when packed for shipment it weighs about 30 pounds.

Our special price upholstered in grade E.......**$12.75**
Our special price upholstered in grade L....... 14.50

## Our $2.00 Napoleon Chair.

**No. 9511** There has been a steadily increasing demand for chairs similar to the one which we show in the accompanying illustration. We have taken particular pains to contract this season with the manufacturer for a line of these chairs such as will enable the man of limited means to be **strictly up to date in** his furniture, and we have succeeded in making the price so attractive that the purchase will not interfere materially with the condition of his pocket book. **This handsome chair** is best known as the **Napoleon Design,** and is finely constructed of selected material, thoroughly well put together and very substantial. The size of the seat, which is upholstered in various grades of material, is 18 inches square. We pack the chair very carefully for shipment and it is bound to reach you in first class condition. **This article will be an ornament to any home** and is a most desirable purchase.

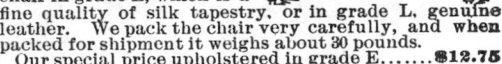

Our special price upholstered in fine silk tapestry...........**$2.00**
Our special price upholstered in silk brocatell or damask...........**$2.95**

# STYLISH FANCY PIECES.

## Our Wonderful $8.75 Bargain.

No. 9512 It is impossible for us in a short description to give you any more than a faint idea of the elegance and desirability of the handsome divan shown in the accompanying illustration. It is made of the very choicest curly birch in either natural finish or imitation mahogany with a beautiful hand polish which renders it very attractive. You can get some idea from the illustration of the style and ornamental designs of the wood work. The corners on the seat and back are decorated with the richest and most tasty hand carving. The fancy pattern back is odd shaped, which makes it striking in appearance. It is thoroughly well made by the best cabinet makers that money can employ. The easy spring seat is upholstered in either grade G, silk brocatell, grade H, satin damask, or in grade I silk damask. In this divan you will have one of the handsomest pieces of furniture that can be put in the parlor, or that will be far handsomer than any thing your neighbors may have bought at 50% more than our factory-to-consumer price. We pack this divan with the utmost care to insure its reaching you in perfect condition.

Our special price upholstered in grade G or H...................$8.75
Our special price upholstered in grade I............................. 9.50

## Our $6.00 Corner Chair.

No. 9514 The Corner Chair which we illustrate is a particularly artistic piece of workmanship, handsome in design and remarkably well constructed and durable. It is made of selected birch in natural finish or imitation mahogany, as desired, and its attractive appearance is added to by the very fine hand polish. The easy seat is upholstered in grade G, silk brocatell, H, satin damask, or I, silk damask. In any grade the chair is one which will be admired by all your friends and an article of which you will never become tired. This corner chair is one that ordinarily retails at at least $9.00, and, in fact, it is very seldom you will find it in a retail store. We are exceedingly anxious to get you started buying your furniture from us for we know we can give you better service than you could secure anywhere else, and that each piece of furniture sold will be an advertisement for us, and secure for us increased trade. Remember we allow a discount of 3 per cent when cash in full accompanies order. If you wish we shall be glad to send the chair C. O. D. subject to examination on our liberal C. O. D. terms. We pack all our furniture carefully and it is sure to reach you in perfect condition.

Our special price in grade G or H upholstering......................$6.00
Our special price in grade I upholstering.............................. 6.50

## Our $11.25 Tabouret Chair.

No. 9513 The Tabouret Chair which we illustrate is made in very handsome curly birch in either natural finish or imitation mahogany. In the finishing, the wood receives a beautiful hand polish, making the finish equal to that of the finest piano. This chair is an odd design which is so popular and fashionable, and one that is exceedingly ornamental anywhere it may be placed. In making the chair the manufacturers have paid attention to comfort and not lost sight of the fact that the chair is to be used instead of to be looked at, and hence in offering you this Handsome Tabouret Chair we do so with the double assurance that it will give satisfaction, not only by its elegant appearance, but by reason of its unusual comfort and durability. In construction it has no rival. Only the most expert cabinetmakers are employed in work of this kind, and hence you may depend upon it that this purchase will be one for a lifetime. It will be a chair that will give long service. It has an easy seat and is upholstered in either grade, G, H or I. Grade G is a very fine silk brocatell; grade H is a satin damask, and grade I is the choicest quality of silk damask. In any of the grades of upholstering mentioned you will be delighted with the chair. The handsome hand carving on the front panel and back add wonderfully to the appearance.

Our special price in grade G or H....................................$11.25
Our special price in grade I............................................. 12.00

## Special Bargain For $3.98.

No. 9575 The Single Lounge which we illustrate is made on a solid oak frame, handsomely decorated with hand carving and is very ornamental in appearance. It is a thoroughly substantial lounge, will stand a lifetime's usage, and at our factory-to-consumer price is remarkably cheap. It has an easy spring bed with hard edges and is upholstered in various grades of material at the prices below. We pack this lounge very carefully for shipment, and it weighs when packed about 85 pounds.

Above lounge upholstered in Brussels carpet, our special price $3.98.
Above lounge upholstered in velvet carpet, our special price.......$4.50
Above lounge upholstered in grade B or D. our special price........ 5.50
Grade B upholstery is a No. 2 corduroy or a nice kizer plush.
Grade D is brocoline crush plush.

OUR MAMMOTH SPECIAL FURNITURE CATALOGUE is very complete, containing as it does every conceivable line of House and Office Furniture, illustrated elaborately with very large cuts. THIS CATALOGUE IS FREE.

---

## LATEST STYLES COUCHES DIRECT FROM THE FACTORY.   THE MOST COMFORTABLE AND DURABLE MADE.

### An $8.00 Couch for $5.50.

No. 9516 This is a couch that is made a leader of by one of the largest manufacturers of the country, and is contracted for by us in large quantities. It is substantially made with very heavy and strong frame, made of the best seasoned material, and is a purchase that will give you satisfaction, not only upon its immediate receipt but after years of usage. It is upholstered in various grades and materials, and is one of the best

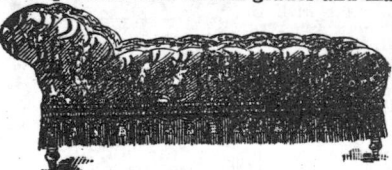

bargains in the furniture line ever offered. It has an easy spring seat, making it very comfortable. In size it is 27 inches wide by 74 inches long. We pack it very carefully for shipment, and when packed it weighs about 90 lbs.

Above Couch upholstered in grade A. Our special price $5.50
Same, upholstered in grade B. Our special price..............$6.00
Same, upholstered in grade C. Our special price.................... 7.00
Same, upholstered in grade D. Our special price.................... 7.00
Grade A upholstering is a nice cotton tapestry; grade B, a No. 2 corduroy or Kizer plush; grade C is an extra quality No. 1 high grade corduroy or very nice Normandie plush; grade D is a first-class grade of brocoline crushed plush. Always state what grade of covering you want.

### Our Great Bargain $6.75 Couch.

No. 9517 The Couch which we show in the illustration is one which has had a very large sale, and the demand has been so unusually great that we have deemed it necessary to continue its sale for this season. Anticipating a continued demand we have increased our contracts with the manufacturers, and by so doing have been able to reduce the price considerably. We make it a point whenever lower prices are secured by us to give our customers immediate and direct benefit of same. This couch is one that will please you, not only by reason of its appearance, but because of its comfort and durability. It is substantially made on an excellent frame, is 28 inches wide by 80 inches long, has easy spring seat, is upholstered in various grades of material and is handsomely ornamented with tassel fringe. It weighs about 95 lbs.

Our special price, upholstered in grade A.....................$ 6.75
Our special price, upholstered in grade B......................... 8.50
Our special price, upholstered in grade C......................... 10.50
Our special price, upholstered in grade D......................... 10.75
Grade A is an excellent cotton tapestry; grade B a No. 2 corduroy or kizer plush; grade C a choice grade extra quality No. 1 corduroy or very fine Normandie plush; grade D is a popular material known as brocoline crushed plush.

### Our Great Bargain Couch For $7.75.

No. 9568 We offer this Couch as a decided bargain at the price named above, and can only make such offer by reason of large contracts with the leading manufacturer. The frame of this couch is made of selected kiln dried lumber and is thoroughly substantial in every respect. It has full spring seat and edges corded all around and at head. The seat is deep tufted and the couch is further decorated with a handsome fringe. The size is 38 inches by 78 inches. It weighs when packed for shipment about 150 pounds. On our liberal terms you can see and examine this couch before paying for it in full. If you wish to send cash in full with order we allow a discount of 3 per cent. We guarantee the couch to be entirely satisfactory or it may be returned to us. Made as follows:

Our special price in cotton tapestry............................$7.75
Upholstered in No. 2 corduroy or kizer plush...................... 11.95
Upholstered in nice grade imported corduroy ...................... 12.75
Upholstered in first quality brocaline crushed plush or silk tapestry.................................................. 13.50
Upholstered in a choice grade of brocatelle or a very superior quality of satin damask........................................ 14.50

### A $12.00 Couch for $8.00.

No. 9519 The Turkish Couch which we show in the illustration is one of the latest styles and is very handsome and graceful in appearance and unusually easy and comfortable. It is 30 inches wide by 80 inches long, and the seat is made with deep tufts and is fitted with best Bessemer steel springs, the seat and edges consequently being very soft and comfortable. This is one of the most desirable couches made, and we have contracted for it in large quantities, thus enabling us to sell it to you at about the price which the local retail dealer would pay for it. We offer it on our liberal C. O. D. terms, or if desired full cash can be sent with order and 3 per cent. can be deducted. Weight, when packed

for shipment, 175 lbs. Prices as follows:
Upholstered in nice Cotton Tapestry............................$ 8.00
Upholstered in No. 2 Corduroy or Kizer Plush..................... 11.50
Upholstered in Choice Imported Corduroy......................... 12.50
Upholstered in Brocaline Crushed Plush or Silk Tapestry.......... 13.75
Upholstered in very Select Brocatell or Stylish Satin Damask..... 15.00

WOULD YOU SELL YOUR WHEAT FOR 50 CENTS, IF THE MARKET PRICE WAS 70 CENTS? WHY PAY THE DEALER $1.00 FOR AN ARTICLE WHEN YOU CAN GET IT OF US FOR 75 CENTS OR LESS.

# GREATEST VALUES THE WORLD HAS EVER SEEN.

### THESE COUCHES ARE BEYOND COMPETITION IN

# COMFORT, QUALITY AND BEAUTY.

### Our Great Bargain $9.50 Couch.

**No. 9525** A wonderful opportunity is offered to secure a most desirable piece of furniture in the shape of the couch which we illustrate. The price which we name is one that will astonish the customer best versed in furniture values. Its actual worth can only be known after examination, and we should be only too glad to ship you one of these couches C. O. D. subject to examination on our liberal terms, for we know that you would

be highly delighted with it, and that one of these articles of furniture introduced into your neighborhood would result in very largely increased sales for us, We undertake to handle only such goods as will give satisfaction, and this is a representative of the line which we carry. The

**Turkish couch is 27 inches wide and 76 inches long.** It has easy and comfortable spring seat and edges and is upholstered in a variety of first-class materials. **It is decorated with a handsome fringe** and is very ornamentally made. We cannot speak too highly of the wonderful value we offer in this article. We urge a trial order in the furniture line to convince you that we are headquarters for the best goods at the lowest possible prices. **It is packed carefully, wrapped in burlap,** and weighs, when packed for shipment, about 100 lbs.

Above Lounge upholstered in grade B, our special price........... $ 9.50
Same upholstered in grade C, our special price...................... 10.65
Same upholstered in grade D, our special price...................... 10.75

**Grade B** is a No. 2 corduroy or kizer plush; grade C a No. 1 high-grade corduroy or Normandie plush; grade D, a choice grade of brocoline crushed plush. Always be explicit to state what upholstering you desire when ordering.

### Our Special $14.00 Turkish Couch.

**No. 9521** The design of Couch which we show in the illustration is one of the newest things on the market, a couch that will beyond doubt have an enormous sale. Anticipating a large demand for this particular couch we have placed very large contracts for it and shall carry in our wareroom such a supply as will undoubtedly meet the demand. By reason of these **large cash contracts** we have been able to hammer the price down to a lower point than we thought possible to secure. This elegant Turkish

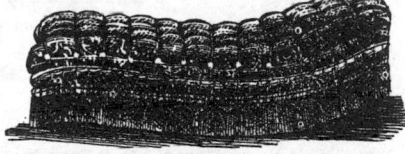

Couch is made on a **very stylish oak frame,** thoroughly substantial in every respect, and is 30 inches wide by 72 inches long. It has an **easy spring seat with fancy ruffled sides and ornamented with a beautiful fringe.** It is a very comfortable couch, one that is guaranteed to remove that "tired feeling," and a couch you would not be without for double the money if you could not get another. It is upholstered in excellent grades of material; **is thoroughly substantial and durable,** and will be an ornament to any home. We pack it very carefully, wrapping it in burlap to prevent damage, and it weighs, when packed, about 100 lbs.

Above Lounge, upholstered in grade B. Our special price........... $14.00
Same, upholstered in grade C. Our special price...................... 15.95

**Grade B** is an excellent No. 2 Corduroy or Kizer Plush; grade C is a No. 1 High Grade Corduroy or Normandie Plush. Be sure to state what upholstering you want.

### A $25.00 Box Couch For $16.75

**No. 9522** A Box Couch is an unusually desirable article of furniture. The box underneath the couch is very convenient and handy for use as a wardrobe, and in it may be laid away winter garments during the summer time, or summer garments during the winter. The box is lined with flannel. **The seat is very soft and easy,** made so by means of the best Bessemer

steel springs. It is deep tufted and the couch is further decorated with a handsome fringe all around. In addition to the couch are furnished two handsome pillows, which will in all cases be covered with the same quality of upholstering as that on the couch itself. Weight, when packed for shipment,

about 100 lbs. Our prices are as follows:

Upholstered in nice cotton tapestry................................$16.30
Upholstered in an excellent grade of corduroy or kizer plush..... 20.75
Upholstered in a very fine imported corduroy...................... 22.50
Upholstered in choice brocaline crushed plush or silk tapestry... 22.50
Upholstered in very fine brocatelle or very handsome satin damask. 25.50

### Latest Style Sofa Bed at $10.75.

**No. 9523** The Sofa Bed has become a most popular piece of furniture. It deserves to be for the simple reason that it is not only comfortable but decidedly handsome and striking in appearance. The one which we show in illustration is the leading product of one of the best manufacturers in this line of goods, and we offer it as a particularly desirable bargain. It is thoroughly well constructed of the **very best seasoned material** and is covered with various grades

of upholstering, all being of **superior quality.** This sofa bed has an **advantage over the ordinary** couch from the fact that the back is made to drop down and part of the head falls over, all resting on the iron feet, making a **large and comfortable** bed when opened. When the bed is opened it is 4 feet 2 inches wide by 6 feet 4 inches long. When closed it makes a handsome and desirable sofa. The desirability of such an article of furniture is so obvious that it needs no argument. So far as the quality is concerned we offer it as superior in every respect and recommend its purchase, knowing it will give entire satisfaction. **Remember our liberal C. O. D. terms** or 3 per cent discount if full cash accompanies your order. Weight, when packed for shipment, 200 lbs. Made in the following grades of upholstering:

Our special price, in cotton tapestry........... ......................$10.75
Same in No. 2 corduroy or kizer plush............................. 13.00
Same in handsome imported corduroy............................. 14.00
Same in choice grade brocaline crushed plush or very handsome
   silk tapestry.............................................. 15.00
Same in very stylish brocatelle or beautiful and expensive satin
   damask.................................................. 15.75

---

**WE GUARANTEE SATISFACTION OR FULL CASH WILL BE REFUNDED.**

# BED LOUNGES.

**3 PER CENT. DISCOUNT WHEN FULL PRICE IS SENT WITH ORDER.**

## THE NEWEST DESIGNS ON THE MARKET.

### A $10.50 Bed Lounge for $7.25.

**No. 9524** A Bed Lounge is a very convenient article of furniture, as those who have used them have learned. Those who have never had them cannot appreciate their convenience until one is purchased. We guarantee that you will be pleased with the one which we show in the illustration. It

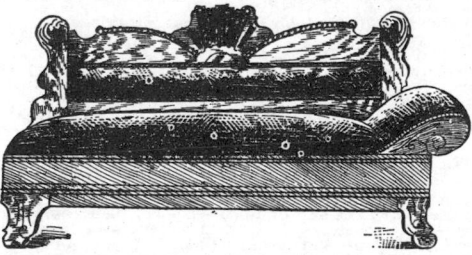

is thoroughly well made, made by one of the best manufacturers in the country, **with a solid oak frame,** very handsomely finished, hand carved and beautifully decorated on the back. The back panel is covered with the same quality of upholstery as the bed. It has an **easy spring bed,** and when opened up it is 4 feet by 6 feet in size. It is fitted with wire

**springs and a cotton top mattress.** We pack these lounges very carefully, wrapping them in burlap. When packed they weigh about 150 lbs. This lounge is made for service, and will be an ornament to any home as well as a convenience. Upholstered as follows at the prices named:

Lounge as above described, in Brussels carpet, our special price....$7.25
Same, upholstered in velvet carpet, our special price.............. 7.75
Same, upholstered in B or D grade of upholstering, our special price 8.50

**Grade B** upholstering is a nice curduroy or an excellent kizer plush. **Grade D** is a brocoline crushed plush. In ordering always state what upholstering you desire.

### Our $8.65 Bed Lounge.

**No. 9525** To Obtain an Idea of the General Superiority of this lounge over anything else on the market at 50 per cent. more than our price, the article must be seen and

examined. We shall be glad to ship the lounge C. O. D, subject to examination on our regular liberal terms, and if it is not all we represent it to be it can be returned to us at our expense and money will be refunded. It is very large, easy and comfortable, upholstered in a variety of materials at the various prices named below. When opened out it forms a large bed with

**woven wire bottom and cotton top mattress** with good ticking. The frame is of best solid oak, either natural or imitation mohogony finish as may be desired. It has an extra high back handsomely decorated with tasty carving and piped rolls upholstered in plush. It is also plush banded in front. Legs are strong and well braced. Fitted with casters. Size when opened. 4 feet wide, 78 inches long. Weight when packed for shipment about 250 lbs. Our Special prices are as follows:

Upholstered in cotton tapestry............................. $ 8.65
Upholstered in No. 2 corduroy or kizer plush............... 9.75
Upholstered in fine imported corduroy...................... 10.00
Upholstered in handsome brocaline crushed plush or fine grade
  silk tapestry............................................ 10.25
Upholstered in choice brocatelle or satin damask........... 11.25

---

**OUR SPECIAL MAMMOTH FURNITURE CATALOGUE WILL BE MAILED FREE TO ANY ONE ON APPLICATION. EVERYTHING KNOWN TO THE FURNITURE TRADE IS QUOTED IN GREAT VARIETY.**

## Our Special $8.75 Bed Lounge.

**No. 9526** This Bed Lounge is made with a solid oak frame, very substantial and constructed by the best workmen that money will employ. It has easy **spring seat** when closed. When opened out it makes a large comfortable bed 48 in. wide and 78 in. long, with wire bottom and cotton top mattress. Fancy piped and corded in back, upholstered same as seat. Fancy pattern back with tasty covering, silk plush banded front.

Weight, packed 130 pounds.   Prices as follows:

| | |
|---|---|
| Upholstered in brussels carpet | $8.75 |
| Upholstered in velvet carpet | 9.50 |
| Upholstered in No. 2 Corduroy or brocoline crushed plush | 9.65 |

Be sure to state covering wanted.

## Our Special Bargain Bed Lounge for $11.50.

**No. 9527** This Bed Lounge, like all our upholstered furniture, is made by a leading manufacturer who employs only the most skilled upholsterers and best cabinet makers, who construct the goods after designs of leading artists. The result is that we are in a position to **offer you artistic furniture** which will not be found in ordinary retail stores, or if to be secured there the prices will be entirely beyond your reach. This lounge, like the others, is made of superior quality **solid oak**. The extra high **back** is decorated with **very fancy and artistic hand carving,** and with the center piece upholstered in the same quality of covering as in the seat. The legs are strong and well braced and handsomely carved. The front is banded.   Easy spring

seat and head.   Size of bed when lounge is opened is 4 feet wide by 78 inches long.  It is made extra easy and comfortable by reason of the superior quality woven wire spring and cotton top mattress with excellent ticking with which it is fitted.  It is finished in either antique oak or imitation mahogany finish.  Weight when packed for shipment, about 250 lbs.  We can furnish this lounge in a variety of popular shades, and when ordering you should indicate what color is particularly desirable.

| | |
|---|---|
| Our special price in excellent corduroy or kizer plush | $11.00 |
| Same in a very fine imported corduroy | 11.50 |
| Same in a choice brocaline crushed plush or very handsome silk tapestry | 11.75 |
| Same in a high grade brocatelle or very expensive satin damask | 13.75 |

## Latest Style Bed Lounge for $11.50.

**No. 9528** The Bed Lounge which we show in the illustration is constructed of the very finest solid oak either in natural finish or imitation mahogany as may be ordered.  When closed it makes a very comfortable and desirable piece of furniture, and when opened out it is a large easy bed 4 feet wide by 78 inches long fitted with woven wire bottom and cotton top mattress with excellent grade of ticking.  The covering is the various grades is first class, very durable and handsome in design.  The fancy

pattern back is extra high, elegantly carved by hand and with fancy tufted ornamentation.  The front is banded and is handsomely carved, while the legs are of unusual strength.  We pack these bed lounges very carefully so that they may reach our customers in the best possible condition.   We ship on liberal C. O. D. terms, and if desired you have the privilege of examining before paying for them.  Remember that we allow a discount of 3 per cent for full cash with order.  Made in the following grades at the prices named below:

| | |
|---|---|
| Above bed lounge upholstered in cotton tapestry | $11.50 |
| Same upholstered in No. 2 corduroy or kizer plush | 12.00 |
| Same upholstered in very choice grade of imported corduroy | 12.50 |
| Same upholstered in fine grade brocoline crushed plush or fine silk tapestry | 13.75 |
| Same upholstered in the very choicest brocatelle or high grade satin damask | 15.00 |

## An $18.00 Bed Lounge For $11.75.

**No. 9529** Our artist has not been able to give you more than a slight idea of the elegance and desirability of the unusually handsome bed lounge which is shown in the cut.  This bed lounge is made of very fine solid oak with handsome pattern back, decorated with **corded and piped ornamentation.**  The decoration is in the highest style of the art, and is after designs executed by the leading designers for the largest manufacturers.  The seat and head are fitted with **springs,** making them **easy and comfortable,** while the

lounge when opened out as a bed is 4 feet wide and 78 inches long.  Fitted with a **woven** wire spring and cotton top mattress, covered with an **excellent grade of** ticking.  This is a durable and handsome piece of furniture that is a necessity for every household.  After purchasing one of these desirable articles of furniture you will wonder how it has been possible for you to do without it.  We offer it at unusually close prices, shipping direct from the factory and giving the privilege of examination on our liberal C. O. D. terms if you desire.  Three per cent. discount allowed if cash in full accompanies your order.

| | |
|---|---|
| Above bed lounge in No. 2 corduroy or an excellent grade of kaizer plush | $11.75 |
| Same in first-class imported corduroy | 12.00 |
| Same in brocoline crushed plush or nice silk tapestry | 12.50 |
| Same in a very select brocatelle or high grade satin damask | 13.00 |

## Our Special $12.00 Bed Lounge.

**No. 9530** The bed lounge which we illustrate is one of the new designs for 1897 trade. It is just on the market, and doubtless will not be seen in your retail stores for a year, if at all. It is seldom if ever carried by small retail dealers. We give you great advantages in purchasing furniture from the fact that our contracts with the manufacturers are equal to the entire yearly purchase of large numbers of retail dealers combined. We are hence in a position to secure net spot cash prices and furnish you the goods at about what your retail dealer would himself have to pay. This is a great advantage to you, and, if you are ever in the market for furniture, we can please you. We guarantee all goods to be **exactly as represented** or money will be refunded. The lounge which we show in the illustration is one of the choicest bed lounges that can be produced. You will get some idea from the cut of the beautiful appearance it presents. It is **unusually large**, has a high back, beautifully hand carved and fancy shaped. It is further decorated with corded silk plush, upholstered panels and top. The bed is fitted with **wire springs** and cotton top matress, making it, when opened, just as comfortable a bed as you can desire. This is a convenient article of furniture and no one who can take advantage of our low price should be without one. We pack it very carefully, and when packed for shipment it weighs about 165 lbs.  We furnish it upholstered as follows at the prices named:

| | |
|---|---|
| **Bed Lounge,** upholstered in velvet carpet.  Our special price | $10.20 |
| Same, upholstered in B or D grade upholstering | 14.75 |
| Same, upholstered in E grade upholstering | 13.85 |

Grade B is a fine No. 2 corduroy or kizer plush.  Grade D is a superior quality brocoline crushed plush.  Grade E is a very rich and handsome silk tapestry.  In ordering, state explicitly what grade of covering you want, and we will please you.

---

# WHAT THE PEOPLE SAY.

---

# The Choicest Hall Trees Ever Manufactured.

**MONEY WON'T BUY MORE STYLISH GOODS.**

## A $15.00 Hall Rack for $9.75.

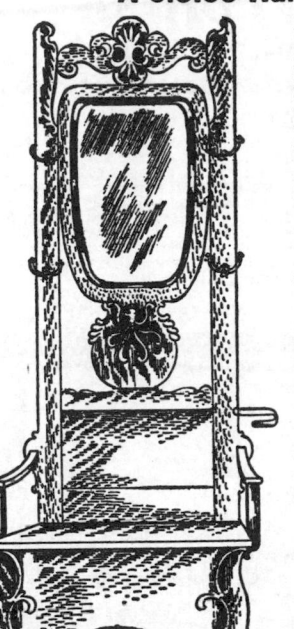

**No. 9533** This Hall Rack has hitherto been held by manufacturers at from $11.25 to $12.00 net jobbing price. We have placed large contracts for these goods, and are able to offer them at the exceedingly low price named, knowing that it is the best value ever offered for the money. We are willing to send these goods C. O. D. subject to examination on our liberal C. O. D. terms described elsewhere with our guarantee that if the article is not entirely desirable in every respect and just as represented it may be returned to us and we will promptly refund the money. This Hall Rack stands 6 feet 10 inches high and 2 feet 9 inches wide, made of the very finest quarter sawed oak with an elegant hand polished finish, and when placed in your hall will be one of the most attractive articles of furniture you could place there. It has handsome hand carvings throughout, box seat with lid and made to hold rubbers, etc., metal umbrella stand is very convenient while the bevel plate mirror is fancy pattern shaped and 14 x 24 inches in size. This rack weighs complete packed for shipment about 100 lbs., and at our factory to consumer price is an unheard of bargain. Our special price, each ............ $9.75

### A $25 HALL TREE FOR $17.90

## This Hall Tree is Yours for $7.50.

**No. 9532** This Hall Tree is specially manufactured for the finest furniture trade, and naturally would be bought by retail stores in large cities for wealthy purchasers, but with our enormous facilities for disposing of large quantities of these goods we are able to bring the price down within the reach of the most limited means. We have heretofore been unable to secure a Hall Tree of equal value to sell at less than $9.50. We are offering this Hall Tree at the unusually low price named, and we believe you will consider it equal to anything you can secure from a local dealer at double the money. It is made of the best quarter sawed oak with a very fine polished finish, with box seat and with a handsome bevel plate mirror 12x20 inches in size. The box seat has lid, and is made to hold rubbers, etc. Fancy metal umbrella holder and new style coat and hat hooks. Height of the case is 6 feet 10 inches and the width is 2 ft. 6 in. The weight packed for shipment is about 85 lbs. Our special price, each .................... $7.50

☞ **OUR C. O. D. TERMS** are very liberal. Any Hall Tree subject to examination on receipt of $5.00. 3 per cent. off for full cash with order.

**No. 9535** It is seldom or never that you will find a Hall Tree of equal value in any retail store, in fact, they are compelled to pay so high a price for such goods and exact so large a profit that their sales would be very few and far between, hence they can not afford to carry them. By buying at the closest spot cash with order price and by adding our narrow margin of profit we are able to place these goods in your hands at a less price than you would have to pay for inferior goods from your local dealers. This Hall Tree is made of quarter sawed oak with very fine hand polished finish. It is impossible for us to give you anything but a faint idea in the illustration of the very choice hand carving with which this Hall Tree is decorated. You can gain some idea however, from the cut, of what appearance it will present when in your hall. The fancy pattern mirror is made of the choicest extra heavy French beveled plate. The wide box seat has lid and is made to hold rubbers, etc. Heavy metal umbrella stand and holder. The height of the rack is 6 feet 10 inches and it is extra wide, the width being 3 feet 6 inches. Weight packed carefully for shipment is 150 lbs. Our special price........ ............. ........................ $17.90

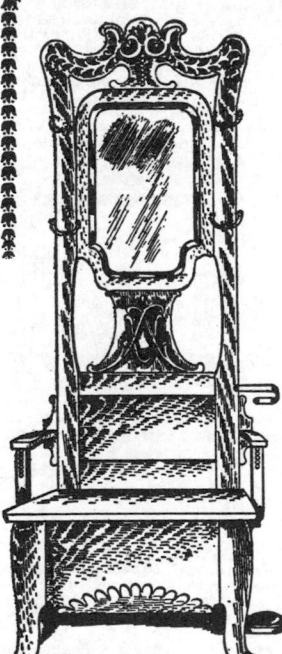

## A Special Bargain for $10.95.

**No. 9534** We ship this elegant Hall Tree to any address C.O.D. subject to examination on our liberal C. O. D. terms on receipt of a small deposit. Only a concern who has absolute confidence in the goods it sells can possibly afford to make such liberal C. O. D. terms. If cash in full accompanies order we allow a discount of 3 per cent. Under our guarantee goods shall be exactly as represented or they may be returned to us and money will be refunded. This hall tree is made of the finest quarter sawed oak with a beautiful hand polish finish. Elegant French bevel plate mirror is pendant shaped and 14 x 24 inches in size. Box seat with lid made to hold rubbers, etc. Fancy pattern front. Heavy metal umbrella stand and holder. Height of hall tree is 6 feet 10 inches; width is 36 inches; weight packed for shipment about 100 lbs. We pack and crate these hall trees very carefully so that they will reach you in perfect condition. Our C. O. D. terms are very liberal. Send $5.00 with your order and we will send this beautiful hall tree subject to examination. Our special price, each................ $10.95

## $5.45 Buys an $8.00 Hall Tree.

**No. 9531** For a very desirable and well made article of furniture, we can recommend nothing that will be more substantial and more satisfactory than the hall tree which we show in the illustration. This article is made of the best quarter sawed oak and has a very handsome polished finish. The German beveled plate mirror in the back is 10½ by 17 inches in size. The hall tree stands 6 feet 9 inches high and 2 feet 2 inches wide. It is very handsomely decorated with fancy ornamentations and has metal umbrella holder and fancy coat and hat hooks. It combines the very necessary qualities of elegance and durability as well as cheapness. In compiling our list of furniture it is not a question of how cheap but how good, and in securing such goods as we list herein at the prices named we believe that we have reached the highest points in our expectations, and are able to give you better value for the money in the furniture line than you have ever been able to secure. This hall rack is carefully crated for shipment and will reach you in perfect condition. Weighs about 75 lbs. Our special price.......................... $5.45

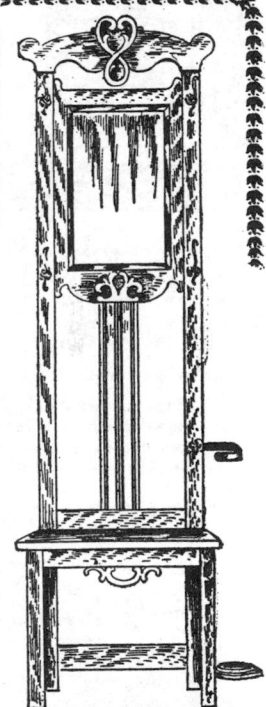

## JARDINIER STANDS.

### Our $1.70 Stand.

### A Very Stylish Ornament for any Parlor.

**Just The Thing For Flowers.**

**No. 9538** The Jardinier Stand which we show in this illustration is 22 inches high and the top is 13x13 inches in size. The stand is made in oak or imitation mahogany finish, as may be desired. This stand is unusually well made, the top is fancy pattern and shape, sides are handsomely Carved and decorated. Our Special Price........................... $1.70

## Our $2.10 Jardinier Stand.

### No. 9539.

### In Offering This Stand at our Low Price Named Below

we feel certain that our customers will be able to effect a saving of from 40 to 50 per cent. The quality of these goods is very high, they being made by a manufacturer whose reputation is second to none for the quality of goods he turns out. We are fortunate in having placed a large contract for these goods, and are able to make a very low price. The stand is 22 inches high, the top is 13x13 inches in size, finished in oak or imitation mahogany as desired. You can get some idea of the fancy ornamentation in the way of turned spindles and balls from the cut, but you must see the stand in order to appreciate its general excellence. Our special price.......................... $2.10

**WHEN YOU SEE ANYTHING IN THE FURNITURE LINE AS GOOD AS OURS IN A RETAIL STORE, YOU'LL FIND THE PRICE ABOUT 50 PER CENT. HIGHER THAN OURS.**

# SPECIAL SALE OF FINE FRAMED PICTURES.

## Reproductions from many of the World's most Famous Paintings at Enormous Reductions in Prices.

1840

### A $5.00 Picture for $2.00.

No. 9540. While the artist has done the best he could to give you some idea of the handsome fac-simile of the water color drawing, the illustration can not do it half justice. As stated, this is what nine out of ten would say is a genuine water color, so near has the original been imitated. The cut shows one of a **variety of 8 different landscape studies**, and should you order from us we will give you such a bargain in the way of a beautiful landscape as you have never seen or heard of. It is mounted in a 4-inch frame, finished in **ivory enamel** with tinted edges and gold-tipped ornaments. We believe this to be the greatest bargain ever offered in the way of a picture. It is something that agents and picture dealers would ordinarily ask $5.00 to $5.50 for. We solicit your trade on this line of goods, knowing that we could give you better terms than you could secure anywhere else. We know that we can please you and only ask a chance to give you such goods as you can obtain from no other concern at anything like our price. Remember our 3 per cent discount when cash in full accompanies order. Our special price...................................$2.00

### A $2.50 Picture for $1.25.

No. 9541. This is a very large size oil painting, painted on heavy canvas with stretcher. Size is 28 x 36 inches. We furnish the picture in selected studies of landscapes, water views, castles, etc. The illustration shows one of a large variety which we carry. They are very well executed oil paintings, and are not to be compared with the cheap, common lithographs for which you are asked a very large price. The frame is made of very handsome 3-inch gold leaf molding in raised figures and pebbled surface. We desire to call your attention to the fact that the **frame is not covered with cheap gold screwings** but covered with **genuine metal leaf.** We are able to offer such bargains in this line from the fact that we buy from one of the largest manufacturers of frames in this country. The pictures are artistic in workmanship and finish. The prices we name are based on our one small profit plan.
Our special price.................... ..........$1.25

1841

### A Wonderful Bargain for $1.00.

No. 9542. We undertake to give you some idea in the illustration of a very superior fac-simile pastel picture which will be an ornament to any home. We give you an opportunity to adorn your home at a very small outlay, and there is no reason why the poorest may not have as handsome pictures as those who are more wealthy. Such a picture as we illustrate is equal to anything you **will ordinarily pay $2.50 to $3.00 for** to agents or dealers. This very handsome picture is furnished with glass, and is 16x20 inches in size inside. The frame is finished in ivory enamel, with tinted edges and gold-tipped ornament. We furnish this picture in a large variety of new and desirable studies in landscapes and fruits. The illustration shows one of our very large assortment.
Our special price... ....................................$1.10

1842

### WALL POCKETS AND MIRRORS.

We offer this desirable line of goods at about half Dealer's prices. Each article is a Gem. The choicest leaders from these different manufacturers. **WE PACK OUR GOODS WITH CARE** and they will reach you in perfect condition.
A Discount of 3% allowed for full cash with order.

### A Special Bargain for 69 Cents.

No. 9545 This Wall Pocket is one of the choicest designs made by one of the leading manufacturers with whom we have placed contracts for large quantities, enabling us to give an **unheard of bargain.** This wall pocket at 69c. would not ordinarily be sold by retailers at less than double our price. It is 19 inches high by 22 inches wide, outside measurement, and is fitted with a **fac-simile pastel landscape** 11 by 14 inches in size. The illustration shows one design, and we have over 60 sets which are all desirable. The frame is made of very handsome moulding and you cannot help but be pleased with this unheard of bargain.
Our special price, each.........................$0.69

### Our 45c Wall Pocket.

No. 9543 Almost every housekeeper knows what a **convenient receptacle** a wall pocket is. It is well known that dealers make very large profits on this class of goods from the fact that they are accustomed to double the money on everything of the kind they sell. By our economic system we are able to furnish these goods to our customers at about what a dealer himself would have to pay. The wall pocket which we show in illustration is made from imitation **oak finely reeded,** made in either light or dark finish. It is fitted with a 10x14 inch hand **painted Japan panel** in assorted designs, of which the illustration shows a very handsome one. It is full size, the outside measurement being 13½x17½ inches. They are so inexpensive and so convenient that you can not afford to be without one or more of them.
Our Special Price, each ...........................$0.45

### Wall Pocket for 80 Cents.

No. 9544 This Wall Pocket is made of handsome **reeded hardwood,** finished in beautiful white enamel and handsomely brass trimmed. We doubt if you could match this article at twice our factory

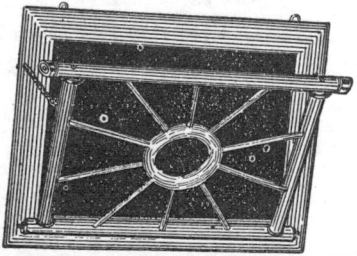

to consumer price. It is 16 inches wide by 20 inches high, and the handiest thing in the world for papers, magazines, etc. **Brass chain** on pocket. It is very neat and substantial, as well as attractive and convenient. Our special price....................$0.80

**OUR PIANO AND ORGAN CATALOGUE** Is the most elaborate and best illustrated ever published.

No. 9546 The handsome mirror which we show in the illustration is very convenient for bath rooms or bed rooms, and at our factory to consumer price the cost is very small. **No house is complete without a number** of small mirrors which are handy in so many rooms, and we offer this one as the choicest bargain in the way of small mirrors we have ever had the pleasure of cataloguing. It is made with a very handsome solid oak frame, beautifully polished and finished, and is fitted with the best **French bevel plate or French plain plate,** as may be desired. It is made in the following sizes at the prices named below:

| Size of Glass. | Plain. | Bevel |
|---|---|---|
| 10x10 | $0.50 | $0.75 |
| 12x12 | .75 | 1.00 |
| 14x14 | 1.08 | 1.42 |
| 16x16 | 1.35 | 1.80 |

### A Heavy Pier Mirror for $6.50.

No. 9550 The handsome and thoroughly well constructed **heavy Pier Mirror** shown in the illustration is quoted at a price far below anything for sale at retail, and at the same time is thoroughly well made and fitted with the very finest plate glass. The frame is made of oak, very handsomely decorated with hand carving, with a fancy pattern top, and in size is about 22x50 inches. The very **fine French plate mirror** is 18x40 inches in size. We pack these mirrors with the utmost care, and aside from accidents they are sure to reach you in the most **perfect condition.** We guarantee that you will be pleased with this article, and feel sure after you have received it you will find it one of the most convenient and desirable pieces of furniture you could add to your home. We allow a discount of 3 per cent. when full cash accompanies order. Our special price, with heavy French plain plates............$6.60
Our special price, with extra heavy French bevel plate.................................$7.50

**OUR SPECIAL FURNITURE CATALOGUE CONTAINS A FAR MORE COMPLETE LINE WITH LARGE ILLUSTRATIONS.**

## A $1.50 Mirror for 86c.

No. 9549 A handsome mirror fitted with fine, clear glass is seldom if ever purchased at a retail store without paying exorbitant profits. Dealers take advantage of the fact that mirrors are easily broken to make the claim that extra high prices must be charged to cover the breakage occasioned by shipping. As we pack all our mirrors in the very best possible shape, and box each one separately, there is no danger whatever of breakage, and consequently we do not have to charge extra to cover losses. Furthermore, by contracting at unusually low prices for large quantities we are able to offer you these mirrors at about half the ordinary retail prices. This pier mirror is made with a solid oak frame with handsome carved top, and presents a very handsome appearance. We fit the mirror with nothing but the best French plate glass, which is of unusual quality and the finest that is imported. It is well known the cheap mirrors found in retail stores are fitted with very imperfect glass, which is entirely unsatisfactory. We guarantee satisfaction in all our mirrors and that the glass shall be perfect in every respect. We make these mirrors in various sizes, and fit them with either plain or bevel plate glass, as may be desired.

| Size of Glass. | Plain. | Bevel. |
|---|---|---|
| 14 x 14 | $ .86 | $1.08 |
| 14 x 17 | 1.08 | 1.35 |
| 12 x 20 | 1.42 | 1.75 |
| 14 x 24 | 1.98 | 2.48 |
| 17 x 30 | 3.28 | 4.05 |
| 18 x 36 | 3.64 | 5.18 |
| 18 x 46 | 4.50 | 5.65 |

## Our Special $9.75 French Pier Mirror.

No. 9551 There is perhaps nothing that adds more to the elegant appearance of a room than a handsome and stylish pier mirror such as we show in the illustration. This article of furniture is made by a manufacturer who caters perticularly to the best trade, and the article, reaching the consumer through the retailer, is necessarily held at such an unusually high price that it is scarcely within the reach of the average man's means. By contracting for a large supply of these mirrors, we are in a position to offer them at a price at least 33⅓ per cent. below any retail price which you can possibly secure. It is very heavy and massive in appearance, and at the same time, elegant in outline and rich in ornamentation. The height of the frame is about 6 feet 4 inches. The frame is made of the best solid oak, with very handsome finish and fitted with a shelf below the mirror. The mirror itself is made of the very best French plate glass imported to this country, and is 18 inches wide by 40 inches high. It is consequently very large in size. We pack these mirrors very carefully and they are sure to reach you in the very best condition and give you the highest satisfaction.

Our special price with plain French plate ..... $9.75
Our special price with finest imported French bevel plate ................................ 10.75

## A Fine Plate Mirror for 30 Cents.

No. 9547 Dealers make a very large profits on this class of goods. They are compelled to from the fact that they sell at such high prices that their sales are comparatively small, hence they make up for their small sales by large profits. This mirror is made with a handsome solid oak frame, beautifully polished, and very finely fitted by the best workmen. We fit the mirror with the best French glass made, in the following sizes at the prices named below:

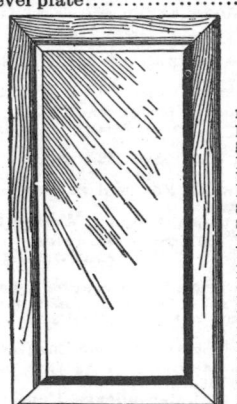

| Size of plate. | Plain. | Bevel. |
|---|---|---|
| 7x 9 inches | $ .30 | $ .38 |
| 8x10 inches | .45 | .58 |
| 9x12 inches | .55 | .75 |
| 10x17 inches | .86 | 1.20 |
| 12x20 inches | 1.10 | 1.50 |
| 14x24 inches | 1.62 | 2.12 |
| 17x30 inches | 2.90 | 3.70 |
| 18x40 inches | 3.82 | 5.05 |

## Fine French Plate Mirror for $6.50.

No. 9548 It is impossible to conceive of a more handsome and attractive design of mirror frame, or a more superior quality of bevel plate glass than that contained in the beautiful mirror which we show in illustration. The frame is made of the very finest selected material, finished in olive and gold, or in white and gold, as may be desired, with ornamental gold burnished corners. This frame is 6 inches wide, and you can judge of the beautiful appearance which it presents by the illustration and by the style of ornamentation. This mirror is fitted with an 18x40 inch French plate glass of the very best imported quality.

Our special price with fine French plate mirror, 18x40 inches .................................. $6.50
Our special price for special quality heavy French bevel plate mirror, 18x40 inches ........... $7.50

## Our 48 Cent Easel.

No. 9552 The Easel which we show in the illustration is made by expert workmen, and while plain in design it is decidedly handsome. It is well constructed from the best selected material, has stationary solid brass easel rests and is 60 inches in height. The rear support is connected with the frame by a handsome chain. For parlor decoration with drapery and picture nothing can be more handsome.
Our Special Price ................ $0.48

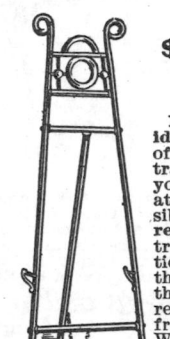

## A $2.00 Easel for $1.20.

No. 9553 You can get but little idea of the handsome appearance of this beautiful easel from illustration, but it is such an easel as you will pay from $2.00 to $2.50 for at any local store where it can possibly be found. It is made of reeded enamelled poles neatly trimmed with brass and has stationary brass easel rests. It is further decorated with a beautiful three inch paneled mirror. The rear support is connected with frame by chain. Height is 60 inches. Weighs but little. costs little, and is an attractive ornament.
Our Special Price .......... $1.20

## Our 50c Fire Screens.

No. 9554 The Fire Screen which we show in the illustration is one of those little articles of furniture which through our economic methods we secure at an unheard of price, and which are so desirable and ornamental. The screen which we show is made of fine light oak, is 36 inches high by 22 inches wide. It is thoroughly well put together, very strong and substantial, and ornamented with turned balls.
Our special price, frame only ...... $0.50
Our special price, filled with pongee drapery as shown in illustration .................... $0.85

## Elegant Fire Screen for $1.50.

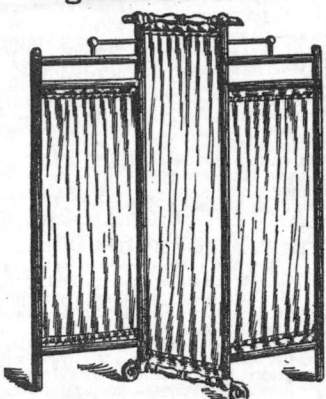

No. 9555 This is a very desirable screen, and is made of the most select light oak, handsomely finished and artistically made. It is constructed in a thoroughly substantial manner and is very desirable both as an ornament and as a useful article of furniture. It stands 44 inches high and its entire width is 40 inches. Outside panel, 12x30 in. in size; center panel, 12x40 in. We can furnish this handsome screen either with or without drapery,
Our special price, frame only ............... $1.50
Our special price, pongee drapery .......... 2.25

## Office or Bath Room Toilet

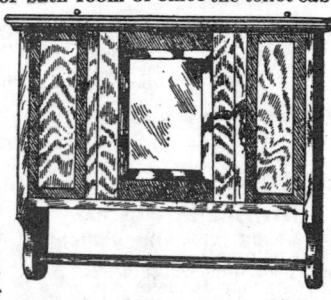

No. 9556 For bath room or office the toilet cabinet which we show in the illustration is a very desirable addition. It is fitted with roomy compartment for soap, comb, brushes. etc. The door has a beautiful French bevel plate mirror 6x8 inches in size. Towel rack for towel. The interior of the toilet measures ten inches nigh, sixteen inches wide and four inches deep, fitted with shelf. It is made of solid oak, very handsomely finished and a most desirable piece of furniture. Our special price, $1.50

## Our Special Bathroom Supply Cabinets.

No. 9557 This Cabinet is one of the handiest and most complete accessories for bathroom or office. It is not only convenient, but splendidly made, and very fine in appearance; constructed of solid oak; handsomely finished. Fancy swell front of patent design. Elaborate hand-carved top. 3 Size, outside, 19x23 inch. Inside, 15x16x4½ inches deep. Complete with shelving, etc., for towels, soap, combs, brushes, and other articles. The door is fitted with a heavy French bevel plate mirror, 8x12 inches in size; very handy for shaving or dressing. Adjustable towel roller at bottom, 16 inches long. Onr special price, each .................. $2.85

## Clock Shelf for 48 Cents.

No. 9558 We make this Clock Shelf of solid ash with a dark antique finish. It is handsomely carved and decorated throughout.

thoroughly well constructed and heavily braced brackets. Size of shelf 7½ inches by 24½ inches. It is a very desirable article of furniture, and it will pay you if you need anything of this kind to include one in your next freight order.
Our Special Price .................. $0.48

No. 9559 Our Mantel and Clock Shelf which we show in illustration is made in three sizes and can be taken apart for shipment. It is very excellent in construction, being made of solid oak, very handsomely finished and ornamented and decorated throughout. We furnish screws so that it can be put together very easily, and it is a very desirable shelf either for mantel or for clock. We quote prices as follows:

Size, 7 inches wide by 24 inches long, price .....$0.53
Size, 8 inches wide by 28 inches long, price ..... .74
Size, 8 inches wide by 36 inches long, price ..... 1.00

## Special Bargains in Bracket Corners.

**No. 9560** The Corner Bracket which we show in illustration is made of solid ash with handsome dark antique finish. It is 18 inches high by 12½ inches wide, and is made to fit the corner perfectly, taking up very small space and being unusually convenient.
Our special price, each....**$0.54**

**No. 9561** We have the same Corner Bracket only smaller in size, 11½ inches high by 8 inches wide. Our special price................**$0.18**

## A $1.50 Corner Bracket for 95cts.

**No. 9562** The corner bracket which we show in this illustration is one of those small articles of furniture which are so convenient and which take up so little room and are unusually inexpensive. The one which we quote here is made of selected ash with a very nice dark finish and is 36 inches high by 12 inches wide, having 3 shelves. A house is never complete without small articles of this kind for they always come in handy as receptacles for such articles as sewing materials, medicine, brushes, etc.
Our special price, each.... **$0.95**

**No. 9562½** We have corner bracket exactly the same as the one illustrated and described above but having only two shelves, and being 26 inches high by 12½ inches wide. Our special price........**$0.50**

## Our $2.00 Solid Oak Umbrella Stand.

**No. 9563** This very desirable piece of furniture is offered by us at an unheard of price. We are only able to make this price by buying in large quantities direct from the manufacturer and closing them out to our customers at the lowest possible margin of profit. This stand is made in oak with very fine polish finish, and is handsomely decorated with spindle work. The brass bostom piece for drippings is securely attached to the frame.
Our special price, each....**$2.00**

## A $4.00 Uubrella Stand for $2.50.

**No. 9563½** This is a New Pattern in the way of an Umbrella Stand and has just been put on the market. It is made in a unique design and is very pleasing in appearance as well as most valuable article of furniture. Has brass bottom piece for drippings. The stand is made of choicest oak with fine polished finish and is very ornamental throughout. Our Special Price, each. **$2.50**

## Our 21c Towel Holder.

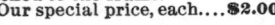

**No. 9564** The Towel Holder illustrated is made of the best selected hard wood, carefully constructed and throughly substantial. Length of arm is 19 inches.
Our special price, each...........................**$0.21**

**No. 9565** The Towel Arm which we show in the above illustration is an old standby, very convenient, desirable and well made. It is constructed of the best seasoned wood, the three arms being 15 inches long, fitted with nickel tips and securely attached to metal base. Can be Swung against the Wall, taking up practically no space.
Our Special Price, each...................**$0.10**

**No. 9566** We have the Same Towel Arm as above illustrated and described but without the nickel tips. Our Special Price, each.......**$0.08**

## A Special Bargain for 9 cents.

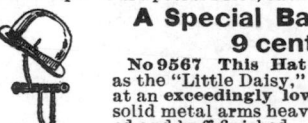

**No 9567** This Hat Rack is known as the "Little Daisy," and is a beauty at an exceedingly low price. It has solid metal arms heavily nickel plated and buff finished.
Our special price, each.........**$0.09**

**ALWAYS ORDER BY NUMBER.**

## Special Bargain for 58 Cents.

**No. 9568** The very ornamental combination rack which we illustrate is made of the finest oak, finished handsomely in antique, decorated with turn ball.
It is unique in design and thoroughly substantial and will prove an ornament to any house.
Our special price, each......................**$0.58**

## Ideal Blacking Cabinet for 50 Cts.

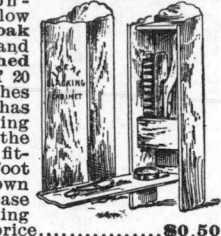

**No. 9569** The Ideal Blacking Cabinet shown in illustration is a very convenient and exceedingly low price. It is made of solid oak or solid birch, as desired, and is very handsomely finished in antique. In height it if 20 inches. the width is 6 inches and the depth 5 inches. It has a convenient rack for holding brush, blacking, etc., and the front, which drops down, is fitted with malleable iron foot rest. The lid folds up as shown in the cut illustrating the case closed. Brush and blacking not included. Our special price................**$0.50**

## A $3.50 Blacking Case for $2.40.

**No. 9570** We Show in the Illustration a Very Handsome and useful article which is necessary in every household, a blacking case that is thoroughly well made of the Best Seasoned Hard Wood, finished in antique oak and handsomely carved. It has a large space below for slippers, brush, blacking, polishes, etc. Strong iron hold fitted on top. Strongly constructed throughout with hinged lid. In size it is 11x15 inches and 16 inches high.
Our Special Price, each, .....................**$2.40**

## A $1.25 Table for 68 cents.

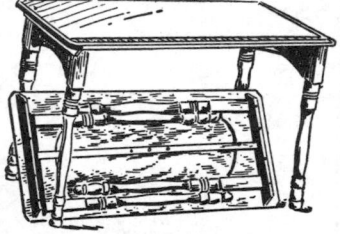

**No. 9571** This Table is made of carefully finished ash with hard wood turned legs. When opened the legs are held perfectly rigid and firm by means of strong wooden springs at each end. It is opened and closed readily and takes up very little space when closed. The top has a yard measure on one side, and the table is the best seller we have ever handled. Size of top is 18 inches wide by 36 inches long, and the height is 25 inches. One of these tables is a great convenience in a household, as those who have them know, If you are without one, we can recommend nothing more highly as an article of furniture. Our special price, each. **$0.68**

## A $1.50 Table For $1.00.

**No. 9572** We have contracted for these handsome tables in very large quantities, and hence are able to offer them at the very low price named above. They are made of solid ash, the best selected material only being used in their construction. When the table is opened the legs are held rigidly in place by means of adjustable braces, and it can be opened or closed in an instant, When closed the legs fold against the bottom of the table, and hence when laid away it takes up very little space. This makes an elegant card table, being handsomely finished and thoroughly substantial. Size, 24 inches by 32 inches; height, 28 inches.
Our special price, each.........................**$1.00**

## WHAT THE PEOPLE SAY.

# WHAT THE PEOPLE SAY

**We always Please our Customers.**

Sirs: Wagon and Harness received all right, every thing in good shape, am' well pleased. I think road wagon will stand our rough lumber country roads all right. I consider those long side springs just the thing for rough roads, the Wilson bit I got from you fills the bill excellently, I never used a bit I liked so well before, it is as easy as a common bit, still in an emergency will control any horse.
JOHN PAULSON,
Gordon, Wis.

**Cannot see how we do it.**

Shiloh, Ala.

Sears, Roebuck & Co.
Dear Friend: The order of Feb. 1st has been received and I like them far better than I expected, I can not see how you do it. The package was at the office but the agent did not notify me, please excuse me for blaming you for it when it was not your fault in the least. Yours truly,
W. J. TUCKER.

**"I Do Not Know a More Fair or Honorable Firm."**

Mound Station, Brown Co., Ill.

Sears, Roebuck & Co.
Dear Sirs: I received the $15.95 parlor suit and am very much pleased with it. I know it is a bargain. I do not know a more fair and reliable firm. I hope the rest of the money will reach you in safety. Wishing you success for your square dealing, I remain, Yours truly, ALBERT BOND.

**"Will Recommend Your House to My Friends."**

Granite, Colo.

Sears, Roebuck & Co., Chicago, Ill.
Dear Sirs: Received suit all right, was much pleased with it, will recommend your house to my friends and hope to favor you with more orders in the future, Thanking you for your kindness.
Resp'y yours, MRS. LAURA GARRISON.

**Well Pleased With Jacket.**

Colorado Springs, Colo.

Sears, Roebuck & Co.
Dear Sirs: I received my jacket all right and I am well pleased with it. It gave good satisfaction. Shall favor you with another order in the future.
Yours respectfully, MISS ANNIE BANDTELL.

**Perfectly Satisfactory in Every Way.**

Braden. I. T.

Sears. Roebuck & Co., Chicago, Ill.
Gentlemen: I received my suit of clothes and I am perfectly satisfied in every way, and will do all I can for your firm. I will send you another order soon and will cheerfully recommend your to all.
Yours truly, A. J. COLLINS.

**Delighted with the Furniture.**

Avon, Ky.

Sears, Roebuck & Co., Chicago, Ill.
Gentlemen: The bed room suit and dinning room table received all O. K. and I must say we are delighted with them. The table is just a beauty, something that would retail here at not less than $15.00. We take great pleasure in speaking a good word for your house, and if at any time we can be of service to you, we will be more than glad to do so. Thanking you for past favors, we remain,
Yours very truly, S. E. STEVENS,
Agt. Adams Exp. Co., Avon, Ky.

**Everybody says the Watch is a Dandy.**

Morristown, Ohio.

Sears, Roebuck & Co.
Sir: Received Watch No. 12015, was well pleased with it, showed it to several, they say it is a dandy, will send for some more goods shortly.
Yours respectfully, WILLIAM DAVIS.

**"Will talk for S. R. & Co. Whereever and Whenever we can."**

Bivins, Texas.

Sears, Roebuck & Co.
Dear sirs: The Sewing Machine, Iowa, No. 91006, $13.25 received last week in good shape, we consider it a daisy, my wife has being using it and says it is all right, will talk for S. R. & Co., whenever and wherever we can. I think this machine will sell others here, when people see it, and see it work. Will do all we can for you, will send you another order for clothing, etc, as soon as we can, thanking you for your promptness in sending the machine and for the very good quality of machine.
I remain your friend,
FRANK HORTON, Bivins, Texas.

**Well Pleased with Suit.**

Mt. Pocono, Pa.

Dear Sirs: I received my suit in good order and am well pleased with it.
Yours truly, MARCUS L. BARTHOLOMEW.

**Never Before Received Satisfactory Results from Other Houses.**

Cherry Valley, N. Y.

Sears, Roebuck & Co.
Gents: The suit I ordered of your house was received in good shape and I beg to say that I am highly pleased with them. The fit is perfect and I am agreeably disappointed from the fact that I have never before succeeded in ordering in this way and received satisfactory results. I wish to compliment you on your credibility and reliability in fully carrying out your statements to those who patronize your house. I am so well pleased that I shall soon give another order for a suit for extra wear and shall, when I am ready, send for samples.
PHILIP R. WALES.

**"Your Kindness Shall Not Be Forgotten."**

Fort Wayne, Ind.

Dear Sirs: I received the watch which you so kindly sent me. I am very well pleased with it. Your kindness shall not be forgotten.
Yours truly, JAMES GLEND.

**Well Pleased With Machine.**

Evansville, Ind.

Messrs. Sears, Roebuck & Co.,
Gentlemen: I received the machine ordered from you April 6, 1896, and gave it a fair trial and will say that I am well pleased with it. I instructed the bank to forward you the balance on same. If I ever need anything in your line you will be favored with my order. Thanking you for your promptness in filling the order, I remain, yonr customer,
J. WINGURTER.

**Will Encourage His Friends to Buy of Us.**

Paris, Tenn.

Sears, Roebuck & Co.
Gentlemen: I received suit a few days ago and am much pleased, as it gives entire satisfaction in every respect. So far I am much encouraged to order from you again, and will encourage my friends like wise. DENNIS WADDY.

**Watch is O. K.**

Newton, Mo.

Sears, Roebuck & Co.
I received the watch O. K. and I believe it is all right. I am well pleased with it.
I remain yours, F. M. NOWTIN,
Newtown, Sullivan Co., Mo.
P. S. Please send me your big catalogue.

**Will Recommend To His Friends.**

Crenshaw, Pa.

Dear Sirs: I received the goods; they are better than I expected. I will recommend you to all my friends for your honesty and nice goods.
Yours truly,
MISS BARBARA SIMBECK, Crenshaw, Pa.

**Sewing Machine Excels All Others.**

Ventland, Pa.

Sears, Roebuck & Co.,
Dear Sirs: I received the machine in good order and am perfectly satisfied with it. It excels all others and is certainly a bargain for the money. My wife has tried it on all kinds of work and we are now able to recommend it to any one. I will hereafter patronize you in anything that I can. I am,
Yours Respectfully,
J. F. WITHEROW, Ventland, Clearfield Co., Pa.

**Will Hear From Him Again.**

Grand Rapids, Mich.

Sears, Roebuck & Co.,
Suit of clothes come all right and am very much pleased with them. You will hear from me again.
Yours respectfully, ED. TAYLOR.

**Well Pleased with Baby Carriage.**

Epperson, McCracken Co., Ky.

Sears, Roebuck & Co.
Sirs: I have received the baby carriage that I ordered and am well pleased with it. Have also received your refund of the 7 cents. Receive my thanks for your prompt action.
Very resp'y, J. H. MOSELEY.

**"Thanks for so Faithfully Filling My Order."**

Bethel, Vermont.

Sears, Roebuck & Co.
Messrs: It is with great pleasnre that I write you this time, for I have received my second "Holman Bible" and it is a beauty. Very many thanks to you for so faithfully filling the order.
Yours very truly, MRS. C. E. FOSTER.

**Has Dealt with us for 18 Months and is Always Surprised at Quality of Goods.**

Pollock, La.

Sears, Roebuck & Co.
Gentlemen: The clothes and shoes I ordered of you have been received and am well pleased with your fair and honest dealings. Have been trading with you for eighteen months and am always surprised when I receive goods from you, as they are so good for such little money. Wishing you many better customers than myself, I am,
Yours truly, D. J. MEADE.

**Will order two more Suits just like it.**

Sears, Roebuck & Co.
Gentlemen: My suit of clothes just received, am highly pleased with it, it fits excellent, will send in an order the 25th of this month for two suits of the same goods. one suit, style 4, at $12.75 and style, 1 at $11.75. Thanking you for past favors I beg the honor to remain. Yours truly. L. P. SHOEMAKER,
Ft. Monroe, V. A.

**Pleased with the Waist.**

Shamer, Okla.

Sears. Roebuck & Co.
I have received the waist which I ordered, invoice, No. 206468, am very well pleased with it.
Yours respectfully,
MISS MATTIE BOSTON.

**You may look for another order.**

Crystal River, Fla.

Sears, Roebuck & Co.
Dear Sir: Your goods were gladly received and in good order and was satisfied, you may look for another order in short time.
Oblige, FLORENCE BAILEY.
N. B.—Ship goods at the earliest date possible.

**Pleased With the Watch.**

Milligan, Fla.

Sears, Roebuck & Co., Chicago. Ill.
Dear Sirs: I received the watch and have it now. I am very much pleased with it, and others are as well pleased with it as myself. I got the watch as soon as it came to the office and paid the agent the price. Hope the money has been sent safely to you.
Yours truly, JOSEPH C. JANDAN.
P. S.—I am going to move my business to Gold City, Saint Rose Co. Fla.

**Promptness in Shipping.**

Manson, Iowa.

Messrs. Sears, Roebuck & Co., Chicago, Ill.
Gentlemen: Replying to your favor of the 11th inst., enclosing your bill and bill of lading for the goods ordered of you, will say that I have received the goods all O. K. and thank you very much for your promptness in filling the order.
Yours truly, DAVID P. SMITH.

**Well Pleased With Pants.**

Packsville, S. C.

Dear Sirs: The suit and pair of pants by express C. O. D. came in to-day. I am well pleased with them and shall favor you with future orders.
Yours respectfully,
J. M. BRADHAM, Packsville, S. C.

**"I Am Very Well Pleased With Your Firm."**

Telluride, Colo.

Sears, Roebuck & Co.,
Dear Sirs: The suit arrived here to-night and I am very much pleased with it. I am very well pleased with your firm and hope we may continue our friendly relations. Hoping your business will increase and you will prosper, I remain as ever,
Truly yours,
J. E. MAYERS, Telluride, Colo.

**Well Pleased with Our Treatment.**

Nashville, Ind.

Sears, Roebuck & Co.
I received invoice 205173 all O. K. Can say I was well pleased with quality and treatment of your house in regard to the matter. WM. C. KELLER.

**Everyone That Looks at the Buggy Pronounces it a Great Bargain.**

Farmersville, Tex.

Gentlemen: The buggy, harness, etc., came to hand all right and in good order; I am well pleased with it. Everyone that has looked at it pronounces it a great bargain and I think it will induce others here to patronize your house. Wishing you great success in your business, I am,
Yours truly,
REV. W. D. CHAPMAN.

**Suit Even Better than Advertised.**

Point View, Kans.

Sears, Roebuck & Co.
Dear Sirs: I want to order another suit and would like to have catalogue and samples.
P. S, I was much surprised at the suit I received from you. It was even better than advertised; which is not often the case.
Very respectfully, EDWARD COOPER.
Frick, Douglass and Danks say they saved $4.00 apiece on the suits they ordered from you.
Yours truly, E. S. COOPER.

**Will Send Another Order Soon.**

Harding.

Sears, Roebuck & Co.
Goods received, everything all right. Think I will send another order soon, expect to get an organ this fall. Yours truly, MRS. SALMON LEWIS.

**Pleased With Shoes.**

Libert, S. C.

Sears, Roebuck & Co.
Dear Sirs: Shoes were received all right; I am well pleased, with thanks for your prompt attention to my order. Resp'y. MRS. JANE SMITH.

**"Your Prices for Clothing are Far Below All Other Concerns,"**

Healing Springs, Ala.

Dear Sir: I received the suits of clothes you sent me the second week in June, according to my request; thank you kindly for the same; were just as represented. Your price for clothes is far below all other concerns. Look for another order soon.
Yours Resp'y, V. LEVI FULLER.

**Proud of the Buggy.**

Rose Hill, Jasper County, Ill.

Sears, Roebuck & Co.
I received the buggy yesterday evening, also harness, lap robe, sweat pad, fly net; I will say I am well pleased with them, the agent said it is the best buggy that has been shipped this season at this place, there was thirty of forty people gathered around it on the platform while I was setting it up together, all looking how nice and good it was; I am so proud of the buggy and when we get anything we always try to get something that shows out right well. Will show this buggy and harness and will do all I can for you. MISS MARY PRICE.

**Goods are Extra Good.**

Lawler, Iowa.

Sears. Roebuck & Co.
Gents: Yours received and must say goods is very good, extra good. I shall recommend you and remain
Yours, W. G. CLAPPER.

**Perfectly Satisfied with Revolver.**

Palestine, Texas.

Messrs. Sears, Roebuck & Co.
Gentlemen. Received my revolver and was perfectly satisfied. Those revolvers cost $2.50 in our city today. I couldn't find any fault if I would try.
Yours truly, J. H. BAREFIELD.

**Takes Pleasure in Recommending Us.**

North Madison, Ohio.

Messrs. Sears, Roebuck & Co.
Gents: I have received the Columbus buggy I ordered of you, invoice 205,496. It came through in perfect order. I am very much pleased with my purchase, and thank you for your courteous treatment. I shall take pleasure in recommending your house in this vicinity. I am, yours respectfully,
J. D. BROWN,
North Madison, Lake Co., Ohio.

# OUR CROCKERY AND GLASSWARE DEPARTMENT.

Our stock of tableware includes only the finest selection of crockery from the **best European manufacturers**. American made crockery is well known to be inferior to the English and French manufacture. Our orders have hence been placed in Europe for the best and most select patterns, with manufacturers whose goods are known the world over as the finest it is possible to produce. **Importing our own stock,** we are not only offering a line that has no superior on the market, but we are in a position to name prices against which the retailer cannot compete. You pay what he himself pays, for we sell to the consumer just as any other importer sells to the retail dealer. The advantage of our Factory-to-Consumer system is apparent. We are constantly breaking down the wall between maker of merchandise, and the actual user.

In connection with our crockery, we desire to say that **every set is most carefully packed** in barrels and casks, and we seldom or never hear of any breakage. The freight is a very small item indeed, when the great saving in price is considered. This class of goods ships as first-class freight.

It is impossible to examine these goods satisfactorily at your depot. Hence we request full cash in advance on all orders. However, we practically ship **subject to your approval.** Any goods not found as represented, or unsatisfactory, may be returned to us and money refunded.

## GENUINE ENGLISH STONE WARE CHINA.
### Manufactured by J. & H. MEAKIN, Hanley, England.

**No. 9610.** Plain white. We guarantee these goods to be the finest and most durable earthen ware made in the world. Warranted not to craze. One set of the above will out-wear three sets of the domestic goods, and will cost but a trifle more.

☞ We Accept No Order for Chinaware Amounting to Less than $2.50. ☜

**Open Stock Prices of this White Granite Ware Set.**

|  | |  |
|---|---|---|
| Tea cups and saucers | per doz., | $1.00 |
| Coffee " " | " | 1.20 |
| Plates, 8 inch " | " | .95 |
| " 7 " " | " | .80 |
| " 6 " " | " | .70 |
| " 5 " " | " | .55 |
| " 7 " soup | " | .80 |
| Fruit saucers, 4 inch | " | .40 |
| Individual butters | " | .25 |
| Oyster bowls | " | 1.00 |
| Tea pot | each, | .35 |
| Sugar bowl | " | .30 |
| Cream pitcher | " | .13 |
| Bread plate | " | .17 |
| Bowls, 1 pint | " | .08 |
| " 1 quart | " | .10 |
| Platters, 4 inch | " | .07 |
| " 8 " | " | .11 |
| " 9 " | " | .13 |
| " 10 " | " | .13 |
| " 12 " | " | .32 |
| " 14 " | " | .50 |
| " 16 " | " | .70 |
| Bakers, 3 inch | " | .08 |
| " 7 " | " | .13 |
| " 9 " | " | .25 |
| Scollops, 6 inch | " | .11 |
| " 7 " | " | .13 |
| " 8 " | " | .19 |
| " 9 " | " | .25 |
| Soup tureen and ladle, (no stand) | " | 1.60 |
| Sauce tureen, complete | " | .65 |
| Sauce boat | " | .17 |
| Covered dish, 8 inch | " | .50 |
| Casseroles, 8 inch | " | .65 |
| Covered butter dish, 5 inch | " | .38 |
| Pickle dish | " | .13 |
| Pitcher, 1 gallon | " | .38 |
| " 2 quarts | " | .25 |
| " 1 " | " | .15 |
| " 1 pint | " | .13 |
| " ½ " | " | .10 |

## $7.95 BUYS A $20.00 IMPORTED 100-PIECE DINNER SET.
### Manufactured by W. H. WETHERBY & SON, Hanley, England.

**No. 9220.** While this Dinner Set retails at $20, we succeeded in making an arrangement with the manufacturers which enables us to sell the complete set at the heretofore unheard of price for $7.95. This set is suitable to decorate the tables of the wealthy, and in price is within the reach of all.

**BARGAINS** are what our customers expect of us, and even in this line we cannot afford to disappoint them. This genuine English semi-porcelain ware, not first or second grade American, but the genuine English, decorated with delicate spray of anemone flowers and leaves, put on under glaze, which prevents its wearing off. We can furnish two colors: Blue and Brown. **Be sure to state** which color is wanted in ordering. They are the latest style and consist of the following 100 pieces: 12 Teacups with handles; 12 Tea Saucers; 12 5-inch Plates; 12 6-inch Plates; 12 7-inch Plates; 12 Fruit Saucers; 12 individual Butters; 1 8-inch Baker; 1 10-inch Platter; 1 12-inch Platter; 2 8-inch Covered Dishes; 1 Sauce Boat; 1 Pickle Dish; 1 Covered Butter Dish; 1 Covered Sugar Bowl; 1 Cream Pitcher; 1 Slop Bowl.

Only .................................. **$7.95**

**Cash in full must accompany your order.** We pack the set carefully in a barrel and deliver to any depot in Chicago free of charge. Our price—$7.95 covers everything. The dishes will reach you in good order. We have never yet heard of a broken piece from any we have shipped. **This is a Rare Bargain.**

As soon as our present contract expires we will not be able to furnish any more at this price.

**You should take advantage of this Special Offer while it lasts...**

# IMPERIAL SET.

The Napoleonic and Trilby fads are dead. The latest fad is Green Table Decorations, and by far the handsomest of the many beautiful designs in fine dinner ware, made to fill this want, is our IMPERIAL DINNER WARE, manufactured by Dunn, Bennett & Co., Burslen, England. It is a very handsome decoration in Olive Green, heavily traced with gold, and will not fail to please the most fastidious.

Wherever one of these sets is sold we shall expect an immediate increase in trade. We make it a practice to advertise ourselves by the value we give for the least money. One of these Elegant Imperial Patterns in a neighborhood is bound to attract great attention to our House, not only as the Cheapest Supply House on Earth, but as a House that is in a position to supply the very latest and best goods to be found in the markets of the World.

9665-9670. Order by number.

**No. 9665. 44 Piece Tea Set:** 12 tea plates; 12 tea-cups; 12 tea saucers; 1 tea pot (2 pieces); 1 cream pitcher; 1 slop bowl; 2 cake plates, and 1 sugar bowl (2 pieces). Our special price, full set............$ 5.80

**No. 9666. 56 Piece Tea Set:** Same composition as 44 piece set, with 12 sauce plates added. Our special price, full set.................................$ 6.57

**No. 9667. 55 Piece Dinner Set:** 6 dinner plates; 6 breakfast plates; 6 pie plates; 6 sauce plates; 6 individual butters; 6 teacups; 6 tea saucers; 1 open vegetable dish, 8 inch; 1 covered vegetable dish, 8 inch, (2 pieces); 1 platter, 12 inch; 1 sugar bowl (2 pieces); 1 cream jug; 1 pickle dish; 1 slop bowl; 1 covered butter dish (3 pieces), and 1 sauce boat. Our special price, full set....................................$ 8.40

**No. 9668. 100 Piece Dinner Set:** 12 dinner plates; 12 breakfast plates; 12 tea plates; 12 sauce plates; 12 individual butters; 12 teacups; 12 tea saucers; 1 open vegetable dish, 8 inch; 2 covered vegetable dishes, 10 inch, (4 pieces); 1 platter, 10 inch; 1 platter, 12 inch; 1 sugar bowl (2 pieces); 1 cream jug; 1 pickle dish; 1 slop bowl; 1 covered butter dish (3 pieces), and 1 sauce boat. Our special price, full set...........$13.75

**No. 9669. 112 Piece Dinner Set:** 12 dinner plates; 12 tea plates; 12 pie plates; 12 soup plates; 12 sauce plates; 12 individual butters; 12 teacups; 12 tea saucers; 1 platter, 10 inch; 1 platter, 12 inch; 1 platter, 14 inch; 2 open vegetable dishes, 8 inch; 2 covered dishes, 8 inch (4 pieces); 1 sauce boat; 1 pickle dish; 1 sugar bowl (2 pieces); 1 cream jug. Our special price, full set...........$15.75

**No. 9670. 124 Piece Dinner Set:** 12 dinner plates; 12 breakfast plates; 12 tea plates; 12 soup plates; 12 individual butters; 12 sauce plates; 12 teacups; 12 tea saucers; 4 platters; 2 open vegetable dishes; 1 soup tureen and ladle (3 pieces); 1 sauce tureen and ladle and stand (4 pieces); 1 sauce boat; 2 covered dishes, 8 inch, (4 pieces); 1 covered butter dish (3 pieces); 1 pickle dish; 1 sugar bowl, and 2 cake plates. Our special price, full set.............................$24.20

# VICTOR PATTERN.

THIS PATTERN IS A HIGH GRADE PRINT ON ENGLISH SEMI-PORCELAIN WARE; the shape is NEW AND TASTY; the plates have FESTOONED EDGES; the decoration is a very neat border design with leaves and flowers, delicate and pretty, under the glaze. WARRANTED NOT TO WEAR OFF. This set comes in two colors, Brown and Blue. In ordering please state which color you prefer. WARRANTED NOT TO CRAZE.

Such a set as the Victor Pattern is one that will set off any dining table to perfection. It is impossible for you to form more than a faint idea of the beauty and daintiness of the elegant decoration. The shape is an entirely new one, the pattern being an entirely new importation from Europe.

The purchaser of one of these sets will be sure of having something entirely different from any thing else ever seen in their locality, and far superior to most sets for which neighbors have paid from 50 to 75 per cent. more.

**No. 9626. 44 Piece Tea Set:** 12 tea plates; 12 tea cups; 12 tea saucers; one tea pot (2 pieces); one cream pitcher; one slop bowl; 2 cake plates and one sugar bowl (two pieces). Our special price, full set....$3.72

**No. 9627. 56 Piece Tea Set:** Same composition as 44 piece set with 12 sauce plates added. Our special price, full set.......................$4.20

**No. 9628. 55 Piece Dinner Set:** 6 dinner plates; 6 breakfast plates; 6 pie plates; 6 sauce plates; 6 individual butters; 6 tea cups; 6 tea saucers; one open vegetable dish, 8 inch; one covered vegetable dish, 8 inch (2 pieces); one platter, 12 inch; one sugar bowl (2 pieces); one cream jug; one pickle dish; one slop bowl; one covered butter dish (3 pieces), and one sauce boat; Our special price, full set.......................$5.40

**No. 9629. 100 Piece Dinner Set:** 12 dinner plates; 12 breakfast plates; 12 tea plates; 12 sauce plates; 12 individual butters; 12 tea cups; 12 tea saucers; one open vegetable dish, 8 inch; two covered vegetable dishes, 8 inch (4 pieces); one platter, 10 inch; one platter, 12 inch; one sugar bowl (2 pieces); one cream jug; one pickle dish; one slop bowl; one covered butter dish (3 pieces), and one sauce boat. Our special price, full set.......................$8.85

**No. 9630. 112 Piece Dinner Set:** 12 dinner plates; 12 tea plates; 12 pie plates; 12 soup plates; 12 sauce plates; 12 individual butters; 12 tea cups; 12 tea saucers; one platter, 10 inch; one platter, 12 inch; one platter, 14 inch; 2 open vegetable dishes, 8 inch; 2 covered dishes, 8 inch (4 pieces); one sauce boat; one pickle dish; one sugar bowl (2 pieces), and one cream jug. Our special price, full set...................$10.20

**No. 9631. 124 Piece Dinner Set:** 12 dinner plates; 12 breakfast plates; 12 tea plates; 12 soup plates; 12 individual butters; 12 sauce plates; 12 tea cups; 12 tea saucers; 4 platters; 2 open vegetable dishes; one soup tureen and ladle (3 pieces); one sauce tureen and ladle and stand (4 pieces); one sauce boat; 2 covered dishes, 8 inch (4 pieces); one covered butter dish (3 pieces); one pickle dish; one sugar bowl and 2 cake plates. Our special price, full set .................................$15.54

ALL GOODS FROM THIS DEPARTMENT WILL BE SENT BY FREIGHT C.O.D., SUBJECT TO EXAMINATION, ON RECEIPT OF $2.00. THERE IS 3 PER CENT. DISCOUNT FOR CASH IN FULL WITH ORDER.

# PRINCESS PATTERN.

Equal to the finest French China sold at double the cost. Manufactured by Alfred Meakin, Tunstall, England. This is the finest semi-porcelain set produced by any maker in the world. The ware is very light and the shape new, and all the pieces embossed with raised work traced in gold. The decoration is a delicate spray of flowers in natural colors, blue, brown and pink.

Lovers of Artistic Designs in tableware will find the Princess Pattern to their entire liking. Only those who are expert in judging different qualities and makes can possibly detect the difference between this pattern and the genuine finest French china, which wholesales at twice our Special Importers' Prices.

The Pattern is one of which you will never tire, as in the case of the common, and in most cases inartistic patterns usually carried in retail Stores.

A trial order on these goods will be sure to please you and lead to continued trade.

9680–9685. Order by number.

**No. 9680. 44 Piece Tea Set:** 12 tea plates; 12 teacups; 12 tea saucers; one teapot (2 pieces); one cream pitcher; one slop bowl; two cake plates, and one sugar bowl (2 pieces). Our special price, full set......$ 6.20

**No. 9681. 56 Piece Tea Set:** Same composition as 44 piece set, with 12 sauce plates added. Our special price, full set......$ 7.05

**No. 9682. 55 Piece Dinner Set:** 6 dinner plates; 6 breakfast plates; 6 pie plates; 6 sauce plates; 6 individual butters; 6 teacups; 6 tea saucers; one open vegetable dish, 8 inch; one covered vegetable dish, 8 inch (2 pieces); one platter, 12 inch; one sugar bowl, (2 pieces); one cream jug; one pickle dish; one slop bowl; one covered butter dish (3 pieces), and one sauce boat. Our special price, full set......$ 9.00

**No. 9683. 100 Piece Dinner Set:** 12 dinner plates; 12 breakfast plates; 12 tea plates; 12 sauce plates; 12 individual butters; 12 teacups; 12 tea saucers; one open vegetable dish, 8 inch; two covered vegetable dishes, 10 inch (4 pieces); one platter, 10 inch; one platter, 12 inch; one sugar bowl (2 pieces); one cream jug; one pickle dish; one slop bowl; one covered butter dish (3 pieces), and one sauce boat. Our special price, full set......$14.75

**No. 9684. 112 Piece Dinner Set:** 12 dinner plates; 12 tea plates; 12 pie plates; 12 soup plates; 12 sauce plates; 12 individual butters; 12 teacups; 12 tea saucers; one platter, 10 inch; one platter, 12 inch; one platter, 14 inch; two open vegetable dishes, 8 inch; two covered dishes, 8 inch (4 pieces); one sauce boat; one pickle dish; one sugar bowl (2 pieces), and one cream jug. Our special price......$16.90

**No. 9685. 124 Piece Dinner Set:** 12 dinner plates; 12 breakfast plates; 12 tea plates; 12 soup plates; 12 individual butters; 12 sauce plates; 12 teacups; 12 tea saucers; 4 platters; two open vegetable dishes; one soup tureen and ladle (3 pieces); one sauce tureen and ladle and stand (4 pieces); one sauce boat; two covered dishes, 8 inch (4 pieces); one covered butter dish (3 pieces); one pickle dish; one sugar bowl, and two cake plates. Our special price......$25.90

# GENUINE HAVILAND CHINA.

This set is the Finest French China, manufactured by CHAS. FIELD HAVILAND, Limoges, France, they being the largest manufacturers of china in the world. Their name alone is sufficient guarantee of quality. The china is thin and transparent, the shape entirely new; every piece is embossed heavily and traced with gold. Plates have fluted edges. The decoration is a very beautiful design, being a spray of pink roses, handsomely executed. This set is a decided bargain, being sold at a price which dealers ordinarily ask for common earthen ware.

We can only make such low prices on this, the choicest of makes and patterns, by importing in large quantities from France and accepting a very small margin of profit. We prefer to sell at smallest margins, increasing our trade thereby, and thus receiving a fair return on an enormous business rather than the same amount of profit on a small business. That our patrons appreciate our fair and honorable dealings, is proven in no better way than by the fact that twice within fifteen months have we been absolutely compelled to seek larger buildings.

On this basis of One Small Profit from factory to consumer, we offer the following assortments of finest Haviland China at about one-half retail prices.

**No. 9695. 56 Piece Tea Set:** 12 tea plates; 12 teacups; 12 tea saucers; 12 sauce plates; one teapot (2 pieces); one cream pitcher; one slop bowl; 2 cake plates, and one sugar bowl (2 pieces)......$14.65

**No. 9696. 55 Piece Dinner Set:** 6 dinner plates; 6 breakfast plates; six pie pie plates; 6 sauce plates; 6 individual butters; 6 teacups; 6 tea saucers; one open vegetable dish, 8 inch; one covered vegetable dish 8 inch (2 pieces); one platter, 12 inch; one sugar bowl (2 pieces); one cream jug; one pickle dish; one slop bowl; one covered butter dish (3 pieces) and one sauce boat......$20.55

**No. 9697. 100 Piece Dinner Set:** 12 dinner plates; 12 breakfast plates; 12 tea plates; 12 sauce plates; 12 individual butters; 12 teacups; 12 tea saucers; one open vegetable dish, 8 inch; 2 covered vegetable dishes, 10 inch (4 pieces); one platter, 10 inch; one platter, 12 inch; one sugar bowl (2 pieces); one cream jug; one pickle dish; one slop bowl; one covered butter dish (3 pieces), and one sauce boat. Our special price......$33.75

**No. 9698. 112 Piece Dinner Set:** 12 dinner plates, 12 tea plates; 12 pie plates; 12 soup plates; 12 sauce plates; 12 individual butters; 12 teacups; 12 tea saucers; one platter, 10 inch; one platter, 12 inch; one platter, 14 inch; 2 open vegetable dishes, 8 inch; two covered dishes, 8 inch (4 pieces); one sauce boat; one cream jug. one pickle dish; one sugar bowl, 2 pieces. Our special price......$39.45

# DECORATED DINNER-WARE.   Patterns Sold in Open Stock.

**PLEASE TAKE NOTICE** that we will not accept of any orders sent to us, for goods on this page, unless same amount to $2.50 or over,

**No. 9701 GERTRUDE PATTERN.** A beautiful under glazed print in a neutral tint of Bader & Co.'s celebrated English-ware, new embossed shape. Your choice of selection of any of below named pieces at prices quoted.

| | | | | |
|---|---|---|---|---|
| Tea Cups and Saucers..Per doz.$1.35 | Bakers, 3 inch | Each | $0 10 |
| Coffee Cups and Saucers.. " 1 60 | Bakers, 7 inch | " | 17 |
| Plates, 8 inch " 1 27 | Bakers, 8 inch | " | 25 |
| Plates, 7 inch " 1 10 | Bakers, 9 inch | " | 35 |
| Plates, 6 inch " 95 | Scallops, 6 inch | " | 15 |
| Plates, 5 inch " 76 | Scallops, 7 inch | " | 17 |
| Pletes, 7 inch, soup " 1 10 | Scallops, 8 inch | " | 25 |
| Fruit Saucers, 4 inch " 50 | Scallops, 9 inch | " | 35 |
| Individual Butters " 34 | Soup Tureen and Ladle | | |
| Oyster Bowls " 1 35 | (no stand) | " | 2 20 |
| Cream Pitcher Each.. 18 | Sauce Tureen, complete.... | " | 90 |
| Tea Pot " 45 | Sauce Brats | " | 25 |
| Sugar Bowl " 38 | Covered Dish, 8 inch | " | 70 |
| Bread Plate " 18 | Casseroles 8 inch | " | 90 |
| Bowls, 1 pint " 11 | Covered Butter Dish, 5 inch " | 50 |
| Bowls, 1 qt " 14 | Pickle Dish | " | 17 |
| Platters, 8 inch " 14 | Pitchers, 1 gal | " | 50 |
| Platters, 9 inch " 17 | Pitchers, 2 qts | " | 35 |
| Platters, 10 inch " 25 | Pitchers, 1 qt | " | 20 |
| Platters, 12 inch " 43 | Pitchers, 1 pt | " | 18 |
| Platters, 14 inch " 60 | Pitchers, ½ pt | " | 15 |
| Platters, 16 inch " 95 | | | |

**No. 9603 LUSTER BAND,** open Meakin's English-ware. This ware is so well known that a description is hardly necessary, the decorations are of a heavy luster band and a flower sprig in luster which resembles gold very closely, but will not wash off as gold is apt to do. Your choice of selection of any of below named pieces.

| | | | | |
|---|---|---|---|---|
| Tea Cups and Saucers....Per doz.$1 80 | Bakers, 3 inch | Per doz.$1 60 |
| Coffee Cups and Saucers.. " 2 10 | Bakers, 7 inch | Each. | 25 |
| Plates, 8 inch " 70 | Bakers, 8 inch | " | 35 |
| Plates, 7 inch " 1 45 | Bakers, 9 inch | " | 45 |
| Plates, 6 inch " 1 25 | Scallops, 5 inch | " | 15 |
| Plates, 5 inch " 1 00 | Scallops, 6 inch | " | 20 |
| Plates, 7 inch, soup " 1 50 | Scallops, 7 inch | " | 25 |
| Fruit Saucers, 4 inch " 78 | Scallops, 8 inch | " | 35 |
| Individual Butters " 45 | Scallops, 9 inch | " | 45 |
| Oyster Bowls " 1 80 | Soup Tureen and Ladle | | |
| Tea Pot Each.. 60 | (no stand) | " | 3 00 |
| Sugar Bowl " 50 | Sauce Tureen (complete) | " | 1 15 |
| Cresm Pitcher " 25 | Sauce Brals | " | 35 |
| Bread Plate " 25 | Covered Dish, 8 inch | " | 90 |
| Bowls, 1 qt " 20 | Casseroles, 8 inch | " | 1 18 |
| Bowls, 1 pt " 15 | Covered Butter, 5 inch | " | 70 |
| Platters, 8 inch " 20 | Pickle Plates | " | 25 |
| Platters, 9 inch " 25 | Pitcher, 1 gal | " | 70 |
| Platters, 10 inch " 35 | Pitcher, 2 qts | " | 45 |
| Platters, 12 inch " 55 | Pitcher, 1 qt | " | 30 |
| Platters, 14 inch " 80 | Pitcher, 1 pt | " | 25 |
| Platters, 16 inch " 1 25 | Pitcher, ½ pt | " | 20 |

# DECORATED DINNER-WARE.   Patterns Sold in Open Stock.

**No. 9705 ROYAL BLUE SET.** This set has an under glazed decoration on English semi-porcelain ware, with full gold trimmings on edges, handles and embossed parts. This is one of the brightest in appearance and popular patterns in the market this day. The decorations are a deep cobalt blue. You can make your own selection of prices quoted.

| | | | | |
|---|---|---|---|---|
| Tea Cups and Saucers....Per doz.$2 25 | Bakers, 3 inch | Per doz.$2 00 |
| Coffee Cups and Saucers.. " 2 50 | Bakers, 7 inch | Each.. | 30 |
| Platters, 8 inch " 2 00 | Bakers, 8 inch | " | 40 |
| Platters, 7 inch " 1 80 | Bakers, 9 inch | " | 55 |
| Platters, 6 inch " 1 50 | Scallops, 5 inch | " | 20 |
| Platters, 5 inch " 1 30 | Scallops, 6 inch | " | 25 |
| Platters, 7 inch, Soup " 1 80 | Scallops, 7 inch | " | 30 |
| Fruit Saucers, 4 inch " 80 | Scallops, 8 inch | " | 40 |
| Individual Butters " 60 | Scallops, 9 inch | " | 55 |
| Oyster Bowls " 2 20 | Soup Tureen and Ladle | " | 3 60 |
| Tea Pot Each.. 75 | Sauce Tureen, (complete) | " | 1 40 |
| Sugar Bows " 60 | Sauce Brat | " | 35 |
| Cream Pitcher " 25 | Covered Dish, 8 inch | " | 1 10 |
| Bread Plate " 25 | Casseroles, 8 inch | " | 1 40 |
| Bowl, 1 Qt " 25 | Covered Butter Dish, 5 inch " | 85 |
| Bowl, 1 Pt " 20 | Pickle Dish | " | 30 |
| Platters, 8 inch " 25 | Pitcher, 1 Gal | " | 85 |
| Platters, 9 inch " 30 | Pitcher, 2 Qt | " | 60 |
| Platters, 10 inch " 40 | Pitcher, 1 Qt | " | 35 |
| Platters, 12 inch " 70 | Pitcher, 1 Pt | " | 30 |
| Platters, 14 inch " 1 00 | Pitcher, ½ Pt | " | 25 |
| Platters, 16 inch " 1 50 | | | |

**No. 9703 BIJOU PATTERN** is one of this season's novelties, shape is entirely new, the decorations consist of small sprays of flowers in natural colors under glaze, gold trimming on all covered pieces, a pattern that will please most any one for style and quality. You can make your own selection of pieces wanted.

| | | | | |
|---|---|---|---|---|
| Tea Cups and Saucers....Per doz.$2 00 | Bakers, 3 inch | Per doz.$1 80 |
| Coffee Cups and Saucers.. " 2 35 | Bakers, 7 inch | Each.. | 25 |
| Plates, 8 inch " 1 90 | Bakers, 8 inch | " | 40 |
| Plates, 7 inch " 1 70 | Bakers, 9 inch | " | 50 |
| Plates, 6 inch " 1 40 | Scallops, 5 inch | " | 17 |
| Plates, 5 inch " 1 25 | Scallops, 6 inch | " | 21 |
| Plates, 7 inch Soup " 1 70 | Scallops, 7 inch | " | 25 |
| Fruit Saucers, 4 inch " 75 | Scallops, 8 inch | " | 40 |
| Individual Butters " 50 | Scallops, 9 inch | " | 50 |
| Tea Pot Each.. 70 | Soup Tureen and Ladle | " | 2 00 |
| Oyster Bowls Per doz. 2 00 | Sauce Tureen, (complete) | " | 1 25 |
| Sugar Bowl Each.. 53 | Sauce Brat | " | 35 |
| Cream Pitcher " 25 | Covered Dish, 8 inch | " | 1 00 |
| Bread Plate " 25 | Casseroles, 8 inch | " | 1 20 |
| Bowl, 1 Qt " 20 | Covered Butter Dish | " | 75 |
| Bowl, 1 Pt " 20 | Pickle Dish | " | 25 |
| Platters, 8 inch " 20 | Pitcher, 1 Gal | " | 75 |
| Platters, 9 inch " 25 | Pitcher, 2 Qt | " | 50 |
| Platters, 10 inch " 40 | Pitcher, 1 Qt | " | 30 |
| Platters, 12 inch " 65 | Pitcher, 1 Pt | " | 25 |
| Platters, 14 inch " 90 | Pitcher, ½ Pt | " | 20 |
| Platters, 16 inch " 1 40 | | | |

☞ **WE WILL ACCEPT NO ORDERS FOR CHINA OR GLASSWARE AMOUNTING TO LESS THAN $2.50. THE ORDER MAY BE A MIXED ONE, HOWEVER, INCLUDING BOTH CHINA AND GLASSWARE.**

# DINNER SETS.

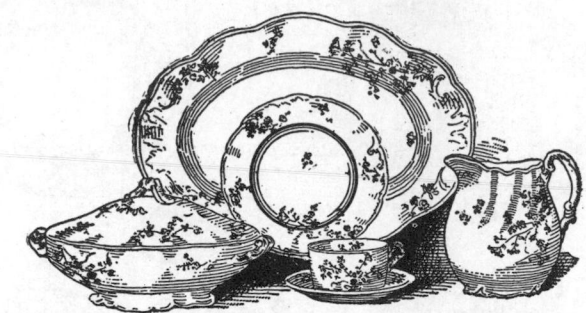

## "GRAY DELHI" PATTERN OF J. & G. MEAKIN'S ENGLISH SEMI-PORCELAIN WARE.

**Gold on Knobs and Handles.**

No. 9727. This is a handsome gray border decoration, offset by gold trimmings, which produce an effect always sought for by potters on wares of the very highest grade. The name of the maker is a guarantee that the goods and decoration are first-class in every respect. Set consists of 100 pieces. Price................$11.50

| | |
|---|---|
| 12 Dinner Plates. | 2 Covered Dishes. |
| 12 Breakfast Plates. | 1 10-inch Platter. |
| 12 Tea Plates. | 1 12-inch Platter. |
| 12 Sauce Plates. | 1 Sugar Bowl. |
| 12 Individual Butters. | 1 Cream Pitcher. |
| 12 Tea Cups. | 1 Pickle Dish. |
| 12 Tea Saucers. | 1 Soup Bowl. |
| 1 Baker. | 1 Sauce Bowl. |
| 1 Covered Butter Dish. | |

## "BEAUTY" PATTERN OF J. & G. MEAKIN'S ENGLISH SEMI-PORCELAIN WARE.

No. 9728. The style of decoration used on this pattern is of the same order as employed by Haviland and other makers of French china dinner ware. A delicate brown spray, filled in with pink and light blue buds, gold on knobs and handles, creates a most pleasing effect, and it cannot fail to satisfy and charm the most fastidious. The ware is of an exceptionaly brilliant finish and shape of the latest of the new designs recently brought out. Set consists of 100 pieces, same as No. 9727. Price....$13.50

## HENSHALL TOILET SET.

This is a high grade English toilet set. The decorations are grand, being a floral design in natural colors, and trimmed with gold. This set will harmonize with the furnishings of any room.

No. 9730. **12 piece Set:** Basin and pitcher, mug, brush vase, hot water pitcher, soap dish, cover and drainer, chamber and cover, and slop jar and cover. Our special price.................................$7.15

### SEE SPECIAL GLASSWARE SETS BELOW.

**Prices Reduced 33⅓ per cent. below former Wholesale figures.**

## BROOKLYN TOILET SET.

**A $15.00 Toilet Set for $8.25. You can't buy anything finer at any price.**

This is the finest set we carry. English semi-porcelain, large shape, decorations under glaze. Comes in two colors, Royal Blue and Dove, heavily stippled with gold. Nothing better in the market for twice the money.

No. 9735. **12 piece Set:** Basin and pitcher, mug, brush vase, hot water pitcher, soap dish, cover and drainer, chamber and cover and slop jar and cover. Our special price.................................$8.25

**The Greatest Bargains of the Century in Glassware.**

ALL CROCKERY IS CAREFULLY BOXED OR PACKED IN BARRELS, AND ONLY EXPERT PACKERS ARE EMPLOYED, THUS INSURING SAFE CARRIAGE. WE HAVE YET TO HEAR OF A SHIPMENT ARRIVING IN BAD SHAPE.

## TOILET SETS.

We admit no competition in this class of goods. To sell such high grade ware at our prices simply means the smallest possible margin of profit to ourselves, and a positive doing away with the profits and expenses of middlemen, through whose hands the goods must pass before you buy over the counter. The illustrations do not do these elegant toilet sets justice. We only ask a trial order to convince you that you can only obtain genuine bargains through us. A 12-piece toilet set, packed, weighs about 60 lbs., and is shipped as first-class freight. Three per cent discount for full cash with order.

### AZALEA ENGLISH SEMI-POR-CELAIN TOILET SET.

#### A $5.00 TOILET SET FOR $2.25.

The shape is new and full size; the decoration is a handsome design of Azaleas, under glaze print, brown, pink or blue. We carry this set in the following assortments:

No. 9710. **6 Piece Set:** Composed of basin and pitcher, chamber and cover, soap block and mug. Our special price......................................$2.25

No. 9711. **10 Piece Set:** Basin and pitcher, mug, brush vase, hot water pitcher, soap dish, cover and drainer, and chamber and cover. Our special price, ...............................................................$2.85

No. 9712. **12 Piece Set:** Same assortment as 10 piece set, with slop jar and cover added. Our special price................................................$4.75

**You can pack many small articles with a Toilet Set and the freight will be no more.**

### THIS TOILET SET $2.25 TO $4.35.
**10 Piece Toilet Set for $2.25. 12 Piece (exactly like illustration) $4.35.**

For $2.25 or $4.35 you can get an elegant Toilet Set that will befit any bedroom. The manufacturer of this ware has a reputation second to none, and no customer will have reason to be displeased in any way with his purchase.

This toilet set is of high-grade white granite, latest style, shape and finish, and guaranteed in every respect. Our special price, packed and shipped to any address, for 12 piece set, exactly as illustrated...............$4.35 For 10 piece set, same as cut without the slop bowl and cover.........................................................$2.25

Order these goods direct from us and you get them at what your retail dealer has to pay.

No. 9718. **10 Piece Set:** Basin and pitcher, mug, brush vase, hot water pitcher, soap dish, cover and drainer, chamber and cover. Our special price ..$2.25

No. 9720. **12 Piece Set:** Same assortment as 10 piece set with slop jar and cover added. Our special price........................................................$4.35

**If you have been accustomed to buy your crockery at home, you can figure up how much profit you have been paying the retailer, if you buy one of these High Art Sets.**

**AN $8.00 SET FOR $4.35.**

**A $12.00 SET FOR $6.75.**

### CHRYSANTHEMUM TOILET SET.

This is an extra large toilet set, English ware. The decoration is a floral design, which is new and very pretty and elegantly trimmed with gold. Can be had in any of the following colors: Brown, Royal Blue and Dove.

No. 9725. **10 piece Set:** Basin and pitcher, mug, brush vase, hot water pitcher, soap dish, cover and drainer, and chamber and cover. Our special price..........$4.35

No. 9726. **12 piece Set:** Same assortment as 10 piece set, with slop jar and cover added. Our special price.$6.75

**If you have any reason to be justly dissatisfied with any purchase from us, you are free to return it and get your money.**

**MAKE UP AN ORDER FOR 100 POUNDS OF GROCERIES, INCLUDE THE NEEDED CROCKERY, AND LET US SHOW YOU WHAT A SAVING THERE IS IN BUYING DIRECT.**

# THE CHOICEST GLASSWARE OF TWO FACTORIES.

**A BARREL OF GLASSWARE FOR $1.90.** ...WHO EVER HEARD OF THE PRICE?..

**FULL CASH MUST ACCOMPANY ORDER. SPECIAL DISCOUNT FOR CASH.**

WE ALLOW A DISCOUNT OF 3 PER CENT WHEN FULL CASH ACCOMPANIES ORDER, WITH THE UNDERSTANDING THAT IF GOODS ARE NOT UP TO VALUE AS REPRESENTED, WE WILL REFUND MONEY.

## A GREAT CUT IN GLASSWARE.

The price of Glassware has been wonderfully reduced. We are on the bottom. We have two outfits at prices never before heard:

### $1.90 AND $2.75.

The above prices are about one-half the retail price. No wholesale house can meet our cut prices of.......

### $1.90 AND $2.75.

No. 9755. This complete outfit for $1.90. No charge for barrel; we pack and deliver at depot free of charge a complete outfit, consisting of the following 36 pieces: 6 tumblers, 6 goblets, 12 4-inch berry saucers, 1 8-inch berry dish, 1 sugar bowl, 1 butter dish, 1 spoon holder, 1 cream pitcher, 1 ¼-gallon water pitcher, 1 celery dish, 1 pickle dish, 1 tall open fruit bowl. The complete outfit for.....................$1.90

Freight will be very little. 25 cents will take a barrel 500 miles; 50 cents will pay the freight to most any point. Send $1.90 and the outfit will be sent to you at once.

Decorate your table with one of our sets of glassware and you will surely say: "Never before were such goods sold for so little money."

No. 9755. (Order by number.)

WE PACK OUR GLASS WARE INBARRELS, EMPLOYING ONLY SKILLED PACKERS, AND WE HAVE YET TO HEAR OF SHIPMENT BEING DAMAGED UNDER ORDINARY CIRCUMSTANCES.

# OUR $2.75 GLASSWARE OUTFIT -- 39 ELEGANT PIECES.

## JUST LIKE CUT GLASS, AT ABOUT 7 CENTS APIECE ON AN AVERAGE.

**Many a Rich Man's Table is Decorated with Glassware no handsomer than this pattern. We make it a point to carry a line that is just as handsome and stylish as the markets afford.**

Would retail at $10.00 and upward. OUR SPECIAL CUT PRICE is $2.75. No charge for packing or delivering to depot. We do that free. An expert only could tell it from a $100 glass outfit.

No. 9757. This elegant 39 piece set must be seen to be appreciated. It is an exact reproduction of the celebrated English "Prism" cut glass and is finished so that it requires an expert to detect the difference. The large pitcher, in particular, is a very handsome piece of glass, and, if it were genuine cut, would alone be worth $20.00, but the glass manufacturers have so improved that we are able to sell this assortment at a fraction of the cost of a single item of the genuine cut glass, and very few could possibly tell the difference. Your neighbors will pronounce it genuine cut glass. These goods are very heavy, beautifully finished, and each piece is a work of art. This outfit consists of 1 butter dish, 1 sugar bowl, 1 spoon holder, 1 cream pitcher, 12 berry saucers, 1 8-inch berry or salad dish, 6 water tumblers, 1 ¼-gallon pitcher, 1 celery tray, 1 silver plated salt shaker, 1 silver plated pepper shaker, 1 large footed fruit bowl, 1 molasses pitcher, 1 vinegar bottle, 1 toothpick holder, 6 goblets. Every one who sees this set will want one. Our price for the complete outfit.............................$2.75

No. 9757. (Order by number.)

A COMPLETE LINE OF SILVERWARE IS QUOTED IN THIS CATALOGUE AT PRICES ABSOLUTELY BEYOND COMPETITION IN GOODS OF EQUAL VALUE. REFER TO INDEX.

SEARS, ROEBUCK & CO., (Incorporated), Cheapest Supply House on Earth, Chicago.

695

# ❋ A TEMPTING SALE OF GLASSWARE. ❋

### We Illustrate on the following pages the Newest Things in Fancy Glassware, products of Leading Makers.

## ELECTRIC GOLD SETS.

This pattern has the most Exquisite Cut Glass Effect. In fact, none but an expert could tell that it is not genuine cut glass. The brilliancy of these pieces is greatly enhanced by finishing the plain parts in gold.

**NOTE**—We accept no orders for Glassware or China amounting to less than **$2.50.** Full cash must accompany the order, and a cash discount of 3 percent is allowed

WE GUARANTEE SATISFACTION, OR GOODS MAY BE RETURNED AND MONEY REFUNDED.

**9812 Electric Gold Berry Set.**
1 Bowl, 6 Saucers. Price.....$1.75
Same as above, 1 Bowl, 12 Saucers.
Price.............................$2.90

**9813 Electric Gold Four-Piece Set,** consisting of Cream Pitcher, Butter Dish, Sugar Bowl and Spoon Holder.
Price......................................$1.50

**9815 Electric Gold Lemonade Se**
consisting of 1 Jug, 6 Tumblers, and 1 Nickel Tray.
Price.............................$1.95

**9817 Four-Piece Glass Set,** extra heavy, imitatian cut glass; none but an expert can tell the difference between this set and the genuine article.
Price per set........................................$0.90

**9819 Four-Piece Glass Set,** is a wonder of brilliant, sparkling imitation cut glass, and worth double amount that we ask for it.
Price, only........................................$0.29

**9821 Lemonade or Water Set,** consisting of 1 jug, 6 tumblers and brilliant tray.
Price.................... $0.48

**9822 4-Piece Plain Glass Set,** very neat and tasty in appearance. A good set at price.............. $0.75

**9823 Lemonade or Water Set,** consisting of 1 jug, 6 tumblers and brilliant tray. Very handsome in design,
Price.................... $0.50

**9800 Child's Cup, Saucer and Plate,** English ware, very fine make and pretty design.
Price, per set...........$0.15

**9801 Extra Fine Decorated Mustache Cup and Saucer,** German transparant china, heavily gold lined. Price, per set. $0.38

**9802 Extra Fine Ladies' Tea Cup and Saucer,** beautiful flower decorations, very pretty, new design.
Price, per set........$0.35

**9803 Gents' Mustache Cup and Saucer,** German china, decorated, very neat.
Price per set........$0.18

**9404 Ladies' Fine Tea Cup and Saucer,** German china, gold lined.
Price, per set...........$0.15

**9805 German China Shaving Mug,** neat and pretty.
Price............. $0.15

**9806 A, B, C, Mug,** English Earthen ware, assorted play scenes.
Price.............$0.05

**9807 Bohemian Glass Vase,** 7 inches high, pretty flower decorations, gold trimmed.
Price, each......$0.18

**9800 Bohemian Flower Vase,** 10 inches high, bright flower decorations and gold trimmed. Price, each.$0.35

**9809 Carlsbad China Fancy Plate,** flowered and gold line decorations.
Price, each ......$0.10

**9810 German China Fancy Dessert Plate,** flowers and gold decorations.
Price, each......$0.17

**WE ACCEPT NO ORDER FOR GLASSWARE AMOUNTING TO LESS THAN $2.50.**

**4829 Glass Tumblers,** full size, plain. Price, per doz...$0.30

**9820 Glass Tumblers,** full size, fluted bottom. Per doz..........$0.32

**9833 Glass Tumblers,** full size, finely engraved Per doz.........$0.60

**9834 Jelly Tumblers,** full size, with tin top. Per doz......$0.30

**9836 Fine Blown** Flint Glass Tumblers, full size. Per doz..........$0.50

**9839 Fine Blown Flint** Glass Tumblers, with rich engravings. Per doz.............$0.70

**9841 Glass Table** Goblets, plain. Per doz..........$0.80

**9843 Glass Table** Goblets, large size. Per doz..........$0.90

**9845 Glass Table** Goblets, large size. Per doz.........$0.92

**9347 Wine Glass,** mottled shaped. Per doz..........$0.38

**9849 Wine Glass,** finely engraved, new pattern. Per doz..$0.60

**0851 Wine Glass,** Im. cut, very light weight. Per doz...........$0.65

**9813 Glass** Toothpick Holder, shaped glass. Price per dozen ..........$0.60

**9855 Salt and** Pepper Shaker, with nickel top. Price per dozen .........$0.65

**9857 Salt and** Pepper Shaker, large silver plated top. Price per dozen..... $1.20

**9859 Fancy Col-** ored Glass Toothpick Holder. Price per dozen.....$0.98

**9861 Plain Glass Salver.** Price for 9 inch....$0.30
"   " 10 " ....38
"   " 12 " ....65

**9863 Glass Salver.** This is without question the handsomest salver yet made in pressed glass. It is well finished, good size and will make first-class piece on banquet tables, etc. Price for 9 inch..................$0.30
"   " 10 " ..................35

**9865 Cruet,** plain glass, very neat and pretty. Price, per doz...$2.85

**9867 Cruet.** Im. cut glass, handsome at price per doz. ,..........$1.55

**9869 Water Jug,** ½ gallon. Im. cut glass. Price, each......$0.28

**9871 Water Jug,** ½ gallon, made of best fine polished glass. Price, each......$0.55

**9873 Syrup Can.** Plain glass, tin top lid. Price.............$0.12

**9875 Syrup Can.** This is an "imitation cut" pattern, extra heavy, with very handsome nickel top. Price, each......$0.25

**9877 Fruit Bowl,** fine imitation cut glass, very pretty in design. Size, 9 inches. Price, each...........................$0.38

**9879 Berry Dish,** a beautiful new pattern, clear glass. Size, 8 inches. Price, each.....................$0.30

**9881 Berry Set,** best in the world for the money. 1 large dish and 6 saucers. Price.........$0.30
Same as above. 1 large dish and 12 saucers. Price............$0.45

**9883 Berry Set,** extra heavy imitation cut glass, equal to the finest crystal made.
1 bowl and 6 saucers.......$0.70
1 bowl and 12 saucers....... .95

# FOUR SPECIAL BARGAINS IN CHINA.

**9824 German China Egg,** white with gold decorations, Sugar Bowl and Creamer. Price, per pair ..............$0.40

**9825 Cream China Pitcher,** flower decorations, gold trimmed. Price........................$0.15

**9826 German China Fancy Shape** Salad, with spray and gold decorations. Price............................$0.75

**9827 Rebecca Tea Pot.**
Price for 2-pint size................$0.15
"   " 3-pint " ..............0.18
"   " 4-pint " ..............0.20
"   " 5-pint " ..............0.25

NO ORDER FOR GLASSWARE AMOUNTING TO LESS THAN $2.50 WILL BE ACCEPTED. YOUR ORDER MAY INCLUDE BOTH CROCKERY AND GLASSWARE.

# REGULAR
# ANNUAL LAMP SALE

## The Lamp Season with Us Means a Season of Rare Bargains.

**OVER 10,000 LAMPS TO BE SOLD** at prices never before heard. If there is a forced sale in any of the markets of the country our buyers are always on the spot. There was a big Lamp sale and our buyers were there and secured all the desirable goods at their own price, a price much less than actual cost to manufacture, hence OUR ANNUAL SALE will be greater than ever.

**OUR TERMS ARE LIBERAL.** Any lamps will be sent to any address by express, C. O. D., subject to examination, on receipt of a sufficient deposit to cover transportation charges both ways, balance and express charges payable at express office.

**THREE PER CENT. DISCOUNT** allowed if cash in full accompanies your order. Your money refunded immediately if you are not perfectly satisfied.

No. 95003.      No. 95004.

**No. 95003. Vase Lamp.** Extra large size. Nicely proportioned and an ornament to any parlor, large climax burner. The decoration is a finely executed design of flowers in natural tints and colorings. Price ...................$1.78

**No. 95004. Vase Lamp.** A very stylish lamp. Decoration is similar to No. 5, except that it is on a matt ground which gives a much richer appearance. Price.................................................................$2.00

No. 95000.     No. 95001.     No. 95002.

**No. 95000. Lamp.** 19 inches to top of chimney. Decorated shade to match fount. Cast metal base. This is the best and cheapest lamp in the market. Price .................$1.20

**No. 95001. Lamp.** This is an extra value. 19 inches high, decorated shade and fount to match. Cast metal base. Price.................$1.35

**No. 95002. Lamp.** With extra large top shade. The lamp is tinted in nice colors and decorated with flowers in natural tints. Price...................$1.65

No. 95007.     No. 95005.     No. 95006.

**No. 95005. Vase Lamp.** This lamp combines beauty with utility. Center draught burner, giving a light equal to 65 candles. The decorations are very rich and finely executed. This is fit to grace any drawing room. Price.................................................................$3.35

**No. 95006. C. Lamp.** This is one of the most staple lamps in the market. Is very strong and substantial, and will last a lifetime. You need no chimney with this lamp, the shade and the illuminator taking the place of chimney, and thus saving you from the breakage of chimneys. Price.................88c

**No. 95007. Study Lamp.** This is an elegant lamp for reading or sewing, or for any purpose where a strong light is desired. Center draught burner, giving a light equal to 65 candles. Lamp is made of brass, heavily nickel plated, and trimmed with a plain white dome shade. Will never get out of order. Price .................$1.75

**No. 95008. Perfection Student Lamp.** This lamp has been used for so many years that a description of it is unnecessary. It is, without a doubt, the peer of all study lamps. Perfectly safe and reliable. Lamp can be adjusted to any height.

Nickel plated, plain white shade.......$3.50
Nickel plated, green shade.............$3.75

No. 95008.

No. 95009.

**No. 95009. Banquet Lamp.** This lamp is of brass with large cast open work vase and No. 2 center draft burner, and finished in gilt. The shade is of silk, in red, orange, lemon, or Nile green, with lace flounce, and in size is well proportioned to the lamp. It will make a very pretty, as well as useful, parlor ornament, and is of much better value than one really expects to get for the price. We include with this, and all the other Banquet lamps we show, a chimney that will not break from heat. Height of lamp is 19 in. to top of burner.

Lamp complete, as shown.................$3.25
Lamp only.................................. 2.00
Shade only................................. 1.25

No. 95010. Banquet Lamp. We offer the No. 95010 lamp, which has American porcelain onyx column, and cast open work base, No. 2 center draft burner, complete, with a beautiful six point silk shade, in either orange, lemon or Nile green color, with lace flounce, at less than one-half price this lamp has always sold at. The lamp stands 18 in. to top of burner.

| | |
|---|---|
| Lamp complete | $3.25 |
| Lamp only | 2.00 |
| Shade only | 1.25 |

No. 95010.

No. 95014. Banquet Lamp. The reason for the great popularity that this lamp has attained is the excellence of the finish and great lighting capacity of the burner. The Cupid is finished in silver, balance of the lamp in gold. The burner is of the latest design of the celebrated "B. & H." pattern, and is bound to give entire satisfaction. We complete the lamp with a handsome silk shade having a deep lace flounce. We can furnish the shade in red, orange, lemon, old rose, pink or Nile green. In ordering please state color of shade desired.

| | |
|---|---|
| Lamp complete | $4.50 |
| Lamp only | 2.85 |
| Shade only | 1.65 |

95014.

No. 95011. Banquet Lamp. The most popular of the many styles of Banquet lamps at a moderate price is the Cupid, and the one we illustrate is unquestionably the best of the many varieties produced to supply the demand. The base is of extra size, of open work embossed design, and the oil fount is also handsomely embossed, and has latest style of No. 2 center draft burner with screw wick movement. Height to top of burner 19 in. The silk shade has lace flounce, and is of a very handsome design. We furnish it in red, orange, pink, old rose, lemon or Nile green. In ordering please state the color desired.

| | |
|---|---|
| Lamp complete | $3.25 |
| Lamp only | 2.00 |
| Shade only | 1.25 |

No. 95011.

No. 95015. Banquet Lamp. Porcelain Banquet Lamps have been exceedingly popular for some time, but on account of price have not come into general use. This year, however, we are enabled to offer one within the range of the "poor man's purse." The No. 95015 is a "gem" in value. The column and oil fount are beautifully embossed, forming panels which are filled in with flowers and leaves in natural colors. The embossed parts are tinted in soft colors. The globe is an exact match in decoration of balance of the lamp. We complete the lamp with large No. 3 burner. The base is richly embossed and finished in gilt. The lamp stands 26 in. to top of globe.

Lamp complete ... $2.79

No. 95012. Banquet Lamp. A lamp having the appearance, as well as the essential points of the highest grade lamps at a popular price, cannot but be the popular lamp in these days. The No. 95012 is just that lamp. It has American porcelain onyx column, cast base and open work head, with removable oil fount and latest style of No. 2 center draft burners. Height to top of burner, 19 in. The silk shade has chiffon flounce, embroidered to match the color of silk in the shades. We can furnish the shade in red, orange, pink, old rose, lemon, or Nile green. In ordering please state color of shade desired.

| | |
|---|---|
| Lamp complete | $5.25 |
| Lamp only | 3.25 |
| Shade only | 2.00 |

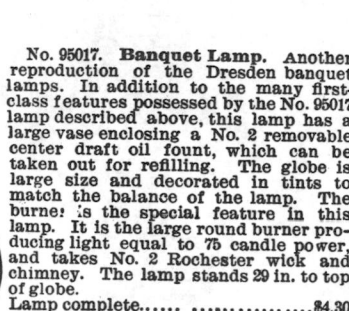

No. 95012.

No. 95016. Banquet Lamp. This is a reproduction of the famous Dresden banquet lamps that have been produced in the highest grades only. The lower column is enclosed by a beautiful cast brass wreath, and both oil fount, vase and column are embossed in handsome designs. All porcelain parts are decorated in pleasing tints, and the flowers are a copy of the genuine Dresden designs. The globe is of extra size, and the lamp is completed with a large No. 3 burner. The lamp stands 27 in. to the top of globe. The base is extra large in cast open work design, and finished in gilt.

Lamp complete ... $3.15

No. 95015.

No. 95017. Banquet Lamp. Another reproduction of the Dresden banquet lamps. In addition to the many first-class features possessed by the No. 95017 lamp described above, this lamp has a large vase enclosing a No. 2 removable center draft oil fount, which can be taken out for refilling. The globe is large size and decorated in tints to match the balance of the lamp. The burner is the special feature in this lamp. It is the large round burner producing light equal to 75 candle power, and takes No. 2 Rochester wick and chimney. The lamp stands 29 in. to top of globe.

Lamp complete ... $4.30

No. 95016.

No. 95013. Banquet Lamp. This is another of the beautiful and popular styles of Cupid banquet lamps. The Cupid is of extra size, silver plated, and mounted on a very large cast open work base. The head is handsomely embossed and has No. 2 center draft burner. Both head and vase are finished in gilt. The lamp is completed with an elegant silk shade, in three colors; lemon, orange, or Nile green, with deep lace flounce. Height of lamp to top of burner is 20 in.

| | |
|---|---|
| Lamp complete | $5.65 |
| Lamp only | 3.30 |
| Shade only | 2.35 |

No. 95013.

No. 95018. Banquet Lamp. With a massive Louis XV base in cast brass 4 in. genuine Mexican onyx column, and beautiful cast open work, designed to match the embossed base. This lamp presents a handsome appearance. It has a No. 2 removable center draft oil fount, and is completed with a large 9 in. Dresden globe. The globe is of pure white opal glass decorated with moss roses and leaves in their natural color. The lamp stands 22 in. to top of burner.

| | |
|---|---|
| Lamp complete | $5.95 |
| Lamp only | 4.55 |
| Globe only | 1.40 |

No. 95017.

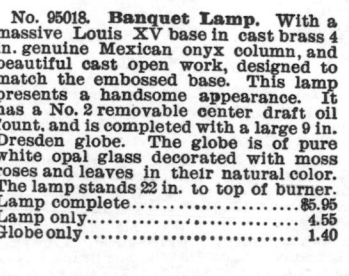

No. 95018.

**TAKE NOTICE—All Globes on Our Banquet Lamps are Interchangeable.**

No. 95019.

No. 95020.

No. 95019. Banquet Lamp. An extremely handsome lamp of an entirely new design. The center column is treated in a French olive green, with cast ornaments in old ivory. The rest of the lamp is of cast brass finished in genuine gold plate. The oil fount is detachable for re-filling and burner is the famous "Miller," conceded by experts to be the best center draft burner on the market. The globe is a copy of the popular "Holland Blue Delft" design, well executed and harmonizes with the lower column of the lamp.
Lamp complete.......................$12.75
Lamp only............................ 10.25
Globe only............................ 2.50

No. 95020. Banquet Lamp. This is the best proportioned lamps ever made, and handsome enough to grace the parlor of a millionaire. The column is of turned Mexican onyx of the very highest grade. with garlands of cast drapery enclosing the lower part. The cast head and base are embossed in Egyptian design, and gold plated. The lamp has removable Miller fount with all the latest devices to make it first-class in every respect. The globe has groups of Cupids on four sides, and is stippled with gold, giving a beautiful effect. Height to top of burner, 22 inches.
Lamp complete........................$13.50
Lamp only............................ 10.45
Globe only............................ 3.05

The silk shades and decorated globes are interchangeable and if one desires a particular lamp with a shade or globe shown on another lamp, we can furnish just what is wanted.

No. 95021.

No. 95021. Library Lamp. No. 2 Sun burner. 14 in. Plain White Shade. Ball weight extension.
Price, complete......$2.00

No. 95022. Library Lamp. Has extra heavy frame, handsomely decorated shade and fount to match automatic spring extension length, closed 25 in. extended 61 inches. Extra large No. 3 burner.
Price..............$3.75

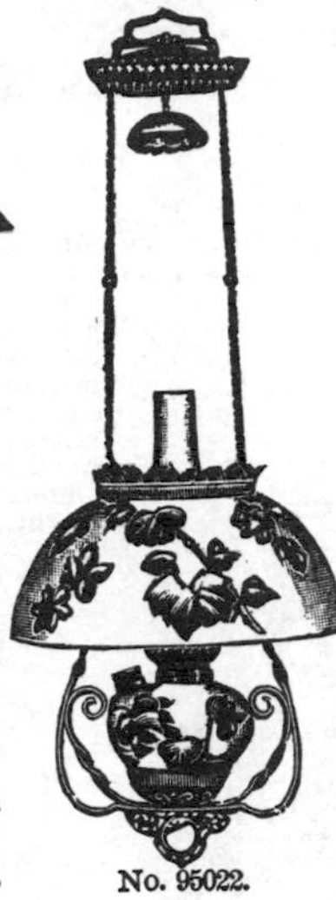

No. 95022.

No. 95023.

No. 95023. Library Lamp. This is one of the best Lamps ever offered for the money. The frame is extra heavy, finished in rich gold. The shade and fount are full tinted and decorated with flowers and heavily stippled with gold, trimmed with genuine cut glass, prisms, automatic spring extension, length closed 25 in., extended 61 in., center draft burner, 65 candle power.
Price complete......$5.65

No. 95029. Complete as illustrated, 20-inch tin shade, suitable for factories, sawmills or any place where a strong light is needed.
Price, brass finish..,...$3.25
Nickel finish.............$3.75

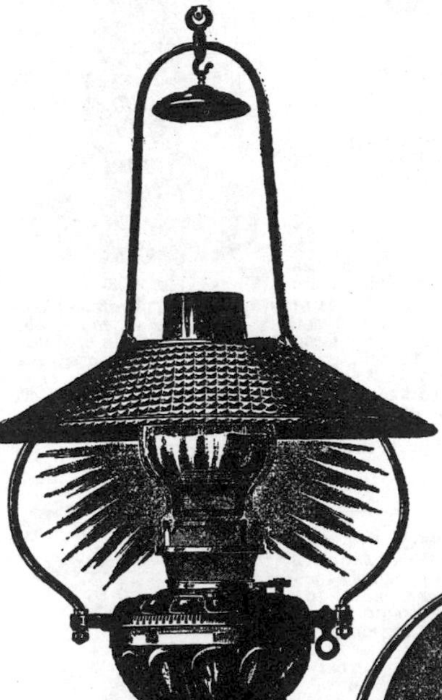

No. 95030. B. & H. Mammoth Store and Hall Lamp. 400 Candle Power. The strongest

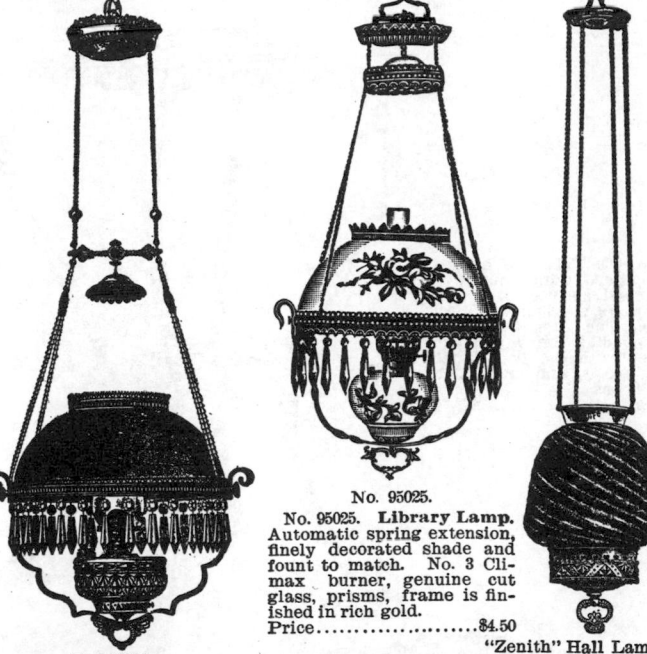

No. 95024.

No. 95024. Library Lamp. Automatic spring extension, plain dome shade, genuine cut glass prisms. Frame is finished in rich gold. No. 2 Sun burner. Price......$3.75

No. 95025.

No. 95025. Library Lamp. Automatic spring extension, finely decorated shade and fount to match. No. 3 Climax burner, genuine cut glass, prisms, frame is finished in rich gold.
Price....................$4.50

"Zenith" Hall Lamp.

No. 95026. Zenith Hall Lamp. Just the thing for a small hall. Ruby, opal, or pink globe. This is the cheapest and best hall lamp in the market. In ordering state which color globe you prefer.
Price.................................$1.45

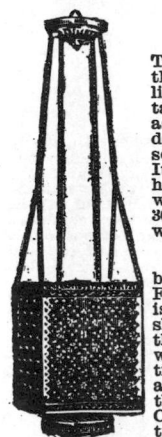

No. 95027. Square Hall Lamp.

No. 95027. Square Hall Lamp. This is a larger and better lamp than the Zenith and costs very little more. In two colors, crystal etched or ruby etched glass, as desired. Be sure to state color desired. This hall lamp is handsome enough for any dwelling. It is an exact reproduction of the high priced gas lamp that has always been so popular. Length 36 inches. Our price complete with burner and chimney...$3.00

No. 95028. Store Lamp. The best and cheapest in the market. For large areas where good light is required only the best lamps should be procured. We keep them, and guarantee every lamp we sell to give perfect satisfaction. The "Juno" gives a steady and white light. Just the thing to throw light on a window display. Complete as illustrated, 15-inch tin shade, suitable for store or window lights, 65 candle power.
Price, brass finish............$2.00
Price, nickel finish...........  2.25

No. 95028.

No. 95029.

and best finished lamp on the market. The wick movement is perfect and so simple that a child can re-wick the lamp. Patent lock ring to hold fount in ring obviates all danger of fount jarring out of frame. Fount taken out from below for filling. You are taking no chances with this lamp, as we guarantee every one to give perfect satisfaction or we will replace them and pay all expenses. Just the lamp for churches and halls, where the ceilings are high. Does away with use of step ladders and chairs in lighting or cleaning. The lock ring used to hold the "B. & H." is a great convenience. The fount can easily be taken out from below for refilling. Complete, as illustrated, spring extension, 14-inch plain dome shade, suitable for churches, halls, stores etc.
Price, brass finish, $6.25, nickel finish, $6.75

No. 95030.

Radiant Wall Lamp.

No. 95032. This very useful lamp jumped into popularity at once because of its great utility and low price. It has removable glass founts and reflector, No. 2 Sun burner and chimney. Is made to hang on a wall or rest on a table and reflector can be taken off if desired.
Each................................38c

Bracket Lamp.

No. 95033. Too well known to need further introduction, the kitchen bracket lamp still keeps in popular favor. The No. 95033 is finished in French bronze, has glass fount, No. 2 Sun burner and 7-inch silvered glass reflector and No. 2 Sun chimney. Each...................................55c

No. 95034. The most popular kitchen and hall lamp ever made and our style is the strongest and best finished on the market. We complete it with No. 2, glass fount having outside filler, No. 2 Sun burner and chimney and 8-inch silvered glass reflector.
Each...........................75c

Bracket Lamp.

No. 95035. Glass Stand Lamps, priced with Sun burners, wicks and chimneys. In this grade we show only the heavy plain style having sunk top to catch overflow of oil
O. (height to collar 9 in) No. 1 burner, each......28c
A. (height to collar 9½ in) No. 1 burner, each.....30c
B. (height to collar 10 in) No. 2 burner, each.....35c
C. (height to collar 10¼ in) No. 2 burner, each...40c
D. (height to collar 11 in) No. 2 burner, each.....45c

No. 95035.

No. 95036. Glass Stand Lamps, shrunk-on-collars; no plaster, collars cannot work loose, and lamps are stronger and heavier than the ordinary grade. Priced with Sun burners, wicks and chimneys.
O. (height to collar 9½ in) No. 1 burner, each....40c
A. (height to collar 10 in) No. 1 burner, each....45c
B. (height to collar 10¼ in) No. 2 burner, each..50c
C. (height to collar 11 in) No. 2 burner, each.....55c

No. 95037. Footed Glass Hand Lamp. Just the thing for bedrooms and to carry around the house into closets, etc. Priced with No. 1 Sun burner, wick and chimney.
Each..............24c

Footed Hand Lamp.

No. 95036.

No. 95038. Footed Hand Lamp. "Shrunk-on-collar," no plaster. A lamp to last must be made well. On this style the collars are pressed on by machinery and cannot work loose. The lamps are heavier and less liable to break. Price includes No. 1 Sun burner, wick and chimney.
Each...................................30c

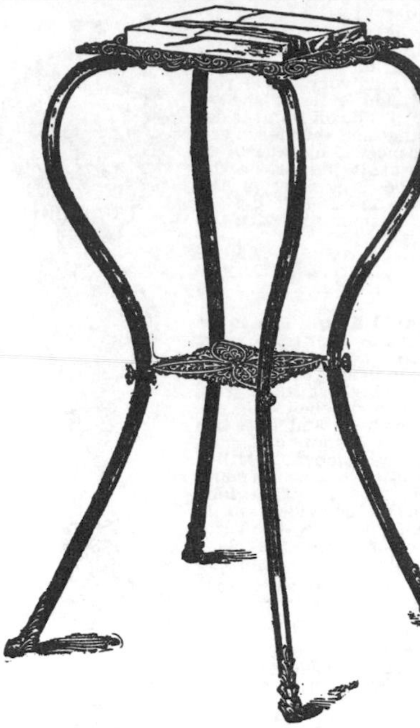

No. 95038. Flat.

No. 95038. In purchasing a table you should get one that will not tarnish. We can guarantee that this table will not, as all metal parts are of genuine brass, finished in gilt. The top is of genuine Mexican Onyx, 8x8 inches
Each.............. ........$7.50

No. 95039. This is a specially good table and will wear well and look like new for years if given ordinary care. The cast borders surrounding the Onyx slabs are extra deep. Top slab is 10x10 inches and lower slab 5x5 inches.
Each...... ..............$13.75

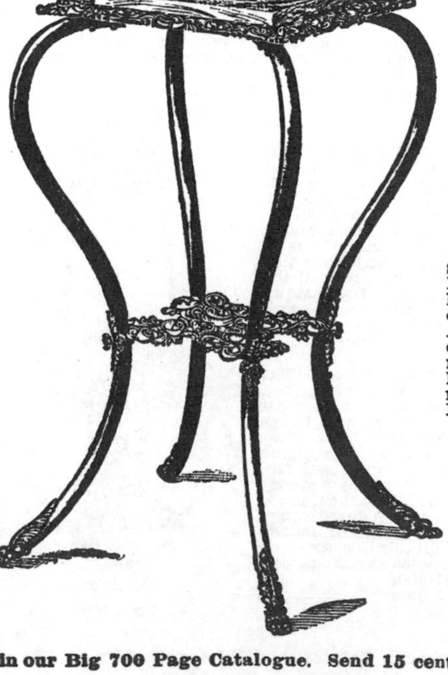

No. 95040. A beautiful heavy scroll top surrounding the Mexican Onyx slab of the highest grade makes this one of the most beautiful tables. All metal parts are gold plated and guaranteed not to tarnish. The shape of top and legs is correct. Top slab measures 10x10 inches.
Each....................$15.25

MOST SURPRISING BARGAINS in Crockery and Glassware will be found in our Big 700 Page Catalogue. Send 15 cents to partly pay postage.

## Parlor Chandeliers.
**With Patent Automatic Extension for Raising and Lowering.**

No. 95042.

**No. 95042. Chandelier.** With patent automatic extension for raising or lowering. This chandelier, the most popular ever put on the market, still retains its place in general favor. It is finished in rich gold bronze, and the center band has cut glass colored jewels. As shown in the illustration, we trim it with cut glass colored jewels suspended on the oil-fount cups, center band, and two rows around the center rod. This gives a very brilliant effect when lighted. The globes are colored opalescent effects, and correspond with the colored jewels. The burner can be lighted without removing globes or chimneys. We furnish the chandelier in two and three lights as follows:
No. 95042 Chandelier, 3 light, complete, as shown......$14.98
No. 95042 Chandelier, 4 light, complete, as shown. .... 18.00

No. 95044.

**No. 95044. Chandelier.** With patent automatic extension for raising and lowering. This chandelier is finished in rich gold bronze, and has cast silver ornaments on the supports which extend from the center rod to the arms. In addition there are straps on the under side of the arms giving a finished effect. The globes are bell shape, and etched in handsome designs. The burners can be lighted without removing globes or chimneys, a great convenience as well as saving the breakage of globes and chimneys in handling. We carry this fixture in two sizes.
No. 95044, 3 light, complete as shown.................$12.00
No. 95044, 4 light, complete.......................... 14.25

**No. 95041.** For an extremely handsome wedding present this table cannot be excelled. All metal parts are of genuine brass, gold plated and the design is exceedingly bold. There are cast ornaments on the legs and in every respect this table ranks with those of the highest grade. The Onyx slabs are of genuine Mexican Onyx and measure 9x9 inches on top and 5x5 inches below.
Each...........................................................$18.25

No. 95041.

No. 95043.

**No. 95043. Chandelier.** With patent automatic extension for raising and lowering. A beautiful parlor chandelier fit to grace the parlor of a millionaire. It is finished in rich gold bronze, with cast silver ornaments on the supports between the center rod and arms, also on the under side of the arms. The scroll straps give a very finished effect to the fixture. The globes are of the latest design with genuine acid etched patterns. The burners can be lighted and trimmed without removing the globes or chimneys, thereby avoiding the chances for breakage in handling. We carry this fixture in three and four lights.
No. 95043, 3 light, complete as shown...........$14.50
No. 95043, 4 light, complete as shown................ 17.25

No. 95045.

**No. 95045. Chandelier.** With patent automatic extension for raising and lowering. A handsome chandelier at a price that puts it within the reach of all. This beautiful parlor fixture, useful as well as ornamental, is finished in rich, gold bronze and completed with etched globes of a very popular shape. The burner is of a new design, that can be lighted and trimmed without removing the globe or chimney, thus avoiding the possibility of breakage in handling them. We furnish this fixture in the following sizes.
No. 95045, 2 light, complete as shown........................$ 6.90
No. 95045, 3 light, complete as shown........................ 9.40
No. 95045, 4 light, complete as shown........................ 11.90

**NO BETTER OR MORE DESIRABLE GOODS ARE MADE THAN THOSE WE ILLUSTRATE AND DESCRIBE.**

# Baby Carriage Department of Sears, Roebuck & Co., Inc.

**FOR THE COMING SEASON WE WILL SHOW THE MOST COMPLETE LINE OF BABY CARRIAGES EVER OFFERED. WE HAVE CONTRACTED** with one of the largest manufacturers in Chicago for a very extensive line, embracing almost everything conceivable in baby carriages from the cheapest to the very best. There is nothing desirable omitted from this line. The manufacturer of these carriages is one of the oldest and most reliable in the country, a concern which has established a reputation for making only the **highest grade work.** Our contract is for such a quantity on a cash basis that we can, after adding our one small percentage of profit, offer you a baby carriage for less money than local dealers can buy in quantities. You will find in the carriages we offer a distinctiveness in quality of materal, style and general construction which is superior to the goods carried in stock by the average retail dealer or other catalogue houses.

**OUR BINDING GUARANTEE.** We guarantee every carriage for **two years,** and during this time if any piece or part gives out by reason of defect in material or workmanship we will replace it free of charge

**WE ISSUE A SPECIAL BABY CARRIAGE CATALOGUE.** If you do not find listed and described in this, our General Catalogue, the baby carriage wanted, please send for our Baby Carriage Catalogue which will be mailed to any address free on application. This catalogue is in pages 9x11¼ inches, and one large illustration on each page. The illustrations are engraved directly from photographs, and being so large they bring out every little detail. **The Special Catalogue shows our complete line** of everything conceivable in strictly high grade carriages at from $2.50 for the cheapest carriage we offer to $33.50 for the finest carriage on the market at any price. The illustrations shown in this catalogue are engraved from photographs taken directly from the carriages, and will give you a very good idea of the general appearance, though a better idea can be had from the large illustrations in the special book.

**WE ARE EXTREMELY ANXIOUS** to receive your order if in want of a Baby Carriage, not so much for the little profit there will be in it for us as for the good it will do us as an advertisement. We know that we can send you a better carriage than you could get from your local dealer at within 33⅓ per cent. more than our price, and we know that you will be so well pleased with it that you will not hesitate to recommend us to your friends and neighbors, and in this way we will receive more orders. If you will favor us with your order we will endeavor to send you such a carriage as has never been seen in your section at anything like the price.

**OUR LIBERAL TERMS.** To any point within 700 miles of Chicago we will send any Baby Carriage you may select by freight or express, **C. O. D., subject to examination,** on receipt of $2.00 as a guarantee of good faith. **You can examine the Carriage at your freight depot,** and if found perfectly satisfactory and exactly as represented, pay the freight agent our price and charges, less the $2.00 sent with order, and the carriage is yours. We believe our binding two years guarantee and our liberal terms of shipment emphasize the fact that our prices are beyond competition.

**DISCOUNT FOR CASH.** We allow a discount of **3 per cent. if cash in full accompanies your order.** If you send the full amount of cash with your order you may deduct 3 per cent. from our price. Nearly all our customers send cash in full. By sending us cash in full you not only save the 3 per cent. discount but you also save return charges on the money to us and the inconvenience of settling the C. O. D.

We crate all our Carriages carefully and the prices quoted are for the carriages carefully taken apart, crated and delivered on board the cars at Chicago.

**RUBBER TIRES FOR $1.00 ONLY.** At $1.00 extra we will furnish any carriage listed below with rubber tired steel wheels complete. We believe we are the first to offer rubber tires at $1.00, and we wish to say that the rubber tires we furnish are the highest grade. We can buy rubber tires, such as are used by many, at 30 per cent. less than we pay, but we believe our customers are entitled to the very best.

If you are in want of anything in this line we hope you will favor us with your order, at least give us the privilege of sending you a carriage to examine for we feel confident we are in a position to **serve you as no other concern** can.

Please observe the different **Trimmings** in which the different carriages come, and in ordering be sure to state the trimming and finish wanted. We are anxious there should be no mistake and that you will not only be satisfied but will receive a carriage even better than described or expected.

**COLOR OF UPHOLSTERING.** We furnish our Carriages upholstered in all of the standard colors, such as **dark peacock blue, coral, pomegranate. Nile green, cardinal, wine, olive, golden brown, bronze gold and steel blue.** In ordering be sure to state color wanted and we will send you the exact color desired.

We can furnish any of the following special finishes at the additional prices named:

Any carriage can be furnished in **cherry, antique** or **sixteenth century** finish without extra charge.

Shellac and varnish or antique finish trimmed with gold leaf, body and gear, except wheels, extra..............**$1.50**

Shellac and varnish or antique finish trimmed with gold leaf, wood wheels, extra .............**$0.45**

Shellac and varnish or antique finish trimmed with gold leaf, good extra..................**$0.70**

Enameled and gold leaf body and gear, except wheels, extra......**$2.60**

Enameled and gold leaf wood wheels, extra..................**$0.65**

Enameled and gold leaf hood, at..................**$1.10**

Flat spoke wood wheels on any carriage without extra charge.

Best flat spoke wood wheels, nickel trimmed, on any carriage......**$0.55**

**Prices of Parts.** We will furnish the following parts to baby carriages at the prices named:

| Part | Price |
|---|---|
| Axles, tinned, each | $0 18 |
| Braces, tinned, each | 8 |
| Carriage Straps, good quality, each | 10 |
| Carriage Straps, extra trimmed, each | 16 |
| Handles, finished, per set | 60 |
| Hub Caps, tinned, each | 5 |
| Hub Caps, nickeled, each | 8 |
| Nuts, axle | 7 |
| Parasol Rod, tinned | 20 |
| Parasol Rod, nickeled | 32 |
| Parasol Rod, top pole nickeled | 8 |
| Patent Rod Clamp, each | 28 |
| Springs, front, C, tinned | 20 |
| Springs, front, C, nickeled | 38 |
| Springs, back, C, tinned | 15 |
| Springs, back. C, nickeled | 32 |
| Wheels, common oval spoke, finished and trimmed, per set of 4 | 1 35 |
| Wheels, best flat spoke. finished and trimmed, per set of 4 | 1 85 |
| Wheels, tinned, steel tire, per set of 4 | 1 30 |
| Wheels, tinned, rubber tire, per set of 4 | 2 60 |

## Our $2.45 Baby Carriage.

**No. 9900** At $2.45 We Offer You a Baby Carriage which you can not duplicate in your local market at less than $4.50 to $5.00. While this is undoubtedly **The Best Carriage** that was ever offered at anything like the price, we are extremely anxious that our customers should order **Carriages at from $6.00 upwards.** $6.00 to $7.00 buys a carriage that we are proud to send out and our carriages at $10.00 and upwards are works of art. **This, Our $2.45 Carriage,** is made with a maple frame body, **Well Finished.** The bottom is 13x25 inches in size with oil cloth bottom. Best steel wheels. The carriage is exactly as illustrated above, without parasol. Made of white reed and maple, upholstered seat, solid bent handles, steel reach, steel braces, steel axles, 4 Bessemer steel springs, trimmings all well finished. Our special price without parasol and upholstering except seat........ **$2.45**

**No. 9901** Same Carriage as above furnished **With Silesia Parasol** with scalloped edge.... **$3.25**

**No. 9902** Same Carriage as above only lined throughout with cretonne, with full upholstered seat, silesia parasol with scalloped edge.... **$3.60**

**No. 9903** Same Carriage as above but upholstered throughout in cretonne with plush roll, silesia parasol with scalloped edge..................**$3.90**

Extra for Rubber-tired Steel Wheels instead of steel tire wheels, **$1.00** Weight of carriage, 40 lbs.

## Our Special $5.95 Baby Carriage.

**No. 9906** This is a very stylish carriage. an entirely new pattern, just out, and one that is sure to please. It is exactly as illustrated in the accompanying cut. From this illustration you can form some idea of the appearance. It is equal to any carriage you would buy in your local market at double the price. **Has very finest reed body, solid maple frame,** elegantly finished, **Brussels carpet** in bottom, our special patent gear with the very best Bessemer steel wheels. It is furnished with the very best patent automatic selflocking brake; **upholstered in cretonne,** buttoned; has a fancy scalloped edge silesia parasol. Our price........**$5.95**

**No. 9907** Same carriage as above, upholstered in damask, fancy buttoned, tufted, sateen parasol with lace or ruffle edge, as desired. Our special price, **$6.60**

The above described carriages are **furnished complete with automatic brake.** Extra for **full rubber tires** throughout, when desired, **$1.00.**

**SEND FOR OUR SPECIAL BABY CARRIAGE CATALOGUE FOR OUR COMPLETE LINE, THE FINEST CHILDREN'S CARRIAGE CATALOGUE PUBLISHED.**

## Our Special $7.50 Baby Carriage.

No. 9912 We offer at $7.50 a baby carriage which you cannot duplicate in any market at less than $12.00. Understand we ship any carriage to any address within 700 miles of Chicago on receipt of $2.00 as a guarantee of good faith, balance and express charges payable at express office. **Three per cent. discount for cash allowed if cash in full accompanies your order.** In selecting a baby carriage from us do not overlook our binding two years' guarantee, nor the fact that every carriage is furnished complete with the **very best self-acting safety brake.** We furnish **rubber tires at only $1.00 extra.** This is a very fancy reed body carriage, made of fancy reed and maple, elegantly finished, Brussels carpet in bottom, our fine patent gear, with the very best Bessemer steel springs. Is made of the best material throughout; body is varnished and finished. Solid bent handles, steel reach, steel braces, steel axles, four strong Bessemer steel springs, best steel wheels. **Upholstered in the highest style of the art in damask,** with plush roll and beautiful sateen Parasol with either ruffle or lace edge, as desired. Our special price................$7.50

No. 9913 **Same carriage, upholstered with extra quality figured plush,** with roll of same, and with sateen parasol with ruffle or lace edge.........$8.25

Understand you can select any color of upholstering wanted, dark peacock blue, cardinal, wine, olive, golden brown, bronze gold, steel blue, coral, pomegranate and Nile green. **The price is the same.**

## Our $8.40 Carriage.

No. 9922 While we offer as low as $2.45 a Carriage that we can guarantee in every respect, and one that is guarranteed in every respect and better than you buy elsewhere at within 33⅓ per cent. more than the price, **and our carriages from $6.00 and upwards are really the most artistic on the market at 50 per cent. of the prices,** we are extremely anxious that our customers should buy our higher grade work, carriages like this one at $8.40, and from that up to $12.00. **We are proud of the carriages that we can offer at from $8.00 to $12.00,** and we know that if you decide to purchase such a high grade you will be more than pleased, your neighbors will envy you, and the result will belt will advertise us and lead to more sales. With that end in view we figure our profit on the higher grade work at the very smallest percentage possible. This beautiful carriage is one of the **very latest designs.** From the illustration you can form some idea of the appearance, although a

No. 9922.

## Our Special $6.35 Carriage.

No. 9909 The illustration, engraved from a photograph, will give you an idea of the appearance of one of the **handsomest carriages** that will be on the market for this season. It is an entirely new pattern that has never been offered for sale before, and is very similar to the higher priced carriages which have been **sold at more than double our price.**

It has a very fine reed body, elegantly finished, fine Brussels carpet in bottom. Our special patent gear with the best Bessemer steel wheels made. Frame is made of the best reed and maple, **strong and well braced.** Solid bent handles. **Bessemer steel reach,** steel braces, steel axles, 4 strong Bessemer steel springs. Best wheels made and all metal parts are nicely plated. Comes complete with our automatic safety brake. Is upholstered in the very **finest style in damask** with plush roll. Beautiful sateen parasol with **ruffle or lace edge.**

Our special price..$6.35

No. 9910 **Same Carriage as above,** upholstered with extra quality figured plush with roll of same. Satin parasol with fancy ruffle or lace edge.

Our price..........$7.50

At the above prices we furnish the carriage **complete with brake.**

Extra for **rubber tires** in place of metal tires.

....................$1.00

We make no charge for packing and crating, and we do our work well, so that the carriage is sure to reach you in perfect order.

## Our Special $7.90 Baby Carriage.

No. 9915 Something Entirely New. This is one of the handsomest designs the manufacturer has been able to offer for this season. It is a thoroughly substantial **high grade carriage,** and is sure to give entire satisfaction to the purchaser. The very latest patent **self-acting lock brake** with every carriage. Rubber tired steel wheels at $1.00 extra when desired. This carriage is made of the very best material, fancy reed body, **high grade Brussels carpet** on bottom. The body is varnished and finished. Solid bent handles, steel reach, **steel axles, four strong Bessemer steel springs,** best steel wheels all nicely plated. Is upholstered in the very latest style of upholstering, **fine damask plush roll** and ribbon bows, beautiful sateen parasol with lace or ruffle edge. The carriage comes complete with our latest and best patent self-acting **automatic brake.**

Our special price....$7.90

No. 9916 **Same carriage as above** described, upholstered with **figured plush** with roll of same and beautiful ribbon bows, beautiful sateen parasol with lace or ruffle edge. Our price............................$8.50

We will furnish these carriages with the best quality rubber tires throughout at $1.00 extra. Please note that you can have the upholstering in any of the colors previously mentioned, viz: dark peacock blue, cardinal, wine, olive, golden brown, bronze gold, steel blue, coral, pomegranate and Nile green. In ordering be sure to state color wanted. We send this carriage anywhere within 700 miles C. O. D. on receipt of $2.00 with order.

better idea can be had from the large full page illustration we show in **Our Baby Carriage Catalogue,** which we will mail free on application. This carriage has the very finest reed body, elegantly finished, very best steel springs, steel axles and wheels. Is fitted with the highest grade self-locking automatic steel brake. **Fine Brussels carpet** in bottom; upholstered in genuine damask with fancy silk plush roll, sateen parasol with ruffle or lace edge.

Our price.....................$8.40

No. 9923 Same carriage as above upholstered in genuine silk plush with fancy roll of same, beautiful silk satin parasol, lined, with ruffle or lace edge, as desired. Our price....................$10.25

With rubber tired wheels, $1.00 extra.

When ordering be sure to state color of trimming wanted. We furnish the carriages in a great variety of colors as previously described. The parasols are always furnished in a shade to match the upholstering.

## Our $8.40 Baby Carriage.

No. 9918 $8.40 is our price when shipped by freight or express C. O. D., subject to examination, to any point within 700 miles of Chicago, on receipt of $2.00, balance of $6.40 and charges payable when received. **Three per cent. discount allowed if cash in full accompanies your order,** when $8.15 pays for the carriage. This is a **very beautiful carriage,** an entirely new design, the latest style for the coming season. The illustration will give you an idea of the appearance. A better idea can be had from our **large full plate illustration** as shown in our **baby carriage catalogue,** which will be mailed free on application. This carriage is made from the very best material throughout, beautiful reed body, elegantly finished; full Brussels carpet in bottom; solid bent wood handles; springs, wheels and axles of the **best Bessemer steel,** nicely plated; and is fitted with our self-acting automatic brake, the best brake made. Upholstered with genuine damask, with beautiful silk plush roll and fancy ribbon bows. Sateen parasol with lace or ruffle edge.

Our price..........$8.40

No. 9919 Same carriage as above, upholstered with **genuine silk plush,** with beautiful roll of same, fancy ribbon bows, fine silk satin parasol, lined throughout, and with lace or ruffle edge.

Our price.......$10.25

This carriage will be fitted with rubber tired wheels if desired, at $1.00 extra.

# FIVE GREAT LEADERS.

## Our $8.50 Baby Carriage.

The Parasol is sateen with lace or ruffle edge, as desired. Price......**$8.50**

**No. 9925  $8.50 is our Price when Shipped by Freight, C. O. D.** subject to examination; $8.25 if cash in full accompanies your order. We would ask you to compare this carriage with those sold at retail at $15.00 and **If You do not Consider Our Carriage** in every way equal we will not expect your order.

**This Carriage** is made of the very best material throughout. It is an entirely new design, the very latest style for the season. If you buy this carriage we assure you there will be **Nothing Like it in Your Neighborhood.** Body is made from the **Finest Reed,** elegantly finished; has full Brussels carpet; wheels, four springs and axles are extra strong and made of the Best Bessemer steel, nicely plated. **Carriage is Fitted With Self Locking Automatic Brake,** our own patent, the best brake made. It is upholstered with genuine damask, with fancy silk plush roll and tassels.

**No. 9926** Same Carriage upholstered in Genuine Silk Plush with fancy roll of same and ornamented with tassels; parasol of fine silk satin, lined throughout, with ruffle of lace edge. Our Price.............................**$10.50**
**In Ordering be Sure to State Color Wanted.** We can furnish these carriages in any color of upholstering or trimming desired, and the parasols are always furnished in a color to match the upholstering.
Extra for Rubber-tired Wheels..........**$1.00**

## Our $8.60 Baby Carriage.

**No. 9928.  $8.60 if seht** by freight C. O. D. subject to examination on receipt of $2.00; **$8.32 if cash in full accompanies your order.** Where cash in full accompanies an order we allow a discount of three per cent. This carriage is also one of the very latest designs for this season. It is something entirely new; there is no other carriage on the market of the same style, and we believe it is in quality, durability, and above all, style of appearance equal to any carriage you can buy in any local market at double the price. This carriage has a **highly ornamented, artistic, elegant reed body,** handsomely finished; full Brussels carpet; springs, wheels and axles are of the best Bessemer steel and nicely plated; has solid bent wood handles; is fitted with our own patent **self-locking automatic brake,** the best brake made; is upholstered in fine damask, beautifully piped, silk plush roll; parasol of sateen **with ruffle or lace edge,** as desired. Our price, **$8.60**
We can furnish these carriages in any color of upholstering desired.

**No. 9929** Same carriage as above, upholstered in fine silk plush with piped roll of same, parasol of fine silk satin, lined throughout, trimmed with fancy ruffle or lace edge, as desired. Our price.............................**$10.50**
Any of these carriages furnished with **rubber tire at $1.00 extra.**
You can have any popular shade of upholstering in this carriage. Colors are pomegranate, olive, steel blue, old rose, golden browu, etc. In ordering, be sure to advise us what color yeu wish.

## Our New Fancy Hood Top Carriage for $10.25.

**No. 9930** We offer for $10.25 a carriage that you cannot buy in your local market at less than **$15.00 to $18.00.** Remember our very liberal terms. Any one of these carriages will be sent to you by freight or express C. O. D., subject to examination, on receipt **of $2.00 as a guarantee of good faith,** balance payable at your freight depot. The illustration engraved from a photograph will give some idea of the **appearance of this new** hood carriage. It is one of the most convenient, comfortable and durable carriages made. The hood can be removed when desired, and will be found the best **protection against sun and wind.** It is adjustable to any position desired. This carriage is made from the very best material. The body is of the highest grade of reed, elegantly finished; fine Brussels carpet on bottom; has the very best bent wood handles; 4 steel springs; **steel axles; steel braces;** is fitted with the best self-locking automatic brake; upholstered in fine damask with plush roll. Our price.................**$10.25**
**No. 9931** Same carriage as above, but upholstered, with beautiful figured plush, with roll of same.......................**$11.55**
Extra charge for rubber tired wheels, **$1.00**
Do not fail to state the color of upholstering wanted. We can furnish any color.

## Our $10.50 Baby Carriage.

**No. 9933** $10.50 is the price when sent by freight C. O. D., subject to examination on recept of $2.00; **$10.18 if cash in full accompanies your order.** If you send the full amount of cash with your order we allow a 3 percent cash discount. In ordering do not fail to **state color of trimming wanted.** We upholster these carriages in all the standard colors, including **dark peacock blue, cardinal, wine, olive, golden brown, bronze gold, steel blue, coral, pomegranate** and Nile green. **This carriage** is made of the very **best material** throughout, **and is** guaranteed in every respect. The body is made from the best reed, elegantly finished; has full Brussels carpet in bottom; the wheels, axles and springs are of the best **Bessemer steel, all plated;** it is fitted with our own patent self-locking automatic brake; has the best bent wood handles **nicely polished** and is upholstered in fine figured plush with pillow of same and ornamented with **fancy cords and tassels.** The parasol is of fine silk satin, lined throughout and trimmed with ruffle or lace edge, as desired. Price, **$10.50**
This carriage will be furnished with rubber tires at $1.00 extra.

graved from a photograph **this beautiful carriage.** For a more complete description you should see the full page plate in our **special baby carriage catalogue,** which we will send free on application. This carriage is made of the **best material throughout.** Finest quality reed body, elegantly finished; full Brussels carpet; solid bent wood handles; steel springs; **steel axles nicely plated;** is upholstered with **silk brocatelle** with fancy **silk plush roll;** fancy parasol of silk satin, lined, with lace or ruffle edge, as desired.
Our price...........**$11.50**
**No. 9936** Same carriage as above, upholstered with **genuine silk plush,** otherwise the same as above.
Our price.......... **$11.75**
These carriages are furnished with our **patent self-locking automatic brake.**
Extra for **rubber tires throughout, $1.00.**
In ordering be sure to state the color of trimming wanted. We can furnish any color.

## Our New Model $11.50 Carriage.

**No. 9935** We would ask you to compare this carriage which we offer at $11.50 on our regular C. O. D. terms, or with a discount of 3 per cent. if cash in full accompanies your order, with any carriage you can buy anywhere at within 50 per cent. of the price. The illustration engraved will give you some idea of the **appearance of**

## Our $11.75 Baby Carriage.

No. 9938 $11.75 is the price when shipped by freight or express C.O.D. subject to examination on receipt of $2.00; $9.75 and freight charges payable when received. $11.40 pays for the carriage if cash in full accompanies your order, as we allow a discount of three per cent. for cash in full with order.

**This is something entirely new in design** for the baby carriage is finished in antique and presents a very rich appearance. The body is made from the very best reed, elegantly finished in antique; **has full length Brussels carpet** in bottom; wheels, springs and axles are of the **best Bessemer steel**, nicely plated; our own patent self-locking **automatic brake.** Is upholstered in fine silk brocatelle with fancy rolls of silk plush and parasol of silk, satin lined throughout with ruffle or lace edge.

Our price........$11.75

No. 9939 Same carriage os above upholstered in fine silk plush, therwise the same as above.

Our price...................$12.00

**Extra for rubber tired wheels**........ 1.00

You can have any popular shade of upholstering in this carriage. Colors are pomegranate, olive. steel blue, old rose, golden brown, etc. In ordering advise us just what you wish. We crate our carriages with great care, so that they will not be marred in shipping. Our prices of $11.75 and $12.00 are subject to a disconnt of 3 per cent. when cash in full accompanies the order, when they will cost you but $11.40 or $11.64 net. **Most of our customers send cash in full.**

## Our $11.90 Baby Carriage.

No. 9941 $11.90 is the price if sent by freight or express C. O. D., subject to examination, on receipt of the required $2.00 deposit, balance of $9.90 and freight charges payable when received. $11.54 pays for the cariage if cash in full accompanies your order. Three per cent. discount is allowed for all orders accompanied by cash in full. The accompanying illustration, engraved from a photograph, does not do justice to this carriage. A better idea of its appearance may be had from the large full plate engraving shown in **our baby carriage catalogue,** which we will be pleased to mail free on application. This carriage is something entirely new in design, made expressly for this season, and if you buy it you can be sure of having the most stylish carriage **in your neighborhood.** It is made from the very best material throughout; the body is of the best quality reed, elegantly finished; has full length Brussels carpet in the bottom; the wheels, axles and springs are made of the best **Bessemer** steel, highly plated; is fitted with our own patent self-locking automatic brake; has the very best bent wood handles, nicely finished; is upholstered in a fine quality of **figured plush pillows,** fancy buttoned with fancy cords and tassels. The parasol is of fine silk satin, lined throughout and trimmed with beautiful lace or wide ruffle edge as desired.

Our price......................$11.90

No. 9942. Same Carriage as above illustrated, upholstered in the very finest silk brocatelle, otherwise same as above...................$12.15

**Extra for rubber tired wheels when desired.** $1.00

---

$20.00
Buys a regular
$35.00
Carriage.
No. 9950.

**No. 9950** We doubt if you can buy a carriage to match this in quality of material, style and finish **in any local market for $35.00.** This is one of the finest carriages the manufacturer has turned out, and far superior to the best carriages made by other manufacturers. In order to make the price of $20.00, we are compelled to buy **these carriages in large quantities for spot cash,** and offer them on a very small percentage of profit, and yet we make you very liberal terms. We will send the carriage to any address within 700 miles of Chicago by freight, C.O.D. **subject to examination** on receipt of $2.00. You can examine the carriage at your freight depot, and if found perfectly satisfactory and exactly as represented, pay the freight agent our price and freight charges less the $2.00 sent with order.

The above illustration, engraved from a photograph will give you some idea of the appearance of this carriage, although it must be seen to be appreciated. From the full plate engraving which we show in our **special free baby carriage catalogue**

you can form a better idea, but we question if you will find a carriage that will begin to compare with it in your local market. It is made of the very **best material** in **every piece and part; has a beautiful** reed body, elegantly finished and ornamented; very fine Wilton carpet in the bottom; solid bent wood handles; finets Bessemer steel wheels, axles and springs fitted with our own patent self locking automatic brake; is upholstered in the very finest style with genuine **silk damask,** piped, beautiful silk **plush pillow** with silk cores and tassels. The parasol is a very fine quality of silk satin, lined, with flounced ruffle and Valenciennes edge.

Our special price...................$20.00

No. 9951. Same carriage as above, upholstered **genuine silk plush,** otherwise the same as above.

Our special price...................$20.50

**Rubber Tires,** $1.00 **extra.**

In ordering be sure to state color of upholstering wanted. We can furnish it in any color.

## Our New $13.25 Baby Carriage.

**No. 9944 This Carriage is entirely new. We will control this design for the season,** and we think it is one of the handsomest carriages that has been shown this season regardless of price. When we can offer you such a carriage as this at $13.25, and send it to you by freight or express C. O. D., subject to examination, or at a discount of 3 per cent. if cash in full accompanies your order, if you are in the market for a strictly high grade carriage we think we are entitled to your order. By the illustration shown above, which is engraved by an artist, direct from the photograph, you can form some idea of the general appearance of this buggy. A better idea can be gained from one of the large page plates as shown in our special **free baby carriage catalogue.** This carriage is made of the very finest material, has a fine reed body, elegantly finished; **extra** quality Brussels carpet in bottom; solid bent wood handles; **high grade Bessemer steel axles;** our own patent automatic self-acting brake; is beautifully upholstered in **genuine silk** brocatelle, with very **fancy corded rolls** of same and cords and tassels; beautiful parasol of silk satin, lined throughout, and with ruffle or lace edge, as desired.

Our price.........$13.25

No. 9945 Same carriage as above, upholstered with genuine silk plush, otherwise same as above.

Our price...................$13.50

We furnish **rubber tired wheels** at $1.00 **extra** when wanted. When ordering be sure to state color of upholstering wanted. We can furnish it in any color.

## One of the Newest Things for $16.

**No. 9947 We Offer You at $16.00** One of the **Finest Carriages** turned out at the factory, and equal to carriages that are retailed in many of the largest cities at more than double our price; in fact, our general line is a line that is **Manufactured Exclusively for the Finest City Trade,** and at the special prices which we are able to make by reason of our large contract and economic method of doing business, and on our one small profit plan we can sell you for less than you can buy inferior goods at home. Note carefully the illustation and full description of this carriage, and for further information send for our free **special baby carriage catalogue,** showing a very large full plate illustration of this buggy. It is a beauty in every respect.

This carriage is very artistically designed and made from the very **finest material throughout; has a beautifully ornamented** reed body, elegantly finished; fine Wilton carpet in bottom; solid bent wood handles; finest Bessemer steel springs, axles and wheels; furnished with our patent self-locking **automatic brake.** It is elegantly upholstered in fine silk damask with piped silk plush rolls. The parasol is of a fine quality of silk satin, flounced ruffle and Valenciennes edge. Parasol is lined.

Our Special Price.. $16.00

No. 9948 Same Carriage as above, only upholstered in very fine silk plush, otherwise the same as above. Our price.......... $16.25

**Rubber tired wheels** furnished at $1.00 extra. When ordering be sure to state the color wanted. We can furnish this carriage in all colors.

## $20.50 Buys a Regular $35.00 Carriage

**No. 9953** We feel safe in saying this is a regular $35.00 carriage, safe in saying that we can furnish you at $20.50 such a carriage as you could not buy in your local market at less than $35.00. The reason we are safe in saying this is that we know we are offering a line of baby carriages direct to our customers at 20 to 30 per cent. less than the same carriages are being sold in large quantities to dealers. **Figuring on the profit that the retail dealer must make, we are sure that this carriage could not retail at less than $35.00.**

The above illustration will give you an idea of the **beautiful appearance of this buggy.** It is the very latest design, brand new for this season. There will be nothing like it in your neighborhood. You will have the **finest baby carriage for miles around** if you order this. It is made from the very best material throughout, gotton up in a very artistic manner. The body is the finest quality **reed**, elegantly finished; has the very finest Wilton carpet in the bottom; solid bent wood handles; **highest grade Bessemer steel wheels, axles and tire; our own patent self-locking automatic brake; all beautifully plated; upholstered in very fine silk damask with fancy silk plush side rolls and silk plush pillow with silk cords and tassels;** parasol of very fine silk satin, lined, flounced ruffle and Valenciennes edge. We can furnish this carriage in **any color of upholstering desired.** When ordering be sure to state color wanted. Our special price ................................................$20.50

**No. 9954 Same carriage upholstered in finest silk plush,** otherwise same as above. Our special price...........................................................$21.50

**Rubber tires** furnished on any carriage in this catalogue for $1.00 extra. Be sure to state when rubber tire is wanted and never fail to state color of upholstering desired. We take the Carriage apart and crate it carefully, so that it is sure to reach you in perfect condition.

**No. 9964** This carriage is for two, and while we **could furnish a carriage much cheaper and last year did quote one as low as $8.95,** we have decided to offer only a high grade job, one we can safely guarantee for two years and we know with care it will last much longer. From the above illustration you can form some idea of the appearance of this carriage, and better from our full plate illustration as shown in our free baby carriage catalogue which we mail to you free on application. **This carriage is made of the very best material throughout.** Body is of best quality reed, elegantly finished; has an extra quality Brussels carpet in bottom; solid bent wood handles; four very heavy springs made of the best Bessemer steel; heavy Bessemer steel

## Our Finest Carriage for $33.00.

**No. 9961** For $33.00 we believe we show the **Finest Carriage** that will be offered this season. Like our cheapest carriage, which we sell at $2.45, we believe our finest carriage at $33.00 is the best carriage ever offered at within 25 per cent. of the price. We do not believe the same carriage can be be had from any retail dealer at less than $45.00 to $50.00. The style is entirely new. It is the first season that anything of this design has been shown, and if you are in the market for **something extraordinary in a Baby Carriage,** we recommend this as the finest carriage we handle, the finest the manufacturer makes, and, we believe, the finest in the market at any price. The illustration above engraved from a photograph, will give you some idea of the appearance of this carriage. From the **large, full-plate page in our Baby Carriage Catalogue** you can form a better idea of this wonderful $33.00 bargain. Everything about this carriage is of the very finest. **The body is a work of art, made of the finest grade of reed,** elegantly finished; has a strong cane bottom, closely **woven;** solid bent wood handles; **finest steel axles,** wheels and springs; also has our own patent, self-locking automatic brake, the best made; is upholstered in the very finest quality imported brocatell, or the finest **imported silk novelty tufted in diamonds with piped rolls of** extra quality silk plush. The back lining is of very fine silk satin; has a very beautiful parasol of extra quality silk satin, lined with satin, flounced ruffle and puffing at top with Valenciennes edge.

Our price ............$33.00

**No. 9962** Same Carriage upholstered in the very finest quality silk plush, otherwise the same as above ..........$33.50

**Very finest rubber tires included free at the price above named. Any special discount of 3 per cent.** for full cash with order, or we ship on very liberal C. O. D. terms.

## Our Special $13.40 Twin Carriage.

## Our Most Stylish $28.90 Beauty.

**No. 9959** To supply such of our customers as desire as fine a carriage as it is possible to build **regardless of price,** a carriage that is equal to anything that can be found in any market at any price, we arranged with the manufacturer to get out three or four special designs, something **entirely new for this season,** and such as we consider without an equal in any market at any price. This is one of the beautiful designs. Our special price is $28.90. **We allow a discount for cash in full with order,** or at our regular price of $28.90 we will send it by freight C. O. D. subject to examination. It can be examined at your freight depot, and if found exactly as represented you can pay the freight agent our price and freight charges less the amount sent with order. From the above illustration engraved from a photograph you can get as good an idea of this carriage as it is possible to give in the space allowed, but in **our free baby carriage catalogue** we show a very **large full plate illustration** which brings out all the details very nicely, and if you are interested in so fine a buggy it would be well for you to send for this book. This carriage is gotten out practically **without regard to expense.** The reed in the body is of a very high grade. **beautifully finished,** has an extra strong closely woven cane bottom; solid bent wood handles; very finest grade Bessemer steel wheels, axles, springs and brake, which are highly plated; **brake is our own patent self-locking automatic brake, the best made.** This carriage is upholstered with an extra quality imported brocatell or very fine imported silk novelty tufted in diamonds. **Parasol** of extra quality silk satin, elegantly lined, flounced ruffle, puffing at top, with Valenciennes edge. Our special price ....................$28.90

**No. 9960** Same carriage as above, upholstered with extra quality silk plush, otherwise same as above. Our price....................$29.40

**Rubber tire on any of our carriages, $1.00 extra.**

wheels and axles; our patent self-locking automatic brake, the best brake made. Is upholstered in fine damask with plush rolls and ribbon bows. Two parasols of extra quality sateen with ruffle or lace edge as desired. Price..................$13.40

**No. 9965 Same carriage as above, upholstered in very fine quality figured plush** with rolls of same quality, ribbon bows, two beautiful parasols of silk satin, lined, with ruffle or lace edge.

Our special price....................$16.50

**Rubber tire to the wheels when wanted, $1 extra.**

In ordering be sure to state color of upholstering. We can furnish these carriages in any color of upholstering. For different colors see introductory to this department.

## $23.50 Buys a $40.00 Carriage.

**No. 9956** From the best information we can get this is a Baby Carriage that generally retails in the finest stores at $35.00 to $40.00. You will find nothing finer in the market. The manufacturer has gotten out this design for this season, an entirely new thing, in competition with the finest work that will be shown by anyone, and it is made specially for fine city trade, although at our price it will come within the reach of many of our customers. The illustration, engraved from a photograph, will give you an idea of the beautiful appearance of this fancy carriage. **A still better idea can be had from the large, full-**page plate as shown in our special free **Baby Carriage Catalogue** which will be mailed to anyone on application. This carriage is made from the very best material in every piece and part; is gotten up in the very finest style; body is from the **finest grade of reed,** elegantly finished; has beautiful **closely woven cane seat bottom;** bent wood handles; finest grade Bessemer steel **wheels,** axles and springs; is fitted with our own patent, self-locking automatic brake. Upholstered in the highest style of the art in extra quality **imported brocatel** made of fine imported silk novelty in combination with an extra quality of silk plush. The back lining is the very finest quality of silk satin. **The parasol furnished** with this carriage is of extra quality silk satin, lined, flounced ruffle and puffing at top with Valenciennes edge.

Our special price......$23.50

**No. 9957.** Same Carriage Upholstered with very fine imported silk plush, otherwise same as above..........$23.75

**Rubber tires on any carriage, $1.00 extra.**

We furnish these carriages with any color of upholstering desired. In ordering, be sure to state color wanted. Remember our C. O. D. terms, or 3 per cent. for **full cash.**

# Sewing Machine Headquarters.

## We Say Headquarters

because we honestly believe we are prepared to furnish Sewing Machines direct to the family for less money than any other concern in existence. **We guarantee our prices** to be lower than any competitors, and we have many competitors.

**FIRST.** We have the country retail dealer, canvasser or peddler. **He will charge you three prices for a sewing machine,** and then try to convince you that you are getting value received. **Don't be deceived.** He is compelled to sell a machine for **three times it's value.** No wonder he talks. He has to. Why? The wholesaler sells him the machines on long time at a big profit, profit enough to pay for the risk taken. To the big price already paid the agent must add enough to pay all his expenses for traveling on the road, rent, help, etc., etc. To all this he must add his profit, for he must look to his sewing machine for a living. **No wonder you pay $40.00, $50 00 or $60.00** for a sewing machine worth $15.00. He may tell you that his machine at $60.00 is better than ours at $18.50. **Don't believe him. We say it is not and we guarantee our statements.** Whose guarantee is the best?

**NOTE OUR REMARKS AS TO RELIABILITY ON ANOTHER PAGE.**

**ANOTHER COMPETITOR** is the various catalogue houses, some of which are reliable, many are not. The reliable ones will sell you a good machine far cheaper than your retail dealer. The unreliable ones you can not afford to patronize. About this class of competition we have something to say. In quality and price they can not compete with us. **Our prices are far below all others.** If we were to depend on the sales of sewing machines alone to defray all expenses, including rent, salaries, etc., we perhaps would be compelled to ask as much as our competitors, but we do not depend on sewing machines to defray this expense. **It costs us very little to sell them.** When the expense of selling our merchandise is divided up, we find it necessary to charge but very little to the sewing machine department. We have nothing to charge for bad debts, no traveling men's expenses, no interests, no additional rent, very little additional help, and, what is of equal importance, **a small conservative profit.** Thus, while we believe we sell more sewing machines than any other advertising house, our profit on each machine is so little that in the aggregate it would not pay even the clerk hire and the rent of some of our competitors, who of necessity must ask more for their machines to defray this expense, as they do almost if not quite an exclusive sewing machine business.

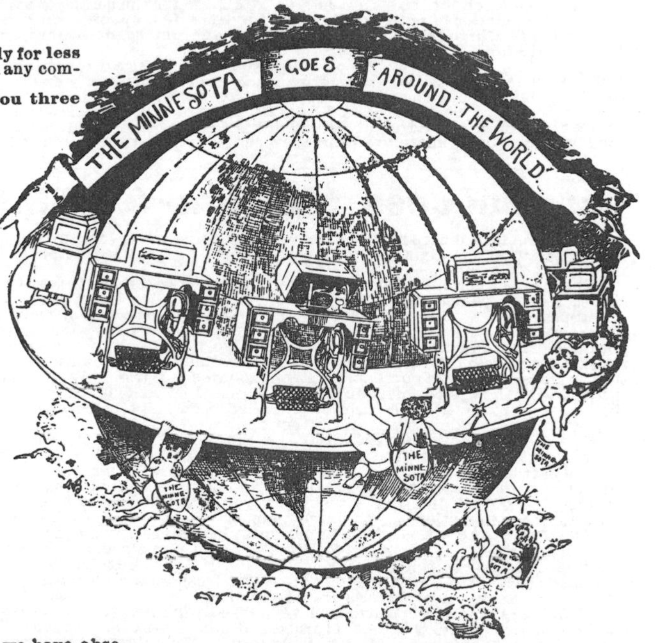


## For the Season of 1896

**We have many special bargains to offer in Sewing Machines,** bargains against which we have absolutely no competition. Our contracts for the season of 1896 are larger than ever, and on our system of selling direct from the manufacturer to the consumer, on our small-profit plan, we are able to offer the highest grade of work it is possible for mechanical genius to produce and at lower prices than ever before. **We have in our employ one of the best sewing machine experts in the country.** He has devoted a great deal of time in going over the different machines manufactured, with a view to offering our customers the best machine it is possible to produce—machines which embrace the good qualities of all with the defects of none, and we believe without dispute that we have the best line of sewing machines on the market regardless of price. In verification of our belief we are perfectly willing to send our machines to any address subject to examination and trial, and send with every machine a most binding ten years' guarantee, not only agreeing to make good any piece or part that may give out by reason of defective material or workmanship, but guaranteeing our machine to be equal to any machine made by any concern in existence, and our prices to be less than the same machine can be produced by any other concern.

**IN OUR DESCRIPTIONS WE HAVE ENDEAVORED TO HONESTLY AND CLEARLY REPRESENT AND DESCRIBE EACH MACHINE.**

By use of the engravings, which are made from photographs taken directly from the machines, we have endeavored to show you exactly what our line is. **We have no one on the ground** to talk for us, no one to repair our machines, consequently every machine we send out must be fully up to the representation and even better than we have described it, in strictly first-class condition, ready to run perfectly from the start and never get out of order. **We must also send a better machine** in appearance and finish than your dealer's machine. **This we always do. Our binding ten years' guarantee** accompanies each machine. It is the **honest, strongest and most binding** guarantee issued by any sewing machine concern. Before we would affix our signatures to such a guarantee we had to be satisfied that the machine was so constructed as to quality of material, workmanship and finish, that it would not only wear and give perfect satisfaction for ten years without expense of repairs, but it would with ordinary usage last a lifetime. We have handled these machines for about ten years, and so far have been put to no expense whatever for repairs. **This most extraordinary record** insures us of the safety of doing what we believe no other thoroughly reliable house has ever done, viz.: **Send a ten years' binding guarantee** with every sewing machine we sell, covering every piece and part in its construction. **Many irresponsible concerns** issue guarantees regardless of the quality of the goods and with no thought of protecting same. For that reason we would urge you to investigate any sewing machine manufacturers who are advertising extensively and learn what their responsibility is. **Unless a concern is honest** and reliable their guarantee is worthless.

**OUR RELIABILITY** can be ascertained by writing to any Express Company in Chicago, any National Bank in Chicago, any old reliable business house in Chicago, or you are at liberty if you choose to send your order and money to the National Bank of Illinois in this city, with instruction not to turn it over to us unless they know us to be perfectly reliable. Ask your nearest express agent about us. Nearly every express agent in the United States delivers our goods and knows of our reputation for fair and honorable dealing. We are authorized and incorporated under the laws of the State of Illinois **with a cash capital of $150,000 paid in full.** We have just moved into our entire new building, built especially for our exclusive use, one of the largest business blocks in Chicago, **six full stories and basement;** 100 feet wide by 180 feet deep, with 110,000 square feet of floor space. We employ over 500 clerks, **and are in a position to serve you as no other concern can.**

**A Special Twenty Days' Trial Offer.** We are so confident that our sewing machine will please you, that you will agree with us to its being **as fine a machine** as it is possible to produce, equal to any machine on the market at any price, finished in the highest style of the art, a machine possessing the good points of every machine with the defects of none, and you will agree the price is below competition, **that we make the following special offers:**

**Send Us $3.00** **AS A GUARANTEE OF GOOD FAITH** and we will send any machine you may select by freight. You can examine it at the freight depot, and if found perfectly satisfactory and exactly as represented, pay the agent our price and freight charges, less the $3.00, and the machine is yours. Then give the machine a thorough trial for 20 days, and if not found perfectly satisfactory, return it at our expense and we will refund your money.

**Another Way.** **Go to your nearest banker,** deposit with him the price of the sewing machine, take his receipt, which should read as follows: "Received of Mr.................., $........, for one of Sears, Roebuck & Co.'s..........Sewing Machines, No..... I agree to hold this money until the machine has been received by Mr..........and he has given it a 20 days' trial, when I shall forward the money to Sears, Roebuck & Co., unless in the meantime Mr.......... becomes dissatisfied with the machine, in which case he can return it to Sears, Roebuck & Co., and take receipt from the railroad agent, and on presenting the receipt to me I will return to Mr..........all the money deposited."

**Another Way.** **If you live within 500 miles of Chicago,** we will, on receipt of $3.00, send the sewing machine to you by express C. O. D. subject to examination. You can pay the express agent our price for the sewing machine and express charges, less the $3.00 sent with order, and take the machine. We will instruct the agent to hold the money 20 days, during which time you can give the machine a thorough trial. If not found entirely satisfactory and exactly as represented, you may return the machine any time within 20 days to the express agent, and he will refund all your money. The machine will be returned to us at our expense, and on receipt of same **we will return you your $3.00.**

**We allow a discount of 3 per cent. when cash in full accompanies your order.** If you send the full amount of cash with your order you may deduct 3 per cent. from our price. The best way is to send cash in full, for you not only save the 3 per cent. discount, but save express charges on return of money to us. Nearly all of our customers send cash in full. You take no risk, for we will immediately refund your money if you are not perfectly satisfied.

**We want you to give our sewing machine a trial. Give the machine a fair trial** in competition with any sewing machine made regardless of price. **Compare it as to general appearance,** finish, construction, durability, easy running, simplicity in operation, noiselessness, for variety of common and fancy stitching that can be done, and if you do not say it is the best machine you ever saw at any price, **return it at our expense.**

**Accept one of our propositions for sending the machine on trial. With us a trial means a sale.** In spite of local agents who would try to convince you that we can not sell you the best machine made for so little money, in spite of all competition, when our machine is placed side by side with any other machine in the market regardless of price, it requires no explanation, no instruction, our machine will always be accepted regardless of price. But when the price is considered, when you consider you can buy from us for $18.55 our highest grade Minnesota machine, a machine which you can not equal from any dealer at three times the price, and when **we only ask the privilege of sending the machine to you on 20 days' trial,** we believe we should have the opportunity of placing one of our machines in your house to examine.

**Read the Descriptions Carefully.** We have carefully and thoroughly described each machine we handle, the **Success,** the **Iowa** and the **Minnesota,** and in the different cabinets. **We offer the Success** in competition with the many cheap machines which are being so extensively advertised by catalogue houses. While we guarantee it to be equal to any of the so-called Singer machines and other cheap machines so extensively advertised, we do not especially recommend it. **On the contrary, we prefer to sell the Minnesota.** Not that there is any more profit in the machine to us, but because we know it will give the best satisfaction, and the best is always the cheapest in the end. **The Iowa is a high grade machine** which we guarantee in every respect, and which will give the best satisfaction; a machine that is thoroughly modern, and as you will find the description, possesses the good points of the best machines made. **It is equal to the best machines** that are being advertised by catalogue houses to-day, and far superior to the cheaper grades advertised by many concerns.

**The Minnesota we describe in various styles as follows:** / **Or in a special finished cabinet.**

| | | | |
|---|---|---|---|
| Our No. 91009 at | **$16.55** | Our No. 91012 at | **$18.55** |
| Our No. 91010 at | **17.55** | Our No. 91013 at | **19.55** |
| Our No. 91011 at | **18.55** | Our No. 91014 at | **20.55** |

**In the Automatic Drop Desk Cabinet $27.45, or in fancy latest style New Drop Head Stand at $21.75 and $24.75,** is our finest machine, and the

**WE ALLOW 3 PER CENT. DISCOUNT ON ALL CASH ORDERS UP TO $50.00. 4 PER CENT ON ALL CASH ORDERS OF FROM $50.00 TO $100.00, AND 5 PER CENT. ON ALL CASH ORDERS OF OVER $100.00. IT WILL PAY YOU TO CLUB WITH YOUR NEIGHBORS.**

machine which we are specially anxious to sell you. The head is exactly the same in all the different styles of woodwork, and whether you buy a No. 91009 regular at $16.55 or the Automatic Drop Desk Cabinet at $27.45, you get the **exact same machine.** The same head is used in all the different cabinets, the same work can be accomplished, the one is as durable as the other.

### The Greatest Bargain, However, is in Our Fancy New Style Drop Head Stand at $21.75 and $24.75.

They combine a very beautiful piece of furniture, a library stand, desk or writing stand, with a thoroughly first-class sewing machine, and as a special inducement to push the sale of this style we have made an extraordinary low price. In fact, a price heretofore never heard of, and other manufacturers would ask as much for the stand alone as we charge for the complete machine. As a special inducement to get you to take what we consider the finest complete machine possible to produce, we have made a special offer on our Drop Head Stand Machines, by offering to send a machine to any address within 700 miles of Chicago by freight C. O. D., subject to examination without one cent in advance. Note the special terms and conditions offered on the New Drop Head Stand Machine.

**About the Freight.** We pack, crate and deliver all machines on board the cars in Chicago free of charge. We exercise more care in crating and packing sewing machines than is usually done, and we guarantee every machine to reach destination in perfect order. A machine crated weighs about 120 pounds, and the freight will average about as follows: 100 miles or less, 30c.; 200 miles or less, 50c.; 300 miles or less, 60c.; 400 miles or less, 75c.; 500 miles or less, 80c.; 600 miles or less, 85c.; 800 miles or less, $1.00; 1,000 miles or less, $1.25; 2,000 miles or less, $2.00. Sewing machines crated are accepted by railroad companies as first-class freight. In the introductory pages of this catalogue we give a complete schedule of rates to all sections of the country. By referring to this schedule you can estimate to within a few cents just what the freight will be.

## Our Success Machine for $8.50.

While we do not care to recommend this machine too highly, we do not hesitate to say it is fully equal to machines generally advertised at $18 to $25 and retailed at $25 to $35.

These machines are made after the latest models of the Singer Co.'s machines, and are perfect fac-similes of their machine in shape, ornamentation and appearance, with the exception of the lettering on the arm of machine and the trade mark. All the parts are made to gauge exactly the same as the Singer Co.'s parts, and are constructed respectively of precisely the same materials. The utmost care is exercised in the selection of the metals used, and only the very best quality is purchased. Each machine is thoroughly well made and is fitted with the utmost nicety and exactness, and no machine is permitted to do perfect work, and run light and without noise.

NOTE.—**Self-Threading Shuttle.** A perfect steel shuttle with delicate and perfect tension opened to allow the bobbin to be inserted without displacing any part of the shuttle; holds more thread than any Singer machine shuttle; runs loose in shuttle with spring center and point bearings, thus insuring an even tension and all annoyance resulting from shuttle thread breaking while the machine is in motion, which is common to many machines, is entirely obviated. **The Stand** is among the handsomest in design. Finely japanned. Has large drive wheel. It rests on four casters and can be easily moved. The treadle is set on anti-friction bearings that run light and never need oil, thus saving the carpet from grease and spots. The dress guard over band wheel is large and protects the operator's dress from oil.

With every machine is furnished registered warranty for **ten years.** Any machine not satisfactory can be returned and money will be refunded. Where can you buy a machine on more favorable terms? Complete set of best attachments with each machine without extra charge, as mentioned hereon.

**Quick Sales and Small Profits** are the proper principles on which to do business, and we are determined to see how much the people will appreciate it.

**Each Machine** is nicely packed in a wooden crate, free of charge, also the following attachments free, accompany each machine, of whatever style. Is furnished with the following equipment of tools and accessories: One Foot Hemmer, one Screw Driver, one Wrench, one Oil Can and Oil, one Gauge, one extra Throat Plate, one extra Check Spring, one package of Needles, six Bobbins and one Instruction Book. In addition to the above we furnish with each machine an extra set of attachments, **free of charge,** consisting of the following: One Tucker, one Foot Ruffler, one set of plain Hemmers, five different widths up to ⅜ of an inch, one Binder and one Thread Cutter.

The Success is a perfect working Sewing Machine in every particular. It is finely finished, the wood being of the best seasoned walnut or oak, and the greatest care is exercised in the manufacture of each part. Money will be refunded if not just as represented.

Remember, the Success is not a cheap machine in quality, but in price. Our great reduction in prices is to increase the demand for our goods.

When ordering give plain shipping directions, giving the Town, County and State, the number and price of the machine, and where to ship machine. You can send money by P. O. Money Order, Registered Letter or Bank Draft, any one of which is perfectly safe.

## The Iowa for $13.25.

Guaranteed equal to machines retailed at from $35.00 to $45.00, far better than machines advertised by other houses at from $20.00 to $30.00. Everything about this machine is strictly first-class.

### Read the Description.

The "Iowa" has been manufactured in order to meet a growing demand for a machine of this kind. **The Iowa is made with great care.** The special points claimed for it are as follows: **Double eccentric** on main shaft for operating the shuttle and feed levers, **made of one piece,** and so perfectly balanced that vibration is reduced to the minimum, requiring but one adjustment, **no slipping of eccentrics,** and therefore throwing machine out of time. Feed mechanism much lighter; less material to be vibrated by springs; mechanical in construction; no knocking or "side lash;" hence no **rawhide** to deaden sound required. **Double feed,** so operated that whether long or short stitch is used the middle section of teeth always starts from immediately behind the needle, insuring thereby a **perfect and uniform stitch.** Also, so arranged that the feed does not fall until point of needle enters the goods, the benefit of which is obvious. The guard for thread controller on inside of face plate prevents injury or displacement, a frequent source of annoyance in some machines. **Loose pulley device,** easily and quickly adjusted, relieving the shaft from friction and all wing shaft end to be neatly finished off, avoiding the unsightly "wabbling" of balance wheel which in time wears out of true. **Cylinder shuttle,** self-threading, large loose bobbin, a delicate and perfect tension; oil holes large and free. ☞**The stand is beautiful in design,** light and graceful in appearance, and at the same time strong and substantial. **The belt replacer is simple and effective,** the utility of which the ladies will fully appreciate. Treadle hung on ball bearings, requiring no oil, hence no soiled carpets. ☞**The Iowa is a perfect working Sewing Machine** in every particular, and is equal to any $45.00 machine in the market. It is finely finished, the wood being of seasoned walnut or oak, and the **greatest care** is exercised in the manufacture of each part.

**STYLE No. 91005. LOW ARM SUCCESS.**

| No. 91001. | Low Arm Success, with one drawer, no cover. | | | Price | $ 8.50 |
| No. 91002. | " | " | " | and cover. | " | 10.00 |
| No. 91003. | " | " | " | 3 drawers and cover. | " | 11.90 |
| No. 91004. | " | " | " | 5 " " " | " | 12.90 |
| No. 91005. | " | " | " | 7 " " " | " | 13.90 |

**READ AND REFLECT!** Ornamented head, nickel-plated balance wheel, handsome oil-polished best walnut or oak woodwork of the latest design; gothic cover, with beautiful veneered panels, convenient drawers, with nickel drop-ring handles and good locks; iron stand and casters, as illustrated above, with all the attachments.

**THIS IS A PICTURE OF OUR No. 91008 IOWA ENGRAVED FROM PHOTOGRAPH.**

### Our Special Price.

| Style No. 91006 Iowa, with 3 drawers and cover | $13.25 |
| Style No. 91007 " " 5 " " " | 14.25 |
| Style No. 91008 " " 7 " " " like machine illustrated above | 15.25 |

**OUR MINNESOTA MACHINE IS THE MOST POPULAR AND THOROUGHLY RELIABLE SEWING MACHINE ON THE MARKET. WE GUARANTEE IT EQUAL TO THE BEST AND HIGHEST PRICED OF THE SO-CALLED STANDARD MAKES.**

## THE IOWA HEAD

Is shown in picture. Has a very high arm, it is beautifully **finished** in every way, very **simple** as shown in cut, almost **impossible to** get out of order. It is constructed on superior mechanical **principles**. The **lever** and **eccentric** which, as is well known, are used **only** in the first-class, high grade sewing machines. This combination requires but four working parts, and is the simplicity of **sewing** mechanism.

This is a picture of the under part of the head, showing the mechanical construction of the **Iowa**. Very simple, consequently easy running, no noise, no danger of getting out of order. Made of the best material and every part true to gauge. The **Iowa** uses the same needles as all first-class machines so you can get them anywhere.

**THE IOWA'S ATTACHMENTS.** We furnish a more complete and better outfit of attachments with the **Iowa** than you will get with other machines. The following attachments are furnished. One foot hemmer, one screw driver, one wrench, one oil can and oil, one gauge, one extra throat plate, one extra check spring, one package of needles, six bobbins, one instruction book, one tucker, one foot ruffler, one set of plain hemmers, 5 different widths up to ⅞ of an inch, one binder and one thread cutter.

There are many inferior attachments, but we furnish only the best, a set you will never wear out.

**Can you run it?** Anyone can operate the **Iowa**. Our book of instructions makes it very plain, and as all is so simple even a child could run it.

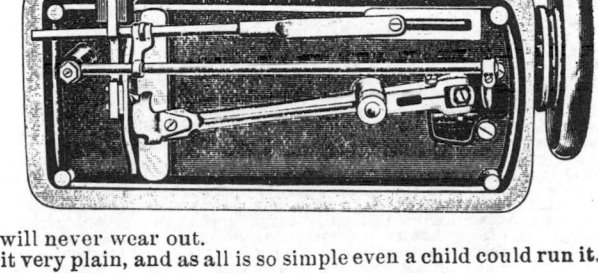

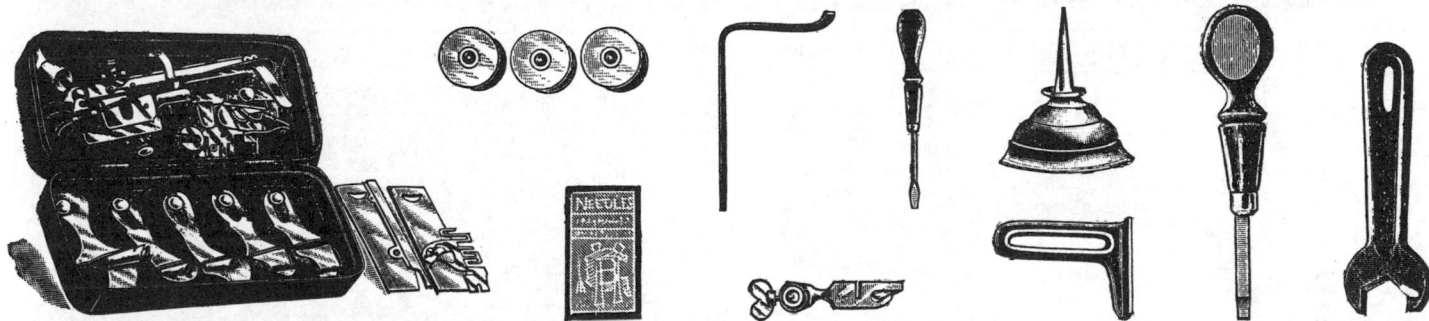

**ABOUT THE FINISH.** Our machines are all the best constructed in every way, heavy antique oak or black walnut cabinet, as desired, beautifully finished, paneled, carved, ornamented and polished, heavy iron frame, hard enameled, standing on four casters, all trimmings nicely nickeled. **Our 10 year guarantee** goes with the **Iowa**. We guarantee safe delivery to any station in the Union, and guarantee the machine to do perfect work for ten years. ☞It will last a lifetime. **Cash in Full** must accompany all orders for sewing machines. **If** not found satisfactory, you can return the machine and we will refund all your money.

## BUY THE MINNESOTA.

It is the **best machine on earth**. The Minnesota No. 91011 at $18.55 and the Minnesota Special No. 91014 at $21.55 are wonders. By all means buy the best, the Minnesota No. 91014. The **Minnesota** is a superior machine in many ways. First: The **attachments** are the best **and** most complete made.

**THE MINNESOTA ATTACHMENTS** Illustrated above, consisting of one foot hemmer, two screw drivers, one wrench, **one** oil can and oil, one gauge, one extra throat plate, one extra check spring, one package of needles, six bobbins, one instruction book, **one** tucker, one foot ruffler, one set of plain hemmers, different widths up to ⅞ of an inch, one binder, one thread cutter and quilter. These attachments are the highest grade made, nicely finished and polished, with a view of doing the finest work.

**READ THE DETAILED DESCRIPTION OF THIS BEST AND CHEAPEST MACHINE ON EARTH. THE FOLLOWING PAGES TELL ALL ABOUT IT.**

# THE MINNESOTA HEAD.

WE use this engraving of our Minnesota Machine to point out to you as clearly as possible the many advantages possessed over the ordinary sewing machine. From the marks indicated by the ciphers and by dotted lines, we point out the special features of the Minnesota as a confirmation that the machine possesses the good points of all the high grade machines with the defects of none, and if there is anything omitted in the construction of the head—the all essential part to a sewing machine, we are not aware of it. Every piece and part that enters into the construction of the head is the best that money can buy. By this cut we wish to point out to you the best self-threading vibrating shuttle action ever produced; the most simple and best double thread lock stitch made; the most simple and durable automatic tension and stitch regulator, which is equaled by no other machine; a tension liberator which is one of the greatest improvements over other machines; an adjustable and automatic improved take-up; the latest style loose wheel; noiseless wear-resisting shuttle carrier; adjustable bearing needle bar which can never get out of order; an automatic bobbin winder, the best automatic winder made. The Minnesota head is constructed on the most simple, wear-resisting, anti-friction eccentric principle, which makes the machine run almost entirely noiseless and lighter than any other machine made, so light, in fact, that a child can operate it, and the machine can hardly be heard in a room when running to its full capacity. For general appearance the cut does not in any way do the head justice, as it is very elaborately finished, highly enameled and ornamented, nickel plated and decorated. In fact, we believe we produce in the Minnesota the handsomest head which is made by any sewing machine concern. It is also very high, being somewhat higher than any other machine made, thus permitting the sewing of bulky goods with perfect ease. There is no machine made which will do as great a variety of work as satisfactorily as the Minnesota. You can, with the same needle, sew the finest fabrics or the coarsest woolens. In fact, one of our customers in writing says it will sew anything from the finest tissue paper to sheet iron. Don't be deceived by the many flattering advertisements that are circulating throughout the country from concerns who pretend to be sewing machine manufacturers, and who would endeavor to lead you to believe that they can furnish you a high grade sewing machine for less money than the Minnesota. If you send for their machine, send for ours also. Put them side by side, pass judgment on their general appearance and construction, then put them to the more important test of the work. The result will be our machine will stay in your house, the other will go back. We could fill a large volume and then not use all the testimonials we have received from customers who have purchased the Minnesota Machine and unsolicited have, of their own free will, written us strong letters of testimonial, and in every case report it the finest machine they have ever seen; nothing finer made at any price. When you can save $30.00 to $40.00 and get the best machine it is possible to produce regardless of price; have it sent to you subject to examination with privilege of 20 days' trial, a machine backed by a most binding guarantee for ten years, during which time a concern with a capital of $150,000 guarantees to replace any piece or part which may give way by reason of defective material or workmanship. We think you must agree it is a proposition you cannot afford to ignore.

## MINNESOTA HEAD.
Picture of the Minnesota head engraved from a photograph.

Is high, strong and substantial with large space under the arm for sewing bulky goods, such as cloaks, dresses, coats, etc. The space under the arm is 5½ inches high by 9 inches long; bed plate, 7 inches wide; total length of head, 16 inches; height of head from bed plate to top of needle

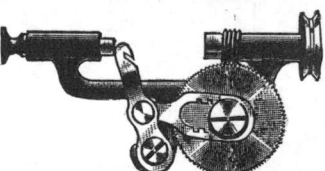

bar, 8½ inches. You will thus see the Minnesota has the highest arm, it is neat and handsome in design, finely polished, japanned and protected by a hard finish. ☞ It is ornamented in gold with enough delicate color to relieve it of plainness.

## Improved Automatic Bobbin Winder.

☞ The best bobbin winder made, and only furnished with the Minnesota. So simple that a child can easily operate it. Winding the thread on the bobbin automatically as evenly and regularly as the thread on a spool. This valuable attachment renders possible a perfect control of the shuttle tension, and thereby prevents the breaking of the lower thread which often occurs in other machines on account of not having the bobbin properly wound. ☞ Machine does not run while winding bobbin.

Minnesota Automatic Bobbin Winder.

## SIMPLE IN CONSTRUCTION

The Minnesota has 28 parts less than any other first-class shuttle machine made. What's the result? Runs the lightest, makes the least noise, less liable to get out of order, easy to repair, more simple, anyone can operate it. ☞ The parts which make up the sewing mechanism, such as the needle bar, cross head, thread controller (or take-up), shaft, eccentric lever,

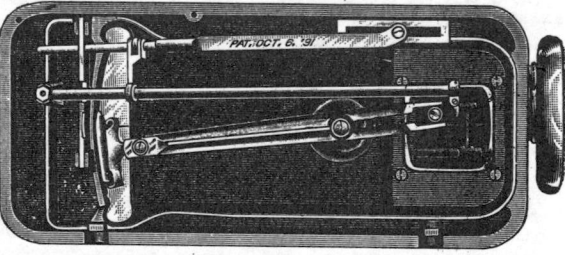

etc., are piece for piece, measurement for measurement with and like those used in other well known sewing machines. The Minnesota uses the same needles as the Domestic and other first-class machines, so you can get them anywhere. Any dealer keeps them. MOVEMENT—Double eccentric on main shaft for operating the shuttle and feed levers, made of one piece and so perfectly balanced that the vibration is reduced to a minimum, requiring but one adjustment, no shifting of eccentrics, hence impossible to throw machine out of time. ADJUSTABLE BEARINGS—All bearings are case-hardened steel and can be easily adjusted with a screw driver, no set screws, all lost motion can be taken up, therefore the machine will last a lifetime. POSITIVE FOUR MOTION DROP-FEED—The latest patent, absolutely positive, no springs. ☞ The feed on a sewing machine is the most important part of its mechanism. You can readily understand that a spring adjusted for heavy sewing cannot be adjusted properly for light sewing and vice versa. The Minnesota never misses a stitch. It has a double feed without springs which extends on both sides of the needle and permits a greater variety of work than any other, never fails to take the goods through, never stops at seams, no rattling springs to break or get out of order, can be lowered and raised at will. The movement being positive and having no springs, it has a great power and never fails to perform its duty, will feed the lightest or heaviest goods with equal precision and will cross seams and hard places without missing or changing the length of stitch. It makes a double thread lock-stitch, which can be made either long or short by simply moving a thumb screw on the bed of the machine, it will not break needles when sewing heavy goods, or pucker the cloth when sewing light goods.

## Self-Threading Vibrating Shuttle.

Picture of Shuttle engraved from a Photograph.

A perfect cylinder steel shuttle, opened at one end, entirely self-threading, easy to put in and take out, holds a bobbin that carries a large amount of thread. There are no holes to thread through, no springs to thread under, no latches to open or turn, making it the most easily threading shuttle in use. It is so simple that it can be threaded in the dark by two motions of the hand, backward and forward. The tension is even and perfect, and can be changed without removing the shuttle from the machine, thereby saving much time and avoiding trouble and annoyance. Owing to its simplicity it is impossible to thread the shuttle wrong.

SELF-THREADING NEEDLE,—Both as to height and position with reference to shuttle with short blade and large shank, insuring great strength. By means of a simple device the needle can not be set wrong, thereby saving time and trouble and preventing the breaking of needles.

THE STITCH is a double-thread lock stitch, the same on both sides, will not unravel and can be made either long or short. By simply moving a thumb screw the stitch can be changed without stopping the machine, a feature not possessed by other machines.

AUTOMATIC TENSION,—The Minnesota has the improved tension on top of the machine, easily adjusted and always reliable. Both threads have practically the automatic tension, thereby preventing the breaking or bending of needles, also breaking of thread in removing the work. The upper tension will admit thread from 8 to 150 spool cotton without changing. ☞ Never gets out of order.

## Stitch Regulator.

The length of stitch is regulated by a thumb screw located on the bed plate directly in front of the upright arm, convenient for the operator, and does not vibrate with the motion of the machine and can not come loose, hence the length of the stitch can not vary; it also has a scale and can be changed from 6 to 32 stitches to the inch. The length of stitch on the Minnesota can be regulated while the machine is in motion. You can also stop the feed by pushing back the stitch regulator, thereby enabling the operator to do darning without attachments.

**TENSION LIBERATOR.** The latest and one of the most useful improvements ever added to a sewing machine. By its use all tension upon the upper thread is relieved by simply pressing down on a convenient lever adjusted to the tension plate, so that work can be withdrawn from under the needle without slackening the thread by hand. By this ingenious little device all danger of breaking or bending the needle, and of breaking the thread when removing the work, is avoided. Improved Take-up is adjustable and Automatic, controlling the thread perfectly on all grades of work.

**IMPROVED LOOSE WHEEL** Enables the operator to wind the bobbin without running the machine. This saves unnecessary wear of the machine and the trouble of unthreading and removing the work while the bobbin is being filled.

**LIGHT RUNNING** Is a great feature of the Minnesota machine. It does not fatigue the operator, makes little noise, sews rapidly and is acknowledged the easiest running shuttle sewing machine on the market.

**ADJUSTABLE PRESSER FOOT.** By simply turning a screw cap on the top of the face plate, back of the needle bar, the entire pressure can be taken off the goods, thereby enabling the operator to do all kinds of art work, including embroidery, aresene, etching, chenille, zephyr, worsted, tinsel, etc. Any fancy work that can be done on any other sewing machine is easily accomplished on the Minnesota.

**IMPROVED SHUTTLE CARRIER.** This has heretofore been the cause of nearly all the noise and racket made by a sewing machine in motion. We use the improved shuttle carrier, reducing the friction to a minimum, thereby making the Minnesota almost noiseless.

**NEEDLE BAR.** It is made of the finest steel carefully hardened, with adjustable bearings, thereby insuring great durability and requiring but little oil. The needle bar is fitted with our improved oil cup at bottom, preventing the oil from soiling goods while sewing. It is self-threading. There are no holes to thread through excepting the eye of the needle.

**THE STAND** Is handsome in design. It rests on four casters and can be easily moved about. The treadle is hung on adjustable, anti-friction, hardened steel centers or bearings that run very light. The pitman has "ball-joint" connections, no side draft. Our stand is the most perfect ever invented.

**PIVOTED BALANCE WHEEL AND TREADLE.** Each machine is fitted with our new style Pivoted Balance Wheel and Treadle. The former is adjusted on two hardened steel centers the object of which is to give a more steady motion, also to facilitate the light-running qualities.

**THE DRESS GUARD** Over band wheel is large and prevents contact of the dress with the wheel, thus preventing soiled or torn garments.

**CABINET WORK.** We furnish the Minnesota in two styles of wood work, viz.: The "Regular" and the "Special." ☞ See full description under following illustrations.

# Our Minnesota No. 91011,

## "REGULAR GRADE."

### Our Special Prices:

No. 91009...........................$16.55
No. 91010...........................17.55
No. 91011...........................18.55

No one meets our prices. Remember our 10-year binding guarantee which is sent with every machine we sell. All machines are crated and delivered on board cars at Chicago without extra charge.

All Minnesota machine cabinets are made of solid antique oak or black walnut, as desired, with drop leaf table, beautifully carved, nickel plated locks and ring pulls

### Our Price for the Regular Minnesota:

No. 91009. "Regular" Style Minnesota, with 3 drawers and cover and drop leaf..........................$16.55
No. 91010. "Regular" Style Minnesota, with 2 drawers and cover and drop leaf..........................17.55
No. 91011. "Regular" Style Minnesota, with 7 drawers and cover and drop leaf..........................18.55

(Same as illustration.)

Our "Special" MINNESOTA grade is in every way the same as the regular grade with the exception of the cabinet which is more elaborate and better finished.

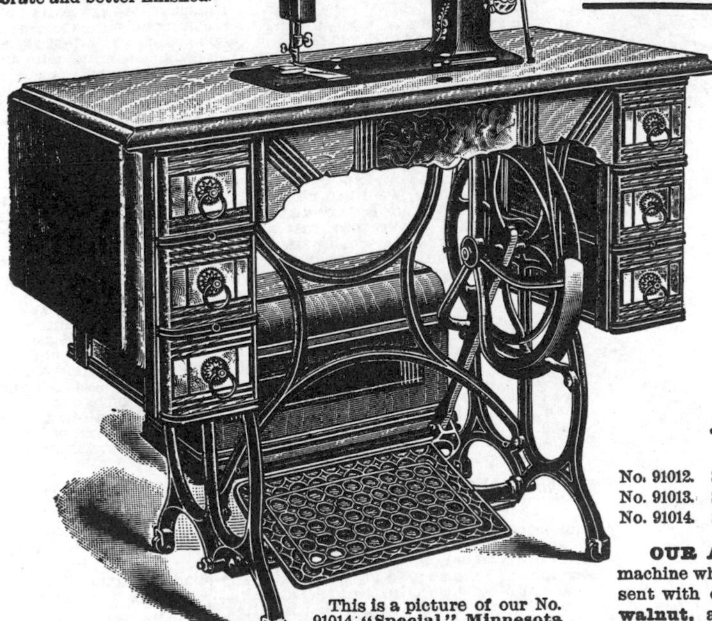

This is a picture of our "Regular" Style No. 91011 Minnesota Machine engraved from a photograph. Solid Antique Oak Finish.

This is a picture of our No. 91014 "Special" Minnesota engraved from a photo.

# OUR MINNESOTA No. 91014.

## "SPECIAL GRADE."

Our "Special" grade is very elaborate in style and finish, finest nickel plated Locks and Ring-Pulls. The cover is the handsomest bent wood style, and the frame work of the drawers is of the latest skeleton design, beautifully paneled, as shown in cut, nicely carved and joined together. It has a long center pull-out drawer instead of the swing drawer, making it the most expensive and richest machine cabinet work that can be secured, and heretofore has been used only on the highest priced machines, gotten up for exhibition at fairs, expositions, etc.

### REMEMBER

This machine is no better than our Regular Minnesota, the head, and in fact all mechanism is exactly the same, it will wear no longer or give no better satisfaction than the regular Minnesota, the only difference is in the cabinet. This cabinet is a work of art and at the slight difference in cost is sure to please.

## OUR PRICE FOR THE SPECIAL MINNESOTA.

No. 91012. Special Style Minnesota, with 3 drawers, cover and drop leaf...............$18.55
No. 91013. Special Style Minnesota, with 5 drawers, cover and drop leaf...............19.55
No. 91014. Special Style Minnesota, with 7 drawers, cover and drop leaf, (same as cut) 20.55

OUR ADVICE is to order the Special Minnesota. You will then have a sewing machine which excels all others. REMEMBER our ten years' binding guarantee which is sent with every machine we sell. ALL MACHINES finished in solid antique oak or walnut, as desired. All shipped from Chicago. ALL MACHINES are crated and delivered on board cars at Chicago without extra charge.

THE THREE PER CENT. CASH DISCOUNT WHICH WE ALLOW ON ALL FULLY PAID ORDERS, WILL VERY FREQUENTLY PAY TRANSPORTATION CHARGES ON THE ORDER. WE ARE ANXIOUS FOR YOU TO SAVE AS LARGE A PERCENTAGE ON YOUR PURCHASE AS POSSIBLE.

# OUR SPECIAL BARGAINS.

We are anxious to increase the sale of our latest style New Drop Head Stand Minnesota Sewing Machines, because we believe they are the most perfect machines it is possible to make. As stated before, they combine in one the finest sewing machine possible to produce with a very elegant piece of highly finished furniture, an ornament for any library or sewing room, finished as they are in quartered antique oak, highly polished, carved, decorated and ornamented. They are especially recommended to your favorable consideration.

## WE MAKE SPECIAL TERMS ON OUR NOS. 91016 AND 91018 NEW DROP-HEAD MINNESOTA SEWING MACHINES.

If you live anywhere within 700 miles of Chicago send us your order for the No. 91016 or the No. 91018. Send no money with your order and we will send the machine by freight. You can examine it at the freight depot, and if found perfectly satisfactory and exactly as represented, pay the agent our price and freight charges and the machine is yours. Then, after you have given the machine 30 days' trial, if the work is not satisfactory and you do not conclude it is the greatest bargain you have ever seen, return the machine at our expense and we will refund your money. If you live more than 700 miles from Chicago send us $3.00 as a guarantee of good faith and we will send the machine by freight and you can examine it at the freight depot, and, if found perfectly satisfactory and exactly as represented, pay the agent our price and freight charges, less the $3, and the machine is yours. After you have given the machine 30 days' trial, if not entirely satisfactory you may return it at our expense and we will refund your money and the freight charges you have had to pay. Or you can deposit the price of the machine with any bank with the understanding that the bank is to hold the money until you have received the machine and given it a 20 days' trial, the money then to be forwarded to us if the machine is satisfactory; if the machine is not satisfactory it may be returned to us and the bank will return the money to you. We are anxious for you to see and examine our special drop-head machine, and with that end in view we are willing to make almost any kind of an arrangement that the machine can be placed in your home along side of any machine made. As pictured in illustrations made from actual photographs, we have endeavored to show the construction of our special drop cabinet. While the pictures in no way do the machine justice, as you must see it in order to appreciate it, you can form some idea of the appearance and the way in which they are constructed.

The above cut represents our No. 91016 in drop head stand, which we are offering on very liberal terms at $21.75. By comparing our price with those of any other reliable house who sell at wholesale to dealers, you will find that we make a lower price on this machine complete with an elegant stand than is made by the largest manufacturers and wholesale houses on their cheapest stands. As you will see by the above cut, the head of the machine is closed from view as it sinks

**OUR No. 91016—SPECIAL OFFER, LIBERAL TERMS. PRICE, $21.75.**

into the stand and is covered by the hinge table, and as shown in the cut, affords a very nice piece of furniture when not in use for sewing, and can be used as a center table, library stand or writing desk. It is made of solid oak, quartered and finished antique, highly polished, elegantly carved and ornamented, and comes complete with every known modern attachment which is furnished with any machine. In fact, with the Minnesota we furnish a more complete set of attachments than is furnished with any other machine made. At $21.75 we furnish this machine with 2 drawers as shown in cut. We have the same machine, our 91017, $23.25, with 4 drawers, 2 drawers on each side.

**No. 91018 AT $24.75.**

The head and working parts of our new drop-desk cabinets are just the same as in our Minnesota attachments with our best machines are included with the Special drop-head stand cabinet machines.

## Our $24.75 New Drop-Head Stand Minnesota.

This is the highest grade drop-head stand made. It is covered by patents which we control, and while there are many imitations, there is no such a stand on the market as the one we offer at $24.75. It works automatically, and when open affords plenty of room for work: when closed, makes a very nice writing desk, library stand or table, and is in itself an elegant piece of furniture, being made of solid oak, quartered, finished antique, elaborately carved, paneled, ornamented and decorated; comes complete with 5 drawers, two on each side and one center drawer, furnished with the finest and most complete set of attachments given with any machine made, and is a machine that the owner may well be proud of. While our Minnesota heads, as before explained, are alike, and you can produce exactly the same results from our No. 91009 regular style Minnesota, at $16.65, as you can with those at $24.75, we by all means recommend our latest new drop-head stands at $21.55 and $24.75. They are the very latest style, and are being adopted by all the standard sewing machine companies. If you buy the old style sewing machine stand you will, in a few years, have an old style machine, as far as appearance is concerned. With a few dollars added now, you get the very latest thing out, and in all probability it will be many years before any sewing machine stand is brought out that will excel, if indeed equal, our special new drop-head stand, which we offer at the extraordinarily low prices of $21.75 and $24.75.

This illustrates our No. 91018 $24.75 new drop-head stand Minnesota Sewing Machine, closed, and, as you see, it would be an ornament to any room in the house. Illustrated in picture made from photograph, you see how easily the machine is brought in place for use. It works automatically and it is only necessary to raise the leaf, when the head automatically comes to its position. You have then the machine extended with a large table, and can proceed with your work. The bracket, which may from the above illustration look as though it would be an obstruction in operating the machine, raises automatically when the machine head is raised and brought into use. In addition to the better appearance one of our drop-head stands makes, in addition to the different uses to which it can be put, we also recommend it as a better protection to the machine against dust and dirt. The machine, when not in use, is securely encased and free from any dust or dirt, and for that reason the chances of getting out of order are next to impossible. In fact, if you buy a Minnesota machine, one of our latest style drop-head stand cabinets, it will last a lifetime, and the probabilities are it will never require a moment's time for repairs.

### WE MAKE SPECIAL TERMS ON THE DROP-HEAD STAND MINNESOTAS

not because we make any more profit on the machine, but because of their many advantages and the general satisfaction they give. From every one to whom we have sold this machine we receive letters saying: "I am so glad I bought your drop-head machine. The cost was but little difference, and the machine is so much nicer, so much more convenient, and I am so much better pleased." The best sewing machine head made. All special

**THE FREIGHT ON A SEWING MACHINE TO ANY POINT IN THE UNITED STATES SINKS INTO INSIGNIFICANCE WHEN YOU CONSIDER THE $20.00 OR $30.00 WE SAVE FOR YOU. AND SPEAKING OF SAVING MONEY, WE WOULD AGAIN POINT TO OUR GUN AND SPORTING GOODS DEPARTMENT.**

# ...Automatic Drop Desk Cabinet...

## MINNESOTA SEWING MACHINE.

### $27.45 Buys a $100.00 Sewing Machine

### READ OUR OFFER.

No. 91015.

This is a picture of our 91015, $27.45, **Automatic Drop Desk Cabinet Minnesota Machine**, engraved from a photograph (showing machine when closed). Closed as seen in this cut, it makes a beautiful writing desk. There is ample drawer space and receptacle for writing material.

To outdo others, we have had made for our **MINNESOTA**, a special automatic drop desk cabinet which we furnish in either solid antique oak or black walnut, as desired. No cabinet made will compare with it. Closed, it has the appearance of a beautiful writing desk and can be used as such. It has a green cloth covered top and makes a nice attractive piece of furniture for any drawing room. By a peculiar and patented device when you lift and turn the top over to the left the sewing machine head will rise to the surface of the table ready for sewing. The machine head moves up and down, and as it is counter balanced it requires but little or no exertion to put it in place. Connected with the two doors closing the front are drawers, pockets, etc., for attachments and accessories. Each cabinet is provided with lock and key, so that the two front doors, as well as the cover, can be securely locked. They are highly polished, beautifully paneled, carved, ornamented and decorated.

> **EVERY KNOWN SEWING MACHINE ATTACHMENT OF THE HIGHEST GRADE IS SENT WITH EACH MACHINE.**

**THIS MACHINE IS OUR LEADER** for the reason you get a regular $100.00 sewing machine for $27.45. Our customers reason like this: A machine as good as a Minnesota with the cheapest kind of cabinet would cost at retail AT LEAST $45.00. HERE IS A CHANCE to get a regular $100.00 machine for $27.45—$17.55 less than the cheapest machine to be had at retail.

This is a picture of our No. 91015, $27.45 Automatic Drop Desk Cabinet Minnesota Machine, engraved from a photograph, (showing machine opened). You will observe, when open, cover forms a large table for work.

No. 91015.

## THE GRANDEST BARGAIN....

We have to offer is this **our Minnesota** complete with the **Automatic Drop Desk Cabinet** with all modern attachments, everything that goes with a **sewing machine**, and all for $27.45, crated, packed and delivered on board the cars in Chicago, free of charge. **You take no risk. Our binding 10 years' guarantee** covers everything. If machine is not perfectly satisfactory, return it at our expense and we will refund all money you have paid, including freight and drayage.

## WHAT THE PEOPLE SAY.

**"Such an Elegant Machine."**
KOUNTZE, TEXAS.
*Gents.*—A few days since I received your "Certificate of Guarantee," guaranteeing the machine purchased of you for a period of ten years. The machine arrived in good order, and I must say I was indeed surprised—agreeably—at receiving such an elegant machine. Have tested it thoroughly and find it all you represented, and far superior to what I expected. Yours,
J. R. DAVENPORT.

**"Used Them on all Kinds of Work."**
LAKE FORK, ILLINOIS.
*Gents.*—The two Minnesota Sewing Machines bought of you are giving entire satisfaction. Could not better ourselves for double the price paid for them. Have used them on all kinds of work. Yours truly, M. F. TARBOX,
Agt. Am. Ex. Co. & I. C. R. R. Co.

**"A No. 1 in Every Respect."**
FOSTER, MISSOURI.
*Gents.*—The small foot hemmer received this A. M. This was all that was needed to make the machine A No. 1 in every respect. I thing I will be able to sell several of your machines here as everyone who sees this one thinks it is first-class. Yours truly, W. S. JAMES.

**"Couldn't Ask Anything Better."**
GLENDIVE, MONTANA.
*Gents.*—We have had the sewing machine you sold us, since Dec. 20, 1890, and are well pleased with the work it does. Couldn't ask for anything better.
Yours truly, JOHN HARPSTER.

**"I can Recommend You."**
WAKEFIELD, VIRGINIA.
*Gents.*—This is to say your machine does just as you recommend it. I have had it about ten months, and have found no fault with it. I feel that I can recommend you to the public, and would do you any favor that I can in selling a machine. Yours truly, MRS. A. W. HOLLOWAY.

**"Truthful Representations."**
RINGWOOD, NORTH CAROLINA.
*Gents.*—The machine I purchased from you gives, and has been giving, satisfaction. I found you truthful in your representations of the same.
Very truly, WM. C. FINCH,
Attorney at Law.

**"Perfectly Square and Honest."**
ALLENTOWN, RHODE ISLAND.
*Gents.*—I had a sewing machine from your place nearly two years ago, and I like the machine very much. It is just what it was said to be. Your manner of doing business with me was perfectly square and honest. Yours truly,
MRS. JENNIE L. ARNOLD.

**"Well Pleased With It."**
WESTMINSTER, SOUTH CAROLINA.
*Gents.*—We received our sewing machine December 15th, 1890, and are well pleased with it. We have found no fault with it so far.
Respectfully yours, W. N. WILSON.

**"It Does Work Beautiful."**
BELLEVIEW, GEORGIA.
*Gents.*—My wife is well pleased with her machine, has done a good deal of sewing and found it does work beautifully. She is charmed with the ease of running and says she hardly knows she is sewing. Have just sent another order to your Chicago house. Yours, JAS. H. FREEMAN.

**"A Splendid Machine for the Price."**
MERIDIAN, TEXAS.
*Gents.*—In stating how I am pleased with the machine I received, I can say it is a splendid machine for the price and is giving perfect satisfaction. It has now been in use about seventeen months. I think your manner of doing business is splendid. Yours truly, A. McCURRY.

**WHILE WE ARE TALKING ABOUT THE HOUSEHOLD SEWING, WE WANT TO REMIND YOU AGAIN OF OUR VERY EXTENSIVE DRY GOODS DEPARTMENT, UNDER THE SUPERVISION OF OUR EXPERIENCED MANAGER.**

# OUR $19.50 AND $22.50 NEW QUEEN SEWING MACHINES

## ♦ GUARANTEED ♦

### THE GREATEST VALUES EVER OFFERED.

### JUST THINK

A High Grade Modern Drop Desk Cabinet Machine for $19.50 and $22.50.

**A BINDING TEN YEAR'S GUARANTEE** accompanies each machine by the terms and conditions of which if any piece or part gives out by reason of defect in material or workmanship, we will replace it FREE OF CHARGE. THE NEW QUEEN will last a lifetime.

**OUR LIBERAL TERMS.** Send us $3.00 as a guarantee of good faith and we will send the machine to you by freight C. O. D. subject to examintion, you can examine it at your freight depot and if found perfectly satisfactory and exactly as represented, pay the freight agent our price and freight charges less the $3.00 sent with order.

**THREE PER CENT. DISCOUNT** allowed if cash in full accompanies your order, if you send the full amount of cash with your order you may deduct 3% from our prices. Nearly all our customers send cash in full.

As will be seen from the illustrations, we furnish our "NEW QUEEN" high grade sewing machine only in drop desk stand cabinets. This being a strictly high grade modern sewing machine, we think it more appropriate to fit it complete with the very latest, handsomest and best cabinet even at a slight addition in cost. From the illustrations you will observe we show the machine when closed and also open for work. The machines illustrated are exactly alike, the only difference being in the number of drawers to the cabinet.

**Our $22.50 New Queen** HAS A FOUR-DRAWER CABINET, WHILE OUR **$19.50** HAS A TWO-DRAWER CABINET.

**Our "New Queen" Sewing Machine** possesses the good points of all first-class machines with the defects of none. It is equal to any machine you can buy at retail at $50.00. Everything that enters into the construction of this machine is of the very best.

**THIS "NEW QUEEN" SEWING MACHINE IS MADE FOR US UNDER CONTRACT BY ONE OF THE** largest and most reliable sewing machine manufacturers in the United States, a concern located at Belvidere, Ill., where they have gained a reputation for making as fine a machine as can be made. The "New Queen" is our trade mark, and the name by which this machine will always be known. Before getting out the "New Queen" we looked over all the high grade machines, and endeavored to combine in this every modern point of value. We can say in our guarantee that it is not only made of the very best material and by skilled mechanics, but it possesses every modern feature.

**Among the Special Advantages of the "New Queen,"** it will be found very light running; almost noiseless, has double eccentric on main shaft for operating shuttle and feed levers made of one piece and so perfectly balanced that the vibration is reduced to the minimum, requiring but one adjustment; no slipping of eccentric and thereby throwing the machine out of order. Feed mechanism much lighter, less material to be vibrated by springs; no knocking or side lash, hence no raw hide required to deaden the sound. Double feed, so operated that whether long or short stitch is used, the middle section of teeth always start immediately behind the needle, insuring thereby a perfect and uniform stitch; also so arranged that the foot does not fall until point of needle enters the goods, the benefit of which is obvious. The guard for thread controller on inside of face plate prevents injury or displacement, a frequent source of annoyance in some machines. Loose pulley device, easily and quickly adjusted, avoiding unsightly wabbling of balance wheel which in time wears out of true. **Adjustable Bearings.** All bearings are case hardened steel and can be easily adjusted with a screw driver. Self-threading, vibrating shuttle, a perfect cyclinder steel shuttle. open at one end and entirely self-threading, easy to put on and take off; holds a bobbin which carries a large amount of thread.

There are no holes to thread through, no springs to thread under, no latches to open or turn, making it the most easily threaded shuttle in use. It is so simple that it can be threaded in the dark by two motions of the hand, backward and forward. The tension is even and perfect and can be changed without removing the shuttle from the machine, thereby saving much time and avoiding trouble and annoyance.

### THIS IS A HIGH ARM MACHINE.

The head is beautifully ornamented, all usual parts nickel plated; in fact, it is as handsome a machine as is turned out.

**CABINET WORK.** WE OFFER IN THIS, OUR "NEW QUEEN" MACHINE AT $19.50 AND $22.50, the finest cabinet work on the market. As will be seen from the illustrations this machine cabinet, which is made of solid quartered oak, finished antique, highly polished, beautifully carved and ornamented. The stand is very strong, well braced and guaranteed in every respect.

**THE "NEW QUEEN" HAS EVERY LATE ATTACHMENT OF THE VERY HIGHEST GRADE.** On our $22.50 machine we show an illustration of the extra set of attachments which accompanies every "New Queen" Machine, and the very best attachments made. Among the attachments we furnish free with every "New Queen" machine will be: One foot hemmer; one screw driver; one wrench; one oil can and oil; one gauge; one package of needles; six bobbins; one instruction book; one tucker; one foot ruffler; one set fine hemmers of different widths up to ⅝ of an inch; one binder; one thread cutter and quilter.

**OUR INSTRUCTION BOOK MAKES EVERYTHING PLAIN.** By carefully reading our instruction book you will find you can operate the machine and do any class of work that can be done on any machine even by an expert.

**PLEASE COMPARE OUR PRICES, VIZ., $19.50 AND $22.50,** with those of any other concern for a strictly high grade ten year guaranteed sewing machine complete with drop desk stand cabinet, and if you do not say that we are saving you from 25% to 50% in price, in fact, if after you have seen and examined this machine, you do not say that it is equal to any machine retailed in your section at $50.00 and upwards, we will not ask you to take it. You can return it at our expense and we will cheerfully refund any money you have paid.

### ↗↗↗ A FURTHER GUARANTEE ↗↗↗

If you send to us for a Sewing Machine we will allow you to use the machine in your own home for thirty days, and after thirty days trial, after you have put it to every possible test and tried every attachment which is furnished with the machine, compared it with the highest grade machines in your neighborhood regardless of what they cost, if you do not say our machine is equal to the very best and in many respects better, you can return it to us and we will cheerfully refund your money.

**OUR $22.50**

**4 DRAWER DESK STAND**

**New Queen Sewing Machine**

No. 91020

This illustration engraved from a photograph shows the machine when open for work. The most simple, handsomest, strongest and best **DROP DESK STAND MADE.**

**OUR $19.50 TWO DRAWER DESK STAND**

**NEW... QUEEN SEWING MACHINE**

No. 91021

The above illustration engraved from a photograph shows the machine when closed, with head dropped under and in the shape it can be used as a table or ordinary desk.

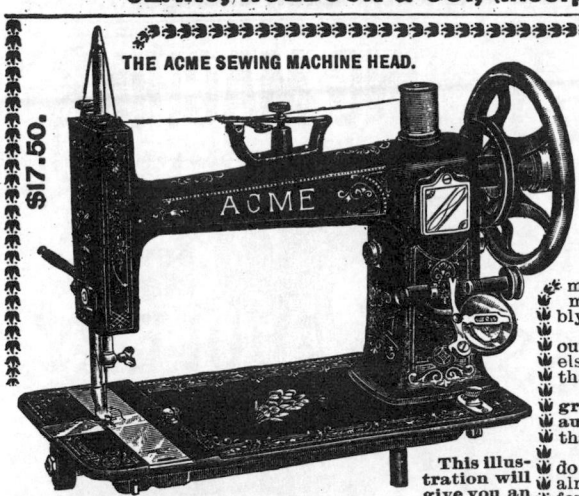

**THE ACME SEWING MACHINE HEAD.**

$17.50

This illustration will give you an idea of the appearance of the Acme Sewing Machine head. The picture shown is engraved from a photograph. You will see that this is one of the highest sewing machine heads made, strongly and substantially built, with very large space under the arms for sewing bulky goods such as cloaks, dresses, coats, etc. The space under the arm is 5¾ inches by 9¼ inches. Bed plates are 7 inches wide. Total length of head, 16¼ inches. Height from bed plate to top of needle bar, 8¾ inches. You will see the Acme has the highest arm, is neat and handsome in design, highly polished, japanned, and protected by hard finish; is ornamented in gold with enough delicate color to relieve it of plainness. All the usual parts are highly nickel plated, in fact, there is no more handsome sewing machine made by any concern.

you have ever seen, that it is equal to any machine on the market at any price. If you would like to know what others think of our sewing machines, if you would like to read concerning the good qualities of our different machines and the amount of money they have saved by sending their orders to us, Send for Our Free Sewing Machine Catalogue. In this catalogue we have printed hundreds of testimonials from customers who have, of their own free will, written to us, telling of the satisfaction our machine has given them and the amount of money they have saved by sending their orders to us. Limited space will not permit our describing all the little points of superiority in this Acme sewing machine, but we can sum it up in this, that every modern improvement, every special attachment, every patent of merit that will be found on any strictly high grade machine will be found in the Acme.

## A FEW OF THE MANY GOOD POINTS.

The Acme is Simple in Construction, has less parts than most first class sewing machines, hence not easy to get out of order, no sewing machine runs lighter, no machine makes less noise. Very simple in construction—a child can operate it. By following our instruction book which goes with each machine no teaching is necessary. Even if you have never seen a sewing machine you can use the Acme from the start. The Acme uses the same needle as the Domestic or any other first class machine, so you can get them anywhere, every dealer keeps them.

**MOVEMENT.** Double Eccentric on Main Shaft for operating shuttle and feed levers made of one piece, and so perfectly balanced that the vibration is reduced to the minimum. Positive four motion drop feed, the latest patent and absolutely positive.

**TENSION LIBERATOR.** The latest and one of the most useful improvements ever added to a sewing machine. By its use all tension on the upper thread is relieved by simply pressing down the convenient lever adjusted to the tension plate, so that the work can be withdrawn from under the needle without slacking the thread by the hand. The Improved Loose Wheel enable the operator to wind the bobbin without running the machine.

**ADJUSTABLE PRESSER FOOT.** By simply turning the screw cap on top of the face plate back of the needle bar, the entire pressure can be taken off the goods, thus enabling the operator to do all kinds of art work including embroidery, arasene, etching, chenille, zephyr, worsted and tinsel. Any fancy work that can be done on any other machine is more easily accomplished on the Acme.

**IMPROVED SHUTTLE CARRIER.** This has heretofore been the cause of nearly all the noise and racket made by a sewing machine. This improved shuttle carrier reduces the friction to the minimum, thereby making the Acme almost noiseless.

**CABINET WORK.** The Cabinet We Use on the Acme is the very highest grade of cabinet made. It comes in either solid black walnut or solid oak, quarter sawed and finished antique, highly polished, beautifully carved, decorated and ornamented. We furnish it with a special finish. The cover is the handsomest bent wood style. The frame work of the drawers is of the very latest skeleton design, beautifully paneled, nicely carved and joined together. It has a long center pull out drawer instead of a swing drawer, making it the most expensive and richest machine cabinet work that can be secured, and such as has been used only on the highest priced machines gotten up for exhibition at fairs, expositions, etc. The drawers are fitted with the finest nickel plated locks and ring pulls.

**STAND.** We Furnish the Handsomest Design, Strongest and Best Iron Stand Made. The stand rests on four casters and can be easily moved. The treadle is hung on adjustable anti-friction, hardened steel centers or bearings, that run very light. The pitman has ball-joint connections, no side draft. Our stand is the most perfect ever invented.

**IMPROVED AUTOMATIC BOBBIN WINDER.** With the Acme machine we furnish the best bobbin winder made—so simple that a child can operate it, winding the thread on the bobbin as evenly and regularly as the thread on a spool, and thereby prevents the breaking of the lower thread which often occurs on other machines on account of not having the bobbin properly wound. The machine does not run while winding the bobbin.

**SELF-THREADING VIBRATING SHUTTLE.** A perfect cylinder steel shuttle, very simple and the best sewing machine shuttle made.

**SELF-THREADING NEEDLE.** Double thread lock stitch. Self-acting automatic tension, in fact, everything that goes to make up the finest machine that can be made is combined in this, our strictly high grade $17.50 Acme Sewing Machine.

Every known modern Sewing Machine attachment and of the very highest grade is furnished with our Acme machines. The following are the attachments: One Foot Hemmer, Two Screw Drivers, One Wrench, One Oil Can and Oil, One Gauge, One Package of Needles, Six Bobbins, One Instruction Book, One Tucker, One Foot Ruffler, One set Plain Hemmers of different Widths up to ⅞ of an inch, One Binder, One Thread Cutter and Quilter and all of the highest grade.

The Acme Sewing Machine, crated and ready for shipment, weighs about 110 lbs. By referring to the freight rates on pages 5 and 6 you can find exactly what the freight will amount to. Sewing machines are accepted by all railroad companies at first-class freight rate, and you will see that the freight will amount to next to nothing as compared with what you will save in price.

In addition to our binding ten years' guarantee, bear in mind that you can return our machine to us after you have used it 30 days if you are not perfectly satisfied. If you do not decide that it is the best machine you ever saw regardless of price, that it is even better than any other machine which you can buy in your local market at $50.00, simply return it to us by freight at our expense and we will pay the freight charges and immediately refund your money.

## ....OUR NEW $17.50 HIGH GRADE....

# HIGH ARM ACME SEWING MACHINE.

**THE ACME** IS A NEW MACHINE, made at Rockford, Ill., by a concern which has been manufacturing high grade sewing machines for the last twenty-five years. They have just put the Acme machine on the market, a machine to supersede all others, the highest grade sewing machine they have ever made.

**THE ACME SEWING MACHINE** possesses the good qualities of every high grade machine this manufacturer has made with the defects of none. 25 years of uninterrupted and successful sewing machine experience have gone into this high grade Acme Machine to make it one of the very best on the market. The little defects of other machines that this maker has made in the past 20 years have been eliminated from our Acme until there is nothing about this machine but what is strictly modern, thoroughly up to date, of the highest grade that can possibly be made, and equal to any machine on the market regardless of price.

The demand we have received for Sewing Machines the past year has caused us to enlarge our line of machines and increase the variety to an extent that no customer need buy a machine elsewhere. It is ever our aim to make our different lines of merchandise so thoroughly complete that no one need be compelled to look elsewhere for the goods wanted.

As for Sewing Machines, we offer you what we believe to be the most complete line of high grade Sewing Machines on the market. From our Success machine at $8.50 to our Minnesota automatic drop desk cabinet machine at $27.45, we show such a variety of high grade goods that we feel confident you will be able to make a suitable selection.

**WE HAVE NOT INCLUDED MANY OF THE CHEAPER MAKES** which we might do and thus reduce the price, but we believe our customers are entitled to the very best. We are almost daily interviewed by sewing machine manufacturers who are anxious to contract with us for sewing machines at even lower prices than those we offer you, but knowing that we own these machines for as little money as it is possible to build them and use only the very latest plans with all improvements, finish them in a first class manner and guarantee them in every respect, we do not care to entertain any proposition from any manufacturer for a lower price machine.

**OUR ACME MACHINE AT $17.50** WILL COMPARE FAVORABLY with the highest grade machine on the market at any price. We Issue a Binding Ten Years' Guarantee, by the terms and conditions of which if any piece or part gives out by reason of defect in material or workmanship we will replace it free of charge. With care this machine will last a lifetime.

**WE ARE ANXIOUS TO RECEIVE YOUR ORDER** and that you may see and examine our Acme machine before paying for it we make you this proposition; Send Us $3.00 as a Guarantee of Good Faith, and we will send the machine by freight C. O. D., subject to examination. You can examine the machine at your freight depot, and if found perfectly satisfactory and exactly as represented, pay the freight agent our price and freight charges, less the amount sent with order, and the machine is yours. After you have used the machine 30 days, if you are not then thoroughly satisfied that it is exactly as represented, that it is the grandest bargain you have ever seen, that it is equal to any machine on the market...

**THIS ILLUSTRATION OF OUR ACME SEWING MACHINE AS IT APPEARS WHEN SET UP.**

**THIS ILLUSTRATION IS ENGRAVED FROM A PHOTOGRAPH, AND SHOWS YOU JUST WHAT THE MACHINE IS.**

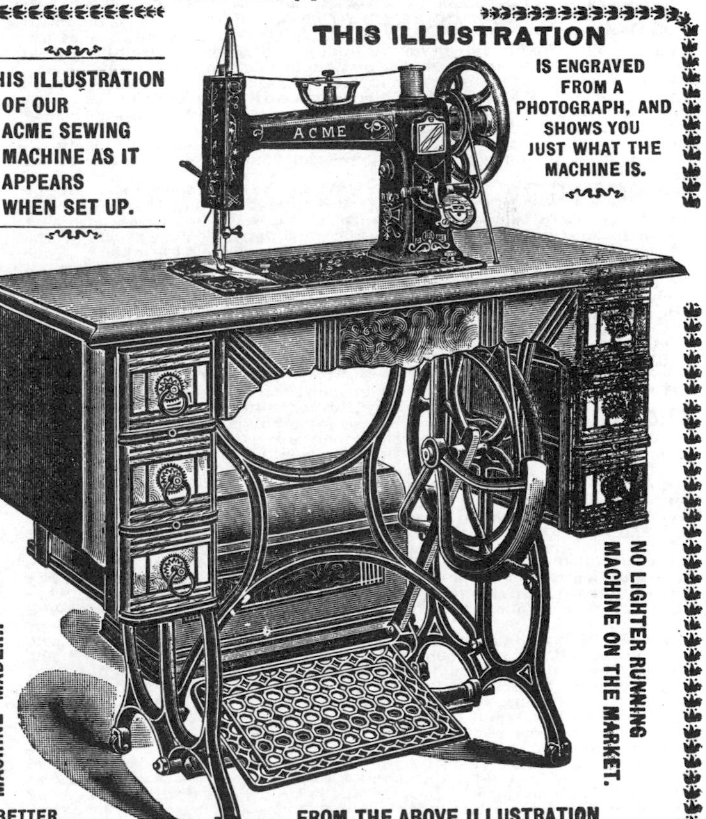

THERE IS NO FINER SEWING MACHINE MADE...

NO LIGHTER RUNNING MACHINE ON THE MARKET.

NO BETTER CABINET WORK

**FROM THE ABOVE ILLUSTRATION** You can see the appearance of our high grade Acme Sewing Machine when set up and ready for use. No machine has a more complete set of attachments.

No. 91024 Our special price for the Acme with 2 drawers, cover and drop leaf.................$17.50
No. 91025 Our special price for the Acme with 5 drawers, cover and drop leaf.................$18.50
No. 91026 Our special price for the Acme with 7 drawers, cover and drop leaf, same as illustrated above.................$19.50

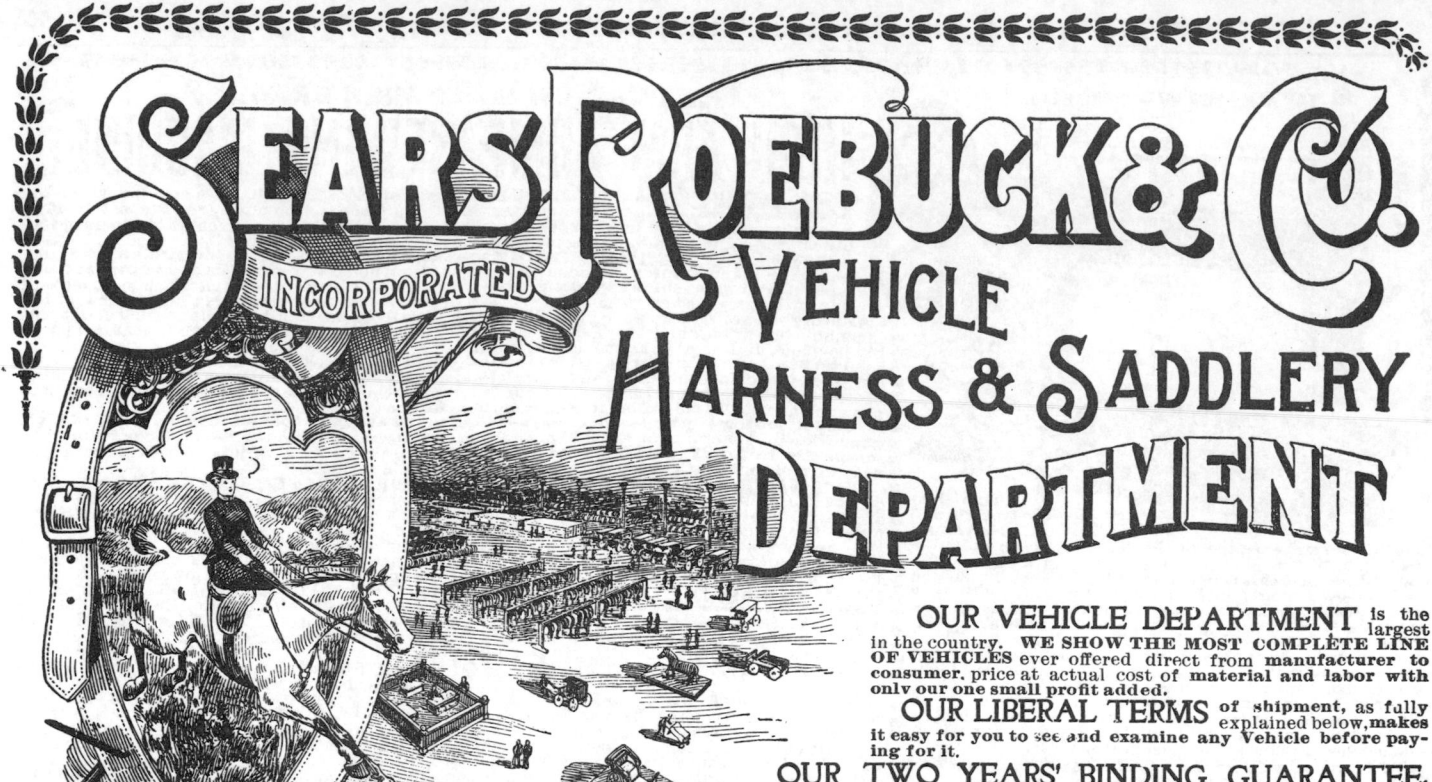

# SEARS ROEBUCK & CO. INCORPORATED VEHICLE HARNESS & SADDLERY DEPARTMENT

**OUR VEHICLE DEPARTMENT** is the largest in the country. **WE SHOW THE MOST COMPLETE LINE OF VEHICLES** ever offered direct from **manufacturer to consumer**, price at actual cost of **material and labor** with only our one small profit added.

**OUR LIBERAL TERMS** of shipment, as fully explained below, makes it easy for you to see and examine any Vehicle before paying for it.

**OUR TWO YEARS' BINDING GUARANTEE,** as fully explained at bottom of page, makes you absolutely safe at all times.

**OUR COLUMBUS, OHIO, VEHICLES** are the greatest values at anything like the price. OUR COLUMBUS, OHIO BUGGIES, PHAETONS, SURRIES and CARRIAGES are equal to those sold by others at more than DOUBLE THE PRICE.

**OUR MICHIGAN, OHIO, AND INDIANA VEHICLES** are of the highest grade made in these states, and our contracts are such that we can name you prices 30 per cent. lower than any dealer can buy in car load lots.

**COMPARE OUR PRICES** with those of other houses and decide for yourself. IF WE CAN'T SAVE YOU MONEY and furnish you a BETTER MADE VEHICLE than you can buy elsewhere DON'T ORDER FROM US.

**ABOUT OUR COMPETITORS.** We have first the retail dealer whose prices are in many cases double the price we quote, and who will use all possible means to discourage our customers from buying; will question our responsibility; will claim that we furnish inferior work; and, in fact, will resort to almost any means to discourage a customer from sending us an order. Concerning this class of competition we would say, we are willing to send any vehicle to any address C. O. D. subject to examination, allow you to compare it with any job you can get from your local dealer at 50 per cent. more money, and if our vehicle is not superior you can return it, and all at our expense.

**ANOTHER COMPETITOR** is the advertiser, or catalogue house, of which there are many reliable, and unfortunately, many unreliable ones. The reliable ones as a rule do an exclusive vehicle business and must depend on the profits of the vehicles alone to defray their running expenses, and look to vehicles alone for their profits, adding a large percentage to the cost in order to defray all this expense. Then, there are the unreliable advertisers who will promise much and do little. We are anxious to put our vehicles into competition with those of any reliable concern, and if we cannot sell you a better job for less money than you could possibly buy it elsewhere, we are willing to stand the expense of sending the vehicle to you and returning it to us.

**HOW WE MAKE THE PRICE SO LOW** WE DO NOT CLAIM TO BE ABLE TO DO WONDERS, but we do claim to be able to sell vehicles direct from the manufacturer to the consumer for less money than any other concern in existence. We cannot produce a strictly high grade vehicle for less money than the other concerns, but we do have facilities for marketing our goods direct to the consumer at a smaller expense and on a larger scale than any other house, which alone enables us to make our incomparably low prices. At the beginning of the season we contract with different manufacturers for a large number of vehicles selected from their line. We make this contract on the basis of the actual cost of the material used and the labor, with a small manufacturing profit added. To this we add our one small profit, and ship the job direct from the manufacturer to the consumer. There is no rehandling, no transportation charges, no traveling men's expenses, no rents, no storage, no bad debts, but you buy your vehicle for as little money as it is possible to produce under contracts for large numbers with but the manufacturer's and our one small profit added.

**WE CAN FIGURE OUR PROFIT LOWER THAN ANY OTHER HOUSE** for the reason that it costs us but little to conduct a vehicle department. We require such an organization for conducting our regular business that the adding to it of the vehicle department necessitates no additional rent, very little additional advertising, very little additional clerk hire, and consequently the allowance for expense for this department is next to nothing. On arriving at a price we do not figure on how much we can get, but we figure on how cheap we can sell. Neither do we figure on the profit of a single vehicle, but we use as a basis for calculation a thousand vehicles. A local dealer may sell you a vehicle and make $50. We may have to sell a great many vehicles to make $50, but in so doing we are constantly advertising our house. Every one who sees a vehicle from us and learns of the extraordinary value we are able to give; finds that he can get such a vehicle as he could not buy elsewhere within 50 per cent of the price; he is sure to show it to his friends, tell them where he bought it and what he paid for it, speaking a kind word in our behalf, and in that way our vehicle business grows to such proportions that we are able to take the entire product of a number of factories on certain selected lines, and in so doing reduce the cost to manufacture, reduce the cost of selling, and thus reduce the price at which we can market the goods to a point where we have no competition to fear.

**WE BELIEVE YOU WILL AGREE** when we have gotten into a position that we can offer you a good grade Columbus top buggy at $39.90, and send it to any address C. O. D.. subject to examination on receipt of a small deposit, the balance and freight charges to be paid after the vehicle is received, we are offering a buggy at less than the price charged by other dealers; and while the Columbus buggy at $39.90 is an extraordinary bargain it is nothing extraordinary as far as our line is concerned. We have figured every job on the same basis of profit. We have gone over the cost to manufacture on each vehicle, taking each one piece for piece and part for part, and no matter whether you buy our cheapest road wagon or our highest grade job, you get the same intrinsic value for your money as in our Columbus top buggy at $39.90.

**OUR BINDING TWO YEARS' GUARANTEE.** On all AA, A and B grade vehicles (see full descriptions of grades further on) WE ISSUE A TWO YEARS' BINDING GUARANTEE. By the terms and conditions of this guarantee if any piece or part gives out by reason of defective material or workmanship we will replace it free of charge. This is the longest, strongest and most binding guarantee given with any vehicle, and furthermore, our guarantee properly signed is FULL PROTECTION, for we will not only cheerfully make good the conditions of the same, but we are legally holding and FINANCIALLY RESPONSIBLE. This part should command your consideration.

**OUR SPECIAL B GRADE WORK** (as fully described further on) we do not guarantee, but offer it for what it is in competition with the cheap class of work that is now being so extensively advertised; work that we cannot guarantee nor can we afford to sell except with the plain understanding that you take it for what it is and hold us in no way liable for any dissatisfaction arising from material or construction.

## OUR TERMS AND CONDITIONS OF SHIPMENT.

**OUR TERMS ARE PRACTICALLY CASH.** In order to maintain our reputation as the CHEAPEST SUPPLY HOUSE ON EARTH it is necessary for us to adhere to certain fixed rules, terms and conditions which prevent our meeting with any loss from any cause whatsoever. But realizing as we do the excellency of the work we offer and knowing that our prices are far lower than those of any other house, on the same class of goods.

**WE MAKE THIS EXTRAORDINARY OFFER.** We will ship any one seated road wagon, one seated buggy or road cart on receipt of $5.00, or any two seated vehicle on receipt of $10.00 to any address in the following states: **Illinois, Indiana, Iowa, Kentucky, Michigan, Minnesota,** South of St. Paul; **Maine, Maryland, Massachusetts, Connecticut, Delaware, New Jersey, New York, Ohio, District of Columbia; Pennsylvania, Tennessee, Virginia, West Virginia, Wisconsin, Rhode Island, Vermont and New Hampshire. YOU CAN EXAMINE THE VEHICLE AT THE DEPOT AND IF FOUND PERFECTLY SATISFACTORY AND EXACTLY AS REPRESENTED,** and the grandest bargain you ever saw or heard of, pay the agent our price and freight charges less the amount sent with your order and the vehicle is yours. Understand, each vehicle, except our Special B grade, will be covered by a **BINDING TWO YEAR'S GUARANTEE,** during which time if any piece or part gives out by reason of defective material or workmanship, we will replace it free of charge, and at any time within 30 days if you find the vehicle is not entirely satisfactory, you may return it at our expense and we will cheerfully refund your money.

SEND FOR OUR SPECIAL VEHICLE CATALOGUE. THE MOST COMPLETE CATALOGUE OF BARGAINS IN VEHICLES AND HARNESS EVER PUBLISHED.

**WE WILL SHIP ANY ONE SEATED ROAD WAGON,** one seated buggy or road cart C. O. D. subject to examination on receipt of **$10.00, or any two seated vehicle** on receipt of **$20.00,** to the following states: **Alabama, Arizona, Arkansas, Colorado, Florida, Georgia, Indian Territory, Kansas, Louisiana, Mississippi, Nebraska, Wyoming, North Carolina, North Dakota, Oklahoma Territory, South Carolina, South Dakota and Texas. To the above states** we will ship any vehicle you may select, by freight, C. O. D. subject to examination. You can exanine it at the freight depot, and if found perfectly satisfactory and exactly as represented, pay the agent our price and freight charges, less the amount sent with order, and the vehicle is yours. **If not found satisfactory** you can return it at our expense and we will refund your money.

**ALL ORDERS FROM CALIFORNIA, Oregon, Washington, Nevada, Utah, Idaho and New Mexico, must be accompanied by cash in full,** in which case you are entitled to our cash discount. ☞ **Note the discount of 3 per cent. for cash.**

## CASH DISCOUNT.

**WE WILL ALLOW A DISCOUNT OF 3 PER CENT. on all vehicles where cash in full accompanies order. If you send the full amount of cash with your order you may deduct 3 per cent. from our price. NEARLY ALL OUR CUSTOMERS SEND CASH WITH ORDER.**

## YOU TAKE NO RISK IN SENDING CASH IN FULL.

You not only **save the 3 per cent. discount, save return express charges on money to us,** and the little inconvenience always connected with a C. O. D. shipment, but you always save a few days' unavoidable delay. **YOU TAKE NO RISK,** for if the vehicle is not perfectly satisfactory and you do not find it exactly as represented you may return it at our expense and we will cheerfully refund your money. We would recommend every one ordering to send cash in full with order.

### A Beautiful Carriage Sun Shade or Pair of Leather Kick Pads or Foot Protectors Free With every Canopy Top Surrey or Piano Box Top Buggy Where Cash in Full Accompanies Order.

**As an inducement in addition to our 3 per cent. cash discount for our customers to send cash in full with their orders, we have decided to send free with every order for A CANOPY TOP TWO-SEATED SURREY, a beautiful SUN SHADE; WITH EVERY PIANO BOX TOP BUGGY a pair of fine LEATHER KICK PADS OR FOOT PROTECTORS, provided cash in full accompanies the order. In order to supply those who will order top buggies and surreys** with the foot protectors named and the sun shades, we have arranged with a very large manufacturer in Michigan for a season's supply of these goods. The sun shade will be found not only beautiful but a very convenient attachment for a canopy top surrey, the kick pads a great protection to a piano box buggy.

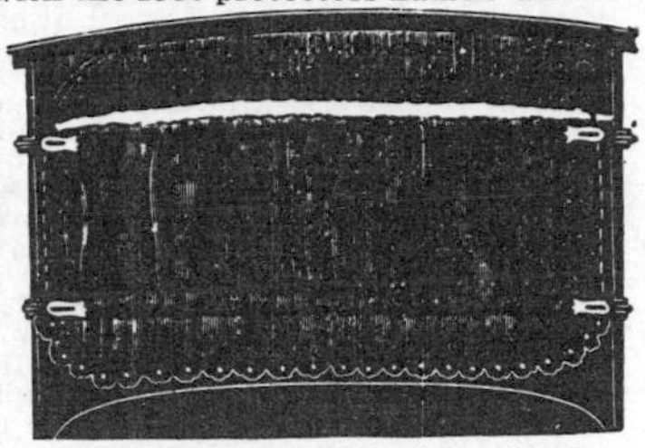

**THIS ILLUSTRATION, ENGRAVED FROM A PHOTOGRAPH,** will give you an idea of the appearance of this beautiful sun shade which we send free as a present with every canopy top two-seated rig when the order is accompanied by cash in full. These shades are adapted to canopy top surreys. They will fit on posts from 26 to 60 inches apart. They are hooked up with rubber covered hooks and easily adjusted, can be changed to either side or rear in five seconds without moving from the seat. They shield the occupant from the sun and are ornamental and a great luxury. No canopy top carriage is complete without one.

**THIS ILLUSTRATION** will give you some idea of the appearance of the pad when on a piano box buggy. **They are not only ornamental** and tend to put a neat finish to the box, but they are also very useful as a protection in getting in and out. **You will often notice that a fine buggy has become scratched or marred from the foot when getting in or out.** This will always be prevented by the use of a pair of our kick pads or foot protectors.

**WE SEND A PAIR OF THESE KICK PADS FREE** with every piano box buggy where cash in full accompanies order.

**IF YOU SEND CASH IN FULL WITH YOUR VEHICLE ORDER,** you not only save the three per cent. cash discount but you also receive either of the above descriced articles free, **you save some time in the shipment, save express charges on money to us, and you take no risk whatever, for we will immediately refund your money** if you are not satisfied and if you do not find the vehicle exactly as represented. **NEARLY ALL OUR CUSTOMERS SEND CASH IN FULL.**

## ABOUT THE DIFFERENT GRADES.

**We have arranged to handle such a high quality of work, so much better than has heretofore been offered by any catalogue house,** that we are compelled to make the following grades:

## AA, A, B AND SPECIAL B.

## OUR AA, A, AND B GRADES ARE GUARANTEED FOR TWO YEARS,

but with care will last a lifetime. **OUR SPECIAL B GRADE WORK WE DO NOT GUARANTEE,** yet many manufacturers guarantee it for one and two years. It is a class of work generally advertised at prices 25 to 50 per cent. in advance of ours. We sell it for what it is. If you want it we will be pleased to supply you, but if you want first-class guaranteed work for wear and service, buy our AA, A or B grade.

## AA GRADE.

**The AA grade is the best work that money can buy;** best A grade wheels; best finish in every respect; only the best material that can be bought is used in AA grade. While it costs more it is really the cheapest in the end.

## THE A GRADE.

**The A grade is a strictly high grade work.** No. 1 wheels are used, first class material and first class workmanship throughout. Our A grade work will compare favorably with the very best grades that can be bought from retail dealers, and is better than is carried by most dealers.

## B GRADE.

**This is a standard grade, the same as is usually carried by all wholesale houses,** repositories and first class retail dealers, and the highest grade carried by many. Well finished, good, honest guaranteed work. No. 2 wheels. We do not use a No. 3 or No. 4 wheel in any of our guaranteed work. These wheels are sold by many as No. 1. A good, honest hickory wheel, much better than the poorest, in fact, in quality far above the average.

## THE SPECIAL B GRADE.

**A very showy work, in fact, made more for show than for service.** Guaranteed by many for two years but not guaranteed by us at all. This is a class of work offered by many houses in top buggies and sold under very glowing colors and descriptions at from $33.00 to $45.00. It has No. 4 or D grade wheels in all this work. Some will give fair service, some will not. Usually an inferior material is used throughout on this class of work and then well covered up with paint and putty. The painting is not first class and liable to crack or wear off. We offer this class of work for just what it is to meet a certain class of competition.

**Please consider the different grades our work is made in in placing your order. Bear in mind the AA grade is the finest work that can be built. The A grade will compare favorably with the finest work carried by most dealers. Our B grade is standard quality that is sold in all small markets generally for their best grade work, and handled as such by most wholesale repositories. The Special B grade work is made more for show than for wear,** and is not guaranteed and the sale of same is not urged.

## WHERE OUR BUGGIES ARE MADE, WHERE SHIPPED FROM AND WHAT THE FREIGHT CHARGES AMOUNT TO.

**Our vehicles are made in Columbus, Ohio; Jackson, Pontiac and Charlotte, Mich., Racine, Wis., Indianapolis, Ind., Abingdon, Ill., and Cincinnati, O., and by the representative factories in the several cities. The prices quoted herein are for the buggies carefully packed, crated and delivered on board the cars at factory.**

## WE DO NOT SHIP VEHICLES FROM CHICAGO.

In order to make these most extraordinary prices we are compelled to relieve ourselves of the expense of drayage, handling, and storage in Chicago, and you have this advantage, i. e., that **every vehicle is fresh from the factory,** has not been handled, consequently is not marred or scratched, but is sure to reach you in the same perfect condition in which it leaves the factory. **We have all of our vehicles packed and crated in the smallest possible space** in order to secure the lowest freight rate possible, and to all points east and south of Chicago our vehicles go at first class freight rate under the ruling of the Southern and Eastern classification. To all points west and north of Chicago they go at one and one-half times first class freight rate.

**AS ALL VEHICLES ARE SHIPPED FROM THE FACTORY,** and a large proportion of our goods are shipped from **Columbus, O., Jackson, Mich.,** and **Indianapolis, Ind.,** to parties living east and south of Chicago we are able to secure a lower freight rate than from Chicago unless they purchase goods made at Racine, Wis., when the freight will be somewhat more than from Chicago, but we have secured an extraordinarily low freight rate from the factory to this city, and it adds but very little to the cost of the vehicle going to points west, even if shipped from Columbus, O., Indianapolis, Ind., or Jackson, Mich. But in every case it should be plainly understood that our vehicles are priced f. o. b at factory.

## ABOUT PROMPT SHIPMENTS.

**WE AIM TO SHIP GOODS IMMEDIATELY UPON RECEIPT OF ORDER,** or as soon thereafter as is consistent with filling your order exactly and giving you a throughly first class job in every respect. We usually complete the upholstering and give the job a final coat of varnish before shipping, and to do this requires at least five days delay for the upholstering to be done and the varnish to dry. **As all vehicles are shipped by freight and freight is comparatively slow,** the customer frequently becomes impatient, thinking we are putting him to an unnecessary delay, but we can assure you such is never the case. **We aim to have large stocks on hand at the factory at all times,** and the moment your order is received we immediately proceed to put the job in shape to ship within five days, and it is carefully crated in our own way of crating as fully described in this book on another page, and delivered to the railroad company. **By reason of the large amount of freight we give the railroad companies** our business is usually given the preference, and in consequence you can expect the goods ordered to reach you in a much shorter time than from almost any other concern, and to receive the goods not only in perfect condition by reason of our special care in crating and packing, but by reason of the fact that the buggy will be furnished with the last coat of varnish and upholstered after your order is received, you will get a buggy which is very much nicer in appearance than when it is carried in stock in the different repositories or held for sale by the different dealers.

## WE CAN SAVE YOU MONEY

**IN FREIGHT BY CRATING OUR VEHICLES in as small a compass as possible.** The smaller the crate we make the lower rate the railroad company gives, and in order to secure the minimum rate we crate our vehicles closer and better than any other concern. They are thoroughly wrapped, packed and crated, and no matter how far they have to be shipped they invariably reach their destination in the same perfect condition in which they leave the factory. **In our Special Vehicle Catalogue we show illustrations of our vehicles as they are crated and shipped;** we ask you to note the difference in the **care** bestowed in crating our vehicles and others you have seen.

## WE GIVE IN FRONT OF BOOK THE FIRST-CLASS FREIGHT RATES PER 100 LBS.

On vehicles from Chicago to several points in the different states and territories, and under the description of each vehicle we give the shipping weight. From this you can calculate very closely what the freight will amount to. As most railroad companies accept the freighton the basis of first class, by multiplying the weight in pounds by the rate per 100 lbs. to the nearest point mentioned in your state, you can ascertain the freight on the vehicle you have selected. If you live west or north of Chicago it will be safe for you to add 30 cents per 100 lbs. to the rate quoted. If you live east or south of Chicago you can safely deduct about 30 cents per 100 lbs., and in this way you can arrive at what the vehicle will cost you delivered at your own station.

**WE CAN ASSURE YOU THE FREIGHT AMOUNTS TO NEXT TO NOTHING compared with what you save on our one small profit basis direct from manufacturer to consumer.** The rates quoted on another page are in force at the time this catalogue is issued, and while they are changed from time to time by the different railroad companies the variation will be very little one way or the other, and we are often able to secure a special rate or take advantage of some cut rate, which we are always glad to do when possible and give our customers the benefit. Where a party lives in the south and we can ship by boat, Ohio or Mississippi river, unless otherwise instructed we do so and secure a rate about one-half the railroad rate.

## ABOUT WIDTH OF TRACK.

**Be sure to state width of track wanted.** We furnish vehicles in both **wide** and **narrow** track. The wide track is **5 feet 2 inches** from wheel to wheel; narrow track **4 feet 8 inches** from wheel to wheel. **We have had no end of trouble** owing to customers failing to specify the width of track wanted. **Where the width is omitted we use our best judgment** and endeavor to send the width most commonly used in the section to which the vehicle is going, but as both wide and narrow tracks are used in some sections we frequently err and that gives rise to unpleasant complaints, so be sure to state the width of track wanted. **The wide tracks, 5 feet 2 inches,** are used very extensively in the following states: Alabama, Arizona, Arkansas, California—all points north of the Tehacapi mountains, Delaware, Florida, Georgia, Indiana (south half), Idaho, Maryland, New Jersey (south half), Nevada, North Carolina, Ohio (eastern half), South Carolina, Texas, Virginia, West Virginia and Wyoming. **Narrow track, 4 feet 8 inches,** are used very extensively in California south of the Tehacapi mountains, Colorado, Connecticut, Indiana, Iowa, Kansas, Kentucky, Maine, Massachusetts, Michigan, Minnesota, New Hampshire, New York, New Mexico, Nebraska, North Dakota, Rhode Island, South Dakota, Tennessee, Vermont and Wisconsin.

**BOTH WIDE AND NARROW TRACK** are used extensively in Delaware, District of Columbia, Indian Territory, Lousiana, Mississippi, Missouri, Oregon and Illinois. In states where both tracks are used extensively, and especially Illinois, where one track is used as much as the other, you can see the great importance of your being explicit in your order for it is impossible for us to determine which track is wanted. The price is always the same. **We will furnish any vehicle in either 5 feet 2 inches or 4 feet 8 inches track, as desired.**

## Our Special B Grade $28.95 Top Buggy.

**To meet a class of competition** in the vehicle line which is offering the cheapest work that can be produced, goods that are made to sell and not to wear, we have been induced to get out what we term a **Special B Grade of work** which we have in **Top Buggies, Phætons and Surreys.**

**We offer them for just what they are** and just what they are worth. **We cannot afford to deceive our customers.** If you want the cheapest kind of a vehicle we can supply you, but if you buy one of the Special B Grade jobs it should be distinctly understood that it is bought without guarantee and entirely at your risk.

**We guarantee every Special B Grade vehicle** to be exactly as represented. Further than that we do not hold ourselves responsible.

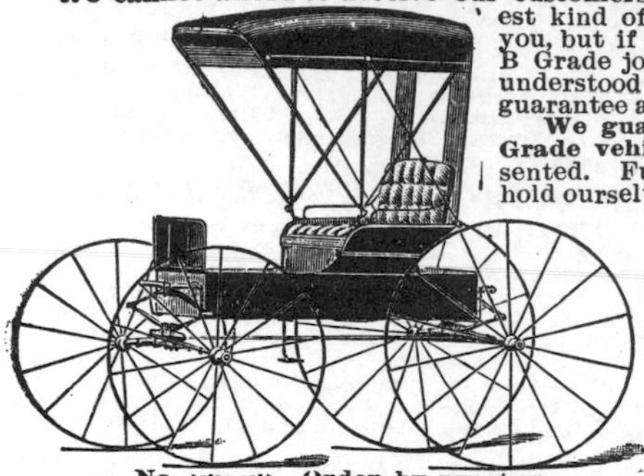

No. 92800. Order by number.

**This $28.95 Top** Buggy will compare favorably with buggies offered by many houses at from $35.00 to $45.00. They are advertised by some concerns in very glowing colors and descriptions, but our customers are entitled to the truth and on this basis we earnestly speak for your trade.

**Above is an illustration of our $28.95** top buggy, which we will furnish in either End Spring or Brewster side bar spring as desired.

**This buggy is made at Cincinnati, O.,** and the price quoted is for the buggy carefully crated, complete with shafts, delivered on board the cars at Cincinnati, and the freight must be calculated from that point.

### Description.

**BODY**—Full size 23x52, round corners, swell panels, panels 8 inches deep with two braces, seat 27 inches wide at bottom, 15 inches deep, 38½ inches to top of seat panel. Seat panel 6 inches deep; 11 inches from the floor to bottom of seat and 15 inches from floor to top of cushion. The seat is held to the body by two wrought iron rods going through the sills. The frame of the body is made of ash, mortised, glued and screwed. Panels and seat are made of poplar, screwed, plugged and glued.

**GEAR**—15-16 inch double collar steel axle; hickory axle caps; double perch of hickory with steel plates running entire length. The gear is well braced by wrought iron stays running from perch to rear axle. Full half circle fifth wheel, End Spring like cut or Brewster side bar as desired.

**WHEELS**—Sarven's patent, 38 or 42 inch front, 40 or 44 inch rear; ⅞ or ¾ inch tread as desired.

**TRIMMINGS AND PAINTING**—Cushions and back are trimmed in imitation leather or 12 oz. dark green cloth in biscuit pattern with a roll.

**TOP**—3-bow, steel sockets, enamelled drill top with good head lining and padded and lined back stays. Green back, side and back curtains. Brewster curtain fasteners for back curtain and black carriage knobs neatly fitted for side curtains. Stitched imitation leather valance and leather roll-up straps.

**PAINTING**—Body black, gear dark green with suitable gold stripe.

**WIDTH OF TRACK**—4 feet 8 inches or 5 ft. 2 inches, as desired.

☞ **In ordering be sure to state width wanted.**

**These Buggies** come complete with **toe carpet, boot, wrench, anti-rattlers, storm apron and shafts.**

| | |
|---|---|
| ☞ Extra for pole with neckyoke and whiffletrees complete in place of shafts | $2.00 |
| Extra for both pole and shafts | 4.00 |
| Extra for leather quarter top | 3.00 |
| Extra for full leather top | 5.00 |
| Extra for genuine leather cushions and back, or 16 oz. English wool dyed body cloth cushions and back | 2.00 |
| Extra for solid panel back | 1.00 |
| Extra for silver plating throughout, including hub bands, top prop nuts and seat handles | 1.00 |

**Do not expect too much of our Special B Grade work.** Note our full description of AA, A and B grades, and note they are guaranteed for two years and are goods of standard make and well known reputation.

**Our Special B Grade work cannot** be guaranteed, and is only sold to compete with low priced work on the market.

**Cash in full** must accompany all orders for **Special B grade** vehicles. **No Cash Discount.**

## Our $39.90 Phaeton.

**Special B Grade Not Guaranteed.**

**We offer this phaeton at $39.90** in competition with the class of cheap work that is being manufactured and sold at prices ranging from $48.00 to $60.00.

**This work looks all right.** In appearance it will pass for a very fair vehicle. See our description of the Special B Grade. Very showy work, made for show, not for service.

**The accompanying illustration engraved** from a photograph, will give you an idea of the appearance of our Special B Grade $39.90 top phaeton.

**This phaeton is made in Cincinnati, O.,** and the price quoted is the net cash with order (no discount) price for the phaeton crated and delivered on board the cars in Cincinnati. **Understand that no guaranty goes with this job.** We guarantee it to be exactly as represented; further than that we can not be held responsible.

No. 92801. Order by number.

### Description.

**BODY**--28 inches wide at the bottom.

**SEAT**--33½ inches at bottom, 17 inches deep, back 20 inches high.

**WHEELS**--36x42 or 38x44 as desired.

**TIRES**--¾, ⅞ or 1 inch as desired.

**AXLES**--15-16 inch, fan tail, double collar steel.

**SPRINGS**--3 leaf front, 4 leaf rear, 36 inches long.

**TOP**--3 or 4 bow, drill, with rubber roof, back and side curtains.

**TRIMMINGS**--12 oz. all wool broadcloth, or imitation leather, as desired.

**PAINTING**--Body black, gear dark green with neat stripe.

We furnish the phaeton complete with storm apron, carpet and shafts.

| | |
|---|---|
| For leather quarter top, add | $3.00 |
| For full leather top, add | $5.00 |
| For pole, neckyoke and whiffletrees complete in place of shafts, add | $2.00 |
| For both pole and shafts, add | $4.00 |

**Be sure to state width** of track wanted, 4 feet 8 inches or 5 feet 2 inches.

**Remember this is our Special B Grade** work, not guaranteed, offered at $39.90 net cash in full with order, no discount and no C. O. D. shipment allowed. We offer you this work simply to show you that we are headquarters for vehicles and can supply you with the cheapest as well as the best.

**During the past season** we have been called upon a great many times to quote lower prices in competition with some house that would be selling cheap work, and to meet this competition we include the cheap work along with our guaranteed AA, A and B grades,

## $44.00 Net Cash with Order for Our Special B Grade Surrey.

**To show how cheap a good looking two seated surrey can be produced** where quality of material and workmanship are sacrificed to appearance only, and in order that we may compete with others who offer this class of work almost exclusively, we offer you this **Special B Grade Canopy Top Surrey for the heretofore unheard-of price of $44.00.**

**Understand our Special B Grade is not guaranteed,** although many concerns issue very strong and binding guaranties as far as the paper is concerned. We mean to protect our guaranties to the letter and consequently can only guarantee work which is safe to guarantee.

No. 92802. Order by Number.

**Our AA, A and B Grades are the highest standard,** and every job is covered by a binding guaranty, but our Special B Grade like all cheap work on the market has a No. 4 or D grade wheel which is not safe to guarantee. The painting cannot be guaranteed, nor do we want to be responsible for any part of it. It is very showy and so far as show is concerned will give you satisfaction.

**The above illustration engraved from a photograph** will give you some idea of the appearance of our Special B Grade $44.00 Top Surrey.

**Note—Illustration shows fall fenders and lamps, which are extra. See extras below. At $44.00 surrey comes with half fenders and no lamps.**

**This surrey is made at Cincinnati,** and the price quoted is the net cash, no discount, cash in full with order price for the surrey crated and delivered on board the cars at Cincinnati, and you must figure the freight from that point.

### Description.

**BODY**—27 inches wide and 5 feet 10 inches long. Size of canopy top, 6 feet long and 46 inches wide. Body has full length Norway iron body loops and steel rockers running inside full length.

**GEAR**—1 1-16 inch steel drop axles and hickory axle caps clipped to the axle with iron clips. Double perch hickory, re-enforced steel plates running full length, iron stays running from the rear axle to the perches. Springs 7 inch opening, 1½ inches wide, 4 and 5 plate, 36 inches long.

**WHEELS**—Sarven's patent, 38x40, ⅞ or 1 inch tread, as desired.

**TRIMMINGS AND PAINTING**—Cushions and back trimmed in 14 oz. dark green cloth or imitation leather. Seat panels are lined full length, wool carpet, canopy top, drill curtains, storm apron and fenders over the back wheel coming down to the step. Shafts are trimmed in leather.

**PAINTING**—Body has dark green olive panels with black seat panels and molding, handsomely striped with a fine line of gold. Gear is a dark green with three lines striped. All complete makes a handsome light surrey.

**Our net cash with order price of $44.00** is for the surrey complete with canopy top, curtains, full length carpet, storm apron, ½ fenders, no lamps, and with anti-rattlers and shafts.

| | |
|---|---|
| Extra for full double fenders and broad step | $6.00 |
| Extra for leather quarter extension top | 9.00 |
| Extra for full leather cushions and backs | 2.50 |
| Extra for pole with neckyoke and whiffletrees complete in place of shafts | 2.00 |
| Extra for lamps | 3.50 |

**In ordering be sure** to state width of track wanted, whether 4 feet 8 or 5 feet 2, and do not expect us to guarantee the rig. Don't look for it to be any different than as represented.

**Read well our descriptions of grades AA, A, B and Special B, and if** you are willing to take the cheap work we are perfectly willing to furnish it if relieved of the responsibility of breakage or wear.

**Cash in full** must accompany all orders for **Special B grade** vehicles. **No Cash Discounts.**

## What the People Say.

**We Always Please the People.**

SHELBURN, (SULLIVAN CO.) IND., Jan. 5, 1897.

SEARS, ROEBUCK & CO., Chicago, Ill.

GENTLEMEN: I can say that my carriage has given me satisfaction, and the several other orders the same. If you continue sending your goods as you have been, you may consider me as your continual customer. If you will send me one of your 1897 Catalogues I shall be very much obliged.

Yours respectfully, FRANCIS WOODSMALL.

**Saddle will Last a Lifetime.**

BRIGHTON, JEFFERSON CO., ALA., Jan. 2, 1897.

SEARS, ROEBECK & CO.

GENTLEMEN: I received my saddle and I must say that I am so well pleased and satisfied with my saddle, words cannot express my thanks for the benefit that I received from the pleasure and satisfaction given me. I know that I have a saddle that will by ordinary care last a lifetime, and all of my neighbors are pleased as well, and I am satisfied so well that you shall have more of my orders in the near future. Yours truly.

LEWIS THOMAS.

**Harness and Suit Even Better than Represented.**

EAST BENTON, LACKA. CO., PA., Jan. 4, 1897.

SEARS, ROEBUCK & CO.

DEAR SIRS:—Goods received, am highly pleased. Harness and suit is as represented, only better in quality. Harness out here would cost $30 to $35. You may look for more orders in the future. Yours, W. W. STATES.

SEARS, ROEBUCK & CO.

**Mackintosh Much Better Than Expected.**

JUNCTION CITY, OREGON, Jan. 6, 1897.

GENTS: I received the two mackintoshes yesterday, they were very satisfactory in every particular, much better than I expected. More orders will follow soon. Very truly yours, LEE W. CLARK.

**SEE OUR COLUMBUS, OHIO VEHICLE, BEST IN THE WORLD FOR THE MONEY. AA, A AND B GRADE WORK IS GUARANTEED TWO YEARS. ☞ SEND FOR OUR FREE VEHICLE CATALOGUE.**

## Our Special B Grade $21.00 Road Wagon.

**Elliptic end Spring or Brewster sidebar spring,** as desired. $21.00 is our net cash with order price. **No discount.**

**Cash in full must accompany your orders** for these Special B Grade $21.00 road wagons.

**We offer these road wagons at $21.00** in competition with wagons that are being offered by catalogue houses at from $25.00 to $30.00, wagons that are made more for appearance than for service. While some concerns sell them under very lengthy guaranties, we cannot guarantee the work and do not consider it safe to do so.

**We sell these wagons for what they are.** We sell them because we are compelled to do so to meet competition on this class of work. If we do not put a low priced vehicle in our catalogue, customers are sure to write in and tell us they can buy road wagons at $25.00, $27.00 or $30.00 elsewhere. To show just what this work is and what it can be sold for, for that reason and that only, we offer the work at all.

**We advise our customers to buy a good substantial vehicle** when buying. Buy our regular B, A or AA grades. Buy a vehicle that is made by a concern whose reputation is established and is now at stake, a vehicle which we can guarantee. It costs but a few dollars more.

**The illustration** engraved from a photograph will give you some idea of the appearance of this road wagon. It is made in either elliptic End Spring or Brewster sidebar spring, as desired. The body is 25 inches wide. 52 inches long; convex panels on seat and body; width of seat at bottom, 27½ inches, outside measurement; width of seat at top, 33½ inches, outside measurement. It is upholstered in enameled duck or imitation leather; has a padded lazy back, as illustrated.

**No. 92804. Order by Number.**

**GEAR**—The gear is made from hickory, has a double reach, ironed full length, rear king bolt, ⅝ inch iron tire, crimped, half bolted.

**SPRINGS**—Made from spring steel of fair grade, not such as we can guarantee.

**WHEELS**—Our special B grade wheel, either Sarven's patent or shell band hub, as desired, but not guaranteed.

**PAINTING**—Body is painted black, gear carmine, yellow or Brewster green. These road wagons weigh about 300 pounds. Crated for shipment, about 350 pounds. Claimed capacity, about 500 pounds.

**Our special price of $21.00 includes the Wagon Complete with** oil cloth carpet, whip socket, foot rail, wrench, washers, anti-rattlers and shafts.

| | |
|---|---|
| For pole with neckyoke and whiffletrees complete in place of shafts add | **$1.75** |
| For both pole and shafts, add | **3.25** |

**These $21.00 road wagons** are made by three different manufacturers, one in Indiana, one in southern Ohio and one in southern Michigan. We ship from the most convenient point, thus securing for you the lowest freight rate.

**If you buy one of our Special B Grade** buggies, road wagons or surreys, we will guarantee it to look all right on arrival, and we have no doubt, in quality it will compare favorably with the rigs you would pay 50 per cent. more for, but remember it is sold by us without any guarantee whatsoever, and if any part breaks or gives way by reason of defective material or workmanship, if the paint does not hold or you meet with any accident, do not blame us. Remember we advise you to buy a B grade, A grade or AA grade; work that we guarantee in every particular.

A more complete line of this work is found in our special Vehicle Catalogue, which we will mail free on application.

YOUR CHOICE OF THE FOLLOWING . . . .

## TWO YEAR GUARANTEED B GRADE TOP BUGGIES FOR $32.98 CASH IN FULL WITH ORDER,

### OR FOR $34.00 ON REGULAR TERMS

**Our special price for this work is $34.00.** We allow a discount of 3% if cash in full accompanies your order, making the price $32.98 for cash in full.

**Your choice of End Springs, Brewster Side Bar, or Jackson Side Bar, or Thomas Coil Springs.**

**Your choice, Piano Box or Corning Body.**

**Our B grade work is guaranteed for two years.** We issue a special binding two years' guaranty with every rig, though with care they will last a natural life time.

**Our B grade is a standard grade of goods** such as is generally carried by wholesale houses, repositories and first class retail dealers, and the highest grade carried by many. Well finished, guaranteed, honest work. **No. 2 wheels;** not a No. 3 or 4 wheel in any of our guaranteed work. Wheels sold by many as No. 1. **A good, honest, hickory wheel,** much better than the poorest, in fact, in quality far above the average.

**If you want a good honest low priced top buggy** we can recommed these at our special price of $32.98 cash **in full with order.**

**If you would like to see a better selection we would refer you to our Special Vehicle Catalogue,** which will be mailed free to any address on application. This shows a very complete line of vehicles.

**At our special $34.00 price you have** the privilege of C. O. D. shipment as explained in the introductory pages.

**No. 92805.**

**No. 92806.**

**No. 92807.**

**The above Illustrations, Engraved from Photographs, will give you an idea of the appearance of these rigs.**

## THEY ARE THE BEST TOP BUGGIES EVER OFFERED AT ANYTHING LIKE THE PRICE....

**AND ARE EQUAL TO BUGGIES** that are being sold by retail dealers at $50.00 to $60.00, Equal to Buggies that are being advertised by many catalogue houses at $50.00 to $60.00; THOROUGHLY HONEST MEDIUM PRICED CLASS OF GOODS.

### Description of Work.

**BODY—Full size, outside measurement 22 inches wide at bottom,** 23 inches at top, 52 inches long, round corners, swell panels. Panels 8 inches deep with two braces for the panel inside in addition to the seat frame braces. Seat, 27 inches wide at bottom, 15 inches deep, 38½ inches wide at top of seat panel. Seat panel 6 inches deep. 11 inches from floor to bottom of seat and 15 inches from floor to top of cushion. The seat is held to the body by two wrought iron seat rods going through the sills. The frame of the body is made of the best seasoned white ash, mortised, glued and screwed. Panels and seat are made of the best seasoned poplar, screwed, plugged and glued. The sill is rabbetted out and the floor sets in this rabbet, letting the floor down even and flush with top sill. The step bar is seasoned oak and gained in the sill from the under side, making it impossible to break through the bottom when putting your weight on the step. Has full length Norway iron body loops and 6 inch rub irons. Distance from top of cushion to roof of top 39 inches; inside measurement 37 inches; between the bows at top is 44 inches. We can also furnish these jobs in what we call three-quarter jobs or smaller sizes For three-quarters job the body is 19 inches wide at the bottom, 20 inches at top, outside measurement. Seat, 24 inches at bottom and 30¼ inches at top. Seat panels 6 inches wide and 34 inches between the bows. Height of back, depth of panels, length of top, distance between cushion and roof are the same as the regular sized buggy, and it is constructed in the same substantial and workmanlike manner.

**GEARS—On regular Buggy, 15-16** double collar, best steel axle with graceful downward sweep. Hickory axle cap closely fitted to the axle, double perch of best hickory with steel plates running the entire length. The gear is substantially braced by wrought iron stays running from perch to rear axle. We use the full half circle fifth wheel, the best known to the carriage trade with king bolt back of axle. The spring bars are of good hickory with a handsome scroll cut on the ends. Springs are of the best tempered steel with Berlin head, making it the easiest rider on the market.

**WHEELS**—Good, honest No. 2 wheels, Sarven's patent or shell band hub as desired; 38 by 42 or 40 by 44 inches, as desired; ⅞ or ¾ inch tread, as desired. Good, honest wheels, having 16 spokes and bolted between each spoke; ¼ inch round edge steel tire.

**TRIMMING AND PAINTING**—Cushions and back trimmed in imitation leather or 12 oz. dark green cloth, biscuit pattern, with a roll. When especially ordered we trim cushions and back with leather, and when leather trimmed we upholster the seat panels. See extras below.

**TOP**—3 bow, steel sockets, enamelled drill top with a good head lining and padded and lined back stays. Green back, side and back curtains. Brewster curtain fasteners for back curtains and black carriage knobs neatly fitted for side curtains. Stitched imitation leather valance and leather roll up straps. For leather quarter, full leather top and lined curtains see extras below.

**PAINTING**—We use the old standby system of oil and lead in forming the groundwork for our painting, which insures durability as well as retaining the luster of the varnish when finished. The body is jet black while the gear is a dark Brewster green with a line of carmine and a line of gold striping and maple leaf gold touch up, making a rich combination.

**We furnish** the buggy with nickel dash rail when desired. See extras.

**Width of track,** 4 ft. 8 in. or 5 ft. 2 in., as desired.

**Our special price, $34.00 or $32.98** for cash in full with order, is for the buggy complete with toe carpet, wrench, storm apron, anti-rattlers and shafts.

| | |
|---|---|
| Extra for pole with neckyoke and whiffletrees complete in place of shafts | **$2.00** |
| Extra for both pole and shafts | **4.00** |
| Extra for leather quarter top | **3.00** |
| Extra for full leather top | **5.00** |
| Extra for leather cushions | **1.50** |
| Extra for silver plating throughout, including hub bands, top prop nuts and dash rail | **1.00** |
| Extra for full length Brussels carpet, side panels lined and bound with Brussels carpet | **1.00** |

**These buggies are made in southern Michigan, central Indiana and southern Ohio.** We have contracts with several of the largest manufacturers in America; concerns whose well earned reputation for the manufacture of first class work is **a guaranty** for the quality. The prices quoted are for the buggies carefully crated and delivered on board the cars at the factory. We will ship from the factory nearest to our customer's railroad station. This buggy is accepted by the railroad companies at 350 pounds though it weighs nearer 400. The carrying capacity of this buggy is about 450 pounds.

**You cannot afford to buy a cheap showy buggy** with a D grade wheel and second quality material covered up with putty and paint, made for show and not for service, when for a few dollars more you can get an honest rig that is guaranteed and will give satisfaction.

**BUY A COLUMBUS, OHIO, VEHICLE. IT WILL PAY YOU. A BIG LINE SHOWN IN OUR FREE VEHICLE CATALOGUE.**

# OUR $35.90 TOP BUGGIES.

**This is our regular B Grade work, guaranteed for two years. A written binding guarantee accompanies each vehicle.**

By the terms and conditions of this guarantee if any piece or part gives out within two years by reason of defective material or workmanship we will replace it free of charge. With care one of these buggies will last a natural life-time.

**These buggies are made for us under contract** in various factories in southern Ohio, central and southern Indiana and southern Michigan. **They are made by concerns of established reputation** and are a high standard of work. For more complete information concerning our B grade work please refer to description of grades AA, A and B.

**The freight on these buggies will amount to next to nothing** as compared with what you will save in price. The net weight of the buggy is 380 lbs.; when crated 430 lbs. Carrying capacity, 500 lbs. As a rule railroad companies will accept these buggies at 350 lbs., and by referring to our freight classification in the front part of this book you can calculate very closely what the freight will amount to to your place. If you live east or south of Chicago the freight will be less than from Chicago as the distance is less.

**By sending us $35.90 cash in full with your order** you will get such a buggy as you could not buy at retail at $50.00, in fact, a buggy equal to those often retailed at $75.00 and upwards. We furnish this buggy in end spring, Brewster sidebar spring, Jackson sidebar spring or Thomas Coil spring, as desired. We furnish this buggy in imitation leather, leather quarter or full leather top.

We offer these buggies at $37.00 on our regular terms, C. O. D., subject to examination on receipt of the required amount of deposit. If cash in full accompanies your order you can deduct 3 per cent. or $35.90 will pay for the rig.

**THE ILLUSTRATIONS** engraved from photographs will give you an idea of the appearance of these buggies. They are thoroughly honest, up to date, well finished work, made for service as well as for appearance.

### GENERAL DESCRIPTION.

**BODY**—The frame of the body is made of the best seasoned white ash, mortised, glued and screwed. **THE PANELS and SEATS** are made of the best seasoned poplar, all screwed, plugged and glued. **THE SILL** is rabbeted out and the floor sets in this rabbett, letting the floor down even and flush with top sill. **THE STEP BAR** is of seasoned oak and gained in the sill from the under side, making it impossible to break through the bottom when putting your weight on the step. Has full length Norway iron **BODY LOOPS,** 6 inch **RUB IRONS. THE BODY** is 52 inches long, 22 inches wide at bottom, 23 inches at top. **PANELS,** 8 inches deep. Made with two braces to the panel inside in addition to the seat frame brace. **SEAT** is 27 inches wide at the bottom, 15 inches deep, and 38½ inches to top of seat panel. **SEAT PANEL** is 26 inches deep, 11 inches from the floor to the bottom of seat and 15 inches from the floor to the top of cushion. **THE SEAT** is held to the body by two wrought iron seat rods going through the sills. Distance from top of cushion to roof of top, 39 inches; inside measurement 37 inches; between the bows at top is 44 inches.

We can furnish any of these rigs in three-fourths size when desired, making the **BODY** 19 inches wide at the bottom and 20 inches at the top; **SEAT** 24 inches at bottom and 34½ inches at top. Height of back, depth of panels, length of top, distance between top cushions and roof are the same as the regular sized buggy, and constructed in the same substantial and workmanlike manner.

**GEARS**—These buggies have our regular 15-16 inch double collar, best **STEEL AXLE** with a graceful downward sweep; **HICKORY AXLE CAPS** closely fitted to the axle, double perch of best hickory with steel plates running the entire length. **THE GEAR** is substantially braced by wrought iron stays running from perch to rear axle. We use the full back circle fifth wheel, the best known to the carriage trade, with king bolt back of axle. The **SPRING BARS** are of good hickory with handsome scroll cut on the ends. **SPRINGS** are

See list of additions and extra prices below.

**No. 92808. Order by Number.**

of the best tempered steel with the Berlin head, making it the easiest rider on the market.

**WHEELS**—Sarven's patent or shell band hub, as desired, 38 or 40 front, 40 or 44 inch rear; ⅞ or ¾ inch tread, as desired; 16 spokes, bolted between each spoke. This is a good, honest No. 2 wheel and warranted in every respect.

**TRIMMING AND PAINTING**—**CUSHIONS** and **BACK** are trimmed in imitation leather or 12 oz. dark green cloth in biscuit pattern with a roll. We can furnish this rig with any style trimming at additional cost. See extras below.

**TOP**—3 or 4 bow, **STEEL SOCKETS,** enamelled drill top, good head lining and padded and lined back stays. Green back, side and back curtains. **BREWSTER CURTAIN FASTENERS** for back curtain and black carriage knobs neatly fitted for side curtains. Stitched imitation leather valance and leather roll up straps. For leather quarter or full leather see extras below.

**PAINTING**—We use the old standby system of oil and lead in forming the groundwork for our painting, which insures durability as well as retaining the luster of the varnish when finished. **THE BODY** is jet black while **THE GEAR** is a dark Brewster green with a line of carmine and a line of gold striping and maple leaf gold touchup, making a rich combination.

Our special offer price of $35.90 cash with order, or $37.00 on C. O. D. terms, includes your choice of the above buggies complete with imitation leather top, spring boot, storm apron, jute toe carpet, wrench, anti-rattlers and shafts.

These buggies can be had with the following extras at the additional prices named.

| | |
|---|---:|
| For leather quarter top, add...... ..................... | $3.00 |
| For full leather top, add...... | 5.00 |
| For leather cushions or 16 oz. English wool dyed body cloth, add...... | 1.50 |
| For solid panel back, add...... | 1.00 |
| For nickel trimmings, including hub bands, prop nuts, and dash rail...... | 1.00 |
| For full length Brussels carpet and Brussels carpet lined side panels ,add...... | 1.00 |
| For pole with neckyoke and whiffletrees complete in place of shafts, add...... | 2.00 |
| For both pole and shafts, add...... | 4.00 |

**No. 92809. Order by Number.**

**Be sure to state width of track wanted, 4 ft. 8 inches, or 5 ft. 2 inches.**

We would especially invite your attention to the catalogues issued by other houses and ask that you make a careful comparison of our prices and the goods we offer. If you do not find we are not only lower but far lower in price we will not expect your orders. We know we are in a position to give you such values in the vehicle line as can be had from no other concern. Send for our special free Vehicle Catalogue, if you do not find in this book the vehicle wanted. Our special Vehicle Catalogue is the most complete book of the kind published, and includes about everything made that runs on wheels.

**WE ARE HEADQUARTERS FOR COLUMBUS, O., VEHICLES. THERE ARE NO BETTER.**

# $37.83
## FOR A
# B GRADE
# TOP
# BUGGY.

**Our Special Price of $37.83 is for this Buggy, cash** in full with order. **$39.00 is our regular price,** and at $39.00 we will send the buggy to any address, C. O. D., subject to examination when our regular terms of shipment are complied with, the necessary deposit received, etc.

**Where cash in full accompanies** your order we allow a discount of 3%, in which case $37.83 pays for the buggy.

**A binding 2 years' guarantee goes with every buggy.** By the terms and conditions of this guarantee if any piece or part gives out by reason of defective material or workmanship, we will replace it free of charge. With care these buggies will last a life-time.

**See full description of Grades AA, A, B and Special B** on previous pages.

**Our B Grade Vehicles are thoroughly** good honest made work. They are made in southern Ohio, central Indiana and southern Michigan by manufacturers of established reputation, and will compare favorably with vehicles you would be asked nearly double the price for from retail dealers.

**We furnish these Buggies** in either End Spring, Brewster Side bar, Jackson Side bar or Thomas Coil, as desired; in Piano Box or Corning body, as desired. Be sure to state style wanted and in ordering never fail to state width of track, whether 4 feet 8 inches, or 5 feet 2 inches.

**We furnish this rig with extra trimming when wanted.** See full particulars concerning extras and changes at bottom of page.

**T**HE Illustrations engraved from Photographs will give you some idea of the appearance of this work. The buggies we offer you at $39.00 C. O. D., OR $37.83 CASH WITH ORDER, are such buggies as were never before offered at anything like the price. We are able to make these extraordinarily low prices only by reason of our very large output and the big contracts we make with manufacturers, always on a spot cash basis.

## GENERAL DESCRIPTION.

**THE FRAME OF BODY** is made of the best seasoned white ash, mortised, glued and screwed. Panels and seats are made of the best seasoned poplar, all screwed, plugged and glued. The sill is rabbeted out and the floor sets in the rabbet, letting the floor down even and flush with the top sill. The step bar is of seasoned oak, and gained in the sill from the under side, making it impossible to break through the bottom when putting your weight on the step. The body is 52 inches long by 23 inches wide; round corners, swell panels. Panels 8 inches deep. The seat is held to the body by two wrought iron seat rods going through the sills. Body has full length Norway iron body loops and 6 inch rub irons. Distance from top of cushion to roof of top, 39 inches; inside measurement 37 inches between the bows. Top is 44 inches long. We also furnish these rigs in three-quarter size when so desired, in which case the body is 19 inches wide at bottom and 20 inches at top outside measurement, 34 inches between the bows. Height of back, depth of panels, length of top, distance between top of cushion and roof are all the same as the regular sized buggy, and it is constructed in the same substantial and workman like manner.

## GEAR.

**WE USE OUR REGULAR 15-16** double collar best steel axle, fantail and swedged, with graceful downward sweep. Second growth hickory axle caps closely and securely fitted to the axle by Norway wrought iron clips, including the shackles and saddle clips. Double perch, best hickory, steel plates running entire length. The gear is substantially braced by wrought iron stays running from perch to rear axle. We use

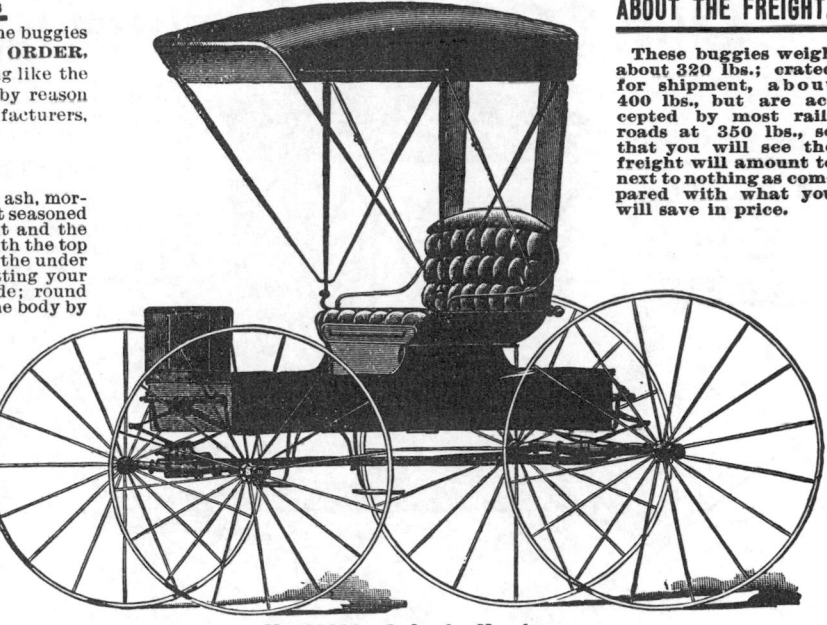

No. 92810. Order by Number.

full back circle fifth wheel, the best known to the carriage trade, with king bolt back of axle. The spring bars are of second growth hickory with handsome scroll cut on the end. Springs are of the best oil tempered steel.

## WHEELS.

Sarven's patent or shell band hub, as desired; 38 and 42 inches, or 40 and 44 inches, as desired; 1 inch, ⅞ inch or ¾ inch tread, as desired; 16 spokes and bolted between each spoke. A good, honest, guaranteed wheel.

## TRIMMING AND PAINTING.

Cushions and backs are trimmed in 16 oz. wool dyed body cloth of a fine texture, dark green, in diamond pattern; upholstered seat. This buggy has solid panel back, soft springs. When so specified we will trim these buggies with leather throughout. Brussels carpet full length, toe pad, also inside panels with same carpet, No. 1 dash, patent leather, 11x24 inches, storm apron and boot.

## TOP.

3 or 4 bow, steel sockets, imitation leather. (Full leather or leather quarter can be had; see extras below.) Good weight, very dark green head lining, back stays are padded and lined with body cloth. Brewster curtain fasteners for back curtain and black carriage knobs neatly fitted for side curtains. Stitched patent roll up straps, stitched valance, front and rear.

## NICKEL PLATED.

This buggy is full nickel trimmed, including hub bands, seat handles, prop cuts and dash rail.

## PAINTING.

We use the old standby system of oil and lead in forming the ground work, which insures durability as well as retaining the luster of the varnish when finished. The body is jet black, gear, dark Brewster green, ornamented with gold line and maple leaf gold touch up, making the richest combination possible finishing a buggy. When so desired, we will finish the gear in carmine.

No. 92811. Order by Number.

**Our Special Price of $37.83 Cash with Order, or $39.00 C. O. D.** subject to examination, is for any one of the above described buggies complete with storm apron, full length carpet, nickel plated trimmings throughout, imitation rubber top and shafts complete.

Extra for leather quarter top................................................$3.00
Extra for pole with neckyoke and whiffletrees complete in place of shafts .................................................................. 2.00

Extra for full leather top and back curtains......................$5.00
Extra for both pole and shafts........ ........... .................. 4.00

By adding any of the above amounts to our special price, $37.83, cash in full with order, or $39.00 C. O. D., you will get the cost of the complete rig trimmed as you like it.

OUR COLUMBUS AA, A AND B GRADE VEHICLES LEAD ALL OTHERS. IT WILL PAY YOU TO GET A COLUMBUS JOB.

# WE ARE HEADQUARTERS FOR COLUMBUS, O. BUGGIES

**AND WE RECOMMEND THE COLUMBUS, O. BUGGIES ABOVE** all others. For the coming season we have made our contract with one of the oldest, largest and most reliable manufacturers in America, at **Columbus, Ohio,** a concern with a world-wide and enviable reputation for their complete line, including open buggies, top buggies, phaetons, surreys, carriages, etc.

**FOR THE FIRST TIME THIS WORK WILL BE** put on the market at a price within easy reach of all. Never before has this class of work been sold, even in a wholesale way and in carload lots, at anything like the prices we are now able to offer.

**THERE WERE SO MANY FAILURES LAST YEAR** among carriage manufactnrers that the Columbus concern decided to make its contract with us, and as we take all their surplus product they were willing to figure on the basis of actual cost that they might keep their factory running. To this we add our one small percentage of profit and this is all you have to pay.

**ALL COLUMBUS VEHICLES ARE QUOTED F. O. B. FACTORY AT COLUMBUS, OHIO,** from which point you must figure the freight. If you live east or southeast of Chicago the freight will be less than from Chicago. If you live west or northwest of Chicago, the freight will be about 40c per cwt. more than from Chicago. In ordering it will pay you to select a Columbus vehicle, even at the slight additional cost, as you will have a rig that will give you the best service and one that will be far cheaper in the end than the cheaper grade of work which is generally offered by wholesale and retail dealers.

**UNDERSTAND THE COLUMBUS WORK** heretofore has only been handled by comparatively few dealers in large cities, and there almost exclusively by the Columbus company's own representatives.

# OUR $39.90 COLUMBUS, O. TOP BUGGY.

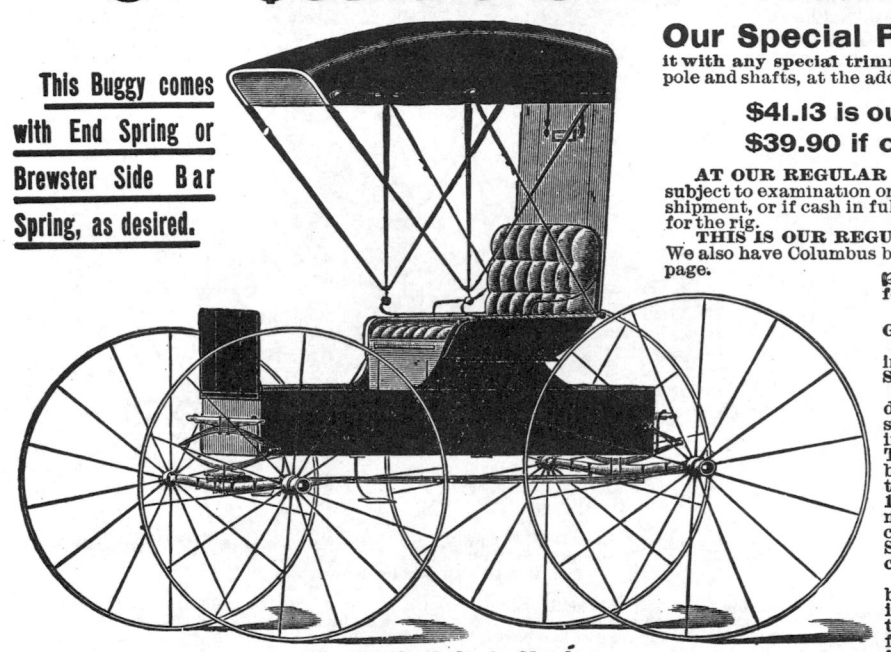

This Buggy comes with End Spring or Brewster Side Bar Spring, as desired.

No. 92812. Order by Number.

**Our Special Price of $39.90** is for the Buggy as illustrated and described. We can furnish it with any special trimming, any special finish, with either pole or shafts, or both pole and shafts, at the additional prices named at the bottom of page.

**$41.13 is our regular price for this Buggy,**
**$39.90 if cash in full accompanies the order.**

AT OUR REGULAR PRICE $41.13, we will ship the buggy by freight C. O. D. subject to examination on receipt of the required deposit as explained in our terms of shipment, or if cash in full accompanies your order you can deduct 3%, or $39.90 pays for the rig.

THIS IS OUR REGULAR B GRADE BUGGY. We also furnish it in A grade. We also have Columbus buggies in AA grade as illustrated and described on another page.

☞ For more complete Descriptions, Illustrations, etc., send for our Free Vehicle Catalogue.

THE ILLUSTRATIONS ENGRAVED FROM PHOTOGRAPHS will give you some idea of the appearance of this rig.

We furnish this buggy in either square piano box or Corning body as illustrated; in **End Spring** or **Brewster Side Bar Spring,** as desired.

**GEAR.**—We build this job on an end elliptic spring with drop axles, or **Brewster Side Bar Spring** with arch axles, as desired. Make it either in 4 feet 4 inch., 4 feet 8 inch., or 5 feet 2 inch. track, as desired. Be sure to state the track wanted. The fifth wheel is full wrought Derby with double king bolt braced. Axles are all steel, spindles steel converted, making them very hard and impervious to wear. Size of axles, ⅞ and 1 inch. All gear woods, axle caps, spring bars and reaches are made of selected second growth hickory. Axle caps are cemented firmly to each axle. Reaches ironed full length. Springs of the best steel, oil tempered and tested. All bolts, clips and forgings of best Norway iron.

**WHEELS.**—We use either Sarven's patent or compressed band wheels, as ordered; ¾ or ⅞ inch tread. Tire on all wheels is steel and round edge projecting over the felloes just enough to protect the wood from wear. We use wheels in height as follows: 3 feet front, 3 feet 4 inches rear; or 3 feet 2 inches front, 3 feet 6 inches rear; or 3 feet 4 inches front, 3 feet 8 inches rear. The tire is bolted between each spoke.

**SHAFTS.**—All are made of selected second growth hickory and of the latest design. They are substantially ironed with heavy iron so that the heels will not straighten out in use.

**BODY.**—We furnish this buggy with a body 22 inches wide only and 52 inches long with concave seat raisers. All bodies and seats are made with the best yellow poplar panels and second growth ash sills, put together in the best possible manner, screwed and plugged from the outside and inside. The seat in width, measuring over top of cushion, is 31½ inches, depth 16½ inches, height of back of cushion 14½ inches.

**TRIMMINGS.**—In this our regular B grade, the seat and back are trimmed in either green cloth or green leather. We make it with both spring back and spring cushion. The cushion has wings on the sides covering inside of seat. The back of the seat is wood, painted the same as the body. We use a full length carpet and also a heavy rubber boot over back of body. The dash frame is made of the best steel and covered with a good quality enameled leather.

**MOUNTINGS.**—We furnish this buggy with silver mountings if desired, such as dash rail, hub bands, hand holds and top prop nuts without extra charge.

**TOP.**—Made with a full leather top excepting half rubber side curtains, or with top made of leather quarter, or with heavy rubber imitation leather throughout.

At our special price of $41.13 we furnish the imitation leather. **For leather quarter and full leather see extras below. The shifting rail is so arranged** that the top can be taken off the seat without any trouble whatever, making an open buggy.

**PAINTING.**—All bodies are painted black regularly with gears of Brewster green, although if desired we can paint the gears either black or carmine. Gears, wheels and shafts striped in an artistic and elegant manner. In painting this buggy we use the best material to be obtained in leads and oils and give the work plenty of time to dry so that the paint will stand in any climate.

Our special price, $41.13 C. O. D. or $39.90 cash in full with order, is for the buggy complete in our regular B grade with full length carpet, anti-rattlers and shafts.

**EXTRA FOR POLE WITH NECKYOKE** and Whiffletrees in place of shafts, $2.00. Extra for both pole and shafts, $4.00. Extra for leather quarter top, $4.00. Extra for full leather top, $6.00.

## THE SAME BUGGY IN OUR A GRADE,

which is a better finished rig, having the very best No. 1 wheels, painted in 13 coats, the first coats rubbed out with pumice stone, cushions, back and top lined with 18 ounce English wool dyed body cloth or machine buffed leather, genuine machine buffed leather quarter top, nickel plated throughout, full length Brussels carpet, panels lined with Brussels carpet, a strictly fine Vehicle in every particular.

**OUR PRICE FOR RIG COMPLETE WITH SHAFTS** and leather quarter top, $49.00.
For Full Leather Top, $52.00. 3 per cent discount if cash in full accompanies your order.

No. 92813. Order by Number.

☞ **Be Sure to State the Width of Track Wanted.** ☞ **Be Sure to State whether B or A Grade. BOTH A and B GRADES are Guaranteed for Two (2) Years, and will Last a Lifetime.** ☞ **Buy the Columbus, O. Buggies.**

# OUR $55.00 A GRADE AND $65.00 AA GRADE TOP BUGGY

**$55.00 IS THE PRICE OF OUR A GRADE COLUMBUS TOP BUGGY IN LEATHER QUARTER.**
**$65.00 IS THE PRICE OF OUR AA GRADE COLUMBUS TOP BUGGY IN LEATHER QUARTER.**

FOR FULL LEATHER TOP ADD $5.00.

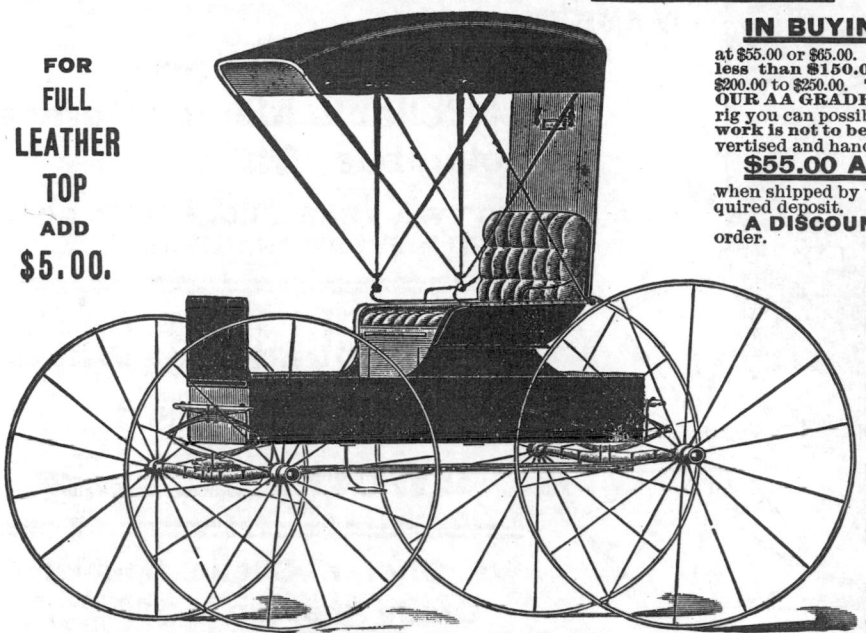

No. 92814. Order by Number.

The above illustration engraved from a photograph will give you some idea of the appearance of our AA and A grades of Top Buggies.

3 feet 2 inch and 3 feet 6 inch, or 3 feet 4 inch and 3 feet 8 inch in height. The material in the wheels is strictly second growth hickory of the very finest quality, and they are put together in the most approved manner possible. Tire is carefully bolted between each spoke. A set of the wheels used in this buggy is worth five sets of the commen Special B grade.

**SHAFTS.** Shafts are all made of selected second growth hickory, of the latest design. They are substantially ironed with heavy irons so that the heels will not straighten out in use.

**BODY AND SEAT.** WE FURNISH THIS JOB IN EITHER PIANO BOX BODY, as illustrated, or CORNING BODY, and can furnish the body in either 20, 22 or 25 inch width. ALL BODIES are 52 inches long. The CORNING BODY is 23 inches wide and 50 inches long. All bodies and seats are made of the best poplar panels second growth ash sills, are put together in the best manner, screwed and plugged from inside and outside. WIDTH OF SEAT, on 20 inch body, measuring over top of cushion, 26 inches; depth, 16 inches; height of back over cushion, 14 inches. WIDTH OF SEAT on 22 inch body, 30 inches; depth, 16 inches; height of back above cushion, 14½ inches. WIDTH OF SEAT on 25 inch, or regular sized body, measuring over top of cushion, 31 ins. Depth, 16 inches; height of back over cushion, 14½ inches. On the Corning body, width of seat measuring over top of cushion, 31 ins.; depth 17 inches; height of back above cushion, 15 inches.

**TRIMMINGS.** We trim the Seat and back in either the very finest imported all wool English green or blue body cloth, or green genuine machine buffed leather. We use the very best spring back and spring seat cushions. The back of the seat is also wood painted same as body. We use a full length velvet carpet, heavy rubber boot over back of body, and dash frame is made of best steel, covered with the very finest enameled leather.

**MOUNTINGS.** We furnish this Buggy with silver mountings throughout.

**PAINTING.** Our AA grade buggies are painted in the very highest style of the art, in 13 coats of paint, the first coats rubbed out with pumice stone. Nothing but the very best grade of paints, oils and varnishes are used, and they are given ample time to dry in a dark, dust proof room, which is kept at an even temperature. Bodies are black, gear dark green with suitable gold stripe.

**IN OUR AA GRADE BUGGIES** we furnish the very best machine buffed leather quarter top, or at $5.00 extra, full leather top. All tops have machine buffed solid leather valance, front and rear, sewed on. The head lining is of the very best imported all wool English green dyed body cloth.

**IN BUYING A TOP BUGGY** it will pay you to buy the highest grade COLUMBUS work either at $55.00 or $65.00. You will get such a buggy as you could not buy at retail at less than $150.00, a buggy equal to those which have been retailed at even $200.00 to $250.00. THERE IS NOTHING FINER IN A TOP BUGGY THAN OUR AA GRADE COLUMBUS TOP BUGGY AT $65.00, and it is the cheapest rig you can possibly buy when you consider the quality. Our A and AA grade work is not to be compared with cheap work that is being so extensively advertised and handled through the regular wholesale trade.

**$55.00 AND $65.00 ARE OUR REGULAR PRICES** when shipped by freight C. O. D. subject to examination on receipt of our required deposit.

**A DISCOUNT OF 3%** will be allowed if cash in full accompanies your order.

☞OUR SPECIAL $65.00 TOP BUGGY, is the finest buggy we make and the best buggy turned out by the manufacturer at Columbus, O. YOU WILL GET NOTHING BETTER NO MATTER HOW MUCH YOU MAY PAY.

## DESCRIPTION OF OUR AA GRADE $65.00 TOP BUGGIES.

**GEAR.** We build this job either with a piano box body as shown in the cut, or with a Corning body, as desired. We build it with arch axles and Brewster springs, or with drop axles and elliptic end springs, as desired. The fifth wheel is full wrought, the finest grade; axles all of steel, highest grade; spindles, steel converted, making them very hard and impervious to wear. Size of axles, ⅞ by 1 inch. All gear wood, such as axle caps, spring bars, side bars and reaches are of the very best, carefully selected second growth Michigan hickory. Reaches are ironed full length with the very best Norway iron. Springs of the best tool steel, oil tempered and tested. All bolts, clips and forgings are of the very best Norway buggy iron.

**WHEELS.** We use the highest grade wheel we can get in this grade work, either Sarven's patent or compressed band wheel as ordered. The wheels on our A or AA grade work will be as good as new when the cheaper grade of wheel will have long since been worn out. ¾ or ⅞ inch tread, tire is of the very best tire steel, round edge projecting over the felloes just enough to protect the wood from wear. We can furnish wheels for this job either

Be sure to state width of track wanted, 4 feet 8 ins. or 5 feet 2 inches.

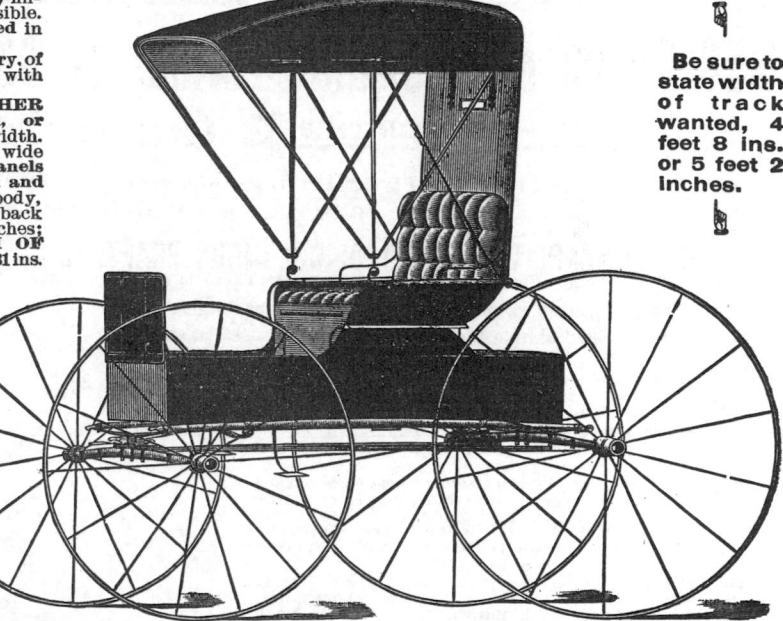

No. 92815. Order by Number.
The above illustration engraved from a photograph will give you some idea of the appearance of our AA and A grades of Top Buggies.

The Bows to the Top are Leather Covered, the Top Prop Nuts are Leather Covered, the Seat Handles are Leather Covered, the Steps have Rubber Covered Step Pads. All these features only to be found on the very finest work. It is not only these little points alone that go to make this Buggy the very best, but the fact that only the most skilled mechanics are allowed to work on the AA grade, nothing but the very finest material enters into every piece and part of the work, and when completed there is nothing finer in appearance, more durable or better made at any price.

**AT $65.00 LEATHER QUARTER TOP, OR $70.00 IN FULL LEATHER TOP,** we furnish the AA Grade Columbus Top Buggy with full length Velvet Carpet, Toe Carpet, Panel Carpet, Full Length Side and Back Curtains, Storm Apron, Leather Foot Protectors to both sides of box, Anti-Rattlers and Shafts.

**FOR POLE WITH NECKYOKE AND WIFFLETREES** complete, in place of Shafts, add $3.50.
**FOR BOTH POLE AND SHAFTS** add $6.00.

**OUR A GRADE AT $55.00 IN FULL LEATHER QUARTER TOP, OR $60.00 IN FULL LEATHER TOP** is a buggy exactly like the illustration above, and a buggy that will compare in every way with any buggy you can buy elsewhere at from $75.00 to $100.00. It has the highest grade wheel, the very best material in every piece and part. The leather is all genuine machine buffed leather. The difference in price to you is only the difference in cost to us, and that is in trimmings and workmanship. This A Grade Buggy at $55.00 and $60.00 does not have the leather covered bows and leather covered prop nuts, the leather covered seat handles, the rubber covered step pads; it is not painted in 13 coats, nor made and finished by the same class of workmen. It is, however, A STRICTLY HIGH GRADE BUGGY, one that we can recommend in every way, and a buggy we GUARANTEE FOR TWO YEARS, and one that will last a natural life time. We would recommend by all means you buy OUR COLUMBUS, O., A GRADE BUGGY AT $55.00 OR $60.00 if you do not buy our AA GRADE COLUMBUS AT $65.00 OR $70.00.

**FOR ADDITIONS TO THE A GRADE COLUMBUS AT $55.00 AND $60.00,** add for pole with neckyoke and whiffletrees, in place of shafts, $2.50. For both pole and shafts, $4.50.

**THE BUSINESS WE DO IN WATCHES, JEWELRY, ETC., WOULD BE CONSIDERED LARGE FOR THE BIGGEST WHOLESALER IN THE COUNTRY. NO WONDER WHEN YOU SEE OUR PRICES AND LIBERAL TERMS,**

# OUR $58.00 B GRADE COLUMBUS PHAETON.

## This is a Genuine Columbus, O. Phaeton,

With
care they
will
Last a
Lifetime.

**MADE BY**

**One of the Oldest and Most Reliable Manufacturers in Columbus, Ohio.**

A BINDING TWO YEAR'S GUARANTY GOES WITH EVERY PHAETON.

## OUR REGULAR B GRADE
## Guaranteed
## Work

**We Offer a Cheap Special B Grade Phaeton at $39.90.**

No. 92816. Order by Number.

We have many other grades of Phaeton's in our Special Vehicle Catalogue which will be mailed free to any Address upon application.

# $58.00 on our Regular Terms, or $56.25 Cash in Full with Order,

### IS OUR PRICE FOR THIS B Grade Columbus Phaeton.

**The Illustrations Engraved from Photographs** will give you some idea of the appearance of these Phaetons. They come in either **CANOPY** top or **LEATHER QUARTER** extension top, as illustrated.

**DO NOT COMPARE THESE B GRADE COLUMBUS PHAETONS** with the cheap work that is being offered at from $45.00 to $60.00. There is no comparison.

These Phaetons will Compare Favorably with any Phaeton you can Buy at Retail at from $100.00 to $125.00.

These Phaetons have the very latest style body.
**The Body is** 28½ inches wide; **Seat is** 32½ inches wide at bottom and 37 inches at top; **Depth of Seat** inside, 20 inches; **Height of Seat** from bottom to top, 22 inches; **Height of Panel**, inside measurement, 9½ inches.

**UPHOLSTERING.**—They are Upholstered in genuine machine buffed leather, or all wool imported green English body cloth, full spring back, tufted seats and backs.

**GEAR.**—The Gear is from the very best selected second growth Hickory, ironed throughout with Norway iron, **Reaches** ironed full length. **Springs** are of the best Crucible steel, tempered in oil. **Wheels** are thoroughly first class standard grade, guaranteed for two years, either Sarven's patent or shell band hub as desired.

**PAINTING.**—The painting on this Phaeton, like all our B grade work, is done with the very best of materials, including the best paints, oils and varnishes. **BODY** black, gear dark Brewster green with suitable gold stripe.

**This Phaeton comes complete** with whip socket, Brussels carpet, anti-rattlers and shafts.

You will observe this Phaeton is hung very low, the bottom of step being but 15 inches from the ground. It is one of the most stylish phaetons on the market, regardless of price.

**TOP.**—At our special price of $58.00 C. O. D., or $56.25 cash in full with order, we furnish this phaeton in either **LEATHER** quarter top with full length side and back curtains or with **Canopy** top with full length side and back curtains, as desired. **OUR** price includes very fancy nickel plated lanterns and wide fenders.

No. 92817. Order by Number.

**Extra for Pole** with Neckyoke and Whiffletrees complete in place of shafts, $2.00. **EXTRA FOR BOTH POLE AND SHAFTS, $4.00.**

**Extra for Full Leather Top** in place of Leather Quarter Top, $4.00. **Extra for very Large Swell Wing Dash,** in place of Dash above Illustrated, $3.50.

## We Show a very Extensive Line of AA, A, B and Special B Phaetons in Our Special Vehicle Catalogue

### WHICH WE WILL MAIL FREE TO ANY ADDRESS ON APPLICATION.

NEVER WAS CLOTHING SEEN OR HEARD OF SO CHEAP AS YOU FIND IT ILLUSTRATED AND DESCRIBED ON THE CLOTHING PAGES OF THIS CATALGUE. WE DO A LARGER BUSINESS IN CLOTHING THAN ANY THREE MAIL ORDER HOUSES IN CHICAGO.

# Our $76.63 Columbus A Grade Canopy Top Park Wagon Surrey.

**$76.63 is our Net Cash with Order Price with Cash Discount Taken Off.**

**$79.00 is our Regular Price when Shipped on Regular C. O. D. Terms.** SEE SPECIAL C. O. D. TERMS.

## WE HAVE CHEAPER SURREYS, and we also Show a very Extensive Line of Higher Grade Surreys In OUR SPECIAL VEHICLE CATALOGUE.

### For A More Complete Line You Should Send For Our Special Vehicle Catalogue.

No. 92818. Order by Number.

**Remember**

**This is a Genuine Columbus, O. Buggy**

Made by One of the Largest and Most Reliable Manufacturers at Columbus, O.

**A BINDING**

**Two Year's Guarantee Goes with Every Vehicle**

By the Terms and Conditions of which if any piece or part gives out by reason of defective material or workmanship we will replace it free of charge.

With care this Surrey will last a natural lifetime.

**THE ABOVE ILLUSTRATION, ENGRAVED FROM A PHOTOGRAPH,** will give you some idea of the appearance of this surrey. We describe it as follows.

## DESCRIPTION.

**GEAR.** We build this vehicle in two elliptic end springs only, as shown in cut. Both axles are drop. We make it with 4 ft. 8 in. or 5 ft. 2 in. track, as desired. The fifth wheel is full wrought with heavy king bolt braced. Axles are all steel. Spindles, steel converted, making them very hard and impervious to wear. Size of axles, 1 1-6 by 1⅛ inches front and rear. All gear wood, such as axle clips, spring bars and reaches are selected hickory. Axle caps are cemented firmly to each axle. Reaches are ironed full length in the most substantial manner. Springs are of the very best steel, oil tempered and tested. All clips, bolts and forgings are of the best Norway iron.

**WHEELS.** We use either Sarven's patent or compressed band wheels, as desired, and they are strictly first class guaranteed goods, ⅞ or 1 inch tread, as desired. Tire on all wheels is steel, electric welded, round edge, projecting over the felloes just enough to protect the wood from wear. The material in the wheel is strictly first class in every respect, made in the most approved manner and guaranteed to stand any climate. Tire is bolted between each spoke.

**SHAFTS.** All shafts are made of selected hickory and of the latest design. They are substantially ironed with heavy irons so that the heels will not straighten out in use.

**BODY AND SEATS.** We furnish this surrey with a body exactly like that shown in cut, 70 inches long and 24 inches wide. In making the same we use the best selected yellow poplar for panels and second growth ash for sills, put together in the securest manner possible, screwed and plugged from inside and outside. Seats measure in width over top of cushion, 34 inches. Depth of front seat, 16 inches; of rear seat, 17 inches. Height of back above cushion, front seat, 17 inches; height of back above cushion, rear seat, 18 inches. The body of this vehicle is constructed in such a manner that the back seat can be removed in an instant, making a light buggy or delivery wagon.

**TRIMMINGS.** The seat and backs are trimmed in either green cloth or green leather. We make the vehicle with spring backs and spring cushions to both seats, use a full length carpet and style of dash shown in cut. We cannot furnish this job with lamps or fenders as it is not adapted to receive them.

**MOUNTINGS.** We can furnish silver mountings if desired, such as dash rail, or hub band; no extra charge.

**TOP.** Canopy only with heavy fringe. We cannot furnish an extension top with this vehicle on account of the back seat being removable. Side curtains and back curtains are all made of heavy rubber.

**PAINTING.** All bodies are painted black regularly, with gears a Brewster green, although if desired we can paint the gears either black or carmine. The gears, wheels and shafts are striped in an artistic and elegant manner. In painting this vehicle we use the best material to be obtained in lead, oils and varnishes, and give the work plenty of time to dry in a dark room so that the paint will stand in any climate.

THIS RIG WEIGHS ABOUT 600 POUNDS. Shipping weight, 750 pounds. Capacity, 800 pounds. The price is for Surrey complete with Canopy Top, full length side and back curtains and shafts. Extra for Pole with Neckyoke and Whiffletrees complete in place of shafts, $2.50.

THIS IS OUR REGULAR A GRADE SURREY. Remember we have Surreys for less money, and for cheaper work and a great variety of A and AA work we would refer you to our Special Catalogue, which we will mail free on application.

**YOU CAN SAVE PART OF YOUR CARPENTER'S BILL BY BUYING YOUR HARDWARE, BUILDER'S HARDWARE, SASH, DOOR, AND BLINDS. SEE INDEX OF THIS CATALOGUE AND COMPARE OUR PRICES WITH THOSE OF ANY OTHER HOUSE ON EARTH.**

# OUR AA GRADE COLUMBUS, O. EXTENSION TOP SURREY

## AT $87.00 and $99.00.

### $87.00 for Canopy Top.
### $99.00 for Full Extension Leather Quarter Top.

No. 92819. Order by Number.

**Our Prices $87.00 and $99.00** are on our regular C. O. D. terms, 3 per cent discount allowed if cash in full accompanies your order.

**THESE SURREYS ARE OUR VERY FINEST AA GRADE COLUMBUS, O. WORK,** and such surreys as were never before offered at less than double the price, in fact, equal to surreys that retail at from $200.00 to $250.00.

**YOU WILL FIND NOTHING FINER THAN THE AA GRADE** genuine Columbus, O. work. There is nothing better on the market. We offer an endless variety of Surreys at all prices to suit all customers, but we cannot possibly offer anything better than this high grade AA Columbus, O. Work. Nothing but the very best material enters into the construction of these vehicles and only the most skilled mechanics are employed.

The Columbus Vehicles are too well known to require very much elaboration. They have been made for a great many years and have stood the test of time and wear, and we are the first catalogue house to offer this work at popular prices.

**THE ILLUSTRATIONS ENGRAVED FROM PHOTOGRAPHS** will give you some idea of the appearance of our Highest Grade AA Columbus, O. straight sill extension top or canopy top surreys.

### DESCRIPTIONS.

**GEAR.** We build this surrey with two elliptic end springs as shown in cut, and drop axles, or with Brewster springs, arch axles. In ordering, be sure to state which are wanted. We make it with 4 feet 8 inch, or 5 feet 2 inch, track. Be sure to state width of track wanted. The fifth wheel is full wrought iron with heavy king bolt braced. Axles are all of the finest axle steel, spindles steel converted, making them very hard and impervious to wear. Size of axles 1 1-16 inch by 1¼ inch front and rear. All gear woods, such as axle caps, spring bars and reaches are of selected second growth hickory. All axle caps are cemented firmly to each axle. Reaches are ironed full length in the most substantial manner. Springs are of the best spring steel, oil tempered and tested. All clips, bolts and forgings are of the very best Norway iron.

**WHEELS.** We use either Sarven's patent or compressed band hubs, as ordered; ⅞ inch or 1 inch tread. Tire on all wheels is steel, electric welded, round edge, projecting over the felloes just enough to protect the wood from wear. The material in the wheels is strictly first-class in every respect, and they are made in the most approved manner and are guaranteed to stand in any climate. Tire is bolted between each spoke. These wheels are No. 1, high grade, every wheel thoroughly tested, will outwear half a dozen sets of the ordinary cheap grade work.

**SHAFTS.** Are all made of selected second growth hickory, the very latest design. They are substantially ironed with heavy irons so that the heels will not straighten out in use.

**BODY AND SEATS.** The body furnished on this vehicle is exactly the same design as shown in cut. Body and seats are made only with the best selected yellow poplar panels and second growth ash sills, put together in the best possible manner, screwed and plugged from inside and outside. Seats measure in width over top of cushion. 33 inches. Depth of front seat, 16 inches; depth of rear seat, 17 inches; height of back above cushion on front seat, 16 inches; height of back above cushion on rear seat, 18 inches. The body is ironed with rail over each side panel as shown in cut in the most substantial manner.

**TRIMMINGS.** The seats and backs are trimmed in either fine imported all wool English green body cloth or green machine buffed leather. Both front and back seats have full spring backs and spring cushion, carpet front and back, and latest pattern, best quality dash. Lamps hung on body only as shown in cut. Very wide extra quality, double fenders as shown in cut.

**MOUNTINGS.** We furnish this rig with silver mountings if desired, including full silver plated hub bands, prop nuts, dash rail, etc.

**TOP.** Canopy or extension, as desired, according to price. Canopy top is the very best and strongest made, has a very heavy fringe, full side and back curtains made of heavy rubber. The extension top comes regularly in leather quarter, heavy rubber side curtains, heavy rubber roof, lined throughout with English wool dyed body cloth. The leather in this top is machine buffed and of the very best grade.

**PAINTING.** All bodies are painted black regularly with gears a Brewster green although if desired we can paint the gears either black or carmine. The gears, wheels and shafts are striped in an artistic and elegant manner. In painting this vehicle we use the best material to be obtained in leads, oils and varnishes, give the work plenty of time to dry and that in a dark dust proof room so that the paint will stand in any climate. These rigs are painted in the highest style of the art in 13 coats, the first coats rubbed out with pumice stone. The painting alone on the AA work requires an expense in material and labor sufficient to paint half a dozen of cheap grades of work.

No. 92820. Order by Number.

## The special price named above, $87.00, for canopy top,

or $99.00 for leather quarter extension top surrey, includes the surrey complete with extra wide full fenders, full length side and back curtains, extra fine lamps, silver plated trimmings when desired, and shafts.

Extra for pole with neckyoke and whiffletrees complete in place of shafts, $3.50.
Extra for both pole and shafts. $5.00.
Extra for full leather top in place of leather quarter top, $7.00.

Understand this is our very finest work, the AA grade genuine Columbus, Ohio manufacture, and as good a surrey as you can buy, no matter how much you may pay.

This rig weighs about 500 lbs., capacity 800 lbs., shipping weight 650 lbs. The price quoted is for surrey crated and delivered on board the cars at Columbus, Ohio. If you live east or south of Chicago you will save the difference in freight; if you live west or northwest of Chicago you will have to add about 40 cents per 100 lbs. to Chicago freight rates.

**IT WOULD BE A SERIOUS LOSS TO US SHOULD WE NAIL TO PLEASE YOU. WE WANT YOUR TRADE AND WANT IT SO BAD THAT WE WILL DO ALL IN OUR POWER TO GIVE YOU GOOD SERVICE.**

# The Highest Grade Columbus Carriages At $150.00 and $175.00...

**3 PER CENT DISCOUNT** ALLOWED IF CASH IN FULL ACCOMPANIES YOUR ORDER

## THIS IS POSITIVELY THE FINEST WORK THAT IS TURNED OUT

**By One of the Largest and Most Reliable Manufacturers there.**

IN ... **COLUMBUS, OHIO.**

## You Can Buy Nothing Better at Any Price.

This is a Class of Work that is handled almost Exclusively in Large Cities, where it is Sold at very fancy Prices, Retailing at $300.00 and $375.00.

### AT OUR SPECIAL PRICE OF $150.00 AND $175.00

We believe we bring the highest class of work within reach of all. We believe our customers are willing to buy the **finest work** possible to produce when they can buy it on the basis of the actual cost of material and labor with only our one small percentage of profit added.

**EVERY RIG IS GUARANTEED BY A SPECIAL BINDING GUARANTEE FOR TWO YEARS.**

If any piece or part gives out by reason of defect in material or workmanship, it may be returned to us and we will replace it free of charge. With care these rigs will last a lifetime.

### This is Our Very Finest AA Grade,

The finest that men and money can make. **Nothing but the very finest material** enters into the construction, not the slightest piece or part has been overlooked.

**THE ILLUSTRATIONS ENGRAVED FROM PHOTOGRAPHS** will give you an idea of the appearance of our highest grade Columbus Carriages which we offer at $150.00 in Canopy Top and $175.00 in Full Leather Extension Top.

No. 92824. Order by Number.

## DESCRIPTION.

THESE CARRIAGES ARE HUNG ON THREE SPRINGS ONLY. THE SPRINGS are made of the very finest crucible steel. THE AXLES are 1 1-16 by 1⅛ inches; finest steel converted spindles. THE GEAR is made from the very best selected **second growth hickory**, ironed throughout in the most artistic manner and only with the very best Norway iron. THE WHEELS are of the finest grade that can be produced. Nothing but the very best selected **second growth hickory**. We furnish them in either Sarven's patent or compressed band hub, as desired. ⅞ inch steel tire electric welded. Height, 2 feet 10 inches in front, 3 feet 8 inches in rear. These buggies have leather covered bows, all trimmed with the very finest all wool 18 oz. extra heavy **English body cloth** or genuine hand buffed leather, as desired. Full spring seat and back, upholstered seat risers, very large wide full fenders. Beautiful Silver Plated French Beveled Glass Lamps. Track 4 feet 8 inches or 5 feet 2 inches, as desired.

No. 92825. Order by Number.

**The $175.00 Extension Top Rig has Full Leather Extension Top**——

Made of **hand buffed leather** throughout, with **English wool** dyed body cloth full back and side curtains.

**The $150.00 Canopy Top Rig is exactly the Same Except Canopy Top.**

IT HAS THE BEST CANOPY TOP THAT CAN POSSIBLY BE BUILT with full length side and back curtains. These rigs come complete with all accessories and shafts.

**Extra for Pole with Neckyoke and Whiffletrees** complete in place of shafts, **$5.00.**

We can furnish the Extension Top Carriage with leather quarter top instead of full leather, at **$165.00.**

**Too much cannot be said in favor of these carriages.** The manufacturer has established almost a world wide reputation for making the finest carriage at Columbus, Ohio, that is made in America, and when we are able to make the price $150.00 and $175.00, we believe our customers will appreciate it. We believe those who can possibly afford to invest the amount in a vehicle will buy one of our finest grade jobs in preference to cheaper work. If you buy the finest two-seated carriage that is made in Columbus, O., you will undoubtedly have the finest rig in your neighborhood. We know you will be so well pleased with it that you will recommend it to your friends, tell them where you got it and what you paid for it, and in this way we will be sure to make many more customers in your neighborhood.

## DON'T FORGET THIS IS THE HIGHEST GRADE COLUMBUS, O. TWO-SEATED CARRIAGE ON THE MARKET.

### No One Can Possibly Have Better--They Cannot Be Made.

# New Fancy Columbus Vehicles

## A and B Grades -- $29.90 to $46.90

These Buggies are covered by a binding two years guarantee During which time if any piece or part gives out by reason of defect in material or workmanship we will replace it free of charge.

### OUR SPECIAL PRICE

**B Grade, Open, $29.90**
**Canopy Top, $39.90**

**A Grade, Open, $35.90**
**Canopy Top, $46.90**

No. 95073

Three per cent discount allowed if cash in full accompanies your order. If you send the full amount of cash with your order, you may deduct 3 per cent from our prices. Nearly all our customers send cash in full.

These buggies are made in Columbus, Ohio, by one of the largest and most reliable manufacturers there, a concern whose enviable reputation for the manufacture of high class work is a sufficient guarantee for the quality. We believe it will pay you to order one of these rigs in preference to saving a few dollars in the purchase of a cheap road wagon which will last but for a few years at the most. One of these rigs will with care last a lifetime.

## DESCRIPTION.

These buggies have solid panel back, built on elliptic end springs, axles 15-16ths inch, swedged and fan tail. Body, 24 inches wide, 50 inches long; wheels, ⅞ inch tread; ⅞ inch steel tire; height of seat, 17 inches; 28 inches on bottom.

**GEAR**—Gear is made of the best selected second growth hickory, ironed throughout with Norway iron. Reaches run full length. Has Columbus patent double circle fifth wheel, front and rear safety bolts.

**WHEELS**—These are thoroughly first-class second growth hickory wheels; our regular B grade wheels in the cheaper grade and the A grade wheel in the better grade.

**UPHOLSTERING**—These buggies are upholstered in a first-class manner, either in imported English wool body cloth or Evans leather. For genuine machine buffed leather, see extras below.

**PAINTING**—They are painted in a first-class manner, bodies black, gears dark green with suitable gold stripe, or carmine, as desired.

**TOP**—Fancy canopy top, fastened to body with strongest patent standards made. Full fringe, nicely trimmed and ornamented. Top can be removed instantly, making an open buggy.

These buggies come complete with carpet, toe carpet, wrench, spring boot, anti-rattlers and shafts.

**EXTRA FOR POLE WITH NECKYOKE AND WHIFFLETREES COMPLETE IN PLACE OF SHAFTS, $2.00**

**EXTRA FOR BOTH POLE AND SHAFTS, $4.00**

**EXTRA FOR GENUINE MACHINE BUFFED LEATHER TRIMMING, $1.00**

**These buggies weigh net about 300 lbs.** Crated for shipment, 350 lbs.; carrying capacity, 500 lbs.

**The prices quoted are for the buggies crated** and delivered on board the cars at Columbus, Ohio, from which point you must pay the freight, but you will find the freight will amount to next to nothing as compared with what you will save in price.

No. 95054

# Our $25.00 Michigan B GRADE Spindle Body Road Wagon

## THIS IS OUR REGULAR B GRADE TWO YEAR GUARANTEED WORK.

With every one of these road wagons we send a written binding two years guarantee by the terms and conditions of which if any piece or part gives out by reason of defect in material or workmanship we will replace it free of charge.

**OUR SPECIAL PRICE ON THIS WAGON IS $25.00** on our regular terms of shipment.

We will ship this wagon to any address, anywhere in the United States by freight C. O. D. subject to examination on receipt of required deposit as fully explained under terms in front of book. You can examine it at the freight depot, and if found perfectly satisfactory and exactly as represented, pay the freight agent our price, $25.00 and freight charges, less the amount sent with order.

No. 95075.

**$24.25 PAYS FOR THE WAGON IF CASH IN FULL ACCOMPANIES YOUR ORDER.** If you send the full amount of cash you may deduct 3 per cent from our price. NEARLY ALL OUR CUSTOMERS SEND CASH IN FULL. This wagon is made in southern Michigan by one of the largest and most reliable Michigan manufacturers, a concern whose reputation alone is a guarantee for the quality of the work.

**DESCRIPTION. BODY**—This is a very neat Spindle Body Road Wagon. The body is made of the very best material, well ironed, braced and stayed throughout and is very showy.
**GEAR**—The gear is from the best selected second growth hickory. Best steel axles, steel tires, crimped and full bolted, full length side springs, combination gear, very strong and easy riding.
**WHEELS**—Are B grade, guaranteed in every respect, Sarven's patent.
**TRIMMINGS**—We furnish this buggy in either cloth trimming or Evans leather. Genuine leather trimming, $1.00 extra.
This wagon comes in either 4 feet 8 inch or 5 feet 2 inch track. In ordering, be sure to state width of track wanted.
**PAINTING**—It is painted in a first-class manner, body black with suitable stripe, gear dark green or carmine with suitable striping. The wagon weighs net about 300 lbs.; crated, 350 lbs.; carrying capacity, 500 lbs.
We feel we are entitled to your favorable consideration, for we have placed before you the most complete line of vehicles from the best makers in America at prices that have heretofore been unknown, and on terms so liberal that no one could ask more. We only want our work to be placed side by side with that of any other in the market and we do not ask you to accept our work if it is not just as good.
We guarantee our work to be not only better, but at least 25 per cent better for the same money. Further, we guarantee to furnish first-class guaranteed work for less money than the cheapest work could be furnished by others, and if we can not show this difference in our favor we will not ask you to take our goods.

## OUR FINEST

# Michigan A Grade Spindle or Solid Body Road Wagon for $32.50

## SPINDLE OR SOLID BODY, END OR SIDE SPRING, AS DESIRED.

**WE OFFER THE FINEST MICHIGAN SPINDLE BODY ROAD WAGON ON THE MARKET FOR $32.50**

**At $32.50, our regular price,** we will send this wagon to any address anywhere in the United States subject to examination on receipt of the required deposit as explained under terms in front of book, the wagon to be examined at your freight depot, and if found perfectly satisfactory and exactly as represented, pay the freight agent our price and freight charges less the amount sent with order.

**$31.50 pays for the wagon if cash in full accompanies your order.** We allow a discount of 3 per cent for cash in full with order, in which case $31.50 pays for the rig.

No. 95076.

WE CONSIDER THIS THE BEST SPINDLE BODY MICHIGAN ROAD WAGON on the market, and we believe the best road wagons in the country are made in Michigan, where they have the advantages of the best quality of wood material and where mechanical labor of this class is perhaps as cheap if not cheaper than elsewhere.

No. 95077.

**DESCRIPTION. BODY**—Body is made from the very best selected material, thoroughly air seasoned. It is strongly ironed throughout, and is probably as handsome a spindle body as has ever been made.
**GEAR**—Is made from the very best selected second growth hickory, ironed throughout with Norway iron, steel axles, steel tire, wrought fifth wheel, reaches ironed full length. Wheels are our regular A grade, guaranteed in every respect, Sarven's patent. They are full bolted and tired with the best steel tire, full crimped and bolted.
**TRIMMING**—This buggy is full trimmed with imported English wool dyed body cloth or Evans leather. Genuine leather trimming, $1.00 extra.
**PAINTING**—The job is thoroughly well painted, body painted black with suitable striping, gear Brewster green or carmine.
AT OUR PRICE OF $32.50 C. O. D. or $31.50 cash in full with order we furnish the wagon in either 4 feet 8 inch or 5 feet 2 inch track, with carpet, wrench, anti-rattlers and shafts.
Extra for pole with neckyoke and whiffletrees complete in place of shafts, $2.00   Extra for both pole and shafts, $4.00
The wagon weighs about 300 lbs.; crated, about 350 lbs.; carrying capacity, about 500 lbs.
The price quoted is for this wagon crated and delivered on board the cars at the factory in southern Michigan, from which point you must pay the freight.

# A GRADE MICHIGAN SURREY AT $70.00 AND $80.00

## THIS STRICTLY A GRADE SURREY . . .

Is Made in Southern Michigan by one of the Largest and Most Reliable Manufacturers there. It is a very neat, light and attractive vehicle for a one horse rig, and is especially recommended as such though we furnish it with pole when desired.

### It is Covered by a Binding Two Years Guarantee,

By the terms and conditions of which if any piece or part gives out by reason of defect in material or workmanship we will replace it free of charge.

$70.00 is Our Price for Canopy Top

$80.00 for Leather Quarter Extension Top

If cash in full accompanies your order $67.90 pays for the Canopy Top, $77.60 pays for the Leather Quarter Extension Top. Further, if cash in full accompanies your order we send free a beautiful sun shade as is fully illustrated and described in front of book.

From the illustration shown you can form a very good idea of the appearance of this rig. It is one of the neatest surreys that has been turned out.

### DESCRIPTION.

**BODY.** Body is made of the best selected material, ironed throughout with the very best Norway iron, 24 inches wide on bottom, two beautiful scrolls on each side, solid panel backs, seats beautifully curved, steel dash covered with very best enameled leather.

**GEAR.** Gear is made from the very best selected second growth hickory ironed throughout with Norway iron; has 1 1-16 inch axles, wrought iron fifth wheel, single reach ironed full length.

**WHEELS.** Sarven's patent wheels, full bolted, guaranteed in every respect, ¼ inch steel tire.

**TRIMMINGS.** We trim this in either extra quality imported all wool English body cloth or genuine leather, as desired; Brussels carpet in bottom; large, wide double fenders; beautiful silver trimmed lamps.

**PAINTINGS.** This job is painted in the highest style of the art, body black, gear dark green with suitable striping in gold.

THE PRICE IS FOR THE RIG COMPLETE WITH Carpet, Lamps, Double Fenders, full length side and back Curtains, Wrench, Anti-Rattlers and Shafts.

**Extra for Pole with Neckyoke and Whiffletrees, complete in place of shafts, $3.00.**

**Extra for both Pole and Shafts, $5.00**

No. 95108.

---

# OUR A GRADE MICHIGAN CUT UNDER SURREY at $79.00 and $89.00

We believe we are Offering a Strictly High Grade Michigan Cut Under Surrey for less money by 33⅓ per cent. than the same has ever been sold in carload lots to dealers. XXXXXXXX

**Our Special Price . . .**
FOR THIS BEAUTIFUL CUT UNDER SURREY IN CANOPY TOP IS . . .
**$79.00**
WITH LEATHER QUARTER EXTENSION TOP,
**$89.00**

WE WOULD ASK YOU TO COMPARE THIS ILLUSTRATION AND description with anything you can buy in your local market at $150.00. If you do not consider our surrey in every way equal, do not give us your order.

### Every Surrey is Covered by a Written Binding Two Year's Guarantee . . . .

During which time if any piece or part gives out by reason of defect in material or workmanship we will replace it free of charge. With care it will last a lifetime.

THREE PER CENT DISCOUNT will be allowed if cash in full accompanies order, in which case $76.60 pays for the canopy top, $86.30 for the leather quarter extension top.

In addition to saving the three per cent cash discount we will also send you free with the surrey if cash in full accompanies your order a beautiful sun shade, which is fully illustrated and described in front of book.

### Description of this Beautiful Light High Grade Michigan AA Grade Surrey.

**BODY.** Body is made of the very best selected material, ironed throughout with Norway iron, has full solid panel seats, 24 inches wide at bottom,

**GEAR.** 1 1-16 inch steel axles, wrought iron fifth wheel, single reach ironed full length, hung on the very best elliptic end springs.

**WHEELS.** Sarven's patent of the very best grade, full bolted throughout.

**TRIMMINGS.** We trim this buggy in either heavy imported all wool English body cloth, green, or genuine leather, as desired. Full spring backs.

**PAINTING.** Body is painted black with suitable striping and ornamentation, gear dark green with suitable gold stripe.

No. 95109.

AT OUR SPECIAL PRICE THIS CUT UNDER SURREY comes complete with beautiful silver plated lamps, full length side and back curtains, very large wide double fenders. carpet, toe carpet, anti-rattlers, wrench and shafts. Extra for pole with neckyoke and wiffletrees, complete in place of shafts, $3.00. Extra for both pole and shafts, $5.00.

We furnish this surrey in either 4 feet 8 inch or 5 feet 2 inch track, as desired. In ordering be sure to state width of track wanted. The Surrey weighs complete about 500 pounds. Shipping weight, 600 pounds. Capacity, 800 pounds.

The price quoted is for surrey crated and delivered on board of cars at the factory in southern Michigan, from which point you must pay the freight, but you will find the freight will amount to next nothing as compared with what you will save in price.

# OUR $67.00 OHIO A GRADE TRAP

## $67.00 FOR THE OPEN TRAP
## $82.00 WITH CANOPY TOP

No. 95092

The above are our regular prices when sent by freight C. O. D. subject to examination on our regular terms.

**$64.90 Pays for the Open Trap**
**$79.55 with Canopy Top,**

If cash in full accompanies your order.

If you send cash in full with your order you may deduct 3 per cent from our regular prices, in which case you own the open trap at $64.90 and the canopy top at $79.55. Nearly all our customers send cash in full.

On traps we are ready to furnish you strictly up to date city work, at prices that will extend this class of goods into all sections, the smaller cities, towns and country as well as the metropolis.

We furnish at $64.90 and $79.55 traps that have been retailed in the best city establishments in the past for $100.00 and $150.00, and on our one small profit plan direct from manufacturer to consumer, we are able to furnish a wealthy man's rig at a poor man's price, able to bring within reach of our many patrons such vehicles as have heretofore been in possession of the wealthy only.

This trap is a strictly modern vehicle, all the rage in large cities, and destined to become very popular everywhere, as it makes a very serviceable, stylish, good everyday use carriage.

The illustration shows the rig open and in docedo form, but as shown in our trap No. 95089, you can see how it will appear when used as a two-seated surrey in the regular way, also the construction of the front seat and its appearance as a canopy top rig. This rig must be seen to be appreciated. It is made by one of the largest and most reliable trap manufacturers in the country, a concern whose reputation for the manufacture of trap work is without an equal. Nothing but the very best material enters into the construction of this work. The makers employ only skilled mechanics and no job is allowed to leave the factory until it has received the final critical inspection of an expert to know that it is perfect in every detail.

**DESCRIPTION.** **BODY**—The body of this rig is beautifully finished, 62 inches long, 28 inches wide at bottom; distance from front cushion to dash is 24 inches; end rail dash with silver plated line rail. Body is nicely paneled, lower panel and main body painted black; upper panel, fancy color. Front cushion is 32 inches wide and 15 inches deep; rear cushion, 33 inches wide, 14 inches deep.

**TRIMMING**—It is upholstered in the highest style of the art with English wool dyed body cloth, fine grade imported corduroy or select leather, as desired.

**GEAR**—Gear is the very best selected second growth hickory, ironed throughout with Norway iron. Single reach ironed full length, bottom and sides with Norway iron. Length of gear from center to center of axles, 54 inches.

**WHEELS**—No. 1 grade the very best that we can buy; either Sarven's patent or shell band hub, as desired. One inch tread, crimped tire, round edge, bolted between each spoke. Axles are 11-16ths inch of the very best steel; front axle arched, rear axle coached. Elliptic springs of the highest grade made.

This rig is finished and furnished complete with beautiful silver plated and highly ornamented oil burning lamps, full length velvet carpet, toe carpet, storm apron, wrench, anti-rattlers and shafts. For pole with neckyoke and whiffletrees complete in place of shafts, add $2.00.

At $82.00 on our regular terms or $79.55 cash with order, we furnish this rig with a very fine canopy top, the most stylish canopy top made; coupe shape, gathered, festooned and fringed, lined throughout, complete with full length side and back curtains.

We furnish this rig in either 4 feet 8 inches or 5 feet 2 inches, as desired. In ordering be sure to state width of track wanted.

The price quoted is for the rig crated and delivered on board the cars at Cincinnati, Ohio, where it it is made, and from which point you must pay the freight. To estimate freight, refer to general information on freight rates in front of book.

# Our $48.40 B Grade Michigan Canopy Top Surrey.

## SO MUCH HAS BEEN SAID BY OUR COMPETITORS

As to how cheap a two seated surrey can be had that we have decided to make arrangements to show a surrey we can sell and guarantee for two years, and yet at a price that would defy competition

WHILE WE SHOW A SURREY UNDER OUR SPECIAL B GRADE AT $44.00 and a surrey that is being extensively advertised and sold under glowing descriptions with very long and promising guarantees, it is not a surrey that can be relied upon, not one that we can guarantee; but we are able to offer you at $48.40 on our regular terms, or $46.95 cash with order, a farmer's two seated surrey which we can guarantee in every respect, and with this surrey we send a written binding two years' guarantee, by the terms and conditions of which if any piece or part gives out by reason of defective material or workmanship, we will replace it free of charge,

$48.40 is our regular price, and at which price we will send the surrey to any address anywhere in the United States, C. O. D. subject to examination on receipt of the required deposit.

Three per cent cash discount brings the surrey down to $46.95, and we invite a comparison of this price with any price you can get from any house for any kind of a surrey, guaranteed or otherwise. This surrey is made in southern Michigan by a very reliable maker,

No. 95093

**DESCRIPTION.** **BODY**—Is made from selected material, ironed throughout with Norway iron in a thoroughly substantial manner. It is 25 inches wide, with removeable back seat. The seat can be removed without disturbing the canopy top. Solid panel spring backs.

**TRIMMING**—Trimmed with good cloth, corduroy or Evans leather. For genuine leather trimming, add $2.00.

**GEAR**—Is from the best selected second growth hickory; 1⅛ inch fan tail swedged axles, wrought iron fifth wheel, with king bolt back of axle. Good hickory spring bars, and axle caps well fitted and cemented to axles.

**WHEELS**—Our regular B grade, thoroughly guaranteed, Sarven's patent, ⅞ inch tire, full bolted.

**TOP**—Good canopy top, lined with good cloth, deep fringe, full length side and back curtains.

At our special prices of $48.40 or $46.95 we furnish this buggy complete with carpet, wrench, anti-rattlers and shafts.

Extra for pole with neckyoke and whiffletrees complete in place of shafts, $2.00    Extra for both pole and shafts, $4.00

# $39.90 MICHIGAN A GRADE FAMILY WAGON.

## AT 39.90 IT LEADS THE WORLD.

**$39.90 is Our Regular Price for this Wagon when Shipped by Freight, C. O. D., Subject to Examination on Our Regular Terms.**

No. 95122.

### Three Per Cent Discount

IS ALLOWED if cash in full accompanies your order, when $38.70 pays for the wagon.

### When we Can Furnish

YOU SUCH A WAGON AS ILLUSTRATED and described at $38.70, we believe we are entitled to your order. We only ask you to compare it with anything on the market at anything like the price, and leave you to be the judge.

### Our Binding Guarantee.

Every wagon is covered by a binding two years' guarantee, during which time if any piece or part gives out by reason of defect in material or workmanship we will replace it free of charge.

**WE SHOW AN ILLUSTATION OF THIS WAGON** hung on Half Plattorm Springs, also the Three Spring Gear. The price is the same. You can have your choice. In ordering be sure to state which is wanted.

## We Must Sell 1000 of these Vehicles Before the Close of the Season.

**IN ORDER TO MAKE THE PRICE WE ARE COMPELLED TO TAKE THE ENTIRE OUTPUT OF THE FACTORY,** and by doing so we are able to offer the wagon direct to our customers at 25 per cent less than the same wagon has ever been sold in carload lots to wholesale dealers.

**THIS WAGON IS MADE IN JACKSON, MICH.,** by one of the most reliable manufacturers of road wagons in America, is made where the factory is convenient to the best material that can be procured, where labor is cheap, and where the highest grade work can he produced at the minimum cost.

**DESCRIPTION.** BODY.—Body made of the very best selected material, 7 feet long, 32 inches wide, 8½ inches deep, full frame ironed throughout in a substantial manner with the best Norway iron, has drop tail gate, round corners, well ironed, well braced inside and out. The seats are adjustable to any position, and can be removed instantly.

**GEAR.**—Gear is made from the very best selected second growth hickory, ironed throughout with No. 1 Norway iron; double perch; rear king bolt; 1⅛ inch axle, Tifford springs, made from the best spring steel.

**WHEELS.**—Wheels are No. 1 grade, Sarven's patent, full bolted; extra heavy tire bolted to wheels.

**TRIMMING.**—Backs are full padded. Backs and seats are trimmed in English wool dyed body cloth, corduroy, or Evans leather. For genuine leather trimmings, add $2.00.

**PAINTING.**—These wagons are painted in a thoroughly first class manner; body black, handsomely striped and ornamented; gear dark green with suitable gold stripe.

This wagon weighs complete about 500 lbs. Crated about 600 lbs. Carrying capacity, 1000 lbs.

WIDTH OF TRACK, 4 feet 8 inches or 5 feet 2 inches. In ordering be sure to state width of track wanted.

No. 95123.

**THE WAGON COMES COMPLETE WITH TWO SEATS** as illustrated, either Three Spring Gear, or Half Platform Gear, as illustrated, wrench, whip socket, anti-rattlers and shafts.

## Extra for Pole with Neckyoke and Whiffletrees Complete in Place of Shafts, $2.00. Extra for Both Pole and Shafts, $4.00.

**IN COMPARING THIS WAGON WITH THOSE OFFERED BY OTHERS,** we would ask you to observe the size of the body, 7 feet long and 32 inches wide, and notice that the seats have full padded back and seat. We furnish either the half platform or three spring gear. Be sure you get a Michigan Wagon and that it is guaranteed for two years by a firm whose guarantee is a protection to the purchaser.

# OUR $34.00 MICHIGAN A GRADE COMBINATION
## Market and Pleasure Wagon.

### This is a Strictly A Grade Wagon,
**GUARANTEED BY A BINDING GUARANTEE FOR TWO YEARS.**

**THIS WAGON IS MADE IN JACKSON, MICH.**

**By One of the Largest and Most Reliable Wagon Manufacturers in America.**

**OUR SPECIAL PRICE IS**

## $34.00
**On Regular C. O. D. Terms.**

**THREE PER CENT DISCOUNT**

Allowed if cash in full accompanies your order, in which case $33.00 pays for the rig.

No. 95142.

{ DESCRIPTION. }

**BODY.** Body is made from the very best selected material, heavily ironed throughout with Norway iron; is 7 feet long, 34 inches wide and 8 inches deep. Comes with a foot board, one seat, long 13 inch riser, and flare boards.

**GEAR.** Gear is from the best selected second growth hickory; combination single perch; 2 elliptic springs in rear of same; elliptic spring in front; 1⅛ inch axle.

**WHEELS.** Sarven's patent, 1⅛ inch tread; ¼ inch tire, full bolted. Wheels are guaranteed in every respect.

**TRIMMINGS.** Imitation leather or corduroy, as desired.

**PAINTING.** It is painted in a thoroughly first class manner, body dark green, handsomely striped; gear dark green or red with suitable striping

**WEIGHT OF WAGON, 500 POUNDS. CRATED IT WEIGHS ABOUT 550 POUNDS. CAPACITY, 1200 POUNDS.**

At the Special Prices Named of $34.00 on Regular Terms or $33.00 Cash with Order we Furnish the Wagon Complete with Shafts.

THE PRICE QUOTED IS FOR THE WAGON CRATED and delivered on board the cars at Jackson, Michigan, from which point you must pay the freight. By referring to the freight rates in front of book you will see that the freight will amount to next to nothing as compared with what you save in price.

Extra for pole with neckyoke and whiffletrees complete in place of shafts, $2.00. Width of track, either 4 feet 8 inches or 5 feet 2 inches, as desired. In ordering, be sure to state width of track wanted.

---

# OUR $34.00 MICHIGAN A GRADE COMBINATION
## Market and Pleasure Wagon.

### A Thoroughly First Class Rig
**GUARANTEED FOR TWO YEARS.**

**IF CASH IN FULL**
Accompanies your Order we will Allow you a
**DISCOUNT OF THREE PER CENT**
In which case $33.00 Pays for the Rig.

**...MADE AT...**
**JACKSON, MICH.**
By One of the Most ....Reliable Wagon Makers in America.

**Our Special Price** ✦

$34.00 on Regular Terms when Shipped by Freight C. O. D. subject to Examination; $33.00 if Cash in Full Accompanies your Order.

No. 95143.

## DESCRIPTION.

**BODY.** Made from the very best material, heavily ironed throughout, 7 feet long, 34 inches wide and 8 inches deep; made with flare boards, wood dash, regular seat with 6 inch lazy back.

**GEAR.** Gear is made from the very best selected second growth hickory; combination single perch; two elliptic end springs in the rear of same; elliptic spring in front; 1⅛ inch axle.

**WHEELS.** Sarven's patent, 1⅛ inch tread, ¼ inch steel tire. Wheels guaranteed in every respect.

**TRIMMING.** Imitation leather or corduroy, as desired.

**PAINTING.** Body dark green, handsomely striped, gear dark green or red with suitable striping.

At the above Special Prices, $34.00 on our Regular Terms and $33.00 if Cash in Full Accompanies Order, WE FURNISH THE WAGON COMPLETE WITH SHAFTS.

Extra for Pole with Neckyoke and Whiffletrees complete in place of Shafts, $2.00　　Extra for Both Pole and Shafts..............................$4.00

The price quoted is for the wagon crated and delivered on board of cars at Jackson, Michigan, from which point you must pay the freight.

# Our $35.00 Michigan A Grade Combination Market and Pleasure Wagon

No. 95144

## This wagon is a thoroughly first-class rig . . .

GUARANTEED FOR TWO YEARS, WILL LAST A LIFE-TIME. MADE AT JACKSON, MICH., BY ONE OF THE OLDEST AND MOST RELIABLE MANUFACTURERS IN AMERICA.

### DESCRIPTION

**BODY**—Body is 7 feet long, 34 inches wide, 8 inches deep, drop tail gate, two regular seats and 6 inch lazy back. Flare boards furnished without charge when desired. Steel dash covered with the best enameled leather.

**GEAR**—Gear is made from the best selected second growth hickory; combination single perch, two elliptic springs in rear of same, elliptic spring in front; 1⅛ in. axle.

**WHEELS**—Sarven's patent, 1⅛ inch, ⅛ inch tire. These are thoroughly first-class wheels, guaranteed in every respect.
**TRIMMINGS**—Imitation leather or corduroy, as desired.
**PAINTING**—Body dark green with suitable stripe, gear dark green or carmine nicely striped. Width of track, 4 feet 8 inches or 5 feet 2 inches. **At the above price** we furnish this rig complete with shafts.
Extra for pole with neckyoke and whiffletrees complete in place of shafts, $2.00    Extra for both pole and shafts, $4.00

# ROAD CARTS

There has been a great demand for road wagons the past few years and many manufacturers have turned their attention to this class of vehicles. The competition has been such that many inferior grades of work has been turned out by some factories. In arranging for our line of road wagons for the coming season we decided to handle nothing but thoroughly high grade work and endeavor, by entering into a large contract with the manufacturers, to produce a road wagon which we can fully recommend and guarantee, and yet bring it within the limit of price at which other dealers are selling inferior work. The result is we are able to furnish a thoroughly first-class line of road wagons at lower prices than our competitors are offering an inferior grade of vehicles. Our road carts are all made by the largest road cart manufacturer in the world at Indianapolis, Ind. We make no charge for crating or cartage, but deliver f. o. b. cars at Indianapolis free of charge, and road carts, like all other vehicles, we ship to any address C. O. D., subject to examination, on receipt of a small deposit, as heretofore explained. You can examine them at the freight depot, and, if not perfectly satisfactory and exactly as represented, they can be returned to us. If they are found perfectly satisfactory you can pay the agent our price and freight charges, less the amount sent with order, and the cart is yours. By reason of our most extraordinary terms, high standard of quality and our prices, which are about one-half that charged by other concerns for the same class of goods, our trade has been something phenomenal.

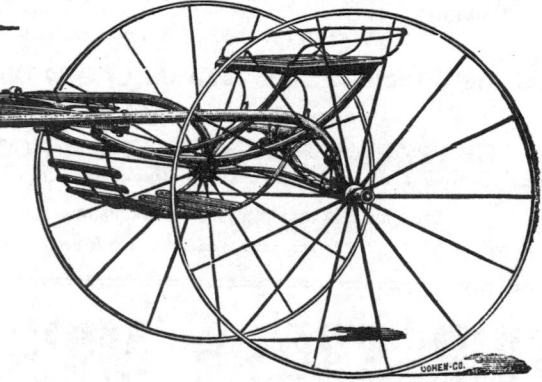

No. 95145. Order by Number.

## OUR $8.45 ROAD CART

You may wonder how it is possible for us to produce such a road cart for such a small amount of money, but a road cart is light, it only weighs about 125 pounds, and while there is nothing but the very best material used in this class of vehicles, the manufacturer has equipped himself with automatic machinery for turning most of the parts for this rig fitted with an exactness which can not possibly be done by the most skilled workman by hand; the result is we have this high class of road carts at the lowest possible prices, and we can assure you our profit is figured so close that it is only by selling these carts in untold quantities that we are able to maintain the prices we do. The carts are very strong and thoroughly well made and nicely finished in natural wood and carries two passengers. All second growth hickory, 1 inch double collar steel axle, square at shoulders, octagon and square in center, steel tire bolted on, low bent seat arms, perfectly balanced, long, easy-riding, oil tempered springs, Sarven's patent wheel with tire 1 inch wide. Width of seat from rail to rail, 30 inches; weight, 125 pounds; shipping weight, 140 pounds.

In offering this cart at $8.45 we accept as our profit but a few cents, but do it with the knowledge that the sale of one cart effects another, by which we mean that the sale of one cart in a neighborhood will cause the sale of many more. It frequently happens that we sell a vehicle in a neighborhood where we have heretofore made no sales, and the result is in a few months our vehicles can be seen on the village streets every day, and as soon as the people learn of the manner in which we treat our customers and the values we are able to give we receive all their trade. Our profit is not so much in dollars and cents as it is in advertising. We make our goods do nearly all our advertising.

# OUR $13.85 LEADER.

This cart at $13.85 is a bargain. It is a special offer and on which we are having a great sale. It is in every way equal to carts that are being retailed throughout the country at from $22.00 to $25.00. Is a first-class job in every respect, covered by a binding two years' guarantee, during which time if any piece or part gives out by reason of defect in the material or workmanship we will replace it free of charge. We will send it to any address by freight, C. O. D., subject to examination, on receipt of a small deposit, as heretofore explained. You can examine it at the freight depot, and, if you find it exactly as represented and perfectly satisfactory in

No. 95147. Order by Number.

every respect, pay the agent our price, $13.85 and freight charges, less the amount sent with order, and the cart is yours.

This cart is made of thoroughly first-class material, wheels and shafts are made of best selected second growth hickory and the body of selected white wood. It is the easiest riding road cart made; has oil tempered springs hung in loops under shafts; body is large and roomy; painted in wine, green or natural wood finish, as desired; shafts, seat and back are nicely trimmed, as shown in the cut; and a handy box is provided underneath the seat for packages, tools, hitch reins, etc. Weight is 140 pounds; shipping weight, 160 pounds. It is sometimes difficult to convince a party at a distance of the extraordinary values we are able to give. We are working at a disadvantage in this respect, as we can only show a picture, while your retail dealer has the cart on the floor to show. We can only ask the privilege of sending ours to you C. O. D., subject to examination, but when you have given us this privilege, and you see and examine our work at your freight depot, and compare it with anything you have ever seen at anything like the price, we are not only sure of selling you, but of also securing your influence in our behalf, and in this way we will get more orders.

# OUR ABINGDON, ILLINOIS, LINE OF HIGH GRADE FARM WAGONS.

**THE FOLLOWING LINE OF FARM WAGONS** is made at Abingdon, Illinois, by a concern whose enviable reputation for the manufacture of high class work is a guarantee for their quality. **The wood material is air seasoned, bone dry.** The iron and steel are of best quality. Wheels are well ironed and boiled in hot oil. Hubs are best oak and black birch. Spokes are strictly select. Felloes finest white oak. Axles select young hickory. Gear select white oak. Boxes are made of clear yellow poplar. Bottom boxes made of long leaf yellow pine. Paint is strictly pure and carefully applied by brush and positively no dipping of any kind.

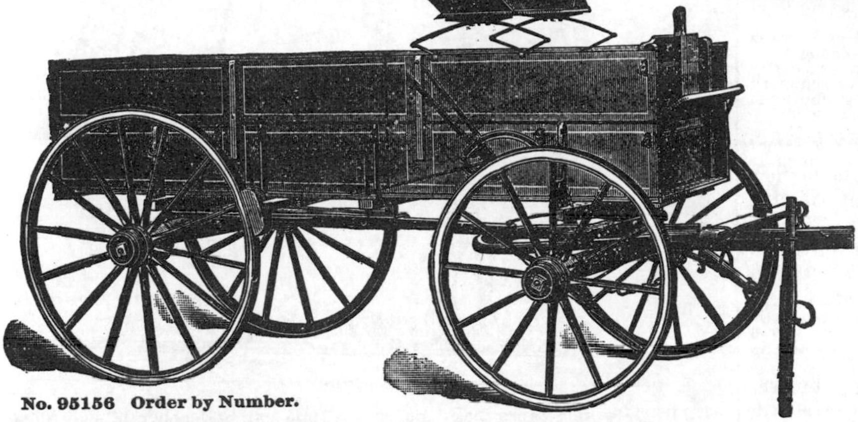

No. 95156 Order by Number.

**The above cut represents our Box Brake Wagon with thimble box is desired. Regular farm sizes 2¾x8¼, 3x9, 3¼x10, 3½x11. Cast thimble skeins. A thribble box comes in as an extra.**

## Explanations and Extras for Our No. 95156 Wagon.

**READ THIS CAREFULLY BEFORE ORDERING** and save mistakes and misunderstandings. Different widths of tracks are used in different localities. **Always state whether you want a wide or a narrow track wagon.** Our wide track wagon is 5 feet and our narrow track wagon is 4 feet 6 inches from center to center of tire. The box on a wide track wagon is 3 feet 6 inches wide outside. On a narrow track wagon it measures 3 feet 2 inches outside. We can furnish a narrow box on a wide track wagon if you so order it. The tongue on this wagon is either a stiff or a drop tongue. Order it as you want it. On all farm wagons size 2¾x8½ skein and larger we can furnish any width tire wanted. The tires are regular, as quoted below. If you want wider tire add to the price of the wagon 65 cents for each ¼ inch wider than regular width. That is, if you want a 2-inch tire on the 2¾ x 8½ wagon you will add $1.30 to the price of the wagon, as the regular tire is 1½ inches, and you hence have added ½ inch or 2-4 inch to the width. The height of wheels on 2¼ and 2½ wagon is, front 3 feet 6 inches, rear 4 feet. On larger sizes the front wheels are 3 feet 7 inches high and rear 4 feet 4 inches high. Beds on 2¾ and 2½ inch wagons are 10 feet long. Beds on 2¾ inch and larger wagons are 10 feet 6 inches long. At bottom beds are 14 inches deep. All top boxes are 12 inches deep. If you want box brake extra, add $2.50 to the price of whichever size wagon you order. If you want gear brake add $5 to the price of whichever size wagon you order. If you want both gear and box brake add $7.50.

**WE ALSO FURNISH** a third box, or triple box, which is often called a corn box, and will be found very convenient when you desire to haul a big load of light, loose material, such as corn, oats, barley or potatoes, in bulk.

**Our special price for third box to fit any wagon is $2.00.** If the third box is desired be sure to so state in your order and add $2.00 extra for same. Understand the extra boxes are separable and need be used only when so desired.

| | | | | | |
|---|---|---|---|---|---|
| Size of skein | 2½x8 | 2¾x8½ | 3x9 | 3¼v10 | 3½x11 |
| Size of tire | 1⅜x ⅜ | 1½x ½ | 1½x9-16 | 1½x9-16 | 1⅝x ⅝ |
| Capacity of wagon | 1,500 lbs. | 2,000 lbs. | 2,500 lbs. | 3,800 lbs. | 4,500 lbs. |
| Price of running gear only, together with neckyoke, whiffletrees and stay chains | $23.95 | $26.50 | $27.95 | $30.45 | $32.45 |
| Price of bottom bed only | 6.25 | 6.25 | 6.25 | 6.25 | 6.25 |
| Price of top box only | 2.25 | 2.25 | 2.25 | 2.25 | 2.25 |
| Price of spring seat only, with two-leaf spring | 2.50 | 2.50 | 2.50 | 2.50 | 2.50 |
| Price of wagon complete, with all of above parts, but with no brake | 34.95 | 37.45 | 38.45 | 41.45 | 43.45 |
| Weight of running gear complete | 575 lbs. | 625 lbs. | 700 lbs. | 725 lbs. | 750 lbs. |
| Weight of box, seat and brake | 215 lbs. | 215 lbs. | 215 lbs. | 300 lbs. | 335 lbs. |
| Weight of complete wagon | 799 lbs. | 840 lbs. | 915 lbs. | 1,025 lbs. | 1,085 lbs. |
| Feed box, extra | $1.00 | $1.00 | $1.00 | $1.00 | $1.00 |
| Bows and staples, per set, extra | 1.50 | 1.50 | 1.50 | 1.50 | 1.50 |
| Steel skeins instead of cast skeins, extra | 4.00 | 4.50 | 5.00 | 6.00 | 6.00 |
| Tubular steel axles, extra | 2.50 | 3.50 | 4.25 | 7.00 | 7.00 |

# OUR NO. 95156 FARM WAGON--$23.95 TO $43.45.

**See full description and prices of running gear and all parts under description of our No. 95156 Farm Wagon.**

**This cut shows running gear only of our No. 95156 Abingdon, Ill., Farm Wagon. We sell it as wanted, gear, with or without boxes, etc., any size wheel, any width tire.**

**Make your order plain.**

**We will guarantee to please you.**

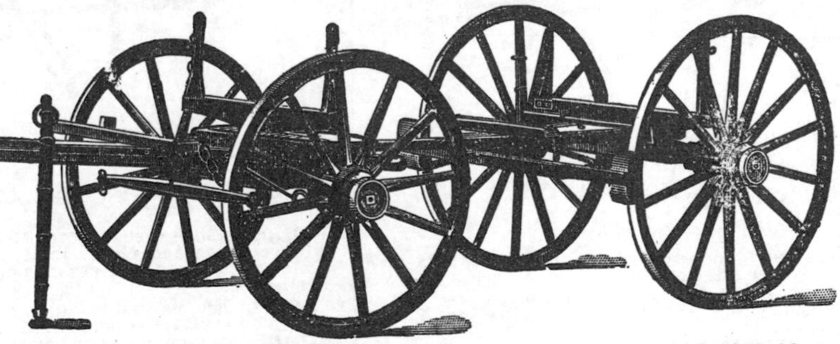

No. 95156 Running Gear

**The above picture shows the Running Gear complete of our No. 95156 Wagon. This gear can be purchased as shown, with or without gear brake. Note quotations on gears, whiffletrees, stay chains and neckyoke, as stated in connection with No. 95156 wagon.**

**UNDERSTAND, WE CAN FURNISH** you the Running Gear alone, with or without brake, as desired, and in any size skein or tire, with neckyoke and whiffletrees complete, at prices quoted under description of our No. 95156 wagon at from $23.95 to $43.45, according to size of skein and tire.

**We can furnish you any piece or part of a FARM WAGON at factory price and save you at least 25 to 33 per cent.**

**IN ORDERING be sure to state just what is wanted, say whether you wish wide or narrow track, 4 feet 6 inches from center of tire to center of tire, or 5 feet wide, center of tire to center of tire, the price is the same.**

**BE SURE TO STATE size of skein and width of tire wanted, and also say whether you wish tubular steel axles or steel skeins in place of wooden axles and cast skeins. Note difference in price under description of OUR No. 95156 WAGON.**

# DEPARTMENT OF HARNESS.

**This Department is Complete with a full line of Harness,** and our prices are as low as the same goods are ever sold by the largest manufacturers to the largest retail trade, and in many cases we have been able to make lower prices than the same class of goods were ever before sold at wholesale.

**You can save the profit of the Retail Dealer** on everything in this line; in other words, at from 60c to 75c you buy from us what your local dealer would ask you $1.00 for.

**We handle nothing but the Best Grade.** All our harness are made from carefully selected oak tanned stock. Our hand made harness is of especially fine quality and far superior to the harness made by the average country harness maker. Our machine made harness are made on the most improved machines, and we guarantee them equal to the average hand made goods.

**We make to order anything in the harness line.** If you want anything special, anything different from that listed in our catalogue, write for prices. We are prepared to furnish you anything in this line.

**Our Harness are made in Chicago by one of the oldest and most reliable makers here,** a concern who for thirty years have had the reputation of making the best grade buggy, farm and team harness, and on this class of goods we invite the closest comparison of quality and price, and earnestly solicit your trade.

**How to Order.** **Always give the weight and height** of the horse the harness is intended for. If the harness is ordered with collar and hames be sure to give the size of collar. See Horse Collars for rules of measurement. All styles of harness in this catalogue are made in full size and will fit any average sized horse up to 1200 lbs.

**Always state the Style of Mountings or Trimmings wanted,** also whether side rein or overcheck is wanted with the bridle, and whether you want the lines russet or black color. If nothing is mentioned concerning the lines or reins it is understood we have the privilege of using our own judgment, in which case we will do our best to please you.

**Our Terms and Conditions of Shipment.** Orders for single harness on receipt of $1.00, and orders for double harness on receipt of $2.00, will be sent to any address by express C.O.D., subject to examination. You can examine the goods at your express office, and if found perfectly satisfactory and exactly as represented. pay the express agent the balance and express charge and the goods are yours. **THIS DOES NOT APPLY** to points in California, Washington, Oregon, Idaho, Montana, Utah, Nevada, Arizona, New Mexico, Colorado, Wyoming, Texas or Florida. From these states and territories cash in full must accompany your order.

**Cash Discount.** We allow a discount of 3% if cash in full accompanies your order. If you send the full amount of cash you may deduct 3% from our price. You take no risk. If the goods are not perfectly satisfactory and exactly as represented, we will refund your money. Nearly all our customers send cash in full.

**We make no charge for boxing,** crating, packing or cartage, but deliver all goods at any express office or freight depot in Chicago free of charge.

Any questions you may wish to ask pertaining to goods in this line will be promptly and cheerfully answered by an expert saddlery man. Whether you write with a view to purchasing or not makes no difference.

## SINGLE BREAST COLLAR BUGGY HARNESS.

## $6.95.

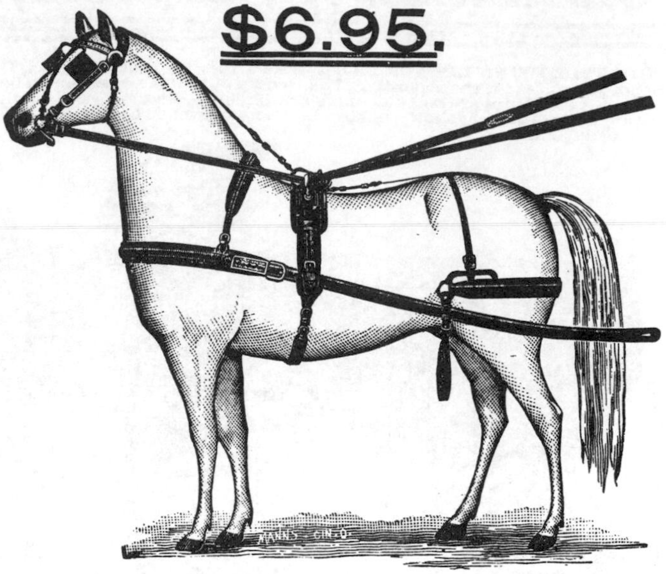

No. 92906.

**BRIDLE**—⅝ inch fancy box loop cheeks, fine patent leather blinds, round winker braces, made with over-check.
**BREAST COLLAR**—1⅞x36 inches, folded and stitched and fancy box loop, raised layer.
**TRACES**—Extra heavy, 1⅛ inches wide, rounded and smoothed edges, raised, double and stitched and made to buckle into breast collar.
**SADDLE**—Has 2 inch single strap skirts, 3 inch leather bottom pad, and is one of the best finished and most durable and showy saddles made.
**BELLY BANDS**—Griffith style, 1½x21 inches.
**TURN BACK**—¾ inch with flax seed crupper.
**HIP STRAP**—⅝ x 50 inches.
**BREECHING**—1¾x39 inches, folded and stitched, raised layer.
**LINES**—⅞ inch hand parts, ⅞ inch checks.
**TRIMMINGS**—Best quality nickel plate on composition throughout, warranted not to rust or tarnish, large flat band, nickel hook and terrets. This harness is made from oak tanned stock, is well finished, smoothed down by hand, blackened on the flesh throughout.
Price........................................$6.95

**No. 92907** Same as the description of 92906, with the exception of collar and hames in place of breast collar. 3½ lb. iron hames, box loop, hame tugs, kip collar, 1⅛ inch trace, double and stitched with round edge.
Price........................................$7.95

### Single Breast Collar Buggy Harness.

Our $3.87 HARNESS.

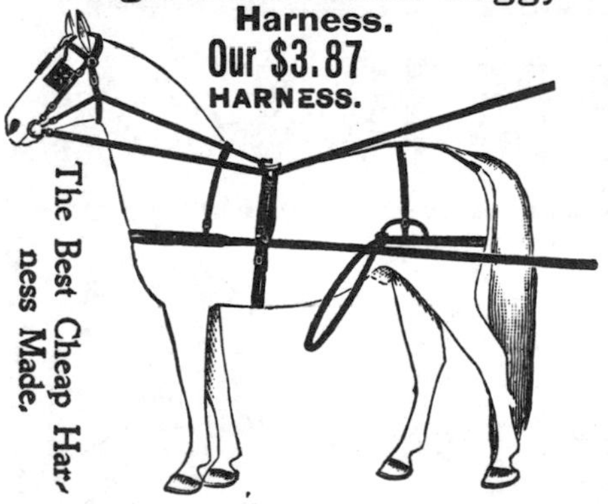

The Best Cheap Harness Made.

No. 92900.

**BRIDLES**—⅝ inch over-check, flat winker stay, patent leather blinds.
**BREAST COLLAR**—Folded with layer.
**TRACES**—1 inch, double and stitched to Breast Collar.
**BREECHING**—Folded with layer.
**SIDE STRAPS**—¾ inch.
**HIP STRAP**—⅝ inch
**TURN BACK**—¾ inch with folded crupper sewed on.
**SADDLE**—2½ inch Patent Leather. Iron Jockey full padded.
**BELLY BANDS**—Griffith style.
**LINES**—¾ inch to loop in bit, X C Trimmings throughout.
Price........................................$3.87

**No. 92901.** Same as the above description, with the exception of Collar and Hames in place of Breast Collar.
Price........................................$4.87

**ANY HARNESS** Sent C.O.D., subject to examination.

### Single Breast Collar Buggy Harness.

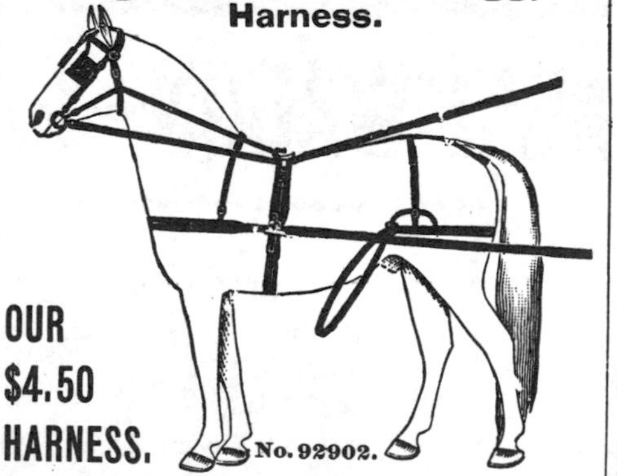

OUR $4.50 HARNESS. No. 92902.

**BRIDLE**—⅝ inch cheeks, patent leather blinds, flat winker brace and check reins, ring bits. fancy fronts and rosettes. Over checks or side reins, as desired.
**LINES**—¾ inch, flat, all black, to loop in bit.
**BREAST COLLAR**—Folded and stitched.
**SADDLE**—2½ inch, enameled cloth bottom, doubled and stitched bearers.
**SHAFT TUGS**—1 inch, with ⅞ inch buckles and ¾ inch belly band billits.
**BELLY BANDS**—⅝ inch flat.
**BREECHING**—Folded and stitched, ⅝ inch flat hip strap, ¾ inch turn back, lapped and stitched to crupper pieces, folded crupper, docks sewed on breeching straps, ¾ inch.
**TRACES**—1 inch doubled and stitched to breast collar.
This single buggy harness comes in full X. C. plate only, imitation hand sewed.
Price........................................$4.50

**No. 92903.** Same as the description of 92902 with the exception of collar and hames in place of breast collar, kip collar, any size, traces attached to hames.
Price........................................$5.50

### Single Breast Collar Buggy Harness.

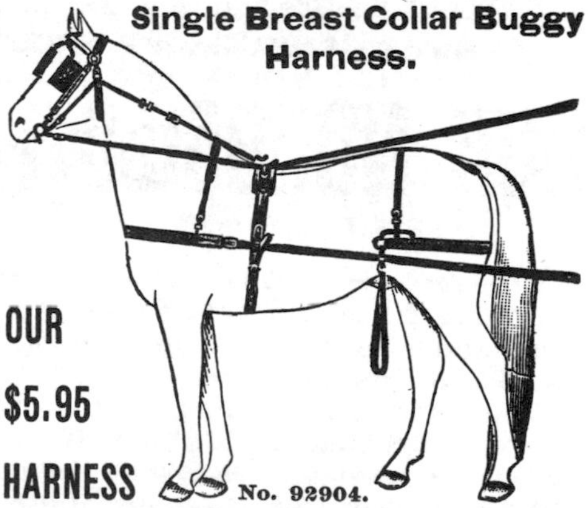

OUR $5.95 HARNESS No. 92904.

**BRIDLE**—⅝ inch over-check, box loops, flat winker stay.
**BREAST COLLAR**—Folded with wide layer and box loops.
**TRACES**—1 inch, double and stitched, round edge.
**BREECHING**—Folded with wide layer.
**SIDE STRAPS**—¾ inch.
**HIP STRAPS**—⅝ inch.
**TURN BACK**—¾ inch, round crupper.
**SADDLE**—2½ inch, single strap, all leather skirts and bottom.
**BELLY BANDS**—Griffith style.
**LINES**—⅞ inch to loop in bit, X C Trimmings throughout.
Price........................................$5.95

**No. 92905** Same as the description of No. 92904 with the exception of Collar and Hames in place of breast collar, 3½ lb. iron hames, box loop, hame tugs, kip collars, 1 inch trace, double and stitched with round edge.
Price........................................$6.95

**3 PER CENT.** DISCOUNT when cash in full accompanies order.

OUR HARDWARE DEPARTMENT GIVES YOU A GREAT OPPORTUNITY TO SAVE FROM 25 TO 50 PER CENT. ON YOUR PURCHASES. IT IS EASY TO MAKE UP A FREIGHT ORDER BY JOINING WITH YOUR NEIGHBORS.

## Single Breast Collar Buggy Harness.

### Our Special $7.95 Harness.

$7.95

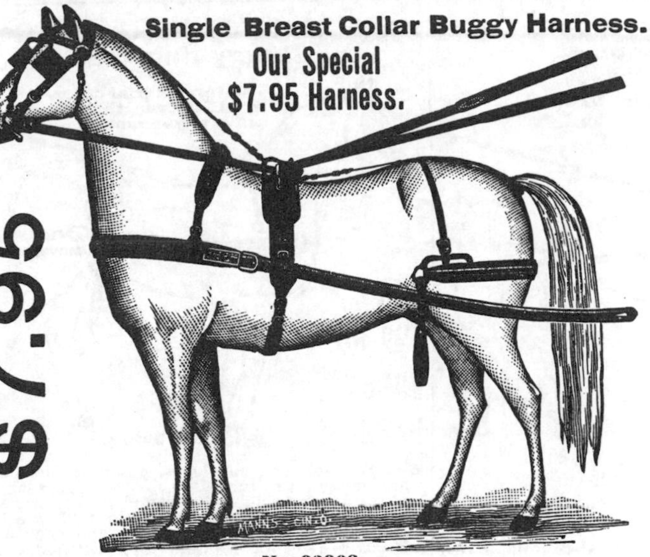

No. 92908.

**BRIDLE**—⅝ inch fancy box loop cheeks, fine patent leather blinds, round winker braces, made with over-check and layer on crown, fancy nickel chain front, fancy rosettes, fancy silver nickel jointed bit.

**HIP STRAPS**—⅝x50 inches.

**TURN BACK**—¾ inch, fancy, creased and finished, flax seed crupper.

**BELLY BAND**—Griffith style, folded, such as is used in all first class harness, 1½x21 inches.

**BREECHING**—1¾x39 inches, folded and stitched, raised layer.

**BREAST COLLAR**—1⅞x36 inch folded and stitched, with box loops and raised layer. In keeping with the traces, the breast collar is also made very strong from selected heavy stock.

**SADDLE**—A genuine full leather single strap saddle, 2½ inch single strap skirts, 8 inch leather bottom pad, nicely stitched and ornamented. The saddle is A1 stock and shows for itself. The most showy and durable saddle made.

**TRACES**—The most important parts of a harness are the traces. This has not been over-looked in special No. 92908 at $7.95. They are extra heavy and made from selected stock, full 1⅛ inches wide, 6 feet long, double and stitched, finely raised, rounded edges worked down smooth, and made to buckle into breast collar. The regular size trace is 1 inch. You will notice this 1⅛ inch trace harness has been built for service.

**LINES**—⅞ inch with 1 inch hand parts; the lines are made from select stock.

**TRIMMINGS**—Finest quality silver nickel throughout, including hooks, terrets, buckles, etc. By the best quality, we mean silver nickel on a patent composition that will wear for years and never tarnish. Very fancy hooks and terrets of the latest and most fashionable pattern; in fact the trimmings used on this harness will compare favorably with those used on the highest priced harness on the market.

Price........ ........................................ **$7.95**

**No. 92909.** Same as the description of No. 92908, with the exception of collar and hames in place of breast collar. 3½ lb. iron hames with nickel spot box loop hame tugs. Kip collar, any size wanted, 1⅛ inch traces, double and stitched, round edge.

Price..... ........................................ **$8.50**

## Single Breast Collar Buggy Harness.

Our Special Single Buggy Harness for $8.65.

$8.65.

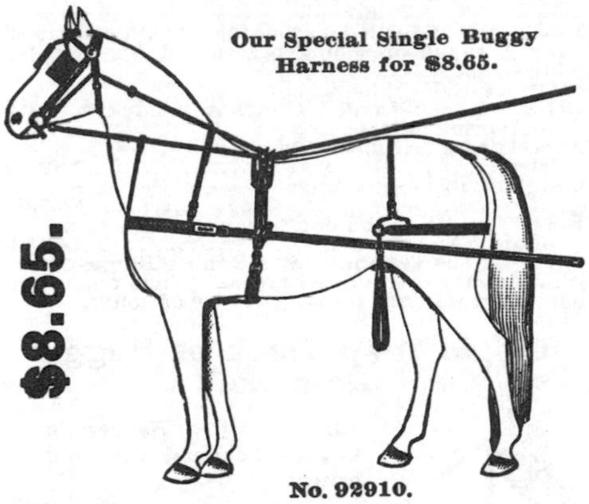

No. 92910.

**BRIDLES**—⅝ inch cheeks, full box loops, fancy creased, finished and polished patent leather blinds, with fancy carving, round winker braces, layer on crown pieces, half check bits, fancy chain fronts and fancy rosettes, flat over-checks or side-reins, as desired.

**LINES**—⅞ inch flat, all black, to buckle into bit.

**BREAST COLLAR**—Folded with straight raised layer and box loops throughout, folded neck strap, with ¾ inch raised lay, doubled and stitched points.

**TRACES**—1⅛ inch solid raised, double and stitched.

**SHAFT TUGS**—⅞ inch double and stitched, ⅞ inch belly band billits.

**BELLY BANDS**—Griffith style folded and stitched.

**BREECHING**—Extra heavy and wide, folded and stitched, with straight lay stitched to breeching, ⅝ inch flat hip straps, ¾ inch turn backs, lapped and stitched to crupper pieces, best quality flax seed stuffed round crupper docks, sewed on breeching straps, ⅞ inch.

**No. 92910.** Price.................................... **$8.65**

**No. 92910½.** The same harness with full Patent leather Saddle ........................ **9.75**

Extra for Collar and Hames in place of Breast Collar .................................. **1.50**

## Single Breast Collar Buggy Harness.

### Our $10.50 Buggy Harness

You can save 33⅓ per cent. by buying this harness at our price.

No. 92911.

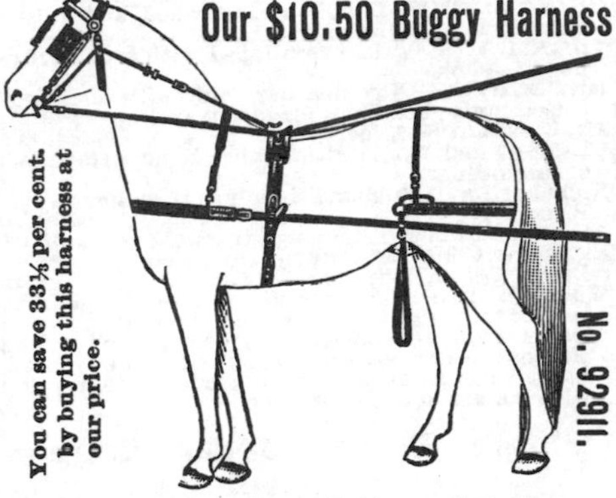

Full Nickle or Davis Rubber as desired.

**BRIDLE**—⅝ inch over-check, box loops, round winker stay, layer on crown pieces, nose band, or side rein, as desired.

**BREAST COLLAR**—Folded with scalloped raised layer, box loops and safe under buckles.

**TRACES**—1⅛ inch, double and stitched, round edge.

**BREECHING**—Folded with scalloped raised layer.

**SIDE STRAPS**—⅝ inch.

**HIP STRAPS**—⅝ inch.

**TURN BACK**—⅞ inch scalloped, round crupper.

No. 92911, Price.................................... **$10.50**

Single Strap Saddle, 2½ inch. Single Strap Skirts, 3 inch leather bottom pad, nicely stitched and ornamented, if desired, at the above price.

Extra for collar and hames in place of breast collar..................................... **$1.50**

## Single Breast Collar Buggy Harness.

### Our $11.45 Single Harness.

Our harness is all made of best selected stock.

We guarantee all our Harness to be strictly first-class.

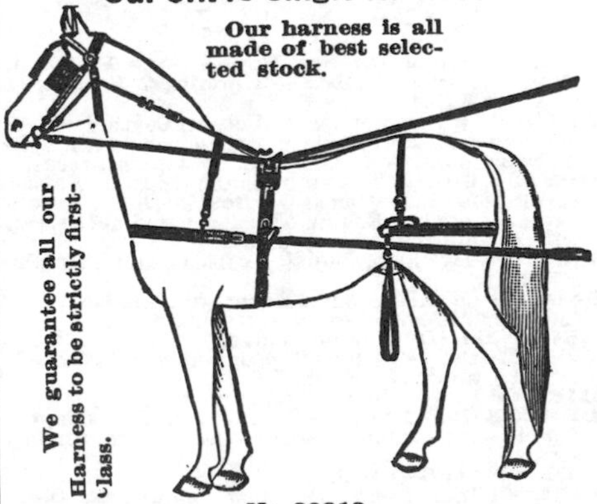

No. 92912.

Nickel or Davis rubber trimmings throughout.

**BRIDLE**—⅝ inch, box loops, patent leather winkers, over-check with nose band, or round side reins, round winker stay, layer on crown.

**BREAST COLLAR**—Oiled leather, (or glove finished fold leather) fold with wide raised layer. Box loops for traces and neck strap, safe under buckles.

**(No. 92912. Harness—Continued.)**

**TRACES**—1⅛ inch, double and stitched, center raised and round edge finished.

**SADDLE**—3 inch, single strap (or full patent leatner padded).

**BELLY BANDS**—Oiled leather fold with wide layer. Griffith style.

**TURN BACK**—¾ inch scalloped with round crupper.

**HIP STRAPS**—⅝ inch.

**BREECHING**—Oiled leather (or glove finished) fold, wide raised layer.

**SIDE STRAPS**—⅝ inch.

**LINES**—1 inch throughout (or ⅞ inch fronts with 1⅛ inch handparts) to loop in bit, or with steel spring billets.

**No. 92912.** Price.............. .............. **$11.45**

Extra for full genuine rubber trimmings throughout.............................. **2.25**

Extra for collar and hames in place of breast collar....................................... **2.00**

When collar and hames are wanted on genuine rubber harness, we use the best quality of Davis Rubber Hames.

## Single Breast Collar Buggy Harness.

### Our $14.00 Buggy Harness.

We guarantee satisfaction or money refunded.

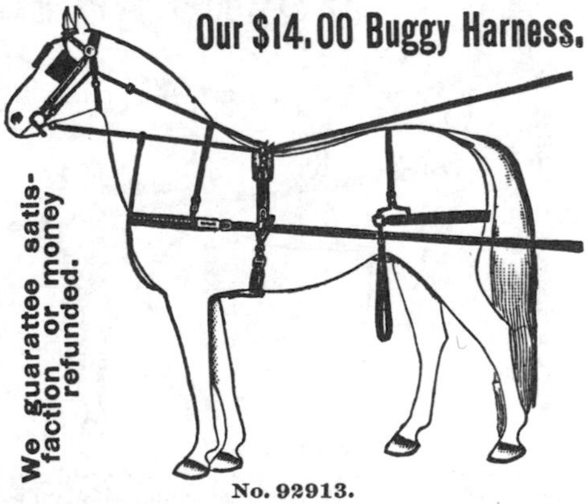

No. 92913.

**BRIDLE**—½ inch, box loops, patent leather winker over-check with nose piece, layer on crown, round winker stay, or side rein, as desired.

**BREAST COLLAR**—Enameled leather fold with scalloped raised layer.

**TRACES**—1 inch double and stitched, raised with round edge, attached to breast collar, (or 1⅛ inch single strap trace as desired).

**BREECHING**—Enameled leather fold with scalloped raised layer.

**SIDE STRAPS**—⅝ inch.

**HIP STRAPS**—⅝ inch.

**TURN BACK**—¾ inch, scalloped with round crupper sewed on.

**SADDLE**—Full patent leather skirts, enameled leather pad laced in, (or single strap saddle, as desired).

**BELLY BANDS**—Inside folded, outside single, attached with billits, (or Griffith style.)

**LINES**—⅞ inch fronts, 1⅛ inch handparts, with steel spring billits.

Nickel or Davis Rubber Trimmings throughout.

**No. 92913.** Price.............. .............. **$14.00**

**No. 92913½.** Genuine Rubber trimmings throughout.......................................... **16.00**

We can also furnish this harness with buckle on the breast collar to buckle trace on, at same price.

Extra for Collar and Hames in place of Breast Collar, (patent leather collar)........ **2.25**

## WE SELL STOVES

### And Dealers Despair at Our Prices.

**Our stoves and ranges have no superiors, and our customers think there are none equal to them. Freight is only 4h-class on stoves and costs little.**

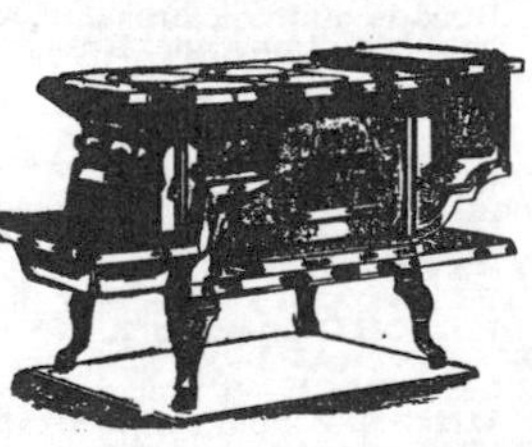

**Every Stove Absolutely Warranted.**

DON'T BUY A 5 CENT ITEM ALONE FROM US, UNLESS YOU CAN'T GET IT AT HOME. BUY ALL YOUR 5 CENT, 50 CENT AND $10.00 ITEMS THAT YOU WILL NEED, AT ONCE, SHIP BY FREIGHT AND SAVE ALL THE MORE.

## Single Breast Collar Buggy Harness.

### Our $14.50 Buggy Harness.

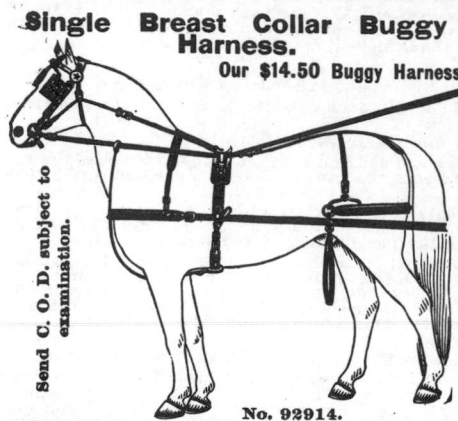

*Send C. O. D. subject to examination.*

No. 92914.

**BRIDLES**—⅝ inch, box loops, Patent Leather winkers, over-check with nose piece or round side reins as desired. Round winker stay.
**BREAST COLLAR**—Glove finished fold leather, fold with safe under buckles, wide raised layer. Box loops for traces and neck strap.
**TRACES**—1⅛ inches, double and stitched, raised with round edge.
**SADDLE**—Single strap, or full Patent Leather padded.
**BELLY BANDS**—Glove finish fold with layer, Griffith style.
**TURN BACK**—¾ inch scalloped, with round crupper sewed on.
**HIP STRAPS**—⅝ inch.
**BREECHING**—Glove finished leather fold, wide raised layer.
**SIDE STRAPS**—⅝ inch.
**LINES**—1 inch throughout, or ⅞ inch fronts and 1⅛ inch handparts, to loop in bit or with steel spring billets.
Nickel or Davis trimmings throughout.
Price......................................$14.50
Genuine Rubber trimmings throughout.
Price..................................$17.00
Extra for Collars and Hames (any size) in place of Breast Collar....................$2.00
When Collar and Hames are wanted on Genuine Rubber Trimmed Harness, we use the best quality of Davis Rubber Hames. In ordering harness with collar and hames, always give size of collar wanted, measuring collar as shown in cut in connection with collars in this catalogue.

## Single Breast Collar Buggy Harness.

### Our $17.50 Buggy Harness

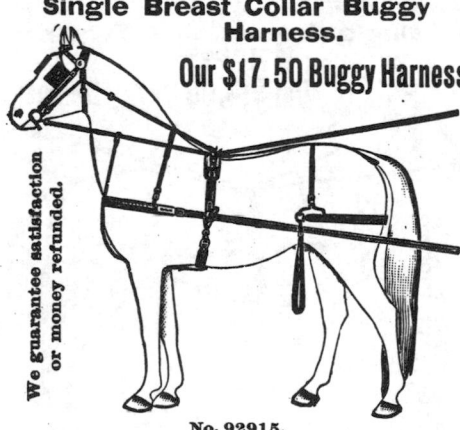

*We guarantee satisfaction or money refunded.*

No. 92915.

**BRIDLE**—⅝ in., box loops, patent leather winkers, over-check with nose piece, or round side reins, round winker stay.
**BREAST COLLAR**—Glove finished leather fold, with scalloped layer, box loops for traces and neck strap, safe under buckles.
**TRACES**—Double and stitched, raised with round edge finish.
**SADDLE**—3 inch, single strap or full padded. Patent leather skirt.
**BELLY BANDS**—Glove finished fold leather with layer, Griffith style.
**TURN BACK**—¾ inch scalloped with round crupper sewed on.
**HIP STRAPS**—⅝ inch.
**BREECHING**—Glove finished leather fold, with scalloped layer. Box loops for hip strap.
**SIDE STRAPS**—⅝ inch.
**LINES**—1 inch fronts with 1⅛ inch handparts, with steel spring billits.
Nickel or Davis rubber trimmings throughout.
Price.............................$17.50
Genuine rubber trimmings throughout.
Price.............................$19.75
Extra for collar and hames, (full patent leather collar, any size) in place of breast collar......................... 2.25
When collar and hames are wanted on genuine rubber trimmed harness, we use the best grade of Davis rubber hames. In ordering harness with collar and hames, always give the size of the collar wanted, measuring collar as shown in cut in connection with collars in this catalogue.

## Hand Made Single Breast Collar Buggy Harness.

### This Buggy Harness for $20.50

*Do You Want Our Best?*

No. 92916

**BRIDLE**—⅝ inch, box loops, patent leather winkers, over-check with nose piece or round side reins, round winker stay.
**BREAST COLLAR**—Oiled leather fold, with scalloped raised layers and box loops for traces and neck strap.
**TRACES**—1⅛ inches, double and stitched, raised round edge finished.
**SADDLE**—Single strap or full padded, patent leather skirt.
**BELLY BANDS**—Double and stitched and raised on the inside, Griffith style.
**TURN BACK**—¾ inch scalloped with round crupper sewed on.
**BREECHING**—Oiled leather fold, with scalloped raised layer; box loops for hip straps.
**SIDE STRAPS**—⅝ inch.
**LINES**—1 inch fronts with 1⅛ inch handparts; steel spring billits.
Nickel or Davis Rubber Trimmings throughout.
Price...........................$20.50
Genuine Rubber Trimmings throughout.. 23.00
Extra for Collar and Hames in place of Breast Collar, (any size)................... 2.25
When Collar and Hames are wanted on genuine rubber trimmed harness, we use the best grade of Davis rubber hames, always give size of collar wanted, measuring collar as shown in cut in connection with collars in this catalogue.

## Single Breast Collar Buggy Harness.

### Our $22.50 Buggy Harness.

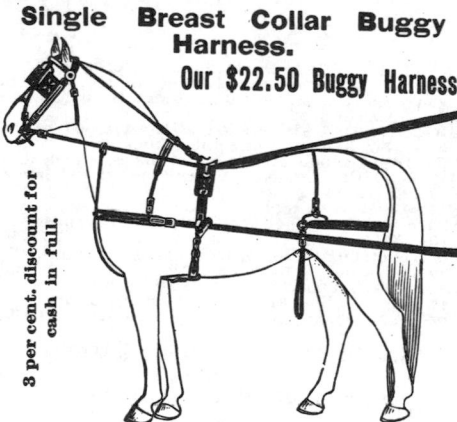

*3 per cent. discount for cash in full.*

No. 92917

**Imitation, Hand Stitched, Round Edge Finished. Full Genuine Rubber Trimmings, Enameled Leather Folds.**
**BRIDLE**—⅝ inch box loops, Patent Leather winkers, layer on crown piece, over-check with nose piece or round side reins. Round winker braces.
**BREAST COLLAR**—Patent enameled fold. Raised layer, safe under buckles. Box loops for traces and neck strap. Enameled leather fold neck strap with double and stitched points.
**TRACES**—1⅛ inch, double, raised and straight stitched.
**SADDLE**—A full patent leather, genuine Kay, the finest saddle made.
**BELLY BANDS**—Double folded.
**TURN BACK**—¾ inch scalloped, double and stitched, round crupper sewed on.
**HIP STRAPS**—⅝ inch, double and stitched.
**BREECHING**—Enameled leather fold, raised layer, double and stitched braces, box loops for hip straps.
**SIDE STRAPS**—⅝ inch.
**LINES**—1 inch fronts, 1⅛ inch handparts. Steel spring billits.
Price...........................$22.50
Extra for Collar and Hames in place of Breast Collar....................$3.00
Collar, a fine Patent Leather, French rim. Hames, Davis Rubber, best quality. Collar any size wanted.
If you order Harness with Collar and Hames, be sure to give size of Collar.

## Hand Made Single Breast Collar Buggy Harness.

*We urge a trial order, to satisfy you that we can save you money.*

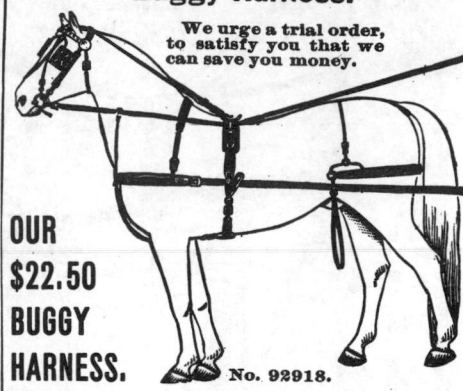

### OUR $22.50 BUGGY HARNESS.

No. 92918.

**BRIDLE**—⅝ inch box loops, patent leather winkers, layer on crown piece, over-check with nose piece, or round side reins, round winker braces.
**BREAST COLLAR**—Oiled leather fold, scalloped raised layer, box loops for traces and neck straps.
**TRACES**—1⅛ inch, double and stitched, raised and round edge finished.
**SADDLE**—Full padded patent leather skirt or a fine grade of single strap saddle.
**BELLY BANDS**—Harness leather, doubled and stitched, raised on inside, Griffith style.
**TURN BACK**—¾ inch scalloped, with round crupper sewed on.
**HITCH STRAP**—Round.
**BREECHING**—Oiled leather fold. Scalloped raised layer, round breeching braces and box loop for hip strap.
**SIDE STRAP**—⅝ inch.
**LINES**—1 inch front, 1⅛ inches handparts, with steel spring billets.
Nickel or Davis rubber trimmings.
Price...........................$22.50
Genuine rubber trimmings.
Price...........................$25.00
Extra for collar and hames in place of breast collar. (Any size collar)............$3.00
We use the genuine Davis Rubber Hames on the genuine rubber trimmed harness. When collar and hames are wanted, always give size of collar.

## Single Strap Track or Buggy Harness.

*One of these Harness in a neighborhood will sell others for us.*

*The Finest $7.50 Single Strap Harness Ever Made.*

No. 92919.

**BRIDLE**—⅝ inch Patent Leather winkers, box loop cheeks, over-check or ride rein, as desired.
**BREAST COLLAR**—1⅛ inch, heavy stock.
**TRACES**—1⅛ inch, heavy stock.
**BREECHING**—1⅛ inch.
**SIDE STRAPS**—¾ inch.
**HIP STRAPS**—⅝ inch.
**TURN BACK**—¾ inch, scalloped with round crupper sewed on.
**SADDLE**—2½ inch, single strap harness leather skirts, leather bottom.
**BELLY BAND**—Griffith style.
**LINES**—⅝ inch
All made plain, no creasing, an extra good harness. Nickle or imitation Rubber Trimmings throughout.
Price...........................$7.50

### No. 92920.

Same harness and description as No. 92922, except that the straps are heavier and are cut wider.
**TRACES**—1⅛ inch.
**BREAST COLLAR**—1⅛ inch.
**BREECHING**—1⅛ inch.
**SIDE STRAPS**—⅝ inch.
**TURN BACK**—⅞ inch.
**SADDLE**—3 inch, single strap swell skirt.
**LINES**—1 inch.
This is a good single strap breast collar harness for a surrey or extra heavy buggy.
Nickel or imitation rubber trimmings throughout.
Price...........................$8.25

**IF EVERY CUSTOMER WHO IS PLEASED WITH OUR MANNER OF DOING BUSINESS WILL TELL A NEIGHBOR ABOUT US, OUR BUSINESS WOULD BE DOUBLED IN TWO WEEKS.**

## Single Strap Track or Buggy Harness.

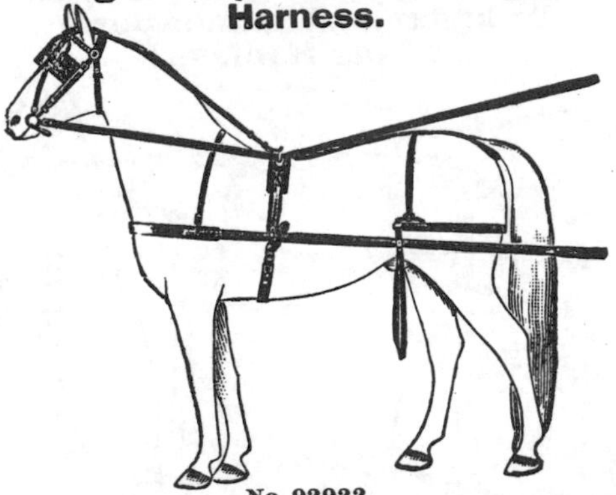

No. 92922.

**BRIDLE**—⅝ inch patent leather winkers, box loop cheeks, over-checks or flat side reins, as desired, round winker stay.
**TRACES**—1⅛ inch, heavy single strap.
**BREAST COLLAR**—1⅝ inch, heavy single strap.
**SADDLE**—2½ inch, single strap, harness leather skirts, leather bottom.
**BREECHING**—1⅛ inch, heavy single strap.
**SIDE STRAPS**—¾ inch.
**HIP STRAPS**—⅝ inch.
**TURN BACK**—¾ inch, scalloped round crupper, stitched on.
**BELLY BAND**—Wide single strap, Griffith style.
**LINES**—⅞ inch to loop in bit, fancy creased.
Nickle or Davis rubber trimmings throughout.
Price........................................$6.00

No. 92923.

Description same as No. 92919, except made plain, round edge in place of fancy creased.
Price........................................$6.00

## Single Strap Track or Buggy Harness.

**Our enormous contracts for harness put us in a position to name rock bottom prices.**

NEW V-SHAPED.... BREAST COLLAR

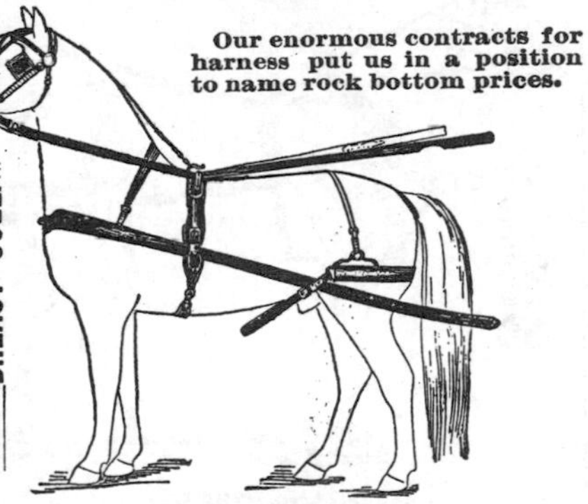

No. 92924.

**BRIDLE**—⅝ inch, patent leather blinds, box loops, round winker stay, layer on crown, over check with nose piece or round side reins.
**BREAST COLLAR**—Extra wide, V shaped.
**TRACES**—1¼ inch single strap, stitched to breast collar with scalloped points.
**BREECHING**—1¾ inch.
**SIDE STRAPS**—⅞ inch.
**HIP STRAPS**—¾ inch.
**TURN BACK**—⅞ inch scalloped with round crupper sewed on.
**SADDLE**—3 inch, single strap, swell padded patent leather jockey, harness leather skirts, leather bottom or full patent leather skirts, full padded leather, lined and laced.
**BELLY BANDS**—Wide, single strap, Griffith style.
**LINES**—1 inch with buckle and billits.
Harness made plain, single edge crease, a very popular harness.
Nickle or imitation rubber trimmings throughout.
Price........................................$11.00

## Single Strap Track or Buggy Harness.

No. 92925.

**BRIDLE**—⅝ inch, patent leather blinds, round winker stays, layer on crown, over check with nose band.
**BREAST COLLAR**—1⅞ inch.
**TRACES**—1⅛ inch stitched to Breast Collar, with long tapering points.
**BREECHING**—1⅝ inch.
**SIDE STRAPS**—⅝ inch.
**HIP STRAPS**—⅝ inch.
**TURN BACK**—¾ inch scalloped, with round crupper sewed on.
**SADDLE**—2½ inch single strap. Patent leather jockey, harness leather skirts, leather bottom, or a patent leather skirt, laced in and leather lined. (Your choice.)
**BELLY BANDS**—Wide, single strap, Griffith style.
**LINES**—⅝ inch fronts, 1⅛ inch handparts, with steel spring billits.
Nickel or imitation Rubber trimmings throughout.
Price........................................$12.00
Genuine rubber trimmings throughout..... 14.00

## Single Strap Track or Buggy Harness.

**$8.75.**

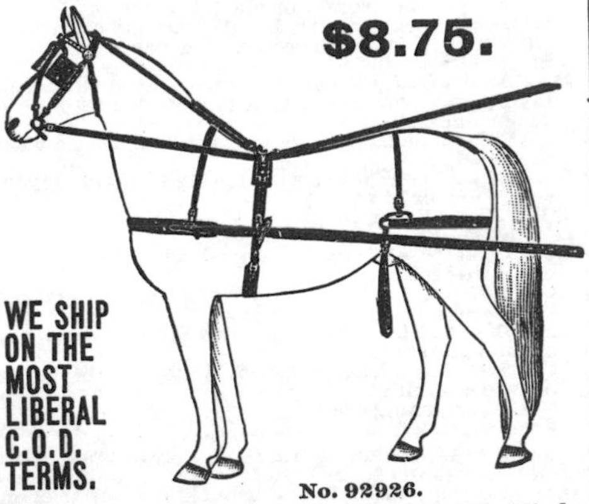

WE SHIP ON THE MOST LIBERAL C.O.D. TERMS.

No. 92926.

**BRIDLE**—⅝ inch, over check, patent leather blinds, box loops, round winker stays, layer on crown, nose piece on over-check.
**BREAST COLLAR**—1¾ inch.
**TRACES**—1⅛ inch, stitched to Breast Collar.
**BREECHING**—1⅝ inch.
**SIDE STRAPS**—⅞ inch.
**HIP STRAP**—⅝ inch.
**TURN BACK**—¾ inch, scalloped with round crupper sewed on.
**SADDLE**—2¼ inch, single strap, Patent Leather Jockey, Harness leather skirts, enameled leather bottom, or full patent leather skirts, full padded saddle, as desired.
**BELLY BANDS**—Griffith style.
**LINES**—1 inch buckle or billit ends or to loop in bit.
Harness all made plain with single edge crease.
Nickel or imitation rubber trimmings throughout.
Price........................................$8.75

## Single Strap Harness for Track or Buggy Use. Extra Heavy.

**Our $10.00 Bargain.**

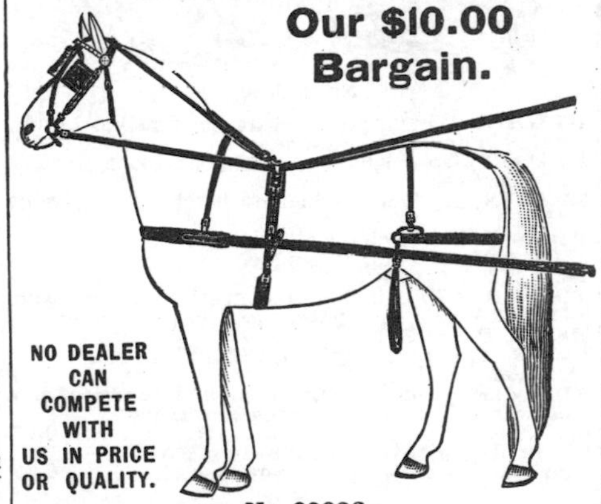

NO DEALER CAN COMPETE WITH US IN PRICE OR QUALITY.

No. 92928.

**BRIDLE**—⅝ inch, box loop, layer on crown, round winker braces, over-check with nose piece or round side reins.
**BREAST COLLAR**—2 inch.
**TRACES**—1¼ inch, scalloped points, stitched to breast collar.
**BREECHING**—1¾ inch.
**SIDE STRAPS**—⅞ inch.
**HIP STRAP**—¾ inch.
**TURN BACK**—⅞ inch scalloped, with round crupper stitched on.
**SADDLE**—3 inch, single strap, swell padded, patent leather jockey, harness leather skirts, leather bottom, or full patent leather skirt, full padded leather lined laced in.
**BELLY BANDS**—Griffith style, wide single strap.
**LINES**—1 inch to loop in bit,
Harness all wave creased. An extra heavy harness for surry or heavy buggy.
Nickel or imitation rubber trimmings throughout.
Price........................................$10.00

No. 92929.

Same description as above, except made extra large for stallions or large horses, weighing from 1300 to 1500 pounds.
Nickel or imitation rubber trimmings throughout.
Price........................................$11.50

**WE ARE JUST AS ANXIOUS to fill your order right, as you are. If you have any cause for complaint, you will do us a favor by notifying us promptly, and giving all necessary information. We are anxious to please you.**

## Single Strap Track or Buggy Harness.

**Our enormous contracts for harness put us in a position to name rock bottom prices.**

$14.00 C. O. D. or $13.58 cash with order.

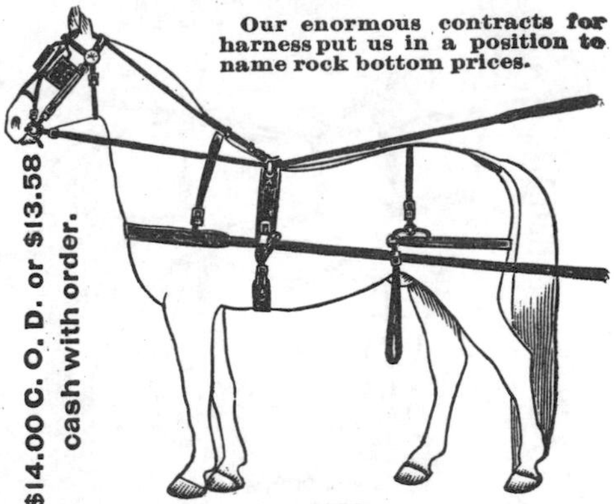

No. 92933.

**BRIDLE**—⅝ inch, patent leather winkers, box loops, round winker stay, layer on crown, over-check with nose piece or round side check, as desired.
**BREAST COLLAR**—1¾ inch, single strap.
**TRACES**—1⅛ inch, single strap, attached to breast collar, with scalloped points.
**BREECHING**—1⅝ inch, single strap.
**SIDE STRAPS**—⅞ inch.
**HIP STRAPS**—⅝ inch.
**TURN BACK**—¾ inch scalloped, with round crupper sewed on.
**SADDLE**—3 inch, full patent leather, leather lined and laced in, covered seat, terrets low down. ½ inch track.
**BELLY BANDS**—Wide single strap, Griffith style.
**LINES**—1⅛ inch handparts, ⅞ inch fronts, with steel spring billets.
This harness is made smooth, round edge, no creasing.
Nickel or imitation rubber trimmings throughout.
Price........................................$14.00
Genuine rubber trimmings throughout.
Price........................................$16.00

## Single Strap Surrey or Heavy Buggy Harness.

NEW V-SHAPED.... BREAST COLLAR.

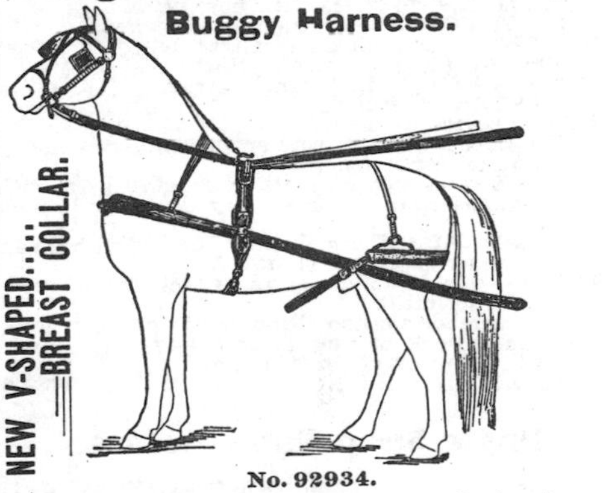

No. 92934.

**BRIDLE**—⅝ inch, patent leather blinds, box loops, round winker stay, layer on crown, over-check with nose piece or round side check as desired.
**BREAST COLLAR**—Single strap, V shaped, extra wide.
**TRACES**—1¼ inch, single strap, attached to breast collar with scalloped points.
**BREECHING**—1¾ inch, single strap.
**SIDE STRAPS**—⅞ inch.
**HIP STRAPS**—¾ inch.
**TURN BACK**—⅞ inch scalloped, with round crupper sewed on.
**SADDLE**—Full, patent leather skirts, full padded and laced in, covered seat low down, or half track terrets, continuous bearer running through the tree of saddle without any holes, making the strongest possible saddle on the market.
**BELLY BANDS**—Flat with billets to wrap around the shafts.
**LINES**—1⅛ inch handparts, 1 inch fronts, with steel spring billets.
Entire harness made smooth,, round edge, no creasing.
Nickel or imitation rubber trimmings.
Price........................................$15.50
Genuine rubber trimmings.
Price........................................$17.50

## SHIRTS AND SWEATERS....

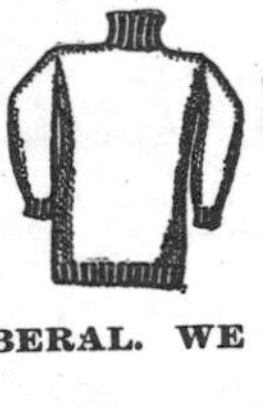

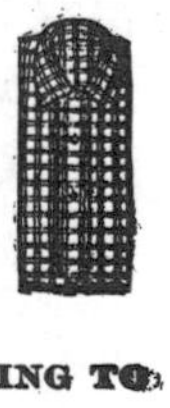

**See Our Gents' Furnishing Goods Dep't. PAGE 206.**

**Latest Styles and Prettiest Designs.**

**LOWEST PRICES.**

## Single Strap Track Harness.

### $17.50.

**A Wonderful Bargain.**

No. 92936.

**BRIDLE**—½ inch, patent grain track leather blinds, box loops, round winker stay, layer on crown, over check with nose piece.
**BREAST COLLAR**—1¼ inch, single strap.
**TRACES**—1½ inch, single strap.
**SIDE STRAPS**—⅝ inch.
**HIP STRAPS**—⅝ inch.
**TURN BACK**—¾ inch scalloped with round crupper sewed on.
**SADDLE**—Full patent leather skirt full padded, laced in and leather lined, with leather covered seat and continuous bearer.
**BELLY BANDS**—Flat, with billits to wrap around the shafts.
**LINES**—1⅛ inch hand parts, ⅝ inch fronts, with steel spring billits.
Made smooth, round edge, no creasing.
Nickel or imitation rubber trimmings throughout.
Price....................................$17.50
Genuine rubber trimmings throughout.
Price....................................$19.50

## Single Strap Track Harness.
No. 92937.

**BRIDLE**—½ inch, grain leather track blinds, round winker stay, crown piece, enameled leather fold with layer, over check with nose band.
**BREAST COLLAR**—1⅝ inch, single strap.
**TRACES**—1 inch, single strap, attached to breast collar, with long tapering points.
**BREECHING**—1½ inch, single strap.
**SIDE STRAPS**—¾ inch.
**HIP STRAPS**—½ inch.
**TURN BACK**—⅝ inch, scalloped, with extra heavy round crupper sewed on.
**SADDLE**—Full patent leather, genuine Kay, with continuous bearer, terrets low down, or ½ inch track.
**BELLY BANDS**—Enameled leather fold with layer, billits to wrap around shafts.
**LINES**—1⅛ inch, hand parts, ⅝ inch fronts with steel spring billits.
Harness made smooth throughout and very light, for track work or very light buggy only. Made only in genuine rubber trimmings.
Price.................................$25.50

## Single Strap Pony Harness.

**Retailers charge 50 per cent. more for this Harness.**

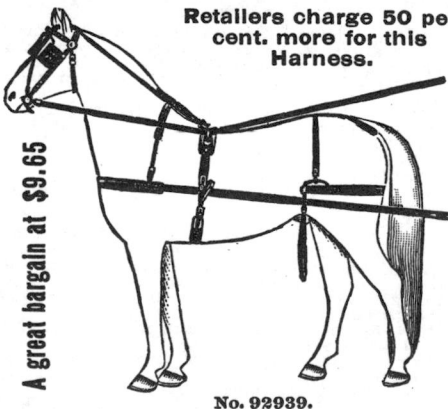

**A great bargain at $9.65**

No. 92939.

**BRIDLE**—½ inch with russet leather blinds or patent leather blinds on black harness, box loops, round winker stay, layer on crown, over-check.
**BREAST COLLAR**—1¼ inch, single strap.
**TRACES**—1 inch, stitched to breast collar.
**BREECHING**—1⅛ inch, single strap.
**SIDE STRAPS**—¾ inch.
**HIP STRAPS**—½ inch.
**TURN BACK**—⅝ inch, scalloped with round crupper, sewed on.
**SADDLE**—2¼ inch, single strap, harness leather skirts, leather bottom.
**BELLY BANDS**—Griffith style.
**LINES**—⅝ inch fronts, 1 inch hand parts.

## Single Strap Pony Harness.
No. 92940.

Either russet or black leather.
**BRIDLE**—½ inch, with blinds, box loops, round winker stay, layer on crown, over-check with nose piece.
**BREAST COLLAR**—Folded with scalloped raised layer, box loops for traces and neck strap, safe under buckles.
**TRACES**—1 inch, double and stitched, raised with round edge.
**BREECHING**—Folded with scalloped raised layer, box loops for hip strap.
**SIDE STRAPS**—¾ inch.
**HIP STRAPS**—½ inch.
**TURN BACK**—⅝ inch scalloped, with round crupper sewed on.
**SADDLE**—2½ inch, full padded skirts, leather lined and laced in covered seat.
**BELLY BANDS**—Folded with billets to wrap around the shafts.
**LINES**—1 inch handparts, ⅝ inch fronts, with buckle and billets.
Nickel trimmings only.
Price....................................$11.00
No. 92941. Same harness as No. 92940 with collar and hames; full plated hames, hame tugs with box loops and safe under buckles. Collar open or closed top. Nickel trimmings only.
Price....................................$14.50

## Single Barouche or Grocery Harness.

☞ $10.00

No. 92946.

**BRIDLE**—¾ inch, patent leather, sensible blinds, flat rein and winker stays.
**HAME TUGS**—with swell ends, box loops, 3¼ lbs. iron hames.
**TRACES**—1¼ inch, double and stitched, round edge finish.
**BREECHING**—Folded with wide layer.
**SIDE STRAPS**—1 inch double.
**HIP STRAP**—(2) ¾ inch.
**TURN BACK**—1 inch round crupper to buckle on.
**SADDLE**—3½ inches, patent leather, full padded.
**BELLY BANDS**—Folded.
**LINES**—1 inch thoroughout, to buckle in bit.
**COLLAR**—Full Kip.
In ordering this harness, always state size of collar wanted. X. C. Trimming throughout.
Price....................................$10.00
If wanted with breast collar in place of collar and hames, the price would be............$8.75

## Single Barouche or Grocery Harness.

$13.50

No. 92947.

**BRIDLE**—⅝ inch, patent leather, sensible blinds, box loops, round rein and winker stays.
**HAME TUGS**—Swell ends, box loops, 3½ lb. iron hames.
**TRACES**—1¼ inch, double and stitched, round edge finish.
**BREECHING**—Folded with layer.
**HIP STRAP**—¾ inch, double.
**SIDE STRAPS**—1 inch.
**TURN BACK**—⅝ inch, round crupper to buckle on.
**SADDLE**—3½ inch, patent leather skirt, full padded.
**BELLY BANDS**—Inside folded, outside single strap.
**LINES**—1 inch, buckles and billits.
**COLLAR**—Patent leather, full nickel or brass trimmings.
Price....................................$13.50

## Great Bargain in Genuine Nickel or Imitation Trimmed Surrey or Trap Harness.

$12.57　GREAT BARGAIN

No. 92948.

**BRIDLES**—⅝ inch, large square patent leather blinds, round side reins, round winker braces, full box loops.
**HAME TUGS**—Patent Leather, swell ends, box loops, safe under buckles.
**HAMES**—Full Nickel Plated.
**TRACES**—1¼ inch, double and stitched, round edge finish.
**BREECHING**—Folded, with scalloped layer.
**HIP STRAP**—⅝ inch full length.
**SIDE STRAPS**—One inch, full length and heavy.
**TURN BACK**—⅝ inch, round crupper to buckle on.
**SADDLE**—3½ inch, full patent leather skirts, full padded, enameled leather, laced in.
**BELLY BANDS**—Full one inch with slide.
**LINES**—1 inch, with spring and loops.
**COLLAR**—Patent leather, open top.
Price....................................$12.57
In ordering always give size of collar wanted.

## Single Surrey Harness.

$16.50

No. 92949.

**BRIDLE**—⅝ inch, patent leather, round corner winkers, round side rein, round winker stays, box loops.
**HAME TUGS**—Patent leather swell ends; full plated hames, 4 lbs.
**TRACES**—1¼ inch, double and stitched, round edge finish.
**BREECHING**—Folded with scalloped raised layer, ⅝ inch double hip strap.
**SIDE STRAPS**—⅝ inch.
**TURN BACK**—⅝ inch, scalloped with round crupper.
**SADDLE**—Full patent leather skirts, full padded, with enameled leather, laced in.
**BELLY BANDS**—Inside one folded, outside one single attached.
**LINES**—1⅛ inch hand parts, ⅝ inch fronts, with steel spring billits.
**COLLARS**—Patent leather. Either open or closed top. In ordering, always give size of collar wanted. Nickle wire, or Imitation Rubber Trimmings throughout.
Price....................................$16.47

## Single Surrey Harness. $21.25

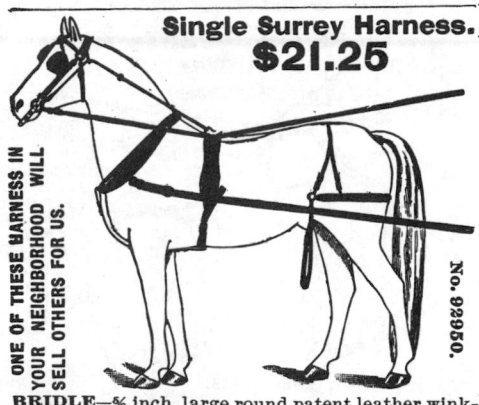

ONE OF THESE HARNESS IN YOUR NEIGHBORHOOD WILL SELL OTHERS FOR US.

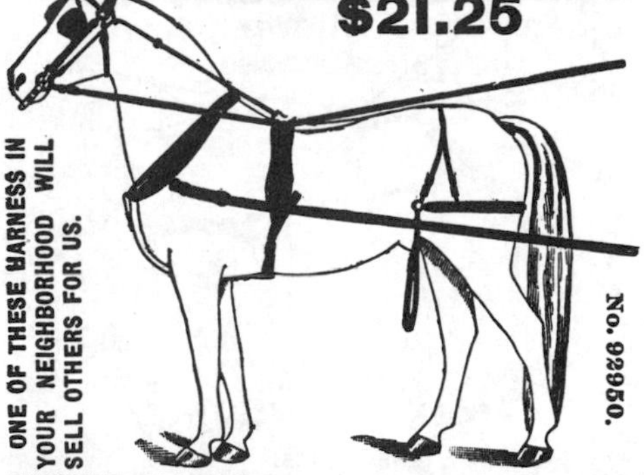

No. 92950.

**BRIDLE**—⅝ inch, large round patent leather winkers, round side rein, box loops, gag chains, nose band.
**HAME TUGS**—Swell patent leather ends, safe under buckles, box loops, 4 lb. full plated hames with fancy draft eye.
**TRACES**—1¼ inch, double and stitched, raised with round edge.
**BREECHING**—Folded with scalloped raised layer.
**HIP STRAPS**—⅝ inch double.
**SIDE STRAPS**—1 inch.
**TURN BACK**—⅞ inch, double reversed, English style. Round crupper to buckle on.
**SADDLE**—4 inch, full patent leather skirts, full padded, enameled leather lined, laced in, covered seat.
**BELLY BANDS**—Folded.
**LINES**—1⅛ inch hand parts, ⅞ inch fronts.
**COLLAR**—Full Patent Leather. Either open on top or closed top. In ordering this harness, always give size of collar wanted. Nickel or Brass center bar trimmings throughout. Price ... $21.25

## Single Surrey Harness. $24.00

Our factory-to-consumer system is a death blow to high prices.

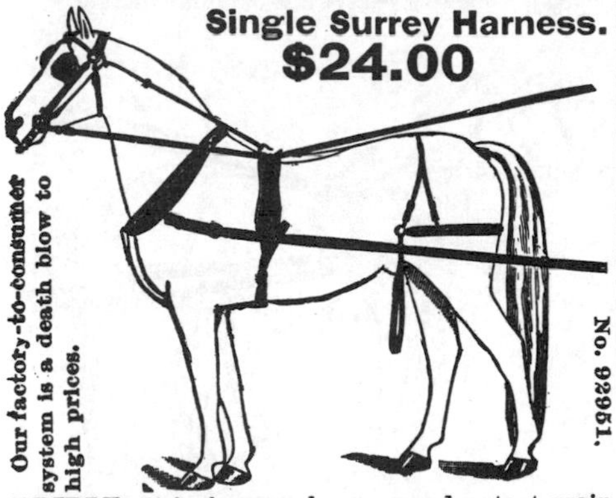

No. 92951.

**BRIDLE**—⅝ inch, very large, round patent grain leather winkers, round rein and winker stays, box loops, gag chains, nose band.
**HAME TUGS**—Large swell patent leather ends, box loops or metal loops, safe under buckles, 4 lb., full plated hames, with fancy draft eye.
**TRACES**—1¼ inch, doubled and stitched, raised with round edge finish.
**BREECHING**—1⅜ inch, doubled and stitched, raised on inside.
**SIDE STRAP**—1 inch.
**HIP STRAP**—⅝ inch double.
**TURN BACK**—⅞ inch, double, reversed English style, extra large round crupper to buckle on.
**SADDLE**—4 inch, full patent leather, swell skirt, full padded enameled leather lined, laced in, covered seat.
**BELLY BANDS**—Inside folded, outside single attached.
**LINES**—1⅛ inch hand parts, 1 inch fronts, with steel spring billits.
Full patent leather surrey collar, either open or closed top. In ordering, always give size of collar wanted. Nickel English swedge trimmings throughout. Price ... $24.00

## Single Surrey Harness.

$19.60

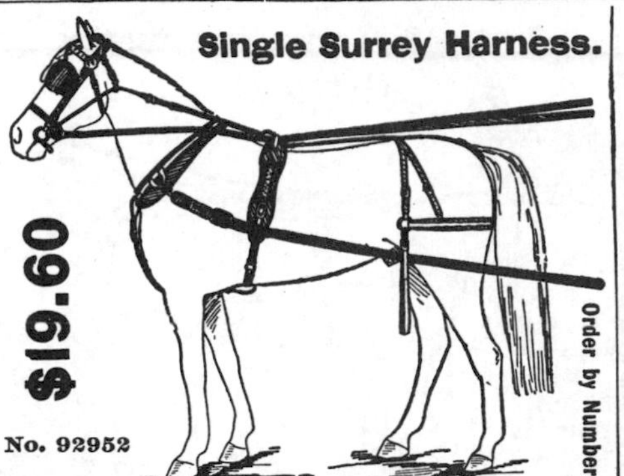

No. 92952

Order by Number.

**BRIDLE**—⅝ inch, large round patent leather blinds, round side reins, round winker stays. Box loop and nose band.
**HAME TUGS**—Patent leather, swell ends, box loops, safe under buckles; 3½ lb. full plated hames.
**TRACES**—1¼ inch, double and stitched, raised, round edge finished.
**BREECHING**—Folded with scalloped raised layer.
**HIP STRAP**—⅝ inch double.
**SIDE STRAPS**—⅞ inch.
**TURN BACK**—¾ inch, English style, round crupper to buckle on.
**SADDLE**—3½ inch, full patent leather skirts, full padded with enameled leather, laced in.
**BELLY BANDS**—Inside folded with layer, outside single attached.
**LINES**—1⅛ inch, hand parts, ⅞ inch fronts, with steel spring billits.
**COLLAR**—Full patent leather. Nickel or Brass Wire Trimmings throughout. Price ... $19.60
In ordering always give size of collar wanted.

## Single Express Harness. $15.50

Our Leather Goods are the Best on the Market.

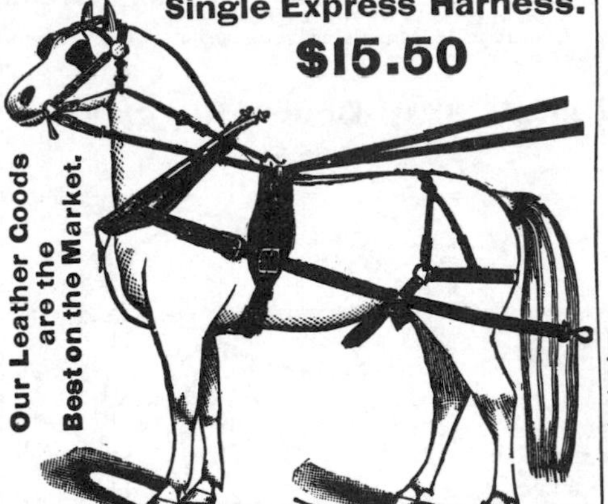

No. 92953.

**BRIDLE**—¾ inch, patent leather blinds, box loops, round rein and winker stay.
**HAME TUGS**—Box loops, Champion trace buckle.
**HAMES**—High ball wood or low top, 4 lb., iron.
**TRACES**—1¼ inch, heavy double and stitched, round edges with cock eyes.
**BREECHING**—Folded with wide layer, with box loops for hip straps.
**HIP STRAP**—¾ inch double.
**SIDE STRAPS**—1 inch.
**BACK STRAPS**—⅞ inch, with round crupper to buckle on.
**SADDLE**—Full padded, harness leather skirts, Kersey pad.
**BELLY BANDS**—Folded.
**LINES**—1 inch.
**COLLAR**—Full Kip.
Nickel or brass trimming throughout.
Price ... $15.50
The same harness, without collars ... 14.20
The same harness as above with 1½ inch traces and 5 inch saddle ... 17.60
Less collars, with 1½ inch traces and 5 inch saddle ... 16.00
We have finer grades at $20.00, $22.00 and $24.00

## Double Buggy Harness.

$13.95

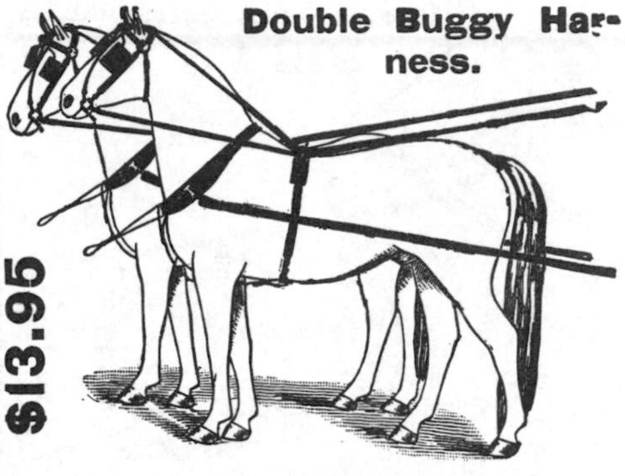

No. 92953½.

**BRIDLE**—⅝ inch patent leather blinds, box loops, over check, flat winker stays.
**HAME TUGS**—Box loops. 7 lb. iron hames.
**PADS**—Straight coach, enameled leather bottoms, skirts and bearers single strap.
**TURN BACK**—¾ inch with round crupper sewed on.
**BELLY BANDS**—Single strap.
**TRACES**—1⅛ inch, 6 feet 4 inches long, double and stitched, round edge finish.
**LINES**—¾ inch throughout.
**NECK YOKE STRAPS**—1¼ inch.
**CHOKE STRAPS**—¾ inch.
Kip buggy collars.
X C trimmings only.
Price ... $13.95

## Our Great Drive for 1897 in Genuine Davis Imitation of Rubber or Full Nickel Double Driving Harness.

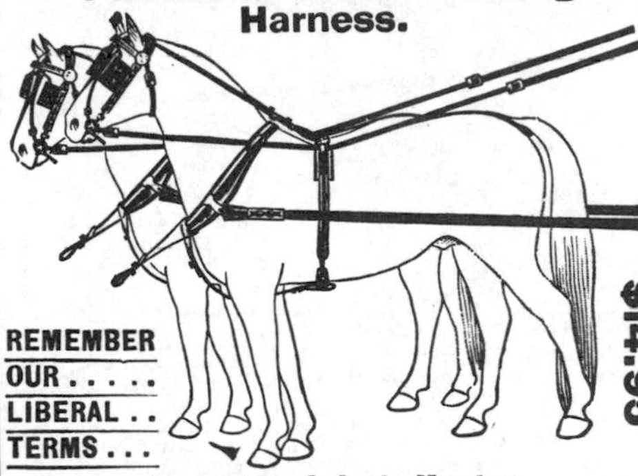

REMEMBER OUR ..... LIBERAL .. TERMS ...

$14.95

No. 92954. Order br Number.

This is the greatest bargain ever offered in a double driving harness and at the price we are offering it, trimmed in the style described above, we are certain there is no concern that can compete with us for the money asked.
**BRIDLES**—⅝ inch, patent leather blinds, box loops, over or side checks, flat winker stays, fancy fronts and rosettes.
**HAMES**—7 lb. iron, imitation of rubber or nickel trimmed, as desired.
**HAME TUGS**—Full length heavy box loops.
**PADS**—Straight coached, enameled leather bottoms, skirts and bearers heavy, double and stitched with layers.
**TURN BACKS**—¾ inch scalloped, with crupper dock sewed on.
**BELLY BANDS**—Heavy, full length, finished.
**TRACES**—1⅛ inch, full length, 6 feet 6 inches long, double and stitched, nicely finished.
**LINES**—⅝ inch, cut full length, heavy stock, neck-yoke straps.
**BREAST STRAPS**—1¼ inch.
Price, with genuine Kip Buggy Collars ... $14.95
Price of same without collars ... 13.35
When ordering, please be sure to state size of collars wanted.

## Single Goat Harness.

Red Leather, Fire Department Style.

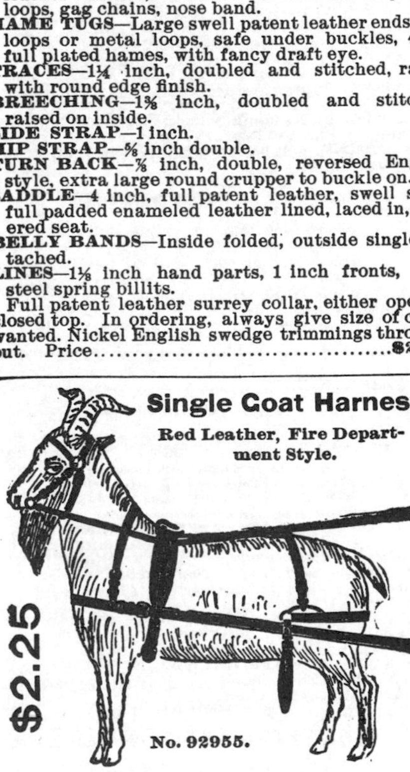

$2.25

No. 92955.

**DESCRIPTION OF GOAT HARNESS. BRIDLE**—½ inch, with bit to snap. **BREAST COLLAR**—1¼ in flat with plain layer point. **TRACES**—1 inch, flat, sewed to breast collar. **SADDLE**—2 inch, flat, no tree, full lined, with loose ring terrets. **SHAFT TUGS**—⅝ inch. **HIP STRAP**—½ inch. **BELLY BAND**—Double with snaps. **SIDE STRAPS**—⅝ inch. **TURN BACK**—⅝ inch. plain with safe. **BREECHING**—1¼ inch, flat with plain layer point. **LINES**—⅝ inch to snap in bit. Price per set ... $2.25

## Single Dog Harness.

**No. 92956. BRIDLE**—⅝ inch, open, adjustable at the top, all around nose band. Rings in cheeks for lines, no bit **BREAST COLLAR**—1¼x17 inches long, with neck strap. **TRACES**—⅞ inch x 3 ft., single strap, sewed to breast collar with a plain splice. **SURCINGLE**—1¼ inch x 3 ft. 3 inches long with shaft tug attached. **BACK STRAP**—⅝ inch. **HIP STRAP**—½ inch. **BREECHING**—1¼x17 inches. **SIDE STRAPS**—⅝ inch. **LINES**—⅝x6 ft. with snaps. Price per set ... $1.50

THE CAREFUL BUYER **WATCHES**

For our Prices on Timepieces and Jewelry before he buys. Our bargains are well known.

HE WHO would buy **CLOCKS** will protect his pocket book by consulting this Catalogue. Refer to pages 438 to 456 for the finest **SILVERWARE** EVER SOLD AT 50 PER CENT. MORE THAN OUR PRICES.

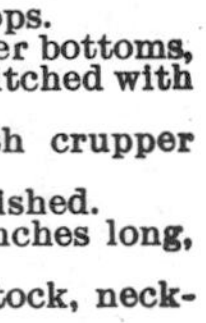

WE PACK ALL OUR GOODS WITH THE UTMOST CARE AND YOU MAY BE SURE THAT THEY WILL REACH YOU IN PERFECT CONDITION. WE DO ALL WE CAN TO PROTECT OUR CUSTOMERS.

## Double Buggy Harness.

**$16.88**

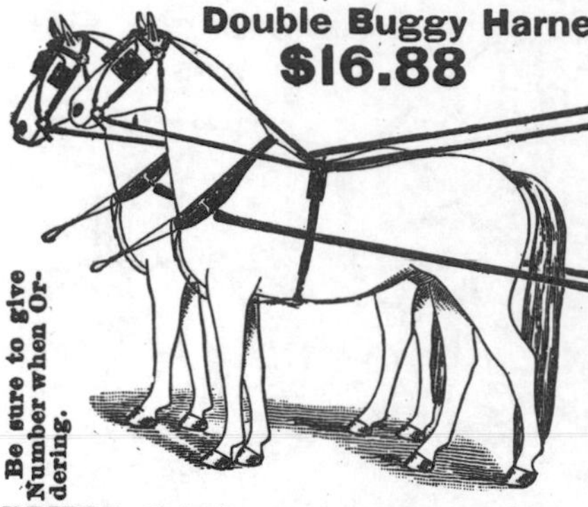

Be sure to give Number when Ordering.

No. 92957

**BRIDLE**—⅝ inch, patent leather winkers, over check reins or side check if desired, round wink r stays.
**HAME TUGS**—With box loops and 7 lb. iron hames.
**COACH PADS**—Straight leather bottoms and housings, skirts and bearer single strap.
**TURN BACK**—¾ inch with round crupper.
**BELLY BANDS**—Single strap.
**TRACES**—1⅛ inch, 6 feet 4 inches long, double and stitched with round edge.
**LINES**—⅞ inch throughout.
**NECK YOKE STRAP**—1¼ inch.
**CHOKE STRAP**—¾ inch. Full Kip collars.
X C or japanned trimmings throughout.... **$16.88**
Nickel or imitation rubber trimmings...... **$18.13**
Breast collars same price as collar and hames.

## Double Buggy Harness.

**$19.90**

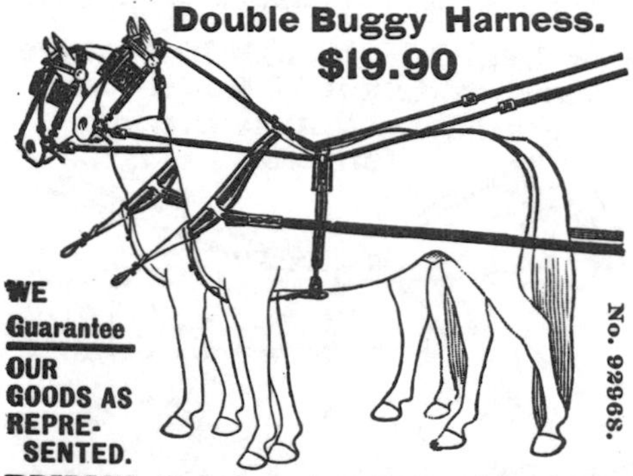

**WE Guarantee OUR GOODS AS REPRESENTED.**

No. 92958.

**BRIDLES**—⅝ inch, patent leather blinds, box loops, overcheck or round side reins as desired, round winker stay.
**HAME TUGS**—Box loops, 7lb iron hames.
**PADS**—Straight leather bottoms and housings, skirts single strap, bearers raised, doubled and stitched.
**TURN BACK**—¾ inch scalloped and wave stitched; round cruppers sewed on.
**BELLY BANDS**—Folded.
**TRACES**—1⅛ inch, 6½ feet long, double and stitched, raised with round edge.
**LINES**—1 inch hand parts, ⅞ inch fronts.
**NECK YOKE STRAPS**—1¼ inch.
**CHOKE STRAPS**—⅞ inch.
Full Kip Collars or Half Patent Leather.
Nickel or imitation Rubber Trimmings throughout.
Price........................................ **$19.90**
Same with breast Collars, same price....... **19.90**

## Double and Stitched Trace Attached to Hame Double Driving Harness.

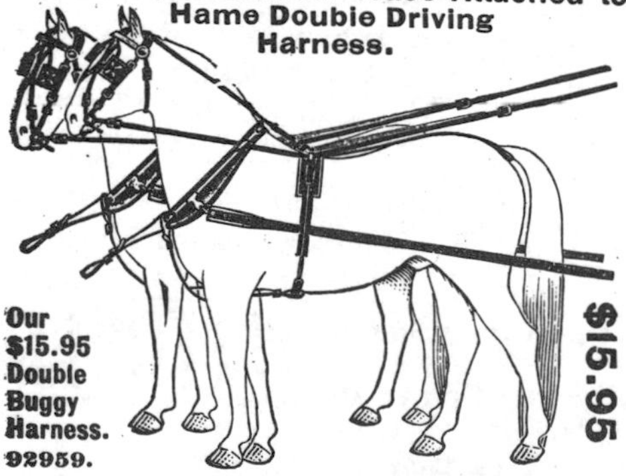

**Our $15.95 Double Buggy Harness.**

**$15.95**

**92959.**

Collars and all included. 3 per cent discount or **$15.47** if cash in full accompanies your order. C. O. D., **$15.95** on receipt of $2.00, balance payable at express office.
**TRIMMINGS**—XC (or for $1.95 extra, full nickel or Davis rubber trimmings as desired).
**PADS**—(Without plates), fancy housings.
**BRIDLES**—⅝ inch checks, patent leather blinds, flat winker braces, flat over draw checks.
**TRACES**—1⅛ double and stitched, attached to hames.
**LINES**—¾ inch, ⅞ inch hand parts.
**HAMES**—7 pound iron.
**BELLY BANDS**—Folded.
**MARTINGALES**—⅞ inch, 1 inch breast straps, plain turn backs, with folded crupper.
**COLLARS**—Plain leather. Our special price. **$15.95**

## Single Strap Double Buggy Harness.

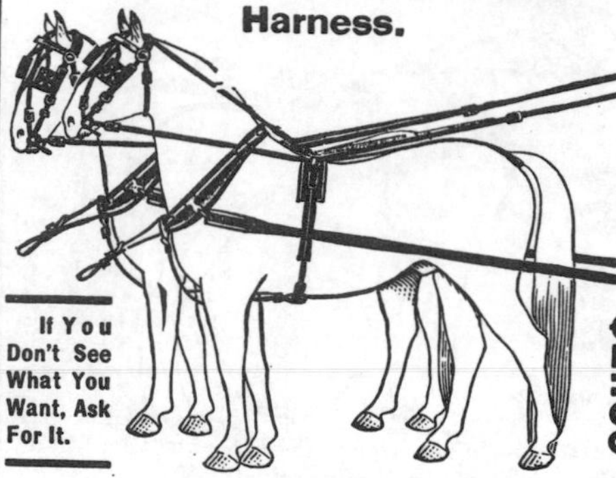

**If You Don't See What You Want, Ask For It.**

**$21.60**

No. 92960. Order by Nunber.

**BRIDLES**—Patent leather blinds, box loops, over checks, with nose pieces, round winker stays, layer on crown.
**HAMES**—7 lb. iron.
**TRACES**—1¼ inch single strap, 7 feet, 2 inches long, attached to hames.
**COACH PADS**—Straight leather bottom, chain housings, skirt single strap, bearers raised, double and stitched.
**TURN BACK**—Single strap, scalloped, round crupper sewed on.
**BELLY BANDS**—Single strap.
**LINES**—1⅛ inch hand parts, 1 inch fronts.
**NECK YOKE STRAPS**—1¼ inch.
**CHOKE STRAPS**—1 inch.
Full Kip collars.
Nickel or imitation rubber trimmings throughout.
Price ................................................ **$21.60**
This harness is wave creased.
Breast collars furnished same price as collars and hames.

## Single Strap Double Buggy Harness.

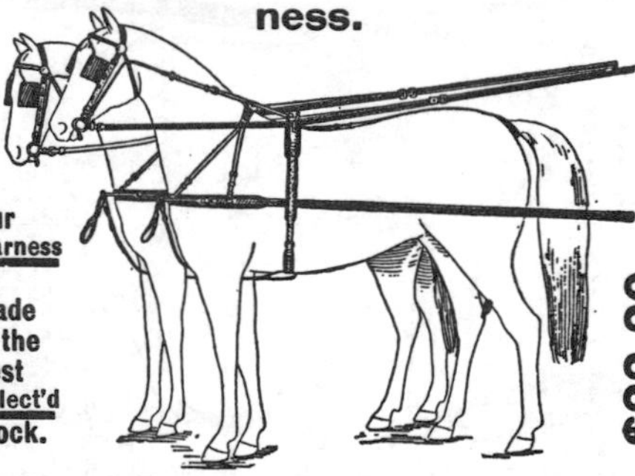

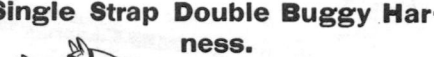

**Our Harness is Made of the Best Select'd Stock.**

**$22.20**

**No. 92961.**

Complete with Breast Collar, like cut.
**BRIDLES**—⅝ inch patent leather blinds, box loops, overcheck or side check, round winker stay, layer on crown.
**BREAST COLLARS**—2 inch, single strap with wide folded neck strap.
**TRACES**—1¼ inch single strap stitched to breast collars.
**PADS**—Coach, straight raised patent leather top, leather bottoms, beaded edge housings, skirts, single strap, bearers raised, double and stitched.
**TURN BACKS**—⅞ inch single strap, scalloped round crupper sewed on.
**BELLY BAND**—Single strap.
**LINES**—1⅛ inch hand parts, 1 inch fronts.
**NECK YOKE STRAPS**—1¼ inch.
**CHOKE STRAPS**—1 inch.
Made smooth, round edge, not creased.
Nickel or Imitaticn Rubber Trimmings throughout.
Price........................................ **$22.50**

## Double Buggy Harness.

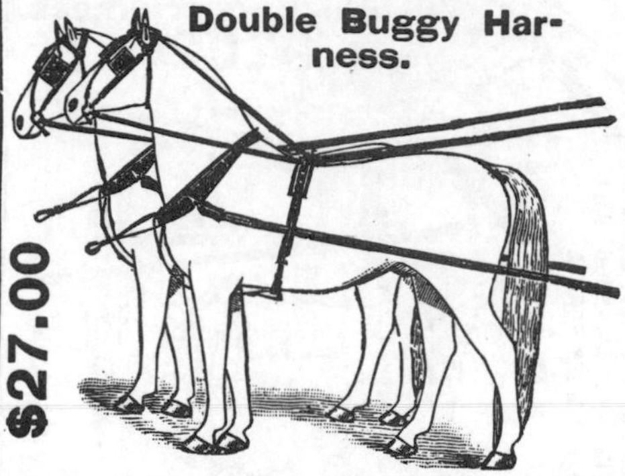

**$27.00**

**No. 92962.**

**BRIDLES**—⅝ inch, patent leather winkers, loops, over check with nose piece, or round side reins as desired. Round winker stays, layer on crown.
**HAME TUGS**—Swell patent leather ends, box loops, safe under buckles, 7 lb. iron hames.
**TRACES**—1⅛ inch, 6½ feet long, double and stitched, raised with round edge finish.
**PADS**—Coach straight, raised patent leather tops, leather bottoms, 3 inch beaded edge housings, skirts single strap, bearers raised, double and stitched.
**TURN BACKS**—⅞ inch scalloped and wave stitched, round crupper sewed on.
**BELLY BANDS**—Folded.
**LINES**—1¼ inch handparts, 1 inch fronts.
**NECK YOKE STRAPS**—1¼ inch.
**CHOKE STRAPS**—1 inch.
**COLLARS**—Patent leather, either open or closed top.
Nickel or imitation rubber trimmings throughout.
Price ................................................ **$27,00**
Breast collars finished same price as collar and hames.

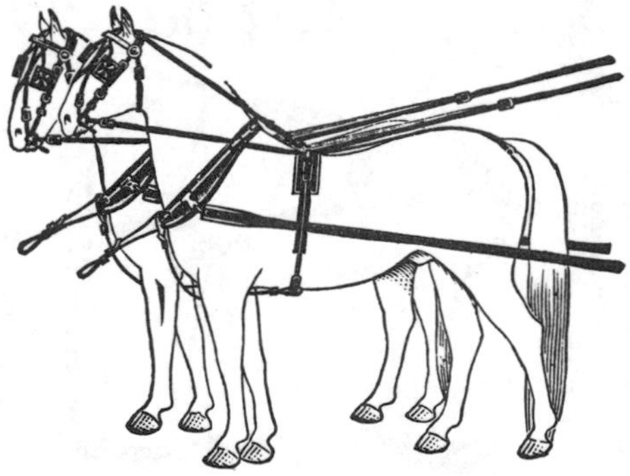

**No. 92963.**

**BRIDLES**—Patent leather blinds, box loops, over checks with nose piece if wanted. Round winker stays. layer on crown or side checks.
**HAMES**—7 lb., iron.
**TRACES**—1¼ inch single strap, 7 feet 2 inches long, attached to hames.
**COACH PADS**—Straight, raised patent leather tops, leather bottoms and facings, 3 inch beaded edge housings, skirts and bearers single strap.
**TURN BACKS**—¾ inch scalloped, with round crupper sewed on.
**BELLY BAND**—Single strap.
**LINES**—1⅛ inch hand parts, 1 inch fronts.
**NECK YOKE STRAPS**—1¼ inch.
**MARTINGALES**—1¼ inch.
**COLLARS**—Patent leather. Made smooth, round edge, no creasing.
Nickel or imitation rubber trimmings throughout.
Price ................................................ **$28.00**
Genuine rubber trimmings throughout.
Price ................................................ **$33.33**

## Double Buggy Harness.

**No. 92964.**

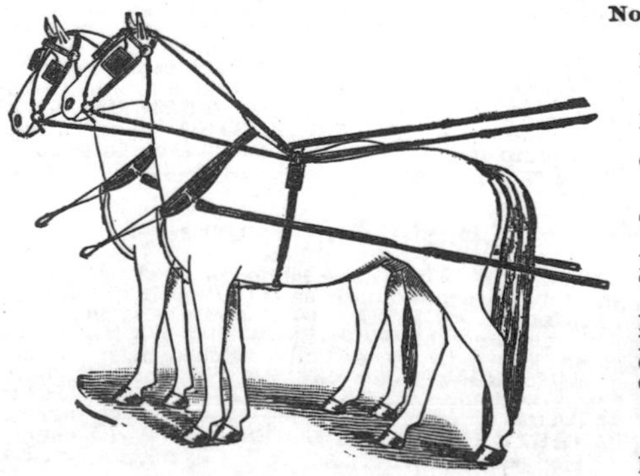

**BRIDLES**—⅝ inch, patent leather winkers, box loops, over check, or round side checks, as desired, round winker stays and layer on crown piece.
**HAME TUGS**—Swell patent leather ends, box loops. 7 pound iron Hames.
**COACH PADS**—Straight, patent leather, raised top. leather bottom, beaded edge housings, skirts, single strap. Bearers raised, doubled and stitched.
**TURN BACKS**—⅞ inch scalloped and wave-stitched, round crupper sewed on.
**BELLY BANDS**—Folded.
**TRACES**—1⅛ inch, 6½ ft. long, double and stitched, raised with round edge.
**LINES**—Round, 1⅛ inch Russet hand parts.
**NECK YOKE STRAPS**—1¼ inch.
**CHOKE STRAPS**—1 inch.
**COLLARS**—Patent leather.
Nickel or Imitation Rubber Trimmings throughout.
Price ................................................ **$23.75**
Breast Collars furnished same price as collars and hames.

**WHEN YOU ORDER GOODS FROM US, YOU WILL PREVENT MOST OF THE FEW ERRORS THAT OCCUR BY USING CARE IN ALL DESCRIPTIONS AND SIZES. DO NOT FAIL TO GIVE CATALOGUE NUMBER AND PAGE.**

## Double Spring Wagon Harness.
## $20.50

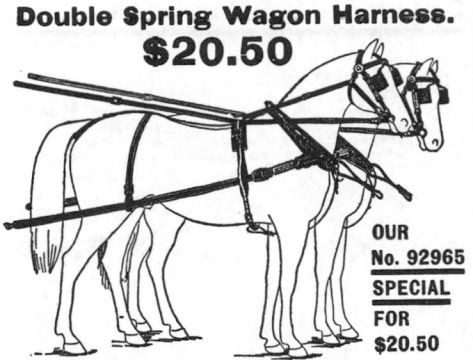

OUR
No. 92965
SPECIAL
FOR
$20.50

### No. 92965.

**BRIDLES**—¾ inch square or sensible patent leather blinds, box loops. flat rein and winker stays.
**HAME TUGS**—Box loops, 8 lb. iron hames or low top wood gig hames.
**PADS**—Straight, leather bottoms, patent leather housings, skirts and bearers double and stitched.
**TURN BACKS**—⅝ inch, round crupper to buckle on.
**HIP STRAPS**—¾ inch, with patent leather drops.
**BELLY BANDS**—Folded.
**TRACES**—1¼ inch by 6 feet 4 inches, double and stitched, round edge with cockeyes.
**LINES**—1⅛ inch hand parts. 1 inch fronts.
**NECK YOKE STRAPS**—1¼ inch.
**CHOKE STRAPS**—1 inch.
**COLLARS**—Kip.
**TRIMMINGS**—X C throughout.
Price ................................................... $20.50

## Double Spring Wagon Harness.
## $22.40

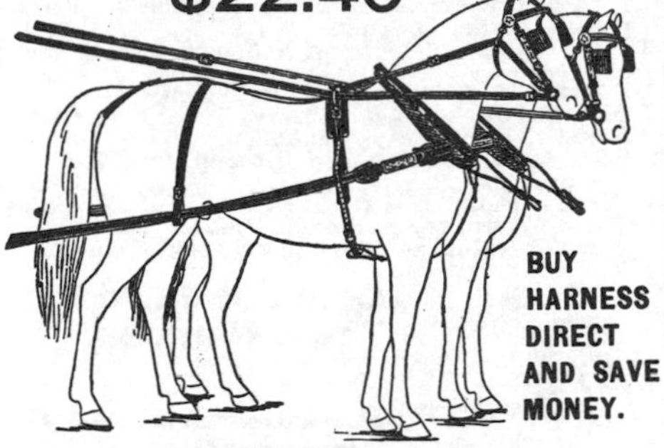

We urge a trial order, to satisfy you that we can save you money.

### No. 92996.

BUY
HARNESS
DIRECT
AND SAVE
MONEY.

**BRIDLES**—⅝ inch, patent leather sensible or square blinds, box loops, round winker stays.
**HEME TUGS**—Box loops, champion trace buckles. oval iron wood coach hames.
**COACH PADS**—Swell inserted housings, leather bottoms. Skirts and bearers single strap.
**TURN BACK**—⅝ inch scalloped and wave stitched, round crupper sewed on.
**BELLY BANDS**—Folded.
**TRACES**—1¼ inches by 6½ feet, double and stitched, raised with round edge, with cockeyes.
**LINES**—1 inch hand parts, ⅞ inch fronts.
**NECK YOKE STRAPS**—1¼ inch.
**CHOKE STRAPS**—⅝ inch.
**COLLARS**—Full kip.
**TRIMMINGS**—X C.
Price ....................................... $22.40
Nickel trimmings throughout.
Price ....................................... $22.45

---

## Double Spring Wagon Harness.

Three Per Cent Discount for Cash.

### No. 92967.

**BRIDLES**—Patent leather sensible blinds. box loops, round side reins, round winker stay.
**HAME TUGS**—Box loop, champion trace buckles, oval iron wood coach hames.
**PADS**—Heavy coach, inserted housings. leather bottoms, single strap skirts, round bearers.
**TURN BACK**—⅝ inch scalloped and wave-stitched, round cruppers sewed on.
**BELLY BANDS**—Folded.
**TRACES**—1¼ inch, double and stitched, raised round edge, 6½ feet long with cockeyes.
**LINES**—1⅛ inch hand parts, 1 inch fronts.
**NECK YOKE STRAPS**—1¼ inch.
**CHOKE STRAPS**—1 inch.
**COLLARS**—Heavy full Kip.
  X C trimmings throughout. Price......... $25.50
  Nickel trimmings throughout. Price....... 28.00
  If furnished with breeching.
  X C trimmings, price......... ............. 29.25
  Nickel trimmings, price..................... 31.75

## Double Surrey or Carriage Harness.

### No. 92968.

**BRIDLES**—⅝ inch, patent leather grain blinds, round side reins, round winker stays, box loops. layer on crown.
**HAME TUGS**—Swell patent leather ends, box loops, safe under buckles, 8 lb. iron hames, full plated.
**COACH PADS**—Straight, raised patent leather tops, patent collar leather bottoms, 4 inch beaded edge housings, skirts, single strap, bearers raised, double and stitched.
**TURN BACK**—⅝ inch scalloped and wave-stitched, with round cruppers sewed on.
**BELLY BANDS**—Folded, with layer.
**TRACES**—1¼ inch. by 6½ feet, double and stitched, raised with round edge.
**LINES**—1⅛ inch hand parts, 1 inch fronts.
**NECK YOKE STRAPS**—1¼ inch.
**CHOKE STRAPS**—1 inch.
**COLLARS**—Heavy patent leather.
Nickel or imitation rubber trimmings throughout.
Price............................................. $30.60
If furnished with breeching................. 34.75

## Heavy Carriage or Light Hack Harness.
### No. 92969.

**BRIDLES**—⅝ inch, patent leather, square or horseshoe blinds, round reins, double and stitched winker stays and nose bands, box loops. patent leather face, drop chain or fancy leather fronts.
**HAME TUGS**—Box loop or metal loops as desired, safe under buckles, close plated hames, with links and rings in place of hame straps at bottom.
**COACH PADS**—Straight raised patent leather tops, leather facings, patent collar leather bottoms, chain housings, skirts and bearers double and stitched.
**TURN BACKS**—⅝ inch, double reversed English style, heavy round cruppers to buckle on.
**HIP STRAPS**—⅝ inch, with two patent leather drops.
**TRACES**—1¼ inch. by 6½ feet, double and stitched, raised round edge.
**LINES**—1⅛ inch hand parts, 1 inch fronts.
**MARTINGALES**—1 inch with patent leather drops.
**BELLY BANDS**—Folded with layer.
**NECK YOKE STRAPS**—1¼ inch, double and stitched.
Heavy patent leather coach collars.
Nickel trimmings, plain wire. Price........ $42.75

## Chain Harness, Commonly known as Plow Harness.

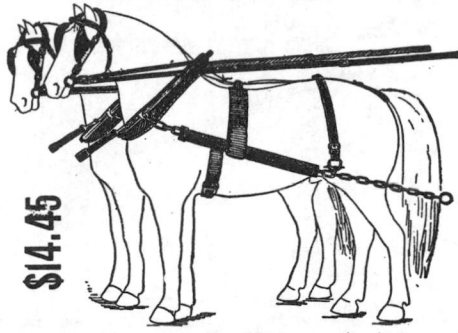

$14.45

### No. 92971.

This Harness is a grand, good article for the purpose for which it is intended, making a very cheap farm or plow harness for people who do not wish to invest any great amount in an article which will give them plenty of service.
**BRIDLES**—⅝ inch, Jenny Lind or Sensible Blinds.
**HAMES**—With varnished iron over top with hooks.
**BACK BAND**—4 inch wide, with back strap loops.
**BELLY BANDS**—1½ inch wide.
**BACK STRAPS**—2½ inch, connecting with hip strap, 1¼ inch with snaps.
**TRACES**—7 ft. chains, with 30 inch leather piping, covered.
**LINES**—⅝ inch. 15 ft. long, with snaps.
**BREAST STRAPS**—1½ inch, with slides and snaps.
**COLLARS**—Good Kip.
  Price, complete with collars................ $14.45
  Price, without collars... .................... 12.20
When ordering, be sure to give size of collars wanted. The weight of the harness is about 50 lbs.

## Short Tug Farm Harness, Made for Two Horses Only.
## $14.00.

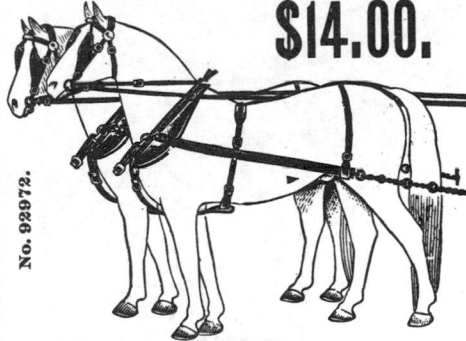

### No. 92972.

This is a very desirable harness for one wanting a stocky and not too cumbersome set of harness for ordinary farm work.
Price, complete with collars.................. $14.00
Less three per cent. discount for cash in full with order. The lowest price on record.
**TRIMMINGS**—Full XC plate.
**TRACES**—1½ inch, 4 ft. long with 3½ ft. stay chains.
**PADS**—Folded with loops for back straps.
**LINES**—⅝ inch, 18 ft. long, with snaps.
**BRIDLES**—¾ inch cheeks, either pigeon wing or Concord blinds, flat cheeks, neck-yoke straps, 1¼ inch, with snaps and breast strap slides.
**HAMES**—Wood, varnished, with iron over top.
**BACK STRAPS**—⅝ inch, with folded crupper.
**HIP STRAPS**—⅝ inch, flat belly bands.
**WEIGHT**—40 pounds.
In ordering this harness be sure to state size of collars wanted.

## A SEWING MACHINE

## Flat Pad Farm Team Harness.

$15.75.

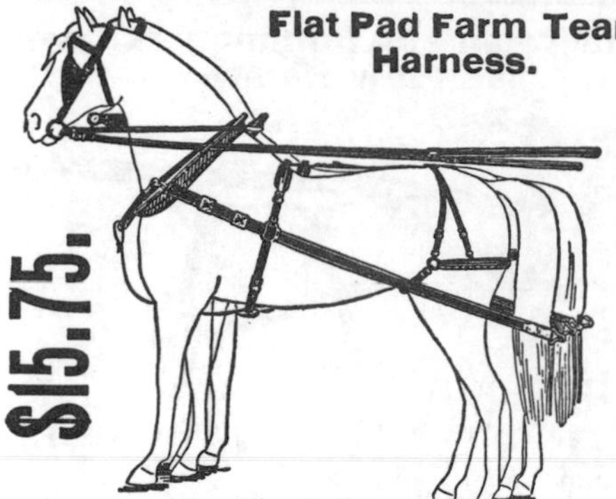

No. 92974.

**This is probably the cheapest all leather farm harness in the market.** We are making a great run on this harness, and will sell it this season, complete, with good Kip Collars for $15.75 per set.
**TRIMMINGS**—Full XC plate.
**BRIDLES**—¾ inch. Jenny Lind or pigeon wing.
**HAMES**—Varnished, with iron over top.
**PADS**—Flat, with 1⅛ inch billets.
**BREECHING**—Folded with layer, 1 inch back strap; ¾ inch double hip straps.
**TRACES**—Folded 1½ inch points with layer, and stitched full length of traces, with clip cockeys.
**LINES**—⅞ inch, 15 ft. with snaps.
**BREAST STRAPS**—1¼ inch with breast strap slides and snaps.
**POLE STRAPS**—1½ inch.
**COLLARS**—No. 1 Kip farm collars.
Price, complete with collars................ $15.75
Price of same without collars.............. 13.75
The weight of this harness is about 45 lbs. In ordering be sure to mention size of collars wanted.

## Full Length Tug Farm Team Harness.

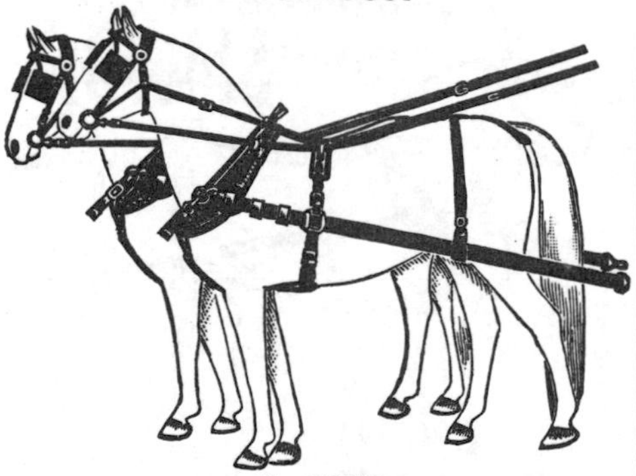

No. 92976.

**This is a big drive in a hook and terret double Farm Harness for 1897.** We consider it of unexceptional value and a harness well worth the attention of any man who wants a first class job for very little money.
**TRIMMINGS**—XC plate, best quality.
**BRIDLES**—¾ inch cheeks, square or sensible blinds, round side checks and round winker braces, fancy fronts and nickel rosettes.
**LINES**—1 inch, flat, 18 ft. long, with snaps complete.
**HAMES**—Wood, painted red, iron over top, combination loops with two hold backs.
**TRACES**—1½ inch, doubled and stitched full length with clip cockeys; Champion trace buckles.
**PADS**—Flat, 3 inch harness leather, furnished with heavy skirts.
**TURN BACKS**—1 inch heavy stock with crupper dock buckled on.
**HIP STRAPS**—1 inch, with three inch patent safety carriers.
**BREAST STRAPS**—1½ inch, with breast strap slides and snaps.
**POLE STRAPS**—1½ inch, heavy.
Price, with genuine pop stitched collars, heavy collar leather, complete...................... $19.75
Price, without collars, per set............. 16.60
Weight, about 50 pounds.
Extra for 1¾ inch traces on above harness. 1.00
Extra for good heavy breeching........... 2.75



## Full Length Tug Farm Team Harness.

$20.75

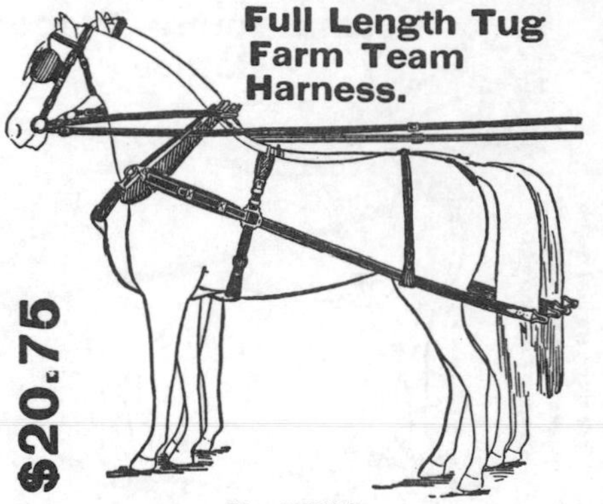

No. 92977.

**This is a special drive of a good one, which, for the money, is a great bargain for anyone who may purchase it. Made of good Pittsburg stock. Everything about this harness is made upon merit.**
**TRIMMINGS**—Japanned or X C Mountings.
**BRIDLES**—⅞ inch, either square or Concord sensible blinds.
**HAMES**—Red, iron over top.
**PADS**—Harness leather, flat, folded; 1¼ inch heavy billets.
**BACK STRAPS**—1¼ inch.
**HIP STRAPS**—1 inch.
**TRACES**—1½ inch, doubled and stitched full length, with clip cockeyes.
**LINES**—⅞ inch with snaps. Breast straps, 1½ inch, with breast strap slides and snaps.
**POLE STRAPS**—1½ inch, cut full length.
**COLLARS**—No. 1 team collars.
Price...................................... $20.75
Price of above harness with collars......... 17.70
If 1¾ inch traces are wanted, add $1.00 per set to the above.
Extra for breeching.......................... $2.75
Weight per set, about 45 lbs.
In ordering be sure to state size of collar wanted.



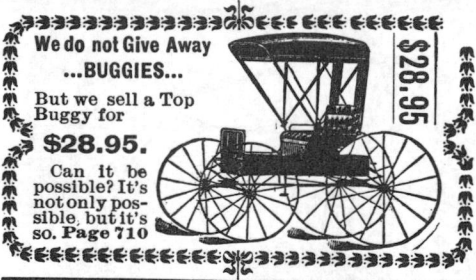

## Extra Fine Farm Team Harness.

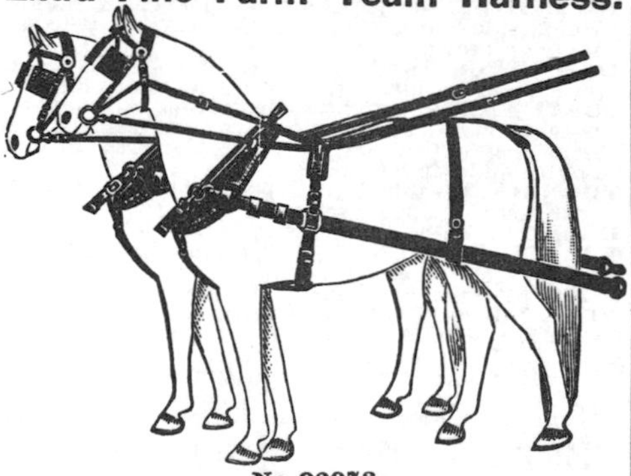

No. 92978.

**TRIMMINGS**—X C plates, best quality.
**BRIDLES**—¾ inch cheeks, round check reins and winker braces; square or rounded Concord blinds, fancy fronts, nickeled rosettes.
**LINES**—1 inch, flat, 18 ft. long with buckles and snaps.
**HAMES**—Wood painted red, iron over top, combination loops with two holdbacks.
**TRACES**—1½ inch, doubled and stitched, full length, with cockeyes and Champion trace buckles.
**PADS**—Flat, 3 inch, folded, hook and terret, skirts 1¾ inch, X C adjustable tree, raised layer and skirts doubled and stitched.
**TURN BACKS**—1 inch, with crupper dock buckled on.
**HIP STRAPS**—1 inch, with 3 inch patent safety trace carriers.
This is one of the best farm harnesses in the United States for the money, and we will guarantee to give you good satisfaction.
Price, complete, with genuine pop-stitched collars............................. $21.87
Price of same, without collars............... 18.68
Extra, for good, heavy breeching........... 2.75

## Genuine Hand Made Full Length Tugs Farm Team Harness.

$23.50

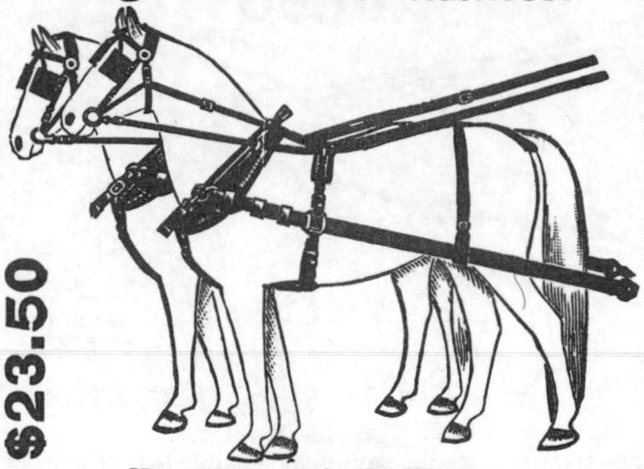

No. 92980. Order by Number.

This will be the only strictly hand made farm team harness which we shall make a leader of and offer this season at anywhere near the price at which we are offering this one. **Remember, this piece of goods is strictly gurranteed as hand made.** The leather is made of the **best Pittsburg oak stock**, hand stuffed. Do not think for a moment that on account of the **exceedingly low price** the stock is inferior or the work slighted.
**TRIMMINGS**—All X C plate, best quality.
**BRIDLES**—¾ inch, with ⅝ inch throat latch; square or sensible blinds, hand stitched, round cheeks and winker bows.
**LINES**—1 inch, flat, 20 ft. long with snaps.
**HAMES**—Wood, painted red, iron over top; combination loops with two hold backs.
**TRACES**—1½ inch, 6 ft. long, 3 ply, with triangular cockeyes.
**PADS**—Either flat, 3 inch harness leather, finished with heavy skirts, or the Perfection Adjustable patent leather housings.
**TURN BACKS**—1 inch, with 3 inch patent safety carriers.
**BREAST STRAPS**—1½ inch with snaps.
**POLE STRAPS**—1½ inch, heavy, with collar strap. Also two hitch straps included.
Price, with genuine pop-stitched collars, complete.......................................... $23.50
Price, without collars ........................ 20.50
The weight of the harness is about 60 lbs.
When ordering, be sure and give size of collars.

## Concord Farm Team Harness.

$23.05

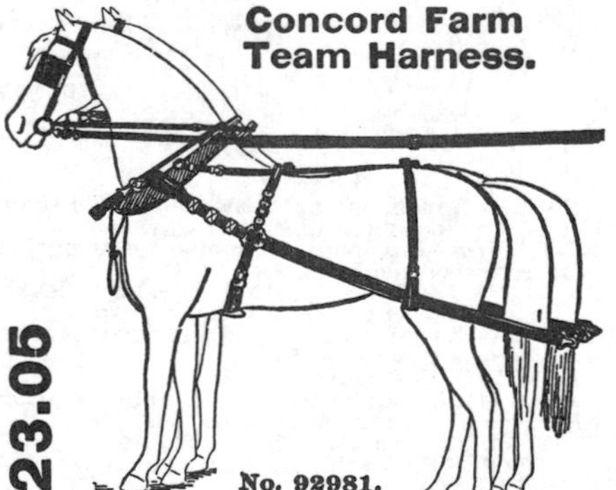

No. 92981.

**TRIMMINGS**—Full X C plate.
**BRIDLES**—¾ inch cheeks, square or Concord sensible blinds.
**HAMES**—No. 5 Concord, long staple.
**PADS**—Flat, folded, two loops, 1¼ inch billets.
**BACK STRAPS**—⅞ inch, doubled, running to rings in hames.
**HIP STRAPS**—⅞ inch.
**TRACES**—1½ inch, 6 ft., doubled and stitched throughout.
**LINES**—⅞ inch, 20 ft. long, with snaps.
**BREAST STRAPS**—1½ inch, with breast strap slides and snaps.
**POLE STRAPS**—1½ inch, cut full length.
**COLLAR STRAP**—⅞ inch.
**COLLARS**—Fine imitation of Scotch, best quality.
Price, complete with collars.................. $23.05
Price of same, less collars.................. 19.82
Extra for first class heavy breeching........ 2.75
Weight, about 40 lbs.
In ordering be sure to state size of collars wanted.

**SEE PAGE 758 FOR BRIDLES.**

**A NEW LINE, The Best Line Ever on the Market.**

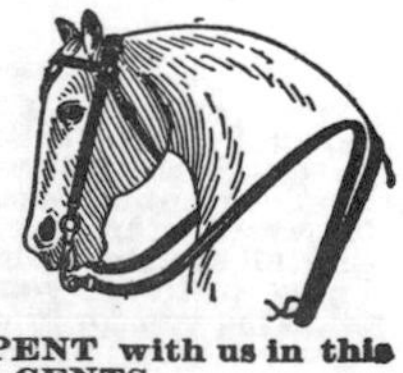

We carry a full line of Harness and Saddlery Sundries, Strap Work, Snaps, Stirrups, Spurs and Bits, as well as Lap Robes, Dusters, etc.
**FOR EVERY DOLLAR SPENT with us in this Line WE SAVE YOU FIFTY CENTS.**

## Slip Tug Farm Team Harness.

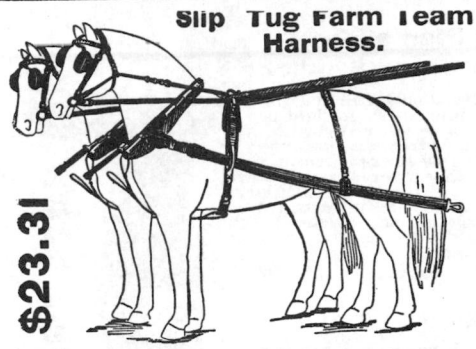

**$23.31**

No. 92983.

In this harness we try to present the very best 1½ inch doubled and stitched tug farm team harness, which can be made for anything like the price at which we offer it. We guarantee the stock to be of the best Pittsburg oak, the workmanship the very best and, in fact, every part of this harness comes to you guaranteed throughout. We make this harness, either in slip tug, or in the regular way, with champion trace buckles for the same price.

**TRIMMINGS**—Full XC plate.
**BRIDLES**—¾ inch cheeks, round reins and winker stays, square or sensible Concord blinds. Hames, black, iron over top or low wood top.
**PADS**—Hook ank terret, or self-adjusting slip tug.
**BACK STRAPS**—1 inch, cut full length.
**TRACES**—1½ inch, 6½ ft. long, doubled and stitched throughout, with cockeyes. Lines, 1 inch, 20 ft. long, with snaps. Breast straps, 1½ inch, with breast strap slides and snaps.
**POLE STRAPS**—1½ inch, cut full length.
**COLLAR STRAPS**—⅝ inch.
**COLLAR**—Imitation Scotch, made of the very best quality of stock.
Price, complete with collars,............$23.31
Price, without collars,.................. 20.12
Weight about 49 lbs.
In ordering this harness, be sure to state the size of collars wanted.

## Crotch Strap Farm or Team Harness.

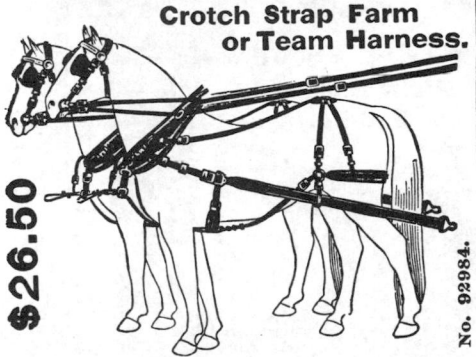

**$26.50**

No. 92984.

**TRIMMINGS**—Full XC Plate,
**BRIDLES**—¾ inch, box loops, round reins and winker braces or Concord sensible binds.
**HAMES**—No. 5 Concord, long staple.
**BREECHING**—Folded, 1¼ inch layer, ⅝ inch double back straps, running to rings in hames. ⅝ inch hip straps; ⅝ inch side straps.
**TRACES**—1½ inch, 6 ft., doubled and stitched.
**LINES**—1 inch, 20 ft., long, with snaps.
**BREAST STRAPS**—1½ inch, with breast strap slides and snaps.
**POLE STRAPS**—1½ inch.
**COLLAR STRAPS**—⅝ inch.
**COLLARS**—No. 1 imitation Scotch, extra value.
The above harness is also made with flat pads, folded, 2 inch loops, 1¼ inch billets for 75 cts. extra.
Price, complete with collars.............$26.50
Price, without collars.................... 24.05
Weight, about 50 lbs.
In ordering, be sure to state size of collars wanted.

## Concord Team Farm Harness.

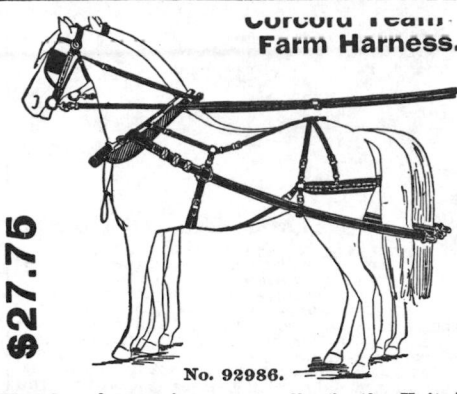

**$27.75**

No. 92986.

The above harness is a great seller in the United States, and in a great many localities they will use no other style of harness. The stock and workmanship in this harness is as fine as can be had for the price we quote. We consider it one of the best and most popular harnesses on the market.
**TRIMMINGS**—Full XC Plate.
**BRIDLES**—¾ inch cheeks, box loops, short round reins, round winker braces, fancy face pieces, square or sensible Concord blinds.
**HAMES**—No. 5 Concord, long staple.
**BREECHING**—Folded, with 1 inch layer, ⅞ inch double back straps, running to hames; ⅞ inch double hip straps; ⅞ inch side strap.
**TRACES**—1½ inches, 6 ft., doubled and stitched throughout.
**LINES**—1 inch, 20 ft. long, with snaps.
**BREAST STRAPS**—1½ inch, with breast strap slides and snaps.
**POLE STRAPS**—1½ inch, cut full length.
**COLLAR STRAPS**—⅝ inch.
**COLLARS**—Imitation Scotch, extra value.
Price, complete with collars. .............$27.75
Price, less collars.......................... 24.25
Weight, about 48 lbs.
In ordering, be sure to state size of collars wanted.

## Genuine Concord Team Harness.

**$30.31.**

No. 92988.

**TRIMMINGS**—X C Plate,
**BRIDLES**—¾ inch box loops, Concord team blinds.
**HAMES**—No. 5 bolt hames, hame tugs, with box loops. Pads, Concord or flat pads, 1¾ inch billets.
**BREECHING**—folded, 1¼ inch layer, 1¼ inch back straps, ⅞ inch double hip straps, ⅞ inch side straps.
**TRACES**—6 ft. single strap, heavy with cockeyes, 1½ inch at points X, 2½ inches wide.
**LINES**—1 inch, 18 ft. long, with snaps.
**BREAST STRAPS**—1½ inch, with breast strap slides and snaps.
**POLE STRAPS**—1½ inch, cut full length.
**COLLARS**—Genuine Concord, wool faced. extra heavy.
Price, complete with collars.............$30.31
Price, less collars.......................... 26.75
Price, with 1¾x2½ inch traces, with collars complete....... 31.65

## Harness.

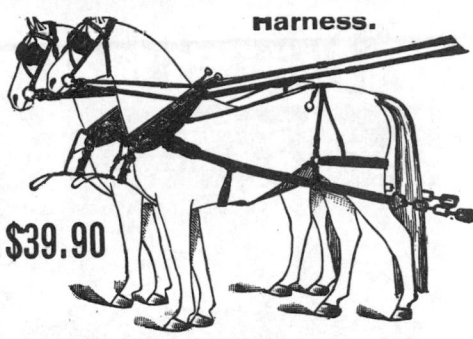

**$39.90**

No. 92990.

As a general teaming, truck, or farm harness you can't buy better. Everything strictly first-class.
**TRIMMINGS**—full brass, highly polished and finished.
**TRACES**—1¾ inch, doubled and stitched, 3 rows stitching, scalloped safes, 6 link heel chains.
**LINES**—1 inch, 18 feet, with snaps
**BRIDLES**—⅞ inch cheeks, with patent leather blinds, round winker braces, fancy face pieces with brass spots.
**MARTINGALES**—1½ inch, doubled and stitched with chafe under ring, with single strap, pole and choke straps.
**BREAST STRAPS**—1¾ inch, with short breast strap or spreader with ring, snaps and breast strap slides.
**BACK STRAPS**—1 inch, split, running to side of hames.
**BREECHING**—heavy folded, with 1½ inch layer.
**BELLY BANDS**—folded, with 1½ inch buckles and billets.
**HIP STRAPS**—⅞ inch, split, sewed in ring on rump, with padded safes under ring, with brass buckle shields.
**SIDE STRAPS**—1 inch, with snaps.
**LAZY STRAPS**—⅞ inch.
**SPREADER STRAPS**—with polished brass rings.
**DROP HIP STRAP**—with polished brass rings.
**HAMES**—red, Concord brass plated, large balls, brass plated. Brass fronts, rosettes, bits, spots and buckle shields, Be sure to state size of collars wanted when you include collars in your order.
Our special price, complete with breeching, $39.90
Extra for heavy solid leather thong sewed collars...................................... 5.25
3 per cent. discount if cash in full accompanies your order.

## We have ~~~ a thoroughly Equipped.

And We Can Save You Money.

**Veterinary DEPT.**

Refer to pages 30, 31 and 3:

We quote Homeopathic remedies for Far and Stable, the best veterinary remedie sheep dip etc. Every variety of veterina instruments. Forceps, castrating knive dehorning saws, poultry instruments, et

**OUR PRICES ARE LOWEST, AN YOU CANNOT AFFORD TO B WITHOUT CERTAIN NECESSAR REMEDIES AND INSTRUMENT**

# DEPARTMENT OF SADDLES

## SEARS ROEBUCK & CO

### In Our Saddle Department

we have endeavored to show everything in the Saddle line, including all the very latest styles and most desirable goods.

Our Saddles are all made by one of the largest and most reliable manufacturers in the country, a concern whose reputation for the manufacture of the highest grade work is everywhere recognized.

If you buy your Saddles from us you will be sure of not only getting lower prices than you could possibly get elsewhere, but the best grade work on the market.

Our Saddle trade has grown until we are now among the largest dealers in this line in this country. We are daily shipping saddles to almost every state and territory in the Union as well as foreign countries.

The low prices we offer, the quality of goods we handle, and our liberal terms of shipment commend our line to your favorable cosideration.

Saddles will be shipped by Express C. O. D. subject to examination on receipt of $1.00 as a guarantee of good faith to all points except in the states of California, Washington, Oregon, Idaho, Montana, Utah, Nevada, Arizona, New Mexico, Colorado, Wyoming , Texas and Florida. From these points cash in full must accompany your order, which will entitle you to a discount of 3%. We allow a discount of 3% where cash in full accompanies an order. You take no risk for we will cheerfully refund your money if goods are not perfectly satisfactory.

**ABOUT OUR PRICES.** We advertise hand made Saddles at from $1.60 upwards, and we believe a careful comparison of our prices with those of any other concern will convince you that we can save you from 25% to 50% in price.

The Freight or Express Charges will amount to next to nothing as compared with what you will save in price.

We are extremely anxious to receive your order, not so much for the little profit there is in it to us as for the good it will do us as an advertisement, and will endeavor to send you a saddle with which you will be so well pleased that your friends will also order from us.

Our line of Stock Saddles we believe is the handsomest line on the market, and the prices certainly are below any possible comparison. Our Western and Southwestern trade has been so very large that we have felt justified in making very extensive preparations in the stock saddle line for the coming season, and if you are in the market for this class of goods we are sure that one trial order will convince you that you cannot afford to place your orders elsewhere.

## Men's $2.40 Morgan Saddle.

No. 93004 This Morgan Saddle comes in light or black leather as desired. 13 inch tree, genuine hide covered Morgan horn, half leather covered seat, stirrup leather 1 inch wide with large fenders, girth of super cotton with 1¼ inch billets, 3 inch wood stirrup. Weight about 7 pounds.

Our special price........$2.40

**No. 93004, $2.40.**

## Men's $2.45 Plain English Saddle.

No. 93005. We furnish this Saddle in either russet or black leather, as desired. Has 15½ inch tree, full leather covered seat, fancy pig skin impression skirt, full padded, sheepskin face, drill lined, ⅞ inch stirrup leathers, No. 4 cotton girth, 3 inch wood stirrups, weighs about 6 ℔s.

Our price.............$2.45

**No. 93005, $2.45.**

## Men's $4.00 Plain English Saddle.

NO. 93006 This saddle comes in russet leath'r only, has a 15½ inch Somerset tree, Shab rack plain leather covered seat, fancy pig skin impression skirts, full padded, cotton flannel lined, ⅞ inch stirrup leathers, super cotton girth, 3 inch wood stirrups, weight about 8 ℔s.

Our Price....,..........$4.00

**No. 93006, $4.00.**

No. 93007. This saddle comes in fair leather only, has 15½ inch Somerset tree, pig skin covered seat, seamed seat and jockey. Pig skin impression skirts, full padded, cotton flannel lined, 1 inch stirrup leathers, super cotton girth, 3 inch wood stirrups. Weight about 7 ℔s.

Price.....................$4.95

**No. 93007, $4.95.**

## Men's $4.95 Plain English Saddle.

## Men's $5.80 English Saddle.

No. 93008. This saddle comes in russet leather only, has 16 inch Somerset tree, pig skin impression skirts with genuine pig skin knee and thigh puffs. Pig skin covered seat. Full padded, cotton flannel lined. 1 inch stirrup leathers, super cotton girth. Stirrups are 3 inch wood, not iron as shown in cut. Weight about 8 ℔s.

Our price.. ......$5.80

**No. 93008, $5.80.**

## MEN'S SADDLES.

### Men's $1.60 Morgan Saddle.

No. 93000 For $1.60 we offer a Morgan saddle, which you would pay your retailer double the price for. This saddle comes in fair or black leather, as desired. 13 inch tree, Morgan horn, hide covered, stirrup leathers are ⅞ inch., girth is from super cotton, stirrups 3 inch wood. The saddle weighs about 5 pounds. Our $1.60 saddle has been advertised extensively and a large number have been sold in every state, and from everywhere we are receiving the most flattering testimonials. The sale of one of these saddles almost invariably leads to the sale of more. If you favor us with your order, we can guarantee that you will be thoroughly satisfied with the saddle received.

**No. 93000, $1.60.**

### Men's $5.35 Morgan Saddle.

No. 93001 This Saddle comes in russet leather only, has the very latest Muley Morgan tree, 1½ inch stirrup leathers, 1½ inch tie straps, 4 inch solid woven hair sinch, 4 inch Texas stirrups, regular single sinch rigged saddle. Weighs about 9 lbs.

Our price ...$5.35

**No. 93001.**

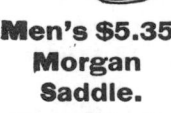
### Men's $3.75 Morgan Saddle.

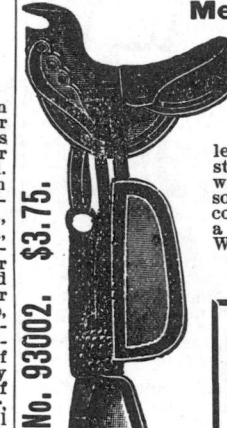

No. 93002 This Saddle is made of russet or black leather as desired. 13 inch tree, genuine hide covered Morgan horn. Seat is half leather covered, has 1½ inch tie straps, 1 inch stirrup leather with large fancy fenders, 4 inch soft woven hairs inch, leather covered wood stirrups. This is a single sinch rigged saddle. Weight about 9 pounds.

Our special price.......$3.75

**No. 93002, $3.75.**

### Men's $3.50 Morgan Saddle.

No. 93003 This Saddle is made from russet or black leather, as desired. Has a 13 inch, Muley Morgan, hide covered tree; half leather covered seat, 1½ inch tie strap, 1 inch stirrup leathers with large fancy fenders, 4 inch soft woven hair sinch, wood stirrups. We can furnish this saddle stamped or carved, as desired. A regular single sinch rigged saddle. Weight about 8 pounds.

Our price... ..$3.50

**No. 93003, $3.50.**

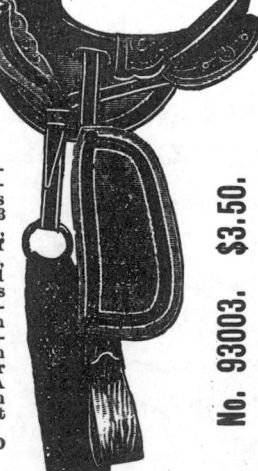

No. 93009 $10.85

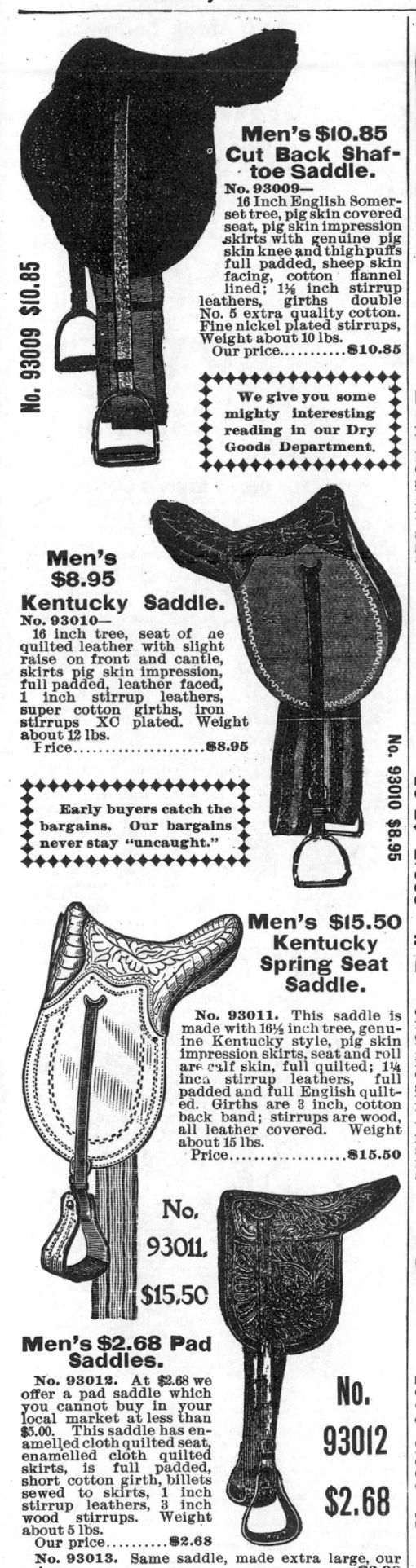

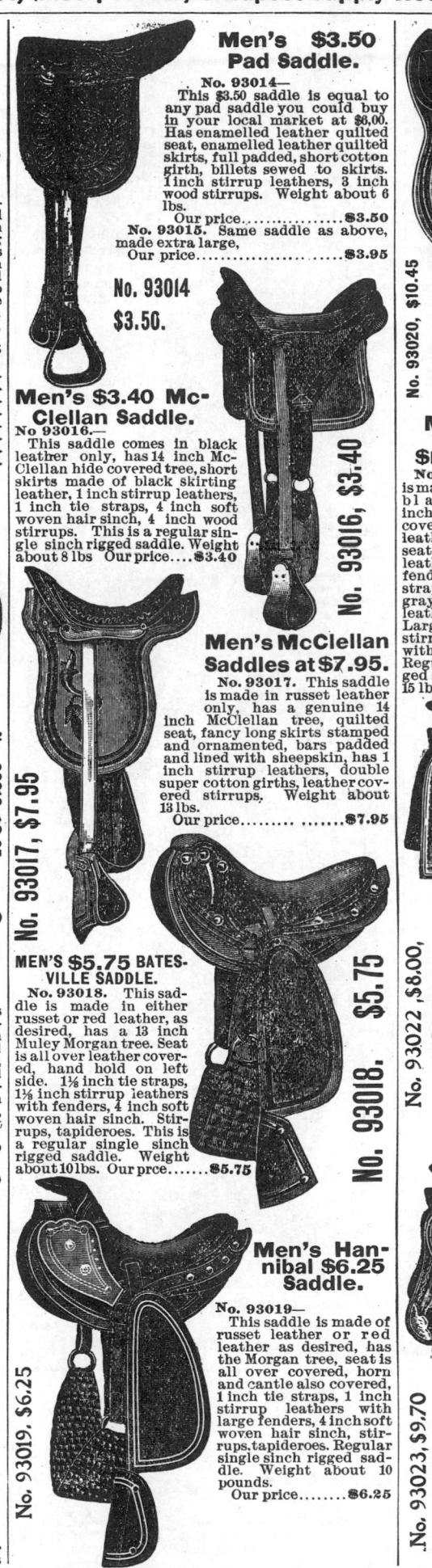

## Men's $10.85 Cut Back Shaftoe Saddle.

**No. 93009—** 16 Inch English Somerset tree, pig skin covered seat, pig skin impression skirts with genuine pig skin knee and thigh puffs full padded, sheep skin facing, cotton flannel lined; 1⅛ inch stirrup leathers, girths double No. 5 extra quality cotton. Fine nickel plated stirrups, Weight about 10 lbs.
Our price..........$10.85

**We give you some mighty interesting reading in our Dry Goods Department.**

No. 93010 $8.95

## Men's $8.95 Kentucky Saddle.

**No. 93010—** 16 inch tree, seat of one quilted leather with slight raise on front and cantle, skirts pig skin impression, full padded, leather faced, 1 inch stirrup leathers, super cotton girths, iron stirrups XC plated. Weight about 12 lbs.
Price....................$8.95

**Early buyers catch the bargains. Our bargains never stay "uncaught."**

No. 93011. $15.50

## Men's $15.50 Kentucky Spring Seat Saddle.

**No. 93011.** This saddle is made with 16½ inch tree, genuine Kentucky style, pig skin impression skirts, seat and roll are calf skin, full quilted; 1¼ inch stirrup leathers, full padded and full English quilted. Girths are 3 inch, cotton back band; stirrups are wood, all leather covered. Weight about 15 lbs.
Price....................$15.50

No. 93012 $2.68

## Men's $2.68 Pad Saddles.

**No. 93012.** At $2.68 we offer a pad saddle which you cannot buy in your local market at less than $5.00. This saddle has enamelled cloth quilted seat, enamelled cloth quilted skirts, is full padded, short cotton girth, billets sewed to skirts, 1 inch stirrup leathers, 3 inch wood stirrups. Weight about 5 lbs.
Our price..........$2.68

**No. 93013.** Same saddle, made extra large, our price.......................$2.98

No. 93014 $3.50.

## Men's $3.50 Pad Saddle.

**No. 93014—** This $3.50 saddle is equal to any pad saddle you could buy in your local market at $6.00. Has enamelled leather quilted seat, enamelled leather quilted skirts, full padded, short cotton girth, billets sewed to skirts. 1 inch stirrup leathers, 3 inch wood stirrups. Weight about 6 lbs.
Our price................$3.50

**No. 93015.** Same saddle as above, made extra large,
Our price..........................$3.95

No. 93016, $3.40

## Men's $3.40 McClellan Saddle.

**No 93016.—** This saddle comes in black leather only, has 14 inch McClellan hide covered tree, short skirts made of black skirting leather, 1 inch stirrup leathers, 1 inch tie straps, 4 inch soft woven hair sinch, 4 inch wood stirrups. This is a regular single sinch rigged saddle. Weight about 8 lbs Our price....$3.40

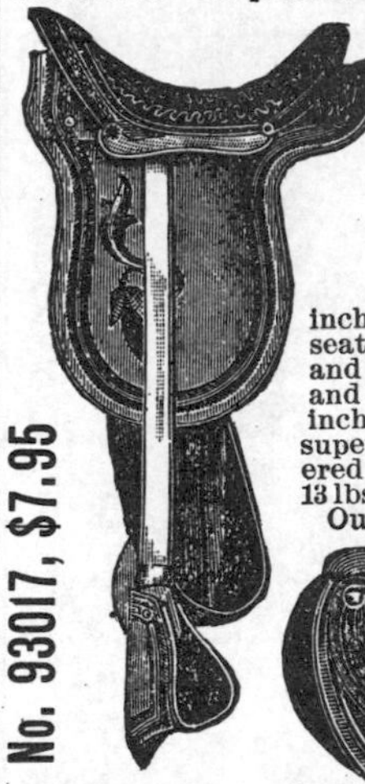

No. 93017, $7.95

## Men's McClellan Saddles at $7.95.

**No. 93017.** This saddle is made in russet leather only, has a genuine 14 inch McClellan tree, quilted seat, fancy long skirts stamped and ornamented, bars padded and lined with sheepskin, has 1 inch stirrup leathers, double super cotton girths, leather covered stirrups. Weight about 13 lbs.
Our price........ .......$7.95

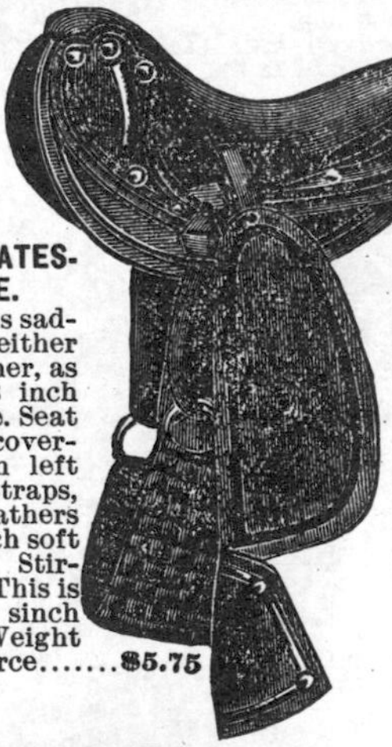

No. 93018. $5.75

## MEN'S $5.75 BATESVILLE SADDLE.

**No. 93018.** This saddle is made in either russet or red leather, as desired, has a 13 inch Muley Morgan tree. Seat is all over leather covered, hand hold on left side. 1⅛ inch tie straps, 1⅛ inch stirrup leathers with fenders, 4 inch soft woven hair sinch. Stirrups, tapideroes. This is a regular single sinch rigged saddle. Weight about 10 lbs. Our prce.......$5.75

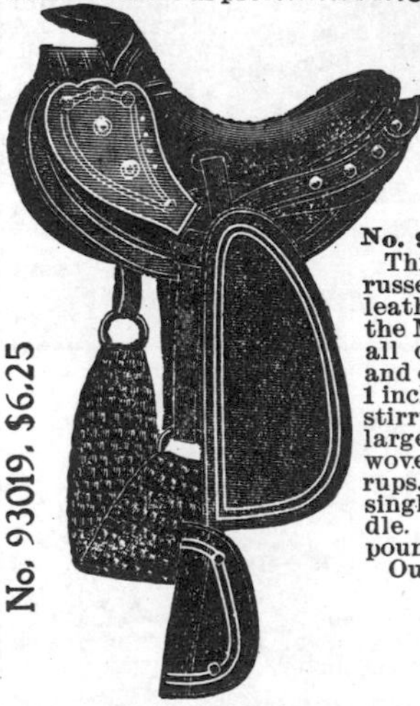

No. 93019, $6.25

## Men's Hannibal $6.25 Saddle.

**No. 93019—** This saddle is made of russet leather or red leather as desired, has the Morgan tree, seat is all over covered, horn and cantle also covered, 1 inch tie straps, 1 inch stirrup leathers with large fenders, 4 inch soft woven hair sinch, stirrups, tapideroes. Regular single sinch rigged saddle. Weight about 10 pounds.
Our price........$6.25

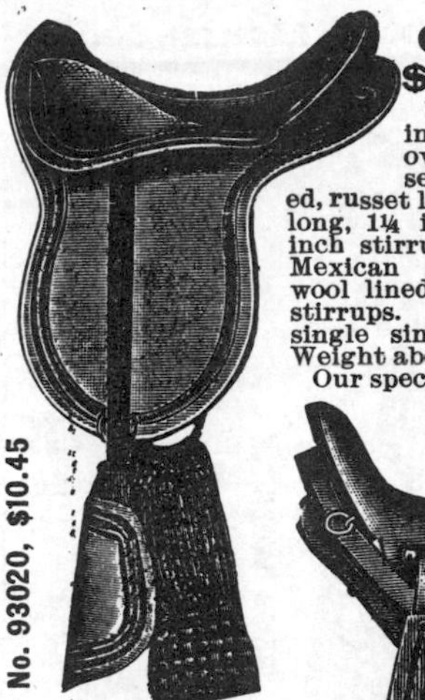

No. 93020, $10.45

## Our Special $10.45 Saddle

**No. 93020.** 15¼ inch sport tree, all over leather covered, seat open and stitched, russet leather skirts, extra long, 1¼ inch tie strap, 1¼ inch stirrup leathers, 6 inch Mexican string hair sinch, wool lined chafes, tapideroes stirrups. This is a regular single sinch rigged saddle. Weight about 14 lbs.
Our special price....$10.45

No. 93021, $10.50

## Men's Black McClellan $10.50 Saddle.

**No. 93021.** This saddle is made of an extra quality black leather, has 1 inch McClellan tree, all covered over with black leather, open and stitched seat. 1¼ inch stirrup leathers with very large fenders. 1¼ inch tie straps. Sinch is 20 strand gray California hair with leather wool lined chafe. Large leather covered stirrups. Saddle is finished with brass rings and nails. Regular single sinch rigged saddle. Weight about 15 lbs. Our price..$10.50

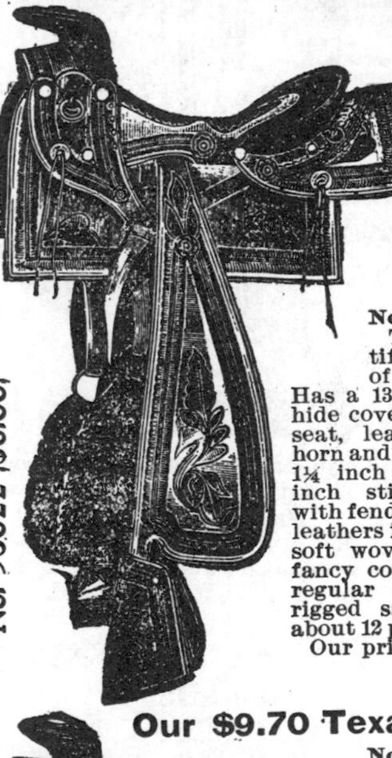

No. 93022, $8.00,

## Men's Western $8.00 Saddle.

**No. 93022—** This is a beautiful saddle, made of russet leather. Has a 13 inch Jackson hide covered tree, open seat, leather covered; horn and cantle covered, 1¼ inch tie straps, 1¼ inch stirrup leathers with fenders and stirrup leathers in one. 5 inch soft woven hair sinch, fancy covered stirrups, regular single sinch rigged saddle. Weight about 12 pounds.
Our price........$8.00

No. 93023, $9.70

## Our $9.70 Texas Saddle.

**No. 93023—** This saddle is made from an extra quality black saddle leather, has the regular Mexican hide covered tree leather covered seat. Horn and cantle leather covered. Skirts are fancy carved with fancy corner ornamentations. 1¼ inch tie straps, stirrup leathers are all 1¼ inch with large fenders. 6 inch Mexican string hair sinch. Stirrups, tapideroes. Regular single sinch rigged saddle. Weight about 14 pounds.
Our price............$9.70

**OUR GUN DEPARTMENT SHOWS AN ASSORTMENT OF THE BEST MAKES AT JUST SUCH PRICES AS PROVE OUR CLAIM TO BEING THE CHEAPEST SUPPLY HOUSE ON EARTH.**

## Men's $4.25 Morgan Saddle

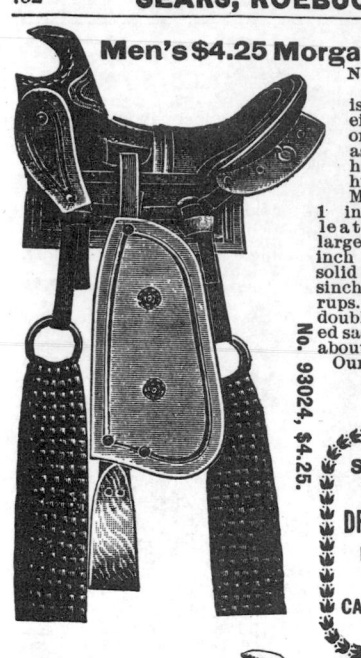

No. 93024— This Saddle is made of either russet or red leather, as desired. It has a 13 inch hide covered Morgan tree; 1 inch stirrup leathers with large fenders; 1 inch tie straps; solid woven hair sinches; wood stirrups. This is a double sinch rigged saddle. Weight about 10 pounds. Our price. $4.25

No. 93024, $4.25.

SELECT YOUR DRY GOODS FROM OUR CATALOGUE

## Men's $5.75 Morgan Saddle.

No. 93025— This saddle is made of russet saddle leather, has a Morgan tree, unlined skirts, 1 inch sinches; 1 inch stirrup leathers with fenders, 1 inch tie straps, solid woven hair sinches, very strong wood stirrups. We can also furnish this saddle made of cherry red leather, if desired. Weight about 11 lbs. Our Price......$5.75

No. 93025, $5.75.

BUY YOUR HARDWARE FROM US.

## STOCK SADDLES.

We wish to call your attention especially to our line of stock saddles, which we believe is the most complete line offered. We guarantee there is nothing on the market that will compare with them in quality of material or make, and our prices you must admit are below any kind of competition.

## Our Special $6.00 Stock Saddle.

No. 93026. 13 in. Morgan tree, hide covered; 21 inch skirts, 1⅛ inch stirrup leathers to buckle, 1¼ in. tie straps, 4 in. woven soft hair sinches, 3 in. wood stirrups. This is a good, substantial well made saddle. Weight about 11 lbs. Price......$6.00

No. 93026 $6.00.

♦♦♦♦♦♦♦♦♦
♦ BUY...
♦ Groceries
♦ FROM
♦ US
♦ And SAVE MONEY

## Our $7.50 Stock Saddle.

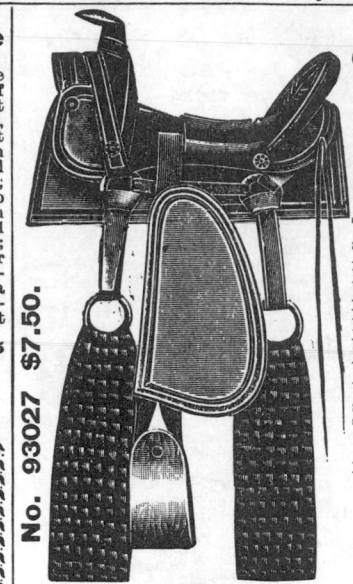

No. 93027. This saddle has a 13½ in. steel fork tree, 21 in. unlined skirts, 1½ inch stirrup leathers to buckle, 1⅛ inch tie straps, solid woven hair sinches, 4 inch Texas stirrups. Weight about 15 lbs. Price...$7.50

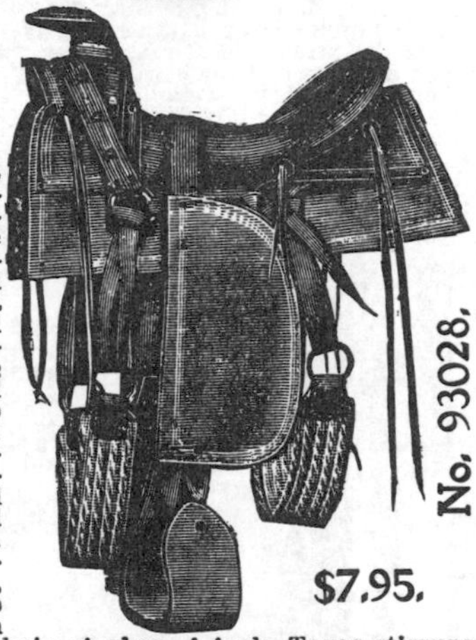

No. 93027 $7.50.

## Our $7.95 Stock Saddle.

No. 93028. This is a thoroughly first-class saddle made of genuine oiled skirting, has a 13½ in. solid fork hide covered tree, 22½ in. unlined skirts. The seat is of solid leather, handsomely stamped flower, steel strainer, roll cante. 1¼ in. stirrup leathers to buckle, 1⅛ inch tie straps, 4 inch solid woven hair sinches, 4 inch Texas stirrups. Weight about 15 lbs. Our price.......................................$7.95

No. 93028.

$7.95.

## Our $8.50 Stock Saddle.

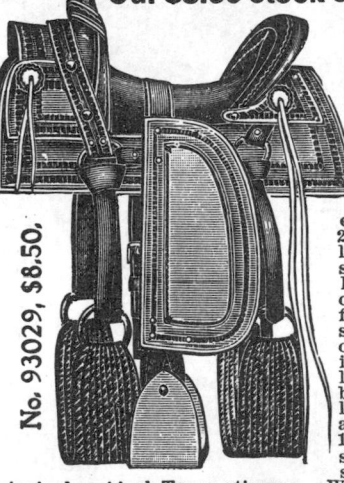

No. 93029 This is a thoroughly first-class saddle, made of extra quality oil'd skirting. Has a 14½ inch steel fork hide covered tree; 22½ inch unlined skirts, seat of solid leather, fancy stamped flower, steel strainer, roll cantle, 1⅛ inch stirrup leathers to buckle, gullet raised and beaded, 1⅛ inch tie straps, 4 inch solid woven hair sinches, 4 inch Texas stirrups. Weight about 16 lbs.

Our price........................$8.50
No. 93030. Same saddle with wool lined skirts......................................$9.75

No. 93029, $8.50.

We Sell A COLUMBUS TOP BUGGY For $39.90

Other Top Buggies Down To $28.95.

For Full Particulars: See Vehicle Department or send for mammoth Special Free Vehicle Catalogue.

## Our $10.25 Stock Saddle.

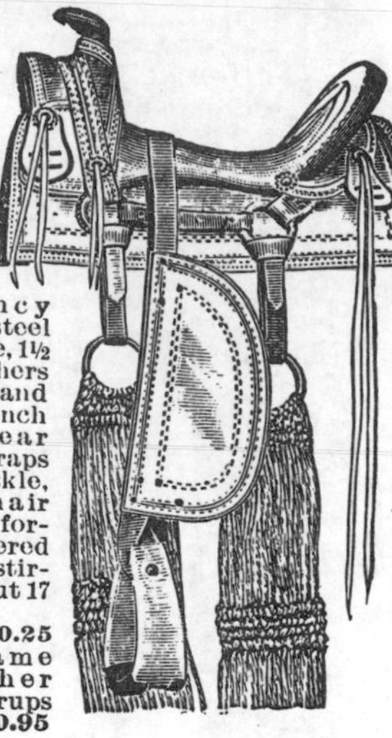

No. 93031. This saddle will compare favorably with anything offered by local dealers at double the price. It is made of oiled skirting, has a 14½ inch steel fork tree, 22½ inch unlined skirts, solid leather seat, fancy stamped flower, steel strainer, roll cantle, 1½ inch stirrup leathers to buckle, raised and beaded gullet, 1¼ inch tie straps on near side, 1½ latigoe straps on off side to buckle, solid woven hair sinches, 3 inch California pattern leathered bar and bottom stirrups. Weight about 17 lbs.

Price......$10.25
No. 93032. Same saddle with leather covered steel stirrups................$10.95

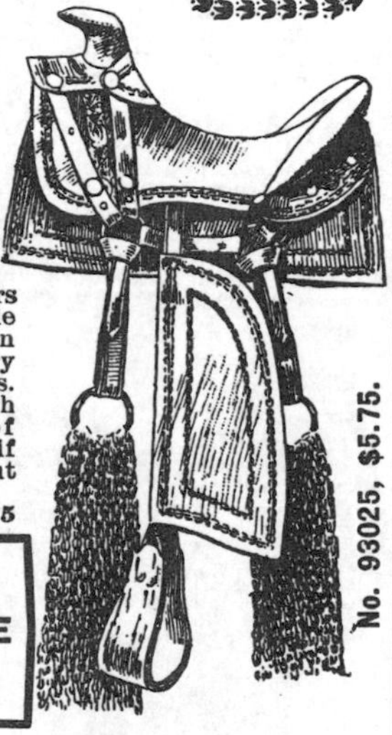

No. 93031, $10.25.

## Our Stout Men's Saddle.

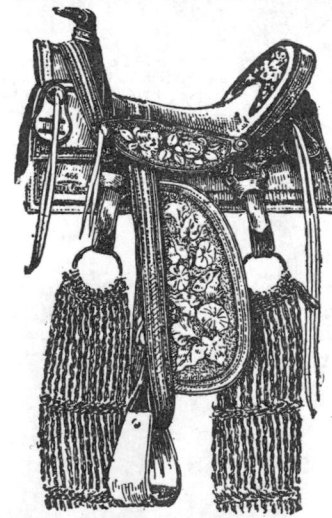

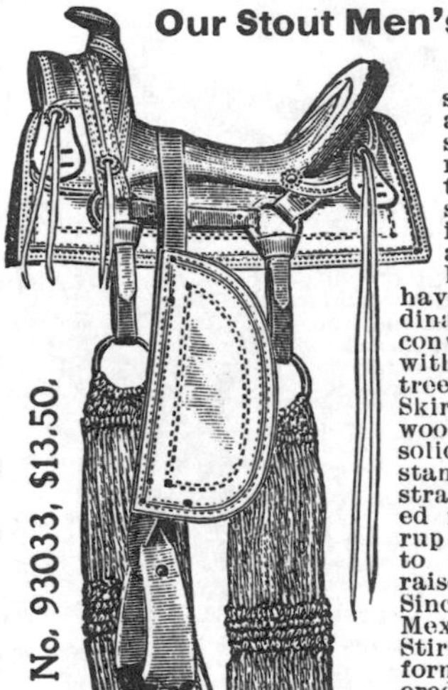

No. 93033. The actory makes up specially for us an extra large stock saddle. It is made larger than the ordinary stock saddle, and it will be appreciated by unusually large men who have found the ordinary size saddle inconvenient. Made with 16 in. steel fork tree, hide covered. Skirts are 25 in. and wool lined. Seat is solid leather with stamped flower, steel strainers and beaded roll cantle. Stirrup leathers are 1¾ in to buckle. Gullet raised and beaded. Sinches of the best Mexican string hair. Stirrups 3 in. California pattern, leathered bar and bottom. Made of oiled California skirting. Our price..........$13.50
No. 94034. Same with wool lined chafes and connecting straps on sinches................$14.50

No. 93033, $13.50.

## Our $11.75 Stock Saddle.

No. 93035 This Saddle is made of genuine oiled California skirting; has a 14½ inch steel fork hide covered tree; 22½ inch wool lined skirts; solid leather, stamped flower, steel strainer, beaded roll cantle seat; 1½ inch stirrup leathers; raised and beaded gullet; 1¼ inch tie straps on near side, 1½ inch latigoe straps to buckle on off side. Genuine Mexican string hair sinches; 3 inch California pattern leathered bar and bottom stirrups. Weight about 18 lbs.
Our price....................................$11.75
No. 93036 Same Saddle with leather covered steel stirrups......................12.50
Add for wool lined chafes and connecting strap on sinches................................1.00

No. 93036. $11.75.

## Our $12.00 Stock Saddle.

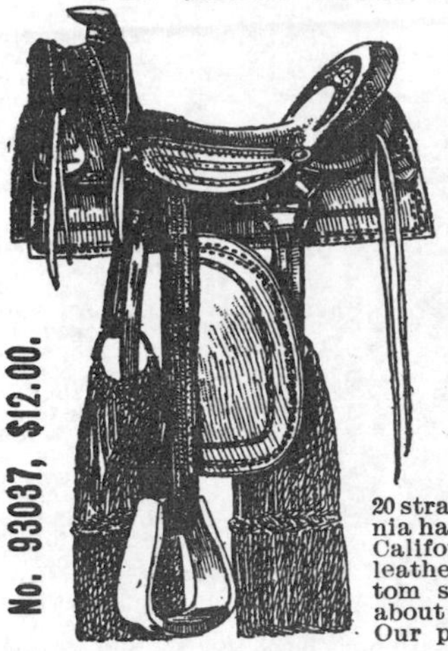

No. 93037, $12.00.

**No. 93037** This Saddle is made of genuine oiled California skirting; has 14½ inch steel fork hide covered tree; 22½ inch wool lined skirts; solid leather, stamped flower, steel strainer, beaded roll cantle seat; 1⅛ inch stirrup leathers raised and beaded gullet; 1½ inch tie straps on near side, 1¼ inch latigoe straps off side to buckle; 20 strand gray California hair sinches; 3 inch California pattern leathered bar and bottom stirrups. Weight about 19 pounds.
Our price......$12.00

**No. 93038** Same Saddle with leather covered steel stirrups ........................ 12.65

Add for all wool lined chafes and connecting strap on sinches........................ 1.00

## Our $13.25 Stock Saddle.

**No. 93039** This Saddle is made of genuine oiled California skirting; has a 14½ inch steel fork hide covered tree; 23 in. wool lined skirt solid leather seat, stamped flower, steel strainer, beaded roll cantle; 1⅝ inch stirrup leathers, raised and beaded gullet; 1¼ inch tie straps on near side. 1⅛ inch latigoe straps to buckle on off side; 20 strand white California hair sinches; 3 inch California pattern leathered bottom and bar stirrups. Weight about 20 lbs.
Our price...$13.25

**No. 93040** Same Saddle with leather covered steel stirrups.........$13.90

Add for wool lined chafes and connecting strap on sinches.........................$1.00

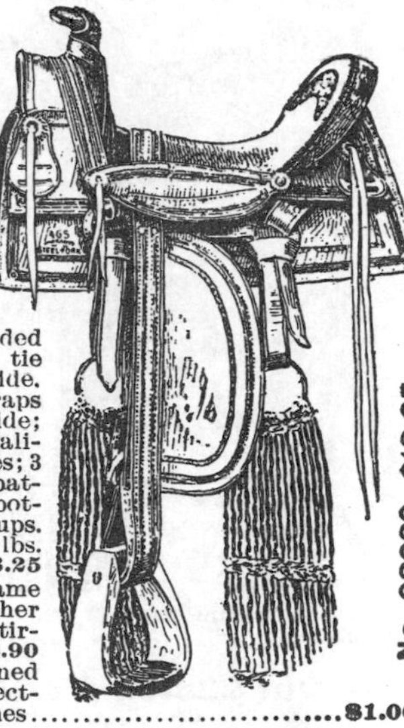

No. 93039, $13.25.

## Our $12.65 Stock Saddle.

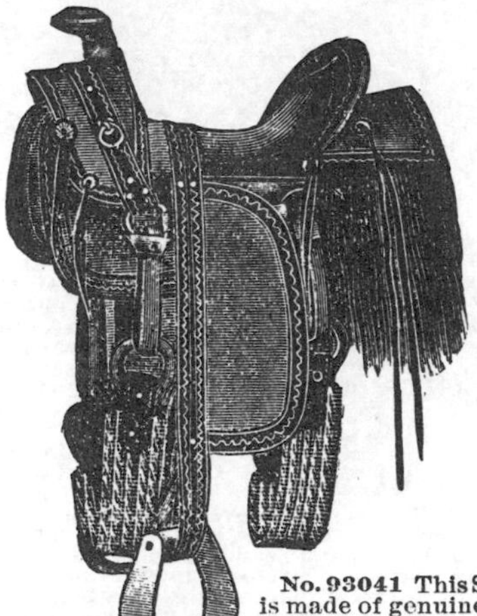

No. 93041, $12.65.

**No. 93041** This Saddle is made of genuine oiled California skirting; has 14½ inch steel fork hide covered tree; genuine Llama skin housing; seat is solid leather, has steel strainer and roll cantle; 1¾ inch stirrup leathers; 1⅛ inch tie straps. Sinches are genuine Mexican string hair; 3 inch California pattern stirrups. Weight about 15 pounds.
Our price........................$12.65

**No. 93042** Same Saddle, leather covered steel stirrups........................$13.30

Add for wool lined chafes and connecting straps on sinches........................$1.00

## Our $13.95 Stock Saddle.

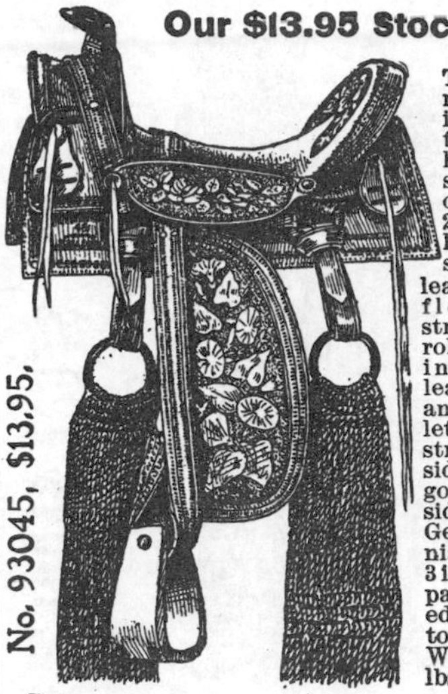

No. 93045, $13.95.

**No. 93045.** This saddle is made of genuine oiled California skirting, has 14½ inch steel fork hide covered tree; 23 inch wool lined skirts; seat of solid leather, stamped flower, steel strainer, beaded roll cantle; 1⅝ inch stirrup leathers; raised and beaded gullet; 1¼ inch tie straps on near side, 1½ inch latigoe straps on off side to buckle. Genuine California hair sinches. 3 inch California pattern leathered bar and bottom stirrups. Weight about 20 lbs.
Price........................$13.95

**No. 93044.** Same saddle with leather covered steel stirrups........................$14.60

Add for wool chafes and connecting strap on sinches........................$1.00

## Our $15.25 Stock Saddle.

**No. 93045.** This saddle is made of genuine oiled California skirting; has 14½ inch steel fork hide covered tree; 24 inch wool lined skirts. Seat is of solid leather, stamped flower, steel strainer, beaded roll cantle. Stirrup leathers, 2 inch, gullet raised and beaded tie straps 1½ inch on near side, latigoe straps to buckle are 1¾ inch, has genuine Mexican string hair sinches, leathered wool lined and connecting straps, 3 inch California pattern leathered bar and bottom stirrups. Weight about 21 lbs.
Price........................$15.25

**No. 93046.** Same saddle with leather covered steel stirrups........................$15.90

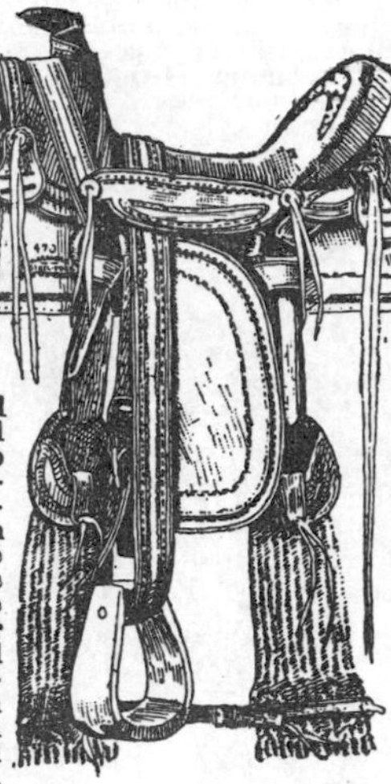

No. 93045, $15.25

## Our $16.75 Stock Saddle.

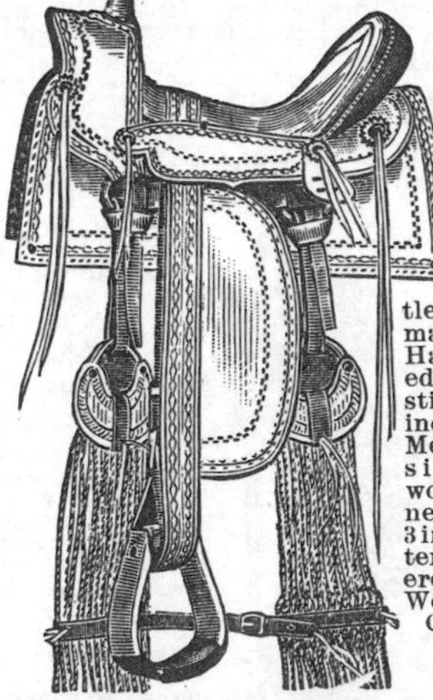

**No. 93047.** This is an exceptionally fine saddle, made of genuine oiled California skirting. Has a 15 inch steel fork hide covered tree; 24 inch wool lined skirts; seat is solid leather, beaded roll cantle, seat and jockey made in one piece. Has raised and beaded gullet, 2 inch stirrup leathers, 1¼ inch tie straps. 6 inch Mexican string hair sinches, leathered, wool lined and connecting strap. Has 3 inch California pattern stirrups, leathered top and bottom. Weight about 21 lbs.
Our price..$16.75

## OUR MAN-SHOEING DEPARTMENT

Shows the best-wearing Footwear at close profit prices.

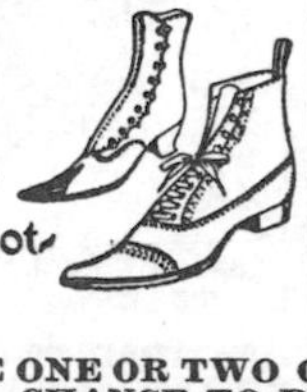

## Our $15.25 Stock Saddle.

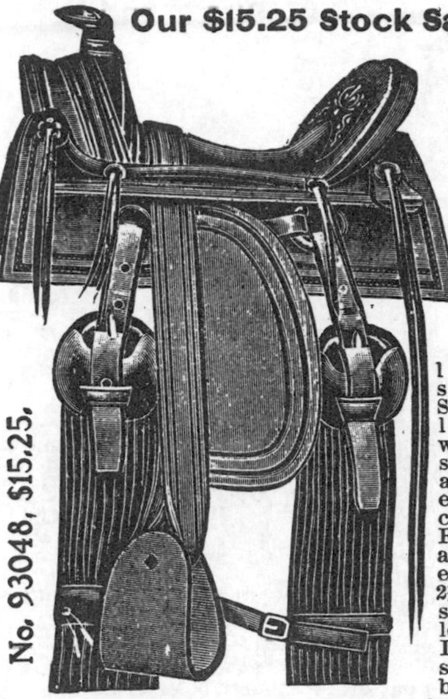

No. 93048, $15.25.

**No. 93048.** This saddle is made from genuine oiled Califor'ia skirting has 15 in. steel fork hide covered tree, 24 in. wool lined skirts. Seats sol'd leather with steel strainer and beaded roll cantle. Raised and beaded gullet. 2¼ inch stirrup leathers. Latigoe straps to buckle on near side, 1½ inch; on off side, 1¾ inch. Sinches are 6 inch Mexican string hair, leathered, wool lined, and connecting strap. Stirrups, 5 inch Texas. Saddles weigh about 24 lbs.
Price........................$15.25

**No. 93049.** Same saddle as above only with tie latigoes 1¼ inch and unlined skirts with tapideroes.
Price........................$14.50

**No. 93050.** With 3 inch California stirrups.
Price........................$13.70

## Our $18.00 Stock Saddle.

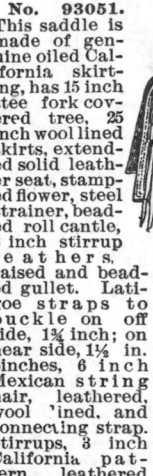

**No. 93051.** This saddle is made of genuine oiled California skirting, has 15 inch stee fork covered tree, 25 inch wool lined skirts, extended solid leather seat, stamped flower, steel strainer, beaded roll cantle, 2 inch stirrup leathers, raised and beaded gullet. Latigoe straps to buckle on off side, 1¾ inch; on near side, 1½ in. Sinches, 6 inch Mexican string hair, leathered, wool lined, and connecting strap. Stirrups, 3 inch California pattern, leathered bar and bottom. Weight about 24 lbs.
Our price........................$18.00

**No. 93052.** Same saddle with leather covered steel stirrups........................$18.69

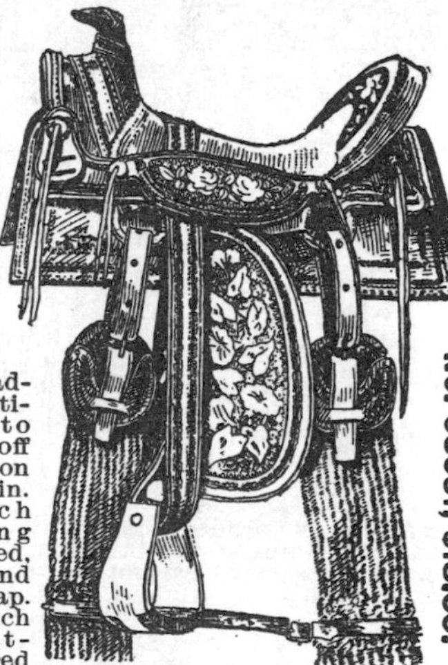

No. 93051, $18.00.

## Our $18.25 Stock Saddle.

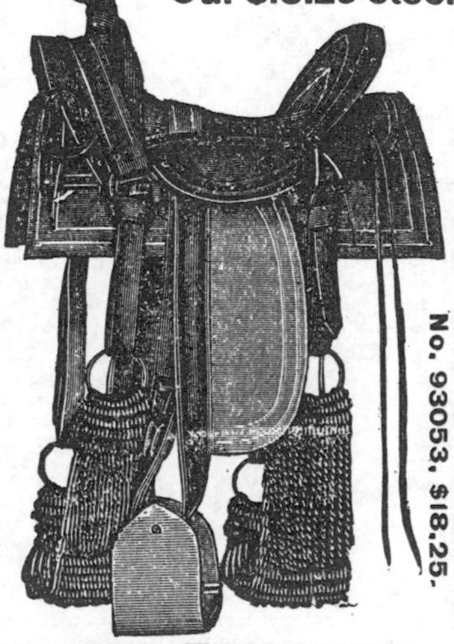

No. 93053, $18.25.

**No. 93053.** This saddle is made of genuine oiled California skirting, has 15½ inch steel fork hide covered tree, 25½ inch wool lined skirts. Seat is solid leather, seat and jockey made in one piece, steel strainer, beaded roll cantle, raised and beaded gullet. Stirrup leathers, 2¼ inch. Tie straps, 1¼ in. Sinches 6 in. Mexican hair leathered, wool lined chafes. Stirrups, 4 inch. Flora's stationary block. Weight about 24 lbs.
Our price........................$18.25

WE ARE NOT THE ONLY MAIL ORDER HOUSE IN EXISTENCE. THERE ARE ONE OR TWO OTHERS. WE ONLY LAY CLAIM TO GENERAL AND SUPERIOR EXCELLENCE. WE ONLY ASK A CHANCE TO PROVE IT. TRY US.

## Our $17.00 Stock Saddle.

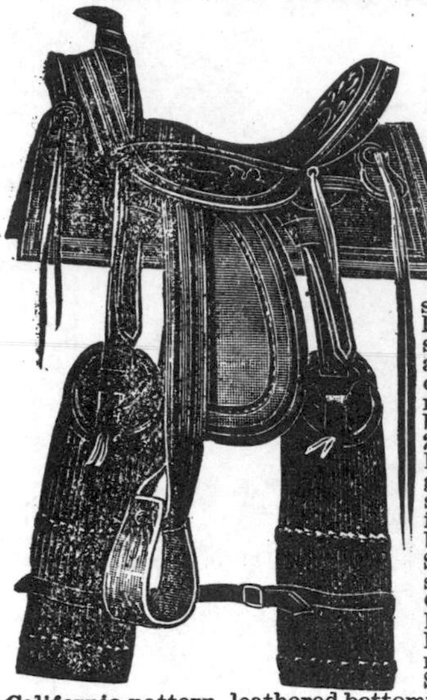

**No. 93054.** This saddle is made from genuine oiled California skirting; has a 15 inch steel fork hide cover'd tree; 25½ inch wool lined skirts; seat, solid leather, with steel strainer and beaded roll cantle. Has raised and beaded gullet. 2¼ inch stirrup leathers. Latigoe straps, near side, to tie, 1½ inch; off side to buckle, 1¾ inch. Sinches, 20 strand gray California hair, leathered, wool lined, and connecting strap. Stirrups, 3 inch California pattern, leathered bottom. Saddle weight about 23 lbs.
Our price........................................$17.00

## Our $20.25 Stock Saddle.

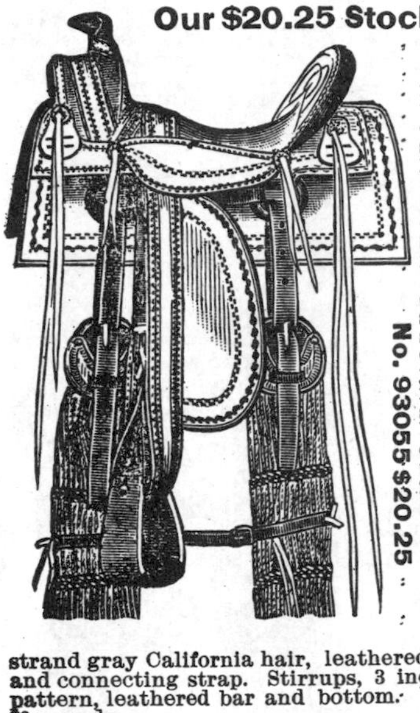

No. 93055 $20.25

**No. 93055.** This saddle is made of the very best oiled Colifornia skirting; has 15½ inch tree with steel fork, hide covered. Skirts are 27 inches, wool lined. Seat extended, solid leather, stamped flower, seat and jockey made in one piece, steel strainer, beaded roll cantle. Stirrup leathers, 2½ inch. Gullet raised and beaded. Latigoestraps to buckle on near side, 1⅝ inch; on off side, 1¾ inch. Sinches, 20-strand gray California hair, leathered, wool lined, and connecting strap. Stirrups, 3 inch, California pattern, leathered bar and bottom. Weight about 26 pounds.
Price........................................$20.25
**No 93056.** Same Saddle with leather covered steel stirrups........................................$20.95

## Our $21.90 Stock Saddle.

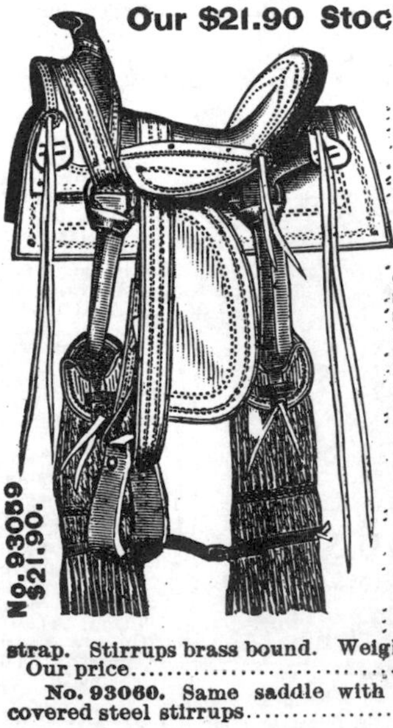

No. 93059 $21.90.

**No 93059.** This saddle is made of genuine oiled California skirting; has 15½ inch tree with steel fork, hide covered; 27 inch wool lined skirts; seat of solid leather, stamped flower, seat and jockey in one piece, steel strainer, beaded roll cantle. Gullet raised and beaded. Stirrup leathers 2½ in. Latigoe straps to buckle on near side, 1⅝ inch; on off side 1¾ inch. Sinches 20 strand white California hair, leathered, wool lined, and connecting strap. Stirrups brass bound. Weight, about 28 lbs.
Our price........................................$21.90
**No. 93060.** Same saddle with leather covered steel stirrups........................................$22.55

## OUR $18.50 STOCK SADDLE.

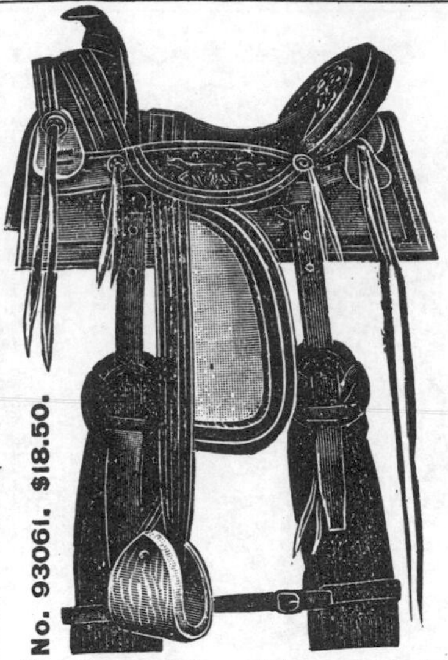

No. 93061. $18.50.

**No. 93061.** This saddle is made from genuine oiled California skirting, has 15½ inch steel fork hide covered tree, skirts are 25 inch, wool lined. Seat is solid leather, seat and jockey in one piece. steel strainer, beaded roll cantle. Gullet raised and beaded. Stirrup leathers, 2½ inch. Latigoe straps to buckle near side, 1⅛ inch by 6 feet; on off side, 1¾ inch by 16 inches double. Sinches 6 inch Mexican string, leathered, wool lined chafes and connecting strap. Stirrups, 4 inch, Flora's stationary block. Weight about 25 lbs.
Our price........................................$18.50

## Our $24.38 Stock Saddle.

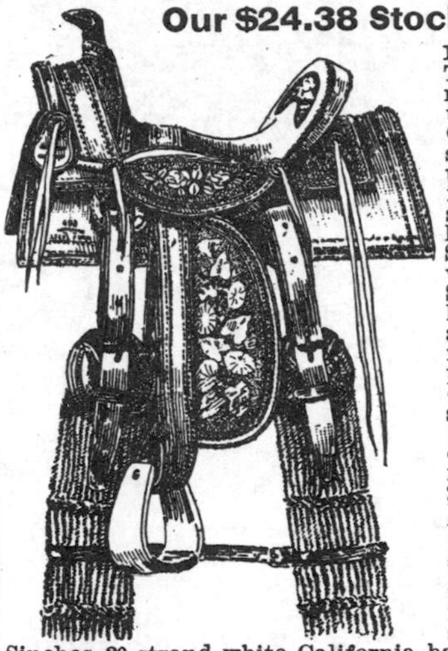

**No. 93062.** This saddle is made of genuine oiled California skirting leather. Has 15½ inch tree, steel fork, hide covered. Skirts 28½ in., wool lined. Seat, solid leather, seat and jockey made in one piece, stamped flower, steel strainer, beaded roll cantle. Stirrup leathers 2½ inch. Gullet raised and beaded. Latigoe straps to buckle on near side, 1¾ inch; on off side, 1⅞ inch. Sinches, 20-strand white California hair, leathered, wool lined, and connecting straps. Stirrups, 3 inch California pattern leathered bar and bottom. Weight of saddle about 26 pounds.
Our price........................................$24.38
**No. 93063.** Same saddle with leather covered steel stirrups........................................$25.03

## Our $30.18 Stock Saddle.

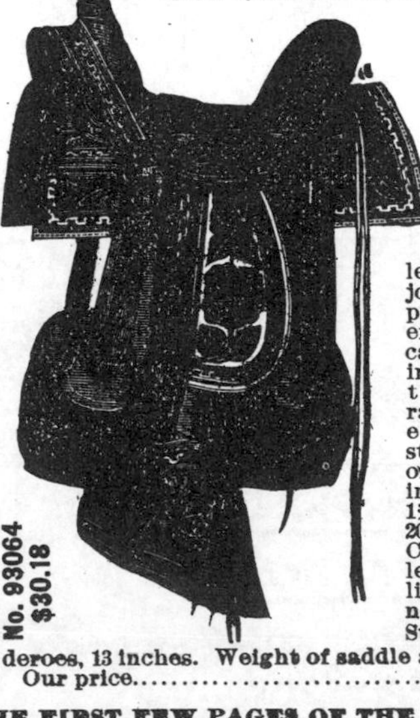

No. 93064 $30.18

**No. 93064.** This saddle is made of the very best oiled California skirting leather; has 15½ inch tree with steel fork. 26 inch wool lined skirts. Seat is solid leather, seat and jockey in one piece, steelstrainer, beaded roll cantle. Has 2½ inch stirrup leathers. Gullet raised and beaded. Latigoe straps to buckle on near side, 1⅝ inch; on off side, 1¾ inch. Sinches 20-strand white California hair, leathered, wool lined, and connecting straps. Stirrups, tapideroes, 13 inches. Weight of saddle about 28 pounds.
Our price........................................$30.18

## Our $32.27 Stock Saddle.

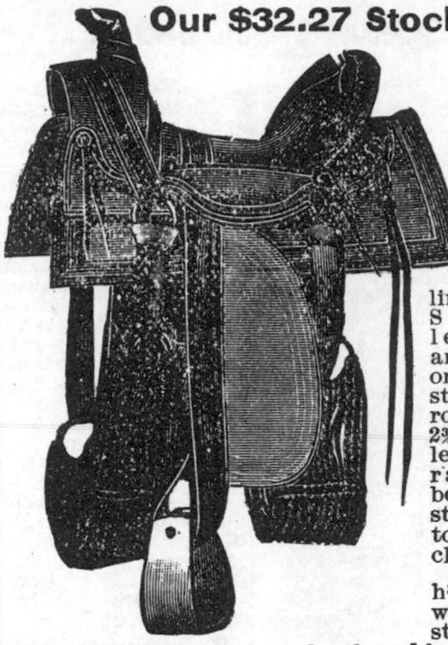

**No. 93067.** This saddle is made from the very best oiled California skirting leather. 16 inch tree, steel fork, hide cov'r'd. 29 inch wool lined skirts. Seat, solid leather, seat and jockey in one piece, steel strainer, bead'd roll cantle. Has 2¾ inch stirrup leathers. Gullet raised and beaded. Latigoe straps 1⅞ inch to buckle. Sinches, California hair, leathered, wool lined, and connecting straps; made with solid block stirrups, leathered bar and bottom.
Our price........................................$32.27
**No. 93068.** Same saddle with leather covered steel stirrups........................................$32.70

## Our $37.25 Stock Saddle.

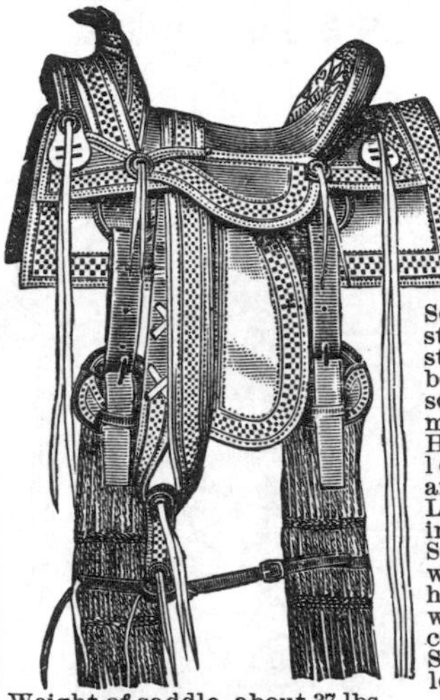

**No. 23069.** This saddle is made from the very finest genuine oiled California skirting leather. Has 16 inch tree, steel fork, hide covered; 30½ inch skirts wool lined. Seat, solid leather, stamped flower, steel strainer, beaded roll cantle, seat and jockey made in one piece. Has 3 inch stirrup leathers, raised and beaded gullet. Latigoe straps, 2 inches, to buckle. Sinches, 20 strand white California hair, leathered, wool lined, and connecting strap. Stirrups, steel, leather covered. Weight of saddle, about 37 lbs.
Our price........................................$37.25

## Our $38.50 Stock Saddle.

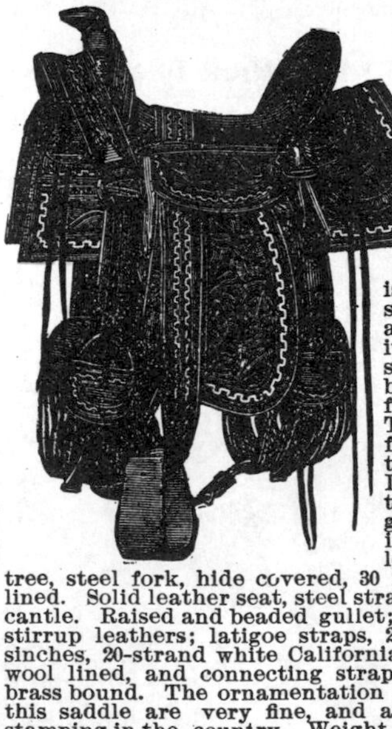

No. 93071, $38.50

**No. 93071.** This is the finest stock saddle we handle, and we guarantee it equal to any saddle you can buy elsewhere at from $50.00 to $60.00 There are very few saddles made that will equal it. It is made from the very finest genuine oiled California skirting leather. 16 inch tree, steel fork, hide covered, 30 inch skirts, wool lined. Solid leather seat, steel strainer, beaded roll cantle. Raised and beaded gullet; 2¾ inch double stirrup leathers; latigoe straps, 2 inch to buckle; sinches, 20-strand white California hair, leathered, wool lined, and connecting straps. Stirrups are brass bound. The ornamentation and stamping on this saddle are very fine, and are equal to any stamping in the country. Weight of saddle about 33 lbs.
Our price........................................$38.50
**No. 93072.** Same saddle with leather covered steel stirrups........................................$38.90

**Take a dose of economy as prescribed in this book and cure the flat pocket book.**

BEFORE SENDING IN YOUR ORDER, READ THE FIRST FEW PAGES OF THE CATALOGUE. OUR TERMS ARE MOST LIBERAL, AND SUCH SUGGESTIONS AS WE MAKE ARE FOR YOUR BENEFIT, THAT YOU MAY SECURE THE GREATEST BENEFIT.

## Our $26.38 Stock Saddle.

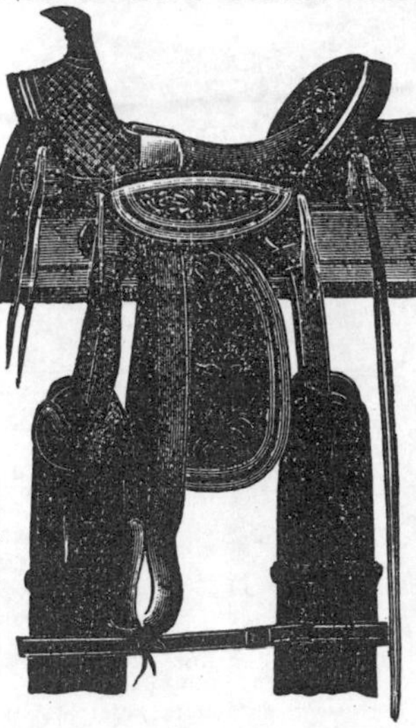

No. 93063 $26.38.

No. 93063 $26.38

**No. 93063.** This saddle is made from the very best oiled California skirting leather. Has 16 inch tree with steel fork, hide covered. Skirts are 28½ inch, wool lined. Seat and jockey in one piece, steel strainer, beaded roll cantle, fancy flower ornamentations. Gullet raised and beaded, basket stamped. Stirrup leathers, 2½ inch. Latigoe straps to tie on near side, 1½ inches by 6 feet; on off side 1¾ inch to buckle. Sinches, 20-strand white California hair, wool lined chafes and connecting straps. Stirrups, steel, leather covered. Weight of saddle about 29 pounds.
Our price.......................................... $26.38

# BOYS' SADDLES.

We show an assortment of eight boys' saddles of the most desirable pattern, and in order to make the prices below any competition we have arranged for a large number of these saddles. They are made by the same manufacturer who makes our men's saddles, and for quality of material, workmanship and price we guarantee they cannot be equalled by anything in the market.

Our terms are the same on these saddles. They will be sent C. O. D. subject to examination on receipt of $1.00 as a guarantee of good faith, balance and express charges payable at express office.

3% discount allowed if cash in full accompanies your order.

## Our $2.45 Boys' Saddle.

**No. 93076.** This is a plain English saddle, made from either russet or black leather, as desired, a saddle you could not buy in your local market at less than $4.00 or $5.00. It has a 13½ inch Somerset tree, the seat is full leather covered, has pigskin impression skirts, it is full padded, faced, drill lined, has ⅝ inch stirrup leathers, girth cotton web, 2½ inch wood stirrups, weighs about 5 lbs.
Our price.......... $2.45

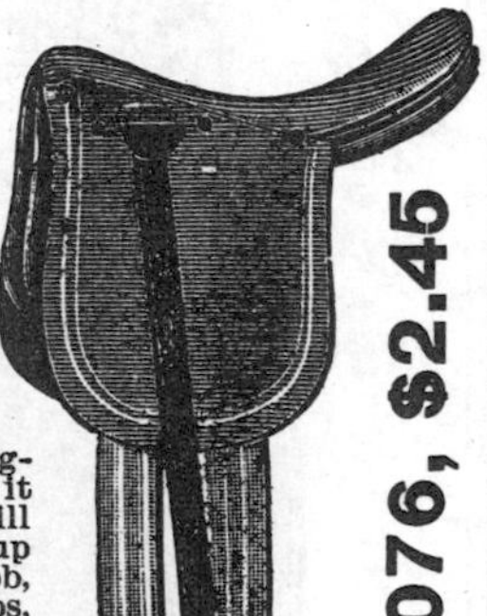

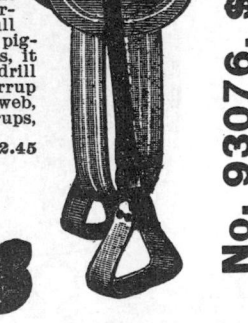

No. 93076, $2.45

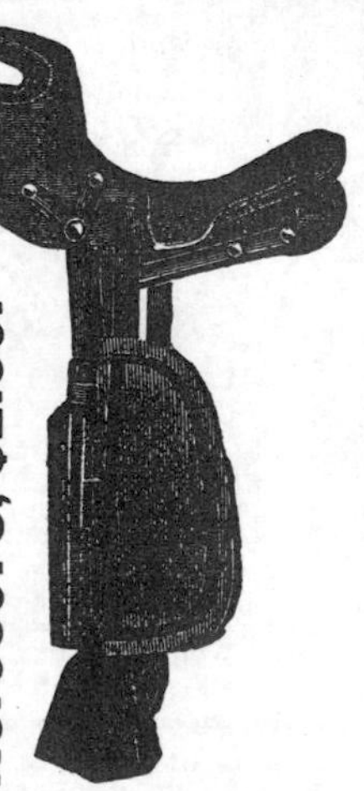

No. 93078, $2.50.

## Boy's $2.50 Morgan Saddle

**No. 93078.** This saddle is made of russet or black leather, as desired, 11 inch hide covered Morgan tree, stirrup leathers are ⅝ inch, fenders riveted on, girth of super cotton, 2½ inch stirrups, and the saddle weighs about 5 lbs.
Our price.... ...$2.50

Guard Against **OVERCHARGE** by Buying from US. . . .

## Boys's $3.25 Morgan Saddle.

**No. 93080.** This saddle is made of russet or black leather as desired, has 11 inch hide covered Morgan tree, stirrup leathers, 1 in. to buckle, fenders riveted on. Has 1 inch tie strap, 4 inch soft woven hair sinch, 2½ inch wood stirrup.
Weight about 6 lbs.
Our price........ $3.25

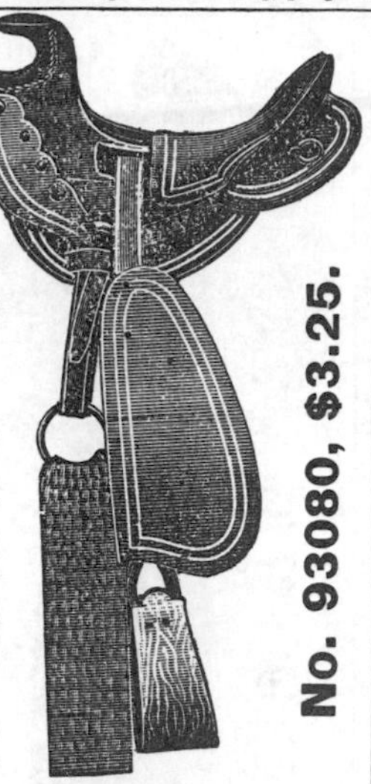

No. 93080, $3.25.

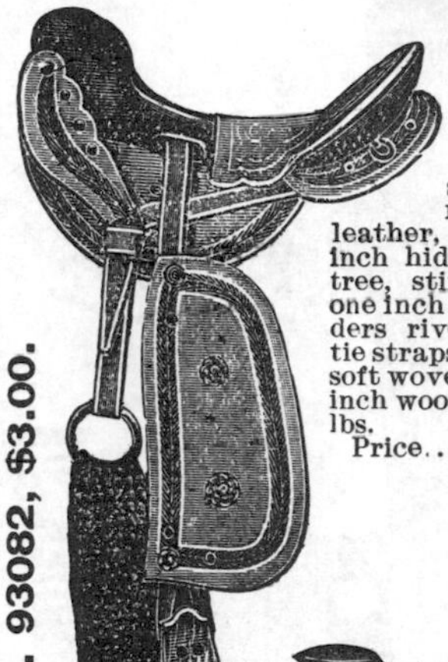

No. 93082, $3.00.

## Boy's $3.00 Morgan Saddle.

**No. 93082.** This saddle is made of russet, or black leather, as desired, has 11 inch hide covered Morgan tree, stirrup leathers are one inch to buckle with fenders riveted on. One inch tie straps. Sinch is 4 inch soft woven hair, stirrups 2½ inch wood. Weight about 5 lbs.
Price.................. $3.00

## Boy's $5.45 Hannibal Saddle.

**No. 93084.** This saddle is made of fair or black leather, as desired, has 11 in. Morgan tree, stirrup leathers are one inch to buckle, one inch tie straps, 4 inch soft woven hair sinch, covered wood stirrups.
Weight about 7 lbs.
Our price . $5.45

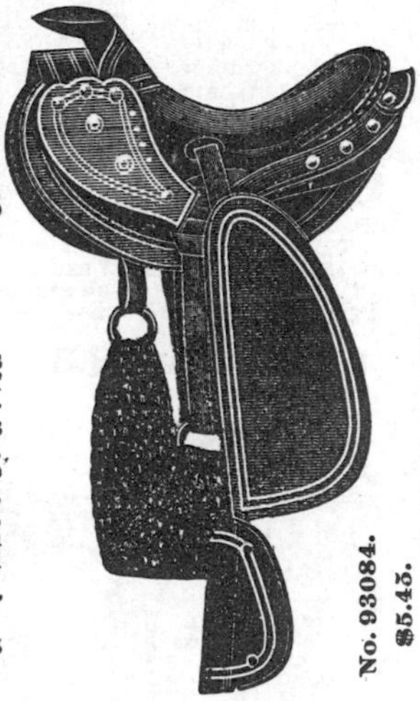

No. 93084. $5.45.

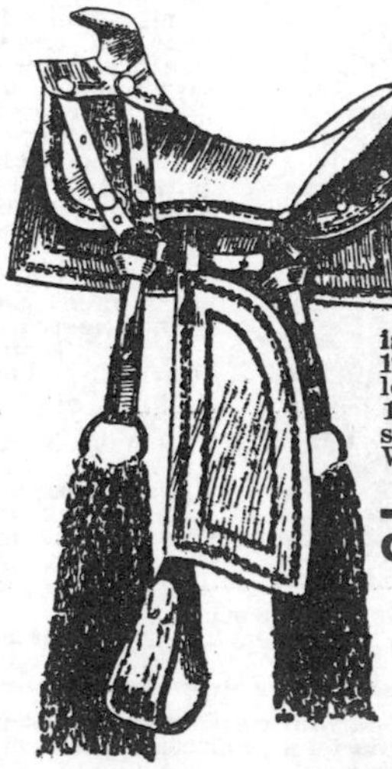

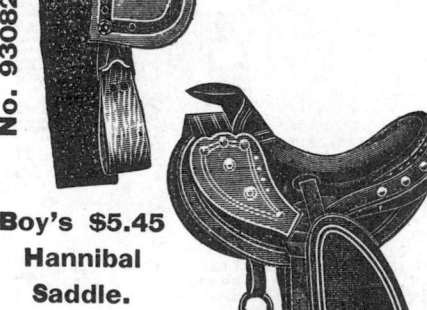

## Boy's $6 Morga Saddle

**No. 93086.** saddle is made o. .u leather, has 11 inch Morgan tree, the seat is all covered over, has 19 inch skirts, stirrup leathers 1 in. to buckle, 1 inch tie straps, 4 inch soft woven hair sinches. Weight about 9 lbs.
Our price........ $6.00

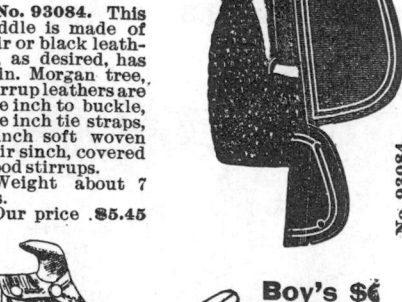

Get Your **Neighbor** TO JOIN YOU IN CLUB ORDERS.

## Boy's $8.25 Saddle.

No. 39090.

**No. 93090.** This saddle is made from genuine oiled California skirting, has 11 in. steel fork hide covered tree, 20 inch unlined skirts, solid leather roll cantle seat, 1⅜ inch stirrup leathers, 1⅛ inch tie straps, 4 inch solid woven hair sinches, boy's California pattern stirrups. Weight about 10½ lbs.
Our price..... $8.25

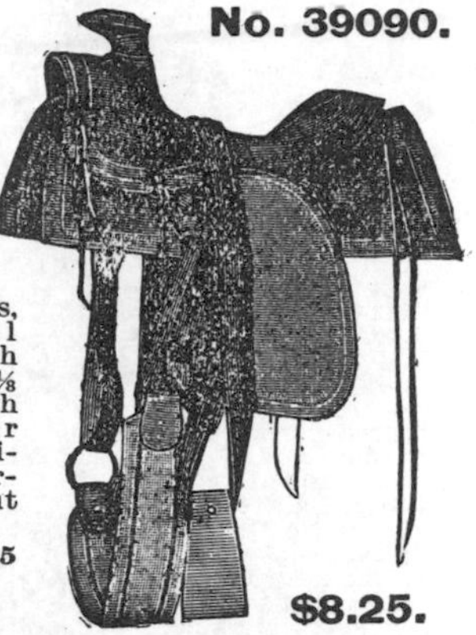

$8.25.

## Boy's or Youths' $12.75 Saddle.

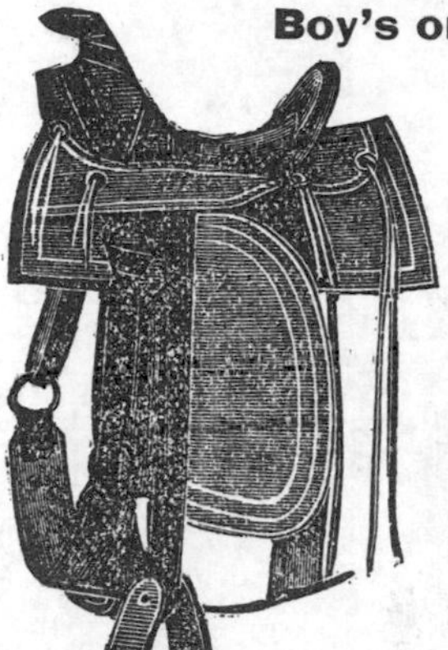

**No. 93092.** This saddle has a 13½ in. steel fork hide covered tree, 23 inch unlined skirts, seat solid leather, beaded roll cantle, gullet raised and beaded, 1¾ in. stirrup leathers, 1⅛ in. tie straps. Sinches 6 in. Mexican string hair, leathered, wool lined and connecting strap. Stirrups, 3 in. California pattern.
Weight about 18 lbs.
Our price. $12.75

# LADIES' SADDLES.

We believe we show the most complete line of ladies' saddles that are manufactured this season. There is nothing omitted in this line, and no one should have any difficulty in making a selection and getting exactly the style wanted. For quality of material, workmanship and price you will find nothing that will compare with the saddles we offer in this catalogue.

Our terms are very liberal. Any saddle will be shipped by freight or express C. O. D. subject to examination on receipt of $1.00, balance and express charges payable at express office. 3% discount allowed if cash in full accompanies order.

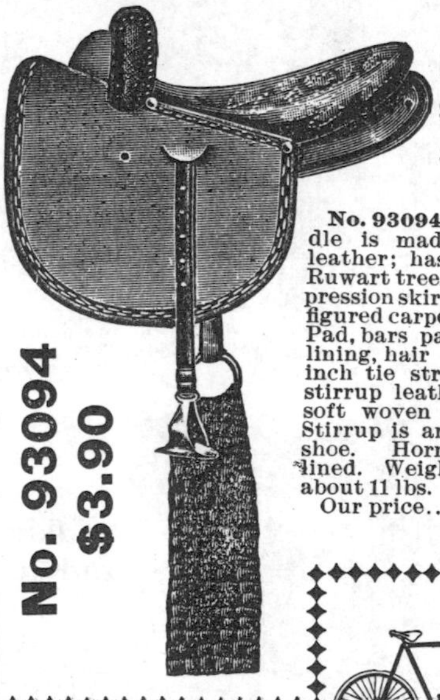

No. 93094 $3.90

## Ladies' $3.90 Saddle.

**No. 93094.** This saddle is made of russet leather; has an 18 inch Ruwart tree, pigskin impression skirts; seating of figured carpet with roll. Pad, bars padded, duck lining, hair stuffed. 1⅛ inch tie strap, ¾ inch stirrup leather, 4 inch soft woven hair sinch. Stirrup is an XC plated shoe. Horn is carpet lined. Weight of saddle about 11 lbs.
Our price......... $3.90

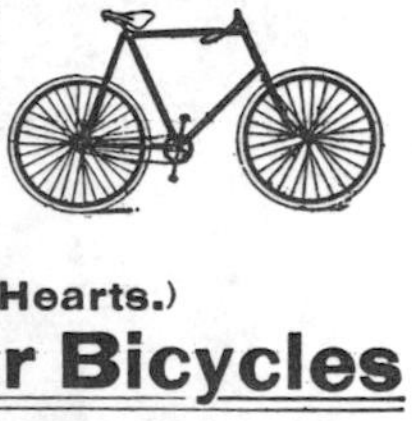

THE LADIES (Bless Their Hearts.) **Prefer Our Bicycles To All Others.**

Special Catalogue Free.

YOU OWE NO MAN A LIVING. DO NOT BE IMPOSED ON BY RETAIL DEALERS. GET THE GOOD END OF BARGAINS AND BUY WHERE YOU CAN BUY THE CHEAPEST.

## Ladies' $5.25 Saddle.

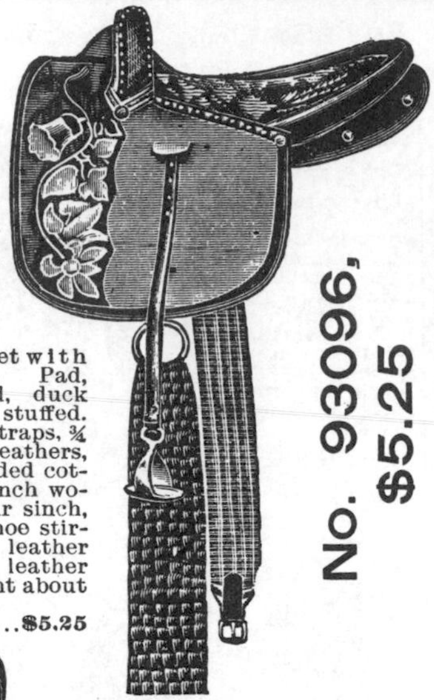

**No. 93096**
This saddle is made of russet leather, has an 18 inch Ruwart tree. skirts pig skin with fancy impression; seating of figured carpet with leather roll. Pad, bars padded, duck lining, hair stuffed. 1⅛ inch tie straps, ¾ inch stirrup leathers, 2½ inch corded cotton girth, 4 inch woven soft hair sinch, XC plated shoe stirrup, horn leather lined and leather faced Weight about 12 lbs
Our price....$5.25

**No. 93096, $5.25**

## Ladies' $6.25 Saddle.

**No. 93098.** Tree common side 18 inch. pig skin fancy impression skirts, seating of figured carpet, leather cantle. Pad, full padded, hair stuffed. ¾ inch stirrup leather. No. 5 extra cotton surcingle, No. 5 extra cotton girth. XC plated shoe. Weight of saddle about 12 lbs.
Our price..........$6.25

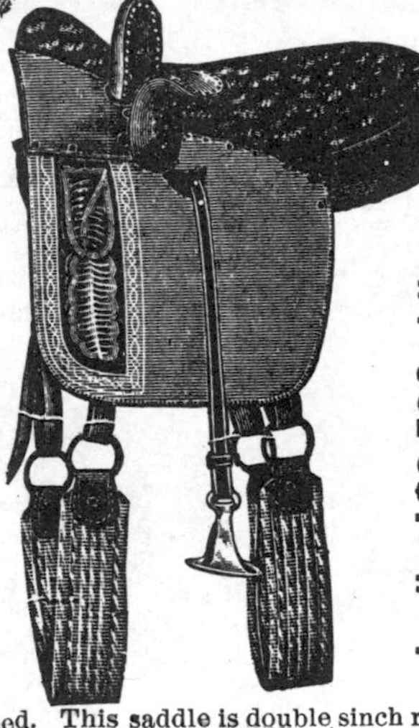

**No. 93100.**
This saddle is made on an 18 inch Ruwart tree, skirts are fancy pig skin impression with raised figure on forepiece; seating of figured plush. Pad, bars padded, sheep skin lined, 1⅛ inch tie straps, ¾ inch stirrup leather, 4 inch soft woven hair sinches or 3 inch No. 2 white back band web sinches, XC plated shoe stirrups, leaping horn, buck skin lined and seamed. This saddle is double sinch rigged, and weighs about 13 pounds.
Our price...................$6.50

**Ladies' $6.50 Saddle.**

## Ladies' $7.75 Saddle.

**No. 93102—**
This saddle is made on an 18 inch Ruwart tree has fancy pig skin, impression skirts; seating of pig skin, seat and roll ornamentally stitched, saddle horn buck skin lined, has 1⅛ inch tie straps, bars padded, sheepskin lined, hair stuffed; has ¾ inch stirrup leathers, 4 inch woven soft hair sinch; XC plated shoe; leaping horn, buck skin lined and seamed, single sinch rigged. Weighs about 13 pounds.
Our price........$7.75

**No. 93102. $7.75.**

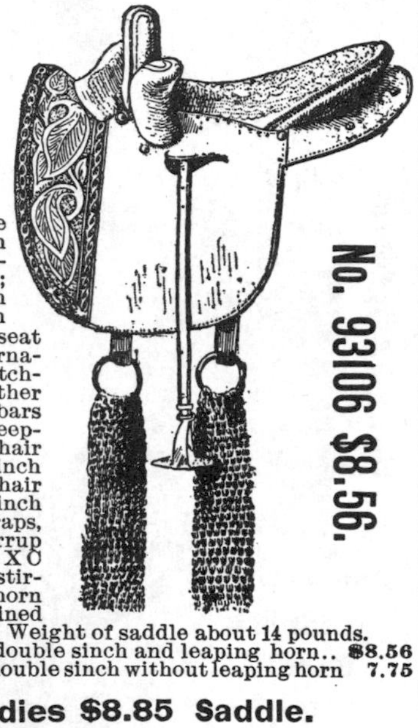

## Ladies' $7.95 Saddle.

**No. 93104.**
This saddle is made on an 18 inch Ruwart tree; fancy pig skin impression skirts. Seating of genuine pig skin ornamentally stitched. Pad, bars padded, sheepskin lined, hair stuffed;1⅛ inch tie straps, ¾ inch stirrup leather, 4 inch solid woven hair sinch, XC plated stirrup. Leaping horn buck skin lined and seamed. Saddle is single sinch rigged and weighs about 12 lbs.
Our price... $7.95

**No. 93104 $7.95.**

## Ladies' $8.56 Saddle.

**No. 93106.**
This saddle is made on an 18 inch Ruwart tree; fancy pig skin impression skirts. The seat is leather ornamentally stitched, cantle leather bound. Pad, bars padded, sheepskin lined, hair stuffed, has 4 inch solid woven hair sinches, 1⅛ inch leather tie straps, ¾ inch stirrup leather, XC plated shoe stirrup, leaping horn buck skin lined and seamed. Weight of saddle about 14 pounds.
Price with double sinch and leaping horn.. $8.56
Price with double sinch without leaping horn  7.75

**No. 93106 $8.56.**

## Ladies $8.85 Saddle.

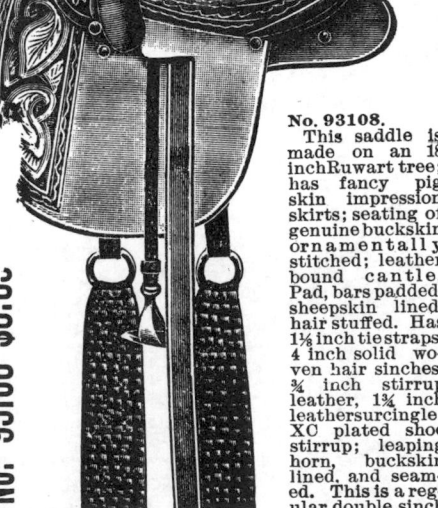

**No. 93108.**
This saddle is made on an 18 inch Ruwart tree; has fancy pig skin impression skirts; seating of genuine buckskin ornamentally stitched; leather bound cantle. Pad, bars padded, sheepskin lined, hair stuffed. Has 1⅛ inch tie straps, 4 inch solid woven hair sinches, ¾ inch stirrup leather, 1¾ inch leather surcingle; XC plated shoe stirrup; leaping horn, buckskin lined, and seamed. This is a regular double sinch rigged saddle. Weight about 15 pounds.
Our price.................................$8.85

**No. 93108 $8.85**

## Ladies' $9.80 Saddle

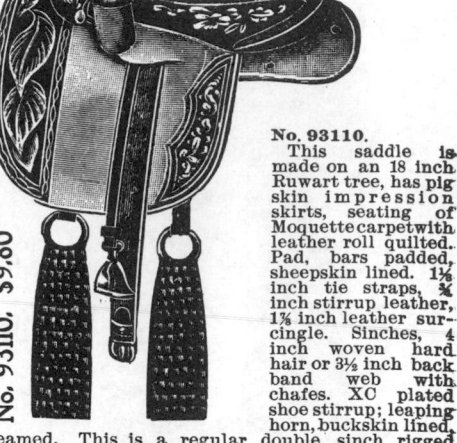

**No. 93110.**
This saddle is made on an 18 inch Ruwart tree, has pig skin impression skirts, seating of Moquette carpet with leather roll quilted. Pad, bars padded, sheepskin lined. 1⅛ inch tie straps, ¾ inch stirrup leather, 1⅛ inch leather surcingle. Sinches, 4 inch woven hard hair or 3½ inch back band web with chafes. XC plated shoe stirrup; leaping horn, buckskin lined and seamed. This is a regular double sinch rigged saddle. Weight about 15 pounds.
Our price...................................$9.80

**No. 93110, $9.80**

## Ladies' $10.00 Saddle.

**No. 93112.** This saddle is made on an 18 inch Ruwart tree. Pig skin impression skirts, seating of leather ornamentally stitched with roll. Pad, bars padded, sheepskin lining, hair stuffed, 1⅛ inch tie straps. Sinches 5 inch. solid woven hard hair or 3½ inch No. 1 red BB web with chafe, ¾ inch stirrup leather, 3 inch fancy cotton surcingle, buckskin seamed leaping horn. Weight, about 16 lbs.
Price... $10.00

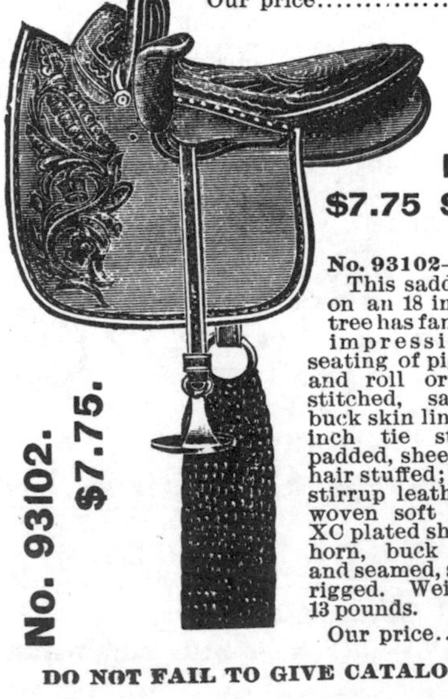

**No. 93112, $10.00**

## Ladies' $12.50 Saddle.

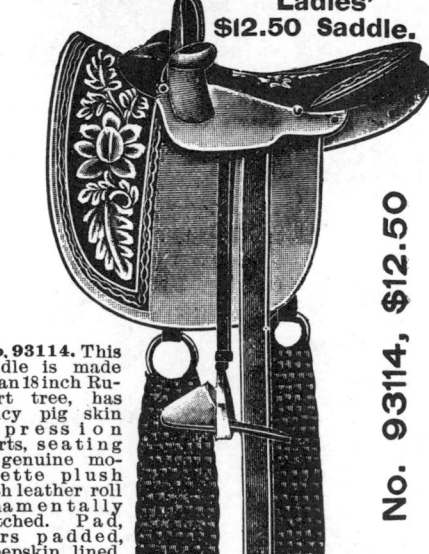

**No. 93114.** This saddle is made on an 18 inch Ruwart tree, has fancy pig skin impression skirts, seating of genuine moquette plush with leather roll ornamentally stitched. Pad, bars padded, sheepskin lined. 1⅛ inch tie straps. Sinches 6 inch, solid woven hard hair. ¾ inch stirrup leather, 2 inch leather surcingle. Buckskin slipper stirrup, buckskin seamed leaping horn. Weight about 18 lbs.
Our price.................................$12.50

**No. 93114, $12.50**

**DO NOT FAIL TO GIVE CATALOGUE NUMBER AND PRICE AS WELL AS NAME AND DESCRIPTION OF THE GOODS YOU ORDER. BE CAREFUL TO AVOID MISTAKES IN ORDERING.**

## Ladies' $8.35 Saddle.

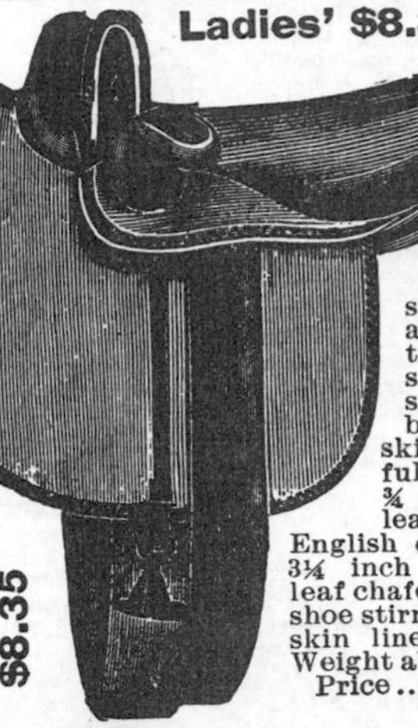

No. 93116 $8.35

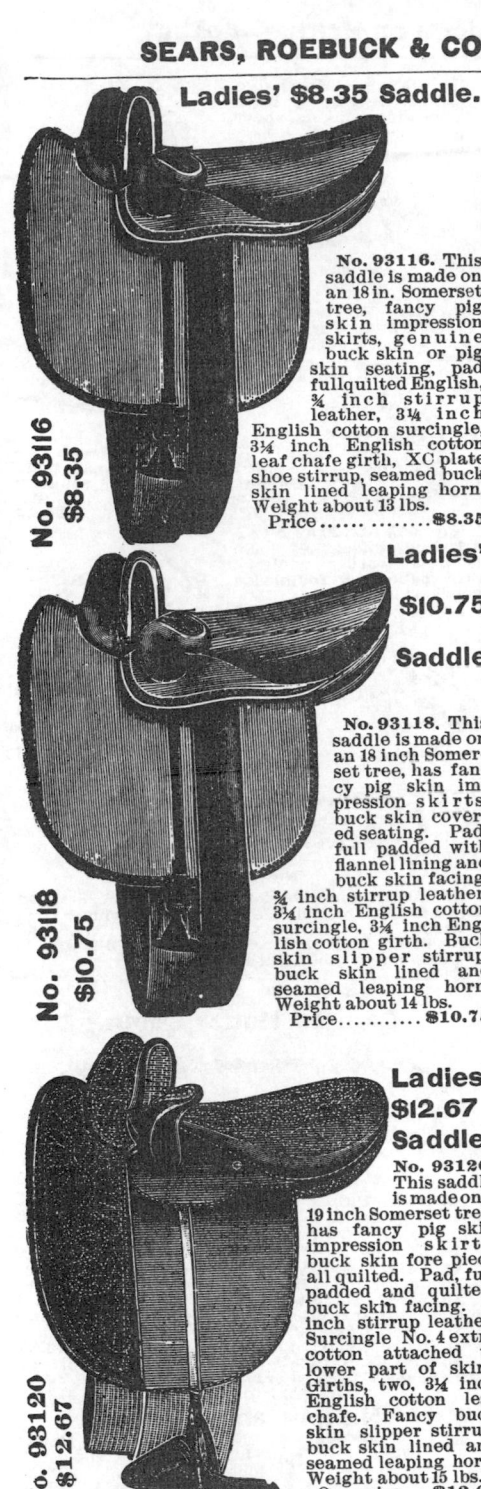

**No. 93116.** This saddle is made on an 18 in. Somerset tree, fancy pig skin impression skirts, genuine buck skin or pig skin seating, pad fullquilted English, ¾ inch stirrup leather, 3¼ inch English cotton surcingle, 3¼ inch English cotton leaf chafe girth, XC plate shoe stirrup, seamed buck skin lined leaping horn. Weight about 13 lbs.
Price ........ ........$8.35

## Ladies' $10.75 Saddle

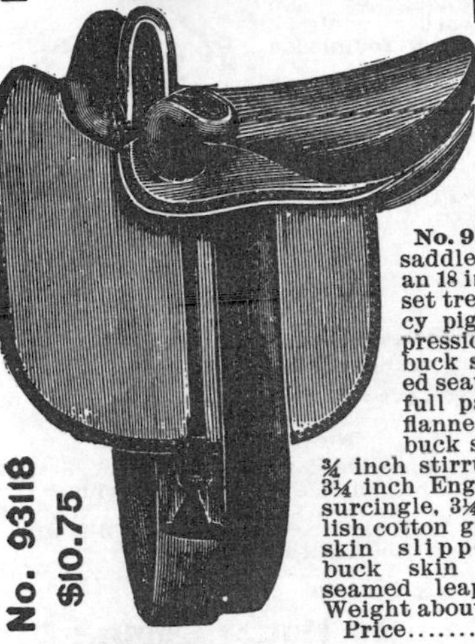

No. 93118 $10.75

**No. 93118.** This saddle is made on an 18 inch Somerset tree, has fancy pig skin impression skirts, buck skin covered seating. Pad, full padded with flannel lining and buck skin facing. ¾ inch stirrup leather, 3¼ inch English cotton surcingle, 3¼ inch English cotton girth. Buck skin slipper stirrup, buck skin lined and seamed leaping horn. Weight about 14 lbs.
Price.......... $10.75

## Ladies' $12.67 Saddle.

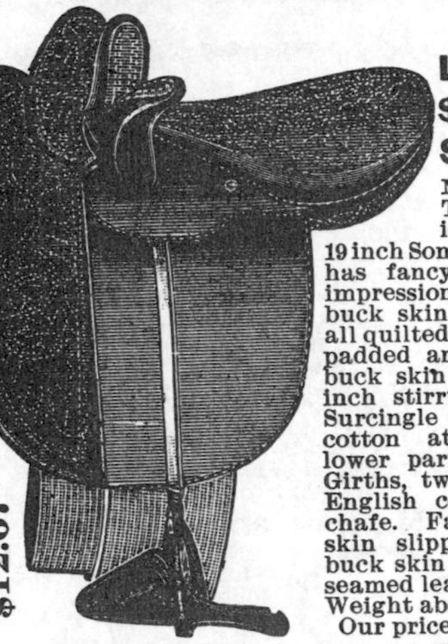

No. 93120 $12.67

**No. 93120.** This saddle is made on a 19 inch Somerset tree, has fancy pig skin impression skirts, buck skin fore piece all quilted. Pad, full padded and quilted, buck skin facing. ⅞ inch stirrup leather. Surcingle No. 4 extra cotton attached to lower part of skirt. Girths, two, 3¼ inch English cotton leaf chafe. Fancy buck skin slipper stirrup, buck skin lined and seamed leaping horn. Weight about 15 lbs.
Our price.... $12.67

## Ladies' $13.10 Saddle.

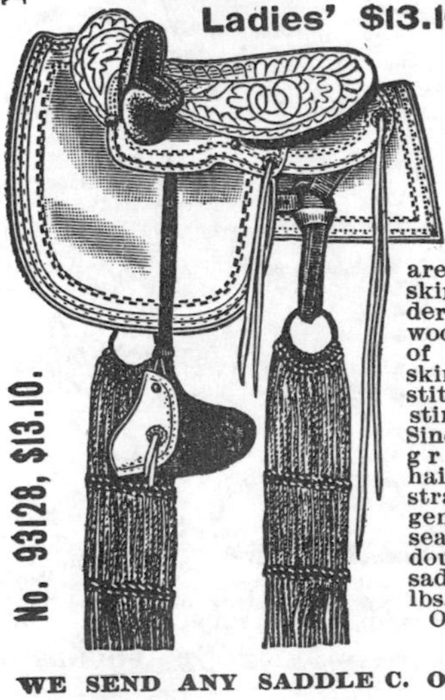

No. 93128, $13.10.

**No. 93121.** This is a regular western style side saddle, and one of the best on the market. It is made on a 18 inch Ruwart tree, skirts are of California skirting, plain, underskirts square, wool lined. Seating of genuine buckskin, ornamentally stitched, has ⅞ in. stirrup leather. Sinches, 20-strand gray California hair. 1¼ inch tie straps, leaping horn genuine buckskin seamed. A regular double sinch rigged saddle. Weight 19 lbs.
Our price, $13.10

## Ladies' $11.90 Saddle.

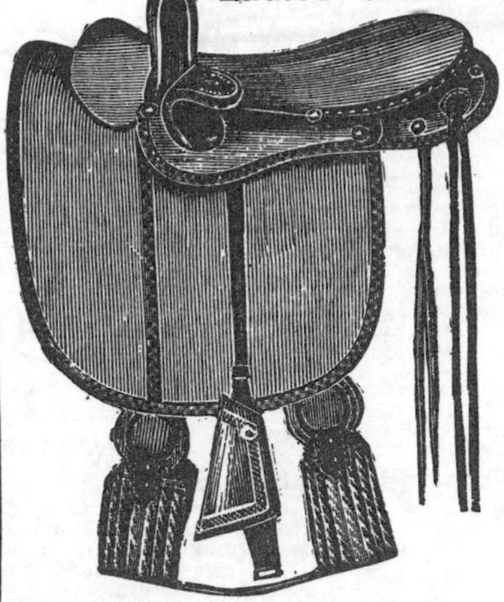

No. 93124, $11.90

**No. 93124.** This is an extra fine western style side saddle, made on an 18 inch Ruwart side tree. Skirts of California plain skirting. Seating of genuine buck skin, leather bound cantle. Pad, bars covered with wool sheepskin, stirrup leathers ⅞ inch; 1¾ inch leather surcingle. Sinches of Mexican string hair or 3½ inch No. 1 red BB web chafe and connecting strap. Stirrup, hooded, wool lined. Tie straps, 1¼ inch. Leaping horn, genuine buck skin, seamed. This saddle is regular double sinch rigged. Weight about 18 lbs.
Price ................ ....................$11.90

## Ladies' $12.45 Saddle.

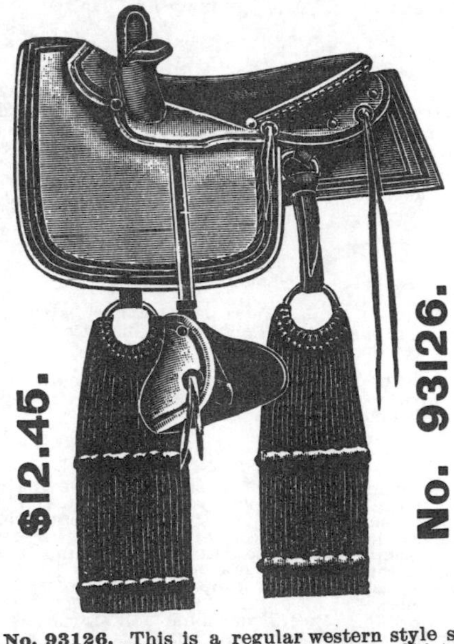

$12.45. No. 93126.

**No. 93126.** This is a regular western style side saddle, made on an 18 inch Ruwart tree. Skirts of California skirting, plain. Underskirts square, wool lined. Seating of genuine buck skin, leather bound, 1¼ inch tie straps, sinches 20-strand gray California hair, stirrup leathers ⅞ inch, stirrup hooded, wool lined. Leaping horn buckskin, seamed. Weight about 19 lbs.
Price... ........................ ......$12.45

## Ladies' $9.50 Princess Saddle.

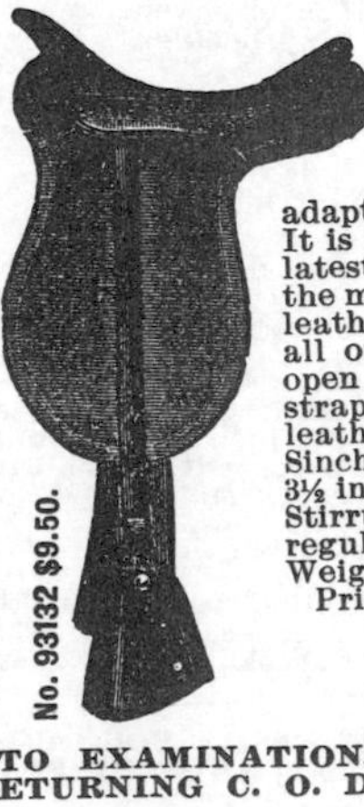

No. 93132 $9.50.

**No. 93128.** This saddle is especially adapted for ladies riding astride. It is the neatest, best made and latest style saddle of the kind on the market. It is made of russet leather, made on an Alexis tree, all over leather covered; seat is open and stitched; has 1⅛ inch tie straps, skirts of russet skirting leather; 1⅛ inch stirrup leathers. Sinch 6 inch Mexican string hair or 3¼ inch No. 1 white back band web. Stirrups tapideroes. This is a regular single sinch rigged saddle. Weight about 11 pounds.
Price ...................... $9.50.

## Ladies' $19.36 Saddle.

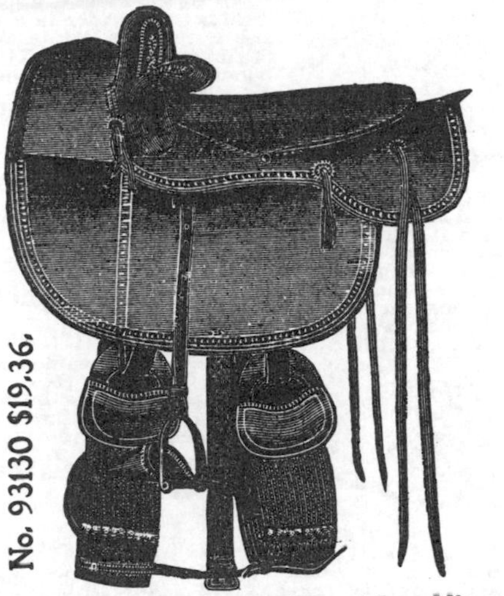

No. 93130 $19.36.

**No. 93130.** This is a western style saddle and the very finest saddle that we handle. We offer you at $19.36 a saddle which your retail dealer would not sell for less than $30.00. It is made on an 18 in. Morgan tree. Skirts of California oiled skirting leather, large pockets on off side. Seating, genuine buckskin, and knee pieces. Pad, wool sheepskin lined bars, 1¾ inch tie straps, ⅞ inch stirrup leather, 2 in. leather surcingle, Sinches, 15-strand white California hair, chafes and connecting straps. Stirrup, buckskin slipper or No. 9 hooded, as desired. Leaping horn, buckskin lined and seamed. Regular double sinch rigged saddle. Weight about 21 lbs.
Our price........................................ $19.36.

## Our $3.50 Misses' or Girls' Saddle.

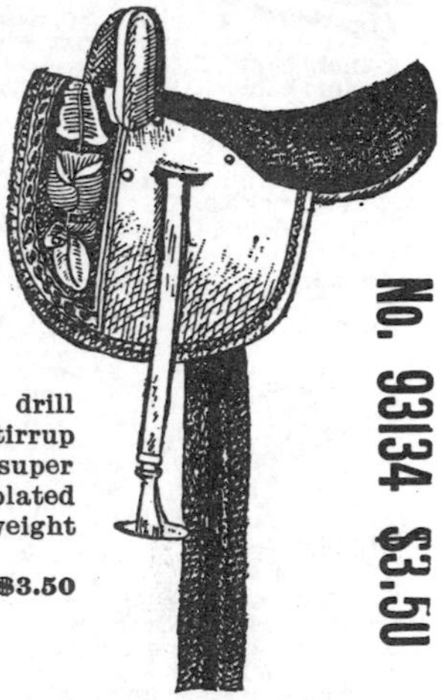

No. 93134 $3.50

**No. 93134.**
This saddle is made on a 15½ in. English tree. Skirts fancy pig skin impression, carpet seating, pad full English, drill lined, ¾ inch stirrup leather, 3 inch super cotton girth, XC plated shoe stirrup, weight about 8 pounds.
Price. ..........$3.50

## Misses' or Girls $6.90 Saddle.

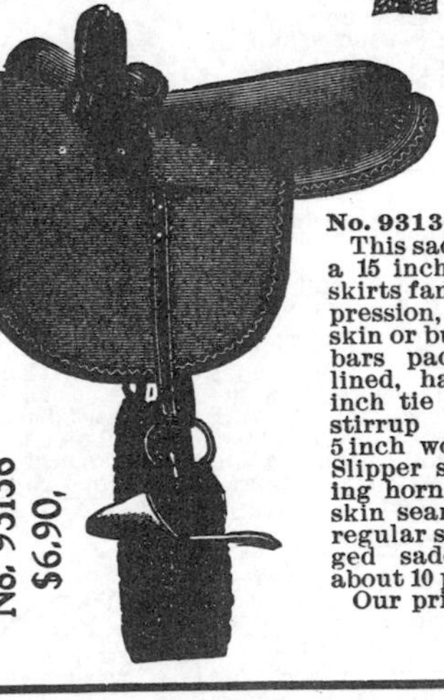

No. 93136 $6.90,

**No. 93136.**
This saddle is made on a 15 inch Ruwart tre skirts fancy pig skin in pression, seating skin or buck skin. Pa bars paded, sheepsk lined, hair stuffed, inch tie straps, ¾ in stirrup leather, sin 5 inch woven soft ha Slipper stirrup. Lea ing horn, hog or bu skin seamed. This is regular single sinch r ged saddle. Weig about 10 pounds.
Our price...... $6.



WE SEND ANY SADDLE C. O. D. SUBJECT TO EXAMINATION. MOST OF OUR CUSTOMERS SEND CASH IN FULL, SAVE COST RETURNING C. O. D. AND GET 3% DISCOUNT.

## Riding Bridles.

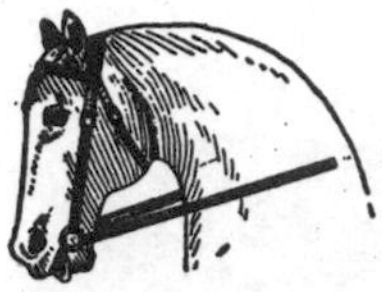

No. 93300. **Flat Bradoons. This is Our Leader in a Full Leather Riding Bridle.** Made of russet leather with XC bar buckles, XC ring bradoon, bit sewed in.
¾ inch, each..........$0.62
⅞ inch, each.......... .70

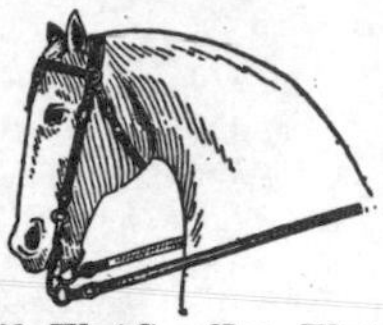

No. 93301. **Flat Snaffle. Flat Head and Reins,** solid crown piece, leather front. Made of good russet leather with XC bar buckles and XC 2 ring port bit and ⅝ inch curb strap.
¾ inch, each..........$0.70
⅞ inch, each.......... .75
1 inch, each.......... .85

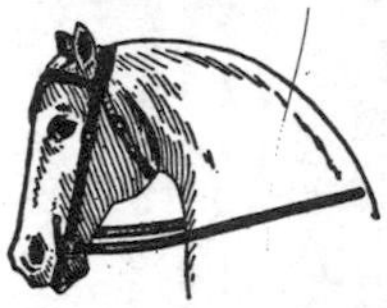

No. 93302. **Flat Snaffles. Flat Russet Leather Head and Reins with XC bar buckles,** head stall and reins sewed into a full cheek XC snaffle bit.
¾ inch, each..........$1.10
⅞ inch, each.......... 1.20

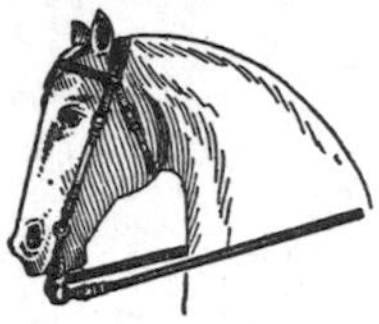

No. 93304. **Flat Snaffle. Extra Fine Russet Leather, all hand sewed flat checks and reins,** imitation leather covered or XC bar buckles, XC port bit with curb strap.
¾ inch, each..........$1.25
⅞ inch, each.......... 1.33
1 inch, each.......... 1.45

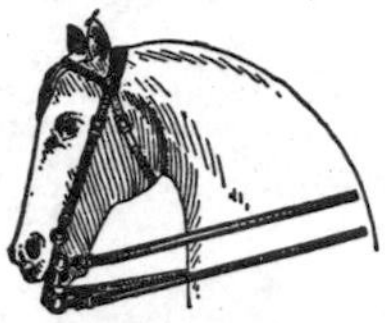

No. 93306. **Superfine Flat Pelham Bridle,** choice russet leather, all hand sewed, flat head stall with two reins, leather covered English buckles, nickel bit and curb strap.
¾ inch, each..........$1.85
⅞ inch, each.......... 2.00

No. 93307. Same bridle as above with single rein.
¾ inch, each..........$1.38
⅞ inch, each.......... 1.43

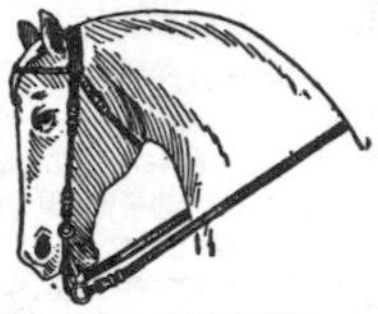

No. 93309. **Round Bridle.** Extra fine Round Russet leather bridle, round cheeks and reins, imitation leather covered buckles, XC port bit and curb straps.
Each..........$1.70

No. 93310. Same bridle as above with two reins.
Each..........$2.33

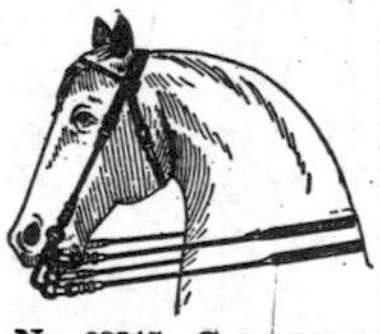

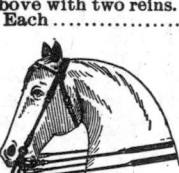

No. 93312. **Round Pelham.** Superfine Round Russet leather bridle, round cheeks, front and two round reins, narrow loops, leather covered buckles, fine nickel port bit and curb strap.
Each..........$3.45

No. 93313. Same bridle as above with single rein.
Each..........$2.40

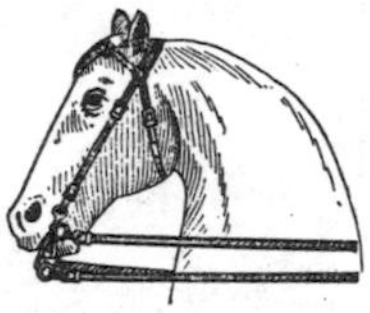

No. 93315 **Genuine Imported English "Pelham" Riding Bridle,** hand made, best English russet leather, with russet leather covered buckles, single head stall, two reins, fine four ring nickel port bit and curb strap. Each..........$3.20

No. 93316 Same Bridle as above with one rein..$2.85

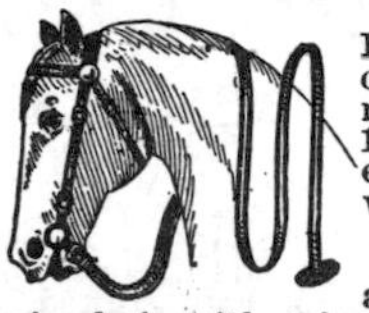

No. 93317 **Stallion Lead Bridle,** heavy black leather, flat cheeks, fancy leather front and nickel rosettes, 1 inch lead rein, 13 ft. long with stopper on end. XC buckles and heavy wrought ring bit.
Each..........$2.38

No. 93318 Same Bridle as above with fine polished English rein chain with swivel. Each..........$2.75

No. 93319 **Fawn Web Riding Bridles,** adjustable for any size horse or pony, 1¼ inch head piece. Flat snaffle, with solid crown, ¾-inch cheeks and reins, XC buckle, full cheek snaffle sewed in. Not sold without bit. Each..........$0.90

## Cow Boy Bridles.

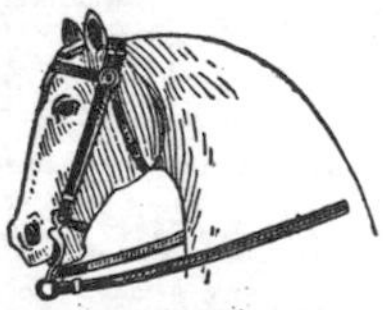

No. 93321. **Made of Oiled Russet Leather,** with double head stall to buckle on top, reins 4½ ft. long to loop in bit, XC bar buckles, port bit and curb strap ¾ inch
Each..........$0.75

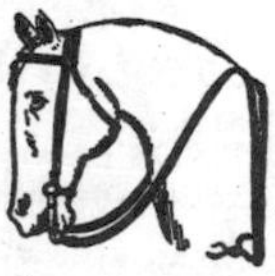

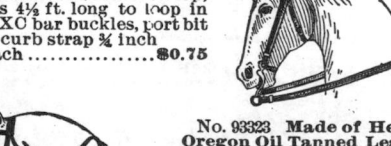

No. 93323 **Made of Heavy Oregon Oil Tanned Leather,** ¾ inch double head stall to buckle on top, ¾ inch reins 6 ft. long to loop in bit, XC buckles, port bit and curb strap. Each ....$1.20
Without bit.......... 1.10

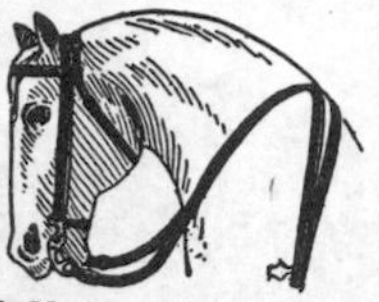

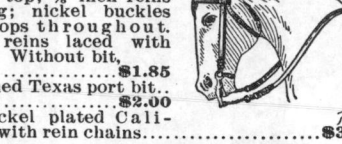

No. 93325 **Made Extra Heavy and Strong, Oregon Oiled Tanned Leather,** 1 inch double head stall to buckle on top, ⅞ inch reins, 6 ft. long, XC buckles and curb strap.
Without bit, each..........$1.40
With XC port bit.......... 1.50
With Blued Texas port bit.......... 1.65

## Cowboy Bridle.

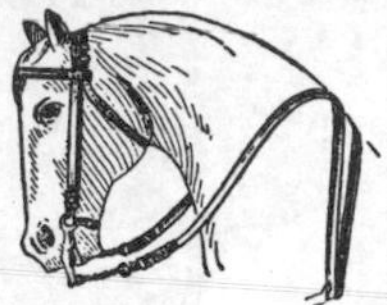

No. 93327 **Extra fine and durable.** Made of Oregon oiled tanned leather, ⅞ inch double head stall to buckle on top; ⅞ inch reins 6 feet long; nickel buckles and box loops throughout. Ends of reins laced with buckskin. Without bit,
Each..........$1.85
With blued Texas port bit..........$2.00
With nickel plated California bit with rein chains..........$3.60

## Fringed Cowboy Bridle.

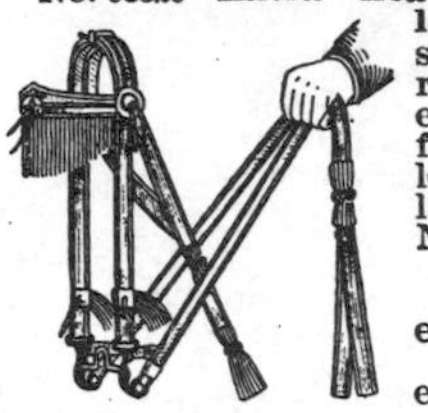

No. 93329 **Extra heavy Oregon oiled tanned leather.** 1 inch double head stalls to buckle on top; 1 inch reins 6 feet long, laced at ends with buckskin. Heavy fringed front, fringed slide loops on cheeks and throatlatch. ⅝ inch curb strap. Nickle buckles.
Without bit, each.....$2.15
With blued Texas port bit, each..........$2.25
With nickle Texas port bit, each..........$2.85

## Rawhide Cowboy Bridle.

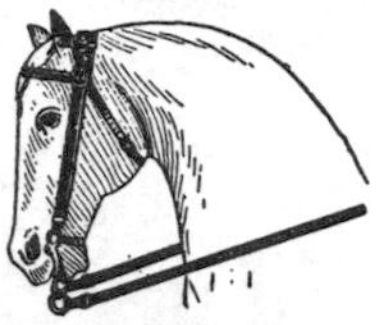

No. 93330 **Rawhide Cowboy Bridle.** Made of the best oiled tanned rawhide. ⅞ inch cheeks and reins, 5 feet long, with XC port bit and curb strap.
Each..........$1.35

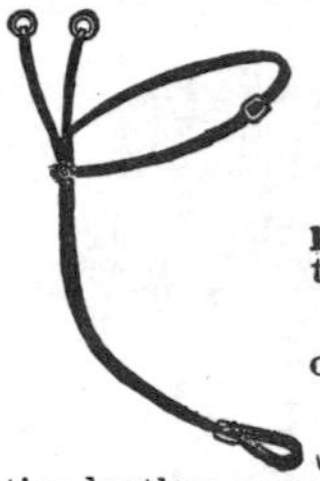

## Riding Martingales.

No. 93331 **Made of russet leather,** with neck strap. XC center bar buckles and rings.
Each..........$0.35

No. 93332 Same as above, made of oiled leather.
Each.......... 0.40

No. 93333 **Heavy russet leather,** with flat neck strap. XC or imitation leather covered buckles and rings.
Each.......... 0.55

No. 93334 **Extra fine russet leather,** with neck strap, round forks, balance flat. Imitation leather covered buckles and rings.
Each.......... 1.00

No. 93335 **Round russet leather forks and neck straps,** with flat body piece. Leather covered English buckles and rings.
Each.......... 1.50

## Buggy Bridles.

The manufacturers of these Bridles have a national reputation for the quality of their work. Only the finest stock is used and we guarantee these Bridles the best in the world, and any that is not up to our representation may be returned to us, and money will be refunded. **3% discount when cash in full accompanies order.**

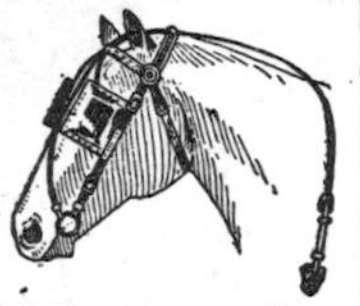

No. 93337. **Buggy,** machine stitched, cheeks ⅝ inch, no box loops, patent leather winkers, flat winker brace, flat side or over check, C plate buckles, ring bit.
Each..........$1.10

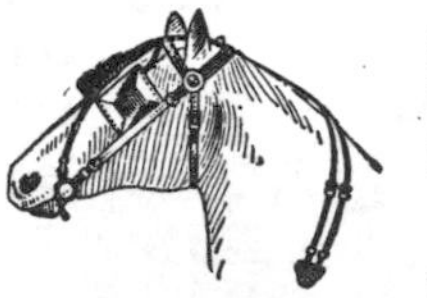

No. 93339. **Buggy,** machine stitched, cheeks ⅝ inch, box loops, patent leather winkers, round winker braces, round side or over check, half cheek snaffle.
C plate buckles,
Each..........$1.85

No. 93340 Nickle or imitation rubber buckles,..$1.95

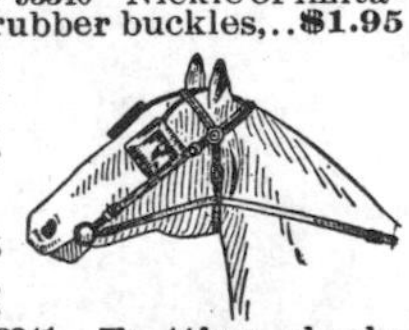

No. 93340½ **Buggy,** machine stitched, cheeks ⅝ inch, box loops, patent leather winkers, flat winker brace, flat side or over check, ring bit.
C plate buckles,
Each..........$1.25
Nickel buckles, per dozen, ..........$1.35

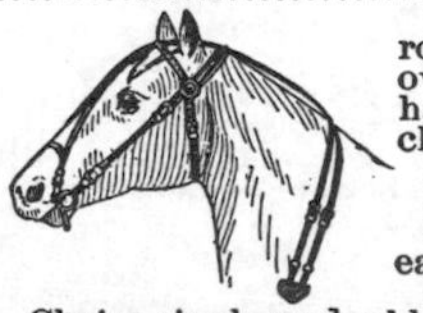

No. 93341. **Trotting,** cheeks round, ⅝ inch billets, double over check with nose band, half cheek snaffle and over check bit.
Nickel buckles,
Each..........$1.75
Imitation rubber buckles, each..........$1.75
Flat cheeks.......... 1.25
Choice single or double cheeks.

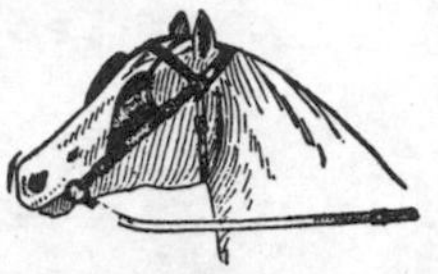

No. 93342. **Machine stitched,** cheeks ¾ inch, pigeon wing winkers, short flat checks, ring bit.
Each..........$0.75

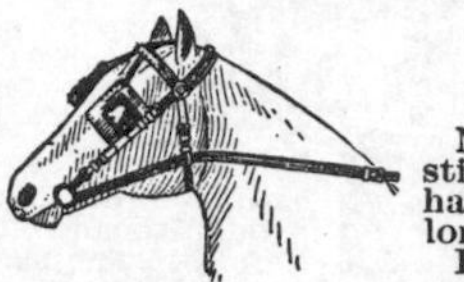

No. 93343. **Team,** machine stitched, cheeks ¾ inch, harness leather winkers, long flat checks, ring bit.
Each..........$1.72

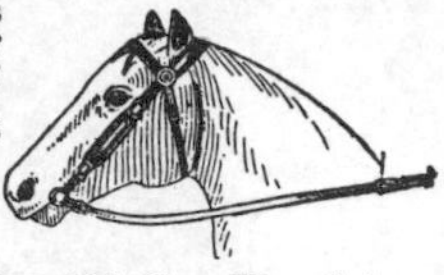

No. 93345. **Riveted,** cheeks ⅞ inch, scalloped safe under cheeks, short cheeks, ring bits.
Each..........$0.88

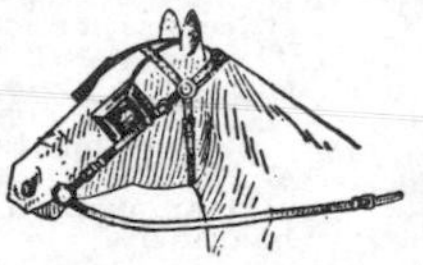

No. 93347. **Machine Stitched,** cheeks ¾ inch, harness leather winkers, short flat checks, ring bits.
Each..........$1.40

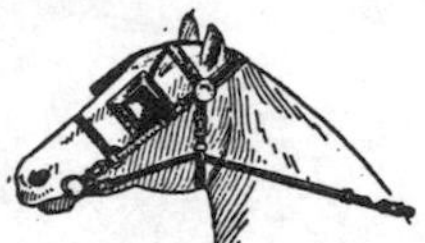

No. 93349. **Machine Stitched,** cheeks ¾ inch, harness leather winkers, nose band long round side check, ring bit.
Each..........$1.50

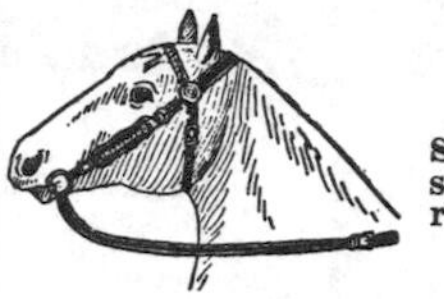

No. 93350, **Machine Stitched,** cheeks ¾ inch, scalloped safe under cheeks, ring bits.
Each..........$1.35

## Stallion Lead Chains.

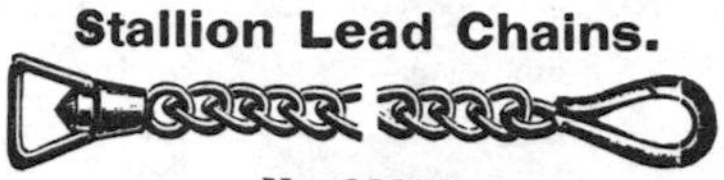

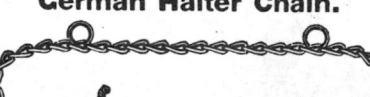

No. 93352.

No. 93352. **American Company Steel Stallion Lead Chain,** steel snap, swivel and "D" ring.
Each..........$0.40

No. 93353. **English Steel Lead Chains,** 3-16 wire, 18 inches long, polished, with snap and swivel.
Each..........$0.50

**Postage, 12 cents.**

## German Halter Chain.

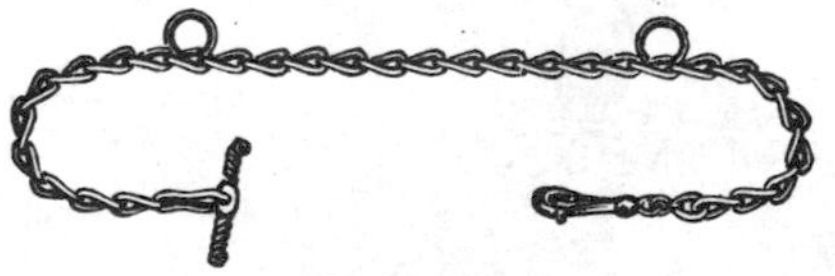

No. 93354.

No. 93354. **Halter Chain,** 4½ feet long, nicely polished. Each..........$0.20

## Safety Bridle Rein Chain.

No. 93356. **Safety Bridle Rein Chain,** nickel plated, with snaps, 11 inch. Per pair..........$0.90
No. 93357. **Regular Bridle Rein Chain,** nickel plated, with snaps, 10 inch. Per pair..........$0.50
No. 93358. **Regular Bridle Rein Chain,** polished, with snaps, 10 inch. Per pair..........$0.35
No. 93359. **Corent's Bridle Rein Chain,** XC plated, with snaps, 11 inch. Per pair..........$0.25
(Weight 6 to 10 ounces.)

## Halters and Ties.

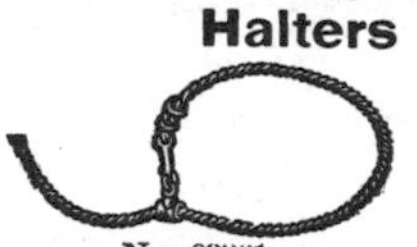

No. 93361.

No. 93361. **Covert's Cattle Tie,** ½ inch jute rope, full length. Each..........$0.12
Per dozen.......... 1.30

No. 93362.

No. 93362 **Covert's Horse Tie,** ½ inch jute rope.
Each..........$0.15
Per dozen.......... 1.62

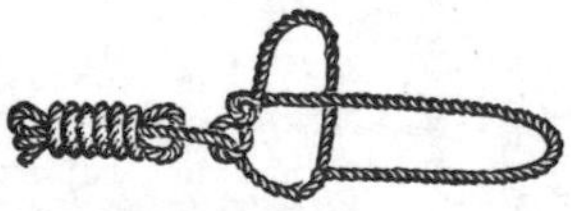

No. 93364 **Round Rope Halter,** ⅝ inch sisal.
Each..........$0.15
Per doz... 1.50
¾ in., each 0.19
Per doz... 1.85

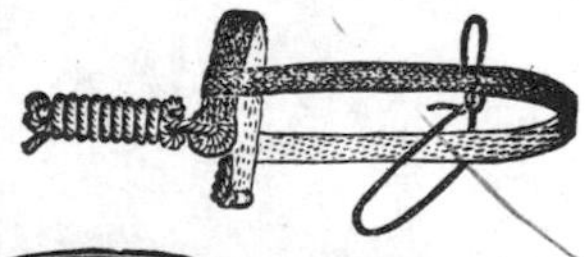

No. 93365 **Braided Rope Halter,** fancy woven.
Each......$0.15
Per doz... 1.70
Better quality.. 0.18
Per doz... 2.00

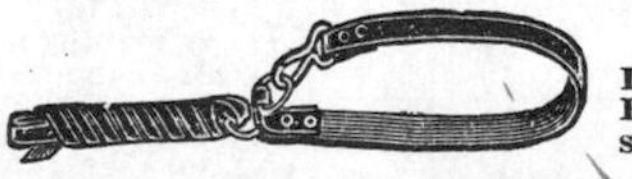

No. 93367 **Solid Leather Neck Halter,** 1 in. neck strap, 1 in. stale.
Each..........$0.58
1¼ inch neck strap, 1 inch stale, each.......... 0.62
1½ inch neck strap, 1¼ inch stale, each.......... 0.75

No. 93368.      No. 93371.

No. 93368  English Tube Web Halter, leather filling, long throat latch, front and nose piece, leather stale. Each ............................................. $1.00
No. 93370  Thirteen-cord Web Halter, rope stale. Each ................................................. $0.16
No. 93371  Solid Leather Halters, five ring riveted, with leather stale. Each ...................... $0.90
No. 93372  Five Ring Hand Sewed Halter, with leather stale. Each .............................. $1.10
No. 93373  A  Hand Sewed, Five Ring, Black Leather Halters, extra heavy, 1¼ inch head, without tie straps. Each ............................... $1.15
No. 93374  B  Hand Sewed, Five Ring, Black Leather Halters, heavy, 1¼ inch head, with heavy tie strap. Each .................................... $1.25
No. 93376  C  Hand Sewed, Five Ring, Black Leather Halters, standard weight, 1 inch head, with tie strap. Each ............................ $1.10
No. 93378  D  Black Leather Halters, Copper Riveted, Five Ring, 1¼ inch head, with heavy tie strap. Each ...................................... $1.05
No. 93379  E  Black Leather Halters, Copper Riveted, Five Ring, 1 inch head, with tie strap. Each ............................................... $0.90
No. 93380  F  Hand Sewed, Five Ring, Black Leather Halters, heavy, 1¼ inch head, without tie straps. Each .................................... $0.95
No. 93381  G  Hand Sewed, Five Ring, Black Leather Halters, 1 inch head piece, without tie straps. Each ...................................... $0.82
No. 93383  H  Black Leather Halters, Five Ring, Copper Riveted, 1 inch without tie strap. Each ...................................... $0.60
No. 93384  I  Black Leather Halters, Five Ring, Copper Riveted, 1¼ inch head, without tie strap. Each ...................................... $0.68
No. 93386  K  Rawhide Halters, Chicago Rawhide, all hand Riveted, 1 inch head, double crown, snap on jaw, with rawhide tie strap. Each ... $0.85
No. 93388  L  Rawhide Halters, Chicago Rawhide, all hand Riveted, 1¼ inch head, double crown, snap on jaw, with rawhide tie strap. Each ........ $1.10
Weight, each, 1½ to 2¾ pounds.
No. 93390  O  Colt Halters, Black Leather, 1 inch, five ring, riveted, without stales.
Each $0.56, per dozen ............................... $6.10
Our stock of halters as to quality and variety is unlimited. Want of space prevents our quoting the entire line, of which there are a hundred styles. If you can't select a halter to suit you write us and we will guarantee to please you.

## Saddle Blankets.
### Ladies' Saddle Blankets.

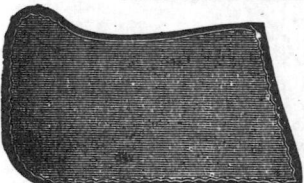

No. 93398.  Ladies' side saddle blankets, heavy brown, blue or gray felt, long on one side, has wide fancy weaved binding, with braid inlay, weight, 16 ounces. Each ........ $1.00

## Men's Saddle Blankets.

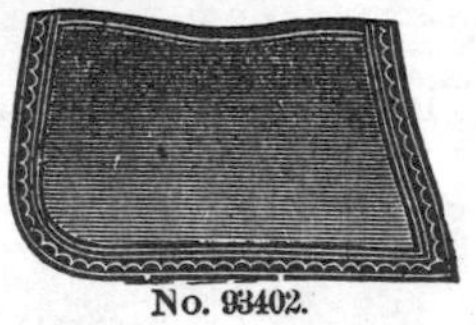

No. 93400.  Made of dark felt, light in weight but good value; weight 15 oz. Each ............................ $0.38
No. 93401.  Felt cloth saddle blanket, medium grade; has fancy colored braid border. Each .......... $0.50
No. 93402.  Good weight felt in dark colors, fancy border and band all around, extra quality. See cut. Each .................................. $0.90

No. 93402.

## Graduated Saddle Blankets.
Thickest in parts where the hardest wear comes.

No. 93404.  Blue heavy graduated felt, scalloped and pinked edge. Each ......................... $1.05
No. 93405.  Yellow heavy graduated scalloped edge. Each ............... $1.10
No. 93406.  Red heavy graduated, scalloped, pinked edge. Each, $1.15
No. 93407.  Spencer's graduated felt, plain gray, plain edge. Each ............................ $1.25
No. 93408.  Spencer's graduated felt, plain gray, medium weight. Each ....................... $1.60
No. 93409.  Spencer's graduated felt, plain gray, extra heavy; weight from 1½ to 2½ pounds. Each ...................................... $2.00

## Woven Hair Saddle Blanket.

No. 93412.  Woven hair, 25x36 inches, web bound; weight 3 pounds. Each ........................ $1.00

## Stirrups.
### Ladies'.

No. 93419.  Ladies' Metal Shoe Stirrups, for side saddle XC plated. Each .... $0.15
No. 93420.  Ladies' Metal Stirrups, (men's pattern) XC plate. Each .... $0.07
No. 93422.  Same XC men's size. Each .... $.023

No. 93419.                No. 93420.

No. 93423.  Ladies' Slipper Stirrup for side saddle, sole or shank, is of steel, covered with leather stitched on, heavy hogskin vamp, strong iron swing, comfort and security combined. Each .......... $0.85

No. 93423.

## Men's Wood Stirrups.

No. 93424.  Boy's size. common wood, 2 rivets, per pair ....... $0.08
No. 93425.  Men's size, 2½ inch, common wood, 2 rivets. Per pair ................. $0.19
No. 93427.  Men's size, common 3 inch, wood, 2 rivets. Per pair ................. $0.10
No. 9343C  Men's Texas wood, solid bent stirrups, strongly bolted, suitable from 1½ to 2½ inches wide. Weight per pair 1¾ lbs. Price, per pair,
4 inches, 15c;
5 inches, 17c;
6 inches, 20c.

## Brass Clad Stirrups.
### Knight's Patent.

No. 93432  2 inch, brass bound, per pair ........................... $0.95
No. 93433  2½ inch, brass bound, per pair ..... $1.00
Weight, per pair, 2 to 2¼ lbs.

## Steel Stirrups.

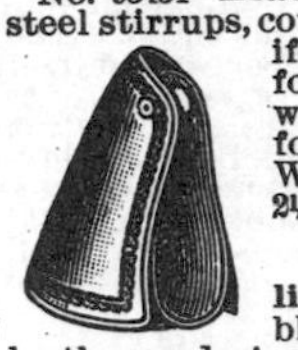

No. 93434  Leather covered. 2 inch steel stirrups, covered with oiled California leather, California pattern. Bars will admit 3 inch California stirrup straps. Weight per pair 2 to 2½ lbs. Per pair ...... $1.45
No. 93435  Covered light wood stirrup, black, russet or red leather as desired, will take stirrup straps from ⅞ to 1¼ inches wide. Price, per pair ................. $0.60

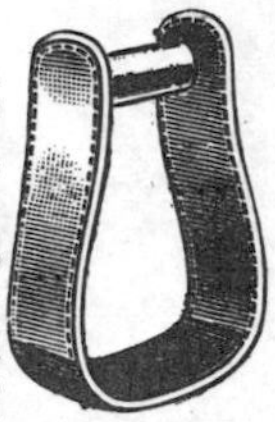

## Stirrup Straps.

No. 93436.  4 feet 6 inches long, with buckle, either black or russet leather.
Price per pair, 1 inch ........................... $0.60
1¼ inch .......................................... .75
No. 93437.  California style stirrup straps, cut from the best Oregon oiled skirting leather, 5 feet 6 inches long, with lace strings.

| | 2 in. | 2¼ in. | 2½ in. | 2¾ in | 3 in. |
|---|---|---|---|---|---|
| Per pair... | $1.38 | $1.50 | $1.85 | $2.20 | $2.50 |

## Latigoes.

No. 93438.  Latigo straps, 2 inches wide, for buckle cinch rig, cut from the best Oregon oiled skirting leather, with lace string to fasten.  Length for draw side, 5 feet 6 inches.  Per pair ...... $1.35
Length for off side, 2 feet 8 inches.  Per pair.. 0.75
No. 93439.  Latigoes for tie cinch rig, with lace strings to fasten to saddle rings, 1¼ inches, 5 feet long.  Per pair .................................. $0.85
1½ inches, 5 feet long.  Per pair ............... .95

## Cantanas.

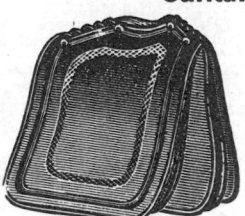 

No. 93440.                No. 93441.

No. 93440  Cantanas, can be hung on horn of saddle, solid leather, outside size 10x13 inches.  Each, $4.00
We also have fancy stamped cantanas, $6.75 to $9.00 each.
No. 93441  Llama Skin Cover, Cantana, very fancy, stamped.  Covered with long black Angora fur. Each ............................................. $4.60

FULL LINE OF
....COWBOY RIDING OVERALLS....
ON PAGE 168.

## Saddle Bags.

No. 93442  Heavy Solid Leather Saddle Bag, to be fastened to skirts of saddle behind cantle. Price per pair ......... $2.90
No. 93443  Fancy Raised Stamped Saddle Bag, with fancy trail border Price per pair... $6.78
No. 93442.

No. 93444  Fancy Llama Skin Cover Saddle Bag. Price per pair ........... $5.58
No. 93445  Fancy Saddle Bag, very fancy, patent leather cover, with handles. Each ............................... $7.20

No. 93445

N. B.—We will attach Saddle Bags or Cantanas or both to any saddle for prices quoted, no charge for extra labor.

## Tapideroes.

No. 93446  Oiled leather, wood stirrups.  Price, per pair... $2.10
No. 93439  (Like cut).  Oiled leather, wood lined, solid block stirrups Price, per pair ........ $3.50

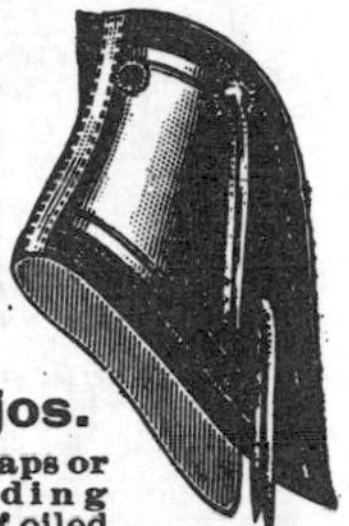

## Chaparejos.

No. 93447  Chaps or Cowboy's riding pants, made of oiled chaparejos leather, stock being specially prepared for this purpose, solid leather waistband, laced together, fringe on outside of each leg, two pockets. Made for service. Sizes 28 to 34 inches; waist measurement not necessary. Weight 5½ to 6½ lbs. according to length.  Price, per pair .................................. $8.50
No fringe ................................... 6.00

## Horse Hobbles.

No. 93448  Front hobbles, two leather anklets connected by a short swivel chain, to be attached to the fore legs of a horse to prevent running or straying away when loose. Weight, 1½ lbs.  Per pair ........ $0.60
No. 93449  Side hobbles, with chain and strap to be attached from one fore-leg to one hind leg.  Weight 2¼ lbs.  Per pair ..... $0.70

## Lariats.

No. 93450  Rawhide lariats, 4 plaits, best quality of oil tanned, rawhide center, all hand plaited and whole strands from end to end without splicing; rawhide hondas; length 40 ft., weight, 2¼ lbs. each, $7.20.  Length, 43 ft., weight 2½ lbs., each, $7.74.  Length, 45 ft., weight, 3 lbs., each, $8.10.  Any length lariats made to order.
No. 93451  Cotton lariats, extra quality braided cotton rope. ½ inch diameter, honda of same, securely fastened; length 35 ft., each .......................... $1.50
Length 50 ft., each .................................. 2.00
No. 93452  Linen Lariats, extra quality braided linen rope, ⅜ inch in diameter, with rawhide honda; have been boiled in oil, which keeps them soft and pliable, and renders them water proof; will not kink or snarl, and will hold anything that runs on hoof. Ends are patent grip fastened.
Length forty feet, each ....................... $2.20
Length fifty feet, each .......................... 2.60
No. 93452½  Hondas for Lariats, firmly pressed rawhide.  Each ................................... $0.20

WHEN YOU COME TO CHICAGO YOU MUST NOT FAIL TO DROP IN AND SEE OUR BIG ESTABLISHMENT.  USHERS WILL TAKE PAINS TO SEE TO YOUR WANTS.

## Bridle Bits.

We always carry a large stock of bits on hand as we do the largest business in this line to the consumer of any house in America.

No. 93453 **Fine Blued Mexican Curb Bits**, with short port on mouth bar. Weight 11 ounces. Price ........ **$0.15**

No. 93454 **Fine Nickel Plated Maud S. Port Bit.** Plain finish, patent roller in post. Price each.............**$0.75**

No 93455 **Two ring Port Bit**, with short post on mouth bar. Price, each XC plate 15c; nickel... **$0.35**

No. 93456 **English Riding Bits.** Two rings, port mouth, fine nickel plated. Each ........ **$0.75**

**Three Per Cent. Discount for Cash.**

## Racking Bits.

No. 93457 **XC Plated Kentucky Short Racing Bits**, with short port on mouth bar. Each........ **$0.10**

No. 93458 **Two Ring XC Plated Riding Bits** with straight round cheeks and short port. Each **$0.11**

No. 93459 **Two Ring Port Racking Bit**, made from best Daniels steel. Nickel plated; sabre bent. Each... **$0.75**

No. 93460 **Four Ring Port Bit.** Made from finest Daniels steel, nickel plated, sabre bent or straight, as desired. Price, each. **$1.00**

No. 93461. **The Patent Double Hand Forged Bit**, with roller, fine nickel steel curb bits and chased with swivels and rings for reins. Weight 17 ounces. Price.............**$4.50**

No. 93462 **Mexican Curb Bit.** Patent filled and chased, with trinkets, rein chain and roller; weight 18 ounces. Each.. **$1.70**

## The Cowboys' Favorites.

chains; weight 18 ounces. Each ...........

No. 93464 **Fine nickel plated, leg pattern bit, patent port mouth**, with roller in port—9 inch rein chains. Beautifully engraved and finished. Weight, 22 ounces. Each.....................**$2.50**

No. 93463 **California Cowboy Bit.** Fancy filled and chased, spade mouth, with roller and rein. Each ............ **$1.00**

No. 93465 **Fine nickel plated leg pattern bit, patent port mouth**, with roller in port—9 inch rein chains. Each.........**$1.75**

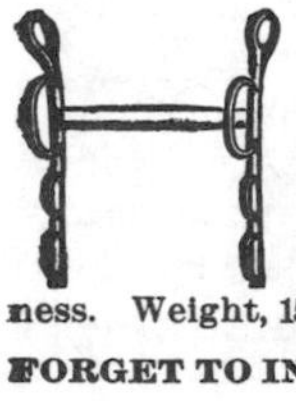

No. 93466 **Hanoverian Coach Bit**, fine nickel plated curb, with wrought mouth and steel cheeks. This bit used largely in fine carriage, coach and double buggy harness. Weight, 15 ounces. Each..................**$0.75**

---

## CALIFORNIA BIT.

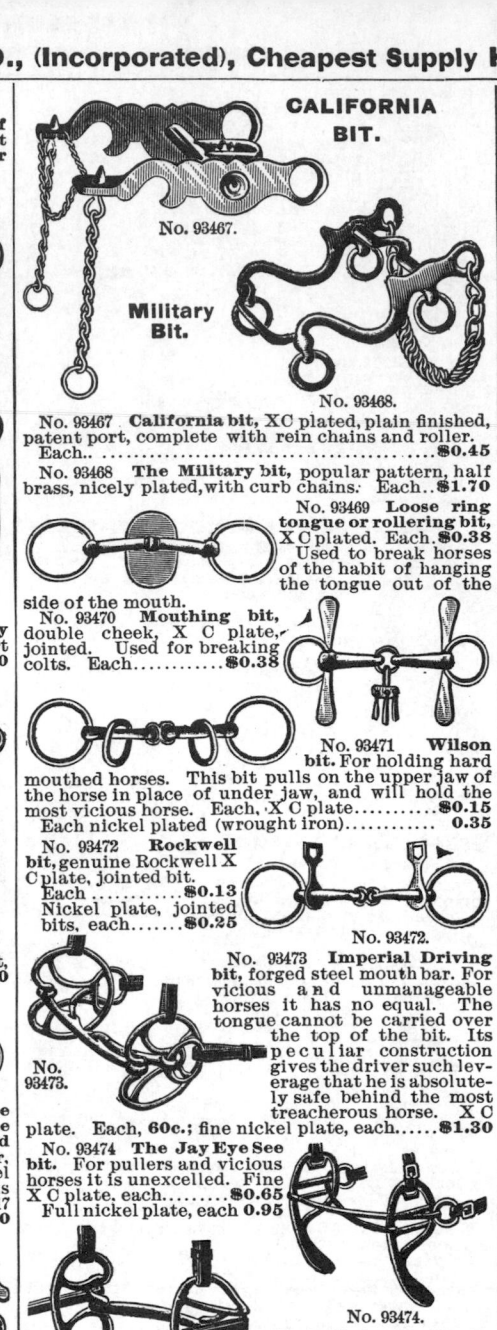

**Military Bit.**

No. 93467. **California bit**, XC plated, plain finished, patent port, complete with rein chains and roller. Each..................................**$0.45**

No. 93468. **The Military bit**, popular pattern, half brass, nicely plated, with curb chains. Each.. **$1.70**

No. 93469 **Loose ring tongue or rollering bit**, XC plated. Each.**$0.38** Used to break horses of the habit of hanging the tongue out of the side of the mouth.

No. 93470 **Mouthing bit**, double cheek, XC plate, jointed. Used for breaking colts. Each.............**$0.38**

No. 93471 **Wilson bit.** For holding hard mouthed horses. This bit pulls on the upper jaw of the horse in place of under jaw, and will hold the most vicious horse. Each, XC plate..**$0.15**
Each nickel plated (wrought iron)........... 0.35

No. 93472 **Rockwell bit**, genuine Rockwell X C plate, jointed bit. Each .............**$0.13** Nickel plate, jointed bits, each.......**$0.25**

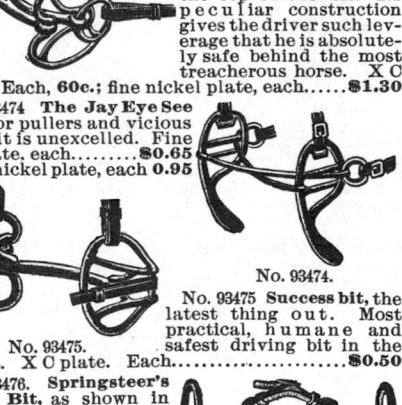

No. 93473 **Imperial Driving bit**, forged steel mouth bar. For vicious and unmanageable horses it has no equal. The tongue cannot be carried over the top of the bit. Its peculiar construction gives the driver such leverage that he is absolutely safe behind the most treacherous horse. XC plate. Each, 60c.; fine nickel plate, each......**$1.30**

No. 93474 **The Jay Eye See bit.** For pullers and vicious horses it is unexcelled. Fine XC plate, each........**$0.65**
Full nickel plate, each 0.95

No. 93475 **Success bit**, the latest thing out. Most practical, humane and safest driving bit in the Market. XC plate. Each.........................**$0.50**

No. 93476. **Springsteer's Patent Bit**, as shown in cut; extra fine finish, nickel plated, **$1.50**. There is comfort and control in this bit and it is guaranteed to cure the worst side puller.
Price each, XC......90c

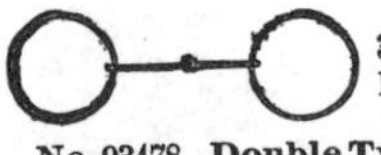

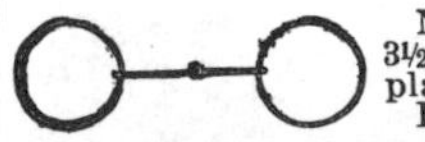

No. 93477. **Jointed Race Bit**, 3½ inch rings, all steel, nickel plated. Each ........**$1.00**

No. 93478. **Double Twisted Wire Bit**, jointed mouth (see cut), XC plate. Each.................**$0.11**

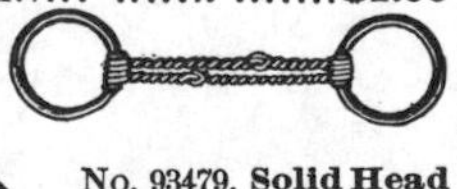

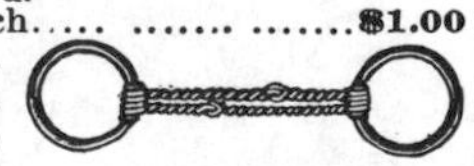

No. 93479. **Solid Head Stiff Ring Bit**, 3 inch ring. XC plate. Each.........**$0.15**

No. 93480. **Stiff or Jointed Bridle Bit**, 2 or 2¾ inch ring, XC plate. Each.................**$0.08**

No. 93481. **Overcheck Bit**, to be used as a separate bit on draw check reins, XC plate. Each, 5c; nickel plated

No. 93482. **Squire's Flexible Rubber Mouth**, nickel, half cheek snaffles. Each.....................**$0.45**

---

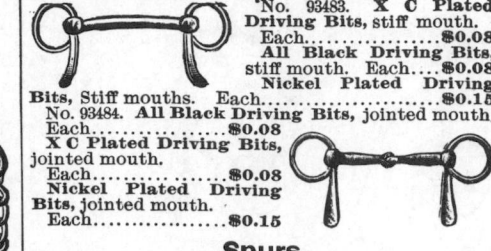

No. 93483. **X C Plated Driving Bits**, stiff mouth. Each.................**$0.08**
**All Black Driving Bits**, stiff mouth. Each.... **$0.08**
**Nickel Plated Driving Bits, Stiff mouths.** Each............**$0.15**

No. 93484. **All Black Driving Bits**, jointed mouth. Each.................**$0.08**
**X C Plated Driving Bits**, jointed mouth. Each.................**$0.08**
**Nickel Plated Driving Bits**, jointed mouth. Each.................**$0.15**

## Spurs.

Spurs are quoted by the pair, make no mistake, single spurs will cost just one-half the price given per pair.

Our stock of spurs is the most complete and we are prepared to serve you better and cheaper than any other concern.

No. 93497 **English Pattern XC Plate Spurs.**
Light per pair..............**$0.15**
Medium weight per pair.. .20
Extra heavy per pair......................25

No. 93497

No. 83498. **English Pattern Spur**, solid brass, extra heavy heavy oval heel band, 1⅜ inch rowel shank, ⅝ in. steel plate rowel, regular military style, without straps. Per pair.............**$0.30**

No. 93498

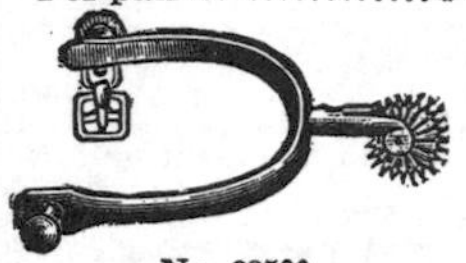

No. 93500 **English Pattern**, solid steel, nickel plated, heavy oval, with knob and buckle. Per pair.................**$1.00**

No. 93500.

No. 93502 **Eureka Spurs**, wide steel heel band, nickel plated 1¼ inch malleable rowell, two buttons, without straps. Per pair.. 0.50

No. 92502.

No. 93503 **Thompson's Pocket Spurs**, made of the best material and nickel plated; can be attached or detached in a moment, and can be carried in a vest pocket when not in use. No straps required. Per pair.............**$1.20**
**Always give number when ordering.**

No. 93503.

No. 93505 **Mexican Spurs**, fine steel, nickeled, filled, engraved and ornamented, chain and trinkets, 1½ inch rowel. Per pair......**$0.30**

No. 93505.

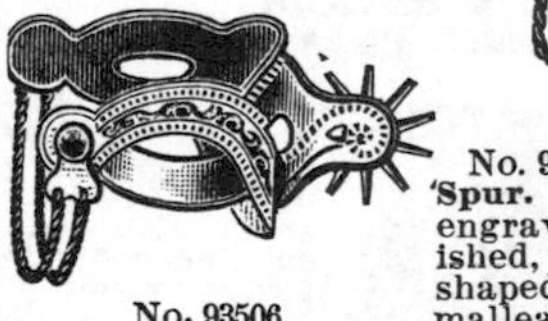

No. 93506 **Excelsior Steel Spur.** Nickel plated and engraved, very finely finished, extra wide, fancy shaped heel band, 1½ inch malleable rowel, 1 button and chain, without straps. Per pair.....**$1.35**

No. 93506.

No. 93508 **California Spur.** Hand forged steel nickeled and chased, leather lined, 2 inch rowel, without strap, one button and chain. Per pair.............**$2.40**

No. 93508.

No. 93509 **California Spur.** Hand forged steel, nickeled and chased, leather-lined, 2½ inch rowel, without strap, one button, chain and trinkets. Per pair.......**$2.90**

No. 93509

No. 93511 **California New Patent Steel Spur**, with chains, burnished and engraved, solid, medium weight heel band, 1⅜ inch rowel. Per pair ...**$0.95**

No. 93511.

No. 93513 **California Spur**, hand forged steel, silver inlaid, blued finish, medium weight heel band, one button and chain, 2½ inch rowel with steel bells or danglers, without straps. Per pair.....................**$5.50**

No. 93513.

No. 93514 **California Spurs**, hand forged steel, silver inlaid, blued finish, extra heavy heel band, one button and chain, 2¾ inch rowel, with steel bells or danglers, without straps. Weight, per pair, 24 ounces. Per pair...................**$9.50**

---

**Three Per Cent. Discount for CASH.**

**ORDER BY NUMBER.**

## Spur Straps.

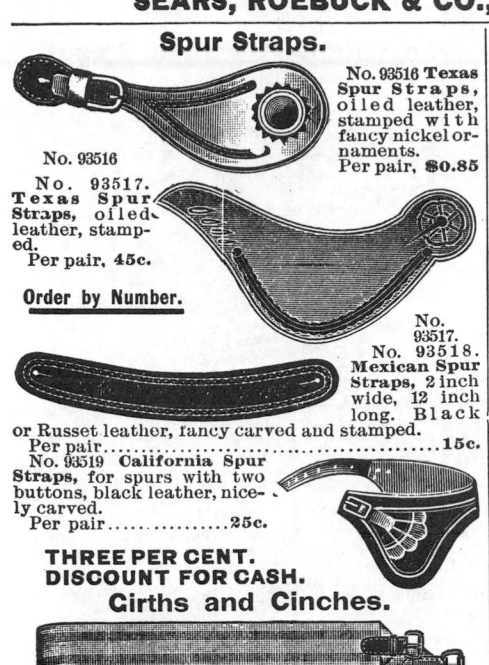

No. 93516 **Texas Spur Straps,** oiled leather, stamped with fancy nickel ornaments. Per pair, $0.85

**No. 93517. Texas Spur Straps,** oiled leather, stamped. Per pair, 45c.

Order by Number.

No. 93517. No. 93518. **Mexican Spur Straps,** 2 inch wide, 12 inch long. Black or Russet leather, fancy carved and stamped. Per pair..............15c.

**No. 93519 California Spur Straps,** for spurs with two buttons, black leather, nicely carved. Per pair..............25c.

### THREE PER CENT. DISCOUNT FOR CASH.

## Girths and Cinches.

**No. 93521**

No. 93521. **Super Cotton Web,** 3 inches wide, 3½ feet long, with 1¼ buckle on each end. Each, $0.20

No. 93523. **Extra Fancy Union Web,** 3¼ inches wide, 3½ feet long, with 1⅛ inch buckle on each end. Weight, 7 ounces. Each..............$0.30

## Cotton Web Cinches.

**No. 93526**

No. 93524. **Heavy Cotton Web Cinches,** 3½ inches wide, with leather chafes on each end. Weight 10 ounces, Each..............$0.40

No. 93526. **Heavy Cotton Web Cinches,** 3½ inches wide, with leather chafes and connecting straps, Weight 21 ounces. Per pair..............$0.90

## California Hair Cinches.

No. 93527. **20-Strand, 4-Cord, 2-Bar Buffalo Hair,** weight 10 ounces. Each, 35c

No. 93528. **20-Strand, 4-Cord, 2-Bar, White Hair,** weight 10 ounces. Each, 60c

No. 98529. **20-Strand, 6-Cord, 2-Bar Fancy White Oblock Hair,** weight 10 ounces. Each..............68c

No. 93531. **32-Strand, 6 Cord, 2-Bar, White Hair,** weight 20 ounces. Each..............$1.35

No. 93532. **24-Strand, 8-Cord, 2-Bar Diamond Center White Hair,** weight 30 ounces. Each..............$1.60

No. 93533. **30-Strand, 8-Cord, Diamond Center White Hair,** weight 32 ounces. Each..............$2.25

## Mexican String Cinches.

No. 93535. **Pure Gray Hard Hair.** Each, 6 inch, 35c; 8 inch, 45c; 9 inch..............50c

No. 93537. **Fancy Cotton.** Each, 4 inch, 21c; 5 inch, 23c; 6 inch..............25c

No. 93527 No. 93535

## Double California Cinches.

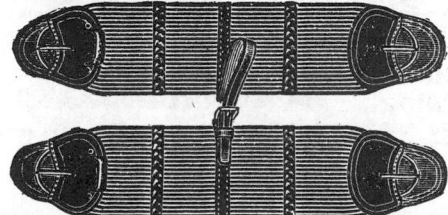

No. 93538. **Gray California Cinch,** with chafes, tongues and connecting straps (like cut). Per pair..............$3.00

No. 93539. **White California Cinch,** wool lined chafes, fancy stamped connecting straps, with buckles. Per pair..............$3.50

## Horse, Mule and Ox Collars.

**HOW TO MEASURE A COLLAR.**

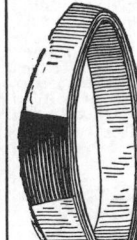

The above cut shows the method to be employed to measure a horse collar. If in ordering collars, you measure the old collar which the illustration shows, giving the inside measurement of the collar, by following this rule, your collar will always be the size which is wanted.

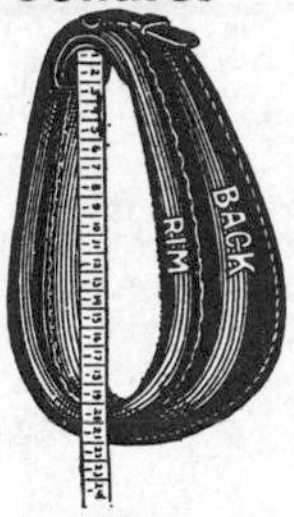

## Horse Collar Couplings.

No. 93541. **Common Sense Collar Couplings.** Can be used either on new collars or on old collars that have been broken through constant handling. No springs or straps required to keep them fastened. They are easily adjusted. Each..............$0.15 Per dozen..............1.65

## Horse and Mule Collars.

When ordering horse or mule collars be sure and mention size wanted. Prices given here are for collars from 17 to 21 inch; collars 22 to 23 inches in size cost 25 per cent more; collars 24 inches and larger cost 40 per cent extra. To get the size of collar in inches, measure in a straight line from top to bottom on the inside.

## Team Collars.

No. 93542. **Draft all kip welted,** all thread sewed, black rim and shoulder, flat top finished. Each..............$1.25

No. 93544. **Imitation Full Case Collar.** Medium, all kip, all thong sewed, made all black or black with fair belly, flat finished top. This is a first-class team collar, thoroughly well made and guaranteed to give the best of satisfaction. Price, each..............$1.75

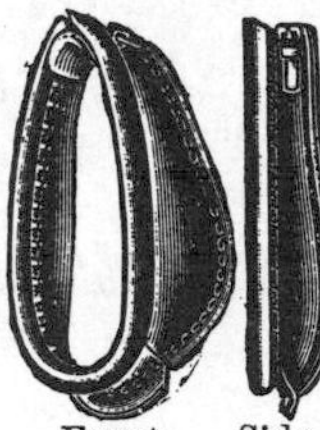

No. 93545. **Our Special Team Collar.** Wool stuffed patent double grip stitched rim, adding double strength and more hame room than any collar which makes it the most perfect collar ever placed on the market. The double grip stitched rim and body of collar is all hand thong stitched. The collar embodies every good and practical principal a horse collar can have. Price, each..............$2.50

Front. Side.

93546. **Fine all black Concord** wool faced team collar. Heavy stock, all thong sewed. Each..............$2.35

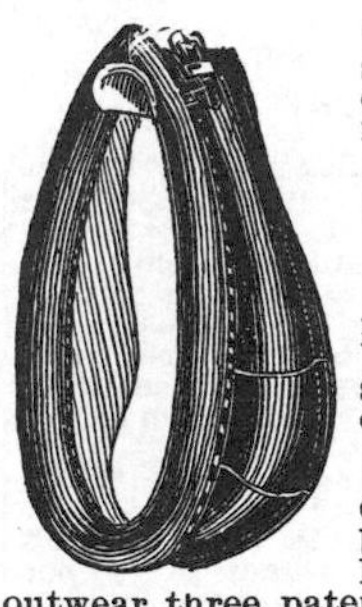

No. 93547 **Imitation Case Collar.** Extra heavy, thong sewed, wood faced. Just the collar for heavy teaming or farm work. Each..............$2.00

## Buggy Collars.

No. 93548. **Common grade,** all black leather, spliced shoulders, one buckle on top. Each..............$1.00

No. 93549 **Buggy Collar,** made of the best kip leather, light and neat; will outwear three patent leather collars. Each..............$1.20

No. 93550 **Extra quality fine half patent leather collar,** russet belly. Best and cheapest buggy collar evre offered for the money. Each..............$1.75

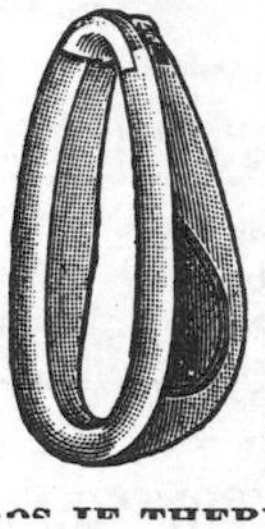

No. 93551 **Plain Duck Collars,** made of cotton duck with leather chafes on side, and leather pad on top, and leather welt all around. Price, each..............$0.35

## Ox Collars.

No. 93552. **Extra heavy,** made of heavy cotton duck. Each..............$0.50

No. 93554 **Ox Collar,** extra heavy cotton duck, with split leather rim. Each..............$0.60

No. 93555 **Made of all kip leather.** Extra heavy. Each..............$1.40

### ....We carry in stock a....

## FULL LINE OF ALL GRADES,

### AND MAKES OF COLLARS

and are prepared to furnish anything a customer may want. If you don't find listed the collar wanted, write for prices.

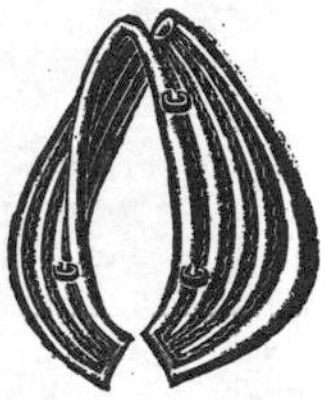

No. 93556 **Patent Sweat Collars.** Made of heavy white drill stuffed with hair, lower ends open, three patent hooks. Size 17 to 23 inches. Each..............$0.25 Per doz..............2.85

No. 93557 **Same Pad as Above.** Top side brown drill. Each..............$0.28 Per doz..............3.00

No. 93558 **Patent Sweat Collars.** Made of heavy white drill, stuffed with deer and goat hair mixed; three patent hooks; lower ends open; 10½ inches wide on shoulder where the draft comes. Sizes 17 to 24 inches. Each..............$0.30 Per doz..............3.40

No. 93561 **Same Pad as Above.** Top side brown drill. Each..............$0.35 Per doz..............3.60

No. 93562 **Extra Heavy Lumberman's Patent Sweat Collars.** 11½ inches wide on shoulder where the draft comes; stuffed with deer and goat hair mixed; three patent hooks; lower ends open. Sizes 18 to 24 inches. Each..............$0.38 Per doz..............4.00

No. 93563 **Same as Above.** With top side brown drill. Each..............$0.42 Per doz..............4.50

No. 93566 **Same as Above.** With top and bottom side brown drill. Each..............$0.45 Per doz..............5.00

No. 93568 **Patent Sweat Collars.** Heavy white drill, stuffed with pure deer hair; lower ends open; three patent hooks; 10½ inches wide on shoulder where the draft comes. Sizes 18 to 24 inches. Each..............$0.38 Per doz..............4.00

No. 93569 **Same as Above.** With top side brown drill. Each..............$0.38 Per doz..............4.00

No. 93570 **Lumberman's Extra Heavy and Wide Sweat Collar.** Made of heavy white drill, stuffed with pure deer hair; lower ends open; three patent hooks. These sweat collars are 11½ inches wide and made specially for heavy teaming. Sizes 19 to 24 inches. Each..............$0.50 Per doz..............5.50

## Top Collar Pads.

The different styles of Collar Pads quoted below, are to be used on top of the horses' neck, under working collar. They effectually prevent pinching or galling. If your horse has a sore neck, the use of one of these collar pads will heal it rapidly.

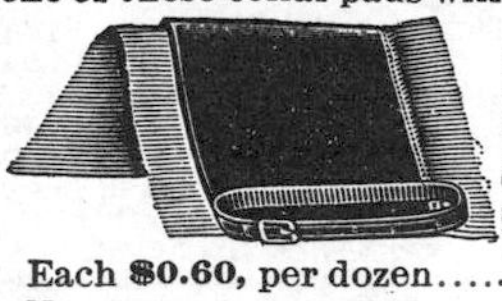

No. 93576 **Collar Pad,** made of heavy harness leather, lined with deer skin tanned with the hair on; 12½ inches long, 6 inches wide, 2⅝ inch straps, 18 inches long to buckle around collar. Each $0.60, per dozen..............$7.00

No. 93578 **Collar Pad,** sheep skin lined, stuffed with deer hair medium size. Each, $0.45, per dozen..............$5.20

No. 93579 **Same pad,** large size, each, $0.50 per dozen..............5.25

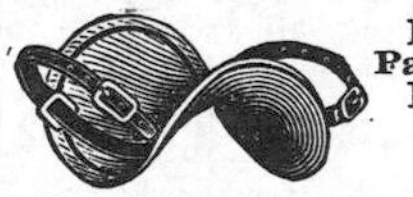

No. 93581 **Curtis Zinc Collar Pad.** Size 6 to 7½ inches. Each, $0.45, per dozen, $5.00

No. 93582 **Sole Leather Collar Pads,** for light team collars. Each..............$0.20 Per dozen..............2.00 For heavy team collar, cach..............$0.22 Per dozen..............2.30

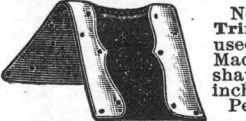

No. 93584 **Brass or Nickel Trimmed Housing,** to be used on top of horse collars. Made of black leather, shaped center. Size, 7½ x 14 inches. Per pair..............$1.90

☞ **All Sorts of Harness Mending Tools on Page 766.**

**WE HELP YOU TO HELP YOURSELF.**

## Breast, Collar, or Gig Housings.

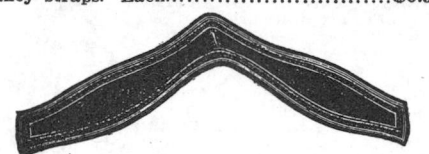

No. 93585  Gig or Saddle Housing, patent leather, sheep wool lined, fancy bound straps can be used under saddle on any single or double buggy harness. Each.................$0.40

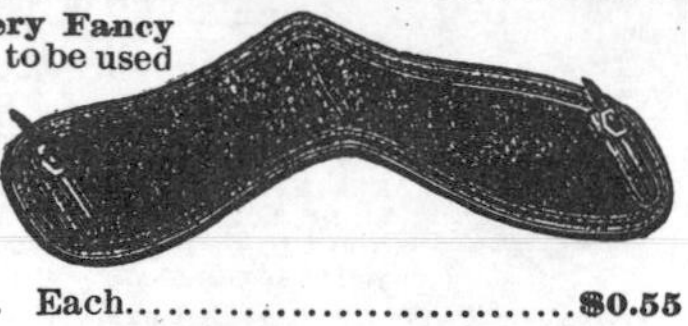

No. 93587  Very Fancy Gig Housing, to be used under buggy harness saddle. Double japanned, patent leather, fancy inlaid border, fancy straps. Each.................$0.55

No. 93589  Fancy Coach Pad Housing, to be used under any double buggy harness. Shaped, cut center, double japanned enameled, fancy bound and inlaid, black center.  Per pair.................$1.20

## Gig Sweat Pad.

No. 93591  Fancy Felt Gig Sweats, strictly first-class quality, strapped.

4x14 inches, each.............$0.15, per dozen, $1.65
5x14 inches, each............. .17, per dozen, 1.87
6x14 inches, each............. .25, per dozen, 2.25
7x15 inches, each....... ... .25, per dozen, 2.75

No. 93593  Fancy Gig Sweat Pad, patent leather top, felt bottom. 4x14 inches. Each..... $0.40
Per dozen.......... 4.50
4x18 inches, each.... 0.45
Per dozen.......... 5.00

## Breast Collar Housings.

No. 93594  Fancy Felt Housings, fawn color, size 3½x36 inches, five straps on each side.
Each, $0.25, per dozen.................$2.75
No. 93596  Fancy Felt Breast Collar Housings, pinked, patent leather covered.
Each, $0.45, per dozen .................$4.90

## Breechings.

No. 93597 Breeching for buggy harness, machine stitched folded, with straight layer, one ring stay, ⅝ inch hip strap, plain turn back, with round crupper sewed on, ¾ inch side straps, nickel or Davis rubber trimmings. Each.........$2.04

We have higher grade breechings for buggy harness at $2.50, $3.00, $3.50 and $4.00.

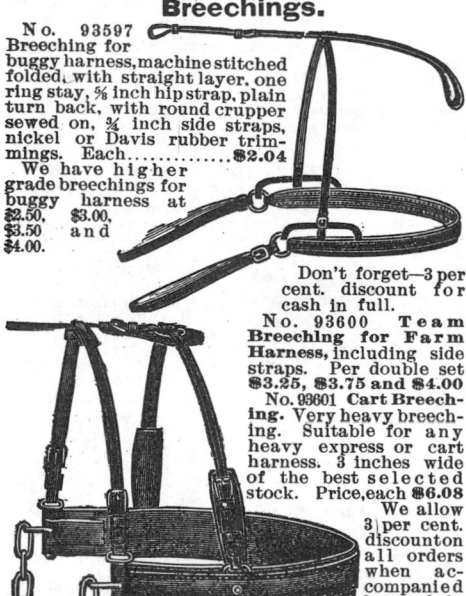

Don't forget—3 per cent. discount for cash in full.

No. 93600  Team Breeching for Farm Harness, including side straps.  Per double set $3.25, $3.75 and $4.00.
No. 93601  Cart Breeching. Very heavy breeching. Suitable for any heavy express or cart harness. 3 inches wide of the best selected stock. Price, each $6.08

We allow 3 per cent. discount on all orders when accompanied by cash in full.

No. 93601.

## Double Lines.

Flat black leather for farm harness, per pair for two horses.  All hand sewed and made from No. 1 selected stock.

| No. 93604 ⅞ in. | 15 ft. | 18 ft. | 20 ft. | 22 ft. | 28 ft. |
|---|---|---|---|---|---|
| Price, per pair... | $1.80 | $2.10 | $2.25 | $2.50 | $2.90 |
| No. 93605  1 in. | 15 ft. | 18 ft. | 20 ft. | 22 ft. | 28 ft. |
| Price, per pair... | $2.05 | $2.30 | $2.60 | $2.85 | $3.10 |

No. 93606  Extra Heavy Double Team Lines, 1⅛ inch wide, 20 feet long, choice selected stock and hand made.  Per set.................$3.60
Double Driving Lines.  Flat for double buggy harness.
No, 93607  Flat Double Driving Lines, ⅞ inch front. with 1 inch russet or black leather hand parts, nickel buckles.  Length 14 feet.  Per set...$2.55
No. 93608  Flat Double Driving Lines, ⅞ inch fronts, with 1⅛ inch russet or black leather hand parts to buckle on cross rein.  Nickel or Davis rubber buckles.  Length 14 feet.  Per set.........$3.00

## Single Driving Lines.

Flat for single buggy harness.
No. 93609  Single Flat Driving Lines, ⅞ inches front, with billets to buckle in bits, 1 inch russet or black leather hand parts.  Length 12 feet, 6 inches. Price .................$1.45
No. 93611  Single Flat Driving Lines, 1 inch fronts. with billets to buckle in bits, 1⅛ inch russet or black leather hand parts.  All hand made.  Price...$1.90

## Loops, or Rein Holder.

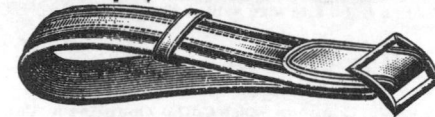

No. 93612  Russet Leather Rein Holder, folded, double stitched layer, nickle loops.  Can be attached to any driving lines.  Per pair.................$0.70

## TRACES.
### Single Buggy Harness.

No. 93613  Machine Stitched Traces, 6 feet long, good sound stock.  Per pair, 1 inch...........$1.20
Per pair, 1⅛ inch, $1.35, 1¼ inch, 1.45
No. 93615  Best Machine Stitched Traces, 6 feet long, raised center, hand smoothed round edge, selected stock.  Per pair, 1 inch, .................$1.35
Per pair, 1⅛ inch, $1.50, 1¼ inch..... 1.65

### Double Buggy Harness.

No. 93616.  Machine Stitched Traces, 6 feet 4 inches long, selected stock.  Per pair, 1 inch........$1.40
Per pair, 1⅛ inch, $1.60,  1¼ inch........ 1.80
No. 93617  Best Machine Stitched Traces, 6 feet 4 inches long, raised center, hand finished round edge.
Per pair, 1 in., $1.55; 1⅛ in., $1.75; 1¼ in..$1.95

### Double Team Farm Harness.

No. 93618  Machine Stitched, 6 feet long.
Per set of four, 1½ inch, $4.95; 1¾ inch.......$5.75
No. 93619  Hand Stitched, 6 feet long.
Per set of four, 1½ inch, $6.05; 1¾ inch.......$6.90

### Breast Collars.

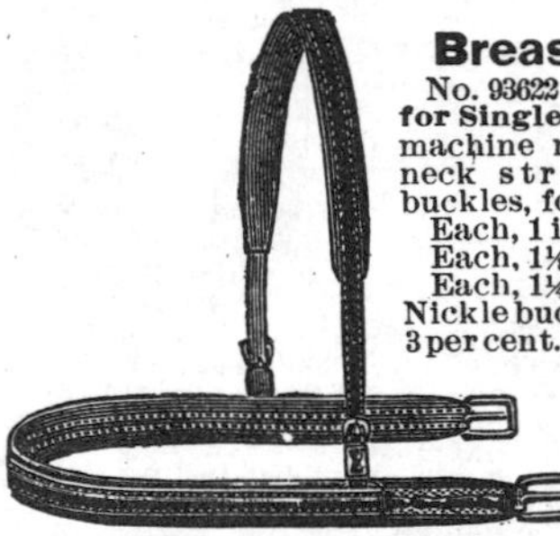

No. 93622  Breast Collar for Single Buggy Harness, machine made, including neck strap, all black buckles, for one horse.
Each, 1 inch.................$1.25
Each, 1⅛ inch ...... 1.35
Each, 1¼ inch...... 1.45
Nickle buckles, $0.15 extra 3 per cent.discount for cash.

No. 93622.   Order by Number.

### Single Strap Breast Collar.

No. 93625  Single Strap Breast Collar, with traces for single buggy harness, best machine made, plain round edge finished, 1¾ breast collar, 1⅛ inch traces, stitched to breast collar with scalloped splice, single strap, neck strap, nickeled or Davis rubber buckles.
Each.................$2.50

We can furnish breast collar with traces in higher grade and hand made work, $3.00 to $3.75

No. 63625.   Order by Number.

### Double Buggy Breast Collars

No. 93627  Double Buggy Breast Collars.  This cut represents breast collar to be used in place of hames and collars on double buggy harness.  When ordering breast collars be sure to give size of buckles, as they come in three sizes, viz: 1, 1⅛ and 1¼ inches, according to size of traces used.  With nickel or black buckles.

Per pair 1 inch.....$6.25
Per pair 1⅛ inch.... 6.30
Per pair 1¼ inch.... 6.35
Don't forget the 3 per cent. discount.

No. 93627.

## Van Wagnen's Patent Breast Collars.

Van Wagnen's Patent Breast Collars.  The best double buggy breast collars made.
No. 93629  Folded, Scalloped Layer, Fancy Box Loops, full nickel trimmed.
Price, per pair, 1 inch.................$9.00
Price, per pair, 1⅛ inch, $9.25, 1¼ inch..... 9.75

### Breast Straps.

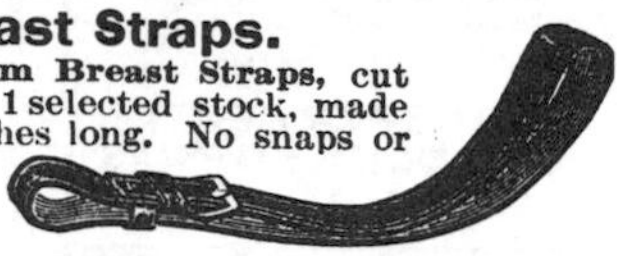

No. 93640  Team Breast Straps, cut from heavy No. 1 selected stock, made up four feet 8 inches long.  No snaps or slides.  Each 1½ in.. 45c; 1¾ in., 50c; 2 in., 58c.

### Martingales.

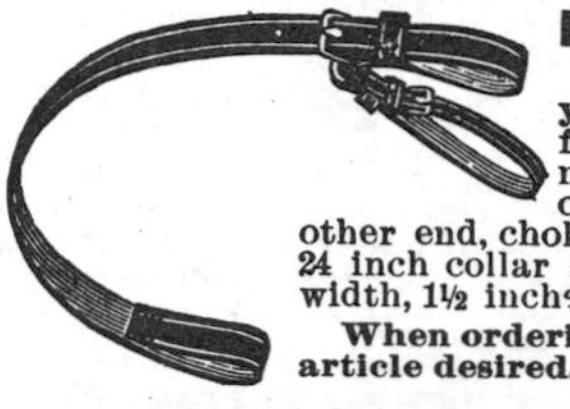

No. 93642  Neckyoke Martingales, for heavy team harness, buckled loop at one end, ring at the other end, choke ring stitched on; 24 inch collar strap with buckle; width, 1½ inches.  Each.........58c
When ordering give number of article desired.

### Pole or Neckyoke Straps.

No. 93643  Pole or Neckyoke Straps, buckled loop at one end, sewed loop at the other end, with ring or breeching side straps.  No collar straps.  Each, 1½ inch, 40c; 1¾ inch, 45c; 2 inch.................59c.

### Hame Straps.

No. 93645  Hame Strap, hand sewed, buckle and leather loops.  Made up 21 inches long. Each ⅞ inch, 10c; 1 inch.................12c.
No. 93646  Rawhide Hame Straps, best quality oil tanned rawhide.  Each, ⅞ inch, 12c; 1 inch..14c.

### Spreader Straps.

No. 93648  Leather Spreader Straps, without rings or loops, with ⅝ inch buckle, 24 inches long, black leather.  Each.................10c.

### Halter or Hitching Straps.

No. 93650  Black Leather Hitching Straps, 7 feet long, ¾ inch wide, with German snaps riveted on.
Each.................20c
No. 93651  With loops, ⅞ inch, 25c; 1 inch.....30c
No. 93652  With buckles, ¾ inch, each, 26c; ⅞ inch 30c; 1 inch, 35c; 1¼ inch.................44c.

### Belly Bands.

No. 93654  Buggy Belly Band, folded and stitched, buckle on each end.  Each, ¾ inch, 41c; ⅞ inch..42c 
No. 93655  Team Belly Band, folded and stitched, 1 ft. 9 inches long, with 1¼ inch buckle on each end. Each.................50c
No. 93657  Griffith Style Belly Band, for buggy harness, single strap, handsome long billets, nickel or Davis rubber buckles.  Each..65c

### Back Bands.

No. 93658  Leather Back Bands, with patent hooks to fasten in trace chains, for horse or ox plow harness.  Each, 3 in.. 58c; 4 in..79c
No. 93659  Cotton Back Bands, with patent hooks to fasten in trace chains, for horse or ox plow harness.  Each, 3 inch, 32c; 4 inch.................40c

### Chain Piping.

No. 93660  Leather Pipes, 24 inches long, to cover trace chains for plow harness.  Per set of four for two horses.................$1.30

### Side Straps.

No. 93662  Side Straps for breeching on double team harness.  Length, 6 feet. Per pair, ⅞ inch, 65c; 1 inch, 75c; 1¼ inch.................95c.
No. 93663  Side Straps for Single Buggy Harness, 4 feet long, either nickel or Davis rubber buckles. Per pair, ¾ inch, 46c; ⅞ inch, 56c; 1 inch..... 68c

## Team Harness Pads.

**No. 93665. Summit City Team Pads,** made with plates. Pads stuffed with housings and dee-rings. This makes a good repair pad as you can use a strap with a buckle for the skirt or flap. Japan or XC trimmed.

Per pair.. **$1.70** Please mention whether black

No. 93665. or white trimmings are wanted.

**No. 93666. Perfection Team Pads,** with patent leather housings and stuffed leather pads to be used where skirts or flaps are screwed on. Japan or XC trimmed.

Per pair.........**$1.75**

## Gig Saddles.
### For Single Harness.

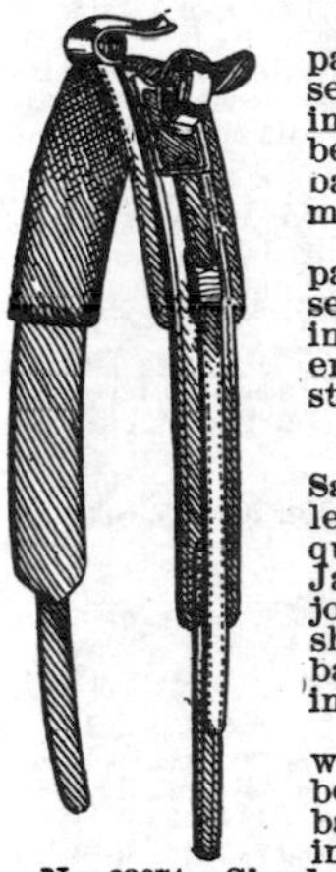

**No. 93668. Gig Saddles,** made of patent leather, Japanned metal seats, enameled cloth pads, 2½ inches wide with ⅝ inch shaft bearer straps and ⅝ inch belly band straps. Japan or XC trimmed. Each............**$1.10**

**No. 93669. Gig Saddles,** made of patent leather, Japanned metal seats, enameled cloth pads, 3 inches wide, with 1 inch shaft bearer straps and ⅝ inch belly band straps. Japan or XC trimmed. Each............**$1.25**

**No. 93670. Fine hand laced Gig Saddle,** 2½ inch tree, full patent leather skirts, enamel leather pad, quilted and laced in by hand. Japanned seat and patent leather jockey, ⅝ inch double and stitched, shaft bearer straps, ⅝ inch belly band straps, trimmed in nickel or imitation. Each............**$2.75**

**No. 93671.** Same style as above with three inch tree, 1 inch shaft bearer straps and ⅝ inch belly band straps. Trimmed in nickel or imitation rubber. Each....**£2.95**

**No. 93674. Single Strap Gig Saddle,** 2½ inch with harness leather skirts and enamel leather pad, ⅝ inch double and stitched shaft bearer straps, ⅝ inch belly band straps. Trimmed in nickel or imitation rubber. Each.....**$1.75**

**No. 93676.** Same saddle as above with patent leather jockey. Nickel or imitation rubber. Each............**$2.00**

Please state which mounting is wanted,

## Shaft Tugs.

**No. 93680. Shaft Tugs,** nickel or Davis rubber buckle, ⅞ inch, per pair.......................**$0.44**
1 inch, per pair.......................**$0.48**

## Cook's Rein Button.

**No. 93681. Rein Button,** briar wood per pair......**$0.20**
Black, per pair............**$0.20**
We allow 3 per cent discount when cash in full accompanies order.

No. 93681.

## Riding Bridle Reins.

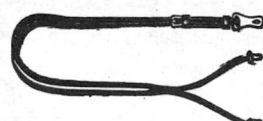

**No. 93682. Flat Reins,** riveted; XC plate, center bar buckles. Each ¾ inch............**$0.35**
⅞ inch....... 0.45
1 inch....... 0.50
Better quality reins furnished at 75c, 85c, 90c and............**$1.00**

## Check Reins.
### For Single and Double Buggy Harness.

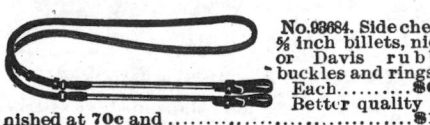

**No. 93683. Over Checks,** 3 buckels, 2 billets, nickel or Davis rubber buckles. Each....**$0.68**
Better quality furnished at 95c, $1.10 and.... $1.35

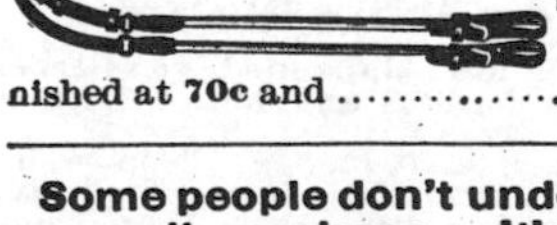

**No.93684.** Side checks, ⅝ inch billets, nickel or Davis rubber buckles and rings. Each.........**$0.55**
Better quality furnished at 70c and..........................**$1.00**

---

## Bolt Hames.

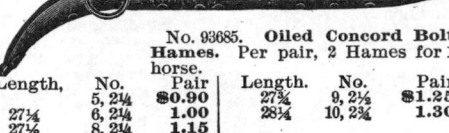

**No. 93685. Oiled Concord Bolt Hames.** Per pair, 2 Hames for 1 horse.

| Length, | No. | Pair | Length. | No. | Pair |
|---------|-----|------|---------|-----|------|
| 27¼ | 5, 2¼ | $0.90 | 27¾ | 9, 2½ | $1.25 |
| 27¼ | 6, 2¼ | 1.00 | 28¼ | 10, 2¾ | 1.30 |
| 27½ | 8, 2¼ | 1.15 | | | |

**No. 93686. XC Tinned, full steel clad Hames,** with bolt. Per pair of 2 hames for 1 horse. Pair...... ...............**$1.25**

**No. 93687. XC Trimmed, full steel clad Hames,** ball top with breast rings. Per pair, 2 hames for 1 horse......**$1.00**

**No. 93688. X C Ball and Plate Hames,** red with breast rings, 2 hames for 1 horse. Per pair....**$0.80**

**No. 93689. All Black Iron Over Top Hames,** with breast rings and patent combination loops for hames straps. Per pair, two hames for one horse...........**$0.45**

**No. 93690. Same Hames as 93678,** with the upper half XC or bright plated. Per pair, two hames for one horse.........**$0.50**

**Low Top Hames For Team Harness** Per pair, two hames for one horse............**$0.45**

**No. 93692 Low Top Hames,** for team harness, with breast rings.

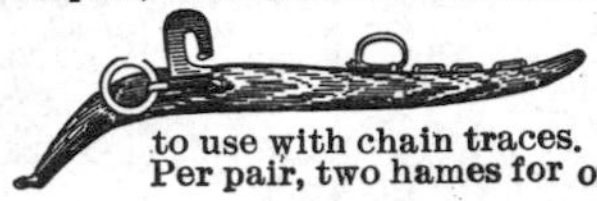

**No. 93692 Varnished I. O. T. Hook Hames,** with breast rings. to use with chain traces. Per pair, two hames for one horse... **$0.40**

**Oiled High Top Concord Hook Hames.**

**No. 93694 Oiled, High Top Concord Hook Hames,** with breast rings, to use with chain traces. Per pair, two hames for one horse............ **$0.80**

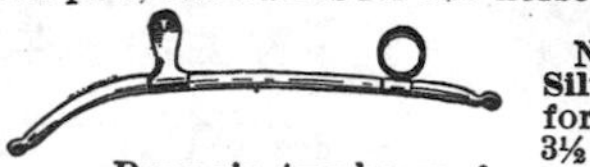

**No. 93696 Full X Silver Iron Hames** for buggy harness. 3½ lbs.; from 17 to 21. Per pair. two hames for one horse...... **$0.50**
**No. 93697 Same Hames as Above,** full jap all black, same price.
**No. 93699 Same as Above** with nickel Terret. Per pair...... **$0.75**

**ORDER BY NUMBER.**

## Iron Hames and Tugs.

**No. 93700. Iron Hames. No. 1,** full japanned (black) 3½ lbs. iron hame with hamestraps; box looped hame tugs and 1 inch trace buckles, per pair.........**$1.00**
With 1⅛ inch trace buckles, per pair.....................**$1.10**
With 1¼ inch trace buckles, per pair.....................**$1.25**
Sizes 17 to 21 inches; mention length. 
**No. 93702. Iron Hames. No. 1,** full XC plated (white), 3½ lbs. iron hames any size from 17 to 21 inches, with hame straps, box looped hame tugs, and 1 inch trace buckles.
Per pair............................**$1.00**
With 1⅛ inch trace buckles, per pair........ 1.10
With 1¼ inch trace buckles, per pair........ 1.25

---

## Horse Clippers, New Line, All American Made.

**Reasons why they should sell and give good satisfaction:** The plates are made from the best English tool steel, are highly tempered and perfectly ground, insuring the best cutting results. They all have the nut directly over the teeth, which prevents the plates from spreading in thick hair and also a tension spring under the nut, which allows the cutters to adjust themselves when cutting.

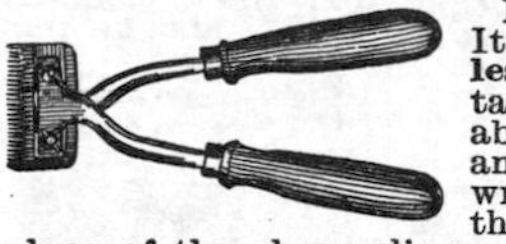

**No. 93710. The Herald.** It is a new clipper and a leader. The plates are detachable and interchangeable, has two thumb nuts and tension springs; no wrench needed to adjust this clipper. It takes the place of the cheap clippers which we formerly imported, weight, 14 oz. Each...............**$0.90**

**No. 93711. The Lenox.** This is a standard clipper and a great favorite with horsemen; has bright red handles, it is well finished and attractive. Cutting plates are detachable and interchangeable; weight, 20 oz. Top plate, 50c; bottom plate, 60c; each, **$1.20**

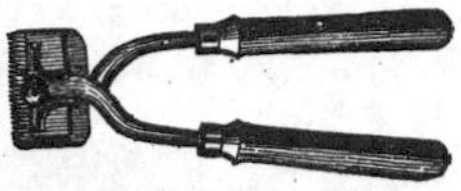

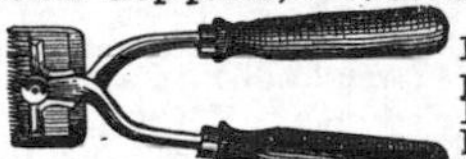

**No. 93712. The American Horse.** A handsome and popular clipper, similar to Lenox, except that it has large oval handles, oil finished, which feature makes this clipper well liked by experts. Plates detachable and interchangeable and highly tempered. Weight, 20 ounces. Top plates, 75c; bottom plate, $1.00; each............**$1.35**

**No. 93713. The New Market Pattern.** It is carefully constructed, handsome in appearance, has bright red handles; there is no clipper made so well known to professional horse clippers as the New Market pattern; the name sells it. All parts are detachable and interchangeable; weight, 18 ounces. Top plates, 75c; bottom plates, $1.00; each............**$1.55**

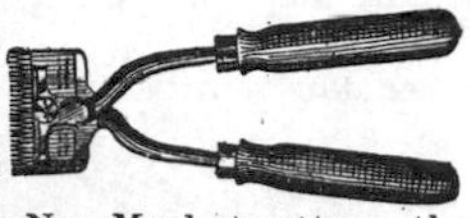

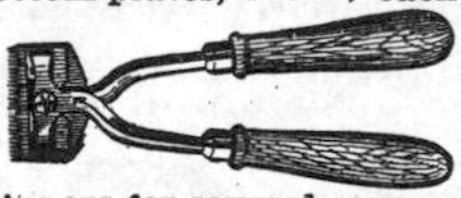

**No. 93714. The O. K. No. 62.** Our old reliable, nickel plated; an excellent cutter, bright polished handles, and has had the lead of all other clippers for several seasons. Cutting plates detachable and interchangeable; weight 20 ounces. Top plates, 75c; bottom plates, $1.25; each......**$1.90**

**No. 93715. French Horse Clippers.** These are imported goods, which we can sell for about the price of a single cutting plate. They have self-adjusting set screws. We positively cannot furnish any extra parts. Length, 10⅝ inches; weight, 14 oz. Each, **$0.95**

**No. 93716. The B. B. (Ball Bearing).** New this season. Has antifriction ball bearings, finest nickel finish, bright polished handles, and by all odds, the easiest cutting and the best clipper ever offered to the public. Cutting plates detachable and interchangeable; weight 21 ounces. Top plates, 75c; bottom plates, $1.25; each............**$2.25**

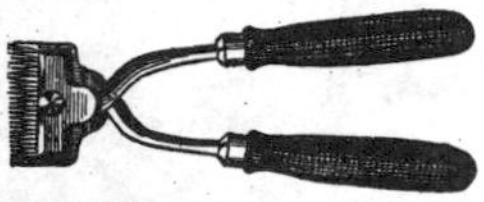

**No. 93717. No. 64. One Handed Horse or Dog Clipper.** For trimming about the ears and fetlocks requires a keen cutting one handed clipper with strong elastic spring. You will find this is the one that is sought after. Plates detachable and interchangeable; Weight, 12 ounces. Each....**$1.45**
Extra springs, each,............... .15
The parts of all our Clippers are interchangeable and can be promptly duplicated.

## English Clipping Shears.

**No. 93718.** With leather covered bows, 7½ inches long. Each, 90c.

No. 93718.

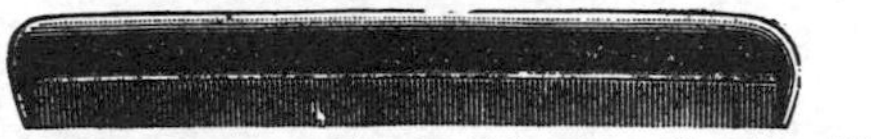

**No. 93719** German Silver Clipping Combs, 7½ inches long. Weight, each, 2 oz. Each........**$0.50**

## Bridle Plumes.

**Bridle Plumes. Curled Horse Hair Plumes, or Tassels for team harness.**
**No. 93720.** Bridle Plumes, colors red or yellow, 9 inches long. Per pair.............**$0.25**
**No. 93721.** Bridle Plumes, colors red or blue, 11 inches long. Per pair.............**$0.30**
**No. 93722.** Bridle Plumes, colors red or green, 13 inches long. Per pair.............**$0.35**
Mention color wanted. Weight, per pair, 3, 4. 5 oz.

---

**Some people don't understand how we can sell so cheap. It's easy to understand. We buy big, buy close, and sell on the narrowest margin of profit.**

**Make up a freight order and save more money.**

THERE'S NOTHING DIFFICULT ABOUT MAIL ORDER BUYING. THE MAIN THING TO CONSIDER IS THE HOUSE YOU BUY OF. IF YOU BUY OF US, AS WE HOPE, YOU WILL FIND COMPLETE INSTRUCTIONS IN FRONT OF THIS BOOK. WE WANT YOUR TRADE AND WILL TREAT YOU RIGHT.

## Curry Combs.

A horse well curried not only looks sleek and attractive, but his health is greatly improved by keeping his skin clean and pliable. Careful grooming saves much feed.

**We do not break dozens at dozen prices on curry combs.**

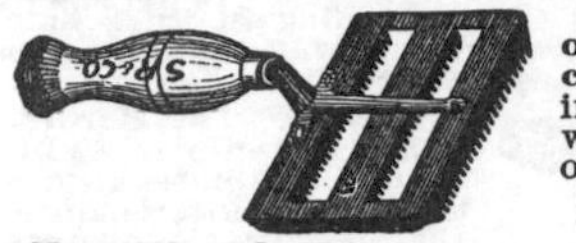

No. 93730 **6 bars open back curry combs.** Japanned iron, wood handle, weight about four ounces.
Each........$0.04
Per doz...... 0.35

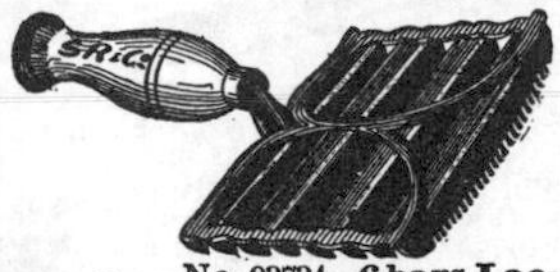

No. 93732 **8 bars Japanned open back curry combs.** Wood handle with double brace running over top of comb. Weight about 10 ounces. Each, 9c; per doz.......$1.00

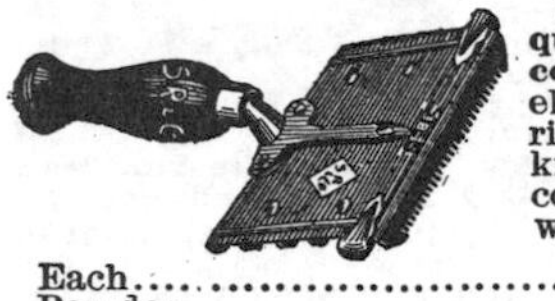

No. 93734 **6 bars Lacquered steel curry combs.** Black enameled handle, strongly riveted on. Heavy knockers. Best cheap comb in the market. weight about 10 ounces.
Each........................$0.10
Per doz........................ 1.10

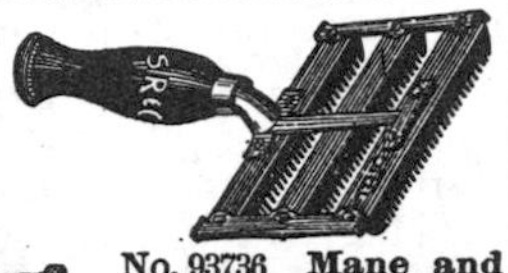

No. 93735 **6 bars open back steel curry comb.** Strongly riveted, wood handle, well made and a bargain. Weight about 10 ounces.
Each..........$0.10
Per doz........ 1.00

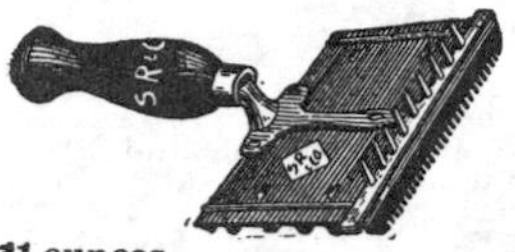

No. 93736 **Mane and curry comb combined.** Lacquered steel, 6 bars, with comb on top for carding the horse's mane. Enamel handle. Extra value for the money. Weight about 11 ounces.
Each........................$0.12
Per doz........................ 1.25

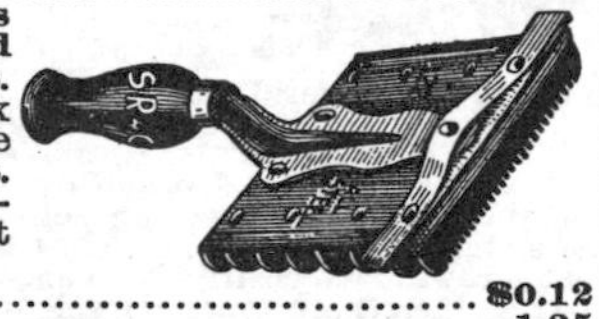

No. 93738 **8 bars Japanned closed back curry combs.** Extra strong shank with heavy brace across the front. Strong and durable. Weight about 13 ounces.
Each........................$0.12
Per doz........................ 1.25

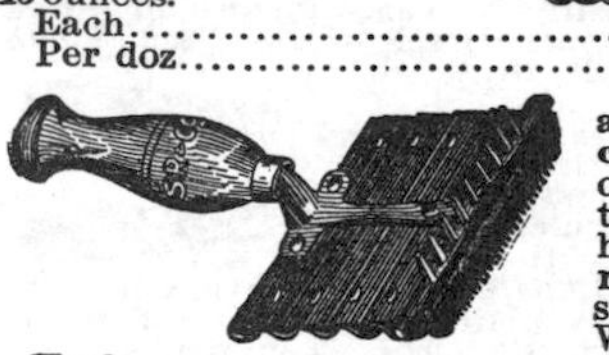

No. 93739 **Mane and curry comb combined.** Made of heavy metal tinned, 6 bars, wood handle, strongly riveted. Extra strong and durable. Weight about 10 oz.
Each........................$0.13
Per doz........................ 1.40

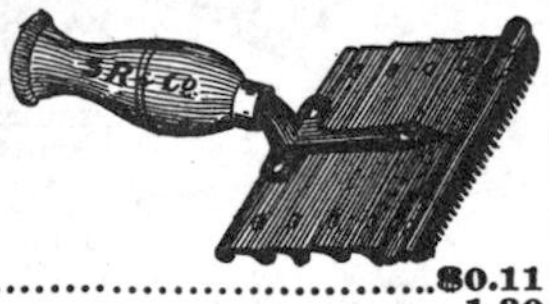

No. 93741 **6 bars, Japanned shingle back curry combs.** Strong wood handle, riveted. Knocker on each side. Good value. Weight about 9 ounces.
Each........................$0.11
Per doz........................ 1.30

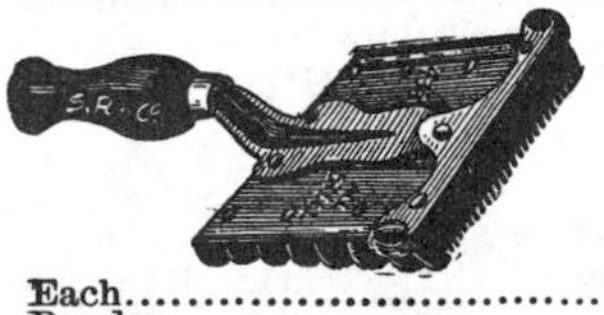

No. 93742 **8 bar all steel,** lacquered solid back, with strong shank, wood handle. A first-class comb. Weight about 10 ounces.
Each........................$0.15
Per doz........................ 1.50

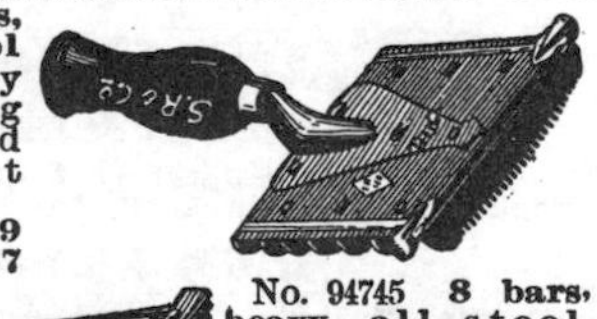

No. 93743 **8 bars, lacquered steel curry combs.** Heavy knockers, Strong and durable. Wood handle. Weight about 10 ounces.
Each...... $0.19
Per doz...... 1.67

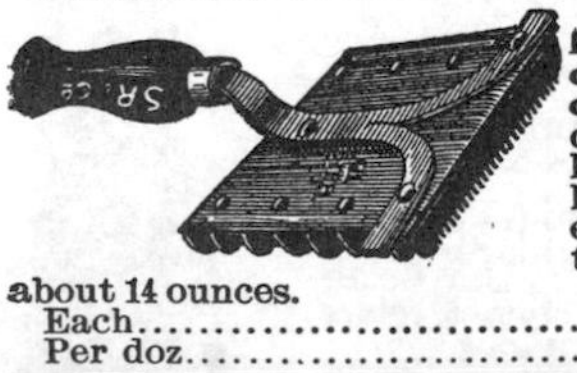

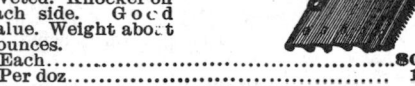

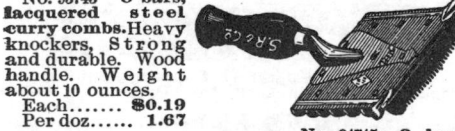

No. 94745 **8 bars, heavy all steel, closed back curry combs.** Strong handle, well riveted, heavy shank and knockers. Best comb ever produced for the money. Weight about 14 ounces.
Each........................$0.20
Per doz........................ 1.70

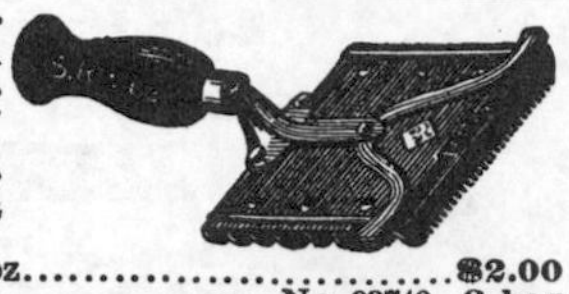

No. 93747 **8 bar blued steel, closed back curry combs.** Wood handle, heavy shank, well riveted, an elegant comb for the money. Weight about 10 ounces.
Each, 20c.; per doz........................$2.00

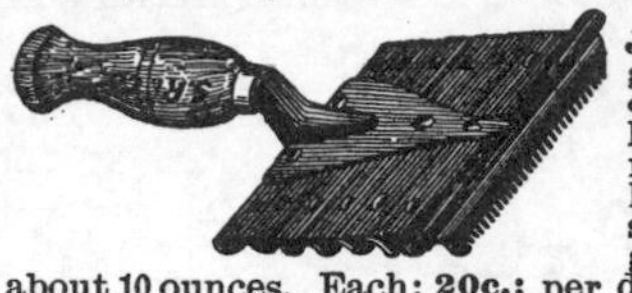

No. 93749 **8 bar Japanned, shingle back curry combs.** Wood handle, strongly riveted. Heavy knockers. Extra strong and a bargain. Weight about 10 ounces. Each; 20c.; per doz........$2.00

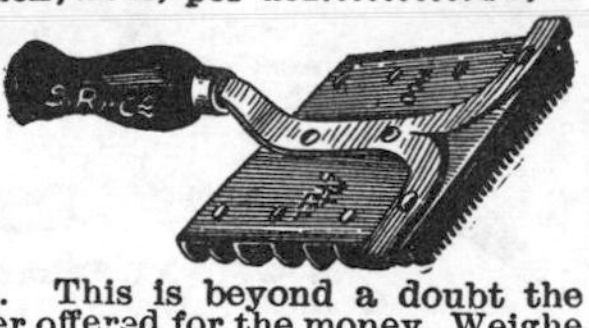

No. 93751 **Fine forged steel curry combs.** 8 bars, solid blued backs. Enamel wood handle. Wrought shank, running through handle, and extra strong brace and knockers. This is beyond a doubt the best curry comb ever offered for the money. Weighe about 15 ounces. Each, 25c.; per doz........$2.75

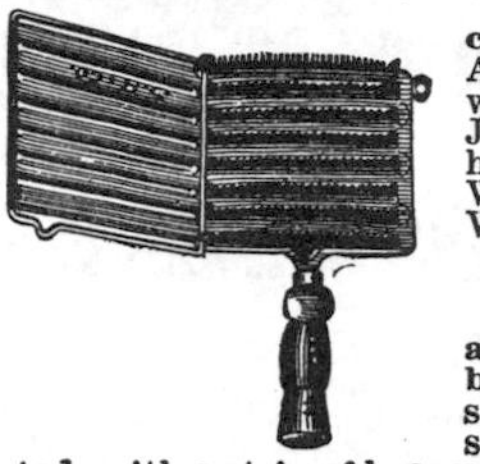

No. 93752 **The self-cleaning curry comb.** A great favorite with all who have used it. 8 bars, Japanned iron, wood handle, strongly riveted. Will give satisfaction. Weight about 15 ounces.
Each..........$0.30
Per doz.......... 3.25

No. 93754 **Curry comb and horse shedder combined.** 7 bars, Japanned shingle back with extra strong handle, well riveted; with a strip of heavy rubber securely fastened on top of comb, which will easily remove the hair in the shedding season. No horseman should be without this comb. Weight about 15 ounces.

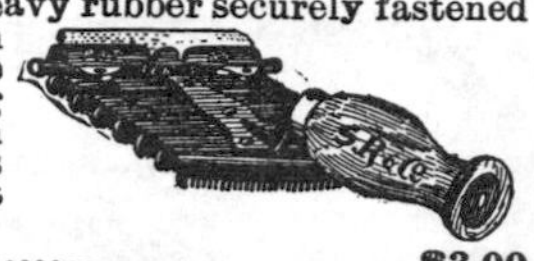

Each, 30c.; per doz........................$3.00

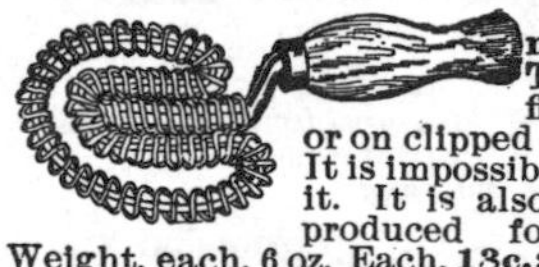

No. 93755 **The "Humane" Curry Comb.** This is the only comb fit to use on horses legs or on clipped or short haired horses. It is impossible to hurt a horse with it. It is also the best thing ever produced for a cattle cleaner. Weight, each, 6 oz. Each, 18c.; per doz........$1.95

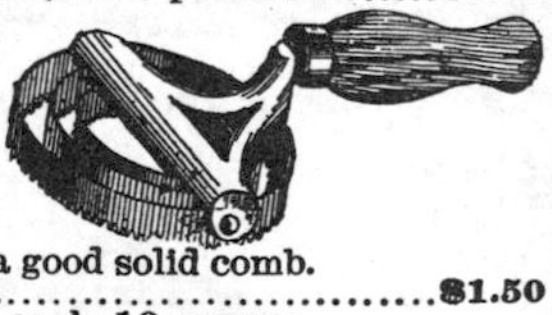

No. 93756 **Circular Steel Spring Curry Combs,** three complete circles of steel working independent of each other, attached to an iron back by a hinged joint, wood handles; a good solid comb.
Each, 14c.; per doz........................$1.50
**Weight, each, 10 ounces.**

## Horse Curry Cards.

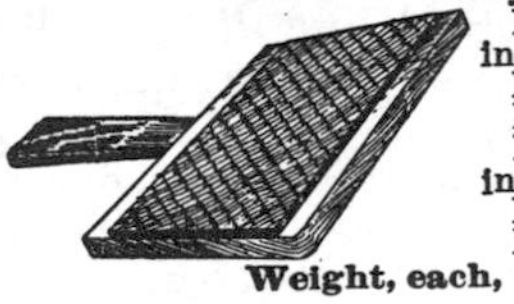

**Weight, each, 8 ounces.**

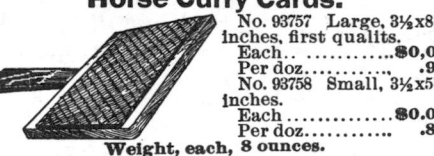

No. 93757 Large, 3½x8¼ inches, first qualits.
Each..........$0,09
Per doz.......... .95

No. 93758 Small, 3½x5½ inches.
Each..........$0.08
Per doz.......... .85

## Pad Hooks and Terrets.

No. 93790 **Check Hooks** for pads on team harness, japanned finish. Each 4c. Per doz..........$0.45

No. 93791 **Check Hooks** for pads on team harness, X C plated. Weight, each, 3 oz. Each........$0.05
Per doz........................ 0.54

No. 93792 **Heavy Band Terrets** for pads on team harness, 1¾ inch, japanned finish. Each, 5c. Per doz..$0.54

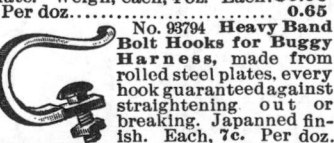

No. 93793 **Heavy Band Terrets** for pads on team harness, 1¾ inch, X C plate. Weigh, each, 4 oz. Each.$0.06
Per doz........................ 0.65

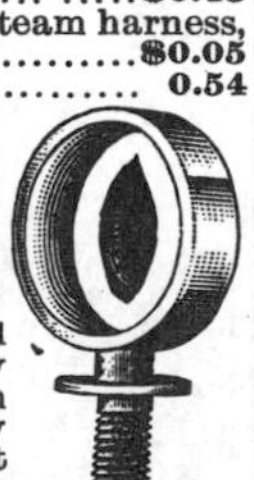

No. 93792.

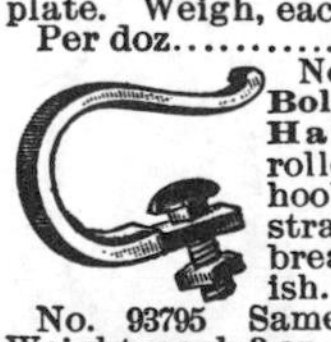

No. 93794 **Heavy Band Bolt Hooks for Buggy Harness,** made from rolled steel plates, every hook guaranteed against straightening out or breaking. Japanned finish. Each, 7c. Per doz........$0.75

No. 93795 Same as No. 93794, but X C plated. Weight, each 3 oz. Each 7c. Per doz........$0.75

No. 93796 **Heavy Band Terrets** for reins to run through on saddle used for buggy harness. Size 1⅜, 1½. Japanned or X C. Each, 6c. Per doz....$0.70

No. 93797 **Nickel or Imitation Rubber Bolt Hooks for Gig Saddle,** either band or wire pattern.
Each........................$0.12

No. 93798 **Nickel or Imitation Rubber Terrets for Gig Saddle,** either band or wire pattern.
Each........................$0.12

## Trace Chains.

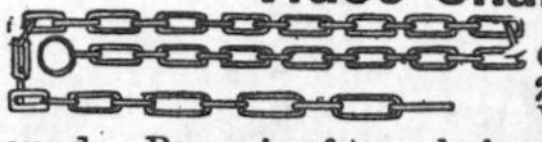

No. 93800 **Trace Chains,** made of size 2 iron, 7 feet long. Weight, per pair, 6½ pounds. Per pair of two chains for one horse..$0.50

## Trace Splicers.

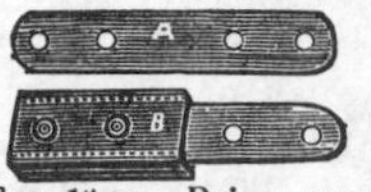

No. 93802 **Malleable Iron Trace Splicers** for mending traces; simple, quick, cheap and durable. They can be used for buggy, express or farm harness. Weight, per doz. 16 oz. Price, per doz........................$0.40

## Whip Racks.

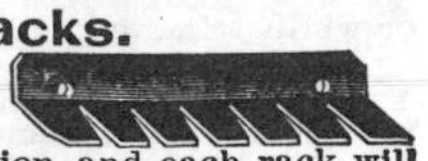

No. 93804 **Hall's Whip Racks,** Japanned sheet iron, 6 inches long, two nails or screws will hold one in position and each rack will hold a dozen whips. Weight 2 oz. Each.......$0.08
Per doz........................ 0.85

## Harness Snaps.

By size of snap we mean the width of snap that can be used.

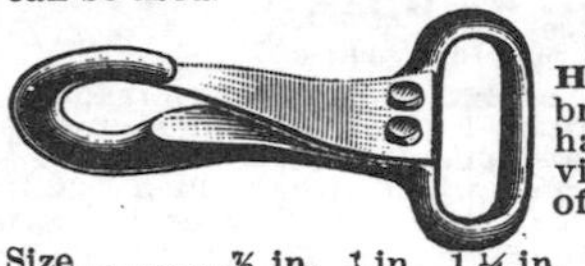

No. 93805 **German Harness Snaps,** bronzed finish. We handle only the heaviest and best snaps of this style made.

| Size | ⅞ in. | 1 in. | 1¼ in. | 1½ in. | 1¾ in. | 2 in. |
|---|---|---|---|---|---|---|
| Per doz | $0.16 | $0.16 | $0.25 | $0.35 | $0.45 | $0.50 |
| Weight, doz | 13 oz. | 18 oz. | 26 oz. | 32 oz. | 40 oz. | 50 oz. |

## Champion Harness Snaps.

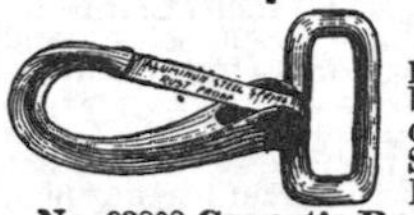

No. 93806 **This snap is very popular** and is considered the best snaps on the market today.

| Size | ¾ | ⅞ | 1 | 1¼ | 1½ | 1¾ |
|---|---|---|---|---|---|---|
| Price | 18c. | 20c. | 20c. | 30c. | 40c. | 48c. |

No. 93808 **Covert's Banner Bolt Snaps.** The principal feature of the snap lies in the spring being entirely covered, shutting out all foreign substance.

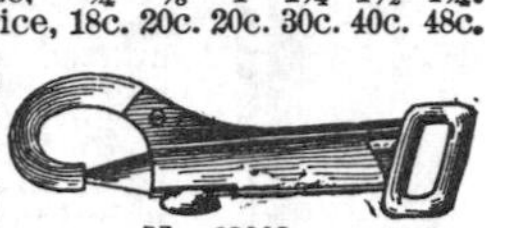

No. 93808.

| Size | ⅞ in. | 1 in. | 1¼ in. | 1½ in. | 1¾ in. | 2 in. |
|---|---|---|---|---|---|---|
| Per doz | $0.24 | $0.26 | $0.40 | $0.44 | $0.48 | $0.52 |

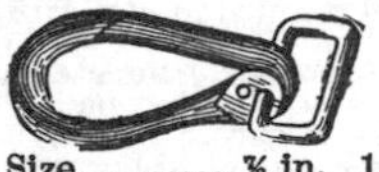

No. 93810 **Bristol's Patent Snaps,** strictly first quality. Every snap is thoroughly tested in the factory before being packed.

| Size | ⅞ in. | 1 in. | 1¼ in. | 1½ in. | 1¾ in. | 2 in. |
|---|---|---|---|---|---|---|
| Per doz | $0.28 | $0.30 | $0.39 | $0.45 | $0.48 | $0.58 |

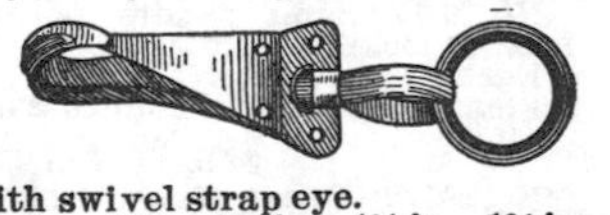

No. 93811 **The American Wrought Steel Harness Snaps** are strong competitors for public favor. All made with swivel strap eye.

| Size | ⅞ in. | 1 in. | 1¼ in. | 1½ in. | 1¾ in. |
|---|---|---|---|---|---|
| Per doz | $0.35 | $0.37 | $0.45 | $0.52 | $0.60 |

No. 93812 **The American Wrought Steel Snap,** for rope halters or cow ties, the strongest made.
Each, $0.04.......... Per doz..........$0.45

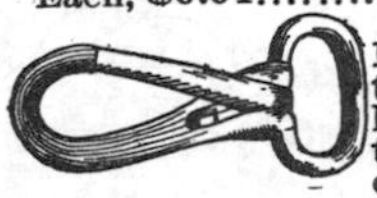

No. 93813 **Bristol's Patent Round Eye Snaps for rope,** tinned finish. Polished on the loop and milled at the nose of the hook. Every snap is thoroughly tested.

| Size | ⅝ in. | ¾ in. |
|---|---|---|
| Per doz | $0.45 | $0.50 |
| Weight, per doz | 15oz. | 25 oz. |

No. 93814 **Bag Snaps,** nickel-plated bag or baby snaps. Will take straps ½ inch.
Per doz....................$0.25

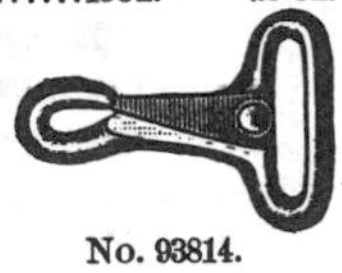

No. 93814.

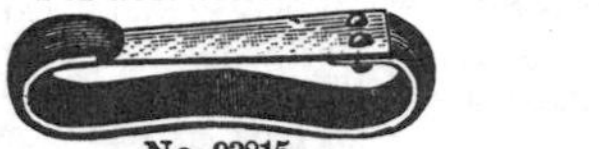

No. 93815.

No. 93815 **Buffalo Patent Snap,** 2 in. long, japanned, can be used for halter, bridle and bit. Weight, per doz. 44 oz. Each, 5c. Per doz................$0.50

## Trace Buckles.

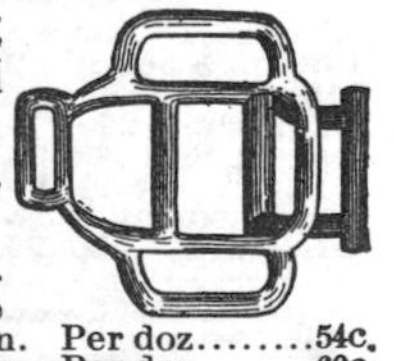

No. 93816 **Three-Loop Champion Trace Buckles,** made of best malleable Iron, japanned finish.
1½ in. Each....................5c.
1¾ in. Each....................5½c.
1½ in. Per doz....................54c.
4¾ in. Per doz....................60c.

No. 93819 **Three-Loop Champion Trace Buckles,** X C plate
1½ in. Each........5c. 1½ in. Per doz........54c.
1¾ in. Each........5½c. 1¾ in. Per doz........60c.

## Harness Buckles.

(Black.)

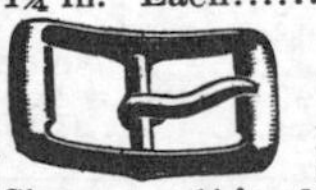

No. 93821 **Japanned Iron Center Bar** harness and halter buckles for straps,

| Size | ½ in. | ⅝ in. | ¾ in. | ⅞ in. | 1 in. | 1¼ in. | 1½ in. |
|---|---|---|---|---|---|---|---|
| Per doz | 6c. | 8c. | 10c. | 12c. | 14c. | 18c. | 25c. |
| Wt. per doz. | 2 oz. | 4 oz. | 6 oz. | 9 oz. | 12 oz. | 16 oz. | 22 oz. |

**POSTAGE MUST BE INCLUDED For mail Shipments. Orders by mail cannot go C. O. D.**

**..See Our Veterinary Department..**
**For Full Line of Instruments and Remedies.**

**Don't Forget the Index,**
**WHEN YOU FAIL TO SEE WHAT YOU WANT.**

WE MAKE YOUR WHEAT WORTH TWICE AS MUCH AS YOU NOW GET, BY MAKING YOUR DOLLAR GO TWICE AS FAR AS WHEN YOU BUY AT RETAIL.

No. 93822 **X C Plate** (white) **Iron Center Bar Harness and Halter Buckles for Straps.**

| Size | ½ in. | ⅝ in. | ¾ in. | ⅞ in. |
|---|---|---|---|---|
| Per dozen | 6c. | 8c. | 10c. | 12c. |
| Weight | 2 oz. | 4 oz. | 6 oz. | 9 oz. |
| Size | 1 in. | 1¼ in. | 1½ in. | |
| Per dozen | 14c. | 18c. | 25c. | |
| Weight | 12 oz. | 16 oz. | 22 oz. | |

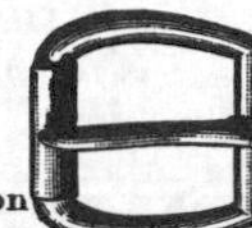

No. 93824 **Japanned** (black) **Iron Barrel Roller Buckles.**

| Size inches | ½ | ⅝ | ¾ | ⅞ | 1 | 1¼ | 1½ | 1¾ | 2 |
|---|---|---|---|---|---|---|---|---|---|
| Per doz | 4c. | 6c. | 8c. | 10c. | 12c. | 14c. | 16c. | 18c. | 20c. |
| Wt. per dz. in. oz. | 3 | 5 | 6 | 8 | 10 | 12 | 15 | 18 | 22 |

No. 93826 **X C Plated** (white) **Iron Barrel Roller Buckles.**

| Size inches | ½ | ⅝ | ¾ | ⅞ | 1 | 1¼ | 1½ | 1¾ | 2 |
|---|---|---|---|---|---|---|---|---|---|
| Per doz | 4c. | 6c. | 8c. | 10c. | 12c. | 14c. | 16c. | 18c. | 20c. |
| Wt. per dz. in. oz. | 3 | 5 | 6 | 8 | 10 | 12 | 15 | 18 | 22 |

## Harness Rings.

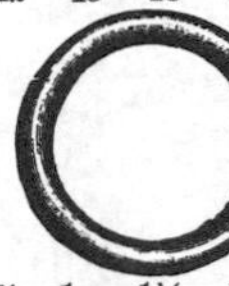

No. 93830 **Breeching and Halter rings, japanned iron, black finish.**

| Diameter, inches | ½ | ⅝ | ¾ | ⅞ | 1 | 1⅛ | 1¼ |
|---|---|---|---|---|---|---|---|
| Per dozen | 4c. | 4c. | 5c. | 5c. | 6c. | 8c. | 10c. |
| Weight per doz. in oz. | 3 | 4 | 5 | 6 | 7 | 8 | 10 |
| Diameter, inches | 1½ | 1¾ | 2 | 2¼ | 2½ | 3 | |
| Per dozen | 12c. | 14c. | 20c. | 24c. | 30c. | 35c. | |
| Weight per doz. in oz. | 16 | 18 | 22 | 32 | 35 | 37 | |

No. 93831 **X C plated white iron breeching and halter rings.**

| Diameter, inches | ½ | ⅝ | ¾ | ⅞ | 1 | 1⅛ | 1¼ |
|---|---|---|---|---|---|---|---|
| Per dozen | 4c. | 4c. | 5c. | 5c. | 6c. | 8c. | 10c. |
| Weight per doz. in oz. | 3 | 4 | 5 | 6 | 7 | 8 | 10 |
| Diameter, inches | 1½ | 1¾ | 2 | 2¼ | 2½ | 3 | |
| Per dozen | 12c. | 14c. | 20c. | 24c. | 30c. | 35c. | |
| Weight per doz. in oz. | 16 | 18 | 22 | 32 | 35 | 37 | |

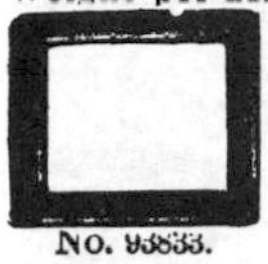

No. 93833.

No. 93833 **Halter Squares. Japanned malleable iron.**

| Sizes | 1x1¼ in. | 1¼x1½in. | 1½x1¾ in. |
|---|---|---|---|
| Per doz | 10c. | 12c. | 15c. |
| Wt. pr. dz. | 10 oz. | 14 oz. | 18 oz. |

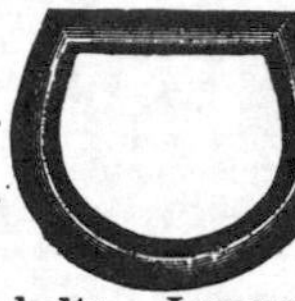

No. 93834 **Halter Dees. Japanned malleable iron.**

| Sizes | 1¼ in. | 1½ in. | 1¾ in. |
|---|---|---|---|
| Per doz | 10c. | 15c. | 20c. |
| Wt. per doz. | 10 oz | 14 oz. | 18 oz |

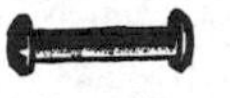

No. 93836.

No. 93836 **Halter bolts. Japanned iron.**

| Sizes | 1 in. | 1¼ in. | 1½ in. |
|---|---|---|---|
| Per doz | 6c. | 8c. | 10c. |
| Weight, per doz. | 10 oz. | 14 oz. | 18 oz. |

## Martingale Rings.

**These are inside measurements.**

No. 93837 **Genuine black rubber rings,** plain, light in weight, but strong. Per doz .......... **$0.50**

No. 93839 **Genuine black rubber rings,** imitation stitched edge; light but strong; diam. 1⅝ in.; weight per doz., 7 oz .......... **$0.65**

No. 93840 **Red Duranoid Rings,** 1⅝ in .......... 0.30

No. 93841 **White Duranoid Rings,** 1⅝ in .......... 0.30

No. 93842 **Blue Duranoid Ring,** 1⅝ in .......... 0.30

**Weight per doz., 14 oz.**

No. 93843 **Bone Rings,** red, 1 inch in diam .......... 0.40

No. 93844 **Bone Rings,** white, 1 inch in diam. .......... 0.40

No. 93845 **Bone Rings,** blue, 1 inch in diam .......... 0.40

**Weight per doz., 3 oz.**

No. 93846 **Celluloid Spreaders,** composed of three solid celluloid rings in assorted fancy colors. Weight each, about 4 oz.

Per string, **50c.**; per dozen strings .......... **$5.40**

## Celluloid Rings.

**Red, White and Blue.**

**Unless color is mentioned, we invariably send white.**

**Diameter, inches.**

| No. 93850 | 1¼ | 1⅜ | 1½ | 1⅝ | 1¾ | 2 | 2¼ |
|---|---|---|---|---|---|---|---|
| Each | $0.10 | $0.13 | $0.16 | $0.19 | $0.22 | $0.25 | $0.28 |
| Per doz | 1.00 | 1.40 | 1.75 | 2.15 | 2.50 | 2.80 | 3.15 |

## White Zylonite Rings.

**Diameter, inches.**

| No. 93852 | 1¼ | 1⅜ | 1½ | 1⅝ | 1¾ | 2 | 2¼ |
|---|---|---|---|---|---|---|---|
| Each | $0.09 | $0.11 | $0.13 | $0.16 | $0.19 | $0.22 | 0.25 |
| Per doz | .90 | 1.15 | 1.45 | 1.70 | 2.10 | 2.40 | 2.65 |

Weight on celluloid and zylonite rings, 5 to 17 oz. per dozen, according to size.

## Celluloid Loops.

No. 93854 **Celluloid Loops,** red, white, or blue (state color wanted), diam .......... ⅝ in. ¾ in.

Per dozen .......... **$0.30 $0.32**

**Weight per dozen, 2 oz.**

The above loops are used for connecting any size rings for making spreader straps.

## Morsman Buckel Shields.

**Buckle Shields are very ornamental on harness and protects the horse's tail from being pulled out on the buckle tongues.**

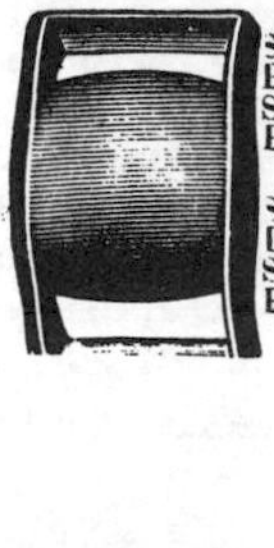

No. 93958 **Brass.**

| Size | ½ in. | ⅝ in. | ¾ in. |
|---|---|---|---|
| Per dozen | .70 | .80 | .90 |
| Size | ⅞ in. | 1 in. | 1⅛ in. | 1¼ in |
| Per doz. | $1.00 | $1.10 | $1.45 | $1.70 |

No. 93859 **Same in Nickel.**

| Size | ½ in. | ⅝ in. | ¾ in. |
|---|---|---|---|
| Per dozen | .75 | .85 | .95 |
| Size | ⅞ in. | 1 in. | 1⅛ in. | 1¼ in. |
| Per doz | $1.05 | $1.15 | $1.50 | $1.75 |

Weight per dozen, 6, 8, 10, 12, 14, 16, 18

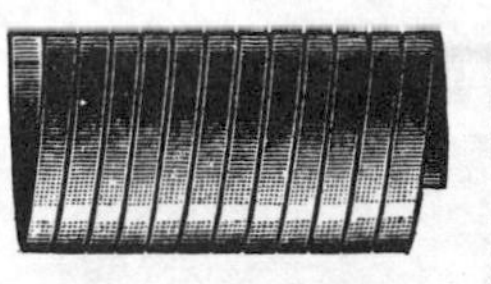

No. 93861. **Adjustable Axle Washers;** are made from the best oak tanned stock, durable and satisfactory; can be cut out to fit any nut or collar, have been thoroughly tested, and are superior to all others. Put up 100 washers in a box.

| Size | ⅝ in. | 1 in. | 1⅛ in. | 1¼ in. | 1½ in. |
|---|---|---|---|---|---|
| Per 100 | **15c.** | **18c.** | **22c.** | **26c.** | **32c.** |

## Crystal Rosettes.

No. 92862. **Pflueger's Fancy Crystal Rosettes,** for bridles, 1¾ inches in diameter. Put up six pairs on a card especially for **Sears, Roebuck & Co.** No two pair on the card alike, all being of different colors and different designs. All new patterns. Ornamental, strong and durable.

Price, per pair **15c**; per card of 6 pairs .......... **$0.82**

**Postage, per pair 3c; per card 20c.**

No. 93864 **Sterling Silver Rosettes,** solid metal (18 per cent. silver), ⅛ inch thick. Hard brazed loop, absolutely non-pull-off, mirror finish, smooth, plain surface, two inches in diameter.

One pair on card, per pair .......... **$0.30**

No. 93865 **Black Terraloid Bridle Rosettes,** commonly called rubber; neat and tasty and nothing to soil or tarnish; require no cleaning. Diameter, 1⅝ inches; weight per pair 2 oz.

Per pair, **10**; per doz. pair .......... **$1.00**

## Hame Tops

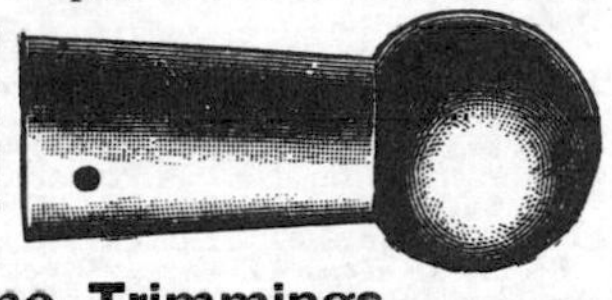

No. 93866 **Brass Ball Hame Tops,** can be used on any Concord Hames; weight per pair, 7 oz.

Per pair... **$0.30**

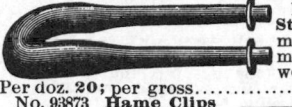

## Hame Trimmings.

No. 93869 **Hame Line Rings,** with studs and burrs; weight, per doz. 18 ounces. Per doz .......... **$0.25**

No. 93870 **Hame Breast Strap Rings,** with studs and burrs; weight per doz., 30 oz. Per doz .......... **$0.35**

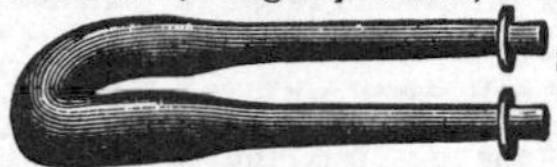

No. 93871 **Hame Staples** with burrs, made of best quality malleable iron; weight per doz., 30 oz.

Per doz. **20**; per gross .......... **$2.00**

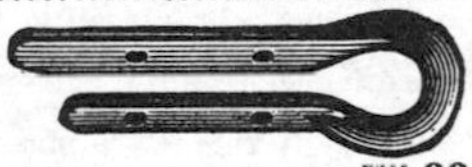

No. 93873 **Hame Clips** made of best quality wrought iron without rivets; weight per dozen 38 oz.

Per doz. **20c**; per gross .......... **$2.00**

No. 93874 **Hame Rivets,** put up in one pound packages. We do not break packages. Per pound **$0.15**

## Hame Loops.

No. 93875 **Screw Hame Bottom Loops;** loop will admit 1 inch strap; weight per doz. 14 oz.

Per doz .......... **$0.35**

## Cockeys.

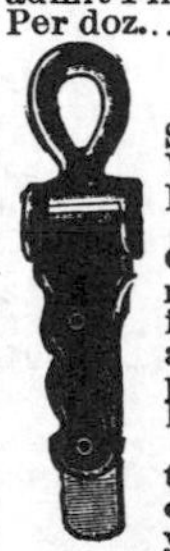

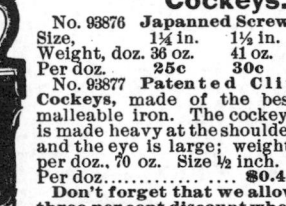

No. 93876 **Japanned Screw Cockeys.**

| Size, | 1¼ in. | 1½ in. | 1¾ in. | 2in |
|---|---|---|---|---|
| Weight, doz. | 36 oz. | 41 oz. | 45 oz. | 56oz. |
| Per doz. | **25c** | **30c** | **35c** | **50c** |

No. 93877 **Patented Clip Cockeys,** made of the best malleable iron. The cockeye is made heavy at the shoulder and the eye is large; weight, per doz., 70 oz. Size ½ inch.

Per doz .......... **$0.40**

**Don't forget that we allow three per cent discount when cash in full accompanies your order.**

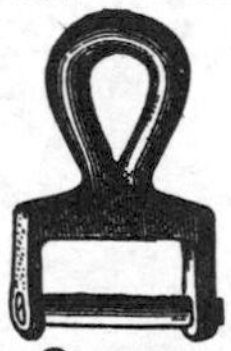

## Breast Strap Rollers with Snap.

No. 93880 **Breast Strap Roller,** with snap, 1½ inch, tinned. Each, **12c**; per doz .......... **$1.30**

No. 93881 **Breast Strap Roller,** with snap, 1¾ inch, tinned. Each, **14c**; per doz .......... **$1.52**

No. 93882 **Breast Strap Roller,** with snap, 2 inch, tinned. Each, **17c**; per doz .......... **$1.85**

Weight per pair, 18 oz., 20 oz., 22 oz.

## Combination Neck Yoke Snap.

No. 93883 **Combination Neck Yoke Strap and Breast Strap Slide.** The strongest, safest and most durable snap made. It is indispensable to the farmer, as it is the only snap that can be used successfully on farm machinery. Tinned finish.

| Sizes | 1½ in. | 1¾ in. | 2 in |
|---|---|---|---|
| Weight, each | 10 oz. | 11 oz. | 12 oz. |
| Each | $0.15 | $0.16 | $0.17 |
| Per doz. | 1.75 | 1.80 | 1.85 |

## Breast Strap Slides.

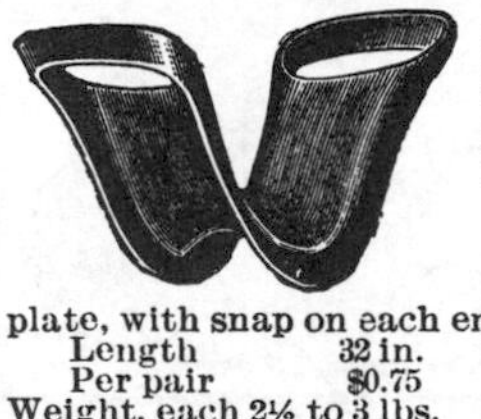

No. 93885 **Breast Strap Slides.** Japanned iron.

| Size | 1½ in. | 1¾ in. | 2 in |
|---|---|---|---|
| Wt. pr. | 10 oz. | 12 oz. | 15 oz |
| Each | $0.03 | $0.04 | $0.06 |
| Per doz | .33 | .43 | .65 |

## Breast Chains.

No. 93887 **Covert's Patent Breast Chains.** XC plate, with snap on each end, extra strong.

| Length | 32 in. | 36 in. | 40 in. | 44 in. |
|---|---|---|---|---|
| Per pair | $0.75 | $0.85 | $1.00 | $1.15 |

Weight, each 2½ to 3 lbs.

No. 93888 **S. R. & Co's Fancy Chain Martingales,** for buggy or carriage use. Finely nickel plated. Each, **$1**; per doz .......... **$11.50**

No. 93889 **S. R. & Co's. Fancy Chain Martingales.** All steel, brightly polished. Weight, each, 6 oz. Each, **50**; per doz .......... **$5.75**

## Heel Chains.

No. 93892 **Heel Chains for Ends of Traces.** Four links and dee, 5-16 inch wire. For 1½ inch traces, per set of four, **35c**; for 1¾ inch traces, per set of four, **38c**; for 2 inch traces, per set of four, **40c.** Weight, per set, 3 to 3¾ pounds.

## Horse Tooth Rasps.

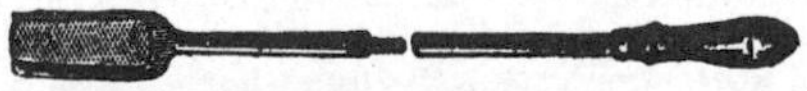

No. 93893. **House's Patent Horse Tooth Rasps,** with handle, fine polished, complete and ready for use. Each .......... **$0.90**

No. 93894. **Extra Steel Files,** 3½ inches long, for horse tooth rasps. Weight, each, 4 oz. Each, **$0.18**

## Horse Tail Holder.

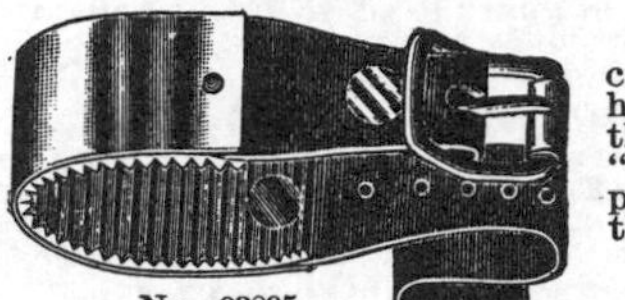

No. 93895.

No. 93895. For clasping and holding together the hair of the "horse's tail," protecting it from the mud.

Each .......... **$0.18**

Per doz .......... **2.00**

## Common Sense Horse Tail Clasp.

No. 93896. This is a simple device for holding the hair of a horse's tail. It is made of one piece of spring brass, without buckles or other contrivances.

Weight, each, 2 oz.

Each .......... **$0.14**

Per dozen .......... **1.50**

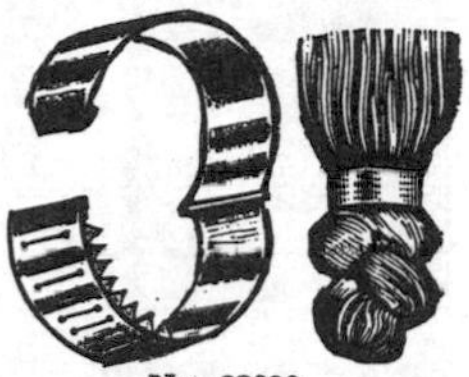

No. 93896.

## Sweat Scrapers.

No. 93897 **Brass Sweat Scrapers,** 1½ inches wide, 20 inches long, with wood handles on each end.

Each .......... **$0.40** Per doz .......... **$4.50**

No. 93898 With wood handles on each end. Weight, each, 12 oz.

Each .......... **$0.55** Per doz .......... **$6.00**

No. 93899 **Wood Scrapers.** Weight, each, 4 oz.

Each .......... **$0.15**

## Hoof Picks.

No. 93900 **Hoof Pick and Cork Screw,** combined. Each .......... **$0.35**

No. 93901 **Hoof Pick,** single instrument. Each .......... **$0.25**

Weight, each, 4 oz.

## Horse Blanket Pins.

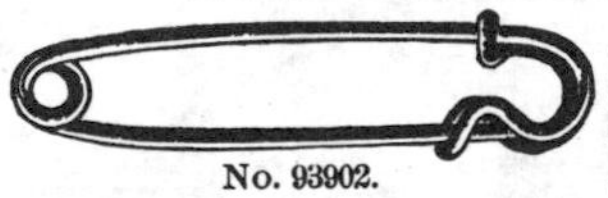

No. 93902.

No. 93902 **Blanket Pins,** protected points, Size, 3½ in.

Per doz .......... **$0.40**

Weight per dozen, 8 oz.

## Cribbing Muzzles.

No. 93906. **Wire Cribbing Muzzle,** complete with headstall. Each .......... **$1.50**

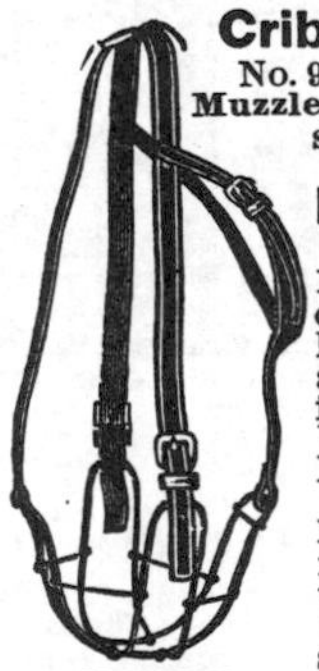

No. 93907

## Horse Muzzles

No. 93907. **Leather Horse Muzzle,** made of No. 1 russet leather having 1⅛ inch halter attachment, and ⅝ inch throat latch. Weight, each, 25 oz.

Each .......... **$1.25**

No. 93908, **Wire Horse Muzzle.** Is made of woven wire and bound with wooly sheepskin, having 1¼ inch halter attachment and ⅝ inch throat latch. Weight, each, 36 oz.

Each .......... **$1.50**

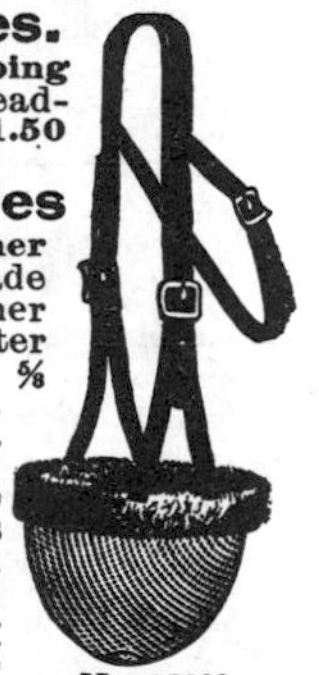

No. 93908

☞ When ordering always give number of article required.

☞ We allow 3 per cent. discount when cash accompanies the order.

No. 93910 **Horse Muzzle,** made of black leather, with head piece and throat latch. Just the thing for vicious horses, also prevent them from eating the corn etc., when working. Weight, about 20 ounces.

Each .......... **$0.80**

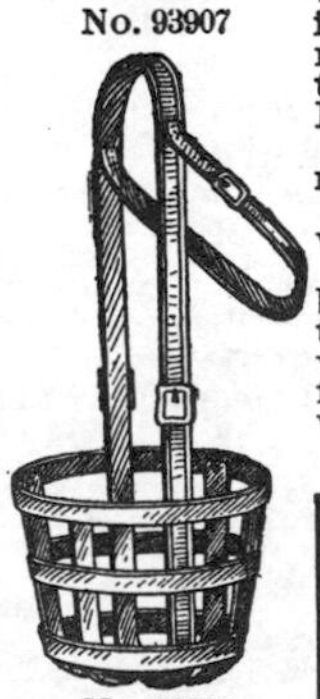

No. 93636.

**Our Hardware Department, shows a complete line of Woven Wire Fencing and Poultry Netting.**

**HOW ABOUT YOUR ORDER?**

## Stallion Support.

For Track or Road Use.

No. 93913 This support is manufactured from the purest quality of rubber made, and has met with universal success with all horsemen and stallion owners. Weight, each, 10 oz. Each............**$1.85**

**Directions.**—When not in use, keep in a cool, dark place. Before applying, wring out pouch in water. When ordering state size, small, medium or large.

## The Perfection Stallion Guard.

No. 93914. **Perfection Stallion Guard.** Patented in U. S., Canada and all the leading countries in Europe. 3,000 sold in first season. All molded rubber; no metal or rigid material, no tacks, torture or chafing, no irritation or danger. They are flexible, simple, humane, clean and safe. Interferes with none of nature's functions. Fits like a glove. One buckle attaches or detaches, puts on or off in thirty seconds. Weighs less than two pounds complete. The perfection is guaranteed to be all and do all that is claimed or money refunded. No stallion owner should be without it. Price, each.............**$5.30**

## Singeing Lamps.

No. 93915. **Singeing Lamps,** for removing hair from horses ears and other places where clippers cannot be used to advantage; use kerosene oil; wick furnished with lamp, Each............................**$2.50**

## Carriage Top Dressing.

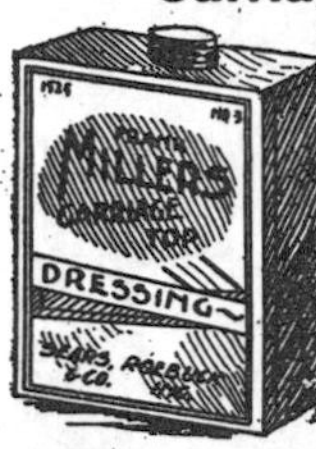


No. 93916 **Frank Miller's Dressing** for buggy and carriage tops. Gives an elastic, durable, jet black, waterproof gloss. Can be easily used on the finest stock. Directions on each can.

Pint cans. Each........ **60c**
Per dozen............ **$6.50**

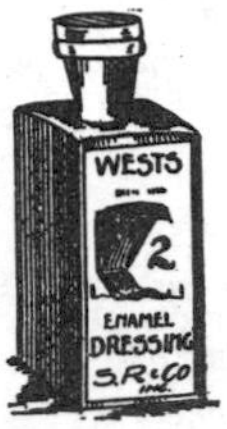


No. 93917 **"West's" Celebrated Top Dressing.** Best ever used for preserving the tops of buggies and carriages. Gives an elegant gloss and makes the leather waterproof.

½ Pint cans............................**45c**
Pint cans..................................**70c**

## Harness Dressing.

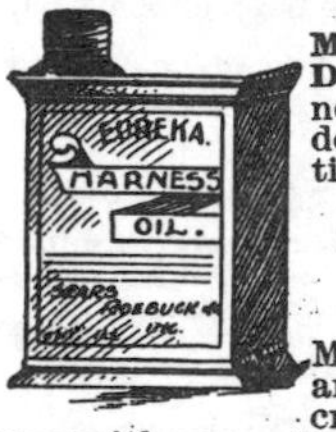


No. 93918. **Frank Miller's Harness Dressing** for harness, saddles, fly nets, etc. Gives a beautiful finish, does not lose its luster. Directions tions for use on every package.

Pint cans, each.... ........**25c**
Quarts ........................**42c**

## Harness Oils.

No. 93919 **Eureka Harness Oil.** Makes the leather soft and glossy and prevents the harness from cracking. Put up in lithographic cans with screw top.

½ Pint can..............**18c** Pint can...............**25c**
Quart can.................**35c** ½ Gallon can............**65c**
Gallon can.......**90c**

## Axle Oils.

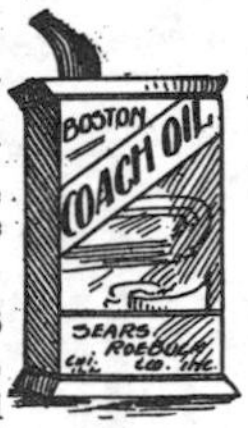


No. 93920 **The Well-known Boston Coach Oil** for all kinds of vehicles. Does not gum or corrode. Good in winter. Put up in spout top cans.

Pint can.....**25c** Quart can......**35c**
½ Gallon can **65c** Gallon.........**90c**

## Harness Soap.

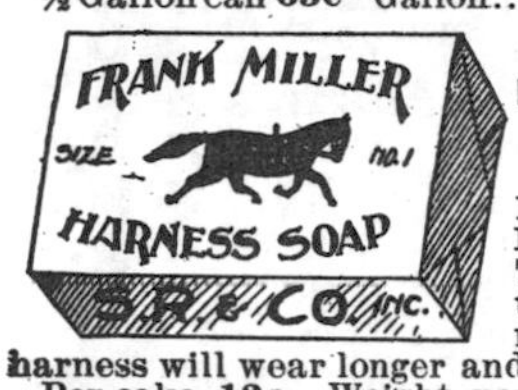


No. 93921 **Frank Miller's Harness Soap.** This is without question the best harness soap made. By using it your harness will wear longer and look better.

Per cake, 12c. Weight, per cake, 12 ozs.

No. 93922 **Crown Soap.** The Chiswick Pure English Crown Soap.

Pint jars, each......**45c** Quart jars, each......**65c**

No. 93923 **Bonner Harness Soap.** One of the most reliable soaps in the market. Cleans quickly and makes the leather soft and pliable. Put up in tin pans with cover.

1 ℔ pans..............**25c** 2¼ ℔ pans..............**35c**
5 ℔ pans..........**70c**

## Peruvian Horse Salve.

No. 93924 **The only true Healing Salve** in the market. Cures all galls from saddle or collar and can be used while working the horse. Best thing in the world for stock cut by wire fences. Put up in tin boxes. 2 ozs.........**20c** Per dozen..........**$2.00**

## Horse Foot Remedy.

No. 93926 **Baum's Horse Foot Remedy** is a sure cure for all ailments of horses feet, and for cuts or wounds, soreness over the kidneys, etc. Full description on can, also a brush for applying the remedy. Quart can, each......**50c** Per dozen......**$5.50**

No. 93928 **Neatsfoot Oil.** Quart cans.................**35c**

No. 93929 **Gladding's Hoof Dressing.** Quart cans, with brushes, each.............................**56c**

No. 93930 **Continental Hoof Ointment.** ¼ ℔ cans, each.....**18c** Per dozen...........**$2.00**

**Special Vehicle and Harness Catalogue free**

# Leather

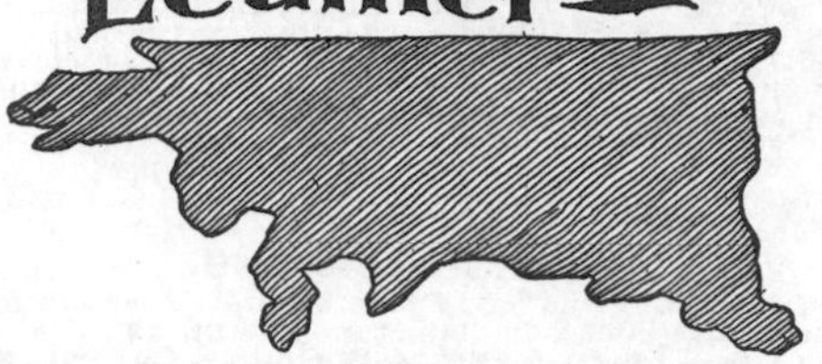

**We sell Harness Leather and Findings at the closest margin, in fact we look for no profit in handling it. We offer genuine High Grade Stock only, and it must not be confused with the cheaply tanned and inferior leather so frequently sold.**

## Harness, Leather, Etc.

No. 94000. **Hemlock Tanned Black Harness Leather,** B grade, whole sides only; sides weighing from 17 to 21 lbs. Per lb.................................**$0.29**

No. 94001. **No. 1 Hemlock Black Harness Leather,** extra quality; weight per side from 17 to 22 lbs. Per lb..................................................**$0.31**

No. 94003. **Pure Oak Harness Leather,** good B grade, whole sides only; sides weigh from 17 to 22 lbs. Per lb.................................................**$0.32**

No. 94004. **Extra Quality No. 1 Oak Tanned Leather,** black; weight per side from 17 to 22 lbs. Per lb..................................................**$0.34**

No. 94006. **Russet Leather Sheep Skins,** good quality, medium size. Price each.............**$0.75**

No. 94007. **Russet Leather Sheep Skins,** good quality, large size. Price each...............**$0.90**

Fo. 94009. **Russet Leather Sheep Skins,** good, large size, for blacksmith's and lumbermen's aprons, etc. Price each.............................................**$1.00**

No. 94011. **Sheep Skins Tanned with the Wool** on, used for lining saddles, harness breeching and breast collars, extra large. Price each........**$1.00**

**NOTE.—All of our different grades of Harness Leather are carefully selected from packer's steer hides.**

No. 94014. **Deer Skins Dressed with the Hair on.** Guaranteed to be No. 1 quality. These skins are used for carriage or floor rugs, for binding harness, facing harness collars and making collar pads, and it is especially valuable for use by bed-ridden invalids, being placed under the sheets to prevent or cure bed-sores, and are frequently ordered by physicians for that purpose. They are graded very closely in regard to size on account of their value. **The price is regulated by the size, ranging from $3.75 to $5.25 each.**

**NOTE.—Owing to the uncertainty of the leather and hide market, the prices on these goods are subject to change without notice.**

## Saddle Strings and Lacing for Heading.

No. 94016. **No. 1 Raw Hide Lace or Whang Leather,** oiled and tanned. One side measures from 7 to 18 square feet.
Per square foot.......................................**$0.27**

No. 94018. **Belt Lacing or Saddle Strings,** cut from No. 1 oak tanned raw hide or whang leather, put up in bunches of 50 feet each,

Per bunch, ½ inch.......... .........**$0.53**
" " ⅝ " ....................... **68**
" " ¾ " ....................... **90**

## Steel Thong Awls.

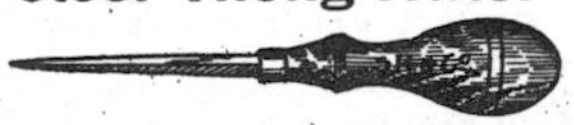

No. 94020 **A very handy tool for mending harness** and repairing belts and heavy strap work of any kind. Made very strong, with round handles. Length of awl, 7 inches.

Price, each.............................................**$0.22**
Price, per dozen..........................................**2.35**

## Harness Maker's Collar Awls.

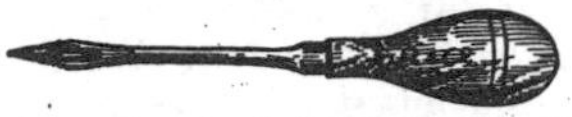

No. 94022 **Drawing Awls or Collar Awls,** as they are called, are made with large eye for sewing horse collars with leather thongs or whangs. The awl is made of the best tool steel, highly tempered. Length from 8 to 9 inches.

Price, each.............................................**$0.35**
Price, per dozen..........................................**3.75**

## Leather Gauge Knife.

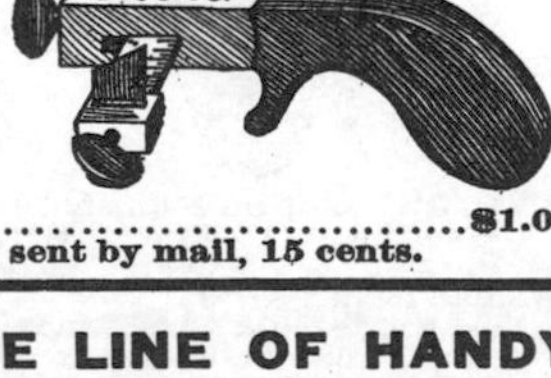


No. 94024 **This is the best hollow iron handle Guage Knife in the market.** Will cut from ⅛ to 4 inches in width. It is the same knife used by all practical harness makers.

Price each..............................................**$1.00**

**Postage, if sent by mail, 15 cents.**

**A COMPLETE LINE OF HANDY COBBLER'S OUTFITS ON PAGE 197.**

## Harness Maker's Round Knife.

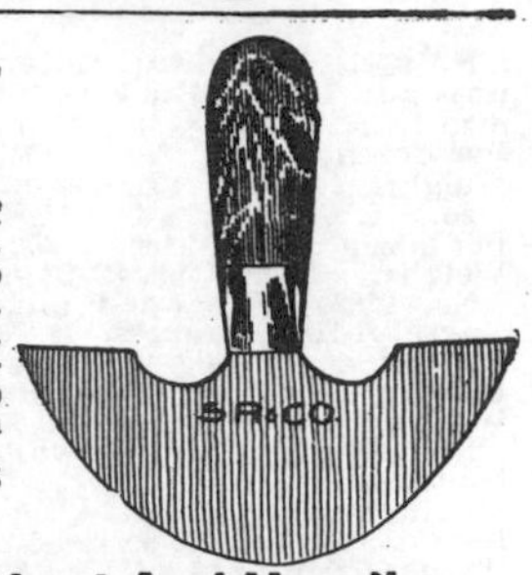


No. 94025 **Made of the best tool steel,** elegantly tempered to take a very sharp edge. Rosewood handles. Every one is guaranteed. Blades measure 5 inches across from point to point.

Price, each....**$1.05**

## Osborne's Patent Awl Handles.

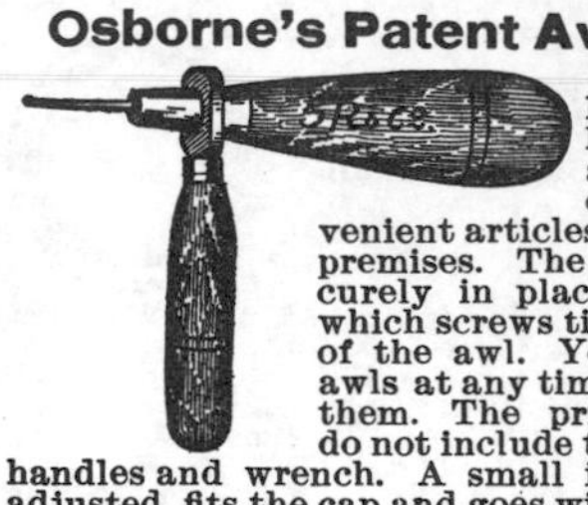

No. 94027. **This handy little tool has a large sale,** and is considered one of the most convenient articles to have about the premises. The awls are held securely in place by a metal cap, which screws tightly on the socket of the awl. You can change the awls at any time without breaking them. The prices quoted below do not include the awls, simply the handles and wrench. A small iron wrench, nicely adjusted, fits the cap and goes with each handle.

Price, each.............................................**$0.20**
Price, per dozen..........................................**2.15**
Weight, each, 4 oz.

No. 94028 **Revolving Spring Punch,** with four tubes of different sizes. Weight, 14 oz.
Price, each.............................................**$1.10**

No. 94029 **Revolving Spring Punch,** with six tubes of different sizes. Weight, 14 oz.
Price, each.............................................**$1.50**

## Harness Maker's Edging Tool.

No. 94030 **A very handy Tool** for removing the sharp corners of any new strap work. Made 5 in. long, nicely polished.

Price each,.............................................**$0.15**
Price, per doz.............................................**1.60**

## Harness Needles, Awls and Handles.

No. 94031 **We have Harness Needles** put up in packages of 25 needles, in assorted sizes from No. 0 to No. 4.

Per Paper.............................................**$0.12**
Per dozen Papers..........................................**1.28**

No. 94032 **Common Turned Wood Sewing Awl Handles.** Nicely finished and smooth.
Price per dozen.........................................**$0.16**

## Harness Repair Outfit.

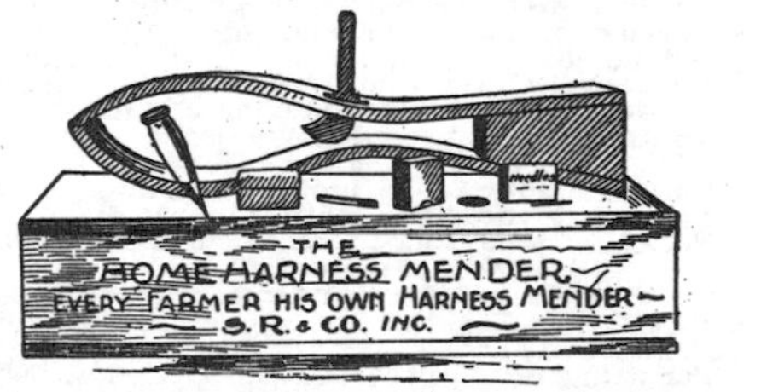


**This is a very convenient assortment of tools to have on any farm or business place.** It can also be used around mills for mending belts, etc. It contains the following articles: One strong lever clamp, round punch, sewing awl and handle, rivet set, ball of wax and a ball of thread, package of assorted needles, and one paper of copper rivets and burrs. These goods are all put up the same and it is inconvenient to break sets, as the prices are so low. Each outfit is nicely packed in a wooden box, with hinged lid. Weight, about 10 lbs.

No. 94034. Price, each...................................**$1.45**

## Leather Splitting Machine.

No. 94037 **This is the Genuine Osborn Splitting Knife,** which has a wide reputation and is considered the best article in the market for the purpose intended. They are made with iron frames, latest pattern. Can be set to any gauge you desire, and can be fastened to any table or work bench with the utmost ease.

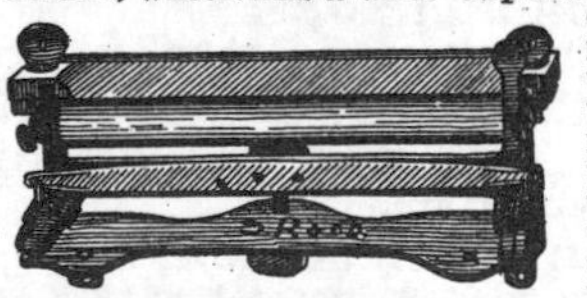

| | | | |
|---|---|---|---|
| Sizes | 5 inch. | 6 inch. | 7 inch. |
| Weight, each | 6 lbs. | 7 lbs. | 8 lbs. |
| Price, each | **$4.10.** | **$4.50.** | **$4.65** |

**We can make you prices on larger machines, from 8 to 12 inches, upon application.**

**When buying Hardware from our Catalogue, you have practically the same advantage as the retailer who selects from a complete wholesale stock. . . . . . . . . . . . . . .**

## Farmer's Handy Repair Kit.

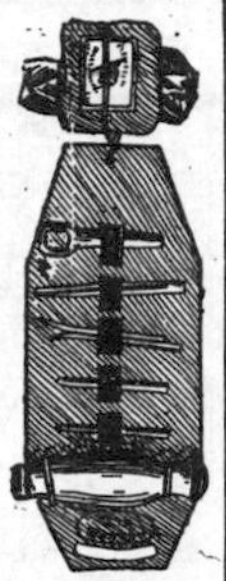

No. 94038 **This is a most convenient assortment of tools** for repairing harness and other leather work around a farm. It contains handle wrench, two dozen large harness needles, two crooked awl blades, two harness awl blades, a ball of thread and a ball of wax.
Price, each........................**$0.50**

## Harness Horse.

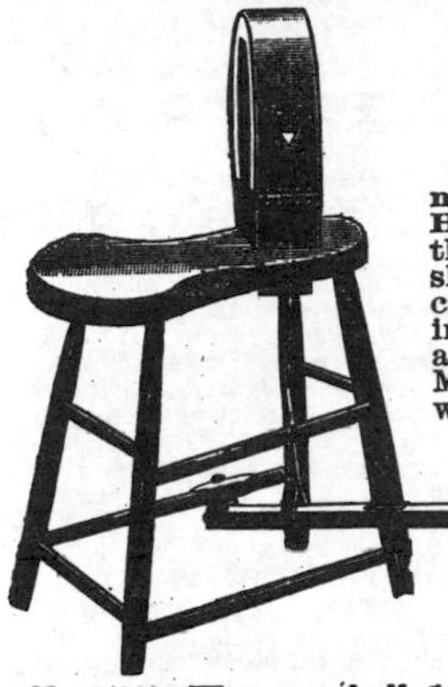

No. 94040 **Harness maker's Stitching Horse.** This is something every horse owner should have. Any man can do his own repairing and save his time, as well as his money. Made of good sound wood.
Without jaw strap, each........**$2.75**
Weight, 18 lbs.
Price for stitching horse with jaw strap........**$3.00**

No. 94041 **Wax,** per ball, 1c; per doz.......**$0.10**
No. 94043 **Harness Thread,** best No. 10 "H. B." thread, natural linen color, 2 oz. balls.
Per ball 12c; per pound (8 balls)..........**$0.90**

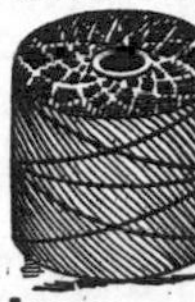

No. 94044 **No. 10 "H. B." Super Thread,** wound on tubes; waste by snarling, or tangling prevented. Natural linen color, 2 oz. balls.
Per ball 15c; per lb. (8 balls) **$1.05**
No. 94045 **No. 12 "H. B." Devonshire Thread,** wound on tubes. natural linen color, 2 oz. balls.
Per ball 16c; per lb. (8 balls) **$1.15**

## Rapid Harness Menders.

No. 94047 **Rapid Harness Menders.** Simple, practical and cheap. Repair your own harness, halters and straps. No punch, rivet set or anvil required; just drive them in and clinch them. Put up in tin boxes, assorted sizes in each box. Regular retail price, 25 cents per box.
Our price, per box 15c; per doz. boxes........ **$1.62**
Weight, per box, about 7 ounces.

## TURF GOODS.

**It will be to your interest to look over our line of Turf Goods illustrated below.** We have made a special effort to offer this year the best line of these goods ever put on the market. They are **strictly guaranteed in regard to quality and workmanship,** and you will notice that they are made especially in three sizes. **Be sure and state the size wanted when ordering.**

## Ankle Boots.

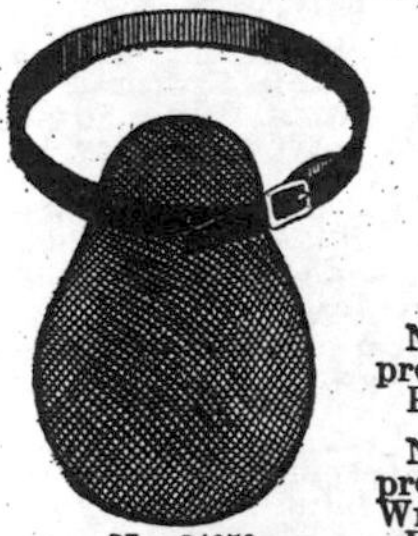

No. 94050.

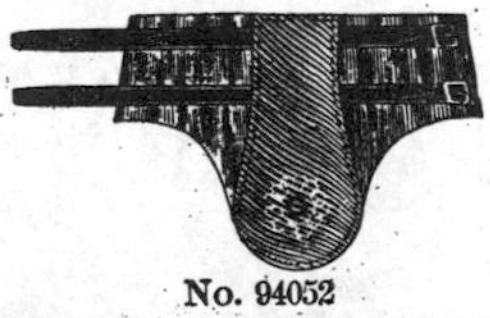

No. 94052

No. 94052 **Russet Sole Leather,** pressed, one strap with pad,
Price, each..............**$0.25**

No. 94052 **Russet Leather,** pressed, two straps; Kersey Wrapper.
Price, each..............**$0.35**

## Ankle Boots.

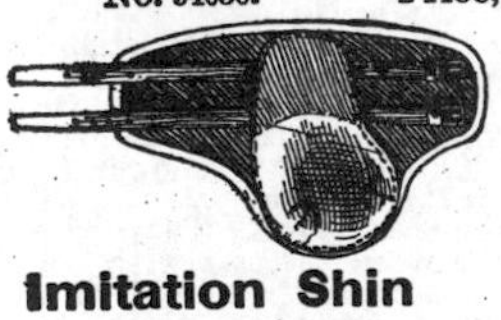

No. 94054 **Russet or Black Leather,** two straps, blue felt wrapper, chamois bound; heel extension.
Price, each....**$0.50**

## Imitation Shin Boots.

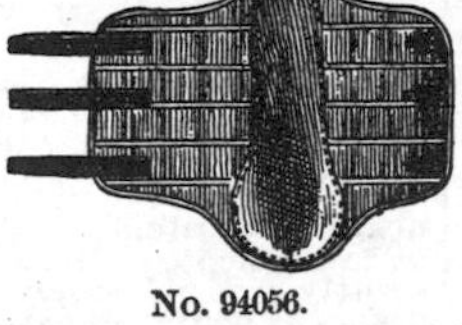

No. 94056.

No. 94056 **Front Shin and Ankle Boots,** three straps, English Kersey wrapper, chamois bound.
Per pair........**$1.30**
No. 94058. **Hind Shin and Ankle Boots,** Russet Leather, three straps, English Kersey wrapper, chamois bound.
Per pair.........**$1.50**

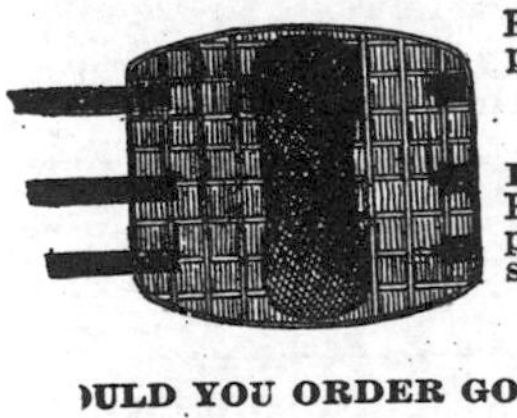

No. 94059 **Front Shin Boots,** Russet Leather, English Kersey wrapper, chamois bound, 3 straps.
Per pair.........**$1.70**

## Road Knee Boots.

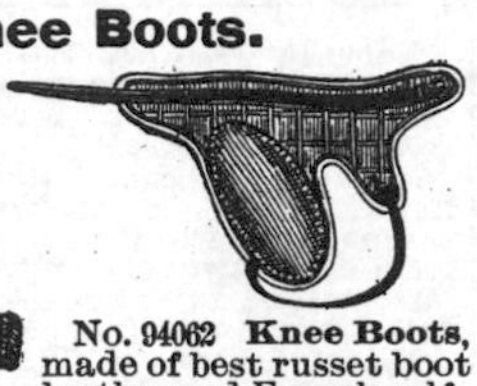

No. 94061 **Made of Solid Russet Leather,** kersey wrapper, chamois bound, two straps; small, medium and large.
Per pair..........**$1.90**

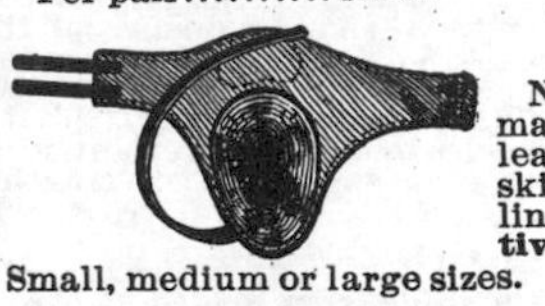

No. 94062 **Knee Boots,** made of best russet boot leather and French calfskin. Heavy blue, felt lined, 3 straps. **Positively all hand made.** Small, medium or large sizes. Per pair.......**$3.00**

## Quarter Boots.

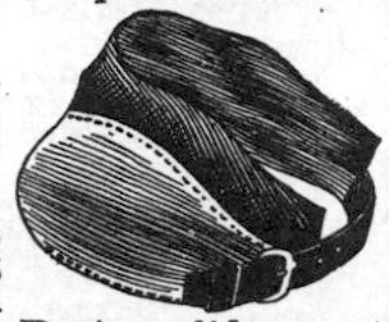

No. 94064 **Close Fitting Quarter Boots,** solid leather quarters and heels, blue heavy felt body, one strap. Small, medium and large sizes.
Per pair..............**$1.40**

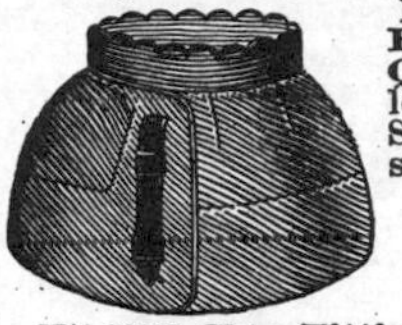

No. 94065 **Bell Quarter Boots,** solid russet leather, brown felt lined. Small, medium and large sizes.
Per pair..............**$1.90**

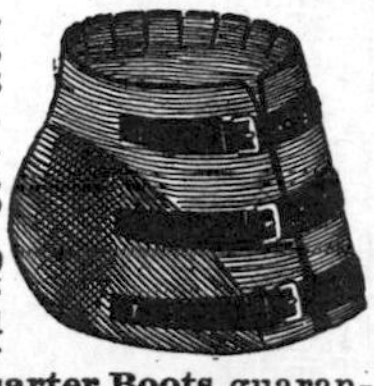

No. 98068 **Close Fitting Quartes Boots,** extra heavy russet stock, solid elkskin body, 3 rawhide billets, extra heavy. Positively all hand made. Small, medium and large sizes.
Per Pair..............**$2.80**

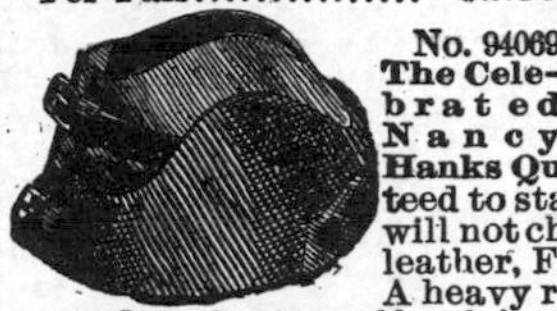

No. 94069 **The Celebrated Nancy Hanks Quarter Boots,** guaranteed to stay on and positively will not chafe. Made of solid leather, French Calfskin lined. A heavy rawhide strap passes around the bottom of hoof; has inside steel protection to quarters. **Positively all hand Made.** Small medium and large sizes.
Per Pair..............**$3.60**

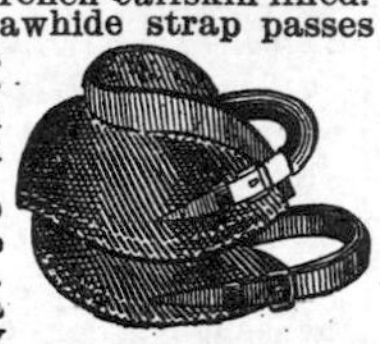

No. 94070 **California Style Quarter Boots,** side hinge, No. 1 russett boot leather, extra heavy elkskin body. **Positively all hand Made.** Small medium and large sizes.
Per pair..............**$3.70**

## Shoe Boil Roll.

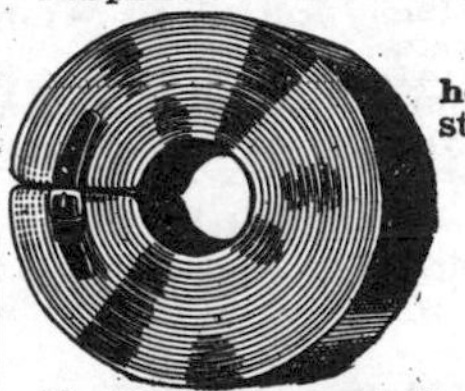

No. 94072. **Made of extra heavy sail duck,** very strong and serviceable.
Price, each..........**$0.95**

## Scalping Boots.

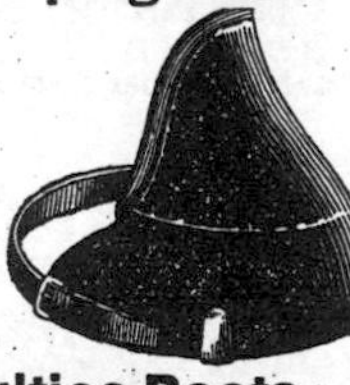

No. 94073. **Boots made of best sole leather,** with steel spur (or strap if so ordered) heavy felt lined. Small, medium or large sizes.
Per pair..............**$1.45**

## Poultice Boots.

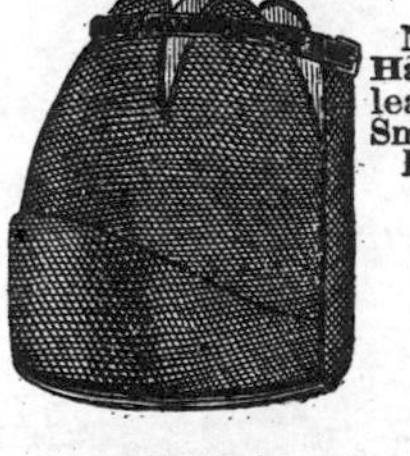

No. 94075 **Made of Heavy Harness Leather,** extra heavy leather bottom, riveted on. Small, medium or large sizes.
Per pair..............**$3.70**

## Trotting Balls.

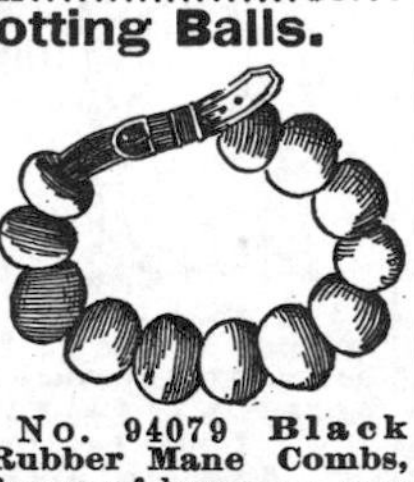

No. 94077 Rubber Trotting Balls. Per string.....**$0.16**
Per dozen strings ...**1.75**
Weight, per string, 7 oz.

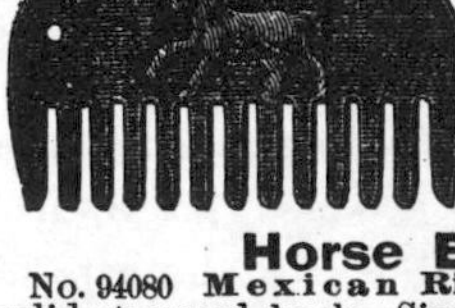

No. 94079 **Black Rubber Mane Combs,** figure of horse on one side, extra quality. Size, 2¾ x 4½ inches. Each, **13c**; per dozen, **$1.50.** Weight, each, 2 ounces.

## Horse Brushes.

No. 94080 **Mexican Rice Root Horse Brushes** solid strapped back. Size, 2¾ x 7 inches. Weight, each, 7 ounces. Each, **12c**; per dozen..........**$1.35**

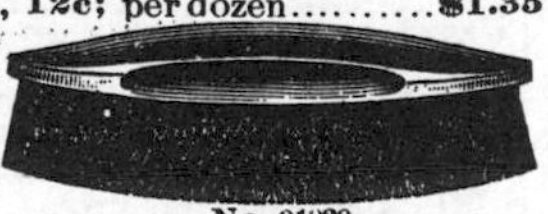

No. 91829

No. 94081 **Mexican Rice Root,** round back, pointed ends. Size, 2½ x 11 inches.
Each..............**$0.15**
Per dozen...... **1.65**

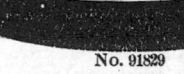

No. 94082 **Dandy, Strictly High Grade Rice Root,** warranted in every particular, round back and pointed ends. Size, 2½ x 11 inches.
Each............................................. **$0.30**
Per dozen........................................ **3.00**

No. 94083 **This is One of the Very Best Brushes Made.** Italian Rice root, drawn with brass wire, block 11x2½ inches, round back. This brush is particularly adapted to stock farms and livery trade, being capable of great service and without a doubt is the **Strongest and Best Rice Root Brush in the Market Today.**
Each............................................. **$0.50**
Per Dozen........................................ **5.38**

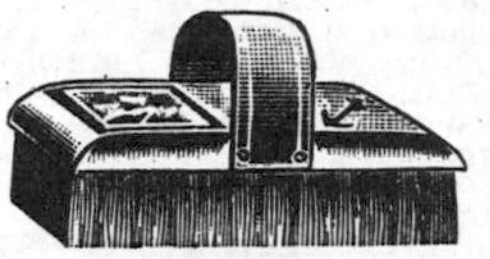

No. 94084.

No. 94084 **The Famous "Anchor" Brand Horse Brush.** All Palmetto fibre, solid back, with hand strap (see cut). Size, 3¾ x 7 inches. Weight, each, 10 oz.
Each, **18c**; per doz. **$1.95**

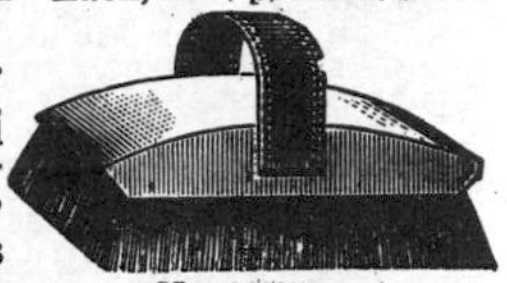

No. 94085.

No. 94085 **All Palmetto,** rounded, solid back, beveled ends, hand strap (see cut); size 3¼x6½ inches. Weight, each, 11 oz.
Each, **20c**; per doz. **$2.16**

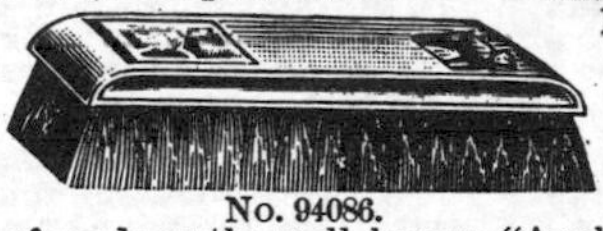

No. 94086.

No. 94086 **"Pug" Horse Brushes.** All Palmetto, solid back, face size 2¾x10 inches. This is the same grade of goods as the well-known "Anchor" and "Ruf and Redy" brushes. Weight, each, 13 oz.
Each, **22c**; per dozen.............................. **$2.40**

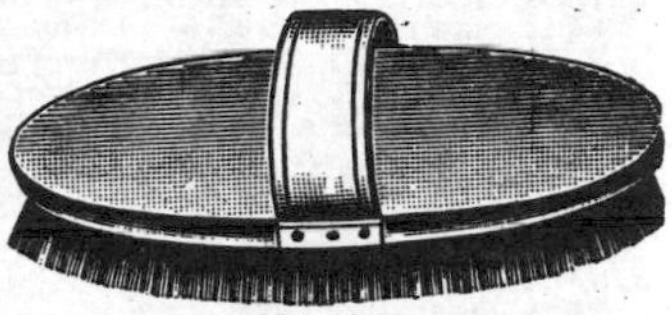

No. 94087.

No. 94087 **The Celebrated "Ruf and Redy,"** solid wood back, all Palmetto horse brush; size 4½x10 in.; weight, each, 15 oz.
Each.....**$0.25**
Per doz.. **2.70**

No. 94088 **Italian Rice Root,** solid back, hand strap, same shape as No. 94087; size 5x10 inches, excellent value. Weight, each 10 oz. Each......**$0.35**
Per doz........................................... **4.00**

No. 94089 **Dandy Brushes.** Fine imported Dandy horse brushes, made of the best selected Italian rice root, with English wood backs; length of fiber 2 inches, length of brushes 10½ inches. Weight, each, 12 oz. Each............................................. **$0.50**
Per doz........................................... **5.40**

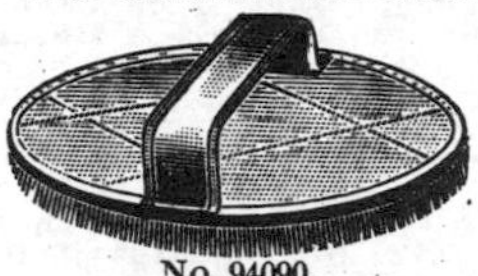

No. 94090.

No. 94090 **Horse Brushes.** Wood backs, oval shape, all tampico, gray center with white row outside. A large and well filled brush. Weight, each 11 oz.
Each..............**$0.13**
Per doz........... **1.40**

No. 94091 **Horse Brushes.** Leather backs; oval shape, gray tampico stock with white outside row. Weight, each, 7 oz. Each..............**$0.32**
Per doz........................................... **3.60**

No. 94092 **Horse Brushes.** Leather backs, oval shape, gray tampico center, with an outside row of black bristles. Weight, each, 9 oz. Each......**$0.30**
Per doz........................................... **3.40**

No. 94093 **Horse Brushes,** grain leather back, army pattern, gray center, outside row of white bristles. Weight, each, 10 oz.
Each....................**$0.48** Per doz............**$5.35**

No. 94094 **Horse Brushes,** leather back, oval shape, flat face, all black bristles. A large, sightly brush that will give good service. Weight, each, 12 oz.
Each....................**$0.45** Per doz............**$5.15**

No. 94095 **Horse Brushes,** grained leather back, army pattern, best grade of gray tampico center, with an outside row of white bristles. Weight, each, 10 oz. Each....**$0.50** Per doz............**$5.80**

No. 94097 **Horse Brushes,** grained russet leather back, oval shape, all white American bristles. Weight, each, 12 oz. Each, **60c**; per doz........**$6.50**

No. 94099 **Horse Brushes,** oval face, solid leather backs, 15 rows all black bristles. Weight, each, 10 oz.
Each...................**$0.80** Per doz............**$8.65**

No. 94101 **Horse Brush,** oval shape, leather backs, gray bristles. This brush is the very best value we have, warranted in every particular and especially adapted for livery trade and heavy farm work. We consider this to be the best brush we have in the catalogue for anywhere near the price. The bristles are very long. Price, each............................**$ 1.00**
Per dozen......................................... **10.50**
**This brush is our leader for this year.**

No. 94102 **Horse Brushes,** oval face, solid leather backs, all brown bristles. Weight, each, 10 oz.
Each..............**$1.25** Per dozen........ **14.50**

No. 94104 **Horse Brushes,** solid leather backs, oval shape, 15 rows all white Russia bristles, oval face. Weight, each, 11 oz. Each........................**$ 1.50**
Per dozen......................................... **16.20**

No. 94105 **Horse Brushes,** oval face, solid leather backs, 19 rows extra length, brown Russia bristles. Weight, each, 11 oz. Each........................**$ 1.90**
Per dozen......................................... **21.60**

No. 94106 **Horse Brushes,** solid leather backs, oval shape, 19 rows of natural yellow Russia bristles. This grade will wear as well as anything money can buy. Weight, each, 13 oz. Each..................**$ 2.50**
Per dozen......................................... **27.00**

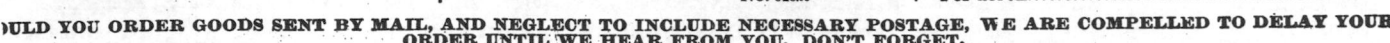

## Whips, Buggy or Carriage.

**Our Stock of Whips is Very Complete and We Can Save You at Least 50 Per Cent. on Anything in This Line. The Fact is We Will Sell You One Whip as Cheap as Dealers can Buy in Dozen Lots,**

No. 94110 **Plain Black,** Platted thread cover. Well finished, 6 ft., each 10c; Per dozen ........... **$1.00**

No. 94112 **Strongest and Best Whip Made in the World for the Money.** Black platted thread cover, Overin's patent linen thread lined, making the whip practically unbreakable, with a fancy nickel mount. Length 6 feet, each **18c.**; Per doz... **$2.00**

No. 94113 **Black Platted Thread Cover, Satin Finish,** with a beautiful chased and beaded nickel head, and one nickel ferrule; phil snap; length 6 feet. Each **25c.**; Per dozen................ **$2.88**

No. 94115 **Old-Fashioned Hand Made Stock Java,** Metal and linen lined, two English buttons, smooth finish, Philidelphia snap, can give either in wine or black color. A beauty for the price, 6 ft.; each **40c.** Per Dozen.............................. **$4.25**

No. 94117 **Black Metal and Buck-skin lined,** double thread cover, two English textile buttons, fine finish, best stock Java whip made, 6 or 6½ feet. Each.............. **$0.50** Per dozen......... **$5.25**

No. 94119 **Black, Thread Cover,** smooth finish, buckskin lined, handsomely mounted either in nickel or gilt, length 6 feet. Each............ **$0.60** Per dozen ..................................... **$6.00**

No. 94121 **Rawhide Whip,** with rawhide running one-half the length of the whip, best quality, black, thread cover, water-proof finish, either with nickel mounts, or with handsome buttons, in lengths:
5½ ft., each ....... **$0.60** 6 ft., each......... **$0.70**
6½ ft., each.......... **.80** 7 ft., each.......... **.80**

No. 94122 **Rawhide Whip,** with rawhide running the entire length of the whip from the snap, and extending out of the butt end of the whip, rawhide one piece not spliced, best that can be made, double thread cover, smooth finish, two buttons.
6½ ft., each........ **$0.75** Per doz............. **$8.50**

No. 94124 **One-half Whalebone,** metal and buckskin lined, black, smooth finish, two English buttons, English silk snap. 6 ft., each............ **$0.75**
6½ ft., each........................................ **.80**

No. 94125 **No. 1 Whalebone through from snap to handle,** not spliced, black thread cover, smooth finish, buck-skin lined, three English buttons, Philadelphia silk snap, 6 ft., each ..................... **$1.25**
6½ ft., each........ **$1.37** 7 ft., each.............. **1.50**

No. 94127 **Rawhide Sulky or Cart Whip,** in wine color or black, with two beautiful buttons, or with nickel head and ferrule, length 4½ ft., each.. **$0.50**

No. 94128 **Ladies' Riding Whips, 25c., 50c., 75c., $1.00, $1.25** and **$1.50** each, according to style and quality.

## Riding Crops.

No. 94130 **Gentlemen's Imported Hunting or Riding Crops,** made of Malacca, with English buck horn hooks and elk skin loops. Each............ **$2.00**

No. 94132 **Ladies' Imported Hunting or Riding Crops,** Malacca stocks, with English buck horn hooks and elk skin loops. Each.................. **$1.60**

## Express Whip.

No. 94134 **Express Whips,** Java stock handle, black thread cover, one nickel ferrule, white horse hide, braided drop top. Length, 6 feet.
Each ................................................... **$0.40**

## Solid Leather Team Whips.

No. 94135 **Team Whips,** body is made of solid leather cover of oil tanned leather, thong stitched, snake style XX. Length, 5 feet.......................... **$0.58**

No. 94137 **Team Whips,** body of solid leather, cover of oil tanned leather, thong stitched, snake style, (XX). Length, 5½ feet.............................. **$0.63**
6 feet.......................................................... **0.70**

No. 94138 **Colorado Team Whips,** made of oil tanned kip, double covered, sewed with buckskin. one-half kip and one-half eight plaid buckskin, shot loaded, 6½ feet long. Weight, 28 oz. Each.... **$1.40**

No. 94139 **Colorado Team Whips,** made of oil tanned kip, double covered, sewed with buckskin, one-half kip and one-half eight plaid buckskin, shot loaded, 7 feet long. Weight, 32 oz. Each...... **$1.65**

## Drovers' Whips.

No. 94141 **Boys' Drover Whips,** 6 plait, whip lash 6 feet long, wired on 9 inch revolving handle, California style. Each.......................... **$0.42**

No. 94142 **Boys' Drover Whips,** 6 plait, 7 feet long, 9 inch handle, California style; lash fastened securely. Each.............................................. **$0.50**

No. 94143 **Boys' Drover Whips,** 8 feet long, 9 inch revolving handle, 6 plait lash finely attached to handle. Each................................................ **$0.60**

No. 94144 **Drovers' Whips,** revolving handle, Jacksonville knot, 8 plait kip, puck point; length, 9 feet. Each.................................................. **$0.75**

No. 94146 **Drovers' Whips,** 10 inch revolving handle, lace fastener, 6 plait kip, buck point; length, 10 feet. Each................................................ **$1.10**

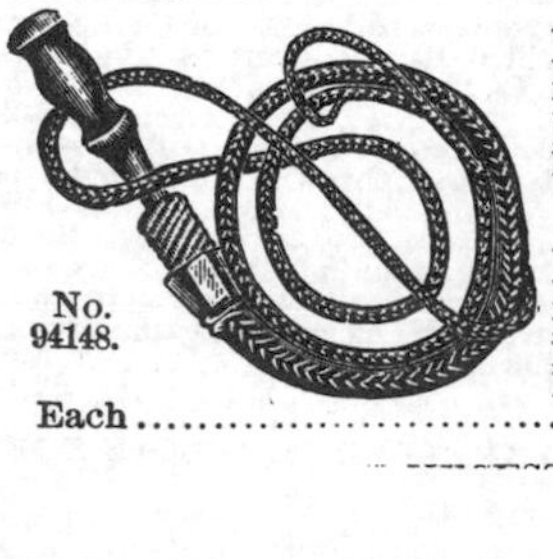

No. 94148.

No. 94148 **Drovers' Whips,** 8 plait, oiled kip, buckskin point, full Jacksonville knot and revolving handle. Length 10 ft. Each............ **$1.25**

No. 94149 **Drovers' Whips,** 8 plait oiled kip, buckskin point, full Jacksonville knot and revolving handle. Length 12 ft. Each ......................................................... **$1.35**

No. 94151 **Drovers' Whips,** 8 plait oiled kip, buckskin point, revolving handle and full Jacksonville knob. Length, 14 ft. Each........................ **$1.58**

No. 94152 **Drovers' Whip,** shot leaded, 12 plait, genuine buckskin, full Jackson knob, revolving handle; length 10 ft. Nothing neater, finer or better made. Each......................................... **$2.51**

No. 94154 **Drovers' Whips,** shot loaded, 8 plait, oiled calfskin with buckskin point, revolving handle, full Jacksonville knot; length, 10 feet. Each.. **$1.40**

No. 94155 **Drovers' Whips,** shot loaded, 12 plait, oiled calf lace leather, with long buckskin point, full Jacksonville knot and revolving handle; length, 10 feet. Each............................................ **$1.70**

## Quirts.

No. 94157 **Braided Rawhide,** shot loaded, 12 plait, no tassel. Each.............................................. **$1.35**

No. 94158 **Braided Buckskin,** shot loaded, with 3 tassels, 12 plait. Each................................. **$1.25**

No. 94161 **Braided Calfskin,** shot loaded, 12 plait. Each ........................................................ **$1.13**

No. 94162 **All Leather Covered,** buckskin stitched, 3 tassels. Weight, 16 oz. Each................ **$0.65**

## Whip Lashes.

**Weight 3 to 6 Ounces.**

No. 94164 **Six-Plait Genuine Buck Lashes.**

| | | | | | | |
|---|---|---|---|---|---|---|
| Length.... | 5 ft. | 6 ft. | 7 ft. | 8 ft. | 9 ft. | 10 ft. |
| Per doz.... | $4.30 | $5.10 | $5.85 | $6.70 | $8.30 | $9.75 |
| Each......... | .40 | .45 | .50 | .60 | .75 | .90 |

No. 94165 **Four-plait Genuine Buck Lash.**

| | | | |
|---|---|---|---|
| Length........ | 5 ft. | 6 ft. | 7 ft. |
| Per doz........ | $3.64 | $4.20 | $4.90 |
| Each........... | .32 | .36 | .44 |

No. 94166 **Eight-plait California Stage Lashes. Genuine Buck.**

| | | | | |
|---|---|---|---|---|
| Length.............. | 10 ft. | 12 ft. | 14 ft. | 16 ft. |
| Per doz.............. | $12.40 | $15.80 | $17.00 | $20.00 |
| Each .................. | 1.15 | 1.40 | 1.60 | 1.80 |

No. 94167 **Four-plait Imitation Buck Lashes.**

| | | | |
|---|---|---|---|
| Length.............. | 4 ft. | 5 ft, | 6 ft. |
| Per doz.............. | $1.08 | $1.40 | $1.70 |
| Each................. | .10 | .14 | .18 |

No. 94168 **Six-plait Imitation Buck Lashes.**

| | | | | |
|---|---|---|---|---|
| Length.............. | 5 ft. | 6 ft. | 7 ft. | 8 ft. |
| Per doz.............. | $2.50 | $3.00 | $3.25 | $3.80 |
| Each................. | .25 | .30 | .35 | .40 |

No. 94169 **White Hickory Whip Sticks.**

| | | | | |
|---|---|---|---|---|
| Length.............. | 3½ ft. | 4 ft. | 4½ ft. | 5 ft |
| Per doz.............. | $1.00 | $1.10 | $1.20 | $1.30 |
| Each................. | .10 | .12 | .13 | 15 |

## Whip Crackers.

**We do not break dozens.**

No. 94170 **Cotton Whip Crackers,** 7 inches long. Per dozen................................................... **$0.08**

No. 94171 **Whip Crackers,** half silk and half cotton, 7 inches long. Per dozen........................ **$0.20**

No. 94172 **Whip Crackers,** all silk, best quality, 7 inches long. Per dozen................................ **$0.30**

## Patent Whip Sockets.

**These sockets will admit any ordinary size whip. They have nickel plated steel spring on side. The top half opens at the entrance of the whip, then closes tightly, always holding the whip in position.**

No. 94174 **Sockets for Wood Dash.** Each... **$0.20**
No. 94175 **Sockets for Leather Dash.** Each. **$0.25**

## Common Iron Whip Holders.

No. 94177 **Holders** for either wood or leather dash. Each, 10c; per dozen..................................... **$0.90**

## Fly Nets.

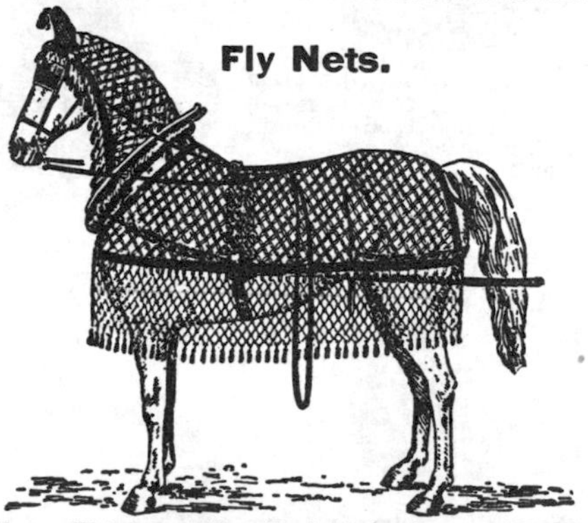

**You will take notice that the price on Fly Nets are not by the pair, but for one single for one horse. Our Nets are all made from selected stock, by experts of many years experience.**

**Upper Leather Team Nets to Head.**

No. 94180 Medium weight, 5 bars.
60 Lashes. 72 Lashes. 84 Lashes. 100 Lashes.
Price, each...$1.90 $2.15 $2.40 $2.75

No. 94182 Heavy weight, 5 bars.
60 Lashes. 72 Lashes. 84 Lashes. 100 Lashes.
Price, each...$2.15 $2.45 $2.70 $3.00

**Upper Leather Team Nets Body and Breast.**

No. 94184 Medium weight, 5 bars.
48 Lashes. 55 Lashes. 60 Lashes.
Price, each.......................$2.00 $2.20 $2.50

**Black Belt Leather Team Nets.**

No. 94186 Heavy all leather Patent net, 5 bars, 60 lashes to head. Price, each............................ **$1.25**

No. 94187 5 bars, 40 lashes, body and breast.ea. **$1.10**

**Fine Black Round Leather Express Nets. Patented. Every Net Guaranteed.**

No. 94188 Body and breast, 5 bars. 50 Lash. 60 Lash.
Price, each. ........................................$2.00 $2.37

**Fine Round Black Calfskin Buggy or Carriage Nets. Two Braided Ends.**

No. 94189 Body and breast, 5 bars.
40 Lash. 50 Lash. 60 Lash. 70 Lash.
Price, each........$1.65 $1.83 $2.00 $2.30

No. 94190 Flank Nets, 5 bars.
40 Lash. 50 Lash. 60 Lash.
Price, each.................$1.40 $1.70 $1.90

No. 94192 **Russet Leather Fly Net,** heavy 5 bar, 60 strings, all leather team nets with metallic fasteners on bars. The cheapest all leather net on the market, made in body, neck and breast; 5 bars and 60 strings, not counting breast strings; weight each, 53 oz. Each................................................. **$1.10**

No. 94193 **Russet Leather Team Nets,** body and breast, with metallic fasteners on bars, 5 bars, 42 lashes in the body and breast piece. Weight, 44 oz. Each.......................................................... **$1.00**

No. 94194 **Combination Nets,** Indestructable Nets, body and head, leather tops, extra large bottoms, heavy cotton cord meshed. Color—Black, with canary bottoms. Each................................ **$1.20**

No. 94196 **Triumph Team Nets,** body and head, 5 heavy cotton bars, 72 lashes, russet in color. Each .......................................................... **$1.15**

No. 94197 **Non-Tangler Team Nets,** 5 bar, 72 strings, body, neck and breast, web bars, with leather strings hanging from lower bar, thus preventing the tangling of strings; weight, 42 oz. Each... **$0.90**

No. 94200 **Combination Nets for Team Use.** Heavy Cotton Mesh Back with Leather Lashes, fastened with patent straps. Each........................... **$1.00**

## Cotton Mesh Nets.

No. 94202 **Cotton Mesh Team Nets,** white body, neck and ear tips. Each .......................... **$0.85**

No. 94204 **Cotton Mesh Team Nets; Colors,** blue, orange, scarlet or black. Body, neck and ear tips. Each......................................................... **$0.95**

No. 94206 **Heavy Cotton Mesh Team Nets,** white; body, neck and ear tips. Price, each........... **$0.97**

No. 94208 **Heavy Cotton Mesh Team Nets.** Fancy colors, with contrasting colored trimmings. Each .......................................................... **$0.95**

No. 94210 **Extra Heavy and Extra Large Cotton Mesh Team Net.** Fancy colored body with contrasting colored borders and tassels. The heaviest and largest net made. Body, neck and ear tips. Each........................................................... **$1.13**

No. 94212 **Extra Heavy and Extra Large Variegated Double Cord Meshed Cotton Team Net.** Body, neck and ear tips; scarlet body, green border and yellow tassels. The best selling cotton net made. Each ............................................ **$1.25**

## Cotton Mesh Buggy Shaft Nets.

No. 94214 **White Shaft Nets,** 1 inch mesh, colored trimmings, body, neck and ear tips made to fit around breast. Each.................................. **$0.90**

No. 94216 **Fancy Colored Variegated Shaft Nets,** 1 inch colored body with contrasting borders and tassels. Body, neck and ear tips made to fit around breast. Each............................................... **$1.00**

Can be had in the following combinations:
Scarlet body, green border, lemon tassels.
Black body, lemon border, black tassels.
Orange body, black body, orange tassels.
Brown body, cream border, brown tassels.

## CARRIAGE ROBES.

## Momie Lap Robes.

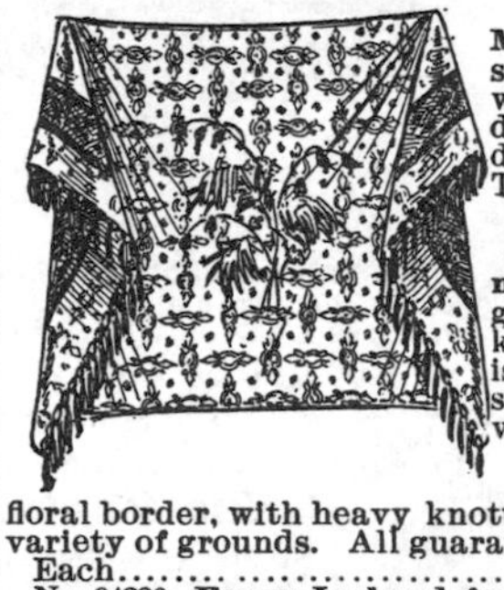

No. 94220 **Fancy Momie Dusters.** Assorted, with basket weave and fancy border. A very sightly duster for the money. This duster is full size. Each........ **$0.35**

No. 94222 **Plain Momie Weave,** drab ground, with heavy knotted fringe. This is always a standard staple article and rare value for the money. Each........ **$0.50**

No. 94224 **Jackard,** floral border, with heavy knotted fringe. Made in a variety of grounds. All guaranteed full size. Each.......................................................... **$0.60**

No. 94226 **Fancy Jackard,** fancy border all around, heavy knotted fringe. This duster is made in fancy grounds. Guaranteed full size. Each........ **$0.75**

No. 94228 **Heavy Jackard Fancy Warp,** Large Grecian border, heavy knotted fringe, with fancy design in center. This is our leader in a first-class duster for 1897. Extra value and extra size. Each........................................................ **$1.00**

## Noveltles or Fancy Momie Lap Robes.

**We have them in a large variety of new and beautiful designs.** It is not always convenient for us to duplicate patterns, as manufacturers are constantly procuring new designs, but we try to fill orders as nearly to pattern as possible.

No. 94230 **Fancy Momie Dusters.** zig-zag pattern, embroidered, blue spray and white lily. Each, **$0.30**

No. 94232 **Fancy Dotted Momie,** with knotted fringe, embroidered, blue spray and flower. Each......................................................... **$0.35**

No. 94234 **Fancy Diamond Pattern,** with fancy border and knotted fringe. Embroidered, oak leaf spray to match border. Each........................ **$0.44**

No. 94236 **Assorted Patterns,** drab, purple and green brown, fancy Jackard weave, heavy knotted fringe. Garnet spray with purple flower. This is great duster for the money. Each............ **$0.[illegible]**

## Momie Lap Robes Continued.

No. 94240 **Gold or Olive Grounds,** fancy Jackard ends, knotted fringe. Wild daisy spray embroidered in center. Each........................$0.60

No. 94241. **Plain Drab Momie,** with marine scenes embroidered in center, and knotted fringe. This is a great duster and one of the very best which we handle. Each........................$0.70

No. 94242 **Fancy Jackard Drab Momie,** with heavy knotted fringe and wide fancy border. An elopement bicycle scene embroidered in center. This is a great novelty and one which is this year enjoying a very large sale. Each..............$0.80

No. 94243 **Fancy Weave,** new Jackard border, drab ground and knotted fringe. Spray of moss rose-buds embroidered in silk. Each..........$0.90

No. 94245 **Our Celebrated $1.00 English Jackard,** corduroy pattern, with fancy colored 10 inch flowered border, extra heavy knotted fringe, large braided flower in center. This is a wonderful duster, and it is certainly worth the while for any person who wants a good article to buy one of these. Each........................$1.00

No. 94247 **Fancy Tinted Grounds in Jackard Weave,** four inch triple border, in fancy Jackard patterns. Heads of Pharaoh's horses, surrounded by a wreath and flowers. This is an extra fine heavy knotted fringe duster and very cheap at the price. Each........................$1.10

No. 94248 **Fancy Jackard Pattern,** assorted grounds. Extra heavy platted fringe, embroidered in a spray of shaded leaves and lemon flower. This is an exceptionally good value. Each.........$1.25

No. 94249 **Small Jackard Seal Pattern,** in dark drab color, heavy knotted fringe. embroidered potted palm in center. A very artistic and beautiful design. Each........................$1.50

## Linen Lap Dusters.

**We are Offering this Year a Very Elegant Line of Genuine Imported Linen Lap Robes, in the Very Best Weights and Designs, and at Prices Considerably Lower than they have ever been Sold for Before.**

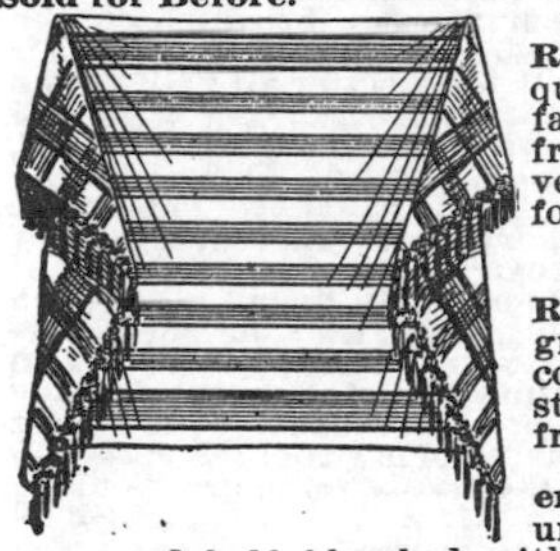

No. 94250 **Linen Lap Robe,** large size, close quality of weave, fancy stripes, only fringed on one end. A very desirable robe for the money. Each........$0.60

No. 94251 **Linen Lap Robe,** common size, ground of natural color, with fancy stripes and plain fringe. Each...$0.50

No. 94252 **Fancy Linen Lap Duster,** medium grade, natural linen ground, half bleached with fancy stripes and checks, wide hem-stitched border. Something entirely new this year, good value. Each......$0.85

No. 94254 **Close Weave Linen Lap Robe,** plain center, extra quality of linen, extra heavy with fancy striped border, heavy knotted fringe. Each........................$1.00

No. 94255 **Imported Linen,** all plain, momie style, very heavy, large size, with knotted fringe. A very desirable robe. Each........................$1.00

No. 94256 **Half Bleached Irish Linen Lap Duster,** one of the most substantial and best wearing linen robes made. Plain, neat and durable, with wide hemstitched border. This robe will give good service. Each........................$1.00

No. 94257 **Genuine Russia Pattern,** imported linen, made in half bleached, solid color. A very stocky, heavy and durable lap duster, one of the best wearing dusters put on the market; with platted and knotted fringe. Each........................$1.25

No. 94258 **Plaid Linen Duster,** made in a variety of fancy plaids, beautifully shaded with fancy wide border; also platted and knotted fringe. A very showy and stylish robe, excellent value. Each........................$1.35

No. 94259 **This is the best genuine Lap Duster we can offer, being genuine Russia finish** in appearance; of the best Irish linen. All plain, with platted heavy knotted fringe. Nothing better in the market at any price, or that will give more service. Each........................$1.65

## Green Fabric and Broadcloth Summer Lap Robes.

**Embroidered Wool Broadcloths.** This class of goods is becoming very fashionable and of late years has been in great demand. We are prepared this year to offer an elegant line, at prices as low as the grade can be produced for.

No. 94260 **Dark Green Ground,** embroidered with green tufted spray and magenta flower. Full size. Each........................$1.00

## Plain Fabric and Broadcloth Lap Robes.

No. 94261 **Fancy Green Twill Cloth,** with wide turned border, patterns are fancy checks, very handsome in design and a very attractive robe. Each........................$0.75

No. 94262 **Genuine English Dyed Cloth,** with an entire pinked edge. Fine value for the money. Each........................$0.90

No. 94264 **Genuine Fabric Cloth,** all wool, representing a very heavy beaver cloth, with full turned edge, all around. A very sightly and heavy carriage robe. Each........................$1.15

No. 94265 **Large Size, Genuine Twill Fabric Cloth,** with a wide border of the same material, 3 rows of silk stitching. A showy and strong lap robe, and elegant value for the money. Each.........$1.25

No. 94266 **This Robe is one of the best sellers we have,** being a dyed body beaver, which makes a very strong and durable robe. It has a nice wide border all around of the same material, 2 rows of silk stitching. A very stocky and showy robe, extra value. Each........................$1.50

No. 94267 **Genuine Wool Dyed, Leather Bound Carriage Robe.** This is a novelty, being bound all around with a border of leather, and two rows of silk stitching. A very desirable and serviceable robe. The pattern is a new feature for this year. Each$1.75

No. 94268 **Heavy wool dyed beaver fabric cloth.** This is a new thing in carriage robes for this year. The body of the robe being heavy beaver finish, very wide border of the same material all around and 5 rows of silk stitching. A very attractive and serviceable robe and extra value for the money. In fact, it is the most showy robe we have. Each......$2.00

No. 94269 **Genuine broadcloth.** wool dyed, extra value and extra heavy. Made extra large, wide border all round, 3 rows of silk stitching. A robe that will give grand good service, almost impossible to wear out. This robe sold last year for **$3.50. We make a price this year of $2.50 each.**

## Waterproof Lap Robes.

**Rubber One Side Only.**

No. 94271 **Gossamer Rubber Lap Robes.** These goods are dust, wind and waterproof, made mostly in slate and brown shades, and can be used at any time of the season. Very desirable in rainy weather. Weight about 16 oz. Each................$1.12

No. 94273 **Gossamer Rubber Waterproof Lap Robes.** This robe can be used either side, one being with a silk finish rubber cloth and the other side a pepper and salt colored cloth, making a very rich and comfortable lap robe for protection against dust wind or rain. Weight 20 oz.. Each...... $1.80

No. 94275 **Heavy Rubber Positive Waterproof Lap Robes.** This is undoubtedly one of the very **best robes** that has ever been offered for the purpose for which it is intended. **Heavy storm rubber** used on one side and an **extra quality of fine mohair** on the other side, very large and **just the robe for rough and stormy weather. This robe is even warmer than a buffalo robe,** because the wind cannot penetrate through it, and it will give a great amount of service. Each........................$2.75

## Baby Carriage Robes.

No. 94278 **White China Goat Baby Carriage Robes,** suitable for an ordinary size baby carriage, with plain white wool eider-down lining and felt border. Size 27x32 inches. Each..............$2.55

No. 94279 **White Lamb's Wool Baby Carriage Robe,** made of a fine quality of white lamb-skin. with selected soft wool pelts, plain white eider-down lining and felt border. Each............$3.50

## Wool Lap Robe.

**We have one of the most desirable lines of Wool lap robes, medium and heavy weights, that can be be found in the market. These goods are fully guaranteed to be just as represented.**

No. 94281 **Media Wool Lap Robe,** a good sightly wool robe, 48x60, weight, about 3 lbs. will give good service, nicely bound all around. Each........$1.00

No. 94282 **Bengal Wool Lap Robe,** brown and gray ground, with border and colored stripes, bound all around, good, stocky and a very popular robe. Each........................$1.35

No. 94283 **Princeton Wool Lap Robe,** made in handsome design, reversible, colors being different on each side; size 52x62 inches and of extra value. Each........................$1.65

No. 94284 **Scotland Wool Lap Robe,** fancy square woven patterns, best quality of wool stock, bound all round, 54x62 inches. Very sightly and serviceble. Each........................$1.90

No. 94286 **Premier Wool Lap Robe.** This is one of the best wool robes made, being made of selected lamb's wool, patterns are a variety of handsome and rich designs, principally dark ground, bound all around, This is a grand good robe for a family or for livery trade. Each........................$2.85

No. 98288 **Imported Scotch Wool Lap Robe.** This robe is made of Imported Scotch wool. The robe itself is imported direct by us, and can be used for a number of purposes; lap robes, couch covers, traveling blankets or storm shawls, Size 64x74 inches, and they are made in very pretty Scotch plaids, with 3 inch fringe. **A very desirable article for any family to own.** They are sold in every market at from $6.00 to $8.00, but we will close out what we have at the wonderfully low price of........................$3.00

## Plush Lap Robes.

**We can save you money on all lines of plush robes.** We have made arrangements with one of the largest mills of the country **to sell their entire output,** who value our large orders and give us **the very best goods** which they can produce. These goods are **strictly guaranteed.** We intend to sell this year to our customers in any quantity about **as cheap as dealers can buy them.** When you buy this robe of us you do not pay jobber's prices. **These are all new goods and colors strictly of the best dyes.**

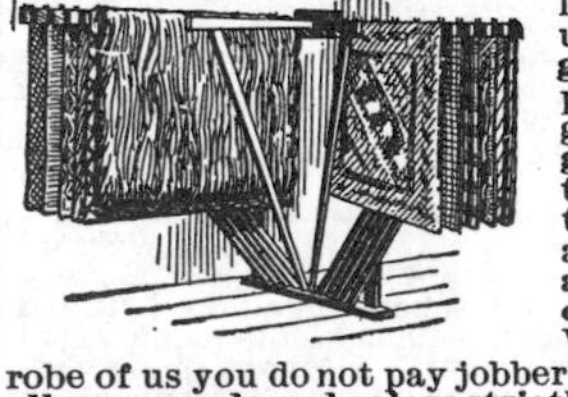

No. 94290 **Single Plush Robes,** finished one side, best whip finish. The other side plain plush finish, in the following colors: black, green, ruby and gold. Each........................$1.30

No. 94292 **Heavy Single Plush Robes,** made in one pattern only, blue ground, handsome gold border, elegant value for the money. Each........... $1.50

No. 94294 **Extra heavy,** made in one pattern only, medallion mechanical pattern, light center and dark border. A rich robe for the money. Each.... $2.50

No. 94295 **Fancy Reversible Heavy Robe.** Plush both sides, fancy stripe patterns. assorted colors. A very sightly and showy robe, suitable for almost any use. Each........................$3.00

No. 94296 **This is a very showy Double Plush Robe.** Black one side, yellow face, with stag's head in center, fancy border. Same as above, in a brown and yellow skin stripe, representing the tiger's skin. A very handsome and showy robe. Each........$3.25

No. 94297 **This is an Extra Large, heavy Double Plush Robe,** black one side and green the other, a robe of great service and utility. Wonderful value. Each........................$3.00

No. 94298 **Large Double Plush Robe.** black one side, soft shades of light and dark brown, with diagonal bar running through the center, from corner to corner, making a most catchy and showy robe. This is an entirely new design. Each.........$3.75

No. 94300 **Fine Double Plush Robes,** black one side, the other side in yellow ground, in jumping medallion patterns. This is a robe of exceptional value. Each........................$3.87

No. 94302 **Extra Fine Double Plush Robes,** black one side, the other side animal skin and fancy leaf patterns. A very new and handsome design. Each........................$4.00

No. 94303 **Large, Heavy, Fine Double Robes,** black one side, fancy animal pattern on face. This is one of the most showy robes shown this year, and is sure to give universal satisfaction. Each...$4.20

No. 94305 **This is an Extra Large Double Plush Robe,** black one side, the other side fancy design, dog and lion heads in medallion. This is very rich and new in design, and extra value for the money. Each........................$5.00

No. 94306 **This is an Exceptionally Large and Heavy Double Robe,** pattern finish, plain black on one side, the other side in mottled animal skin effects, medallion with soft shaded border; a most attractive robe. Each........................$7.15

No. 94308 **A Very Extra Heavy Fine Robe,** with Sultan crushed plush mohair face. One side of this robe can be furnished in imitation of leopard spots. A most attractive and desirable robe. This robe is the finest which is produced in plush goods, and one which of late years sold at $18.00 each. Each..$9.25

## Genuine Goat Fur Lap Robes.

**We shall offer for this season one of the best lines of genuine Japanese Goat Fur Robes ever placed in the market.** Fur robes have never been as cheap since they have been manufactured as they have been in 1896 and 1897. These skins are **all imported in the natural and in black.** They are of the **best American dyes.** These robes can easily be sold as bear robes, and are today, without question, **the most popular fur robes in the market** at a medium price. **Every robe is guaranteed** to be just as represented, and they are all composed of the best skins, with the best grade of plush lining, when the description calls for same.

No. 94310 **Gray Japanese Goat Robes,** lined with fancy felt, scalloped borders. Size, 48x60; weight, 6½ lbs. Each........................$2.67

No. 94312 **Gray Fur Japanese Robes,** the regular standard size, lined with the best grade of heavy plush, fancy borders, scalloped all around. Size 48x60; weight, 8 lbs. Each........................$3.65

No. 94314 **Large Gray Fur Japanese Robes,** deodorized, lining of extra quality plain plush, trimmed with fancy scalloped border. in fancy colors. Size, 54x66 inches; weight, about 10 lbs. Each......$5.00

No. 94316 **Extra Large Size Gray Fur Lap Robes,** deodorized, elegant quality of Japanese goat skins, lined with extra quality of plain plush, fancy scalloped border. Size, 58x68 inches; weight, about 12 lbs. Each........................$6.30

No. 94317 **Gray Japanese Fur Robes,** the largest size made, 60x70 inches, **extra heavy** hides, deodorized, lined with the best **quality of** fancy plush, in fancy designs, double **scalloped borders,** very heavy and extra quality. Each........................$7.70

## Genuine Black Japenese Fur Lap Robes.

No. 94320 **Black Japanese Fur Lap Robes,** best American dyed black skins, **felt cloth** lining, fancy scalloped borders; size, 48x60 **inches;** weight, about 6 lbs. Each........................$3.42

No. 94322 **Black Fur Lap Robes,** regulation size, lined with an elegant quality of pale green plush, fancy scalloped borders. This is an extra good robe, and there is more of this style sold than any other robe made. Size, 48x60 inches; weight, 8½ lbs. Each........................$4.70

No. 94323 **Japanese Black Fur Lap Robes,** large size, dyed a fine imitation of bear, with a fine quality of plain plush linng. double scalloped border; size, 54x66 inches; weight, about 10 lbs. Each......$6.00

No. 94325 **Black Japanese Fur Lap Robes,** large size, extra long hair, dyed a fine imitation of bear, extra quality of fancy green plush lining, in bright fancy designs and double borders. This is a very elegant and sightly robe; size, 54x66; weight, about 11 lbs. Each........................$7.45

No. 94326 **Extra Large Size Black Fur Lap Robes,** made of selected black Japanese goat skins, an elegant imitation of bear, with the best quality of plain plush lining and a double scalloped border. This is an elegant robe and the largest size made; size, 60x70 inches. Each........................$8.00

No. 94327 **Extra Large size Black Fur Lap Robes,** made of selected black Japanese goat skins, an elegant imitation of bear, with the best quality of black Melton lining, and double scalloped border. Size, 60x70 inches. Each........................$8.00

No. 94329 **Extra Large Size Black Fur Lap Robes,** made of selected black Japanese goat skins and an elegant imitation of bear, lined with the best quality of fancy medallion plush and with double scalloped border; size, 60x70 inches. Each........................$8.50

**YOU WILL MAKE A MISTAKE IF YOU OVERLOOK THE LIBERAL TERMS WE OFFER FOR CLUB ORDERS, ON PAGE 4. THE ADVANTAGES ARE NUMEROUS. YOU SAVE ON FREIGHT, GAIN EXTRA DISCOUNTS AND CAN ORDER MORE FREQUENTLY.**

## Dog Skin Robes.

No. 94330 **Large Fawn Dog Robes**, lined with a fine quality of green plush, with fancy double border; size, 54x66 in. Weight, about 9 lbs. Each....................**$6.60**

No. 94332 **Black Dyed China Dog Robes**, elegantly made, have fine, close fur, plush lined; size, 54x66 in. Weight, 7½ lbs. Each....................**$8.00**

No. 94333 **Genuine Gray Siberian Dog Robes**, plain plush lined, fancy double scalloped border; size, 48x60 in. Weight, about 8 lbs. Each......**$6.70**

No. 94334 **Extra Large Gray Siberian Dog Robes**, largest size made, plain plush lined, fancy scalloped double border; size, 54x66 in. Each..........**$8.37**

## Galloway Robes.

No. 94335 **Genuine Black Galloway Fur Robes.** These robes are the natural color, just as taken from the animal, and first class in every respect. Each robe is made from the hide of one animal. The skins are elegantly tanned, very soft in finish and are very durable, lined with green plush, scalloped border; size, 54x60 in. Weight, 10 lbs. Each.....**$13.25**

No. 94337 **Black Galloway Fur Robes**, natural color, green plush lined, with scalloped border; size, 60 in. square. Weight, about 12 lbs. Each...**$15.00**

No. 94339 **Brown Galloway Fur Robes**, same grade as the black, with the exception that they are not absolutely black; some of them show a reddish shade of color along the center of the hide, some at the end, and again, some of them along the flanks. Green plush lined, scalloped border; size, 54 inches square. Weight, about 10 lbs. Each..........**$11.50**

## Prairie Wolf Robes.

No. 94340 **Prairie Wolf Robes**, 8 skins to the robe, selected stock, green plush lined and double border; size, 54x66 in. Weight, about 7 lbs. Each....**$12.50**

No. 94342 **Prairie Wolf Robes**, very choicest skins, 8 skins to the robe, fancy medallion plush lined and double border; size, 54x66 in. Weight, about 11 lbs. Each....................**$13.50**

## Horse Covers.

### Waterproof.

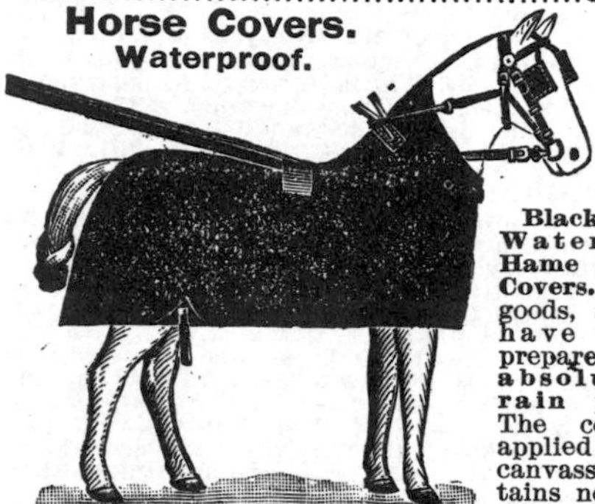

**Black Oiled Waterproof Hame Horse Covers.** These goods, as we have them prepared, are **absolutely rain proof.** The coating applied to the canvass contains nothing that will in any way injure the fabric, but is rather a preservative. Our covers extend on the neck 12 inches in front of the collar. and can be used over either single or double harness. They are made with hame leathers, trace straps and straps across the breast.

No. 94346 **Made of black oiled 8-ounce duck** in sizes from 5 feet to 5 feet 6 inches from collar to tail. Weight, each, about 8 lbs. Each..............**$1.90**

No. 94347 **Made of black oiled drill**, in sizes from 4 feet 8 inches to 5 feet 4 inches, from collar to tail. Weight, each, about 5 lbs. Each..............**$1.60**

No. 94348 **Made of black oiled sheeting**, medium or large sizes. Weight, each about 4 lbs. Each, **$1.50**

## Rubber Horse Blankets.

No. 94349 **(Pure Gum) Rubber horse covers or blankets**, dull finish, all seams both gummed and stitched to neck only. The best made, small, medium or large sizes. Weight, 4 to 5 lbs. Each........**$3.25**

No. 94351 **Luster sheeting rubber horse covers or blankets**, to collar only, small, medium or large. Weight, 3 to 4 lbs. Each....................**$2.50**

No. 94352 **Long luster sheeting, covers to head**, made in one piece, with holes for ears, strapped, holding securely in place, small, medium or large. Weight, 5 lbs. Each....................**$3.50**

## Horse Fly Covers.

**All made with ear, hame and terret holes, reinforced; the strongest cover on the market.**

No. 94353 (Z) **Heavy Plain Burlap.** Price, each....................**$0.40**

No. 94354 (A) **Fancy Corded Scrim**, light but strong. Each....................**$0.50**

No. 94355 (B) **Heavy Striped Burlap**, 100 inches long. Each....................**$0.55**

No. 94356 (H) **Fancy Checked Sheeting**, Each....................**$0.60**

No. 94357 (I) **Heavy Fawn Sheeting**, 40 in. deep, 100 in. long. Each....................**$0.60**

No. 94358 (L) **A Knotted Open Cover**, 40 in. deep, 100 in. long. Each....................**$0.75**

## Horse Sheets.

**All horse sheets are quoted with two surcingles attached.** They can be furnished without surcingles, if so desired for 10 cents less than the price named below. **Don't let your horse stand in misery fighting flies** when you can buy sheets at the below prices.

No. 94360 **Striped burlap**, hemmed. Each.. **$0.50**

No. 94362 **Fancy burlap**, bound. Each...... **.67**

No. 94363 **Fawn sheeting**, a very sightly and good wearing sheet. Each....................**$0.85**

No. 94364 **Brown duck**, very strong, bound on ends, extra deep. Each....................**$1.00**

No. 94365 **English twill in fancy patterns**, very fine. Each....................**$1.25**

No. 94367 **Pure heavy linen**, white ground, blue check. Each....................**$1.35**

## "Stay-On" Burlington Sheets.

**The best materials and finest workmanship on the market. The name vouches for their excellence.**

No. 94370 **Extra Heavy Burlap**, bright Hessian mangled finish, two corded web surcingles, bound around neck and down the front. Each......**$0.87**

No. 94372 **Stone Ground Fancy Plaided Sheeting**, two heavy corded web surcingles, bound around neck and down front. Each....................**$1.00**

No. 94374 **Brown Duck**, two heavy corded web surcingles, bound around neck and down front. Each....................**$1.25**

No. 94376 **Extra Heavy English Twills**, in fancy patterns, bound around neck and down front, a beautiful sheet and very strong. Each........**$1.50**

No. 94378 **Pure Linen Bleached Ground**, fancy plaid, two heavy corded surcingles, bound all around. Each....................**$1.75**

## "Stay-on" Cattle Cover.

**Made and cut to fit cattle.** They are made in three sizes—small, medium and large; have two surcingles attached, and are the only protection against flies, and just the thing when showing cattle at fairs, etc.

No. 94380 **Heavy Plain Burlap**, 40 in. deep. Each....................**$0.50**

No. 94382. **Heavy Brown Canvas**, 40 in deep. Each....................**$0.65**

No. 94384 **Heavy Plaid Sheeting**, 40 in. deep. Each....................**$0.75**

No. 94386 **Heavy Plaided Linen**, 40 in deep. Each....................**$1.00**

## HORSE BLANKETS.

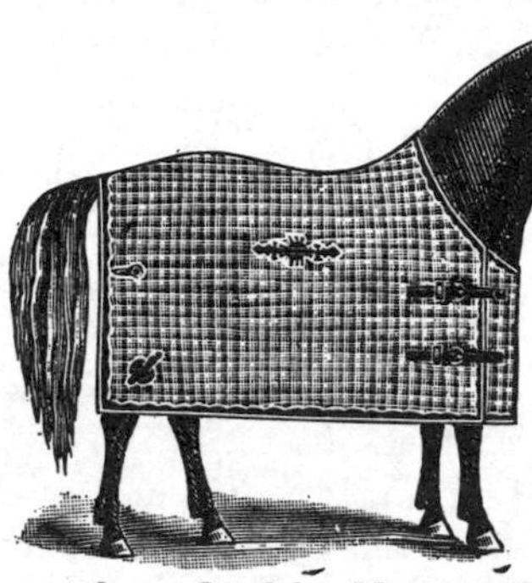

## Shaped or Stable Horse Blankets.

**Please note that horse blankets are not sold by the pair. The prices quoted are for single blankets.**

No. 94390 **Shaped or Stable Blanket**, full size, dark fancy checks, fancy bound on both ends and back, doubled in front, one strap. Each.......**$0.75**

No. 94391 **Same Blanket as above**, with two fancy surcingles attached. Each....................**$1.00**

No. 94392. **Shaped or Stable Blanket**, with orange ground and black plaid, fancy bound all around, leather pockets, all new patterns. Each......**$0.95**

No. 94393. **Same as above**, fancy trimmed, extra wide surcingles attached, special stay on the neck, elegant value. Each....................**$1.25**

No. 94394. **Shaped or Stable Blanket**, buff ground, brown plaids, bound all round, figure 4 stay, adjustable snap strap. A very heavy and stocky blanket. Each....................**$1.10**

No. 94395. **Same blanket as above**, with extra stays on the neck, extra wide surcingles with adjustable snap strap, elegant value. Each..........**$1.25**

No. 94396. **Shaped or Stable Blanket**, made up only in blue ground. red and black plaids, figure 4 stay, bound all around, two patent fasteners on a double stayed neck. This is a grand good blanket for a person who **wants** one that will give him good service. Each....................**$1.35**

No. 94397. **Same blanket as above**, with figure 4 stay, two wide surcingles attached and two patent fasteners. Each....................**$1.50**

No. 94398. **Shaped or Stable Blanket**, patent double weave, giving a blanket with a duck finish outside and a wool finish inside, made extra deep, making a most desirable blanket, black and gold plaid, striped inside, two surcingles, with patent swell sewed straps. This is something new. Each.........**$1.65**

No. 94399. **Shaped or Stable Blanket**, extra large, 78 in. long. A very desirable blanket for people who have large horses. Made in brown plaid, scarlet trimmed, with Chicago stay, one swell sewed strap. extra stay on neck. with two surcingles and patent snaps. Each....................**$1.60**

No. 94400 **Shaped or Stable Blanket.** This is the genuine imitation of Baker plaid blanket, known to the world as being one of the best and most serviceable blankets made; 40 in. deep, extra heavy, fancy grounds, boot web bound, **very large and very strong.** Each....................**$1.75**

No. 94401 **Same Blanket as above**, with two surcingles attached. Each....................**$2.00**

No. 94402 **Shaped or Stable Blanket.** A very fancy and striking blanket, being made well stayed around the neck with two inch binding and extra heavy two-inch surcingles, with patent snaps, adjustable round strap, with snap and ring in front, black and scarlet bright plaid, red duck bound, wide neck stay. This is a blanket that will give universal satisfaction. Each....................**$1.70**

**HORSE REMEDIES** IN VETERINARY DEPARTMENT...

☞ THE BEST. See Page 30.

No. 94403 **Shaped or Stable Blanket.** This is a new design, being made with wool lining, cotton out-side, with adjustable neck, so that it can be fitted to different size horses, two very wide adjustable surcingles attached with two snaps. Colors, brown and black plaids, duck trimmed, adjustable breast, woven double and altogether a very elegant blanket, which we fully guarantee. Each....................**$1.85**

No. 94405 **Shaped or Stable Blanket.** Regular full size. This is a very handsome blanket, being made **extra stout and stocky.** Doubled in front with heavy swell strap and buckles, bound all around neck, extra wide binding so as not to tear, two wide surcingles attached with patent snaps. Colors, light brown plaid in a variety of shadings. This is a grand good blanket and one that we like to sell. Each **$1.68**

No. 94407 **Shaped or Stable Blanket. This is one of the best blankets we handle.** It is made of **extra strong warp**; two swell sewed straps, double neck with Chicago stay, two extra heavy wide surcingles attached with patent snaps. Size, 40 x 75 inches. Scarlet trimmed all around. This is undoubtedly one of the best stable blankets which can be bought. Each....................**$2.10**

No. 94410 **Shaped or Stable Blanket.** This blanket is known the world over, and is considered one of the best stable blankets ever made, being 40 inches deep; made with boot web binding all around, swell strap, English brace, heavy stay champion warp, with two wide surcingles attached with patent snaps. **This blanket is too well known to need any comment, fully guaranteed.** Each..........**$2.25**

No. 94412 **Shaped or Stable Blanket.** This blanket is made with patent champion warps, 2 inches apart throughout the blanket, adding 33⅓ per cent. more strength than any other similar blanket pattern. Baker plaids, extra bound, English brace, double stayed at neck, champion warps and altogether the most durable shaped horse blanket on the market to-day. Each....................**$3.25**

No. 94414 **Kersey Shaped or Stable Blanket**, 40 inches deep. This is strictly an all wool stable blanket, and it will pay anyone who can afford to own a **first-class all wool blanket** to buy this one. Fancy gray plaid ground, **extra heavy**, boot web bound all around, with English brace and leather pocket. We cannot sell you a better all wool stable blanket. Each....................**$3.00**

No. 94415 **Same blanket as above**, duck bound, with two wide surcingles attached. Each.......**$3.25**

No. 94416 **Shaped or Stable Blanket.** This is the only blanket that will dry a horse thoroughly. They are made in 3-ply, are extra stayed and doubled at the neck with the same material, bound all around with heavy red webbing, two extra wide heavy surcingles with patent snaps, reinforced in front with the same material, **the most stocky and durable stable blanket** to put on a horse made. It is almost impossible to tear them; color fawn only. Each **$2.50**

No. 94417 **Same blanket as above**, in grays only. Each....................**$2.00**

## Square Horse Blankets.

**Please note that Horse Blankets are not sold by the pair. Price quoted is for Single Blankets.**

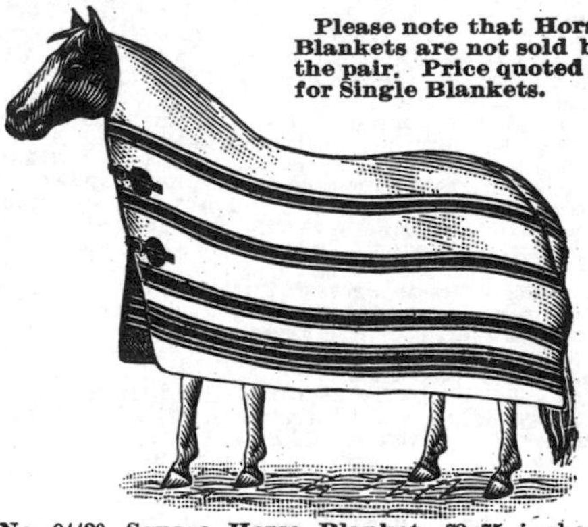

No. 94420 **Square Horse Blanket**, 72x75 inches, one strap. This is one of the best and cheapest square blankets in the market. It is made in blue and gold plaids. We are offering this blanket this year at the unheard of price of..............**$0.75**

No. 94422 **Square Horse Blanket**, 74x76 inches. This is a very durable blanket, made in gray ground, bright fancy headings, and altogether a very stocky and desirable blanket; one strap. Each..........**$0.85**

No. 94423 **Square Horse Blanket**, 74x76 inches, This is one of the best sellers in the market to-day and is a blanket made upon honor; dark brown wool body, with fancy headings, round sewed strap. A very sightly blanket. Each....................**$0.95**

No. 94424 **Square Horse Blanket**, 74x76 inches. This is a very showy blanket and excellent value for the money, being made in snuff ground and yellow plaids, bound straps and fancy striped headings. Altogether a very serviceable blanket. Each...**$1.10**

No. 94426 **Square Horse Blanket**, 76x80 inches, 5 lbs., made of hair and wool; colors, wine and red; Kersey bound, with fancy yellow stripes at heading, round strap, and it is one of the best blankets on the market for the money. Each....................**$1.25**

No. 94427 **Square Horse Blanket**, 80x84 inches, 6½ lbs. This is one of the best wool blankets made by any concern, and has proved itself to be a great seller; extra strong warp, made in red Kersey and snuff body; also navy blue stripes with adjustable snap straps, A very stocky and serviceable blanket. Each....................**$1.65**

No. 94428 **Square Horse Blanket**, 80x84 inches, 6½ lbs., double weave, very strong, dark green grounds, fancy plaids, round strap, fancy headings, and altogether a very desirable blanket. Each.........**$1.75**

SHOULD YOU EVER HAVE OCCASION TO RETURN GOODS TO US, ALWAYS MARK YOUR NAME AND ADDRESS ON ARTICLES OF PACKAGE, AND WRITE US FULLY REGARDING THE RETURN, GIVING INVOICE NUMBER OF ORIGINAL SHIPMENT.

## Square Horse Blankets, Continued

No. 94429 **Square Horse Blanket,** 84x90 inches. This is the largest cheap square horse blanket made, and one of unusual value, taking into consideration the size; made in gray grounds, white stripes, fancy headings, round strap. A great bargain for the money. Each ..................... **$1.35**

No. 94430 **Square Horse Blanket,** 84x90 inches. This blanket has had a phenomenal sale. It is made in brown ground, cinnamon stripes, round strap, a good looker and a great seller. Each ....... **$1.45**

No. 94431 **Square Horse Blanket,** 84x90 inches, 7 lbs. This is an extra heavy, double warp square blanket of unusual value, made in snuff ground, cinnamon and orange stripes, fancy headings, crowded with extra heavy warp, making a very strong and durable blanket. Each ....................... **$2.00**

No. 94432 **Square Horse Blanket,** 84x90 inches, 8 lbs. This is undoubtedly the best 8 lb. blanket made, colors, fawn and brown, fancy stripes, woven double thickness with round strap. This is a great blanket for the money. Each ........ ....... **$2.10**

No. 94434 **Square Horse Blanket,** 90x96, 10 lbs. The largest cheap blanket ever made, and one that is sure to give satisfaction. Crowded with extra heavy warp and a good wearer. Fawn and brown ground, fancy stripes, double woven, extra heavy and extra large. We know of no blanket that will compare with this in value or size for the money. Each ........................................ **$2.75**

No. 94435 **Square Horse Blanket,** 76x85 inches, genuine wool body with extra strong warp, fancy stripes and headings, round strap. A very sightly and showy blanket. Each .................. **$1.65**

No. 94437 **Square Horse Blanket,** 84x90 inches, 8 lbs. Same as above, with heavy double weave. A very superior blanket and capable of good service. Each ........................................ **$2.25**

No. 94438 **Square Horse Blanket,** same as above, only larger and heavier, being 90x96 inches, 10 lbs. Nothing better made for the money. Each... **$3.00**

No. 94439 **Square Horse Blanket,** 76 x 80 inches. A cheap all wool square blanket. This is a great seller and a grand blanket for any one who wants a wool blanket at a low figure. Made in fancy plaids, with round strap. Each ....................... **$1.85**

No. 94440 Same blanket as above, 84x90 inches, same pattern. Each ................................ **$2.50**

No. 94441 **Genuine "J. I. C." Square Wool Horse Blankets.** Brown, gray ground with bright narrow stripes and wide fancy border; sewed straps. Size 84x90 inches; weight, 7 lbs. Each .............. **$2.90**

No. 94442 **Wool Square Horse Blanket,** 76x80, strictly all wool, good quality. Made in **very fancy wool plaids,** round strap, a very sightly, showy and serviceable blanket. Each ..................... **$2.75**

No. 94443 **Same Blanket as above,** only 84x90 inches, in a variety of plaids, round strap. **A great bargain.** Each ................................ **$3.15**

No. 94444 **Square Horse Blanket,** 76x80, 5 lbs. This is without a doubt one of the best all wool fancy plaid, square blankets made, and is **guaranteed to be first class in every respect.** Made in a variety of fancy patterns. round strap, with neck buckles, and is a very serviceable and fancy blanket. Each. **$3.10**

No. 94445 **Same as above,** only larger and heavier, being 84x90 inches, 6½ lbs. Same pattern and same finish. Each ................................ **$4.00**

No. 94446 **Square Horse Blanket,** 75x80 inches. Warranted extra serviceable, all wool, in a variety of fancy plaids, round straps, with neck buckles. This blanket is made up by one of the best mills in the country and we will **warrant it to give perfect satisfaction.** Each ........................ **$3.25**

No. 94449 **Square Horse Blanket.** Same as used by all the leading Express Companies in the U. S., with fawn bodies and bright red headings, round sewed strap. The very best horse blanket made. Size, 84x90 inches. Weight, 6½ and 7 lbs. Extra quality wool. Each ........................ **$5.50**

No. 94450 **Same as above,** 90x96 inches. Weight, 9 lbs. Each .................................... **$5.75**

No. 94452 **Square Horse Blanket,** 3-ply, very heavy. The only blanket that will dry a horse thoroughly. This is without a doubt **one of the strongest blankets made,** and will give perfect satisfaction. Solid fawn color. Each .......... **$3.65**

## Special Drive in Horse Blankets

### FOR 1897.

**If you are interested in Horse Blankets we can save you from 33 1-3 to 50 per cent.; in fact, you can not afford to pay retail prices for Horse Blankets when you can buy them in any quantity for as little or even less money than your retailer can buy.** This is a **special sale** of the celebrated **Burlington stay-on Stable Blankets.** They are the only Blankets that remain securely in place on the horse without a surcingle. **You will never find a horse wearing this Blanket under his feet.** It is the only Blanket which protects at all times the horse's tail from rubbing and injury. There are no leather straps to become hard or buckles to be torn off. **It is the most durable, economical, and best Blanket on the market.**

## Instruction for Measurement.

**We here give you schedule of sizes of blankets to fit horses of different weights.**

Size 20 will fit medium size yearlings.
Size 22 will fit a horse weighing from 750 to 900 lbs.
Size 24 will fit a horse weighing from 900 to 1,050 lbs.
Size 26 will fit a horse weighing from 1,050 to 1,250 lbs.
Size 28 will fit a horse weighing from 1,250 to 1,400 lbs.
Size 30 will fit a horse weighing from 1,400 to 1,500 lbs.

In order to get good satisfaction, be sure and get a fit. Regular stock sizes in all our **"Stay-on" Blankets** are 22, 24, 26, 28 and 30; any blankets larger **than 30 will have to be made to order, at an additional cost of $3.00 per dozen.**

**In ordering state size wanted.**

No. 94460 **Burlington No. 6.** made of very heavy and fine 2 ounce bright Hessian, mangled finished burlap, the best made. Without lining. The best and strongest burlap stable blankets on the market. Please state sizes wanted. Each ............... **$0.85**

No. 94461 **Burlington No. 1,** made of heavy 11 ounce white canvas, without lining; well stayed with heavy and strong corded webbing. A very durable blanket. Please state sizes wanted. Each ........................................ **$1.85**

No. 94462 **Burlington No. 0,** made of heavy 11 ounce brown canvas, without lining; well stayed with heavy and strong corded webbing, and equipped with the best and most easily adjusted fastenings. Please mention sizes wanted. Each ........................................ **$1.95**

No. 94463 **Burlington No. 8,** made of same material as No. 6, and in same style, with heavy brown ribbed wool lining. Please mention sizes wanted. Each ........................................ **$2.20**

No. 94464 **Burlington No. 60,** made of fawn-colored canvas in the well-known Burlington "Stay On" style, with a heavy brown ribbed wool lining. Please mention sizes wanted. Each ............ **$1.30**

No. 94466 **Burlington No. 10,** Made of the same material as No. 94464, and in same style, but with a heavy ribbed wool lining. Please mention sizes wanted. Each ................................ **$3.00**

No. 94467 **Extra heavy burlap,** two surcingles, with best hardware snaps, etc. 72 inch ......... **$0.65** 76 inch .......... **$0.60** 80 inch ............ **$0.65**

No. 94468 **Extra Heavy Burlap,** lined with a heavy wool, two surcingles, a strong, heavy blanket, Price. 72 inch, **$1.00;** 76 inch, **$1.27;** 80 inch ........... **$1.35**

No. 94469 **Heavy Brown Duck,** lined with gray or brown wool, two surcingles. Price, 72 inch, **$1.30;** 76 inch. **$1.40;** 80 inch ...................... **$1.50**

No. 94470 **Heavy Fancy Plaid,** Sandow pattern, lined with a heavy ribbed wool, two heavy corded web surcingles, adjustable strap and snap in front. Price, 72 inch, **$1.50;** 76 inch, **$1.60;** 80 inch.. **$1.70**

No. 94472 **Heavy, Fancy Colored Stable Blanket for $1.00.** Extra quality, wool lined, two surcingles, patent fastening, double stitched, reinforced in every strap and buckle. Best on earth for the money. Price ................................ **$1.00**

## Special Drive in Genuine "Stay-on" Blankets.

No. 94473 **Extra heavy,** 12 ounce mangled fancy burlap, lined to the bottom of blanket with a heavy brown wool, two heavy corded webbed stays and surcingles, leather shield in front. The best blanket of the kind on the market. Price ............. **$1.84**

No. 94474 **Heavy brown duck,** lined with a heavy ribbed wool, two heavy corded web stays, and surcingles, leather shield in front. Price ......... **$1.90**

No. 94476 **Heavy brown duck,** lined with a heavy brown wool to the bottom of blanket, two heavy corded webbed stays and surcingles, leather shield on front. This is a hummer. Price ........... **$2.00**

## Lumbermen or Storm Blankets.

No. 94477 **Martin,** heavy brown Blanket, lined with a nice brown ribbed wool lining, adjustable fastenings in front. The best Blanket ever made for the money. Size, 72x80. Price ............. **$1.40**

No. 94479 **Sable,** heavy fancy plaid duck, very heavy brown ribbed wool lining, adjustable fastenings in front, turned up at bottom. A superior Blanket at the price. Size, 76x80. Price ......... **$1.67**

No. 94480 **Zebra,** extra heavy brown duck with a fawn border which gives it a very fine appearance, lined with a heavy wool lining to the bottom, adjustable fastenings in front, extra rows of stitching and goring. A great Blanket. Size, 80x80. Price ........................................ **$1.00**

No. 94482 **Arabian,** fancy check, duck lined with a very fancy heavy lining, adjustable fastenings in front, fine close stitching, turned up at bottom. A splendid blanket. Price ........................ **$2.00**

No. 94483 **Beaver,** extra heavy, 13 ounce, brown duck lined with a very heavy fancy blanketing, two adjustable fastenings in front, extra goring and extra stitching. The best blanket made of its kind, Price ........................................ **$2.50**

No. 94485 **Heavy Brown Duck,** waterproof down the back, lined with a heavy brown wool ribbed lining, hame leathers, trace carriers and adjustable fastenings in front. Size, 80x84. Price ......... **$2.60**

**All our Storm Blankets are as perfect as skilled labor can produce them. They are all made of the very best Canvas and No. 1 Wool Linings and all have Raw Hide Hame Leathers and Trace Straps.**

No. 94490 **No. 2 Blanket,** size 80x84, covered with 8 oz. brown duck and lined with fancy grey wool blanket. Double all around edge hame leather and tug snaps. Each ................................ **$2.25**

No. 94492 **No. 1 Blankets,** size 76x84, covered with 8 oz. brown duck and lined with good mixed wool blanket, rawhide hame leather and trace straps. Each ........................................ **$1.90**

No. 94494 **No. 3, same as No, 2,** only 84x90 in. Each ........................................ **$2.37**

No. 94496 **No. 4 Extra Heavy Brown Duck,** 82x84, extra heavy, wool lined, heavy striped all around. Turned back at front and bottom. This is an extra heavy and strong blanket. Each ............... **$3.00**

No. 94498 **No. 10. 12 oz. heavy Paraffine Duck,** lined with heavy wool lining. Rawhide hame leather and trace straps, size 76x84. Each............ .... **$2.50**

No. 94499 **No. 7. 12 oz. heavy Paraffine Duck,** lined with extra heavy mixed wool blanket, all heavy striped rawhide hame leather and trace straps. This is the best storm blanket made, size 84x90. Each ................................ **$3.15**

No. 94500 **No. 12.** Size 76x84, covered with heavy 12oz praffine duck and lined with fawn wool blanket, rawhide hame leather and trace straps. Each, **$3.00**

No. 94502 **No. 13.** Size 84x90, covered with extra heavy 12 oz. paraffine duck and lined with heavy fawn wool lining, double all around edge, rawhide hame leather and trace straps. Each .......... **$3.75**

## Horse Suits.

**Blankets with folded breast to button. Hoods with jowl to button.**

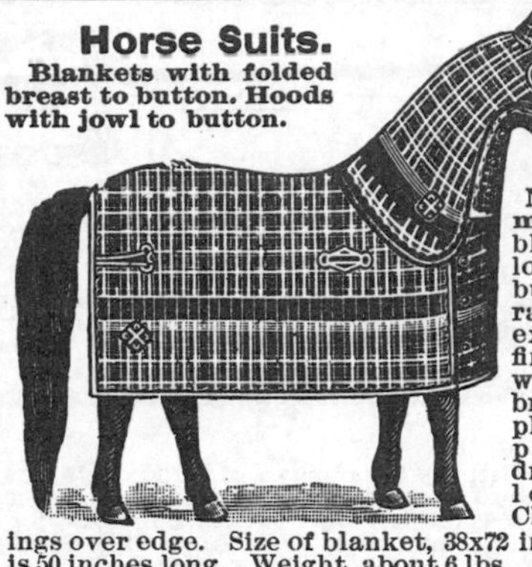

No. 94510 **Belmont Suit,** blanket and long hood to button, warranted to be extra superfine, all wool, woven in bright fancy plaids of a new pattern in drab and scarlet grounds. Chinese bindings over edge. Size of blanket, 38x72 inches. Hood is 50 inches long. Weight, about 6 lbs. Each.. **$8.00**

No. 94512 **Brighton Suit,** blanket and long hood to button; superfine, all wool, in red and blue fancy plaids. Chinese binding over edge. Size of blaknet, 38x72 inches. Hood is 50 inches long. Weight, about 6½ lbs. Each ................................ **$6.25**

No. 94514 **Linsey-Woolsey Horse Suits,** square blanket and long hood, both to tie. Blanket is 40 inches deep, 72 inches long. Whole suits, blue and red stripes, scarlet bound. Price, per suit..... **$5.50**
**Weight, per suit, 4 lbs.**

No. 94515 **Linen Horse Suits,** fancy plaid, shaped blanket, extra deep to buckle over the breast, long hood to tie. Flat web bound and well stayed. Price per suit, ................................ **$2.67**
**Weight per suit 2¾ lbs.**

## Sweat Blankets.

No. 94517 **Extra superfine all-wool Coolers,** in fancy plaids, in handsome drab grounds. Nothing better made. Size, 90x89 inches; weight, 5 to 5½ lbs. Each ........................................ **$5.25**

## Cooling Blankets.

No. 94519 **Extra superfine all-wool Coolers,** in fancy plaids of assorted colors. First-class goods in every respect. Size, 84x90 inches; weight. 2¼ lbs. Each ........................................ **$3.00**

No. 94520 **Union Cooler.** Fancy plaids with brown grounds; medium grade, full value. Size, 84x90 in.; weight, 2¾ lbs. Each ................................ **$2.25**

No. 94521 **Imitation Wool Cooler.** These are really cotton stock, but have a nappy surface and fine finish, and closely resembles all wool goods. Assorted grounds and plaids in small checks. Size, 84 x 90 inches; weight, 2½ lbs. Each ........... **$1.35**

## Sweat Hoods.

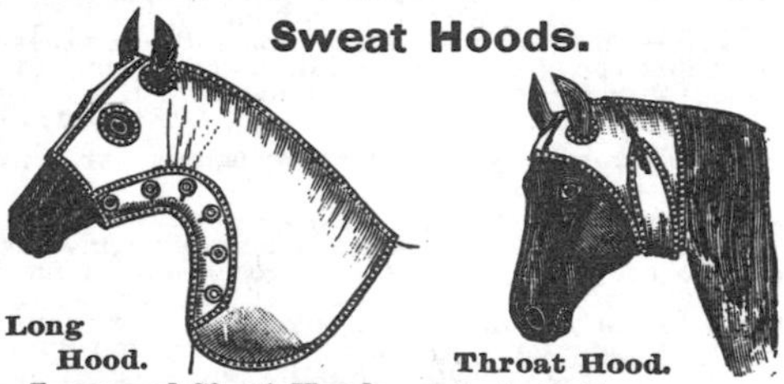

**Long Hood.** **Throat Hood.**

**Long and Short Hoods made to button.**
**Throat Hoods made to strap.**

No. 94523 **Plain white sweat hoods warranted all wool, finely bound.**

| | Long. | Short. | Throat. |
|---|---|---|---|
| Each | $3.35 | $1.65 | $0.90 |
| Weight | 35 oz. | 18 oz. | 8 oz. |

No. 94524 **Fancy plaid sweat hoods, warranted all wool.**

| | Long. | Short. | Throat. |
|---|---|---|---|
| Each | $3.75 | $1.90 | $1.00 |
| Weight | 35 oz. | 18 oz. | 8 oz. |

## Surcingles.

**Weight, each, 10 to 18 ounces.**

No. 94526 **Superb Cotton Web,** 3 inches wide, 1 inch strap and buckle. Each ........................ **$0.20**

No. 94527 **Extra Cotton Web,** 3¼ inches wide, 1 inch buckle and strap, regular size. Each.. **$0.25**

No. 94528 **Extra Fancy Union Web,** 3½ in. wide, 1⅛ in. buckle and strap, regular size. Each... **$0.35**

No. 94529 **Padded Surcingles,** super cotton web, 3 n, wide, super cotton web, 1 in. strap. Each.. **$0.35**

No. 94531 **Padded Surcingles,** twilled cotton web, 3¼ in. wide, 1¼ in, strap. Each ................ **$0.45**

No. 94532 **Padded Surcingle.** extra cotton web, 4 in. wide, 1¼ in. strap. Each ........................ **$0.55**

No. 94534 **Extra Cotton Web,** 4 in. wide, 1¼ in. strap and buckle, 8 feet long. Extra length for large horses. Each ........................................ **$0.40**

No. 94535 **Padded Surcingles for large horses,** extra cotton web, 4 in. wide, 1¼ in. strap and buckle, 8 feet long. Each ................................ **$0.60**

## ....IF YOU SELL YOUR HORSE....

**BUY A BICYLE.**

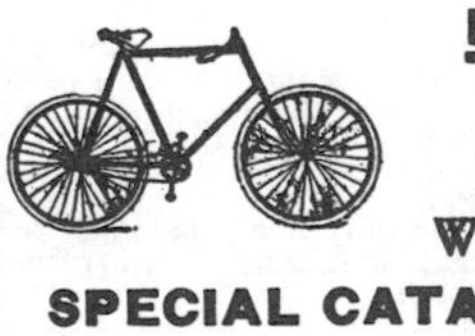

Buy Ours and Get What You Pay for.

**SPECIAL CATALOGUE FREE.**

**FINIS—THE END OF THIS CYCLOPEDIA OF MERCHANDISE. IT IS OUR SINCEREST WISH THAT THIS CATALOGUE HAS BEEN AND CONTINUES TO BE OF GREAT AND LASTING SERVICE TO YOU. WE ARE YOUR SERVANTS. OUR BEST EFFORTS ARE AT YOUR COMMAND.**

# WHAT THE PEOPLE SAY.

**Saved $20.00. No Wonder the People think He Got a Bargain.**

Ashland.

Dear Sir: My surrey I received all right, and I am very well satisfied with it and think I must have saved something near $25.00 in trading with you people. There have been some here looking at it, they think I got a bargain considering the way they sell rigs here. Yours truly,
WM. WILKINSON.

**Buggy Takes the Lead for Style and Strength and Costs Half Retail Price.**

Stubenville, Ohio.

Mr. R. W. Sears,

Dear Sir: Will say the buggy I ordered of you came in good shape and I have used it and I think it takes the lead for easy riding, strength and style. I know I saved one-half the price by ordering from you.
Yours truly, ALONZO B. GRAFTON, Stubenville, O.

**Buggy Worth $10.00 More Than One Bought at $10.00 Higher Price.**

Lutes, Neb.

Sears, Roebuck & Co., Chicago, Ill.

Dear Sirs: In regard to the buggy I purchased from you, will say I am well satisfied with it. It reached me in good shape. I think it is a first-class rig in every respect and as good as there is in the county. I can't say how much money I saved by buying from you, as I know of only one new buggy being bought here lately. My buggy was $10.00 cheaper, and I consider it worth about $10.00 the most money. I received the harness from you all O.K. and it is giving good satisfaction also. Very respectfully yours,
H. D. LEWIS.

**Well Pleased with Buggy and the Saving of $10.00.**

Pompey Center, N. Y.

Sears, Roebuck & Co.

Dear Sirs: Will say in reply that the buggy reached me all right and am well suited with it. I consider that I saved $10.00 by buying of you.
Yours, W. W. JENNINGS.

**He Has Paid Double for a Less Desirable Rig.**

Bradford, Pa.

Sears, Roebuck & Co.

Gents: The carriage I purchased of you came well packed and in good order. It is a surprise to me and others how a carriage can be sold at such a price. I have paid double for a less desirable one. It seems to be strong, of good material and stylish. Respectfully yours, A. W. NEWELL.

**Pays $63.00 for a Carriage That Retails at $85.00.**

Hardinsburg, Ky.

Messrs. Sears, Roebuck & Co.,

Dear Sirs: Some time about the first of August, I ordered one phaeton No. 125, price $63.00, full leather top and back curtain, lamps and fenders left off. The buggy came all right and I have no hesitancy in saying that I have one of the best, neatest and easiest riding buggies, and everyone that rides in it says the same thing. I think the same vehicle would cost about $80.00 or $85.00, some say it would cost $100.00. It comes fully up to my expectations and I am well pleased with my bargain.
Respectfully your friend, ALFRED MILLER.

P. S.—I may send an order for a suit of clothes or a box mackintosh if you think you can give a bargain as well as a fit. I think I would like sample C40 or C26 clothes and No. 431 box mackintosh; you can send your lowest price if it is not asking too much. Respectfully, A. M.

**Has Everybody Else's Catalogue, but Our Prices Beat Them All.**

Great Falls, Mont.

Sears, Roebuck & Co., Chicago, Ill.

Gentlemen: I take pleasure in acknowledging the receipt of buggy shipped me last, and like the other, it reached me in fine shape, and is giving excellent satisfaction. I feel that I can make a saving of from $15.00 to $30.00 in buying from you instead of buying here, or sending to other like firms. I have catalogues from all over the country, but your buggy, made at Columbus, Ohio, beats them all in quality and price. Wishing you success, I am,
Yours very truly, W. J. STONE.

**We Made it Worth $25.00 to Him to Buy His Vehicles of Us.**

Jelloway, Ohio.

Messrs. Sears, Roebuck & Co., Chicago, Ill.

Gentlemen: The vehicle purchased of you several months ago, reached me in good order and is giving perfect satisfaction. Can safely say that I have saved $25.00 by buying it from you. Since then I have made other purchases, all of which have proved entirely satisfactory.
Yours respectfully,
J. H. TILTON, Jelloway, O.

**Buggy More Than He Expected for the Money and He Saved $25.00.**

Westford, N. Y.

Sears, Roebuck & Co.

Dear Sirs: I was well pleased with the vehicle which you shipped me a short time ago. I wish to state that it was more than I expected for the money, and I saved at least $25.00 in purchasing from you, as I could not buy such a wagon of retail dealers any less than $70.00. It has been run about 500 miles this season and not a break or weak spot on it. I think you are the cheapest house with whom I have ever dealt, and shall favor you with any orders which I may have in the future.
Yours with respect, L. L. JENKINS.

**Friends Never Believe the Price When Told.**

Sanford, N. Y.

Sears, Roebuck & Co.

Messrs: The surrey I bought of you came to hand in good condition and according to agreement, and all perfectly satisfactory. I am well pleased with it and think I got full value for my money. I do not think I could have bought it of any agent here for less than $90.00. One man asked me how much I paid for it and I asked him how much he thought I paid for it, and he said $125.00. I saw several at a fair this fall but I did not think any of them came any where near competing with the one I bought from you. Thus far all satisfactory. Yours respectfully, JOEL CRANE.

**Buggy Worth $15.00 More Than He Paid.**

Shady Plain, Pa.

Sears, Roebuck & Co.

Gentlemen: The buggy you shipped me some time ago arrived safely, and I consider it worth fully $15.00 more than I paid for it. I fully intended to write previous to this time to express my entire satisfaction. I now have perfect confidence in regard to the truthfulness of your claims of large values for small money. I have just sent money for other goods and enclosed please find order for watch. I intend to buy harness, and, in fact, everything I use in your line. You may use this letter for reference or in any way that would benefit your firm, as fair and honest dealers deserve the patronage of the public. Yours truly, W. T. STARK.

**The Vehicle is Fine and He Saved $25.00 By Buying of Us.**

Navasota, Tex.

Sears, Roebuck & Co.

Sirs: With the vehicles I bought I am well pleased and I think I saved at least $25.00 by purchasing the same of you. Everyone who sees the vehicles says they are "fine." I am, yours respectfully, B. W. BURROW.

P. S.—There are one or two slight breaks in iron work about the wagon which I shall mention later. B. W. B.

**$25.00 Difference Between Our Price and Retail Prices.**

Fayette, Howard Co., Mo.

Sears, Roebuck & Co.

Dear Sirs: I can say so far as the buggy and harness purchased from you are concerned they are better than I expected. I am well pleased with same. In purchasing from your house I can say I have saved $25.00 in your price and the prices of our houses. Hoping the above will prove satisfactory to you I remain, Yours respectfully,
H. S. CASHELL.
Box 42 Fayette, Howard Co., Mo.

**Worth His While to Order His Buggy of Us and Save $10.00.**

McComb City, Miss.

Sears, Roebuck & Co.

Gentlemen: The vehicle I purchased of your firm reached me all O. K. I am well pleased with it. Think from the expression of others that I saved at least $10.00 by purchasing the same from you. I anticipate ordering a suit of clothes for myself and son soon. Truly,
R. P. MARTIN.

**Saves $25.00 and Tells His Friends of His Bargain.**

Oakville, Ky.

Sears, Roebuck & Co.,

Dear Sirs: The buggy came up all right in good condition; it has given entire satisfaction. I saved $25.00 by buying of you. My brother bought a buggy here that cost him $65.00; I think mine as good as his. I tell all my friends of your house and the way you do business.
Yours truly, W. O. PRICE, Oakville, Ky.

**Buggy Costs $20.00 Less than at Retail.**

Clifton, Lincoln Co., O. T.

Messrs. Sears, Roebuck & Co., Chicago, Ill.

Dear Sirs: I like the vehicle I ordered from you. It has proved entirely satisfactory to me. I saved about $20.00 by ordering from you. The vehicle reached me in good order. I am well pleased with it and other things I have ordered from your house, and give you my thanks for the bargains you have give me. Yours truly,
W. N. WALTSON.

**A $75.00 Buggy for $55.75. A $35.00 Road Cart for $16.95.**

New Durham, N. H.

Messrs. Sears, Roebuck & Co.

In relation to the Columbus Silver King Buggy, bought of you for $55.75, and freight of $2.36, will say I am well satisfied and feel that I have received full value for my money, and I certainly could not have bought one here as good for $75.00. And in relation to road cart No. 91,224, bought of you for $16.95, will say I am well pleased with it, and the man I got it for told me that he tried to get one at Rochester, N. H., and could not get one to satisfy him as well any less than $35.00. I will also say that all the goods received from you have been of better value than I could get here for the same money, by from 15 to 50 per cent. PERCY C. BERRY.

**Road Cart Better Then He Expected.**

Forest City, Ark.

Sears, Roebuck & Co.,

Gentlemen: I have been thinking I would write to you ever since I received the cart, but have neglected until now. I received the cart in good order and am well pleased with it; it is much better than I expected at the price. The harness is all O. K. Please send me your big catalogue.
Yours truly, D. W. INGRAM.

**Buggy Cost Him $20.00 Less Than at Retail.**

Ragan, Nebr.

Sears, Roebuck & Co., Chicago, Ill.

Gents: Am well pleased so far with my rig; think have saved $20.00 at the least. If the buggy is what I think it is, am not ashamed of it or afraid to recommend it to any one. Will speak a good word for you whenever the opportunity presents itself. Yours very respectfully, W. E. GOWER.

**$50.00 Saved on the Surrey.**

Mobile, Ala.

Mr. R. W. Sears.

Dear Sir: The vehicle you shipped me some time ago reached me in safety, and has proven entirely satisfactory. I do not think you can be excelled anywhere in this line. I am well pleased with the surrey and think I got more than full value for the money. I feel that I have saved at least $50.00 by ordering the vehicle from you, and in future if I have or can get orders in this line, I will cheerfully place them with you. Thanking you for your prompt shipments and kind attention, I remain,
Yours truly, F. A. SCHILLING.

**"Your House is Reliable, Prompt, and Straightforward, as well as Exceedingly Low Priced."**

Brighton, Lorain Co., Ohio.

Gentlemen: In reply to your letter of a recent date, will say; the vehicle referred to reached me well known he saved money, and thanked me for my kindness, as I now thank you for yours, and for your promptness while attending to this matter. I feel free to say that I believe your house to be a reliable, prompt and straightforward as well as an exceedingly low priced business house. Thanking you for past favors, I remain.
Yours very truly,
W. O. COOKE, Agent.

**Lowest Estimate is a Saving of $30.00.**

Narragansett Pier, R. I.

Sears, Roebuck & Co.

Dear Sirs: Vehicle reached me in good order, and was pleased with my purchase; also that I saved $30.00 at the lowest estimation. A number of my friends and people have admired it; and the lowest guess was $65.00. I also have made some other purchases from your firm and feel fully satisfied, and I have saved money on articles that I purchased. I speak a good word for you at every opportunity.
Yours truly,
LEROY E. THOMPSON.

# WHAT THE PEOPLE SAY.

### Our Buggies Give Good and Long Service.
Amherst, Va.

Sears, Roebuck & Co., Chicago, Ill.
Gentlemen: The Columbus Buggy which I ordered from you last August reached me in good shape, and now after several months usage I feel perfectly satisfied with it and consider it a good bargain. Wishing you a pleasant X-mas and a prosperous New Year, I am. yours truly, E. B. McGINNIS.

### Saves $25.00 or $30.00 on a Buggy that Retails at From $65.00 to $70.00.
Ulysses, Pa.

Sears, Roebuck & Co., Chicago, Ill.
The buggy that I bought of you reached me in due time and in good condition; was a better buggy than I expected. Such a buggy sells here for $65.00 to $70.00; it cost me $41.90 freight and all, so that I saved $25.00 to $30.00. I would have sent you another order, but it was so late before you got it ready that the man said wait until spring. Will you please quote me bob runners to slip on buggy axle. MARTIN LEWIS, Ulysses, Pa.

### Satisfied he saves 50 per cent. on the Buggy.
Gents: The buggy reached me all right, and is giving universal satisfaction. I could not get one in my town for anything like the money; i e, the same grade of buggy that I got of you. I advise all wishing to buy a buggy to buy of you; they can save 50% by buying of you. There is no better buggy than the Columbus buggy. Yours truly, E. S. VINSON.

P. S. Gents: The twenty year gold filled watch is at hand and is giving entire satisfaction. Nothing like the money would buy it; i e, I would have to pay twice as much here for one. E. S. V.

### Buys his Buggy of us and Saves $20.00.
Mountainburg, Ark.

Mr. R. W. Sears, Chicago, Ill.
Dear Sir: In reply to yours of the 16th, I will say in regard to the buggy I received from you I was pleased with it. It was received in good condition; my father bought the buggy, he says he saved not less than $25.00 by ordering from you. I remain yours truly, W. M. H. EARLY.

### "Your Honest way of doing Business Speaks for you in the Highest Praise."
Trempealeau, Wis.

Mr. Sears, Roebuck & Co.
Dear Sirs: The buggy has arrived O. K. I am more than satisfied with it, it also contained lap robe, strom apron, stay straps and side curtains, more than I sent for; many thanks for same. Your gentlemanly honest way of doing business, speaks for you the highest praise. Yours respectfully, S. E. HOUGHTON.

### A Great Bargain and $15.00 Cheaper than at Retail.
Echo, Wayne Co., W. Va.

Messrs. Sears, Roebuck & Co., Chicago, Ill.
Dear Sirs:—Will say that vehicle purchased on June 2 of you has given entire satisfaction, and is a great bargain; will positively say that I saved $15.00 clear by buying from you. I will sure give you all orders for Mdse. Yours truly, R. C. DILLON.
P. S.—Please send me price of a suit of clothes, Corduroy, medium grade, style I.

### We Ship with the Greatest Possible Promptness.
Corning, Iowa.

Sears, Roebuck & Co., Chicago, Ill.
Dear Sirs: I have received the cart in good shape and the warrant. Thanks for your promptness. Respectfully yours, ERNST KLEBENON.

### Our Vehicles Are Always Advertisements for Us.
Canton, Lewis Co., Mo.

To Messrs. Sears, Roebuck & Co.
I want to tell you I am well pleased with the wagon. Those who have seen it speak highly of it. One man said it was immense; it is quite an advertisement for you. There are other things I would like to buy of you, if I can manage it, but produce is low and money hard to get. Hope you will be prosperous and happy. I am yours truly, W. H. LOWN.

### Our Vehicles are Made for Wear, Not for Mere Show,
Pleasant Hill, Ky.

Sears, Roebuck & Co.
Gentlemen: I purchased a buggy and harness from you last year about this time, and have been waiting to see how the buggy was going to wear before writing to you. I can now say that they have given satisfaction beyond all expectations. I feel like doing all in my power to help you and the people who need such goods by telling them how much they can save and at the same time get first class goods by purchasing from you. If this will help you any you can copy it and use my name to it. Wishing you a prosperous year, I remain, Very truly yours, R. T. SMITH.

### Buggy Cheaper by $26.00 Than Retailers Sell at.
Carmi, Ill.

Sears, Roebuck & Co., Chicago, Ill.
Dear Sirs: Replying to the letter on the reverse side of this sheet I will say that the vehicle ordered from you last fall reached me all right and that I am more than pleased with it. It is standing hard running fine; the paint is holding well and everything is simply first class. I consider that I saved just $26.50 in buying from you. I appreciate the binding written guarantee you give with your vehicles. I will give you my orders so long as I can secure such bargains from you and receive such fair and prompt treatment. Yours respectfully, DR. W. W. APPLE.

### Our Customers Become Our Friends Because of the Money We Save Them.
Leander, Tex.

Messrs. Sears, Roebuck & Co.,
Dear Sirs: I received my buggy and harness and was well pleased with them. I think it is very nice for the price I paid for it. I appreciate the lap robe and saddle pads. I think you will have some more orders from some of my neighbors. Yours truly, W. R. WALSTON.

### Columbus Buggy Would Have Cost Him $23.00 More At Home.
Kickbusch, P. O.

Sears, Roebuck & Co., Chicago, Ill.
Gentlemen: The Columbus buggy ordered of you came July 20. Am more than pleased with it; is exactly as represented in every respect. The same buggy bought here would cost me $23.00 more than I paid you, including freight charges. I fail to see how you can sell such high-grade vehicles at such low prices. The harness is far better than I expected it to be. OTTO A. MILLER.
P. S.—Please accept sincere thanks for robe, When in need of anything in your line you will hear from me. O. A. M.

### We Give Our Customers their Full Money's Worth in Vehicles.
Grimes, Ala.

Sears, Roebuck. & Co., Chicago, Ill.
Dear Sirs: Some time ago you shipped a vehicle and it reached me in good order and proved satisfactory; and in fact I am well pleased with it, and I feel like I got the worth of my money. I saved money by buying from you. Yours truly, J. T. VICKERS.

### A Saving of $48.00 on Two Wagons.
Kennett Square, Chester Co., Pa.

Mssrs. Sears, Roebuck & Co., Chicago.
Dear Sirs: I will say that the wagon reached me safely and it is entirely satisfactory. As to how many dollars I saved, I will say $24.00, or $48.00 on the two. One that my friend, Mr. Davis, ordered through me, and other parties that I have recommend your firm to, have been well satisfied with the goods ordered—Harness, Clothes, etc. I always find it a pleasure to recommend your firm to anyone wanting anything in your line. We all want to get the best and cheapest, and Sears, Roebuck & Co. is the place. I liked the wagon that Mr. Davis got better than mine. My number was No. 6661; I do not know what his number was. Can you furnish me with his make of wagon with side bar in carmine or any good red. If so, please inform me. I want to be prepared for the spring trade. Respectfully, CHARLES W. GILLEN.

### Our Buggies Are Always Advertisements for Us.
Brownsville, Tennessee.

Sears, Roebuck & Co.
Dear Sirs: We received the buggy in good shape and are more than pleased with it; in fact, every one who has seen it thinks it a tip top buggy for price. I have had good many to say when they needed a new vehicle they were going to order from you. I think I saved about $15.00. Yours truly, J. M. DARNABY.
P. S.—My wife wants a catalogue—clothing of all kinds.

### Buggy Much Better Than Expected. Saved $20.00.
Ferrum, Franklin Co., Va.

Gents: The buggy reached me in good order, and I am well pleased; it is much better than I expected for the price, and I feel sure that I saved at least $20.00 by buying from you. I have recommended your house to several of my friends and think you will receive more orders from this county soon. You may expect my future orders for anything that I buy in the line of vehicles or clothing. Please accept many thanks for your kindness. Yours very respectfully, C. A. HICKMAN.

### Road Cart Cost Him $6.00 Less Than At Retail.
Corning, Wis.

Sears, Roebuck & Co.,
Dear Sirs: I am very much pleased with the cart you sent me. I saved about $6.00 by ordering of you. Yours truly, ERNEST KLEBENON.

### Made a Clear Saving of $13.00 on His Buggy.
Rockport, Ind.

Sears, Roebuck & Co.,
Dear Sirs: I liked the buggy; it is far better than I expected. I made at least $13.00 by ordering it from you. I thank you for the way you have treated me in the past and if you do business in the future as in the past, you may recive some more orders from me. Truly yours, WM. H. FRESHLY, Rockport, Spencer Co., Ind.
P. S.—I received the buggy June 27, 1896, and it looks as neat as ever. It reached me without a scratch and in good order. W. H. F.

### Buggy Came Without a Scratch.
Belpre, Kan.

Sears, Roebuck & Co., Chicago, Ill.
Gentlemen: In reply to yours of recent date would say the buggy I ordered from you came to hand O. K. and without a scratch; I am well pleased with it. I saved about $7.00 by buying from you and think I got very good value for my money. Very truly yours, THOMAS GARRARD.

### Everyone Who Sees the Buggy Thinks it a Great Bargain.
Anthony, Athens Co., Ohio.

Sears, Roebuck & Co., Chicago.
Dear Sir: I received the buggy in good shape and am 'highly pleased with it. I saved from $10 to $15 in buying of you. Everyone who sees the buggy thinks it is a great bargain. You will receive my future orders, and anyone I see wanting to buy anything in your line I will direct them to you. Yours truly, MOLLIE MOORE.

### Saved $20.00 on His Buying and Got a Neat Job.
Mt. Williams, Va.

Messrs. Sears, Roebuck & Co.
Gents: In regard to the vehicle received some time ago from you. Received it in good condition without any defect and am very much pleased with the vehicle and harness in every respect. Priced one in Winchester, not as good apparently, and not near as neat at $65.00. Believe we saved $20.00 by purchasing from your company. Neighbors very much pleased; have had calls to examine catalogue. Think some will send orders next season. You kindly sent me, some time ago, a coupon for $6.00 to allow that much on a $12.00 suit of clothes; procrastinated making use of it; still have the conpon and if the limit of time has not expired, please send me sample of said suit by return mail and you will much oblige. Very truly yours, JOSEPH F. BEAN.

### Buggy Gave Perfect Satisfaction and Cost $15.00 Less than Retail.
Greenville, Ala.

Messrs. Sears, Roebuck & Co., Chicago, Ill.
Dear Sirs: I will say that the buggy I ordered from you gave perfect satisfaction in every way. No doubt I saved at least $15.00 dollars by making the order. Yours truly, R. G. SHANKS.

### He is $10.00 Better Off by Getting His Vehicle of Us.
Gleam, Tex.

Sears, Roebuck & Co., Chicago, Ill.
Kind Friend: Will say I am well pleased with the vehicle I received from you, and think I saved $10 anyhow, or more, and any order I can get I will surely favor you with them. Accept my thanks for your past favors. I remain, sir, yours very truly, O. ROBBINS.

### "Easiest Riding Vehicle I Have Ever Seen. Saved Ten to Fifteen Dollars."
Dunkirk, N. Y.

Dear Sir: The vehicle reached us in good order and were well pleased with it, and in fact we saved from $10.00 to $15.00 in buying from your firm, and it is the easiest riding vehicle that I have seen. I would like to see the prices of your cutters. Yours truly, JAMES MOODY, 23 Talcott St., Dunkirk, N. Y.

# WHAT THE PEOPLE SAY.

### We Save Him $20.00 and Give Him a Fine Rig.

Aucilla, Fla,

Messrs. Sears, Roebuck & Co., Chicago, Ill.
Gentlemen: Replying to yours of recent date, beg to say I received the vehicle shipped me in good order, and I am well pleased with it. I find the buggy all that it should be in every respect, and I think you saved me at least $20.00 on this purchase. In fact, I have seen buggies that cost $60.00 that I would not exchange mine for. Yours truly, A. A. BISHOP.

### Pleased with Vehicle and Saved a Great Deal of Money.

Scranton, Miss.

Sears, Roebuck & Co.
Dear Sirs: I must say am sorry that I have neglected letting you know that the vehicle reached me all right and has proved to be as represented, was received in good condition, freight costing $4.98. I have saved a great deal by ordering of you, and expect to give you my future orders.
Yours respectfully, WALTER K. HAVENS.

### Columbus Buggy came in Perfect Condition and with a Saving of $20.00.

North Madison Lake, Ohio.

Sears, Roebuck & Co,
Gents: Yours of Dec. 15th at hand. In reply the Columbus buggy I received of you came all right, there was not a marred shop on it. I wrote you when I received it in June, we are very much pleased with our bargain and the courtious treatment and in the thorough manner it was crated for shipment, we have never had any cause for complaint, but think I saved $20.00 by buying of you. I take pleasure in refering others to you.
Respectfully, J. H. BROWN.

### Saved $17.00 on this Buggy and Sold it at Once.

Justus, Ind.

Sears, Roebuck & Co.
Dear Sirs: The buggy I bought of you came all right. I was satisfied and feel that I saved about $17.00 by ordering from you. I sold the buggy at once. If you will look over your books you will find you sold a buggy to W. S. Smith, of Justus, Ind. I got him to order for me. I have been running it for 2½ years, and offer to put it against any of their buggies sold around that they sell for $65. Please send me your catalogue for '97. Yours truly, JACOB SHEPHERD, Justus, Ind.
P. S.—I try to get orders for you, and if you send me your catalogue I will still do so. I know parties wanting wagons. Yours, J. S.

### Saved Money On Rig and Harnsss.

Bancroft, Mich.

Mr. Sears: Yours at hand; will say I am well satisfied with the buggy I purchased from your house. I am using the buggy myself and we think we got a bargain at $10.00 less than we could have got the rig here. Anyone wishing a vehicle will get a bargain; also in a harness. I think I saved $3.00 in buying my harness of you. I remain yours, CHAS. H. KENT.

### Could Not Duplicate the Columbus Buggy for Twice the Amount.

Centreview, Missouri.

Sears, Roebuck & Co.
Dear Sirs: The Columbus buggy I ordered from you some time ago, came all O. K., and am well pleased with it. I don't think it could be duplicated here for twice the amount it cost me. I will order for two more in the spring as I have three sold. Yours truly, G. L. BAIRD.

### Saved $50.00 on Vehicle and Can't Find Its Equal.

DeForest, Wis.

R. W. Sears, Chicago.
Dear Sir: I received the vehicle promptly and it gave perfect satisfaction and how much money I saved by sending the order to your house, and shall state also that I have not seen one equal to this one since I received it, in fact I saved $50.00 on that one order. Yours very truly, CLAUS E. ROISUM.

### Thoroughly Pleased with the Vehicle and with the $20.00 Saved.

Rehobth, Del.

Dear Sir: The carriage that you shipped me reached here safely and I am thoroughly pleased with the quality of the vehicle, but it was shipped before the varnish was dry and consequently soiled the appearance by the accumulation of dust in transit. I may say also that in my opinion I saved at least $20.00 in purchasing of you. Yours, A. W. DICK.

### This is the Way to Save Money.

Madison, Ga.

Sears, Roebuck & Co., Chicago, Ill.
Gentlemen: The road cart ordered from you some time ago received, and I will say I am more than pleased with it. In my business I have lots of hard trips to make, and have given it a good test. The same cart here sells for $28.00. I bought from you, freight and all. for $9.00. Wishing you success. Yours, LEN C. BALDWIN, Mgr. Madison Music House.

### Much Pleased With Road Wagon.

N. Georgetown, O.

Sears, Roebuck & Co.
Kind Sirs:—I received the road wagon I ordered of you in good condition, and I am much pleased with it. Thanking you for prompt attention to my order. Yours truly, HARVEY MOUNTZ.
P. S.—Please send the grocery catalogue to me.

### Saved $15.00 or $20.00 on Buggy.

Grand Rapids, Ohio.

Sears, Roebuck & Co.
Gentlemen: I would just say the buggy was received all right and I am well pleased with it, and I think I saved $15.00 or $20.00 on buggy and harness, and if I can do you any good I will try and do so. How do you sell lap robes, black or gray and plush lined? Please let me hear from you.
Yours truly, JUSTIN JENNINGS.

### Likes His Buggy First Rate.

Hammondsville, Ohio.

Sears, Roebuck & Co.
Dear Sirs: I like my buggy first rate and I know I got a good buggy for the money. I couldn't have got a better running or riding buggy if I had paid $60.00 for it. I am more than satisfied for what I got for the money. Yours truly, J. C. WARDEZKE.

### Saved $30.00 on His Vehicles.

Bertram, Texas.

Sears, Roebuck & Co., Chicago, Ill.,
Dear Sirs: Have purchased three vehicles from you and think I can safely say that I saved about $10 each, on them, making a total saving of $30.00. Yours truly, B. F. ELLIS.

### Vehicle Came in Perfect Order and Saved $12.00.

Jenkinsville, S. C.

Sears, Roebuck & Co., Chicago. Ill.
Gentlemen: I received the vehicle which you shipped me in perfect order, and up to date it has proved to be all that I could desire. I consider that I not only got the value of my money but that I saved at least $12.00 by the transaction. I will be glad if you will send me a catalogue of furniture at your earliest convenience. Respectfully, J. C. McMETKIN.

### Saves $35.00 on Two Rigs and Sends an Order for His Neighbor.

Export, Pa.

Sears, Roebuck & Co., Chicago, Ill.
Gentlemen: Some time ago I purchased from your company a buggy. It is not only what you represented it to be, but much better to say the least. I am very much pleased with my bargain, not only in quality but in price. I saved $15.00 by purchasing from your company. I also purchased one two horse wagon which could not be improved on for quality and price. I saved at least $20.00 by purchasing of your company. My neighbor was so pleased with my wagon that he requested me to order him one. The order for same sent you a few days ago. Wishing you success in all your business transactions. Respectfully, J. T. LONGHRY.

### A Saving of $60.00 on Buggies and Harness is Enough to Convince any one that Sears, Roebuck & Co. is the House to Deal with.

McClure, Ohio.

Sears, Roebuck & Co.
Gentlemen: Can say that I have bought two of your $39.90 Columbus buggies, also two set of buggy harness and all are giving entire satisfaction. A buggy of the same style would cost me here $65.00 and guaranteed for only one year. I can truthfully say that I have saved at least $25.00 on each rig and $10.00 on harness, making a total of $60.00. I think that is enough to convince any one that Sears, Roebuck & Co. is the house to deal with. You can expect more orders from me, as I have five names now who intend to order rigs as soon as spring opens up. I am yours respectfully, JAMES WEAVER.

### Wagon Far Better than Expected. Saved $10.00 or $15.00.

Callin, Illinois.

Sears, Roebuck & Co., Chicago, Ill.
Dear Sirs: I received the wagon all right and everything was all O. K., and was far better than I expected for the money, and think I can be justified in saying I saved from $10.00 to $15.00 on the same wagon at Danville, and do hope it will be the means of selling more vehicles in this neighborhood.
I remain yours truly, hoping this may be the means of selling many more. JNO. CARBY.

### Even in the Midst of the Sharpest Competition We Save 25 per cent. on Vehicles.

Don Juan, Ind.

Sears, Roebuck and Co., Chicago, Ill.
Gentlemen: The buggy was received in good condition and has given perfect satisfaction so far. I think I can safely say that, notwithstanding the sharp competition between vehicle dealers here, I have saved at least $10.00 by purchasing of you, and not improbably $15.00 or $20.00. I will purchase of you again if you happen to strike me with the right thing at the right time. Yours respectfully, W. F MENNER.

### It Pays to Buy of Us and Save $20.00 on a Vehicle.

Pawnee City, Neb.

Sears, Roebuck & Co.
Sirs: Would say that I am well pleased with my buggy up to date, and if it proves to be as good in the future would say that I saved at least $20.00 in the purchase. Yours truly, T. B. WHURTON.

### Pleased With the Buggy and $15.00 Saved.

Kopperl, Texas.

Sears, Roebuck & Co.
I am glad to say buggy came to hand all right, and I am well pleased with it. I consider I have saved about $15.00 in purchasing buggy from you. Yours truly, W. A. STASEY.

### A $65.00 Buggy Costs Him Only About $40.00.

Peterson, Iowa.

Kind Friends: I received your letter in regard to that vehicle I ordered of you in June last. I received it the 3d of July last in good shape. I tried to buy one here and could not get it for less for than $65 00 cash, and I think I saved about $24.00, and we have received other goods from you in good shape and saved money on them all. I think we can favor you with more orders in the future than we have in the past; as I am a small farmer and your prices are below our home dealers, you can look for more of my trade. Yours truly, H. E. WEBSTER, Peterson, Clay Co., Iowa.

### Pays $75.00 for a Wagon that Would Cost Him $150.00 at Home.

Gale, Oregon.

Sears, Roebuck & Co.
Dear Sirs: I am well pleased with my wagon. I have shown it to all my friends; every one says it is a cheap wagon, the paint is coming off the wheels, but that is caused by the alkali dust, it just cost me $75.00 laid down at Montague. I have made one trip to Montague and all my friends there say if I had bought it at Montague or Yreka I would have paid $150.00 for it. I want to get me a cart in the next year. My wagon came through in good shape; there was not a scar on it. The harness would have cost me $20.00 here. I am well satisfied with my rig. Respectfully, MRS. F. M. BARNUM.

### We Pack All Our Articles With Care.

Colchester, McDonough Co., Ill.

Sears, Roebuck & Co., Chicago.
Gentlemen: The buggy I bought of you some time ago was received in good condition, it was packed and crated in good condition and was not scuffed or scratched at all. I bought the buggy for another person, he says it is giving good satisfaction and he thinks he saved about ten dollars by having me send for it. He thinks he got full value for the money and I know he did get value received. Yours respectfully, ALLEN G. HUMMER.

### It's Easy to Save $20.00 or $25.00 on a Vehicle.

Mexico, Mo.

Sears, Roebuck & Co.,
Sirs: I received the vehicle in good order; am very well pleased with it. I saved about twenty or twenty-five dollars by buying from you. Respectfully, GEO. BOOMER.

# INDEX.

**The following pages,** devoted to a most complete index, wil be found **an accurate guide** to the **countless bargains** contained in the catalogue.

We urge our customers to anticipate their needs. There are **numerous supplies** that have to be bought **each month,** supplies that can be ordered at the same time from us, and **shipped by freight** at very **little expense.** Hence, we deem the index of great importance to you. Many items which you need will be overlooked, but for this part of the book.

**Refer to it constantly,** make up your order intelligently, paying attention to the great advantage of freight shipping, and we will guarantee to render you such satisfactory service and enable you to save such a large percentage on each purchase, that you will **prize this catalogue** as an actual necessary of life, and one that you will never be without.

## A

Abdominal Corsets ..... 306
Abdominal Supporter ... 32
Absorbent Cotton, Photographic ........ 479
Absorbent Pads.... ... 32
Accordeon ........ 525-526
Accordeon Flute ...... 528
Accordeon Instruction Books ........ 541
Achromatic Spy Glasses. 465
Achromatic Telescopes .. 465
Acme Transparent Water Colors ........ 480
Adjustable Auger Handles ........ 80
Adjuster's, Chain ......619
Adjustable Drawing Knives ........ 79
Adjustable Handle Bars 616
Adjustable Planes .....74-77
Adjustable Thimbles ... 128
Adze, Carpenter's ...... 78
Adze, Cooper's ........ 79
Agricultural Implement Department ......148-165
Agate Buttons ......... 320
Ague Pills........ 26
Air Cocks ........ 55
Air Cushions ........ 329
Air Pumps ........ 594
Air Rifles ........ 574
Air Tight Stove ...... 127
Alarm Clocks ........ 475
Alaska Silverware ..... 438
Albums ........ 349
Albums, Photographic .. 481
Alcohol Stove ........ 112
Ale, Ginger ........ 11
Alligator Bag ........ 252
Alligator Skins ........ 208
Alligator Wrenches ..... 178
Alpaca Coats, Men's..... 176
Alpaca Dress Goods..... 254
Allspice ........ 11
Alto Horns ..........530-531
Aluminum Combs ..... 326
Aluminum Opera Glasses 464
Aluminum Ware .....135-136
Aluminico Spectacles ..462-463
Amber Necklaces ...... 430
American A Grain Bags 293
American Flags ....... 293
American Laces ....... 264
Ammonia ........ 28
Amoskeag Apron Gingham ........ 291
Ammunition ........580-585
Anchors, Boat ........ 606
Aneroid Barometer ..... 470
Angelica Organs ...... 524
Angle Valves ........ 54
Angular Borers ........ 81
Animal Cake Cutters..... 133
Animal Pokes ........ 46
Animal Traps ........ 100
Anti Rattlers ........ 61
Annunciators, Call ..... 471
Annunciator Wire ...... 471
Anvils, Blacksmith .... 65
Anvils, Plow ........ 65
Anvil Tools ........ 68
Anvils and Vise ....... 65
Apple Butter ........ 12
Apples, Canned ........ 11
Apple Corer ........ 134
Apples, Dried ........ 12
Apple Parer ........ 102
Apollo Harps ........ 521
Apricots, Canned ...... 11
Apricots, Dried ........ 12
Aprons ........ 309
Aprons, Buggy ........ 58
Apron Fabrics, White .. 293
Apron, Gingham ........ 291
Apron Overalls ........ 178
Aquarium Stand ........ 45
Arctics, Men's and Women's ........ 204
Arctic Sleeping Bags... 610
Architect's Compass .... 467
Architects' Rules ...... 73
Arm Bands ........ 335
Arm Bandages ........ 597
Arrowroot ........ 15
Arsenic Complexion Wafers ........ 26
Art Embroidery Materials ........ 332
Art Squares ........ 300
Artificial Bait ........603-604
Artistotype Paper ...... 480
Artists' Materials ...360-361
Asbestos Stove Mats ... 129
Ash Sifters ........ 129
Astronomical Telescopes 465
Athletic Goods ......593-597
Athletic Shoes ........203-206
Athlophloros ........ 29
Atomizers ........ 329
Atlases ........ 37
Attachments, Neckyoke . 62
Attachment, Three-horse 62
Auger Bits ........ 81
Auger Handles ........ 80
Augers ........ 80
Augers, Hollow ........ 81
Augers, Post Hole ..... 50
Australian Wool Underwear, Men's ........ 239
Autoharps ........ 322
Autoharp Cases ........ 536
Autoharp Picks ........ 536
Autoharp Springs ...... 533
Autoharp Tuning Hammer ........ 536
Automatic Pencils ..... 353
Awl Blades ........ 207
Awl Handles ........ 207
Awl Sets ........ 82
Awls ........ 82
Awls, Collar ........ 766
Awls, Peg ........ 207
Awls, Sewing ........ 207
Awls, Steel Thong ..... 766
Awnings ........ 608
Awning Pulleys ........ 96
Axe Handles ........ 77
Axe Sheaths ........ 590
Axe, Stone ........ 50
Axe, Stones, Emery .... 71
Axe Wedges ........ 77
Axes, Boys' ........ 77
Axes, Broad ........ 78
Axes, Double Bitted ... 77
Axes, Hand ........ 78
Axes, Hunters' ........ 77
Axes, Hunter's .......77, 590
Axes, Woodchoppers' ... 77
Axle Clips ........ 61
Axle Grease ........ 23
Axle, Wagon ........ 62
Axles, Iron ........ 59
Axminister Rugs ....... 300

## B

Babcock Milk Tests.... 145
Baby Carriages ......692-696
Baby Cloaks ........ 283
Baby Dresses, Skirts and Sacques ........ 309
Baby Foods ........ 28
Baby Medicines ........ 28
Baby Ribbons ........ 263
Baby Swings ........ 142
Back Combs ........ 326
Back Flaps ........ 86
Back Saws ........ 70
Bacon Cured ........ 13
Badger Hair Brushes ... 113
Bags, Arctic Sleeping ... 610
Bags, Banjo ........ 535
Bags, Camphor Clothes. 610
Bags, Carryall ........ 610
Bags, Game ........ 588
Bags, Guitar ........ 535
Bags, Kit ........ 610
Bags, Ladies' Shopping. 335
Bags, Laundry ........ 322
Bags, Mandolin ........ 536
Bags, Saddle ........ 759
Bags, School ........ 355
Bags, Shell ........ 588
Bags, Striking ........ 593
Bag Strings ........ 20
Bags, Traveling ....... 252
Bags, Violoncello ...... 534
Bailey Planes .........74-75
Bait, Artificial .......603-604
Bait Boxes ..........604-605
Bake Dish, Silver ..... 451
Bake Oven ........ 129
Bake Pans ......130, 133, 136
Baking Powder ........ 10
Baking Powder Cans ... 35
Balances, Sash ........ 89
Balbriggan Underwear.. ......237-238
Balers' Hay ........ 151
Ball, Base ..........594-595
Ball Bearing Ratchet Braces ........ 80
Ball Bearing Shoes ..... 203
Ball, Foot ........ 594
Balls, Ox ........ 46
Ball Pene Hammer ..... 78
Ball Shoes ..........203, 596
Ball, Trotting ........ 767
Balusters ........ 95
Bamboo Fishing Rods.598-599
Band Instruments ......530-531
Band Instrument Mouthpieces ........ 537
Band Instrument Mutes. 537
Band Instrument Music Racks ........5, 30, 532
Bandages, Ankle ....... 597
Bandages, Elastic ...... 32
Bandages, Elastic ...... 597
Bandages, Elbow ....... 597
Bandages Forearm ..... 597
Bandages, Knee-Cap ... 597
Bandages, Shoulder .... 597
Bandages, Suspensory .. 597
Bandages, Wrist ...... 597
Bands, Back ........ 762
Bands, Belly ........ 762
Bangs, Human Hair .... 330
Band Rings ........ 417
Bands, Rubber ........ 355
Baritone Horns ........ 530
Banks, Toy ........ 99
Banjo Bags ........ 535
Banjo Brackets ........ 535
Banjo Bridges ........ 535
Banjo Cases ........ 535
Banjo Heads ........ 537
Banjo Instruction Books 541
Banjo Music ........ 539
Banjo Patent Heads..... 535
Banjo Pegs ........ 535
Banjo Strings ........ 533
Banjo Tailpieces ...... 535
Banjo Thimbles ........ 535
Banjo Wrenches ........ 535
Banjos ........ 528
Banjorines ........ 519
Baptismal Pants ....... 206
Barbed Wire ........ 41
Barbers' Combs ........ 326
Barbers' Shears ....... 109
Barley ........ 15
Barley Forks ........ 49
Barn Door Hangers .... 86
Barn Door Latch ....... 86
Barn Door Pulls ....... 86
Barn Door Rails ....... 86
Barometers ........ 470
Barometers, Mercurial .. 470
Barometers, Pocket .... 470
Barrel, Churn ........ 143
Barrel Carts ........ 164
Barrels for Carts ...... 164
Bars, Clothes ........ 141
Bars, Crow ........ 50
Bars, Horizontal ....... 594
Bars, Shutter ........ 91
Bars, Trapeze ........ 594
Base Balls ..........294, 595
Base Ball Bats ........ 595
Base Ball Belts ........ 596
Base Ball Gloves ...... 595
Base Ball Masks ....... 595
Base Ball Mitts ....... 595
Base Ball Pants ....... 596
Base Ball Protectors ... 595
Base Ball Shirts ...... 596
Base Ball Shoes......203,596
Base Ball Stockings .... 596
Base Blocks ........ 596
Base Blocks ........ 95
Base Molding ........ 95
Bastard Files ........ 71
Basins, Wash ........ 56
Baskets ........ 142
Baskets, Trout ........ 605
Bass Drums ........ 529
Bass Drum Slings ..... 536
Bass Drum Sticks ..... 536
Bass Flies ........ 603
Bass Viols ........ 517
Bass Viol Resin ....... 534
Bass Viol Instruction Books ........ 541
Bass Viol Strings ..... 533
Bath Brick ........ 19
Bath Brushes ........ 33
Bath Brushes ........ 326
Baths, Fixing ........ 478
Bath Room Cabinet .... 671
Bath Thermometer ..... 470
Bath Tubs ........ 134
Bathing Trunks ........ 597
Batteries, Dry ........ 471
Battery, Edison ........ 471
Batteries, Electro-Medical........ 472
Battery, Gravity ....... 471
Batteries, Open Circuit. 471
Batteries, Renewal Parts 471
Batting, Cotton ........ 292
Bats, Base Ball ....... 595
Bay Leaves ........ 11
Bead Trimmings ....... 319
Bead Garniture ........ 319
Bead Planes ..........76-77
Beans, Dried ........ 15
Beans, Canned ........ 11
Bear Hair Brushes ..... 103
Bear Traps ........ 100
Beaters, Dulcimer ...... 537
Beattle Rings ........ 77
Beater, Egg ........ 134
Beaver Shawls ........ 305
Beaver Shoes, Child's... 196
Beaver Shoes, Ladies'... 196
Beaver Boots, Men's .... 202
Beaver Shoes, Men's .... 196
Beaver Traps ........99-100
Bed Blankets ........ 288
Bed Casters ........ 98
Beds, Camping ........ 610
Bed Cots ........ 661
Beds, Child's Folding.... 660
Beds, Child's Iron ..... 660
Beds, Folding ........656-657
Beds, Iron ..........658-660
Bed Lounges ........666-667
Bed Pans ........ 132
Bed Quilts and Comforters ........ 288
Bed Sets, Lace ........ 298
Bed Spreads, Colored ... 289
Bed Spreads, White .... 289
Bed Sheets, Stockmen's. 610
Bed Springs ........ 661
Bed Ticking ........ 292
Beds, Wood ........ 656
Bedroom Sets ........654-655
Bedroom Sets, Iron ..... 658
Beef, Chipped ........ 14
Beef Corned, Canned.... 14
Beef, Cured ........ 13
Beef, Dried ........ 13
Beef Scraps ........ 23
Beef Scraps for Poultry. 30
Beef, Wine and Iron.... 26
Belgian Prints ........ 291
Bells ........ 106
Bells, Door ........ 93
Bells, Electric ........ 471
Bell Harmonicas ....... 527
Bells, Iron Box ....... 471
Bevel Jacks ........ 150
Bells, Musical Sleigh ... 532
Bells, Orchestra ....... 532
Bells, Parlor ........ 532
Bellows, Blacksmith .... 65
Bellows, Molders' ...... 65
Belt, Base Ball ....... 596
Belt Buckles ........ 331
Belt Buckles, Silver .... 432
Belt Holders and Pins.. 331
Belt Lacing ........ 56
Belt, Ladies' Dolly .... 32
Belt, Money ........589-590
Belt Pins, Silver ....... 429
Belt Punches ........ 83
Belt Rivets ........ 83
Belt Studs ........ 56
Belts, Cartridge .....589-590
Belts, Ladies' ........ 331
Belts, Men's ........ 218
Belts, Ladies' Bicycle ... 436
Belts, Life ........ 606
Benders, Tire ........ 66
Bench Drills ........ 65
Bench Screws ........ 83
Bench Stops ........ 83
Bench Vise ........ 65
Bent Cutter Stuff ...... 63
Bent Rims ........ 60
Benzine ..........20-21
Berry Dishes, Silver Plated ........ 449
Berry Spoons ........441-444
Berry Sets ........ 441
Berry Sets, Glass....... 686
Belting, Cotton ........ 56
Belting, Endless ....... 56
Belting, Leather ....... 56
Belting, Rubber ....... 56
Belting, Silk ........229, 331
Belting, Thresher ...... 56
Bevels ........ 73
Bevel Blades ........ 85
Bevel, Machinist ...... 85
Bevel Protractor ...... 85
Beverages ........ 11
Bib Plus ........ 429
Bibles ........ 348
Bicycle Boots, Ladies'.. ........Colored Pages
Bicycle Leggings ....... 206
Bicycle Shoes ........ 206
Bicycle Screw Plate .... 67
Bicycle Suits ........ 177
Bibs, Infant's ........ 309
Bibs, Stamped ........ 332
Bibs, Rubber ........ 329
Bicycle Balls ........ 619
Bicycle Bells ........ 617
Bicycle Belts ........ 218
Bicycles, Boy's .....614-615
Bicycle Bugles ........ 618
Bicycle Bundle Carriers 616-618
Bicycle Carriers .....616-618
Bicycle Cements ....... 619
Bicycle Chains ........ 619
Bicycle Chain Adjusters 619
Bicycle Chain Parts ... 619
Bicycle Child's Seat ... 618
Bicycle Clothing ...213-215
Bicycle Coasters ....... 617
Bicycle Cork Grips .... 618
Bicycle Cyclists' Cape.. 618
Bicycle Cyclometers ... 617
Bicycle Department.611-619
Bicycle Enamel ........ 619
Bicycle Enamel Brush.. 619
Bicycle Enamel Varnish 619
Bicycle Foot Rests .... 617
Bicycle Fluxine ....... 619
Bicycle, Girls .......614-615
Bicycle Goods .......611-619
Bicycle Grips ........ 618
Bicycle Guards ........ 618
Bicycle Handle Bars ... 616
Bicycle Hats ........232-236
Bicycle Horns ........ 618
Bicycle Hose
Bicycle Hose Supporters 619
Bicycle Hubs
Bicycle Lamps ........ 617
Bicycle Lamp Brackets. 617
Bicycle Leggings .....
Bicyle Locks ........ 618
Bicycle Lunch Boxes .. 616
Bicycle Oil ........ 619
Bicycle Pedals ........ 617
Bicycle Pants Guards .. 619
Bicycle Parcel Carriers 616-618
Bicycle Parts .......611-615
Bicycle Patching Plugs. 619
Bicycle Patching Rubber ........ 619
Bicycle Pumps ........ 617

Bicycle Repair Outfits... 618
Bicycle Rims ........ 619
Bicycle Saddles ........ 616
Bicycle Seat ........ 618
Bicycle Shoes ........ 266
Bicycle Siren Whistles.. 617
Bicycle Spoke Grips.... 618
Bicycle Spokes ........ 619
Bicycle Suits, Men's.... 177
Bicycle Suits, Ladies'... 281
Bicycle Tires ........ 616
Bicycle Tire Tape...... 618
Bicycle Toe Clips...... 618
Bicycle Tool Bags ...... 616
Bicycle Tourists' Cases. 616
Bicycle Valises ........ 616
Bicycle Valves ........ 617
Bicycle Valve Stems.... 617
Bicycle Wrenches ...... 618
Bicycle Wheels ........ 619
Bicycle Wheel Parts.... 619
ment ........ 619
Bicycle Whistles ........ 618
Bicycles, Women's.611-612-613
Bicycle Wood Rims..... 619
Bicycle Wood Rim Ce-
Bi-Focal Spectacles ........ 463
Bill Books ........324-325
Bill Poster's Tacks...... 39
Bindings ........ 263
Binders, Photo Album .. 480
Bird Cages ........ 89
Bird Cage Hooks........ 89
Bird Cage Springs...... 89
Bird Seed ........ 16
Biscuits ........ 16
Biscuit Cutters ........ 133
Biscuit Jars, Silver...... 454
Bit Boxes ........ 81
Bit Braces ........ 80
Bit Gauges ........ 82
Bit Sets ........ 81
Bit and Square Levels... 72
Bits, Auger ........ 81
Bits, Bridle ........ 760
Bits, Car ........ 81
Bits, Counter Sink...... 81
Bits, Drill ........ 81
Bits, Expansive ........ 81
Bits, Gimlet ........ 81
Bits, Imperial ........ 760
Bits, J. I. C. ........ 760
Bits, Overcheck........ 760
Bits, Mexican ........ 760
Bits, Military ........ 760
Bits, Racking ........ 760
Bits, Reamer ........ 81
Bits, Rubber Mouth..... 760
Bits, Screw Driver...... 81
Bits, Wilson ........ 760
Bitters, Stomach ........ 26
Black Berlin Gloves, Men's ........ 228
Black Chantilly Lace.... 268
Black Dress Goods.256-257-259
Black Land Plow........ 156
Black Lawns ........ 291
Black Shoe Buttons..... 207
Black Silks ........ 257
Black Tennis Shoes..... 203
Blackberries, Canned ... 11
Blackberries, Dried ..... 12
Blackberry Balsam ..... 26
Blackberry Brandy ..... 11
Blackboards ........ 356
Blacking ........ 19
Blacking Cases ........ 672
Blacking Sets ........ 114
Blacking, Shoe ........ 209
Blacksmith Tools ......64-68
Bladders, Foot Ball and
Blankets, Bed ........ 288
Blankets, Cooling ........ 771
Blankets, Horse .....770-771
Blankets, Lumberman's Storm ........ 771
Blanket, Rubber Horse.. 770
Blanket, Saddle........ 759
Blankets, Sweat ........ 771
Striking Bag ........ 594
Blatchford's Calf Meal. 30
Blatchford's Calf Meal. 23
Blazer Bicycle Suits, Ladies ........280-281
Bleached Cotton Flannel 288
Bleached Cottons ..... 292
Bleached Sheetings ... 292
Bleached Table Damask 294
Blenders ........ 113
Blinds, Fixtures ........ 93
Blinds, Fasts ........ 93
Blinds, Hinges ........ 96
Blocks, Tackle ........ 96
Block Planes ........ 75
Bloomer Suits, Ladies.. 281
Blotting Pads ........ 355
Blotting Paper, Photographic ........ 479
Blow Pipe or Torch ... 84
Blower, Portable ........ 65
Blouse, Waists, Boy's.. 247
Blouse, Hunting ........ 591
Blue Denim ........ 292
Blue Flame Stoves .... 118
Blue Flannel ........ 288
Blueing ........ 19
Boards, Bread ........ 140
Board Clips ........ 355
Boards, Drawing ........ 358
Boards, Ironing ........ 140
Boards, Lap ........ 140
Board Rules ........ 73
Boards, Stove ........ 129
Boats ........ 610
Boat Anchors ........ 606
Boat Compasses ........ 467
Boat Oars ........ 606
Boat Oar Locks ........ 606
Bob Beams ........ 63
Bob Benches ........ 63
Bob Knees ........ 63
Bobs, Plumb ........ 72
Bob Racers ........ 63
Bob Reaches ........ 63
Bob Rollers ........ 63
Bob Runners ........ 63
Bob Saddles ........ 63
Bob Shoes ........ 63
Bob Sleds ........ 63
Bob Woods ........ 63
Bodies, Buggy ........ 58
Body Brussels Carpet... 285
Boilers, Coffee ........130-132
Boilers and Engines.... 151
Boilers, Farmers' ........ 127
Boilers, Rice ........130-136
Boilers, Wash ........ 132
Bolero Fronts ........ 311
Boleros ........ 318
Bolster, Wagon ........ 63
Bolster Plates ........ 62
Bolts, Carriage ........ 39
Bolts, Chain ........ 92
Bolt Clippers ........ 67
Bolts, Clip King ........ 61
Bolts, Door ........88-92
Bolt Ends.... ........ 39
Bolts, Flush ........ 93
Bolts, Foot ........ 92
Bolts, King ........ 62
Bolts, Machine ........ 39
Bolts, Sleigh Shoe ........ 63
Bolts, Stove ........ 39
Bolster Spring ........ 60
Bolts, Tire ........ 59
Bolt Tongs ........ 67
Bolts, Window Springs.. 89
Books ........337-348
Books, Bill ........324-325
Book Cases ........652-653
Books on Electricity ........ 472
Books, Gospel Hymn.538-539
Book Holders ........ 336
Books, Homeopathic .... 30
Book of the Lantern (Magic) ........ 484
Book Slates ........ 356
Book Straps ........ 355
Books, Musical Instruction ........538-540
Books, Pin ........ 322
Books, Pocket ........ 325
Bookkeeping Blanks .... 349
Bootees, Infants' ........ 309
Bootees, Lumberman's.. 206
Boot Calks ........ 207
Boots, Boys' ........ 203
Boots, Horse ........ 767
Boot Jacks ........ 99
Boots, Ladies' Rubber.. 205
Boots, Men's ........ 202
Boots, Rubber ........ 205
Boots, Paultice ........ 767
Bone, Cracked for Poultry ........ 30
Bones, Ground ........ 23
Bones, Rattle ........ 532
Bonnets, Infants' ....319-320
Bonnets, Ladies' ........ 302
Bon Bon Dishes, Silver Plated ........ 450
Bordeaux Mixture ........ 22
Borated Talcum Powder. 28
Borax ........ 28
Borax ........ 19
Boring Machines ........ 80
Boring Machine Augers. 80
Bosom Boards ........ 140
Buttons, Bone ........ 319
Bottles, Glass ........ 35
Bottles, Nursing ........ 329
Bottles, Rubber ........ 329
Bottles, Rubber Water.. 32
Bouquet Holders, Silver Plated ........ 449
Bows, Double Bass ........ 534
Bow Frogs, Double Bass 534
Bow Frogs, Viola ........ 534
Bow Frogs, Violin ........ 533
Bows, Wagon ........ 62
Bow Hair, Double Bass. 535
Bow Hair, Viola ........ 534
Bow Hair, Violin ........ 534
Bow Hair, Violoncello.. 535
Bows, Ox ........ 46
Bow Pins ........ 46
Bowls and Pitchers..... 134
Bow Resin, Violin ........ 534
Bow Resin, Violoncello.. 535
Bowls, Scotch ........ 129
Bow Screws, Violin..... 533
Bows, Violin, etc. ........ 532
Bowls, Wooden ........ 140
Boxes, Bait ........604-605
Boxes, Bread ........ 135
Boxes, Cash ........ 135
Box Churn ........143-144
Box Couches ........ 667
Boxes, Deed ........ 135
Boxes, Dredge ........ 134
Boxes, Feed ........ 46
Boxing Gloves ........593-594
Box Graters ........ 134
Box Hooks ........ 99
Box, Ice ........ 104
Boxes, Knife and Fork.. 135
Boxes, Lunch ........ 133
Box Mackintosh ........ 187
Box, Mail ........ 98
Boxes, Match ........ 334
Boxes, Meter.... ........ 69
Boxes, Music ........523-524
Box, Negative ........ 479
Boxed Paper ........ 350
Boxes, Puff ........ 28
Boxes, Puff, Silver Plater 456
Boxes, Shell ........ 589
Boxes, Snuff ........ 334
Boxes, Soap ........ 328
Boxes, Spice ........ 135
Box Straps ........ 62
Boxes, Tackle ........604-605
Boxes, Tin ........ 35
Box, Twine ........ 98
Boxes, Vaseline, Silver Plated ........ 456
Boxes, Wood ........ 35
Boxwood Rules ........ 73
Boys' Air Rifles ........ 574
Boys' Blouses and Waists 247
Boys' Clothing ........ 176
Boys' Clothing........179-180
Boys' Hats ........ 235
Boys' Hoes ........ 49
Boys' Hose ........ 246
Boys' Leather Stockings. 246
Boys' Long Pants...... 180
Boys' Mackintoshes .... 187
Boys' Overalls ........ 178
Boys' Overshoes .....204-206
Boys' Reefer Suits...... 183
Boys' Sailor Suits...... 182
Boys' Shirts ........ 213
Boys' Shoes ........ 203
Boys' Shotguns ........ 538
Boys' Wagons ........ 143
Boys' Wash Sailor Suits. 182
Boys' Watches .......369-371
Brace, Lightning ........ 82
Bracelets, Gold Filled and Silver ........ 415
Brackets, Banjo ........ 535
Bracket Clock ........671-672
Brackets, Corner.... ........ 672
Bracelets, Diamond ........ 403
Brackets, Flower Pot... 88
Bracket Saws ........69-70
Brackets, Shelf ........88-92
Brackets, Shingling ..... 74
Bradawl ........ 82
Brads, Wire ........ 38
Braids, Dress ........ 332
Braids, Feather Stitched 323
Braid, Gold Tinsel ........ 319
Braids, Hercules ........ 319
Braid, Skirt ........ 323
Braid, Soutache ........ 319
Braid, Tubular ........ 319
Bran Middlings ........ 23
Brass Band Harmonicas. 526
Brass Band Instruments ........530-531
Brass Band Music...... 540
Brass Box Books ........ 88
Brass Kettles ........ 129
Brass Curtain Rings.... 299
Brass Rods ........ 299
Brass Screws ........ 40
Brass Shells ........ 584
Brass Shoe Nails ........ 208
Brass Stair Rods ........ 300
Brass Watches ........ 376
Brass Wire ........ 41
Braziers ........ 84
Bread Boards ........ 140
Bread Boxes ........ 135
Bread Knives ........ 108
Bread Raisers ........ 132
Bread Pans........133-136
Bread Trays, Silver.... 454
Breaking Plows ........ 156
Breast Drills ........ 82
Breast Pins, Silver...427-430
Breast Pump ........ 32
Breast Pumps ........ 329
Breech-loading Guns..531-571
Breeching ........ 762
Briar Pipes ........333-334
Bridal Night Gowns.... 282
Bridal Sets, Floral ........ 303
Bridal Wreaths ........ 303
Bridges, Banjo ........ 535
Bridges, Double Bass.... 534
Bridges, Guitar ........ 535
Bridges, Mandolin ........ 536
Bridge Pins, Guitar.... 535
Bridges, Viola ........ 534
Bridges, Violin ........ 534
Bridges, Violoncello.... 535
Bridles, Buggy ........ 758
Bridles, Cowboy ........ 758
Bridles, Riding ........ 758
Bridles, Rawhide ........ 758
Bridles, Open ........ 758
Bridles, Open Team.... 758
Bridles, Stallion Lead.. 758
Bridles, Team ........ 758
Brilliantine Dress Goods. 259
Brilliantine Skirts ........ 271
Bristles, Shoemakers' ... 209
Broadaxe ........ 78
Broadcast Seeders ........ 155
Broad Hatchet ........ 78
Brocaded Satins ........ 261
Brocaded Silks ........ 261
Broilers ........129-135
Broom Holders ........ 98
Bromide Paper ........ 480
Bromo Vichy ........ 26
Brooms ........ 20
Bronze Clock Ornaments. 459
Bronze Dividers ........ 85
Brooch Pins ......428-429-430
Brooches, Diamond .... 403
Brooches, Garnet.... ........ 430
Brooches, Mourning .... 430
Brownie Suits ........ 181
Brushes, Bath ........33-327
Brushes, Bristle, Gun.587-588
Brush Broom Holders .. 135
Brussels Carpet ........ 285
Brushes, Clothes ........ 327
Brushes, Complexion ... 33
Brush Department ....113-114
Brushes, Hair ........ 327
Brushes, Hand ........ 327
Brushes, Horse ........ 767
Brushes, Photographic .. 479
Brush Plows ........ 156
Brushes, Rice Root...... 767
Brushes, Scrub ........ 20
Brush Sets ........ 328
Brush, Shaving, Silver.. 436
Brushes, Sterling, Silver Handle........ 437
Brushes, Toilet ........33-327
Brushes, Tooth ........34-327
Brushes, Wire Gun....587-588
Buck Saws ........ 69
Buckles and Loops ........ 58
Buckles, Belt ........ 331
Buckles, Pants ........ 321
Buckles, Garter ........435-436
Buckles, Harness ....764-765
Buckets, Minnow........ 605
Buckles, Trace ........ 764
Buckles, Ladies' Belt.... 432
Buckles, Vest ........ 321
Buckskin Gloves ........ 228
Buckwheat ........ 15
Buff Shoes, Men's ........ 199
Buffets ........ 650
Buggy Shafts ........ 63
Buggy Singletrees ........ 63
Buggy Poles ........ 63
Buggy Neck Yokes........ 63
Buggy Paint ........ 22
Buggy Tops ........ 57
Buggy Cushions ........ 58
Buggy Aprons ........ 58
Buggy Dashes ........ 58
Buggy Bodies ........ 58
Buggy Seats ........ 58
Buggy Wheels ........58-59
Buggy Hubs ........ 59
Buggy Spokes ........ 60
Buggy Steps ........ 61
Buggies, Baby ......692-696
Buggies and Carriages..
Builders' Compasses.... 467
Builders' Hardware ...86-93
Building Paper ........95-96
Building Paper ........ 23
........708-723
Bull Rings ........ 46
Bull Snaps ........ 46
Bullseye Lens ........ 137
Bullet Dippers ........ 587
Bullets, Grooved........ 582
Bullet Molds ........586-587
Bullets, Patched........ 582
Bullnose Rabbet Plane.. 76
Bunting ........ 293
Bureaus ........ 650
Burglar Alarms ........ 471
Burlap Bags ........ 293
Burlap Sacking........ 292
Burners, Lamp ........ 137
Burners, Lantern ........ 137
Burnishers ........ 479
Burnishine ........ 19
Burrs, Riveting ........ 61
Bush Hooks ........ 50
Bush Scythes ........ 51
Bust Pads ........ 307
Butchers' Cleavers ..... 103
Butcher Knives ........ 108
Butcher Refrigerators .. 105
Butcher Linen ........ 295
Butcher Saws ........ 69
Butchers' Scales ........ 47
Butcher Steels ........ 108
Butter Boxes ........146-147
Butter Cloth ........ 292
Butter Cloth ........ 147
Butter Color Laces ........ 265
Butter Color ........ 14
Butter Color ........ 147
Butter Dishes ........ 448
Butter Knives ........438-445
Butter Ladles ........ 147
Butter Molds........ 146
Butter Paper ........ 147
Butter Sizers ........ 586
Butter Trays ........ 146
Butter Triers ........ 146
Butter Tubs ........ 147
Butter Workers ........ 144
Buttress ........ 67
Buttons, Agate ........ 320
Butts, Cast ........ 91
Buttons, Collar ........ 425
Buttons, Cuff ........ 424
Buttons, Door ........ 88
Buttons, Dress ........ 320
Buttons, Emblem ....422-423
Button Fastening Machine.... ........ 207
Buttons, Gold........ 320
Buttons, Hand Snap .... 320
Button Hole Scissors, Silver ........ 435
Button Hooks, Silver ... 435
Button Hooks ........ 209
Buttons, Horn ........ 320
Buttons, Mohair ........ 320
Button Overshoes ........ 204
Buttons, Pants ........ 320
Buttons, Pearl........ 319
Buttons, Rein ........ 763
Buttons, Shirt ........ 320
Button Shoes ........ 207
Buttons, Silk Covered .. 320
Buttons, Silver ........ 320
Buttons, Solid Gold Cuff. 425
Buttons, Tufting ........ 58
Buttonholes ........ 58
Buttonhole Scissors .... 109
Butts, Wrought ........ 86
Buzzers.... ........ 471


## C


Cable Cord, Silk........ 319
Cabin Bags ........ 253
Cabinet Rasps........ 71
Cabinet Scrapers........ 77
Cabinet Photographs........ 469
Cabinets, Bathroom..... 671
Cable Chain........ 97
Cachous for the Breath.. 28
Cages, Bird ........ 89
Cake Cutters........ 133
Cake Dishes, Silver..... 450
Cake Forks........ 444
Cake Knives........ 444
Cake Pans........131-136
Cake Turner........ 132
Calf Shoes, Men's... .197-201
Calf Skins ........ 204
Calf Weaners........ 46
Calendar Clocks......460-461
Calendar Watches ........ 374
Calfskin Gloves, Men's.. 228
Calks, Toe ........ 68
Calks, Boots ........ 207
California Flannel........ 288
California Bed Blankets. 288
Calicos and Prints ........ 291
Caliper Square ........ 85
Caliper........74, 84-85
Caliper Rules ........ 73
Call Annunciators........ 471
Calls ........ 618
Calls, Bird........ 590
Calls, Dog........ 590
Calls, Duck........ 590
Calls, Goose........ 590
Calls, Police........ 592
Calls, Snipe........ 590
Calls, Turkey........ 590
Cambric Drawers........ 308
Cambric Dresses, Child's. 278
Cambric Nightgowns.... 282
Cambric Skirt Linings.. 258
Camels Hair Underwear, Child's........ 242
Camels Hair Underwear, Men's ........ 239
Camels Hair Underwear, Ladies'........ 242
Camel Hair Brushes..... 113
Cameo Drapery........ 291
Camera Tripods ........ 477
Camera Shutters........ 478
Camera Printing Frames. 478
Cameras, Photographic ........473-477
Camp Lamp........ 610
Camp Stoves........ 610
Camphorated Oil........ 28
Camphor, Spirits........ 27
Camping Cots ........ 610
Camping Chairs ........ 610
Camping Outfits........ 610
Can Meats........ 14
Can Fish........ 14
Can Goods........ 11
Can Openers........ 23
Can Openers........ 98
Candles........ 20
Candy........ 17
Canes........ 248
Canes, Gold........ 436
Cane Mills........ 154
Canes, Walking........ 436
Cans, Oil........ 135
Cans, Baking Powder... 35
Cans, Oil........ 84
Canisters........ 134
Cantanas ........ 759
Canvas Belts, Men's..... 218
Canvas Boats........ 610
Canvas Cots........ 610
Canvas Gun Cases........ 598
Canvas Gymnasium Shoes........ 203
Canvas Hunting Clothing........588-589
Canvas Hats and Caps.588-589
Canvas Shoes, Base Ball. 596
Canvas Stools........ 610
Canvas Slippers, Men's.. 209
Canvas for Tents, etc... 293
Canvas Telescope Cases. 253
Canvas Traveling Bags.. 253
Canopy Tops ........ 57
Cap Badges, Metal ........ 236
Cape Mackintosh Coat.. 187
Capers........ 12

Capo D'Astros, Guitar.. 535
Capes, Ladies'.. .......273-276
Caps....... .................. 536
Caps, Base Ball.......... 596
Caps, Canvas............. 591
Caps, Corduroy.......... 591
Caps, Children's.......236-237
Caps, Gun.................. 584
Caps, Hunting............ 591
Caps, Infants'............309-310
Caps, Men's and Boy's.235-236
Caps, Pole............... 62
Capsules, Empty Gelatine .................. 35
Car Inspectors' Lanterns. 137
Car Bits ................... 81
Carbo Wafers............ 26
Carbon Paper............ 359
Carbolic Soap............. 33
Card Mounts..........481-482
Card, Curry ............. 764
Card Receivers, Silver Plate ................... 449
Cards, Fancy............. 332
Cards, Playing........... 356
Carpenter Adze.......... 78
Carpenters' Augers...... 80
Carpenters' Overalls.... 178
Carpenter Pencils....... 74
Carpenters' Pincers..... 82
Carpenters' Squares.. .. 73
Carpenters' Slick......... 79
Carpets.... .........284-285
Carpet Binding.. ........ 300
Carpets and Rugs........ 300
Carpet Linings........... 300
Carpet Slippers, Ladies'. 196
Carpet Slippers, Men's.. 200
Carpet Stretchers.... ... 78
Carpet Sweepers.......... 101
Carpet Tacks ............ 38
Carpet Warp.............. 292
Carriage Bolts........... 39
Carriages, Baby.......692-696
Carriage Department. .708-727
Carriage Fringe........... 58
Carriage Hardware.....57-63
Carriage Knobs........... 58
Carriage Knobs........... 58
Carriage Lamps........... 58
Carriage Springs.......... 60
Carriage Steps............ 61
Carriage Top Prop Nuts. 58
Carriers ................. 618
Carriers, Game.. ........ 590
Carriers, Hay............. 165
Carrying Case for Graphophone ................ 485
Carrying Cases........616-618
Cartridges ............580-583
Carts, Barrow............ 164
Carts, Hand.............. 164
Carts, Road...........723-727
Carving Tools............ 80
Carving Knives and Forks ................. 108
Cash Boxes............... 135
Cash Drawers............. 99
Cashmere Dress Goods.254-256
Cashmere Cloaks, Infants'................... 283
Cashmere Shawls......... 305
Casters, Bed.............. 98
Casing, Molding.......... 95
Casings, Outer........... 616
Casters, Plate............ 98
Casing, Whalebone....... 323
Cases, Autoharp......... 536
Cases, Blacking.......... 672
Cases, Banjo............. 535
Cases, Clarionet......... 536
Cases, Cornet............ 536
Cases, Egg............... 141
Cases, Fish Rod.......... 599
Cases, Flute.............. 536
Cases, Gun............588-589
Cases, Guitar............ 535
Cases, Gold Filled Watch, How Made .............. 372
Cases, Medicine.......... 30
Cases, Mandolin.......... 536
Cases, Needle............ 322
Cases, Piccolo.... ....... 536
Cases, Reed.............. 599
Cases, Viola.............. 534
Cases, Violin............. 533
Cases, Violoncello....... 532
Cases, Zither............. 536
Casters, Silver Pickle.... 448
Casters .................. 617
Casters, Silver Plated Table ..................... 447
Cassia Buds.............. 9
Cassimeres and Cloths.. 289
Cast Bob Shoes........... 63
Castinets................. 533
Castor Oil................ 21
Castor Oil................ 27
Castroline..............26-28
Catarrh Snuff............ 26
Catches, Cupboard.... ..88-91
Catches, French Window. 91
Catches, Screen Door... 92
Catchers' Masks......595-996
Catchers' Mitts........... 595
Catchers' Protectors..... 595
Catches, Screen Door.... 44
Cathartic Pills........... 26
Catheters ................ 32
Catholic Bibles.......... 348
Catsup ................12-13
Cattle Leaders........... 46
Cattle Tie Irons.......... 46
Cattle Powders........... 30
Cattle or Horse Powder. 23
Caviar, Canned........... 14
Cedar Churn ............ 144
Cedar Tubs and Pails .. 138
Celery Salt.... ......... 13
Celerite Paper .......... 480
Celery Holders.... ...... 449
Celluloid Combs.. ....... 326
Celluloid Collars and Cuffs.................... 219
Celluloid Films ......... 480
Celluloid Rattles......... 328
Celluloid Shirt Bosoms.. 219
Cements, Bicycle ....... 619
Cement (Liquid) .......21-22
Cement and Lime........ 23
Cement Leather.. ........ 208
Cement, Rubber ........ 303
Center Clips ............ 62
Center Punch ........... 82
Cerealine................. 15
Chain Door Fasteners... 93
Chain Adjusters ......... 619
Chain Mountings ....... 413
Chain, Picket ........... 46
Chain Pump ............. 53
Chain Bolts ............. 92
Chains, Trace .......... 764
Chains, Tie.............. 46
Chains, Heel ............ 765
Chains, Breast .......... 765
Chairs, Camp ........... 610
Chains, Bicycle .......... 619
Chains, Key.............. 321
Chains, Stallions' Lead.. 758
Chains, Halter .......... 758
Chains, Safety Bridle .. 758
Chains.. ................. 97
Chains, Well ............ 99
Chains, Fob.............. 408
Chains, Hair ............ 409
Chains, Silk, Vest....... 409
Chains, Silver ........... 409
Chains, White Metal..... 409
Chains, Ladies' Silk...... 409
Chains ................404-409
Chains, Solid Gold....... 406
Chains, Ladies' Victoria..... ............410-411
Chains, Ladies' Solid Gold.................... 413
Chains, Bracelet. Gold Filled and Silver...... 415
Chain Mountings, Gents' and Ladies' .......... 413
Chains, Lorgnettes, Gold Filled and Solid Gold 412
Chains, Neck, Solid Gold and Gold Filled....... 414
Chains, Gents' Gold Filled ...............404-406
Chains and Loops for Curtains ............... 298
Chair Drops ............ 297
Chair Seats ............. 142
Chair Hammock ......... 142
Chairs, Assorted .....642-648
Chairs, Dining ........642-643
Chairs, Bedroom ......642-643
Chairs, Child's .......645-647
Chairs, Youths' ......... 645
Chairs, Misses' ......... 645
Chairs, Invalid .......... 645
Chairs, Office.. ......... 646
Chairs, Library .......644-646
Chairs, Lawn ........... 646
Chairs, Rattan .......... 647
Chairs, Reception ....... 648
Chairs, Folding ......... 648
Chairs, Child's Cabinet. 648
Chairs, Step Ladder .... 648
Chairs, Camp ........... 648
Chairs, Upholstered .... 665
Chairs, Wire ............ 45
Chalk Crayons .......... 355
Chalk Line, Reel and Awls .................... 74
Chalk Lines ............. 74
Chalk ................... 74
Challies ................ 262
Chambers ............... 132
Chamber Pails .......132-134
Chamber Sets ........... 134
Chamber Sets ........654-655
Chamfer Plane ......... 76
Chamfer Gauge ......... 79
Chamois Skins ......... 208
Chamois Skins ......... 330
Chamois Gloves, Ladies'. 231
Changeable Silks ....... 261
Chantilly ............... 265
Chandeliers ............ 691
Chaparejos ............. 759
Chapel Organs ......... 514
Charcoal Irons ......... 100
Charms, Diamond ...... 403
Charms, Watch .......419-420
Charms, Emblem, Gold Filled ................... 421
Charms, Emblem, Solid Gold .................... 421
Chatelaine Watches ....391-399
Check Door.............. 44
Check Valves ........... 54
Chelsea Cloth Wrappers.. 272
Chemical Thermometers. 470
Chemicals, Photographic. 308
Chemise ................ 308
Chenille Balls.... ....... 332
Chenille Table Covers... 298
Choppers' Mittens ..... 229
Chocolate ............... 9
Chow-Chow ............. 13
Chopping Knives ....... 102
Chopping Trays ........ 140
Cherries, Dried.. ....... 12
Cherries, Canned ...... 11
Cheroots ..............23-24
Cherry Phosphate ...... 12
Cherry Stoners ......... 102
Chest Handlers ......... 99
Chest Hinges ........... 86
Chest Locks ...........87-88
Chesterman's Tape ..... 73
Cheese Vats ............ 144
Cheese Making Outfit... 145
Cheese Press Screws.... 145
Cheese Color ........... 147
Cheese .................. 16
Cheese Coloring ........ 14
Cheese, Butter and Dairy Cloth ................... 292
Cheviot Shirtings ....... 292
Cheviot Suitings .......289
Chewing Gum ........... 17
Chicory ................. 9
Chiffoniers ............. 658
Child's Toilet Sets, Silver 435
Child's Seat ............ 618
Children's Shoes ....... 194
Child's Overshoes ...... 204
Child's Oxfords.. ....... 195
Child's Beaver Felt Shoes.................. 196
Child's Cribs and Folding Beds ............. 660
Child's Straw Hats ..... 303
Child's Trays ........... 134
Child's Cups, Silver..... 446
Child's Table Sets.......439
Child's Waists .......... 307
Children's White Dresses 278
Children's Union Suits.. 240
Children's Seamless Waists .................. 241
Children's Underwear..241-242
Children's and Misses' Caps ..................236-237
Children's Wool Mittens 231
Children's Kid Mittens.. 231
Children's Parasols .... 250
Children's Handkerchiefs ................... 227
Children's Hose ........ 246
Children's Shawls ...... 305
Children's Ready-Made Dresses..............304-305
Children's Oilcloth Mats. 309
Children's Sun Hats .... 310
Children's Military Reefer Suit .............. 184
Children's Kilt Suit .... 185
Children's Head to Foot Combination Suit ..... 186
Children's Clothing ..179-181
Children's Department.... 181
Children's Junior Suits.. 183
Children's Zouave Suits.. 183
Children's Jackets and Reefers ..............277-278
Chili Sauce ............. 12
Chimney Thimbles ...... 128
Chimneys, Lamp ........ 137
Chin Rests, Violin ...... 534
China Matting .......... 300
China Silks............... 257
China Silks, Colored.... 261
China Closets ........... 650
China Cups and Saucers.. ...........678-681, 685
China Vases ............ 685
China Plates .....678-681, 685
China Shaving Mugs .... 685
China Pitchers ....678-681, 685
Chips, Poker ............ 356
Chipper, Ice ............ 103
Chisels .................. 79
Chisel Handle .........79-80
Chisel Grinder .......... 80
Chisel Gauge ........... 80
Chisel, Ice .............. 103
Church Bells ............ 106
Church Service Sets..... 455
Chronographs ........... 377
Churn Thermometers ... 470
Churns ................143-144
Cider Mills .............. 154
Cigar Holders ........... 334
Cigar Cases, Fancy...... 437
Cigars ..................23-24
Cigarettes................ 24
Cinches, Cotton Web ... 761
Cinches, California Hair. 761
Cinnamon ............... 9
Circular Saws .......... 68
Circular Plane.......... 75
Circles, Paper .......... 147
Citron .................. 12
Clams, Canned ......... 14
Clamp Rests for Telescopes .................. 465
Clamps, Saw ........... 70
Clamps .................. 83
Clamp Head ............ 83
Clamps, Hose ........... 56
Clamps, Trap Setting.... 100
Clapboard Gauge ....... 74
Clapboard Marker....... 74
Clappers and Bones......532
Clarionet Cases ........ 536
Clarionet Mouthpieces .. 536
Clarionet Mouthpiece Cases .................. 536
Clarionet Mouthpiece
Clarionet Reeds ........ 536
Clarionet Reed Holders. 536
Clarionet Reed Trimmers 536
Clarionets.... .......... 528
Clariophones ........... 528
Clasps, Corset .......... 323
Claw Hatchet ........... 78
Clay Worsted Suits, Men's ................... 170
Cleaners, Window ...... 102
Cleaning Rods .......587-588
Cleaners, Lamp Chimney 98
Cleaners, Pot ........... 98
Cleaners, File .......... 71
Cleaner, Drain ......... 49
Cleavers, Butcher's ..... 103
Cleats, Line ............ 89
Clevises ................ 62
Clinch Shoe Nails........ 208
Clinch Rivets ........... 83
Clinical Thermometers .. 470
Clip Files .. ............ 355
Clip Yokes ............. 61
Clips, Axle ............. 61
Clips, Photographic ..... 479
Clips, Toe .............. 618
Clipper, Grinding ....... 111
Clippers, Hair .......... 111
Clippers, Spring........ 111
Clippers, Bolt .......... 67
Clippers, Horse ........ 763
Cloaks, Infants' Long Cashmere ............... 283
Cloaks and Wraps.....273-277
Clock Shelves .......... 671
Clock Bronze Ornaments. 459
Clocks..................457-461
Clog Shoes, Men's....... 206
Cloths, Turkish Face ... 297
Cloth, Table Linen ..... 294
Cloth and Cassimere Suitings ................... 289
Cloth, Ladies' .......... 255
Cloth, Black Jacquard... 259
Cloth, Madras .......... 262
Cloths, Stamped ......331-332
Cloth Brushes ......... 327
Cloth, Sanitary ........ 323
Clothes Lines .......... 20
Cloth, Emery ........... 77
Cloth Circles .......... 147
Cloth Top Shoes, Ladies'. ......................191-192
Clothes Bars ........... 141
Clothes Baskets ........ 142
Clothes Line Hooks..... 89
Clothes Line Pulleys.... 89
Clothes Line Reels..... 100
Clothes Lines, Wire..... 100
Clothes Pins ........... 139
Clothes Sprinkler....... 134
Clothes Wringers .....100-101
Clothing, Athletic ....596-597
Clothing, Boys' ..176, 179, 186
Clothing, Children's ...179-181
Clothing Department. ..166-186
Clothing, Hunter's.. ..590-592
Clothing, Juvenile ...... 181
Clothing, Men's ......166-177
Clothing, Oil ........188-189
Clothing, Summer, Men's 176
Clothing, Youths'.....179-180
Club House Ties .....223-224
Club Spokes............. 60
Clubs, Indian .......... 594
Clout Nails ............ 38
Cloves ................. 9
Clover Seed ............ 25
Coach Oil .............. 21
Coal Oil ............... 20
Coal Hods .............. 129
Coal Chisels ........... 80
Coats, Alpaca, Men's.... 176
Coat, Rubber ........... 189
Coat Cape Mackintosh .. 187
Coat, Combination Mackintosh ................. 187
Coats, Cotton, Men's.... 176
Coat Hanger ........... 135
Coat Hangers, Silver.... 436
Coats, Hunting .......590-591
Coats, Linen, Men's..... 176
Coats, Ministers' ....... 176
Coats, Mohair, Men's.... 176
Coats, Men's ........... 173
Coat Mackintosh ....... 187
Coats, Serge, Men's..... 176
Coats and Vests, Men's.. 173
Cobweb Brusher......... 114
Cobblers' Tools ......208-209
Cockeyes ............... 765
Cocoa Door Mats........ 300
Cocoa Shells ........... 9
Cocoa .................. 9
Cocoanut ............... 11
Codfish ................ 14
Cod Liver Oil........... 26
Cod Liver Oil........... 21
Coddington Magnifiers .. 466
Coffee .................. 9
Coffee Boilers .......130-132
Coffee Canisters ....... 134
Coffee Essence ......... 9
Coffee Flasks .......... 133
Coffee Mills ........... 103
Coffee Pots ..........132, 136
Coffee Pots, Silver...... 453
Coffee Sets, Silver...... 454
Coffee Spoons.....438, 442, 445
Colanders ............... 132
Cold Cutter ............ 68
Colored Silks and Satins 257
Colored Silk Velvet...... 256
Colored Bosom Shirts, Men's ................... 212
Colored Shoe Buttons.... 207
Colored Shoe Laces..... 209
Colored Dress Sateens... 290
Cologne ................ 19
Colognes ..............33-34
Cottosuet .............. 14
Colt Skin Shoes......... 198
Columbia Zithers ....... 522
Collars, Buggy ......... 761
Collars, Breast ......... 762
Collar Buttons, Gold.... 425
Collars and Cuffs, Ladies' 311
Collars and Cuffs, Men's. 219
Collars and Cuffs, Boys'. 219
Collars, Double Breast.. 762
Collars, Horse ......... 761
Collars, Ox ............ 761
Collars, Sweat ......... 761
Collars, Stovepipe ..... 128
Collapsing Cups ........ 136
Combs .................. 326
Comb, Black Mane....... 767
Comb and Brush Case.... 135
Comb, Curry ............ 764
Combs, Dog ............. 592
Comb, German Silver.... 592
Combs, Graining ........ 113
Combs, Side, Silver..... 437
Combined Drill ......... 161
Combination Mackintosh
Combination Squares ...73-85
Combination Suits ...... 184
Comforters and Quilts.. 288
Comic Songs ........... 538
Compasses, Architects' .. 467
Compasses, Boat ....... 467
Compasses, Miners' .... 467
Compasses, Pocket .... 467
Compasses, Surveyors' .. 467
Compasses, Woodman's .. 467
Compass Saws .......... 70
Combination Planes...... 76
Compasses ...........353-357
Complexion Wafers ..... 26
Complexion Brush ...... 33
Common Diapers ....... 323
Communion Sets ....... 455
Concert Roller Organs... 524
Concertinas ............ 526
Condensed Milk ........ 15
Conductors' Caps ...... 236
Conductors' Lanterns... 137
Condition Powders ..... 30
Conductor Pipe ........ 96
Conductor Punch ....... 83
Condensing Lenses ..... 484
Confectioners' Thermometers ................... 470
Confirmation Suits ...... 186
Congo Canes ........... 248
Congress Shoes, Ladies'. 192
Cook Books ............. 346
Cook Stoves ..........119-124
Cooking Outfit, Camping. 610
Coolers, Water ......... 135
Cooley Creamer ........ 145
Cooley Cans ........... 145
Copper Rivets ......... 83
Copper Kettles ........ 130
Coppers, Soldering ..... 84
Copper Tea Kettle....... 132
Copper Tacks .......... 39
Copper Wire ........... 41
Coopers' Adze ......... 79
Coopers' Hoop Knives .. 79
Coopers' Fraes......... 79
Cord Silk Cable......... 319
Cord Silk Lacing........ 319
Cord for Pictures...... 298
Cord, Sash ...........89-90
Cordage ..............89-90
Corded Pique ........293-296
Cordial Neutralizing ..293
Corduroy Boys' Suits ..................181-186
Corduroy Bicycle Leggings .........181-186
Corduroy Caps ........236
Corduroy Caps, Men's..236
Corduroy Caps, Boys'... 236
Corduroy Caps, Child's.. 236
Cordovan Shoes, Men's. 197
Corduroy Suits ......... 591
Corduroy ............... 289
Cork Floats............ 602
Cork Grips ............ 618
Cork Insoles ........... 209
Cork Sole Shoes, Men's. 198
Corks .................. 35
Corn and Cotton Stalk Cutter ................. 159
Corduroy Suits, Men's.... 174
Corduroy Vests, Men's.. 175
Corer, Parer and Slicer.. 102
Corer, Apple ........... 134
Corn Popper ........... 135
Corn Sheller ..........153-154
Corn Planters ......... 155
Corkscrews ............ 98
Corn Beef ............. 13
Corn and Bunion Plasters ..................... 35
Corn, Canned .......... 11
Corn Cure Shoes, Men's. 198
Corn Hooks ............ 51
Corn Knives ........... 51

Corn Knife 33
Corn Meal 15
Corn Starch 16
Corn and Bunion Remover 26
Corner Brackets 672
Corner Blocks 95
Corner Brace 80
Corner Chisels 79
Cornet Cases 536
Corner Irons 61
Corner Irons, Screen 44
Corner Trowels 84
Cornets 530-531
Corset Clasps 323
Corset Covers 308
Corset Department 306
Cornet Instruction Books 541
Corset Laces 308
Cornet Music 540
Cornet Mouth Pieces 537
Corset Waists 307
Cotton Coats, Men's 176
Cotton Plow 156
Cosmetics 34
Cot Beds 661
Cots, Folding 610
Cottage Organs 512-513
Cotton Batting 292
Cotton Belting 56
Cotton Blankets 288
Cotton Crepon 290
Cotton Crash Toweling 295
Cotton, Crochet 320-321
Cotton Duck 290
Cotton Diapers 295
Cotton Darning 321
Cotton Duck Tidies 321
Cotton Embroidery 321
Cotton Elderdown 288
Cotton Flannel 288
Cotton Knitting 321
Cotton, Spool 320
Cotton Towels 296
Cotton Underwear, Ladies' and Misses' 240-241
Cotton Worsted Pants Goods 289
Cotton Weaving 292
Cotton Wadding 292
Cotton Yarn 292
Cottolene 14
Couches 667
Cough Syrups 26
Counter Scales 47
Counter Sink Bits 81
Couplings, Hose 56
Couplings, Dog 592
Couplings, Whiffletree 62
Coupling Shaft 61
Cove Planes 77
Covert Cloth 255
Covers, Emigrant 608
Covers, Fly 770
Covers, Gun 588-589
Covers, Horse 608
Covers, Horse 770
Covers, Machine 608
Covers, Merchandise 608
Covers, Pot 130
Covered Pails 131
Covers, Stack 608
Covers, Wagon 608
Cow Ties 46
Cowboy Boots 201-202
Coat 187
Cowboys' Gloves 229
Cowboys' Hats 234
Crabs, Deviled 14
Crack Proof Shoes 197
Crackers, Nut 98
Crackers 16
Cracked Bone 23
Cracked Wheat 15
Cradles, Child's 661
Cradles, Grain 50
Cranberries, Canned 11
Crash Hats, Men's 233
Crash Suits, Ladies' 281
Crash Suits, Men's 176
Crash Toweling 295
Crayon Pencils 353
Cream Colored Laces 265
Cream, Cold 26, 34
Cream, Evaporated 15
Cream Separator 143
Cream Setters 145
Creams, Toilet 34
Cream Tartar 10
Cream, Witch Hazel 27
Creameries 143
Creamers, Silver 451-453
Creole Shoes, Men's 200-201
Crepon Cotton 290
Crepe Tissue Paper 333
Creedmoors, Men's 201
Creek Seines 606
Creels, Trout 605
Cribs, Child's 660
Crimpers, Hair 322
Crimpers, Shells 587
Crochet Cotton 320-321
Crochet Needles 322
Croquet Sets 593
Crowbars 50
Crooks, Shepherds' 46
Cross-Cut Saws 69
Cross-Cut Saw Handles 62
Cross Links 62
Cross Valves 54
Crosses, Gold-Filled, Gold and Silver 429
Crumb Pan and Brush 134
Crumb Sets, Silver Plated 448
Crusher Hats, Men's 233
Crutches 33
Cuff Buttons 424-425
Cuff Holders, Men's 221
Cuff Links, Diamond 403
Cuff Links, Gold and Silver 424-425
Cup, Grease 21
Cup Hooks 99
Cup, Tin Palette 360
Cups 131, 133, 136
Cups, Child's, Silver 446
Cups and Saucers 131
Cups and Saucers 446
Cupboard Catches 88-91
Cupboard Locks 88
Cupboard Turns 91
Curd Knives 145
Curd Pails 145
Curd Scoop 145
Cure to Stop Drinking 26
Curling, Hair, Sets 456
Curling Irons 102
Curling Iron Heater 112
Curling Irons 322
Curtains, Chenille and Tapestry 297
Curtain Lights 58
Curtains, Lace 286-287
Curtain Loops and Chains 298
Curtains, Mull and Lace 297
Curtain Poles 298
Curtain, Sash 297
Curtain Straps and Fasteners 58
Currants 12
Curry Powder 13
Cushions, Sofa 331
Cushions, Buggy 58
Cuspidors 134
Cut Lacings 56
Cut Nails 38
Cutter Stuff 63
Cutter Shoes 63
Cutters, Cold 68
Cutters, Glass 84
Cutters, Hot 68
Cutting Pliers 82
Cutters, Washer 82
Cutters, Wad 585
Cutting Nippers 68, 82
Cuttle Bone 21
Cutters, Bone 153
Cutters, Feed 152-153
Cutters, Kraut 140
Cutters, Meat 102
Cutters, Slaw 140
Cutlery 107-112
Cyclists' Cape 618
Cycle Shoes 206
Cyclometers 617
Cymbalets 532
Cymbals 529

## D

Dairy Cloth 292
Dairy Pans 130
Dairy Supplies 143-147
Dairy Thermometers 470
Damask Table Cloth 294
Damask Towels 295-296
Dampers, Stovepipe 128
Dance Music 538-541
Dancing Shoes, Men's 200
Dancing Slippers, Ladies 196
Dark Lanterns 138
Darners, Egg 321
Darning Cotton 221
Darning Needles 322
Dash Churns 144
Dashers, Buggy 58
Dash Lanterns 137
Dates 12
Daubing Brushes 114
Dead Locks 90
DeBeige Cloth 255
Decoration Bunting 293
Decoy Ducks 590
Decoy Geese 590
Decoy Whistles 590
Deed Boxes 135
Dehorners 46
Dehorning of Cattle 32
Dehorning Saws 46
Denim Drapery 298
Denison's Tissue Paper 332
Dentifrice Liquid 34
Depilatory 34
Depth Gauge 85
Desks, Ladies' 653
Desks, Office 653-654
Desk Telephones 472
Dessert Forks 438-445
Dessert Sets, Silver-plated 454
Dessert Spoons 438-445
Developing Outfits 482
Developing Trays 478
Deviled Crabs 14
Derby Hats, Men's 232
Derby Ribbed Underwear, Men's 237
Diagonal Cloth, Ladies' 255
Dialogues and Recitation
Dials, Blacksmiths' 65
Diamond Bracelets 403
Diamond Brooches 403
Diamond Charms 403
Diamond Ear Drops 402
Diamond Lace Pins 403
Diamond Links 403
Diamond Lockets 403
Diamond Rings 401
Diamond Scarf Pins 402
Diamond Set Watches 397-399
Diamond Studs 402-403
Diamonds 401-403
Diamonds, Glaziers' 84
Diapers 295
Diapers, Common Sense 323
Dictionaries 337
Dictionaries, Bible 347
Dictionary Holders 336
Dies, Blacksmiths' 67
Diggers, Post-hole 50
Dimity, Lace-striped 262
Dimity Shirt Waists 268
Dimity, Washable 290
Dining Tables 643-649
Dinner Castors 447
Dinner Pails 133
Dinner Sets, China 678-682
Dinner Sets, Glass 685-687
Dip Nets 605
Dippers 132, 133, 136
Dip, Sheep 30
Dishes, Bake, Silver-plated 451
Dishes, Berry, Silver-plated 449
Dishes, Bon-bon 450
Dishes, Butter 448
Dishes, Cake 450
Dishes, Fruit 449-456
Dish Pans 131-136
Disk Cultivators 159
Disk Harrows 159
Disk Sharpeners 159
Divans 666
Books 341-342-343
Divided Sauce Pans 132
Dividers 74, 84-85
Dog Cakes 593
Dog Collar Locks 592
Dog Collars 592
Dog Combs 592
Dog Couplings 592
Dog Leads 592
Dog Medicines 592
Dog Muzzles 592
Dog Powders 143
Dog Remedies 592
Dog Soap 33, 592
Dog Whips 592
Dog Whistles 592
Domestics 291
Dongola Kid Leather 208
Dongola Oxfords, Ladies' 195-196
Dongola Oxfords, Men's 200
Dongola Shoes, Ladies' 190-195
Door Bells 93
Door Bells 471
Door Bolts 88-92
Door Buttons 88
Door Butts 86, 91
Door Calls 471
Door Catches, Screen 44
Door Check and Springs 45
Door Clamps 83
Door Knobs 90
Door Locks 90-91-92
Door Mats 300
Door Mats, Wire 45
Doors 93-94
Door Screens 44
Door Springs 44
Door Stops 88
Double-acting Spring Hinges 44
Double Barrel Shotguns 562-569
Double Bass Viols 517
Double Bass Viol Bows 534
Double Bass Viol Bow Bridges 534
Double Bass Viol Bow Finger Boards 534
Double Bass Viol, Bow Frog 534
Double Bass Viol Bow Hair 534
Double Bass Viol Bow Rosin 534
Double Bass Viol Mutes 535
Double Bass Viol Pat. Heads 534
Double Bass Viol Strings 533
Double Ender Files 71
Double Gauges 74
Double-pointed Tacks 38
Double Square 85
Double Wheel-hoe 161
Doughnut Cutters 133
Dotted Swiss 293-294
Down Sofa Cushions 662
Doylies 295
Doylies, Stamped 331
Drag Seines 606
Drain Cleaners 49
Drain Spades 48
Drapers, Rubber 329
Drapery Prints 291
Drapery Silks 257
Drapery, Turkish 297
Drawer Pulls 88-92
Drawers, Money 99
Drawers, Ladies, white 308
Drawer Supporters 320
Drawing Boards 358
Drawing Inks 358
Drawing Instruments 357
Drawing Knives 78
Drawn Locks 88
Drawing Paper 359
Drawing Pencils 359
Drawing Pens 359
Drawing Scales 358
Dredge Boxes 134
Dresden Flannelettes 258
Dresden, Shirtwaists 269
Dress Boots, Men's 202
Dress Buttons 320
Dress Buttons, Bone 319
Dresser, Emery Wheel 72
Dressers 657
Dresses, Children's and Misses' 304-305
Dresses, Infants', Long 309
Dresses, Infants', White 278
Dresses, Night 282
Dress Ginghams 289
Dress Goods 254
Dress Goods, Alpaca 254
Dress Goods, Black 259
Dress Goods, Broadcloth 255
Dress Goods, Cashmere 254
Dress Goods, Henrietta 255
Dress Goods, Serge 254-255
Dress Goods, Summer 262
Dress Goods, Washable 289
Dressing Combs 326
Dressing, Harness 766
Dressing, Shoe 209
Dress Linens 293
Dress Linings 258
Dress Loops, Silk 319
Dress Sateen 290
Dress Shields 321
Dress Stays 323
Dress Suit Cases 253
Dress Trimmings 318-319
Dried Fruits 12
Drifting Picks 50
Drill Bits 81
Drill, Brace 80
Drilling Hammers 50
Drilling, Unbleached 292
Drill, Rubber 58
Drills, Breast 82
Drills, Grain 155-159-160
Drills, Hand 82
Drinking Cups 131, 133, 136, 593
Drinking Flasks 593
Dripping Pans 133-136
Drivers, Screw 80
Drive Well Points 54
Driving Batteries 471
Driving Gloves, Men's 228
Driving Lamps 137-138
Driving Mittens, Ladies' 231
Driving Shoe, River 201
Driving Spectacles 463
Drop Plates 93
Dr. Riehl's Health Underwear 239
Drug Department 26-35
Drum Heads 537
Drum Keys 536
Drum Major's Batons 537
Drums, Bass 539
Drum Slings 536
Drums, Snare 529
Drum Sticks 536
Dr. Warner Corsets 306
Dryers, Clothes 141
Dry Plates 480
Dry Plates, Seed's 480
Duchess Silks 257
Dutch Prints 291
Duck, Brown 292
Duck Calls 590
Duck Coats 178, 590-591
Duck Coats, Farmers' 178
Duck Coats, Fishermen's 178
Duck Coats, Hunters' 178
Duck Coats, Miners' 178
Duck Coats, Prospectors' 178
Duck Coats, Teamsters' 178
Duck Coats, Trappers' 178
Duck Decoys 590
Duck, for Tents, etc 293
Duck Overalls 178
Duck Pants 590-591
Duck Suiting 262
Duck Tennis Shoes 203
Duck Vests 590-591
Dulcimer Beaters 536
Dulcimers 522
Dulcimer Tuning Hammers 536
Dulcimer Tuning Pins 536
Dumb Bells, Iron 594
Dumb Bells, Wood 594
Dust Brushes 114
Dust Pans 134
Dust Protectors 464
Dusters, Linen, Men's 176
Dutch Oven 129
Dyes, Family 29
Dyspepsia Powders 27

## E

Ear Cleaner 34
Ear, Labels 46
Ear Tubes 464
Ear Trumpets 464
Eardrops, Diamond 402
Eardrops, Garnet 430
Earrings 431
Earrings, Mourning 431
Easels 361, 478, 671
Eaton Suits, Ladies' 280
Eave Troughs 96
Edging, Mohair 319
Edison Battery 471
Egg Beaters 134
Egg Cases 141
Egg Case Fillers 141
Egg Darners 321
Egg Poachers 129
Elderdowns 288
Elastic Bandages 32
Elastic Cement 23
Elastic Web Truss 323
Electric Cycle Oil 21
Elastic, Garter 323
Elastic Goring 208
Elastic, Hat 323
Elbows, Conductor 96
Elbows, Stovepipe 128
Electric Bells 471
Electric Motors 472
Electric Medical Batteries 472
Electric Ring 28
Electric Switches 471
Electric Matting 471
Electrical Goods 470
Electricity, Books on 472
Elixirs 29
Embroideries 266
Embroidered Flannels 288
Embroidery Cotton 321
Embroidered Handkerchiefs, Ladies' 226-227
Embroidery Materials 332
Embroidery Silk 321
Emblem Charms 421
Emblem, Pins 422-423
Emblem Rings 417
Emery Cloth 77
Emery Goods 71-72
Emery Wheel Stands 72
Emery Wheel Dresser 72
Empire Night Gowns 282
Empire Suits, Ladies' 280
Empty Shells, Brass 584
Empty Shells, Paper 583
Enamel 619
Enamel Iron Clocks 458-459
Enamel Paint 22
Enameline 19
Enameler, Photographic 479
End Clevises 62
End Cutting Nippers 82
End Pins, Guitar 534
End Pins, Violin 534
Engine Oil 21
Engines and Boilers 151
Engineers' Caps 236
Engineers' Jackets 178
Endless Belt 56
English Novelty Dress Goods 259
English Cashmere Dress Goods 254
Engraved Rings 417
Erasers 353-354-355, 559
Escutcheons 88
Essences 10
Estimate for Telegraph Line 471
Envelopes 350
Envelopes, Photographic 479
Evaporators 154
Evaporating Thermometer 470
Eveners, Iron 63
Eveners, Plow 63
Evener, Wood 63
Everlasting Shells 582
Exercisers, Whitley's 597
Expansive Bits 81
Express Wagon Bows 62
Extension Ladders 142
Extension Tables 643-649
Extension Tops 57
Extension Top, Surreys 711, 723
Extra-sized Colored Shirts, Men's 213-217
Extracts, Beef 14
Extracts, Flavoring 10
Extract, Lemon 27
Extracts, Medicinal 29
Extracts, Perfumes 33
Extract, Vanilla 27
Extractors, Shell 588
Eye Glasses 462-463
Eye Glass Cases 464
Eye Glass Chains 464
Eye Glass Cords 464
Eye Shades 464
Eye Protectors 463
Eye Water 26
Eyes, Screw 99
Eyelets 209
Eyelets, Carriage Knob 58
Eyelet Sets 209
Eyelet Set and Punch 208

## F

Fabrics, Washable Dress Goods 289
Face Cloths 297
Face Powder 34
Face Washes 34
Fall and Winter Underwear, Ladies' 242
False Mustaches 334

Fall and Winter Underwear, Men's ... 239
Family Bibles ... 348
Family Cobbler ... 207
Family Remedies ... 27
Fancy Black Silks ... 257
Fancy Boxes ... 350
Fancy Calipers ... 74
Fancy Cheviot Shirtings.. 292
Fancy Dress Shirts, Boys' 213
Fancy Dress Shirts, Men's ... 213
Fancy Hose, Ladies' ..244-245
Fancy Iron Planes......74-76
Fancy Neckwear, Ladies' ...310-311
Fancy Percale Shirts, Men's ... 213
Fancy Shirt Waists, Ladies' ...268-269
Fancy Vest, Men's ... 175
Fancy Work ...331-332
Fancy Wood Planes ... 77
Fanfares ... 532
Fanning Mills ... 163
Fans ... 335
Fans for Motors ... 472
Fargo's Bicycle Shoes...
Farina ... 15
Farinaceous Goods ... 15
Farm Bells ... 106
Farmers' Boilers ... 127
Farmers' Duck Coats ... 178
Farmers' Satin ... 258
Farm Wagons, Boys' ... 143
Farriers' Tools ...67-68
Fascinators ... 305
Fasteners, Chain ... 93
Fasteners, Paper ... 355
Fasts, Sash ...89-92
Fat-Ankle Shoes, Ladies' 192
Fat Baby Shoes ... 194
Faucets ... 99
Faucets, Brass ... 55
Faucets, Wood ... 141
Feather Pillows ... 662
Feathers ... 662
Feather Stitched Braid.. 323
Feather Ticking ... 292
Fedora Hats, Men's ... 232
Feed Boxes ... 46
Feeding Bottles ... 28
Feed Cutters ...152-153
Feed Steamer ... 163
Felloe Plates ... 61
Felloes, Sawed ... 60
Felloe Saws ... 70
Felt Building ... 23
Felt Roofing ... 95
Felt Shoes and Slippers.. 196
Female Pills ... 27
Fence Ornaments ... 42
Fence Posts ... 43
Fence Staples ... 43
Fencing Foils ... 597
Fencing Gloves ... 597
Fencing Masks ... 597
Fencing Sticks ... 597
Fencing Wire ... 41
Fern Dishes ... 456
Ferro-Prussiate Paper .. 480
Ferrotype Plates ... 479
Ferrules and Rings, Neck-Yoke ... 62
Ferrules, Fish Rods ... 605
Ferrules, Whiffletree ...41-43
Feverine ... 147
Fiber Lining ... 258
Fiber Lunch Boxes ... 259
Field Glasses ... 464
Field Rollers ... 162
Fife Instruction Books... 541
Fife Mouthpieces ... 528
Fifes ... 528
Fifth Wheels ... 61
Figs ... 12
Fig Laxative ... 27
File Cleaners ... 71
File Handles ... 71
Fillers, Egg Case ... 141
Files ... 355
Files ... 71
Filers, Saw ... 70
Films, Celluloid ... 480
Fillister, Plane ... 75
Filtering Paper ... 35
Filtering Paper, Photographic ... 479
Findings, Shoe ...207-209
Fine Combs ... 326
Fine Cut Tobacco ... 24
Finger Boards, Bass Viol 534
Finger Boards, Guitar... 534
Finger Boards, Viola ... 534
Finger Boards Violin ... 534
Finger Boards, Violoncello ... 535
Finger Tips, Photographic ... 479
Finishing Nails ... 38
Fire Backs ... 129
Fire-fly Single Wheel Hoe 162
Fire Kindlers ... 98
Fireman's Lantern ... 137
Fireproof Gloves, Men's ...228-229
Fire Screens ... 671
Firmer Chisels ... 79
Firmer Gauges ... 79
Fish, All Kinds ... 14
Fish, Canned ... 14
Fish Bait, Artificial...603-604
Fish Hooks ...601-602
Fish Hook Extractors ... 604
Fishermen's Duck Coats.. 178
Fishing Books ... 605
Fishing Boxes ...604-605
Fishing Lamps ... 610
Fishing Lines ...600-601
Fishing Reels ...599-600
Fishing Reel Cases ... 599
Fishing Rod Cases ... 599
Fishing Rod Cement ... 606
Fishing Rod Ferrules ... 605
Fishing Rod Holders ... 599
Fishing Rod Mountings.. ...605-606
Fishing Rods ...598-599
Fishing Rod Varnish ... 606
Fishing Rod Winding Silk 606
Fishing Sinkers ... 602
Fishing Swivels ... 602
Fishing Tackle Department ...
Fishing Torches ... 118
Fish-Net Curtains ... 297
Fish-Net Undershirts, Men's ... 238
Fish Scalers ... 99
Fish Scale Scrapers ... 605
Fish Stringers ... 604
Fish Weighing Scales ... 606
Fittings for Nursing Bottles ... 330
Fittings, Bicycle ...617-619
Fixings, Bath ... 478
Fixtures, Grindstone ... 84
Flageolet Accordions ... 528
Flageolet, Nightingale ... 528
Flageolets, Clark's, London ... 528
Flageolet Mouthpiece ... 526
Flageolets ... 528
Flageolets, Piccolo ... 528
Flagons, Silver, for Church Service ... 455
Flags ... 293
Flannel, Blanketing ... 288
Flannel Department ... 258
Flannel, Embroidered ... 288
Flannelettes ... 258
Flannelette Underskirts. 305
Flannel Shawls, Infants'. 278
Flannel, Shaker ... 288
Flannel Skirts, Infants'. 309
Flannel Shirting ... 258
Flannels, Bleached and Unbleached Cotton ... 288
Flannels, Outing and Twilled ... 258
Flannels, Wool and Cotton ... 288
Flash Lamps ... 478
Flasks, Drinking, Silver. 456
Flasks, Shoo Fly ... 35
Flat Bastard Files ... 71
Flat Head Screws ... 40
Flat Irons ... 100
Flatters ... 68
Flavor Extracts ... 10
Floor Hooks ... 165
Floor Oil Cloth ... 301
Floor Scrapers ... 102
Floral Sets ... 49
Florida Water ... 33
Flour ... 15
Flour Bin and Sifter ... 134
Flour Sifters ...133-134
Flower Pot Brackets ... 88
Flower Pot Shelves ... 45
Flower Pot Stands ...44-45
Flowers ... 303
Flue Stoppers ... 128
Flush Rings ... 87
Flush Bolts ... 93
Flute Cases ... 536
Flute Harmonicas ... 528
Flute Mouthpieces ... 536
Flutes ... 528
Fluxine ... 916
Fob Chains, Watch ..408, 436
Focusing Cloth ... 479
Foils, Fencing ... 591
Folding Beds ... 657
Folding Chairs ... 648
Folding Drawing Knives. 79
Folding Ironing Boards. 141
Folding Lap Boards ... 141
Folding Lunch Box ... 133
Folding Tables ...141, 672
Folios, Vocal and Instrumental ...538-540
Folios, Music ... 537
Food, Infants' ... 28
Food, Mocking Bird ... 29
Foot Balls ... 594
Foot Ball Inflators ... 594
Foot Baths ... 134
Foot Bolts ... 92
Foot Rests ...300, 617
Foot Scrapers ...88-89
Foot Valves ... 54
Force Pumps ...52-53
Forges, Blacksmiths' ...64-65
Forks, Coke ... 49
Forks, Barley ... 49
Forks, Cake, Silver ... 444
Forks, Hay ... 49
Forks, Kraut ... 140
Forks, Manure ... 49
Forks, Meat, Silver ... 441
Forks, Spading ... 49
Forks, Weeding ... 49
Forks, Table, Silver Plated ...438, 445
Fountain Pens ...354, 433
Four-piece Combination Suits ...183-184
Fox Traps ...99-100
Frame, Window Screen. 44
Frames, Wire, for Lamp Shade ... 333
Freezers, Ice Cream ... 103
French Briar Pipes...333-334
French Calf Skins ... 208
French Corsets ... 307
French Penang Waists, Ladies' ...268-269
French Shoe Blacking .. 209
French Window Catches. 91
Fringe, Carriage ... 58
Fringe for Window Shades ... 299
Fringe, Linen ... 332
Fringes, Rug and Curtain ... 298
Fringes, Tablecloth ...294-295
Frock Suits, Men's...168, 173
Froes ... 79
Front Door Lock ... 91
Fruit Butter ... 12
Fruit Evaporators ... 154
Fruit Jar Funnels ... 133
Fruit Press ... 102
Fruits, Canned ... 11
Fruits, Dried ... 12
Fry Pans ...130, 136
Fullers ... 68
Funnel, Fluted ... 478
Funnel Nets ... 607
Funnel, Rubber ... 478
Funnels ...131, 133, 136, 478
Furnishing Goods ...210, 253
Furnishings, Stove ...128-136
Furniture Gimp ... 298
Furniture Handles ... 88
Furniture Nails ... 38
Fyke Nets ... 607

G

Gable Ornaments ... 95
Gaff Hooks ... 605
Gallery Targets ...285-586
Galvanized Pipe ... 54
Galvanometers, Pocket .. 471
Galvanized Wire ... 41
Game Calls ... 590
Game Carriers ... 590
Game Bags ... 588
Game Skirts ... 590
Game Traps ...99-100
Gang Plows ... 157
Garden Hose ... 56
Garden Rakes ... 49
Garden Seeds ... 25
Garden Sets ... 49
Garden Trowels ... 49
Garnet Jewelry ... 430
Garnitures Bead ... 319
Garter Buckles ...435-436
Garter, Elastic ... 323
Garters, Ladies' Fancy .. 323
Garters, Men's ... 221
Garters, Silver Mounted. ...435-436
Gasoline ... 20
Gasoline Stoves ...115-116
Gasoline Torches ... 118
Gasmaking Outfits ... 484
Gate Hinges ... 87
Gate Latches ... 87
Gates' Molasses ... 99
Gates, Wire ...42-43
Gauges, Bit ... 82
Gauges, Butt ... 74
Gauges, Chamfer ... 79
Gauges, Chisel ... 80
Gauges, Clapboard ... 74
Gauges, Depth ... 85
Gauges, Double ... 74
Gauges, Joiner ... 77
Gauges, Marking ... 74
Gauges, Mortise ... 74
Gauges, Panel ... 74
Gauges, Slitting ... 74
Gauges, Screw Pitch ... 85
Gauntlet Gloves, Ladies'. 231
Gelatine ... 12
Gelatine Capsules ... 35
Gem Pans ... 129
Gents' Chains ...404-409
Gents' Rings ...416-418
German Bits ... 81
German Dictionaries ... 337
German Henriettas ... 256
German Socks ... 203
Gherkins ... 13
Gilling Twine ... 608
Gill Nets ... 607
Gill Netting ... 607
Gimlet Bits ... 81
Gimp, Black Silk ... 319
Gimp, Furniture ... 298
Gimp, Silk ... 319
Gimp Tacks ... 39
Ginger ... 9
Ginger Ale ... 11
Ginger Essence ... 27
Ginger Snaps ... 16
Gingham ... 291
Gingham Aprons ... 309
Glass Cruets ... 686
Glass Cutters ... 84
Glasses, Eye ...462-463
Glasses, Measuring ... 35
Glasses, Graduated ..35, 478
Glass Forms, Photographic ... 479
Glass Funnels ... 35
Glass Goblets ... 686
Glass Jugs ... 686
Glass Milk Jars ... 145
Glass Mortars and Pestles ... 478
Glass Salt and Peppers. 686
Glass Salvers ... 686
Glass Spirit Lamps ... 478
Glass Stoppered Bottles. 35
Glass Syrup Cans ... 686
Glass Towels ... 296
Glass Trays ... 478
Glass Tumblers ... 686
Glassware Outfit.684, 685, 686
Glass Water Sets ... 685
Glazed Dongola Kid ... 208
Glazier Points ... 39
Globes ... 336
Globe Valves ... 54
Glove Boxes ...350-351
Gloves and Mittens, Men's ... 228
Gloves, Base Ball ... 595
Gloves, Boxing ...593-594
Gloves, Cowboy's ... 229
Gloves, Fencing ... 597
Gloves, Husking ... 229
Gloves, Men's, Gauntlets. 229
Gloves, Rubber ... 329
Glue Brushes ... 113
Glue, Liquid ... 21
Glycerine ...21, 27
Glycerine and Rose Water ... 27
Goatskin Gloves, Men's. ...228-229
Goblets, Silver ... 446
Goggles ... 463
Gold Buttons ... 320
Gold Canes ... 436
Gold Crosses ... 439
Gold Filled Watches..369, 399
Gold Pencils ... 433
Gold Pens ... 433
Gold Plating Outfits ... 472
Gold, Quality and Grade. 372
Gold Rings ...416-418
Gold Spectacles ... 462
Golf Stockings, Men's... 218
Gold Thimbles ... 435
Gold Tinsel Braid ... 319
Goodyear's Syringes and Rubber Goods ... 329
Goodyear Welt Shoes, Ladies' ... 191
Gooseberries, Canned ... 11
Goose Calls ... 590
Goring, Shoe ... 208
Gospel Hymn Books..538-539
Gouges ... 79
Gouge Slips, Emery ... 71
Gowns, Ladies' Night ... 282
Graduates ...35, 478
Grain Bags and Sacks .. 293
Grain Cradles ... 50
Graining Brushes ... 113
Graining Combs ... 113
Grain Leather ... 208
Grain Sickles ... 50
Grain Slippers ... 196
Grain Slippers, Men's .. 200
Grand Army Suits, Men's 173
Grand Army Hats ... 233
Granula ... 15
Grape Juice ... 11
Grapes, Canned ... 11
Grapple Hooks ... 165
Graphophones ... 485
Graphophone Carrying Case ... 485
Graphophone Musical Records ... 485
Graphoscope Views ... 469
Grass Catches ... 51
Grass Edger ... 161
Grass Hooks ... 50
Grass Linen Lawns ... 289
Grass Scythes ... 50
Grass Seeders ... 155
Grass Shears ... 50
Grass Suits ... 590
Graters ... 134
Grates, Revolving ... 102
Gravity Battery ... 471
Gravy Boats, Silver ... 455
Gravy Ladles, Silver ... 444
Gravy Strainers ... 132
Gray Bed Blankets ... 288
Gray Flannel ... 288
Grease, Gun ... 590
Grease Paints ... 330
Grenadine Silks ... 257
Grenadine Skirts ... 270
Griddles ... 129
Grinders, Chisel ... 80
Grindstones ...83-84
Grindstone Filters ... 84
Grist Mills ...149-150
Grocers' Refrigerators .. 105
Grocers' Scoops ... 134
Gros Grain Silks ...257, 261
Ground Bone ... 23
Ground Oyster Shells ... 23
Grove Guards ... 45
Grub Hoes ... 50
Guards ... 618
Guards, Grove ... 45
Guards, Ladies' Silk ... 409
Guards Stallion ... 766
Guards, Trouser ... 619
Guards, Watch Chain ... 409
Guards, Wire Spork ... 45
Guitar Bags ... 534
Guitar Bridge Pins ... 534
Guitar Bridges ... 534
Guitar Capo D'Astros ... 534
Guitar Cases ... 534
Guitar End Pins ... 534
Guitar Finger Boards ... 534
Guitar Frets ... 534
Guitar Instruction Books. 541
Guitar Music ... 539
Guitar Patent Heads ... 535
Guitars ... 518
Guitar Strings ... 533
Guitar Tail Pieces ... 534
Gum Chewing ... 17
Gun Department ...562, 591
Gun Implements ...586-588
Gun Oil ... 590
Gun Wads ...584-585
Gymnasium Shoes ...203-206

H

Habutai Silks ... 257
Hack Saws ... 70
Hair Brushes ... 327
Hair Clippers ... 111
Hair Crimpers ... 322
Hair Curlers ... 112
Hair Curlers, Silver, ... 456
Hair Curling Fluid ... 34
Hair Dye ... 34
Hair Goods ... 330
Hair Oils ... 34
Hair Pins ... 322
Hair Pins, Garnet ... 430
Hair Pins, Gold and Silver ... 435
Hair (Plaster) ... 23
Hair Preparation ... 34
Hair Regenerator ... 330
Hair Restorer ... 34
Hair Shampoo ... 34
Hair, To Make Blonde ... 34
Hair Watch Chains ...409-413
Half-Round Files ... 71
Half Soles ... 208
Half Wool Novelty Goods 259
Half Wool Twilled Flannel ... 288
Hall Trees ... 669
Halters and Ties ... 758
Halters, Leather ... 759
Halters, Rope ... 758
Halters, Solid Leather Neck ... 758
Halters, Web ...758-759
Ham, Canned ... 14
Hamilton Prints ... 291
Hams ... 13
Hamburg Edging ... 266
Hamburg Insertion ... 266
Hames, Bolt ... 763
Hames, Hook ... 763
Hames, Iron and Tug ... 763
Hammer Straps ... 62
Hammers, Ball Pene ... 78
Hammers, Drilling ... 50
Hammers, Farriers' ... 67
Hammers, Blacksmith .. 67
Hammers, Nail ... 78
Hammers, Nail Holding.. 78
Hammers, Riveting ... 78
Hammers, Shoe ... 207
Hammers, Spalling ... 50
Hammers, Striking ... 50
Hammers, Tack ... 78
Hammers, Turning ... 67
Hammock Hooks ... 608
Hammock Chairs ... 142
Hammock Ropes ... 608
Hammocks ... 608
Hammock Spreaders ... 608
Hand Beader ... 76
Hand Bells ... 106
Hand Brushes ... 327
Hand Drills ... 82
Hand Drills ...168-169
Hand Mirrors ... 328
Hand Peg Breaks ... 208
Hand Pump ... 617
Hand Saws ...69-70
Hand Screws ... 83
Hand Sewed Shoes, Men's ...197-198
Hand Seed Sower ... 155
Hand Snap Buttons ... 320
Handle Bars ... 616
Handles, Awl ... 766
Handles, Axe ... 77
Handles, Auger ... 80
Handles, Chest ... 99
Handles, Chisel ...79-80
Handles, Cork ... 618
Handles, Cross-Cut Saw.. 69
Handles, File ... 71
Handles, Furniture ... 88
Handles, Hand Saw ... 69
Handles, Lifting ... 88
Hand Organs ... 524
Handles, Plane ... 75
Handkerchief Boxes ..350-351
Hangers, Barn Door ... 86
Hangers, Coat ... 139
Hangers, Parlor Door ... 91
Hanging Hooks ... 165
Hangings, Grindstone ... 84

Hard Cash Shoes, Men's.. 197
Hard Knock Shoes, Boys' 203
Hardies 68
Hardware Department..38-165
Harmonica Instruction Books 541
Harmonica Holders ...527-528
Harmonica Pouches 527
Harmonicas ....526-527
Harmonicas, Flute 528
Harness, Awl Set 82
Harness, Single Buggy.736-741
Harness, Surrey ......740-741
Harness, Express 741
Harness, Goat 741
Harness, Dog 741
Harness, Double Buggy.. ........741-743
Harness, Double Breast Collar 742
Harness, Double Farm Chain 743
Harness, Concord Farm.. ......744-745
Harness, Farm Double.744-745
Harness, Heavy Carriage 743
Harness Hooks 89
Harness, Light Hack 743
Harness Oil 21
Harness, Slip Tug Farm. 745
Harness, Concord Team.. 745
Harness, Chicago Truck. 744
Harps, Apollo 521
Harps, Jews' 531
Harrow Teeth 158
Harrows ......157-158
Harvester Oil 21
Hasps and Staples 86
Hassocks 300
Hat Elastic 323
Hat Marks, Silver 436
Hat Pins ......322, 435
Hat Badges 236
Hat Bands, Leather 234
Hat Racks 89
Hat and Coat Hooks....89-92
Hats, Children's 310
Hats, Hunting 592
Hats, Ladies' ......301-302
Hatchets 78
Hatchets, Ice 103
Hawns, Wagon 62
Hay Carriers 155
Hay Covers 609
Hay Forks 165
Hay Fork Pulleys 165
Hay Loaders 155
Hay Tedders 155
Hay Rakes, Horse ....154-155
Hay Presses 151
Hay Hooks 99
Hay Rakes, Hand 46
Hay Knives 51
Hazel Hoes 50
Head Blocks 95
Head Lamps 610
Head Lights 138
Head Nets 605
Headache Cure 27
Health Exercisers 597
Health Underwear 239
Heaters, Curling Iron 112
Heaters, Oil 118
Heaters, Tent 610
Heavy Boots, Men's 202
Heavy Shoes, Ladies' 193
Heavy Shoes, Men's...199-201
Hedge Shears 50
Heel Lifts 208
Heel Plates 208
Heel Plates 596
Heel Protectors 209
Heel Stiffeners 208
Hemp Carpets 300
Hemlock Calfskins 208
Hemlock Shoe Leather 208
Hens' Nests 43
Henrietta Dress Goods.254-255
Henrietta Skirts 270
Herb Tea 27
Herbs 11
Hercules Braids 319
Herring, Dried 14
Herring, Spiced 14
Hickory Canes 248
High Cut Shoes, Men's 201
Hill Dropping Seed Sower ......160-161
Hinge Hasps 86
Hinge Strap and T 86
Hinges, Double Acting 44
Hinges, Gate 87
Hinges, Chest 87
Hinges, Spring 44
Hip Baths 134
Hip Pads 307
Hip Boots, Rubber 205
Histories 339
Hitching Rings 86
Hob Nails 208
Hobbles, Horse 759
Hods, Coal 129
Hoes, Hand 49
Hoes, Mortar 49
Hog Rings and Ringers 45
Hog Scrapers 98
Hog Skin Gloves, Men's. 228
Hog Tamers 46
Holders, Belt and Skirt. 331
Holders, Bouquet 449
Holders, Broom 98
Holders, Celery 449
Holders, Cigar 334
Holders, Pen .....353-354
Holders, Pencil 353
Holders Pencil 74
Holders, Silver Toothpick 446
Holders, Tail, Horse 765
Holostine Barometer 470
Holland Shade Cloth 299
Hollow Augers 81
Hollows and Rounds....76-77
Holsters, Pistol ......589-590
Hollow Punch ......82-83
Homeopathic Books 30
Homeopathic Cases 30
Homeopathic Remedies..29-30
Homeopathic Specialties. 30
Homeopathic Syringes 32
Hominy 15
Hones, Emery 71
Hones, Pocket 111
Honey 18
Honiton Lace Braids 332
Hoods and Fascinators 305
Hoods, Sweat 771
Hoof Dressing 21
Hoof Nippers 68
Hooks, Box 99
Hooks, Box 88
Hooks, Brush 50
Hooks, Button 209
Hooks, Bird Cage 89
Hooks, Corn 51
Hooks, Clothes Line 89
Hooks, Cup 99
Hooks and Eyes 323
Hooks, Fish ......601-602
Hooks and Ferrules 62
Hooks, Grass 50
Hooks, Harness 89
Hooks, Hat and Coat..89-92
Hooks, Hammock 608
Hooks, Lamp 92
Hooks, Meat 102
Hooks, Manure 49
Hooks, Seat Spring 62
Hooks, Potato 49
Hooks for Pictures 299
Hooks and Staples 86
Hooks and Turrets 764
Hooks, School House 89
Hooks, Screw 99
Hooks, Well Wheel 99
Hooks, Whiffletree 61
Hoop Knives 79
Hops 11
Horizontal Bars 594
Horn Buttons 320
Horns (Band Instrument) ......530-531
Horns, Bicycle 618
Horns (Bugle) 531
Horns (Hunting) 531
Horns, Tin 133
Horse Covers 609
Horse and Cattle Powder 23
Horse Hoe ......161-162
Horse Nails 68
Horse Pitching Tools 165
Horse Powers 150
Horse Rasps 71
Horse Shoes 68
Horse, Stitching 767
Horseradish 12
Horses, Rocking 142
Horseshoers' Hammers 67
Hose, Bicycle 218
Hose Clamps 56
Hose Couplings 56
Hose Darners, Silver 436
Hose, Extra Size, Ladies'. 245
Hose, Infants' 247
Hose Nozzles 56
Hose Pipe Tires 616
Hose Reels 56
Hose, Rubber 56
Hose, Suction 53
Hose Supporters 619
Hose Supporters, Ladies'. 322
Hosiery Department..243-246
Hot Bed Thermometer 470
Hot Cutter 68
Hot House Pulleys 96
Hot Water Bottles 329
House Bells 106
House Numbers 99
Housekeeping Linens 294
How to Measure for a Hat 232
Howard Bookholder 336
Housing, Breast Collar 762
Housing, Gig 762
Hungarian Nails 208
Huckaback Towels 296
Hunters' Axes 590
Hunters' Axe Sheaths 590
Hunters' Belts 589
Hunters' Blouses 591
Hunters' Capes 591
Hunters' Clothing 591
Hunters' Camp Outfits 610
Hunters' Duck Coats 178
Hunters' Hats 591
Hunters' Knives 590
Hunters' Knife Sheaths. 590
Hunters' Lamps 610
Hunters' Skiffs 610
Hunters' Tent Heaters 610
Hunters' Vests 591
Hunters' Whistles 590
Hunting Horns 531
Hunting Lamp 138
Hunting Shoe ......201-202
Husking Gloves 229
Husking Pins 229
Hubs, Wagon 59
Hubs 619
Hurons (Men's) 206
Hydrometer Jars 470
Hydrometers 470
Hydrometers, Gauge 470
Hydrometers, Photographic 479

**I**

Ice Balances 48
Ice Boxes 104
Ice Chippers 103
Ice Chisels 103
Ice Cream Freezers 103
Ice Hatchets 103
Ice Picks 103
Ice Shaves 103
Ice Skates 97
Ice Tongs 103
Ice Wool 332
Ice Wool Shawls 305
Illuminating Oil, Bicycle. 619
Imported Dress Goods.254-256
Imported Lace Curtains. ......286-287
Imported Sateen 290
Inclinometers ......72, 85
Incubating Thermometers 470
Indelible Ink 359
India Linen ......291-293
India Lawn, Black 290
India Mull 293
Indian Clubs 594
Indicators, Speed 85
Induction Coil 472
Infants' Bibs 309
Infants' Bootees 309
Infants' Caps ......309-310
Infants' Cambric Slips 309
Infants' Flannel Shawls. 278
Infants' Foods 28
Infants' Hose 247
Infants' Long Cloaks 283
Infants' Sacques 309
Infants' Shoes ......194-195
Infants' Skirts 309
Infants' White Dresses 278
Infants' Undershirts 241
Inflators, Foot Ball 594
Ingrain Art Squares 300
Ingrain Carpets ......284-285
Initial Handkerchiefs, Men's and Ladies'...226-227
Injection 27
Ink Erasers ......353-355
Inks ......19, 351
Inner Tubes 616
Insect Powder 28
Inserting ......264-265
Inside Calipers.....74, 84, 85
Insoles, Cork 209
Insoles, Lambs Wool 209
Insoles, Leather 209
Inspectors' Lanterns 137
Instruction Books, Music. ......540-541
Instrumental Music Folios ......539, 541
Insulator Brackets 472
Insulator Pins 472
Insulators 472
Invalid Air Cushions 329
Irish Butcher Linen 295
Irish Point Lace Curtains 287
Iron Beds ......658, 660
Iron Bound Mallets 78
Iron Box Bells 471
Iron Clamps 83
Iron Dumb Bells 594
Ironed Eveners 63
Ironed Neck Yokes 63
Ironed Shafts 63
Ironed Single Trees 63
Ironing Boards 141
Iron Kettles ......129, 130
Iron Levels 72
Iron Pipe 54
Iron Pipe Fittings 54
Iron Planes ......74, 75, 76
Iron Rakes 49
Iron Ribbed Hose, Boys'. 246
Iron Roofing 96
Irons, Curling 322
Irons, Cattle Tie 46
Irons, Charcoal 100
Irons, Corner 61
Irons, Curling 112
Iron Shoe Lasts ......207-208
Iron Shoe Nails 208
Irons, Pinking 98
Irons, Plane 75
Irons, Polishing 100
Iron Squares 73
Irons, Sad 100
Irons, Screen Corner 44
Irons, Soldering 84
Irons, Rub 62
Irons, Toy 99
Irons, Waffle 129
Irons, Wear 62
Iron Thresholds 99
Isinglass Plaster 35
Italian Cloths 258
Ivory Bead Sights 579
Ivory Ear Cleaners 34
Ivory Rules 73

**J**

Jack Buck Gloves and Mittens ......228-229
Jack Chain 97
Jackets, Engineers' 178
Jackets, Hunting 591
Jackets, Ladies' ......273-276
Jackets, Oil 189
Jackets, Smoking, Men's 177
Jacks, Bevel 159
Jack Screw 165
Jack Knives 109
Jacks, Pumping 149
Jack Spur 150
Jacks, Speeding 150
Jacks, Wagon 59
Jacquered Cloth 259
Jacquered Cloth Novelties 260
Jamaica Ginger 11
Jams ......11-12
Japanese Silks 257
Japanned Tinware ....134-135
Japanese Fish Rods 598
Japanese Loofah 32
Japanese Matting 300
Japanese Tooth Brushes 34
Jardiniere Stands 669
Jars, Cold Cream 35
Java Oil 21
Jeans, Kentucky 289
Jellies ......11-12
Jelly Cake Pans ......131-136
Jelly Tumblers 23
Jersey Bicycle Leggins.. ......206-207
Jet Pins 322
Jews Harps 531
Jig Saws 69
Jointer Gauges 77
Jointers, Saw 71
Jones' White Cambric 292
Jumbo Soles 208
Jumpers, Baby 142
Jumpers, Painters' 178
Jumpers, Paper Hangers' 178
Junior Children's Suits 183
Juvenile Bicycles ......614-615
Juvenile Clothing 181

**K**

Kalsomine 22
Kalsomine Brushes 113
Kangaroo Shoes, Men's.. ......197-198
Kazoos 532
Kazoo Cornets 532
Kean's Drawing Instruments 357
Kentucky Jeans 289
Kerosene Emulsion 22
Kerosene Oil 20
Kettles, Brass 129
Kettles, Copper 130
Kettles, Iron ......129-130
Kettles, Porcelain 130
Key Chains 321
Key Rings, Silver 435
Keys, Drum 536
Kid Gloves, Ladies' and Misses' ......230-231
Kid Gloves, Men's 228
Kidney Cure 27
Kid Skins 208
Kilt Suits, Children's 185
Kindlers, Fire 98
King Bolts ......61-62
Kip Boots, Men's 202
Kit Bags 610
Kitchen Forks 131
Kitchen Knives 108
Kitchen Saws 69
Kitchen Sinks 55
Kitchen Tables 648
Kits, Camping 610
Kits, Repair ......618, 767
Knee Pants, Children's Combination Suits 184
Knee Protectors 598
Knees, Bob 63
Knee Shields 209
Knee Tights 597
Knife and Fork Boxes 135
Knife Hones 111
Knife Sharpeners ....71, 108
Knit Fascinators 305
Knitting Cotton 321
Knitting Needles 322
Knitting Silk 321
Knitting Yarns 332
Knives and Forks ....107-108
Knives, Bread 108
Knives, Butcher 108
Knives, Butter ......438-445
Knives, Carving 108
Knives, Corn ......33, 51
Knives, Drawing 79
Knives, Farriers' 67
Knives, Gauge 766
Knives, Hay 51
Knives, Hoop 79
Knives, Hunting 590
Knives, Kitchen 108
Knives, Mincing 102
Knives, Palette 361
Knives, Pie, Plated 442
Knives, Pocket ......109-111
Knives, Poultry 32
Knives, Putty 108
Knives, Round 766
Knives, Sheath 590
Knives, Shingle 79
Knives, Shoe 208
Knives, Silver Plated Fruit 439
Knives, Silver Plated Table ......438-445
Knives, Skinning 108
Knives, Solid Silver, Pen 436
Knives, Sticking 108
Knobs, Door 90
Knobs, Eyeret 58
Kraut Cutters 140
Kraut Forks 140

**L**

Lace Bed Sets 298
Lace Braids 332
Lace Curtains ....286-287, 297
Lace Collars and Yokes. ......310-311
Lace Lambrequins 298
Lace Pins, Diamond 403
Lace Pins, Mourning 430
Lace Pins, Plated and Gold ......427-428-429-430
Laces ......264-265
Laces, Corset 321
Lace Sets, Ladies' 311
Lace, Shoe 209
Laces, Shoe 321
Lace Striped Dimity 262
Lace Striped, Lawn 290
Lace Striped Lawns 262
Lacing Cord, Silk 319
Lacing Cutter 56
Lacing Leather 56
Lactometer 470
Lacquering Brushes 113
Ladders ......141-142
Ladies' Aprons 309
Ladies' Antiseptic Pads 32
Ladies' Belts 331
Ladies' Boots ......191-193
Ladies' Cloth 255
Ladies' Collars and Cuffs. 311
Ladies' Corset Covers 308
Ladies' Doily Belt 32
Ladies' Extra Size Vests. 241
Ladies' Fabric Gloves 231
Ladies' Fancy Garters 323
Ladies' Felt Slippers and Shoes 196
Ladies' Fine Shoes ...191-193
Ladies' Gauntlet Gloves. 231
Ladies' Handkerchiefs.226-227
Ladies' Hats ......301-302
Ladies' Hose Supporters. 322
Ladies' Hosiery 244
Ladies' Leggins ......206-207
Overshoes ......205-206
Ladies' Mackintoshes 188
Ladies' Muslin Drawers. 308
Ladies' Muslin Skirts.307-308
Ladies' Neckwear ......310-311
Ladies' Night Gowns 282
Ladies' Overgaiters 206
Ladies' Overshoes ......204-206
Ladies' Oxfords ......195-196
Ladies' Ready-to-Wear Clothing ......267-276
Ladies' Rings ......416-418
Ladies' Rubber Boots and
Ladies' Safety Belts 323
Ladies' Shawls 305
Ladies' Shoe Dressing 209
Ladies' Shoe Laces 209
Ladies' Shoulder Braces. 221
Ladies' Silk Gloves 231
Ladies' Spring and Summer Wraps ......273-276
Ladies' Summer Underwear ......240-241
Ladies' Tool Sets 335
Ladles 131
Ladies' Tailor Made Suits ......279-281
Ladies' Undershirts 305
Ladies' Union Suits 240
Ladies' Violins 515
Ladies' Waists ......268-269
Ladies' Watch Chains.410-413
Ladies' Watches..376, 391, 399
Ladies' Winter Underwear 242
Ladies' Wrappers 272
Ladle, Gravy, Silver 444
Ladle, Oyster 444
Ladles, Soup, Silver Plated 444
Lag Bolts 39
Lake and River Seines.606-607
Lambrequin Lace 298
Lambs Wool Slipper Soles 209
Lamp Bracket 617
Lamp Burners 137
Lamp, Camp 610
Lamp Chimney Cleaners. 98
Lamp Chimneys 137
Lamp Chimney Stoves 98
Lamp Hooks 92
Lamps, Banquet...687-688-689
Lamps, Bicycle 617
Lamps, Bracket 690
Lamps, Carriage 58
Lamps, Fishing 610
Lamps, Flash ......478-479
Lamps, Hanging 689
Lamps, Hunting 610
Lamp, Singeing 766
Lamps, Spirit 35

Lamps, Stand.... 690
Lamp Stoves.... 117
Lamps, Student.... 687
Lamps, Vase.... 687
Lamp Wicks.... 137
Lancewood Rods.... 598-599
Landing Net Rings.... 605
Landing Nets.... 605
Landscape Telescopes.... 465
Lantern Burners.... 137
Lantern Holders.... 137
Lanterns.... 136-138
Lantern Slides, Magic.... 482-483
Lanterns, Magic.... 482, 485
Lap Boards.... 141
Lapel Buttons.... 423
Lap Lasts, Iron.... 208
Lard.... 14
Lard Press.... 102
Lard Oil.... 21
Lariats.... 759
Lariat Swivels.... 46
Latches, Gate.... 87
Latches, Mortise.... 90
Latches, Night.... 90
Latches, Thumb.... 90-92
Lathes, Turning.... 69
Lath Hatchet.... 78
Lath Wire.... 43
Latigos.... 759
Laudanum.... 27
Laundered White Shirts, Men's.... 211
Laundry Bags.... 332
Laundry Starch.... 18
Laundry Stoves.... 124
Laundry Wax.... 16
Lawn Aprons.... 309
Lawn Chairs and Settees.... 45
Lawn Dress Goods, Lace, Striped.... 262
Lawn Grass Seed.... 25
Lawn Mowers.... 51
Lawn Rakes.... 49
Lawn Shirt Waists.... 268-269
Lawn Sprinklers.... 56
Lawn Tennis Racquets.. 593
Lawns, Victoria.... 293
Lawn Swings.... 142
Lawn Tennis Balls.... 593
Lawn Tennis Forks.... 593
Lawn Tennis Goods.... 593
Lawn Tennis Markers.... 593
Lawn Tennis Poles.... 593
Lawn Tennis Rope.... 593
Lawn Tennis Sets.... 593
Lawn Tents.... 609
Lead Bar.... 585
Leaders, Cattle.... 46
Lead Pencils.... 252-253
Lead Pipe.... 56
Leads, Dog.... 592
Lead Sinkers.... 606
League Tires.... 616
Leather.... 766
Leather Belting.... 56
Leather Belts, Hunting. 589
Leather Belts, Men's.... 218
Leather Capped Chisel Handles.... 79
Leather Cement.... 208
Leather Coats.... 589
Leather Gloves and Mittens, Men's and Boys'.... 228-229-230
Leather Gun Cases.... 588-589
Leather Hat Bands.... 234
Leather Holsters.... 589-590
Leather Insoles.... 209
Leather Lacing.... 56, 766
Leather Leggins.... 589-590
Leather Punch.... 82-83
Leather Shawl Straps.... 253
Leather Shell Bags.... 588-589
Leather Shoe Laces.... 209
Leather Shoe Laces.... 209
Leather Shoes.... 208
Leather Stockings, Boys'. 246
Leather Straps for Club Bags.... 253
Leather Suspenders.... 221
Leather Traveling Bags. 252
Lecturers' Lamp for Magic Lantern.... 484
Leggins, Canvas.... 589-590
Leggins, Corduroy.... 589-590
Leggins, Hunting.... 589-590
Leggins, Knee.... 589-590
Leggins, Ladies'.... 206
Leggins, Leather.... 589-590
Leggins, Military.... 589
Leggins, Thigh.... 590
Lemonade Shakers.... 133-136
Lemon Extract.... 27
Lemon Juice.... 11
Lemon Peel.... 12
Lemon Squeezers.... 140
Lemon Squeezers.... 98-99
Lemon Sugar.... 11
Lentils.... 15
Lenses, Photographic. 477-478
Letter Drop Plates.... 93
Lettering Pencils.... 113
Letter Scales.... 47
Levels.... 72
Level Sights.... 72
Library Furniture.... 652
Library Tables.... 652
Lice Destroyer.... 30
Licorice Lozenges.... 28
Licoric Powder.... 27
Life Belts.... 606
Life Preservers.... 606
Lifters, Stove.... 128
Lifters, Transom.... 91
Lifting Handles.... 88
Lifts, Sash.... 91
Lightning Arrester.... 471
Lightning Brace.... 82
Lime.... 23
Lime Juice.... 11
Line Cleats.... 89
Linen Coats, Men's.... 176
Linen, Collars and Cuffs, Ladies'.... 311
Linen Dip Nets.... 605
Linen Dusters, Men's.... 176
Linen, Fringe.... 332
Linen Handkerchiefs.. 225-227
Linen Hats, Men's.... 233
Linen Netting.... 607
Lines, Chalk.... 74
Lines, Double Team.... 762
Linens, Dress.... 293
Lines, Fishing.... 600-601
Linen Shoe Thread.... 209
Linen, Spool.... 321
Linens, Table.... 294
Linen, Stamped.... 331-332
Linen Suits, Men's.... 176
Lines, Single.... 762
Lines, Tape.... 73
Liniments.... 26-30
Lining Nails.... 58
Linings, Dress and Waist 258
Linings for Carpets.... 300
Linings, Skirt.... 258
Lining, Stove.... 129
Links, Cross.... 62
Links, Cuff, Gold Filled. 424
Links, Diamond.... 403, 425
Links, Pearl.... 425
Links, Silver.... 425
Links, Solid Gold.... 425
Linoleum.... 300
Linon, India.... 293
Linseed Oil.... 21
Lister.... 157
Lithium Paper.... 479, 480
Live Nets.... 605
Liver Pills.... 27
Lizard Cloth, Black.... 259
Lizard Cloth Skirts.... 270
Loaded Canes.... 248
Loaded Shells.... 583
Loaders, Hay.... 155
Loading Tools.... 586-588
Lobsters, Canned.... 14
Lockets.... 403
Locks, Bicycle.... 618
Locks, Chest.... 87-88
Locks, Cupboard.... 88
Locks, Drawer.... 88
Locks, Mortise.... 90-91
Locks, Pad.... 87
Locks, Pad, "Dog Collar" 592
Locks, Rim.... 90
Locks, Sash.... 89
Locks, Sliding Door.... 91
Locks, Store Door.... 90-91-92
Locks, Trunk.... 88
Log Chains.... 97
Log Rules.... 73
Long Cloth.... 293
Long Distance Telephone. 472
Long Sleigh Runners.... 63
Loofah.... 33
Loofah Bath Brush.... 33
Loofah Mitten.... 33
Looking Glasses.... 670-671
Loops and Buckles.... 58
Loops, Celluloid.... 765
Loops, Hame.... 765
Loop Sets, Ladies'.... 381
Loops, Silk Dress.... 319
Lounges, Bed.... 668
Lubricating Oil, Bicycle. 619
Lumberman's Overshoes.... 204-206
Lumberman's Pacs.... 201
Lumberman's Socks.... 203
Lumber Pencils.... 352
Luminous Alarm Clocks. 457
Luminous Fish Bait.... 605
Lunch Boxes.... 133, 253, 616
Lye.... 19

## M

Macaroni.... 16
Mace.... 9
Madras Cloth.... 262
Magic Lanterns.... 482-485
Magic Lantern Book.... 484
Magic Lantern, Lecturer's Lamp.... 484
Magic Lantern Professional.... 483
Magic Lantern Slides. 484-486
Magic Lantern Secret Society Views.... 485
Magic Lantern Screens.. 484
Magic Lantern Views.. 485
Magnets.... 472
Magnetic Tack Hammers. 78
Magnifiers, Coddington.. 466
Magnifying Glasses.... 466
Machine Bolts.... 39
Machine Covers.... 609
Machine, Slitting.... 766
Machines, Boring.... 80
Machinists' Levels.... 72
Machinists' Tools.... 84-85
Mackerel.... 14
Mackerel, Canned.... 14
Mackinaw Flannel.... 288
Machine Oil.... 21
Machines, Sewing.... 697-705
Mackintosh Wading Pants 206
Mackintoshes, Boys'.... 187
Mackintoshes, Cape.. 187-188
Mackintoshes, Ladies'.. 188
Mackintoshes, Misses'.... 188
Mackintoshes, Box.... 187
Mackintoshes, Men's.... 187
Mail Box.... 98
Mailing Envelopes, Photographic.... 479
Malt Extract.... 15
Malleable Dees....
Mallets.... 78
Mandolin Bags.... 536
Mandolin Bridges.... 536
Mandolin Cases.... 536
Mandolin Instruction Books.... 541
Mandolin Music.... 539-540
Mandolin Patent Heads.. 536
Mandolin Picks.... 536
Mandolin Strings.... 533
Mandolin Tailpiece.... 536
Mandolins.... 520
Mandrils, Saw.... 68
Mangles.... 140
Manicure Scissors.... 109
Manila Rope.... 97
Manioca.... 16
Manuals.... 338
Maps, Pocket.... 337
Maps, School.... 336
Maple Syrup.... 18
Marine Glasses.... 464-465
Marjoram.... 11
Marks, Stock.... 45-46
Markers, Poultry.... 46
Market Baskets.... 142
Marking Brushes.... 114
Marking Gauges.... 74
Marseilles Bed Spreads.. 289
Martingales, Team.... 762
Martingales, Riding.... 758
Mashers, Potato.... 140
Mason Fruit Jars.... 23
Masons' Trowels.... 84
Matamora Sole Leather.. 208
Mats for Children.... 309
Mats, Wire Door.... 45
Match Planes.... 76
Match Safes.... 135, 334
Matches.... 20
Matched Table Cloth Sets 295
Mathematical and Drawing Instruments.... 357
Matting, Floor.... 300
Mattings, Electric.... 471
Mattocks.... 50
Mattresses.... 662
Mauls, Post.... 50
Mauls, Steak.... 140
Measures.... 133-136
Measurements, Ladies' Apparel.... 267
Measures, Powder and Shot.... 588
Measures, Tape.... 322
Measures, Wood.... 141
Measuring Glasses.... 35
Measuring Tapes.... 73
Meat Cutters.... 102
Meat Hooks.... 102
Meats, Canned.... 14
Meats, Cured.... 13
Meats, Pickled.... 13
Medical Books.... 346
Medical Atomizers.... 329
Medicine Cases.... 30
Medicine Cabinets.... 145
Medicines.... 26-30
Medicines, Homeopathic. 29-30
Medicines, Patent.... 29
Medicines, Veterinary.... 30
Mending Outfits.... 335
Mending Yarn.... 321
Meerschaum Pipes.... 333-334
Melting Ladles.... 587
Melting Pots.... 587
Melting Tubes.... 32
Men's Boots.... 202
Men's Bicycle Shoes.... Colored Pages.
Men's and Boys' Suspenders.... 220-221
Men's and Boys' Sweaters.... 217-218
Men's Celluloid Cuffs and Collars.... 219
Men's Celluloid Shirt Bosoms.... 219
Men's Clothing.... 166-177
Men's Coats.... 173
Men's Colored Bosom Shirts.... 212
Men's Crash Suits.... 176
Men's Crusher Hats.... 233
Men's Cuff Holders.... 221
Men's Duck Coats.... 178
Men's Duck Pants.... 178
Men's Duck Vests.... 178
Men's Extra Sized Colored Shirts.... 213-217
Men's Fancy Percale Shirts.... 213
Men's Felt Shoes and Slippers.... 196
Men's Fine Shoes.... 197-201
Men's Flannel Overshirts.... 216-217
Men's Garters.... 221
Men's Golf Stockings.... 218
Men's Golf Caps.... 235-236
Men's Jersey Overshirts. 217
Men's Laundered Negligee Shirts.... 213-214
Men's Laundered White Shirts.... 211
Men's Leather Belts.... 218
Men's Linen Suits.... 176
Men's Linen Cuffs and Collars.... 219
Men's Linen Dusters.... 176
Men's Furnishing Goods.... 210-253
Men's Hats.... 232-235
Men's Half Hose.... 243-244
Men's Handkerchiefs.. 225-226
Men's Hunting Shirts.... 591
Men's Ideal Outing Shirts 214
Men's Jumpers.... 178
Men's Mufflers.... 226
Men's Neckwear.... 222-223-224
Men's Night Shirts.... 212
Men's Overalls.... 178
Men's Overcoats.... 175
Men's Overgaiters.... 207
Men's Overshoes.... 204-206
Men's Serge Coats and
Men's Straw Hats.... 235
Vests.... 176
Men's Silk Vests.... 175
Men's Shoes.... 196-201
Men's Shoe Laces.... 209
Men's Shoe Polish.... 209
Men's Shoulder Braces.. 221
Men's Slippers.... 200
Men's Smoking Jackets.. 177
Men's Sweaters.... 591
Men's Soft Neglige.... 215-217
Men's Tailor-Made Pants. 174
Men's Top Soles.... 208
Men's Underwear.... 237
Men's Unlaundered White Shirts.... 210
Men's Unlined Gloves. 228-229
Men's Wigs.... 330
Men's White Cotton Military Gloves.... 228
Metal Hat and Cap Badges.... 236
Metal Keyed Faucets.... 141
Metal Wheels.... 59
Metallic Points.... 479
Metallic Tape Lines.... 468
Mercurial Barometer.... 470
Merino Underwear, Ladies'.... 242
Merino Underwear, Gents' 239
Merino Underwear, Children's.... 242
Merchandise Covers.... 609
Merrimac Prints.... 291
Microbe Killers.... 27
Microscopes.... 465-466
Microscopes, Students'.. 466
"Midway" Musettes.... 533
Military Caps.... 236
Military Cord Loop Sets. 318
Military Suit, Children's. 184
Milk Cans.... 146
Milk, Condensed.... 15
Milk Pans.... 130
Milk Skimmers.... 131
Milk Strainers.... 132
Mill Files.... 71
Millinery Department. 301-302
"Mills'" Belts.... 589
Mills, Bone.... 153
Mills, Coffee.... 103
Mills, Feed.... 149-150
Mills, Wind.... 148
Mince Meat.... 13-14
Mincing Knives.... 102
Miner's Compass.... 467
Miners' Duck Coats.... 178
Miner's Tents.... 608
Mining Shoes, Men's.... 201
Mink Traps.... 99-100
Minnow Buckets.... 605
Minnow Boxes.... 605
Minnow Dip Nets.... 605
Minnow Netting.... 607
Minnow Seines.... 606-607
Minnows, Casting.... 604
Minnows, Fly, Artificial.... 603-604
Minnows, Phantom.... 604
Minnows, Rubber.... 603-604
Mirrors.... 670-671
Mirrors, Hand.... 328
Ministers' Coats.... 176
Minstrel Wigs.... 330
Mint.... 11
Misses' Caps and Hats.. 236
Misses' Gloves and Mittens.... 230-231
Misses' Hose.... 246-247
Misses' Jackets.... 275
Misses' Shawls.... 305
Misses' Shoes.... 194
Mitre Boxes.... 69
Mitts, Catchers'.... 595
Mittens, Men's.... 229-230
Mittens, Ladies' and Children's.... 230-231
Mittens, Rubber.... 329
Mixers, Liquor.... 133-136
Moccasins, Infants'.... 195
Moccasins, Men's.... 201
Mohair Buttons.... 320
Mohair Coats, Men's.... 176
Mohair Dress Goods.. 255-259
Mohair Edging.... 319
Moire Silks.... 257
Molasses Gates.... 99
Molasses.... 18
Molders' Bellows.... 65
Molding Planes.... 77
Moldings.... 95
Molds, Bullet.... 587-588
Mole Traps.... 100
Money Belts.... 589
Money Drawers.... 99
Monkey Wrenches.... 78
Moose Hide Moccasins.... 201
Mop Dish.... 98
Mop Handles.... 102
Mop Wringers.... 140
Mops, Self-Wringing.... 140
Moquette Rugs.... 300
Moreen Underskirts.... 298
Moquette Carpets.... 285
Mortar Hoes.... 49
Mortars, Druggists'.... 35
Mortars and Pestles, Glass.... 478
Mortise Gauge.... 74
Morton's Supporters.... 597
Mosquito Head Nets.... 605
Mosquito Netting.... 292
Motor Fans.... 472
Motors, Electric.... 472
Mottling Brushes.... 113
Mouse Traps.... 100
Mountain Plows.... 156
Mounts, Card.... 481-482
Mounts, Stereoscopic.... 482
Mouthpieces, Clarionet.. 536
Mouthpiece Caps, Clarionet.... 536
Mouthpiece Cases, Clarionet.... 536
Mouthpieces, Band Instrument.... 536
Mouthpieces, Fife.... 536
Mouthpieces, Flageolet.. 536
Mouthpieces, Flute.... 536
Mouthpieces, Piccolo.... 536
Mourning Bonnets.... 302
Mourning Handkerchiefs. 226
Mourning Sprays.... 303
Mourning Prints.... 291
Mower, Lawn.... 51
Mowing Machines.... 155
Mucilage.... 21
Mucilage.... 351
Mud Guards.... 618
Muffin Pans.... 131, 136
Mufflers, Men's.... 226
Mulhouse Percales.... 290
Mull Ties.... 311
Mull, Curtain.... 297
Mull, India.... 293
Musette, Midway.... 532
Mushrooms, Canned.... 11
Music Boxes.... 523-524
Music Cabinet.... 655
Music Folios.... 537
Music Paper.... 538
Music Racks.... 537
Music Stands.... 537
Music Wrappers.... 537
Musical Records Graphophone.... 485
Musical Sleigh Bells.... 532
Musical Goods Department.... 510, 541
Muslin Chemises.... 308
Muslin Night Gowns.... 282
Muslin Underwear.... 282-308
Muslin Bibs.... 306
Mustard Plasters.... 35
Mustard.... 9-10
Mutes, Band Instrument 537
Mutes, Bass Viol.... 534
Mutes, Viola.... 534
Mutes, Violin.... 534
Mutes, Violoncello.... 534
Muzzles, Dog.... 592
Muzzle, Cribbing.... 765
Muzzle, Horse.... 76

## N

Nail Brushes.... 328
Nail Holding Hammers.. 78
Nails.... 38
Nail Scissors.... 109
Nail Sets.... 82
Nails, Horse.... 68
Nails, Lining.... 58
Nails, Wagon Box.... 61
Nainsook.... 293
Nainsook Embroidery.... 266
Naphtha.... 20
Napkin Rings, Wood.... 140
Napkins.... 295
Neatsfoot Oil.... 21
Necks, Viola.... 534
Necks, Violin.... 534
Neckties, Ladies'.... 223-224
Neckwear, Ladies'.... 310-311, 334-335
Neckwear, Men's.... 222-224
Neck Yoke Attachments. 62
Neck Yokes, Buggy.... 63
Neck Yoke Ferrules.... 62
Neck Yokes, Iron.... 63
Neck Yoke Woods.... 63
Nectarines.... 12
Needle Cases.... 322
Needles, Crochet.... 322
Needles, Darning.... 322

Needles, Knitting ....... 322
Needles, Sacking ........ 98
Needles, Seine.... ...... 608
Needles, Sewing......... 322
Needles, Shoemakers'.... 207
Negative Racks...... .... 479
Negative Boxes.......... 479
Negligee Shirts, Men's.215-217
Nerve Medicines...... ... 27
Nests, Wire Hens'........ 43
Net Rings................. 605
Nets, Cotton Mesh....... 768
Nets, Dip ............... 605
Nets, Fish..........606-608
Nets, Fly...... ........ 768
Nets, Funnel............ 607
Nets, Fyke.............. 607
Nets, Gill................ 607
Nets, Leather, Team..... 768
Nets, Mosquito Head.... 605
Nets, Quail.............. 607
Nets, Trammel.......... 607
Netting, Cotton......... 606
Netting, Gill............ 607
Netting, Minnow.....606-607
Netting, Mosquito ....... 292
Netting, Wire ........... 42
Newhouse Traps .......99-100
Nickel Plated Coffee-pots.............. 132
Nickel Plated Screws.... 43
Nickel Plated Tea Kettles.................. 132
Nickle Plated Teapots.. 132
Night Gowns, Ladies' ... 282
Nightingale Flageolets.. 528
Nightingale Shoe Laces. 209
Night Latches............ 90
Night Shirts, Men's..... 212
Nippers, Cutting..... ... 68
Nipples, Rubber......28, 329
Nipple Shields............ 32
Non-Achromatic Spy Glasses............ 465
Non-Elastic Webbing.... 223
Non-Holation Plates.... 480
Note Books, Photographic........... 479
Note Paper.............. 350
Notion Department...320-323
Nottingham Lace Curtains.............286-287
Nosing Plane........... 77
Nosing Tools...... ...... 76
Novelty Cloth........... 255
Novelty Dress Goods.... 260
Noyes' Dictionary Holders............... 336
Nozzles, Hose .......... 56
Numbers, House......... 99
Nursing Bottles.......28, 329
Nursing Bottle Fittings. 330
Nursing Corsets ......... 306
Nursery Goods Department............. 28
Nut Crackers .......... 98
Nutmegs................ 9
Nutmeg Graters......... 134
Nutria Fur Hats.....232-234
Nuts.................... 17
Nuts, Violoncello.. .... 532

O

Oak Blocks ............ 208
Oak Sole Leather....... 208
Oak Tanned Calfskins.... 208
Oar Locks.............. 606
Oars, Boat.... ......... 606
Oat Sieves.............. 141
Oatmeal................. 15
Obesity Powders........ 27
Ocarina Instruction Books.... .... ...... 541
Ocarinas ............... 533
Odorless Chamber Pails. 134
Odd Jobs................ 73
Office Furniture........ 652
Officers' Bugles........ 531
Officers' Coats......... 189
Ogee Planes............. 77
Oil, All Kinds........20-21
Oil, Axle............... 766
Oil, Bicycle............ 619
Oil Cake Meal........... 23
Oil, Camphorated........ 28
Oil Cans..............84, 135
Oil Cans, Bicycle....... 618
Oil, Castor............. 27
Oil Clothing.........188-189
Oil Cups................ 55
Oil Faucets............. 99
Oil Grain Shoes, Ladies' 193
Oil Grain Shoes, Men's..........200-201
Oil, Gun................ 590
Oil, Hair............... 34
Oil, Harness.......21, 766
Oil Jackets............. 189
Oil, Kerosene........... 20
Oil, Lamp..........20, 619
Oil Pants............... 189
Oil Stones.............. 84
Oil Stones, Emery....... 71
Oil Stoves.........117-118
Oil Tanks............... 20
Oil Troughs............. 66
Oilers, Pocket, Gun .... 590
Oilcloth Mats, Children's. 309
Oilcloth, Floor and Table.............. 300
Ointment Pots........... 35
Olive Oil.... ....... .... 13
Olives ................. 13
One-Man Saws........... 69
Oneita Union Suits...... 240
Onion Seed.............. 25
Opaque Attachments for Magic Lantern........ 483
Opaque Shade Cloth..... 299
Open Bells............. 106
Open Buggies........711-723
Open Circuit Batteries.. 471
Open Work Embroidery. 266
Opera Boots, Men's ..... 202
Opera Glass Bags....... 464
Opera Glass Handles.... 464
Opera Glasses.......... 464
Opera Length Hose...... 244
Opera Slippers, Ladies'.. 195
Opodeldoc .............. 28
Openers, Can........... 98
Optical Goods Department.............462-485
Orange Blossoms........ 303
Orange Peel............. 12
Orchestra Bells......... 532
Orchestra Music........ 539
Organ Stools........... 537
Organ Instruction Books 540
Organ Music Folios..... 539
Organs and Pianos....510-514
Organs, Roller.......... 524
Organdies............... 290
Organdies, Fancy Figured................ 262
Oriental Laces.......... 265
Oriental Fiber Lining... 258
Ornaments, Gable....... 95
Ornaments, Fence....... 42
Ortho-Chromatic Plates. 480
Ostrich Tips............ 303
Otter Trap...........99-100
Out Size Hose.......... 245
Outfits, Camping........ 610
Outfits, Violin.......... 516
Outfits, Cooking........ 610
Outfits, Harness Repair. 766
Outfits, Shoe Repair..... 207
Outing Shirts, Men's..213-215
Outing Flannels......... 258
Outside Calipers....74, 84-85
Ovens, Gasoline........ 113
Ovens, Oil Stove ....... 117
Overalls, Apron......... 178
Overalls, Boys'......... 178
Overalls, Duck.......... 178
Overalls, Carpenters' ... 178
Overalls, Mechanics' ... 178
Overalls, Men's......... 178
Overalls, Painters'...... 178
Overalls, Riding........ 178
Overgaiters..........206-207
Overcoats, Men's ....... 175
Overshoes and Rubbers...........204-205
Ox Balls............... 46
Ox Bow Pins........... 46
Ox Bows............... 46
Ox Hair Brushes........ 113
Ox Yokes............... 46
Oxford Laces........... 209
Oxfords, Child's........ 195
Oxfords, Ladies'......195-196
Oxfords, Men's......... 200
Oyster Shells, Ground.20, 30
Oysters, Canned......... 14
Ozaline................ 147

P

Pacs, Lumberman ...... 201
Padlocks ............... 87
Pads, Blotting ......... 355
Pads, Buggy ........... 58
Pads, Gig .............. 762
Pads, Hip and Bust .... 307
Pads, Ladies' Absorbent. 32
Pads, Recoil ........... 590
Pads, Team ............ 763
Pads, Top Collar ...... 761
Pails, Minnow ......... 605
Pails, Tin ...........132-133
Pails, Wood ........138-139
Paint Brushes ......113-114
Painters' Dusters ...... 114
Painters' Jumpers ..... 178
Painters' Overalls ..... 178
Paints, Artists' ......360-361
Paints, Dry Color....... 22
Paints, Grease .......... 330
Paints, House ........21-22
Paints in Oil .......... 22
Palette Cups .......... 360
Pancake Griddles ...... 129
Panel Gauges .......... 74
Panel Protectors ...... 58
Pans, Evaporator ...... 154
Pans, Gem ............. 129
Pants, Boys' Long ..... 180
Pants Buckles ......... 321
Pants Buttons ......... 320
Pants, Duck ........... 178
Pants Goods ........... 289
Pants, Hunting ........ 591
Pants, Oiled .......... 189
Pants, Tailor-Made Men's 174
Paper, Aristotype ...... 480
Paper Bags ............ 23
Paper, Bromide ........ 480
Paper, Building ........ 95
Paper, Carbon ......... 359
Paper Carpet Lining .... 300
Paper, Celerite ........ 480
Paper Clips ........... 355
Paper, Drawing ........ 359
Paper Fasteners ........ 355
Paper, Ferro-Prussiate .. 480
Paper, Filtering ........ 35
Paper Hangers' Brushes 114
Paper Hangers' Jumpers 178
Paper, Lithium ......... 480
Paper, Music .......... 538
Paper Patterns ........ 324
Paper (Roof) ........... 23
Parers, Apple .......... 102
Paper, Sand ........... 77
Papers, Drawing ....... 350
Paper Sheathing ....... 23
Paper Shells .........583-584
Paper, Tissue ......... 332
Paper, Tissue Crepe .... 333
Paper (Toilet) ......... 23
Paper, Wall ........... 299
Paper (Wrapping) ...... 23
Papeteries ............ 350
Parasols ............249-250
Parchment Paper ....... 147
Paregoric ............. 27
Paris Green Sprinkler .. 162
Parisian Bangs ........ 330
Park Wagons .......... 717
Parlor Cabinets ....... 653
Parlor Door Hangers ... 91
Parlor Furniture .....663-668
Parlor Organs ........512-514
Parlor Suits ..........663-665
Parlor Tables ......... 651
Parting Stops ......... 95
Partridge Nets ........ 607
Paste, Library ........ 351
Pastry Boards ......... 140
Patched Bullets ....... 582
Patching, Rubber Tire... 619
Patent Dog Remedies .. 592
Patent Leather Polish .. 209
Patent Leatner Shoes, Patent Medicine ...... 29
Patent Heads, Banjo..... 535
Patent Heads, Double Bass .................. 535
Patent Heads, Guitar ... 535
Patent Heads, Mandolin 536
Patent Heads, Violin ... 533
Patent Heads, Violoncello ................. 535
Patent Heads, Zither ... 536
Patterns, Paper ........ 324
Patterns, Skirt ........ 306
Patty Pans ............ 131
Paulins ............... 609
Men's .................. 200
Peach Butter .......... 12
Peaches, Canned ...... 11
Peaches, Dried ........ 12
Pearl Buttons ......... 319
Pearl Opera Glasses ... 464
Pears, Dried .......... 12
Pears, Canned ......... 11
Peas, Canned .......... 11
Peas, Dried ........... 15
Pedals, Bicycle ........ 617
Peep Sights .........579-580
Peg Breaks ............ 208
Pegs, Banjo ........... 535
Pegs, Shoe ............ 208
Pegs, Viola ........... 534
Pegs, Violin ........... 533
Pegs, Violoncello ...... 535
Pellissiers ........... 252
Pencil Holders ......74, 353
Pencil Sharpeners ..... 353
Pencil Tablets ........ 349
Pencils, Automatic .... 353
Pencils, Carpenter .... 74
Pencils, Crayon ....... 353
Pencils, Drawing ...... 359
Pencils, Lead ......... 352
Pencils, Retouching ... 479
Pencils, Slate ........ 353
Pen Holders ........353-354
Pen Racks ............ 354
Pens, Steel ........... 354
Pepper Boxes ......... 134
Pepper ................ 9
Pepperell Sheetings ... 292
Pepper Sauce ......... 13
Pepper Sauce, Tobasco.. 12
Pequot Sheetings ...... 292
Percale Dress Goods ... 290
Percalines ............ 258
Percale Shirt Waists, Ladies' .................. 269
Percale Wrappers ..... 272
Perfections, Lumberman's .................. 206
Perfume ..........19, 33, 329
Perfume Atomizers .... 329
Persian Flannelette .... 258
Persian Shirt Waists, Ladies' ...............268-269
Persian Wrappers ..... 272
Petroleum Jelly ....... 27
Phaetons ..........710, 723
Phantom Minnows ..... 604
Photo Album Binders ... 480
Photinto .............. 480
Photograph Albums..... 349
Photographic Absorbent Cotton ................ 479
Photographic Albums.349, 481
Photographic Brushes ... 479
Photographic Blotting Paper ................ 479
Photographs, Cabinet .. 469
Photographic Cameras ............473-477
Photographic Clips ..... 479
Photographic Chemicals.............480-481
Photographic Colored Glasses............. 479
Photographic Easel ..... 478
Photographic Enameler.. 479
Photographic Envelopes.. 479
Photographic Filtering Paper ................ 479
Photographic Finger Tips 479
Photographic Focusing Cloth ................ 479
Photographic Glass Forms ................ 479
Photographic Hydrometers ................... 479
Photographic Lenses .477-478
Photographic Litmus Paper ................... 479
Photographic Mailing Envelopes ............... 479
Photographic Metallic Paints ................ 479
Photographic Note Books 479
Photographic Outfits ... 477
Photographic Plate Lifters .................. 479
Photographic Polishes .. 479
Photographic Ruby Paper ................... 479
Photographic Solutions ... 480
Photographic Trimmers. 479
Photographic Vignettes... 478
Photographic Yellow Paper ................... 479
Piano Instruction Books 751
Piano Music............ 539
Piano Scarfs........... 537
Piano Stools........... 537
Pianos..............510-511
Pianos (Toy)........... 532
Piano Tuning Hammers. 538
Piccolo Cases.......... 536
Piccolo Flageolets...... 528
Piccolo Instruction Books 541
Piccolo Mouthpieces.... 536
Piccolos .............. 528
Picket Chains.......... 46
Picket Pins............ 46
Pickles................ 13
Pick Mattocks.......... 50
Picks.................. 50
Picks, Autoharp........ 536
Picks, Mandolin........ 536
Picks, Zither.......... 536
Picture Cord........... 299
Picture Hooks.......... 299
Pictures............... 670
Picture Wire........41, 299
Pie Plates.........131-136
Pier Mirrors.......670-671
Pigs' Feet............. 13
Pig Troughs............ 163
Pile Remedy............ 27
Pillows ............... 62
Pillows, Down ......... 662
Pillow Shams........... 332
Pillow Slips........... 292
Pills, Ague............ 26
Pills, Cathartic....... 26
Pills, Female.......... 27
Pills, Nerve and Brain.. 27
Pills, Pink............ 27
Pills, Little Liver..... 27
Pills, Quinine......... 28
Pills, Tansy........... 29
Pins................... 322
Pin Books.............. 322
Pincers, Carpenters'.... 82
Pincers, Farriers'..... 67
Pincers, Shoemakers' ... 207
Pineapple Candy........ 11
Pine Tar............... 23
Pin Fasteners.......... 358
Pinking Irons.......... 98
Pins, Belt ............ 331
Pins, Bow.............. 46
Pins, Hair............. 322
Pins, Hat.............. 322
Pins, Horse Blanket.... 765
Pins, Husking.......... 229
Pins, Jet.............. 322
Pins, Picket .......... 46
Pins, Safety........... 322
Pins, Shawl............ 322
Pipe Black ............ 54
Pipe Clevis............ 55
Pipe Cutters........... 55
Pipe Fitters' Tools..... 55
Pipe Fittings........... 54
Pipe, Galvanized....... 54
Pipe, Iron ............ 54
Pipe, Lead ............ 56
Pipe Lifter............ 55
Pipes and Smokers' Goods ................333-334
Pipe Screw Plate...... 55
Pipe Stands........... 334
Pipe Stock and Dies.... 55
Pipe, Stove........... 128
Pipes, Tuning.......537-538
Pipe Tongs............ 55
Pipe Vise ............ 55
Pipe Wrench........... 55
Piping, Chain.......... 762
Pique, White Corded.... 293
Pistol Holsters........ 589
Pistols............571-574
Pitchers .............. 131
Pitcher Tray........... 134
Pitch Gauges .......... 85
Plaid Dress Goods...255-260
Plain Calico........... 291
Plane Handles.......... 75
Plane, Irons........... 75
Planes.............74-75-76-77
Planet Jr. Garden Tools
Planter Hats, Men's.... 234
Plant Sprinklers....... 329
........................160-162
Plaster Board.......... 95
Plaster, Court......... 28
Plaster, Medicated..... 35
Plaster, Mustard....... 35
Plaster of Paris....... 23
Plaster, Porous ....... 35
Plate Holders, Photographic ............... 477
Plate Lifters, Photographic ............... 479
Plates, Bolster ........ 62
Plates, Dry............ 480
Plates, Felloe ........ 61
Plates, Ferotype....... 479
Plates, Letter Drop..... 93
Plates, Non-Halation.... 480
Plates, Ortho-Chromatic. 480
Plates, Sash Pull...... 92
Plates, T.............. 61
Plates, Transom........ 89
Plates, Whiffletree..... 61
Platform Scales........ 47
Plating, Outfits ....... 472
Platting Scales........ 358
Playing Cards.......... 356
Pliers................. 82
Plow Boots, Men's..... 202
Plow Clevises......... 62
Plow Evener........... 63
Plow Handles.......... 65
Plows..............156-157
Plows, Carpenters' .....76-77
Plow Shares........... 158
Plow Shoes, Boys'...... 203
Plow Shoes, Men's....200-201
Plow Singletrees....... 63
Plugs, Rubber Tire .... 619
Plug Tobacco........... 24
Plumb and Levels....... 72
Plumb Bobs
Plumes, Ostrich........ 303
Plumes, Bridle......... 763
Plum Pudding........... 11
Plums, Canned.......... 11
Plums, Dried........... 12
Plush.................. 256
Poachers, Egg ......... 129
Poke Bonnets, Infants'...........309-310
Pocket Barometers ..... 470
Pocket Books.......324-325
Pocket Combs.......... 326
Pocket Compasses ..... 467
Pocket Galvanometer ... 471
Pocket Goods, Handy.... 28
Pocket Hones .......... 71
Pocket Hones .......... 111
Pocket Knife .......... 111
Pocket Knives ....109-110-111
Pocket Levels ......... 72
Pocket Oilers.......... 590
Pocket Scales ......... 48
Pocket Scissors ....... 109
Pocket Spy Glasses .... 465
Pocket Stove........... 28
Pocket Tape Lines ..... 73
Pocket Wrenches ....... 78
Pointers, Spoke ....... 81
Pointing Trowels ...... 84
Points, Trammel ....... 74
Points, Well .......... 54
Pokes, Animal ......... 46
Poker Chips ........... 356
Pokers, Stove ......... 128
Pole Caps.............. 62
Poles, Buggy .......... 63
Poles, Curtain ........ 298
Pole Tips ............. 61
Police Lanterns ....... 138
Police Whistles........ 592
Polishers, Photographic.. 479
Polishers, Shoe .....109-209
Polyopticians ......... 483
Pomatum ............... 34
Pomatum Wax .......... 112
Pommel Slickers......188-189
Popcorn ............... 15
Poppers, Corn ......... 135
Porcelain Kettles ..... 130
Porch Trimmings ....... 95
Pork .................. 13
Porpoise Shoe Laces .... 209
Portable Forges .......64-65
Portiere Curtains...... 297
Portland Cutter Stuff... 63
Postal Scales ......... 47
Post Drills ........... 65
Post Hole Augers ...... 50
Post Hole Diggers ..... 50
Post Mauls ............ 50
Postman's Boxes ....... 98
Posts ................. 43
Post Spade ............ 48
Posts, Stair .......... 95
Posts, Street Lamp .... 138
Potash ................ 19
Potato Bug Sprinklers... 162
Potato Forks .......... 48
Potato Masher ......... 140
Potato Scoop .......... 48
Pot Cleaners .......... 98
Pot Covers ............ 130
Pots, Ointment......... 35
Pots, Stove ........... 130

Punches, Shot.... 588
Punches, Tobacco.. 324
Poultry Instruments. 32
Poultry Knife.... 32
Poultry Marker.. 32
Poultry Marks 46
Poultry Netting 42
Pounders, Steak 98
Powder and Shot Measures. 588
Powder, Black 585
Powders, Dog 143
Powder, Obesity 27
Powder, Smokeless 585
Prescription Department. 29
Preservaline 147
Preserves 12
Preserving Kettles.129-130, 135
Presses, Cider 154
Presses, Fruit 102
Presses, Hay 151
Presses, Lard 102
Presses, Wine 102
Press Screws 165
Pretzels 16
Prick Punches 82
Primers, Gun 584
Prince Albert Suits 171
Prince Albert Shoes, Ladies' 191
Printing Frame, Camera 478
Print Rollers 479
Prints, Drapery 291
Prints, Dress 256
Professional Magic Lanterns 483
Professional Men's Suits 171
Proprietary Articles 29
Prop. Nuts 53
Protectors, Panel 58
Protractors 85, 358
Pruners, Tree 50
Prunes 12
Pruning Hooks and Saws 50
Pruning Shears 50
Pudding Pans 131, 136
Puff Boxes 28
Puffs, Powder 28
Pullers, Tack 78
Pulley Blocks 96
Pulleys 96
Pulleys, Clothesline 89
Pulleys, Sash 89
Pulls, Barn Door 86
Pulls, Door 92
Pulls, Drawer 88-92
Pumice Stone 22
Pump Cylinders 53
Pump Department 52-53
Pumping Jacks 148
Pumpkin, Canned 11
Pump Oil Cans 135
Pumps, Bicycle 617
Pumps, Breast 32, 329
Pumps, Spray 162
Punches, Center 82
Punches, Conductors' 83
Punches, Eyelet 208
Punches, Hollow 82-83
Punches, Prick 82
Punches, Shoemakers' 207
Purses 325
Push Buttons 471
Putty 22
Putty Knives 108

**Q**
Quackenbush Rifles 574-575
Quail Nets 607
Quarter Boots 767
Quarter Round Planes 77
Quartette Books 528
Quilt Frame Clamps 83
Quilts and Comforters 288
Quinine Pills 28

**R**
Rabbit Gauges 74
Rabbit Planes 75-77
Racing Shoes, Men's 206
Racing Skates 97
Racks, Clothes 141
Racks, Hat 89
Racks, Music 537
Racks, Negative 479
Racks, Whip 764
Racquets, Tennis 593
Rafter Irons 165
Rakes, Garden 49
Rakes, Hay 154-155
Ram's Horn Handle Bars 616
Rasps, Horsetooth 765
Rasps, Wood 71
Rail, Barndoor 86
Rail, Stair 95
Railroad Cap Badges 236
Railroad Men's Hats 233
Railroad Lanterns 137
Railroad Spectacles 463
Rain Gauges 470
Raisers, Bread 132
Raisin Seeder 102
Raisins 12
Ranch Hats, Men's 234
Ranges 121-124
Rasps 71
Raspberries, Dried 12
Raspberry Vinegar 12
Raspberries, Canned 11
Rat Killer 28
Rat Traps 99-100
Ratchet Braces 80
Ratchet, Fence 43

Ratchet Screwdrivers 80
Rattles, Celluloid 328
Rattle and Whistle 13b
Rawhide Lace Leather 56
Raves, Bob 63
Razor Hones 71
Razor Grinding 112
Razor Hones 112
Razor Strops 112
Razors 111-112
Reading Glasses 466
Ready-Made Dresses, Children's 304-305
Ready-Made Sheets 292
Ready-Made Skirts 270-271
Ready-Made Tablecloths 294-295
Reaches, Bob 63
Reaches, Wagon 62
Ream Paper 350
Reamer Bits 81
Rear Sights 579-580
Recappers 587
Receivers for Telephones 472
Recoil Pads 589-590
Rectangular Churn 144
Red Bed Blankets 288
Red Flannels 288
Reed Trimmers 537
Reed Holders, Clarionet 536
Reeding Tool 76
Reeding Planes 77
Reeds, Clarionet 536
Reefer Jackets, Children's 277-278
Reefer Jackets, Ladies'' 273-276
Reefer Jackets, Misses' 273-276
Reels, Chalk Line 74
Reel Bands 605
Reels, Clothes Line 100
Reels, Fishing 599-600
Reels, Hose 56
Reference Books 336
Refreshment Tents 608
Regenerator, Hair 330
Refrigerators 104-105
Regina Music Boxes 523
Regulator, Clock 461
Reins, Check 763
Reins, Riding Bridle 763
Religious Works 347
Reloading Tools 586-587
Remedies, Dog 593
Remedies, Family 27
Remedies, Homeopathic 29-30
Remedies, Horsefoot 766
Remedies, Veterinary 30
Remnants, Dress Goods 255
Renewal Parts for Batteries 471
Rennets 147
Rennet, Butter 14
Rennet Tablets 147
Repair Cloths 209
Repair Kits, Bicycle 618
Repair Links 97
Resin, Double Bass 534
Resin, Violin 534
Resin, Violoncello 535
Resizing Tools 208
Retouching Pencils 479
Reversible Shawls 305
Revolvers 571-574
Revolver Cartridges 580-583
Revolver Holsters 559-560
Revolving Eyelet Set and Punches 208
Revolving Grater 102
Revolving Slicer 102
Revolving Spring Pounches 83
Revolution Counter 85
Rheumatism Cure 27
Rheumatism Ring 28
Rhubarb, Canned 11
Ribbons 263
Ridge Roll 96
Riding Cultivators 158-159
Rim Locks 90
Rims, Bent 60
Rings, Baby, Engraved Band 417
Rings, Beetle 77
Rings, Bull 46
Rings, Celluloid 765
Rings, Child's Set 416
Rings, Diamond 401
Rings, Flush 87
Rings, Gent's Set 418
Rings, Gold Filled 416
Rings, Harness 765
Rings, Initial and Emblem 417
Rings, Key Silver 435
Rings, Lady's Engraved Band 417
Rings, Lady's Set 418
Rings, Martingale 765
Rings, Misses' Engraved Band 417
Rings, Plain Solid Gold 417
Rings and Ringers, Hog 45
Rings and Staples 86
Rings, Silver 416
Rings, Silver Napkin 446
Rings, Teething 328
Rings, Wood Napkin 140
Rings, White Zylonite 765

Rice 16
Rice Flour 16
Rifle Cases 588-589
Rifle Cartridges 580-583
Rifle Cleaning Rods 588
Rifles 574, 580
Rigged Fish Lines 601
River Boats 202
River Seines 606-607
River Shoes 201
Rivets, Copper 83
Rivets, Slotted 83
Rivets, Wagon Box 61
Riveting Burrs 61
Riveting Hammer 78
Road Carts 723-727
Road Wagons 711, 723
Roasting Pans 133
Robes, Black Japanese Fur 769
Robes, Carriage 768-769
Robes, Dog Skin 770
Robes, Galloway 770
Robes, Goat Fur 769
Robes, Prairie Wolf 770
Robes, Plush 769
Robes, Wool 769
Rockford Socks 243
Rocking Chairs, Cane Seat 644-645-647
Rocking Chairs, Leather Seat 644-645
Rocking Chairs, Rattan 647
Rocking Chairs, Upholstered 644-645
Rocking Chairs, Wood Seat 644
Rocking Horses 142
Rod Varnish 606
Rods, Fishing 594-599
Rods, Cleaning 587-588
Rods, Saw 69
Rods, Wagon Box 62
Roofing 96
Roofing Brushes 114
Roofing Felt 23
Roofing Cement 23
Rolled Oats 15
Rolled Wheat 15
Roller Organs 524
Rollers, Bob 63
Rollers, Land 162
Rollers, Print 479
Rolling Pins 140
Root Beer 27
Root Beer Extract 11
Root Cutters 152
Rope 20
Rope, Hitch 165
Rope, Manila 97
Ropes, Tennis 593
Rope, Wire 97
Rosin 18
Round Files 71
Round Head Screws 40
Round Leather Shoe Laces 209
Round Nose Pliers 82
Rouge 34
Roses 303
Rosettes, Crystal 765
Router Planes 76
Rub Irons 62
Rubber Anti-Rattlers 61
Rubber Bands 355
Rubber Belting 56
Rubber Bibs 329
Rubber Bladders 594
Rubber Boots and Shoes 204-206
Rubber Brushes 33, 327
Rubber Cement 22, 208
Rubber Diaper Drawers 329
Rubber Drill 58
Rubber Crutch Bottoms 33
Rubber Dog Combs 592
Rubber Erasers 354-355
Rubber Foot Balls 594
Rubber Gloves and Mittens 329
Rubber Hair Pins 322
Rubber Hose 56
Rubber Mending Tissue 333
Rubber Nipples 329
Rubber Pants 206
Rubber Patching 208
Rubber Recoil Pads 589-590
Rubber Soles 208
Rubber Sole Shoes 208
Rubber Soling 208
Rubber Sundries 32-35, 329
Rubber Trays 478
Rubber Tubing 56, 333
Rubber Water Bottles 329
Rubber Finger Tips 479
Ruby or Orange Glass, Photographic 479
Ruby Paper, Photographic 479
Rug Fringes 298
Rugs and Carpets 300
Rules, Architects' 73
Rules, Board 73
Rules, Boxwood 73
Rules, Caliper 73
Rules, Ivory 73
Rules, Log 73
Rules for Measurement, Ladies' 267
Rules for Measurement, Men's 170
Rules, Slide 73

Rulers 353
Ruling Pens, Music 528
Runners, Bob 63
Runners, Long Sleigh 63
Running Shoes 206
Russian Colt Skin Shoes 198
Russet Polish 209
Russian Shoemakers' Bristles 209
Rust Remover 590
Rust Preventer 590

**S**
Sack Suits, Men's 168-173
Sacks and Bags 23
Sacks, Grain 293
Sacks, Wool 293
Sacking, Burlap 292
Sacking Needles 98
Sacques, Infants' 309
Sad Irons 100
Saddle Pads 751
Saddle Rifle Sheath 588-589
Saddle Bags 751
Saddle, Bicycle 616
Saddles 750-757
Saddles, Gig 763
Saddles, Ladies' 759
Safes, Match 334-437
Safes, Steel 97
Safes, Toy 99
Safety Belts, Ladies' 323
Safety Pins 322
Safety Razors 112
Sago 16
Sailor Caps, Children's 236-237
Salad Dressing 12
Salaratus 10
Salmon 14
Salt 13
Salt Bores 141
Salt Shakers 439
Salts, Epsom 18
Salts, Rochelle 28
Salts, Smelling 28
Salve, Horse 769
Salvation Army Tambourines 532
Sandpaper 77
Sand Screens 45
Sap Pails 133
Sardines 14
Sarsaparilla 27
Sarven Wheels 58
Sarven Spokes 59
Sash 94-95
Sash Balances 89
Sash Centers 89
Sash Cords 20
Sash Curtains 297
Sash Locks 89-92
Sash Lifts 89
Sash Planes 77
Sash Plates and Hooks 92
Sash Pulleys 89
Satchel Tags, Silver 437
Sateens 290
Sateens, Black and Colored 262
Sateen Linings 258
Sateen Shirtwaists 269
Sateen Tennis Shoes 203
Sateen Wrappers 272
Satin, Brocaded 262
Satin Calf Shoes, Men's 198-199
Satin, Farmers' 258
Satin Slippers, Ladies' 195
Satins and Silks 257
Sauce Pans 130-135
Sauces 12
Sausage Choppers 102
Sausage Stuffers 102
Saws 68-69-70
Saw Blades 69-70
Saw Clamps 70
Saw Files 70
Saw Handles 69
Saw Jointers 71
Saw Machines 152
Saw Mandrils 68
Saw Sets 70-71
Saws, Drag 152
Saws, Dehorning 46
Saws, Pole 152
Scale Beam 48
Scales, Fish 606
Scales, Prescription 35
Scales and Weights 478
Scales, Fish 99
Scales 47
Scalloped Pans 131
Scarfs 134
Scarf Pins, Gold 426
Scarf Pins, Diamond 402
Scarfs 537
Scarfs for Fancy Work 331
Scarlet Bed Blankets 288
Scarlet Flannel 288
School Bags 355
School House Bells 106
School Hats, Boys' 235
School Shoes 194
School Supplies 351-356
Scissors 109
Scissors, Silver 454
Sciopticon 483
Scotch Bowls 129
Scotch Plaid Dress Goods 260

Scotch Wool Plaids 255
Scoops 48
Scrapers, Cabinet 77
Scrapers, Floor 102
Scrapers, Hog 98
Scrapers, Meat 765
Scrapers, Plane 76
Scrapers, Steel 164, 363
Scratch Awls 82
Screw, Cork 98
Screw Eyes 99
Screw Hooks 99
Screw Pitch Gauge 85
Screw Pulleys 96
Screw Pin Clevises 62
Screw Plates 67
Screws 40
Screws, Bench 83
Screws, Brass 40
Screws, Drive 40
Screws, Flat Head 40
Screws, Jack 165
Screws, Nickel Plated 40
Screws, Round Head 40
Screws, Press 165
Screwdrivers 80
Screwdriver Bits 81
Screens 671
Screen Corner Irons 44
Screen Cloth 43
Screen Doors 44
Screen Door Catches 44
Screen Door Springs 44
Screen Door Catches 92
Screen Frames 44
Screens for Magic Lanterns 484
Screens, Sand 45
Screens, Window 43
Scriber 85
Scythe Snaths 51
Scrub Brushes 20
Scrub Brushes 114
Scythe Stones 51
Scythes 50
Scythe Stones, Emery 71
Seals 354
Sealing Wax 354
Seam Binding 263
Search Light 138
Seat Spring Hooks 62
Seat, Spring 60
Seats, Buggy 58
Seats, Chair 142
Secret Society Views of Magic Lantern 485
Seed Sowers 155
Seed Droppers 160-162
Seeds 16
Seeder, Raisin 102
Seine Needles 608
Seine Twine 608
Seines, Creek 606-607
Seines, Drag 606
Seines, Fyke 607
Seines, Hoop Net 607
Seines, Lake and River 606
Seines, Minnow 606
Seines, Straight 606
Seidlitz Powders 27
Self Rising Foods 15
Self-Fastening Clevis 62
Self-Registering Thermometers 469
Sen Sen 28
Separator, Cream 143
Serge Coat Lining 258
Serge Coat and Vest, Men's 176
Serpentine Crepe 290
Serge Skirts, Black 271
Serge Slippers, Ladies' 196
Set Nets 607
Sets, Croquet 593
Sets, Chamber 134
Sets, Dessert 454
Sets, Nail 82
Sets, Reloading 586-587
Sets, Rings 401, 416-418
Sets, Saw 71
Sets, Tennis 593
Sets, Tray Silver Pot 451-452-453
Sets, Water 455
Settees, Lawn 646
Setting Clamps 100
Setting Tanks 144
Settees, Wire 45
Sewing Needles 322
Sewing Machine Oil 21
Sewing Machines 697-705
Sewing Silk 321
Shade Cloth 299
Shade Fringe 299
Shade Pulls 299
Shades, Window 299
Shaft Tips 61
Shaft Irons 61
Shaft Coupling 67
Shafts, Buggy 63
Shafts, Ironed 63
Shams, Pillow 332
Sharpeners, Scissors 109
Sharpeners, Knife 71
Shaving Brushes, Silver 436
Shaving Brushes 323
Shaving Brushes 112
Shaving Mugs, Silver 456
Shaving Soap 112
Shaving Sets 330
Shawl Pins 322

Shawl Straps ... 535
Shawls ... 305
Shawls, Infants' ... 278
Shears ... 109
Shears, Grass ... 50
Shears, Hedge ... 50
Shears, Pruning ... 50
Shearer, Sheep ... 46
Sheaths, Axe ... 590
Sheaths, Gun ... 588-589
Sheaths, Knife ... 589
Sheathing Paper ... 95
Shelves, Clock and Man-
Shelves, Flower Pot ... 45
Shell Band Spokes ... 60
Shell Bags ... 589
Shell Boxes ... 589
Shell Closers ... 587
Shell Crimpers ... 587
Shell Extractors ... 587
Shell Loaders ... 588
Shell Reamers ... 587
Shells, Brass, Empty ... 582-583
Shells, Empty, Rifle ... 582
Shells, Loaded ... 583
Shells, Paper, Empty ... 583-584
Shepherd Plaid Skirts ... 271
Shepherd Plaids ... 255
Shetland Shawls ... 305
Sheep Lined Boots ... 202
Sheep Dip ... 30
Sheepskin Slippers ... 209
Sheets, Stockmen's Bed ... 609
Sheet Lead ... 56
Sheets, Ready-Made ... 292
Sheeting ... 291-292
Sheets, Horse ... 770
Sheeting Paper ... 23
Shields ... 765
Shields, Dress ... 321
Shields, Knee ... 209
Shingling Brackets ... 74
Shrimp, Canned ... 14
tel ... 671-672
Shirt Buttons ... 320
Shirts, Hunting ... 591
Shirt Studs ... 402, 425
Shirt Waists, Ladies' ... 268-269
Shirting Prints ... 291
Shirtings, Fancy Cheviot ... 292
Shoe Buttons ... 207
Shoe Brushes ... 114
Shoe Brush Sets ... 328
Shoe Blacking ... 209
Shoe Brush Cabinet ... 114
Shoe Dressing ... 19
Shoe Dressing ... 209
Shoe Hammers ... 207-209
Shoe Knives ... 207
Shoe Laces ... 209
Shoe Lasts, Iron ... 207
Shoe Laces ... 321
Shoe Nails ... 208
Shoe Pacs ... 201
Shoe Polisher ... 209
Shoe Pegs ... 142
Shoe Pockets, Stamped ... 332
Shoe Pegs ... 208
Shoe Stretcher ... 208
Shoe Thread ... 209
Shoe and Boot Department ... 190-209
Shoes, Boys' ... 203
Shoes, Base Ball ... 596
Shoes, Beaver ... 196
Shoes, Bicycle ... 266
Shoes, Bob ... 63
Shoes, Cutter ... 63
Shoes, Child's ... 193-195
Shoes, Gymnasium ... 203-206
Shoes, Horse ... 68
Shovel Handles ... 49
Shoes, Ladies' ... 191-196
Shoes, Men's ... 197-201
Shoes, Misses' ... 194-195
Shoes, Sporting ... 201-206
Shoes, Youths' ... 194-195-203
Shoemakers' Bristles ... 209
Shoemakers' Hammers ... 207
Shoemakers' Needles ... 207
Shoemakers' Pincers and Punches ... 207-208
Shoemakers' Tools ... 207-209
Shoemakers' Repair Outfits ... 207
Shoemakers' Wax ... 209
Shopping Bags ... 335
Shot ... 585
Shot Cartridges ... 583
Shot Guns ... 562-571
Shot Gun Sights ... 579
Shot Gun Shells ... 583-584
Shooting Creedmoors ... 201
Shooting Spectacles ... 463
Shovels ... 48
Shovel Plows ... 158
Shoulder Shawls ... 305
Shoulder Braces ... 221
Shoveling Boards ... 165
Shredder, Ice ... 103
Shrinkers, Tire ... 66
Shutters, Camera ... 478
Sickle Grinders ... 165
Sickles, Grain ... 50
Side Boards ... 650
Side Combs ... 326
Side Pulleys ... 96
Side Rabbit Plane ... 76
Sieves, Oat ... 141
Sieves, Flour ... 133
Sifters, Ash ... 129
Sights, Level ... 72
Sights, Rifle ... 579-580
Silesias ... 258
Silk Belting ... 331
Silk Belting ... 263
Silk Covered Buttons ... 320
Silk Drapery ... 257
Silk Dress Goods ... 261
Silk Dress Loops ... 319
Silk Dress Goods Novelties ... 261
Silk, Embroidery ... 321
Silk Embroidered Flannels ... 288
Silk Gloves ... 231
Silk Gimp ... 319
Silk Gimp, Black ... 319
Silk Handkerchiefs ... 226-227
Silk, Japanese ... 257
Silk, Knitting ... 321
Silk Lacing Cord ... 319
Silk Laces ... 265
Silk Mufflers ... 226
Silk Mittens ... 231
Silk Neckties ... 222-223-224
Silk Ribbon ... 263
Silk Stockings ... 245
Silk Suspenders ... 220-221
Silk, Sewing ... 321
Silk Skirts ... 270-271
Silk Tassels ... 332
Silk Twist ... 321
Silk Trimmings ... 257
Silk Underwear ... 241
Silk Veiling ... 318
Silk and Velvet Flowers ... 303
Silk Velvet ... 256
Silk Waists ... 268
Silk Watch Chains ... 408-409
Silks, Brocaded ... 261
Silks, Changeable ... 261
Silks, China ... 257
Silks, Washable ... 256
Silkaline ... 293
Singletree Woods ... 63
Singletrees, Ironed ... 63
Singletrees, Buggy ... 63
Singletrees, Plow ... 63
Sinks, Kitchen ... 55
Silver Buttons ... 320
Silver Bake Dish ... 451
Silver Belt Buckles ... 432
Silver Casters ... 447-448
Silver, Child's Toilet Sets ... 435
Silver Coat Hangers ... 436
Silver Ink Sets ... 456
Silver Mounted Purses ... 437
Silver Novelties ... 435
Silver Perfume Bottles ... 456
Silver Rings ... 416
Silver, Smoking Sets ... 456
Silver Thimbles ... 435
Silver Watches ... 373-378
Silver Watch Chains ... 409
Silverine Watches ... 373-377
Silverware, Alaska ... 438
Silverware Department ... 438-456
Silverware, Rogers Bros. ... 434-444
Skates ... 97
Skeins, Cast ... 59
Skeins, Steel ... 59
Skirt Braid ... 323
Skirt Binding ... 323
Skirt Linings ... 258
Skirt Patterns ... 306
Skins, Chamois ... 330
Skirts, Infants' Flannel ... 309
Skirts, Ladies' White ... 307-308
Skirts, Ladies' Sateen ... 305
Skirts, Ready-Made ... 270-271
Slates, School ... 356
Slaw Cutters ... 140
Sleds, Bob ... 63
Sledges, Stone ... 50
Sledges, Blacksmiths' ... 67
Sleigh Gearing ... 63
Sleigh Shoe Bolts ... 63
Sleigh Runners ... 63
Sleeping Bag, Arctic ... 610
Sleeve Supporter ... 335
Slick, Carpenters' ... 79
Slickers, Men's ... 188-189
Slide Rule ... 73
Slides, Breast Strap ... 765
Slides for Stereopticons ... 484-486
Slides for Magic Lanterns ... 484-486
Sliding Door Lock ... 91
Sliding Door Locks ... 91
Sliding Bevels ... 73
Slim Taper Files ... 71
Sling Shot ... 98
Sling Pulleys ... 165
Slings, Wagon ... 165
Slings, Drum ... 536
Slotted Rivets ... 83
Slips, Pillow ... 292
Slips, Emery ... 71
Slippers, Ladies' ... 191-196
Slippers ... 209
Slitting Gauge ... 74
Slitting Plane ... 76
Silver Plating Outfits ... 472
Smokers' Articles ... 333-334
Smokeless Powder ... 585
Smokeless Shells ... 584
Smoking Jackets ... 177
Smooth Wire ... 41
Smyrna Rugs ... 300
Snare Drum Wrenches ... 536
Snare Drums ... 529
Snare Drum Slings ... 536
Snare Drum Sticks ... 536
Snare Drum Keys ... 536
Snap Breast Strap Roller ... 765
Snaps, Bull ... 46
Snip Snaps ... 98
Snips, Tinners' ... 84
Snuff Boxes ... 334
Soap ... 18
Soap Boxes ... 328
Soap Brackets ... 135
Soap, Dog ... 30
Soap Dish ... 133
Soap, Harness ... 30
Soap, Sulphur ... 33
Soap, Shaving ... 33
Soap, Toilet ... 33
Soap, Harness ... 766
Soaps ... 328
Socks, Men's ... 243-244
Socks, Lumbermen's ... 203
Socket Oar Locks ... 605
Soda Mint Tablets ... 28
Soda ... 10
Sofa Cushions ... 391, 662
Soft Sole Shoe, Infants' ... 194-195
Soldering Coppers ... 84
Sole Leather ... 208
Soles ... 208
Solid Gold Watches ... 389-390
Solo Cornets ... 531
Sombreros ... 234
Stools, Organ ... 537
Stools, Piano ... 537
Soup Ladles, Silver ... 444
Soup Tureens, Silver ... 454
Soups, Canned ... 15
Soutache Braid ... 319
Spades ... 48
Spalling Hammers ... 50
Spanish Lace ... 265
Spangle Trimming ... 319
Spears, Fish ... 604
Spears, Frog ... 604
Speed Indicators ... 85
Special Family Remedies ... 27
Special Veterinary Remedies ... 30
Specifics, Homeopathic ... 29
Spectacles ... 462-463
Spectacle Frames ... 463
Spectacle Cases ... 463
Spiral Screwdrivers ... 80
Spice Cabinets ... 141
Spices ... 9-10
Spiders ... 129
Spigots ... 141
Spirit Lamps, Glass ... 478
Spirit Levels ... 579
Spirit Lamps ... 35
Spirits ... 11
Spirits of Camphor ... 27
Spirits of Nitre ... 27
Spirits of Turpentine ... 28
ers ... 142
Split Shot Sinkers ... 602
Split Bamboo Rods ... 598-599
Splashers, Stamped ... 331
Spoke Grips ... 618
Spoke Shaves ... 79
Spoke Pointers ... 81
Spokes, Bicycle ... 619
Sponges ... 330
Sponge Baskets ... 135
Sporting Sights ... 579-580
Spool Cotton ... 320
Spool Linen ... 321
Spoon Fish Bait ... 603-604
Spoons, Berry ... 441
Spoons, Bon-Bon, Silver ... 445
Spoons, Orange ... 441
Spoons, Silver-Plated ... 438-445
Spoons, Wood ... 140
Spoons, Tin ... 131
Spoonholders, Silver ... 451-455
Spray Pumps ... 162
Spray Pumps ... 53
Sprays, Floral ... 293
Spreads, Bed ... 289
Spreaders, Hammock ... 608
Spring Balances ... 48
Spring Clothespins ... 139
Spring Fish Hooks ... 604
Spring Heel Plow Shoes ... 201
Spring Heel Shoes, Ladies' ... 192
Spring Hinges ... 44
Spring Heel Shoes, Misses' and Childs' ... 194
Spring Overcoats ... 175
Spring Punches ... 82-83
Spring and Summer Wraps, Ladies' ... 273-276
Spring and Summer Clothing, Men's ... 266-288
Spring Tooth Harrows ... 158
Spring Wire ... 41
Springs, Bolster ... 60
Springs, Bed ... 661
Springs, Bird-Cage ... 89
Springs, Carriage ... 60
Splicers, Hose ... 56
Springs, Seat ... 60
Sprinkler, Lawn ... 56
Springs, Screen Door ... 44
Springs for Baby Jump-
Sprinklers, Plant ... 329
Spur Straps ... 761
Spurs ... 760
Spy Glasses ... 464-465
Spy Glasses, Pocket ... 465
Square Churns ... 143
Square Body Cutter Stuff ... 63
Squares, Steel ... 73
Squares, Iron ... 73
Squares, Tory ... 73
Squares, Tory and Meter ... 73
Squares, Combination ... 73
Squares, Machinists' ... 85
Squares, Caliper ... 85
Squeezers, Lemon ... 98-99, 140
Stable Pails ... 139
Stable Brooms ... 20
Stable Fittings ... 46
Stack Covers ... 609
Stake Mallets ... 140
Stakes ... 62
Stains, Wood ... 22
Stair Carpet ... 300
Stair Rods ... 300
Stair Posts and Rails ... 95
Stamped Tidies ... 335
Stamped Linens ... 331-332
Stamping Pattern Outfits ... 332
Stands, Emery Wheel ... 72
Stands, Umbrella ... 672
Stands, Jardiniere ... 669
Stanley Planes ... 74-77
Stands, Wire Flower Pot. ... 44-45
Staples ... 43
Staples, Wire Cloth ... 43
Staples, Wagon Bow ... 62
Staples, Wrought ... 87
Star Heel Plates ... 208
Starch ... 16
Starch, Laundry ... 16
Starch, Corn ... 16
Stark, A., Grain Bags ... 293
Stateroom Trunks ... 252
Stays, Dress ... 323
Stays, Barn Door ... 86
Steak Pounders ... 98
Steel Axles ... 59
Steel Beam Cultivators ... 158
Steel Beam Plows ... 156
Steel Churns ... 143
Steel Fence Posts ... 43
Steel Harrows ... 157
Steel Lamps ... 138
Steel Pens ... 354
Steel Roofing ... 96
Steel Rakes ... 49
Steel Ranges ... 123-127
Steel Stamps ... 83
Steel Safes ... 97
Steel Squares ... 73
Steel Tape Measures ... 468
Steel Traps ... 99-100
Steel Tape Lines ... 73
Steel Tanks ... 163
Steel Wire ... 41
Steelyards ... 48
Stems, Pipe ... 334
Steam Engines ... 151
Steamers ... 133
Steamers, Feed ... 163
Stencil Sets ... 83
Step Ladders ... 648
Steps, Buggy ... 61
Stereoscopes ... 468
Stereo-Graphoscope ... 468
Stereopticon Slides ... 484-486
Stereoscopic Views ... 468
Stereoscopic Mounts ... 482
Sterling Silver Flatware ... 445
Stetson Hats ... 233-234
Sticks, Drum ... 536
Stirrups, Steel ... 759
Stirrup Straps ... 759
Stirrups, Ladies' ... 759
Stirrups, Men's Wood ... 759
Stirrups, Brass Clad ... 759
Stock Covers ... 609
Stock Fountain ... 163
Stock Food ... 23
Stocks and Dies ... 66
Stocking Heel Protectors ... 209
Stocking Supporters ... 322
Stockings, Bicycle ... 218
Stockings, Ladies' ... 244
Stockings, Golf ... 218
Stockmen's Bed Sheets ... 609
Stockings, Misses' and Children's ... 244
Stocking, Knee Protectors ... 209
Stone Axes ... 50
Stones, Emery ... 71
Stones, Scythe ... 51
Stonecutters' Spectacles ... 463
Stools, Camp ... 610
Stools, Wood and Cane Seat ... 646
Stops, Bench ... 83
Stops, Door ... 58
Stoppers, Flue ... 128
Store Door Locks ... 90-92
Storm Thresholds ... 99
Storm Overshoes ... 204-206
Storm Glass and Thermometer ... 469
Stove Bolts ... 39
Stove Brushes ... 20
Stove Boards ... 129
Stove Backs ... 129
Stove Furniture ... 128-134
Stove Kettles ... 129
Stove Lining ... 129
Stove Mats ... 129
Stove Polish ... 9
Stove Poker ... 128
Stove Shovels ... 128
Stoves, Cook ... 119-124
Stoves, Camping ... 610
Stoves, Gasoline ... 115-116
Stoves, Heating ... 124-127
Stoves, Lamp Chimney ... 98
Stoves, Oil ... 84
Stoves, Oil ... 117-118
Stoves, Pocket ... 28
Stoves, Tent Heating ... 610
Stovelid Lifter ... 128
Stovepipe ... 128
Stovepipe Damper ... 128
Stovepipe Shelves ... 128
Stovepipe Collars ... 128
Straight Seines ... 606
Strap, Breast ... 762
Strap Hinges ... 86
Strap Sandals, Ladies' ... 195-196
Strap Spreaders ... 762
Strap, Side ... 762
Straps, Hammer ... 62
Straps, School ... 355
Straps, Wagon Box ... 62
Boys' ... 243
Straw Hats, Ladies' ... 293
Straw Hats, Men's and
Straw Matting ... 300
Straw Ticking ... 292
Strawberry Cultivators ... 161
Strawberry Forks ... 49
Strawberries, Canned ... 11
Stretchers ... 43
Striking Bags ... 593
Striking Bag Platform ... 593
String ... 20
Strings, Autoharp ... 533
Strings, Banjo ... 533
Strings, Double Bass ... 533
Strings, Guitar ... 533
Strings, Mandolin ... 533
Strings, Violin ... 533
Strings, Violoncello ... 533
Strings, Zither ... 533
Striking Hammers ... 50
Stringers, Fish ... 604
Striped Dimity ... 290
Stubble Plows ... 156-157
Studs, Belt ... 56
Studs, Diamond ... 402-403
Studs, Shirt ... 425
Sub-Soil Lister ... 157
Succotash ... 11
Sugar ... 17
Sugar Bowls, Silver ... 451-453
Sugar Shells ... 438-445
Suits, Boys' Wash ... 182
Suits, Bicycle ... 177
Suits, Bicycle ... 297
Suits, Boys' Sailor ... 182
Suits, Base Ball ... 596
Suits, Boys' ... 179
Suits, Brownie ... 181
Suits, Crash, Men's ... 176
Suits, Children's ... 181
Suits, Corduroy, Boys' ... 184
Suits, Children's Kilt ... 185
Suits, Confirmation ... 186
Suits, Corduroy, Men's ... 174
Suits, Children's Military Reefer ... 184
Suits, Children's Head to Foot Combination ... 186
Suits, Children's Combination, Four-Piece ... 184
Suits, Four-Piece Combination, Boys' ... 183
Suits, Fancy Worsted, Men's ... 172
Suits, Grass ... 590
Suits, Grand Army, Men's ... 173
Suits, Junior, Children's ... 183
Suits, Knee-Pants, Children's Combination ... 184
Suits, Linen, Men's ... 176
Suits, Ladies' Bicycle ... 281
Suits, Ladies' Tailor-Made ... 279-281
Suits, Professional, Men's ... 171
Suits, Prince Albert, Men's ... 171
Suits, Reefer, Boys' ... 183
Suits, Sailor, Boys' ... 182
Suits, Sailor Wash, Boys' ... 182
Suits, Two-Piece, Boys' ... 181-182
Suits, Two-Piece, Blouse, Boys' ... 182
Suits, Youths' ... 180
Suits, Zouave, Children's ... 183
Suiting, Ladies' Wool and Silk ... 260
Suiting, Duck ... 261
Suiting and Pants Goods ... 289
Sulky Lister ... 157
Sulky Plows ... 157
Sulphur ... 28
Summer Clothing ... 176
Summer Dress Goods ... 262
Summer Overcoats ... 175
Summer Skirts ... 270-271
Summer Sports ... 593-598
Summer Wash Goods ... 289
Summer Underwear,
Summer Underwear, Ladies' ... 241
Supplies, Base Ball ... 594-597
Supports, Tongue ... 66
Supporters, Athletic ... 597

Supporters, Abdominal .. 32
Supporters, Drawer .... 320
Supporters, Morton's .... 597
Supporters, Sleeve ..... 335
Surah Silk ..... 257
Men's ..... 238, 273
Surgical Instruments (Veterinary) ..... 31-32
Surreys ..... 710-723
Surveyors' Compasses... 467
Surveyors' Tapes and
Suspenders, Men's ..... 221
Chains ..... 468
Suspensory Bandages ... 32
Suspensory Bandages ... 595
Swabs, Gun ..... 587
Swages ..... 68
Sway Bar ..... 62
Sweaters ..... 591
Sweaters, Men's and Boys' ..... 217-218
Swell Body Cutter Stuff. 63
Swell Sized Gloves, Men's 229
Sweet Oil ..... 21
Sweet Potatoes ..... 11
Swing Rocking Horse.... 142
Swings ..... 142
Swiss Embroidery ..... 266
Swiss Handkerchiefs ..... 227
Swiss, Dotted ..... 293-294
Switches, Hair ..... 330
Switches, Electric ..... 471
Swivel Hook Clevis ..... 62
Swivels, Brass Fishing... 602
Swivels, Rope Hitch..... 165
Swivels, Lariat ..... 46
Syringes, Bulb ..... 32, 329
Syringes, Family ..... 32
Syringes, Fountain ..... 32
Syringes, Hypodermic .. 32
Syringes, Hard Rubber.. 32
Syringes, Ladies' ..... 32
Syringes, Veterinary ... 31
Syrup, Cough ..... 26
Syrups and Molasses.... 18
Syrup Pitchers ..... 449-454

## T

T-Bevels ..... 73
T-Hinges ..... 86
T-Shaft Irons ..... 61
T-Plates ..... 61
Tables, Brass ..... 690-691
Table Casters ..... 447
Table Covers ..... 298, 331
Table Cutlery ..... 107-108
Table Forks, Silver.. 438-445
Table Knives, Silver.. 438-445
Table Linens ..... 294-295
Table, Oilcloth ..... 300
Tables, Breakfast ..... 648
Tables, Drawing ..... 358
Tables, Extension ..... 643-649
Tables, Folding ..... 141
Tables, Folding ..... 672
Tables, Kitchen ..... 648
Tables, Library ..... 652-654
Tables, Parlor ..... 651
Tables, Toilet ..... 652
Tablespoons, Silver .. 438-445
Tablets ..... 349
Tablets, Soda Mint..... 28
Tablets, Chlorate Potash. 28
Tablets, Pepsin ..... 28
Tabouret Chairs ..... 666
Tacks ..... 38-39
Tack Hammers ..... 78
Tack Pullers ..... 78
Tacks, Thumb ..... 358
Tackle Blocks ..... 96
Tackle Books ..... 605
Tackle Boxes ..... 604-605
Tackle, Fishing ..... 598, 609
Taffeta Silks ..... 257
Tags, Satchel, Silver.... 439
Tailor-Made Suits, Ladies' ..... 279-281
Tailor Pants.. ..... 174
Tailpieces, Banjo ..... 535
Tailpieces, Double Bass.. 534
Tailpieces, Guitar ..... 535
Tailpieces, Mandolin .... 536
Tailpieces, Violin ..... 534
Tailpieces, Violoncello .. 534
Tailpieces, Viola ..... 534
Talking Machine ..... 485
Tam O'Shanter Caps.. 236-237
Tamers, Hog ..... 46
Tambourine Heads .... 537
Tambourines ..... 532
Tan Nullifiers, Men's.... 200
Tan Oxfords ..... 195
Tan Shoes....Colored Pages
Tan Shoe Buttons....... 207
Tan Shoe Polish....... 209
Tank Heater ..... 163
Tank Pumps ..... 53
Tanks, Steel ..... 163
Tanks, Wood ..... 163
Tap Soles ..... 208
Tape Measure, Steel.... 468
Tape Measure ..... 322
Tape, Metallic Linen.... 468
Tape Lines ..... 73
Taper Files ..... 71
Taper Taps ..... 67
Tapestry, Brussels Carpet ..... 285
Tapestry Curtains ..... 297
Tapioca ..... 16
Tapideros ..... 759
Tar Soap ..... 33
Tar (Pine) ..... 23
Targets ..... 587-588
Tarletan ..... 293
Tarpaulins ..... 609
Tassels ..... 332
Tattoo Marker ..... 45
Teas ..... 8-9
Tea Cannisters ..... 134
Tea Kettle Iron ..... 129
Tea Kettle ..... 129-136
Tea Pots ..... 130-136
Tea Pots, Silver..... 453
Tea Pot Stands..... 135
Tea Steeper ..... 130-136
Tea Sets, Silver Plated. 451-453
Tea Tray ..... 134
Teachers' Bibles ..... 348
Teaspoons, Silver ..... 438-445
Telegraph Line Estimate 471
Telegraph Wire ..... 471
Telephones ..... 472
Telephones, Desk ..... 472
Telephones, Long Distance ..... 472
Telephone Receivers ..... 472
Telescope Cases ..... 253
Telegraphic Instruments ..... 470-471
Teething Rings ..... 28, 328
Tenor Drums ..... 529
Tenor Horns ..... 530
Tenor Trombones ..... 530-531
Tenor Violins ..... 515
Tennis Balls ..... 593
Tennis Marks ..... 593
Tennis Nets ..... 593
Tennis Poles ..... 593
Tenis Racquets ..... 593
Tennis Ropes ..... 593
Tennis Sets ..... 593
Tennis Shoes ..... 203
Tests for Sight..... 462
Tents, Duck ..... 608-609
Tents, Lawn ..... 608-609
Tents, Miners' ..... 608
Tents, Oblong ..... 608-609
Tents, Palmetto ..... 608
Tents, Photographers' .. 609
Tents, Refreshment .... 608
Tents, Wall ..... 609
Tents, Wedge ..... 608
Thermometers ..... 469-470
Thermometers, Bath .... 470
Thermometers, Chemical. 470
Thermometers, Churn ... 470
Thermometers, Confectioners' ..... 470
Thermometers, Clinical... 470
Thermometers, Dairy ... 470
Thermometers, Evaporating ..... 470
Thermometers, Hot Bed. 470
Thermometers, Incubating ..... 470
Thermometers, Clinical.. 33
Thermometers, Chemical 33
Thermometers, Self-Registering ..... 469
Thermometer and Storm Glass ..... 469
Thermometers, Veterinary 31
Thigh Boots, Rubber.... 205
Thigh Leggins, Ladies'... 207
Thimbles, Adjustable .. 128
Thimbles, Chimney .... 128
Thimbles, Gold and Silver 435
Thimble Skeins ..... 59
Thimbles, Steel ..... 322
Three Horse Attachments 62
Thread Gauges ..... 85
Thread, Shoe ..... 209
Thresher Belt ..... 56
Thresher Pumps ..... 53
Thresholds ..... 99
Thumb Latches ..... 90-92
Thyme ..... 11
Ticking, Bed ..... 292
Tidies, Turkish ..... 297
Tie Chains ..... 46
Ties, Cow ..... 46
Tights, Athletic..... 597
Tights, Bathing ..... 597
Tights, Ladies' Equestrian ..... 241
Tile Handler's Gloves... 229
Tiling Spades ..... 48
Timothy Seed ..... 25
Tin Horns ..... 133
Tinsel Braid ..... 319
Tinsel, Drapery ..... 298
Tinners' Snips ..... 84
Tinware Assortments .... 128
Tinware Department . 130-136
Tills, Case ..... 98
Tips, Ostrich ..... 303
Tips, Pole ..... 61
Tips, Shaft ..... 61
Tips, Whiffletree ..... 61
Tire Benders ..... 66
Tire Bolts ..... 59
Tire Casing ..... 616
Tire Measuring Wheel.. 66
Tire Tape ..... 618
Tire Shrinkers ..... 66
Tired Wheels ..... 59
Tires, Iron ..... 58
Tires, Steel ..... 59
Tires, Bicycle ..... 616
Tissue Paper ..... 332
Tissue Paper Outfits.... 333
Tobacco ..... 24
Tobacco Pouches ..... 324
Toe Calks ..... 68
Toe Pads ..... 58
Toilet Articles ..... 33
Toilet Articles ..... 335
Toilet Paper ..... 23
Toilet Preparations .... 34
Toilet Sets ..... 682-683
Toilet Soaps ..... 33
Toilet Stands ..... 134
Toilet Water ..... 19
Toilet Waters ..... 33
Toilets, Bathroom ..... 671
Tomatoes (Canned) ..... 11
Tongs, Blacksmiths' .... 67
Tongs, Ice ..... 103
Tongs, Silver Sugar .... 445
Tongue Supports ..... 60
Tongueless Cultivators . 158
Tongues, Wagon ..... 63
Toning Trays ..... 478
Tool Sets ..... 82
Tools, Carving ..... 80
Tools, Harness Mending. 766
Tools, Reloading ..... 586-588
Tools, Watchmakers' ... 400
Tooth Brushes ..... 34
Tooth Planes ..... 76
Tooth Brushes ..... 328
Tooth Preparations ..... 34
Tooth Soap ..... 34
Toothache Drops ..... 27
Toothache Wax ..... 27
Toothpick Holders ..... 446
Toothpicks, Gold ..... 433
Top Buggies ..... 708-721
Top Lifts ..... 208
Tops, Buggy ..... 57
Tops, Hame ..... 766
Torch, Blow ..... 84
Torches, Gasoline ..... 118
Torchon Laces ..... 264
Towel Holders ..... 672
Towels ..... 295-296
Toy Brooms ..... 20
Toy Carpet Sweepers .... 101
Toy Safes ..... 99
Toy Sad Irons ..... 99
Toy Trunks ..... 252
Toy Wagons ..... 143
Traces, Double Buggy... 762
Traces, Double Farm.... 762
Traces, Single Buggy .. 762
Tracing Paper and Cloth. 359
Tracing Wheels ..... 109
Track, Barn Door ..... 86
Traction Engine Headlights ..... 138
Trammel Nets ..... 607
Trammel Points ..... 74
Trapeze Bars ..... 594
Transmitters, Telephone. 472
Transom Lifters ..... 91
Transom Plates ..... 89
Trap-Setting Clamps .... 100
Traps, Driving ..... 721-725
Traps, Steel ..... 99-100
Traps, Shooting ..... 587-588
Traveling Bags ..... 252-253
Tray Cloths ..... 331
Trays, Child's ..... 134
Trays, Chopping ..... 134
Trays, Glass ..... 478
Trays, Developing ..... 478
Trays, Rubber ..... 478
Trays, Silver Plated..... 454
Trays, Toning ..... 478
Trays, Water Pitcher ... 134
Tree Pruners ..... 50
Tread Powers ..... 150
Triangles, Musical ..... 532
Triangular Scales ..... 358
Trimmed Hats ..... 301-302
Trimmed Neckyokes .... 63
Trimmings, Bead ..... 319
Trimmings, Dress ..... 318-319
Trimmings, Hame ..... 765
Trimmings, Spangle.. .. 319
Tripe, Spiced ..... 13
Tripods for Cameras.... 477
Tripods for Telescopes... 465
Trimmers, Photographic.. 479
Trix ..... 28
Trocars, Cattle ..... 31
Troughs, Pig ..... 163
Trombones ..... 531
Trot Lines ..... 607
Trout Baskets ..... 605
Trout Flies and Tackle. 602-607
Trowels Garden ..... 49
Trowels, Masons' ..... 84
Troughs, Oil ..... 66
Trucks, Hand ..... 164
Trucks, Farm ..... 723-727
Trunks ..... 250-252
Trunk Locks ..... 88
Trunk Nails ..... 38
Try Squares ..... 73
Try and Mitre Squares.. 73
Tubs, Bath ..... 134
Tubs, Galvanized Iron... 132
Tubs, Wood ..... 138-139
Tubed Cake Pans ..... 131-136
Tubing, Rubber ..... 58
Tubing, Rubber ..... 333
Tubular Braid ..... 319
Tubular Lanterns ..... 137
Tufting Buttons ..... 58
Tugs, Shaft ..... 763
Tuning Hammers, Autoharp ..... 536
Tuning Forks ..... 537
Tuning Hammers, Dulcimer ..... 536
Tuning Hammers, Piano. 538
Tuning Hammers, Zither 538
Tuning Pins, Dulcimer.. 536
Tuning Pipes ..... 537-538
Turkey Calls .....
Turkey Red Damask .... 294
Turkey Red Prints..... 291
Turkey Red Handkerchiefs ..... 225
Turkish Towels ..... 296
Turkish Tidies ..... 297
Turkish Stand Covers... 297
Turns, Cupboard ..... 91
Turning Chisels ..... 79
Turning Gouges ..... 79
Turning Hammers ..... 69
Turpentine ..... 21
Tweed Suitings ..... 289
Twine Boxes ..... 98
Twist Drills ..... 81
Twine ..... 20
Twine, Cotton Hammock 608
Twine, Cotton Netting... ..... 607-608
Twine, Gilling ..... 608
Twine, Seine ..... 608
Twilled Flannel ..... 288
Twist, Silk ..... 321
Tuyer Irons ..... 65

## U

Umbrella Stands ..... 672
Umbrellas, Wagon ..... 57
Umbrellas, Gents' and Ladies' ..... 248-249
Umpires' Indicators .... 596
Umpires' Protectors .... 596
Unbleached Balbriggan Hose ..... 245
Unbleached Cotton Flannel ..... 288
Unbleached Drilling .... 292
Unbleached Sheetings.... 291
Underskirts ..... 305
Underwear, Men's ..... 237-239
Underwear, Ladies' and Misses' ..... 240-241
Union Churn ..... 144
Union Suits, Ladies'..... 240
Union Syringes ..... 329
Universal Bevel ..... 85
Universal Grips, Bicycle. 618
Universal Plane ..... 76
Unlaundered White Shirts 210
Untrimmed Hats, Ladies' 302
Upholstered Furniture. 663-668
Upholsterers' Tacks ... 39
Upsetters, Tire ..... 66
Urinals ..... 56
Urinometers ..... 35, 470
U. S. A. Cavalry Hats.. 233

## V

Vacation Rubber Boots... 205
Vegetables, Canned .... 11
Vegetable Boilers ..... 133
Vegetable Strainers .... 132
Vaginal Syringes ..... 32
Vehicle Department ... 708-727
(Send for free Special Vehicle Catalogue.)
Valenciennes Laces .... 264
Valises ..... 252-253
Valises, Bicycle ..... 616, 618
Valve Stems, Bicycle .... 617
Valve Trombones ..... 530-531
Valves, Angle ..... 54
Valves, Bicycle ..... 617
Varnish Brushes ..... 113-114
Valves, Check ..... 54
Valves, Cross ..... 54
Valves, Foot ..... 54
Valves, Globe ..... 54
Varnishes ..... 22, 361
Vaseline ..... 28
Veiling Department ..... 318
Velvet Flowers ..... 303
Velvet Carpets ..... 285
Velvet Ribbons ..... 263
Velvets and Velveteens.. 256
Velveteen Shirt Binding 323
Ventilated Health Underwear, Men's ..... 237
Ventilators ..... 128
Vermicelli ..... 16
Vestibule Rods ..... 299
Vest Buckles ..... 321
Vests, Corduroy, Men's... 175
Vests, Duck ..... 178
Vests, Fancy, Men's..... 175
Vests, Hunting ..... 591
Vests, Ladies' Summer.. ..... 240-241
Vests, Men's ..... 175
Vests, Serge, Men's ..... 176
Vest Pocket Dictionaries. ..... 338-339
Vests, Silk, Men's ..... 175
Veterinary Catheters ... 31
Veterinary Ecraseurs ... 31
Veterinary Files ..... 31
Veterinary Instruments.. 31
Veterinary Needles ..... 31
Veterinary Remedies..... 30
Veterinary Silk ..... 31
Velvet Slippers, Men's.. 200
Veterinary Thermometers 31
Veterinary Trocars ..... 31
Vials, Homeopathic ..... 35
Vibrating Cultivators.... 158
Vici Kid Polish ..... 209
Vici Kid Shoes, Ladies'... 191
Victoria Lawns ..... 293
Victoria Gun Cases .. 588-589
View Finders ..... 477
Views for Magic Lanterns ..... 485
Vignettes, Photographic 478
Vinegar, Raspberry .... 11
Vinegar, Cider ..... 13
Viola Bow Frogs..... 534
Viola Bow Hair..... 534
Viola Bridges ..... 534
Viola Cases ..... 534
Viola Fingerboards .... 534
Viola Mutes ..... 534
Viola Necks ..... 534
Viola Pegs ..... 534
Viola Tailpieces ..... 534
Violins ..... 515-516
Violin Bows ..... 533
Violin Bow Hair ..... 534
Violin Bow Frogs ..... 533
Violin Bow Resin ..... 534
Violin Bow Screws ..... 533
Violin Bridges ..... 534
Violin Cases ..... 533
Violin Chin Rests ..... 534
Violin End Pins ..... 534
Violin Fingerboards .... 534
Violin Instruction Books ..... 540-541
Violin Music ..... 539-540
Violin Mutes ..... 534
Violin Necks ..... 534
Violin Outfits ..... 516-517
Violin Patent Heads .... 533
Violin Pegs ..... 533
Violin Strings ..... 533
Violin Tailpieces ..... 534
Violoncellos ..... 517
Violoncello Bags ..... 534
Violoncello Bows ..... 534
Violoncello Bow Frogs.. 535
Violoncello Bow Hair.. 535
Violoncello Bow Resin.. 535
Violoncello Bridges .... 535
Violoncello Cases ..... 534
Violoncello Fingerboards. 535
Violoncello Mutes ..... 535
Violoncello Nuts ..... 535
Violoncello Patent Heads 535
Violoncello Pegs ..... 535
Violoncello Strings ..... 533
Violoncello Tailpieces .. 535
Viols, Double Bass ..... 517
Violets ..... 303
Violet Extract ..... 33
Vises ..... 65-66
Vises, Saw ..... 70

## W

Wad Cutters ..... 585
Wads, Gun ..... 584-585
Wading Pants, Men's.... 206
Wadding, Cotton ..... 292
Wafers ..... 16
Waffle Irons ..... 129
Wagon Axles ..... 62
Wagon Bolster ..... 63
Wagon Bow Staples .... 62
Wagon Bows ..... 62
Wagon Box Nails ..... 61
Wagon Box Rivets ..... 61
Wagon Box Rods ..... 62
Wagon Box Straps ..... 62
Wagons, Boys' ..... 143
Wagons and Carriages. 708-727
Wagon Covers ..... 609
Wagon Eveners ..... 63
Wagons, Farm ..... 722-727
Wagon Gearing ..... 62
Wagon Hubs ..... 59
Wagon Jacks ..... 59
Wagon Neck Yokes .... 63
Wagon Reaches ..... 62
Wagon Rims ..... 60
Wagon Singletrees ..... 63
Wagon Slings ..... 165
Wagons, Road ..... 711-723
Wagon Scales ..... 47
Wagon Spokes ..... 60
Wagon Storm Tops ..... 57
Wagon Sunshades ..... 57
Wagon Tongue ..... 63
Wagon Umbrellas ..... 57
Waists and Blouses, Boys' ..... 247
Waists, Ladies' ..... 268, 269
Waist Linings ..... 258
Walking Cultivator ..... 158
Walking Plows ..... 156
Walking Sticks ..... 248
Wall Maps ..... 337
Wall Paint Brushes ..... 113
Wall Paper ..... 299
Wall Paper Cleaner..... 22
Wall Pockets ..... 670
Warehouse Trucks ..... 164
Warren Hoes ..... 49
Warp, Carpet ..... 292
Warranted Shoes ..... 190-209
Wash Basins ..... 56
Wash Bench ..... 139
Wash Boards ..... 139
Wash Boilers ..... 132
Wash Bowls ..... 131-136
Wash Bowls and Pitchers 134
Wash Dress Goods.... 262, 289
Wash Dimity ..... 290
Wash Silks ..... 256, 261
Wash Tubs ..... 132

| | | | | | | | | | |
|---|---|---|---|---|---|---|---|---|---|
| Wash Tubs | 138, 139 | Wheat Germ Meal | 15 | Whitewash Brushes | 114 | Wire Potato Scoop | 48 | Wool Shawls | 305 |
| Washable Neckties | 224 | Wheelbarrows | 164 | Wide Tire Wheels | 59 | Wire Rakes | 49 | Wool Socks | 29 |
| Washer Cutters | 82 | Wheels, Bicycle | 619 | Wigs | 330 | Wire Ratchets | 43 | Wool Suitings, Ladies' | 289 |
| Washers, Iron | 39 | Wheels, Buggy | 58-59 | Wild Cherry Phosphate | 11 | Wire Rope | 97 | Wool Swabs | 587 |
| Washers, Leather | 765 | Wheels, Emery | 72 | Wind Gauge Sights | 580 | Wire Sash Cord | 97 | York Shoes, Ladies' | 193 |
| Washing Machines | 139 | Wheels, Fifth | 61 | Windmill Pumps | 52-53 | Window Screens | 43 | Wormers, Gun | 586 |
| Washing Powder | 18 | Wheels, Metal | 59 | Windmills | 148 | Wire Shoe Nails | 208 | Worsted Cloth, Ladies' | 255 |
| Watchmen's Eyeglasses | 466 | Wheels, Tire | 59 | Window Brushes | 114 | Wire, Smooth | 41 | Worsted Suits, Men's | 170 |
| Watchmen's Lanterns | 138 | Wheels, Tire Measuring | 66 | Window Cleaners | 102 | Wire, Spring | 41 | Woven Wire Fencing | 41-48 |
| Water Bottles | 32, 329 | Wheels, Tracing | 109 | Windows | 94-95 | Wire Stretchers | 43 | Wrappers, Ladies' | 273 |
| Water Can | 138 | Whiffletree Couplings | 62 | Window-Screen Frames | 44 | Wires Nails | 38 | Wrappers, Music | 537 |
| Water Coolers | 135 | Whiffletree Ferrules | 61 | Window Shades | 299 | Wire Spark Guards | 45 | Wraps, Ladies' Spring | |
| Water Pails | 131 | Whiffletree Hooks | 61 | Window Spring Bolts | 89 | Wire, Steel | 41 | and Summer | 273-276 |
| Watered Silks | 257 | Whiffletree Hooks | 62 | Windsor Ties | 224 | Wire, Telegraph | 471 | Wreaths, Floral | 303 |
| Watering Pots | 133 | Whiffletree Plates | 61 | Wing Caliper | 74-84-85 | Wire, Woven | 42-43 | Wrenches, Banjo | 536 |
| Watering Tanks | 163 | Whiffletree Tips | 61 | Wire Cloth Staples | 43 | Witchhazel Extract | 27 | Wrenches, Bicycle | 618 |
| Waterproof Bibs | 309 | Whiffletree Tongues | 62 | Wing Dividers | 74-84-85 | Witchhazel Cream | 27 | Wrenches, Drum | 536 |
| Waterproof Clothing, | | Whip Crackers | 768 | Wine, Beef and Iron | 26 | Wolf Traps | 100 | Wrenches, Monkey | 78 |
| Men's | 187-189 | Whip Holders | 768 | Wine Corks | 35 | Women's Fancy Work | 331 | Wringers | 100-101 |
| Waterproof Dress Goods | | Whip Lashes | 768 | Wire, Annunciator | 471 | Women's Tap Soles | 208 | | |
| | 255-259 | Whips, Buggy | 768 | Wire Arm Bands | 333 | Wooden Ware | 138, 141 | **X** | |
| Waterproof Shoe Polish | 209 | Whips, Carriage | 768 | Wire, Barbed | 41 | Wood Faucets | 141 | | |
| Waving Irons | 112 | Whips, Dog | 592 | Wire, Brads | 38 | Wood Filler | 22 | Xylophones | 532 |
| Wax, Upper Leather | 208 | Whips, Drover's | 768 | Wire, Brass | 41 | Wood Handscrews | 83 | | |
| Wax, Laundry | 16 | Whips, Riding | 768 | Wire Broilers | 135 | Woodman's Compasses | 467 | **Y** | |
| Wax, Moustache | 112 | Whips, Team | 768 | Wire Brushes, Gun | 587 | Wood Rasps | 71 | Yeast | 10 |
| Wax, Sealing | 354 | Whisk Brooms | 20 | Wire Button Hooks | 209 | Wood Rim Cement | 619 | Yellow Paper, Photo- | |
| Wax, Shoemakers' | 209 | Whiskers and Whigs | 330 | Wire Coat Hangers | 135 | Wood Rims, Bicycle | 619 | graphic | 479 |
| Waxed Butter Paper | 147 | Whistles, Bicycle | 617-618 | Wire Chairs and Settees | 45 | Wood Rim Washers | 619 | Yokes, Axle Clip | 61 |
| Wear Irons | 62 | Whistles, Dog | 592 | Wire Clothes Pins | 139 | Woods Bob | 63 | Yokes, Neck | 63 |
| Webbing, Non-Elastic | 323 | Whistles, Hunting | 592 | Wire Clothes Lines | 100 | Woods Evener | 63 | Yokes, Ox | 46 |
| Weaners, Calf | 46 | Whistles, Police | 592 | Wire Cloth | 43 | Woods Singletree | 63 | Youths' Clothing | 179-180 |
| Weaving Cotton | 292 | White Bed Spreads | 289 | Wire, Copper | 41 | Woods Neckyoke | 63 | | |
| Wedges, Ax Handle | 77 | White Blankets | 288 | Wire Dish Cloth | 98 | Wood Stains | 22 | **Z** | |
| Wedges, Woodchoppers' | 77 | White Dresses, Children's | 278 | Wire Door Mats | 45 | Wool Boots, Men's | 202-203 | Zinc in Oil | 22 |
| Weeding Hoes | 49 | White Flannels | 288 | Wire, Fencing | 41 | Wool Elderdown | 288 | Zither Brushes | 536 |
| Weeding Hooks | 49 | White Goods Department | 293 | Wire, Galvanized | 41 | Wood Enamels | 360 | Zither Cases | 536 |
| Weed Scythes | 51 | White Kid Slippers, La- | | Wire Gates | 42-43 | Wooden Measures | 141 | Zither, Columbia | 522 |
| Well Buckets | 139 | dies' | 195 | Wire Hen's Nests | 43 | Wooden Rules | 354 | Zither Instruction Books | 541 |
| Well Chains | 99 | White Laces | 265 | Wire Lamp Shade Frame | 333 | Wool Flannel Shirting | 258 | Zither Patent Heads | 536 |
| Wells, Ink | 351-352 | White Lawn Ties | 224 | Wire Lath | 43 | Wool Hose, Ladies' | 245-246 | Zither Rings and Picks | 536 |
| Well Wheel Hooks | 99 | White Lead | 22 | Wire on Spools | 333 | Wool, Ice | 332 | Zithers | 522 |
| Well Wheels | 99 | White Long Cloth | 293 | Wire Palm Gloves | 229 | Wool Mittens, Ladies' | 231 | Zither Strings | 533 |
| Whalebone Casing | 323 | White Mull Ties | 311 | Wire, Picture | 41 | Wool Underwear, Men's | | Zither Tuning Hammers | 536 |
| Whang Leather | 56 | White Tennis Shoes | 203 | Wire, Picture | 299 | | 238-239 | Zouave Suits, Child's | 183 |
| Wheat Bags | 293 | | | | | | | Zulu Gun | 572 |

# INDEX

## YOU WILL FIND THE ARTICLE YOU ARE LOOKING FOR IN THE INDEX PAGES 775 TO 786.

IF YOU DON'T FIND IT UNDER THE NAME YOU ARE LOOKING FOR YOU MAY FIND THE ARTICLE INDEXED UNDER ANOTHER NAME.

## Don't Say it Is'nt in the Catalogue

If you don't find the article indexed under the name you are looking for, LOOK CAREFULLY through the index under every name the article could possible be listed.

## .......IF YOU DON'T FIND IT IN THE INDEX......

LOOK VERY CAREFULLY THROUGH THE ENTIRE CATALOGUE.

NEARLY EVERYTHING IN MERCHANDISE CAN BE FOUND IN THIS BOOK.

Customers often Write for Prices on Goods that are Plainly Illustrated, Described and Priced in the Catalogue which Shows the Very Article they Want has been Overlooked by them.

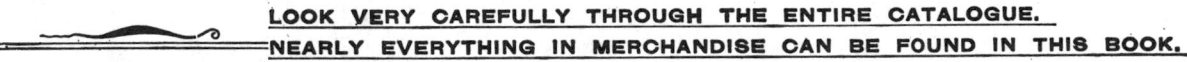

# SEARS, ROEBUCK & CO., Incorporated.

## Cheapest Supply House on Earth,

82 TO 96 FULTON STREET,
73 TO 87 DESPLAINES STREET,
17 TO 31 WAYMAN STREET,

# CHICAGO, ILL., U. S. A.